QFINANCE

THE ULTIMATE RESOURCE

QFINANCE

THE ULTIMATE RESOURCE

BLOOMSBURY

First edition published in 2009
Second edition published in 2011
Third edition published in 2012
Fourth edition published in 2013 by

Bloomsbury Information Ltd
50 Bedford Square
London
WC1B 3DB
United Kingdom

Bloomsbury Publishing, London, New Delhi, New York, and Sydney
www.bloomsbury.com

A CIP record for this book is available from the British Library.

Standard edition
ISBN-10: 1-84930-062-3
ISBN-13: 978-1-84930-062-9

Middle East edition
ISBN-10: 1-84930-063-1
ISBN-13: 978-1-84930-063-6

E-book edition
ISBN-10: 1-84930-064-X
ISBN-13: 978-1-84930-064-3

Page design by Fiona Pike, Pike Design, Winchester, UK
Typeset by OKS Prepress Services, Chennai
Printed and bound in Italy by L.E.G.O. S.p.A.

MIX
Paper from responsible sources
FSC www.fsc.org FSC® C023419

  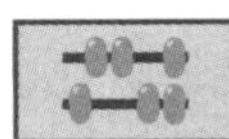   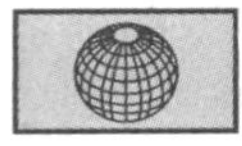   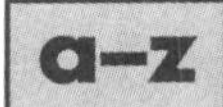

Contents

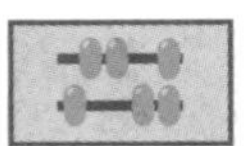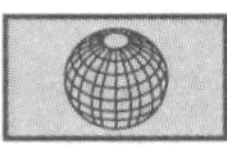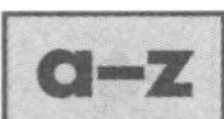

Financial Regulation and Compliance

Funding and Investment

     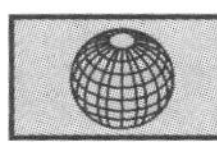   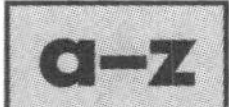
a–z

  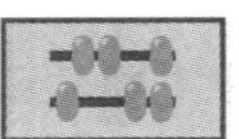         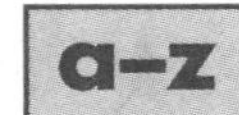

        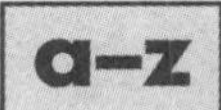

a–z

  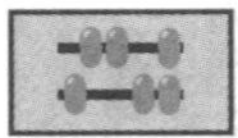      

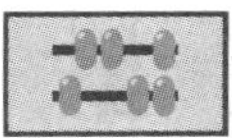

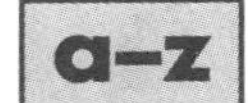
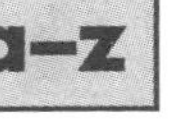
a–z

     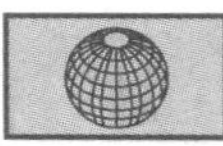   

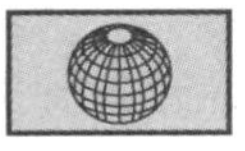

COUNTRY AND SECTOR PROFILES

Country Profiles

  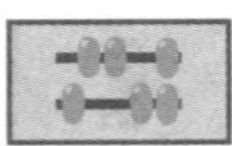      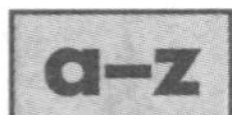
a–z

a–z

     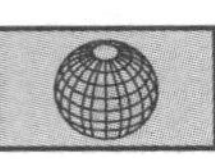   

Foreword

by HE Yousef Hussain Kamal, Minister of Economy and Finance of the State of Qatar and Chairman of the Qatar Financial Centre Authority

The world of finance is changing dramatically, but despite its current challenges finance remains the bedrock of global development. Never in this generation's lifetime has best financial practice needed to be reinforced so clearly.

Qatar Finance: The Ultimate Resource (*QFINANCE*) is a project of immense dimensions and scope. It combines the vast experience and knowledge of some 300 experts in the world of finance and provides a wealth of examples of best practice, an understanding of basic and applied principles of finance, and a financial reference point on which users can depend.

The State of Qatar, through the Qatar Financial Centre Authority, is proud to partner Bloomsbury Publishing in the creation of *QFINANCE*. This project reflects everything that Qatar is striving for as a nation. It is progressive in that it gives to the world of finance a platform of knowledge that does not exist in one place anywhere else. It is reliable in that those who have supported *QFINANCE* and contributed to it as it has come into being are all recognized as experts in their respective fields. And it is educational, to ensure that this and future generations have the best sources of learning at their disposal.

As a young but dynamic country, Qatar represents the future. We are investing in our financial sector to help us develop Qatar into an economy that is fully diversified and which can sustain itself for generations to come. The contribution that we believe *QFINANCE* will make to the world's financial practitioners, students, and commentators is a gift which we believe goes well beyond the investment we have made in it.

        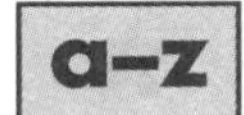

Advisory Panel

HE Sheikh Hamad bin Jabor bin Jassim Al-Thani was appointed director-general of the General Secretariat for Development Planning (GSDP) and acting chairman of the Qatar Statistics Authority in 2007. At GSDP, Sheikh Hamad is in charge of day-to-day management and, with the secretary-general, provides leadership on strategic direction. Sheikh Hamad also takes a keen interest in GSDP's project work and has played an instrumental role in projects such as the KBE and SMEs projects. Sheikh Hamad serves as a member of the board of directors of Hamad Medical Corporation, Qatar Chemical Company, Qatar Electricity and Water Company, Qatar National Bank, and ictQatar. He is also a member of the board of trustees of Qatar University, chairman of the Permanent Population Committee, a member of the governing board for the UNESCO Institute for Statistics, and a deputy chairman of the AIDS Control Committee. Previously, Sheikh Hamad was the secretary-general of the Planning Council for four years, which had the responsibility for planning Qatar's social and economic policies. Sheikh Hamad earned his managerial skills from working at Qatar Petroleum for fifteen years, including a position as a Manager of Human Resources and Director of Administration.

Zvi Bodie is professor of finance and economics at Boston University School of Management. He holds a PhD from the Massachusetts Institute of Technology, has served on the finance faculty at the Harvard Business School and MIT's Sloan School of Management, and is a member of the Pension Research Council of the Wharton School, University of Pennsylvania. Professor Bodie has published widely on pension finance and investment strategy in leading professional journals. His books include *The Foundations of Pension Finance*, *Pensions in the US Economy*, *Issues in Pension Economics*, and *Financial Aspects of the US Pension System*. His textbook *Investments* is the market leader and is used in the certification programs of the Financial Planning Association and the Society of Actuaries. His textbook *Finance* is coauthored by Nobel Prize-winning economist Robert C. Merton. His latest book is *Worry-Free Investing: A Safe Approach to Achieving Your Lifetime Financial Goals*.

Ian Cormack is a senior non-executive director at the Pearl Group, a non-executive director at the Qatar Financial Centre Authority (QFCA), and a non-executive director of Bloomsbury Publishing. He was a senior partner in Cormack Tansey Partners, a strategic consulting firm for financial institutions, from 2003 to 2005. He was chief executive officer of AIG, Inc's insurance financial services and asset management in Europe from 1997 to 2000, chairman of Citibank International plc, and co-head of the Global Financial Institutions Client Group at Citigroup. He was also country head of Citicorp in the UK from 1992 to 1996. He now holds a number of non-executive positions with various companies (public and private) and charities in the UK and abroad.

Florence Eid, PhD, is managing director for MENA at Passport Capital, having previously been vice president and senior economist for MENA at JP Morgan and professor of finance and economics at the American University of Beirut. She has worked for the World Bank, the Ford Foundation, and with Save the Children.

Hatem El-Karanshawy is the founding dean of the Qatar Faculty of Islamic Studies (QFIS). His efforts have been instrumental in building the faculty from the ground up. He came to QFIS after a long and distinguished career both in academia and policy. Before joining QFIS, Dr El-Karanshawy was professor of finance and director of the Public Administration Program at the American University in Cairo. He was also dean at the Faculty of Commerce in Al Azhar University. Dr El-Karanshawy was also a member of the board of directors of the Central Bank of Egypt. He continues to advise extensively on Islamic finance and economic development. In addition to advising the Prime Minister of Egypt and other senior cabinet members, he has contributed to negotiations with the World Bank, the African Development Bank, the International Monetary Fund, and the US State Department.

Robert Gray is chairman of Debt Finance & Advisory at HSBC Bank. He joined HSBC in 1994 as chairman of HSBC Markets Ltd, with particular responsibility for developing HSBC's capital markets capabilities globally. In 1999, he was appointed vice chairman of Client Development at HSBC Investment Bank, and to his current position in March 2001. Prior to joining HSBC, Gray was head of JP Morgan's capital markets (Europe). Previously he was president and Tokyo branch manager of JP Morgan Securities Asia Ltd. He also headed JP Morgan's worldwide loan syndication group and was responsible for their Eurobond underwriting activities.

Hasung Jang is a professor of finance and an executive director of the Asian Institute of Corporate Governance at Korea University. Since 1996, Professor Jang has been the leader of a minority shareholder activist's civil group (PSPD) in Korea and has been at the forefront of improving the corporate governance in Korea. In recognition of his contributions, he, with two other distinguished figures, Sir Adrian Cadbury and Ira Millstein, was given the first Annual Award from the International Corporate Governance Network (ICGN) in July 2001. The *Financial Times* selected him as one of five "prominent figures in the world of corporate governance" in December 2004, and *Business Week* recognized him by placing him among the Asian Star 50 in 1998 and 1999. He and his group were given the Economic Justice Citizen's Award in 1998.

Robert C. Merton is currently the School of Management Distinguished Professor of Finance at the MIT Sloan School of Management. After receiving a PhD in Economics from the Massachusetts Institute of Technology (MIT) in 1970, he served on the finance faculty of MIT's Sloan School of Management until 1988 when he moved to Harvard. Professor Merton is past President of the American Finance Association, a member of the National Academy of Sciences, and a Fellow of the American Academy of Arts and Sciences. He received the Alfred Nobel Memorial Prize in the Economic Sciences in 1997.

Jim O'Neill is chairman of Goldman Sachs Asset Management, having been head of global economics research since 2001. In this role, he oversees the firm's economic research globally. He joined Goldman Sachs in 1995 as a partner, co-head of Global Economics and Chief Currency Economist. Prior to this, he was head of research at Swiss Bank Corporation (SBC), which he joined in 1988 to set up the fixed income research group in London. O'Neill moved to Goldman Sachs from International Treasury Management, a division of Marine Midland Bank and worked for a brief spell at Bank of America in 1983. O'Neill received his PhD in 1982 from the University of Surrey after graduating in economics from Sheffield University in 1978.

Michael K. Ong is the director of the finance program at Illinois Institute of Technology. He was executive vice president and chief

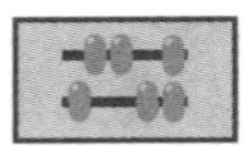

risk officer for Credit Agricole Indosuez in New York, where he held enterprise-wide responsibility for all risk management functions for corporate banking, merchant banking, asset management, capital markets activities, and the Carr Futures Group. He was a member of the executive committee and chaired the Risk Management Committee, Credit Committee, Market Risk Committee, Equity Investment Committee, and the Operational Risk Committee. Dr Ong was also head of Enterprise Risk Management for ABN-AMRO Bank. He was responsible for management information and decision support function for the Executive Committee regarding enterprise-wide market, credit, operational, and liquidity risk, as well as RAROC, ROE, and related optimization models. Previously, Dr Ong was head of the Corporate Research Unit for First Chicago NBD Corporation (now Bank One).

Sir John Stuttard has spent his career with accountants PricewaterhouseCoopers, and is now deputy chairman of the firm's advisory board. He has focused on auditing, acquisitions, stock exchange listings, and privatizations for UK, US, and Scandinavian companies. He was made a Knight, and then a Commander, of the Order of the Lion of Finland and has been chairman of the Finnish-British Chamber of Commerce. He served in the Cabinet Office for two years and spent five years in China as PwC executive chairman. He has also been a director of the China Britain Business Council. He is currently pro-chancellor of City University London, a trustee of Charities Aid Foundation and of Morden College, a governor of King Edward's School Witley and on the board of other charities. He served as Sheriff of London in 2005–2006 and Lord Mayor in 2006–2007.

Jackson Tai was made a member of the supervisory board at ING in 2008, and has served as a director of NYSE Euronext since April 2010. He is former vice chairman and CEO of DBS Group Holdings and former managing director in the Investment Banking Division of JP Morgan, where he held senior management positions in New York, Tokyo and San Francisco. He also holds a number of non-directorships including MasterCard Incorporated, CapitaLand, and non-executive chairman of Brookstone, Inc. He is a member of the Bloomberg Asia-Pacific Advisory Board, Harvard Business School Asia-Pacific Advisory Board and a trustee of Rensselaer Polytechnic Institute.

Laura Tyson is the S. K. and Angela Chan professor of global management at the Haas Business and Public Policy Group at UCLA, and is a member of President Obama's Economic Recovery Advisory Board. Professor Tyson was dean of the London Business School from January 2002 to 2006, and was previously dean of the Walter A. Haas School of Business at the University of California, Berkeley, where she had been professor of economics and business administration. Professor Tyson served in the Clinton administration from 1993 to 1996. Between February 1995 and December 1996 she served as the President's National Economic Adviser and was the highest-ranking woman in the Clinton White House. A key architect of President Clinton's domestic and international policy agenda during his first term in office, she also served as a member of the President's National Security Council and Domestic Policy Council. Prior to this appointment Laura Tyson was the sixteenth chairman of the White House Council of Economic Advisers, the first woman to hold that post.

  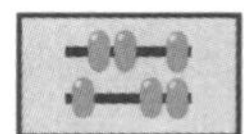      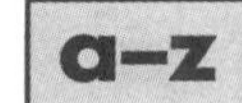

Publishing, Editorial, and Production Staff

Chief Executive
Nigel Newton

Publisher
Kathy Rooney

Project Director
Conrad Gardner

Project Manager
Ben Hickling

Senior Production Controller
Paul Nash

Database Manager
Martin Dowling

Consultant Editor
Amarendra Swarup

Commissioning Editors
Ian Fraser
Conrad Gardner
Anthony Harrington
Wendy Morris
Tim Penn
Stuart Rutherford
Dave Stauffer
Amarendra Swarup

Marketing Manager
Sophia Blackwell

Copy Editors
Romilly Hambling
Corinne Orde
Paul Lewis
Claire Annals
Louise Bolotin
Adèle Linderholm
Val Rice
Deborah Smith
Frances Worlock

Proofreaders
Sheila Cameron
Ann Ridgway
Corinne Orde
Lisa Cordaro
Nathan Joyce
Joel Simons
Oli Lurie

Other Contributors and Advisers

Checklists
Anthony Beachey
Michael Beachey
Louise Bolotin
David Thomson
Anca Toma-Thomson

Calculations and Ratios
Sally Whittle

Finance Thinkers and Leaders
Laurie Donaldson
Stuart Rutherford
Lauren Mills

Finance Library
Laurie Donaldson
Anthony Beachey
Stuart Rutherford
Lauren Mills

Country and Sector Profiles
Whitaker's Almanack
Anthony Beachey
Anthony Harrington

Finance Information Sources
Laurie Donaldson
Chartered Management Institute

Quotations
Market House Books

Dictionary
Susan Jellis
Lesley Brown
John Butler
Faye Carney
John Y. Fishman
Stephen Handorf
Marcus Johnson
Julie Plier
David Pritchard
Howard Sargeant
Ruth Hillmore
Sandra Anderson

Referees
Habib Ahmed
Manzurul Alam
Seth Armitage
Buddy Baker
Ruth Bender
Paul Beretz
R. Brayton Bowen
Janusz Brzeszczyński
Terry Carroll
David Coderre
Andrew Cox
Paul Davies
Shane Edwards
John Ferry
Jonathan Fletcher
Norman Goldstein
Ashish Gupta
Kamal Hassan
Andrew Higson
Hylmum Izhar
Andy Jobst
Vijyata Kirpalani
Leslie Kossoff
Vinod Lall
Tanja Maffei
Roger Mattar
Tom McKaig
Nigel Morgan
John Mosher
Kristian Niemietz
Martin O'Donovan
Justin Oliver
Emilia Onyema
Jeremy Phillips
Ramesh Pillai
Bilal Rasul
David Sadtler
Olgun Fuat Sahin
Shireen Smith
Gabriel Stein
Pearl Tan Hock Neo
Siri Terjesen
Steve Wallace
Véronique Weets
Juergen Weiss
Lawrence White
Suzanne White
Priscilla Wisner

  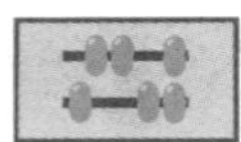      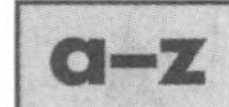

Contributor Biographies

Georgia Aarons currently leads strategy and business development for Halpern, one of London's leading communications consultancies. Prior to joining Halpern, she spent six years working as a recruitment and talent management consultant for Wall Street investment banks. Aarons has worked with Professor Argenti and Dartmouth's Tuck School of Business on consulting and training programs for clients such as Shell, Novartis, Freddie Mac, and Citibank. She holds an undergraduate degree from Columbia University and a graduate degree from the University of Cambridge.

Reena Aggarwal is the Robert E. McDonough professor of business and professor of finance at Georgetown University's McDonough School of Business in Washington, DC. She specializes in international stock markets, demutualization of stock exchanges, initial public offerings, international investments by mutual funds, and international corporate governance and market valuation. She has been named among "outstanding faculty" in the *Business Week Guide to the Best Business Schools*. She is also a faculty associate of the Capital Markets Research Center. Dr Aggarwal is a frequent guest on local and international radio and television stations. Her research and comments have been cited in the *Wall Street Journal*, the *Washington Post*, *Business Week*, and the *Financial Times*, among other media outlets.

Andrew Ainsworth is a lecturer in the finance discipline at the University of Sydney Business School. He received a bachelor of economics degree with first-class honours from the University of Western Australia, and a master of finance and PhD from the University of New South Wales. He has previously worked at the Reserve Bank of Australia. His current research interests include investments, the role of information in fixed income and equity markets, ex-dividend trading behavior, and market microstructure.

Amjid Ali, senior manager at HSBC Amanah Global is recognized as one of the most influential Muslims in the United Kingdom by the Muslim Power 100 awards, and has 22 years of branch banking experience with Midland Bank and HSBC in the United Kingdom. He joined HSBC Amanah UK in 2003 as senior business development manager, and took over as UK head in January 2005 with responsibility for strategy, distribution, and sales. He was appointed as senior manager, HSBC Amanah Global, in August 2008, where he works as part of the HSBC Amanah central team headquartered in Dubai.

Paul A. Argenti has taught management, corporate communication, and corporate responsibility starting in 1977 at the Harvard Business School, from 1979 to 1981 at the Columbia Business School, and since 1981 at Dartmouth's Tuck School of Business. He is currently faculty director for Tuck's Leadership and Strategic Impact Program and its custom executive programs for Novartis. His latest book (coauthored with Courtney Barnes) is *Digital Strategies* and he is currently working on the sixth edition of his *Corporate Communication* textbook. Professor Argenti is a Fulbright scholar and winner of the 2007 Pathfinder Award from the Institute for Public Relations. He has consulted and run training programs for many companies, including General Electric, ING, Sony, Novartis, and Goldman Sachs.

Mehmet Asutay is senior lecturer in Middle East and Islamic political economy and finance at the School of Government and International Affairs, Durham University. He teaches and supervises masters and doctoral research on various aspects of Islamic economics, banking, and finance; economies of the Middle East and Muslim countries; and political economy and economic development related subjects. He is a co-director of the Durham Islamic Finance Programme and course director of the MA/MSc in Islamic finance at the Durham Islamic finance summer school. He is managing editor of the *Review of Islamic Economics*, and associate editor of the *American Journal of Islamic Social Sciences*. He has published articles and books on Islamic moral economy and finance, and on issues in Turkish and Middle Eastern political economy.

Philipp Bagus is a professor of economics at King Juan Carlos University in Madrid. He is also assistant editor of the journal *Procesos de Mercado: Revista Europea de Economía Política*. His main research areas are monetary theory and business cycle theory. He has published articles in numerous academic journals and other scholarly outlets. Bagus is author of *The Tragedy of the Euro* and, with David Howden, of *Deep Freeze: Iceland's Economic Collapse*.

Angela Baron is a chartered member of the Chartered Institute of Personnel and Development (CIPD), for which she is currently an adviser on organization and resourcing. She has been responsible for numerous research programs including corporate culture, psychological testing, counseling in the workplace, performance management, HR strategy and recruitment practice. Her current research covers investigating the underlying links between people management, productivity, and profitability. She is also steering work on human capital, developing measures and reporting systems for practitioners. Baron has coauthored a number of books in the field, including *The Job Evaluation Handbook* and *Strategic HRM*.

Paul Barrett is AIG's EMEA chief operating officer for ERM. He is responsible for the risk management operations in the company, with a central analytics and governance team, plus risk officers reporting to him from key countries and hubs across EMEA. He has been leading on the development of the ORSA, Risk Appetite Framework, Risk Register, and governance processes, and leads the independent validation exercise for the internal model. Until July 2013 he also fulfilled the role as head of operational risk for AIG Europe. Previously he was assistant director, Solvency II at the Association of British Insurers. Prior to that he worked at the Financial Services Authority.

Wim Bartels has been global head of KPMG's sustainability services network since October 2007. He studied business economics and accountancy at Amsterdam's Vrije Universiteit before qualifying as a chartered accountant in 1993. In 2001 he became a KPMG partner with overall responsibility for the group's sustainability services, including the provision of sustainability assurance services to multinational businesses such as BASF, DSM, Heineken, KLM, Philips, and Rabobank. Bartels is closely involved with the UN's Global Reporting Initiative, and he sits on the council of AccountAbility. In his spare time he sings and plays trumpet in a band that performs cover versions of 1970s and 1980s hits and which performs for good causes.

Ilias G. Basioudis is senior lecturer in financial accounting and auditing at Aston Business School. He is also chairman of the Auditing Special Interest Group of the British Accounting Association, a fellow of the UK Academy of Higher Education, and an adjunct senior lecturer at the University of South Australia. Dr Basioudis has published widely in academic and professional journals and his textbook Financial Accounting: a Practical Introduction is recently published by Pearson. His research interests lie primarily in the area of empirical auditing, corporate governance, and accounting education. He is a member of various international accounting associations and is on the editorial board of the *International Journal of Auditing*.

Jeremy Beckwith joined Kleinwort Benson in April 2003 as chief investment officer and is responsible for all aspects of the investment process and investment performance of discretionary portfolios. He introduced

  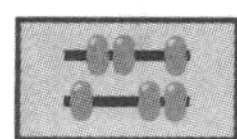      

multi-asset class investing to Kleinwort Benson and is regularly invited on to Bloomberg TV to give his views on markets and economics. Prior to this, he was a managing director and head of EAFE Equities (non-US equities for American retail and institutional clients) at Merrill Lynch Investment Managers. Before joining the EAFE team in 1988 he was managing director of Merrill Lynch Global Asset Management, managing the portfolios of high net worth private clients and small institutions from Europe and the Middle East, and also chaired the Global Investment Committee. Prior to 1990 he was head of equities for Mitsubishi Finance International and a portfolio manager for Manufacturers Life Insurance Company. From 2006 to 2008 he was chairman of the FTSE Private Banking Index Advisory Board, and was named on the Citywealth Private Banking Leaders List for 2008.

Ruth Bender is a senior lecturer at Cranfield School of Management. She joined the faculty in 1994, having completed her MBA there. Prior to this she was a partner in Grant Thornton, where latterly she specialized in corporate finance, including a time on secondment as a private equity investment manager in the City of London. She is a chartered accountant, and was a committee member of the Institute of Chartered Accountants in England and Wales' Faculty of Finance and Management. Other outside roles have included non-executive directorships of a health authority and an NHS trust. Bender's main teaching areas include financial strategy, working capital management, and corporate governance. Her doctorate is in corporate governance.

Samy Ben Naceur is associate professor of finance at ESSEC Tunis. Ben Naceur is a consultant in finance and economics and has previously worked with the Economic Research Forum, the European Union, and the World Bank. He was previously associate professor of finance at Bouabdelli University, Tunisia. Ben Naceur's main areas of academic research cover accounting, financial structure, corporate valuation, and economics, with particular emphasis on Middle Eastern and North African financial markets.

Barruch Ben-Zekry is a manager in Ernst & Young LLP's Americas climate change and sustainability services practice with expertise in strategy, carbon footprinting, energy management, environmental performance improvement, and lifecycle analysis. Prior to joining Ernst & Young, Barruch was the manager of environmental sustainability at Levi Strauss & Co. based at its San Francisco, CA, headquarters. Ben-Zekry holds a BS in environmental economics and policy from the University of California, Berkeley.

Paul Beretz, CICE (Certified International Credit Executive), is managing director of Pacific Business Solutions, Clayton, CA, a company he created in 1999. In addition, he is a partner of Q2C (Quote to Cash) Solutions. He brings over 30 years of global management experience in telecommunications, semiconductors, forest products, and chemicals. His faculty postings include St Mary's College, California (MA in leadership), University of California, Berkeley, Michigan State University, and Dartmouth College. He has designed and facilitates online courses in international credit and general business. He currently serves on the advisory committee of the Export–Import Bank of the United States.

Harold Bierman, Jr, is Nicholas H. Noyes professor of business administration at the Johnson Graduate School of Management, Cornell University, New York. Professor Bierman's interests are in investment and corporate financial policy decisions. He has consulted for many public organizations and industrial firms and is the author of more than 150 books and articles in the fields of accounting, finance, investment, taxation, and quantitative analysis. In 1985 he was named winner of the prestigious Dow Jones Award of the American Assembly of Collegiate Schools of Business for his outstanding contributions to collegiate management education.

Keith Black is associate director of curriculum, CAIA Association, Massachusetts, USA. He was formerly an associate of Ennis Knupp + Associates, a member of the opportunistic strategies group, advising foundations, endowments, and pension funds on their asset allocation and manager selection strategies in the alternative investment space. His professional experience prior to this includes commodities derivatives trading at First Chicago Capital Markets, stock options research and trading for Hull Trading Company, building stock selection models for Chicago Investment Analytics, and teaching finance at the Illinois Institute of Technology. He has earned the Chartered Financial Analyst (CFA) and the Chartered Alternative Investment Analyst (CAIA) designations. Black is the author of the book *Managing a Hedge Fund*.

Björn Bloching is a senior partner at Roland Berger Strategy Consultants where he is responsible for global business in the areas of marketing and sales, and retail and consumer goods. Besides brand management, quantitative marketing, and sales strategies, his consulting focuses on a range of topics from creative urban development and tourism to projects involving culture, education, academia, and professional sports. Professor Bloching has dealt extensively with data and their use, including writing the book *In Data We Trust*.

Lena Booth is associate professor of finance at the Thunderbird School of Global Management and served as the first executive director of the Thunderbird Private Equity Center (TPEC). Dr Booth has been a member of the Thunderbird faculty since 1995 and has taught and presented research in many countries around the world. Her research interests lie mainly in capital raising and security issuance by firms, with the primary focus on initial public offerings. She has received several teaching and research awards during her tenure at Thunderbird. Born and raised in Malaysia, Dr Booth holds a BBA from the National University of Singapore, an MBA from Northern Arizona University, and a PhD (finance) from Arizona State University.

R. Brayton Bowen is author of *Recognizing and Rewarding Employees* (McGraw-Hill) and leads the Howland Group, a strategy consulting and change management firm committed to "building better worlds of work." His documentary series *Anger in the Workplace*, distributed to public radio nationally in the United States, continues to be regarded as a benchmark study on the subject of workplace issues and change. A *Best Practice* editor and contributing author to the hallmark work *Business: The Ultimate Resource* (Bloomsbury Publishing and Perseus Books), he has written for *MWorld*, the online magazine of the American Management Association. He currently serves as executive adviser for the Center for Business Excellence at McKendree University.

Paul Brain is investment leader of the fixed-income team at Newton Investment Management. He joined Newton in 2004, and manages a range of global bond funds. He is also the lead manager of Newton's global dynamic bond strategy. Paul is chairman of the bond/foreign exchange strategy group and is a member of the macro strategy group and the investment committee. He has held a number of senior fixed-income positions within the industry and has acquired a wide breadth of knowledge and experience in managing fixed-income portfolios. As head of retail fixed income at Investec (formerly Guinness Flight), Paul led the team that won the International Money Marketing "Fixed Interest Manager of the Year" award in 2000.

Stavros Brekoulakis, LLB (Athens), LLM (London), and PhD (London) is a lecturer in international dispute resolution. Dr Brekoulakis lectures at Queen Mary, University of London, on the Master of Laws (LLM) courses on international comparative and commercial arbitration, international commercial construction, international commercial litigation, and conflict of laws. He is also academic director of the diploma course (taught by distance learning) on international arbitration. His academic research focuses on international commercial arbitration, conflict

  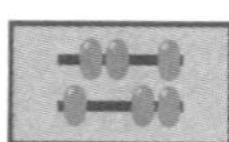      

of laws, multiparty and complex dispute resolution, issues on jurisdiction of tribunals and national courts, and enforcement of awards and national judgments. He is a member of the Athens Bar, having practiced shipping law and dispute resolution.

Ian Bremmer is the founder and president of Eurasia Group, a leading global political risk research and consulting firm. He created Wall Street's first global political risk index, and has authored several books, including *Every Nation for Itself: Winners and Losers in a G-Zero World* (2012), on risks and opportunities in a world without global leadership, and *The J Curve: A New Way to Understand Why Nations Rise and Fall*, which *The Economist* named one of the best books of 2006. He contributes to the *Financial Times* A-List, Reuters.com, and ForeignPolicy.com. Bremmer has a PhD in political science from Stanford University (1994), and he teaches at Columbia University. His analysis focuses on global macro political trends and emerging markets.

David Bresch has headed the sustainability unit at Swiss Re since 2008. His previous roles there include head of university and risk research relations, head of atmospheric perils group, and chief modeler for natural catastrophe risk assessment. He has been member of the deal teams for many innovative risk transfer transactions, like cat bonds and weather index solutions. He has been a member of the official Swiss delegation to the UNFCCC climate negotiations in Copenhagen (2009), Cancun (2010), Durban (2011), and Doha (2012). He is a member of the adaptation board of the global network for climate solutions of the Earth Institute at Columbia University, a steering committee member of ProClim, and a member of the advisory board of the INSEAD energy club. He holds a PhD in physics from the Swiss Federal Institute of Technology (ETH) and lectures on the economics of climate adaptation there.

Lawrence Brotzge's business background includes 11 years with Ernst & Young, 10 years as corporate controller and CFO for two major divisions of Providian Corp (a Fortune 500 financial services company), and five years as a founder of a corporate venturing project, which resulted in Providian establishing an entirely new business. Since 1994, Brotzge has been an independent consultant and an angel investor. He has an ownership position in several small/start-up businesses and consults with a number of other companies.

Janusz Brzeszczynski is a senior lecturer in the Department of Accountancy, Economics and Finance at Heriot-Watt University, Edinburgh, and specializes in international finance, financial markets, and financial econometrics. Before joining Heriot-Watt, he held a Fulbright scholarship in the United States and worked as a visiting professor in the Department of Economics, Arizona State University. He was also a visiting scholar at the Swiss Institute of Banking and Finance, University of St Gallen, Switzerland, and assistant/associate professor at the Chair of Econometric Models and Forecasts, University of Lodz, Poland. Besides the Fulbright scholarship, he was also awarded an ESKAS post-doctoral scholarship at the Swiss Institute of Banking and Finance and a DAAD doctoral scholarship at Kiel University, Germany. Dr Brzeszczynski has published in a number of finance journals.

Daniel Byrne is a risk analyst within the ERM department at AIG Europe Ltd. He specializes in developing and embedding key aspects of AIG Europe's risk management framework, including Risk Appetite, Own Risk and Solvency Assessment, Internal Model Uses, and Stress and Scenario Testing. Prior to this role he was the lead subject matter expert for the AIG Solvency II program. He had previously worked on the FSA Solvency II program, implementing Solvency II into the Supervisory Framework. He holds a BSc in economics from the London School of Economics.

Sir Adrian Cadbury studied economics at Cambridge before joining the Cadbury business in 1952. He became chairman of Cadbury Ltd in 1965 and retired as chairman of Cadbury Schweppes in 1989. He was chairman of the UK Committee on the Financial Aspects of Corporate Governance, which published its *Report and Code of Best Practice* in December 1992. Sir Adrian received the International Corporate Governance Network Award in 2001. His book, *Corporate Governance and Chairmanship—A Personal View*, was published by Oxford University Press in 2002 and has been translated into Japanese, Chinese, and Italian. In 2005 he was awarded the Laureate Medal for Corporate Governance.

Mark Camp is director of institutional liquidity funds for Henderson Global Investors, where he is responsible for marketing a comprehensive range of such funds. He was formerly a business development manager for AIM Global money market funds, part of the Amvescap Group. Camp joined the Amvescap Group soon after its inception and made a significant contribution to getting money market funds accepted for regulatory purposes for the insurance and public sectors. Before that, he worked for over 10 years in the UK insurance market with banking and investment responsibilities.

Janet Campagna is the CEO of QS Investors, a 100% employee-owned, majority woman-owned investment management company based in New York and founded in 2010. Prior to founding QS Investors, Janet was a managing director at Deutsche Asset Management serving as the global head of quantitative strategies and a member of the global operating committee. She was a principal at Barclays Global Investors (1994–99) and an associate at First Quadrant and director of asset allocation research (1989–94). She is a board member of the Mott Haven Academy in the South Bronx, a charter school for at-risk students in the foster care and child welfare system, and a member of the MFE Steering Committee for the Haas Business School, UC Berkeley. Janet has a BS from Northeastern University, an MS from California Institute of Technology, and a PhD from the University of California, Irvine, in 1990.

Laurie Carroll is executive vice president and the global short-duration strategist for BNY Mellon Cash Investment Strategies (CIS), a division of the Dreyfus Corporation. Carroll is responsible for the global strategic direction and product development for the short-duration products of CIS. She is an active member of CIS's fiduciary risk committee and has over 29 years of industry experience. Her career at BNY Mellon spans 24 years, during which she has held positions of increasing responsibility for a number of company affiliates. Most recently, she served as managing director of short-duration, index, and stable value strategies for Standish Mellon Asset Management, a BNY Mellon company. Carroll has an MBA from the University of Pittsburgh and a BA from Seton Hill University. She is a member of the board of trustees of Seton Hill University.

Terry Carroll headed up corporate finance and advisory services for Broadhead Peel Rhodes, following a highly successful career as finance director and CEO of a range of businesses. He was also for some years a business and financial consultant, working especially with SMEs and growing businesses. A qualified banker, corporate treasurer, and chartered accountant who trained with KPMG, Carroll has experience of many different corporate finance projects, including banking, financing, business restructuring, mergers and acquisitions, MBO/MBI, and venture and private capital. With five books and scores of published articles, he is also an established business author.

Susan Cartwright is professor of organizational psychology and well-being and director of Centre for Organizational Health and Well-Being, having previously been a professor at Manchester Business School. She worked in industry for 12 years before joining the Manchester School of Management (now MBS) in 1987, where she completed a master's degree in 1988 and a PhD in 1990, which was supported by an ESRC competitive scholarship. Professor Cartwright is a fellow of

     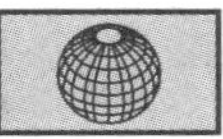   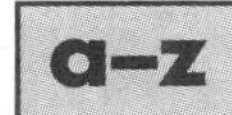

the British Academy of Management, of which she is currently president. She has been an associate editor of the *British Journal of Management* for more than seven years, is a past editor of the *Leadership & Organization Development Journal*, and is the recipient of the first Meritous Reviewer Award presented by Human Relations.

Richard E. Cascarino is CEO of Richard Cascarino & Associates, based in Colorado, with over 26 years' experience in audit training and consultancy. Well known in international auditing circles as one of the most knowledgeable practitioners in the field, he is a regular speaker at national and international conferences and has presented courses throughout Africa, Europe, the Middle East, and the United States. He is a past president of the Institute of Internal Auditors (IIA) in South Africa, was the founding regional director of the Southern African Region of the IIA, and is a member of ISACA and the American Institute of Certified Fraud Examiners. He is also a visiting lecturer at the University of the Witwatersrand.

Peter Casson is a senior lecturer in accounting at the School of Management of the University of Southampton. He graduated with BTech and PhD degrees in psychology from Brunel University and an MSc in occupational psychology from Birkbeck College, University of London. He is a fellow of the Institute of Chartered Accountants in England and Wales. After holding a number of research posts in psychology, he trained as a chartered accountant before starting an academic career in accounting. His research interests are mainly in accounting for financial instruments, stock option compensation, corporate governance, and company taxation.

James Chadwick qualified as a chartered accountant in 2003 and is a member of the Institute of Chartered Accountants of Scotland. In 2004 he joined Grant Thornton, where he has performed a number of different roles and undertaken a six-month secondment into industry. In January 2011 he became associate director and head of Grant Thornton's audit practice for the Scottish region. Chadwick has a wide and varied client base that includes some of Scotland's highest-profile businesses across a number of different sectors. He is head of the food and drink team for Scotland.

Andrew Chambers works for Management Audit LLP advising on corporate governance and internal auditing, and is also a professor at London South Bank and Birmingham City universities. Described in an editorial in The Times (September 15, 2006) as "a worldwide authority on corporate governance," until 2010 he chaired the Corporate Governance and Risk Management Committee of the Association of Chartered Certified Accountants. Professor Chambers was dean of what is now the Cass Business School, London where he is professor emeritus. He is a member of The Institute of Internal Auditors' international Internal Audit Standards Board.

Moorad Choudhry is managing director, head of business treasury, global banking and markets at Royal Bank of Scotland, UK. He was formerly head of treasury at Europe Arab Bank in London, prior to that head of treasury at KBC Financial Products, and has worked at JP Morgan Chase, ABN Amro Hoare Govett, and Hambros Bank. Dr Choudhry is visiting professor at the Department of Economics, London Metropolitan University, visiting research fellow at the ICMA Centre, University of Reading, and a fellow of the Securities and Investment Institute. He is on the editorial board of the *Journal of Structured Finance*.

Yves Choueifaty built TOBAM in 2006, when he was managing director, head of Lehman Brothers's quantitative asset management business in Europe. He was also previously head of Lehman Brothers Asset Management France. Prior to joining Lehman Brothers, he was CEO of Credit Lyonnais Asset Management (CLAM), with assets under management of €70 billion. Mr Choueifaty graduated in 1992 from ENSAE in statistics, actuarial studies, finance, and artificial intelligence.

Subir Chowdhury is chairman and CEO of ASI Consulting Group, LLC. A respected quality strategist, Chowdhury's clients include global Fortune 100 companies as well as small organizations in both the public and private sectors. He is the author of 12 books and has received numerous international awards for leadership in quality management and major contributions to various industries worldwide. He has a graduate degree in aerospace engineering from the Indian Institute of Technology, Kharagpur, a postgraduate degree in industrial management from Central Michigan University, and an honorary doctorate in engineering from Michigan Technological University. Chowdhury is frequently cited in national and international media.

Diana Choyleva joined the World Service at Lombard Street Research (LSR) in 2000 after graduating with a master's degree in economics from the University of Warwick. She was promoted to the position of director and head of the UK Service in 2005. Choyleva's work covers global issues, with a particular focus on the United Kingdom and Chinese economies. In 2006 she published her first book, *The Bill from the China Shop*, coauthored with Charles Dumas. She has also specialized in research on monetary and financial flows, and her work on estimating potential output and output gaps is the basis for producing LSR's proprietary global leading indicators. Choyleva's research has been extensively quoted in the international press and she gives regular TV and radio interviews.

Denise Cicchella is a recognized expert in construction audit, protecting owners from the overpayment of construction costs due to fraud, error, or negligence by contractors. She is a Certified Internal Auditor, Certified Fraud Examiner, Certified Construction Auditor, and Project Management Professional, and a fellow of the Life Management Institute. She holds an MBA in international business from Fairleigh Dickinson University and a BBA in accounting from Loyola University. She is president of the New York/New Jersey Chapter of the National Association of Construction Auditors. Cicchella is author of the Institute of Internal Auditor's handbook *Construction Audit Guide: Overview, Monitoring, and Auditing*.

Tony Clare is a pensions partner at Deloitte's North West office. He has over 22 years' experience in the sector and is an associate of the Chartered Insurance Institute and a fellow of the Pensions Management Institute. Working across all industries in both the public and private sectors, Tony leads teams advising on transactions and pensions strategy as part of overall reward reviews. He has helped many clients deal with transitions from defined benefits to defined contribution schemes, including leading negotiations with public-sector unions and employees. Tony has also led employee communication programs regarding changes to pension arrangements.

Eddie Cochrane is executive development manager at the University of Edinburgh Business School. Currently studying for a PhD in the area of emotional management, he holds the British Psychological Society Certificate of Competence in Occupational Testing (Level A & B). He delivers and manages external executive programs to corporate clients, with recent clients including RBS, NPower, BP, and Nucleus. He has featured regularly in the UK press, most recently for his work on emotional engagement in organizations. He also has responsibility for the design and delivery of leadership and management skills throughout the various MBA programs. He has 15 years' experience in HR Management where he managed a variety of HR teams in both the private and public sectors.

Andrew Cox is a corporate governance professional who currently works as an independent consultant, primarily in Australia and the United Arab Emirates. His specialty areas are internal audit, quality assessment of internal audit functions, risk management, business continuity and IT disaster recovery planning. His professional experience also covers other areas including project management, change and capacity building programs, security, strategic planning, IT planning, and industrial relations. His career

includes roles as chief audit executive at high profile organizations. He has given presentations on auditing in forums both in Australia and internationally, and has taught auditing in Australia and overseas.

Tom Coyne has been a chief investment strategist at the Index Investor since 2000. He received a BS in economics from Georgetown University and MBA from Harvard University. He began his career at Chase Manhattan Bank in South America, and for many years specialized in turnaround and growth consulting at the MAC Group in London and Bristol Partners in San Francisco. He has also been both the CFO and CEO of a publicly traded environmental technology company in Canada.

Susi Crawford is a senior associate in Clifford Chance's finance practice. She has worked on a number of projects, project financings, and financings in Europe and the Middle East and specializes in Islamic finance. She advised on the first ever *shariah*-compliant swap to use the *wa'ad* structure and continues to advise a number of financial institutions on this structure. In addition to her structured finance practice, she has been the lead associate on a number of significant Islamic finance transactions and continues to work on Islamic finance transactions that use new and innovative structures.

Henrik Cronqvist is the McMahon family chair in corporate finance, George R. Roberts fellow, and associate professor of financial economics at the Robert Day School of Economics and Finance, Claremont McKenna College (CMC), California. He received his PhD in finance from the University of Chicago. Prior to joining CMC, he served on the faculty at the Fisher College of Business, Ohio State University, where he was a recipient of the Pace Setters Research Award. His research and teaching interests are empirical corporate finance, behavioral finance, and individual investor behavior. His work has been published in the top journals in economics and finance, and based on his research he is regularly invited to give seminars at academic conferences and to policy makers, executives, and investment managers, in the United States and overseas. His research has been featured in *The Economist*, the *Financial Times*, and the *Wall Street Journal*.

Angelos Damaskos is founder and CEO of Sector Investment Managers (SIM), an FSA-authorized and regulated investment advisory company, and portfolio manager for SIM's Junior Oils Trust. Junior Oils Trust, launched in October 2004, focuses its investments in smaller oil and gas equities and grew from a launch net asset value size of £3.7 million to in excess of £67 million by February 2011. In 2009 Damaskos and SIM launched Junior Gold, an FSA-authorized and regulated open-ended investment company concentrating on gold and other precious metals mining equities. Damaskos graduated in 1985 from the University of Glasgow with a degree in mechanical engineering and in 1989 obtained a MBA from the University of Sheffield. He has more than 14 years' investment banking experience with major banks in London, concentrating on natural resources. Most recently he worked with the European Bank for Reconstruction and Development with responsibility for some of the bank's equity investments in Russia.

Aswath Damodaran is a professor of finance at the Stern School of Business at New York University, where he teaches corporate finance and equity valuation. He also teaches on the TRIUM Global Executive MBA program, an alliance of NYU Stern, the London School of Economics, and HEC School of Management. Professor Damodaran is best known as author of several widely used academic and practitioner texts on valuation, corporate finance, and investment management. He is also widely published in leading finance journals, including the *Journal of Financial and Quantitative Analysis*, the *Journal of Finance*, the *Journal of Financial Economics*, and the *Review of Financial Studies*.

Simon D'Arcy was until recently head of internal audit for a joint venture between two global banks. He began his career in internal auditing in 1986 with the UK Department of the Environment. Later he joined Abbey National, where he spent 14 years fulfilling a variety of roles. In 2003 he left Abbey National to become associate director, audit services, for the Portman Building Society, where he remained until its merger with Nationwide. D'Arcy has been a volunteer member of the Institute of Internal Auditors UK and Ireland (IIA) since 1996, and he was president of the IIA in 2007/08. He regularly speaks on a range of governance, risk management, and internal audit subjects and contributes on the same topics to professional publications and periodicals.

Rod Davidson, head of the fixed-income team at Alliance Trust Asset Management, has been managing money, teams, and businesses in the global fixed-income arena for more than 20 years. Prior to joining Alliance Trust Asset Management he held similar posts at Scottish Widows Investment Partnership, Aberdeen Asset Management, and Murray Johnstone. He specializes in managing global bond and currency portfolios and has responsibility at Alliance Trust Asset Management for macroeconomic research, duration strategy, and currency strategy.

Andy Davies joined Terra Nova in 1994 as group financial controller of Terra Nova Bermuda Holdings. In 2000 he became finance director at Markel International, with responsibility for reporting into Markel Corporation and overseeing the operations of the finance and RAO departments.

Paul Davies is managing director of Onshore Offshore Ltd. He has been responsible for a wide range of business transformation projects, whether establishing companies offshore, providing consultancy for entering offshore markets, creating the most appropriate offshoring approaches and environments, recruiting the appropriate staff and management, managing the procurement of offshore services, providing interim management, transferring contracts under employment legislation, or creating new business strategies. With a management background in the United Kingdom and India and sales and marketing experience across Europe, Dr Davies has formed a team of professionals who can address a wide range of business issues and provide solutions in management, finance, business efficiency, and global talent management.

Robert E. Davis obtained a bachelor of business administration degree in accounting and business law and an MBA in management information systems from Temple and West Chester Universities, respectively. During his 20 years of involvement in education, he acquired postgraduate and professional technical licenses in computer science and computer systems technology. He also holds Certified Information Systems Auditor (CISA) and Certified Internal Controls Auditor (CICA) certificates. Since starting his career as an information systems auditor, Davis has provided data security consulting and information systems auditing services to the US Securities and Exchange Commission, Raytheon Company, Dow Jones, and other organizations. He has authored articles addressing IT issues for the IIA, IT Governance, and ISACA, as well as writing Internet content for Techtarget.com, Toolbox.com, and Suite101.com.

Graham Dawson studied philosophy, politics, and economics at University College, Oxford, and holds a PhD in philosophy from the Keele University. He is the author of *Inflation and Unemployment: Causes, Consequences and Cures*, and of articles in journals including *Philosophy and Economics*, *Risk, Decision and Policy*, *Philosophy*, the *Review of Austrian Economics*, and *Economic Affairs*. He recently retired from the post of senior lecturer in economics at the Open University and is currently visiting fellow at the Max Beloff Centre for the Study of Liberty at the University of Buckingham.

Augusto de la Torre is the chief economist for Latin America and the Caribbean at the World Bank. Since joining the Bank in 1997, he has held the positions of senior adviser in the

Financial Systems Department and senior financial sector adviser for the Latin American and Caribbean regions. From 1993 to 1997 he was the head of the Central Bank of Ecuador, and in November 1996 *Euromoney* nominated him as the year's "Best Latin American Central Banker." From 1986 to 1992 he worked at the International Monetary Fund, where, among other positions, he was the IMF's resident representative in Venezuela (1991–1992). De la Torre has published on a broad range of macroeconomic and financial development topics. He is a member of the Carnegie Economic Reform Network.

Bert De Reyck is a professor of management science and innovation at University College London and adjunct professor at the London Business School. Previously, he held positions at the Kellogg School of Management, Northwestern University, and the Rotterdam School of Management. He is an authority on decision-making, risk management, project management, and project portfolio management. Professor De Reyck's awardwinning research has been published in numerous scientific and professional journals, and applications of his work can be found in industries such as pharmaceuticals, energy, and aerospace. He is also a multiple award-winning educator. He is a member of the Institute for Management Science and Operations Research (INFORMS), the Institute of Industrial Engineers (IIE), and the Project Management Institute (PMI).

Hernando de Soto is president of the Institute for Liberty and Democracy (ILD), headquartered in Lima, Peru. He is focused on designing and implementing capital formation programs to empower the poor in Africa, Asia, Latin America, the Middle East, and former Soviet nations. He also co-chaired the Commission on Legal Empowerment of the Poor, and currently serves as honorary co-chair on the World Justice Project. De Soto has served as an economist for the General Agreement on Tariffs and Trade, as president of the executive committee of the Copper Exporting Countries Organization (CIPEC), as CEO of Universal Engineering Corporation, as a principal of the Swiss Bank Corporation Consultant Group, and as a governor of Peru's Central Reserve Bank.

Thibault de Tersant has been executive vice president and CFO of Dassault Systèmes since joining the company in 1988 and was appointed senior executive vice-president in 2006. He is responsible for finance, investor relations, legal affairs, sales business administration, information technology, and internal controls for the company. He was elected to the board of the company in 1993 and currently holds directorships of various subsidiaries. He is also responsible for mergers and acquisitions and has conducted more than 20 successful acquisitions totaling around $2 billion over the last ten years. He oversaw Dassault Systèmes' successful initial public offering on the Paris and Nasdaq stock exchanges in 1996, as well as a secondary offering in 1997. Prior to joining the company, he served as a finance executive in export financing at Dassault Aviation from 1983 until 1988. The recipient of France's prestigious Chief Financial Officer of the Year award in 2002, de Tersant is a graduate of the ESSEC Business School and of the Institut d'Etudes Politiques de Paris.

Gary M. Deutsch is founder and president of BRT Publications LLC, a professional education and training company that has served the financial industry for over 10 years. He has written numerous publications for Sheshunoff and A. S. Pratt on topics such as risk management, credit management, asset and liability management, and accounting and internal auditing. He also consults on credit risk management and allowance for loan and lease loss regulatory compliance and accounting issues. Prior to founding BRT Publications, Deutsch worked extensively in management positions with regional financial institutions and community banks in audit, lending, financial, and operational areas. He is a licensed CPA in Maryland and has a BA in accounting and an MBA in finance from Loyola University Maryland. He holds certified management accountant, certified internal auditor, and certified bank auditor designations.

Todd DeZoort is professor of accounting and accounting advisory board fellow at the University of Alabama. He joined the university's accounting faculty in 2001 and has published 40 articles with many in top academic journals such as *Accounting, Organizations and Society*, *Contemporary Accounting Research*, *Auditing: A Journal of Practice & Theory*, *J ournal of Accounting Literature*, and *Behavioral Research in Accounting*. He also has received several research grants from the American Institute of Certified Public Accountants, KPMG's Audit Committee Institute, and the Institute of Internal Auditors. Dr DeZoort is currently a member of the AICPA's reliability task force and an advisory council member at the Academy for Ethics in Financial Reporting.

Daniel Diermeier is the IBM professor of regulation and competitive practice, a professor of managerial economics and decision sciences at the Kellogg School of Management, and a professor of political science at the Weinberg College of Arts and Sciences, all at Northwestern University. He is director of the Ford Motor Company Center for Global Citizenship and co-creator of the CEO Perspective Program (Kellogg's most senior executive education program). Professor Diermeier's work focuses on reputation management, political and regulatory risk, crisis management, and integrated strategy. He was named Kellogg Professor of the Year (2001) and received the prestigious Faculty Pioneer Award from the Aspen Institute (2007). In December 2004 he was appointed to the Management Board of the FBI.

Eric R. Dinallo has been superintendent of insurance for New York State since January 2007. During his tenure the New York State Insurance Department has been given the 2008 Esprit de Corps award by the National Association of Insurance Commissioners (NAIC) for outstanding service to state insurance regulation. He has worked with the United States Treasury Department, the Federal Reserve Bank of New York, and others in the rescue of financial services giant AIG. He is chair of the 50-state task force of the NAIC charged with safeguarding AIG insurance interests during the federal government's stewardship of the company. He has served as chair of the NAIC's Life and Annuities Committee since January 2008.

Rajiv Dogra is a diplomat by profession, an engineer by training, a writer by choice, and an artist by inclination. Currently he is based in New Delhi and is a well-known commentator and columnist. He became a member of the Indian Diplomatic Service in 1974. During the course of a wideranging professional career he was India's ambassador to Italy, Romania, Moldova, Albania, and San Marino. He was also India's permanent representative to United Nations agencies in Rome (FAO, WFP, and IFAD) and India's last full-time consul general in Karachi. He is the author of two novels, *Footprints in Foreign Sands* and *Almost an Ambassador*. Among the honors he has received is an honorary doctorate.

David A. Doney is vice-president of internal audit for SIRVA, Inc., a global moving and relocation services company, where he oversees the audit team and is the coordinator for the company's Sarbanes– Oxley (SOX) compliance efforts. Prior to SIRVA, Doney led the SOX assessment efforts for Bally Total Fitness from 2004 to 2007. He has also worked for Sears, Roebuck & Company in the internal audit and financial planning areas, and for Ingersoll-Rand Company as a financial management trainee. He is a frequent speaker at the MIS Training Institute on internal audit and SOX and gave presentations at the Institute of Internal Auditors' international conferences in 2002 and 2008. Doney is a registered Certified Public Accountant (CPA) and a Certified Internal Auditor (CIA).

Emma Du Haney is senior fixed-income product specialist on the fixed-income team at Insight Investment. Previously she worked at Henderson Global Investors as investment director. Her focus now is Insight's developing client base outside the United Kingdom,

  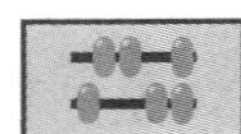      

especially in Europe. Emma has over 20 years of fixed-income experience in both fund management and product specialist roles. Before Henderson she spent most of her career at Credit Suisse Asset Management.

Sudhir Singh Dungarpur is partner and head of the development sector practice at KPMG in India. He has over 18 years' global experience working in both start-ups and large multinational corporations in the areas of technology, education, and consulting. Sudhir's strength lies in developing new businesses and he has successfully built new divisions and businesses in highly competitive environments. Building strong relationships and networks, a clear control on market dynamics, and creating the best teams has ensured that Sudhir has delivered consistent results in growth, revenue, operational performance, and profitability.

Simon Earp is director of corporate development and director of the University of Edinburgh Business School's part-time MBA program. He has a BSc Dip. Marketing and obtained his management science degree at Warwick University. In addition to running several TCS programs he has overall responsibility for TCS programs throughout the university. Prior to becoming Director of Corporate Engagement and Marketing he was a marketing lecturer in the department. His research interests include relationship marketing, customer service, marketing strategy, and marketing information systems.

Shane Edwards is managing director and global head of equity structuring at the Royal Bank of Scotland. His team has won numerous "best in country" and innovation awards and is responsible for structured products across the entire client spectrum from retail investors to large institutions and major hedge funds. Edwards's research on derivatives markets has been published in industry and academic journals, and he is frequently a speaker at derivatives conferences and interviewed by journalists. Prior to the Royal Bank of Scotland, he worked in a similar capacity and as an algorithmic trader at Deutsche Bank, Macquarie Bank, and a private hedge fund. He is one of the youngest ever winners of the Dow Jones' *Financial News* Top 100 Rising Stars in Europe Award.

Richard Ellis, Director of corporate social responsibility (CSR) at Alliance Boots Group, has spent the past 30 years working for a range of companies on all aspects of the CSR agenda. The early part of his career was spent in banking, before he became involved in CSR after the inner city riots of the early 1980s. After this involvement he held CSR-related positions at HSBC, TSB, and British Aerospace, and ran his own CSR consultancy for five years. In 2003 he joined Boots and became responsible for all of the company's CSR activities. Following the merger between Boots and Alliance UniChem and the subsequent private equity buyout, he was appointed to his current role.

Peter Elston is head of Asia-Pacific Strategy and Asset Allocation, responsible for Aberdeen's multi-asset business in the region as well as articulating and communicating investment strategy. He has lived in Asia since 1988, joined Aberdeen in 2008, and is based in Singapore. Peter began his career at UK pension fund manager Mercury Asset Management, where he spent 11 years. For most of this time he managed Asian equity funds from Tokyo, Hong Kong, and Singapore. Peter appears regularly on TV, and has had numerous articles published. He graduated with a BA in mathematics and Oriental studies from Cambridge University.

Rainer Ender is managing director of Adveq. Before joining Adveq in 2001, he was an underwriter for alternative risk transfer at Zurich Reinsurance Company. From 1997 to 2000 he was a manager in the financial risk management practice at Arthur Andersen. He also served for several years on the board of DTS, a regulated derivatives trader in Switzerland. Dr Ender holds an MSc in physics and a PhD in natural sciences from the Swiss Federal Institute of Technology (ETH), and he is a CFA charter holder.

Marc J. Epstein is distinguished research professor of management at Jones Graduate School of Management at Rice University, Houston, Texas. He was also recently visiting professor and Wyss visiting scholar at Harvard Business School. Prior to joining Rice, Dr Epstein was a professor at Stanford Business School, Harvard Business School, and INSEAD (European Institute of Business Administration). He has completed extensive academic research and has extensive practical experience in the implementation of corporate strategies and the development of performance metrics for use in these implementations. Dr Epstein has extensive industry experience and has been a senior consultant to leading corporations and governments for over 25 years.

Javier Estrada, professor of financial management at Barcelona-based IESE Business School, set the cat among the pigeons with his ground-breaking research, *Black Swans and Market Timing: How Not to Generate Alpha*. Published in 2008, this revealed that investors who seek to time the market are unlikely to reap rewards. His research focuses on risk, portfolio management, investment strategies, emerging markets, and insider trading. The founding editor of the *Emerging Markets Review*, he also has several visiting professorships in Scandinavia and Latin America. His first degree, a BA in economics, was from the National University of La Plata in Buenos Aires, and he has an MSc and PhD from the University of Illinois at Urbana-Champaign.

Frank J. Fabozzi is professor of finance at the EDHEC Business School, France, having previously been at Yale School of Management from 1994 to 2011. He is editor of the *Journal of Portfolio Management* and has authored and edited many acclaimed books, three of which were coauthored with the late Franco Modigliani and one coedited with Harry Markowitz. Professor Fabozzi is a consultant to several financial institutions, is on the board of directors of the BlackRock complex of closed-end funds, and is on the advisory council for the Department of Operations Research and Financial Engineering at Princeton University. He was inducted into the Fixed Income Analysts Society Hall of Fame in November 2002 and is the 2007 recipient of the C. Stewart Sheppard Award given by the CFA Institute.

Alain Fayolle is professor and director of the entrepreneurship research center at EM Lyon Business School, France. He is also visiting professor at Solvay Brussels School of Economics and Management, Belgium, and HEC Montréal, Canada. His current research work focuses on the dynamics of entrepreneurial processes, the influence of cultural factors on organizations' entrepreneurial orientation, and the evaluation of entrepreneurship education. Professor Fayolle's most recent books are *Entrepreneurship and New Value Creation: The Dynamic of the Entrepreneurial Process* (Cambridge University Press, 2007) and *The Dynamics between Entrepreneurship, Environment and Education* (Edward Elgar, 2008).

Peter Firestein is author of the book *Crisis of Character: Building Corporate Reputation in the Age of Skepticism*. He serves as strategic advisor to senior corporate managements in all major world markets, helping them to build market value and sustainability by strengthening support among investors and social stakeholders. He is originator of the "Investor valuation analysis/Open perception study," a methodology for developing market intelligence that reveals how investors make decisions to buy and sell the shares of a particular company. Firestein also serves as advisor to senior executives and boards on strategies for developing sustainable reputations as well as crisis avoidance and management. He speaks and writes widely on these matters.

Omar Fisher is managing director of Khidr Solutions, an advisory service concentrating on *takaful* (Islamic insurance), Islamic finance, and risk management. He was a founding member and managing director of Unicorn Investment Bank of Bahrain from

2004 until 2008 and previously deputy head of Takaful Taawuni at Bank Al Jazira, where he launched the first family (life) *takaful* business in Saudi Arabia. He also established the first commercial/general *takaful* business in the United States. He is author of numerous books and articles on cross-border financing, hedging political risks, Islamic leasing, and *takaful*. Dr Fisher was awarded a PhD jointly by the International Islamic University of Malaysia and Camden University of Delaware (USA) for research on operational and financial performance characteristics of *takaful* companies in the GCC states. He is an adviser to the International Council of Mutual/Cooperative Insurers (UK) and a board member of Family Bank, an Islamic microfinance bank licensed in Bahrain. The Hult International Business School's Dubai campus awarded Dr Fisher its first Global Alumni Achievement award in August 2010.

Björn Flismark is a senior vice president, product management (and development), within Global Transaction Services at Skandinaviska Enskilda Banken (SEB). Formerly he was responsible for infrastructure projects on payments, securities, and foreign exchange, and he is now involved in SEB's preparations for the Single Euro Payments Area (SEPA) and for complying with the related legal requirements. Flismark is deputy chairman of the Euro Banking Association (EBA) and chairs the SEPA and PSD compliance working group, which produced "Banks preparing for SEPA," "Banks preparing for PSD," and "Banks fine-tuning their PSD preparations." He was a member of the European Payments Council and the Coordination Committee 2002–2010 and was chairman of the Information Security Support Group (ISSG).

Hung-Gay Fung is a professor of Chinese studies at the College of Business Administration of the University of Missouri, St Louis. He holds a BBA (1978) from the Chinese University of Hong Kong and a PhD (1984) from Georgia State University, in both cases majoring in finance with a minor in economics. His teaching areas are investments, risk management, corporate finance, and international investments. His research focuses on international finance, banking, derivative markets, and small business finance. In 1999 he won a best paper award (with G. Lai, R. MacMinn and Bob Witt) given by the Committee on Online Services (COOS) of the Casualty Actuarial Society.

Leslie Gaines-Ross is Weber Shandwick's chief reputation strategist and one of the world's most widely recognized experts on reputation. She spearheaded the first comprehensive research on CEO reputation and its impact on company reputation and performance. She developed Weber Shandwick's global reputation studies "Safeguarding reputation," "Risky business: Reputations online," and "Socializing your CEO." Her article "Reputation warfare" was published in the *Harvard Business Review*. Gaines-Ross is the author of *CEO Capital: A Guide to Building CEO Reputation and Company Success* and *Corporate Reputation: 12 Steps to Safeguarding and Recovering Reputation*. She writes a blog on reputationXchange and tweets as @ReputationRx.

Stuart Gardner has more than 20 years of audit and corporate experience in a variety of sectors and industries, including government, publishing, and financial services. His experience combines audit of numerous largescale construction projects, internal controls and audit reviews, information security, relocation planning, and project risk management. He was director of risk assessment for the McGraw-Hill companies. Gardner is a Chartered Public Finance Accountant (UK government and healthcare), Certified Construction Auditor, Certified Information Systems Auditor, and Certified Information Systems Security Professional. He holds a bachelor's degree in computer science from the University of Swansea.

James Gifford is executive director of Principles for Responsible Investment (PRI) and has been guiding the initiative since its inception in November 2003. He was also a member of the Global Reporting Initiative working group that developed the environmental sector supplement for the finance sector. As well as leading the PRI, he has recently completed a PhD at the Faculty of Economics and Business, University of Sydney, on the effectiveness of shareholder engagement in improving corporate environmental, social, and corporate governance performance. He has degrees in commerce and law from the University of Queensland, and a master's in environment management from the University of New South Wales.

John Gilligan is a corporate finance partner in PKF (UK) LLP and has worked in the private equity and venture capital industry for 24 years. He started his career in 1988 at 3i Group plc as a financial analyst. He joined what is now Deloitte in 1993 and was a partner from 1998 to 2003. He is a special lecturer at Nottingham University Business School and has also taught at Cranfield University Business School. He has a degree in economics from Southampton University and an MBA in financial studies from Nottingham University. He is the coauthor with Mike Wright of *Private Equity Demystified*.

Annette Godart-van der Kroon is president of the Ludwig von Mises Institute Europe, having taken up the position in 2001. Since then the Institute has hosted a large number of events on various topics that influence politics in Brussels. Previously she worked as adjunct referendary at the Ministry of Defence in the Department of Judicial Affairs at the Hague and as a lawyer at the Court of Utrecht and in Roermond in the Netherlands, specializing in civil affairs. She has given numerous speeches on juridical, philosophical, and economic issues and has published books, articles, and comments on these topics. Her publications include two books on the theories of von Hayek and articles on Schopenhauer's theory of law published in the *Schopenhauer-Jahrbuch* in 2003. She is also a member of the Mont Pelerin Society and has participated in Liberty Fund meetings. She enjoys opera, reading, and horseback riding.

Martin Gold is a senior lecturer at the Sydney Business School, University of Wollongong, having joined academia after a successful career in the investment industry. He is an experienced funds manager and investment analyst who has held senior analytical and managerial positions in financial institutions and investment research firms. Dr Gold coauthored *Corporate Governance and Investment Fiduciaries* (Thomson Lawbook Co., 2003), and he has also published a number of articles on innovative investment products and the related fiduciary obligations of fund managers and pension fund trustees.

Beverly Goldberg is senior fellow and editor-at-large at the Century Foundation. She is the author of *Age Works: What Corporate America Must Do to Survive the Graying of the Workforce* (Free Press, 2000) and *Overcoming High-tech Anxiety: Thriving in a Wired World* (Jossey-Bass, 1999) and coauthor of *Corporation on a Tightrope: Balancing Leadership, Governance, and Technology in an Age of Complexity* (Oxford, 1996) and *Dynamic Planning: The Art of Managing Beyond Tomorrow* (Oxford, 1994). Goldberg was the former vice president and director of publications at the Century Foundation.

Erik Gosule is a director, and head of Client Solutions and Investment Strategy at PanAgora Asset Management. As such, he is responsible for assisting in the development and implementation of investment strategies across the firm, including customized solutions that combine multiple investment capabilities designed to meet clients' specific needs. Prior to joining PanAgora, Mr Gosule worked at the D. E. Shaw Group, where he was most recently a member of their Institutional Asset Management team, focused on systematic equity strategies. Prior to joining D. E. Shaw, Mr Gosule held investment oriented roles at Putnam Investments and Fidelity Investments.

Vidhan Goyal is a professor of finance at the Hong Kong University of Science and

  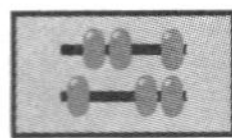   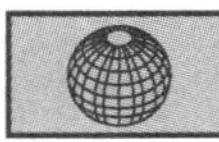   

Technology. His research interests are in empirical corporate finance, with an emphasis on capital structure and corporate governance. His research papers have been published in the *Journal of Finance*, *Journal of Financial Economics*, *Journal of Business*, *Journal of Financial Intermediation*, *Finance Research Letters*, *Journal of Corporate Finance*, and the *Pacific Basin Finance Journal*. Professor Goyal is a member of the American Finance Association, the Western Finance Association, and Beta Gamma Sigma.

Michelle Greene is vice president and head of corporate responsibility for NYSE Euronext, also developing programs to leverage and enhance efforts of NYSE Euronext-listed companies, promoting collaboration and cooperation on issues of common interest. She is also executive director of the NYSE Foundation. Until 2012, she was deputy assistant secretary for financial education and financial access at the US Department of the Treasury, advising on financial access and financial education, and helped drive the development of major new policy initiatives in this area. She was also executive director of the President's Advisory Council on Financial Literacy and a member of the White House Council on Women and Girls. She was a consultant for McKinsey & Co. and Blaqwell, and executive director of the Carr Center for Human Rights Policy at the John F. Kennedy School of Government, Harvard University. She has a JD from Harvard Law School and an AB from Dartmouth College.

John C. Groth is professor of finance in the Department of Finance, Mays Business School, at Texas A&M University. He has received many teaching awards, authored numerous publications, and been cited as a major contributor to the finance literature. Dr Groth received his PhD from the Krannert School, Purdue University. He also holds degrees in physics and in industrial administration. He serves as a consultant in the areas of corporate finance and management education and conducts executive development programs. In addition to his work in finance, he researches and speaks on human capital and creativity and is a keynote speaker. In 2006 he was designated a Mays Faculty Fellow in Teaching Innovation.

Ben Gunnee is European director of the Mercer Sentinel Group, a specialist group within Mercer's investments business that advises clients on investment operations and investment execution, including custodian reviews, investment manager operational due diligence, transition manager operations, and transaction cost analysis. Based in London, he is responsible for the group's overall business strategy within Europe and is part of its global management committee. Before joining Mercer in 2002, Gunnee worked for the Financial Services Authority and a major life assurance company. Holding a master's degree in accounting and finance and an honors degree in accounting and financial management, he has more than 14 years of experience in the investment and pensions sector. He is a fellow of the Institute of Actuaries.

Raj Gupta is research director of the Center for International Securities and Derivatives Markets (CISDM) at the University of Massachusetts, Amherst. He is also a visiting faculty at Clark University and has taught finance at the University of Massachusetts, Amherst. Gupta is assistant editor for the *Journal of Alternative Investments* and has published articles in the *Journal of Portfolio Management*, *Journal of Alternative Investments*, *Journal of Investment Consulting*, *Journal of Trading*, *Alternative Investment Quarterly*, *IMCA Monitor*, and the *Journal of Performance Measurement*. He is a frequent speaker at industry conferences on topics such as performance measurement, asset allocation, and risk management. He holds a PhD in finance from the University of Massachusetts, Amherst.

Keith Guthrie is chief investment officer at Cardano, where he heads the investment team responsible for investment strategy, portfolio construction, and manager selection for pension fund clients. From 2002 to 2007 he worked as an investment manager at GAM, responsible for US$6 billion in arbitrage related fund-of-hedge fund strategies and US$500 million in multi-asset-class portfolios. He started his career in the corporate actuarial department of the First Rand group. In 1999 he became head of long-only manager research and an investment committee member at RMB International, a subsidiary of First Rand. He joined Cardano in January 2008. Guthrie graduated from the University of Witwatersrand with a BSc in statistics and actuarial science and BSc (Hons) in actuarial science. He qualified as an actuary in 1997.

Steven Haasz leads Prudential UK's wholesale business, which provides solutions for Prudential's corporate clients, working with businesses, insurance companies, and their advisers to help manage the investment and longevity risks associated with their pension funds and in-force portfolios of policies. Before joining Prudential, Haasz was a director at Lloyd's of London for five years, overseeing a variety of functions including strategy, business planning, change management, business process transformation, and human resources. He began his financial services career at the actuarial and consulting firm Bacon & Woodrow. He was also an independent consultant for clients including J.P. Morgan, Royal & Sun Alliance, Equitas, and Lloyd's.

Stephen Haddrill took up his post as director general of the Association of British Insurers in 2005, focusing on maintaining and developing its influential relationship with government and regulators. Previously he was a civil servant, joining UK government service in 1978 and ultimately rising to the position of director general, Fair Markets Group, at the Department of Trade and Industry (DTI). Between 1990 and 1994 he worked for the Hong Kong government as a member of the Governor's central policy unit. Haddrill was recently appointed chief executive of the Financial Reporting Council, and will begin this new role in November 2009.

Roszaini Haniffa is professor of accounting at the Bradford University School of Management, where she is also head of the accounting and finance group. Prior to joining Bradford she taught at Exeter University, where she received her PhD. She has also taught professional and academic courses in accounting and finance at several higher education institutions in Malaysia. Her research interests focus on corporate governance, voluntary disclosure, corporate social and environmental reporting, auditing, business ethics, international accounting, and the Islamic perspective on accounting. Professor Haniffa is moderator and examiner for the Association of International Accountants and the Bahrain Institute of Banking and Finance. She is also the joint editor of a newly launched specialist journal, the *Journal of Islamic Accounting and Business Research* (JIABR) and is a member of several other editorial boards. She was included in the Muslim Women Power List 2009 of the UK Equality and Human Rights Commission.

Gail Harden is internal audit manager with Specialized Technology Resources, Inc. (STR). She created the internal audit function at both STR and her previous employer, United Natural Foods, Inc. Harden has been the sole internal auditor at each company, utilizing creative and insightful ways to meet the demands and standards of the internal audit profession with limited resources. At United Natural Foods she was responsible for implementing the Sarbanes–Oxley compliance process. Gail has seven years' experience in internal audit and 13 years' experience in accounting. She holds a bachelor's degree in accounting and MS in business administration and is a certified internal auditor (CIA).

Robert P. Hartwig is president of the Insurance Information Institute, where for the last 11 years he has focused on improving the understanding of key insurance issues across all industry stakeholders. He previously served as director of economic research and senior economist with the National Council on Compensation Insurance (NCCI). He has also worked as senior economist for the Swiss

Reinsurance Group and as senior statistician for the US Consumer Product Safety Commission. Dr Hartwig is a published author and is frequently quoted in leading publications such as the *Wall Street Journal* and *The Economist*. He has a PhD and MSc in economics from the University of Illinois and a BA in economics cum laude from the University of Massachusetts.

Kamal Abdelkarim Hassan is involved in structured products as part of the Treasury, Financial Institutions, and Debt Capital Markets at Kuwait Finance House (Bahrain). He is the former director of technical development at the Accounting and Auditing Organization for Islamic Financial Institutions (AAOIFI), the international self-regulatory organization for the Islamic finance industry. Hassan has over 10 years' experience working in the Islamic finance industry. He holds a MBA in Islamic banking and finance from the International Islamic University Malaysia and a BSc in economics from the London School of Economics. He is a sought-after speaker on Islamic finance, having delivered presentations and lectures at various international conferences.

M. Kabir Hassan is a financial economist with consulting, research, and teaching experience in development finance, money and capital markets, Islamic finance, corporate finance, investment, monetary economics, macroeconomics, and international trade and finance. He has provided consulting services to the World Bank, the International Monetary Fund, the Islamic Development Bank, the African Development Bank, USAID, the Government of Bangladesh, the Organisation of the Islamic Conference, and many private organizations and universities around the world. Dr Hassan received a BA in economics and mathematics from Gustavus Adolphus College, Minnesota, US, and a MA in economics and a PhD in finance from the University of Nebraska-Lincoln, US. He is now a professor in the Department of Economics and Finance at the University of New Orleans, Louisiana, USA. He has more than 100 papers published in refereed academic journals to his credit. He is editor of the *Global Journal of Finance and Economics* and the *Journal of Islamic Economics, Banking and Finance*, and co-editor of the *Journal of Economic Cooperation and Development*. Dr Hassan has edited and published many books along with articles in refereed academic journals. A frequent traveler, Dr Hassan gives lectures and workshops in the United States and abroad, and has presented more than 150 research papers at professional conferences.

Renee Haugerud is the founder, chief investment officer, and managing principal of Galtere, a registered investment adviser that manages approximately US$1 billion across several commodity-focused products. During her 30-year investment career she has acquired expertise across all asset classes in posts throughout the world. She began by trading cash commodity markets in the United States and Canada for Cargill and Continental Grain, before serving as Cargill's foreign exchange trading manager in Geneva, Switzerland, then vice president/structural trading manager at corporate headquarters in Minneapolis. After 13 years at Cargill she managed proprietary trading desks at institutions including NatWest Markets in Hong Kong and Hunter Douglas in the United States. She is a sought-after speaker and panelist, is active in the community of women business leaders, and is an advocate for numerous global education initiatives. Haugerud received her BS in forest resource management from the University of Montana in 1980.

Rita Herron Brown has been a business educator and editor for more than 25 years. She is editor-in-chief at BrownHerron Publishing and an editor of *Business Strategy Review*, the quarterly journal of the London Business School. Previously she developed the curriculum for marketing programs at Honeywell's Aerospace Management Development Center in Minneapolis. She also served as associate director of the executive program at Indiana University's Kelley School of Business, where she was involved in both curriculum development and marketing. She gained her BA and MBA degrees from Indiana University.

Andrew Hiles is founding director of Kingswell International, consultants and trainers in crisis, reputation, risk, continuity, and service management. He has conducted projects in some 60 countries. Kingswell International can be found at www.kingswell.net. He was founder and, for some 15 years, chairman of the first international user group for business continuity professionals, and founding director of the Business Continuity Institute and the World Food Safety Organisation. He has contributed to international standards and is the author of numerous books. He edited, and is the main contributor to, *The Definitive Handbook of Business Continuity Management*. Hiles has delivered more than 500 public and in-company workshops and training courses internationally and broadcasts on television, radio, webinars, and podcasts.

Tim Hindle is a freelance writer and editor. Educated at Worcester College, Oxford, and Heriot-Watt University, Edinburgh, he was a research analyst in the City of London before joining *The Banker* magazine as deputy editor. He subsequently wrote for *The Economist* for many years, acting as finance editor in the 1980s before taking on the new role of management editor. He launched *EuroBusiness* magazine in the early 1990s and then relaunched the Institute of Directors' magazine, *Director*, later that decade. He has written a number of books. *The Essential Manager's Manual*, published by Dorling Kindersley, was a worldwide bestseller. His latest book, *Guide to Management Ideas and Gurus*, was published in 2008 to widespread acclaim.

Dan Hird is head of corporate finance at Triodos Bank and has more than 20 years experience as a lead adviser. Since joining Triodos four years ago, he has built a corporate finance team at the bank that has completed 12 capital-raising transactions over the last two years for clients in the social and environmental sectors. Hird is a chartered accountant and spent seven years with KPMG Corporate Finance before establishing his own corporate finance business. He also has operational experience and spent six years as finance director in two medium-sized private companies in the retail and manufacturing sectors.

Sir Christopher Hogg was chairman of the UK Financial Reporting Council from January 2006 to May 2010. He began his career in industry with Courtaulds in 1968, was a nonexecutive director and subsequently chairman of Reuters Group, SmithKline Beecham, and then GlaxoSmithKline, and Allied Domecq. He has also been a member of the UK Department of Industry's Industrial Development Advisory Board and a nonexecutive director of the Bank of England. Sir Christopher is a graduate of Oxford University and Harvard and saw active service with the Parachute Regiment in Cyprus and Suez while on National Service. Before his career in industry he worked for three years in corporate finance in the City and for two years in the public sector.

Mark Hogg joined RBC Dexia in February 2010. As Director for FX Product Development, Mark has overall responsibility for driving foreign exchange product strategy and growth for RBC Dexia. Prior to this appointment, Mark spent 9 years with Fidelity International and progressed to the overall responsibility for all FX hedging and currency overlay activity for all Fidelity International Investment funds and products globally. Mark spent his early career in various analyst, trading, and market risk roles with the Bank of Ireland, Barclays, and ANZ. Mark is a graduate of Dublin City University, holding a BSc in business and finance and an MSc in investment and treasury.

Zahirul Hoque is associate dean (research) and professor of accounting in the Faculty of Law and Management of La Trobe University in Australia, where he is also deputy director of the Public Sector Governance and Accountability Research Centre. Prior to that he held a number of faculty posts at

     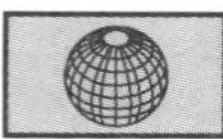   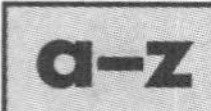

universities in Australia, New Zealand, Bangladesh, and Saudi Arabia. His research interests include accounting and organizational change, management accounting, performance management, public sector accounting, and a general interest in the interdisciplinary research in organizational designs. Professor Hoque has published widely, including two books, *Handbook of Cost and Management Accounting* and *Strategic Management Accounting*. He is founding editor of the *Journal of Accounting and Organizational Change*.

Catherine Howarth has been chief executive of FairPensions since July 2008. Established in 2005, FairPensions is the United Kingdom's only charity that is devoted to campaigning for responsible investment in the pensions industry. It aims to mobilize the financial power of pension investments to improve corporate behavior. Howarth was previously employed at London Citizens. During seven years there she developed a high-profile campaign for a London living wage, successfully influencing a broad cross-section of stakeholders, including companies, investors, public bodies, and politicians. Previously she was senior researcher at the New Policy Institute, London. Howarth has a first-class BA in modern history from Oxford University and an MSc in industrial relations from the London School of Economics. She is a member-nominated trustee at the Pensions Trust and a member of the Pensions Trust's investment committee.

Andrew Howie is the managing partner of Grant Thornton in Scotland and has been with the firm since 2005. During his career with Grant Thornton he has worked within Assurance and now heads up the Audit practice. Andrew acts for some of the largest privately held business in Scotland and his client base covers a wide variety of sectors including property and construction, food and drink, and AIM. Since joining the firm, he's also been responsible for business development in Scotland.

Peter Howson is a director of AMR International, a London-based strategic consultancy that specializes in commercial due diligence. His particluar focus is on manufacturing, building, and construction. He has over 20 years of M&A experience, gained both in industry and as an adviser. Previously he worked in corporate finance at Barings, where he focused on domestic and cross-border deals in manufacturing industries. He has also worked for TI Group plc, transforming the company from a UK supplier of mainly commodity engineering products into a global specialist engineering company through a series of acquisitions and disposals. He has also held senior finance and M&A roles with British Steel and T&N.

Jesús Huerta de Soto holds a PhD in economic science and a PhD in law from the Complutense University of Madrid. He is also a mathematical actuary and holds a MBA from Stanford University. He is a member of the Mont Pelerin Society, the Royal Economic Society (London), the American Economic Association, and the Spanish, Portuguese, and Swiss Associations of Actuaries. He has been awarded the King Juan Carlos International Prize for Economics (Madrid, 1983), the Adam Smith Award (Brussels, 2005), the Franz Cuhel Memorial Prize for Excellence in Economic Education (Prague, 2006), and the Gary G. Schlarbaum Prize for Liberty (Salamanca, 2009), as well as honorary doctorates by Francisco Marroquín University (Guatemala, 2009) and Alexandru Ioan Cuzá (Romania, 2010). Since 2000 he has been professor of political economy at the King Juan Carlos University of Madrid. Huerta de Soto is currently considered to be one of the most representative exponents of the Austrian School of Economics and has published numerous research works and articles on subjects related to his specialty.

Duncan Hughes has 25 years' experience in the City of London in specialties ranging from fund management to investment banking. During his career he has held senior roles at NM Rothschild & Sons and Threadneedle Asset Management, and recently he has focused on private equity and corporate financing and structuring with specialist boutiques. He is a guest lecturer in finance at London Metropolitan University and the London Financial Academy, and he is author of the book *Asset Management in Theory and Practice* . He is also a managing director of Global Analytics, an international financial training and consultancy firm. Hughes won the Chartered Financial Analysts (CFA) Institute's prize for statistics and financial mathematics in 1994 and he now sits on the Institute's UK examination panel.

Christopher Humphrey is a professor of accounting in the Manchester Accounting and Finance Group (MAFG) at Manchester Business School. His main research interests are in the areas of auditing, international financial regulation, public sector financial management, accounting education, and qualitative research methodologies. He is an associate editor of the *European Accounting Review* and sits on a number of editorial boards for international academic journals in accounting, business, and management. He is a co-opted academic member of the Council of the Institute of Chartered Accountants in England and Wales and is currently writing the official history of the International Federation of Accountants (IFAC) (jointly with Anne Loft, Lund University, Sweden).

Bridget Hutter is chair of risk regulation at the London School of Economics and Political Science and former director of the ESRC Centre for Analysis of Risk and Regulation (CARR), a multidisciplinary research center which focuses on the organizational and institutional settings of risk management and regulation. She has held research and teaching appointments at the universities of Oxford and London and is former editor of the *British Journal of Sociology*. Professor Hutter is author of numerous publications on the subject of risk regulation and has an international reputation for her work on compliance, regulatory enforcement, and business risk management. She is regularly involved with policy-making and business discussions, particularly with international bodies such as the World Economic Forum and with business organizations and regulatory agencies.

Antoine Hyafil is the Deloitte professor of finance and energy at HEC and a former dean of the faculty at the HEC School of Management, Paris. He has been on the visiting faculty at the Sloan School of Management, MIT, and at INSEAD in Singapore. He teaches both intermediate and advanced courses in corporate finance, and he has taught executives in Brazil, Bahrain, China, Lebanon, Lithuania, India, Japan, Poland, Russia, and the United States. More recently, he has been commissioned to develop a portfolio of courses linking financial and strategic issues in the field of energy within the context of climate change economics. Professor Hyafil has been an officer of the First National Bank of Chicago and an academic in residence with Merrill Lynch Investment Banking Department.

Bill Janeway is senior adviser at Warburg Pincus. He received his doctorate in economics from Cambridge University, where he was a Marshall scholar. He was valedictorian of the class of 1965 at Princeton University. Prior to joining Warburg Pincus in 1988, where he was responsible for building the information technology practice, he was executive vice president and director at Eberstadt Fleming. Janeway is a director of Nuance Communications, O'Reilly Media, and Wall Street Systems, and he is a member of the board of managers of Roubini Global Economics. He is also chairman of the board of trustees of Cambridge in America, co-chair of Cambridge University's 800th anniversary capital campaign, and a member of the board of managers of the Cambridge Endowment for Research in Finance. Janeway is a member of the board of directors of the Social Science Research Council (SSRC), the board of governors of the Institute for New Economic Thinking, and the advisory boards of the Bendheim Center for Finance (Princeton University) and the MIT Sloan Finance Group.

Hao Jiang is assistant professor of finance at Rotterdam School of Management, Erasmus

    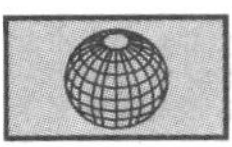   

University. Dr Jiang's main research areas include asset pricing, investments, the behavior of institutional and individual investors, and international finance. At Erasmus he teaches portfolio management, investments, advanced asset pricing, and behavioral finance. His work will appear in the *Journal of Financial Economics* and he has conducted industry and academic presentations across Europe, the United States, and Asia.

Irena Jindrichovska is a Head of the Department of Business Economics at the University of Economics and Management in Prague, Czech Republic. She has a broad experience in the financial sector and in consulting and executive training. Previously she worked at several British and European universities. She was a program director of successful MSc programme in Accounting and Finance at University of Buckingham, UK. She acts as a lead researcher in British and international projects. She is an author of academic articles in the field of market-based accounting and a coauthor of books on corporate finance, financial derivatives, and financial statement analysis. Her current academic interests include corporate financing decisions and corporate governance in transitional countries.

Andreas Jobst is an economist in the Monetary and Capital Markets Department of the IMF in Washington, DC. His work focuses on structured finance, risk management, sovereign debt management, financial regulation, and Islamic finance. As part of IMF missions, he has been responsible for the financial sector coverage of Costa Rica, the Dominican Republic, Germany, Honduras, India, Panama, Switzerland, and the United States. He previously worked at the Federal Deposit Insurance Corporation, Deutsche Bundesbank, the Center for Financial Studies, the European Central Bank, the Bank of England, the Comisión Económica para América Latina y el Caribe of the United Nations, the European Securitization Group of Deutsche Bank, and the Boston Consulting Group. Jobst holds a PhD in finance from the London School of Economics. He has published widely and is associate editor of the *International Journal of Emerging Markets* and the *Journal of Islamic and Middle Eastern Finance*.

Christopher Johnson is a senior partner at Mercer, a leading international provider of HR and related financial advice, products, and services. He is responsible for developing Mercer's reputation for human capital services and the provision of human capital strategy, talent, and reward services in the UK market. He has been in consulting for nearly 25 years, supporting private and public-sector organizations in managing human resource issues. Before joining Mercer in 2008, he worked for the UK government's Cabinet Office, where he was responsible for employee relations and rewards across the Civil Service. Prior to that, he was with the Hay Group, Kinsley Lord, and Towers Perrin.

Scott S. Johnson is the CEO of SJ Partners, LLC, a middle-market leveraged buyout group. He is on the boards of portfolio companies European Soaps LLC and Audio Messaging Solutions LLC. He previously worked in equity research at Salomon Smith Barney and Merrill Lynch. Johnson earned his BA, MIA (Master of International Affairs), and MBA from Columbia University.

Tim Johnson is chief operating officer of Regester Larkin and oversees its international operations. He advises FTSE 100 and Fortune 500 companies and high-profile public organizations on how to earn, maintain, and expand their licenses to operate. Risk management and organizational resilience is Tim's specific area of expertise. He advises clients on the procedural, behavioral, cultural, leadership, and communication aspects of crisis preparedness and reputation management. He has supported clients facing allegations of fraud and senior management malpractice, industrial accidents leading to multiple fatalities, high-profile litigation, sensitive asset divestments, controversial market withdrawals, organizational restructuring, and supply chain failures.

Andrew Kakabadse is professor of international management development at Cranfield University School of Management. He was the H. Smith Richardson Fellow at the Center for Creative Leadership, North Carolina, in 2005–06 and is a visiting professor at the University of Ulster, Ireland, Macquarie Graduate School of Management, Australia, Thunderbird School of Global Management, Arizona, Université Panthéon-Assas (Paris II), France, and Swinburne University of Technology, Australia. His research covers boards, top teams, and the governance of governments. He has published 37 books, more than 220 articles, and 18 monographs. Kakabadse is coeditor of the *Journal of Management Development* and *Corporate Governance: The International Journal of Business in Society*. Among his most recent books are *Bilderberg People: Elite Power and Consensus in World Affairs* (with Ian Richardson and Nada Kakabadse), *Rice Wine with the Minister: Distilled Wisdom to Manage, Lead and Succeed on the Global Stage* (with Nada Kakabadse), and *Global Boards: One Desire, Many Realities* (with Nada Kakabadse).

Dean Karlan is professor of economics at Yale University, president of Innovations for Poverty Action, a research fellow at MIT's Jameel Poverty Action Lab, cofounder and president of StickK.com, and codirector of the Financial Access Initiative, a consortium with funding from the Bill and Melinda Gates Foundation. He holds a PhD in economics from MIT, MBA and MPP from the University of Chicago, and BA in international affairs from the University of Virginia. In 2007 he was a recipient of the Presidential Early Career Award for Scientists and Engineers and in 2008 was awarded an Alfred P. Sloan research fellowship. His research employs experimental methodologies to examine what works and what doesn't in interventions in microfinance and health internationally, and, domestically, in voting, charitable giving, and commitment contracts. Karlan consults for many organizations, including the World Bank, the Asian Development Bank, FINCA International, and the Guatemalan government.

Jonathan M. Karpoff has a particular interest in what drives executives to commit corporate crimes and misdemeanors, believing that a breakdown of trust can have long-term repercussions for individual corporations and that it contributed to the wider financial collapse of 2007–08. A professor of finance at the University of Washington's Michael G. Foster School of Business, Karpoff is also associate editor of a number of academic journals including the *Journal of Finance*. He won the best paper award in the CRSP Forum at the University of Chicago in 2006 and 2008 for his research into corporate and financial scandals. He was founding director of the University of Washington's environmental management program and was director of its CFO Forum in 2004–07.

Paul Kasriel joined the economic research unit of the Northern Trust Company in 1986 as vice president and economist, and was made senior vice president and director of economic research in 2000. In 2006 he received the prestigious Lawrence R. Klein Award for making the most accurate economic forecast among the Blue Chip survey participants for the years 2002 through 2005. The accuracy of Kasriel's 2008 economic forecast was ranked in the top five of the *Wall Street Journal* survey panel of economists. In January 2009, the *Wall Street Journal* and *Forbes* cited him as one of the few who identified early on the formation of the housing bubble and foresaw the economic and financial market havoc that would ensue after the bubble burst. Kasriel began his career as a research economist at the Federal Reserve Bank of Chicago. He is coauthor of a book entitled *Seven Indicators that Move Markets*, and he serves on the Economic Advisory Committee of the American Bankers Association.

Giles Keating is a managing director of Credit Suisse in the Private Banking Division. He is head of private banking research and also responsible for the research groups of asset management. He is also chair of the Global

  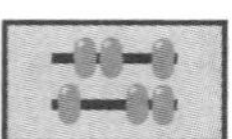      

Economics and Strategy Group of Credit Suisse. Before joining Credit Suisse First Boston in 1986, Keating was a research fellow at the London Business School Centre for Economic Forecasting, where he built an econometric model of the UK financial system. He spent six years at the Confederation of British Industry, finishing as head of the Economic Forecasting Department. He has published widely in academic and general media on macroeconomics, financial markets, and public policy.

Alison Kemper is completing her PhD in strategic management under the supervision of Roger Martin. She is studying the impact of social ratings on the behavior of firms. For many years she was a leader and activist in the nonprofit sector. She completed her BA in religious studies at Yale College, her MDiv and MTh at Trinity College, Toronto, and her MBA at the Rotman School of Management, University of Toronto.

Mark Kenber is CEO of international NGO The Climate Group. He has worked on climate change for fifteen years and is an expert on international climate policy. Before becoming CEO, he was The Climate Group's deputy CEO (2010) and international policy director (2004–10). Mark advised former UK Prime Minister Tony Blair in the joint policy initiative Breaking the Climate Deadlock. He is also a carbon markets expert and cofounded the Voluntary Carbon Standard (VCS), now the most popular kitemark for the US$400 million voluntary market. He continues to be involved as deputy chair of the VCS Association. Prior to joining The Climate Group, Mark worked for WWF and Fundacion Natura, Ecuador's largest environmental organization. Mark currently sits on the Climate Change Advisory Council at Zurich Insurance (since 2009), BP's targetneutral Assurance and Advisory Panel (since 2007), the Climate Policy Editorial Advisory Board (since 2005), and the Institutional Investors Group on Climate Change Steering Committee (since 2005). Mark has a degree in economics and an MPhil in development studies.

Shân Kennedy is an independent consultant who advises on IFRS and valuation issues. Her background includes more than 20 years with Ernst & Young and Deloitte. She has also spent four years working at the UK Accounting Standards Board developing UK GAAP guidance on accounting for goodwill and intangible assets; this included developing the impairment test. Kennedy has presented at many IFRS conferences in London and Europe. She has recently acted as technical consultant to the International Valuation Standards Council to develop its guidance on the valuation of intangible assets, both generally and for IFRS purposes.

Peter Killing is professor of strategy at IMD, Lausanne, Switzerland. His major interest is the interface between strategy and leadership. His teaching, research, and consulting activities focus on leaders who are working with their teams to create the right strategy and at the same time set the ground for effective implementation. In the area of mergers, acquisitions, and alliances, Professor Killing has written and edited four books and several articles, including one in the *Harvard Business Review*. He also runs in-company programs for a variety of clients including BMW, Allianz, Sika, and Vestas, the Danish wind turbine company.

Kelvin King 's early career was spent with the UK government division responsible for private company, business, intellectual property, and intangible asset valuation. He established a valuation unit for an accountancy practice. Before the founding of Valuation Consulting, a BNP Paribas company, he was managing director of a specialist valuation company within an international Swiss bank. Since 1996 he has been a separately listed UK expert witness in intellectual property, intangible asset, and unquoted company valuation. King is a founder of the Society of Share and Business Valuers, founding expert of Lord Woolf's Expert Witness Institute, associate member of the Licensing Executive Society, Chartered Institute of Patent Agents, fellow of the Royal Institution of Chartered Surveyors, and a member of the International Association of Consultants, Valuers and Analysts.

Joachim Klewes is honorary professor at the Heinrich Heine University, Düsseldorf, and senior partner at Ketchum Pleon, the leading communications consultancy in Europe. In addition, he is the founder of the Change Centre Foundation, an independent think-tank focused on scientific research and concept development in the field of change and transformation in business and society. His consulting expertise covers the fields of strategic communications, including corporate communications, and board/CEO positioning and coaching, crisis and issues management, public affairs, and change management.

Ruud Kleynen is professor of asset– liability management in the Faculty of Economics and Business Administration at the University of Maastricht. His main areas of research cover the risk management and asset–liability management for pension funds and insurance companies. He also runs his own consultancy bureau, Kleynen Consultants, which aims to apply knowledge in the field of asset–liability management to offer state of the art solutions to large clients.

Leslie L. Kossoff is an internationally renowned executive adviser specializing in next generation thinking and strategy for executives and their enterprises. For over 20 years she has assisted clients ranging from start-ups to Fortune 50's across industries and sectors in the United States, Japan, and Europe. Her clients include Fidelity Investments, Sony, TRW, Kraft Foods, Baxter Healthcare, the UK National Health Service, Seiko/Epson, 3M, Infonet and GM/Hughes. A former executive in the aerospace/defense and pharmaceutical industries, Kossoff enjoys an outstanding reputation as an invited speaker at conferences worldwide. She is the author of the *Executive Field Guides*, the award winning book, *Executive Thinking*, and more than 100 articles in journals and newspapers, including the *Financial Times* and *CEO Magazine*.

Peter Koveos is professor and chair of the Finance Department at the Whitman School of Management, Syracuse University. He is also the Kiebach chair in international business, director of the Kiebach Center, and executive director of the Africa Business Program at the Whitman School. As director of ExportNY, an institute for international business executives, and the International Business Forum he works closely with New York companies to develop their international business strategies. He is also president of the Central New York International Business Alliance and has worked extensively in Asia. Professor Koveos is editor of the *Journal of Developmental Entrepreneurship* and his work has appeared in numerous professional journals.

Klaus Kremers is a partner at Roland Berger Strategy Consultants in London. He is also a member of Berger's Restructuring & Corporate Finance Competence Center. Kremers has more than 10 years' experience in strategic, operational, and financial restructuring in turnaround situations. He advises international sponsors/financiers and European corporate clients across a range of industries. Prior to joining Roland Berger in 2000, he worked for KPMG Transaction and Corporate Recovery Services in Frankfurt. He has studied in Germany, the United States, the Netherlands, and the United Kingdom. He holds a degree in international business administration and a master's in business administration with special focus on finance.

Satya Kumar is an associate at Ennis Knupp and manages consulting assignments for several retainer and project clients. Prior to joining Ennis Knupp in 2004, he served as a research associate involved in risk management and quantitative strategy development with a proprietary options trading firm. Kumar holds a BComm degree from the University of Madras and earned a MS degree in finance from the Illinois Institute of Technology. He is a CFA charterholder and a member of CFA Institute and the CFA Society of Chicago. He is also an associate member of the Institute of Chartered Accountants of India.

  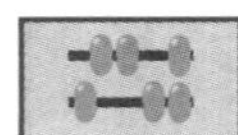      

Chiraz Labidi is assistant professor of finance at the College of Business and Economics, United Arab Emirates University in Al Ain. She was previously assistant professor of finance at IHEC Carthage. Her areas of academic research cover international financial markets, emerging markets, and dependence structures.

Vinod Lall is a professor in the School of Business at Minnesota State University Moorhead, teaching supply chain management, operations management, management science, project management, and management information systems. Lall has developed and taught online and face-to-face graduate courses at business schools in Bulgaria, Ecuador, India, Thailand, and the United States. Active in research, he has published numerous papers in peer-reviewed journals and presented at conferences. He is a certified supply chain professional (CSCP) by APICS, the American Association for Operations Management, and is the vice president of education for the Red River Valley chapter of APICS, leading certification training for a number of regional manufacturing and service organizations.

Morton Lane is director of the Master of Science in Financial Engineering program at the University of Illinois. He is also an independent consultant and president of Lane Financial, LLC, a broker-dealer operating at the intersection of the reinsurance and capital markets. Previously, he has been president of Sedgwick Lane Financial, senior managing director of the capital markets division at Gerling Global Financial Products, president of the Discount Corporation of New York Futures, senior managing director and head of commodities at Bear Stearns & Co., president of Lind-Waldock, investment officer for the World Bank, and lecturer at the London Graduate School of Business Studies. Lane has been awarded the Charles A. Hachemeister prize for his article on “Pricing risk transfer transactions” published in the *ASTIN Bulletin*. He has coauthored two books, *The Treasury Bond Basis* and *Eurodollar Futures*, and edited a third, *Alternative Risk Strategies*. He has designed and taught courses at the University of Chicago Graduate School of Business and at the University of New South Wales. Lane earned his BSocSc from Birmingham University and his PhD in mathematics, business administration, and computer science from the University of Texas.

Meziane Lasfer is professor of finance at Cass Business School, London, which he joined in 1990. He has written extensively on corporate finance, capital markets, and corporate governance issues. His research is widely reported in the financial press and is published in top academic journals such as the *Journal of Finance*, the *Journal of Finance and Quantitative Analysis*, the *Journal of Banking and Finance*, the *Journal of Corporate Finance*, the *Journal of Business Finance and Accounting*, *Financial Management*, the *National Tax Journal*, and *European Financial Management*. He is a visiting professor at University Paris-Dauphine. He teaches extensively masters, PhDs, and executives at Cass and abroad.

Qudeer Latif is head of Islamic finance at Clifford Chance. He has worked with Chance in London, Dubai, and Riyadh, and his practice covers structuring and implementing Islamic instruments across a number of asset classes including those in the capital markets, project finance, acquisition finance, structured finance, and asset finance fields.

Brendan LeBlanc is the assurance leader in Ernst & Young LLP’s Americas climate change and sustainability services practice. In this role he oversees the development and implementation of related competencies throughout the United States, extending to clients through the firm’s core services. Previously, he founded LeBlanc & Associates, a niche CPA firm focused on corporate social responsibility assurance services. In this capacity, he issued the first reasonable assurance opinion on a sustainability report in the United States in 2008. He received a BA in accounting from Gordon College, Wenham, MA. He is a certified internal auditor and a certified public accountant licensed in Massachusetts and New Hampshire.

Peter, Lord Levene started his career in the UK defense industry with United Scientific Holdings. He was then appointed personal adviser to Defence Secretary Michael Heseltine in the Ministry of Defence and later permanent secretary in the role of Chief of Defence Procurement. Subsequently he held a number of government posts, as adviser to the Secretary of State for the Environment; to the President of the Board of Trade; and to the Chancellor of the Exchequer. From 1992 to 1997 he was adviser to Prime Minister John Major on efficiency and effectiveness. During this period he was also chairman and chief executive of Canary Wharf Ltd. He received a knighthood in 1989 and became a life peer in 1997. Later he became vice chairman of Deutsche Bank in the United Kingdom, having also been at Wasserstein Perella and Morgan Stanley. Lord Levene was elected chairman of Lloyd’s, the world’s leading specialist insurance and reinsurance market, in 2002. In this role, he chairs the Council of Lloyd’s and Lloyd’s Franchise Board. He is a member of the House of Lords Select Committee for Economic Affairs.

Frederick D. Lipman is a partner with Blank Rome, an international law firm, and specializes in mergers and acquisitions. He has appeared as a television commentator on CNN, CNBC, Bloomberg, and Chinese television. He was previously a lecturer in the MBA program at the Wharton School of Business and is the author of *Valuing Your Business: Strategies to Maximize the Sale Price* (Wiley, 2005).

Joseph LiPuma is an affiliate professor in strategic management at EM Lyon Business School. He has a BS in mathematics and an MBA from SUNY Buffalo, and received his doctorate in business strategy and policy from Boston University. LiPuma has nearly 20 years of professional experience, including senior management, operating committee and board-level roles. He has established new businesses (information technology consultancies) in both US domestic and international environments. His research focuses on international entrepreneurship, specifically new venture internationalization and its relationship to the manner in which ventures are capitalized. He teaches masters-level courses in strategy, international business, and entrepreneurship.

Roger Lister is a chartered accountant and a professor of finance at Salford University. After reading modern languages as a major open scholar at Oriel College, Oxford, he worked for international accounting firms KPMG and PwC, specializing latterly in corporate taxation with particular interest in the taxation of groups. In his academic posts at Liverpool and Salford universities, Lister has taught accounting, corporate finance, and corporate tax and given specialized courses on capital structure. His research and publications have focused on corporate finance. Recent work has included an interdisciplinary perspective in which he examines alternative cultural models and advocates a role for the arts in business education.

Gilad Livne has been a senior lecturer at City University’s Cass Business School since May 2005. Prior to that he was an assistant professor of accounting at the London Business School. He received his MSc in 1994 and PhD in 1996, both in accounting, from the University of California at Berkeley. He is a CPA (Israel) and worked for several years as a senior auditor in Israel after completing his BA in accounting and economics at Tel Aviv University. Livne’s research focuses on understanding how capital markets react to accounting information and the role of auditors.

Anne Loft is professor of accounting at Lund University in Sweden. Gaining a PhD from the London Business School in 1986, she moved to Denmark, becoming professor of auditing there in 1997, moving to Lund University in 2005. She was one of the founder editors of the *European Accounting Review* (1992–2000), and is currently an editor of the *International Journal of Auditing*. At present she is writing

  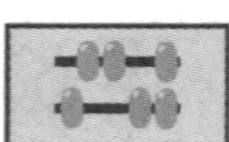   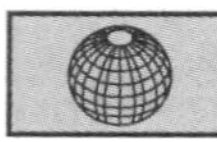   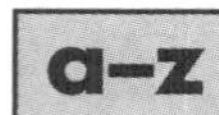

the official history of the International Federation of accountants (IFAC) jointly with Christopher Humphrey. Her main research interests are in the accounting profession and in auditing regulation—from both historical and contemporary perspectives.

Jay W. Lorsch is Louis Kirstein professor of human relations at Harvard Business School and chairman of the School's global corporate governance initiative. As a consultant, his clients have included Citicorp, Deloitte & Touche, DLA Piper Rudnick, Goldman Sachs, Tyco International, and Shire Pharmaceuticals. He is currently a director of Computer Associates. Lorsch graduated from Antioch College in 1955 and has an MSc in business from Columbia University and a doctorate in business administration from HBS. He is a fellow of the American Academy of Arts and Sciences.

Steven Lowe is client portfolio manager at JP Morgan and a partner at Pension Corporation Investments. Previously he was a senior credit portfolio manager with Legal and General Investment Management (LGIM), where he focused on structured solutions, derivatives, and investment-grade credit for pension fund clients. Before working at LGIM, he worked at Barclays Global Investors, State Street Global Advisors and Baring Asset Management. Lowe has 15 years of investment experience and was awarded the Chartered Financial Analyst designation in 1997.

Robin Mann is head of the Centre for Organisational Excellence Research, New Zealand, chairman of the Global Benchmarking Network, advisory board member of the Hamdan bin Mohammed e-University, and cofounder of BPIR.com Ltd. Dr Mann's experience includes managing the UK's Food and Drinks Industry Benchmarking and Self-Assessment Initiative (1995–98), the New Zealand Benchmarking Club (2000–04), the Sheikh Saqr Government Excellence Program, UAE (2005–07), and leading TRADE benchmarking projects in Singapore (from 2007 on). He worked in Edinburgh (1992–95) for Burton's Biscuits as a process improvement manager and obtained his PhD in total quality management at Liverpool University in 1992.

Steven V. Mann is professor and chair of the finance department at the Moore School of Business, University of South Carolina. He has coauthored and coedited several books on the bond market. He is also associate editor of *The Handbook of Fixed Income Securities*, the eighth edition of which was published in January 2012. Professor Mann is an accomplished teacher, having won more than 20 awards for excellence in teaching, including the two highest awards given by the University of South Carolina. He is an active consultant to clients that include some of the largest investment/commercial banks in the world, as well as a number of Fortune 500 companies. He also serves as an expert witness in court cases involving fixed-income-related matters.

Jyothi Manohar serves as a director for a CPA and consulting firm in the United States that has international affiliations. She is an accounting, audit, and consulting professional focusing on the community banking industry. Her experience covers US banking regulations, risk management, internal controls, accounting, financial, and regulatory reporting, and audit committee responsibilities. She also has experience writing articles and presenting relevant topics for community bankers at industry conferences and on webcasts. She has assisted in creating staff training material and providing training for staff and senior auditors serving the banking industry.

Aldo Mareuse has been chief financial officer of Orascom Telecom Holding since 2002. He is also CFO of Weather Investments SpA, a private company that owns a majority stake in Orascom Telecom. Prior to joining Orascom Telecom, Mareuse worked in various positions for the investment bank Credit Suisse First Boston. He holds an engineering degree from Ecole Centrale de Lyon. When he is not traveling between Islamabad, Cairo, Rome, or New York, in the winter he enjoys back-country skiing in the Alps or the Rockies and in the summer he likes to cruise on the Mediterranean on his boat. He is married and has three children.

John L. Mariotti is the president, CEO, and founder of the Enterprise Group, a coalition of time-shared executive advisers. Mariotti is a director on corporate boards, including World Kitchen, LLC. Previously he was president of Rubbermaid Office Products Group (1992–94), leading nine divisions spanning four continents, and president of Huffy Bicycles (1982–92), the world's largest bicycle company in that era. Mariotti has written nine business books, a novel, thousands of articles, columns, and blog posts, and is a highly regarded keynote speaker. His book *The Complexity Crisis* received awards as one of 2008's best business books. He was previously a contributing editor for *Industry Week* magazine and he currently writes for Forbes.com. He can be found at www.mariotti.net.

Norman Marks is vice president, governance, risk, and compliance at SAP, focusing on thought leadership around internal audit, governance, risk management, compliance, enterprise performance, and business intelligence. Marks has been chief audit executive of major global corporations since 1990 and is a recognized thought leader in the profession of internal auditing. He is the author of two of the most downloaded Institute of Internal Auditors (IIA) products: a guide for management on Sarbanes–Oxley s. 404 and the GAIT methodology for defining the scope for Sarbanes–Oxley of IT general controls. He is the editor of the corporate governance column in the IIA's *Internal Auditing* magazine, a member of the review boards of several audit and risk management publications, a frequent speaker internationally, the author of several award-winning articles, and a prolific blogger. He is a fellow of the Open Compliance and Ethics Group.

Robert Marquardt is founder, chairman, and co-head of investment management at Signet Group, responsible for overall portfolio management and for development of the group's investment strategy. He is a member of Signet's investment committee and leads the group's top-down process of identifying investment opportunities while focusing on the most pertinent investment risks; he is also intimately involved in hedge fund due diligence. Marquardt has two decades of experience with alternative investments. Before founding Signet in 1993, he was an independent investment manager based in Luxembourg (1990–93). This followed a successful career as a credit analyst and lending officer with Chase Manhattan Bank (1979–90) in London and Bahrain, and in Luxembourg, where he was the director in charge of private banking.

Neil Marriott, BSc, MBA, PhD, DipM, CPFA, FHEA, is dean of the Winchester Business School and in 2008 and 2009 was chair of the British Accounting Association (BAA). Professor Marriott has also been the chair of the BAA's Special Interest Group in Accounting Education for 10 years. His publications include five textbooks and tutor manuals covering financial and management accounting, as well as a specialized work for NHS financial managers. His research interests include small business financial management and auditing, public sector accounting, and accounting education. Marriott is editor of the *International Journal of Management Education*, published by the Higher Education Academy.

Duncan Martin is a partner and managing director in the risk management practice at the Boston Consulting Group (BCG), based in London. Prior to joining BCG, he was the head of Wholesale Credit Risk Analytics at the Royal Bank of Scotland in London, the director of Strategic Risk Management at Dresdner Kleinwort, and a senior manager at Oliver Wyman & Company. Martin was educated at Cambridge University and the Wharton School of the University of Pennsylvania. He is the author of the book *Managing Risk in Extreme Environments* (2008).

Roger Martin has served as dean of the Rotman School of Management since 1998. He

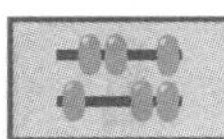

also serves as an adviser on strategy to the CEOs of several major global corporations. He has published two books: *The Opposable Mind* (2007) and *The Responsibility Virus* (2002). His third book, *The Design of Business: Why Design Thinking is the Next Competitive Advantage*, will be published in November 2009 (Harvard Business School Press). In 2007, *Business Week* named him one of the 10 most influential business professors in the world. He received his AB from Harvard College, with a concentration in economics, in 1979, and his MBA from the Harvard Business School in 1981.

María Soledad Martínez Pería is a senior economist in the finance team of the Development Economics Research Group of the World Bank. Her published research has focused on currency and banking crises, depositor market discipline, and foreign bank participation in developing countries. Currently she is conducting research on financial sector outreach and on the impact of remittances on financial development. Prior to joining the World Bank, she worked at the Brookings Institution, the Central Bank of Argentina, the Federal Reserve Board, and the International Monetary Fund. She holds a PhD in economics from the University of California, Berkeley, and a BA from Stanford University.

John Mauldin is president of Millennium Wave Investments and is a renowned financial expert, a many-times *New York Times* best-selling author, and an online commentator. His weekly e-newsletter, *Thoughts from the Frontline*, was one of the first publications to provide investors with free, unbiased information and guidance. Today it is one of the most widely distributed investment newsletters in the world, with a subscriber base of more than one million readers. It appears in English, Chinese, Spanish, and Italian. He is called on to comment regularly by TV and national media.

Thomas McKaig is a widely recognized Canadian author with 30 years of international business experience in 40+ countries. He delivers quality business solutions to clients in five languages. He owns Thomas McKaig International, Inc., found at www.tm-int.com. He speaks internationally on quality management and international trade, and is an adjunct professor, teaching Global Business Today in the Executive MBA program at the University of Guelph. His most recent book is *Global Business Today* (3rd ed, 2011). He has served as executive in residence at the University of Tennessee and Universidad de Montevideo, and was worldwide strategic marketing adviser to the United States Treasury Department Bureau of the US Mint's Gold Eagle Bullion coin program.

Michael D. McKenzie is a professor of finance and the chair of discipline at the University of Sydney, Australia, and a research associate at the Centre for Financial Analysis and Policy, Cambridge University, England. During his time as an academic he has published numerous books and journal articles on a wide range of topics. His main research interests encompass the areas of risk management, market volatility, price discovery, and market microstructure analysis. Prior to joining academia McKenzie was a treasury analyst for Deloitte Touche Tohmatsu, and he currently works as a consultant with the Midwine Financial Risk Management Consulting group, Australia, which specializes in the areas of strategic asset allocation and financial risk management.

Alex McNeil is the Maxwell professor of mathematics at Heriot-Watt University, Edinburgh. He was formerly assistant professor at ETH Zurich. Professor McNeil has a BSc from Imperial College, London, and a PhD in mathematical statistics from Cambridge University. He has published papers in leading statistics, econometrics, finance, and insurance mathematics journals and is a regular speaker at international risk management conferences. He is joint author of the book Quantitative Risk Management: Concepts, Techniques and Tools (2005). Professor McNeil is the director of the Scottish Financial Risk Academy, which aims to provide financial service companies with an efficient, streamlined framework for exploring complex issues of risk and related topics, in partnership with academia.

Damian Merciar is managing director of Merciar Business Consulting, www.merciar.com, a niche business economics consultancy founded in 1998. He has twenty years experience in the areas of commercial Business Strategy. He is experienced in the transition environments of nationalized to private sector state utilities and the senior practice of commercial management, advisorial consultancy, and implementation. He has carried out policy advisory work for government ministries and been an adviser to institutional bodies proposing changes to government. He holds an MBA from the University of Kent at Canterbury (1993), attended the leading University in the Middle East, studying International Relations and Language (1992), for which he won a competitive international scholarship, and has a BA (Hons) in Economic History and Political Economy from the University of Portsmouth (1991). He is currently based in London.

Lauren Mills is a senior financial journalist with 17 years' experience working for business publications and national newspapers. She was retail correspondent for the *Sunday Telegraph* for more than five years and went on to become enterprise editor at the *Sunday Express*, before joining the *Mail on Sunday*'s financial desk covering a range of sectors that now includes banking, insurance, private equity, mining, pharmaceuticals, and manufacturing. She has also contributed business articles to the *Sunday Times*, the *Daily Telegraph*, the *Daily Mail*, the *Financial Times*, and the *Independent on Sunday*.

Scott Moeller is the director of the M&A Research Centre at Cass Business School, London, and a former senior executive at Deutsche Bank and Morgan Stanley. While at Deutsche Bank, Professor Moeller held roles as global head of the corporate venture capital unit, managing director of the Global eBusiness division, and managing director responsible for worldwide strategy and new business acquisitions. Prior to his career in investment banking he was a management consultant with Booz, Allen & Hamilton (now Booz & Co). He is a non-executive director of several nonprofit and financial services companies in the United States, the United Kingdom, and Continental Europe.

Marcus Mollan is head of strategy in the Pension Solutions Group at Legal & General Investment Management (LGIM), one of the leading managers in the field of liability-driven investment, with more than £90 billion in derivatives under management. His role is to design and implement risk management solutions, involving both derivatives and physical assets, for pension schemes and other institutional investors.

James Montier, an expert in behavioral finance, argues that investors would have a greater chance of spotting the formation of bubbles if they could only brush up on their history and have a greater awareness of human psychology. Co-head of global strategy at Société Générale, he has been described as an "enfant terrible" by *Frankfurter Allgemeine Zeitung*, an "iconoclast" by the *Financial Times*, a "maverick" by the *Sunday Times*, and "a prophet" by *Fast Company*. Montier has been a top-rated strategist in the annual Thomson Reuters Extel survey for the last five years. When not reading, writing, or speaking, Montier can usually be found swimming with sharks and blowing bubbles at fishes.

Pau Morilla-Giner oversees alternative investments at London & Capital and is also the manager of London & Capital's equities and commodities funds. He started his career at JP Morgan Asset Management in Madrid and New York. In 2001 he joined Omega Capital, a multibillion investment company, where he became head of traditional investments and senior hedge fund analyst. From 2005 he was investment manager and head of research at Pragma Wealth Management, a London-based alternative investment company. Pau obtained his BA summa cum laude in economics from

  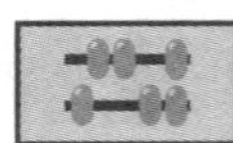   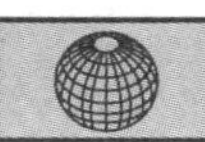   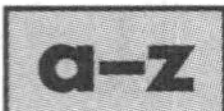

Universitat Pompeu Fabra, Barcelona, in 1999, followed by a masters degree in finance from CEMFI (Bank of Spain) in 2001. He has been a visiting professor of finance at the RiskLab School of the Spanish Financial Futures and Options Exchange (MEFF).

Rod Morris is vice president in charge of the political risk insurance program for the Overseas Private Investment Corporation. He first came to OPIC in 2000 after serving as a senior vice president at CNA Insurance Company, where he was in charge of a number of products and divisions as well as the branch offices in Omaha and Phoenix. He has also served as the chief regulator for the captive insurance program in Arizona and has authored a number of articles and training texts on underwriting and captives. Morris has been a member of the United Nation's Expert Group on Public-Private Risk Sharing.

Arun Motianey is director of fixed-income strategy for Roubini Global Economics (RGE). Prior to joining RGE, he worked for two decades at Citigroup in a variety of roles, including head of macro research and strategy for global wealth management, head of investment research and cohead of asset allocation at Citigroup Private Bank Asset Management, and economist in the office of the chairman during the restructuring of Latin American sovereign debt under the Brady Plan, which involved liaising with the IMF. Most recently he has authored *SuperCycles: The New Economic Force Transforming Global Markets and Investment Strategy*. He received his bachelor's degree at the University of Bombay and participated in a graduate exchange fellowship at Princeton University. He received his doctorate in mathematics and economics from King's College, Cambridge.

Sendhil Mullainathan is a professor of economics at Harvard University and a director of ideas42, a center devoted to taking insights about people from behavioral economics and using them to create novel policies, interventions, and products. He received his BA in computer science, mathematics, and economics from Cornell University and PhD in economics from Harvard. He conducts research on development economics, behavioral economics, and corporate finance. Professor Mullainathan has published extensively in top economics journals including the *American Economic Review*, the *Quarterly Journal of Economics*, and the *Journal of Political Economy*. He is the recipient of a MacArthur Foundation "genius grant" and of other grants and fellowships from the National Science Foundation, the Olin Foundation, the Alfred P. Sloan Foundation, and the Russell Sage Foundation.

Arun Muralidhar is cofounder and chairman of AlphaEngine Global Investment Solutions (AEGIS) and its parent company, Mcube Investment Technologies. Muralidhar earned an undergraduate degree in economics in 1988 from Wabash College in Indiana. After gaining a PhD in managerial economics at the Sloan School of Management he joined the World Bank, where he rose to become head of investment research for the bank's pension fund. He has also worked as managing director and head of currency research at JP Morgan Investment Management and FX Concepts.

Sanjay Muralidhar, cofounder and CEO of AlphaEngine Global Investment Solutions (AEGIS) and its parent company, Mcube Investment Technologies, is devoted to helping clients to make better investment decisions and improve returns. Muralidhar earned an undergraduate degree in accounting in 1984 from Bombay University and an MBA from the University of Pennsylvania. He has worked in senior finance positions at Bristol-Myers Squibb, Reader's Digest, and iVillage.

Richard Murphy is a graduate in economics and accountancy from Southampton University, and was then articled to Peat Marwick Mitchell & Co., a forerunner of KPMG in London. Since 2003 he has been researching and campaigning on economic and taxation policy issues. He founded the Tax Justice Network and is director of Tax Research LLP, which undertakes work on taxation policy for aid agencies, unions, NGOs, and others. Murphy has helped to reshape the debate on international tax policy, for example through the creation of country-by-country reporting. As principal researcher of the Tax Justice Network until 2009, he helped to put tax havens on the international agenda. He is a coauthor of *Tax Havens: How Globalization Really Works* (2009) and the author of *The Courageous State: Rethinking Economics, Society and the Role of Government* (2011).

Russell Napier is an Edinburgh-based consultant for Asia-focused brokerage CLSA Asia-Pacific Markets who writes about issues impacting the global equity markets. With more than two decades in the industry, he has contributed to the development and scope of CLSA's equity research. He started his career in investment at Edinburgh-based asset managers Baillie Gifford before joining CLSA in 1995 as an Asian equity strategist based in Hong Kong. He remained in that post until 1999 and was ranked number one for Asian strategy in the *Asiamoney* and *Institutional Investor* polls from 1997 to 1999. Napier is a nonexecutive director of the Scottish Investment Trust and the Mid Wynd International Investment Trust. His book *Anatomy of a Bear* was published to critical acclaim in 2005 (an updated edition was published in 2009). He created and runs a course for finance professionals at the Edinburgh Business School called "A practical history of financial markets."

Andy Nash is a serial entrepreneur and has chaired 12 management buyouts and buyins since 1996. During this period he has also successfully chaired two FTSE plcs. He was one of three principles of the Taunton Cider MBO which, at £72 million in 1991, was one of the first big private equity deals in the United Kingdom. The exit via flotation and a recommended takeover for almost £300 million four years later achieved a handsome return for shareholders. His book, *The Management Guide to MBOs*, was published to acclaim in 2005 and is due to be revised and updated in late 2009. Nash also chairs Somerset county cricket club and, with friends, has built a new day hospital in Zanzibar. In later life he qualified as a ski guide, and he occasionally lectures at Nottingham University's Business School. He is married with four grown-up children and the family has homes in Somerset and Spain.

Ravi Nedungadi is president and group CFO of Bangalore-based United Breweries (UB) Group. From the start of his career in 1990, he has held various positions from corporate treasurer to finance director of the group's international businesses. Appointed president and group CFO in 1998, he has led the way to sharpening the group's focus on areas of core competence and global reach. Under his leadership the market capitalization of the three principal group companies has grown to US$7.7 billion, up from $145 million three years earlier. Nedungadi's achievements have been recognized by many awards, including the Udyog Ratan Award and the IMA Award for CFO of the Year (2007). He lives in Bangalore with his wife and two children.

Sue Newell is Cammarata professor of management at Bentley University in Waltham, Massachusetts, and a part-time professor of information management at Warwick University in the United Kingdom. She gained her BSc and PhD from Cardiff University and is currently PhD director at Bentley University. Professor Newell's research focuses on understanding the relationships between innovation, knowledge, and organizational networking (IKON)—primarily from an organizational theory perspective. She was one of the founding members of IKON, a research center based at Warwick University. Newell has published more than 80 journal articles on organizational studies and management and information systems, as well as numerous books and book chapters.

Hansjörg Nymphius is director of market infrastructures at Deutsche Bank's Global Transaction Bank, and global product manager for financial supply chain management. He previously held the position of global head of methodologies and performance management. Over the course of his career he has actively participated in various domestic and international industry bodies, both at working group level and in policy-making. Currently he is chairman of the board of the Euro Banking Association (EBA), Paris. Nymphius has been a key driver behind the integration of EU payments markets over the past decade. As a senior manager he has made significant contributions to the successful deployment of euro market infrastructures, business rules, and standards.

Martin O'Donovan is assistant director, policy and technical, at the Association of Corporate Treasurers (ACT). The ACT is the international body for finance professionals working in treasury, risk, and corporate finance. With 3,600 members in over 60 countries, the ACT defines and promotes best practice in treasury and is the world's leading examining body for treasury. O'Donovan qualified as a chartered accountant and has spent his career working in treasury at Redland, Hertz, BTR, and, most recently, as group treasurer of National Grid Group. He is a fellow of the Association of Corporate Treasurers.

Umar Oseni is a solicitor and advocate of the Supreme Court of Nigeria. He completed the Bachelor of Laws program in 2005 and proceeded to the Nigerian Law School. He successfully completed the Bar Part II program in 2007 and was called to the Nigerian Bar later that year. He is a member of the Peace and Collaborative Development Network, the Young International Arbitration Group, the London Court of International Arbitration, the Nigerian Bar Association, and the Association of Professional Negotiators and Mediators. Oseni has written 15 academic papers, 10 of which have been published in academic journals and books. He has also presented papers at international conferences on Islamic banking and finance. He won the Best Student Award for Masters of Comparative Laws during the 25th Convocation Ceremony of the International University Malaysia (IIUM) in 2009. He is currently a PhD research scholar and part-time lecturer at the Faculty of Law, IIUM. His areas of research include Islamic banking and finance, alternative dispute resolution, contemporary application of Islamic law, and international trade law.

Krzysztof M. Ostaszewski holds a PhD in mathematics from the University of Washington in Seattle. He is a chartered financial analyst, a member of the American Academy of Actuaries, a fellow of the Society of Actuaries, a chartered enterprise risk analyst, and a fellow of the Singapore Actuarial Society. He is a professor of mathematics and the actuarial program director at Illinois State University, a center of actuarial excellence. Ostaszewski is also the research director for life insurance and pensions at the Geneva Association, International Association for the Study of Insurance Economics.

Amitendu Palit is an economist specializing in comparative studies of China and India, international trade and investment, political economy, and public policy. Currently he is a senior research fellow of the Institute of South Asian Studies at the National University of Singapore. He has a decade's experience handing macroeconomic policy issues at India's Ministry of Finance. His latest book is *China–India Economics: Challenges, Competition and Collaboration* (Routledge, 2012) and his forthcoming book is on the Trans-Pacific Partnership (TPP) and its implications for China and India. His work has been published in peer-reviewed academic journals and he writes regularly for India's *Financial Express*, *China Daily*, and *The Business Times*.

Mona Pearl is founder and COO of BeyondAStrategy, based in Chicago, IL. Mona Pearl's experience in international strategic development and global entrepreneurship has been vital in helping companies design and execute their global strategies. From operations to organization to top-line growth strategies, Mona has initiated and executed cost-effective and creative opportunities for companies to make money. She has helped companies increase global market share, enhance leadership, and engage the stakeholders along the value chain. She is multi-lingual and has lived in 3 continents. She holds a Master's Degree focused on global business from DePaul University in Chicago.

Stephen H. Penman is the George O. May professor in the Graduate School of Business, Columbia University. Prior to this he was the L. H. Penney professor in the Walter A. Haas School of Business at the University of California at Berkeley, and has served as a visiting professor at London Business School and Stockholm School of Economics. He has a first-class honors degree in commerce from the University of Queensland, Australia, and MBA and PhD degrees from the University of Chicago. His research is on equity valuation and the role of accounting information in security analysis. He is managing editor of the *Review of Accounting Studies* and is on the editorial board of the *Schmalenbach Business Review*, and in 2002 he was awarded the Wildman Medal for his book, *Financial Statement Analysis and Security Valuation*.

Jeremy Phillips is an intellectual property consultant, author, lecturer and commentator on patents, trademarks, copyrights, and most contemporary issues involving intellectual property rights. He is an intellectual property consultant at Olswang LLP solicitors, honorary research fellow at the Intellectual Property Institute, and visiting professorial fellow, Queen Mary Intellectual Property Research Institute, Queen Mary, University of London. Cofounder and blogmeister of the IPKat weblog, Phillips is currently involved in the development of weblog-based intellectual property communities.

Lawrence Phillips, visiting professor of decision science at the London School of Economics and a director of Facilitations Ltd, is a leading expert on ways in which organizations can improve their decision making. He has long been fascinated by the challenges associated with deciding how best to deploy limited resources across a range of projects and getting people to buy into the outcome—the quintessential budgeting and, indeed, management problem. Dr Phillips teaches decision science to graduates and undergraduates at the LSE and conducts training courses on decision science and facilitation skills to external organizations. In 2005 he was awarded the Frank P. Ramsey medal for distinguished contributions to decision analysis by the Decision Analysis Society of INFORMS.

Ramesh Pillai is CEO and group managing director of Friday Concepts (Asia). He is also the risk management adviser to AmanahRaya/KWB and a nominee director for Bank Negara Malaysia (Central Bank of Malaysia). Previously he was the risk management adviser to Tabung Haji. He holds a bachelor of economics with accountancy (honours) degree from Loughborough University. A member of the Institute of Chartered Accountants in England and Wales and the Malaysian Institute of Accountants, as well as a Certified Risk Professional, Pillai was also a regional director for the Global Association of Risk Professionals and is one of the founding members of the Malaysian chapter of the Professional Risk Managers International Association.

Robin Pritchard is professor of internal audit, governance and risk management at Birmingham City University and a nonexecutive director with a number of UK government agencies. He is chairman of Severnside Housing and a specialist adviser to three further audit committees. Robin has developed a number of outsourced internal audit practices and was UK public sector internal audit partner with Arthur Andersen. Recognizing that there is a diverse understanding of what represents good governance and world-class internal audit, Robin has recently started his own consultancy business providing external quality assessment of internal audit teams and governance reviews in association with the Governance Forum.

Price Pritchett is founder and CEO of Pritchett LP, a Dallas-based consulting firm recognized internationally for its expertise in

  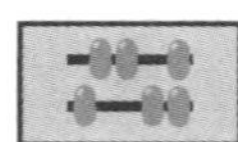      

mergers, culture, and organizational change. Dr Pritchett's book, *After the Merger: Managing the Shockwaves*, named one of the 10 best business books of the year, was the first ever written on merger integration strategy. He is also author of the all-time best seller on mergers, *The Employee Guide to Mergers and Acquisitions*, plus various other titles. More than 20 million copies of his books are in print worldwide, with translations into many foreign languages. Almost all of the Fortune 500 have used some combination of Pritchett LP's consulting, training, and handbooks.

Marc Quintyn has been division chief, Africa, at the IMF Institute since 2006, where he teaches macroeconomics and more specialized topics. He has been with the IMF since 1989 and worked most of his career on monetary and financial sector issues in surveillance and program missions, financial sector assessment programs (FSAPs), and technical assistance work. He received his PhD from the University of Ghent, Belgium. Before joining the IMF, he held various positions at the University of Ghent (1979–83), the Research Department, National Bank of Belgium (1984–89), and the University of Limburg, Belgium (1986–89). Dr Quintyn is a published author of numerous books, papers, and articles.

Shamus Rae is lead partner in charge of KPMG Europe's sourcing advisory team. This team provides outsourcing, shared services, and offshoring advice and support for clients across financial services, consumer and industrial markets, information, communications and entertainment, and government and business support sectors. He has more than 18 years' experience of making investments and achieving benefits through sourcing (shared services, offshoring, and outsourcing) both in emerging market countries such as India, the Philippines, China, and Central and Eastern Europe, and in Western Europe and the United States.

Sridhar Ramamoorti has a blended academic–practitioner background spanning over 25 years of academic, auditing, and consulting experience. He earned his BCom from Bombay University, India, and his MAcc and PhD from Ohio State University. Dr Ramamoorti was on the University of Illinois accountancy faculty prior to returning to professional practice with Andersen Worldwide, Ernst & Young, and most recently as a corporate governance partner with Grant Thornton. Widely published, Dr Ramamoorti is a coauthor of the best-selling IIA textbook on internal auditing, *The Audit Committee Handbook*, and served on the COSO (2009) and ISACA (2010) monitoring guidance development teams. A prolific and sought-after speaker, he has presented in over a dozen countries. Dr Ramamoorti was co-chair of the IIA's 2010 Global CBOK Study (2008–11).

Bilal Rasul is the registrar of modaraba companies and of the Modarabas, Securities and Exchange Commission of Pakistan (SECP). A British Council (Chevening) scholar, Rasul gained his master's degrees in public administration and in economics and finance in the United Kingdom. He has 15 years of varied experience in capital market regulation, including the securities market and nonbanking and finance companies, as well as the nonfinancial sector. As registrar, he is responsible for heading the Islamic finance initiative for the capital market in Pakistan. He is also the focal person of the Islamic Financial Services Board (IFSB) at SECP, responsible for the implementation and adoption of IFSB standards and principles.

Philip Ratcliffe left Oxford University to start his life-long career in internal audit with Unilever, where he qualified as a chartered management accountant. He later became head of internal audit at a number of large multinational companies involved in manufacturing, distribution, and natural resources. He was then chief audit executive at a publicly quoted UK paper and packaging company. A long-term member and fellow of the Institute of Internal Auditors (in the United Kingdom, Brazil, and Belgium), Ratcliffe joined the UK council in 2006, serving as president for 2008–09.

Riccardo Rebonato is global head of market risk and global head of the Quantitative Research Team at the Royal Bank of Scotland (RBS). He also sits on the Investment Committee of RBS Asset Management. Dr Rebonato is a visiting lecturer at Oxford University and adjunct professor at Imperial College's Tanaka Business School. He sits on the board of directors of ISDA (International Swaps and Derivatives Association) and the board of trustees for GARP (Global Association of Risk Professionals). He is an editor for several financial journals, and has written several books. He holds a doctorate in nuclear engineering and a PhD in condensed matter physics/science of materials from Stony Brook University, NY.

Luc Renneboog is a professor of corporate finance and director of graduate studies at Tilburg University, the Netherlands. Before joining Tilburg, he taught at the University of Leuven and at Oxford University. Dr Renneboog graduated with a BSc/MSc in management engineering from the University of Leuven, followed by an MBA from the University of Chicago, a BA in philosophy from Leuven, and a PhD in financial economics from the London Business School. He has also been a visiting researcher at the London Business School, HEC Paris, and Venice University. He is a widely published author, with research interests are corporate finance, corporate governance, mergers and acquisitions, and the economics of art.

Jeffrey Ridley is visiting professor of auditing at London South Bank University. He teaches and researches internal auditing, corporate governance, corporate social responsibility, and quality management. His experience spans both the public and private sectors over 40 years. Formerly he was manager of internal auditing at Kodak UK, an operational auditor at Vauxhall Motors, and a member of the British colonial audit service in Nigeria. He is a past president of the Chartered Institute of Internal Auditors (UK and Ireland) and in 2010 was awarded its distinguished service award. He has been a member of the IIA's international board of regents and of its international committee on quality. Currently he is a member of the IIA Research Foundation's board of research advisers and also of the editorial advisory board for the IIA's journal *Internal Auditor*. Ridley's books include *Leading Edge Internal Auditing* and *Cutting Edge Internal Auditing*.

James Roberts is a senior audit partner at BDO LLP. After training with Binder Hamlyn he became a partner there in 1986 and in Arthur Andersen when it acquired the firm. His audit clients have always included a mix of public and private clients across a broad range of sectors and he has been responsible for the accounting work on over 20 IPOs. At BDO, James is responsible for the firm's Gatwick office and is public policy spokesperson on audit and accounting matters. James is married with two student children and lives in West Sussex in the United Kingdom. His interests outside business include music, gardening, and reading.

Steve Robinson was director of open executive programs at Henley Business School until the end of 2007. Previously he was with Ashridge Business School for 14 years, latterly as director of executive MBA programs. Robinson has designed and taught on a variety of management development and qualification programs in the United States, Europe, Asia, and Australia. He is the author of the *Financial Times Handbook of Financial Management* and is an external examiner at the Cass Business School, City University, London. He is now an independent educator, writer, and consultant working closely with Duke Corporate Education and with the Henley, Warwick, and Kingston Business Schools.

Gerasimos G. Rompotis is a senior auditor at KPMG Greece and also a researcher at the Faculty of Economics of the National and Kapodistrian University of Athens. His main areas of research cover the evaluation of mutual fund managers' selection and market timing skills, the performance of exchange-traded funds, calendar effects on the performance and volatility of equity investments, and intervaling effects on the systematic risk of ETFs. His work has been published in a number of industry journals

  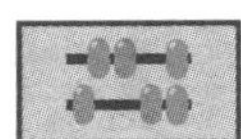      

such as the *Journal of Asset Management*, the *Guide to Exchange Traded Funds and Indexing Innovations* issued by Institutional Investor Journals and the *International Research Journal of Finance and Economics*, including the European conferences.

Alan Rugman holds the L. Leslie Waters Chair of International Business at the Kelley School of Business, Indiana University, where he is professor of international business and professor of business economics and public policy. He has also been Thames Water Fellow in strategic management at Templeton College, University of Oxford. Dr Rugman has published widely and has served as a consultant to major private sector companies, research institutes, and government agencies, and as an outside adviser on free trade, foreign investment, and international competitiveness to two Canadian prime ministers. Dr Rugman was president of the Academy of International Business from 2004 to 2006.

Tarun Sabarwal is assistant professor of economics and Oswald Scholar at the University of Kansas. He received his doctorate from the University of California at Berkeley. His research interests include microeconomic theory and financial economics. Dr Sabarwal's work has been published in a number of academic journals, most recently in *Economic Theory*, in *Regional Science and Urban Economics*, and in *Annals of Finance*, among others. He has presented his work at conferences around the world.

David Sadtler is an associate of the Ashridge Strategic Management Centre. His research, teaching, consulting, and writing activities are concentrated on questions of corporate-level strategy. A graduate of Brown University (mathematics and economics) and of Harvard Business School, his career has been divided between consulting and industry. Sadtler was the corporate development director and a main board director of London International Group plc, a diversified healthcare company, for eight years and is a two-time alumnus of McKinsey & Company, having served a broad range of clients on questions of strategy in the New York, Amsterdam, and London offices.

Shahzada Omar Saeed has an MBA in financial management and is head of the high-yield team at Swisscanto Asset Management, where he is responsible for overseeing investments of US$1 billion. He is lead manager for the Swisscanto (CH) Institutional Bond Fund—Global High Yield I and the Swisscanto (LU) Bond Invest Short Duration Global High Yield fund. Under his leadership, Swisscanto has experienced exponential growth of greater than 300%, along with achieving top-quartile ranking for its flagship institutional bond fund. Before Swisscanto, Saeed worked for Western Asset in London, where he was responsible for co-managing some €750 million of high-yield and leveraged-loan portfolios. Prior to that he held a similar position with F&C Asset Management.

James S. Sagner is an internationally recognized expert in financial management and economic analysis. He teaches undergraduate and MBA-level management, finance, and international business courses in the School of Business at the University of Bridgeport, Connecticut, and is currently a lecturer in the Executive Education Finance Program at the University of North Carolina. He has written six business finance and economics books and dozens of papers and articles, and is a former editor of *Treasury Views*. He is a graduate in accounting of Washington and Lee University, Lexington, Virginia, has an MBA from the Wharton School of the University of Pennsylvania, holds a PhD in business and economics from the American University in Washington, DC, and has been a Rockefeller Foundation fellow. He holds CCM and CMC certifications. His book *Cashflow Reengineering* (1997) was selected as a most influential finance book of all time by *QFinance* Business Library.

Richard Sambrook was an influential and senior BBC executive and leading manager of its news services before joining the Edelman public relations company in 2010. Born in 1956, he was educated at Maidstone Technical High School, the University of Reading (where he gained a BA in English), and Birkbeck College, University of London. He joined BBC Radio News as a subeditor in 1980. He was a BBC journalist and news executive, becoming successively director of BBC Sport, BBC News, and, latterly, director of the BBC World Service and Global News. During this time he was responsible for merging radio and television news, as well as domestic and World Service news-gathering, resulting in the world's largest broadcast news operation. He oversaw a major restructuring of the World Service and the opening of Arabic and Persian television, as well as of commercial interactive services.

Paul J. Sanchez conducts a CPA practice in Port Washington, New York. He is the owner of Professional Service Associates (PSA), a consulting and professional training and development business servicing financial services companies, CPA firms, and professional associations. Prior to starting PSA he was vice president, professional development, for the audit division of a regional bank, served on the technical staff of the auditing standards and examinations divisions of the AICPA, and practiced public accounting in the New York office of Deloitte. Sanchez is a frequent lecturer and seminar leader for accounting, auditing, banking, and other professional presentations. He also is the author of a textbook, *Accounting Basics for Community Financial Institutions*, and the monthly "Ideas and analysis letter: The Sanchez take."

John A. Sandwick moved to Geneva in 1993, first working at Deutsche Bank (Suisse), and then at Banque Leu, a unit of Credit Suisse Private Banking. In 1999 he started his own conventional wealth management company, but in 2009 he converted his practice to entirely *shariah*-compliant asset management. Sandwick has been called a pioneer of Islamic banking by *Schweizer Bank* magazine and has appeared in numerous venues worldwide, including the World Islamic Economic Forum and many International Islamic Finance Forum events. He has a master's degree in development banking from the American University in Washington, DC, and is author of numerous works on Islamic banking in the Western and Arabic press.

Hans-Dieter Scheuermann has extensive experience at SAP, the business software developer, in the areas of financials and insurance solutions. Since 2003 he has headed the SAP Business Solution Architects Group, deploying his 30 years of experience directly in strategic customer relationships. Before assuming his current post, he had global responsibility for the General Business Unit (GBU) Financials. In 1998–2000 he was director of the Industry Business Unit (IBU) Insurance. Prior to that, from 1991 he was head of development for the financials and accounting application. He started his career at SAP in 1978 as a developer for financial accounting solutions. Scheuermann studied mathematics at the University of Heidelberg.

Sergio Schmukler is lead economist with the Development Research Group of the World Bank. He has also worked continuously for the Office of the Chief Economist for Latin America and for the East Asia and South Asia regions. Besides his work for the World Bank, he has been treasurer of LACEA (Latin American and Caribbean Economic Association) since 2004, was associate editor of the *Journal of Development Economics* (2001–2004), taught in the Department of Economics, University of Maryland (1999–2003), and worked in the International Monetary Fund Research Department (2004–2005). He gained his PhD at the University of California at Berkeley.

David Schofield is president of the international division of INTECH. He holds an joint honors MA in French and German from Oxford University. Formerly he was European business head of Janus Capital Group and before that he had 15 years in investment banking with Salomon Brothers, Lehman Brothers, and UBS, in New York, London, and Frankfurt.

  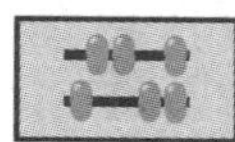      

Leonard Seabrooke is a professor at the International Center for Business and Politics of the Copenhagen Business School and also professor of international political economy and director of the Centre for the Study of Globalisation and Regionalisation at the University of Warwick. His publications include *The Social Sources of Financial Power* and *US Power in International Finance*, and he has coedited *Everyday Politics of the World Economy* (with John M. Hobson), *Global Standards of Market Civilization* (with Brett Bowden), and *The Politics of Housing Booms and Busts* (with Herman M. Schwartz). Professor Seabrooke is coeditor of the international journal the *Review of International Political Economy*. He was also the director of studies of the Warwick Commission on International Financial Reform.

Neil Seitz is professor of finance and prior dean at the John Cook School of Business, Saint Louis University. He holds a PhD in finance from Ohio State University (1973) and an MBA from the University of Hawaii (1969). He worked on consulting and executive development programs for AT&T, Barclays, Caterpillar Inc., Citicorp, Household International, and Standard Chartered Bank. He has also done acquisition planning for Telecheck International (1969) and inventory planning and long-range forecasting for the Cooper Tire and Rubber Company (1966–1968). He has published six books, including two on capital budgeting.

Bill Sharon has been conducting seminars, workshops, and consulting assignments in the area of risk management for the past 14 years. He has 30 years' experience in the financial services and marketing/communications industry in a variety of C-level positions and consultancies. He has been featured in numerous industry magazines (*Intelligent Risk*, *CIO Magazine*, *Business Finance*, and *Business Credit Magazine*) and has authored numerous articles. Bill holds a clinical degree, and for the first 10 years of his professional life he worked with adolescents—an experience that taught him the very difficult skill of how to listen. His website, Strategic Operational Risk Management Solutions, can be found at www.sorms.com.

David Shimko holds a PhD in finance from Northwestern University. He has taught finance at the Kellogg Graduate School of Management at Northwestern University, the Marshall School of Business at the University of Southern California, the Harvard Business School, and the Courant Institute at New York University. His professional career included positions at JP Morgan, Bankers Trust, and Risk Capital, an independent risk advisory firm that was sold to Towers Perrin in 2006. Currently, Shimko sits on the board of trustees of the Global Association of Risk Professionals (GARP). He acts as an independent financial consultant and continues to teach part-time at the Kellogg School.

Jonathan Silberstein-Loeb is a research fellow at the Oxford University Centre for Corporate Reputation. Before moving to Oxford, he was an Alfred Chandler Jr traveling fellow at Harvard Business School, a fellow at the Newberry Library, Chicago, a fellow of the Lilly Library at the University of Indiana, Bloomington, a Deutscher Akademischer Austauschdienst fellow in Berlin, and a Fulbright Fellow in Kyoto, Japan. He received his doctorate from the University of Cambridge.

Gary Silha has more than 25 years of treasury management experience and is currently assistant treasurer at Tenneco Inc., where he has responsibility for worldwide treasury operations. Prior to joining Tenneco in 2000, he was the director of worldwide treasury operations at the American National Can Company, the largest beverage can manufacturer in the world. Silha holds bachelor's and master's degrees in business from Illinois State University, is a Certified Treasury Professional, and is a former president of the Treasury Management Association of Chicago.

Robert, Lord Skidelsky is emeritus professor of political economy at the University of Warwick. He read history at Oxford University, and from 1961 to 1969 he was successively research student, senior student, and research fellow at Nuffield College, Oxford. In 1970 he became an associate professor at the School of Advanced International Studies, John Hopkins University. In 1978 he was appointed professor of international studies at the University of Warwick, where he has remained since, joining the Economics Department as professor of political economy in 1990. In the 1980s he began to take a more active interest in politics, becoming a founder member of the Social Democratic Party and remaining in the party until its dissolution in 1992. He was made a life peer in 1991. His three-volume biography of John Maynard Keynes, published between 1983 and 2000, has received numerous prizes and wide acclaim. He is currently Andrew D. White Professor-at-Large at Cornell University.

Chris Skinner is well known as an authority on the future of banking. He chairs the Financial Services Club, a European networking group, works with the media, and presents extensively at conferences globally, speaking about the future of banking. He has written several books on the subject and keeps a daily blog at www.thefinanser.co.uk. Previously, he was vice president of marketing and strategy for Unisys Global Financial Services and strategy director with NCR Financial Services. Skinner is also a cofounder of the website for strategists www.shapingtomorrow.com.

Shireen Smith founded Azrights in 2005, having worked as an in-house lawyer at media organization Reuters for five years. She has also held positions at Coopers & Lybrand and Eversheds, and she was a part-time in-house counsel for a small IT company for more than seven years. She has over 20 years' experience as a commercial solicitor and is particularly interested in new technologies, the Internet, and social media. Working closely with Ferreter, an IT business run by her husband Paul, the firm is able to assist clients with the full range of technical expertise required to provide a comprehensive reputation management service to clients.

Edib Smolo is a researcher and coordinator of the Islamic Banking Unit at the International Shari'ah Research Academy (ISRA) for Islamic Finance. He received a double bachelor's degree in economics and Islamic revealed knowledge and heritage, as well as a master's degree in economics, from the International Islamic University Malaysia. He also holds a Certificate for Professional Specialization in Political Management from the Bulgarian School of Politics, jointly organized by the New Bulgarian University and the Council of Europe. Prior to joining ISRA, Smolo worked for an insurance company in Bosnia and Herzegovina, and at the same time he was assistant professor at the Faculty of Economics, Sarajevo School of Science and Technology. He is features editor of the *ISRA Bulletin*. Smolo has authored and coauthored several papers on Islamic microfinance, economics, and finance.

Erik Stern, president international of Stern Stewart & Co., has advised numerous organizations on their implementation of EVA. He coauthored the EVAluation report on cascading EVA to shop-floor employees, "The capitalist manifesto," and has written for many publications, including the *Financial Times*. A global value ranking based on his pioneering metric, the Wealth Added Index (WAI), was highlighted in the *Economist* (December 1, 2001). His book *The Value Mindset* was published in 2004. Stern has an MBA from the University of Chicago and a BA (Hons) from Brown University.

John Surdyk is director of the Initiative for Studies in Transformational Entrepreneurship at the Wisconsin School of Business in Madison, Wisconsin. He has advised companies bringing emerging technologies to market for international consultancies for 10 years. Surdyk spent more than a decade consulting with high-technology start-ups, Fortune 500 firms, and nonprofit organizations at SRI International in Menlo Park and, later, Navigant Consulting in

Chicago. He has also evaluated policy initiatives at the National Center for Environmental Economics at the US Environmental Protection Agency. He now teaches on social entrepreneurship at the University of Wisconsin, Madison.

Amarendra Swarup is a respected commentator and expert on financial markets, alternative investments, asset–liability management, regulation, risk management, and pensions. He was formerly a partner at Pension Corporation, a leading UK-based pension buyout firm, and was at an AAA-rated hedge fund of funds in London before that. Swarup is a CAIA charter-holder and sits on the CAIA examinations council, the AllAboutAlpha.com editorial board, and the Adveq advisory board. He was a visiting fellow at the London School of Economics, setting up the Pensions Tomorrow research initiative, and a member of the CRO and Solvency II committees of the Association of British Insurers. Swarup holds a PhD (cosmology, Imperial College, London) and an MA (natural sciences, University of Cambridge). He has written extensively on diverse topics and is currently writing a book on financial crises throughout history and the common human factors underlying them, to be published by Bloomsbury in 2013.

Solomon Tadesse is a financial economist, investment professional, educator, and financial sector policy expert. He holds a PhD in finance and graduate degrees in accounting, operations research, and financial economics, as well as CMA and CFM designations. His career has spanned banking, academia, and financial sector policy. He is a vice president at State Street Global Advisors, designing and developing quantitative investment strategies primarily in global macro tactical asset allocation areas. Dr Tadesse has held faculty positions at the University of Chicago, University of Michigan, University of South Carolina, and Penn State University. He is a fellow of the Wharton Financial Institutions Center, and research fellow at the William Davidson Institute. Dr Tadesse's expertise encompasses financial system design, international asset allocation and security selection, and global capital markets. He is the author of numerous scholarly research published at top-tier academic journals. He has given invited expert testimony before the US–China Economic and Security Review Commission of the US Congress, and served as an adviser and fellow at the House Committee on Small Business.

Aziz Tayyebi works as head of international development for the Association of Chartered Certified Accountants (ACCA), having previously been financial reporting officer for ACCA. Tayyebi is the key technical contributor to ACCA's thought leadership in the field of Islamic finance, contributing articles and discussion papers on the subject and responding to external consultations in this area. He represents the ACCA on the Federation of European Accountants (FEE) task force on XBRL and on the UKTI accounting subgroup on Islamic finance. Previously, he worked as a manager with Ernst & Young, managing a portfolio of audit clients ranging from large privately owned companies to listed companies.

Siri Terjesen holds a PhD from Cranfield School of Management (2006), a master's in international business from the Norwegian School of Economics and Business Administration (Norges Handelshùyskole), where she was a Fulbright scholar (2002), and a BS in business administration from the University of Richmond, Virginia (1997). She is an assistant professor in the Kelley School of Business at Indiana University and a visiting research fellow in the entrepreneurship, growth, and public policy group at the Max Planck Institute of Economics in Jena, Germany. She has been widely published in leading journals and is a coauthor of *Strategic Management: Logic & Action* (Wiley, 2008).

Stuart Thomson graduated from Edinburgh University in 1985 with an MA honors degree in economics. He began his career in 1985 as a junior economist with Britannia Asset Management and a year later joined Chase Manhattan Securities. In 1988 he took up the post of chief international economist at Nikko Europe Plc, and in 1997 moved to Credit Agricole Indosuez, where he worked as chief market strategist. In 1999 he joined Sutherlands Limited as a senior economist, and from there went on to be founding director and investor of RIA Limited. Thomson joined Charles Stanley Sutherlands as a senior economist in 2003, remaining there until he joined Ignis Asset Management in August 2006, where he is responsible for international bonds and currencies.

Peter Tickner is sole director of Peter Tickner Associates Ltd, and has 38 years' experience as a public sector auditor. In his early career he was an external auditor for the National Health Service in the United Kingdom. From 1988 to 1995 he was head of internal audit at Her Majesty's Treasury, and was then director of internal audit for the Metropolitan Police (Scotland Yard), London, between 1995 and 2009. He also spent five years as a lecturer in internal audit at the Civil Service College. Tickner is the author of *How to be a Successful Frauditor*, published by Wiley in 2010.

Edmund Truell is the founder of Pension Corporation, a leading provider of risk management solutions to defined benefit pension funds, which was established in 2006. Pension Corporation has £5bn of pension assets under stewardship and amongst other achievements was the first to insure the benefits of a public sector pension scheme, as well as transacting the largest ever UK corporate pension insurance buyout. Edmund has twenty two years' experience in private equity and debt markets. He was appointed chief executive of Hambro European Ventures in 1994; led the 1998 buyout and formation of Duke Street Capital; and was responsible in 2000 for creating and building Duke Street Capital Debt Management. Edmund was chairman of the British Venture Capital Association 2001–02. He is a trustee of the Truell Charitable Foundation and of the Galapagos Conservation Trust.

Jon Tucker is professor of finance at the Bristol Business School of the University of the West of England and is director of the Centre for Global Finance there. He holds a PhD in European corporate finance (1995) and a BSc in applied economics (1991), both from the University of Plymouth. He has published frequently in leading finance journals and is associate editor of the *Journal of Finance and Management in Public Services*. He is a former chief examiner in investment analysis for the Securities and Investment Institute, a Member of CISI (MCSI), and visiting professor at Universitatea Babes-Bolyai, in Romania.

Bruce Turner has been chief internal auditor at the Australian Taxation Office since February 2007. As chief audit executive at one of Australia's largest and most prestigious public sector agencies, he provides strategic leadership for the Tax Office's internal audit activities and works closely with the audit committee. He has extensive experience in leading and managing internal audit areas, having previously held chief audit executive roles in the energy and transport sectors in Australia. In 2008 the Institute of Internal Auditors Australia presented him with the Bob McDonald Award in recognition of his contribution to internal audit services and the profession.

Shaun Tyson is emeritus professor of human resource management at Cranfield University. He holds a PhD from the London School of Economics and is a fellow of the Chartered Institute of Personnel and Development, a fellow of the Royal Society of Arts, and a member of the British Psychological Society. He has written 19 books on human resource management and has published extensively on human resource strategy and policies. He has carried out consultancy assignments and research with a wide range of public and private sector organizations in the United Kingdom and overseas. He chaired the remuneration committee of the Law Society for four years.

Roger Urwin is global head of investment content at Watson Wyatt after having been global head of the investment practice from

  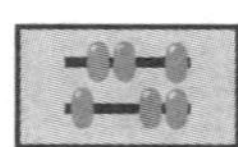 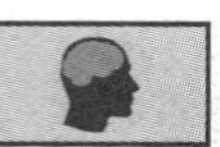     

1995 to 2008. He joined Watson Wyatt in 1989 to start the firm's investment consulting practice. His prior career involved investment consulting for Hewitt, heading the investment practice at Mercer, and leading the business development and quantitative investment functions at Gartmore Investment Management. He is author of a number of papers on asset allocation policy, manager selection, and governance. Urwin is on the boards of the Chartered Financial Analyst Institute and the Institute for Quantitative Investment Research (INQUIRE), and also on the editorial board of MSCI.

Sheryl Vacca is the senior vice president/chief compliance and audit officer at the University of California (UC). Previous to UC, she served as the West Coast practice leader and national lead for internal audit, life sciences and healthcare. She was also the vice president of internal audit and corporate compliance officer for a large healthcare system in northern California. Vacca has published and presented nationally in the fields of healthcare compliance and internal audit to professional organizations such as the Institute of Internal Auditors, Health Care Compliance Association, Healthcare Financial Management Association, and the Practising Law Institute.

John Vail is Nikko Asset Management's head of global macro strategy and asset allocation and also chairs the group's global investment committee. Before joining Nikko AM in 2006, he was chief Japanese equity strategist for JPMorgan Securities Japan from 2004 and chief strategist at Mizuho Securities USA from 2000. He also held various senior research and strategy positions at Fidelity from 1985 to 1992, based in Hong Kong, Taiwan, and Japan, and covered pan-Asia equities at his own firm, Asia House Funds, for five years from 1993. Vail holds a BA from the University of Chicago.

Jos van Bommel is associate professor at CEU Cardenal Herrera University, in Valencia, Spain. He was formerly a lecturer in finance at Oxford University's Said Business School and conducts empirical and theoretical research in various areas of corporate finance. He has completed several studies on IPOs, but is also interested in private equity, venture capital, and international finance. He also studies the market's microstructure and investigates the strategic behavior of informed and less informed traders to better understand how information is incorporated into market prices. Dr van Bommel holds a university degree in engineering from the University of Eindhoven, an MBA from the IESE Business School, and a PhD in finance from INSEAD. In between his studies he worked in international sales and marketing.

Valentijn van Nieuwenhuijzen is head of strategy for the strategy and tactical asset allocation group at ING Investment Management. He is responsible for formulating the firm's macroeconomic outlook and fixed-income tactical asset allocation. Focused on tactical allocation between cash, fixed-income, equities, real estate, and commodities, and more particularly between specific fixed-income markets such as treasuries, intergovernmental credits, high-yields, and emerging market debt, his research supports the ING Investment Management global asset allocation team's allocation decisions. He is a recognized expert on growth, inflation, and central bank policy in the major economic blocks and the global dynamics that influence different regions. Until 2008, as a member of the global fixed-income team he was responsible for formulating the team's macroeconomic outlook. van Nieuwenhuijzen specialized in international macroeconomics at the University of Amsterdam, where he took his degree in 1998.

Jayanth R. Varma holds a doctorate in management from the Indian Institute of Management, Ahmedabad, and is a professor of finance and accounting at the same Institute. During the last 25 years as an academic he has worked mainly in the field of financial markets and their regulation. He has served on the board of the Securities and Exchange Board of India, on several government committees concerned with risk management and financial sector reforms, and also on the boards of a couple of Indian banks.

Theo Vermaelen is the Schroders professor of international finance and asset management at INSEAD, Fontainebleau, where he teaches Corporate Financial Strategy in Global Markets. He is a graduate of the Department of Applied Economics at the Catholic University of Leuven and obtained an MBA and PhD in finance from the Graduate School of Business, University of Chicago. He has taught at the University of British Columbia, the Catholic University of Leuven, the London Business School, UCLA, and the University of Chicago. Vermaelen has published articles on corporate finance and investment in leading academic journals, including the *Journal of Finance*, the *Journal of Financial Economics* and the *Journal of Banking and Finance*. He is coeditor of the *Journal of Empirical Finance* and associate editor of the *Journal of Corporate Finance* and the *European Financial Review*. He is also a consultant to various corporations and government agencies and program director of the Amsterdam Institute of Finance.

Curtis C. Verschoor is the emeritus Ledger and Quill research professor at the School of Accountancy and Management Information Systems and honorary senior Wicklander research fellow in the Institute for Business and Professional Ethics, both at DePaul University. He is also CEO and chair of C. C. Verschoor & Associates. His career in industry included service as the corporate controller of Colgate-Palmolive Company and of Baxter Laboratories, as vice president of finance and certified financial planner of a diversified public corporation, and as the chief internal auditor and assistant controller of the Singer Company. Professor Verschoor has written articles in many prominent journals. His most recent books are *Internal Auditing: Fundamental Principles and Best Practices*, *Audit Committee Essentials*, and *Ethics and Compliance: Challenges for Internal Auditing*.

Daud Vicary Abdullah is the managing director of DVA Consulting. Since 2002 he has focused exclusively on Islamic finance. He is a distinguished fellow of the Islamic Banking and Finance Institute Malaysia (IBFIM), a Chartered Islamic Finance Professional (CIFP), and a former board member of the Accounting and Auditing Organization for Islamic Financial Institutions (AAOIFI). He was the first managing director of Hong Leong Islamic Bank, after which he became chief operating officer and ultimately acting CEO at the Asian Finance Bank. He is now engaged by Deloitte to assist in the setting up of their global Islamic finance practice. Abdullah is a frequent speaker and commentator on matters relating to Islamic finance.

Stéphane Voisin is head of Sustainability Research and Responsible Investment at CA Cheuvreux. He also teaches sustainable finance at Paris Dauphine University and chairs the scientific committees of Good Planet. Stephane is a board member of Eurosif, the FIR, and Agrisud. Prior to joining CA Cheuvreux in 2005 to start and develop the Sustainability Research service, he was a vice-president at JP Morgan, at Paribas in London, and at Barclays and Natwest. Stéphane Voisin has authorised a number of Sustainability Research reports and articles from both equity markets and sustainability perspectives. He contributed to the "Finance and sustainable developments" Europlace work published by Economia ed.

Hans Vrensen is global head of research at DTZ. He is responsible for leading DTZ research worldwide and has launched the company's "Great wall of money" and "Global debt funding gap" reports and the DTZ Fair Value Index. Prior to joining DTZ, he was head of European securitization research at Barclays Capital, where he managed a team of analysts covering European asset-backed securities, and he has held several positions in the property sector. In particular, he has focused on bringing rigor to the research teams he has run. At Barclays Capital his team consistently received top three rankings in its area by *Institutional Investor* and *International Securitisation Report*. He is a

  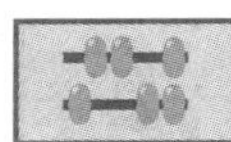      

chartered financial analyst and holds master degrees in both real estate and in economics.

Steve Wallace joined the Chartered Alternative Investment Analyst (CAIA) Association as associate director of industry relations in June 2008 and is based in England. Prior to joining the CAIA Association he managed client relations for several UK firms—most recently with an emerging market equity hedge fund as well as ING Wholesale Banking and Société Générale Corporate & Investment Banking. In addition, he spent seven years working in the private wealth management sector in Australia, primarily in investment strategy for high net worth individuals at firms, including the private bank division of National Australia Bank and AXA Australia.

Peter Walton is a professor of accounting at ESSEC Business School, Paris. He is IFRS director at the ESSEC–KPMG financial reporting chair. After working for British and French multinational companies, he became a journalist and researcher. He is a chartered certified accountant and has a PhD from the London School of Economics. His consultancy firm provides reports on the evolution of international financial reporting standards for audit firms, standard-setters and companies.

Wang Jiwei is a professor of accounting at Singapore Management University. He graduated with honors from Xi'an Jiaotong University with a bachelor's degree in economics and obtained his PhD in accounting from Hong Kong University of Science and Technology. He has many years of industry and academia experience in auditing, corporate reporting, financial statements analysis, and equity valuation. Dr Wang has been doing practical research on Chinese accounting standards and securities regulation. He has published research papers in prestigious international journals and serves on the editorial board of the *Singapore Accountant*. His research has also been profiled in the *Financial Times* and the *Straits Times*.

Véronique Weets is founder and managing partner of Cethys. She is a professor of international accounting and a faculty member of the Vrije Universiteit Brussel (VUB) and the University of Antwerp. She has several years of practical experience in one of the big four firms, where she was involved in client work on matters such as the transition to IFRS and the subsequent application of IFRS by listed companies. Weets also facilitates IFRS-related training programs for organizations such as IASeminars, Euromoney, and Quorum Training, and is a widely published author. She holds an IFRS certificate from the Association of Chartered Certified Accountants.

Juergen Bernd Weiss worked for almost 11 years at SAP AG in the SAP ERP (enterprise resource planning) financials area. In his last position he was consulting director for financial supply chain management and corporate performance management. He also worked as director of application solution management ERP and held global responsibility for financial supply chain management, particularly for SAP solutions in the areas of electronic bill presentment and payment, dispute management, credit management, in-house cash, and customer and vendor accounting. Prior to joining SAP in 1997 he worked for Westdeutsche Landesbank in Dösseldorf, Germany. He has degrees in economics and business.

Paul Wharton is chief investment strategist for Deutsche Bank Private Wealth Management UK, responsible for economic and market strategy and the income-oriented portfolios within the bank's UK onshore discretionary portfolio service. He serves on both the UK and the global investment committees of Deutsche Bank Private Wealth Management. A passionate student of economic history, he has more than 20 years' experience of investment markets and management. He graduated from University College London in 1985 and trained with Fidelity. He subsequently completed a diploma in business studies before establishing a pensions management business in conjunction with Norwich Union. In the early 1990s Wharton was recruited by Société Générale to develop a UK division serving the rapidly growing market for investors in self-invested personal pensions. In 2003 this business was sold to Tilney Investment Management, which was itself subsequently acquired by Deutsche Bank Private Wealth Management in 2006.

Jon White is a consultant specializing in the application of psychological thinking to the problems of organizational communication, working internationally for clients such as the European Commission and Shell. He is associated with Henley Business School, Cardiff University, the University of Central Lancashire, and universities in Germany and Switzerland, for teaching, research, and special projects. He has written books and articles on public affairs, public relations, and corporate communications practice, and management case studies for teaching purposes on organizations such as Dunhill, Lloyds of London, AEA Technology, Diageo, and the South African company Barloworld. He is a fellow of the UK's Chartered Institute of Public Relations.

Suzanne White, FCII, is chief executive officer of JWZ Solutions. Before founding JWZ Solutions, Dr White's most recent position was at a banking and finance institute in the Gulf, where, in addition to leading the insurance and accounting teaching teams, she was involved in other projects for the Chartered Insurance Institute as a member of the senior management team. A major responsibility and achievement was to establish the CII Academy at the Bahrain Institute of Banking and Finance (BIBF). Dr White has over 15 years of consultancy and training experience with educational and corporate entities, and she holds a PhD in educational research.

Philip Whittingham is European chief enterprise risk officer at XL Group, where he is responsible for developing risk management policy and approaches to meet the regulatory requirements of Solvency II and the Bermuda Monetary Authority. He started his career broking general insurance business in the London market before moving into risk management at a large UK insurer. He subsequently has had industry and consultancy roles centered on risk management, including at two Big Four firms, before joining XL in 2010. Whittingham is chairman of the Institute of Risk Management's Solvency II special interest group and is course developer and lead examiner of its risk management in financial services paper. He is a regular speaker on Solvency II and risk management.

Gervais Williams is managing director of Miton Group plc, and co-manages Miton's UK Smaller Companies Fund with Martin Turner. He has been an equity portfolio manager since 1985. His career includes five years with Throgmorton Investment Management (later part of the Framlington Group), three years with Thornton Investment Management (part of Dresdner Bank), and 17 years with Gartmore Group, where he was head of UK Small Companies. He won Investor of the Year as awarded by Grant Thornton at their Quoted Company Awards in both 2009 and 2010. He has sat on two UK Department of Trade and Industry committees in the quoted small-cap sector, is a member of the AIM Advisory Group of the London Stock Exchange, and has joined the board of the Quoted Companies Alliance.

Neil Williams is responsible for global economic research at Hermes Fund Managers and Hermes Asset Management. He has more than 20 years' experience of providing economic analysis and he generates investment strategy ideas for the fixed-income team. He adopts a top-down approach involving macro and market analysis to identify interest rate, credit value, and sovereign default risk. He began his career in 1987 at the Confederation of British Industry (CBI), becoming its youngest-ever head of economic policy. He went on to hold a number of senior positions at investment banks, including director of bond research at UBS, head of research at Sumitomo International, global head of emerging markets research at PaineWebber International, and, before

joining Hermes, head of sovereign research and strategy at Mizuho International, the London-based securities arm of one of Japan's largest banking groups.

Toby Willson was appointed finance director of Microsoft UK in July 2008. In this role he is responsible for all finance and accounting operations in Microsoft's UK subsidiary and is a member of the subsidiary leadership team. He has performed a number of finance roles within Microsoft UK, including those of financial controller and manager of the business control team. During the previous three years he has been based in Amsterdam performing the role of finance director Netherlands, and most recently he has spent six months as acting controller Western Europe. Prior to joining Microsoft he worked for Xerox and Centerprise International. Wilson has an economics degree and is a member of the Chartered Institute of Management Accountants.

Richard Wilson is a senior audit partner with Ernst & Young. He qualified as a chartered accountant in 1976 and became a partner in the firm in 1985. He has worked predominately with large listed companies in sectors such as oil and gas, media, and transportation. He was global head of Ernst & Young's energy and utilities practice from 1998 to 2003. He became a member of the Institute of Chartered Accountants in England and Wales (ICAEW) audit and assurance faculty in 2008 and a member of the Financial Reporting Council (FRC) financial reporting review panel in 2011.

Priscilla Wisner is a distinguished lecturer at the University of Tennessee. She formerly taught at Montana State University and the Thunderbird School of Global Management, and her research has been widely published in journals and books, including *Management International Review* and the *Harvard Business School Balanced Scorecard Report*. She also has more than 15 years' experience of consultancy with corporations. Dr Wisner earned her PhD at the University of Tennessee, an MBA degree from Cornell University, and a BA in international economics from the George Washington University.

Robert Wreschniok is managing director at Emanate in Germany. Before that he was business director at Pleon KohtesKlewes, responsible for reputation management and strategic stakeholder dialog. Together with Joachim Klewes, he is coeditor of the management book *Reputation Capital: Building and Maintaining Trust in the 21st Century*. After completing his MA in international relations at the University of Sussex, he received a certification in strategic foundation management from the University of Basel. He is a board member of the European Centre for Reputation Studies and spokesman of the Private Institute of Foundation Law.

David Wyss is chief economist at Standard & Poor's. He is responsible for S&P.'s economic forecasts and publications. Wyss joined Data Resources, Inc., in 1979 as an economist in the European Economic Service in London, which was acquired by McGraw-Hill. He returned to the United States in 1983 as chief financial economist for DRI/McGraw-Hill, became chief economist for Standard & Poor's DRI in 1992, and chief economist for Standard & Poor's in 1999. Wyss holds a BS from the Massachusetts Institute of Technology and a PhD in economics from Harvard University.

S. David Young is a professor at INSEAD (France and Singapore), holds a PhD from the University of Virginia, and is both a certified public accountant (United States) and a chartered financial analyst. His main research interests are value-based management, executive compensation, and corporate financial reporting. Most of his efforts focus on how businesses can align key management systems with the value creation imperative. His research has appeared in a wide range of academic and professional journals, including the *Harvard Business Review*. He is also a consultant, having advised many firms in Europe, North America, and Asia.

Pierre Yourougou is associate professor of finance at the Whitman School of Management, Syracuse University. He is also managing director of the Africa Business Program at the Whitman School. His research and teaching interests are in the areas of corporate finance, financial institutions and markets, and emerging markets. Prior to joining Syracuse University in 2006, Professor Yourougou worked for the World Bank, where he held various senior level positions in the corporate finance, financial products development, and public debt management departments. He received his PhD in banking and finance from New York University's Stern School of Business.

Abdel-Rahman Yousri Ahmad, PhD in economics (1968) from St Andrews University, Scotland, is professor and exchair of the Department of Economics at Alexandria University. He is a former director general of the International Institute of Islamic Economics at the International Islamic University, Islamabad, Pakistan. He is a member of the Economic Research Council and the Academy of Scientific Research and Technology, Ministry of Higher Education and Scientific Research, Egypt, and is a deputy and visiting professor to many universities and institutes in the Middle East, Asia, and Europe. Professor Yousri Ahmad is the author of nine textbooks and of 30 articles, most on Islamic economics and Islamic finance.

Hassan Ahmed Yusuf is operational risk manager at Masraf Al Rayan (Al Rayan Bank), an Islamic financial institution in Qatar. Currently a PhD candidate in Islamic finance at the International Islamic University Malaysia, he holds a MSc in economics from that university. He also holds a MBA in finance from the University of Poona and a BComm degree from Osmania University. He has written a number of published and unpublished articles on Islamic finance, *shariah*, and risk management in economic development. Yusuf is also a member of several risk management associations.

Chendi Zhang is assistant professor of finance at Warwick Business School. His main areas of research include corporate finance, behavioral finance, ethical/social investments, and emerging economies. He is junior extramural fellow of the CentER for Economic Research, Tilburg, the Netherlands, and was previously lecturer in finance at the University of Sheffield. He has also held positions as consultant/researcher at the World Bank and the International Finance Corporation (IFC), Washington, DC. Dr Zhang has published in academic journals such as the *Journal of Corporate Finance* and the *Journal of Banking and Finance*. He holds a PhD in financial economics from Tilburg University, the Netherlands.

Guofu Zhou is professor of finance at Olin Business School, Washington University. His teaching and research interests include asset pricing tests, asset allocation, portfolio optimization, Bayesian learning and model evaluation, econometric methods in finance, futures, options, and derivatives, the term structure of interest rates, and the real option valuation of corporate projects. Before joining Olin Business School in 1990, Zhou studied at Duke University for his PhD in economics and MA in mathematics, at Academia Sinica for an MS in numerical analysis, and at Chengdu College of Geology for a BS.

  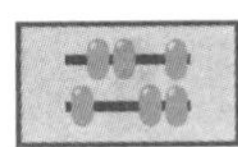      

QFINANCE User Guide

QFINANCE is a one-stop guide for finance professionals, compiled by 300 + expert advisers and contributors, covering topics such as Balance Sheets and Cash Flow, Financial Markets, Financial Regulation and Compliance, Funding and Investment, Governance and Ethics, Mergers and Acquisitions, and Operations and Performance.

QFINANCE includes:

- 300+ original best practice essays written by leading international finance experts and market movers
- 300+ step-by-step guides to solving everyday problems and making calculations
- analysis of 105 countries and 26 industry sectors
- definitions for 9,000 + financial terms
- 113 influential finance books summarized
- 2,000 + insightful quotations
- coverage of subject areas ranging from accounting to wealth management
- concise biographies of the world's key thinkers behind modern finance

The material is split into nine distinct sections to ensure ease of navigation. Each section is extensively cross-referenced across and within topics.

BEST PRACTICE

Putting the expertise of the world's leading finance writers, educators, and practitioners to work for you

The **Best Practice** section presents a powerful array of practical advice and fresh thinking reflecting the full spectrum of issues that define finance today.

Internationally renowned finance leaders, experts, and educators distil the most important aspects of finance best practice. Contributors include Riccardo Rebonato, James Gifford, Ian Bremmer, James Montier, Scott Moeller, and John Mauldin.

Essays

Each essay begins with an **Executive Summary** for quick reference, outlining the main points in the article. The **Making It Happen** feature illustrates practical applications of the principles and concepts, and where relevant authors have provided illustrative case studies and definitions of technical terms. In addition the **More Info** section includes recommendations of related books, articles, reports, and websites, and is linked to detailed hands-on advice in the **Checklists, Calculations and Ratios**.

Viewpoints

Viewpoints have been contributed by some of the world's most prominent financial minds. The articles and interviews are forward-looking and agenda-setting explorations of personal perspectives on the future of finance in an environment of constant challenge and change.

CHECKLISTS

Finding practical solutions to everyday finance problems

The **Checklists** section provides a comprehensive handbook of practical answers to the daily challenges of modern finance. Each checklist is a step-by-step guide to achieving the best results in areas including hedging interest rate risk, governance practices, project appraisal, estimating enterprise value, and managing credit ratings. Each checklist reflects current thinking and best practice, and includes a list of "dos" and "don'ts" as well as critical reflection on the topic at hand.

CALCULATIONS AND RATIOS

The **Calculations and Ratios** section presents the essential mathematical tools the finance professional needs for finding solutions to daily numerical problems. This section includes how to calculate return on investment, return on shareholders' equity, working capital productivity, EVA, risk-adjusted rate of return, CAPM, and many more.

FINANCE THINKERS AND LEADERS

Profiling the top finance thinkers and leaders

This section provides over 50 profiles of the most influential or controversial finance writers, thinkers, and entrepreneurs; those who shaped modern finance through their contributions to both theory and practice. These profiles offer insights into the background, defining moments, and legacies of each of the key characters including Joseph de la Vega, Franco Modigliani, Louis Bachelier, Warren Buffett, Paul Samuelson, and Myron Scholes.

FINANCE LIBRARY

Summarizing the most influential finance books

The canon of finance literature is vast, with hundreds more publications emerging every year. This section distils the main lessons from most influential finance books both past and present, from the cornerstones to the most popular reads, from *Against the Gods* to *Portfolio Theory and Capital Markets* and *The Great Crash*.

Each summary includes a concise overview and analysis of the book's most distinctive contributions to finance thinking and practice, along with bibliographic information for the featured title and related works by the author.

COUNTRY AND SECTOR PROFILES

Country and Sector Profiles provide an in-depth analysis of 105 countries comprising EU, OECD, and OPEC members, and composites of MSCI, emerging markets, and MENA indexes, plus coverage of 26 industry sectors from automobiles to water.

FINANCE INFORMATION SOURCES

Providing the quickest and easiest route to the best financial information available

Finance Information Sources brings together the best financial information sources from around the world. Organized into over 60 subject areas, this carefully selected list includes authoritative books, magazines, journals, and websites, as well as key organizations.

QUOTATIONS

This section includes more than 2,000 quotations on finance, management, leadership, money, and business.

  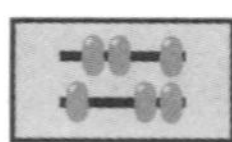      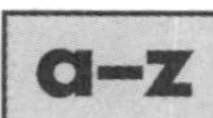

DICTIONARY

The most up-to-date global finance dictionary

Over 9,000 terms providing a comprehensive global dictionary of finance and banking vocabulary. See p. 1926 for further details of the dictionary.

QFINANCE ONLINE

To complement your print copy of *QFINANCE*, a fully searchable electronic version can be found at **qfinance.com.** The online edition of the book will be regularly updated to incorporate the very the latest developments in this fast-moving area.

FEEDBACK

We welcome any comments you may have about how ***QFINANCE*** might be improved. Let us know, too, if you disagree with any of the points made, or have any corrections, we welcome your views. Write to us at qfinance@bloomsbury.com.

BEST PRACTICE

Best Practice

Putting the expertise of the world's best business thinkers to work for you

The purpose of the Best Practice section is to provide you with incisive information covering key problems and finance-related issues you are likely to face during your working life.

With over 250 contributors, this section presents a powerful array of practical advice and thinking from some of the world's leading finance authors, educators, and practitioners.

However, don't expect easy answers to every problem. These essays are not designed to be the last word on the subject, but an easy-to-read and practical introduction. There are extensive links to detailed hands-on advice on "how to do it" in later sections.

We have tried to organize these essays so you can browse them quickly. The section is therefore divided into seven broad themes: Balance Sheets and Cash Flow, Financial Markets, Financial Regulation and Compliance, Funding and Investment, Governance and Ethics, Mergers and Acquisitions, and Operations and Performance.

At the beginning of each essay is an **Executive Summary** for quick reference, outlining the key areas in the article

The **Making It Happen** section shows you how you can apply what has been discussed in practice. Where relevant, authors have provided examples to show how theories have been implemented.

Most essays provide you with a short directory entitled **More Info**, as well as quick links to other sections in *QFINANCE*.

We have also provided a number of distinguished **Viewpoints**, which provide you with perspectives on a number of finance-related themes including the corporate social responsibility, the future of asset management, and financial regulation. These are based on a number of exclusive interviews and essays contributed by some of the world's leading finance thinkers such as Janet Campagna, Catherine Howarth, John Mauldin, Arun Motianey, Stephen Penman, Robert, Lord Skidelsky, and Paul Wharton. Our aim here is to stimulate, to provoke, and to inspire.

Contents

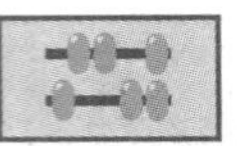

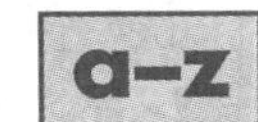

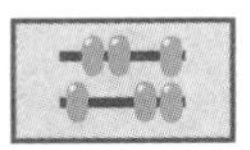

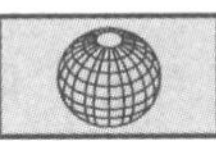

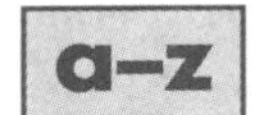

QFINANCE

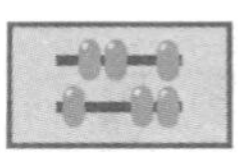

     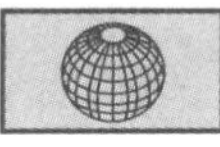   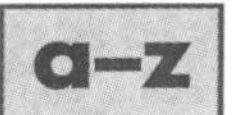
a–z

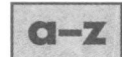

Advantages of Finance Best Practice Networks

by Hans-Dieter Scheuermann

EXECUTIVE SUMMARY

The article describes the needs of complex finance transformations projects and how finance best practice networks can help an organization find the best practices that fit its specific requirements.

- Most business transformation projects require that the finance function is prepared to enable and accompany change.
- Governance and stewardship is one role. Finance excellence in operations and business partnering is the second one.
- Finance best practice networks are the platform to exchange experiences: Examples from Roche, BHP Billiton, Nestlé, BP, and Philips illustrate such projects.

INTRODUCTION

The Best Practice Network for Finance and HR is a network for senior executives and best practice leaders at the senior executive level—spanning nations and industries. The goal is to facilitate networking, and allow the business leaders of large customers to exchange experiences and their use of best practices. The Best Practice Network for Finance and HR injects ideas and concepts into a cross-company network of professionals to identify best practices, disseminate information members can learn from, test new ideas, and develop practical solutions that work in specific company environments.

By tapping into the vast amount of experiences out there, and a new willingness to share and connect, companies stand to gain. Why not learn from an insurance company how best to prepare for risk, and why not talk to an oil company to learn how to handle the current trend to be green?

FINANCE TRANSFORMATION PROJECTS

Many companies currently undergo big projects such as a finance transformation, responding to the needs of corporate governance, and, at the same time, optimizing the organization of their finance functions. Finance transformation projects typically follow four main areas for improvement: Processes, organization, information systems, and people. From the viewpoint of an IT (information technology) company, it is of utmost importance that the goal, the process, and the organizational structure are clearly laid out, agreed on, and planned, before they are set in stone by the implementation of an IT system. What is required is a multi-step process towards management of information management—according to Peter Drucker "focusing on the 'I' in 'IT,' not on technology first." First, it is important to understand the critical business and chief financial officer (CFO) issues, and their mission. The second step is to design or redesign the finance and/or business architecture, and its processes. The final step, only after completion of the first two, is to design or re-engineer the IS architecture and solutions. Only by integrating all three views, can IT/IS (information system) create maximum value, enabling the possibility for optimal trade-off decisions.

The structure and goals of finance transformation projects reflect what the production and supply-chain side of companies have already addressed under the umbrella of "lean manufacturing"–the acceleration, automation, and simplification of processes; the reduction of working capital; the implementation of centers of expertise; the saving on labor costs; etc. It is possible to create more value with less work, by dispensing with wasteful activities, and applying best practices. On the financial side, companies look at shared services, simplify the charts of accounts, optimize their financial supply chain, put their management reporting on a diet, and implement employee and manager self-services. Reporting does happen in a "pull mode" by the business user instead of being "pushed" on a periodic schedule.

As financial transformation most often leads to automation and efficiency gains as well, financial capacity is freed to support the business in a different way from before. Where better analytics and real-time business insight become available in an ever-more complex world, the finance function can and must develop from a bean-counting report provider into a trusted, well-equipped, knowledgeable, and respected business partner. "If we are honest, most finance professionals are still at the backend of the pipeline, still analyzing what others have done. The challenge in the future will be to help to develop the pipeline rather than reporting on the pipeline and on the ideas of others," says Paul Koppelman, CFO of BHP Billiton Marketing, in his presentation at the European CFO Roundtable on July 9–10, 2007, in Hamburg, Germany.

FINANCE AS THE BUSINESS PARTNER

Dominic Moorhead, head of finance and accounting at F. Hoffmann-La Roche Pharma, and his team put the following quote rather nicely into their finance credo, which he presented at the European CFO

Figure 1. General Electric (Jeff Immelt's view). (*Source*: Björn Bergabo, CFO of GE Commercial Finance, SAP Finance Best Practice Workshop, September 22, 2005, Barcelona)

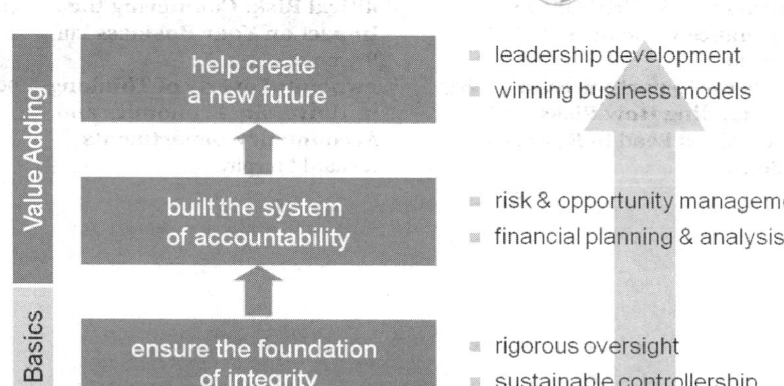

"For top executives to award themselves these kinds of compensation packages in the midst of this economic crisis is not only bad taste, it's bad strategy—and I will not tolerate it as president." Barack Obama

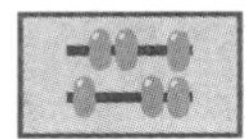

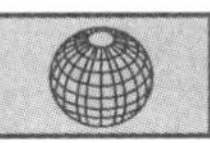

Roundtable in Hamburg, Germany: "Our winning finance team will navigate the path to new heights of business performance, leading with our partners in crafting and executing value enhancing decisions, while ensuring financial peace."

At the basic level, finance transformation requires a secure foundation of rigorous oversight and sustained controllership to ensure integrity of the function. It adds value as soon as a system of accountability is built, by introducing risk and opportunity management, and financial planning and analysis. However, the greatest step towards the creation of a new future is being done by leadership-development and winning-business models, where finance comes in as the business partner, according to Jeff Immelt, chief executive officer (CEO) of General Electric.

The result can be a "house of finance," as described, for example, by the former CFO of Nestlé, Paul Polman. Polman established four pillars that support profitable growth: Co-pilots/business partners (grouped along countries, product lines, etc.); specialist services (for example, for tax); business services (for example, for accounting), and decision-support services (for example, costing).

In the networked business environment of today, many have come to the conclusion that you can no longer be excellent on your own. A. G. Lafley, CEO of P&G, said: "In 2000, a little more than 10% of our innovation was partnered... last year, a bit more than 40% of what we commercialized had at least one external partner." So, apart from optimal processes, a stable infrastructure, and an effective leadership development program, intelligent business networks could be an important element of what a high-performing organization requires.

FINANCE BEST PRACTICE NETWORKS

There are a number of business networks out there that may support an organization's striving for learning and exchange, and help it to cope with the challenges ahead.

The Conference Board, for example, runs regular meetings that focus on IT, shared services, and other topics with attendees from multinational organizations.

The Corporate Executive Board reports on case studies and presents the results at conferences.

Hackett and other benchmark providers run surveys and share the resulting studies in annual conferences.

And also the major consulting companies offer a variety of events to enable networking among peers.

Figure 2. Nestlé's house of finance. (*Source*: Paul Polman, CFO of Nestlé, SAP CFO Round Table, July 2007, Hamburg)

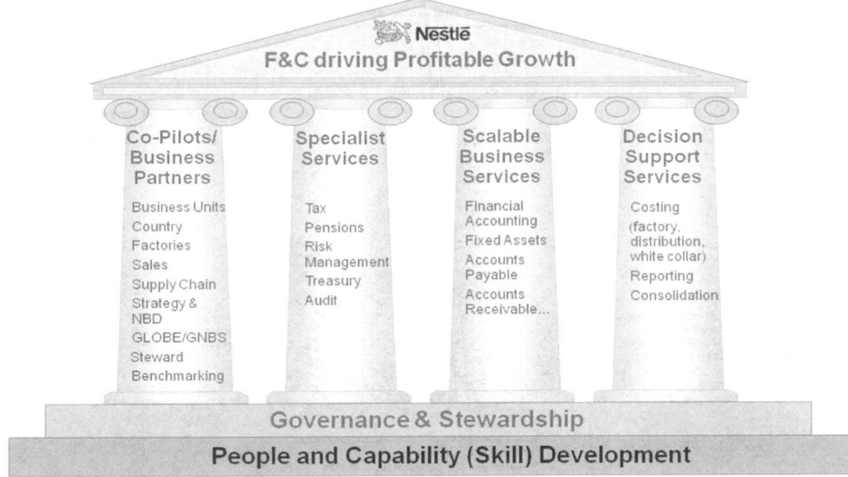

Figure 3. The different roles of finance. (*Source*: Daum, J. H. *ZfCM—Zeitschrift für Controlling & Management* 52 [June 2008])

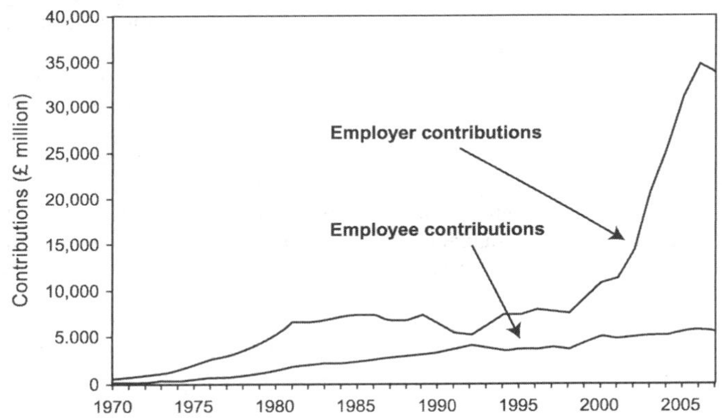

Figure 4. The multi-level finance best practice network. (*Source*: H. D. Scheuermann, SAP CFO Round Table, July 2007, Hamburg)

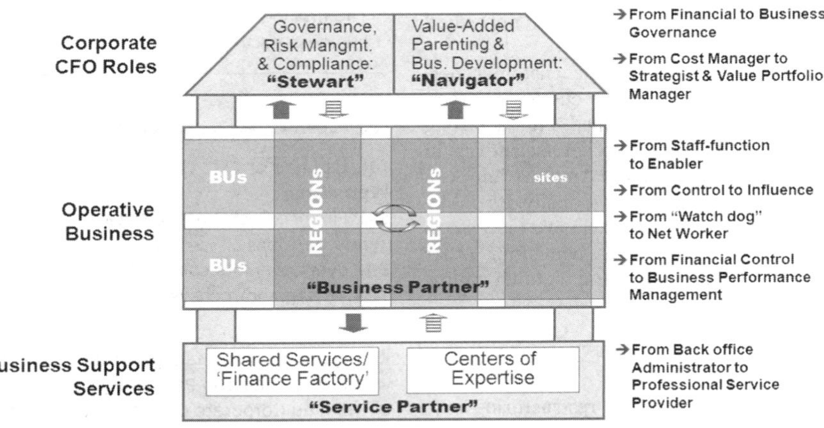

"The bonus system has proved to be wrong. Substantial cash bonuses do not reward the right kind of behaviour."
Andy Hornby

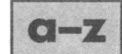

Figure 5. Value delivery. (*Source*: Amy Senew Brown. "Value delivery." Presentation for the Value Management Office at SAP, November 2008)

THE SAP FINANCE BEST PRACTICE NETWORK

The SAP Finance Best Practice Network offers peer-to-peer exchange of experiences and learning, with a special focus on three dimensions of the aforementioned complex projects. First, the green light and budget typically come top-down from the CFO, who can also give the necessary management backing when it comes to politically difficult decisions and measures, such as staff reductions. Second, a project manager is needed who can set priorities for the whole program, align its different parts, including aligning it with the organization, and, as in our example, also align business needs and IT capabilities. Third, an expert is needed to look at the detail. Ideally, an exchange of experiences takes place on all three levels, thus providing a complete picture of the project, from the strategic to the tool view. The SAP Finance Best Practice Network offers a whole set of events targeted at each management level participating in a finance transformation program, as described earlier.

It is a business-specific customer network, with customer-to-customer-driven events that has developed into a strong and vibrant community of executives in Europe, North and Latin America, and Asia who share best practices globally. Its online community enables exclusive access to case studies, as well as contacting other community members and holding online discussions.

BP'S FINANCE TRANSFORMATION PROGRAM

BP underwent a major restructuring process of its enterprise resource planning (ERP) systems in the early 2000s. BP had suffered from a plethora of different systems and processes, stemming from its extensive mergers and acquisitions during the 1990s. Through outsourcing of IT and finance operations, BP lost a lot of knowledge, and was heavily dependent on external consultants. As part of a five-year plan, BP was looking at a whole finance transformation program, including processes, analytics, management reporting, shared services, risk management, charts of accounts, master data management, and so on. Clive Thomas, then financial solutions director, found out about the SAP Finance Best Practice Network at an early stage, and became a regular and enthusiastic attendee, as the topics in the meetings fitted his needs perfectly. Away from consulting spin and sales pitches, he was able to learn and research how organizations from his own and other industries had conquered the same unknown lands. "Many great companies have done many great things—we needed to filter these and see which areas were appropriate for BP," Thomas says. Among the case studies Thomas looked at, in the exclusive circle of companies gathered in the network round him, were how Siemens had solved the puzzle of complex organizational models, how Philips in the Netherlands had harmonized its multitude of charts of accounts, and how BHP Billiton had got to grips with risk management. BP, in return, shared its Sarbanes–Oxley activities with Shell, helped Nestlé to consolidate its African banking and treasury operations, and helped Barclays set up operations where currencies run into too many digits. After the first two meetings, Thomas even arranged his travel to Singapore, London, and Houston to match the schedule of the sessions. He wanted to: "listen to real-life customer experiences, and look and see what went well and what didn't."

Networking helped BP to compare itself to other customers, and find out about innovations and opportunities within its own organization, while benchmarks gave reliable figures that helped to create a sense of urgency to change. BP was able to access a collaborative platform online with all past case studies, and even find out about relevant solutions and roadmaps from an IT perspective, by using the SAP network. All that knowledge helped BP to prioritize and plan the project, knowledge which was also an important cornerstone in the sense of being effective risk management for the endeavor.

MAKING IT HAPPEN

- Start with end-to-end finance processes and a bridge to IT before starting an IT project.
- The finance function, led by the CFO, has a strong role in business change projects as a business partner.

MORE INFO

Websites:

SAP Finance Best Practice Network, for finance professionals: www.sap.com/community/private/fbpn

SAP overview of its communities for different information needs and target groups: www.sap.com/ecosystem/communities

See Also:

★ Engaging Senior Management in Internal Control (pp. 336–337)
★ Internal Audit and Partnering with Senior Management (pp. 368–371)
✔ Defining Corporate Governance: Its Aims, Goals, and Responsibilities (p. 1115)

"You can blame it on me and close the book, but it doesn't come close to explaining what happened." Sir Fred Goodwin

  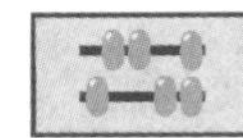   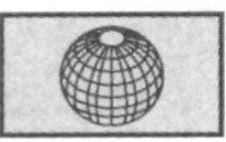   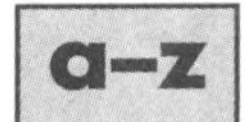

Allocating Corporate Capital Fairly by John L. Mariotti

EXECUTIVE SUMMARY

- The principal job of management is the allocation of scarce resources—people, time, and money—to opportunities that yield the greatest returns.
- There is always a shortage of capital and an excess of worthy projects. There are many methods of capital allocation, but most do not fund the best opportunities.
- The key task is to allocate capital to support the greatest opportunities, those that match strategic objectives.

INTRODUCTION

The appetite of organizations for capital is insatiable. Understanding the nature of capital and its effective allocation is essential to organizational success. Classical economics defines land, labor, and capital as the determinants of wealth, each being exclusive to its owner. Now there is a fourth determinant of wealth—information—and it is nonexclusive. The more information is shared, the more valuable it becomes. Business is a competition in which the score is kept in money, and thus allocation of capital, in all its forms, is a critical success factor.

The challenge is to decide which division, project, or acquisition gets the scarce capital. The challenge varies with the source of capital. Venture capitalists' and hedge funds' tolerance for risk is offset by their high return expectations. The low risk of municipal bonds and banks is matched by low returns. Hedge funds make increasingly larger "bets," while equity investors carefully consider exit strategies in capital allocation decisions. Privately owned companies strive to enhance shareholder value, matching investment choices to their investors' expectations. Public companies are servants of the public stock markets and investment analysts. Each master has different expectations, and thus capital allocation must vary accordingly.

ALLOCATING CAPITAL

If capital is allocated foolishly, or to poorly defined projects, it is wasted. The game is a simple one: invest the least possible amount, borrow the rest, and put it in projects with the greatest potential return (or occasionally the lowest risk). Deciding which ventures to invest in has always occupied management attention. There are many quantitative methods for allocating capital. Most of these remain valid, but they share one problem: they all depend on a forecast of future events, which is uncertain. The challenge is to allocate capital to the best opportunities, given the risk-reward profile of the investors, and to choose projects that have the best chance of earning good returns.

The Typical Plan: Allocation for Strategic Purposes and Objectives

Capital allocation must be aligned with the strategic purposes and objectives of the investor. The implication is that these are well defined and clearly understood. However, this is frequently not the case. Often the strategies and goals are unclear or poorly understood.

MAKING IT HAPPEN

The Capital Appropriation Process

When management has determined what it believes is an effective use of capital, it must find a means to communicate that need and its worthiness relative to other needs. Larger organizations use a formal capital appropriation process. This process involves documentation of the intended use, description of the assets to be acquired, time frames for the investments, and benefits to be gained. A financial analysis is a required part of the capital appropriation request

The methods used to compare and evaluate capital investments are based on projections of future revenue streams and a calculation of some combination of:

- internal rate of return (IRR);
- net present value (NPV);
- breakeven;
- economic value added (EVA);
- economic profit created (EP);
- risk-adjusted return on capital (RAROC).

This approach rewards the best analysts, politicians, and sycophants, but not the best projects. The most innovative, high-potential projects are seldom easy to analyze and quantify. Yet these are the very ideas that turn out to be outstanding—but only in retrospect—and only if they ever get funded. In traditional allocation, the capital tends to be spent either protecting the past or perfecting the present, with precious little left for funding the future. For reasons of personal or organizational pride, differing goals, or political power, appropriation requests often do not match corporate goals. Competing executives or organizations will scuffle for scarce capital, and even if their intentions are good (which they usually aren't) the resulting conflicts can be ugly. Who is to resolve these conflicts

Approvals and the Capital Appropriation Committee

In some companies the authority level for heads of business units is high—assuming funds have been budgeted—in the category needed. This means there is a chance that good, innovative ideas might receive financing. In central-control-oriented companies spending approval levels are kept low, forcing corporate reviews of most investments.

Appropriation requests go up the ladder to be approved by successively higher levels of management, and the higher one goes, the less informed the management tends to be. The originator's chain of command includes gatekeepers from finance and accounting. Other functions affected often have sign-off rights, too. This creates a time-consuming, bureaucratic, and often contentious process that wrings the creativity out of any proposal, replacing it with conservatism, caution, and capital "constipation."

After running the divisional bureaucratic gauntlet, the appropriation goes to the corporate capital appropriation committee, where it is subjected to more scrutiny by even less informed people. This review is supposedly based on alignment with corporate strategies, return versus competing capital needs, and the requesting unit's budget. The larger the organization the more levels there may be, but the process varies surprisingly little from company to company.

When small companies grow rapidly, capital allocation is efficient and effective—and involves only a few well-informed people. As the company gets larger or is acquired by a larger entity, it implements a more formal capital approval process. This process now includes approval at higher authority levels. While this is considered necessary, it is noticeably slower and less efficient. The successive layers of capital appropriation processes and committees can slow down or even kill most creative projects and divert capital to safer, less rewarding uses.

Historically, depreciation was designed to fund the replacement of assets by expensing non-cash charges, thereby reserving the cash (capital) for new expenditures. Thus the norm was

"What is the first duty—and the continuing responsibility of the business manager? To strive for the best possible economic results from the resources currently employed or available." Peter F. Drucker

  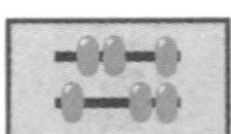      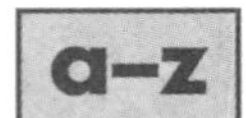

The Typical Practice: An Artifact—The Capital Budget

Organizations develop capital expenditure budget needs for annual review by boards and lenders. A common breakdown of a capital budget is by category or type of expenditure—for example, new products, new facilities, maintenance of existing products or facilities, and infrastructure needs. This is a theoretically sound method since each category has a different strategic purpose: for example, sustaining current activities or revenue streams, creating new revenue streams, or providing infrastructure to support current or new business needs. These category splits are intended to allow senior management and boards to allocate capital fairly according to the company's strategic needs. The problem is that there is an enormous gap developing those artifacts of bygone eras—capital budgets—and the actual intent of the investments. This traditional route is a sure path to sustained mediocrity or steady decline.

CONCLUSION

Companies usually allocate capital on the basis of one of three mindsets.

- The first is protecting the past, in which case they will always be following the competition and reacting to a leader's moves, simply trying to hang on to past glories.
- The second mindset is the attractive trap of perfecting the present. Such moves are always easier to analyze, and make short-term goals, except when new, disruptive technology or a competitor enters the fray, upsetting the applecart.
- The third mindset is the critical one—to allocate capital by investing in funding the future. This is harder and riskier, but it is the only true path to success. The capital need must attract the needed capital based on its potential success.

Few traditional appropriation processes accommodate this approach, which is why so few companies succeed over the longer term. Companies trying to fund the future are often led by "escapees" from the other kind of companies—people seeking outlets for creative brilliance and thwarted by bureaucratic, inwardly focused capital appropriation processes, policies, and committees. The best rule for capital allocation is to allocate very little to protecting the past and just enough to perfecting the present, leaving plenty to spend on funding the future. That is where real wealth and excitement lies—if only management and boards will finance it.

for capital allocation to equal depreciation. To spend more is equivalent to putting in new money, and to spend less is in effect using up the business. Many lending agreements also contain restrictive covenants that limit capital spending to formulae—the right spending level is a function of what happened in the past adjusted by management's or investors' wishes. The obvious corollary is that, if the company is struggling, it is often starved of the necessary capital to rebuild itself.

Other Challenges in Capital Allocation

Cash-rich companies also have a problem. A low return on conservatively invested cash reduces overall returns. Companies are expected to earn higher returns than banks. A common alternative is to repurchase stock, a less than exciting capital allocation. In other cases, company treasurers are tempted to use high-risk investments like derivatives to elevate returns on excess cash. Multinational companies encounter another issue: currency exchange rate fluctuations, which can negate the best analyses. Hedging currency by buying futures can protect the downside, but, like all insurance, this too comes at a cost. Then there are fiascos in which capital allocation is based on equity markets and stock prices. The dot-com deals involving stock swaps quickly revealed the flaws here: huge profits disappeared overnight, replaced by unexpected write-offs. Misadventures like the Enron illusion or the subprime mortgage fiasco clearly illustrate how easily a bogus capital structure can tumble like a house of cards.

Furthermore, what happens to budgeted but unspent money? The government model—use it or lose it—is often used. The rush to spend unused budgeted capital results in waste, misallocation, or both. Alternatively, a passive indecision deprives the enterprise of funding for its growth or rejuvenation.

Nonmoney "Capital"

Finally, there are critical non-capital resources to be allocated—people, knowledge, or time. The people part is often called "human capital," an appropriate name. If this human capital is in short supply, all the monetary capital in the world will not help. Capital must be spent wisely or allocating it well is useless. People spend the capital, and thus the most important question to ask is not what it will be spent on, but who will be spending it and what is their track record? Choosing the right people to bet on is the critical decision.

An Alternative to Allocation?

In the bubble era of 2000–2001 capital flowed freely to those perceived to deserve it; those perceived as undeserving were starved. Many decisions were bad, but consider the concept. Instead of allocating capital, think of "earning it and/or deserving it." Innovative ideas seldom survive bureaucratic battles, particularly if they threaten to cannibalize existing businesses. Harvard's Clayton Christensen has written at length about "disruptive technologies" and their impact on markets. In the real world, an idea should either be able to attract capital or not. No corporate committee says yea or nay. The idea must prove that it deserved the capital by being successful. That is capital allocation's model for the 21st century.

MORE INFO

Books:

Drucker, Peter F. *Management Challenges for the 21st Century*. New York: HarperBusiness, 1999.

Hamel, Gary. *Leading the Revolution*. Cambridge, MA: Harvard Business School Press, 2000.

Hamel, Gary, and C. K. Prahalad. *Competing for the Future*. Boston, MA: McGraw-Hill, 1996.

Selden, Larry, and Geoffrey Colvin. *Angel Customers & Demon Customers*. New York: Portfolio, 2003.

Websites:

The Enterprise Group: www.mariotti.net

Telling It Like It Is, John L. Mariotti's blog: mariotti.blogs.com/my_weblog

See Also:

★ Capital Budgeting: The Dominance of Net Present Value (pp. 20–23)
★ Comparing Net Present Value and Internal Rate of Return (pp. 30–32)
★ Managing Capital Budgets for Small and Medium-Sized Companies (pp. 68–70)
✔ Understanding Economic Efficiency Theory (p. 1126)
✔ Understanding the Relationship between the Discount Rate and Risk (p. 1001)

"The majority of products in most companies are cash traps. They will absorb more money forever than they will generate." Bruce Henderson

  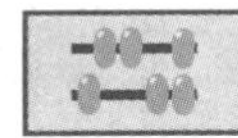      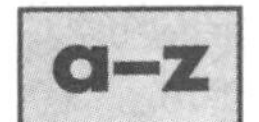

Asset Liability Management for Pension Funds

by Ruud Kleynen

EXECUTIVE SUMMARY

- Asset liability management (ALM) is an overall risk management technique for pension funds.
- ALM requires the board to formulate guidelines for its strategy on contribution and indexing levels, and its attitude to risk.
- ALM is based on stochastic simulation and is used as a basis for decisions on the distribution of future contributions, funding, and indexing levels.
- Practicing ALM requires an assets and liabilities committee (ALCO). An ALCO consists of senior pension fund management, with the chief risk officer as chairman. The committee converts the guidelines into formal proposals on the investment strategy and the contributions and indexing policies.
- ALM does not predict the future, but it gives insight into the possible risks a pension fund is exposed to and how to handle them.
- An ALM model should be as parsimonious and uncomplicated as possible. The purpose of such models is to act as a tool to help management understand what is really going on, and how to reach responsible and internally consistent decisions.

INTRODUCTION

The management of a pension fund has to make decisions about its strategic asset allocation, its contributions policy, and its indexing policy in a context of acceptable financial risk. It has to meet the return requirements necessary to improve benefit payments on the one hand, and to stay in line with the solvency requirements of the regulator on the other. But what is an acceptable contributions and indexing policy, and how is an acceptable risk attitude defined? ALM forces the board to think about these aspects, and to quantify them. That is not an easy job. But only by giving clear guidelines does risk management have practical and measurable value. Putting ALM into practice is not a solo achievement but requires a multidisciplinary team of specialists who are willing to work together. Formalization normally results in the so-called assets and liabilities committee, or ALCO, with the chief risk officer as chairman.

THE AIM OF ALM

A crucial stage in the exploration of an ALM strategy is the development of the funding level. The funding level is the ratio of the market value of the assets and the market value of the liabilities. Funding levels below 100% are disliked because the assets do not cover the total value of the liabilities. So management of the funding level in general, and the possibility of underfunding in particular, is of primary importance. Generating high funding levels is easy to accomplish. Just increasing the contributions and investing them in low-risk assets will generate attractive funding levels. However, neither employers nor employees will be too enthusiastic about this solution because they are faced with high pension contributions.

Another important concern is the indexing policy. Pension funds aim to index their benefit payments based on the price inflation of the previous year to protect pensioners from loss of purchasing power. Such indexing clauses are conditional, as full indexing can only be implemented if the funding level is high enough. The closer the funding level falls to the 100% mark, the less the benefits will be increased. If benefit payments are to be made inflation-resistant, adequate indexing levels are very important.

ALM, therefore, is the search for a balanced perspective. By practicing ALM we want to find a balance between future contributions on the one hand and future funding and indexing levels on the other. To accomplish this, the choice of strategic asset allocation plays an important role, as Figure 1 shows.

WHY IS ALM IMPORTANT?

Within a pension fund, investment managers, risk managers, accountants, actuaries, CEOs, and CFOs have to communicate, and communication is not that easy. How nice it would be if we all spoke the same language. ALM helps us. ALM is a technique that pension funds employ in coordinating the management of assets and liabilities. An ALM approach forces all parties to quantify the relevant factors and bundles them into an overall framework. The effects of separate decisions are analyzed in an overall context. Isolated decision-making is no longer possible. ALM is therefore a financial risk assessment and asset planning tool used by pension funds to help them choose the strategic policy under uncertainty, and in a coherent and consistent balance sheet approach.

ALM MODELING

In the complex environment in which pension funds have to operate, ALM requires an instrument to identify and manage risks. Such an instrument is a stochastic simulation model, which mimics the behavior of a pension fund by incorporating randomness to obtain a statistical sample of possible outcomes. ALM modeling is thus a key method in strategic risk management. It involves developing mathematical scenarios of the future evolution of

Figure 1. The impact of asset allocation on returns. © Kleynen Consultants bv

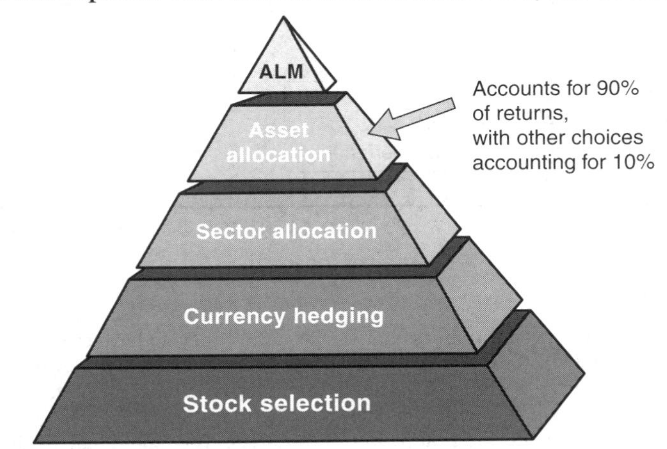

“Companies that have been around for 50 years are another world to me. I entered the technology arena the same year that Microsoft was started. And the arena has always felt like a meritocracy, though there were never many women.”
Ann Winblad

Figure 2. Examples of pension fund cash flow and term structure. © **Kleynen Consultants bv**

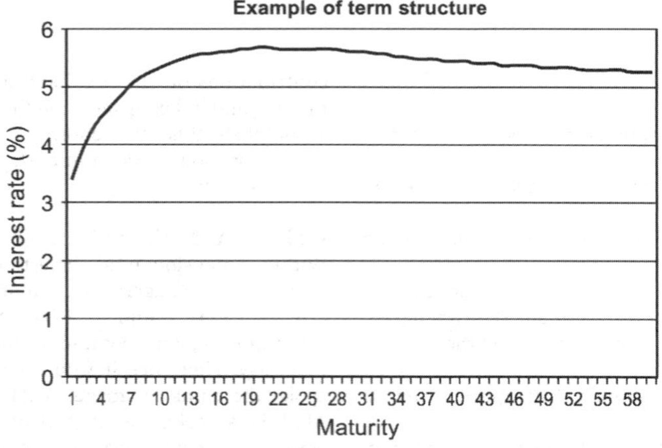

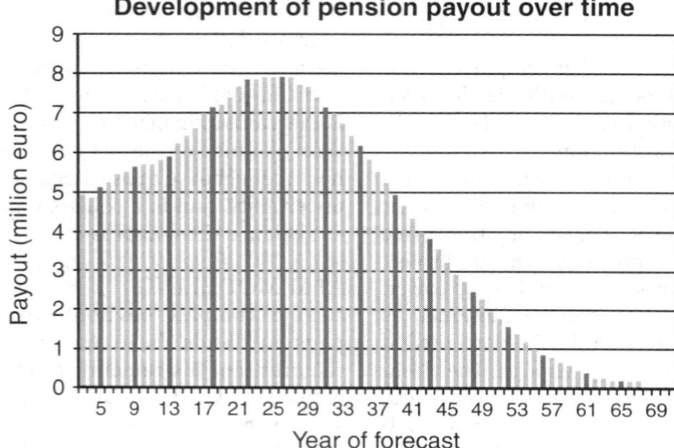

Figure 3. Main characteristics of the probability of underfunding. © **Kleynen Consultants bv**

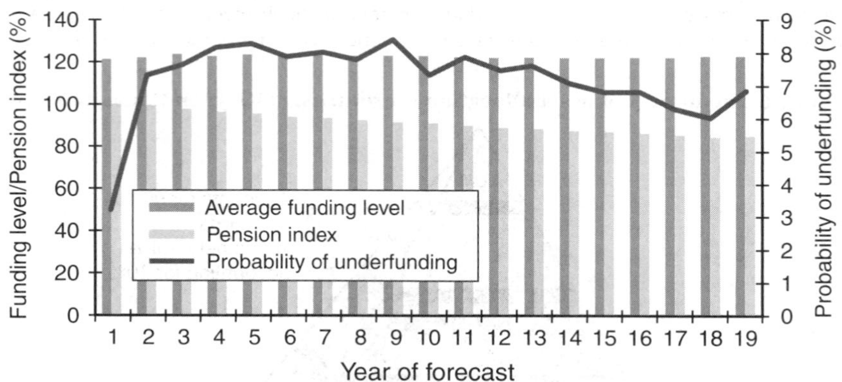

assets and liabilities, given certain assumptions about the statistical properties of the variables that affect the evolution of assets and liabilities. Though dynamic models have proven a better fit for real world scenarios, they do have their drawbacks, as due to their complexity they may be harder to understand and interpret.

There are many ways to generate these scenarios. The traditional method was to create a central scenario, and to carry out some stress testing around it. With time the models have become more sophisticated, involving stochastic simulation of assets and liabilities. Modern ALM studies rely on stochastic models that generate thousands of scenarios, with different probabilities attached to each. While the traditional ALM studies focused on asset optimization with a deterministic view of liabilities, today ALM is increasingly used to simulate the consequences of policies for different stakeholders while complying with the requirements of the regulatory authorities. In this sense, ALM systems are used as integrated planning systems to simultaneously determine investment, funding, and—if applicable—indexation policies, thereby balancing the goals of the different stakeholders. Each ALM system has its own unique characteristics, principally governed by the underlying stochastic processes and distribution functions.[1] The main financial uncertainty comes from changing asset prices and interest rates, and from transition probabilities. But how do they behave? Questions such as "Are there differences between short-term and long-term behavior?"[2] have to be asked, and if the answer is yes, they should be modeled. Furthermore, modeling normally concentrates only on stocks and bonds, so the question arises whether investment products should also be included.[3]

Pension Fund XYZ: Some Characteristics

The ALM study for pension fund XYZ starts with assumptions about investments, participants, financial construction, contribution policy, and indexing.

Investments: The total value of the investment portfolio at year-end is 150,000 million euros. The structure of the portfolio is assumed to be the same as that of the strategic investment portfolio. This implies a portfolio based on a constant mix of 65% fixed income, 25% equity, and 10% real estate.

Charges: The charge for solvency, set by the rules formulated by the pension regulator De Nederlandsche Bank, is equal to 23% of the net reserve. The charge is based on the portfolio structure, the cash flow scheme of payouts, and the term structure.

Contributions: Contributions are assumed to be equal to 35% of the contribution base. The contribution base equals the salary minus an offset of 15,000 euros.

Indexing: Indexing is based on price inflation in the previous year. Indexing policy is as follows:

- if the funding level is less than 110%, there is no indexing

"If anything terrifies me, I must try to conquer it." Francis Charles Chichester

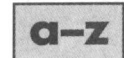

- between 110% and 130% indexing is increased linearly
- between 130% and 135% there is full indexing
- above 135% any lost indexing is restored
- if funding levels remain below 105% for more than a year, pension rights are cut until they reach 105% again

Economy: In order to make forecasts, assumptions with respect to the future risk/return profiles of economic variables have to be made. The regulator has given guidelines on the mean values of these variables. With regard to these basic risk characteristics, the pension fund has made its own assumptions, as set out in the table below.

Table 1. Pension fund risk–return assumptions

Category	Return (%)	Standard deviation (%)
Stocks	7.5	18.5
Bonds	4.5	8.5
Real estate	6.0	14
Wage inflation	3.0	2.0
Price inflation	2.0	2.0

Test statistic: The resulting risk/return profile is accepted if the probability of underfunding (meaning when the funding level is below 100%) at year ten is less than 2.5%.

A Survey of Pension Fund XYZ

A prime concern for pension funds is the cash flow scheme of the benefit payments, as the development of this scheme over time, in combination with the term structure, determines the required reserve. An example of such a cash flow and term structure is given in Figure 2.

Based on this information, profiles of contribution levels, probabilities of underfunding, and indexing levels can be derived. The probability of underfunding is now considered in more detail; it has the characteristics shown in Figure 3.

We see that after ten years the probability of underfunding exceeds the limit of 5%. Therefore one has to conclude that the policy of this pension fund will have to be changed if it is to meet its requirements.

CONCLUSION

ALM is not just an analytical tool that generates suitable strategies for pension fund management—it also forces departments to cooperate and to reach joint conclusions. It makes decision-making very transparent, and it helps pension funds to maneuver in a consistent way in uncertain and sometimes difficult times. ALM is all about understanding what is really going on and how to make responsible decisions. It is not some technical *tour de force*, but rather a practical tool that assists management in making systematically sound strategic decisions under conditions of uncertainty.

CASE STUDY

ALM is a widely accepted risk management tool in the Netherlands. The new regulatory framework introduced in January 2007 requires the use of ALM studies, with stochastic analysis prescribed as of 2010. Although these stochastic analyses are voluntary until 2010, most pension funds have already integrated this kind of analysis into their daily practice. But how is this done? The example below gives an idea of how an ALM study is structured and the results presented.

MAKING IT HAPPEN

- Implementation of ALM is a top-down process.
- The board formulates the required contribution and indexing levels.
- The ALCO transforms these requirements into a practical proposal that outlines the pros and cons of the possible ALM strategies.
- The board formulates an investment strategy and sets contribution levels and any increase in pension payouts.
- Investment strategy is implemented in daily practice—contributions are collected and pensions are indexed.
- The control cycle starts. The ALCO monitors the environment to see if expectations and reality still meet. If not, alternatives are presented and the board reconsiders its earlier decisions.

MORE INFO

Articles:

Campbell, John Y., and Luis M. Viceira. "The term structure of the risk–return trade-off." *Financial Analysts Journal* 61:1 (January/February 2005): 34–44. Online at: dx.doi.org/10.2469/faj.v61.n1.2682

Gerstner, Thomas, Michael Griebel, Markus Holtz, Ralf Goschnick, *et al*. "A general asset-liability management model for the efficient simulation of portfolios of life insurance policies." *Insurance: Mathematics and Economics* 42:2 (April 2008): 704–716. Online at: dx.doi.org/10.1016/j.insmatheco.2007.07.007

Gibbs, S., and E. McNamara. "Practical issues in ALM and stochastic modelling for actuaries." Institute of Actuaries of Australia Biennial Convention, September 23–26, 2007.

See Also:

★ Pension Schemes: A Unique and Unintended Basket of Risks on the Balance Sheet (pp. 87–90)
★ Valuing Pension Fund Liabilities on the Balance Sheet (pp. 122–124)
✔ Preparing Financial Statements: Balance Sheets (p. 1046)
✔ Understanding Asset–Liability Management (Full Balance Sheet Approach) (p. 996)

NOTES

1 See Gibbs and McNamara (2007).

2 See e.g. Campbell, John Y., and Luis M. Viceira. *Strategic Asset Allocation: Portfolio Choice for Long-Term Investors*. Clarendon Lectures in Economics. Oxford: Oxford University Press, 2002.

3 Hoevenaars, Roy P. M. M., R. Molenaar, Peter C. Schotman, and Tom Steenkamp. "Strategic asset allocation with liabilities: Beyond stocks and bonds." Working paper. Maastricht University, 2007.

  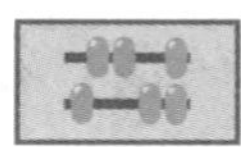      

Best Practices in Cash Flow Management and Reporting by Hans-Dieter Scheuermann

EXECUTIVE SUMMARY

The article compares classical ex post cash flow reporting with modern ex ante cash flow analysis and management. It sets focus on integrated cash management and cash flow forecast and explains how integrated data management works. Insights in optimization of financial supply chains complete the picture.

INTRODUCTION: BENEFITS OF INTEGRATED CASH FLOW INFORMATION

With margins getting squeezed, the optimized use of the resource known as capital has never been more important for companies. At the same time, the globalization of the markets means that new risks must be hedged due to volatile currencies. Risks from interest rates, supply, and quality must become transparent. Customer and vendor credit risk with their link to dependent "risk family trees" after the subprime crisis is obvious. Company performance hinges to a great extent on an efficient and effective internal treasury. Managers need to access accurate company data at the "push of a button," complete transparency and disclosure of risk factors, and integration with all relevant business processes.

CASH FLOW REPORTING

The importance of cash-flow management with the components of cash-flow reporting and cash-flow monitoring has changed dramatically. Cash-flow monitoring has been an important part of managing a company for years, but it always was an ex-post view on the balance sheet. The structure was defined by legislation. So, IAS7 defines indirect cash flow with:

- Annual net profit/loss;
- Cash flow from operating activities;
- Cash flow from investing activities;
- Cash flow from financing activities

representing the cash flow. So, cash flow reporting is an established part of a corporate's period end reporting.

CASH FLOW ACCOUNTING AND LIQUIDITY PLANNING

Cash-flow reporting is aided by cash-flow accounting, which records changes in cash flows directly. Incoming and outgoing payments of liquid funds, such as cash in hand and bank savings, are analyzed in real time and recorded according to their cash flow classes in revenues and expenditures.

The primary task of cash accounting is to provide information on a corporate's solvency and internal financing potential. It delivers the actuals and is, therefore, the basis for cash flow analysis and liquidity planning. (Liquidity planning, and its potential integration with sales, personnel, production and investment plans, is beyond the scope of this article.)

INTEGRATED CASH FLOW MANAGEMENT

Modern cash-flow management is based on an ex-ante principle with current information on the cash position and short/medium-term cash forecast. This article focuses on the integration of cash-flow management and optimization of working capital by means of financial supply-chain management.

Integrated Financial Infrastructure

As integrated IT systems map the entire logistical and accounting business process, in terms of its impact on liquidity as well as its risk, they provide crucial benefits for short-term and medium-term liquidity management. Each business transaction is still processed in the company department to which it is functionally assigned. However, different integration levels are updated and aggregated in the background, so that the information can be viewed by the relevant people in the appropriate form. These levels are:

- Integration of values and quantities;
- Integration of deadlines and time requirements;
- Integration of commitments and availabilities;
- Cash-flow integration.

This means, for example, that all the stages in the cash-relevant business processes in an integrated accounting system are evaluated in real time, and the expected cash flow can be forecast using information that is always up to date. This is shown in the example of the sales order–invoicing–incoming payment process chain (Figure 1) below. In the sales department, the order is managed using a purely logistical approach.

At the same time, the forecast for the expected cash inflow runs in the background, based on the agreed delivery data and terms of payment. Every

Figure 1. Integrated views on order to cash process. (*Source*: Finance Best Practice Network Workshop, Milan, January 2009, Hans-Dieter Scheuermann, SAP)

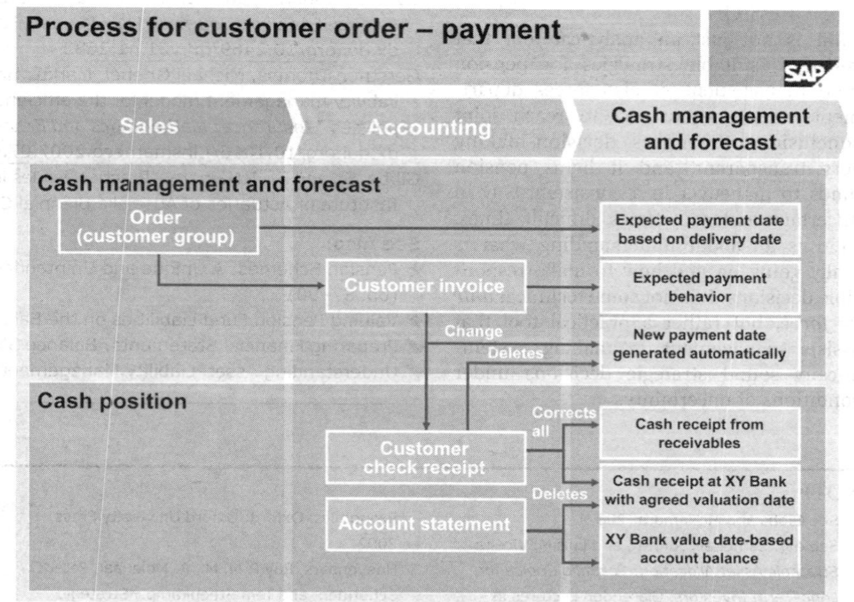

"**A debt may get mouldy, but it never decays.**" Chinua Achebe

  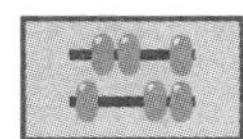      

commodity transaction change that results in a change to the value (through delivery quantity, price, or term of payment) or to the forecast cash-flow date is immediately and automatically updated in the cash forecast.

When the order is billed, the actual terms of payment and billing amounts as well as the customer's payment history (for example, taking advantage of discounts, tendency to delay payments) are used. This makes the forecast even more accurate. In the cash forecast, the updated values appear in the forecast from invoices process step.

When the actual payments arrive from the customer, for example, as checks, the cash forecast is updated again, this time with the agreed valuation date at the presenting bank. This example shows just how much transparency in terms of cash flow and risk (according to currency, countries, or creditworthiness of customer groups) can be achieved. This forecast accuracy offers great opportunities for intra-enterprise risk netting and managing short term financial transactions.

Integrated Business Partners of Supply & Delivery Chain

Like the tight integration of commodity transactions in the logistical supply chain, the exchange of accounting and financial data also becomes more important. By merging traditionally separate financial functions such as accounting and treasury, financial information is obtained. This means that payment advice information, particularly from large customers, is integrated into active cash management at an early stage—and before the actual payment is received—so that planning can be done using reliable data. For the day-to-day processing of accounting functions, data is passed on with the required level of detail, and with the partner assignment characteristics and references, using electronic payment advice notes, and then automatically processed using the recipient's IT system. Standardized encryption and message standards (for example, REMADV in EDIFACT and now XML SEPA Bank Transfer Standards) enable this rationalization at an international level. Electronic connectivity thus becomes an important qualification criterion when companies choose their vendors.

Integrated Bank Partners

Whatever applies to partners in commodity transactions applies to an even greater extent to the bank—the partner in financial transactions—because here, a financial transaction must be up-to-date and secure for it to be successful. The company can thus participate in the information services offered in the area of financials and, at the same time, meet the need for information required by an active in-house treasury. Electronic communication with the financial partner ensures market transparency and the availability of up-to-date external market data for the company's own computer systems. In addition to providing information on financial market data and the company's own offering, day-to-day processing in money-market and foreign-exchange trading, as well as financial transactions for financial assets and raising cash are predestined for the electronic exchange of information. The flow of information in a money-market transaction is used here as an example:

Money market → Payment order → (Confirmation) → Account statement

Performing a money-market transaction from quotation through to conclusion is still supported for the most part by traditional means of communication such as telephone, telex, and fax. With electronic connectivity, the transaction can be completed more reliably. FOREX marketplaces, such as "360°" in Germany, in which the bank customer triggers the automatic execution of money-market transactions, are becoming more and more relevant. The electronic payment order with non-repudiation status management enables financial transactions to be executed in a timely manner within the planning and value-date deadlines. Reference information is sent with the order and, with confirmation from the bank via the account statement, this information results in reduced administration expenses. Automated controls ensure that the information flow complies with security regulations.

Integrated Cash Management & Treasury and Accounting Within your Corporation

Powerful bank accounting functions are required as the basis for intra-enterprise financial controlling. Using a standardized, integrated data basis, processes optimized for accounting are combined with cash-management analyses. Highly developed bank accounting with detailed structuring using subaccounts (settlement accounts) is characterized by:

- Administration on an open account basis;
- Value-date-based recording of values;
- The storing of parallel currencies;
- Automated posting using automatic payment transactions;
- Automated processing of money-market and foreign-exchange trading transactions in the treasury back office;
- Automatic clearing using electronic bank transactions.

These functions enable the permanent reconciliation, balance-sheet assignment, and evaluation of all items, and are integrated with the automated processing of all payment transactions for the relevant cash and subledger accounts.

In addition, the following options exist for payment transactions:

- Manual fast entry of bank statements with the option of clearing current account items;
- The entry, management, and deletion of payment advice notes as value-date-based (pre-) information for all payment orders and/or incoming payments in the form of incoming checks, bank statements, and bill of exchange discounting;
- The creation of check deposit lists with posting proposal, management of outstanding checks, and returns monitoring;
- Billing holdings management and commitment management;
- An interest scale calculation with automatic interest settlement and costing-based interest calculation.

The key factor here is that the bank accounting functions are integrated with the general ledger. The networking of cash flows and the customer and vendor processing that is closely linked with this create the integrated database for cash management and forecast, and financial planning.

In the interfaces to modern electronic banking services, manual entry work is further reduced to get closer to the goal of being able to plan ahead as early as possible. Automated controls require human intervention only if defined rules apply or in defined exceptional circumstances.

Specifically, this leads to a key improvement in organizational processes through:

- Automated posting of the account statement;
- Statement entry with automatic management of the settlement accounts;
- Transfer to automatic incoming payments processing in accounts receivable;
- Automatic posting of the costs of the payment transaction (bank charges, fees);
- Maintaining foreign currency accounts with automatic posting of exchange rate differences.

This enables payment transactions in many areas to be processed more securely, faster, and more effectively. Automatic cash concentration represents a considerable improvement to short-term balance management and planning in the area of bank accounts. Financial transactions can be configured using advice notes and can thus be planned in advance—individually

"Accountants are the witch-doctors of the modern world and willing to turn their hands to any kind of magic."
Sir Charles Eustace Harman

and to the exact day—for the participating accounts.

The following specific features are especially worth mentioning:

- Consideration of payment methods and core deposits;
- Cross-company summaries;
- Multiple levels enabled by grouping accounts;
- Possibility to make manual corrections;
- Creation of correspondence.

Of course, postings are also made directly to the general ledger accounts, if posting-relevant clearing activities are involved.

In the cash position, you can see all incoming and outgoing payments updated on a daily basis. It comprises all bank-related transactions, differentiated according to the sources of information. To create a planning- and value-date-based cash position over the short term (nought to five days), the actual data must be entered dependent on the value date. This is ensured by integrating bank accounting.

Short-Term and Medium-Term Cash Management and Forecast

In financials, the tasks of adequate and orderly accounting merge with the functions for controlling and safeguarding liquidity and profitability. By including all of a company's payment-related and planning-relevant transactions, and consolidating them across all the corporate functions and units, the cornerstone is set for sound evaluations and analyses.

As an integral part of the application software, Treasury is integrated with the logistical and financial processes. Based on the financial results (banking, accounting and receivables, and collections management), the disclosure of the actual bank balance leads to the cash position.

If you take this observation further and include:

- The expected cash flows from completed or planned capital-market-driven foreign-exchange transactions;
- The interest-rate adjustment schedules/repayment schedules from granted and received loans;
- The receivables and payables;
- The planned items available;
- The open sales orders;
- The current purchase orders

you can extend liquidity forecasting, step by step, into the medium term. As a result of modern transmission technologies and end-to-end partner relationships between the customer, vendor, and bank, the information is available at short notice to any desired degree of detail (for example, automatic transfer and clearing of payment advice notes). The displays in cash management and forecast can be set to any degree of detail and show the development of:

- Liquidity as a whole;
- The planned amounts;
- The risk classes

in local and foreign currencies.

Modern financial supply-chain management presents a good opportunity to test traditional payables and receivables processes in accounting, and to design a meaningful and affordable distribution of tasks as part of an integrated approach to process optimization in O2C (order to cash) and P2P (purchase to pay).

OPTIMIZATION OF WORKING CAPITAL THROUGH FINANCIAL SUPPLY CHAIN MANAGEMENT

The CFO is at the heart of complex internal and external relationships that need to be connected intelligently. As the company's integrating force, they must also take care of all the individual aspects of the financial supply chain (FSC). This chain encompasses all processes and transactions that have a direct impact on cash flow and working capital. As the diagram below illustrates, the financial supply chain starts with the selection of business partners and continues with the payment process, draw-

Figure 2. The Structure of the Financial Supply Chain (based on a concept by the Aberdeen Group). (*Source*: CFO—The CFO as Business Integrator, Cedric Read, Hans-Dieter Scheuermann)

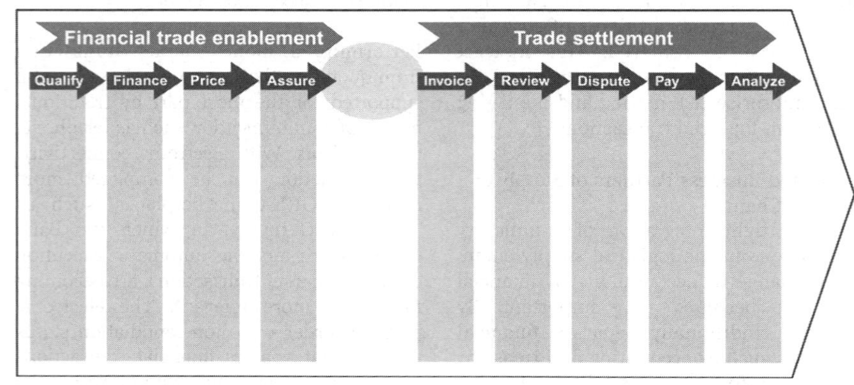

Figure 3. Financial Supply Chain Management Overview. (*Source*: Finance Best Practice Network Workshop, Milan, January 2009, Hans-Dieter Scheuermann)

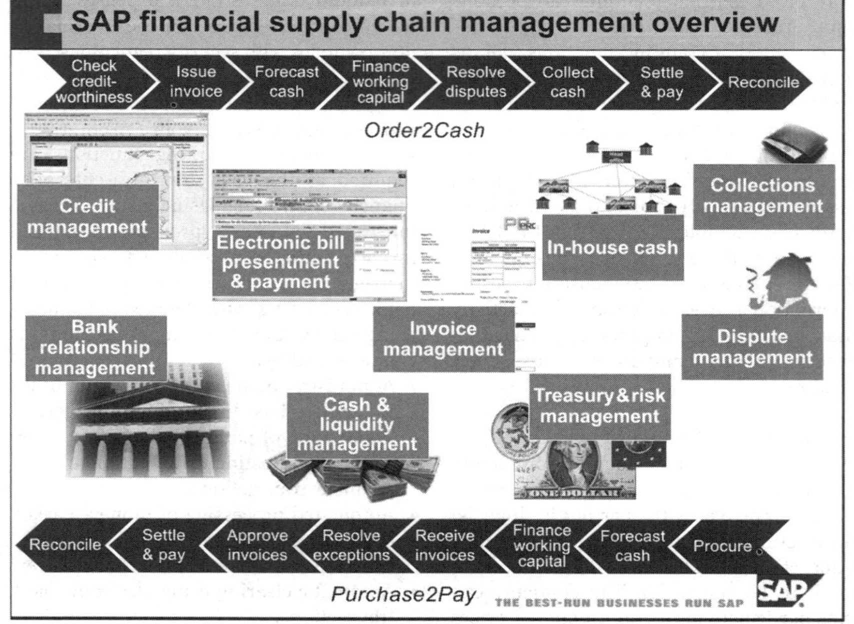

"All money nowadays seems to be produced with a homing instinct for the Treasury." Prince Philip

ing up reports and analyses, and making cash-flow forecasts.

Effective FSC management can be a great blessing for the CFO, because it can positively influence customers, financial forecasting, and working capital. The advantages of successful FSC planning for your company include:

- Improved inventory monitoring and cash-flow management;
- Reduction in the working capital by 20% and more;
- Lower installment payments for the required working capital;
- Earlier identification of problems with business transactions;
- More efficient, automated financial systems.

Until recently, the individual financial functions were usually regarded by CFOs not within the context of an integrated supply chain, but rather as separate entities. An integrated approach enables better resource management and makes it easier to adjust the financial supply chain to operational requirements. Such an approach offers CFOs the following benefits:

- Integrated cash-flow management;
- More exact profitability forecasts through more up-to-date and precise information about customers;
- Better use of the working capital and avoidance of an expensive working capital float;
- Greater drilldown depth in financial reports;
- Faster and more efficient resolution of payment problems;
- Comprehensive overview of business partners;
- Improved support for strategic planning.

Moreover, an integrated financial supply chain accelerates the processes between the vendor and the customer, which represents a decisive competitive factor in today's transient business environment.

Financing and invoice processing are usually the most expensive factors in financials, and tie up large amounts of capital. Traditional ERP systems can accompany these processes, but are often not yet integrated with the related systems to customers, vendors, and banks. SAP® Financial Supply Chain Management (FSCM) is a concept that encompasses the entire process—from selecting vendors and customers, through the payment process, reporting, and analysis—in other words, all processes that directly have an impact on cash flow and working capital, and not just within the company, but also throughout the business partner network. A Swiss SAP customer stated: "The SAP solution supports, improves, and optimizes the business processes in the financial supply chain by drastically cutting the days of sales outstanding (DSO), and reducing the cost of finance, ultimately optimizing the working capital."

CONCLUSION

SAP FSCM can greatly simplify financial supply-chain management in an organization. With this set of applications, companies can more easily address the multifaceted challenges of managing cash flow and optimizing working capital—two critical elements for successful financial performance today.

The outcome of the experience of this Finance Best Practice Network (see also the article, "Advantages of Finance Best Practice Networks") shows clearly that traditional cash-flow reporting is "out" and only seen as a complementary communication to stakeholders with no impact on the cash-flow management on an operational level, which is key in today's turbulent financial environment.

CASE STUDY

A Swiss pharmaceutical company provides a strong example of modern cash-flow management and reporting beyond traditional boundaries.

A centralized treasury function based on SAP Technology Infrastructure was not the subject of these experiences, but helped as an enabler. The company saw treasury as a central service provider with the goal of cost reductions and efficiency gains for finance and IT.

The core tasks are providing optimal funding and safeguarding business from forex exposures.

In relation to Bank Relationship Management they achieved the goal of reducing bank fees and increasing automation in Bank Communication.

The ease of communication with bank partners, business wise and IT wise was an additional value add.

In protecting the internal supply chain from external challenges (such as financing fees and exchange rates) they secured the Supply Chain Finance.

The company considers Treasury as a financial supply-chain-oriented one and its inhouse bank concept is based on the management mission, which sees the Treasury as a service provider for the business, its vision to partly internalize business of external banks, and its strategic decision for central Treasury to run SAP and "pick up your customer at his front door."

In 2004, the company started the global rollout of InHouse Bank with key enablers of physical cash pooling with non-resident and Bank streamlining to three global cash-management banks with strong IT automation and standardization.

The InHouse Bank achieved classical benefits in Cash pooling by more than 150 affiliates participating with 42 countries, 34 currencies

- by Interest savings > CHF5 million
- by ST Cash reduced by 80%.

Intercompany payments initialized (volume > CHF22 billion pa)

- Interest savings and lower bank fees > CHF1 million

Forex hedging internalized (volume > CHF30 billion pa)

- Netting gains & margin savings > CHF1 million

Streamlined Banking

- Fewer bank accounts, fewer Treasury HQ headcount etc.

Additional benefits for the financial supply chain included:

- Automation of bank postings and Automated EBS upload and Payment File upload host to host
- Intercompany invoicing and reconciliation upgrade by currency streamlining and elimination of local FX P&L, automation of payment allocation (850,000 invoices p.a.) and local finance headcount reduction
- Communication with banks (IT) through elimation of local EBS interfaces, process automation and standardization. Payment interfaces are standardized and file upload is automated.

On their radar screen, they define the outlook towards a payment and collection factory, with further benefits for the financial supply chain. Cross-border payments can be turned into domestic payments, saving bank fees, Forex spreads and value-dated, as well enabling the closing of more than 100 bank accounts. IT complexity can be reduced—no more interfaces from local SAP to banks, routing of electronic payments and collections can be done via IHB, and payment workflow can be streamlined and concentrated onto SAP. Centralized cash flow becomes information and transactional-wise. A centrally controlled standardized disbursement channel aids compliance & security when it is Swift & SAP-based.

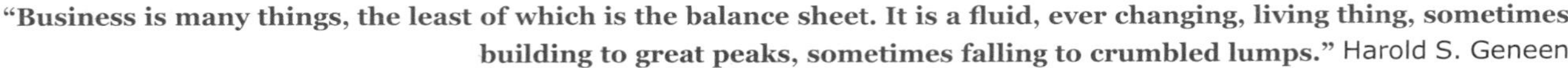

"**Business is many things, the least of which is the balance sheet. It is a fluid, ever changing, living thing, sometimes building to great peaks, sometimes falling to crumbled lumps.**" Harold S. Geneen

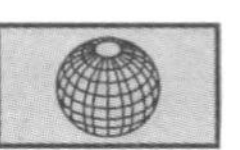

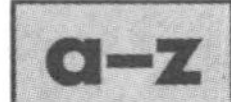

Capital Budgeting: The Dominance of Net Present Value by Harold Bierman, Jr

EXECUTIVE SUMMARY

- The time value of money is highly relevant.
- Net present value (NPV) is a very reliable method of analysis.
- Use incremental cash flows.
- NPV profile is an excellent summary.

INTRODUCTION

A capital budgeting decision is characterized by costs and benefits that are spread out over several time periods. This leads to a requirement that the time value of money be considered in order to evaluate the alternatives correctly. Although to make decisions we must consider risks as well as time value, I restrict the discussion to situations in which the costs and benefits are known with certainty. There are sufficient difficulties in just taking the time value of money into consideration. Moreover, when the cash flows are allowed to be uncertain, I would suggest the use of procedures that are based on the initial recommendations made with the certainty assumption, so nothing is lost by making the assumption of certainty.

A financial executive made the following interesting observation (Bierman, 1986): "The real challenge is creativity and invention, not analysis. Timely execution of projects by entrepreneurial managers is also more critical than sophistication of analytical budgeting techniques."

RATE OF DISCOUNT

We shall use the term time value of money to describe the discount rate. One possibility is to use the rate of interest associated with default-free securities. This rate does not include an adjustment for the risk of default; thus risk, if present, would be handled separately from the time discounting. In some situations, it is convenient to use the firm's borrowing rate (the marginal cost of borrowing funds). The objective of the discounting process is to take the time value of money into consideration. We want to find the present equivalent of future sums, neglecting risk considerations.

Although the average cost of capital is an important concept that should be understood by all managers and is useful in deciding on the financing mix, I do not advocate its general use in evaluating all investments. Different investments have different risks.

DEPENDENT AND INDEPENDENT INVESTMENTS

In evaluating the investment proposals presented to management, it is important to be aware of the possible interrelationships between pairs of investment proposals. An investment proposal will be said to be economically independent of a second investment if the cash flows (or equivalently the costs and benefits) expected from the first investment would be the same regardless of whether the second investment were accepted or rejected. If the cash flows associated with the first investment are affected by the decision to accept or reject the second investment, the first investment is said to be economically dependent on the second.

In order for investment A to be economically independent of investment B, two conditions must be satisfied. First, it must be technically possible to undertake investment A whether or not investment B is accepted. Second, the net benefits to be expected from the first investment must not be affected by the acceptance or rejection of the second. The dependency relationship can be classified further. In the extreme case where the potential benefits to be derived from the first investment will completely disappear if the second investment is accepted, or where it is technically impossible to undertake the first when the second has been accepted, the two investments are said to be mutually exclusive.

STATISTICAL DEPENDENCE

It is possible for two or more investments to be economically independent but statistically dependent. Statistical dependence is said to be present if the cash flows from two or more investments would be affected by some external event or happening whose occurrence is uncertain. For example, a firm could produce high-priced yachts and expensive cars. The investment decisions affecting these two product lines are economically independent. However, the fortunes of both activities are closely associated with high business activity and a large amount of discretionary income for the "rich" people. This statistical dependence may affect the risk of investments in these product lines because the swings of profitability of a firm with these two product lines will be wider than those of a firm with two product lines having less statistical dependence.

INCREMENTAL CASH FLOWS

Investments should be analyzed using after-tax incremental cash flows. Although we shall assume zero taxes so that we can concentrate on the technique of analysis, it should be remembered that the only relevant cash flows of a period are after all tax effects have been taken into account.

The definition of incremental cash flows is relatively straightforward: If the item changes the bank account or cash balance, it is a cash flow. This definition includes opportunity costs (the value of alternative uses). For example, if a warehouse is used for a new product and the alternative is to rent the space, the lost rentals should be counted as an opportunity cost in computing the incremental cash flows of using the space.

The computations in this article make several assumptions that are convenient and that simplify the analysis:

- Capital can be borrowed and lent at the same rate.
- The cash inflows and outflows occur at the beginning or end of each period, rather than continuously during the periods.
- The cash flows are certain, and no risk adjustment is necessary.

In addition, in choosing the methods of analysis and implementation, it is assumed that the objective is to maximize the wellbeing of stockholders, and more wealth is better than less.

TWO DISCOUNTED CASH FLOW METHODS

The two primary discounted cash flow investment evaluation procedures are net present value (NPV) and internal rate of return (IRR). We shall conclude that the net present value method is better than the other possible methods of analyzing investments.

Net Present Value

The two most important measures of investment worth are called the discounted cash flow (DCF), measures. It is desirable to explain the concept of the present value of a

"Large firms rely heavily on present value techniques and the capital asset pricing model, while small firms are relatively likely to use the payback criterion." John R. Graham and Campbell R. Harvey

future sum because in one way or another this concept is utilized in both these measures.

The present value of $100 payable in two years can be defined as that quantity of money necessary to invest today at compound interest in order to have $100 in two years. The rate of interest at which the money will grow and the frequency at which it will be compounded will determine the present value. I shall assume that funds are compounded annually. Assume that we are given a 0.10 annual rate of interest. Let us examine how the present value of a future sum can be computed by using that rate of interest.

Suppose that an investment promises to return a total of $100 at the end of two years. Because $1.00 invested today at 10% compounded annually would grow to $1.21 in two years, we can find the present value at 10% of $100 in two years by dividing $100 by 1.21 or by multiplying by the present value factor, 0.8264. This gives $82.64. Therefore, a sum of $82.64 that earns 10% interest compounded annually will be worth $100 at the end of two years. By repeated applications of this method, we can convert any series of current or future cash payments (or outlays) into an equivalent present value. Because tables, hand calculators, and computers are available that give the appropriate conversion factors for various rates of interest, the calculations involved are relatively simple.

The net present value method is a direct application of the present value concept. Its computation requires the following steps:

1 Choose an appropriate rate of discount.
2 Compute the present value of the cash proceeds expected from the investment.
3 Compute the present value of the cash outlays required by the investment.
4 Add all the present value equivalents to obtain the net present value.

The sum of the present values of the proceeds minus the present value of the outlays is the net present value of the investment. The recommended accept or reject criterion is to accept all independent investments whose net present value is greater than or equal to zero and to reject all investments whose net present value is less than zero.

With zero taxes, the net present value of an investment may be described as the maximum amount a firm could pay for the opportunity of making the investment without being financially worse off. If no such payment must be made, the expected net present value is an unrealized capital gain from the investment, over and above the cost of the investment used in the calculation. The capital gain will be realized if the expected cash proceeds materialize.

The following example illustrates the basic computations for discounting cash flows—that is, adjusting future cash flows for the time value of money, using the net present value method.

Assume that there is an investment opportunity with the cash flows given in Table 1.

Table 1. An investment's cash flows

Period	0	1	2
Cash flow	–$12,337	$10,000	$5,000

We want first to compute the net present value of this investment using 0.10 as the discount rate. The present value of $1 due zero periods from now discounted at any interest rate is 1.000. The present value of $1 due one period from now discounted at 0.10 is 0.9091 or $(1.10)^{-1}$. The present value of $1 due two periods from now discounted at 0.10 is 0.8264 or $(1.10)^{-2}$.

The net present value of the investment is the algebraic sum of the three present values of the cash flows (Table 2).

The net present value is positive, indicating that the investment is acceptable. Any investment with a net present value equal to or greater than zero is acceptable using this single criterion. Since the net present value is $886, the firm could pay an amount of $886 in excess of the cost of $12,337 and still break even economically by undertaking the investment. The net present value calculation is a reliable method for evaluating investments.

Internal Rate of Return

Many different terms are used to describe the internal rate of return concept. Among these terms are: yield, interest rate of return, rate of return, return on investment, present value return on investment, discounted cash flow, investor's method, time-adjusted rate of return, and marginal efficiency of capital. IRR and internal rate of return may be used interchangeably.

The internal rate of return method utilizes present value concepts. The procedure is to find a rate of discount that will make the present value of the cash proceeds expected from an investment equal to the present value of the cash outlays required by the investment. Such a rate of discount may be found by trial and error. For example, with a conventional investment, if we know the cash proceeds and the cash outlays in each future year, we can start with any rate of discount and find for that rate the present value of the cash proceeds and the present value of the outlays. If the net present value of the cash flows is positive, then using some higher rate of discount would make them equal. By a process of trial and error, an approximately correct rate of discount can be determined. This rate of discount is referred to as the internal rate of return of the investment, or its IRR.

The IRR method is commonly used in security markets in evaluating bonds and other debt instruments. The yield to maturity of a bond is the rate of discount that makes the present value of the payments promised to the bondholder equal to the market price of the bond. The yield to maturity on a $1,000 bond having a coupon rate of 10% will be equal to 10% only if the current market value of the bond is $1,000. If the current market value is greater than $1,000, the IRR to maturity will be something less than the coupon rate; if the current market value is less than $1,000, the IRR will be greater than the coupon rate.

The internal rate of return may also be described as the rate of growth of an investment. This is more easily seen for an investment with one present outlay and one future benefit. For example, assume that an investment with an outlay of $1,000 today will return $1,331 three years from now.

Table 3 shows a 0.10 internal rate of return, and it is also a 0.10 growth rate per year.

The internal rate of return of a conventional investment represents the highest rate of interest an investor could afford to pay, without losing money, if all the funds to finance the investment were borrowed and the loan (principal and accrued interest) was repaid by application of the cash proceeds from the investment as they were earned.

We shall illustrate the internal rate of return calculation using the example of the previous section where the investment had

Table 2. Present value calculations

	(1)	(2)	(3)
Period	*Cash flow*	*Present value factor*	*Present value (col. 1 × col. 2)*
0	– $12,337	1.0000	– $12,337
1	$10,000	0.9091	$9,091
2	$5,000	0.8264	$4,132
	Net present value =		**$886**

        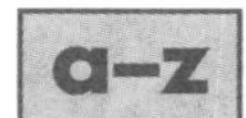

Table 3. Cash flow

Beginning-of-time period	Growth of cash investment	Growth	Growth divided by beginning-of-period flow investment
0	$1,000	$100	100 ÷ 1,000 = 0.10
1	$1,100	$110	110 ÷ 1,100 = 0.10
2	$1,210	$121	121 ÷ 1,210 = 0.10
3	$1,331	—	—

Table 4. NPV using 0.20

Period	Cash flow	Present value factor	Present value
0	– $12,337	1.0000	– $12,337
1	$10,000	0.8333	$8,333
2	$5,000	0.6944	$3,472
	Net present value =		**$532**

Table 5. NPV using 0.16

Period	Cash flow	Present value factor	Present value
0	– $12,337	1.0000	– $12,337
1	$10,000	0.8621	$8,621
2	$5,000	0.7432	$3,716
	Net present value =		$0

a net present value of $886 using 0.10 as the discount rate.

We want to find the rate of discount that causes the sum of the present values of the cash flows to be equal to zero. Assume that our first choice (an arbitrary guess) is 0.10. In the preceding situation, we found that the net present value using 0.10 is a positive $886. We want to change the discount rate so that the present value is zero. Since the cash flows are conventional (negative followed by positive), to decrease the present value of the future cash flows we should increase the rate of discount (thus causing the present value of the future cash flows that are positive to be smaller).

In Table 4 we try 0.20 as the rate of discount.

The net present value is negative, indicating that the 0.20 rate of discount is too large. We shall try a value between 0.10 and 0.20 for our next estimate. Assume that we try 0.16 (Table 5).

The net present value is zero using 0.16 as the rate of discount, which by definition means that 0.16 is the internal rate of return of the investment.

Although tables give only present value factors for select interest rates, calculators and computers can be used for any interest rate.

NET PRESENT VALUE PROFILE

The net present value profile is one of the more useful devices for summarizing the profitability characteristics of an investment. On the horizontal axis we measure different discount rates; on the vertical axis we measure the net present value of the investment. The net present value of the investment is plotted for all discount rates from zero to some reasonably large rate. The plot of net present values will cross the horizontal axis (have zero net present value) at the rate of discount that is called the internal rate of return of the investment.

Figure 1 shows the net present value profile for the investment discussed in the previous two sections. If we add the cash flows, assuming a zero rate of discount, we obtain

$$-\$12,337 + \$10,000 + \$5,000 = \$2,663$$

The $2,663 is the intersection of the graph with the y-axis. We know that the graph has a height of $886 at a 0.10 rate of discount and crosses the x-axis at 0.16, since 0.16 is the internal rate of return of the investment. For interest rates greater than 0.16, the investment's net present value is negative.

Figure 1. Net present value profile

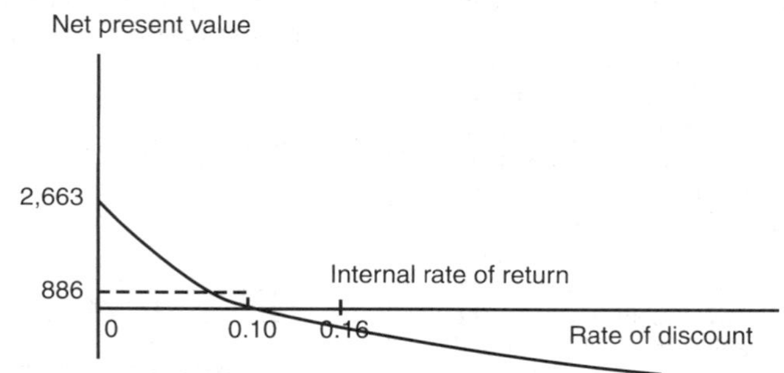

Note that for a conventional investment (negative cash flows followed by positive cash flows), the net present value profile slopes downward to the right.

THE ROLLBACK METHOD

On a simple hand calculator that lacks a present value button, it is sometimes convenient to use a rollback method of calculation to compute the net present value of an investment. One advantage of this procedure is that the present values at different moments in time are obtained. Consider the investment in Table 6.

Table 6. The rollback example

Time	Cash flow
0	– $7,000
1	5,000
2	2,300
3	1,100

Assume that the discount rate is 0.10.

The first step is to place the cash flow of period 3 ($1,100) in the calculator and divide by 1.10 to obtain $1,000, the value at time 2. Add $2,300 and divide the sum by 1.10 to obtain $3,000, the value at time 1. Add $5,000 and divide by 1.10 to obtain $7,273, the value of time 0. Subtract $7,000 to obtain the net present value of $273.

CONCLUSION

There are many different ways of evaluating investments. In some situations, several of the methods will lead to identical decisions. We shall consistently recommend the net present value method as the primary means of evaluating investments.

The net present value method ensures that future cash flows are brought back to a common moment in time called time 0. For each future cash flow, a present value equivalent is found. These present value equivalents are summed to obtain a net

"If you dislike change, you're going to dislike irrelevance even more." General Eric Shineski

present value. If the net present value is positive, the investment is acceptable.

The transformation of future flows back to the present is accomplished using the mathematical relationship $(1 + r)^{-n}$, which we shall call the present value factor for r rate of interest and n time periods.

In cases of uncertainty, additional complexities must be considered, but the basic framework of analysis will remain a discounted present value method.

A Stanford Research Institute publication (1966) stated the situation well (p. 3): "The growth in corporate long range planning has intensified interest in corporate objectives, and has created a critical need to evaluate the financial impact of alternative courses of action."

Table 7. Financial analysis for the chemical company

	NPV (0.15)	*IRR*
Most probable outcome	$80,000,000	0.38
A 20% decrease in expected volume	$50,000,000	0.30
A 10% decrease in gross margin	$70,000,000	0.35
A 20% decrease in volume and 10% decrease in gross margin	$44,000,000	0.20

CASE STUDY

A chemical company had sales of $14 billion and net earnings of $380 million in 20X1. Sales grew at 8% in the period 2001–20X1 and earnings at 10%.

Management was concerned that the firm's growth rates would fall as its product lines were maturing and the firm was finding it difficult to develop desirable investments. Management wanted the firm to grow at least 10% per year.

The firm used a 15% (after tax) hurdle rate as the required return.

The European plant was designed to manufacture a new proprietary polyethylene terephthalate (PET) that could be used, if successful, to package bottled water. A test tube quantity had been prepared but the new product had never been manufactured.

Demand for water bottles was expected to double in the next six years. The materials currently being used were neither environmentally sound nor safe. The new bottle would also have a better appearance. The average European drinks three times as much bottled water as the average resident in the United States.

The economic analysis presented for this plant was as given in Table 7.

Question: Should the plant being considered be accepted?

Answer: The plant has risk (the product has never been manufactured), but the likely profits look good. Accept. For all the listed events, the outcomes are acceptable.

MORE INFO

Books:

Bierman, Harold. *Implementation of Capital Budgeting Techniques*. Financial Management Survey & Synthesis Series. Tampa, FL: FMA, 1986.

Bierman, Harold, Jr, and Seymour Smidt. *The Capital Budgeting Decision*. 9th ed. New York: Routledge, 2007.

Bierman, Harold, Jr, and Seymour Smidt. *Advanced Capital Budgeting*. New York: Routledge, 2007.

Stanford Research Institute. *Financial Management in Transition*. Menlo Park, CA, 1966.

Articles:

Graham, John R., and Campbell R. Harvey. "The theory and practice of corporate finance: Evidence from the field." *Journal of Financial Economics* 60:2–3 (May 2001): 187–243. Online at: dx.doi.org/10.1016/S0304-405X(01)00044-7

Hastie, K. L. "One businessman's view of capital budgeting." *Financial Management* 3:4 (Winter 1974): 36–44.

See Also:

★ Allocating Corporate Capital Fairly (pp. 11–12)
★ Comparing Net Present Value and Internal Rate of Return (pp. 30–32)
★ Corporate Finance for SMEs (pp. 33–35)
✔ Appraising Investment Opportunities (p. 1143)
✔ Managing the Time Value of Money (p. 979)
✔ Options for Raising Finance (p. 1081)
✔ Understanding the Relationship between the Discount Rate and Risk (p. 1001)
Net Present Value (pp. 1237–1238)

"Don't say yes until I finish talking." Darryl Zanuck

  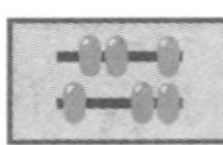      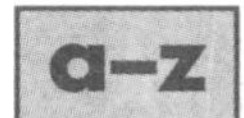

Capital Structure: Perspectives by John C. Groth

EXECUTIVE SUMMARY

- Capital structure reflects the financing strategy and potentially influences the value of a company.
- The potential value to shareholders of capital structure depends on the tax environment.
- Understanding the logic of capital structure and the origin of potential value is of import to leaders, strategists, and managers.
- The greater the business risk, the lower the optimal debt/equity (D/E) ratio.
- Tax strategy and management should consider capital structure. The higher the expected tax rate, the more important are capital structure decisions and management.

INTRODUCTION

Capital has three forms: human, tangible, and financial. In this article, we focus on how financing choices influence the cost of financial capital and company value. Capital structure focuses on the sources of financial capital. The choice of structure affects firm value in some economies.[1]

The seminal works of Nobel laureate Franco Modigliani conceived important relationships and issues in capital structure. Subsequently, researchers have nourished the development of capital structure theory and the related literature, and they have influenced practice. Many companies follow the prescriptions of capital structure theory, and create value for stockholders and society.[2]

We do not have the "perfect" capital markets described by economists, and key factors influence the choice of capital structure. For example, investors are concerned with the potential for, and cost of, bankruptcy. If a company disappoints investors by using too little or too much debt, its stock price will suffer. Understanding exactly how the use of some debt may add to company value is essential to understanding capital structure.

First, we will clarify the meaning of capital structure. Then we will address other issues.

CAPITAL STRUCTURE

The decision on capital structure is the choice of how to finance a company. Capital structure represents the proportion of each source of financing relative to total financing. Types of financing fall into broad categories: equity, representing ownership; debt; and preferred financing. Interestingly, in some economies the concept of equity or ownership was unfamiliar until recently, as historically individuals did not enjoy the privilege of ownership.

Capital structure is about dividing up expected economic returns (not accounting returns) and risk, in exchange for providing capital. Those divisions are specific. For example, a pecking order exists amongst the different creditors. The "covenants" of debt arrangements, as well as precedent in practice and legal arrangements, address these relationships. For example, in practice "normal" trade credit is often not formalized, and the company routinely pays trade creditors.[3]

In the context of capital structure and an "ongoing enterprise," equity ownership is last in line with a claim on what others have not claimed of the returns. Equity holders also bear the risks which the creditors and preferred shareholders (if present) have not accepted. In the event of financial distress or bankruptcy, in most economies very specific rules apply to dividing up the carcass.[4]

In Figure 1, the balance sheet depicts the "assets" and the source of financing, and, consequently, the claim on the assets. For simplicity, we will focus on financing with a combination of debt and equity, ignoring preferred shares as a source of capital. In fact, many firms do not have preferred shares.

The choice of assets, how well we manage the assets, and the nature and success of our providing product/services to markets, taxes, and other factors determine the business risk of the company. The business risk influences the cost of equity capital. For a firm without debt, or an "unlevered" firm, the cost of equity equals the risk-free rate of interest plus a premium for business risk. Collectively, the business risk factors will determine the expected level and risk of cash flows that originate in the asset side of the company. These expected cash flows that come from the asset side of the company must service any debt. After debt service and the payment of taxes, the net remaining cash flows provide the expected returns to equity holders.

The higher the business risk of a company—and hence, the greater the uncertainty in cash flows from the asset side of the business—the less financial risk a company should have, and the lower the optimal D/E ratio.

Consequently, the more uncertain the environment, and the greater the sensitivity of the business side of the company to the economic environment, the more important it is that one select a capital structure with care. Companies with high sensitivity to the cyclical effects of the economy should consider a more conservative capital structure, and have a strategy to manage the structure across economic cycles.

For the purposes of discussion, Figure 1 shows four alternative financing arrangements. In financing alternative A, only equity holders provide capital. In finance jargon, situation A represents an unlevered firm. Each equity holder has a claim on the after-tax benefits of owning and operating the assets, as well as on the assets

Figure 1. Alternative capital structures

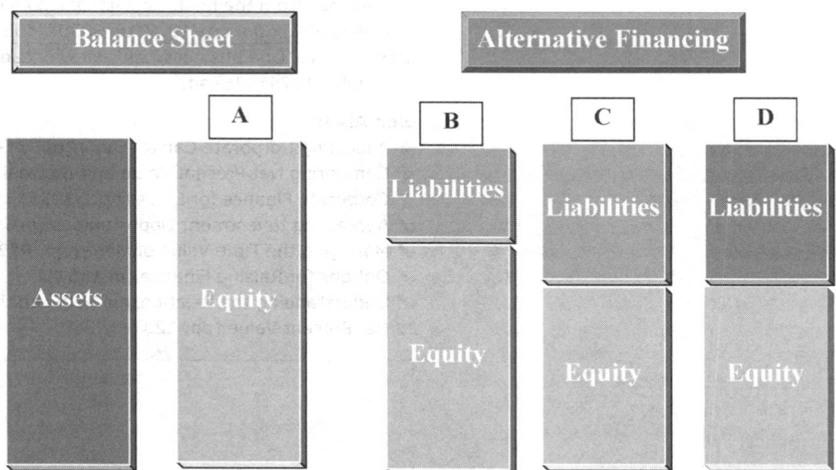

"Haggling over every ounce in purchasing may not reduce one's cost of capital." Tao Zhu Gong

themselves. The proportion of total shares owned determines the claims of each. In some instances, different classes of equity exist, with the rights of each class defined accordingly.

Alternatives B and C represent different ways of financing the same assets, with C having a higher debt/equity ratio than B. Assuming that the nature of liabilities (discussed shortly) for B and C are the same, C, which has the higher debt/equity ratio, has greater financial risk. We will explain alternative D later in the chapter.

Relative Position and Risk

Capital structure does not involve sharing, but dividing and ordering. Deciding to use debt and/or preferred ownership entails dividing expected returns and risk, and ordering claims—both for "normal" times, as well as in the event of bankruptcy. Think of a line of people, an uncertain future, and expected benefits that may stem from the operation or sale of a company's assets, or benefits that might arise from the financing of the company.

A metaphor helps in understanding the issues and relationships. Imagine an apple orchard. Uncertainty exists about future crops in terms of the size, and quality, of the apples. Variance in quality means not all apples in a crop have equal value. Let's see how the ordered line works.

Governments are first in line, taking the most certain and best apples for taxes. Some taxes are ardent claims, which are due independent of the sufficiency of the crop. Equity holders bear this tax responsibility. However, tax circumstances also affect creditors and other providers of capital.

Fundamental Principle: The Division of Risk and Expected Return

A position first in line gives first access to the orchard, and the right to take the best apples. Others enter the orchard according to their order in the line, each taking the apples they are allowed—if apples are available. The average quality of the remaining apples declines with the successive removal of the best of the remaining crop, as those in line are careful and claim the best apples to which they are entitled. Remove the best, and the quality of what remains must be lower—and the risk that insufficient or no apples remain increases.

After the tax authorities, creditors are next in line, with multiple creditors each careful to specify and protect their position in the line. Sometimes creditors limit the number and/or magnitude of other credit claims in line. Preferred stockholders (if the company has any) have a position in line ahead of common stockholders, but behind creditors. A company may have different classes of stockholders, with the classes also ordered.

Equity holders are last in line, expecting to get the lower-quality (higher-risk) apples that are left, and having a claim on all that are left. Equity holders, last in line, have the most risk, but also the possibility of unlimited returns. Equity holders bear the risk that others have not accepted, and they get what is left over. Different classes of equity holders may exist, with these classes differentiated and "labeled," for example, class A. The classification scheme specifies the positions, potential rights, and claims of each class.

With distress or bankruptcy, the provisions of the various sources of financing specify the relative position and claims of each party, but with one usual modification: tax liabilities, attorneys, and related costs often take first from the carcass. After that, an ordered picking over the corpse follows.

Motivation for Using Debt

A logical question surfaces: why would equity holders allow others to go ahead of them in the line? There are two main reasons for this: garnering incremental value; and/or issues of control.

Increased Value

Potential increases in value stem from "leveraging effects" (stockholders) and tax effects (total firm value). Capital structure theory generally focuses on the value that may originate in tax effects that result from the use of debt. This article focuses on capital structure, but we will first briefly comment on the classic financial leverage reasons for using debt.

Equally Clever Creditors and Stockholders Have Implications

The presence of astute creditors and stockholders will result in no bargains or favors in terms of dividing up expected returns and risks. Creditors will not give stockholders a bargain just to be nice. Absent control issues, capital structure is only important if interest on debt is tax-deductible, and dividend payments are not deductible.

TAX-DEDUCTIBLE INTEREST

In some economies, interest is tax-deductible. The expected deductibility of interest payments provides opportunity for value. The expected benefit of this deduction flows to stockholders, which is best illustrated with an example.

Example

A company borrows money at a fixed rate of 10%. The tax rate is 30%. The company expects to have sufficient pretax income to allow the deduction of the interest before calculating taxes. The net effects are:

- Lenders expect payment of 10%, whether the company has taxable income or not.
- If the company realizes the tax deduction, the after-tax cost = 10% (1 − 0.3) = 7%.
- The expected benefit of the tax deduction goes to stockholders.
- The stockholders have increased financial risk that stems from the borrowing—and letting creditors precede them in line.
- Stockholders are astute. Increased risk increases the cost of equity capital.
- However, if the expected value of the tax savings is attractive to stockholders relative to the added risk of borrowing, stockholders are happy, and the share price increases.
- The right choice of capital structure will result in a reduction of the weighted cost of capital—even though the cost of both equity and debt capital increase with debt, as Table 1 illustrates, and we discuss below.

Importantly, the tax deduction and its benefit is an expected benefit, as the uncertain pretax income (EBIT or NOI in several economies) must be large enough to allow the interest deduction.

Tax Rate and Implications

Notice that the higher the tax rate, the greater the potential impact of the deductibility of interest on the after-tax cost of debt. For example, with the same 10% borrowing rate but a 40% tax rate, the after-tax cost is 10% (1 − 0.4) = 6%.

We take care not to confuse issues. We don't benefit from higher tax rates. However, the higher the tax rate we endure, the more important becomes the choice of capital structure.

To reiterate, the tax benefits of using debt do not alter the promised cash flows in the form of interest or principle to creditors. Any tax benefits therefore precipitate to stockholders, and that is core to understanding how capital structure can create value.[5]

Asymmetry of Effects

The use of some debt in place of some equity will lever up (down) the expected returns to stockholders. If interest is tax-deductible, the potential good or bad leveraging effects are asymmetric. If the company has returns on its assets that exceed the cost of debt, a positive leveraging effect accrues to stockholders. If stockholders view these returns as attractive, given the financial risk of the added debt, the stock value increases.

  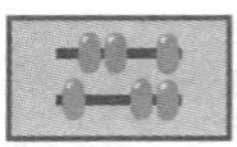   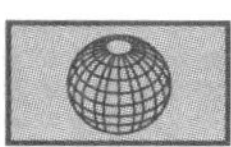   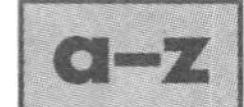

Table 1. Calculation of weighted cost of capital (WCOC)

Source of capital	Relative proportion	Cost of component	Weighted cost of component	Weighted cost of captial
Debt	0%	5.40%	0.00%	
Equity	100%	13.00%	13.00%	
				13.00%
Debt	10%	5.40%	0.54%	
Equity	90%	13.40%	12.10%	
				12.64%
Debt	20%	6.10%	1.22%	
Equity	80%	13.90%	11.12%	
				12.34%
Debt	**30%**	6.60%	1.98%	
Equity	**70%**	14.50%	10.15%	
				12.13%
Debt	40%	7.60%	3.04%	
Equity	60%	15.50%	9.30%	
				12.34%
Debt	50%	9.00%	4.50%	
Equity	50%	17.20%	8.60%	
				13.10%

If the EBIT for tax accounting is insufficient to allow the deduction of interest, stockholders must now bear the full cost of debt rather than benefit from a lower after-tax cost.[6] This shift in tax impact results in a greater and adverse leveraging effect on returns to stockholders, as equity investors must now cover the full cost of debt, rather than the after-tax cost of debt. Using the original example above, the cost of debt rises from the after-tax 7% to the full 10%. The inability to realize the interest deduction results in an asymmetric effect on expected returns to stockholders.

BEHAVIOR OF WEIGHTED COST OF CAPITAL

An example showing the behavior of the component costs of capital and the weighted cost of capital (WCOC) appears in Table 1. For simplification, we consider only equity and debt sources of capital. One might employ one or more models, or different forms of models, as well as alternative econometric procedures to estimate the costs of the components of capital for different levels of leverage.[7]

Entries reflect the raising of money from debt and equity in different proportions. The more debt that is used as a proportion of the total, the less equity (and fewer shares). Costs are after-tax costs to the company. The cost of debt represents the weighted cost of debt, reflecting the fact that first-in-line creditors have lower risk, and the borrowing cost is lower. Creditors that follow in line have greater risk, and demand a higher rate. The chapter, "The Weighted Cost of Capital: Perspectives and Applications," addresses issues related to the WCOC.

For all entries in this table, the company is getting the same amount of money. The values show the effects of getting this money in different proportions from debt and equity, which is the capital structure decision.

Choices of capital structure seek to increase the value of the firm. Hence, in Table 1 and all discussion in this chapter and the chapter, Capital Structure: A Strategy that Makes Sense, debt and equity refer to the market values of debt and equity. Hence, the D/E ratio we calculate uses the market values of the debt and equity.

Note in Table 1 that the weighted cost of capital (WCOC) at first decreases, reaching a minimum when about 30% of capital comes from debt and 70% from equity. Observe also that this decrease occurs even though the weighted cost of debt increases with the use of an increased proportion of debt capital. Recognize that successive increments of debt cost more, as successive creditors in the line of claimants demand higher expected returns to compensate for their higher risk.

With an increase in the use of debt, the cost of equity increases as well. Equity holders recognize the greater financial risk attendant with a higher D/E ratio, and demand increased expected returns.

Seemingly, the WCOC could not decline if the cost of components increased. The reason for the decline stems entirely from the expected tax-deductibility of debt, and equity holders think the value of the tax benefit is attractive compared to the added risk. As the D/E ratio increases, the amount of equity decreases because we are raising the same amount of capital everywhere in Table 1. If we raise more from debt, less comes from equity. The use of some debt rather than all equity amplifies the effect on a per-share basis, as the company needs fewer shares for the same amount of capital. The result is that with an increasing D/E the expected tax benefits increase, and these are spread over fewer shares.

In the example in Table 1, note that obtaining more than 30% of capital from debt results in an increase in the WCOC. Above 30% debt, stockholders do not think that the incremental tax benefits of more debt are attractive enough to compensate them for the incremental financial risk, and the uncertainty of realizing the tax benefits. Hence, the demanded rate of increase in the cost of equity and debt overpowers the effects on value of the expected incremental tax benefits of employing more debt.

Summary

Given a particular business risk of a company, determined by the asset side of the business and how well the company employs its assets, an optimal capital structure exists—optimal, as it lowers the WCOC of the company. For example, in Table 1, using about 30% from debt and 70% from equity will result in the lowest weighted cost of capital.[8] Note in the table that the cost of components increases in a nonlinear manner as the use of debt increases. This behavior is related to several factors, including: the risk of realizing the expected tax benefit of debt; potential distress caused by excess debt, and its effects on operations as well as opportunities and investments; and possible bankruptcy with attendant loss.

OTHER ISSUES

The Nature of Liabilities and Optimal D/E

The nature of the liabilities influences the choice of capital structure. Let alternative D in Figure 1 represent the same capital structure as in alternative C. Suppose that certain characteristics of the liabilities for C and D differ. To illustrate, assume that the weighted maturity of liabilities in D is less than that in C, and/or that C represents borrowing at a fixed rate while some debt in D has a variable rate of interest.

Despite the same D/E ratio, the financial risk of D is greater than that of C because D is bearing interest-rate risk if the debt has a variable rate of interest, and D has more risk as it faces refunding of debt sooner. Less flexibility in the timing of refunding the debt is a potentially important issue, as capital market conditions vary over time. The developments and difficulty for firms of obtaining "replacement" credit in the 2008 crisis illustrate this refunding risk.

  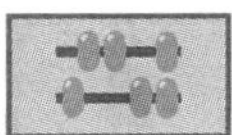      

Logically, the nature of the liabilities therefore affects the optimal D/E ratio. For A, B, C, and D, the business risk is still the same. The use of liabilities with greater risk (in this scenario, maturity and interest rate risk) results in a lower optimal D/E, despite the same business risk on the asset side of the company. Thus, if the structure shown for C is optimal, the structure shown for D is incorrect. D should have a lower optimal D/E ratio than C, as the nature and structure of liabilities for D results in higher risk on the financing side of the company.

CONCLUSION

The tax deductibility of interest provides the opportunity to add to company value by employing the correct amount of debt relative to equity. The underlying relationships that cause this potential increment in value rest on the logical behavior of informed investors who agree to divide risks and expected returns. The deductibility of interest has expected economic benefits that flow to equity holders. Consequently, the use of debt is logical if interest is tax deductible and we expect to realize the benefit of that deduction. The higher the corporate tax rate we must endure, the greater the value of issuing debt.

The choice of how to finance the company, and its resulting debt/equity ratio, is the capital structure decision. Issues relating to the strategy and management of capital structure are discussed in the article, "Capital Structure: A Strategy that Makes Sense."

MAKING IT HAPPEN

- Remember that the expected tax deductibility of interest is the origin of any value that arises from the choice of capital structure.
- In capital structure decisions, the examination focuses on the market value of debt and equity.
- Changes in the tax rate will influence the optimal capital structure.
- The greater the business risk, the lower the optimal D/E ratio.
- The choice of capital structure will influence the cost of the individual sources of capital, and, in turn, the weighted cost of capital.
- "Real world" considerations argue for a target capital structure, and a strategy to pursue that structure. The chapter, "Capital Structure: A Strategy that Makes Sense," examines these issues and offers guidance on a strategy.

MORE INFO

Articles:

Groth, John C., and Ronald C. Anderson. "Capital structure: Perspectives for managers." *Management Decision* 35:7 (1997): 552–561. Online at: dx.doi.org/10.1108/00251749710170529

Miller, Merton H. "The Modigliani–Miller propositions after thirty years." *Journal of Applied Corporate Finance* 2:1 (Spring 1989): 6–18. Online at: dx.doi.org/10.1111/j.1745-6622.1989.tb00548.x

Website:

Weighted average cost of capital: en.wikipedia.org/wiki/Weighted_average_cost_of_capital

See Also:

★ Capital Structure: A Strategy that Makes Sense (pp. 710–714)
★ Capital Structure: Implications (pp. 715–718)
★ Optimizing the Capital Structure: Finding the Right Balance between Debt and Equity (pp. 543–545)
✔ Investors and the Capital Structure (p. 1120)
✔ Options for Raising Finance (p. 1081)
✔ Understanding Capital Structure Theory: Modigliani and Miller (p. 997)
Debt/Equity Ratio (p. 1215)
Franco Modigliani (p. 1296)
Merton Miller (p. 1294)
Taxes and Business Strategy: A Planning Approach (p. 1420)

NOTES

1 Issues of control can influence choice of capital structure, for example, with current managers not willing to issue equity as the issuance would dilute management's "personal" control percentage, or alter the distribution of shares in float.

2 Actions that lower the cost of capital result in benefits to individuals in economies and societies. In contrast, in 2008 we have witnessed the adverse and spreading effects that result from interruptions in the availability and/or cost of capital in economies.

3 If suppliers perceive unnecessary risk or the likelihood of financial distress, suppliers may demand trade notes payable. Trade notes payable formalize trade credit, and seek to clearly identify the obligation. Hence, requiring formalization of obligation with trade notes payable clarifies as well as "perfects" the supplier's interest, and relative claimant position. This formalization can alter the risks to the suppliers of receipt of payment, both during ongoing operations as well as in the case of bankruptcy. Normally, the existence of trade notes payable on a balance sheet signals concerns by trade creditors of the financial viability of the company.

4 Multiple classes of equity may exist, with specified relative claimant positions during normal operations as well as in bankruptcy.

5 In imperfect markets with multiple periods, and with certain tax rules, the risk of promised cash flows to creditors may be reduced by the tax-deductibility of interest in previous periods or by carry-back tax effects. These issues are beyond the scope of this article.

6 In some environments, differences exist in accounting for taxes, and accounting for financial reporting.

7 The most common approaches include several different model forms based on the capital asset pricing model, multi-factor models, discounted cash flow models, risk-premium models, and other pricing models.

8 This is an approximation. Estimating the WCOC curve and finding the minimum point is not a precise science.

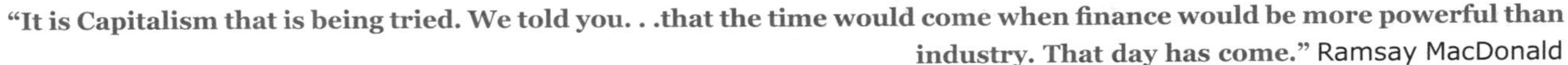

  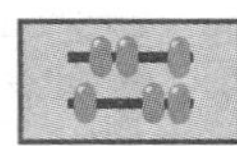      

Cash Flow Best Practice for Small and Medium-Sized Enterprises by Rita Herron Brown

EXECUTIVE SUMMARY

- Cash is the oxygen of a business: it must have cash in order to operate.
- Cash flow management entails measuring cash coming in (receivables) and cash going out (payables).
- It's not uncommon for smaller businesses to need a line of credit to bridge the gap between receivables and payables—but this facility comes at a cost.
- Many cash flow issues are due more to inattention or sloppy management than to problems with customers. Nonetheless, it's important for managers to know who they are doing business with, and customers need to know the terms of any sales transactions.

INTRODUCTION

In late summer 2008, a Californian company that helped businesses to cut their power consumption costs, BluePoint Energy, found itself in very hot water. BluePoint's CEO, Guy Archbold, had stated a year earlier that the company would soon lock down contracts to bring in more than US$50 million in revenue. However, this didn't happen. And when newspapers reported that Archbold had been suspended, they also reported that the company had lost US$14.3 million on sales of only US$1.3 million. The story ended unhappily for all involved, and there are many management lessons that could be learned from it—with the importance of cash flow management at the top of the list. A 2008 survey by Discover Financial Services showed that some 44% of small-business owners said they had experienced cash flow problems.[1] In a tough economy, that number is assuredly higher. What can a manager do?

MASTER DAY-TO-DAY FINANCIAL METRICS

Every business needs a budget that allocates income and outgoings in well-defined categories. The best budget system is based on the history of the business, i.e. a detailed listing of where money was earned and spent in the past; but, essentially, what a manager is trying to do is pin down (on at least a quarterly basis) his yearly receivables, and from whom and where, and his yearly expenditures. Then, against that budget, the manager should track business operations to see whether budget projections are turning out to be reality. It's important for a manager to account for every dollar that comes into the business and every dollar that goes out. And, in a pinch, he needs to know where the business is, against budget, *right now*.

TRACK AND FORECAST RECEIVABLES

The part of any budget that is most critical, of course, is the cash coming in—not the cash that might possibly come in (projected or booked business), but the cash for which a business has performed work, or for which it has a contract with a firm payment schedule. Yet here too, the tieback to a budget is quite important: Every manager needs to know (based on past experience as well as future plans) *when* he can reasonably expect those dollars to be in the mailbox or, better, electronically transferred to a business bank account. Thus, managers need to know on a weekly (some say daily) basis whether the to-date income projected is actually in hand. If it is, a manager can then start to disburse payments (salaries, supplier invoices, and so forth); if the business is running short of income, a manager needs to take other forms of action (as will be discussed later).

KNOW THE CUSTOMERS AND SET TERMS

It's not hard to find stories of businesses that did work for a new customer only to have the order canceled just as the product is about to be shipped. Worse still is the customer who takes delivery and pays with a check without having enough cash in the bank to cover it. On any substantial customer order, it's not improper to ask for references (which must be checked!)—and, on any order, it's not unusual to state before beginning the work how the business expects to be paid and when. Does a customer pay on completion of work? If the customer takes 30 days or more to pay, are there any penalties? What if a customer pays immediately or within a week: Is there a discount? Is the amount due the same if the bill is paid with cash rather than a credit card, or in installments? Knowing the customer—and making sure that each customer knows the terms of any business transaction—is key to cash flow management.

BILL PROMPTLY AND OFFER DISCOUNTS

Many businesses, of course, do the work and bill later. Amazingly, many businesses are lax when it comes to cutting the invoice, and often this is because it's viewed as too much work to take time to raise invoices when there's "real" work to be done. Nonsense. The quicker a business bills for completed work (no matter what the terms of payment are), the quicker that business can expect cash to show on the balance sheet. That's why many businesses offer incentives to customers to pay earlier. Incentives can be as high as 3%, although a manager needs to decide the discount rate by judging how much it's worth to receive payment sooner rather than later.

DON'T LET CASH SIT AROUND

It's easy to allow the work in process to dominate one's attention, yet there's no excuse for allowing checks received for past work to lie in an inbox, unattended for days. But a manager doesn't have to have checks sitting on a desk to be guilty of cash flow dereliction. Even if all receivables arrive on time and are deposited in the bank promptly, many businesses allow their cash to sit in business checking accounts that often pay *zero* interest. This, too, is letting cash sit around. Depending on when a business will need the cash to pay its own

MAKING IT HAPPEN

- Create systems for budgeting, receivables, and payables to establish how healthy the business is in a financial sense. Create a cash flow statement.
- Don't perform work for customers that can't be relied on to pay promptly. Share with all customers the terms of payment, including any incentives and penalties.
- Keep a close eye on both payments the business will be required to make and payments that could be delayed or deferred because they are not essential to current business operations.
- When the business is cash negative, don't panic. As long as the business has predictable, reliable income from customers in the near future, a manager can access lines of credit—if he has been wise enough to establish those before they become a critical need. And when income arrives, such short-term debt should be paid down immediately.

"Civilization and profits go hand in hand." Calvin Coolidge

     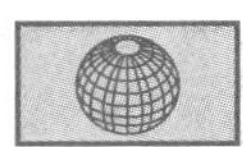   

bills, there are ways to put that money to work, via short-term certificates of deposit or other financial instruments that bankers can quickly explain.

TRACK AND FORECAST PAYABLES

Each time a manager pays anything, it should be logged properly via a chart of accounts that lists the category of the expense and ties it to a specific business check or direct-from-bank payment. There are many software programs that can help a small business to manage these details. Yet the most important thing is that a business has a precise plan in place for any expense that a manager can project. When a manager is surprised that "payroll ran so high this month," or complains that "energy prices are way out of line," such comments reveal that his attention to cash flow detail is lacking. If, in fact, the business is large enough that such details can't be managed by the senior manager, they should be delegated to someone who can report on income and outgoings—in precise detail—at a moment's notice. The list of payables should be divided into those that must be paid (required spending) and those which can be deferred or delayed (discretionary spending). Payroll and rent are required payments; new carpeting for the manager's office is discretionary.

WHEN CASH FLOW DIPS

In 1997, Francine Glick started a company, Hands2Go, that sells hand-sanitizing products. Glick says that, from day one, she was on top of the financials of her successful business. But has her company always had more cash on hand or coming in than it needed to operate? As with the vast majority of businesses, she'd be the first to say hers did not. For those times when she might need cash in a downturn, or when receivables were running late, Glick set up credit lines *before* she needed to draw on such resources. "As long as you only use it for emergencies and don't become dependent on it, a line of credit is a useful tool," she says.

The key, of course, is to use a line of credit (a company credit card is, in essence, the same thing) only when a manager can, with certainty, pinpoint when the business will receive income that can be used to pay down that credit line. Otherwise, one is borrowing blindly or on faith; either way, that's not good business. One more point: Many a small business has borrowed liberally when facing a cash flow dip, received income in due course, and then failed to pay down its debt. Cash that comes from a line of credit should be considered as receivables that have already been spent. Keeping credit line balances close to zero will mean that a business has full access to dollars it may critically need during even tougher times to come.

CASE STUDY

Omni Graphics Printing & Copying

Jim Hahn runs Omni Graphics Printing & Copying in Kentucky, a small firm that handles all kinds of printing jobs—from business cards to publishing booklets such as annual reports for sports teams. In business since the mid-1980s, Hahn's operation increased its year-on-year revenues by 3–5% without the need to market extensively. His five-man business serves both walk-in customers and large business-to-business clientele. Word of mouth sustained his business growth; and, as his business grew, he added printing equipment and employees to boost his productivity and profits.

Yet, by the end of 2008, Hahn could sense that something was wrong. As the American economy started to tank, Hahn could feel that his revenue was sliding and that his bills and payroll were starting to exceed income. But he didn't know exactly what was happening. That's because Hahn did not really use a budget or cash flow tracking. "For years, I didn't need to worry about such things," he says. "Revenues always handily exceeded expenses."

The economic downturn has actually helped to make Hahn an even better businessman. "Now, I have a budget that pins down all my expenses; I've even listed how much my advertisement in the local phone book costs me. More than that, I have identified where 80% of my income has been coming from, so I know who my best customers have been, their industries, and thus, the probable source for potential future income."

Hahn's cash flow management is now a daily activity. First, Hahn has quadrupled the amount of time he is spending on marketing; he now personally checks on his top customers and is attending group business luncheons and making dozens of cold calls to attract customers with a profile that matches those of his best customers in the past. Second, on payables, Hahn has been reducing expenses by tracking every dollar that flows out of his business. He has found that employees have been flexible in temporarily reducing work hours and salaries, that he doesn't need to stock as much paper and other supplies, that his expensive advertisement in the local phone book doesn't have the return on investment that he thought, that every large equipment purchase planned for the next year can be deferred, and that numerous other expenses—once deemed essential, such as four telephone lines—can be cut back. Third, Hahn is documenting his case to establish a business line of credit at his bank, so as to be ready to handle downturns in the future.

Hahn admits that this new attention to cash flow management has not been easy. Nevertheless, although these practices were implemented during harsh business times and have boosted his chances of sustaining his business for another 20 years, the exercise in cash flow management has taught him an enormous lesson: "If I can find ways to eke out a profit using these techniques in tough times, imagine how much more profitable my business can be if I manage exactly the same way when the good times return."

MORE INFO

Books:

Forsyth, Patrick, and Frances Kay. *Tough Tactics for Tough Times: How to Maintain Business Success in Difficult Economic Conditions.* Philadelphia, PA: Kogan Page, 2009.

Jordan, Caroline Grimm. *Stop the Cash Flow Roller Coaster, I Want to Get Off! What Every Small Business Owner Should Know About Cash Flow... But Most Don't.* Lincoln, NE: iUniverse, 2007.

Article:

Bernabucci, Bob. "Improving your cash flow problems." *Entrepreneur.com* (August 2, 2005). Online at: tinyurl.com/5zghay

Websites:

About.com Small Business Resource Center: smallbusiness.specials.about.com

Business Owner's Toolkit, "Managing your cash flow": tinyurl.com/3njnbr5

Inc. "Cash management basics": www.inc.com/guides/start_biz/20675.html

NOTE

1 "Small business economic confidence continues to slide. 2 in 3 small business owners rate economy as poor; 3 in 4 see it getting worse." Discover Financial Services Small Business Watch, November 2008.

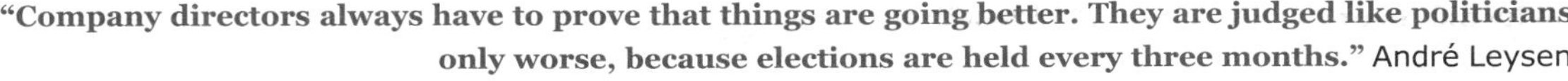

"Company directors always have to prove that things are going better. They are judged like politicians, only worse, because elections are held every three months." André Leysen

  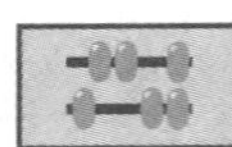      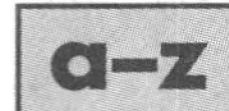

Comparing Net Present Value and Internal Rate of Return by Harold Bierman, Jr

EXECUTIVE SUMMARY

- Net present value (NPV) and internal rate of return (IRR) are two very practical discounted cash flow (DCF) calculations used for making capital budgeting decisions.
- NPV and IRR lead to the same decisions with investments that are independent.
- With mutually exclusive investments, the NPV method is easier to use and more reliable.

INTRODUCTION

To this point neither of the two discounted cash flow procedures for evaluating an investment is obviously incorrect. In many situations, the internal rate of return (IRR) procedure will lead to the same decision as the net present value (NPV) procedure, but there are also times when the IRR may lead to different decisions from those obtained by using the net present value procedure. When the two methods lead to different decisions, the net present value method tends to give better decisions.

It is sometimes possible to use the IRR method in such a way that it gives the same results as the NPV method. For this to occur, it is necessary that the rate of discount at which it is appropriate to discount future cash proceeds be the same for all future years. If the appropriate rate of interest varies from year to year, then the two procedures may not give identical answers.

It is easy to use the NPV method correctly. It is much more difficult to use the IRR method correctly.

ACCEPT OR REJECT DECISIONS

Frequently, the investment decision to be made is whether to accept or reject a project where the cash flows of the project do not affect the cash flows of other projects. We speak of this type of investment as being an independent investment. With the IRR procedure, the recommendation with conventional cash flows is to accept an independent investment if its IRR is greater than some minimum acceptable rate of discount. If the cash flow corresponding to the investment consists of one or more periods of cash outlays followed only by periods of cash proceeds, this method will give the same accept or reject decisions as the NPV method, using the same discount rate. Because most independent investments have cash flow patterns that meet the specifications described, it is fair to say that in practice, the IRR and NPV methods tend to give the same accept or reject recommendations for independent investments.

MUTUALLY EXCLUSIVE INVESTMENT

If undertaking any one of a set of investments will change the profitability of the other investments, the investments are substitutes. An extreme case of substitution exists if undertaking one of the investments completely eliminates the expected proceeds of the other investments. Such investments are said to be mutually exclusive.

Frequently, a company will have two or more investments, any one of which would be acceptable, but because the investments are mutually exclusive, only one can be accepted. Mutually exclusive investment alternatives are common in industry. The situation frequently occurs in connection with the engineering design of a new installation. In the process of designing such an installation, the engineers are typically faced at a great many points with alternatives that are mutually exclusive. Thus, a measure of investment worth that does not lead to correct mutually exclusive choices will be seriously deficient.

INCREMENTAL BENEFITS: THE SCALE PROBLEM

The IRR method's recommendations for mutually exclusive investments are less reliable than are those that result from the application of the NPV method because the former fail to consider the size of the investment. Let us assume that we must choose one of the following investments for a company whose discount rate is 10%: Investment A requires an outlay of $10,000 this year and has cash proceeds of $12,000 next year; investment B requires an outlay of $15,000 this year and has cash proceeds of $17,700 next year. The IRR of A is 20%, and that of B is 18%.

A quick answer would be that A is more desirable, based on the hypothesis that the higher the IRR, the better the investment. When only the IRR of the investment is considered, something significant is left out¾and that is the size of the investment. The important difference between investments B and A is that B requires an additional outlay of $5,000 and provides additional cash proceeds of $5,700. Table 1 shows that the IRR of the incremental investment is 14%, which is clearly worthwhile for a company that can obtain additional funds at 10%. The $5,000 saved by investing in A can earn $5,500 (a 10% return). This is inferior to the $5,700 earned by investing an additional $5,000 in B.

Table 1. Two mutually exclusive investments, A and B

	Cash flows		
Investment	**0**	**1**	**IRR (%)**
A	–$10,000	$12,000	20
B	–$15,000	$17,700	18
Incremental (B–A)	–$5,000	$5,000	14

Figure 1 shows both investments. It can be seen that investment B is more desirable (has a higher present value) as long as the discount rate is less than 14%.

We can identify the difficulty just described as the scale or size problem that arises when the IRR method is used to evaluate mutually exclusive investments. Because the IRR is a percentage, the process of computation eliminates size; yet, size of the investment is important.

TIMING

Assume that there are two mutually exclusive investments both requiring the same initial outlay. This case seems to be different from the one we have just discussed because there is no incremental investment. Actually, the difference is superficial. Consider investments Y and Z, described in Table 2. Suppose that Y and Z are mutually exclusive investments for a company whose cost of money is 5%. The IRR of Y is 20%, whereas that of Z is 25%. If we take the present value of each investment at 5%, however, we find that the ranking is in the opposite order. The present value of Z is less than the present value of Y.

Suppose that we attempt to make an incremental comparison, as shown in Table 3. We see that the cash flow of Y is $80.00 less in year 1 and $88.75 more than Z in year 2. As before, we can compute the IRR on the incremental cash flow. An outlay of $80.00 that returns $88.75 one year later has an IRR of 10.9%. An investment such as this would be desirable for a company whose cost of money is less than 10.9%.

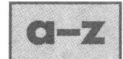

Figure 1. Two mutually exclusive investments, A and B

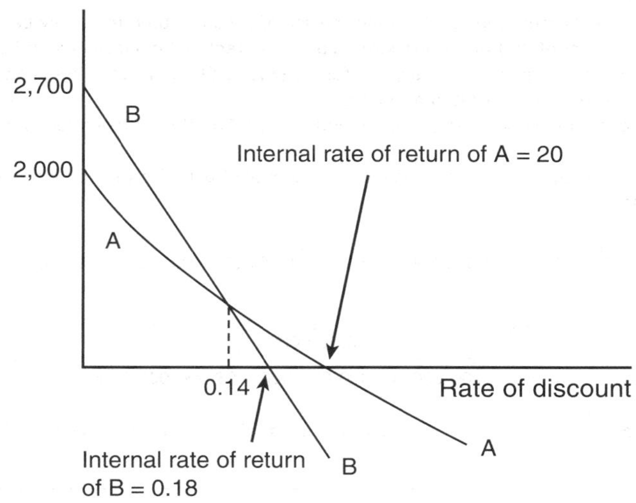

Table 2. Cash flows for two investments, Y and Z

	Cash flows for period			IRR (%)	NPV at 5%
Investment	0	1	2		
Y	– $100.00	$20.00	$120.00	20	$27.89
Z	– $100.00	$100.00	$31.25	25	$23.58

Table 3. Incremental comparison of cash flows for investments Y and Z

Period 0	$0.00	Cash flows identical
Period 1	– $80.00	Cash flow of Y is less than that of Z
Period 2	$88.75	Cash flow of Y exceeds that of Z

Again, we are really dealing with a problem of the scale of the investment, but in this case, the opportunity for the additional investment occurs one year later.

The same result can be reached by a somewhat different route if we ask how much cash the company would have on hand at the end of the second year if it accepted investment Y or if it accepted investment Z. Both investments give some cash proceeds at the end of the first year. The value of the investment at the end of the second year will depend on what is done with cash proceeds of the first year. Assume that the cash proceeds of the first year could be reinvested to yield 5%. Then investment Y would result in a total cash accumulation by the end of the year of $141 (105% of $20 plus $120). Investment Z would result in a cash accumulation of only $136.25 (105% of $100 plus $31.25).

Figure 2 shows that investment Y is to be preferred as long as the appropriate discount rate is less than 10.9%. If the rate is in excess of 10.9, then Z is to be preferred.

One disadvantage associated with the use of the IRR method is the necessity of computing the IRR on the incremental cash proceeds in order to determine which of a pair of mutually exclusive investments is preferable. If there are more than two mutually exclusive investments, we shall have to conduct an elimination tournament among the mutually exclusive investments. Taking any pair, we compute the IRR on the incremental cash flow and attempt to decide which of the two investments is preferable. The winner of this round would then be compared in the same manner with one of the remaining investments until the grand champion investment is discovered. If there are 151 investments being considered, there will have to be 150 computations, because 150 investments would have to be eliminated.

WHY IRR IS POPULAR

Managers like the IRR method, since they consider it important to know the differential between the proposed investment's IRR and the required return. This is a measure of safety that allows an evaluation of the investment's return compared to its risk. If an investment has an IRR of 0.30 when the required return is 0.12, this is a large margin that allows for error. An NPV measure does not give the same type of information to management.

CONCLUSION

An effective understanding of present value concepts is of great assistance in the understanding of a wide range of areas of business decision making. The concepts are especially important in managerial decision making, since many decisions made today affect the firm's cash flows over future time periods.

It should be stressed that I have only discussed how to take the timing of the cash

Figure 2. Two mutually exclusive investments, Y and Z

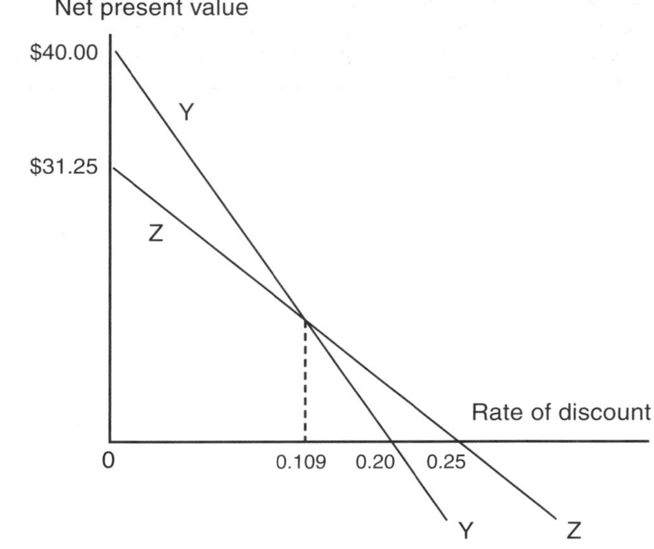

  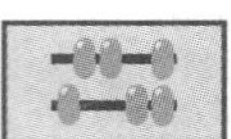   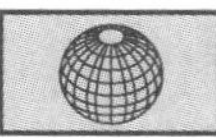   

flows into consideration. Risk and tax considerations must still be explained before the real-world decision maker has a tool that can be effectively applied. In addition, there may be qualitative factors that management wants to consider before accepting or rejecting an investment.

It is sometimes stated that refinements in capital budgeting techniques are a waste of effort because the basic information being used is so unreliable. It is claimed that the estimates of cash proceeds are only guesses and that to use anything except the simplest capital budget procedures is as futile as using complicated formulas or observations of past market levels to determine which way the stock market is going to move next. For example, in 1974 K. Larry Hastie published his classic paper, "One Businessman's View of Capital Budgeting." His position is that firms should avoid excessively complex measurement techniques. He states: "Investment decision making could be improved significantly if the emphasis were placed on asking the appropriate strategic questions and providing better assumptions rather than on increasing the sophistication of measurement techniques" (1974, p. 36).

It is true that in many situations reliable estimates of cash proceeds are difficult to make. Fortunately, there are a large number of investment decisions in which cash proceeds can be predicted with a fair degree of certainty. But even with an accurate, reliable estimate of cash proceeds, the wrong decision is frequently made because incorrect methods are used in evaluating this information.

While it is not possible to make a single estimate of cash proceeds that is certain to occur, it does not follow that incorrect methods of analysis are justified. When all the calculations are completed, judgmental insights may be included in the analysis to decide whether to accept or reject a project.

CASE STUDY

A Decision in Mexico

A major Mexican steel corporation had a major decision. It could stand relatively pat (a marginal investment of $50,000,000) with its present steel making facilities and earn indefinitely (after maintenance capital expenditures) $8,000,000 per year. This is an IRR of 0.16. The pesos have been translated to dollars.

The alternative is to invest $10,000,000,000 and earn $1,500,000,000 per year indefinitely, an IRR of 0.15.

What should the corporation do if it has a cost of capital of 0.10 for steel making facilities? The solution is:

$$\text{NPV(standpat)} = \frac{8,000,000}{0.10} - 50,000,000 = 80,000,000 - 50,000,000 = \$30,000,000$$

$$\begin{aligned}\text{NPV(majorinvestment)} &= \frac{1,500,000,000}{0.10} - 10,000,000,000 \\ &= 15,000,000,000 - 10,000,000,000 = \$5,000,000,000\end{aligned}$$

IRR says stand pat (0.16 is larger than 0.15). NPV says rebuild ($5 billion is larger than $30 million).

MORE INFO

Books:

Bierman, Harold, Jr. *Implementation of Capital Budgeting Techniques*. Financial Management Survey & Synthesis Series, FMA, Tampa, FL, 1986.

Bierman, Harold, Jr, and Seymour Smidt. *Advanced Capital Budgeting*. New York and London: Routledge, 2007.

Bierman, Harold, Jr, and Seymour Smidt. *The Capital Budgeting Decision*. 9th ed. New York and London: Routledge, 2007.

Article:

Hastie, K. L. "One businessman's view of capital budgeting." *Financial Management* 3 (Winter 1974): 36–44.

See Also:

★ Allocating Corporate Capital Fairly (pp. 11–12)
★ Corporate Finance for SMEs (pp. 33–35)
★ Creating Value with EVA (pp. 814–816)
★ Valuing Start-Ups (pp. 769–771)
✔ Options for Raising Finance (p. 1081)
✔ Preparing a Budget (p. 985)
✔ Understanding the Relationship between the Discount Rate and Risk (p. 1001)

"Harvey & Thompson, the UK's largest listed pawnbrokers, yesterday announced good trading and a record number of store openings." Anonymous

  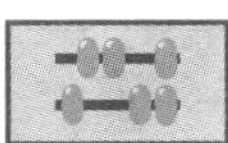   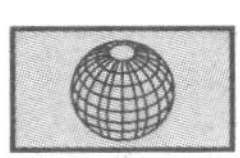   

Corporate Finance for SMEs by Terry Carroll

EXECUTIVE SUMMARY

- Corporate finance has evolved over many years to become a sophisticated specialism, for which the fees may be substantial.
- The principles are the same for SMEs (small and medium enterprises) as for any larger company.
- Often transaction-led, it is recommended that a wider full balance sheet approach be adopted because of the strategic financial significance.
- SMEs often originate as owner/proprietor businesses, and this structure can often trigger transactions such as change of ownership or disposal for tax purposes.
- By applying the same basic principles, there is no reason why similar sophistication should not be available to SMEs at affordable rates.
- Working capital is a fundamental need in a recession. In order to survive, SMEs should strategically review and simplify the business, exploring all available sources of capital.

INTRODUCTION

The term "corporate finance" is widely, and sometimes loosely, used in business. In accounting firms it typically relates to a department or function that primarily deals with:

- mergers, acquisitions, and disposals (M&A);
- raising finance (early stage through to mature businesses);
- flotations;
- management buyouts and buy-ins;
- business valuations;
- due diligence;
- succession planning and exit strategies.

These might represent the practical application of corporate finance. In theory, however, its primary role is to maximize the value of the business while minimizing the financial risks. The essence of the present article is that the practice of corporate finance has become oversimplified—potentially to the detriment of the business.

Furthermore, while corporate finance is usually a specialized department in larger accounting firms and in some smaller ones, its application in SMEs can often be quite different. Here, accessing and managing sources of working capital becomes a fundamental need, especially in a recession.

We shall propose a wider approach to corporate finance, based on asset/liability management principles and the *full balance sheet approach*, that is just as applicable to SMEs as it is to larger, more sophisticated companies.

A FULL BALANCE SHEET APPROACH

A full balance sheet approach is recommended as the underlying principle of applying corporate finance. This involves looking at each and every asset in the context of the liabilities that actually or notionally finance them. Two key measures are:

- The amount by which the profit would increase or decrease as the overall result of a 1% change in interest rates.
- The difference between the average duration (i.e. asset life weighted by value) of the assets and the average duration of the liabilities that fund them. The importance of this is that, if the duration of the liabilities is shorter than that of the assets and, for example, interest rates rise, there will be an additional cost to the profit and loss account that cannot be recovered by the assets.

A MORE SOPHISTICATED APPROACH TO CORPORATE FINANCE FOR SMES

SMEs are often started and/or owned by owner/entrepreneurs. Corporate finance transactions may be precipitated by owners, their bankers, accountants, or lawyers, or by approaches from elsewhere. For example, two sets of circumstances have recently led to a flurry of transactions:

1. The British Government changed the capital gains tax (CGT) arrangements for businesses from April 6, 2008, ending taper relief. One result was that, leading up to this date, accounting and law firms were deluged by a spate of entrepreneurs seeking advice on financial restructuring or sale of their businesses to children, managers, and other interested parties so as to minimize CGT.
2. A growing number of owner/entrepreneurs are approaching retirement age and want to pass their businesses on to their children or managers.

Both of these typical situations create the need for advice and support on corporate finance, funding, and tax and legal advice.

The transactions referred to in points 1 and 2 are circumstantial. Other typical examples are refinancing the business, management buyouts and buy-ins, and M&A. These are routine corporate finance transactions, but if we return to the theory and apply it there are many more sophisticated possibilities which can be more appropriately driven by business or financial strategy, rather than circumstance. One of the less obvious times to consider these is during a recession or economic slowdown.

BUSINESS IN THREE BOXES

Entrepreneurs who have started their own business often end up trying to juggle all of what are known as the "three boxes," though such a simplified approach is entirely appropriate in a recession. The three boxes are:

- business development, which includes both sales and marketing and the development of the business itself, whether organically or by acquisition;
- operations, including delivery;
- finance and administration.

It has been possible to outsource the last of these for at least 20 years. Not every business can afford or justify the appointment of a full-time finance director, but even that function can be contracted out these days at an economic cost—creating the "virtual F.D." By doing so, the entrepreneur is able to focus on those aspects where his or her skills and experience are usually best applied—in the first two boxes. These should go hand in glove, as together they represent the "end to end" customer-focused processes.

RECESSION, REVIEW, AND THE APPLICATION OF CORPORATE FINANCE

A recession or similar downturn is absolutely the time to do a root and branch review, "lift the drains," and spring-clean the business. Why? Two reasons: First, because you have more time to do it during a recession; and second, because having done so, you will emerge lean and mean when the economic cycle turns favorable once more.

So often, corporate finance is transaction-led. Most accountants routinely offer the corporate finance services listed at the top of this article, but (and not just in the application of theory) there are many more opportunities, both holistically and in detail, to add measurable and lasting value to the business—and better understand it—if a

"We will take all measures necessary to help small businesses get the loan capital they need." Gordon Brown

     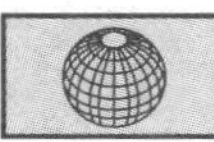   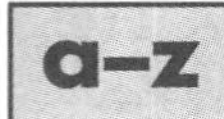

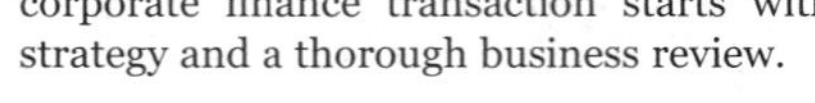

corporate finance transaction starts with strategy and a thorough business review.

BUSINESS AND FINANCIAL REVIEWS

Any accountancy firm worth its salt can do a financial review of sorts. This would probably focus on the profit and loss account, or tax, and how you can thereby save money. But the central focus of corporate finance is much more on the balance sheet. For example, an acquisition needs financing, either by debt or equity, or by both. Both need to be seen in the context of and integrated into the existing financial structure of the balance sheet.

A thorough financial review should ideally begin with a thorough *business* review. Every financial transaction is the consequence of a business decision. The business review starts with a review of strategy—especially the marketing strategy. It can go all the way through to the business processes and the systems that support them.

It's rather too simplistic to think that corporate finance transactions result solely from a need such as raising more working capital, financing capital expenditure, saving tax, selling or passing the business on, etc. Even if these are the circumstances that trigger a corporate finance transaction, each transaction should still be preceded by a thorough business and balance sheet review to see how it fits into the whole and ensure that the overall goal of *maximizing the return on the balance sheet at a managed level of risk* can be achieved.

CORPORATE FINANCE IN A CREDIT CRUNCH

Credit shortages and squeezes are not unusual; they typically follow a credit "bubble," where credit has grown so fast that it necessitates an economic readjustment. More importantly, the recent credit crunch has actually been a liquidity shortage. Funds have been scarce and the cost of borrowing has gone higher because the banks could not raise sufficient, or even any, longer-term funds to lend to business.

The smaller the enterprise, the harder it is to raise sufficient funds and the higher the likely cost. It's hard enough that the economic slowdown has squeezed financial performance. Being unable to find additional funds readily when they are most needed can all too often lead to business failure. It's not lack of capital but lack of cash that busts businesses. So creativity in corporate finance becomes even more important.

SO WHAT CAN SMES DO?

Few SMEs have the opportunity to float via either an Alternative Investment Market (AIM) or full listing on the London Stock Exchange. Furthermore, the new issues market is unlikely to return to anywhere near normal before 2010. Most corporate finance transactions for SMEs involve rather less finance than might be raised through an IPO (initial public offering, or flotation).

One factor that unites all SMEs is the need to find and manage working capital. Many are wedded to the idea of unsecured debt—usually an overdraft. Some will even resort to moving banks just to get a bigger unsecured overdraft facility.

This may not be the most efficient or, especially, the cheapest means, however. The credit crunch produced some fundamental changes in the commercial and corporate banking markets (many UK bankers refer to finance for companies with turnovers of up to $1.5 million as "commercial" and above that level as "corporate"; there is no real difference in principle). First, it accelerated the transition from overdraft finance to invoice discounting. One of the key reasons for this was because in most cases banks wanted security for the debt.

This security can take many forms. The most common is assets—property, machinery, other capital assets, cash, stock, receivables, etc. The practice of taking unsecured personal guarantees has decreased, but banks may routinely ask for a statement of personal assets and liabilities. Ideally, they prefer to take a charge on personal assets, such as the owner's or director's house.

Parallel with these changes has been the move away from base rate related finance. At the worst of the credit crunch, Libor (the London Interbank Offered Rate, i.e. the rate at which banks lend each other money) diverged by up to 1.6% from base rate (usually equal to the Bank of England Base Rate as reviewed and set by the FOMC monthly), so banks preferred to use Libor as the basis for their lending rates. It also allowed them to blur the edges from one bank to another, as opposed to the common metric of the base rate.

So unsecured overdrafts became relatively dearer (up to 5% or more above base rate) and invoice discounting relatively cheaper (as low as 1.2% over base rate, although it rose as high as 2% above as Libor diverged).

THE CHEAPEST FORM OF WORKING CAPITAL

The cheapest form is that generated by the business itself, i.e. from sales. It is amazing how many SMEs approach their advisers or bankers seeking to borrow more money for working capital purposes when they could devote more time to selling and less to administration. This is the principle of working *in* the business rather than *on* the business. Sir Alan Sugar, the British entrepreneur and businessman, is not alone in referring to the concept of the "busy fool"—someone who works long hours and makes little or no profit.

OTHER FORMS OF FUNDING

Beyond sales and shorter-term borrowing, banks offer several other forms of financing, at various cost levels:

Asset-backed

- property finance;
- asset finance, including leasing, HP, etc.;
- stock finance.

Quasi-secured

- payroll finance;
- invoice discounting (not the same as factoring, but similar).

Unfortunately, as the credit crunch deepened, the availability of finance fell and the price increased. In particular, property finance became scarcer, with much lower loan-to-value (LTV) rates, as banks found they were yet again overcommitted to commercial property finance less than 20 years after the last property crash.

In summary, therefore, funding has always been available for well-run, profitable companies of any size generating regular cash flows and with assets to act as collateral. With little interbank lending taking place, resulting in shrinking wholesale funding and a liquidity squeeze, it has been no surprise that banks in general became more cautious about the scale and security of their lending.

TRANSACTION-BASED CORPORATE FINANCE

As in the wider markets, M&A activity has slowed dramatically, due both to a shortage of funds and to the greater overall perceived risk of corporates in a slowdown. In the case of both M&As and management buyouts/buy-ins, the transaction is primarily based on the track record of sales and profit generation and the capability of the business being acquired.

The more doubtful the recent and projected profit record, the more likely it is that the majority, if not all, of the funding will need to be based on assets and/or quasi-assets.

TAX, LEGAL, AND PROFESSIONAL ADVICE

Some may think that corporate finance is an industry invented by professionals to generate fat fees. However, there are many pitfalls in trying to do it yourself. The

"We face prolonged tough times." Paul Williams

finance director or owner is generally unlikely to get the best terms possible, even if they run a competitive auction.

Professional advisers, such as the accountancy firms, will usually have better and more banking and financing contacts. They should also be able to exert more leverage on the banks, as they have their whole clientele as the lever, rather than the business and assets of a single company or business.

Many people also resent paying what they regard as high or exorbitant fees, especially to lawyers. While there may be the odd less scrupulous professional adviser, in the main you will be paying for massive accumulated experience of the best and most efficient ways to source, transact, and document the finance, as well as avoiding myriad pitfalls.

While sale and purchase agreements and shareholder agreements may have a standard form at their core, each company and set of directors is different. Finally, there will be tax implications for every corporate finance transaction, whether for the organization or the individuals concerned. If you have the right advisers, there is no harm in taking a degree of responsibility on yourselves, but your advisers can save you money and help you avoid penal costs and consequences.

CONCLUSION

Corporate finance can mean different things to different people; even the banks divide it into at least three categories: commercial finance, corporate finance, and structured finance. In truth, however, it is about just one thing—how the business is financed. The key is the *whole balance sheet approach*, looking not only at the optimum mix of short- and longer-term finance, but also at the overall picture: which liability funds which asset, at an optimum balance of cost and risk.

At its best in practice, corporate finance can be a sophisticated science. This does not make it any less applicable to SMEs. While the scale and nature of transactions may often be smaller or simpler, there is no reason why similar principles and practices shouldn't be applied. Equally, for firms that have the necessary breadth of skills, the fees do not need to be exorbitant either.

MORE INFO

See Also:

★ Capital Structure: A Strategy that Makes Sense (pp. 710–714)
★ Investing in Structured Finance Products in the Debt Money Markets (pp. 510–513)
★ Managing 21st Century Finances (pp. 66–67)
✔ Investors and the Capital Structure (p. 1120)
✔ Options for Raising Finance (p. 1081)
✔ Using Mezzanine Financing (p. 1105)
Joseph Schumpeter (p. 1308)
Financial Management for the Small Business (p. 1358)

"Drive-in banks were established so most of the cars today could see their real owners." E. Joseph Cossman

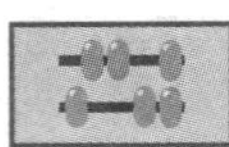

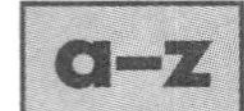

Dangers of Corporate Derivative Transactions

by David Shimko

EXECUTIVE SUMMARY

- Derivatives can be extremely effective risk management tools when used correctly.
- Used incorrectly, derivatives can cost firms hundreds of millions of dollars and damage the hard-won reputations of firms and managers.
- Most derivative debacles could have been avoided had appropriate checklists been followed and corrective action taken.
- Successful derivative transactions require significant analysis, senior management understanding and judgment, and due skepticism regarding advice from conflicted counterparties.

OVERLOOKED RISKS

It's easy for managers to overlook risks. Financial risk managers may ignore non-financial risks. Business managers responsible for a particular line item (such as costs) may downplay risks unrelated to their particular line item. Firms often manage their risks compartmentally—for example: the treasury department for foreign exchange and interest rates; the procurement department for commodity purchases; and the insurance department for catastrophic risks.

By its nature, any derivatives transaction introduces an enterprise-wide risk, even if it has a narrow purpose. Therefore, derivative transactions must be analyzed and managed systematically to ensure consistency with corporate objectives, suitability of the transaction, and avoidance of unintended consequences of the process.

Many soft risks can be avoided by following the steps on this derivatives transaction checklist:

- Verify consistency with risk policy and corporate objectives. Has the risk policy been updated to reflect current business strategy?
- Consider the impact of potentially offsetting risks on the balance sheet.
- Examine legal and regulatory requirements to assure compliance.
- Anticipate possible future legal and regulatory changes.
- Simulate possible outcomes of the derivative transaction under many scenarios.
- Establish the correct accounting treatment.
- Ensure the accounting treatment has the desired result in all scenarios.
- Understand when the desired accounting treatment cannot be attained.
- Make sure the firm has the personnel and systems to trade, monitor, and report derivatives activity.
- Communicate objectives to all stakeholders.
- Plan communication strategies for alternative future outcomes.
- Anticipate reputational risk due to possible adverse outcomes.
- Predetermine performance measurement criteria.
- Undertake review by audit committee (some firms will have a risk management committee).
- In the absence of sufficient internal expertise, seek outside evaluation.
- Determine in advance how ongoing valuations and risk assessments will be performed.
- Provide updated performance reports referencing communicated objectives.
- Study exit strategies in the event that conditions change materially.
- Consider personal political risk to managers under different outcome scenarios.

FAILURE TO REDUCE RISK

Although a derivative usually meets its narrow goal of reducing a particular risk, it is often the case that the derivatives transaction fails to reduce corporate risk materially. Indeed, some may actually increase the overall net risk profile.

For example, many firms hedge their foreign exchange risk carefully, perhaps not realizing that foreign exchange risk may be a very small part of the overall corporate risk profile.[1] In many cases, tacit speculation occurs under the guise of hedging, particularly if the trading activity gets hedge accounting treatment.

More generally, derivative transactions supported by a particular department will likely reduce departmental risk but may not reduce the overall risk of the firm. For example, a large software firm may want to hedge its interest rate risk, without realizing that the interest rate risk pales in comparison to the business risks of software development and sales.

The only remedy for this problem is to build a firm-wide risk model, even if it is approximate in many ways, to understand the impact of a particular derivatives strategy on the firm. The firm-wide risk model should include market, credit, operational, and event risks in order to be as complete as possible. With this kind of model in place, the benefits of risk management can be more precisely measured in order to compare the benefits to the costs. The following steps may be added to the checklist above:

- Build a model of the firm that simulates all material risks.
- Overlay the proposed derivative on the firm model.
- Test cash margin requirements, credit exposures, and accounting outcomes from the model.
- Document courses of action for select scenarios.

CREATION OF NEW RISKS WITH DERIVATIVES

There is a kind of law of conservation of risk in the universe. Risk is neither created nor destroyed, merely transformed into different risks.[2] Hedging market risk creates margin risk if hedging is done on exchanges, and it creates counterparty risk if it is done over-the-counter. Hedging also creates operational risks if the hedger is ill-prepared to manage the unanticipated consequences of hedging. In this section we will describe the three major risks created by derivative transactions.

Market risk. Hedging creates incremental market risk in many different scenarios. For example, most hedgers cannot hedge their risk perfectly—a corn farmer in Vermont may hedge with Illinois corn futures, exposing the farmer to fluctuations in corn value between Vermont and Illinois. Market risk is also created when the hedger overhedges, such as when an oil producer hedges planned production from a well to find out that the well does not end up producing oil. Finally, market risk is created when the underlying risk profile of the company changes and its derivative contract does not. For example, the size of an exposure to counterparty default will generally vary with changes in market prices. If the company hedges counterparty risk but the exposure doubles, it is no longer hedged.

"Many . . . corporations use derivatives conservatively, to offset risks from fluctuating currency and interest rates. But over the years, companies . . . have run into serious financial trouble using derivatives in a more dangerous fashion—to speculate." Knowledge@Wharton

Credit risk. Hedging creates credit risk whenever a specific counterparty is involved. This may be a bank party to an OTC derivatives trade, or it may be an insurance company. A company's own credit may be impaired by hedging if hedging creates future cash margin requirements that compromise the company (see box).

Operational risk. The large number of soft risks may be inferred from the list above. Here we emphasize that even a firm that hedges may find it does not have the valuation, validation, monitoring, reporting and execution skills to maintain derivative strategies. In some cases, strategies were designed poorly because of the unfamiliarity of the analysts with the risks they were modeling.[3] Particularly when a company chooses to reverse a particular strategy, it is prone to losing significant sums due to trading with sophisticated counterparties.

Several of the world's largest and most successful companies have suffered derivative disasters of one form or another. One such listing is the "Wheel of Misfortune" on a website provided by Sungard (see Table 1 and More Info section).

Table 1. Disasters cited in Sungard's "Wheel of Misfortune"

	Credit risk	Market risk	Operational risk
Allied Irish Banks		•	•
Bank of Credit and Commerce International			•
Bankers Trust		•	•
Bankgesellschaft Berlin	•		
Barings		•	•
Bausch and Lomb			•
California power crisis 2000–2001	•	•	
Cendant			•
Confederation Life	•		•
Continental Illinois	•		•
Credit Lyonnais			•
Daiwa			•
First National Bank of Keystone	•		•
HIH Insurance			•
Lloyd's	•		•
Long-Term Capital Management	•	•	•
Metallgesellschaft (MG)		•	•
Morgan Grenfell		•	•
NatWest Markets			•
Orange County		•	•
Power Company of America (PCA)	•	•	
US savings and loan crisis	•	•	

These debacles are documented on Sungard's website. The most important thing for the CFO is to be aware of the dangers in order to manage them. Derivatives comprise a specialized subfield of financial management requiring specialized skills. A CFO with analytic support from people experienced in derivative transactions and risk management stands a better chance of executing derivative strategies successfully than one who does not have this support.

FITCH RELEASE ON SEMGROUP ENERGY PARTNERS LP

Corporate CFOs often enter derivative transactions with the best of intentions, but leave them as unintended consequences develop. As an example, in 2008, SemGroup suffered significant financial distress as a result of its hedging activities.

"The downgrades and Watch Negative status reflect liquidity pressures related to the sustained elevated level of crude oil prices and SemGroup's ability to continue its marketing and storage businesses in the current price environment. Spot prices for WTI crude at Cushing, OK have increased by as much as 43% since April 1, 2008. SemGroup hedges a large percentage of its inventories and would be required to post additional margin to increase the collateral support for its hedging program. Specifically, Fitch is concerned that the company may not have sufficient available capacity from its bank facilities to meet requests for additional margin. SemGroup is a privately held midstream energy partnership focused primarily on providing gathering, transportation, processing, and marketing services for crude oil and refined products in the US Midcontinent region and Canada." (July 17, 2008)

REGRETS EXPRESSED BY CFOS WHO HAVE HEDGED WITH DERIVATIVES

To understand the dangers of corporate derivatives transactions, it is useful to share the personal experiences of CFOs who have hedged using derivatives. While there are many success stories, here are some

CASE STUDY

We consider the case of a US-based petroleum refinery seeking to reduce its net income variations with a strategy using either exchange-traded or OTC derivatives. What are the problems the refinery may have?

- It may not consider all risks in its derivatives strategy. For example, the risk of plant failure due to operational failures may end up not being factored into the analysis, causing the refinery to over-hedge.
- A transaction designed to reduce the risk surrounding crude oil purchases may actually end up increasing risk for the refinery. This happens because the margin between crude and crude products becomes more variable if costs are hedged but revenues are not.
- New risks may be introduced by hedging. If the refinery hedges on a futures exchange, it is subject to cash margin calls it may not have anticipated. If the refinery transacts on the OTC market, it can expect to take additional risk due to potential counterparty failure.
- As the refiner's risk profile changes, the derivative strategy may be discovered to be inappropriate. For example, if refinery margins shrink and become negative, it may make more sense for the refinery to stop producing rather than continuing to produce at a loss for the purpose of honoring a delivery contract, especially if the delivery requirement can be arranged elsewhere more cheaply. Clearly, the refinery must consider its entire risk profile if it seeks to manage one of its risks.

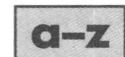

paraphrased quotes from CFOs that have not been as successful:

"When we make money on the hedge, we are told we are doing our jobs. When we lose money on the hedge, we are responsible. Management should realize the purpose of the hedge is to reduce risk, not make money."

"Are we really hedging, or are we speculating under the guise of hedge accounting treatment?"

"We had no idea how bad the margin requirements could get. This trade may bankrupt us."

"Is this risk really material to our business? We spend 80% of our time hedging 20% of our risk, exactly the wrong way around."

CONCLUSION

Unfortunately, many CFOs have nowhere to turn but to their counterparties for advice. This is like asking the wolf to guard the sheep. The counterparty has a position of conflict and, even if qualified, should not advise a corporation on derivatives strategy.

Another problem CFOs have is that senior management expect them to have the skills necessary to evaluate and execute derivative transactions, even though this is a highly specialized subfield of financial management. Yet, the best source of advice is an independent adviser who is familiar with the company's risk policies and profile, and familiar with the markets and instruments under consideration for the hedge.

It is tempting to think that a financial executive need only read a textbook on derivatives to be effective, but this could not be further from the truth. In fact, unscrupulous counterparties can take advantage of executives whose knowledge is textbook-oriented.

Nothing beats practical experience. Nevertheless, there are some excellent textbooks where the financial executive should begin. These are listed in the More Info section.

MAKING IT HAPPEN

The checklist items given earlier would surely need to be completed in an exhaustive derivatives analysis. The most important steps for minimizing derivative dangers are summarized below:

- *Risk Policy*. Risk policy must be consistent with shareholder and board preferences, and with corporate strategy generally. Risk governance must be clear; risk control must be independent; and standards for derivatives performance need to be articulated precisely in advance of the transaction.
- *Risk Measurement*. Risk must be measured in the context of the entire firm and reported in terms familiar to managers.
- *Scenario analysis*. The derivative outcomes should be analyzed under many different scenarios to ensure the firm has created a contingency plan for management of the transaction under these scenarios.
- *Suitability*. It should be determined that the type of transaction and its terms are suitable for the company, given its level of experience and expertise.
- *Performance*. Performance must be consistent with policy goals, rather than just the profit or loss of the hedge program in isolation.

MORE INFO

Books:

Brown, Gregory W., and Donald H. Chew (eds). *Corporate Risk: Strategies and Management*. London: Risk Books, 1999.

Hull, John C. *Options, Futures and Other Derivatives*. 7th ed. Harlow, UK: Prentice Hall, 2008.

Kolb, Robert W., and James A. Overdahl. *Understanding Futures Markets*. 6th ed. Malden, MA: Blackwell, 2006.

McDonald, Robert L. *Derivatives Markets*. 2nd ed. Boston, MA: Addison-Wesley, 2005.

Smithson, Charles W. *Managing Financial Risk: A Guide to Derivative Products, Financial Engineering, and Value Maximization*. 3rd ed. New York: McGraw-Hill, 1998.

See Also:

★ Credit Derivatives—The Origins of the Problem (pp. 156–157)
★ A Total Balance Sheet Approach to Financial Risk (pp. 113–114)
★ Using Structured Products to Manage Liabilities (pp. 115–117)
✔ Derivatives Markets: Their Structure and Function (p. 1007)
✔ Sarbanes–Oxley: Its Development and Aims (p. 1052)
✔ Swaps, Options, and Futures: What They Are and Their Function (p. 988)
Futures, Options, and Swaps (p. 1366)
Options, Futures, and Other Derivatives (p. 1405)

NOTES

1 Copeland, Thomas E., and Yash Joshi. "Why derivatives don't reduce foreign exchange risk." *McKinsey Quarterly* (February 1996): 66–79.

2 Shimko, David. "As if by magic." *Risk Magazine* 11:10 (1998): 45.

3 Edwards, Franklin R., and Michael S. Canter. "The collapse of Metallgesellschaft: Unhedgeable risks, poor hedging strategy, or just bad luck?" *Journal of Futures Markets* 15:3 (1995): 211–264.

"Derivatives are financial weapons of mass destruction." Warren Buffett

     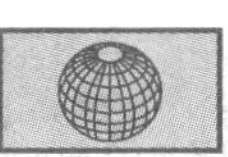   

Factoring and Invoice Discounting: Working Capital Management Options by Irena Jindrichovska

EXECUTIVE SUMMARY

- Factoring is often understood by businesses to be invoice discounting. However, it is, in fact, the sale of receivables, whereas invoice discounting is borrowing, where receivables are used as collateral.
- In recent years, factoring has experienced substantial growth, as it has become an important source of financing for both small and medium-size enterprises (SMEs), as well as for export corporations.
- Both factoring and invoice discounting are methods that help to speed up the collection of receivables, and thus increase asset turnover and profit generation for corporate shareholders.
- Both factoring and invoice discounting directly affect the performance of corporations as they impact on working capital, and affect the performance of asset turnover and profit generation.

FACTORING

Factoring is provided by financial institutions, for example banks and individual factoring brokers. It is a form of asset-based financing, where the factor provides funding based upon the values of a borrower's accounts receivable, i.e. corporate debtors. The receivables are purchased by the factor rather than used as collateral for a loan. This means that the ownership of receivables shifts from the seller to the factor. Factoring generally includes more than just financing, and it also includes funding and collection (Booth and Cleary, 2007).

Factoring and invoice discounting in the UK is being used by more than 47,000 companies, with a total volume of €170,000 billion in 2003 (Bakker *et al.*, 2004). It is a popular method of working capital management in many countries, and is especially helpful for start-up companies, as well as small and medium-size corporations, to use their working capital more effectively.

Factoring offers some advantages for the factor over lending, and is likely to become more important in transitional and developing countries. The funding provided to the customer is explicitly linked to the value of their underlying assets (working capital), and not to the borrower's overall creditworthiness. This portfolio of assets (receivables) is being continuously managed, to ensure that the value of the underlying assets always exceeds the amount of credit.

FEATURES AND PARAMETERS OF FACTORING

Factoring can be done on both a recourse and non-recourse basis. In developed financial markets, factoring is done on a non-recourse basis. The factor does not have a claim against its client (the borrower) if the accounts default. In less-mature financial markets, recourse factoring is used, where the factor has a claim against its borrower for deficiencies of purchased receivables. Therefore, the factor would suffer a loss only if the underlying accounts are not paid, while, at the same time, the borrower cannot cover the deficiency. In recourse factoring, all the debts are at the client's risk in the event of customer failure. The factoring company is taking little risk. In these cases, one might expect that the factor would not be restrictive as to whom the company is selling the product. However, factors impose credit risks and concentration limits that restrict the funding of their clients. This is also an important aspect of risk management on the part of factors.

Factoring can be also be done on a notification and a non-notification basis. Under notification, the debtors are notified that their payables have been sold to a factor. In general, factoring with recourse does not include notification, but factoring without recourse does. (In many countries, factoring has a negative connotation, so some clients prefer factors that do not notify their debtors.)

In reality, a factor provides three linked services: financing, assuming credit risk, and a collection service. The collection service involves collecting current accounts, and the collecting of non-performing accounts. This helps to minimize losses associated with bad debts to the client.

Factors typically pay less than 100% of the face value of receivables, even though they take ownership of the whole amount. The difference between those amounts creates a reserve held by the factor. This reserve will be used to cover deficiencies in the payment of invoices.

In world trade, factorable products often flow from developing countries to developed countries. This creates opportunities for export factoring. Export factoring is the principal type of factoring in most developing and transitional countries because it is, in many cases, easier and safer to factor export receivables than domestic receivables. Obviously, in these cases, all parties to the transaction will face an exchange-rate risk, which needs to be mitigated with the help of financial institutions.

FACTORING EXAMPLE AND THE COST OF FACTORING

Factoring represents a sale of accounts receivable to a financial institution, which acts as a factor. This may be a bank, or an independent factoring broker. There are three parties to this transaction: a client company (a producer that has provided services or produced goods, and issued invoices to its debtors, who need to pay invoices to the company under certain conditions); a debtor (the company that ought to pay the invoice to the producer in due time); and a factor that facilitates the transaction through buying the invoice from the client, and finances the amount over an agreed period.

Simple Illustration

The factor purchases £100 from its client under a factoring contract. The client company (borrower) receives, from the factor, 70% of the value of the invoice minus interest and service fees, and minus a factoring commission of, say, 2%. The client receives the remaining 30% upon receiving the payment from its customer. The amount of £30 serves as a reserve amount, and is kept by the factor until the invoice is paid.

At the beginning of the transaction, the factor advances £68 and acquires ownership of the whole receivable. When the invoice is paid in 31 days, the factor sends £30 to the client on day 31. The size of the reserve depends on the perceived risk of the client. There will be an additional cost, which will be the interest on the outstanding balance of receivables. The interest can be deducted at the beginning, at the same time as factoring the commission.

The client company pays a commission fee for the factoring service to the factor, as well as interest for the period of financing. The factor bears the risk of non-paying customers. The factor buys the receivable at a discount, which ranges from 0.35% to 4%.

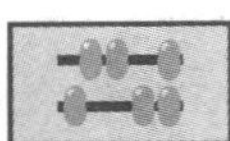

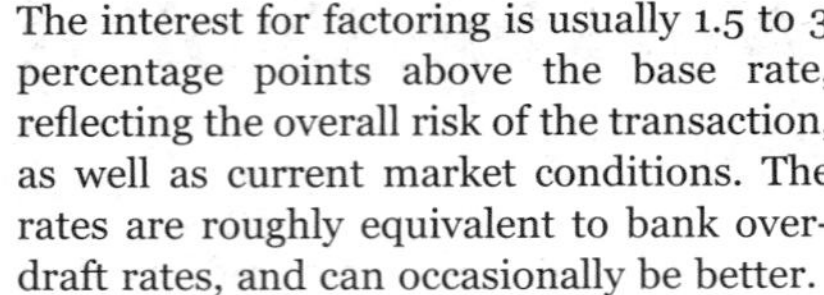

The interest for factoring is usually 1.5 to 3 percentage points above the base rate, reflecting the overall risk of the transaction, as well as current market conditions. The rates are roughly equivalent to bank overdraft rates, and can occasionally be better.

REGULATION OF THE INDUSTRY

Company cash flow, and its financial health, are very much affected by performance of its short-term assets. In this regard, the way factoring is arranged and managed is extremely important, as it directly affects the cash flow and financial health of a client company. Companies, therefore, need to pay close attention to choosing a good quality factor, because selecting the wrong factor can have a damaging effect on the company.

"Unfortunately, there isn't any regulation of factoring companies, and equally unfortunately, as any knowledgeable factoring insider will tell you, the industry is badly in need of regulation, as currently the factoring companies exercise far too much power, and on the occasions when they abuse that power, the poor client has no one to complain to." (*Source*: www.factoring-broker.org.uk, accessed December 9, 2009.)

Factoring is a complex, long-term agreement that could have major effects on the management and development of the client company. It is, therefore, advisable to take legal advice on the legal and financial implications of factoring.

INVOICE DISCOUNTING

Invoice discounting is another policy used by firms to speed up collection of receivables. Invoice discounting is an alternative way of drawing money against a company's receivables, i.e., issued invoices. In this case, the business retains control over the administration of receivables. It provides a cost-effective way for profitable businesses to improve their cash flow.

There are two parties to this transaction: the client company and the invoice discounter.

This service is provided by banks and financial institutions to businesses that sell products or services on credit to other businesses. It is normally available to businesses with a proven track record, and annual turnover of at least £500,000, and is usually a long-term relationship between the business and the invoice discounter.

The Mechanics of Invoice Discounting

The invoice discounter first checks the client company, its accounting, and production systems. It reviews the client's accounting system, its customers, and its overall creditworthiness, and will then agree to pay a certain percentage of its total outstanding receivables.

The client company pays a monthly fee and interest on the net amount advanced. Typical fees range from 0.2% to 0.5% of discounted receivables. These fees are less than factoring fees, because only the financing service is provided.

"For example, if the invoice discounter agrees to advance 80% of the total owing, and the total of outstanding invoices is steadily changing, then so will the amount you receive. If the outstanding debt drops month on month, you must repay 80% of the fall in debt. If the debt rises month on month, you will receive 80% of the increase." (*Source*: Adapted from Business Link, www.businesslink.gov.uk, accessed December 9, 2009.)

SHORT-TERM FINANCE AND WORKING CAPITAL MANAGEMENT

Short-term finance consists of the management of short-term assets and liabilities. Both methods—factoring and invoice discounting—reduce the cash cycle in the business, and the need to finance short-term assets of the company. The shortcomings of these methods are that if the factor is not a good-quality organization, the corporate client will suffer and have problems with cash flow. Lack of regulation in the industry may also be a problem in using factoring. Invoice discounting is less complex as the discounter provides only

CASE STUDY

The Cost of Factoring: A Short Summary

Background: The turnover of a client company is £750,000 per year, and debtors are taking an average of 50 days to pay on commencement of the factoring agreement.

The factoring company provides the following conditions:

Factoring commission:	1.25%
Factoring interest:	7.0% pa
Average credit period:	50 days
Convention 360 days in a year	
Factoring commission cost:	
1.25% x £750,000	£9,375
Factoring interest cost:	
(£750,000 – £9,375) × 7% × 50 ÷ 360	£7,200
Total factoring costs:	£16,575

The total cost of funding over the period of 50 days is £16,575. This needs to be compared with other funding options (e.g. bank loan) for optimization. (Adapted from Factoring solutions: www.factoringsolutions.co.uk, accessed December 9, 2009.)

MAKING IT HAPPEN

Factoring services in particular are provided by many companies and therefore it pays to look around for the best deal. Financial companies usually provide both factoring and invoice discounting services. Factors are usually linked with bigger banks to provide secure funding. Some examples of providers of commercial finance and asset financing are provided in the next section.

MORE INFO

Books:

Bakker, M., L. Klapper, and G. Udell. *Financing Small and Medium-size Enterprises with Factoring: Global Growth and Its Potential in Eastern Europe*. Washington, DC: World Bank, 2004.

Booth, L., and W. S. Cleary. *Introduction to Corporate Finance*. Toronto, ON: Wiley, 2007.

Klapper, L. *The Role of Factoring for Financing Small and Medium Enterprises*. Washington, DC: World Bank, 2005.

Meckin, D. *Naked Finance: Business and Finance Pure and Simple*. London: Nicolas Brealey Publishing, 2007.

"I don't want to do business with those who don't make a profit, because they can't give the best service." Lee Bristol

financing, while the company retains total control over its sales ledger.

There are also many other services provided by the financial sector that can improve the use of cash in a company, including debt factoring, invoice factoring, and asset-based lending. The topic remains the same: turn the company's unpaid invoices into cash that can be put to work immediately. An invoice-discounting facility grows with the volume of issued invoices. Therefore, there is no need to renegotiate funding or increase the overdraft facility to free business capacity in order to enable a quick reaction to market opportunities.

For export financing and advising on overseas invoices, there is the Asset Based Finance Association. The ABFA represents the interests of UK and Republic of Ireland based companies, providing factoring, invoice discounting and other forms of asset based finance (*Source*: www.abfa.org.uk, accessed December 9, 2009)

Article:

Soufani, K. "Factoring as a financing option: Evidence from the UK." Working paper, Concordia University, 2003.

Websites:

Asset Based Finance Association: www.abfa.org.uk

Factoring Solutions, independent factoring firm: www.factoringsolutions.co.uk

HSBC, information on factoring: tinyurl.com/3g5h3pa

Independent Factoring Brokers Association: www.factoring-broker.org.uk

Lloyds TSB, information on factoring: www.ltsbcf.co.uk/factoring

Royal Bank of Scotland, information on factoring: www.rbsif.co.uk/invoice-financing/factoring

UK government-sponsored advice agency, Business Link: www.businesslink.gov.uk

See Also:

★ Corporate Finance for SMEs (pp. 33–35)
✔ Hedging Foreign Exchange Risk—Case Studies and Strategies (p. 970)
✔ How to Use Receivables as Collateral (p. 1074)
✔ Invoicing and Credit Control for Small and Medium-Sized Enterprises (p. 976)
✔ Understanding and Using the Cash Conversion Cycle (p. 995)

"I feel these days like a very large flamingo. No matter what way I turn, there is always a very large bill." Joseph O'Connor

  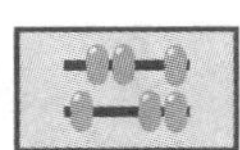      

Formulating a Contingency Funding Plan to Manage Liquidity Risks by Gary Deutsch

EXECUTIVE SUMMARY

- How financial institutions can use their liquidity risk management program as the launch point for developing a comprehensive contingency funding plan (CFP) to address potential adverse liquidity events and emergency cash flow requirements.
- Guidance on establishing a CFP, management strategies for implementing a CFP, and steps for developing CFP liquidity needs and availability based on stress-testing.
- Conclusions and next steps, as well as an extensive list of reference sources for those looking to delve into this topic in more detail.

INTRODUCTION

Managing the funding activities of a financial institution has become quite challenging as the global economy continues to develop economic linkages that can lead to unexpected volatility and systemic problems. The European Union, the United States, Asia, and other world economies have become connected through trade and currencies, and changing cultures and demographics such that it is no longer possible to focus solely on local or regional markets when planning for liquidity risk management.

Liquidity risk measurement and monitoring systems must, of necessity, look to worldwide economic linkages to understand how to assess current and prospective cash flows and to establish plans for funding sources and uses. Financial institutions need to establish a forward-looking approach to developing liquidity management strategies, policies, procedures, and limits to ensure that they draw on a diverse mix of existing and potential future funding sources.

Moreover, to protect against unexpected economic volatility and systemic problems, financial institutions need to hold adequate levels of highly liquid financial instruments free of legal, regulatory, or operational impediments to meet liquidity needs in stressful situations.

THE IMPORTANCE OF A CONTINGENCY FUNDING PLAN

A contingency funding plan (CFP) should describe the procedures that a bank or financial institution will implement to fund cash flow shortfalls that could occur in situations of stress or liquidity crises. To develop effective stressed or crisis-based CFP procedures, institutions must create plausible scenarios that simulate what could happen in various stress or crisis conditions.

CFP procedures must outline in sufficient detail areas such as:

- specific tasks and responsibilities, including decisions that must be made;
- timely and detailed liquidity information;
- alternative contingency funding measures.

CFP procedures cannot be passive. The procedures have to be tested, adjusted, and updated as market conditions, regulations, funding sources, business operations, and the capabilities of internal systems change over time.

Furthermore, because CFP procedures are derived from a financial institution's liquidity risk management (LRM) program, the procedures must be coordinated with the institution's overall asset–liability management program as well as with its central bank to avoid possible contagion effects that could disrupt the efficiency and stability of money market channels.

Consider the scenario presented in the case study as an example of how a minor problem can grow into a liquidity crisis if not handled according to a properly developed and executed CFP. This example will then be discussed in the remainder of the section.

DISCUSSION

In the example described in the case study, Bank A did not have a plan to contain the liquidity risk that it encountered. In developing CFPs, many institutions focus on methods to contain or limit liquidity risks so that they will not grow and get out of hand, as they did for this bank. Ideally, Bank A should have expanded its liquidity risk limits to go beyond just containing the risks that it encountered. It should have considered various types of liquidity shocks and how it could set CFP procedures in motion to absorb those shocks.

An effective CFP will consider the types of shock that could result in a liquidity crisis using scenarios like the one in the example. Often, describing possible scenarios can help management to think through what it would do if specific events occurred. For instance, when Bank A had a capital shortfall and obtained regulatory approval to seek new capital, it is unlikely that it would have associated a liquidity crisis with its capital plan. Yet, if it had used its cumulative experience to describe a sequence of events that could lead to a liquidity crisis stemming from a capital event, it would have been able to evaluate plausible ways to limit the impact of a minor liquidity problem and avoid a more severe problem that could lead to contagion effects. Each step in this process can be balanced against the institution's tolerance for dealing with related risks.

Overall, a CFP should address two major questions:

- Does management have a strategy for handling a crisis?
- Does management have procedures in place for accessing funds in an emergency?

A CFP should be required as part of a comprehensive liquidity risk management (LRM) program. A financial institution's LRM program should be based on comprehensive cash flow projections together with a funding plan that forecasts funding needs and funding sources under various market scenarios. If the LRM is forward-looking, a CFP will also be designed to deal with future events. Past liquidity crises are important to gaining an understanding of what could happen, but future events may not follow the same pattern. CFPs that are derived from forward-looking LRM programs work much better in the real world.

Given a forward-looking approach, the CFP should evaluate an institution's estimate of potential balance sheet changes that may result from various liquidity or credit events. The idea is to develop specific plans that uncover early warning signals of a potential liquidity crisis. Early warning signals are essentially a way to anticipate what could happen if events A, B, C, or D occur.

For instance, in the above example scenario for Bank A, event A was a capital deficiency. What could happen if Bank A experienced a capital deficiency was probably not a question that arose because the bank did not create a CFP. If it had, it would have explored the possible scenarios that could arise if a capital deficiency occurred. Although it may seem unlikely that a capital deficiency would trigger a liquidity crisis, one seemingly controllable event led to another which, in a short time, progressed into a serious liquidity crisis. It is the steps that lead to this possible progression that institutions must discuss and evaluate when formulating their CFP.

Once possible events and steps leading to a potential liquidity crisis have been evaluated, financial institutions should develop detailed strategies and tactics to prevent the escalation of liquidity concerns. If Bank A had initiated a public relations campaign to proactively dispel rumors of financial problems, it might have prevented the build-up of negative market impressions that eventually led to its liquidity crisis.

There should always be more than one alternative for dealing with events, especially considering that liquidity events may be taking an institution into uncharted waters. CFPs should highlight possible strategies for dealing with different levels of severity and types of liquidity stress events that may cause liquidity shortfalls. Ideally, institutions will link their CFP to specific stress-testing scenarios and proposed actions for accessing liquidity under each scenario. The proposed actions should be translated into specific procedures that should be followed in the attempt to close liquidity shortfalls, particularly in emergency situations.

MANAGEMENT STRATEGY FOR IMPLEMENTING CFP PROCEDURES

There are five key areas that management must focus on when developing a CFP implementation plan.

- *Policies and procedures*to ensure that information-flows to senior management remain timely and uninterrupted.
- *Division of responsibility*to ensure that all personnel understand exactly what is required of them during a period of liquidity strain or a stress event.
- *Information provided to markets and relevant parties*should be covered in a clear and decisive strategy that ensures a continuous stream of information to manage perceptions during times of stress.
- *A press and broadcast media communications strategy*should cover how management is to deal with press and broadcast media when negative information about the institution is disseminated.
- *A public relations strategy*should set out how management can deploy an effective program to counter rumors about the financial institution that may result in significant withdrawals of deposits.

When considering the division of responsibility, one alternative is to establish a crisis management team chaired by the institution's treasurer or chief financial officer or as part of the institution's asset and liability management committee (ALCO). Functional participants could include representatives from treasury, finance, risk management, ALCO, funding desks, and other significant business functions or geographic areas. This team should be responsible for implementing liquidity stress scenario simulations, developing market insight reports, conducting liquidity monitoring, and analysis and updating of the institution's liquidity management strategy.

Good communications are essential to ensuring that this team functions effectively and is prepared to defend the institution against a potential liquidity crisis. Therefore, the CFP should include the following information in the section on administrative policies and procedures:

- specific senior management responsibilities during a funding crisis;
- names, addresses, and telephone numbers of members of the liquidity crisis team;
- team members' assignments based on their office locations and functions.

If the liquidity crisis management team has to be activated, designated members should be contacted to initiate actions included in the CFP procedures. It may also be beneficial to conduct periodic tests or "dry runs" so that everyone has the opportunity to practice their role in the event of a liquidity crisis.

STEPS FOR DEVELOPING CFP LIQUIDITY NEEDS AND AVAILABILITY

Developing a CFP is a relatively new requirement for many financial institutions. As an extension of liquidity risk management practices, a CFP should be designed to help an institution to deal with both pre-crisis and crisis situations. Therefore, there are some basic concepts that need to be included in a CFP. These include determining how to measure the current availability of liquidity and routine needs, identifying and generating stress scenarios that could adversely impact the institution's funding availability and needs, and identifying indicators that can be used to establish an early warning system consistent with the stress scenarios.

Determining How to Measure Current Liquidity Availability and Routine Needs

When evaluating how liquidity should be measured, a financial institution can start by looking to its liquidity risk management (LRM) program to assess current risks. Here are some risk assessment questions to consider:

- Are liquidity needs and availabilities clearly identified and reported?
- Do reports related to liquidity needs and availabilities assist management with identifying liquidity vulnerabilities?
- Does the liquidity reporting system address how credit risk exposure, spread, and spread volatility impact market, funding liquidity, and counterparty risks?
- Are collateral, counterparty, regulatory, and legal entity issues updated routinely?
- Does the LRM program look to capital as a potential means of correcting or mitigating exposure to liquidity risk?

Expanding the risk assessment into the development of a CFP, here are some additional questions to address:

- Does the CFP stress-testing consider how financial and nonfinancial risks are often interconnected in unexpected, but significant, ways?
- Do scenario analyses and stress-testing analyses consider plausible but extreme circumstances?

When determining how to measure current liquidity availability and routine needs, institutions must consider their unique internal and external environment as well as the interconnectedness of financial markets. Despite the complexities that can arise, the measurement process ultimately is focused on an institution's ability to raise cash quickly at a reasonable cost. If asset sales are involved, there should be minimal loss of principal.

As stated earlier in this chapter, when measuring liquidity risks during development of a CFP, an institution is best served by adopting a forward-looking approach. An effective liquidity measurement process should therefore start with the institution's balance sheet and capture the following monthly and quarterly data:

- overnight funds sold;
- short-term investments;
- market value of securities less securities pledged;
- overcollateralized securities;
- government- and agency-guaranteed loans;
- cash flow due in 30 days or less from other securities;
- other liquid assets, such as interest-bearing deposits or money-market mutual funds.
- *Less*: Funds purchased, contingencies for deposit withdrawals (maturing certificates of deposit (CDs) and other withdrawals), and other liquidity reserves needed.

These balance sheet items represent the institution's core surplus or deficit of available funds to meet routine or emergency cash needs. When considering emergency needs in a CFP, the core surplus or

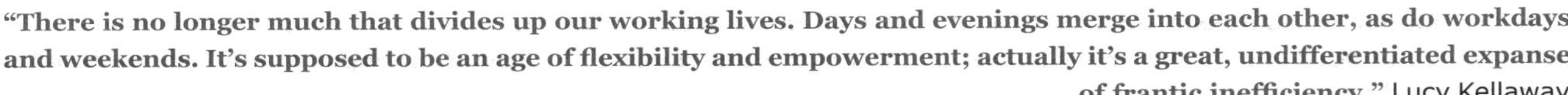

deficit can then be enhanced with such items as:

- additional borrowing capacity;
- available board-authorized broker deposits;
- secondary collateral (municipal securities, corporate securities, equities);
- borrowing capability from the central bank.

Once the core and enhanced surplus or deficit are known, the next step is to determine how this number could change in the future. To address this issue, consider the following analysis of cash flow and availability of funds.

Cash Inflows

These balance sheet items are the core cash inflows that impact most financial institutions:

- loan payments and prepayments;
- loan sales;
- investment coupon payments and maturities;
- investment sales;
- new nonmaturity deposit balances;
- new CD balances;
- wholesale funding drawdowns.

As institutions grow larger, the list may become more detailed and complex, but the cash flow concepts remain the same. These cash inflows must be tracked over time and under various economic conditions to determine their sensitivity to market liquidity risks. This tracking could be as simple as producing graphs of these transactions, or the transaction data (cash flows) could be correlated with economic data to determine if there is a positive or negative correlation between the institution's cash flows and specific economic factors. Institutions often rely on judgment in this analysis process, especially since liquidity risk management should be forward-looking and not be solely based on historical data that may be misleading should market conditions shift beyond what the institution has previously experienced.

Cash Outflows

The same type of analysis as described above should be conducted for cash outflows. Here are the core cash outflow transactions to consider:

- investment purchases;
- loan originations and purchases;
- the decay of nonmaturity deposits (annual decay as a percentage);
- CD withdrawals;
- CD maturities less retention of CD maturities;
- wholesale funding maturities (borrowings with bond or loan collateral, brokered CDs, other borrowings).

When the cash inflows and outflows are added together, they reflect the institution's proforma cash surplus or deficit. These data should be tracked monthly and quarterly and on a cumulative basis.

The proforma net cash flow can then be compared to the institution's primary, secondary, and other funding sources. For instance, primary funding sources may include the cash inflows described above plus any collateral available to support additional funding or any remaining approved broker deposit cap. This availability of primary funds can be calculated as a percentage of the institution's total assets to provide management with a benchmark that can be tracked over time and possibly tied to the institution's liquidity risk management policy guidelines.

Secondary funding resources can include the current line availability and maximum line capacity for borrowing sources and availability of funding from the central bank. In addition, institutions may receive funding support from their holding company if the organization is so structured.

Any other borrowing capacity not mentioned above should also be factored into the funds availability analysis process.

Identifying Indicators that Can Be Used to Establish an Early Warning System Consistent with the Stress Scenarios

Stress scenarios are discussed later in this chapter, but before evaluating what to stresstest, institutions must settle on how they will interpret what they learn. For instance, if under stressed conditions it appears that the institution would deplete its available collateral to support wholesale borrowing, should management consider the collateral situation as a warning sign that CFP procedures should be invoked? Or are there other cash flow trends and fund availability issues that need to be considered before CFP procedures are initiated?

Warning signals or risk indicators can be triggers for CFP actions, but institutions must think through which indicators work best for them and when an indicator represents a trigger or call to action. There is no one-size-fits-all approach that management can use to decide on indicators and triggers. This is because a CFP should not be a boilerplate rehash of what another institution decided worked for them. CFPs should be institution-specific and be tailored to operating systems, management philosophies, local, regional, national, and international market conditions, and customer demographics. Each institution will have a unique balance sheet risk profile, so choose measures that work best in your environment.

In fact, appropriate indicators and triggers may already be in use in your management and board meeting reports. For instance, a liquidity early warning system could consider such operating liquidity measures as loan and investment collateral levels, as discussed in the previous section. Institutions that need to maintain access to brokered deposit markets should track their regulatory capital status. If increased funding needs are projected in stress scenarios,

CASE STUDY

Bank Without an Effective Contingency Funding Plan

Bank A did not have an effective CFP. Negative news related to the bank's capital position caused sufficient concern about its viability that some depositors decided to move their accounts to a more stable bank. Although Bank A had plans approved by its regulator to raise additional capital, the limited run on its deposit base left it with a funding shortfall for which it had no prepared response. As a result, the press reported that the bank might not be able to fund a new loan to XYZ Corporation. As a result of the latest new report, the bank pressured its correspondents to assist with temporary credit lines, but since it did not have prior arrangements in place for this funding, it had to turn to its central bank for emergency funding. However, without an emergency funding plan, Bank A did not have sufficient collateral to support its funding shortfall.

More negative news was published and deposit withdrawals began to accelerate. Without an emergency funding source, the bank's correspondents were not able to support its deposit clearing activities or overnight cash needs. With matters growing worse by the day, and without detailed procedures to handle the growing funding shortfall, negative news prompted still more depositors to move their accounts and a run on the bank ensued. The run escalated and created a public relations problem for other banks in Bank A's markets. Bank A, unable to find funding sources to deal with its liquidity crisis, resorted to selling assets at fire-sale prices. What started as a minor capital problem for the bank became a liquidity crisis in its wholesale and retail markets and led to increasing uncertainty as to the viability of the bank.

"The domination of capitalism globally depends today on the existence of a Chinese Communist party that gives delocalized capitalist enterprises cheap labour to lower prices and deprive workers of the rights of self-organization."
Jacques Rancière

then deposit trends compared to loan growth could be a useful indicator and potential trigger within the CFP.

Here are some sample indicators to consider when evaluating liquidity risk stress tests to use in developing and updating an institution's CFP.

Cash flows:

- cash flow surplus plus additional availability from wholesale borrowing and brokered deposit lines;
- cash flow surplus plus available loan collateral;
- net cash flow surplus as a percentage of total assets.

Investment securities:

- total available investment securities collateral plus short-term investments divided by total assets;
- increases or decreases in the fair value of investment securities available as collateral.

Loans:

- total available loan collateral for wholesale borrowing divided by total assets;
- material short-term increases in the loan-to-deposit ratio;
- significant increases in loan line of credit utilization as a percentage of committed amounts;
- significant increases in the amount of adversely classified loans for regulatory purposes;
- material increases in the amount of nonperforming loans as a percentage of total loans by category;
- material increases in the amount of nonperforming loans as a percentage of tangible capital.

Deposits:

- material increases or decreases in nonmaturity deposit balances.

Capital:

- Basel II, Basel III, and regulatory capital ratios.

On the negative side of stress tests, if credit conditions are projected to worsen, then track loan impairment, loan loss provisions, troubled debt restructurings, foreclosures, and related collateral sales and charge-offs and include them in your liquidity risk management analyses.

Stress tests should be updated when market and economic conditions change and the CFP should be modified to include the results of these new stress tests when warranted.

Institutions that show net operating losses in stress scenarios should consider the possibility that they may also suffer from a reduced availability of funds due to a decline in the value of collaterals, among other factors. When the quality of assets on an institution's balance sheet deteriorates, there is often a greater potential for regulatory intervention. If stress scenarios indicate this potential, this situation could represent a red-flag trigger that should be integrated into the CFP, along with detailed procedures for risk mitigation alternatives. Some early warning indicators that could be considered red-flag indicators that may significantly reduce fund availability include:

- material adverse changes in wholesale borrowing lines, such as line reductions, increased collateral restrictions, or term-to-maturity restrictions;
- a downgraded credit rating or regulatory risk rating;
- inability to access the brokered CD market.

Institutions will need to experiment with the above indicators by conducting multiple stress tests to determine which represent the best triggers to use when implementing CFP emergency procedures. Also, stress tests should be updated when market and economic conditions change, and the CFP should be modified to include the results of these new stress tests when warranted.

Creating Stress Scenarios that Could Adversely Impact the Institution's Funding Availability and Needs

Stress tests should be conducted to determine how and when the institution's liquidity position may become impaired. Guidelines for developing stress tests will

MAKING IT HAPPEN

Developing an effective CFP is an important extension of an institution's liquidity risk management program. Issues that should be considered in structuring a CFP include the following.

- Ensuring that the organizational level at which the CFP is set up does not leave any gaps in the coverage.
- Establishing procedures that stress the importance of prompt decision-making.
- Making sure that decision-makers have quick access to timely and detailed liquidity information.
- Including diversified funding sources and funding maturities in the CFP.
- Giving consideration to the potentially destabilizing second-round effects on markets from liquidity-saving measures and asset sales.
- Reducing or avoiding potential contagion effects at the money-market level that stem from liquidity problems at money-center banks by maintaining the institution's role at the money-market level even in times of stress.
- Providing for and testing credible communication strategies and effective internal procedures consistent with cash flow projections and stress tests.
- Ensuring timely and comprehensive communication with regulators and central banks in periods of stress.

According to the ECB (2008) report referred to earlier in the chapter, experiences with liquidity stress tests and CFPs during the severe recession indicated that there was substantial room for improvement. Some of the areas where improvement was warranted are listed here.

- Recourse to central bank liquidity facilities in CFPs should be limited only to those which are routinely provided. Emergency facilities should not be relied on in CFPs. In addition, potential reputational costs associated with borrowing from the central bank in stress situations should be taken into account.
- When identifying "fail-safe" refinancing sources for inclusion in CFPs, the necessary operational arrangements have to be in place in order to access those sources easily during episodes of market turbulence. This implies regular and thorough testing and plausibility checks, with a view to potentially revising and updating the CFP in the light of changing conditions inside or outside the bank.
- During the recent turmoil some banks encountered difficulties in selling assets or pledging assets in secured lending. Regularly testing the capacity of liquid assets to actually generate positive cash flows might not only prove useful in its own right, but should also improve the identification of available and easily locatable liquid assets within a banking group in times of stress.

Institutions that are creating or updating their CFPs should give consideration to these liquidity risk issues. More resources are given in the More Info section to assist readers in developing an effective CFP.

depend on the institution's risk profile based on current assessments of interest rate risk, liquidity risk, earnings performance, and regulatory capital position. Tests should be designed to review the impact of specific liquidity events that may occur at various crisis levels, such as moderate, significant, and severe. To do this, one liquidity assumption at a time is input into the institution's asset–liability management (ALM) model. This is called sensitivity testing—only one assumption is changed and all other model assumptions remain the same. Therefore, the model output tests the sensitivity of the institution's liquidity to that single assumption. Here are some examples of assumptions that can be changed in an ALM model:

- a significant decline in investment security collateral values;
- credit issues that result in the need to sell loan assets at a substantial loss;
- significant tightening by wholesale lenders of collateral standards that reduce borrowing capacity;
- a material increase in deposit outflows;
- a significant reduction in capital that reduces access to brokered CD markets.

In addition to changing just one assumption at a time to conduct sensitivity stresstesting, consider inputting several of the types of assumptions listed above to determine if and when the institution may have a severe liquidity need that would require borrowing from the central bank.

Other sample stress test assumptions to consider are as follows:

- reductions in the correspondent credit lines available and counterparty limits;
- inability to draw down on precommitted lines;
- increased "haircuts" and collateral calls;
- increased utilization of credit commitments;
- currency conversion issues.

According to the European Central Bank's (2008) report "EU banks' liquidity stress testing and contingency funding plans," institution-specific assumptions should be supplemented with stress assumptions related to market-wide events such as:

- geographical liquidity issues during local, regional, and global liquidity crises;
- systemic issues in major financial centers, emerging markets, local money markets, or retail deposit markets such as the closure of key funding markets—including bond and covered bond markets, unsecured and secured interbank markets, and securitization markets;
- negative economic indicators related to an increase in bond yields, a drop in stock prices, a rise in credit spreads, a rise in short-term interest rates, or appreciation/depreciation of the domestic currency;
- a market perception that can lead to an acceleration of stress severity from mild to severe without a clear underlying cause;
- a clarification in the market perception of causes of stress based on such events as a subprime market liquidity crisis, government crisis or change in monetary policy, sudden and deep economic recessions, or the default of a primary market counterparty.

Furthermore, as liquidity risk increases, an institution may be faced with stress assumptions such as:

- repo markets and unsecured interbank markets are closed;
- marketable securities cannot be sold immediately—and when a sale takes place the price is lower than a recent fair-market value estimate;
- credit lines granted are drawn by corporate clients;
- loan securitizations cannot be completed;
- the commercial paper and certificate of deposit markets are in turmoil and not accessible as a source of funds;
- large demand deposit accounts are drawn down;
- the stability of retail deposits decreases substantially;
- foreign exchange markets create cross-border liquidity risk issues;
- no access to capital market funding.

The time horizon for stress tests with the types of assumptions described above should cover from one month up to 12 months in the future. Generally, a CFP should look out over a one- to six-month time period since that time horizon defines the amount of time it may take to evaluate CFP indicators, identify a trigger, and initiate procedures as defined in the CFP. It is important to be prepared to take quick, decisive actions based on predetermined and preapproved CFP plans that have been tested often to ensure their viability should there be a call to action.

Assumptions for longer time periods will become more strategic and should only be considered in the context of the institution's liquidity risk management program and strategic plans.

Overall, the information you should expect to derive from stress-testing is rooted in what can go wrong, how it can go wrong, and how badly can it go wrong in terms of your institution's liquidity. Through stress-testing, you should be able to determine what your institution can do well in advance of a severe liquidity crisis to

MORE INFO

Articles:

Longstaff, Francis A. "The flight-to-liquidity premium in U.S. Treasury bond prices." *Journal of Business* 77:3 (July 2004): 511–526. Online at: www.jstor.org/stable/10.1086/386528

Huberman, Gur, and Dominika Halka. "Systematic liquidity." *Journal of Financial Research* 24:2 (Summer 2001): 161–178. Online at: www.gsb.columbia.edu/whoswho/getpub.cfm?pub=1815 [PDF].

Reports:

Basel Committee on Banking Supervision. "Principles for sound liquidity risk management and supervision." Bank for International Settlements, September 2008. Online at: www.bis.org/publ/bcbs144.htm

Basel Committee on Banking Supervision. "Principles for sound stress testing practices and supervision." Bank for International Settlements, May 2009. Online at: www.bis.org/publ/bcbs155.htm

Bühler, Wolfgang, and Monika Trapp. "Time-varying credit risk and liquidity premia in bond and CDS markets." Working paper no. 09-13. Centre for Financial Research, October 2009. Online at: tinyurl.com/7k629v7 [PDF].

European Central Bank. "EU banks' liquidity stress testing and contingency funding plans." November 2008. Online at: tinyurl.com/84q2efd [PDF].

Financial Services Authority. "Strengthening liquidity standards, including feedback on CP08/22, CP09/13, CP09/14." Policy statement 09/16. October 2009. Online at: www.fsa.gov.uk/pubs/policy/ps09_16.pdf

Kunghehian, Nicolas. "Stress testing for liquidity risk: The impact of the new regulations." Moody's Analytics, November 2010. Online at: tinyurl.com/7zdecqo [PDF].

Matten, Chris. "Stress testing liquidity and the contingency funding plan." PricewaterhouseCoopers, PRMIA members' meeting, February 2009. Online at: tinyurl.com/cyq73p [PDF].

"Put a bunch of confident, aggressive men in the same room and reward them for taking risks, and you create a pressure cooker, from which probity and prudence evaporate like steam." Ian Leslie

   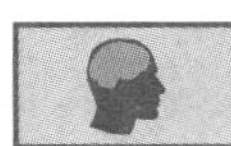  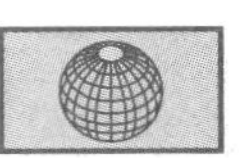   

minimize the damage that may result from even the worst-case scenario. The CFP should use stress-test results together with risk indicators, red flags, and triggers to identify opportunities for rapid and effective responses to liquidity risks. This process should assist management in making a smooth transition from benign conditions to stress conditions and help to identify the suitability and adequacy of resources available to deploy during a stress event until planned remedial actions are implemented.

Schwarz, Krista. "Mind the gap: Disentangling credit and liquidity in risk spreads." October 2010. Online at: finance.wharton.upenn.edu/~kschwarz/Spreads.pdf

Zhen Qi, Claudia, K. R. Subramanyam, and Jieying Zhang. "Accrual quality, bond liquidity, and cost of debt." Marshall School of Business, University of Southern California, August 2010. Online at: tinyurl.com/6ngrje9 [PDF].

See Also:

★ Managing Liquidity Risk in a Financial Institution: The Dangers of Short-Term Liabilities (pp. 74–76)
★ Navigating a Liquidity Crisis Effectively (pp. 82–84)
✔ Developing a Contingency Funding Plan (p. 966)
✔ Hedging Liquidity Risk—Case Study and Strategies (p. 972)

  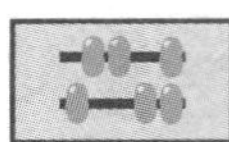   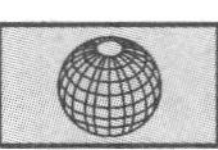   

How Taxation Impacts on Liquidity Management

by Martin O'Donovan

EXECUTIVE SUMMARY

- Efficient cash and liquidity management will involve centralizing cash within a single entity, on a country, regional, or even global basis.
- The movement of cash between entities and between countries will create complex tax considerations, so that all loans and rates of interest applied must be at arm's-length pricing.
- The cash centralization is normally arranged with the group's bankers who can offer a notional pooling or a physical movement of cash.
- Interest payable on the balances arising from the cash centralization or from the overall funding structure of the group can be subject to withholding tax (WHT), which may be reduced to zero by tax treaties or may be reclaimable through a variety of mechanisms.

THE BASIS FOR TAXATION

Taxation is highly dependent on the specifics of the companies concerned and the tax jurisdictions to which they are subject. Nonetheless, there are sufficient structural similarities between countries so that background generalizations can be made, although the specific rules and tax rates vary over time and will need to be verified with local tax experts.

Tax is initially assessed on the basis of each legal entity in isolation, but various allowances exist that enable operations to be examined from a group or subgroup perspective.

The legal grouping of companies, the managerial grouping, the accounting grouping and taxation group may each be on a different basis.

Taxable profit is not calculated in the same way as accounting profit. The latter may be generated using IFRS (International Financial Reporting Standards) or local GAAP (Generally Accepted Accounting Principles) using cash accounting or some taxation specific rules.

Efficient liquidity management for an international group involves making best use of the cash resources existing or being required or generated across the group.

In order to manage the daily flows of cash across the group there are normally efficiencies to be gained by centralizing cash flows within a central entity for each country or region, or, if practical, globally. The consequent movement of cash around the group, whether buying and selling goods between companies, or lending cash backward and forward, have significant tax consequences, made complicated by the interaction of different national and international rules.

Tax is therefore a major issue in the selection of a treasury center location. Areas set up specifically to attract treasury may be located in tax environments where local taxes are low and where there is special treatment of foreign earnings. They will be located in countries with extensive tax treaties, and there will be no WHT on interest earned or paid, or on income from dividends. These locations should also enable the repatriation of profits without tax deductions. Note, however, that in common with many business decisions, tax is not the only factor. Issues over staff availability and retention, proximity to management and major investors (for example, in London) are equally important factors.

TRANSACTING WITH CONNECTED PARTIES

Transfer Pricing

Most developed tax systems contain provisions that allow the tax authorities to increase the taxable profit, or reduce the allowable loss, of an entity which has entered into transactions with affiliates on non-arm's-length terms. In some jurisdictions, including the United Kingdom, this now includes domestic transactions as well as cross-border items. The concern for tax authorities is that profits are artificially moved between countries and, in particular, from a high tax area to a lower tax area.

Transfer pricing rules concern the provision of services as well as goods, and so they affect not only intragroup funding and hedging arrangements but also the provision of centralized treasury services. From a practical perspective, this means that apart from keeping contemporaneous documentary evidence of group transactions:

- all intercompany loans should carry a market rate of interest or other finance charge;
- commercial foreign exchange rates should be used when transacting between group companies;
- central treasury services should be recharged among those group members that benefit from them.

In-house re-invoicing and factoring centers usually receive particular scrutiny from the tax authorities of all the countries where participating group members are based.

Thin Capitalization

A company is said to be "thinly capitalized" where it is particularly highly geared. The tax authorities are concerned to ensure that companies do not receive debt funding from affiliates at levels that mean their profits are largely sheltered by interest expense. Many jurisdictions have now passed rules that set out what they consider to be an acceptable level of gearing for tax purposes. In some cases, for example in the United States, Germany, or Australia, the rules prescribe a maximum debt/equity ratio or required interest cover, and in others, such as the United Kingdom, the rules restrict finance charges by reference to the company's capacity to borrow from a third party on a stand-alone basis. Where the acceptable level of debt is based on subjective tests, it is frequently possible to secure advance clearance from the fiscal authorities on the proposed level of gearing.

In the United Kingdom a new debt cap takes effect for accounting periods beginning on or after January 1, 2010, running in parallel with the arm's length principle. The debt cap applies to limit the tax deduction for finance expense payable by UK group companies by reference to the consolidated worldwide gross finance expense of that group. This is intended to counter the risk that groups with little or no external debt may nevertheless leverage their UK operations to reduce UK corporate taxes. There is a risk that interest deductions on intragroup loans could be denied in the United Kingdom, while the corresponding receipt remains taxable in a foreign country.

For companies, the downside is that if transfer pricing or thin cap rules are breached a tax deduction for interest expense may be denied, while at the other end of the transaction the lending company is still taxed on the interest income.

WITHHOLDING TAXES

WHT is a tax that is deducted at source on earnings, which include employment income, dividends, and interest payments, and can also include intangible services. It is a charge on the recipient. It is not tax that is charged on the remitter and has no effect on tax payable by the latter. This tax is withheld by the remitter and is paid over to the domestic tax authority in which the income arose. A tax treaty may lower the withholding rate between certain countries—sometimes

"If Thomas Jefferson thought taxation without representation was bad, he should see how it is with representation."
Rush Limbaugh

  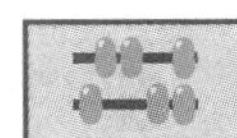      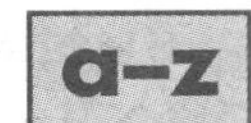

to zero. Double tax relief may also be available to offset WHT against a domestic tax liability. It may be necessary to apply in advance in order to obtain the reduced rate. As there are considerable differences in WHT rules between countries, companies need to carry out due diligence at the country level first and then look at the tax treaties that are available in order to obtain a full appreciation of the impact of WHT on their activities.

From a liquidity perspective, the major areas where withholding taxes can be an issue are:

- Dividends and royalties.
- Bank interest applied at source: The company may, or may not, be able to reclaim or deduct the WHT from income when the corporate tax return is filed, but there is inevitably a cash flow delay.
- Deemed bank interest applied by the corporate treasury, for example when reallocating interest on deemed bank interest arising from a notional pool. In some countries, such as the United Kingdom and the Netherlands, banks pay corporate interest gross, i.e. without deduction of WHT. This is one of the reasons why these countries are popular as cash pool centers.
- Interest on intercompany loans applied by the corporate treasury or created by cash concentration sweeping.
- Payments considered "in lieu of interest," such as guarantee and arrangement fees. The tax is due irrespective of whether or not an actual payment was received or a charge made for the service.

The WHT tax paid may become a final tax burden for the lender if it cannot be refunded or claimed as a tax credit or deduction. In some countries the WHT can be offset against corporate taxes due.

TAX TREATIES/DOUBLE TAX RELIEF

Tax treaties (also known as double taxation treaties) are a set of bilateral agreements between two countries that set out the taxation rights of each country in respect of tax charged in the other.

When a company receives income from overseas that has been taxed at the local level there are three options in dealing with the potential for double taxation. In order of most advantageous to the company:

- If the tax treaty calls for participation exemption (which prevents the same income from being taxed twice), the income may not be taxed again at the shareholder level.
- The overseas tax is used to offset and reduce any domestic tax liability, i.e. the amount of the tax already paid reduces the amount of the tax due at home by an equal amount.
- The overseas tax may simply be allowed as a tax deduction against domestic tax liability, i.e. the tax paid overseas is used as a deduction against income, thereby reducing taxable income.

TAX IMPLICATIONS OF NOTIONAL POOLING

Notional pooling means that credit and debit balances of various companies are notionally aggregated and netted by the group's bank, without actual transfer of ownership of the funds taking place. The following issues are associated with notional pooling:

- Notional pooling is usually considered to be a form of bank lending and treated as if interest is paid to the bank, although in fact the interest may actually be paid through intercompany transactions.
- Transfer pricing regulations require that any interest paid as an intercompany transaction is reallocated to the subsidiaries on an arm's-length basis.
- Transfer pricing will also look into the issues of pricing for the value of cross-guarantees that would normally be paid to a third party.
- There may be withholding tax (WHT) on the interest paid through intercompany transactions.
- A debit balance in a notional pool may also be used to calculate thin capitalization ratios.
- Notional pooling requires cross-guarantees and a legal right of offset to secure the position of creditors. Strictly, both these should be charged for.
- Legal constraints, such as not allowing cross-border legal right of offset, prohibiting the co-mingling of resident and nonresident accounts or requiring central bank reporting and reserves to be maintained on a gross basis, render pooling unviable or difficult in some countries.

TAX IMPLICATIONS OF CASH CONCENTRATION

With cash concentration, the funds move physically into the concentration account, with a resulting change of ownership. These are the major issues that arise from cash concentration:

- It creates intercompany loans and is taxed accordingly.
- No cross-guarantees or legal right of offset are required.
- Transfer pricing regulations require that any interest paid as an intercompany transaction is reallocated to the subsidiaries on an arm's-length basis.
- There may be WHT on the interest paid through intercompany transactions.
- Thin capitalization is likely to be an issue.
- It may attract deemed dividends.
- In some countries there may be additional stamp duties on cross-border intercompany loans (for example Austria, Italy, Portugal).
- Regulations prohibiting cross-border transfers will restrict participation in an overseas concentration scheme.
- Reference accounts are a way to pool cash without transfer of ownership.

MAKING IT HAPPEN

- Taxation considerations should be built in at an early stage in the planning of liquidity management structures and processes.
- The best location for a cash management center will often be within a country with an extensive network of tax treaties and with no WHT on interest or dividends.
- Intra-group financial transactions should be priced at market prices (including margin where appropriate), and there should be contemporaneous independent documentation in place to support the prices used (for example, Reuters, Bloomberg, or the *Wall Street Journal*). Justification of margin can be more subjective. Possible comparators might be alternative facilities offered by banks locally or perhaps bond spreads, or credit default spreads (from Markit for instance).
- Where there is a central treasury operation or an in-house bank, borrowing rates and other terms and conditions should be formalized in the same manner as they would be with an external commercial bank.
- The same applies where a parent company is obliged to guarantee a subsidiary as a means of securing the subsidiary a lower borrowing rate. The parent should charge a guarantee fee.
- Structures such as "shared service centers," where a centralized group resource provides services to affiliates, also attract particular attention from tax authorities. Pricing and service levels should be similar to those that might be offered by a third-party provider.

MORE INFO

Websites:

Deloitte International Tax and Business Guides: www.deloitte.com

GT News on how to manage your global liquidity: www.gtnews.com/feature/85.cfm

"Everyone wants a more simple tax system. But if this means that certain tax breaks have to be cut, people are no longer so enthusiastic." Angela Merkel

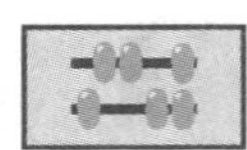

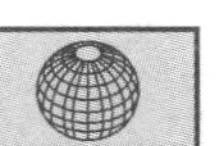

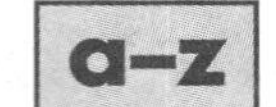

How to Assess a Company's Global Treasury Needs and Objectives Successfully by Gary Silha

EXECUTIVE SUMMARY

In order to identify the most effective global liquidity management structure for a company:

- Develop a detailed understanding of the company's local cash management needs and relationships.
- Develop an understanding of the company's current and future credit and/or investment strategies.
- Develop an understanding of the company's current and future tax strategies.
- Research using the internet.
- Utilize the money center banks that provide global liquidity management services.
- Benchmark companies that have implemented successful global liquidity management solutions.
- Utilize the availability of treasury conferences.
- Do the work yourself.

DOING YOUR HOMEWORK

Since Tenneco is in the auto industry, there is an analogy I often use when I am asked what is the best global liquidity management structure. There is a reason that auto manufacturers make cars in different shapes and colors: Consumers all have different needs and desires. Similarly, corporations have different objectives when implementing a global liquidity management structure. Identifying a company's needs and objectives is the first step in the development of an effective worldwide liquidity management structure.

The trick when accessing a company's global treasury needs is to determine the structure that best coincides with the company's objectives, geographic footprint, bank relationships, current and future credit and/or investment positions, and current and future tax strategies. The task can be daunting, often resulting in the project never quite getting off the ground. Detailed below are eight tips to assist in identifying a company's most efficient global liquidity management structure.

Develop a Detailed Understanding of the Company's Local Cash Management Needs and Relationships

There is no substitute for a face-to-face meeting with the company's subsidiaries to understand the basis for their local bank relationships and the services provided by those banks. Keep in mind, however, that these bank relationships have been cultivated over the years by the local corporate treasury personnel. Replacing their local bank relationship with a global bank with which the subsidiary has no relationship will not be received as a positive strategy by the company's local personnel. Resistance should therefore be anticipated.

By the same token, while many global banks will have brick and mortar operations in the countries in which the company operates, you will need to acknowledge that the company's global bank may not be able to provide coverage for all the services currently provided by the local banks. For example, although it will vary from bank to bank and country to country, global banks have considerable difficulty competing with local banks in the areas of payroll and payroll-related taxes. It is necessary to sell the idea of a global structure and the worldwide benefits the structure will generate for the company while simultaneously gaining an understanding of the subsidiary's cash management needs. Such a strategy will provide the foundation for the development and implementation of the company's global liquidity management structure.

Develop an Understanding of the Company's Current and Future Credit and/or Investment Strategy

Despite all of the technological advances introduced over the years, corporate treasury and banking continue to be relationship-based businesses. In fact, many companies practice relationship-based banking whereby only banks that are lenders to the company are considered when awarding auxiliary service business. However, what happens when the small group of worldwide banks that offer global liquidity management solutions are not in the company's bank lending group, forcing the company to remove service-based business from a lender and award it to a nonlender?

This scenario will most likely occur either with respect to the bank that is selected as the company's global provider or in the replacement of a local subsidiary cash management provider. Determining how the company will respond to this scenario when confronted by a current lender will dictate to a large extent the service providers considered for the company's global liquidity management business.

Develop an Understanding of the Company's Current and Future Tax Strategies

Although corporate treasury careers have been built on the premise that "cash is king," it has become increasingly clear over the years that large corporate decision-making is more often driven by taxes, and in particular the minimization of taxes to boost profitability. A review with the company's tax department, to gain an understanding of how a global liquidity management structure may impact the company from a tax perspective, will aid greatly in the selection of the most efficient global liquidity management structure. Tax departments usually appreciate global structures, since the standardization they provide facilitates their own understanding and management of each operation's local tax position. If approached wisely, the tax department could become the company's biggest supporter of the global liquidity management structure project.

Research Using the Internet

Global liquidity management structures come in various forms. There are zero-balance-based structures which are implemented through the use of a single bank, notional-based structures that simultaneously manage a company's liquidity and foreign exchange exposures created by the centralization of this liquidity, and combination structures which adopt pieces of each structure in the countries where they are most effective or where current structures already exist. There is therefore a learning curve that can be achieved via some basic internet searches.

An understanding of the basic global liquidity management structures, their advantages and disadvantages, their acceptability by the central bank in each country in which the company operates, and their ease of implementation can be easily attained via an internet search. These will provide the company with a foundation for discussing these structures in greater depth with potential service providers.

"The secret of getting ahead is getting started." Agatha Christie

Figure 1. The global liquidity management structure review process

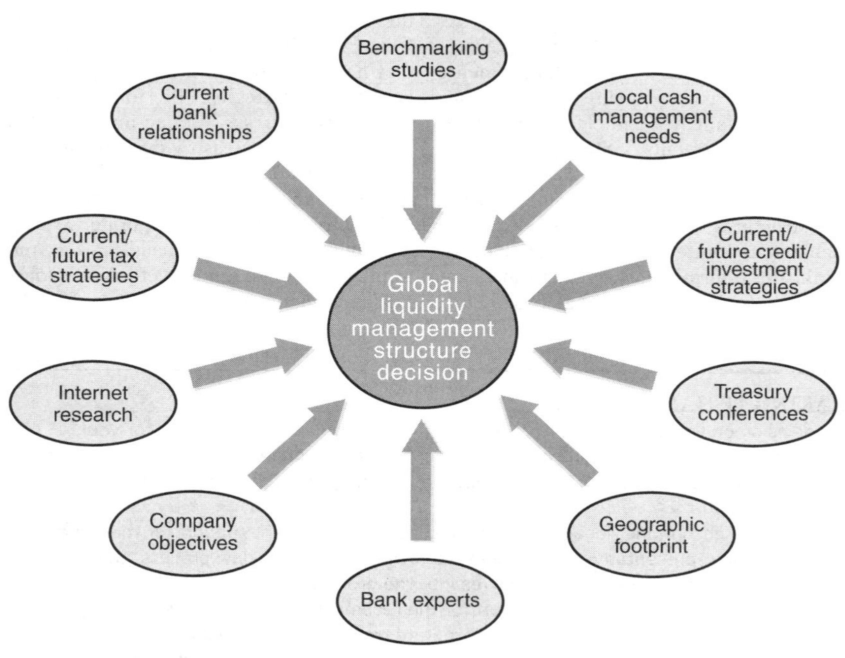

Utilize the Money Center Banks that Provide Global Liquidity Management Services

As of this writing there are only a handful of banks that can provide a true global liquidity management solution. These banks have staffs of experts who live, breathe, and sleep these structures. These bankers are more than willing to assist companies in developing a global liquidity management structure that best fits a company's needs and objectives.

The more experienced banks will have implemented similar structures for other companies and are therefore able to provide firsthand knowledge of the twists and turns of implementation in each country in which the company operates. Although for liability reasons most banks will defer to the company's own tax, legal, insurance, audit, and accounting departments on specific issues, the more experienced banks will be able to demonstrate how other companies faced with exactly the same issues were able to resolve them.

Benchmark Companies that Have Implemented Successful Global Liquidity Management Solutions

Experience usually does not come cheap, although it is attainable by finding companies that are willing to benchmark their successes. The global liquidity management providers which a company considers for its business should be able to set up several benchmark meetings with companies that have similar footprints, needs, and objectives.

Through these meetings a company will be able to attain an understanding of, among other things, why these companies ended up with the service provider they selected, how they went about managing their implementation, the issues that caught them by surprise, the specific successes and failures they experienced in their implementation, and the ease of managing their structure on an ongoing basis.

Utilize the Availability of Corporate Treasury Conferences

There are several large corporate treasury management conferences where, for a nominal fee, an attendee will gain access to presentations of case studies of companies that have implemented successful global liquidity management structures. These conferences also offer one-stop shopping in their exhibit halls with banks that offer global liquidity management solutions. Although the amount of information an attendee will receive at these conferences can be overwhelming, the greatest benefit of attending one is the ability to introduce the company to the banks and to establish follow-up meetings with potential service providers. Having access to these banks within a day, or over a couple of days, will greatly accelerate the attendee's global liquidity management review process.

Do the Work Yourself

Shortcuts taken in managing the review process will inevitably return to haunt a company in the end. Though there are consultants that will manage the review process, the client will end up either implementing or managing on an ongoing basis the global solution that is developed. A thorough understanding of why specific aspects of the structure were adopted or excluded is necessary to ensure the successful implementation and management of the structure. There is no substitute for hands-on learning. Outsourcing the review process to a consultant will leave the company at a disadvantage when issues arise down the road.

SERVICE PROVIDER REVIEW

The process of understanding the various forms of liquidity management structures and identifying the company's global liquidity management needs and objectives can take several months to complete. Once the company's needs and objectives are finalized, the company is in a position to entertain presentations by potential service providers. Detailed below are three tips related to comparing the various bank-provided solutions:

Spend Most of the Review Period Evaluating the Reporting Systems Provided by the Global Service Providers

When reviewing the various reports provided by the global service providers, drill down on each individual field within each report. Although this can make for a very tedious meeting, it is the only way to determine whether the timeliness of the information being reported meets the company's needs.

Inquire where each field of information in each report comes from, how often these systems are updated, and how often these systems feed each other. Inquire about each system's downtime and recovery time, when the last upgrade to the system was implemented, the changes that were made in the last upgrade, and how long it has been since the previous upgrade. Finally, inquire about whether the reporting system can accommodate value-dated transactions without human intervention, whether the system has ad-hoc reporting capabilities, and whether the system can provide interest accrual reports during the company's accounting close.

  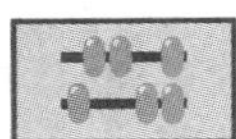   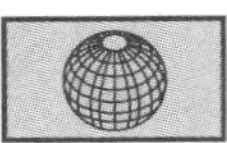   

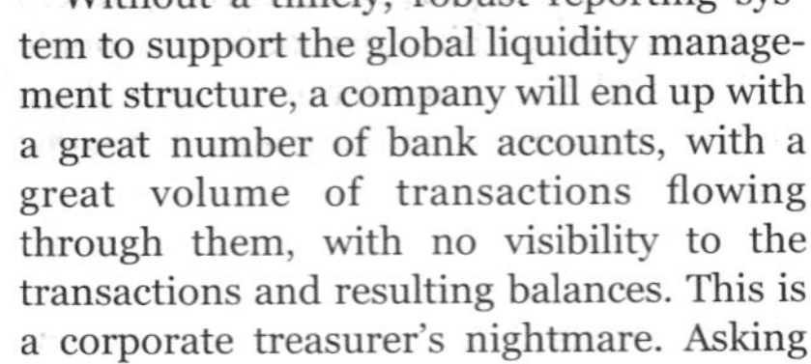

Without a timely, robust reporting system to support the global liquidity management structure, a company will end up with a great number of bank accounts, with a great volume of transactions flowing through them, with no visibility to the transactions and resulting balances. This is a corporate treasurer's nightmare. Asking about the specifics of the bank's reporting system will reveal those banks that have truly invested in their global liquidity management reporting systems—in other words, who are the true players and who are the posers.

Evaluate the Bank's Commitment to Their Global Liquidity Management Structure

Global liquidity management solutions require the support of enhanced electronic reporting systems. The investment to develop and maintain these systems is substantial. These products therefore need to be core to the bank's overall global cash management strategy. The last thing you want to do is align the company with a service provider that is not going to keep pace with the market on a product that can take the company up to a year to implement.

Get to Know the People on the Company's Account

Depending on the number of entities in the pool the worldwide implimentation of the structure could take up to a year to complete. The bank's implementation team, in coordination with the company's in-house project manager, will have the greatest impact on the success of the implementation.

An experienced bank implementation manager will have already implemented several similar structures for companies with a similar geographic footprint, thereby ensuring knowledge of the specific local customs and hurdles which will need to be addressed. Just as important, this individual must have a thorough understanding of the internal processes needed to open bank accounts and set up the services required from the global structure.

Ask about the background of the implementation manager who will be assigned to the company. Meet specifically with this individual to discuss the implementation plan that will be developed. Ask for references from clients for which this manager has previously worked. The bank's implementation manager will be working with the company on a daily basis. Making sure the company is comfortable with this individual's abilities is imperative to the ultimate success of the company's implementation.

CONCLUSION

According to the 2007 JP Morgan Asset Management Global Cash Management Survey, cash management remained the most important function for corporate treasury departments, with 53% of the respondents assigning it the top score, up from 45% in 2006. Fortunately, systems and structures have been developed that enable a corporate treasury department to obtain the information needed to manage this daily activity on a global basis in a timely and efficient manner.

The challenge in implementing a global liquidity management structure is in being able to focus the company's attention on the key drivers that will dictate the worldwide liquidity management structure that best coincides with its own goals and long-term strategies. By following the suggested courses of action detailed above, corporate treasury departments can turn the review process—which can be daunting in scope—into a manageable activity. In this way the corporate treasury will be prepared for deciding on and implementing the most effective global liquidity management structure for the company.

MAKING IT HAPPEN

The decision on the most appropriate global liquidity management structure for your company must coincide with the overall company, treasury/finance department, business unit, and local facility/plant goals and objectives. To build consensus for the recommended structure:

- Obtain tax, accounting, legal, audit, and insurance department support for the structure by involving representatives from these departments in the review process, thereby incorporating their needs and objectives into the process.
- Obtain senior treasury/finance support for the recommended structure by identifying how the structure meets the company and corporate treasury department goals and strategies.
- Obtain senior business unit support by identifying how the recommended structure will improve operations at the business unit level.
- Obtain facility/plant support for the recommended structure by considering its local cash management needs and identifying how the structure will improve its local operations.

MORE INFO

Book:

van der Wielen, Lex, Willem van Alphen, Joost Bergen, and Phillip Lindow. *International Cash Management: A Practical Guide to Managing Cash Flows, Liquidity, Working Capital and Short-Term Financial Risks*. 2nd ed. Treasury and Management Finance Series. Driebergen, Netherlands: Riskmatrix, 2006.

Articles:

gtnews with ABN AMRO. "How to manage your global liquidity—Part 2: Cross-currency pooling." *gtnews* (September 28, 2005). Online at: www.gtnews.com/feature/85_2.cfm

gtnews with ABN AMRO. "How to manage your global liquidity—Part 4: The next wave of enhancements." *gtnews* (January 24, 2006). Online at: www.gtnews.com/feature/85_4.cfm

Hawser, Anita. "Bringing it all together." *Global Finance* (December 2005). Online at: www.gfmag.com/2005/Dec/c_ci/fe_art03.php

Seifert, Erik, and Robert Pehrson. "Corporate cash management trends—Part 4: Liquidity management." *gtnews* (March 4, 2008). Online at: www.gtnews.com/feature/225_4.cfm

Skerritt, Susan. "European treasury structures: Compare and contrast." *Treasury Management International* (February 2003): 14–18. Online at: www.treasurystrat.com/resources/articles/EuropeanTreasuryStructures.pdf

Reports:

Diamond, Nick, and Michael Golden. "Achieving new heights through a truly global liquidity structure." Online at: www.ibm.com/us (search on "Diamond Golden").

Potter, St John. "Global provider: Do all banks live up to the label?" JP Morgan Treasury Services. Online at: www.jpmorgan.com (search on "Potter global provider").

Website:

Association for Financial Professionals (AFP), Bethesda, MD: www.afponline.org

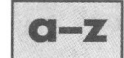

How to Better Manage Your Financial Supply Chain

by Juergen Bernd Weiss

EXECUTIVE SUMMARY

- Financial supply chain management (FSCM) addresses a number of initiatives that can help to make finance organizations more efficient and improve the working capital position of an enterprise.
- There are a number of indicators for an inefficient financial supply chain including low straight through processing rates and a high amount of uncollectible receivables on the balance sheet.
- Key performance indicators such as days sales outstanding or days in receivables can be used by companies to benchmark themselves with their peers.
- Microsoft decided to improve its financial supply chain to better utilize working capital, to reduce bank fees, to process payments more effectively and to gain better control of cash flows.

INTRODUCTION

Benchmarks of business performance indicate that enterprise resource planning (ERP) systems and other enterprise technologies have transformed customer and supply chain processes but that the performance of the finance function has hardly changed. Although some companies have managed to improve the performance of their financial processes profoundly, financial functions are still neglected in many businesses, and days sales outstanding (DSO) and working capital needs are very high in several industries. The working capital scorecard for 2008 from *CFO Magazine* demonstrates that there are significant differences between high and low performers within an industry. In the automotive industry, for example, the best score in DSO was 44, while the worst score was 241—five times more than the sector median of 47. Research from the Hackett Group indicates that finance department costs continue to consume more than 1% of revenues in many companies, and CFOs struggle with poor transparency of their daily cash flows.

In times when unprecedented economic uncertainty and soaring stockholder expectations are putting every function under closer scrutiny than ever before, the finance function should be driving business, not holding it back. Financial supply chain management (FSCM) can help companies to remove some of the inefficiencies in operational processes in order to become more effective.

DEFINITIONS OF FINANCIAL SUPPLY CHAIN MANAGEMENT

There are different definitions of the term *financial supply chain*, which appeared for the first time in 2000 and 2001. According to the research company Killen & Associates (2001), the financial supply chain "parallels the physical or materials supply chain and represents all transaction activities related to the flow of cash from the customer's initial order through reconciliation and payment to the seller." The Aberdeen Group, another research company, calls the financial supply chain "a range of B-to-B trade-related intra- and inter-company financial transaction-based functions and processes [which] begin before buyers and suppliers establish contact and proceed beyond the settlement process." The two definitions emphasize different topics. Killen's focuses on the parallelism between the physical and the financial supply chain, and it stresses a section of the cash flow cycle that I'll discuss in more detail below. The Aberdeen Group's definition focuses on the collaborative nature of financial supply chain management and reveals that the financial value chain isn't limited to the inner walls of a company but includes communication and cooperation with business partners.

Both definitions focus on a process-oriented view of the financial supply chain that is basically correct; however, in many respects the explanations do not go far enough:

- They focus very much on the collaboration between companies—specifically, suppliers and customers—and they do not consider other important business partners within the financial supply chain, such as banks.
- They describe primarily the status quo, and do not stress the various dimensions for the optimization of business processes within the financial supply chain.
- The motivation, as well as the key performance indicators, for an efficient financial supply chain are not obvious.

Another definition that includes these three aspects is the following: Financial supply chain management (FSCM) is the holistic and comprehensive planning and controlling of all financial processes which are relevant within a company and for communication with other enterprises. The goal of FSCM is to increase the transparency and the level of automation of business processes along the financial value chain. The purpose is to save processing costs and reduce the working capital of the company. This definition doesn't consider where the financial supply chain actually begins and ends, because there are also analytical processes that are not directly related to a business process but which belong nonetheless to the financial supply chain. Let's now have a closer look at the indicators of an *inefficient* financial supply chain.

INDICATORS OF AN INEFFICIENT FINANCIAL SUPPLY CHAIN

As we have seen, the financial supply chain is different from the physical supply chain because it deals with the flow of cash instead of goods. Just as in the physical supply chain, though, every day that's lost in the cash-to-cash cycle equals lost revenue. But how do you know that your financial value chain isn't working properly? Besides a number of rather operational problems, there are also several concrete key performance indicators and metrics that you can use to analyze your financial supply chain. You are most likely aware of the fact that the financial supply chain stretches across many different business processes. These are, in a broader sense, the two processes *order-to-cash* and *purchase-to-pay*, which consist of various sub-processes that are relevant to the financial aspects of the value chain.

The order-to-cash process includes, from the perspective of a supplier (or creditor), the following business process steps:

1 Creditworthiness check.
2 Invoice creation.
3 Cash forecast.
4 Financing of working capital.
5 Processing of dispute cases.
6 Cash collection.
7 Settlement and payment.
8 Account reconciliation.

From the perspective of a customer (or debtor), the purchase-to-pay process consists of the following business processes:

1 Procurement.
2 Cash forecast.

"In the foundation and development of a successful enterprise there must be a single-minded pursuit of financial profit."
C. Northcote Parkinson

3 Financing of working capital.
4 Receipt of invoices.
5 Resolution of discrepancies or exceptions.
6 Invoice approval.
7 Settlement and payment.
8 Account reconciliation.

There are a number of operational factors within the order-to-cash and purchase-to-pay processes that can serve as indicators of a suboptimal financial supply chain. Some examples are:

- The number of paper-based business processes is very high and there are several changes in medium (for example, the creation of invoices).
- The straight-through processing rate is low, which means that there are multiple manual interventions and process steps.
- Companies struggle with a large number of dispute cases during the creation of invoices, and it takes them a lot of time to process these.
- There is a large amount of uncollectable receivables on the balance sheet, and many employees in receivables or collections management are involved in the resolution process.
- Enterprises haven't implemented a consistent credit management policy, which results in a number of bad debt losses.
- Management has difficulties in predicting cash flows.
- There is no centralized cash management to control payment streams, and the company maintains too many bank connections.

KEY PERFORMANCE INDICATORS

There are various key performance indicators that are relevant for measurement in financial supply chain management. One key metric is the cash flow cycle, which defines the period from delivery by suppliers until the cash collection of receivables from customers (Figure 1). It is the time period required for the company to receive the invested funds back in the form of cash. The cash flow cycle can be divided into the *operating cycle*—which is the time period between delivery by suppliers and the actual cash collection of receivables, and the *cash flow cycle*—which is the time period between the cash payment for inventory and the cash collection of receivables. The longer the cash flow cycle, the greater is the working capital requirement of a company, which means that a reduction of the cash flow cycle will immediately free up liquidity.

Within the cash flow cycle we can differentiate the following parameters, which are delimited in Figure 1 with curly brackets:

Figure 1. The cash flow cycle

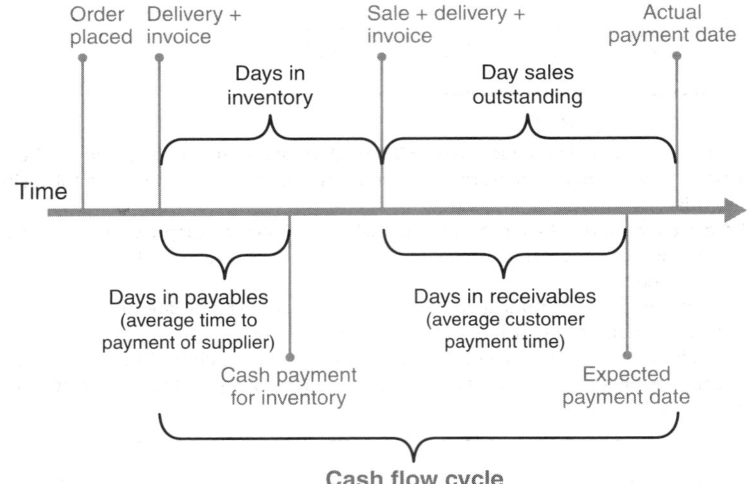

- Days in inventory: This is the length of time between the delivery of the goods and the invoice from the supplier, and the sale of the goods and the invoice to the customer. It describes the average number of days the goods of a company remain in inventory before being sold. This metric is the focus for all activities around classical supply chain management.
- Days in payables: This is the length of time between delivery of the goods and the invoice from the supplier, and the actual payment for the inventory. This figure describes the average time it takes to pay a supplier. The parameter considers the outstanding receivables of a company, and is an important metric for debtors concentrating on their efforts to optimize the purchase-to-pay cycle.
- Days sales outstanding: This is the length of time between the sale of the goods and the invoice to the customer, and the actual payment date of the customer. This metric measures the average number of days companies need to collect revenue after a sale has been

CASE STUDY

Microsoft

US company Microsoft decided to improve its financial supply chain by replacing third-party and in-house developed legacy software systems that were very costly to maintain. Microsoft, which is headquartered in Redmond, Washington, provides information technology, operating systems, middleware solutions, small/mid-size business applications, professional services, and other software solutions. The company reported annual sales in 2008 of more than US$60 billion and had more than 90,000 employees worldwide.

The main business drivers for the company were:

- Better data integration between applications.
- Elimination of manual intercompany processes and month-end bank account reconciliation.
- More transparent accessibility to real-time data such as bank account balances, financial transactions, and accounts receivable and payable.
- More efficient usage of excess funds and better working capital management.
- Increased straight-through processing of foreign exchange trading.
- Reduction of bank fees and more cost-effective processing of payments.
- Risk reduction and better control of cash flows.
- Better utilization of human resources.

Microsoft decided to implement a vendor's financial supply chain management solution to complement its existing enterprise resource planning (ERP) landscape. The company realized a number of benefits from the project and was, for example, able to automate the confirmation process in the foreign exchange settlement fully. Exception rates are now smaller than 5%, the settlement process went from four hours to less than 15 minutes, and the percentage of settlement errors is approaching 0%.

"Income tax has made more liars out of the American people than golf." Will Rogers

made. A high DSO number means that an enterprise is selling to its customers on credit and taking longer to collect money. The figure is an important figure for creditors, to optimize the order-to-cash cycle.

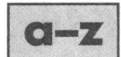

- Days in receivables: This is the length of time between the sale of the goods and the invoice to the customer, and the expected payment date. This key performance indicator is similar to DSO, and indicates the average time, in days, that receivables are outstanding. Days in receivables can also be called best possible DSO, since the company would collect all receivables before the due date.

Within the cash flow cycle there is potential to reduce both days in inventory and days sales outstanding. Days in payables can be reduced but should be monitored carefully to avoid putting supplies at risk. Days in receivables can be reduced by optimizing cash collection. Another important indicator for an efficient financial supply chain management is working capital, which is a balance sheet metric and part of the liquid assets. Working capital is calculated as current assets less current liabilities, and is a measure of the liquid reserve and short-term solvency of an enterprise, available to satisfy contingencies and uncertainties. One of the key objectives of financial supply chain management is to optimize the working capital by reducing, for instance, outstanding receivables.

MORE INFO

Books:

Bhalla, V. K. *Working Capital Management: Text and Cases*. New Delhi: Anmol Publications, 2006.

Horcher, Karen A. *Essentials of Managing Treasury*. Hoboken, NJ: Wiley, 2006.

Salek, John G. *Accounts Receivable Management Best Practices*. Hoboken, NJ: Wiley, 2005.

Schaeffer, Mary S. *Essentials of Credit, Collections, and Accounts Receivable*. Hoboken, NJ: Wiley, 2002.

Scheuermann, Hans-Dieter, the Mysap Financials Team, and Cedric Read. *The CFO as Business Integrator*. Hoboken, NJ: Wiley, 2003.

Articles:

Hartley-Urquhart, Roland. "Managing the financial supply chain." *Supply Chain Management Review* (2006). Online at: www.scmr.com/article/CA6376439.html

Karaian, Jason. "Working capital scorecard 2008." *CFO Europe Magazine* (July 7, 2008). Online at: www.cfo.com/article.cfm/11661239?f=search

Websites:

CFO—News and insight for financial executives: www.cfo.com

gtnews—Library for finance and treasury professionals: www.gtnews.com

The Hackett Group: www.thehackettgroup.com

See Also:

★ Factoring and Invoice Discounting: Working Capital Management Options (pp. 39–41)

★ Payment Factories: How to Streamline Financial Flows (pp. 85–86)

✔ Building an Efficient Credit and Collection Accounts System (p. 1148)

✔ Choosing the Right Payment Policy (p. 1151)

✔ Key Components of an Optimal Enterprise Resource Planning System (p. 997)

✔ Understanding and Using the Cash Conversion Cycle (p. 995)

✔ Understanding Key Performance Indicators (p. 1180)

Cashflow Reengineering: How to Optimize the Cashflow Timeline and Improve Financial Efficiency (p. 1340)

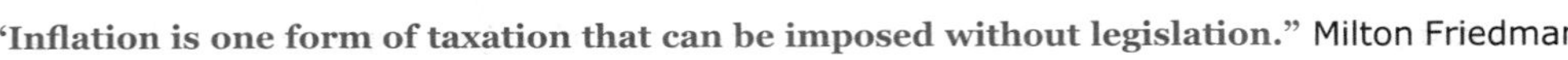

How to Manage Pension Costs by Edmund Truell

EXECUTIVE SUMMARY

- The financial implications of rising longevity, in particular with regard to pensions, pose significant challenges to society. The re-allocation of the financial burden among governments, businesses, and individuals will significantly affect pension systems.
- The upward trend in life expectancy and the consequent aging population has led to large unanticipated retirement costs for businesses and governments, particularly in developed countries.
- Governments have increased the long-term sustainability of the public finances by reducing the future generosity of state pension entitlements and encouraging greater private-sector involvement.
- In response to government initiatives, corporate sponsors have closed their defined benefit pension schemes, and moved employees into defined contribution schemes—thus shifting investment and longevity risk onto individuals.
- To deal with the legacy of previous commitments, managers have created a range of new solutions for the financial markets, from hedging liabilities to passing all or part of the risk and responsibility to specialist third-party providers.

INTRODUCTION

A huge increase in life expectancy is one of the great achievements of the human race over the past two centuries. Increased longevity has transformed both individuals' lives and their societies, with the most marked changes taking place in the developed world. Actual increases in life expectancy have been far more substantial than previously projected, with the result that governments, businesses, financial markets, and individuals must radically readjust their plans.

Moreover, the current trend shows no sign of leveling off. For example, between 1981 and 2000 the life expectancy for 65-year-old males in the United Kingdom increased by approximately three months for every year, and future life expectancy is widely expected to continue to increase. Therefore, it is increasingly important that governments, businesses, and individuals consider the economic, societal, and financial implications of an aging society in diverse but important policy areas such as pensions, health care, and long-term care provision. For example, pension liabilities increase by 3% or more for every added year of life expectancy.

CHANGES TO THE PENSIONS LANDSCAPE

Pension reform has been high on the political agenda in most Organizations for Economic Co-operation and Development (OECD) countries during the past decade. In most instances the key objective of reform has been to increase the long-term sustainability of public finances in the light of an aging population. Governments have frequently reduced the future generosity of state pension entitlements through several means, such as indexing future pension increases to inflation rather than earnings growth, increasing the official pension age to compensate for expected longevity increases, and, in some cases, developing new measures to automatically reallocate the financial burden of unexpected future increases in longevity between the state and the individual.

To compensate for planned reductions, most reform packages also include measures aimed at encouraging greater private-sector involvement. This shift has led to a reallocation of risk, including longevity risk, away from the state and onto businesses and individuals. However, shifting the responsibility of future pension provision to businesses or individuals does not solve all the problems.

Countries such as the United States, the United Kingdom, and the Netherlands, with traditionally larger private-sector involvement in pension provision, face unique challenges due to the defined benefit (DB) nature of their pension schemes. In these countries, DB pensions are linked to the salary earned by the individual, and are often index-linked and passed on to dependents in the event of death. Although DB schemes are attractive and arguably help to foster employee loyalty, they have become increasingly onerous for companies to maintain. The United Kingdom, the United States, and the Netherlands have all witnessed an accelerated closure of DB schemes, as businesses respond to new accounting standards and recognize more clearly the substantial longevity risk borne with DB schemes.

Some firms have opted for defined contribution (DC) schemes, in which a contribution of salary is paid regularly into the scheme by the individual and typically is matched by an employer contribution. The contributions are then invested, with the assumption that the compounded return on these investments over time will be sufficient to provide a pension in retirement. The shift from DB to DC schemes places more risk on individuals. Taken together with less generous state pensions, this move raises the question: Will future pensioner incomes be sufficient to meet the expectations of future pensioners? There is an additional danger for companies in some countries, where planned compulsory pensions for all employees are likely to lead to large costs because of the significant increase in employer contributions.

LEGACY ISSUES

There is also another issue. Although closing DB pension schemes to new entrants means that no new liabilities will be added to the existing stock, dealing with the legacy issues still remains a formidable challenge for companies and pension fund trustees. Today's corporate pension managers face the problem of maintaining a set of financial commitments made in another era, when assumptions and expectations were vastly different. These commitments are difficult to measure, let alone anticipate, and are tied to the health and well-being of the corporate sponsor of the fund, which is required to underwrite any deficit.

Similarly, pension fund trustees are attempting to steer a secure course through a sea of investment strategies, taking account of increasing longevity exposure, while also keeping an eye on the financial robustness of their corporate sponsor. The issue is further complicated by the fact that the time horizon within which most companies operate will generally be much shorter than that covered by pension funds, with the result that corporate sponsors are also charged with maintaining open-ended commitments for a very long period ahead. These obligations frequently stretch beyond the tenure of current managers or stockholders.

Corporate sponsors that initiated DB pension funds in the past now find their pension-inflated balance sheets at the mercy of volatile markets. These inflated balance sheets can dramatically affect share price, ability to maneuver, and, ironically, the very security of the pension commitments they are obliged to maintain.

"Investing is an activity of forecasting the yield over the life of the asset; speculation is the activity of forecasting the psychology of the market." John Maynard Keynes

SOLUTIONS AND CASE STUDIES

There are a number of different approaches to dealing with pension cost issues in the private sector. The overriding prerequisite is for assets and liabilities to be run as a combined analysis. This is because the true benchmark for any pension scheme is the liabilities that have to be paid out over time. Managers should also be cognizant of the risks associated with these liabilities, particularly the effect of interest rates and inflation, in addition to the better understood market risks present within the assets.

Over the last few years, the financial markets have innovated and provided a range of tools and solutions. For example, the liabilities can be hedged against the effect of interest rate changes and inflation through traditional instruments such as government securities and corporate bonds, or through interest rate and inflation swaps. Interest rate and inflation swaps are often preferable and more efficient from an asset–liability management standpoint, as they free up assets for investment in a diversified pool of return-seeking assets: This can then help schemes potentially turn around a deficit over time.

Large companies may choose to embrace the risks and potential returns offered by the pension fund, establishing asset and liability teams to understand, coordinate, and manage asset–liability and balance sheet risk.

CONCLUSION

The exponential increase in life expectancy over the last century is a staggering achievement. However, the experiences of economies with strong private-sector involvement in pensions show that a mixed system poses its own complex challenges. For example, in the United Kingdom many firms have concluded that they are not well placed to deal with these challenges and have closed their defined benefit schemes as a result. Although such a move deals with the accrual of future liabilities, it does not address legacy issues. Businesses have turned to the financial markets to offer innovative solutions, though here cost will be a critical factor in dealing with future pension provision. Nevertheless, these new approaches have expanded the choice set available to policymakers, businesses, and individuals, and as, such, are likely to play an important role in designing a sustainable pension environment for the future.

CASE STUDY 1

Large UK Corporate, Dutch Pension Schemes and Insurance Options

One large UK corporate chose to establish its own asset and liability management team in order to manage inhouse its pension obligations and assets. The team was so successful that demand for its services increased and the corporate created a separate fund management entity, predominantly owned by the sponsor's Pension Scheme. However, the risks taken by this team were larger than originally identified, and the team is now being dismantled. In some countries, such as the Netherlands, interest in managing assets and liabilities as a holistic entity has also led to the advent of third-party fiduciary managers, who take on the responsibility of hedging the liabilities and managing the assets to help trustees and companies meet their funding targets.

A permanent solution that is gaining increased attention in Anglo-Saxon economies, notably the United Kingdom, is to pass the risk and responsibility to a specialist third-party pension solutions provider. A third-party insurer can provide members with improved security through a bespoke insurance solution, securing member benefits for the long term. Furthermore, the sponsor company removes all future pension uncertainties from its balance sheet. This route also has the advantage that the liabilities are covered for all risks, including longevity risk. The most common mechanism is a pension insurance buyout—a bulk annuity policy secured with an insurer, which ensures that all benefits are met in exchange for an upfront premium. Historically, this route was used as part of insolvency procedures or in the case of a winding-up. However, increasing scrutiny of the health of corporate sponsors by financial markets and the practical difficulties associated with DB schemes for companies have meant that, in recent years, many companies have sought to transfer the liabilities to specialists. This usually increases the security for scheme members. Traditionally, operating businesses have been perceived to provide security for the promise of future contributions. In contrast, insurance companies have no such operating assets and, under FSA rules, need to hold assets and regulatory capital in excess of the accounting liabilities. Moreover, pension insurance buyout costs are typically higher than pension liabilities on an accounting basis, due to the more conservative assumptions used for the assessment of liabilities and projected asset returns. As a result, there has also been rapid recent growth in more cost-effective alternatives such as partial buyouts, where only part of the liabilities is insured, and buyins, where an insurance policy is purchased as an asset to precisely match some proportion of the liabilities.

CASE STUDY 2

Thorn Pension Scheme

An alternative approach was followed by UK-based Thorn Ltd. Thorn's active business was sold off and gradually reduced over time, to end up with a large £1.2 billion pension fund supported by a very small corporate covenant. In this situation, the trustee decided that the safest way to secure the 24,000 pensioners' obligations was to buy out their current and future obligations with a registered insurance company, using all the assets in the pension fund.

But not all firms are necessarily interested in fully shedding their pension liabilities, particularly in the case of pension schemes where there are strong reasons not to sever links with the sponsoring employer. Although many firms have managed everything themselves along the approaches discussed earlier, these firms are still faced with the key outstanding risk of increased future longevity. Though nascent, the insurance industry that is now developing aims to decouple longevity risk and investment risk. Some financial services companies, such as J.P. Morgan, have sought to construct longevity indices that can be used as the basis for hedging longevity, while others have sought solutions tailored to the specific longevity profile of a particular scheme. Either way, the common mechanism is a longevity swap, which allows the scheme to lock into an agreed level of future longevity. The cost of any future pension payments that arises from pensioners living longer than expected is swapped by the pension fund for fixed annual premiums set at the inception of the swap. This can also be structured as an insurance contract, removing the counterparty issues and the limited time frame enshrined in most derivative contracts.

  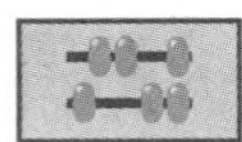      

MAKING IT HAPPEN

- Understand the nature of your liabilities and how long they go out for, as this is critical to managing them.
- Catalog and quantify the risks you are exposed to, such as interest rates, inflation, and longevity.
- De-risk if possible, though this will depend on cost and what solutions exist for transferring the risk in your jurisdiction.
- If that's not possible, hedge out or mitigate those risks for which you are not rewarded, such as inflation risk. Only take on those where you can hope to manage and improve the funding position, such as market risk.

MORE INFO

Articles:

Eich, Frank, and Amarendra Swarup. "Pensions tomorrow: A white paper." London School of Economics, 2008. Online at: tinyurl.com/4yeym5x [PDF].

Eich, Frank, and Amarendra Swarup. "Longevity: Trends, uncertainty and the implications for pension systems." London School of Economics, 2009. Online at: tinyurl.com/3zaf6rx [PDF].

Website:

London School of Economics—Pensions Tomorrow: tinyurl.com/3qey89z

See Also:

★ Asset Liability Management for Pension Funds (pp. 13–15)
★ The Origins and Current State of the Buyout Market for Pension Funds (pp. 224–225)
★ Pension Schemes: A Unique and Unintended Basket of Risks on the Balance Sheet (pp. 87–90)
★ Valuing Pension Fund Liabilities on the Balance Sheet (pp. 122–124)
★ Viewpoint: Yet Another Nail in the Final Salary Scheme Coffin (pp. 275–276)

Introduction to Islamic Financial Risk Management Products by Qudeer Latif and Susi Crawford

EXECUTIVE SUMMARY

- The main features of Islamic finance and *shariah* scholars are introduced.
- Conventional financial risk management products are viewed as non-*shariah*-compliant, which means that such products are not available to Islamic investors.
- The popularity of Islamic finance has given rise to a demand for *shariah*-compliant financial risk management products for underlying Islamic investments.
- A number of structures of *shariah*-compliant financial risk management products are available in the marketplace, all based around a *murabaha* sale structure.
- The rising popularity of the *wa'ad* structure is discussed.
- The article concludes with a brief summary of the future of *shariah*-compliant financial risk management products including an introduction to the ISDA/IIFM Tahawwut Master Agreement.

INTRODUCTION: THE MAIN FEATURES OF ISLAMIC FINANCE

To consider the basics of Islamic financial risk management products it is helpful to summarize the Islamic principles and jurisprudence on which Islamic finance is based.

- **Speculation**: contracts which involve speculation (*maysir*) are not permissible (*haram*) and are considered void. Islamic law does not prohibit general commercial speculation, but it does prohibit speculation which is akin to gambling, i.e. gaining something by chance rather than productive effort.
- **Unjust enrichment**: contracts where one party gains unjustly at the expense of another are considered void.
- **Interest**: the payment and receipt of interest (*riba*) are prohibited, and any obligation to pay interest is considered void. Islamic principles require that any return on funds provided by the lender be earned by way of profit derived from a commercial risk taken by that lender.
- **Uncertainty**: contracts which contain uncertainty (*gharar*)—particularly when there is uncertainty as to the fundamental terms of the contract, such as the subject matter, price, and time for delivery—are considered void.

To ensure adherence to these underlying principles, most banks that sell Islamic products have a board of *shariah* scholars (or will appoint a *shariah* scholar on a product-by-product basis) to ensure the bank's (or product's) compliance with the Islamic precepts.

On the whole, *shariah* scholars in the financial field hold the view that financial risk management products (commonly referred to as hedging arrangements) in the conventional finance space fall into the category of speculation (*maysir*) and uncertainty (*gharar*), both of which are prohibited under the *shariah* and cannot therefore be marketed as *shariah*-compliant products or used in conjunction with Islamic financing.

With the rise in sophistication of Islamic finance in recent years, however, a school of thought has emerged among pre-eminent *shariah* scholars that Islamic investors should be able to enter into hedging arrangements, provided that the financial risk management product is itself structured in a *shariah*-compliant manner and that there is genuine underlying risk arising from an Islamic investment.

The conventional financial risk management products have become an intrinsic part of the mechanics of banking finance and are, to a large part, documented by standard documentation and negotiated without recourse to lawyers. Any *shariah*-compliant financial risk products have to strike the balance of being faithful to the principles of *shariah* while maintaining the user-friendly structure of their conventional counterparts.

THE CONVENTIONAL PRODUCTS

Financial risk management products in the conventional world are, in their basic form, a derivative, and each product is based on the principles that a derivative is a financial instrument whose value derives from that of an underlying asset, and the underlying asset must be capable of being ascribed a market value.

The number of "assets" that can be ascribed a market value and from which, therefore, a derivative can be derived has resulted in a variety of financial risk management products. The commonly known structures are those based on interest and currency rates: i.e. interest rate swaps, cross-currency swaps, and foreign exchange forwards. There are also commodity derivatives based on gold, steel, and other metals. More recently, products known as "exotics" based on the weather and carbon emissions have appeared in the market in response to the requirements of a changing environmental as well as financial climate.

HOW A *SHARIAH*-COMPLIANT PRODUCT IS STRUCTURED

The starting point in structuring an Islamic financial risk management product should be an understanding of the commercial purpose of its conventional counterpart. For example, when structuring an Islamic-compliant profit rate swap, one must examine the use and structure of its equivalent in the conventional space: the basic interest rate swap. The interest rate swap is a hedging arrangement that is used to limit exposure to possible losses of expected income due to interest rate movements, and there is a similar demand for *shariah*-compliant products to limit exposure in Islamic investments where the profit, rent, or commission payable is linked in part to interest rate movements.

One must also must consider the non-*shariah* aspects of a conventional financial risk management product and address the same in the Islamic structure. As noted in the introduction, a principle of Islamic finance is that any profit must be earned through trade and taking a risk in a transaction. A common reason why hedging arrangements are seen as non-compliant is that although a financial risk management product is linked to the value of an asset, it does not always require ownership risk in the asset itself and any profit earned is earned independently of trade, ownership, or investment in such an asset.

Conventional risk management products are structured along the lines of a synthetic trade that occurs on each payment date. The elements of this synthetic trade are that:

- a party will be obliged to carry out an action (such as the delivery of an asset or the payment of a price) on a certain date; and
- the obligation to carry out such action will vary in accordance with the value of the underlying asset.

This structure has provided the framework for *shariah*-compliant financial risk management products by replacing the synthetic trade with an actual commodity (or any

"**If we listened to our intellect, we'd never have a love affair. We'd never have a friendship. We'd never go into business. Well, that's nonsense. You've got to jump off cliffs all the time and build your wings on the way down.**" Ray Bradbury

other asset) trade structured along the lines of a *murabaha*. This is a common Islamic structure under which assets can be sold for a determined profit and the payment can be deferred.

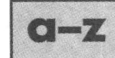

By using commodity trades, the banks and the counterparty expose themselves to ownership, if only briefly, of an underlying asset. The value of the traded commodity represents the principal amount of the underlying Islamic investment (the "cost price") and is sold at a profit, which is calculated by reference to an interest rate and, if applicable, a margin or spread (the "profit"). As the bank has taken ownership in the underlying asset, it is permitted to on-sell this at the profit, the calculation of which must be agreed upfront.

A number of structures of *shariah*-compliant products all based on the *murabaha* have appeared in the marketplace with varying degrees of success. A description of the main structures, using the example of a profit (interest) rate swap, are set out below, together with the advantages and disadvantages of each.

Profit Rate Swap Structure No. 1

As in a conventional trade the parties, namely the "bank" and the "counterparty," agree the commercial terms of the future transaction i.e. the trade dates, the fixed rate, the floating rate, the assets to be traded, and the notional cost price. On each trade date, the bank and counterparty will enter into two *murabaha* agreements.

Under the first *murabaha* agreement (the "floating leg"):

- the counterparty will sell to the bank an amount of commodities, the value of which will be the notional cost price;
- the sale price for these commodities will be cost price + profit;
- the profit element will represent the floating rate (calculated against the notional cost price).

Under the second *murabaha* agreement (the "fixed leg"):

- the bank will sell to the counterparty an amount of commodities the value of which will be the notional cost price;
- the sale price for these commodities, will be cost price + profit;
- the profit element will represent the fixed rate (calculated against the notional cost price).

The structure is shown in Figure 1. The net result of these trades is that on each trade date: the amount of commodities sold under each *murabaha* will be the same and the cost price will be the same, and these will effectively be netted off by way of on-sales to a third-party broker; only the profit element will differ; and, as in a conventional interest rate swap, the net beneficiary (of the difference between the fixed and floating rate) is dependent on whether the fixed or floating rate was higher.

The risks associated with this *murabaha* structure are as follows:

Commodity risk. This arises from the bank's and the counterparty's ownership of the commodity. To mitigate this risk, although the ownership lasts for a short period only, many banks require the counterparty to indemnify them against any losses incurred due to ownership of the commodity. Some Islamic institutions see this as undermining the principles of *shariah*, which require that full ownership risk is taken.

Execution risk. This arises due to the fact that, under Islamic principles, parties cannot agree to a future sale (where delivery of the asset and payment of the price are both deferred to a later date). Therefore, the delivery of a commodity must occur on the same day that the *murabaha* contract is concluded. The result of this "parallel *murabaha*" structure depends on both parties' willingness to enter into the *murabaha* agreements on each trade date (whether or not they are the net beneficiary).

Costs. These costs arise from the fact that two new *murabahas* are entered into at the beginning of each "profit" period (with deferred payment provisions) or on the trade date itself (with immediate delivery and payment provisions), throughout the term of the profit rate swap. This exposes each party not only to ownership risk, but also to the brokerage costs associated with a commodity trade (normally the brokerage fees are the liability of the counterparty, who would then be liable for two sets of brokerage fees on each trade date).

Profit Rate Swap Structure No. 2

In recognition of the risks set out above, the "parallel *murabaha*" structure has been developed in such a way as to limit the bank's and the counterparty's exposure to these risks, the key of which is that the fixed-leg *murabaha* is only entered into on day 1 and runs for the life of the profit rate swap, with "fixed" profit under the day-one *murabaha* being paid in installments over a number of deferred payment dates (with no need for further commodity trades to take place or *murabaha* agreements to be entered into).

The deferred payment dates under the fixed-leg *murabaha* will match the trade dates of each floating-leg *murabaha*. Because the floating-leg *murabaha* resets the profit rate a number of times, it has to be re-executed in relation to each trade date in order to give the parties certainty of the cost price + profit, which results in a commodity trade being carried out. The way that structure 2 operates is illustrated in Figure 2.

This structure reduces the ownership risk (by reducing the number of commodity trades that are carried out) and the associated costs. It also reduces the execution risk as one half of the trade is entered into on day 1. The parties are, however, still exposed to some execution risk: for example, a party not benefiting

Figure 1. *Murabaha* structure no. 1

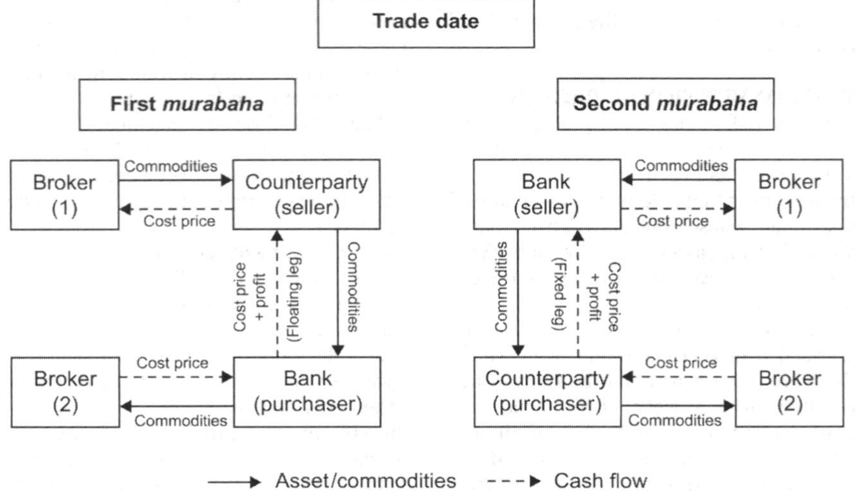

"My argument is: keep the bloody bottom line at the bottom. That's where it should be." Dame Anita Roddick

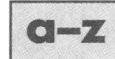

Figure 2. *Murabaha* structure no. 2

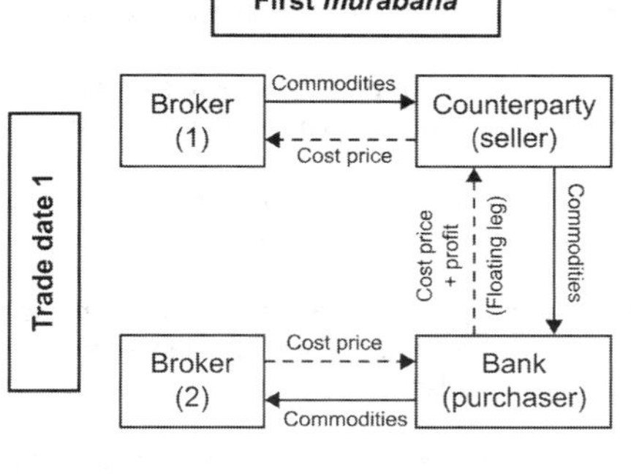

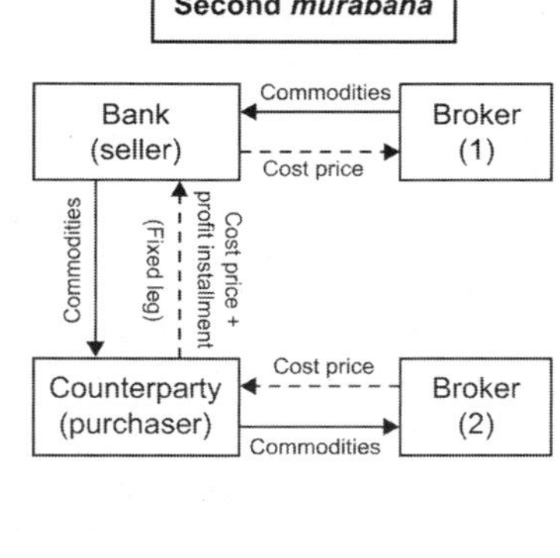

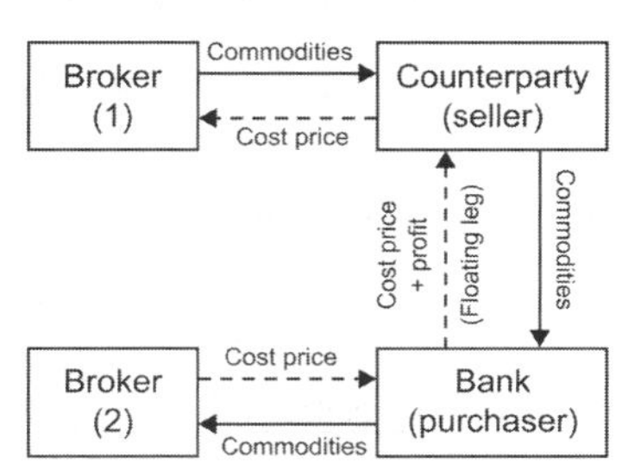

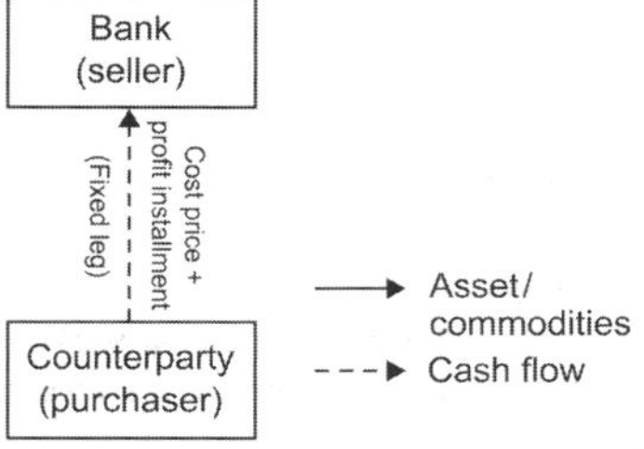

from a trade could walk away from the trade and the bank would remain liable to pay out under the fixed-leg *murabaha*.

Profit Rate Swap Structure No. 3

A structure that addresses the execution risk associated with structures 1 and 2 (and mitigates the ownership risk associated with structure 1) has been adopted in the market with great success and is known as the *wa'ad* structure (Figure 3).

Wa'ad is the Arabic word for promise. A promise, though commonly thought of as a moral obligation, is in most legal systems also a legal one. The *wa'ad* structure is based on each party (as promisor) granting the other (as promisee) a unilateral and irrevocable promise to enter into a trade on certain dates for a certain price in the future (effectively a put option). The trade that takes place on a trade date is, as in structures 1 and 2, a *murabaha* trade of commodities (or other assets), whereas the promise to enter into the trade is documented by way of a purchase undertaking (or put option).

These two purchase undertakings are documented separately so that each "promise" is a standalone, unilateral obligation of the promisor, but they can and do contain similar terms such as the trade dates and the commodities to be purchased. So that when read together, they represent the two sides of a profit rate swap. The only main difference is the price, which consists of cost price and profit (which will be calculated to reflect the difference between the fixed and floating rates).

The main aspect of the purchase undertaking is the conditions attached to its exercise by the beneficiary, the promisee. The conditions attached to the exercise mirror those in the conventional hedge that determine which party benefits on a trade date. In an interest rate swap, this would be whether the fixed rate or the floating rate were higher. Depending on which is higher, only one party is able to exercise the purchase undertaking under which they are promisee and require the promisor to carry out a trade, purchase commodities, and pay the promisee the cost price + profit. The net result of the trade mirrors that of structures 1 and 2 in that the cash flows are gained through the purchase and on-sale of commodities, but also that of a conventional trade, where there is only one cash flow representing the difference in the profit.

Figure 3. The *wa'ad* structure

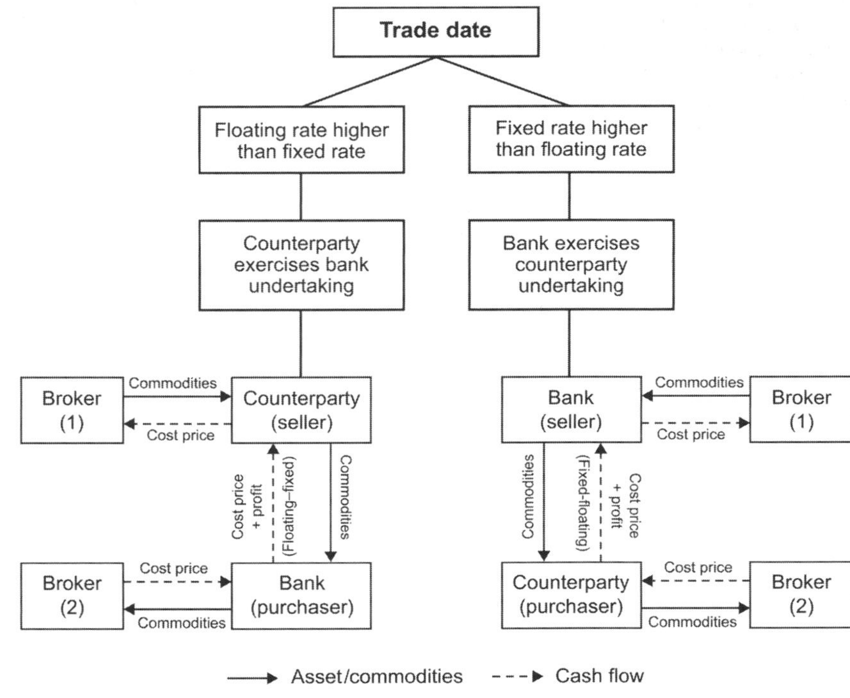

As is the case with structure 2, the benefits are that there is only one trade on any trade date, which lowers the ownership risk and associated costs. The real advantage, however, is that it resolves the issue of execution risk as the party in the money is in "control" of the trade, and once the promise is exercised by the promisee, the contractual obligation to purchase the commodities and pay the cost price + profit arises without need for further execution.

The flexibility of the *wa'ad* structure makes it suitable for a number of products beyond profit rate swaps, as it can be adapted as a foreign exchange forward (with only one purchase undertaking) or cross-currency swap. It can also be drafted as a master agreement together with purchase

"One can't say that figures lie. But figures, as used in financial arguments, seem to have the bad habit of expressing a small part of the truth forcibly, and neglecting the other part, as do some people we know." Fred Schwed

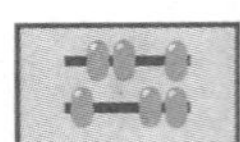

undertakings, bringing it in line with its conventional counterparts.

THE FUTURE

The Islamic financial risk management products market has gathered such momentum in recent years that the favored structures are constantly under review and revision. Satisfied that the Islamic structure allows payments that mirror those of the conventional trades, bankers are now looking at the other International Swaps and Derivatives Association (ISDA)–style provisions, such as right to terminate, termination events, tax events, and calculation of close-out amounts, and they are demanding the same level of sophistication in the Islamic financial risk management products.

In March 2010, ISDA and the International Islamic Financial Market (IIFM) launched the ISDA/IIFM Tahawwut Master Agreement. Taking an approach similar to that of the ISDA 2002 Master Agreement (a market standard agreement used for conventional financial risk management products), the Tahawwut Master Agreement is a framework agreement under which a range of *shariah*-compliant financial risk management products, such as the profit rate swap, can be documented. As well as containing "master terms" such as tax, representations, events of default, and termination events, the ISDA/IIFM Tahawwut Master Agreement contains a *shariah*-compliant method of close out which can be used across product groups.

In 2012, ISDA and IIFM released the first template product documentation designed to be used with the ISDA/IIFM Tahawwut Master Agreement, which was for the profit rate swap. The templates known as the Mubadalatul Arbaah used the *wa'ad* structure documented by way of purchase undertakings, though the ISDA/IIFM Tahawwut Master Agreement is designed to be used with other types of structures such as *murabaha*.

It is hoped that the ISDA/IIFM Tahawwut Master Agreement and its related documentation will be adopted by the market as industry standard documentation for Islamic financial risk management products.

MAKING IT HAPPEN

Before structuring or entering into an Islamic financial risk management product, consider the following points.

- What is the commercial objective of the transaction: i.e. what position should the parties be in on a trade date and at the end of the transaction? Does the Islamic structure reflect this?
- Which structure is more suitable, considering the costs and the risks involved? This may be determined more by the *shariah* board of the financial institution involved than by commercial preference.
- How should the trade be documented? Who will be carrying out the day-to-day mechanics of the underlying trades, and will they understand the documentation? Conventional financial risk products are often based on ISDA documentation and are carried out by bankers without recourse to lawyers.
- What jurisdiction are you dealing in, and will the documentation be enforceable? What is the situation on insolvency? This will have to be considered when drafting the close-out or unwind mechanics.

MORE INFO

Websites:

International Islamic Financial Market: www.iifm.net
International Swaps and Derivatives Association (ISDA): www.isda.org

See Also:

★ Identifying the Main Regulatory Challenges for Islamic Finance (pp. 358–360)
★ Procedures for Reporting Financial Risk in Islamic Finance (pp. 394–396)
★ Risk Management of Islamic Finance Instruments (pp. 94–97)
★ Viewpoint: *Shariah* Law—Bringing a New Ethical Dimension to Banking (pp. 242–243)
✔ Key Islamic Banking Instruments and How They Work (p. 1010)
✔ Key Principles of Islamic Finance (p. 1011)
✔ An Overview of *Shariah*-Compliant Funds (p. 1083)
✔ The Role of the *Shariah* Advisory Board in Islamic Finance (p. 1015)

"One must have some sort of occupation now-a-days. If I hadn't my debts I shouldn't have anything to think about." Oscar Wilde

Investment Risk in Islamic Finance

by Kamal Abdelkarim Hassan and Hassan Ahmed Yusuf

EXECUTIVE SUMMARY

- The unique risks within the Islamic finance investment space are described, along with the challenges faced in developing procedures and processes to address those risks.
- The categories of *shariah* risk, and the means available to mitigate this risk, are considered.
- Investment opportunities are limited due to the restricted nature of the Islamic investment universe.

INTRODUCTION

At the inception of Islamic finance, Islamic economists advocated change and developed a policy for Islamic banking practice and process, arguing that the main aspect of conventional banking—*riba* (interest)—required immediate rectification if Islamic banking was to exist. To achieve this goal, profit and loss sharing methods were introduced, along with other products such as *ijarah* (lease) and *murabahah* (cost plus). The rest of the technical banking operational procedure remained almost the same, especially in areas where there was no immediate solution, such as the application of the London Interbank Offered Rate (LIBOR) as a benchmark. This was based on the Islamic maxim *al daruuriyaatu tubihu al mahdurat* (necessity permits the unlawful). Likewise, the application of risk management within Islamic finance is not completely different from its conventional counterpart. Similarly, both Islamic and conventional financing apply the same methodology and technique in regard to risk management. It is essential to note that there are elements of risk, such as *shariah* risk, associated with Islamic finance that do not exist in its conventional counterpart due to the nature of Islamic finance and investment. As such, the challenge for the *shariah*-compliant investment and finance industry is to have procedures and processes in place to deal with risks unique to Islamic finance instruments. Based on the above, we discuss below types of Islamic investment risks unique in Islamic finance, as shown in Table 1.

UNIQUE RISKS IN ISLAMIC FINANCE

There is no the doubt that the recent financial crisis and the rapid development of financial innovation and engineering of Islamic investment instruments necessitate the need for risk management, control, and vigilant supervision. Islamic finance investment is different from its conventional counterpart because it is required to comply with *shariah* rules and guidance or it could lose its legitimacy, thereby constituting a *shariah* risk. *Shariah* risk has a deeper, more profound meaning than its current use in the Islamic finance literature, and its scope is changing relative to the pace of Islamic finance development.[1]

SHARIAH RISK AND ITS CATEGORIES

Shariah risk can occur in different stages in Islamic investment. It has subcategories and the impact of each category is different. To understand this better, *shariah* risk can be categorized as follows.

Category 1 relates to the minimum requirements for an investment to be deemed *shariah*-compliant and forms important distinctions between conventional and Islamic investment. Those features that are to be avoided are interest, gambling, and uncertainty. All Islamic investments should be free from dealings with interest, gambling, and excessive uncertainty. Additionally, *shariah* compliance requires abstention from investing in industries where the core business is considered illicit in Islam, such as alcohol, pork, cinemas, gambling industries, and items that are regarded as prohibited in *shariah* (Figure 1).

Failure to comply with the minimum parameters in the first category of *shariah* risk with respect to any potential Islamic investment could have a huge impact, possibly resulting in the dissolution of the invested entity, and could cause huge reputational risk. Hence, the important responsibility of the *shariah* board to check and ensure the details of the investment and declare it legitimate before any investment commitment.

Category 2 of *shariah* risk relates to the process and implementation mechanism of finance investment products. Generally, the process starts with presentation of the financial product to the *shariah* board by the developer of the product. The product description and structure, its underlying asset securities (if any), different types of contracts, charges, fees, and other necessary details are examined by the *shariah* board. Following detailed discussions, the *shariah* board renders its advice.[2] Once the product is completed as the *shariah* board has advised, legitimacy is given and it hits the market. *Shariah* risk in this category would arise if the product failed to conform to the process approved by the *shariah* board (for instance, the procedure advised by *shariah* is sequential in order, where one step follows its predecessor, while in contrast the implementation team may feel it irrelevant that step 3 should preceed step 4).[3] This type of risk is mitigated through a *shariah* auditor or supervisor review of the process and mechanism implemented during the operational process of any product launch.

This type of risk is limited as long as *shariah* audit reviews and corrections are applied immediately. An example of this type of risk is in a *wakalah* contract offer where money is received by a *wakil* (agent)

Table 1. Risks specific to Islamic investment

Shariah risk	Risk associated with not implementing Islamic investment and finance products in accordance with *shariah* principles.
Asset concentration	Investing, financing, or drawing earnings and income in a single market or a single asset class.
Default risk	Risk that a counterparty fails to meet its financial obligations as they fall due.
Rate of return risk	Risk of fluctuations in earnings where expected income targets may not be achieved due to market conditions as Islamic finance and investment concentrates more on equity.
Transparency risk	Risk of not disclosing information necessary for users in regard to financial data, risk management, business conditions, and other necessary information.
Equity investment risk	Risk associated with holding equity investment during unfavorable situations, where decline in investment caused by market conditions in turn gives volatility of earnings of *musharakah* and *mudarabah* investments. (This definition needs more clarity as it appears to include rate of return risk as well.)

"Eagles may soar but weasels don't get sucked into jet engines." Anonymous

        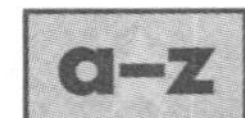

Figure 1. The investment selection process

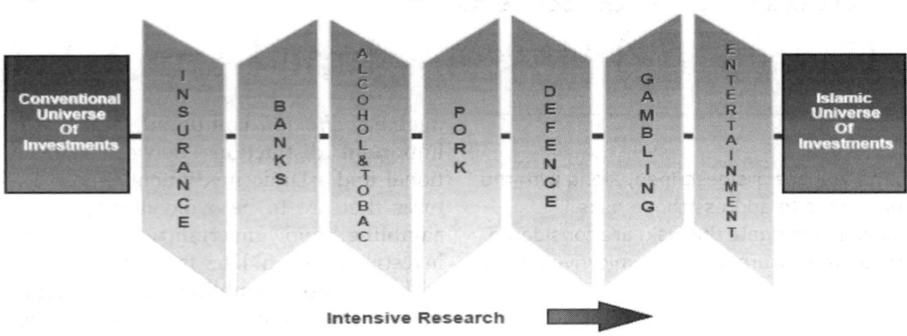

before the offer is accepted by the *muwwakil* (principal). The money cannot be invested before the acceptance of offer is signed, according to the *shariah* guidelines.

Category 3 refers to the situation where the process of a structured product presented to the *shariah* board may not be implemented as advised by the board. Here there could be some additions and/or deletions of the process by the developers which were not included in the information initially presented to the *shariah* board. Such a risk is mitigated by employing a *shariah* auditor review, or additionally making it the practice of *shariah* boards to review products after launch and during normal operations. An example of this type is a structured product approved by *shariah* but where the board has not approved part of the fees or commission received as these were not presented to the board during the initial product presentations. The impact and the risk are that the generated fees or profit not approved by the *shariah* board during that period could be canceled.

Category 4 risk is that some investments may be declared null and void by another group of scholars or a regulatory body, based on the lack of accurate product formulation or their own differing interpretation of *shariah* principles, procedures, and processes. An example of this type is *tawwaruq*,[4] as the legitimacy and the approval of the investment product was based on the *fatwa* given by the *shariah* board. Since the *fatwa* itself is in the form of *ijtihad* (the process of making a legal decision by independent interpretation of the legal sources of the scholar), there are no problems if it is right. If it is wrong, the appropriate corrections will need to be applied thereto without necessarily outlawing the product or the interpretation. This is based on the well-known principle of *fiqh* in Islamic jurisprudence (i.e. if a scholar offers a correct *fatwa*, he or she receives two rewards; if he or she gets it wrong, they get one reward only). In contrast, declaring a product illegitimate requires research and evidence, as financial transactions in Islamic investment are based on what is known. Permissibility of origin[5] and the burden of proof lie with the person asserting that the product is not permissible.

ASSET CONCENTRATION

The Islamic investment universe offers a limited choice of investment products that meet *shariah*-compliant guidelines. As a result, a primary Islamic investment vehicle for many Islamic financial institutions tends to be real estate. This type of concentration leads to risky circumstances, particularly in unfavorable market conditions as we have seen in the subprime mortgage crisis of 2008. Unsurprisingly, within the Gulf Cooperation Council (GCC), banks reached the ceiling investment limit of real estate portfolio. Such a situation clearly highlights asset concentration due to the limited choice of Islamic investment products. Currently, Islamic investment is moving toward more mature levels, and therefore is in dire need of product innovation. The impact of this type of risk could be enormous if there is a sudden change of microeconomic conditions. There are defined guidelines for addressing this risk concentration and controls that can reduce exposure to risk if properly applied and managed.

DEFAULT RISK

Default risk is when a counterparty fails to pay its investment or finance obligation. This is also classified as credit risk in conventional terminology. Similar mitigating frameworks applied in conventional finance may be applied within Islamic investment and finance. Nevertheless, within the conventional investment system, the procedure for granting credit facilities includes background checks and credit history of the past performance of applicants that is facilitated by maintaining good quality data (credit agencies). Within Islamic investment and finance, trust by way of name-lending supersedes conventional credit examination—particularly in the GCC, where a developed credit bureau does not exist. The significant downside of name-lending has long been established (for example, investments without collateral). Risk of default may be higher and, even in the face of existing genuine collateral, issues may arise in determining the real market value when required, and any liquidation of assets could entail a lengthy legal process.

RATE OF RETURN RISK

Islamic investments face rate of return risk due to the fluctuations in microeconomic conditions. Islamic investment could experience greater fluctuations and volatility in rate of return risk due to limited product choices and prefixed income, which are absent in conventional investment. Furthermore, asset classes within Islamic investment are not easily converted to cash and may be subject to commodity price risk, as some of these assets do not have ready or deep secondary markets (*sukuk*—Islamic bonds) and, as such, must be held until maturity.

OTHER RISKS

Investment in Islamic finance faces equity investment risk, largely due to the application of both *mudarabah* and *musharakah* investments. Likewise, there are other risk elements that are interrelated in Islamic investments. For instance, the lack of a wide range of *shariah*-compliant products to absorb the liquidity of Islamic investments could result in an opportunity loss for the investment. Islamic investment products are few considering the amount of available funds available for Islamic investment. This results in a low return on investment as it is invested in short-term products and thus creates mismatch problems, since Islamic investments are in long-term opportunities such as project finance, real estate, and *sukuk*. Furthermore, the lack of tradable instruments in secondary markets could also play a role. The scope of transparency risk in Islamic investment is not confined to lack of reliability, nondisclosure, and inadequate information, but can also include the process of the approval of products in case of dispute, as we have seen in recent court cases. It also includes the stock selection process and details and strategies for stringent risk management process employed to safeguard the interests of all parties—shareholders and depositors alike.

"If you are scared to go to the brink you are lost." John Foster Dulles

RISK IMPACT OF ISLAMIC FINANCE

The subprime mortgage and subsequent financial crisis in 2008 were blamed on the lack of risk management and the complete ignoring of signs of risk by senior management within financial institutions. Nevertheless, recent cases in the Islamic finance sector highlight that lapses in risk management could have detrimental results on the stability of Islamic finance institutions and damage the reputation of the industry.

The troubled Bahrain-based Gulf Finance House (GFH), once the darling of Islamic finance in the Kingdom, suffered from severe lapses in risk management.[6] Within GFH there was an absence of real diversification. In 2008 and 2009, 78.5% and 83.4% respectively of GFH's assets were concentrated in Gulf countries and were primarily real estate in nature. Furthermore, the fact that the business and earnings of GFH were directly linked to a single asset class (real estate) was a recipe for disaster. One could also argue that the presence of *shariah* risk, evident in methods of implementing *murabahah* transactions within GFH, was not complete given that the basic conditions to disclose price and markup were violated. Likewise, in the case of Dato' Haji Nik Mahmud bin Daud vs Bank Islam Malaysia,[7] *shariah* risk occurred due to the nontransferrence of ownership. This also violated the *shariah* requirement that a seller must own the title of the asset. In the Symphony Gems case,[8] the *murabahah* contract was not a valid *murabahah* contract according to the testimony of Dr Al-Samaan. In a recent case involving the Investment Dar Company (TID) vs Blom Development Bank,[9] TID's legal counsel used *shariah* noncompliance of the contract as a defense—highlighting the significance of *shariah* risk.

MAKING IT HAPPEN

- The risks faced by Islamic investments, such as *shariah* risk and equity investment risk, are unique due to the nature of such investments. Inadequate and insufficient observation of *shariah* investment guidelines could cause a risk that results in the dissolution of the investment and leads to loss of confidence, trust, and reputation of the institution. Consequently, there is a lack of development in the Islamic risk management framework that would enable it to identify, assess, and measure the risks unique to Islamic investment. Even the analysis and structure of presentation of *shariah* risk are borrowed from conventional risk management.
- There is a dire need to have a complete and comprehensive *shariah* risk management framework for Islamic finance that can capture the current process of the Islamic finance structure. Other risks faced by Islamic investment, such as rate of return, credit risk, asset concentration, commodity risk, and market volatility, can have a huge impact if not managed properly. Contained within the *shariah* principles are adequate measures that provide effective safeguards for Islamic investment.
- However, there remains a need for *shariah* to show adaptability in the face of phenomenal growth, the sophistication of product innovation, and financial engineering. This should hasten changes and the development of a suitable risk management framework that is compatible with the *maqasid al-shariah* (objective of *shariah*).

MORE INFO

Books:

Archer, Simon, and Rifaat Abdelkarim. *Islamic Finance: The Regulatory Challenge*. Singapore: Wiley, 2007.

Iqbal, Zamir, and Abbas Mirakhor. *An Introduction to Islamic Finance Theory and Practice*. Singapore: Wiley, 2007.

Article:

Moghul, Umar F., and Arshad A. Ahmed. "Contractual forms in Islamic finance law and Islamic Investment Company of the Gulf (Bahamas) Ltd. v. Symphony Gems N.V. & others: A first impression of Islamic finance." *Fordham International Law Journal* 27:1 (December 2003): 150–194. Online at: ir.lawnet.fordham.edu/ilj/vol27/iss1/7/

Reports:

Bälz, Kilian. "Sharia risk? How Islamic finance has transformed Islamic contract law." Occasional Publications 9. Islamic Legal Studies Program, Harvard Law School, September 2008. Online at: www.law.harvard.edu/programs/ilsp/publications/balz.pdf

Khnifer, Mohammed, Aatef Baig, and Frank Winkler. "The rise and fall of Gulf Finance House." Design, Implementation and Risk Aspects of Islamic Financial Products and Services module, Reading University, 2010.

Saiful, Azhar Rosly. "*Shariah* compliant parameters reconsidered." Paper presented at the Annual Malaysian Finance Association Conference, Kuching, Malaysia, June 4–5, 2008.

NOTES

1. The scope of *shariah* risk currently applied is often limited to financial transactions, but, given that *shariah* compliance is the distinctive characteristic of Islamic finance, a much broader application of this unique risk is required. As *shariah* should encompass all of an Islamic financial institution's activities, from transactional contracts to staff and vendor contracts, a broader approach to *shariah* risk is required.
2. This is one of the processes for obtaining approval of Islamic finance and investment products from the *shariah* board. Different banks have different processes for obtaining product approval from the *shariah* board. Sometimes a *shariah* compliance officer may make the presentation to the *shariah* board.
3. There was a case in a Gulf bank where written acceptance of an offer was received after the profit of that period was realized, and the *shariah* board canceled the profit from that period.
4. *Tawwaruq* is a controversial product among scholars. Recently a Gulf central bank issued written advice on the use of *tawwaruq* products, the permissible percentages of these relative to other products, and even advising that *tawwaruq* should not be used on credit cards.
5. Under *shariah* law, legality and illegality are based on either prohibition or permissibility. For example, all forms of worship are illegitimate except those allowed by *shariah*. This means that no one can use any form of worship unless that form is permitted by *shariah*. This is unlike the situation with food, where all kinds are permissible except what has been prohibited. That is why, when *shariah* considers items of food, it starts with prohibitions, as permissibility is the basis in matters of food. Similarly, financial transactions are based on permissibility. The outcome is that if the usage of something is based on permissibility, the burden of proof is on the party rejecting such permissibility, and if it is based on prohibition, the burden of proof is on the party permitting such actions.
6. Khnifer *et al.*, 2010.
7. Saiful, 2008.
8. Moghul and Ahmed, 2003.
9. Investment Dar Company vs Blom Development Bank case.

  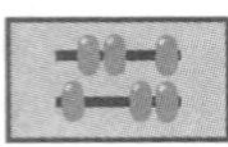      

Managing 21st Century Finances by Terry Carroll

EXECUTIVE SUMMARY

- CFOs have to balance long-term planning with short-termist behavior in the markets.
- In order to do this, it's essential to have a good business model, a clear understanding of business risk, sustainable revenues, and proper communication.
- Failing to manage the financial information systems well can seriously damage your brand. Getting it right will please both short- and long-term investors.
- Matters have been complicated by the globalization of standards and reinterpretation of company accounts.
- Tangible value creation remains top of the agenda. When investors are frightened or lose faith, they can destroy value much faster than you can create it.
- Relationship management is one of the most important new skills to acquire on the road to success.

INTRODUCTION

Corporate purpose, for most companies, is to create and sustain long-term stockholder value. However, markets can be driven by fear or euphoria. Stuck in the middle are top managers, especially the CFOs. They have to balance long-term planning with "short-termist" behavior in the markets. How can this be achieved? What are the new metrics for survival and sustainable prosperity?

As some companies have destroyed value, some have begun to question whether stockholder value should be a goal, or rather a consequence of excellence. In both quoted and private companies you need a clear, understandable business model that works; to be able to explain it easily and consistently; to understand strategic business risk and make it work for you; to generate sustainable revenues, income, and cash with rapid and reliable reporting; and no surprises!

MANAGING INVESTORS' EXPECTATIONS

Managing stockholder value is also about managing expectations. The major long-term players (institutions, pension, investment, and insurance funds) are advised by analysts. Short-term investors, traders, and the public are more influenced by news flow and market movements. How can we reconcile these forces? By timely financial information, "no surprises," always having cash, and finally, having a credible, understandable business model.

FINANCIAL REPORTING IN THE COMMUNICATIONS AGE

Great companies produce rapid, reliable, succinct, simple, usable financial information. Internally, more than three days to report is too long. The Internet or intranets can provide "always-on," real-time connection for the whole company. Management and financial reporting tools and technology allow fast collection, collation, interpretation, and distribution of results. Now, three factors are converging internal with external reporting: urgency, transparency, and consistency.

Global markets and the pace of change mean that management needs reliable financial feedback, fast. Meanwhile, external reporting periods are shortening. This is spilling into Europe. Information is a global property, especially when it "leaks." Global brand management demands control of your own destiny. The market wants information as fast as you get it. Too much conversion for external consumption takes time, unsettling management and investor alike. Meanwhile, market regulation requires transparency and "equality" of distribution.

Investors want financial information that is consistent with expectations. The more frequently it is released, the smaller the mismatch. Regular, progressive business and financial news flow, along with rational enhancements to the business model, can lead to outperformance. When there are surprises, markets wonder whether management is competent.

Uneven information flow; profit warnings or their lack; information released to analysts before the market; lack of comment on speculation; all these unsettle investors and regulators, sometimes causing sharp movements in stock prices. News and specialist market services supply corporate information 24 hours a day. Analysts interpret it as fast as it is produced. The changes in Accounting Standards, Sarbanes–Oxley, Basel II, and other complications mean more reliance on expert interpretation. While some have argued about the validity of new standards, industry leaders and others have got on with it to create a sustainable advantage.

Some CFOs may need to wake up to the new paradigm. Others will see it as an opportunity for skilled relationship management, making the financial information systems work for the company as another weapon in the public relations armory. The swift can capitalize on the lethargy of the slow. Brand is everything. Failing this new challenge can seriously damage yours. The right approach will please both short- and long-term investors.

CASH IS KING

Investors will demand that companies report quicker. This is a challenge for accounting standards and governance. Historic price/earnings multiples have been replaced by forecast revenues and EBITDA (earnings before interest, tax, depreciation, and amortization) as the currency of decisions. As accounts become almost impenetrable, the metric we all understand is cash. How much cash was generated in the last period; how much remains in the balance sheet; what is the NPV of sustainable future cash flows?

EVERYBODY NEEDS A BUSINESS MODEL

Apart from cash, the other factor that brings together short- and long-term interests is a credible, explainable business model. If you don't have one, analysts will create their own (or worse still, transport one from another company unlike your own). For example, good TMT (technology, media, telecommunications) stocks have floated up and down with the bad on the waves of market volatility. Some values were absurd, for good or ill.

Nortel (US) and Bookham (UK) were both top 100 stocks in their own markets. They were both linked to building communications networks. Nortel's market capitalization peaked at around $282 billion in 2000. It collapsed in value after the dot-com bubble burst and in January 2009 Nortel filed for protection from its creditors. Bookham Technology was a darling of the FTSE, floated in July 2000 at roughly $18. Its shares rocketed to $94 in a few months, based on the NPV of forecast revenues for a business model that few people understood. The price was driven by over-optimistic analyst estimates, blind faith, and greed. Its price fell 99% and its market capitalization from $11.4 to around £88 million. Like Nortel, it was buffeted by fear and optimism. Unlike Nortel, it had never made any money and it moved to the NASDAQ to try and escape its past. In 2004 it became a US domiciled company and recently produced its best ever quarterly profit.

"Money is better than poverty, if only for financial reasons." Woody Allen

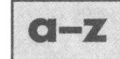

There are other examples: insurance companies have ebbed and flowed with each other, washed by pension fund and capital adequacy fears. In personal finance, Cattles' and Provident Financial's recent fortunes have been very different. Both are described as "doorstep lenders" even though this is now less than 10% of Cattles' business. Unless you regularly communicate a clear differentiation and a plausible business model, you may remain at the whim of the market.

So it's the financial model that really counts, especially generating and sustaining cash. It's lack of cash that busts companies, not lack of capital. When you don't have enough cash to survive a recession and the market isn't receptive to new issues, you have to start slashing costs—"eating yourself"—to stay alive. This can damage the business model, undermine the stock price, and become a vicious spiral toward death, or at best consumption by a sounder business model.

VALUING THE BUSINESS

There has been much theoretical talk in the past about "value added." The theory is that every company should be focused on protecting, creating, and sustaining value. Failure could mean stock price falls, cash calls, unwelcome bids, or business failure.

So the CEO, CFO, and colleagues need vision and courage. Value creation is top of the agenda. It involves generating the value and protecting it. Brand, fear, technical, and fundamental analysis of markets have assumed more significance than the internal business plan, budgets, and the annual report. When investors are frightened or lose faith, they can destroy value much faster than you can create it.

This is why cash generation is critical. Stock prices that are already eroding due to poor results or loss of confidence in a business model fall dramatically faster when you have to raise cash in an unreceptive market. Investors share your wish to sleep easy at night.

Some CFOs therefore cite short-termism as the real driver of value. They castigate "teenage scribblers" and analysts for not understanding their business. Some make errors of judgment, not only in their handling of such relationships, but also in silence or, worse still, nasty surprises.

Marconi was the classic case in the United Kingdom. For months investors expected a profit warning. The company continued to make reassuring noises. Investors continued to sell against an expectation of bad news. Eventually trading in the stock was suspended. Dreadful news was released. Returning from suspension the price was savaged. It had fallen from over $20 to under 35 cents in a year. In early 2004, it was recapitalized by its bankers, a shadow of its once great self. In October 2005 the Marconi name and most of the assets were bought by Ericsson.

CONCLUSION

All companies can follow this best practice to prosper in the 21st century:

- fast, reliable reporting against a sound business model;
- proactively anticipating and managing investor interest;
- investing in relationships to differentiate your company;
- being clear, informed, and consistent;
- creating and sustaining long-term corporate and brand value.

MAKING IT HAPPEN

Messages for Managers

Creating and protecting stockholder value are even more important in the 21st century. Volatility, expectations, speed of reporting, and a hungry investor demand for "real-time" information have changed the dynamics. The CFO needs new skills. These include strategic thinking, proactive risk management, and communication and interpersonal skills of a high order.

Value creation is about having a clear strategic and business focus, flexible and adaptable as appropriate. The CFO and executive colleagues must recognize the importance of having a sound, understandable business model. The financial model must be based on value creation, ideally measured in sustainable revenues, income, and especially cash. Reporting should be rapid and transparent, using the speed of technology, with no surprises.

You can create long-term value, but investors can take it away in the short term when fear overrides faith if you don't heed these messages. Relationship management with analysts, investors, and the media is the critical skill that wasn't mentioned when the CFO trained as an accountant. When you understand and manage strategic business risk and the macroeconomic factors, you may at least anticipate the challenge of analysts, whether or not they understand your own unique business model. If the unforeseen occurs, report it rapidly and accurately, with a clear understanding of the factors and a plan to manage the consequences.

Finally, much of this message relates to private companies too. Investment of private capital is accelerating. A clear business model is fundamental to accessing the cash for investment and growth, especially if you plan eventually to come to market.

MORE INFO

Books:

Bierman, Harold, Jr. *Corporate Financial Strategy and Decision Making to Increase Shareholder Value*. New Hope, PA: Frank J. Fabozzi Associates, 1999.

Carroll, Terry. *The Role of the Finance Director*. 3rd ed. Englewood Cliffs, NJ: FT Prentice Hall, 2002.

Conger, Jay A., Edward E. Lawler III, and David L. Finegold. *Corporate Boards: New Strategies for Adding Value at the Top*. San Francisco, CA: Jossey-Bass, 2001.

Moore, Geoffrey A. *Living on the Fault Line: Managing for Shareholder Value in Any Economy*. Revised ed. New York: HarperBusiness, 2002.

Website:

CFO.com: www.cfo.com

See Also:

★ Comparing Net Present Value and Internal Rate of Return (pp. 30–32)
★ Corporate Finance for SMEs (pp. 33–35)
★ Creating Value with EVA (pp. 814–816)
★ Dividend Policy: Maximizing Shareholder Value (pp. 667–670)
★ Why EVA Is the Best Measurement Tool for Creating Shareholder Value (pp. 952–953)
✔ Assessing Business Performance (p. 1144)
✔ Investors and the Capital Structure (p. 1120)
✔ Options for Raising Finance (p. 1081)

  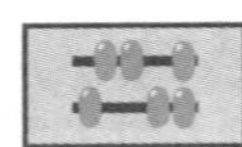      

Managing Capital Budgets for Small and Medium-Sized Companies by Neil Seitz

EXECUTIVE SUMMARY

- Small and medium-sized enterprises have distinct capital budgeting best practices, distinct because they result from top management's intimate knowledge of the business.
- The search for investment opportunities depends on effective communication of strategy.
- Best practice in capital investment analysis starts with strategic importance, followed by profitability and risk assessment.
- Funding decisions must consider cost, control, flexibility, and risk.
- Monitoring capital investments is the essential, but frequently neglected, final phase.

INTRODUCTION

Capital budgeting irrevocably shapes the direction of a business, and our collective capital budgeting decisions "determine the kind of society that we and our children will live in—not just this year but many years from now as well."[1] Investment of revenue from their oil industry by Gulf countries is "profoundly reshaping global capitalism."[2] More than 15 years ago, Peel and Bridge published a study showing that SMEs with formal processes for planning and capital budgeting report improved profitability.[3] Best practice tools for these critical decisions are essential, and available.

All corporate finance books, including books by the present author, offer the same advice: Choose investments with positive net present values. The NPV rule is important, but it is only one element of best practice. This article highlights best practices in four phases of managing capital budgets for small and medium-sized businesses (SMEs):

- Create proposals;
- Select investments;
- Fund investments;
- Monitor results.

THE NPV RULE

Net present value (NPV) is the present value of cash inflows minus the present value of cash outflows. A capital investment is desirable if the NPV is positive, and the greater the NPV, the more desirable is the investment. Let us say that a proposed project generates a cash inflow of $1,100 in one year. Suppose that the *hurdle rate*, the rate investors could earn elsewhere with similar risk, is 10%. The present value—the amount you would have to invest elsewhere at 10% to get $1,100 in one year—is $1,000. The proposed project happens to cost only $950, which is $50 less than the present value; the NPV of the project is $50. The internal rate of return (IRR) is the rate of return actually earned on the investment. For this example, the IRR is 15.8%: $950 invested at 15.8% would grow to $1,100 in one year. If the NPV is positive, the IRR is greater than the hurdle rate, and vice versa.

CREATE PROPOSALS

The results of capital budgeting cannot exceed the set of capital investment proposals. Some large bureaucracies announce a process for submitting proposals—and then wait passively. The shape and direction of a company are determined by capital budgeting decisions, so a passive approach gives the CEO little role in shaping the future of the business.

An *active capital budgeting approach* is best practice, and it starts with strategy. Strategy creates competitive advantage, and therefore adds value. Without competitive advantage there are no projects with positive NPV. Managers in a position to identify capital investment opportunities must understand the company's strategy, and how capital investments are a major part of strategy implementation.

A second aspect of the active approach is that many people have vested interests in the status quo. A new strategic direction requires aggressive top management involvement to identify investment opportunities.

An advantage of a SME is that the CEO is generally close to the action. The CEO is well positioned to communicate strategy, spot opportunities, and evaluate investments. A potential weakness of a SME is failure of the CEO to maintain a disciplined, strategic approach, and failure to communicate strategy to other managers. Best practice responsibility in generating proposals in a SME falls heavily on top management. Strategy, communication, and discipline are key elements.

SELECT INVESTMENTS

General rules for capital investment decisions are the same at global conglomerates and SMEs. Application of the rules is different at a SME, because the CEO is usually not far removed from the person proposing an investment. The CEO is often the originator of a large project, particularly one of strategic importance.

Strategy is the best place to start. Clever wordsmiths can explain why anything and everything is consistent with the company's strategy. It is the job of top management to make a critical, independent judgment of the strategic importance of the project. To aid in that judgment, Carroll and Mui (2008) stress that "Reviewers should ask for a detailed written description of the strategy—not spreadsheets and slides."[4]

The second step in the capital budgeting process is NPV analysis. Project proponents will compute an NPV if asked, and will generally predict positive NPV. Herein lies a subtle danger. If a pet project has a negative NPV, there is a temptation to adjust the sales forecast enough to make it positive. Studies have shown that, on average, proposals overestimate NPV.[5]

What are best practices for avoiding excess optimism? First, know the people in your company well enough to know who is likely to be overly optimistic. The SME has an advantage in this regard because of its size. Second, seek independent input on critical assumptions for major investments. Third, and this is essential, establish an effective monitoring system, so that managers expect to be accountable for their forecasts.

One reason for starting with strategy rather than NPV is that there are strategic decisions for which accurate NPV estimates are virtually impossible. One example is the Scott Seed Company, which invests in research to maintain its enviable brand recognition for the best lawn grass seed. It would be difficult for Scott to measure the NPV of a particular research project. The project approval process must allow for the funding of critical activities of this type, even though they would lose out if the first hurdle was *proven* NPV.

Decision speed is another best practice. Many organizations still use an annual budget cycle, in which all proposals for the year are considered together. This might be consistent with the speed of business in another century, but not today. The process must be open to respond to rapidly changing challenges and opportunities. SMEs have a capital investment decision speed advantage, because fewer layers of management are involved.

Risk analysis is different for SMEs compared to large, publicly traded compa-

"One of the most important responsibilities of corporate managers is to evaluate and choose among major investment projects." Laughton *et al.* (2008)

  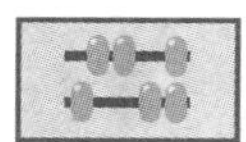      

nies, which are typically owned by diversified investors who are concerned about risk to their portfolio. For large companies, sensitivity to overall market conditions is the relevant risk, and risks unique to one company will average out across their portfolio. Owners of SMEs may have most of their wealth in one company, so the welfare of the company is of importance to them. For SMEs, the relevant risk of a particular capital investment is its impact on the overall health of the company.

Stress testing is a best practice for risk assessment. Identify possible problems, such as a recession or loss of a major customer. Prepare pro forma financial statements for the company in these unfortunate scenarios, with and without the proposed capital investment. Although income is important, the critical variable is cash: Will the proposed capital investment push the company into a vulnerable cash position in difficult times?

FUND INVESTMENTS

Funding is an essential part of the decision for a large capital investment. Availability of funding has always been a challenge for SMEs, and the challenge is growing. Small business loans by banks fell by half in the financial crisis, and have not come close to fully recovering.[6] The prediction of a US$7 trillion long-term developed country funding gap for capital investments suggests that the problem will not go away.[7] Credibility of proposals will be key to competing for scarce funds.

The major considerations in funding, after availability, are cost, control, flexibility, and risk. Debt is often seen as less expensive than equity, partly because the cost of debt is tax-deductible. Sale of new equity is often seen as undesirable, because it dilutes ownership and weakens management control. The trade-offs are in flexibility and risk. Heavy debt levels reduce financing alternatives and have been shown to limit companies' ability to maintain their capital investment plans.[8] An often ignored best practice is always to maintain some unused borrowing ability so you can respond to changing circumstances.

The risk associated with debt is determined primarily by the cash flow needed to service the debt, not the amount of debt. Risk analysis using pro forma financial statements highlights the combined impacts of the proposed investment and its funding on the risk of running out of cash. A project funded with intermediate-term debt may raise the risk of a cash crisis to an unacceptable level, though the same project funded with long-term debt or equity would not be excessively risky.

MONITOR RESULTS

The most common deviation from best practice is a failure to monitor capital investments after the decision is made. First, the expectation of monitoring helps control excess optimism about costs and benefits. Second, deviations are more likely to be correctable if detected early. Third, monitoring is a learning tool for improving the capital budgeting process.

The first stage of monitoring occurs as the capital investment is being acquired and

CASE STUDY

Bass Family Electric

Bass Family Electric (the name has been changed for confidentiality) was an electronic contractor with a 20-year history of success in small commercial building projects. The founder made a strategic decision to leapfrog into much larger projects, increasing debt to fund the needed capital investment. Small projects typically lasted a few weeks, but big projects stretched over a couple of years. The sad result of expansion was a series of losses and looming bankruptcy.

The problem was failure to fully implement the strategic decision. The company continued to prepare bids as it had done for small projects, ignoring the fact that long-term projects were capital investments. One capital investment that was not made was a monitoring system for long-term projects. A brief study of past projects made clear which types of projects and conditions were leading to losses.

The prescription was to avoid the types of projects that created losses temporarily, modify the bid process to recognize large projects as capital investments, and institute monitoring that allowed a rapid response to deviations. Bass was then positioned to expand its range of business, including the types of projects that had previously contributed to losses.

MAKING IT HAPPEN

- Determine who will be responsible for managing the capital budgeting process (typically the CFO). In addition to managing the process, the CFO will recommend financing.
- Communicate business strategy clearly to everyone involved.
- Establish and publish hurdle rates.
- Create standards with regard to what must be in capital investment proposals, including general description, strategic impact, NPV, and risk analysis.
- Establish responsibility for capital investment decisions. Managers at various levels may be given authority to decide on smaller investments, while large, strategic investments are decided by top management. A capital investment committee is frequently used, with membership including the CEO, CFO, and other senior managers.
- Establish a time schedule and process for monitoring. The monitoring process may be done as often as once a week during implementation, and may be part of the annual review thereafter.

MORE INFO

Books:

Baker, H. Kent, and Philip English (eds). *Capital Budgeting Valuation: Financial Analysis for Today's Investment Projects*. Hoboken, NJ: Wiley, 2011.

Seitz, Neil, and Mitch Ellison. *Capital Budgeting and Long-Term Financing Decisions*. Cincinnati, OH: Cengage, 2005.

Articles:

Laughton, David, Raul Guerrero, and Donald Lessard. "Real asset valuation: A back-to-basics approach." *Journal of Applied Corporate Finance* 20:2 (Spring 2008): 46–65. Online at: dx.doi.org/10.1111/j.1745-6622.2008.00180.x

Ruback, Richard S. "Downsides and DCF: Valuing biased cash flow forecasts." *Journal of Applied Corporate Finance* 23:2 (Spring 2011): 8–17. Online at: dx.doi.org/10.1111/j.1745-6622.2011.00322.x

"In most instances, the avoidable fiascos resulted from flawed strategies—not inept execution." Carroll and Mui (2008)

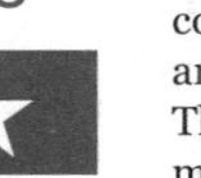

made operational. Are costs and timing consistent with the proposal? If there are deviations, can they be corrected? The second stage is monitoring the investment once it is operational. Are results what we expected, can we make improvements, and what can we learn from the experience?

CONCLUSION

Capital budgeting is the implementation of strategy, and it commits the firm to directions that are not easily changed. Best practice requires that strategy determines capital investments, not the other way round. Best practice requires a disciplined process, with the involvement of the CEO and CFO, and clear communication from proposal development through capital budgeting, funding, and monitoring.

Website:

Best practices for planning and budgeting: www.prophix.com

See Also:

★ Allocating Corporate Capital Fairly (pp. 11–12)
★ Banks and Small and Medium-Sized Enterprises: Recent Business Developments (pp. 138–140)
★ Capital Budgeting: The Dominance of Net Present Value (pp. 20–23)
★ Cash Flow Best Practice for Small and Medium-Sized Enterprises (pp. 28–29)
★ Comparing Net Present Value and Internal Rate of Return (pp. 30–32)
★ How to Set the Hurdle Rate for Capital Investments (pp. 737–739)
✔ Preparing a Budget (p. 985)
✔ Understanding the Relationship between the Discount Rate and Risk (p. 1001)
Financial Management for the Small Business (p. 1358)

NOTES

1 *Report of the President's Commission to Study Capital Budgeting*. Washington, DC. February 1999. Online at: clinton3.nara.gov/pcscb/report_pcscb.html
2 Abdelal, Rawi, Ayesha Khan, and Tarun Khanna. "Where the oil-rich nations are placing their bets." *Harvard Business Review* (September 2008): 119.
3 Peel, Michael J., and John Bridge. "How planning and capital budgeting improve SME performance." *Long Range Planning* 31:6 (1998): 848–856.
4 Carroll, Paul B., and Chunka Mui. "7 ways to fail big." *Harvard Business Review* (September 2008): 82–91.
5 Malmendier, Ulrike, and G. Tate. "CEO overconfidence and corporate investment." *Journal of Finance* 60 (2005): 2661–2700.
6 Koopytoff, Verne. "Looking beyond banks for financing." *Bloomberg BusinessWeek* (February 5, 2013).
7 Moshiinsky, Ben. "World must bridge $7 trillion long-term financing gap, G30 says." *Bloomberg BusinessWeek* (February 11, 2013).
8 Marchica, Maria-Teresa, and Robert Mura. "Financial flexibility, investment ability, and firm value: Evidence from firms with spare debt capacity." *Financial Management* 39:4 (2010): 1339–1365.

"Post-audits generally reveal that actual project costs exceed their forecasts, and actual project revenues fall short of their forecasts." Statman and Tyebjee (1985)

     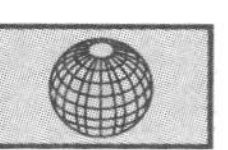   

Managing Counterparty Credit Risk by David Shimko

EXECUTIVE SUMMARY

- Counterparty risk exposure is the financial measure of performance risk in any contract.
- Many contract exposures are managed through operational or legal means; this article focuses on financial risk management.
- Counterparty credit exposure equals *current exposure* (accounts receivable minus collateral) plus an adjustment for *potential future exposure* based on possible increases in future net receivables.
- A comprehensive credit risk management policy addresses counterparty initiation and monitoring, contracting standards, credit authorities and limits, the transaction approval process, credit risk reporting, and reserving and capital policy.
- Credit risk mitigation is best handled through collateral, but there are legal and financial means to mitigate credit risk as well.
- Credit insurance can fit the exposure perfectly, but may be costly.
- Credit default swaps are linked to credit events and payments that may not correspond exactly to counterparty exposures, but may be cheaper than credit insurance.

DEFINING COUNTERPARTY RISK

Counterparty risk is the risk to each party of a contract that the counterparty will not live up to its contractual obligations; it is otherwise known as default risk.

Counterparty risk relates closely to performance risk. It arises whenever one entity depends on another to honor the terms of a contract. If a parts supplier fails to provide steering wheels to General Motors, GM will be damaged because of its inability to deliver complete cars. The resulting profit reduction is defined as the *exposure* that GM runs to its supplier. Similarly, GM runs a credit exposure to its customers who have not yet paid for their cars. This would include dealers and end customers who are financed by GMAC, GM's financing subsidiary.

Normally, performance risk is managed operationally—i.e., GM would use alternative suppliers, reserve supplies of steering wheels, and contractual nonperformance remedies to manage its performance risk. Also, to manage risk to its dealers, it may retain title to vehicles, verify insurance coverage, obtain some advance payment, and use legal means to minimize their collections risk. In addition to these counterparty risk situations, GM will experience counterparty risk from its derivative contracts.

Suppose GM wanted to purchase steering wheels on an ongoing basis from a European supplier, and protect itself from devaluation of the US dollar. It would likely enter a foreign exchange swap transaction with a bank. After entering the contract, rates would continue to change, bringing the contract in-the-money to either GM or the bank. If the dollar were to devalue, the contract would move in-the-money to GM, which would expose GM to the possible failure of the bank to honor its contract. Conversely, if the dollar were to strengthen, the bank would have an in-the-money contract with GM, and subsequently become concerned about GM's possible default risk.

MEASURING COUNTERPARTY RISK

Counterparty risk exposure can be divided into accounts receivable exposure and potential future exposure. If collateral is held as a bond for performance risk, the amount of the collateral is deducted from the gross exposure calculation. If the collateral itself is risky, such as a deposit of traded securities rather than cash, the collateral may not get full credit. Therefore, total credit exposure can be defined as follows:

Current exposure = Maximum of {Accounts receivable (A/R) − discounted collateral value} and 0

Potential future exposure = Current credit exposure + maximum likely increase in future credit exposure

The maximum likely increase in future credit exposure is defined relative to a timeframe and relative to a statistical confidence interval, typically 95%. To demonstrate this concept simply, assume a potential foreign exchange transaction as an expected value of zero with an annual standard deviation of σ, a duration of τ, and a normally distributed risk. This is illustrated in Figure 1.

Figure 1. Exposure distribution for GM

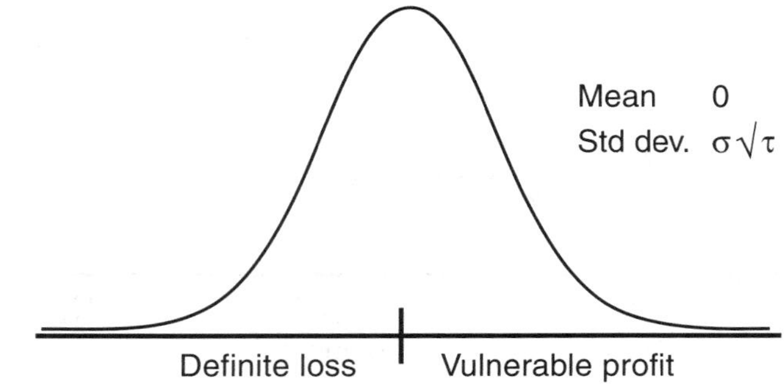

The *definite loss* shows in which cases GM will owe money to the bank, while *vulnerable profit* shows cases where the bank may owe money to GM. It is called vulnerable on account of the default risk of the bank. Although the current exposure is zero, the vulnerable profit could be as great as 1.65 standard deviations using a 95% confidence interval. This is also known as the *peak exposure*. The probability-weighted average of all the exposure figures, both zero and positive, is known as the *expected exposure*. For the normal distribution case, the expected exposure is 0.40 times the standard deviation.

To determine the expected loss conditional on default, we need to have two more pieces of information. One is the probability of default, which we will call π. The other is the *loss given default*, i.e., the percentage of the exposure that we never recover, even after settlement or bankruptcy. We call this estimate λ. Given these assumptions, we may summarize:

$$\text{Peak exposure} = 1.65\sigma\sqrt{\tau}$$

$$\text{Expected exposure} = 0.40\sigma\sqrt{\tau}$$

$$\text{Expected loss} = 0.40\pi\lambda\sigma\sqrt{\tau}$$

For example, if GM determines the euro volatility to be 15% per year, the contract to be three months in duration (0.25 years), its bank to have a default likelihood of 10%, and the loss given default to be 50%, its expected loss is (0.40 × 0.10 × 0.50 ×

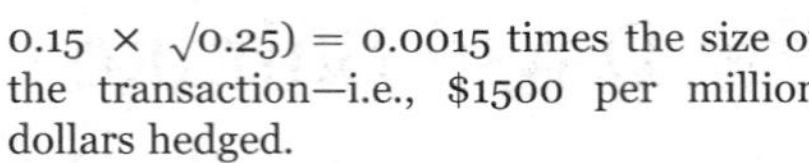

$0.15 \times \sqrt{0.25}) = 0.0015$ times the size of the transaction—i.e., $1500 per million dollars hedged.

In the case of a swap rather than a single forward transaction, the amortization of the swap payments reduces exposure over time, so that it does not necessarily rise with the square root of time. In this case, the peak and expected exposure can be determined as in Figure 2.

The peak exposure can be used to understand how much risk is being taken with respect to the counterparty, whereas the expected exposure is an indicator of expected losses.

CREDIT RISK MANAGEMENT POLICY

Best practice credit risk management policy includes the following items:

- counterparty initiation and monitoring;
- contracting standards;
- credit authorities and limits;
- transaction approval process;
- credit risk reporting;
- a reserving and capital policy.

Counterparty initiation refers to the first time a company wishes to enter a transaction with a proposed counterparty. The credit department typically reviews available public information, credit agency reports, and counterparty financials before agreeing to trade with the counterparty. The financial status of the counterparty should be continually monitored to detect proactively situations where counterparty credit quality might deteriorate. It is also important to segregate counterparties according to legal entities; trading with a subsidiary of a triple-A company may provide little or no financial protection in the event of a default. Furthermore, one should assume in general that a benefit of trading with one legal entity *cannot* be netted against a loss to another legal entity of the same firm. For example, if a company is owed $1 million by subsidiary X, and owes $1 million to subsidiary Y of the same counterparty, and X defaults, it will still have an obligation to Y.

Contracting standards refer to the types of contracts that may be entered with an appropriately initiated counterparty. For example, in most derivative contracts, a standard contract such as the International Swaps and Derivatives Association (ISDA) contract is used. Even standard contracts require customization, however. The Credit Support Annex (CSA) of the ISDA details the unilateral or bilateral collateral posting requirements of the counterparties. It also typically contains provisions for Material Adverse Changes (MAC) in the credit quality of the counterparties, perhaps calling for more collateral when credit ratings downgrade. Finally, the CSA details rules for termination of contracts—for example, upon failure to supply collateral. ISDA Master Agreements should be established to guarantee netting across different legal entities of the same counterparty.

Credit limits refer to the amount of credit risk that may be taken to approved counterparties with approved contract forms. In most firms, credit limits are set on an aggregate basis by counterparty or credit rating—for instance, the firm is unwilling to take more than $100 million in credit risk to any one bank with a AA rating.

Credit authorities refer to the ability of any individual trader or trading desk to enter into new transactions with a counterparty, considering the possible impact on current or future credit exposure. Best practice firms use some measure of *potential future exposure* in setting their credit limits, although many focus only on *current exposure*. Some firms will also set portfolio concentration limits, for example, restricting the company's credit exposure to a particular industry. In all cases, firms must establish exception policies to deal with situations where credit limits are inadvertently or deliberately breached.

Transaction approval is a verification process to ensure that, before an individual transaction is executed, all of its requirements have been met: Counterparty initiation, contracts, collateral provisions, collateral collection if applicable, and compliance with authorities and with limits. Some firms allow slack in the process, such as transactions under a given materiality threshold with an uninitiated counterparty. These are a practical consequence of business dealings, but credit risk departments should strive to minimize these occurrences.

Credit risk reporting should address credit risk across the firm, whether risk is run in treasury, procurement, or sales. Aggregate receivables, potential future exposure, and aggregate collateral should be brought together in a comprehensive report by a non-netted legal entity. Best practice reporting includes portfolio risk measures, such as aggregate credit exposure, concentrations, and sensitivity of exposure to key economic drivers.

A reserving policy for expected credit losses– to be taken as a charge against earnings and reversed if losses never materialize–should be established by the office of the chief financial officer. This practice ensures that business units are held responsible for credit risk in their contracting processes. Some firms also charge business units for credit risk usage, but practices vary considerably. As a general statement, if a firm puts a price on credit risk, then business units must ensure that the profitability of their projects includes a cost factor for the credit risk being used. In general, the formula to adjust project NPV (net present value) for credit is as follows:

$$\text{Project NPV} = \text{Starting NPV} - \text{Expected PV of credit losses} - \text{Cost of credit risk} \times \text{PV of credit risk consumed for unexpected credit losses}$$

In the marketing department, credit risk calculations are sometimes used as a determinant in product pricing. For example, credit card companies will factor expected collection costs and losses into its fee structure for retail clients.

Figure 2. Exposure of a swap

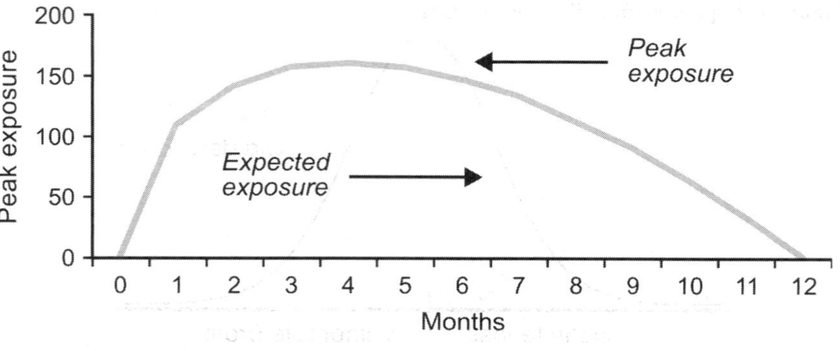

CREDIT RISK MITIGATION

The most important credit risk mitigation tool is the collection of collateral and ongoing diligence with respect to enforcing collateral requirements. This may include the threat of forced terminations for failure to provide collateral. If collateral is not an option, due to contract limitations, then there are other options.

When a company determines that it has too much exposure to a single counterparty,

"Receivables and payables by the billions become concentrated in the hands of a few large dealers who are apt to be highly leveraged in other ways as well ... It's not just whom you sleep with, but also whom they are sleeping with."
Warren Buffett

  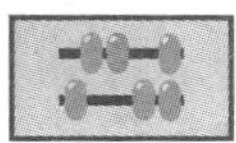      

and it is unable to collect collateral, it may undertake several actions. First, attempts may be made to close out some trading positions with the counterparty, or initiate new trading positions that have the effect of reducing the risk. Second, the company may attempt to novate a contract—i.e., reassign the contract to a different counterparty for some consideration. Third, a firm may try to "book out" a trade if it finds it has identical and offsetting trades to two different counterparties. All of these options require counterparty agreement.

Barring these operational strategies, there are two financial strategies for mitigating credit risk. One is to obtain credit insurance for the actual realized loss to a defaulting counterparty. The other is to enter a credit default swap (CDS), which is essentially a contingent payment triggered by a counterparty credit event and made by a third-party derivatives trading counterparty.

Insurance can be tailored to provide specific coverage of the actual realized loss, but because of its specificity, the insurance company margin can be seen as being excessive by some corporations. Credit default swaps can be cheaper, since they trade in broader over-the-counter (OTC) markets.

Using CDSs to manage credit risk creates three problems. First, in most trading situations, the actual exposure is variable, making it difficult to target 100% protection. Second, in CDS markets, the payment-triggering event may not correspond exactly to a counterparty's default event. For example, when Fannie Mae and Freddie Mac were put into receivership by the US government in 2008, this was classified as a default event in CDSs and synthetic collateralized debt obligations (CDOs), which were built from those CDSs—even though there was no default. Third, as we learned in 2008, CDS spreads can become extremely high and can be subject to their own performance risk, as Lehman Brothers' counterparties discovered.

OTHER CONSIDERATIONS

Contagion. Most models of credit focus on bilateral credit arrangements, without recognizing that credit relationships are multilateral. For example, GM's supplier mentioned above may depend on other suppliers for parts. While the supplier itself may be creditworthy, its own suppliers may not be creditworthy. GM may not know how vulnerable it is to its counterparty's counterparty.

Consequences. While counterparty risk is often measured in terms of the counterparty's failure, it may be the case that default by a counterparty leads to much greater damage for a company. Many financial institutions were compromised in 2008 when the credit crisis caused a domino-like effect of systemic corporate collapse. Counterparty credit risk assessment, therefore, must include all the costs of counterparty failure, including the cost of lost reputation, lower credit rating, and, in the most extreme cases, bankruptcy.

CONCLUSION

Although a relatively young discipline, credit risk management has matured rapidly. Improved risk measurement and reporting techniques paired with comprehensive credit risk policies can provide extremely effective protection against credit risk losses. The best risk management techniques are operational and legal, with collateral providing the best financial risk mitigation. Credit insurance and credit default swaps offer financial protection against default, but each at its own cost—which must be compared to the benefits of reducing the specific risk it is intended to mitigate.

MAKING IT HAPPEN

- Set a corporate policy for credit risk management that recognizes the links to financial strategy.
- Identify corporate contracts and relationships with credit or performance risk.
- Model and quantify the organization's exposure to credit losses.
- Consider operational and financial credit risk mitigation where appropriate.

MORE INFO

Books:

Saunders, Anthony, and Linda Allen. *Credit Risk Measurement: New Approaches to Value at Risk and Other Paradigms*. 2nd ed. New York: Wiley, 2002.

Servigny, Arnaud de, and Olivier Renault. *Measuring and Managing Credit Risk*. New York: McGraw-Hill, 2004.

See Also:

★ Credit Ratings (pp. 478–480)
★ Investing Cash: Back to Basics (pp. 502–504)
★ Minimizing Credit Risk (pp. 540–542)
✔ Derivatives Markets: Their Structure and Function (p. 1007)
✔ Hedging Credit Risk—Case Study and Strategies (p. 969)
✔ Managing Your Credit Risk (p. 981)

"Never cheat, but do not be soft. It is a hard world. Be harder. But, and this is the test, at the same time, obviously, a good fellow." Gerald Sparrow

     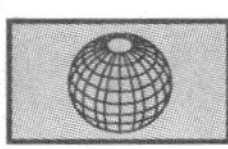   

Managing Liquidity Risk in a Financial Institution: The Dangers of Short-Term Liabilities by David Shimko

EXECUTIVE SUMMARY

- Organizations fail if they do not have access to sufficient cash to meet their short-term liabilities as they fall due.
- As long as short-term assets exceed short-term liabilities, companies face minimal liquidity problems.
- Fluctuations in margining requirements from lenders and trading counterparties can cause short-term liabilities to rise sharply, precisely when assets fall, leading to costly and sudden liquidations.
- Collateral haircuts, discretionary interest rates, and material adverse change clauses exacerbate liquidity risk.
- Ironically, lenders make "bank runs" on liquidity-stressed funds and corporations, each lender securing its own interest while collectively destroying value.
- Enron's demise was triggered by fraud, but caused by inability to manage liquidity risk.
- Financial institution bankruptcies and restructurings in 2008 were accelerated by the inability or failure to manage liquidity risk.
- Corporations must manage these risks through better contracting and precommitted contingency plans.

THE BALANCE SHEET AND SHORT-TERM LIABILITIES

The assets and liabilities of a firm can be segregated into their short-term and long-term components. Short-term assets include cash, cash equivalents, marketable securities, and marketable inventories—i.e., any asset that can be converted in a short period of time to cash. Long-term assets include assets that cannot easily be converted to cash, such as plant and equipment, reputation, good will, and the present value of future growth opportunities. Short-term liabilities include short-term debt and liabilities which can be converted to debt, such as lender margin calls and trading counterparty collateral calls. Long-term liabilities include long-term debt and equity, or other long-term funding mechanisms. The basic schematic is shown in Figure 1.

Figure 1. When short-term liabilities exceed short-term assets, to prevent bankruptcy, long-term assets must be converted to short-term assets, or long-term liabilities must be increased, with funds being used to retire short-term liabilities

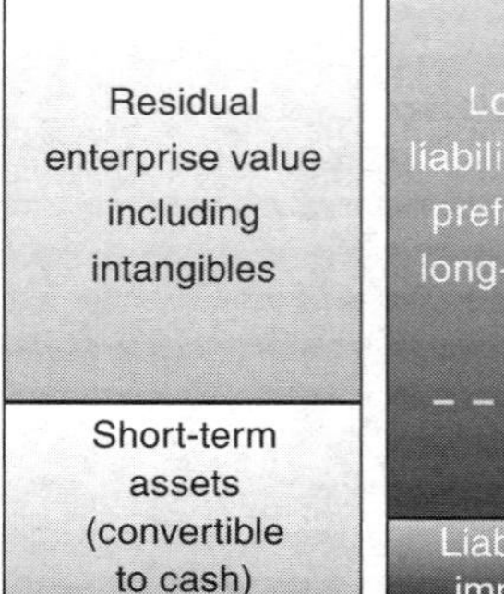

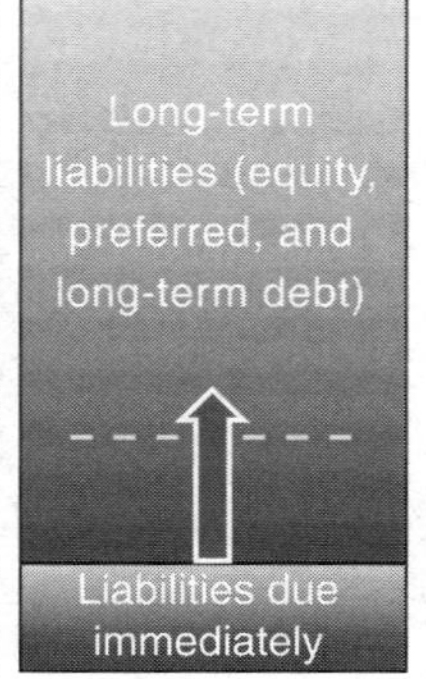

As long as short-term assets exceed short-term liabilities, companies will not have many liquidity problems, finding resources or engaging in short-term borrowing to offset liabilities as they become due. A serious problem arises, however, when short-term assets or short-term liabilities are stochastic, or unpredictably variable. In these situations, its short-term liabilities can suddenly exceed short-term assets, forcing the company to liquidate long-term assets, increase long-term liabilities, or face bankruptcy. When these events take place, the company enters "financial distress," and can find that the market for both its assets and liabilities has diminished or disappeared.

CONTRIBUTORS TO LIQUIDITY RISK

The term *liquidity risk* is meant to capture the risks to a corporation of having its short-term liability funding requirements unmet by its short-term assets. In essence, this is the risk that the company will not have sufficient cash to meet its liabilities as they fall due. *Liquidity risk* is also used to describe the risk of an increase in a security's bid–offer spread or a reduction in market depth for a traded security. The two types of liquidity risk are related yet distinct. In this article, we focus on the first definition.

Liquidity risk arises from the variable components of short-term assets and liabilities. On the asset side, security values may fall. On the liability side, lenders may make margin calls on security loans, trading counterparties may make collateral calls on repurchase agreements and over-the-counter (OTC) derivative trades, and futures exchanges may make mark-to-market cash demands. In the case of a commercial bank, when depositors demand their funds, they are converting longer-term bank liabilities into shorter-term liabilities. In a classical "bank run," the short-term liabilities exceed the available liquid assets of the bank, and the bank is forced into liquidating assets, restructuring, or going bankrupt.[1]

Therefore, liquidity risk includes the add-on losses experienced by banks and corporations as a result of failure to pay short-term liabilities. Most significantly, these losses include:

- the discount accepted by the company for selling its assets in a "fire sale";
- the increased cost of funding liabilities in a financially distressed situation;
- a reduction in the value of reputation, good will, and present value of future growth opportunities in the event of financial distress;
- the loss of all intangible corporate assets in the event of a bankruptcy.

Example Using a Margin Loan

Suppose a fund has \$100 to invest. It borrows \$100 on a margin loan and invests \$200 in securities with a 25% volatility factor. Within a month's time, if the security moves downward by \$23.74, or 11.9%,[2] the fund will receive a margin call from its lender. At the time of the margin call, the fund can either liquidate assets or increase its equity by adding cash. If it liquidates assets, it must sell an amount equivalent to the drop in the market value of the securities to pay down the debt. Once this is done, the debt and equity are balanced, and the size of the fund is reduced. This can be seen in Table 1.

If the fund addresses the margin call by bringing in additional funds equal to the drop in value of the securities, the accounts unfold as shown in Table 2. Even if the cash is used to pay down debt, the effect is not exactly the same as the first case, since the security position did not have to be liquidated in this case.

"A liquidity crisis ... may, in some cases, trigger still more downgrades. It all becomes a spiral that can lead to a corporate meltdown." Warren Buffett

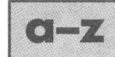

Table 1. Asset sale

Event	Assets		Liabilities	
	Securities	Cash	Loan	Equity
Before investment	0.00	100.00	0.00	100.00
Initial investment	200.00	0.00	100.00	100.00
Asset value falls	176.26	0.00	100.00	76.26
After asset sales	152.51	23.74	100.00	76.26
Pay down loan	152.51	0.00	76.26	76.26

Table 2. Equity infusion

Event	Assets		Liabilities	
	Securities	Cash	Loan	Equity
Before investment	0.00	100.00	0.00	100.00
Initial investment	200.00	0.00	100.00	100.00
Asset value falls	176.26	0.00	100.00	76.26
Call equity investment	176.26	23.74	100.00	100.00

OTHER VARIABLE SHORT-TERM LIABILITIES

Repurchase Agreements

A repurchase agreement, or "repo" amounts to using a security as collateral to obtain a loan. The counterparty sells the securities to the lender and agrees to repurchase them at a later date at a fixed price or interest rate formula, allowing the lender to earn a rate of return on the loan. The loan amount is typically less than the value of the security by a percentage *haircut*, which can be quite small for government securities or quite large for very risky securities.

Repos behave like margin loans except that the implicit leverage is much greater. Since the lender takes significant risk in these transactions, they reserve the right to change the interest rate formula, the amount of the haircut, or other credit terms to increase their margin calls when they feel it is appropriate. For example, the lender may reserve the right to increase margin calls if a counterparty's credit rating declines. Collectively, these features can lead to rapidly rising liquidity demands in times of financial distress.

Futures Margins

While futures markets can reduce price risk for those who need to hedge, many hedgers do not understand or measure the liquidity risk created by futures contracts. While trading on a futures exchange mitigates price risk for hedgers, and reduces counterparty risk, it actually increases the risk that a hedger will go bankrupt due to unforeseen liquidity demands.[3] Since those demands must be met on a one-day notice, hedgers can find themselves scrambling for funds, faced with the prospect of liquidating a losing position, selling other assets to raise cash, or finding other sources of short-term liquidity. Failing these remedies, firms that hedge may actually go bankrupt in doing so.

Futures margins may vary with prices, but exchange margin requirements can also change unexpectedly, either for individual contracts or for futures portfolios. This is an additional source of risk to futures hedgers and speculators alike.

OTC Collateral Calls

OTC derivative positions that move against a counterparty in excess of their credit lines usually require collateral to be posted. They can behave like futures margins when the derivative positions resemble futures contracts. They can also behave like repos in some cases. Therefore, all the liquidity risks affecting repos and futures apply to OTC contracts as well.

There is at least one important incremental risk associated with OTC contracts. If a firm wishes to take risk in excess of its counterparty credit lines, it will seek to spread its position over several counterparties. Normally, this would not be a problem except that the counterparties are in general unaware of the aggregate risks being taken, and thereby underestimate the firm's performance risk. Therefore, if a firm's position starts to move adversely, it can expect simultaneous collateral demands from all of its counterparties, forcing a reckoning with asset sales, liability issuance, or bankruptcy.

Many market participants have argued that the cause of Enron's demise in 2001 was due to illiquidity caused by simultaneous OTC counterparty demands. This argument was made in *The Economist*, together with an analogy to the credit crisis of 2008.

"For many people, the mere fact of Enron's collapse is evidence that Mr Skilling and his old mentor and boss, Ken Lay, who died between his conviction and sentencing, presided over a fraudulent house of cards. Yet Mr Skilling has always argued that Enron's collapse largely resulted from a loss of trust in the firm by its financial-market counterparties, who engaged in the equivalent of a bank run. Certainly, the amounts of money involved in the specific frauds identified at Enron were small compared to the amount of shareholder value that was ultimately destroyed when it plunged into bankruptcy.

"Yet recent events in the financial markets add some weight to Mr Skilling's story—though today's credit crunch creates a far more hostile environment that the one Enron faced and nobody is (yet) alleging the sort of fraudulent behaviour on Wall Street that apparently took place at Enron. The hastily arranged purchase of Bear Stearns by JP Morgan Chase is the result of exactly such a run on the bank, as Bear's counterparties lost faith in it. This has seen the destruction of most of its roughly $20 billion market capitalisation since January 2007. By comparison, $65 billion was wiped out at Enron, and $190 billion at Citigroup since May 2007, as the credit crunch turned into a crisis in capitalism."

Source: "Enron Revisited." *Economist.com* (March 18, 2008).

QUANTIFYING LIQUIDITY RISK

Any model that is used to measure market price risk can be adapted to measure margin risk. To do so, one simulates the effect of changes in market prices and the resultant impact on cash requirements in any given time period. If the simulation yields instances where short-term assets cannot pay short-term liabilities becoming due, there is a potential liquidity problem.

There are several modeling challenges, however. For example, one cannot confidently model lender behavior in increasing haircuts and lending rates. It is also difficult to model the risk of changes in one's own credit rating. Even if a firm can successfully model all three of these factors, it would be remiss without addressing the inherent correlations between them.

Finally, simulation models usually address liquidity requirements by establishing a 99% confidence interval for cash requirements. This suffers from the obvious problem that given the model, there is a 1% chance of exceeding this requirement. The less obvious problem is that the model itself may be wrong. Therefore, while it is incumbent on firms to build models for liquidity risk, they must also understand the severe limitations of these models.

MANAGING LIQUIDITY RISK

The best way to minimize liquidity risk is to negotiate it out of all lending and counterparty agreements. For example, an OTC contract may be priced by the dealer so that

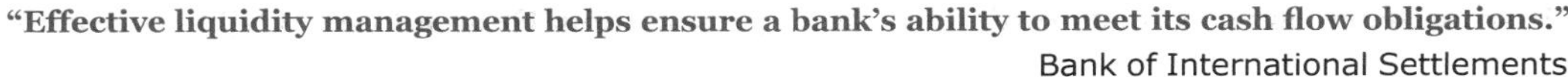
"Effective liquidity management helps ensure a bank's ability to meet its cash flow obligations."
Bank of International Settlements

  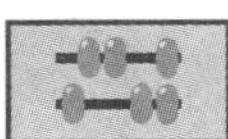   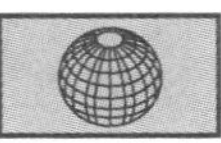   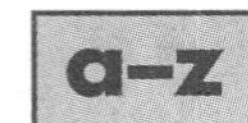

the corporate customer never has to provide collateral. Alternatively, the deal can be struck to have a maximum payout by the corporate customer that never exceeds its credit line. Companies should strive to eliminate lender discretion in setting margining terms. In recognition of the fact that this presents a greater risk for lenders, companies should expect the terms to be less favorable with these protections included.

Other effective methods for managing liquidity risk include precommitted contingent asset sales and liability issuances. One example is a line of credit, which could be established solely for the purpose of funding margin calls. Another example is an equity commitment, wherein an investor can be called to purchase equity at a price specified in advance. The importance of precommitment cannot be overstated. The bank will not offer letters of credit, and investors will not offer cheap support, in times of financial crisis.

CONCLUSIONS

Liquidity risk was a footnote in many treatments of risk management until the credit crisis of 2008. While the crisis may have been triggered by bad mortgage debt, it was accelerated and brought to a head by unanticipated cash demands that caused bankruptcies (Lehman), fund dissolutions (too many to mention), bank reorganizations (too many to list), forced sales (Bear Stearns), distress aversion (Merrill Lynch), asset sales (the original program of the US Treasury), and equity infusions (Goldman and GE Capital).

Liquidity risk comes from fluctuations in the prices of either short-term assets or short-term liabilities, or both. It is typically manifest in margin lending, futures contracts, and OTC derivative contracts. Nonprice risk factors include lender-determined haircuts, subjective interest rates, material adverse credit quality changes, "me first" credit terms, herd behavior, and market panic. As such, quantitative liquidity modeling is both critically necessary and extremely difficult. Best practice liquidity risk management takes place at the point of contracting. In the absence of contractual protections, firms need to provide precommitted solutions to solve liquidity problems. If they wait for a liquidity shortfall to occur, it is already too late to undo the damage.

MAKING IT HAPPEN

- Identify sources of potential cash demands and cash supplies.
- Develop models to quantify the risk of unknown cash demands.
- Assess the company's ability to sustain extreme cash requirements.
- If necessary, secure additional liquidity or contingent financing sources to protect against financial distress.

MORE INFO

Books:

Banks, Erik. *Liquidity Risk: Managing Asset and Funding Risks.* Finance and Capital Markets Series. Basingstoke, UK: Palgrave Macmillan, 2005.

Matz, Leonard, and Peter Neu (eds). *Liquidity Risk Measurement and Management: A Practitioner's Guide to Global Best Practices.* Singapore: Wiley, 2007.

Persaud, Avinash D. (ed). *Liquidity Black Holes: Understanding, Quantifying and Managing Financial Liquidity Risk.* London: Risk Books, 2003.

Tirole, Jean. *Financial Crises, Liquidity, and the International Monetary System.* Princeton, NJ: Princeton University Press, 2002.

Report:

Basel Committee on Banking Supervision. "Liquidity risk: Management and supervisory challenges." Bank for International Settlements, February 2008. Online at: www.bis.org/publ/bcbs136.htm

See Also:

★ How Taxation Impacts on Liquidity Management (pp. 48–49)
★ How to Assess a Company's Global Treasury Needs and Objectives Successfully (pp. 50–52)
★ Navigating a Liquidity Crisis Effectively (pp. 82–84)
★ Political Risk: Countering the Impact on Your Business (pp. 902–904)
✔ Hedging Liquidity Risk—Case Study and Strategies (p. 972)
✔ Measuring Liquidity (p. 983)
✔ Understanding and Using the Repos Market (p. 1098)
Cashflow Reengineering: How to Optimize the Cashflow Timeline and Improve Financial Efficiency (p. 1340)

NOTES

1 Arguably, the FDIC exists partially to protect US depositors, but it also protects banks by reducing the incentives of depositors to make runs on the bank.

2 This is determined by multiplying as follows: 1.645 standard deviations times the 25% volatility factor times the square root of 1/12, the number of years in one month. Given a normal distribution, 1.645 standard deviations corresponds to a 95% confidence worst case outcome.

3 For a number of examples of liquidity risk failure, see "Dangers of Corporate Derivative Transactions."

  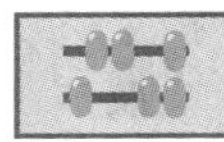   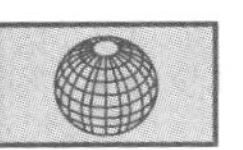   

Managing Retirement Costs by Beverly Goldberg

EXECUTIVE SUMMARY

- The large generation of baby boomers born in the years after World War II is nearing retirement age, and the generation that follows is far smaller.
- Although the aging of the workforce may not affect every business, or every area of a business, management should, at the very least, conduct demographic surveys of their workforces, discover the retirement plans of older employees, and explore the skills needed to remain productive.
- The costs of recruiting and training new workers must be evaluated and measured against the costs of programs aimed at retaining older workers to decide what approach, or mix of approaches, should be taken to ensure that major problems do not develop.
- If necessary, retention programs aimed at convincing employees with needed skills to remain longer should be put in place. Among the programs already being used across the G7 nations (with varying degrees of success) are phased retirement, flexible hours, working from home, temporary work, job sharing, and consulting.

INTRODUCTION

The industrialized nations of the world are getting grayer. In the United States some 76 million individuals, known as the baby boomers, were born between World War II and 1964, wheareas the generation that followed numbered only 66 million. One-fifth of current workers in the United States will reach retirement age by 2020, and some industrialized nations, such as Japan, are graying even faster. This means that the number of people in the workforce available to replace the boomers as they reach retirement is much smaller than the number that will be leaving the workforce. Moreover, the trend to smaller families, which means smaller populations of younger people available to employers, has been continuing (Table 1), indicating that the problem of fewer replacements for retiring workers is one that will not disappear.

Although some analysts dismiss the warning that labor shortages will be a major problem—citing increased productivity and immigration as mitigating factors—others predict that the lack of skilled workers to replace retirees, a phenomenon that is often called the "boomer brain drain," will be devastating. The truth is that the retirement of this huge cohort of workers will affect different nations, different regions within nations, different industries, and different companies in different ways.

Table 1. Fertility rates* in the industrialized nations. (*Source*: United Nations Population Division)

Country	1960	2000
Canada	3.6	1.6
France	2.9	1.8
Germany	2.5	1.3
Italy	2.5	1.2
Japan	2.0	1.4
United Kingdom	2.8	1.7
United States	3.3	2.0

*Average number of children born to a woman over her lifetime

Unfortunately, in large organizations, human resources and personnel managers—who were the first to feel the effects of this trend—have found it difficult to convince senior management of its importance, primarily because the problem is not immediate. In smaller organizations, where dealing with issues about employees may be in the hands of the finance department, the issue often does not surface as a problem, because hiring is done on an individual basis by those needing to find replacements for employees who leave. In the case of large organizations, the head of human resources should ask the CFO to help by conducting an in-depth analysis of the actual costs of an older workforce, as well as the costs of recruiting replacements. In smaller organizations, the CEO, COO, and CFO should work together to determine whether they are facing problems due to the age and composition of the workforce.

WILL BOOMER RETIREMENTS ADVERSELY AFFECT YOUR BUSINESS?

When matched to a skills survey, a demographic profile of your organization as a whole, and of specific departments and teams, will help to determine whether or not it needs to develop programs to forestall major problems. For example, in the United States, according to a recent Hay Group study, "a substantial number of mission-critical employees in the utilities industry from the executive suite down to the lineman are rapidly approaching retirement age in the next four years." As a result, according to a Hay Group spokesman, "The electric and gas industries could easily collapse if they don't put a plan in place for staffing, retention, recruitment, and training."[1] In the United Kingdom, a similar report to the Scottish Parliament indicates that there are likely to be recruitment problems in the electro-technical sector because there are not enough qualified workers to replace those who are due to retire in the next few years.[2]

In general, the companies that should be most concerned about the fact that a fifth of current workers will reach retirement age by 2020 are those that have the highest concentration of older employees, such as utilities, manufacturing, health care, and retail. All companies, however, may have certain groups of employees whose skills may not be easy to replace. Or they may have large numbers of employees in certain functional areas who may be eligible for retirement at about the same time.

So the sensible approach is to assemble a profile of the ages of the current workforce, the skills needed by workers in each job category, and the retirement plans of older workers to determine when they plan to retire, as well as what it might take to entice them to stay. At the same time, companies should examine whether younger people in the region are acquiring the skills that will be needed when older workers retire. If they find that this is not happening, companies must see what measures they can take to induce the current workforce to undertake additional skills training and to convince high school students to pursue those skills and vocational schools and colleges to provide training in them.

ASSESSING THE COSTS OF RETIREMENT

Companies facing the loss of employees to retirement must factor in the costs of hiring workers to replace those who leave when deciding how to deal with the issue of retirement. Among the costs to be analyzed are:

- lost productivity during the time it takes to find a suitable replacement;
- the costs of finding a replacement for the departing worker;
- the time needed for the new employee to adapt to the culture and become fully proficient at the job;
- ancillary costs due to productivity losses by colleagues of the retiring employee as they adjust to the departure and then to working with the new hire.

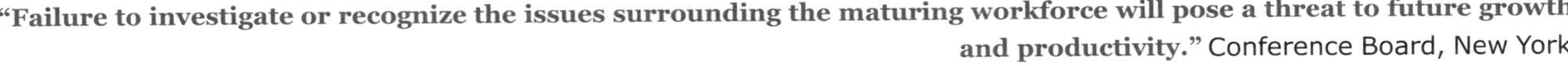

"Failure to investigate or recognize the issues surrounding the maturing workforce will pose a threat to future growth and productivity." Conference Board, New York

Measuring the costs of lost productivity during the search for a replacement requires having records (or management knowledge) of the amount of work usually completed by employees in the same position over a given period. Management then must look at the amount of work not being done by the person leaving to determine how much can be taken over by others in the department. In addition, it may be necessary to hire temporary workers from an agency to do much of the work until the replacement is found. Taken together, the loss of completed work, the overtime put in by others in the department, and the cost of temporary workers provides a measure of the costs of the lost productivity.

Analyzing the costs of finding the replacement includes examining the costs of advertising the job opening; agency fees, or bonuses for referrals from current employees; time spent by managers on interviews; and, sometimes, costs of relocation (usually for highly skilled workers).

In general, the cost of replacing an experienced worker averages about 50% of the employee's annual salary, but that proportion (and cost) rises dramatically for those with specialized skills. For example, according to *InformationWeek* magazine, "IT employee replacement costs are 2.5 times the annual salary of an IT professional leaving the organization."[3] In addition, this rule of thumb understates the cost of lost productivity when many employees in any given functional area must be replaced over a short period.

Some observers contend that the costs of replacing older workers may be largely or wholly offset by younger workers' lower pay and benefits (although that assumes that younger workers with the needed skills are available). While some costs, such as higher salaries due to seniority, more accrued vacation time, and larger contributions to pension plans (and in the United States higher health care premiums) are real, many others that are given as reasons not to retain older workers are myths.[4] For example, some claim that older workers take more sick days than younger workers. According to the US Bureau of Labor Statistics, in 2007 the absence rate of full-time workers aged 25 to 54 was 3.2 per 100, and workers aged 55 and over were absent at only a marginally higher rate: 3.6 per 100.

PROGRAMS AIMED AT RETAINING OLDER WORKERS

Solutions to the problem posed by the likelihood that large numbers of baby boomers will retire simultaneously include keeping a portion of these would-be retirees in the workforce by modifying traditional work rules. A Towers Perrin survey of workers in the G7 countries found that, while about 40% of workers over age 50 indicated that they plan to retire from their current positions in the next five years, almost the same number stated that they plan to work in some capacity after retiring from their current jobs.[5]

The same study found that almost half of workers nearing retirement find the

CASE STUDY

A Midwestern US Nursing School

One of the major causes of the general nursing shortage in the United States is the shortage of nursing faculty to train those who wish to enter the field. This shortage is the result of both the retirement of older tenured faculty and the lack of interest of nurses with advanced degrees in teaching rather than nursing, primarily because nurses with specialized skills earn more than nursing faculty.

In the case of this Midwestern state university-based nursing school, the problem was particularly severe because of the aging of the state's population: like many other states in the northern Midwest, the population in general is older, with a consequent increase in the demand for nurses. The university's board of regents asked the nursing school to increase the number of nurses they graduated each year and made available some funding for the effort.

After careful examination of the issue, a program was developed that included the following actions:

- Recruiting recently retired faculty to teach as adjuncts at a salary higher than that usually paid to part-time university faculty.
- Working with hospital administrators in the region to find out which current older nurses were planning to retire in the next two to five years because the work had become too physically demanding. These nurses were offered scholarships for advanced degrees in exchange for promises to join the faculty for a given number of years.
- Meeting with principals of high schools in the region to see whether they knew of older teachers, especially science teachers, who were planning to retire because of burnout or boredom. Such teachers were offered scholarships for degrees that would enable them to pursue a new career teaching nursing students (a more dedicated and mature student body), again in return for a promise to teach at the university's nursing school.
- Running advertisements in other regions promoting the advantages to nursing teachers of relocating to the region and offering them relocation expenses and recruitment bonuses.

Each of these approaches had some degree of success. Only a small number of new faculty were recruited as the result of seeking adjuncts and placing advertisements in other regions. However, the number of soon-to-retire nurses and teachers who applied for and were granted scholarships gives promise that the needed expansion of the faculty will occur over the next five years. The time frame is longer than expected because those who accepted are, for the most part, attending school only part time. The reason for this is that the scholarships only provide tuition and do not cover such things as living expenses.

MAKING IT HAPPEN

Because senior management often dismisses the issue of the aging of the workforce, the CFO, along with the heads of human resources and personnel, must formally evaluate the likelihood that major problems will develop and estimate the costs of programs aimed at addressing such problems. Only by presenting hard evidence will they be able to convince senior management to take action aimed at eliminating these threats to the long-term success of the business. Such evidence should include:

- a general demographic profile of employees, as well as profiles of various divisions, functional areas, and teams;
- a catalog of specialized skills and educational levels of current employees in various divisions, functional areas, and teams;
- the retirement plans of current employees, matched to their areas and skills;
- when these analyses indicate a future skills shortfall, a further analysis should be carried out to determine:
  - recruitment costs when it comes to difficult-to-replace skills;
  - the general availability of people with those skills;
  - the costs of training people in those skills;
  - the costs of various programs aimed at retaining retirees with those skills for a period of time.

"Work needs to be made a more attractive and rewarding proposition for older workers." OECD

possibility of part-time work and flexible work for their present company enticing, while a little more than a third would be attracted by the possibility of working from home. About a fourth of those planning to retire say they would stay on if they were offered retention bonuses, credits to pension benefits for delaying retirement, or the ability to collect partial pensions while working. The same proportion would be interested in returning as contractors.

Many companies that already have encountered problems due to retirements have instituted programs both to develop replacements and to hold on to some older workers, including:[6]

- training programs for younger workers who have the basics they need to acquire the specific skills that will be lost;
- mentoring programs to transfer specialized knowledge from retiring workers to younger staff;
- phased retirement policies that enable employees to reduce the number of days they work each week gradually over a period of years;
- flexible work options that would allow employees to job share (two older workers sharing a single job) or to work on a reduced schedule;
- telecommuting programs that allow people to work from home either a few days a week or full time;
- consulting and contracting arrangements that can be used to increase staff at the busiest time of the year;
- keeping in touch with retirees and offering them special bonuses for returning in some capacity after sampling retirement.

CONCLUSION

Senior managers cannot bury their heads in the sand when it comes to the issue of the approaching retirement of baby boomers, which will begin in earnest in 2010. Analyzing the possibility of shortfalls of needed skills now will give businesses time to put in place programs to prevent the loss of employees with those skills and to develop plans that will ensure that new employees with those skills will be available when needed.

MORE INFO

Books:

DeLong, David W. *Lost Knowledge: Confronting the Threat of an Aging Workforce.* New York: Oxford University Press, 2004.

Dychtwald, Ken, Tamara J. Erikson, and Robert Morison. *Workforce Crisis: How to Beat the Coming Shortage of Skills and Talent.* Boston, MA: Harvard Business School Press, 2006.

Goldberg, Beverly. *Age Works: What Corporate America Must Do to Survive the Graying of the Workforce.* New York: The Free Press, 2000.

Report:

Towers Perrin. "Perspectives of employers, workers and policymakers in the G7 countries on the new demographic realities." September 2007.

Websites:

Aging Workforce News for developments, tools, and resources for managing older workers and boomers in the workplace: www.agingworkforcenews.com

American Association of Retired Persons, now just AARP: www.aarp.org. See especially the section on employee retention: www.aarp.org/money/careers/employerresourcecenter/retention; and the Towers Perrin report listed above.

See Also:

★ Corporate Responsibility in a Global World: Marrying Investment in Human Capital with Focus on Costs (pp. 661–663)

★ Return on Talent (pp. 927–928)

NOTES

1 Hay Group. "Study says utility industry faces severe manpower shortage as majority of its workforce plans retirement": www.jobbankusa.com/news/business_human_resources/utility_industry_faces_severe_manpower_shortage.html

2 Submission by National Electrotechnical Training (NET): www.scottish.parliament.uk/business/committees/historic/x-enterprise/inquiries-01/lli-submissions/ell-010.pdf

3 Luftman, Jerry with Rajkumar Kempaiah. "Tips for recruiting and retaining IT talent." *Information Week*: www.informationweek.com/news/management/trends/showArticle.jhtml?articleID=201807942

4 Grossman, Robert. "Keep pace with older workers." *HR Magazine*: www.shrm.org/Publications/hrmagazine/PastIssues/2008/Pages/20085.aspx

5 Towers Perrin (2007).

6 Goldberg (2000).

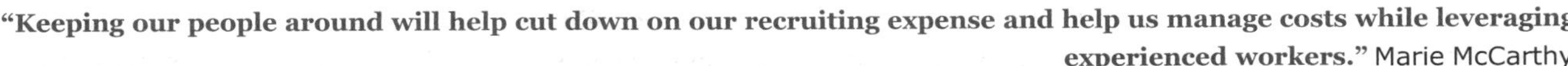

"Keeping our people around will help cut down on our recruiting expense and help us manage costs while leveraging experienced workers." Marie McCarthy

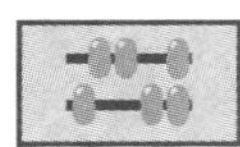

Viewpoint: Moving Away from Traditional Budgeting

by Lawrence Phillips

INTRODUCTION

Dr Lawrence Phillips, Visiting Professor of Decision Science at the London School of Economics and a director of Facilitations Ltd, is a leading expert on ways in which organizations can improve their decision-making. He has long been fascinated by the challenges associated with deciding how best to deploy limited resources across a range of possible projects and getting people to buy into the outcome—the quintessential budgeting and indeed management problem. He teaches decision science to graduates and undergraduates at the LSE and conducts training courses on decision science and facilitation skills to external organizations. His expertise is in applying a wide variety of approaches, particularly decision and risk analysis, to issues of strategic and operational management, option evaluation, prioritization, resource allocation, and crisis management. In November 2005, Dr Phillips was awarded the Frank P. Ramsey Medal for distinguished contributions to decision analysis by the Decision Analysis Society of INFORMS.

TRADITIONAL BUDGETING AND ALTERNATIVES

Every organization has finite resources and must, therefore, assign priorities to a range of possible options when allocating its budget. However, in my experience, very few organizations do this particularly well.

The traditional approach to budgeting invariably leads to "silo decisions," in which resources are allocated on a project-by-project basis. The individual judgments that are being made preclude any coherent analysis of the wider options available, often resulting in missed opportunity for the organization concerned. However, by applying the principles of decision analysis, it becomes possible to create a portfolio of options that really do make the best use of the available resources.

Budgeting is generally an exercise in balancing costs, benefits, and risks. It involves persuading a wide constituency of stakeholders to sign up to these decisions. In the process, multiple stakeholders with different agendas will compete for limited resources. A classic example is the UK government spending round, in which different spending departments slug it out for a slice of the Treasury's pie.

Resource allocations that are optimal to the individual organizational units are rarely collectively optimal, and those who are dissatisfied with the outcome can become jaundiced and resistant to implementation. In this article, I explain three current approaches to resource allocation, taken from the worlds of corporate finance, operational research, and decision analysis; the latter is one of my expertizes. I draw heavily on an earlier paper coauthored with Carlos A. Bana e Costa in 2007, entitled "Transparent prioritisation, budgeting and resource allocation with multi-criteria decision analysis and decision conferencing."

What I want to sketch out is a technical process, multi-criteria portfolio analysis, which makes it possible to balance the conflicting elements, and a social process, decision conferencing, which ensures that all relevant players are engaged in the modeling process, ensuring their ownership of the model and their satisfaction when it comes to implementation.

The essence of much decision-making, including budgeting, is that, when presented with a large number of opportunities, decision-makers have insufficient knowledge of each option to be able to make informed choices. Another problem is that the benefits associated with these opportunities are typically characterized by multiple objectives, which themselves often conflict.

A DELICATE BALANCE

What is needed is an approach that enables decision-makers to balance costs, risks, and multiple benefits; to construct portfolios of investments across different areas to ensure that collective best use is made of the limited total resource; to consult the right people in a structured, coherent way, so that their multiple perspectives can be brought to bear; and to engage with key players to ensure they are aligned with the way forward, while preserving their individual differences of approach.

That may sound a tall order. But it can be accomplished by blending a technical solution that captures the differing perspectives with a social process that engages with the people concerned. The technical solution I am suggesting is multi-criteria decision analysis (MCDA), blended with decision conferencing.

We need to distinguish between resource allocation, which is done by a manager bearing the responsibility for this allocation (ultimately the responsibility is borne by the board in a public company) and resource prioritization, which can involve input from multiple line-management functions. It is also useful to distinguish between two prioritization tasks: the appraisal of options, and the construction of portfolios. The former orders options within an area, the latter refers to the appraisal of options across multiple areas (a portfolio of options), with the aim of finding the best combination of options for a given level of resource.

The three main perspectives on portfolio resource allocation decisions are derived from the worlds of corporate finance, operations research optimization, and decision analysis. Each places a different emphasis on how benefits, costs, and risks can best be handled.

In the corporate finance perspective, it is assumed that benefits are expressed in monetary terms and that the appraisal of a project's worth is determined by calculating its net present value (NPV). One of the commonest budgeting techniques is to select from a universe of options by ranking them in terms of highest to lowest NPV, and assigning the budget to options until the resource reaches zero.

It seems logical and it is widely deployed in the finance departments of major corporations. But this approach conceals a schoolboy howler. The essence of the howler is that the method uses a simple "screen" that masks out the possibility that other budget combinations, based on a ratio of NPV over cost, will deliver far better returns.

There is no substitute, in short, for carrying out a scoring and weighting

"**Exactly 5,126 attempts to make the first bagless vacuum cleaner were failures—some catastrophic disappointments, some minor defects. It took 15 years. Prototype 5,127 was the success ... Failure is painful, but it spurs on improvement like nothing else.**" James Dyson

analysis of all the options. In all cases with finite budgets, which effectively means in all budgets, the appropriate criterion is not just a positive NPV (or highest ranking NPV), but rather the ratio of NPV to the investment cost. This is a profitability index that represents value for money.

THE BINARY KNAPSACK

Unlike the corporate finance perspective, the optimization perspective of operations research takes the "binary knapsack" approach. This casts the problem as one of maximizing the sum of the benefits of all investments subject to the constraints of the budget. Each chosen project is put into the "knapsack" and when this is full, it's full. The challenge is to fill it with the most valuable projects. The hidden "risk" in this approach is that in the real world, it is more realistic to think of the options as varying degrees of funding the projects, not as "go, no-go" alternatives for each project. In this way, allocating more resources to the more promising projects can be accomplished by spending less on the projects that are characterized by lesser opportunities.

The third perspective, decision analysis, comes in two flavors. In the first flavor, each project's risks can be modeled using "decision trees," as can the possible future decisions. Typically, NPV is used to provide a "score" with the discount rate set as "risk-free."

Why? The answer is simple and straightforward. All the uncertainties about future events are intended to be fully modeled as probabilities in the decision tree (what else is it?). This point is missed again and again, even by academics who really ought to know better.

I have lost count of the number of times that I have found people building risk into NPV discount rates in decision trees. Uncertainty about the future is better modeled by probabilities of later events, followed by downstream decisions, a true options analysis that provides expected (weighted average) monetary values as the basis for valuing the options, and, when divided by costs, providing indices for constructing portfolios.

The second flavor relies on multi-criteria decision analysis for placing values on the consequences of the options. In this way, monetary and nonmonetary values can be incorporated in the model, with common units of added-value across all the criteria. Thus, it is not necessary to use money as the common unit, easing the process of valuation. Risks here often become criteria, which many people find congenial because they think of risks as negative values rather than as probabilities.

All three approaches, financial modeling, operations research, and decision analysis, conform to the principle that the correct basis for prioritization in budgeting, the one that ensures that the best value is obtained for the available resource, is risk-adjusted benefit divided by cost.

WEAKNESS REMAINS WIDESPREAD

However, in practice, I and the coauthor of the original paper, who have amassed some 35 years of experience working with organizations between us, have not once come across an organization that really makes this principle work in practice.

What they actually do amounts to a variant of the following five steps:

1 List the projects they wish to support;
2 Determine the benefit that each project is expected to create;
3 Rank the projects from most to least benefit;
4 Associate a forward cost to each project;
5 Go down the list, choosing projects until the budget is exceeded.

In short, projects are prioritized on the basis of benefits only. It is easy to show that this does not make the best use of the budget and that choosing on the basis of the benefit-to-cost ratio is always a better way of maximizing the total benefit.

One further important point needs to be made. Insofar as future benefits are uncertain, then the benefits should be risk-adjusted. In decision theory, this is accomplished by multiplying the benefits by the probability of realizing them, a necessary step to ensure consistency of preference between projects with different benefits and probabilities of success.

To be useful to decision-makers, models need to be able to accommodate all of the following: financial and nonfinancial benefit criteria, risk and uncertainty, data, and judgment. They should also be transparent (in a way that real-option analysis, for example, most certainly is not), and should provide an audit trail which enables a review, after the fact, of how particular decisions were reached and what the underlying assumptions were. Decision analysis does all this exceptionally well.

Allow me to provide a perhaps grossly oversimplified example of decision analysis.

A tossed coin has a 50–50 probability of landing heads or tails up. If I offer you a ticket that entitles you to one toss of the coin to win £10,000, you will judge yourself to have a one in two chance of winning. A risk-adjusted view of the benefit conferred on your ticket would value it at £5,000. If we say that the ticket is transferable, it immediately has a value, probably some value less than £5,000, unless the buyer happens to be a Muggins.

How much would you sell that ticket for, trading off a potential win which you only have a 50–50 chance of securing, in return for real cash in your pocket now? The answer you give places a cash weighting on the decision, and indeed the difference between your minimum selling (or reserve) price and £5,000 gives a measure of your risk aversion. If we imagine a collection of people with a stake in the ticket, then their collective answer provides a group view of the value, which would probably be different from most of the individual views, and this gives us the basis for a decision conference. Note that the whole process builds in the possibility that the coin toss will not be favorable and so the consequence of the coin toss will turn out to be valueless in reality when that moment of truth arrives.

BUILDING CONSENSUS

Today decision conferences, where all the key players in a decision process come together to work on an issue of concern to their organization, are becoming best practice in many organizations. They create a model of their decisions, which always involves assigning values to the consequences of the options and taking account of uncertainty that the consequences may or may not occur.

It is a highly effective way of ensuring that everyone buys into the final decisions that inform a budget. Assisted by a decision conference facilitator, who is a specialist in decision analysis, and whose job it is to help people in how to think about the issues, and not what to think, the process aims to get the whole group thinking more clearly about the issues involved.

The model represents the collective view of the group at any point during its generation and modification, and serves as a way of examining the impact of differences in perspective or vagueness in the data. Everyone should understand the formation of the model as it is constructed, so that they can see and understand the impact of their own participation in it. In practice, we have discovered that decision conferences are a tremendous way of getting organizations to think creatively and to move away from merely pumping resources into maintaining or slightly adjusting the status quo.

It generally takes around two weeks for senior staff to digest the results of the decision conference fully. For larger problems, a sustained workshop approach is often required, utilizing several decision conferences along with workshops, interviews, and individual meetings. But one outcome is certain—better decisions, and decisions in which the participants really believe, will be achieved.

"Sex and taxes are in many ways the same. Tax does to cash what males do to genes. It dispenses assets among the population as a whole." Steve Jones

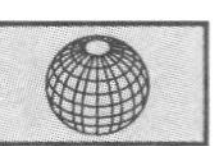

Navigating a Liquidity Crisis Effectively

by Klaus Kremers

EXECUTIVE SUMMARY

- Liquidity crises are usually the symptoms of underlying strategic and operational crises that must be tackled to avoid repeated cash crises.
- The levers to address liquidity crises are not just operational and financial but also behavioral.
- CFOs must recognise the liquidity crisis and communicate openly to crucial stakeholders as a first step; they need to build trust with current and new financing stakeholders by producing a predictable rolling liquidity forecast.
- Cash constraints can be addressed by collecting and controlling existing cash, reducing net working capital, and restructuring the balance sheet.
- The control of cash requires very conservative cash authorizations and aggressive control from the financial team on all operations.
- Reducing net working capital is a well-known source of cash, but requires care to avoid deteriorating relationships with clients or suppliers.
- Restructuring the balance sheet is a medium/long-term solution. It mainly involves selling assets and raising/refinancing debt and/or equity.

INTRODUCTION

Until 2007, debt had become very cheap and accessible. Most companies sharply increased their leverage. In Germany, for example, the net-debt-to-EBITDA ratio extremes moved from around 3 in 2002 to around 7 in early 2008. However, a downturn in company performance or an external financial crisis—where lending becomes scarce and borrowing expensive—can make this approach risky.

WHAT IS A LIQUIDITY CRISIS?

A company's liquidity is its ability to quickly pay off its short-term debts as they fall due, and still have enough cash to keep operating. Liquidity crises can be broadly split into company-specific crises, and those driven by external factors—by market or general economic changes. In both cases, the company experiences a loss of investor confidence, making it difficult to raise further cash. If the company has insufficient cash reserves, it can very quickly run into serious difficulty. A familiar vicious circle takes hold, where a company cannot pay its debts because it has no funds, but cannot raise funds as its financial difficulties result in the downgrading of its debt.

HOW TO RESPOND TO A LIQUIDITY CRISIS

Once a company finds itself struggling to meet its short-term obligations, it needs to urgently access sources of cash, both internal and external. The following five-step approach covers the key elements of any response:

1. Tackle the Root of the Crisis

Normally, a liquidity crisis is only the last symptom of pre-existing root issues such as strategic or profitability crises (for example, losing one key customer contract, misalignment of product portfolio and market, a company overstretching itself by entering too many markets). A liquidity crisis needs to be addressed right away, but ignoring the crisis' root causes will merely postpone the next liquidity crisis. In these times of urgency, the support of external advisers can bring highly needed extra resources, experience of crisis management, and an independent perspective.

2. Be Honest

It is essential that a company is honest about its current situation, and creates a climate of transparency. It must comply with any regulatory requirements to inform the market, which can be applicable to listed companies. A CFO only has one chance to put things right with the banks:

- Give an honest assessment of the situation;
- Communicate appropriate information to all stakeholders; banks, shareholders, employees, suppliers, credit insurers, etc. so as not to mislead, or make fraudulent misrepresentations. Be sure to present an accurate picture of the current situation; account for all received bills (from experience, purchase ledgers do not include all received invoices, with many invoices hidden in staff drawers).

3. Gain or regain trust

Regaining the trust of banks, shareholders, and other stakeholders is a prerequisite to maintaining, or raising external funding. This requires communicating robust and realistic plans, delivering on these plans and building relationships.

- The main tool for trust building is a bullet-proof rolling liquidity forecast on which you will deliver (see Rolling Liquidity Forecast).
- In a liquidity crisis, a company's usual banking relationship can be replaced by a workout banker with different expectations and greater experience of liquidity crises.

4. Harvest Cash

There are three main ways to improve cash position:

1. Collect and control existing cash
2. Reduce working capital
3. Restructure the balance sheet

4.1. Collect and control existing cash

Companies usually have large amounts of cash spread across business entities and regions:

- Know where the cash is and who is responsible for it;
- Establish cash pooling: minimise cash held by operational entities (no cash constraint on operational entities means no tough cash discipline);
- Make managers ask for cash if they want to spend;
- If the company has one main bank lender, try to keep all the company's cash within this bank, to increase transparency.

4.2. Reduce net working capital

Working capital reduction obviously uses three levers: receivables, inventories, and payables. Keep some key points in mind while reducing working capital:

- Fix a deadline for finalizing collection and deciding on write-offs for receivables;
- Promptly claim refunds of taxation, if due;
- Reduce inventories by both reducing replenishment of production inventories, and by selling low-rotation inventories to generate cash;
- Be careful when extending payment conditions for suppliers, and keep in touch with the credit insurer—if they pull the cover, the company would have to prepay its suppliers, with disastrous consequences for its liquidity.

The potential for reduction in working capital is also very much industry-specific, depending on the make-up of the industry's working capital requirements. For example:

- The construction industry has far greater potential for cash realization (up to 20%

"CFOs live and die by liquidity. While CEOs may be able to talk themselves out of their strategic miscalculations, CFOs do not survive the loss of a company's liquidity." Klaus Kremers

of working capital employed) than the oil and gas industry (far less than 10% of working capital employed).

- This difference is from the type of long-term contracts normally used in the construction industry, creating significant work in progress and inventory balances.

4.3. Restructure balance sheet

Restructuring the balance sheet is a medium/long-term option, and usually involves third parties. Three main approaches exist:

1 *Reduce investments*: short-term solution of freezing or cancelling investments:
   - Before freezing expenditures, critically analyze impacts on future earnings;
   - Investments should be modular as far as possible, so that if a project is curtailed or postponed, the investment already made is itself still viable;
   - The cash return on investment should be a maximum of three years for generic industries (longer for asset intensive industries).

2 *Sell fixed assets*: medium/long-term solution. A liquidity crisis gives the opportunity to redefine the core businesses and sell non-core activities:
   - Selling assets always takes much longer than planned—consider it an upside rather than part of the main solution;
   - Within the core business, consider the sale and leaseback of assets.

3 *Raise debt and/or equity*: medium to long-term solution. This approach may seem the easiest solution, but at the end of 2008, banks reduced credit lines, and stock markets closed to capital increases.

4 Following the aforementioned steps will better enable the company to raise finance in the future. Remember, too, that keeping the supplier insurers on side and informed indirectly generates a source of credit through creditor balances.

5. Manage Cash Sustainability

Finally, a company needs to ensure a sustainable liquidity position. As mentioned above, strategic and operational root causes for the last crisis must be understood and tackled to avoid reoccurrences of liquidity crises; then companies can implement the following techniques to keep control of liquidity:

- Implementation of KPI-based management that includes liquidity and capital tied-up indicators.
- Active risk management of the business, including operations, legal contracts, financing decisions and structure, investments, and image/reputation. For example, a European pharmaceutical company lacking cash flows decided to finance a €80m factory with short-term loans. Due to poor performance, banks decreased the credit facility, causing a liquidity crisis which forced the company to restructure.
- Change of the company culture:
  - Encourage staff to take care of the company's cash as if it were their own;
  - Encourage realistic forecasts and planning: use scenario modelling techniques to limit future surprises;
  - Change employees' incentivization (long-term focus).
- Ongoing communication with internal and external stakeholders to further build trust and confidence.
- Continuous implementation of a "tool box" of operational measures to optimize cash management, working capital, and information accuracy.
- Further operational, financial and strategic flexibility to enable the company to react early and quickly once issues become apparent.

CASE STUDY

Roland Berger

- A mid-sized mechanical engineering company with assets of €500m was in a liquidity crisis following two years of losses. External funding sources had dried up due to poor performance. Our project focused on generating cash from internal sources. A team of four consultants released €51m cash in around six months. The methods used for extracting cash included:
- In the first two months:
  - Putting a cash control and liquidity plan put in place
  - Selling raw materials back to suppliers (€6m)
  - Postponement of non-essential projects (€4m)
  - Review of accounts receivable (€16m) and accounts payable (€2m)
- Over the course of the next four months:
  - Cash pooling across sites
  - Giving site managers targets for raising cash – further cut in inventories (€12m)
  - Operational and strategic restructuring defined and implementation started, for example loss making activities identified and plans put in place for site and product rationalizationIn the first 12 months, an additional €11m of liquidity was generated through asset disposal, as well as sale and leaseback of fixed assets. Short-term measures allowed the company some breathing space to enable it to find an investor; longer-term measures provided the negotiation basis for the entry of an additional investor. The company is now trading profitably and has a new investor, brought in on reasonable terms.

MAKING IT HAPPEN

A few dos and don'ts that management should bear in mind during a liquidity crisis:

Do

- Announce problems early and honestly to all relevant stakeholders.
- Build and monitor a reliable rolling liquidity forecast.
- Develop an action plan early on to demonstrate control of the situation.
- Empower managers to look for potential to extract cash in their areas from the bottom up.
- Maintain regular and open contact with external stakeholders.
- Be honest with employees and involve them in the process.
- Perform financial restructuring in conjunction with operational restructuring.
- Always prepare for the worst: in a crisis situation the worst case is always the real case.

Don't

- Ignore the situation hoping that things will turn themselves around.
- Look for profit instead of liquidity: avoid paying early for cash discounts, and collect value adjusted receivables rather than keep your write-offs down.
- Throw good money after bad: accept sunk cost rather than continuously burn new cash.
- Forget to include an additional buffer for peaks in cash requirements in your liquidity forecast: there will always be unexpected events, and most will hit you.
- Stop spending and investing completely: do not risk a complete breakdown of operations.
- Look for perfect solutions: take a practical approach, and react quickly to avoid rumours spreading and a domino effect.

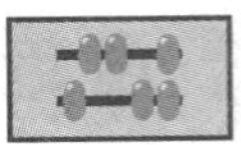

ROLLING LIQUIDITY FORECAST

- This is not "just another financial report": it shows where your company liquidity is—and will be—when negotiating with external and internal parties.
- All departments communicate their cash impacts (purchasing, sales, operation/investment, etc) and are responsible for impacts and timing.
- Obviously, take into account business seasonality and a reasonable buffer. Avoid surprises, as one cannot ask twice for an extension of credit lines: the CFO's credibility would not survive.
- The frequency with which the forecast is updated depends on the liquidity stretch: daily rolling liquidity plans are usual during periods of high crisis.
- Carrying out these simple steps properly will put the company in favourable light with banks: a Roland Berger study showed that only 30% of companies with a liquidity crisis have implemented a rolling liquidity forecast.

CONCLUSION

The outlined approach to a liquidity crisis describes the worst-case scenario. In less severe cases, not all levers need to be utilized. Even in good times, however, the best companies are already using most of these tools.

MORE INFO

Books:

Blatz, Michael, Karl-J. Kraus, and Sascha Haghani. *Corporate Restructuring: Finance in Times of Crisis.* New York: Springer, 2006.

Graham, Alistair. *Cash Flow Forecasting and Liquidity.* Chicago, IL: AMACOM, 2001.

Websites:

Association of Corporate Treasurers, contingency planning: www.treasurers.org/contingencyplanning

Roland Berger, restructuring: www.rolandberger.com/expertise/functional_issues/restructuring

Turnaround Management Association: www.turnaround.org

See Also:

★ How Taxation Impacts on Liquidity Management (pp. 48–49)
★ How to Assess a Company's Global Treasury Needs and Objectives Successfully (pp. 50–52)
★ Managing Liquidity Risk in a Financial Institution: The Dangers of Short-Term Liabilities (pp. 74–76)
✔ Managing Working Capital (p. 980)
✔ Measuring Liquidity (p. 983)
✔ Options for Raising Finance (p. 1081)
✔ Understanding Key Performance Indicators (p. 1180)

"Lack of money is the root of all evil." George Bernard Shaw

Payment Factories: How to Streamline Financial Flows by Chris Skinner

EXECUTIVE SUMMARY

- The world's largest businesses and their banks have been bringing their major global payments structures together into a rationalized, single platform known as a "payment factory."
- This platform is not a single system, but a single payments application that runs across multiple centers around the world.
- These payment factories replace the previously disparate, fragmented, and nonintegrated payments applications that businesses ran historically, whereby every country had its own system and operation.
- The aim is to gain the efficiencies and cost savings that such global integration can deliver through economies of scale, alongside fault-tolerant, mission-critical operations because each technical center now provides a real-time backup to the others.
- The single payments platform also allows all payment transactions and currencies put through it to be managed globally in real time, which helps greatly with managing a firm's cash position, liquidity, and risk.

INTRODUCTION

During the past few years, banks and their clients have been consolidating their payments infrastructures into single, global platforms. Payment consolidation helps to overcome the issues of fragmentation between systems that have been set up over the years. For large international banks and businesses in particular, having duplicate systems in different geographies just does not make sense. As a result, international banks and companies have been transforming their back-office operations with streamlined services based on refreshed processes and the latest technologies.

THE CHALLENGE

When you consider any large bank or global corporation, you think of multiple operations in multiple countries. Now think of a business and how it began, and you will probably think of one office in one town. There lies the challenge for any business: How can it grow operations effectively?

Growth may require new offices in new locations with new staff, and throughout the 20th century it often meant implementing more robust systems to handle payroll, general ledgers, and general office support. The problem is that, as the business expands, managers are forced to implement hundreds of systems to handle payments. The systems are often incompatible because they have been implemented at different times, to handle different currencies, and in different countries with differing tax regimes over a long period of time.

In the payments world, there are also many payment instruments and processes, covering cash, checks, and electronic payments, as well as accounts payable and receivable, with all of these differing domestically and internationally. This is why historically the payments world has been such a mess for multinational businesses—a mess of payments practices, processes, and systems, across the world.

THE SOLUTION

Over the past decade, many firms have decided to rationalize their payment infrastructures and to consolidate all of their payment applications, systems, and services into a single, global platform. This has been prompted by a range of factors, including the increasing costs and risks of regulatory exposures created by Sarbanes–Oxley.

A single, global platform does not mean a single computer, as that would create too much risk exposure should such a system fail. It means bringing together all the payments for a function or instrument, such as all cash management, into a single application. This application will often operate on three or more physical computer sites globally, with each site copying the others to replicate all data and applications. The result is that one has a single view of the data on a single application, working in real time, with fault tolerance and backup across systems in case any of the physical operations fail.

Banks and financial departments call this a payments factory. The phrase is a loose term that covers the rationalization and consolidation of a payment service into these global hubs. The aim is to have a single track of payments for invoices, purchase orders, payroll, cash management, and more, that can be easily managed, tracked, and changed regardless of where these are happening.

WHAT IS IMPLEMENTED?

There are many suppliers of payments factory services in the technology industry. The usual method of implementing such a capability is to analyze what a firm has in place today, and then put into play a rationalization plan. This plan would normally be based on putting in place a new payments platform as the first global hub near the firm's home office. The reason is that this makes the first project highly controllable, with the firm's main resources and expertise available.

The reason for it being near the home office, rather than within head office, is due to the risks of changing all the key payments applications: invoicing, purchase orders, receivables, payroll, and so on. These are all applications that are fundamental to an organization's financial health, and therefore nothing should be changed too fast. A typical project runs for 18 to 24 months.

Once this is achieved, however, the rationalization can be started much more rapidly because the risks are now known and controllable. Change can therefore be implemented reasonably rapidly thereafter.

Within this context, it should be borne in mind that not all implementations are the same. In some instances, firms will replace their local system with an approved corporate package, which is integrated across the network into the head office, to ensure that a single view of payments data is available. In other instances, some businesses will take out the local payments system and use networking services to allow local business users to access the payments hub in their nearest regional hub center.

In all implementations in a business context, one of the primary drivers for making the changes from local payment systems to a global payment factory is to control payment inflows and outflows more effectively so as to reduce costs. Another driver is to gain efficiencies through removing fragmented and incompatible systems, ensuring that there is a single and consistent approach worldwide that is compliant with regulations.

In the context of removing costs, one of the biggest cost-reducing factors is the ability to work closely with a bank. As mentioned, many corporations have local currency systems with differing tax implications. The result is that most businesses have a different bank in every country of operation. In part, this has also been due to the lack of availability of global banking

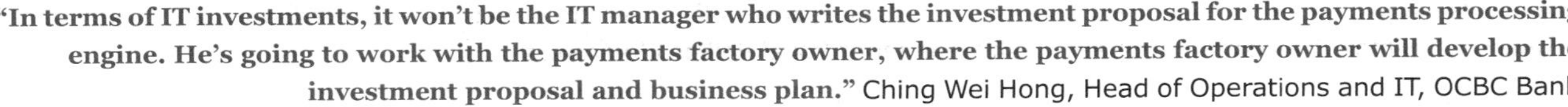
"In terms of IT investments, it won't be the IT manager who writes the investment proposal for the payments processing engine. He's going to work with the payments factory owner, where the payments factory owner will develop the investment proposal and business plan." Ching Wei Hong, Head of Operations and IT, OCBC Bank

services, but today, with HSBC, Deutsche Bank, Citibank, JPMorgan, and others offering globalized account services, this is possible.

Therefore, as another key part of the change process, corporations will work closely with a global bank partner in their implementation of a payments factory, as illustrated by P&O and others. The reorganization undertaken by Philips is described in the case study that follows. The importance of a strong banking partner in this context cannot be underestimated. For example, just as a technology firm understands the technological requirements of change, a bank understands payment processes, practices, and instruments. With the right bank partner working with the corporation, moving all payment instructions from a smaller, local bank to a global facility becomes routine. The bank will take over most of the responsibilities of making the transition.

The result is that a company can reduce its bank accounts throughout the world from hundreds down to just a few, although it is worth noting that most corporations will rarely consolidate all global payments to a single bank partner as they do not want to be exposed to a single dominant bank for fees and charges purposes. In other words, they like to maintain some form of competitive relationship with banks.

WHAT NEXT?

After the implementation of a payments factory, which focuses on consolidation, costs savings, and a centralized platform, most firms develop more sophisticated functions of risk management. This means that new processes and functions are integrated into the core system, for example real-time cash management reporting. This requires even more focus on technology, as the integration required across many different systems, formats, and services—both internal and external, including the banks—is considerable.

Therefore, most firms would partner with technology organizations, and possibly their number one global bank partner, to implement this range of services. Following this, the more information services and reporting a corporate can provide to its treasury, finance, and end-user population the better.

CASE STUDY

Philips

gtnews reported Philips' major reorganization of disparate systems into a single payments factory between 1998 and 2004.[1] In 1999 the first replacement system was implemented near Philips' main office at Eindhoven in the Netherlands. In the second year 40 sites were replaced, and in the third year a further 100. In each instance, replacing the local facilities did not necessarily entail removal of their payment systems. Six years after the project's commencement, 630 sites around the world had migrated to the new global payments factory platform, which was processing 70,000 payments per month.

A range of benefits was gained from consolidating payments into a payments factory. For example, it is believed that a typical company with annual revenues of around $1 billion would save over 1% of its costs per year (i.e. $10 million per annum through such consolidation. Certainly, the Philips case study bears this out, with savings of around 50 staff, bank fees and netting fees down by almost €7 million per annum, and systems maintenance savings of around €1 million per annum.

Other benefits include:

- Real-time management of all cash and netting positions.
- An accurate picture of risk and liquidity.
- Improved bank relationships and transaction management.
- More effective negotiation of cross-border positions and currency transactions.

MAKING IT HAPPEN

Any organization considering the implementation of a payments factory should take the proven path of consolidation by following these steps:

1 Consider the costs of processing payments based upon the range of systems and processes involved and discuss with senior management the rationale for maintaining such a range;
2 Agree to move towards a payments factory approach and invite key providers of such services to discuss what would be involved;
3 Based upon the firms you invite to discuss this with your firm, identify up to six organizations that may be appropriate to deliver a payments factory solution;
4 Ask each firm to outline the approach they would take and then invite two or three to prepare a formal proposal;
5 Review each proposal and ensure that:
   a they clearly articulate how they will identify the global structure of payments processes across the corporation;
   b they explicitly identify how they will audit the systems, software and platforms involved including their age, resilience and compatibilities, or incompatibilities;
   c the benefits and issues of consolidation are clear;
   d you are comfortable they can do the job and have strong references to prove they have worked with similar organizations to your own.

As long as all of the above are clear and proven, select an organization to work with and make it happen.

MORE INFO

Book:

Skinner, Chris. *The Future of Finance after SEPA*. Chichester, UK: Wiley, 2008.

Websites:

Financial Services Club (UK): www.fsclub.co.uk
Financial Services Club blog: www.thefinanser.com
gtnews.com—treasury and finance network: www.gtnews.com
PaymentsNews.com: www.paymentsnews.com

NOTE

1 Capachin, Jeanne. "Implementing a payments factory at Philips." gtnews (November 15, 2004). Online at: www.gtnews.com/article/5678.cfm

"One of the objectives was to achieve one way of working across the product divisions, simplifying accounts payable processes." Simon Braaksma, European Cash Manager at Royal Philips Electronics

Pension Schemes: A Unique and Unintended Basket of Risks on the Balance Sheet by Amarendra Swarup

EXECUTIVE SUMMARY

- Pension schemes are often the most overlooked part of a company's balance sheet, despite the large hidden and complex risks they can pose. Some of the unique risks within pension schemes are exposure to interest rates, inflation, market risk, and longevity.
- The problem is particularly acute for defined-benefit pension schemes—common in many developed countries—where the benefits are predetermined, are often index-linked, and can be passed on to dependents. The present cost of bearing these risks has risen sharply in recent decades, and many companies have closed their pension schemes to new members.
- In the short term, changing economic, financial, and demographic perceptions can materially alter the valuation of a pension scheme's assets and liabilities from one day to the next, potentially leaving many finance directors with an uncontrolled liability on otherwise well-managed balance sheets.
- The waters can be muddied further by another fundamental problem: for most schemes, liabilities are calculated infrequently using ad hoc or out-of-date assumptions, which can often present a less than prudent valuation of the true costs.
- Options to manage and even reduce these uncertainties are now appearing. The key is to have a proactive and realistic approach to the risks that are being carried on the balance sheet.

INTRODUCTION

The only function of economic forecasting, the late American economist J. K. Galbraith once noted, was to make astrology look respectable. And, knowingly or not, it's a belief that's endemic in the corporate world.

The overriding concern is to find the hidden value in companies—whether in their balance sheet or in their intellectual property—and extract it in the most efficient way possible. Every financial and operational risk is carefully studied and, where possible, mitigated. Lines of credit are negotiated at known terms to suit the company's horizon. Capital structures are continually redrawn to maximize efficiency. Balance sheets are scrutinized line by line and operations are streamlined.

There is no obsession with predicting GDP, or agonizing over the evolution of the labor market over the next decade, for example. No, these are all nebulous questions for economic forecasters to ponder. For the seasoned financial director, the wider economy only matters insofar as it affects that all important cash flow.

Yet, hidden in that otherwise well-managed balance sheet might be a host of unconstrained liabilities that threaten to undo the most meticulous business plan and expose companies to a whole host of unknown risks—all housed within an often overlooked pension plan.

The problem is particularly acute for defined benefit schemes—occupational schemes where the pension benefits are fixed in advance and are often calculated as a proportion of an employee's final salary. Many include provision for dependents such as widows, and can even be indexed to inflation. These proved to be enormously popular in the aftermath of the Second World War, when many companies saw them as an effective way to defer compensation for workers to future years. However, these schemes placed a host of unintended and poorly understood risks with the sponsoring employer, such as exposure to longevity, to future interest rates, and to the capricious whims of financial markets.

In recent decades, as companies found themselves confronted with declining employment and a growing retiree problem, the present cost of bearing these risks has escalated sharply, and many have closed their pension schemes to new members. Furthermore, pension schemes and, in some jurisdictions, their associated health-care liabilities, are increasingly a growing factor in corporate finance transactions.

A potentially attractive merger or acquisition may become unstuck because of the pension fund, or, worse still, an existing company may hit difficulties as the full cost of the pension obligation becomes known. The abortive takeover of Sainsbury's in the United Kingdom and the well-publicized troubles at General Motors in the United States are but the most visible tip of the proverbial iceberg, and are indicative of a problem that can consign businesses to a slow decline.

But more than just eroding stockholder value in the present, defined benefit schemes are also a danger to a company's long-term survival in an increasingly competitive global economy. Many management teams now face the problem of maintaining a set of financial commitments made in another era, when assumptions and expectations were vastly different. These commitments are difficult to measure—let alone anticipate—and they are tied to the health of the corporate sponsor of the pension fund, which is legally required to underwrite any deficit. If the company does go under, the responsibility of meeting at least part of these liabilities may then be transferred to governments and taxpayers. This may create additional problems, as pension scheme members will likely receive reduced benefits, and the addition of significant numbers of liabilities to the government balance sheet is eventually likely to become politically unpalatable.

A GROWING PROBLEM

Anyone who doubts the potential scale of the problem only has to look at the case of the American Civil War veterans' pension fund—one of the earliest defined benefit schemes. Originally set up during the war to pay pensions to disabled veterans, the scheme was gradually extended to include all veterans and their dependants, making its final payment only in 2004—nearly 140 years after the war ended. By then, the scheme had cost the US government hundreds of billions in today's dollars, and at its peak in the early 1890s, it had even constituted over 40% of the annual federal budget.

It's a stark warning for many pension schemes and their corporate sponsors today.

Any views on interest rates over the next decade? Your debt financing may have excellent terms, and it may seem a moot point, but the pension fund's liabilities and their associated accounting costs will swing violently over the next few decades with movements in the prevailing interest rates. By some estimates, the drop in long-term interest rates from 1999 to 2002 increased the value of pension liabilities by 30–40%.

How about inflation—any thoughts on how it might evolve over the next half century? Many scheme members, particularly in the United Kingdom, have index-linked pensions, and the burden of payments can quickly become onerous. Figures from the UK's Office for National Statistics show that from 1970 to 2007, annual employer contributions to pension schemes

went up a factor of 53, and they trebled over the last seven years alone of that period (Figure 1). Wage inflation too can rapidly push up costs.

And what about people living longer? For individuals and society, increased longevity is desirable, but living longer can often also create large unanticipated costs. Ever since German Chancellor Otto von Bismarck thought he'd pulled off a politically brilliant move back in 1889, by promising pensions at 70 when the average German lived to less than 50 years of age, the continual improvements in life expectancies have rapidly unraveled the best-laid pension plans. Even more troubling, the current upward trend shows little sign of leveling off, and it is increasingly clear that this is the most significant risk to the finances of pension schemes and their sponsors. The rising life expectancies for males and females in the United Kingdom are shown in Figure 2.

In a field typified by extremes, the case of Jeanne Calment is a situation that's humorlessly reminiscent of reality for many pension schemes. When Madame Calment's lawyer agreed in 1965 to pay her an annual income worth one-tenth of the value of her flat on the understanding that he would inherit the property on her death, it seemed like a shrewd bargain. Madame Calment was then 90 years old, and it seemed unlikely that she had much longer to go on this particular journey. Unfortunately, bearing testament to perhaps one of the most misjudged investment decisions ever, Jeanne went on to live to the ripe old age of 122. Along the way, she also became the oldest rap artist ever, releasing an album at 121, but that is unlikely to have provided much consolation to her poor aforementioned lawyer. By then, he was long dead and his widow was still making the payments.

THE DANGERS OF VOLATILE MARKETS

It's a complex basket of risks and, in the short term, changing economic and demographic perceptions can materially alter the valuation of a pension scheme's liabilities from one day to the next. Even the assets are not immune, as many pension schemes have more than half their assets in equities—a consequence of their long-term perspective, adherents argue. In the short term, however, volatility in the markets can materially alter the valuation of a pension scheme from one day to the next. It's a headache for many finance directors, who are left with an uncontrolled liability on otherwise well-managed balance sheets.

It becomes extremely difficult under these circumstances to determine the ability of a defined benefit pension scheme to pay its annuities 40 years down the track. Throw in the increasingly common belief that the economic environment in the coming years is likely to be far less favorable than in recent years, and increased volatility seems inevitable.

In early 2008, for example, Aon Consulting estimated that sharp falls in the FTSE caused UK pension schemes to lose $60 billion in just a single week, wiping out all the gains made in 2007. More worryingly for companies, equity markets have declined significantly since their highs in mid-2007. Given that these companies are often older, and therefore have a much greater role as pension sponsors than the percentage of market capitalization that they represent, sponsor risk is also an increasingly major concern across the board.

It's a growing headache for many firms, for whom such risks often lie far from familiar territory and who are charged with looking after a broad church of stakeholders, not just pensioners. Though the increased pension fund liabilities are often longer term than most corporate horizons, they must be carried on the company's balance sheet, reducing net asset value and increasing financial leverage. As the corporate sponsor, they generally also have an obligation to fund at least part of these unexpected costs, giving them an uncertain command over their own cash flow and reducing future distributions to investors. The impact can go far beyond the immediate cash flow hit—filtering through to the P & L, lowering profits, hurting competitiveness, and, ultimately, even impacting the share price.

In the case of General Motors, for example, net obligations are estimated to be about $170 billion across all of GM's US operations, dwarfing its current market cap of $3 billion. To meet its soaring obligations, the company contributed an astonishing $30 billion to its US pension plans in 2003 and 2004, but the accounts are still tens of billions of dollars in deficit. Now, pension and healthcare costs make up more of the average GM vehicle's price tag than the steel used to build it. Consequently, the company is inexorably losing ground to a wave of foreign competitors with lower cost bases and less debt on their balance sheets—resulting in a catastrophic decline in stock price for investors, from $55 in January 2004 to under $10 today.

MUDDY WATERS

The waters are muddied further by another fundamental problem. For most schemes, liabilities are calculated infrequently, using out-of-date longevity assumptions and ad hoc discount rates, and often presenting a less than prudent valuation of the true costs of delivering pensioners full financial security. As people live longer—15 minutes more for every passing hour by some estimates—and accounting standards move more toward valuing balance sheets on a mark-to-market basis, the immediately calculable costs can rise dramatically as outdated assumptions are revised.

Many pension schemes value their liabilities by using a discount rate that is implicitly linked to the assumed return on their assets. The problem is that they are effectively banking on an uncertain set of future gains to pay off their obligations to millions of current and future pensioners. Even worse, the discount rates vary from scheme to scheme. Some may choose a point in time and a single discount rate for all their liabilities, while others may choose to be more sophisticated and look at evolving discount rates over time. Regardless, most discount rates are ultimately linked to AA-rated corporate bond yields—the result of an

Figure 1. Increasing life expectancy in the United Kingdom for 65-year-olds. (*Source*: Office for National Statistics)

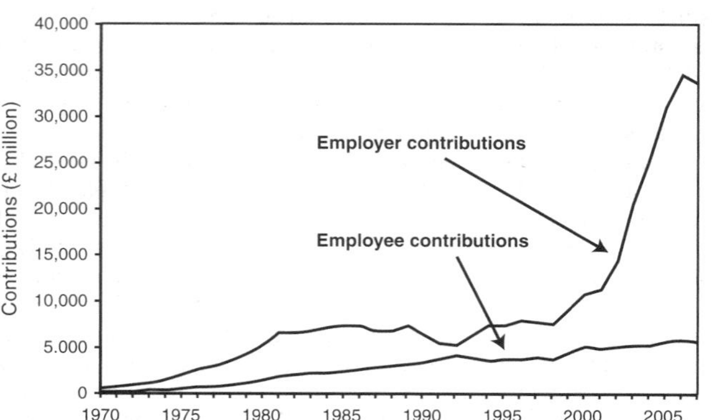

"The bottom line is in heaven." Edwin Land

Figure 2. Annual contributions to UK pension schemes by employers and employees 1970–2007. (*Source*: Office for National Statistics)

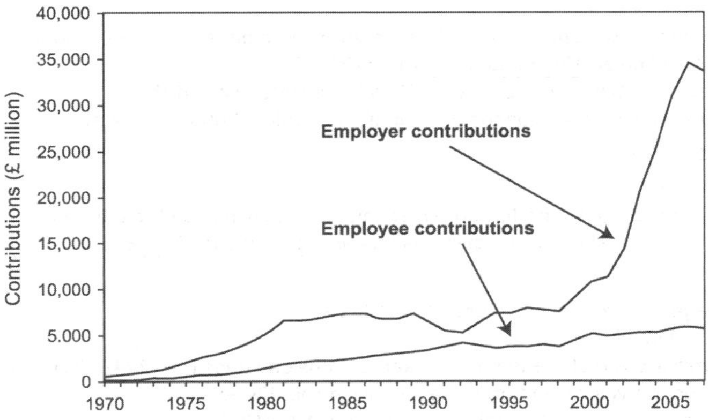

implicit belief that returns of this order can be harvested without difficulty.

This is not to say that corporate bonds are not good investments. They are an investment staple with good reason and can provide low-risk returns. However, they are not risk-free, and any prudent investor needs to be cognizant of the default, credit, and liquidity risks that go with the asset class. In recent months, the problem has been highlighted by the credit crunch, which has seen prices of AA corporate bonds collapse and their yields soar. No wonder many schemes were feeling pleasantly flush and in surplus over the last couple of years—their liabilities dramatically lessened over the same time period!

It's a false optimism. The downturn in prices reflects the increasing fear that some of these corporate bonds might default. Even if one claimed that investing everything in AA corporate bonds today could still provide these returns at low risk, there simply aren't enough around. Taking the United Kingdom as an example, the total value of AA corporate bonds floating around the UK financial markets at last count was just over $142 billion—a fraction of the some $1,200 billion of liabilities they are supposed to underpin.

It's a troubling mismatch problem. Although there is a tradition of pension schemes and insurers "booking" some potential asset gains in advance, it is important for companies not to bank on future gains to work out their liabilities. An unembellished picture of the liabilities, stripped of any assumed risk premiums, can often be a good guide when setting investment targets and managing the risk on your balance sheet.

The area is also coming under increased regulatory scrutiny, with more stringent accounting standards being imposed. For example, the pensions regulator in the United Kingdom is now pushing schemes to adopt more realistic mortality assumptions that reflect the latest scientific evidence—a change that could equate to an additional cost of $40 billion for the UK defined benefit industry with every added year of life expectancy. This also presents additional shorter-term risks for sponsors, as they may have to divert extra cash into the scheme to meet these future liabilities via a contribution notice.

SOLUTIONS ON THE HORIZON

Company finance directors must feel victimized. Constrained by ever-growing liabilities on the balance sheet and a volatile pension asset portfolio, they often find themselves on the wrong side of the window when it comes to securing their retirees' benefits. Changing interest rates, rising inflation, and ever-increasing allowances for longevity mean that the liabilities are often a fast-moving target. Throw in a worsening economic environment, and keeping apace is complicated by potentially thorny negotiations with trustees and retirees for additional injections.

So how are trustees and sponsors to manage these new, troubling risks? It's hard enough to judge market returns over the next few years, without crystal ball gazing to estimate the lifespan of all the scheme members under your responsibility—past, present, and future.

The answer today is that it is largely a dark art. The current trend is unlikely to be your friend here; longevity improvements have repeatedly defied the hopeful shackles of successive actuarial models, despite the most Orwellian filtering of data by job, medical history, and even postcode. The latest models—even if true—give scant comfort. For example, by 2050 a 65-year-old UK male might live to be between 86 and 97 years old, up from 83 today.

However, there are options. Like any other risk, these uncertainties can be managed, and even reduced, once understood. The key is to have a proactive and realistic approach to the risks that are being carried on the balance sheet. Sponsors need to engage actively with trustees and walk a fine line between investors' expectations and the funding needs for the pension scheme.

Unique solutions are now appearing in the market. A whole industry has now sprung up in the United Kingdom offering full insurance buyouts, where the pension liabilities are transferred away to dedicated specialists. This can often improve the situation for pension scheme members, as these specialist insurers are tightly regulated, operate within strict investment and asset/liability guidelines, and have to hold capital against any extreme losses.

It also helps troubled sponsors: Securing pension liabilities away from balance sheets improves their ability to raise finance, and removes the situation where, in a falling equity market with a commensurate fall in the valuation of a scheme's assets, a sponsor looking to invest in the business might also find trustees coming cap in hand. Above all, it enables management to get on with running the business, free from the peripheral distractions of administering a pension scheme.

However, insurance buyout valuations use more cautious longevity assumptions and paint a truer picture of the hidden arrears, increasing the liabilities and the premiums required significantly. Like customers outside a Ferrari showroom peering in through the window, it is simply unaffordable for many companies and not available in many countries.

But there are alternatives to help transfer risk. Schemes can execute partial buyouts for some of their liabilities, such as current pensioners. If that overshoots the budget and the deficit is still too large, or the options are not available in your jurisdiction, there are now innovative corporate solutions to help transfer risk, ranging from taking on the entire scheme and its myriad liabilities, to specific solutions for specific risks.

For example, trustees and sponsors can implement bond or swap-based hedging strategies to nullify the impact of interest rates and inflation on their liabilities, and thereby on the balance sheet. There is even a growing market in longevity swaps, allowing people also to hedge this idiosyncratic risk. Although they introduce new risks in lieu, such as the health of the counterparties on the other side of the swap, these steps are cost-effective and can ensure that the larger part of a scheme's risk—its volatile liabilities—is better constrained, while precious assets are freed up to invest in assets with higher returns.

"The City is a machine miraculously organized for extracting gold from the seas, airs, clouds, from barren lands, holds of ships, mines, plantations, cottage hearth-stones, trees and rock." Christina Stead

Another alternative is to delegate the holistic management of all the scheme's assets and liabilities to a third-party fiduciary manager, who will manage them on a real-time basis within tight guidelines agreed with the trustees. These specialists will typically hedge all the liabilities where possible and diversify the assets among a range of best of breed providers. This ensures that the funding position is improved, and its ultimate targets, such as a full buyout, are reached in an efficient and structured manner. The asset/liability management approach has proved popular in countries such as The Netherlands, where it has significantly improved funding positions.

It's a rapidly evolving environment, and, with new solutions appearing fast, corporate sponsors can be hopeful of finding innovative ways of managing these new risks on their horizon. Most importantly, they can go back to finding and building businesses—not reading horoscopes.

MORE INFO

Reports:

Eich, Frank, and Amarendra Swarup. "Pensions tomorrow: A white paper." London School of Economics, 2008. Online at: tinyurl.com/4yeym5x [PDF].

Eich, Frank, and Amarendra Swarup. "Longevity: Trends, uncertainty and the implications for pension systems." London School of Economics, 2009. Online at: tinyurl.com/3zaf6rx [PDF].

Website:

London School of Economics—Pensions Tomorrow, an initiative launched by the LSE to stimulate debate on how to take pension systems forward: tinyurl.com/3qey89z

See Also:

★ Asset Liability Management for Pension Funds (pp. 13–15)
★ Mixflation (pp. 215–218)
★ The Origins and Current State of the Buyout Market for Pension Funds (pp. 224–225)
★ The Role of Institutional Investors in Corporate Financing (pp. 589–592)
★ Valuing Pension Fund Liabilities on the Balance Sheet (pp. 122–124)
✔ Preparing Financial Statements: Balance Sheets (p. 1046)
✔ Understanding Asset-Liability Management (Full Balance Sheet Approach) (p. 996)
✔ Understanding the Balance Sheet (p. 999)
✔ Understanding the Relationship between the Discount Rate and Risk (p. 1001)

"The debt is like a crazy aunt we keep down in the basement. All the neighbors know she's there, but nobody wants to talk about her." H. Ross Perot

  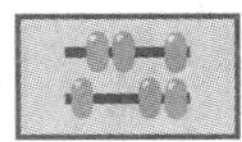   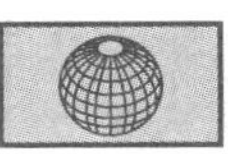   

Quantifying Corporate Financial Risk

by David Shimko

EXECUTIVE SUMMARY

- Standard pro forma cash flow analysis considers risk in a crude way, usually with a subjectively determined upside and downside to cash flows.
- Stochastic analysis generates a large number of scenarios to give a better understanding of risk interactions, business linkages, optionality, and contracts designed to mitigate risk.
- Simple models can be built in spreadsheets, but one must take care to model financial assets, commodity prices, interest rates, and exchange rates appropriately.
- Stochastic pro-formas can lead to better capital budgeting, valuation, and risk management decisions, particularly when risk is important to decision-making.
- Even the most sophisticated models are still subject to model risk; and they do not likely capture all the risks affecting an enterprise.

EXAMPLE OF A STOCHASTIC PRO FORMA

Consider the case of a company that has experienced six months of cash flows this year and wants to forecast the next six months. The usual way to do this is to predict a cash flow growth rate—expected, high, and low—and to base the analysis on these choices. A sample cash flow projection might be illustrated graphically in Figure 1.

In reality, of course, several different cash flow patterns might emerge for the last six months of the year. Using the same risk model, we could run a large number of simulations and see what the outcomes might be. Eight possible outcomes are plotted in Figure 2.

Clearly the stochastic analysis, albeit more realistic, is not as simple and not as attractive at first blush as deterministic analysis. And there are many situations where stochastic analysis is not needed. Yet there are certain results that one can get from stochastic analysis that cannot be gained from deterministic analysis. Table 1 gives some examples.

Stochastic analysis is needed in situations where risk assessment is required, where the future company decisions depend on an unknown variable, where options are present, and when the company wants to study risk mitigation strategies.

Stochastic modeling of the income statement can be done at the aggregate level as it has been demonstrated here, or the components can be broken down into smaller components, such as the prices of products, inputs, interest rates, foreign exchange rates, and the like. The benefit of breaking down the income statement into its market-driven components is that we can find much more information on market-quoted prices and rates. This historical information is usually used as a starting point in determining how best to model these prices and rates.

MODELING MARKET RISK

Risk analysts need to spend significant time and effort to model the risk of the inputs to their stochastic models correctly. Incorrect specifications for market prices will lead to incorrect results. There are several models available to model market price risk. The choice of the best model generally is made by looking at the market's historical performance and making judgments about market price behavior.[1]

For example, if our risk model depends on fluctuations in the stock market index, a popular approach is to represent the index as following a random walk in percentage terms. Thus, any given day's return is normally distributed with a constant mean and standard deviation, and statistically independent from the previous day's return. This approach was popularized in the Black–Scholes (1973) and Merton (1973) papers on option pricing. The random walk works reasonably well, except that with specialized knowledge one could argue that the average return should not be constant, the volatility should not be constant, and there are sometimes events which cause stock prices not to be normally distributed. For this reason, the S&P 500 index may reasonably follow a random walk, but the stock of a small pharmaceutical company will not, since it is prone to occasional major

Figure 1. Deterministic cash flow forecast for last six months

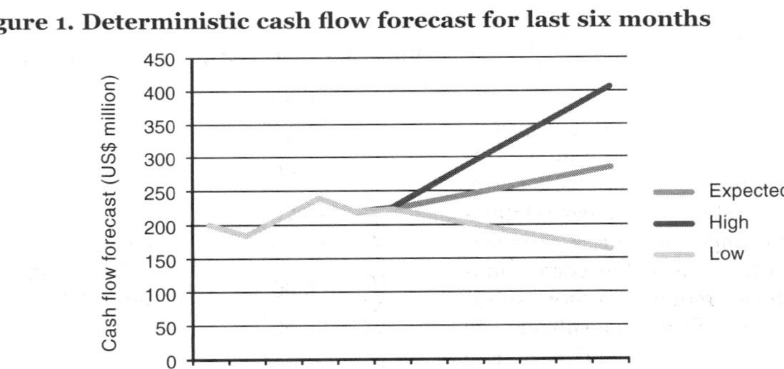

Figure 2. Stochastic cash flow projection for last six months

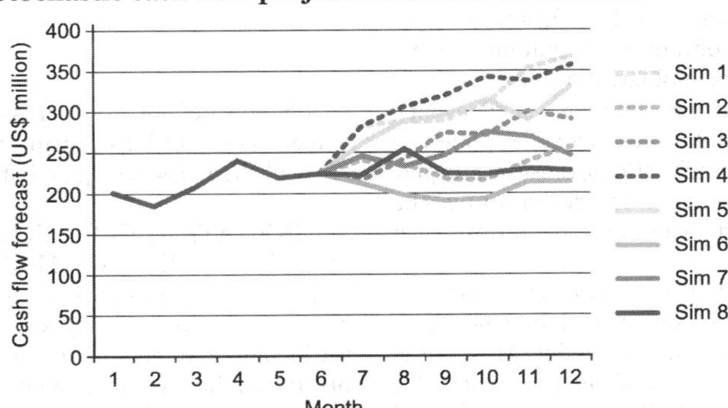

events such as FDA drug approval or discovery of legal liability.

Other market prices, such as interest rates, do not follow random walks. Overly high and overly low interest rates tend to correct over time to equilibrium levels. Although that equilibrium level may change over time, the general character of interest rates is that they are *mean-reverting*—i.e., they revert to a long-run mean over time. The same is true of commodity prices. High commodity prices stimulate production, which causes future prices to fall. Low prices discourage production, causing future prices to rise. Therefore, interest rates and commodities need to be modeled in a similar way. Some currencies exhibit mean-reverting behavior and some do not.

Finally, every market price may have unique characteristics. The volatility of natural gas and heating oil changes by season. Power prices spike rapidly when generation fails and bounce back immediately as generation comes back on line. Careful modeling of critical market price inputs will lead to the best models of stochastic results.

MODELING RISK INTERACTIONS

It is not enough to have good models of security prices, interest rates, foreign exchange rates, and commodity prices. We must also understand how those prices and rates interact. For example, higher security prices are generally correlated with low interest rates. The Australian dollar exchange rate is correlated to gold prices, due to the importance of gold mining in its economy. In many cases, simplistic correlation is fine to establish a linear relationship between changes in the risk variables. However, in other cases, the correlations may not be linear, requiring a more subtle approach. For some firms, that subtlety will be important enough to build a precise model of the interaction between two risks of importance to the company.

MODELING EVENT RISK

Every corporation is subject to risks from significant events, such as losing a major lawsuit, or obtaining a patent on its proprietary technology. Also, the company can be affected by market-related events, such as the bankruptcy of a key supplier. In many modeling situations, these events play an important role in determining the probability distributions of future cash flows.

It is tempting to think of event risks as being random outcomes, independent of everything else in the model. This is the biggest mistake a modeler can make. The credit crisis of 2008, for example, showed vividly how default risks across investment banks were correlated, owing to the similarity of their risk-taking activities.

Table 1. Incremental analyses produced by stochastic pro formas

Analysis	Sample question
Probabilities of outcomes	What is the likelihood we will need to borrow?
Risk of outcomes	What is the most likely range for annual cash flows at year-end?
Interactions	If we invest more in capital expenditures only when cash flows are up, how do we reflect that in the analysis, and what impact does it have?
Options	Our loan contracts have floating rates, but the rates are capped. How does this affect the probabilities of different cash flow levels?
Worst case	We probably won't have the worst case revenues and the worst case costs in the same year; how does that reflect on our expectation of the worst case?
Events	There is a 10% chance we get a major contract that will increase our cash flows significantly. How do we incorporate this in the model?
Risk mitigation	The treasurer wants to lock in foreign exchange rates for our foreign buyers. How will this affect cash flow volatility?
Capital structure	What is our capacity to make interest payments on debt with 99% certainty?

Figure 3. Current EBIT stochastics

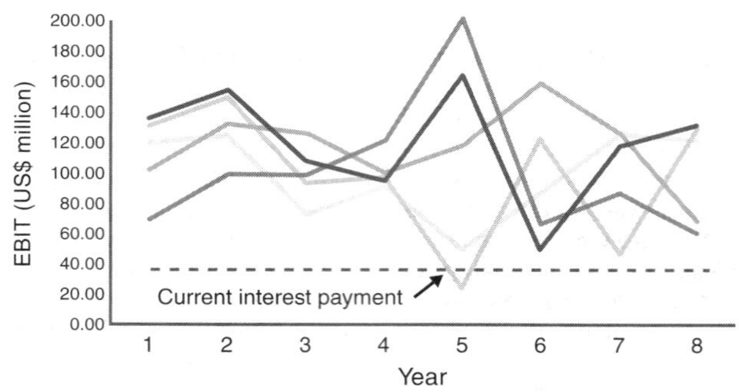

Figure 4. EBIT stochastics post-hedging

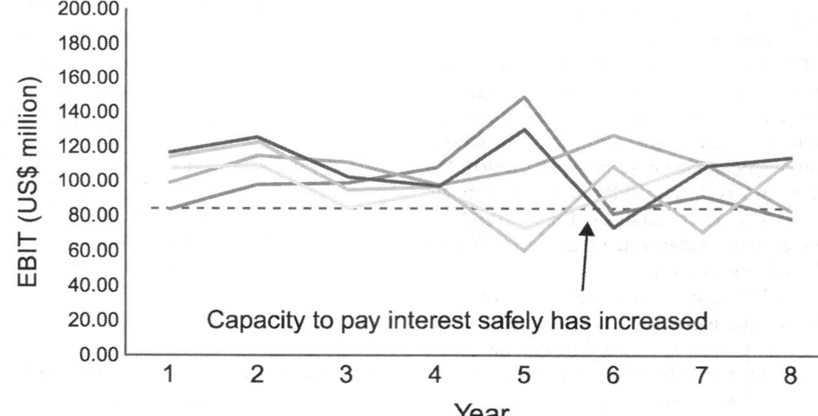

AGGREGATING CASH FLOW RISKS TO THE INCOME STATEMENT

Once all the drivers of the income statement have been modeled, they are compiled to the income statement in the same way that a pro-forma income statement would normally be generated. For example, suppose a refinery in Brazil buys crude oil in dollars, sells products in reais, shuts down production when it is not profitable to produce, and runs the risk of operational failures according to some statistical model. In this case, the modeler could build stochastic formulas for the price of crude, the price of products, the dollar foreign exchange rate, the shutdown policy of the firm, and the unplanned outage rates due to operational risk. The result is a determination of net

  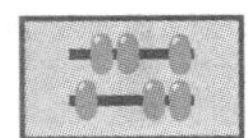   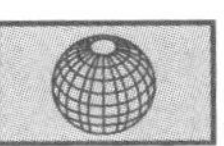   

income for each particular simulated environment. These net income numbers can be simulated as many times as required to determine the volatility of cash flows, the value of the shutdown option, and the answer to any of the questions posed above.

MODELING RISKS OTHER THAN CASH FLOW

Some risks may not affect cash flows but could affect earnings, such as a mark-to-market liability. In these cases, similar risk models can be built to model earnings risk, or to model the likelihood of a credit downgrade. Stochastic models can be simple or extremely complex, but they all are built fundamentally to make deterministic models more realistic and able to answer questions related to risk, risk management, optionality, capital structure, and much, much more.

CONCLUSION

Stochastic pro-forma analysis answers many financial questions that cannot be addressed with usual deterministic pro-forma analysis. The case study demonstrates how hedging and capital structure may be evaluated using stochastic pro formas. Other applications include evaluation of real options,[2] the study of credit ratings, and the development of probability statements around cash flow or earnings.

Like any other type of analysis, poor assumptions lead to poor conclusions. Good simulation models take a great deal of care in specifying the correct models for all the risk drivers and the interactions between them. Finally, more realistic risk-based models lead to better corporate financial decisions.

In the final analysis, however, even a very sophisticated model is still a model, and is therefore subject to model risk. Thus, the model may not fully identify or quantify all risks that affect an enterprise, and can thereby lead to a false sense of security. Accordingly, decision-makers should consider model risk as one of the components of any financial decision based on stochastic pro-forma analysis.

CASE STUDY

An ethanol-producing company may be reluctant to issue more debt because of the high volatility of its cash flows and the increased risk of being put into bankruptcy.

A bank has proposed a transaction where the company would reduce its risk by selling its ethanol to customers at a price agreed today—i.e., entering forward contracts. If it did so, the bank would lend additional funds at the same rate. The company is reluctant to accept the bank's proposal because the sales price falls below the level at which the company thinks it can sell ethanol, costing the company $2 million per year. How can the company compare the benefit of higher debt with the cost of selling at a distressed price? And how can the company and the bank determine an appropriate level of additional debt?

A stochastic pro forma analysis could be done for the company before and after the proposed transaction. Before the transaction, the average earnings before interest and tax (EBIT) is estimated at $100 million with a standard deviation of $50 million. Shown in Figure 3 are five outcomes simulated over an eight-year period. The current annual debt service is $49 million.

By selling its ethanol forward, the company expects to lose $2 million per year, but to reduce the standard deviation to $25 million. The resulting stochastics demonstrate that the company can now prudently afford to make higher interest payments without having much risk of failure to pay (Figure 4).

The company can afford to pay $65 million in interest safely, after hedging its results. Should the company accept the hedging program? The answer depends on taxes. If the ethanol company is not in a tax-paying situation, it has lost an expected $2 million per year in value, so it should not hedge unless there are other reasons to do so. A taxpaying firm in the 40% bracket, however, will be able to deduct the interest expense from taxable income, saving $6.4 million per year (40% of 65 minus 49). The taxpaying firm should hedge, barring other considerations that might cause the firm not to want to hedge.

MAKING IT HAPPEN

- Begin with a project or corporate pro forma.
- Consider every assumption and ask if it is vulnerable to risk.
- Produce a risk model to simulate all the assumptions consistently and simultaneously.
- Use this model (stochastic pro forma) to design best and worst cases.
- Simulate outcomes of all key financial variables and communicate the risks.

MORE INFO

Articles:

Black, Fischer, and Myron Scholes. "The pricing of options and corporate liabilities." *Journal of Political Economy* 81:3 (May–June 1973): 637–654. Online at: www.jstor.org/stable/1831029

Merton, Robert C. "Theory of rational option pricing." *Bell Journal of Economics and Management Science* 4:1 (Spring 1973): 141–183. Online at: www.jstor.org/stable/3003143

Websites:

Most of the literature in "stochastic processes" is extremely technical and not suitable for the average business reader. Even "stochastic processes in finance" tends to lead to models of security prices and interest rates for building value-at-risk models and option pricing models.

The topic "financial statement simulation" in an internet search engine leads to simulation software providers, such as Palisade, Finance 3.0, and @Risk. These providers offer written materials to supplement their software services. In addition, the reader is invited to request additional materials from the author.

NOTES

1 Analysts should never expect that historical price behavior will represent future price behavior—only to realize that there is usually no better source of information for modeling purposes.

2 See the article on "Real Options: Opportunity from Risk" in this volume.

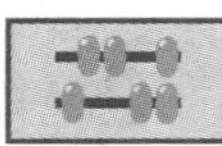

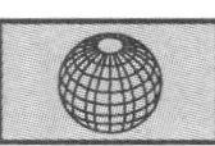

Risk Management of Islamic Finance Instruments by Andreas Jobst

EXECUTIVE SUMMARY

- Derivatives are few and far between in Islamic countries. This is due to the fact that the compatibility of capital market transactions with Islamic law requires the development of *shariah*-compliant structures that guarantee certainty of payment obligations from contingent claims on assets with immutable object characteristics. Notwithstanding these religious constraints, Islamic finance can synthesize close equivalents to conventional derivatives.
- Based on the current use of accepted risk transfer mechanisms, this article explores the validity of risk management in accordance with fundamental legal principles of *shariah*, and summarizes the key objections of *shariah* scholars that challenge the permissibility of derivatives under Islamic law.
- In conclusion, the article offers suggestions for the *shariah* compliance of derivatives.

TYPES OF ISLAMIC FINANCE

Since only interest-free forms of finance are considered permissible in Islamic finance, financial relationships between financiers and borrowers are not governed by capital-based investment gains but by shared business risk (and returns) in lawful activities (*halal*). Any financial transaction under Islamic law implies *direct participation in performance of the asset*, which constitutes entrepreneurial investment that conveys clearly identifiable rights and obligations for which investors are entitled to receive a commensurate return in the form of state-contingent payments relative to asset performance. *Shariah* does not object to payment for the use of an asset as long as both lender and borrower share the investment risk together, and profits are not guaranteed *ex ante* but accrue only if the investment itself yields income—subject to the intent to create an equitable system of distributive justice and promote permitted activities in the public interest (*maslahah*).

The permissibility of risky capital investment without explicit earning of interest has spawned three basic forms of Islamic financing for both investment and trade: (1) synthetic loans (*debt-based*) through a sale–repurchase agreement or back-to-back sale of borrower- or third-party-held assets; (2) lease contracts (*asset-based*) through a sale–leaseback agreement (operating lease) or the lease of third-party-acquired assets with purchase obligation components (financing lease); and (3) profit-sharing contracts (*equity-based*) of future assets. As opposed to equity-based contracts, both debt- and asset-based contracts are initiated by a temporary (permanent) transfer of existing (future) assets from the borrower to the lender, or the acquisition of third-party assets by the lender on behalf of the borrower.

"IMPLICIT DERIVATIVES" IN ISLAMIC FINANCE

From an economic point of view, the "creditor-in-possession"-based lending arrangements of Islamic finance replicate the interest income of conventional lending transactions in a religiously acceptable manner. The concept of *put–call parity*[1] illustrates that the three main types of Islamic finance outlined above represent different ways of recharacterizing conventional interest through the attribution of economic benefits from the ownership of an existing or future (contractible) asset by means of an "implicit derivatives" arrangement.

In *asset-based* Islamic finance, the borrower leases from the lender one or more assets A, valued at S, which have previously been acquired from either the borrower or a third party. The lender allows the borrower to (re-)gain ownership of A at time T by writing a call option $-C(E)$ with time-invariant strike price E subject to the promise of full repayment of E (via a put option $+P(E)$), plus an agreed premium in the form of rental payments over the investment period. This arrangement amounts to a *secured* loan with *fully collateralized* principal (i.e. full recourse). The present value of the lender's *ex ante* position at maturity is $L = S - C(E) + P(E) = PV(E)$,[2] which equals the present value of the principal amount and interest of a conventional loan. In a more realistic depiction, this put–call combination represents a series of cash-neutral, maturity-matched, risk-free (and periodically extendible), *synthetic* forward contracts

$$\Sigma_{t=1}^{T}[P_t(E) - C_t(E)]$$

over a sequence of rental payment dates t. By holding equal and opposite option positions on the same strike price at inception, there are no objectionable zero-sum gains or uncertainty of object characteristics and/or delivery results.

Overall, the put–call arrangement of *asset-based Islamic lending implies a sequence of cash-neutral, risk-free (forward) hedges of credit exposure*. Since poor transparency of S in long-dated contracts could make the time value of $+P(E)$ appear greater than its intrinsic value, long-term Islamic lending with limited information disclosure would require a high repayment frequency to ensure efficient investor recourse. In *debt-based* Islamic finance, borrower indebtedness from a sale–repurchase agreement ("cost-plus sale") of an asset with current value $PV(E)$ implies a premium payment to the lender for the use of funds over the investment period T and the same investor payoff L.[3] In Islamic profit-sharing (*equity-based*) agreements, the lender receives a payout in accordance with a pre-agreed disbursement ratio only if the investment project generates enough profits to repay the initial investment amount and the premium payment at maturity T. Since the lender bears all losses, this equity-based arrangement precludes any recourse in the amount $+P(E)$ in the absence of enforceable collateral.

"EXPLICIT DERIVATIVES" AND *SHARIAH*-COMPLIANT RISK MANAGEMENT

Amid weak reliance on capital market financing in many Islamic countries, risk transfer mechanisms are subject to several critical legal hindrances that impact on the way that derivatives redress perceived market imperfections and financing constraints. Although "implicit derivatives" in the form of synthetic forward contracts (see above) are essential to profit generation from temporary asset transfer or profit-sharing in Islamic finance without creating the potential of unilateral gains, and thus are not deemed objectionable on religious grounds, the *explicit* use of derivatives remains highly controversial (Jobst, 2008b).

While "explicit derivatives" remain few and far between in Islamic finance, the implicit forward element of Islamic lending contracts, like forwards in conventional finance, involves problems of double coincidence and counterparty risk due to privately negotiated customization. Parties to forward agreements need to have exactly opposite hedging interests, which *inter alia* coincide in the timing of protection sought against adverse price movements and the quantity of asset delivery. More-

"Permissibility to conventional options is generally denied by a majority of scholars on the ground that these involve *gharar* and are primarily transacted for speculative gains." Mohammed Obaidullah

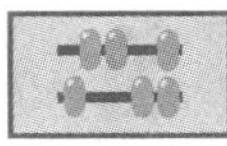

Figure 1. *Murabaha*-based cross-currency swap. (Numbers indicate sequence in which transactions are executed. GCC indicates country in Gulf Cooperation Council)

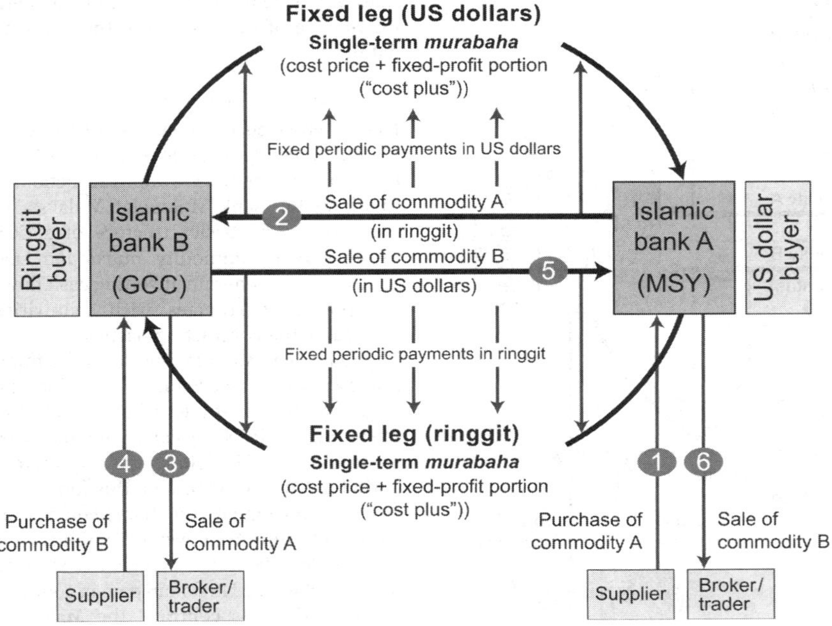

over, forward contracts elevate the risk of one counterparty defaulting when the spot price of the underlying asset falls below the forward price prior to maturity, rendering the contract "out-of-the-money" and making deliberate default more attractive.

Although the premise of eliminating these risks is desirable *per se* under Islamic law, the assurance of definite performance through either cash settlement (in futures), or mutual deferment (in options), as in conventional derivatives contracts, is clearly not, as it supplants the concept of direct asset recourse and implies a zero-sum proposition (Usmani, 1999). Instead, in Islamic finance, the bilateral nature and asset-backing *ensure definite performance* on the delivery of the underlying asset (unlike a conventional forward contract). By virtue of holding equal and opposite option positions on the same strike price, both creditor and debtor are obliged to honor the terms of the contract irrespective of changes in asset value. Unlike in conventional options, there are no unilateral gains from favorable price movements (for example, "in-the-money" appreciation of option premia) in the range between the current and the contractually agreed repayment amount. Any deviation of the underlying asset value from the final repayment amount constitutes shared business risk (in an existing or future asset).

Shariah scholars take issue with the fact that futures and options are valued mostly by reference to the sale of a nonexistent asset or an asset not in the possession (*qabd*) of the seller, which negates the *hadith* "sell not what is not with you." *Shariah* principles, however, require creditors (or protection sellers) to actually own the reference asset at the inception of a transaction. Futures and options also continue to be rejected by a majority of Islamic scholars on the grounds that "... in most futures transactions, delivery of the commodities or their possession is not intended" (Usmani, 1996). Derivatives almost never involve delivery by *both* parties to the contract. Often parties reverse the transaction and cash-settle the price difference only, which transforms a derivative contract into a paper transaction without the element of a genuine sale. Given the Islamic principle of permissibility (*ibahah*), which renders all commercial transactions *shariah*-compliant in the absence of a clear and specific prohibition, current objections to futures and options constitute the most discouraging form of religious censure (*taqlid*).

Besides the lack of asset ownership at the time of sale, other areas of concern shared by Islamic scholars about *shariah* compliance of derivatives have centered on: the selection of reference assets that are nonexistent at the time of contract; the requirement of *qabd* (i.e. taking possession of the item prior to resale); mutual deferment of both sides of the bargain, which reduces contingency risk but turns a derivative contract into a profitable sale of debt; and excessive uncertainty or speculation that verges on gambling, resulting in zero-sum payoffs of both sides of the bargain (Mohamad and Tabatabaei, 2008; Kamali, 2007; Khan, 1991).

Although Khan (1995) concedes that "some of the underlying basic concepts as well as some of the conditions for [contemporary futures] trading are exactly the same as [those] laid down by the Prophet Mohammed for forward trading," he also acknowledges the risk of exploitation and speculation, which belie fundamental precepts of *shariah*. For the same reasons, several scholars also consider options in violation of Islamic law. Nonetheless, Kamali (2001) finds that "there is nothing inherently objectionable in granting an option, exercising it over a period of time or charging a fee for it, and that options trading like other varieties of trade is permissible *mubah*, and as such, it is simply an extension of the basic liberty that the Qur'an has granted."

However, so far only a few explicit derivative products have been developed by various banks for managing currency and interest rate risk. While recent innovation in this area has focused mostly on highly customized option contracts as well as commodity hedges, cross-currency swaps and so-called "profit-rate swaps" constitute the most widely accepted forms of newly established *shariah*-compliant derivatives (see next section). Given the prohibition of interest income and the exchange of the same assets for profit (which includes the cost-plus sale of debt), for Islamic investors to execute a swap both parties instead agree to sell assets, usually commodities, to each other for deferred payment. In the case of cross-currency swaps, the contractual parties exchange commodities in the form of a cost-plus sale and settle their mutual payment obligations in different currencies according to a predefined installment schedule.

Nonetheless, governance issues—especially *shariah*-compliance of products and activities—constitute a major challenge for the Islamic finance industry in general and risk management in particular. Although *shariah* rulings (*fatwas*) and their underlying reasoning are disclosed, there are currently no unified principles (and no precedents) on the basis of which *shariah* scholars decide on the religious compliance of new products. *Fatwas* are not consolidated, which inhibits the dissemination, adoption, and cross-fertilization of jurisprudence across different countries and schools of thought. Therefore, the fragmented opinions of *shariah* boards, which act as quasi-regulatory bodies, remain a source of continued divergence of legal opinion. In particular, there is considerable heterogeneity of scholastic

"Business, in the Qur'anic sense of 'profitable trade' or *tijarat'un rabiha*, is business that brings blessings to those who conduct it. Obviously, profits are important as ends, but the means by which those profits are earned are even more important." Sheikh Yusuf Talal DeLorenzo

Figure 2. *Murabaha*-based profit-rate swap[5]

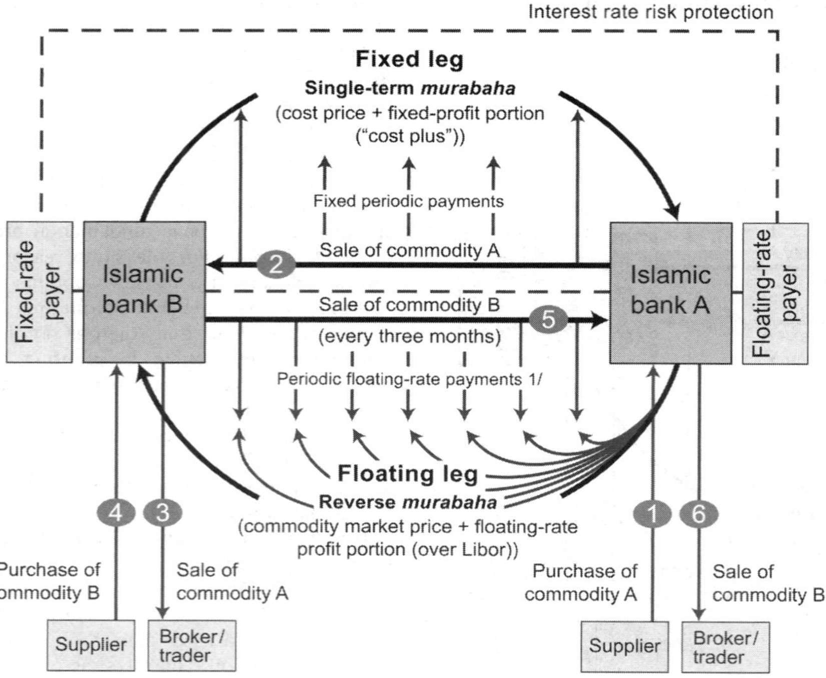

opinion about the *shariah*-compliance of derivatives, which testifies to the general controversy about risk management in Islamic finance. In particular, it underscores the difficulties of reconciling financial innovation and greater flexibility in the principled interpretation of different modes of secondary sources supporting religious doctrine: i.e. analogous deduction (*qiyas*), independent analytical reasoning (*ijtihad*), and scholarly consensus (*ijma*).

Recent efforts of regulatory consolidation and standard-setting have addressed the economic constraints and legal uncertainty imposed by both Islamic jurisprudence and the poorly developed uniformity of market practices. Private-sector initiatives, such as an Islamic primary market project led by the Bahrain-based International Islamic Financial Market (IIFM) in cooperation with the International Capital Markets Association (ICMA), have resulted in the adoption of a memorandum of understanding on documentation standards and master agreement protocols for Islamic derivatives. Also, national solutions are gaining traction. In November 2006, Malaysia's only fully fledged Islamic banks, Bank Islam Berhad and Bank Muamalat Malaysia Berhad, agreed to execute a master agreement for the documentation of Islamic derivative transactions (Jobst, 2007 and 2008a). Therefore, market inefficiencies and concerns about contract enforceability caused by heterogeneous prudential norms and diverse interpretations of *shariah*-compliance are expected to dissipate in the near future.

ISLAMIC SWAP TRANSACTIONS: CROSS-CURRENCY AND PROFIT-RATE SWAPS

Shariah-compliant swap transactions are traded bilaterally and combine opposite, maturity-matched *murabaha* contracts with instantaneous (or periodic) transfer of similar assets and delayed payment of the sales price (inclusive of a premium payment for the use of the asset until the maturity date).[4]

Islamic Cross-Currency Swap

Islamic cross-currency swaps (CCS) debuted only recently when Standard Chartered executed the first ever swap transaction of this kind for Bank Muamalat Malaysia in July 2006. The basic structure of a CCS matches two commodity *murabaha* sale contracts that generate offsetting cash flows in opposite currencies with maturities desired by the contracting parties.

The following example illustrates the functioning of a CCS (see Figure 1). Consider the case of a Malaysia-based Islamic bank that raises revenue in Malaysian ringgit but faces payments in US dollars over a certain period of time. To eliminate this forseeable currency mismatch, the bank could substitute its future outflows in US dollars for outflows in Malaysian ringgit by entering into a CCS with a US dollar-paying counterparty. Under this contract, the Malaysia-based Islamic bank purchases an amount of commodity A on a *murabaha* basis (i.e. against future installments) denominated in Malaysian ringgit. Simultaneously, an Islamic bank based in a Gulf Cooperation Council (GCC) country buys an amount of commodity B, also under a *murabaha* agreement but denominated in US dollars. By combining the two *murabaha* contracts,

MAKING IT HAPPEN

Possibilities for Establishing *Shariah*-Compliance of Derivatives and Risk Management

The heterogeneity of scholastic opinion about the *shariah*-compliance of derivatives is largely a reflection of individual interpretations of *shariah* and different knowledge of the mechanics of derivative structures and risk management strategies. Many policymakers, market participants, and regulators are unfamiliar with the intricate mechanics and highly technical language of many derivative transactions, which hinder a more comprehensive understanding and objective appreciation of the role of derivatives in the financial system and their prevalence in a great variety of business and financial transactions. Risk diversification through derivatives contributes to the continuous discovery of the fair market price of risk, improves stability at all levels of the financial system, and enhances general welfare.

In principle, futures and options may be compatible with Islamic law if they: (1) are employed to address a genuine hedging demand on asset performance associated with a direct ownership interest; (2) disavow mutual deferment without actual asset transfer; and (3) eschew avertable uncertainty (*gharar*) as prohibited sinful activity (*haram*) in a bid to create an equitable system of distributive justice in consideration of the public interest (*maslahah*). *Shariah*-compliant derivatives would also maintain risk sharing that favors win–win situations from changes in asset value. For instance, the issuance of stock options to employees would be an ideal candidate for a *shariah*-compliant derivative. By setting incentives for higher productivity, firm owners reap larger corporate profits that offset the marginal cost of greater employee participation in stock price performance. However, the *de facto* application of many derivative contracts is still objectionable due to the potential for speculation (or deficient hedging need) to violate the tenets of distributive justice and equal risk sharing subject to religious restrictions on lending and profit-taking without real economic activity and asset transfer.

"Innovation will never stop. God will not create a genuine human need within society and not give a genuine means to fulfil that need, whether in the area of finance or marriage." Muddassir Siddiqui

     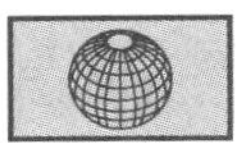   

each denominated in a different currency, each party will be able to receive cash flows in the desired currency. Finally, both banks sell their respective commodities in order to recoup their initial expense, where the fair value of each commodity (A and B) should wash out at the prevailing exchange rate.

If the parties wanted to hedge term risk (i.e. the risk of the fair market values of the exchanged assets diverging over the life of the transaction), either in addition to the cross-currency swap or as a separate transaction, they would enter into a profit-rate swap. In this Islamic version of an interest-rate swap, the two sides exchange periodic fixed-rate for floating-rate payments. After selling a designated commodity to the protection seller, the protection buyer receives periodic fixed-rate payments in return for floating-rate installments.

Islamic Profit-Rate Swap

This instrument, pioneered by Commerce International Merchant Bank of Malaysia in 2005, allows financial institutions to manage their exposures to fixed and floating rates of return. That is, through the profit-rate swap (PRS), institutions can restructure the nature (fixed vs. floating) of their existing rates of return. As in the CCS, profit-rate swaps are based on the combination of two commodity *murabaha* contracts (see Figure 2). The floating-rate leg involves the periodic *murabaha* sale of a commodity by the protection seller in exchange for future installments at the fair value (market) price plus a *floating-rate profit portion* ("cost-plus") that varies according to changes in some pre-agreed benchmark (for example, some interbank funding rate such as the London or Kuala Lumpur Interbank Offered Rate). The fixed-rate leg stipulates the one-off sale of a commodity by the protection buyer in exchange for a stream of future predetermined payments. As in the cross-currency swap, both parties may sell their commodities in order to recoup their initial disbursement. Note that the floating-rate payer (or interest rate protection buyer) purchases commodity B in periodic increments—unlike the fixed-rate payer (or interest rate protection seller), who receives commodity A in full at inception.

Attempts to design other *shariah*-compliant derivatives, such as total return swaps, have been mired in controversy. One particularly contested structure is based on a dual *wa'ad* (or promise) contract, which swaps the returns of a *shariah*-compliant asset portfolio with those of a designated index or reference investment portfolio, which can contain conventional assets. This Islamic total return swap would allow investors to access returns from assets that are prohibited under *shariah* principles. DeLorenzo (2007) has argued that, in practice, this swap structure does not conform to *shariah* norms, because the returns from the alternative portfolio are not derived from religiously acceptable activities.

MORE INFO

Books:

Jobst, Andreas A. "Derivatives in Islamic finance." In Syed Salman Ali (ed). *Islamic Capital Markets: Products, Regulation and Development*. Jeddah, Saudi Arabia: Islamic Research and Training Institute, 2008a; 97–124.

Kamali, Mohammad Hashim. *Islamic Commercial Law: An Analysis of Futures and Options*. Cambridge, UK: Islamic Texts Society, 2001; ch. 10.

Khan, Muhammad Akram. "Commodity exchange and stock exchange in an Islamic economy." In A. H. M. Sadeq *et al.* (eds). *Development and Finance in Islam*. Kuala Lumpur: International Islamic University Press, 1991; 191–212.

Articles:

Jobst, Andreas A. "The economics of Islamic finance and securitization." *Journal of Structured Finance* 13:1 (Spring 2007): 6–27. Online at: dx.doi.org/10.3905/jsf.2007.684860

Jobst, Andreas A. "Double-edged sword: Derivatives and Shariah compliance." *Islamica* (July–August 2008b): 22–25.

Kamali, Mohammad Hashim. "Commodity futures: An Islamic legal analysis." *Thunderbird International Business Review* 49:3 (May/June 2007): 309–339. Online at: dx.doi.org/10.1002/tie.20146

Usmani, Maulana Taqi. "Futures, options, swaps and equity investments." *New Horizon* 59 (June 1996): 10.

Usmani, Maulana Taqi. "What shariah experts say: Futures, options and swaps." *International Journal of Islamic Financial Services* 1:1 (April–June 1999): 36–38.

Reports:

DeLorenzo, Yusuf Talal. "The total returns swap and the 'Shariah conversion technology' stratagem." December 2007. Online at: www.dinarstandard.com/finance/DeLorenzo.pdf

Khan, M. Fahim. "Islamic futures and their markets." Research paper no. 32. Islamic Research and Training Institute, Jeddah, Saudi Arabia, 1995, p. 12.

Mohamad, Saadiah, and Ali Tabatabaei. "Islamic hedging: Gambling or risk management?" Islamic Law and Law of the Muslim World Paper no. 08-47, New York Law School, August 27, 2008. Online at: ssrn.com/abstract=1260110

NOTES

1 The relation between the put and call values of a European option on a nondividend-paying stock of a traded firm can be expressed as $PV(E) + C = S + P$. $PV(E)$ denotes the present value of a risky debt with a face value equal to exercise price E, which is continuously discounted by $\exp(-rT)$ at a risk-free interest rate r over T years. In our case of a lending transaction, the share price S represents the asset value of the funded investment available for the repayment of terminal value E.

2 The lease payments received from the borrower wash out in this representation.

3 However, some debt-based financing with deferred payment of future claims on existing assets (*salam*), predelivery finance for future assets (*istisna*), or the deferred cost-plus sale of a third party-held asset imply counterparty and market risks from lost recovery value, which could translate to a lower strike price F on the call or put option respectively.

4 The degree of collateralization of each leg of the swap depends on the original ownership of the transferred asset (or, in this case, the exchanged commodities), defining the level of creditor indebtedness. In the standard *murabaha* sales contract, the creditor has either full recourse to the underlying asset and periodic payments (in a sale–repurchase agreement at an initially discounted sales price (cost-plus sale)), or limited recourse to periodic payments only (in a back-to-back cost-plus sale of an asset which the seller acquired previously from a third party). In a *murabaha*-based swap transaction the restrictions on recourse apply, even though both contract parties hold mutually offsetting payment obligations against each other, preventing speculative interest and mitigating the contingency risk of periodic payments.

5 This includes full payment and physical settlement in each period. This structure was pioneered by the Commerce International Merchant Bank of Malaysia in 2005.

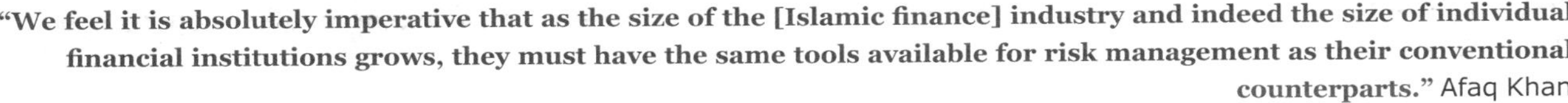

"We feel it is absolutely imperative that as the size of the [Islamic finance] industry and indeed the size of individual financial institutions grows, they must have the same tools available for risk management as their conventional counterparts." Afaq Khan

  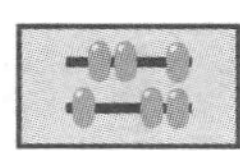      

Small and Medium-Sized Enterprises and Risk in the Gulf Cooperation Council Countries: Managing Risk and Boosting Profit by Omar Fisher

EXECUTIVE SUMMARY

- Small and medium-sized enterprises (SMEs) are a major pillar of the market economy and an essential building block of economic development in the Gulf Cooperation Council (GCC) region.
- Banks in the GCC region are reluctant to lend to SMEs due to higher risk and applicants' failure to meet loan conditions, meaning that 55% of SMEs do not have credit available to them.
- Effective risk management enables the avoidance of losses and maximization of the potential of opportunities. Both business and nonbusiness risks can be protected against by insurance.
- In order to assess the effect of the risks impacting your business, an internal risk audit can be performed. The benefits of this are increasing revenue, saving time, improving safety, and protecting company value.
- Risk management can be a business enabler and aid business value creation by delivering more stable earnings, resources during an emergency, and a tighter grip on the value drivers of your business.
- Implementation of these practices by SMEs will impress bankers, demonstrating a reduced risk profile, and can result in wider access to capital and/or lower cost of funds.

INTRODUCTION

Small and medium-sized businesses (SMEs) across the Gulf Cooperation Council (GCC) region, many of which are family-owned enterprises, bear the same risks as Fortune 1000 companies. A common definition of a SME is a business with fewer than 250 employees and revenues below US$68 million (Dhs 250 million), whereas the real difference lies in scale and complexity. We have found in working with many types of business that most business owners in the Middle East do not fully comprehend insurance and the importance of risk management. Yet, every day, these business owners confront risk—both business risk and nonbusiness risk. This article explores what, in the SME context risk is and some methods to better manage nonbusiness risks to yield sustained cash flows and boost SME profitability.

PROFILE OF SMES IN THE GCC

It is well accepted that SMEs generally are a major pillar of the market economy and supply the following:

- a source of vitality and innovation;
- a pool of skilled and semi-skilled workers;
- a driver for job creation;
- promotion of economic stability as a complement to large corporations;
- a broadening and diversification of the basis of competition within the economy.

A recent research report confirms that SMEs in the GCC region are an essential building block for economic development. "Both in the European Union and the Gulf region, small and medium-sized enterprises (SMEs) are the main drivers of job creation, growth and economic diversification."[1]

Official data suggest that some 40,000 SMEs operate in Bahrain, 85,000 in Dubai/United Arab Emirates (UAE), and 700,000+ in the Kingdom of Saudi Arabia. On average, SMEs employ between 10 and 50 workers, so their impact on employment across the GCC is above 8.5 million jobs. Table 1 summarizes the size and scope of SMEs in the GCC countries.

Table 1. Size and scope of SMEs in GCC countries. (*Sources*: Hertog (2010) and research by the author)

	Micro-enterprise	*Small enterprise*	*Medium enterprise*
Bahrain			
Employment	Up to 10	Up to 50	Up to 150
Assets	BD20,000 (US$53,000)	BD20,000–500,000 (≤ US$1.3 million)	BD500,000–2,000,000 (≤ US$5.3 million)
Saudi Arabia			
Employment	n/a	Fewer than 60	Fewer than 100
Revenue/turnover			Less than SR20 million (US$5.3 million)
Assets	n/a	Less than SR5 million (US$1.3 million)	SR5–20 million (≤ US$5.3 million)
UAE*			
Trading			
Employment	Fewer than 9	Fewer than 35	Fewer than 75
Revenue/turnover	Less than Dhs9 million (US$2.5 million)	Less than Dhs50 million (US$13.7 million)	Less than Dhs250 million (US$68.5 million)
Manufacturing			
Employment	Fewer than 20	Fewer than 100	Fewer than 250
Revenue/turnover	Less than Dhs10 million (US$2.7 million)	Less than Dhs100 million (US$27.4 million)	Less than Dhs250 million (US$68.5 million)
Services			
Employment	Fewer than 20	Fewer than 100	Fewer than 250
Revenue/turnover	Less than Dhs3 million (US$0.82 million)	Less than Dhs25 million (US$6.8 million)	Less than Dhs150 million (US$41 million)
EU definitions of SME			
Employment	Fewer than 10	Fewer than 50	Fewer than 250
Annual sales/revenue	Less than US$3 million	Less than US$13 million	Less than US$67 million

* Estimate by Muhammed bin Rashid for SME development.

Currencies: Dh, United Arab Emirates dirham; BD, Bahraini dinar; SR, Saudi Arabian riyal.

"How many millionaires do you know who have become wealthy by investing in savings accounts? I rest my case."
Robert G. Allen

  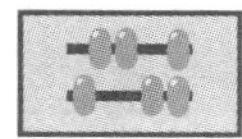   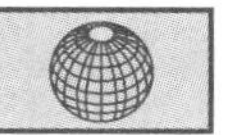   

Table 2. Summary of value drivers

Cash inflows	Cash outflows
Core revenues	Operations/raw materials
Investment income	Capital costs (financing costs)
Supporting business income (royalties, intellectual property)	Capital expenditures
Other incone	Advisory costs (legal, accounting)

Table 3. Summary of risk drivers

Risks to cash inflows	Risks to cash outflows
Pricing and customer behavior	Emergency resources, credit lines
Fluctuations in cost of funds	Natural disasters, catastrophes
Credit and payables	Competitive pressures
Business processes	Supervision, management, plans
	Corporate governance, decision making

As reported by David Morgan in *Arab–British Business* (April 2010), across the GCC region "47% of SMEs are engaged in commercial, trading and hotel businesses, 27% in construction, 12% in industry/manufacturing, 6% in social services and 8% in sundry other sectors."

The top three challenges facing SMEs in the GCC area are: (1) administrative hurdles and lack of enabling regulations; (2) limited or scarce financing; and (3) weak corporate governance and poor bookkeeping and accounting practices. Points 2 and 3 are related and, when combined, explain why banks in the Gulf region are generally reluctant to lend to SMEs. According to a study by Dun and Bradstreet, banks in the UAE in 2008 rejected 50–70% of credit applications from SMEs due to the higher risk and applicants' failure to meet basic loan conditions.[2] Because most SMEs in GCC countries have been in business for less than seven years, and many cannot muster credible financial statements for at least three years, bank loans and lines of credit are unavailable for more than 55% of SMEs.

Although the limited access to financing constrains SME growth, it also causes heightened emphasis on the cash flows that are generated and the necessity to reinvest these earnings to bolster growth. Therefore, any interruption of expected earnings and, of course, any disaster or unforeseen circumstance will seriously impact a SME's situation as a going concern. This is precisely where risk management comes in.

WHAT IS RISK?

Risk is "the possibility of something happening that impacts on your business objectives. It is the chance to either make a gain or a loss. It is measured in terms of likelihood and consequence."

The effective management of risk enables the business owner to avoid losses, maximize the potential of opportunities, and achieve the desired outcomes. SME owners and managers face both business (application of technology, skills, pricing, packaging, distribution choices, competitive positioning, etc.) and nonbusiness (compliance, legal, disasters, liability, product warranty, etc.) risks. Thus, the proactive management of an enterprise to anticipate risks is essential to creating and nurturing core business value.

Business value creation[3] occurs in the interaction between value drivers and risk drivers (Tables 2 and 3). Value drivers are simply cash inflows balancing against cash outflows.

For many SMEs, the main response to risk is to purchase insurance—i.e. protection against risk. However, insurance cannot be viewed as just another commodity, where buying at the lowest possible price means good value. Rather than approach risk as an exercise in cost containment, the SME owner or manager should adopt an attitude of becoming risk smart.

WHY SHOULD AN SME BOTHER TO LEARN ABOUT RISK AND INSURANCE?

The purpose of insurance is risk protection—to transfer a risk that you can afford (i.e. the payment of a premium with no guarantee that it will be returned) to cover a risk whose consequences you cannot afford. To help calculate the cost–benefit of insurance, your business should have access to a dedicated and knowledgeable risk manager. Typically, the revenue of a SME does not justify hiring a full-time, in-house risk manager or insurance expert. Therefore, many businesses seek the services of an insurance broker or an insurance agent. However, a broker or agent may not be qualified in risk assessment and may not always negotiate insurance prices in the

Table 4. Examples of SME risks. (*Source*: European Agency for Safety and Health at Work, 2010)

Risk type	Examples	Possible consequences
Personnel risks	An accident A key person leaves An entrepreneur is overburdened	Loss of work input The company loses important expertise Ability to work is reduced
Business risks	Demand for a product decreases Disruption in a customer's payments Production capacity does not correspond to a customer's needs	The company finances cannot take it Anticipated income does not arrive The customer changes supplier
Property risks	A fire in a production facility or shop Water leakage spoils the company's stocks A machine breaks down	Substantial damage, business operations are interrupted for several months Production and deliveries are disturbed Production is interrupted
Information risks	A computer hard disk breaks down The customer register is sold without permission The company's information is accidentally leaked	Order data are lost The company's reputation suffers. A competitor steals the customers The company's competitiveness suffers
Operational liability risks	An employee makes a mistake with a product or service An agreed delivery is delayed	Liability for damages to a third party The company has to pay a contract penalty
Product liability risks	A product causes damage A faulty product has to be withdrawn from the market	The company has to pay compensation Financial loss, the company's reputation suffers
Interruption risks	A power cut interrupts production A delivery from a subcontractor is delayed A load of raw material is stopped at a neighbouring country's customs	The company's operations are interrupted Production is interrupted Capital is tied up, production is interrupted
Transport risks	A product is broken durring transport A transport vehicle is stolen	Financial loss Deliveries are disrupted
Environmental risks	An oil container breaks Packaging proves to be unsuitable for recycling	The company's reputation suffers and it becomes liable for damages Sales to an important export country are interrupted

"If you only take small risks, you are only entitled to a small life." Robin S. Sharma

  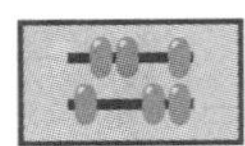      

Table 5. Ranking of risks of business disruption

Risk	%
Failure of computers and data loss	74%
Communications and network failure	59%
Power breakdown	47%
Fire	44%
Computer hacking	21%
Natural disasters	21%
Internal security breaches/ theft	18%
Terrorist attacks	12%
Pandemic diseases/flu	3%
Strikes and riots	3%

best interest of your business (because typically the insurance company will pay him or her a commission). Nowadays, when all businesses are seeking ways to reduce expenses, to lower the cost of insurance, and to boost their bottom line/profitability, it certainly would be advantageous to have a risk assessment (internal audit) performed, and to re-examine the business risks and existing insurance program in light of this risk assessment. The main goals for a SME must be to avoid overinsuring the misalignment of risks and risk protection, incorrect limits, exclusions, and so on.

Insurance is not only very important for you and the company's assets, it is also critically important to business relationships. Your customers, suppliers, employees, and bankers will all feel more comfortable in doing business with your company when there is a solid, well-structured insurance program in place. This provides the assurance to stakeholders that your business will not disappear overnight or fail to pay for goods or services in the event of a loss that may afflict the business.

Figure 1. Significant business disruptions in GCC countries and Jordan, 2009. (*Source*: Khan, 2009)

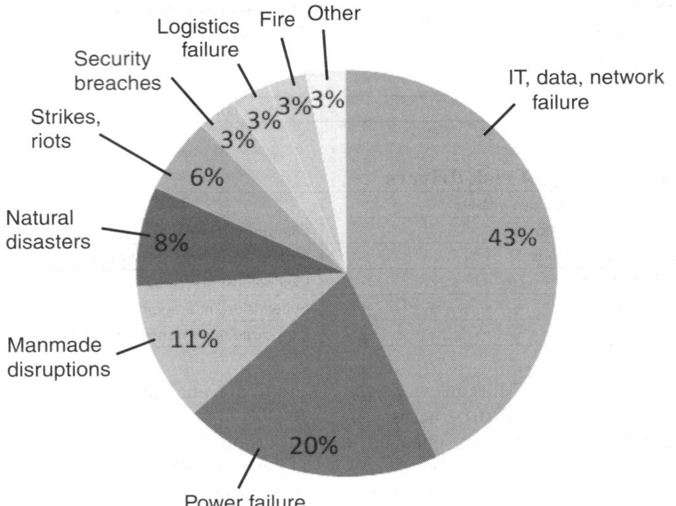

Table 6. What are the alternatives?

Options	*Cost*
Hiring a full-time, professional risk manager	Average base salary for 2009 is US$ 51,852 (Dhs 190,000)
Buying/leasing risk software	Purchase costs can be US$250,000 and above plus annual maintenance fees
Hiring a consultant/adviser	Variable costs depending on the consultant, usually $150 to $250 per hour
Figuring it out on your own—"go it alone"	Wasted work hours and reduced productivity. Most likely not up to industry best practices
Do nothing	Costs nothing, until serious loss...

EXAMPLES OF RISKS AFFECTING SMES

Although not exhaustive, Table 4 describes numerous textbook types of risk that can hamper or destroy a SME business. Among the risks highlighted are: personnel risks, business risks, property risks, IT and information risks, operational and liability risks, machinery breakdown and interruption risks, transportation and delivery risks, and environmental risks.

As suggested earlier, to capture the effect of the risks that could impact your business, a risk assessment, or internal risk audit, should be performed. The benefits of an internal risk audit are as follows.

- *Increase revenue*. Formalizing risk management practices helps to improve risk assessment, identify real exposures, reduce claims costs, and lower insurance premiums, leading to more predictable cash flows, increased revenues, and a better bottom line.
- *Save time*. With plans, maps, risk tools, and more, an audit can bring structure and timeliness to all your risk management activities, improving operational efficiency and overall profitability.
- *Improve safety*. Actively managing risk reduces the frequency and severity of accidents, resulting in safer customers and employees and fewer claims against the organization.
- *Protect company value*. An audit can help organizations to safeguard their assets, build stronger employee loyalty, and protect themselves from reputational damage.

In December 2009, more than 75 organizations in the GCC region and Jordan were surveyed[4] to see how many had a strategy to deal with disasters. 70% admitted to not having done any contingency planning. Risks and business survival were simply ignored. The perceived risks threatening continuation of business are set out in Table 5.

Figure 1 displays the categories of actual risks that adversely affected businesses in the GCC–Jordan region during 2009.

This survey provides insight into the types of occurrence that can temporarily or permanently set back SME earnings. Owners and managers should ask themselves whether they have examined these risks in relation to their business operations. The options open to them are set out in Table 6.

CONCLUSIONS

SMEs in the GCC region today confront huge business and nonbusiness challenges: limited access to financing, higher borrowing costs, limited collateral resources, and poor bookkeeping and accounting practices, to name a few. Risk management can be a business enabler, not just another cost item to be controlled. Owners and managers of SMEs are advised to adapt their attitude to risk to shift toward business value creation and to focus on how risk management can deliver more stable earnings, much-needed resources to cover emergencies, and a tighter grip on value drivers. A periodic internal risk audit can be performed by a risk professional in order to:

- ensure that the business assets are properly protected;
- secure the stability of cash flows;

"You want a valve that doesn't leak and you try everything possible to develop one. But the real world provides you with a leaky valve. You have to determine how much leakiness you can tolerate." Arthur Rudolph

- underpin the longevity of the young SME business;
- enhance the bookkeeping and strengthen corporate governance;
- align the risk–reward calculation of buying insurance coverage.

In addition, the implementation of risk management practices by SMEs will impress their bankers, demonstrate that their business presents a reduced risk profile, and can result in the easier access to capital and/or lower cost of funds that is so crucial to acceleration of the growth of the core business of SMEs.

MORE INFO

Book:

Pickford, James (ed). *Mastering Risk: Volume 1—Concepts*. Harlow, UK: Pearson Education, 2001.

Reports:

Deloitte. "Guide to risk: Intelligent governance." 2009.

European Agency for Safety and Health at Work. "Risk management basics for SMEs." UK and Finland report. 2010.

Hertog, Steffen. "Benchmarking SME policies in the GCC." European Union–Gulf Cooperation Council Chamber Forum, April 2010.

IBM Global Business Services. "Risk management." 2007.

Khan, Zarina. "Risky business: Contingency planning in the Gulf." Gulf Business.com, December 2009.

Massachusetts Division of Insurance. "Small business guide to commercial insurance." 2009.

Small Business Centre, Government of Australia. "Small business bizguide." 2010.

See Also:

★ Banks and Small and Medium-Sized Enterprises: Recent Business Developments (pp. 138–140)

★ Growing and Maximizing SME Profitability Without Compromising ROI (pp. 859–860)

NOTES

1 Hertog, 2010.

2 *Ibid.*, p. 9.

3 Adapted from IBM Global Business Services. "Risk management." 2007.

4 Khan, 2009.

"Creditors have better memories than debtors." Benjamin Franklin

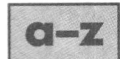

Viewpoint: Sustainability Reporting and Assurance—A Market-Driven Transformation

by Brendan Le Blanc and Barruch Ben-Zekry

INTRODUCTION

Brendan LeBlanc is the assurance leader in Ernst & Young LLP's Americas climate change and sustainability services practice. In this role he oversees the development and implementation of related competencies throughout the United States, extending to clients through the firm's core services. Previously, he founded LeBlanc & Associates, a niche CPA firm focused on corporate social responsibility assurance services. In this capacity, he issued the first reasonable assurance opinion on a sustainability report in the United States in 2008. He received a BA in accounting from Gordon College, Wenham, MA. He is a certified internal auditor and a certified public accountant licensed in Massachusetts and New Hampshire.

Barruch Ben-Zekry is a manager in Ernst & Young LLP's Americas climate change and sustainability services practice with expertise in strategy, carbon footprinting, energy management, environmental performance improvement, and lifecycle analysis. Prior to joining Ernst & Young, Barruch was the manager of environmental sustainability at Levi Strauss & Co. based at its San Francisco, CA, headquarters. Ben-Zekry holds a BS in environmental economics and policy from the University of California, Berkeley.

GOING BEYOND THE FINANCIAL STATEMENTS

Companies today are looking for ways to measure and report more than just their financial statements. To increase profits and build transparency and accountability with their customers, employees, suppliers, boards, investors, and the public, companies are also looking to measure and report on their environmental, social, and governmental performance.

To understand sustainability reporting, we need to look back at its evolution. Sustainability reporting has its roots in corporate citizenship, sometimes called corporate social responsibility (CSR), a practice that is as old as trade and business. Businesses—in particular larger companies that have a larger impact on their communities—have long sought to ensure good corporate stewardship through creating philanthropic programs. Historically, businesses engaged in these types of practices to be good local community partners and to help to build, maintain, or repair their reputations. And, for many years, these activities were kept separate from what were the perceived costs of doing business—materials, property, cash, transportation—and, as such, the financial reporting mechanisms.

As the world has become more interconnected, the lens viewing the real costs of products and services has widened its scope. Companies of all sizes—but particularly multinational corporations—are seeking to better understand their externalized costs, meaning they are now considering the costs borne by the environment, community, employee treatment in their supply chains, and the respective risks. This paradigm shift has demonstrated a need for a change in the ways companies gather and report their "value creation story". Since this change involves topics that traditionally are relegated to the world of CSR, those practices and processes have also needed to evolve. Socially responsible investors, active nongovernmental organizations (NGOs), and a few values-led companies have been clamoring for this kind of information for decades.

ENTER SUSTAINABILITY REPORTING

The guidelines for sustainability reporting have largely come out of the Global Reporting Initiative (GRI). The GRI developed and, in 2000, launched a widely adopted and comprehensive sustainability reporting framework that enables measurement and reporting on the key areas of sustainability: economic, environmental, social, and governance performance. This framework allowed companies to have a common language and a way to present a large volume of information about the aforementioned topics in a succinct way.

The framework had another impact, though: it gave companies and their stakeholders a wide view into all aspects of business operations and, therefore, the true costs and drivers of profits. Suddenly, there were more reported-upon factors that impacted the value of an organization: people, natural resources, intellectual capital, market and regulatory context, competition, and security. Suddenly, too, there were more risks to consider. As a result, companies are responsible not only for making and delivering products and services, but also for managing every aspect of that product or service's creation through every avenue of the supply chain down to, for example, a mineral's extraction from the earth.

To keep up with this expansion, the GRI has routinely adapted and updated its framework. Currently, the organization is in the process of asking for comment on G4, the latest version of its sustainability reporting framework. Among the chief differences from GRI version G3.1, which is the framework that most use today, is the way in which supply chains are considered and treated. G4 focuses much more on the sustainability performance all the way through the supply chain, and that promises to be very useful for larger

"There are 300,000 accountants in Britain, which means that, as with rats, you're never less than a few feet from one."
Jolyon Jenkins

companies with extended global or regional supply chains.

When we look at what is driving sustainability reporting, what is particularly noteworthy is that it isn't a process that is being mandated by regulation. Instead, this is a process that is largely driven by the increasing sophistication of company stakeholders, which include customers, employees, communities, NGOs, suppliers, and providers of financial capital. Stakeholders want relevant information. They want to understand how the company is identifying and managing risk in the widest dimension. A company following GRI will attempt to report on material items of importance to these multiple stakeholders.

THE WORK OF THE INTERNATIONAL INTEGRATED REPORTING COUNCIL (IIRC)

To focus this lens of additional disclosed information for the providers of financial capital, some companies are working toward the creation of a framework that integrates sustainability and financial reporting. The IIRC was set up in 2008 by the joint efforts of the Prince's Accounting for Sustainability Project (A4S), the International Federation of Accountants (IFAC), and the GRI to create a common language that enables companies to communicate how value is created and will be preserved through time. More than 80 companies—including Clorox, Cliffs Natural Resources, Coca-Cola, Microsoft, and Prudential—and accounting firms, including Ernst & Young LLP, have signed up for a pilot program that is seeking to evolve corporate reporting, building on developments in both financial and sustainability reporting. Ultimately, the desire is to be able to provide comprehensive communication about the factors that are most relevant to the creation and preservation of company value.

Currently, there is increasing global interest in exploring integrated reports. In South Africa, for example, it is now a listing requirement of the Johannesburg Stock Exchange that companies produce an integrated financial and sustainability report, or explain why they have not. There are also interesting developments now in Sweden, Denmark, Singapore, and France, so the pace is definitely quickening. In the United States movement toward integrated reporting is slower than in other parts of the world.

Clearly, most companies are some distance from producing an integrated report. In fact, many are in the beginning stages of their own sustainability journeys and are unclear about exactly how and where to begin this process. That's where accounting firms can help.

As our clients report more nonfinancial information, they are increasingly turning to us to provide assurance that the information that they are reporting is credible. To support this growing part of our business, we have been developing sustainability-related assurance and advisory services that are an extension of the financial assurance services we provide. Our role is to help management to assess and report on the risks associated with actions or inactions around sustainability.

Reputation, and the idea of mitigating the risk to reputation, is one driver to creating these complex reports, but this is certainly not just about branding. Sustainability reporting speaks to access to capital and identifies opportunities for increased revenue and cost reductions. In fact, some corporations are now using sustainability reporting as a means to make crucial business decisions, such as choosing suppliers. Moreover, analysts and investors are making decisions based on the data in sustainability reports, as is evidenced by the fact that environmental, social, and governance reporting data are available on the more than 300,000 Bloomberg terminals around the world.

CONCLUSION

What does this all mean for how corporations conduct their business? We see sustainability reporting and its extensions becoming an ingrained part of corporate decision-making at the strategic level. We see management asking the questions: "Does this capital expenditure make sense in terms of the way we want to deliver profits into the future? Where do we build our next plant? How do we react to and make use of hotter summers? How big an issue is water scarcity?" These questions are all a part of the future of good corporate decision-making, which is good for the environment and even better for business.

MORE INFO

Books:

Chouinard, Yvon. *Let My People Go Surfing: The Education of a Reluctant Businessman*. New York: Penguin Press, 2005.

Esty, Daniel C., and Simmons, P. J. *The Green to Gold Business Playbook: How to Implement Sustainability Practices for Bottom-Line Results in Every Business Function*. Hoboken, NJ: Wiley, 2011.

Friedman, Thomas L. *Hot, Flat, and Crowded: Why We Need a Green Revolution—And How It Can Renew America*. New York: Farrar, Straus and Giroux, 2008.

Kurlansky, Mark. *Cod: A Biography of the Fish That Changed the World*. New York: Walker & Co., 1997.

Werbach, Adam.*Strategy for Sustainability: A Business Manifesto*. Boston, MA: Harvard Business Press, 2009.

Websites:

Global Reporting Initiative (GRI): www.globalreporting.org
International Integrated Reporting Council (IIRC): www.theiirc.org
The Prince's Accounting for Sustainability Project (A4S): www.accountingforsustainability.org

See Also:

★ Improving Corporate Profitability Through Accountability (pp. 685–686)
★ Internal Auditing's Contribution to Sustainability (pp. 687–691)
★ Viewpoint: The Growth of Sustainability Reporting (pp. 680–681)
✔ The Triple Bottom Line (p. 1125)

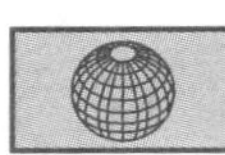

To Hedge or Not to Hedge by Steve Robinson

EXECUTIVE SUMMARY

- How currency risks are created and managed and the types of risk inherent in international trading.
- The techniques for managing currency risks.
- A framework for selecting appropriate techniques in specific business situations.
- An outline and illustration of the use of the main financial derivatives.

INTRODUCTION

Business has become increasingly international, and companies cannot ignore the impact of currency changes on cash flows, profitability, and their asset and liability position. No company is wholly immune—the cash received from exporting is affected by the relationship between the currency used by the customer to pay and the currency in which the cost of providing the product or service is denominated.

Many commodity prices have been volatile, rising and falling dramatically in recent years—driven by exploding or plummeting demand from fast-developing countries. Copper, tin, wheat, platinum, and of course oil, have risen dramatically, and this has had a significant impact on costs for many industries. Declines can be equally sudden, although falling costs often take more time to work through to market prices.

A spectacular result was the sudden collapse of several airline businesses in late 2007 and early 2008. Among them was EOS, a business-class only carrier operating mainly between London and New York, which started only in 2005. Also, Oasis Hong Kong Airlines, an innovative long-haul discount operator between Hong Kong, London, and Vancouver, MAXjet Airways, and some smaller low-cost US carriers, have all ceased trading very suddenly. Although other factors, such as reduced business travel and turbulent financial markets, have had an impact, the price of aviation fuel is the main cost driver, closely followed by the impact of currency changes—airlines pay all their costs in US dollars.

The risks extend beyond the trading sphere. Many banks have had to write down the value of their assets—largely complex "trading" securities. Finance is a global industry, and companies borrow and invest in many currencies. It is not sufficient that only financial people know how currency risks are created and managed.

WHAT ARE THE RISKS?

Currency risk is the net potential effect of exchange rate movements on the cash flow, profit, and balance sheet of a business. There are three types of currency risk:

Economic, Strategic, or Competitive Risk

Economic exposure covers the indirect risk to the profitability and cash flow of a company that arises from changes in exchange rates. It is likely that ultimately a resultant transaction exposure will arise.

An illustration, relating to the US dollar, the euro, and sterling, could be holidays. For British holidaymakers, holidays in the euro zone and the US dollar zone become more expensive if sterling weakens. The UK holiday industry could benefit from the euro exchange rate if more British stayed in the United Kingdom for their holidays.

Translation Risk

Translation risk arises when amounts denominated in foreign currency are converted to domestic equivalents for financial reporting purposes. There is no immediate cash impact. Translation can affect both the profit and loss account and the balance sheet. Increasingly, converging accounting standards under International Financial Reporting Standards (IFRS), which do not apply to unquoted companies, are removing some previous distortions. The most common accounting policy is to convert trading profit and loss numbers at an average exchange rate during the accounting period, and to convert assets and liabilities at the year-end rate.

Profit and Loss Statement Translation

The profit and loss translation is only a paper figure initially, but it may become a real transaction exposure if cash interest or dividends need to be paid. A company with a large proportion of its income, or of its cash, in other currencies, will have a translation issue, but this can be helped by effective communication to investors, persuading them that short-term currency fluctuations will not necessarily lead to reduced long-term stockholder value creation.

Balance Sheet Translation

The foreign currency assets of the company are not exposed to currency fluctuations unless they are to be sold and the cash converted to another currency. Liabilities denominated in foreign currencies will represent a real exposure when they are due for repayment.

The impact of translation on the gearing level has to be evaluated to ensure that no covenants are breached, even if only technically. A very simple way around this is to match investment in foreign currency assets with loans dominated in equivalent currencies.

The practical difficulty is how far the company can go to protect *reported* earnings, while incurring a cost that will impact on the bottom line. It is also possible that a *real* transaction exposure could be created by a currency borrowing. Also to be considered is the impact of a fair value adjustment, on both the profit and loss bottom line and on reserves in the balance sheet.

Transaction Risk

This risk is that exchange rate movements affect the value of foreign currency cash flows. It is the only risk that has a direct and immediate impact on cash, and arises when a transaction is entered into to convert from one currency to another.

The most common trading situation creating this exposure is the sale or purchase of goods or services on extended payment terms in foreign currencies. Another common situation arises when dividend or interest payments are paid or received.

This type of risk is usually predictable and quantified, making the protection or hedging process straightforward. Really successful management of currency exposures needs to cope with transactions that have not yet been identified but are likely to occur.

SPECIFIC SITUATIONS

Price List Exposure

Scenario: An exporting company publishes a price list in a local currency. It is commercially impractical to change prices in less than six months.

Risk: A potential exposure is created for up to six months, plus any extended payment term. Actual exposure arises when an invoice is issued.

Possible solutions:

- Small print "right to impose surcharges" clauses. This is legally possible, but commercially highly damaging. Airlines have had to resort to this, but it is easier for them given the high profile of oil price

"The system of book-keeping by double entry is, perhaps, the most beautiful one in the wide domain of literature or science. Were it less common, it would be the admiration of the learned world." Edwin T. Freedley

movements and the fact that almost all of the competitors are doing it!

- Hedging a proportion of projected sales, from the date of publication of the price list, is advisable. What proportion is a risk management decision, dependent on the corporate attitude to risk, the corporate memory of past situations, and the degree of volatility between currencies.

Capital expenditure: This investment is usually planned and committed over a long period. There may be no actual transaction exposure until purchase contracts are awarded, so the exposure can be identified, quantified, and handled by a hedging technique.

Tender to Control Exposure

Scenario and risk exposure: Companies that regularly submit tenders for the supply of goods and services are exposed from the date of submitting the tender to the date(s) cash is received. Until an order has been received, this is potential exposure; after that event there is real exposure, and from the invoice date transaction exposure exists.

Possible solutions:

- Using historic data for guidance, assess the success rate from tender to contract. Apply that rate—with a value weighting—to all tenders issued, hedging the proportion that's likely to be successful. Additionally, where good market intelligence exists, add in those contracts likely to be won.
- Treat the exposure after winning the contract as a transaction, and hedge using an appropriate technique.
- Try to offset as many costs as possible by buying in the currency of the payer.

MANAGING CURRENCY RISKS

A range of techniques exists that enable companies to limit their exposure to the effect of fluctuating exchange rates. The decision to protect or hedge is made after an assessment of the significance of the risk to the business of exchange rate movements. The selection of hedging technique is made for each specific situation, following a risk assessment of the impact on the business. Factors considered in the risk assessment are:

- The percentage of the company's turnover that is exposed to currency risk. The greater the proportion of sales paid in international currencies versus the home currency, the greater the risk to the business.
- The individual size of a single exposure. Depending on the volatility of the currency, this could be a very high risk, even threatening the continuity of the business.
- The market position of the company. This is its financial strength and consequent ability to react to competitive pressures.
- The portfolio of currencies in which the company trades, and whether there are potential offsetting transactions.
- The relationship of cost to sales within trading blocs, particularly currencies that move in lockstep with the US dollar—those of Canada, Hong Kong, Malaysia, Singapore, and Saudi Arabia.
- The ability to match the currency of sales with the currency of costs.
- The previous experience of the company in relation to currency losses, and its forecasting experience.
- The level of currency management expertise within the company.

HEDGING TECHNIQUES

Internal

Sometimes known as commercial or natural, these techniques are within the internal management control of the company.

Pricing:

- In the currency in which the majority of the costs are incurred.
- In the domestic currency of the main competitors, so that comparative prices are less affected by exchange rate variations.
- Inserting an exchange rate variation clause (always difficult commercially) to protect margins.

Matching:

- Setting up an equal and opposite commercial transaction when the original exposure is created—for example, using the currency of a receivable to buy a commodity used by the business.
- Borrow in the same currency as that needed to complete the asset purchase.

Netting:

- A partial alternative to matching—a net amount is still left exposed, but the overall risk is reduced.

Leading and lagging:

- Simply, either delaying payment, or settling early, in anticipation of falling or rising exchange rates. Safe, and simple to manage, but there is a reliance on the accuracy of a forecast.

Intercompany payment discipline:

- Intercompany payables and receivables are real exposure and should be ranked equally for settlement with external liabilities.
- There is no canceling gain or loss situation within a group. When the transaction interacts with the market there will be a gain or a loss—and it will be real.

External

When the use of internal techniques has been exhausted, external ones should be used. There are four main instruments:

- Forward contracts;
- Lending and borrowing;
- Options;
- Swaps.

Forward Contracts

A forward contract is an agreement to exchange a fixed amount of one currency for a fixed amount of another currency at an agreed date in the future. The effective exchange rate is derived from the comparative interest rates of the two currencies being exchanged. Its suitability depends on being able to forecast the currency flows confidently. If the forecast proves not to be accurate, the business has in reality created an exposure rather than protected an existing one, because the forward contract is a binding agreement to deliver a quantity of one currency and receive a quantity of another. The key features of a forward contract are:

- Certainty and simplicity—enabling good cash management;
- Off balance sheet—it does not count as borrowings that affect gearing;
- Normally sourced from a bank.

Lending and Borrowing

As an alternative to a forward contract, the currency could be exchanged immediately in the spot market, i.e. where the transaction is agreed on the "spot" and takes place immediately. The exchange rate is known as fixed, the transaction immediate (two days delivery normally), and the administration and monitoring of forward contracts are avoided. The currency is normally deposited in an interest-bearing currency account until needed.

Illustration: A forward transaction to buy yen for a capital equipment purchase has been made. Delivery will be late. A way around this problem would be to take delivery of the yen as agreed and put the amount on deposit until needed. As yen interest rates are lower than for sterling, there will be an effective interest cost. If delivery was available earlier and agreed to by the company, yen could be borrowed short term and repaid when the forward contract matured.

Options

An option is the right, but not the obligation, to exchange a fixed amount of one currency for a fixed amount of another within, or at the end of, a predetermined period. In effect, it is a forward contract that can be walked away from, where you lose only the cost of the option, which could be

"The world of finance hails the invention of the wheel over and over again, often in a slightly more unstable form."
J. K. Galbraith

3–5% of the contract value. It therefore has the advantage of limiting the downside, as the maximum cost is known at the beginning, while leaving unlimited profit potential. These options are ideally suited to translations, where the size or existence of the exposure is uncertain, for example tender-to-contract or price list exposures.

Illustration: A quantity of a commodity (or currency to pay for it) is needed in three months' time. A dealer is willing to accept US$100 per ton to supply a predetermined quantity at US$2,000 per ton. If the price of this commodity in three months' time is US$1,700 per ton, then the option would be thrown away, the product bought in the spot market, and the cost to the company would be US$1,800 per ton. The tender-to-contract or price list item would have been safeguarded, and the price could even be reduced by US$200 per ton if competitive conditions demanded. If the price of the commodity rose, the cost to the company would be contained. The option could be sold at a profit if the product was not needed, or the loss would in any event be limited to US$100 per ton.

There are two types of option:

- **Calls**—giving the right to buy a currency;
- **Puts**—giving the right to sell a currency.

Currency Options

The exchange rate (known as the strike price) and the expiry date of the option are chosen by the customer at the outset. The cost (known as the premium) of the option is calculated based on these decisions and the volatility of the currency involved. Options can be exchange-traded where they exist in standardized form, or bought over the counter, where they are written to fit a customer's particular circumstances.

There are two styles of option:

- **American option**. The buyer can exercise the option (make the exchange of currencies) at any time up to the expiry date.
- **European option**. This can be exercised on the expiry date only, and is slightly cheaper because of its lack of flexibility.

Options may have a resale value, determined by the same criteria as the original cost. When the exercise price of an option is better than the current spot exchange rate, it is called "in the money"; when it is the other way round, it is "out of the money."

Swaps

Swaps are like long-dated forward contracts. They involve the exchange of a liability now, with the exchange back at a predetermined future time, and the compensation of the other party for costs in the intervening period. Swaps are used primarily to protect an investment or portfolio of borrowings. They involve a back-to-back loan between companies with a matching but opposite need. What is "swapped" is essentially a series of cash flows.

Illustration: A UK company wishes to raise cash to invest in developing its business in the United States. It is quoted in the United Kingdom only, which means it does not have access to US capital markets and it does not have a rating, so it would be extremely difficult to borrow in the United States.

What sources of funds are available?

- Raise equity via a UK rights issue;
- Borrow sterling from a UK bank;
- Borrow in US dollars.

The first two of these options will appear on a balance sheet as sterling liabilities, but the asset will appear as a dollar asset, creating a translation exposure. The returns from the investment will be in dollars, which will create a translation exposure when they are converted to sterling income in the profit statement, and a transaction exposure when they need to be converted to pay interest or dividends in sterling.

A solution is to swap the currency flows for the duration of a loan, paying or receiving a sum of money from the other party, leaving both sides in an equivalent cash flow position but having avoided specific payments in another currency. The loan would revert to the borrowing currency on maturity.

CONCLUSION

Managing currency and related transactions is a core part of corporate risk management within the treasury function. Its importance will continue to demand boardroom time and the highest standard of corporate governance. Massive and unpredictable fluctuations in currency markets have made forecasting more difficult and the need to safeguard the value of assets, liabilities, and transactions is paramount.

MORE INFO

Books:

Arnold, Glen. *Corporate Financial Management*. 4th ed. Harlow, UK: FT Prentice Hall, 2008.

Boakes, Kevin. *Reading and Understanding the Financial Times*. Harlow, UK: FT Prentice Hall, 2008.

Matza, Peter (ed). *The International Treasurer's Handbook 2009*. 19th ed. London: Association of Corporate Treasurers, 2008.

Shomah, Shani Beverley. *A Foreign Exchange Primer*. 2nd ed. Chichester, UK: Wiley, 2009.

Slatyer, Will. *The Debt Delusion: Evolution and Management of Financial Risk*. Boca Raton, FL: Universal Publishers, 2008.

Websites:

DailyFX: www.dailyfx.com

Reuters Business and Finance: www.reuters.com/finance

TMI Online: www.treasury-management.com

See Also:

★ Political Risk: Countering the Impact on Your Business (pp. 902–904)
★ A Total Balance Sheet Approach to Financial Risk (pp. 113–114)
✔ Building a Forex Plan (p. 965)
✔ The Foreign Exchange Market: Its Structure and Function (p. 968)
✔ Hedging Foreign Exchange Risk—Case Studies and Strategies (p. 970)
✔ International Financial Reporting Standards (IFRS): The Basics (p. 1039)
✔ Key Accounting Standards and Organizations (p. 1040)
✔ Understanding and Using Currency Swaps (p. 992)

"There are two times in a man's life when he should not speculate: when he can't afford it and when he can." Mark Twain

  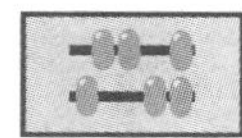   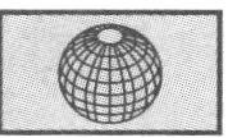   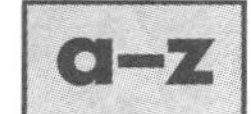

Tools for Measuring Interest Rate Risk

by Steven V. Mann

EXECUTIVE SUMMARY

- The two dimensions of interest rate risk: level risk and curve risk.
- The two approaches for measuring interest rate risk: duration/convexity and full valuation.
- The valuation of any security involves determining the present values of expected cash flows and figuring out how much the embedded options are worth.
- Four attributes govern a bond's response to a yield change: the remaining term to maturity, the level of the coupon rate, the level of the yields, and the presence of embedded options.
- Duration can be defined as the average percentage price change for a 100 bp movement in the reference yield curve.
- Convexity measures the magnitude of the error of linear approximation by duration of the price–yield relationship.
- The full valuation approach performs a full valuation of a bond (or bond portfolio) for each of the chosen interest rate scenarios.

INTRODUCTION

One can understand risk intuitively as the chance of an unpleasant surprise. Financial institutions must be able to manage their exposure to risk. To accomplish this task, they must be able to identify the risks to which they are exposed and measure that exposure. Numerous types of risk put a financial institution in harm's way. One major exposure is to interest rate risk. Interest rate risk has two dimensions—*level risk* and *curve risk*. Level risk is the chance of an adverse movement in the price of a bond owing to a parallel shift in the reference yield curve. Curve risk is the prospect of an adverse movement in the price of a bond owing to a change in the shape (i.e. slope and curvature) of the reference yield curve. To manage their exposure to interest rate risk, financial institutions must be able to measure both level and curve risk. The purpose of this chapter is to introduce the tools for measuring both types of interest rate risk. Most of the time will be spent discussing level risk, while curve risk will be covered to a lesser extent.

We will discuss two approaches for assessing the interest rate risk exposure of a bond or bond portfolio. The first approach entails the computation of measures that approximate how a bond's price or the portfolio's value will change when interest rates change. The most commonly used measures are *duration* and *convexity*. We will discuss duration and convexity measures for bonds and bond portfolios. The second approach is the *full valuation approach*, which involves selecting possible interest rate scenarios for how interest rates and yield spreads may change and then revaluing the bond position.

WHY DO BOND PRICES CHANGE?

Any security can be thought of as a package of one or more cash flows. A complicated security is a package of cash flows with one or more options attached. The option attached to the security gives its owner (either the holder or the issuer) the right to alter the security's cash flows at an optimal time. That said, the valuation of any security involves determining present values and figuring out how much the embedded options are worth.

To determine present values, a discount rate is employed. Simply put, a discount rate is an exchange rate across time. A discount rate translates the value of a set of cash flows scattered across time and with different exposures to risk into a single sum. In general, discount rates are driven by two factors—a default-free benchmark interest rate and a risk premium. A default-free benchmark interest rate reflects the risk-free interest rate. Even in a world without risk, interest rates are positive. The reason is that human beings would prefer to consume now as opposed to later. Interest rates are bribes designed to quell our impatience to consume. Correspondingly, risk premiums are bribes that are designed to neutralize our risk-aversion. As a general description of how human beings behave, we operate under the assumption that investors are risk-averse. Risk-aversion does not mean that investors shun risk, merely that one must compensate them for taking it. The risk premium is the spread over the risk-free rate required to induce an investor to hold a risky security as opposed to a safe one. For a given level of risk, the risk premium is time-varying. The size of the risk premium depends on both the level of interest rates and investors' willingness to bear risk.

Given this background, we can now address the question of why bond prices change. First, any factor that results in a change in the bond's required yield will result in a change in the price of an option-free bond in the opposite direction. Second, the mere passage of time will push all bond prices to the par values. Bond prices that trade at a premium will be pulled to par without any change in required yield. Although we are cognizant of the second factor, our focus in this chapter is the first factor—specifically, the immediate response of the bond price to an instantaneous change in the bond's required yield.

THE PRICE–YIELD RELATIONSHIP OF A BOND

Figure 1 depicts the relationship between the price of a default-free, option-free bond and its required yield. Here, 30-year, 10-year, and five-year US Treasury notes were chosen as examples of such bonds, paying coupons of 4.375%, 3.375%, and 1.5% respectively.[1] Note the features that all three curves in Figure 1 have in common—namely, each relationship is downward-sloping and curved (more or less). The downward slope is courtesy of the inverse relationship between bond prices and their required yields. As for the curvature, it is a byproduct of the mathematics of the bond-pricing formula. The relationship is said to be convex as it bends toward the origin and out toward the horizontal axis. Bond market participants use the term "positive convexity." It turns out that the slope and curvature give us important information about the exposure of a bond to interest rate risk.

A bond has four attributes that impact its response to a given change in required yield:

- the remaining term to maturity;
- the level of the coupon rate;
- the level of the yields;
- the presence of embedded options.

These four attributes affect the slope and curvature of the price–yield relationship.

The price–yield relationship for an option-free bond is downward-sloping and curved. A bond's interest rate risk depends on the slope of this relationship and the degree of the curvature.

Four Observations About the Shape of the Curve

The first observation we put forward is that the percentage change in price, given a

"If the argument is that failure helps you succeed, well, so does success and it's quicker. This suggests at least one reason for trying to succeed." Norman Geras

  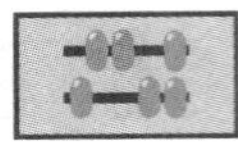      

Figure 1. The price–yield relationship

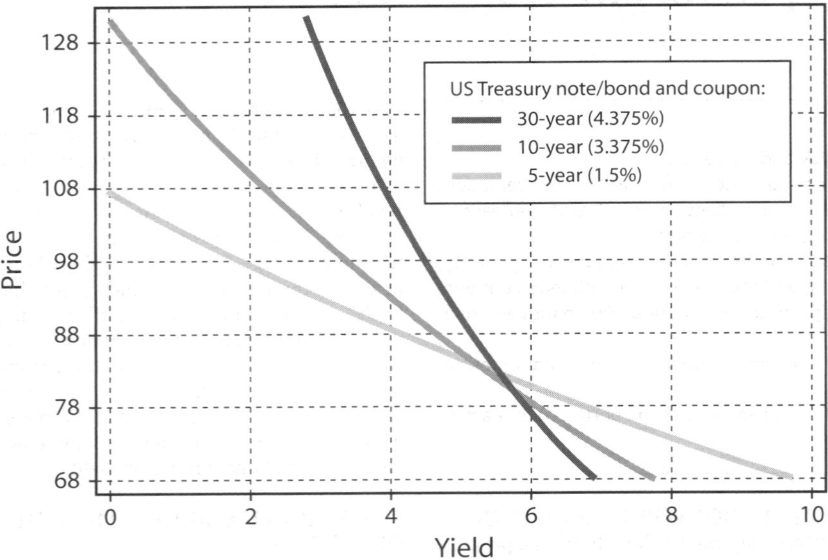

change in yield, is not the same for all bonds. Looking back at Figure 1, this certainly rings true. The price–yield relationships for the three Treasury notes/bonds have different slopes and curvatures, so equal yield changes of, say, 100 bps will evoke different percentage price changes.

The second observation is that, for small changes in yield, the percentage price change for a particular bond is approximately the same whether the yield increases or decreases. Let us demonstrate this with some numbers. Consider a 30-year, 10% coupon bond priced to yield 10% so that the bond trades at par. Now we reprice the bond at yields one basis point higher and lower. At a yield of 10.01%, the price falls to 99.9054. At a yield of 9.99%, the price rises to 100.0947. The dollar value of a 1 bp change if the yield increases by 1 bp is 100 − 99.9054 = 0.0946. The dollar value of a 1 bp change if the yield decreases by 1 bp is 100.0947 − 100 = 0.0947. These changes are almost exactly the same in absolute value. For small changes in required yield, we can treat the curved price–yield relationship as if it were linear. As a result, the amount that the bond price rises or falls is almost exactly the same.

The third observation states that for large changes in yield the previous result no longer holds. For large changes in yield, the percentage price change for a yield increase is different from that of a yield decrease. The curvature influences the magnitude of the price changes for larger changes in yields.

The fourth and last observation takes the third observation one step further. For large changes in yield, the percentage price increase is greater than the percentage price decrease. We will demonstrate this result with some numbers. Once again we employ our 30-year, 10% coupon bond initially priced to yield 10%. We now consider dramatic changes in the bond's required yield. First, let us reprice the bond at 8%, which represents a 200 bp reduction in yield. The resulting price is 122.6235, which reflects a percentage change in price of 22.6235%. Now let us reprice the bond at 12%, which represents a 200 bp increase in yield from the initial yield of 10%. The resulting price is 83.8386, which reflects a percentage price change of −16.1614%. Note that the percentage increase (22.2635%) when yields fall is greater in absolute value than the percentage price decrease (−16.1614%) when yields rise. This result is attributable to positive convexity. Indeed, these four observations can be explained by the convex shape of the price–yield relationship.

We turn now to the question of which attributes affect a bond's sensitivity to a change in yield. In other words, what attributes explain the slope and curvature of the price–yield relationship? Consider the four hypothetical bonds with an initial yield of 8% in Table 1—two five-year notes with coupons of 7% or 10% and two 30-year bonds with coupons of 7% or 10%. The first column shows the different levels of required yield in increments and decrements of 50 bps, with the initial yield being 8%. Accordingly, each cell in the table represents a percentage change in price for a given level of required yield.

We see two factors at work here. First, when yield and maturity are held constant, the lower the coupon, the greater the sensitivity of the bond price to a given change in required yield. Coupon payments lessen the impact of a given change in required yield. As we move in Table 1 between the two five-year bonds, we see that for the higher-coupon bond all the percentage price changes are lower in absolute value. The same pattern is evident when one compares the percentage price changes of the two 30-year bonds. The second factor at work is the impact of maturity when yield and maturity are held constant. Other things being equal, the longer the maturity, the greater the impact of a given change in required yield. The reasoning is straightforward: cash flows more distant from the present are affected more dramatically by a given change in required yield.

Table 1. Percentage change in bond price for a given level of required yield

Yield (%)	Note/bond and coupon			
	5-year, 7%	30-year, 7%	5-year, 10%	30-year, 10%
6.0	8.67	28.36	8.28	26.69
6.5	6.42	20.15	6.13	19.02
7.0	4.23	12.75	4.04	12.06
7.5	2.09	6.06	1.99	5.75
8.0 (initial)	0.00	0.00	0.00	0.00
8.5	−2.04	−5.51	−1.94	−5.24
9.0	−4.02	−10.52	−3.84	−10.03
9.5	−5.96	−15.08	−5.69	−14.42
10.0	−7.85	−19.26	−7.50	−18.45

INTRODUCTION TO DURATION

In general, duration measures the sensitivity of the price of a bond (in percentage terms) to a change in yield. Here we are trying to measure the slope of the price–yield relationship at a particular point on the curve. Let us introduce the following notation:

Δy= Change in the bond's yield (decimal)

P_+= Bond price if the yield increases by Δy

P_-= Bond price if the yield decreases by Δy

"I think if your goal is for everything to be okay, that's a mistake. To achieve that goal, the only obstacle you'd have to face tomorrow is to eliminate all risk ... I've made the decision that I'm never trying to make everything okay. I'm trying for there to be more loose ends, not fewer loose ends." Seth Godin

P_0= Initial price of bond (per $100 of par value)

Duration is a linear approximation to the price–yield relationship, which is non-linear. If the change in rates is considerable or the price–yield relationship is more curved, the linear approximation will be less reliable.

We develop the duration measure under the assumption that the reference yield curve is flat and moves by way of parallel shifts. As a result, the yield for all maturities changes by the same number of basis points.

The duration measure that we will develop is a linear approximation to the current price–yield relationship. To obtain the slope of a line we need two points. The first point is the percentage price change for a 1 bp increase in yield, which is given by the expression Similarly, the second point is the percentage price change for a 1 bp decrease in yield, which is given by the expression

$$(P_- - P_0) \div P_0(\Delta y)100$$

Similarly, the second point is the percentage price change for a 1 bp decrease in yield, which is given by the expression

$$(P_0 - P_+) \div P_0(\Delta y)100$$

These two numbers are close to each other in absolute value but are not exactly the same because the price–yield relationship is a curve. Suppose that we wanted to know the average percentage price change for a 1 bp movement in the yield regardless of the direction. We would simply add the percentage price change expressions together and divide by two:

$$\frac{1}{2}[(P_- - P_0) \div P_0(\Delta y)100 + (P_0 - P_+) \div P_0(\Delta y)100]$$

Simply put,

$$(P_- - P_+) \div P_0(\Delta y)100$$

This expression tells us the average percentage price change for a 1 bp movement in the reference yield curve. Duration gives us the average percentage price change for a 100 bp movement in the reference yield curve. To move from the expression we have to the expression we want, simply multiply by 100. Duration can be computed using the following formula:

$$\text{Duration} = (P_- - P_+) \div 2P_0(\Delta y)$$

Example

Let's put the formula through its paces. Consider a 10%, 30-year bond priced to yield 8%. We need to choose a value for Δy in order to compute P_+ and P_-. The bigger the value of Δy, the greater the difference between P_+ and P_-. It turns out that the choice for $\Delta y$is somewhat arbitrary as the duration computed is almost exactly the same regardless of the value of Δy chosen. The important point to remember is that the choice of Δy does not affect the interpretation of the formula. Duration is the average percentage price change for a 100 bp change in the reference yield curve. Let Δy be 20 bps. We reprice the bond at a yield of 7.8% and a value for $P_-$of 125.3646. Perform the same operation with a yield of 8.2% to obtain a value of 119.9815 for P_+. Inserting these values into the duration formula results in

$$\begin{aligned}\text{Duration} &= (125.3646 - 119.9815) \div 2(122.6235) \times (0.002) \\ &= 10.97\end{aligned}$$

That is, when the reference yield curve shifts by 100 bps, we would expect this bond to change in value by approximately 10.97% in the opposite direction.

The advantages of duration being a linear approximation are manifest. We can easily approximate how much the bond value will respond to different interest rate shocks. If the reference yield curve shifts by 200 bps, the bond value will move by twice the duration's value in percentage terms. If the reference yield curve shifts by 50 bps, the bond's value is projected to change by half the duration, and so on.

Our next task is to expand our tool duration to three specific applications. First, what if we are dealing with expected dollar price changes as opposed to percentage price changes in response to interest rate shocks? Second, how does one compute the duration of a portfolio of bonds? Third, how does one extend the notion of duration to a bond with one or more embedded options?

Dollar Duration

When a financial institution is managing its exposure to interest rate risk, it is often useful to think in terms of dollar changes in value as opposed to percentage changes in value. For example, suppose that a trader wants to hedge the interest rate risk of a short position in a bond which he or she believes to be overvalued. The trader is concerned with offsetting adverse changes in the value of the position rather than percentage price changes. This brings us to dollar duration. Duration tells us the approximate percentage price change for a 100 bp shift in the reference yield curve.[2-] Two bonds with the same duration will not experience the same dollar price change. The approximate dollar price change for a 100 bp shift in the reference yield curve is given by the expression

$$\text{Dollar price change} = \text{Duration} \times \text{Bond price} \times 0.01$$

Portfolio Duration

Investors almost always hold a portfolio of bonds as opposed to a single bond. Thus, we are interested in measuring the interest rate risk exposure of a portfolio. A portfolio's duration is simply the weighted average of the durations of the individual bonds that comprise the portfolio. Each portfolio's weight is the proportion of the portfolio that is attributable to each security. Consider the hypothetical three-bond portfolio detailed in Table 2.

The portfolio duration is 4.987. The question arises as to how this number is to be interpreted. A portfolio duration measures the approximate percentage change in the portfolio's value if the yield for each of the bonds changes by 100 bps.

Effective Duration

The approximation formula for duration assumes that the bond's cash flows are invariant to parallel shifts in the reference yield curve. For an option-free bond this condition holds. A parallel shift in the reference yield curve does not engender a change in the expected size and timing of an option-free bond's cash flows. For bonds with embedded options, the cash flows are interest rate-dependent. Simply put, when interest rates change, the cash flows change. Duration (as calculated above) is not an appropriate measure of interest rate risk sensitivity for bonds with embedded options: callables, putables, structured products, etc. The presence of the embedded call option changes the convexity of the price–yield relationship.

Table 2. Portfolio duration example

Bond	Full price	Duration	Portfolio weight
A	100.6555	1.886	0.489
B	101.5119	7.518	0.394
C	60.1730	9.421	0.117

"Obvious almost always isn't. With the sheer number of different world views people have these days one person's obvious is another person's revelation." Joshua Porter

  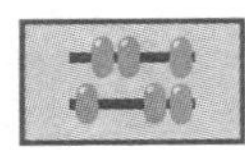      

Figure 2. Price–yield relationship for option-free bond and callable bond

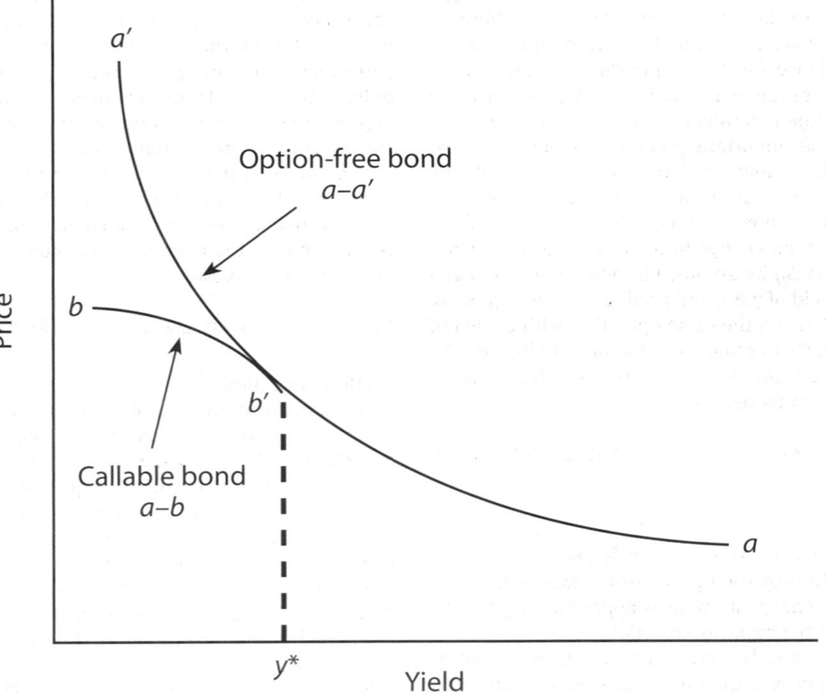

Figure 2 shows the price–yield relationship for an option-free bond and a callable bond. The curve labeled *a–a′* is the price–yield relationship of an option-free bond. Correspondingly, the price–yield relationship for a callable bond is given by the curve *a–b*. An embedded call option causes the price–yield relationship to bend back the opposite direction (curve *b–b′*) relative to an option-free bond. The reason for this effect is that as yields fall the value of the embedded call option increases. The bondholder is short the call option, so the increase in its value causes the callable bond's price to appreciate at a decreasing rate.

To account for embedded options, analysts often employ a so-called *effective* or *option-adjusted* duration using our approximation formula developed earlier. The only difference is in how $P_-$and P_+ are computed. These terms are computed using a valuation model that is designed to incorporate the impact of the shift in the reference yield curve on the cash flows of a bond with an embedded option. Thus, the interest rate dependence is incorporated directly into the calculation of P_- and P_+. Many analysts believe that the duration and effective duration of option-free bonds should always be the same. This is strictly true only when the reference yield curve is flat and moves with parallel shifts. The reason for this is that the par and spot curves do not shift by the same amount except when the yield curve is flat.[3]

INTRODUCTION TO CONVEXITY

Duration is a linear approximation to the relationship between bond prices and yield, which is inherently nonlinear (see Figure 1). The question is under what conditions this linear approximation is viable. To answer this question, we need to be able to measure the curvature of the price–yield relationship. Using the same notation as before, we employ the following formula to approximate the curvature or convexity of the price–yield relationship:

$$(\text{Convexity} = P_+ + P_- - 2P_0) \div P_0(\Delta y)^2$$

We will use the approximation formula to compute the convexity of a 30-year US Treasury principal STRIPS valued at 25.088 and yielding 4.692%.[4] Assume that*y*is 20 bps, as before, and reprice the bonds at lower and higher yields. The following are the inputs to be inserted into the formula:

$\Delta y = 0.002$
$P_+ = 23.669$
$P_- = 26.594$
$P_0 = 25.088$

The convexity is computed as follows:

$$\text{Convexity} = [23.669 + 26.594 - 2(25.088)] \div 23.088(0.002)^2 = 870$$

Duration and convexity are complements, not substitutes. One either uses duration alone when interest rates are stable, or duration and convexity together when interest rates are volatile.

This number, 870, represents the degree of curvature of the price–yield relationship. Larger convexity values represent greater curvature. A larger curvature translates into a larger error from using a linear, duration-based approximation to estimate a nonlinear relationship. Convexity is used to measure the magnitude of that error. Duration provides a first approximation of a bond's sensitivity to change in yield. Convexity gives a finer, second approximation. The approximate percentage change in price due to convexity, or the so-called convexity correction, is given by the expression

$$\text{Convexity correction} = 0.5 \times \text{Convexity} \times (\Delta y)^2$$

Let us return to our Treasury STRIPS to illustrate. If the yield increases from 4.692% to 7.692%, what is the percentage price change due to convexity?

$$0.5 \times 870 \times (0.03)^2 = 0.3915$$

Thus, the percentage price change due to convexity is 39.15%. This is the error due to using duration alone. Now let us put duration and convexity together.

The duration of this Treasury STRIPS is 29.157. The percentage change in the bond price predicted using duration alone is computed as follows:

$$\text{Percentage change} = -29.157 \times 3 = -87.47\%$$

This is the price change predicted using duration, which is a linear approximation. The convexity correction adjusts the linear approximation to take into account the effect of the curvature of the price–yield relationship. The approximate percentage change in the bond price using both duration and convexity is summarized as follows:

Linear approximation estimated by duration:	−87.45%
Convexity correction:	+ 39.15%
Total:	−48.30%

The convexity correction adjusts for the error from using duration alone. The

“**Know what you want—and remember that whatever your bottom line is, there's always another line below that.**”
Anonymous

correction will be larger when the convexity is large and interest rates are volatile.

THE FULL VALUATION APPROACH

An alternative method to measure the interest rate risk exposure of a bond position or a portfolio of bonds is to revalue it assuming different hypothetical yield levels. For example, a manager may want to measure the interest rate exposure to instantaneous shifts of 50, 100, and 200 bps in the reference yield curve. This approach comprises the valuation of a bond or bond portfolio for multiple interest rate scenarios and is referred to as the *full valuation approach*. It is sometimes referred to asscenario *analysis*.

The full valuation, or scenario analysis, approach is the most flexible method for assessing a portfolio's exposure to curve risk because any change in the reference yield curve can be simulated.

To illustrate this approach, suppose that a portfolio manager has a US$50 million par value position in US principal STRIPS (i.e. a zero-coupon investment) that matures on May 15, 2041.[5] The price is 26.7928, with a corresponding yield of 4.471%. The market value of the position is US$13,396,400. Since the manager has a long position in this issue, he/she is concerned with a rise in yields since this will reduce the position's market value. To assess the portfolio's exposure to a rise in yields, the manager decides to examine how the STRIPS' value will change if yields increase instantaneously by 50, 100, 150, and 200 bps—i.e. four scenarios. Because this zero-coupon bond is optionfree, valuation is straightforward. The STRIPS' price per US$100 of par value and the market value of the US$50 million par position are shown in Table 3. Also presented are the change in the market value and the percentage change.

The full valuation approach can also handle scenarios where the yield curve does not change in a parallel fashion. Here, the scenario analyzed is for a change in the slope of the yield curve combined with changes in the levels of the yields. As a result, the portfolio manager can measure the exposure of a portfolio to yield curve risk.

A common question that often arises when using the full valuation approach is which scenarios should be evaluated to assess exposure to interest rate risk. For some regulated entities specified scenarios are established by regulators. For example, it is common for regulators of depository institutions to require entities to determine the impact on the value of their bond portfolio for 100, 200, and 300 bp instantaneous changes, both up and down, in interest rates. Risk managers and highly leveraged investors such as hedge funds tend to look at extreme shocks to assess exposure to interest rate changes. This practice is referred to as stress testing.

Of course, in assessing how changes in the yield curve can affect the exposure of a portfolio, there are an infinite number of scenarios that can be evaluated. The state-of-the-art technology involves using a complex statistical procedure[6]to determine a likely set of yield curve shift scenarios from historical data.

In summary, we can use the full valuation approach to assess the exposure of a bond or portfolio to interest rate shocks, assuming that the manager has a good valuation model to estimate what the price of the bond will be in each interest rate scenario. Moreover, we recommend use of the full valuation approach for assessing the position of a single bond or a portfolio of a few bonds. For a portfolio with a large number of bonds and/or bonds containing embedded options, the full valuation process may be too time-consuming.

CASE STUDY

You are given the task of demonstrating that the proper method for approximating a portfolio's internal rate of return is through the use of dollar duration weights and not market value weights. Dollar durations are simply the product of a bond's full price and its duration. Consider the following hypothetical spot rates out to two years:

Maturity (years)	Spot rate (%)
0.5	3.0
1.0	3.30
1.5	3.55
2.0	3.85

Treat this coupon note as if it were a portfolio of zero-coupon securities which should be discounted using Treasury spot rates. Use these spot rates to price a 4% coupon, two-year note and answer the following questions.

- What is the yield to maturity of the note?
- What is the market value-weighted yield of a portfolio of zero-coupon bonds with identical cash flows that replicates the two-year note? Assume that there is no arbitrage.
- What is the dollar duration-weighted portfolio yield?

Table 3. Illustration of full valuation approach to assessing the interest rate risk of a bond position for four scenarios. (Adapted from Fabozzi and Mann, 2010, p. 331)

Scenario	Yield change (bp)	New yield (%)	New price	New market value (US$)	Change in market value (%)
1	50	4.971	23.1650	11,582,500	−13.540
2	100	5.471	20.0355	10,017,750	−25.221
3	150	5.971	17.3349	8,667,450	−35.300
4	200	6.471	15.0035	7,501,750	−44.002

Current bond position: US principal STRIPS maturing May 15, 2041. Price: 26.7929; yield to maturity: 4.471%; par value owned: US$50 million; market value of position: US$13,396,400.

MAKING IT HAPPEN

- Interest rate risk is one of the most important risks with which a financial institution must contend.
- The slope and curvature of the price-yield relationship of a bond determines the exposure to interest rate risk.
- Duration is a first (i.e. linear) approximation to the price-yield relationship.
- Convexity is a finer second approximation that takes into account the degree of curvature of the price-yield relationship.
- The full valuation approach is the most general, accurate, and flexible approach for measuring interest rate risk.

"Ideals may tell us something important about what we would like to be. But compromises tell us who we are."
Avishai Margalit

  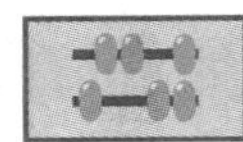      

MORE INFO

Books:

de La Grandville, Olivier. *Bond Pricing and Portfolio Analysis: Protecting Investors in the Long Run*. Cambridge, MA: MIT Press, 2001.

Fabozzi, Frank J., and Steven V. Mann. *Introduction to Fixed Income Analytics: Relative Value Analysis, Risk Measures, and Valuation*. 2nd ed. Hoboken, NJ: Wiley, 2010.

Fabozzi, Frank J., and Steven V. Mann (eds).*The Handbook of Fixed Income Securities*. 8th ed. New York: McGraw Hill, 2012.

Fabozzi, Frank J., Steven V. Mann, and Moorad Choudhry. *Measuring and Controlling Interest Rate and Credit Risk*. 2nd ed. Hoboken, NJ: Wiley, 2003.

Golub, Bennett W., and Leo M. Tilman. *Risk Management: Approaches for Fixed Income Markets*. New York: Wiley, 2000.

Ilmanen, Antti. *Expected Returns: An Investor's Guide to Harvesting Market Rewards*. Chichester, UK: Wiley, 2011.

See Also:

✔ Hedging Interest Rate Risk—Case Study and Strategies (p. 971)

✔ Identifying and Managing Exposure to Interest and Exchange Rate Risks (p. 974)

Portfolio Analysis: Duration, Convexity, and Immunization (pp. 1241–1242)

NOTES

1 Currently, the only difference between US Treasury notes and bonds is the initial term to maturity.

2 Dollar duration for a 1 bp change in yield is to all intents and purposes the same as the dollar value of a 1 bp change in yield.

3 For more on this issue see Golub and Tilman (2000).

4 A 30-year US Treasury principal STRIPS is a zero-coupon security created by dealers from the principal payment of a 30-year bond. STRIPS is an acronym for "separate trading of registered interest and principal of securities."

5 A principal STRIPS is a zero-coupon bond created from a bond's principal payment.

6 The procedure used is principal-component analysis.

"Bad ideas are so widespread because those who have good content don't take seriously the task of charming others into trusting in it." Alain de Botton

A Total Balance Sheet Approach to Financial Risk

by Terry Carroll

EXECUTIVE SUMMARY

- Because the oil price rose rapidly and the wider commodities market followed suit, inflation rose to its highest level for many years. Following a protracted boom, property prices have been savaged. Only interest rates have remained comparatively benign.
- Protecting or insulating yourself or your company against financial risks is known as "hedging." Most businesses use a transaction-driven approach. The generic name often used by bankers for these hedging instruments is "treasury products."
- Bankers can provide a derivative-based hedge to reduce or neutralize an interest rate, inflation, or commodity price risk. A derivative is a financial instrument whose value changes in relation to an underlying variable such as interest rates, commodity prices, or house prices.
- Price increases and currency fluctuations, as well as interest rate movements, can be hedged. The most common source of long-term capital, fixed by nature, is retained profits. A mismatch between, say, fixed-rate assets and variable-rate liabilities may cause you to want to hedge or renegotiate more fixed-rate liabilities to produce a better match and more overall certainty, with, by definition, lower overall risk.

INTRODUCTION

We are living in some of the most volatile times in the history of the global financial markets. One of the reasons is exactly because they have become truly global. As banks seek to restore profitability, they may increase their offering of "treasury products" to customers. This article argues that these should be considered only in the context of a total balance sheet approach rather than transaction by transaction.

MANAGING INCREASED FINANCIAL RISK

We have seen a period in which the oil price rose to $147 a barrel and then fell back dramatically. The wider commodities market followed suit. Inflation rose to its highest level for many years before easing back. Property prices have been savaged, following a protracted boom. Only interest rates have remained relatively benign compared to the extremes of the past.

Volatility has been traded as a market index for many years, but in 2008 alone it hit several spikes. It has become a fact of life. Markets are now driven mainly by fear—fear of being caught out when prices fall or fear of not being in the market as prices rise. Add to that the power of short sellers and you have a scary scenario for borrowers and investors, whether individuals or corporate.

Protecting or insulating yourself or your company against financial risks is known as "hedging." The principle of hedging is easily understood—it's like an insurance premium. In practice, the instruments generally used are known as "derivatives." These are poorly understood and, given the recent financial mess, probably viewed with fear or trepidation.

This article attempts two things: first, to put forward a more objective approach for companies wishing to improve their financial efficiency at a managed level of risk; and second, to demystify financial risk, making it a more approachable topic for the average manager or director.

WHAT IS A DERIVATIVE?

A derivative is a financial instrument whose value changes in relation to an underlying variable, for example: interest rates, the rate of inflation, commodity prices, share or bond prices, house prices, etc. Its most general use is for the purpose of "hedging" a given risk, i.e. neutralizing or taking the opposite position to a given risk, such as commodity prices, exchange or interest rates.

The problem with derivatives is that although they were created for the primary purpose of insuring against financial risks, the proportion of derivatives trading done for speculative purposes now dramatically outweighs that for ordinary trade purposes.

MOST HEDGING IS TRANSACTION-BASED

In this article we shall be proposing a "full balance sheet approach" to the management of financial risk. Most businesses currently use a transaction-driven approach. This could result in overall risk being increased rather than decreased.

By a transaction-driven approach, we mean that each transaction or set of similar transactions is individually hedged. This is the most common situation, whether the use of derivatives is recommended by a bank or requested by the customer. The generic title often used by bankers for these hedging instruments is "treasury products."

Trading and managing the use of derivatives is a highly skilled and often complex process. They are usually created and dealt with by the treasury or special products division of a bank. In the United Kingdom, these "rocket scientists," as they are sometimes known, are usually based in the City of London, embedded within the financial markets.

If you wish to hedge a risk, your bank will usually put you in touch with such a treasury specialist. Alternatively, the bank may make the first move. Not surprisingly, banks have increasingly been offering these products in the climate of increasing volatility for all the commodities and financial facilities that companies use.

A TRANSACTION-BASED APPROACH CAN ACTUALLY INCREASE OVERALL RISK

There is an important difference between the profit and loss account approach and the balance sheet approach to improving financial efficiency. Any accountant or banker worth their salt can look at the profit and loss account and come up with suggestions on how to improve profitability or reduce risk. If you fear interest rate, inflation, or commodity price risks, your banker can provide you with a derivative-based hedge to reduce or neutralize that risk. Accountants like certainty, so that they can sleep easy at night.

The danger of this approach is that it can actually increase the risk of loss for the company. Take a simple example:

Suppose you have a commercial property—the business premises for example—that you own and plan to keep for the long term. It is by nature, therefore, a fixed asset. It has a fixed notional return, i.e. its long-term value to the business. You wouldn't think of financing it out of short-term overdraft. You want a long-term debt, ideally, to finance it. This may well be at an interest rate linked to bank base rate.

Your bank draws your attention to the possibility that interest rates may increase. Wouldn't you like to hedge that risk? Their treasury products division can sell you an interest rate hedge that swaps the variable-rate risk into a fixed-rate risk, thereby insulating you against the cost of rising interest rates.

"They are a special breed-like normal accountants, but without the soppy sentimentality. These are the oncologists of market capitalism." Sean O'Grady

Now consider two worrying circumstances. The first is that interest rates actually fall. In those circumstances you have not only lost the value of the "premium" you paid, i.e. the cost of the derivative contract, but you've also lost the opportunity to gain from the interest rate falls, because you're now effectively stuck with a stream of fixed-rate payments.

So the first and most important consideration is not to use hedging on a transaction by transaction basis, because you may actually be increasing the overall risk profile of the company.

Take another example: sterling is falling against the dollar and, because commodities are usually priced in dollars, the effective cost you are paying for your raw materials is increasing. So you decide to hedge against the risk of a rising dollar. But suppose you also sell much of your finished product overseas. Whether or not you are invoicing in dollars—but especially if you are—the currency you receive will be exchanging into more and more pounds. This could be counterbalancing your raw material price increases.

Of course, you could decide to hedge the raw material currency risk alone and profit from the widening margins in sterling. But again, if the currency rates swing round the other way, your sales income in sterling will be falling and you won't benefit from the fact that raw material prices are also falling. This again illustrates the importance of looking at both sides of the trading account or balance sheet.

A HOLISTIC OR FULL BALANCE SHEET APPROACH

So, the first point we are making is that when you are looking at your trading, before entering into a hedge on one side of the transaction, i.e. the buying or selling side, you should also consider what is happening on the other side. You can hedge price increases and currency fluctuations, as well as interest rate movements.

There is also a range of products that can make the holistic hedging approach even more effective. As well as swapping variable interest rate payments for fixed, you can also buy what is called a "cap" or a "collar." A cap protects you from interest rate increases above a certain level but enables you still to benefit if rates fall; and a collar gives you protection from interest rate fluctuations both up and down, outside of a given band of rates, and may be cheaper.

Having considered trading transactions on both sides of the equation (such as the inflation of selling prices matching out the inflation of raw material costs), the most significant and generally underexploited area is the balance sheet.

Many of you will have come across fixed-rate mortgages for home purchase. Although 25-year fixed-rate mortgages have been available in recent years, few have been taken out to date. Normally fixes are for up to five years. The problem is that, on a 25-year mortgage term, after five years you are exposed to the risk of rising rates again. In other words, you don't have a perfect hedge.

And so with balance sheets. It would seem to be folly to fund long-term fixed assets from overdrafts, but that is exactly what some businesses effectively do. By taking the whole balance sheet perspective, you can not only ensure that you reduce overall financial risk, but you can also increase profitability without increasing risk.

EFFECTING THE FULL BALANCE SHEET APPROACH

You may still wish to seek the help of a treasury specialist, but here you want them to look at the whole balance sheet.

To take the earlier example: you may have funded the purchase of a commercial property that you intend to use and keep indefinitely, by borrowing on a five-year term at a margin over bank base rate. There is certainly logic in swapping this into a fixed rate if you think interest rates may rise, but this can also be a gamble because if they fall, you are not gaining the benefit.

Furthermore, the most common source of long-term capital, fixed by nature, is retained profits. So, suppose that your retained profits are at least as great in value as the cost of the property. Given that both are retained for the long term, they could be said to match each other. This leaves the cash that you have borrowed on a variable rate free to fluctuate. If you also generate spare cash on the other side of the balance sheet, then, in order not to increase the overall financial risk in the balance sheet, either this should be invested at a variable rate, or, if it is at a fixed rate, then the cost of the debt should be swapped to variable.

When you put all those assets and liabilities together in the balance sheet, you have not only reduced the financial risk in the balance sheet, but you have also significantly improved the certainty of the net cost or profit arising from those matched transactions.

THE CONCEPT OF DURATION RISK

The final piece of the jigsaw is known as "duration." In simple terms, duration is the length of the life of the particular asset or liability. The importance of this is as follows.

Most people understand the likely folly of borrowing short to lend long. You wouldn't borrow money for six months to buy your house. You might borrow money for 25 years with a fixed rate for the first five to give you relative certainty, but because of the constant risk of rising interest costs it is no surprise when people are looking to refix the rate for another two, three, or five years—for example, when the first fixed rate runs out. It may cost more, but that is the price of certainty.

So, the final piece is duration, and we bring this together with the whole balance sheet approach. First, you analyze your whole balance sheet by looking at each of the assets and determining which liabilities are funding which assets. If you have a mismatch between, say, fixed-rate assets and variable-rate liabilities, you may want to hedge or renegotiate more fixed-rate liabilities to produce a better match and more overall certainty, with, by definition, lower overall risk.

The next stage is to look at the average duration (or maturity/life) of the assets and the same for the liabilities. If there is a mismatch, either you will have greater overall certainty and lower risk because the average duration of the liabilities is longer than that of the assets, or you may have greater overall risk and less certainty if the balance is the other way. In the latter case, you may wish to increase the average duration of the liabilities, perhaps by refinancing.

CONCLUSION

We have introduced some complex concepts here, but this is for at least two important reasons: first, if you have, or know of, a risk that you face and choose to do nothing about it, that decision alone increases the risk to the corporation. Hedging through the use of the increasingly sophisticated range of derivative-based products can both reduce risk and increase either or both the overall return and the certainty of costs or return.

This can only be guaranteed if you use the full balance sheet approach or look at both sides of the transaction. If you allow yourself to be persuaded to hedge individual transactions, you may by definition actually be speculating and, worse still, increasing the overall risk profile of the business.

Any worthwhile treasury products specialist at your bank should understand all the principles and concepts introduced in this article and would find it hard to disagree with the overall premise. Business finance should be about improving returns and the certainty of returns and reducing or neutralizing risk. Never has this been truer than in these increasingly volatile times.

"To tax and to please is no more given to man than to love and be wise." John, Viscount Simon

Using Structured Products to Manage Liabilities

by Shane Edwards

EXECUTIVE SUMMARY

- Structured products (SPs) are derivative contracts that are tailored for a specific purpose, such as hedging the value of an uncertain future liability.
- The value of a SP is derived from one or many underlying reference asset values, which causes uncertainty in the value of the liability to be hedged.
- SPs are typically transacted between a client and an investment bank, and can take various legal forms.
- The fact that SPs are flexible and can be tailored to client needs distinguishes them from standard derivatives, which have generic fixed terms.
- However, SPs tend to be regarded as more complex financial instruments, and they are more difficult to value than vanilla derivatives.

INTRODUCTION

Only a decade ago, the use of structured products (SPs) was largely confined to sophisticated institutions that used them for risk management purposes. Now SPs are embraced across the client spectrum and are owned by millions—from retail individuals investing in capital-protected equity products, to global corporations that tailor SPs to meet their often complex and highly specific liability management needs.

In the liability management arena, SPs have an important role to play due to their highly customizable nature. They are used by corporate treasurers as a way of actively managing borrowing costs and hedging foreign exchange liabilities. Many companies have also embraced SPs, outside of treasury, to manage expected future liabilities (for example, airlines hedging the price of jet fuel or importers/exporters hedging the foreign exchange rate). SPs are also used by many pension funds as a strategic initiative to manage the asset–liability mismatch and tailor the pension deficit risk profile.

The increased appetite for SPs is a result of improved client education and the rapid pace of innovation at investment banks, where SPs have become a major source of business. The growth in SP volumes is expected to continue its rapid pace in the years ahead.

ANATOMY OF A STRUCTURED PRODUCT

A derivative is a financial instrument that derives its value from one or more underlying reference asset values. Derivatives can range in complexity from very simple with standardized terms (vanilla derivatives), to very complex with highly customized features (exotic derivatives). Broadly, there are three levels of complexity in derivatives, listed here in order of complexity:

Linear derivatives (for example, futures, forwards, zero strike calls), which reflect the performance of an underlying asset on an almost one-to-one basis but without legal ownership of the underlying asset. These derivatives can be simply priced through arbitrage (cost of carry) arguments.

Nonlinear derivatives (for example, call options), where at expiry the price of the derivative will vary linearly with the underlying asset price if the underlying is above a predefined strike level. If this is not the case, the option price will be worth zero. Well-understood models are available that rely heavily on the volatility of the underlying asset to determine the derivative price.

Exotic derivatives, which have path-dependent payouts, restriking features, or hybrid (multiasset class) characteristics. They require sophisticated mathematical models to price and are highly sensitive to calibrations of the underlying probability distribution and correlation assumptions (in the case of multiasset underlyings).

Any of the three derivative types may be regarded as structured products due to the amount of customization that is contained in the contract terms. Common customizations include:

- Underlying assets (underlyings): These may include anything that is transparent and tradable, such as equities, interest rates, foreign exchange rates, commodities, and inflation. Hybrid SPs can be created where multiple asset classes are used.
- Tenor: Clients are able to tailor the maturity of a SP to any extent where the counterparty providing the hedge allows it, which in turn is dictated by the liquidity of the underlying asset. SPs can include features that allow early maturity, such as: puttability (where the client may choose to early-terminate the structure with preagreed payout), callability (where the hedge counterparty can terminate at its discretion), or automatic termination (where maturity will occur once a predefined event has occured).
- Path dependency: The payouts of many SPs are determined with reference to how the underlyings have performed through the life of the product, and not simply as a function of the final underlying asset level. Examples are Asian options (where the average level of an underlying is calculated) and lookback or barrier options (where the highest or lowest observed levels of an underlying determine the payout).
- Payouts: SPs can have interim payouts (coupons) and/or a final payout at maturity as specified.
- Currency: SP payouts are often requested in currencies other than the currency of the underlying asset; such products are known as quanto or composite options.

LEGAL FORM

A structured product is a legally binding financial contract between a client and an investment bank, stating the specific terms that have been agreed. The legal form of the transaction is referred to as a wrapper, and the most common wrappers are:

Over-the-counter (OTC). This typically means that a client makes an upfront payment equal to the offer price of the SP. In return, the bank (as per the terms of the SP) may pay the client coupons and/or a payment at maturity, all of which are typically dependent on the performance of the underlying reference assets.

Structured note. The client pays the principal amount to the bank at inception. In return, the bank sells the client a note, which is typically a senior unsecured debt obligation of the bank. The note will reflect the terms of the transaction and specify payments, normally including the return of the principal amount at maturity (for principal protected notes), or possibly some principal loss (in the case of non-principal protected notes), depending on the performance of the underlying.

Swap. In a swap there is no exchange of principal. Typically, the client will pay floating Libor (minus a spread) and the investment bank will pay periodic amounts

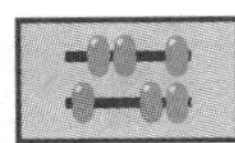

contingent on the performance of the underlying.

Other forms. There are myriad wrappers that find preference with certain clients or in certain jurisdictions, depending on the tax consequences, counterparty risk exposure, and local regulation. Other wrappers include structured deposits and UCITS III funds,[1] for example.

CLIENT TYPES AND COMMON USES OF STRUCTURED PRODUCTS IN LIABILITY MANAGEMENT

Due to their flexibility, SPs are chosen in a variety of liability management situations and by an array of users. They are implemented as both a proactive (value enhancing) and a reactive (risk hedging) tool. Some examples are given below for corporate treasurers who manage interest rate exposure, borrowing requirements, and currency exposure, and for pension managers who employ SPs in the asset–liability management framework.

Managing interest rate exposure (reactive example). A corporation has existing floating-rate debt and is concerned that interest rates will increase. It may buy a cap with the same remaining debt maturity, which means it will pay a premium upfront and will receive periodic payments if the floating reference rate is above the agreed cap rate. Thus the company can ensure that its net floating payments will not exceed a capped rate.

Managing interest rate exposure (proactive example). A corporation is aware that its business revenue varies inversely with the level of prevailing interest rates. Working with an investment bank, the treasurer decides to restructure its borrowing and issue an inverse floater, which means that its interest payments will decline as the floating reference rate rises (and its business revenues contract), and its interest payments will rise if floating reference rates fall (and business revenues expand), providing profit stabilization through the economic cycle.

Using SPs for new borrowing requirements (hybrid example). A Japanese company could borrow in US dollars to establish a US-based distribution center for products it manufactures in Japan for a fixed cost in Japanese yen. A major threat to profit is the selling price, which is fixed in US dollars. Again, looking to stabilize profit, the company could buy a SP where it will receive coupons if the dollar depreciates or if the US interest rate rises.

Hedging input prices. Steel is a vital input for automobile manufacturers. In forecasting the budget, auto makers will estimate the number of cars they need to complete over the following period and the associated revenues and costs. Clearly, fluctuating input prices could threaten the bottom line. A variety of SPs can hedge this risk, including a forward purchase agreement that guarantees a fixed price or an option to buy steel at a fixed price in the future, for which the company could pay an upfront premium.

Pension asset–liability management. Pension managers receive plan contributions and must grow the asset base so that it exceeds the expected liabilities that arise from funding the future retirement benefits of fund members. The desire to invest in higher-growth assets (for example, equities) is tempered by the knowledge that they are also higher risk. The fund could invest in low-risk assets (for example, government bonds) and gain exposure to the outperformance of an equity index over a bond index, floored at zero, through a tailored hybrid SP. This would allow it to substantially outperform fixed-income investments during good times, though it would slightly underperform during bad times since the SP premium paid would detract from a bond-only portfolio.

PRACTICAL CONSIDERATIONS

The attributes that make SPs so desirable—namely their flexibility and highly customizable nature—may also be their biggest disadvantage. Some predominant practical considerations are:

- Pricing: This can be complicated and requires mathematical models and computing power. Most structured products are priced in a Monte Carlo framework, which is a statistical technique involving the simulation of many paths for each underlying to assess the expected payout of the SP.
- Mark-to-market valuation: Although many SPs have a clearly defined payout at maturity (intended to match a specific liability, for example), the fluctuations in mark-to-market valuations also depend on other variables. Such variables include changes in the underlying's volatility, correlation, or interest rates. Mark-to-market fluctuations can cause balance sheet volatility, depending on how hedge accounting is implemented.
- Secondary market: A client wishing to terminate an SP before its maturity date may be granted an unwind price from the bank it originally traded with, or enter into a directly opposite trade with another investment bank. This may leave residual credit risk.
- Asset mismatch: Sometimes the precise underlying that constitutes the source of a future liability cannot be used as the underlying for the SP because it is not readily tradable. This is a particular concern with commodity SPs, which are often linked to commodity futures rather than physical commodities.
- Counterparty risk: Many of the typical SP wrappers, such as OTC, note, and swap, contain credit risk—that is, the investment bank may not be able to fulfill its obligations when they fall due. This can be mitigated by requiring the bank to post high-quality collateral against mark-to-market valuations.

CONCLUSION

Structured products represent a powerful instrument for the active management of specific liabilities, a liability portfolio, or asset–liability dilemmas. They can be linked to a wide variety of underlying assets and are fully flexible with regard to maturity date and conditions observed throughout the term. However, there are a number of practical issues that need to be understood, including valuation difficulties, counterparty risk, and mark-to-market fluctuations.

MAKING IT HAPPEN

Most SP experts are found at the major investment banks. As a potential client, a useful starting point is to have clarity on a specific liability or liability portfolio, and an objective that the company would like to achieve—for example, hedging of price uncertainties, smoothed performance over business cycles, or achieving a higher return with less risk on surplus funds. Clients can approach this in a number of ways:

- Advanced clients will often propose the details of an SP to investment banks and ask for pricing and trade terms to see whether they are favorable.
- Less-experienced clients will request a meeting with a bank at which SP experts will propose a range of potentially appropriate products and indicative terms.
- Always conduct a scenario analysis of how the liability portfolio behaves before and after the inclusion of an SP that is being considered, and consider mark-to-market and accounting effects.
- Many courses are available that teach elementary SP pricing. This knowledge will help you to understand how different variables may affect a valuation.

"We at Chrysler borrow money the old-fashioned way. We pay it back." Lee Iacocca

     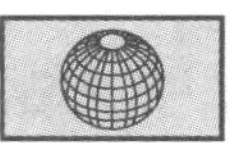   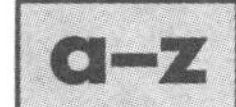

MORE INFO

Books:

Adam, Alexandre. *Handbook of Asset and Liability Management: From Models to Optimal Return Strategies*. Chichester, UK: Wiley, 2007.

Hull, John C. *Options, Futures, and Other Derivatives*. 8th ed. Upper Saddle River, NJ: Pearson, 2011.

Rebonato, Riccardo. *Volatility and Correlation: The Perfect Hedger and the Fox*. 2nd ed. Chichester, UK: Wiley, 2004.

Wilmott, Paul. *Paul Wilmott on Quantitative Finance*. 2nd ed. Chichester, UK: Wiley, 2006.

Articles:

Black, Fischer, and Myron Scholes. "The pricing of options and corporate liabilities." *Journal of Political Economy* 81:3 (1973): 637–654.

Dupire, B. "Pricing with a smile." *Risk* 7:1 (1994): 18–20.

Heston, Steven. L. "A closed-form solution for options with stochastic volatility with applications to bond and currency options." *Review of Financial Studies* 6:2 (1993): 327–343.

Magazines:

Risk, *Structured Products*, *Euromoney*, *Derivatives Week*.

See Also:

★ Dangers of Corporate Derivative Transactions (pp. 36–38)
★ A Total Balance Sheet Approach to Financial Risk (pp. 113–114)
✔ Analysis Using Monte Carlo Simulation (p. 1062)
✔ Derivatives Markets: Their Structure and Function (p. 1007)
✔ Hedging Foreign Exchange Risk—Case Studies and Strategies (p. 970)
✔ Hedging Interest Rate Risk—Case Study and Strategies (p. 971)
✔ Understanding Asset-Liability Management (Full Balance Sheet Approach) (p. 996)
John C. Cox (p. 1276)
Stephen A. Ross (p. 1302)

NOTE

1 Undertakings for Collective Investments in Transferable Securities (UCITS) are a set of European Union directives that allow compliant collective investment schemes to operate freely throughout the European Union. These funds are a versatile legal structure that often includes embedded structured products.

"What's the difference between Enron and Fannie Mae? The guys at Enron have been convicted." Anonymous

  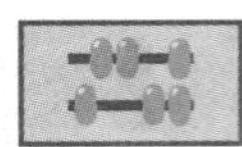      

The Value and Management of Intellectual Property, Intangible Assets, and Goodwill by Kelvin King

EXECUTIVE SUMMARY

- Intellectual capital is recognized as the most important asset of many of the world's largest and most powerful companies.
- It is the foundation for the market dominance and continuing profitability of leading corporations.
- It is often the key objective in mergers and acquisitions, and knowledgeable companies are increasingly using licensing routes to transfer these assets to low-tax jurisdictions.
- Accounting standards have traditionally not been helpful in representing the worth of intellectual property rights (IPR) and intangible assets in company accounts.
- Future winners will be those who own and effectively manage intellectual capital, which asset—such as a brand, patent portfolio, etc.—has become possibly the most critical success factor. No sector has been untouched by IPR.

INTRODUCTION

The role of IPR in business is insufficiently understood. It is probably undervalued, undermanaged or underexploited, and there is little coordination between the different professionals dealing with an organization's IPR. You probably need to have a better understanding about intellectual capital and its ownership, acquisition, and use. You probably need a practical source of knowledge and guidance about intellectual property and other intellectual capital in a commercial context. You might be a chief executive of an intellectual capital company, or a brand-based business, or both. You might be a manager of such a business, or a research director, or academic. Maybe you are a student on a management program, or an accountant, a corporate finance professional, an investor, or a venture capitalist. In your studies intellectual capital will not have been a core subject. Whatever the reason, you need to understand intellectual capital, especially IPRs, to do your job better or to be more successful in your career. IPRs are both important and complex. Therefore the questions to be addressed are often:

- What are the IPRs used in the business?
- What are their value (and hence level of risk)?
- Who owns it (could I sue or could someone sue me)?
- How may it be better exploited (e.g. licensing in or out of technology)?
- At what level do I need to insure the IPR risk?

THE BENEFITS OF IPR MANAGEMENT

You cannot "manage" without having some understanding of value, and the benefits of good IPR management include:

- Increased returns on capital invested in the business, particularly capital tied up in intellectual property.
- Increased shareholder value.
- A thorough understanding of the alignment of intellectual property development or acquisitions and business strategic objectives.
- The ability to make informed decisions about intellectual property development or acquisition.
- The creation of new and diverse revenue streams from intellectual capital, and especially from underused intellectual capital.
- The ability to distinguish between valuable intellectual capital (perhaps within a large portfolio) and so protect it fully, and intellectual capital of no significant value, which might be sold or abandoned.
- Achieving lower overall costs associated with intellectual capital development or acquisition, protection, and utilization.
- Creating internal awareness of the importance of intellectual capital to success.

CURRENT BIG ISSUES FOR IPR VALUATION

- Accounting standards.
- Corporate governance.
- Litigation (defence and attack).
- Fairness opinions.
- In-process R&D.

IFRS 3 Business Combination Valuation Allocations, IAS 38 Recognition of IPR in Accounts, and IAS 36 Valuation Impairment Tests

Purchase accounting must be applied to all acquisitions (business combinations are also treated as acquisitions, and there is no more merger accounting). Many intangible assets that would previously have been subsumed within goodwill must be separately identified and valued. Explicit guidance is provided for the recognition of such intangible assets, and IFRS 3 includes a list of assets that are expected to be recognized separately from goodwill.

The valuation of such assets is a complex process and nearly always requires specialist intellectual property (IP) valuation skills, and frequently an IP lawyer to undertake the categorization which the valuer requires. Examples of intangible assets to be separately recognized and categorized within the purchase cost are set out in the regulations and include those which are: marketing-related (trademarks, brands, domain names, newspaper mastheads), customer-related (customer lists and contracts), artistic-related (television programs, photographs, films, publications), contract-based (e.g. licensing and royalty agreements, contracts for numerous situations such as advertising, construction and supply), and technology-based (patents, computer software, databases, trade secrets, etc.).

IFRS 3 is mandatory for all new transactions from March 31, 2004.

Additionally, under IAS 36 valuations need to be independently tested for impairment by the valuer on a regular basis. Obviously one of the valuer's first questions will be (with advice from the IP lawyer, or patent or trademark attorney): Has there been any diminution of the legal nature of the originally categorized IP?

Corporate Governance

Statute and case law is being developed which will compel boards of directors to accept that they must undertake and lead IP decisions rather than leave them to management.

- Sarbanes–Oxley: The provision of valuation services for audit clients is prohibited.
- Caremark International 1996 imposed on directors the duty to ensure adequate reporting.
- A Walt Disney case in 2003 and Research in Motion (the Blackberry case) establish the potential liability of directors in respect of IP.
- Find case references at www.valuation-consulting.co.uk/services/oxley_act.html

IPR AND THE VALUATION EXPERT

For the valuer, this process of understanding is not usually a problem when these rights have been formally protected through trademarks, patents, or copyright. This is

"Our data shows that capital markets will reward companies that focus on the intangible assets of innovation and intellectual property." J. M. Torres and N. Kossovsky

not the case with intangibles such as know-how (which can include the talents, skill, and knowledge of the workforce), training systems and methods, designs, technical processes, customer lists, distribution networks, etc. These assets are equally valuable but more difficult to identify in terms of the earnings and profits they generate. With many intangibles a very careful initial due diligence process needs to be undertaken together with IP lawyers and in-house accountants.

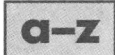

Overall risk affects valuation analysis; corporate valuation must reflect risk, and, most importantly, risk assessment should reflect IPR value.

One of the key factors affecting a company's success or failure is the degree to which it effectively exploits intellectual capital and values risk. Management obviously need to know the value of the IPR and those risks for the same reason that they need to know the underlying value of their tangible assets; this is because business managers need to know, or should know, the value of all assets and liabilities under their stewardship and control, to make sure that values are maintained. Markets (restricted or otherwise), institutions, and shareholders need to be educated. Exploitation can take many forms, ranging from outright sale of an asset, to a joint venture or a licensing agreement. Inevitably, exploitation increases the risk assessment.

The valuation procedure is, essentially, a bringing together of the economic concept of value and the legal concept of property. The presence of an asset is a function of its ability to generate a return and the discount rate applied to that return. The cardinal rule of commercial valuation is: the value of something cannot be stated in the abstract; all that can be stated is the value of a thing in a particular place, at a particular time, in particular circumstances. The questions "to whom?" and "for what purpose?" must always be asked before a valuation can be carried out. This rule is particularly significant as far as the valuation of intellectual property rights is concerned. More often than not, there will be only one or two interested parties, and the value to each of them will depend on their circumstances. Failure to take these circumstances, and those of the owner, into account will result in a meaningless valuation.

There are four main value concepts, namely, owner value, market value, tax value, and fair value. *Owner value* often determines the price in negotiated deals and is often led by a proprietor's view of the value if he or she were deprived of the property. The basis of *market value* is the assumption that if comparable property has fetched a certain price, then the subject property will realize a similar price. The *fair value* concept is essentially the desire to be equitable to both parties. It recognizes that the transaction is not in the open market and that vendor and purchaser have been brought together in a legally binding manner. *Tax valuation* has been the subject of case law worldwide since the turn of the century and is an esoteric practice. There are also quasi-concepts of value which impinge on each of these main areas, namely, investment value, liquidation value, and going-concern value.

METHODS FOR THE VALUATION OF IPR

Acceptable methods for the valuation of identifiable intangible assets and intellectual property fall into three broad categories. They are either *market-based*, *cost-based*, or *based on estimates of future economic benefit*. In an ideal situation an independent expert will always prefer to determine a market value by reference to comparable market transactions. This is difficult enough when valuing assets such as bricks and mortar because it is never possible to find a transaction that is exactly comparable. In valuing an item of intellectual property, the search for a comparable market transaction becomes almost futile. This is not only due to lack of comparability, but also because intellectual property is generally not developed to be sold, and many sales are usually only a small part of a larger transaction and details are kept extremely confidential. There are other impediments that limit the usefulness of this method, namely, special purchasers, different negotiating skills, and the distorting effects of the peaks and troughs of economic cycles. In a nutshell, this summarizes my objection to such statements as "this is a rule of thumb in the sector."

Cost-based methodologies, such as the cost to create or the cost to replace, assume that there is some relationship between cost and value, and the approach has very little to commend itself other than ease of use. The method ignores changes in the time value of money, and maintenance.

The *method of valuation flowing from an estimate of past and future economic benefits* can be broken down into four limbs: (1) capitalization of historic profits, (2) gross profit differential methods, (3) excess profits methods, and (4) the relief from royalty method.

Discounted cash flow (DCF) analysis sits across the last three methodologies. DCF mathematical modeling allows for the fact that one euro in your pocket today is worth more than one euro next year or one euro the year after. The time value of money is taken into account by adjusting expected future returns to today's monetary values using a discount rate. The discount rate is used to calculate economic value and includes compensation for risk and for expected rates of inflation.

The *capitalization of historic profits* arrives at the value of IPRs by multiplying the maintainable historic profitability of the asset by a multiple that is assessed after scoring the relative strength of the IPR. For example, a multiple is arrived at after assessing a brand in the light of factors such as leadership, stability, market share, internationality, trend of profitability, marketing, and advertizing support and protection. While this capitalization process recognizes some of the factors which should be considered, it has major shortcomings, mostly associated with historic earning capability. The method pays little regard to the future.

Gross profit differential methods are often associated with trademark and brand valuation. These methods adopt the differences in sale prices, adjusted for differences in marketing costs. That is, the difference between the margin of the branded and/or patented product and an unbranded or generic product. This formula is used to drive out cash flows and calculate value. Finding generic equivalents for a patent and identifiable price differences is far more difficult than for a retail brand.

The *excess profits method* looks at the current value of the net tangible assets employed as the benchmark for an estimated rate of return to calculate the profits that are required in order to induce investors to invest into those net tangible assets. Any return over and above those profits required to induce investment is considered to be the excess return attributable to the IPRs. Although theoretically relying on future economic benefits from the use of the asset, the method has difficulty in adjusting to alternative uses of the asset.

Relief from royalty considers what the purchaser could afford, or would be willing to pay, for the licence. The royalty stream is then capitalized, reflecting the risk and return relationship of investing in the asset.

Discounted Cash Flow Analysis

Discounted cash flow analysis is probably the most comprehensive of appraisal techniques. Potential profits and cash flows need to be assessed carefully and then restated to present value through use of a discount rate, or rates. With the asset you are considering, the valuer will need to

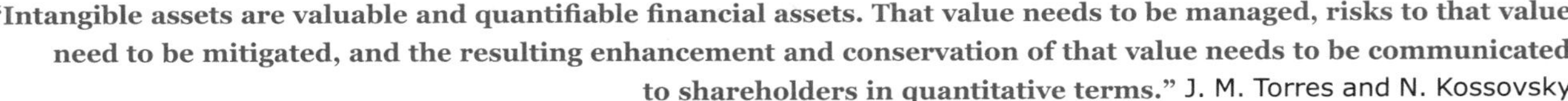

"Intangible assets are valuable and quantifiable financial assets. That value needs to be managed, risks to that value need to be mitigated, and the resulting enhancement and conservation of that value needs to be communicated to shareholders in quantitative terms." J. M. Torres and N. Kossovsky

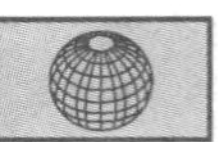

consider the operating environment of the asset to determine the potential for market revenue growth. The projection of market revenues will be a critical step in the valuation. The potential will need to be assessed by reference to the enduring nature of the asset and its marketability, and this must subsume consideration of expenses together with an estimate of residual value or terminal value, if any. This method recognizes market conditions, likely performance and potential, and the time value of money. It is illustrative, demonstrating the cash flow potential of the property, and is highly regarded and widely accepted in the financial community.

The discount rate to be applied to the cash flows can be derived from a number of different models, including common sense, the build-up method, dividend growth models, or the capital asset pricing model (CAPM), utilizing a weighted average cost of capital. This appraisal technique will probably be the preferred option.

These processes lead one nowhere unless due diligence and the valuation process quantify remaining useful life and decay rates. This will quantify lives such as the following, and which is the shortest: physical, functional, technological, economic, and legal. This process is necessary because, just like any other asset, IPR has a varying ability to generate economic returns that depend on these main lives. For example, in the discounted cash flow model it would not be correct to drive out cash flows for the entire legal length of copyright protection—which may be 100 plus years—when a valuation concerns computer software with only a short economic life span of one to two years. However, patent legal protection of 20 years can prevent infringement situations which may be important, as is often illustrated in the pharmaceutical sector where generic competitors enter the marketplace at a speed that dilutes a monopoly position when protection ceases. The message is that, when undertaking DCF modeling, never project longer than is realistic by testing against these major lives.

It must also be acknowledged that, in many situations, after these lives have been examined carefully to produce cash flow forecasts it is often not credible to forecast beyond, say, four to five years. The mathematical modeling allows for this by using, at the end of the period when forecasting becomes futile but clearly the cash flows will not "fall of a cliff," a terminal value that is calculated using a modest growth rate (say inflation) at the steady state year but also discounting this forecast to the valuation date.

Valuation is more an art than a science and is an interdisciplinary study drawing on law, economics, finance, accounting, and investment. It is rash to attempt any valuation adopting so-called industry/sector norms in ignorance of the fundamental theoretical framework of valuation.

CASE STUDY

IP financings can unlock value that markets and capital providers have overlooked. Tax-effective strategies concerning the management of IP, and the attendant ability for structures to provide attractive securitization prospects, have become more widely known. As reported by *Business Week* in 2007, the largest ever IP-backed securitization, US$1.8 billion for Sears' Kenmore Craftsman and DieHard brands, may be a harbinger of things to come for IP as an asset class.

Sears has disclosed that it created a "separate, wholly owned, bankruptcy-remote subsidiary"—essentially a company within a company. Called KCD IP (for Kenmore, Craftsman, DieHard, intellectual property), the entity issued US$1.8 billion worth of bonds backed by the intellectual property of Sears' three biggest brands, according to filings with the Patent & Trademark Office.

Sears, in essence, created licensing income. First it transferred ownership of the brand names into KCD, which charges Sears royalty fees to license bonds to the insurance subsidiary, where, like any other security on an insurer's books, it serves as protection against future loss. The insurer, meanwhile, protects Sears from financial trouble—and, because it is a subsidiary, it does so at a lower cost than Sears could get from an outside party.

The payments net out to zero because Sears owns every piece. But that would change if Sears were to sell the bonds to outsiders. Sears would be holding up to US$1.8 billion in case, and investors would be holding the bonds.

The KCD bonds have a higher credit rating than Sears' regular bonds. Moody's Investors Service gave KCD an investment-grade rating of Baa2, four rungs better than Sears' junk rating of Ba1. How so? If Sears were to go bankrupt, bondholders wouldn't be able to get their hands on Kenmore, Craftsman and DieHard trademarks, the company's crown jewels.

Following this, Eric Hedman, a director in S&P's Structural Finance Group, said "interest [in intellectual property deals] is exploding."

MAKING IT HAPPEN

In the book I coauthored with John Sykes, an IP lawyer (Sykes and King, 2003), we established a number of general principles concerning the management and valuation of intellectual property:

- Make intellectual capital a part of the business's strategic thinking and planning. For example, risk control, maximizing value, being aware of emerging technologies, seeking appropriate legal protection, etc.
- Understand the role of intellectual capital. This involves assessing the importance of intellectual capital now and in the future to the market position and future success of your business. Part of this is the challenge of identifying the intellectual property of others and avoiding infringement of the associated legal rights.
- Be aware of competing intellectual capital.
- Know your own intellectual capital. Use rigorous processes to identify and evaluate the existing intellectual capital in the business, creating a comprehensive record of results, and developing a process for identifying future IPR. Carry out positive due diligence. Success or not is dependent on a management process to do the aforementioned.
- Identify required intellectual capital, which is a process of forecasting future needs.
- Acquire any required intellectual capital.
- Think tax and balance sheet.
- Be ready to protect your rights.
- Measure improvements as an essential part of good intellectual capital management, to develop measures of success for the management and evaluation of IPR.
- Spread the message, because just as important as measuring improvements is communicating a strategy and a process, not least via financial PR, etc.
- Know the cost and value of your intellectual capital.

"Companies, like people, cannot be skillful at everything. Therefore, core capabilities both advantage and disadvantage a company." Dorothy Leonard

MORE INFO

Books:

King, Kelvin. *The Valuation and Exploitation of Intangible Assets*. Welwyn Garden City, UK: EMIS Professional Publishing, 2003.

Sykes, John, and Kelvin King. *Valuation and Exploitation of Intellectual Property and Intangible Assets*. Welwyn Garden City, UK: EMIS Professional Publishing, 2003.

Articles:

Sexton, Donald E. "Valuing brand equity." *The Advertiser* (March 2000).

Torres, J. M., and N. Kossovsky. "Intangible assets and shareholder value." *Intellectual Asset Management* 32 (October/November 2008): 18–22.

Websites:

American Society of Appraisers (ASA): www.appraisers.org

International Asset Management magazine: www.iam-magazine.com

International Valuation Standards Committee (IVSC): www.ivsc.org

Society of Share and Business Valuers (SSBV): www.ssbv.org

Valuation Consulting, the website of the author's company: www.valuation-consulting.co.uk

See Also:

★ Protecting Your Intellectual Property—Nonregistered Rights (pp. 911–912)
★ Protecting Your Intellectual Property—Registered Rights (pp. 913–914)
✔ Intellectual Property—Copyright (p. 1162)
✔ Intellectual Property—Patents—An International Overview (p. 1163)
✔ Intellectual Property—Registered Designs and Trademarks (p. 1164)
✔ The Rationale for an Acquisition (p. 1134)
Intellectual Capital: The New Wealth of Organizations (p. 1376)

"Companies with consumer products or service; the value of all their brands is typically 50 to 70% of the firm's market capitalization . . . Companies with industrial products or services [it is] about 10 to 20% of the market capitalization."

Donald Sexton

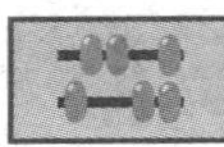

Valuing Pension Fund Liabilities on the Balance Sheet by Steven Lowe

EXECUTIVE SUMMARY

- Accounting standards affect how pension liabilities are reported in company accounts. FAS 158 requires that the net of pension fund assets and liabilities are reported in the main accounts. Traditional accountancy measures allow a more subjective measurement, and relegate pension information to the accounting notes.
- The real issue is how a company calculates and values the projected liability—which depends on the discount rate selected, the actuarial assumptions relating to future inflation, wage increases, and, most importantly, the expected longevity of employees.
- Different pension stakeholders will favor different liability measures, resulting in differing investment risk tolerances and strategies, which in turn can impact the corporate balance sheet.
- Accounting measures and buyout measures of pension liabilities differ. Finance directors need to be aware of both types of measure, their assumptions, and the interaction between them, as they can impact pension strategies and, consequently, financial reporting.

INTRODUCTION

With a pension plan, companies agree to provide certain benefits to their employees, by specifying either a defined contribution (where a fixed contribution is made to the plan each year by the employer, with no promises as to the future benefits that will be delivered by the plan) or a defined benefit (where the employer undertakes to pay a certain benefit to the employee at some point in the future).

With a defined contribution plan, the firm meets its obligation once it has made the prespecified contribution to the plan, and its valuation on the balance sheet is reasonably straightforward. With a defined benefit plan, the employer has to put sufficient money into the plan each period such that the amounts, with reinvestment, are sufficient to meet the defined benefits due as plan members retire. Here, the firm's obligations are much more difficult to estimate, since they will be determined by a number of variables, including the benefits that employees are entitled to (which will change as their salary and employment status change), the prior contributions made by the employer (and the returns they have earned), the expected retirement date of employees, and the rate of return that the employer expects to make in the future on current contributions.

As these variables change, the value of the pension fund assets can be greater than, less than, or equal to the pension fund liabilities (which include the present value of promised benefits). Recent changes to accounting regulations have increased the transparency of pension funding, and this has sparked an increased debate about the goals of defined benefit pension funds. The stakeholders of a pension fund (sponsor, trustees, and the various classes of pensioner) often have different goals, and therefore require the asset and liability information to be presented using different assumptions. These assumptions can materially affect both profit and loss (P&L) and balance sheet statements.

A pension fund whose assets exceed liabilities is an overfunded plan, whereas one in which assets are less than liabilities is underfunded, and disclosures to that effect have to be included in financial statements. When a pension fund is overfunded the firm has several options: It can withdraw the excess assets from the fund, it can discontinue contributions to the plan, or it can continue to make contributions on the assumption that the overfunding is a transitory phenomenon that could well disappear by the next period. When a fund is underfunded, the firm has a liability that must be recognized on the balance sheet.

ACCOUNTING STANDARDS

In late 2006, the Financial Accounting Standards Board issued its final Statement of Financial Accounting Standards No. 158 (FAS 158), which deals with the rules for reporting the obligations and expenses of pension plans, retiree health plans, nonqualified deferred compensation plans, and other post retirement benefits. Among many changes, FAS 158 moved information about the funded status of pension plans and other postretirement employee benefit plans from the footnotes of the financial statements to the balance sheet itself. The idea behind FAS 158 was to create more transparency and to make information about pension plans and other postretirement employee benefit plans available to investors. It requires companies to include on the balance sheet the full net value of pension assets and obligations. These are to be measured as the difference between the fund assets and the projected benefit obligations. A company does not have to show the full value of assets and the full value of liabilities—just the net of the two. If the fund assets are higher than the pension obligation, it will show as an asset; if not, it will be a liability.

Before FAS 158, the effects of certain events, such as plan amendments or actuarial gains and losses, could be given delayed recognition in the balance sheet. Alternatively, market returns could be smoothed over several years rather than recognized at once. As a result, a plan's funded status (plan assets less obligations) rarely reflected the true position and so was not reported on the balance sheet. FAS 158 requires companies to report their plan's funded status, which is likely to cause reported pension liabilities to rise significantly. The traditional actuarial approach is incorporated to a degree in International Accounting Standard 19 (IAS 19), which means that the balance sheet generated on an IAS 19 basis does not necessarily reflect the full net asset or liability position of the pension plan. Whichever accountancy basis is adopted, the real issue is how to identify the projected benefit obligation.

Typically, the assets held by the sponsor's pension fund are liquid, have publicly accessible pricing data, and are subject to market value fluctuations. The liabilities, however, are rarely traded, are particular to the individual pension scheme, and, depending on the valuation method adopted, can be considerably less volatile. Assets are measured at market value, whereas the discount rate for valuing liabilities is based on the actuaries' assessment of long-run returns on the assets in the pension fund.

CALCULATING ACCOUNTING LIABILITIES

The projected benefit obligation is the actuarial present value of the benefit obligations made by the pension plan. This liability, according to most accounting standards (FRS 17, FAS 87, IAS 19), is calculated by reference to the yield on AA corporate bonds. These in turn are affected by movements in interest rates, and also variations in the cost of credit.

This accounting measure of liabilities makes no allowance for the actual invest-

"Where profit is, loss is hidden nearby." Japanese proverb

ment policy pursued by the pension scheme. It does, however, include actuarial forecasts of inflation, expected future salary increases, and current longevity assumptions. These assumptions are taken as being best-guess estimations, and often cause keen debate between a corporate sponsor's actuaries and those advising the trustees during the triennial funding discussion. The rate of inflation and forecast salary increases are usually fairly straightforward and based on recent experience, but forecasts of longevity lead to more discussion.

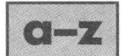

Longevity has been increasing exponentially since the Second World War, and actuaries have consistently underestimated life expectancy. Any increase in assumed life expectancy will increase the liability of the pension fund and thus increase the annual contributions required by the sponsor, as well as increasing the total liability on the balance sheet. It is estimated that an increase of one year of life expectancy will add approximately 7% to pension liability. Given that life expectancy for a 65-year-old male is improving at the rate of one year's increase in life expectancy in every five years, this has the potential to have a huge impact on corporate investment plans.

The assumptions made about inflation, salary increases, and longevity are a key subject of discussion when trustees and sponsor debate proposed future funding strategies for the pension plan. The other key topic for discussion should be the expected investment returns from the asset strategy undertaken by the trustees. Both the actuarial assumptions and the investment risk assumed by the pension fund are likely to greatly influence the size and scale of future sponsor contributions.

The funding strategy is normally assessed on a going concern principle, resting on the assumption that the sponsor will be around for many years and is able and willing to provide the support necessary to the pension scheme if the investment strategy produces returns below those expected, or if life expectancy or any of the other actuarial assumptions exceeds the forecast.

DECIDING APPROPRIATE INVESTMENT RISK

There are a number of factors that should be considered by both sponsor and trustees in determining how much risk there is to the ability of the pension fund to meet its future liabilities:

- Covenant or sponsor business risk: The stronger the covenant (the lower the business risk), the more risk can be taken with the pension fund investment and the less conservative the actuarial assumptions need to be.
- Maturity of pension scheme: The longer the funding period (i.e., the younger the potential beneficiaries or pension scheme membership), the more investment risk can be taken without compromising the security of the final benefit payments. Conversely, the higher the longevity risk which a younger scheme incorporates, the greater is the risk that even minor improvements in life expectancy will cause a large movement in the value of future pension promises and, hence, liability on the balance sheet.
- Surplus: The larger the accounting surplus, the more investment risk can be taken. Conversely, with a large deficit there will also be pressure to take increased investment risk.

The minimal risk approach argues that assets should be valued at market prices and that liabilities should be valued consistently using the market returns on appropriate assets and conservative longevity assumptions. The optimal asset allocation would then be determined using horizon matching. This uses bonds, with their reliable cash flows, to meet current and near-maturing pension obligations (using a strategy called cash flow matching), and equity and property, with their growth potential, to match long-maturing liabilities that grow in line with earnings (using a strategy called surplus management). This second strategy is justified because of the long-run constancy of factor shares in national income (which makes capital and land ideal long-term matching assets for a liability that is linked to the return on labor), and because of the positive long-run equity risk premium and mean-reversion in equity returns (which implies that long-run equity returns are more stable than short-run returns). Such an asset allocation should mean that changes in pension liabilities caused by moves in interest rates, inflation, or longevity are matched by a mixture of bond and equity returns, thus immunizing the balance sheet from any unexpected changes in value of either asset or liability metric. With a stable balance sheet, planning future pension contributions can be done with more certainty, thus limiting the impact of volatile contributions on the P&L.

BUYOUT LIABILITY

Another, different, way of calculating the pension position is based on the assets required to "buy out" the pension liabilities at a specific point in time. This can be thought of as the market price of passing all the liabilities of a pension fund to a specialist insurer. Five years ago, this only happened in the case of insolvency, but increasingly niche insurers are starting to specialize in pooling longevity risk and offering prices to remove all pension assets and liabilities from a sponsor's balance sheet. The buyout deficit shows the additional funds needed if the accrued liabilities were to be settled by purchasing matching annuities from these insurers. Under UK legislation, this is also the contingent debt that could be served on the sponsor by the trustees of the pension scheme, should the sponsor decide to discontinue the scheme.

The volatility of this measure is dictated by the terms on which insurance companies are prepared to deal. Annuities are usually priced at yields well below the prevailing yields on government bonds and with a cautious view of future longevity trends. Therefore, the liabilities assessed on this measure are significantly higher than those assessed on the accounting and funding measures.

ACCOUNTING IMPACT

The current accounting methodology has three main impacts. First, balance sheets have become more volatile due to the inclusion of net pension assets or liabilities, which are dependent on publicly traded debt prices. This volatility may trigger loan covenants or borrowing limits, or otherwise affect corporate behavior. Second, the P&L retains some volatility due to pension impacts, since changes in the balance sheet funding position affect the level of sponsor contributions and, hence, flow through to the P&L. Finally, financial statements have increased in complexity as noncash pension items are now included. Some items, such as the current service cost and amortization of past service costs within operating cost, the unwinding of the pension liability discount, and the expected return on assets within financing costs, are highly complex in themselves.

CONCLUSION

There is no doubt that the accounting measure has been, and continues to be, hugely influential in corporate decision-making and short-term risk management. It provides the basis for funding discussions with the trustees and is therefore important for cash flow management, particularly in companies where the corporate covenant is not strong. The buyout measure of pension liabilities is becoming more important, since the discharge of all pension obligations by the sponsor is growing in desirability as the full risks of longevity increases are increasingly recognized. Additionally, trustees often find that a buyout, with the security provided by a

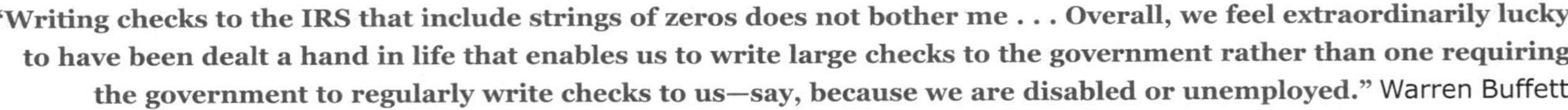

  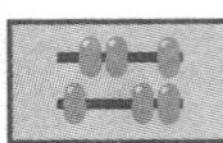   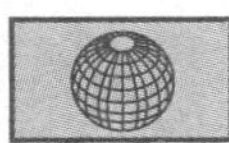   

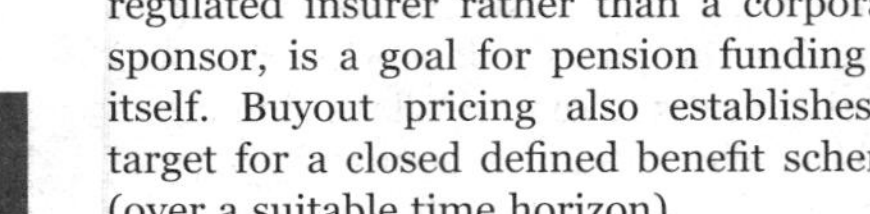

regulated insurer rather than a corporate sponsor, is a goal for pension funding in itself. Buyout pricing also establishes a target for a closed defined benefit scheme (over a suitable time horizon).

Therefore it is vital that finance directors monitor the development of assets and liabilities using both accounting and buyout measures, as well as understanding the assumptions that each employs and interactions between them.

MAKING IT HAPPEN

- A defined benefit pension scheme is one where the employer promises to pay a certain benefit to the employee on retirement. It is funded by contributions to a pension plan and the investment return on those contributions while the employee is working, which, over time, the employer hopes will match the benefits promised.
- Both the assets and liabilities are accounted for on the corporate balance sheet, introducing a complicated variable into financial reporting that usually has little to do with the main business of the employer.
- Assets are valued using market rates, but future liabilities are valued by selecting a discount rate and making assumptions about future inflation, wage increases, and longevity.
- Each of these factors (inflation, wages, and longevity) can have a large influence not only on the financial information reported, but also on the strategy and risk tolerance of the pension fund and its stakeholders.
- Because of this, it is vital that the employer understands a variety of different measures for the pension liabilities, such as the accounting/funding basis and the buyout liability, as these can impact how the pension fund assets and liabilities are ultimately reported on the balance sheet each year.

MORE INFO

Book:

Fridson, Martin, and Fernando Alvarez. *Financial Statement Analysis: A Practitioner's Guide*. 3rd ed. New York: Wiley, 2002.

Articles:

Financial Education. "Balance sheet recognition of pension liabilities under International Accounting Standards (IAS)." Online at: tinyurl.com/anupfb

JP Morgan. "Implementing FAS 158 for year-end financial reporting." January 18, 2007. Online at: tinyurl.com/dj7mrq

Juliens, Dennis. "The impact of pension accounting on financial statements and disclosures." CFA Institute Publications. Online at: www.cfapubs.org/doi/abs/10.2469/cp.v2005.n3.3484

Riley, Leigh C., and Katherine L. Aizawa. "Pension fund issues in the boardroom: Is your pension plan becoming too expensive?" Chicago, IL: Foley & Lardner, 2007. Online at: tinyurl.com/3vyrssp [PDF].

Zion, David. "Beginning to overhaul the pension accounting rules." *CFA Institute Conference Proceedings Quarterly* 24:2 (2007): 38–44.

See Also:

★ Asset Liability Management for Pension Funds (pp. 13–15)
★ Pension Schemes: A Unique and Unintended Basket of Risks on the Balance Sheet (pp. 87–90)
★ The Role of Institutional Investors in Corporate Financing (pp. 589–592)
★ A Total Balance Sheet Approach to Financial Risk (pp. 113–114)
✔ Key Accounting Standards and Organizations (p. 1040)
✔ Preparing Financial Statements: Balance Sheets (p. 1046)
✔ Understanding Asset–Liability Management (Full Balance Sheet Approach) (p. 996)
✔ Understanding the Balance Sheet (p. 999)
✔ Understanding the Relationship between the Discount Rate and Risk (p. 1001)
Peter L. Bernstein (p. 1271)

"Proficient is defined with one word: skilled. In order to become skilled you must have more than knowledge, you need to apply that information." Jac Fitz-Enz

ALM in Financial Intermediation: The Derivatives Business by Krzysztof M. Ostaszewski

EXECUTIVE SUMMARY

- Asset-liability management (ALM) is often viewed as a methodology for hedging risks—or even of eliminating them—to lock in the spread earned by the business.
- But ALM is not that. Risks in financial intermediation cannot be eliminated; they are an intrinsic part of the business of banks and insurance companies.
- The worlds of traditional banking and insurance and derivatives markets seem very different but they are merely different expressions of the same business process.
- In reality, financial intermediation is conceptually equivalent to dealing in derivatives.
- The bar for ALM must be raised to that of managing a complex portfolio of derivative securities, as that is the underlying nature of the business.

INTRODUCTION

The headlines about the credit crisis of 2008 and the subsequent downturn in the global economy often name the exploding trade in derivative securities as the villain in this economic calamity. This attribution of the cause of the crisis is related to the perception that derivatives are somehow new, mysterious, and incomprehensible to the clients of banks, insurance firms, and other financial intermediaries. I consider this perception not only incorrect, I view it as distorting. By association, major dealers in derivatives are also viewed as villains, and are subject to increased scrutiny. In this chapter I propose that this view is misguided, as the growth of derivative instruments represents merely a new form of traditional financial intermediation. Although the investment bankers might be villains in their own right, they earned that distinction the old-fashioned way, not through the use of new financial technologies.

Derivative securities are not villains, they are tools.

In other words, I claim here that the wave of financial innovation we have experienced over the last three decades—with the vast expansion of new derivative instruments, such as futures, options, and swaps—is essentially not a new reality, but rather that this new technology is just a new expression of the same reality that has always existed.

When I want to challenge my students to have a more general perspective on financial issues, I ask them: "How was this done in the year 1000?" I propose that it is quite helpful to pose that challenge when facing a decision on financial matters. For example: How was executive compensation handled in the year 1000? Obviously, we have developed a more sophisticated theoretical base than that existing a millennium ago. With the contribution to understanding of the agency problem by Becker and Stigler (1974) and Shapiro and Stiglitz (1984), and see also Myerson (2011), we have understood that dynamic moral-hazard problems with limited liability, of which the executive compensation problem is the most significant manifestation, are efficiently solved by promising large end-of-career rewards for agents who prove good performance. For example, an efficient solution to moral hazard in banking involves long-term promises of large rewards at career-end for successful bankers. Interestingly enough, the medieval system of transferring the business from master to apprentice was very similar. The reward came in the form of ownership of the business, and it came only after many years of service proving good long-term performance. We now have new ways of expressing this idea, and new technologies, but the idea remains basically the same.

WHAT ARE DERIVATIVE SECURITIES?

A derivative security is defined as a financial instrument whose cash flows are *derived* (hence the name) from some other financial instrument (Hull, 2012; also Ostaszewski, 2002, 2003). They are, completely unnecessarily, often presented as mysterious and mathematically complex. The three core types of derivatives are described below.

The core types of derivatives—forwards, futures, options, and swaps—are building blocks for more complex portfolios.

Forward Contracts

Forward contracts are agreements to buy (for the party long forward) and sell (for the party short forward) an asset or financial instrument (called the *underlying*) at a future date but at a price specified today. A forward contract is a private agreement between two parties about the transaction just described. Thus it involves substantial risk of nonperformance by the other party. That risk is remedied in *futures contracts*, which are standardized, written by a clearing house that operates an exchange where the contract can be bought and sold. Notably, the clearing house imposes the requirement that parties involved in the transaction post a security deposit, i.e. a *margin deposit*, which serves as collateral for performance of the contract obligation. Let us also observe that when the transaction is consummated in the future, the market price may be different than the one named in the contract, and because the two parties to the contract trade between themselves, the benefit of one party is the cost of the other party.

Options

Options are contracts that give the owner (party long the option contract) the right, but not the obligation, to buy (in this case the option is called a *call option*) or the right to sell (known as a *put option*) an asset (called the *underlying*). The transaction takes place at a specific time, or in a specified time period, at a price also specified in the contract (known as the *strike price* or *exercise price*). The right acquired by the owner of an option does not appear miraculously out of nowhere, it is actually created by the other party to the contract, the party that assumes the obligation to deliver the promise embedded in the option contract. Thus, the right to buy gold at a price of $1,500 per ounce embedded in a call option on gold is also an obligation to sell gold at $1,500 for the party on the other side of the transaction. That party on the other side is said to *write* the option, is short the option contract, and actually creates it out of nowhere. For that service, the short party is paid the *premium*, which is a certain amount of money representing the market price of the option, by the long party (the party that owns the option). Whereas the long party has the right, but not an obligation, the short party does have an obligation when the right of the long party is exercised.

This situation is not unusual, and not just mathematical: a right of one person is always an obligation of other people. For example, when a person arrested by authorities has the right to remain silent, this is just another way of saying that the authorities have an obligation to respect that silence and not to try to break it by force. Because the short party in an option contract assumes an obligation to either sell (in the case of a call option) or buy (in the case of a put option), that party has substantial risk. Because of that high risk, most option contracts are traded on exchanges, and the short party is required to post a margin deposit, with the exchange also guaranteeing performance. The only cost to the long party is the premium paid for the option, but the long party enjoys all benefits in the case of a price increase of the underlying (in the case of a call option) or price decline (in the case of a put option). The only benefit to the short party is the premium received for the option, with the entire risk of a price increase of the underlying (in the case of a call option) or decline in the price of the underlying (in the case of a put option) borne by that party. Note again the phenomenon of the benefit of one party being the cost of the other party; this is an important principle, which I will discuss further later in this chapter.

Swaps

Swaps are contracts to exchange cash flows between two parties on or before a specified future date based on the underlying value of currencies/exchange rates, bonds/interest rates, commodities, stocks, or other assets. The cash flows exchanged may be in different currencies, or may even be cash payments by one side and physical commodity payments by the other side. Until the 2008 credit crisis debacle these transactions were largely unregulated and treated as private transactions between two parties. But such private transactions are subject to the risk of nonperformance by the other party to the contract, and without any regulation or exchange where swaps are traded no mechanism exists to protect against the credit risk of such nonperformance. As in the case of forwards/futures and options, the gain of one party to the transaction is a loss to the other party in the transaction.

Other Derivatives

While forward contracts, options, and swaps are the three main types of derivative securities, over time market participants have been active in creating a variety of other derivatives. The credit crisis of 2008 made *mortgage derivatives* famous—or, to be more precise, infamous. Mortgage derivative securities have their cash flows derived from payments made by a specified pool of mortgage loans. When borrowers make payments of principal and interest, such payments are received by a processing agent and then distributed to investors according to formulas specified in the documents describing the derivative structure (formulated and distributed on its creation and, in the United States, also filed with the Securities Exchange Commission).

The simplest mortgage-backed securities were basically pro-rata shares of payments. Subsequently, more complex securities, called *collateralized mortgage obligations* (CMOs), were subsequently created. In the United States the Tax Reform Act of 1986 allowed the creation of tax-free real estate mortgage investment conduits (REMICs), which are special-purpose vehicles created for the express purpose of issuing mortgage derivatives (Fabozzi and Modigliani, 1992; also Haubrich, 1995). Let us note that, in a manner similar to swaps, these were not traded on an exchange and no margin requirement exists for them, although dealers in these securities have been subject to regulatory capital requirements.

A representative of a dealer in those derivatives who spoke at a meeting of a local society of financial analysts which I attended in the 1990s provided an interesting comment on the marketing of these securities. CMOs have been generally structured as a series of *tranches* of differing levels of security. Conservative investors buy the most secure of those tranches. A person present at the meeting asked the representative of a dealer who in that case bought the riskiest tranches. The representative responded that many purchases were made by speculative investors, but that sales people had also created what was known as the "slow deer theory" about the sales of the risky tranches. What was the slow deer theory? When one drives on country roads in upstate New York, Michigan, or rural Pennsylvania one occasionally encounters deer crossing the roads. Some deer are fast and run away when they see a car approaching. Others become fascinated by the headlights, carefully observing them while slowly crossing the road. Those slow deer have significantly lower chances of survival.

MR FILIP'S PRINCIPLE

A derivative security is basically a bet on the underlying. By itself, a bet does not affect the outcome of the underlying economic process.

I attended high school in Poland during the Soviet occupation of the country (an occupation that lasted from 1945 until 1989). We did not hear much about derivative securities or financial markets. We did know, from experience, a great deal about the permanent economic crisis under communism, and we heard a lot about the permanent economic crisis in the capitalist countries of the decadent West. Our physics teacher, Mr Filip, was very demanding, quite strict, and not very popular among students, even though he did offer us a substantial knowledge of his field. The boys in the class were far more interested in the better parts of life, such as soccer and the European Champion Clubs' Cup, in which professional soccer teams competed for the title of the best team in Europe.

We had an extensive betting scheme on those games. One day, Mr Filip caught the bookie with all the incriminating details written in his books, which the outraged and principled educator confiscated. Subsequently, Mr Filip gave us a stern speech in our next physics class. He said: "I am shocked. I can't believe that you are making bets on soccer games. Don't you know that when two people make a bet, one of them is a pig and the other one is stupid?" I still remember thinking (but not saying): "Mr Filip, but that's precisely the point!" Mr Filip's outrage and indignation were caused by the fact that, in a bet like this, the amount gained by the winning party is exactly the amount lost by the losing party (with adjustments for any compensation of the bookies). No actual value is created.

Recall our discussion of derivative securities from the previous section. In every case, we pointed out that any gains from the transaction to one party were balanced by the losses to the other party. A derivative security is in fact a bet on the underlying—nothing more, nothing less. Politicians, activists, and the like argue that this makes derivatives markets into one big gambling house that contributes nothing, and which in fact extracts value in the process because bookies need to be paid, the house needs its profits, and excessive betting may develop that causes addictions and personal financial tragedies.

But do we really know whether the process of gambling in the derivatives markets affects the real economy? Mr Filip probably did not assume that our betting would affect the outcomes of soccer games. He was, however, worried about our character. After all, there are two ways to think about the ways we obtain money. The first is that money comes from work and the second is that money comes from other people. If we believe the first, we are inclined to work. If we believe the second, we are inclined to seek ways to squeeze money from other people. Of course, both perceptions are correct on the microeconomic scale, but Mr Filip was right to be indignant, because on the macroeconomic scale only the first way is true. The mere receipt of money does not mean that one has created value in return for the funds, but in order for the money to have value, the good or service received for it later on must be produced.

There are typically three perspectives on the relationship between the derivatives markets and the real economy. I propose that they be called:

- the Wall Street value creation theory;
- the Main Street irrelevance theory;
- the Washington greed theory.

The Wall Street value creation theory proposes that by creating derivative securities—and in fact by all of its functions—Wall Street, and financial intermediaries in general, add value because they allocate capital efficiently. The Main Street irrelevance theory proposes that the only true value added to the economy is that created by work, in the real business world, and that what Wall Street, bankers, insurance firms, and investment gurus do is just shuffle paper (or, to be more precise, shuffle electronic entries) with no relevance to the real world. The Washington greed theory takes it one step further by claiming that the shuffling of paper (or electronic entries) is, at best, costly beyond any reasonable level and, at worst, outright fraud, where the finance gurus use the access they have to other people's money to enrich themselves immensely, without any consideration for the economic pain they inflict on the unsuspecting public. Of course, the supreme irony of this third theory lies in the fact that when the greedy finance gurus were caught with their pants down in 2008, they were saved by the political system and offered bailouts, often by the same political agents that once were quick to condemn them.

The Modigliani–Miller theorem implies that a method of financing affects an economic process if it affects tax costs, bankruptcy costs, or agency costs.

The issue raised by these three theories had been addressed by financial theory. Modigliani and Miller (1958), in a secular work of modern finance, showed that, under specific conditions, the value of the firm does not depend on its leverage policy, or the method of financing of the firm in general. The answer provided by them was that, in the absence of taxes, bankruptcy costs, or agency costs, the value of the firm is fundamentally determined by its earnings, and not by the way the firm is financed. Subsequent research (for example, Miller and Modigliani, 1961; and Stiglitz, 1969, 1974) has pointed out that taxes, bankruptcy costs, and agency costs do affect the value of the firm; and if the method of financing influences the tax costs, bankruptcy costs, or agency costs (especially the incentives of all the stakeholders of the firm, or the structure of distribution of information among those stakeholders, given information asymmetries among them), then the leverage policy or dividend policy becomes relevant. Over time, more specific research on how these factors affect the value of the firm developed.

WHAT DO FINANCIAL INTERMEDIARIES DO?

The old adage about the work of a banker is: "Borrow at 3%, lend at 5%, be on the golf course at 4." This concept of financial intermediation presents it basically as a *spread business*, i.e. a business of living off the difference between the cost of funds and investment returns. While this adage is very old indeed, it evolved in the modern financial world into the idea that financial intermediation is basically an *arbitrage business*. Arbitrage (Delbaen and Schachermayer, 2006) is defined as the creation of a short/long portfolio without an outlay of capital and without any risk of loss, yet earning income with positive probability. We tend to expect markets to be arbitrage-free, because arbitrage opportunities would be exploited until they disappeared. In the case of the banker, we do not expect the bank's customers to ignore the existence of the investment opportunities that would allow them to earn the full 5%, instead of the 3% offered by the bank.

But if financial intermediaries do not do arbitrage, what do they do? In a world without financial intermediaries, the economy's flow of funds would be between the household sector, which contains net savers, or equivalently, net purchasers of securities, and the production (i.e. business) sector, which contains net borrowers, or net providers of securities, and users of funds. However, because of price risk, monitoring costs, liquidity costs, etc., the typical household saver may view investment in the securities provided by the business sector as unattractive. Financial intermediaries step in between and "grease the wheels of commerce." They provide products (financial assets, even though typically not traded) that are accepted by the household sector (thus financial intermediaries assume a short position in those financial assets), which uses the funds to

CASE STUDY

Writing CDSs on Risky Bonds, or Buying Risky Bonds with Borrowed Money

Let us illustrate the functioning of the CDS market with a simple case. Imagine that you are an investment actuary in a hypothetical Swiss life insurance company. You notice that the country of Freedonia issues 10-year bonds denominated in Swiss francs and which currently pay a 3% annual coupon. The Swiss franc is not the currency of Freedonia. In fact, Freedonia uses its own currency, the *freebie*. The government of Freedonia plans to pay the interest and principal by collecting tax revenues in freebies and converting them at the market rate into Swiss francs to make payments. Since the interest rate offered is quite attractive (in the second half of 2011, the Swiss National Bank kept its interest rate target band at 0.00–0.25%, an extremely low level), you consider this an attractive investment and purchase SFr 1 million worth of those bonds. Subsequently, you are approached by a CDS dealer, Really Smart Investment Bank, Inc. (RSIB). RSIB offers you insurance against a default by Freedonia. In return for an annual fee, RSIB will pay you the full principal amount of the loan in case of default by the government of Freedonia, if such a default happens. This transaction is of course a standard credit default swap, written by the RSIB and purchased by you.

At the same time another company—let us call it the Swiss Medieval Bank (SMB)—accepts a deposit from a customer in the amount of SFr 1 million and buys the same amount of Freedonia's bonds with the funds. SMB pays its customer a rate of 0.25% annually. The conditions of the customer's deposit contract state that the customer will withdraw funds immediately if Freedonia's bond purchased by SMB defaults (a simple model to represent the risk of a run on a bank). Every year, SMB has a net profit of 2.75%, but if Freedonia defaults on its bond SMB must collect the market value of the now defaulted bond and then top it off with its own capital to repay SFr 1 million to its depositor.

The key point of this story is that, all other factors being equal, the situations that the RSIB and the SMB find themselves in are identical. The RSIB operates in the new sophisticated derivatives markets with fancy mathematical models, while the SMB might as well be doing its business in the year 1000. But their payoffs, and hence spreads collected, must be identical. Specifically, in the case of the RSIB transaction:

- before bond default, the RSIB is paid 3% − 0.25% = 2.75% (the CDS spread) on the principal of SFr 1 million;
- upon default, the RSIB pays SFr 1 million less the market value of the defaulted bond.

In the case of the SMB:

- before bond default, the SMB is paid 3% − 0.25% = 2.75% (the spread between the bond yield and the deposit rate) on the principal of SFr 1 million;
- upon default, the SMB pays SFr 1 million less the market value of the defaulted bond.

"**Retirement kills more people than hard work ever did.**" Malcolm S. Forbes

purchase securities supplied by the corporate sector (therefore assuming a long position in those securities) and other net issuers of securities (governments, government-sponsored enterprises, and even consumers themselves when they borrow). I submit that the creation of such a short/long portfolio is the essence of the intermediation business and, therefore, the essence of asset–liability management (ALM).

It is now generally acknowledged that financial intermediaries write options that are included in their products and in their portfolios in general. For example, the minimum interest rate guarantee, so common in long-term savings products, is a form of a put on the interest rate and a call on a fixed-coupon bond paying that interest rate. What I would like to point out is that the products of banks, insurance companies, and investment companies in general are in fact conceptually equivalent to derivative securities. For example, banks and insurance companies invest in a portfolio of certain assets and pay their customers cash flows derived from those created by that asset portfolio. The resulting short/long portfolio payments are not substantially different from the payments of a swap. In fact, an interest rate swap in which a swap dealer pays a variable interest rate and receives a fixed interest rate on a specified notional amount is exactly equivalent to borrowing the notional at a fixed interest rate (the one named in the swap) and investing it in a bond paying a floating interest rate named in the swap contract. An insurance company that issues a guaranteed investment contract at a fixed interest rate paid at regular intervals and invests in an asset paying a variable rate is in an exactly equivalent position. Ostaszewski (2003) also points out that the life insurance business can be viewed as a form of a derivative security based on human capital.

ALM is about restructuring asset cash flows into liability cash flows. That's basically the same business as that of writing derivative securities.

Thus, financial intermediaries effectively restructure cash flows provided by securities of the business sector into the cash flows demanded by the household sector. The derivative created by a financial intermediary, however, must be understood in a much broader sense than is commonly used—i.e. not one restricted to just options, or futures, or swaps. In the popular perception it is often assumed that derivatives increase risk. One of the most common features of the derivatives issued by financial intermediaries is that they actually reduce the risk faced by their customers. But the risk does not disappear—in fact it is retained by the financial intermediary. This perspective implies that financial intermediaries *always face financial risks*, i.e. risks caused by changing values of market variables, such as interest rates, credit risk, share prices, liquidity, etc.

CREDIT DEFAULT SWAPS (THE *VILLAIN EXTRAORDINAIRE*), AND MR ANSZPERGER'S STRAWBERRY PRINCIPLE

The ideas presented here are illustrated very well by the credit default swaps market and its role in the credit crisis of 2008, as well as in the subsequent sovereign debt crisis seen in Europe. A credit default swap (CDS) is a transaction between a buyer of a CDS and a seller of a CDS. Of course, as you should realize by now, it is a bet. The buyer of a CDS makes a series of payments (each of which is called a *fee*, or a *spread*) to the seller. The seller, in return, is required to make a full payoff of the loan, or other credit instrument named in the contract, when that loan goes through a specified *credit event* (which could be a default, but could also be a ratings downgrade, or any event specified in the contract). In the case study below I show that a CDS is, in fact, identical to a package of transactions carried out in traditional banking.

The price of a derivative security is determined from the price of a *replicating portfolio* of cash and the underlying.

The idea of equivalence illustrated in the case study lies behind the use of the concept of arbitrage (or, more precisely, the lack of it) for the pricing of derivative securities (Delbaen and Schachermayer, 2006). To put it simply: two financial instruments that make identical payments, no matter what the circumstances, must have the same price. In fact, if they make identical payments no matter what the circumstances, they are the same thing, regardless of what we choose to call them. I call this the "strawberry principle." I learned it from my elementary school mathematics teacher, Mr Anszperger. As you already know, I attended elementary school in Poland under communist Soviet occupation. Mr Anszperger was not only an excellent mathematics teacher in my school, he was an amateur stand-up comedian, and he usually started every class with an anticommunist joke. We pupils were very worried about his safety, but apparently nobody in the school was a rat because he was not arrested during my years there. A very important part of our education was learning about the great achievements of the Soviet Union and of Russia in the pre-Soviet period. We were taught (by other teachers more dedicated to the cause than Mr Anszperger) that all great inventions and scientific discoveries (the light bulb, radio, electricity, etc.) had been made by Soviet and Russian scientists. We did not treat this propaganda too seriously, and I still remember how astonished I was when I learned that Dmitri Mendeleev actually did invent the periodic table. One day, Mr Anszperger came to class and very seriously announced that Soviet scientists had just invented a new and revolutionary type of raspberry. It was revolutionary because it was as big as a strawberry. It also smelt like a strawberry, looked like a strawberry, tasted like a strawberry, and had the same consistency as a strawberry. Thus, Mr Anszperger had independently discovered the fundamental theorem of asset pricing (Delbaen and Schachermayer, 2006), though I much prefer to refer to his discovery as the Strawberry Principle.

MAKING IT HAPPEN

The modern financial world has brought about intense competition and financial innovation. But the essence of the business has not changed. Derivative securities allow simpler and more direct risk and financing transfers, but they are still financial products and work well or badly because the underlying business model or finance structure works well or badly, respectively.

Thus, in asset–liability management, we should remember that:

- ALM is not about hedging risks, or arbitrage, it is about managing risks.
- A financial intermediary who does not take risks should not earn any profits.
- Risks of ALM are functionally equivalent to risks of derivatives market maker.
- Derivative securities are equivalent to packages of simpler, underlying securities, and do not create value by their mere existence.
- Derivatives may even destroy value, especially when their complexity is not appreciated and not studied with appropriate mathematical models.
- ALM is not an esoteric speculative endeavor where money is made through miracles of smart arbitrage.
- ALM serves the underlying real business, and it should be structured to increase its value.

  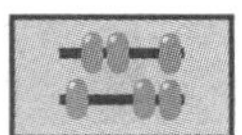      

IMPLICATIONS OF ALM

In the story of Freedonia's bond purchase told in the case study, the key insight is that the cash flows of the transactions of the RSIB and SMB are identical—thus must have the same price, and are in fact the same transactions. Why then do we have a CDS market when the same transaction can be created by a standard short/long portfolio of a financial intermediary? The answer is obvious: regulatory requirements for those two transactions are different. This represents a stern warning for regulators, who somehow believe that they can control financial markets through accounting entries and not by paying attention to real economics, especially to risk-taking, of financial institutions.

But this observation also provides important advice for the management of financial institutions. Asset–liability management cannot be viewed as a process of eliminating risks in order to earn a riskless spread. Such a perspective, while often exhibited by ALM, contradicts the very nature of financial intermediation. Financial intermediaries are not in a spread business; they are, and always have been, in a derivatives business. We have developed new technologies for creating derivatives. But our sophisticated mathematical models for pricing derivatives rely on one underlying (strawberry) principle: in order to price a derivative we seek to replicate it (often dynamically, in continuous time) with cash and the underlying. Although the derivative may not have existed in the year 1000, cash and the underlying (maybe in somewhat different form) did. Thus, risk management and pricing issues in banking, insurance, and finance in general must be viewed in the same light and with the same frame of mind—as risk management and pricing in derivatives markets, and vice versa. Granted, it was actually the derivatives dealers who gave us the worst examples of "spread business mentality" in the recent crisis. But their debacle also gave us examples of how this spread business mentality (which is really an arbitrage-seeking mentality) ALM has failed. We must become much more serious about the representation of the risk of extreme events in our models, pay attention to how that risk is priced by the markets, and not fall prey to simplistic models that avoid deeper mathematical questions, the way investment bankers did.

When in doubt, let us ask ourselves again: How was this done in the year 1000? The central issue of the recent crisis was credit risk. How was credit risk addressed in the year 1000? Let us note that derivatives traded on the exchanges—where credit risks are mitigated by design—came through the credit crisis smoothly. The blowup happened in privately traded derivatives and in the short/long derivatives portfolios of financial institutions. The mechanisms used to mitigate credit risk on the exchanges are actually the same as those used in the year 1000. There are only two such mechanisms. If a young entrepreneur with no established credit or reputation in the year 1000 wanted to borrow some money from a wealthy merchant in his/her town, two credit enhancement procedures existed. The entrepreneur could offer collateral—for example a cow, or a piece of land—or the entrepreneur could have the loan cosigned by his/her wealthy uncle. Nowadays, everybody wants theirs cosigned by Uncle Sam, who may not turn out to be as wealthy as expected, but the principle remains the same.

Say goodbye to the "spread business" mentality. Say hello to derivatives.

The most stunning phenomenon to be brought into daylight by the credit crisis was, as I see it, the hubris of investment bankers, satisfied by simplistic models that avoid any humbling mathematics. If the perspective of this chapter is correct, then all financial intermediation is a complex process, with many risks of extreme events, and where mathematical models must be used extensively, with extreme humility, and updated continuously to fit with the changing world. If we are serious about risk, this is how we must price derivatives, and this is how we must approach ALM in financial institutions.

MORE INFO

Books:

Delbaen, Freddy, and Walter Schachermayer. *The Mathematics of Arbitrage*. Berlin: Springer, 2006.

Fabozzi, Frank J., and Franco Modigliani. *Mortgage and Mortgage-Backed Securities Markets*. Boston, MA: Harvard Business School Press, 1992.

Hull, John C. *Options, Futures, and Other Derivatives*. 8th ed. Upper Saddle River, NJ: Pearson, 2011.

Ostaszewski, Krzysztof M. *Asset–Liability Integration*. Society of Actuaries (SOA) monograph M-FI02-1. Schaumberg, IL: SOA, 2002. Online at: tinyurl.com/7lfz89k

Ostaszewski, Krzysztof M. "Modigliani, Miller, and Mortgages." In *Housing in Retirement*. Society of Actuaries (SOA) monograph M-FI09. Schaumberg, IL: SOA, 2009. Online at: tinyurl.com/7ebt5ww [PDF].

Articles:

Becker, Gary S., and George J. Stigler. "Law enforcement, malfeasance, and compensation of enforcers." *Journal of Legal Studies* 3:1 (January 1974): 1–18. Online at: www.jstor.org/stable/724119

Haubrich, Joseph G. "Derivative mechanics: The CMO." *Economic Commentary* (Federal Reserve Bank of Cleveland), Issue Q1 (September 1, 1995): 13–19. Online at: tinyurl.com/7pv68ot [PDF].

Miller, Merton H., and Franco Modigliani. "Dividend policy, growth, and the valuation of shares." *Journal of Business* 34:4 (October 1961): 411–433. Online at: www.jstor.org/stable/2351143

Modigliani, Franco, and Merton H. Miller. "The cost of capital, corporation finance and the theory of investment." *American Economic Review* 48:3 (June 1958): 261–297. Online at: www.jstor.org/stable/1809766

Myerson, Roger B. "A model of moral-hazard credit cycles." Working paper. March 2010, revised September 2012. Online at: tinyurl.com/7t43lw2 [PDF].

Ostaszewski, Krzysztof. "Is life insurance a human capital derivatives business?" *Journal of Insurance Issues* 26:1 (2003): 1–14. Online at: www.insuranceissues.org/PDFs/261O.pdf

Shapiro, Carl, and Joseph E. Stiglitz. "Equilibrium unemployment as a worker disciplinary device." *American Economic Review* 74:3 (June 1984): 433–444. Online at: www.jstor.org/stable/1804018

Stiglitz, Joseph E. "A re-examination of the Modigliani–Miller theorem." *American Economic Review* 59:5 (December 1969): 784–793. Online at: www.jstor.org/stable/1810676

Stiglitz, Joseph E. "On the irrelevance of corporate financial policy." *American Economic Review* 64:6 (December 1974): 851–866. Online at: www.jstor.org/stable/1815238

See Also:

★ Asset Liability Management for Pension Funds (pp. 13–15)
★ Dangers of Corporate Derivative Transactions (pp. 36–38)
✔ Derivatives Markets: Their Structure and Function (p. 1007)
✔ Understanding Asset–Liability Management (Full Balance Sheet Approach) (p. 996)

"Till old experience do attain / To something like prophetic strain." John Milton

  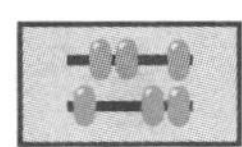      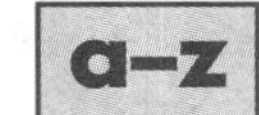

Analyzing a Bank's Financial Performance

by Jyothi Manohar

EXECUTIVE SUMMARY

- The key components of a bank's basic financial statements.
- A description of each of the components.
- How relationships between components are measured and analyzed.
- The conclusions that can be reached as a result of analyzing these relationships.
- The capital, asset, management, earnings, liquidity (CAMEL) methodology of analyzing a bank's financial performance.

INTRODUCTION

Individually and collectively, the financial health of banks and the banking system is critical to national and global economies. Central banks or other regulators in various countries monitor financial institutions using rating and evaluation systems that may be unique to those countries. However, there are certain common measures of financial performance and the safety and soundness of a financial institution. No one measure, by itself, is an indicator of the financial health of a bank. It is important to understand each and the interplay among all or many of these measures to properly evaluate a bank's financial performance.

ANALYZING A BANK'S FINANCIAL PERFORMANCE

It is necessary to understand the composition of a bank's basic financial statements (this is itemized in detail in the Appendix to this chapter) and the business of banking (described in the section "Earnings" below). It is difficult to analyze a bank's financial performance merely by looking at financial information at a particular point in time. Essential to this analysis is a review of how similar components of a bank's financial information have trended over time, compared to its own past performance as well as the performance of its peers.

Common measures of financial performance are capital adequacy, asset quality, liquidity, earnings, management capability, risk management, and critical key ratios that serve as tools to analyze a bank's financial performance.

COMMON MEASURES OF FINANCIAL PERFORMANCE

Capital Adequacy

How do banking regulators measure, evaluate, and rate the quality of a bank's financial stability or, in industry parlance, the safety and soundness of a bank? Capital adequacy is a keystone. The Basel Committee on Banking Supervision of the Bank of International Settlements (BIS) has established minimum capital standards that are widely followed by banks across the world. (In September 2010 higher global minimum capital standards were announced that will be phased in over a period of time.) Capital adequacy is generally measured in the following categories.

- *Tier I capital* generally consists of common equity, disclosed reserves, and retained earnings (excluding other comprehensive income) and is calculated as Tier I capital/Total risk-weighted assets. All assets on a bank's balance sheet are risk-weighted based on the respective credit risk as defined by the respective central banks; for instance, cash on hand has a risk weight of 0, whereas a commercial advance may carry a risk weight of 100%. Tier I minimum capital ratios are generally established at 4%.
- *Total risk-based capital* includes Tier I capital plus certain other eligible items up to limits specified by regulatory guidance. Minimum capital ratios are generally established at 8%.
- *Leverage ratio*: Calculated as Tier I capital/Average total assets, with the minimum established at 4%.

Capital adequacy helps to sustain a bank's growth and protect it from the consequences of the risks represented by its various lines of business. For instance, if a bank makes a strategic decision to expand its lending operations in a new geography, it will need to ensure that any impairment losses inherent in the new operations can be adequately absorbed by retained earnings while still maintaining healthy capital ratios.

These ratios are a necessary disclosure in any bank's financial statements. Once a bank's key capital ratios start to hover near or sink below the minimums required, alarm bells sound, hinting to analysts and regulators that the financial institution requires closer monitoring. In the United States, starting in 2009, peaking in 2010, and continuing today have been numerous bank failures that resulted in closure by the Federal Deposit Insurance Corporation (FDIC). A common thread among these failures is credit losses so excessive that they eroded retained earnings, and hence capital, to below the minimum or to such critically deficient levels as to threaten the very existence of the financial institution. Analyses of several of these bank failures can be read on the FDIC's website (see More Info section at the end of the chapter).

Asset Quality

The asset quality measure largely addresses the quality of the loans and advances of a bank, although the quality of investment securities has also come into play. While all banks have credit policies that provide a framework within which the bank limits its lending operations, the varied nature of the loans made by a bank, the vast geographies over which they are spread, the varied nature, characteristics, and demographics of the borrowers, and the collateral underlying the loans present risks of nonperformance and collectability that are difficult to measure and quantify. Hence, credit risk is among the most critical risks that a financial institution must manage. Banks must necessarily have risk management systems in place to continuously monitor their loan portfolios.

The notes to a bank's financial statements detail a bank's credit risk management policies, the types of loans it makes, policies related to when nonperforming loans (NPLs) are placed on nonaccrual status (usually at 90 days of delinquency), charge-off (write-off as losses) policies, when loans are deemed impaired, policies related to the evaluation and measurement of impaired loans, and what factors are considered by the bank in establishing reserves (or allowances) for credit impairment and losses. Key asset quality ratios include the following.

- *Loan by type/Total loans and advances.* Reflects the composition of the loan portfolio and growth rate of each in relation to total loans and advances, showing which sector of the portfolio is increasing rapidly and how credit risk might be impacted as a result.
- *Reserve (allowance) for credit losses/Total loans and advances.* Presents the reserve for loan losses as a percentage of total loans.
- *NPL/Total loans and advances.* Presents the proportion of the total loan portfolio that is nonperforming, i.e. no longer accruing interest since collection is in doubt.
- *Loans and advances charged off (written off)/Average total loans and*

  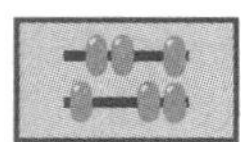      

advances. Represents actual losses incurred as a result of loans written off in proportion to average total loans.
- *Reserve for credit losses/NPL*. Coverage represented by the reserve or allowance for credit losses to the existing level of nonperforming loans.

Liquidity

At any given point in time, a bank must have the necessary funds to make loans and advances to borrowers, meet the demands of customers for deposit withdrawals, and pay other obligations. Although a bank can project some of these requirements based on loan commitments in the pipeline, upcoming maturities of loans and deposits, and known obligations, unanticipated demands and contingencies must be met as well. A necessary byproduct of asset liability management processes is liquidity management. All banks have liquidity policies that allow them to meet known and unexpected liquidity requirements. Sources of liquidity are:
- cash and cash equivalents;
- core deposits;
- reserve balances;
- assets available for sale that can be disposed of quickly and converted to cash;
- borrowing sources that include lines of credit that can be drawn on.

Essential to this analysis is that a bank has access to diverse sources of liquidity and can answer the following questions.
- Is there a stable base of core deposits, or is it shrinking?
- Is there reliance on short-term, volatile sources of funds to meet long-term obligations, or vice-versa?
- Is there ready access to money and capital markets in the event that additional funds must be raised?
- Does the bank have enough diversification among assets on its balance sheet that can be quickly converted to cash?
- Does management have enough policies and processes in place to evaluate its liquidity position funds management and contingency funding strategies on an ongoing basis?
- What picture is the cash flow statement presenting that will impact the bank's liquidity position?
- Is the loan-to-deposit ratio satisfactory? Calculated as Total loans and advances/Total deposits, this is a measure for assessing a bank's liquidity.

If the ratio is too high, the bank might not have enough liquidity to cover unanticipated funding requirements; if the ratio is too low, the bank may not be earning as much as it could be.

Earnings

How Does a Bank Generate Net Income?

Banks lend money and accept deposits, invest excess funds, generate fee income, and pay bills. On the face of it, and through a quick perusal of a bank's income statement, the concept appears straightforward enough—generate a healthy net interest income and enough noninterest income to cover all noninterest expenses and then some. It is easier said than done, however.

The next sections describe the different components that go into the calculation of a bank's net income.

Net Interest Income

Managing and monitoring a large variety of interest-bearing assets and interest-bearing liabilities in a constantly changing interest rate environment is no easy task. When one thinks of the variety of interest-bearing assets (primarily investment securities and loans and advances) that carry a multitude of interest rates (fixed rate or variable rates tied to indices such as Libor, Treasury rates, prime rates, bank rates) and a multitude of maturities and the variety of interest-bearing liabilities (primarily customer and bank deposits and borrowings) that also carry a plethora of interest rates and span maturities from "on demand" to 10 years or more and everything in between, managing the balance sheet and interest rate risk is a challenging, complex, ongoing exercise.

The proportion of noninterest income to total income speaks volumes as to the sources of revenues for a bank and its reliance on ancillary services versus traditional banking services.

Throw into the mix the vagaries of consumer and business demand for funds, national and world events that impact the financial markets and economies locally, nationally, and internationally, and a bank's ability to meet all of those demands while still generating income for its shareholders, and it becomes obvious that remaining financially healthy is a highwire act. Asset liability management, liquidity management, interest rate risk and sensitivity analysis, duration and maturity gap analysis are all inextricably intertwined.

The interest rate environment has been at historical lows these past few years. It has been especially challenging for banks to maintain consistently healthy net interest margins (NIM, measured by net interest income as a percentage of average interest-earning assets). Ideally, banks will strive for a NIM better than 3%.

It has been especially challenging for banks to maintain consistently healthy net interest margins (measured by net interest income as a percentage of average interest earning assets).

Noninterest Income

To meet the objective of consistent net income and earnings per share (EPS), the other alternatives for banks have been either to generate as much noninterest revenue as possible through fees, service charges, and gains on sale of assets or to reduce operating expenses. Reducing provisions for losses and asset impairments is not a prudent option, particularly in a troubled world economy. To augment revenues from traditional banking services, more and more banks are generating fee and service revenue from private banking, trust and wealth management, financial advice, sale of non-deposit investment vehicles, insurance products, and other such ancillary services. The proportion of noninterest income to total income speaks volumes as to the sources of revenues for a bank and its reliance on ancillary services versus traditional banking services. It should help to focus an analyst's attention on the viability of these revenue sources for the bank.

Provisions for Impairment and Other Losses

Though all banks have lending and investment policies that purport to be prudent and establish parameters as to the types of loans, advances, and investments they will make and their relative concentrations, both as a proportion of the respective totals and of equity, it is difficult for any bank to accurately anticipate economic downturns and financial meltdowns (as have been experienced since 2007 and are continuing to impact several countries across the globe). These events are, to a fair degree, outside a bank's control, yet they have an adverse impact on the collateral value of loans and advances and the quality and collectability of its assets. Many banks across the world have experienced losses as a result of nonperforming loans, toxic investments, and other asset write-downs, particularly during the trough year 2009. Analyzing the carrying value of its assets is an ongoing risk management activity for every bank. This includes the valuation of goodwill and intangibles as well, some of which have suffered in the recent crises and been written down or charged off through profit and loss as being impaired.

Noninterest Expense

Most operating costs, with the exception of discretionary spending such as marketing and advertising, represent fixed costs that a bank must incur to operate its business efficiently. Depending on how internal and external factors impact other components of the financial statements, a bank may

  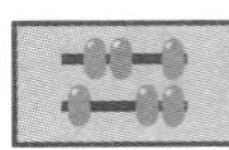      

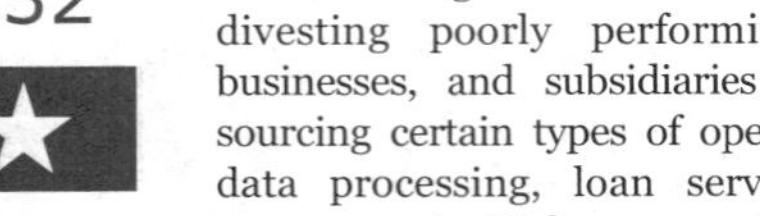

make strategic decisions to cut costs by divesting poorly performing branches, businesses, and subsidiaries and by outsourcing certain types of operation such as data processing, loan servicing, human resources, etc. Risk management techniques that include close monitoring of planned (budgeted) performance against actual results are another tool used by a bank to manage its financial performance. The efficiency ratio is a measure of how well a bank is controlling its operating costs. While there are variations in how banks compute the efficiency ratio, it is generally calculated as:

$$\text{Noninterest expense} \div (\text{Net interest income} + \text{Noninterest income} - \text{Gains on investment securities})$$

The lower the efficiency ratio, the better the bank's performance. Ideally, banks will strive for efficiency ratios of 50–55% or less.

The efficiency ratio is a good measure of how well a bank is controlling its operating costs. The lower the efficiency ratio, the better the bank's performance.

Net Income and Earnings Per Share

Sustained positive earnings and earnings per share are among the planned primary objectives for any company's business plan—and no less so for a bank. Net income helps to build retained earnings, which in turn sustains healthy capital ratios. For a bank, maintaining better than minimum capital ratios (as we have already seen in this chapter) is the lifeblood for survival. Net income keeps stockholders happy by providing a source of continued dividends on their investment. EPS is a common measure of a company's profitability and is well known to anyone who invests in company stock.

In analyzing net income, however, it is important to understand which components of the income statement are major contributors to the net income or net loss—whether these be core operations, ancillary services, gains from investment securities sales or other asset disposals, or increases in noninterest expenses or provisions for loan losses or other asset impairments. Is net income or loss being generated by a one-time event that will not recur? Looking at the cause of changes in net income or loss over a period of time will help an analyst to focus on what events are shaping a bank's financial performance.

No one measure by itself is an indicator of the financial health of a bank. It is important to understand each, and the interplay among all or many of these measures, to properly evaluate a bank's financial performance.

Summary

In summary, analyses of a bank's earnings encompass:

- the consistency, quality, and adequacy of earnings;
- sources and levels of earnings;
- the ability to bolster retained earnings and capital through earnings;
- levels of provision required for impaired loans and assets;
- net interest margins;
- the return on assets (ROA): Net income/Average assets;
- the return on equity (ROE): Net income/Average equity;
- the dividend payout ratio: Dividends/Net income.

In analyzing net income, it is important to understand which components of the income statement are major contributors to the net income or net loss.

Management Capability

This intangible measure encompasses the qualifications of board members, the level of participation of each, the level of collective oversight provided by board committees and the board over the critical operating, accounting, and financial reporting policies of the bank, as well as the qualifications of key members of management, their experience and capability in executing board-approved policies, and their oversight of the day-to-day operations of the bank.

Although it is difficult to quantify this measure, the annual reports of all public banks include discussion and disclosures related to board members, executive management, the level of shareholdings of each, the remuneration received, the qualifications, and the specific position each holds in relation to the bank. In addition, significant related party transactions—i.e. transactions that board members, executive management, or their affiliated interests have with the bank—will be disclosed. All of these disclosures point an analyst to the potential for conflicts of interest and the level of objectivity with which board members and executive management execute their responsibilities in protecting the interests of the bank, its customers, and its stockholders.

Risk Management

In this chapter we have alluded to varied risks in several aspects that must be managed in order to achieve positive financial performance. The typical risks listed below have direct or indirect effects on a bank's financial performance and should be addressed by all banks. Banks' annual reports detail the risk management activities that are applicable to the organization.

- *Credit risk*: Credit risk is addressed in the section "Asset quality" above and encompasses more than the traditional definition associated with lending activities. Credit risk is found in all activities where success depends on counterparty, issuer, or borrower performance.
- *Interest rate and market risk*: Interest rate risk is addressed under "Ne interest income" above. Market risk is the risk to a bank's financial condition resulting from adverse movements in market rates or prices, such as interest rates, foreign exchange rates, or equity prices. Changes in interest rates may have a significant effect on other areas of risk. For example, market risk can impair the bank's liquidity position.
- *Liquidity risk*: This is addressed under "Liquidity" above.
- *Operational and transaction risk*: Operational risk arises from the potential that inadequate information systems, operational problems, breaches in internal controls, fraud, or unforeseen catastrophes will result in unexpected losses. Transaction risk is pervasive to an organization. It is the risk to earnings or capital arising from problems with service or product delivery and may include potential financial losses from human error or fraud, incomplete information, and related decision-making or operational disruption.
- *Compliance and legal risk*: All banks must operate in compliance with a myriad of laws, rules, and regulations. Compliance risk arises from potential violations of or nonconformance with those laws, regulations, or prescribed practices which govern the bank's activities. Legal risk arises from the potential that unenforceable contracts, lawsuits, or adverse judgments can adversely affect the operations and financial performance of the bank.
- *Strategic risk*: Strategic risk results from adverse business decisions or the improper implementation of those decisions. Examples include the misalignment of business and technology strategic plans, improper market positioning (e.g. retail delivery strategies, geographic positioning, etc.) and pricing of products and services.
- *Reputation risk*: Reputation risk is the potential that negative publicity regarding a bank's business practices will cause a decline in the customer base, costly litigation, or revenue reductions,

often as a result of poor earnings, regulatory censure, significant fraud or litigation, or failure to provide services or products in conformity with the local market. Reputation risk exposure is driven to a large extent by the bank's actions to manage other categories of risks.
- *Foreign exchange risk*: Tied to market risk above.
- *Technology risk*: Technology risk is the potential that the bank has an inadequate technology infrastructure and related technical support to properly process daily transactions, keep customer information private, provide timely and accurate board and management information for key decision-making, thereby disabling the bank in the event of a catastrophe.

Critical Key Ratios: Risk-Adjusted Performance Measures (RAPMs)

We have seen that the safety and soundness of banks and the banking system are reliant on maintaining levels of capital that will see a financial institution through adverse periods and sustain it over the long run. Given the many tangible and intangible risks facing the banking industry today, protecting capital through risk-adjusted performance measures is of increasing importance. The most common RAPM is risk-adjusted return on risk-adjusted capital (RARORAC), which goes beyond the earnings measures represented by return on assets (ROA) and return on equity (ROE). RARORAC takes into consideration anticipated returns adjusted for expected future losses (credit losses, declines in interest income or noninterest income, contingencies, etc.). In addition, capital-at-risk represents not just equity (the difference between total assets and total liabilities) but the estimated funds required to protect against expected losses as well as unexpected losses—i.e. losses that could result from each of the risks identified in "Risk management" above. Hence, RARORAC is a marked change from traditional measures of return on equity not only with respect to computation, but also to measurement and complexity. RARORAC is measured as:

Risk-adjusted return ÷ Capital-at-risk

SUMMARY

Analyzing a bank's financial performance requires a holistic approach. It involves an understanding not only of the numbers that comprise the nancial statements, but also of the various intangible or qualitative factors both internal and external to the financial institution that have a direct or indirect impact on the numbers. Banks are in a unique position in the world economy such that the performance of each can be significantly affected by external market forces, many of which are outside the banks' control. Like all other business organizations, however, internal risk management policies and the quality of management and board oversight that are within the organization's control have an impact on financial performance. An analyst needs to understand that there are interrelationships among all or many of the varied financial and performance indicators and the intangible factors that must be evaluated in concert in order to reach accurate conclusions.

APPENDIX: BASIC BANK FINANCIAL STATEMENTS

Balance Sheet

As with any business organization, a bank's balance sheet comprises assets, liabilities, and capital (stockholders' equity). The nature of these items reflects the uniqueness of the business of banking.

Assets

- *Cash*. The cash on hand (usually at various branch locations, in vaults, and in automated teller machines (ATMs)) and required reserves maintained with the respective central bank of the country.
- *Balances maintained with other financial institutions*. Includes short-term investments with original maturities of 90 days or less.

The above two balances are aggregated as "Cash and cash equivalents" (CCE).

- *Federal funds sold*. Temporary (often overnight) investments of excess funds with other banks.
- *Investment securities*. Debt or equity securities held for interest earnings, liquidity, or gains trading. There may be regulatory restrictions on the types of investment a bank can hold.
- *Derivatives*. Financial instruments whose price or value is dependent on the changes in value of other underlying assets, which may be stocks, bonds, currencies, commodities, etc. Banks generally use derivative instruments as a means of protecting themselves from interest rate or international currency exchange rate fluctuations. Due to the sophisticated nature of derivative instruments both from a risk and an accounting perspective, derivatives are typically entered into only by those banks that have the resources and expertise to handle them.
- *Advances or loans to customers*. Loans made to individuals, businesses, and other organizations for a whole plethora of reasons, ranging from buying a car to funding working capital for business organizations, construction projects, and the like.
- *Advances or loans to banks*. Typically, loans made by larger banks to other banks for a variety of reasons; accounted for in much the same manner as advances or loans to customers.
- *Property, plant, and equipment*. The bank's holdings of real estate (the bank's various locations may be leased or owned), furniture, fixtures, equipment, technology hardware, capitalized leases, or other similar assets that have an estimated useful life and which are used on an ongoing basis.
- *Goodwill and intangible assets*. Goodwill arises from the acquisition of another business where the consideration paid exceeds the assets acquired and the liabilities assumed. For a bank, intangibles usually represent items like loan-servicing rights, core deposit premiums, and customer lists, although trade names and computer software (purchased or internally generated) may also be included as intangible assets.
- *Deferred taxes*. These balances arise due to temporary differences in the carrying value of assets and liabilities for financial reporting purposes versus tax reporting purposes. Deferred tax assets represent temporary differences that will result in future tax benefits for the bank.
- *Other assets*. This could include a multitude of balances including accrued interest receivable, prepaid assets, investments in joint ventures, miscellaneous receivables, and repossessed assets.
- *Off-balance sheet items*. Includes items such as commitments, letters of credit, debt financing, off-balance sheet exposure to derivatives, etc.

Liabilities

- *Deposits*. These include deposits by customers (current or demand accounts, savings accounts, fixed deposits, also known as term deposit receipts or certificates of deposit) and other banks.
- *Borrowings*. These include short- and long-term borrowings from other banks, repurchase agreements, and federal funds purchased. Repurchase agreements are short-term arrangements to sell investment securities with an agreement that they will be repurchased at pre-set prices and in pre-set time frames. Federal funds purchased are temporary (usually overnight)

  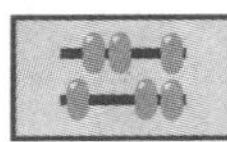      

borrowings of excess funds from other banks.

- *Debt securities issued.* These are generally longer-term borrowings for specific purposes and include trust preferred issuances and corporate bonds. The debt issuances of larger banks frequently trade on a regular basis and may be readily purchased and sold through investment brokers.
- *Derivatives.* See "Assets" section above for definition. Fair-value fluctuations may cause derivative instruments to be classified as liabilities.
- *Deferred taxes.* See "Assets" section above for definition. Deferred tax liabilities represent temporary differences that are currently taxable.
- *Accounts payable and accrued expenses.* Current liabilities arising out of the routine day-to-day operations of a bank such as bills payable, salaries payable, professional fees payable, etc.
- *Pension and retirement liabilities.* Depending on the type of employee benefits plans adopted by a bank, these may represent the actuarial valuation of future benefits payable.

Capital (or Equity)

- *Common capital (or stock).* The par value of common shares issued and outstanding.
- *Surplus (share premium or additional paid-in capital).* Excess over par of common shares issued and outstanding.
- *Other equity instruments.* Typically, different classes of preference (or preferred) shares.
- *Other comprehensive income.* This includes net income or loss for the current fiscal period. It also represents an account through which changes in fair values of certain items (e.g. investment securities that are classified as available-for-sale, derivatives that qualify for hedge accounting, foreign currency exchange rates, or actuarial valuations for certain types of deferred compensation plan) are recorded.
- *Retained earnings.* The cumulative amount of net income earned or loss incurred since the bank's inception, adjusted for cash or share dividends paid.
- *Reserves.* Banks in some countries are required to maintain statutory reserves as mandated by their regulators or central banks.

Income Statement

The presentation of a bank income statement varies widely from one country to another. Nevertheless, the components are generally the same.

- *Interest income.* Interest earned on all interest-bearing assets.
- *Interest expense.* Interest paid on all interest-bearing liabilities.
- *Net interest income.* The difference between interest income and interest expense.
- *Noninterest income.* Income from other sources such as service charges, fee income from the sale of trust services, wealth management services, etc., and gain on sale of investment securities, loans, or other assets.
- *Noninterest expense.* Operating expenses such as personnel costs, occupancy expenses, professional services, insurance, data processing, etc., and losses from the sale of investment securities, loans, or other assets.
- *Provisions for losses.* Losses such as loan losses, provisions for liabilities such as actuarial liabilities, and provisions for impairment losses such as investment or other asset impairment.
- *Net income or loss before taxes.* The excess of total income over total expense or vice-versa.
- *Provision for income taxes.* Current tax expense plus changes in deferred tax expense.
- *Net income or loss after taxes.* The excess of total income over total expense or vice-versa adjusted for tax expense or tax benefit.

Statement of Changes in Stockholders' Equity

The statement of changes in stockholders' equity comprises the activity during the year that resulted in changes in each of the components of capital (or equity) described under "Balance sheet" above.

Cash Flow Statement

The cash flow statement gives a telling picture of how a bank's cash and cash equivalents changed during the year as a result of the cash inflows and outflows affecting each component of the balance sheet. The cash flow statement is segregated into three sections that indicate the bank's cash flows generated by or used in operating activities, investing activities, and financing activities. Focusing on the individual components in the cash flow statement gives the analyst an indication of the sources of the bank's business that are generating cash flows and those that are draining cash. Excessive cash outflows over cash inflows could have an adverse impact on the bank's liquidity position.

Notes to the Financial Statements

Basic financial statements for any business organization are accompanied by notes to the financial statements. Audited financial statements usually include an indicator that "the accompanying notes are an integral part of the financial statements." Each account balance on the financial statements is referenced to a note number. Notes to the financial statements usually lead with a summary of the bank's accounting policies as it relates to all key financial accounts. Thereafter, individual notes detail what comprises the account balance and how the carrying amount of the account came about.

Notes to financial statements contain all the relevant disclosures required by the Generally Accepted Accounting Principles (GAAP), such as International Financial Reporting Standards (IFRS), under which it is presented and enable a financial statement user to better understand the bank's financial condition and its operations. It is easy to access and read the audited financial statements of most banks across the world under the "Annual report" caption on their respective websites. An example would be www.hsbc.fr, where the annual report for HSBC France can be located by following the link "Informations financières."

MORE INFO

Book:

Golin, Jonathan. *The Bank Credit Analysis Handbook: A Guide for Analysts, Bankers and Investors*. Singapore: Wiley, 2001.

Article:

Basel Committee on Banking Supervision. "Basel III: A global regulatory framework for more resilient banks and banking systems." Bank of International Settlements. Updated June 2011. Online at: www.bis.org/publ/bcbs189.htm

Websites:

Credit and Finance Risk Analysis: credfinrisk.com/bank.html
Federal Deposit Insurance Corporation (FDIC): www.fdic.gov
FitchTraining: tinyurl.com/ckh54pn

See Also:

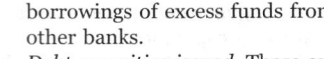

Banking and Financial Services (pp. 1612–1614)

"We hate inflation, but we love everything that causes it." William Simon

Banking Transparency and the Robustness of the Banking System by Solomon Tadesse

EXECUTIVE SUMMARY

- The global financial crisis of the new millennium has brought to light the inherent fragility of the financial system and made more urgent the need for policy reforms to enhance its robustness against future shocks.
- The opaque world of securitization and credit derivatives in subprime mortgages, which served as the breeding ground for the crisis, has brought attention to the age-old question of whether enhancing transparency can promote the stability of the financial system.
- The objective of this article is to provide a short review of the issues surrounding the relationship between banking transparency and the stability of the banking system.
- The theoretical as well as the empirical case for transparency as an enhancer of banking system robustness is not without controversy.
- However, despite conflicting views, there is a consensus that transparency, while not a panacea against systemic turbulence in financial systems, plays a significant role in enhancing banking system stability.

INTRODUCTION

Crises have been a common feature of banking systems for a long time—the United States alone experienced 11 banking panics between 1800 and the beginning of World War I (Beim and Calomiris, 2001). The crises of recent times have, however, been rather severe. The full range of costs linked to the 2007–09 financial crisis may not be easily estimable. While initial gross government commitments to deal with the crisis have reached between 20% and 30% of GDP in developed markets (Schildbach, 2010), the effective fiscal outlays so far have amounted to 3.5% of GDP in G20 countries, with gross output losses projected to be much higher. In earlier crises the costs of bailing out troubled banks in a banking crisis ranged between 20% and 50% of a country's GDP, with a resolution time that could extend up to nine years (Honohan and Klingebiel, 2000). Hoggarth and Saporta (2001) report the average fiscal costs of resolving a banking crisis to be about 16% of GDP, with cumulative real output losses stemming from a banking crisis put at more than 17% of GDP. As an example, the cost to Indonesia of resolving the crisis of 1997 is estimated to have been 50% of its GDP.

The global crisis, coupled with the massive recurrent financial turbulence of the late 1990s, brought to the fore the public debate on the potential role of increased disclosure and transparency in strengthening market discipline in relation to the financial sector. In its report to the G7 finance ministers, the Financial Stability Forum (FSF), for example, calls for financial institutions to strengthen their risk disclosure and for supervisors to improve risk disclosure requirements under Pillar 3 of Basel II (FSF, 2008). Enhanced transparency via greater disclosure of accurate and timely information about constituent financial institutions is believed to facilitate an objective assessment of the financial health of banks by market participants, inducing market discipline that could reduce the likelihood of systemic turbulence in the banking sector.

BANKING TRANSPARENCY

The Bank for International Settlements (BIS) defines transparency as public disclosure of reliable and timely information that enables users to make an accurate assessment of a bank's financial condition and performance, business activities, risk profile, and risk management practices (Basel Committee on Banking Supervision (BCBS), 1998). Information that induces transparency is believed to have the characteristics of being comprehensive, timely, reliable, comparable, and material. Enhanced disclosure may improve bank performance and banking system stability for a number of reasons. First, disclosure and transparency prevent banks from taking excessive risks, as market discipline reduces the funding base of imprudent banks. Second, if crises happen, losses would be less costly in high-disclosure regimes than otherwise. Disclosure of bank problems could lead to quick recovery from crisis, thus reducing realized losses (see, for example, Rosengren, 1999). It would force banking consolidation, transfer of problem assets, and closure of insolvent banks, speeding the recovery of the banking sector.

In general, disclosure is regulated in both the corporate and banking sectors. Regulated disclosure is justified by the existence of market failure that results from either asymmetry of information or externalities. Bank runs and panics have been attributed to informational asymmetries between banks and depositors (Bryant, 1980; Bernanke and Gertler, 1990), where uninformed depositors precipitate a bank run due to fear of real or imagined bank failure. This can then be spread, again due to asymmetry, to other banks—even healthy ones—endangering stability. Mandated disclosure places bank depositors, other market participants, and insiders on an equal footing, thereby reducing runs and panics. At the same time, disclosure would also reduce the incentives for banks to undertake excessive risk through the mechanism of market discipline.

Information can be viewed as a public good subject to free-rider problems. In banking, due to the central role the banking system plays in the economy, the social benefits of bank-specific information outweigh the private benefits to the bank, generating externalities. Greater disclosure may, however, also engender negative informational externalities. Disclosure may lead to an interpretation of bank information as indicative of widespread problems in the banking sector, leading to bank runs and collapses in stock markets.

TRANSPARENCY AND BANKING SYSTEM STABILITY: THE ISSUES

The role of disclosure in relation to the stability of the banking system is thus not very clear-cut. Anecdotal historical evidence suggests that banking crises have been rampant even during regimes of increased disclosure. During the deregulated "national banking" era in the United States (1863–1913), banks practiced extensive disclosure, and yet the banking system was routinely paralyzed by periodic panics (Gorton, 1988). On the other hand, some argue that panics were a particularity of the US structure at that time, as they were less frequent in Europe, where banking had a longer tradition, perhaps with much less transparency. Furthermore, the disclosure regime was voluntary rather than mandatory, which may not have been an optimal arrangement to address the public-good nature of information production, and reporting by banks was selective.

Nonetheless, economic theory also provides conflicting predictions with regard to the benefits of greater transparency. The "disclosure-stability" view holds that greater disclosure and its consequent

"We were at the stage where in a very short period of time, one of the world's biggest banks would have to shut the door and switch off the electricity." Alistair Darling

transparency facilitate efficient allocation of resources by improving market discipline. Increased transparency permits greater market discipline, whereby strong banks are rewarded for their risk management and performance, while weak banks are penalized by higher costs of raising capital, thereby enabling early detection of weak banks before they drag the entire banking system into crisis. That is, market discipline provides incentives for banks to manage their risks prudently and to operate efficiently, thus reducing the severity and frequency of bank failures.

On the other hand, the "disclosure-fragility" view holds that disclosure may lead to interpretation of specific information about banks' financial conditions unjustifiably as indicators of widespread problems in the banking system, thereby leading to bank runs or stock market collapses (Calomiris and Mason, 1997; Kaufman, 1994). Disclosure of financial problems at a bank may lead to the bank's failure through a bank run. It may also lead to an overreaction in the financial markets, jeopardizing the ability of the bank to raise capital. This lack of investor confidence could spread to the entire banking system, causing systemic failure. In that case, rather than providing market discipline to improve resource allocation, more disclosure may lead to the collapse of the banking system, causing failure of both strong and weak banks alike.

These ambiguities surrounding the impacts of greater disclosure on bank stability are reflected in the public policy debate and the reluctance of countries to adopt pro-disclosure policies. Bank transparency is a centerpiece of international regulatory regimes for the banking industry. The Basel Committee's global risk-based capital regime, Basel II (which is now quickly being superseded by Basel III in the wake of a rewriting of the rules to reflect the financial crisis), relies on minimum capital requirements (Pillar 1) and supervisory review of banks' assessments of capital relative to risk (Pillar 2), complemented by market discipline through greater bank disclosure (Pillar 3) (see BCBS, 2003). By providing flexibility for banks when it comes to measuring their risk and capital adequacy, the Basel rules bring market discipline into focus as a supplementary tool in bank capital regulation. International organizations such as the World Bank and the International Monetary Fund also recommend that countries enhance the transparency of their banking sectors by improving disclosure. Yet despite these calls, disclosure and transparency are not always the hallmark of banking sector reform policies in the implementing countries. Japan, for example, adopted a policy of less disclosure recently while undergoing a protracted period of banking crisis.

TRANSPARENCY AND BANKING ROBUSTNESS: THE EVIDENCE

Despite the importance of transparency to banking system stability, empirical research in the area has not been extensive. One line of research investigates the efficacy of market discipline in banking. Bliss and Flannery (2002) identify two components for the effectiveness of market discipline: investors' ability to accurately assess the financial health of a bank based on disclosure (market monitoring); and investors' ability to actually effect changes in managerial behavior (influence). A lack of discipline proper (influence) in the presence of market monitoring is possible due to agency problems between bank management and market participants exasperated by poor regulation and supervision.

While there is an increasing consensus that disclosure-induced market discipline operates in banking in general, the evidence is stronger on market monitoring. Nier and Baumann (2006) find that information disclosure induces banks to hold larger capital buffers, indicating lower risk-taking and probability of default. They report, however, that government safety nets and lack of competition in the interbank markets reduce the effectiveness of these market mechanisms. In a study of Turkish banking, Penas and Tümer-Alkan (2010) find evidence of strong reactions of bank stock prices in response to disclosure of increased financial fragility, which indicates market monitoring, but warn that this may not have translated into increased bank safety and soundness. Others find evidence of market monitoring in bank debt markets (for example, DeYoung *et al.*, 2001, and Krishnan, Ritchken, and Thomson, 2006). Jordan, Peek, and Rosengren (2000) suggest that market participants find supervisory information useful in pricing bank securities, particularly for those banks that do not fully report their true conditions in prior disclosures. Thus, the effectiveness of market discipline may depend on the regulatory environment, and may need to complement supervisory actions and prudential regulation that also retain responsibilities in influencing bank behavior. This is in line with the spirit of the Basel framework, in which market discipline is positioned as a complement to strengthening supervisory actions under Pillar 2.

Alternatively, bank disclosure and transparency should be viewed as part and parcel of the regulatory regimes underlying the banking system. Few studies provide cross-country comparison of disclosure requirements as part of the regulatory regimes, or of the impact of variation in required transparency on banking system stability. Barth, Caprio, and Levine (2004), for example, explore the relation between bank regulation in general and banking system stability. In the context of the effectiveness of banking regulation, they examine the degree of private monitoring, not mandatory disclosure, on bank performance and fragility. They find that although private monitoring increases individual bank performance, it has little association with banking fragility. Tadesse (2006), in a cross-country setting, addresses the role of increased regulatory disclosure, controlling for other aspects of bank regulation, on banking system stability directly, and reports a robust positive relation between mandated disclosure requirements and national banking system stability. Defining banking transparency broadly to include disclosure requirements, the degree of information-gathering activity by investors. and the extent of information dissemination in the country, the study reports strong evidence that increased transparency is related to a lower likelihood of banking system fragility.

CONCLUSION

The recurrent banking crises of the 1990s that culminated in the global financial crisis of 2008–09 have heightened the debate on the role of increased transparency in promoting banking system stability. In the aftermath of the crises, and with the realization of the opaqueness and complexity of the underlying system, policymakers have increased their advocacy for more disclosure as an enhancer of the system's future robustness. In its report to the G7 finance ministers, the Financial Stability Forum calls for financial institutions to strengthen their risk disclosure and for supervisors to improve risk disclosure requirements under Pillar 3 of the Basel Accord. The role of increased disclosure in banking system stability is not, however, without controversy. As more information is associated with both positive and negative externalities, economic theory provides conflicting predictions about the benefits of greater disclosure for banking stability. Disclosure and transparency may affect prudent bank risk-taking through facilitation of market discipline. It also enables quick recovery from a crisis, if that happens. On the other hand, greater disclosure has the potential to undermine stability by

  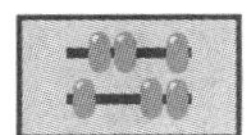   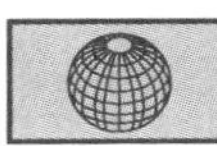   

propagating negative information spillovers through the banking system.

The bulk of the evidence suggests that increased banking disclosure promotes stability of the banking system. More transparent systems that are supported by regulatory regimes that mFandate greater disclosure both in quantity and quality of information tend to be more robust to the turbulence that periodically seizes the banking system. The evidence is mixed as to the exact mechanisms, however. Although disclosure enhances market discipline, particularly in facilitating monitoring, it is not clear whether this translates to changes in bank behavior. Nonetheless, the impact of increased transparency as part of the overall regulatory regime appears to be robustly positive for the system's stability.

Needless to say, banking transparency is not a panacea for instability in the banking system. As US banking history shows, systemic banking crises have been rampant even during regimes of greater disclosure in the nineteenth century. Furthermore, the efficacy of increased transparency in promoting banking stability critically depends on the regulatory environment, and it needs to be complemented by supervisory actions and prudential regulation that retain responsibility for influencing bank behavior. This is in line with the new international regulatory regime, the Basel Committee's risk-based capital regime (Basel II—now commonly referred to in its latest forms as Basel III), in which the role of disclosure is viewed as an enhancer of market discipline that complements bank capital regulation (Pillar 1) and supervisory review of bank assessment of capital relative to risk (Pillar 2). The Basel Accord aims to encourage market discipline by developing a set of disclosure requirements that let market participants assess bank risk positions and capital adequacy. The Accord's initiatives in requiring greater disclosure are consistent with the broader regulatory objectives of promoting banking system stability. In light of what we know in the aftermath of the global crises, the objectives of the Basel rules could be greatly enhanced by expanding the scope of bank disclosure to include bank activities in the areas of securitization, credit derivatives, and off-balance-sheet financings and vehicles.

MORE INFO

Books:

Beim, David O., and Charles W. Calomiris. *Emerging Financial Markets*. New York: McGraw-Hill/Irwin, 2001.

Rosengren, E. "Will greater disclosure and transparency prevent the next banking crisis?" In William C. Hunter, George G. Kaufman, and Thomas H. Krueger (eds). *The Asian Financial Crisis: Origins, Implications and Solutions*. Boston, MA: Kluwer Academic, 1999.

Articles:

Barth, James R., Gerard Caprio, Jr, and Ross Levine. "Bank regulation and supervision: What works best?" *Journal of Financial Intermediation* 13:2 (April 2004): 205–248. Online at: dx.doi.org/10.1016/j.jfi.2003.06.002

Bernanke, Ben, and Mark Gertler. "Financial fragility and economic performance." *Quarterly Journal of Economics* 105:1 (February 1990): 87–114. Online at: www.jstor.org/stable/2937820

Bliss, Robert R., and Mark J. Flannery. "Market discipline in the governance of U.S. bank holding companies: Monitoring vs. influencing." *Review of Finance* 6:3 (2002): 361–396. Online at: dx.doi.org/10.1023/A:1022021430852

Bryant, John. "A model of reserves, bank runs, and deposit insurance." *Journal of Banking and Finance* 4:4 (1980): 335–344. Online at: dx.doi.org/10.1016/0378-4266(80)90012-6

Calomiris, Charles W., and Joseph R. Mason. "Contagion and bank failures during the Great Depression: The June 1932 Chicago banking panic." *American Economic Review* 87:5 (December 1997): 863–883. Online at: www.jstor.org/stable/2951329

DeYoung, Robert, Mark J. Flannery, William W. Lang, and Sorin M. Sorescu. "The information content of bank exam ratings and subordinated debt prices." *Journal of Money, Credit and Banking* 33:4 (November 2001): 900–925.

Gorton, Gary. "Banking panics and business cycles." *Oxford Economic Papers* 40:4 (December 1988): 751–781. Online at: oep.oxfordjournals.org/content/40/4/751.full.pdf+html

Jordan, John S., Joe Peek, and Eric S. Rosengren. "The market reaction to the disclosure of supervisory actions: Implications for bank transparency." *Journal of Financial Intermediation* 9:3 (July 2000): 298–319. Online at: dx.doi.org/10.1006/jfin.2000.0292

Kaufman, George G. "Bank contagion: A review of the theory and evidence." *Journal of Financial Services Research* 8:2 (April 1994): 123–150. Online at: dx.doi.org/10.1007/BF01053812

Krishnan, C. N. V., P. H. Ritchken, and J. B. Thomson. "On credit-spread slopes and predicting bank risk." *Journal of Money, Credit and Banking* 38:6 (September 2006): 1545–1574.

Nier, Erlend, and Ursel Baumann. "Market discipline, disclosure and moral hazard in banking." *Journal of Financial Intermediation* 15:3 (July 2006): 332–361. Online at: dx.doi.org/10.1016/j.jfi.2006.03.001

Penas, María Fabiana, and Günseli Tümer-Alkan. "Bank disclosure and market assessment of financial fragility: Evidence from Turkish banks' equity prices." *Journal of Financial Services Research* 37:2–3 (June 2010): 159–178. Online at: dx.doi.org/10.1007/s10693-009-0076-5

Tadesse, Solomon. "The economic value of regulated disclosure: Evidence from the banking sector." *Journal of Accounting and Public Policy* 25:1 (January–February 2006): 32–70. Online at: dx.doi.org/10.1016/j.jaccpubpol.2005.11.002

Reports:

Basel Committee on Banking Supervision (BCBS). "Enhancing bank transparency: Public disclosure and supervisory information that promote safety and soundness in banking systems." Bank for International Settlements, September 1998. Online at: www.bis.org/publ/bcbs41.htm

BCBS. "The new Basel capital accord." Consultative document, Bank for International Settlements, April 2003. Online at: www.bis.org/bcbs/bcbscp3.htm

Financial Stability Forum (FSF). "Report of the Financial Stability Forum on enhancing market and institutional resilience." FSF, April 7, 2008. Online at: www.financialstabilityboard.org/publications/r_0804.pdf

Hoggarth, Glenn, and Victoria Saporta. "Costs of banking system instability: Some empirical evidence." In *Financial Stability Review*. Bank of England, June 2001. Online at: www.bankofengland.co.uk/publications/fsr/2001/fsr10.htm

Honohan, Patrick, and Daniela Klingebiel. "Controlling the fiscal costs of banking crises." Policy Research Working Paper 2441. World Bank, 2000. Online at: tinyurl.com/5t6bfp5

Schildbach, Jan. "Direct fiscal cost of the financial crisis: Probably much lower than feared." Deutsche Bank Research, May 14, 2010. Online at: tinyurl.com/6ezbxd2 [PDF].

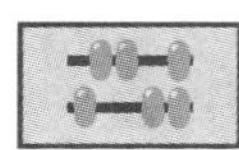

Banks and Small and Medium-Sized Enterprises: Recent Business Developments

by Sergio Schmukler, Augusto de la Torre, and María Soledad Martínez Pería

EXECUTIVE SUMMARY

- Banks consider SMEs to be core strategic businesses with a high profit potential.
- To serve SMEs, banks are now establishing separate dedicated units, standardized processes, and risk-management systems.
- The relationship manager's role is crucial for attracting new customers, and selling products to existing SME customers.
- Banks are increasingly serving SMEs through different transactional technologies. which emphasize cross-selling.
- Large, multiple-service banks are the main players in the SME market.

INTRODUCTION

A common perception is that small and medium-sized enterprises (SMEs) cannot access appropriate financing. This perception is often supported by academic and policy circles' "conventional wisdom" that banks are generally not interested in dealing with SMEs, mainly due to SMEs' perceived opaqueness[1] and higher informality.[2] As capital markets do not compensate for these deficiencies in the banking sector, the need to receive special assistance, such as government programs to increase lending, has been suggested.[3] In recent years, SME financing initiatives included government-subsidized lines of credit and public guarantee funds.[4]

In the academic literature, there is evidence that banks (especially small and niche players) engage with SMEs through relationship lending. Relationship lending can overcome opaqueness due to the primary reliance on "soft" information gathered by the loan officer through continuous, personalized, direct contacts with SMEs.[5] However, in a series of studies recently conducted by the World Bank, new stylized facts point to a gap between the conventional view and the way banks are actually interacting with SMEs.[6]

First, new evidence suggests that most banks, including large and foreign banks, indeed serve SMEs, finding this segment very profitable.[7] Second, different transactional technologies that facilitate arms-length lending (such as credit scoring and significantly standardized risk-rating tools and processes, as well as special products such as asset-based lending, factoring, fixed-asset lending, and leasing) are increasingly applied to SME financing (Berger and Udell, 2006). Third, banks try to serve SMEs in a holistic way through a wide range of products and services, with fee-based products rising in importance, placing cross-selling at the heart of their business strategy.

Under this new model of bank engagement with SMEs, larger, multiple-service banks exhibit, through the use of new technologies, business models, and risk-management systems, a comparative advantage in offering a wide range of products and services on a large scale, becoming leaders in this business segment.

NEW BUSINESS MODEL

Banks' high level of interest towards SMEs has, consequently, brought major changes to business models. First, as SMEs have become a strategic sector, banks are changing their organizational set-up to approach and serve this segment efficiently. Two main structures can be broadly categorized. The first combines the work of a commercial and credit risk team established at headquarters, with relationship managers distributed throughout the branches. The second consists of business centers or regional centers that operate as mediators between headquarters and branches, with a team leader or regional manager who controls and trains the relationship managers of the corresponding branches. In addition, banks are establishing separate, dedicated units with new strategies to cater adequately for the specific needs of SMEs. These dedicated business units approach SMEs in an integrated way, offering them a wide variety of products and services, including both deposits and loan products. In this set-up, relationship managers (RMs) are instrumental in attracting new customers, and selling products to existing ones. RMs look for new clients and prepare the information of each SME that is presented at the regional centers or at headquarters. They develop a relationship with the client, and, in some cases, RMs are allowed to express their opinion, make recommendations, or even present the case to the credit committee.

Second, the new model serves SMEs at all branches, and with standardized processes, facilitating the reduction of the high transaction costs that dealing with each SME entails. In most cases, branches and headquarters complement each other and undertake different functions. The initial stages of granting loans to SMEs are decentralized in most banks, while later stages, such as risk analysis or loan recovery, are usually centralized. In addition, banks exploit the synergies of working with different types of clients. Using information from existing firm databases, such as credit bureaus, relying on existing deposit clients, and attracting clients with bank credit are also common approaches that banks use to identify prospective SMEs.

Third, regarding credit-risk management, banks are reorganizing their systems, with a greater degree of sophistication among international banks and the leading, large domestic banks. Typically, risk management is a process that is organizationally separated from sales, and primarily done independently at headquarters. In most large banks, credit-risk management is not automated. Furthermore, in most cases, credit-risk management involves a credit-risk analyst, who is in charge of conducting both qualitative and quantitative risk assessments on the SME. The quality rating of SME management and SWOT (strengths, weaknesses, opportunities, and threats) analysis are the main components of qualitative assessments, while the financial analysis and projections of the SME firm and the SME owner are the main quantitative assessments. Qualitative assessments usually include an analysis of the SMEs' products, their demand and market structure, the quality of the owners and managers (including the degree of separation between management and owners), the degree of informality, the years of activity in the sector, and the vulnerability to foreign-exchange-rate fluctuations. Quantitative assessments entail an analysis of profitability, cash-flow generation capacity, solvency, quality of assets, structure of balance sheets, and global guarantees. Moreover, scoring models are still being developed, and primarily applied to small loans.

Monitoring of the credit-risk outlook is standardized at the majority of banks. Some monitoring mechanisms used frequently are preventive triggers and alerts automatically generated to signal the deterioration of the SMEs' payment capacity. However, credit-risk monitoring still depends on the diligence of the relationship manager or the credit-risk

"**What is robbing a bank compared with founding a bank?**" Bertolt Brecht

analyst. Some banks use a system that allows different individuals to provide input on each enterprise (such as auditors, back-office staff, sales personnel, and risk analysts).

The business and risk-management models described above can be better pursued by large universal banks, especially foreign ones, which can be more aggressive in reaching out to SME clients, and are better suited to conduct lending based on automated scoring models for small loans (as they have the know-how and models to do so) and template-type rating systems for larger loans (based on streamlined, standardized versions of corporate rating).

SME EVIDENCE

SMEs interact with banks using a variety of products, mostly checking and savings accounts, as well as term loans.[8] Furthermore, SMEs do not exclusively obtain financing via "relationship loans." SMEs access financing products that do not depend on the bank processing soft information on the firm.[9] An interesting finding is that the provision of loans through public programs or guarantees is low. The highest usage of public programs observed is in Chile, with 8% of SMEs reporting using them; other countries are reporting percentages of around 3% (World Bank, 2007a).

Nonetheless, while SMEs increasingly interact with banks to purchase a range of products and services, SMEs still appear unable to obtain access to crucial products such as loans secured by certain forms of collateral (for example, accounts receivable, inventories, equipment, cattle, and intangible assets), or long-term, fixed-interest rate loans in domestic currency. However, it is still unclear how much SMEs in developing countries would be able to rely on banks to obtain those products. As the US literature indicates (Carey *et al.*, 1993; and Berger and Udell, 1996), SMEs might have to rely on private placements and non-bank institutions. Bank financing for certain SMEs, such as start-ups (in particular, those in high-tech or research-based industries), is also likely to remain limited, as has proven to be the case in developed markets such as the United States.

CONCLUSION

In summary, the new evidence shows that the whole spectrum of private banks (large and small, domestic and foreign) has started to perceive SMEs as a strategic sector. Banks are aggressively expanding, or planning to expand, their operations in the SME segment. As a consequence, the SME market is becoming increasingly competitive, although far from saturated. The evidence suggests that banks are learning how to deal with SMEs, and, at the same time, making the investments to develop the structure to deal with a growing market in the years to come. As banks have recently discovered a key, untapped segment, it is likely that the models to work with SMEs will evolve significantly as the involvement with the SME segment increases.

However, there are issues that remain for future work. Although banks appear to have become more involved with SMEs, banks may not be able to measure comprehensibly their exposure to the segment in terms of income, costs, or risk. Furthermore, banks are not adequately tracking their loan-loss experiences. We might be witnessing a process in which banks are only now developing the structure to deal with SMEs, and, through their interactions with the segment, they will be able to reduce the involved costs and risks.

CASE STUDY

Government Interventions in Colombia[10]

While direct government funding programs have been described as relatively unsuccessful, policy innovations could still prove important for SME financing. For example, in Colombia, several policy measures targeted towards the micro and SME segments have been introduced since 2004. On the one hand, non-financial instruments have been implemented, including training programs to increase competitiveness, and promote technological development and exports. On the other hand, financial instruments have been introduced, including the further expansion of existing government programs, and promoting the development of alternative financing instruments (investment funds, factoring/supplier financing, fiduciary structures, etc).

Colombian government programs include long-term development funds and partial credit guarantees. Longer-term development funding is mainly provided in the form of rediscounting lines at below-market rates by the state-owned, second-tier credit institutions, Bancóldex,[11] Finagro,[12] and Findeter.[13] Partial credit guarantees—typically around 50% loan-loss coverage—are provided by FNG,[14] as well as by FAG[15] for the agricultural sector. The role of these institutions—particularly Bancóldex and FNG—has been cited as instrumental in promoting access to credit for SMEs.

The authorities have recently embarked on an initiative to improve financial access, including for SMEs. The low level of financial penetration in Colombia, both in response to pre-crisis levels and in comparison to regional peers, has prompted the authorities to take measures to expand access to credit and other financial services. Both demand- and supply-side barriers have been identified, and will be tackled via regulatory reforms and the *Banca de las Oportunidades* initiative. Recent policy measures include the introduction of correspondent banking arrangements, changes in the definition of the interest-rate ceiling, the passage of legislation on credit reporting, and the strengthening of creditor rights via a new bankruptcy law. Additional proposed reforms include changes to the civil code on enforcement procedures and to the financial system structure, as well as plans for the introduction of a special savings account for low-income households. In addition, the *Banca de las Oportunidades* initiative aims to design and propose measures to stimulate financial access, particularly for low-income households.

MORE INFO

Books:

Berger, Allen N., and Gregory F. Udell. "Universal banking and the future of small business lending." In Anthony Saunders and Ingo Walter (eds). *Financial System Design: The Case for Universal Banking*. Burr Ridge, IL: Irwin, 1996; 559–627.

de la Torre, Augusto, Maria Soledad Martínez Pería, Mercedes Politi, Sergio Schmukler, and Victoria Vanasco. "How do banks serve SMEs? Business and risk management models." In Benoît Leleux, Ximena Escobar de Nogales, and Albert Diversé (eds). *Small and Medium Enterprise Finance in Emerging and Frontier Markets*. IMD and IFC, 2008a.

DeYoung, Robert, and William C. Hunter. "Deregulation, the internet, and the competitive viability of large and community banks." In Benton E. Gup (ed). *The Future of Banking*. Westport, CT: Quorom Books, 2003; 173–202.

Organisation for Economic Co-operation and Development (OECD). *The SME Financing Gap: Volume I—Theory and Evidence*. Paris: OECD Publishing, 2006.

Articles:

Berger, Allen N., and Gregory F. Udell. "A more complete conceptual framework for SME finance." *Journal of Banking and Finance* 30:11 (November 2006): 2945–2966. Online at: dx.doi.org/10.1016/j.jbankfin.2006.05.008

Carey, Mark, Stephen Prowse, John Rea, and Gregory Udell. "The economics of the private placements: A new look." *Financial Markets, Institutions and Instruments* 2:3 (August 1993): 1–66.

Carter, David A., James E. McNulty, and James A. Verbrugge. "Do small banks have an advantage in lending? An examination of risk-adjusted yields on business loans at large

"Economics is as much a study in fantasy and aspiration as in hard numbers—maybe more so." Theodore Roszak

  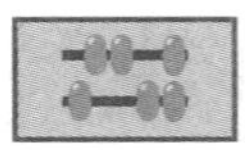      

and small banks." *Journal of Financial Services Research* 25:2–3 (April 2004): 233–252. Online at: dx.doi.org/10.1023/B:FINA.0000020663.21079.d2

DeYoung, Robert. "Mergers and the changing landscape of commercial banking (part II)." *Chicago Fed Letter* 150 (February 2000). Online at: tinyurl.com/33afmy7

DeYoung, Robert, William C. Hunter, and Gregory F. Udell. "The past, present, and probable future for community banks." *Journal of Financial Services Research* 25:2–3 (April 2004): 85–133. Online at: dx.doi.org/10.1023/B:FINA.0000020656.65653.79

Reports:

Beck, Thorsten, Asli Demirgüç-Kunt, and María Soledad Martínez Pería. "Bank financing for SMEs around the world. Drivers, obstacles, business models, and lending practices." Policy Research Working Paper 4785. World Bank, November 2008. Online at: dx.doi.org/10.1596/1813-9450-4785

de la Torre, Augusto, Juan Carlos Gozzi, and Sergio L. Schmukler. "Innovative experiences in access to finance: Market friendly roles for the visible hand?" Policy Research Working Paper 4326. World Bank, November 2007. Online at: dx.doi.org/10.1596/1813-9450-4326

de la Torre, Augusto, María Soledad Martínez Pería, and Sergio L. Schmukler. "Bank involvement with SMEs: Beyond relationship lending." Policy Research Working Paper 4649. World Bank, June 2008b. Online at: dx.doi.org/10.1596/1813-9450-4649

Stephanou, Constantinos, and Camila Rodriguez. "Bank financing to small and medium-sized enterprises (SMEs) in Colombia." Policy Research Working Paper 4481. World Bank, January 2008. Online at: dx.doi.org/10.1596/1813-9450-4481

World Bank. "Bank financing to small and medium enterprises: Survey results from Argentina and Chile." 2007a. Online at: tinyurl.com/26eu78q

World Bank. "Bank lending to small and medium enterprises: The Republic of Serbia." 2007b. Online at: tinyurl.com/22supx6

World Economic Forum (WEF). "World Economic Forum on Latin America: Securing a place in an uncertain economic landscape—Cancún, Mexico 15–16 April 2008—Report." Online at: tinyurl.com/2vlgmq7

NOTES

1 Opaqueness means that it is difficult to ascertain if firms have the capacity to pay (for example, viable projects) and/or the willingness to pay (due to moral hazard). For example, lack of audited financial statements prevents banks from engaging in what is known as financial-statement lending, by which the loan contract terms are set on the basis of the company's expected future cash flow and current financial condition, as reflected in audited statements (see Berger and Udell, 2006).

2 If firms do not reliably report their full financial activity on their financial statements, banks do not count, for example, with complete information on warranties for lending. See OECD (2006) for more on the factors that drive SMEs to operate in the informal economy, especially in emerging economies.

3 The need to provide support to SMEs through critical government investments was stated at the World Economic Forum on Latin America Summit in 2008. In addition, re-examination of tax regimes, regulatory reforms, and provision of capital through public-private partnerships were mentioned. See WEF (2008).

4 Chile's *Fondo de Garantía para Pequeños Empresarios* (FOGAPE) is a fund created to encourage bank lending to SMEs through partial credit guarantees. The Colombian *Fondo Nacional de Garantías* (National Guarantee Fund) provides similar partial credit guarantees. Structured finance transactions arranged by FIRA, a Mexican development financial institution focused on the agricultural sector, are another example of a government effort to provide financing to rural SMEs. Furthermore, the Mexican development bank, NAFIN, has initiated a reverse factoring program to provide working capital financing to SMEs through a process of online sale of receivables from large buyers. See de la Torre *et al.* (2007).

5 See DeYoung (2000), DeYoung and Hunter (2003), Carter *et al.* (2004), and DeYoung *et al.* (2004) for a discussion of the comparative advantages that small community banks have in lending to small firms through relationship lending.

6 See de la Torre *et al.* (2008a, 2008b) for a comprehensive analysis. Case studies are also available for Argentina, Chile, Colombia, and Serbia, describing the institutional and macroeconomic contexts, their banking industries and trends, and the data in detail. See World Bank (2007a and 2007b) and Stephanou and Rodriguez (2008).

7 Using data from 91 banks in 45 countries, Beck *et al.* (2008) found that all banks in the sample have SME customers, over 80% perceive the market to be big and prospects to be good, and more than 60% have a separate department managing their relations with SMEs. On average, the share of bank loans to small (medium) enterprises averages 11% (13%), compared to 32% in the case of large firms. The share of non-performing loans for small (medium) enterprises is 7.4% (5.7%), compared to 4% in the case of large firms.

8 Banks have developed a wide range of fee-based, non-lending products and financial services for SMEs. Loans are not all always the main product offered to SMEs. Moreover, loans are often offered as a way to cross-sell other lucrative fee-based products and services. See de la Torre *et al.* (2008a, 2008b).

9 de la Torre *et al.* (2008b) argue that banks are developing new technologies and business models to serve the SME segment, reducing their dependence on "relationship lending" and the gathering of "soft" information, which is costly and time-consuming.

10 This case study can be found in Stephanou and Rodriguez (2008).

11 Bancóldex's main aim is to provide low-interest lines of credit via first-tier credit institutions for exporters and SMEs.

12 Finagro's main aim is to provide low-interest financing for agriculture, livestock, forestry, and related rural projects.

13 Findeter was set up in order to lend (via first-tier banks) to subnational entities for infrastructure and other development projects.

14 FNG is a guarantee fund that "backs" credits to all economic sectors (except agriculture) with the primary objective of facilitating access to credit for micro enterprises and SMEs.

15 FAG is a guarantee fund that "backs" working capital and investment loans for the agricultural sector that are financed either with Finagro discounting, or with a credit institution's own funds.

"Unsustainable situations usually go on longer than most economists think possible. But they always end, and when they do, it's often painful." Paul R. Krugman

     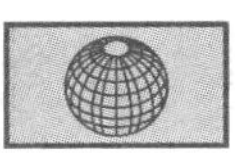   

Capital Adequacy Requirements for Islamic Financial Institutions: Key Issues

by M. Kabir Hassan and Ebid Smolo

EXECUTIVE SUMMARY

- The global financial crisis revealed many flaws in the conventional financial system, and many identified the Islamic financial system as a viable alternative.
- Both the Basel I and Basel II Accords were devised with an aim of improving the credibility and soundness of the financial system globally.
- The differences between conventional and Islamic banks are apparent on both the liabilities and the assets sides. Although Basel II was never intended for the Islamic financial industry, it can be taken as the foundation and improved upon with respect to the nature and characteristics of Islamic banking.
- Both the Accounting and Auditing Organization for Islamic Financial Institutions (AAOIFI) and the Islamic Financial Services Board (IFSB) tried to develop capital adequacy ratio (CAR) guidelines for Islamic banks, taking into account Basel II recommendations as their basis.
- While the AAOIFI's recommendations are biased toward the liabilities side of the balance sheet, the IFSB's recommendations consider the assets as well.
- There is a dire need to differentiate between financial instruments in order to come up with an appropriate CAR for Islamic banks.
- Proper measurement of CAR and the meeting of international standards will foster the credibility and soundness of the Islamic financial system worldwide. This will lead to the future growth of the industry.

INTRODUCTION

The Islamic financial industry (IFI) has grown tremendously in the last two to three decades. In short, Islamic finance refers to financial activities that are guided by the teachings of *shariah* (Islamic law), which strictly prohibits the payment and receipt of interest. Today, Islamic finance attracts both Muslim and non-Muslim market participants. The worldwide market for *shariah*-compliant Islamic financial products is estimated to be between US$800 billion and US$1 trillion. According to International Financial Services, London (IFSL), *shariah*-compliant assets had grown to US$951 billion by the end of 2008, which is a 25% increase from US$758 billion in 2007, and about 75% up from US$549 billion in 2006. The IFI is growing at 15–20% per annum—a rate that is much greater than the growth rate of the traditional (conventional) financial industry.

While the global financial crisis revealed serious weaknesses in the international financial system around the globe, the IFI showed signs of relative resilience to the shocks. It is even argued that if the principles of Islamic finance had been followed, the financial crisis would have been prevented. Nevertheless, some impact has been felt within the industry, revealing vulnerabilities that need to be addressed urgently in order to sustain the growth of the IFI.

Despite the fact that there is no consensus on the causes of the global financial crisis, various authors have highlighted several culprits. Some argue that the complexity and intensive use of structured financial products, derivatives, and other assets with uncertain fundamentals are to blame for the current financial crisis. Others say that easy monetary policy, financial supervision, and regulation, combined with excessive leveraging and credit growth, are fundamental factors that ignited the crisis.

All of the above brought the need for prudent regulation and supervision into the limelight. Lack of both supervision and regulation of the financial sector played an important role in the crisis. This led to the growth of unregulated exposures, which in turn led to excessive risk taking and weak liquidity risk management.

Being a niche industry, Islamic finance faces considerable challenges. For example, the lack of an efficient legal framework, standards and procedures, qualified manpower, effective government support, prudential regulations and supervision, internal controls, risk management, and external audits of Islamic banks are some of the challenges confronting the future growth of IFI.

Apart from the extraordinary growth and multiple challenges faced by the IFI, one daunting challenge is the compliance of Islamic banks with international standards and guidelines. Meeting international standards, such as the capital adequacy requirements set by the Basel II Accord, is not an easy task, as Islamic banks face different types of risks. For this reason, this article discusses the key issues in capital adequacy requirements for Islamic financial institutions.

CAPITAL ADEQUACY RATIO FOR ISLAMIC FINANCIAL INSTITUTIONS

An Overview of the Capital Adequacy Ratio

Capital adequacy is a measure of the adequacy of an entity's capital resources in relation to its current liabilities and also in relation to the risks associated with its assets. An appropriate level of capital adequacy ensures that the entity has sufficient capital to support its activities and that its net worth is sufficient to absorb adverse changes in the value of its assets without it becoming insolvent.

The initial Basel Capital Accord (known as Basel I) was concluded in 1988 with the aim of developing standardized risk-based capital requirements for banks across countries. Its aim was to encourage banks around the world to retain strong capital positions and to reduce the inequalities in this regard across countries. This fairly basic framework had many weaknesses, such as the limited use of risk-mitigating techniques—there was no distinction between high and low-quality borrowers and no distinction between long and short-term loans. Due to these and other shortcomings, the Basel I Accord was replaced by a new capital adequacy framework, Basel II, published in June 2004.

Basel II is still used as the basis for defining and maintaining capital for Islamic banks. Furthermore, it kept a minimum capital adequacy ratio (CAR) of 8% as an indication that a bank is adequately capitalized (although the methodology for calculating the CAR is completely different between the two accords). This new framework, apart from emphasizing credit risk measurement and mitigation techniques, introduces two additional types of risk: market risk and operational risk. In short, the Basel II Accord is based on three mutually reinforcing pillars that allow banks and supervisors to properly evaluate the various risks that banks face. These three pillars are as follows.

"**No bank should be allowed to become so big that it can blackmail governments.**" Angela Merkel

Pillar 1: minimum capital requirements, which seek to refine the present measurement framework.

Pillar 2: supervisory review of an institution's capital adequacy and internal assessment process.

Pillar 3: market discipline through effective disclosure to encourage safe and sound banking practices.

The above pillars, taken together, should lead to a greater level of safety and soundness of a financial system.

Capital Adequacy Requirements and Islamic Financial Institutions

Conventional and Islamic banks face different types of risks in their everyday operations. Nevertheless, the risks faced by Islamic banks are somewhat different from those faced by their conventional counterparts. When it comes to the conventional banks, Basel II provides a detailed framework for the calculation of risk-weighted assets, taking into account different types of risks related to their activities. However, this framework does not address the risks pertinent to the nature of Islamic banks' activities. Islamic banking goes beyond the traditional role of banks, which only provide financial intermediation. The role of an Islamic bank and the modes of financing available to it are manifold. Depending on the situation and the customer's demands, it may act as an investor, a trader, a financial adviser, or an agent. Each and every role it takes, as well as the mode of financing it chooses, has its own risk characteristics that need to be taken into account. The sharing of risk with its customers distinguishes Islamic banking from conventional banking.

Up until now, several proposals for a capital adequacy framework for Islamic banking have been devised. The first initiative came in 1999 from the Accounting and Auditing Organization for Islamic Financial Institutions (AAOIFI). In its "Statement on the purpose and calculation of the capital adequacy ratio for Islamic banks," the AAOIFI proposed a method based on Basel II standards, but with slight modification with regard to the liabilities side of Islamic banks' balance sheets. Nevertheless, this proposal was biased toward the liabilities side of Islamic banks, without paying due attention to the calculation of risk-weighted assets.

This limitation of the AAOIFI proposal led others to come up with other proposals, such as one that suggested treating Islamic banks as mutual funds whose obligation is to pay the residual amount after taking into account gains and losses. Another proposal, which went a step further, was issued by the Islamic Financial Services Board (IFSB). This proposal was detailed in the "Capital adequacy standard for institutions (other than insurance institutions) offering only Islamic financial services," issued in December 2005. It not only focuses on the liabilities side of Islamic banks—as was the case with the AAOIFI proposal—but also on the assets side, by assigning appropriate risk weight to each item on the asset side.

CHALLENGES IN IMPLEMENTATION OF CAR FOR ISLAMIC BANKS

As already mentioned, Islamic banking activities differ to a great extent from those of conventional banks. As such, Islamic banks generally have different risk profiles altogether. In fact, when we look into the balance sheets of Islamic banks, we find that on the liabilities side there is a mix of contracts with investment deposits that are quasi-equity in nature. These deposits are based on profit and loss sharing principles. There are demand deposits whose capital is guaranteed by Islamic banks. Based on the AAOIFI's standards, the risk of investment deposits should be shared equally by depositors and investors. Thus, the capital requirements for investment deposits are assigned a weight of only 50%. However, it is argued that this weight should be raised to 100% to determine capital adequacy, as per Basel II.

One suggestion to address this issue is to apply different capital standards for demand and investment deposits. Since demand deposits are guaranteed and need more protection than investment deposits, the capital requirements for these deposits should be higher that those for investment deposits. According to Hassan and Chowdhury (2010), the demand deposits should be kept in the banking book and the investment deposits in the trading book, or the investment deposits should be pooled into securities with different capital requirements. This would, ultimately, enhance the transparency and address several issues with regard to the nature and practice of Islamic banks.

Similarly, on the asset side of the balance sheet, Islamic banks have at their disposal a number of modes of financing that differ to a great extent to those available to conventional banks. The financing and investments of Islamic banks, therefore, can be structured based on profit and loss sharing, equity, sales, and/or lease-based contracts—with each one having different risk exposures.

Besides credit risk, market risk, and operational risk, which are covered by the Basel II framework, Islamic banks are faced with other risks such as price risk, rate of return risk, fiduciary risk, and displaced commercial risk. In order for us to determine a proper CAR for Islamic banks, we need to adequately measure these risks as well. In other words, CAR has to be adjusted to accommodate the different risk profiles of Islamic banks.

Under the Basel I accord, the individual risk weights depend on the category of the borrower—whether it is sovereign, bank, or corporate. On the other hand, when Basel II is applied, these weights are refined based on a rating provided by an external rating agency. Now the issue arises of when we are to apply these standards to Islamic banks, as they differ from conventional counterparts. Furthermore, the rating agencies themselves need to be familiar with principles of Islamic finance in order to make an accurate rating of Islamic financial institutions. Inaccurate ratings would lead to wrong impressions about Islamic banks in general.

One of the critical issues with regard to the risk management of Islamic banks is

MAKING IT HAPPEN

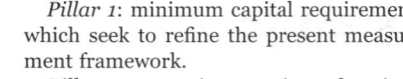

The current global financial system is in need of an overall restructuring. Islamic finance differs from conventional finance both in substance and form. Although the Basel II Accord improved a great deal on Basel I, it does not cater for the unique characteristics of the Islamic financial system. Not only that, but the global financial crisis revealed that Basel II also failed to devise the good market practice and discipline that was its initial objective. Therefore, many suggest that we need to come up with Basel III to enhance further the principles elaborated in Basel II.

Islamic finance, which showed great resilience to the global financial meltdown and is a viable alternative, should play a greater role in coming up with a new Basel Accord that will address the issues highlighted in this article. In this regard, the AAOIFI and the IFSB could assist the Bank for International Settlements in drafting the future accord. This will be beneficial not only to the Islamic financial industry, but also to the conventional one, as it can learn some lessons from Islamic finance.

"The problem with the bank managers was not that they were malevolent but that they were mediocre."
Christopher Caldwell

how to measure and manage the risk characteristics of profit-sharing investment accounts, which constitute one of the sources of funding of Islamic banks. Here, displaced commercial risk is introduced, i.e. the extent of credit and market risk is shifted to banks instead of being borne by the investment account holders.

Apart from the issues highlighted above, regional differences play another role in trying to set up a standard approach to CAR for Islamic banks. Not only do Islamic banks operate under different regulatory regimes, but they are also faced with different views on many Islamic financial products. In other words, there is a disagreement among *shariah* scholars on what is and what is not *shariah*-compliant. This makes the job of regulatory agencies harder when trying to evaluate the performance of Islamic banks and *shariah*-compliance risk.

CONCLUSION

The Islamic financial system differs to a great extent from the conventional one. As discussed, the deposits placed in Islamic banks are exposed to risks that are not faced by those in conventional banks. At the same time, the assets of Islamic banks are utilized in a different way from the assets of conventional banks. Depending on the role that an Islamic bank assumes, the risks faced by that bank will differ. As a result, due to these structural differences between Islamic and conventional banks, the risk weights set by Basel II need to be amended in order to take these differences into account.

The AAOIFI's recommendations address only the liabilities side of the balance sheet, and as such do not offer comprehensive guidelines for calculating CAR for Islamic banks. Nevertheless, these recommendations, combined with the IFSB's guidelines, are a very good starting point for Islamic banks.

The special nature of investment accounts and the different types of risk faced by Islamic banks make the implementation of Basel II a difficult task. However, amending these standards to accommodate the nature of Islamic financial systems would bring credibility and soundness to the Islamic finance industry and foster its future growth worldwide.

MORE INFO

Books:

Balthazar, Laurent. *From Basel 1 to Basel 3: The Integration of State of the Art Risk Modeling in Banking Regulation*. Basingstoke, UK: Palgrave Macmillan, 2006.

Schoon, N. "Basel II and capital adequacy." In Habiba Anwar and Roderick Millar (eds). *Islamic Finance: A Guide for International Business and Investment*. London: GMB Publishing, 2008; pp. 169–175.

Articles:

Archer, Simon, Rifaat Ahmed Abdel Karim, and Vasudevan Sundararajan. "Supervisory, regulatory, and capital adequacy implications of profit-sharing investment accounts in Islamic finance." *Journal of Islamic Accounting and Business Research* 1:1 (2010): 10–31. Online at: dx.doi.org/10.1108/17590811011033389

Hassan, M. Kabir, and M. A. Mannan Chowdhury. "Islamic banking regulations in light of Basel II." *American Journal of Islamic Social Sciences* 27:1 (2010): 74–101.

Hassan, M. Kabir, and Mehmet F. Dicle. "Basel II and regulatory framework for Islamic banks." *Journal of Islamic Economics and Finance* 1:1 (July–December 2005): 17–36.

Reports:

Accounting and Auditing Organization for Islamic Financial Institutions (AAOIFI). "Statement on the purpose and calculation of the capital adequacy ratio for Islamic banks." 1999.

Basel Committee on Banking Supervision. "International convergence of capital measurement and capital standards: A revised framework." 1988.

Basel Committee on Banking Supervision. "Amendment to the capital accord to incorporate market risks." 1996.

Chapra, M. Umer, and Tariqullah Khan. "Regulation and supervision of Islamic banks." Occasional paper no. 3. Islamic Research and Training Institute, Islamic Development Bank, 2000.

Islamic Financial Services Board. "Capital adequacy standard for institutions (other than insurance institutions) offering only Islamic financial services." Standard IFSB-2. December 2005. Online at: www.ifsb.org/standard/ifsb2.pdf

Islamic Financial Services Board. "Guidance note in connection with the capital adequacy standard: Recognition of ratings by external credit assessment institutions (ECAIs) on shari'ah-compliant financial instruments." Guidance note GN-1. March 2008. Online at: www.ifsb.org/standard/eng_IFSB_Guidance_Note_CAS.pdf

Islamic Financial Services Board. "Guiding principles of risk management for institutions (other than insurance institutions) offering only islamic financial services." Standard IFSB-1. December 2005. Online at: www.ifsb.org/standard/ifsb1.pdf

Sundararajan, V., and Luca Errico. "Islamic financial institutions and products in the global financial system: Key issues in risk management and challenges ahead." Working paper WP/02/192. International Monetary Fund, November 2002. Online at: www.imf.org/external/pubs/cat/longres.cfm?sk=16109.0

Websites:

Accounting and Auditing Organization for Islamic Financial Institutions (AAOIFI): www.aaoifi.com

Bank for International Settlements (BIS): www.bis.org

Islamic Financial Services Board (IFSB): www.ifsb.org

See Also:

★ Auditing Islamic Financial Institutions (p. 289)
★ Rules versus Discretion in Supervisory Interventions in Financial Institutions (p. 239)
✔ Regulatory and Capital Issues under *Shariah* Law. (p. 1050)
✔ Solvency II: Its Development and Aims (p. 1053)
✔ Understanding the Internal Capital Adequacy Assessment Process (ICAAP) (p. 1058)

"We have a good deal of comfort about the capital cushions at these firms at the moment." Christopher Cox

  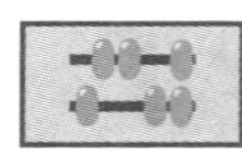      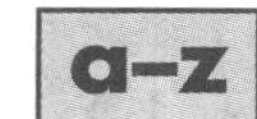

Viewpoint: Challenges in Global Energy and Their Potential Impact on the Cost of Energy

by Pau Morilla-Giner

INTRODUCTION

Pau Morilla-Giner oversees alternative investments at London and Capital and is also the manager of London and Capital's equities and commodities funds. He started his career at JP Morgan Asset Management in Madrid and New York. In 2001 he joined Omega Capital, a multibillion investment company, where he became head of traditional investments and senior hedge fund analyst. From 2005 he was investment manager and head of research at Pragma Wealth Management, a London-based alternative investment company. Pau obtained his BA summa cum laude in economics from Universitat Pompeu Fabra, Barcelona, in 1999, followed by a masters degree in finance from CEMFI (Bank of Spain) in 2001. He has been a visiting professor of finance at the RiskLab School of the Spanish Financial Futures and Options Exchange (MEFF).

Energy has always been both a fundamental issue for nations and an extremely volatile commodity. What are the implications for energy markets following the Japanese earthquake and tsunami and the Libyan war and unrest in the Persian Gulf?

It is already abundantly clear that the Japanese earthquake has created problems for the global nuclear industry. Going forward, industry regulators will pay much more attention at the planning stage to issues such as the location of nuclear plants and how many of them it is sensible to put in the same locality. On older nuclear plants, which is to say plants where the basic design is more than 20 years old, governments are going to have a much more difficult job granting end-of-life extensions. I cannot for a minute think that this will be the end for the nuclear industry, but it does mean that a highly regulated industry is going to become even more intensely regulated, which adds an additional layer of difficulty for potential investors in new nuclear plant.

In Germany, for example, the average age of nuclear plant is 23 years, and Germany has already called a halt to any license extensions while the issue is reconsidered. The United States too is reassessing the way it uses nuclear. The danger for business, in all of this, is that countries could hit periods of brownouts and blackouts if aging nuclear plant is retired on safety grounds before there is adequate alternative generating capacity.

China has given some mixed signals. The ruling State Council suspended all new approval for nuclear plants on March 16, 2011, pending an inspection of existing plants and the issuing of revised safety rules. However, according to an article in the *Washington Post* of April 2, Xie Zhenhua, vice chairman of the National Development and Reform Commission, told a meeting on climate change in Australia that China's nuclear goals remained unchanged. The article's author was deeply unimpressed by China's current safety planning and noted the absence of real or workable evacuation plans for people living within a mile or two of existing nuclear plant facilities.

However, when all is said and done, nuclear remains one of the most efficient ways of generating a large component of base-load electricity. The "easy" alternative, namely massive coal-fired power plants, is either environmentally unacceptable, or, if clean-burning technologies and carbon capture are introduced, becomes hugely expensive. Which brings us back to the impossibility over the next 30 years of moving away from nuclear.

There will be serious questions around design issues, however. We have not yet seen a great deal of technical information coming out of Japan, but there were clear concerns about the ability of the elderly reactor design to provide unambiguous temperature readings in the core as the crisis developed. This same design technology has been used a great deal in Europe, and if it shows real deficiencies, then that is going to pose some real problems.

By the same token, nuclear power's difficulties smooth the way for other technologies, and one of the fastest and safest replacement technologies available is natural gas. By fast, I do not mean overnight. It takes a lot of time to switch electricity generation capacity from one technology to another.

If we look at the situation in North Africa, it seems clear that the price of oil is destined to be somewhere between US$110 and US$115 or more for some considerable time. This is high enough to bring projects forward that were impossible at sub-US$85 oil. In Canada, the oil tar sand deposits contain huge reserves, but this is very heavy oil and is very expensive to refine. Unit production costs are around US$85 to US$90 a barrel, and the further north in Canada you go, the higher the cost of production. Northern Canada requires US$110 a barrel before companies can break even. Clearly, if we had stable pricing at US$125 a barrel, there would be a real incentive for projects to go forward here.

What this tells us is that the "peak oil" story is not the full picture. There does not have to be less oil available in the world for prices to climb. The determining factor is not just available supply, but how expensive, effectively, oil drilling becomes. Oil, in other words, is expensive not simply because of demand dynamics or inventory dynamics, but because of supply dynamics, which are all about the marginal costof extracting additional oil from sources that are nontraditional, more expensive to get at, and more expensive to produce and refine.

There is a huge amount of oil still in the ground, but the technology to get at it is fiercely expensive, so for this reason, once these technologies begin to be deployed in any scale, you will not see much retrenchment of oil prices below the breakeven costs for these nontraditional reserves. On the same theme, there is a huge amount of oil in offshore Brazil, but this is deep-water drilling and the cost of extraction is very high. You would not see breakeven with oil at US$110, which, again, points to oil moving higher in the near future.

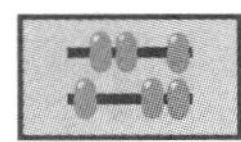

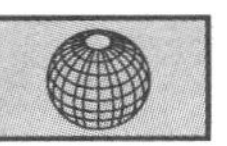

On top of all this, if you add instability in the Middle East into the equation, the problems are compounded. Bahrain is looking difficult, but without doubt the last barrier holding back the oil price from going beyond US$120 a barrel is Saudi Arabia. Today, Saudi Arabia can absorb any dislocation to world supplies coming from disruption to Libyan oil production. Libya produces less than 2% of world oil and replacing it absorbs about 12% of Saudi surplus capacity. So it is not a problem for them. But this means too that they are not in a position to absorb further shocks to production from the Middle East. If another major country in the Persian Gulf reduced supply, or if there were to be a problem which impacted the passage of oil tankers through the Suez Canal, that would be a huge event for global oil prices.

The key point to grasp here is that as we near the end of March 2011, we are seeing unusually high, cyclically high, inventories in oil stocks coinciding with the oil price at very high levels above US$100 a barrel. If there were no instability in the Middle East, at current inventory levelsoil would not be above US$85 a barrel.

The Bahrain situation is not that big an issue purely from the standpoint of the country's oil reserves. But it is a highly dangerous issue from another standpoint, and in fact is far more dangerous than either Libya or Egypt. The issue with Bahrain is not a population that is revolting against a leader. It is the fact that it is a minority Sunni ruling elite being confronted by a majority Shiah population that is being stirred up by Iran. The big fear in the market is that this will lead to a direct confrontation between Sunni Saudi Arabia, which is committed to defending the Sunni regime in Bahrain, and Shiah Iran. That would be catastrophic for the oil and gas sector. Bahrain itself is not the issue. It is the fact that it could create a domino effect, drawing more and more parties reluctantly into a conflict that no one country wants to precipitate.

Both oil and natural gas are hugely important fuels for industry. If we look at the relationship between the price of oil and the price of natural gas, that relationship varies dramatically from one region to the next. What are the implications for natural gas pricing in the medium term?

The place to start any analysis of the relationship between the price of oil and natural gas is to look at their energy equivalence. A barrel of crude oil is equivalent to about 5.8 thousand cubic feet of gas in energy terms. So the price of gas per 1,000 cubic feet should logically be about one-sixth the price of a barrel of oil. If you owned an oil-fired generation plant and a gas-fired plant, you would arbitrage any price differentialbetween the two fuel types. So when the spread widens between the logical price and the actual price, what is happening is that you are looking at real difficulties for particular markets in arbitraging away that energy/price equivalence. I make this point for illustrative purposes, but it is important to realize that in many instances there is no arbitrage possibility because the two fuels are not equivalent in their use. Natural gas is primarily used in heating and power generation, and oil is very important for transport. Of course, the further the price ratio between the two tips out of balance, the more pressure there is to explore direct equivalences, such as the use of compressed natural gas for transport, or as a feed to hydrogen fuel cell-driven vehicles.

Now let us look regionally. In Europe, Russian gas is hugely important and the Russians have pegged the price of gas very solidly to the price of oil. I see nothing to change this in the medium term. In Asia there is a shortage of natural gas for power generation, so there is a very big global business shipping liquefied natural gas (LNG) to Asia. Demand outstrips supply, so this maintains the price of gas at high levels.

Then you have the third region, North America. Here you have exactly the reverse set of conditions. The United States has seen a massive ramp-upin the production of shale gas, or the extraction of gas from hydrocarbon-bearing shale, of which it has huge deposits, running to more than 1 trillion cubic feet. Advanced extraction techniques in the United States based on hydrofracturing of the shale and a combination of deep vertical drilling and horizontal drilling out from the bottom of the well have considerably extended production capacity from shale.

It is important to realize that shale gas is a complete game-changer for the United States. It takes the country in one bound, as it were, from being a massive importer of oil and gas to being energy self-sufficient for potentially the whole of the next century—a time frame that is more than sufficient for other sources of energy generation, such as nuclear fission from deuterium and tritium (hydrogen isotopes found in seawater and common right across the planet) to become mainstream, commonplace technologies. Nuclear fission is probably three to four decades away from being a commercial reality and it has the potential, again, to be a complete game-changer, making energy self-sufficiency much easier for countries to acquire.

I take it that the United States is not unique in having shale gas reserves. What are the implications for other regions?

The reserves in the United States are on a different scale to those elsewhere. Russia has some shale gas reserves, and there are some in the Middle East, in Iran, and off the coast of Venezuela. But the key point is that shale gas in the United States and Canada can really change the balance of power among energy producers. Today we have OPEC as a cartel dictating oil pricing to some extent to the world. The United States could have an impact on this pricing. Another important factor is that natural gas is a very clean fuel. It will make it much easier for the United States to lower its carbon footprint and get closer to the Kyoto Protocol.

There are issues with the hydrofracturing, or hydrofracking, techniques used, with claims that the chemicals in the hydrofracking mix are environmentally damaging. Will that become a major stumbling block to the development of shale gas?

The background to the hydrofracking controversy was fully aired in a series of articles in the *New York Times* recently. There are two major issues. One concerns the additives mixed in with the water and sand that are pumped down the well. The additives are only a very small component, typically around 0.5%, but the charge is that they contain toxic elements which, if they escape to the surface, will pollute and poison the soil and the environment. This is very difficult to establish since the production companies take a very proprietary attitude to their formulae for the additives, claiming that the right mix conveys a competitive advantage, so they should not be forced to disclose it to their competitors. The other problem is that a percentage of the water that is pumped down the well to fracture the rock flows back out again. In the Marcellus Shale area, which is both the second largest shale gas reservoir in the world and is located in and near densely populated areas, these controversies will run and run and they look certain to impose some kind of additional regulatory cost on the industry. It seems unlikely though, that the protests will stop gas shale from being produced.

Another key point to grasp about US shale gas is that it confers a tremendous competitive advantage to US industry at a time when the US deficit is a serious cause for concern. US companies that are heavy energy users can save considerably on their production and manufacturing costsby switching from oil at US$120 or more a barrel to natural gas at US$4–$5 per 1,000

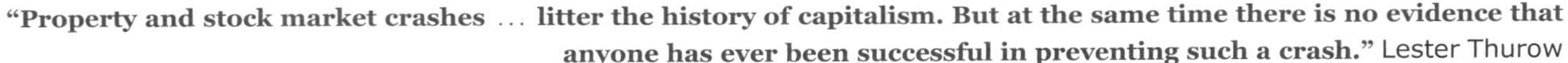

cubic feet instead of US$20, which would be the logical price if the gas price had not decoupled from oil. Although shale gas prices will go up over the next few years, gas futures pricing even going out 20 years is still very low.

However, there is an issue with distribution. The United States is poorly served as far as coast-to-coast and state-to-state distribution pipelines are concerned, and there are huge planning and permission obstacles in the way of private companies-wanting to build new pipelines. No town or city wants a pipeline running near it or through any scenic spot. So it is hard to retrofit a national gas distribution network on to the country. The other point is that baseload electricity generation in the United States is very solidly predicated on coal-fired power stations. Gas-fired generation plants are there in plenty, but they are used to meet peak demand, since they can be powered up very quickly. Switching from coal- to gas-fired stations designed to run 100% of the time is going to be a challenge. On the plus side, in a speech at the end of March 2011 President Obama announced a number of new energy policy goals, including making much more use of shale gas and using compressed natural gas to drive bus fleets and heavy transport fleets. That will be a very positive boost for natural gas. It will also help the United States to go some way toward meeting its carbon reduction obligations under the Kyoto Agreement.

MORE INFO

Books:

Cassidy, John. *How Markets Fail: The Logic of Economic Calamities*. New York: Farrar, Straus and Giroux, 2009.

Sorkin, Andrew Ross. *Too Big to Fail: The Inside Story of How Wall Street and Washington Fought to Save the Financial System—and Themselves*. New York: Viking/Penguin, 2009.

Ward, Nick, with Sinéad O'Brien. *Left for Dead: The 1979 Fastnet Race—One Man's Epic Story of Survival*. London, UK: A&C Black, 2010.

Article:

Richburg, K. B. "China expanding nuclear power but lacks emergency planning." *Washington Post* (April 2, 2011). Online at: tinyurl.com/3t8blf5

See Also:

★ Viewpoint: Energy Self-Sufficiency through Shale Gas Changes the Game for the United States (pp. 170–172)

Energy (pp. 1624–1626)

Oil and Gas (pp. 1638–1639)

"Unsustainable situations usually go on longer than most economists think possible. But they always end, and when they do, it's often painful." Paul R. Krugman

  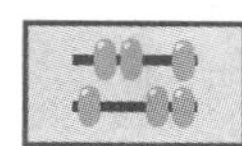      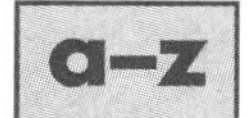

Viewpoint: The Challenges to Slow Growth in the Advanced Economies Just Keep Coming

by Stuart Thomson

INTRODUCTION

Stuart Thomson graduated from Edinburgh University in 1985 with an MA honors degree in economics. He began his career in 1985 as a junior economist with Britannia Asset Management and a year later joined Chase Manhattan Securities. In 1988 he took up the post of chief international economist at Nikko Europe Plc, and in 1997 moved to Credit Agricole Indosuez, where he worked as chief market strategist. In 1999 he joined Sutherlands Limited as a senior economist, and from there went on to be founding director and investor of RIA Limited. Thomson joined Charles Stanley Sutherlands as a senior economist in 2003, remaining there until he joined Ignis Asset Management in August 2006, where he is responsible for international bonds and currencies.

There is a lot of concern that developed economies are finding it extremely difficult to generate any real, sustained growth. Do you see a third round of quantitative easing as a possibility?

We have seen a marked slowdown in the economic data since the middle of 2010, with another distinct slowdown in May 2011. The 2010 slowdown prompted the president of the St Louis Federal Reserve, James Bullard, to warn that there was a very real danger that US consumers, corporates, and investors could all become accustomed to low nominal GDP growth and a quiescent central bank. That kind of attitude is already a few steps along the path to a pernicious deflationary era, and the Federal Reserve will do all it can to avoid the US economy falling into that trap.

As we saw with the second round of quantitative easing, QE2, which ended in June 2011, it is not necessary for the US economy to be seen to be sinking back into a double-dip recessionfor the Fed to resume quantitative easing. It remains an option if the US economy stalls. The Federal Open Market Committee (FMOC) will keep this under review. (The FMOC consists of 12 members, including the seven members of the board of governors of the Federal Reserve System, the New York Fed president, and a rotating quorum of four of the remaining 11 Fed presidents. At its eight annual meetingsthe FMOC reviews economic and financial conditions and determines monetary policy, including whether or not to proceed with more quantitative easing.)

Quantitative easing, or QE, is designed to produce effective negative interest rates, which is a disincentive to hold dollars. It has the side effect of exporting deflation to those high-saving economies which do not link their currencies to the dollar. For high-saving, mercantilist economies that do link to the dollar, the inevitable result of the United States rolling the printing presses is inflation.

One country with a great deal of experience of deflation in the modern era is Japan. It is a major exporter, and the yen strengthening even as Japan's interest rates hit zero in real terms is crippling the country's economy. What is your view of Japan's prospects?

Japan is confronted by persistent and stubborn deflation and when, in 2010, we saw Japan's overnight ratecut by the Bank of Japan from the ultra low rate of 0.1% to effectively zero, this was a signal that the Bank of Japan itself intended to engage in QE, which it initiated by mid-October 2010. This should have the spin-off benefit of weakening the yen, the current strength of which is undoubtedly crippling Japanese export trade.

Japanese nominal GDP has averaged –0.2% since 1995. In the first quarterof 2010, however, a recovery in Japan's export markets enabled the country to become, briefly, the world's fastest growing economy. However, currency appreciation has undermined all the growth the economy achieved in that first quarter, and by the end of the second quarter of 2010 Japan had become one of the world's slowest growing economies.

To make matters worse from the Japanese perspective, China has been diversifying its foreign reservesby buying yen in substantial quantities, in the shape of Japanese government bonds. As an appreciating currency, the yen provides China with a welcome diversification of a small part of its reserves (3% according to Chinese officials) away from depreciating US Treasury bills, which could be further impacted by the next round of QE from the United States. Japan is countering China's impact on the yen in two ways—by calling for talks with China, and by intervening directly in the markets to weaken the yen by buying dollars aggressively.

This is in the teeth of explicit warnings by the US Treasury back in autumn 2008. At that time, in its semiannual currency report, the US Treasury called on Japan not to intervene directly in the currency markets. The crisis at that point was a surge in the yen in the wake of the collapse of Lehman Brothers. The United States was worried, and still is, that intervention in the currency markets by a leading global economylike Japan sends the worst possible signal to the developing nations, which the United States is trying to move away from mercantilist currency intervention policies—i.e. deflating their currencies to make their goods more acceptable to foreign buyers. For a while Japan heeded the United States' warning, but its domestic concerns have now apparently overridden its anxiety not to upset the United States. This also represents a real change of heart by the Japanese Ministry of Finance, which had viewed currency intervention as the kind of thing that developing nations indulged in to assist their weak economies. It was thought of as beneath the dignity of a mature, developed economy. However, the Japanese coalition government's position is fragile, and it has to respond to pressure to improve the prospects of the country's exporters by acting against what many see as the "unfair" manipulation of Japan's currency by China.

"The recession debate is over. It's not gonna happen ... The Bush boom is alive and well. It's finishing up its sixth splendid year with many more years to come." Lawrence Kudlow

In this spat between Japan and China, are we seeing yet another instance of the protectionist mood that seems to be sweeping across the globe as a reaction to the global recession of 2008–09?

Protectionism has been admirably restrained through the credit crunch, but there is no doubt that it has the potential to break out in many different directions. It is merely resting, not gone. There is considerable pressure from Western economies for emerging marketeconomies to buy more of their goods. Not only would this help to rebalance global trade flows, it would give Western economies, which are struggling to achieve even very low growth rates, access to demand from countries that are growing in the high single figures.

However, this will be very difficult to achieve. Chinese consumer spendinghas fallen as a percentage of GDP to a record low of 36% from a more respectable 46% in 2000. The United States' second round of full QE forced China to hike rates continuously as it tried, and continues to try, to dampen down rampant domestic inflation without allowing its currency to appreciate against the dollar. Neither option is particularly palatable to the Chinese authorities, and geopolitical tensions are on the rise as a result.

In the United Kingdom the coalition government is committed to cutting the country's deficit, which means steep public-sector cuts despite warnings, not least from the United States, that austerity now could push the country into a double-dip recession. How do you see the UK austerity measures impacting the economy?

The UK economy performed exceptionally well during the second quarterof 2010. This was due in no small part to the economy benefiting from an unprecedented monetary, fiscal, and foreign exchange stimulus. This strength continued into July, helped by strong demand through the Football World Cup. However, leading consumer, construction, housing, and business sentiment indicators turned weaker in the wake of the election, and there is no doubt that the first hundred days of the coalition government passed in a blaze of austerity.

We are now seeing a marked weakness in the economy that will get worse as cutbacks in the public sectorstart to bite. By mid-2011 the coalition government was already being faced with waves of strikes and protests from the public sector, which will further depress consumer confidence. I do not expect these strikes to deter the government from pursuing its austerity program, but it seems inevitable that they will weaken sterling still further, and taking money out of the public sector will dampen economic activity.

We have already seen warnings from the European Central Bank (ECB) president Jean-Claude Trichet that ECB rate rises are possible. Bundesbank members on the ECB governing council are very much in favor of tightening monetary policy. We saw German GDP growth for the full year 2010 come in at 3%, well above earlier estimates of 1.5%, and in the light of that withdrawing liquidity from the Eurozone as early as possible will be attractive to the Bundesbank. However, we have to remember that it was the ECB decision, made at the behest of the Bundesbank, to signal the withdrawal of liquidity at the end of 2009 that triggered the sovereign debtcrisis in Greece.

In light of this it seems clear that the situation of peripheral Europe is set to worsen substantially. Growth is already contracting in those countries. The Irish position is particularly desperate, with deflation being imposed by fiscal austerity. If we look to the sovereign bondmarket, it is clear that the next stage of peripheral bond spread widening is already upon us.

One of the problems with QE, apart from the potential long-term and largely unpredictable impact on inflation, is that the new regulatory demands in banking and insurance will act to deter banks from selling their triple AAA holdings. The impact of QE2, therefore, as we saw, was to drive down yields and returns, which in turn prompted central banksto run the printing presses even harder. The laws of economics dictate quite straightforwardly that if you pump enough money at an economy, it will grow.

On the positive side for the UK government, it has already made clear its intention for debt issuance in 2011 to be less than Germany's. This would be a remarkable achievement if it were able to hit this target, though there is considerable execution risk here. One area where the United Kingdom gains is that it turns over its debt on a 14-year cycle. Most other countries, including the United States, are on a far shorter debt cycle of six to seven years. This gives the United Kingdom a great deal of protection against having to go to the market to refresh debt when conditions are highly unfavorable.

What is the impact of QE on the debt markets?

Clearly, if you are a creditor to a particular sovereign state, you do not want to see its currency depreciate. About 35% of UK debt is held by foreign investors, and through the Bank of England's first phase of QE we saw a sharp drop in the three-month rolling demand. It fell to about £11 billion, and after the election of the coalition government, with its commitment to austerity, demand rose to £20 billion. The government's commitment to cutting the deficit improved investor confidence in the United Kingdom's ability to maintain its triple AAA sovereign rating. This in turn made investors more willing to hold UK bonds.

In summary, it is quite clear that deflationary forces are still dominant in the developed economies, despite the optical illusion created by such factors as the United Kingdom's rather "sticky" 3.1% rise in inflation over the last year. This has been driven by several factors that are unique to the UK context, including the VAT increase, the lagged impact of the weakness of sterling, which pushes up import prices, and the general effect of higher global commodity prices. Much more important for the deflation/inflation debate is the slowdown in global trade, which remains quite palpable in mid-2011. The stimulus-induced bounce in global trade has now largely faded away, and the risk is much more that domestic fiscal tightening at a time when unemployment is high and there is overcapacity in the market will create deflationary pressures and a significant risk of a double-dip recessionin the year ahead.

QE2 was a rising tide that lifted all boats in the investment universe as far as asset classperformance is concerned, until a fresh and rather intense bout of European sovereign debtworries troubled the markets in May 2011. Further out, at around 2015, the QE that we have already seen may well generate an inflationary risk. The logic here is that, since debt deflation is so depressing to the economy, it is likely that central bankswill err on the side of too much QE rather than too little—and too much QE can drive inflation quite sharply. We are definitely in for an interesting few years ahead.

  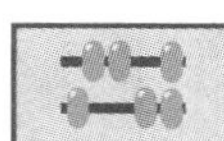      

Climate Change and Insurance by Stephen Haddrill

EXECUTIVE SUMMARY

- A discussion of the likely impact of climate change
- The scenario 50 years on
- Present responses to extreme weather
- Insurance sector agreements with government
- The limits to insurance

INTRODUCTION

Starting from the fact that climate change is a reality that is happening now, and that we can see its impact across the world, what role does the insurance sector have in covering this? There is no doubt that climate change is of enormous importance to the insurance industry. The costs of flooding, wind damage, and abnormal heat are all huge, and climate change threatens to increase all those costs.

Work done so far on climate change shows the threat has arrived. The carbon produced in the last century is already causing extreme weather. The scientific consensus is that flooding has increased in severity due to sea level rises and more rain. Wind-storms are fiercer. Heat waves are more intense. Again, the scientific consensus is that reducing carbon emissions will not reverse this trend for decades. More extreme views, such as that by the founder of Gaia theory, James Lovelock, argue that we have probably already gone past the point of no return, but this pessimistic approach is not mainstream thinking. What is clear is that both the insurance sector and the world at large have to adapt and look to protect themselves.

Failure to adapt will generate extreme economic costs. Even relatively low percentage increases in weather phenomena, such as the footprint of a flood area, lead to massively increased costs. For example, a 5% increase in the footprint of a flood can lead to a 75% increase in the consequent bill for damages.

EXTREME WEATHER CONDITIONS

Over the next 50 years, we expect to see:

- Windstorm losses increase by two-thirds to US$27bn per year worldwide.
- Additional flooding costs of €100–120 billion a year in Europe.
- A 15-fold increase in UK flood costs, to £22 billion.
- Subsidence costs increasing by 50% in average clay-soil areas.

At the same time, heat stress on people, animals, machinery, and property will also increase. It is quite possible that by the 2040s, the summer of 2003 will be regarded as normal. If this becomes reality, then a quarter of working hours will be hotter than "comfort levels" in London offices, increasing the demand for air conditioning, and creating heat islands.

Last year's floods in the United Kingdom present a good example of our concerns. While it is difficult to point to one isolated storm or flood and say conclusively, "there we have proof of climate change", the floods of 2007 nevertheless give us a picture of the effects we are facing. Torrential rain did not just lead to rivers bursting their banks. Crucially, the drains failed also, as flash flooding overwhelmed them. In all, some 180,000 people made claims, or four times the annual average of flood claimants. Another way of putting this is that the industry experienced four years' worth of claims in just two months.

At the same time, the floods put a significant percentage of the United Kingdom's infrastructure at great risk. Reservoir banks threatened to fail. The electricity supply to 600,000 homes was almost lost, and the water supply to those homes was in fact lost for a while—this despite the fact that the insurance industry has issued repeated warnings to government about the vulnerability of critical infrastructure.

THE RESPONSE OF INSURANCE COMPANIES

To date, the insurance industry has coped with extreme weather events extremely well. In the 2007 floods in the United Kingdom, most insurers had loss adjusters on the ground within 24 hours, often calling in staff from overseas. People were put in temporary housing within days, and almost all are now back in their homes. Two hundred families were still displaced at the end of September, but virtually all because they required special building work.

There are, however, some lessons to learn. People talk to each other in a crisis. If a loss adjuster representing one insurer gives information to one household, while another gives different information to a neighbor, people get confused. The sector therefore came together to standardize the process of communicating with citizens in an afflicted area after an extreme weather event.

People in hard-hit areas worry greatly whether they will be able to obtain insurance again. The industry has been tremendously resourceful in continuing to provide insurance cover in "at-risk" areas, and it has done so at very reasonable premium prices. However, there is a need for governments around the world to be alert to the dangers of allowing building on flood plains and low-lying coastal areas in an era of rising sea levels.

Insurance covers risk. It is not there to cover loss that is absolutely certain to be incurred—you cannot insure your house once it is on fire! It is a fact that, in both America and the United Kingdom, and in many European countries, some of the most valuable properties, infrastructure assets, and concentrations of people live in areas that are going to be more at risk from tidal surges, flooding, and rising sea levels in the years and decades ahead.

The 2007 floods were the result of extreme rainfall. Water also threatens us from the seas, particularly as sea levels are expected to increase by at least a meter this century. If nothing is done, the risk of the 1953 flood being repeated will increase from 1 in 1000 in 2000, to 1 in 100 by 2100 (figures from the UK Environmental Agency).

The financial cost of a major storm on the UK east coast, for example, could reach £15–20 billion, as quoted in an Association of British Insurers report, "Coastal Flood Risk—Thinking for Tomorrow, Acting Today," published in November 2006. This is not a fantastical, or a remote possibility. In 2008, the United Kingdom was just hours away from a combination of a tidal surge, strong east winds, and high water levels in the Thames causing flooding in London, according to the London Meteorological Office. The ABI report used insurance catastrophe models to examine the effects of a rise in sea levels on flood risk.

Handling such an event would be extremely difficult. A high proportion of our emergency facilities are on the coastal flood plain. It is worth bearing in mind that the number of people over the age of 75 (the least-mobile members of our community) living on the UK coast is expected to double in the next 30 years, according to ABI research.

Taking all this together, the adaptation of homes, business, and the infrastructure economy is vital for every country. Adaptation requires concerted action at an international level, and at the national level, as well as by the global insurance

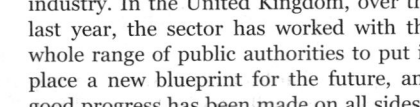

industry. In the United Kingdom, over the last year, the sector has worked with the whole range of public authorities to put in place a new blueprint for the future, and good progress has been made on all sides.

INTERNATIONAL AND BRITISH STRATEGIES

First, the international dimension: There is already international action on carbon reduction. That international cooperation needs to be repeated for adaptation. Globally agreed principles need to feed into EU strategic plans. Storms do not respect borders, nor do rivers in flood. Across the EU, we need a better understanding of risk, and we need agreement on the standard of protection required across Europe.

Such international strategies must, however, promote and encourage national and local action. Successful adaptation requires a framework that allows regional and local authorities to develop their individual action plans, responding to the specific threats affecting each locality.

The UK government has proposed new legislation to start creating this framework. We need to see two fundamental measures. First, there needs to be a commitment to a properly coordinated flood-management system in the United Kingdom, with clarity about who will be responsible for drainage. The government is talking here about a new strategic role for the Environment Agency, but the details will be critical.

Secondly, the United Kingdom and Europe need a commitment to a new, long-term, flood-management strategy, with a commitment to invest consistently over the long term. The industry needs to ensure that flood insurance remains as affordable and widely available as possible, so that consumers and small businesses can continue to be able to protect themselves from the financial cost of flooding.

Since 2000, this has been achieved in the United Kingdom through the "Statement of Principles on Flood Insurance," which commit insurers to provide flood insurance to homes that are already covered, provided the risk is not worse than 1:75, or if flood protection works are planned within five years. Under this arrangement, half a million homes at high risk of flooding have been protected. In fact, the sector is probably protecting an additional 400,000 homes that are not strictly covered by the agreement.

The statement has been a good deal for consumers in many respects, but it has not been entirely good for the market. The cost has fallen on existing insurers alone. New entrants to the market have no obligation to existing customers, and so are not affected. Specialist insurance for higher-risk customers has not developed, and because insurers have insured more people than they need to, inappropriate new property developments have secured insurance cover.

In its latest agreement with the UK government, the UK insurance industry has addressed these points. The new agreement sets out a series of government actions that are necessary to enable flood insurance to continue to be as widely available as possible in the future.

These include:

- Agreement by government to move away from a short-term, three-year approach to flood-risk management. Instead, the Environment Agency will publish next year a paper setting out a range of options for protecting the country over the next 25 years. This will facilitate a full debate about the best way forward. The government will then publish its response by the next spending review, setting out long-term aims and the associated funding.
- Risk data will be improved by the Environment Agency, and these will be made more readily available.
- Planning policy will be evaluated by early 2009, to ensure the new planning rules are delivering at both strategic and practical levels (it must be said that the early evidence is positive).
- Properties built from 2009 onwards are now explicitly excluded from the statement so that the onus clearly lies on developers to ensure their development is insurable.

Another important feature of this agreement is that it sets an end-date for the insurer commitments of June 30, 2013, after which what is, after all, a market distortion, will be removed. This instance shows how national governments can cooperate with the insurance industry to provide insurance, even under difficult circumstances.

However, the ABI and the industry are very keen to ensure that it is made obvious whether a new development is a good flood risk or not. We are working with the Royal Institute of Chartered Surveyors to develop a kitemark that can be applied to new homes. This will assure prospective owners whether their new home will be insurable or not. In this way, the market can be made to work for adaptation. Second, both the ABI and the industry will do more to promote better understanding of climate risk among the general population.

To this end, we will be publishing research on the economic costs of climate impacts. We will disseminate new climate data within the industry by hosting discussions among insurers and scientists about new climate science scenarios. We will also be working with government to educate the general public, by offering advice and tools for individuals to understand climate risks.

Home owners can also be encouraged to make their homes more resilient to flooding, and the ABI will produce new guidance for property developers about making new developments more climate-resilient. It will also research the cost of resilient repairs, and will continue to work with the industry and government on options for increasing the take-up of cost-effective resilience measures.

ClimateWise

Finally, the ABI is a strong supporter of the ClimateWise initiative. ClimateWise is a set of principles that commits insurers and the wider insurance industry to build climate change into their business operations. ClimateWise was developed by the UK industry, with the support of the Prince of Wales, to strengthen efforts to tackle climate change, including carrying out further research into climate change, and to promote the findings.

The insurance industry reaches into millions of homes and businesses, and has a key role to play in enabling customers to prepare for changing weather, as well as encouraging them to reduce their own emissions.

CONCLUSION

The UK sector has had warning of the scale of the threat. The floods of 2007 showed that new effort is needed. It did not tell us exactly what to do, nor where or how to do it. Since then the industry, and those outside the industry, have come up with many good ideas for a safer future. These ideas now need to be acted on.

MORE INFO

Reports:

Association of British Insurers. "Climate adaption—Guidance on insurance issues for new developments." Online at: tinyurl.com/3mtrt45

Haddrill, Stephen. "Preparing the UK for climate change." Speech, January 27, 2009. Online at: tinyurl.com/3gfa5u8 [PDF].

Viewpoint: The Corporate Bond Markets in 2012 and Beyond by Shahzada Omar Saeed

INTRODUCTION

Shahzada Omar Saeed has an MBA in financial management and is head of the high-yield team at Swisscanto Asset Management, where he is responsible for overseeing investments of US$1 billion. He is lead manager for the Swisscanto (CH) Institutional Bond Fund—Global High Yield I and the Swisscanto (LU) Bond Invest Short Duration Global High Yield fund. Under his leadership, Swisscanto has experienced exponential growth of greater than 300%, along with achieving top-quartile ranking for its flagship institutional bond fund. Before Swisscanto, Saeed worked for Western Asset in London, where he was responsible for co-managing some €750 million of high-yield and leveraged-loan portfolios. Prior to that he held a similar position with F&C Asset Management.

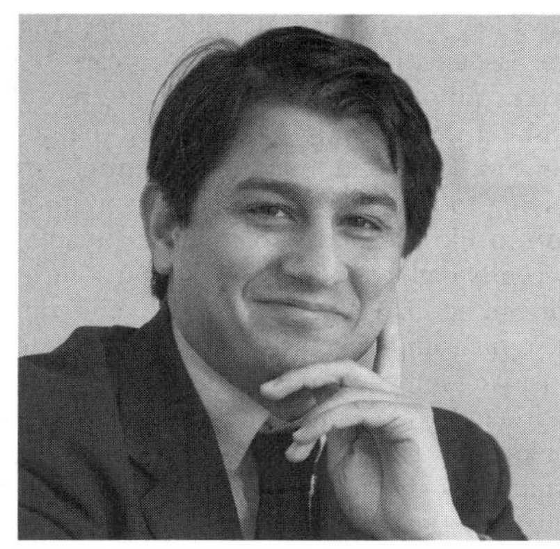

The collateralized loan obligations (CLO) market was a major source of funding in the European capital markets for companies looking to raise debt. What is likely to happen to this market through 2012?

There is no doubt that demand for CLOs is diminishing. Until 2008 they made up about two-thirds of the European leveraged-loan market. However, after the crash of 2008 and the collapse of collateralized debt obligations (CDO) or structured debt in general, demand for CLOs has virtually disappeared. A CLO is a bundle, or pool, of corporate loans made by a bank or a group of banks. Like CDOs, which were backed by mortgage securities and which are now regarded as a major toxic element in the crash, a CLO is a structured investment vehicle. It is divided into tranches of increasing risk and increasing reward. The most senior tranche of a CLO pays a modest rate on the debt, and investors holding the senior tranche are paid off first on the maturity of the CLO. The investors holding the next tranche are paid a higher premium and are paid off after the senior investors, assuming that there is sufficient money remaining in the CLO. The same for the next tranche, and so on.

Investors holding the tranche with the highest premium are the last to be paid, so their money is the most at risk. However, a significant proportion of leveraged loans within the CLO would have to default and pay very little in the pound, euro, or dollar before this class of investor took serious capital losses. For this reason, the higher-risk layers of CLOs were seen as attractive by institutional investors across Europe until the 2008 crash. However, CLOs are, by their nature, structured investment vehicles, and these vehicles are to a very large extent no longer viewed as feasible options by European investors.

Another point is that CLOs are inherently leveraged vehicles. Prior to 2008 leverage multiples were very aggressive (10–15 times) and the cost of financing this leverage was very low (Libor + 20 bps). This low cost was because the bulk of the CLO tranches were rated AA and above. With diminished demand for structured debt, leverage multiples drastically reduced to three to six times and cost of financing moved significantly higher compared to the past (Libor + 300 bps). As a result, the only survival option for the remaining vehicles is if spreads for leveraged loans remain significantly wider on a sustainable basis. Hence, European CLO markets are likely to shrink by some 75% as a consequence.

The troubles of the CLO markets play very well for the high-yield corporate bond market in Europe, which is now growing as companies look to renew debt that used to be serviced by CLOs. However, the general lack of appetite for CLOs in Europe, which makes them nearly impossible to roll over as new CLOs, creates a further problem. The maturity profile of most of the CLOs that are still running has a maturity date that is around the same time as the loans themselves become due. The banks cannot sell the CLOs on since there is very little duration left, so they are going to have to find the money to pay out to the investors on the maturity of the CLO and then hope that corporate borrowers can meet their debt at maturity or the CLO investors could lose significantly. With the diminished appetite in the market, it is clear that when current CLOs reach their maturity that will effectively be the end of the CLO market in Europe for the foreseeable future.

What does the diminished appetite of the CLO market mean for investors in high-yield corporate bonds?

Inevitably, the proportion of leveraged loans to high-yield corporate bonds is increasingly switching in favor of bonds. Given that a significant maturity wall of leveraged loans is due over the next two years, in the face of this demand for credit high-yield bond investors have been able to secure better terms for themselves than has historically been possible.

To put some color on this, since the Lehman Brothers crisis in September 2008, 50% of all new debt issuance has been as secured high-yield bonds, which means that the bond is backed by assets of one sort of another, be they security against property, cash flows, or whatever. The historic position was that secured high-yield bonds were a rarity. Intuitively, bond investors securing better terms should have a lower premium, but, to the contrary, bond coupons have actually moved slightly higher. Before the move from CLO to bonds began, the coupon averaged 7.25%. Today the average coupon is 7.4–7.5%, so not only do the bonds come with securities that guarantee that a high percentage of the capital will be recovered in the event of a default, but the investor gets a good coupon rate as well. What this means is that if you make four years of coupons and you get a 70% recovery on a default in the fifth year, you have, from an economic standpoint, lost nothing on that particular bond and your portfolio of bond holdings is not damaged. The 70% return on capital in a default is the history of the index for defaults, so that is not an unreasonable assumption. For me, in an era of low returns, this makes the return from investing in high-yield corporate bonds very attractive.

To what extent are you seeing pension funds switching their investment strategies to take advantage of corporate bonds as an asset class?

The big surprise of 2011 and the early part of 2012 is that pension funds are not yet

"Capitalism is a forest fire that is never extinguished, only contained." Bryan Appleyard

beating their way into this to any really noticeable extent. My estimation is that, on average, 2% of their funds are allocated in this asset class. However, I foresee issuance in Europe remaining above average levels for a few years ahead, despite the fact that the issuance over the last two years has been quite high relative to the recent past. At the same time, companies that are new to the bond market in Europe are having to pay a new issuance premium of 100 to 150 bps on top of what is already a decently high coupon, plus offering security for the bond. This is a very attractive rate of return and represents a fundamentally positive shift for investors in the bond market. In my opinion, investment managers really have to capture this trend if they want performance in their portfolios, considering the low interest rate and low-inflation environment.

How do you see the new capital requirements on banks affecting the corporate debt market?

There is no doubt that companies whose debt is rated as single B and below by the ratings agencies are going to be pushed away from the banks and toward the bond markets. This will be an inevitable effect of the new capital requirements under Basel III. In the past, before Basel III, $2 of CCC-rated debt meant that a bank had to apportion $2 of equity to cover that risk. Basel III demands that they apportion $9 of equity for every $2 that they lend to CCC-rated company. This means that for a bank the cost of having CCC leveraged loans on the balance sheet is astronomically high. This is why you are seeing governments setting up mechanisms to guarantee loans to small to medium-sized enterprises. Without this, lending to a vital sector of the economy would simply dry up.

However, this issue is mitigated as, for borrowers of this type, loans are usually well secured against assets, so banks can be expected to continue to support this vital part of the economy because such loans are already well collateralized. Where the real squeeze is going to be felt is in the middle bit. Corporates with turnovers of US$200 million and more, but outside the big-company bracket, will find that debt is now significantly more expensive—which, of course, is good for high-yield bond investors. However, there is now a necessity for companies in the US$200 million and above bracket to put in place the fiscal discipline internally that will enable them to bear the higher cost of debt. For a few years they have been enjoying ultra-low rates that were not reflective of their actual credit standing, and that position has now changed for the foreseeable future.

The transition is going to be difficult for some. We have seen instances of companies preparing to approach the bond market and then backing out when they discover the coupon expectations of potential investors. If they are unable to tap the bond markets, they are going to have to try to restructure their existing debt by agreement with their banks, or else default outright.

The amount of high-yield corporate debt that has to be rolled over in Europe through 2012 and 2013 amounts to €5 billion. This is not of itself an issue for the global high-yield asset class. But the real drama will start in the second half of 2013 through to 2015, when the debt that requires rolling over will amount to some €76 billion. I do not see the market being able to self-finance that level of debt. So new money is going to have to be found. That new money will come from the bond markets, and to a lesser extent from hedge funds and private equity houses. However, corporates are going to have to offer attractive premiums to tap these sources. My feeling then is that despite the fact that coupons are already very attractive, they are going to go still higher through to 2015.

How is the low growth and deleveraging scenario expected to affect bond markets in developed countries?

The volatility experienced in the last four to five months of 2011 had a severe impact on growth expectations. We forecast a mild recession in Europe for 2012 and attach a 95% probability to such a scenario materializing. The inevitable and obvious result of a recession in Europe will be an increase in default levels, which we expect to rise to between 5% and 7% from their current historic lows. The default level in global high yield we expect to be less, at around 4%, though the market currently anticipates defaults of no more than 3%. However, the price of high-yield corporate bonds is such that you are currently being compensated for at least twice as many defaults as we expect in Europe. So if the question is whether or not the high-yield asset class offers protection against volatility and defaults, in my view the answer to that question is absolutely yes. However, what it does not offer protection against is an Armageddon scenario where Europe breaks apart ungracefully. Cumulative default levels would rise to around 45–50%, a level similar to the Great Depression in the 1930s. In such a case all risk asset classes, including high-yield bonds, will suffer heavy losses.

There are things to watch for, of course, particularly in financial-sector bonds. Some bank bonds pay 14%, but they tend to be what are known as "COCO" bonds, or contingent convertible bonds. They are straight bonds with a high coupon, but there is an agreement in the bond that if the capital ratio of the bank concerned falls below a certain level, the bond will be converted into equity. Suddenly, instead of holding a bond that puts you ahead of the equity-holders in the event of a default, you are left as just another equity-holder and all the protection of the bond goes out the window. If that happens, 14% will not look at all like an attractive recompense. These bonds, however, are worth considering as a way of adding extra performance to a high net worth individual's portfolio. So far there have been about five or six COCO bond issuances in Europe, but the market for these bonds is expected to grow to some half a trillion euros over the next five to six years as European banks refinance themselves. Any stressed bank will be interested in this, but you have to consider the investment case very carefully.

There is no doubt that this is an exceptional period for any fund manager in the high-yield corporate bond space. We are going through a multiyear period of high volatility and massive deleveraging by both the finance sector and governments, which is very painful for economies. The geopolitical risk is huge, too. If you look back at history, it is very clear that periods of massive deleveraging and high volatility have tended to coincide with major wars, so political risk is extremely high. To prevent a major accident in the market, the European Central Bank (ECB) and Europe's political leaders have so far built a liquidity "trauma center." Soon they will have to convert this into a full-blown "liquidity hospital," and it is highly unlikely that we will see this happening in a "single-shot, big bazooka" move such as was being spoken of toward the close of 2011. The politicians have been tested by the markets again and again, and each time they have balked at coming up with a two trillion euro-type rescue package. So support will come in a variety of different forms instead.

On a positive note, we have seen political changes in Greece, Italy, Spain, Ireland, and Portugal that are clearly stepping-stones toward tighter fiscal union. We saw action by six major central banks at the end of 2011 to reduce interest rates for interbank lending. We saw the ECB confirming that it would be the lender of last resort for banks. And in addition there has been the recent very successful LTRO (long-term

"Less than seventy-five years after it officially began, the contest between capitalism and socialism is over: capitalism has won." Andrew Carnegie

repo operation) program, which was viewed very positively by the market. All of this has helped to keep the interbank market functioning—and more will be needed to keep it functioning. The "liquidity hospital" that Europe is going to have to set up to prevent a total liquidity freeze will need to provide each and every type of therapy that is required in the months and years ahead.

Peripheral Eurozone countries have realized that they have to swallow their austerity medicine. We saw Ireland leading the way. The Irish have realized that they have to take hits on pensions and on property, and they are delivering admirably. Ireland continues to have a higher premium on its debt than core countries, but there is no run on Irish sovereign debt because they have shown that they have the resilience and the maturity to deal with these matters. Portugal and Spain are now also working very hard to implement austerity. Italy, too, is coming into line. Governments in peripheral countries now realize that whereas in the past you could fund a 100% debt to GDP ratio at 4%, those days are gone. As a result of this level of realization by politicians, I put the chances of a major implosion of the Eurozone at only 5%.

Although it will not be a smooth ride going forward, investors will find that high yield really is a good hedge against both inflation and volatility. If you are getting 9% plus your capital back, that is a level of return that is unmatched by most other investment options. At the same time, investor appetite for the high-yield market will keep funds flowing to corporates, which has to be a very good thing for the global economy at a time when bank credit is drying up.

MORE INFO

Books:

Bernanke, Ben S. *Essays on the Great Depression*. Princeton, NJ: Princeton University Press, 2004.

Taleb, Nassim Nicholas. *The Black Swan: The Impact of the Highly Improbable*. 2nd ed. New York: 2010.

Article:

Bernanke, Ben S. "The macroeconomics of the Great Depression: A comparative approach." *Journal of Money, Credit, and Banking* 27:1 (February 1995): 1–28. Online at: www.jstor.org/stable/2077848

See Also:

★ Issuing Corporate Debt (pp. 522–524)
★ Securitization: Understanding the Risks and Rewards (pp. 598–600)
★ Viewpoint: Reflections on the Fixed-Income Market in Difficult Times (pp. 573–575)
✔ The Bond Market: Its Structure and Function (p. 1064)
✔ Trading in Corporate Bonds: Why and How (p. 1094)

"Private property is a necessary institution, at least in a fallen world; men work more and dispute less when goods are private than when they are in common." Richard Tawney

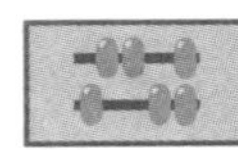

Viewpoint: Corporate Responsibility in a Community of Companies by Michelle Greene

INTRODUCTION

Michelle Greene is vice president and head of corporate responsibility for NYSE Euronext, also developing programs to leverage and enhance efforts of NYSE Euronext-listed companies, promoting collaboration and cooperation on issues of common interest. She is also executive director of the NYSE Foundation. Until 2012, she was deputy assistant secretary for financial education and financial access at the US Department of the Treasury, advising on financial access and financial education, and helped drive the development of major new policy initiatives in this area. She was also executive director of the President's Advisory Council on Financial Literacy and a member of the White House Council on Women and Girls. She was a consultant for McKinsey & Co. and Blaqwell, and executive director of the Carr Center for Human Rights Policy at the John F. Kennedy School of Government, Harvard University. She has a JD from Harvard Law School and an AB from Dartmouth College.

SUSTAINABLE BUSINESS

As an international exchange that is home to the world's leading brands, including 89% of this year's Dow Jones Sustainability Index companies, and 87% of the companies on *Corporate Responsibility* magazine's "100 best corporate citizens list," NYSE Euronext's approach to corporate responsibility (CR) and sustainability plays an integral role in the identity of our global exchange group. Not only are we are in an ideal position to bring together thought leaders from corporations, academia, and nonprofit organizations to discuss the challenges and emerging trends in the field of sustainability, but we also guide our listed companies on their sustainability journey by providing connections and resources, as well as leading by example through our environmental, social, and governance (ESG) initiatives.

As a financial services company, we do not engage in manufacturing or other large-scale operations that greatly affect the environment. So, while we must begin by leading through example, in many ways our greatest potential impact comes through working with our listed companies, and our role varies quite widely from sector to sector. We celebrate the good work of companies leading the way, we provide tools and resources for companies advancing on their own sustainability paths, and we promote collaboration across companies and across sectors.

We want to go beyond ourselves to celebrate those among our community of companies who are at the forefront of sustainability practices. We do so by hosting events that feature exemplary company efforts, as well as regularly profiling leading programs on our own CR website. We provide resources to companies by hosting workshops with our partners, including the Global Reporting Initiative (GRI) and the Carbon Disclosure Project (CDP), to bring together sustainability executives from various companies to share ideas on sustainability and on mitigating their organization's environmental impact. The GRI is a nonprofit organization that works towards a sustainable global economy through its sustainability reporting guidelines, which it pioneered and which are used around the world. The aim of the GRI guidelines is to bring a set of commonly accepted standards that enables all organizations to measure and report their economic, environmental, social, and governance performance, with these four areas taken as key to sustainability. NYSE Euronext is an Organizational Stakeholder of GRI, and we both provide input on the development of GRI frameworks and help companies communicate with each other about how they are best implemented in their particular sectors and organizations.

Sustainability is a natural area for us to seek to connect with listed companies. In addition to hosting workshops, one of the ways that NYSE Euronext can be of service to our community of companies in the CR area is to advise and support those who are interested in getting involved with sustainability, or by helping companies that have established sustainability practices but have specific issues and challenges. We constitute a community of companies and we are active in helping information about sustainability practices flow among our listed companies. To do this, we convene events and meetings on those issues relevant to our companies to help them discuss and establish best practices.

The meaning of "being a good corporate citizen," as well as the expectations companies face from their customers, suppliers, peers, and the wider society have changed. Sustainability is no longer simply a defensive issue used to protect an organization's reputation. What we see from many of our companies is that they treat sustainability as a critical part of the way they do business. It is seen positively as a way of differentiating themselves to customers and of meeting employee and community expectations.

LEADING BY EXAMPLE

To play such a role in the sustainability sphere amongst our global companies, we must lead by example with our internal ESG initiatives. As an exchange, we have a longstanding tradition of good governance, transparency, and a strong ethical stance, so adopting the sustainability philosophy is a natural fit for us. One area where we have been able to take practical steps ourselves is in lowering our environmental footprint. We are the first global exchange group to become 100% carbon-neutral beginning in 2010 with an ongoing commitment to be a carbon-neutral company. Our Global Real Estate Team took the lead in this effort, starting with reviewing how to maximize our own energy efficiency.

We have two major data centers (one in Basildon in the United Kingdom and the other in Mahwah in the United States) and we have gone to considerable lengths to ensure that green energy and clean energy play a major role in powering these centers. We commissioned two on-site photovoltaic solar energy generation plants on the roofs of the data centers. These two plants put out a peak output of 2.1 megawatts of electricity and enable us to reduce our carbon emissions by some 1,554

  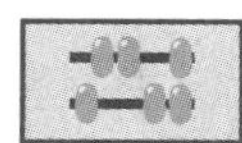   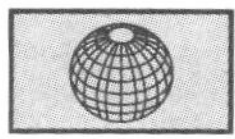   

metric tons of CO_2. This amount that we have saved would take 331 acres of pine or fir forest to sequester. When we launched our UK data center the solar power generation capacity was the largest in the country at that time.

We recognize the importance of actively involving our employees in the sustainability efforts, and we have local "green teams" throughout our global offices. These teams help to develop environmental efficiency initiatives such as swapping out personal printers for communal printing as well as promoting recycling awareness to reduce, reuse, and recycle. To help increase awareness among our employees of how much energy our offices consume, the Global Real Estate Team now tracks energy use and emissions output in all our global offices and regularly reports this data in the NYSE Euronext annual global carbon footprint report. Our overall environmental mission is to reduce office energy usage by 15% by 2015 relevant to occupancy and the 2010 baseline GHG data.

We have also implemented waste audits which analyze each office's waste stream, which helps offices identify ways to reduce waste, enhance their recycling efforts, and to work out the potential for further cost savings. By designing a more-efficient waste disposal program, NYSE Euronext has been able to increase the amount of paper, plastic, and metals that we recycle, which in turn reduces air and water pollution, and helps to curb global warming and conserve natural resources. Our target here was to meet a goal of 70% waste diversion (70% of waste does not enter landfills) by the end of 2013 and we are on track to achieve this. Additionally, we emphasize the use of food items that are in season, locally produced, and use minimal product packaging, while aiming to reduce our impact on the potable water supply and reducing the amount of waste water that we generate.

Of course, we still have to buy power, so it was an honor to be added as a member to the Environmental Protection Agency's (EPA) Green Power Partnership. We are ranked 17th on the EPA's 100% Green Power Users list, which records the largest green power purchasers in the United States that use 100% green power. In 2012, NYSE Euronext received a Green Power Leadership Award from the EPA. NYSE Euronext was the only global exchange operator and one of only 12 US organizations to earn the award for purchasing power generated by environmentally preferable, renewable resources. Our green power purchasing has a surprisingly substantial impact on the environment. These purchases are equivalent to avoiding the CO_2 emissions of more than 15,000 passenger vehicles per year. It is also the equivalent of avoiding the CO_2 emissions from the electricity use of over 9,000 average American homes each year. NYSE Euronext purchases more than 100 million kilowatt-hours (kWh) of green power annually in the United States alone, which meets 100% of our power requirements there. To achieve carbon neutrality, we also buy a combination of renewable energy certificates (RECs) and carbon offsets from Green Mountain Energy and 3Degrees.

RESPONSIBLE INVESTMENT

On a different track altogether, NYSE Euronext helps to raise the profile of leading renewable energy companies. In partnership with Bloomberg New Energy Finance, NYSE Euronext runs a family of investable clean energy indexes, known as NYSE Bloomberg. Bloomberg New Energy Finance analysts track well over 1,000 non-OTC quoted organizations who have at least 10% of their activity in clean energy and these organizations are combined into the unique basket of companies making up the various indexes. This group of indexes has shown real value for investors, highlighting the different geographical and sector trends within the increasingly massive and diverse global clean energy industry. Over the 12 months to March 2013, the NYSE Bloomberg Americas Clean Energy Index and the NYSE Bloomberg Global Energy Smart Technologies Index have outperformed very successfully. The latter comprises companies active across the advanced transportation, digital energy, energy efficiency, and energy storage sectors, and is an investable, modified market-cap-weighted index. The former follows a basket of between 125 and 325 companies with a moderate or greater exposure to renewable energy and allows investors to take a view on the ability of this sector—which has enjoyed very rapid growth in capital spending—to outperform.

In addition, with a rise of investments being made with ESG criteria, NYSE Euronext has teamed up with Vigeo, Europe's leading rating agency for social responsibility, to launch a portfolio of ESG indexes on March 20, 2013. The Euronext Vigeo ESG indexes focus on the three ESG pillars of responsible investment and include Euronext Vigeo World 120, Euronext Vigeo Europe 120, Euronext Vigeo France 20, and Euronext Vigeo United Kingdom 20. The Euronext Vigeo family of indexes are positioned to serve as genuine benchmarks for socially responsible investors looking to invest in the most sustainable companies in Europe, Asia-Pacific, and North America. This recent move by NYSE Euronext demonstrates our commitment to enabling investors to buy shares in companies that meet globally recognized standards for corporate social responsibility.

In summary, NYSE Euronext looks to take a leadership position for our companies in sustainability issues, to contribute to the development of the field more broadly, and at the same time we are very committed to managing our own environmental impact in a truly responsible fashion.

MORE INFO

Websites:

Environmental Protection Agency (EPA; US) Green Power Partnership: www.epa.gov/greenpower/

NYSE Euronext: www.nyx.com

What is the Global Reporting Initiative (GRI)?: tinyurl.com/7oeu2dg

See Also:

★ Best Practices in Corporate Social Responsibility (pp. 636–638)
★ CSR: More than PR, Pursuing Competitive Advantage in the Long Run (pp. 664–666)
★ Viewpoint: Embedding CSR and Sustainability in Corporate Culture: The Boots Experience (pp. 671–672)
★ Viewpoint: The Growth of Sustainability Reporting (pp. 680–681)
★ Viewpoint: Sustainability Reporting and Assurance—A Market-Driven Transformation (pp. 102–103)

"The only statistics you can trust are those you have falsified yourself." Winston Churchill

  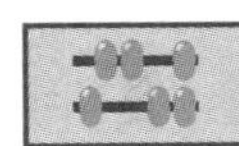      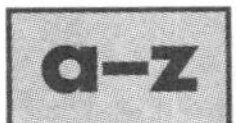

Credit Derivatives—The Origins of the Problem

by Eric R. Dinallo

EXECUTIVE SUMMARY

The nature of credit swaps explained:

- The difference between insurance and speculation in CDSs.
- "Anti-bucket shop" legislation as a precursor to the CDS debate.
- The origins of the exemption for CDSs.
- The role of the New York Insurance Department.
- Steps to bring CDSs under control.

INTRODUCTION

There is no doubt that credit default swaps (CDSs) have played a major role in the financial problems the world now faces. As the insurance regulator for New York, the New York Insurance Department had a role to play in the development of CDSs. As they developed, there was a question about whether or not they were insurance. As they initially were used by owners of bonds to seek protection or insurance in the case of a default by the issuer of the bonds, this was a reasonable question. In 2000, under a prior administration, the New York Insurance Department was asked to determine if swaps were insurance, and said no. That is a decision the department has since revisited and reversed as incomplete. We are now unambiguously in favor of the regulation of CDSs.

Since 2007, when the author took office, the impact of CDSs has been one of the major issues the department has had to confront. In the first instance, the department tackled the problems of financial guarantee companies, known as bond insurers. CDSs were a major factor in their difficulties. More recently, the department was involved in the rescue of AIG. Again, credit default swaps were the biggest source of that company's problems.

WHAT IS A CREDIT DEFAULT SWAP AND HOW MANY VARIETIES ARE THERE?

A CDS is a contract in which the seller, for a fee, agrees to make a payment to the protection buyer in the event that the referenced security, usually some kind of bond, experiences any number of various "credit events," such as bankruptcy, default, or reorganization. If something goes wrong with the referenced entity, the protection buyer can put the bond to the protection seller and be made whole. Or a net payment can be made by the seller to the buyer. Originally, credit default swaps were used to transfer, and thus reduce risk, for the owners of bonds. If you owned a bond in company X and were concerned that the company might default, you bought the swap to protect yourself. The swaps could also be used by banks who loaned money to a company. This type of swap is still used for hedging purposes.

Over time, however, swaps came to be used not to reduce risk, but to assume it. Institutions that did not own the obligation bought and sold credit default swaps to place what Wall Street calls a directional bet on a company's creditworthiness. Swaps bought by speculators are sometimes known as "naked credit default swaps" because the swap purchasers do not own the underlying obligation. The protection becomes more valuable as the company becomes less creditworthy. This is similar to naked shorting of stocks.

I have argued that these naked credit default swaps should not be called swaps, because there is no transfer or swap of risk. Instead, risk is created by the transaction. For example, you have no risk on the outcome of the third race until you place a bet on horse number five to win.

WHEN IS A SWAP INSURANCE AND WHEN IS IT PURE SPECULATION?

We believe that the first type of swap—let's call it the covered swap—is insurance. The essence of an insurance contract is that the buyer has to have a material interest in the asset or obligation that is the subject of the contract. That means the buyer owns property or a security and can suffer a loss from damage to, or the loss of value of that property.

With insurance, the buyer only has a claim after actually suffering a loss. With the covered swaps, if the issuer of a bond defaults, then the owner of the bond has suffered a loss and the swap provides some recovery for that loss. The second type of swap contains none of these features.

Because the credit default swap market is not regulated, there is no valid data on the number of swaps outstanding, and how many are naked. Estimates of the market were as high as US$62 trillion. By comparison, there is only about US$6 trillion in corporate debt outstanding, US$7.5 trillion in mortgage-backed debt and US$2.5 trillion in asset-backed debt. That's a total of about US$16 trillion in private-sector debt.

BUCKET SHOPS AND ANTI-BUCKET SHOP LEGISLATION IN THE US—AN IMPORTANT PIECE OF HISTORY IN THE CDS DEBACLE

Some history here would be useful. Betting or speculating on movements in securities or commodities prices without actually owning the referenced security or commodity is nothing new. As early as 1829, "stock jobbing," an early version of short selling, was outlawed in New York. The Stock Jobbing Act was ultimately repealed in 1858 because it was overly broad and captured legitimate forms of speculation. However, the issue of whether to allow bets on security and commodity prices outside of organized exchanges continued to be an issue.

"Bucket shops" arose in the late 19th Century. Customers "bought" securities or commodities on these unauthorized exchanges, but, in reality, the bucket shop was simply booking the customer's order without executing on an exchange. In fact, they were simply throwing the trade ticket in the bucket, which is where the name comes from, and tearing it up when an opposite trade came in. The bucket shop would agree to take the other side of the customer's "bet" on the performance of the security or commodity.

Bucket shops sometimes survived for a time by balancing their books, but were wiped out by extreme bull or bear markets. When their books failed, the bucketeers simply closed up shop and left town, leaving the "investors" holding worthless tickets. The Bank Panic of 1907 is famous for J. P. Morgan, the leading banker of the time, calling all the other bankers to a meeting and keeping them there until they agreed to form a consortium of bankers to create an emergency backstop for the banking system.

At the time there was no Federal Reserve. However, a more lasting result was the passage of New York's anti-bucket shop law in 1909. The law, General Business Law Section 351, made it a felony to operate or be connected with a bucket shop or "fake exchange." Because of the specificity and severity of the much-anticipated legislation, virtually all bucket shops shut down before the law came into effect, and little

"Unfortunately monetarism, like Marxism, suffered the only fate that for a theory is worse than death: it was put into practice." Ian Gilmour

enforcement was necessary. Other states passed similar laws.

Section 351 prohibits the making or offering of a purchase or sale of a security, commodity, debt, property, options, bonds, etc., without intending a bona fide purchase or sale of the security, commodity, debt, property, options, bonds, etc. If you think that sounds exactly like a naked credit default swap, you are right. What this tells us is that back in 1909, 100 years ago, people understood the risks and potential instability that comes from betting on securities prices, and outlawed it.

HOW CDSS CAME TO BE EXEMPT FROM ANTI-BUCKET-SHOP LEGISLATION

With the growth of various kinds of derivatives in the late 20th Century, there was legal uncertainty as to whether certain derivatives, including credit default swaps, violated state bucket-shop and gambling laws. The Commodity Futures Modernization Act of 2000 (CFMA), signed by President Clinton on December 21, 2000, created a "safe harbor" by (1) pre-empting state and local gaming and bucket-shop laws, except for general antifraud provisions; and (2) exempting certain derivative transaction on commodities and swap agreements, including credit default swaps, from CFTC regulation.

CFMA also amended the Securities and Exchange Acts of 1933 and 1934 to make it clear that the definition of "security" does not include certain swap agreements, including credit default swaps, and that the SEC is prohibited from regulating those swap agreements, except for its anti-fraud enforcement authority.

So, by ruling that credit default swaps were not subject to state laws or SEC regulation, the way was cleared for the growth of the market. But there was one other issue. If the swaps were considered insurance, then they would be regulated by state insurance departments. If this were the case, then the capital and underwriting limits in insurance regulation would have curtailed the rapid growth in the market for these derivatives.

THE ROLE OF THE NEW YORK INSURANCE DEPARTMENT

So, at the same time, in 2000, the New York Insurance Department was asked a very carefully crafted question. "Does a credit default swap transaction, wherein the seller will make payment to the buyer upon the happening of a negative credit event, and such payment is not dependent upon the buyer having suffered a loss, constitute a contract of insurance under the insurance law?"

Clearly, the question was framed to ask only about naked credit default swaps. Under the facts we were given, the swap was not insurance, because the buyer had no material interest and the filing of claim does not require a loss. However, the entities involved were careful not to ask about covered credit default swaps. Nonetheless, the market took the Department's opinion on a subset of credit default swaps as a ruling on all swaps.

In sum, in 2000, as a society we chose not to regulate credit default swaps. Why did that matter? As we have seen, the financial system has been placed in peril because there was no comprehensive management of counterparty risk. Deals were made privately between two parties. These bilateral arrangements mean that there are no standards for the solvency of counterparties. The buyer does not know how much risk the seller is taking on. And there are no requirements for the seller to hold reserves or capital against the risks it is taking on by selling swaps.

None of this was a problem as long as the value of everything was going up, and defaults were rare. But the problem with this sort of unregulated protection scheme is that when everyone needs to be paid at once, the market is not strong enough to provide the protection everyone suddenly needs.

CDSS AND MARKING TO MARKET

Unlike insurance, credit default swaps are marked to market. That means the value of the swap reflects the current market value, which can swing sharply and suddenly. Value changes require the sellers to post collateral. Sudden and sharp changes in the credit rating of the issuer of the bonds, or of the bonds themselves, can produce large swings in the value of the swaps, and thus the need to post large and increasing amounts of collateral. That capital strain can produce sudden liquidity problems for sellers. The seller may own enough assets to provide collateral, but the assets may not be liquid, and thus not immediately accessible.

When many sellers are forced to sell assets, the price of those assets falls and sellers are faced with taking large losses just to meet collateral requirements. As the prices of the assets are driven down by forced sales, mark-to-market losses increase, and the collateral posting cycle continues. Meanwhile, the underlying assets may continue to perform, paying interest and principal in full.

STEPS TO BRING CDSS UNDER CONTROL

On September 22, we announced that New York State would, beginning in January 2009, regulate the insurance part of the credit default swap market, which has, to date, been unregulated—the part which the Insurance Department has jurisdiction to regulate.

That announcement played an important role in spurring national discussion about a comprehensive regulatory structure for the CDS market. The result has been exactly what was envisioned—a broad debate and discussion about the best way to bring controls and oversight to this huge and important market, and concrete progress toward a centralized risk management, trading, and clearing system.

After our announcement, SEC Chairman Cox asked for the power to regulate the credit default swap market. The New York Federal Reserve began a series of meetings with the dealer community to discuss how to proceed. We believe that there are appropriate uses for credit default swaps.

CONCLUSION

We acknowledge that some amount of speculation can provide useful information and market liquidity. We also recognize that the best route to a healthy market in credit default swaps is not to divide it up among regulators. It would not be effective or efficient for New York to regulate some transactions under the insurance law, while other transactions are either not regulated or regulated under some other law. The best outcome is a holistic solution for the entire credit default swap market.

MORE INFO

Article:

Dinallo, Eric. "We modernized ourselves into this ice age." *Financial Times* (March 30, 2009). Online at: tinyurl.com/d6kt2o

Report:

Testimony by Eric Dinallo to the US House of Representatives: Hearing to review the role of credit derivatives in the US economy. Online at: www.ins.state.ny.us/speeches/pdf/sp0811201.pdf

NOTE

1 This article is drawn from Dinallo's testimony to the US Congress on November 20, 2008, at a hearing to review the role of credit derivatives in the US economy.

"An economist is a man who states the obvious in terms of the incomprehensible." Alfred A. Knopf

  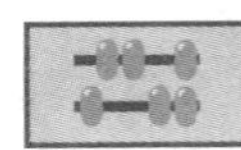      

Viewpoint: Deleveraging, Deflation, and Rebalancing in the Global Economy by Paul Brain and Laurie Carroll

INTRODUCTION

Paul Brain is investment leader of the fixed-incometeam at Newton Investment Management. He joined Newton in 2004, and manages a range of global bondfunds. He is also the lead managerof Newton's global dynamic bond strategy. Paul is chairman of the bond/foreign exchangestrategy group and is a member of the macro strategy group and the investment committee. He has held a number of senior fixed-incomepositions within the industry and has acquired a wide breadth of knowledge and experience in managing fixed-incomeportfolios. As head of retail fixed incomeat Investec (formerly Guinness Flight), Paul led the team that won the International Money Marketing "Fixed Interest Manager of the Year" award in 2000.

Laurie Carroll is executive vice president and the global short-duration strategist for BNY Mellon Cash Investment Strategies (CIS), a division of the Dreyfus Corporation. Carroll is responsible for the global strategic direction and product developmentfor the short-duration products of CIS. She is an active member of CIS's fiduciary risk committee and has over 29 years of industry experience. Her career at BNY Mellon spans 24 years, during which she has held positions of increasing responsibility for a number of company affiliates. Most recently, she served as managing directorof short-duration, index, and stable value strategies for Standish Mellon Asset Management, a BNY Mellon company. Carroll has an MBA from the University of Pittsburgh and a BA from Seton Hill University. She is a member of the board of trusteesof Seton Hill University.

As global short-durations strategist, you have an eye to what is likely to happen over anything from a month to a year. That gives you a very keen sense of near-term trouble for developed and developing markets. How do you view the strength of the current recovery from the global crash of 2008?

Laurie Carroll: It seems as if every week brings some fresh piece of drama. I do not think we have been in a period where we have been flooded so continuously with mixed economic news, with market commentators oscillating between fears of a double-dip recessionand signs of growth. What is certain is that we are still very much in the repair phase of the financial services sectors in the United Kingdom, the eurozone, and the United States, and that the re-regulation of the sector still has a long way to run.

Basically, one has to go back to the savings and loan crisis in the United States to find anything similar to the current position. That crisis was confined to the United States and ran through the 1980s and early 1990s. It took banks a very long time then to repair their balance sheets, and that tells us that this time round it is likely to take many banks a number of years to get back to where they were. At the same time, through the savings and loan crisis there was not the same appetite on a global scale for regulatory change that we are now seeing.

Already we are seeing real contradictions emerging from different regulators. The Securities and Exchange Commission (SEC) in the United States is producing regulations that are asking money marketsto move to shorter-duration issues. At the same time we have emerging banking regulations asking the banks to go for longer-duration issues and to buy more government securities. The idea is that if banks issue longer-dated paper, they will not be so much at risk of coming to the market for refunding when the market is not willing or able to satisfy that funding requirement. All of this makes the short-duration space—and, indeed, every part of the financial market—very interesting indeed.

On top of all this we have pressure on the ratings agencies to rethink their methodologies after the mistakes made in rating residential mortgage-backed securitizations. So there are an awful lot of things going on simultaneously, all of which have some bearing on prices going up and down.

One result of this is that there is a degree of cloudiness about what portion of any price movement is being determined by the market reacting to actual or potential regulatory moves, and what portion of the price bears on the inflation/deflation debate.

This is particularly unhelpful to anyone who is trying to develop strategies to deal with either inflation or deflation. The key point here, of course, is that the defense against inflation is very different from the defense against deflation. If you had been devising strategies to protect a portfolio from inflationary trends over the last year, it is very likely that those strategies would have been losing rather than winning strategies since we have undoubtedly seen more deflation than inflation over the course of the last 12 months.

There seems to be some market confusion as to whether the United States in particular is in more danger from deflation than from inflation, at least in the short term. What is your view?

Laurie Carroll: The United States is right to be particularly concerned about deflation. Japan is still trying to deal with deflation after 20 years. There is no doubt that we have seen a dramatic reduction in house sales in the United States as a direct result of the withdrawal of tax creditsto home buyers there. This could be regarded as a fiscal tightening measure, and although it was probably inevitable, it has hammered the US housing market, which now remains a very significant drag on growth. You can see the danger signs too in consumer attitudes, with people being very keen on cutting their borrowing and increasing their savings. This deleveraging by the consumer takes money directly out of the economy. The US economy needs the consumer to spend to drive real GDPgrowth.

I do not think that anyone, prior to the crash, appreciated the extent to which the consumer would shift into deleveraging. Consumer spendinghas been a very reliable component, accounting for around two-thirds of GDP, and now people are talking about a generation that has shifted toward short-term retail funds and is not investing much in equity or longer fixed-interestassets. We don't yet have the "depression baby," but we have people who have become attuned to the shock of the recession, and it takes a long time to change.

When people switch from spending to saving they have to be strongly incentivized to spend again. The United States did this on housing and new house building, and government stimulus worked until it was withdrawn, but it seems to have had little carry-through after the withdrawal. Of course, in countries with no social safety net, such as China, it is very difficult to get strong consumer spendingsince people place a very high priority on saving sufficient to get themselves through any emergency that might come along. This generates a very persistent habit of saving, and you get very high savings rates precisely when you want to encourage much higher levels of domestic consumerspending. China is going to have to spend vast sums putting in place a much more trusted social safety net as part of its ambition to build up consumer spending, but that is going to take a number of years to come through.

However, these are longer-term plays, and my focus is on short-term strategies. Key for me is the behavior of central banks. With deflation seen as the bigger near-term threat, the US Federal Reservewill be keeping short-term rates low for a long while yet. We could see some movement from the Bank of England, given the higher rateof inflation in the United Kingdom and the fact that it has proved "stickier" than many anticipated. But we do not expect to see any raising of rates from the European Central Bankfor a long while yet.

In October 2010 we saw some price action in the two-year bond space, but strong demand brought the price down again. Corporate bondspreads gapped out just a bit in September, but again, it is hard to see us moving too far from where we are right now, given the level of uncertainty in the markets. We now have the Dodd–Frank Act, but much of the detail work still has to be drafted, so we will be well into 2011 before we get any clarity on the regulatory front. This being so, I do not see people changing their strategies a lot much before the first quarterof 2011. If anything, I would expect market thinking to become more conservative.

Right now we are in a very neutral stance. It is very difficult to put a position on one way or another at this point as far as government bondsare concerned. There is still value in investment-grade corporate bonds, so we are overweight in corporate credit. We do not see any point in hedging against interest rate riskright now since it is still very unclear what is happening, and a hedge just becomes yet another risk that you are assuming. The simplest strategy right now is to continue investing in corporate credit. There is a great deal of new paper coming on to the market, particularly in the financial sector as the banks look to shore up their books.

As to sovereign debt, we are very selective in the countries we want to go into. Some of the bigger, better trading nations are giving cause for concern, and this saga has by no means run its course. Much of the future difficulty for European politicians lies in trying to reduce the scale of public benefits, such as pensions, in an effort to cut government deficits. It is very hard to get people to accept a decrease in lifestyle. Increases are easily absorbed, but decreases are fiercely resisted.

The US administration has just added another very difficult-to-pay-for social layer, in the shape of the healthcare acts of 2010, and that will doubtless cause the United States further difficulties going forward.

Another very significant factor in the equation is the potential fallout from the competitive deflation that various countries are now engaging in against the dollar. In some senses this is the same conflict as that between tight and loose monetary policy-playing out in the realm of currencies. Developing countriesare experiencing above-trend growth that threatens to boost their currencies against the dollar. This hurts their export markets, so they seek to devalue their currencies downward against the dollar, which itself is weakening through a combination of weak US growth and the impact of the first round of quantitative easingand market fears over the inflationary impact of the much anticipated second round of quantitative easing, which is now scheduled to run through 2011 and to be worth around US$600 billion. This "competitive devaluation" of currencies is creating something of a "race to the bottom."

Do you see scope for any positive outcomes or corrections to the global dislocations that are producing these currency tensions?

Paul Brain: We believe that the realignment of the world's major economies relies on economic growthand debt repayment in the West, coupled with economic growthand increased domestic demand in the East. To achieve the first of these, the West will need to maintain a degree of stimulus as far as monetary policyis concerned. This inevitably leads to some undermining of currency values. The emerging economiesnaturally see this as a form of currency debasement. The natural response is going to be to want to limit " hot money" flows into their economies by applying measures such as capital controls, taxes on foreign investment, and perhaps even currency controls.

The problem the West has is that the repair of bank balancesheets is going to be a long, slow affair, and while this is happening the velocity of money in society—the speed at which money is exchanged, which is a gauge of liquidity—is unlikely to rise sufficiently to enable the monetary stimulus-induced recovery to gain traction. If policy-makers manage to raise velocity, then we believe that the currency war could be won before it really gets going.

Quantitative easingcan be positive in the real economyby, for example, lowering the cost of credit to consumers and lowering mortgage costs, which makes homes more affordable and creates more surplus income. However, this requires some appetite for borrowing on the part of consumers. Again, we need more job creation to lower unemployment for consumer demandto make itself felt.

It seems clear that the liquidity created by quantitative easingis likely to only partially offset the money wiped out by the credit crisis, which means that the inflationary consequences of quantitative easingmay well be minimal. Effectively, the use of quantitative easingmeans that bond marketsare being used as a monetary policytool. We believe this is set to continue until economies are able to cope without unconventional monetary and fiscal support. There will be a time to be bearish, but we are not there yet.

We maintain a positive stance on government bondmarkets, but expect this to be severely challenged during 2011. With a steadily developing markets-led economic recovery, a pickup in investment could be possible should equity markets stabilize. What will give us the signal that things are changing? Much rests on the velocity of

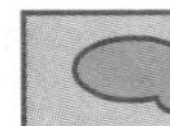

money. Signs of a return to normal borrowing and lending conditions in the banking sector would suggest that the emergency funding measures are no longer required, and that the use of bond market-sas a policy tool is at an end. It is clear that other asset classeswill need to stabilize before we see any material rise in bond yields. Equities seem set to remain volatile in the face of higher bond yieldsdue to fears of higher ratesquelling the recovery and denting corporate profits.

If we manage to find our way to a period of sustained equity market strength and it becomes clear that the banking systemis fixed, plus we get an increase in the velocity of money, then we will be able to declare with some confidence that we have beaten off the specter of deflation. However, we are in for a period of prolonged low bond yieldsuntil central bankers are confident that they can withdraw unconventional monetary and fiscal support to their various economies.

MORE INFO

Books:

Ahamed, Liaquat. *Lords of Finance: The Bankers Who Broke the World*. New York: Penguin, 2009.

Friedman, Thomas L. *The World Is Flat: A Brief History of the Twenty-First Century*. New York: Picador, 2007.

Gladwell, Malcolm. *Outliers: The Story of Success*. New York: Little, Brown, 2008.

Reinhard, Carmen M., and Kenneth S. Rogoff. *This Time Is Different: Eight Centuries of Financial Folly*. Princeton, NJ: Princeton University Press, 2009.

Sorkin, Andrew Ross. *Too Big to Fail: The Inside Story of How Wall Street and Washington Fought to Save the Financial System—And Themselves*. New York: Penguin, 2009.

Tett, Gillian. *Fool's Gold: The Inside Story of J. P. Morgan and How Wall St Greed Corrupted Its Bold Dream and Created a Financial Catastrophe*. New York: Free Press, 2010.

See Also:

★ The Globalization of Inflation (pp. 184–185)
★ Mixflation (pp. 215–218)
★ Viewpoint: Steering Between Deflation and Inflation—A Troubled Road for Developed Economies (pp. 604–606)
✔ The Bond Market: Its Structure and Function (p. 1064)
✔ Building a Forex Plan (p. 965)
✔ Methods for Dealing with Inflation Risk (p. 984)

"Spread the truth–the laws of economics are like the laws of engineering. One set of laws works everywhere."
Lawrence H. Summers

  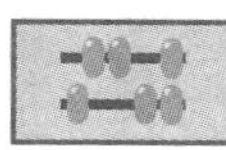      

Viewpoint: Derivatives Regulation Threatens to Damage Pension Funds and Pensioners across Europe by Ben Gunnee

INTRODUCTION

Ben Gunnee is European director of the Mercer Sentinel Group, a specialist group within Mercer's investments business that advises clients on investment operations and investment execution, including custodian reviews, investment manager operational due diligence, transition manager operations, and transaction cost analysis. Based in London, he is responsible for the group's overall business strategy within Europe and is part of its global management committee. Before joining Mercer in 2002, Gunnee worked for the Financial Services Authority and a major life assurance company. Holding a master's degree in accounting and finance and an honors degree in accounting and financial management, he has more than 14 years of experience in the investment and pensions sector. He is a fellow of the Institute of Actuaries.

As a principal consultant for Mercer, you have warned that the new banking regulatory regime set out in Basel III, together with aspects of the US Dodd–Frank Act, is likely to harm pension funds and so, ultimately, pensioners. What are the dangers?

It seems clear that capital charges on banks brought in by the new Basel III banking regulations are going to have a profound impact across Europe on pension funds that use over-the-counter (OTC) derivatives programs. If we break this down step by step, it becomes clear why this should be so. Pension funds that have achieved a degree of balance between their assets and their liabilities are very keen to take further risk off the table. The sponsoring companies behind these final salary pension schemes are also very keen not to expose themselves to continued volatility, so derisking schemes makes sense both from the point of view of the trustees and from that of the scheme sponsors.

Trustees, then, need tools that will enable them to "hedge out" unwanted risk, particularly risk that lies in possible interest rate movements and in inflation, neither of which are within their control and both of which can have a major impact on increasing their liabilities. So pension funds want to hedge out this risk, typically through a series of bilateral swaps with a number of counterparties. So far so good. This kind of swap has been used increasingly by pension funds over the last five to 10 years. There is no argument by any regulator against this, and it is considered to be an important tool for pension funds to have as they seek to meet the obligations they have to their members.

However, swaps are derivatives products and there is no doubt that derivatives—or, more specifically, the lack of transparency in derivatives trading—played a major role in the global financial crash of 2008. Because so much of derivatives trading was conducted away from recognized stock exchanges—taking place on a bilateral basis between two counterparties, with no visibility of how such deals were building up into a systemic risk—regulators and even the banks themselves were taken by surprise by how toxic derivatives turned out to be in the 2008 crash. Naturally enough, once the role that the lack of transparency in derivatives trading had played in the crash came to light, there was massive pressure to bring more transparency to the derivatives market. It seemed to both regulators and politicians that forcing as much as possible of the OTC derivatives market to be traded on recognized exchanges, or move to central clearing, would create transparency. The idea was that regulators should be able to have somewhere where they could go to check on any bank's global OTC exposure, and since a central clearing counterparty (CCP) acts as a repository of all trades by standing between buyers and sellers this seemed to solve the transparency issue.

What they did not take fully into account is that OTC derivatives constitute a very complex area, and when you try to approach complexity with a rigid rule book the law of unintended consequences tends to run riot.

Can you spell out how the law of unintended consequences has made itself felt so far?

Certainly. Let us go back for a moment to the world of the final salary defined-benefit pension fund, which was already a difficult enough world before the current wave of enthusiasm for reregulation. For schemes that are in deficit, the sponsor company has two basic choices. They can either urge the scheme trustees to take on more risk (note that this decision lies with the trustees, not with the scheme sponsor) or the sponsor can put more cash into the scheme. If a sponsor puts more cash into the scheme, it is going to be very interested in derisking the scheme going forward, so that it will not have to repeat the cash injection at regular intervals. Companies would much rather use surplus cash to invest in new projects or boost the share price by increasing dividend payments to shareholders.

The new regulatory environment for OTC derivatives, which includes swaps, is then layered in on top of the world of the final salary pension scheme, not because the regulators want to regulate pension funds but because they want to regulate derivatives exposures. Under the proposed regulations there is a requirement for cash collateral, an asset class that is not typically held by investors with long-term liabilities such as a pension fund.

So, as the logical way of preventing pension funds from having an unwarranted and quite substantial additional layer of costs imposed on schemes by the new OTC regulation, the European Union has decided to allow pension schemes an exemption for three years. The idea is that they have three years when they can put all the swaps they want or need in place on a bilateral basis just as they have always done, and thus they will not be caught out by the cash collateral requirements once they too are included in the OTC regulations.

However, this exemption is granted to pension funds via the European Union's proposed European Market Infrastructure Regulation (EMIR). This would be all fine but for the fact that the exemption is eroded by the provisions in a different piece of regulatory legislation, namely the new Basel III regulatory framework for banks. Basel III doesn't address the needs of pension funds, instead requiring banks that are trading on a bilateral basis (i.e. with pension funds) to hold substantially more capital for these types of trades, which increases the overall cost of execution. It does this by imposing very stringent capital and margin requirements on any bilateral trades that banks do outside a CCP framework. So Basel III provides a disincentive for banks to do bilateral swaps with pension funds, which means that the three-year exemption for pension funds will not be as useful as originally intended.

The problem right now is that a large number of pension schemes are presuming that, as they have an exemption from central clearing, they do not need to make any of the operational changes that will be necessary for them to interact with a clearing house. They are also not taking the necessary steps to minimize the impact of the additional collateral they are going to be required to post in order to engage in swaps.

EMIR was supposed to be introduced at the end of 2012, so what do you think will happen to the deadline? Will EMIR come in on time?

I very much doubt it. Our expectation is that implementation is much more likely to take place around the second quarter of 2013—that is, if there is no further slippage, which is possible. EMIR has been a long time getting to the final draft stage, and contradictions between EMIR and Basel III, such as I have just highlighted, are symptomatic of how difficult this piece of legislation is to get right. We fully expect to see the emergence of a two-tiered pricing structure, which pension funds are going to have to get to grips with. There will be one price for OTC-cleared swaps and another price for uncleared contracts. The difference between the two could be significant, and that will make it necessary for pension schemes to look to pass their swaps through CCPs, which contradicts the purpose of the exemption granted to them under EMIR.

What is the problem with pension funds deciding to do all their swaps through CCPS? There is no compulsion for them to avail themselves of the three-year exemption if doing so will make it more expensive for them.

Under the existing, uncleared arrangements the securities that will constitute the collateral that is posted by the pension fund to support a swap are a matter for agreement between the bank and the pension fund under their International Swaps and Derivatives Association (ISDA) contracts. Under the CCP model initial margin will be required, which is not currently a requirement, and also ongoing margin. The CCPs will require high-quality bonds for initial margin and will only currently accept cash for ongoing margin. Pension funds tend to invest in a wide range of asset classes but do not typically hold significant allocations to cash, nor do they want their high-quality bonds tied up in a collateral pool.

So what is likely to happen is that we will see the emergence of a thriving new market aimed at "improving" collateral. The pension funds will swap some of their assets and have the assets transformed into cash, something that is referred to as collateral transformation. One market we expect to expand rapidly as a result is the repo market. However, there will inevitably be a charge for doing this, so the swap will still be more expensive to do than it is at present, before EMIR kicks in.

The CCP model eliminates counterparty risk for the seller and the buyer, since the CCP is deemed to be a "deep-pockets" organization that is unlikely to fail and has a well-controlled process in place to minimize the loss from counterparty failure. But it does mean that all the counterparty risk is then concentrated in the CCP. EMIR lays down that any prospective CCP has to be able to show that it could withstand the failure of its largest clients. The CCP can only do this by imposing a levy on each of its direct members, which is how it gathers the resources needed to meet the operating criteria for CCPs laid down by EMIR. The size of these "deposits" by direct clearing members is of a scale that makes it impossible for any but the large global banks to become direct clearing members.

This in turn means that where a European pension fund, for example, was accustomed to going to one of the local national banks when it wanted to write an interest rate or an inflation rate swap contract, those banks might not be able to offer cleared trades. Instead the pension fund is going to have to forge new relationships if it wishes to clear centrally. This is not impossible for the pension fund to do, of course, but the regulators, one imagines, never set out to take business away from local national banks and give it instead to the big global banks. This is just another unintended consequence of the move to regulate the swaps market.

There has been talk of people looking to push through various regulatory arbitrage plays based on the fact that Asia is moving at a different pace from both Europe and the United States on pushing swaps through CCPs. Do you see regulatory arbitrage as a route for pension funds to follow?

I don't see this working for pension funds. If you are trading sterling interest rate swaps, for example, and you only have a certain, very limited tolerance for risk, do you really want to trade those swaps through some offshore location which, at the very least, looks likely to increase your risk? Moreover, the mainstream large banks like JP Morgan, for example, might in theory be able to use, say, their Singapore desk to write bilateral swaps for their European pension clients, but even if they found some way of servicing their pension fund clients outside the OTC regulations, you have to question whether they would have the appetite to push ahead with that kind of deal. The new environment, especially post the LIBOR scandal, is not exactly conducive to banks signing off on a process to navigate around the rules.

If one was cynical, it would be easy to suggest the regulators' underlying aim is to reduce the use of derivatives. But all of this will take time to play out. Interest rate swaps will be the first to be cleared, and it could be at least two years before we see inflation swaps being brought into central clearing.

In the wake of the collapse of Lehman it was easy to make a case for more transparency—and, yes, that helps to monitor counterparty risk more effectively. However, it introduces secondary risks into the swap process in several areas, including in the amount of funding that has to be put up for margin calls to support hedges, and in pension funds tapping the repo market for securities lending in order to upgrade collateral. With CCPs, as many people have pointed out, you have a concentration of risk on the CCP when it used to be spread between all the bilateral players.

So have the regulators managed to bring about a net reduction in risk? Only time will tell, but what we are certainly seeing is a number of unforeseen consequences—and one of these unforeseen consequences is to make swaps more expensive for pension funds. Some funds may well decide not to put hedging strategies in place as a result, and that, too, introduces another dimension of risk. The jury is going to be out on the effectiveness of the new OTC derivatives regulatory framework for a long time to come.

"Prosperity or egalitarianism—you have to choose. I favor freedom—you never achieve real equality anyway: you simply sacrifice prosperity for an illusion." Mario Vargas Llosa

  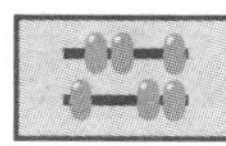   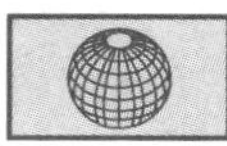   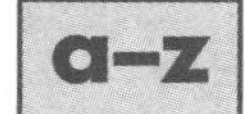

Viewpoint: Disinflation and Low Growth versus Inflation and Reasonable Growth

by Valentijn van Nieuwenhuijzen

INTRODUCTION

Valentijn van Nieuwenhuijzen is head of strategy for the strategy and tactical asset allocation group at ING Investment Management. He is responsible for formulating the firm's macroeconomic outlook and fixed-income tactical asset allocation. Focused on tactical allocation between cash, fixed-income, equities, real estate, and commodities, and more particularly between specific fixed-income markets such as treasuries, intergovernmental credits, high-yields, and emerging market debt, his research supports the ING Investment Management global asset allocation team's allocation decisions. He is a recognized expert on growth, inflation, and central bank policy in the major economic blocks and the global dynamics that influence different regions. Until 2008, as a member of the global fixed-income team he was responsible for formulating the team's macroeconomic outlook. van Nieuwenhuijzen specialized in international macroeconomics at the University of Amsterdam, where he took his degree in 1998.

What is your view of the growth prospects for developed and emerging economies?

By the start of the fourth quarter of 2010, the global economy, which had picked up to the high single digits following the 2008 crash, had begun to decelerate. Much of that early growth was inventory-driven as companies restocked. As the positive impact from inventories started to wane, fiscal policy, too, turned from a boost to a drag. Developing economies started to tighten fiscal policy to combat inflation, while developed economies in Europe moved to implement fiscal austerity to claw back very substantial deficits.

This left private demand to take over the baton. While the prospects for emerging markets continue to be good, with signs of increased private consumption, developed economies have been struggling as far as both the consumer and private enterprise are concerned.

Over the past two years savings rates in the developed countries have increased substantially, taking money out of the economy, while the corporate sector has witnessed sharp improvements to its collective balance sheet. This leaves the private sector in a position to produce a cyclical increase in demand as low stocks of capital and durable goods come up for replenishment.

However, there are clear signs that this cyclical increase is having trouble getting off the ground. Business confidence remains weak, especially in the United States, which suggests that companies will be reluctant to drive demand via investment. This creates a difficult set of self-reinforcing circumstances, with the soft labor market conditions in the United States in particular causing consumers to worry about unemployment, while businesses are not hiring due to worries about final demand.

Some room for hope has emerged, however, as US labor market and consumer spending dynamics have improved recently. Moreover, fiscal policy will be more supportive in 2011 than was expected until recently. This suggests that growth will be above 3% this year. Importantly, however, this will not bring the US economy back to equilibrium any time soon, and therefore disinflation will likely persist.

Also positive is that the Eurozone economy has proved to be surprisingly resilient in the face of sovereign turmoil, with Germany as the clear outperformer. We expect momentum in the Eurozone to get some headwinds from fiscal austerity in the peripheral countries. However, this could be cushioned somewhat by preliminary signs of life in core domestic demand.

We hear a great deal about global imbalances. Do these look set to continue, or do you see some rebalancing taking place?

The global economic system remains out of balance in many respects. Interestingly enough, stronger global growth and a more shock-resilient financial system are beneficial to all countries in the long run. Policy decisions, however, are not taken by countries, but by the officials who are employed by the governments or policy institutes of these countries. These policymakers have a far shorter horizon as their incentives are determined by election cycles, personal career motives, and/or personal PR opportunities.

Similarly, corporate decision-makers very often have incentives that are more focused on the short term than is optimal for the long-term growth objectives of the firms involved. With these barriers preventing any easy alignment of individual interests (at either the country or the personal level) with the "common good" for the medium to long term, finding the right antidote to correct the imbalances in the system is going to be extremely difficult.

Even at the academic and theoretical level, economists and policymakers have widely divergent views on how to address problems of overleverage, lack of final demand, and/or shock-resilience. In economic "science" it is impossible to isolate certain policy actions and observe outcomes in a controlled environment. It follows that empirical analysis nearly always leaves room for debate and differences in interpretation.

This leads in turn to widely different policies and variations on them as countries conduct their own, "test tube" policy experiments. These policy innovations are often partially driven by personal incentives and partially based on cultural and academic convictions. They generally consist of a trial-and-error process in which unprecedented policy settings are tested in the real world for effectiveness. As any competent laboratory scientist knows, such ad-hoc experiments entail significant risks.

Indeed, it is possible, if not probable, that policy experimentation of this sort, as typified by low central bank interest rates in developed markets and pegged currencies in emerging markets, has exacerbated the global imbalances that lie behind the 2008 crash and which remain a continuing challenge to the global economy.

"A free market was never meant to be a free licence to take whatever you can get, however you can get it." Barack Obama

Do you see the latest round of quantitative easing in the United States and Japan, and possibly also in the United Kingdom and Europe, as ultimately inflationary?

We see little risk that quantitative easing measures by developed market central banks will lead to a sustained rise in inflation over the next year or two. In fact our concerns are more tilted toward quantitative easing being not effective enough to stimulate final demand, especially as the current*experiment du jour* for developed markets is austerity and more austerity. We remain convinced that fiscal tightening will depress final demand in most places, and therefore we continue to believe in a low-inflation and disinflating growth environment in the developed world.

The tension this creates in foreign exchange markets might be labeled a "currency war" by some, but we see little likelihood of change in the short term. The big downside risks are an escalation into a trade war between the United States and China or serious overheating in the emerging world, but in the short term—over the next three to six months—there is little sign of this.

The boring message for markets from all this is that risks are building, but are unlikely to explode in the near term. This suggests that a combination of ample liquidity and cyclical bottoming in a low-growth range remain the most likely drivers of financial markets.

How does this impact investment markets?

For fixed-income this backdrop is constructive as the easy monetary policy stance anchors treasury yields at historically low levels and reduces the probability of a sustained sell-off in these markets. Persistent disinflation also helps, as it suggests that the risks to (market-implied) inflation expectations are tilted downward. This leads us to hold on to a modest overweight in treasuries and a preferences for nominal paper (standard bonds with no index-linking) over inflation-linked bonds, which we are neutral on.

Higher-yielding corporate credit and emerging market debt are attractive at present on the back of ample market liquidity and strong corporate and emerging market fundamentals. One has to be cautious over the prospects for investment-grade corporate credit since this sector has considerable exposure to the financial sector, which is peculiarly sensitive at present to event risks and has little capacity to absorb surprise shocks.

Signs of cyclical bottoming in the global economy, with many economies now showing at least weak growth, are likely to continue to benefit emerging market debt and high-yield corporate bonds.

This return to some growth momentum in the global economy is supported by data in recent months which show that global retail sales have started to reaccelerate again somewhat. In fact retail sales are increasing at a pace that is now well above the momentum in global industrial production. This means that production growth should soon start to follow the pickup in sales, and recent rises in the global purchasing managers' indexes (PMI) are a good sign here.

From a developed world perspective, it is particularly reassuring to see the momentum in the US economy improving somewhat from the lull observed between May and September 2010. Third-quarter GDP growth was revised up from 2.0 to 2.5% on an annualized quarter-on-quarter basis (which we view as being around potential growth) and fourth-quarter GDP growth will probably print around 4% on the back of stronger consumer demand.

In fact the level of net exports is now almost exactly following the script laid out by the recoveries in the early 1990s and early 2000s. This still implies a substantial underperformance relative to the average post-recession recovery in domestic final sales between 1950 and 1982.

With global sales showing gains, are you encouraged by the levels of consumer spending in developed markets?

By far the biggest component of final sales is, of course, consumer spending. In the third quarter this advanced by 2.8% quarter-on-quarter, annualized. The prime driver behind the improved consumption outlook is probably the improvement in personal income growth in the United States, which in nominal terms reached 4.1% year-on-year in October, the fastest pace in more than two years. If the recent improvement in the labor market continues (and the trend decline in initial claims suggests that it will!), then US households may well continue to benefit from further gains in real income growth—which is also supported by the fact that inflation continues to slide further. Recent gains in asset prices could even induce a moderate decrease in the savings rate, which currently stands at 5.7%.

Is there any evidence of inflation attending these growth signals?

The existence of a large amount of slack, in terms of overcapacity, means that the economy can grow well above potential for a very long time before price pressures start to build. Disinflation continues unabated. In October 2010, the core consumer price index fell by 0.01% month-on-month, driving the year-on-year rate down to just 0.6%, the lowest rate of inflation in the United States since the series began in the 1950s.

The tail risks in the global economy mentioned earlier are actually a question of a double impossible trinity. Such a trinity consists of three things that are considered desirable, but of which only two can be realized simultaneously. On the global level emerging market economies struggle with the trinity of free capital flows, (semi-) fixed exchange rates, and monetary independence. The risks attached to this stem from their dealing with surges in capital inflows on the back of the US quantitative easing via capital controls and sterilized interventions.

In the medium term, capital flows could create asset price bubbles and inflation in some emerging markets. Also, there is a medium-term risk of a proliferation of protectionism.

Meanwhile, the European Economic and Monetary Union (EMU) struggles with its own impossible trinity of sovereign debt as policymakers try to position themselves on the triangle of "no exit", "no default," and "no bailout." The crisis forced policymakers to give up on the "no bailout" corner of the triangle. Funds disbursed by the European Financial Stability Facility (EFSF) are formally a loan, but because there is no seniority with respect to existing debt-holders it may still turn into a (partial) one-off fiscal transfer in the case of a sovereign default. Also, the European Central Bank (ECB) was forced into (indirect) monetary financing of peripheral debt, which is of course a form of bailout by the central bank.

EMU policymakers clearly feel that this is not a permanent solution. The ECB wants to prevent sovereign and financial sector addiction to central bank-provided liquidity. This explains its desire to tighten fiscal policy by stealth and to push the peripheral ball firmly into the court of fiscal policy. Meanwhile, nonperipheral governments would probably have a very hard time explaining a further bailout to their voters.

The "no exit" principle will probably also be maintained because of the political will to move forward with the European project. One should not underestimate the importance the European political leaders and intellectual elite attach to political reconciliation and integration. This desire appears to be passed from one generation of leaders to the next. In this respect we do well to

"There are different ways to organise capitalism. Free-market capitalism is only one of them and not a very good one at that." Ha-Joon Chang

remember the words of Jean Monnet, one of the founding fathers of the European Union, who said: "Europe will be forged in crises, and will be the sum of the solutions adopted for those crises." All this is not to say that there will never be an exit. However, we regard this as a tail risk which could, for instance, be triggered by the rise of populist governments that take nonrational decisions.

So it seems that by default EMU policymakers have ended up scrapping the "no default" principle. It has now been decided that the European Stability Mechanism (ESM) will be installed as a successor to the EFSF in 2013. Actually, the ESM seems to be very much a continuation of the EFSF. The difference from the current liquidity mechanism is that, on application, there will be a rigorous analysis of debt sustainability by the EC, the IMF, and the ECB. On that basis the Euro Group (consisting of the finance ministers of Eurozone countries) will then decide by unanimous vote whether to provide assistance or whether the debt should be restructured.

All post-2013 EMU debt will be subject to standardized and identical collective action clauses to facilitate orderly restructuring. Also, and in contrast to the current EFSF, any loans will enjoy preferred creditor status. The ESM will only apply to debt issued after 2013, because of which no defaults should be expected until that date.

All in all, the ESM should be seen as an important step forward, consistent with the political will among Europe's leaders to preserve EMU. The situation is reminiscent of the exchange rate mechanism (ERM) crisis of the early 1990s, when many pundits thought that European monetary integration would morph into substantial disintegration. Europe defied those expectations and moved forward instead!

However, there are still risks. Politicians try to separate two things: resolution of the current crisis; and creation of a framework to deal with future crises in an orderly way. However, in practice the separation between pre- and post-2013 debt is to some extent artificial. By 2013 many peripheral states will not yet have achieved debt sustainability (defined as a primary balance that stabilizes the debt-to-GDP ratio), and part of the existing debt will need to be rolled over to after 2013. Because of this, there is a risk that the ESM will cause risk premia to rise, eliciting the kind of self-fulfilling prophecies that we have seen this year.

As a result, there is still a risk that the current outstanding debt cannot be serviced fully, which is exactly what makes market participants so nervous. It is not yet clear how the European Union will deal with this. In the end, some kind of subsidy by core Europe to the periphery will probably be inevitable. The question is what form of subsidy will be politically feasible. We would argue that an implicit subsidy in the form of extended cheap borrowing costs (cutting the rates of EFSF/ESM) is more likely than a direct fiscal transfer.

What is your opinion of the Irish bailout in November 2010?

It was encouraging to see that policymakers are demonstrating an increasing degree of flexibility. The details of the Irish bailout were disclosed on the same day that the ESM was announced. Probably because Ireland had already put a lot of effort into reining in its deficit, no further conditionality was imposed and the Irish government was given one more year to bring its budget deficit below 3%. Furthermore, the external part of the €85 billion support package will only be €67.5 billion, with the remainder coming from the Irish government's cash reserves and the National Pension Reserve Fund. An amount of €10 billion will be used for immediate further bank recapitalization, thus putting the total bill at 35% of Irish GDP, while €25 billion will be put into a contingency fund which can be tapped for possible further bank recapitalization in the future.

The concerns with the Irish bailout, however, lie in the way the dynamics play out between Ireland's program of austerity and its hopes for generating some economic and revenue growth to pay down its debt. If the austerity package crushes growth and shrinks revenues to the government, it is difficult to see how Ireland could avoid default short of an outright transfer of funds from the European Union. As we have said, the run-up to 2013 is going to create some interesting tensions for European debt.

MORE INFO

Books:

Akerlof, George A., and Robert J. Shiller. *Animal Spirits: How Human Psychology Drives the Economy, and Why It Matters for Global Capitalism*. Princeton, NJ: Princeton University Press, 2009.

Kindleberger, Charles P., and Robert Z. Aliber. *Manias, Panics, and Crashes: A History of Financial Crises*. 6th ed. Basingstoke, UK: Palgrave Macmillan, 2011.

Koo, Richard C. *The Holy Grail of Macroeconomics: Lessons from Japan's Great Recession*. Singapore: Wiley, 2008.

Krugman, Paul. *The Return of Depression Economics and the Crisis of 2008*. London: Penguin, 2008.

Krugman, Paul R., Maurice Obstfeld, and Marc J. Melitz. *International Economics: Theory & Policy*. 9th ed. Boston, MA: Pearson Addison-Wesley, 2011.

Mankiw, N. Gregory. *Principles of Economics*. 6th ed. Mason, OH: South-Western Cengage Learning, 2011.

Reinhart, Carmen M., and Kenneth S. Rogoff. *This Time Is Different: Eight Centuries of Financial Folly*. Princeton, NJ: Princeton University Press, 2009.

See Also:

★ The Globalization of Inflation (pp. 184–185)

★ Viewpoint: The Challenges to Slow Growth in the Advanced Economies Just Keep Coming (pp. 147–148)

★ Viewpoint: Deleveraging, Deflation, and Rebalancing in the Global Economy (pp. 158–160)

★ Viewpoint: Steering Between Deflation and Inflation—A Troubled Road for Developed Economies (pp. 604–606)

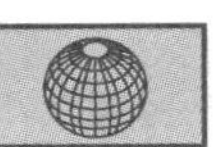

The Emergence and Development of Islamic Banking

by Umar Oseni and M. Kabir Hassan

EXECUTIVE SUMMARY

- Islamic banking is an interest-free banking system which emerged on the global scene barely four decades ago.
- The definition of the Islamic banking system is essentially a banking system that complies with the economic value system of Islam.
- The Islamic banking business has emerged as an ethical banking system which is designed to cater for the interests of about a quarter of the world's population.
- Islamic banks engage in three major services: free services; services rendered by banks on fixed exchange, commission, or discount; and creation and development of funds.
- The development of the Islamic banking system has demonstrated its potential to be used as a viable global financial intermediary.
- The crystallization of the Islamic banking system in the 21st century has made it a force to be reckoned with to avert any future global economic crunch.

INTRODUCTION

As an alternative banking system, Islamic banking emerged in the global landscape with the advent of Islam. This form of interest-free banking has developed over a long period of time with the introduction of new products in the industry. The crystallization of interest-free banking based on Islamic legal principles has won a positive global image for Islamic banking in the modern world. The underlying philosophy in Islamic banking is to facilitate financial intercourse and spur symbiotic commercial relations that will ultimately bring benefit to the parties involved. One must work for whatever he or she earns in the long run. According to Rodney Wilson, "The Islamic banking industry has grown rapidly since the 1970s, reflecting the demand by pious Muslims to manage their finances in a way that avoids interest and complies with Islamic law" (Wilson, 2006). This emerging discipline of banking business in the modern world has reached a crescendo where it has become a force to be reckoned with in the global banking business. The best practices in the Islamic banking industry are worth exploring with a view to harmonizing practices in global banking to strengthen the world economy.

It is, however, important to emphasize that Islamic banking and Islamic finance are two inextricable disciplines in Islamic commercial law, but it is believed by most experts that the former is a subset of the later. Meanwhile, the global banking business needs several alternative banking models in order to cushion the effects of economic meltdown that may arise in the future. The experiences of Islamic banking in Muslim countries as well as Muslim-inhabited countries in Europe and America have been very encouraging, even though some problems were encountered at the outset (Hassan, 1999). The emergence and development of Islamic banking in the modern world has witnessed dramatic changes, especially in the recent global financial plummet. As an urgent step toward cushioning the effects of the global financial crisis, American International Group Inc. (AIG) had to offer Islamic insurance to the United States. This was after it had earlier reached two major bailout agreements, worth US$152.5 billion in taxpayer dollars. As a further move to step up its deals, AIG has established subsidiaries in some Muslim-majority countries such as Bahrain, Malaysia, and the United Arab Emirates. It is axiomatic to observe that Islamic insurance (*takaful*) is an aspect of Islamic finance which was one of the Islamic financial mechanisms embraced during the troubled times that engulfed most financialcum-insurance heavyweights in recent years.

EMERGENCE OF ISLAMIC BANKING

Although Islamic banking was practiced during the classical period, the modern experiment of profit and risk-sharing business, which is the cornerstone of Islamic banking business, was first undertaken in 1963 in Mit Ghamr, a city in the Nile Delta in Egypt. "Its purpose was to explore the possibilities of mobilizing local savings and credits as an essential requirement for socioeconomic development in the area." (El Naggar, 2005). The ripple effects of this successful experiment were felt in some other Muslim countries after some years. "Few years before the bank consolidated its services in 1981, other banks such as the Islamic Development (IDB) and Dubai Islamic Bank opened their doors to customers in 1975. Also, Malaysia followed suit with the enactment of the Islamic Banking Act 1983. This brought about the establishment of the first formal financial institution in Malaysia in 1983 known as the Bank Islam Malaysia Berhad (BIMB)" (Oseni, 2009). The Islamic banking and finance industry has continued to grow in leaps and bounds over the years. The industry grows at a rate of 10–15% per year (Khan *et al.*, 2007). It is now the fastest-growing segment of the global financial system, with the unremitting establishment of Islamic banks in the Muslim world and beyond.

WHAT IS ISLAMIC BANKING?

In simplified form, Islamic banking and finance can be defined as "banking and finance in consonance with the ethos and value system of Islam. Hence, it is governed, in addition to the conventional good governance and risk management rules, by the principles laid down by the Islamic *Sharī'ah*" (Ayub, 2007). In a similar vein, it has been described as "a financial institution whose statutes, rules and procedures expressly state its commitment to the principles of Islamic *Sharī'ah* (Jurisprudence) and forbids of the receipt and payment of interest on any of its transaction" (Islam, 2006). This is the nature of the Islamic banking business. Although interest is proscribed in Islamic banking business, there are specific avenues through which the bank gets its returns. One may wonder how Islamic banks make profits and ensure that they stay in business. In general, banking services can be classified into three categories: free services; services rendered on fixed exchange, commission, or discount; and the creation and development of funds. In Islam, free services are part of the role of banks, so they are required to render this service as part of their customer care service, which is in line with the spirit of Islamic commercial transactions (for example, benevolent loans without interest). The second category of services, which attract some sort of commission, fixed charge, or fee, is considered an important source of income for banks. Therefore the sources of funding for Islamic banks are mainly owner's equity, deposits, and special funds. This is illustrated in Table 1.

     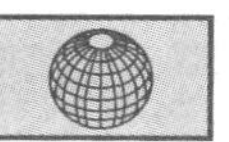   

Table 1. Sources of deployment of bank funds. (*Source*: Islam, 2006)

Sources of funds	Use of funds
1. Owner's equity } = Total fund	
2. Deposits }(a) Current account	1. Deployment of funds (a) *Qard al-hasanah* (i) Overdraft } = Where PLS method is not possible (ii) Cash credit application } (iii) Demand loan (iv) Priority sectors, individuals, and the poor
(b) Profit/loss sharing accounts	(b) Profit/loss sharing investments (i) Equity financing (ii) Leasing (iii) Hire purchase (iv) Normal rate of return
	(c) Direct investment by banks (i) Bank's own projects (ii) Investment auctioning (iii) Commodity trade (iv) Spot transaction in foreign exchange (v) *Bai-muajjal* (vi) *Bai-salam* (vii) Discounting equity
Special 3. (a) *Zakat* (c) Social welfare fund	2. *Zakat* (a) Charity to target groups (b) Project for eligible target groups

WHY THE ISLAMIC BANKING SYSTEM?

The Islamic banking system is unique, with its own features. Even though some of the products look similar to conventional modes of finance, there is a need for an alternative banking system to suit the needs of Muslims and non-Muslims alike who prefer the interest-free option. The global banking system must have alternatives for all sorts of customers with different religious and sociocultural backgrounds. Against this backdrop, the Islamic banking business has emerged as an ethical banking system that is primarily intended to cater for the interests of about one-fourth of the world's population. The universal welfare and profit and loss sharing principles of Islamic banking are meant for humankind. The need for Islamic banking in the modern world cannot be overemphasized. "Modern businesses need huge amounts of funds, while people at large have mostly small savings. This necessitates the presence of such financial intermediary institutions through which business needs can be directly and indirectly fulfilled with savers' pooled money in such a way that savers/investors can also get a just return on their investments and business and industry can get the funds required for ensuring a sufficient supply of goods and services for the welfare of mankind" (Ayub, 2007). This is the value-added feature of Islamic banks that makes them a socially responsible financial intermediary within the economy.

ESSENTIAL REQUIREMENTS FOR ISLAMIC BANKING

The Islamic banking system is an integral part of the Islamic economic system. Provided that certain key requirements are complied with, Islamic banking can be established in any part of the world. Hussain Lawai identified nine essential requirements for a successful Islamic banking system. According to him, for a successful Islamic banking system, there must be: a supportive legal framework and swift judicial system; disciplined entrepreneurship; a conceptual change from credit risk to overall risk management; strong ethical values; a Supreme *Shariah* Council; uniform accounting standards, committed management, and a progressive and modern outlook; and a body to evaluate Islamic financial institutions (Lawai, 1994). The principles of Islamic banking as contained in the Qur'an and the *Sunnah* are summarized thus: any predetermined payment over and above the actual amount of principal is prohibited, and the lender must share in the profits or losses arising from the enterprise for which the money was lent (except in benevolent loans). Making money from money is not allowed since it is a mere medium of exchange that has no value in itself, transactions involving *gharar* (deception) and *maysir* (gambling) are prohibited, and investments should only support practices or products that are not forbidden or even discouraged by Islam (Ahmad and Hassan, 2007).

BRIEF OVERVIEW OF MODES OF FINANCING IN ISLAMIC BANKING

There are numerous modes of financing in Islamic banking. Many more products are being certified periodically by the *shariah* advisory councils of the banks to meet the modern challenges posed by the conventional banking system. The modes of financing in Islamic banking are based on certain terminologies introduced by Muslim jurists. Although it may not be necessary to examine each of the modes of financing in Islamic banking, it suffices to give an overview of some of the notable modes of financing. Table 2 gives a general outline of some basic terminologies in Islamic

MAKING IT HAPPEN

The Islamic banking business is becoming more complex, with new products appearing from time to time. Stakeholders in the Islamic financial industry must face the challenges headlong if contemporary demands are to be met. The process begins with the introduction of a robust legal framework to strengthen Islamic financial houses.

- The regulatory challenges posed by the Islamic banking business must be addressed to further enhance the productivity of the business.
- The duties of the *shariah* advisory councils should be properly defined to ensure the efficiency of their work.
- A proper framework must be formulated to ensure a sustainable means of dispute resolution for the banks. Legal reforms may be required here to further streamline practices in the industry.
- Amicable resolution of disputes arising from customer–banker relationships should be encouraged, backed up by an arbitral tribunal of industry experts.
- Support should be given to a degree of standardization in the Islamic banking industry through uniform practices that are generally agreed by Muslim jurists and experts in the field.
- Care should be taken to see that products are genuine and do not simply mimic conventional products.

"Economists may not know how to run the economy, but they know how to create shortages or gluts simply by regulating prices below the market, or artificially supporting them from above." Milton Friedman

  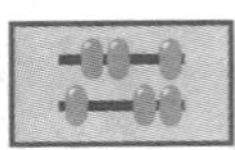   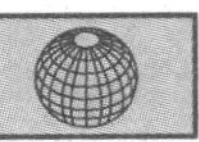   

Table 2. Islamic banking: basic terminology. (*Sources*: Errico and Farrahbaksh, 1998, and El-Hawary *et al.*, 2004)

Term	Explanation
Amanah (Demand deposits)	Deposits held at the bank for safekeeping purposes. Their capital value is guaranteed and they earn no return.
Bay mu'ajal (Predelivery, deferred payment)	The seller can sell a product on the basis of a deferred payment, in installments or in a lump sum. The price of the product is agreed upon between the buyer and the seller at the time of the sale and cannot include any charges for deferring payment.
Bay salam (Prepayment, deferred delivery)	The buyer pays the seller the full negotiated price of a product that the seller promises to deliver at a future date.
Ijarah (Lease, lease purchase)	A party leases a particular product for a specific sum and a specific time period. In the case of a lease purchase, each payment includes a portion that goes toward the final purchase and transfer of ownership of the product.
Istisna'a (Deferred payment, deferred delivery)	A manufacturer (contractor) agrees to produce (build) and to deliver a certain good (or premise) at a given price on a given date in the future. The price does not have to be paid in advance (in contrast to *bai salam*). It may be paid in installments or part may be paid in advance with the balance to be paid later, based on the preferences of the parties.
Ju'ala (Service charge)	One party pays another a specified amount of money as a fee for rendering a specific service in accordance with the terms of the contract stipulated between the two parties. This mode usually applies to transactions such as consultations and professional services, fund placements, and trust services.
Kafalah	A pledge given to a creditor that the debtor will pay the debt, fine, or liability. A third party stands surety for the payment of the debt if unpaid by the person originally liable.
Mudarabah (Trustee finance contract)	The *Rabb-ul-mal* (owner of the capital) provides the entire capital needed to finance a project, while the entrepreneur offers his or her labor and expertise. Profits are shared between them at a certain fixed ratio, whereas financial losses are exclusively borne by the *rabb-ul-mal*. The liability of the entrepreneur is limited only to his/her time and effort.
Murabahah (Markup financing)	The seller informs the buyer of his or her cost of acquiring or producing a specified product. The profit margin is then negotiated between them. The total cost is usually paid in installments.
Musharakah (Equity participation)	The bank enters into an equity partnership agreement with one or more partners to jointly finance an investment project. Profits (and losses) are shared strictly in relation to the respective capital contributions.
Qard hasana (Beneficence loans)	These are zero-return loans that the Qur'an encourages Muslims to make to the needy. Banks are allowed to charge borrowers a service fee to cover the administrative expenses of handling the loan. The fee should not be related to the loan amount or maturity.

banking upon which the modes of financing are built.

BEST PRACTICE: THE CRYSTALLIZATION OF ISLAMIC BANKING

It goes without saying that best practice in the Islamic banking industry must be standardized and universalized with a degree of benchmarking. The development of the Islamic banking system has demonstrated its potential to be used as a viable global financial intermediary (Siddiqi, 1988). The sustainable and profitable practice of Islamic banking is based on ethical norms of Islamic financial transactions (*fiqh mu'amalat*). The banking operations have "positive socio-economic implications through real sector development and just and equitable pricing policies, in addition to cost efficiency and profit adequacy" (Ayub, 2007).

CONCLUSION

With the gradual shrinking of world banking toward a global hamlet, it is important to emphasize the growing need for the recognition of more Islamic banking products to prepare for the likelihood of any future economic crunch. The crystallization of the Islamic banking business in the 21st century has made it a force to be reckoned with in the world economy. The Islamic banking business is not only meant for Muslims; non-Muslims have patronized Islamic banks as shareholders and customers in many countries across the world, and many are still transacting business with them. The recent global economic crunch, and the quick adoption of some Islamic finance products by some giant corporations, is an important example of the dire necessity and unfeigned relevance of Islamic banking and finance in global finance. Islamic banking has indeed survived the test of time as a viable global financial intermediary in the world economy.

  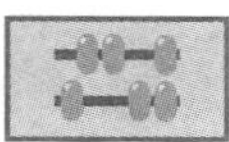      

MORE INFO

Books:

Ayub, Muhammad. *Understanding Islamic Finance*. Hoboken, NJ: Wiley, 2007.

El Naggar, Ahmed A. "Islamic bank in Egypt: A model and the challenge." In Ataul Huq Pramanik (ed). *Islamic Banking: How Far Have We Gone?* Kuala Lumpur: International Islamic University Malaysia, 2006; 247–259.

Iqbal, Munawar, and David Llewellyn (eds). *Islamic Banking and Finance: New Perspectives on Profit-Sharing and Risk*. Cheltenham, UK: Edward Elgar, 2002.

Islam, Tajul. "Mechanics of Islamic banking." In Ataul Huq Pramanik. *Islamic Banking: How Far Have We Gone?* Kuala Lumpur: International Islamic University Malaysia, 2006; 127–142.

Lewis, Mervyn, and Latifa Algaoud. *Islamic Banking*. Cheltenham, UK: Edward Elgar, 2001.

Oseni, Umar A. *Dispute Resolution in Islamic Banking and Finance: Common Trends and Future Perspectives*. Kuala Lumpur: International Islamic University Malaysia, 2009.

Siddiqi, Muhammad Nejatullah. "Islamic banking: Theory and practice." In Mohamed Ariff (ed). *Islamic Banking in Southeast Asia*. Singapore: Institute of Southeast Asian Studies, 1988; 34–66.

Vogel, Frank, and Samuel Hayes. *Islamic Law and Finance*. The Hague, The Netherlands: Kluwer Law International, 1998.

Articles:

Ahmad, Abu Umar Faruq, and M. Kabir Hassan. "Riba and Islamic banking." *Journal of Islamic Economics, Banking and Finance* 3:1 (2007): 1–33.

Hassan, M. Kabir. "Islamic banking in theory and practice: The experience of Bangladesh." *Managerial Finance* 25:5 (1999): 60–113.

Khan, Mohammad Saif Noman, M. Kabir Hassan, and Abdullah Ibneyy Shahid. "Banking behavior of Islamic bank customers in Bangladesh." *Journal of Islamic Economics, Banking and Finance* 3:2 (2007): 159–194.

Khan, Mohsin S., and Abbas Mirakhor. "The framework and practice of Islamic banking." *Finance and Development* 23:3 (1986): 32–36.

Lawai, Hussain. "Key features of Islamic banking." *Journal of Islamic Banking and Finance* 11:4 (1994): 7–13.

Wilson, Rodney. "Regulatory challenges facing the Islamic finance industry." *Journal of Financial Transformation* (2006): 140–143.

Reports:

Chapra, M. Umer, and Tariqullah Khan. "Regulation and supervision of islamic banks." Occasional paper no. 3. Islamic Research and Training Institute, Islamic Development Bank, 2000.

Čihák, Martin, and Heiko Hesse. "Islamic banks and financial stability: An empirical analysis." Working paper 08/16. International Monetary Fund, 2008. Online at: www.imf.org/external/pubs/cat/longres.cfm?sk=21594.0

El-Hawary, Dhalia, Wafik Grais, and Zamir Iqbal, "Regulating Islamic financial institutions: The nature of the regulated." Policy research working paper WPS3227. World Bank, March 2004.

Errico, Luca, and Mitra Farrahbaksh. "Islamic banking: Issues in prudential regulation and supervision." Working paper 98/30. International Monetary Fund, 1998.

Iqbal, Zubair, and Abbas Mirakhor. "Islamic banking." Occasional paper no. 49. International Monetary Fund, 1987.

See Also:

★ The International Role of Islamic Finance (pp. 192–195)
★ Islamic Finance and the Global Financial Crisis (pp. 199–201)
★ Viewpoint: *Shariah* Law—Bringing a New Ethical Dimension to Banking (pp. 242–243)
✔ Key Islamic Banking Instruments and How They Work (p. 1010)
✔ Key Principles of Islamic Finance (p. 1011)

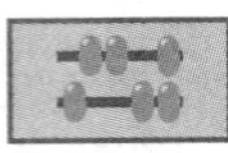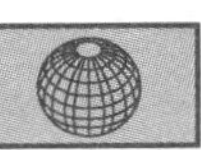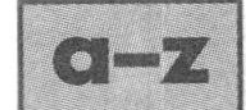

Viewpoint: Energy Self-Sufficiency through Shale Gas Changes the Game for the United States

by Angelos Damaskos

INTRODUCTION

Angelos Damaskos is founder and CEO of Sector Investment Managers (SIM), an FSA-authorized and regulated investment advisory company, and portfolio manager for SIM's Junior Oils Trust. Junior Oils Trust, launched in October 2004, focuses its investments in smaller oil and gas equities and grew from a launch net asset value size of £3.7 million to in excess of £67 million by February 2011. In 2009 Damaskos and SIM launched Junior Gold, an FSA-authorized and regulated open-ended investment company concentrating on gold and other precious metals mining equities.

Damaskos graduated in 1985 from the University of Glasgow with a degree in mechanical engineering and in 1989 obtained a MBA from the University of Sheffield. He has more than 14 years' investment banking experience with major banks in London, concentrating on natural resources. Most recently he worked with the European Bank for Reconstruction and Development with responsibility for some of the bank's equity investments in Russia.

The radiation leaks at Japan's Fukushima reactors following the earthquake and tsunami in March 2011 appear to be causing several countries to rethink their attitude to nuclear power. How do you view the potential impact on industry, which needs reliable power generation?

The possibility of a reactor meltdown has always been the worst nightmare of everyone in the nuclear industry and, indeed, outside it. We have to understand, though, that the Fukushima reactors were an old design, one that has been in operation since the 1970s. This design requires electrical pumps to drive the coolant water, and when power was lost after the tsunami took out the backup diesel generators, coolant could not be pumped and the reactors began to overheat. In the modern design you have a passive cooling system that works on the basis of conduction and by recirculating the water within the reactor using latent heat.

Germany has suspended operations at six nuclear reactors and is going to tighten up heavily on safety requirements, which may well delay the construction of new reactors. China is building 45 reactors of the passive cooling type. However, it has now announced that it wants to shift some of its future generation capacity away from nuclear, as a direct reaction to the Japanese crisis. Instead it will look to renewable generation, primarily wind, to make up the difference. But nuclear continues to be a significant part of their generation plans, so this is certainly not the end for nuclear power.

The point, however, is that nuclear power plants are hugely expensive, costing anything between US$4 and 5 billion to build, and they take up to eight years to complete. And by the time they are completed, whatever design they are based on will have been to an extent superseded by newer technology. So "old" is not necessarily the same as "bad." What is clear is that modern economies need electricity and power if they are going to thrive, and if we want to reduce carbon emission, nuclear power looks like a very big part of the equation. For fast-growing economies like China there is no alternative other than to incorporate nuclear into the mix, or their carbon emissions will grow at a frightening pace.

The Japanese situation was unprecedented. We now know that, because of the contours of the land, the tsunami was 14.5 m high when it struck the plant, and not just 7.6 m, as it was when it hit the coast. Who could have envisaged such a wave swamping and devastating the Fukushima pumping system?

From the perspective of the oil and gas industry, the positive thing to emerge from this disaster is that there will be an increased demand for gas-fired electricity generation. We can expect Japanese imports of liquefied natural gas (LNG) to go up as a result, and that demand in other Asian countries will grow too. There are very big LNG export facilities in the Middle East, and Australia is building some massive LNG terminals to meet demand from China. These should come onstream in the next few years. Whether the United States, with its vast shale gas reserves, will move into LNG export is very difficult to predict. Some licenses have already been granted, but building new plant to liquefy natural gas is hugely expensive. However, if the US production of shale gas ramps up massively, the economics might justify export.

At the same time, given the revolutions that are spreading through the Arab world—rocking even such an autocratic and despotic regime as Syria and disturbing Saudi Arabia—it seems clear that a generation of internet-aware citizens in that part of the world is much less inclined to accept arguments appealing to religion and tradition to explain their exclusion from the decision-making process. Over time the whole of the Persian Gulf area is likely to get caught up in this process of change. One result is that oil companies with reserves in safe political regions will attract an increasing premium as the turmoil in the Middle East grows. One obvious strategy for investors, and certainly one that we have been following, is to invest in such companies while holding significant reserves of cash to enable one to buy in to such weaknesses as might appear. Oil company bonds with a low risk of default are another way of generating reliable returns, with aggregate yields of 12.5% very achievable, along with lower volatility than one would get from an equity portfolio.

In Europe the gas price is quite tightly coupled to the price of oil. What would more gas generation plant being installed as older nuclear plants are retired do to the price of gas?

There is no one global price for gas. The gas futures industry draws its pricing from the Henry Hub futures exchange in the United States. In June 2008, when we saw oil at US$147 per barrel, gas prices were at a high of US$13.00 per 1,000 cubic feet. They have been declining ever since, to an all-time low of US$2.4 in August 2009.

"This administration made decisions that allowed the free market to operate as a barroom brawl instead of a prize fight." L. William Seidman

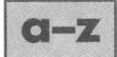

However, this is a purely North American phenomenon, and the low gas prices—somewhere around US$4 in March 2011—are a function of too much supply. Gas and a range of oil companies, including the majors such as Exxon, are competing for prime position in the US shale gas market, and acquiring shale gas acreage is now a big part of the game. In Europe and the United Kingdom, natural gas is the fuel of choice for power generation as well as for residential and industrial heating, so we see gas prices remaining firm there for the foreseeable future. Russia has huge supplies of natural gas, so supply is not an issue for Europe, other than the political risk. However, the United Kingdom, which is now a net importer of natural gas, is presently constrained by the capacity of the pipelines that bring gas into the country. There have been several initiatives to develop temporary gas storage capacity to offset this, primarily underground in depleted oil fields, to help cope with peak demand. There may also be projects coming forward for more permanent gas storage terminals. The point about gas, versus oil, is that it is a very easy fuel to handle and is easy to distribute to many consumer points. Moreover, unlike oil, it does not have to go through an expensive refining process. However, you need big infrastructure changes before it can be used as a fuel for transport.

To what extent do you see renewables playing a major role in US power production through the next decade or so?

There is strong support right now for solar power in the United States and we are seeing some quite extensive new installations for solar generation. Clearly this has all the advantages of a "home-grown" industry and acts to reduce energy imports, which is positive for the US balance of trade, although currently not in a hugely significant way. But we see the cost of solar panels dropping significantly over the next year or two. This will make it much more economically viable for industrial premises and residential estates to do a lot more local power generation. What goes for the United States goes for many other parts of the world too, so we see solar power becoming increasingly important. We think that wind power, while important, is probably limited in terms of its share of global power generation since it is expensive and more difficult than solar power both to push through planning and to install. Without quite high subsidies, much of the currently installed base of wind farms around the world does not make economic sense. This is not true of solar power, and as the cost of solar panels falls it will be even less so. The United States already has massive fields of solar panels, and you get a direct and immediate input into the local grid. If the power is consumed by local industry and population centers, it makes excellent economic sense, particularly in states with plenty of sun like Texas.

On shale gas, how do you see this being played as an investment proposition?

One way of taking a position would be to invest in the oil majors, most of which are involved in and very committed to shale gas extraction. However, we do not particularly like investing in oil majors for the simple reason that much of their balance sheet is invested in the associated infrastructure that goes with oil and gas production. This infrastructure is completely unresponsive to upward movements in the oil price, which means that a large chunk of their balance sheets does not respond to increased oil prices. That acts as a drag on returns from an investor's perspective.

For this reason we prefer to invest in oil companies that are at a much earlier stage in their development, with less infrastructure on their balance sheets, such as Talisman Energy. We have exposure to that type of company. There has been a great deal of corporate activity across the United States buying or leasing land that has potential for shale gas production, and that too provides investment opportunity.

However, one has to be aware that the market is very much at a positioning stage right now. Analysis shows that from a production perspective the marginal profitability of shale gas is US$5–6 per 1,000 cubic feet, so, considered purely from a present-day standpoint, shale gas is not profitable. In order to invest in this sector you have to take a long-term view and wait for the gas price to recover.

For those companies that want to be big players in shale gas there is no option. They have to invest right now and take an early position or they simply will not be able to get into the game. So they are looking to their operations in a few years time to subsidize their current production and asset acquisition phase. However, with a positive view of gas prices over the next few years, they can continue to accelerate their production and their shale reserves. So we look to hold companies that have a large acreage in shale gas plays, knowing that this acreage will make them very attractive as acquisition targets for the majors over the next few years. We have seen transactions done in areas neighboring these companies' holdings at high multiples, so we are very optimistic.

Environmentally, shale gas production is attracting considerable controversy, with allegations that it pollutes the water table, the rivers, and the local environment. Could that be a "show stopper" going forward?

If we start from the basics, shale gas is held in dense, relatively impermeable rock formations, so the gas is trapped in the rock and unable to flow to the surface. Many of the biggest reserves of shale gas in the United States, such as the belt running from Louisiana through to Texas, are typically far away from residential areas. However, the Marcellus Shale in New York State, on which much of the controversy over shale gas production centers, is different. Much of the production there is very close to residential areas and protests were inevitable. The controversy centers on the production technique, known as hydrofracturing, or "hydrofracking." This involves drilling a deep vertical well, then drilling a long horizontal hole through the shale at the bottom of the vertical drop. Water is then pumped at high pressure down the well into the horizontal hole, where it fractures the shale.

The water contains a "filler," sand, which stops the cracks in the shale from resealing and allows the gas to flow from the shale. However, it also contains additives, and the shale gas production companies do not like to reveal their individual formulae for the fluids that are pumped down the well. They claim that this protects their competitive advantage and that the formulations are their intellectual property, much as Coca-Cola claims that its recipe for Coke is its unique property. The protestors claim that the formulae used in hydrofracking are hazardous to health and to the soil. In our view, however, it is clear that extensive studies on the potential dangers from hydrofracking have provided no conclusive evidence of damage to health or the environment. Indeed, since the vertical wells go way down below the porous rock layers into the dense shale, the only possibility of, say, methane, one of the most potent of the greenhouse gases, escaping is if the upper few hundred feet of the well is poorly cemented in.

Given industry best practice, we do not see substantive issues—and given that, thanks to the sheer scale of the country's shale gas reserves, we are talking here about energy self-sufficiency for the United States for the next 100 years, we cannot see protests proving a serious block to production. As Talisman points out in its account of hydrofracking, the additives typically amount to 0.5% of the total fluid used and are there to prevent bacteria building up, to lubricate the fracking

process, and to prevent scale deposits that could otherwise build up on piping and equipment. A portion of the water used in hydrofracking flows back to the surface and there have been protests, particularly in the Marcellus Shale area, around sites that have allowed runoff of this water into the Delaware River. However, best practice is to capture the emerging water and to remix and reuse it to cut down on the total water requirements involved in hydrofracking. So a good part of what we will probably see going forward will be regulations to enforce codes of best practice on producers. That may raise costs slightly, but we do not see it being a show stopper.

One of the difficulties for producers is that shale lease licenses typically have a "use it or lose it" clause, since the owner of the land, who is also the owner of the mineral rights, naturally wants to see the earliest possible returns from granting the license. However, a reasonably high percentage of the gas from a shale gas well is extracted within the first year or two, with subsequent annualized flows tailing down to a steady, but much lower, percentage. This creates a dilemma when gas prices are as low as at present, since producers from new wells are faced with having to take a significant percentage of their production to market at a time when prices are depressed, thereby contributing to the very gas glut that is depressing prices! So they are truly between a rock and a hard place at the moment, and there are going to be many producers that will not make it through gas prices that are below production costs to a period where they can expect US$7–8 per 1,000 cubic feet.

The reverse of this is that the United States has a once-in-a-lifetime year or two of extremely cheap energy prices at a time when the price of oil looks set to go much higher than US$120 a barrel in the near future—and prices of US$150 a barrel are possible if Saudi Arabian production is threatened by a spread of the unrest in North Africa. The next few years are going to be very interesting for energy analysts and for businesses that are large consumers of energy.

MORE INFO

Books:

Collins, Jim. *Good to Great: Why Some Companies Make the Leap ... And Others Don't*. New York: HarperCollins, 2001.

Fisher, Ken, with Jennifer Chou and Lara Hoffmans. *The Only Three Questions That Count: Investing by Knowing What Others Don't*. Hoboken, NJ: Wiley, 2007.

Rogers, Jim. *Adventure Capitalist: The Ultimate Road Trip*. New York: Random House, 2003.

Rogers, Jim. *Hot Commodities: How Anyone Can Invest Profitably in the World's Best Market*. New York: Random House, 2004.

Yergin, Daniel. *The Prize: The Epic Quest for Oil, Money & Power*. New York: Free Press, 2008.

See Also:

★ Viewpoint: Challenges in Global Energy and Their Potential Impact on the Cost of Energy (pp. 144–146)

Energy (pp. 1624–1626)

Oil and Gas (pp. 1638–1639)

  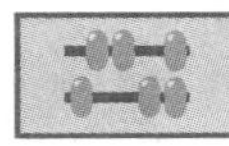   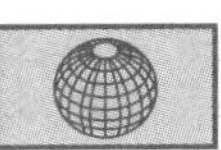   

Enterprise Risk Management and Solvency II

by Andy Davies

EXECUTIVE SUMMARY

- The key components of ERM;
- The dangers of overcomplicating processes;
- How policies, risk strategy, and risk appetite are set;
- Capital allocation and management;
- The implications of Solvency II.

INTRODUCTION

There is a great deal that the insurance sector has to come to terms with as it addresses the implications of Solvency II. There are broad general questions such as: What does it all mean? How will it be achieved and its requirements met? How much will it cost both from a capital and a monetary perspective? What resources are required? Then there is the related issue of how the International Financial Reporting Standards will fit with Solvency II.

ENTERPRISE RISK MANAGEMENT: CULTURE IS THE KEY

Rating agencies, analysts, shareholders, and regulators are all taking more interest in capital models and enterprise risk management (ERM). Effective ERM acts as the common thread that links balance sheet strength, operating performance and business profile." [1]

In an ideal ERM model, the risk management group will work with the board and all employees to ensure that their organization has effective ERM. It is fair to say that the majority of companies today have some form of ERM, but it is also true that for many this is an area that needs further development.

ERM is not about finding the perfect model; it is about having a strong risk-management culture which ensures that risk is understood, controlled, and effectively communicated. Effective ERM should be part of an insurance company's DNA.

The key components of ERM are:

- Aligning risk appetite and strategy;
- Enhancing risk response decisions;
- Reducing operational surprises and losses;
- Identifying and managing multiple and cross-enterprise risks;
- Seizing opportunities;
- Improving the deployment of capital.

Management should consider the company's risk appetite in evaluating its strategy, setting objectives, and developing mechanisms to manage related risks. ERM provides the rigour to identify and select alternative responses to risk—such as risk avoidance, risk reduction, risk sharing, and risk acceptance. Through ERM, companies enhance their ability to identify potential events and establish responses, thereby reducing surprises and associated costs or losses.

Every company faces a variety of risks that affect different parts of the organization, and ERM facilitates effective responses to such multiple risks. By considering a full range of potential events, management can identify and proactively realize opportunities.

Finally, obtaining robust risk information allows management to assess overall capital needs effectively and enhance capital allocation.

ERM AND SOLVENCY II

Solvency II is based on three "pillars." Pillar 1 is about capital requirements and the triggers for supervisory action. Pillar 2 focuses on the supervisory activities of regulators, based on organizational and governance requirements. Pillar 3 covers additional disclosures that supervisors may need to carry out their regulatory function. Under Solvency II, the concept of an "internal model" effectively refers to an enterprise-wide risk management framework. It covers both the quantitative requirements of Pillar 1 and the organizational and governance requirements of Pillar 2.

The broad thrust of an internal model is to use an economic capital model, accompanied by the embedding and effective management of risk, driven from the board to the front line.

It is important to remember the context and immediate historical backdrop against which the insurance sector is working. It is undeniable, for example, that the industry has had problems with risk assessment and modeling in recent years. The 2005 hurricane damage payouts and the current credit crisis put significant stress on capital and liquidity requirements for many companies. This makes discussion of capital adequacy regimes a very strong necessity, not just an academic exercise.

However, as insurance company boards try to square up to these issues—and there are many of them—there is a real danger of overcomplicating certain processes and of critical data being obscured by information overload. Having a complex model is no guarantee of success, as the crises experienced by several banks will testify. Instead, what is really critical is to ensure that the insurer's approach to risk management is simple enough for all staff to understand and engage with, and that it is also effective enough to add real value. The concept of "proportionality" is specifically enshrined within the proposed European Directive for Solvency II, so there is regulatory recognition that we do not need to overelaborate.

Risk management will only be fully effective if people throughout the organization receive clear, consistent messages from leadership and understand what they need to do. It starts at the top, and senior management need to develop a unified view, common language, policies, and appropriate governance structures.

The recent testimony of Paul Moore, former head of Group Regulatory Risk at HBOS, makes clear the importance of culture in risk management. Moore commented that: "Being an internal risk and compliance manager at the time felt a bit like being a man in a rowing boat trying to slow down an oil tanker." [2] If the culture is wrong, then even the most sophisticated model will be ineffective.

Markel Corporation, the company for which I work, is a relatively small company with 400 employees.[3] It therefore has a very flat organization structure, enabling close interaction between board and employees. This is very helpful as all employees can be given clear and consistent messages in a common language. We are committed to creating an environment in which risk is managed effectively. The Markel style, which articulates our core values, includes statements that "we will build the financial value of our company," which implies a steady, cautious approach to risk, and "we are encouraged to challenge management...we have the ability to make decisions or alter a course quickly," which empowers discussions of strategy. As both US and UK management "walk the talk," this culture facilitates a risk-focused approach for all employees.

"It's one of life's ironies that the more you can prove that you don't need a loan, the better your chances usually are of getting one. This is especially true for start-up businesses." Lillian Vernon

Figure 1 highlights that a clear articulation of risk strategy and risk appetite is an essential starting point in embedding risk management across an organization. These statements of corporate objectives act as the fundamental reference point against which all risk-taking and risk-mitigation activity within an organization should be benchmarked. They provide governance and define boundaries within which risk-based decision-making can occur, and provide a clear framework for the selection of one course of action over another.

Policies, risk strategy, and risk appetite are set at board level, and this is embedded into the annual and day-to-day activities of the business. These activities are analyzed through various risk maps, capital models, and sensitivity metrics. In addition, external factors such as market movements and the actions of competitors are communicated to the business. The model at Markel that is shown in Figure 2 splits the business into two components—underwriting and investing. As a consequence there are several key committees and meetings. These are:

- IBNR (incurred but not reported losses) and P&L meetings, at which all aspects of underwriting and reserving are discussed.
- Investment Committee meetings, where all aspects of the company's investment performance and strategy are discussed.
- And in the middle there are the Capital and Risk Committees, which look at the company's risk and capital management.

The IBNR and P&L meetings are crucial to the way Markel operates. A thorough and robust reserving process is the cornerstone of a successful organization. It is important that underwriters and management agree on the IBNR results as this ensures that there is one version of the truth. Having two sets of numbers causes confusion, wastes time, and results in poor decision-making.

The meetings need to be held on a consistent and regular basis. At Markel, IBNR meetings are held quarterly, and the P&L meetings are held on a monthly basis. The IBNR packs and P&L statements show the combined ratio and the required return on risk-adjusted capital by line of business. They include all allocated expenses so that the underwriters understand the full cost of writing their business.

The IBNR and P&L meetings are attended by senior management and underwriters and are a crucial part of the business culture at Markel. They are used to identify lines of business that are not achieving profitability and required return on capital targets so that appropriate action can be taken at the earliest opportunity.

It is crucial that the results of all these meetings are embedded in the management and financial reporting and also in the capital management of the business.

Finally, the activities and results of the business are fed back to the board through effective risk management and reporting.

The results are a key driver in deciding the remuneration of underwriters. Part of our underwriters' remuneration is phased over a period of years, which thus provides a safeguard against underwriting strategies that appear profitable in the short term but ultimately deteriorate. The alignment of risk management with remuneration strategy is an essential part of the effective embedding of ERM.

CAPITAL ALLOCATION AND MANAGEMENT

The standard model for the majority of companies in the United Kingdom today is a product of the Individual Capital Assessment (ICA) regime, introduced by the Financial Services Authority while it waited for Europe to refine and introduce Solvency II. The implementation of ICA has been a significant step forward in delivering more risk-based capital management and has gone a good way to help meet the challenges of Solvency II.

Figure 3 highlights that for a nonlife company the basic capital requirement is split into four risk categories:

- Insurance risk;
- Liquidity risk;
- Market risk;
- Credit risk.

The capital assigned to these risk categories is used to produce the basic capital requirement of the company, and in most cases the capital required is calculated through a combination of stress and scenario tests and a capital model. Operational and group risk are added to the basic capital requirement to produce the company's total capital requirement.

Although this model has been successful in getting companies through the ICA regime, it will not be sufficient to meet the requirements of Solvency II. In addition, ICA models suffer from the fact that for the most part they have been developed and owned by the finance and actuarial departments in companies. As a consequence, there has been minimal embedding into the rest of the business. At Markel, our ICA process has always been multi-disciplined, with a number of stakeholders involved. However, we are embedding the process further. Individual members of the Capital and Risk Committee work with the board, underwriters, and investment managers to ensure that they understand the capital being allocated to them and the risk-adjusted returns required.

The key to effective capital management is to ensure:

- that it drives the decision-making process, ensuring optimal use of capital;
- that it is embedded into the business. It needs to be a key driver in strategy and planning, acquisitions, new lines of business, and legacy claims management. This is an area that needs a considerable amount of effort, but the

Figure 1. Insurer of the future with integrated model

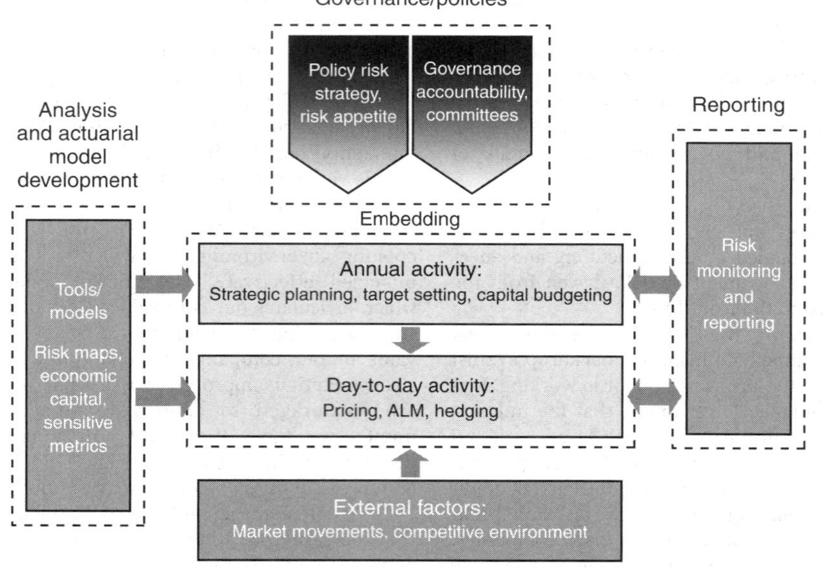

"Consumer spending is now plunging at serious-recession rate ... even if the rescue now in train succeeds in unfreezing credit markets, the real economy has immense downward momentum. In addition to financial rescues, we need major stimulus programs." Paul R. Krugman

        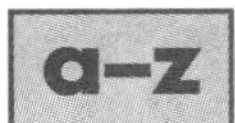

Figure 2. Model used at Markel

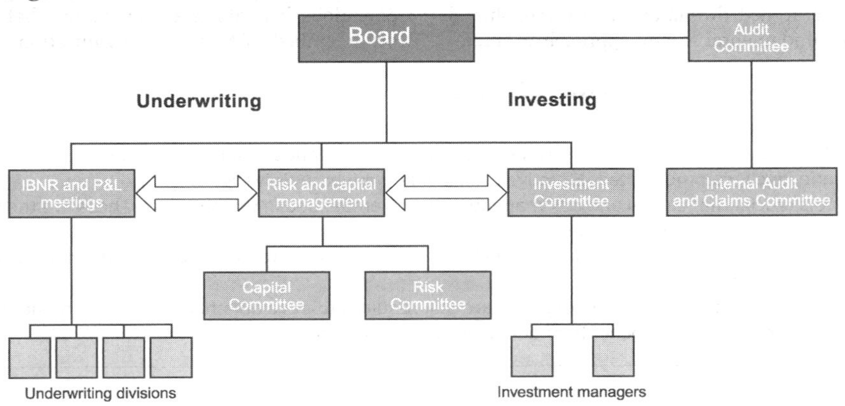

benefits are considerable. This area is key to achieving the objectives of Solvency II;

- that people are rewarded by return on capital. People will take more of an interest if their bonuses are dependent on it, so ensure that the bonuses of underwriters and senior management are calculated by return on capital;
- that the model is transparent and well documented. Too many models act as a black box whose results cannot be explained;
- that financial and nonfinancial information used by the model and the capital management team is consistent with the information used by the business. Different information causes confusion, wastes time, and will result in poor decisions being made. An organization cannot have a model that operates with stand-alone information—it needs to be embedded into all aspects of the business.

The goal should be to minimize group and operational risk through effective ERM. A prudent approach is to have minimal appetite for credit and liquidity risk and a reasonable appetite for market risk.

The last and most significant risk is reserve and underwriting risk. A sound approach here is to split the capital required for reserve and underwriting risk into two components: prior-year reserve risk and current business risk. Here one allocates capital to cover the uncertainty on prior-year insurance reserves. Again, one can try to reduce this capital requirement by establishing prudent case and IBNR reserves so that reserves are more likely to be redundant than deficient.

Capital is also allocated to underwriting the current business. This capital is allocated to each product line, enabling management to set combined ratio targets that achieve the required return on risk-adjusted capital. These combined ratio targets will vary according to the volatility, length of tail, and reinsurance usage of the product line. In addition, the combined ratio target will take into consideration diversification with other classes of business.

The combined ratio targets are used to benchmark underwriting performance, and they act as a key driver in the setting of underwriter and management bonus targets.

Figure 3. Capital allocation

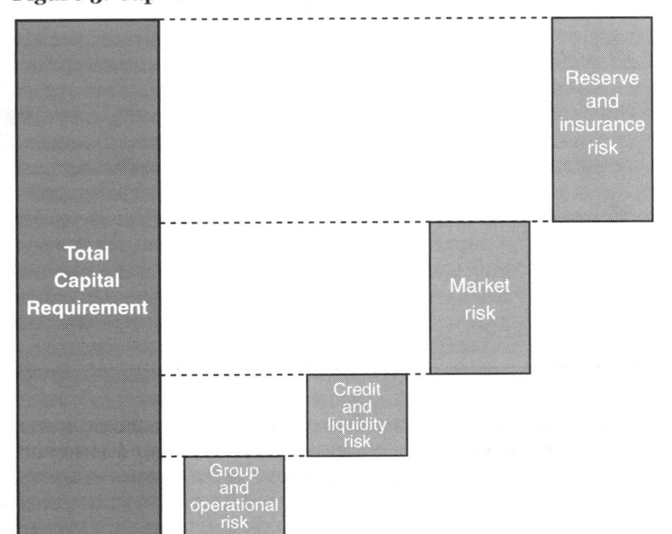

WHAT ARE THE IMPLICATIONS OF SOLVENCY II?

The three-pillar approach of Solvency II works as follows. Pillar 1 deals with the quantitative capital requirements. It ensures that the valuation of assets and liabilities, and the calculation of capital requirements, are standardized. The areas covered are:

- Valuation of technical provisions;
- Minimum capital requirement;
- Solvency capital requirement;
- Investment rules

Pillar 2 deals with the qualitative side of Solvency II and focuses on

- The principles of internal control and risk management;
- Individual risk and capital assessment;
- The supervisory review process.

Pillar 3 deals with disclosure requirements discipline and covers:

- Transparency and disclosure and the support of risk-based supervision through market mechanisms.

So what are the implications of Solvency II for capital management? Already we can see that there are problems.

Within Pillar 1 it is clear that the technical provision under Solvency II and International Financial Reporting Standards (IFRS) is calculated differently. This difference will be a potent source of confusion, additional cost, and wasted effort—and it needs to be resolved.

It is also clear that the communications effort required to implement Pillar 1 will not be trivial. How are the new technical provisions to be communicated and embedded in the business? How do you explain to underwriters that their loss ratio reflects discounting and a cost-of-capital adjustment? It took a long time for underwriters to understand combined ratios, so this will be a challenge.

The minimum capital requirement (MRC) set out in Solvency II fails to reward appropriate risk management due to its formulaic approach. It is also clear that in the majority of cases an internal capital

"If economists could manage to get themselves thought of as humble, competent people on a level with dentists, that would be splendid." John Maynard Keynes

  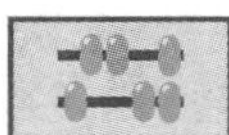      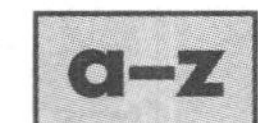

model produces a lower solvency capital requirement, which means that there is a significant advantage to an organization in having its model approved. Finally, there are also significant implications for IT and data collection.

With Pillar 2 it is crucial that a company can demonstrate that it has effective ERM and that it is embedded in the business. Meeting the embedding or "use test" requires significant time and resources.

The main focus of Pillar 3 is disclosure, and therefore the implications of these disclosures need to be carefully thought through. These disclosures will include a report on:

- Governance and risk management;
- Valuation principles applied for solvency purposes;
- The internal model: methodologies, assumptions, and validation;
- Capital requirements, with an account of the company's minimum capital requirement and solvency capital requirement (SCR) and any breaches during the year, plus a breakdown of the SCR standard formula and internal model calculations.

CONCLUSION

So how does the road ahead look? It is clear that the sector has a number of challenges to overcome and that a period of hard work lies ahead. An effective ERM model, as we have argued throughout this piece, should be fundamental to any approach to implementing Solvency II and will, of itself, bring tremendous benefits to organizations that work to embed ERM in their organization.

MAKING IT HAPPEN

- A strong management culture will ensure that risks are understood, controlled, and effectively communicated. Effective ERM is a key driver in Solvency II.
- It is crucial that capital and risk management are embedded in the business. These are the DNA of an insurance company.
- Return on risk-adjusted capital should be a key driver in the remuneration of underwriters and management.
- Considerable resources and expense are still required to develop a fully integrated model; however, the capital benefits of doing so will be significant.

MORE INFO

Websites:

European Commission collection of documents on various aspects of Solvency II: ec.europa.eu/internal_market/insurance/solvency/index_en.htm

Financial Services Authority (FSA) section on Solvency II: www.fsa.gov.uk/pages/About/What/International/solvency/index.shtml

Solvency II Association training and presentations: www.solvency-ii-training.com

See Also:

✔ Solvency II: Its Development and Aims (p. 1053)
✔ Stress Testing to Evaluate Insurance Cover (p. 1016)
✔ Understanding and Calculating Probable Maximum Loss (PML) (p. 1019)
✔ Understanding Asset–Liability Management (Full Balance Sheet Approach) (p. 996)
Insurance (pp. 1633–1635)

NOTES

1 AM Best. "Risk management and the rating process for insurance companies." January 25, 2008. Online at: www.ambest.com/ratings/methodology/riskmanagement.pdf

2 Paul Moore, HBOS, "Man in a rowing boat."

3 Markel International comprises the international operations of Markel Corporation, a US property casualty company listed on the New York Stock Exchange. It writes a variety of property, casualty, and marine insurance and reinsurance business through its two London-based platforms: Markel International Insurance Company and Markel Syndicate 3000.

Viewpoint: Finance Teaching After the Global Financial Crisis by Jayanth R. Varma

INTRODUCTION

Jayanth R. Varma holds a doctorate in management from the Indian Institute of Management, Ahmedabad, and is a professor of finance and accounting at the same Institute. During the last 25 years as an academic he has worked mainly in the field of financial markets and their regulation. He has served on the board of the Securities and Exchange Board of India, on several government committees concerned with risk management and financial sector reforms, and also on the boards of a couple of Indian banks.

OVERVIEW

I argue that we must rethink the way finance is taught because the global financial crisis has revealed deep-seated problems with older, oversimplified models that used to be popular in the classroom. I believe that newer and more nuanced models became well established in finance theory in the last couple of decades, and the crisis has not done anything to discredit these models. Finance teaching must therefore start shifting toward these more modern and sophisticated models so that our students are better able to cope with the post-crisis world.

RISK MEASURES MUST BE MULTIDIMENSIONAL AND FORWARD LOOKING

The capital asset pricing model (CAPM) was developed half a century ago, but it remains the workhorse model in the classroom even today. The CAPM is popular because it is simple and easy to use: there is only one source of risk (market risk or beta), and there is a practical way to measure this risk. Modern finance theory, on the other hand, has moved on to multifactor models where the measure of risk is multidimensional:

- *size*: small-cap stocks are riskier than large-cap stocks;
- *value*: value stocks differ systematically from growth stocks;
- *momentum*: prices trends cannot be ignored;
- *liquidity*: illiquid assets are more risky.

Today, although no serious finance journal would publish a paper that relied exclusively on the CAPM to measure risk, many finance MBAs probably believe that the CAPM is the best way to measure risk.

The CAPM makes the simplifying assumption that all investors have identical beliefs about the probability distribution of future stock prices—investors are assumed to agree on the means and the variances of the returns. While the modern models in finance theory assume that probabilities are subjective and are estimated using optimal Bayesian methods, classroom practice is dominated by classical statistics. Students therefore easily fall into the trap of believing that means, variances, and betas are objective facts to be revealed by statistical estimation from historical data instead of being subjective judgments about the future.

Finance professors like to joke that accounting is about the past, while finance is about the future. However, when it comes to risk measurement, we have allowed students to uncritically imbibe a backward-looking methodology that failed so disastrously in the crisis—VaR models based purely on recent past data led to catastrophic underestimates of the true risk.

I think that finance teachers must now bring modern risk models to the classroom in a much bigger way.

PRICES MAY NOT BE RIGHT, BUT THERE IS STILL NO FREE LUNCH

The efficient markets hypothesis (EMH) has two important components, and the global financial crisis has led to diametrically opposite conclusions regarding these two:

- There is no free lunch—or it is not possible to beat the market in risk-adjusted terms. If something is too good to be true, it probably is not true. The global financial crisis has strengthened this claim. All those apparently low-risk, high-return investments turned out to be high risk.
- Prices are "right" in the sense that they reflect fundamentals. The global financial crisis has weakened this claim. Many prices were clearly not right.

Limits to arbitrage imply that prices are not always "right," but limits to arbitrage also tell us that the prices are wrong for a reason. The no free lunch argument remains true: there are anomalies, but no easily exploitable anomalies.

What appears like a free lunch is just the reward for a hidden tail risk. The unhedgeability of this risk (possibly a liquidity risk) means that the apparent free lunch can be exploited only by those who can back their bets with a nearly infinite pool of liquidity and capital. Pre-crisis, the "too big to fail" (TBTF) banks with implicit sovereign support might have thought that they had infinitely deep pockets, but the crisis blew the illusion away.

Finance courses need to teach more about the limits to arbitrage, with proper attention paid to transaction costs, leverage, and collateral requirements. The important stream of recent literature linking funding liquidity and market liquidity needs to be part of the core courses in financial markets.

MARKET MICROSTRUCTURE HAS MACRO-CONSEQUENCES

The study of market microstructure has become one of the most exciting fields in finance, and a vast literature of elegant models has emerged. In finance teaching, however, market microstructure is covered only in specialized courses, if at all. The dominant thinking seems to be that microstructure is important only to securities brokers and dealers who are focused on extremely short-term movements in prices. It was thought that the weird phenomena that take place at the short time scales relevant to market microstructure wash out over longer time periods and become irrelevant for mainstream finance.

The global financial crisis and subsequent events like the flash crash of May 2010 in the United States have taught us that this is not so. Quite often, market microstructure has macro-consequences and, perhaps, a financial crisis is simply market microstructure writ large.

Over the short time intervals of microstructure events (a few minutes), sharp and rapid price declines (market meltdowns) and the converse ("meltups") happen all the time. For example, any sell order large enough to sweep through the whole or a major fraction of the bid side of the order book would cause

        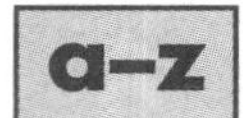

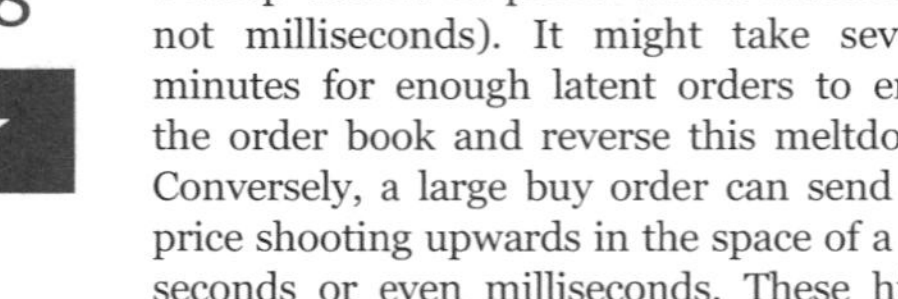

a steep decline in prices within seconds (if not milliseconds). It might take several minutes for enough latent orders to enter the order book and reverse this meltdown. Conversely, a large buy order can send the price shooting upwards in the space of a few seconds or even milliseconds. These high-frequency price movements are several times the range that would be expected from a Gaussian distribution.

Although fat tails are very common in high-frequency price data, microstructure theorists do not regard these markets as dysfunctional or irrational. On the contrary, the self-correcting ability of the market restores equilibrium over the space of several minutes or hours. Taking into account the various frictions (search and information costs, transaction costs, and leverage restrictions), we should probably consider a market which experiences (and then quickly recovers from) such microstructure meltdowns or meltups to be an efficient market.

During the crisis, booms and busts happened at a macro-scale (over time frames of several months instead of minutes), but it is possible that the phenomenon differed from microstructure events only in their scale and duration. A financial crisis may simply be a market microstructure event that has gone macro. Perhaps the complexities of "microstructure noise" persist at longer time scales as well, and the market is in a perpetual state of chaotic movement toward an ever-changing equilibrium instead of being in a continuous state of equilibrium.

The hypothesis that financial crisis is simply market microstructure writ large implies that markets are messier and more complex than the ideal friction-free market that is typically taught in finance courses. On the flip side, it means that we have the theoretical tools and techniques (of microstructure theory) to study crises.

ECONOMETRICS MUST BE GROUNDED IN FINANCIAL HISTORY

The global financial crisis and its aftermath evoked parallels with:

- the Great Depression of the 1930s;
- the panic of 1907;
- the sovereign defaults of the 1890s and 1930s;
- the financial (and sovereign debt) crises of the 1830s and 1870s.

From a long historical perspective, the financial crisis does not appear to be an aberration at all. On the contrary, it is the so-called Great Moderation of the late 1990s and early 2000s that appears to be an aberration. For example, Haldane (2009) provides the data given in Table 1 for macroeconomic volatility in the United Kingdom.

Table 1. Volatility of UK macroeconomic variables during the Great Moderation compared with 150-year average

Variable	*Volatility, 1998–2007*	*Volatility, 1857–2007*
GDP growth	0.6%	2.7%
Earnings growth	0.5%	6.4%
Inflation	0.9%	5.9%
Unemployment	0.6%	3.4%

Source: Adapted from Haldane (2009), Annex Table 1.

A key mistake prior to the crisis was the assumption that the Great Moderation was a permanent structural change in the world economy that implied a permanently reduced volatility. The crisis has taught us that the statistical processes that we observe during any particular period should be viewed as just one of several possible regimes. There is always a nontrivial probability of shifting to a different regime. The "new normal" in this sense is that there is no unique and stable "normal."

I see financial history as providing powerful inputs into the econometric procedures that we use. Since high-quality data do not usually go back more than a few decades, we do not have the option of fitting econometric models directly to centuries of data. Yet it is not sensible to limit the estimation process to only the limited sample duration that is available. Students should be encouraged to favor robust models that are qualitatively consistent with decades, if not centuries, of historical experience.

Students taking advanced courses should be exposed to powerful econometric techniques like Markov switching models, but much simpler approaches may also be sufficient. Haldane's table reproduced above involves only a simple tabulation of means and standard deviations for different sample periods, but it provides very valuable information. This means that a significant amount of financial history should be a part of the finance curriculum.

THE NORMAL DISTRIBUTION IS COMMON IN NATURE BUT RARE IN FINANCE

The Gaussian (normal) distribution is found everywhere in nature, but nowhere in finance. Theoreticians and practitioners use various tricks to correct for nonnormality—for example, the smile in a Black–Scholes option pricing model accounts for the fat tails of asset prices. Finance teaching tends to underemphasize this, and students tend to think of the Gaussian distribution as the default assumption in finance.

I think that finance teaching should include more discussion of fat-tailed distributions as well as copulas and other tools for dealing with non-Gaussian data. Similarly, courses on stochastic calculus should not be focused only on the mathematics of Wiener processes, but must also cover Lévy processes, which have non-Gaussian increments.

FINANCE MUST DRAW FROM OTHER DISCIPLINES

Insights from psychology in the form of behavioral finance are now an integral part of the standard finance curriculum, but it is necessary to seek inputs from other disciplines as well. Neuroscience tells us a lot about the cognitive capability of the human mind as well as the nature of risk and time preferences. The sociology of finance asks us to look at markets as complex socio-technical systems that overcome some of the limitations of bounded rationality. Network theory provides powerful theoretical tools to understand highly interconnected financial markets and institutions. Finance students should be exposed to all these important perspectives.

Some of these ideas would surely lead to changes in finance theory itself. But even before this happens, finance teachers can prepare their students for a post-crisis world by discussing the more robust models that already exist in the literature.

MORE INFO

Books:

Easley, David, and Jon Kleinberg. *Networks, Crowds, and Markets: Reasoning About a Highly Connected World*. New York: Cambridge University Press, 2010.

Glimcher, Paul W. *Foundations of Neuroeconomic Analysis*. New York: Oxford University Press, 2011.

Reinhart, Carmen M., and Kenneth S. Rogoff. *This Time is Different: Eight Centuries of Financial Folly*. Princeton, NJ: Princeton University Press, 2009.

Articles:

Haldane , Andrew G. "Why banks failed the stress test." Bank of England, February 13, 2009. Online at: tinyurl.com/aztdqc [PDF].

MacKenzie, Donald. "The credit crisis as a problem in the sociology of knowledge." *American Journal of Sociology* 116:6 (May 2011): 1778–1841. Online at: tinyurl.com/pfglcl2

"Economics is as much a study in fantasy and aspiration as in hard numbers–maybe more so." Theodore Roszak

  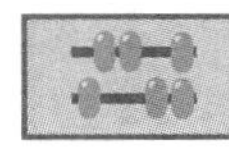   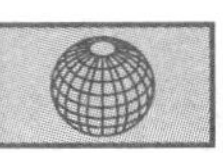   

Viewpoint: Future Directions: The Global Economy After the Crash by Arun Motianey

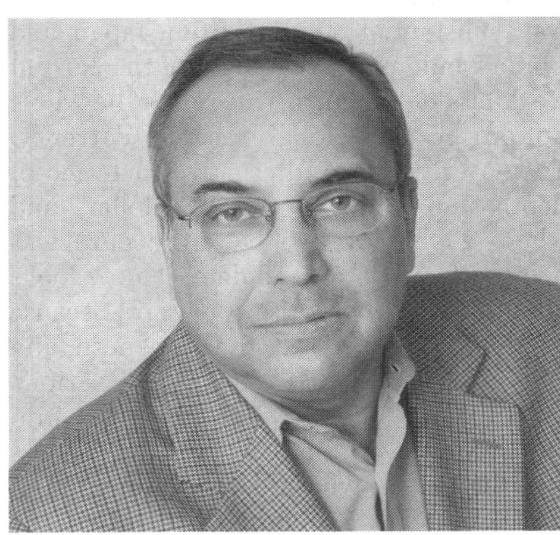

INTRODUCTION

Arun Motianey is director of fixed-income strategy for Roubini Global Economics (RGE). Prior to joining RGE, he worked for two decades at Citigroup in a variety of roles, including head of macro research and strategy for global wealth management, head of investment research and cohead of asset allocation at Citigroup Private Bank Asset Management, and economist in the office of the chairman during the restructuring of Latin American sovereign debt under the Brady Plan, which involved liaising with the IMF. Most recently he has authored *SuperCycles: The New Economic Force Transforming Global Markets and Investment Strategy*. He received his bachelor's degree at the University of Bombay and participated in a graduate exchange fellowship at Princeton University. He received his doctorate in mathematics and economics from King's College, Cambridge.

When, from the perspective provided by your theory of supercycles, you take a global view of growth and the risks to growth, how do you see the interplay of the various regions and what factors are you focusing on currently?

In its essentials the supercycle thesis has two parts: first, the downleg, which we have been experiencing for the last 30 years or so and which is characterized by powerful disinflationary tendencies that take us to the very brink of deflation. This is the result of falling input costs that temporarily widen profit margins in output, but the overcapacity that then follows leads to a crash in the output industry, and so on until the end of the pipeline. The second component is the upleg, where input costs push upward, overcoming the resistance of weak demand until inflation is admitted into the system.

We are now in the earliest stages of the upleg. Keep in mind that these forces play out slowly and are met with significant resistance both in the sluggishness of the economy as well as from central banking ideology, which has intolerance for inflation. We are, however, seeing the ideological resistance breaking down (though for different reasons) in the Bank of England, the US Federal Reserve, and several of the important emerging economy central banks. The European Central Bank, on the other hand, maintains a fortress-like commitment to price stability. But the far more interesting question—and highly relevant to where we find ourselves today in the modern supercycle—is exactly how does inflation seep back into the system?

The sharp rise in commodity prices (due to zero-cost money seeking out "hard" assets) in *relative price terms*, i.e. against the price of goods and services broadly, implies a reversal of the forces that appear in the downleg. In both legs the cost of inputs drives the movement of prices through the pipeline, but in the downleg the direction is toward deflation, and in the upleg it is toward inflation or possibly stagflation.

Because of the surge in commodity prices, the major developed economies of the world—especially those that suffered most during this supercycle, i.e., the service-dominated economies of the United States and the United Kingdom—will experience a terrible squeeze in margins (in contrast to the widening during the downleg) now that labor costs have been cut to the bone. On the upside, their weakening currencies are giving them some breathing room. However, in order to export their way out of trouble the existing manufacturing points on the pipeline must now become service-led economies. What this means is simply that places need to be swapped in the pipeline.

Nominal exchange-rate appreciation and higher inflation in the emerging markets are already taking us in that direction. Today, the most important thing to watch (far more important, in my opinion, than Federal Reserve policy on interest rates or quantitative easing) is the monetary policy stance of the major emerging economies of the world. If China, India, Brazil, Turkey, and Indonesia (to name just five of the most important) show signs of tolerating higher inflation in their economies and, in fact, allow inflation to slip into wages (which appears to be the case with all of them), the upleg of the supercycle will have begun.

Once inflation comes into these economies you will begin to see signs of inflation in goods everywhere. Rising goods prices globally will give a boost to the tradables sector in the developed world and, provided that this is accompanied by rising wages in these economies, we shall see a return to recovery, though with rapidly rising nominal rates and possibly higher real rates. The risk is that corporations in the developed world may wish to choke off wage increases—so as to rebuild profits—in which case we will get stagflation.

Where do quantitative easing and other kinds of unconventional policies fit into all this?

These are essentially monetary policy measures driven by central bank policymaking. They have no role to play in the supercycle other than weakening the dollar, sterling, yen, etc., and so pushing up commodity prices and thereby imparting a "lift" to the upleg of the supercycle. This is, of course, not the intention of the central banks that launch these policies, but it is the inescapable effect.

We have seen statements from both China and Japan that they are prepared to buy eurozone debt in order to play their part in helping to stabilize Europe and the euro. What is your reaction to this?

I think that Chinese and Japanese money will be largely symbolic here, but the Japanese have been down this road before. During the worst of the Asian crisis, in late 1998, the Asian Development Bank convened a special meeting at which the Japanese finance minister offered to provide around US$100 billion in seed capital to create an Asian Monetary Fund. At the time this made the United States very nervous at the prospect of Japan increasing its influence in Asia, and the Clinton administration sent their man to stop the proposal in its tracks. The Clinton administration argued that markets had to find their natural equilibrium.

That argument, of course, will not work with the eurozone crisis, and we may find that Europe's appetite for Japanese and Chinese money turns out to be much stronger than anyone anticipates. That raises the question of Asian influence in Europe, but you also have to look at the way substantial support from Japan and China would play in the light of the current weakness of the euro. This raises the whole notion of the global reserve currency. Today, there is no alternative in terms of depth and scale to the US dollar, and where a year or two back the euro was being offered as a candidate, it now looks far too much the worse for wear. Because of this I cannot see the Japanese and Chinese wanting to transfer serious amounts of their dollar reserves into euros. Moreover, the Germans, the French, and the Dutch, who are very influential in the European Economic and Monetary Union (EMU) are historically very suspicious of Chinese intentions and are likely to want to persuade the Greeks and the Portuguese not to depend too heavily on the magnanimity of the Chinese and Japanese, especially the former. However, we have already seen China making very substantial investments in Greece through the crisis.

It has been suggested that some of the wobblier EU states could start issuing Samurai bonds or Panda bonds (renminbi-denominated bonds from foreign issuers). Would that make it easier for Japan and China to weigh in?

The moment you start to issue debt in the creditor's currency, you are at the mercy of the other party's exchange rate. So what could look like reasonably priced debt could turn, in a few years, into very expensive debt—and even into ruinous debt if the renminbi went from, say, 7.5 to the euro to four. That would create a crisis rather than solve one. However, there are routes by which the Chinese could end up making the renminbi a global reserve currency. We are seeing retrenchment in Europe and the United States, and the Chinese are being urged to consume more and export less to assist global trade balancing. They could turn around and say, all right, we will now run fiscal deficits, which would be easier than getting Chinese households to buy more (the Chinese household is a small player by comparison with the government sector). If they moved from a large current account surplus to a deficit and financed this by issuing renminbi bonds, that would provide central banks around the world with a way of holding renminbi. That could scale up to being a rival to the US dollar over time. I am reasonably confident that by 2020 things will have developed along these lines.

This could be supplemented by a logical extension to an order that went out from the central government in China at the end of 2010, namely for public-sector companies in China to think about paying out more in dividends and to invest less. Many of these companies are joint public- and private-sector companies whose shares are held by banks and households, so that would help household wealth. It is also possible that the Chinese will open up some of this shareholding to foreign investors. That would be the right way for China to grow into a world economic power. To my way of thinking, the development of share ownership in China is one of the most underreported and underanalyzed stories about the country. It will unfold very gradually, I anticipate, with plenty of pitfalls along the way, but it is very important. The trickle-down of wealth will stimulate household consumption and reduce savings, which will help to diminish China's current account surplus. It is important to realize that China has learnt the lessons of history. It cannot allow its currency to be forced into a maxi-appreciation, because when that happens it will usher in a Japan-style deflation. So they are committed to very gradual internal adjustments.

Do you see a rise in protectionist sentiment in the global economy?

There is a real risk that we will see the rise of protectionist sentiment not just in the United States but everywhere, because we know from history that free trade is something of a house of cards and can collapse whenever any major component of the global trading system is removed or collapses. In this connection, I would look at the threats that we heard coming from Brazil in particular, and more generally from other emerging economies, to the effect that the United States' unconventional policies are a kind of currency war. I worry a great deal about that. As I explained earlier, the success of the supercycle theory is to allow inflation to come back into the global economy, and the emerging markets have a key role to play in that. Easy money in the developed world serves no purpose other than to weaken developed world currencies and strengthen those of the emerging markets. Any pushback on that front means that we have a policy coordination problem of the greatest severity. Luckily, as of now, it seems to be mostly rhetoric.

Having said that, the US appetite for taking out the protectionist knives is worryingly strong. Protectionism, or phases of protectionism, in small economies is not particularly alarming. If South Korea or Indonesia suddenly started to raise tariff barriers, it would not necessarily be the start of a major trend. The United States is definitely the one to watch. It is given to fits of protectionism, and we have seen the resurgence of this tendency throughout its history. If the US economy stalls, the risk of protectionism and the potential for a breakdown of world trade would rise sharply. If you look at the World Trade Organization's Doha Round talks, the two countries that have always tried to put sand in the gears of the world trade machine have been India and Brazil. However, the rhetoric of both has always been far more severe than any concrete acts of theirs, and both countries are moving rapidly into current account deficits (which by definition means that they are tolerating a much higher volume of imports, which in turn means that more countries have access to their markets). The United States is a much scarier proposition when it comes to protectionism.

Among all the talk of the possible breakup of the European Union, do you see scenarios where Germany could walk away?

It is very clear that the Germans recognize that they have enjoyed huge gains from being part of a Europe-wide fiscal currency. The exchange rate gains for Germany have been huge, disproportionately large. They came into the European Union at an overvalued level, given the cost of production. Germany went through a very painful process through the 1990s with reunification and also went through very significant structural reforms in the labor market after the launch of the euro in 1999, as a result of which the country became profitable again. That was a very creditable adjustment, and they are reaping the gains of this. They are now very much more productive and competitive than their EU neighbors, and every time the euro weakens it boosts German exports still more. Germany provides the highest-quality capital and consumer goods, and this makes them the natural beneficiaries of the strong "animal spirits" in emerging markets, so they are in a very sweet spot right now. It is true that the interbank linkages in the European Union are a deep source of concern for them, but in the global market Germany has never had it so good. So membership of the European Union is a double-edged sword for them. They have to remember that

---

"Our belief in salvation through the market is very much in the Utopian tradition. The economists and managers are the servants of God. Like the medieval scholastics, their only job is to uncover the divine plan. They could never create or stop it. At most they might aspire to small alterations." John Ralston Saul

when they were rebuilding and the dollar was weakening steadily against the euro, the United States ceased to be their major export market and Europe filled that gap. Germany would not be in the position it is in today if it were not for Greece, Spain, Portugal, and the rest buying German goods and creating large trade imbalances with Germany. So some help from Germany is in order. Unfortunately, although this is realized in Germany, the moral hazard question stands in the road and has yet to be properly resolved. The next year is going to be very interesting on this question and on just about everything we have touched on. The big danger, however, has to be how gracefully the European Union manages to deal with what looks like an inevitable default of one or more of its members.

MORE INFO

Books:

Eichengreen, Barry. *Exorbitant Privilege: The Rise and Fall of the Dollar and the Future of the International Monetary System*. Oxford, UK: Oxford University Press, 2011.

Gamble, Andrew. *The Spectre at the Feast: Capitalist Crisis and the Politics of Recession*. Basingstoke, UK: Palgrave Macmillan, 2009.

Motianey, Arun. *SuperCycles: The New Economic Force Transforming Global Markets and Investment Strategy*. New York: McGraw-Hill, 2010.

Reinhart, Carmen M., and Kenneth S. Rogoff. *This Time Is Different: Eight Centuries of Financial Folly*. Princeton, NJ: Princeton University Press, 2009.

Skidelsky, Robert. *Keynes: The Return of The Master*. London, UK: Penguin, 2010.

See Also:

★ Viewpoint: The Challenges to Slow Growth in the Advanced Economies Just Keep Coming (pp. 147–148)

★ Viewpoint: Deleveraging, Deflation, and Rebalancing in the Global Economy (pp. 158–160)

★ Viewpoint: Disinflation and Low Growth versus Inflation and Reasonable Growth (pp. 163–165)

★ Viewpoint: Governments of All Stripes Still Have Much to Learn from Keynes (pp. 187–189)

★ Viewpoint: Nothing but Painful Choices Ahead as the Global Debt Supercycle Ends (p. 219)

  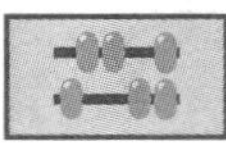   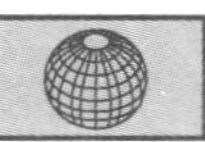   

Viewpoint: The Global Risk Map and the Current Credit Crunch by Peter, Lord Levene

INTRODUCTION

Peter Levene started his career in the UK defense industry with United Scientific Holdings. He was then appointed personal adviser to Defence Secretary Michael Heseltine in the Ministry of Defence and later permanent secretary in the role of Chief of Defence Procurement. Subsequently he held a number of government posts, as adviser to the Secretary of State for the Environment; to the President of the Board of Trade; and to the Chancellor of the Exchequer. From 1992 to 1997 he was adviser to Prime Minister John Major on efficiency and effectiveness. During this period he was also chairman and chief executive of Canary Wharf Ltd. He received a knighthood in 1989 and became a life peer in 1997. Later he became vice chairman of Deutsche Bank in the United Kingdom, having also been at Wasserstein Perella and Morgan Stanley. Lord Levene was elected chairman of Lloyd's, the world's leading specialist insurance and reinsurance market, in 2002. In this role, he chairs the Council of Lloyd's and Lloyd's Franchise Board. He is a member of the House of Lords Select Committee for Economic Affairs.

A CHANGED LANDSCAPE

The last decade was, by any standards, an insurance challenge. The tragedy of the World Trade Center followed by the unprecedented losses of hurricanes Katrina, Rita, and Wilma, followed by the worst global recession since 1929 meant that many ended the decade battered and bruised. But this was also the decade when Lloyd's re-emerged, phoenix like, from what had seemed not so long ago to be an impossible situation, to become, once again an icon of the industry. The story of Lloyd's should reassure governments and regulators that root and branch reform can come from within. Financial service industries *can* be responsible and prudent risk managers. Lloyd's has a specific view of the major features of the global risk map ahead.

First, let us turn to the outlook for the insurance industry in the context of a difficult global economy. Redundancies, cutbacks, insolvencies—this is hardly the finest hour for the financial services sector. And the dramatic bailout of America's largest insurer, AIG, proves that it would be foolish to pretend that the insurance industry can expect to be insulated from what is happening elsewhere. The industry is very much engaged and needs to contribute vigorously to the debate about the new architecture needed for its markets.

Financial services must take stock and get back to basics. It exists to provide services to keep wider society and business moving. And there is a clear consensus for change. Over two-thirds of global business leaders surveyed at the end of last year said that complex financial instruments require better regulation, more restrictions, and greater disclosure.

Regulation certainly needs to be more effective. We need to have more oversight over what we are doing. But I must sound a word of caution at this point: Better regulation does not simply equate to more regulation. It does not mean knee-jerk reactions or equate to vast new rafts of legislation. We need change, but we definitely do not need another Sarbanes–Oxley.

What the current crisis proves is that we are all part of a global market in which global systemic risk is now very much to the fore. What we therefore need—for insurance and reinsurance too—is closer cooperation across borders, more harmonization of standards, and greater mutual recognition between different territories. We also need company boards everywhere, as part of a more robust system of checks and balances, to demonstrate that they are focused on rewarding performance, considered as a whole, and not just short-term risk-taking.

Much is currently being made of the bonus culture associated with short-term risk taking. While there is much to be said here, we also need to insist that not to reward our people fairly would be ludicrous. Those who perform well must be properly rewarded, and we would simply lose them if we did not do so. But in order to retain public trust we must demonstrate that we are not part of a "culture of excess" and that we do not reward failure.

It could be argued that, with hindsight, too many personal compensation structures in the financial services sector have pushed people into taking bets on positions which, if they were thinking long term, and in the true interests of their businesses, they might well not have done.

However, it is important here to draw a crucial distinction between the insurance industry and wider finance. Despite the high-profile casualties in the financial sector, the overall impact of recent events on the general insurance industry has been limited. Recent months have shown quite clearly that the whole financial sector is not a house of cards that is destined to fall when some parts are shaken. Insurers and bankers are not joined together in an unholy matrimony.

First and foremost, insurance is an economic necessity, not a discretionary purchase. And although insurance is not immune from what is going on elsewhere in the economy, the fact that it is an economic necessity largely holds true even as the recession bites.

Certainly, buyers will seek to cut costs during difficult times, and history shows us that fraud may rise during a steep downturn. Yet it remains true that people's homes, automobiles, and businesses all need to be insured, irrespective of the state of the economy. A decline in construction and automobile manufacture will have some negative impact on the insurance industry's medium-term growth prospects. However this will impact mainly at the margins because so much of the growth of insurance exposure is linked to renewal business.

SURVIVING THE "TOXIC LIABILITIES" EXPERIENCE

Lloyd's itself has had considerable and painful experience of dealing with its own "toxic liabilities" in the past, and it has learnt some important lessons. Indeed, since the transfer of approximately $20 billion of liabilities to Equitas in the 1990s, (a business since bought by Berkshire

"Did you ever think that making a speech on economics is a lot like pissing down your leg? It seems hot to you but it never does to anyone else." Lyndon Baines Johnson

Hathaway), Lloyd's has changed almost every aspect of its business. The creation of a new franchise structure in particular has led to fundamental changes in the Lloyd's business model, and these changes have helped to keep Lloyd's members on course despite record insurance losses in recent years.

Another key reason why Lloyd's in particular has not been greatly impacted by the current crisis is that it has stuck firmly to what it knows—and that is the business of underwriting. A few years ago, the fact that Lloyd's turned its back resolutely on complicated financial products must have appeared highly unadventurous. Similarly, in the middle of the bull market, Lloyd's conservative investment strategy must have seemed full of missed opportunity. In hindsight, however, it was clearly the right strategy, and the impact of recent events has therefore not been nearly as pronounced on Lloyd's as it has been elsewhere.

If we have learnt one thing from the financial crisis it is that poor risk management was a big part of the problem. Risk is not and should not be a dirty word for the reinsurance sector. However, we need to work to understand risk. Only when we understand it can we start to manage it.

DEALING WITH THE THREE MAIN RISK ISSUES

Today there are three particular risk issues which business and society perhaps need to work to understand better. These are liability risk, climate risk, and political risk.

It seems clear that the credit crunch, followed by a deep recession, has created a perfect breeding ground for a new increase in litigation activity. There is typically a delay before claims tend to materialize from an economic downturn. Economic activity fell sharply in 1990 to 1991, but it was not until 1992 and 1993 that the raft of new claims arrived.

Research carried out by Lloyd's with global business leaders shows that boards are once again spending an increasing amount of time discussing litigation and liability risk. With the growth of globalization, companies outside the United States are becoming more disposed to litigate generally. There is also a perception among larger European companies that US courts are increasingly being asked to rule on cases that might have once been considered extraterritorial.

In these testing times, it is very important not to allow litigation and the fear of it to stifle the innovation that business needs to survive and succeed. Insurers and intermediaries are well placed to help boards to focus on these important areas. It is vital that companies carefully consider whether they have the right processes in place to manage liability risk.

A majority of global business leaders would admit that they have not yet adopted formal policies and procedures to respond to liability risk, although they have done so for other types of risk.

Another area of concern right now is climate change. The economics of climate change are not yet entirely clear, but the indications are extremely worrying. It is already clear that weather-related catastrophes are costing the insurance industry more than ever before. Despite the economic challenges, it would be an environmental and a business disaster for the industry, and indeed for nation states, to lose their strategic vision on climate change now.

The climate also needs to be a factor within every corporate risk management strategy. The insurance industry has a key role to play in helping to change attitudes. Debates on important issues like flood defence, how we can best adapt buildings and infrastructure, and the necessity of regulating development in high-risk zones are all vital.

As well as significant challenges, climate change also presents the world with real opportunities. Ultimately, society will adapt to the climate. It has no choice. And new technologies will be developed that will create huge opportunities for business—and indeed for insurers too.

In the United Kingdom, it is already clear that consumers expect to see much more in the way of climate-friendly behavior from their favorite brands. As a result, how business responds to climate change will start to have a tangible impact on corporate reputation and brand image for companies all around the world.

The third issue involves terrorism and political risk. Home-grown terrorism is probably the greatest security threat developed nations now face.

Yet research by Lloyd's in the United Kingdom and the United States suggests that only one in three business professionals thinks that enough has been learned from events like 9/11 in the United States and 7/7 in the United Kingdom, or that we will be better prepared next time.

In other words, a gap has emerged between the heightened awareness of the risk of home-grown terrorism and our understanding of how to tackle it. This gap needs to be closed urgently. This will inevitably become more urgent and more important as the impact of recession begins to bite. In the United States and the United Kingdom rising unemployment and economic hardship mean that the number of young people susceptible to extremist doctrines is likely to increase.

Another risk area concerns emerging markets. Should the downturn in emerging markets be sustained, there is little doubt that it could result in greater tensions and instabilities in some regions.

The director general of the security service in the United Kingdom recently confirmed that he thinks the global economic crisis will increase the security threat to Britain, and it seems clear that the same logic can be applied elsewhere.

Against this background, the insurance industry can help in at least two ways. Insurers and intermediaries can work with their clients to improve their information gathering and planning.

Getting the right information from the right sources is critical. Today, too many business leaders rely on media reports for their knowledge of terrorism and political violence, and not enough use other sources, such as bought-in research, reports from "think tank" organizations, and/or in-depth in-house research. Companies must also make sure they have in place an up-to-date business continuity plan which reflects the changing reality and strengths of the risks they face.

A growing body of opinion now suggests that closer engagement with groups at risk of being radicalized by terrorists makes a good deal of sense for both businesses and local communities. Now, more than ever we need to expect the unexpected. As business faces one of its most difficult years in memory, a strong and stable insurance industry has a unique opportunity to help to develop the risk solutions that the struggling economy needs.

MORE INFO

See Also:

★ Climate Change and Insurance (pp. 149–150)
★ How to Manage Emerging Market Risks with Third Party Insurance (pp. 866–868)
★ Insurance—Bruised, Not Crushed (pp. 190–191)
★ Political Risk: Countering the Impact on Your Business (pp. 902–904)
Insurance (pp. 1633–1635)

"Inflation might be called prosperity with high blood pressure." Arnold H. Glasgow

  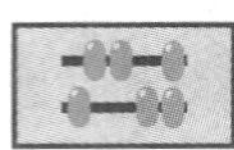   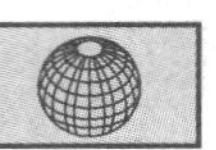   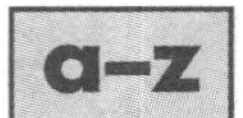

The Globalization of Inflation by Diana Choyleva

EXECUTIVE SUMMARY

- The past ten years saw the clash between China's semi-command saver economy and the market economies of the West. Interaction between supply and demand for goods, services, factors of production, and assets has been polarized on a global scale. Inflation or deflation in the modern world has to be analyzed in the framework of the balance between global demand and supply.
- The low-inflation decade that preceded the overheating of 2007 and early 2008 gave central bankers God-like status. But they fell seriously behind the curve by failing to grasp the profound global changes at play and their implications for economic, financial, and price developments. The central bankers' mistakes could cost the world a dangerous lurch into deflation.

INTRODUCTION

The surge in global consumer price inflation in 2007 and most of 2008 caught many by surprise. The low-inflation decade that preceded this overheating had given central bankers God-like status. But improved monetary policy had at best a supporting role in the global Goldilocks story. The protagonist was the Eurasian savings glut. The setting was the process of globalization. Central bankers across the world fell seriously behind the curve by failing to grasp the profound global changes at play and their implications for economic, financial, and price developments. Their mistakes could cost the world a dangerous lurch into deflation.

The past ten years saw the global clash between China's semi-command saver economy and the market economies of the West. China's supersonic expansion turned it into the manufacturing hub of the world. But final demand for manufacturing goods came from the developed borrower countries. China provided the world with an endless supply of low-cost labor and mispriced, cheap capital. Developed countries provided most of the supply of real and financial assets. Interaction between supply and demand for goods, services, factors of production, and assets has been polarized on a global scale. Globalization did not alter the nature of inflation. But inflation in the context of the modern world has to be analyzed in the framework of the balance between global demand and supply.

THE IMPACT OF CHINA'S ECONOMIC EXPANSION

China's reawakening has transformed the global economy. For many centuries it was the world's greatest. Chinese steel production in 1066, using blast furnaces, exceeded Britain's in 1866. But China ignored the 18th and 19th century Industrial Revolution. It then failed to tackle its 20th century weakness, culminating in the 30-year economic catastrophe of Mao's leadership. Since 1978, China has gone down the export-led, catch-up path pioneered by Japan and Korea, with a similar annual growth rate of almost 10%. Growth of GDP per capita at purchasing power parity averaged a huge 12%, meaning the standard of living doubled every six and a bit years. In 2007 China was the second largest manufacturer, after the United States. Much of China's manufacturing is low value-added assembly, where China now dominates both global output and capacity.

While China was fast becoming the world's manufacturing powerhouse, the emergence of the Chinese consumer remained a chimera. Final demand for manufacturing goods came from the developed, especially the borrower, economies. The reason is that China saves excessively out of its income, more than a half. This negates the possibility of a mass consumer market. Savings are high for structural reasons. These reasons include the lack of universal social security, pension provision, and poor health care; the one-child policy, which has destroyed family security; migration into cities, which has broken up families; and limited financial products to channel savings between the old and the young, or into the private corporate side of the economy.

Instead, China provided the world not only with what seemed like an endless supply of low-cost labor, but also with mispriced, cheap capital. China's high savings cannot be invested profitably in the domestic economy. In a command economy they have no need to be. Profitability and return on capital are irrelevant. Instead, command economies are incredibly good at wasting savings through misallocating investment. China can waste its excess savings either domestically or abroad.

In the first half of this decade its excess savings went into a massive domestic investment boom. There was a huge buildup of excess capacity. The mainly state-owned banking system played an instrumental role in this. It has the bulk of the domestic savings, and the bulk of its lending goes to state firms and local governments. It is not done according to market principles and proper credit risk assessment. State banks are unwilling or unable to provide much finance to private firms or households. Access to cheap money gave state firms an unfair competitive advantage over private firms. But for private firms, China's incorporation into the global economy, especially since its entry in the World Trade Organization (WTO) in 2001, was a boon, providing both the markets and a source of funds. Moreover, Beijing kept its exchange rate fixed to the dollar and the capital account closed.

Unsurprisingly, overinvestment and a pegged currency led to falling global manufacturing goods prices. Meanwhile, energy and commodity prices surged on the world market as China's production was extremely energy-inefficient. But this was not reflected in the price of manufacturing goods because Beijing does not allow domestic energy prices to be set by the market. Ultimately, China could not escape the business cycle. By mid-2004 it had run into severe energy and transport shortages, which curbed its investment frenzy. Over the next two years domestic demand growth slowed significantly. China was still saving excessively, but now it had to find another channel to waste the savings—this time exporting them to the Americans. The yuan–dollar peg had also forced the Tigers and Japan, which had excess savings for their own reasons, to do the same.

China's current account surplus surged. Beijing was investing its huge savings in low-risk, low-yield dollar assets, and so did most of the other Asians. Globally this led to a collapse in real yields. But while China was providing the world with the excess savings, developed countries provided most of the supply of real and financial assets. In simplistic terms, when the huge population of China was bolted onto the global economy, the demand for assets shot up. Naturally, the supply of assets shot up in response. The booms in real estate and in mergers and acquisitions in the borrower economies were an expression of that. They were also the source of yet another boom—that of a purely financial type of asset: the asset-backed security and its derivatives.

BANKERS FAILED TO CURB AN OVERHEATING MARKET

Unfortunately, central bankers across the world fell seriously behind the curve by failing to grasp the profound global changes at play. In the developed countries they believed that globalization meant a change in relative prices. Eventually, they started to talk about China "exporting deflation" and then "exporting inflation." But in terms of their remit, their focus remained firmly at home. They failed to realize how manufacturing prices were set globally; where the "low bond yield conundrum" came from; and why the surge in energy prices did not translate into higher domestic wage inflation. Importantly, they did not pay attention to money and asset price developments.

But the harbingers of the global overheating that began in 2006 came in the form of above-trend broad money growth and asset price inflation. Central banks in the developed economies ignored their message and kept policy rates too low for too long, spawning asset price bubbles and the buildup of excessive debt. The Chinese authorities also made a mistake. They allowed some appreciation of the yuan versus the dollar, but in effective exchange rate terms the yuan was up by a lot less as Beijing was taking advantage of the stronger euro and stronger growth in euroland. Beijing thought the yuan–dollar peg was serving China well. The economy industrialized at breakneck speed, and international influences were kept at bay. The authorities failed to realize that China could no longer be immune to global developments. If Beijing did not allow the exchange rate to appreciate, inflation had to accelerate.

By 2006 most developed and developing economies were overheating. At the start of 2008 the global economy was still operating above its capacity, but the developed and the developing economies had distinctly different cyclical positions. The borrower economies' ability to take up debt was exhausted. The trigger was the emergence of the US subprime mortgage problems in early 2007. This caused global risk-aversion to surge, leading to a global liquidity crunch, followed by a fundamental failure of the banks' funding model, and severe deleveraging. By the middle of 2008 most developed economies were already operating below capacity—the United States, the United Kingdom, and Japan—or close to their capacity in the case of euroland.

However, most developing economies, led by China and India, were still operating above capacity. Their overheating and the oil and commodity bubbles, which were stoked by investment demand and the Fed's misguided early slashing of policy rates, exacerbated the hit from the credit crunch. Developed economies saw cost-push inflation cutting into real incomes. But spare capacity in their economies suggested that a wage-inflation spiral like the 1970s was unlikely to ensue. For the borrower economies this meant they could not rely on inflating away their excessive household debt. The workout had to involve rising defaults, domestic demand deflation, currency depreciation and falling asset prices. The borrower economies, with the most conspicuous big ones being the United States, the United Kingdom, and Spain are in for a prolonged period of significantly below-trend growth.

About 60% of Western Europe and Japan does not suffer from excess household debt. But these countries have been primarily export-led and are also in for a sharpe cyclical growth correction. Both the developing and the developed countries are likely to see headline inflation start to ease sharply in 2009 as the oil and commodity bubbles burst. While lower headline inflation will not help revive the battered consumer in the excess debt countries, where any increase in real income is likely to be saved rather than spent, it could help kick-start a domestic demand recovery in the countries where excess debt is not a problem. Lower interest rates should also lend support. But in both of the borrower and saver economies, willingness to boost public spending substantially will be needed to pull them out of the doldrums in 2010.

In terms of the overall global story, China is crucial. It seems that slumping external demand has finally pulled the rug from under China's expansion. The crucial question is how drastic the externally driven slowdown is set to be. Ever since China joined the WTO, external demand has provided the main genuine source of final demand. The share of exports in output was 36% in 2007. But the share of exports tells you about the composition of output, not about the cause of growth. To determine the cause of growth one has to look at the change in the shares of output of the various expenditure components.

Exports were indeed a key growth driver in the early stages of China's boom. Over the past two years consumer spending has taken over. But the increase in the propensity to consume came on the back of strong export income growth and accelerating wage inflation in the context of overheating. Going forward, with incomes hit and unemployment on the rise, it is difficult to see the Chinese consumer becoming an independent source of final demand. Moreover, the change in investment is determined by the change in the growth of demand, making investment the most volatile component of output. In China the share of investment in output remains ridiculously high at 40%. Consequently, slumping external demand should present a serious hit to China's economy.

CONCLUSION

By the middle of 2009 the global economy is likely to be operating significantly below its potential, pointing to severe disinflation—in other words minimal rises in core prices. For the medium term, China's policy choices will be crucial for the world. China is currently at a major crossroads. The positive path is turning into a fully fledged market economy that allocates its savings efficiently, whether domestically or abroad, and invests its wealth and savings in search of high returns. This involves reforming the banking sector, allowing the yuan to move freely, opening up the capital account, and supporting consumer spending.

The negative path is a return to the bad old ways—state resources thrown into wasteful domestic investment to counteract the global downswing. Public infrastructure spending is the least bad option, but you cannot turn the state spending tap on fast. The worst option will be to force banks to lend support to the struggling manufacturing sector. If Beijing goes for a state-directed investment binge that boosts manufacturing capacity and production when global consumer demand is flagging, there is even the possibility that price deflation—a sustained fall in the price level—could rear its ugly head.

MORE INFO

Books:

Congdon, T. *Keynes, the Keynesians and Monetarism*. Cheltenham, UK: Edward Elgar Publishing, 2007.

Dumas, C. *China and America: A Time of Reckoning*. London: Profile Books, 2008.

Dumas, C., and D. Choyleva. *The Bill from the China Shop: How Asia's Savings Glut Threatens the World Economy*. London: Profile Books, 2006.

Pepper, G., and M. Oliver. *The Liquidity Theory of Asset Prices*. Chichester, UK: Wiley, 2006.

"It is a common fault of men not to reckon on storms in fair weather." Niccolò Machiavelli

Report:

Beyer, A., and L. Reichlin (eds). "The role of money—Money and monetary policy in the twenty-first century." Fourth ECB Central Banking Conference, November 2006. Frankfurt am Main, Germany: European Central Bank, 2008. Online at: www.ecb.int/press/pr/date/2008/html/pr080225.en.html

Articles:

Ball, L. M. "Has globalization changed inflation?" NBER working paper 12687, 2006. Online at: ideas.repec.org/p/nbr/nberwo/12687.html

Borio, C. E. V., and A. Filardo. "Globalization and inflation: New cross-country evidence on the global determinants of domestic inflation." Bank for International Settlements working paper 227, 2007. Online at: ideas.repec.org/p/bis/biswps/227.html

Choyleva, D. "US liquidity crunch—The slow motion crisis." *Lombard Street Research Monthly Review* 219 (August 2007).

Choyleva, D. "The globalisation of inflation." *Lombard Street Research Monthly Review* 234 (October 2008).

Congdon, T. "Money and asset prices in boom and bust." Institute of Economic Affairs, 2005. Online at: accessible.iea.org.uk/record.jsp?type=book&ID=291

Guilloux, S., and E. Kharroubi. "Some preliminary evidence on the globalization-inflation nexus." Federal Reserve Bank of Dallas, Globalization and Monetary Policy Institute working paper 18, 2008. Online at: www.dallasfed.org/institute/wpapers/2008/0018.pdf

International Monetary Fund. "How has globalization changed inflation?" IMF World Economic Outlook, Chapter III, April 2006: 97–134. Online at: imf.org/external/pubs/ft/weo/2006/01/pdf/c3.pdf

Loungani, P., and A. Razin. "Globalization and disinflation: The efficiency channel." CEPR discussion paper 4895, 2005. Online at: ideas.repec.org/p/cpr/ceprdp/4895.html

Pain, N., I. Koske, and M. Sollie. "Globalization and inflation in the OECD economies." OECD Economics Department working paper 524, November 2006. Online at: ideas.repec.org/p/oec/ecoaaa/524-en.html

Rogoff, K. "Globalization and global disinflation." Paper presented at Federal Reserve Bank of Kansas City conference on "Monetary policy and uncertainty: Adapting to a changing economy." August 2003. Online at: www.kc.frb.org/publicat/sympos/2003/pdf/Rogoff.0910.2003.pdf

Wynne, M. A., and G. R. Solomon. "Obstacles to measuring global output gaps." *Federal Reserve Bank of Dallas Economic Letter* 2:3 (March 2007). Online at: www.dallasfed.org/research/eclett/2007/el0703.html

See Also:

★ Mixflation (pp. 215–218)
★ Viewpoint: Steering Between Deflation and Inflation—A Troubled Road for Developed Economies (pp. 604–606)
✔ Methods for Dealing with Inflation Risk (p. 984)
✔ Understanding and Using Inflation Swaps (p. 993)
Joseph Stiglitz (p. 1313)
Globalization and Its Discontents (p. 1368)

"Without humanity a man cannot long endure adversity, nor can he long enjoy prosperity." Confucius

  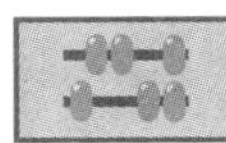   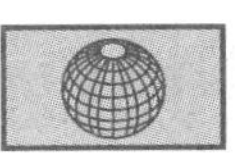   

Viewpoint: Governments of All Stripes Still Have Much to Learn from Keynes by Robert, Lord Skidelsky

INTRODUCTION

Robert, Lord Skidelsky is emeritus professor of political economy at the University of Warwick. He read history at Oxford University, and from 1961 to 1969 he was successively research student, senior student, and research fellow at Nuffield College, Oxford. In 1970 he became an associate professor at the School of Advanced International Studies, John Hopkins University. In 1978 he was appointed professor of international studies at the University of Warwick, where he has remained since, joining the Economics Department as professor of political economy in 1990. In the 1980s he began to take a more active interest in politics, becoming a founder member of the Social Democratic Party and remaining in the party until its dissolution in 1992. He was made a life peer in 1991. His three-volume biography of John Maynard Keynes, published between 1983 and 2000, has received numerous prizes and wide acclaim. He is currently Andrew D. White Professor-at-Large at Cornell University.

You have written and spoken on what you see as the false logic of austerity for the United Kingdom and other debt-laden developed economies. Could you explain your views on this?

Sometimes, when politicians think they are devising fresh economic policy, they are, in reality, simply applying—usually incorrectly—the theories of dead economists. This is not my idea; Keynes said it first. His comment was: "Practical men, who believe themselves to be quite exempt from any intellectual influences, are usually the slaves of some defunct economist." In the case of the United Kingdom I have argued before, in an article in the *New Statesman* in March 2011, that the present coalition government is following the precepts of the 19th century thinker David Ricardo. A brief summary of Ricardo's position would be that the private sector creates wealth and the government squanders it, so the smaller the government, the less it taxes and spends, and the better it is for the economy.

Ricardo argued that government borrowing—the issuing of bonds—is just a form of deferred taxation which has to be paid in the fullness of time. In the Ricardian view of things, individuals and companies know that this borrowing is happening and that it is creating a deferred tax burden, so they set aside funds to pay this tax when it is due. That holds back the economy, because the money is not available for investment. In the Ricardian view, by cutting public-sector spending you lower government debt, and the public, freed of its fear of future additional taxes, can spend more, creating more productive private-sector jobs to replace the less productive public-sector jobs that are shed in the public spending cuts.

In the view of Keynes, however, Ricardian theory only makes sense when the economy is running at full capacity. At that point public borrowing can be seen to crowd out private spending. However, when the economy has been dealt a massive shock, that theory is not only dead wrong, it has got things backwards. It is not the deficit that causes private spending to fall. It is the fall in private spending that causes the deficit to rise, and it is the deficit that is keeping the economy just about alive and growing. Plain logic tells you that any policy that encourages the economy to grow will automatically shrink the deficit.

At the height of the 2008 crash, liquidity in the world's banking systems dried up. The pumping of money into businesses and households, which is what banks do, stopped. So businesses and households reduced their spending dramatically. That put the economy into a downward spiral. If there were no government to act, then the economy would die. That is a pretty dramatic state of affairs, but we saw something very like it for a few years in Russia following the collapse of communism in the early 1990s. Wages were unpaid and people grew their own food and resorted to barter. What happens in the West is that as the private sector reduces its spending, the government continues to spend to fulfill its function. As businesses fail, government pays unemployment benefits to more people while its tax revenues decline, which means that government deficits automatically rise. Judicious stimulus of the economy at this point, according to Keynes, will bring the slump to an end and will provide enough liquidity to enable businesses to start to recover some momentum.

This is how, in the Keynesian view, you end recessions. Cutting government spending at this point just exacerbates the problem. The huge, coordinated stimulus measures that were taken between the autumn of 2008 and the spring of 2009 were successful in cutting off another great depression. On this view, the G20 governments were wholly mistaken when they agreed in June 2010 to proceed with "fiscal consolidation," which meant slashing budget deficits and imposing austerity programs even before their economies had recovered to anything like prerecession levels.

There is, in actual fact, nothing in economic theory which says that a country should aim to eliminate its deficit in four years rather than five or ten. The urgency felt by the G20 can doubtless be laid at the door of the sovereign debt crisis that erupted in Greece at the end of 2009 and which spread, by contagion, to Ireland and then to Portugal. The cost of debt for these countries rose and rose, to the point where, by Easter 2011, Greek three-year bonds were attracting interest payments of 21%. Naturally, the bailout conditions imposed by the European Central Bank and the International Monetary Fund imposed severe austerity measures on the recipient countries. So austerity came to be seen as an essential step on the road to recovery—instead of the stumbling block that it undoubtedly is. In the United Kingdom George Osborne and the coalition government claimed that austerity was essential to prevent the country from becoming another Greece, but that was always a nonsense. It appealed to the public feeling that the boom had been a debt-fueled illusion and that the slump was essential to purge the system of its rottenness. Austerity was the cure. This kind of reasoning, well divorced from economic reality, took control of policy.

"To speak of limits to growth under a capitalistic market economy is as meaningless as to speak of limits of warfare under a warrior society." Murray Bookchin

If there were some economic reality behind this 21st century form of Ricardianism, then with some £70 billion of cuts scheduled to be made over four years the United Kingdom should already be enjoying the benefits. People should be starting to spend, knowing that the deficit, which is just deferred taxation, is vanishing, and since the taxes associated with it will vanish along with it, there is no need to save for those taxes. We should, therefore, be seeing the pace of recovery picking up. In reality, the economy has flat-lined, which says volumes for the limitations of the Ricardian view. A healthy recovery should bring the economy back to full employment and normal growth within four to five years of the onset of a recession. There is no sign of this happening on the basis of present policy.

If austerity is not the way forward, what would you advocate?

The main need, as I see it, is to channel surplus cash to finance long-term investment. The government is already overborrowed, so it can't put funds directly into the economy. A reasonable alternative would be a national investment bank. In my *New Statesman* article I argued that, with some seed capital from government, such a bank could attract open market funds to support long-term private investment. It could offer interest rates that are slightly higher than the risk-free long-term bond rate and use the moneys it attracts to finance long-term investment in transport systems, green technology, and social housing, offering better terms than commercial banks. We have something like this coming along in the shape of the Green Investment Bank announced in the 2011 budget, and there are many successful examples that one can point to elsewhere. These include the German KfW Banking Group, the Development Bank of Japan, and of course the European Investment Bank. The EIB was initially funded by member governments to the tune of €50 billion and the bank then went on to raise a further €420 billion on the capital markets.

Your three-volume biography of John Maynard Keynes has been richly and deservedly praised. We touched on Keynes' fiscal theories earlier. Is the requirement for stimulus in a downturn the crux of Keynesian thought for you?

Keynes was sucked into economics by the global disorder that followed the First World War. I wrote in an essay for *The Economist* that economics, as Keynes practiced and transformed it, offered a way of reconciling his ethical and aesthetic commitments with the mastery of an external world which menaced them. In 1930 he defined the purpose of economics as the endeavor to solve the "economic problem" so that mankind could live "wisely, agreeably and well." At the time that I wrote the second volume of my trilogy we were in the Thatcherite 1980s, and by that point it was reasonable to ask whether Milton Friedman had more to offer us than Maynard Keynes.

Certainly Keynes' great work *The General Theory of Employment, Interest and Money*, which had been published in 1936, was no longer immediately relevant in the sense of being "holy writ," since it was clearly the product of the special conjucture that produced the Great Depression. In thinking about this I drew heart from Keynes' own comments to his Cambridge students in 1933, when he said: "When you adopt perfectly precise language you are trying to express yourself for the benefit of those who are incapable of thought."

It seems clear that we suffer from an overelaboration and pseudo-precision in economics today, to the point where the subject has become so formal and mathematicized that even economists "lose the plot." The financial engineering around subprime mortgages, which was supposed to diversify away all risk (subprime being by definition high risk), is a wonderful case in point. I came to see Keynes' general theory as a macroeconomic model of his long-standing concern with the effects of uncertainty on business expectations. In fact, I saw that this concept of Keynesian uncertainty lies at the heart of his work and at the heart of his relevance today. It ties together the connections between uncertainty and money, the psychology of money, and Keynes's long-standing advocacy of the government's role in stabilizing the economy.

For Keynes, uncertainty is a fundamental condition of all human life. This is a line of thought that goes back to his early work on probability theory. In economic terms, all agents have to grapple with incomplete knowledge about the future, and they devise a range of quasi-rational strategies to cope with this. Holding money is the key strategy. Devising ways of deploying it follows from this. Having money means that you can postpone decisions to invest and consume. It is an escape from the necessity of an immediate commitment to action. This is one of Keynes' deep, original contributions to economics.

This view takes into account the propensity to hoard money. Depressions, then, become the fruits of sin, just as the classical economists taught, but they are a sin not of extravagance, but of usury. This medieval concept Keynes identified with his own "liquidity preference" theory of the rate of interest. As I have said before, like all properly educated atheists, Keynes was steeped in theology!

From the uncertainty principle, Keynes rejected the idea that an economy has a natural tendency to full employment. The analytical model that he chose to embody his vision of uncertainty saw any economy as having multiple "equilibrium" levels, with different degrees of employment at each level. Money enables expectations about the future to influence the decisions that agents make about production in the present. Keynes took a technical tool invented by Richard Kahn—the multiplier—and used it to show that following a shock to demand in the economy, the diminution of income would lead to reduced incentives to invest and a concomitant increase in the propensity to save. This in turn would balance out at a lower level of employment and output than before the shock. Hence, to shift the economy back to the levels of employment prior to the crash, some form of government stimulus to the economy is essential, otherwise the state of equilibrium at the lower level of employment continues indefinitely.

Dubbed the "income-expenditure model" this became the core of "scientific" Keynesianism and became, too, the policy tool which governments could use at any moment to adjust levels of aggregate expenditure in the economy to any desired level of employment.

The third volume of your biography of Keynes deals with events after the Second World War. How did Depression-era Keynesian theory cope with postwar events?

Through the "golden age" of the 1950s and 1960s, when rearmament, the Cold War, and the construction of the welfare state dragged the world back to full employment, Keynes' scientific model was applied not so much to output as to inflation. What is left to us of Keynes' thought today, I would argue, is not the "scientific" demonstration that underemployment equilibrium is possible, but his intuition that a market economy is inherently unstable, and that this instability is deeply rooted in the logic of financial markets. It follows from this not that market capitalism should be left alone or abolished, but rather that it needs constant intervention to stabilize it.

Most macroeconomic models still have Keynes' "aggregates" (prices, output, savings, investment) and their relationships at their heart, but governments no longer try to fine-tune these relationships so persistently.

You are now involved with the Institute for New Economic Thinking (INET), the body sponsored by George Soros and tasked with stimulating a revolution in economic thinking around the world. How is that progressing?

INET was launched in October 2009 with a US$50 million grant from George Soros. The dominant form of economics prior to the crash was based on the "perfect knowledge" assumption. As I said at the Government Economic Service conference in January 2011, economics is an axiomatic discipline. It starts with a very small number of assumptions, such as equilibrium, stable preference, and maximization, and then deduces a very large number of conclusions from these. Ideally these should be seen as heuristics—moves to get the argument in motion. However, most economists tend to see them as the basis for their explanations of real-world behavior. The "perfect knowledge" assumption underlies all these assumptions, as a kind of super-axiom. Agents not only know what they want, they know how to get it. The real world is much messier.

The "perfect knowledge" axiom also conflicts directly with Keynes's uncertainty principle. However, it has been much more powerful, before the crash, than any opposing theory in defining economics. The crash was a vivid demonstration of the limitations of this model, hence the need for new economic thinking. The best approach, and the one taken by INET, is to encourage the development of new research and to promote changes to the way economics is taught. This is INET's purpose. I am on the advisory council and chair a task force to work out a new economics curriculum. We presented a draft of a reformed economics degree program at the second general meeting of INET, at Bretton Woods, in April 2011.

British participation in INET was triggered by the now famous question put by Queen Elizabeth when she asked the London School of Economics why so few economists had foreseen the credit crunch. The US Nobel laureate economist and *New York Times* columnist Paul Krugman had already written of "the profession's blindness to the very possibility of catastrophic failures in a market economy." The central idea of our reform is to reconnect the teachings of economics with the workings of the actual economy—and to begin at the beginning, with the reform of the undergraduate curriculum.

MORE INFO

Book:

Skidelsky, Robert. *John Maynard Keynes*. 3 vols. New York: Penguin Group, 1994 (vol. 1), 1995 (vol. 2), and 2002 (vol. 3).

Articles:

Krugman, Paul. "How did economists get it so wrong?" *New York Times Magazine* (September 2, 2009). Online at: www.nytimes.com/2009/09/06/magazine/06Economic-t.html

Skidelsky, Robert. "The Osborne ultimatum." *New Statesman* (March 24, 2011). Online at: www.skidelskyr.com/site/article/the-osborne-ultimatum

Website:

Institute for New Economic Thinking (INET): ineteconomics.org

See Also:

John Maynard Keynes (p. 1289)

Insurance—Bruised, Not Crushed by Robert P. Hartwig

EXECUTIVE SUMMARY

- Compared with the banking sector, the insurance industry has been able to continue business as usual through the crash thanks to some crucial differences between the two sectors.
- The sector faces some specific challenges posed by "long-tailed" business in the downturn as it seeks to match assets against liabilities.
- Low returns in an era of near zero interest rates will push up premium prices.
- The sector has a number of anxieties concerning potential regulatory responses to the crash.
- Risk appraisal is a key differences between banks and insurance companies.

INTRODUCTION

There is no doubt that, compared with the banks and the investment banks, the insurance sector has come through the crash in relatively good order. The sector has not escaped entirely. AIG, the world's biggest insurer, needed a US$85 billion bailout from the Federal Reserve to help the company unwind its credit default swap (CDS) positions "in an orderly manner," without precipitating one of the biggest insolvencies ever in US insurance history. However, it is important to realize that AIG was a very unusual insurance company, and a leader in the CDS market, which went sour when the liquidity crunch set in. AIG's business model and profile of operations have no real parallel in the rest of the sector.

The vast majority of what the United States calls property and casualty insurers, and Europe terms general insurers, are working through the current deep recession with the fundamental business of insurance operating normally, with the transfer of risk from client to insurer and from insurer to re-insurer continuing as normal, and with no shortage of capacity.

None of this is true of the banking market, and this is where the fundamental difference between these two components of the financial services sector manifests itself most strikingly. In the banking sector, of course, loan activity has been greatly reduced, and, by early 2009, there was really very little that could be termed "normal" about many of the world's major banks.

Of course, the insurance sector as a whole is not immune to a general economic downturn, and particularly not to a full-blown, deep, global recession. The sector is less sensitive to fluctuations in the economy than most industries, as in many instances insurance is not an option but a necessity. However, to the extent that economies are not growing, the sector cannot advance.

A RISK-AVERSE MARKET

We have a more general challenge, however, in the sector, and this has to do with the fact that many insurance risks are "long-tailed;" they run for many years into the future. In an ideal world, you would look to match your liabilities with your assets. Today, however, there is very little yield available on long-term instruments, and we even had the bizarre situation on December 4, 2008, when long-dated Treasury bills slipped into nominal negative returns. This kind of position shows a tremendous level of risk aversion in the market, with short-term fear outweighing long-term needs. It created a bubble in the price of Treasuries that leads to unsustainable programs.

What all this means is that insurers are not going to tie up their investment money in a 20-year yield at these very low rates, as, if the rates went up in a few years' time, these instruments would sustain a significant loss. This, in turn, means that investment income will decline in the medium term for insurers, as short-term investments are likely to provide very meagre rates of return.

A "SOFT MARKET"

For the insurance sector, there are only two possible sources of income. These are investment income premiums on business written, and low investment returns have a very direct impact on premium prices, which will almost certainly rise. There is very little option about this for the industry. The sector's anticipated losses are not going to be any the less because investment yields are down. Natural catastrophes happen every year, and they cost a great deal, whatever the investment climate.

This, then, creates a fear that insurance prices will become too high for the market to bear. We are currently in a period of declining prices for insurance premiums; what the industry calls a "soft market." Prices have been declining for four straight years, and the price of many types of insurance in the United States today are below where they were in 2004. This is one of the features of the sector. Insurance is nothing if not cyclical, and every player in the sector knows this very well.

However, even if rising prices cause the insurance sector to "flip flop" from a declining price market to a rising price market, the cost of premiums, despite the current difficult economic circumstances, is highly unlikely to become an onerous burden on an individual's or a company's budget. The last "hard market," when the industry was able to charge high prices because the market in general was pricing high, was in the period 2000–2003, and we could be seeing a return to that period.

To understand how pricing affects the industry, it is worth pointing out, perhaps, that the hard pricing of 2000–2003 brought the industry through the 9/11 period with its massive payouts, and, when insurers experienced record catastrophe losses in 2004 and 2005, the industry had to build up sufficient capital to come through in good shape. At the same time, 2006 and 2007 were low loss years as far as natural disasters were concerned. That all turned around in 2008, where we had poor investment returns and high catastrophe payouts.

It is probably too soon, at the time of writing in February 2009, to say that insurance markets are definitely heading back to a hard market, with a rapid and sustained price rise ahead. The industry globally needs to take a very severe hit before that happens, and we are possibly not there yet.

Despite the adverse features of 2008 for the industry, the underwriting performance was not that bad, and was consistent with four years of a soft pricing market. The problem the sector has is that, with the economic downturn, asset categories that were thought of as safe have lost significant amounts of value, and the sector has to invest its premium income to generate returns.

To sum up then, the industry went into the financial crisis extremely well capitalized. However, much of that surplus capital has been eroded through the underwriting and investment losses 2008. So now, instead of being extremely well capitalized, the industry is merely adequately capitalized.

One of the common misconceptions about the challenges facing the industry is that global warming, and the more energetic and extreme weather events that are predicted to follow from this, will be too much for the sector to handle. In actual fact, extreme weather conditions are nothing new for the sector. It has been dealing with the consequences of extreme weather

"The four most expensive words in the English language are, This time, it's different." Sir John Templeton

events for centuries. The key here, as elsewhere, is to be able to price the business appropriately. The increased risk has to be priced into the cost of insurance.

The insurance sector has been extremely strong in Europe and, more recently, in the United States, in voicing its concerns about global warming and the need for concerted action. However, it is undoubtedly true that the current crisis has somewhat overwhelmed environmental concerns.

REGULATORY RESPONSE

A great source of anxiety, going forward, is how the regulators will respond. There is no doubt at all that there will be a change in the regulatory environment faced by the industry. In the United States, regulation has traditionally been carried out on a state-by-state basis, and there is now speculation that we could be seeing the end of a 135-year tradition of state-based regulation in favor of centralized federal regulation. Smaller insurers, particularly, would much rather continue to be faced with local regulators, than some central regulator in far-away Washington, DC.

Another unknown is whether any new federal regulatory structure would regulate for solvency, or for rates and forms. Many larger multinational insurers would prefer that solvency regulation be moved to the federal level and that there be no regulatory hand on the price of insurance. The remaining months of 2009 will see a good deal of debate on these themes.

On top of all this, we have new regulations, such as Solvency II and the international accounting standards. It seems clear from the current financial crisis that accounting systems were clearly not up to the task. There were also undoubted problems, both in the United States and in Europe, in the regulation of financial services, and there will need to be a good deal of discussion here before some kind of a global regulatory system can be imposed. The regulatory and oversight regimes in both the United States and Europe have been shown to be faulty, so no one, at this point in time, has a template without its shortcomings.

CONTROLLING SYSTEMATIC RISK

As far as the United States is concerned, it is already clear that the focus will be on controlling systemic risk, and on identifying points across the financial services sector that have the potential to bring down the system, as was the case with poorly priced credit derivatives products. The insurance sector invested in some of these instruments, but, by and large, with the exception of AIG, it was not deeply involved. It seems a reasonable guess, therefore, that the general insurance sector will emerge from this crisis with its risk management model more intact than any other sector of the financial service industry.

A key reason for this is that, unlike banks, which spun off risks away from themselves by wrapping the risk up in securitized products and selling it on, the insurance sector retains in whole or in part the risks associated with the business it writes. Therefore, it does not have the "out of touch," "out of control" motivation to keep on creating very risky products to maximize volume, fees and profitability, *á la* the banks. The endpoint of all this for the banks was a total collapse of risk management, and catastrophic losses.

With hindsight, now that we know both how reliant many banks were on liquidity in the credit markets to sustain their business models, and how subprime mortgages were used in asset-backed securities on a grand scale (securities that were taken up, also on a grand scale, by the banks themselves), the collapse does not appear that surprising. What was surprising was the fact that this out-of-control model in the banking world could continue for so long, and that it was able to blow the bubble up to such a proportion without check.

Not only do insurance companies retain a stake in every contract they write, the operating model in the sector is not based on debt. We now see that the model for some of the best-known investment banks was to have one dollar of capital for US$30 of debt, and then to invest most of it in highly risky assets. The equivalent behavior in the insurance world would be for an insurer to leverage up their capital by a factor of 30, and then to use the money to write insurance policies on every home on the coast of Florida.

Again, the key difference with the banks is that, in insurance, there is an alignment of interests between the insurer and the consumer—the insurer bears the risk if the contract does not perform. In a securitization deal, the bank that originates the deal has sold the risk on to the investor, and the risk becomes the investor's risk. The bank is "free" from the risk. Whether selling "toxic" products was an appropriate way to treat one's investors seems not to have been considered. Of course, not all sellers of structured credit products knew they were toxic before the collapse of the asset-backed market, but with hindsight one has to question the due diligence model being used.

Another point to stress is that insurers are accustomed to applying a great deal of care, discipline, and accuracy to the treatment and pricing of risk. Underwriting is a real discipline, and no organization survives the challenges involved in being an underwriter if there is anything loose or sloppy in its approach and methodology. You have to be focused on managing your potential loss exposure, or it will destroy you. The model adopted by the banks emphasized leverage, volume, and short-term rewards, and was blind to any risk that was not immediate, or that did not have an impact on the banks' regulatory capital requirements.

CONCLUSION

Off-balance-sheet special purpose vehicles (SPVs) had no impact on bank capital adequacy requirements, and the potential impact on bank solvency of the business written by such entities was not considered. The insurance sector is more stringently regulated than the banking sector, and the focus is much more on transparency. In 2008, there were 25 bank failures in the United States, including the largest bank failure in history, Washington Mutual, with US$307 billion in assets. No insurer has, so far, failed in the current credit crunch and downturn.

MORE INFO

Presentation:

Hartwig, Robert. "Financial crisis, economic stimulus and the future of the P/C insurance industry: Trends, challenges and opportunities." Online at: www.iii.org/media/presentations/westchester

Website:

Insurance Information Institute: www.iii.org

See Also:

★ Credit Derivatives—The Origins of the Problem (p. 156)
★ Enterprise Risk Management and Solvency II (p. 173)
✔ Key Accounting Standards and Organizations (p. 1040)
✔ Solvency II: Its Development and Aims (p. 1053)
✔ Understanding Asset–Liability Management (Full Balance Sheet Approach) (p. 996)
Insurance (pp. 1633–1635)

"**Except for the con men borrowing money they shouldn't get and the widows who have to visit with the handsome young men in the trust department, no sane person ever enjoyed visiting a bank.**" Martin Mayer

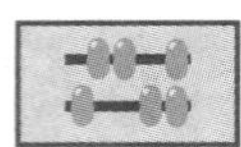

The International Role of Islamic Finance

EXECUTIVE SUMMARY

- Islamic finance has become mainstream, with more than US$800 billion of assets worldwide. However, it still faces distinct developmental challenges from economic and legal constraints associated with *sukuk*, banking-specific issues, and fragmented financial regulation.
- Although Islamic capital markets and banking have defied the impact of the financial crisis, some negative effects were felt in 2008 and are likely to inhibit further expansion.
- Despite current challenges, most of which arise from the infancy of the industry, Islamic finance has promising long-term prospects.

INTRODUCTION

Since the summer of 2007 the global financial system has undergone a period of dramatic turbulence, which has caused a widespread reassessment of risk in both developed and emerging economies and the price it should command across different asset classes. After a rather painful reckoning, policymakers and regulators are hastening a redesign of the financial sector architecture afflicted by the demise of self-regulation and a failure of market efficiency. As the global credit crisis continues to deepen, with investment banks and finance houses worldwide still reeling from the collapse of the US subprime mortgage market and the breakdown of the wholesale money markets, soul-searching in conventional finance has directed attention to alternative modes of finance. In this context new investors, unsettled by excessive risk-taking and asset price volatility, are turning to Islamic finance as market ruptures caused by the headlong flight to safety during the initial phase of the credit crisis seem to be receding only slowly.

Although Islamic finance did not entirely escape the implications of persistent counterparty risk concerns and deep-seated investor distrust of credit-sensitive assets, it managed to harness the current market adversity as a result of greater focus on collateralization, the contempt for excessive leverage, and the near absence of "distressed legacy assets," such as mortgage-backed securities. Islamic finance is driven by the general precept of extending religious doctrine in the *shariah* to financial agreements and transactions. Islamic finance is distinct from conventional finance insofar as it substitutes the (temporary) use of assets (or services) by the borrower for a permanent transfer of funds from the lender as a source of indebtedness. Predatory lending, empty short-selling, and a series of incentive problems between originators, arrangers, and sponsors, of which all have infested the conventional capital markets, go against fundamental Islamic principles which ensure that contractual certainty and a mutually beneficial balance are maintained between borrowers and lenders (Wilson, 2008).[1]

Until the onset of the credit crisis at the end of 2007, the Islamic finance industry was in an expansionary phase, exhibiting average annual growth rates of about 15% in recent years. This rapid growth has been fueled by surging demand for *shariah*-compliant products not only from Muslim financiers, but also by investors around the world. Besides its wide geographical scope, the rapid expansion of Islamic finance is also taking place across the whole spectrum of financial activities, ranging from retail banking to insurance and capital market investments. There is currently more than US$800 billion worth of deposits and investments lodged in Islamic banks, mutual funds, insurance schemes (known as *takaful*), and Islamic branches of conventional banks.

The rapid evolution of Islamic finance points to the considerable profit opportunities, which have prompted a vetting process among a number of jurisdictions around the world to establish themselves as leading Islamic financial centers. In this regard, the case of London is perhaps the most remarkable insofar as it has managed to extend its leading position in world financial markets to become a center for Islamic finance. Similarly, Hong Kong, New York, and Singapore are making important advances to accommodate Islamic finance within their jurisdictions, and they aspire to join the ranks of the more established Islamic centers such as Bahrain, Dubai, and Kuala Lumpur. These developments underscore the fact that Islamic finance has established itself as a permanent element of the global financial landscape. Nevertheless, despite the recent advances, important challenges lie ahead.

Against this background, the present article first reviews the current situation of Islamic finance before discussing some of the challenges going forward. For expository purposes, the article follows a two-pronged approach in considering these challenges through a discussion of key banking issues and then selected capital market issues.

ISLAMIC BANKING

As mentioned above, Islamic banks have increased their presence in conventional financial systems. Typically, this process has taken place in two ways: either conventional banks have increasingly tested the waters of *shariah*-compliant banking activities by opening an Islamic "window," and/or they have offered specific Islamic financial products, or fully fledged Islamic banks have been licensed as such.

One of the first concerns that arise as Islamic banking emerges within a conventional system is how to embed Islamic activities into the existing juridical and supervisory frameworks. To think about this issue, it is useful to adopt a two-tier perspective and address, first, the *legal* aspects of Islamic contracts, and, second, the *regulatory* aspects of Islamic financial transactions.

In other words, on the one hand there is the legal question of whether the existing laws in a secular jurisdiction allow financial transactions to be governed by *shariah* principles. On the other hand, there is the regulatory question of whether Islamic institutions require the same intensity and kind of prudential supervision as conventional institutions.

First, regarding the place of Islamic contractual arrangements within secular jurisdictions, it is likely that the existing legislation in conventional jurisdictions does not include all the *shariah* principles that should govern Islamic financial transactions. However, as DeLorenzo and McMillen (2007) point out, in most of the jurisdictions with modern legal systems the legal set-up is typically flexible enough to allow the parties involved to write their own contracts. Thus, in these contracts, the signing parties could explicitly specify the desired principles by which their transactions should be governed. By doing this, both parties would ensure that the principles to which they wish to adhere would be upheld in the jurisdiction where the contract is enforced.

"Islamic finance should still be able to combat the crisis better than conventional banks but big problems loom if liquidity remains tight." Sohail Zubairi

Second, a key aspect is whether Islamic institutions require levels of supervision similar to those applied to conventional institutions. In this regard, a somewhat common misunderstanding is that, since Islamic banking is largely based on profit and loss sharing agreements, Islamic institutions do not need to be supervised at the same level as conventional banks. In fact, as pointed out by Errico and Farrahbaksh (1998), El-Hawary *et al.* (2004), and Solé (2007), there are certain features of Islamic banks that warrant a similar degree of prudential regulation as traditional banks. These considerations include moral hazard considerations, safeguarding the interests of demand depositors, and systemic considerations.

There are specific risks that need to be taken into account both by financial institutions and regulators to foster an environment where Islamic banking can offer a suitable response to investors' and depositors' demands for Islamic products (Bhambra, 2007; Sundararajan, 2007). Recognizing the need for guidance on these issues, in 2002 a number of central banks and national monetary authorities of Islamic countries inaugurated the Islamic Financial Services Board (IFSB) in Malaysia as an international standard-setting body. The IFSB's mandate is to ensure the stability and soundness of the Islamic financial services industry by developing new, or adapting existing, international finance standards consistent with *shariah* principles, and by harmonizing industry practices. In fact, parallel to the revision of the Basel Capital Accord in 2005, the IFSB issued regulatory standards on capital adequacy and risk management for Islamic institutions (IFSB, 2005a, b). It has also issued additional standards in other important areas, such as corporate governance and the supervisory review, and most recently on capital adequacy of *sukuk*.

ISLAMIC CAPITAL MARKETS

Amid a growing demand for alternative investments, there has been a surge in recent years in the issuance of Islamic capital market securities by corporates and public-sector entities, owing in large part to enabling capital market regulations, a favorable macroeconomic environment, and financial innovation aimed at establishing *shariah* compliance. In some cases, governments have taken a greater role in shaping the growth prospects of the fledgling Islamic capital market (which is largely sponsored by banks). Asset securitization plays a special role in this regard.

Although the concepts of asset-backing and absolute transfer of ownership are inherent to Islamic finance, very few structured credit transactions have been executed following the precepts of the *shariah*. Islamic securitization transforms *bilateral risk sharing* between borrowers and lenders in Islamic finance into *market-based refinancing*. Although the religious prohibition of the exchange of debt and the required conferral of ownership interest to participate in business risk still pose challenges to the development of Islamic securitization, the gradual acceptance of Islamic investment certificates, so-called *sukuk* bonds, in particular represents a successful attempt to overcome these impediments (Oakley *et al.*, 2008; Jobst, 2007a, b).

Since conventional securitization is virtually absent in Islamic countries, considerable demand for *shariah*-compliant investment assets, such as *sukuk*, has provided an untapped market for structured finance as a means to advance capital market development. While *sukuk* are structured in a similar way to conventional asset-backed securities or covered bonds, they can have significantly different underlying structures and provisions. *Sukuk* commoditize capital gains from bilateral risk-sharing between borrowers and lenders in *shariah*-compliant finance contracts—such as lending transactions (installment sale) or trust-based investments in existing or future assets—into marketable securities.

Before the financial crisis, the *sukuk* market soared in response to surging demand for *shariah*-compliant products. Gross issuance rose from US$7.2 billion in 2004 to close to US$39 billion by the end of 2007 (Moody's Investors Service, 2008). At the end of 2007, the outstanding volume of *sukuk* globally exceeded US$90 billion. However, in 2008, *sukuk* volumes declined sharply to US$17.2 billion (about 50%) as a result of challenging market conditions, liquidity constraints, and the presentation of new rules on the *shariah* compliance of *sukuk* (Jobst *et al.*, 2008). In particular, the less supportive economic environment in the Gulf Corporation Council countries, and the regional real estate sector troubled by the slowdown of global trade and foreign direct investment, have contributed to this development. Even countries that have been driving forces in the *sukuk* market in recent years witnessed sizable declines. Amid a gradual normalization of credit conditions in early 2009, incipient demand helped, stabilize the primary market for *sukuk*. During the first seven months of 2009 new issuance exceeded US$9 billion, compared with US$11.1 billion during the same period in 2008 (Damak *et al.*, 2009).

In spite of having been hemmed in by the credit crisis, the *sukuk* market is expected to gain momentum again over the medium term, with an estimated US$50 billion worth of planned transactions in the pipeline. With more than US$2 trillion of credit demand projected to be unmet in the next three years as the conventional private-label securitization market remains dysfunctional, the current market situation provides a window of opportunity for *sukuk*. Given the ongoing efforts to resolve the major difficulties impeding market development, *sukuk* is likely to register ever more as an alternative and diversified funding option that broadens the pricing spectrum and asset supply.

GENERAL CHALLENGES

What are the current challenges for Islamic finance and its continued above-average growth rates in the different regions, and across banks and products?

Recent regulatory changes concerning the structure of *sukuk* warrant careful

Figure 1. Global issuance of *sukuk*, 2005–08. (*Source*: IFIS, Bloomberg, Dealogic, Datastream)

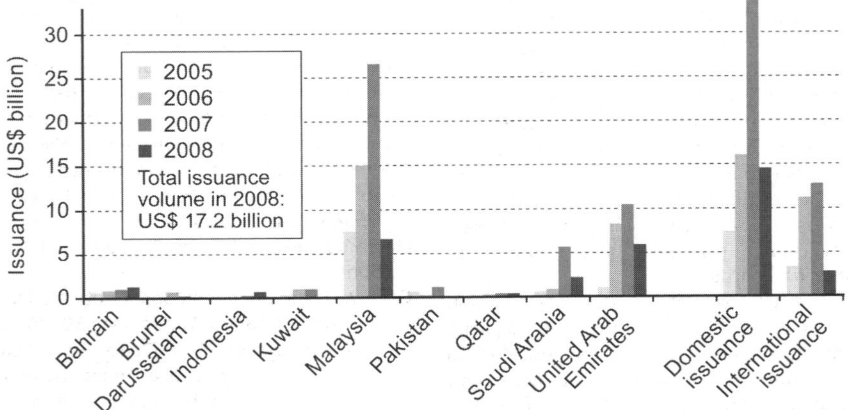

"As investors and issuers become more comfortable with [. . .] *sukuk*, the industry will be able to take advantage [. . .] of their quasi-equity qualities." Blake Goud

consideration and might mute some of the recent enthusiasm for Islamic capital market products. In February 2008, the *shariah* committee of the Accounting and Auditing Organization of Islamic Finance Institutions (AAOIFI) issued new recommendations regarding the role of asset ownership, investment guarantees, and the *shariah* advisory and approval process in *sukuk* origination and trading. Most *sukuk* issued in the GCC have explicit repurchase agreements that guarantee the repayment of principal but violate the profit and loss sharing features of *shariah* law. Discussions are currently underway between the various stakeholders and some market participants to gauge the potential of these recommendations to cause permanent damage to the *sukuk* market.

The liquidity risk management of Islamic banks is an important challenge and is constrained due to the limited availability of tradable Islamic money market instruments and weak systemic liquidity infrastructure. At the moment, there is no *shariah*-compliant short-term Islamic money market (of less than one-week maturity) in local currency or in US dollars, and Islamic reposession markets (for funding liquidity) have not yet developed. Islamic money markets with longer maturities sometimes suffer from an unreliable clearing and settlement process. Islamic banks also have a competitive disadvantage compared to conventional banks, as they deposit their overnight money with their domestic central bank at no interest.

The future development of Islamic capital markets could be arrested by insufficient supervisory and legal harmonization across national boundaries and the ongoing controversy about financial innovation. Governance issues, especially the *shariah* compliance of products and activities, constitute a major challenge for the Islamic finance industry. Although *shariah* rulings (*fatwas*) by legal scholars are disclosed, there are currently no unified principles on the basis of which *shariah* scholars decide on the *shariah* compliance of new products and subsequently convey their assessment. These rulings are not consolidated, which inhibits the dissemination, adoption, and cross-fertilization of jurisprudence across different countries and schools of thought. As a result, there is still considerable diversity and inconsistency in corporate governance principles and opinions of *shariah* boards.

The heterogeneity of scholastic opinion about *shariah* compliance and disparity among national supervisors continue to undermine the creation of a consistent regulatory framework. That said, recent standard-setting efforts have addressed the legal uncertainty imposed by Islamic jurisprudence and the poorly developed uniformity of market practices. Leading international organizations in Islamic finance, such as AAOIFI, have been working on aligning *shariah* principles on a consistent basis. In this regard, a fine balance is required between collective initiatives and regulatory revisions to ensure that standardization is achieved without staving off financial innovation. Also, efforts to achieve regulatory consolidation and standard setting are underway. The AAOIFI and the IFSB have moved ahead with their standardization efforts in relation to the Islamic financial services industry.

CONCLUSION

This adversity of current economic conditions is likely also to prolong the recovery of Islamic finance. As policymakers in mature markets enter the uncharted territory of dealing with troubled banks, restoring confidence in financial markets, and restarting economic growth, heightened risk-aversion and depressed asset prices portend a further contraction of credit in the near future. Islamic finance is not insulated from these fundamental developments in conventional finance. For Islamic banks in particular, the absence of government guarantees (which would violate the basic tenets of *shariah* law), and the cannibalization of term markets by an avalanche of sovereign debt, might exacerbate long-term funding pressures to overcome chronic maturity mismatches while slowing the rebuilding of their capital base and raising the risk of displaced commercial interest for depositors.

Many challenges still lie ahead, but the banks' search for profitable opportunities and the ensuing financial innovation process, in tandem with favorable regulatory developments at the domestic and international levels, will ensure that the Islamic finance industry continues to develop at a steady pace in the long run. For instance, the development of Islamic derivatives bodes well for the Islamic insurance (*takaful*) industry, whose *shariah* compliance has traditionally resulted in overdependence on equity and real-estate investment, restricting the potential of risk diversification from a wider spectrum of available assets. From a more strategic perspective, financial institutions in countries such as Bahrain, Qatar, the United Arab Emirates, and Malaysia continue to register considerable demand for *shariah*-compliant investments and structured finance on both the asset and liability sides. The jury is still out on how strongly Islamic finance will be affected by the repercussions of the global financial crisis.

MORE INFO

Books:

Bhambra, Hari. "Supervisory implications of Islamic finance in the current regulatory environment." In Rifaat Ahmed Abdel Kareem and Simon Archer (eds). *Islamic Finance: The Regulatory Challenge*. Singapore: Wiley, 2007; 198–212.

DeLorenzo, Yusuf T., and Michael J. T. McMillen. "Law and Islamic finance: An interactive analysis." In Rifaat Ahmed Abdel Kareem and Simon Archer (eds). *Islamic Finance: The Regulatory Challenge*. Singapore: Wiley, 2007; 132–197.

Sundararajan, V. "Risk characteristics of Islamic products: Implication for risk measurement and supervision." In Rifaat Ahmed Abdel Kareem and Simon Archer (eds). *Islamic Finance: The Regulatory Challenge*. Singapore: Wiley, 2007; 40–68.

Articles:

Jobst, Andreas A. "A primer on structured finance." *Journal of Derivatives and Hedge Funds* 13:3 (2007a): 199–213. Online at: dx.doi.org/10.1057/palgrave.jdhf.1850070

Jobst, Andreas A. "The economics of Islamic finance and securitization." *Journal of Structured Finance* 13:1 (2007b): 6–27. Online at: dx.doi.org/10.3905/jsf.2007.684860. Also published as IMF working paper 07/117.

Jobst, Andreas A., Peter Kunzel, Paul Mills, and Amadou N. R. Sy. "Islamic bond issuance: What sovereign debt managers need to know." *International Journal of Islamic and Middle Eastern Finance and Management* 1:4 (2008): 330–344. Online at: dx.doi.org/10.1108/17538390810919637

Moody's Investors Service. "Inside Moody's: Focus on the Middle East." *Inside Moody's* (Spring 2008): 4.

Oakley, David, Shannon Bond, Cynthia O'Murchu, and Celve Jones. "Islamic finance explained." *Financial Times* (May 30, 2008). Online at: www.ft.com/cms/s/0/5067aace-2e67-11dd-ab55-000077b07658.html

Wilson, Rodney. "Islamic economics and finance." *World Economics* 9:1 (2008): 177–195. Online at: www.world-economics-journal.com/Contents/ArticleOverview.aspx?ID=327

"Shariah principles would help asset managers to step back from financial engineering and shift toward risk and profit sharing, which is much healthier." Toby Birch

  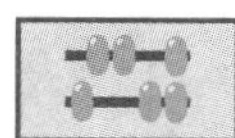   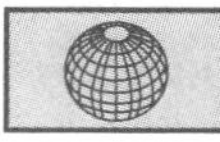   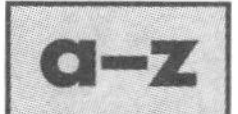

Reports:

Damak, Mohamed, Emmanuel Volland, and Ritesh Maheshwari. "The sukuk market has continued to progress in 2009 despite some roadblocks." Paris: Standard & Poor's, September 2, 2009.

El-Hawary, Dahlia, Wafik Grais, and Zamir Iqbal. "Regulating Islamic financial institutions: The nature of the regulated." World Bank policy research working paper 3227, Washington, DC: World Bank, 2004.

Errico, Luca, and Mitra Farrahbaksh. "Islamic banking: Issues in prudential regulation and supervision." International Monetary Fund working paper 98/30, Washington, DC: IMF, 1998.

Islamic Financial Services Board (IFSB). "Capital adequacy standard for institutions (other than insurance institutions) offering only Islamic financial services." Kuala Lumpur: IFSB, December 2005a. Online at: www.ifsb.org/standard/ifsb2.pdf

Islamic Financial Services Board (IFSB). "Guiding principles of risk management for institutions (other than insurance institutions) offering only Islamic financial services." Kuala Lumpur: IFSB, December 2005b. Online at: www.ifsb.org/standard/ifsb1.pdf

Solé, Juan A. "Introducing Islamic banks into conventional banking systems." IMF working paper 07/175. Washington, DC: IMF, July 2007.

See Also:

★ Identifying the Main Regulatory Challenges for Islamic Finance (pp. 358–360)
★ Introduction to Islamic Financial Risk Management Products (pp. 59–62)
★ Islamic Modes of Finance and the Role of *Sukuk* (pp. 520–521)
★ Risk Management of Islamic Finance Instruments (pp. 94–97)
★ Viewpoint: *Shariah* Law—Bringing a New Ethical Dimension to Banking (pp. 242–243)
✔ Key Islamic Banking Instruments and How They Work (p. 1010)
✔ Key Principles of Islamic Finance (p. 1011)
✔ Regulatory and Capital Issues under *Shariah* Law (p. 1050)
An Introduction to Islamic Finance Theory and Practice (p. 1380)

NOTE

1 Any financial transaction under Islamic law implies *direct participation in asset performance* ("asset layer") and assigns to financiers clearly identifiable rights and obligations for which they are entitled to receive a commensurate return in the form of state-contingent payments. *Shariah* law prohibits the sale and purchase of debt contracts with the aim of obtaining an interest gain (*riba*) or profit-taking without real economic activity and asset transfer, as well as legal uncertainty surrounding the enforceability of contractual claims.

"All the great economic ills the world has known this century can be directly traced back to the London School of Economics." N. M. Perera

Viewpoint: Investment Lessons from the Crash

by Jeremy Beckwith

INTRODUCTION

Jeremy Beckwith joined Kleinwort Benson in April 2003 as chief investment officer and is responsible for all aspects of the investment process and investment performance of discretionary portfolios. He introduced multi-asset class investing to Kleinwort Benson and is regularly invited on to Bloomberg TV to give his views on markets and economics.

Prior to this, he was a managing director and head of EAFE Equities (non-US equities for American retail and institutional clients) at Merrill Lynch Investment Managers. Before joining the EAFE team in 1988 he was managing director of Merrill Lynch Global Asset Management, managing the portfolios of high net worth private clients and small institutions from Europe and the Middle East, and also chaired the Global Investment Committee. Prior to 1990 he was head of equities for Mitsubishi Finance International and a portfolio manager for Manufacturers Life Insurance Company. From 2006 to 2008 he was chairman of the FTSE Private Banking Index Advisory Board, and was named on the Citywealth Private Banking Leaders List for 2008.

From the perspective of portfolio management and investment strategy, what lessons can we learn from the 2008–09 financial crash, which was characterized by a high degree of correlation among a diverse range of asset classes?

Hindsight is a wonderful thing. The near total collapse of the world's financial system in October 2008, and the volatility that this triggered off across all types offinancial markets, offer us many lessons that have a recurring value and are not just specific to this last crash. Even a cursory study of economic history shows that financial collapses recur at regular five or six yearly intervals, although really major collapses tend to come in about 50- to 100-year cycles. 2008 was a major collapse because it was at heart abanking systemcollapse, which leads to high correlations among all financial assets. The precise events that trigger each one are never identical, but there are similarities.

The four major lessons that I draw from this were set out in a chapter that I contributed to theInstitute of Directors' 2010 *Handbook of Personal Wealth Management*. The first lesson we should take away from the latest crash is that where you have an explosive growth of cheap debt, you are going to have an asset price bubble that will end up being unsustainable and which will implode, with massive and often unlooked-for results. In the last cycle this showed up most clearly in two areas, namely the US housing market and the "shadow banking" sector. In the former, a continuing fall in USinterest rates, as set by theFederal Reserve, added fuel to a popular political agenda committed to extending home ownership to "every American," including the poorer sections of the community, thus setting the scene for the US subprime debacle.

The fact that US economic data prior to 2008 showed that US house prices had never declined boosted the confidence of both borrowers and lenders, leading them to believe that there was no downside to housing debt. This confidence, allied to very attractiverates of returnfor investors in subprime-backed securities, set the scene for a massive toxic asset bubble.

On top of this, financial innovation in the shadow banking sector greatly extended the toxic power of the subprime asset bubble. Billions of dollars of new products, such ascollateralized debt obligations(CDOs), predicated onmortgage-backed securities-were seen by household-name institutions in Europe and the United States as "safe," high-yieldinginvestments, and they were given AAA ratings by the ratings agencies. This, coupled with a huge expansion of existing practices such as the writing ofcredit default swaps(CDSs) that purported to insure investing institutions against losses, amplified enormously the eventual losses that were associated with the subprime market.

The shadow banking sector grew substantially over the middle part of the decade of the "noughties." It consisted of special purpose vehicles (SPVs) owned and constructed by banks but which were not consolidated on tobank balancesheets, so putting them outside regulatory capital requirements. There was also a sharp increase in the number ofhedge fundsas investors, faced with low returns on cash, chased after higher yields from specialist funds. What was not well realized at the time was that a substantial number of hedge fund managers were inflating fairly modest, market-average returns through leverage. The ready availability of very cheap funding enabled these funds to invest heavily in securitized and structured investments, adding to their "mystique" and aura of specialist know-how. These investments promised very attractive yields but were so complex that few investors really understood the risks associated with theunderlying assets.

Once the easy credit stopped, everyone wanted to sell the same assets at once and the value of these investments plummeted. The lesson we all take away from this is that an era of easy, cheap, and plentiful credit will generally create an asset bubble in someasset classor other. The second lesson is that the exuberance that accompanies the inflating of a bubble, with many people reaping large profits through the up-cycle, makes the bubble extremely difficult to control. No one is able to marshal enough political will to kill the party.

The third major lesson the crash teaches us is that if you are going to act to mitigate the effects of an investment that is turning sour, you must act quickly and before the bad news becomes widespread. It is easy to see now that thecredit marketshad already begun to exhibit signs of difficulty in late 2006 and early 2007. One of the first signs was HSBC announcing substantial provisions for credit losses in its US consumer financing business. This was followed in relatively short order by cracks inmoney market fundsin the summer of 2007 and by the collapse of Northern Rock in September 2007. Despite all this, a number of markets reached new highs as late as October 2007.

From late 2007 banks began to announce significant losses, but the effect of these was shielded by the fact that the equity markets were still buoyant and banks were able to

"The system of private property is the most important guarantee of freedom, not only for those who own property, but scarcely less for those who do not." Friedrich August von Hayek

raise as much new capital as they were writing off. This had the paradoxical effect of making it even easier for investors and the markets to discount bad news in the belief that nothing could break the positive cycle.

This effect can be seen very clearly when, in March 2008, Bear Stearns collapsed. Today this is seen as the forerunner of the collapse of Lehman Brothers, and as signaling the start of the crash. At the time, however, Bear Stearns was rescued almost immediately by JP Morgan, and this sparked a strongstock marketrally. The market took the rescue as a sign that no serious bankruptcy would be allowed in the US banking sector. With the government seen as backing everything, the party resumed—albeit briefly.

By the early summer of 2008, markets had risen to within 10% of their October 2007 peaks. Then, in September, Lehman Brothers collapsed, and in October it became clear that in the United Kingdom both the Royal Bank of Scotland and Halifax Bank of Scotland were about to go under, which probably would have caused the collapse of theglobal bankingsystem. They were rescued by the UK government and theBank of England, but theFTSE 100Index had already crashed to 4,000. The point here is that, under this deluge of bad news, investors who had ignored all the warning signs in the run-up to these events were now panic-selling their equity holdings at a time when it was clearly far too late to sell.

In reality, the smart move in October 2008 would have been to buy rather than to sell. The time for "panic-selling" was at the time of those early warning signs. At that point it actually would have been sensible to move out of equities into cash—or even better, into short-dated government gilts (since cash itself became wobbly as the banks looked like failing). Sellers then would have been able to take advantage of the overconfidence of other investors who were blithely ignoring the cumulative bad news. The moral of the story here is that panic-selling when the bad news has reached the point where it is making media headlines is always going to be very expensive.

The third lesson, and the hardest of all for people to absorb, is that gut feel and "instinct" make very bad guides to investment. Some very interesting research by neuroscientists has shown that when we do not conform to the group mindset or the conventional wisdom, the same sense of failure is triggered that we experience when we make a prediction that fails. Similarly, if we make a prediction that turns out to be valid, the brain's reward system is activated and we are made to feel good by the release of dopamine. This is an inbuilt system of reward and punishment that guides the way we accumulate knowledge and strategize about our environment.

Going against the tide in investing is therefore particularly tough to do. It literally makes us feel bad unless and until we train ourselves to see through the immediate "gut feelings" and generate the more lasting rewards that come from buying when prices are falling, instead of selling when they are tumbling. That "gut feel" and the good feeling that going with the crowd generates are also at the root of asset bubbles, and they go a long way toward explaining why bad news is so ineffective at stopping the continuing climb of a bubble price until the imminence of disaster simply cannot be ignored. Then the whole thing goes into reverse, with the difference being that fear is an even more effective driver than greed, so crashes occur much more quickly than bubbles form.

This, too, is what makes it so very difficult even for professional wealth managers to make the right decisions at the right time. The pain of losing a certain sum of money is at least twice as intense as the pleasure that comes from making the same amount of gains. So not selling when everyone else is selling and sitting on assets whose value is dropping is difficult and actually feels unpleasant. The need to avoid the painful possibility of further losses becomes a real driver. If not selling is difficult, it is easy to see that actually buying at such a time takes considerable self-confidence and experience.

Between October 2008 and February 2009, as we know from our own experience with clients (which is to say, those who insisted on selling despite our advice to sit tight), almost everyone who was going to sell sold. That left very few sellers in the market. At that point, all it took was a few active buyers and a few items of reasonably good news—the so-called "green shoots" stories—to start the markets moving upward again. Many of those investors who sold at the worst point in the market continue to feel pleased that they "got out" instead of putting more of their wealth at risk. However, it is clear that in reality crystallizing their losses like that was a very expensive mistake.

The fourth lesson we can draw from the crash is that one should always keep an eye on what it is that those with the power to make policy are setting out to achieve. Whencentral banksand governments intervene they can do so massively, and smart investing will be aware of those goals as things that will shape the markets. The phrase for this in the United States is "Don't fight the Fed." If fighting inflation becomes the driving goal, then inflation will get squeezed out. If recessionary forces are too strong and it becomes necessary to stimulate the economy, growth will be boosted, at least in the short term.

Unfortunately for the consistency of our "teaching," the final lesson to be drawn is that regulators are never smart enough after a crash to prevent the next one from happening. This appears to fly in the face of lesson four, but the contradiction is resolved when we point out that lesson four is a short-term thing, whereas lesson five looks to the medium term. What creates difficulties for regulators in the medium term is that the rules they devise to improve matters after the last crisis lose their effectiveness as the industry innovates its way around them.

The saga of bank re-regulation is being played out against a backdrop of a stuttering recovery, with European governments apparently turning their backs on the lessons of the Great Depression and opting for fiscal tightening. Surely this makes for a very difficult set of conditions for anyone concerned with evaluating the respective returns possible from different asset classes?

There is no doubt that the Western world now finds itself in a real mess. Decades ofdeficit spendingand borrowing have created a debt overhang that governments seem afraid to add to by furtherquantitative easingand stimulus packages. In practice we are now seeing a reverse of Keynes' argument that government deficits can be used to bring economies to a new state of equilibrium, at which point the new growth can be used topay downthe deficit. Instead, what we are seeing is that in order to retain sufficient credibility to finance their existing debt loads, governments are having to make substantial cuts to their spending programs precisely at a time wheneconomic growthis weak.

Keynes' theory tells us that this runs the risk of sending economies back into recession. The problem with the Keynesian model, however, is that it was not designed to operate in an environment where governments are already running record levels of debt. There is no clear theoretical answer to our current dilemma—or, if there is one, the world has not yet found the genius to spell it out for the rest of us.

Looking back at the data post the crash, what we can now see is that the modest recovery that happened was driven in part by the recovery of the Chinese economy, which began to pick up in thefirst quarterof 2009, while the US economy picked up in thethird quarterof 2009. However, while the infrastructure spending in both economies revived demand for commodities and for labor, which had a positive impact

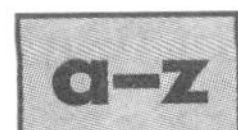

onprivate sectorincomes and consumption, that impetus is now waning.

The US unemployment statistics are showing a weakness that will not go away. House prices in the US are very weak. Withcentral bankbase ratesat zero, nothing can be done to make mortgages more attractive, and the enormous volumes of unsold properties in the US are clogging up the housing market. Moreover, banks have more than enough mortgage debt on their books and are reluctant to make new loans.

China is tightening its lending regime to combat a potential asset bubble in its own property market and to prevent inflation, and that too has a depressing effect on those countries that trade with China. In short, we have had the good news on the economic front as far as 2010 is concerned, and there is not much to get excited about in the medium term either. As far as bank re-regulation is concerned, it will probably enable banks to argue against the imposition of more onerouscapital buffersfor a long time to come.

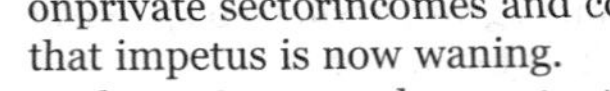

MORE INFO

Books:

Beckwith, Jeremy. "How to be a smarter investor: What to learn from 2008–09." In Jonathan Reuvid (ed). *The Handbook of Personal Wealth Management: How to Ensure Maximum Investment Returns with Security*. 6th ed. London: Kogan Page, 2010; 17–24.

Fergusson, Adam. *When Money Dies: The Nightmare of the Weimar Collapse*. London: Kimber, 1975.

Kindleberger, Charles P., and Robert Z. Aliber. *Manias, Panics, and Crashes: A History of Financial Crises*. 6th ed. Basingstoke, UK: Palgrave Macmillan, 2011.

Lewis, Michael. *The Big Short: Inside the Doomsday Machine*. New York: WW Norton, 2010.

Montier, James. *Value Investing: Tools and Techniques for Intelligent Investing*. Chichester, UK: Wiley, 2009.

Sorkin, Andrew Ross. *Too Big to Fail: The Inside Story of How Wall Street and Washington Fought to Save the Financial System—And Themselves*. New York: Viking, 2009.

See Also:

★ Navigating a Liquidity Crisis Effectively (pp. 82–84)
★ Viewpoint: Investing in a Volatile Environment: A Black Swan Perspective (pp. 505–506)
★ Viewpoint: Lessons from the Credit Crisis: Governing Financial Institutions (pp. 694–695)
★ Viewpoint: Understanding the Risks and Opportunities in Recession-Hit Markets (pp. 611–613)

"Capitalism, wisely managed, can probably be made more efficient for attaining economic ends than any alternative system yet in sight." John Maynard Keynes

  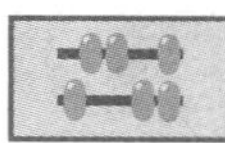   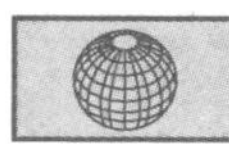   

Islamic Finance and the Global Financial Crisis

by Bilal Rasul

EXECUTIVE SUMMARY

- The growth of Islamic financial institutions (IFIs) has been steady but the full potential for deposit-raising remains untapped.
- The resilience of IFIs is a direct consequence of transactions being backed by real assets and prescribed financing contracts/agreements.
- Disparity between the creation of wealth and underlying real assets is countered through socially and ethically responsible investments propagated by Islamic finance.
- The report of the IFSB–IRTI Task Force on Islamic Finance and Global Financial Stability gives recommendations for keeping vigilant and creating global financial stability through IFIs.
- The participatory/risk-sharing nature of Islamic finance is the mainstay of the system.
- The projection and promotion of Islamic finance philosophy is the key to success.
- Emphasis should be on the fiduciary responsibility of IFIs to market products that are authentic (*shariah*-compliant) so that wealth and the distribution of profits is equitable.

ISLAMIC FINANCE

Islamic finance is a safe financial doctrine that promises justice and equity. The theme of Islamic finance is popular among those economies that are either interested in following the *shariah* tenets or are exploring alternative investment opportunities that have a sound basis and a promising potential.

The principles of Islamic finance fundamentally uphold the corporate governance and social responsibility philosophies: that is, accountability, transparency, and equitable distribution of wealth. They are derived from the *shariah* and the financial laws enabled by the Qur'an. The Qur'an, a complete code of life, is not just for the believers or for Muslims; it is for all mankind *(linnaas)*:

"The month of Ramadan in which the Qur'an was revealed, a guidance for mankind, [a Book of] clear proofs of guidance and the criterion [distinguishing right from wrong]..." *Sura Al-Baqarah, ayat 185. (English translation by the Nawawi Foundation, Chicago/Ibn Khaldun Foundation, London).*

The stipulations of the Qur'an pertaining to the economic and financial system, too, are for the benefit of all mankind. Adherence to this conduct may not necessarily mean adhering to the faith—a misconception that needs to be addressed in the most benign manner.

Islamic finance is a subject that has reached out to a reasonable number of Muslims, as well as non-Muslims and financial planners. It is now accepted as an international form of financial intermediation. The growth of the industry, 20% annually, [1] has been the swiftest seen by any industry in the last few years. The innovation and product development have been dynamic.

In order to exploit the versatility of the corporate sector, an appropriate strategy is required to reveal the window of opportunity that exists for investors which, undoubtedly, would also launch Islamic finance to larger proportions. The practitioners and scholars of Islamic finance are expected to devise an unprejudiced approach for the purpose. Under the auspices of the Islamic Development Bank (IDB), the Task Force on Islamic Finance and Global Financial Stability was formed in October 2008, on the recommendation of the Forum of the Global Financial Crisis and its Impact on the Islamic Financial Industry, organized by the IDB Group. The Task Force was mandated to: (1) examine the conceptual aspects of Islamic finance and its role in enhancing financial stability; (2) conduct a stocktaking of the state of the Islamic financial services industry following the global financial crisis; and (3) examine the financial architecture of the Islamic financial industry amid the more challenging post-crisis environment.[2] Since then the Task Force has thoroughly examined these areas and documented them in a report submitted to them by the three working groups. The report is a public document and can be accessed for a better understanding of the current stability issues that Islamic finance addresses, the state of the Islamic financial industry, and the challenges that lie ahead.

The events transpiring in the last two years leave little doubt that Islamic finance is the way forward and that the discipline should be explored. The role of the IFIs and Islamic regulatory organizations is critical in promoting an ethics-based financial system to provide the solution for the ailing conventional financial system.

RESILIENCE THROUGH THE CRISIS

The resilience of the Islamic financial system has been put to the test at the evolutionary stage of its life. The incidence of default and financial instability in IFIs was significantly reduced due to the nature of Islamic finance, which is manifested in limited debt leverage, risk and profit sharing, and financial transactions backed by real assets, coupled with legislative restrictions on derivative-like products. Written contracts that emphasize the possession and ownership of real assets are a fundamental source of credibility for transactions and provide disclosure and transparency for investors to *shariah* standards. "The Islamic financial system is driven by trade and production and is intimately linked to the real sector ('Main Street' and not 'Wall Street')." [3]

Regulatory oversight, absence of governance, and pitiable rating structures failed the conventional financial system. Lapses in prudential standards and risk mitigating factors added to the tribulations. The hedging instruments that were designed to absorb the risk ended up manufacturing risk. By and large, however, the IFIs remained resilient.

EXTRACT FROM ERNST & YOUNG REPORT

- Market capitalization of the top 10 conventional banks declined by 42.8%, in contrast to the 8.5% decline of that of Islamic banks between 2006 and 2009.
- The profits of conventional banks fell from US$116 billion in 2006 to a net loss of US$42 billion in 2008. By comparison, Islamic banks' net profits increased 9% during the same period, from US$4.2 billion to US$4.6 billion. No Islamic bank suffered a loss in 2008.
- The total assets of conventional banks grew by 36% to US$17.4 trillion, whereas assets of the Islamic banks grew by 55% from US$94 billion to US$147 billion between 2006 and 2008. The growth in total equity during this period was 24% and 36% for conventional and Islamic banks, respectively.
- Conventional banks' leverage ratio (assets/equity) was 16.6 times in 2006,

"There's a whole branch of economics devoted to proving that ... what most of us would consider humankind's cardinal virtues—love, honor, compassion—do not actually exist." Philipp Meyer

  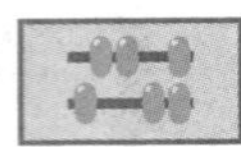      

which increased further to 18.2 times in 2008. This was nearly three times the leverage ratio of Islamic banks, which was 5.8 times in 2006 and 6.6 times in 2008.

- Five of the top 10 conventional banks received government financial assistance to the extent of US$163 billion in aggregate, while only one IFI required government assistance to restructure. No Islamic bank needed any support from government for bailout.

(From the "Report of the Task Force on Islamic Finance and Global Financial Stability," Ernst & Young, 2009.)

IS ISLAMIC FINANCE A CLEAR WINNER?

The bailout of international financial institutions by way of acquisitions by the government, capital injection, and liquidity injection is unprecedented. In the new global financial and economic scenario IFIs may have survived the 2008–09 financial crisis, but whether they have capitalized on the remnants of the defunct capitalist financial system is a question that needs to be probed.

Is it a foregone conclusion that Islamic finance has appeared as the panacea to the collapsed global financial system? Theoretically, the answer is in the affirmative, but realistically and practically, the size of the industry suggests otherwise. A trillion dollar industry though it may be, the asset base of the IFIs figures minutely against the gargantuan conventional financial industry. It would be naive to think that the IFIs survived the financial crisis due to their authentic product lines, good governance, and regulatory frameworks. Systematic risks such as exchange rate risk, market risk, and liquidity risk are externalities that cannot be isolated from IFIs and have a spillover effect, and must be managed by them.

Nevertheless, the Islamic financial paradigm may be the long-term solution. "The solution lies in disciplining the creation of money, limiting the self-interest with social aspects and the business ethics, transforming the corrupt financial system to make it free of exploitation and games of chance and thus enabling mankind to optimally use the resources for benefits at a larger scale." [4]

POST-CRISIS RELAUNCHING OF ISLAMIC FINANCE

While the conventional banking and finance industry recuperates from the exigencies of the global financial crisis, this is the opportune time for Islamic finance to prove its competitiveness and enhance its profile. The pull-factor must be rediscovered and employed to attract investors and borrowers toward IFIs to service their financial requirements and avoid the risk-sharing, highly complex hedging investment opportunities offered by the conventional banking institutions.

Researchers and scholars of Islamic finance are endeavoring to create products that are equitable and attractive. However, the discord in transactional issues presented by the varied interpretations of the various schools of thought prevents this system from evolving and being effectively marketed. It must be truly understood and implemented in substance that adoption of the Accounting and Auditing Organization for Islamic Financial Institutions (AAOIFI) standards is a precursor to claiming *shariah*-compliant status. This cardinal principle, in itself, is the key for the harmonization issue.

The Islamic Financial Services Board (IFSB), being the international Islamic financial regulator, also shoulders the responsibility for playing the lead role in marketing and establishing credibility for Islamic finance. International summits and conferences are consistently held around the financial centers of the world to promote and enhance the image of Islamic finance as an ethical and stable financial system. While awareness creation may no longer be the need of the hour, what is required are measures to incentivize IFIs at an industry-wide level: for example, the provision of corporate tax relief to IFIs; capital gains tax exemptions on *shariah*-compliant securities; withholding of tax exemptions on dividends of *shariah*-complaint companies; etc. These incentives require the patronization of those governments interested in adopting Islamic finance. Memoranda of Understanding should be inked through the regulatory agencies acting as representatives of their respective countries on the Islamic Financial Services Board (IFSB).

THE WAY FORWARD

The lessons for IFIs and Islamic financial markets are clear. If financial stability is to be achieved, the separation of risk from the real asset, as embodied in the conventional system, needs to be countered. Adherence to the risk-sharing philosophy preached by Islamic finance needs to be marketed, and the Islamic infrastructure has to place clear and unambiguous restrictions on questionable transactions. The Task Force has recommended that an Islamic Financial Stability Forum (IFSF) be established to serve as a platform for the deliberation of issues relevant to the ensuring of financial stability in the Islamic financial system.

To grow, adoption of the best practices and international standards prescribed for IFIs is a priority. The intrinsic principles of Islamic finance ensure that the allocation of resources is efficient and equitable, which inexorably will prevent exposure to the market shocks that have afflicted the conventional banking and finance sector. Islamic finance is rationally the next dimension of the financial world.

CASE STUDY

Camouflage

A commonplace apprehension among the general public toward IFIs, and Islamic finance in general, is the authenticity issue. This is due to the mimicking or camouflaging of conventional products by the IFI. Although some mimicking may be justified, products need to be totally aligned to the *shariah* framework that regulates them.

The worker vs his/her tool dilemma presents itself here again, where the tool is the Islamic finance philosophy, which lays down the roadmap for just and equitable distribution of wealth, and the worker is the IFI manager. It is the workman who has to reposition his or her attitude and *niyah* (intent) toward achieving the prescribed goal of Islamic finance. Highlighting and redefining the fiduciary responsibility of the IFI is critical. The fiduciary responsibility adds another component over and above the regular role of the corporate manager—that is, accountability and subscription to the prescriptions of the *shariah*. Dubious products marketed by IFIs undermine the credibility of the system. Exploitative and unjust products that disguise *riba* (usury), *gharar* (uncertainty), and *maysir* (gambling) need to be identified, and the *shariah* boards must censure those who promote them. The *shariah* boards also need to be regulated by the overseeing regulatory authority to ensure that they are not simply rubberstamping products.

The *sukuk* (Islamic bonds) issuances around the world, now a popular Islamic financial product, are also not devoid of structural issues. Similarly, *tawarruq* (reverse *murabahah* or monetization), wherein a sale is made for deferred payment, has been held as impermissible by the OIC Fiqh Academy.[5]

"The Robert Mugabe school of economics provides a salutary warning about uncontrolled monetary expansion in generating hyper-inflation. The road to Harare is not as long as we might hope." Vince Cable

     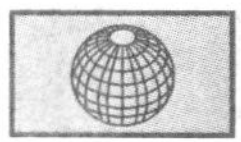   

MORE INFO

Books:

Archer, Simon, and Rifaat Karim. *Islamic Finance: The Regulatory Challenge*. Singapore: Wiley, 2007.

Askari, Hossein, Zamir Iqbal, Abbas Mirakhor, and Noureddine Krichenne. *The Stability of Islamic Finance: Creating a Resilient Financial Environment for a Secure Future*. Singapore: Wiley, 2010.

Venardos, Angelo M. *Current Issues in Islamic Banking and Finance*. Singapore: World Scientific Publishing, 2010.

Article:

Tayyebi, Aziz. "Eclipsed by the crescent moon: Islamic finance provides some light in the global financial crisis." *Financial Services Review* 90 (June 2009): 14–16.

Reports:

Ernst & Young. "Islamic funds and investments report 2009: Surviving and adapting in a downturn." 2009.

Islamic Development Bank. "Report of the Task Force on Islamic Finance and Global Financial Stability." April 2010.

Websites:

Accounting and Auditing Organization for Islamic Financial Institutions (AAOIFI): www.aaoifi.com

Islamic Financial Services Board (IFSB): www.ifsb.org

See Also:

★ The Emergence and Development of Islamic Banking (pp. 166–168)
★ The International Role of Islamic Finance (pp. 192–195)
★ Viewpoint: Lessons from the Credit Crisis: Governing Financial Institutions (pp. 694–695)
★ Viewpoint: *Shariah* Law—Bringing a New Ethical Dimension to Banking (pp. 242–243)

NOTES

1 Islamic Development Bank, 2010.
2 *Ibid.*, p. 34.
3 Venardos, 2010, p. 2.
4 Ayub, Mohammad. "Islamic finance must turn to the roots." *Journal of International Banking and Finance*, p. 27.
5 Resolution 179 (19/5), 19th session, April 2009, Organisation of the Islamic Conference (OIC) Islamic Fiqh Academy.

  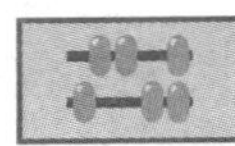      

Islamic Insurance Markets and the Structure of *Takaful* by Suzanne White

EXECUTIVE SUMMARY

- Islamic scholars object to the concept of conventional insurance due to three key elements: *riba* (usury), *gharar* (uncertainty), and *maysir* (gambling).
- Islamic insurance or *takaful* operators have therefore redesigned their management and accounting practices to comply with *shariah* law.
- *Takaful* and conventional or traditional insurance policy wordings both operate in a similar way, with the protection that is provided to the client being exactly the same.
- The differences between Islamic and conventional insurance lie in the ownership and financing of the company, in the management and accounting systems, and in the entities in which the premiums are invested.
- Islamic insurance is a very close concept to that of "mutual insurers" in the West and, in particular, to those we call "ethical" insurers.

INTRODUCTION

Insurance plays a vital role in supporting both national and international economic development and growth. Islamic countries are no exception. The main issue for insurers in the Islamic world is that many Islamic scholars view conventional insurance as prohibited by Islam.

Muslim scholars are not against the concept of risk mitigation, risk sharing, or risk management, including risk financing, *per se*. In fact, they support the compensation of victims of misfortune. However, many scholars consider some aspects of conventional insurance contracts as being prohibited from a *shariah* (Islamic law) point of view. *Shariah* covers all aspects of a Muslim's life, not just worship.

PROHIBITED FACTORS OF INSURANCE

Several *fatawa* (the plural of *fatwa*, meaning an answer to a question related to an issue of *shariah*) have been issued by eminent Muslim scholars on the subject of insurance. The objections tend to relate to the insurance contract itself or to insurance market practice in general.

Objections relating to the insurance contract itself are those of *riba* (usury), *gharar* (uncertainty), and *maysir* (gambling). The other objections relating to market practice are usually concerned with two issues: the first is that insurance companies' investment policies are generally interest-bearing (which is not acceptable in Islam); and the second issue is the fact that life assurance is considered to breach Islamic inheritance rules by distributing the sum assured among beneficiaries. These objections relating to market practice can be easily overcome by the insurer making changes to their company policy, as they do not affect the insurance contract itself.

The objections related to the contract itself, however, require the restructuring of insurance contracts to be in line with *shariah*.

Riba (Usury)

Under a conventional insurance contract, the insured pays the insurance company a premium (either as a lump sum in general insurance or as installments in life insurance), in exchange for financial compensation at the time of a claim, subject to the happening of an insured occurrence or event. Claims are generally larger amounts than the premium paid. Islamic law objects to this payment on the grounds that a small amount of money (premium) is being exchanged for a larger amount of money (claim). Scholars consider this an unjustified increase of money, and therefore *riba*. Islamic insurers therefore have to structure their operations and investments to avoid *riba*.

Gharar (Uncertainty)

Gharar can be defined as uncertainty or ambiguity. Islamic law seeks to avoid ambiguity in contracts in order to prevent disputes and conflict between parties. This is a general Islamic principle that must be applied to all contracts, including insurance.

In the case of conventional insurance, neither the insurer nor the insured knows the outcome of the contract (i.e. whether a loss will occur or not). The insurer is entitled to get the premium in all cases, whereas the insured may not receive a claim because the payment of claims depends on the probability of loss occurrence (which is a random variable). Other uncertain elements are as to when the claim may be paid and how much the insured may receive.

In life assurance contracts, *gharar* can be seen to exist even in the premium, as the insured party does not know how much he will pay to the insurance company each year, or for how many years. The insured may know the monthly or yearly premium, but he does not know how much he will pay to the insurer before he dies. In general insurance (nonlife insurance), the premium is pre-agreed, but there is *gharar* in the claim amount. Therefore *gharar* exists in all insurance contracts, either in premiums or in claims. In Islamic insurance, scholars agree that engaging in *takaful* transactions, with a donation element as part of their contribution, offsets *gharar*.

Maysir (Gambling)

Some arguments against conventional insurance are based on the grounds that insurance contracts are basically gambling contracts. Islam rejects any contract where financial gain comes from chance or speculation. Insurance, however, needs to comply with the principle of insurable interest. This principle requires a financial and legal relationship between the insured and the subject matter of insurance. The insured is only entitled to get a claim if he proves his insurable interest, and this feature therefore nullifies the notion that insurance is a gamble.

The other difference between gambling and insurance is that the first is a speculative risk (which is uninsurable), while the latter consists of pure risk only (i.e., the insured should not make a gain but should be put back into the same financial position as before the loss occurred).

THE CONCEPT OF ISLAMIC INSURANCE

The first Islamic insurance company was set up in Sudan in 1979. Today there are many Islamic insurance operators in Muslim as well as non-Muslim countries. The main concept of Islamic insurance is that it is an alternative to conventional insurance, with characteristics and features that comply with *shariah* requirements. This is done by eliminating the objections against conventional insurance. "The term *takaful* is an infinitive noun which is derived from the Arabic root verb *kafal*' or *kafala*, meaning to guarantee or bear responsibility for" (Kassar *et al.*, 2008, p. 26).

The main features of Islamic insurance are:

- cooperative risk sharing by using charitable donations to eliminate *gharar* and *riba*;
- clear financial segregation between the participant (insured) and the operator (insurance company); and

"You have to eventually nationalize US banks, you have to take the problem by the horns. In my view actually most of the US banking system is insolvent." Nouriel Roubini

        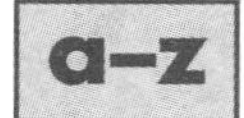

- *shariah*-compliant underwriting policies and investment strategies.

Cooperative Risk–Sharing

The characteristics of a cooperative include self-responsibility, democracy, equality, equity, solidarity, honesty, openness, social responsibility, and caring for others. While mutuality or cooperative risk-sharing is at the core of Islamic insurance, it cannot alone create an Islamic insurance operation. Islamic insurance is based on more than one contractual relationship: the first relationship is a mutual insurance contract between policyholders (contributors) and each other. This is similar to a pure mutual insurance relationship, taking into consideration the concept of donation *(tabarru)* instead of premiums and an ethical framework of Islamic transactions. The main features behind cooperative insurance are as follows.

- Policyholders pay premiums to a cooperative fund with the intention of it being a donation to those who will suffer losses (*tabarru*).
- Policyholders are entitled to receive any surplus resulting from the operation of the cooperative insurance fund.
- Policyholders are liable to make up for any deficits that result from the operation of the cooperative insurance fund.
- The amount of contribution (premium) differs from one participant to another, based on the degree of risk in general insurances and actuarial principles in life assurance.
- There is no unified system to operate the treatment of surplus and deficit. There is therefore more than one model accepted by *shariah* scholars being used in practice.

Clear Segregation Between Participant and Operator

In conventional insurance, the insurance company is a profit-making organization that aims to maximize profit by accepting the financial burden of others' losses. The insurance company is owned by shareholders who are entitled to receive any profit and are responsible for financing any deficit. Under Islamic insurance, the system is that the insurance company's role is restricted to managing the portfolio and investing the insurance contributions for and on behalf of the participants. The relationship between the participants and the insurance company (as an operator, not as an insurer) is different. There are four different models in operation: The *mudarabh* model, the *wakalah* model, the hybrid *mudarabh–wakalah* model, and the pure cooperative model (nonprofit). "The overarching goal of Takaful is brotherhood, solidarity, protection and mutual cooperation between members" (Kassar *et al.*, 2008, p. 66).

Shariah-Compliant Policies and Strategies

Ethical insurers invest money in a responsible way in industries that are ethically sound and do not harm the environment or people. Islamic insurance is similar, except that the ethical considerations are extended to those which do not contravene the religion of Islam and are monitored by a *shariah* board, which is part of the company structure. In particular, the investment and underwriting policies need to be free of any involvement with the prohibited activities of gambling, alcohol, pork, armaments, tobacco, and interest-bearing activities, loans, and securities.

CONCLUSION

Islamic insurance has grown out of the need of many stakeholders in the Islamic world to have protection for assets and liabilities. This protection was required in a similar fashion to that provided by conventional insurance which, for a variety of reasons, was often viewed as prohibited in Islam. *Takaful* or Islamic insurers have been structured in such a way that Islamic scholars are satisfied that the main objections to insurance, which are *riba, gharar,* and *maysir*, have been addressed.

CASE STUDY

American Insurance Group

The potential for *takaful* business is evidenced by the fact that almost all new insurance license applications in the Middle East region are for *takaful* companies. Even many Western insurers, such as American Insurance Group (AIG), have realized the potential of *takaful* and have set up their own *takaful* operations. AIG Takaful, known as Enaya, which means "care," was established in 2006 in Bahrain with a US$15 million paid-up capital and licensed by the Central Bank of Bahrain. Enaya's plan was to start business in the Gulf region and then expand into the Far East and Europe.

MAKING IT HAPPEN

Islamic insurance is the fastest-growing area of insurance throughout the world, including in Western countries. In order to call a company Islamic, there are features that need to be built into the structure:

- cooperative risk-sharing, by using charitable donations to eliminate *gharar* and *riba;*
- clear financial segregation between the participant (insured) and the operator (insurance company);
- *shariah*-compliant underwriting policies and investment strategies.

MORE INFO

Books:

El-Gamal, M. *A Basic Guide to Contemporary Islamic Banking and Finance*. Houston, TX: Rice University, 2000.

Jaffer, S. (ed). *Islamic Insurance: Trends, Opportunities and the Future of Takaful.* London: Euromoney Books, 2007.

Kassar, Khaled, Omar Clark Fisher, *et al. What's Takaful—A Guide to Islamic Insurance*. Beirut: BISC Group, 2008.

Ma'sum Billah, M. *Islamic Insurance (Takaful)*. Kuala Lumpur: Ilmiah Publishers, 2003.

Websites:

Institute of Islamic Banking and Finance: www.islamic-banking.com
Islamic Banking and Finance: www.islamicbankingandfinance.com
Middle East Insurance Review: www.meinsurancereview.com

See Also:

★ Identifying the Main Regulatory Challenges for Islamic Finance (pp. 358–360)
★ Islamic Modes of Finance and the Role of *Sukuk* (pp. 520–521)
★ Procedures for Reporting Financial Risk in Islamic Finance (pp. 394–396)
✔ Regulatory and Capital Issues under *Shariah* Law (p. 1050)
✔ The Role of the *Shariah* Advisory Board in Islamic Finance (p. 1015)
✔ Stress Testing to Evaluate Insurance Cover (p. 1016)
🌐 Insurance (pp. 1633–1635)

"Bankers regard research as most dangerous and a thing that makes banking hazardous due to the rapid changes it brings about in industry." Charles Franklin Kettering

  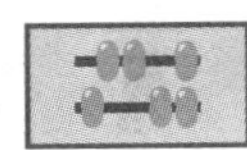   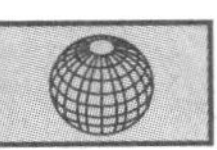   

Issues in Issuing Insurance-Linked Securities

by Morton Lane

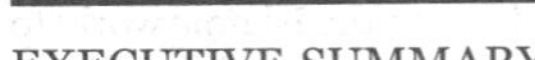

EXECUTIVE SUMMARY

The checklist of considerations for insurers planning to issue insurance-linked securities (ILS) into the capital markets includes the following:

- Identify risk concentrations;
- Quantify the loss consequence of such concentrations;
- Design offsetting structure to transfer risks to capital markets with the help of agents;
- Engage a placement agent or investment banker—essential to fruitful design;
- Engage a risk modeling firm—essential to fruitful design;
- Decide on denomination of loss measures: indemnity or index;
- Choose SPV location and attendant experts in those locations;
- Review structure, design, price, and alternatives to ensure the ILS suitability;
- Execute.

INTRODUCTION

The first insurance-linked security (ILS) was conceived in 1992, three months before Hurricane Andrew. However, perhaps to the chagrin of the potential issuer, AIG, the deal was not consummated. Had it been, the issuer would have collected for both Hurricane Andrew and the Northridge earthquake of 1994. The first executed ILS took place two years later, but it and some subsequent issues were relatively small in size. Two years after that, the first sizable issue of a catastrophe ILS (usually referred to as "Cat ILS") heralded the beginning of the modern era. The cedant was the United Services Automobile Association (USAA), the placement agent was Goldman Sachs, and the issue size was US$500 million.

Since that beginning the market has steadily expanded to the undisputed advantage of investors and issuers alike. Almost US$45 billion in risk has been transferred from issuers of ILS to the capital markets (of which US$40 billion is Cat). Furthermore, every time there is another catastrophe, the revealed utility of ILS to cedants leads to increased adoption by traditional risk transferees in the insurance market. To date, issuance has been consummated by insureds (e.g. Tokyo Disneyland, Universal Studios), insurance companies (e.g. USAA, Hartford), reinsurers (e.g. Swiss Re, Munich Re), retrocessionaires (e.g. Montpelier Re, PXRE), official institutions (e.g. IBRD) and sovereigns (e.g. Mexico, North Carolina).

While each different type of issuer has particular needs, many elements of issuance are common to each. Our purpose here is to list the elements to consider when issuing ILS. These elements, listed by importance, are: risk concentration, effect on the overall portfolio of the ILS risk, the investment banker, the risk-modeling agency, denomination, choice of additional agents, the structure of the bond, and the law firm, as well as other factors. We discuss each element below.

THE IMPORTANT ELEMENTS OF ILS ISSUANCE

Risk Concentration

The first item on any issuer's checklist must be to identify the need to transfer risk. This means being able to describe and quantify exposures and the resulting concentrations. The concentrations in the exposures are where protection is needed. It is no accident that the biggest such concentration in many portfolios are wind events in the US. The US home-owners market is the biggest in the world. Scattered wind storms are not the concern; rather it is the concentrated devastation from a major hurricane. Such events generate huge numbers of claims for insurers with attendant large losses. But identification is not enough in itself.

Effect of ILS Risk on the Overall Portfolio

The second essential element is to be able to quantify the concentration exposure and the effect the concentration has on the overall portfolio. This means employing a risk quantifying model. This can be done by a DFA [Dynamic Financial Analysis] analysis or some other portfolio analysis techniques, such as optimization. Now, such analysis is not just essential for issuers of ILS, it is a requirement of any purchaser of protection whether in the traditional reinsurance market or the capital markets. It also ought to be an essential ingredient in constructing an underwriting portfolio, whether or not one is buying protection. Thus, for most issuers part of the analysis is already in place. That will be especially true if the coverage for which protection is sought is an "indemnity" protection. Traditional reinsurance is by definition indemnity-based, and it means that the protector will protect the cedant for the exact amount of loss (or at least that part of the loss contracted for) that the cedant itself suffers.

In many traditional cases brokers will be partly familiar with the exposures and portfolio of the cedant. As a result the broker comes with products that are: available in the traditional market; and fit with the broker's perception of the cedant's needs. They will also present an analysis to fit. There is nothing wrong with this, but it is a model of behavior that has to be amended in interacting with capital markets. Cedants must take more initiative themselves in identifying the protection they need, rather than being reactive to broker's pitches. This should not be misunderstood. Brokers do provide valuable information about what is available in the market and what is the likely cost. However, simply identifying unattainable protection desires without knowing what is possible and at what price is as undesirable as simply reacting to whichever broker knocks on the door.

The Investment Banker

The point to start at is to identify your own perceived needs and then to engage a placement agent to effect those needs, as best is practical, in the chosen market. If the risk is to be placed in the capital market, that means that the third important choice for an issuer is the choice of investment banker. Well-known names such as Goldman Sachs and BNP Paribas operate in the ILS market, as do reinsurer capital market subsidiaries such as Swiss Re Capital Markets and Aon Benfield Securities. These and several other names come with their own skill sets and investor bases. They all also have different fee schedules. New issuers might well want to place investment bankers in competition (sometimes referred to as a beauty parade) before making their choice. They will be looking for cost differences, experience, market insight, and investor base—who can do the best job of helping to structure and distribute the securities. Often it is the case that two or more managers are chosen: one to lead, the others to co-manage.

The Risk-Modeling Agency

Having settled on an investment bank, the next important choice is the risk-modeling agency. Three firms share the bulk of the market: AIR Worldwide, RMS, and EQECAT. Investors are familiar with these

"Economics, as it has been practised in the last three decades, has been positively harmful for most people."
Ha-Joon Chang

  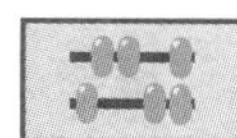   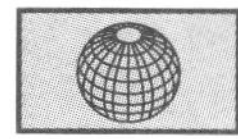   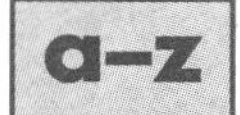

firms, and while others are not excluded (indeed, Swiss Re and others have offered their own risk analysis to investors), investor comfort presently resides with these three firms. Also, each has its own approaches and its own strengths. It is best to choose the firm whose strengths most closely align with the peril against which protection is sought.

In the choice of either investment banker or risk modeler it is best not to be "penny wise and pound foolish." The investor will react to sloppy work, and it will cost the issuer to overcome unknowns or questionable work.

Denomination

The fifth important decision is how the protection is to be denominated. Indemnity cover is what most cedants want, but it is not most popular with investors. There is a feeling that there is an asymmetry of information between issuer and investor. The issuer knows the whole book; the investor does not. The investor could be taken advantage of, i.e., "selected against." Obviously this has echoes in the recent consternation about adverse selection of mortgages in the CDO market, but it is an issue that insurers have dealt with for centuries. If indemnity is the way in which losses are to be denominated, then most investors will require an "alignment of interest." In other words, the issuer must be alongside for part of the risk. As a rule, the higher the alignment retained by the issuer, the greater is the investor comfort. In ILS a 10% share is common, and 20% and 50% are frequently seen, as is 5%, but the latter does not have a good record. Moreover, the alignment should be permanent for the life of the ILS. Investors will not take kindly to an issuer who starts with a 10% alignment and then retrocedes it away. If the issuer does retrocede his share, for whatever good reason, the investor will want to be protected as well for the same good reason. At least the investor should have that option.

The other, much more common way to assure that the investor is not selected against is to base the loss on an index of loss or equivalent. To provide a specific example, if an earthquake risk is denominated on the Richter scale (the bigger the reading, the bigger the loss payment), it is hard to argue that the issuer has any more information than the investor—certainly he cannot select the exact reading. Independent scientific measuring stations will do that. Furthermore, the issuer will have engaged an independent risk modeler to assess the nature of the risk. Similar arguments apply to other indices—industry loss, wind speed, temperature, etc. Indeed, these days very sophisticated loss models can be built, archived on a computer, and used to calculate investor loss. These models can be constructed and weighted in such a way as to closely replicate cedant portfolios without having the perceived risk of indemnity cover. Any index solution will mean that the cedant will not have its loss exactly recompensed. For that he must gauge whether the benefit in investor acceptance is worth it.

Choice of Additional Agents

Beyond the choice of protection needs and appropriate selection of the most important agents, a host of smaller agent choices must be made. Which domicile should be used for the issuing special purpose vehicle (SPV)? Which manager should run the SPV? Who is the trustee and investment manager, the accountant, and the indenture agent? In dollar terms these decisions do not appear important, but sloppy choice here can have important consequences. In recent years the phrase "brain-dead SPV manager" has entered the ILS language. The task of running the SPV is relatively easy—except when it is not. The manager, as with all agents, must be sufficiently alert to unusual circumstances to be able to adjust intelligently to the letter of his mandate. Similarly, the trust must be one that protects both the issuer and investor alike. Issuers will want to be assured that the money to compensate them for loss is available when needed. This means making sure that it is invested in only the most secure collateral. They should also want a structure that is cancelable if, for whatever reason, the value of their protection diminishes. Investors also want their investment to be returned if the ILS runs loss-free and is protected against improper collection by the cedant.

Structure of the Bond

Another raft of decisions concerns the structure of the bond itself. Should the issue be a one-off transaction, or should it be part of a regular program? Each will have an impact on documentation. Should the term of the bond be one year or multiple year? Should the bond risk be resettable, or coupon-adjusted? There are many such structural decisions that the banker, the risk modeler, and the cedant will need to decide on. And when all are put together they will have to be enshrined in a legal private placement memorandum. Thus the legal firm is also a most important choice.

The Law Firm

The sponsor, in conjunction with the investment bankers, will select attorneys to represent its interests and draft the transaction documents. It will also need a law firm in the jurisdiction of the chosen SPV to contend with local issues. These firms should be experienced in insurance law as well as securities law. There are a number of firms in New York and Chicago (such as Cadwalader, Wickersham & Taft LLP, or Sidley Austin LLP), as well as in the most common SPV jurisdictions—Bermuda, Cayman Islands, and Dublin.

CONCLUSION

Compare the Alternatives

Best practice requires that the cedant compare and contrast the ILS alternative with more traditional protection possibilities. This goes beyond just checking for one deal; it means doing the comparison on a regular and consistent basis. This ensures that the best deal is acquired for shareholders or policyholders. There is one firm that has set the gold standard in this regard—USAA. It has issued for 16 years in a row. It has always issued indemnity cover, after building trust in its first few years with an

CASE STUDY

United Services Automobile Association (USAA)

- First issuance: 1996
- Original issue size: US$500 million
- Original issue structure: double trigger with indemnity and index contingents
- Subsequent issues: all indemnity
- Initial coverage: coastal wind
- Subsequent coverage: all US Wind and Quake
- Most tranches occurrence-based, some aggregate
- Maturity of typical structure: 3 years
- Typical number of tranches annually: 4
- Number of years of consecutive issuance: 16
- Total issuance to date: US$4.8 billion
- Smallest issuance year: US$125 million
- Largest issuance year: US$700 million
- Currently outstanding: approximately US$1.3 billion

"Like other branches of the study of society, economics remains culturally parochial, and its underlying concepts based on a few centuries of Western experience." John Gray

event cover. And it has always simultaneously bought protection in both the traditional market and the ILS market. Finally, it has displayed great adaptability in its coverage, responding to its own needs, presumably with the trust of its investors.

Reiterate

No securitization forms perfectly the instant after an initial decision to proceed has been made. It requires going back over the analysis and double checking the assumptions, prices, etc., to see if it still meets objectives before moving to the "execute" decision. The last step in the process must therefore be the step of rechecking and reiterating through the procedures.

As the market grows and reissues take place, the practice elements listed here become more routine. Persistent issuers such as USAA will follow a regular procedural calendar over several months. They know where they are going and the touch points that must be visited. They know the speed at which they are comfortable putting the components together. First-time issuers will likely need to spend a period of up to six months to go through a thorough process, but depending on the simplicity of the structure, the whole process can be accomplished in as little as 10–12 weeks. If we think of protection buying as raising surrogate capital, these times and procedures compare favorably with other markets that raise debt, equity, or indeed traditional reinsurance protection.

MORE INFO

Books:

Lane, Morton (ed). *Alternative Risk Strategies*. London: Risk Books, 2003.

Kunreuther, Howard C., and Erwann O. Michel-Kerjan, with Neil A. Doherty *et al*. *At War With the Weather: Managing Large-Scale Risks in a New Era of Catastrophes*. Cambridge, MA: MIT Press, 2009.

Himick, Michael (ed). *Securitized Insurance Risk, Strategic Opportunities for Insurers and Investors*. Chicago, IL: Glenlake Publishing, 1998.

Culp, Christopher L. *Structured Finance and Insurance: The ART of Managing Capital and Risk*. Hoboken, NJ: Wiley, 2006.

Froot, Kenneth A. (ed). *The Financing of Catastrophe Risk*. Chicago, IL: University of Chicago Press, 1999.

Tang, Kenny (ed). *Weather Risk Management: A Guide for Corporations, Hedge Funds and Investors*. London: Risk Books, 2010.

Websites:

Artemis : www.artemis.bm
Aon Benfield Securities: www.aon.com/reinsurance
Global Reinsurance: www.globalreinsurance.com
Guy Carpenter & Company: www.guycarp.com/portal/extranet/insights/insights.html?vid=5
Insurance Insider: www.insuranceinsider.com
Lane Financial: www.lanefinancialllc.com
Reactions: www.reactionsnet.com
Swiss Re Sigma: www.swissre.com/sigma
Trading Risk: www.trading-risk.com

See Also:

★ Building Potential Catastrophe Management into a Strategic Risk Framework (pp. 785–787)
★ Climate Change and Insurance (pp. 149–150)
✔ Catastrophe Bonds: What They Are and How They Function (p. 1006)
✔ Understanding and Calculating Probable Maximum Loss (PML) (p. 1019)
Insurance (pp. 1633–1635)

"An economist is a man who states the obvious in terms of the incomprehensible." Alfred A. Knopf

  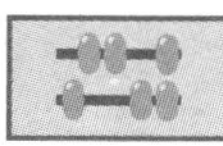      

Viewpoint: A Lesson in Austrian School Economics: The Real Cause of the Crash by Jesús Huerta de Soto

INTRODUCTION

Jesús Huerta de Soto holds a PhD in economic science and PhD in law from the Complutense University of Madrid. He is also a mathematical actuary and holds a MBA from Stanford University. He is a member of the Mont Pelerin Society, the Royal Economic Society (London), the American Economic Association, and the Spanish, Portuguese and Swiss Associations of Actuaries. He has been awarded the King Juan Carlos International Prize for Economics (Madrid, 1983), the Adam Smith Award (Brussels, 2005), the Franz Cuhel Memorial Prize for Excellence in Economic Education (Prague, 2006), and the Gary G. Schlarbaum Prize for Liberty (Salamanca, 2009), as well as honorary doctorates by Francisco Marroquín University (Guatemala, 2009) and Alexandru Ioan Cuzá (Romania, 2010). Since 2000 he has been professor of political economy at the King Juan Carlos University of Madrid. Huerta de Soto is currently considered to be one of the most representative exponents of the Austrian School of Economics and has published numerous research works and articles on subjects related to his speciality.

In your 2010 Hayek Memorial Lecture to the London School of Economics and Political Science, you suggested that the laws governing banking had gone wrong way back in 1844—that the West missed an opportunity then to put itself on a sound economic path. Can you take us through this?

I began by saying that without doubt the recent financial crisis and the subsequent worldwide recession constitute the most challenging problem that we, as economists, now face, and I suggested that the problems we are struggling with today are the result, in one way or another, of something that happened in England on July 19, 1844. On that date Sir Robert Peel's Bank Act, also known as the Bank Charter Act, was approved. This approval followed years of debate between two schools of thought, the Banking School theorists and the Currency School theorists, on the true causes of the artificial economic booms and the subsequent financial crises that had been affecting England, especially since the beginning of the Industrial Revolution.

On the plus side, the Act successfully incorporated the sound monetary theoretical insights of the Currency School. This school argued, in my view completely correctly, that the origin of the country's boom and bust cycles lay in the artificial credit expansions orchestrated by private banks and financed not by the prior or genuine savings of citizens, but through the issue of huge doses of fiduciary media—in those days mainly paper banknotes, or certificates of demand deposits issued by banks for a much greater amount than the gold originally deposited in their vaults.

Accordingly, Peel's Bank Act brought in a requirement for banks to hold 100% gold reserves on all banknotes issued. This goes back to the most elementary general principles of Roman law concerning the need to prevent forgery; issuing more banknotes than you hold gold for is nothing short of a sleight-of-hand or confidence trick played on your customers. It was a first and positive step in the right direction in order to avoid endlessly recurring cycles of boom and depression.

Unfortunately, while bolting one door, the Act left another door wide open, and this rendered it a disastrous failure, notwithstanding the good intentions behind the Act, and in spite of its sound theoretical foundations. It failed to extend the 100% reserve requirement to demand deposits. The originators of the Act failed to see that demand deposits were also part of the money supply. This had been clear to the scholars of the Spanish Golden Century, the *Siglo de Oro*, three hundred years earlier, but the knowledge had been entirely forgotten. As a result the Act opened the way, after 1844, for bankers to continue the practice of keeping fractional reserves—creating new credit by *fiat*, by issuing demand deposits that are not 100% backed by reserves.

Thanks to the Act, they could no longer issue profligate amounts of banknotes, but there was nothing to stop them from switching their attention to demand deposits, which they rapidly did. From an economic point of view, this gave the banks the power to create vast amounts of new credit at will, exactly as issuing banknotes unsupported by reserves would have done. So, of course, artificial credit expansions and economic booms continued, and these led in turn to financial crises and economic recessions. Despite all the hopes and good intentions originally put into Peel's Bank Act, this piece of legislation soon lost all of its credibility and popular support.

Worse, the failure of the Bank Act conditioned the evolution of financial matters up to the present time and fully explains the incorrect institutional design that afflicts the financial and monetary system of the so-called free market economies. In that sense it underpins the dreadful economic consequences that we are currently suffering.

Fractional-reserve banking is the normal state of affairs. Even the new regulatory regime that is now being worked out stops far short of demanding 100% reserves. How then does this impact the economy negatively?

There is all the difference in the world between a healthy process of capital accumulation based on true savings and a central bank-inspired expansion of credit. Central banks came into existence because of the way fractional-reserve banking led to constant traumas in the banking sector. The mission of central banks was to "smooth" the economy and save the banking community. In an unhampered free market, specific entrepreneurial, spontaneous, and microeconomic processes tend to ensure that all funds previously saved by economic agents are correctly invested. This is worth explaining in some detail, because only this knowledge permits us to understand the huge differences with respect to what happens if investment is financed not by true savings, but by the mere creation out of thin air of new demand deposits that simply materialize in the entries of banks' accounting books. Crucially, this

  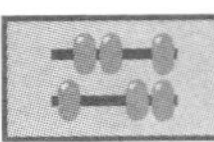      

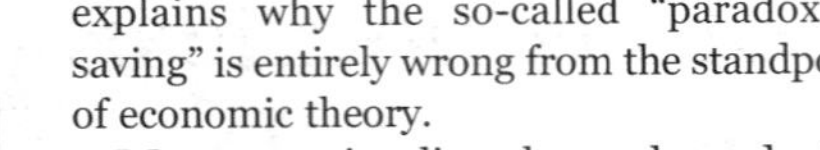

explains why the so-called "paradox of saving" is entirely wrong from the standpoint of economic theory.

We must visualize the real productive structure of the market as a temporal process composed of many very complex temporal stages in which most labor, capital goods, and productive resources are devoted not to producing consumer goods maturing this year, but to producing consumer goods and services that will mature two, three, four years, or even further into the future. For instance, a period of several years elapses between the time engineers begin to imagine and design a new car and the time when it appears in the sale showrooms. In the meantime, a whole range of processes are required, from the iron ore being mined and converted into steel, to the different parts of the automobile being produced and ultimately assembled in the factory. Only then can the new cars be distributed, marketed, and sold.

This period, clearly, consists of a very complex set of successive temporal stages of production. So, what happens if during this process consumers begin to show an increased preference for saving rather than spending? (In economic terms, the subjective time preference of economic agents decreases and, instead of wanting to spend now, they increasingly favor deferring spending.) Say that consumption falls by 10%; in that instance, three key spontaneous microeconomic processes are triggered which tend to guarantee the correct investment of the newly saved consumer goods.

The *first effect* is the new disparity in profits between the different productive stages: immediate sales in current consumer goods industries will fall and profits will decrease and stagnate compared with the profits in other sectors further away in time from current consumption. We refer here to industries which produce consumer goods that mature anything from two to five or more years from now. Their profitability will not be affected by the negative evolution of short-term current consumption since these transactions are business-to-business and are already set in train for the longer term. Entrepreneurial profits are the key signal that moves entrepreneurs in their investment decisions, and the relatively superior profit behavior of capital goods industries, which help to produce consumer goods that will mature in the long term, tells entrepreneurs all around the productive structure that they must redirect their efforts and investments from the less-profitable industries closer to consumption, to the more profitable capital goods industries situated further away in time from consumption.

The *second effect* of the new increase in savings is the decrease in the interest rate and the way it influences the market price of capital goods situated further away in time from consumption: as the interest rate is used to discount the present value of the expected future returns of each capital good, a decrease in the interest rate increases the market price of capital goods. This is self-explanatory since you are discounting the return by a lower figure; similarly, a decrease in the interest rate is also a self-explanatory consequence—with more people wanting to save, borrowers need to offer less interest to attract loans.

Importantly, since the discount rate is applied to each of the relevant years, this increase in the price of capital goods is greater the longer the capital good takes to reach maturity as a consumer good. It follows that you will have a significant increase in the market prices of capital goods compared with the relatively lower prices of consumer goods (which are less in demand due to the increase in savings). For entrepreneurs, switching investment from the underperforming consumer-related industries to the outperforming capital goods industries is an obvious move.

Finally, as our *third effect*, we should mention what Friedrich Hayek called the *Ricardo effect* (Hayek, 1990), which refers to the impact on real wages of any increase in savings. Whenever savings increase, sales and market prices of immediate consumer goods relatively stagnate or even decrease. If factor incomes (those, like wages or rent, derived from selling the services of factors of production) remain the same, this means that people will in effect enjoy higher real wages (since their purchasing power has improved). But at the same time the reality of higher wage costs will push entrepreneurs to try to see where they can substitute the now relatively cheaper capital goods for labor.

What the Ricardo effect explains is that it is perfectly possible for entrepreneurs to earn profits even when sales (of consumer goods) go down, provided that their costs decrease even more via the replacement of labor, which has become more expensive, with machines and IT. So now we need to ask: who produces these machines, computers, and capital goods that are newly demanded? Precisely those workers who have been dismissed by the stagnating consumer goods industries and who have relocated to the capital goods industries, with their longer-term focus, where there is new demand for them to produce the newly demanded capital goods. This third, Ricardo effect, along with the other two mentioned above, promotes a longer productive process with more stages, which are further away from current consumption. And this new, more capital-intensive production structure is fully sustainable, since it is fully backed by prior, genuine, real savings.

Furthermore, and this is key to our argument, it can also significantly increase, in the future, the final production of consumer goods and the real income of all economic agents (a bigger, more efficient capital goods base equates to a more productive economy and to more consumer goods at lower prices—so everyone gains). These three combined effects all work in the same direction; they are the most elementary teachings of capital theory; and they explain the secular tendency of the unhampered free market to correctly invest new savings and to constantly promote capital accumulation, together with the corresponding sustainable increase in economic welfare and development.

So then, central banks stimulating the economy with cheap credit via ultra-low interest rates must necessarily be a bad thing for the economy?

If you keep this explanation in mind, it becomes very clear why, by contrast with the above process of healthy capital accumulation, when investments are financed not by prior genuine savings but by a process of artificial credit expansion, orchestrated by fractional-reserve banks and directed by the lender of last resort, or central bank, things go very wrong indeed.

Unilateral credit expansion pushed along by the central bank means that new loans are provided by banks and recorded on the asset side of their balance sheets, against new demand deposits that are created out of thin air as collateral for the new loans, and these new deposits are automatically recorded on the liability side of banks' balance sheets. So new money—or I should say new "virtual money" because it only "materializes" in bank accounting book entries—is constantly created through this process of artificial credit expansion. In fact, only around 10% of the money supply of most important economies is in the form of cash (paper bills and coins), while the remaining 90% is this virtual money that only exists as written entries in banks' accounting books. This is precisely what the Spanish scholars termed, more than 400 years ago, *chirographis pecuniarum*, or "virtual" money that exists only in writing in an accounting book.

It is easy to understand why credit expansions are so tempting and popular and the way in which they entirely corrupt the behavior of economic agents and deeply demoralize society at all levels. To begin with, entrepreneurs are usually very happy with expansions of credit, because they make it seem as if any investment project, no matter how crazy it would appear in other situations, can easily get financing at very low interest rates. The money created through credit expansions is used by entrepreneurs to demand factors of production, which they employ mainly in capital goods industries that are more distant from consumption. As the process has not been triggered by an increase in savings (with the consequent fall in demand for consumer goods), no productive resources are liberated from consumer industries, and the prices of commodities, factors of production, capital goods, and the securities that represent them in stock markets tend to grow substantially.

What you then have is the creation of a market bubble. Everyone is happy, especially because it looks as if wealth can be increased easily, with no prior sacrifice in the form of savings (deferred consumption) and honest, hard, individual work. Near the high point of the bubble, society seems to have moved into the so-called "virtuous circle of the new economy," in which recessions seem to have been avoided forever. Investors are very happy looking at stock market quotes that grow day after day; consumer goods industries are able to sell everything they bring to the market at ever increasing prices; restaurants are always full, with long waiting lists just to get a table; workers and their unions see how desperately entrepreneurs demand their services in an environment of full employment, wage increases, and immigration; political leaders benefit from what appears to be an exceptionally good economic and social climate, which they invariably sell to the electorate as the direct result of their leadership and good economic policies; state budget bureaucrats are astonished to find that every year public income increases at double-digit figures, particularly the proceeds from value-added tax; and the whole show is artificially financed by credit expansion!

So, how long can this party last? How long can there continue to be a huge disconnect between the behavior of consumers, who do not wish to increase their savings, and that of investors—mainly financial institutions, which continuously increase their investments financed by the artificial creation of virtual money and not by citizens' prior genuine savings? How long can this illusion that everybody can get whatever he or she wants without any sacrifice last?

In fact, not that long. The unhampered market is a very dynamically efficient process. Sooner or later it inevitably discovers (and tries to correct) the huge errors that have been committed. There is always a set of spontaneous microeconomic reactions that occur to halt and reverse the negative effects of the bubble years.

What are these microeconomic reactions that lead to the bursting of the cheap credit bubble?

In my book *Money, Bank Credit, and Economic Cycles* (2009, pp. 361–384), I analyze in detail the six spontaneous and inevitable microeconomic causes of the reversal of the artificial boom that aggressive expansion of bank credit invariably triggers in the market. Let me briefly summarize these six factors.

1. *The rise in the price of the original means of production* (mainly labor, natural resources, and commodities). This rise appears when these resources have not been liberated from consumer goods industries (because savings have not increased) and the entrepreneurs of the different stages in the production process compete with each other to obtain them.

2. *The subsequent rise in the price of consumer goods at an even quicker pace than that of the rise in the price of the factors of production.* This happens when consumers' time preferences remain stable (buy now!) and the new money created by banks reaches the pockets of the consumers in an environment in which entrepreneurs are frantically trying to produce more for distant consumption and less for immediate consumption of all kinds of goods. Demand for goods is stronger than supply, so prices rise.

This also explains the next factor, namely:

3. *The substantial relative increase in the accounting profits of companies that are closest to final consumption*, especially compared with the profits of capital goods industries, which begin to stagnate when their costs rise more rapidly than their turnover.

4. *The Ricardo effect*, which exerts an impact that is exactly opposite to the one it exerted when there was an increase in voluntary saving. Now the relative rise in the prices of consumer goods (or of consumer industries' turnover in an environment of increased productivity) with respect to the increase in original factor income begins to drive down real wages, motivating entrepreneurs to substitute cheaper labor for machinery, which lessens the demand for capital goods and further reduces the profits of companies operating in the stages furthest from consumption.

5. *The inevitable subsequent increase in the loan rate of interest, pushing it beyond even pre-credit expansion levels.* This happens when the pace of credit expansion stops accelerating, something that always occurs sooner or later. Interest rates significantly increase due to the higher purchasing power and risk premiums demanded by the lenders. Furthermore, entrepreneurs involved in malinvestments start a "fight to the death" to obtain additional financing to try to complete their investment projects (Hayek, 1937 1990?), so banks are able to charge them more for their loan money.

These five factors provoke the following combined effect.

6. *Companies that operate in the stages that are relatively more distant from consumption begin to discover that they are incurring heavy accounting losses.* These accounting losses, when compared with the relative profits generated in the stages closest to consumption, finally reveal beyond a doubt that serious entrepreneurial errors have been committed and that there is an urgent need to correct them by halting and liquidating investment projects that were mistakenly launched during the boom years.

The financial crisis begins the moment the market, which is very dynamically efficient, discovers that the true market value of the loans granted by banks during the boom is only a fraction of what was originally thought. In other words, the market discovers that the value of bank assets is much lower than previously thought and, as bank liabilities (which are the deposits created during the boom) remain constant, the market discovers that the banks are in fact bankrupt. At this point, were it not for the desperate action of central banks—as lenders of last resort—in bailing out the banks, the whole financial and monetary system would collapse.

What is critical here is to recognize that unlike the popular account of the 2008 crash, the financial and banking crisis *is not* the cause of the economic recession *but one of its most important first symptoms.*

Economic recessions—and the 2008 crash was no different—begin when the market discovers that many investment projects launched during the boom years are not profitable. And then consumers demand liquidation of these malinvestments which, it is now discovered, were planned to mature in a too-distant future considering the true wishes of consumers. The recession marks the beginning of the painful readjustment of the production structure, which consists of withdrawing

  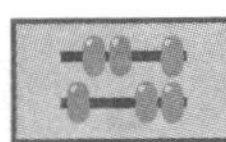      

productive resources from the stages furthest from consumption and transferring them back to those closest to it.

Both financial crisis and economic recession are unavoidable once credit expansion has begun, because the market sooner or later discovers that investment projects financed by banks during the boom period were too ambitious due to a lack of the real saved resources that would be needed to complete them. In other words, the expansion of bank credit during the boom period encourages entrepreneurs to act as if savings had increased when in fact this is not the case. A generalized error of economic calculation has been committed, and sooner or later it will be discovered and corrected spontaneously by the market.

MORE INFO

Books:

Hayek, F. A. *The Fatal Conceit: The Errors of Socialism*. W. W. Bartley, III (ed). Chicago, IL: University of Chicago Press, 1990.

Huerta de Soto, Jesús. *Money, Bank Credit, and Economic Cycles*. 2nd English ed. Auburn, AL: Ludwig von Mises Institute, 2009a.

Huerta de Soto, Jesús. *The Theory of Dynamic Efficiency*. Abingdon, UK, and New York: Routledge, 2009b.

Huerta de Soto, Jesús. *Socialism, Economic Calculation and Entrepreneurship*. Cheltenham, UK, and Northampton, MA: Edward Elgar Publishing, 2010.

Mises, Ludwig von. *The Theory of Money and Credit*. Auburn, AL: Ludwig von Mises Institute, 2009.

See Also:

★ Viewpoint: Lessons from the Credit Crisis: Governing Financial Institutions (pp. 694–695)

★ Viewpoint: Why the Thinking of the Austrian School of Economics Matters in Today's Economy (pp. 269–271)

"Except for the con men borrowing money they shouldn't get and the widows who have to visit with the handsome young men in the trust department, no sane person ever enjoyed visiting a bank." Martin Mayer

  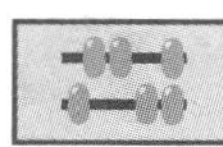   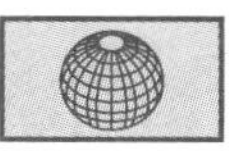   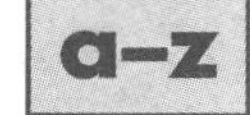

Middle East and North Africa Region: Financial Sector and Integration

by Samy Ben Naceur and Chiraz Labidi

EXECUTIVE SUMMARY

- With a population of 345.5 million and a GDP of about US$1,593 billion in 2007, the Middle East and North Africa (MENA) region has great potential, but faces major challenges.
- By reforming their economies, most of the MENA countries have achieved macroeconomic stability, and increased their growth.
- A more developed and well-functioning financial sector is essential to boosting sustainable economic growth in the region.
- Given the existing complementarities between MENA countries, there are numerous possibilities for intra-regional integration. Financial integration within the region will also help deepen financial markets, and increase their efficiency.

INTRODUCTION

The Middle East and North Africa region, as defined by the World Bank in the MENA 2008 Economic Developments and Prospects (EDP) report,[1] comprises Algeria, Bahrain, Djibouti, Egypt, Iran, Iraq, Jordan, Kuwait, Lebanon, Libya, Morocco, Oman, the Palestinian Territories (West Bank and Gaza), Qatar, Saudi Arabia, Syria, Tunisia, the United Arab Emirates, and Yemen.

The World Bank classifies these countries within three groups: resource-poor, labor-abundant economies (Djibouti, Egypt, Jordan, Lebanon, Morocco, Tunisia, and the West Bank and Gaza); resource-rich, labor-abundant economies (Algeria, Iran, Iraq, Syria, and Yemen); and resource-rich, labor-importing economies (Bahrain, Kuwait, Libya, Oman, Qatar, Saudi Arabia and the United Arab Emirates).

In 2007, these 19 countries and territories represented about 5% (345.5 million) of the world's population. The region's GDP was approximately US$1,593 billion (at current exchange rates), or about 3% of world GDP.

The Gulf Cooperation Council (GCC) countries—Bahrain, Kuwait, Oman, Qatar, Saudi Arabia, and the United Arab Emirates—account for fewer than 11% of the population of MENA countries but for some 49% of the region's GDP and around 80% of the area's stock-market capitalization.[2] The GCC region's wealth is, in large part, a product of its petroleum resources.

In 2007, the MENA region experienced GDP growth of 5.7% (see Table 1), and five years of growth at a rate higher than 5%. This performance occurred in the context of a continued rise in the oil price in recent years having important spillover effects on the financial and real-estate sectors, as well as on job creation. It has also brought more interest in intraregional integration as a means of sharing prosperity within the region, and as a catalyst for global integration and competitiveness.

However, the increased interests of MENA banks and investors in the volatile equity and real-estate markets have made some economies more vulnerable to contagion effects. During 2008, the recession in developed economies, and the slowdown in emerging markets, affected some MENA countries. More precisely, the region, and especially GCC countries, experienced reduced financial liquidity, and a sharp drop in share values.

FINANCIAL SECTOR

A well-developed and dynamic financial sector is essential to achieve sustainable economic growth. Many attempts have been made in the last decade to improve the performance and efficiency of the MENA financial sector. However, there still exists a wide gap if compared to other developed and emerging regions. Although MENA countries present different levels of the financial sector's development, some broad generalizations can be made. Overall, the banking sector dominates MENA's financial system, and stock and bond markets remain a minor alternative option for raising funds.

Banking Sector

Banks dominate MENA's financial systems, and, over the past years, the exceptional increases in liquidity stemming from oil revenues have fed a rapid rise in bank deposits, and a growing demand for credit from the real economy. The credit growth has supported real-estate loans and mortgage lending. This has been complemented by housing finance reform efforts throughout the region. Particularly in the Gulf economies, the banking sector has increased credit and relaxed financing terms to the real-estate sector.

The MENA financial sector is also experiencing prodigious growth in the Islamic banking sector (15–20% over the past decade), which is based on the principles of Islamic law (also known as *shariah* law). Two basic principles behind Islamic banking are the prohibition of the collection and payment of interest (known as *riba*), and the prohibition of profit-sharing or leasing without underlying tangible assets. These principles contribute to make lending more prudent and linked to real economic activity, and explain the resiliency of the sector to the credit crunch crisis.

However, according to the MENA 2008 EDP report, "These positive developments are overshadowed by a number of factors. The financial sector in MENA is still dominated by commercial banks that are vulnerable to shocks from the equity and the real markets. A disconnect between the financial sector and the real economy is still observed, public-sector ownership is high, and access to banking services is low." Indeed, heavy public-sector ownership, as well as limited openness in some countries, had had a significant impact on the direction of credit in MENA, as well as operating efficiency and the ability of the banking sector to conduct robust risk analysis.

Table 1. Real GDP growth (US$ '000s). (*Source*: World Bank)

	2000–04	2005	2006	2007
MENA region	4.6	5.8	5.8	5.7
Resource-poor, labor-abundant*	4.2	3.7	6.3	5.4
Resource-rich, labor-abundant†	5.1	6.5	5.7	5.8
Resource-rich, labor-importing‡	5.1	7.3	6.2	5.8

* Djibouti, Egypt, Jordan, Lebanon, Morocco, and Tunisia (West Bank and Gaza are excluded because of data limitations).
† Algeria, Iran, Iraq, Syria, and Yemen.
‡ Bahrain, Kuwait, Libya, Oman, Qatar, Saudi Arabia and the United Arab Emirates.

  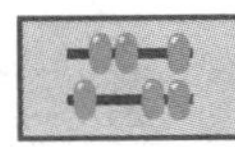      

Table 2. Stock market indicators. (*Source*: World Bank and Arab Monetary Fund (AMF))

Indicator	2003	2004	2005	2006	2007	2008
Market capitalization (US$ millions)	361,078	620,364	1,287,696	883,497	1,333,620	765,784
Value traded (US$ millions)	230,417	568,158	1,434,908	1,684,029	1,107,177	997,331
Number of listed firms	1,723	1,549	1,616	1,571	1,498	1,503

Capital Markets

The MENA capital markets are generally perceived as less developed than other emerging markets.

The privatization process launched during the 1990s has been slow, and has not reached its promise with regard to capital markets development. There are many reasons for the markedly slow privatization in the region, and its consequences in terms of capital markets underdevelopment. In some cases, there is evidence of a lack of political will, and some pressure by interest groups. More generally, the considerable involvement of governments in economic activities and related overstaffing, as well as the slow pace of job creation in the private sector, represent barriers to a rapid privatization process.

However, following continuous liberalization efforts and improvements to the underlying legal framework, some MENA stock markets have been successfully revitalized during the last few years. As shown in Table 2, market development indicators such as market capitalization, value traded, and number of listed firms have significantly increased. GCC capital markets can be considered as the most developed, and they account for about 73% of the region's stock-market capitalization (see Figure 1), but for only 40% of the total number of listed companies. There are also bond markets in almost all MENA countries, but they have not yet reached a sufficient level of development due to low governmental and institutional investors' participation, and to the relative scarcity of large private corporations able to issue debt.

Overall, a key challenge for capital markets in the MENA countries is to channel available liquidity into the real economy, boosting sustainable and efficient growth. However, academic research shows that stock-market informational efficiency (in the sense defined by Eugene Fama) is essential to achieve this goal. Lagoarde-Segot and Lucey (2008)[3] investigated informational efficiency in a set of seven MENA stock markets, excluding GCC countries, while other studies focused on the GCC stock markets. (See, for example, Abraham et al., (2002),[4] Al Loughani (2003),[5] and Al Saad and Moosa (2005).[6]) Most of these studies found evidence of a significant departure from the efficient market hypothesis. After constructing an efficiency index, Lagoarde-Segot and Lucey highlighted heterogeneous levels of efficiency in the MENA stock markets. Their results indicate that informational efficiency in the MENA markets is primarily affected by market depth, and corporate governance factors.

Figure 1. Relative market capitalization (2008). (*Source*: AMF)

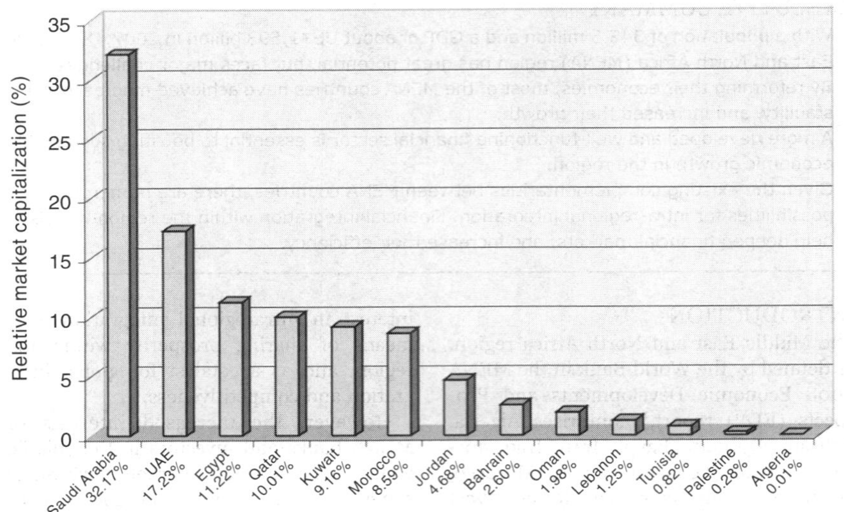

Indeed, in most MENA countries, stock markets are characterized by the concentration of ownership and the limited role of market forces. These aspects, among others, have a negative impact on transparency and disclosure standards, in particular, and on corporate governance practices in general.

CASE STUDY

Tunisia's Stock Exchange

Overview

Tunisia's Stock Exchange (TSE) is composed of an equity market and a bond market, while there are no derivative instruments traded. The equity market consists of an Official Market, which contains 51 listed firms, and an Alternative Market, which was set up in 2007 and has one listed firm. There is also an unlisted market comprising four companies. Two-thirds of the stocks, representing 63% of the market capitalization by the end of 2007, are continuously priced.

Institutions

TSE is managed by the Bourse des Valeurs Mobilières de Tunis (BVMT), which is owned by 24 financial intermediaries, supervised by the Conseil du Marché Financier, and for which stock and bonds transactions are deposited and cleared by the Société Tunisienne Interprofessionnelle de Compensation et de Dépôt des Valeurs Mobilières.

Markets

TSE is dominated by retail investors, and foreign participation stood at 28% of the whole market by the end of 2007. Any foreign participation above 50% of a firm's capital needs authorization. There are two market indices. The unweighted BVMT index, created in September 1990, includes the most liquid stocks on the market with at least six months' listing. The other index is TUNINDEX, which has been published since 1998 and is weighted by market capitalization. It also covers listed firms that have at least six months' of quotations. TSE implemented in December 2007 a new electronic trading platform, which

  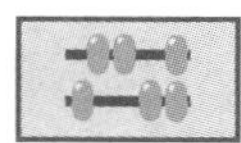   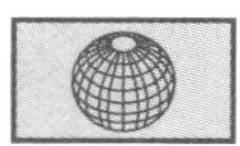   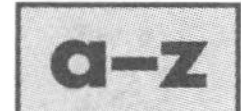

Recent surveys[7] show evidence of a corporate governance gap in the MENA region, if the benchmark of the Organisation for Economic Co-operation and Developement (OECD) corporate governance principles and practice in developed countries are considered. Despite the fact that the corporate governance framework is already in place, there is still room for improvement with respect to transparency, disclosure, protection of non-controlling shareholders, directors' independence, qualifications, and compensation. The challenges that the region is still facing regarding legal and regulatory frameworks, and in the property rights area, can also be considered as barriers to proper corporate governance.

FINANCIAL INTEGRATION

The MENA countries share geographical, cultural, and economic similarities and, at the same time, present complementarities providing a favorable context for intraregional financial integration. Some countries in the region export capital, while others are capital importers. Some countries have small populations, are major oil exporters, and typically import labor, whereas others have large populations and face unemployment issues.

Moreover, the wealthiest countries had traditionally invested their surpluses in the major international financial centers, and are now seeking to diversify their investments by placing an increased share of their funds in the region. As a consequence, intraregional foreign direct investments (FDI) and portfolio investments have risen in many MENA countries. In particular, between 2002 and 2006, about US$60 billion, or 11% of total GCC capital outflows, went to other MENA countries.[8]

Direct foreign investment flows have been boosted by the improved business climate in some MENA countries, and many GCC investors, operating in several sectors (telecommunications, real estate, tourism, banking), are targeting countries such as Egypt, Lebanon, Syria, and Tunisia.

As for capital market integration, the amount of funds that actually flows intraregionally depends on regulatory aspects related to stock markets and foreign investments. Investors from the GCC are showing interest in stocks of non-GCC countries. However, most countries impose barriers and restrictions on foreign investments in domestic equities, preventing deeper capital market integration (for example, Amman Stock Exchange imposes a ceiling of 50% foreign ownership for companies operating in some specific sectors, foreign investors are allowed to own a maximum of 49% of United Arab Emirates corporations, and foreign ownership in Omani companies is generally limited to 70%).

CONCLUSION

The structural and institutional reforms undertaken by many MENA countries, as well as the oil boom, have contributed to the substantial development of the financial system in the MENA region in the last decade. Despite this progress, much remains to be done, and the region is still facing a number of issues with regard to its banking sector and capital markets. Good corporate governance practices are also essential in ensuring efficient access to financing, in attracting foreign investors, and, more generally, in promoting sustainable development. In addition, more pronounced intraregional integration should enable investors throughout the region to achieve more portfolio diversification, and improve resources allocation. Hence, deeper regional cooperation should be encouraged if MENA is to keep up in an increasingly competitive global environment.

uses the same trading system as the New York Stock Exchange. New trading rules have been introduced, such as the increase in the minimum daily trading margin from 4.50% to 6.09% on the equity market.

The debt market is small compared to the equity market, as it represents fewer than 10% of market transactions in the period 2003–07. Bond issues reached US$1.2 billion in 2007, with the state representing 83.4% of bond issues by value in 2007. The corporate bond market is monopolized by financial institutions. Banks tend to use it to finance mortgages, and leasing companies to balance their books. New legislation allowing foreign investors to own up to 20% of government bonds from January 2007 will certainly stimulate trading in the debt market.

Challenges

The main challenge for the TSE is to increase the number of listed firms, and the contribution of the capital market to finance the economy[9] from 8% in 2007 to 20% by the end of 2009. The recent reallocation of the privatization program towards the stock exchange will certainly have a strong impact on developing the TSE. Besides, the creation of the Alternative Market in 2007 is expected to boost the capital market, as 100 companies from the Tunisian Modernization Program have been identified for listing in this market. Finally, the willingness of the Maghreb countries' authorities to spur regional financial integration will be another contributor to the development of the Tunisian Stock Exchange.

MAKING IT HAPPEN

- A healthy and dynamic financial sector entails achieving sustainable and efficient economic growth in the MENA region.
- Good corporate governance is crucial for the region to achieve its challenge of becoming a global player.
- The efficiency of the banking system is one of the key aspects that the MENA countries need to face the challenges of globalization, and support economic growth. A more developed capital markets infrastructure should make it easier for borrowers and investors to operate.
- Economic and financial integration within the region could represent stepping stones towards the ultimate goal of development and global competitiveness.

MORE INFO

Books:

Molyneux, Philip, and Iqbal Munawar. *Banking and Financial Systems in the Arab World*. New York: Palgrave Macmillan, 2005.

Noland, Marcus, and Howard Pack. *The Arab Economies in a Changing World*. Washington, DC: Peterson Institute for International Economics, 2007.

Websites:

Arab Monetary Fund: www.amf.org.ae
International Monetary Fund: www.imf.org
OECD information on MENA: www.oecd.org/mena
World Bank's MENA site: go.worldbank.org/DT45JDVOK0

"A very powerful and durable rally is in the works. But it may need another couple of days to lift off. Hold the fort and keep the faith!" Richard Band

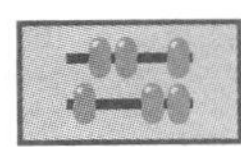

See Also:

NOTES

1 Middle East and North Africa Region. "Economic Developments and Prospects: Regional Integration for Global competitiveness." World Bank, 2008.
2 Excluding Tehran's stock exchange capitalization.
3 Lagoarde-Segot, T., and B. M. Lucey. "Efficiency in emerging markets: Evidence from the MENA region." *International Financial Markets, Institutions and Money* 18 (2008): 94–105.
4 Abraham, A., F. J. Seyyed, and S. A. Alsakran. "Testing the random walk behavior and efficiency of Gulf stock markets." *The Financial Review* 37:3 (2002): 469–480.
5 Al Loughani, N. E. "The seasonal characteristics of stock returns in the Kuwaiti stock market." *Journal of Gulf and Arabian Peninsula Studies* 29: 109 (2003): 15–40.
6 Al Saad, K., and A. I. Moosa. "Seasonality in stock returns: Evidence from an emerging market." *Applied Financial Economics* 15:1 (2005): 63–71.
7 See, for example, "Advancing the corporate governance agenda in the Middle East and North Africa: A survey of legal and institutional frameworks." MENA-OECD Investment Program.
8 Source: World Bank.
9 Three possible sources of financing are considered: bank credits, bonds, and equity.

"What a country calls its vital economic interests are not the things that enable its citizens to live, but the things that enable it to make war." Simone Weil

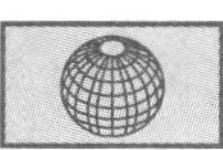

Mixflation by Giles Keating

EXECUTIVE SUMMARY

- Mixflation is the deflation or rapid disinflation of one large and important block of prices, occurring simultaneously with the rapid inflation of another similarly large block. The collapse of manufactured good prices and surge in commodity prices over much of the last 10 years is a key example. This has now reversed rapidly, suggesting that monetary policy is a crucial driver of mixflation, and not just structural forces (urbanization, industrialization).
- We take a stylized description of global monetary policy (inflation targets, plus output for the Fed, in developed countries and exchange rate targets in emerging countries). We argue this encouraged excess investment in manufacturing etc., and insufficient consumption, in emerging countries. This exaggerated the divergence between manufactured and commodity prices, and created a savings glut, depressing long-term interest rates, and leading to excess risk-taking and asset price bubbles globally, which have now burst.
- A new global monetary regime is needed, with developed countries explicitly targeting asset price volatility alongside inflation, and emerging countries accepting a flexible system for adjusting exchange rates to avoid growing imbalances.

INTRODUCTION

Previous eras—viewed through the simplifying lens of history—seem often to fall into periods of inflation and deflation: the great falling-price boom of the 1880s; The deflationary slump of the 1930s; the inflationary 1970s. But modern times are more mixed. Over much of the last 10 years, manufactured goods prices have fallen while commodity prices soared. During 2008, this bifurcation seemed to briefly give way to a more generalized inflation, until the intensifying credit crisis suddenly instead suggested the risk of deflation. Meanwhile, for the second time within a decade, asset prices have moved in wild gyrations between boom and slump. We could describe this modern era as a phase of mixflation.

A LONGER-TERM PERSPECTIVE

There is considerable evidence to suggest that the experience of the last 10 years in relative price movements has been markedly greater than the preceding decades. Figure 1 shows the Reuters CRB commodity index, deflated by the US CPI and covering the period since the First World War. This shows a far larger percentage rise from the start of the current decade until the peak in July 2008 than recorded at any earlier point. This has been followed by a percentage decline that is also the largest on this data set.

Figure 2 provides evidence of increased volatility in real US house prices. It shows median US house prices (Census Bureau data, one family homes), deflated by core CPI. Following a sharp surge in the 10 years to the late 1970s, there was a period of some two decades of relative stability. Then, in the decade to 2008, there was a major surge. This took the peak growth to its highest peak in this data set. Moreover, it was followed by a sharp reversal down.

Looking at equity markets, Figure 3 shows the total real return (calculated using headline US CPI) on the US S&P 500 index and its predecessors, back to the middle of the 19th Century, and expressed as a deviation from trend. This illustrates that movements in real equity returns over the last 10 years have been more extreme than the past in certain respects. During the dotcom bubble, the index showed its highest ever deviation to the upside, in early 2000. The crash, partial recovery, and then renewed crash since then have taken the index close to the most extreme downside deviations previously recorded. The peak to trough movement is also the largest recorded apart from one event during the Great Depression.

ANALYSIS: MIXFLATION AND MONETARY POLICY

Why are we now living in times where rapidly rising prices in one major part of the economy coexist with falling prices in another, and where inflation can switch so suddenly to deflation? One driving force is global structural change, as demographic expansion in lower-income countries, and the logical and natural move of such countries to higher living standards, puts

Figure 1. Reuters CRB commodity index, deflated by US CPI

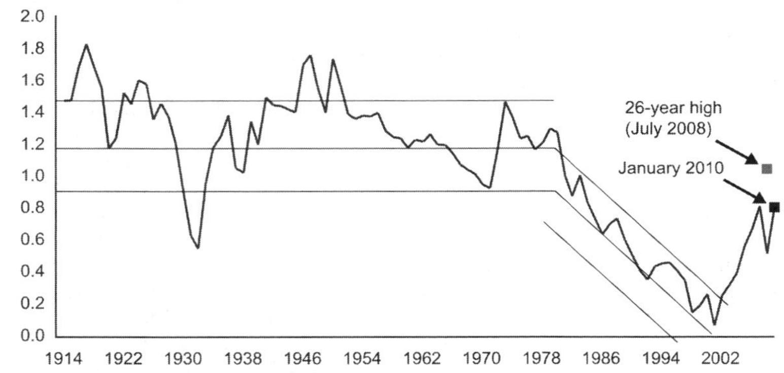

CASE STUDY

A few key figures will help to illustrate the recent experience of mixflation. Over the 10 years to December 2009, US manufactured consumer import prices (excluding autos) increased by a compound rate of 0.3% per annum, while prices of traded commodities (CCI index) rose by 9% annually. During the same period, US core consumer prices increased at a rate of 2.1% (and the headline rate by 2.6%) annually.

There were also very wide gyrations in share prices. Over the 10 years to the end of 2009, the US S&P 500 index changed relatively little (its annualised total return was −0.9%). However, there were two calendar years when it fell more than a fifth (2002 and 2008 with 23% and 38% falls, respectively) and two years when it rose more than a fifth (2003 and 2009 with a 26% and 26% rise, respectively).

"The banking crisis may not have been caused by the internet but it was certainly fuelled by the way connectivity and speed created a market in which everybody was gripped by the hysteria of the herd." Bryan Appleyard

Figure 2. US house prices relative to core CPI

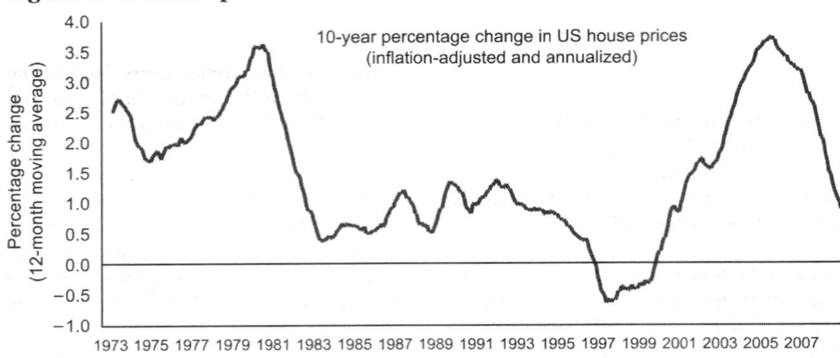

Figure 3. US real equity returns—deviation from trend. Latest data point: January 2010. (*Source*: DataStream, Credit Suisse)

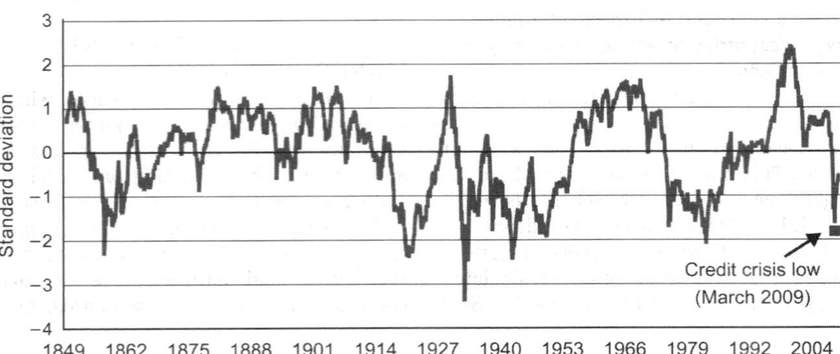

upward pressure on the prices of natural resources, especially when those had previously seen two decades of decline (see Figure 1). But while such long-term forces can point to a long-term mixflation price trend, it is difficult to see them as the main driver of the speed and violence of the relative price moves of recent years. To explain this, we need to look at the role of monetary policy, and consider how the interaction of this across different countries may have influenced the relative prices of manufactured goods and commodities.

The range of factors that make up monetary policy in an integrated global economy includes, first and foremost, central banks' macromonetary policies, but the context in which these operate is also critical. This includes financial regulation, fiscal policy, and exchange rate policy (including capital controls). The context also includes other key variables, influenced by past policy actions: The structure of the financial industry; the pace of financial innovation; the pattern of global capital flows; and the risk appetite of investors.

Looking back over the last decade, central banks' macromonetary policies can be divided into, broadly, three types, varying across countries. First, the US Fed, in line with its mandate, has simultaneously targeted consumer price inflation and output growth. Second, a large group of central banks have essentially targeted (anticipated) consumer price inflation, including those that explicitly have this as their sole target (for example, New Zealand and the United Kingdom), but also the ECB, which technically also targets monetary growth. Third, many central banks in China and many other countries across Asia, as well as in many other emerging markets, have, in practice, based monetary policy around an explicit or implicit exchange rate target. The Bank of Japan, wrestling with deflation for a decade, does not fit neatly into this framework, but can perhaps be described as nominally targeting price stability while *de facto* targeting an exchange rate characterized by long phases of depreciation or (more recently) stability, punctuated by occasional violent appreciations.

While these policy regimes were individually based on objectives that were sensible from a national perspective, when interacting together they have caused a range of outcomes that are highly undesirable.

In particular, exchange rate targets were typically set at a relatively low level, so the countries concerned saw high levels of net exports, and supernormal returns on real estate and industrial investment projects. The resulting distortions seem to have been one of the major causes of mixflation. The high rates of net exports boosted the global supply of (mainly lower-end) manufactured products, putting downward pressure on their prices. Simultaneously, the prospect of high returns encouraged large and arguably excessive investment in factories, infrastructure, and real estate, which in turn boosted demand for many commodities, ranging from base metals like copper through to oil and other energy sources. This contributed to surges in their prices, providing the other half of the mixflation phenomenon.

These policies also had distortive effects on international capital flows. Buoyant net exports, combined with large net capital inflows encouraged by the high investment returns, implied a large surplus on basic balance for many of these fast-growing emerging countries. The same occurred in Japan for slightly different reasons, with the basic balance surplus there mainly reflecting depressed consumption. To prevent these surpluses causing unwanted currency appreciation, the local central banks accumulated large foreign exchange reserves, much of which was invested in US government debt or near substitutes. This drove down yields on government debt to levels that appeared low on a theoretical basis (for example, if compared to trend nominal GDP growth).

These low yields were unattractive to many investors, including those like pension funds and insurers with clear future liability streams. Such investors responded by switching into higher-risk, lower-credit quality investments, including tranches of securitised structures with apparently good credit ratings. This lowered the cost and increased the availability of credit, which underpinned the expansion of subprime mortgages and general consumer credit in the United States and, to a varying extent, in many other countries, including the United Kingdom. It also fueled consumer booms and worsened trade deficits in these countries, as well as gradually boosting equity prices. With consumer prices kept under control by mixflation, being the main target of central banks, interest rates were set at a low enough level to accommodate this credit-induced boom, rather than ending it.

The excesses of the pre-crisis years have now been exposed. House prices, equity markets, and many credit assets rose to unsustainable levels and then collapsed; many individuals took on excessive loan commitments; banks took on high levels of

"The business of banking ought to be simple. If it is hard it is wrong. The only securities which a banker, using money that he may be asked at short notice to repay, ought to touch, are those which are easily saleable and easily intelligible."
Walter Bagehot

risk and, eventually, public confidence in them began to be threatened as the extent of losses became clear. Expansionary monetary policy helped avert a prolonged global recession, but if policy remains loose for too long, new asset price bubbles could be created, and already commodity prices and real estate in some Asian centres have rebounded very sharply from their lows. Meanwhile, consumer price inflation remains subdued due to high levels of spare capacity and unemployment. Mixflation is thus once again very prominent

Much of the commentary on the credit crisis has focused on issues such as the regulatory framework and capital requirements for banks, the possible perverse remuneration incentives for bank officers, and the role of the rating agencies. The above description suggests that each of these may have played some role, but it also implies that their importance was secondary, compared to the much more fundamental issue of global monetary policy having quite the wrong objectives. On the one hand, a key cause of the credit crisis was that emerging countries and Japan had their monetary policies influenced or dominated by exchange rates. This generated mixflation and perverse capital flows, which then made it inappropriate to focus monetary policy on consumer price inflation in the United States and elsewhere.

There are several rationales for targeting consumer prices, rather than variables, with the potential to be more forward looking (asset prices, credit, or money growth, etc.). First, the forward information content of such variables is meant to be difficult to quantify, especially as institutions change, and indeed some variables tend to become less relevant, precisely because they are targeted. Second, consumer prices are meant to be the ultimate anchor for asset prices. Third, central banks target forecasts of future consumer prices, rather than current levels, allowing them in principle to incorporate forward-looking indicators as appropriate. Fourth, there have been instances (the 1987 stock market crash being an example) where violent movements in key asset prices have occurred with apparently very little impact on the real economy, or on the general price level.

However, as the credit crisis has illustrated, asset price movements often do embed information about the future, even if the signal is not straightforward. For example, a high price for equities or debt may not be signaling robust income streams ahead as a simple time discount model might imply, but instead may be indicating a severe excess demand that over time will become unstable. Extracting this information certainly cannot be done by a crude rule but, nevertheless, it may be very important. Moreover, the path of asset prices clearly does matter in certain circumstances. Some assets (often the case with equities) are held by unleveraged end investors, or on their behalf by entities like pension funds, against very long-term future liabilities. In this case, rather substantial fluctuations may have relatively little feedback to the real economy. But other assets (such as many credit instruments) are held by highly leveraged institutions such as banks, which typically under the pre-crisis Basel II regime could have a ratio of assets to equity capital of 30 times or more, and will still be able to have a ratio up up to about 20 to 25 even under new proposed rules. Fluctuations in the prices of such assets can clearly have major feedthrough to the real economy.

APPENDIX: REVIEW OF LITERATURE

While the term "mixflation" has not been used in the academic literature, it has long been acknowledged that monetary policy may have to be set against the background of widely divergent price signals, especially when consumer prices and asset prices are behaving in a very different way.

The feedback between asset price fluctuations and real economic activity has long been acknowledged by economists (for example, Fisher 1930, Keating 1987), but it has tended to be argued that their influence on monetary policy should, at most, be secondary and indirect. Bernanke and Gertler (2000) suggest that while there is a case in principle for monetary policy to respond directly to "nonfundamental" moves in asset prices, in practice such effects are difficult to identify and therefore asset prices should be used only as an indirect input, via their impact on inflation projections. Subsequent debate has sometimes leant to a greater role for asset prices, with, for example, Borio (2005) advocating that policy be based on multi-year inflation projections, where asset prices play a greater role, while Ingves (2007) gives a practioner's description of (limited) targeting of asset price volatility at the Sveriges Riksbank.

For emerging market monetary policy, it has long been understood that the ability to set domestic interest rates and the exchange rate independently depends inversely on the amount of capital account mobility, and recent work (for example, Saxena 2008) provides some empirical estimates. Such discussions tend to assume that the countries involved are small, relative to the global financial system, but Greenspan (2007) notes that the savings glut in larger emerging countries was large enough to

MAKING IT HAPPEN

The implication is that a new regime for central bank monetary policy is needed. For emerging countries, a global initiative should aim to de-politicize the delicate issue of exchange rate targets. It should establish the principle that the short-term gains to one country from an undervalued currency are outweighed over time by the pressures that build up, and should agree a flexible system for adjusting rates on a technical rather than political basis.

For the developed countries, consumer price forecasts should be only one pillar of a broader targeting, which should also include a mandate to dampen extreme fluctuations in asset prices. This mandate should not attempt to define asset price level targets, but rather should have a broad set of targets that included a range of valuation measures, and a range of measures of speed of movement. In short, it should acknowledge that there are severe limits to the signal, which can be extracted from asset prices, while at the same time making use of the crucial information that does lie buried in the noise. Such an approach, known as "leaning into the wind," immediately faces the criticism that it is not a clear and simple rule, but unfortunately we do not live in a simple world, and in any event, existing approaches, based on consumer price inflation, include complex modeling processes. Moreover, in determining the points at which verbal or actual exchange rate intervention is applied, central banks around the world already have experience in operating a regime with some of these characteristics, since the intervention points are often based on a combination of level and rate of change.

With hindsight, the era of mixflation, and the credit crisis with which it is intimately linked, seems to have been driven by unforeseen interactions between monetary policies in different countries across the world. There are powerful structural trends, tending to drive up commodity prices from the low relative levels they reached at the start of this decade. But they have been exaggerated, distorted, and reversed, probably temporarily, by the effects of monetary policy. A new regime is now needed to allow the mixflation era to resume in a more sustainable and ordered way.

force down long-term US government bond yields (so that a crucial asset price was influenced by, in Bernanke's terminology, a "nonfundamental" factor). A number of studies have looked at this "conundrum," for example, Warnock and Warnock (2006) conclude that it may have depressed yields by up to 90 basis points. Finally, a recent analysis by Frankel (2006) finds a clear empirical link between real interest rates and commodity prices, and concludes that the latter should be a key monetary condition indicator.

Meanwhile, key monetary policymakers seem to be moving only slowly towards the analysis and conclusions set out here. Ben Bernanke (2010), chairman of the Federal Reserve Board, in a major post-crisis speech stated "That conclusion suggests that the best response to the housing bubble would have been regulatory, not monetary...," although he does concede, "...However, if adequate reforms are not made, or if they are made but prove insufficient to prevent dangerous buildups of financial risks, we must remain open to using monetary policy as a supplementary tool for addressing those risks–proceeding cautiously and always keeping in mind the inherent difficulties of that approach."

MORE INFO

Books:

Frankel, J. "The effect of monetary policy on real commodity prices." In J. Campbell (ed). *Asset Prices and Monetary Policy*. Chicago, IL: University of Chicago Press, 2008.

Greenspan, A. *The Age of Turbulence, Adventures in a New World*. New York: Penguin Press, 2007.

Articles:

Bernanke, B. Speech to Annual Meeting of American Economic Association, Atlanta, Georgia, January 3, 2010, "Monetary policy and the housing bubble." Online at: www.federalreserve.gov/newsevents/speech/bernanke20100103a.htm

Bernanke, B., and M. Gertler. "Monetary policy and asset price volatility." National Bureau of Economic Research, Working paper 7559, 2000.

Borio, C. "Monetary and financial stability: So close and yet so far?" *National Institute Economic Review* 192:1 (2005): 84–101.

Fisher, I. "The debt-deflation theory of great depressions." *Econometrica* 1 (1993): 337–357.

Ingves, S. "Housing and monetary policy: A view from an inflation-targeting central bank." Remarks at the Federal Reserve Bank of Kansas City's Economic Symposium, Jackson Hole, Wyoming, 2007: 433–443.

Keating, G. "A two-good model with capital accumulation and a real balance effect." *Oxford Economic Papers* 39 (1987): 481–499.

Saxena, S. "Capital flows, exchange rate regime and monetary policy." In *Transmission Mechanisms for Monetary Policy in Emerging Market Economies*, BIS Papers No 35, January (2008): 81–102.

Warnock, F., and V. Warnock. "International capital flows and U.S. interest rates." National Bureau of Economic Research, Working Paper 12560, 2006.

See Also:

★ The Globalization of Inflation (pp. 184–185)
★ Viewpoint: Steering Between Deflation and Inflation—A Troubled Road for Developed Economies (pp. 604–606)
✔ Methods for Dealing with Inflation Risk (p. 984)
✔ Understanding and Using Inflation Swaps (p. 993)
Joseph Stiglitz (p. 1313)
When Markets Collide: Investment Strategies for the Age of Global Economic Change (p. 1436)

"We are in the midst of a once-in-a-century credit tsunami. Central banks and governments are being required to take unprecedented measures. Those of us who have looked to the self-interest of lending institutions to protect shareholders' equity are in a state of shocked disbelief." Alan Greenspan

        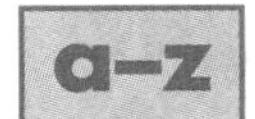

Viewpoint: Nothing but Painful Choices Ahead as the Global Debt Supercycle Ends by John Mauldin

INTRODUCTION

John Mauldin is president of Millennium Wave Investments and is a renowned financial expert, a many-times *New York Times* best-selling author, and an online commentator. His weekly e-newsletter, *Thoughts from the Frontline*, was one of the first publications to provide investors with free, unbiased information and guidance. Today it is one of the most widely distributed investment newsletters in the world, with a subscriber base of more than one million readers. It appears in English, Chinese, Spanish, and Italian. He is called on to comment regularly by TV and national media.

In your most recent book, *Endgame: The End of the Debt Supercycle and How It Changes Everything*, with Jonathan Tepper, you argue that developed economies are facing the end of a 60-year-long debt supercycle. Can you take us through your view of this debt cycle?

The concept of the debt supercycle probably goes back to the famous economist Irving Fisher in 1933, when he talked of the long debt cycle leading up to the Great Depression. The term "supercycle" was originally developed by the Bank Credit Analyst (BCA) more than 50 years ago. A. Hamilton Bolton, the founder of BCA, used the word to refer to a cluster of things, including money velocity, bank liquidity, and interest rates. Then Tony Boeckh used the term in the 1970s, in a simpler form, to refer to what he saw as spiraling private debt. The current editor of the BCA, Martin Barnes, took up the concept and expanded it greatly. Back in 2007, the BCA pointed out that "the history of the US is characterised by a long run increase in indebtedness, punctuated by occasional financial crises and subsequent policy reflation."

It warned that the supercycle would end if foreign investors ever turned their backs on US assets, but added that this would probably not happen in the immediate future. Barnes argues that because the government has stepped in to ratchet up debt as private debtors begin to deleverage, there is no immediate end in sight to the debt cycle. Jonathan Tepper and I argue in our book that although the end has not yet happened, the signs of the end are now starting to be visible. Greece matters. The case of Greece is a highly visible instance of the fact that there is a limit to how much debt any country can pile on. Without massive assistance, Greek debt would be unmarketable and, even with that assistance, by April 2011 the interest on Greek three-year bonds had reached an unsustainable 21%.

What that tells you is that, even with the inducement provided by the opportunity to earn astounding rates of interest for holding Greek debt, investors are seeing the writing on the wall. They expect Greece, despite the support of the European Central Bank (ECB) and the International Monetary Fund, to be unable to repay its debts in full, and they are turning away. What is a 21% return if you are likely to suffer a 50% or greater loss of capital? For Greece, the debt cycle is already in its endgame, and the Greeks now have nothing but extremely painful choices ahead of them.

This was the point of *Endgame*, to warn that as the crunch moment approaches a country rapidly runs out of reasonable choices, and those options left to it become more and more painful. The state of being in the endgame is a qualitatively different state from the one we are used to. It is akin to what scientists call a "phase transition," as when water turns to ice. Different rules apply, and they mean that life becomes much tougher. Greece is already in the endgame. It is close to ungovernable, and if the present socialist government is unseated and a more radical left-wing government is able to use public discontent at austerity to get itself elected, the country's position will become even more painful. You cannot vote yourself more debt once the markets are closed to you. Even austerity doesn't help that much because massive cutbacks provoke a deep depression, and that hammers government tax revenues—which makes it even harder to service debt interests. The market sees this and raises the interest rates that it wants to hold more debt, which makes the debt still harder to repay.

In the end the only options are default, which shuts the country out of the debt market until it has got its house in order, or hyperinflation. Greece does not have the option of hyperinflation since it cannot print euros. That is the privilege of the ECB. The Greeks are out of good choices. Our concern is that the United States and many European countries also face some painful choices. They are not as painful, by a long stretch, as those facing Greece—and now Ireland—but they need to be made while there is still time to make them.

It follows from our argument that the worst option of all is to postpone decisions and do nothing. Time does not heal here. Doing nothing means that the deficit grows, while the passage of time means that the not-so-painful choices vanish and all you are left with is a handful of really painful choices. In the case of Greece, this will inevitably mean not just a diminution in the standard of living for many, but also the dismantling of much of their social welfare system. This is happening now, but the cuts will deepen as the state becomes clearly unable to pay for anything like the current level of benefits. That will be extremely painful for many, but particularly for the old and the vulnerable. Unemployment levels will soar. That is what we mean by painful choices.

There are those who argue that the US debt could just be rolled on until it is brought somewhat more under control by some combination of growth, inflation, and budgetary restraint. Yet *Endgame* expresses a real sense of urgency. Why?

What was key for Tepper and myself in analyzing the current state of things in our book is the speed with which investor attitudes to a country's creditworthiness can change. The work of Carmen Reinhart and Ken Rogoff in *This Time Is Different* demonstrates some fundamental facts that have a direct bearing on our situation. These are, first, history shows that no country, no matter the size of its economy, is immune from a debt crisis, and second, there is no one event that triggers a loss of investor confidence—it just happens, and when it happens it does so suddenly, with little prior warning.

Let me quote from the conclusions of Reinhart and Rogoff on the subject of financial fragility in economies with massive indebtedness:

"... highly leveraged economies, particularly those in which continual rollover of short-term debt is sustained only by confidence in relatively illiquid underlying assets, seldom survive forever, particularly if leverage continues to grow unchecked."

If public debt is unsustainable and the burden on government budgets is too great, what does this mean for government bonds? It means that, in effect, they are a Ponzi scheme and that governments are banking on investors not realizing this. Like all Ponzi schemes, that position ends badly.

One of the most important papers of recent years is a report by the Bank of International Settlements (BIS) written in 2010 by Stephen Cecchetti, M. S. Mohanty, and Fabrizio Zampolli. Entitled "The future of public debt: Prospects and implications," the report uses the distinction between cyclical and structural deficits. Cyclical deficits relate to whether an economy and a government have had a good or a bad year as far as tax receipts are concerned. In a good year the government might have a surplus of revenue over expenditure, and in a bad year it might have a deficit. That is a cyclical deficit. Structural deficits are the enduring deficits that build up irrespective of the economic cycle because the government is consistently spending more than it collects in taxes. The primary balance of government spending is related to the structural and cyclical deficits. The primary balance is achieved when total government expenditure, except for interest payments on debt, equals government tax revenues. The twist here is that if a country's debt interest rates go up faster than its economy is growing, the deficit can only increase and you are in a debt spiral with no happy solution.

As the BIS report shows, the US deficit has exploded from 2.8%, which was sustainable, to 10.4% today, and the Obama administration's plan for deficit reductions in 2011 and onward is about cuts in *increases* to the budget, not real reductions. For the BIS the question is when markets will start putting pressure on governments, not if. It warns that if the industrialized economies fail to address deficit reduction, this will raise the chances of unexpected and abrupt rises in government bond yields at medium to long maturities. We have already seen Standard & Poor's put US debt on negative watch, in April 2011, as far as the United States' AAA rating is concerned.

Reinhart and Rogoff showed in their 800-year data set that when the ratio of debt to GDP rises above 100%, GDP drops by about 1%. According to the BIS, this probably comes about because the cost of public debt starts to suck funds away from productive private debt. If we turn from the US fiscal debt to look at official US government debt, this will shoot from 62% of GDP to an estimated 100% of GDP by the end of 2011. Moreover, the figures do not take into account the huge unfunded costs of social security and Medicare programs. Total US debt, public and private, is already more than 300% of GDP. At the same time, trend GDP growth in the United States has fallen to 2.5% from 3.5%, which means that we are locking in high unemployment for a very long time.

In the United Kingdom the government debt to GDP ratio has doubled from 47% in 2007 to 94% in 2011 and is set to rise by 10% a year unless the coalition government's austerity measures really bite, which will probably put the country back into recession. Portugal's debt is going from 71% to 97%, and there is almost no way that Portugal can grow its way out of its problems.

The BIS then offers a 30-year projection for the path of the debt/GDP ratio for a dozen major industrial economies. It calculates three scenarios: the path if current policies are maintained; the path if minor debt reductions are implemented; and the path that reflects severe austerity. The results are truly alarming. Never mind 30 years, within the next decade the BIS study sees deep trouble ahead on the "business as usual" path. Japan is the out and out front runner here, reaching a 300% debt to GDP ratio. The United Kingdom hits debt to GDP of 200%, while Belgium, France, Ireland, Greece, Italy, and the United States all go through 150%. Even with draconian cost-cutting measures, the BIS predicts US debt going through 200% in 30 years.

As the debt to GDP ratio rises, bondholders will demand higher and higher rates of interest. The BIS and the OECD projections show bond market interest rates on medium-term debt going up steadily from their current levels of 3–5% to higher than 10% by 2025 for the United States and over 20% some time between 2035 and 2040. Of course, these are just projections. In reality, it is clear that bond markets would revolt long before these levels were even approached.

What can be done? What every country with a spiraling debt to GDP ratio wants to do is to grow its exports, but it is an obvious mathematical fact that not every country can be a net exporter. Some have to be buyers. Countries have to look seriously at their welfare and entitlement programs. We have got into the position, or more accurately, the habit, of voting ourselves more than we can pay for, and there is no magic formula to deliver this. None of the countries in the BIS survey, including the United States, will be in a position to fund entitlement growth at the present expected levels. This is one of the major reasons why we say that there are very painful choices ahead for the developed economies.

One of the weakest points in the current debt cycle is the level of foreign investment in developed country debt. Bonds are issued for various periods. When they become due, typically they are not repaid out of revenues. Instead, the country concerned rolls over the debt by issuing new bonds. If the party that originally bought your debt no longer wants to hold it, you have to find someone else to buy your new bond so that the first party can cash up and get out. If there are no takers for your new debt, you fall into default, and that absolutely guarantees that you will not be able to raise further debt until the markets see that you have sorted out your problems. About 45% of Spain's debt is held outside Spain, which had to refinance 190 billion euros of debt in 2010, or more than the entire GDP of Portugal. It managed to do this in 2010 and has so far managed to roll over its debt in 2011, but it is getting tougher. The euro crisis is not going away any time soon.

How does this impact the global banking community?

Of course, we also have to consider the impact on global banks when sovereign debt becomes shaky. Prior to 2007 sovereign debt was very attractive to banks. They could take cheap money from their central bank, lever up, and make a nice spread on the difference between what they were paying for their debt and what they were earning on the sovereign bond. Moreover, since their central banks generally accepted sovereign debt as collateral, these transactions did not impinge that much on their capacity to lever up still further.

We are on a journey here to a Minsky moment. Hyman Minksy famously taught that the longer a period of stability continues, the more it breeds instability and the larger the ensuing crisis. The Minsky journey goes from where an investment is its own source of repayment, which Minsky called a hedge unit, to a

"It has been the bankers' destiny ... to find themselves on the dangerous edge of the world, pointing up the contradictions and cross-purposes. They are not often loved for it." Anthony Sampson

        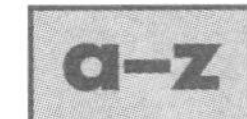

speculative unit, where the investment only pays the interest. The next stage is where the investment turns into a Ponzi unit, where the only way to repay the debt is for the value of the invested unit to rise. The end of the journey is always the Minsky moment of violent markets and unwanted, intense volatility.

The United States had its Minsky moment and Minsky journey in 2008 when no one wanted US mortgage debt and every financial institution worried about what was on the balance sheet of other financial institutions, so interbank lending froze, and credit froze with it. Bank holdings of sovereign debt now look like the next Minsky journey is already well under way.

What is certain is that we will see increasing attempts to monetize deficits and to reduce the future value of government liabilities through inflation. The results will not be pretty.

What are the options in your view apart from drastic budget cuts?

I have been giving a lot of thought since the publication of *Endgame* to what could be done. Clearly we need growth, but we need to stop trying to inflate our way out of our problem. The problem any democracy with an ageing population faces is that people are not going to voluntarily vote away their benefit entitlements, yet our entitlement programs are on an impossible trajectory. So the longer you delay revising entitlements, the more ageing voters you have and the more impossible it becomes to address the issue. David Walker, the founder and CEO of the Comeback America Initiative (CAI) and a former comptroller general of the United States, has a deep understanding of public finances at both the federal and state level. In a recent article entitled "Restoring fiscal sanity in the US: A way forward," he offers three pie charts showing the extent to which the share of US spending taken by mandatory programs like Medicare and social security, as against discretionary programs, has grown and grown. In 1970, when total spending was US$909 billion, discretionary programs amounted to 62% of this, while mandatory programs were 31% and net interest on debt was 7%. In 2011, when total spending is US$3.8 trillion, discretionary programs are down to 37%, while mandatory programs get 57% of the budget and interest is down to 5%. By 2040, if we follow the present path, mandatory programs will have dropped to 47% while discretionary programs will have more or less held steady at 35% (down 2%).

That might look like some kind of balance is being achieved, but the only reason mandatory programs will have fallen back some 10% will be that interest payments on US debt by 2040 will be a staggering 35% of a US$12.4 trillion budget, so these programs will be forced to give up some ground. Since 1917, when Congress passed the Second Liberty Bond Act, there has been a statutory limit restricting total federal debt, which includes government bonds and the debt held by government accounts, such as the social security, Medicare, and transportation trust funds. These two elements combined—bonds and the government accounts—comprise the total federal debt. By 2008 Congress had raised the debt ceiling five times since 2001, and it looks certain to have to raise the debt ceiling again, largely because of the persistent increase in mandatory program debt. The point of the debt limit is to provide Congress with the strings to control the federal purse, allowing Congress to assert its constitutional prerogatives to control spending (I'm referring here to a Congressional Research Service report on the debt limit prepared for Congress by D. Andrew Austin in 2008). What David Walker would like to see is Congress getting a lot tougher about demanding meaningful spending cuts and tax rises in return for raising the debt ceiling the next time the Treasury finds itself bumping up against the ceiling, which it certainly will. Spending cuts alone won't get us where we need to go. The Government needs to generate additional revenues. Some of that will come from increased growth, but we should not look to try to grow our way out of our present unsustainable path. As Walker says, we need to return to fiscal sanity.

MORE INFO

Books:

Bernstein, Peter L. *Against the Gods: The Remarkable Story of Risk*. New York: Wiley, 1998.

Easterling, Ed. *Probable Outcomes: Secular Stock Market Insights*. Fort Bragg, CA: Cypress House, 2011.

Ferguson, Niall. *The Ascent of Money: A Financial History of the World*. New York: Penguin Press, 2008.

Kurzweil, Ray. *The Singularity Is Near: When Humans Transcend Biology*. New York: Penguin Group, 2005.

Mauldin, John, and Jonathan Tepper. *Endgame: The End of the Debt Supercycle and How It Changes Everything*. Hoboken, NJ: Wiley, 2011.

Reinhart, Carmen M., and Kenneth S. Rogoff. *This Time Is Different: Eight Centuries of Financial Folly*. Princeton, NJ: Princeton University Press, 2009.

Reports:

Austin, D. Andrew. "The debt limit: History and recent increases." Congressional Research Service (CRS) Report for Congress RL31967. April 29, 2008. Online at: fpc.state.gov/documents/organization/105193.pdf

Cecchetti, Stephen G., Madhusudan Mohanty, and Fabrizio Zampolli. "The future of public debt: Prospects and implications." Working paper no. 300. Bank of International Settlements (BIS), March 2010. Online at: www.bis.org/publ/work300.htm

Walker, David M. "Restoring fiscal sanity in the United States: A way forward."

Websites:

Author's website: www.johnmauldin.com

Bank Credit Analyst (BCA) Research: www.bcaresearch.com

*Thoughts from the Frontline*newsletter: www.frontlinethoughts.com

See Also:

★ Viewpoint: The Challenges to Slow Growth in the Advanced Economies Just Keep Coming (pp. 147–148)

★ Viewpoint: Deleveraging, Deflation, and Rebalancing in the Global Economy (pp. 158–160)

★ Viewpoint: The Unintended Consequences of Globalization (pp. 260–262)

Irving Fisher (p. 1282)

"Our banking system grew by accident; and whenever something happens by accident, it becomes a religion."
Walter Wriston

  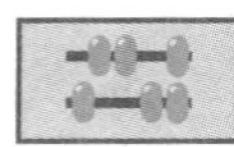      

Viewpoint: Only White Swans on the Road to Revulsion by James Montier

INTRODUCTION

James Montier, an expert in behavioral finance, argues that investors would have a greater chance of spotting the formation of bubbles if they could only brush up on their history and have a greater awareness of human psychology. Co-head of global strategy at Société Générale, Montier has been described as an "enfant terrible" by Frankfurter *Allgemeine Zeitung*, an "iconoclast" by the Financial *Times*, a "maverick" by the *Sunday Times* and "a prophet" by Fast Company. Montier, who formerly worked as an equity strategist at Dresdner Kleinwort Wasserstein, NatWest Markets, and Bankers Trust, has been a top-rated strategist in the annual Extel survey for the last five years. He began mining behavioral economics, then an emerging discipline, to explain investors' irrational behavior during the dotcom bubble. He is a visiting fellow of Durham University and a Fellow of the Royal Society of Arts. When not reading, writing, or speaking, Montier can usually be found swimming with sharks and blowing bubbles at fishes.

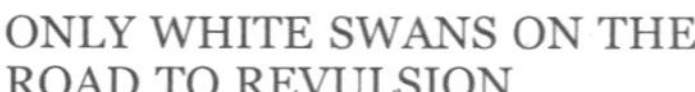

ONLY WHITE SWANS ON THE ROAD TO REVULSION

The destruction of the US economy, its housing market, its credit markets, its commodity market, and its equity markets has frequently been blamed on or described as a "black swan."

My friend Nicholas Nassim Taleb defines a black swan as a highly improbable event that has three main characteristics: (1) It is unpredictable; (2) It has a massive impact, and (3) *ex post*, explanations are concocted that make the event appear less random, and more predictable than it was.

However, it is wholly wrong to characterize what happened to the US economy and markets as a black swan. To do so is, in fact, an abdication of responsibility. If these extraordinary events were totally unpredictable, then there would have been nothing we could have done to prevent them.

The events of 2003–2008 were not black swans at all. They were "predictable surprises." The term was first coined by Michael Watkins and Max Bazerman. A predictable surprise also has three characteristics: (1) At least some people are aware of the problem; (2) The problem intensifies over time, and (3) Eventually the problem explodes into a crisis, much to the "shock" of decision-makers. As Bazerman says: "The nature of predictable surprises [is that] while uncertainty surrounds the details of the impending disaster, there is little uncertainty that a large disaster awaits."

What evidence do I have that the current mess was a predictable surprise? The *New York Times* ran a fascinating article in mid-December 2007. This noted that, seven years earlier, Edward Gramlich, a governor of the Federal Reserve, had warned that a fast-growing new breed of lenders was luring many households into risky mortgages they couldn't afford. The article also cited the Herculean efforts of Sheila C. Bair, a senior Treasury official, to persuade subprime lenders to adopt a code of practice and to let external monitors verify whether they were complying with these standards.

Robert Shiller, a professor at Yale and founder of the investment management firm MacroMarkets, even went so far as to re-issue his 2000 book, *Irrational Exuberance*, with a special chapter dedicated to the US housing market. Even yours truly (not renowned for having my finger on the pulse) wrote a note on June 20, 2005, entitled *Pictures of a Mania?—US Housing Special* which concluded "All the criteria of a speculative mania seem present to me." So a cacophony of Cassandras were clearly warning of dangers, and these dangers clearly existed.

All this discussion about "foreseeing" future risks might seem odd coming from someone who is known to be openly hostile to the notion of forecasting (see The Folly of Forecasting, Chapter 9 of Behavioral Investing). However, I think a clear line can be drawn between analysis and forecasting. As Ben Graham, the original proponent of value investing, stated: "Analysis connotes the careful study of available facts with the attempt to draw conclusions there based on established principles and sound logic."

So the big question is this: What prevented us from reacting to the predictable surprise? I can think of five major psychological hurdles that hampered us in this regard. Firstly, there is an ever-present over-optimism. Everyone assumes that they are less likely than average to have drinking problems, to get divorced, or be fired, etc. It is highly likely that the same over-optimism applies when it comes to predictable surprises; we expect them to affect others but not us.

In addition to over-optimism, we suffer from the illusion of control. This refers to people's belief that they have influence over the outcome of uncontrollable events. For instance, E. Langer has shown (1975, "The illusion of control," *Journal of Personality and Social Psychology*, 32) that people will pay four and half times more for a lottery ticket that contains numbers they choose rather than a random draw of numbers.

The same study demonstrated that people will bet more on a coin toss before the coin is actually tossed, rather than after. Perhaps they believe they can influence the spin of the coin in the air! The illusion of control is exacerbated by information. The more you think you know, the more likely you are to suffer the illusion of control.

So-called risk management techniques have clearly fostered the illusion of control. The idea that, if we can quantify risk, we can also control it is deeply flawed. In fact, we can neither measure nor control risk. Simply by providing a number, we fool ourselves into thinking we are in control.

The third psychological barrier to recognizing predictable surprises is self-serving bias. This is the innate desire to interpret information and act in ways that are supportive of our own interests.

So estate agents are unlikely to tell you that real estate is too expensive, just as companies will always tell you that everything is fine and dandy. A classic example of self-serving bias can be found in a recent Bloomberg story on the ratings agencies Moody's and Standard & Poor's. None of the 80 'AAA' securities in the ABX indices meets the criteria that S&P themselves define. Yet only one of these bonds had

"Last year this was a financial crisis that we thought with a bit of luck would be over by Christmas..." Charles Bean

been downgraded by S&P, and none were downgraded by Moody's.

The penultimate hurdle is myopia (or "hyperbolic discounting," if you happen to be a geek). This reflects the idea that consequences, which occur at a later date, tend to have much less bearing on our choices the further into the future they fall.

This can be summed up as "Eat, drink and be merry, for tomorrow we may die." Of course, this ignores the fact that on any given day we are roughly 26,000 times more likely to be wrong than right with respect to making it to tomorrow. Or, if you prefer, this myopic bias can be summed up by Saint Augustine's plea: "Lord, make me chaste, but not yet." In a world in which short-term profits are so highly prized, it is exceptionally difficult to focus on the longer-term picture.

The final barrier to spotting predictable surprises is inattentional blindness. This refers to the fact we don't see the things we don't look for. The classic experiment in this area concerns watching a video of two teams playing basketball. One is dressed in black, the other in white, and a person is asked to count the number of times the players in white pass the ball amongst themselves. Half way through the video, a man in a gorilla suit walks on, beats his chest and then walks off. Whilst watching the video, around 80% of people fail to spot the gorilla. Why? Because they were distracted with the task of counting the ball passes.

Bubbles are a by-product of human behavior, and human behavior is (sadly) all too predictable.

The details of bubbles change, but the general patterns remain very similar. Such events are clearly not black swans. Of course, the timing of the eventual burst remains as uncertain as ever, but the events themselves are all too predictable. We have long been proponents of the Kindleberger and Minsky framework for analyzing bubbles. Essentially, this model breaks a bubble's rise and fall into five phases as shown below.

Displacement
↓
Credit creation
↓
Euphoria
↓
Critical stage/Financial distress
↓
Revulsion

1. Displacement—The Birth of a Boom

Displacement is generally an exogenous shock that triggers the creation of profit opportunities in some sectors, while closing down profit availability in other sectors. As long as the new opportunities created are greater than those that get shut down, investment and production will pick up to exploit these new opportunities. Investment in both financial and physical assets is likely to occur. Effectively, we are witnessing the birth of a boom

2. Credit creation—The Nurturing of a Bubble

Just as fire can't grow without oxygen, so a boom needs liquidity on which to feed. Minsky argued that monetary expansion and credit creation are largely endogenous to the system. That is to say, not only can money be created by existing banks ("inside money"), but also by the formation of new banks, the development of new credit instruments, the use of leverage, and the expansion of personal credit outside the banking system ("outside money").

As J. K. Galbraith writes: "As to new financial instruments, however, experience establishes a firm rule ... that financial operations do not lend themselves to innovation. What is recurrently so described and celebrated is, without exception, a small variation on an established design ... The world of finance hails the invention of the wheel over and over again, often in a slightly more unstable version."

3. Euphoria—The Acceptance of the Bubble as Norm

Everyone starts to buy into the new era. Prices are seen as only capable of ever going up. Traditional valuation standards are abandoned and new measures are introduced to justify the current price. A wave of over-optimism and over-confidence is unleashed, leading people to overestimate potential gains, underestimate the risks, and generally deceive themselves into thinking they can control the situation.

4. Critical Stage/Financial Distress

The critical stage is often characterized by insiders cashing out, and is rapidly followed by financial distress, in which the excessive leverage built up during the boom becomes a major problem. Fraud often emerges during this terminal stage of the bubble's life.

5. Revulsion

This is the final stage of a bubble's lifecycle. Investors are so scarred by the events in which they participated that they can no longer bring themselves to participate in the market at all. Revulsion is characterized by exceptionally cheap asset prices and bargain basement valuations, often bought about by forced sellers.

A through understanding of history and human psychology should better equip investors to understand the warning signs, the opportunities, and the pitfalls associated with the formation of bubbles. But as J. K. Galbraith notes: "There can be few fields of human endeavor in which history counts for so little as the field of finance."

MORE INFO

Books:

Galbraith, John Kenneth. *A Short History of Financial Euphoria*. London: Penguin Books, 1994.

Graham, Benjamin. *Security Analysis*. 6th ed. Maidenhead, UK: McGraw-Hill.

Montier, James. *Behavioral Investing: A Practitioner's Guide to Applying Behavioral Finance*. Chichester, UK: Wiley, 2007.

Montier, James. *Behavioral Finance: Insights into Irrational Minds and Markets*. Chichester, UK: Wiley, 2000.

Shiller, Robert. *Irrational Exuberance*. 2nd ed. New York: Broadway Books, 2006.

Watkins, Michael, and Max Bazerman. *Predictable Surprises: The Disasters You Should Have Seen Coming, and How to Prevent Them*. Cambridge, MA: Harvard Business Press, 2004.

Article:

Langer, Ellen J. "The illusion of control." *Journal of Personality and Social Psychology* 32:2 (August 1975): 311–328. Online at: dx.doi.org/10.1037/0022-3514.32.2.311

See Also:

★ Viewpoint: Nothing but Painful Choices Ahead as the Global Debt Supercycle Ends (pp. 219–221)

✔ Stock Markets: Their Structure and Function (p. 1091)

The Black Swan: The Impact of the Highly Improbable (p. 1335)

"Like other branches of the study of society, economics remains culturally parochial, and its underlying concepts based on a few centuries of Western experience." John Gray

The Origins and Current State of the Buyout Market for Pension Funds by Steven Haasz

EXECUTIVE SUMMARY

The article looks at the way the market for annuities buyout activity has developed over the last decade and at the stresses that market is experiencing as a result of the global downturn through 2008/2009. The following topics are covered:

- The origins of the buyout market as a "rescue" for distressed companies, now taken over by the Pensions Protection Fund
- The risks facing annuities providers, that the assets will be insufficient to meet the liabilities, and the longevity risk
- The pressures in the market pushing companies towards pensions buyout, despite the high relative cost of this solution
- Different types of providers in the market
- The dynamics of buyout pricing
- The trend for larger and larger schemes to adopt a buyout solution

INTRODUCTION

The buyout market for final salary pension or defined benefit (DB) schemes began more than a decade ago in the UK, with Legal & General as the sole provider. At the time, the focus was on distressed companies going into insolvency or administration. A buyout enabled the liquidator to separate off the company's pension scheme, with its statutory obligations to pay benefits to members, from the company. Instead, the buyout provider would take over responsibility for the scheme and the liquidator would be free to sell on the viable parts of the company, unencumbered by the liability constituted by its pension scheme.

In this context, it is important to remember that, from the company's perspective, while a DB pension scheme might be a very important part of its overall reward package for employees, the pension fund is, ultimately, just another debt on the company's books.

For taking over the scheme, the provider would charge the company a fee, and the fee would cover any shortfall between the company pension-scheme's assets (which would be transferred to the provider) and its liabilities. The liabilities are the totality of the benefits that the scheme is obligated to pay to members for the life of the scheme (i.e. until the last scheme member dies). Often, though, the company was unable to pay the fee because of insolvency, and so the member benefits would be reduced. This line of business from insolvent companies is effectively closed now, as a result of the introduction of the Pension Protection Fund (PPF). The main lines of business are with solvent companies looking to de-risk their liabilities.

RISKS FACING PROVIDERS

There are two major classes of risk involved in a provider taking over the liabilities and assets of a pension scheme. The first involves the risk that the future returns on the assets of the scheme will not be sufficient to meet the expected payments when they fall due, and the second is the longevity risk.

This is the risk that members in the scheme will live longer than expected. When calculating whether a scheme is fully funded or is in deficit, actuaries have reference to the average or expected lifespans of all the members of the scheme, in order to calculate the benefits the scheme is going to have to pay out over its lifespan.

As providers are in business, ultimately, to add value for their shareholders, Legal & General, and then Prudential, which was the second player to enter this market in 1997, took—and still take—a very prudent view of these risks. The returns risk was managed by investing in low-to-negligible-risk securities, such as government bonds, with some investment-grade corporate bonds.

The second risk is something of a movable feast, as longevity at present is on the increase, and no one knows where that process will end. That risk was, and is, managed by charging a premium which allows for longevity to improve in the future. For many companies, however, the combination of low-yielding assets and the buyout premium made the buyout just too expensive to contemplate.

PRESSURES IN THE MARKET PUSHING FOR DB SCHEME BUYOUTS

However, several things have happened which, combined together, have predisposed many financial directors and CEOS of companies with final salary schemes to be much more energized about finding ways to close their final salary schemes—something that they can only do in law by effecting a buyout (or a buy-in) with a provider. Without retelling the whole saga of the decline of the final salary scheme market in the UK, which is a fairly well known and well documented story, it is fair to say that a combination of accounting changes, which look to reflect scheme deficits much more prominently on a company's balance sheet, and legislative changes, which have considerably added to the burden final salary schemes impose on companies, have effectively sounded the death knell for the vast majority of UK final salary schemes.

Other countries have tended to go much more towards defined contribution schemes. Again, in brief, the difference between the two types of scheme—a final salary scheme and a defined contribution (DC) scheme—is that in the former, the employer makes a promise that they will pay x proportion of an employee's final salary, and then takes on the responsibility for funding that promise. In a DC scheme, on the other hand, the employee builds up his or her own "pension pot," and it is the employee who takes the risk that that pot will not be big enough to provide a decent pension for them on retirement. As no "promise" has been made about the level of benefit that will result, there are no funding issues, and a DC scheme cannot be in deficit in the same way that a final salary scheme (DB scheme) can. Nor does it import any market volatility into a company's balance sheet—all market volatility resides with the member.

The total final salary scheme liability on the books of UK companies is estimated at around £800 billion. A figure on that scale, once it became clear that companies would increasingly be exploring the buyout of their scheme as an option, is sufficiently large to attract new players into the buyout market. This is exactly what we have seen over the course of the last few years.

DIFFERENT TYPES OF PROVIDERS: INSURERS VERSUS THE REST

It is worth pointing out that where a provider is an insurance company, such as L&G or Prudential, it is subject to regulation, and the regulator will want to see that the company is in a position to remain solvent throughout the projected life of the liabilities that it is taking on. This precludes an insurance company buyout provider from using non-matching assets, such as exposure

"In economics, hope and faith coexist with great scientific pretension and also a deep desire for respectability."
J. K. Galbraith

to the equity markets, for example, as an asset class in which to invest to meet scheme liabilities. Given the ups and downs of the equity market, a provider can expect that, from time to time, the value of equities in their portfolio could dip below their acquisition value, rendering the scheme technically insolvent—which is not a position an insurance company could adopt.

However, a non-insurance company provider that is not subject to the same regulatory regime, might take a view that, while equity markets can show extreme volatility over the short term—the state of the markets at the end of 2008 and the start of 2009 being a spectacular case in point—over a 20-to-30-year period, equities, so the argument goes, generally deliver a very stable level of returns, well in excess of bonds. The non-insurance player can do a number of things differently. They can buy the entire company, and, as the employer, they then have wider options as to what contribution decisions they take, and can engage with scheme trustees in a way that would not be appropriate for an insurance company. The point is that they are very different from insurance companies, and they can engage with the trustees and seek to influence them on issues such as investment decisions.

This opens the way for providers from outside the insurance sector to be very competitive on their pricing of alternative buyout solutions. Their offer is different, but it may seem to be a very attractive option for the corporate, as it is not just the pension scheme that they are potentially buying, but the whole subsidiary. If it was not performing well, that could be very attractive to the corporate. However, employers who are looking at risk management of their DB schemes have a number of options, and they need to be mindful of the ultimate risk to members. There may well be considerable risks to a company that disposes of its pension fund to a provider who later fails, and leaves pensioners bereft of benefits. At the very least, the prospect of large numbers of angry former employees mobbing the company's premises would constitute a formidable "hit" to the company's reputation and brand.

In practice, the arrival of new entrants to the market tended to drive down buyout prices. In the main, the business that has been done to date has been written at what we would regard as reasonably sensible levels. However, there have been one or two instances where the buyout has been done by a new entrant at a level that seems to underprice the risks involved quite significantly. It is not unusual for new entrants to some markets to seek to "buy" market share by discounting product, but the pensions market is not a market where discounting to buy business makes sense. While price is clearly an important factor, and driven by an assessment of longevity risk and assumptions about future investment returns, the pension-scheme trustees will also want to satisfy themselves that the provider they are doing a transaction with is financially strong, and will be around for the lifetime of the pension scheme.

THE DYNAMICS OF BUYOUT PRICING

Interestingly, during 2008, the premium over and above the value of scheme assets that financial directors had to find in order to dispose of their final salary schemes shrank quite remarkably. This had very little to do with competition among providers, and much more to do with the behavior of pricing in the corporate-bond markets. Basically, as the risk of defaults has increased in the corporate-bond markets, it has become more risky to hold these bonds, so the returns for holding them have had to climb. Yields on corporate bonds are now at record levels. For a pension-scheme buyout, if we assume the simplistic example of a fund that holds all its assets in cash, the higher the corporate-bond spread goes, the lower the price on the buyout will be.

When finance directors are asked how much of their time they find they have to devote, on average, to managing issues related to their final salary scheme, the answer tends to be more than they actually want to. It also restricts the company's ability to do certain things, it could influence merger decisions or divestments, or even listings or delistings. Again, this demonstrates why so many finance directors feel some urgency about disposing of their final salary schemes, if they can do so at affordable prices.

One of the consequences of this has been an enormous growth in the number of buyout quotations providers are being asked to produce. In almost all instances, requests for buyout quotations do not come directly from the companies themselves. These requests are "intermediated" by EBCs (employee benefit consultancies). In a large number of instances, the requests turn out to be more of the nature of exploratory queries. This is to be expected, as it is a very big decision for a corporate, but it does mean a great deal of work for providers who want to turn all quotes around quickly.

One option for the provider is to provide an initial "fast track" or indicative response, which does not guarantee a premium and makes some approximations based on the fairly limited level of information provided by the company (for example, "for a scheme of this size, with 200 employees, with this age profile, and with this kind of asset base, we would be likely to charge a figure of x." Once a company has demonstrated that its interest is real and serious, then a guaranteed quotation would be provided.

BUYOUTS MOVE UP THE SCALE

One definite trend that can be seen from the early days of the buyout market to today is a definite "surge" in the size of schemes being proposed for buyout. During 2008, some of the largest pension buyout and buy-in deals ever were completed (in fact, eight of the 10 largest bulk-purchase annuity transactions completed in 2008 were buy-ins). Until 2008, the largest buyout deal done involved a scheme with liabilities of £400 million. Prudential did a buy-in in 2008 for £1 billion, as did another provider, and the market is aware of enquiries concerning schemes for £3 billion-plus worth of liabilities.

CONCLUSION

One obvious direction for the bulk-purchase annuity market to go in, as the deal sizes increase beyond the £1 billion mark, is a move to syndication, as one sees in the corporate finance arena, where a "club" of financial services providers get together to share the risk and debt in a large deal. Conversations in principle have already taken place between major providers in this space, and there is no reason why providers cannot compete vigorously on some deals, and work in conjunction with others on other deals. In conclusion, one can expect the pressure of the recession to focus the minds of company boards yet more firmly on the challenges presented by the pensions debt on their books, and the ongoing, long-term drain on their resources that this debt represents. Consequently, all the signs are that we expect the bulk-purchase annuity market will continue to grow in the years ahead.

MAKING IT HAPPEN

Any company interested in pursuing a buyout solution will want to talk first of all to a consultancy, such as Watson Wyatt or Mercer and will want to get a range of quotations from insurance providers. It is then a matter of weighing up the advantages of "escaping" from the continuing obligations associated with running an in-house Final Salary Scheme, versus the cost of a buyout and the surety being offered to members.

"As the economy gets better, everything else gets worse." Art Buchwald

     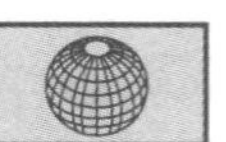   

Outsourcing and the Banks by Shamus Rae

EXECUTIVE SUMMARY

The article examines the growth of the outsourcing phenomenon in the financial services sector and looks at the next wave of "value-added" outsourcing, where banks seek to outsource more highly skilled jobs done by higher-paid employees, thus gaining more from wage arbitrage. The emphasis is on:

- The benefits of taking the long view (strategy) rather than looking for quick piecemeal gains (tactics).
- The value to be gained from outsourcing more highly paid work.
- The erosion of the benefits of "simple" process outsourcing due to rising salaries in major outsource markets like India.
- The impact of consolidation through M&As, when several outsourcing contracts may need to be rationalized.
- The differences between onshore, near-shore, and offshore outsourcing.

INTRODUCTION

The major banks in developed markets have been extensive users of outsourcing and have been at the forefront of pushing the boundaries of outsourcing onshore, near-shore, and offshore (near-shore in this context refers to outsourcing to a country location that has a time differential of not more than three hours from the bank's main business locations). High-profile examples here include Barclays Bank's outsourcing arrangement with Accenture, and Citibank's outsourcing operations, which it sold to the Indian outsourcing giant, Tata Consultancy Services (TCS), in October 2008 in a deal worth US$505 million.

In 2004 Barclays signed a £400 million deal with Accenture to outsource applications development for its UK banking systems. A year earlier, in a £230 million deal, it outsourced its desktop management to IT services firm EDS.[1] Citibank's sale of its outsourcing arm was planned prior to the global downturn, since in the spring of 2007, while the world was still in a boom phase, Citigroup said that it wanted to cut US$10.4 billion off its spending over the next three years. This would be achieved by disposing of its own outsourcing operations and instead moving more of its jobs to outsourcing providers offshore. As part of the deal with Tata, it was agreed that TCS would provide offshore services to Citi, using Citi's former operation, in a contract reportedly worth US$2.5 billion over nine and a half years.[2]

Today it would be difficult to find a major or even a mid-range bank that does not have fairly extensive outsourcing at least of its IT function, and generally of some business processes as well.

THE DEVELOPMENT OF THE NEXT WAVE OF OUTSOURCING

The development of the next wave of outsourcing centers on the idea of moving up the value chain and outsourcing higher-end, more highly skilled work. Much of the impetus for this came from the big investment banks just prior to the current global banking crash. There was tremendous pressure on banks to increase margins and profitability and to cut costs, and the way to do this was seen to be to move more highly skilled work offshore. There are very substantial salary savings to be made by organizations that can achieve high-value outsourcing to low-wage economies.

The challenges are formidable, but the process is now well underway and it seems inevitable that there will be a greater use of shared service centers—locations that support more than one department or business unit for the same organization. In the late 1990s and until around 2000–02, banks found that they could outsource moderately skilled parts of retail banking offshore and achieve savings of the order of 40–50%, as reported by market analyst organizations such as Gartner and Forrester Research.

Salary pressures in offshore countries like India and the Philippines have reduced the level of savings that can be achieved for moderately skilled outsourcing arrangements. On top of this, for UK banks, the depreciation of the pound has further eroded savings from overseas outsourcing (translating pounds into almost any other currency requires more pounds today than it did two years ago, so those contracts have become more expensive).

LARGE SAVINGS LIE AHEAD IN NEW WAVE OUTSOURCING

However, price pressures simply add to the banks' incentive to move more highly skilled, and therefore higher-paid, work offshore, since this is the area where really substantial savings can be made. In the case of banks involved in securitization and merger and acquisition (M&A) work—in other words the old-style investment banks, and whatever may come along to replace them, since they have now all switched to become deposit-taking institutions—the high fees and high remuneration structures in those banks could generate savings of up to 65% through offshoring. Although bank remuneration packages have come under pressure due to the economic downturn, the salary differences between more highly skilled functions and clerical functions are still considerable. From the banks' point of view, another really attractive feature of offshore working environments is that they are free of the bonus culture that permeates the financial services sector in developed economies.

Generating maximum savings, however, is not always the major driver for offshoring. Increasingly, particularly in a world driven by compliance issues, organizations are looking to achieve greater standardization of processes—i.e. having all operations of a certain kind run from a shared services center, or "center of excellence." This term is used for a specialized central function with a developed ability to execute specific business processes, such as accounts payable, to a high level. By using such a center to service many business units, the company gains efficiencies and economies of scale. A center of excellence enables standardized procedures to be shared throughout a global organization. At KPMG we are talking to global chief finance officers (CFOs) about outsourcing to Asia precisely in order to drive greater compliance and control. That such an arrangement does also produce cost savings is seen by some organizations as a secondary rather than as the primary benefit.

RATIONALIZATION OF EXISTING ARRANGEMENTS REMAINS A KEY DRIVER

Another major trend is the rationalization of existing outsourcing arrangements. The world has just passed through a boom period of M&A activity. As a consequence, large organizations have acquired businesses which themselves have outsourcing contracts of one type or another. When sales activity is high, companies tend not to have the time to undertake the rationalization exercises that everyone involved can see would make sense—if only the management resources were available to tackle these projects. However, in a sharp downturn, sales pressure evaporates and rationalization moves up the agenda.

What we have seen—and will continue to see as a consequence of the turmoil in the global banking market—is a number of acquisitions and mergers as the sector consolidates and weak banks are bought by stronger banks. Again, this means that the acquirer finds itself inheriting a range of outsourcing arrangements, some of which might be better, or more far-reaching in scope, than it has so far initiated itself. All of this tends to stimulate management thinking in the sector about the role of outsourcing at a global level. One inevitable consequence of this as we go through 2009 and into 2010 is that there will be a step increase throughout the sector in outsourcing, together with a good deal of retendering activity as companies look to rationalize and get best value from existing contracts.

At the same time as this is going on, at the national level there are already the usual recessionary calls for protectionist measures. The outsourcing industry is going to have to make its case in the teeth of government, political, and public pressures for jobs to be kept onshore. In the case of banks that are in receipt of public funds, with government bailout packages of one kind or another, there is already considerable pressure for them to spend money "at home" rather than on jobs in Asia. These pressures can be expected to have a dampening effect on the global outsourcing market, though how far they will offset the strong drivers toward outsourcing remains to be seen.

A RETURN TO TACTICAL OUTSOURCING

We can expect a short hiatus in outsourcing over the spring and possibly summer of 2009 as financial services organizations across the developed world take stock of where they are and formulate their strategies for going forward. Having made some huge mistakes in their investment strategies, many organizations will be very mindful of some of the classic mistakes in outsourcing that have been made over the last 10 years.

Tactical outsourcing, for example, where an isolated function such as credit card payment collections, was "lifted out" of the organization and placed offshore, is now demonstrably not the way forward. This kind of outsourcing may well have achieved short-term savings of the order of 40% for the parent organization. However, it did so at the cost of creating dislocations in "ownership" and responsibility for the function that in many instances have come back to haunt the company concerned. The process, once isolated in this way, stops growing and evolving along with the parent organization, and it stops improving. Also, you get divergence away from developing group policies and standards, and returning to such a function and bringing it back up to best-practice levels becomes a real challenge.

Instead of this tactical approach to outsourcing, management teams are now thinking much more strategically. Does a bank simply outsource its accounts payable function and gain a quick return from that, or does it sketch out a model for the next three to five years that will see it moving 60% of its finance function out of a high-cost arena? Taking this second approach gives it the chance to create a more globally integrated operation, and this in turn allows management to start thinking about driving global compliance and global design and delivery of processes. Instead of outsourcing a bit here and a bit there, the organization can start to think about generating a much more coherent and strategic approach.

THE FUTURE LIES WITH STRATEGY RATHER THAN TACTICS

It is important to realize here that, for a large organization, this need not mean outsourcing everything to one location. What it means is having a governance model that is coherent and makes sense for the medium term. Under this kind of model, management can ensure that there are named, responsible teams for each of the sub-functions and that their linkages and dependencies with the rest of the organization are fully understood. It is crucial that sub-processes and functions like this are owned by particular senior management parties end to end across the globe.

Once an organization starts to take this strategic approach, it becomes clear that there are various options for outsourcing, including:

- *Onshore*, with a shared service center, say, in the same country.
- *Near shore*, where the service center is within two or three hours' reach of the home country, which makes it easy for management to commute and keep close contact with an evolving function. Often with accounts preparation and management accounting, for example, the finance function will need to go to subsidiaries to help the management teams there to understand what the numbers are doing. Again, near-shoring keeps the function within reach of this kind of activity.
- *Offshore*, where parts that can be done much further off are outsourced to distant centers, although as part of a coherent overall design.

It is often the case that when large organizations in the financial services sector begin to take a strategic view of their business processes, it becomes clear that a great deal of work is being done at very high cost within the business. This is because it is being done by very expensive people located in some of the highest-cost office premises in the world. By moving the work to a shared service center onshore, which may well still be wholly owned by the organization, management can start to take a more holistic view about how their business—including the finance function, the design function, the product origination function and so on—should look in three to five years.

It has taken banks a decade to get round to the idea of combining shared service centers with outsourcing to generate a more complete picture of what the organization could look like in the medium to long term. It is quite possible, for example, for an organization without a strategic vision to take too much work out of a country. There is a lot to be said for keeping a critical mass of expertise in any function within the country.

One of the difficulties with outsourcing to multiple foreign centers is that much of the responsibility for operations delivery moves away from the core business, so you lose some of the benefits that come from the cross-fertilization that happens when units interact. Another difficulty is that there is much less scope for local deviations away from the standard. What rapidly becomes clear is that the cost of deviating from a proven standard rapidly outstrips whatever local advantages people think they are deriving from allowing the deviation. Businesses, in other words, get much better at weighing the cost and the risk impact of deviations from standard processes, so centers of excellence tend to bear down hard on parts of the business that want to go their own way. It is still possible to accommodate this, but it has to be signed off by people with authority at a very senior level in the organization.

Another difficulty has to do with change management. Often projects are properly scoped at the outset, but things go wrong because the company undergoes fundamental changes and the way the organization then interacts with the outsourcing provider causes costs to ramp sharply. At its worst, this moves us back to the 1970s model of IT, for example, where what IT can or cannot do constrains the business's ability to grow. This is why it is vital for the service-level agreements and support agreements that frame outsourcing arrangements to be properly constructed.

  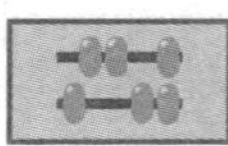 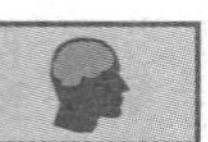     

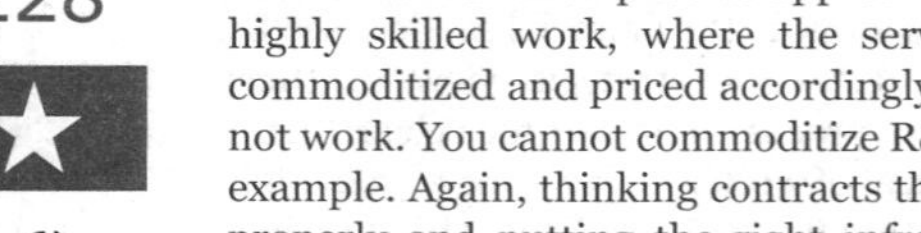

The standardized process approach with highly skilled work, where the service is commoditized and priced accordingly, does not work. You cannot commoditize R&D for example. Again, thinking contracts through properly and putting the right infrastructure in place is critical.

CONCLUSION

There are still tremendous gains to be made from outsourcing and some very powerful drivers continue to push financial service organisations to intensify their use of outsourcing to generate both profitability and organisational control. However, the process takes real commitment and skill to achieve the target savings that organisations are looking for. This is an area where strategic planning really does pay dividends.

MAKING IT HAPPEN

Any move to outsource a major function requires considerable work and planning, together with the appropriate consultancy support. Key decisions include:

- The control and responsibility of delivery to service-level agreements.
- The shape and location of the outsource contract.
- The relationship between what is being outsourced and the rest of the client's business.
- The flow of data.

Outsourcing is a challenging project and requires top-rate project management and planning skills to generate the full range of expected benefits.

MORE INFO

Report:

KPMG. "Exploring global frontiers: The new emerging destinations." KPMG International, 2009. Report on the various outsourcing locations around the world. Online at: www.kpmg.co.uk/news/docs/Exploring%20Global%20Frontiers.pdf

Websites:

Accenture: www.accenture.com
EDS: www.eds.com

See Also:

★ Considerations when Outsourcing Internal Audit (pp. 312–314)
★ Reducing Costs and Improving Efficiency by Outsourcing and Selecting Suppliers (pp. 918–920)
✔ Assessing the Value of Outsourcing and Offshoring (p. 1146)
Banking and Financial Services (pp. 1612–1614)

NOTES

1 www.vnunet.com (June 23, 2004).

2 *Information Week* (October 8, 2008).

"Global capital markets pose the same kinds of problems that jet planes do. They are faster, more comfortable, and they get you where you are going better. But the crashes are much more spectacular." Lawrence H. Summers

  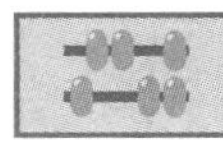      

The Payment Services Directive: A Crucial Step Toward Payment Harmonization Across the EU

by Björn Flismark

EXECUTIVE SUMMARY

This article looks at the impact and implications of the Payment Services Directive (PSD), which has been transposed into national law across the European Union. The implementation of the PSD requirements marked another step on the road to an integrated Europe-wide payments market. The article considers:

- The objectives of the PSD;
- Its scope and impact;
- The differences between SEPA (Single Euro Payments Area) and the PSD;
- The benefits of the PSD for customers;
- The impact of the PSD on banks.

INTRODUCTION

The Payment Services Directive (PSD) provides a legal framework for payment services in the internal market of the EU and the European Economic Area (EEA). It was adopted by European legislators on November 13, 2007, for transposition into national law by the 27 EU member states by November 1, 2009 (about half of the EU countries took a bit longer than foreseen by the official deadline and completed their transposition in 2010) . The three non-EU EEA countries—Iceland, Liechtenstein, and Norway—are also committed to transposing the PSD into their national law; Iceland was the last of these countries to complete its transposition process in November 2010. The EU and EEA countries plus Switzerland together form the Single Euro Payments Area (SEPA) for euro payments.

The PSD is one additional step in the efforts of the European legislators to achieve an integrated payments market. This process started with the introduction of the euro in 1999 (as an electronic currency) and 2002 (notes and coins), the implementation of new payments-related legislation at EU level, such as Regulation EC2560/2001, and the launch in 2008 of the first Single Euro Payments Area (SEPA) instrument for handling credit transfers as well as of the SEPA Cards Framework. In November 2009, SEPA Direct Debit Schemes (Core and B2B) were launched. At the same time Regulation EC924/2009 on cross-border payments in the Community replaced Regulation EC2560/2001 and extended the principle of equal charges for national and cross-border payments in euro to direct debits.

In November 2012, the EU Commission will publish a report reviewing the functioning of the PSD. This review will also focus on whether the scope of the PSD should be expanded with regard to non-EU/EEA currencies and to transactions where only one of the payment service providers involved is located in the EU/EEA. The EU Commission is also working on a proposal for a regulation setting end dates for the migration of national credit transfers and direct debits to SEPA. Thus, the PSD should be seen as one major step, rather than as the final step, in Europe's drive for harmonization.

OBJECTIVES OF THE PSD

The PSD has five main objectives:

- To establish a single payments market in the EU;
- To provide the regulatory framework for a single payments market;
- To create a level playing field and to enhance competition;
- To ensure that there is consistent consumer protection and improved transparency;
- To create the potential for greater efficiency in EU payments systems.

By removing legal barriers to the provision of payment services across Europe and fulfilling these objectives, the PSD has paved the way for citizens and businesses to make all kinds of intra-EU/EEA payments—at both national and cross-border level—easily, safely, efficiently, cost-effectively, and in a timely manner. The legal framework provided by the directive supports the SEPA payment instruments, particularly the SEPA Direct Debit Scheme, and removes barriers to entry into new markets within the EU/EEA.

The PSD has also introduced a clear set of rules for payment institutions (PIs), a new category of payment service providers. Once authorized to provide and execute payment services in one member state, a PI can operate throughout the EU/EEA. PIs have to meet specific capital requirements and fulfill a number of other requirements, such as specific obligations related to record keeping.

THE SCOPE AND IMPACT OF THE PSD

As the PSD applies to payment services between payment service providers (PSPs) and payment service users (PSUs) within the EU/EEA, its requirements have affected everyone carrying out payment transactions, from private banking customers to businesses and corporates, as well as financial institutions, governments, local authorities, merchants, credit card providers, and so on.

The PSD has had a particularly far-reaching impact on the way banks process payments. It is relevant not only for euro payments, but also for payments carried out in non-euro currencies of all EU/EEA countries. SEPA instruments, as well as existing national payment instruments, fall under the provisions of the PSD. The PSD covers credit transfers, direct debits, card payments, and some cash transactions such as cash deposits. Excluded are a number of paper-based instruments, as well as some transactions that do not fall directly under the PSP–customer relationship.

DIFFERENCES BETWEEN SEPA AND THE PSD

The building of the Single Euro Payments Area (SEPA) is an initiative to establish a truly integrated European payments landscape, where euro payments are subject to a uniform set of standards, rules, and conditions and can be executed as easily, quickly, securely, and efficiently as in national markets. SEPA was launched in January 2008 with the SEPA Credit Transfer and the SEPA Cards Framework.

Although both the PSD and the SEPA initiatives were launched in order to enable and facilitate the integration of the European payments market, their scope and areas of impact differed from the start, in spite of some overlap. The PSD is a European directive that was transposed into national law across the EU/EEA, whereas SEPA is a self-regulatory initiative of the European Payments Council. While SEPA focuses only on the euro, the PSD embraces all currencies within the EU/EEA. SEPA coverage is slightly wider than the

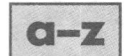

PSD in that it includes Switzerland. Most importantly, the main focus of the PSD is the payment service users (the customers) and their relationship to the PSP, whereas the main focus of the initial SEPA initiative was to establish binding standards and business practices for the bank-to-bank relationship. The PSD also covers a wider range of transaction types, including cash deposits and withdrawals.

With SEPA migration end-date legislation under preparation at the level of the European Commission, the SEPA project is about to expand in scope. The aim of the new legislative effort is to achieve a fully integrated and highly standardized euro payments market for all actors involved, including customers. That is why the legislation is expected to define a number of key requirements for the whole end-to-end processing chain, which would directly affect payments customers as well.

BENEFITS OF THE PSD FOR CUSTOMERS

The implementation of the PSD has delivered significant benefits to customers as the directive contains a number of protective measures that have been applied uniformly across the EU/EEA to payment services offered to private consumers and, to some extent, corporate customers. The directive spells out in detail the obligations of payment service providers (PSPs) with respect to customers. Among others, it stipulates maximum execution times for the banks' payment processes and imposes strict rules on value dating.

In general, customers should expect a more harmonized and transparent service now that the PSD is in place, since the directive mandates full transparency of conditions and requires the PSP to provide a high standard of information to the customer. Key provisions include:

- PSPs have to provide a great deal of payment-related information to the customer free of charge.
- In some countries, PSPs have been required by the different EU/EEA member states to provide paper information updates to customers once a month free of charge.
- PSPs need to be given a unique identifier by the customer for a payment to be properly executed.
- PSPs must provide full transparency to customers before and after a payment is executed, i.e., inform customers of the maximum execution time and of all charges payable, provide a breakdown of charges, and confirm any exchange rate that may apply.

BENEFITS AND CHALLENGES FOR BANKS

The Payment Services Directive has had a major impact on the banks' payments business, as it has brought about changes to many payment-related processes. All banks operating in the EU/EEA have had to undergo the costly exercise of adjusting their existing internal systems and platforms, as well as their services and underlying terms and conditions, to the PSD requirements.

Beside the cost of compliance, the PSD has also imposed an additional burden on banks. The directive has negatively impacted some of the revenue streams of the banks because there are provisions, such as the requirement to provide some information services free of charge, that have reduced the banks' ability to charge for certain services. Bank revenues have also been impacted by increased obligations vis-à-vis customers, such as the responsibility to inform customers of the PSD, and by the maximum execution times and value dating rules stipulated by the PSD.

The articles on maximum execution times and on obligations with regard to value dating have had the most significant impact on banks. Among others, they detail that:

- The payer's PSP may set a cutoff time toward the end of its business day, after which a payment order can be treated as if it had been received on the following business day.
- Payments within the EU/EEA should generally be subject to a D + 1 execution time, with up to D + 3 being a possible exception until January 1, 2012, if agreed between PSP and payer.
- Longer execution times of up to D + 4 may be applied to a number of transaction scenarios involving currency conversions—but only if they have been agreed on between PSP and PSU.
- The debit value date of a payment is no earlier than the point in time at which the payment is debited to a payer's account.
- The credit value date of a payment is no later than the business day on which the PSP's own account has been credited with the amount of the payment and the PSP has to put the amount at the PSU's disposal immediately after the PSU has received it in its own account.

The PSD has also opened new business opportunities for banks. For example, the fact that the PSD has led to a harmonization of legislation concerning payment services across the EU/EEA makes it easier for banks to develop new products and services that can be offered at a pan-European level. This has opened up the possibility of expanding into new markets without having to establish a physical presence in those new markets. Standardized service offerings also provide the opportunity to simplify both account documentation and terms and conditions for customers across Europe. What is more, the necessary investments in the adjustment of payment processes that banks had to undertake also provided the opportunity to modernize and streamline these processes.

THE PSD'S IMPACT ON BANKS: A HIGH-LEVEL OVERVIEW

On a practical level, the PSD impacted the following areas and functions within a bank:

Figure 1. Value dating and availability of funds when both payer's and payee's banks are located in the EU/EEA. (*Source*: Euro Banking Association, "Banks preparing for PSD," 2008)

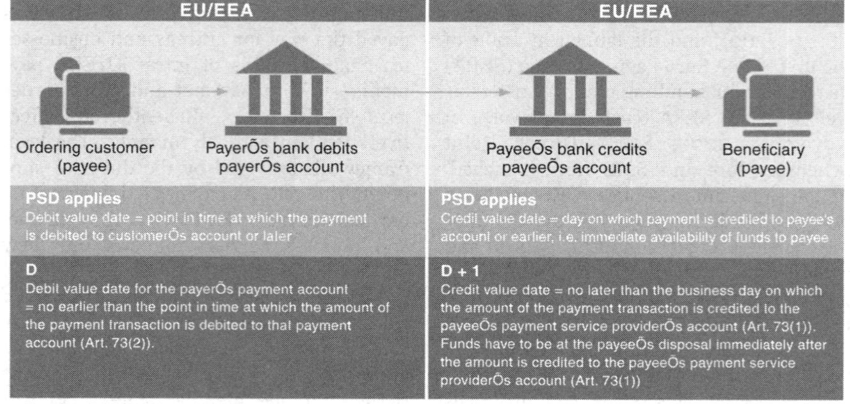

Note: D + 3 is possible until January 1, 2012, if there is an agreement between ordering customer (payer) and payer's bank (+1 possible in case of paper-initiated transactions).

"My problem lies in reconciling my gross habits with my net income." Errol Flynn

        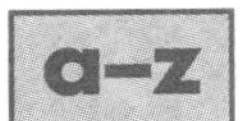

- In the area of payment products and cash management businesses, there was a need to implement changes in product offerings to ensure PSD compliance.
- IT systems had to be modified to ensure that shortened execution time requirements can be met (further changes might still be needed to meet the 2012 deadline for D + 1 processing of credit transfers).
- Information channels, including electronic banking systems, had to be adjusted.
- Additional operational procedures, including enhanced risk management, had to be put in place where current procedures did not cater for the compliance with the new requirements. For example, if a payment service provider refuses to execute a payment, the reason for the refusal and the procedure for correcting the problem needs to be notified to the customer within the time frame specified in the PSD (normally D + 1).
- Banking documentation (account opening documentation, framework contracts, etc.) had to be adjusted.
- Customer communication had to reflect the impact of the PSD.
- Staff education and training was needed to ensure that customer service staff, as well as product, sales, operational, and IT staff, were able to communicate with customers and make the necessary internal bank changes.
- Third-party agreements (existing agreements with technical providers, intermediaries, clearing houses, correspondents, etc.) had to be reviewed and/or renegotiated.
- Financial planning (revenue and cost budgets have been impacted because of reduction of float, full amount to be paid, investments in system changes, etc.).

On a strategic level, the PSD has to be considered in terms of:

- The opportunity it offers to agree that certain articles should not apply when the customer is not a consumer; this opportunity, which is called the corporate opt-out, is detailed in Article 51.
- The competitive environment in which a bank operates.
- The impact of new market entrants (for example, the PIs, which to some extent today are still in the accreditation process or preparing for accreditation) and their product offering on a bank's current client base.
- Potential changes in strategy regarding products and services, expansion into new markets, and targeting of customer segments.

Overall, the implementation of the PSD has required a major effort involving many different functions and areas. It has undoubtedly generated an increased demand for skilled resources, funding of systems enhancements, and legal and compliance expertise and has taken up a significant amount of senior managements' attention and focus. As a result of changes in execution times (with the final deadline mandating the D + 1 processing of credit transfers still ahead of us), banks have had to review their operational risk management procedures and will potentially still need to further change existing processes before January 2012.

CONCLUSION

The PSD required banks to make considerable and costly changes to their processes and procedures in order to conform to the requirements of the directive. However, it also brought opportunities, particularly for national players to move into pan-European and EEA markets, without having to establish a physical presence in those markets. The proposed regulation on migration End dates aims at finally delivering the Single Euro Payments Area. The realization of SEPA will offer banks many new opportunities as a single payment offering will be possible. On the other hand competition is certain to increase and banks need to carefully assess the strategies in this new environment.

MORE INFO

Reports:

Euro Banking Association (ABE/EBA). "Banks preparing for SEPA: Issues to be addressed to achieve SEPA compliance." Version 2.2. Paris: ABE/EBA, May 25, 2007. Online at: tinyurl.com/2fs3avk

Euro Banking Association (ABE/EBA). "Banks preparing for PSD: A guide for bankers on the Payment Services Directive." Version 1.1. Paris: ABE/EBA, November 2008. Online at: tinyurl.com/274blq6

Euro Banking Association (ABE/EBA). "Banks fine-tuning their PSD preparations: A selection of key details to be addressed on the way to PSD compliance." Version 1.0. Paris: ABE/EBA, June 2009. Online at: tinyurl.com/2byhdgh

Website:

Euro Banking Association (ABE/EBA): www.abe-eba.eu

See Also:

★ Electronic Invoicing in the European Union (pp. 832–833)
★ How to Assess a Company's Global Treasury Needs and Objectives Successfully (pp. 50–52)
★ Payment Factories: How to Streamline Financial Flows (pp. 85–86)
✔ Building an Efficient Credit and Collection Accounts System (p. 1148)
✔ Building an Electronic Invoicing System (p. 1149)
✔ Choosing the Right Payment Policy (p. 1151)
✔ Efficient Invoicing Procedures (p. 1158)
✔ Invoicing and Credit Control for Small and Medium-Sized Enterprises (p. 976)

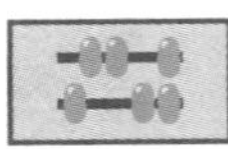

Viewpoint: Pension Funds—The Dangers of Taking Off-Benchmark Foreign Exchange Risk by Mark Hogg

INTRODUCTION

Mark Hogg joined RBC Dexia in February 2010. As Director for FX Product Development, Mark has overall responsibility for driving foreign exchange product strategy and growth for RBC Dexia. Prior to this appointment, Mark spent 9 years with Fidelity International and progressed to the overall responsibility for all FX hedging and currency overlay activity for all Fidelity International Investment funds and products globally. Mark spent his early career in various analyst, trading, and market risk roles with the Bank of Ireland, Barclays, and ANZ. Mark is a graduate of Dublin City University, holding a BSc in business and finance and an MSc in investment and treasury.

Pension funds in the United Kingdom with substantial investments in overseas equities have to take foreign currency risk into account. How should they approach this?

If you are investing in a foreign asset or basket of assets, whether you like it or not your investment return is going to come from two different sources. You will see a return or a loss on theunderlying asset, of course. But when you sell that asset you will also see a gain or a loss on the translation back into your home currency. A UK investor buying Apple also buys exposure to the dollar, whether they are aware of this or not. When you are faced with that opportunity set you have a choice to make—in fact, three choices. You can ignore thecurrency risk, which is very much an active decision that has consequences. Second, you can hedge a portion, or almost all, of the risk away. And finally, you can try to actively manage the risk in pursuit of an enhanced return.

This decision matrix can and should only be resolved with reference to the unique requirements of each fund. The underlying question you are asking is: how do we view this risk in relation to our investment policy or objectives? There are plenty of academic studies that demonstrate that unmanaged currency risk has no inherent positive value. So if you manage global equities as afund manager, and if you believe that if that risk is left unattended it has no inherent value, the obvious decision to take is to hedge it out, since the only thing that is likely to emerge from it is damage. If you are unsure of the potential outcome, then one decision could be to hedge out half the risk. The downside of hedging away all the currency risk is that the fund cannot then benefit from currency swings that move in its favor. The downside of not hedging at all is that adverse currency movements can kill your performance.

Between these two extremes, a 50% "passive" hedge (passive in that it is set and then left to operate) may be termed the "least-regret"currency hedgingpolicy. You get half the upside and protect against half the downside of currency movements. With a 50% hedge in place you could then choose to tactically tilt the hedge by either increasing or reducing the percentage, based on your strategic directional views of the currency exposures. On a quarterly review of the hedge, you might, for example, decide to tilt it 5% or 10% away from the mid-point if you were bullish on the movement of theforeign currencyagainst the pound. This is a reasonable way of combining a passive "overlay," as it is called, with some active management.

However, the question then is whether the fund manager should manage the hedging in-house, including putting in place the necessaryforeign exchangetrading infrastructure, or whether to outsource the maintenance of the hedge to an external provider. The question equity orbond fundmanagers have to ask themselves is: do they want to morph into being currency managers as well? It is a very different skill set. Many managers will simply want the currency risk managed in a sensible way that is aligned with their overall investment strategy. In this case, outsourcing can make perfect sense.

There is another major point to take into account here, and that is the view the fund manager's investorclient baseis likely to take of the currency element. Investors are becoming much more savvy about interpreting the attribution of returns from the fund. If the investor looks within the returns and sees that they are getting random currency returns that are giving them off-benchmark exposure, they are going to be asking some sharp questions. They will want to know how your currency exposure aligns to your investment strategy.

Can you give an idea of the scale of the risk potential contained in currency exposures?

Anasset managerlooking at a G5[1] investment in either bonds or equities has inherent price volatility in equities or bonds to contend with. That is where their core skill set usually lies. However, the underlying volatility of theasset classmay, in some cases, be less than theforeign exchangerisk in the portfolio and can easily end up dominating your returns. That is not going to make investors happy even if it is positive. They key is to ensure that you have a clear strategy that aligns yourcurrency riskpolicy with your overall investment strategy.

If you want to take active off-benchmark currency risk, you need to ensure that you have the right to do this by agreeing your strategy with your investor base. And if you are going to go down this route, you need to maintain a really sound, competent analysis of your performance. Over and over again I see situations where managers take unstructured and random foreign exchange risk over time without doing the post-mortem analysis to ensure that the decisions they have been taking really do add risk-adjusted value to the portfolio. Remember that the concept of a risk-adjusted return is that you expect a proportionately higher return for ahigher rateof risk. Plus you want that higher rate of risk to be factored in to your overall risk budget so that it is part of your strategic approach. If you do not analyze the risk and monitor your risk performance, you are simply flying blind.

Often, when people get around to doing this analysis, they are surprised by the outcome. They may well have put a lot of thought and effort into putting their foreign

  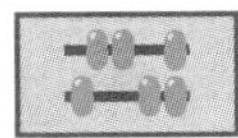      
a–z

exchange decisions in place with respect to their portfolio and at the end of the year they find that all their efforts have canceled out to zero. From a technical perspective, all they have succeeded in doing is adding some additional variance to their portfolio, which is not a happy outcome when you are presenting to investors. So afund managerneeds to ask him- or herself if they really do have a proven ability to add active value in the foreign exchange space that can stand the test of time. They need to make a conscious decision about the extent of their risk allocation to active currency management.

That raises the question of whether currency can in fact be successfully and consistently traded as an alpha generator for a portfolio.

The investment world is conditioned to look for diversification betweenasset classesand to go for a well-constructed portfolio that delivers returns above the risk-freerate of return. These are well-established, fundamental axioms in investment management. Then you come to currency and you have to ask if the unavoidable, embeddedcurrency riskin an overseas portfolio has any value. Many studies show that it does not. In a bond portfolio it can dominate the returns of the portfolio. Often, withgovernment bonds, you are trying very hard to protect your performance against your benchmark in terms ofbasis points, or hundredths of a per cent. You can end up giving back 10 or 20 times your portfolio outperformance because you did not get your currency house in order.

There are many different ways of trading currency. You can take your own strategic and tactical views and be deliberately over- or underweight in particular currencies with respect to your benchmark. Or you can go with some of the more well-established traditional active currency styles. These boil down to carry, trend, and value strategies. Carry is where you borrow in a lowinterest ratecurrency and buy a high interest rate currency. A value strategy is where youtake a viewthat, because of macroeconomic fundamentals, one currency is going to appreciate in value against another currency.

A simple G10[2] carry strategy, for example, involves ranking the currencies by, say, three-month interest rate differentials and then buying the top five and selling the bottom five. You are essentially betting against theforward-raterealization. That strategy has for a long time been the backbone of the active currency world.

There are lots of ways to go about generating alpha inforeign exchangetrading. However, you really do have to go back to basics and ask what your currency risk policy is. Is it risk reduction? Is it to generate a diversified source of return? Is it a combination of both? If it is a combination of both, you need to be aware that risk reduction and generating outperformance are two entirely different things, and each needs to be managed separately.

To what extent are equity and bond fund managers focused on currency risk?

The investment market is becoming more and more aware ofcurrency risk. Over the last 12–18 months we have seen rising interest in passive currency management, withfund managersreally wanting to understand the nuts and bolts of it. Many of them are looking at their passivecurrency hedgingmanagement and coming to the conclusion that they are not getting the results they wanted from those programs. What they want to know is where they are going wrong and what they have to do to put things right. Even passive hedges require the rules of the program to be set with care.

In a global equities portfolio you have to decide which currencies you want to hedge and how much of each you want to hedge. You also need to decide what your tolerance band is around that hedge. Remember, your assets are moving in value all the time and the currencies are fluctuating against each other. So if you have a policy of being 50% hedged, the underlying movements in value will mean that in reality your hedge will fluctuate in a range around 50%. Your tolerance level will determine how active you have to be in making adjustments in order to restore your hedging level. If you decide to be exactly 50% hedged, you are going to be chasing a moving target. Similarly, if you set a 1% "collar"—meaning that you want to be between 49.5% hedged and 50.5% hedged—you will break your heart since you will end up adjusting the hedge every day!

So the question is: how big a discrepancy in your hedging policy are you comfortable with before you feel you have to bring it back to a neutral point? You also have to take into account the cost of the hedge and what makes economic sense. The other aspect about setting unrealistically tight levels, like trying to be 100% hedged 100% of the time, is that you would need a team of people to accomplish this—and they are going to be generating a stream of trading tickets. The cost of the hedge is going to be exorbitant.

All these factors need to be considered when the fund manager is deciding whether to run theforeign exchangepolicy in-house or to outsource the hedge and the active currency management to a specialist house. With a hedge, you are hedging away a translation gain or loss on theasset value. The hedge gain or loss has to be realized periodically into acash flow. If it is a loss, you will have to sell some of theunderlying assetsto cover the loss, and if it is a gain, then it has to be reinvested. The fund manager needs to decide whether he or she is equipped to manage incoming and outgoing cash flows from the hedge.

Hedges are most often achieved withforward contractsthat reflect theinterest ratedifferentials between the two currencies being hedged. For G10 currencies the trading cost of the hedge will only be a fewbasis points, since bid–offer spreads in forward foreign exchange rates for major currencies are very tight.

Given that the cost is low and that hedging can be outsourced, you have to have a very good reason not to hedge or, conversely, to do any hedging that you are going to do in-house. However, the most important point is that the fund manager should have a currency management strategy that he or she can speak about and the necessary expertise to consult with. You should not just treat currency risk as an inevitable byproduct of buying an overseas asset. You can't avoid the risk, which is embedded with the asset, so you need to make a conscious decision to understand it and to rationalize your treatment of it.

One of the really strong benefits of having a coherent, active currency hedging and currency management program is that it can demonstrably increase yourSharpe ratio.[3] Since unmanaged currency risk does not add long-term risk-adjusted returns to the portfolio, hedging this risk out may improve the risk-adjusted returns within the portfolio. For fund managers this is a very strong marketing point with potential investors. New and existing investors will pay attention to the Sharpe ratio, and this can help to bring investment flows toward that product.

How easy is it for funds to get access to active currency management?

In today's markets the staple styles of active currency trading have become commoditized and very easy to access. Evenretail investorswith modest sums to invest can buy units in funds that offer access to the various currency styles. For years currency managers made a good living out of trading these styles and charging large fees for access to the product. Now the specialist houses are having to look hard for ways to differentiate themselves. So we are seeing a number of different trading models springing up and the market has become pretty murky. You can't readily build a benchmark for many of the strategies, so it is very difficult to compare the performance of managers. The best guide is to look at the performance over time to demonstrate consistency.

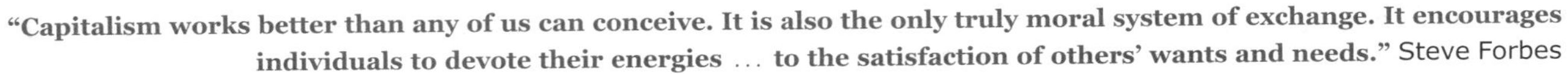
"Capitalism works better than any of us can conceive. It is also the only truly moral system of exchange. It encourages individuals to devote their energies ... to the satisfaction of others' wants and needs." Steve Forbes

MORE INFO

See Also:

★ How to Manage Pension Costs (p. 56)
★ Pension Schemes: A Unique and Unintended Basket of Risks on the Balance Sheet (pp. 87–90)
✔ Hedging Foreign Exchange Risk—Case Studies and Strategies (p. 970)
✔ Identifying and Managing Exposure to Interest and Exchange Rate Risks (p. 974)
Exchange Rate Risk (pp. 1224–1226)

NOTES

1 G5 refers to the Group of Five countries: the United States, the United Kingdom, Japan, Germany, and France. It has since become theGroup of Eight, or G8, with the addition of Italy, Canada, and Russia.

2 G10, orGroup of Ten, refers to the group of countries that have agreed to participate in theGeneral Arrangements to Borrow(GAB), established in 1962. The group now consists of 11 members: Belgium, Canada, France, Germany, Italy, Japan, the Netherlands, Sweden, Switzerland, the United Kingdom, and the United States.

3 A measure of risk-adjusted performance developed by Nobel laureate William F. Sharpe. The ratio indicates how well the return of an asset compensates the investor for the risk taken, higher values of the ratio being better.

"The man who accepts the laissez-faire doctrine would allow his garden to grow wild so that roses might fight it out with the weeds and the fittest might survive." John Ruskin

  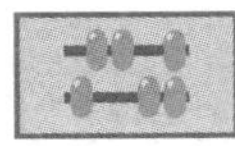      

Viewpoint: The Role of Insurance in Bringing Resilience to Societies Challenged by Global Warming by David Bresch

INTRODUCTION

David Bresch has headed the sustainability unit at Swiss Re since 2008. His previous roles there include head of university and risk research relations, head of atmospheric perils group, and chief modeler for natural catastrophe risk assessment. He has been member of the deal teams for many innovative risk transfer transactions, like cat bonds and weather index solutions. He has been a member of the official Swiss delegation to the UNFCCC climate negotiations in Copenhagen (2009), Cancun (2010), Durban (2011), and Doha (2012). He is a member of the adaptation board of the global network for climate solutions of the Earth Institute at Columbia University, a steering committee member of ProClim, and a member of the advisory board of the INSEAD energy club. He holds a PhD in physics from the Swiss Federal Institute of Technology (ETH) and lectures on the economics of climate adaptation there.

How does Swiss Re approach sustainability? Is it very different as a concept for a reinsurer, given that by definition what you manufacture is a technical insurance solution, not a tangible widget that takes a set number of carbon units to produce?

The key point to grasp is that for every reinsurer, the nature of the game has to be long-term. You have to take a long-term view of risk, since this is fundamental to the idea of insuring insurers and large corporates against specific risks for moderately long periods. Much of what stood against sustainability—and which the whole sustainability effort was partly aimed at redressing—was the myopic dash after short-term profits regardless, for example, of long-term environmental damage caused in the pursuit of those profits. Since Swiss Re was founded 150 years ago, we've worked together to find smarter ways to manage risk sustainably, so that people all over the world can turn pioneering ideas into reality or get back on track when things go wrong.

Risk for us comes in two flavors, both of which have to do with "sustainability" in that they are about sustainable growth over time. First, there is the emergence of new technologies and the risks associated with managing new technologies, which for us means assessing how to provide cover for these new technologies and their inherent risks. The second is more directly associated with climate change and has to do with development in hazard-prone areas, such as coastal plains. This is where a lot of our focus is and our aim here is to make societies and communities more resilient by providing them with natural-catastrophe cover.

"Resilience" differs from "sustainability," but they imply each other. A "fragile" society will not be very sustainable. However, in helping societies to be more resilient you must look closely at their exposure to environmental risk. I imagine this also means looking at what they must do to mitigate risk?

Absolutely. We must have a sustainable business, since we are engaged and committed for the long term. So we have to make sure that we do not engage in transactions that we would later regret. We use our in-depth knowledge of risk and our capacity to model a wide range of environmental risks to evaluate specific opportunities to see if they fit within acceptable parameters, or, if they don't, what would be needed to bring the risk within acceptable parameters. It is often not helpful simply to refuse a proposal. The better approach is to engage in a conversation with the client to see what we would require to be changed for the risk to be insurable. Take a ouse that is on the edge of a crumbling cliff, for example. That is not an insurable proposition as it stands, but a serious consideration would want to look at whether the cliff top could be stabilized, or the cliff supported, perhaps for other reasons such as coastal defense that would justify the cost. To explore these kinds of issues we formed the Economics of Climate Adaptation working group in 2008 with a view to forming partnering relationships with communities, cities, and regions There are large numbers of cities or regions that would be in a better position if they could get some of the risk volatility out of their balance sheets, with much of that volatility coming from the stresses that follow "acts of God."

The best example of this is the Caribbean Catastrophe Risk Insurance Facility (CCRIF). The CCRIF is a risk-pooling facility owned, operated, and registered in the Caribbean for Caribbean governments. It is designed to limit the financial impact of catastrophic hurricanes and earthquakes to Caribbean governments by quickly providing short-term liquidity when a policy is triggered. It is the world's first and, to date, only regional fund utilizing parametric insurance, thus giving Caribbean governments the unique opportunity to purchase earthquake and hurricane catastrophe coverage with lowest-possible pricing. The CCRIF represents a paradigm shift in the way governments treat risk. The facility was developed through funding from the Japanese Government, and was capitalized through contributions to a multi-donor Trust Fund by the Canadian Government, the European Union, the World Bank, the governments of the United Kingdom and France, the Caribbean Development Bank, and the governments of Ireland and Bermuda, as well as through membership fees paid by participating governments.

Sixteen governments are currently members of the CCRIF, namely: Anguilla, Antigua and Barbuda, Bahamas, Barbados, Belize, Bermuda, Cayman Islands, Dominica, Grenada, Haiti, Jamaica, St Kitts and Nevis, St Lucia, St Vincent and the Grenadines, Trinidad and Tobago, and the Turks and Caicos Islands. In 2007, the CCRIF paid out almost US$1 million to the Dominican and St Lucian governments after the November 29 earthquake in the eastern Caribbean; in 2008, the CCRIF paid out US$6.3 million to the Turks and Caicos Islands after Hurricane Ike made a direct hit on Grand Turk; and in 2010, the CCRIF made a payment of US$7.75 million to the government of Haiti after the January 12 earthquake. Swiss Re provides the reinsurance for the fund and was instrumental in its establishment.

We got together with the World Bank and others to look at how we could combine to help Caribbean communities deal in a better way with hurricanes and earthquakes in a forward-looking manner, instead of having the world community provide aid after the event. The key here was to find ways of structuring the finances of these countries so that they would be able to get fast access to relief money and to provide an insurance mechanism that would make funds available to all the affected governments rapidly. The mechanism we came up with means that the scale of the payout is precisely calibrated to the intensity of the disaster.

What this shows is that even if the world does move into a more unstable, more volatile phase, if global warming takes hold it will still e possible to model potential events and to plan for them in a coherent fashion. However, we have to engage and develop the dialogue with various regions, cities, and communities because if matters are left to local insurers, they very often simply do not have the capacity to deal with the scale of what is being envisaged. We also find that there are a great many public infrastructure exposures that are not being insured, and these too represent opportunities.

We have a similar example to the Caribbean fund that we can point to, namely the Mexico catastrophe bond. This has a similar logic behind it, in that if there is a large earthquake or hurricane, then the bond pays out. This is not reinsured by us, but it was brought to the capital markets and was very well received by investors. It might seem odd that investors would want to take on the risk of insuring against catastrophes, but you have to remember that the risk is well-rewarded and that it is not correlated with any other risk in the investor's portfolio, so it adds considerably to their diversification.

Another strong argument in favor of investing in catastrophe bonds for many investors is that this is an investment that is a good thing in and of itself. It does good in the world by helping to make a particular area or region more resilient and better able to recover should disaster strike. Many investors want to secure some ethical dimension for at least a portion of their investment and they can therefore justify the investment on two grounds: on the probable returns, and on the fact that this is an investment that does good. This is well beyond aid, in that investors are not just giving away money. They are entitled to a share of the profits if things go well and they have the satisfaction of knowing that the fund they are creating will do good if things go badly.

Since catastrophe bonds address the capital markets, what role is there for Swiss Re in this side of the sustainability initiative?

There are a lot of technical issues that have to be overcome in the structuring of a catastrophe bond. Above all, you need it to be supported by a really good modeling system. We do all our disaster modeling in-house and employ some 30 scientists for this purpose. We are very transparent in how we go about building these models and we make them available for studies on the economics of climate change, so that institutions, both academic and financial, can understand the economic risks associated with global warming and the additional risks of further economic development.

Obviously, catastrophe bonds are a very good innovation in that they bring the capital markets into play and they broaden the capital base of the insurance industry very substantially. However, structuring a catastrophe bond so that it is transparent to all the stakeholders, so that everyone knows what the bond's purpose is when it is triggered, and what their liability is, is critical. We see a very strong role for Swiss Re in structuring these bonds properly, so that they can be renewed and replenished. The deeper understanding of risk is at the core of what we do.

When you have models of the comprehensive risk landscape, you can start to assess the nature of the risk and how you can reduce and manage it. From a community's point of view, they can pinpoint specific actions, such as the impact of building a dam, or how zoning and building restrictions on certain kinds of land might reduce risk. Higher standards in building or flood-proofing could be called for. The Netherlands is an extremely good example of how a whole country has dealt with natural-disaster threats in a very resilient, long-term fashion.

Is your initiative in the direction of sustainability wholly dependent on the realities of climate change?

There is a tremendous body of evidence pointing to climate change being both a fact and man-made, Even if all emissions could be stopped today, the climate will continue to alter in the coming decades. This means we need to reduce emissions as quickly as possible and deal with the impact of climate change by making our societies more resilient. We employ a scenario approach to imagine how various futures might look. When you look at the economics of climate adaptation, then you start figuring out what would constitute the basket of measures that societies need to undertake in order to increase, strengthen, or at least maintain their resilience against possible future challenges. Above all, we need to transform our energy and transportation systems. In doing this we encounter some of those technological challenges I mentioned. There are risks, for example, in moving from traditional electric grids to smart grids. It is a huge step to take and one that comes with a lot of opportunities and some risks, and we are willing to take on some of those risks in order to enable the change to happen. There are lots of opportunities, but you need a deep understanding of the driving forces and you have to dig through the complexity to provide viable solutions. Our approach is to collaborate very strongly with the various stakeholders, since no one organization can provide a solution in isolation any more.

The global society should do the utmost to avoid the unmanageable—that is, global greenhouse gas emissions need to be drastically reduced. Only if this is achieved, can the insurance sector help to manage the unavoidable—that is, the increase in risk associated with a changing climate. If matters are well organized, it is possible to manage risk at a reasonable cost, with the aim to keep societies resilient and robust. The challenge for some of these societies, particularly low-lying islands, for example, is that if catastrophes happen too often, the people become desperate and lose trust in institutions and society. The social fabric starts to unravel, so you need to address these matters with quite some urgency. As a single actor we can by no means provide resilience single handedly; but we do play a role in helping communities to strengthen their resilience.

MORE INFO

See Also:

★ Climate Change and Insurance (pp. 149–150)
★ The Impact of Climate Change on Business (pp. 875–877)
★ Viewpoint: Leveraging Influence to Impact Climate-Change Policy (pp. 696–697)

"Like other branches of the study of society, economics remains culturally parochial, and its underlying concepts based on a few centuries of Western experience." John Gray

  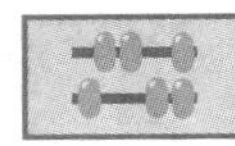      

Viewpoint: The Role of the Global Property Markets Since the Crash by Hans Vrensen

INTRODUCTION

Hans Vrensen is global head of research at DTZ. He is responsible for leading DTZ research worldwide and has launched the company's "Great wall of money" and "Global debt funding gap" reports and the DTZ Fair Value Index. Prior to joining DTZ, he was head of European securitization research at Barclays Capital, where he managed a team of analysts covering European asset-backed securities, and he has held several positions in the property sector. In particular, he has focused on bringing rigor to the research teams he has run. At Barclays Capital his team consistently received top three rankings in its area by *Institutional Investor* and *International Securitisation Report*. He is a chartered financial analyst and holds master degrees in both real estate and in economics.

The global residential and commercial property market has to be viewed on a regional basis since it is moving at different speeds in different regions. How do you view things at present?

These markets do indeed break down regionally. Asia is barrelling ahead, with Chinese GDP growth, for example, topping 9.5% in 2011. So the issue in Asia is strong growth against a background of concerns over inflation. The real worry, however, is the ongoing sovereign debt crisis in Europe and the way that is playing out in the property markets there. With the focus so much on European risk through the mid-part of 2011, people are, to a large extent, taking their eye off the risks to the US economy. However, we could well see downgrades of US debt by the ratings agencies, given the scale of the debt and ongoing difficulties in trimming back ever-growing US fiscal and public-sector debt. The United States has one of the biggest public deficits globally, yet the administration is unwilling to increase taxes and to tackle the task of reducing that deficit meaningfully. So one has to keep in mind, with all the focus on the European issues, that the US deficit has the potential to move to center stage at any point, with fairly dramatic consequences for the global economy.

Naturally, real estate markets are affected by some of these trends. Most notably, uncertainty has a very negative effect on both commercial and residential markets. Faced with uncertainty, companies delay plans to expand or to move to new headquarters. They also delay expansion plans and hold back on growth, which pushes uncertainty through to households via job insecurity.

Many commentators have been concerned about what they see as a dangerous bubble in the Chinese real-estate market. Do you share their anxiety?

It seems to us that these commentators are not looking closely enough at the data. We did quite a bit of work in this area a year ago, and the results did not support the idea of a bubble. Of course, there is good evidence to show that the average nominal growth in house prices in China has been significantly ahead of inflation for the last decade, with the year-on-year average increase being 5.4%, as against an inflation rate of 1.9%. By mid-2011, inflation in China was running at a much higher level, somewhere above 9%, and considerably higher for food price inflation.

The growth in house prices was triggered by the mass influx of people from rural areas to the cities, which put huge stresses on China's capacity to provide sufficient levels of affordable housing, particularly in the country's tier-one cities. Price increases were inevitable in that scenario, and prices were driven up by demand from investors speculating on future increases in residential property in these cities.

However, there is also a very strong local savings factor playing in here. The Chinese have one of the world's highest savings rates, driven by the absence of any meaningful state-provided safety nets by way of health, pensions, and social security. There are very few alternative investment opportunities that can serve as a home for savings, since bank deposits attract very low rates of interest and it is difficult for ordinary citizens to invest in China's emerging stock markets. The mutual fund industry in China is embryonic at present. So property is widely seen as the logical option—which, again, increases the flow of cash into property.

We would argue, however, that if you look at long-term affordability—in other words at wages growth and the growth of disposable surplus income—this is running comfortably ahead of house price increases. In other words, viewed against the backdrop of long-term affordability, which is an excellent measure to use when evaluating residential property trends in a country, there is no house price bubble in mainland China, not even in the first-tier cities like Beijing and Shanghai.

In fact the affordability trend across most Chinese cities shows an improvement over the last 10 years. Nominal household income growth has, on average, been around 11.4% annually in the period from 2000 to 2009, which is more than double the year-on-year growth in house prices over the same period. That said, affordability has worsened slightly in both Beijing and Shanghai recently, but overall, in comparison to other countries, the Chinese house price affordability trend has been very favorable over the last decade. This means that in the long term the residential market looks sound, despite rapid rises in the prices of one- and two-bedroom flats in the big metropolitan areas.

Also, China has some advantages that are simply not there for developed markets in the West. For a start, the use of mortgages in China is quite limited by comparison. Fewer than half of all residential purchases are enabled by mortgages. The rest are cash transactions. This has huge implications for household indebtedness and means that more than half of Chinese property owners are not exposed to interest rate rises via increases in the monthly cost of their mortgages. That position compares very favorably to the position of home owners in say, the United Kingdom or the United States.

The other major advantage that China has—and not just in the property field—is that because it is not a democracy it can make policy changes very rapidly. In a democracy politicians have to worry about adverse public reaction to strong policy measures. To a large extent, the Chinese

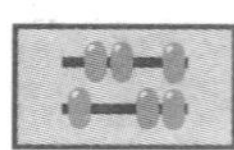

government is much freer when it comes to pushing through such measures. So the government can decree, for example, that people are not allowed to buy second and third homes, thereby taking a huge slice of demand out of the property market and taking a lot of pressure off prices. Imagine how much of the heat in the subprime property bubble in the United States would have vanished if the government had been able to push through such an impossible edict! We would not have had the absurd position of people with very low incomes being granted 110% mortgages on third homes, and the toxic element in the US securitized mortgage market would have been greatly diminished.

Such things are impossible in a democracy but are easy for the Chinese government to implement, and this is exactly what it has done. People are simply not allowed to invest in more than one home. Commentators who worry about the so-called Chinese real-estate bubble do not factor things like this into their thinking. Moreover, the Chinese state tends to be quite precise in the measures it introduces when making policy changes, and that, too, speaks against a "hard landing" for the Chinese property market.

MORE INFO

Books:

Smith, David. *The Dragon and the Elephant: China, India and the New World Order.* London, UK: Profile Books, 2008.

Walter, Carl E., and Fraser J. T. Howie. *Red Capitalism: The Fragile Financial Foundation of China's Extraordinary Rise*. Singapore: Wiley, 2011.

Website:

DTZ: www.dtz.com

See Also:

Real Estate (pp. 1641–1642)

"**A bank is a place that will lend you money if you can prove that you don't need it.**" Bob Hope

     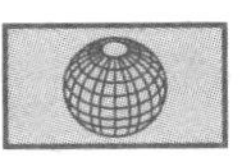   

Rules versus Discretion in Supervisory Interventions in Financial Institutions by Marc Quintyn[1]

EXECUTIVE SUMMARY

- One of the most critical moments in financial-sector supervision is when supervisors need to decide if they should "intervene" in a "problem bank" (a bank that is gliding towards insolvency or is already insolvent). This decision is critical because, if supervisors wait too long to intervene, the worth of the bank will continue to erode, losses to depositors may increase, and systemic risks may increase, ultimately leading to high costs to the government and, thus, the taxpayers.
- In the wake of every banking crisis, the debate about "rules versus discretion" in supervisory intervention flares up. This discussion regarding supervisory intervention in problem banks focuses on the incentives for supervisors to act swiftly and decisively in order to minimize losses to depositors, and society more widely.
- In this debate, rules are often proposed as the preferred solution (with some discretion left), because the closure of a financial institution remains a tricky event where many interests collide (private, political, business), and even independent supervisors can be seduced by self-interest if the stakes get high. The rules-based intervention system in the United States (prompt corrective actions) has proven many of its merits over the years, and made the product ready for export to other jurisdictions around the world. Until recently, most European supervisory frameworks relied more on discretion than rules, but the 2007–08 financial crisis seems to change the mood, and more voices are being heard in favor of a rules-based system.

INTRODUCTION

Financial supervisors' main task is to monitor the behavior and actions of the institutions under their area of responsibility. They check compliance with the regulatory framework, and, when necessary, impose sanctions and enforce them. So, in every jurisdiction, a key component of the regulatory and supervisory framework is the nature, timing, and form of intervention by the supervisors in case the health of an individual institution fails. The supervisors step in to address the problems in the financial institution in an effort to protect the depositors of this institution and of other institutions, as well as the taxpayers' money by avoiding or limiting contagion (the systemic risk).

Supervisors typically have a toolbox of instruments and sanctions at their disposal, ranging from orders to comply with specific rules, over monetary fines, to the ultimate sanction, closure of a financial institution. Typically, these sanctions are graded. They start from small corrections when the problems are still minor, in the hope the bigger interventions can be avoided.

Practice around the globe has amply shown that the decision as to when and how to intervene in a problem bank is the Achilles heel of the supervisory process. Reasons abound for this! Firstly, a weak regulatory framework inherently leads to weak supervision and lack of enforcement rules. For instance, the regulatory framework may lack pointers for supervisors regarding the timing of an intervention, may not be specific enough regarding the intervention instruments, or may leave the supervisors without the power to collect the critical data to properly analyze a financial institution's health. Secondly, politicians may dissuade supervisors from intervening in a problem institution for fear that this (connected) institution gets a bad press, or worse.

Judgment is another factor that could influence the supervisory decisions. Supervisors faced with bank problems may believe that these problems are temporary, and will go away without supervisory action. Finally, some form of self-interest may also be at play. Supervisors faced with a problem bank may take a "not on my watch" approach, and hide the problems as long as possible. This behavior can be explained by the fact that society may see the problems in a bank as a reflection of weak supervision, which is damaging for the supervisor's reputation.

Whatever their cause, these situations typically lead to forbearance, i.e., refraining from addressing an institution's problems head-on. Such forbearance is bound to lead to a deepening of the problems in that specific institution, and ultimately to an increase in the costs of addressing them, among others, because these problems could be contagious. These costs will eventually fall on the shoulders of the depositors, the government, and ultimately the taxpayers.

Starting from this reality, the "rules versus discretion" debate in supervisory intervention is about the question: in order to limit political interference, reduce the risk of judgmental errors, and self-interested behavior, and thus forbearance, should the supervisor, when intervening in an individual bank, be bound by strict rules, or have the discretion to take action when deemed necessary?

ORIGIN OF THE DEBATE: HOW TO DEAL WITH TIME-INCONSISTENCY IN POLICIES?

The "rules versus discretion" debate in economic policy goes back to the seminal paper by Kydland and Prescott (1977). They introduced the distinction between time-consistent and time-inconsistent policies. The issue with time-inconsistent policies is that they produce good results in the short run, but will ultimately fail to produce the long-run policy goals set forth. Politicians have a tendency to renege on their long-term commitments for short-term gain, for example, in the run-up to elections. A key issue in settings where the time-consistency problem arises is the ability or inability of the government to make binding commitments about future policy. The authors argued that in such situations policies should be bound by rules, which is superior to leaving discretion to policymakers. Rules imply commitment, and therefore produce time-consistent policies, while discretion implies the absence of commitment, and therefore opens the door to time-inconsistencies. The issue has been widely debated with respect to monetary policy (with the emergence of the independent central bank as a broadly accepted institutional solution to the time-inconsistency problem, rather than the strict imposition of a monetary rule) and fiscal policy (fiscal rules).

From the above examples, it can be seen that bank supervision faces similar risks of time-inconsistency, when it comes to dealing with weak or ailing institutions. Bank liquidations are typically politically unpopular, as they can result in genuine hardship for depositors and other creditors, many of whom will also be voters. Vote-maximizing politicians with short time horizons may be concerned about the short-term costs of bank closure, whether fiscal, in terms of lost votes, or in terms of lost campaign contributions. So they will be sensitive to demands of these groups, particularly if these are politically well organized. Politicians may be tempted, as a result, to put pressure on supervisors to organize a bailout, exercise forbearance or grant dispensations from regulatory requirements to avoid short-term costs. But short-term forbearance may be the cause of higher longer-term resolution costs.

To eliminate time-inconsistency in bank resolution, it has also been proposed that bank supervisors are granted a fair degree of independence from the politicians, for the same reasons as central banks in matters of monetary policy. It has been argued that independent supervisors would not fall into the trap of time-inconsistent policies. Their reaction functions would differ from those of their political masters. So supervisors will act decisively, and without interference from politicians, when they need to deal with an ailing bank. However, some have argued that this is not enough because the incentives faced by supervisors differ from those faced by central bankers. This critique of regulatory forbearance was mainly developed in reaction to the observed behavior of regulators during the S&L problem in the United States in the 1980s. In this account, regulatory forbearance arises not only from political influence but also from the self-interested actions of supervisors. The incentive structure they face encourages them to "sweep problems under the carpet," at least until they have left office. Supervisors face more complex pressures than monetary policy-makers, because so many (private, public and political) interests are at stake when the decision is taken to close and liquidate a financial institution. Thus, even an independent supervisor could come under pressure when faced with an ailing bank, particularly if that bank is politically connected or is a national champion (or both).

"PROMPT CORRECTIVE ACTIONS"—A RULES-BASED SOLUTION

This above analysis highlights the need to pay close attention to the regulators' incentive structures, remuneration arrangements, and accountability measures. More specifically, the view emerged that supervisors, even politically independent ones, would benefit from the presence of intervention rules to avoid succumbing to political and other pressures. An influential proposal by Benston and Kaufman (1988) promoted a system of predetermined capital/asset ratios that would trigger structured actions by supervisors. They called it structured early intervention and resolution (SEIR). Their proposal opened the rules versus discretion debate for supervisory intervention. Instead of leaving the decision as to when and how to intervene in ailing banks (discretion) in the hands of supervisors, they proposed rules specifying when and how supervisors need to intervene. A version of SEIR was adopted by the United States as "prompt corrective action (PCA) in the 1991 Federal Deposit Insurance Corporation Improvement Act (FDICIA) (see Making It Happen). The main objective behind systems of SEIR is to minimize the losses for depositors, deposit insurance, and, by extension, taxpayers.

Since the adoption of PCA in the United States, a number of countries, including Japan, Korea, and Mexico, have followed this example. Many more are contemplating the adoption of such an approach to supervisory intervention. In the aftermath of the 2007–08 financial crisis, the debate has been vividly reopened with calls from various circles, academic and policy, for more rules in the intervention process. So, given this growing appetite for rules-based systems, the question really is: are rules-based systems so much superior to discretion? Let's have a look at advantages and disadvantages of both in order to draw some conclusions.

Rules-Based Systems

- By determining the pace and nature of intervention, rules-based systems can prevent excessive forbearance, so action is taken in a timely way, when the bank's obligations can probably still be met, thus limiting the costs to depositors and/or taxpayers, and forestalling contagion.
- Indeed, PCA starts when the regulatory capital ratio is still positive, giving the bank managers incentives to recapitalize the bank or look for a suitable merger partner.
- A rules-based system, by its nature, provides better (or additional) protection for supervisors against political influence, or legal action. The supervisor's defense would simply be: "I was doing what the law told me to do." This is, in general, a useful buffer against political interference, and is particularly important in countries where supervisors do not have a great deal of political independence (such as many middle- and low-income countries).
- A rules-based system provides clear signals to the banks and to the public what to expect. It provides clear incentives to banks to comply with rules designed to protect their solvency; it is a public promise that the supervisor will intervene in a timely way to avoid losses. It thus promotes public confidence.

Discretion-Based Systems

- A discretion-based system provides the supervisor with the flexibility to pursue an optimal solution in terms of timing, cost, and type of action. All bank failures are different, and *ex ante* legislative criteria for bank intervention are too crude to provide an effective and low-cost system of bank intervention.
- Discretion could also avoid that capital is destructed when intervention is unnecessarily rapid and intrusive. The supervisory authority is a better judge of the actual situation, and the most adequate remedial measures, than any *ex ante* legislator. In some cases, exercising forbearance may increase the probability that a distressed bank may recover.
- By being able to operate more discreetly, unnecessary unrest in the markets and with depositors, and other creditors can be avoided.
- Rules-based systems such as PCA rely on regulatory measures of a bank's capital. Such measures may deviate significantly from the bank's economic capital. Bank capital is also a backward-looking policy instrument. For these reasons, judgment, rather than rules may be better to make a proper assessment of a bank's situation.

Clearly, both approaches come with advantages and disadvantages. So, drawing a clear-cut conclusion is not all that simple. A rules-based system is clear and able to shape anticipations of all stakeholders, but it is also rigid. A discretion-based system offers more flexibility but may be insufficiently proactive and transparent, and may provide insufficient incentives for prudent behavior of banks. So, perhaps, for a complex operation such as financial supervision and intervention, it is dangerous to think too much in "either/or" terms, particularly because every case for intervention is different. It seems more prudent to think of an intervention strategy that is based on a fair dose of both discretion and rules.

In that regard, reliance on discretion is more desirable at the beginning of the process, when problems are first detected, giving supervisors leeway to adjust measures to specific circumstances. Rules-driven interventions have more merits once the situation becomes more urgent. How would such an intervention strategy operate?

In a "normal times" situation, supervisors evidently watch a bank's capital adequacy ratio, as well as other ratios. However, given the complex nature of financial operations, these days their attention goes more to a financial institution's risk-management systems and strategies. This approach to

        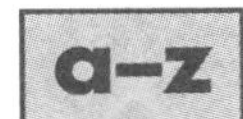

supervision gained more weight since the adoption of the Basel II framework (Pillar 2). The point of gravity of supervision is on qualitative assessments of risk management systems. In the wake of the current crisis, this tendency is likely to continue. Qualitative principles are therefore likely to be elevated relative to mechanical rules that were "gamed" leading up to the current crisis.

The implication of this new approach to supervision is that in the very early stages of emerging problems—the transition from a "normal" situation to one of distress—reliance on rules would not be adequate. Supervisors should assess strategies and mainly rely on their discretion to suggest corrective actions.

However, once it is clear that an institution's situation continues to deteriorate, and quantitative measures point in the same direction, intervention rules should kick in, and supervisory discretion should be reduced and eliminated.

So, we would see a gradual transition from qualitative and discretionary interventions to more rules-based interventions. For such rules to operate effectively, what are the necessary ingredients of an intervention system? Well:

1. first of all, the language in the law should be clear that the supervisor is mandated to intervene;
2. the triggers for action by the supervisors should be clearly defined, objective, and non-debatable;
3. the actions to be taken by the supervisors should also be clearly specified;
4. an indication of the timeframe within which imposed actions should be taken by the supervised entity needs to be given;
5. the law should specify a range of sanctions that should be taken if actions are not implemented.

Furthermore, a rules-based intervention system needs solid, up-to-date financial information on the bank's financial conditions. As indicated earlier, a fair degree of supervisory independence is desirable under a rules-based intervention system, but on the other hand, rules rather than discretion tend to shelter supervisors from political interference. Just like for any supervisory action, supervisors that enjoy legal protection for actions taken in good faith are in a better and stronger position than colleagues that do not enjoy such protection. Legal protection is an important requirement for effective supervision.

MAKING IT HAPPEN

Table 1. The United States FIDICIA system for "prompt corrective action." (*Source*: Board of Governors of the Federal Reserve System)

Capital level trigger	Mandatory and discretionary actions
10% > capital adequacy ratio > 8% or 5% > core capital ratio > 4%	Bank cannot make any capital distribution or payments that would leave the institution undercapitalized.
Capital adequacy ratio < 8% or core capital ratio < 4%	Bank must submit a capital restoration plan; asset growth restricted; approval required for new acquisitions, branching, and new lines of business.
Capital adequacy ratio < 6% or core capital ratio < 3%	Bank must increase capital; restrictions on deposit interest rates and asset growth; may be required to elect new board of directors.
Capital adequacy ratio < 4% or core capital ratio < 2%	Bank must be placed in conservatorship or receivership within 90 days; approval of FDIC required for entering into material transactions other than usual core business, extending credit for any highly leveraged transaction, changes in accounting methods, paying excessive compensation or bonuses.

MORE INFO

Book:

Nieto, Maria, and L. Wall. "Prompt corrective action: Is there a case for an international banking standard?" In D. Evanoff, G. Kaufman, and J. La Brosse (eds). *International Financial Instability: Global Banking and National Regulation*. World Scientific Studies in International Economics Series, Vol. 2. Singapore: World Scientific, 2007; ch. 23.

Articles:

Benston, George J., and George G. Kaufman. "Risk and solvency regulation of depository institutions: Past policies and current options." Federal Reserve Bank of Chicago Staff Memorandum no. 88-1 (1988): 1–67.

Benston, George J., and George G. Kaufman. "FDICIA after five years." *Journal of Economic Perspectives* 11:3 (Summer 1997): 139–158. Online at: econpapers.repec.org/RePEc:aea:jecper:v:11:y:1997:i:3:p:139-58

Kydland, Finn E., and Edward C. Prescott. "Rules rather than discretion: The inconsistency of optimal plans." *Journal of Political Economy* 85:3 (June 1977): 473–491. Online at: www.jstor.org/pss/1830193

See Also:

★ How Much Independence for Supervisors in Financial Market Regulation? (pp. 351–354)
★ Why Organizations Need to be Regulated—Lessons from History (pp. 437–439)
★ Viewpoint: Lessons from the Credit Crisis: Governing Financial Institutions (pp. 694–695)
✔ The EU Regulatory Regime (p. 1029)
✔ Principles of Financial Services Regulation (p. 1048)
John Kenneth Galbraith (p. 1283)
The Age of Turbulence: Adventures in a New World (p. 1329)
Banking and Financial Services (pp. 1612–1614)

NOTE

1 The views expressed in this chapter are the author's and should not be attributed to the IMF, its Executive Board, or its Management.

"It's quite possible that at some point we may get an odd quarter or two of negative growth, but recession is not the central projection at all." Mervyn King

  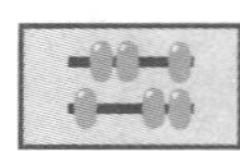      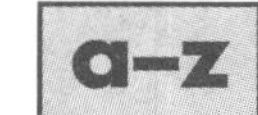

Viewpoint: *Shariah* Law—Bringing a New Ethical Dimension to Banking by Amjid Ali

INTRODUCTION

Amjid Ali, senior manager, HSBC Amanah Global, believes that *shariah* finance is broadening its appeal and reach—both among Muslims and non-Muslims—as a result of the banking and financial crisis. Recognized as one of the most influential Muslims in the United Kingdom by the Muslim Power 100 Awards, Ali has 22 years of branch banking experience with Midland Bank and HSBC in the United Kingdom. In September 2003 he joined HSBC Amanah UK as senior business development manager, with responsibility for raising the profile of Amanah Home Finance in the United Kingdom. He took over as UK head in January 2005, with responsibility for strategy, distribution, and sales, and was appointed senior manager, HSBC Amanah Global, in August 2008. In this role Ali is working as part of the HSBC Amanah central team headquartered in Dubai.

What are the underlying principles of *shariah* law from a financial perspective? In other words, what defines the kind of model to which a financial institution that seeks to offer *shariah*-compliant services to its Muslim customers will have to adhere?

Shariah is the body of Islamic faith and has two main sources. The first is the Qur'an, the sacred book that records the word of God as revealed to the Prophet Mohammed. To quote directly from the Qur'an: "God has permitted trade and forbidden interest," Qur'an, Chapter 2, Verse 275. The fundamental underlying principle is that interest is prohibited.

The second source is the *Hadith*, the body of documents that records the *sunnah* (the practice, or "life example") of the Prophet Mohammed.

From these two sources there are five main prohibitions that must be observed in the creation of a *shariah*-compliant financial services model. They overlap somewhat and are mutually supportive.

1. *Riba*: the prohibition of interest.
2. *Gharar* (translated as "uncertainty" or opacity): there must be a full and fair disclosure (for example, certainty as to the price of a contract before it is concluded).
3. *Maysair*: the prohibition of speculation or gambling ("obtaining something easily or becoming rich without effort").
4. Profit: the Islamic financier should only generate benefit from the project in which they invest and must take some risk, since risk equates to effort and potential loss.
5. Unethical investment: Islam prohibits investing or dealing in certain products such as alcohol, armaments, and pork, and in activities such as gambling, entertainment, and hotels. (Exactly how this last prohibition is interpreted varies widely depending on where one is in the Muslim world.)

Is this list sufficient to define *shariah*-compliant financial services?

No, there are other factors to keep in mind when constructing product offerings. Very importantly, one has to keep in mind the Islamic view of money. In Islam money is not a commodity; it has no intrinsic use and it can only be exchanged for the same par value. Also, Islam allows the use of securities to support a transaction, which guards against the wilful wrongdoing or carelessness of partners.

HSBC, Lloyds, and other banks now offer *shariah*-compliant mortgages for house purchase. How can this be reconciled with the principles you have outlined?

If we are supporting a customer in the buying of a property, it is done under a contract known as diminishing *musharakah*. This translates as co-ownership. In this transaction, the bank and the customer buy the home jointly, in joint names. As time progresses the customer buys more and more of the property from the bank and the bank's share in the home diminishes, until the bank no longer has any stake in the home. It is proper for the bank to take a reward for bearing the initial risk: this reward is not interest on a loan, but a rental charge for the portion, the asset owned by the bank. This method follows the underlying principle that "you cannot make money on money," but it is permissible to "make money on the use or the exchange of an asset."

Can you provide a sense of the growing scale and importance of *shariah* finance around the world?

Islamic banking is already large and it is growing very substantially. The target market is the world's 1.6 billion Muslims, who represent 25% of the world's population, and are largely concentrated in emerging economies. The industry's total funds under management are estimated to be worth around US$450 billion to US$500 billion, excluding Iran. The annual growth rate for Islamic finance is currently running at 30%, which suggests that the market will reach US$1 trillion in funds under management by 2010. These figures were provided in a recent issue of *The Banker*.

While the Muslim community in general views *shariah* banking as the only acceptable method of banking, we have to accept that, when viewed globally, *shariah* banking is an alternative to, rather than a replacement for, the conventional, traditional model of Western banking. The latter has been in existence for centuries and has developed into a very sophisticated global industry. By contrast, Islamic finance is still very much an emerging, developing form of banking, which continues to evolve almost on a daily basis. At this moment, no *shariah* bank has a complete set of products that would mirror the portfolio of products on offer in a traditional bank.

Following the financial crisis, there have been calls for a more ethical financial infrastructure in the West. Does *shariah* banking have anything to offer to non-Muslims on this front?

If you look at the ethical platform of *shariah* banking, it will undoubtedly appeal not only to the Muslim community, but to the wider community as well. The transparency of products and the sharing of risk, together with the emphasis on like-for-like benefits are very appealing universally. What is also very clear is that, with any *shariah* bank, the principle of treating customers fairly must be at the heart of the bank's practice or it cannot be *shariah*-compliant. There are

"Everybody is always in favour of general economy and particular expenditure." Anthony Eden (Earl of Avon)

lessons for all from the credit crisis and subsequent global recession. However, I personally do not believe that Islamic financing can be considered a replacement for traditional banking. However, as it stands today, it is a credible alternative for non-Muslims. And for Muslims, it is really the only way for a Muslim to do business and sleep peacefully at night.

The prohibition against interest is not just an incidental or minor detail. It is the only prohibition in the Quran which is actually specified: to be in breach of this principle is to "make war on God and on his messenger," the Prophet Mohammed. This is a fundamental dividing point between traditional banking practice and *shariah* banking and it is not something that a Muslim can "fudge" and be happy.

I should point out that both the Christian and the Jewish traditions have a long history of being against usury, or the payment and receipt of interest. So the three traditions are not very far apart on this point.

You have provided an example of mortgage finance *shariah*-style. What other products are available?

One that comes to mind is *ijara*, a lease-backed contract, which "mirrors" asset-based finance in traditional banking. In *ijara*, the bank buys the asset in its entirety and then leases it back to the client and charges a rental. With *ijara*, the return going to the bank from the customer is rent, not interest, and Islam is comfortable with the concept of rent. Here, the bank is making money on the use of an asset.

Another product area is pensions. The restrictions of *riba* mean that pensions cannot be invested in government securities, as these are pure interest-bearing investments. However, certain equities are perfectly acceptable because the investor is a partner in the company, so he or she shares its risks and losses. Therefore, our pension product is very heavily based on equities, although property is also allowed as an asset class if the transaction is structured correctly.

The whole pensions area is much undeveloped in the Muslim community. Because of *riba*, Muslims naturally look to rental income and property ownership as the most natural way of funding their retirement. There is a real culture clash in the area of pensions, and it is something that we have been in longstanding discussions with the HM Revenue & Customs about. In the United Kingdom, the law mandates that at the age of 75 you have no other option but to buy an annuity with your pension. And annuities, being interest-based, are not ideal for Muslims. We have made this point through the Islamic Finance Experts Group that the government has set up, in which I participate. But it is not an issue that can be resolved overnight.

Then there are wholesale products, such as support for major corporates that are Muslim-owned. Again, this is very much a developing area in Islamic banking.

It seems that Islamic banks and traditional banks do coexist in some areas, perhaps because they are serving different markets. In others, Islamic financial institutions are predominant. And there are also areas where Western banks are developing Islamic finance arms, such as HSBC's Amanah proposition. Is this how you see things progressing?

Today there are over 500 institutions around the world offering *shariah*-compliant products in 47 countries across the globe. I expect this to continue to expand, particularly in the Middle East, Indonesia, and Malaysia. The market is big enough to accommodate both wholly Islamic financial institutions as well as those who have "window" operations which offer Islamic products through existing branch networks.

At HSBC we have adopted a three-pronged approach.

- Window Model—this offers Islamic products through existing branch networks, and is used in UAE, Bahrain, United Kingdom, and Indonesia.
- Partnership Model—a joint venture between HSBC and Saudi British Bank. This unique partnership has given us access to one of the biggest markets in the Muslim world.
- Islamic Subsidiary—HSBC's Malaysian subsidiary was the first international bank offered this license in Malaysia. This is a unique proposition available for HSBC with the option of opening branches outside Malaysia (Brunei and Bangladesh).

It is all about understanding the local market and deciding which model works best.

The window model, offering *shariah*-compliant products through an existing branch network, works extremely well for us in markets where the idea of *shariah* banking remains unfamiliar. In the United Kingdom, for example, there is not a particularly developed understanding of what makes a product *shariah*-compliant, even among British Muslims. There is also a lack of understanding of how a *shariah*-compliant financial product might benefit a Muslim customer. There are invariably many questions, and one needs the interaction with a customer and trained branch staff who can make clear how a *shariah* product differs from a conventional one.

Is it necessary for a bank wishing to have a *shariah* banking service to have a body of Islamic scholars overseeing its *shariah* products and its operations?

It is absolutely fundamental. It is the key to gaining credibility and integrity in the eyes of the market. Right from the outset, in 1998, when HSBC first set up HSBC Amanah as the Islamic financial services division of the group, we established an independent board of leading Muslim scholars to be our *shariah* advisers. These are very eminent and respected scholars from across the Muslim world. Success in this market depends on a *shariah* bank's ability to deliver in a way that continually demonstrates a respect and understanding of cultural differences, and of the importance of Islam in the daily life of a Muslim.

MORE INFO

Books:

El-Gamal, Mahmoud A. *Islamic Finance: Law, Economics, and Practice*. Cambridge, UK: Cambridge University Press, 2008.

Usmani, Muhammad Taqi. *The Authority of Sunnah*. New Delhi: Kitab Bhavan, 1998.

Usmani, Muhammad Taqi. *An Introduction to Islamic Finance*. New Delhi: Idara Isha'at-e-Diniyat, 1999.

Zarabozo, Jamal Al-Din. *The Authority of and Importance of the Sunnah*. Denver, CO: Al-Basheer Publications, 2000.

See Also:

★ Identifying the Main Regulatory Challenges for Islamic Finance (pp. 358–360)
★ Islamic Insurance Markets and the Structure of *Takaful* (pp. 202–203)
★ Islamic Modes of Finance and the Role of *Sukuk* (pp. 520–521)
✔ Islamic Commercial Law (p. 1166)
✔ Islamic Law of Contracts (p. 1167)
✔ Key Islamic Banking Instruments and How They Work (p. 1010)
✔ An Overview of *Shariah*-Compliant Funds (p. 1083)
✔ The Role of the *Shariah* Advisory Board in Islamic Finance (p. 1015)

"Our workers are no less productive than when this crisis began. Our minds are no less inventive, our goods and services no less needed than they were last week or last month or last year." Barack Obama

Viewpoint: A Single Currency for Asia?

by Amitendu Palit

INTRODUCTION

Amitendu Palit is an economist specializing in comparative studies of China and India, international trade and investment, political economy, and public policy. Currently he is a senior research fellow of the Institute of South Asian Studies at the National University of Singapore. He has a decade's experience handing macroeconomic policy issues at India's Ministry of Finance. His latest book is *China–India Economics: Challenges, Competition and Collaboration* (Routledge, 2012) and his forthcoming book is on the Trans-Pacific Partnership (TPP) and its implications for China and India. His work has been published in peer-reviewed academic journals and he writes regularly for India's *Financial Express*, *China Daily*, and *The Business Times*.

BACKGROUND

Asia's efforts to move toward a common regional currency appear to have stalled. Although the Asian financial crisis of 1997 created the tempo for greater monetary policy and exchange rate coordination in the region, large heterogeneities in economic structures, policies, and institutions among regional economies have prevented decisive moves to a common currency. Asia lacks appropriate institutions for adopting common monetary policies and moving to a single currency. The problems faced by the euro have further diminished the prospects for a single currency in the region.

The key challenges facing implementation of a single currency for Asia are:

- the Asian financial crisis of 1997, the need for greater policy coordination, the Chiang Mai Initiative, and the Asian Currency Unit (ACU);
- ASEAN's centrality in a common Asian currency and its lack of enabling conditions;
- the difference in exchange rate arrangements in the region;
- the question as to whether Asia could even contemplate a single currency, when the euro faces crisis despite covering a more homogeneous economic region.

One of the consequences of the prolonged economic contraction and financial downturn in Europe is the skepticism it has engendered about the prospects of a unified regional currency in Asia. There was a time when Asia was seriously considering the prospect of adopting a common currency. But the troubles of the euro have made the South East Asian economies wary of currency unification. South East Asia, or more specifically the ASEAN group of economies, is central to moves toward a single Asian currency. The lack of enthusiasm of the ASEAN on a common legal tender for the region underscores the erosion in credibility that the concept of a single regional currency has suffered following the European crisis.

THE 1997 ASIAN FINANCIAL CRISIS AND THE BIRTH OF THE CHIANG MAI INITIATIVE

The beginnings of a common currency in Asia can be traced to the Asian financial crisis of 1997. The crisis drove home the importance of greater policy coordination among the regional economies, particularly the large economies of North East, South East and South Asia. These regions comprise several large economies such as Japan, South Korea, China, Taiwan, Hong Kong, Singapore, Malaysia, Indonesia, Thailand, and India. Most of these countries were affected by the crisis of 1997, though not in equal measure. Economies like China and India suffered relatively less because of their limited integration with the global financial system. Nonetheless, the urgency of policy coordination was realized by all the economies notwithstanding the difference in the degree of the difficulty they encountered.

A major driver of greater policy and institutional coordination among the regional economies was their disappointment with the policy responses of the IMF during the crisis. The crisis highlighted the importance of the region being self-sufficient in warding off contagion-type situations precipitated by speculative attacks on national currencies. This realization gave birth to the Chiang Mai Initiative (CMI). The CMI created a pool of reserve currency and extended bilateral credit swaps to participating members. The reserve pool and the swaps are intended to help regional central banks to maintain the stability of their currencies in the event of speculative attacks. The CMI has 13 participating economies, which include the 10 ASEAN members (Brunei, Cambodia, Laos, Malaysia, Myanmar, Indonesia, the Philippines, Singapore, Thailand, and Vietnam), China (including the Hong Kong Monetary Authority), Japan, and South Korea. It has been decided that the current corpus of the CMI should be doubled, from US$120 billion to US$240 billion.

The move on the CMI was accompanied by the first steps for forming an Asian currency unit (ACU) in the middle of the last decade. Following the interest expressed by China, Japan, and South Korea in greater coordination of their currencies at the annual meeting of the Asian Development Bank in May 2006, the idea of an ACU was formally floated. The ACU is statistically conceptualized as a basket of currencies reflecting the movements of various national currencies against a numeraire currency. This was expected to be a precursor to an eventual common currency in Asia. However, the move to a common currency has been sluggish for several reasons. Many of these relate to typical features of the region and its economies.

IS ASIA READY?

On paper, a common currency has several benefits for Asia. These include more seamless integration of trade and capital flows within the region. This follows from avoiding costs of invoicing products and services in different currencies when they cross borders. Apart from cutting transaction costs of paperwork and procedures, a single currency also helps traders to avoid the risks of exchange rate fluctuations. These risks often force traders to hedge against fluctuations by entering into futures contracts. More predictability and less uncertainty are clear benefits of a common currency. Given that the region has extensive intraregional trade, a common currency should ideally be a welcome option.

The early moves toward the ARU involved China, Japan, South Korea, and the 10 ASEAN economies. This is the ASEAN + 3 grouping that spans across South East Asia and North East Asia. How feasible is it for the group to work toward a common currency?

The ASEAN is the most cohesive regional grouping in Asia. But it is different from the European Union in several respects. The most important difference, perhaps, is the lack of regional institutions with the capacity to serve as overarching regulators. The ASEAN secretariat is hardly equivalent

"In the end we beat them with Levi 501 jeans. Seventy-two years of Communist indoctrination and propaganda was drowned out by a three-ounce Sony Walkman." P. J. O'Rourke

  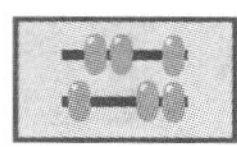   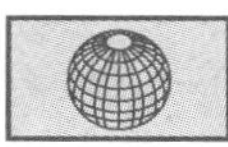   

to the European Commission. More importantly, ASEAN does not have the equivalent of a European Central Bank. Individual ASEAN members continue to retain sovereignty over their monetary policies. Such sovereignty must be sacrificed if the move to a common currency is to be made.

Progress on a common currency is inseparable from progress on regional integration. The conditions for moving to a common currency must take shape within the ASEAN, which is the most visible structure of a regional bloc in Asia. If ASEAN cannot produce the enabling conditions for a common currency, it is difficult to perceive how the ASEAN + 3 can do so. This appears all the more difficult given that South Korea, Japan, and China are unlikely to agree easily on various aspects of convergence of their monetary policies and exchange rate management.

The EU experience shows that some members can retain their individual currencies. Those EU members outside the Eurozone, such as the United Kingdom, Denmark, Switzerland, and Sweden, have different currencies. Can Asia adopt such a system? Reproducing the current EU structure with similar features would require creating a "eurozone" within Asia. More specifically, in the context of the ASEAN + 3, either the ASEAN or a subgroup within ASEAN needs to replicate the "eurozone" by giving up sovereignties on monetary and exchange rate policies and establishing a supranational regulator to manage the group collectively. Such a scenario appears distant within the ASEAN.

The milestones that have been mentioned to achieve the ASEAN Economic Community (AEC) by 2015 do not include steps for moving to a single currency. The plan proposes the establishment of a regional economic zone enabling free flows of goods, services, capital, investment, and labor. But it refrains from proposing more ambitious plans of monetary policy convergence or establishing a regional regulator for managing monetary policy and moving toward a common currency. Indeed, it does not even propose the establishment of a parallel currency on the lines of the ACU. Similarly, the idea of a common currency does not find mention in other regional economic integration initiatives, such as the one being pursued by the East Asia Summit.

It appears that ASEAN and the Asian region are not yet ready to embrace the notion of a common currency. One of the main reasons for the unwillingness is the heterogeneity among the economies. There are considerable differences within the ASEAN economies in the degree of economic development and in their economic structures. The relative differences increase if the pool is enlarged to include China, Japan, South Korea, India, Australia, and New Zealand. Apart from the obvious differences in economic features and the nature of economic institutions, there are noticeable differences in the economic policy management systems as well.

One of the best examples of the heterogeneity in the region in the context of a single currency is the difference between the exchange rate systems of the various economies. While most economies follow the floating exchange rate system, there are variations in the nature of the float. Many prefer the "managed" float where, despite allowing the exchange rates of national currencies to be market-determined, central banks intervene at periodic intervals to influence the values of the currencies through their sales and purchases. The interventions are usually influenced by the desire to control large appreciations of currencies, which can erode the competitiveness of a country's goods and services.

Indonesia, Malaysia, Thailand, and India are examples of managed floats, while Japan and South Korea have more free floats, in contrast to the "peg" arrangements of China and Vietnam. In several countries of South East Asia, such as Cambodia, Myanmar, Indonesia, and Vietnam, the US dollar is unquestionably accepted as the legal tender. With such wide differences in exchange rate regimes and monetary policy frameworks, moving to a common currency through convergence of institutions and systems is seemingly difficult.

THE EFFECTS OF THE EURO CRISIS

The prospects for a common Asian currency have received a considerable setback after the problems experienced by the euro. The financial crisis in the Eurozone—particularly the difficulties suffered by relatively smaller euro economies like Greece, Portugal, and Ireland—has raised serious doubts over the effectiveness of currency integration in facilitating greater integration of trade and investment within a region. If the Eurozone and the euro, with the Eurozone's much greater institutional, systemic, social, and political similarities than the ASEAN + 3, could not avoid a financial catastrophe, then the possibility of any such arrangement in Asia is far less likely.

Indeed, common currencies can probably work only if member countries have a lot in common. There is no denying that noncommonalities among the ASEAN + 3, and among the even greater Asian region that includes India, Australia, and New Zealand, are too much to even contemplate formal and common exchange management structures. Apart from economic dissimilarities, matters are further complicated by delicate political and strategic dynamics. The China–Japan–South Korea grouping, for example, harbors considerable political volatility. The Eurozone was free from such pressures. Even then, the members' economies are finding it difficult to stick to the euro.

The euro crisis also reveals the importance of institutional support in times of trouble. The European Central Bank has tried its best to support the affected countries. But probably that is not enough. It will be unwise of Asia to contemplate a common currency unless the regional institutions are strong enough to sustain multiple bailouts. This will require the growth of contingency measures far larger than the current Chiang Mai corpus.

FINAL THOUGHTS

The outbreak of the global financial crisis and the troubles faced by the euro initially raised hopes for the emergence of a common currency in Asia and its gradual growth as a global reserve currency. However, Asia does not appear to be ready for currency integration. Several limitations are hampering a regional currency union, including the large economic, social, and institutional heterogeneities in the region. Countries seem unprepared to converge on common exchange rate management systems and monetary policy frameworks. The region also lacks strong institutions for coordinating monetary and exchange rate policies. The failure of several Eurozone economies to manage their monetary and fiscal health, despite operating in a far more homogeneous region than Asia, has made the already remote possibility of a single Asian currency even more distant.

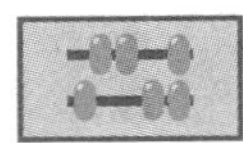

MORE INFO

Book:

Das, Sanchita Basu (ed). *Achieving the ASEAN Economic Community 2015*. Singapore: Institute of Southeast Asian Studies (ISEAS), 2012. Online at: muse.jhu.edu/books/9789814379656

Articles:

Grenville, Stephen. "The euro crisis: Lessons for East Asia." *The Interpreter* (November 29, 2011). Online at: tinyurl.com/q8u6s77

Henning, C. Randall. "The future of the Chiang Mai Initiative: An Asian monetary fund." Policy brief PB09-5. Peterson Institute for International Economics, February 2009. Online at: www.piie.com/publications/pb/pb09-5.pdf

Sen Gupta, Abhijit. "Prospects for a single Asian currency." *Public Policy Review* 6:5 (June 2010): 873–892. Online at: tinyurl.com/oo2kohy [PDF].

Sen Gupta, Abhijit, and Amitendu Palit. "Feasibility of an Asian currency unit." Working paper no. 208. Indian Council for Research on International Economic Relations (ICRIER), March 2008. Online at: tinyurl.com/oyd5drt [PDF].

Website:

Chiang Mai Initiative (Wikipedia): en.wikipedia.org/wiki/Chiang_Mai_Initiative

See Also:

★ Viewpoint: The Tragedy of the Euro (pp. 254–256)

"You cannot go to sleep with one form of economic system and wake up the next morning with another."
Mikhail Gorbachev

     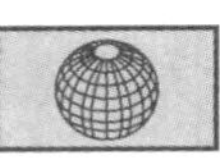   

Solvency II—A New Regulatory Framework for the Insurance Sector by Paul Barrett and Daniel Byrne

EXECUTIVE SUMMARY

This article examines:

- The aims of Solvency II.
- Setting risk-based capital requirements.
- Embedding risk management.
- Current timeline for implementation.
- Solvency II's impact on global insurance supervision.

OVERVIEW

Solvency II is a pan-European regulatory framework which, as described by the now-replaced UK Financial Services Authority (FSA), "aims to establish a revised set of EU-wide capital requirements, valuation techniques, and risk management standards" to replace the current Solvency I regime. It will apply to all insurance companies across the EU with a gross premium income exceeding €5 million.

In being developed at the European level, Solvency II aims to implement a level playing field of insurance regulation (a concept referred to as "maximum harmonization") and as a whole improve the quality and focus of the supervision of the insurance industry across the region.

THE STRUCTURE

One of the features of Solvency II that most have heard of but may not be entirely clear on is the "three pillars" approach. In short, Pillar 1 involves insurance companies demonstrating that they have adequate resources to support the business that they are writing. Pillar 2 revolves around systems of governance and in particular firms fully embedding a comprehensive risk management framework, while Pillar 3 focuses on both regulatory reporting and public disclosure requirements.

The most important feature of Solvency II is that it is a risk-based regulatory regime: Capital requirements are related to the risk profile of an insurance entity, instead of being set in an arbitrary way on a country-by-country basis by the national regulators and legislators. Higher risks will lead to a higher capital requirement. Solvency II allows firms to calculate their risk-based capital requirement (solvency capital requirement, or SCR) either through a set pan-industry calculation (standard formula) or through an "internal model," an entity-specific capital calculation.

It should be noted that firms can only calculate their SCR with an internal model if they have received approval from their local regulator. Given the role capital modeling (under Basel II) had in the 2008 financial crisis, the level of regulatory review (both initially and on an ongoing basis) of firms' internal models will be comprehensive and the burden is placed on the firm to demonstrate their internal model provides an appropriate reflection of their risk profile. The SCR is the first threshold of regulatory capital; the minimum capital requirement (MCR) is the ultimate backstop and is consistently calculated for all firms. Where a firm breaches the MCR it can expect significant regulatory intervention, including being closed to write new business.

A second feature of the Solvency II framework is a greater focus on insurance groups (as opposed to separate legal entities). The existing Solvency I regime, being on a state-by-state basis, finds it impossible to consider groups operating on a pan-European basis, from the perspective of group capital adequacy.

The third key feature is the increased focus on risk management and in particular the development of the "own risk and solvency assessment" (ORSA). The ORSA requires firms to bring together their business planning, capital plan, and risk management framework to assess and understand their key drivers of risk, both at that point in time and on a forward-looking basis (3 to 5-year time horizon).

TIMELINE TO IMPLEMENTATION

In July 2007, the European Union (EU) introduced the Framework Directive for Solvency II (the first of three "levels" of regulatory requirements). The new regulatory regime aims to be a "modern, risk-based, supervisory framework for the regulation of European insurance and reinsurance companies."

Since the publication of the Solvency II Directive there have, however, been multiple false starts in the implementation of Solvency II. Not only have Levels 2 and 3 (the more granular regulatory requirements) not been finalized, but in fact following the ratification of the Treaty of Lisbon, the Level 1 Solvency II Directive itself has had to be redrafted to align with other legislative developments in the EU. What started as a straightforward update to the legalese of the directive has in fact opened a Pandora's Box of national interest and industry uncertainty. The challenges of setting a consistent regulatory framework that improves prudential regulation across the diverse insurance markets of Europe has proved a significant hurdle.

The latest timeline for Solvency II realistically sets implementation at January 2016 or potentially later. In the interim period, the European Insurance and Occupational Pensions Authority (EIOPA) has produced a set of guidelines for national regulators to transition their industries to the Solvency II regime. For example, in the United Kingdom, the Prudential Regulation Authority (PRA), the successor to the FSA, are utilizing their Individual Capital Assessment (ICA) framework to continue to assess firms' internal models and readiness for Solvency II.

The EIOPA guidelines for transitioning to Solvency II focus on a number of the more stable aspects of the regulations, namely, internal model pre-application, systems of governance, the ORSA, and reporting requirements. The guidelines require national regulators to assess firm preparedness from 2014 onwards across each of these areas.

IMPACTS FURTHER AFIELD—SETTING NEW GLOBAL STANDARDS

The key facets of Solvency are at the leading edge of global insurance supervision. Accordingly, the global representative of insurance regulators, the International Association of Insurance Supervisors (IAIS), has utilized aspects of Solvency II within its Insurance Core Principles (ICP) initiative. National regulators that are members of the IAIS are required to comply with these high-level ICPs. As such, one of the Solvency II requirements that has reached the global stage is the ORSA. Countries including the United States, Canada, Bermuda, Singapore, Mexico, and others are currently developing—and in some cases implementing—their own ORSA requirements.

CONCLUSION

Whilst there is still uncertainty around the final implementation date of the full Solvency II regulatory regime, activity at the national supervisory level continues, with local regulators implementing and embedding aspects of the framework in preparation for implementation. In spite of the costs of preparing for Solvency II to date, the benefits it has provided to the industry should not be underestimated. Expediting firms' modeling capabilities, and hence their understanding of their risk profiles, has yielded a powerful tool in the form of the internal model. The ability to more accurately assess and price risk results in real benefits throughout the operations of insurance firms. From being a key input in underwriting decisions to optimizing reinsurance structures and investment portfolios.

As such, aspects of Solvency II such as the internal model and ORSA should be seen as more than just regulatory exercises and more as fundamental risk management tools to aid all aspects of the business. So in spite of the delays and uncertainty in the Solvency II regime itself, the principles that underlie it are already having real impacts in the insurance industry globally.

MORE INFO

Websites:

Association of British Insurers on Solvency II: tinyurl.com/olez42t

European Union guidelines on Solvency II: tinyurl.com/2usz3wb

See Also:

★ Enterprise Risk Management and Solvency II (pp. 173–176)

✔ The EU Regulatory Regime (p. 1029)

✔ Solvency II: Its Development and Aims (p. 1053)

Insurance (pp. 1633–1635)

"Trickle-down theory—the less than elegant metaphor that if one feeds the horse enough oats, some will pass through to the road for the sparrows." J. K. Galbraith

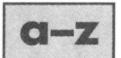

Viewpoint: Staying in the Dark about Derivatives Will Bring Economic Collapse by Hernando de Soto

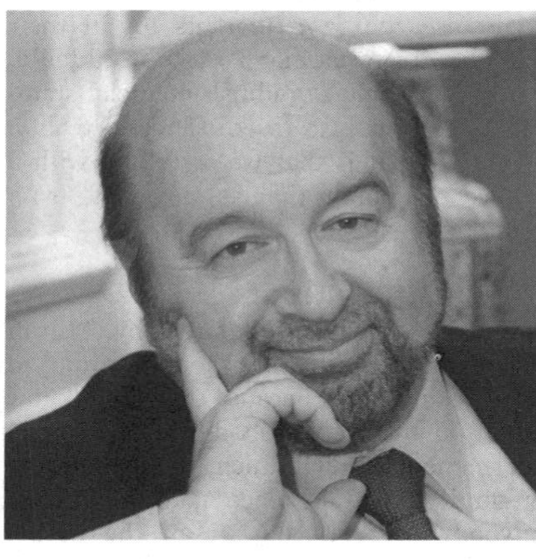

INTRODUCTION

Hernando de Soto is president of the Institute for Liberty and Democracy (ILD)—headquartered in Lima, Peru—considered by *The Economist* as one of the two most important think tanks in the world. Currently, he is focused on designing and implementing capital formation programs to empower the poor in Africa, Asia, Latin America, the Middle East, and former Soviet nations. He also co-chaired the Commission on Legal Empowerment of the Poor, and currently serves as honorary co-chair on various boards and organizations, including the World Justice Project.

De Soto has served as an economist for the General Agreement on Tariffs and Trade, as president of the executive committee of the Copper Exporting Countries Organization (CIPEC), as CEO of Universal Engineering Corporation, as a principal of the Swiss Bank Corporation Consultant Group, and as a governor of Peru's Central Reserve Bank.

De Soto has published two books about economic and political development, *The Other Path* and *The Mystery of Capital: Why Capitalism Triumphs in the West and Fails Everywhere Else*.

CRISIS FROM DERIVATIVES

When US Treasury Secretary Henry Paulson initiated his Troubled Assets Relief Program (TARP) in the midst of the financial crisis in October 2008, most of us thought that the objective was to identify and weed out the nonperforming derivatives (the "troubled assets") held by financial institutions so as to restore trust in the market.

Three weeks later, when I asked my friends in the US government why Paulson had switched his strategy to injecting hundreds of billions of dollars into struggling financial institutions, I was told that there were so many idiosyncratic types of paper scattered helter-skelter around the world that no one had any clear idea of how many there were, where they were, or who was finally accountable for them. So dispersed and jumbled up, these derivative securities were no longer connected to the assets that they had been originally derived from.

To me, this admission was shocking. But an even bigger shock was that my Western friends were not shocked.

Suddenly, I recognized that Western governments had allowed a massive shadow economy to grow up in the heart of Western democracies, crowding out their legal economies. I realized this was probably a turning point for Western civilization, which had beaten back its shadow economies to make way for the Industrial Revolution: many of the gains that they had made in the subsequent centuries were now slipping away.

RECORD-KEEPING IN THE WEST

One of the things that I have long admired about the West was that everything was recorded, on paper, as a piece of property. That included every stretch of land, building, car, plane, home, movie script, every bond, and every stock. It was the main reason why the West became so prosperous in the 19th and 20th centuries. From the development of land registries and a record-keeping system that worked, immense rewards flowed.

Over time, a group of wise men, including Eugen Huber in Switzerland and Charles Coquelin in France, made possible the extended division of labor and specialization by building standardized property recording systems that allowed everyone to know who controlled what and in what manner, and how people were relating to each other economically. They refined that over the years and overlaid it with the idea of further organizing labor and capital through the limited liability corporation. As a result, all that economic information got into the public memory. And it was organized so that you could track all the pieces that entered the market all of the time and could infer what was going on.

This creation of a "public memory system" was essentially an information revolution, just as significant as the one precipitated by Bill Gates. This information revolution was really about how to package information into standard statements that can be tested for truth.

The model was refined as Western economies emerged from feudalism. Everything was reported. And not just reported once. Every time it changed hands, it was reported. It's not just who owns what but who has a vested interest in what and where that's located. And critically this evolving public memory system left space for leveraging, because investors and creditors got a sense of how the value of things could increase if appropriately combined.

OPAQUENESS CREEPS BACK

Finance existed to support production, to back real recorded assets. Adam Smith wrote that finance was the wheel that brings in resources from the savers to the producing people who need it.

Then, along came derivatives, together with the opaqueness they encourage, and this well-tested public memory system was allowed to be turned on its head. Partly, thanks to finance-industry-friendly legislation, such as the Commodity Futures Deregulation Act in 1999, a situation arose where derivative contracts no longer had to be recorded, tracked, or even tied to the assets that represented.

The Basel-based Bank for International Settlements has estimated that there could be more than $1 quadrillion of derivatives in circulation; the US Securities Exchange Commission (SEC) figures the total could be more than $600 trillion. Either way, the value of this paper dwarfs US GDP of $15 trillion and global GDP of $60 trillion. I believe this is the real reason for the developed world's financial crisis. It is an epistemological problem, a problem of knowledge—of no longer having facts to rely on.

An unsupervised derivatives market together with credit default swaps that are impossible to trace, off-balance sheet vehicles, and mathematical models that have replaced record-keeping have made the lives of some financiers so much more exciting.

Add to that the use of swaps employing derivatives, which were used by Greece to push its debts and liabilities forward into the future, and financial institutions

"During its rule of scarce one hundred years, capitalism has created more massive and more colossal productive forces than have all preceding generations together." Karl Marx

were able to pretend that they had something on your books that they didn't—and they could use accounting trickery to downplay their true indebtedness and to inflate the value of their assets. Or they could use the repo markets to fill their banks with imaginary cash. Suddenly, banks were able to publish financial statements that bore no resemblance to reality. The net result is that we ended up with a fantasy economy that is detached from economic reality.

CREDIT CRUNCH

A credit crunch is defined by Milton Friedman as when banks don't want to provide any credit because they don't know whom to give it to. A shadow economy is a "permanent credit crunch," a place where credit does not take place. You cannot trust anybody because you are in the dark—nobody knows the value of anything, where anything is, or who owns what.

Governments in the developed economies still seem to think that they can resolve such a crisis by pumping more stimulus money into the system. But if nobody wants to borrow, this is doomed to fail. Deflation makes people even more reluctant to borrow. The value of buildings continues to fall in the United States. Why would anyone borrow money to buy something the value of which is falling?

Money is not simply created by the printing presses. Ultimately, cash has to represent something real, not because we can actually touch it—you can't after all touch or photograph "energy" or "capital"—but because the levels of certification are such that you know that it's for real. Both credit and capital ultimately depend on this.

THE FUTURE

So the important thing to keep in mind is that, in the period of 1800–1999, Europe, the United States, and other Western countries developed a large market economy that was, to a large extent, based on clear records and laws about who owns what, and what for. But since 1999, you have thrown this legacy out the window. You lost sight of the fact that having a reliable public memory system of record-keeping, to store an enormous amount of factual information on how knowledge and assets are divided worldwide, is critical to economic success.

One day, you're going to have to acknowledge that you have many times the gross national product of the world in pieces of paper that don't correspond to anything that can be meaningfully identified. That is going to lead you absolutely nowhere, except into a deep and lasting crisis.

The only reason the show remains on the road currently is the assumption that government will always be there to backstop the financial system—with further bailouts, further stimulus. But you must understand that the $600–700 trillion in the shadow banking system is much more than all the governments in the world can afford! There's no way they're going to be able to assume all those "assets." And when that truth becomes widely clear, there will be another collapse—unless the world is square.

It would seem that most economists confidently assert that everything will be just fine if we accelerate the printing of money, that everything must be alright given the banks are being cleaned out, that bad banks will be replaced with good ones. But they continue to ignore the elephant in the room.

Government's main duty now is to bring the whole toxic environment under the rule of law. No economic activity based on the public trust should be allowed to operate outside the general principles of property law.

Financial institutions should be forced to serve society and fully report what they own and what they owe—just like the rest of us—so that we get the facts necessary to find a way out of this maze. They must begin learning to put on paper statements about facts, instead of statements about statements.

A friend in the United States claimed to me that it doesn't really matter: "We are a great nation with two oceans, lots of great people, and tremendous natural resources." I said: "Are you talking about the United States or Mexico? Both have these features. What is different between them is that in the United States, everything is recorded, everything is in its place, and you can organize according to paper and according to law. That is what you're losing now. If you go on like that, you will get a lot closer to becoming Mexico!"

SIX STANDARDS TO SAVE FINANCIAL MARKETS

What are the standards behind good property law that are needed in these new, innovative markets?

To bring the financial market out of the shadows, you've got to put it under the rule of law, ensuring that all financial paper relating to assets is in sync with economic reality and follows a set of at least six well-accepted legal standards:

1. All documents and the assets and transactions they represent or are derived from must be recorded in publicly accessible registries.
2. The law must take into account the "externalities" or side-effects of all financial transactions according to the legal principle of *erga omnes* ("toward all").
3. Every financial deal should be tied to the real performance of the asset from which it originates. By aligning debts to assets, it becomes possible create benchmarks for detecting whether a transaction has been created to help production or just to bet on the performance of distant "underlying assets."
4. Governments should never forget that production always takes priority over finance. As Adam Smith and Karl Marx both recognized, finance supports wealth creation, but in itself creates no value.
5. Governments can encourage assets to be leveraged, transformed, combined, recombined and repackaged into any number of tranches, provided the process intends to improve the value of the original asset. This has been the rule for awarding property since the beginning of time.
6. Governments should no longer tolerate the use of opaque and confusing language in the drafting of financial instruments. All obligations and commitments that stick are derived from words recorded on paper with great precision.

This is an edited version of a speech given by Professor Hernando de Soto at the inaugural Zermatt Summit in June 2010.

MORE INFO

See Also:

★ Credit Derivatives—The Origins of the Problem (p. 156)
★ Dangers of Corporate Derivative Transactions (p. 36)
★ Viewpoint: Derivatives Regulation Threatens to Damage Pension Funds and Pensioners across Europe (pp. 161–162)
✔ Derivatives Markets: Their Structure and Function (p. 1007)
Options, Futures, and Other Derivatives (p. 1405)
Traders, Guns, and Money: Knowns and Unknowns in the Dazzling World of Derivatives (p. 1427)

"The twentieth century marks the turning point from the old capitalism to the new, from the domination of capital in general to the domination of financial capital." Vladimir Ilich Lenin

  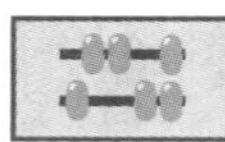   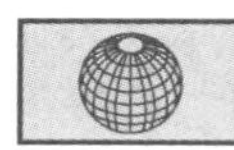   

Viewpoint: Toward a Deeper Understanding of Risk in the Insurance Sector by Alex McNeil

INTRODUCTION

Alex McNeil is the Maxwell professor of mathematics at Heriot-Watt University, Edinburgh. He was formerly assistant professor at ETH Zurich. Professor McNeil has a BSc from Imperial College, London, and a PhD in mathematical statistics from Cambridge University. He has published papers in leading statistics, econometrics, finance, and insurance mathematics journals and is a regular speaker at international risk management conferences. He is joint author of the book Quantitative Risk Management: Concepts, Techniques and Tools (2005). Professor McNeil is the director of the Scottish Financial Risk Academy, which aims to provide financial service companies with an efficient, streamlined framework for exploring complex issues of risk and related topics, in partnership with academia.

In 2010 you were instrumental in the setting up of the Scottish Financial Risk Academy, a forum for academics with expertise in risk management, to work with the finance sector to enhance the understanding of various forms of financial risk. How has that progressed?

In September 2011 the Scottish Financial Risk Academy held its third biannual colloquium, where we had speakers from academia, industry, and regulatory bodies. The focus of the colloquium was Solvency II, the new regulatory standard for the insurance industry. The implementation date for Solvency II is 2013, and institutions across the sector are currently involved in trying to understand both how Solvency II will affect them specifically, and in looking at a number of outstanding issues with Solvency II that have yet to be resolved. What came out of the colloquium was a clear sense that there are still one or two ongoing challenges with Solvency II. We looked at the outstanding technical issues and how they might be best addressed.

In particular there are a lot of questions about MCV, or market-consistent valuation. There are well-known concerns from the regulator on the procyclical effects of marking to current value, where you mark up the value of your liabilities when interest rates are low and mark down the value of your assets in falling markets. The net effect of this when you have a situation such as we saw in October 2011, when falling markets were accompanied by continuing ultra-low interest rate regimes, is of course to make the solvency position of any institution look considerably worse than it might turn out to be. The risk is that the view provided by marking-to-market may prompt dramatic interventions on issues that may well not require action. One result could be that a regulator could end up calling for capital ratios to be enhanced at exactly the time when this would hurt firms the most.

Does the fact that the life sector, for example, writes extremely long-term contracts pose particular challenges?

One of the characteristics of the insurance industry is that organizations have long-term liabilities going into the future, and how they value these liabilities can have a really material impact on views of the solvency of those organizations. No one is arguing that the industry should move away from MCV, but it is recognized that certain kinds of liability are very hard to replicate or hedge, particularly when the maturity date for the liability could be like 30 to 40 years in the future. It is clear that mathematical techniques have a very important contribution to make here.

Another debate in the industry is how to account for liquidity in the valuation of liabilities. There is still some debate as to whether liabilities can in fact be valued in a way that respects the fact that insurance companies will back their liabilities with the cheapest assets possible. They can pursue buy-and-hold strategies with less liquid assets, such as off-the-run securities rather than on-the-run, and they can use the asset cash flows to cover liability outgoings. Because these assets are cheaper for them to obtain, they want to have this taken into account in the valuation of long-dated liabilities. So the question arises as to what value to place on liquidity as an end in itself. There is a tremendous amount of literature on the theme of liquidity premiums.

In essence, the liquidity premium is the difference between the prices of a liquid and an illiquid asset, assuming both to be equivalent. The more liquid asset is easier to deal in and has correspondingly lower dealing costs. It follows from this is that liquid assets trade at a premium over more illiquid assets, and that premium, arguably, needs to be taken into account when matching assets against future liabilities. This is just one complexity among many when computing the solvency position of an insurance company.

Are you satisfied with the approach taken by Solvency II?

Solvency II is all about computing the organization's capital and showing how the company's balance sheet can change over a one-year horizon. To do this, you project the economy forward one year, and within your projections of the economy a whole distribution of scenarios arise as to how fundamental risk factors are likely to impact the organization's solvency. These risk factors include the yield curve for government bonds, the way credit spreads might develop through the year, and anything else that can have a material bearing on assets and liabilities.

Projecting these outcomes one year forward in time allows you to revalue the assets and liabilities that make up your balance sheet. Because there is no simple valuation formula for many balance sheet positions, this means that you have to mark-to-model, based on your model assumptions, in a risk-neutral way. To do this, the most popular method today is to use Monte Carlo valuation techniques, which involves averaging pay-offs and cash flows over many risk-neutral scenarios. The projection of values then becomes a problem in nested simulations, with each of the outer simulation points representing a scenario for the way in which the world might develop over one year and each of the inner simulations relating to a risk-neutral projection into the

"The system of private property is the most important guarantee of freedom, not only for those who own property, but scarcely less for those who do not." Friedrich August von Hayek

more distant future. Moreover, each of these scenarios is inherently multivariate: at the same time as you project forward a possible scenario for the different values that might comprise the yield curve one year on, you will also be looking at dependencies and relationships with stock market valuations and credit risk projections, and so on. This is a very complex, iterative mathematical calculation exercise with many moving parts, as it were.

The ideas that lie behind the famous Black–Scholes formula for valuing derivatives lie behind much of the way the industry approaches this problem. However, with complex insurance products—such as unit-linked products where payouts are linked to stock market returns—there is no simple formula that you just plug the numbers into, in the way that options traders, for example, use Black–Scholes to generate values for call and put options. We are dealing with products like variable annuities, and you have to compute the discounted payouts by simulation. There is no way of avoiding the fact that in projecting values one has to grapple with the problem of nested simulations.

Nested simulations can become very complex very quickly. How tractable is this for modeling the risks facing the insurance sector?

This is a problem that is particularly pertinent to the insurance sector but is not unique to the sector. It also occurs in banking where you have to project the value of derivative contracts that include, for example, structured credit instruments such as credit default obligations (CDOs). Some people argue that it is a problem that will go away as computers get more powerful. The argument is that all that is required is sufficient computing power to run, say, 10,000 nested simulations, which gives you 100 million potential outcomes.

However, at this point in time finding workable mathematical workarounds to do brute-force calculations is both attractive and logically plausible. The brute-force approach means tying up computer resources for long runs, whereas using, say, the least-squares Monte Carlo approach is a neat alternative that delivers acceptable approximations to what you would get with brute force.

Remember that the primary goal of Solvency II is to demonstrate that 99.5% of the time the organization is going to remain solvent over a one-year time frame, given a wide range of potential impacts and scenarios. Solvency II takes as its base criterion the 200-year event—in other words the organization should be able to survive the kind of adverse alignment of negative forces that is likely to occur only once every 200 years. This is equivalent to the capital standards that are used in banking and is the standard of prudence that European regulators feel is right for the insurance sector. Taking this as their guideline, the requirement then is to compute the relevant capital buffer that will enable the organization's balance sheet to be resilient to this once-in-200-years event through the course of a one-year period. The probability of the organization going insolvent, in other words, should be less than 0.5%.

This is the famous Pillar One in Solvency II, which has a three-pillar framework. Does Pillar One, the internal model, all come down to mathematics? And if it does, what is tractable and what is not tractable?

Recreating complex reality exactly is not tractable, not with our current state of technology and knowledge. So then the question is, which approaches to modeling reality, as far as insurance companies are concerned, are both tractable and practical, and at the same time sound enough for the industry to found a regulatory framework on their use?

Incidentally, the other two pillars in Solvency II are the risk culture in the firm, i.e. does it have a good risk governance structure, and the third pillar is disclosure and transparency. You should be able to look up an organization's risk numbers and see how much risk they bear and how they measure that risk.

Solvency II gives insurance companies two options. They can use the standard formula approach to calculate their capital requirements. If they do this, they don't have to do too much modeling and can just apply the formula mandated by their regulator. This formula looks at 200-year stress events for various factors, from equity market events to credit risk events, natural catastrophes, and life underwriting events—where an event would be, for example, a sudden dramatic lengthening of life expectancies, which would create much larger liabilities.

Under the standard formula approach you work out the impact of all of these and then aggregate the results using a formula. However, many companies feel that this approach overstates their capital requirements quite drastically. They prefer the second approach, which permits companies to develop an internal model. A few countries seem very keen on mandating the standard model. The United Kingdom is content to allow companies to develop internal models which are then approved by the regulator.

How does Solvency II relate to past efforts to regulate the sector?

Basel I, the initial regulatory standard for the financial services sector, was very standard formula-based. Basel II allowed some internal modeling, but was quite limited in its approach. It allowed companies to have an internal "value-at-risk" model that analyzed the organization's market risks and an internal model for the losses that might occur given defaults in its lending portfolios. What you could not have was a model that showed how these various factors might interact with each other.

Solvency II takes a different approach. It lays down principles, but it does not mandate the models to be used. This freedom to explore interrelationships in important variables, or what may be important variables, is crucial. The global financial crisis of 2008 taught us that even quite liquid markets can become illiquid and lose their depth under certain conditions. So Solvency II allows room for interpretation. At the Scottish Financial Risk Academy's latest colloquium we had some 100 representatives from some of the largest companies in the insurance industry, and the general impression of Solvency II so far was quite favorable.

However, as I said, there are still challenges to be resolved, not least of which is defining a reliable price for assets and liabilities. Undoubtedly the best approach to valuing liabilities is to look at what you would have to pay a third party to come in and take over those liabilities. Valuation according to transfer value is therefore one of the ideas in Solvency II, but that still leaves open the question of how best to compute this value. If I offered to take over your liabilities for $200 billion, you have to have some way of knowing whether this represents a just price, or an unreasonably exaggerated price. The basic principle is that the transfer value would be composed of the price of the assets that are required to replicate the liability cash flows as well as a risk margin required by the party taking on the liabilities. But of course perfect replication of liabilities is not possible, and the risk margin is also a difficult quantity to determine.

A lot of people are working hard to understand the technical, mathematical details that underlie the models that Solvency II requires. It is a given that there is quite a technical core to Solvency II, irrespective of whether you go down the standard formula approach or the internal model approach.

Do you feel that the regulators proposing Solvency II have a good grip on the challenges involved?

What is clear so far is that the regulators behind Solvency II are very knowledgeable. They have the support of a number of actuaries, and my impression as a mathematician is that they are well up to speed with the technical issues.

What we are seeking to do at the colloquia held by the Risk Academy is to fill a need for technical presentations that address all the components of solvency capital modeling, and these presentations are of benefit to both regulators and the industry. Of course, there is an unavoidable gap between the technical core of the internal models and the second pillar, which goes to the way in which the board of the organization implements the risk governance regime in the organization. One of the things that went so disastrously wrong in the financial crash, as we can now see clearly, is that the boards of major banks did not have a grasp of how badly their organizations were mispricing and undervaluing the risks they were assuming.

How the information derived in the internal models in Solvency II is passed to the board, and how this information then informs the risk governance profile of the organization, is an extremely interesting, but as yet untested, part of the regulatory mechanism. I have some confidence that major insurance companies are already having the right kinds of conversations about this issue. The role of the chief risk officer will be pretty crucial here, and we had an excellent presentation at the colloquium from Tom Wilson, the chief risk officer at Allianz, and interesting insights during the panel discussion from Raj Singh, the founder of the Chief Risk Officer forum.

There is no doubt that as we progress with the implementation of Solvency II across the industry, our understanding of risk and valuation will be considerably enhanced. Whether this will enable the sector to navigate successfully a real 200-year event when it happens remains to be seen. That will be the real test of the effectiveness of Solvency II and all the good work that has been put into it.

MORE INFO

Websites:

Chief Risk Officer (CRO) Forum: www.thecroforum.org

European Commission on Solvency II: tinyurl.com/2usz3wb

Scottish Financial Risk Academy Risk Colloquia: www.sfra.ac.uk/colloquia.php

See Also:

★ Enterprise Risk Management and Solvency II (p. 173)

★ Solvency II—A New Regulatory Framework for the Insurance Sector (p. 247)

✔ Solvency II: Its Development and Aims (p. 1053)

Insurance (pp. 1633–1635)

"Communism has failed, but capitalism has not succeeded." William Keegan

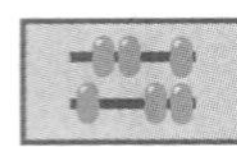

Viewpoint: The Tragedy of the Euro

by Philipp Bagus

INTRODUCTION

Philipp Bagus is a professor of economics at King Juan Carlos University in Madrid. He is also assistant editor of the journal *Procesos de Mercado: Revista Europea de Economía Política*. His main research areas are monetary theory and business cycle theory. He has published articles in numerous academic journals and other scholarly outlets. Bagus is author of *The Tragedy of the Euro* and, with David Howden, of *Deep Freeze: Iceland's Economic Collapse*.

In your book, *The Tragedy of the Euro*, you argue that the euro project actually started out as a Liberal/Christian notion and was then "captured" by the Socialist, Centrist, "big government" viewpoint. What happened?

It is quite clear that from the beginning of the European Union the advocates of two different ideals strove to impose their preferred form on the European project, and the euro is key to understanding how this struggle has played out. As I say in the book, the founding fathers of the European Union, Robert Schuman from France, Konrad Adenauer from Germany, and Italy's Alcide De Gasperi, were all German-speaking Catholics and Christian Democrats. Their ideals were the classical cultural values of Europeans and Christianity, which see sovereign European states as being the defenders of private property rights and the creators of a free market economy in a Europe of open borders. The natural boundaries of Europe, in the liberal vision, were the limits of Christian Europe.

This liberal vision's greatest achievement was the Treaty of Rome in 1957. The Treaty underlined four basic liberties for Europe: the free circulation of goods, the free offering of services, free movement of finance, and freedom of movement for European citizens. These essential rights had been achieved in Europe during the 19th century, but they were then swept aside by the age of nationalism and socialism that ended with the Second World War.

This idea of freedom is extremely powerful as a limit on "big government" philosophies. Citizens who find themselves in a socialist state that is determined to redistribute wealth through "progressive" taxation in order to build a massive welfare state would be able to vote with their feet by moving to a state with a lower tax burden. All you need to achieve this is freedom of movement for goods, people, services, and finance, together with a respect for private property.

In this vision there is not only no need to create a European superstate, such a concept is in fact antithetical to the vision. The classical liberal point of view needs many competing political systems, as had been the case in Europe for centuries. Competition on all levels is essential to the vision. It leads to coherence as product standards, factor prices (factors being all the elements, including labor, needed to create products and services) and especially wage rates, tend to converge.

Capital moves to where wages are low, bidding them up; workers on the other hand move to where wage rates are high, bidding them down. You have the basis for efficient, competitive economies, while political competition ensures the most important European value: liberty.

Self-evidently, the "superstate" approach is very much in favor of "big government," since such a state works to establish a homogeneous set of conditions within its borders. There is nowhere to move to that is different, so the citizens are "captured" and freedom of movement is rendered meaningless. Having different national tax sovereignties is the best protection against the tyranny of "big government."

Politicians who aim for big government have to have policies that appeal to the largest possible base of voters. It is natural and logical therefore for them to offer "redistributive" taxation strategies which promise a socialist "nirvana" of free housing, free education, free healthcare, and early and large pensions to all. This policy garners votes and puts socialist politicians in power, but what this strategy lacks is a way to pay for the socialist vision of a vast welfare state. As we will see, this point has returned to haunt the euro and may well be instrumental in its eventual demise. The current plight of Greece sketches out the possible fate of all.

The time-honored way for politicians—and kings and emperors before them—to pay for unaffordable policies is to produce money. The idea, or rather, the myth, of controlled inflation is therefore deeply embedded in the socialist vision ("control" is illusory since booms and busts are endemic to an inflationary stance, as Austrian business cycle theory demonstrates).

You have argued that the creation of the euro can be seen as an attempt by high-spending, high-inflation countries to get away from the tyranny of the Deutsche Bundesbank. Can you explain this?

Much of the story of the creation of the euro revolves around such high-spending, high-inflationary states—with France the paramount example—struggling to get rid of the limiting power of Germany's Bundesbank. In postwar Europe the Bundesbank—which, for historical reasons (the two periods of hyperinflation endured by Germans in the 20th century) was fixated on stable prices—became the yardstick against which all European economies were measured. It is not that the Bundesbank was not itself inflationary; rather, that it inflated at a lower rate than countries with more overtly socialist governments found desirable.

The inflationary excesses of such countries were highly visible when set against the "stability" of the Deutschmark. The exchange rates against the Deutschmark, especially of the southern European countries which used their central banks most generously to finance deficits, served as a standard of comparison. Their currencies would devalue very visibly against the Deutschmark as they attempted to inflate away their deficits. The euro was a way of ending the embarrassing comparisons and devaluations.

Importantly, although from the outside the new European Central Bank (ECB)

"What is robbing a bank compared with founding a bank?" Bertolt Brecht

would look like a copy of the Bundesbank, from the inside it could be put under political pressure and transformed over time into a central bank more like the Latin central banks. Key here is the fact that voting rights mean that southern Europe actually has control of the ECB. The council of the ECB is composed of the directors of the ECB and the presidents of the national central banks. All have the same vote. Hard-currency countries with low rates of monetary inflation, such as Germany, the Netherlands, Luxembourg, and Belgium, hold the minority of votes against countries such as Italy, Portugal, Greece, Spain, and France. These countries had strong labor unions and high debts, making them prone to wage inflation and inflation generally.

One of the great advantages of the euro to these countries is that its inflation could be conducted without any direct evidence of an appreciating Deutschmark. Under a euro regime, when prices started to rise it would be relatively easy to blame it on externalities. Fiscal mismanagement in Spain or Greece would, initially at least, be much harder to spot.

Giscard d'Estaing, founder of a lobbying group for the euro, explicitly stated in June 1992 that the ECB would finally put an end to the monetary supremacy of Germany, and added that the ECB should be used for macroeconomic growth policies—in other words, inflation. In a similar way Jacques Attali, advisor to François Mitterand, acknowledged that the Maastricht Treaty was just a complicated contract whose purpose was to get rid of the Deutschmark.

The result of the introduction of the euro was the expectation of a more stable currency for southern European countries. As a result, inflationary expectations fell in those countries. When inflation expectations rise, people reduce their cash holdings and buy today as they expect goods to be more expensive tomorrow. When inflationary expectations fall, that pressure to spend evaporates and spending falls marginally, leading to lower price inflation. This was a positive benefit for southern Europe, and these countries began to benefit as soon as it became clear that the euro would be introduced. This in turn helped them to fulfill the Maastricht euro entry criterion of low inflation rates.

Another great benefit the southern European countries enjoyed in the run-up to the euro was that investors became much more willing to buy government bonds issued by these countries. The expectation was that these bonds, which were still denominated in lira, peseta, escudo, and drachma, would be repaid in the more stable euro. As a result of the attractiveness of this proposition to investors, the rates of interest paid by southern European countries for their bonds fell. This in turn helped some of these countries to reduce their debt and helped them to meet the Maastricht entry criteria. Italy, for example, paid around €110 billion in interest on its debts in 1996. By 1999 its interest payments had fallen to €79 billion. The risk premium element of their debts fell, and the partial transfer of the prestige of the Bundesbank to the ECB made the euro a more acceptable currency than southern European national currencies.

If the southern European countries were winners in this process, it looks as if the Germans were set to be net losers. What was the attraction for them?

Germans, of course, feared that the euro would be less stable than the Deutschmark, spurring inflationary expectations. It was plain to all that the German government was in fact using the Bundesbank's monetary prestige to the benefit of the inflationary member states and to the detriment of the general German population. So the question we have to answer next is, why did the German ruling classes agree to the demise of the Bundesbank? Some polls show that up to 70% of Germans wanted to keep the Deutschmark, so why did the politicians override the will of the majority? The most feasible explanation is that giving up the Mark was seen by Germany's political class as the price of achieving reunification in 1990, after the fall of the Berlin Wall.

The negotiators at the time included the two Germanies and the winning allies, namely the United Kingdom, the United States, France, and the Soviet Union. You have to remember that Germany was still subject to domination, since no peace treaty was signed with Germany after World War II. The allies continued to have special control rights after the Potsdam Agreement of August 1945 right up until the Two Plus Four Agreement of 1991. All four occupying powers—Russia in East Germany, the United States, France, and the United Kingdom in West Germany, were atomic powers with vastly superior military forces to Germany. This despite the fact that Germany is the most populated nation in Europe, is the strongest economically, and is located in the strategic heart of Europe.

The French and British governments in particular feared the power of a unified Germany, which they saw as potentially moving to dominate Europe. For more than a decade prior to unification the Bundesbank had repeatedly forced other nations to curtail their printing presses and their inflationary ways, or to realign their foreign exchange rates. There have been a number of press articles (for example, "Mitterand forderte Euro als Gegenleistung für die Einheit" in *Spiegel Online*, September 25, 2010) which show that the French President, François Mitterrand, demanded the single currency as a condition for his agreement to unification.

Horst Teltschik, chief foreign policy advisor to Chancellor Helmut Kohl, told journalists that "the German Federal Government was now in a position that it had to accept practically any French initiative for Europe (Vaubel, 2010, p. 83). Hans Albin Larsson (2004, p. 163) points out that "The European Monetary Union [EMU, the precursor to the euro] became an opportunity for the French to get a share of German economic power. For the German Federal Chancellor Kohl, the EMU was an instrument to make the other EC member states accept the German reunion and consequently a larger and stronger Germany in the heart of Europe."

The ECB was modeled on the Bundesbank, but you suggest that it was flawed from the start. Why?

A key idea here is the "tragedy of the commons" in banking. This is a term coined by the American ecologist Garrett Hardin. First you need to grasp the idea of externalized costs. These are costs that an agent can shift to others because of poorly defined property rights. If a factory can dump waste in a private lake, it externalizes that cost to someone else. In a "tragedy of the commons" multiple agents can externalize costs. Take shoals of fish in the ocean. A fisherman benefits by fishing the shoal but reduces its size for others. Where there are multiple fishermen, they will all seek to grab as many fish as they can before the resource runs out. Hanging back does not conserve the fish since someone else will net them. In a tragedy of the commons, a resource is totally consumed because there is no defined framework for controlling access or allocating rights.

The idea can be applied to our modern banking system, where any bank can produce fiduciary media (i.e. unbacked demand deposits) by expanding its loan-making. Traditional legal principles of deposit contracts are not respected, because the bank lends out demand deposits and earns interest. The temptation to expand credit is almost irresistible. The more credits that get put into circulation, the more prices go up, so everyone in society bears the costs induced by the expansion of bank credit. There are complexities here that have to do with the relationship

"Bankers regard research as most dangerous and a thing that makes banking hazardous due to the rapid changes it brings about in industry." Charles Franklin Kettering

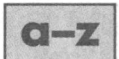

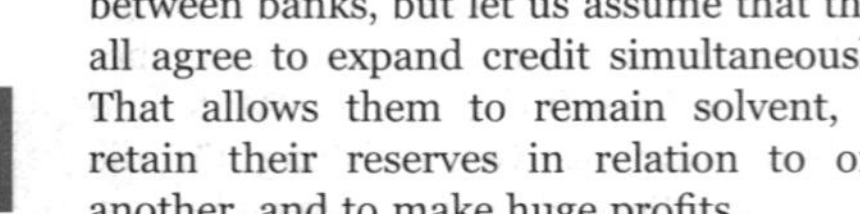

between banks, but let us assume that they all agree to expand credit simultaneously. That allows them to remain solvent, to retain their reserves in relation to one another, and to make huge profits.

Where you have a central bank, it takes over the business of coordinating credit expansion, which allows banks the freedom to expand at will—subject only to two factors. These are: the control of the central bank, which may set limits to credit expansion; and the fear of hyperinflation.

In our fishing example, the ungoverned exploitation of the common resource can be managed through the introduction of monitored fish quotas; similarly, central banks can choose to monitor and regulate the credit expansion of banks. This happens through the requirement to hold minimum reserves, control of interest rates, and so on. Now we have the introduction of the euro, which brings in a third layer to go along with the central bank as monopolistic money producer, and a fractional reserve banking system. The institutional set-up of the euro in the EMU is such that all governments can use the ECB to finance their deficits.

The ECB does this by buying government bonds directly (this policy was started only recently, in May 2010) or, which amounts to the same thing, by accepting them as collateral for new loans to the banking system. The process works like this. When governments in the EMU run deficits, they issue bonds. A substantial portion of these bonds are bought by that nation's banks. They are happy to buy their own government's bonds, because they know that the ECB will accept these bonds as collateral and will then give new money as cheap loans to the banks. What do the banks buy their government bonds with in the first place? They buy them with the new money they have created.

This is a merry-go-round. The governments finance their deficits with new money created by banks, and the banks receive new base money from the ECB by pledging the bonds as collateral. There are brakes on this process, which explains why the euro is still with us and has not yet imploded. There is the not insignificant risk that banks, even local banks, might not want to purchase the bonds of a highly indebted government, or that the ECB will not be accommodative in the production of base money.

This risk is reduced in the eurozone by the fact that the whole project is widely seen as a political project aimed at tighter European integration. The default of a member state and its exit from the euro would be seen as not only a failure of the euro, but also as a failure of the socialist version of the European Union.

We have now reached the point where the implicit guarantee that stronger states would support the weaker and not allow the euro project to fail has transformed into an explicit guarantee. We have the €110 billion bailout fund from the eurozone and the IMF and a pledge of a further €750 billion from EU member states. In addition, from May 2010 the ECB began buying government bonds outright from banks.

What we have here, then, is the tragedy of the euro, which is on a par with the tragedy of the commons. The tragedy is the incentive that governments have to incur higher deficits, and then to issue government bonds that make the whole euro group take on the cost burden of those higher deficits. The costs show up as a diminution of the purchasing power of the euro. The perverse incentive for politicians is easy to state: why pay for higher expenditure by making yourself unpopular through raising taxation? Instead, simply issue bonds that will be purchased by the creation of new money. Ultimately the process drives up prices in the whole of the EMU, but local politicians escape blame since their role in driving up prices is not clearly visible to the public.

In this way the costs of extravagant government are externalized in the EMU. Add in the fact that, in democracies, politicians tend to focus on the next election rather than the long-term effects of their policies, and you have the making of a total disaster. The EMU is, ultimately, a self-destroying mechanism.

MORE INFO

Books:

Bagus, Philipp. *The Tragedy of the Euro*. Auburn, AL: Ludwig von Mises Institute, 2010. Online at: mises.org/resources/6045/The-Tragedy-of-the-Euro

Bagus, Philipp, and David Howden. *Deep Freeze: Iceland's Economic Collapse*. Auburn, AL: Ludwig von Mises Institute, 2011. Online at: tinyurl.com/3qpd5wq

Connolly, Bernard. *The Rotten Heart of Europe: The Dirty War for Europe's Money*. London: Faber & Faber, 1997.

Huerta de Soto, Jesús. *Money, Bank Credit, and Economic Cycles*. 2nd English ed. Auburn, AL: Ludwig von Mises Institute, 2009. Online at: tinyurl.com/2ak9oww

Huerta de Soto, Jesús. *The Theory of Dynamic Efficiency*. New York: Routledge, 2009.

Larsson, H. A. "National policy in disguise: A historical interpretation of the EMU." In Jonas Ljungberg (ed). *The Price of the Euro*. New York: Palgrave MacMillan, 2004; pp. 143–170.

Marsh, David. *The Euro: The Politics of the New Global Currency*. New Haven, CT: Yale University Press, 2009.

von Mises, Ludwig. *Human Action: A Treatise on Economics*. Indianapolis, IN: Liberty Fund, 2010.

Articles:

Anon. "Mitterand forderte Euro als Gegenleistung für die Einheit" [in German]. *Spiegel Online* September 25, 2010. Online at: tinyurl.com/2vxrugn

Vaubel, R. "The euro and the German veto." *Econ Journal Watch* 7:1 (2010): 82–90. Online at: econjwatch.org/447

See Also:

★ Viewpoint: Nothing but Painful Choices Ahead as the Global Debt Supercycle Ends (p. 219)

★ Viewpoint: The Unintended Consequences of Globalization (pp. 260–262)

🌐 Germany (pp. 1496–1497)

"The business of banking ought to be simple. If it is hard it is wrong. The only securities which a banker, using money that he may be asked at short notice to repay, ought to touch, are those which are easily saleable and easily intelligible."
Walter Bagehot

  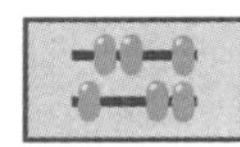      

Viewpoint: Understanding the Implications of Japan's "Two Lost Decades": Lessons for Europe and the United States by John Vail

INTRODUCTION

John Vail is Nikko Asset Management's head of global macro strategy and asset allocation and also chairs the group's global investment committee. Before joining Nikko AM in 2006, he was chief Japanese equity strategist for JPMorgan Securities Japan from 2004 and chief strategist at Mizuho Securities USA from 2000. He also held various senior research and strategy positions at Fidelity from 1985 to 1992, based in Hong Kong, Taiwan, and Japan, and covered pan-Asia equities at his own firm, Asia House Funds, for five years from 1993. Vail holds a BA from the University of Chicago.

Many commentators have warned that advanced economies, particularly in Europe, could be in for a protracted period of near-zero growth, with clear parallels with Japan's "lost two decades." As a fund strategist with deep experience of Japan, what is your view?

The first thing I would point out is that Japan is a very different place, culturally and at the level of people's attitudes and expectations, than anything you will find in Europe or the United States. So the differences between the West and Japan are at least as important as any similarities in their economic positions. Japan's differences have been both a strength and a burden in the way that they have dealt with their crisis over the last 20 years. The Japanese were very slow to recognize the depth of their crisis and slow to react to it, but throughout the people—the general public—have maintained discipline and have been very cautious in the way they deal with their household budgets. To find anything like the same level of thrift in the West you would have to go back to the 1930s and the Great Depression, when everyone was deeply concerned about the future and was counting their pennies.

However, that is certainly not the general way in the United States. There is a good deal of optimism there. Certainly there is some stress in the national psyche in the United States today, but Americans do not react in the same way as the Japanese. Of course, one of the reasons why the policy response by the Japanese has been so conservative is that the country is trapped by its huge deficit, currently around 200% of GDP. If the economy ever got too strong, or inflation rose above 2%, their interest payments would rise sharply and this would aggravate the deficit more than economic growth would help it. That is the crux of Japan's dilemma and explains much about how the Japanese government and the Bank of Japan (Japan's central bank) have conducted economic and monetary policy.

Is there not a significant parallel there with the rising level of debt in the United States? Could the United States be headed into the same trap?

The United States now faces very similar constraints. The boom years for the US economy look to be over for a very long time to come. One significant economic measure that needs to be considered is the NAIRU, or non-accelerating inflation rate of unemployment, which measures how low unemployment can be tolerated before inflation starts to rise. As the economy moves into a growth phase and more jobs are created, unemployment goes down and inflation starts to rise. But what is this rate? Usually it is thought to be a fairly fixed level of unemployment, but what US economists are starting to realize is that, even with a large unemployed base, you can still get inflation if China's growth accelerates. In other words, the level of NAIRU at which you will see inflation starting to rise is a function not just of the US economy but of its interaction with other major economies, so the critical level of NAIRU moves in a way that depends on global growth elsewhere. Experience over the past few years certainly shows that inflation can be high in the United States and Europe even though unemployment is high, and this does not seem likely to change unless global growth turns negative.

This and other factors—notably the monetization of US and European debt—suggests that deflation or zero inflation, which is part of what has characterized the Japanese situation, will not take hold in the same way. In the short term it might look as if the West is "going Japanese," but the intermediate to longer-term view suggests not. Actually, the consumer price index (CPI) in Japan has hovered around zero for a very long time. I call that "no-flation" rather than deflation. It is extremely difficult to imagine the United States tolerating "no-flation" for very long. The chairman of the Federal Reserve, Ben Bernanke, would make sure that this did not happen.

What are the advantages that Europe and the United States can draw on that were not available to Japan?

The central banks in both Europe and the United States have done a very reasonable job of pulling their respective economies out of a complete tailspin, and they did it very quickly. There are, of course, some who say that everything should have been allowed to take its "natural course" and that this would have cleared out "malinvestment" and led to a faster recovery. But apart from those voices, there is general agreement that these central banks did a good job. The same cannot be said for the Bank of Japan in the years after the stock market and property market crash. It was very slow to react, and when it did react it vacillated between tightening and loosening.

Also, the strong yen has been a big deflationary factor for Japan, which accumulated very large net investment positions in terms of ownership of overseas assets. Returning revenue flows from those assets led to large current account surpluses and the inflow of capital into Japan, which is not the same situation that the West faces.

How are Japanese companies and the Japanese stock markets performing?

The first point to be made about Japanese equities is that they have gone through a

"The experience of being disastrously wrong is salutary; no economist should be denied it, and not many are."
J. K. Galbraith

tremendous derating since Japan's bubble burst. At the peak, Japanese equities were on a multiple of 70 to 80 times earnings. Even the United States multiples never got that high. This means, in our view, that Japanese equities are now about as cheap as they are ever likely to get. Earnings multiples are now down to around 12 times earnings, which means that they are approximately one-fifth of what they used to be.

Moreover, earnings multiples are not falling just due to lower stock prices; the average earnings of all nonfinancial stocks just before the 2008 global financial crash were 50% higher than they were in 1989, at the top of the market. By the first quarter of 2011, this average figure had risen to 30% higher than in 1989. So valuations are now very acceptable, even if Japanese stocks may not look overly attractive when compared to the total universe of global stocks. Obviously, the crises of 2011 impacted earnings, but Japan is now bouncing back.

One of the common criticisms of Japanese companies is that they hold too much cash and do not return enough of it to shareholders. Another concerns the standard of corporate governance, with some recent scandals being the obvious cases in point. However, the United States and Europe too have their share of corporate governance issues, not least being executive pay and bonuses at US and European banks. One thing that one can say is that it is extremely rare for Japanese companies to have accounting problems or for Japanese companies to be forced to restate their accounts—something one sees many examples of in US listed companies. Japanese companies are very particular and detailed about their accounting.

On the issue of returning cash to shareholders, there are companies in Japan that are world class in this respect, while there are also some with a long history of being bad eggs. Japan does have a profit motive, but it is a disciplined and tempered profit motive. There is this feeling of social cohesion, and the dominance of the Japanese middle class—and middle-class values—remains strong. The dominant set of attitudes lends itself to the long view, so local investors are not too begrudging about companies retaining cash for investment. Sometimes this is abused, but we are now seeing share buybacks happening in Japan, which, of course, improves the position of anyone holding the stock since their holding is now that bit less diluted. And we have seen a tremendous improvement, dating back to around 2005, in the willingness of major Japanese companies to return value to shareholders. As I said, there are some incredibly good examples of this, and, moreover, the dividend payout ratio in Japan is equivalent to that in the United States. Share buybacks are not at US levels, but you have to remember that share buybacks in the United States are inflated by the buybacks of share options to management.

We often hear about Japan's horrendous demographic position, with the country fast approaching the point where more than 60% of the population will be over 60. Surely that is a huge drag on productivity?

Japan has a severe demographic issue and it is compounded by the fact that, unlike some other advanced economies, which look to solve the problem of too few younger workers by encouraging immigration, the Japanese population is not at all disposed to accept immigrants to any significant extent. They would rather deal with the negative ramifications of an aging population than risk losing social cohesion. This also helps them to avoid the complications that arise from the large divisions of wealth in society that often go along with an influx of immigrant labor.

The Japanese solution to the country's demographic issue has been to shift production overseas. This immediately gives companies access to the labor markets in those countries. On top of this, they are automating everything that can be automated. So an aging population remains an issue, but it is not the end of the world for the country.

The other huge issue, of course, is Japan's debt, which is approaching 200% of GDP. How do you see that playing?

I think that the fiscal deficit is unsustainable at present levels and it needs to be reduced to manageable proportions. There is a global realization among all advanced nations that benefit entitlements have to be reformed so that countries achieve sustainable gross debt positions. In this sense, Japan is a huge warning flag for Europe, but I think that Europe's political classes have achieved a great deal since the start of the sovereign debt crisis. The austerity measures introduced in Italy, Portugal, Spain, Greece, and Ireland are extensive. Greece has even introduced a reduction in the rights of collective bargaining, which is a very difficult measure to get passed in a country with a strongly socialist recent past.

There is no doubt that this is a dangerous period for European economies. It is the most painful part of the cycle. Austerity pushes economies into contraction and recession. Tax revenues go down and generate a need for further cuts, which calls for less public spending, so you get more austerity. This creates a negative cycle that takes a long time to work through. Pushing for too much austerity can create a social backlash that destroys the whole project, so things have to be managed very carefully. In this respect, Japan's social cohesion clearly puts it in a better position than many more socially fragile countries.

What we need to see in Greece, particularly, is more privatization of state-owned enterprises. They should have started with a vigorous privatization programme rather than by cutting the average person's salary. However, now that the "Germans" are running the Greek tax collection system and the budget, and with agreement having been reached on the next tranche of the bailout, there is some reason to think that Greece is on track to solving some of its problems.

"I doubt if there is any occupation which is more consistently and unfairly demeaned, degraded, denounced, and deplored than banking." William Proxmire

  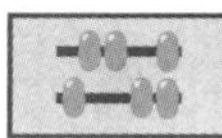      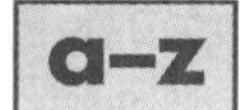

MORE INFO

Books:

Beard, Charles A. *An Economic Interpretation of the Constitution of the United States*. New York: Free Press, 1986.

McCormack, Richard (ed). *Manufacturing a Better Future for America*. Washington, DC: The Alliance for American Manufacturing, 2009.

Prestowitz, Clyde. *The Betrayal of American Prosperity: Free Market Delusions, America's Decline, and How We Must Compete in the Post-Dollar Era*. New York: Free Press, 2010.

Wanger, Ralph. *A Zebra in Lion Country: The "Dean" of Small-Cap Stocks Explains How to Invest in Small, Rapidly Growing Companies Whose Stocks Represent Good Values*. New York: Touchstone, 1999.

Zuckerman, Gregory. *The Greatest Trade Ever: The Behind-the-Scenes Story of How John Paulson Defied Wall Street and Made Financial History*. New York: Broadway Books, 2009.

See Also:

★ Viewpoint: The Challenges to Slow Growth in the Advanced Economies Just Keep Coming (pp. 147–148)

★ Viewpoint: Nothing but Painful Choices Ahead as the Global Debt Supercycle Ends (pp. 219–221)

★ Viewpoint: Steering Between Deflation and Inflation—A Troubled Road for Developed Economies (pp. 604–606)

Conquer the Crash: You Can Survive and Prosper in a Deflationary Depression (p. 1343)

Japan (pp. 1518–1520)

"There's a rumour going around that states cannot go bankrupt. This rumour is not true." Angela Merkel

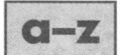

Viewpoint: The Unintended Consequences of Globalization by Paul Wharton

INTRODUCTION

As chief investment strategist for Deutsche Bank Private Wealth Management UK, Paul Wharton is responsible for economic and market strategy and the income-oriented portfolios within the bank's UK onshore discretionary portfolio service. He serves on both the UK and the global investment committees of Deutsche Bank Private Wealth Management. A passionate student of economic history, he has more than 20 years' experience of investment markets and management. He graduated from University College London in 1985 and trained with Fidelity. He subsequently completed a diploma in business studies before establishing a pensions management business in conjunction with Norwich Union. In the early 1990s Wharton was recruited by Société Générale to develop a UK division serving the rapidly growing market for investors in self-invested personal pensions. In 2003 this business was sold to Tilney Investment Management, which was itself subsequently acquired by Deutsche Bank Private Wealth Management in 2006.

Are there any winners or beneficiaries in the "currency wars" that we are currently witnessing?

We are certainly seeing a "race to the bottom" as growth economies dependent on exports try to weaken their currencies even as continuing weakness in the US dollar drives those currencies upwards. Clearly no exporter likes to see their currency strengthening unduly since it damages their ability to sell in to foreign markets. At the moment China and Germany seem to be the main winners, with Germany coming out rather better than China.

The linkage with the dollar means that the yuan weakens as the dollar weakens, and that helps to make Chinese exports even more price-competitive. However, the big negative consequence of this is that it creates serious inflation in food prices in China since the Chinese have to spend more to buy the same amount of grain. Food prices rose by a third in 2010, and this in turn threatens to lead to social unrest in China. So for them there is a very marked downside to the second round of quantitative easing (QE2) in the United States.

Germany also has its difficulties. On the one hand there is a real irony in the fact that the more the European sovereign debt crisis perturbs the markets and weakens the euro, the more it boosts Germany's burgeoning export sector. On the other hand, much of the burden for funding the bailouts falls on Germany as the European Union's biggest economy. However, since the European sovereign debt issues have very little to do with the currency wars, one would have to say that Germany will remain a net beneficiary provided that the dollar doesn't weaken too much against the euro.

Our official view is that we think that China will allow the renminbi to appreciate by around 4% against the dollar in the medium term and will allow wage costs to rise. That will put more money in the pockets of workers and will also help to rebalance the global economy. We have already seen some quite sharp wage rises in China, and more along these lines would be very helpful.

If the Chinese revalued the renminbi upward, that would lower the cost of their food imports and it would also have the beneficial effect of making the Chinese focus more on domestic consumption, since it would generate some falling off in exports. Manufacturers would have to look to sell the extra capacity locally. We have to remember that the Chinese labor force is 850 million strong. That is more than 20 times the size of the entire UK labor force. Moreover, economic commentators are starting to talk about the end of the global export model, since the big "importer of last resort," the United States, is running out of steam. It is just a simple economic fact that no country can both deleverage massively and import strongly.

This could, however, be a good thing for China in the medium term, since it should force the Chinese to become much more effective when it comes to deploying their investment cash. China has really got to stop wasting resources. The country looks like a late-cycle version of the Asian tiger economic boom, the problem there being that ever-increasing investment generated ever-smaller rates of return until we were suddenly hit by the Asian crisis of 1998. All investment booms fizzle out if consumption and final demand are not able to keep pace with the capacity that the investment is generating.

What is particularly interesting for me in all these linkages—which we see particularly vividly in the currency interrelationships—is perhaps the unexpected rather unintended consequences of globalization, where everything ends up being linked to everything else. We saw, for example, a problem in US mortgages along with a problem about excess savings in China generating massive capital flows to peripheral eurozone economies. The debt that generated cannot be revalued away, so we now have a very fragile global model.

What do you see as the route out of the eurozone crisis?

There is considerable consensus around the fact that if you want to have an orderly adjustment of the major developed economies, the fiscal stimulus that we saw in the United States, the United Kingdom, and the European Union, as well as in Japan and China, is important. The next step has to be a reappraisal of the German and Chinese economic models toward much greater domestic consumption and an expanded domestic economy. In Germany, for example, the savings ratio is around 20%. If it was that high in the United States, the United States would be sucked into a depression to rival the 1930s. So you have to get a continued expansion of global trade by growing the amount of consumption in Northern Europe and in China. Without this happening, there really does not seem to be a viable plan B that anyone has come up with.

There are some severe risks for China as well if it cannot get a grip on inflation while maintaining the 7% or so growth that it requires to keep the flow of new jobs in synch with movement of people from the countryside to the cities. Failure here carries a very high risk of social unrest which, at the least, would severely impede China's ability to drive global growth in the medium term. It is a paradox that many in

        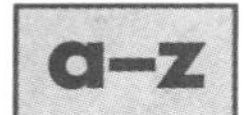

the West who regard liberal free-market capitalism as fundamental to incentivizing innovation and growth are hoping that Chinese economic development will bail out the global economy.

The other side of the coin, of course, is to accept a considerable lowering of living standards. In fact the managing director of the International Monetary Fund, Dominique Strauss-Kahn, recently warned that Europe would have to accept drastic reductions in its social care and benefits systems if it did not undertake very significant reforms that at least prepared the way for fiscal union further down the road. These are very broad-brush sketches, but they fill in a very worrying set of downside scenarios.

How is QE2, the second round of quantitative easing in the United States, going to play against a combination of factors such as the US relationship with China, currency issues, and, of course, the European sovereign debt crisis?

The way we see it is that all these linkages are very difficult to follow and the interactions among them make predicting the outcomes next to impossible. Market participants do not have a clear perspective on how this is going to end up. What we can see is that in the first round of quantitative easing, the cash that the US Federal Reserve pumped in to the system did not find its way into the real economy but instead went to boost risk assets like equities and commodities.

The second round is doing much the same so far. There is no strong demand for borrowing in the corporate sector, and where there is demand the bigger corporates are bypassing the banks and going direct to the capital markets. There is a tremendous demand for corporate debt as investors hunt for higher-yielding assets in an environment of near-zero real returns on bonds and negative returns on cash. The big risk of printing cash is that it fuels rallies in paper assets.

At the same time, by the end of November 2010 we had a resurgence in tension in the eurozone, with Irish, Spanish, Portuguese, and Greek bonds all blowing out as far as their pricing relative to German bonds was concerned.

If you look at the way the bond market is judging the European sovereign debt crisis, by the end of November 2010 you had Spanish 10-year debt at 5.15% interest, Portugal out at 6.38%, Ireland at 8.76%, and Germany at just 2.69%. Another way of summarizing things is that in terms of relative size, Greece is a toothache, Portugal and Ireland are headaches, and Spain is a death blow. There is no doubt that the markets are testing the resolve of the eurozone, and there are definite parallels here with Britain's unfortunate experience trying to defend its membership of the European exchange rate mechanism (ERM). We all know how that ended. However, I do not think that anyone should underestimate the political will in Europe to keep the euro going.

From an investment standpoint, one thing that emerges very strongly from this is that Germany will probably be one of the safest homes for investment for some time to come. We think that the United Kingdom is also well placed, with good exposure to emerging markets through the major players in the FTSE 100. So, in terms of equities, it is a good place for investors to get exposure to fast-growing markets while still having their investments in an environment of enforceable property rights and strong protection for intellectual property (IP).

The big downside risk for the medium term is an outright collapse of the US dollar as a result of rolling the printing presses. The Federal Reserve chairman, Ben Bernanke, is the world's foremost scholar on the US Great Depression. He is determined not to fall into those traps, so everything now is a mirror reverse of the policies that were pursued by the US administrations of the 1930s. This is why we are seeing the world's biggest ever expansion of "fiat" currency through the avowedly unorthodox policy of quantitative easing (a fiat currency being any currency that is not backed by gold, but simply by the market's belief in the government and economy that is issuing the money). On the positive side, it is well understood in the academic literature that those economies which came off the gold standard fastest recovered fastest.

The problem for the eurozone, however, is that the European Central Bank is wholly committed to price stability and keeping inflation close to, but under, 2%. The United Kingdom, on the other hand, has been able to effect a de facto devaluation of sterling with respect to its trade index by some 30%. In fact the monetary policy committee of the Bank of England has made it as clear as it can do that a weak pound is very much part of the United Kingdom's recovery strategy.

If we look at the eurozone, though, it is clear that Germany's extremely high productivity and competitiveness mean that the European Central Bank policy framework is just too tight for southern Europe, which is being asked to come into line with German practice. This is next to impossible. And in the absence of full fiscal union, there is no mechanism—other than the bailout funding—to effect a transfer of payments from stronger eurozone economies to weaker eurozone economies, such as you get in the United States. There really are only two options for southern European countries. Either they should have a second currency regime put in place with a floating currency rate, which would allow a basket of southern European countries to deflate, or there has to be full fiscal union. At present, nothing of the sort is on the table. This makes Europe the next official, major problem since the economic elastic is being stretched ever more tightly. If the eurozone were to split you would see an immediate flight of capital to the north followed by hyperinflation in southern European economies. No one should underestimate the savage economic distress that would result. Our house view, though, is that the chance of Europe breaking up is close to zero. The most likely scenario is bigger and bigger bailout funds to enable Europe to muddle through.

Interestingly, you can paint a pretty bleak scenario for full fiscal union as well, assuming it were even doable. There would have to be tax harmonization across Europe, and that in itself would generate considerable misery. If it happened, you would be selling German bunds and buying peripheral debt that had a much higher yield but would be underwritten by Germany anyway. That is the exact reverse of the picture we have today, and of the investment advice that we would give today. Under full fiscal union Germany would be jointly and severally liable for the debts of Europe as a whole and its bond rate would, in all probability, blow right out beyond 5%.

Turning to investment advice, which do you prefer at present, corporate bonds or equities?

The only reason you would buy short-dated government bonds right now is if you were convinced that we were about to experience some kind of financial deflationary Armageddon. In an inflationary world, corporate bonds provide a relatively secure source of income but with little prospect of capital growth, since by and large bonds are now fully valued. By way of contrast, even though equity markets have in effect gone sideways for a decade—which gives you no capital growth at all—valuation measures have declined throughout, suggesting that current levels do offer the prospect of good economic returns. Another good thing is that equities are well financed right now. Companies tend to have a lot of cash on their balance sheets, having trimmed themselves down through the recession. Finally, equities provide "real returns," so given the balance of probability that the scale of quantitative easing will likely raise inflation (and thereby reduce the

"China embraced capitalism to entrench its socialist elite. The US embraced socialism to entrench its capitalist elite."
Jim Chanos

real burden of outstanding debt), this makes equities a good hedge against a mild upswing in inflation.

Given that, the balance of the argument has to tip strongly in favor of investing directly in equities rather than corporate debt. Innovation and technology are going to be huge differentiators through the coming decade—and here again, corporates that are early adopters and which have good dividend histories are going to be very attractive as equity investments. There is almost a return to 1950s investment thinking here—focus on companies that are well managed and can generate real growth in a low-growth environment. The "great moderation" is over, and along with it the long, steady downswing in Western interest rates and bond yields that have made fixed-income investors so well off. Real needs are served by businesses, and if and when the 1.5 billion or so of emerging consumers begin to spend, that spending will provide healthy profits for investors in business.

MORE INFO

Books:

Bootle, Roger. *The Death of Inflation: Surviving and Thriving in the Zero Era*. London: Nicholas Brealey Publishing, 1998.

Diamond, Jared M. *Collapse: How Societies Choose to Fail or Succeed*. Rev. ed. New York: Viking Penguin, 2011.

Galbraith, John Kenneth. *The Great Crash 1929*. New York: Houghton Mifflin Harcourt, 2009.

Graham, Benjamin. *The Intelligent Investor*. Rev. ed. New York: HarperCollins, 2003.

Jay, Douglas. *Sterling: Its Use and Misuse: A Plea for Moderation*. Oxford: Oxford University Press, 1986.

Kay, John. *Culture and Prosperity: The Truth About Markets—Why Some Nations Are Rich But Most Remain Poor*. New York: HarperCollins, 2004.

Mandelbrot, Benoit, and Richard L. Hudson. *The (Mis)Behavior of Markets: A Fractal View of Risk, Ruin and Reward*. New York: Basic Books, 2006.

Reinhart, Carmen M., and Kenneth S. Rogoff. *This Time Is Different: Eight Centuries of Financial Folly*. Princeton, NJ: Princeton University Press, 2009.

Roubini, Nouriel, and Stephen Mihm. *Crisis Economics: A Crash Course in the Future of Finance*. London: Penguin Books, 2010.

Taleb, Nassim Nicholas. *Fooled by Randomness: The Hidden Role of Chance in Life and in the Markets*. New York: Random House, 2008.

Trevithick, James Anthony. *Inflation: A Guide to the Crises in Economics*. Harmondsworth, UK: Penguin Books, 1977.

See Also:

★ Viewpoint: Deleveraging, Deflation, and Rebalancing in the Global Economy (pp. 158–160)
★ Viewpoint: Investment Lessons from the Crash (pp. 196–198)
★ Viewpoint: Steering Between Deflation and Inflation—A Troubled Road for Developed Economies (pp. 604–606)
Globalization and Its Discontents (p. 1368)

"The fact that global capitalism is flawed does not mean that we should turn to communism or withdraw into national isolation, just as the failure of communism does not mean that markets are perfect." George Soros

  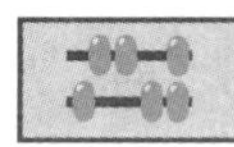   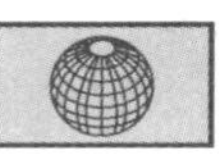   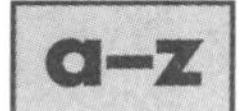

Viewpoint: What Models Do We Need for Risk Management? by Riccardo Rebonato

INTRODUCTION

Riccardo Rebonato is global head of market risk and global head of the Quantitative Research Team at the Royal Bank of Scotland (RBS). He also sits on the Investment Committee of RBS Asset Management. Dr Rebonato is a visiting lecturer at Oxford University and adjunct professor at Imperial College's Tanaka Business School. He sits on the board of directors of ISDA (International Swaps and Derivatives Association) and the board of trustees for GARP (Global Association of Risk Professionals). He is an editor for several financial journals, and has written several books. He holds a doctorate in nuclear engineering and a PhD in condensed matter physics/science of materials from Stony Brook University, NY.

MODELS FOR FINANCIAL RISK MANAGEMENT

"All models are wrong, but some models are useful." Anon

Quantitative models have come under intense scrutiny in the wake of the recent, and still unfolding, financial crisis. And justly so, as the way models have been used in these turbulent times has left a lot to be desired. Much of the criticism, however, has been misplaced, and, often, not even reasonably well-informed. The conspiracy theorists, for instance, who see in the blind acceptance by the "establishment" of the Normal distribution as the root of all evil, have, quite simply, missed the point. Those critics who have complained about "imperfect model assumptions" do not seem to appreciate that, if a model did not have some imperfect assumptions, it would not be a model at all, and that some very successful models in the hardest science of all (physics) often make outrageously unrealistic assumptions, yet can be just as outrageously successful. As I have been involved with models throughout all of my professional life, both as practitioner and academic, I intend to touch on the topic of models from an insider's perspective. However, generalizing about "models in finance" would cause whatever conclusions or suggestions I might reach to be rather bland and generic. I therefore intend to focus on one particular set of applications: i.e., on the use of models for financial risk management.

ONE MODEL OR MANY MODELS?

I intend to argue that there exist a plurality of interpretative models of financial reality, and that each can be adopted or abandoned by market participants in an unpredictable fashion. If this view is correct, the search for the "true" model, for the unique "correct" mapping from information to prices, may be futile and some of the modeling risk-management efforts to date have been misguided. This has important consequences: the existence of competition among models and the resulting "fluctuations" between them can give rise to coordination among agents and feed back mechanisms into prices. This complex dynamic is beginning to be well-understood in some areas of finance and economics, but has not received sufficient attention in financial risk management. This, I believe, is dangerous, and has been one of the contributing factors to the current financial turmoil.

REDUCED-FORM AND MICROSTRUCTURAL MODELS

I referred above to a plurality of interpretative models. What does this mean? Models come in all forms and stripes. The most ambitious are microstructural models that attempt to explain and predict aggregate observables (for example, price movements), starting from the specification of the behavior of individual agents. Traditional micromodels in economics are fully prespecified, i.e. they make strong assumptions about how agents make their choices given inputs (for example, utility functions, etc). They assume the inputs to these models are fixed, and that we know them; there is a "communism of models," the assumption is made that "all agents inside the model, econometricians and God all share the same model." [1] These models can, of course, be stochastic, but, even when they are, they still assume that the nature of the uncertainty (for example, the parameters of the chosen distribution) is perfectly known to all the agents, to the econometrician (and, hopefully, to God).[2]

Reduced-form models are less ambitious. They dispense with the description of the underlying micromechanisms, and simply account for the statistical properties of a phenomenon at an aggregate level. Intensity models of credit default, for instance, where the frequency of default becomes an exogenous quantity, belong to this class. In the risk management domain, all analyses of risk that simply look at price movements, without asking what mechanisms brought about the observed changes, firmly fall in to the reduced-form camp.

Reduced-form models look less assumption-laden (and therefore presumably safer) than the microstructural ones. However, they give no indication as to when their conditions of validity may fail to apply—just because they do not look under the bonnet. Their strength is, in this respect, also their weakness. These reduced-form models are therefore adequate for day-to-day, "nothing-much-has-changed" type of applications. They can also work in the tails of a return distribution if we have enough data and the underlying phenomenon is stationary. But reduced-form models are intrinsically unable to deal with the unexpected, the new—with the real tail event.

Those who preach power laws, more-or-less-truncated Levy flights, Cauchy distributions, or other exotica, without offering a mechanism capable of explaining how and *when* these distributional features occur are therefore still solidly in the reduced-form camp—despite their claims, they are still fundamentally ill-equipped to deal with the unexpected. Unless coupled with model(s) of reality, these distributional suggestions ultimately give us no real handle on black swans.

The microstructural models loved by economists have in principle far more power, because they specify the mechanisms that bring about certain outcomes, and we can therefore ask ourselves whether these mechanisms still apply. They are not without problems, though, and it is to these problems that I now turn.

A DIFFERENT PICTURE OF THE DATA/MODEL INTERACTION

From the discussion above, a strong case can be made that for day-to-day risk management reduced-form models can do a good (and "cheap") job; but if we want to capture truly exceptional risk, microstructural models that link aggregate outputs to the behavior of agents via a simplified mechanism of financial reality, seem to be needed.

For the purpose of financial risk management, the aggregate variables of interest are asset prices. Asset prices are, in turn, determined by the actions of traders. In order to understand how prices evolve, it is therefore essential to understand how traders react to information.

One paradigm (Efficient Market Hypothesis, Rational Expectation Hypothesis) is that of the perfectly efficient Bayesian agent, who (almost) instantaneously updates his prior beliefs in the light of new information. Depending on the application, this picture may or may not be useful as a model that links microbehavior (utility maximization and Bayesian updating) and market institutional set-ups to aggregate outcomes (prices of assets). It certainly leaves behind important features of real price dynamics:

1 overreaction to news cannot happen;
2 traders can adjust their beliefs almost instantaneously;
3 traders are principals, not agents, or, if agents, the principal/agent set-up perfectly aligns the actions of the agent with the interests of the principal;
4 there are no limits to (pseudo-)arbitrage.

For the reasons alluded to above, it is futile and unproductive to say that "these assumptions are not met in practice." The relevant question is whether these simplifications of reality are so strong as to make the predictions uninteresting or useless for the purposes of the management of financial risk. Unfortunately, there is abundant evidence that suggests that important features are left out of the stylized description above, especially in situation of market distress.

A more realistic model of how traders react to information and, by so doing, affect prices, may go along the following lines.

- Traders are agents—with all the problems of incentivization and principal-agent alignment that this entails.
- Traders are smart—they understand that, in order to make sense of the minute-by-minute flow of information, they need "stories" that can help them organize this enormous amount of data. These stories are often very "micro" in nature, in the sense that they assume complex mechanisms to link economic data to aggregate outputs—we have all heard the "stories" (or "rationalizations") that run along the lines of: "pension funds are buying index-linkers to cover their liabilities," "exotic traders are rehedging their negative gamma," "sellers of variance swaps are dumping stock in the last twenty minutes of opening," etc.
- Traders are fickle—each of the above models seems prima facie like a mini microstructural model. However, unlike economists, traders are unashamedly ready to dump their perfect fully prespecified micromodel for the new flavor-of-the-month/week/day fully prespecified micromodel—how quickly did we go from the "oil-at-$300 story" to "oil-at-US$20 story?" From a world with out-of-control inflation to a deflationary world? From a decoupling story to full synchronicity of the world economies?
- Traders are selective in their choice of data—they never let inconvenient data get in the way of today's good story, at least until tomorrow when the new story is all the rage.

The interaction of several competing models into a dynamic, not-fully-prespecified picture of reality has been picked up in the academic economics domain by the Imperfect Knowledge Economics (IKE) school—the approach offers very interesting applications to FX dynamics, and an explanation of how FX rates can stray from "fundamentals" for so long. I suggest that a similar way of looking at financial risk may be very profitable.

From this perspective, for risk management purposes the important observation from the above is that it is advantageous for market participants to coordinate their actions. In many situations, this can give rise to feedback mechanisms that can produce wild moves of prices away from fundamentals and that can ultimately leave a signature in the tail behavior of price returns.

The existence of this competing heuristic to make sense of data cannot, of course, be proven by anecdotes, but a conversation I had with the head of a commodity trading desk in the late summer of 2008, when oil prices were testing US$140, and there were fears that Israel may attempt a preemptive strike on Iran's nuclear facilities, is very telling. I wanted to confirm with the trader my intuition that the feared bombing would send oil prices even higher. "A strike by Israel will have two effects," the trader confidently said: "either the oil price will go up a lot. Or it will go down a lot." His reasoning was that the military action may cause a restriction of supply, or that the action would have such a negative effect on global sentiment, as to tip toward recession a world already shaken by the unfolding financial crisis. The merits of either argument are not the point here. What *is* the point is the readiness of the trader to embrace two such discordant models of reality, and his need to coordinate his action with the perceived interpretation of the other traders. What springs to mind, of course, is Keynes's beauty contest, where the judges have to choose not the most attractive contestant, but the contestant that the other judges will choose as the most attractive.

The view of trading that I propose is therefore consistent with a coordination game played by the market participants; as information arrives, traders have to analyze it and process it in a very short time. It is plausible that they use relatively simple heuristics in doing so. They have to categorize this information in one of the "market modes" they recognize—the inflationary story, the commodity-demand-from-emerging-markets story, the decoupling story. Then they have to coordinate their categorization with what the other market participants are doing, because the worst situation for an individual trader is not to be wrong, but to give the "wrong" (i.e. dissonant) categorization in comparison to the rest of the market. And, in periods of turmoil or great uncertainty, the swings from one temporary paradigm to another can be wild (both in amplitude and in rapidity): "... investors have an incentive to coordinate, *which may generate self-fulfilling beliefs and multiple equilibria.* Using insights from global games, [one can] pin down investors' beliefs, analyze equilibrium prices, and show that *strong feedback leads to higher excess volatility*..."[3] (my emphasis).

In order to anticipate, at least at a qualitative level, how prices might behave tomorrow, an understanding of these imperfect models and heuristics and how they can be temporarily adopted or dropped is therefore indispensable. Blind adherence to any one model, even to the intellectually most satisfactory or the empirically least wrong one, will therefore leave us unprepared to cope with what reality will throw at us tomorrow.

THE CURRENT QUANTITATIVE APPROACH TO FINANCIAL RISK MANAGEMENT

How do these views square with current thinking about quantitative financial risk management? Even a cursory analysis of

"These are not normal circumstances. The market is not functioning properly." George W. Bush

what is presented as best practice immediately shows that the prevailing paradigm is one where reduced-form models reign supreme. The obsessive interest in the study of the return distribution is, of course, the ultimate reduced-form-model approach, with all the limitations highlighted above. The frequently heard statement, "All the statistical information of interest is contained in the multivariate joint distribution of returns—pity that it is so difficult to obtain, and, if we had it, more difficult to interpret" must be strongly qualified. All the statistical information of relevance is indeed in the return distribution, but only for time-stationary phenomena and *over the same time horizon over which the returns have been calculated*.[4] This means that, if I have vectors of daily returns, I can hope to have all the statistical information I need about 1-day changes. But if I am interested in 2-day, 10-day, or 1-year changes there is no sure-proof, model-independent, assumption-free way of aggregating these data for the longer time frames of interest.

Of course, if perfect independence of returns applied and one were dealing with a time-stationary phenomenon, one could in principle obtain the distribution of one-year changes from the distribution of one-minute changes: the way to do it is by convolution. But there is overwhelming evidence that shows that the "synthetic" long-horizon distributions calculated by repeated convolutions starting from the short-horizon distribution are very different from the empirical long-horizon distribution.[5] Why not using the long-horizon distribution to start with? Because the longer the horizon, the fewer the independent observation points, the less we can say about the tails of the distribution, the less confident we can be of the relevance of very "ancient" data to the current market conditions. I have expanded at length on this aspect in Rebonato (2006), and I will therefore not pursue this line here.

Ultimately, the joint distribution of n-day returns does give full information about what n-day returns have been in the past (over the time horizon equal to the frequency of data collection). The link between this information and future n-day returns, however, is not in the data, but in our model(s) of reality. When it comes to financial risk management, are we interested in understanding the past or predicting the future?

DESIGNING A MORE REALISTIC MODELING APPROACH

If these insights are correct, the (self-organizing) switching between modes of understanding reality referred to above should leave a signature in the distribution of returns. To see how this can happen, suppose that one of the prevalent market reactions to very bad economic news is the expectation of a pronounced steepening of the yield curve. Then one would expect to be able to identify a subset of data associated with large downward moves at the short end, high maturity-adjusted volatility, high correlation among short-dated yields, and lower correlation between short and long-dated yields. Or suppose that a mode of reaction to unexpected inflationary evidence is a flattening of the yield curve, with short rates moving up much more than long rates and high maturity-adjusted volatility at the short end. One should be able to identify in a subset of the data the signature of these market responses as well.

As long as there is not an infinity of modes of reaction to economic news (and this is likely to be the case as a result of the traders' need to organize information in digestible soundbites), these modes of deformation should be recognizable in the full time series of returns (but not at all in the cumulative distribution).

As pieces of information do not come with ready-made labels, if different market participants chose their heuristic models independently, there would be little chance for the result of a single mode of organization of reality to become apparent. However, for the reasons explained above, market participants must develop the ability to "lock into" a coordinated market response. The market creates a small number of filters through which information is passed. The filters are changed occasionally (with a frequency ranging from a few days to a few months).

The good news is that the signature onto the prices of the different modes of reaction to economic news *is* detectable. There now exist powerful analytical methods to identify (i) how many modes of deformation exist; and (ii) what happens (to volatilities, correlations, etc.) in each of these modes.[6] It is also often possible to give a narrative interpretation—for example, a flight-to-liquidity mode, for some (or most) of the modes so identified. And, *looking at each mode in isolation*, it is not unreasonable to expect that quantities such as correlations or volatilities might be constant (conditional homoskedasticity).

So, despite recent events, models are not dead. Models don't kill financial systems—people who don't understand how to use models sometimes do. But we must realize that, without an interpretative model of reality, data analysis, however sophisticated, is mute. We will be better served by a plurality of imperfect, but richer, microstructurally inspired models than by a supposedly all-encompassing, reduced-form supermodel. And most of all, we need people—analysts, traders and, yes, also senior managers—who can use models more effectively.

MORE INFO

There are similarities between the views I presented and the much wider reflexivity model proposed by Soros (2003) and Soros (2008). About the shortcomings of fully prespecified microstructural models, and an application to FX rates, see Frydman and Goldberg (2007). About the effect on asset prices of heterogeneous beliefs, see, for example, Shefrin (2008) and Buraschi (2006). The effects of coordination in general are nicely presented in Chamley (2004). The techniques presented in this text do not deal, however, with the case when the actions of the coordinating agents affect the prices. To explore this angle, see Cipriani and Guarino (2008).

Books:

Chamley, Christophe P. *Rational Herds: Economic Models of Social Learning*. Cambridge, UK: Cambridge University Press, 2004.

Frydman, Roman, and Michael D. Goldberg. *Imperfect Knowledge Economics: Exchange Rates and Risk*. Princeton, NJ: Princeton University Press, 2007.

Rebonato R. *The Plight of the Fortune Tellers—Why We Need to Manage Financial Risk Differently*. Princeton, NJ: Princeton University Press, 2007.

Shefrin Hersh. *A Behavioral Approach to Asset Pricing*. 2nd ed. Oxford: Academic Press, 2008.

Soros, George. *The Alchemy of Finance*. 3rd ed. Hoboken, NJ: Wiley, 2003.

Soros, George. *The New Paradigm for Financial Markets: The Credit Crisis of 2008 and What It Means*. New York: Public Affairs, 2008.

"Every banker knows that if he has to prove that he is worthy of credit, however good may be his arguments, in fact his credit is gone." Walter Bagehot

Articles:

Buraschi, Andrea, and Alexei Jiltsov. "Model uncertainty and option markets with heterogeneous beliefs." *Journal of Finance* 61:6 (December 2006): 2841–2898. Online at: dx.doi.org/10.1111/j.1540-6261.2006.01006.x

Cipriani, Marco, and Antonio Guarino. "Herd behaviour and contagion in financial markets." *Berkley Electronic Journal of Theoretical Economics* 8:1 (January 2008): article 24. Online at: dx.doi.org/10.2202/1935-1704.1390

See Also:

★ Risk Management: Beyond Compliance (pp. 929–932)
★ Risk Management of Islamic Finance Instruments (pp. 94–97)
✔ Analysis Using Monte Carlo Simulation (p. 1062)
✔ Calculating Your Total Economic Capital (p. 1005)

NOTES

1 Interview with Thomas Sargent in Frydman (2006).

2 I note in passing that behavioural finance, often offered as a cure to all of our neoclassical woes, is in this respect no exception—it is still a fully pre-specified model that happens to make different assumptions about human "rationality" (for example, it questions the actual prevalence of Bayesian updating of beliefs).

3 Ozdenoren, E., and K. Yuan. "Feedback effects and asset prices." *Journal of Finance* 63:4 (August 2008): 1939–1975.

4 If we are interested in properties such as drawdowns—and, as risk managers, we certainly should—we must also add the assumption of independence of draws for the return distribution to be all-informative.

5 See, for example, Malevergne, Y., and D. Sornette. *Extreme Financial Risks: From Dependence to Risk Management*. Springer Verlag, 2005.

6 See, for example, Doust, Chen, and Rebonato. "Identification of the modes of deformation of the US$ yield curve." RBS Working Paper, 2008.

"A commodity appears, at first sight, a very trivial thing, and easily understood. Its analysis shows that is is, in reality, a very queer thing, abounding in metaphysical subtleties and theological niceties." Karl Marx

  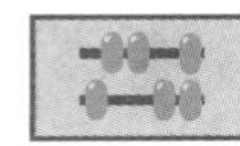      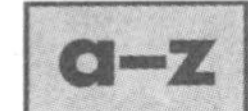

Why Printing Money Sometimes Works for Central Banks by Paul Kasriel

EXECUTIVE SUMMARY

- There is a logical and defensible rationale for running the printing presses in the current economic climate.
- The banks and two-year Treasury notes, how the banks are recapitalized.
- Options that do not involve monetizing the debt–their disadvantages improve the argument for the monetizing approach.
- Why TALF is essentially a Structured Investment Vehicle.
- The possibility of a second recession in 2012.

INTRODUCTION

At the start of March 2009, even after the signing of the US$787 billion fiscal stimulus package from President Obama, doom and gloom was the order of the day from most commentators. The markets were extremely volatile, anticipating the imminent nationalization of one or more major US banks. The US commerce department released its fourth-quarter GDP data for 2008, which showed that the economy had contracted at an annualized rate of 6.2%, the sharpest contraction since the first quarter of 1982, when the economy fell back by 6.4%. In the light of this and the deepening global recession, very few economists were predicting growth restarting in Q4 2009.

RUNNING THE PRESSES AT HIGH SPEED

Yet there is a very clear route and rationale for growth to come about in this sort of time frame. It all depends on how the Obama fiscal stimulus package is put into effect. In explaining this, we will, simultaneously, be demonstrating how it is that for a central bank, with an economy in this kind of difficulty, running the printing presses at high speed can be a highly responsible course of action.

Of course, if printing money were always a good thing, the Zimbabwean economy in 2009 would be a thing of wonder for the world, instead of the unmitigated disaster it certainly is. Printing money ultimately leads to price inflation, and from there, down the slippery slope to hyperinflation. Before things reach this pass, however, in the early stages, good things can be achieved, as we will demonstrate.

The basis for predicting growth in the fourth quarter of 2009 is an anticipation—at the time of writing, this was not yet a certainty—that the effects of increased federal government spending and tax rebates from the fiscal stimulus will come from the stimulus being largely financed by the banking system and/or the Federal Reserve. When the Federal Reserve and the banking system team up to buy debt, in combination they are, in effect, printing money.

GETTING 65 BASIS POINTS FOR FREE—NICE WORK IF YOU CAN GET IT

How does this work? At today's overnight Fed funds market rate, banks can fund themselves at a cost of about 0.25%. At the same time, two-year Treasury securities are yielding approximately 0.9%. So, if the banks load themselves up with two-year Treasury securities, all funded at 0.25%, they generate a healthy 65 basis-point profit for absolutely no risk. By loading up on Treasuries, banks are, in effect, replenishing their depleted capital. It is a "trick" that worked extremely well for the banks in the 1990s, when they needed to repair depleted capital structures, and it will work again this time round.

It is important here to realize that, because of the Federal Government's ability to tax, there is no credit risk involved in the purchase of Treasury securities. So, there is no risk-based capital charge incurred when banks purchase them. The only meaningful constraint on bank purchases of Treasury securities is their respective overall leverage ratios—total assets in relation to their capital.

There is some slight interest-rate risk, in that if the Federal Reserve began to raise the overnight rate, the profitability of the two-year bills to the banks would diminish, and possibly even turn into a loss. But that is the only risk, and it is likely to be well into 2010 before the Federal Reserve will need to worry about inflation, which might cause it to want to push rates up.

There seems little likelihood or risk of stagflation for the US economy. Stagflation usually occurs when there is some supply constraint on the economy; for example, where the economy has run out of labor and cannot grow any faster because it does not have the labor to produce the goods and services, or where there is a sharp reduction in energy supplies, which constrains industry. The United States is a net debtor nation, and falling prices of goods, services, and income make a very hostile environment for debtors. The nominal value of the debt contracted for does not fall, but the revenue of the debtor nation falls, making the debt much harder to pay back. So, the United States has an interest in generating a modest amount of inflation as it restarts the economy. It also has plenty of excess capacity in the economy, with unemployment likely to go above 9% in the months ahead, and underutilized capacity rising in US factories. The real factor holding back GDP growth in the United States right now is the lack of aggregate demand for goods from households and businesses, as well as from state and local government.

How does the monetization of debt (with the Fed printing money to pay the banks and the banks buying Treasury debt) affect the banks' ability to lend? The process of borrowing cheaply and buying debt for a net 65 basis-points profit allows the banks' capital to increase, and that, in turn, allows the banks to start to extend more credit to the private sector. This is exactly what happened during the early 1990s, and although the situation is more severe now, the yield curve is steeper. In the early 1990s, by the second half of 1993, this process of gaining capital through buying Treasuries had recapitalized the banks sufficiently for them to resume near-normal lending.

However, there are two other options where the debt is not monetized, via the banks buying Treasury bills and the Fed printing money. Option one is where the Federal Government acquires funding via increasing the taxes it collects—which does not look to be on the agenda now, despite President Obama's pre-election promise to increase taxes on incomes in excess of US$250,000. Option two is where the Fed increases its bond sales to the non-bank public—a method much used by Argentina after it defaulted on its sovereign debt. Neither of these options, increasing taxes and selling to the non-bank public, lead to any new spending in the economy. In the first option, the private sector cuts back on spending to pay for the new taxes. In the second, it cuts back on spending to pay for the new bonds (in other words it saves, rather than spends, and increased saving at the cost of spending deepens the recession).

"Having a little inflation is like being a little bit pregnant." Leon Henderson

  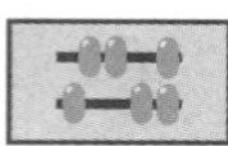      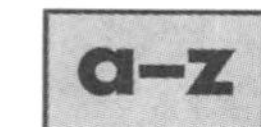

However, where the Fed prints money to fund increased spending, the private sector is not supplied with a new motive for cutting back on spending, so the new spending by the government is a real net additional spend in the economy. That is the first part of the monetization process. The second part is the improvement in bank-retained earnings.

Of course, in addition to taking these measures, the federal government is also doing other things to encourage the economy to move forward. Both TARP (the Troubled Assets Relief Program) and the Federal Reserve's Term Asset-backed securities Lending Facility (TALF) are crucial here. The goal of TALF is to begin a thawing process in the frozen, asset-backed securities (ABS) market. These asset-backed securities involve many types of private-sector credit, such as credit cards, auto loans, student loans, residential real-estate mortgages, and commercial real-estate mortgage debt. The idea is that, through TALF, the Federal Reserve will provide non-recourse financing to entities that purchase newly issued securitized debt with a credit rating of AAA. The term of these loans would be three years. The borrowers could opt for a floating-rate loan, priced at 100 basis points over one-month Libor, or a fixed-rate loan priced at 100 basis points over three-year Libor. The Fed would not lend 100% of the face value of these securities, but would lend an amount something less than face value in order to protect the taxpayer against some future loss in the value of these securities. However, due to the non-recourse nature of the loan, if the value of the securities were to fall below this discounted value, then the Fed would have to accept the credit loss.

When TALF was first proposed, back in November 2008, its funding allocation was US$200 billion. Under the Treasury's new Financial Stability Package (FSP), TALF's funding amount has been increased five-fold, to US$1 trillion.

Interestingly, the TALF program is essentially a structured investment vehicle (SIV), much like the banks' off-balance-sheet SIVs that got us all into this mess in the first place. The one really important distinction, however, is that the Fed, which has the largest capacity in the world to absorb losses, is providing the financing. So, unlike the case with the original SIVs, there are no parties in a position to make margin calls in the TALF version. (It was the margin calls that were triggered as the collateral in the SIVs deteriorated that first opened up the debt abyss for the banks.)

With previous facilities, the Fed had already begun creating credit for the non-bank private sector in the United States. For example, the Fed has been purchasing commercial paper, short-term uncollateralized loans, from corporate issuers (borrowers). TALF expands the capacity for the Fed, in effect, to create credit for the private sector. It is, therefore, very likely that TALF will be the most important element of the federal government's Financial Stability Package, as far as increasing the flow of credit to the private sector over the coming 12 months is concerned.

Another part of the FSP is, as far as can be seen at this stage, a kind of "purge and merge" program, whereby the Fed's "stress test" is supposed to show which banks have a decent chance of surviving the recession, and which do not. The "terminally ill" will be purged of their poisonous assets and merged into those with a better chance of survival. In the process, it is likely that stockholder equity in the terminally ill banks will be wiped out. Taxpayers will bear the costs of any unrecoverable losses of purged assets.

CONCLUSION

There is a reasonable case to be made, as of the beginning of March 2009, that the combination of the US$1 trillion TALF program and the US$787 billion fiscal stimulus program, assuming it is financed by the banking system and the Fed, will have a salutary effect on aggregate real activity in the US economy, with a reasonable chance of inducing an economic recovery by the fourth quarter of 2009.

However, because a key part of this upturn will rely on the Fed running the printing presses as hard as it can, there is also a reasonable likelihood that rising inflation will return as we go through 2010. This, in turn, will prompt the Fed to tighten credit again, which could have a second recessionary impact by 2012. So, one possible shape for the future of the United States, and possibly of the global economy, is not a "V" but a "W." However, that would still, in all probability, be a better outcome than a multi-year recession.

MORE INFO

Websites:

Northern Trust Bank: www.ntrs.com

Paul Kasriel's The Econtrarian: tinyurl.com/yg2vms

See Also:

★ Viewpoint: Deleveraging, Deflation, and Rebalancing in the Global Economy (pp. 158–160)

★ Viewpoint: Steering Between Deflation and Inflation—A Troubled Road for Developed Economies (pp. 604–606)

John Maynard Keynes (p. 1289)

Irrational Exuberance (p. 1385)

Macroeconomics (p. 1388)

"Less of a negotiation, more of a drive-by shooting." Sir Fred Goodwin

  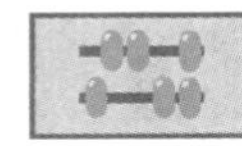      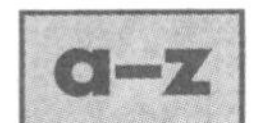

Viewpoint: Why the Thinking of the Austrian School of Economics Matters in Today's Economy

by Annette Godart-van der Kroon

INTRODUCTION

Annette Godart-van der Kroon is president of the Ludwig von Mises Institute Europe, having taken up the position in 2001. Since then the Institute has hosted a large number of events on various topics that influence politics in Brussels. Previously she worked as adjunct referendary at the Ministry of Defence in the Department of Judicial Affairs at the Hague and as a lawyer at the Court of Utrecht and in Roermond in the Netherlands, specializing in civil affairs. She has given numerous speeches on juridical, philosophical, and economic issues and has published books, articles, and comments on these topics. Her publications include two books on the theories of von Hayek and articles on Schopenhauer's theory of law published in the *Schopenhauer-Jahrbuch* in 2003. She is also a member of the Mont Pelerin Society and has participated in Liberty Fund meetings. She enjoys opera, reading, and horseback riding.

We are going through a period where some governments in developed countries are intervening in the markets as never before, with quantitative easing on a massive scale. The failure to intervene, however, is now frequently cited as one of the causes of the crash. How do you view this?

As President of the European Mises Institute I have been able to view the global crash of 2008–09 through the eyes of the Austrian school of economists, who are champions of capitalism and liberalism and who are vigorously against government intervention in the markets. However, we are going through a period of intensive intervention which began around 2009 and which looks as if it will last at least until deep into 2011. The question of how to view all this is a complex one and needs to be answered in several stages. I would start by pointing out that Ludwig von Mises, whose writings and thought lie at the heart of the Austrian school, is against unnecessary government intervention. Period. But one needs to understand what is meant by intervention. Not everything governments do to maintain the freedom of the markets or to maintain individual freedoms is not intervention. That is simply government doing its proper job. What is not the proper job of government, for example, is to intervene to affect prices. I will come back to this point in a moment to explain why the market's ability to set prices through the actions and decisions of individuals is such a fundamental matter in the eyes of the Austrian school.

Let us take an example. Wheat and other grain crops are currently at record highs. There is a long history of governments intervening to set the price of bread, and it has never turned out well. So even though food crop prices are extremely high, we do not hear calls in Europe or the United States for government to set the price of grain. Everyone believes that this would be folly, and unworkable in a global market. What we do have, though, is demands from interventionists—one thinks particularly of President Nicholas Sarkozy of France—for special taxes to be introduced to discourage speculators in commodities. When in doubt, blame "speculators."

Intervention is very popular among the political classes. It enables politicians to be seen to be active, to be doing things, to be seizing the initiative. It is seen as an easy route to votes. However, the problem with intervention, as von Mises pointed out, is that it creates issues which then lead to the need for further intervention, and so on. What the Austrian school shows us is that when you start traveling along this road, you begin to erode personal freedoms and government becomes more and more oppressive.

Now let us look at the 2008 global crash. People, including the media, begin their analysis of the crash from the standpoint that it was all caused by greed and short-sightedness on the part of the bankers, which pushed them to take bigger and bigger risks on derivatives based on the US housing market. Increased foreclosures in the US subprime housing market then triggered losses that were multiples of the underlying sums, resulting in the need for massive government intervention to bail out the "too big to fail" banks.

On this analysis, what was needed—what would have prevented the crash—was more vigorous intervention of a different kind, regulatory intervention, with the regulator as a proxy for government. This regulation did not happen. It failed to happen because the United States was pursuing "light-touch" regulation as advocated by former Secretary to the Treasury Alan Greenspan. Now that the crash has happened, light-touch regulation is out of fashion and we are witnessing a massive wave of reregulation both in the United States and in Europe, aimed at the financial services sector. Again, intervention is seen very much as a positive force, necessary to control an unruly market.

What is not seen in all of this is the deep collusion, interference by the back door, between the bankers and government that created the conditions for the crash. The US administration under President Clinton was on a mission to enable poorer Americans to own their own homes. This is one of the major factors at the root of the US subprime debacle. Banks were positively encouraged to relax lending standards. In other words, where risks would have been properly priced by the market at a certain level, a thumb was put in the scales to drive the cost of mortgages down to the point where it could be deemed to be affordable.

Once you start skewing the market in this way, you lose your frame of reference. From there it was a short hop to self-certified mortgages where applicants were encouraged to misstate their income since no one would check on it. At the same time, the biggest banks in the United States were able to proceed to riskier and riskier lending and more and more opaque derivatives trading precisely because they knew that government would intervene to save them if things

  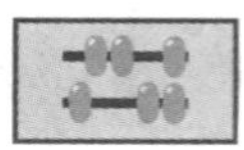      

went wrong. None of this represents the proper functioning of the market. It represents, instead, a market pulled out of shape by interventionism. Let us now look at the importance of allowing the market to set prices. Friedrich Hayek, the Nobel laureate and student of von Mises, put this very well. Economists in the early part of the 20th century liked to talk about the "given" data. Hayek argued that in fact data were never "given" in that easy fashion, since in a complex economy information is complex and dispersed. No one person sees it all or sees all its connections and ramifications. On this basis Hayek created his theory of pricing.

Prices, in a free market, act as a guide to behavior. They enable individuals to make decisions about the resources they have at their disposal in order to achieve whatever goals they have set themselves. However, an individual can only make these decisions freely if he/she is completely free and secure in the possession of those resources. Security of private property, in other words, is fundamental. The proper role of government is to protect individual freedom by ensuring private property rights, whether that property is money, land, a business, or the proceeds from a business. So prices, produced by the operation of a free market, and the security of private property, which gives people an incentive to engage in the market, are the foundations for a thriving capitalist society. Insofar as we move away from this, we start to destroy the foundations that make capitalism possible.

How, then, do you view the current effort being made to devise a framework to monitor systemic risk in the financial sector and to bring in a new regulatory framework?

I believe that, as things now stand, there is a need for well-considered regulation in the financial services sector. In this I believe we are following the likes of Karl Popper, who pointed out in his book *The Open Society and its Enemies* that unlimited freedom is not possible. Freedom defeats itself if it is unlimited. For this reason it is necessary to ensure that the state limits freedom so that no individual is at the mercy of any other. We should be vigilant to limit the power of the state at the right moment, but the financial markets—just like unlimited freedom—have to be supervised and, yes, regulated.

However, an economist such as George Reisman, who follows von Mises very closely and who has worked out a very comprehensive "pro-capitalist" economic theory, is vehemently against all forms of government intervention. He would argue that if the government stopped protecting banks from the consequences of their actions, mismanaged banks would fail and well-managed banks that put the customer first would prosper, so in this regard the market would be able to adjust itself.

One has to put all this in the context of how the Austrian school views capitalism. According to von Mises, "Capitalism is essentially a system of mass production for the satisfaction of the needs of the masses. It has raised the average standard of living to a level never dreamed of in earlier ages." What drives capitalism is the profit motive of individual entrepreneurs and businesses. That is a tremendously powerful force. One has only to look at the emerging economies of China and India, where people are being lifted out of subsistence poverty at a rate never seen before in the history of the world. In the last decade China has succeeded in raising some 400 million people above the poverty line. By contrast, socialism and centrally planned economies have proved devastating to countries that adopted state ownership of the means of production.

When von Mises wrote his famous critique of socialism, what he focused on was the fact that it is impossible for those involved in centrally planning an economy to have access to all the information they need to make accurate planning decisions. By removing private ownership of the means of production, the socialist state destroys the market's ability to generate prices dynamically. Without price information to guide decision-making, central planners lack the vital tools they need to made coherent decisions about how to distribute goods, or even which goods to manufacture and in what quantities. The results were disastrous and explain the economic collapse of the Soviet Union. By switching to a capitalist model that encourages private enterprise—even though substantial state controls remain—China continues to improve the living standards of its 1.2 billion citizens.

The US Federal Reserve is committed to pumping money into the economy to try to stimulate growth in a classic Keynesian policy directly opposed to the Austrian school's principle of nonintervention. The arguement is that if nothing were done, the outcome would be a self-sustaining depression. What is your view?

The debate between Keynes and the Austrian school—or, to put it another way, the Austrian school's analysis of the errors of Keynes's economic theory—has been very fully set out by a number of figures from the Austrian school, including Hayek and Murray Rothbard, and most recently George Reisman, in very substantial works that are available as e-books for downloading (see the More Info section). This is a complex topic and difficult to deal with in a few sentences. On the Keynesian side, in praise of Bernanke, the best-known voice is that of the Nobel laureate economist and *New York Times* columnist Paul Krugman. There are a number of articles that take on Krugman's views directly on the US von Mises site. I would cite in particular the essay "Krugman contra Hayek" by Jonathan Finegold Catalan, or Robert Murphy's essay "My reply to Krugman on Austrian business-cycle theory." (Links for these are given at the end of the article.)

A brief answer, however, concerns the Austrian school concept of the business cycle. The argument is that the boom and bust cycle comes about through creation of the boom phase as a result of government intervention in the markets via the central bank. In the early stages of the cycle, the central bank makes it possible for banks to lend out money to businesses and consumers at lower rates, creating a credit-fueled expansion. The central bank plans to turn off the flow once the economy starts to overheat by raising interest rates. However, the Austrian school analysis, which is based not on models but on a careful study of real decisions by real actors in the economy, shows that what drives the boom period, once it gets going, are multiple projects based on a belief that the low interest rate cycle will endure long enough for long-term capital projects to come to fruition. When the economy overheats and interest rates start to climb, choking off consumption, many of these longer-term investments of capital by businesses turn out to be malinvestments. This creates the bust.

As Paul Johnson says in his introduction to Murray Rothbard's great study of the US Depression (Rothbard, 2000), business and stock exchange downturns serve essential economic purposes. They have to be sharp, but they need not be long, he says, because they are self-adjusting as the malinvestments are cleared out the system. All they require from the government, the business community, and the public is patience. It is government intervention during the bust phase which creates further confusion and prevents the system from clearing and recovering, prolonging either recession or stagnation. So, on this view, Bernanke has it completely wrong.

It seems to me that we cannot separate an analysis of what are the right steps to be taken now from an understanding of how

"Our belief in salvation through the market is very much in the Utopian tradition. The economists and managers are the servants of God. Like the medieval scholastics, their only job is to uncover the divine plan. They could never create or stop it. At most they might aspire to small alterations." John Ralston Saul

we arrived in this mess in the first place. It was government action that prepared the ground for the banking collapse. The Clinton administration repealed the Glass–Steagall Act in 1999. This Act separated deposit-taking commercial banks from investment banks and prevented banks from gambling with investor funding. The repeal enabled commercial lenders such as Citigroup, then the largest US bank by assets, to underwrite and trade instruments such as mortgage-backed securities and collateralized debt obligations. The year before the repeal, subprime loans amounted to just 5% of all mortgage lending. By the time the credit crisis peaked in 2008, they were approaching 30% of all mortgage lending. In 2004, as Thomas Woods pointed out in a blog for the von Mises Group, "Hank Paulson, the current Treasury Secretary, who at the time was chairman of Goldman Sachs, convinced the Securities and Exchange Commission to remove all capital requirements for investment banks." This enabled them to drive up their profits using astonishing amounts of leverage. For example, when Bear Stearns finally went under, it had US$33 of debt for every dollar in equity. Moreover, the ground for this was prepared by the Securities and Exchange Commission!

Now we have the Federal Reserve gambling that adding US$2 trillion—and possibly a great deal more—to the Fed balance sheet will stimulate the economy and drive growth. It is worth remembering that when President Barak Obama was seeking to marshal public opinion in favor of a major stimulus package for the US economy, he gathered 200 economists, including six Nobel prize winners, to endorse his plans. On the other hand, the CATO Institute, a free-market think tank in Washington, marshaled 200 economists against the stimulus, saying: "Despite the fact that now every economist is a Keynesian, we do not believe that more public expenditure can save the economy. That would be a victory of hope over experience. It did not work in the thirties for the USA and it did not work for Japan in the nineties." What seems clear in all the confusion among competing views is that trust between banks and between banks and the general public is vital to a healthy economy. That trust was all but lost because of the crash, and it is going to take a great deal of hard work to rebuild.

MORE INFO

Books:

Hayek, F. A. *Individualism and Economic Order*. Chicago, IL: University of Chicago Press, 1948. Online at: mises.org/books/individualismandeconomicorder.pdf

Rothbard, Murray N. *The Case Against the Fed*. Auburn, AL: Ludwig von Mises Institute, 1994. Online at: mises.org/books/fed.pdf

Rothbard, Murray N. *America's Great Depression*. 5th ed. Auburn, AL: Ludwig von Mises Institute, 2000. Online at: mises.org/rothbard/agd.pdf

Salerno, Joseph T. (ed). *Prices and Production and Other Works: F. A. Hayek on Money, the Business Cycle, and the Gold Standard*. Auburn, AL: Ludwig von Mises Institute, 2008. Online at: mises.org/books/hayekcollection.pdf

von Mises, Ludwig. *Human Action: A Treatise on Economics*. 4th ed. San Francisco, CA: Fox & Wilkes, 1966. Online at: mises.org/Books/humanaction.pdf

von Mises, Ludwig. *The Theory of Money and Credit*. New Haven, CT: Yale University Press, 1953. Online at: mises.org/books/tmc.pdf

Articles:

Finegold Catalán, Jonathan M. "Krugman contra Hayek." *Mises Daily* (July 29, 2010). Online at: mises.org/daily/4578

Murphy, Robert P. "My reply to Krugman on Austrian business-cycle theory." *Mises Daily* (January 24, 2011). Online at: mises.org/daily/4993

Websites:

Ludwig von Mises Institute Europe: www.vonmisesinstitute-europe.org

Ludwig von Mises Institute in United States: mises.org

Mont Pelerin Society: www.montpelerin.org

See Also:

★ Why Organizations Need to be Regulated—Lessons from History (pp. 437–439)

★ Viewpoint: A Lesson in Austrian School Economics: The Real Cause of the Crash (pp. 207–210)

★ Viewpoint: Nothing but Painful Choices Ahead as the Global Debt Supercycle Ends (p. 219)

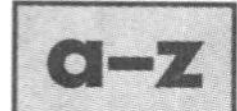

Viewpoint: Why Turning Growth into Profit Is Challenging for Asian Economies by Peter Elston

INTRODUCTION

Peter Elston is head of Asia-Pacific Strategy and Asset Allocation, responsible for Aberdeen's multi-asset business in the region as well as articulating and communicating investment strategy. He has lived in Asia since 1988, joined Aberdeen in 2008, and is based in Singapore. Peter began his career at UK pension fund manager Mercury Asset Management, where he spent 11 years. For most of this time he managed Asian equity funds from Tokyo, Hong Kong, and Singapore. Peter appears regularly on TV, and has had numerous articles published. He graduated with a BA in mathematics and Oriental studies from Cambridge University.

You are based in Singapore and specialize in Asian economies. How much of a slowdown in growth is Asia experiencing now, and what are the impediments to regional growth?

As might be expected, Asia presents a very complex, mixed picture. Asian local currency bond markets performed well through the end of 2011 despite concerns over a sharper slowdown in the region and despite the shadow cast by credit downgrades in the Eurozone. Asian equities saw double-digit losses through 2011, but most stock markets in the region saw stocks rising by the end of the year.

Singapore itself is an interesting case. It has massive government debt, but this debt has been generated in the process of managing its exchange rate. It mops up a lot of current account liquidity by issuing government bonds, which are almost all held by local investors. For much of the time debt issuance in Singapore is not about the government's funding requirements but has to do with managing foreign reserves. Singapore's trade profile is distorted, in a sense, by the fact that the country has a massive refinery capacity. It imports oil to process in its refineries and exports the finished fuel. This is a very deliberate value-added play by the Singapore government. The refinery capacity provides an engine of growth for the economy and helps the country to get round the fact that it is 100% reliant on imported oil for all its energy requirements.

However, because the revenues from refining are very substantial, as are the costs of oil imports to feed the refineries, they distort the picture one gets of the Singapore economy. So the export figures for Singapore are always broken down into oil and nonoil exports, which provides a much better picture of how the economy generally is working.

What we see when we look at the nonoil figures for the economy is that Singapore put in some stunning growth in the initial stages of the recovery after the 2008 crash. In 2009, for example, the economy grew by 20% on an annualized basis. However, by mid-2010 this had started to weaken markedly. More recently, weaknesses in the economy have become more pronounced across Asia, not just in Singapore. Korea released fourth-quarter 2011 numbers in January 2012, and they were pretty weak. China, too, continues to slow, and its growth now looks likely to be just over the 8% mark, well down from the 10–11% growth it posted in 2010.

Is the decoupling of emerging economies a myth then?

The point is that all the major Asian economies are exposed to the advanced economies. There is a long-term decoupling trend, with domestic Asian demand taking over from external demand, but that is a very long-term phenomenon. Medium-term trends in Asia will remain heavily affected by what goes on in advanced economies.

There is a very substantial volume of intra-Asian trade, but what is key is the location of the final demand. If it is all intra-Asian trade making subassemblies for final export to the United States or Europe, then everything fails if Europe and the United States fail. Basically, you export to pay for the imports that you need to develop your own economy. It follows, then, that naturally—over time—you get a deemphasizing of exports.

The world economy has progressed over the last decade or so through globalization. In broad terms, the whole process of globalization so far has been one in which the developed world outsourced a lot of its manufacturing of lower-value goods to emerging countries. That was very advantageous for developed markets. It enabled them to keep their inflation in check and to move their economies in other directions in terms of technologies and services.

The big issue with outsourced manufacturing, however, concerns the consequences of developing a reliance on other countries to do your manufacturing for you. Unemployment in the West did not rise substantially following the start of the process of globalization. It is only in the last four years or so that the cracks have really begun to show. They are visible over the last decade, however, if you look at factors such as wage growth. Wages in the United States, for example, have been flat for a decade or more. The debate now in advanced markets is whether manufacturing jobs should be repatriated—and whether in fact it is possible to reverse the trend. In effect, we are moving into an era when the debate is between globalization and a return to protectionism.

However, trade is very different now to what it was in the 1930s when you had the Smoot–Hawley Tariff Act as a reactive protectionist measure to the Great Depression in the United States. In the 1930s all countries produced pretty much the same kinds of goods, and what was exported was the surplus. Now that is not the case. China specializes in some things, such as low-value manufacturing, Japan does other things, such as auto manufacture, the United States does technology, and so on. Subassemblies and components for these specialisms are sourced globally. So when you start introducing protectionism into this complex web of trade relationships, you really shoot your own feet off. This goes a long way toward explaining why the knee-jerk protectionism that came somewhat to the surface after the 2008 crash failed to gather the momentum that it did in the 1930s. Multiple specialisms keep everyone at the table, playing nicely together.

"It has been the bankers' destiny … to find themselves on the dangerous edge of the world, pointing up the contradictions and cross-purposes. They are not often loved for it." Anthony Sampson

  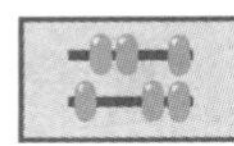      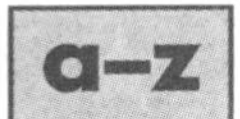

This playing nicely together does not seem to extend to currencies, where we have a number of countries racing to gain export advantage by depreciating their currencies. Do you see this changing?

Clearly, if everyone tries to depreciate, then this is self-canceling. Large-scale macro-factors force some currencies to appreciate despite the fact that their governments would prefer them to be weaker. Running massive trade surpluses is an obvious case in point. Being seen as a "safe haven," and thus attracting huge capital inflows at moments of crisis, is another.

China comes in for a great deal of criticism from the United States for not allowing the renminbi to appreciate faster, but the fact is that it has been appreciating. Moreover, if you factor in inflation, it is plain that it has appreciated quite substantially in real terms. Plus, if you look at wage growth instead of at the official Chinese inflation figures, you can see that its currency appreciation has really been quite extreme. The IMF is currently engaged in carrying out another reassessment of whether or not the renminbi is still undervalued. It says that the case is much less clearcut now than it was two or three years ago.

However, it remains true that following the contraction we had in 2008, the recovery strategy for many countries is still heavily dependent on exporting to boost growth, and relative currency strengths are a key factor in export success. The main point, however, is that it is obvious that not everyone can export their way to growth, just as we can't all devalue simultaneously.

If we go back to the immediate policy responses to the crash, governments everywhere went in for massive fiscal stimulus as a way of preventing continued economic contraction. Clearly, in the case of many Western markets, that stimulus was very justifiable. However, in the case of Asia there were not really the same kinds of underlying problems of public and private overindebtedness, housing bubbles, overgeared property markets, and so on. So once Asian countries got through the initial tough period, when global trade almost dried up, continued stimulus in Asia led directly to overheating.

Economies in Asia recovered very rapidly and growth rates quickly bounced back to levels that exceeded those prior to the crisis. The inevitable result of all this was that the stimulus proved to be inflationary. This, of course, was a problem that Western central bankers would have loved to have had, since their big fear was that their economies would head into a deflationary spiral. Inflation in a number of Western economies is still on the low side, particularly if you strip out commodity price inflation, which is very much an external factor. Among Asian countries, once it became clear that inflation was taking hold, central banks started tightening monetary policy. This in turn goes some way toward explaining the underpeformance of Asian markets in the last part of 2010 and through 2011.

What about the inflows of capital into Asia? How is that affecting regional economies?

Foreign investment into Asian markets is basically hunting returns that are well above the "risk-free" rate, which is set by US Treasuries and, in Asia, by the local prevailing interest rates. What we saw as local interest rates climbed was a lot of domestic investors in Asia pulling their money out of risk assets like equities and putting it into risk-free bonds. By 2012, however, inflation had started to fall in some Asian countries, largely as a result of the continued weakness in Europe feeding through and depressing global demand. This, together with the monetary tightening that Asian economies have gone in for, has had an impact. So local interest rates have eased off a bit and we are now seeing investor interest in Asian equity markets sharpening again.

With Asian equities, the market is still skewed toward Japan. A breakdown of the MSCI World Index for the end of December 2011 shows that Asia-Pacific, excluding Japan, makes up 15% of the World Index, while Japan itself accounts for 8% of the Index. In other words, Japan alone is 50% of the size of the whole of Asia-Pacific ex-Japan. However, if you go back to the late 1980s, when Japan was at the peak of its bubble, it accounted for around 90% of Asia-Pacific market capitalization. By comparison, the United States makes up 23% of the MSCI World Index, and Europe 43%.

If you look at population distribution, Asia-Pacific plus Japan accounts for something like 60–70% of the global population, which gives a pretty clear idea of how much of the potential of this region still has to be realized. There was an excellent report recently by the Organisation for Economic Co-operation and Development (OECD), looking at the rise of the middle classes by region globally. The report pointed out that all the growth in the middle classes is currently coming from Asia. The middle class in Europe is actually slightly on the decline, while its growth in the United States is extremely limited. Other emerging regions, such as Latin America and Africa, are not going to make much of an impact on the overall numbers of the middle class in the near future. It is all about Asia. This is critical because the middle class is where the discretionary spend that boosts economies comes from. Higher-income groups generally invest rather than spend. Once they have hit a certain level of spending, their spend stays constant. The lower-income groups spend only on nondiscretionary items. So the additional, discretionary spend comes almost solely from the middle classes. That makes for a very exciting picture for Asian economies, and these are the things that we are interested in as long-term investors there.

Is investment in Asia all about buy-and-hold in your view, rather than about short-term, active trading? The constant cry from companies in advanced markets is that analysts and investors are far too short-term in their thinking. Is Asia different?

We believe that you have to have a five- to 10-year time frame for investments in Asian equities. This is the time frame in which you can spot trends and inefficiencies. There are very successful short-term traders. Jim Simons at Renaissance Technologies is the master of identifying short-term trading patterns. We prefer to focus on the long-term, and our equity team is much more focused on picking value stocks rather than looking at top-down macro-themes.

However, against the exciting trends I have pointed out, one has also to take into account the fact that in many respects Asian companies have really been a disappointment over the last 20 years. If you look at the Asian MSCI index, it has underperformed the US MSCI index despite the fact that the region has seen about 4% more growth per annum than the United States. So, clearly, Asian companies, on average, have not been particularly successful at translating good economic growth into good profit growth at the bottom line.

Against this, you have to take into account the fact that this 20-year period includes the Asian financial crisis, which blew a lot of promising companies out the water and damaged many others. Growth can lure one into making excessive capital expenditures. These expenditures might be great, short-term, for banks or employees or local suppliers, but they are not great for shareholders, and they are not great for profit unless they translate, later down the line, into a cumulative increase in profit.

In the case of Korea, there was always far too much of an emphasis on market share rather than profits. Companies were heavily focused on being in the top three in their

"We're a me-me-me generation. We're borrowing the savings of every nation in the world. We're … piling up a big tab. Now, I may think we're too big to have a run on us. You may think that. But it's possible that God does not."

Paul Samuelson

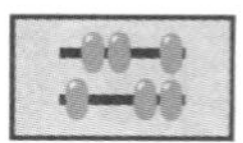

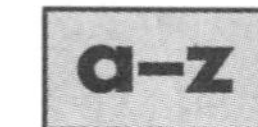

market and paid very little attention to how much profit they were generating. So their return on capital and the cost of capital were of much less concern to them. They would borrow today, invest, and worry about the returns later. This attitude helps to explain why, from an investment perspective, Asian companies have had a less than brilliant record. What we have found is that by taking a long-term view and by picking companies that are careful about spending money we generate better returns. Slow and steady does best for us.

Companies in Asia that are serious about profitability tend to be subsidiaries of the big multinationals. So for us this is a no-brainer. Picking stocks in Asia is not about spotting the next local equivalent of Apple because this is a very hard game to play. It is about recognizing that a strong corporate culture is very hard to create and thus represents a sustainable competitive advantage. There are a number of listed subsidiaries of multinationals across the emerging world, and following them is an excellent way of capturing the growth trends in Asia. They already have the strong governance and reporting traditions of advanced markets and their focus on cash comes from the parent company. In the end their success will pull Asian indigenous companies in the desired direction of better governance and a greater focus on profitability, although this will take time.

MORE INFO

Books:

Kahneman, Daniel. *Thinking, Fast and Slow*. New York: Farrar, Straus and Giroux, 2011.

Latané, Henry A., Donald L. Tuttle, and Charles Parker Jones. *Security Analysis and Portfolio Management*. 2nd ed. New York: Ronald Press, 1975.

Mandelbrot, Benoit B., and Richard L. Hudson. *The (Mis)behavior of Markets: A Fractal View of Risk, Ruin, and Reward*. New York: Basic Books, 2004.

Poundstone, William. *Fortune's Formula: The Untold Story of the Scientific Betting System that Beat the Casinos and Wall Street*. New York: Hill and Wang, 2005.

Smithers, Andrew. *Wall Street Revalued: Imperfect Markets and Inept Central Bankers*. Chichester, UK: Wiley, 2009.

See Also:

China (pp. 1471–1476)

Singapore (pp. 1573–1574)

"In the next economic downturn there will be an outbreak of bitterness and contempt for the supercorporate chieftains who pay themselves millions. In every major economic downturn in US history the villains have been the heroes during the preceding boom." Peter F. Drucker

  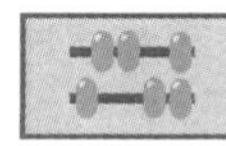   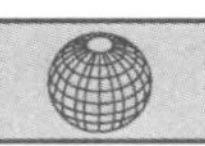   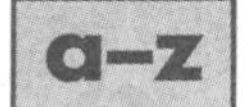

Viewpoint: Yet Another Nail in the Final Salary Scheme Coffin by Tony Clare

INTRODUCTION

Tony Clare is a pensions partner at Deloitte's North West office. He has over 22 years' experience in the sector and is an associate of the Chartered Insurance Institute and a fellow of the Pensions Management Institute. Working across all industries in both the public and private sectors, Tony leads teams advising on transactions and pensions strategy as part of overall reward reviews. He has helped many clients deal with transitions from defined benefits to defined contribution schemes, including leading negotiations with public-sector unions and employees. Tony has also led employee communication programs regarding changes to pension arrangements.

PENSIONS IN THE DOWNTURN

With global equity markets having fallen some 30% since January 2008, and with bond markets in turmoil, it comes as no surprise to find that the assets of final salary pension schemes have taken a battering in the current downturn.

Along with the increased deficit, which will consume yet more of their organization's resources, CFOs are very unhappy about the amount of volatility that is imported into their balance sheets by the current rules for accounting for pension fund liabilities.

Between two and four years ago, a number of finance directors went to their shareholders and convinced them that they had to grasp the nettle on the funding deficit in the final salary scheme. Shareholders agreed to substantial contributions being made over the next year or two so that schemes could be brought back into a fully funded position. If this was achieved, they realized, it would remove a deep source of concern.

However, with the current economic downturn and extreme market volatility, much of this good work has been undone. Matters have been further exacerbated by the impact of increasing longevity.

As people live longer, pension schemes' liabilities increase with each additional average year of life. As a consequence, companies are discovering that any ground they might have made up in terms of improving their scheme's funding position has now more than likely evaporated.

One obvious example here that is in the public domain is British Airways. About four years ago the company began a serious effort to overcome the funding deficit in its pension plan. BA paid in around £900 million in additional contributions. However, a snapshot of the fund today shows that its funding deficit is not significantly less than it was before BA threw a great deal of money at the problem.

MOVING TO A DIRECT CONTRIBUTION SCHEME

There are viable options for employers to lessen or end their exposure. It is reasonable for them to turn to the workforce and to say "let's talk about the problem." If they offer employees a switch to a well-funded defined contribution (DC) scheme, with about the same level of contributions as the defined benefit (DB) scheme, the employer may not save money in the short term but it can at least gain cost certainty. It knows exactly how much the scheme is going to cost and that figure will not mask any nasty surprises, since there is no funding deficit issue in a DC scheme from the employer's point of view.

From the employee's perspective a DC scheme is almost always seen as a lesser one. However, if the pension scheme is genuinely threatening the viability of the company, the employee has the incentive of knowing that the switch could mean the difference between having a job or having no job.

Of course, closing the DB pension scheme to future accruals does not mean that you are getting rid of the scheme. What you are doing is capping your liabilities. You are looking to ensure that the position does not get any worse.

ENHANCED TRANSFER

An option that might be worth considering where a wholesale switch of all the employees from a DB to a DC scheme is not going to work is to offer some members an enhanced transfer to a DC scheme. This has the merit of lowering the DB scheme's liability for every member who leaves. So long as this is done "by the book," with the scheme member being properly advised by an independent financial advisor, it is a viable technique for reducing scheme liabilities.

Employers need to be careful here that they do not run foul of age discrimination legislation by only offering enhanced transfers to certain categories of member based on age-related criteria. Best practice here is to offer an enhanced transfer to all staff, irrespective of length of service and age.

THE BUYOUT MARKET

Another option is to contract with an insurance company for it to take over the scheme liabilities in exchange for the scheme assets and a lump sum cash payment. This last is used to fund any shortfall between the scheme assets and the full buyout value for the liability for each member of the scheme. The drawback here is that buyout is done on a "fully funded" basis with a very conservative measure (government gilts) being used as the basis for the calculation. This makes buyout prohibitively expensive for many schemes.

For years there were only two effective players in the UK pensions buyout market. These were the Prudential and Legal & General. The position improved somewhat two years ago when a number of additional players entered the buyout market and buyout values came down by between 10% and 15%.

However, much of the buyout market was based on the futures swaps market, and the recent market crash with all the associated fears about counterparty risk has made the swap providers very concerned. This in turn had virtually closed the pensions buyout market at the time of writing. Futures swaps are important to the buyout market because they give a better match between investment income and the cash outflows associated with paying pensions. To price such swaps, though, you have to have confidence that the other party is going to be there in 20 years—and that has become much

"I expect there will be some failures ... I don't anticipate any serious problems of that sort among the large internationally active banks that make up a very substantial part of our banking system." Ben Bernanke

  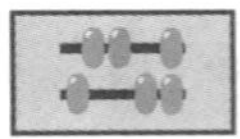   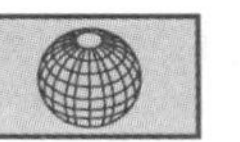   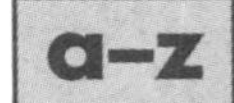

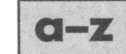

harder to be confident about, given the weakness in the global banking system.

CLOSING SCHEMES TO NEW MEMBERS

One of the first steps a finance director can take to resolve his or her final salary scheme dilemma is to close the scheme to new entrants and to enroll new members in a defined contribution scheme. DC schemes shift the risk from the employer to the employee. In a final salary scheme, the employee's benefit is guaranteed as a set proportion of their final salary and the employer carries the risk that the scheme will not be sufficiently funded to meet its liabilities (i.e. the benefits it will have to pay out to members throughout their retirement). In a DC scheme the employee carries the risk that the amount of money saved in the scheme through their working life will not be sufficient to buy them a reasonable pension in retirement.

This risk has been heightened by the fact that surveys of DC schemes in the United Kingdom show that many employers are treating the move from a final salary scheme to a DC scheme as a cost-cutting exercise and are scaling back their own contribution.

However, in many cases when final salary scheme employer contributions are compared to employer contributions to DC schemes, the people doing the comparison fail to see that they are not comparing like with like. DB schemes are almost always "contracted out" schemes, while DC schemes are "contracted in." In a contracted-in scheme the scheme member retains their entitlement to the state second pension. This is worth 3.4% of band earnings for the employer and 1.6% for the employee. In other words, a combined employer/employee DB contribution rate of 13% is roughly equivalent to a DC rate of 8%. The employee gets additional benefits in the form of the second state pension when they retire.

PERSONAL ACCOUNTS AND THEIR LIKELY IMPACT ON THE PENSIONS LANDSCAPE

With effect from 2012, the British Government's new Personal Account (PA) pension plan aimed at lower-paid employees comes into effect. There has been concern that the PA will initiate a general "leveling down" of pensions to the relatively low mandatory employer/employee contribution levels required by the PA.

However, one needs to remember that in some key sectors the arrival of the PA will actually have the effect of bringing pensions benefits to areas where there are currently no such benefits. Catering, retail, leisure, and the hotels sector all have large numbers of low-paid staff who are either not in any occupational scheme at all or are in very low contribution DC schemes. In those instances, the arrival of the PA will actually represent a leveling up rather than a leveling down.

In the manufacturing sector, it may well be that there will be some leveling down to the requirements of the PA, and in the professional services sector I would anticipate that its introduction would be broadly neutral.

The real question for employers is going to lie in deciding how best to absorb what will be another 4% cost layer on the business. With people on the minimum wage, there is no scope there to cut back on wages to fund the pension. So how will it be funded?

On the more philosophical question of whether the introduction of the PA is a good or a bad thing, much depends on what one thinks government policy will be on pensions in 30 years time, which is about when the first recipients of the PA will be approaching retirement. Without a crystal ball, that is a question that simply can't be answered as we approach the end of 2008.

CONFLICT OF INTEREST

Five years ago it was normal practice for the finance director of a plc to sit on the pension fund trustee board. He or she would bring a level of financial acumen and experience to the board that was highly valued by most trustees. Today, however, there is a widespread realization that the Companies Act makes it quite clear that the finance director's overriding fiduciary duty is to the company's shareholders. Therefore he or she is all too likely to be caught up in a conflict of interest if they try to fulfill both roles simultaneously.

Both the accountancy bodies and the UK Pensions Regulator (TPR) have issued very clear guidance on how finance directors should manage conflicts of interest. The necessary actions range from absenting themselves from meetings on issues where conflicts occur to, in more severe cases of a conflict of interest, resigning from the trustee board.

It is important for finance directors to realize that they cannot, in law, ignore the information they have as a finance director of the company if it is relevant to the trustees. If, for example, you know that the bank has just changed the terms of the company's banking facility to the detriment of the company, that has to be declared to the trustees. Similarly, if you are taking on a new acquisition, the trustees are going to want to know the scale of the debt the company is taking on to make the acquisition, and they are going to want to know how cash-generative the target company is.

Will it leave them in a better or a worse position when it comes to trying to get the company to maintain or increase its payments to the pension fund? As a finance director you cannot pretend that you don't have this information.

The trustees, for their part, will be looking at corporate events of all sorts to try to gauge if any of these events weaken the employer's covenant—in other words, the employer's ability to stand behind and support the fund. One has to remember that the health of a final salary pension scheme very much depends on the financial strength of the employer behind the scheme.

I predict that we will see more and more finance directors and other company officers resigning from their organization's pension fund trustee board through 2010. Their place will increasingly be taken by independent trustees.

THE PENSIONS SHORTFALL

With the average pensions pot in the United Kingdom currently standing at rather less than £50,000 it is quite clear that the majority of scheme members are not saving enough to fund a comfortable retirement. However, that is not the fault of DC schemes per se. One could argue that one of the great merits of DC schemes is that they are transparent. If you put a substantial amount of money into them, you get a decent pension, and if you underfund them, you do not. They are really not that complicated.

There are only two options for resolving the savings deficit. Either employers and employees have to pay in substantially more on a regular basis, or the employee has to consider a later retirement age. The United Kingdom already has a growing proportion of people remaining in work beyond the age of 65, and there is some evidence that more people now expect to have to work until their 70th birthday if they want to avoid a penurious old age.

MORE INFO

See Also:

★ How to Manage Pension Costs (pp. 56–58)
★ Valuing Pension Fund Liabilities on the Balance Sheet (pp. 122–124)

"Waiting for supply-side economics to work is like leaving the landing lights on for Amelia Earhart." Walter Heller

  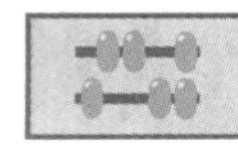   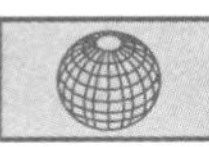   

Viewpoint: Accounting for Value: Why the Accountancy Bodies Are Losing Their Way in the Standard-Setting Process by Stephen Penman

INTRODUCTION

Stephen H. Penman is the George O. May professor in the Graduate School of Business, Columbia University. Prior to this he was the L. H. Penney professor in the Walter A. Haas School of Business at the University of California at Berkeley, and has served as a visiting professor at London Business School and Stockholm School of Economics. He has a first-class honors degree in commerce from the University of Queensland, Australia, and MBA and PhD degrees from the University of Chicago. His research is on equity valuation and the role of accounting information in security analysis. He is managing editor of the *Review of Accounting Studies* and is on the editorial board of the *Schmalenbach Business Review*, and in 2002 he was awarded the Wildman Medal for his book, *Financial Statement Analysis and Security Valuation*.

In your recent book, *Accounting for Value*, you take the accounting standards-setting bodies to task for bringing speculative values into the accounts. Where do you see them going wrong?

I approach accountancy by asking what it measures that is of use to an investor. Basically, I am looking for accountancy to be a set of tools for measuring value—the real value of a business. My book was first and foremost a book on valuation, aimed at investors and those to whom they entrust their savings. This last group includes investment advisors, analysts, and portfolio managers. Beyond them, of course, I hope that it will also be useful to businesses that have an interest in ensuring that investors and their advisors are able to grasp the value of a company and its operations.

With this as my starting-point, I distinguish between accounting techniques for measuring value and models that are aimed at predicting, say, exit values on assets that the business is not actually exiting. I want to use known value as my anchor and then add to that a speculative component about future performance where value is derived from the best information available to me. In investing you are always taking a view of future performance, so a speculative dimension is inevitable. However, this should come only after you have anchored yourself on actual valuation. If your starting-point in appraising a particular company is also speculative, where are you?

With this approach it is clear that historic cost accounting is very useful to investors who like to base themselves on fundamental values, since it grounds itself in prices actually paid. My problem with the accountancy bodies begins at the point where they start to move away from historic cost accounting toward what they define as balance sheet accounting. With balance sheet accounting they are trying to put a present value on all the assets on the balance sheet, including assets such as stock, which the business has no intention of selling, but which, rather, is designated for production purposes. As such, external prices for that stock are completely irrelevant until and unless the company is in the process of winding up —at which point you would be highly unlikely to want to invest in it anyway.

There are very few companies where balance sheet accounting is actually useful for a potential investor. With a pure investment company that holds a large equity portfolio, for example, knowing the present value of that portfolio is excellent information. The company's worth really does go up and down with the market, so you need to know where it stands. A bank's portfolio of mortgage loans, on the other hand, is not, I would argue, something to which you need to apply a moment-by-moment "fair value."

That mortgage portfolio is what drives revenue for the bank, and it is, by its nature, going to be held to termination. Where the bank conducts a securitization of its mortgage book and sells that part of the book, of course you have a present value for the securitized bundle, but that is a special case where the bank is literally turning part of the book into cash and there is nothing speculative about that cash value.

What you would want to know about the bank's mortgage portfolio is not its fluctuating present value, but rather that there has been appropriate due diligence in the granting of the loans that comprise the portfolio. You want to know, in other words, that the bank's business processes are sound and under control. If you conclude that its processes are hugely flawed, then the present value of the bank's book is largely irrelevant since you can assume that the bank is highly likely to experience a much higher rate of default than its competitors—in other words, that the value of its book is likely to be considerably impaired over time, irrespective of what its present value might be—and you would be a fool to invest. This point, clearly, has to do with the importance of information and nothing to do with fair value, or the supposed present value of the bank's mortgage portfolio.

You contend then that taking a "fair-value" view of the assets on the balance sheet does not generate much useful information for investors?

In my view this is a crucial point to make. Fair-value accounting, which is what the accounting standards bodies are now nailing their colors to, by definition sees value as being communicated through the balance sheet. The US Financial Accounting Standards Board (FASB) and the International Accounting Standards Board (IASB), in developing their "conceptual framework" for accounting—which is designed to harmonize the standards-setting process between the two bodies—appear to be committed to this balance sheet focus.

In their view, if you measure value in the balance sheet, then earnings will fall out as simply the change in balance sheet measurement. My contention is that, for anyone interested in a company's value and its actual and potential earnings capability

"Speculation is an effort, probably unsuccessful, to turn a little money into a lot. Investment is an effort, which should be successful, to prevent a lot of money from becoming a little." Fred Schwed

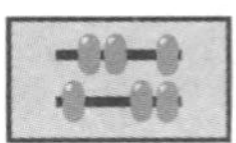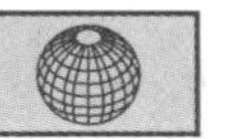

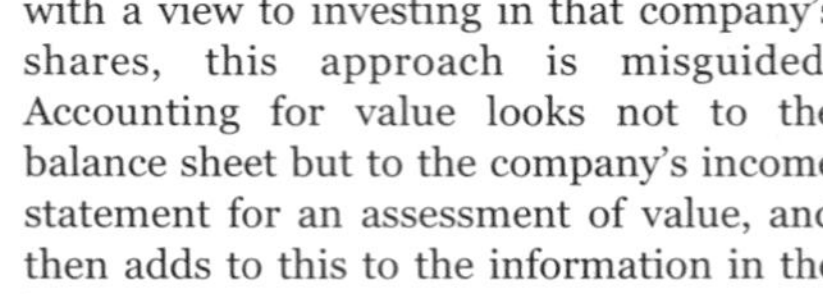

with a view to investing in that company's shares, this approach is misguided. Accounting for value looks not to the balance sheet but to the company's income statement for an assessment of value, and then adds to this to the information in the balance sheet.

It should be clear from what I have said that fair-value accounting is not the same thing as accounting for value except in the case of the example just given of an investment company. An accountant cannot hope to capture value by listing assets and liabilities at their fair value, defined as their present price in the market.

The role of the accountant, then, is to avoid all speculation? Is this possible?

As I say in the book, accounting defines reality by bringing specificity to what would otherwise be speculative generalities. It takes concepts in common use by economists, such as "revenue," "cost," "income," and "assets," and applies measurement to them. "Cost of production" is, fundamentally, an accounting measure, and the figure that emerges depends on how one does the accounting. "Economic profit" is just a phrase, a pretentious label, until accounting gives it content. There is much in accounting that is an art rather than a science, and that relies on professional judgment. How "profit" is determined, for example, depends very much on the accounting conventions that are used, but there is a solid, agreed body of best practice here as far as historic cost accounting is concerned and investors, by and large, are comfortable with this best practice.

Without accounting, concepts such as "profitability," "financial position," and "growth" are just speculative ideas in the mind of the beholder. Accounting forces concreteness—not simply concrete numbers, which are important, but also concrete thinking. It gives investors the chance to ground their analysis of an organization on something solid. In the heyday of "efficient market" theory, accounting was held not to matter. It was said that the market "sees through" the accounting to the future cash flows of the company concerned. When we analyze this idea, however, it turns out that what the market is "seeing" is some form of information that allows it to forecast future cash flows, and ultimately the information that the market is seeing flows from accounting. We can, of course, see factories, employees, the movement of goods, and the delivery of services, but accounting produces a representation of these realities that is appropriate for valuation.

Proponents of the efficient market have a tendency to dismiss accounting as unconnected to reality, an archaic system that is unrelated to cash flows. This is a gross misconception. Accounting forces management to face the numbers when reporting to shareholders, rather than simply delivering platitudes about plans and prospects. Similarly, sound government accounting forces politicians to be straightforward in reporting to taxpayers—to view borrowing as a debt, for example, rather than as a miraculous revenue stream.

For a few quantitative investment techniques that focus purely on stock volatility and the correlation between stocks to build a portfolio, accounting "facts" may not be part of the data sets that the funds look at to pick the stocks to make up their portfolios. This might seem as if accounting has been cast aside, but accounting is still there, of course, in that the vast number of investors who are not "quants" use accounting facts in their investment decisions. Their decisions, informed in part by accounting "facts," set the prices of stocks, and the changes in those prices constitute the volatilities used by quant funds. Volatility, then, is simply a measure of investor and market uncertainty. It is a very useful measure, but it certainly does not supplant accountancy, without which uncertainty would be rampant!

How do you see the interaction between accounting for value and financial engineering, or the building of mathematical models to forecast cash flows and to determine where investment can profitably flow?

Modern finance, and modern financial engineering, begin with the no-arbitrage principle. This principle is the cornerstone of modern finance. Its insight is that prices are set in relation to each other such that there is no profit to be gained from selling at one price and buying at another. Prices cannot be arbitraged. Oil should trade in Rotterdam and New York at the same price, adjusted for transport and other transaction costs. Oil futures trade relative to spot prices such that there is no advantage to arbitraging the two. And the price of a call or put option on a stock must bear a no-arbitrage relation to the stock price.

The power and usefulness of the no-arbitrage principle is that it enables theorists, particularly mathematical modelers, to move much more cleanly towards their goals, unencumbered by a whole collection of assumptions about consumer or investor likes and dislikes. Price and risk can be put into direct relation to each other, with additional risk being rewarded by additional price.

However, although this relationship between price and risk is very useful for fundamental investors, it is important to realize that value investing picks up the no-arbitrage principle from a different standpoint to mathematical modeling. For the value investor, what the no-arbitrage principle speaks to is value, not price, and the principle is really a function or summary of the role that information plays in decision-making. This is what drives it. Prices obey the no-arbitrage rule, as far as fundamental investors are concerned, not because of their relationship to other prices, but because of their relationship to information. As I say in my book, information is the arbitraging mechanism in the market. Prices gravitate to fundamentals as information on which value is based is recognized by the markets.

One of the most important contributions of modern financial engineering is the Black–Scholes formula for pricing derivatives, which was formulated by Fischer Black, Myron S. Scholes, and Robert C. Merton. This rests on the no-arbitrage principle and has been hugely useful as it has enabled financial engineers to develop a wide range of hedging instruments which reach through to the underlying prices of whatever is in question, be it share prices, indexes, commodities, or mortgages. This has had enormous benefits since it has enabled the development of markets in those instruments, enabling enhanced risk-sharing in the economy and greatly improving our understanding of risk.

For the value investor, the positive outcomes of all this are many and various. The investor can now focus on the alpha performance they are after, while specifically identifying and hedging out the risks that they do not want to be exposed to. Of course, there is a cost to buying insurance against those other risks, but evaluating this cost against the benefits of the hedge is now part of the investor's skill set.

Where it all gets tricky, however, is that these new financial instruments can be used as speculative tools as well as being pressed into service as hedging tools. The price at which insurance can be bought can become the prime area for speculation.

There is a more basic problem for the fundamentalist, however, based on the distinction between price and value. The Black–Scholes formula might reach through to the underlying price of the equity in an option contract, but it is silent on its value, assuming that the two are identical. From this standpoint, for funda-

"The responsibility to minimise risks and prevent problems happening in a particular institution lies, first and foremost, with the people who run and own that institution … no government should ever be in the business of using public money to protect executives who make the wrong call or bad decisions." Alistair Darling

mentalists the no-arbitrage principle is no help at all.

So the question then is how should fundamental investors regard financial engineering innovations? It is clear that they should welcome the risk-sharing opportunities that financial engineering products offer, for now (in the language of active investing) investors can be exposed to "alpha" (manager outperformance) while buying insurance against risk factors to which they do not wish to be exposed. But fundamentalists have reservations. They see arbitrage opportunities, so no-arbitrage engineering goes against the grain. If you are buying a business rather than a share, then you recognize that businesses are fundamentally about arbitrage. They trade in input markets (assets, labor) and in output markets (customers) on the basis that they sell high (to customers) and buy low (from suppliers). That is arbitrage. When you buy a share of a business, you are essentially expressing your confidence in its ability to operate the arbitrage principle! The no-arbitrage principle comes in one level above this, as it were, and for the fundamental investor what it states is that information about that business's ability to operate the arbitrage principle is available to the market and therefore determines that business's value to investors. It is that value which the principle is stating cannot be arbitraged. Put like this, the principle is seen as no more than a probability statement about the likelihood of investors all reaching a similar conclusion on value based on identical access to information. Differences between price and value have to do with which kinds of information a market is mainly paying attention to. If fear is driving the markets, then value information often has little traction and whole sectors are marked down. This misalignment of price and value creates opportunities for value investors. What is being arbitraged here is not price, but the misalignment of price and value.

Looking again at the information content, what is clear is that a value investor needs an accounting model that accounts for how the shareholder's value is increased (or diminished) by the business's ability to arbitrage inputs and outputs. This brings us to the negative use of financial engineering. It is clear that for a given accounting system, say US GAAP (Generally Agreed Accounting Principles), financial engineering will be used to structure transactions to get around the requirements of accounting. Lease transactions can be arranged to take leasing contracts off the balance sheet. Assets and liabilities can be moved into "special-purpose vehicles" (SPVs), and borrowing can be restructured to look like an option on stock. Fundamental investors look for ways to finesse these masking activities by bringing that information back into the accounting model. The energies and expertise of the accounting standards bodies would be much better employed focusing on undoing these negative impacts of financial engineering, rather than continuing with their current enthusiasm for balance sheet accounting.

MORE INFO

Book:

Penman, Stephen. *Accounting for Value*. New York: Columbia University Press, 2011.

Articles:

Black, Fischer, and Myron Scholes. "The pricing of options and corporate liabilities." *Journal of Political Economy* 81:3 (May–June 1973): 637–654. Online at: www.jstor.org/stable/1831029

Merton, Robert C. "Theory of rational option pricing." *Bell Journal of Economics and Management Science* 4:1 (Spring 1973): 141–183. Online at: www.jstor.org/stable/3003143

See Also:

★ Origins and Rationale for IFRS Convergence (pp. 385–388)
★ Viewpoint: The "Comply or Explain" Approach to Improving Standards of Corporate Governance (pp. 651–653)
✔ International Financial Reporting Standards (IFRS): The Basics (p. 1039)
✔ Key Accounting Standards and Organizations (p. 1040)

  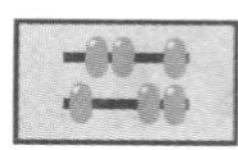      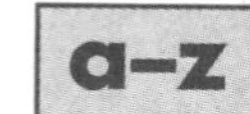

Aligning the Internal Audit Function with Strategic Objectives by Ilias G. Basioudis

EXECUTIVE SUMMARY

- Due to high-profile scandals at the beginning of the century, regulators and the accounting profession worldwide have put forward a series of initiatives to repair the damage and restore faith in corporate governance.
- Globally, more companies are adopting corporate governance best practice.
- An independent internal audit function is widely recognized as an integral part of a company's strategic objectives, corporate governance, and risk management.
- The internal audit standards issued by the Institute of Internal Auditors serve as authoritative guidance for members of the internal audit profession.
- Internal audit's role is to evaluate the appropriateness and effectiveness of companies' systems and processes, and to identify and manage risks present in the normal course of conducting business activities.

INTRODUCTION

Given today's complex and rapidly changing management climate, companies must implement continuous improvements to achieve efficiency, and assure investors and other concerned parties of solid corporate governance.

The recent scandals at Enron, WorldCom, Parmalat, and others have raised the profile of corporate governance across the globe. Trust in the process of financial accounting, corporate governance, and auditing has been undermined by these high-profile corporate scandals. In response, regulators and the accounting profession worldwide have put forward a series of initiatives to repair the damage and restore faith in corporate governance. Furthermore, companies must continuously implement improvements to achieve effective and efficient management in order to assure the investors, other stakeholders, and concerned parties in general of its good and sound corporate governance. Globally, more companies, governments, states, and regulators are adopting corporate governance best practice, and placing more emphasis on improving corporate governance in companies, which in turn improves the confidence of investors and stakeholders in companies.

Worldwide legislative initiatives, of which the Sarbanes–Oxley Act (US) and Directive No. 8 (EU) are the most famous, make senior management responsible for establishing, evaluating, and assessing over time the effectiveness of risk management processes, systems of internal control, and corporate governance processes. In tandem, companies play a critical role in the national economy, or economies, in which they have activities. A country's competitiveness, wealth, efficiency, and high level of economic growth may depend on the competitive nature of its companies. There is no doubt that a transparent and reasonable corporate governance structure has a positive impact on a company.

The audit committee is a subcommittee of the board of directors, and is widely recognized as an integral part of a company's corporate governance, and, together with the internal audit function, they contribute towards the company implementing continuous improvements. In fact, one line of thought claims that the audit committee, especially in large organizations, could not possibly be effective without an efficient, effective, and independent-minded internal audit function.

As a result, the internal audit function has the potential to be one of the most influential and value-adding services available to a company's senior management and board of directors. Furthermore, with the growing focus on corporate governance issues, organizations are increasingly exploring the potential benefits to be gained from establishing an effective and efficient internal audit function. Company boards must identify the opportunities, risks, and exposures that can determine success or failure. The establishment of an internal audit function can become an integral part of overall strategy, and assist in achieving corporate objectives.

THE PURPOSE AND ROLE OF INTERNAL AUDITING

According to The Institute of Internal Auditors' (IIA) definition of internal auditing, the internal audit function should provide independent, thorough, timely, and objective results of quantitative and qualitative testing to senior management, and, in essence, help evaluate organizational risk management. Internal auditing assists public and private organizations to meet overall corporate objectives by establishing a systematic and disciplined approach to assessing, evaluating, and improving the quality and effectiveness of risk management processes, systems of internal control, and corporate governance processes. This systematic approach and analysis is implemented across all parts of an organization, and the internal auditor reports directly and independently to the most senior level of management. The role of the internal auditor, therefore, is to provide an overall assurance to management that all key risks within an organization are managed effectively, so that the organization can achieve its strategic objectives.

An internal audit function should be independent and unbiased, and hold a neutral position within an organization. The audit function looks beyond the narrow focus of financial statements and financial risks (although these risks are included in the remit of the internal auditor's job), and it may, for example, involve auditing reputational, operational, environmental, or strategic risks. Reputational risks could involve labor practices in host countries; operational risks include poor health and safety procedures; environmental risks might involve pollution generated by a factory; while a strategic risk might involve the board stretching company resources by producing too many products.

An internal audit function should have the ability itself to define the scope of internal audits (after consultation with the internal audit's primary stakeholders), the authority to obtain information and resources, and have an appropriate reporting structure to senior management. The internal audit team members do not test their own work, or the work of persons that they report to. Any actual or potential conflicts of interest that hinder an honest, independent, and unbiased assessment must be disclosed.

INTERNAL AUDIT STANDARDS

In order to operate an internal audit function that is objective, independent, effective, and useful to an organization, it is essential that the internal audit function complies with the International Standards for the Professional Practice of Internal Auditing, developed by the Institute of Internal Auditors. The International Standards are authoritative guidance for the internal audit profession, and are

"**Those who invest only to get rich will fail. Those who invest to help others will probably succeed.**" Art Fry

  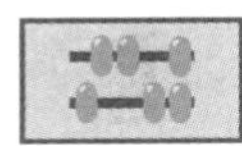      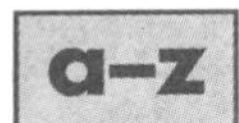

principles-focused. Implementation standards refer to either assurance or consulting activities, and are embedded in the attribute and performance standards. Attribute standards refer to the composition of the audit department in terms of staff expertise and ongoing training, as well as independence and objectivity. Attribute standards also refer to the internal audit department's purpose, authority, and responsibility.

Performance standards refer to how the internal audit function should operate, and how the planning, scope, and reporting activities should be conducted and by whom. The performance standards reflect the purpose of the internal audit function in that they define the activities to be completed, which help make sure that the internal audit function is operating as designed for the benefit of the organization.

Another authoritative guidance issued by the IIA is the Code of Ethics. This is a statement of principles and expectations governing the behavior of individuals and organizations in the conduct of internal auditing, and provides a description of minimum requirements for conduct, and describes behavioral expectations rather than specific activities. The Code of Ethics refers to the integrity, objectivity, confidentiality, and competence of internal auditors.

DESIGNING A STRATEGICALLY FOCUSED INTERNAL AUDIT FUNCTION

How well an organization is able to recognize, understand, and manage its risks plays a critical part in the success, or failure, of the organization, and, consequently, the value it is able to deliver to customers, shareholders, and other stakeholders.

The internal audit function contributes to better overall governance when it operates within a strategic framework established by the audit committee and senior management. Once this strategic framework is in place, the corporation will be well positioned to define the mission, organizational structure, resource model, working practices, and communications protocols for the internal audit function.

Hence, when designing and implementing an effective internal audit function, the corporation's strategic objectives must be followed closely, and not vice versa. In other words, the internal audit's primary stakeholders must determine how the function will deliver the desired value, and what the specified outcomes expected of the new function are to be.

Common internal audit outcomes include:

- assessment of internal control effectiveness and efficiency;
- risk management and control assurance;
- regulatory and corporate compliance assurance;
- legislature readiness assessment and ongoing testing, such as Sarbanes-Oxley Act (US) and Directive No. 8 (EU);
- fostering awareness of risk and control across the organization;
- ability to respond to urgent events.

Once the function is established and the specific outcomes have been identified and defined, the internal audit's stakeholder expectations should be reassessed on a regular basis, and the mission for the internal audit function must be clearly articulated, so that the performance of the function can be evaluated on a regular basis. In addition, a formal mission statement for the internal audit function should be laid out by the head of the audit function, with the cooperation of senior management and the audit committee. The mission statement must also be aligned clearly and directly with stakeholder expectations and the internal audit's specified outcomes, as otherwise it would be of little value and possibly detrimental to achieving corporate strategic performance. Furthermore, the mission statement must be shared and communicated, to achieve full understanding and buy-in among key stakeholders and staff.

Once the mission statement is agreed, a formal strategic plan must be approved. This plan formally defines the value proposition of the new function, the customers it serves, and the value it will create now and into the future. The strategic plan serves as an operational manual of the new function, and as guidance on the key objectives and outcomes of the function, and how they will be achieved. The strategic plan sets a standard against which future decisions and results can be measured. Ideally, the plan should be reviewed at least annually, with changes considered and approved by all primary stakeholders as appropriate. For large companies, a full audit cycle of three years generally may seem appropriate; that is, the whole organization should be audited in an appropriate manner within three years. However, high risk areas should be audited at least annually.

Next, it is critical for the internal audit to develop a systematic process to analyze risk, and ensure that the audit plan is sufficiently broad in scope and executed in a timely manner. Internal auditors should segment the corporation into well-defined, reasonably sized, auditable units (often collectively called the "audit universe"), and then identify, determine, and prioritize/rank the inherent risks in each unit. Even a small business unit is likely to have a range of risks, some of which are higher priority than others. Inherent risks are those present in the normal course of conducting business activities. These include external risks such as changes to global, national, and economic climates, as well as technological, legal, social, and political changes. Inherent risks also include internal factors that warrant special attention, including changes in operating systems, new product launches, entry to new markets, management and organizational changes, and the expansion of foreign operations. Therefore, the risk assessment should evaluate current and prospective risks, particularly where new risks are emerging due to a change in the corporation's strategy or product mix.

The senior management and the audit committee must ensure the risk assessment executed by the audit function is not limited by reference to its own skill sets. In other words, a misalignment must be avoided between the technical competencies necessary to execute the audit plan and the skill sets resident in the internal audit function. An effective way to prioritize processes for audit purposes is to look at a matrix of probability of occurrence versus severity of loss for each of the processes, and develop a risk-based audit plan according to this classification.

Furthermore, other departments and functions within an organization gather intelligence and other important information, and senior management and the audit committee must ensure that the internal auditors are aware of these, and use them accordingly in determining and prioritizing risks. However, it is not necessary that the internal audit's independent view on risks coincide with other functions' perspectives in the organization, and this needs to be recognized and accepted. Senior management and the audit committee should also evaluate whether any "strong" executives or directors outside of the internal audit function, or "strong" business areas within the organization, have played a major role in shaping the internal audit's plan, and, if so, in what way. After the risk assessment is performed and the risk-based audit plan is drawn up, it is then important that timely and comprehensive coverage by the internal audit function is secured in order that the reliability and effectiveness of the internal controls in mitigating the significance and/or likelihood of a risk occurrence are considered. Another step to be taken after the assessment of risks and the audit plan are completed is the creation of current and longer-term budgets for the internal audit function. Budgets must provide sufficient resources for internal auditors to deliver the developed risk-based audit plan, as well

"Make your company stock a consumer product. When consumers buy stock in your company, they'll never buy a competitive product. You've linked their financial future to yours." Faith Popcorn

as the flexibility to respond to changing business needs.

Budgets should be aligned with corporate strategies, and look to internal audit benchmarks developed by the IIA or other third parties to establish a budgetary baseline as compared to similar internal audit functions within the same industry. The budget should be projected on a three-to-five-year horizon.

The fieldwork should begin as soon as possible, even prior to having all staffing and infrastructure in place. Key stakeholders in an organization want to see demonstrable progress promptly, so it is important to begin conducting the audits without delay, in order for the internal audit function to create immediate value. In a start-up internal audit department, the first three months are important in completing the audits of three to five known high-risk areas, such as general computer systems and controls, inventory management, and other business areas with known internal control problems and challenges.

At times, corporations are impatient for results and, thus, they may choose to outsource all, or nearly all, of the internal audit to a third-party specialist firm. This is in contrast to the IIA's recommendation, which states that internal audit activity should never be fully outsourced, but should be managed from within the organization. Outsourcing can have several advantages, including employing professionals who are more independent as they are not beholden to management for their compensation; access to resources necessary to complete specific high-risk audits; access to an array of technical, up-to-date expertise; and, possibly, knowledge transfer to the organization's employees as the function converts into a full in-house or co-sourced resource model.

On the other hand, full or near-full outsourcing brings with it specific governance challenges for senior management and the audit committee. These problems may include the following: limited communication and level of interaction between the organization and the third-party audit professionals; increased difficulty for the third-party auditors to gain sufficient standing in the corporation; outsourcing is significantly more expensive on a per-hour basis than undertaking the function in-house; and, the corporation has limited ability to influence audit team appointments when the internal audit function is fully outsourced. If some level of dependence on third-party firms for specialist audit skills is necessary for a corporation, then selective use of co-sourcing arrangements should be in place.

By revisiting stakeholder-specified outcomes and the internal audit function's mission statement developed earlier in the start-up process, a balanced staffing model must be adapted to each corporation's needs. Best practice requires corporations to staff their internal audit functions with long-tenured audit career professionals, as well as rotating talented executives from across the organization for two-or three-year rotations in internal audit. Furthermore, the necessary internal audit infrastructure and methodologies should be developed at the same time. These will greatly improve the efficiency, quality, and consistency of the internal audit process, and will provide assurance towards compliance with both the organization's methodologies, policies, and desired outcomes, and the standards developed by the IIA. Corporations should establish routine, robust, and frank lines of communication with their key internal audit professionals. It is imperative that an internal audit function communicates effectively and freely with all its internal stakeholders (and, primarily, with senior management and the audit committee). On a regular, if not daily, basis, the internal audit should seek opportunities for dialogue and communication with the corporation's senior management and the audit committee, creating a strong, clear connection between the internal audit mission and the corporation's strategic issues and risks.

In addition, the external auditors also have a role to play in an organization's corporate governance, and, as such, the audit committee should seek to establish and maintain good links and cooperation between internal and external audits.

Finally, it is important that the internal audit demonstrates results, and its reports are actionable and implemented. The reports should be generated and circulated in a timely fashion after the audit is complete, and senior management and the audit committee should ensure that an effective and timely follow-up to the reports has been implemented.

CONCLUSION

Organizations serve their stakeholders. Senior management's role is to ensure that the organization's resources are managed and applied effectively to meet objectives and responsibilities. A crucial part of this process of governance is the design of appropriate systems and processes in order for them to be able to identify and manage risks effectively and efficiently. Internal audit's role is to evaluate the appropriateness and effectiveness of those systems and processes, whether they are related to finance, IT, brand reputation, health and safety, legal and regulatory compliance, human resources, and/or major projects.

Internal auditors perform their role by working with boards of directors, audit committees, and senior managers to help them understand the consequences of risks and ineffective processes to manage them. They encourage and support managers to have appropriate systems in place. Internal auditors then report to senior management and the audit committee on how effectively these systems of control are operating. In such a way, the corporation succeeds in aligning the internal audit function with its strategic objectives.

MAKING IT HAPPEN

Aligning the Internal Audit Function with Strategic Objectives

- Define stakeholder expectations.
- Articulate the mission, structure, resource model, working practices, and communication protocols for the internal audit function.
- Develop a formal strategic plan and assess company risks.
- Establish short- and long-term budgets for the internal audit function.
- Launch fieldwork quickly and, concurrently, assess any further needed skill sets.
- Develop internally or acquire (by outsourcing) enabling internal audit infrastructure, methodologies, and technologies.
- Determine clear lines of communication between the internal audit function and all company stakeholders (primarily, however, with senior management and the audit committee).
- Measure the results of the internal audit function.

MORE INFO

Books:

Pickett, K. H. Spencer. *The Essential Handbook of Internal Auditing*. Chichester, UK: Wiley, 2005.

Pickett, K. H. Spencer. *Audit Planning: A Risk-Based Approach*. Hoboken, NJ: Wiley, 2006.

"My advice to this investor is the same that I give to the young investors in my classes ... Devote the same earnest attention to investing that $50,000 as you devoted to earning it." Ivan Boesky

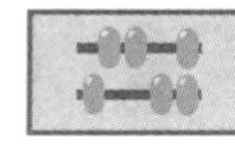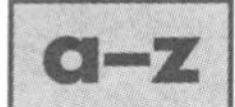

Viewpoint: The Audit Committee and Corporate Governance by Richard Wilson

INTRODUCTION

Richard Wilson is a senior audit partner with Ernst & Young. He qualified as a chartered accountant in 1976 and became a partner in the firm in 1985. He has worked predominately with large listed companies in sectors such as oil and gas, media, and transportation. He was global head of Ernst & Young's energy and utilities practice from 1998 to 2003. He became a member of the Institute of Chartered Accountants in England and Wales (ICAEW) audit and assurance faculty in 2008 and a member of the Financial Reporting Council (FRC) financial reporting review panel in 2011.

Audit committees in large public companies have an essential role as part of the corporate governance regime. How would you sum up the main tasks of the audit committee?

The main role of the audit committee comes down to providing delegated board oversight over financial reporting and financial risk management. Maintaining a continuing dialog with the internal and external auditors is very much a central part of the audit committee's activities, as is its relationship with the finance director and the finance team. Understanding the way risk is identified and managed within the organization is also central. Basically, everything that that is financial in nature that goes to the sustainability of the organization is part of the brief.

In some companies this may go beyond financial. There are a tremendous number of moving parts that define the viability of the organization, with many drivers and a great deal of complexity and interaction between them. The quality of the people involved, the quality of the systems that a company has, and the sector the company is in all play a role and have a bearing on the degree of effort that the audit committee has to put in to satisfy itself that it is on top of the brief assigned to it by the board. It is important to remember that the audit committee is, in one sense, simply a specialist subcommittee of the main board, with its members appointed by the chairman of the board.

The interaction with external auditors is a very interesting and critical part of the brief. The external auditors are there to provide assurance to investors/shareholders that they are receiving the appropriate financial information, free from material error, to allow them to judge whether their money is being well protected and well managed by the directors.

The standards governing the audit process are constantly evolving and being refined. How technically aware does the audit committee need to be?

There is absolutely no doubt that audit standards have been and are evolving. When I look at the audit world today by comparison to, say, 30 years ago, it is quite clear that we now have more clearly defined audit standards and there is a great deal to help auditors to determine how they should go about their work. However, in many areas the quality of the financial information available to the auditor will be dependent on judgments taken by the board in key areas. In these cases, the auditor's role is to judge whether the reported output on those board judgments is clear and understandable.

A great deal of the audit, in other words, is about routine processes, and there is another element that is about exercising sound commercial business and financial judgment in the execution of the annual audit. The external audit firm needs to understand the risk profile of the company and it needs to form judgments on the integrity of management and whether the company has the quality of management to manage the risks that the company, at the direction of the board, is taking on and that this is presented in the financial statements in a way that is true and fair.

There are some important distinctions here that the press and the public often get into a muddle over. It may be very clear in a particular company what its business model is and you can see very clearly what it is setting out to do. The execution of that model might not turn out well in practice, but this is not the same thing as misleading shareholders and creditors as to what the company is doing, or what its aims and objectives are. What is key here is getting some definition and transparency over the risks that are being run. Investors need to be able to form a view about the risks that a company is running in its attempt to make a certain level of returns.

If you invest in an exploration and production (E&P) oil company, for example, you know that the company explores for oil and gas, and you know from the outset that you run the risk as an investor that the company might fail to find reserves. What you need—assuming that you have some confidence in the management team to achieve the company's goals—in order to make your investment decision is some indication or guidance as to the probability of them finding oil. So the financial statements produced by the E&P company should include sufficient information for investors to form a clear view as to the chances of success and the risks associated with achieving that success.

Before signing the audit report the auditors will need to work with the company to see whether it has got it right or not. If not, then since this could go, for example, directly to whether the E&P company can claim to be a going concern or not, the audit firm might well need to revisit its "going concern" opinion. In any event, the external auditor needs to enable shareholders to form a view as to whether they are comfortable or not with the stewardship of the company through the completion of the audit report. The audit committee is there to ensure that the auditors get the level of cooperation from management that they require. So you can see that the audit committee's role is fundamental in ensuring that external auditors can do their job unhindered.

You can extrapolate from this to every shade of enterprise. In any set of financial statements there is an element that is historical, which reports on past numbers, and there is an element that is forward-looking. Everyone knows that the financial statements are struck at a particular point in time, and all the auditor can do is to ensure that the information being included in the report is reasonable and that it complies with the relevant laws, standards, and regulations.

But what we are also seeing is rather more disclosure on business models and on the key risks and uncertainties facing the company. It cannot be the role of the external auditor to second-guess management's judgment of those risks and uncertainties. However, the auditor will challenge management on their assertions and will need to review this information to ensure that it reflects the auditors' knowledge of how the board and management are running the enterprise when it comes to including this information in the financial statements.

The audit committee also has a brief to challenge the financial statements. This is where the audit committee chairperson plays a hugely important role. The committee chair will want to engage in continuing dialog with the finance director and the external and internal auditors. It is therefore very important that the chair of the committee has a strong financial background.

So the audit chairperson will provide guidance to the rest of the audit committee?

Yes, insofar as it is necessary. Clearly, the way the company interprets international financial reporting standards and their acceptability is down to the finance director and the external auditors, but where there are issues to be discussed the chair will brief the other members of the audit committee. At the end of the day the audit committee has to confirm to the board as a whole that it is satisfied with the financial statements and the underlying financial processes and procedures.

It is quite clear that an extraordinary amount of detailed information goes into company reports and accounts these days, either to comply with corporate law or to meet accounting standards, or the listing rules of various stock exchanges. Best practice is continually evolving and it can enhance a company's reputation for it to be seen as at the forefront of best practice.

There is some criticism today that too much information is required to meet the various compliance criteria and that this makes it harder for the investors to focus on the parts of the report that really matter to them. However, a good auditor will always make sure that the company discloses all relevant information and that all relevant information is made available to the audit committee, either by management or by themselves before it becomes part of the published financial statements. Companies will make mistakes in executing on their strategy, and those mistakes will need to be understood in the context of what the company is trying to do and the reasons for their occurrence rectified. Mistakes may indicate a breakdown in risk management processes, so the committee will seek assurances on how they will be prevented from occurring again.

This is an important point to grasp. The audit committee is not there to get involved in the ordinary operational running of the company—and in fact it should not get involved at this level since that would compromise its independence. It is there to provide independent oversight and scrutiny, and it should only get involved via a responsible challenge process, where it is testing the finance director's grip on, and the systems for, monitoring the strategic execution of board policies.

Common sense helps here. Risk is expected to carry a premium, and the company's track record in turning risk into outperformance will be factored into its share price. What you do not want as an investor is to have a company that is at the racier end of the scale from, say, a bog standard utility, yet the accounts seek to convey an impression that there is no added risk over and above that which the utility would experience.

If the chairman of the board has the composition of the audit committee right, the committee will be able to walk the fine line between being independent and being on hand to provide some input into management thinking based on the experience of the nonexecutive directors that comprise the audit committee. Their role as committee members is to bring their experience to bear on responsible challenge. What they must not do is get involved in operational matters. So a nonexecutive director who is, say, a marketing specialist might comment on the company's marketing plans, but he or she certainly should not be providing detailed consultancy support on those plans. Oversight embraces the issue of corporate governance, but seen from a challenge perspective.

For example, where the company is planning to acquire a competitor, it is very much part of the board's role to ask what the finance director and the CEO expect the benefits of the merger to be. The audit committee may be tasked to challenge the evidence of a financial nature which supports the proposal. They might also say, for example, that acquiring that particular company would not be their first choice, but they are not there to second-guess management, they are there to challenge management on their rationale and thinking. If there are concerns, it is legitimate to raise these concerns for full board discussion.

What the audit committee would want to see through its oversight of risk, in the case of merger and acquisition, or in the case of, say, the setting up of a new plant in an emerging market, is that the project has been fully thought through. The committee would want to see that management has the right procedures in place to identify and mitigate risk. This, again, goes to both corporate governance and, ultimately, to the going-concern provisions, which seek to ensure that the company is not jeopardizing its survival by taking on projects that could overbalance it or lead to disaster.

The more technical role of the audit committee will be to ascertain what the expected returns from the project are and then to see that, as this information is developed and reported to shareholders, it matches back to the key decisions that management took and to the goals that were set for the project. So, even if the audit committee feels that the project is not ideal, if the overwhelming consensus of the board is that it should go ahead, the audit committee will have to content itself with monitoring the way the project is reported over its life cycle and to seeing that a fair report is made to shareholders.

You have been joint chair of the Confederation of British Industry/ Ernst and Young forum for the chairs of audit committees. As such you are very well placed to understand what concerns audit committee chairs. How would you characterize these concerns?

There are a number of pressing issues that are concerning audit committee chairs around the country. First and foremost probably, the intervention of regulators and lawmakers and their views on corporate reporting and the quality of boards. This manifests itself in the whole issue of corporate transparency and compliance with international auditing and accounting standards. Then there is the evolving nature of risk and the management of risk. As an audit committee chair you have the classic problems that confront all nonexecutive directors. Your obligations are primarily to the shareholders, but you have far less time than management to grapple with the major

"I am very careful about bringing people into my confidence. I want to see the color of their eyes." E. Gerald Corrigan

issues facing the company. This despite the fact that you are there to provide oversight and challenge on those same issues! It is absolutely key that the audit committee has access to the right level of information to enable it to do its job.

Because the rest of the audit committee may not be from a finance background, they will be looking to the audit committee chair to provide the expertise on accounting standards and to provide guidance on whether or not the company is fulfilling its duties of compliance. The chair needs to recognize that they will be taking a strong leadership role, and it is up to the chair to ensure that members are sufficiently briefed.

What should the relationship be between the audit committee and the finance director?

The chair will want to maintain a continuing dialog with the finance director throughout the year. The relationship should be cordial, but it should also be one of challenge. There are a number of areas where the audit committee will want to probe the finance director. These include the preparation of interim statements and the annual report and accounts, obviously, but the committee will also want to understand and be comfortable with the sorts of financial communication that the finance director and the executive team are having with the market. Plus there will need to be constant dialog on the areas of the accounts where management have to exercise judgment.

What you try to do here is to satisfy yourself that the rationale behind the judgments is sound and that there are processes in place to apply metrics to the results. Also, you are challenging the auditors as to how they got themselves happy with some of these key judgment areas. Examples include the risks on assets, sales expectations, and so on. The audit committee is also very concerned with off-balance-sheet decisions that can affect the financing of the business. It needs to be kept in the loop, and the audit chair's relationship with the finance director is key here.

It is inevitable that more reporting is going to be required from companies, and we may well see a move to requiring some kind of report from the audit committee directed at stakeholders, akin to the remuneration committee report that has been introduced. There is no doubt that there is now much more pressure on the audit committee from regulators for it to probe the external auditors. The responsibilities placed on the committee and on the committee chair just keep growing.

MORE INFO

Website:

CBI/Ernst & Young Audit Committee Chair Forum: www.ey.com/UK/en/Issues/Audit-Committee-Chair-Forum

See Also:

★ Viewpoint: Auditing in Volatile Markets (pp. 286–288)
★ Viewpoint: Challenges Faced by the Audit Profession After the Crash (pp. 306–308)
★ Managing the Relationships between Audit Committees and the CAE (pp. 375–377)
✔ The Role of the Audit Committee (p. 1051)

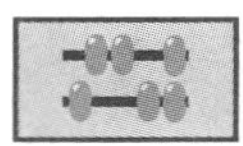

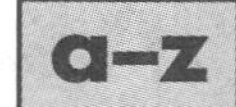

Viewpoint: Auditing in Volatile Markets

by James Roberts

INTRODUCTION

James Roberts is a senior audit partner at BDO LLP. After training with Binder Hamlyn he became a partner there in 1986 and in Arthur Andersen when it acquired the firm. His audit clients have always included a mix of public and private clients across a broad range of sectors and he has been responsible for the accounting work on over 20 IPOs. At BDO, James is responsible for the firm's Gatwick office and is public policy spokesperson on audit and accounting matters. James is married with two student children and lives in West Sussex in the United Kingdom. His interests outside business include music, gardening, and reading.

Being an auditor when markets are falling and companies have become extremely defensive and inward-looking must pose particular challenges?

There is no doubt that everything is much more fraught when markets are crashing. These circumstances make management's life much more difficult. In a very uncertain environment, when all the figures, the key numbers for a company, are in play, it becomes particularly challenging for both management and auditors. For a start, very volatile markets create in turn a great deal of volatility in corporate balance sheets, and users of accounts do not understand as well as they might how to view this volatility when they are looking at the accounts. It becomes very difficult for them to judge what is "real" and actually matters, as against what is simply an artifact of a particular accounting process.

Auditors need to understand these difficulties but there is no doubt that it does take us into difficult philosophical terrain. When you have that much volatility, what are the accounts actually telling you?

Of course, from an investor's perspective, the accounts should only be one among a number of information sources feeding in to the decision-making process. That said, however, users have a right to believe that the accounts will offer something of a guide to future performance and provide a snapshot of the overall position of the company. What they want, in order to get this information from the accounts, is for the accounts to reflect a clear view of the underlying business reality.

If there is a criticism to be made of the current thrust of the accounting standards bodies, with mark-to-market accounting, for example, it is that some of the standards work seems to have gone beyond the underlying business realities. There is a large and growing gulf between accounting standards and the practical reality of business. Buyers of businesses, for example, do not sit down and compile a list that attempts to identify each element of an enterprise individually. They don't say: alright, the brand is worth so much, the current value of contracts is worth so much, so I'll add all these bits together and that is what I will pay. What the potential buyer of a business looks at primarily is future earnings. That determines what they are prepared to pay. Assets may be part of the mix but they have no stand alone meaning. Your focus, as a buyer, is on the return that is capable of being generated by those assets.

This takes us directly to the fact that there is a growing gulf between accounting standards and the business person's perception of what constitutes the realities of business. In general, accounting standards are not intuitively accessible to business people and this is particularly true of the International Financial Reporting Standards (IFRS). The feeling from business is that IFRS introduces a level of complexity that goes way beyond how they have always done business. They have a sense that IFRS is attempting to reach some Nirvana of theoretical perfection in accounting theory that is just irrelevant to their concerns and interests.

The "revolution" in accounting standards began in areas such as share option scheme accounting and share rewards, where the standards setters felt that the real costs of these schemes were not being fully recognized and reported on by companies. From there it has moved on to embrace acquisition accounting and fair value accounting, where the profession is now concerned with attempting to evaluate the market value of a business's assets and liabilities at the point in time where the accounts are drawn up. For business people, in a time where property values, say, are depressed, or even if they are inflated relative to the past year, bringing the new value into the balance sheet has no real meaning if they are not planning to dispose of the asset concerned. And if they are selling the property, then the sales price will provide that value. So they see no or little value from a mark-to-market exercise.

In a sense, it seems that the profession has lost balance between the various principles that underlie any financial reporting framework. Under the old UK Generally Accepted Accounting Principles (GAAP), the concept of Prudence was very much to the fore. Now it is just one of the elements in the new GAAP set by IFRS, rather than being a watchword for accountants and auditors alike.

How does this impact real-world accounting and the work of the auditor?

The effects of this become very clear when you look at accounting through the global crisis. Once the credit crunch hit, many markets became highly illiquid and deriving theoretical values became very hit and miss. This meant that you ended up with a range of possible values for any asset. By definition this imported, and continues to import, a great deal of subjectivity into the balance sheet. It is not at all clear how this is a benefit either to the business or to users of accounts. By comparison, historic cost accounting produces a very reasonable amount of certainty. It does not attempt to tell you what the replacement cost of an asset would be today, but it does give you solid and certain information about the original purchase cost.

Under fair value accounting, if you have a thousand or more assets that you are applying values to, and if you choose values for each asset that are at or near the top end of the range of possible values, then you

"Bureaucracy emerged out of the organization's need for order and precision and the workers' demands for impartial treatment. It was an organization ideally suited to the values and demands of the Victorian age." Warren Bennis

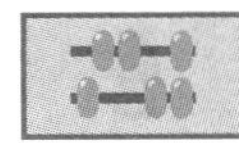

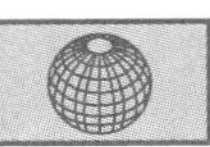

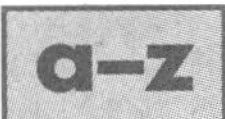

finish up with an answer, once you add all these totals together, that is clearly not supportable. However, if a company chooses to account in that way it can argue that it has followed the spirit and letter of IFRS fair value accounting and it is very difficult for the auditors then to cry "foul" in a way that would have been perfectly proper and straightforward under historic cost accounting.

When we had the Enron scandal in the US, everyone said, "Oh, that couldn't happen in the UK." The thinking then was that because we have principles-based accounting rather than rules-based, prescriptive accounting, all those off-balance sheet structures that Enron used, which evaded the rules-based approach, would have been caught by the UK's principles-based approach. The auditor could have asked: "Yes, but what is your actual exposure? How much are you at risk?"

However, the move to IFRS has seen the UK ditching the principles-based approach. In the past, an auditor would have felt much more comfortable saying to a big corporation, "Alright, you may be inside the rules, but the answer is still no, we don't like the figures you are producing and we can't agree them." Today it is a lot more difficult to say that, not because we need a stronger form of "true and fair" override, but simply because issues of rightness or wrongness were in themselves indistinct. With hard rules it is more difficult to revert to an overall "feel" that something isn't quite right. I am not personally involved in bank audits, but it is easy to see why organizations such as the Financial Services Authority have found it necessary to publicly criticize the report and accounts of major banks while the auditors of the banks concerned have not been able to push back at the banks in a like manner.

There was a good deal of criticism of the audit profession's role following the global crash. Was it all the fault of IFRS?

Undoubtedly one of the big failings that we can now see with hindsight is that before the fall of Lehman Brothers and the onset of the global financial crash, regulators and auditors were not talking to each other. Each went their own way. There are different accounts of why this was so, depending on who you talk to. This was not the case when the Bank of England was the regulator in the UK. At that time the Bank talked to auditors all the time, and now that it is resuming its duties as a regulator the Bank of England has made it clear that the FSA and the audit profession will henceforth talk to each other in a very open way. But if you go back to before the crash, if you talk to auditors they would tell you that in their view the FSA did not really seem to want to talk to auditors. If you talk to the FSA, they will tell you that there was no push from the auditors for it to talk to them. At the same time, if you consider the real world in all of this, the big banks, who are the clients of the Big Four audit firms, would not have been very happy back then to find that their auditors were perpetually popping round for coffee and a chat with the FSA about their accounting practices.

Then there is the fact that with fair-value accounting, even if auditors and regulators are talking together in a reasonable way, there is still nothing to be done if there is a substantial change in current values the day after a big client's accounts are signed off. If you are a big property company, for example, in a depressed market and your accounts are signed off, and then the next day the market bounces back and rises strongly, you are going to be very unhappy at the fact that IFRS and your auditors have made you very significantly undervalue and under-report your property portfolio. Moreover, it is going to be very difficult for users of accounts to compare the report and accounts of the property company in this example with the report and accounts of a very similar property company whose accounts were prepared after the market bounce. An analyst would have to do a lot of work with a spreadsheet translating the values before they could compare like with like. If it was all on historic cost, they would have a perfectly reasonable basis for comparison and could then go on to make any current price adjustments that they wanted to make, depending on where their analysis was going.

We have to ask ourselves why it is the purpose of accounting standards to produce accounts that make it very difficult to compare accounts both between different organizations, and indeed, between one accounting period and another. Today I suspect that analysts spend a great deal more time looking at company cash flow statements rather than at the profit and loss or the balance sheet. What you really want to know is how much cash the business is going to throw off in the longer term. It is all about operating cash flow and cash generation and the current thrust of accounting standards does not tend in this direction.

As auditors you are not required to comment on accompanying narrative, but at the same time you can't ignore it. What is the approach there?

There is currently some interesting movement in terms of all the narrative surrounding a set of accounts. The Department for Business, Innovation and Skills is currently formulating views about how this narrative might look in future. The general idea seems to be to relegate some of the verbiage to company websites and to have the accounts take the time to say what the company's business model is and where it is going. However, for company boards to feel relaxed about making these sorts of statements the UK would need to enact some kind of safe harbor provisions such as they have in the US. These provisions protect the board from litigation by investors if things turn out other than how the board was expecting. Without safe harbor provisions all this will produce is unhelpful "boiler plate" statements.

If we are going to move more towards US practice, do you see the UK adopting the US approach to producing quarterly interim statements?

We have never gone in for quarterly interims in the UK. I can perhaps see it coming in at the top of the market, for the biggest companies. The driver for this may be something that emerges from the European Union, or it might come from investor demand. However, there is no move from official UK sources to push in this direction. The FTSE techMARK index at the height of the dot.com boom encouraged quarterly statements, but it has never really taken off.

The monopoly of the Big Four audit firms (PwC, KPMG, Deloitte, and Ernst & Young) on FTSE 100 audits has come up for scrutiny. What is your view?

The House of Lords Select Committee has been particularly critical on this point. The Office of Fair Trading had a look at the stranglehold of the Big Four on big company audits and said that it intends to refer the matter to the Competition Commission for a full investigation and that is now very likely to happen. We and other firms just outside the Big Four have met with the Competition Commission and have pointed out that as things stand at present it is not a level playing field. The Big Four have 99 out of 100 audits of the FTSE 100. They maintain that there is fierce competition for audit services, but the statistics are not on their side. On average, the big plcs change their auditors once every 43 years!

The point is not particularly whether this has a price implication for audit services. It goes more to choice. A big plc might have one of the Big Four doing tax structuring work for it and the other doing work on its

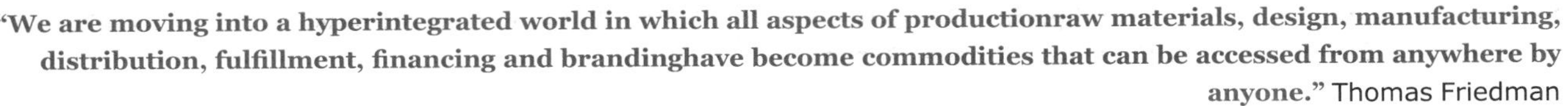
"We are moving into a hyperintegrated world in which all aspects of productionraw materials, design, manufacturing, distribution, fulfillment, financing and brandinghave become commodities that can be accessed from anywhere by anyone." Thomas Friedman

accounting systems. With the current strictures on auditors not providing additional services to clients, and not auditing their own work, this leaves the big plc with a choice of just two for its audit. If one of the Big Four exited the market—and everyone will remember that we saw Arthur Andersen spectacularly implode after the Enron scandal—that would bring the Big Four down to a big three, and in our example there would be no choice at all for that big plc. This is not an entirely satisfactory shape for the audit market and something needs to change. If the exit of one of the Big Four came at a time when the market was highly stressed, that could undermine confidence.

The argument for the Big Four doing the big audits is that they have the range of skills required. Where do you think the limits of your firm would be in top blue-chip audits?

We would need to build substantially before we could audit the oil majors, for example, or the largest UK banks or the biggest insurance companies. Outside of that, there is nothing we could not cope with. However, there is a "hearts and minds" battle to be won by firms outside the Big Four. Many of the finance team in big plc finance departments are alumni of the Big Four firms and there is the old "no one ever got fired for buying IBM" comfort structure to overcome. Unless directors in big plcs actually want to engage with other firms and give themselves a chance to get comfortable with the idea of a change, then all the regulatory pressure in the world is unlikely to change things. As a firm we have some 3% or so of the top 250 audits and one FTSE 100 audit. So we know what it takes to do big company audits. Will the change happen? It is going to take a great deal of work on the part of firms outside the Big Four to demonstrate that real benefits will follow from a more regular change of auditors by top plcs.

MORE INFO

Book:

Scott, David Meerman, and Brian Halligan. *Marketing Lessons from the Grateful Dead: What Every Business Can Learn from the Most Iconic Band in History*. Wiley, 2010.

Websites:

Financial Reporting Council (FRC; UK): www.frc.org.uk

Audit Practices Board (APB), setting auditing standards and ethical standards for the audit profession: www.frc.org.uk/apb/

Financial Accounting Standards Board (FASB), the official accounting standards setting body for the US: www.fasb.org

International Financial Reporting Standards (IFRS) Foundation, the body responsible for setting international accounting standards through the International Accounting Standards Board (IASB): www.ifrs.org

See Also:

★ Considerations when Outsourcing Internal Audit (pp. 312–314)
★ Has Financial Reporting Impacted on Internal Auditing Negatively? (pp. 338–341)
★ Viewpoint: Challenges Faced by the Audit Profession After the Crash (pp. 306–308)

"When the music stops, in terms of liquidity, things will be complicated. But as long as the music is playing, you've got to get up and dance. We're still dancing." Charles Prince

  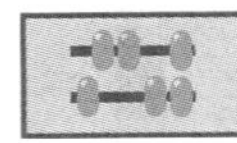   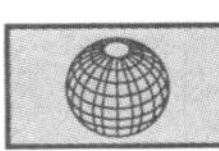   

Auditing Islamic Financial Institutions

by Roszaini Haniffa

EXECUTIVE SUMMARY

- Auditing Islamic financial institutions (IFIs) covers a wider scope than statutory financial statement auditing.
- External auditors of IFIs not only conduct financial audits, but also conduct tests on the *shariah* compliance of IFIs, according to *fatawa* (religious opinions) and guidelines set by the *Shariah* Supervisory Board (SSB).
- *Shariah* review is unique to IFIs, due to the requirement to ensure that all business activities and operations of IFIs adhere to *shariah* precepts.
- Scope of audit of IFIs needs to be comprehensive in order to achieve *maqasid al-shariah* (wider objectives of the *shariah*).
- Challenges in auditing of IFIs include lack of standardized *shariah* guidelines, lack of independence of SSB, and lack of competence of external auditors to conduct comprehensive *shariah* audit.

INTRODUCTION

The purpose of the statutory or financial statement audit is to enhance the degree of confidence of intended users of the financial statements as to whether the financial statements are prepared in accordance with an applicable financial reporting framework. The most widely accepted and adopted auditing standards are those issued by the International Federation of Accountants (IFAC).

Following the emergence and phenomenal growth of Islamic financial institutions (IFIs) in recent years in various parts of the world, the scope of conventional statutory financial audit is inadequate to fulfill the needs of the stakeholders of IFIs. Because IFIs need to adhere to *shariah* principles in all their business transactions and operations, a new dimension in auditing, as well as auditing standards which can cope with such principles, is needed. Recognizing the limitations of the International Standards of Auditing (ISA) in addressing issues related to religious compliance, the Accounting and Auditing Organization for Islamic Financial Institutions (AAOIFI) has taken steps in producing a number of auditing standards and audit methodologies specifically for IFIs.

OBJECTIVE OF AUDITING IFIS

Auditing forms an important element in the process of securing corporate accountability and in enhancing stakeholder faith in management's stewardship. According to AAOIFI's Auditing Standard for Islamic Financial Institutions No. 1 (ASIFI 1), the objective of an audit of financial statements of IFIs "... is to enable the auditor to express an opinion as to whether the financial statements are prepared, in all material respects, in accordance with the Shari'ah Rules and Principles, the accounting standards of the Accounting and Auditing Organization for Islamic Financial Institutions (AAOIFI) and relevant national accounting standards and practices in the country in which the financial institution operates."

Unlike conventional statutory financial audit, which requires auditors to express a true and fair view that the financial statements have been prepared according to relevant auditing standards, the audit of IFIs covers a wider scope. This is because auditors must also attest that management has complied not only with the *shariah* precepts, but also with the wider objective of *shariah* (*maqasid al-shariah*), which is to protect and improve the condition of human life in all dimensions. In other words, auditing of IFIs is not only confined to the statutory financial audit but also to what is known as the *shariah* review, which is the *raison d'être* for IFIs.

Hence, auditing of IFIs can be defined as a systematic process of objectively obtaining and evaluating evidence regarding assertions about religious and socioeconomic actions and events, in order to ascertain the degree of correspondence between those assertions and the applicable financial reporting framework, including the criteria specified based on *shariah* principles as recommended by the *Shariah* Supervisory Board (SSB), and communicating the results to all interested parties. Noncompliance with *shariah* principles is an area of risk for IFIs that could translate into legal, image, and reputational risks, which would have far-reaching consequences not only for the individual IFI but also for the entire Islamic financial system.

CHARACTERISTICS OF THE AUDIT OF IFIS

Role of Key Players in the Audit

Due to the need to ensure proper adherence to the *shariah* principles in operations and activities, external auditors are not expected to conduct both types of audit for IFIs. This is because the criteria in deciding whether an activity complies with *shariah* principles or not are a matter for the SSB of the individual IFI to decide, as they have expert knowledge in Islamic jurisprudence. Given the accepted divergence in *shariah* principles between, and even within, national groups, the additional attestation of *shariah* compliance is measured against the Islamic *shariah* rules and principles, as determined by the SSB in each IFI.

The role of the external auditor with respect to *shariah* compliance is only to test for compliance based on the outlines provided by the SSB. Besides the SSB and external auditors, the other two key players involved in the audit of IFIs are the internal auditors and the Audit and Governance Committees. The role of each key player in the audit of an IFI is illustrated in Figure 1.

Shariah Supervisory Board

The SSB plays a key role in the overall audit and governance framework, both *ex-ante* and *ex-post*. Their role *ex-ante* is to formulate policy and guidelines to be followed by management in their activities, including approval of products. The *ex-post* role is to conduct *shariah* review, which is an examination to ensure that the activities carried out by an IFI do not contravene the principles of *shariah*. The *shariah* review involves three phases: planning and designing the review procedures; executing the review procedures and preparing and reviewing the working papers; and last, documenting the conclusions and producing a comprehensive *Shariah* Supervisory Report. When executing the *shariah* review procedures, a draft report from the external auditor regarding *shariah* compliance testing, and the internal *shariah* review report from the internal auditor, will help the SSB in documenting their conclusions and expressing a *shariah* opinion in their comprehensive report. In short, the *shariah* review is a comprehensive review of not only the financial statements but also of contracts, agreements, and transactions, to ensure *shariah* compliance and to add credibility to management's activities.

Figure 1. Key players and their role in the audit and governance of IFIs

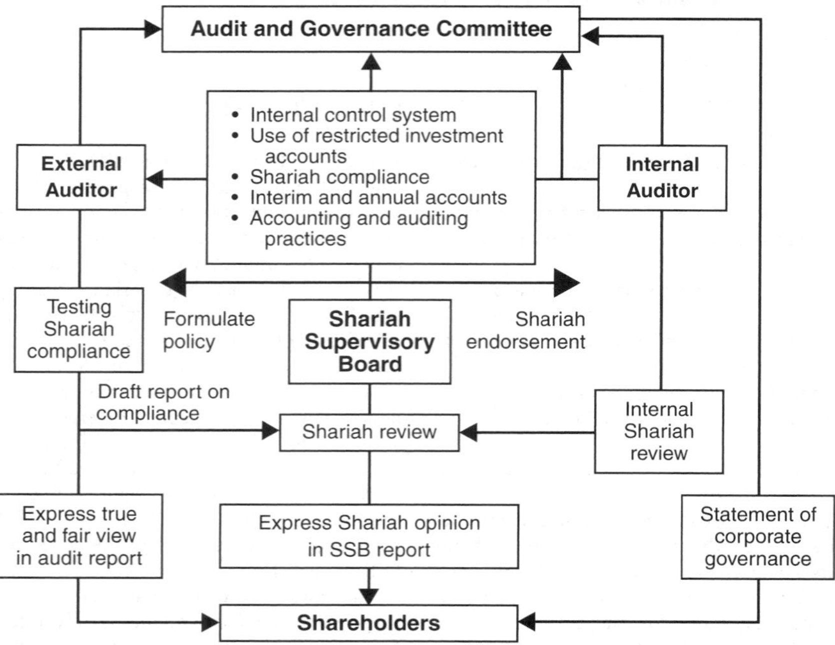

External Auditor

One of the unique roles played by the external auditor of an IFI, besides performing the financial statements audit, is to conduct a test of *shariah* compliance. The audit process involves a structured, documented plan involving a series of steps beginning with planning the audit and ending with expressing an opinion in an external audit report as to whether the financial statements are prepared in accordance with the fatawa (religious opinions), rulings and guidelines issued by the SSB of the IFI, the accounting standards of the AAOIFI, and relevant national accounting standards and practices in the country in which the IFI operates. In order to provide reasonable assurance that the IFI has complied with *shariah* rules and principles as determined by the SSB, the auditor needs to obtain sufficient and appropriate audit evidence. In order to guide the auditor in making judgment as to whether the financial statements of the IFI have been prepared in accordance with *shariah* rules and principles, the auditor will rely on the fatawa, and rulings and guidance issued by the SSB. However, the auditor is not expected to provide interpretation of the *shariah* rules and principles.

Hence, when conducting the audit, the auditor will include procedures in his or her examination to ensure that all new fatawa, rulings, and guidance, and modifications to existing fatawa, rulings, and guidance, are identified and reviewed for each period under examination. The auditor will review the reports issued by the SSB to the IFI concerning *shariah* compliance as well as the SSB's minutes of meetings to ensure that all types of products offered by the IFI have been subjected to a review by the SSB. The auditor must also examine the findings of all internal reviews carried out by the IFI's management, the internal audit, and the report of the internal *shariah* review. The auditor will send his or her draft report and conclusions related to *shariah* compliance to the SSB, and if the SSB's draft report indicates that compliance is lacking, the auditor may modify his or her draft report, providing adequate explanation of the nature of, and reasons for, the modification.

Internal Shariah Review

According to AAOIFI Governance Standards for Islamic Financial Institutions No. 3 (GSIFI 3), the conduct of the internal *shariah* review process may be undertaken by the internal audit department, provided that the reviewers are properly qualified and independent. Before the review process can take place, management prepares a charter containing a statement of purpose, authority, and responsibility, and sends it to the SSB for approval. Once the charter is approved, the board of directors will send the charter to the head of the internal *shariah* review, who will then appoint a team that has competence to carry out the task.

The reviewers will first plan each review assignment and the documentation. Then they will collect, analyze, and interpret all matters related to the review objectives and scope of work, including examination of documentation, analytical reviews, inquiries, discussions with management, and observations to support their review results. Working papers that document the review will be prepared by the reviewer and reviewed by the head of internal *shariah* review, who will then discuss the conclusions and recommendations with appropriate levels of management before issuing the final written report.

Audit and Governance Committee

The role of the Audit and Governance Committee (AGC), comprising nonexecutive directors, is described in detail under GSIFI No.4. It is responsible for checking the structure and internal control processes and ensuring that the activities of the IFI are *shariah*-compliant. The duties of the AGC also include the review of the reports produced by the internal *shariah* review and the SSB to ensure that appropriate actions have been taken.

Scope and Extent of Audit

As mentioned earlier, the scope of audit for IFIs is much broader. AAOIFI defined "scope of an audit" as the audit procedures deemed necessary by the auditor in the circumstances to achieve the objective of the audit for the IFI. It further stated:

"The procedures required to conduct an audit in accordance with ASIFIs should be determined by the auditor having regard to the requirements of appropriate Islamic Rules and Principles, ASIFIs, relevant professional bodies, legislation, regulations, which do not contravene Islamic Rules and Principles, and, where appropriate, the terms of audit engagement and reporting requirements, International Standards on Auditing (ISAs) shall apply in respect of matters not covered in detail by ASIFIs providing these do not contravene Islamic Rules and Principles."

From the above statement, it is clear that external auditors of IFIs are expected to deal with wider rules and guidelines. Since they are expected to conduct tests of *shariah* compliance, they will have to ensure that management has adhered to the interest-free and permissibility (*halal*) principles as specified by the SSBs. External auditors should also be concerned with elements of socioeconomic justice in line with *maqasid al-shariah*, even if they have not been addressed by the SSB.

CHALLENGES ON THE AUDIT OF IFIS

There are currently a number of challenges with regard to the auditing of IFIs,

     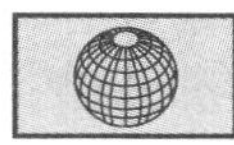   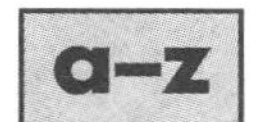

especially in terms of *shariah* compliance audit. First, despite the efforts of AAOIFI in promulgating auditing standards, the focus and scope tend to be on financial statements rather than the broader concept of *shariah* audit, which involves the audit of all activities of IFIs based on *maqasid al-shariah*. Furthermore, the use of the term "*shariah* review" rather than "*shariah* audit" by AAOIFI may implicate a lower level of assurance in the case of the former.

Second, based on AAOIFI's auditing standards, the functions of *shariah* audit or review are distributed to different entities, for example, external auditor, SSB, internal *shariah* reviewer, and the Audit and Governance Committee. While external auditors act as the external mechanism in monitoring compliance, their lack of competence makes them rely heavily on the SSB's *fatawa*, whereas in fact they should be making an independent judgment on the issue of compliance.

Third, the independence of the SSB has been questioned as they are involved in making *fatawa* and in setting up the guidelines on *shariah* compliance as well as in conducting a *shariah* review or audit of the IFI concerned.

Given the rapid growth of IFIs globally, there is little doubt that the auditing of IFIs will have to change to overcome these challenges and, perhaps, a new *shariah* auditing professional body will soon emerge.

MORE INFO

Books:

El-Gamal, M. *Islamic Finance: Law, Economics and Practice*. Cambridge, UK: Cambridge University Press, 2006.

Sultan, S. A. M. *A Mini Guide to Shari'ah Audit for Islamic Financial Institutions: A Primer.* Kuala Lumpur, Malaysia: CERT Publications, 2007.

Article:

Haniffa, R., and M. Hudaib. "A theoretical framework for the development of the Islamic perspective of accounting." *Accounting, Commerce and Finance: The Islamic Perspective Journal* 6:2 (2002): 1–71.

Websites:

Accounting and Auditing Organization for Islamic Financial Institutions (AAOIFI): www.aaoifi.com

Journal of Islamic Accounting and Business Research: www.emeraldinsight.com/products/journals/journals.htm?id=jiabr

See Also:

★ Aligning the Internal Audit Function with Strategic Objectives (pp. 280–282)
★ Capital Adequacy Requirements for Islamic Financial Institutions: Key Issues (pp. 141–143)
✔ Key Principles of Islamic Finance (p. 1011)
✔ The Role of the *Shariah* Advisory Board in Islamic Finance (p. 1015)

"What is really desired, under the name of riches, is essentially, power over men ... this power ... is in direct proportion to the poverty of the men over whom it is exercised, and in inverse proportion to the number of persons who are as rich as ourselves." John Ruskin

  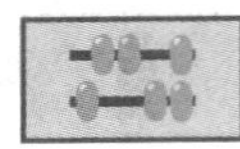      

Auditor Sensitivity to Source Reliability

by Denise Cicchella and Stuart Gardner

EXECUTIVE SUMMARY

- The importance of understanding the source of information and the reliability of that source.
- The challenges and constraints auditors face in current environments.
- The importance of kinesics-based techniques, neurolingusitics, and professional skepticism.
- The role of management in ensuring that audit staff and other resources have the skills necessary to assess reliability of information.
- The importance of techniques necessary to select and interview "experts."

INTRODUCTION

The auditor is always playing catch-up. Both external and internal auditors have to review the work of people who do the same job day-in, day-out and who, if competent, are usually intimately familiar with the processes, systems, and information that are under their control. Looking at the transactions on a historical basis further hampers the certified public accountant, chartered accountant, or other audit professional. These difficulties have been overcome by structured professional training, on-the-job training, and thorough review of audit work.

Auditors face numerous challenges in assessing the evidence behind the statements which they are auditing:

- a constantly evolving landscape of technology that feeds service delivery, distribution, resource management, reporting, decision-making, and a host of other systems;
- regulatory environments that change rapidly and are rarely consistent from jurisdiction to jurisdiction;
- expanded reporting requirements (e.g. corporate social responsibility statements);
- complex new financial products whose risks may not be completely understood;
- assessing the work of nonfinancial staff, who often have an asymmetric advantage in their area of expertise.

What do these challenges have in common? Much of the risk from these areas stems from change, lack of experience, and the unknown. What else do these challenges have in common? Most will result from companywide projects and programs. The project that addresses a new regulatory requirement, product, system, service, or building, places organizations at substantial risk. Key vendors supporting change often possess greater knowledge and experience than internal staff, further increasing the risk of fraud or substandard delivery. Many projects are delivered late, fail to meet expectations, and exceed budget. Such projects need to be included within the audit universe of internal audit. High-risk projects must be audited. External audit, equally, must consider any project that impacts their client as a "going concern."

Project audits provide an opportunity to ensure that appropriate governance is in place to report progress to senior management, ensure effective control of change, and provide quality assurance that, if absent, may well lead to adverse or even disastrous results. An audit of a project should also include an assessment of future audit trails for new products, services, and systems. This should be performed before completion of the project, when any changes or reengineering cost are likely to be far higher. It is at this stage that audit can most readily address the systemic reliability of evidence issues.

A fundamental skill is the ability to quickly assess the reliability of both people and information while applying appropriate "professional skepticism." This chapter will explore the use, evaluation, and assessment of information—how auditors should consider reliability, and the red flags to consider when evaluating information sources in the context of a project audit.

The Institute of Internal Auditors (IIA) states: "Internal auditors must identify sufficient, reliable, relevant, and useful information to achieve the engagement's objectives" (Standard 2310). The Institute further clarifies this to mean: "Sufficient information is factual, adequate, and convincing so that a prudent, informed person would reach the same conclusions as the auditor. Reliable information is the best attainable information through the use of appropriate engagement techniques. Relevant information supports engagement observations and recommendations and is consistent with the objectives for the engagement. Useful information helps the organization meet its goals."

It is often the case that the information obtained or given to an auditor is subject to interpretation. This is particularly true of project audits, where information may be presented as optimistically as possible to present the best possible case rather than the most realistic. There is often external "noise" that may cloud project reporting as various stakeholders interpret results to meet their own agendas, which may or may not be aligned with the goals of the project. Auditors are faced with constraints that may tempt them to jump to conclusions or misinterpret information—or simply to "go with the flow." Audit management should work toward eliminating or mitigating these constraints through a proper structured review of projects and supervision of assignments. Some of the constraints faced by auditors are:

- the time assigned to perform project audits;
- understanding of project processes as written and as practiced, which are often not the same;
- full comprehension of the subject matter being audited—products, lines of business, business constraints, system functions, etc.;
- acceptance of issues with client management, who sometimes force issues to be negotiated for "softer" wording;
- access or ability to get messages fully communicated to an audit committee or senior management with possibly limited time before a project becomes operational (the audit committee may read only the first few lines of an audit report and will not take the time to read all the evidence supporting an opinion).

SYSTEMS AND PROCESSES

As the range of activities that audit reports on is expanded (for example, to include social responsibility reporting) audit is examining many additional nonfinancial systems that historically would not have been subject to detailed audit review—if they were considered at all. Frequently such systems are not overly complex or difficult to understand in principle (e.g. facilities management, nonpayroll human resource systems, records management systems, sales databases, etc.) and should not present a major challenge for an experienced auditor. Areas to consider during review/audit of these systems should include the following.

"You know what a learning experience is? A learning experience is one of those things that says, 'You know that thing you just did? Don't do that.'" Douglas Adams

  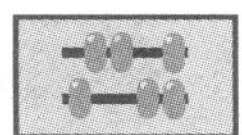   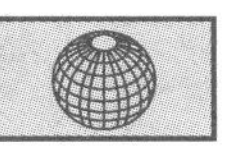   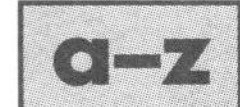

- The impact of additional resources.
- Understanding and interpreting the source and reliability of the data.
- Spreadsheets, end-user databases (e.g. Microsoft Access), internal Wikis, SharePoint, and other information repository/report software developed by end-users to solve project-specific needs may often be encountered. The auditor may have difficulties reconciling information back to reliable sources as these ad-hoc applications frequently lack audit trails or enforce strict accountability. The auditors should look for evidence to assess the sources of information, such as the formulae used for calculations programmed into the reports.

If the auditor is not an expert in the field of the project, this involves additional challenges.

When evaluating systems the auditor should test, or ask an expert to test, for questions such as the following.

- Are "dummy" or test accounts active and, if so, can they be used to conduct "illicit" transactions?
- Are safeguards in place to protect the confidentiality of data or to detect unauthorized access to information? I.e. are data and information held securely to prevent them being manipulated, copied, or stolen? Obviously, the more sensitive the data, the more important these questions become.
- How sensitive are the data and information stored? A leak of customer data can be catastrophic, whereas a database of paint colors used to redecorate a building would be less sensitive.
- Are data stored in such a way that they can be restored if they are hacked or penetrated?
- Are the data backed by source documentation so that they can be authenticated and tested for reliability?
- Does the system track changes and leave a sufficient trail to ensure accountability?
- Are procedures for change sufficient to restore systems back to the original code if necessary?

Auditors may also find it difficult to assess risk in an area unless they are comfortable with such systems. They will often need to rely on programmers, coders, or manuals to truly understand how the systems work.

THE HUMAN ASPECT

People

In many organizations the need to operate in a multicultural environment that may span continents, operate in different languages, encompass different cultural norms, work across multiple time zones, etc., creates a unique challenge to which auditors must adapt and work effectively, efficiently, and economically.

Your Team

It goes without saying that every audit leader must understand the strengths, weaknesses, intellect, skills, and motivation of each team member. Increasingly the staffing of audits is complicated by an increased reliance on temporary staff, cosourcing, outsourcing (possibly even off-shore), and a rising rate of staff turnover.

For audit leadership, the most critical aspect of information reliability is based on understanding the quality of the team it deploys. This understanding impacts every aspect of audit delivery:

- the realism of budgets;
- the identification, classification, and assessment of fundamental risks;
- appropriate high-quality reporting;
- practical and pragmatic solutions to the mitigation of risks;
- the ability of auditors to influence management and staff at all levels;
- the reliability of staff members in executing the work that is planned and to adapt to changing circumstances;
- and, finally, the integrity, honesty, and ethical and professional standards toward which each staff member should work.

Audit leaders must be able to quickly assess their team and ensure that there are the appropriate resources to audit a project effectively and provide adequate supervision. This may be achieved by:

- hiring or contracting a resource with significant audit experience in the project area;
- a selection process that identifies a team with the background, skills, and understanding to ensure the success of the project—possibly including the recruitment and training of professionals from non-audit backgrounds to meet project-specific needs that address critical skill gaps;
- timely performance feedback that is both formal and informal;
- mentoring and on-the-job training that helps non-auditors or junior auditors to adapt to the audit department;
- an understanding of the relative merits of the myriad of professional qualifications and designations;
- project-specific training—for example, application- or system-specific or in project management;
- structured training to ensure core audit, interpersonal (communications, leadership, time management), and technical skills.

Assessing Project Roles and Responsibilities

A fundamental skill that can give the auditor an edge—or at least partly compensate for any skill gap—is the ability to "read" people and a strong social intelligence. Effective interpersonal skills are critical to the success of project audits. With the pressure of project delivery, conducting work in a manner that will not adversely impact the progress of a project is essential. Each team member must be able to effectively interact with third-party vendors, employees from multiple disciplines, coworkers, and management to deliver effective audits. Although this sounds easy enough, along with multiple interaction levels the individual personality traits of these communication channels only adds to the challenge.

The ability to establish credibility, understanding, trust, and rapport with project team members is key. This can be hampered by the overuse of conference calls, e-mails, text messages, and even video conferencing, which, while indispensable and cost-effective, are no substitute for meeting in person. For example, auditors are spending less and less time in the field—an area where valuable insights can often be gained. This can have the effect that clients feel more detached from the audit process and are less open or comfortable with auditors or audit management; and the client's staff may be too relaxed if they do not "see" audit staff in person and the preventive effects of feeling that "the auditors are watching" is therefore diluted. See Appendix 1 for more information on the advantages and disadvantages of alternate means of information gathering.

How might an auditor overcome these issues? Interpersonal skills do make a tacit appearance at the fringes of accountancy education, in MBA schemes, and in professional qualifications, but it would be an understatement to say they are close to being "front and center." Whether or not this should be the case is beyond the scope of this article or the qualifications of its authors. However, practical experience has repeatedly demonstrated to us that the most effective auditors, investigators, and examiners are those who can rapidly develop effective rapport, identify deception, and facilitate the extraction of information. In many instances such techniques have been taught to sales people to help them to identify the needs of customers.

Although these skills are innate in some people, more often than not they can be taught with varying degrees of success to others who do not have them. Some of the fundamental approaches to learning these skills include:

- kinesics-based interviewing techniques (Walters, 2003);

"Powerful people do not have good listening skills. They hate to listen. They succeed by getting good at faking it ... If you're an extrovert, you think while you're talking. And it's impossible to listen to someone if you are thinking of the next thing you want to say." Penelope Trunk

  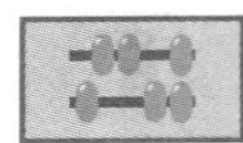 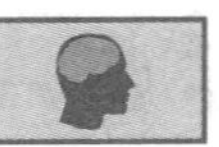     

- an understanding of personality types and of personality types associated with criminality
- neurolinguistic programming (Bandler and Grinder, 1981).

Kinesics-based techniques use the body language of the interviewee as an aid to assessing the truthfulness of information relayed during interviews and conversations. Some of these body cues include:

- shifting of the eyes;
- pupil dilation or other signs of increased heart rate;
- sweating in a cold room or, conversely, acting overly cold in a warm room;
- wringing of hands and excessive movement of feet;
- crossed arms;
- pointing of feet toward doors or windows—as if an interviewee is looking to flee;
- overly physical gestures while talking (being careful not to misinterpret culturally normative gestures as signs of possible deception).

When interviewing experts or sources of information, auditors should look for behaviors above and beyond normal that may indicate deception or misleading information. Remember that outside influences may come into play. Assess behavior over time and against known facts.

These techniques also look for cues in speech patterns and wording to help to pick up on deception. They teach the interviewer to look for signs of changes in vocabulary such as depersonalization, or if an interviewee suddenly shortens his or her answers. They teach the auditor the optimal room set-up and interview positioning to relax the interviewee and obtain optimal benefit from the interview. Aside from looking for cues of deception, an auditor can also assess whether an auditee really understands the audit process, the relative risks, and the scope of the engagement. Please see Appendix 2 for more information of effective interview tips.

Understanding personality types will help an auditor to customize the interview and information-gathering process by understanding what makes the interviewee most comfortable, as well as how to pick up on signs of criminal behavior or personality disorders that may raise flags during an audit. This understanding will also aid an auditor should the audit uncover indications of fraud, criminal behavior, or other irregularities that require an intensification of effort. Knowledge of personality types will also help the auditor to understand certain cues that a person may be giving off.

Neurolinguistic programming (NLP) as a method of interviewing is diminishing in popularity, but an understanding of the method can help an auditor to place reliance on information gathered during the audit. NLP was originally used to create solutions for dealing with phobias. Applied to the field of auditing, it can be used to help an auditor to extract more information from a client and in developing a degree of trust with the auditee.

Formal education and in-depth training in any of these types of interviewing techniques will help an auditor to reduce the "noise" in interpreting what an interviewee is saying and will increase the reliability of the information-gathering process. Along with this training, in a multinational environment auditors should also be trained in cultural sensitivity so that cues are not misinterpreted and relationships are not marred by language or behavior that may be perceived as insulting by the client.

Experts have long known that nonverbal signals (body language) are an important component of communication. Traditionally used by investigators, interrogators, and auditors, whether during initial meetings or in later discussion of control weaknesses, deficiencies, or findings, the use of kinesic techniques can give interviewers valuable insights. During communications and interviews it is important that the auditor has the ability to talk to people on their level and that he or she can listen actively and collate information. This information then needs to be collated with information received outside the course of the interview in the hopes that they are consistent. The goal of the interview is simply to gather the facts and clear up any confusion or inconsistency—not to form conclusions. Active listening is a skill that auditors should learn and practice. I have often seen auditors complete sentences for clients, a practice that can lead to a lack of clarity in the information gathered. Auditors should ensure that interviews are done in such a way that they are free from distractions and create an environment that is neutral for all parties.

Outside Experts

In many instances the organization may need to rely on external professionals to assist in performing audit work, providing audit supervision, training of internal staff, creating audit programs, or assessing the reliability of information received during an audit.

When using external experts, the organization must exercise due professional care in both the selection of and the contracting with these individuals. The case study below illustrates the risks of not doing so. Management should be concerned that the following considerations are given proper attention.

- Management must be able to determine that the expert possesses the knowledge and competency necessary to complete the work in question. This may or may not include specific licensing (which should be verified with relevant licensing boards), expertise (which can be demonstrated and verified through references or personal observations), and other qualifications necessary to ensure competency.
- It must ensure that the relationship with the professional does not hinder the latter's ability to make a sound judgment free of bias or partiality. For example, when a professional is asked to make a value assessment of an asset, his/her fee should not be related to the assessment value arrived at (e.g. a percentage of the value assessed).
- Communication with the expert should be kept formal but frequent to ensure that the work performed is consistent with management expectations and objectives of the assignment. Careful consideration has to be made to ensure that the expert does not scope-creep or create work for him or herself beyond what is necessary to get the job done.
- Management should determine beforehand that the risk of using the outside professional (who will have access to confidential information) is outweighed by the benefit of securing the professional's services.
- Any use of outside experts should be disclosed to and agreed on by key stakeholders, the audit committee, and the board of directors/executive management.

Experts may be used in the performance of audit work. Assurance should be made that experts possess the required experience and training. Key stakeholders should be informed when experts are being used.

The techniques we have described to interview clients should also be applied when interviewing experts. In addition, auditors may wish to consider asking technical questions to ensure that the expert really does have expertise in his or her field. They should make sure that they themselves know the correct answers before doing this, and they may wish to consider contacting their own experts first to help in building and answering such assessment questions.

EVALUATING EVIDENCE OF PROJECT PROGRESS

Often the percentage of completion is used as a basis for paying for services, especially for IT projects and capital improvements. With percentage of completion, invoices come in that need to be paid with reference to an overall contract price on the basis of estimated completion points along the course of the project. The problem comes in estimating how much has been done and what the total costs will be. Coupled with that is that the overall project will most likely include change orders, scope changes, or other requests for changes, so a project that is at one stage of completion may actually go backward, in whole or by line item, as time goes on. Ideally the percentage of completion is assessed by an independent source prior to payment. Auditors need to assess the accuracy of invoices that come in for these services to ensure that due diligence has been done prior to making a payment. This may require an assessment of the current stage of completion and progress over time by comparing with the intended final result (total project completion), an interview with the independent party that certified the estimate, and knowledge of the project at hand. An auditor may not be familiar enough with the project to determine if the estimated percentage of completion is accurate. Auditors may be limited as to what they can verify; they need to trust that the independent assessment was accurate and that the mathematical flow makes sense.

An auditor should concentrate on the control environment around how assessments were made and approved, as well as confirming the independence of the expert who verified the percentage completed. Auditors should examine several other matters related to the use of the expert by:

- obtaining background information on the expert and testing the relevance of their experience;
- checking the contract to ensure that the scope of services includes making independent assessments;
- ensuring that the expert has duly documented the assessment;
- if possible, obtaining the expert's notes and calculations to determine how they made their assessment.

Whether obtained through interview, audit testing, or expert advice, audit evidence from different sources or of a different nature may indicate that a particular item of audit evidence is not reliable. It is then up to the auditor to play an objective role and evaluate the evidence. Additional testing may be required to support the evidence that has been obtained. International audit standards, such as ISA 500, guide an auditor as to how to obtain evidence and how evidence should be used to support audit findings and conclusions. The auditor must determine the relevance and reliability of evidence obtained using several methods:

- audit steps to recalculate or come to the same conclusion as the evidence;
- evaluation of the consistency of audit material;
- identifying the source of audit material, recognizing that the more independent a source is of the audit the more reliable the evidence is likely to be; such independent sources may consist of confirmations, benchmarks, or reports from analysts/appraisers;
- verification of evidence against source documentation, keeping in mind that evidence that is a "copy" or replication is less reliable than original material; such verification may be difficult as it is often difficult or impossible to differentiate between an original and a copy;
- evidence obtained from an environment where an auditor has performed tests of controls and has concluded favorably for that environment.
- Information is only as valuable as its source.
- An auditor must be able to trace sources and originality.
- Understanding independence is key to assessing validity of information.

Conflict occurs when audit evidence contradicts itself or contradicts the conclusions of the audit report. An auditor needs to feel comfortable that his or her interpretation is correct and should be sure that another reasonable person would make the same interpretation. At times, it may be useful for an auditor to ask someone else, independent of the audit, what conclusion they would draw to see if it is in agreement with their own. This independent person should be asked in such a way that bias is eliminated. As an example, the auditor should present the facts and ask "what do you think?" being careful not to say "I concluded such and such, do you agree?" If the independent person cannot draw a conclusion, the auditor may need to gather or present more evidence to both form and justify an appropriate opinion.

CASE STUDY

A Cautionary Tale

A recent client was relocating its corporate headquarters to a number of new and refurbished buildings in the neighborhood as the current facility was being sold. Several locations were scouted out and selected to move into; formerly in one building, headquarters was being moved into six. There was an experienced team of facility managers within the corporate structure, but it was decided that due to the complexity of the project an external project manager would be used. Because of the streamlined design and the priority given to time, the company was looking for a project manager with experience in construction, engineering, and handling large projects.

A formal bidding process was started, firms were eliminated, and a shortlist of qualified candidates followed. The selection committee unanimously selected a firm based on the qualifications of the project manager (Bob), who they wanted to work on this project. The team was particularly impressed by his educational credentials, as he had graduated from the Massachusetts Institute of Technology (MIT), a school well known for its strength in mathematics and engineering. There was no indication that Bob was a licensed project management professional, but during interviewing he was able to list with confidence the many projects he had worked on.

Several months into the project it was obvious that cost overrun was imminent and that the project was falling way behind schedule. Executive management was concerned about the financial impact, and project management was concerned as it feared that employees would not be relocated on time. Audit was called in to investigate.

Audit interviewed the general contractor to find out why the project was so far behind. The general contractor admitted that there were conflicts between himself and Bob and that at times Bob had hindered the project more than helping it. The contractor expressed concern that he was not getting paid on time and that some of his proposed value engineering solutions were ignored or overlooked by Bob.

Audit interviewed Bob, who defended his position by stating that he was a proven expert in the field and should be trusted. However, when asked basic construction questions he seemed confused or answered inaccurately. Audit asked for proof of his expertise and received his résumé, which stated that he had attended MIT. When asked, he would not produce a copy of his diploma. Audit called MIT to verify his attendance. It was confirmed that he had graduated from the university but that his degree was in history. He had received no formal training in engineering or construction while there.

SUMMARY

- Information gathering is a fundamental skill that every auditor must have and is an integral part of every audit.
- Many auditors gather information without taking steps to confirm, validate,

"Keith Richards ... was once asked how he came up with all those amazing guitar riffs. His answer? He just starts playing until he makes the right mistake. In other words he's optimistic he will create something good by virtue of getting something 'wrong.'" Mark Stevenson

  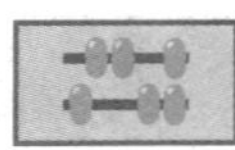      

and give credibility to the information obtained. This can lead to improper conclusions, whether for or against the client. Most clients will likely dispute an unfavorable audit result, but they may not be so quick to question conclusions that suggest they have done a better job than they actually have.

- An auditor needs to have determination and the confidence to persevere in the conclusion they reach. Documentation showing how the conclusions were arrived at should be part of the audit records and should be kept in case the auditor has to defend his or her position at a later time.
- Time needs to be devoted to training staff in interpersonal skills and communication.
- Additionally, audit management should ensure that enough time and resources are allocated to an audit so that audit team members have the time they need to obtain efficient and reliable information during the information-gathering stages of an audit.

APPENDIX 1: ADVANTAGES AND DISADVANTAGES OF ALTERNATE MEANS OF INFORMATION GATHERING

Advantages	*Disadvantages*
Telephone	
Interviewer can clarify questions if answers are not understood	No opportunity to establish rapport with the interviewee
Fastest way to collect information and has better response rate than mail surveys	Scope of interview is not necessarily limited but it may become scripted if conducted by an inexperienced interviewer
Least expensive type of interview	Respondents tire quickly during interviews
	Difficult to schedule in advance
	Difficult to get calls returned
	Respondent's environment may be noisy or distracting
Mailed survey	
Answers are not as susceptible to bias as in phone interviews	No physical connection with auditee
Interviewees can complete in their own time and be more relaxed in giving answers	Information given may be brief and lack sufficient detail
	No opportunity to clarify ambiguous answers
	Answers may be reviewed and reworked so that information is filtered and details are omitted
	Auditor may have to chase up unreturned surveys
Answers are documented and it is easier to keep evidence of what was stated	More difficult to verify source of information as one does not know who completed the survey
Site visit	
Improves interviewer's understanding of the working project environment and he/she sees how it*is*done versus how it *should* be done	Auditor may not fully "get into" the site and may be reluctant to ask questions
Auditor can observe issues as they arise	Time spent on site is limited and auditor may not pick up on key areas where there are defects or missing controls
Validates data gathered from other sources	Time and resource-consuming
	Must be carefully scheduled well in advance
	Allows in a lot of "noise" that may lead to incorrect conclusions or assessments of the environment. Staff are on best behavior while audit is present
	Visits may be distractive to productivity
	Visits may be hazardous for an auditor not trained to be on site

APPENDIX 2: EFFECTIVE INTERVIEW TIPS

- Auditors must be prepared for interviews by gathering background information and knowing as much as possible about the area that is being audited. An interview conducted "blind" will lead to confusion and may cause the auditor to overlook obvious concerns.
- Interviews should be held in a "neutral" area and should be free of distractions. There should be no opportunity for others to stop by and ask questions, nor should there be telephones nearby or an area where phones are constantly ringing. It should be quiet.
- Auditors need to practice active listening techniques and ensure that they do not provide answers or finish sentences for the auditee.
- Auditors must be able to talk to people at all levels without being condescending, rude, or giving offence.
- Interviews should be documented as they proceed. However, the auditor should maintain as much eye contact with the auditee/interviewee as possible. If necessary an additional person should be brought in to note the proceedings. The auditor should give a copy of the notes to the interviewee to review for accuracy.
- Auditors need to collate and corroborate information received during an interview, questioning any inconsistencies as soon as they arise.
- The goal of an interview is to gather facts and clear up inconsistencies. Auditors must focus on this goal.
- The setting or meeting room should be set up so that the auditor has a clear view of the interviewee that allows them to interpret nonverbal clues/body language.
- The auditor should watch for changes in tone of voice or eye contact, which may be a sign of deceitfulness.
- Interviews should be scheduled at a time when neither party has other constraints or schedule conflicts as these will be distracting.

MORE INFO

Books:

Bandler, Richard, and John Grinder. *Trance-formations: Neuro-Linguistic Programming and the Structure of Hypnosis*. Moab, UT: Real People Press, 1981.

Walters, Stan B. *Principles of Kinesic Interview and Interrogation*. 2nd ed. Boca Raton, FL: CRC Press, 2003.

Standards:

Institute of Internal Auditing (IIA). " International standards for the professional practice of internal auditing." Online at: tinyurl.com/7xg5rlw

International Federation of Accountants (IFAC). "International Standard on Auditing 500: Audit evidence." Online at: tinyurl.com/6qph7p2

Website:

International Federation of Accountants (IFAC): www.ifac.org

"An opinion should be the result of thought, not a substitute for it." Jef Mallett

  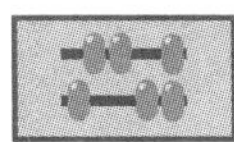   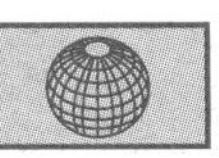   

An Auditor's Approach to Risk-Based Auditing: What to Audit and When by Paul J. Sanchez

EXECUTIVE SUMMARY

- The need for internal auditing professionals to make a serious professional risk assessment about how limited audit resources should be allocated to various corporate activities.
- A risk-based approach and a risk model for prioritizing auditable activities by risk scores.
- The perennial internal audit problem of how to effectively use limited audit resources. It emphasizes that high risk areas require top priority.
- This chapter highlights a model that easily can be used to rank auditable activities.

INTRODUCTION

Each year the senior audit manager in a corporate internal audit department is faced with the difficult task of presenting the audit committee with a schedule of audit coverage for the coming year. The senior audit manager must decide what to audit and when. This crucial assignment for the internal audit function sets in place the audit schedule for the year. The schedule should focus on the areas of risk that, if not controlled, will most likely interfere with corporate objectives. If audit work does not cover such risk areas, the audit function may find itself in the embarrassing position of being in the wrong place at the wrong time. Since the internal audit function is part of the enterprise risk management (ERM) process, the auditor is expected to know the sensitive operations of the entity and to use audit resources to provide efficient audit risk coverage. A proper ERM process will embrace an audit plan that will satisfy the audit committee and will answer the question of what to audit.

INTERNAL AUDITORS CANNOT AUDIT EVERYTHING!

This chapter focuses on each corporation's need for a careful, consistent, professional approach to determining what to audit. The generally limited resources in the corporate internal auditing environment must be used in selected areas on the basis of a risk prioritization exercise. Without a risk-based auditing approach, professional auditors may fall into the trap of trying to audit *all* activities. It is an automatic reaction. Auditors try to do a little audit work in every auditable area. It is usually difficult or inconvenient for management and audit committee members to accept the truth—that there simply are not enough audit resources to audit "everything." Auditors never want to be in a position where they would have to say that there will be no audit coverage in particular areas. It is difficult for auditors to list what will *not* be audited. Accordingly, internal auditors tend to do "a little bit of everything." That is the same as doing "a lot of nothing"—and it is not a helpful approach to applying overall effective audit coverage for the corporation. The modern audit committee wants to know that the limited audit resources are being allocated to the high-risk areas at the expense of the low-risk areas.

INTERNAL AUDITORS MUST RANK AUDITABLE ACTIVITIES

Although internal auditor resources are scarce, corporate management seems to expect auditors to provide audit coverage for "everything that moves." That simply cannot be done! The auditor must be in the right place at the right time. A risk-ranking approach, where high-risk activities are more subject to audit coverage than low-risk areas, is essential. In fact, some low-risk areas will not be covered at all by the internal auditors. Those activities are just not significant, or, as practicing accountants say, they are "not material." A risk assessment approach to creating an audit plan is the logical starting-point for the audit manger who wants to focus audit coverage on high-risk areas.

PROFESSIONAL STANDARDS

The auditing standards (measures of the quality of performances) of the internal audit profession recognize the importance of an audit plan. That fact is clearly stated in the international professional auditing standards promulgated by the Institute of Internal Auditors (IIA).

IIA Standard "2010—Planning" states the following:

"The chief audit executive must establish risk-based plans to determine the priorities of the internal audit activity, consistent with the organization's goals."

Paragraph A1 of Standard 2010 suggests that the risk assessment:

- be based on a documented risk assessment;
- be undertaken at least annually;
- should consider the input of senior management and the board.

Further, the Standard 2010 suggests the internal audit activity have, at a minimum, a carefully prepared annual audit plan based on risk assessment. Audit committees expect such a plan; the professional standards require such a plan; and common sense dictates such a plan.

THE AUDIT PLAN

Designing a Plan

Designing a workable audit plan requires knowledge of all the activities and the related risks and controls throughout the corporation. The audit plan is dependent on the size and capabilities of the audit staff. It must be prepared by the senior audit manager (i.e. the general auditor or director of internal auditing).

The plan should be based on:

- the strategic objectives of the corporation;
- the risk (chance, possibility, or likelihood) of control failures that would impede the achievement of the objectives;
- what activities must be audited based on laws or regulations;
- potential monetary losses;
- the estimated time required to provide audit coverage, taking into account the proposed nature, timing, and extent of the internal auditor's work, and the work that might be done by external auditors or others;
- any changes or proposed changes to controls, automated systems, operations, etc.;
- any changes in the composition of the audit staff;
- the dates and results of previous audits.

Although the audit plan will guide the audit work to be performed, it must be flexible. It must allow the audit staff to react to unforeseen events. Sometimes an unanticipated risk event is encountered that requires the auditor to reconsider the initial risk-based plan and to reallocate audit resources. When this happens, the auditor must adjust the original plan and "give-ups"(the deferral or elimination of what was originally scheduled) must be presented to management. The reallocation of resources will alter the original schedule, but the rescheduling of audit coverage would still be guided by risk concerns.

Use a Systematic Approach

To devise an audit plan, it is best to:

- start analyzing the business functions, goals, risks, and controls of the

  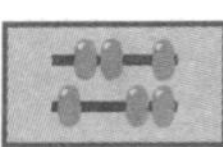      

corporation, which the auditor, as part of the ERM team, is familiar with;
- develop a standardized approach to a systems-based audit.

If the auditor uses a standardized approach to the audit of systems of internal control, the audit plan should develop as follows:

1 Identify the business functions of the entity.
2 Identify auditable activities within the functions.
3 Identify what could go wrong—"Where can the entity get burned?" These are the risks.
4 Identify key controls—"What would prevent the burning?"
5 Use a model that has a scoring scheme for ranking auditable activities from high-risk to low-risk.
6 Decide what to audit, and how and when to audit it.

The important notion to remember is that the starting-point is a list of auditable activities within the business functions of the corporation—one that is not based on accounts, departments or physical locations. Examples of business functions with related, auditable activities might include those set out in Appendix 1 for a retail establishment or a not-for-profit hospital.

It is difficult to sit down and list what should be audited without some formal approach. The tendency is simply to look at last year's audits and expand or contract the coverage. This might have been sufficient in the past. Today, however, businesses and their attendant business risks change frequently. Any audit risk assessment must consider the current business risks in each of the corporation's business functions. A business function approach to determining what should be audited is recommended.

In past years, audits were generally financial in nature. They concentrated on verifying or substantiating the numbers in the accounting records. That approach has changed. Today, audit departments are embracing the IIA standards and are conducting audits that are designed to report on the adequacy, efficiency, and effectiveness of the systems of internal control. These systems-based, operational-type audits are more comprehensive than the "old" substantive test audits. The approach is now standardized and makes audit planning easier, since "how to audit" is not a serious concern.

The basic concerns of the systems-based audit are as follows.

- Are there controls in place that, if they work, will prevent or detect material problems and will help to achieve corporate objectives? I.e. are the controls *adequate*?
- Do the identified controls work? I.e. are the controls *effective*?
- Do the controls provide the best outcomes at the lowest possible cost?

THE RISK ASSESSMENT PROCESS FOR A BANK

In this section we will consider the example of a currently used risk assessment process for a depository institution (i.e. a bank).

Identify the Business Functions

Every depository institution is, for the most part, involved in the following external and internal business functions.

External

Every depository institution is, for the most part, involved in the following external and internal business functions.

- *Funding*: Obtaining funds to do business.
- *Lending*: Temporarily loaning funds to customers.
- *Investing*: Buying and holding government and other securities with funds not loaned out.
- *Trading*: Short-term buying and selling of government and other securities and other financial instruments (foreign exchange, Bankers Acceptances, certificates of deposit, etc).
- *Fee-based customer servicing*: Receiving fees for providing services to customers; other fee-based services.

Internal

- *Support functions for external business*: Internal activities that support the above regular business functions of the bank.
- *Accounting and reporting*: Internal bookkeeping, accounting, and financial reporting activities.

Identify Major Activities Within Each Business Function

After listing the business functions, each auditable activity within the business functions should be identified. Auditable activities will differ from bank to bank. The audit manager must know what his or her bank is doing and must carefully list the major activities within each business function. A generalization of major activities by function might include the following.

Funding

- Deposit-gathering accounts (time, demand, CDs, money market, public, commercial, individual retirement arrangements, etc).
- Issuance of commercial paper.
- Issuance of short-term debt.
- Bank borrowings.
- Federal funds borrowed.
- Repurchase agreements.
- Other.

Lending

- Loans (commercial, personal, agricultural, foreign, real estate, consumer, letters of credit, acceptance financing, etc).
- Federal funds sold.
- Reverse repurchase agreements.
- Outstanding drafts "accepted" by the bank—bankers' acceptances receivable.
- Other.

Investing

- Interest-bearing bank account deposits.
- Security positions (treasuries, agencies, municipal securities, BAs, CDs, etc).
- Float—cash management.
- Advances to (or investments in) affiliates.
- Other.

Trading

- Foreign exchange.
- Securities (treasuries, agencies, municipal securities, BAs, CDs, etc).
- Interest rate futures, interest rate swaps, credit swaps, etc.
- Other.

Fee-Based Customer Services

- Check processing.
- Trust service (corporate and personal).
- Discount brokerage.
- Home banking.
- Lockbox services.
- Safekeeping, safe deposit, custodial.
- Mortgage servicing.
- Money transfer/wire transfer.
- Other.

Internal Business Functions

- Interoffice settlement system (IOS).
- Systems development life cycle (SDLC).
- Asset–liability management.
- Marketing.
- Human resources (personnel).
- General services (security, purchasing, maintenance, etc).
- Insurance.
- Data center management.
- Payroll.
- Legal.
- Audit.
- Other.

Internal Accounting, Reporting, and Compliance

- Loan loss provision and related reserve for loan losses.
- Tax provision and related deferrals.

"Perhaps the greatest pleasure in science comes from theories that derive the solution to some deep puzzle from a small set of simple principles in a surprising way." John Brockman

- Accrued payables.
- Dividend policy and payments.
- Pension, profit-sharing, incentive compensation, etc.
- Other assets, fixed assets, and goodwill.
- Regulatory compliance/regulatory reporting.
- Other liabilities.
- Other.

This categorization could be used by the audit manager to decide on the audit coverage for activities within each business function. Clearly, because of the limited resources not all of the activities can be audited. They must be sorted out. The list of auditable activities should be adjusted as needed based on changes in the business of the bank and changes to the bank's risk exposure. The list of auditable activities is a necessity. Preparing such a list is a simple procedure, that, if properly thought out, can be a valuable part of the planning.

Identify Risks and the Procedures (Control) to Manage the Risks

For each auditable activity within the business functions, the audit manager should identify the major business risks (i.e. "What could go wrong?"). This should be based primarily on the auditor's previous experience with the auditable activity. Input from line management can also be used to obtain an understanding of the activities and the related risks—as long as auditor objectivity is not compromised. A generalized example of major risks and related controls for the bank's auditable foreign exchange activity is shown in the risk/control sheet presented in Appendix 2.

It should be noted that to create a risk calculation worksheet (see Appendix 3) for each auditable activity is a monumental task. But it is necessary if the priorities for the audit plan are to be properly established. Without one the auditor is in the dark. The risk calculation worksheets become a bank-wide inventory of risks and controls that can be updated periodically based on changing business risks and control conditions. The risk calculation worksheet is not unlike the documentation envisioned by the US Sarbanes–Oxley Act of 2002 (SOX). For well-controlled public companies, such documentation should be readily available.

Use a Model to Rank the Risks for the Activities Included in the Audit Plan

The audit manager can use the risk calculation worksheet for each activity to decide what audit coverage is appropriate. The audit manager can then devise a scoring mechanism for the activities, focusing on risks and related controls. The auditable activities can then be ranked from high-risk to low-risk.

Various ranking schemes are in use by banks. As long as the scheme is consistently applied, a fair and reasonable ranking of auditable activities can be achieved. The auditor can then audit, review, or monitor some or all of the activities, or parts of the auditable activities. With currently updated risk calculation worksheets, the auditor is in an excellent position to allocate resources to those activities that are "riskier" than others. The ranking can be based on a simple 1 to 4 scoring scheme based on responses to a standardized questionnaire.

A very simple, currently used model consists of two parts.

- Part 1: Establish "importance weights" for the model's four categories.
- Part 2: Assign risk (scores "0" to "4" for each question indicated in Appendix 4 for each auditable activity; "0" would indicate no risk; "4" would indicate unacceptable risk).

The following text can be read in conjunction with the risk calculation worksheet presented in Appendix 3.

Part 1: Importance Weights

The auditable activities must be examined in greater depth. It is necessary to consider the following four categories for each auditable activity:

- monetary values;
- nature of operations;
- controls and security;
- human resources.

Importance weights can be assigned to these four categories. The importance weights should add up to 100% and can be assigned on the basis of the general auditor's beliefs about which category is most important relative to the other categories.

Typical weights might look like those shown in Table 1, although different companies may have different opinions about the "importance" of each category.

The importance weights are subjective. They are based on the professional judgment and the audit philosophy of the internal audit function. Different audit functions have different philosophies. The importance weights are a matter of opinion about how the four categories relate to each other (in terms of risk) on a scale of 0 to 100.

Table 1. Typical importance weights for categories in each auditable activity

Category	Overall importance weight
1. Monetary values	20%
2. Nature of operations	10%
3. Controls and security	50%
4. Human resources	20%
Total	100%

What the categories stand for, of course, is essential. For each auditable activity the categories must be carefully studied. This requires a good working knowledge of the auditable activity. Exactly what the four major categories stand for in the simple model presented here is explained below.

Monetary values: This category deals with monetary values and the importance of the transaction in terms of the currency (dollar, euro, pound, etc.) amount per transaction, the total daily value of the transaction, the average end-of-day monetary balances (end-of-day balance sheet amounts) and the liquidity of the transaction.

Nature of operations: This category deals with the type of transaction, the time constraints on completing the transaction, the consequences of completing late, the number of transactions in an average day, the complexity of the transaction, and the sophistication of processing.

Controls and security: This category deals with the traditional, long-standing operative objectives of internal accounting controls. It is concerned with the following.

- Are transactions executed in accordance with management's general or specific established lines, limits, etc.?
- Are transactions recorded so that proper accountability for assets is maintained and financial statements that comply with Generally Accepted Accounting Principles (GAAP) or International Financial Reporting Standards (IFRS) are the result?
- Is the recorded accountability for assets compared with existing assets at reasonable intervals, and is appropriate action taken with respect to differences? That is, are balance sheet amounts compared to actual assets or to customer input—cash, investments, loan statements, deposit statements, etc.?

Human resources: This fourth category deals with the quality of management, including experience, awareness, and problem-solving ability. It also deals with the staff—its size, abilities, experience, motivation, and training. In addition, it is concerned with delegation of duties and proper follow-up of findings, exceptions, and so on.

The importance weights for each category must be allocated to subcategories. For example, based on the philosophy of the audit department and of the organization overall, the 20% for the "monetary values" category might be allocated as in Table 2.

  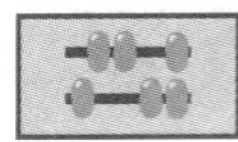   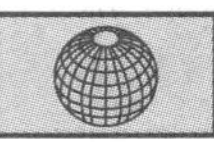   

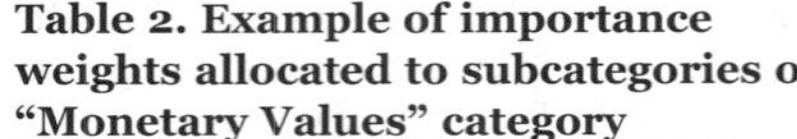

Table 2. Example of importance weights allocated to subcategories of "Monetary Values" category

Subcategory	*Importance weight*
Value per transaction	5%
Total daily value of transactions	5%
End of day balance	5%
Liquidity	5%
Total	20%

Again, the allocation of importance weights to the four categories (monetary values, nature of operations, controls and security, and human resources) is subjective and differs between organizations. Careful consideration in light of the audit philosophy of the internal audit function is required to properly perform the risk assessment.

Each subcategory for each auditable activity requires an intelligent assessment in terms of risk ratings (high, medium, or low) and known or perceived conditions. The ratings are made on a scale of 0 to 4, where 0 is no risk and 4 is high-risk. The 0 to 4 scale must to be established for each sub-category before the assessment begins. The established questions are based on the notion that "0" is no risk, "1" is a very low risk, "2" is moderate risk, "3" is above average risk and "4" is unacceptable risk. The established scale must be used consistently for all auditable activities. The rating multiplied by the importance weight gives an overall risk score for each of the four categories and related subcategories. The risk rating is based on evidence and professional judgment.

The sum of the overall risk scores by category is the total risk score for each auditable activity. How each auditable activity relates to each other auditable activity is then compared and ranked by reviewing absolute total risk scores.

APPENDIX 1: EXAMPLES OF BUSINESS FUNCTIONS AND AUDITABLE ACTIVITIES FOR A RETAIL ESTABLISHMENT AND A NOT-FOR-PROFIT HOSPITAL

Retail establishment	*Not-for-profit hospital*
1. Obtaining working funds Stock issuance Debt issuance Vendor financing Other	1. Gathering funds Grants Patient fees Donations
2. Product acquisition Buying goods R&D Market analysis Cash payments Quality control Product returns	2. Expenditures Plant replacement and maintenance R&D Supplies and materials Professional fees Employee costs (personnel and payroll)
3. Sales Product location Customer credit approval Cash collections Customer satisfaction Customer tracking Shipping	3. Fund balance control Budgeting Float management Satisfaction of donor intent
4. Inventory control Obsolescence review Storage levels	4. Constituency relations Patients Community Brand management
5. Cash management Budgeting Cash flow "float" management Tax management	5. Security and safety Automated Nonautomated Insurance
6. Stockholder relations Dividend maintenance Public relations Brand management	
7. Personnel and payroll Hiring Training Development Payments to employees	
8. Security and safety Automated Nonautomated Insurance	

Part 2: The Detailed Risk Assessment Questionnaire

To develop the risk ratings, detailed questions are asked for each activity. A summary of the questions by category is given in Appendix 4.

The risk calculation worksheet in Appendix 3 is used to score each auditable activity, which then can be listed from high-risk score to low-risk score based on total risk score for each auditable activity.

SUMMARY

The entire assessment process is not time-consuming if the audit manager knows the risks and controls for each auditable activity. A serious attempt to implement this approach will probably result in a question as to why the internal auditors are or are not concentrating efforts in one area versus another. The answer is straightforward—the time and effort spent on any audit area should be based on a careful, consistently applied risk ranking.

A conscientious annual audit risk assessment is a healthy experience for the audit department and for the bank. The approach set forth in this chapter is a simple one, and it costs little to do. The only ingredient needed is knowledge of the bank's business functions, activities, and controls.

The approach makes the difficult decision about differentiating between activities such as:

- wire transfers;
- commercial lending;
- investment of depositor funds;
- trust management (managing other people's money);
- foreign currency trading;
- derivative activities (hedging or trading).

The ranking of these auditable activities and others will differ from bank to bank. That is so because of the different bank audit philosophies that are in place (which will be reflected in the importance weights) and auditor assessments about the risks and control conditions within each auditable activity. Banks will differ on what activities need audit coverage, and what type of audit coverage is needed. That is appropriate since each internal audit function will be

"An elephant is vastly more efficient, metabolically, than a mouse. It's the same for a megacity as opposed to a village. But an elephant can break a leg very easily, whereas you can toss a mouse out of a window and it'll be fine. Size makes you fragile." Nassim Nicholas Taleb

  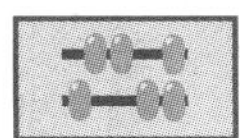   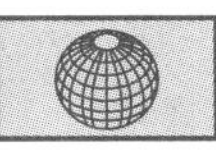   

APPENDIX 2: EXAMPLE OF RISK/CONTROL SHEET—MAJOR RISKS AND RELATED KEY CONTROLS FOR FOREIGN EXCHANGE ACTIVITY

Major risks	*Key control*
Deals could be made with unauthorized parties	Management establishes lists of authorized customers, including brokers
Deals could be made in excess of approved lines and limits	Trading limits are established for customers, currency traded, etc.
Approved customers may not be properly reviewed for overall creditworthiness	Nontrading personnel compare trading activity with authorizations; trading positions are valued daily by nontrading personnel and compared with authorizations
Market risk (daily price changes) for positions held may not be independently monitored	Excessive price changes and authorization violations are reported daily to senior management by nontrading personnel
Unauthorized bank employees could execute trades for the bank	Approved customers (including brokers and dealers) are given specific trading authorizations; authorized bank employee foreign currency dealers are told with whom (which specific person) they can transact business with at the counterparty's company

APPENDIX 3: RISK CALCULATION WORKSHEET

Activity: ____________

Date: ____________

Factor	*Importance weight ×*	*Risk rating (1 to 4) =*	*Risk score*	*Subtotal*
1. Monetary values				
Value per transaction	____	____	____	
Total value of transactions	____	____	____	
End-of-day balances	____	____	____	
Liquidity	____	____	____	____
2. Nature of operations				
Pressure	____	____	____	
Volume	____	____	____	
Complexity of transaction	____	____	____	
Process sophistication	____	____	____	____
3. Controls and security				
Authorization:				
General	____	____	____	
Specific	____	____	____	
Recording:				
Flow of documents and activities	____	____	____	
GAAP or IFRS	____	____	____	
Access:				
Direct	____	____	____	
Indirect	____	____	____	
Comparison:				
Periodicity	____	____	____	
Actions taken	____	____	____	____
4. Human resources				
Management:				
Experience	____	____	____	
Awareness	____	____	____	
Problem solving	____	____	____	
Staffing/motivation	____	____	____	
Training	____	____	____	
Delegation of duties	____	____	____	
Resolution of previous findings	____	____	____	
Staff:				
Experience	____	____	____	
Performance	____	____	____	____
	100 points		**Total risk score**	____

performing its audit coverage based on its own professional risk assessment.

Decisions about allocating resources to the auditable activities are easier and more professional when a simple risk assessment approach is used. The perennial resource allocation headache is less of a problem when a risk-based auditing approach such as the one presented in this chapter is used.

The professional internal auditor who is determining the annual audit plan should implement the following steps outlined in this chapter.

- List the business functions and auditable activities.
- For each auditable activity determine the business risks and related controls.
- Establish importance weights.
- Use the various questions to risk score by category for each auditable activity.
- Calculate overall risk scores by auditable activity.
- Rank the activities by risk score (high to low).
- Based on available resources, determine what to audit and when.

APPENDIX 4: DETERMINATION OF RISK RATINGS FOR EACH ACTIVITY—SUMMARY OF QUESTIONS BY CATEGORY

Category No. 1: Monetary Values:

This category requires the risk assessor to consider the characteristics of the activity and the valuables, if any, that are being handled. (Valuables are items that have monetary worth in their present form or when they are converted.)

Value per transaction: For each activity, what is the risk level (i.e. the chance that there will be a monetary or nonmonetary loss) based on the importance of the average daily monetary amount of each transaction? Use a risk scale of one for low-risk to four for high-risk. Monetary amounts for all activities must be decided upon.

Total daily value of transactions: What is the risk level based on the importance of the total daily value of all transactions? Volume numbers for the 1 to 4 ratings must be established.

End-of-day balances: What is the risk based on the amount of valuables held overnight, i.e. end-of-day balances? Monetary amounts for the 1 to 4 ratings must be established.

Liquidity: What is the risk level based on the ease with which valuables can be converted into cash? Consider the number of activities needed for conversion, the time needed to convert, the expertise required to convert, and the degree of negotiability of the instrument in question.

"All opinions are not equal. Some are a very great deal more robust, sophisticated, and well supported in logic and argument than others." Douglas Adams

Category No. 2: Nature of Operations

This category requires the risk assessor to consider the characteristics of the day-to-day work performed by employees. It requires knowledge of the type of transaction involved, the time needed to finish the transaction, the consequences of completing the transaction late, the average daily number of transactions, the complexity of the transactions, and the sophistication of processing.

Pressure: What is the risk level based on the time constraints on completing the transaction and the consequences if the work is not completed on time?

Volume: What is the risk level associated with the absolute number of units received, processed, or delivered by the activity during the average day?

Complexity of transactions: What is the risk level based on the number of people, the amount of time, the number of steps, and the degree of difficulty involved in completing the transactions?

Processing sophistication: What is the risk level based on the reliability of the technology used for processing?

Category No. 3: Controls and Security

This category requires the risk assessor to consider the "health" of the procedures and activities that safeguard the assets and generate reasonably accurate financial information.

Authorization—general: What is the risk level based on the importance of having written, understandable, properly distributed, and suitably monitored general authorizations (i.e. policies concerned with the definition or identification of general conditions under which transactions are authorized without regard to specific parties or transactions)?

Authorization—specific: What is the risk level based on the importance of having written policies that specify the conditions under which transactions can be undertaken and with whom and at what prices, limits, volume, etc.?

Recording—flow: What is the risk that the flow of documents, activities, procedures, and controls will not record all transactions properly and completely?

Recording—GAAP or IFRS: What is the risk that transactions are recorded in a way that does not easily generate accurate financial statements that are in accordance with Generally Accepted Accounting Principles or International Financial Reporting Standards?

Access—direct: What is the risk that direct access to assets will be achieved by unauthorized employees or others?

Access—indirect: What is the risk that unauthorized personnel can prepare or process documents that will result in improper use of assets?

Periodic comparisons: What s the risk that there is a significant difference between accountabilities for assets and the actual assets?

Follow-up comparisons: What is the likelihood that the differences between accountabilities and actual assets are left long outstanding and not investigated at once?

Category No. 4: Human Resources

This category requires the risk assessor to consider the characteristics that constitute top quality management and staff. It deals with management quality, experience, awareness and problem solving ability. It also deals with motivation, training and the delegation of duties.

Management experience: What is the risk that the appropriate knowledge and skills are lacking?

Awareness: What is the risk that management is not aware of the current state of operations?

Problem solving: What is the risk that management is not able to meet operating problems promptly and effectively?

Staffing/motivation: What is the risk that management does not have an appropriate staff size to inspire staff employees to perform well?

Training: What is the risk that management has not provided appropriate training to appropriate employees?

Delegation of duties: What is the risk that management does not appropriately delegate duties?

Resolution of previous findings: What is the risk that management is not satisfactorily taking action to respond to audit or other "findings?"

Staff experience: What is the risk that the staff does not have a high level of experience?

Performance: What is the risk that the quality of work and the timeliness to which staff carry out their duties is less than standard?

MORE INFO

There are few notable books and/or articles about the specifics of internal auditor risk assessment. The sources given below, however, provide some useful further information.

Standards:

Institute of Internal Auditors (IIA). "International Professional Practices Framework (IPPF)." 2011 edition, updated for 2012. Online at: tinyurl.com/79nzmne

Institute of Internal Auditors (IIA). "2010—Planning." Online at: tinyurl.com/72nbjmx

Websites:

Institute of Internal Auditors (IIA): www.theiia.org

Washington State University Office of Internal Audit on risk assessment: internalaudit.wsu.edu/riskassessment.html

World Intellectual Property Organization (WIPO) on risk assessment methodology: tinyurl.com/83ut78n

"Questions are places in your mind where answers fit. If you haven't asked the question, the answer has nowhere to go. It hits your mind and bounces right off. You have to ask the question—you have to want to know—in order to open up the space for the answer to fit." Clayton M. Christensen

Best Practices in Risk-Based Internal Auditing

by Sheryl Vacca

EXECUTIVE SUMMARY

- Agree on a common framework for the risk-based auditing and monitoring program.
- Assess risks across the enterprise and then prioritize them by looking at the likelihood of occurrence and impact for the organization.
- Develop a risk-based auditing and monitoring plan from the identified risk priorities.
- Execute a corrective action plan developed by management to mitigate risks and/or resolve risks.
- Assess the auditing and monitoring process for effectiveness.

GETTING STARTED

In designing risk-based auditing and monitoring activities, it is important that the internal auditor works closely with the organization's senior leadership and the board, or committee of the board, to gain a clear understanding of auditing and monitoring expectations and how these activities can be leveraged together to help minimize and mitigate risks for the organization. These discussions should also include leadership from the legal, compliance, and risk management functions, if they are not already a part of the senior leadership team.

This process should include performing periodic audits to determine compliance with respect to applicable regulatory and legal requirements, and to provide assurance that management controls are in place for the detection and/or prevention of noncompliant behavior. Additionally, risk-based auditing and monitoring should include mechanisms to determine that management has implemented corrective action through an ongoing performance management process to address any non-compliance.

Once the common framework for the risk-based auditing and monitoring program has been established, four key tasks must be performed:

1 Assessment and prioritization of risks, conducted enterprise-wide;
2 Development of a risk-based auditing and monitoring plan;
3 Execution of a corrective action plan developed by management to mitigate risks and/or resolve risks;
4 Periodic assessment of the overall process for effectiveness.

RISK ASSESSMENT

The Committee of Sponsoring Organizations of the Treadway Commission (COSO) helped to define "risk" as any event that can keep an organization from achieving its objectives.[1] According to the COSO model, risk is viewed in four major areas:

- operational (processes and procedures);
- financial (data rolling up to internal/external statements);
- regulatory (federal, state, local, organizational policy);
- reputation (institutional).

There are several ways in which risk assessments in these areas can be conducted. These include the use of:

- focus groups to assist in the identification of risks;
- interviews of key leadership and the board;
- surveys;
- reviews of previous audit findings, external audits conducted in the organization, and identifying what is occurring within the industry and the local market, etc.

Once risks have been identified, a prioritization process is needed to identify the likelihood of the risk occurring, the ability of management to mitigate risk (i.e. are there controls in place for risk, regardless of the likelihood of those risks of occurring?), and the impact of risk on the organization. Risk prioritization is an ongoing process and should include periodic reviews during the year to ensure that previous prioritization methods, when applied in real time, are still applicable for the risk.

It is important that senior leadership participate in, and agree with, the determination of the high-risk priorities for the audit and monitoring plan. This will ensure management buy-in and focus on risk priorities. Also, with managers involved at the development stage of the plan, they will be educated as to the type of activities being planned and the resources needed to conduct these activities. Hence, during the plan year, if there are changes, management will understand the need for additional resources or a change in focus in the plan as the business environment and priorities may change.

DEVELOPING THE PLAN

The International Standards for the Professional Practice of Internal Audit (IIA), Standard 2120 says "The internal audit activity must evaluate the effectiveness and contribute to the improvement of the risk management processes." [2]

This is done through the development and execution of the risk-based auditing and monitoring plan.

Risk assessments and prioritization are important elements in the development of your risk-based auditing and monitoring plan. Considerations related to the plan should also include:

- Review of other business areas in the organization which may be conducting an audit or monitoring activity in this area:
  - If so, could you leverage this resource for assistance in completing the stated activity, or utilize their activity and integrate the results into the overall plan?
- Resources available to implement the plan:
  - Do you have the appropriate resources for the subject matter as needed within your department? (If not, is there subject matter expertise somewhere else in the organization?)
  - If subject matter requires outsourcing, budget considerations and overall risk priorities may need to be re-evaluated.
- Hours needed to complete the plan.
- Projected timeframes.
- Defined auditing or monitoring activities and determination as to whether they are outcome or process oriented.
- Flexibility incorporated into the plan to address changes in risk priorities and possibly unplanned compliance risks/crises which may need an immediate audit or monitoring to occur.

IIA Standard 2120.A1 identifies the focus of the risk assessment process: "The internal audit activity must evaluate risk exposures related to the organization's governance, operations, and information systems regarding the:

- Reliability and integrity of financial and operational information;
- Effectiveness and efficiency of operations;
- Safeguarding of assets;
- Compliance with laws, regulations, and contracts.

The process of risk assessment continues through the execution of the plan where the

"The only reason to invest in the market is because you think you know something others don't." R. Foster Winans

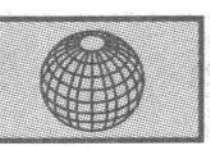

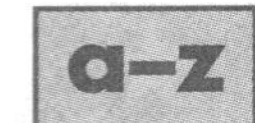

engagement objectives would reflect the results of the risk assessment. Risk-based auditing and monitoring is ongoing and dynamic with the needs of the organization.

EXECUTION OF THE PLAN—MAKING IT HAPPEN

Each activity should have a defined framework which will provide management with an understanding of the overall expectations and approach as you execute the plan. The framework for your activities should include the following actions:

- Set the purpose and goal for the activity (audit or monitoring):
  - Identify the scope from the purpose or goal, but make sure that it is objective, measurable, and concise.
  - Before conducting activities in high-risk priority areas, it is important to consider whether legal advice may be needed in establishing the approach to the activity.
- Conduct initial discussion with the business area for input related to audit attributes, timing, and process:
  - Concurrent vs retrospective status may be determined at this point. (Concurrent is "real time" and before the end point of what you are looking at has occurred. Retrospective is after the end point has occurred, i.e. the claim has been submitted or the research has concluded, etc. Milestones should be determined for rationale as to how far back to go, for example, new law, new system, etc.).
- Finalize the approach and attributes:
  - Sampling methodology will be determined largely by the scope (purpose and goal) of your activity. For example, the sample used in self reporting a risk area to an outside enforcement agency may be predetermined by the precedent that the enforcement agency has set in industry; to determine if education is needed in a risk area, a small sample only may be needed, etc.
  - Consider the audience frame of reference that will receive the results of activity, and then develop an appropriate format for reporting.
  - Data collection and tracking are critical because they provide trend analysis and measurement of progress.
- Conduct the activity.
- Identify preliminary findings and observations.
- Provide an opportunity for findings and observations to be validated by the business area.
- Finalize the report.
- Identify processes for the follow-up after management has taken corrective action related to activity findings and observations.
- Determine the key points of activity that may be provided to leadership and/or in reporting to the board.

Figure 1. Benefits of an effectively executed risk-based auditing and monitoring plan

NO BIG SURPRISES

Early warning systems
- ◆ Systematically identify, assess, and prioritize risks.
- ◆ Avoid unrewarded risks and protect assets in place.

Integrated infrastructure
- ◆ Ensure that bad news travels fast internally first Ñhave early warning systems in place.
- ◆ Prevent and respond rapidly to potential catastrophic failures.
- ◆ Improve ability to anticipate and prepare for change.
- ◆ Establish a risk-based culture.
- ◆ Provide assurance that key risks and exposures are understood and mitigated.

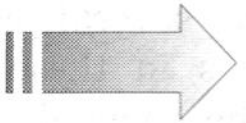

Comprehensive policies and procedures
- ◆ Seek growth, but ensure that strategic and tactical risks are mitigated.
- ◆ Maximize chances of success of achieving business plan goals.
- ◆ Accelerate ability to respond to change and opportunities.

CASE STUDY

Scenario: An organization with multiple businesses in several geographic locations is conducting an enterprise-wide risk assessment. It is noted during the risk assessment that, due to recent financial losses, the organization is going through a consolidation of business units and reduction in workforce. This has been identified as a high-risk priority area for the auditing and monitoring plan for the next fiscal year.

In planning the audit on the risk area of business consolidation, the following considerations should be included:

- The business consolidation could be impacting the organization in various ways—customer base loss, reduced finances, loss of reputation, loss of workforce resulting in loss of controls, etc.
- The risk-based audit will focus on areas of greatest impact: loss of controls in financial areas due to the reduction in workforce.
- The timing of the audit will be negotiated to bring the most value to the organization. This might involve having a two-part audit. Part I could take place after the business consolidation and reduction in workforce have occurred. This would include assessing the consolidated business unit to determine if there are any gaps in the financial controls. For instance, segregation of duties is commonly found in situations with loss of people and consolidation of functions. Any gaps identified would become actions for management to correct before the Part II audit took place.
- Management may also want to set up its own monitoring system to ensure that its corrective actions have resolved any of the gaps identified.
- Part II of the audit would occur after a negotiated period of time with management and would allow the corrective actions to have been in place long enough for their effectiveness to be determined.

The overall purpose of this type of risk-based auditing is to work with management in "real time," to add value to the organization in regard to its strategic and best business interest, and to provide input on processes before they become "fixed." After management believes it has the "fixes" in place, then the second part of the audit will help to provide assurances that the risks identified are no longer risks and that no new gaps or lack of controls have developed around the process of business consolidation and reduction in workforce.

"If investing is entertaining, if you're having fun, you're probably not making any money. Good investing is boring."
George Soros

The overall process of developing the audit and monitoring plan should be documented. This would include a description of how the risk assessment was conducted and the methodology for prioritization of risks. Working papers to support the audit findings, reports, and corrective action plans should be documented and filed appropriately. Prior to the audit activity, be sure to define and document what should be considered as part of the working papers.

At the end of each plan year, it is important to conduct an evaluation of the overall effectiveness of the plan. Questions to consider may include:

- Was the plan fully executed?
- Were appropriate resources utilized for the plan's execution?
- Were the activities conducted in a timely manner?
- Did the plan "make a difference" in regard to the organization's strategy and business?
- Did the plan reach the goal of detecting, deterring, and/or preventing compliance research risks from occurring?

Annual evaluations may be conducted through self reviews or independently of the internal audit function by a third party, i.e. peer review conducted with auditors from other organizations, Quality Assessment Review conducted according to IIA standards (every 5 years), etc. However, while self reviews are less resource intensive, it is recommended that a independent review be conducted at least every other year to assess the effectiveness of your auditing and monitoring efforts. Figure 1 helps to identify the benefits of an effectively executed risk-based auditing and monitoring plan.

In summary, effectiveness in the development and execution of the risk-based audit and monitoring plan will be determined by the integrity and characteristics of the overall audit and monitoring process. Effective audit and monitoring activities will assist in the identification of weaknesses in controls, management's action to correct those weaknesses, and follow-up to ensure that timely mechanisms have been put in place to strengthen controls for mitigating the business risks. Additionally, risks will be detected, deterred and/or prevented with effective auditing and monitoring activities.

MAKING IT HAPPEN

The development of an effective risk-based auditing and monitoring program includes several key elements:

1. Performing an enterprise-wide risk assessment that includes operational, financial, regulatory, and reputational risk (1-IIA).
2. Prioritizing risks identified through measures such as likelihood and impact for the organization.
3. Developing a risk-based auditing and monitoring plan from the identified risk priorities.
4. Determining that corrective action plans which have been developed by management to mitigate priority risks or ensure controls are in place to lower the risk level for the organization.
5. Conducting follow-up activities that validate, monitor, or audit corrective actions to mitigate and/or resolve the identified risks.
6. Re-evaluating risks on an annual basis through a risk assessment process to ensure that the priority risks of the organization have been addressed.
7. Conducting a periodic third-party review of the risk-based auditing and monitoring plan to assess whether:
   a. processes are in place to identify risks;
   b. appropriate resources are utilized to audit and/or monitor risks;
   c. a commitment to reinforcing the need for management to execute plans to mitigate risks is demonstrated by the board and senior management.

MORE INFO

Websites:

Federal Sentencing Guidelines, Chapter 8. US Sentencing Commission's webpage's at www.ussc.gov/general.htm (history and overview of the guidelines) and www.ussc.gov/GUIDELIN.HTM (guidelines and manuals). Chapter 8's provisions can be found at www.ussc.gov/2004guid/tabconchapt8.htm

General Accounting Office (GAO): www.gao.gov

Institute of Internal Auditors: www.theiia.org

Public Company Accounting Oversight Board (PCAOB): www.pcaobus.org

Sarbanes–Oxley Act 2002: www.soxlaw.com

Securities and Exchange Commission: www.sec.gov

Society of Corporate Compliance and Ethics (SCCE): www.corporatecompliance.org

See Also:

★ The Effect of SOX on Internal Control, Risk Management, and Corporate Governance Best Practice (pp. 333–335)
★ New Assurance Challenges Facing Chief Audit Executives (p. 381)
★ Optimizing Internal Audit (pp. 382–384)
★ Risk Management: Beyond Compliance (pp. 929–932)
★ What Is the Range of the Internal Auditor's Work? (pp. 431–434)
✔ Defining Corporate Governance: Its Aims, Goals, and Responsibilities (p. 1115)
✔ Understanding Internal Audits (p. 1057)

NOTES

1. Committee of Sponsoring Organizations of the Treadway Commission. *Enterprise Risk Management Framework: Draft (2003)*. Published in 2004 as *Enterprise Risk Management—Integrated Framework* and available from www.coso.org
2. Institute of Internal Auditors. *Professional Practice Standards. 2120—Risk Management*, Section A1. January 2009.

"I don't invest in anything I don't understandit makes more sense to buy TV stations than oil wells." Oprah Winfrey

Viewpoint: Challenges Faced by the Audit Profession After the Crash by James Chadwick

INTRODUCTION

James Chadwick qualified as a chartered accountant in 2003 and is a member of the Institute of Chartered Accountants of Scotland. In 2004 he joined Grant Thornton, where he has performed a number of different roles and undertaken a six-month secondment into industry. In January 2011 he became associate director and head of Grant Thornton's audit practice for the Scottish region. Chadwick has a wide and varied client base that includes some of Scotland's highest-profile businesses across a number of different sectors. He is head of the food and drink team for Scotland.

In the post-2008 analysis of the crash in the financial sector, auditors were heavily blamed for not flagging up weaknesses in bank practices and for not spotting the mispricing of risk. What has the fallout from this been for the profession?

In a sense, this is part of the larger question about audit quality, which has never gone away and continues to be a perennial concern. To place this in context, the audit profession is subject to continuous review of the quality of its work. This is part of the brief of the Financial Reporting Council (FRC), which is responsible for upholding the quality of the audits of the financial statements of all companies in the United Kingdom. As such, their inspection teams review financial statements and satisfy themselves that all the key questions with respect to risk, controls, and disclosure have been correctly dealt with. If a review of the published accounts does not satisfy the FRC that all the questions it wants answers to have in fact been answered, it will write to the company concerned and ask for a clarification of its position. If it is still not satisfied, the FRC has the power to issue a press notice, which is the equivalent of a public censure, and it creates a furor when this happens. We saw this most recently when Rio Tinto was the subject of a press notice. So the work of auditors is constantly scrutinized not just by the major users of accounts, such as funders, but specifically by the quality control side of the FRC.

However, there remains the ongoing task of rebuilding confidence in audit reports and getting people comfortable again that they can rely on the value of a clean audit report. The audit exercise is not cheap for a large public company and it is compulsory, so value for money is a key criterion. At the same time, there is tremendous price competition in the audit market, as audit firms compete fiercely for clients. This has a bearing on audit quality in a sense, but the entwined notions of price and value are also impacted by at least three other factors. These are: the issue of auditor independence and "other services"; the constant increase in the volume of audit practice standards; and the structure of the market for big company audits.

There is clear and mounting pressure from the Ethical Standards setting body, part of the Audit Practices Board, which is itself part of the Financial Reporting Council, in the direction of proscribing any services for audit clients other than the provision of the audit. Clearly, the more work outside the audit that a firm does for a company, the deeper its knowledge of that company will be—which will ultimately improve the efficiency of the audit process.

There is already a strict rule against a firm auditing work that it has itself had a material influence on. For almost a decade now, audit firms have not carried out IT consultancy for clients because there was a clear conflict of interest in an audit firm both specifying the client's operational accounting systems and then auditing those systems. As a consequence, the big accounting firms spun out their consultancy arms as separate entities.

If we turn to audit standards, the auditor has to take account of both the specific audit practice standards and the full range of accounting standards set by the relevant accounting standards body. With audit standards we have again seen a recent change through the clarification project on International Standards on Auditing (ISA), which has further increased the amount of work required, for example, when groups are audited. The question at issue here is the degree to which an audit firm that is auditing a group of companies where some of the members of the group around the world are audited by third-party firms of auditors can rely on the work of those third-party firms. Whereas in the past the practice has been to place considerable reliance on those audits when the quality of the audit firm responsible for a particular subsidiary company audit is known to be sound, the new audit practice standard demands that the auditor of the parent company carry out a good deal more work to test the quality of the subsidiary audit.

What audit practice standards demand today is that the auditor of a group of companies must do sufficient work at the planning stage to identify for itself all the key risks in all the subsidiary companies. This requires a lot more interaction with the subsidiary auditors to ensure that the work that they have done meets the requirements of the group auditors. Audit firms long ago formed international networks, which helps them to deal with the challenges of auditing multinational companies with subsidiaries in many countries. However, the new audit practices standard on group audits means that even where the audit firms responsible for subsidiary audits belong to the same network as the group auditor, you still need an increased level of involvement in subsidiary audits. You cannot just rely on those audits even though you may have a very good knowledge of the individual audit firms responsible for those audits. There are of course nontrivial cost implications here.

If you think about this for a moment, it means that the client group of companies is having to pay or an element of the work twice. First it pays for the audit of the subsidiary, then it pays for the auditor of the parent company to review the work of the auditor of its overseas subsidiary. It is very difficult for the client company to regard this double payment as value for money since, to the parent company, it looks as if the audit profession is merely doing work to cover its own back if something goes wrong. It would argue that the original subsidiary audit has already been done—and done well.

"You have to be intellectually honest with yourself and others. In my judgment, all great investors are seekers of truth."
Michael Steinhardt

One could argue that since the new audit practice standard is about ensuring the quality of the audit, it is therefore in the interests of both the client and the audit firm, since the interests of both client and auditor are aligned here. They both want the outside world to be able to place a high degree of confidence in the audit. But, on the emotional level, it looks and feels like double checking of the same thing and does nothing to help the relationship between the client company and the audit firm.

In fact, one could make a larger point here about the difficulty clients have in seeing real value in the considerable increase in the volume and detail of required by audit standards. Relating the massive increase in compliance costs back to the actual value that a client organization derives from the audit is difficult, to say the least. It looks to the client—who is generally not shy about making this point to the audit firm—as if what all this is about is the profession covering itself and making sure that it is seen to be diligent. There is no perceived additional value to the client from the increased workload, and the resulting increased fee, since there is no easy way of equating more work by the audit firm with a direct increase in the level of market confidence in audit reports. This is one of the big dilemmas facing the audit profession.

Obviously the audit of a multinational group poses challenges that are of a different order from the audit of a mid-sized or smaller company with no, or only one or two, local subsidiaries. How do the audit practice standards cope with the challenges of this enormous difference in scale?

That is another difficulty. Audit practice standards are the same for, say, the audit of the Royal Bank of Scotland as they are for an owner-managed business with a £6 million turnover. So the relative cost for a small business that requires an audit is considerable. At present the turnover threshold above which a company is required by law to have an audit stands at £6.5 million. There is talk of increasing this threshold, putting it up significantly to, say, turnover above £25 million.

Would that not have a severe impact on the fee earnings of the many smaller firms of auditors, for whom auditing the vast army of smaller private companies constitutes a very significant part of a firm's income?

Clearly, taking large numbers of smaller companies out of the audit net would impact the profession. However, this is not the first time that such an exercise has been carried out. Around six years ago, when the UK government increased the audit exemption threshold from £1 million to £5.6 million, there were predictions that large numbers of companies would do away with having an audit and that this would wipe out large numbers of small, one- to four-partner firms of accountants. However, although there were undoubtedly difficulties for some firms, the profession adjusted and moved to providing a greater range of accounts preparation, payroll, and other services, such as advisory, analysis, and management accounting services. I imagine that the same would be true again if the audit threshold was raised significantly.

Audit has been caught up to some extent in the mark-to-market accounting controversy. How is that playing out?

There is no doubt that mark-to-market as an accounting practice creates huge volatility in any set of accounts. In my view, the best picture of the underlying trading position of a business comes from a perusal of its cash flow statement. Mark-to-market can create some very significant distortions by, for example, turning a loss into a profit. We saw one of the big UK banks, for example, showing a significant profit in an interim set of results purely through the marking-to-market of a financial instrument that was not due through the period in question. This kind of momentary fluctuation in value that is not being realized in the trading profit of the business has nothing to do with underlying trading and can really mask what is going on there.

Accounting standards are continually under development, and we are going through a very demanding period where the International Financial Reporting Standards (IFRS) are developing all the time, while the UK Generally Accepted Accounting Principles (GAAP) are converging steadily toward IFRS best practice. Some of the more contentious IFRS standards, such as the implementation of financial instruments standard, have taken some time to bed down.

What we are seeing is a slow but inescapable change in the UK GAAP. This has implications and consequences for smaller companies, and we are seeing an attempt to address this with the Financial Reporting Standard for Medium Sized Entities, FRSME, which has gone through the exposure draft stage and for which final proposals are now being prepared. The aim is to remove UK GAAP for all but the smallest companies and to move all other companies to either a scaled-down and less demanding version of IFRS or to full IFRS. The Accounting Standards Board in the United Kingdom has seen a lot of push-back from companies and their advisers on the exposure draft and is now in the process of taking those comments on board. Again, this will change things for the audit profession and for those who prepare accounts. It has taken a long time for IFRS GAAP to really settle down, and we have seen some significant changes in the views of accounts preparers as to how some bits of the IFRS should be interpreted. Again, the audit profession has the task of ensuring that it understands what is driving a client company's policies on accounts preparation and how that relates to issues of compliance.

This is addressed through the audit practice standards, and through amendments to those standards over time. We had a new set of audit practice standards released in 2005, which increased the requirement on auditors to document systems and controls, and to understand the risk of fraud and other risks at the overall entity level down to whatever level in the organization those risks could prove to be material to the financial statements. All this added to the work that auditors have to do, and therefore it drives up fees. In fact we saw a round of fee increases after the new audit practice standards were introduced. However, each new addition to the standards inevitably seems to drive the workload, and hence the fees, upward—against considerable push-back from clients.

Your firm has been at the forefront of trying to break the near monopoly of the Big Four audit firms on public company audits. What drives that "monopoly," and how successful have you been in making inroads into it?

The fundamental issue is one of perceived risk. If every large plc uses a big-four audit firm, then by definition a board cannot be faulted on its choice of auditor if it selects one of those firms, even if things go wrong. In reality both my firm and similarly sized firms are able to provide highly competitive services for multinational group audits, and we and they can both point to a track record of successes in auditing blue-chip plc clients. But making inroads is not easy and one has to chip away at the big-four myth on a case-by-case basis. There are instances where a big-four firm will have specialist skills that we do not have, but there are also many large corporations for whom those specialist skill sets are irrelevant and where we can provide a service that is at least as good as would be provided by a big-four firm. What is on our side is the fact that, as I

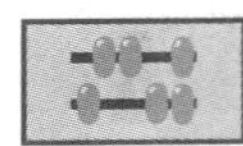

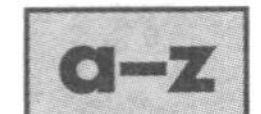

began by saying, audit is fiercely price-competitive and we have a lighter cost base than a big-four firm, which gives us an advantage. However, the inertial drag posed by the truism that "no one ever got fired for using a big-four firm" pulls in the other direction. What is certain is that audit is only going to get more competitive, not less!

MORE INFO

Books:

Johnson, Spencer. *Who Moved My Cheese? An Amazing Way to Deal with Change in Your Work and in Your Life*. London: Vermillion, 1999.

Kline, Nancy. *Time to Think: Listening to Ignite the Human Mind*. London: Cassell Illustrated, 1998.

McLean, Bethany, and Peter Elkind. *The Smartest Guys in the Room: The Amazing Rise and Scandalous Fall of Enron*. New York: Penguin, 2003.

Sorkin, Andrew Ross. *Too Big to Fail: The Inside Story of How Wall Street and Washington Fought to Save the Financial System—and Themselves*. New York: Viking, 2009.

Websites:

Audit Practices Board, sets auditing standards and ethical standards for the audit profession: www.frc.org.uk/apb/

Financial Accounting Standards Board, the official accounting standards setting body for the US: www.fasb.org

International Financial Reporting Standards Foundation, the body responsible for setting international accounting standards through the International Accounting Standards Board: www.ifrs.org

See Also:

★ Considerations when Outsourcing Internal Audit (pp. 312–314)
★ Has Financial Reporting Impacted on Internal Auditing Negatively? (pp. 338–341)
★ Viewpoint: Auditing in Volatile Markets (pp. 286–288)

"A society which reverences the attainment of riches as the supreme felicity will naturally be disposed to regard the poor as damned . . . if only to justify itself for making their life a hell." Richard Tawney

Classification and Treatment of Leases

by Roger Lister

EXECUTIVE SUMMARY

- Accounting bodies, both international and national, require leases to be classified in terms of economic substance rather than legal form.
- Current regulation distinguishes a finance lease from an operating lease. If a lease transfers the risks and rewards of an asset to the lessee, it is a finance lease. Otherwise, the lease is an operating lease. A finance lease appears in the balance sheet; an operating lease may remain off the balance sheet.
- New international and national accounting standards will almost certainly remove the distinction. Except for very short leases, all will go on the balance sheet.
- The change will eliminate a sometimes artificial distinction, but higher reported leverage may have ill effects. Management may avoid otherwise desirable leasing to protect the leverage ratio. Bond covenants may be breached and need to be renegotiated. There may be an incentive to circumvent the standard by taking out a succession of short but renewable leases.
- Tax allowances emphasize legal form, but tax in its detail tends to follow accounting standards. Companies will therefore need to consider the tax impact of the new standard as it solidifies.
- Anti-avoidance tax legislation proliferates daily and will probably increase as governments seek every opportunity to raise revenue in straitened times. At worst, a measure will be retrospective. Planners should monitor discussion and attempt the difficult task of identifying and anticipating the most likely changes, including anti-avoidance legislation.

INTRODUCTION

Lease accounting is nearer than ever to its goal of reporting substance rather than form. International regulators and their national counterparts agree that right-to-use rather than legal title should determine the classification and treatment of leases. The choice is essentially between disclosing a lease as a financial instrument on the balance sheet or as an operating lease on the income statement.

Financial reporting of leases is addressed in the International Accounting Standards Board's International Accounting Standard IAS 17. The International Accounting Standards Board (IASB) benefits from the participation of many countries, including the US Financial Accounting Standards Board (FASB).

Why lease? Management needs to test conventional answers carefully since some have limited relevance, while others are frankly contestable. Leasing is sometimes promoted for its small initial outlay, even as 100% financing. This ignores the fact that a rational lessor like a lender will seek a cushion of equity to protect the finance provided. A more rational answer is that leasing is advantageous if it provides more finance than the borrowing which it displaces. Management is essentially asking how far, for their company, is leasing a substitute for borrowing and how far a complement. Research suggests that leasing tends to be a substitute for borrowing for larger firms and a valuable complement to borrowing for small and medium enterprises (SMEs). Leasing can help to overcome SMEs' difficulty in conveying their quality to would-be financiers.

In the individual case, management has to investigate the impact of the fact that repossession of a leased asset is easier than foreclosure on the collateral of a secured loan, enhancing the debt capacity of leasing over secured lending. They must also consider how far leasing provides a solution to potential mistrust between asset provider and user with respect to the quality of the asset and the costs of maintenance.

CLASSIFICATION

Currently, the essential distinction is between the finance and the operating lease, but it is virtually certain that under the revised international financial reporting standard due about 2011 this distinction will disappear. The new classification will equate finance and operating leases. All but the shortest contracts will be treated like finance leases. New national standards will probably anticipate, accompany, or follow the new international standard.

A finance lease transfers substantially all the risks and rewards of asset ownership to the lessee and features accordingly in the balance sheet. An operating lease remains off balance sheet. If a lease satisfies any one or more of certain criteria, then it may be a finance lease. These are:

- Ownership of the asset is transferred to the lessee at the end of the lease term;
- The lease contains a bargain purchase option to buy the equipment at less than fair market value;
- The lease term is for the major part of the economic life of the asset even if title is not transferred;
- At the inception of the lease, the present value of the minimum lease payments amounts at least substantially to all of the fair value of the leased asset;
- The leased assets are of a specialized nature such that only the lessee can use them without major modification;
- Any cancellation losses are borne by the lessee;
- The lessee takes gains and losses on the asset's residual value;
- The lessee can rent for a secondary period for less than the market rent.

The international standard, unlike some national standards, does not focus on a numerical percentage of fair asset value (typically 90%).

"Asset" means the lower of the fair value and the present value of the minimum lease payments (MLP). MLP are discounted at the interest rate implicit in the lease if practicable, or else at the enterprise's incremental borrowing rate. Depreciation has to be consistent with that for similar owned assets. If ultimate ownership is unlikely, the asset has to be depreciated over the shorter of the lease term and the life of the asset. The income statement includes depreciation and the finance charge. Rental payments are recognized as part finance charge and part repayment of the liability to the lessor. Repayments of the obligation reduce the liability in the balance sheet.

In the case of operating leases, periodic rentals are charged in total against income on a straight-line basis, unless another systematic basis is more representative of the time pattern of the user's benefit. Any outstanding rentals are reported in the balance sheet, distinguishing maturities and categories of activity.

IAS 17 is further explained in SIC 15, SIC 27 and IFRIC 4 and 12. SIC 15 states that any incentives such as rent-free periods or contributions by the lessor to the lessee's relocation costs should be reported as a reduction of lease income or lease expense. IFRIC (a standard issued post 2001) 4 and 12 consider cases where a right to use, while not a lease in form, may amount to a lease

"**You don't own me.**" Bette Midler

for financial reporting purposes. Examples are outsourcing arrangements, telecommunication contracts that provide rights to capacity, and take-or-pay and similar contracts in which purchasers must make specified payments regardless of whether they take delivery of the contracted products or services.

Current classification and treatment of leasing has already brought financial reporting closer to economic reality, and the new standard will continue this progress. It will break down deceptive barriers between economically similar transactions. However, management needs to recognize potentially perverse effects. Reported leverage will increase if finance and operating leases are both on the balance sheet, possibly causing management to avoid otherwise beneficial leases. Bond covenants may be nominally breached and have to be renegotiated. Without suitable safeguards, companies may circumvent the standard by taking out short but renewable leases that will in practice span an asset's useful life.

The underlying principle is that treating lease expenses as financing expenses potentially impinges on reported operating income, capital, profitability and cash flow. It is likely that the market will reassess the value of many companies.

In the case of leveraged leasing (not under discussion here), the lessee gains access to the lessor's leveraged capital. The lessor owns the asset but typically provides only some 25% of capital while garnering any tax allowance in full. Institutional lenders provide the balance of the purchase price to the lessor on a non-recourse basis.

An extract from Christian Dior's 2007 accounts illustrates how lease classification appears in practice:"In addition to leasing its stores, the Group also finances some of its equipment through long term operating leases. Some fixed assets and equipment were also purchased or refinanced under finance leases."

SALE AND LEASEBACK

Extra financial reporting issues arise with sale and leaseback. An owner selling and leasing back an asset should in the first instance revise the recorded value of the asset to its economic value. This avoids distortion of the sale and leaseback transactions.

If the asset is sold at fair value and made the subject of an operating lease, any profit belongs in the year's income statement. If the sale is above fair value, the purchaser will charge higher rentals. In this case, the seller's profit on sale must be set against the high rentals by annual installments over the term of the lease or until the time of any rent review if sooner. If the asset is sold at a loss, the loss must be recognized immediately unless the purchaser compensates by below-market rentals, in which case the loss is amortized over the period of use. If the asset is sold at fair value and made the subject of a finance lease, any excess of proceeds over recorded value is amortized over the term of the lease.

CASE STUDY

Coleman

The British Tax Court imposed the strong proof rule on the taxpayer to show that it was entitled to depreciation deductions on a double-dip leasing transaction, even though the transaction was structured to also obtain a UK tax advantage. Coleman involved a cross-border leasing transaction, in which the parties sought to obtain depreciation deductions on certain leased computer equipment for both UK and US tax purposes. The lease and title to the computer equipment were transferred by a dealer to UK lenders, who were able to write off the computers in one year under UK tax law. The dealer retained an interest in the residual of the lease and (to simplify matters greatly) sold a portion of the residual interest to the US taxpayers. These persons claimed to be the owners of the leased computer equipment for US tax purposes and depreciated their bases in the equipment for US tax purposes. The court held that the record failed, under the strong proof standard, to sustain the petitioners' position that they were the owners of the computer equipment, and that the form of the transaction as a financing should be disregarded.

TAX

Significant tax changes will come with new accounting standards and increasing anti-avoidance legislation. Legislators and avoiders dodge and weave around pitfalls and opportunities. Management has to monitor and even try to influence discussion and hope that anti-avoidance provisions will not be retrospective.

In the United Kingdom, current detailed regulations[1] as administered by HM Revenue and Customs tend to look to the accounting standards subject to the fundamental difference that the tax definition of finance lease is based on legal title. Thus, a taxable lessor can still pass the benefits of capital allowances to a nontaxable lessee in the form of reduced rentals. Other points include:

- Finance charges are deductible according to any method that gives the lessor a constant return on rentals outstanding.
- If premature termination occurs, individual circumstances will determine whether any payment is an adjustment of past rentals (revenue expenditure) or a penal charge (capital expenditure).
- Any rebate or further rental arising on the substitution of one finance lease for another in respect of the same asset will also be a revenue item for tax purposes. Where an operating lease becomes a finance lease any transitional payment is treated as a revenue item.
- Rentals on operating leases are tax-deductible.

The above general rules are subject to a continuing stream of anti-avoidance legislation. For example, on November 13, 2008, the UK government announced that it would take action, effective from that date, to prevent a loss of tax on transactions involving the leasing of plant or machinery under long funding leases, on the sale of a company that is an intermediate lessor of plant or machinery, and on rents payable on long funding leases of films.

Anti-avoidance legislation has countered many traditional tax benefits of leasing such as deferral of income, conversion of income into capital, acceleration of capital allowances, and techniques connected with sales and leasebacks. The cat and mouse anti-avoidance game becomes particularly frenetic when it crosses borders. This arises with double-dip leasing, when differing tax treatment of lessor and lessee under different jurisdictions generates allowances in each country. Anti-avoidance has closed off many such opportunities, and the taxpayer's defeat in the Coleman case (see Case Study) illustrates both the complexity of the taxpayer's attempt and the taxpayer's vulnerability.[2]

OPEN ISSUES

Much will be resolved when the new international standards appear, but in the meantime companies should monitor the IASB's discussions of open issues. Sensitive areas under discussion include the following.

Right of Use

The Board favored reporting the lessee's right of use during the term and the accompanying obligation to make specified payments. This seemingly innocuous definition amounts to a preference for a model that does not take account of an obligation to return the physical item. This may be insignificant for a long lease, but is material for a shorter lease.

Measurement of the Lessee's Asset and Liability Under the Lease

The Board decided to recommend that right to use should be initially measured at the present value of the "expected lease payments." They noted that these may differ from minimum lease payments if they include contingent rentals. The discount rate used in calculating the expected lease payments should be the secured incremental borrowing rate.

Options to Extend or Terminate a Lease

The Board decided to propose that options to extend or terminate the lease should be based on an assessment of the lease term, but it did not express a preference among the various frameworks for assessment, for example, a probability-weighted approach, or as to whether the estimated lease term should be trued up on a regular basis. There was a consensus that all contractual, noncontractual, financial, and business factors should be taken into consideration when determining the lease term.

Purchase Option

The Board favored inclusion of the purchase option if exercise of the option was the most likely outcome.

Residual Value Guarantee

The Board decided to propose that the lessee's liabilities should include the obligation to make payments under a residual value guarantee.

In addition to the above, management need to monitor numerous outstanding issues which are to be addressed in the Board's future discussions. These include accounting for sale-leaseback transactions, accounting for subleases, whether a lease should be recognized on execution or asset-delivery, treatment of payments for services within the lease payments and capitalization of initial direct costs.

MAKING IT HAPPEN

Classification and treatment should not dominate the leasing decision. They should be integrated with the decision to achieve an optimal capital structure, including optimal financial mobility. Six important lessons emerge from the present review:

- It remains important to choose between an operating and finance lease contract, but discussions regarding the revised international standard and evolving national standards must be carefully monitored to see how best to contract the lease.
- Opportunities should be taken to contribute to the discussions, especially if there is a chance to head off a result that will harm the company's interests.
- The tax impact of a leasing decision under current provisions is crucially important even though its impact may be less in the short-term insofar as recession makes more businesses zero tax rated.
- Probable changes of tax treatment in response to the new standard must be monitored.
- Anti-avoidance legislation must be anticipated as far as possible—the content of tax cases may provide a first indication.

MORE INFO

Books:

Epstein, Barry J., Ralph Nach, and Steven M. Bragg. *GAAP 2009*. 6th ed. Hoboken, NJ: Wiley, 2008.

International Accounting Standards Board. *International Financial Reporting Standards IFRS 2008: Including International Accounting Standards (IASs) and Interpretations as approved at 1 January 2008*. London: IASB, 2008.

Articles:

Beattie, V., A. Goodacre, and S. J. Thomson. "International lease-accounting reform and economic consequences: The views of U.K. users and preparers." *International Journal of Accounting* 41:1 (2006): 75–103.

Frecka, T. J. "Ethical issues in financial reporting: Is intentional structuring of lease contracts to avoid capitalization unethical?" *Journal of Business Ethics* 80:1 (2008): 45–59.

Henry, E., O. J. Holzmann, and Y. Yang. "Tracking the lease accounting project." *Journal of Corporate Accounting and Finance* 19:1 (2007): 73–76.

Websites:

Equipment Leasing and Finance Association (ELFA): www.elfaonline.org

Finance and Leasing Association (FLA): www.fla.org.uk

HM Revenue and Customs' information about taxation of leases (UK): www.hmrc.gov.uk/manuals/bimmanual/bim61101.htm

International Accounting Standards Board (IASB): www.iasb.org.uk

International Finance and Leasing Association (IFLA): www.ifla.com

See Also:

★ Understanding the Requirements for Preparing IFRS Financial Statements (pp. 423–424)

✔ Key Accounting Standards and Organizations (p. 1040)

Distinguishing between a Capital and an Operating Lease (pp. 1218–1219)

NOTES

1 HM Revenue and Customs documentation, notably BIM61101–BIM 61185; BLM 00050–38000.

2 *Coleman v. Commissioner*, 87 T.C. 178 (1986).

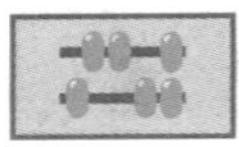

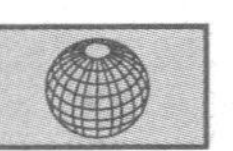

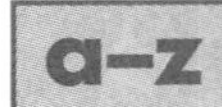

Considerations when Outsourcing Internal Audit

by Peter Tickner

EXECUTIVE SUMMARY

- The key consideration is whether it is better to outsource internal audit, insource to support an existing function, or leave the function inhouse.
- Outsourcing is a valid option when cost or effectiveness is the single most important factor in considering the internal audit function.
- If the key consideration is efficiency, outsourcing may not be the best option.
- Outsourcing a small, existing internal audit function may be counterproductive.
- Outsourcing either a new internal audit function or a weak medium-to-large inhouse audit function is often an effective solution.
- Organizations should only consider outsourcing once they have evaluated the effectiveness of the existing inhouse function and have identified any improvements that they can implement. Only then can the merits of outsourcing be evaluated properly against those of retaining the inhouse function.
- Outsourcing can provide benefits by bringing skills not available to an inhouse team, but it can also risk losing the internal knowledge of the organization.
- A valid alternative for consideration is cosourcing (a partnership between inhouse and external provider), which may confer the advantages of outsourcing while keeping the effective parts of the inhouse function.
- Outsourcing can be to a specialist internal audit provider, a major organization with an audit arm such as one of the "big four" accounting firms, a specialist financial and business services provider, or a consortium formed from several internal audit departments in similar businesses.

INTRODUCTION

Outsourcing the internal audit function is a major step and one that should not be taken for the wrong reasons. Wrong reasons include a personality clash between the chief internal auditor and the person taking the decision to outsource, and a decision based on the perceived ineffectiveness of an under-resourced inhouse audit team that would struggle to perform well even if the most outstanding employees in the organization were assigned to it.

When deciding to outsource internal audit, three options should automatically be evaluated before a decision is taken. First, is the inhouse function fit for purpose? Second, is outsourcing a value-adding solution? Third, is a better option to cosource[1] where skills can be improved or cost savings made?

In some circumstances outsourcing can initially save costs and, in the long term, reduce the pension requirements of internal employees. Before taking such a step, the options must be weighed and a realistic evaluation of the consequences made. What may seem on paper a straightforward way of reducing internal audit costs and increasing the pool of expertise can have unexpected consequences if the starting position is not as the organization imagines it to be.

ASSESSING THE RISKS BEFORE OUTSOURCING INTERNAL AUDIT

For organizations with little or no existing internal audit resource there is often little risk associated with taking on an outsourced provider, particularly where the organization has a need for an effective internal audit function. This is not the case in organizations with any significant existing internal audit service. If the whole function is outsourced and employees, certainly initially, expect to transfer to the audit provider, the organization will need to ensure that the chosen provider can manage the transition and still provide the required level of service.[3]

One of the great mistakes in outsourcing so-called "noncore" services in the dogmatically driven "new management" 1990s was to end up handing over the existing staff to an external management regime that was driven only by its own desire to make as much profit as possible from the contract. This often had the dual impact of demotivating previously loyal staff who no longer felt wanted by the organization and therefore worked less loyally and less hard than before, while at the same time the organization ended up with fewer staff performing the work on the ground as the external management sought to extract maximum profits for their company.

In similar organizational types—for instance public services such as the UK National Health Service, local authorities, and the police—it is not unusual to consider outsourcing to a consortium or a specialist internal audit provider rather than to one of the major accounting bodies.

Although the "big four" and those specializing in providing internal audit services among the larger players in the market place can often provide a lean, high-powered internal audit service, particularly for blue-chip and well-established commercial organizations, they are often a step too far for public bodies with tighter budgets and less flexibility about the existing workforce. Employees at major accountancy firms are generally better paid and rewarded than public-sector equivalents, making genuine cost savings difficult. For some medium-sized and smaller players in the market it is not desirable to take on employees who are unlikely to add to their bottom line or marketability elsewhere. In effect, for many public bodies this can have a significant impact on any perceived savings from outsourcing internal audit, as more specialized, smaller organizations may feel unable to compete for the contract, leaving the field clear for a major player to bid at a less competitive price than might otherwise have been achieved.

MATCHING THE MODEL TO THE RIGHT CIRCUMSTANCES

Outsourcing based on reducing costs and inputs can make a tempting case for those on tight budgets, whether private or public sector, particularly in the current climate. It is important in such circumstances for an organization to think rationally about what it is seeking to achieve by outsourcing internal audit. Reducing costs can be achieved easily in the short term by reducing employees and/or their remuneration. Outsourcing can also help to reduce future pension costs. If the organization needs to pay lip service to an internal audit function only in order to keep its regulator or external stakeholders happy, then outsourcing based purely on lowest cost, regardless of quality, will achieve that objective.

If the existing inhouse service has come in for criticism and outsourcing is seen as the means to raise the internal audit bar, then cost becomes secondary to a visible improvement in quality of service. Here the change can be cost-neutral or even lead to a higher cost, but the decision to outsource will need to be based on the achievement of an expected standard of performance that is measurable and demonstrably better than the existing service, with outcome and output rather than input as the key drivers.

"Quick start-up, variable cost, access to a broader range of resources and more flexibility are some of the benefits of outsourcing." Robert B. Hirth, Jr, Executive Vice President, Global Internal Audit, Protiviti Inc.

  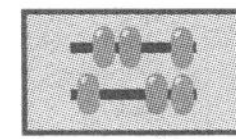      

CASE STUDY

Her Majesty's Treasury

In the 1990s the United Kingdom's HM Treasury embarked on a program of outsourcing noncore functions, including internal audit. An immediate and unexpected snag was hit when the head of internal audit pointed out that the inhouse function had been significantly under-resourced for several years. In order to outsource the function they would need to determine the true need for internal audit resources, as it would be unlikely that an external provider could give the levels of service required with the same or fewer staff than were currently employed. Also, an issue arose as to who was to ensure the quality of an outsourced service provider. The Treasury set standards for internal audit in government and could not be seen to fail to provide the right standard of service for itself. Leaving an outsourced contract to be evaluated by someone with no specific knowledge of the function would leave the Treasury exposed to external criticism. At the time, no senior finance staff outside of the audit department had any specialist knowledge of internal audit.

To ensure that there would be an adequate internal audit, the Treasury had an audit needs assessment prepared to go with the specification for the service to be outsourced. When senior management realized that a significant increase in staff and costs would follow, they opted for a cheaper compromise option of cosourcing specialist skills and retaining a core general audit team. Although this did not fully meet the identified audit need, it enabled the Treasury to demonstrate to external reviewers that it did take the level of resource needed for internal audit seriously. At the same time it enabled the Treasury to implement the extant UK government policy of using the private sector wherever that was the best placed to offer the appropriate skills and add value.

Lessons Learned from the Case Study

The decision to outsource has to be preceded by a thorough analysis of the data available about the existing service, both financial and structural. The 'political' decision in this instance backfired. Ultimately, management spent time and resources to end up with a more effective but more expensive audit service when the strategy had been to cut costs by outsourcing non-core functions. At the time of writing the Treasury's internal audit service is still largely in-house. It is unlikely that there is any meaningful benefit to be gained from outsourcing an existing small inhouse internal audit function. Almost certainly, the chief internal auditor or a senior audit manager will have to be retained to oversee the quality and performance of the outsourced function, and it is likely that the margin for making savings will be small if not nonexistent.[2]

Conclusions from the Case Study

In such circumstances the best option may well be to keep a small cadre of inhouse staff supplemented by an insourced external partner to provide one-off expertise and professional support, thereby avoiding the need to carry the costs of a full-time internal member of staff or a significant overhead to manage an outsourced function.

Getting the basket of performance measures right will be the key for most organizations. Defining an effective internal audit function is not as straightforward as at first it might seem. Describing performance in a rigid or mechanical way, such as an overly systematic approach through ISO standards and the like, can lead to a sterile audit service that fails to pick up the issues of most significance and risk to the organization. What use is an internal audit that routinely checks and reports on standard activities but fails to notice the hurricane waiting to blow the organization away?

UNDERSTANDING THE RISKS

Effective organizations will want an internal audit function that is on the ball and responsive to the "big ticket" issues of concern to top management while at the same time having its ear to the ground for those embarrassing problems that middle management often suppress to avoid blotting their copybook with top management and limiting their careers. There is no reason why a well-chosen outsourced provider cannot provide such a service, but there are risks that the organization needs to know are being effectively managed before they outsource.

First, will the outsourced provider have sufficient knowledge of the innermost parts of the organization? While any skilled internal auditor should be able to conduct a professional audit, half of the skill of an internal auditor is its ability to understand the business and read the people in the organization.

This is not so much a problem where the organization is one of many in a similar industry or public service, but it can be trickier if the organization is specialized or in a niche market with few players from which an outsourced service may have gained appropriate knowledge to understand the business.

Second, will internal audit employees be embedded within the organization? One of the great benefits of an inhouse service is that employees are there on a day-to-day basis and know the undercurrents within the organization. A service provider that sends employees in for one-off assignments or frequently changes the staff or management responsible for providing the outsourced audit is unlikely to retain any corporate inner knowledge of its client. Such organizations are far less likely to spot anomalies or major issues until it is too late.

Finally, will the outsourced provider be able to sustain an effective internal audit over the lifetime of the contract? Once an inhouse team has been outsourced or replaced by a higher-level or different audit function, it can be difficult to "reverse engineer" an inhouse audit team again. Outsourcing should be seen as an irrevocable step that is taken for the right reasons and with the organization's eyes wide open or it should not be taken at all.

Another consideration is to avoid conflicts of interest, either through appointing a contractor that already provides the organization with external audit services or through appointing one that provides an already outsourced financial activity that will be subject to its internal audit.

OTHER CONSIDERATIONS

There are other alternatives to a full outsource that need to be considered here as well. If the inhouse senior management of internal audit are seen as effective, why not look for the best of both worlds? Retain the effective management team but let them cosource skills and knowledge from a suitably priced leading provider of outsourced internal audit services. If the audit requirement is large or diverse enough, the organization can consider using more than one cosource partner to support the internal audit function. This can also often be an effective way to drive out costs and in efficiencies, by playing off the providers against each other for some of the available general audit work. Alternatively, the organization might consider retaining the more general internal audit work inhouse and outsourcing various specialist aspects to different specialist providers—

"Listed companies must maintain an internal audit function . . . A listed company may choose to outsource this function to a third party service provider other than its independent auditor." NYSE Corporate Governance Standard 303A.07

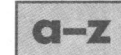

for example IT auditors, treasury audit, investments audit, fraud auditors, or operational auditors.

In either of these partial alternatives to full outsourcing it is possible to try out options to find the best model for the work that can be unwound if a particular option doesn't work out in practice. Equally, if a successful model is found, consideration can be given to a more extensive outsourcing model.

Another alternative to inhouse, outsource, or cosource routes is the use of a consortium, whereby the inhouse team is encouraged to merge with similar inhouse teams in other organizations, creating economies of scale while providing an independent professional internal audit over several similar organizations. Such an approach has worked successfully in the British NHS and among health care providers in the United States, but it can be less viable between rival commercial organizations or those where research or other scientific or security matters could be put at risk by sharing services.

CONCLUSION

Outsourced and cosourced internal audit have worked well in many organizations in the private and public sector. It can ensure a refreshed skill set of professional internal auditors that an inhouse audit setup can find hard to maintain. At its best the organization gains a highly professional expert team to work alongside senior management, one that is proactive and produces clear, succinct reports that help the organization to move forward. At worst, it can lead to a disjointed service that fails to match the needs of the organization and produces meaningless reports that add little or no value, or which fundamentally damages the organization by failing to understand a key issue, missing signs of a catastrophic organizational failure/fraud, or unnecessarily consuming organizational time and resources and frustrating middle management.

MAKING IT HAPPEN

Make sure that internal audit outsourcing is being done for the right reasons.

- The right reasons include: improving the skill set, being "meaner and leaner," reducing the cost for the same or better quality, reducing overheads such as pensions, and buying in specialist help and experience that isn't available inhouse.
- The wrong reasons include: cutting the costs regardless of the impact on the effectiveness of internal audit, looking only at inputs and not at outputs or outcomes, and a vendetta between a senior manager and the chief internal auditor.
- See what improvements can be made inhouse before going to the market place—or you may end up outsourcing the problem and not the solution.
- Where an existing substantial inhouse team will have to be outsourced, don't underestimate the potential damage to employee morale and performance.
- Pick an outsourcing partner that can understand your organization and empathize with its ethics and values.
- In choosing an outsourcing partner, avoid conflicts of interest that may compromise the independence of your external auditors or suppliers of business services that will be audited by the outsourced internal audit provider.
- If possible, try a trial outsourcing of a specialist skill or a one-off audit project before considering outsourcing the whole function.
- Make sure that there are robust management and performance arrangements in place, but don't become obsessed by meaningless minutiae that measure effort but not the value of what that effort has produced.
- Don't overlook alternatives to outsourcing, such as cosourcing and consortia arrangements.

MORE INFO

Articles:

Anon. "Of the risk of internal audit outsourcing." *Free Papers Download Center* (December 1, 2010). Online at: eng.hi138.com/?i270596_Of_the_risk_of_internal_audit_outsourcing. A distillation of previous academic research on outsourcing internal audit by three separate Chinese authors.

Geiger, Marshall A., D. Jordan Lowe, and Kurt J. Pany. "Outsourced internal audit services and the perception of auditor independence." *CPA Journal* (April 2002). Online at: www.nysscpa.org/cpajournal/2002/0402/features/f042002.htm

Report:

Institute of Internal Auditors (IIA). "The role of internal auditing in resourcing the internal audit activity." IIA position paper. January 2009. Online at: www.theiia.org/download.cfm?file=66876 [PDF].

See Also:

★ Aligning the Internal Audit Function with Strategic Objectives (pp. 280–282)
★ Reducing Costs and Improving Efficiency by Outsourcing and Selecting Suppliers (pp. 918–920)
✔ Assessing the Value of Outsourcing and Offshoring (p. 1146)
✔ Quality Assessment of Internal Audits (p. 1049)
✔ Understanding Internal Audits (p. 1057)

NOTES

1 By cosourcing I mean using an external provider to carry out some internal audit activities while leaving the function of internal audit under the control of a reduced inhouse team.

2 The 2009 IIA Position paper on resourcing the internal audit function (see More Info) emphasizes the need to consider how best to discharge the chief audit executive function.

3 This is always the case in the public sector and should be in many private-sector organizations, where the Transfer of Undertakings (Protection of Employment) Regulations 2006, known universally as TUPE, apply to existing staff.

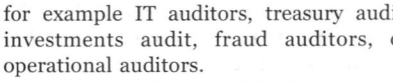

  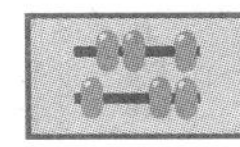      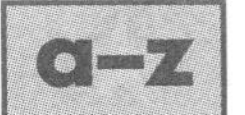

Contemporary Developments in International Auditing Regulation by Christopher Humphrey and Anne Loft

EXECUTIVE SUMMARY

The contemporary development of international audit regulation is connected to the growing significance of international investors who demand financial reports that are prepared and audited in accordance with globally accepted international standards. International Standards on Auditing (ISAs) are set by the International Auditing and Assurance Standards Board (IAASB), an independent standard setting board working within the International Federation of Accountants (IFAC) and subject to public oversight by international regulators. ISAs have been adopted in many countries, but their practical impact depends centrally on how they are implemented and enforced. Recent years have seen a greater emphasis on such issues.

INTRODUCTION

The development of international audit regulation is closely linked to the development of international accounting regulation. Both have been significantly associated with the globalization of capital markets and growth in importance of international investors. Such investors expect the financial reports of the companies they are investing in to be fair and reliable, with auditors playing a critical role—famously categorized by Paul Volcker in 2002—as the "guardians of truth in markets."

Audit regulation is centrally concerned with the issue of ensuring that auditors are competent and independent. These attributes ensure that auditors are both capable of detecting significant errors and omissions in financial status (competent) and faithfully reporting these to investors/stakeholders in the enterprise (independence).

Broadly defined, audit regulation has the same four basic elements of any regulatory system—namely a concern and involvement with the setting, adoption, and implementation of standards and, through monitoring and enforcement processes, ensuring that such standards are applied in practice.

Following this introductory section, the chapter reviews the setting of international auditing standards (ISAs). This includes the role of international regulatory bodies in supporting this process and the demands they have made of the standard setting body and the international accounting profession more generally. In the third section, issues of compliance and oversight are discussed; including recent developments in international coordination through the International Forum for Independent Audit Regulators (IFIAR). The fourth section examines the role of the big audit firms in international audit regulation, and the final section presents conclusions and some thoughts for the future.

SETTING GLOBAL STANDARDS

International Standards for Auditing (ISAs) are set by the International Auditing and Assurance Standards Board (IAASB), which is situated within the International Federation of Accountants (IFAC)—a private body whose member bodies are the national associations of professional accountants in each country. There are currently (December, 2009) 159 member bodies of IFAC, representing 124 countries and around 2.5 million professional accountants worldwide. IFAC recently celebrated its 32nd anniversary, having been formed in 1977, four years after the International Accounting Standards Committee (IASC), which was the predecessor body of the International Accounting Standards Board (IASB).

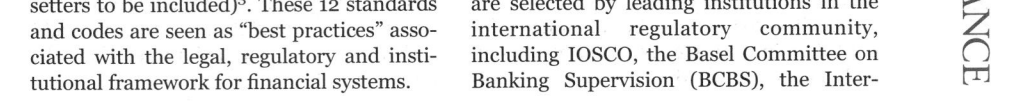

The members of the IAASB are a mixture of practicing professional accountants (especially members of the large audit firms) and persons from outside the profession. A number of important global organizations have supported the development and application of ISAs, which are now used in more than 100 countries around the world[1]. These include the Financial Stability Forum (FSF), a body set up by the G7 Finance Ministers and central bank governors in 1999 in the wake of the financial crisis in Asia in 1997/8—and re-established as the Financial Stability Board (FSB) in April 2009[2]. The objective of the FSF/FSB is to strengthen financial systems and ensure the stability of international financial markets, and as part of this remit it has designated 12 key standards and codes as most relevant to strengthening financial systems. Both International Accounting Standards (IASs/IFRS and ISAs are included in this group (the only private standard setters to be included)[3]. These 12 standards and codes are seen as "best practices" associated with the legal, regulatory and institutional framework for financial systems.

The International Organization of Securities Commissions (IOSCO) is another important organization in this respect. Despite the FSF/FSB's inclusion of ISAs in its leading globally recognized standards and codes, the endorsement of ISAs by IOSCO has proved to be a more problematic and longstanding issue. A 1992 resolution by IOSCO's Presidents' Committee in support of the use of ISAs was subsequently suspended while "negotiations" continued with IFAC over issues such as the quality of ISAs and the degree of public oversight of the standard setting process.

The EU has also continued to review the feasibility of a formal EU endorsement of ISAs. In 2003, the European Commission issued a Communication entitled "Reinforcing the statutory audit in the EU," announcing that it intended that ISAs would apply to all statutory audits in Europe. It emphasized, though, that this required the public interest to be fully taken into account in the IAASB's standard setting processes, with a subsequent communication reiterating that the EU needs to be content that ISAs are "developed with proper due process, public oversight and transparency" and that IFAC's governance arrangements are adequate to ensure the pursuit of the public interest, specifically that the standards are "conducive to the European public good." In the Statutory Audit Directive issued on May 17, 2006, it repeated this message, whilst at the same time the text of the Directive indicated that it was expected that ISAs should become EU's auditing standards, ultimately to be legally binding in all Member States. The European Commission is currently analyzing the responses to its June 2009 formal public consultation on the adoption of ISAs for statutory audits required by European Community Law, having previously commissioned and published an independent study on the relative costs and benefits of adoption[4]. IFAC has moved towards satisfying such demands over its standard setting processes and governance arrangements by establishing, among other things, an active Public Interest Oversight Board (PIOB) and developing ISAs through the IAASB's "clarity project." The members of the PIOB are selected by leading institutions in the international regulatory community, including IOSCO, the Basel Committee on Banking Supervision (BCBS), the Inter-

"Lethargy bordering on sloth remains the cornerstone of our investment style." Warren Buffett

national Association of Insurance Supervisors (IAIS), the European Commission, World Bank and the FSF/FSB. Included in the activities of the PIOB is the monitoring of all meetings of IFAC's public interest standard setting committees, making this a very active process of oversight. With this IFAC appears to have satisfied one of the requirements of the regulators for improving governance arrangements to bring in a clear consideration of the public interest, although it is worth noting that the effectiveness of such governance reforms is currently being evaluated by the above mentioned regulatory and international organizations (commonly referred to as the Monitoring Group.[5]

The IAASB's Clarity Project, started in 2004, and was completed in February 2009.[6] The project's aim was to ensure that ISAs have clear objectives and that each standard distinguishes what the auditor absolutely shall do when carrying out an audit from guidance on how to achieve this.[7] In the process of clarification, some standards were ultimately revised quite considerably (and more than was originally anticipated). In total, the clarity project produced 36 updated and clarified ISAs, together with a clarified International Standard on Quality Control (ISQC). The standards are to be applied to audits of financial statements for reporting periods beginning on or after December 15, 2009.

In June 2009, IOSCO issued a statement that formally encouraged[8] securities regulators to accept audits performed and reported in accordance with the clarified ISAs for cross-border purposes; "recognizing that the decision whether to do so would depend on a number of factors and circumstances in their jurisdiction" (IOSCO, 2009). In much the same way, IOSCO encouraged securities regulators to consider the clarified ISAs when setting auditing standards for national purposes.[9]

According to IFAC, currently 43 countries have adopted ISAs or are required to use them by law, with a further 28 countries having generally adopted them as national standards but with modifications (acceptable to the IAASB) for specific legislative and regulatory requirements.[10] While ISAs are pushing towards the position of being the global standards for auditing, a significant inclusion in the 55 "other/remaining" countries surveyed by IFAC, is the United States of America—which, as yet, has not abandoned its own auditing standards. Up until 2002 the American Institute of Certified Public Accountants (AICPA) was responsible for setting US auditing standards but, in the wake of the Enron scandal, and others like it, this responsibility was given to a new independent body under the supervision of the Securities and Exchange Commission (SEC). This body, namely, the Public Company Accounting Oversight Board (PCAOB), has it its own processes for setting independent audit standards and also has extraterritorial powers of regulatory reach in relation to audits of US quoted companies. Recent speeches by SEC staff at the 2009 AICPA national conference on current SEC and PCAOB developments have confirmed that the PCAOB does maintain an active interest in ISAs and standard setting developments at the IAASB—and that, in their view, the momentum for international convergence in auditing standards is growing.[11] The chances of ISAs becoming truly "world standards" are also likely to be aided by the SEC's approach towards IFRS. The latest indications are that the SEC will shortly update its "roadmap" proposals for US listed companies to move to IFRS.[12] The international pressure on the SEC would seem to have increased recently, with the G20 in September 2009 notably calling for a "redoubling of efforts" by international accounting bodies to achieve a single-set of "high quality global accounting standards" and for the convergence process to be completed by June 2011.[13]

Finally, in relation to global (auditing) standards, it is important to point out that, while scandals such as Enron regularly illustrate the international significance of both auditor independence and competence, international independence standards remain some way off. While IFAC's Code of Ethics for Professional Accountants[14] provides a potential international regulatory solution in this area, the lack of international consensus on the issue of auditor independence is such that regulation here is more likely to be of national or regional orientation, influenced strongly by related legal structures.

COMPLIANCE AND REGULATORY OVERSIGHT

As was noted at the start of this chapter, a regulatory system is not just about standard setting but also the implementation and enforcement of such standards. Historically, issues of compliance with international auditing standards were not given enormous emphasis at the global level—reflecting a range of factors, including desires to grow the numbers of countries adopting such standards, a limited level of available resources, accepted traditions of self-regulation and professional peer review and the clear positioning of responsibilities for compliance, regulation, and oversight activities at the national rather than the international level.

One of the most active and visible initiatives in this area has been the ROSC (Reports on Standards and Codes) program set up by the IMF and World Bank in 1999, which examines the degree to which emerging and developing countries are using key standards and codes (defined to include ISAs and IASs as benchmark standards for each individual country's reports on accounting and auditing practices). The formal remit is to: "analyze comparability of national accounting and auditing standards with international standards" and "assist the country in developing and implementing a country action plan for improving institutional capacity with a view to strengthening the country's corporate financial reporting regime."[15]

IFAC has increased its focus on global compliance issues with the 2004 launch of its Compliance Program, overseen by the Compliance Advisory Panel (CAP), which seeks to ensure that member bodies are meeting their membership obligations. Formally, this program has three main elements, comprising: an assessment by each member body of their country's regulatory and standard-setting framework; a self-assessment questionnaire of the extent to which each member body is using its best endeavors to adopt international accounting and auditing standards and maintain quality assurance and enforcement regimes to ensure such standards are applied in practice; and the development of action plans to further the global accounting and auditing standards convergence process and address any issues/weaknesses identified in the self-assessment questionnaire. IFAC, "in the interests of transparency," has chosen to post all the responses received from member bodies for full public access on its website.[16]

These initiatives are dealing with the general issue of compliance, but not with the actual compliance of a particular audit firm with ISAs and other standards. In reaction to the problematic audits of Enron, Global Crossing and other large companies, in July 2002, the passing of the Sarbanes–Oxley Act replaced the self-regulation of the US auditing profession with the PCAOB-led system of independent inspection. Similar initiatives have followed in other countries and there is a whole new international emphasis on auditor oversight as an essential feature of audit regulation. This oversight is, for obvious reasons, done at local national level. However, the Sarbanes–Oxley Act did not exclude foreign registrants with US stock exchanges from the requirement from oversight by the PCAOB. This appears to have encouraged a number of (large) countries to establish

  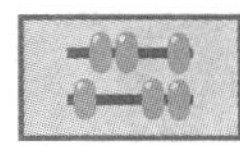      

their own auditor oversight systems in the hope that there will be mutual recognition of each other's systems. This, however, has only occurred to a small extent, resulting in a considerable amount of extra-territorial activity by the PCAOB audit inspectors.

The issue of public oversight has further developed on the international stage through the establishment in September 2006 of the International Forum of Independent Audit Regulators (IFIAR).[17] IFIAR is committed to sharing knowledge and experiences of the audit market and associated regulatory activities between independent national audit regulatory agencies. It seeks to promote collaboration and consistency in regulatory activity and to act as a platform for dialogue with other organizations with an interest in the quality of auditing. There are currently 36 independent national regulators who are members of this new international organization, including the PCAOB. Observers at IFIAR meetings include the FSB, IFAC's PIOB, IOSCO, IAIS, World Bank, European Commission and the Basel Committee, again reflecting the increasingly interlocking nature of international regulatory relationships (for more discussion, see Humphrey *et al.*, 2009).

The multi-layered nature of such regulatory arrangements is well illustrated by the fact that the European Union itself had previously established a European Group of Audit Oversight Bodies (EGAOB) in December 2005—with the specific remit of ensuring effective coordination of new public oversight systems of statutory auditors and audit firms within the European Union.[18] The press release announcing the EGAOB development cited the view of Commissioner McCreevy that this "group will help to make public supervision systems a reality in all 25 Member States, promoting practical day-to-day co-operation as it goes along. It is a key initiative in our drive to bring EU audit rules into the 21st century and restore faith in the profession." The European Commission reiterated its views on the importance of public oversight, with a Recommendation (May 13, 2008) on external quality assurance for the statutory audit of public interest entities. This expanded the responsibilities of public oversight boards and emphasized that they should play an active role in the inspections of audit firms.

THE GLOBAL REGULATORY INVOLVEMENT OF AUDIT FIRMS

An interesting development with respect to public oversight was the presentation by the CEOs of the six largest global auditing firms at IFIAR meetings in Norway (April 2008) and South Africa (September 2008) to consider global quality monitoring arrangements. This section of the chapter explores what is an evidently growing involvement of the large audit firms in international audit regulation.

During the last two decades, there has been a continued increasing concentration in the international auditing profession, with the large firms getting a greater share of the audit market. The Big Eight firms of the past have reduced to the Big Four today of PwC, KPMG, E&Y, and Deloitte—with the next two largest firms, BDO International and Grant Thornton International, relatively speaking, being quite a lot smaller. Gradually, through a variety of pressures, often driven by major corporate collapses and financial crises, such firms have sought to ensure a greater global consistency in auditing practice, such that that an audit, for example, in China by PwC is equivalent to one conducted by the same firm in, say, Sweden. Through internal processes of regulation, they place pressure on parts of their network where audit quality and associated quality control procedures are apparently insufficient, and thus act as an "internal" or "self" regulatory pressure towards harmonizing standards.

The audits undertaken by the, then, Big Five[19] in Asia at the time of the crisis (1997–8) were sharply criticized by the World Bank, and it was this that stimulated the Big Five to set up a Global Steering Committee. One of the aims was to provide a body to deal, on a collective, global basis, with the common professional and regulatory issues they were facing. Another aim was to strengthen IFAC as the global audit standard setter. Under this initiative the large firms supported IFAC financially and were allocated seats on each of IFAC's standard setting boards. In the case of the newly established IAASB (previously the International Auditing Practices Committee) they had 5 seats out of a total of 18. This greater engagement of the Big Firms with IFAC continued to grow, especially in the wake of the Enron scandal and its aftermath, with the establishment of a new organization, the Global Public Policy Committee (GPPC).

The GPPC comprises the six largest international accounting networks and focuses on "public policy" issues for the profession. The GPPC has a Regulatory Working Group and a Standards Working Group and while much of its work is undertaken in private, it does issue policy papers where it expresses its commitment to working in the public interest and facilitating the functioning of global capital markets (see GPPS, 2006). The global firms' involvement in international regulatory affairs has also seen them expand the scale of financial support that they provide to IFAC, which now receives approximately one-third of its funding from the large firms. The firms can also be seen to making substantial efforts to further strengthen their own global organization. For instance, it was reported in the *Financial Times* (August 20, 2008) that a number of them had announced restructuring plans to align more tightly member firms within global structures/networks and introduce "enhanced" audit practice standards.[20] The current financial crisis has witnessed a continuing major involvement with global regulatory matters, driven by the direct consequences that auditing work could have for global financial stability through decisions relating to the valuation of "toxic" assets and the auditor's determination as to whether audited enterprises are "going concerns."

MAINTAINING PUBLIC INTEREST IN GLOBAL REGULATION

While the global audit regulatory arena is complex, it is possible to draw out a number of important characteristics. While contemporary audit regulation engages directly with audit practice at the national level, it is being driven primarily by events and strategic action at the global level. The development in this global regulation of audit has been rapid during the current decade and, associated with the identifi-

MAKING IT HAPPEN

For international audit regulation to meet the claims laid out for it in terms of global scope and consistency of application requires a variety of actions and commitments on the part of the international financial regulatory community. Some of the more frequently mentioned priorities include:

- ISAs to be fully endorsed by international financial regulators;
- ISAs to be adopted globally for listed company audits;
- IFAC to continue to operate as an international organization acting in the global public interest;
- Greater global coordination of the work of audit regulatory and oversight bodies.
- Enhanced visibility of the quality and achievements of audit work.

cation of reliable financial reporting, is becoming an essential part of a wider international financial architecture. Significant strategic actions have been made by international organizations such as the EU, IOSCO, FSF/FSB, and the World Bank, to aid, support and increasingly mandate, the usage of international standards on auditing. While these organizations are primarily governmental in character, the main international audit standard setter, the IAASB—under the auspices of IFAC—is classified as private in nature, as are the large audit firms who are also closely involved, albeit in a less public way. This has placed particular emphasis and significance on the development of public oversight regimes as a way of ensuring that international audit standard setting processes are seen to be globally credible and sufficiently responsive to public interest demands (see IFAC, 2008; PIOB, 2008). The policy recommendations emerging from the November 2008 meeting of the G20 likewise have highlighted the importance of regulators serving the public interest and the global importance of making sure that financial markets operate in the most transparent of fashions. The current financial crisis is testing global regulatory structures to their limit, and it is pretty certain that auditing will remain a fascinating field—both to observe and to debate in an open and constructive fashion. It could be argued that serving the public interest deserves no less.

ABBREVIATIONS

ACCA: Association of Chartered Certified Accountants
AICPA: American Institute of Certified Public Accountants
BCBS: Basel Committee on Banking Supervision
CAP: Compliance Advisory Panel
EU: European Union
FSF/(FSB): Financial Stability Forum/ Board
GPPC: Global Public Policy Committee
GPPS: Global Public Policy Symposium
IAASB: International Auditing and Assurance Standards Board
IAIS: International Association of Insurance Supervisors
IFAC: International Federation of Accountants
IFIAR: International Forum of Independent Audit Regulators
IFRS: International Financial Reporting Standard
IMF: International Monetary Fund
IOSCO: International Organization of Securities Commissions
ISA: International Standard on Auditing
ISQC: International Standard on Quality Control
PIOB: Public Interest Oversight Board
PCAOB: Public Company Accounting Oversight Board
ROSC: Report on Standards and Codes (World Bank)
SEC: Securities and Exchange Commission

MORE INFO

Article:

Humphrey, Christopher, Anne Loft, and Margaret Woods. "The global audit profession and the international financial architecture: Understanding regulatory relationships at a time of financial crisis." *Accounting, Organizations and Society* 34:6–7 (August–October 2009): 810–825. Online at: dx.doi.org/10.1016/j.aos.2009.06.003

Reports:

International Federation of Accountants (IFAC). "Regulation of the accountancy profession." IFAC Policy Position 1. December 2007. Online at: tinyurl.com/2b3wa4e

International Federation of Accountants (IFAC). "International standard setting in the public interest." IFAC Policy Position 3. December 2008. Online at: tinyurl.com/27ohv6l

International Federation of Accountants (IFAC). "International Federation of Accountants 2008 annual report: Transitioning to a global financial system." February 2009. Online at: web.ifac.org/download/2008_AR_IFAC_Full.pdf

International Forum for Independent Audit Regulators (IFIAR). "Charter." Online at: www.frc.org.uk/images/uploaded/documents/IFIAR%20Charter1.pdf

Technical Committee of the International Organization of Securities Commissions (IOSCO). "Contingency planning for events and conditions affecting availability of audit services: Final report." May 2008. Online at: www.iosco.org/library/pubdocs/pdf/IOSCOPD269.pdf

Public Interest Oversight Board (PIOB). "Third public report of the PIOB." May 2008. Online at: tinyurl.com/23byvuu

Public Interest Oversight Board (PIOB). "Fourth public report of the PIOB." May 2009. Online at: tinyurl.com/29bm3q3

NOTES

1 See web.ifac.org/download/2008_IAASB_Annual_Report.pdf
2 See www.fsforum.org/press/pr_090402b.pdf
3 See www.fsforum.org/cos/key_standards.htm
4 ec.europa.eu/internal_market/auditing/isa/index_en.htm#isastudy
5 www.iosco.org/news/pdf/IOSCONEWS162.pdf
6 See web.ifac.org/clarity-center/index
7 www.cnbv.gob.mx/recursos/iosco13.pdf
8 It is an interesting point of debate as to whether such "encouragement" on the part of IOSCO equates with the formal endorsement of ISAs sought, for example, by accounting firms and professional bodies such as PwC, IFAC, ACCA, and the Institut der Wirtschaftsprüfer in Germany—on the grounds that ISAs were already in widespread usage (see IOSCO, 2008).
9 www.iosco.org/library/statements/pdf/statements-7.pdf
10 web.ifac.org/isa-adoption/chart
11 See www.sec.gov/news/speech/2009/spch120709amp.htm
12 The initial proposals suggested an adoption decision in 2011, with mandatory application for US issuers in 2014. The latest indications are that the SEC will announce its current thinking regarding IFRS adoption in early 2010 (see www.sec.gov/news/speech/2009/spch120909ebw.htm).
13 www.pittsburghsummit.gov/mediacenter/129639.htm
14 www.ifac.org/Ethics/Resources.php
15 See www.worldbank.org/ifa/rosc_aa.html
16 See www.ifac.org/ComplianceProgram
17 IFIAR's formal charter can be found at www.frc.org.uk/images/uploaded/documents/IFIAR%20Charter1.pdf
18 europa.eu.int/rapid/pressReleasesAction.do?reference=IP/05/1596&format=HTML&aged=0&language=EN&guiLanguage=en
19 The Big Four plus, the now defunct firm of, Arthur Andersen.
20 See www.ft.com/cms/s/0/198b3e42-6edd-11dd-a80a-0000779fd18c.html?nclick_check=1

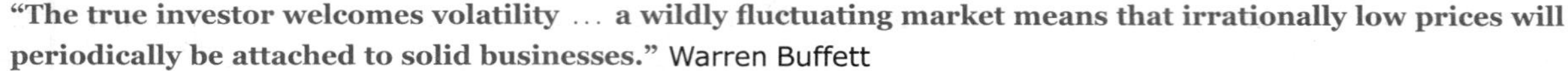

"The true investor welcomes volatility … a wildly fluctuating market means that irrationally low prices will periodically be attached to solid businesses." Warren Buffett

  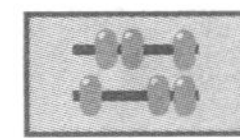      

Continuous Auditing: Putting Theory into Practice by Norman Marks

EXECUTIVE SUMMARY

- Continuous auditing is a topic that is frequently identified as a method for internal auditors to "raise their game" and improve the value they provide to their stakeholders. For example, in their 2010 "State of the internal audit profession" study, PricewaterhouseCoopers identifies the ability to leverage technology (including the use of continuous auditing techniques) as one of the eight attributes of a maximized internal audit function.
- In a 2010 study, "What is driving continuous auditing and continuous monitoring today?," KPMG reports, "In a volatile economic environment, a number of key drivers are prompting companies to employ continuous auditing and continuous monitoring techniques to do more than manage risk, including help reduce cost, improve performance, and create value."
- This article defines continuous auditing, discusses the ways in which continuous auditing techniques can be used to provide value, and shares guidance on how to design an effective program. It advises that only after the objectives of a continuous auditing initiative have been determined, and the program designed, should auditors evaluate and acquire software.

INTRODUCTION

The Institute of Internal Auditors (IIA) has issued an excellent global technology audit guide (GTAG) on the topic of continuous auditing. The guide, which we will refer to as GTAG-3, covers a lot of ground, including this definition of continuous auditing:[1]

"Continuous Auditing is any method used by auditors to perform audit-related activities on a more continuous or continual basis. It is the continuum of activities ranging from continuous control assessment to continuous risk assessment—all activities on the control-risk continuum. Technology plays a key role in automating the identification of exceptions and/or anomalies, analysis of patterns within the digits of key numeric fields, analysis of trends, detailed transaction analysis against cut-offs and thresholds, testing of controls, and the comparison of the process or system over time and/or against other similar entities."

Continuous auditing enables an internal audit function to:

- provide the board and management with assurance on a more frequent, if not continuous, basis;
- monitor risks and adjust the audit program to ensure that it addresses what matters to the organization today;
- improve the level of activity, in terms of both volume and period of time, that is audited.

It is important to consider the use and value of continuous auditing within the context of how the IIA defines an internal auditing function:

"A department, division, team of consultants, or other practitioner(s) that provides independent, objective assurance and consulting services designed to add value and improve an organization's operations. The internal audit activity helps an organization accomplish its objectives by bringing a systematic, disciplined approach to evaluate and improve the effectiveness of governance, risk management and control processes."

Taking these two definitions together enables the following points to be made. Each of these will be discussed in this article.

1. Continuous auditing is a method used by internal auditors in support of their assurance and consulting services.
2. Continuous auditing includes activities related to one or more of the following:
   a. *Continuous risk assessment* (also known as risk monitoring), including the use of analytical techniques to identify trends, etc., to develop and maintain the periodic audit plan;
   b. *Continuous testing of controls* to provide assurance that they operate as intended. GTAG-3 refers to this as "continuous controls assessment";
   c. *Continuous testing of transactions*[2] to identify anomalies, exceptions, and potential problems.
3. Although continuous auditing typically leverages technology, continuous auditing activities may include manual testing, reviews of reports, etc.
4. Despite its name, continuous auditing is not necessarily performed continuously. The frequency will depend on a number of factors, including:
   a. The frequency with which transactions occur (for example, journal entries are predominantly a month and quarter-end activity);
   b. The frequency with which controls are performed;
   c. The level of business risk being addressed;
   d. The risk that the control may not be performed as intended.

However, few internal audit departments have made major moves into continuous auditing. One of the reasons is that the value is not clear to every chief audit executive (CAE)[3] We will discuss that first.

THE VALUE OF CONTINUOUS AUDITING

Imagine that you are the CAE of a global company and you are called in to see the CEO. He asks for your assessment of the quality of controls over the hedging of currency risk—which you identified as a high-risk area in your last report to the audit committee.

Is it acceptable to reply to the CEO that you will be able to tell him when you have completed the next audit, scheduled in three months? Is it acceptable to report, instead, on the audit your team completed a year ago?

The answer is clearly "no." When it comes to the more significant risk areas (such as the hedging of currency risk mentioned above), the CAE should try to provide assurance when it is needed by the primary stakeholders.

Value Proposition 1: Audit at the Speed of Business

This is the first value proposition for continuous auditing: the ability to provide assurance when it is needed. This can be referred to as "audit at the speed of business." The GTAG-3 refers to it as "continuous controls assessment."

What does internal audit provide assurance on? The Institute of Internal Auditors's "International standards for the professional practice of internal auditing" (IIA, 2010) guides us to provide assurance on the "governance, risk management, and control processes for the organization."[4]

Extending that, *continuous auditing enables an internal auditing function to provide assurance, when it is needed, on the more significant areas of the organization's governance, risk management, and related controls processes.* We can

"**I have no interest in celebrities. If all the superrich disappeared, the world economy would not even notice. The superrich are irrelevant to the economy.**" Peter F. Drucker

refer to this as "continuous risk and control assurance."

The value to the board and executive management of continuous risk and control assurance is generally very high. Although this dimension of continuous auditing can require the most resources to develop and maintain, the value will frequently far exceed the cost.

The next section will discuss how an internal audit department can use continuous auditing techniques for each of the value propositions. The second value relates to fraud.

Value Proposition 2: Fraud Detection and Control

Internal audit departments have a keen interest in fraud: in the adequacy of controls that prevent or detect fraud, and in investigating potential fraudulent activities. The second value proposition is that *continuous auditing enables the monitoring of risks for indicators of fraud, and of transactions for potential fraudulent activity.*

Continuous testing of transactions to detect potential errors and possible fraudulent activity is generally considered a management activity. However, many internal audit departments have included in their charter the detection of fraudulent activity. Automated techniques can improve the effectiveness and efficiency of a fraud detection program.

Building a business case for continuous fraud detection will depend on the level of risk that fraud represents to the organization, and the quality of existing controls to either prevent or detect significant fraud. The greater the quality of existing controls that can be leveraged, the lower the total cost of a fraud detection program will be.

Value Proposition 3: Continuous Risk Assessment/Monitoring

The third, but possibly the most important dimension of continuous auditing, is continuous risk assessment or monitoring. The key to an effective internal audit department is to be focused on the risks that are important to the organization *now*. If risk assessment is only performed annually, or even semi-annually, audit engagements may be scoped to address risks that are no longer critical—and the more critical risks may not receive audit attention.

Internal audit departments are moving to more continuous risk assessment, often updating their audit plan on a quarterly basis. Technology can enable many risks to be monitored as frequently as the auditor desires. For example, consider the risk to a global company of sales to customers in Poland. One of the "drivers" of that risk will be the level of sales (or even the pipeline of sales orders) to customers in Poland. As that level rises, so does the risk. Technology can be used to monitor the level of sales or sales orders and send an alert to the audit department if it exceeds a predefined level.

This value proposition can be described as: *continuous auditing can be used to ensure that the internal audit plan remains focused on the more significant risks to the organization as the business changes.* It enables auditing at the speed of business.

Continuous risk monitoring is an essential element in continuous risk and control assurance. Without it, the scope continuous auditing of controls will not be updated as risks change.

Summary

Three value propositions have been identified, each of which will be discussed in more detail below.

- *Continuous risk and control assurance*: Continuous auditing enables an internal auditing function to provide assurance, when it is needed, on the more significant areas of the organization's governance, risk management, and related control processes.
- *Continuous fraud detection*: Continuous auditing enables the monitoring of risks for indicators of fraud, and of transactions for potential fraudulent activity.
- *Continuous risk assessment or monitoring*: Continuous auditing can be used to ensure that the internal audit plan remains focused on the more significant risks to the organization as the business changes.

CONTINUOUS RISK ASSESSMENT OR MONITORING

Although this is the third value proposition, it is a critical element of both continuous risk and control assurance and continuous fraud detection, so it will be covered first. Why is it so critical? Because without continuously updating internal audit's understanding of risks, auditing (whether continuous or not) is likely to remain focused on what used to be important

MAKING IT HAPPEN

A Continuous Risk Monitoring Program

One way to build a continuous risk assessment/monitoring program is as follows.

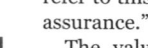

1 Start with the risks you want to monitor. Use the latest risk assessment as a basis.
2 Identify the causes or drivers of the risk. What would cause the risk level (probability or potential impact) to change? For example, if there is a revenue recognition risk related to sales to Thailand, the risk level is likely to rise if the level of sales to Thailand increases.
3 Determine your strategy for monitoring the risk drivers. For example, you can monitor corporate information on orders in the sales pipeline and be alerted when the level (volume or value) is outside a defined range. Why a range? Because if the pipeline is low, the risk level decreases. It is not only increases that should be monitored. The strategy should also include a decision on how often to monitor the risk. If the risk is considered critical and the level is volatile, then monitor more often than if the risk is lower and considered less likely to change.
4 Identify the mechanism(s) that will be used for risk monitoring. Will you rely on existing reports and systems, or will you need to build new capabilities?
5 Define the process for receiving the risk information and responding, generally with updates to the audit plan. How often will you update the plan? Also, a change in a risk level may indicate a need to inquire of management what the causes of the change are—to confirm the risk level and understand whether related controls and/or activity need prompt audit attention. Some changes in risk levels may indicate an increased level of fraud risk, meriting special attention by internal audit or a fraud department.
6 Step back and decide whether the design to date will be sufficient to monitor the risks. Update the plan, or accept the limitations as appropriate.
7 Build and implement the continuous risk assessment program.
8 Consider how to work with management to identify new or emerging risks, and when to add them to the program.
9 Consider metrics with which to monitor whether the continuous risk assessment program is working effectively.
10 Seek to continuously improve. Perform formal reviews on a formal basis to validate performance, including determining whether the program failed to identify risk changes of significance during the period

  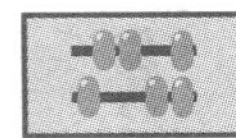   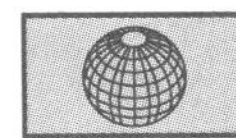   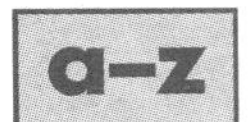

instead of what is important. The same applies to fraud detection, which should also be driven by the types of fraud and fraud schemes that represent a higher level of risk to the organization.

Ideally, internal audit will be able to leverage an effective risk management program (or ERM, for enterprise risk management) that identifies and assesses risks to the strategies and objectives of the organization. The internal auditor should evaluate whether:

- the ERM program can be relied on to identify the more significant risks to the organization;
- the identification of risks is timely, enabling the internal audit department to adjust the audit plan as needed;
- the assessment of risk levels is reliable.

When these conditions exist, the audit department should work with the risk function to ensure that it receives the information it needs, when it needs it, to maintain the risk-based audit plan.

However, many organizations do not have an ERM program that can be relied upon. Presumably, internal audit has raised this as an issue of critical importance with the board and executive management. But internal audit should not use this as an excuse not to try to maintain an audit plan focused on today's risks.

CONTINUOUS RISK AND CONTROL ASSURANCE

The idea behind a continuous risk and control assurance (CRCA) program is that internal audit should provide its stakeholders with assurance that the more critical risks to the enterprise are effectively managed—when that assurance is needed.

Building a CRCA program takes time. A typical organization has multiple risks that internal audit will want to address, each of which relies on multiple controls.

Although the decision could be made to provide continuous assurance on only a very few risks and their controls, a larger program that addresses more risks and controls will generally provide a higher return on the investment.

Before considering tools, the CRCA program must be designed. Some internal audit departments are sold tools before they have designed a program, before they have decided how to use the tools—or even whether they are in fact the tools they need. As a result, most of these departments have had limited success.

Design

A CRCA program will include most if not all of the following components, as shown in Figure 1:

- continuous risk monitoring, including the monitoring of key performance indicators (KPI);
- continuous control monitoring;
- continuous transaction or activity monitoring;
- investigation of potential inappropriate activities that have been detected;
- continuous reporting to stakeholders.

The first step, as discussed above, is to decide which business risks will be included in the CRCA program. These will be subject to continuous risk monitoring (see previous section), which has two aspects:

- Monitoring of key performance indicators. A failure to achieve strategies, goals, or performance targets is a strong indicator that risks were not managed effectively, and that there is a continuing level of risk to achieving goals and objectives.
- Monitoring of risk levels, typically achieved by monitoring the drivers of the risk as discussed earlier. Risk levels are reflected in key risk indicators, or KRI.

Risks are managed through controls. ISO Publication 73 defines a control as a "measure that is modifying risk" and IIA Standard (2010) defines control as "Any action taken by management, the board, and other parties to manage risk and

Figure 1. A continuous risk and control assurance program

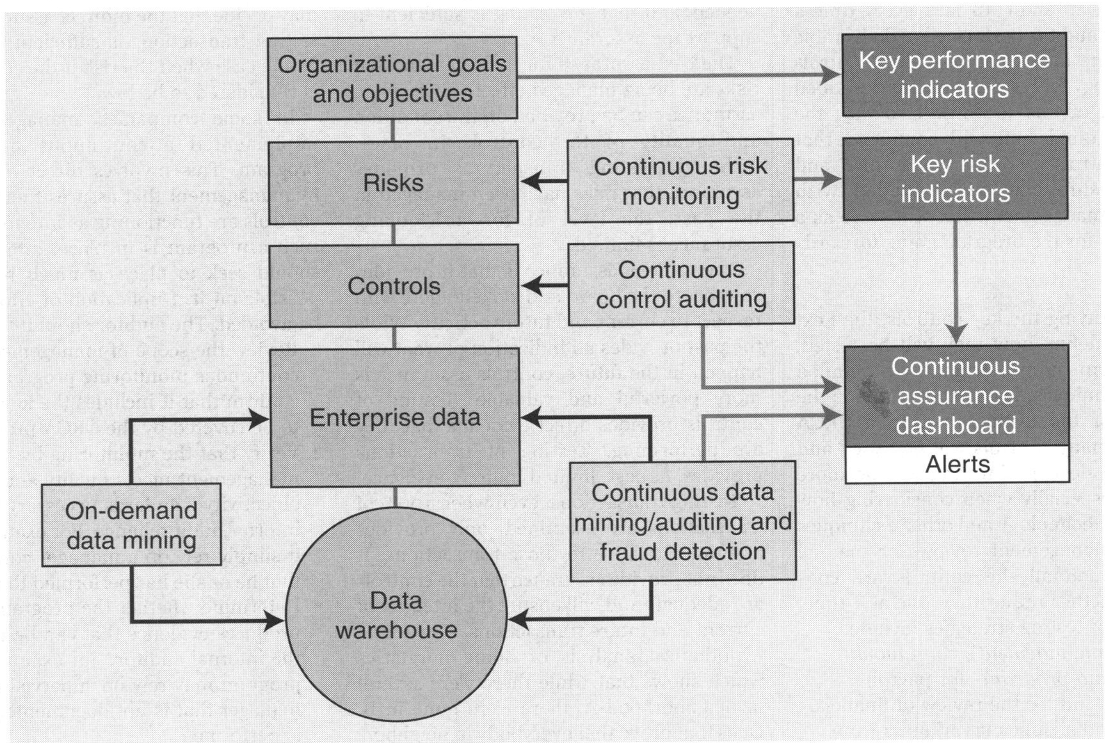

  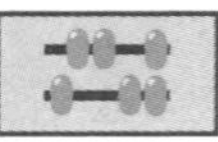 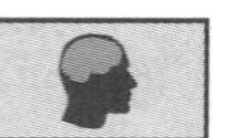     

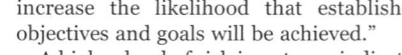

increase the likelihood that established objectives and goals will be achieved."

A higher level of risk is a strong indicator that controls are either not designed or are not working effectively to manage risk within organizational tolerances. The CRCA program should include processes to respond to higher levels of risk, such as reviewing with management the root causes of the higher risk level and whether the system of internal controls remains adequate.

Once the business risks to be addressed are defined, the next step is to identify the controls that are relied on to manage those risks. These are the controls, the *key* controls, that will be tested in the CRCA program. By *key* controls, we mean those controls that have to be in place and operating properly if risks are to be managed. They are not all the controls, just those that if they failed or were not adequately designed would mean that the risks are highly unlikely to be well managed.

Key controls may operate at any level of the organization (corporate, division, location, department, process, etc.) and may be manual or automated. Typically, several controls are required to manage any single risk. If assurance is to be obtained that the risks are well managed, all the key controls have to be addressed in the CRCA program.

If the key controls have not already been identified, consideration should be given to performing an audit. In fact, every time a traditional audit is performed, a deliverable could be the identification of key controls and a strategy for testing them (as described in the rest of this section). This way, the CRCA program is built with confidence that the key controls are properly identified, and a relationship can be developed with operating management that will serve as a foundation for the program going forward.

Testing

After identifying the key controls, the next step is to define how they will be tested. Rather than jump straight to detailed testing techniques, it is better to define the strategy for the testing first. In a CRCA program, many controls will be tested and the overall design of testing will be more efficient—especially when considering how to leverage technology and other techniques (such as management reviews or manual testing)—when all the controls are considered together rather than one at a time. Examples of testing strategies include:

- *Rely on management's continuous monitoring program*—for payroll controls, and for the review of financial trends and significant variances from forecast. Obtain reports monthly to review the results and follow up on any issues.
- *Use software to test controls*—to confirm that all journal entries are approved by a manager, and to verify that all changes to the manufacturing computer system were approved by the IT manager.
- *Use manual testing*—to review actions taken with respect to outstanding items on the bank reconciliation, and to confirm that appropriate cutoff procedures are in place for the annual inventory count.
- *Rely on management self-assessments*—to confirm that the code of conduct has been reviewed with all personnel, and that backup generators are in place and tested periodically.
- *Rely on supervision*—by the IT director of controls over the work of the database administrators, and by the manager of the warehouse of the quality inspection of goods received.
- *Use software to test data*—to validate that all payments to suppliers were consistent with purchase orders and records of goods received, and to identify potential duplicate payments.

One important design considerations is the frequency with which assurance should be provided. Just because it is called *continuous* doesn't mean that the testing and the assurance have to be continuous. They key is that the assurance is provided when it is needed, and that the testing is sufficient to support the assurance.

The best assurance for management that risks are being managed effectively is when assurance can be provided on the condition and quality of the controls in place. Although testing transactions provides assurance that risks have been managed in the past, the level of forward-looking assurance is limited.

The value of assurance is that it provides comfort to the board and stakeholders with respect to current and future activity. While the past provides an indication of what will happen in the future, controls assurance is more powerful and valuable. Testing of controls provides direct evidence that they are performing. Testing of transactions provides, at best, limited indirect evidence.

Testing transactions, even when 100% of transactions are examined, only provides assurance relative to those transactions. It does not provide assurance that the controls are adequate and will ensure the integrity of current and future transactions. Consider a hypothetical analysis of home burglaries which shows that while there were several in neighborhood A, there were none in B. Does that prove that everybody in neighborhood B locked their doors and had effective alarm systems? Clearly not. The fact that transactions were accurate does not prove that there were adequate controls to ensure that they were accurate.

Therefore, a risk and controls assurance program aims to provide as much assurance that the controls are adequate as possible. However, there are limitations, especially to the use of technology to enable the continuous auditing of controls:

- Some controls involve the exercise of judgment, such as the review of journal entries. While technology can test that the journal entries were approved by a manager, they cannot test whether the review was perfunctory or whether appropriate judgment was exercised.
- A number of controls involve physical activities, such as the counting of inventory. Technology can test that a count was taken and adjustments approved by a manager, but it cannot test to ensure that all locations were properly examined.

In many cases these limitations can be addressed by including manual testing as part of the CRCA program. For example:

- a manual review of a sample of journal entries can be performed throughout the year;
- auditors can attend the occasional inventory counting procedure.

Where the limitations involved in testing controls cannot be overcome, the auditor may decide that the indirect assurance from testing transactions is sufficient. This may be the case when the risk if the control fails is considered to be low.

In some companies, management has implemented a continuous monitoring program. This involves direct monitoring by management that assures them that the controls are functioning as intended. When such a program is in place, internal audit should seek to place as much reliance as possible on it. Duplication of effort should be avoided. The auditor should:

- Review the scope of management's continuous monitoring program and confirm that it includes the key controls to be covered by the CRCA program.
- Verify that the monitoring by management meets quality and objectivity standards necessary for internal audit reliance. For example, does it simply rely on a manager confirming that he or she has performed the control?
- Determine whether the program produces evidence that can be used by the internal auditor. For example, the program may rely on supervision by a manager that is not documented when it is performed.

"In every well-governed state wealth is a sacred thing; in democracies it is the only sacred thing." Anatole France

  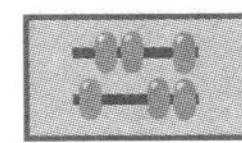   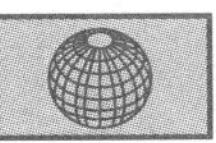   

For some controls, the auditor may decide to rely on a self-assessment program. This can be valuable, especially where the risk is relatively low, or where direct testing is difficult—such as testing employee awareness of the code of ethics.

The CRCA program design must include consideration of how testing exceptions, or indications that controls may be failing, will be addressed. Most of the time the exceptions will have to be reviewed with management, so that explanations can be obtained and a determination made as to whether the controls have in fact failed—and what actions will be taken in response.

In a few cases, especially where the risk of fraud is considered high, the CRCA program might include "alerts," typically but not necessarily automated, informing internal audit of the control or data exception.

The CRCA program design should include how the results of the testing and monitoring will be summarized for use by internal audit management. What will the summary look like, how often will it be produced (or will it be continuously updated and always available), and how will exceptions be highlighted?

Reporting

Finally, the design has to address how stakeholders will be informed of the quality of risk management and the related controls.

- How often do executive management and the board require reports?
- Do they prefer to receive reports (such as dashboards) or to be notified when there are exceptions?
- What information will be provided to operating management? How often will it be provided, and in what form?

Once the design is complete, the tests can be developed. With respect to the use of technology, the design will determine what the technology needs to achieve and will define the requirements for the selection of the appropriate set of tools. Since the program needs to address all forms of controls, it is unlikely that a single software tool will meet all needs and a combination of tools will be required. For example, one tool may be used as a repository of risk and control information to capture and report the results of testing. Another may be used for risk monitoring and data analytics. Yet another may be used to monitor IT activity when testing IT general controls.

Figure 1 summarizes all the elements of a fully-featured CRCA program.

- The first two rows address the monitoring of key performance indicators (for business objectives) and risk indicators (for risks to those business objectives).
- Controls auditing is the preferred testing approach, but where that is not possible the testing of data (either in the enterprise systems or in a data warehouse or similar) may be included. This is especially true when the risk of fraud is considered (see below).
- The results of the CRCA program have to be collected for reporting within internal audit and to stakeholders. This is shown on the right side of the diagram.

CONTINUOUS FRAUD DETECTION

Many internal audit functions have taken on the responsibility for detecting fraud. Even where strong controls are in place, it is prudent to monitor transactions and look for the signs of potential fraud.

A CRCA program will typically include fraud risks, monitoring their level, testing the controls, and examining activity for potential issues of concern.

A continuous fraud detection program will follow some of the same principles and steps as a CRCA program, even if the continuous auditing activity is limited to fraud detection rather than a full CRCA program:

- Design the program and define your needs before selecting software or developing detailed testing techniques.
- Focus on frauds that represent the higher level of risk to the business. According to the Association of Certified Fraud Examiners's latest global fraud study (AC FE, 2010), the average company experiences fraud amounting to 5% of annual revenue. While this is high, care should be taken not to allocate more resources to fraud detection than the risk merits or the detection costs. This can be done by focusing on those fraud risks and schemes that are more likely to be significant to the business.

SUMMARY

There are several ways in which continuous auditing techniques can be used to improve the effectiveness of an internal audit program. They include:

- continuous risk and control assurance;
- continuous fraud detection;
- continuous risk assessment.

Before embarking on the continuous auditing journey, the internal audit department should decide what it wants to use continuous auditing for. Will it be for one or more, or for some variant, of the above purposes?

Some departments review the software marketed for continuous auditing or continuous control monitoring and purchase what appears to be the "best." However, they may do this before deciding on the purpose and objectives of their program, which would enable them to define their needs for technology.

Other audit functions understand continuous auditing to be purely an application of technology and do not therefore consider the use of manual testing. Typically, their program becomes one of testing transactions, primarily for potential fraud. It does not provide assurance on the quality of controls, and does not help them to realize their mission of providing assurance and consulting services relating to the effectiveness of governance, risk management, and related control processes.

MAKING IT HAPPEN

An Effective Fraud Detection Program

The following steps have proven useful in implementing effective fraud detection programs.

1. Identify the fraud risks specific to your organization. Every company is different, and the risks from fraud will vary.
2. Assess each fraud risk for likelihood and potential scale.
3. Select the fraud risks that the program will address.
4. For each risk, identify how the fraud would work: what are the fraud schemes?
5. Determine how an inspection of transactions or other activity (such as trend analysis, comparison of same product margins in different locations, or the detection of transactions approved by the same person who originated the transactions) might detect potential fraud.
6. Design the process for investigating exceptions. Take care to discuss the process with any management personnel who might be involved in reviewing and providing explanations for exceptions.
7. Develop and implement the program.
8. Monitor and adjust the testing procedures as necessary (for example, changing tolerances on any automated tests that are producing false positives).
9. Continue to monitor fraud risks and change the program as needed.
10. Review and continually improve the fraud detection program.

Finally, some audit departments have left the field entirely. They believe that management should be performing continuous monitoring of controls and that continuous auditing is not necessary. This overlooks the potential for internal audit to review and test management's monitoring program and then rely on it (perhaps supplementing it with its own tests as necessary) to provide their stakeholders with assurance when it is needed by the board and management.

Continuous auditing has great potential. It can move an internal audit from providing assurance based on traditional point-in-time audits to providing assurance when it is needed. But to realize that potential, an internal audit department has to be disciplined.

MORE INFO

Reports:

Association of Certified Fraud Examiners (ACFE). "Report to the nations on occupational fraud and abuse: 2010 global fraud study." 2010. Online at: www.acfe.com/rttn/2010-rttn.asp

Coderre, David. "Global technology audit guide (GTAG) 3: Continuous auditing: Implications for assurance, monitoring, and risk assessment." Institute of Internal Auditors, 2005. Online at: www.theiia.org/guidance/technology/gtag3

Ernst & Young. "Escalating the role of internal audit: Ernst & Young's 2008 global internal audit survey." 2008. Online at: tinyurl.com/6frqjad [PDF].

Institute of Internal Auditors (IIA). "International standards for the professional practice of internal auditing (Standards)." Revised October 2010. Online at: www.theiia.org/guidance/standards-and-guidance/ippf/standards

KPMG. "Continuous auditing/continuous monitoring: Using technology to drive value by managing risk and improving performance." June 2009. Online at: tinyurl.com/5w3huxt [PDF].

NOTES

1 Unfortunately, there is no universally accepted definition of continuous auditing. Many (including KPMG in its 2008 publication, "Continuous auditing/continuous monitoring") have limited continuous auditing to the use of technology to collect and analyze transactions. The present essay uses the IIA definition.

2 Any activity may be tested, including not only transactions but changes to application code, router or automated control configurations, master data, etc. The term "transaction" is used generically to include any activity subject to testing.

3 In its 2008 global internal audit survey (the latest), "Escalating the role of internal audit," Ernst & Young reported that 42% of respondents to its survey had implemented some level of continuous auditing, mainly to "identify deficiencies, monitor risks and identify potential fraud activities." Reasons for not having already implemented continuous auditing included a "lack of skill sets within internal audit, budget constraints and no perceived value in the program."

4 From the definition of "assurance services" in the Glossary to IIA Standards (2010), p. 18.

  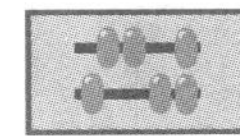   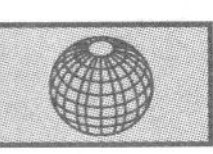   

Costs and Benefits of Accounting-Based Regulation in Emerging Capital Markets by Wang Jiwei

EXECUTIVE SUMMARY

- Securities regulation is vital to the development of an efficient capital market.
- Accounting-based regulation embeds accounting numbers as a threshold.
- There are both benefits and costs to accounting-based regulation.
- The costs of accounting-based regulation include opportunistic behavior by management to manipulate accounting numbers, and capital resource misallocation.
- The benefits of accounting-based regulation include the potential to mitigate resource misallocation by preventing poorly performing firms from entering the market and to avoid "adverse selection problems" by managers.
- Recent Chinese regulations on rights offerings and seasoned equity offerings shed light on the costs and benefits of accounting-based regulation in emerging capital markets.

INTRODUCTION

One of the most controversial debates in economic policy is: Should governments intervene in or regulate capital markets? Pure free-marketeers believe that the "invisible hand" can correct all market failures. However, advocates of intervention characterize the regulation process as one in which government intervention corrects market failures and maximizes social welfare. In the case of regulating stock issuance after initial public offerings (IPO), governments in many countries adopt a "disclosure-based approach" with limited government regulation and intervention. No official approval is needed to issue additional shares as long as companies provide adequate disclosure. There is no accounting-based profitability threshold that the company has to meet before making the stock issuance. The rationale is that such thresholds create additional costs for investors.

COSTS OF ACCOUNTING-BASED REGULATION

In a world without transaction costs, parties will naturally achieve an efficient outcome without any form of intervention. Regulation, then, is only bound to worsen the outcome, at the very least by imposing undue costs. Under regulation, governments must devote tremendous resources of money and time to screen new entrants, thus reducing social welfare. The money and time could have been allocated to other government projects that would enhance social welfare. Applicants also incur costs related to compliance. When an accounting-based threshold is embedded in a regulation, there may be agency problems for investors, as explained in the following paragraph.

Regulations based on accounting numbers, such as a minimum return on equity (ROE) threshold, can provide incentives for contracting parties to manipulate accounting data opportunistically to meet these thresholds. The reason for corporate managers to commit this opportunistic behavior is that they believe it will be costly for regulators to "undo" such behavior. If a manager opportunistically manipulates accounting data to meet criteria for issuing additional shares to the public, this action will trigger inefficient allocation of capital resources and hence diminish the welfare of investors.

BENEFITS OF ACCOUNTING-BASED REGULATION

In efficient capital markets, investors are sophisticated enough to weed out poorly performing firms. Hence there is no need for accounting-based regulations to gauge the performance of new entrants. However, situations in emerging markets may be different. In these emerging market environments, accounting-based regulation may bring benefits that exceed the costs. The following three points explain why accounting-based regulations may be needed in emerging markets.

- Emerging markets are typically portrayed as inefficient. At the early stage of capital market development, investors do not have enough sophistication to screen the "good eggs" and "bad eggs" in the market.
- Firms can manipulate the selling price of stocks at a big discount from the ongoing price. This large discount forces existing shareholders to purchase additional shares irrespective of a firm's performance, as otherwise their ownership will be diluted.
- There are severe "adverse selection problems" in emerging markets, especially by comparison to developed markets. That is managers, as insiders, know more than the market about the true value of the firm and have an incentive to issue additional shares when stock prices are overvalued.

These market failures cannot be automatically corrected by the market because the market *per se* is inefficient. Government should act as a "helping hand" and intervene by imposing accounting-based regulation. This regulation is used to help investors to distinguish good and bad firms on the market and can minimize adverse selection by managers. These benefits may exceed the costs associated with the misallocation of capital resources.

To provide companies with more options to raise additional capital, the CSRC allowed large-scale seasoned equity offerings (SEO) in May 2000 by issuing regulations that were similar to the rights offering regulations of 1993. The CSRC believed that China's capital market had become more efficient during the first seven years and would be able to automatically correct market failures. This regulation did not impose a strict profitability

Figure 1. The distributions of ROEs in China over two periods in 1992–98

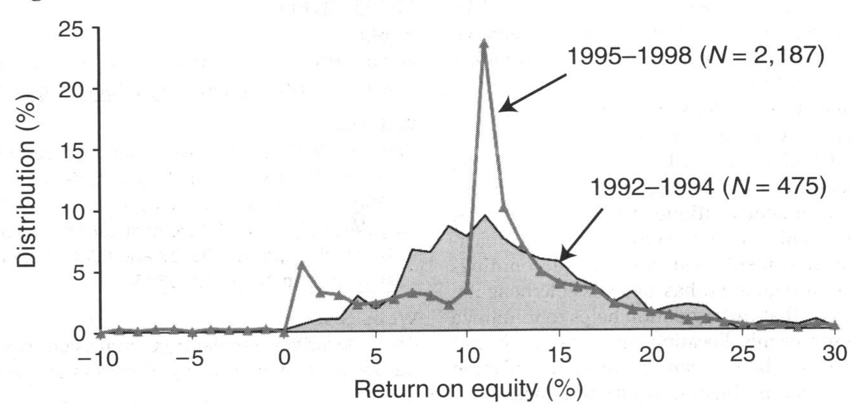

"Letting a hundred flowers blossom and a hundred schools of thought contend is the policy for promoting the progress of the arts and the sciences and a flourishing culture in our land." Mao Zedong

threshold, and any company with profits in the previous three years could apply to the CSRC for SEO authorization. Below we list the major milestones in China's regulations on seasoned equity offerings—it will be seen that they are surprisingly similar to the regulations for rights offerings.

- May 2000: The CSRC issued a regulation that allowed listed companies with three years' profits to apply to the CSRC to conduct seasoned equity offerings.
- March 2001: The CSRC increased the threshold to a three-year average ROE of 6%. This was not a definitive threshold in that companies that did not meet it could qualify under certain conditions—for example, if the management and underwriter provided detailed evidence of the healthy state of the company. Again the CSRC found that the SEO was abused by Chinese listed companies, and therefore increased the threshold to curb excessive abuse.
- July 2002: The CSRC raised the bar to a three-year average ROE of 10% and a minimum ROE of 10% in the previous year. Since the 2001 threshold was not definitive, management and underwriters were able to collude to help poor companies to gain additional market resources. For example, Wuhan Department Store Group Co. Ltd. announced a SEO proposal right after the 2001 Regulation went into effect. Its ROEs in the previous three years (1998 to 2000) had been 3.16%, 2.72%, and 2.41%—all below 6%.

The various regulations on rights offerings and SEOs detailed above imposed at least two types of cost on China's capital markets. The first cost was the earnings "management" needed to achieve the numerical accounting threshold. Managers of poorly performing companies could manipulate accounting numbers to meet the threshold so that they could then raise additional capital from investors. When this happens, investors' capital may be allocated to less efficient projects and their welfare is reduced. The second cost of a numerical threshold was that it had the potential to exclude firms with a potential for good future performance and to allow firms with likely poor future performance to conduct rights offerings or SEOs.

Despite the costs consequent on the adoption of numerical rules, the Chinese government continues to use similar rules to establish rights issues and SEO qualifications. As mentioned above, this accounting-based regulation has two possible benefits: one is that the regulation helps to minimize resource misallocation, and the other is that the regulation can reduce the adverse selection problem in equity offerings.

CASE STUDY

Accounting-Based Regulations in China

The Chinese government has used accounting-based regulation to regulate share issuance by listed companies. China's experience will be considered here because it sheds light on the costs and benefits of accounting-based regulation in emerging capital markets.

In the early 1990s, China's listed companies could only issue additional shares through preemptive rights offered to existing shareholders. Due to the lack of other means of raising capital and the Chinese investing public's insatiable demand for stocks in the early 1990s, rights offerings were excessively abused by listed companies. To curb this activity, the China Securities Regulatory Commission (CSRC) issued a series of regulations to restrict rights issues after November 1993. The following are the major milestones of China's regulations on rights offerings.

- November 1993: Listed companies were allowed to issue rights to existing shareholders if they had been profitable in the previous two years.
- September 1994: The CSRC required listed companies that wished to issue additional shares to have at least three years' profits and a minimum three-year *average* return on equity of 10%. The CSRC found that rights offerings were abused by listed companies in the way they reported profits. In fact it is very simple for companies to manipulate accounting numbers to report a profit.
- January 1996: The CSRC increased the threshold to a minimum ROE of 10% in *each* of the previous three years. Within about 18 months the CSRC found that the accounting-based regulation of 1994 was still not stringent enough to curb the opportunistic behavior of listed companies.
- March 1999: The CSRC lowered the threshold to a minimum three-year average ROE of 10% and a minimum ROE of 6% in each of previous three years. The 10% ROE threshold regulation of 1996 triggered a very large amount of opportunistic earnings manipulation behavior in China. Figure 1 shows the sharp increase in reported ROE between 10 and 11% for 1995–98. However, this pattern was not seen in 1992–94, when there was no ROE requirement. The public criticized the threshold, and the CSRC had to respond by lowering the threshold. Note, however, that the threshold (at the lower requirements) is still embedded in the regulation.

MAKING IT HAPPEN

Governments of emerging economies must have an excellent understanding of the status of their capital markets. The following actions should be considered when policymakers implement accounting-based regulations:

- Promote rigorous capital market research by academics and consultants.
- Understand the demand and supply of capital markets.
- Impose a stringent threshold at the beginning.
- Actively monitor market reactions to government regulations and adjust the regulations accordingly.

MORE INFO

Book:

Pigou, Arthur C. *The Economics of Welfare*. 4th ed. London: Macmillan, 1932. Online at: www.econlib.org/library/NPDBooks/Pigou/pgEW.html

Articles:

Chen, Kevin C. W., and Jiwei Wang. "Accounting-based regulation in emerging markets: The case of China's seasoned-equity offerings." *International Journal of Accounting* 42:3 (2007): 221–236. Online at: dx.doi.org/10.1016/j.intacc.2007.06.001

Zingales, Luigi. "The future of securities regulation." Chicago Booth School of Business Research paper no. 08-27 and FEEM Working paper no. 7.2009, 2009. Online at: ssrn.com/abstract=1319648

Websites:

China Securities Regulatory Commission: www.csrc.gov.cn/n575458/n4001948

US Securities and Exchange Commission: www.sec.gov

"It doesn't matter if a cat is black or white, so long as it catches mice." Deng Xiaoping

Cultural Changes in External Auditing

by Jyothi Manohar

EXECUTIVE SUMMARY

- How external auditing has evolved over the years, and factors that have impacted cultural changes in external auditing over the last century.
- The users of financial statements are now a much wider group. They now include any individual or entity that has a vested interest in a business's financial condition, such as lenders, regulators, or government departments.
- Companies have changed from being focused on one line of business to become more complex organizations with many lines of business through multiple ownership structures and across international borders.
- The globalization of business and information technologies that are advancing by leaps and bounds have dramatically changed the manner in which business is conducted—from paper-based to electronic-based to Internet-based, and now via mobile devices.
- Accounting rules used to be simple. With all the changes in the business world and the development of a single, global marketplace, accounting standards have proliferated into complex requirements that are both rule- and principle-based.
- The clamor for better corporate results, global competition, and a greed for the rewards of corporate success have led to major accounting fraud and company failures. This has resulted in vast changes in the rules of corporate governance and in the role and accountability of both the audit committee and the external auditor.
- Since business was largely male-dominated, auditing used also to be a primarily male-dominated profession. It has evolved into a profession that has competing numbers of male and female professionals and changing perspectives.

INTRODUCTION

This chapter focuses on external audits of financial statements. The objective of an external audit is to conclude that financial statements are, or are not, fairly presented in accordance with appropriate accounting standards. Consequently, a knowledge of accounting is a prerequisite for auditing. An auditor of financial statements must, therefore, have a thorough understanding of the accounting rules and other regulations that impact the financial statements that are being audited. This understanding, in turn, must be preceded by a thorough understanding of the business and industry in which the company presenting the financial statements operates. Cultural changes in auditing have evolved with the multifaceted nature of business, a global marketplace, advancing technologies, a clamor for comparable, timely, and transparent information on which to base business decisions, corporate accounting fraud and corporate failures, and all the consequences that flow therefrom.

THE USERS OF FINANCIAL STATEMENTS

Although audits of exchequers, royal vaults, trusts, bequests, and accounts have a long history in many countries in the world, the modern concept of "independently validating and providing reasonable assurance (positive or negative) as to the accuracy, fairness, reasonableness or compliance with regulations," i.e. the independent audit of a business entity's financial numbers began with the industrial revolution and the founding of formal stock exchanges across the world during the 1800s. The regulatory requirement for external audits of companies whose stock traded on these exchanges generally became prevalent in different countries during the 1930s. This happened when the securities and exchange commissions (or similar regulating authorities) in different countries required that companies listed on public stock exchanges and whose stock traded on those exchanges should, among a myriad of other regulatory requirements, have the "fair presentation" of their financial statements attested by a third party that was fully independent of the management and operations of the company. In other words, an external auditor should have no stake in the ownership of, or receive any other type of benefit or remuneration from, the company he or she was auditing. The intent was that the "users" of the financial statements—in this case, the investors in the respective companies—should have reliable financial information on which to base their investment decisions. Further, independent or "external" auditors were viewed as being qualified in their knowledge of the accounting rules applicable to the company being audited and unbiased in their approach to validating the books, records, and transactions of the company which were translated into financial statements in a manner that was "generally accepted" and understood by the investing public.

Over the years, the "users" of financial statements have mushroomed. Depending on the nature of the business and the industry in which it operates, the individuals, regulatory authorities, governments, financial institutions, funders, and other entities that use and rely on an entity's financial information have changed. For instance:

- A not-for-profit or charitable organization does not have ownership through stock holdings and is not listed on a stock exchange. However, it may receive funding, charitable donations, grants, or bequests from other business entities, individuals, or government agencies. All of these sources of funding (the users) would have an interest in the financial statements of the not-for-profit organization to ensure that the monies they have provided are being used for the purpose intended.
- Companies in regulated industries such as financial institutions, insurance companies, pharmaceutical companies, utility companies, airlines, etc., may or may not be publicly traded on a stock exchange but must follow the regulatory requirements of their respective regulators. In these instances, the regulators, in addition to other stakeholders, are "users" of the company's financial statements. The regulators have an interest in ensuring that reliable financial information is being produced to help them to monitor the stability of the company and to ensure that the company complies with applicable regulations.
- Federal, state, and local governments, municipalities and school districts are all recipients of revenues from individuals and business organizations in the form of levies and taxes. Their expenditures are intended to be for the public good in the form of infrastructure (roads, bridges, waterways, libraries), social programs, education, support for low-income families, healthcare, etc. Members of the general public are "users" of government agencies' financial information in that we are interested in making sure that our tax payments are being put to appropriate use.

"A dozen more questions occurred to me. Not to mention twenty-two possible solutions to each one, sixteen resulting hypotheses and counter-theorems, eight abstract speculations, a quadrilateral equation, two axioms, and a limerick. That's raw intelligence for you." Jonathan Stroud

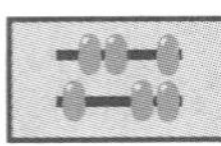

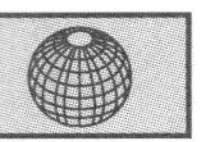

- Small businesses, owned by individuals or families, are the unseen and unheard mainstay of national economies all over the world. These small business entities turn to financial institutions and other funding sources for loans that will fund different aspects of their business. Increasingly, their banks or credit unions have become "users" of financial information and are requiring external auditors to provide reasonable assurance as to the financial condition and income-producing capabilities of the businesses for which they provide financial support.

As the users of financial statements and the corresponding utility of financial information have become more diverse, the method of presentation of financial information has evolved from merely accumulating numbers to also include disclosures relating to the numbers and, in many cases, compliance with relevant laws and regulations that govern the presentation of financial information. It follows, therefore, that accounting standards vary widely from industry to industry and often from country to country. The financial presentation for each is unique. The external auditor has to develop the knowledge and expertise to adapt to the requirements of each type of financial statement presentation in order to provide "reasonable assurance" as to fairness.

ACCOUNTING STANDARDS AND THE GLOBALIZATION OF BUSINESS

In order for the external auditor to effectively conduct an audit and conclude on the fair presentation of financial statements, it is critical that he or she understand the applicable accounting standards. As accounting has changed over the decades, so has the culture of external audit.

Accounting Methods

Accounting has evolved from Luca Pacioli's double-entry system in the late 1400s to modern day approaches. While debits and credits still form the keystones of all accounting standards, the British (and some of the countries that were previously British colonies, like India) use the traditional approach in which accounts are classified by their nature as real, personal, or nominal, while countries like the United States and Canada use the accounting equation approach in which the balance sheet must reconcile, i.e. Assets = Liabilities + Equity. Accounts are classified as assets, liabilities, equity, income, and expense. Irrespective of the approach, the concept is the same: the difference between income (or revenue) and expenses represents net income (or loss), which in turn is absorbed into equity (or capital). The balance sheet represents the financial condition of an entity as of a point in time, while the income statement (or statement of operations) represents the activity for a fiscal year.

What initially started as the cost method of accounting, where all account balances and transactions were stated at cost and recorded on a cash basis—i.e. when cash was actually exchanged—evolved into accrual-basis accounting, i.e. when revenue was earned and expense incurred as opposed to when cash was transacted. With the advent of selling goods and services on credit, accrual-basis accounting became the norm, although cash-basis accounting is still widely prevalent, particularly for tax purposes. Over the years, the carrying (or reportable) value of different assets and liabilities, depending on the nature of each, has also diverged from historical cost to current cost and fair values.

Complexity of Business Organizations

Business organizations are not limited to single entities that conduct one line of business. The purpose and structure of business entities are as diverse as the world itself. Business transactions are not limited to the buying and selling of goods and services. Revenues can be generated from something as trivial as selling paperclips to items such as an office building, a shopping center, artwork, or a group of companies, from selling seats for travel by air, land or water, from renting space, cars, or equipment—in fact from any of a multitude of transactions. Services can be one-time, ongoing, contingent, or for a fixed fee. Assets no longer consist only of tangibles that can be physically perceived, but also of intangibles such as goodwill, trademarks, patents, royalties, intellectual property, and rights to future income streams. Business transactions that at first were generally conducted face to face were later done over the telephone, first nationally, then internationally, then remotely via fax and computers, and now, globally via the World Wide Web and mobile applications. As the complexity of business organizations, industries, and transactions has increased, and the sources and manner of revenue generation, asset, liability, and income creation have increased, so have generally accepted accounting rules and standards. While there are commonalities in accounting rules among industries and companies, there are additional unique accounting standards by industry—for example, airlines, insurance, financial institutions, broker-dealers, investment companies, and utilities.

Diversity in Accounting Standards

Most of the major developed and developing countries in the world have an accounting standard-setting body. For instance, the Accounting Standards Board (ASB) in the United Kingdom, the Financial Accounting Standards Board (FASB) in the United States, the Accounting Standards Committee of Germany (DRSC), and the Accounting Standards Board of Canada (AcSB). As a means of standardizing diverse accounting practices in a global marketplace and for global users of financial information, IFRS, or International Financial Reporting Standards were born, as promulgated by the International Accounting Standards Board (IASB), which replaced the International Accounting Standards Committee in 2001. The IASB was formed in cooperation among various countries in Europe, North and South America, and the Far East, with more and more countries today seeking to adopt IFRS. IFRS are "principles-based" standards as opposed to "rules-based" in that they require financial reporting based on the nature and substance of a transaction rather than following a specific rule related to that transaction. In addition to these standard-setters are governments and government agencies that also set unique government accounting standards.

Estimation in Accounting

It is common knowledge that accounting rules incorporate the use of judgment and estimates in many cases. This is especially true as it relates to the valuation of assets and, in many instances, liabilities. Loss contingencies, reserves for uncollectible receivables (whether accounts receivable or loans receivable), reserves for all types of asset impairment, the estimated useful life of an asset, and inventory valuation are all typical examples of accounting estimates. The introduction of fair value or "mark-to-market" accounting in the 1990s and its burgeoning influence on international accounting and reporting standards has significantly increased the underlying complexity of how certain asset or liability balances are derived. Earlier we made reference to the use of historical cost, current cost, or fair value to report financial statement balances. Relatively speaking, historical cost and current costs may be more readily determinable than fair value. Generally, the FASB has defined fair value as "the exchange price in an orderly transaction between market participants to sell the asset or transfer the liability in the market in which the reporting entity would

  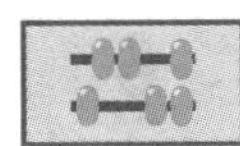      

transact for the asset or liability, that is, the principal or most advantageous market for the asset or liability... the definition focuses on the price that would be received to sell the asset or paid to transfer the liability (an exit price) not the price that would be paid to acquire the asset or received to assume the liability (an entry price)." Depending on where in the global marketplace a transaction is being conducted and who is conducting it, the fair value of an item (an investment security, a piece of real estate, a commodity, a loan, a car, a piece of equipment...you name it) could vary widely. It is easy to see why the fair value of an asset or liability, unless traded on a public exchange such as the stock market, as a basis for reporting would be complex, involving significant judgment and assumptions that must be elaborately explained in financial statement disclosures.

The preceding paragraphs set the tone for what external auditors must know, understand, and indeed specialize in to effectively conduct an audit and issue an opinion on the financial statements prepared by a business.

AUDITING STANDARDS

The primary objective of the standard-setters is to ensure that the user of financial information is properly informed through transparency in financial reporting and that the public interest is served. The goal of the external auditor is to adhere to auditing standards, understand the business, rules, and reporting requirements of the auditee, maintain an unbiased viewpoint (through appropriate professional skepticism), obtain and document all the necessary evidence, and opine on the fairness of the financial information being presented. This not only includes the numbers that make up the account balances being reported, but also the narrative disclosures that accompany the numbers in the form of the "Notes to the financial statements."

As with accounting standards, generally accepted auditing standards (GAAS) in all major countries are issued and monitored by an appropriate standards board. For instance, in the United States the American Institute of Certified Public Accountants (AICPA) issues the standards by which auditors of nonpublic companies must abide.

Public company auditors are governed by the auditing standards (AS) issued by the Public Company Accounting Oversight Board (PCAOB). In Japan, the auditing standards codified by the Business Accounting Council (BAC) and implemented by the Japanese Institute of Certified Public Accountants (JICPA) constitute GAAS. In Canada, the Auditing and Assurance Standards Board (AASB) has adopted International Standards on Auditing (ISA) as GAAS for the audits of financial statements. The International Federation of Accountants (IFAC) issues the International Standards on Auditing with the objective of providing guidance that will ensure high-quality audits. The auditing standards boards of many countries in the world are members of the IFAC.

What the External Auditor Must Know

In order for an external auditor to independently validate a financial statement balance, he or she must first understand the transaction that resulted in the balance. There are many questions to consider.

- In every case, have all the financial transactions impacting the company been captured, and if so, how did the account balance come about?
- If an asset, does it exist, is it complete, is it valued properly, and does the company actually own the asset?
- If a liability, is it valued correctly and is it complete?
- If a capital account balance, does it properly represent the holdings of real shareholders?
- If a revenue or income balance, is it real, is it complete, and was it earned in the reporting period? (And when or how is revenue recognized in a world of eBay, Groupon, Facebook, and Amazon?)
- If an expense account balance, is it complete, and is it being reported in the correct amount and in the proper period.
- Have there been any significant violations of laws or regulations that will have an impact on the financial statements?
- How is the business doing in its industry and in its economic environment? Will it be viable to continue to do business in the near term?
- Do all of the disclosures accompanying the basic financial statements (the balance sheet, the income statement, the statement of equity, the cash flow statement) properly reflect the business of the company, the nature of its transactions, and its business relationships and commitments?

The answers to these questions will vary widely, depending on the type of company or organization under audit, the industry in which it operates, the state of the national or global economy impacting the industry, the complexity of its business transactions, its affiliated entities, whether it is standalone or part of a consolidated group, the number of its locations, its corporate governance, the quality of its management, internal operations and information systems, its technology infrastructure and whether its footprint is national, international, or global. The starting point for the auditor, therefore, is an understanding of each of these aspects of the company which he or she will audit. Needless to say, like the various branches of medicine and affiliated specializations, auditing has become a field where specialized training and expertise are required for an external auditor to meet professional standards and conduct an effective audit.

Cultural Evolution in Auditing

This is a rather dramatic cultural evolution! The very first external auditors likely went to the single location occupied by a company, looked at a few documents to support transactions, examined the assets that were on hand, made inquiries of company management and some external suppliers, asked a few questions and traced amounts of transactions to a handwritten ledger before they were satisfied that the numbers were proper. Auditing standards used to incorporate general standards, fieldwork standards, and reporting standards that have since mushroomed to cover fair-value audit guidance, special circumstances, and rules concerning independence and ethics disseminated by varying governing bodies. Auditing standards now variously address all of the following.

- **Expertise and exercising due professional care**. All external auditors are expected to have the training and expertise necessary to carry out their responsibilities in compliance with GAAS. This standard includes a requirement to execute the audit in an unbiased fashion with appropriate professional skepticism.
- **Arrangement with the auditee to explain the roles and responsibilities of the external auditor and of company management**. Specifically, this elaborates that company management is responsible for the quality of the financial statements and the internal controls that affect the financial statements. The latter requirements evolved with the corporate governance rules of the early 2000s.
- **Independence and accountability**. Typically, the external auditor is evaluated and engaged by and reports to the audit committee of the board of directors or similar governing body that is charged with corporate governance and overseeing the financial reporting of the company. This accountability to a committee that is independent of the management of the company preserves

"I'm the only person I know that's lost a quarter of a billion dollars in one year ... It's very character building." Steve Jobs

the independence of the external auditor and prevents any influence by management over the audit process. As a result of the audit process, therefore, the external auditor is obligated by auditing standards to report specific matters, including deficiencies and exceptions noted, to the audit committee.

- **Quality control**. This concerns the required levels of review within the external audit firm of work performed by an audit team to ensure that auditing standards have been met with respect to the nature of the company under audit.
- **Audit documentation and audit work-paper standards**. What previously used to consist of handwritten sheets of paper supported by paper-based audit evidence has evolved into word-processed documents, spreadsheets, templates, portable document format (PDF) files, and various other electronic documents housed in electronic work-paper databases that can be more readily protected from modification and destruction (see the section "Corporate accounting fraud and corporate failures" below). Audit work-papers are housed on an external audit firm's server in a remote location and are accessible by the firm's authorized audit professionals from anywhere in the world through a personal computer or other portable device. (Gone are the days of files full of paper and audit trunks that were lugged around from one location to the next!)
- **Responsibilities relating to fraud in the financial statements**. This standard has been in existence since the late 1990s and requires external auditors to consider the possibility of material fraud impacting the financial statements, but it has since been modified (in response to some of the major corporate fraud incidents of the early 2000s) to provide more specific guidance relating to the plan and design of external audit procedures to respond to the risk of fraud. Auditors are now required to address the potential for internal or external fraud that could have a material effect on the financial statements. Based on the auditor's understanding of the company being audited, and of the internal and external changes that affect the company, fraud risk must be made part of an audit risk assessment at the entity level, account balance level, and transaction level. Planned audit procedures must include specific procedures to address any potential fraud risks identified in the risk assessment process.
- **Planning and assessing the risk of material misstatement in financial statements**. This standard addresses the requirement for the auditor, as noted previously in this chapter, to gain a thorough understanding of the company under audit, identifying and evaluating all the internal and external factors that impact the company's financial results and the risk that the financial statements may be significantly (or in audit parlance, "materially") misstated. Evaluation of these factors and risks, particularly the design and operating effectiveness of the company's internal controls (system of checks and balances) are expected to dictate the audit procedures that will be performed. This is a far cry from merely examining supporting documentation and vouching for receipts and disbursements.
- **Materiality in planning and performing an audit**. Understanding that an audit of financial statements does not purport to examine all of the company's transactions and does not attest to the financial statements being completely accurate, the concept of "fair presentation" involves testing, through sampling or other means, reasonable auditor assumptions and judgments and a degree of tolerance for potential errors. The level of tolerance is also dictated by the external auditor's perception of how a user's judgment will be affected by reading the financial statements. Materiality thresholds therefore guide auditors' conclusions on whether an account balance is fairly stated (in other words, not materially misstated) and how exceptions and errors in account balances will be resolved.
- **Audit evidence, with specific considerations for certain items such as inventory, claims and litigation against the company under audit, segment information, etc**. The legitimacy and validity of audit evidence has always been a high priority for external auditors. The move from paper-based evidence to electronic and cyber-based audit evidence, and the magnitude thereof, adds complexity to audit procedures. External auditor culture has evolved to adopt electronic audit tools and data-mining technologies and techniques to comply with the requisite auditing standards in a changing business world.
- **Required auditing procedures**, including:
  - external (or independent) third-party confirmation of account balances and transactions;
  - contractual commitments;
  - analytical procedures to examine the interrelationships among different aspects of financial information (e.g. capital ratios, ratios of reserves for loan losses to total loans, gross profit margin, current ratio, working capital ratios, efficiency ratios) as a means of identifying trends and, hence, misstatements in account balances;
  - audit sampling techniques to extract the most representative samples to test the fairness of account balances.
- **Auditing accounting estimates, including fair-value accounting estimates and related disclosures**. The increasing number of estimates in financial reporting and the increasing trend toward fair-value accounting, as noted earlier, has resulted in changes in audit standards that became effective as recently as 2009, providing guidance to auditors on how to audit these estimates and related disclosures. In many instances, external auditors have had to use the expertise of valuation specialists as part of the audit team in order to meet auditing standards requirements to properly evaluate and conclude on the fair value of account balances.
- **Other special considerations**, including special reports and circumstances, using the work of other auditors and experts, evaluating third-party service organizations used by the company under audit, consideration of laws and regulations in an audit of financial statements, additional audit procedures on initial audit engagements, subsequent events, related party transactions, going concern (whether the financial condition and near-term prospects of the company are conducive to the company continuing to be a viable business entity).
- **Content of the representation letter**. Written representations from management have been a standard audit requirement for a long time. The content of the representation letter, however, has evolved with the times. Not only does management now attest to having answered all of the auditors' inquiries and to having provided all the requested information, but, among other things, it also takes responsibility for the preparation of the financial statements and related internal controls, compliance with all applicable laws, regulations, and accounting and financial reporting standards, the evaluation of all appropriate estimates, and the accuracy and completeness of all balance-sheet accounts.

- **Reporting on the audit**. The external auditor's opinion has evolved consistent with the delineation of responsibilities between the auditor and management. The opinion letter clearly addresses the scope of the audit, the relevant accounting and reporting standards, qualifications (or caveats) to the opinion, and a positive or negative assurance as to the fairness of presentation of the financial statement.

Take a look, for example, at the audited financial statements of Médecins Sans Frontières USA (see More Info). This is a not-for-profit organization, with its financial statements presented in accordance with US Generally Accepted Accounting Principles (US GAAP). The auditor's opinion addresses the relevant accounting rules and how the auditor conducted the audit. Contrast these with the annual report of Royal Bank of Scotland (RBS) (see More Info). This is a multicompany parent holding company that is primarily in the financial services business. The financial statements have been prepared in accordance with International Financial Reporting Standards (IFRS). The auditor's opinion addresses the scope of the financial statement audit as well as compliance with applicable regulations. The manner of presentation of the financial information varies with the nature and type of RBS's industry, as does the auditor's report.

CORPORATE ACCOUNTING FRAUD AND CORPORATE FAILURES

The most sweeping reform in external audit culture has been a response to large-scale corporate accounting fraud and corporate failures that resulted either from the fallout from fraud or from the economic and financial crises that have recently been gripping the globe. Accounting irregularities and scandals began in the 1990s and gained momentum to climax with catastrophic results in the early 2000s. The well-publicized incidents involving Enron, Parmalat, WorldCom, Tyco International, and AIG, to name but a few, revealed instances of company management, external auditors, and boards of directors falling down in their respective fiduciary, professional, and oversight responsibilities. External auditors were cited for altering and/or destroying audit work-papers and audit evidence to cover up their blatant failure to adhere to auditing standards. The result: the demise of what had been a prestigious international audit firm and loss of public (investor) confidence in large corporations and their external audit firms. This was the impetus for widespread changes that include, but are not limited to:

- the creation of additional regulatory bodies such as the PCAOB to create new rules for and to monitor the quality of work performed by external auditors of public reporting companies in the United States;
- the prohibition of external auditors from providing non-attest services to the company under audit;
- strict definitions for auditor independence and ethics;
- corporate responsibility, requiring the chief executive officer and chief financial officer to take responsibility for the accuracy and completeness of financial statements and the effectiveness of internal controls over financial reporting;
- additional rules governing conflicts of interest;
- expanded financial reporting disclosures;
- expanded penalties for criminal fraud and white-collar crime;
- expanded disclosures relating to executive compensation.

Although these changes were intended for publicly traded companies and their external auditors, other auditing standards boards that promulgate standards for non-public companies and government agencies have increasingly adopted similar standards, particularly in relation to the ethics, independence, and accountability of external auditors and how they report.

The global interdependence of business, coupled with widespread economic and financial crises, on the other hand, have thrown a spotlight on the ability of business entities, large and small, to survive. In assessing external factors that affect financial statements, auditors have had more occasions in the past few years to "qualify" their audit opinions to alert users of financial statements as to "the company's ability to continue as a going concern." Irrespective of the circumstances, the external auditor has to respond to what is critical for the users of a financial statement.

SUMMARY

External audit firms, whether global, regional or local, have expanded, restructured, affiliated, and positioned themselves to meet the new challenges and demands of a changed external audit environment. The image of a traditional external auditor—a man in a dark suit with a pocket protector—has evolved into competing numbers of men and women in the audit profession, agile with technology, ready to travel the world at a moment's notice and adapting to a myriad of additional requirements and specializations within what was a staid profession. It is not uncommon for external auditors to have served in corporations or in industry, or in other professions such as law or teaching, prior to becoming auditors. The variety and depth of knowledge and expertise required to be an external auditor today necessitates that training for external auditors be ongoing, intense, specialized, and covering a wide variety of relevant subjects that extend beyond traditional accounting and auditing. The ongoing training keeps the auditor able to grapple with the dynamics of a rapidly changing work environment. Increasingly included on external audit teams are asset valuation specialists, actuarial specialists, regulatory compliance experts, and technology specialists. Changes in business culture will, of necessity, continue to spawn cultural changes in external auditing.

MORE INFO

Book:

Girgenti, Richard H., and Timothy P. Hedley. *Managing the Risk of Fraud and Misconduct: Meeting the Challenges of a Global, Regulated, and Digital Environment*. New York: McGraw-Hill, 2011.

Articles, Standards, and Reports:

International Auditing and Assurance Standards Board (IAASB). "The clarified standards." The final set of International Standards on Auditing (ISAs) and the International Standard on Quality Control. Online at: tinyurl.com/6pz48a9

Médecins Sans Frontières USA. "Financial statements and report of independent certified public accountants: December 31, 2010 and 2009." Online at: tinyurl.com/6olgprp [PDF].

Royal Bank of Scotland. "Annual report and accounts 2010." Online at: tinyurl.com/bqhcfwk [PDF].

Wikipedia. "Luca Pacioli." Online at: en.wikipedia.org/wiki/Luca_Pacioli

Websites:

Accounting Standards Board (AcSB; Canada): www.frascanada.ca/accounting-standards-board/

Accounting Standards Board (ASB; UK): www.frc.org.uk/asb/

Accounting Standards Committee of Germany (DRSC): www.drsc.de/service/index_en.php

American Institute of Certified Public Accountants (AICPA): www.aicpa.org

Auditing and Assurance Standards Board (AASB; Canada): tinyurl.com/dyzfy2j

Financial Accounting Standards Board (FASB; US): www.fasb.org

International Accounting Standards Board (IASB) and International Financial Reporting Standards (IFRS): www.ifrs.org

International Auditing and Assurance Standards Board (IAASB): www.ifac.org/auditing-assurance

Public Company Accounting Oversight Board (PCAOB; US): www.pcaobus.org

See Also:

★ Cultural Alignment and Risk Management: Developing the Right Culture (pp. 724–726)
✔ Choosing an External Auditor (p. 1026)

"But many intelligent people have a sort of bug: they think intelligence is an end in itself. They have one idea in mind: to be intelligent, which is really stupid. And when intelligence takes itself for its own goal, it operates very strangely."
Muriel Barbery

The Effect of SOX on Internal Control, Risk Management, and Corporate Governance

Best Practice by David A. Doney

EXECUTIVE SUMMARY

- The effect of the Sarbanes–Oxley Act of 2002 (SOX) has been dramatic and global. SOX enhanced the regulatory framework for investor protection and confidence.
- SOX has required or encouraged a variety of best practices related to management accountability, auditor independence, audit committees, internal control reporting, risk management, and improvement of financial processes.
- One of the important contributions of the regulatory guidance is the "top-down risk-based assessment," a robust framework for identifying and assessing financial reporting risks.
- Compliance approaches, benefits, and costs continue to evolve as practice and regulatory guidance change.

INTRODUCTION

The Sarbanes–Oxley Act of 2002 was passed in the context of a series of high-profile corporate scandals, a brief recession, and the events of 9/11. These factors were cited by President George W. Bush as a threat to investor confidence and the US economy overall. He also declared: "This law says to every dishonest corporate leader: you will be exposed and punished; the era of low standards and false profits is over; no boardroom in America is above or beyond the law."[1]

US Senator Paul Sarbanes stated that during the development of the law, a series of Senate hearings with experts from business, government, and academia resulted in a "remarkable consensus on the nature of the problems."[2] These included inadequate oversight of the accounting profession, conflicts of interest involving auditors and stock analysts, weak corporate governance procedures, inadequate disclosure rules, and insufficient funding for the Securities and Exchange Commission (SEC).

The SOX law, corresponding guidance from regulators, and evolving approaches to implementation have resulted in a variety of internal control, risk management, and corporate governance best practices.

HOLD MANAGEMENT ACCOUNTABLE

The law requires that the CEO and CFO sign certifications quarterly and annually attesting that they have reviewed the financial statements and (to their knowledge) believe them to be fair, accurate, and complete. Penalties for fraudulent certification are severe. This requirement has encouraged such best practices as:

- Disclosure committees: A cross-functional group of top-level managers that meets to discuss pending public disclosures, including quarterly and annual financial reporting.
- Representation letters: To support the certification by the CEO and CFO and ensure that material information is made known to them, a variety of senior finance and operations managers sign representation letters regarding financial reporting matters relevant to their areas of responsibility.
- Improvement of finance organization: Many companies expanded the number and quality of financial personnel, particularly with respect to US Generally Accepted Accounting Principles and SEC reporting requirements.

MAINTAIN AUDITOR INDEPENDENCE

Auditors are the primary watchdogs of the corporation. Prior to SOX, auditors performed significant consulting work for publicly traded companies ("issuers") that they audited. Further, auditors often moved into senior financial management positions in the client company. These factors created at least a perceived conflict of interest.

SOX prohibits auditors from providing many types of consulting services to issuers they audit. The law also prohibits auditors from auditing an issuer if the issuer's CEO or top financial management worked for the audit firm during the past year.

CASE STUDY

SIRVA, Inc.—Implementing a Top-Down Risk Assessment

SIRVA, Inc., is a decentralized global moving and relocation services company with revenues of US$4 billion in 2007. Under new internal audit leadership in 2007, the company implemented a top-down risk assessment, new SOX compliance software, and brought the effort substantially in-house. This resulted in *annual* savings of over US$3 million and brought costs into line with benchmark companies.

First, management completed a risk-ranking of each balance sheet account (and certain sub-accounts) to assess the risk of material misstatement. The ranking was also used to identify key process/location combinations ("processes"). For example, revenue and receivables might be significant (i.e. in-scope) for one location but not another.

Second, processes were risk-ranked. Higher-risk processes or topics included entity-level controls, period-end reporting, revenue, and key accounting estimates and judgments. Other transactional processes such as accounts payable, payroll, tax, and treasury were lower risk and received less assessment effort. Nearly 200 material misstatement risks (MMR) were documented by systematically considering key accounting policies and financial statement assertions for each process or account. Risks represented "what could go wrong" in relation to the account or assertion.

Third, the number of key controls tested was reduced from the prior year by 50% (from nearly 1,000 to 500) by including only those entity-level and transaction-level controls needed to address the MMR. In other words, specific risks determined which controls mattered, as opposed to merely large dollar balances, locations, or systems. Management assigned each control a risk-ranking of high, medium, or low. This ranking was based on a combination of account-specific and control-specific factors in the SOX guidance. Sample sizes used in testing were based on the ranking and the frequency of control operation.

Fourth, SOX compliance software was implemented to document the risks, controls, and tests. Comprehensive status and quality reporting was developed and discussed in weekly meetings with the global audit team and management.

Finally, multiple domestic general ledger systems were consolidated into one system. Further, two major operating platforms were consolidated into one, removing an entire financial process.

"Promote, then, as an object of primary importance, institutions for the general diffusion of knowledge. In proportion as the structure of government gives force to public opinion, it is essential that public opinion should be enlightened."

George Washington

        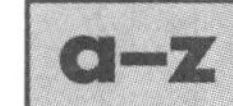

EMPOWER THE REGULATORS

Prior to SOX, the audit industry was self-regulated. SOX also established the Public Company Accounting Oversight Board (PCAOB), a nonprofit, nongovernmental entity, to oversee the audit firms. The PCAOB sets standards and publicly discloses the results of its auditor reviews and any disciplinary action taken.

Critics also argued that the SEC, the regulator tasked with investor protection and corporate disclosure standards, was significantly underfunded and understaffed. The SEC budget was nearly doubled in the wake of SOX and remains at that level today.

ENGAGE AUDIT COMMITTEES

Prior to SOX, former SEC Chairman Arthur Levitt stated that "qualified, committed, independent and tough-minded audit committees represent the most reliable guardians of the public interest."[3] The many scandals that resulted in SOX indicated that audit committees were not performing their financial oversight responsibilities effectively.

SOX mandated that the audit committee, rather than management, be accountable for the relationship with the auditor, including selection, compensation, retention, and review of independence. Issuers are now required to disclose whether or not the audit committee has a financial expert, which has encouraged additional financial expertise on audit committees. Auditors are now required to provide more robust disclosures to the audit committee regarding alternative accounting policies and their discussions with management. Audit committees must also ensure the availability of an anonymous reporting channel for accounting or auditing matters (i.e. a "whistleblower hotline"). The law also expanded protection for whistleblowers and penalties for retaliation against them.

EVALUATE KEY FINANCIAL CONTROLS

The infamous SOX "Section 404" guidance requires both management and the external auditor to provide a report that includes an opinion regarding internal control over financial reporting (ICFR). This is additional to the traditional auditor's opinion on the accuracy of financial statements. It requires management to document and comprehensively test financial controls necessary to address "material misstatement risks."

Any controls that are assessed as not effectively designed (i.e. not capable of addressing the related risk, even if executed) or not operating effectively (i.e. not executed consistently) result in "deficiencies." More serious deficiencies are categorized as "significant deficiencies" or "material weaknesses" and must be reported to the external auditor and audit committee. Material weaknesses require public disclosure during the quarter in which they are identified and, if not remediated as of year-end, an unfavorable opinion on ICFR in the issuer's annual report.

The requirement to perform a comprehensive control assessment has resulted in several improvements in the art and science of financial management. For example, controls related to the "tone at the top," incentives, and conflicts of interest were often not formally assessed prior to SOX. Focus on effective controls has significantly improved. Further, the quality of the SOX assessment (for example, project management, technology use, risk assessment, and quality of presentation materials) is a good proxy for "tone at the top" in the organization and the process management skills of the finance team.

In the aftermath of SOX the focus of internal auditing efforts also shifted significantly to financial controls, as opposed to operational processes. Many issuers expanded the staffing and capabilities of their internal auditing teams to absorb incremental SOX responsibilities. The New York Stock Exchange (NYSE) listing standards now require that all listed companies have an internal audit function. Tracking deficiencies to resolution also establishes good discipline for internal audit follow-up of all issue types, as required by internal auditing standards.

IMPROVE RISK MANAGEMENT

Pressure is increasing on businesses to improve risk management practices. This comes from a variety of sources, including regulators, credit rating agencies, and activist shareholders. Further, the subprime mortgage crisis which became apparent in 2007 has (arguably) exposed systemic risk management concerns.

The 2007 guidance from the SEC and PCAOB regarding SOX Section 404 established a comprehensive framework for conducting a "top-down" financial reporting risk assessment. For example, management is required to identify material misstatement risks and related controls, which then must be tested. (See the Case Study for details.)

Techniques used in top-down risk assessment are applicable to other risk categories. Under the COSO Enterprise Risk Management (ERM) framework, risks fall into strategic, operational, legal/regulatory, and financial reporting categories. SOX compliance implies substantial coverage of financial reporting risks. The SOX compliance process also provides a framework that relates processes, risks, and controls, and the network of managers involved, which can be used to help establish an ERM program.

Many companies also use SOX-compliance database software, which may also be useful for retaining risk information to support an ERM program and as an internal audit workflow tool. For example, as

MAKING IT HAPPEN

SOX regulations and implementation have provided a series of best practices to help companies improve risk, control, and governance, even if technically they are not required to comply.

- Identify and remove conflicts of interest that affect your business. These can involve auditors, management, the board, vendors, outside consultants, etc.
- Ensure that your external auditors and internal auditors are independent by having their continuing employment, performance rating, and compensation determined by the audit committee or board.
- Help to ensure that financial disclosures are transparent and fairly describe the organization's performance by using a disclosure committee and management representation letters.
- Insist on a robust top-down risk assessment of financial reporting processes. The extent of testing to perform (the primary cost-driver) can then be determined appropriately.
- Capture risk and control information in compliance database software. User-friendly software that can be customized and administered by non-IT personnel is available at very reasonable prices.
- Establish risk committees at the senior management and board level. These committees can direct risk management efforts and help the audit committee to focus on financial reporting matters.
- Develop reporting of operating metrics that are predictive of financial results and share it with the audit committee and board.
- Communicate periodically to the audit committee any significant deficiencies identified (financial or otherwise) and management's progress towards remediating them.
- Use the financial reporting effort and framework to initiate or improve an ERM program.

"A business that is too big to fail cannot be run in the interests of shareholders, since it is no longer part of the market. Either it must be possible to close it down or it has to be run in a different way. It is as simple—and brutal—as that."
Martin Wolf

internal audits are completed, the amount of risk and control information expands in such a database, across all risk types.

In response to increased expectations around risk, many audit committees have expanded their scope to include overall risk management. With SOX efforts addressing financial reporting risks, they can focus more attention on strategic and operational risks. Some issuers have also created board risk committees to address non-financial reporting matters.

IMPROVE FINANCIAL PROCESSES

The significant cost of the ICFR assessment required under SOX Section 404 represents a "tax" on inefficiency, providing additional incentives for process improvement. Redundant systems, processes, or locations generally require some type of incremental assessment, increasing the scope and cost of compliance. The Financial Executives International (FEI) survey of SOX 404 compliance costs in 2007[4] indicated that, for companies with average revenue of US$4.7 billion, the costs in *decentralized* companies averaged US$1.9 million, 46% higher than the US$1.3 million in *centralized* companies. The difference is likely to be a fraction of the savings available from addressing the underlying process inefficiency.

In addition, manual control procedures involve substantially higher testing costs. For example, a manual control that operates daily may require a sample size of 30 to be evaluated by an expert. However, the same control if automated requires a sample size of just one and does not have to be evaluated each year if certain criteria are met. Leading companies track the number of manual versus automated controls and seek automation opportunities. Reducing the number of manual journal entries is another means of improving the reliability of financial statements and reducing closing-cycle time, while reducing both compliance and personnel costs.

Section 404 is one of the more contentious elements of SOX, due to the significant cost of compliance. According to a survey by FEI that included issuers with an average revenue of US$4.7 billion, compliance costs were US$1.7 million during 2007, or 0.36% of revenue. The total cost includes internal and external labor and auditor attestation fees.[5]

Compliance costs have continued to decline since 2004, when Section 404 became applicable for most issuers. The 2007 SEC and PCAOB guidance has provided management with additional flexibility in addressing risk and determining the timing, nature, and extent of testing procedures, further reducing costs.

CONCLUSION

SOX has resulted in dramatic changes in internal control, risk management, and corporate governance. Management and audit committees are more focused on financial reporting. The internal control and risk management best practices discussed above continue to evolve in practice. Companies continue to focus and reduce costs in their SOX 404 efforts through top-down risk assessment and compliance software, which have broader applications to other risk management efforts.

MORE INFO

Book:

Farrell, Greg. *America Robbed Blind. How Corporate Crooks Fleeced American Shareholders (and How Congress Failed to Stop Them)*. Buda, TX: Wizard Academy Press, 2005.

Websites:

Committee of Sponsoring Organizations of the Treadway Commission (COSO): www.coso.org. For *Enterprise Risk Management—Integrated Framework (2004)*: www.coso.org/-ERM.htm

Institute of International Auditors (IIA): www.theiia.org. For *The International Standards for the Professional Practice of Internal Auditing*: www.theiia.org/guidance/standards-and-guidance

Public Company Accounting Oversight Board (PCAOB): www.pcaob.org

PCAOB Auditing Standard No. 5, "An audit of internal control over financial reporting that is integrated with an audit of financial statements and related independence rule and conforming amendments" (2007): pcaobus.org/Standards/Auditing/Pages/Auditing_Standard_5.aspx

Sarbanes–Oxley. The text of the Act can be found at: fl1.findlaw.com/news.findlaw.com/hdocs/docs/gwbush/sarbanesoxley072302.pdf

US Securities and Exchange Commission (SEC): www.sec.gov

"Commission guidance regarding management's report on internal control over financial reporting under Section 13(a) or 15(d) of the Securities Exchange Act of 1934." Interpretive guidance release 33-8810, etc. (2007): www.sec.gov/rules/interp/2007/33-8810.pdf

See Also:

★ Engaging Senior Management in Internal Control (pp. 336–337)
★ Has Financial Reporting Impacted on Internal Auditing Negatively? (pp. 338–341)
★ Implementing an Effective Internal Controls System (pp. 361–364)
★ Understanding the Requirements for Preparing IFRS Financial Statements (pp. 423–424)
★ What Are the Leading Causes of Financial Restatements? (pp. 428–430)
✔ International Financial Reporting Standards (IFRS): The Basics (p. 1039)
✔ Key Accounting Standards and Organizations (p. 1040)
✔ Sarbanes–Oxley: Its Development and Aims (p. 1052)

NOTES

1 Office of the Press Secretary, The White House. "President Bush signs corporate corruption bill" (Sarbanes–Oxley Act 2002): www.whitehouse.gov/news/releases/2002/07/20020730.html

2 Lucas, Nance. "An interview with United States Senator Paul S. Sarbanes." *Journal of Leadership & Organizational Studies* (11:1 (January 2004): 3–8.

3 Levitt, Arthur. "The numbers game." Speech dated September 28, 1998. Online at: www.sec.gov/news/speech/speecharchive/1998/spch220.txt

4 Financial Executives International (FEI). News release "FEI survey: Average 2007 SOX compliance cost $1.7 million." Online at: fei.mediaroom.com/index.php?s=43&item=204

5 *Ibid.* A complete cross-referenced index of SEC filers, audit firms, offices, CPAs, services, fees, compliance/enforcement actions, and other critical disclosure information can be found at: www.sarbanes-oxley.com

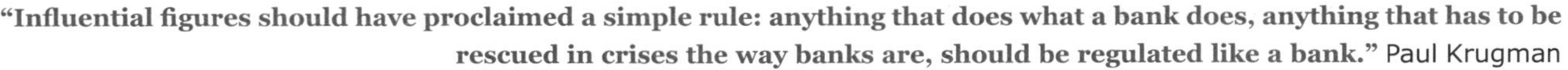
"Influential figures should have proclaimed a simple rule: anything that does what a bank does, anything that has to be rescued in crises the way banks are, should be regulated like a bank." Paul Krugman

  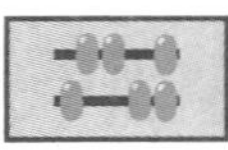      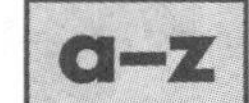

Engaging Senior Management in Internal Control

by Philip Ratcliffe

EXECUTIVE SUMMARY

- Internal control systems must have the backing of senior management to be effective.
- Internal auditors should make management aware of the importance of sound internal controls, and the serious problems that could arise if they are inadequate.
- The benefits of sound internal controls include efficiency and effectiveness, protection against losses and unpleasant surprises, optimum use of assets, and motivated staff—all in all, they make a major contribution to organizational survival and prosperity.
- Key risks resulting from lack of good internal control are fraud, incorrect accounts, inefficiency and ineffectiveness, damage to the reputation of the organization and its management, and a consequent fall in the value of the company.
- Internal auditors should form their own view of the specific risks facing their organization.
- If the internal control system is inadequate, they should meet with senior management to explain the need for strong, sound controls and their benefits for the organization.

HOW TO GET SENIOR MANAGEMENT TO TAKE INTERNAL CONTROL SERIOUSLY

Top managers in any organization have many calls on their time and attention. Vying for their attention will be customers, suppliers, employees, consultants, and many others. Internal controls can easily be squeezed out of their agenda. The problem this can create is that if senior management does not take control seriously, the "tone from the top" will be wrong—and if the people in charge don't care, then why should anyone else in the organization? Rightly or wrongly, this is the message that will be perceived across the organization, and internal control will suffer.

So, as a corporate auditor, how can you push internal control up the priority list? Showing clearly to management the benefits of strong internal control on the one hand, and the consequences of failure of internal control on the other, is one path to this goal.

Benefits of Control

A key message to communicate to management is that effective, active controls give positive benefits as well as avoiding negative outcomes. Having controls that are effective will ensure that the directions of the board and senior management are implemented as intended; that operations and activities are carried out efficiently and meet their objectives; and that the assets used in an organization are not only properly accounted for, but also that they are used effectively and efficiently for the benefit of the organization. Procedures which follow sound control principles enable people to carry out their work in an environment that is orderly and satisfying to work in. Good internal control will also protect an organization and its staff against the temptations of dishonesty, fraud, and theft.

Organizations that have sound internal controls will know where they are, and where they are going, because management information controls will tell the organization's management what they need to know when they need to know it. If the first imperative of most organizations is survival, then good internal control can play a major role in achieving that objective. Additionally, and very importantly, there can also be an efficiency dividend for an organization if good, cost-effective internal control systems are in place; for example, when processes are streamlined and well controlled, fewer people may be needed to do the work.

The Impact of Control Failure Inside the Business

All too often, internal control only becomes a concern to top management after it breaks down. Out of the blue comes the sudden discovery of a massive fraud or a major hole in the accounts, or a business segment that was thought to be profitable is dramatically discovered not to be. There is a myriad of such possibilities. Management discovers, painfully, that when there is such a breakdown of control, almost everything else has to be thrown out of the window while the breakdown is investigated. It has to engage with internal auditors, external auditors, consultants, and specialists to uncover the root causes of the problem, as there is no cure without first making a diagnosis. The managers immediately responsible for the failure must be identified, and a conclusion reached on their degree of culpability. And if someone has to be fired, who is going to take on their responsibilities?

Then, senior managers have to make up their minds what to do about the underlying problem. What changes have to be made to ensure that it can never happen again? Should they commission reviews in other similar parts of the organization to gain assurance that the problem isn't endemic elsewhere? Are major investments in systems or capital items needed to fix things? Should procedures be revised? Do staff need retraining or reorganizing? If so, who is going to implement the changes, and where is the money going to come from?

Control Breakdown Can Have External Implications

Another vital aspect is the impact of a breakdown on external relations. Do investors and the stock markets have to be informed? Is a profits warning necessary? How will stakeholders react? What will the (inevitably negative) impact be on the share price, and therefore the value, of the organization? Often such an announcement will create a loss of shareholder value that is many times the original operating loss. At times like these, an executive director may be lucky to keep his job; at the very least, there is a major risk of loss of personal and corporate reputation.

CASE STUDY

When a new chief executive officer joined his company, the chief audit executive arranged an early meeting with him. The CAE discussed the internal controls in the organization, demonstrated his knowledge of their strengths and weaknesses, and explained his view of the importance of controls and the vital role to be played by the CEO in setting an example—the tone from the top. As a result, the CEO agreed to have regular meetings to discuss internal controls and to review the assurance provided by internal audit and any resultant need for action, undertakings he subsequently fulfilled. Expectation that these meetings would take place helped to ensure that management throughout the organization gave high priority to internal control and to responding to internal audit findings.

"Trust is not a substitute for internal control."

        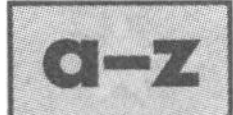

The Opportunity Cost Is Great

On top of this, in a serious case the opportunity cost of the time that management will lose in attending to the consequences of an internal control breakdown can be massive. Strategic issues, tactical issues, business development—all these and many more normal concerns of senior management will have to take a back seat until the problem is resolved. Add to this the loss of reputation and of confidence, inside and outside the organization, because news will inevitably leak out however carefully those involved try to prevent it.

The case here has been made in the context of a commercial organization, but similar considerations apply to all other types of organization, whether governmental, private, or in the not-for-profit sector.

GETTING MANAGEMENT BACKING: WHERE TO START

If the benefits of sound controls are so tangible, and the aftermath of a failure of internal control is so dreadful, how does the corporate auditor make a start on obtaining top management's backing for a regime of sound internal control? Corporate governance regulations in many countries, and best practice, now require organizations formally to analyze and record the risks they face. The purpose of this requirement is, first, to ensure that organizations actually understand their risk profile, as only then can they seriously and properly consider whether they have the right mitigation arrangements in place. Often a management team, in making explicit the risks they face, will discover that initially they do not have a common view as to what the risks are. Only when they have a unified vision can they expect to come up with a coherent and balanced response. Only then can they hope to design and develop a comprehensive internal control system that meets the needs of the organization. The corporate auditor can assist by becoming involved in the risk identification process, by emphasizing to senior management the immediate impact of failure to mitigate the risks (for example, by pointing out that the accounts will be incorrect), and the secondary, but possibly even more drastic, consequences (for example, that a profits warning will have to be issued and the share price will nosedive.)

It is not least by confronting management with the consequences of control failure that it can be helped to take internal control seriously. The internal auditor can help to create an understanding and appreciation of the consequences of control failure by making presentations and having one-to-one meetings with influential people, such as the chairman/president, chief executive, chief financial officer, audit committee chair, other board members, and senior managers. The objective is to create an awareness of internal control in the organization and, through that awareness, to change the attitude to it.

While some risks may be external to the organization and not susceptible to internal control, many can be mitigated by internal controls. In some cultures, management is reluctant to accept the need for internal controls, believing that staff should be trusted. Internal auditors should point out to such management that trust is not a substitute for internal control. A proper system of internal controls should be considered a force for moral good, in that it effectively removes temptation from employees by ensuring that undesirable behaviors will be promptly detected and corrected; if employees understand this, they will be less likely to attempt to defraud their employer.

CONCLUSION

Management's role in ensuring effective internal control is vital. Management sets the tone from the top. Unless management engages and commits, the rest of the organization will not take internal control seriously. The internal auditor can help management to appreciate the importance of internal control by demonstrating its value—not least, the efficiency dividend to an organization if good, cost-effective internal control systems are in place—and by making management aware of the consequences of failures of internal control. The internal auditor can further assist management by highlighting the need to set tone from the top, to allocate sufficient resources for internal control, and to ensure that internal control processes are suitably designed for the needs of the business.

MAKING IT HAPPEN

- Collect evidence about the state of internal controls and any opportunities that exist for improving them.
- Present the benefits of better controls in terms with which management can identify.
- Review the organization's code of conduct or similar document; if none exists, it is worth raising the issue.
- Seek a meeting with the head of the organization and influential members of the board. Have a clear but short agenda. Aim for some specific goals from your meeting. Go prepared with a succinct presentation and some practical recommendations.
- Use the opportunity to argue for the importance of tone from the top where internal control is concerned; if the top people in the company take internal control seriously, so will everybody else. Ask whether they like unwelcome surprises, and what they are prepared to do to avoid them.
- Point up the risks facing the organization, and show how a well-designed control structure can help to avoid or mitigate the worst consequences.
- Don't expect everything to be achieved with just one meeting. Be prepared to keep going back with the same messages until they are not only accepted, but also acted on.

MORE INFO

Book:

Sawyer, Lawrence B., Mortimer A. Dittenhofer, James H. Scheiner, Anne Graham, and Paul Makosz. *Sawyer's Internal Auditing: The Practice of Modern Internal Auditing*. Altamonte Springs, FL: Institute of Internal Auditors, 2003.

Reports:

American Institute of Certified Public Accountants. "Internal control—Integrated framework." May 1994. Order online at: www.theiia.org/bookstore

Financial Reporting Council. "The combined code on corporate governance." June 2008. Online at: www.frc.org.uk/corporate/combinedcode.cfm

See Also:

★ Improving Corporate Profitability Through Accountability (pp. 685–686)
★ New Assurance Challenges Facing Chief Audit Executives (pp. 378–381)
✔ Corporate Governance and Its Interpretations (p. 1111)
✔ Understanding Internal Audits (p. 1057)

"Ensure that your organization really understands its risk profile."

Has Financial Reporting Impacted on Internal Auditing Negatively? by Andrew Chambers

EXECUTIVE SUMMARY

- At the turn of the millennium, the internal auditing profession sought to formally broaden its role for internal audit by embracing "consulting services" that went beyond its traditional assurance role. This move was almost immediately challenged by the collapse of Enron and other large corporations, which led to stockholders and boards demanding more focus not only on the internal audit assurance role but also, more specifically, on the assurance of internal control over financial reporting—at the expense of assurance on operational effectiveness and efficiency and assurance on compliance with laws, regulations, and policies.
- Since then, internal audit has often been commandeered into discharging what should be management's role—for instance, to comply with Section 404 of the Sarbanes-Oxley Act (2002)—whereas the proper internal audit role should be to audit the compliance work that management has done. A better balance is now being achieved, not least as the Sarbanes-Oxley compliance requirements become bedded into companies as well as becoming slightly less onerous.
- The storm that hit the US corporate sector at the turn of the millennium was a salutary reminder of the importance of effective assurance auditing and the need for this to be done in depth. However, it is not only (or even primarily) in financial and accounting matters that assurance is needed. Entities achieve their objectives mainly in the operational areas of their businesses, and they need assurance that operations are effective and efficient. They also need assurance that laws and regulations are being complied with, for instance with regard to the security of personal data in IT.
- Entities can also benefit from the consulting services that internal audit is able to offer, but internal audit is still neglecting these activities by focusing disproportionately on the internal control of financial reporting.

INTERNAL AUDIT'S CONSULTING ROLE

It was unfortunate that The Institute of Internal Auditors (The IIA) released its first consulting implementation *Standards*, to add to its already existing assurance *Standards*, at exactly the time when Enron collapsed. "Implementation Standards" set out how the "Attribute Standards" and "Performance Standards" should be applied in the context of either assurance or consulting work. In 2007 The IIA announced that it had no plans to release further sets of "Implementation Standards."[1]

In spite of its bad timing, the release of the consulting *Standards* was a natural development in the evolution of internal auditing, albeit not one that gained universal approval. This development was the principal driver behind the release in 2000 of a completely revamped set of *Standards* (effective January 1, 2002) to replace The IIA's original *Standards* that had remained unaltered, except in one or two minor details, since their first release in 1978. The main need for new *Standards* arose from a widely held perception that the old *Standards* had ceased to describe either what constituted contemporary best practice in internal auditing or, indeed, how internal auditors spent much of their time. Faced with this challenge, the IIA set out to determine the nature of internal auditing as it currently was. Prior to developing the new *Standards* the IIA invested much effort, including two exposure drafts, in achieving an agreed new definition of internal auditing. The new *Standards* were then modeled around this new definition (see "Optimizing Internal Audit").

"Internal auditing is an independent, objective assurance and consulting activity designed to add value and improve an organization's operations. It helps an organization accomplish its objectives by bringing a systematic, disciplined approach to evaluate and improve the effectiveness of risk management, control, and governance processes."[2]

Prior to this definition and prior to the new *Standards*, internal auditing had been perceived as an assurance service, but now "consulting activity" was added. Some say this definition gives the consulting role equal weight to the assurance role (for example, "the definition gives equal consideration to both assurance and consulting activities").[3] The fundamental challenge was to determine whether all the non-assurance activities that engaged internal auditors' time should continue to be regarded as noninternal audit work or whether they should be brought within the definition of internal auditing. The latter was decided upon. This was hardly surprising as throughout the 1990s there had been some skepticism as to the value of internal auditors' assurance work and a view that their role in providing consulting services was much more constructive and added much more value.

SWING TO MORE EMPHASIS ON THE ASSURANCE ROLE

Then came the spectacular collapses of Enron, Tyco, WorldCom, and others. Almost immediately the pendulum in the internal audit role swung away from offering consulting services toward providing stronger assurance. Audit committees and boards arrived at the painful realization that they had been starved of the independent assurance they needed and they looked to their internal auditors, among others, to provide them with that assurance.

The IIA's Global Auditing Information Network (GAIN) survey found that 36% of a total of 341 respondents fully supported the idea of internal auditors doing consultancy work. Of the remainder, 41% agreed with the statement: "consulting is usually the way to go, but you have to be careful; sometimes it is not a good idea," 7% considered that internal auditors should rarely or never do consulting work, and 16% thought that in theory consulting sounded good, but in practice it was a bad idea more often than not.

An *AuditWire* article[4] quoted two contrasting views about the place of consultancy services in the internal auditor's repertoire:

Against:

"The Andersen debacle drove home the risks to maintaining our independence when we auditors neglect or stray from our primary mission, which should be providing internal control assurance.

When my audit team is approached by management for a consulting project, four red flags are raised in my mind:

- If management is asking the audit group for help, there must be a control concern. As an auditor, my first responsibility is to decide whether an audit or investigation is warranted.
- If there is no control concern, I must wonder whether the manager considers the project too risky for his or her own people to do or whether it's of too little value to engage a third party on the project.
- If it's too risky for the manager's own people to tackle, does this indicate that

        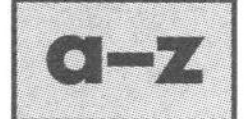

the manager has the wrong people on staff or not enough people? If the project has insufficient value to warrant hiring a third party, why would I want to associate our audit group with the project?

- Finally, I must ask myself whether I believe that I have been so successful in my assurance role that internal auditing has no other risk-based priorities to pursue. If so, the audit group must be overstaffed."

In favor:

"Consulting is one of the most important services we provide for management. We have found a direct correlation between our time spent on consulting and the decrease that we have in investigations. So, when I do my audit plan at the beginning of the year, I save a certain amount of time to do the consulting projects that aren't part of the risk-based audit program ...

"We have an incredibly wonderful, comfortable relationship [with management]. People see the audit staff as peers and feel very comfortable calling and asking them questions ...

"In the next couple of months, I'll be developing an online conflict-of-interest training course, which our federal researchers will be required to take. We'll be doing that with our new whistleblowers policy as well."

The corporate governance debacles at the turn of the millennium, of the United States in particular but of Europe and elsewhere too, therefore heralded a relative swing away from an internal audit emphasis on consulting services back to the more traditional assurance role. As we will see later in this chapter, internal auditors were to prove not entirely effective in this assurance role. There are many internal audit functions, including some of the largest, that reject a consulting role entirely. The heavily revised 2009 *Standards* of The IIA will make that harder, if not impossible, to sustain while still applying the *Standards*.

INTERNAL AUDIT FOCUS ON ASSURANCE OVER FINANCIAL REPORTING

The impact of the corporate governance debacles has been even more extreme than stated above: Not only have management and the audit committee tended to place more stress on the assurance role of internal audit, but beyond that, they have often required internal audit to focus on assurance about financial and accounting matters rather than assurance on operational and other matters. The standard definition of internal control gives three objectives of internal control, and internal audit functions have recently been asked to focus more on providing assurance on the second of these:

"Internal control is broadly defined as a process, effected by the entity's board of directors, management and other personnel, designed to provide reasonable assurance regarding the achievement of objectives in the following categories:

- Effectiveness and efficiency of operations;
- Reliability of financial reporting;
- Compliance with applicable laws and regulations."[5]

and

"Internal control can be judged effective in each of the three categories, respectively, if the board of directors and management have reasonable assurance that:

- They understand the extent to which the entity's operations objectives are being achieved.
- Published financial statements are being prepared reliably.
- Applicable laws and regulations are being complied with."[6]

That the assurance needs of boards extend across all three objectives of internal control and also risk management is illustrated well by a provision within the United Kingdom's corporate governance code:

"The board should, at least annually, conduct a review of the effectiveness of the group's system of internal controls and should report to shareholders that they have done so. The review should cover all material controls, including financial, operational and compliance controls and risk management systems."[7]

IMPACT OF SARBANES–OXLEY ON INTERNAL AUDITING

The Sarbanes–Oxley Act of 2002, itself a direct result of the Enron debacle, has turned the screw further as far as internal audit is concerned. It has been emulated outside the United States with equivalent laws now in Canada and Japan. The Sarbanes–Oxley Act catches US quoted companies, overseas subsidiaries, and operating units of US quoted companies and companies registered elsewhere with secondary listings in the US. Draconian criminal sanctions contained within the Act mean that the criminalization of breaches of corporate governance has arrived in a serious way, and executives across the world are mindful of the global reach of the US Department of Justice. Section 906 on "Corporate Responsibility for Financial Reports" of the Sarbanes–Oxley Act sets out criminal penalties with fines of up to one million dollars or imprisonment of up to 10 years, or both, for chief executive officers and chief financial officers (or equivalent thereof) who certify financial reports in the knowledge that they do not comport with all the requirements; or if the false certification were willful, the penalties may be up to five million dollars or imprisonment for up to 20 years, or both (see "Implementing an Effective Internal Controls System").

CASE STUDY

This case illustrates how internal audit focus has been skewed by recent demands for extra assurance of internal control over financial reporting.

One of the top ten global multinationals came to Sarbanes–Oxley compliance rather later than it should have done. At the time it already had difficulties with the regulatory authorities, in particular the SEC. It was determined not to fail in its compliance with Section 404, having already risked the ire of the SEC with respect to its disclosures under Section 302. The multinational's approach to Section 404 compliance was to set up a dedicated Section 404 compliance team within its internal audit function. The head of this team, recruited from outside, had been a partner at one of the "Big Four" accountancy firms. Worldwide, the company had some 250 internal auditors and 70 became Section 404 specialists, many being recruited from outside. In addition, the company bought in supplementary Section 404 compliance resources from one of the Big Four. These overhead costs for management compliance with Section 404 did not of course include the extra fees paid to the external auditors for their own attestation work under Section 404. Typically, Section 404 has doubled the cost of the external audit.

The team's approach was first to develop a plan, with dates, for rolling out the project. It then identified and documented all the processes that could have a material impact on the multinational's financial statement assertions. This included identifying and documenting the key controls within these processes, and then developing and documenting a program to test the functioning of these controls. The results of all this work were recorded in process maps, narrative writeups and spreadsheet-based control registers.

Following the successful implementation of this part of Section 404 compliance, the emphasis then become to transfer this compliance work to line management, so that line managers themselves became responsible for running the compliance program in the future.

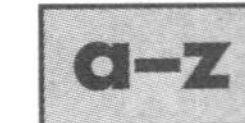

The key certification requirement is set out in Section 404. Subsection (a) requires that each annual report contain an internal control report, which states the responsibility of management for establishing and maintaining an adequate internal control structure and procedures for financial reporting. The annual report must also contain an assessment by management, as of the end of the most recent fiscal year of the issuer, of the effectiveness of the internal control structure and procedures of the issuer for financial reporting. Subsection (b) requires that, with respect to that internal control assessment, each registered public accounting firm that prepares or issues the audit report for the issuer shall attest to, and report on, the assessment made by the management of the issuer in accordance with *Standards* for attestation engagements issued or adopted by the Public Companies Accounting Oversight Board (PCAOB). Such an attestation shall not be the subject of a separate engagement. Section 302 of the Act requires a similar assessment and certification by management of internal control over other disclosures made in the annual report.

"The Sarbanes–Oxley Act was designed in a panic and rushed through in a blinding fervour of moral indignation." *The Economist*

"Sarbanes–Oxley has provided a bonanza for accountants and auditors, the very professions thought to be at fault in the original scandals." Tony Blair[8]

Very frequently, internal audit has been drafted in to undertake much of the assessment work on behalf of management with respect to Sections 302 and 404 compliance, diverting internal audit from other work. This was particularly the case when companies were initially seeking to comply with the Sarbanes–Oxley Act. Over time, companies have been endeavoring to transfer this compliance work to line management, freeing up internal audit to provide assurance that this work is being done effectively rather than doing the work itself.

Measures by the SEC and PCAOB[9] (in 2007), sometimes termed "SOX-Lite," have helped to make compliance less onerous. The definitions of "significant deficiencies"[10] and "material weaknesses"[11] in internal control—both of which have to be reported by management—have been relaxed, and the so-called "triple audit" by the external auditors under Section 404 has now become just a "double audit," though it is the least costly element that has been abandoned under PCAOB Auditing Standard No. 5.[12]

Following the delisting of British Airways in the United States, and thus the end of its requirement to comply with the Sarbanes–Oxley Act, the company's annual report for the year ended 31 March 2008 showed a reduction in external audit fees from £4.3 million to £3 million, and further savings of £1.27 million associated with other costs primarily pursuant to complying with the Sarbanes–Oxley Act.

THE WALKER REVIEW

It is interesting to speculate why internal audit emerged virtually unscathed from the financial crisis that hit the world economy towards the end of the last decade. Was it because they did a good job, or that there were low expectations about their remit? In the wake of this crisis, the Walker Report addressed corporate governance in UK banks and other financial entities. Its analysis and recommendations have much wider relevance than just for the UK. That this report saw internal audit as no part of the solution speaks volumes. The report says:

"Some concern was also expressed at the very limited discussion of audit, in particular internal audit, in the July consultation paper—though this in fact reflected judgement that the principal failures that afflicted problem banks did not principally arise under the rubric of 'audit' ... Discussions in the context of this Review process suggest that failures that proved to be critical for many banks related much less to what might be characterised as conventional compliance and audit processes, including internal audit, but to defective information flow, defective analytical tools and inability to bring insightful judgement in the interpretation of information and the impact of market events on the business model."[13]

On the contrary, we take the position that "defective information flow, defective analytical tools and inability to bring insightful judgement in the interpretation of information and the impact of market events on the business model" are mainstream issues for internal audit to comment upon. It follows that internal audit was ineffective in its assurance role at communicating persuasively to top management and the board the risks that financial institutions were running. Internal auditors in nonfinancial entities were ineffective at communicating to their top managements and boards the risks that those entities were running through their excessive dependence on precarious financial institutions.

MAKING IT HAPPEN

Key "learning" points for finance professionals, as well as ideas and issues for action or further consideration:

- Take compliance requirements seriously.
- Consider the costs of compliance when deciding whether to list or delist in the US.
- Don't leave new compliance requirements to the last moment.
- Consider using your internal audit function in the initial stages of implementing new compliance obligations.
- Remember that internal audit should be independent of the activities upon which it provides assurance.
- In time, transfer compliance responsibilities to line management and away from internal audit.
- Accept that internal audit adds value when assurance over operational efficiency and effectiveness along with assurance of compliance with laws, regulations, and policies are both "in scope"—not just assurance of control over financial reporting.
- Accept that internal audit also adds value when it is available to provide consulting services to management.
- Consider whether internal audit is sufficiently independent of management to provide valuable assurance to the board and its audit committee.

MORE INFO

Reports:

Financial Reporting Council. "The Combined Code on Corporate Governance." June 2008. Online at: www.frc.org.uk/documents/pagemanager/frc/Combined_Code_June_2008

Financial Reporting Council. "Internal control—Revised guidance for directors on the Combined Code." October 2005. Online at: www.frc.org.uk/documents/pagemanager/frc/Revised%20Turnbull%20Guidance%20October%202005.pdf

Financial Reporting Council. "The Turnbull guidance as an evaluation framework for the purposes of Section 404(a) of the Sarbanes–Oxley Act." December 2004. Online at: www.frc.org.uk/documents/pagemanager/frc/draft_guide.pdf

"Bureaucratic and risk-averse environments are career killers because of their impact on learning." John P. Kotter

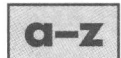

Public Companies Accounting Oversight Board (PCAOB). "Auditing Standard No. 5: An audit of internal control over financial reporting that is integrated with an audit of financial statements." 2007. Online at: www.pcaobus.org/Standards/Standards_and_Related_Rules/Auditing_Standard_No.5.aspx

US Securities & Exchange Commission. "Commission guidance regarding management's report on internal control over financial reporting under Section 13(a) or 15(d) of the Securities Exchange Act of 1934." June 20, 2007. Online at: www.sec.gov/rules/final/2007/33-8809.pdf

Website:

Institute of Internal Auditors: www.theiia.org

This Florida-based website is a fund of information. In particular "Sarbanes-Oxley Section 404: A guide for management by internal controls practitioners" (2nd ed, January 2008) at www.theiia.org/download.cfm?file=31866 [PDF]. The Institute's bimonthly membership newsletter, *AuditWire*, is available in electronic form to IIA members and subscribers on its website and via e-mail. The IIA runs Global Audit Information Network (GAIN)—a very effective and economic online benchmarking service for internal audit functions. More information at www.theiia.org/guidance/benchmarking/gain

See Also:

★ Understanding the Requirements for Preparing IFRS Financial Statements (pp. 423–424)
✔ International Financial Reporting Standards (IFRS): The Basics (p. 1039)
✔ Key Accounting Standards and Organizations (p. 1040)
✔ Sarbanes–Oxley: Its Development and Aims (p. 1052)
✔ The Ten Accounting Principles (p. 1055)
✔ Understanding Internal Audits (p. 1057)
Financial Accounting and Reporting (p. 1356)

NOTES

1 Further sets might, for instance, have been in the areas of fraud investigations, IT auditing, governmental internal auditing, and auditing in financial institutions.

2 The IIA's definition of internal auditing, to be found within its *Standards*.

3 Brune, Christina. "Consulting: Friend or foe?" *AuditWire* 25:1 (January–February 2003).

4 Quotes from Peter Rodgers (vice president and general auditor of BISYS Group Inc. in Columbus, Ohio) as being against consulting services, and Geraldine Gail (director of internal audit, the University of California, Santa Cruz) as being in favor, in: Brune, Christina "Consulting: Friend or foe?" *AuditWire* 25:1 (January–February 2003).

5 Committee of Sponsoring Organizations (COSO) (www.coso.org). *Internal Control—Integrated Framework*. AICPA, 1992. (Available at www.cpa2biz.com).

6 Executive Summary to *Internal Control—Integrated Framework*, p. 4.

7 Financial Reporting Council (2010): The UK Corporate Governance Code, 2010, Code Provision C.2.2 (www.frc.org.uk).

8 Speech on compensation culture delivered at the Institute of Public Policy Research, University College, London, on May 26, 2005. www.number10.gov.uk/output/Page7562.asp.

9 In particular, PCAOB Auditing Standard No. 5 replacing the more demanding Standard No. 2.

10 PCAOB Auditing Standard No. 2 (2004): "A control deficiency (or a combination of internal control deficiencies) should be classified as a *significant deficiency* if, by itself or in combination with other control deficiencies, it results in more than a remote likelihood of a misstatement of the company's annual or interim financial statements that is more than inconsequential will not be prevented or detected." This statement has been replaced by PCAOB Auditing Standard No. 5 (2007): "A *significant deficiency* is a deficiency, or a combination of deficiencies, in internal control over financial reporting that is less severe than a material weakness, yet important enough to merit attention by those responsible for oversight of the company's financial reporting."

11 PCAOB Auditing Standard No. 2 (2004): "A significant deficiency should be classified as a *material weakness* if, by itself or in combination with other control deficiencies, it results in more than a remote likelihood that a material misstatement in the company's annual or interim financial statements will not be prevented or detected." This has been replaced by PCAOB Auditing Standard No. 5 (2007): "A *material weakness* is a deficiency, or a combination of deficiencies, in internal control over financial reporting, such that there is a *reasonable possibility* that a material misstatement of the company's annual or interim financial statements will not be prevented or detected on a timely basis ... A material weakness in internal control over financial reporting may exist even when financial statements are not materially misstated."

12 Until 2007, the PCAOB interpreted Section 404 as requiring a "triple audit"—(1) the traditional audit of the financial statements, (2) an attestation that management have done what they are required to do under SEC rules to assess and certify the effectiveness of internal control over financial reporting, and (3) the external auditor's own assessment of the effectiveness of internal control over financial reporting. In fact, a careful reading of Section 404 indicates that the Act only required (1) and (2). Post 2007 requirements under the SOX-Lite regime mean that PCAOB Auditing Standard No. 5 continues with (1) and (3) (above)—a surprising interpretation by PCAOB, but one that preserves a maximum of the extra fee-earning opportunity that Section 404 has given external auditors.

13 HM Treasury. "A review of corporate governance in UK banks and other financial industry entities—Final recommendations." (Walker Report). November 26, 2009. pp. 90, 93. Online at: www.hm-treasury.gov.uk/d/walker_review_261109.pdf

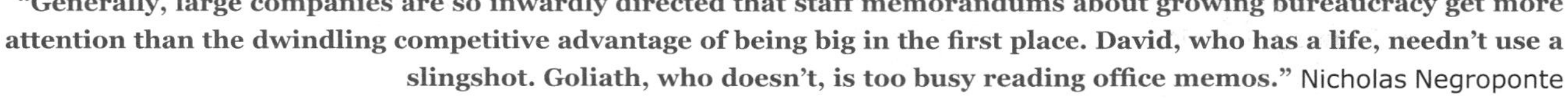

"Generally, large companies are so inwardly directed that staff memorandums about growing bureaucracy get more attention than the dwindling competitive advantage of being big in the first place. David, who has a life, needn't use a slingshot. Goliath, who doesn't, is too busy reading office memos." Nicholas Negroponte

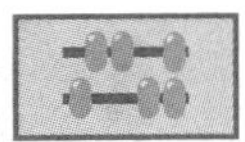

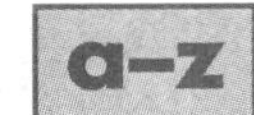

How Can Internal Audit Report Effectively to Its Stakeholders? by Andrew Cox

EXECUTIVE SUMMARY

- Internal audit has a range of stakeholders who rely on its work, seeking assurance that the organization is running well and that there are effective controls in place.
- Internal audit has a responsibility to its stakeholders to provide reports on the operation of the organization's risk management, control, and governance processes. It also has a responsibility to justify the value of its work and the organization's spending on internal audit resources.
- Internal audit can report on its work to its stakeholders by:
  - reporting on the outcomes of its internal audit work;
  - reporting on the quality of its internal audit work.
- Together, these elements combine to provide stakeholders with an overall view of the effectiveness of internal audit; one without the other will only provide a partial reporting structure.

INTRODUCTION

Internal audit has a variety of stakeholders who rely on its work. These include: the board of directors; the audit committee; the chief executive officer; senior executives such as the chief financial officer, chief information officer, chief risk officer, etc.; the external auditors; in some cases, regulatory bodies; and stockholders—who, in the case of government organizations, could be the public.

All these stakeholders are seeking assurance that the organization is running well, and that effective controls are in place and operating properly. Internal audit has an important role to play in providing assurance to these stakeholders, but the trick is how to report the results of its work to them effectively.

ASSURANCE MODELS

Assurance can be equated with the term governance, the four pillars of a good corporate governance framework being—according to the Institute of Internal Auditors—executive management, the audit committee, external audit, and internal audit. Each of these elements relies to an extent on the others, and they all need to be operating effectively to provide overall assurance to stakeholders.

The board of directors will generally want to see a combined assurance model in place for the organization that provides three lines of defense, as shown in Table 1. This demonstrates the interdependencies between the four pillars of good corporate governance and the three lines of defense that go to make up a combined assurance model.

Table 1. Combined assurance model with three lines of defense. (*Source*: National Australia Bank, with amendment)

First line of defense	Second line of defense	Third line of defense
Management controls	**Management of risk**	**Independent assurance**
Real-time focus	Real-time focus + review focus of 1st line	Review focus of 1st and 2nd line
Elements	***Elements***	***Elements***
Policies and procedures Internal controls	Risk management Legal department	External audit Internal audit
Role	***Role***	***Role***
Review compliance Implement improvements	Confirm compliance Recommend improvements[a]	Independently confirm compliance Recommend improvements

REPORTING ON THE OUTCOMES OF INTERNAL AUDIT WORK

A model for reporting the outcomes of internal audit work could be based on the following four elements: internal audit reports, recommendations for improvement, a communication strategy, and an annual internal audit report. These are discussed below.

Internal Audit Reports

Internal audit reports are the most important part of the work of an internal audit function. The report is the culmination of the effort directed toward an audit of a part of the organization. Internal audit can be a costly resource, so reports of its work should demonstrate its value to the organization. Internal audit reports need to be:

- Timely: reports should be issued in a timely manner.
- Accurate: reports should contain accurate information.
- Logical: reports should be logical and valid.
- Clear: reports should be clearly written and easily understood.
- Purposeful: reports should state why the internal audit was performed.
- Written with the audience in mind: reports should be written to suit the intended reader.

The power of a tick cannot be underestimated—it provides balance to an internal audit report. People do not go to work to do a bad job, and they appreciate recognition of good work. What they do not appreciate is an audit report that is negative by exception, says nothing positive, and effectively just gives them stick. So, acknowledge good work, and always say something positive in the report—and not begrudgingly.

Internal audit reports need to tell a story and be insightful. Merely telling people what is wrong cannot be seen as a good use of internal audit resources. That is the easy work, and does not reflect well on internal auditing as a profession. The real value of the work of internal audit comes from an emphasis on cause and effect. It is easy work to find the effect, but much more difficult to ascertain the root cause. Because of this, many internal auditors take the easy way out and just report on what has been found to be operating ineffectively.

Many internal audits could provide additional value to the organization if there was more emphasis on efficiency, effectiveness, economy, and organizational outcomes, with a view to assisting the organization further to improve and streamline business processes.

Recommendations for Improvement

Internal audit reports need to contain recommendations for improvement if they are to have any point. And the recommendations need to be targeted at correcting the root cause.

Locating the cause provides information on accountability relationships, and provides the basis for making improvements. It is important not just to find that something is wrong, but to work out what caused

"Internal auditors now must work to improve the performance of their employer as well as ensuring their conformance." Christopher McRostie

        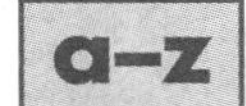

it to be wrong. This can prevent similar problems from happening again. Each recommendation needs to include:

- Whether it is agreed with or not by the audit customer (and if not, why not).
- What the audit customer is going to do about it (action plan).
- By what date the action will be implemented and completed.
- Who will be responsible for implementing the recommendation.

Recommendations contained in internal audit reports also need to be risk rated. In this way, management with the responsibility to implement remedial action will know which recommendations are most important and should be implemented first.

An important task of the internal audit function is to ensure that agreed recommendations arising from internal audit reports are satisfactorily actioned within a reasonable time-frame. If this is not done, its work will be virtually worthless. Many internal audit functions adopt an approach whereby:

- Agreed recommendations from internal audit, external audit, and regulatory bodies are entered into a tracking system and monitored on an ongoing basis by internal audit and the audit committee.
- Management responsible for implementing the recommendations is required to advise internal audit when this is complete, or to provide periodic reports on progress where this may be over a longer period of time.
- Overdue recommendations are reported to the audit committee.
- Internal audit periodically follows up to ensure that implementation has occurred as reported by management. This can be by 100% follow-up, by following up only those recommendations of higher risk, or by following up on a sample basis. A full follow-up audit is not generally necessary.

One point worthy of consideration is the necessity to cover off risks if recommendations are not actioned within a reasonable time-frame. Where a recommendation relates to a higher-risk problem and is not dealt with quickly, the chief audit executive should ask:

- Why has it not been actioned?
- Should the risk rating assigned to the recommendation be increased?
- What fall-back or interim risk management procedures have been put in place to mitigate the risks associated with nonimplementation of the recommendation?
- Should management make a statement accepting the risk associated with nonimplementation of the recommendation?

This information should be reported to each meeting of the audit committee.

Communication Strategy

To develop and maintain a profile within an organization, internal audit should take steps to improve its communication in order to make itself more visible to the wider organization. Some ways in which internal audit might do this include:

Raising awareness

- Have information about internal audit and its achievements posted on the organization's intranet.
- Distribute a small brochure about internal audit, what it does, and its achievements.
- Further develop relationships with stakeholders by making presentations on the work of internal audit to groups within the organization's corporate environment.
- Prepare an annual internal audit report on its activities.

Engaging management

- Consult with internal audit customers prior to the commencement of each internal audit, and request their input to the objectives and scope of the audit.
- Facilitate a risk workshop with internal audit customers in the planning phase of each internal audit.
- When conducting internal audits, internal auditors should spend most of their time in the work areas of their internal audit customers, rather than in the internal audit work area.
- At the completion of internal audit fieldwork, hold a workshop with the audit customer to discuss and agree possible improvement options.
- Provide a balanced reporting format by reporting on what management is doing well, in addition to identifying opportunities for improvement.

Providing value-add

- Plan for each internal audit with a wider view by encompassing objectives relating to efficiency, effectiveness, economy, and organizational outcomes.
- Have involvement in working groups related to strategic developments within the organization in an observer/adviser capacity. It is considered best practice for internal audit to contribute to such forums by providing opinions, and ensuring that controls are considered and built-in to projects and systems under development, rather than after the event via post-implementation reviews, without necessarily compromising the integrity of later audits.

Annual Internal Audit Report

In some organizations, best practice extends to providing the audit committee and management with an annual report of internal audit activities featuring:

- Achievements in the year.
- Analysis of systemic issues identified through the work of internal audit.
- An opinion on the organization's overall risk management, control, and governance environment.

This can provide additional assurance to the audit committee, as well as being beneficial in alerting management to issues and risks identified in internal audits but which may also be occurring in other business areas.

REPORTING ON THE QUALITY OF INTERNAL AUDIT WORK

A model for reporting on the quality of internal audit work could be based on the following four elements: a quality assurance and improvement program, performance

CASE STUDY

Measurement of the Internal Audit Function

The chief audit executive of an organization in Brisbane Australia was seeking ways to measure the work of his internal audit function. He knew that internal audit was doing a good job, but he did not have the evidence to prove it. In thinking how to address this problem, he designed KPIs against which his internal audit function could demonstrate its performance to the audit committee and the organization (Table 2). After all, internal audit assesses the performance of other areas of the organization, so why should it be exempt from having its own performance examined?

The chief audit executive considered these to be the KPIs the audit committee would be interested in to provide an overall assessment of the work of internal audit, and when he asked the audit committee, they agreed. He discounted KPIs such as the number of internal audit recommendations, or the number of internal audit hours delivered, since these can be manipulated and would therefore have little credibility with the committee.

"**Internal audit needs to prove its value to its organization. Otherwise what is the good of it?**" Nigel Morgan

  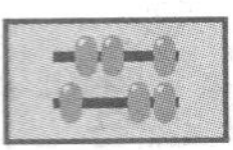   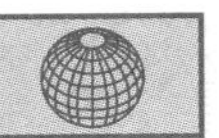   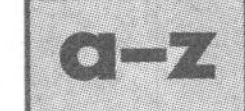

Table 2. KPIs prepared by the chief audit executive to assess internal audit. (*Source*: National Australia Bank, with amendment)

	Key performance indicator	Measure	Target	Frequency
	1. Completion of *Internal Audit Plan*			
1.1	Complete planned internal audits as per the approved *Internal Audit Plan* (subject to approved plan amendments)	% of planned internal audits completed within the financial year	95%	Annually
1.2	Complete special and ad hoc management-initiated internal audits and investigations in addition to scheduled internal audits (an allowance for this is contained in the *Internal Audit Plan*)	% of allowance utilized for unplanned ad hoc and management-initiated internal audits and investigations	95%	Annually
1.3	Approved *Internal Audit Plan* to be completed within the approved internal audit budget	% variance from approved budget for the financial year	5%	Annually
	2. Implementation of internal audit recommendations			
2.1	Internal audit recommendations accepted by management	% of recommendations accepted by management (subject to internal audit independence being maintained)	95%	Annually
2.2	Monitor the implementation status of internal audit recommendations by management and report outcomes to the audit committee	Updated status obtained from responsible managers and reported to the audit committee	Quarterly status reports delivered	Quarterly
	3. Formal survey feedback			
3.1	Results of customer feedback surveys following each internal audit	% of survey responses of good or better (averaged)	90%	Annually
3.2	Result of annual feedback survey of members of the audit committee	% of survey responses of good or better (averaged)	90%	Annually
	4. Independent quality review of internal audit			
4.1	Result of external quality assessment of internal audit in accordance with *The International Standards for Professional Practice of Internal Auditing*	Report issued detailing results of review	Consistent with better practice	Five-Yearly

measures, review by external audit, and review by regulatory bodies.

Quality Assurance and Improvement Program

The "International Standards for the Professional Practice of Internal Auditing" issued by the Institute of Internal Auditors requires every internal audit function to operate a quality assurance program:

"The chief audit executive must develop and maintain a quality assurance and improvement program that covers all aspects of internal audit activity."

A quality assurance and improvement program is designed to enable an evaluation of internal audit's conformance with the Definition of Internal Auditing and the Standards, and an evaluation of whether internal auditors apply the Code of Ethics. The program also assesses the efficiency and effectiveness of internal audit and identifies opportunities for improvement.

This program should include both internal and external assessments. Internal assessments comprise: ongoing monitoring of the performance of the internal audit activity; and periodic reviews performed through self-assessment or by other persons within the organization with sufficient knowledge of internal audit practices.

External assessments must be conducted at least once every five years by a qualified, independent reviewer or review team from outside the organization. The chief audit executive must discuss with the board the need for more frequent external assessments; and the qualifications and independence of the external reviewer or review team, including any potential conflict of interest. The chief audit executive must communicate the results of the quality assurance and improvement program to senior management and the board.

Performance Measures

Best practice in internal auditing suggests that, like most business units in an organization, internal audit should have performance measures or key performance indicators (KPIs) in place to demonstrate its own level of performance. Best practice also suggests that performance measures need to be specific (clear and concise), measurable (quantifiable), achievable (practical and reasonable), relevant (to users), and timed (having a range or time limit). For more on this, see the case study.

Review by External Audit

As part of its annual external audit of an organization, the external auditors will usually assess the internal audit function on such matters as its organizational status, scope of function, technical competence,

MAKING IT HAPPEN

The chief audit executive should develop effective reporting mechanisms with the audit committee and other stakeholders. Key reporting tools include:

- Insightful internal audit reports.
- Monitoring of internal audit recommendations, and periodic follow-up to ensure that recommendations have been implemented effectively and in a timely way.
- An internal audit communication strategy.
- An annual internal audit report that covers achievements in the year, an analysis of systemic issues identified through the work of internal audit, and an opinion
- on the organization's overall risk management, control, and governance environment.
- on the organization's overall risk management, control, and governance environment.
- A quality assurance and improvement program that incorporates both internal and external assessments.
- Key performance indicators measuring the performance of internal audit.
- Periodic review of internal audit by external auditors and, where applicable, regulatory bodies.

"The process of developing and monitoring metrics for internal audit can serve as an effective marketing tool for the internal audit function." *Internal Auditor* magazine

        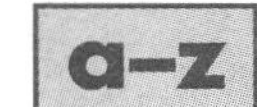

and due professional care exercised in its work.

Review by Regulatory Bodies

In many countries, regulatory bodies review the competency and work of internal audit as part of their periodic regulatory review of an organization. These are generally restricted to particular industry groups, for example financial institutions.

CONCLUSION

Internal audit has a responsibility to its stakeholders to provide reports on the operations of the organization's risk management, control, and governance processes. It also has a responsibility to justify the value of its work and the organization's spending on internal audit resources.

Internal audit can do this in two ways:

- By reporting on the outcomes of its internal audit work.
- By reporting on the quality of its internal audit work.

MORE INFO

Books:

Reding, Kurt F., Paul J. Sobel, Urton L. Anderson, Michael J. Head, Sridhar Ramamoorti, Mark Salamasick, and Cris Riddle. *Internal Auditing: Assurance and Consulting Services*. 2nd ed. Orlando, FL: IIA Research Foundation, 2009.

Sawyer, Lawrence B., Mortimer A. Dittenhofer, and James H. Scheiner. *Sawyer's Internal Auditing: The Practice of Modern Internal Auditing*. Altamonte Springs, FL: IIA, 2003.

Report:

Australian National Audit Office. "Public sector internal audit: An investment in assurance and business improvement." Better Practice Guide. September 2007. Online at: www.anao.gov.au/uploads/documents/Public_Sector_Internal_Audit.pdf

Standards:

Institute of Internal Auditors. "International standards for the professional practice of internal auditing." October 2010. Online at: www.theiia.org/guidance/standards-and-guidance/ippf/standards

Websites:

Institute of Internal Auditors: www.theiia.org

Institute of Internal Auditors—Australia: www.iia.org.au

See Also:

★ Engaging Senior Management in Internal Control (pp. 336–337)
★ Implementing an Effective Internal Controls System (pp. 361–364)
★ Internal Audit and Partnering with Senior Management (pp. 368–371)
★ Managing the Relationships between Audit Committees and the CAE (pp. 375–377)
★ New Assurance Challenges Facing Chief Audit Executives (pp. 378–381)
★ Optimizing Internal Audit (pp. 382–384)
✔ Understanding Internal Audits (p. 1057)

"The bureaucratic method of building an integrated Europe has exhausted its potential." George Soros

How Internal Auditing Can Help with a Company's Fraud Issues by Gail Harden

EXECUTIVE SUMMARY

- Fraud risk exposure should be assessed periodically by an organization to identify specific potential schemes and events for which it needs to have controls in place to mitigate risks.
- Internal audit serves as a critical defense against the threat of fraud, with a focus on assessing and monitoring controls designed to prevent and detect fraud.
- Internal auditors can be part of fraud deterrence by examining the adequacy of the system of internal controls.

INTRODUCTION

Regulatory oversight is increasing, as are penalties. A passive attitude in an organization toward oversight and the topic of fraud, antifraud programs, and controls would be a strong indicator of a significant deficiency in its system of internal controls.

Economic factors can increase the occurrence of fraudulent practices. When the economy is in a downturn the risk of fraud increases due to personal financial pressures, the stagnation of compensation, and corporate stabilization strategies.[1] Problems associated with corporate stabilization strategies include:

- fewer personnel and fear of downsizing;
- increased workloads;
- less accuracy;
- less time to make decisions;
- shortcuts taken to circumvent controls;
- low morale;
- likelihood of "cooking the books" to meet performance goals.

Additionally, corporations expand into foreign markets to reduce costs, which can lead to less transparency, stretched resources, and corrupt practices.

FRAUD AND FRAUD RISK ASSESSMENT DEFINED

Fraud is defined as the use of dishonesty, deception, or false representation in order to gain a material advantage or injure the interests of others. Types of fraud include false accounting, theft, third party or investment fraud, collusion between employees, and computer fraud. Fraud risk assessment is a structured approach to identify and analyze fraud risk and controls in an organization, and to assess whether those controls are working as intended. PricewaterhouseCoopers (PwC) explained:

"Fraud risk assessment expands upon traditional risk assessment. It is scheme and scenario based rather than based on control risk or inherent risk. The assessment considers the various ways that fraud and misconduct can occur by and against the company. Fraud risk assessment also considers vulnerability to management override and potential schemes to circumvent existing control activities, which may require additional compensating control activities."[2]

WHY SHOULD INTERNAL AUDIT PERFORM FRAUD RISK ASSESSMENT?

The Institute of Internal Auditors (IIA) sets forth professional standards that require internal auditors to assess the risks facing their organizations. Furthermore, internal audit is expected to evaluate whether the company's controls sufficiently address identified risks of material misstatement in financial reporting due to fraud.

Internal audit participates in fraud deterrence by examining and evaluating the adequacy of internal controls. By merely asking such questions, internal audit makes it known that it is on the lookout for possible fraud schemes. Internal audit reports to the audit committee and management on the functioning of internal controls in relation to fraud risk, thus facilitating adherence to financial reporting and corporate governance responsibilities.

The audit committee has responsibilities of fiduciary oversight to consider:

- the process utilized to identify, document, and evaluate fraud risk;
- types of fraud identified;
- the level of likelihood and significance of fraud;
- appropriate action taken to close any gaps in the existence and operation of controls;
- opportunities for override of controls by management.

PROCESS OVERVIEW

The fraud risk assessment process is a structured method to identify possible fraud schemes, identify internal controls that help

Figure 1. The fraud risk assessment process

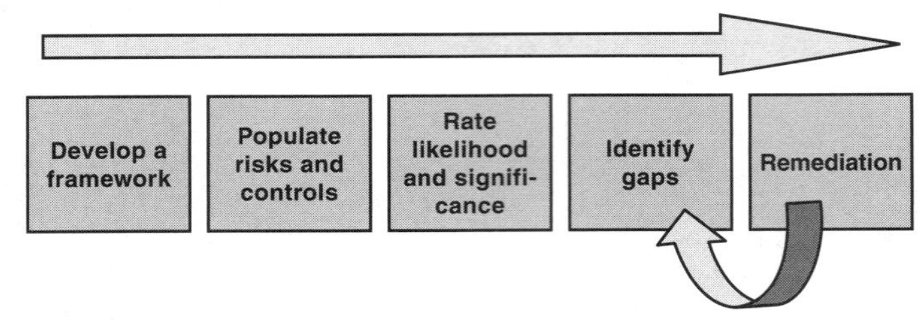

Figure 2. Rating the likelihood and significance of risk

Likelihood and significance
(gray = higher risk)

Risks

#1 – Shell company scheme
#2 – Overpayment scheme
#3 – Phony contractor scheme
#4 – Personal travel expenses
#5 – Fraudulent auditor/inspector expenses
#6 – Check tampering
#7 – Orders for personal supplies

	#6			
			#4	
		#1		
	#2		#5	
#7				

Likelihood (horizontal axis); Significance (vertical axis)

Table 1. Example of a fraud risk assessment framework

Fraud Risk Assessment			Accounts Receivable			Process Owner: < Insert Process Owner Name >		
Fraud Risk	**Likelihood**	**Significance**	**Control Activity**	**Preventive or Detective**	**Has Audit tested Control?**	**Date tested**	**Result**	**Action Plan**
Theft of cash receipts and written off as bad debts.	High	High	Reconciliation of bad debt expense reserve with supervisory review.	Detective	Yes	1/10/06	OK	
Person posting receivables does not also have system access to make journal entries to bad debt expense.	Preventative	Yes	1/10/06	OK				
Procedure exists and is followed to turn over delinquent accounts to a third-party collections agency.	Preventative	Yes	1/10/06	OK				
Accounts receivables reconciled to the general ledger by individual with no conflicting duties.	Detective	Yes	1/10/06	OK				
Accounting Manager authorization required to write off uncollectible accounts.	Preventative	Yes	1/10/06	OK				
Rebilling of past due items to change the # of days past due (To change DSO's for example).	Medium	Medium	Policy disallows cancelling and rebilling invoices unless the original was billed to the wrong client, or some other extenuating circumstances.	Preventative	Yes			
All credits require the use of a request form and approval from management according to an authorization matrix.	Preventative	Yes	1/10/06	OK				
Duties to input billing and credits to the AR system, approvals for credits, and collections activities are segregated.	Preventative	Yes	1/10/06	OK				
Kitting – writing checks against insufficient funds or unavailable funds and hoping the funds are deposited or become available before the checks clear the account.	Medium	Low	The Accounting Manager has a "cash card" where cash receipts and disbursements are logged. He monitors the cash level and transfers money from savings when necessary to cover disbursements. The Controller approves the disbursement batches and also has access to monitor the daily cash position.	Preventative	Yes	1/10/06	OK	
ZBA Accounts – type of bank account where funds are transferred from a deposit account to a disbursement account as disbursements are presented for payment.	Preventative				Company does not currently use ZBA accounts.			
Positive pay set up with the bank. This is a practice where the company sends a file to the bank of all the disbursements generated and the bank will only pay those that are on the file.	Preventative				Company is in progress to set up this type of arrangement.			

Table 2. Identifying control gaps and recommending remediation plans

Control Activity	Preventive or Detective	Has Audit Tested Control?	Date tested	Result	Action Plan
Reconciliation of bad debt expense reserve with supervisory review.	Detective	Yes	1/10/2006	Failed	No supervisory review, effective April 11, 2008, now have supervisory review.
Person posting receivables does not also have system access to make journal entries to bad debt expense.	Preventive	Yes	1/10/2006	OK	
Procedure exists and is followed to turn over delinquent accounts to a third-party collections agency.	Preventive	Yes	1/10/2006	OK	
Accounts receivable reconciled to the general ledger by individual with no conflicting duties.	Detective	Yes	1/10/2006	Failed	AR account reconciled but contained variances. Account to be reconciled and reviewed by August 31, 2008. Owner: Corporate Controller.
Accounting manager authorization required to write off uncollectible accounts.	Preventive	Yes	1/10/2006	OK	
Policy disallows cancelling and rebilling invoices unless the original was billed to the wrong client, or some other extenuating circumstances.	Preventive	No			

to prevent or detect identified fraud schemes, document the results of testing the controls, and implement corrective action plans where needed. The objective of this process is to identify the existence of controls and how they operate, not necessarily to seek out fraud. Adequate controls reduce the opportunities for fraud to be committed. The assessment considers the various ways in which a company can be subjected to fraud and misconduct, along with its vulnerability to management override and other potential schemes to circumvent existing controls.

Fraud risk assessment is a continuous process, as shown in Figure 1.

Process Steps

The steps in the process are:

- develop a framework (i.e. a format);
- identify risks and controls;
- rate the likelihood and significance of the risks;
- identify gaps;
- plan and implement remedial measures.

The process should follow the approach recommended by the Committee of Sponsoring Organizations (COSO).[3] This includes:

- setting the "tone at the top," instituting a code of ethics, and setting up a whistleblower hotline;
- monitoring effectiveness;
- communication;
- identifying risks;
- linking risks and controls.

OTHER FRAUD PREVENTION AND DETECTION ACTIVITIES

The following control activities meet the COSO element of "tone at the top," a code of ethics, and whistleblower hotlines:

- company ethics and anti-fraud policy/program;

CASE STUDY

To understand the process better, consider the following approach taken by a specific company.

Develop a Framework

Development of a framework consists of selecting the business processes to assess, determining the automation tool to use, and setting up the layout using such a tool. The layout should include the identified potential fraud schemes, an evaluation of the likelihood and significance of the risks, controls to prevent or detect the risks, the type of control, whether the control has been tested, the date of the test and the results, and corrective action plans. Table 1 shows an Excel worksheet utilized by the company in our case study.

The business processes assessed by this company were financial reporting, business development, sales, billing, accounts receivable, cash receipts, purchasing, accounts payable, payroll, inventory and shipping, officers' expenses, and entity level controls. Revenue recognition and management override controls are of particular concern, and they fall under financial reporting controls. All processes were also assessed and organized according to the business location to which the processes have been decentralized.

Balance sheet and expense accounts should be identified as they relate to each of the business processes. Mapping accounts to the processes can be useful in determining the financial impact of a particular process by business location. For example, locations with higher revenue have a higher financial impact on the Revenue Recognition Process.

Identify Risks and Controls

The next step is to populate the framework with fraud schemes (risks) and controls. To identify potential fraud schemes and best practice controls requires extensive research. Examples of resources are, but are not limited to, seminars and conferences, articles and white papers from experts such as the Institute of Internal Auditors, Deloitte, KPMG (or other CPA (certified public accountant) firms—these were used in the case example), business periodicals and journals, and the American Institute of Certified Public Accountants (AICPA).

It is important to choose controls that can be tested. For example, a third-party control cannot be tested. Reliance on external audit to find an error, or customer complaints, are examples of inadequate controls. No controls exist that provide absolute assurance against fraud. Individuals who are sufficiently motivated will find a way to override or circumvent controls. Even so, controls are a vital part of fraud deterrence. Auditors should continually ask themselves: "How could someone get around this control?" The general expectation of internal auditors is that they have sufficient knowledge to identify indicators of fraud, but they are not expected to have the expertise of a person whose primary responsibility is detecting and investigating fraud.

Rate the Likelihood and Significance of Risks

Risks should be rated by likelihood and significance. The objective of a risk rating is to narrow down and prioritize the controls to test. Process owners/managers should be interviewed or surveyed to evaluate risk ranking.

"It is always right to detect a fraud, and to perceive a folly; but it is very often wrong to expose either. A man of business should always have his eyes open, but must often seem to have them shut." Philip Stanhope

- fraud response policy and procedure;
- active participation and support from management and the board of directors;
- conducting background investigations prior to employment for senior and sensitive positions;
- ethics and fraud awareness training.

These topics and other related controls constitute what is referred to as "entity level controls." Table 3 shows the fraud risk assessment for entity-level controls.

CONCLUSION

An article in *Business Finance* in May 2008 (Skalak, 2008) stated that the average cost of one incident of fraud is US$3 million. Fast-growing companies are more susceptible to fraud. As they expand into new markets, acquire new operations, and enter joint ventures these companies become more vulnerable.

Internal audit is in a key position to lead the fraud risk assessment process as it has extensive knowledge of the company and direct lines of communication with management and the audit committee, as well as experience, training and a structured approach to identify and evaluate. Internal audit has a responsibility to assist the audit committee to carry out its fiduciary duties. Fraud risk is a key area of responsibility of the audit committee. According to a PwC white paper:

"For internal audit, this environment poses both opportunities and challenges. Corporate auditors who move quickly to develop antifraud action plans will find ample ways to provide added value to their organizations. Conversely, internal audit directors who fail to address rising stakeholder expectations jeopardize their relevance and imperil their job security."[4]

Internal audit's work on fraud risk assessment can add value to the organization. The following comment was cited in a *Business Finance* article in August of 2007. Larry Harrington, Vice-president of Internal Audit at Raytheon, was quoted as saying:

"We're building relationships within the engineering, supply chain, contracts, and other areas of the company that we might not otherwise have worked with that often,

Likelihood can be assessed based on three levels: "remote," "more than remote/reasonably probable," and "probable." Likelihood could be evaluated based on previous experience and past audit results.

Significance can be determined by using the standards "inconsequential," "more than inconsequential," and "material." Materiality can be based on financial impact, reputation risk, and/or shareholder or lender considerations. Management determines the organization's risk appetite—the amount of risk the company is willing to accept as a consequence of doing business.

In our case study, the described levels equated to "low," "medium," and "high."

In our case study, the company rated likelihood and significance on a scale of 1 to 5, 1 representing the least risk or significance. The chart shown in Figure 2 was used to display the rating results graphically. Risks falling in the gray blocks require higher priority. In this example, risk #7, Orders for personal supplies, had a rating of 1 for likelihood and 1 for significance, thus placing it in the lower left-hand corner. Risk #4 had a rating of 4 under likelihood and 4 for significance, and so on. Risks falling closer to the top right-hand corner are the highest risks and should receive highest focus and priority.

Identify Control Gaps

Risks and controls have been identified and populated into the spreadsheet. The next step is to identify control gaps and weaknesses. Identifying control gaps and weaknesses meets the COSO element of "monitoring effectiveness." Generally, the information needed to document whether the controls exist and are working as intended comes from operational internal audits, external audits, direct testing, or any other regulatory testing.

Remediation

Remediation plans meet the COSO element of "communication." Missing controls, or controls not working as intended and the related corrective action plans, are communicated to the process owners and company management, as well as to the audit committee. The case example tracks all the corrective action plans utilizing a Microsoft Access database. Action plans not completed by the due date are reported to the audit committee.

Refer to Table 2 for an example of the section of the fraud risk assessment worksheet (Table 1) related to the testing of controls and setting out corrective action plans for remediation.

Ongoing Monitoring

In order to meet the COSO element of "monitoring effectiveness," the content of the framework should be regularly revisited to determine whether there are any new weaknesses, risks, or controls, and to take into account any changes in the internal and external environments. In conjunction with operational audits and other testing of controls, current data are entered for test results and corrective action plans.

Table 3. Fraud risk assessment for entity-level controls

Fraud Risk Assessment		General Fraud Controls—"Entity Level"		Process Owner: Board of Directors	
Control Activity	**Preventive or Detective**	**Has Audit tested Control?**	**Date tested**	**Result**	**Action Plan**
Code of Ethics—communicated, training, monitoring	Preventive	Yes	2/1/2007	OK	
Background investigation when hiring	Preventive	Yes	2/1/2007	OK	
Ethics hotline and whistleblower program	Detective			OK	
Defined process for investigation of alleged fraud	Detective				
IT controls—system access, fraud detection & monitoring, controls to prevent inappropriate computer modifications and overrides by IT	Both	Yes	Annual	NI	IT Strategic Plan
Documented antifraud policies and procedures, Code of Ethics/Conduct, and hiring and promotion standards	Preventive		2/1/2007	OK	
Promoting antifraud programs through the organization's communication programs	Preventive				
Segregation of duties	Preventive				
Audit Committee is actively overseeing fraud prevention programs and incident investigations	Preventive	Yes	2/1/2007	OK	
Internal Audit assess and tests controls for fraud risk in the organization	Detective	n/a	n/a	n/a	

NI: Needs improvement

"Some cursed fraud of enemy hath beguiled thee, yet unknown, and me with thee hath ruined." John Milton, *Paradise Lost*

  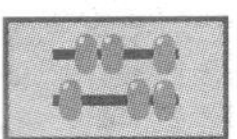      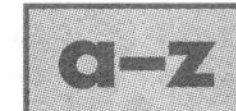

and folks who did not work with us that often might have had a perception of internal audit as the people who stab the wounded and beat up the dead. When you work with the rest of the business on a project like this, they see our talent, energy, and passion in a much more positive light."[5]

MAKING IT HAPPEN

The following are keys for success:

- A planned and documented approach, based on COSO recommendations, that integrates fraud risk assessment with operational and other audits.
- Active involvement from management.
- Consideration of specific potential fraud schemes for each business process and for general ledger accounts.
- Mapping of fraud risks and schemes to control activities.
- Assessment of fraud risks by likelihood and significance.
- Making fraud risk assessment an ongoing process.

MORE INFO

Articles:

Krell, Eric. "The awakening." *Business Finance* (August 2007). Online at: businessfinancemag.com/article/awakening-0801

Skalak, Steven. "Up for grabs." *Business Finance* (May 2008). Online at: businessfinancemag.com/article/grabs-0503

Wells, Joseph T. "New approaches to fraud deterrence: It's time to take a new look at the auditing process." *Journal of Accountancy* 197 (February 2004). Online at: tinyurl.com/ycpd7f2

Reports:

Deloitte Forensic Center. "Ten things about fraud control: How executives view the "fraud control gap'." November 2007.

KPMG. "Fraud risk management: Developing a strategy for prevention, detection, and response." 2006.

PricewaterhouseCoopers. "Key elements of antifraud programs and controls." White Paper. November 2003.

PricewaterhouseCoopers. "The emerging role of internal audit in mitigating fraud and reputation risks." 2004.

Websites:

AICPA antifraud/forensic accounting resources: fvs.aicpa.org/Resources/Antifraud+Forensic + Accounting

Deloitte "Dbriefs" webcasts (US): www.deloitte.com/us/dbriefs. Especially those on "Fraud detection, deterrence, and prevention: Are you doing enough?" (April 11, 2006) and "Fraud risk management: Whose job is it anyway?" (April 9, 2007).

IIA Member Exchange: www.theiia.org/memberexchange

PricewaterhouseCoopers: www.pwc.com

Protiviti risk and business consulting: www.protiviti.com

See Also:

★ Aligning the Internal Audit Function with Strategic Objectives (pp. 280–282)
★ Engaging Senior Management in Internal Control (pp. 336–337)
★ Fraud: Minimizing the Impact on Corporate Image (pp. 856–858)
★ Human Risk: How Effective Strategic Risk Management Can Identify Rogues (pp. 872–874)
★ New Assurance Challenges Facing Chief Audit Executives (pp. 378–381)
✔ Establishing a Framework for Assessing Risk (p. 1028)
✔ Understanding Internal Audits (p. 1057)
✔ What Is Forensic Auditing? (p. 1060)

NOTES

1 "Financial fraud: Does an economic downturn mean an uptick?" Deloitte webinar, July 16, 2008.

2 "Key elements of antifraud programs and controls." PwC, December 11, 2003, p. 12.

3 The Committee of Sponsoring Organizations of the Treadway Commission (COSO) is a US private-sector initiative, formed in 1985. Its major objective is to identify the factors that cause fraudulent financial reporting and to make recommendations to reduce its incidence. COSO has established a common definition of internal controls, standards, and criteria against which companies and organizations can assess their control systems.

4 "The emerging role of internal audit in mitigating fraud and reputation risks." PwC, March 16, 2004, p. 3.

5 "The awakening." *Business Finance* (August 2007).

"The internet was not always the top priority in Microsoft's strategy. Its arrival changed our business and became the biggest unplanned event we've ever had to respond to." Bill Gates

How Much Independence for Supervisors in Financial Market Regulation? by Marc Quintyn

EXECUTIVE SUMMARY

- The degree of political independence that financial supervisors should enjoy is a hotly debated topic.
- This is because financial supervisors are a "one of a kind" breed of regulatory agency. They supervise the sector that is at the heart of the allocation of capital in any society, and therefore attract much political interest, not only in normal times, but even more so in times of crisis.
- While a fair degree of independence is justified—institutionally, in their regulatory and supervisory work, and financially—independence alone will not establish the right incentive structure for supervisors.
- Agency independence is not a goal in itself. It is just one institutional arrangement that should assist in establishing a governance framework that provides the regulatory agency with the right incentives to discharge its delegated powers. The other three elements are accountability, transparency, and integrity.
- Accountability arrangements ensure that the agency maintains legitimacy towards its stakeholders. This legitimacy will support independence, as will accountability.
- Transparency and integrity arrangements play an important role in making independence and accountability effective.
- These four elements of regulatory governance keep each other in equilibrium, and together establish the right incentives for the agency to fulfill its mandate, and for its stakeholders to refrain from interfering.

INTRODUCTION

The concept of independence, and, in particular, political independence is loaded. In a principal–agent relationship, it is associated with (more) power for the agent and a loss of power or grip for the principal. While the notion of an independent central bank is now more or less generally accepted in democratic societies, the broader notion of independent regulatory agencies (IRAs)—agencies that regulate and monitor important parts of social and economic life on behalf of government—is slowly gaining acceptance.

Financial sector supervisors are a "one of a kind" regulatory agency among these IRAs, and the debate about their independence is fairly recent, i.e., since the late 1990s and the turn of the century. Financial supervisors possess some unique features among IRAs that complicate the discussion about their degree of political independence. They are close to the central banks in that they contribute to preserving a country's financial stability by monitoring the health of individual institutions. Yet they differ from most other IRAs (central banks, competition regulators, and utilities regulators) in a number of crucial ways. Most importantly, they monitor a sector that fulfills a central role in the economy as allocator of capital, and as a source of governance for the corporate sector. For these very reasons, the sector has always generated much attention from the political class. This political interest, which is also eagerly exploited by the sector itself, opens the door to constant attempts at political interference and lobbying.

Add to this uniquely distinguishing feature (i.e., the nature of the sector they supervise) a number of other specific characteristics in the content of their supervision job, and it is clear why the independence of financial supervisors is such a much-debated issue. These other characteristics are:

- their mandate contains a great number of contingencies;
- given the sensitivities inherent in the workings of the financial system, transparency in their supervisory operations needs to be weighed against confidentiality more than in any of the other types of regulators;
- they wield wide-ranging judicial powers which include "the coercive power of the state against private citizens," which is more far-reaching than for any other type of IRA.

These features lead to two conclusions regarding their independence. First, a fair degree of regulatory and supervisory independence is needed to insulate them from both political *and* industry interference and lobbying. Second, and equally important, given their job content, the granting of independence alone is most unlikely to provide the right incentive structure to financial supervisors. In order to fulfill their mandate properly, independence arrangements need to be designed in coordination with other features, which together establish a regulatory governance structure that provides the right incentives to the supervisors, as well as to the other stakeholders, in particular their political masters.

Such an incentive-compatible governance structure for financial supervisors should be built around elements of independence, accountability, transparency, and integrity. These four ingredients of a governance framework, if designed properly, tend to reinforce each other, as we shall demonstrate. In the next section, we substantiate the need for supervisory independence, and the subsequent section presents an incentive-compatible regulatory governance framework.

ESSENTIAL ELEMENTS OF INDEPENDENCE

The need for regulatory and supervisory independence in the financial sector stems broadly from the same sources as central bank independence, and finds its origin in the literature on time inconsistency in economic policy.[1] Time inconsistency occurs when the government's optimal long-run policy differs from its optimal short-run policy, leading to situations where the government in the short run reneges on its long-term commitments. Thus, time inconsistency emphasizes the need for a credible and binding precommitment to a particular mandate that prevents violations *ex post*. In the case of monetary policy, Rogoff (1985) argued that one way to achieve policy credibility is to place it in the hands of a person or institution who weighs inflation deviations more heavily than in the social welfare function—the "conservative central banker" whose preferences will differ from those of the government. The need for agency independence follows from this: For the central banker to have a different reaction function, they need to be independent from government.

The analogy with supervisory independence is straightforward. Bank liquidations are typically politically unpopular, as they can result in genuine hardship for depositors and other creditors, many of who will also be voters. Vote-maximizing politicians with short time horizons may be concerned about the short-term costs of bank closures, whether fiscal, in terms of lost votes, or in terms of lost campaign contributions, and

  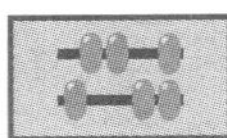   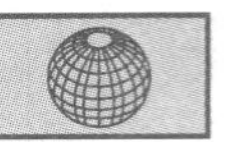   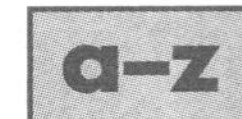

will be sensitive to the demands of these groups, particularly if these are politically well organized. Politicians may be tempted, as a result, to put pressure on supervisors to organize a bailout or exercise forbearance to avoid short-term costs. However, short-term forbearance may be the cause of higher longer-term resolution costs. Accordingly, politicians face the same incentives in relation to failing banks as they do in relation to the goal of price stability. Hence the need for independent regulators whose reaction function differs from that of their political masters.

Let us now define ways in which this independence could be made operational. For financial supervisors, there are actually four dimensions to it—institutional, regulatory, supervisory, and budgetary independence.

Institutional Independence

Institutional independence is achieved if the agency as an institution is separate from the executive and legislative branches of government. Institutional independence encompasses three critical elements:

- the terms of appointment and dismissal of its senior personnel should be clearly defined to avoid political interference, and thus ensure security of tenure;
- the agency's governance structure should favor decision-making by a commission, as opposed to vesting all responsibilities in the chairperson, to reduce external influences;
- decision-making should be as open and transparent as possible, to minimize the risk of political interference.

Regulatory Independence

Regulatory independence refers to the ability of the agency to have an appropriate degree of autonomy in setting prudential rules and regulations for the sectors under its supervision. Autonomy in setting prudential regulations will help in ensuring that the regulatory framework is stable and predictable, complies with international best practices, and is not contaminated with political considerations.

Supervisory Independence

Supervisory independence refers to the degree of independence with which the agency is able to exercise its judgment and powers in such matters as licensing, on-site inspections and off-site monitoring, sanctioning, and enforcement of sanctions (including revoking licenses), which are the supervisors' main tools to ensure the stability of the system.

Supervisory independence is the most difficult of the four dimensions of independence to guarantee. To preserve its effectiveness, the supervisory function typically involves private ordering between the supervisor and the supervised institution. However, the privacy of the supervisory process makes it vulnerable to interference, from both politicians and supervised entities. Political interference (and interference from the industry itself) can take many forms, and can indeed be very subtle, making it difficult to shield the supervisors from all forms of interference.

As the supervisory process starts with the act of licensing a financial institution, supervisors should ideally have the final word on who can enter the system. A typical situation that may lead to problems is one where the government has the final say over the licensing of individual banks and may—either out of self-interest or lack of technical ability to assess business plans—license unviable projects. The same degree of autonomy should apply to exit procedures, based on the same argument that supervisors are in the best position to decide on the viability of individual institutions. Decisions to close or not close an institution that are taken on political, rather than technical, grounds may result in the prolongation of the life of insolvent or corrupt institutions, thus ultimately increasing resolution costs. Moreover, if the power of license revocation is not in the hands of the supervisor, the threat by the supervisor can be empty, and their other powers undermined.

To strengthen supervisory independence, it is recommended that (i) supervisors enjoy legal protection in the performance of their duties. The absence of proper legal protection in many instances has a paralyzing effect on supervision; (ii) supervisors enjoy appropriate salary levels to attract better qualified individuals who may be less prone to bribery; (iii) rules-based system of sanctions and interventions be applied (see Rules Versus Discretion Supervisory Intervention Finacial Institutions).

Budgetary Independence

Budgetary independence refers to the ability of the regulatory agency to determine the size of its own budget, and the specific allocations of resources and priorities that are set within the budget. Regulatory agencies that enjoy a high degree of budgetary independence are better equipped to withstand political interference (which might be exerted through budgetary pressures), to respond more quickly to newly emerging needs in the area of supervision, and to ensure that salaries are sufficiently attractive to hire competent staff.

FROM REGULATORY INDEPENDENCE TO GOVERNANCE

"... governance is an effort to craft order, thereby to mitigate conflict and realize neutral gains. So conceived a governance structure obviously reshapes incentives."[2]

Independence for supervisors is a necessary but insufficient condition when establishing the proper incentive structure for meeting their mandate. When allowed to operate at arm's length of the government, the challenge is to endow them with the right incentive-compatible governance attributes. Following Williamson's definition of governance, the aim of the model of governance arrangements elaborated in this section is exactly to:

- craft order, internally in the agency, and between the agency and its stakeholders (for instance, by identifying mechanisms to avoid capture, see below);
- mitigate conflict between the agency and its stakeholders;
- assist in realizing gains for all stakeholders, i.e., to ensure that the delegation of power to the financial supervisor is a socially optimal solution.

Making Williamson's definition operational, Das and Quintyn (2002) identified four essential pillars of good regulatory governance: Independence, accountability, transparency, and integrity. If well designed, these four pillars can underpin most of the key elements of internal and external governance arrangements for regulatory agencies. They lay down principles for dealing with shareholders (the government) and stakeholders (regulated and supervised entities, customers of the regulated entities, and the public at large), and for setting up *internal* governance arrangements in support of the *external* ones. They underpin mechanisms for attaining the agency's stated objectives and for monitoring its performance.

Although references to these four principles are rare in the corporate governance literature, some parallels can easily be made: The need for an arm's length relationship between managers and shareholders in the corporate sector finds its parallel in the need for independence for the regulator from the share- and stakeholders (government and regulated industry, respectively). Independent regulators have a fiduciary relationship with their stakeholders. To be effective, these fiduciary responsibilities need to be complemented with accountability arrangements towards the stakeholders. Furthermore, transparency mechanisms facilitate accountability, and integrity measures minimize conflicts of interest. As can already be observed from this overview, a major feature of this

  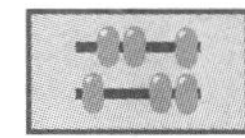      

Figure 1. The four pillars of regulatory governance

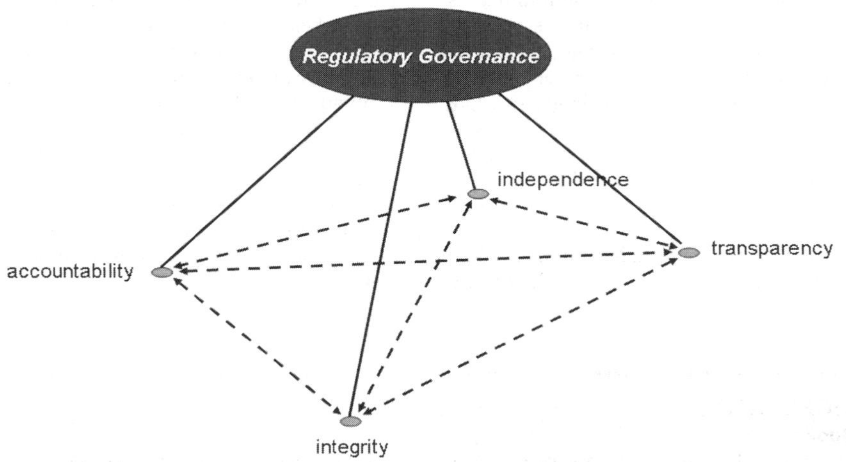

foursome is that they reinforce each other (Figure 1). Weakening one of them tends to undermine the effectiveness of the others, and, in the end, the quality of the agency's governance.

Accountability

Accountability is the indispensable, other side of independence. Yet it is a problematic one, because policy makers and agencies seem to have trouble getting a practical grasp of its workings. One of the problems is that many scholars still tend to refer to narrow concepts of accountability, more or less equivalent to reporting. Another problem is that the line between accountability and control remains very thin, leading to misunderstandings about the true meaning and content of accountability. The purpose of designing accountability arrangements is to put in place a combination of monitoring arrangements and instruments, so as to arrive at a situation where no one controls the agency directly, but the agency is nonetheless under control, i.e., it can be monitored—not just by the government, but by other stakeholders as well—to see if it fulfills its fiduciary obligations.

Modern interpretations of accountability as a mechanism of checks and balances stress that it fulfills at least four functions.

1 To provide public oversight. This is the classical role of accountability.
2 To maintain and enhance legitimacy of the agency. The actions of an agency with delegated power need to have legitimacy in the eyes of the other stakeholders, in order to enjoy the granted independence effectively. If the agency's actions are perceived as lacking legitimacy, its independence will not be long lasting. Legitimacy can be generated through various accountability mechanisms and relations. Once it has been accepted that accountability generates legitimacy, and legitimacy supports independence, it becomes clear that the relationship between accountability and independence does not imply a trade-off, as is often stated, but is one of complementarities. In other words, properly designed independence and accountability arrangements lead to a virtuous interaction between both pillars of governance.
3 To enhance the integrity of regulatory governance. Besides political and industry capture, independent agencies face a third type of capture: Self-interest capture. There are situations in which the powers of the regulatory agency are captured by individual staff pursuing their own self-interest, which may not be consistent with social welfare. Regulatory self-interest can take a variety of forms including, in highly corrupt societies, the abuse of regulatory powers to extract rents. Less blatant, but potentially just as damaging, is the motivation of "not on my watch," i.e., the desire of regulators to delay the emergence of problems until after they have left office. Agency accountability provides society with assurances that regulation is not being manipulated or subverted by private interests.
4 To improve agency performance. Accountability is not only about monitoring, blaming, and punishing. It is also about enhancing the agency's performance. By giving account to the executive and legislative branches of government, the agency provides input to the government as to how to (re)shape its broader economic and financial policies, and receives feedback from the government. In this sense, accountability stimulates coordination with the government and enhances the agency's legitimacy, without encroaching on its independence. Accountability also enhances agency performance by avoiding that the independent agency becomes uninformed and loses touch with the (political) reality of the nation. Accountability forces the agency into a dialogue with all stakeholders, with positive effects on its performance.

Transparency

Transparency refers to an environment in which the agency's objectives, frameworks, decisions and their rationale, data and other information, as well as terms of accountability are provided to the stakeholders in a comprehensive, accessible, and timely manner.

Transparency has increasingly been recognized as a "good" in itself, but it also serves other purposes related to the other components of governance. As a good in itself, policy makers have been recognizing that it is a means of containing market uncertainty. In addition, transparency has become a powerful vehicle for countering poor operating practices and policies. It has become a main conduit of accountability to a large number of stakeholders.

Integrity

Integrity is often the forgotten pillar. Yet it is an essential one, as it provides several underpinnings for good internal governance in support of the external elements. Integrity refers to the set of mechanisms that ensure that agencies' staff can pursue institutional goals without compromising them as a result of their own behavior or self-interest. Integrity affects staff of regulatory agencies at various levels. Procedures for appointing heads, their terms of office, and criteria for removal should be such that the integrity of the board-level appointees (policy-making body) is safeguarded. Second, the integrity of the agency's day-to-day operations is ensured through internal audit arrangements, which ensure that the agency's objectives are clearly set and observed, and accountability is maintained. Ensuring the quality of the agency's operations will maintain the integrity of the institution and strengthen its credibility to the outside world. Third, integrity also implies that there are standards for the conduct by officials and staff of their personal affairs, to prevent conflicts of interest. Fourth, assuring integrity also implies that the staff of the regulatory

  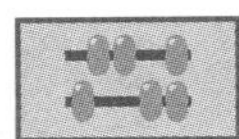      

agency enjoy legal protection while discharging their official duties.

Mutual Reinforcement

A key feature of these four pillars is that they hold each other in balance and reinforce each other as governance pillars. The previous paragraphs have already illustrated this, and a few more examples will reinforce the point. Independence and accountability are two sides of the same coin. Independence cannot be effective without proper accountability. Without accountability, agencies (or their heads) can lose their independence easily in disputes with the government. Transparency is a key instrument to make accountability work. It is also a vehicle for safeguarding independence. By making actions and decisions transparent, chances for interference are reduced. Transparency also helps to establish and safeguard integrity, in the sense that published arrangements provide even better protection for agency staff (against themselves). Independence and integrity also reinforce each other. Legal protection of agency staff, as well as clear rules for the appointment and removal of agency heads, support both their independence and integrity. Finally, accountability and integrity also reinforce each other. Because of accountability requirements, there are additional reasons for heads and staff to keep their integrity. Together, they reduce the risk of self-interest capture.

Accountability is extremely important in the case of a financial supervisor. As stated before, this agency's mandate is much less measurable (such as "to maintain a sound financial system" often in conjunction with other goals such as "consumer protection," "prevention of money laundering," etc.), and cannot be very specific because of all the contingencies involved in financial sector regulation and supervision. Some authors have argued that such a vague mandate precludes proper accountability, and, therefore, that these agencies should not be granted too much independence from government.

The argument developed here states that, on the contrary, these agencies should be able to operate at arm's length from the government (and the industry) for the reasons discussed in the literature, but that accountability arrangements should be such that the agency remains "in check." Given the wide range of contingencies in financial regulation and the large number of stakeholders in financial regulation and supervision, a "360 degree"-type of accountability is required, involving arrangements towards the three government branches, the supervised industry, the customers of financial services, and the public at large. In more general terms, the less specific and measurable the mandate, the more elaborate accountability arrangements should be.

CONCLUSION

In sum, these four underpinnings, taken together, create clarity in the relationship between the financial supervisors and the government (and other stakeholders). With sufficient checks and balances in place, the agency will have assurances that it can operate independently to pursue its mandate, and the government will have assurances that the agency remains "in check," i.e., that its operations remain aligned with the government's broad policy objectives. Referring to Williamson's definition, all this is indeed about shaping and reshaping incentives on both sides.

MORE INFO

Books:

Bovens, Mark. "Public accountability." In E. Ferlie, L. Lynne, and C. Pollitt (eds). *The Oxford Handbook of Public Management*. Oxford: Oxford University Press, 2004.

Das, Udaibir, and Marc Quintyn. "Financial crisis prevention and crisis management—The role of regulatory governance." In Robert, Litan, Michel Pomerleano, and V. Sundararajan (eds). *Financial Sector Governance: The Roles of the Public and Private Sectors*. Washington, DC: Brookings Institution Press, 2002.

Quintyn, Marc, and Michael Taylor. "Robust regulators and their political masters: Independence and accountability in theory." In Donato Masciandaro, and Marc Quintyn (eds). *Designing Financial Supervision Institutions: Independence, Accountability, and Governance*. Cheltenham, UK: Edward Elgar, 2007.

Articles:

Hüpkes, Eva, Marc Quintyn, and Michael Taylor. "The accountability of financial sector supervisors: Theory and practice." *European Business Law Review* 16:6 (2005): 1575–1620.

Kydland, Finn, and E. Prescott. "Rules rather than discretion: The inconsistency of optimal plans." *Journal of Political Economy* 85:3 (1977): 473–491.

Majone, Giandomenico. "Strategy and structure: The political economy of agency independence and accountability." *Designing Independent and Accountable Regulatory Agencies for High Quality Regulation: Proceedings of an Expert Meeting in London, Organization for Economic Cooperation and Development, January 10–11, 2005*: 126–155.

Quintyn, Marc, Silvia Ramirez, and Michael Taylor. "Fear of freedom—Politicians and the independence and accountability of financial sector supervisors." IMF Working Paper 07/25, Washington, DC: International Monetary Fund, 2007. Also in Donato Masciandaro, and Marc Quintyn (eds). *Designing Financial Supervision Institutions: Independence, Accountability, and Governance*. Cheltenham, UK: Edward Elgar, 2007.

Quintyn, Marc. "Governance of financial supervisors and its effects—a stocktaking exercise." SUERF Studies (2007/4): 64

Rogoff, Kenneth. "Optimal degree of commitment to an intermediate monetary target: Inflation gains versus stabilization costs." *Quarterly Journal of Economics* 100 (1985): 1169–1189.

Williamson, Oliver. "The new institutional economics: Taking stock, looking ahead." *Journal of Economic Literature* 38:3 (2000): 595–613.

See Also:

★ Why Organizations Need to be Regulated—Lessons from History (pp. 437–439)
★ Rules versus Discretion in Supervisory Interventions in Financial Institutions (pp. 239–241)
★ Viewpoint: Lessons from the Credit Crisis: Governing Financial Institutions (pp. 694–695)
✔ The EU Regulatory Regime (p. 1029)
Banking and Financial Services (pp. 1612–1614)

NOTES

1 Kydland and Prescott (1977).

2 Williamson (2000).

"Bond investors are the vampires of the investment world. They love decay, recession—anything that leads to low inflation and the protection of the real value of their loans." Bill Gross

  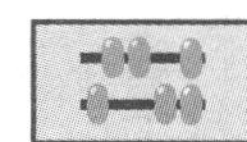   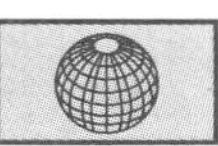   

How to Implement a Standard Chart of Accounts Effectively by Aziz Tayyebi

EXECUTIVE SUMMARY

A chart of accounts (COA), representing a unique set of codes to record all an entity's transactions consistently, is a well-recognised, fundamental accounting need. Whether it concerns a complex organisation with numerous divisions, or an individual applying basic cash accounting, it is essential to be able to collate financial information that is relevant, both for internal management and external parties. This article considers some questions that management should take into account when implementing a standard COA, such as:

- Why update a chart of accounts? An organisation may need to adopt a new COA if its industry or country adopts a new set of specific accounting standards. Furthermore, as organizations evolve, it is vital that the COA keeps pace and stays relevant to management.
- What are the options when implementing a chart of accounts? Implementing a new COA can improve an existing system, or involve a completely new development. Management should take care to incorporate all useful accounts from older systems.
- What are the practical consideration when designing a chart of accounts? Management must consider user needs, detailed design specifications, logistics, cost/benefit analysis, and legal requirements.

INTRODUCTION

A chart of accounts (COA) is essentially a set of codes for the consistent classification of financial information. This allows for the systematic production of decision-useful accounting information for management, such as budgeting, monitoring, and management reporting. Similarly, a standard COA helps to ensure comparability in external financial reporting.

The COA facilitates the recording of all transactions, which are filtered into a unique account code, based on certain criteria. While this criteria is influenced both by internal management needs as well as regulatory requirements, many common types of codes would always be expected, such as revenue, expenses, assets, liabilities, and equity.

WHY UPDATE A CHART OF ACCOUNTS?

A standard COA represents an integral part of an overall financial information system. A COA takes inputs from source accounting documents and journal entries, and allocates that information to a prescribed set of accounts, ultimately producing financial reports, which in turn enable users of that information to track the performance of the business, in a format that best suits their needs.

External Decisions

COAs can change for a number of reasons, including an industry-wide move to standardize accounting terminology. An example of this was the development of a standard COA for not-for-profit organizations (NPOs) in Queensland, Australia. In 2002, Queensland University of Technology (QUT) and Queensland Treasury commenced a project to develop a standard COA for small NPOs that received government funding. The project was commissioned because, at the time, Australia did not provide specific national accounting standards for NPOs. As a result, there was tremendous inconsistency in accounting categories and terms required by government departments in their funding relationships with such organizations. Research from QUT indicated that these inconsistencies created a heavy compliance burden on NPOs when acquitting grants, with many additional costs being incurred in the reporting process . Thus, through an extensive consultation process, a standard COA was launched in Queensland in 2006 . The success of the COA, both for NPOs and the funders, through reducing simplification of the reporting process, increasing understanding, and consistency of accounting practices, led to other Australian jurisdictions subsequently commencing similar projects.[1]

A significant number of companies around the world have recently implemented International Financial Reporting Standards (IFRS). For many of those companies, the IFRS implementation was mandated in national legislation. The transition to IFRS involves significant practical and logistical challenges, especially in upgrading and adapting IT systems across the organization. A recent report by KPMG[2] indicated that, "IT costs are generally over 50 per cent of the cost of IFRS conversion," and that changes to the chart of accounts are inevitable.

Other key regulatory requirements, which can have an impact on the COA, revolve around taxation. For larger companies with overseas subsidiaries that will be using the same general ledger system, it is important to consider country-specific requirements when completing the COA, while providing as much consistency as possible.

Organizational Decisions

More commonly, businesses are likely to go through restructuring, make a strategic decision to implement a new IT system, or simply acknowledge that the current COA is not fulfilling the information needs of the business. Whatever the reasons are for change, management needs to assess both the new business requirements, as well as any that were not being met previously.

Similarly when considering the implementation of new reporting systems, it is essential to ensure that the individual components of the financial system, such as invoicing, stock management, and disbursements, are providing the appropriate support to the wider business objectives. This is often why ERM packages are so useful, as they allow information from a common source to be shared across previously disparate departments of the business.

OPTIONS WHEN IMPLEMENTING A CHART OF ACCOUNTS

Essentially, an organization is faced with three choices.

1 Keep the COA from the legacy system in place;
2 Supplement the existing COA with some additional ones;
3 Overhaul the COA and implement the new, changed structures.

From a practical point of view, moving away from the existing chart of accounts also has the significant advantage of offloading redundant codes and accounts which unnecessarily congest it.

In practice, especially when a comprehensive system such as an ERP package is being implemented, the organization faces limited choices. The chances are management will have to consider a whole-scale overhaul of the current system. Thus, it is also essential to ensure that, while this is an opportunity to cleanse the current COA, it is also vital to ensure that the new COA reflects the realities of the business. All-round general ledger systems are, by their

"Whales only get harpooned when they come to the surface, and turtles can only move forward when they stick their neck out, but investors face risk no matter what they do." Charles A. Jaffe

  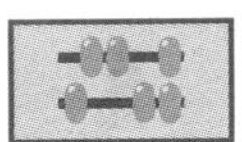      

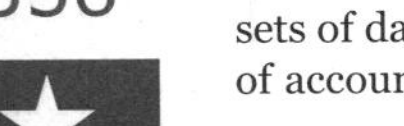

nature, more sophisticated, linking various sets of data. Designing an appropriate chart of accounts is a complex process.

PRACTICAL CONSIDERATIONS WHEN DESIGNING A NEW CHART OF ACCOUNTS

As previously described, the COA is only one element in the information system (manual and automated) which aids management decision-making. The COA is, however, a key part, bringing together financial information held within the general ledger, and filtering it into a format that can be used by managers.

The general considerations for implementing a new COA are, unsurprisingly, akin to those that would be assessed when making any significant system changes. Considerations include an assessment of user needs, a detailed design, potential impact assessment and testing, and simulations prior to final running. By thoroughly considering these basic procedures, it should be possible to complete a relatively risk-free, "big bang" approach to the adoption of the new COA. However, in the case of an overall system change, management may decide to run both systems for a period of time in order to ensure that all data is being captured. While costly and time-consuming, the old COA is then still available for cross-reference.

User Needs

Again, reiterating the main reason for having a standard COA, the initial phase of implementation must begin with a thorough analysis of the organization's information requirements. Thus management will need to consider the existing outputs resulting from their present COA, and ensure that all potential stakeholders, within and outside the finance department, are involved in the process.

Understanding the current condition should ensure that relevant COAs are included in the new version, and that shortcomings are remedied. A simulation of the revised COA can then be produced, allowing the stakeholders to preview the resulting information. The main aim of this phase is not to determine what the final reports may look like, but to confirm that the required information is being generated.

Logistical Consideration

Business analysts tend to want as much information as possible, and then decide which information they really need at any given time. This desire, coupled with the wide range of internal and external stakeholders, may make it tempting to include excessive fields in a COA. However, it is generally the case that by widening the net of accounts, the likelihood of error, as well as underutilized codes, will be greater too. Thus, it is also vital to strike the right balance between the user's often-exhaustive demands, and the limitations of an efficient data-capture system.

Typically management may be interested in analyzing performance based on:

- individual product basis and product class;
- separate cost centers;
- geographical segments;
- legal entities.

However, it is the needs of the business that should ultimately dictate the scope of data requirements.

It is also possible that the difficulty and cost of generating some information might ultimately mean that it is not worthwhile. The tendency is that future preparers of information may find it too difficult to provide the inputs regularly, and, therefore, these accounts would again become vacant. Thus, it is imperative to conduct a careful analysis of the process for data capture. While much reporting information can easily be extracted from basic input data from invoices, etc, the consistent splitting of costs and revenues by appropriate cost and activity centers is more challenging.

In order to maintain a consistent application of the COA, it is also important that a thorough guide is in place, outlining how information should be captured and recorded. Again, a regular review of these guidelines should be conducted.

Manual or Electronic Conversion?

In practice, the choice of manual or electronic conversion will be dictated by the type of system being implemented. If a totally new package is introduced, then the standard COA is already inbuilt, and only the process of identifying and/or adding new accounts is required, as discussed above. If the organization is simply implementing a new standard COA only, then the organization is faced with either a manual or an electronic change. Usually, electronic downloading into the accounting software is straightforward—the relevant file is downloaded from the data file into the existing accounting package, which then essentially overlays the existing COA.

A manual conversion requires a thorough comparison between the new standard COA and the existing COA. The process of identifying relevant accounts is, again, critical, although by virtue of the fact that this is not automated, it can be lengthier. A constant review of output reports, such as trial balances, is required.

If the company's financial statements are audited, it is important to consider any requests from auditors, regardless of whether the process is manual or electronic. It is, therefore, important to document any changes to the COA, with an appropriate audit trail in place.

Balancing Cost-Centre Demands and Legal Entity Requirements

Many large organizations have a number of subsidiaries that are legal entities in their own right. While management may make business decisions on quite different aspects, the financial reporting process demands that a COA is able to meet all external reporting requirements, such as statutory and tax reporting. The COA must be set up so that a full trial balance for that individual entity can be obtained.

MAKING IT HAPPEN

A correctly structured COA should support the financial and management reporting process, enabling the organization to evaluate its performance in a manner that uses information systems efficiently. Ultimately, a good understanding of the business and its future direction ensures that an optimum COA is developed. It is essential that managers are involved throughout the implementation process. At the centre of the considerations should be:

- Appraising the current system, including the relevance of outputs and accessibility of information, by bringing together managers from relevant departments.
- Understanding the current and potential information needs of the organization and focusing on the overall business strategy and processes, while taking into account external reporting and regulatory requirements.
- Designing and assessing the potential impact of the new COA against those user needs, and adopting an appropriate strategy to move from the old chart.
- Balancing the benefits of numerous financial information demands with the finite resources, both time and costs, required to capture that information, and ensure its accuracy.
- Putting in place a robust framework for operating the COA, including guidance on use (for future employees), regular review of outputs, and methodology for inputs.

"Four hundred seventy-three million to one. Those are the odds against George Soros compiling the investment record he did as manager of the Quantum Fund from 1968 through 1993." Paul Tudor Jones

This can lead to possible conflicts and difficulty, especially where corporate cost centers are managed across a number of reporting entities. It may be that, at a cost-center level, additional detail is required on income-statement accounts, but limited detail is required for balance-sheet classifications—there is no compromise on statutory requirements.

Management should carefully consider how best to set up an accounting company, or a cost center for COA purposes. Typically, when businesses have their own general ledger systems or are legal reporting entities, a separate accounting company approach is the optimal solution. A cost-center approach is more appropriate when an organization is reviewed on the basis of divisional performance, which is supervised by individual mangers themselves.

While a standard COA should be comprehensive enough to allow for all divisional requirements, it should not compromise the compliance requirements of statutory reporting, either for the local entity, or the group as a whole.

CONCLUSION

Changing a COA involves a thorough understanding and analysis of the existing business requirements. However, it is equally important to realize that most businesses constantly evolve, and management information needs may also change. It is, therefore, essential that the implementation process includes a clear vision for future years, and makes the most of available technologies such as eXtensible Business Reporting Language (XBRL), for example. XBRL can benefit the dissemination of financial information from various sources, including various charts of account.

Finally, it is important to be mindful that there is no ideal standard COA. What fits the needs of one organization, and indeed one manager within an organization, may be considerably different for another. What is vital is that a thorough investigation of the needs of the organization as a whole is conducted.

MORE INFO

Book:

Potter, Douglas A. *The Automated Accounting Systems and Procedures Handbook*. New York: Wiley, 1991.

Websites:

Queensland University of Technology, experiences of implementing a standard chart of accounts (SCOA): www.bus.qut.edu.au/research/cpns/seminarevent/ExperiencesofimplementingthestandardchartofaccountsSCOA.jsp

Queensland University of Technology, chart of accounts research project: www.bus.qut.edu.au/research/cpns/whatweresear/chartofaccou.jsp

See Also:

★ Reducing Costs and Improving Efficiency with New Management Information Systems (pp. 921–923)
★ Understanding the Requirements for Preparing IFRS Financial Statements (pp. 423–424)
✔ Assessing Business Performance (p. 1144)
✔ International Financial Reporting Standards (IFRS): The Basics (p. 1039)
✔ Key Accounting Standards and Organizations (p. 1040)
✔ The Ten Accounting Principles (p. 1055)

NOTES

1 Queensland University of Technology, research programme, website

2 KPMG, The Effects of IFRS on Information Systems, 2008

"More money is probably lost by people who attempt to invest their money conservatively and sanely, but ignorantly, than is lost by those who enter into frank speculations." John Moody

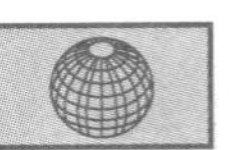

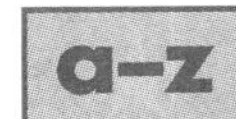

Identifying the Main Regulatory Challenges for Islamic Finance by Bilal Rasul

EXECUTIVE SUMMARY

- Harmonization and standardization within the Islamic financial industry, as well as with the conventional banking and finance industry, are the biggest regulatory challenges.
- *Shariah* rulings in *Fiqh* should be harmonized by central Islamic authorities such as the Islamic Fiqh Academy.
- Pursuit is toward uniform regulatory frameworks which restrict *shariah* arbitrage.
- *Shariah* advisers and advisory boards are indispensable in the regulation of Islamic financial institutions, but there is a dearth of expertise and there are not enough advisers to match growing demand.
- *Shariah*-compliant securities are relatively few and not liquid.
- The Islamic Financial Services Board's Ten-year Master Plan for Islamic financial services is a good starting point to tackle the regulatory challenges.

INTRODUCTION

Globally, Islamic finance has exhibited its potential through the ever-increasing number of Islamic financial institutions (IFIs). Unofficial estimates figure Islamic financial assets of the IFIs at nearly US$1 trillion. The Islamic financial industry is still growing and is finding its niche in many Muslim as well as non-Muslim countries. The growth is swift, but it is accompanied by regulatory issues and challenges that will need to be addressed in order to facilitate and coordinate the innovation and diversity that it brings.

ISLAMIC FINANCE: THE FUNDAMENTAL DIFFERENCE

In order to understand Islamic finance it must be known that the underlying theme of Islamic finance is the *niyah* or "good intention"—the element that drives the Islamic socioeconomic system for ensuring the enhancement of the welfare of society. The *niyah* may represent the Islamic philosophy of conducting life and business, but it is not restricted to Muslims. The tenet pertains to justice and fairness which can be practiced by all, Muslim and non-Muslim alike. The Islamic financial system, therefore, hinges on the *niyah* as an essential ingredient for every contractual transaction that is executed.[1]

For the layman, the fundamental difference between Islamic finance and conventional finance is the feature in the latter to put a cost on money in financial transactions, i.e. interest, or *riba* as it is known in the Islamic financial world. Basically, whatever is borrowed has to be returned but with an increment.

In Islamic finance one of the questions most often visited is: "Money has time value; how can it not have a cost?" The simplest answer is that in Islamic finance there is no concept of money as a commodity: there is always an underlying contract in the form of a partnership or venture that is entered into between the lender and the borrower, with the profits or losses and the risks all being shared. Therefore, a fixed return *per se* cannot be assured. This perspective of Islamic finance confers a "soul" to business activity. The motives are: the welfare of the people; an egalitarian society; the opportunity for all to benefit without being exploited. Islamic finance covers the social aspect of being in enterprise. Above all, it is trust-based.

ISSUES

Harmonization and Standardization

The contracts prescribed in Islamic law provide a significant part of the principles and procedures explicitly laid down in the *Fiqh* (Islamic jurisprudence) which must be observed for *shariah* compliance. For instance, the Qur'an is replete with passages that denounce *riba* as exploitative and against the norms of fairness. The problem arises where the principles and procedures for specifics are not so easily found and therefore have to be derived from the *fatwas*, or interpretations of the *shariah* scholars. The *fatwas* awarded on financial transactions differ amongst scholars and across jurisdictions, which produces the problem of pluralism in *shariah* interpretations.[2] There are mainly five schools of thought in Islamic jurisprudence, for example: *Hanafi, Shafii, Hanbali, Maliki,* and *Ibadi,* among others. Each school of thought has its own set of *muftis* (scholars) on Islamic financial issues which, more often than not, creates conflict and ambiguity in decisions on the veracity of a transaction in terms of its compliance with the *shariah*. In this context the Quran states "As for those who divide their religion and break up into sects, thou hast no part in them in the least: their affair is with Allah: He will in the end tell them the truth of all that they did." The Quran, sura 6 (Al-Anaam) Ayat 159.

So, the biggest challenge faced by the regulators of Islamic finance is harmonizing and standardizing these interpretations into a consistent and efficient regulatory framework that will ensure unimpeded Islamic financial intermediation among the participants.

The process of harmonization and standardization of transactions across and within borders is undoubtedly a daunting one and has to be comprehensive. In some jurisdictions certain transactions are considered *shariah*-compliant, while in others they may not be accepted as so. It is extremely difficult to adjudge as to which is the closest to *shariah*. Consensus in the *fatwas* may be overcome by the centralization of the *shariah* rulings in a central Islamic authority such as the Islamic Fiqh Academy of the Organisation of the Islamic Conference, which is recognized by a large majority of scholars. In the event of disagreement the Academy can give its verdict.

The pursuit should be toward uniform regulatory frameworks based on principles and standards designed by universally accepted organizations such as the Islamic Financial Services Board (IFSB) and the Accounting and Auditing Organization for Islamic Financial Institutions (AAOIFI). The adoption of the guidelines drafted by these institutions is the panacea for the *shariah* arbitrage that exists otherwise.

Not secondary to this issue is the problem of emulating the conventional financial system and applying the Basel II principles.[3] Effective risk management measures applied to the conventional financial system need to be applied to Islamic finance, but with certain modifications and adaptations. The Islamic financial industry has to be adept with techniques and competitive products to improvise and emulate the conventional banking and finance industry. Only then can IFIs compete with the conventional giants and access the international markets while maintaining their Islamic identity.

SHARIAH EXPERTISE

The lack of *shariah* expertise is one of the challenges that face the regulators of the Islamic financial industry. Due to the

"While the industry regulators and supervisors are in the front line facing this challenge, in fact the challenge is much wider, and confronts the firms competing in the industry at the micro level and the governmental and legislative authorities in the host countries at the macro level." The Regulatory Challenge

  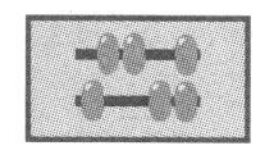      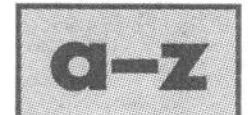

infancy of the system, very few institutions have produced the desired skill set for the Islamic financial and banking industry. While there are plenty of Islamic jurisprudence experts, there is a dearth of Islamic financial experts with a knowledge of the dynamics of conventional finance and its transformation to an Islamic/*shariah*-compliant system. Due to the regulatory obligation of instating *shariah* supervision, IFIs employ less-experienced *shariah* scholars, as only a limited number of professionals are available and they are usually attached to more than one IFI concurrently.

The transition to Islamic finance is highly technical and complex. A balance has to be maintained in order to provide, on the one hand, an adequate return and to remain, on the other hand, within the boundaries of the Quran and Sunna, which cannot be done without quality *shariah* supervision. In order to achieve this, regulators of the capital and money markets will have to encourage the development of educational institutions that offer programs and syllabi for Islamic financial technical skills. The International Centre for Education in Islamic Finance in Malaysia is an example that has designed an outstanding course—namely, CIFA (Chartered Islamic Financial Analyst), which prepares the student for a specialized course in Islamic finance.

Shariah-Compliant Securities

The limited number of *shariah*-compliant securities emanates from the lack of both harmony and Islamic financial prowess, and poses yet another problem in the development of the industry. Due to the paucity of available instruments in the market, investors are constrained to take their funds elsewhere. The limited choices also affect the liquidity of the securities as there is a limited market for them. The buying and selling of such securities is not as lively as in the conventional securities market, possibly due to their non-speculative nature. Nevertheless, investors are eager to place their funds in *shariah*-compliant securities, even for a comparatively lower return, provided that a reasonable degree of assurance can be given with regard to their nearness to *shariah*. The market for *shariah*-compliant securities, in terms of buyers and sellers, quite certainly exists, but it awaits the introduction and innovation of new Islamic instruments. Much of the apprehension that exists in the market with regard to *shariah*-compliant securities, or Islamic banking and finance for that matter, is owed to the slow pace of development of products and awareness-creating endeavors. In this context, the Liquidity Management Centre and the International Islamic Financial Market have a huge mandate and are vigorously involved in bridging the gaps in terms of investment of surplus funds of IFIs and creating Islamic financial markets. "The combination of services offered by operating IFI and the prevailing practices compound the difficulties of designing a regulatory framework to govern them."[5]

CONCLUSION

A purely Islamic financial system would be ideal: one in which the *niyah* and trust are predominant so that a self-perpetuating regulatory system prevails. There would be minimal regulatory interference—only for transparency and disclosure. In such a system, issues of compliance diminish directly with the prevalence of a coherent and trustful financial environment in which profits and risks are authentically disclosed and equitably distributed.

While a conventional financial system cannot evolve into an Islamic one overnight, praiseworthy efforts are being made in terms of bringing the diverging interpretations to a common platform and attempting to accord them congruence. In this context, the contributions of AAOIFI and the IFSB, as conduits for bringing solutions to the problems of standardization and harmonization, and as cornerstones of change and adaptation, must not be undermined in any way. The IFSB's Ten-Year Master Plan for Islamic Financial Services is an excellent precursor to the type of regulatory environment that should prevail in jurisdictions offering Islamic finance.

CASE STUDY

The Case of *Sukuk*

Sukuk, the plural of *suk* meaning Islamic bond, is a case that particularly highlights the divergence in views of Islamic scholars. One of the most popular Islamic financial instruments, the *sukuk* have questions looming over them. The renowned *shariah* scholar Sheikh Muhammad Taqi Usmani believes that the guarantee to pay back the invested capital in *sukuk* undermines the tenets of the *shariah* by compromising on the risk and profit/loss sharing philosophy. Sheikh Usmani contends that the investment must be consequential to the investor where profits and losses both have to be anticipated. The views of Sheikh Usmani are difficult to oppose, but in giving impetus to the Islamic financial industry certain exemptions are in order, for which AAOIFI may well have the solution.[4]

MAKING IT HAPPEN

The solution to the harmonization problem is to design regulatory frameworks that are standard. Thus, all criteria relating to the formation of Islamic financial institutions, the induction of *shariah* experts, the risk management measures, and the various codes should conform to a standard document, such as an enabling Islamic financial services law, which prescribes common Islamic financial accounting standards, corporate governance practices, and prudential regulations for risk management for the industry, and which interfaces with the IFSB's Ten-year Master Plan for Islamic Financial Services.

To bolster the Islamic securities market, companies listed on the stock exchanges (financial or manufacturing) should be encouraged to pursue *shariah* compliance. To achieve these objectives the role of the regulator(s) is emphasized.

MORE INFO

Books:

Karim, Rifaat Ahmed Abdel, and Simon Archer. *Islamic Finance: The Regulatory Challenge*. Singapore: Wiley, 2007.

Mirakhor, Abbas. "General characteristics of an Islamic economic system." In Bakir al-Hasani, and Abbas Mirakhor (eds). *Essays on Iqtisad*. Silver Spring, MD: NUR Corp., 1989; 45–80.

Venardos, Angelo M. *Islamic Banking and Finance in South-East Asia: Its Development and Future*. 2nd ed. Singapore: World Scientific Publishing, 2006.

Articles:

Akhtar, Shamshad. "Islamic finance: Its sustainability and challenges." *Journal of Islamic Banking and Finance* 25:1 (2008).

"Government proposes, bureaucracy disposes. And the bureaucracy must dispose of government proposals by dumping them on us." P. J. O'Rourke

  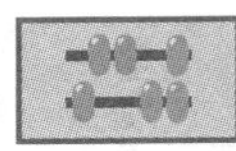      

Thomas, Abdulkader, and Sheikh Muhamed Becic. "Are sukuk Islamic?" *Islamic Business and Finance* 26 (January 2008). Online at: tinyurl.com/yej8x8p

Reports:

Ainley, Michael, Ali Mashayekhi, Robert Hicks, Arshadur Rahman, and Ali Ravalia. "Islamic finance in the UK: Regulation and challenges." Financial Services Authority, November 2007. Online at: www.fsa.gov.uk/pubs/other/islamic_finance.pdf

El-Hawary, Dahlia, Grais Wafik, and Zamir Iqbal. "Regulating Islamic financial institutions: The nature of the regulated." World Bank Policy Research Working Paper 3227, March 2004.

Websites:

Islamic Financial Services Board: www.ifsb.org

Securities and Exchange Commission of Pakistan: www.secp.gov.pk

See Also:

★ Islamic Insurance Markets and the Structure of *Takaful* (pp. 202–203)
★ Islamic Modes of Finance and the Role of *Sukuk* (pp. 520–521)
★ Viewpoint: *Shariah* Law—Bringing a New Ethical Dimension to Banking (pp. 242–243)
✔ An Overview of *Shariah*-Compliant Funds (p. 1083)
✔ Regulatory and Capital Issues under *Shariah* Law (p. 1050)
✔ The Role of the *Shariah* Advisory Board in Islamic Finance (p. 1015)
An Introduction to Islamic Finance Theory and Practice (p. 1380)

NOTES

1 Mirakhor (1989).
2 Venardos (2006).
3 Basel Committee on Banking Supervision. "Consultative document: Overview of the new Basel Capital Accord." Bank for International Settlements, April (2003). Online at: www.bis.org/bcbs/bcbscp3.htm
4 Thomas and Becic (2008).
5 El-Hawary *et al.* (2004), p. 36.

"The speed with which bureaucracy has invaded almost every branch of human activity is something astounding once one thinks about it." Simone Weil

Implementing an Effective Internal Controls System

by Andrew Chambers

EXECUTIVE SUMMARY

- Effective internal control gives reasonable assurance, though not a guarantee, that all business objectives will be achieved. It extends much beyond the aim of ensuring that financial reports are reliable. It includes the efficient achievement of operational objectives and ensuring that laws, regulations, policies, and contractual obligations are complied with.
- There is growing appreciation that effective internal control does not evolve naturally. It requires concerted effort on an ongoing basis.
- Often initially stimulated by the requirements of the Sarbanes–Oxley Act (2002), many more businesses are now systematically documenting, testing, evaluating, and improving their internal control processes. We show how to do this.
- In a large organization this more rigorous focus on internal control is likely to encourage greater standardization of similar processes in use in different parts of the organization.
- More effective internal control does not necessarily cost more. Aside from reducing costly risks of avoidable losses and business failures, it is often no more costly to organize business activities in ways that optimize control.
- Better internal controls may enable a business to engage safely in more profitable activities that would be too risky for a competitor without those controls.

INTRODUCTION

In some jurisdictions law or regulation may require effective systems of internal control, with serious penalties for irresponsible failure. The Sarbanes–Oxley Act (2002) requires CEOs and CFOs of companies with listings in the United States to certify their assessment of the effectiveness of internal control over reported disclosures (s302) and financial reporting (s404), with penalties of up to US$1 million and ten years imprisonment for unjustified certification, or up to US$5 million and 20 years imprisonment for wilful breach of the requirements (s906). The Public Companies Accounting Oversight Board's Auditing Standard No. 5 (2007) requires the company's external auditors themselves to assess the effectiveness of their client's system of internal control over financial reporting, in order to meet the audit requirements of s404 of the Sarbanes–Oxley Act.

Japan and Canada have laws broadly similar to the Sarbanes–Oxley Act. Although not reinforced by the risk of criminal sections, provision C.2.1 of the The UK Corporate Governance Code (2010) requires that the board of a company listed on the main market of the London Stock Exchange should satisfy itself that appropriate systems are in place to identify, evaluate, and manage the significant risks faced by the company; and provision C.2.2 requires that the board should, at least annually, conduct a review of the effectiveness of the group's system of internal controls and should report to shareholders that they have done so. The review should cover all material controls, including financial, operational, and compliance controls, and risk management systems. In addition, the UK Financial Services Authority's Disclosure and Transparency Rule DTR 7.2.5 R requires companies to describe the main features of the internal control and risk management systems in relation to the financial reporting process (see Schedule C).

WHAT "EFFECTIVE" MEANS

Although similar requirements exist in many countries, the principal driver for implementing an effective internal controls system should be the enlightened self interest of the company.

Effective internal control is intended to give reasonable assurance of the achievement of corporate objectives at all levels. An internal control framework should be used for the design and evaluation of an internal control system. The COSO framework is the most widely applied of three published frameworks.[1] COSO (the Committee of Sponsoring Organizations of the Treadway Commission) defines internal control as follows:

"Internal control is broadly defined as a process, effected by the entity's board of directors, management and other personnel, designed to provide reasonable assurance regarding the achievement of objectives in the following categories:
1 Effectiveness and efficiency of operations.
2 Reliability of financial reporting.
3 Compliance with applicable laws and regulations."

Other definitions of internal control categorize the objectives of internal control differently, but fundamentally, effective internal control gives reasonable assurance that all of management's objectives will be achieved. For instance, the King Report (2002)[2] defined internal control as follows:

"The board should make use of generally recognized risk management and internal control models and frameworks in order to maintain a sound system of risk management and internal control to provide a reasonable assurance regarding the achievement of organizational objectives with respect to:
1 Effectiveness and efficiency of operations;
2 Safeguarding of the company's assets (including information);

CASE STUDY 1

A multinational company took the requirement to comply with s404 of the Sarbanes–Oxley Act as an opportunity to assess the effectiveness of its internal control generally, not just internal controls over financial reporting.

First, the accounting processes that could lead to financial misstatements were identified. Second, mission-critical operational processes were identified where there were significant risks of not achieving business objectives and/or risks of misstatement. These accounting and operational processes were documented in process maps (flowcharts), using distinctive symbols to denote what were considered to be key s404 controls, other key financial controls , and key operational controls. These controls were described in a spreadsheet-based control register, supplemented where necessary by further process narrative. From this understanding of each process, deficiencies in control procedures were identified and corrected. Using predetermined, documented test scripts, each key control within a process was then tested for compliance prior to drawing a conclusion about internal control effectiveness of the process.

Initially this work was done by the internal audit function, before being transferred to become an ongoing responsibility of management, working to an annual cycle.

"If companies view the new laws as opportunities—opportunities to improve internal controls, improve the performance of the board, and improve their public reporting—they will ultimately be better run, more transparent, and therefore more attractive to investors." William Donaldson

3 Compliance with applicable laws, regulations and supervisory requirements;
4 Supporting business sustainability under normal as well as adverse operating conditions;
5 Reliability of reporting;
6 Behaving responsibly towards all stakeholders."

Before a conclusion can be reached that internal control is effective, both *results* and *processes* must be considered. For the former, the test is whether there have been any known outcomes attributable to significant breakdowns in internal control. Absence of these does not lead automatically to the conclusion that internal control is effective: it is possible that there may have been breakdowns of internal control yet to be discovered; it is also possible that serious weaknesses exist within the system of internal control that have not yet been exploited. So the second test must also be applied, which is to assess the quality of the control processes or "components."

DESIGN CHARACTERISTICS OF AN EFFECTIVE INTERNAL CONTROLS SYSTEM

The COSO internal control framework recognizes five essential components of any effective internal control system:

- The control environment: Values and culture; tone at the top; policies, organizational structure.
- Information and communication: Reliability, timeliness, clarity, usefulness.
- Risk assessment: Identification, measurement, and responses to threats.
- Control activities: Procedures followed for a control purpose.
- Monitoring: Review of internal control arrangements.

A common failing in designing and evaluating a system of internal control is to focus almost exclusively on control activities, vitally important though they are, overlooking that the other components are also essential. The Securities and Exchange Commission's rule for management's implementation of s404 of the Sarbanes–Oxley Act requires that a recognized internal control framework is applied. Usually it is the COSO framework that is used, and the framework comprises all of these five as being essential components of an effective system of internal control.

General hallmarks of an effective system of internal control include that controls:

- are designed to meet objectives which are clear;
- have regard to competitive issues;
- enable and ensure that performance is measured;
- aid the identification of risks;
- result in unsatisfactory performance being rectified;
- ensure that activities are completed in a timely way;
- mean the right people do the right jobs;
- are cost effective;
- are placed as early in the process as is practical, so that thereafter there is control;[3]
- specify and require appropriate authorization requirements;
- ensure there is an adequate audit trail;
- are "preventative" rather than merely "permissive";
- have no more movements, or steps than are necessary;
- are flexible to allow for adaptation;
- are documented.

Control activities can be categorized as follows:

Preventive controls: *To limit the possibility of an undesirable outcome being realized.* The more important it is that an undesirable outcome should not arise, the more important it becomes to implement appropriate preventive controls. Examples are when no one person has authority to act without the consent of another, or limitation of action to authorized persons (such as only those suitably trained and authorized being permitted to handle media enquiries).

Corrective controls: *To correct undesirable outcomes that have been realized.* Examples are the design of contract terms to allow recovery of overpayment, or contingency planning for business continuity/recovery after events which the business could not avoid.

Directive controls: *To ensure that a particular outcome is achieved or an undesirable event is avoided.* Examples are a requirement that protective clothing be worn, or that staff be trained with required skills before working unsupervised.

Detective controls: *To identify undesirable outcomes "after the event."* Examples are stock or asset checks which

CASE STUDY 2

To be useful, process narrative on internal control must be sufficiently specific to indicate whether control is effective. In the three examples below, only the third is adequate. The reader of the first and second examples will be unclear as to whether it is merely the narrative that is inadequate, or that internal control is inadequate.

Control Documentation Poor

A report on duplicate invoices is produced before payments are made. It is looked at and approved by someone who plays no other part in the order-processing and invoicing procedures.

Control Documentation Average

Each day, before the payments processing run, the senior creditors clerk (SCC) investigates a report on possible duplicate invoices. The SCC signs and dates this report when the check has been completed, and sends the report to James Smith for second review and final approval. James signs and dates the report to indicate completion of his review and approval of the SCC's investigation.

Neither James nor the SCC has access to the purchase order or invoice-processing SAP modules or the manual parts of those subsystems.

Control Documentation Good

Daily, before the IT-based processing of payments, the SCC personally prints out a possible duplicate payments report from the payables module in SAP (SAP report code 9VDFZ3). This report may indicate five possible types of duplicate (refer to details in the process narrative).

The SCC investigates the possible duplicate invoices as indicated in the report by checking the accuracy of invoice data captured in the SAP accounts payable module against original invoices, making sure that each invoice is valid by reference to source documentation, such as purchase orders , as necessary.

The SCC has no responsibility for other elements of this system, not having any involvement in, or other access to, the processing of purchase orders or invoices—these access rights are blocked to the SCC by the accounts payable module.

When the SCC has completed the investigation, he signs and dates the possible duplicate payments report to indicate that the investigation has been completed. His manager then reviews the possible duplicate payments report, together with the relevant, supporting evidence and comments from SCC's investigation. If the manager is satisfied by the investigation and supporting evidence, he signs and dates the possible duplicate payments report to indicate approval of the SCC's investigation.

"Cars have brakes so that they can go faster." Anonymous

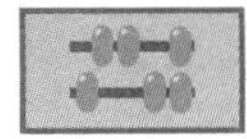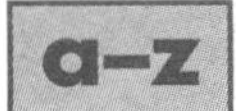

detect unauthorized removals, or post-implementation reviews to learn lessons.

Performance controls: *To orientate and motivate the organization's people to focus on the achievement of targets that are appropriate for the achievement of objectives.* Examples are despatching all orders on the day of receipt of the order, or allowing that less than 2% of production should fail quality control checks.

Investigative controls: To try to understand how the undesirable outcome occurred so as to be able to ensure that it does not happen next time, and to provide a route of recourse to achieve some recovery against loss or damage.[4]

ASSESSING INTERNAL CONTROL EFFECTIVENESS

A widely followed approach to assessing and improving internal control effectiveness has been developed that comprises these steps (see case study 1):

1 Determine the documentation to be used, such as process maps (flowcharts), control registers, and process narratives.
2 Identify the objectives to be achieved.
3 Determine the processes that are key to the achievement of objectives.
4 Learn about each key process, documenting it in narrative, spreadsheet, and/or flowchart form.
5 Within a key process, identify and document the key controls.
6 Judge the potential of each key control to be effective, if followed as intended. Modify the control approach if necessary.
7 Design and document tests to be conducted to assess compliance with each control.
8 Conduct these tests.
9 Interpret the results of these tests. Where necessary, ensure better compliance or modify the control approach if satisfactory compliance is judged impractical.
10 Interpret the control significance of unwanted outcomes that have occurred.
11 Consider the adequacy of the control environment, information and communication, risk assessment, control activities, and monitoring.
12 Conclude on the effectiveness of internal control at the process level.

TESTING INTERNAL CONTROLS

The extent of testing is a compromise between the need for thoroughness and the testing resources available, and will vary according to the criticality of the controls that are being relied upon, the potential for the controls to be circumvented, and the results of initial testing. For controls designed to operate at intervals (such as at week, month, or year ends), initial sample sizes may be as in *Table 1*. For controls that apply to individual transactions *Table 2* may be appropriate, which can also be used for interval controls that are used in multiple locations or on multiple occasions.

Table 1. Sample sizes to be used if the control operates at the frequencies shown

Frequency of control	Sample size
Annually	1
Quarterly	2
Monthly	2
Weekly	5
Daily	20
Many times a day	25

Table 2. Sample sizes for transaction controls

Population size	Sample size
1–3	1
4–11	2
12–50	3
51–100	5
101–200	15
201–300	20
Above 300	25 max

ONGOING MAINTENANCE OF AN INTERNAL CONTROLS SYSTEM

Changing business requirements will result in modified business processes and the risk that controls within those processes may be abandoned or made less effective. Each modified business process that is key to the achievement of a business objective should be reassessed, applying steps 3 to 6 (above), prior to releasing the new or modified business process for operational use.

For established processes, performance criteria should be established to monitor the quality of performance and the extent to which controls fail.

MAKING IT HAPPEN

The approach to follow:

1 Adopt and understand a recognized internal control framework.
2 Engage the board, management, and other personnel in the ownership of internal control.
3 Identify the mission-critical business processes.
4 Consider standardizing processes across the business.
5 Document those processes, highlighting the key controls.
6 Consider the effectiveness of the key controls and improve where necessary.
7 Design tests to confirm satisfactory compliance with key controls, and take remedial action as required.
8 In addition to control activities, consider whether the other essential components of an effective system of internal control are sound—for example, the control environment, information and communication, risk assessment , and monitoring.
9 Draw overall conclusions.
10 Use the results from this process as a continuous improvement tool to improve the internal control system.

MORE INFO

Books:

American Institute of Certified Public Accountants (AICPA). *Internal Control over Financial Reporting: Guidance for Smaller Public Companies.* The Institute of Internal Auditors Research Foundation, 2006. Order from: www.theiia.org/bookstore

Chambers, Andrew. *Tolley's Internal Auditor's Handbook*. 2nd ed. London: LexisNexis Butterworths, 2009. See especially chapter 6.

Committee of Sponsoring Organizations of the Treadway Commission (COSO). *Internal Control—Integrated Framework*. 2 vols, 1992. Order from: www.coso.org/IC-IntegratedFramework-summary.htm

COSO. *Guidance on Monitoring Internal Control Systems*. 2009. See exposure/review link at: www.coso.org

Articles:

Sneller, Lineke, and Henk Langendijk. "Sarbanes-Oxley Section 404 costs of compliance: A case study." *Corporate Governance: An International Review* 15:2 (March 2007): 101–111. Online at: dx.doi.org/10.1111/j.1467-8683.2007.00547.x

Wagner, Stephen, and Lee Dittmar. "The unexpected benefits of Sarbanes-Oxley." *Harvard Business Review* (April 2006). Online at: tinyurl.com/4jewuc5

"In short, if you are looking for leniency you had better be able to show that you cared about preventing corporate misconduct before you discovered it occurred." Cynthia A. Glassman

Reports:

Canadian Institute of Chartered Accountants. A number of publications in the series *Control Environment—Guidance on Control*. Online at: www.rmgb.ca/publications/index.aspx

COSO. "Enterprise risk management—Integrated framework." 2004. Summary and print requests online at: www.coso.org/ERM-IntegratedFramework.htm

Financial Reporting Council (FRC), UK. "The Turnbull guidance as an evaluation framework for the purposes of Section 404(a) of the Sarbanes–Oxley Act." 2004. Online at: www.frc.org.uk/documents/pagemanager/frc/draft_guide.pdf

FRC. "Internal control: Revised guidance for directors on the Combined Code." October 2005. Online at: www.ecgi.org/codes/code.php?code_id=178.

HM Treasury, UK. "The orange book: management of risk—Principles and concepts." October 2004. Online at: www.hm-treasury.gov.uk/d/3(4).pdf

The Institute of Internal Auditors. "Sarbanes–Oxley Section 404: A guide for management by internal controls practitioners." 2nd ed. January 2008. Online at: www.theiia.org/download.cfm?file=31866

Public Company Accounting Oversight Board (PCAOB). "Auditing standard no. 5: An audit of internal control over financial reporting that is integrated with an audit of financial statements." July 2007. Online at: www.pcaobus.org/Standards/Standards_and_Related_Rules/Auditing_Standard_No.5.aspx

Securities and Exchange Commission (SEC). "Commission guidance regarding management's report on internal control over financial reporting under section 13(a) or 15(d) of the Securities Exchange Act of 1934." June 2007. Online at: www.sec.gov/rules/interp/2007/33-8810.pdf. Subject to amendment issued August 2007: www.sec.gov/rules/final/2007/33-8809.pdf

Website:

Institute of Internal Auditors: www.theiia.org

See Also:

★ The Effect of SOX on Internal Control, Risk Management, and Corporate Governance Best Practice (pp. 333–335)
★ Engaging Senior Management in Internal Control (pp. 336–337)
★ How Can Internal Audit Report Effectively to Its Stakeholders? (pp. 342–345)
★ Internal Audit and Partnering with Senior Management (pp. 368–371)
★ Optimizing Internal Audit (pp. 382–384)
★ What Is the Range of the Internal Auditor's Work? (pp. 431–434)
✔ Sarbanes–Oxley: Its Development and Aims (p. 1052)
✔ Understanding Internal Audits (p. 1057)
Managing Financial Resources (p. 1390)

NOTES

1 Other recognized internal control frameworks are the Canadian "CoCo" framework, and the United Kingdom's Turnbull framework.

2 King Report on Corporate Governance for South Africa (March 2002), "King II," Institute of Directors in Southern Africa. "King III Report and Code" (September 1, 2009) did not include this definition of internal control.

3 For instance, incoming cash should be controlled at the point and time of entry into the business.

4 The Institute of Internal Auditors Inc., (May 2009): Practice Advisory 2010-2: *Using the Risk Management Process in Internal Audit Planning*, para 4. The meaning PA 2010-2 gives to 'investigative controls' is not identical to the meaning we have given in this chapter.

"Bureaucracy is ever desirous of spreading its influence and power." Herbert Hoover

  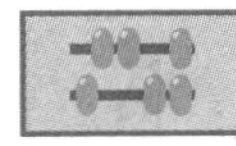   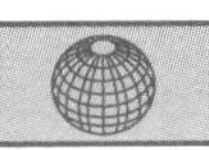   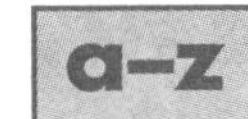

Incorporating Operational and Performance Auditing into Compliance and Financial Auditing

by Andrew Cox

EXECUTIVE SUMMARY

- Almost every audit can also be an operational or performance audit.
- With a bit of creativity, it is not too difficult to include a value-adding element to a compliance or financial audit.
- Operational and performance auditing can provide added value to your organization.
- Including an operational or performance auditing element in your audits can enhance the image of auditing for those being audited and also for management.
- Auditors can increase their job satisfaction through operational and performance auditing.
- The 3Es of economy, efficiency, and effectiveness should be integral components of the internal auditor's work.

INTRODUCTION

"The truth is, "audit gets no respect." Quite frankly, if the audit department in question is using yesterday's approach in today's company, has not manoeuvred top management and the board into focusing on the company's top five or ten risks, has not caused management to quantify these risks, and has not succeeded in developing authorized bounds of risk tolerance, then it doesn't deserve any respect." Larry Small, President, Fannie Mae, 2000.

This is a great quote, but what a pity it was not applied in recent times when this company got into serious financial difficulty. Perhaps a greater focus on operational and performance auditing might have helped.

What are the big risks for management? Are they likely to be immaterial accounting mistakes, a missing signature on a form, an immaterial asset that cannot be located, people not following a procedure exactly, or perhaps petty cash missing?

Or maybe management is more concerned with making sure the organization is running properly, which means focusing on economy, efficiency, and effectiveness—better known as the 3Es.

OPERATIONAL AND PERFORMANCE AUDITING

What is the difference between operational and performance auditing?

- **Operational audit**. Sometimes called program or performance audits, these examine the use of resources to evaluate whether those resources are being used in the most efficient and effective ways to fulfill an organization's objectives. An operational audit may include elements of a compliance audit, a financial audit, and an information systems audit. This term is mainly used in the private sector.
- **Performance audit**. This is an independent and systematic examination of the management of an organization, program, or function to identify whether the management is being carried out in an efficient and effective manner and whether management practices promote improvement. This term is mainly used in the public sector and may be the same as or similar to an operational audit.

While there may be purists who will argue there is a difference, the reality is that they seek to achieve the same objective. Although operational and performance auditing are generally applied to public sector auditing, and operational auditing is usually applied to private sector auditing, both seek to achieve organizational improvement of the 3Es.

THE AUDIT CONTINUUM

The audit continuum is shown in Figure 1. As we move from basic compliance auditing to more complex forms of auditing such as operational and performance auditing, the complexity of the audit and the difficulty in getting agreement to the audit objectives from the audit customer increases.

THE DIFFERENCES

The differences between operational and performance auditing, and compliance and financial auditing, are shown in Table 1. The real difference is that operational and performance auditing will genuinely add value and seek to improve the bottom line of an organization. Compliance and financial auditing cannot make this assertion, since their focus is generally on whether things are being done in accordance with legislation, regulations,

Figure 1. The audit continuum

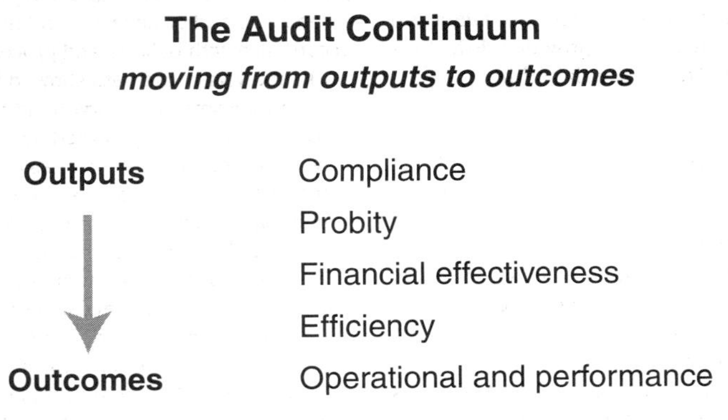

The Audit Continuum

moving from outputs to outcomes

Outputs	Compliance
↓	Probity
	Financial effectiveness
	Efficiency
Outcomes	Operational and performance

Table 1. Differences between operational and performance auditing, and compliance and financial auditing. (*Source*: The State Audit of the United Arab Emirates)

	Operational and performance auditing	Compliance and financial auditing
Purpose	Does performance meet the 3Es?	Is there compliance?
Focus	The organization and its objectives	Accounting transactions
Academic base	Economics, political science, sociology, etc.	Accounting
Methods	Methods vary from audit to audit	Standardized methods
Assessment criteria	Unique for each audit	Standardized criteria
Reports	Varying format	Standardized format

"The new business environment requires an equally new vision for internal audit." KPMG

  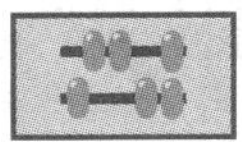      

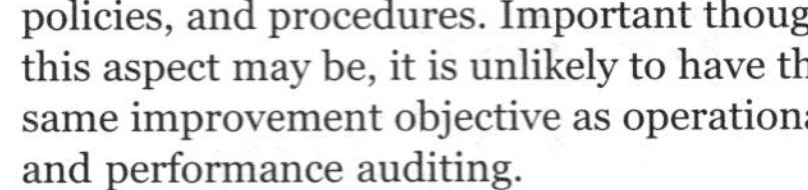

policies, and procedures. Important though this aspect may be, it is unlikely to have the same improvement objective as operational and performance auditing.

ECONOMY, EFFICIENCY, AND EFFECTIVENESS

What are we seeking to achieve by using performance and operational auditing? The aim is to find out whether business operations are being managed in an economic, efficient, and effective manner; whether procedures for promoting and monitoring the 3Es are adequate; and, importantly, whether improvements can be made.

Economy is concerned with minimizing the cost of resources used (people, materials, equipment, etc.), having regard to the appropriate quality required: i.e., keeping the cost of inputs low without compromising quality. An example could be where healthcare supplies or services of a specific quality are purchased at the best possible price.

Efficiency is concerned with the relationship between goods and services produced (outputs) and the resources used to produce them (inputs): i.e., getting the most from available resources. An example could be where the cost of providing healthcare has been reduced over time. Efficiency is about "doing things right."

Effectiveness is concerned with achieving predetermined objectives (specifically planned achievements) and having the actual impact (output achieved) compared with the intended impact (objective): i.e., achieving the predetermined objective. An example could be where disease rates have fallen as a result of the healthcare provided. Effectiveness is about "doing the right things."

WHAT MANAGEMENT WANTS

Although there are many internal auditors who still believe their job is to tell management what is wrong but not how to fix it, many more enlightened internal auditors have worked out what management is really seeking. This includes such things as:

- help in reducing risk;
- help in improving the business;
- assurance that appropriate governance is in place and working properly;
- internal audits that are relevant and timely;
- internal audits that genuinely add value;
- more value for the money spent on internal audits.

THE STEPS IN PERFORMING AN OPERATIONAL OR PERFORMANCE AUDIT

The sequence of an operational or performance audit is likely to be:

- establish what should be done;
- establish what is being done;
- compare "what should" with "what is";
- investigate significant differences;
- assess the effects of the differences;
- determine the cause of the differences;
- develop audit findings and value-adding options and recommendations.

While the initial steps may not be very different from a compliance or financial audit, the crucial and value-adding steps are: determining the cause of the differences; and developing audit findings and value-adding options and recommendations.

These are the difficult parts. Most compliance or financial auditors can work out an effect, but trying to isolate the cause can be much harder. Hence, many internal auditors find it easier just to report on what is wrong and avoid trying to identify the root cause of a problem.

Often an internal audit recommendation will be something like "Employees should follow the procedures." This is lazy internal audit work and not a particularly enlightened recommendation—it is more of a throwaway line. There may be many reasons why an employee is not following

CASE STUDY

It is not difficult to turn a compliance audit into a performance audit. In fact, almost every audit can also be an operational or performance audit. And, by being creative, internal auditors can make their internal audit work more interesting and satisfying.

This case study comes from an internal audit conducted in a utilities company that provides electricity, gas, and water to the community. In this company, field staff work overtime. (Overtime is time worked beyond an established limit: i.e., hours worked in excess of the working hours prescribed in the employment agreement.)

The objectives of the audit were to:

- determine who had responsibility for overtime and assess whether this arrangement was working effectively;
- identify the key risks involved with overtime and the mitigation strategies and controls currently in place to manage those risks;
- identify the extent of overtime worked and test whether the key controls were working effectively to manage the identified risks;
- ascertain whether overtime requirements were being effectively communicated to managers and staff;
- review whether management regularly received and acted on feedback on the need for overtime and periodically examined cost-effective alternatives.

The audit covered all the regular auditing matters such as compliance with policy and procedures, sampling and testing overtime calculations, etc., as you would expect in a compliance audit. Since it found that overtime payments were being made correctly in accordance with policies and procedures, the audit was a nonevent. But, with some extra work, analysis of the data showed that:

- most overtime was worked in the electricity division;
- overtime was being worked by around a third of employees, with the number of employees who worked overtime increasing;
- the overall amount of overtime had been steadily increasing in absolute and payroll percentage terms across the organization over the previous four years;
- the electricity and water divisions had overtime budgets for the next year that were below the budgets for the current year (almost certainly optimistically).

Analysis of the causes revealed that:

- there was a countrywide shortage of line workers, resulting in the electricity division being unable to recruit sufficient numbers of people with these skills;
- the electricity division pole replacement program was difficult to run with the number of line workers currently employed by the organization;
- a serious wildfire had destroyed substantial electricity assets.

Once the causes had been identified, the audit recommendations suggested that the organization consider such things as:

- developing a longer-term perspective when formulating future industrial plans for the workforce;
- extending human resources employee self-service to the field employees;
- extending mobile computing to the field for human resources activities and job costing;
- further annualizing salaries to include an overtime component;
- changing the rostering of work crews to true shift work arrangements over 24/7/365.

This added real value to the audit, rather than being a simple compliance audit approach—which would have merely reported that overtime calculations were being made correctly.

"We will make an impact when we understand and anticipate stakeholder needs, use our core competencies to highlight weaknesses in a timely manner, and provide meaningful recommendations that solve the 'big problems'."
Head of Internal Audit in an Australian Government department

  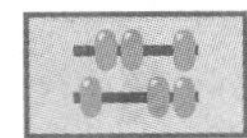      

procedures. But not many employees will deliberately disobey a procedure unless it is a bad procedure, or something else is preventing them from complying with it.

PARTNERING WITH MANAGEMENT

There are a number of ways in which internal auditors can promote their services—in particular the benefits of operational and performance auditing. These may include:

- Develop an engagement model and get management buy-in.
- Closely align your internal auditing with the business.
- Plan a risk-based internal audit program developed with management.
- Aim to become an integral part of the organization and to help management improve the business.
- Plan each internal audit with management.
- Facilitate a frank risk assessment with management and stakeholders for each internal audit.
- Formulate insightful objectives for each internal audit, not just "throwaway lines."
- Ask management to agree and sign off the terms of reference for each internal audit.
- Consider using technical experts where internal auditors may not have all the necessary skills for an internal audit.
- Facilitate a workshop with management and stakeholders at the conclusion of an audit to discuss and agree possible improvement options.

REPORTING

As mentioned previously, the real value in an internal audit report is in determining the cause of the differences between "what is" and "what should be," and developing audit findings and value-adding options and recommendations. This is the essence of what operational and performance auditing is all about.

By working closely with management and stakeholders at the conclusion of the audit to discuss improvement options, possibly using a facilitated workshop approach, a much better outcome can be achieved. After all, the people doing the job know a lot more about it than the internal auditor!

CONCLUSION

With a bit of creativity, it is not too difficult to include a value-adding element in a compliance or financial audit:

- Almost every audit can also be an operational or performance audit.
- You can do operational and performance auditing to provide added value to your organization.
- Including an operational or performance auditing element in your audits can enhance the image of auditing with the people being audited and with management.
- You can increase your job satisfaction through operational and performance auditing.

MAKING IT HAPPEN

- Develop an engagement model for your internal auditing, and get management buy-in.?36;
- Closely align your internal auditing with the business, plan a risk-based internal audit program developed with management, and aim to become an integral part of the organization in order to help management improve the business.
- Plan each internal audit with management, and facilitate an up-front risk assessment with management and stakeholders at the commencement of each internal audit—this is a quick and cost-effective way to determine the business processes, risks, and control procedures in place, as well as getting management buy-in.
- Ask management to agree and sign off the terms of reference for each internal audit—be sure that the objectives of an operational or performance audit are insightful and are not just throwaway lines.
- Consider using experts in technical subject areas where internal audit may not have all the skills required for an internal audit.
- Measurement criteria need to be developed; this is much more difficult than a compliance or financial audit and needs to be objective, understandable, comparable, complete, and acceptable.
- Learn the difference between "hard controls" (existence of policies and procedures, documents, payment approvals, segregation of duties, etc.) and "soft controls" (focus on ethics, integrity, competency, relationship building), and learn how to audit soft controls.
- Go outside the organization to get information and consult with external stakeholders.
- Keep the audit focused and timely, if not properly managed operational and performance audits can take on a life of their own and can end up taking a long time to complete.
- Engage and communicate with management throughout the internal audit.
- Convene a peer review challenge session within internal audit for the draft report; also do this for service providers who perform internal audits for you.
- Get the report "as right as it can be" before taking a draft to management.
- Facilitate a workshop with management and stakeholders at the conclusion of the audit to discuss and agree possible improvement options.

MORE INFO

Books:

Reding, Kurt F., Paul J. Sobel, Urton L. Anderson, Michael J. Head, Sridhar Ramamoorti, Mark Salamasick, and Cris Riddle. *Internal Auditing: Assurance and Consulting Services*. 2nd ed. Orlando, FL: IIA Research Foundation, 2009.

Sawyer, Lawrence B., Mortimer A. Dittenhofer, and James H. Scheiner. *Sawyer's Internal Auditing: The Practice of Modern Internal Auditing.* 5th ed. Altamonte Springs, FL: IIA Research Foundation, 2003.

Standards:

Institute of Internal Auditors. "International standards for the professional practice of internal auditing." October 2010. Online at: www.theiia.org/guidance/standards-and-guidance/ippf/standards

Websites:

Australian National Audit Office: www.anao.gov.au
International Organization of Supreme Audit Institutions: www.intosai.org
Institute of Internal Auditors: www.theiia.org
Office of the Auditor-General of Canada: www.oag-bvg.gc.ca

Training Courses and Postgraduate Qualifications:

University of Canberra. "Graduate certificate in performance audit and evaluation." Details online at: www.canberra.edu.au/courses-units/gc/business/domestic-only/842aa

Institute of Internal Auditors. "Performance based auditing in the public sector." Details online at: www.theiia.org/training/index.cfm?act=seminar.onsitedetail&semID=76

Institute of Internal Auditors. "Operational auditing: An introduction through advanced." Details online at: www.theiia.org/training/index.cfm?act=seminar.onsitedetail&semID=209

"Almost every audit can also be an operational or performance audit." Andrew Cox

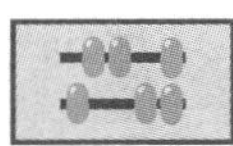

Internal Audit and Partnering with Senior Management by Bruce Turner

EXECUTIVE SUMMARY

- The business world is constantly changing. Internal auditors increasingly need to embrace ongoing changes to the business. They also need to understand changes to key drivers, such as the regulatory environment, the profession, and the social and political landscape.
- To do so, internal auditors must maintain a meaningful dialog with senior management, so as to understand their changing needs and expectations.
- An internal audit work plan that aligns neatly with the primary risk concerns of senior management and other key stakeholders ensures that the audit effort is directed at the areas that are likely to add the greatest value to the organization.
- Because of the increasing complexity associated with running an organization, internal auditors must ensure that their recommendations translate into improved business processes and effective risk management, governance, and control arrangements.
- Internal auditors need to have the capability to deliver a product that meets or exceeds the expectations of senior management.
- Internal auditors must also be able to tell their story to maintain their influence, relevance, and credibility within the organization.

THE CHANGING ENVIRONMENT

"The internal audit function has evolved from corporate cop to that of a savvy in-house consulting service."[1]

Internal auditing in the twenty-first century imposes even greater demands on the professional internal audit staff, whose role has expanded to combine both an assurance and a consulting service to management. Internal audit charters have been broadened considerably to reflect these demands.

The chief executive of the Institute of Internal Auditors in Australia (Christopher McRostie) has reflected:

"In rapidly changing and increasingly complex business and regulatory environments the internal audit function has evolved from corporate cop to that of a savvy in-house consulting service that not only reports problems, but that also gives constructive suggestions to line managers about how to improve the performance of the business."[2]

Internal audit staff are being increasingly relied on to provide organizational expertise in risk management, internal control, and governance processes as a consequence of the emergence of stronger corporate governance demands across the world. Internal auditors need to have strategies in place that allow them to remain abreast of trends and emerging issues within their organization and the broader business community.

Contemporary internal auditing practitioners need to apply a strategic approach to understanding the key organizational value drivers and positioning themselves to meet the expectations of senior management.

Internal auditors are well placed to influence senior management in setting the right tone at the top. This, in turn, is a powerful way to nurture an organizational culture that is consistent with the values, risk tolerance, and strategies of senior management and the board.

WHAT SENIOR MANAGEMENT WANTS

"The Chief Audit Executive should effectively manage the internal audit activity to ensure it adds value to the organization."[3]

Senior management trusts internal auditors to "tell it as it is" by reporting without fear or favor. One company chairman[4] observed that "senior management want much more immediate and informal input on how the corporation is doing ... I'd rather have the internal auditor on my doorstep telling me what I need to know so I can act on it now." His main suggestions for internal auditors were:

- Don't be distracted from good business practice.
- Understand your customer.
- Avoid being too production-oriented.
- Prioritize your activities and coordination role.
- Speak up when others may not.

Senior management is looking for assurance that current business activities meet regulatory and legislative obligations. They are also looking for ideas that drive better business performance in line with their overarching strategies and business model.

Internal auditors are best placed to meet senior management's expectations when they apply a sense of urgency to their work, apply a win–win mindset, and consistently deliver on commitments made. It is imperative that the integrity and credibility of their activities is undoubted, and that they nurture a professional and constructive relationship. The chief audit executive should undertake surveys of senior management to measure the quality of the service and determine how well the internal audit activity is serving their needs.

See below for a perspective on senior management's priorities in one organization in relation to internal auditing.

The chief audit executive ought to maintain regular conversations with senior management with the objective of understanding their business perspectives and expectations of the internal audit activity. This helps to shape the planning, objectives, and scope of individual audits. The relationship should be based on cooperation, collaboration, and mutual respect.

A structured stakeholder relationship program is a useful mechanism to ensure that regular contact is maintained and that the conversations and commitments are appropriately tracked. It needs to be tailored for the business environment by recognizing the areas that need the greatest level of contact.

By way of example, a three-tier stakeholder relationship program schedule might have:

- Quarterly contact with senior managers, such as the chief financial officer and chief risk officer.
- Half-yearly contact with business leaders in remote locations.
- Annual contact with managers of relatively low-risk activities like marketing.

Because of the heavy workload of many senior managers, it may be difficult to get time in their diaries. Get to know who their gatekeepers are and build relationships with them. That can sometimes help to unlock the doors in a more timely manner.

Some larger agencies establish audit liaison officers or champions across their business lines or regional offices as contact points for the internal audit activity. These people can also facilitate audit planning and the conduct of audits, and provide periodic updates on the status of previous audit recommendations.

There are benefits in establishing an internal auditor alumni. Most internal auditors retain their passion for the profession when they leave the area. They represent a fertile avenue across the

"The internal audit function has evolved from corporate cop to that of a savvy in-house consulting service." LexisNexis

  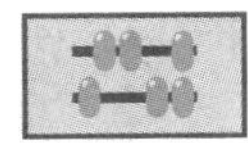      

organization for keeping abreast of what is really going on in the business.

SENIOR MANAGEMENT PRIORITIES

- Accurate reporting, which reflects a business perspective, is well-written, easy to follow, and is consistent with the facts.
- Practical, constructive, and actionable recommendations.
- Proper consideration of business concerns and perspectives.
- Clear communication of objectives and scope at the start of the audit.
- Disruption to daily business operations is minimized.

PLANNING THE INTERNAL AUDIT EFFORT TO DELIVER VALUE

"Begin with the end in mind."[5]

The internal audit effort is underpinned by effective planning that directs audit effort to the higher-risk areas of the business. It is imperative that senior management and other key stakeholders are engaged in the development of the internal audit plan to ensure that it is relevant and consistent with the organization's risk profile.

In addition to looking for feedback on the adequacy and effectiveness of risk management, governance, and internal controls, senior management want recommendations that help to improve business processes. They are no longer satisfied with receiving just the results of individual audits, though these remain important. Senior management are increasingly looking for the internal auditors to provide additional analyses of the results of audits to identify systemic issues and provide insights into the corporate culture of the organization. One way of meeting these expectations is to set "themes" for the various audits contained in the internal audit plan. This facilitates high-level reporting to senior management against each of the themes.

Internal auditors can provide the greatest value to senior management when they:

- Align their activities to their organization's goals and objectives, and periodically review the role of internal audit in the light of changes to the business and global events.
- Understand the business, the key drivers, the impact of developments on the organization's risks, and the mood of senior management.
- Consult effectively with senior management, staff, and other key stakeholders, and contribute ideas and advice on an ongoing basis.
- Elevate the focus of their activities to strategic decision-making and broader risk management strategies and mitigation, while maintaining an appropriate balance with traditional compliance and operational and financial auditing.
- Provide broader information and a deeper insight into emerging governance, risk, and control issues in a timely manner.
- Deliver what they promise.

MAXIMIZING INTERNAL AUDIT'S CAPABILITY

"The vision of the director of auditing and the high expectations of management are merely wistful wishes without the right staff to do the job."[6]

It is the capability of internal audit staff that often determines the level of credibility, trust, and respect that the internal audit activity has within the organization.

Ensure that senior management and the audit committee are kept apprised of the talent within the internal audit activity. Periodically produce a staff profile that sets out the skills, experience, qualifications, and years of audit experience of the internal auditors. This helps to establish or retain credibility, especially when it is combined with benchmarking of other internal audit activities.

At a time in our history when there is a global shortage of professional internal audit practitioners, coupled with a broader internal audit charter, it is imperative to position the internal audit activity as an employer of choice.

To attract the right people, use the results of the periodic external quality assessment reviews to differentiate your internal audit activity from others (these reviews are mandatory under professional internal auditing standards).

Elements that could be considered in building greater internal capability include the following.

- Develop a recruitment strategy based on a skills gap analysis. This will ensure that you have the right multidisciplinary capability to undertake the broad range of audits in the internal audit plan.
- Establish internal audit as a learning environment and encourage innovation. This is a point of differentiation from others that will help to cater for the needs of talented and ambitious individuals.
- Produce a professional development plan for internal auditors that incorporates both a top-down and a bottom-up approach. There are typically three elements: develop the current capability; extend the capability to broaden the circle of influence; and identify future disciplines. The top-down analysis will help to close the gap between current and future staff capability needs. It should also promote continuous learning by encouraging postgraduate studies and the pursuit of professional certifications. The bottom-up element reflects the specific developmental needs of individual internal auditors.
- Recognize that internal auditors must have exceptionally strong communication skills across all areas (especially written, reading, oral, listening, body language, and presentation).
- Promote professional internal auditing standards. Use the results of the periodic external quality assessment reviews to differentiate your internal audit activity from others.
- Build greater awareness of the internal audit activity across the organization, as this will help to attract fresh talent to the area. For instance, many large organizations have a structured graduate recruitment program, which is potentially a rich breeding ground. But graduates often do not understand the nature of internal auditing beyond the basic technical aspects they learned at university.
- Establish a policy that encourages subject matter experts to spend some time in internal audit on a secondment (typically three to six months). Tailor this to attract

CASE STUDY

Misguided Auditing Efforts

On reviewing the audit coverage of the retail loan portfolio of a commercial bank, an auditor discovered that there was broad coverage of personal loans which averaged about US$30,000. The auditors were doing a very thorough audit of the personal loans in line with the content of the internal audit plan, their sampling techniques were effective, their work papers were well-constructed, and the resultant audit report was well written.

However, the auditor also found that there was absolutely no audit coverage of foreign currency loans, although the average loan was around US$750,000 and had a far greater inherent risk. The reason was simple. Foreign currency loans had been introduced the previous year, and internal audit planning had not kept pace with the changing loan product and risk profile of the commercial bank. Consequently, the internal audit effort was misdirected and proved to be of little value to senior management in the overall context of their loan portfolio.

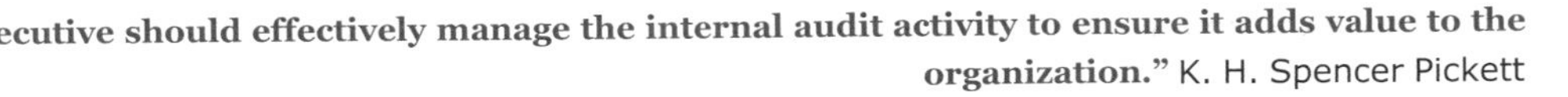

"The Chief Audit Executive should effectively manage the internal audit activity to ensure it adds value to the organization." K. H. Spencer Pickett

people with high potential, on the basis that what they learn in internal audit will help them throughout their career.

TELLING THE INTERNAL AUDIT STORY

"The balanced scorecard can help internal auditing directors achieve superior performance by focusing on value-added services, corporate strategies and priorities."[7]

The internal audit activity influences the business in many different ways, quite apart from producing the traditional audit reports. To this end, it is important that the chief audit executive takes the time to tell the internal audit story.

The balanced scorecard is a contemporary reporting structure that helps to paint a picture of how effectively the internal audit activity is partnering with senior management and driving value for the organization. In addition to periodic reporting throughout the year, the balanced scorecard approach provides a solid foundation for producing an annual report on internal audit aimed at better informing internal stakeholders. The balanced scorecard typically focuses on four elements: partnering with the audit committee; supporting senior management; managing internal audit processes; and managing people and their development.

There is an emerging interest in what internal audit is doing outside the organization. A recent trend has been to include a section in the balanced scorecard on professional outreach (for example, activities with professional associations, presentation of papers at external conferences, and published articles).

There are a range of communication channels that the chief audit executive can use to help build the "audit brand." The strategies will vary depending on the size of the organization. A good starting point is to develop a marketing plan or communication strategy. The intention is to influence people across the organization to embrace appropriate governance and risk management techniques, and to promote an effective control environment. In doing so, it helps to raise awareness about the internal audit activity, which, in turn, helps to garner cooperation and support for internal auditors in the conduct of their work.

Elements that could be included in a communication strategy include:

- Active participation in presenting key messages at the organization's induction, training, and other corporate programs.
- Articles in staff newsletters.
- An interesting, useful, and informative internal audit intranet site.
- Establishment of a network of business unit champions as a conduit for regular communications on audit matters.
- Taking an interest in the organization's graduate programs, so as to help promote ambassadors for internal audit in future leaders.
- Brochures on the internal audit activity.

ELEMENTS OF AN ANNUAL REPORT ON INTERNAL AUDIT

The content of an annual report will be dictated by the needs of senior management and the nature of the internal audit charter. Typical headings include:

- Foreword;
- Summary of internal audit activities;
- Overall conclusion;
- Activity headings.

For each balanced scorecard element there should be:

- A performance summary;
- A meeting attendance summary;
- Highlights;
- Areas for continuing focus.

MAKING IT HAPPEN

The chief audit executive must set the right direction for the internal audit activity in consultation with the audit committee and senior management. This will be reflected in an internal audit charter that outlines the role and responsibilities of the internal audit activity, as well as its vision and mission. The internal audit plan will reflect where internal audit resources are best applied.

At a time when the expectations of senior management and other stakeholders are getting higher, successful internal auditing demands the right people. These people will be intelligent, passionate, and innovative. They will have the knack of communicating well with senior managers and other stakeholders and responding to their needs, without compromising their independence of mind. Their research will alert them to the "next big risk."

Ideas for Further Consideration

There is a strong parallel between factors that result in highly credible internal auditing and those at the heart of a successful small business. Internal auditors will be well placed to partner with senior management when they think like a manager and apply business concepts similar to those outlined below. They are nine easy steps that underpinned a successful franchise business:[8]

- Try different things.
- Try to do everything you do better, and improve what you do in every possible way.
- Try to be more cost-effective.
- Try to keep overheads down.
- Try to give better service to your clients, make them happy, and focus on them.
- Be persistent and never give up.
- Look after your customers obsessively and worry about how you can look after them better.
- Give maximum service for the least cost.
- Listen a lot. Listen all the time. Listen. Listen. Listen.

MORE INFO

Books:

Covey, Stephen R. *The 7 Habits of Highly Effective People: Powerful Lessons in Personal Change*. London: Simon & Schuster, 2004.

Fraser, John, and Hugh Lindsay. *20 Questions Directors Should Ask about Internal Audit*. Toronto, ON: Canadian Institute of Chartered Accountants, 2004.

Frigo, Mark L. *A Balanced Scorecard Framework for Internal Auditing Departments*. Altamonte Springs, FA: Institute of Internal Auditors Research Foundation, 2002.

Pickett, K. H. Spencer. *The Internal Auditor at Work: A Practical Guide to Everyday Challenges*. 2nd ed. Hoboken, NJ: Wiley, 2004.

Sawyer, Lawrence B., Mortimer A. Dittenhofer, and James H. Scheiner. *Sawyer's Internal Auditing: The Practice of Modern Internal Auditing*. 5th ed. Altamonte Springs, FL: IIA Research Foundation, 2003.

Report:

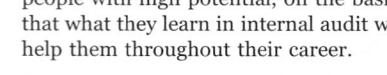

Australian National Audit Office. "Public sector internal audit: An investment in assurance and business improvement." Better Practice Guide. September 2007. Online at: www.anao.gov.au/uploads/documents/Public_Sector_Internal_Audit.pdf

Websites:
Australian National Audit Office: www.anao.gov.au
Canadian Institute of Chartered Accountants: www.cica.ca
Corporate Executive Board: www.audit.executiveboard.com
Institute of Internal Auditors: www.theiia.org

See Also:
★ Engaging Senior Management in Internal Control (pp. 336–337)
★ Financial Reporting: Conveying the Message Down the Line (pp. 677–679)
★ Incorporating Operational and Performance Auditing into Compliance and Financial Auditing (pp. 365–367)
★ The Internal Audit Role—Is There an Expectation Gap in Your Organization? (pp. 372–374)
★ New Assurance Challenges Facing Chief Audit Executives (pp. 378–381)
✔ Corporate Governance and Its Interpretations (p. 1111)
✔ Defining Corporate Governance: Its Aims, Goals, and Responsibilities (p. 1115)
✔ Understanding Internal Audits (p. 1057)

NOTES

1 LexisNexis. *Risk Management* 48 (2008): 12.
2 *Ibid.*
3 Pickett (2004), pp. 60–61.
4 Thomas, R. L. "A chairman's view of internal audit." *Bank Management Journal* (May/June 1996): 28–29.
5 Covey (2004), chapter on habit 2.
6 Sawyer, Lawrence B. *Sawyer's Internal Auditing*. 3rd ed. IIA, 1988, p. 785.
7 Frigo (2002), pp. 43, 50 (slightly edited).
8 Meltzer, G. "Someone else's slip-ups—Minding their own business." *Daily Telegraph (Sydney, Australia)* (October 16, 2001): 34 (edited).

"The vision of the director of auditing and the high expectations of management are merely wistful wishes without the right staff to do the job." Lawrence B. Sawyer

  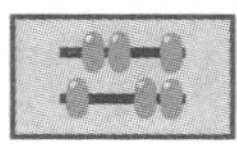   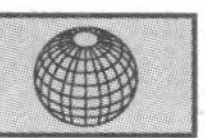   

The Internal Audit Role—Is There an Expectation Gap in Your Organization? by Jeffrey Ridley

EXECUTIVE SUMMARY

- Every internal audit role should be established with a charter approved and reviewed annually at board level.
- The internal audit charter should describe the internal audit role in the organization it serves, including its purpose, authority, responsibility, and relationships with external organizations.
- The internal audit charter should be promoted across the organization at all levels and as appropriate across its supply chains and to its stakeholders.
- Internal audit should have measures in place to demonstrate its level of performance to the organization.
- Expectation gaps at organization and individual customer levels should be identified, and all performance measures continuously monitored if the full added value of the internal audit role is to be achieved.
- New dimensions of the internal audit role in an organization should be continuously explored to ensure that it is at the cutting edge of its professional attributes and in its performance.

INTRODUCTION

Establishing the internal audit role in any organization requires formality to ensure that it is understood not only by the board and management but also by its customers across the organization and, where necessary, those external to the organization. The internal audit assurance and consulting role should be explained clearly in a charter to minimize any expectation gaps at board and organization levels. When the role is being established, it is important that internal audit management should have an input into the formal process through discussion with the board and senior management.

The Institute of Internal Auditors (IIA), as the global professional body representing internal auditing in every country, has always recommended and now requires in its *Standards*[1] the purpose, authority and responsibility of an internal audit activity to be formally approved and kept under review at the highest level in an organization." In some sectors this may also be a requirement of one or more of an organization's stakeholders, such as government or a sector's regulator.

PURPOSE, AUTHORITY, AND RESPONSIBILITY OF THE INTERNAL AUDIT ROLE

Purpose

The purpose of professional internal audit is described in the IIA's 2009 definition as:

"Internal auditing is an **independent objective assurance and consulting activity** designed **to add value and improve** an organization's operations. It helps an organization accomplish its objectives by bringing **a systematic, disciplined approach to evaluate and improve** the effectiveness of **risk management, control, and governance processes**."

Key to this definition of internal auditing are the words in bold:

- Independence of the internal audit and its objectivity are critical for all dimensions of the role practiced by the internal auditor.
- The value it adds to improve an organization's operations should be measured and reported continuously.
- All its services require systematic and disciplined processes.
- It requires a wide and deep knowledge and understanding of risk management, control and governance within the organizations it serves, across their supply chains, and with all their stakeholders.

Writers on internal auditing have been promoting its independent assurance and consulting roles since the first statement of responsibilities of the internal auditor was published by the IIA in 1947. Consultancy and training were never mentioned as such in the IIA's statements but were implied by its scope of responsibilities. The best evidence for this is in the "objective and scope of internal auditing" in its 1957 statement:

"The overall objective of internal auditing is to assist all members of management in the effective discharge of their responsibilities, by furnishing them with objective analyses, appraisals, recommendations and pertinent comments concerning the activities reviewed. The internal auditor therefore should be concerned with any phase of business activity wherein he can be of service to management. The attainment of this over-all objective of service to management should involve such activities as:

- Reviewing and appraising the soundness, adequacy and application of accounting, financial and operating controls.
- Ascertaining the extent of compliance with established policies, plans and procedures.
- Ascertaining the extent to which company assets are accounted for, and safeguarded from losses of all kinds.
- Ascertaining the reliability of accounting and other data developed within the organization.
- Appraising the quality of performance in carrying out assigned responsibilities."

The 1971 revision to this statement changed the fourth activity from "accounting and other data" to "management data," and added a sixth activity—"Recommending operating improvements." This widened the scope of internal audit into all operations. In 1981, the statement was further changed to state that internal auditing is a service to the "organization," not just to "management." This brought the board and all operating levels in the organization into the internal auditing market place.

Lawrence Sawyer[2] supported the role of internal auditors as consultants (and trainers) in his 1979 writings. He draws vivid pictures of "problem-solving internal auditors" providing reviews, appraisals, communications and advice on management: "the [internal] auditor has a duty to know the functions of management as thoroughly as the manager does." He discusses various consulting opportunities for internal auditors in the services they can provide, and he also gives recognition to internal auditors as teachers: "the internal auditor's role as a teacher is little known, insufficiently practiced, and generally not believed or accepted."

As the IIA scope statement was being revised, practicing internal auditors were broadening their services by increasing the number of dimensions in the role they provided in their organizations. Dr James Wilson and Dr Donna Wood[3] researched the behavioral dynamics of internal auditing, recognizing seven dimensions and conflicts in the internal auditor's role at that time (1985):

1. Accountant
2. Policeman
3. Watchdog
4. Teacher
5. Consultant

"**Professional internal auditors are experts in governance and skilled in the strategic, tactical and operational aspects of risk assessment and audit planning.**" *Cutting Edge Internal Auditing* (2008)

  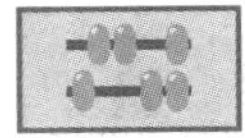      

6 Communicator
7 Future Manager

These dimensions and conflicts still exist in internal auditing. They should all be addressed at board level and, as appropriate, be clearly seen in its charter. They are currently seen in the IIA's definition of internal auditing and in its *Standards*.[4] The two roles in the definition—assurance and consultancy—are defined thus:

- **Assurance services** are an objective examination of evidence for the purpose of providing an independent assessment on governance, risk management, and control processes for the organization.
- **Consulting services** are advisory and related client services, the nature and scope of which are agreed with the client, are intended to add value and improve an organization's governance, risk management and control processes without the internal auditor assuming management responsibility.

The other dimensions can all be seen in these roles in practice and in the *Standards* and supporting guidelines.

Authority

The authority of internal audit should always lie at board level, evidenced by its reporting lines to the board and senior management and reviews of its performance at these levels. That authority may include reporting lines to the chair of an audit committee and presence at its meetings. It should also include open access to all an organization's employees, operations, systems, records, and property.

Responsibility

The responsibility of internal audit should clearly state the scope of its work in the organization and its reporting requirements to the board, senior management, and customers. In some organizations this may also include reference to the internal audit role in the organization's training programs, code of conduct, procedure for dealing with whistleblowing, and fraud prevention, detection, and investigation processes.

PROMOTING THE INTERNAL AUDIT ROLE

The internal audit charter approved by the board is only the beginning of the promotion of the internal audit role throughout an organization. It has to be visible to all its customers in the services it provides and in its planning and engagement processes. Internal auditing has developed many ways to do this through the publishing of internal brochures, intranet websites, and even organization websites. Examples of each can be found in many internal auditing text books.

Cindy Cosmas (1996)[5] studied how internal auditing in North America marketed itself within the organizations to which it provided services. She concluded that it required some initial planning and formality, but that it brought significant benefits:

"A marketing program, or plan, is essential for every internal auditing department. A well-devised plan will direct internal auditors in their quest to provide valuable services to their organization."

Cosmas goes on to say that such a plan should consist of specific objectives, a well-developed customer base, effective promotional tools, a plan of action, and a way to monitor success: in other words, a business strategy. It is not about internal auditing living on an island in an organization, separated from its customers! She discusses internal auditing marketing its creativity in her chapter on internal audit participation in management teams: "Utilizing creative instincts is one of the internal auditor's most powerful marketing tools." She recognized at the time the growing participation by internal auditors in team projects across organizations, working closely with operating staff and management. Seeing internal auditing creativity as an important part of the marketing, she writes:

"As a marketing tool, audit participation on project teams has been beneficial overall in winning management's praise and support. Internal auditing brings a unique perspective to project teams through their background and training."

MEASURING THE INTERNAL AUDIT EXPECTATION GAP

Cindy Cosmas also saw the marketing of internal auditing services as one of its key indicators for success and an important performance measure for assessing its continuous improvement: "The primary purpose of a performance measurement system is to support continuous improvement,"

CASE STUDY

Nine Important Points to Avoid Internal Audit Expectation Gaps[9]

More and more organizations are beginning to benefit from professional internal audit practice. This can be seen from the growing number of internal auditors in Europe that can be found in all sectors, public and private. This growth has been accelerated by legislation and regulation that requires organizations to demonstrate the effectiveness of their governance, risk management, and internal control processes because it is clear that an internal audit activity is uniquely positioned to support management. In the detailed paper,[9] we set out what we consider to be best practice in internal auditing and how organizations should use internal auditing to help achieve good governance and risk management practice. The most important points are:

1 Professional internal auditors will apply and uphold the IIA's Code of Ethics in all circumstances.
2 The audit committee will ensure that the mandate and responsibility of the internal audit activity is formalized in a charter that it approves.
3 The audit committee will ensure that the internal audit activity has a direct reporting line to the chief executive of the organization and an open and direct communication line to the board and itself, in order that it maintains its independence.
4 The chief audit executive will support the board and executive management in fulfilling its responsibilities for the systems of governance, risk management, and internal control.
5 The audit committee will ensure that the internal audit activity is adequately resourced and competently staffed by investing in their qualification and their continuing professional development. The promotion of qualifications, endorsed by the profession of internal auditing, will be central in this approach.
6 The chief audit executive will develop and maintain a quality assurance programme that covers all aspects of the internal audit activity, monitoring its effectiveness by using both internal assessments and assessments by appropriate external review bodies.
7 The chief audit executive will plan the internal audit work on the basis of the risks facing the organization, will make relevant and timely reports to other participants in the governance process, and will follow-up internal audit recommendations to enable the drive for continuous improvement in the organization to be successful.
8 The internal audit activity will promote internal controls that effectively mitigate risks in all activities of the organization.
9 The audit committee and the chief audit executive will work to improve the cooperation between all those active in the field of governance, in particular, optimizing cooperation with statutory auditors to ensure the comprehensive audit of all activity.

Consider

1 Are these nine points all reflected in your internal audit role and charter?
2 Are there any expectation gaps in your organization concerning these nine points?

"It is important that there is agreement in an organization on the roles internal auditors undertake..."
Cutting Edge Internal Auditing (2008)

  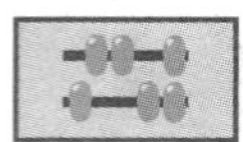      

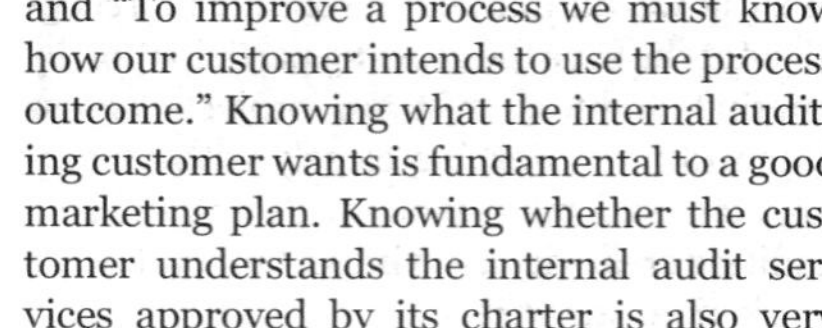

and "To improve a process we must know how our customer intends to use the process outcome." Knowing what the internal auditing customer wants is fundamental to a good marketing plan. Knowing whether the customer understands the internal audit services approved by its charter is also very important.

A current performance measurement tool with many internal audit activities is the use of a questionnaire during its engagements to seek feedback from its customers on the service it provides. Such a questionnaire is an effective way to seek views on how the customer understands the internal audit's role in the organization and whether it is perceived to be as written in its charter. Another practice is to use discussion and training groups within the organization to spread the purpose, authority, and responsibility of the internal audit role.

One example of an expectation gap in the internal auditing role is in the prevention, detection, and investigation of fraud. This is too often not always clear and can cause different perceptions across an organization at all levels. Chambers (2005)[6] recognizes this:

"There is undoubtedly an expectation gap for internal auditors in the area of fraud . . . Other parties expect . . . internal auditors to be effective at detecting significant fraud . . . [and] preventing significant fraud . . . Much effort is needed by the chief audit executive to explain internal audit's interface with fraud."

Today's New Image for Internal Auditing

In my book *Cutting Edge Internal Auditing* I cite an article published in 2005[7] in which I wrote:

"By the late 90s some different aspects of the internal auditor's role were identified in new IIA research—assurers of control, risk facilitators, in-house consultants, business analyst, fraud detectors, innovators, quality advocates, advisers on governance. Later research in the UK[8] in 2002 supported these aspects; showing internal audit in the UK is currently adding value in the following six elements of the governance process, ranked in order of perception by those it serves:

- Assurance that the internal control framework is operating effectively.
- Assurance that major business risks are being managed appropriately.
- Detection and prevention of fraud and irregularities.
- Improving business performance by sharing knowledge of best practices.
- Identification of new business risks.
- Use of knowledge and experience to tackle urgent issues.

The first three are the traditional approaches to internal audit work. Most board members and management recognise these. The last three require a participative teamwork approach and for some internal audit functions are still relatively new services: in some internal audit activities they have been provided for many years. Today's professional internal auditors should be well trained and competent to add all of these values in their organizations. A measure of their professionalism is whether they can and do. Board and audit committee members should expect and ensure that all are well provided."

Since 2005 these new services have changed the internal audit role in many organizations and continue to do so, encouraged at board level and by management. They have also been pioneered by many internal auditors as they develop their professional attributes and practices to increase their value.

MAKING IT HAPPEN

The internal audit role has a variety of independent professional dimensions, created and approved at board level to meet management governance, risk management, and control needs at all levels in an organization, and across its supply chains. To minimize any expectation gaps in the services it provides it is important that:

- the purpose, authority, and responsibility of the role are clearly established in a charter;
- that charter is promoted at all levels across the organizations it serves;
- customer perceptions and expectations of the internal audit role are measured continuously;
- expectation gaps are identified and monitored;
- dimensions of the internal audit role are, and remain, at its professional cutting edge.

MORE INFO

Websites:

Chartered Institute of Internal Auditors (UK and Ireland): www.iia.org.uk
European Confederation of Institutes of Internal Auditing (ECIIA): www.eciia.org
Institute of Internal Auditors (IIA): www.theiia.org

See Also:

★ Engaging Senior Management in Internal Control (pp. 336–337)
★ Internal Audit and Partnering with Senior Management (pp. 368–371)
★ Managing the Relationships between Audit Committees and the CAE (pp. 375–377)
★ New Assurance Challenges Facing Chief Audit Executives (pp. 378–381)
✔ Corporate Governance and Its Interpretations (p. 1111)
✔ Understanding Internal Audits (p. 1057)

NOTES

1 Institute of Internal Auditors (IIA). *International Standards for the Professional Practice of Internal Auditing*. Altamonte Springs, FL: IIA, 2009.

2 Sawyer, Lawrence B. *The Manager and the Modern Internal Auditor.* New York: Amacom, 1979.

3 Wilson, James A., and Donna J. Wood. *Managing the Behavioral Dynamics of Internal Auditing*. Altamonte Springs, FL: IIA, 1985.

4 Anderson, Urton, and Andrew J. Dahle. *Implementing the Professional Practices Framework*. 2nd ed. Altamonte Springs, FL: IIA, 2006.

5 Cosmas, Cindy E. *Audit Customer Satisfaction: Marketing Added Value*. Altamonte Springs, FL: IIA, 1996.

6 Chambers, Andrew. *Tolley's Internal Auditor's Handbook*. 2nd ed. Edinburgh, UK: LexisNexis Butterworths, 2009.

7 "Is internal auditing's new image recognized by your organization?" In Chapter 4 of: Ridley, Jeffrey. *Cutting Edge Internal Auditing*. Chichester, UK: Wiley, 2008.

8 *The Value Agenda*. London: Deloitte & Touche and IIA, 2002.

9 *Internal Auditing in Europe—Position Paper.* Brussels: European Confederation of Institutes of Internal Auditors, 2005.

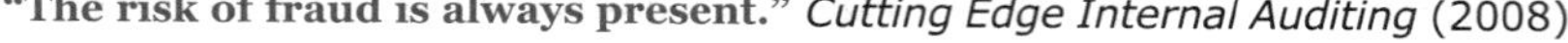

"The risk of fraud is always present." *Cutting Edge Internal Auditing* (2008)

  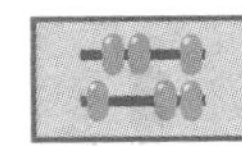   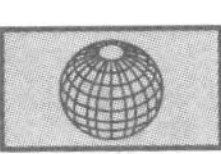   

Managing the Relationships between Audit Committees and the CAE by Richard E. Cascarino

EXECUTIVE SUMMARY

- Audit committees are a fundamental part of the proper governance of any organization, together with executive management and internal as well as external audit.
- An audit committee can only be as effective as is permitted by the information it receives.
- The relationship between the committee and the chief audit executive (CAE) is critical to the successful functioning of the audit committee.
- The relationship will be effective in an environment of mutual trust and common understanding.
- Of all the committees involved in the management and control of an organization, perhaps the audit committee has the most significant impact on the life of the CAE.
- Although, in general, all audit committees fulfill a similar function within the organization, the nature of the organization itself can prescribe a particular emphasis in the working of the audit committee. This, in turn, affects the nature of the relationship between the CAE and the committee as a whole.

THE ROLE OF THE AUDIT COMMITTEE

The audit committee is intended, overall, to assist an organization to achieve an effective internal control structure derived directly from the tone at the top. The authority of an audit committee is drawn from the board of directors, the rules and regulations of the organization, and any relevant governance legislation of the country or countries within which the organization operates.

This role, of necessity, involves ensuring that the risk management process remains both comprehensive and ongoing instead of the annual process that is implemented in many organizations. Corporate policies regarding legal compliance, compliance with corporate codes of conduct, and conflicts of interest must be maintained and policed. In addition, the audit committee has a duty to review both current and pending legislation as it relates to corporate governance within the country or countries wherein it operates. Communication is the key to good governance and includes ensuring that the financial statements presented to the shareholders are both understandable and reliable, and facilitating internal communication with senior management and internal audit. Communication with internal audit should go beyond the scheduled committee meetings, and the CAE should be encouraged to communicate with the chair of the audit committee directly. The audit committee, as a whole, should meet privately with the CAE at least annually to seek assurances about the independence of the internal audit function.

To ensure effective use of internal auditing, the audit committee would normally review internal audit plans as well as reports and significant findings. It would seek to ensure that internal auditing is carried out by professionals with a comprehensive understanding of the business systems and processes as well as of the corporate culture within the organization.

The audit committee relies on the internal audit function to provide objective opinions, information, and, when necessary, education to the audit committee, while the audit committee in turn will provide oversight and validation to the internal audit function. In today's environment this could include the outsourcing or co-sourcing of all or part of the internal audit function; however, the audit committee should ensure that the role of the CAE remains within the organization itself.

Overall, the major purpose of the Board's audit committee is the oversight of the financial reporting of an organization. In the United States, since the 2002 Statement on Auditing Standards No. 99, "Considerations of fraud in a financial statement audit" (SAS 99),[1] auditors have been required to question management's awareness and understanding of fraud. As a result, audit committees have been required to have greater financial expertise, act with a greater level of conservatism, and be cognizant of the need for improved reporting accuracy.

A regular part of the audit committee's agenda should be the evaluation of audit's assessment of fraud risk and the appropriateness of the audit plan to examine the internal controls designed to mitigate these risks.

INTERNAL AUDIT REPORTING STRUCTURE

In order to ensure transparency and to prevent undue influence internally, the Institute of Internal Auditors (IIA) recommends that the CAE maintain a dual reporting relationship. Typically, this would involve the CAE reporting to executive management at as high a level as possible for administrative purposes to ensure alignment with corporate direction, support at a managerial level, and the normal administrative support required for a staff function. The second relationship, with the audit committee, is for operational and functional purposes, to ensure that independence and objectivity is maintained. The audit function's independence and reporting structure are normally laid out in the internal audit charter, which specifies the dual reporting structure as well as the internal auditors' right of access to personnel and records without hindrance or impediment, a critical part of their independence. The charter would normally be signed by both the chief executive and the chair of the audit committee.

The audit committee should provide oversight, strategic direction, accountability, and enforcement where required. Part of such oversight includes ensuring that the internal audit function is properly positioned, resourced, and supported. This involves reviewing and approving:

- the internal audit activity's charter, and mission statement where appropriate, to ensure they meet the needs of the organization;
- the annual work plan to ensure that all significant risk areas are being addressed and that no restrictions are placed on the scope of internal audit activities;
- the resources, skill levels, and budget to ensure that the work plan is achievable within the appropriate time;
- internal audit activities, performance, and recommendations.

At the same time, the audit committee is responsible for providing input into the appointment, dismissal, evaluation, compensation, and succession planning of the CAE. This is a critical activity of the audit committee since the CAE will, of neccessity, have a high degree of interaction with the audit committee. The committee will typically seek to ensure that candidates for a CAE position have distinguished themselves professionally. They would normally have an advanced degree, the appropriate professional designation, and several years experience in an audit supervisory role. Typical professional designations could include the Certified Internal Auditor (CIA), Certified Government Auditing Professional (CGAP), Certified Financial Services Auditor (CFSA), or Certified Information Systems Auditor (CISA) among others.

"Audit committee duty entails significant time and effort and requires accountability when things go wrong."
Curtis C. Verschoor

     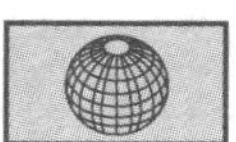   

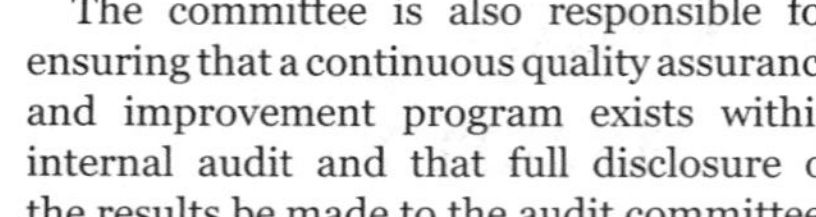

The committee is also responsible for ensuring that a continuous quality assurance and improvement program exists within internal audit and that full disclosure of the results be made to the audit committee.

THE RELATIONSHIP WITH INTERNAL AUDIT

The audit committee chair can foster a healthy relationship with the internal auditors, and particularly the chief internal auditor, by keeping communication channels open, getting to know the CAE as a person, frequently touching base between meetings, and taking an interest in and caring about the internal audit function. It is also a good idea for the audit committee chair to meet with the entire senior internal audit staff from time to time to get to know some of the individuals who report to the CAE, and to thank them for their efforts.

It is critical that the internal audit function be positioned well within the organization so that the internal auditors are not limited in what they can review, and that they, and the recommendations they propose, are respected by line management. It should always be remembered that the accountability for, and ownership of, good internal controls are the responsibility of management—not of the internal auditors and not of the audit committee. The internal auditors, nonetheless, must recognize that theirs is a unique yet critical role.

The CAE needs to be up to date on best practices and trends in governance, as well as on "emerging issues," and the audit committee will seek reassurance in this area. The audit committee also needs assurance that the internal auditors understand the corporate strategy and have the professional judgment to identify all forms of risk at an early enough opportunity to allow management to take appropriate action. In order for the audit committee to be appropriately assured in these areas, performance assessment of both the CAE and internal audit will be required.

MUTUAL TRUST

Most critical to the relationship between the audit committee and the internal audit activity is trust. The audit committee chair needs to be sure that the CAE understands and shares the committee's concerns and priorities. In addition, the CAE must be willing to communicate results and opinions without fear or favor and regardless of who is involved. Due to its unique position and the sensitivity of information passing through its hands, the audit committee needs assurance that the internal audit activity maintains the highest level of integrity and values.

The committee needs to be able to trust that, when confronted with management resistance or a failure of management integrity, the CAE will make the right decision and take appropriate action. By the same token, the CAE must be able to rely on the support and backing of the chair of the audit committee, and the committee as a whole. This ensures that the "internal audit activity [is] free from interference in determining the scope of internal auditing, performing work, and communicating results" (IIA Standards).

Two Cases in Point

In one government department, accusations of corruption were made against the chief executive. The CAE who reported to the chief executive took the accusations directly to the audit committee chair. Although the responsible Minister was notified, it was the audit committee, acting independently, that commissioned an external forensic investigation into the allegations. The external route was chosen so that, regardless of the outcome, the CAE would be able to continue to function effectively within the department. In the event, the allegations proved unjustified, but it was the trust between the CAE and the audit committee chair which made it possible for such allegations to be brought forward without fear of reprisal. In a contrasting case involving a pension fund, allegations of abuse of power by the chief executive were brought to the attention of the CAE. These were taken to the chair of the audit committee, who immediately called the chief executive to discuss them privately. There was no follow-up. The trust between the audit committee and the CAE was destroyed, ultimately resulting in the resignation of the CAE.

ASSESSING PERFORMANCE AND PLANNING AHEAD

The *International Standards for the Professional Practice of Internal Auditing*[2] promulgated by the Institute of Internal Auditors requires that an external assessment, performed by appropriately qualified reviewers and carried out to professional standards, be conducted every five years. This is designed to give the audit committee assurance that the work of the internal audit function is being conducted to internationally accepted standards.

In addition, the CAE is required to ensure quality on an ongoing basis. The CAE may utilize benchmarking to develop an internal auditor balanced scorecard for the audit committee to use for assessing the performance of the internal audit function. An objective evaluation would, nevertheless, include such areas as audit scope and coverage (including financial, compliance, operational, IT, and fraud auditing), audit capabilities, independence, objectivity, supervision, and internal audit assignment quality control. In addition to ensuring the quality of the work of the internal audit function, the audit committee chair will also

MAKING IT HAPPEN

In Order to Manage the Relationship the CAE Must:

- Keep the audit committee informed on risks faced by the organization. Monitor the risk environment for new/changed risks which need to be brought to the audit committee's attention.
- Check that the audit committee's charter, activities, and processes are appropriate. Periodically review the audit committee's practices against international standards and "best practices" on behalf of the chair of the audit committee.
- Educate the audit committee on the internal audit team's charter, role, and activities. The CAE should seek to obtain management and audit committee buy-in on internal auditing's goals, objectives, risk assessments, and audit plan by demonstrating their appropriateness and relevance.
- Ensure that the internal audit function is responsive to the needs of the audit committee and the board. Meet frequently with the audit committee chair to ensure that the committee's needs are fully understood and met.
- Ensure open and effective communication with the audit committee and its chair. Effective communication is one of the best tools for understanding organizational priorities and reinforcing the benefits and value of internal auditing.
- Provide training, when appropriate, to audit committee members on the topics of risk and internal control. Not all committee members will initially be up to speed on the changing needs and legislation.
- Confirm the quality of the services provided. Internal auditing should provide quality performance indicators to show that it complies with the IIA's *International Standards for the Professional Practice of Internal Auditing* and the IIA's *Code of Ethics* and that it adds value on an ongoing basis.
- Provide feedback on the internal audit function's achievement of its operational plans and objectives.

seek assurance on the performance of the audit committee itself. The CAE can assist in benchmarking the committee's performance in terms of committee structure and composition, the role of audit committee members, and leadership of the committee against standards such as The Board Institute's Audit Committee Index[3] on behalf of the chair of the audit committee. The European Corporate Governance Institute (ECGI) has produced an excellent paper on such benchmarking.[4] This presents an opportunity for the audit committee to review and discuss all areas of its performance, as well as to bring to the table items that committee members feel should be covered in the future, and training opportunities that would enhance performance.

It is critical that proactive succession planning for the internal audit function and the CAE be an important area of focus and support by the audit committee. Many organizations use internal audit as a training ground for future executive managers and rotate candidates through the internal auditing function. While this is beneficial to the organization in terms of managers who understand internal control, it can be devastating to the effectiveness of the internal audit function if carried out to excess. One internal audit function lost seven out of eight senior auditors in a six-month period as they were head-hunted by operational areas of the organization. Succession planning is intended to ensure that, while some of the current team may get appropriate and substantive positions in the organization as rotations end, the effectiveness of the internal audit function is not impacted. Professional, career-oriented internal auditors form the backbone of the function and they must see career opportunities with internal audit itself. In addition, succession planning is critical to the organization's ability to attract the right talent into the internal audit activity.

CONCLUSION

The mere existence of the audit committee does not necessarily translate into an effective monitoring body over corporate governance. By the same token, the existence of an internal audit function, in-sourced or out-sourced, does not guarantee the effectiveness of the system of internal controls. It is the combination of the two, both acting in a professional manner for the benefit of the organization as a whole, which contributes significantly to the achievement of sound corporate governance.

Audit Committee Characteristics

- independence
- financial knowledge and experience
- frequency of meetings
- involvement in CAE appointment and dismissal
- reviewing internal audit program and processes
- ensuring internal audit quality

Internal Audit Function Characteristics

- independence and objectivity
- availability of adequate resources
- internal audit staff expertise
- use of external subject matter experts where appropriate

MORE INFO

Books:

Braiotta, Louis, Jr, R. Trent Gazzaway, Robert Colson, and Sridhar Ramamoorti *The Audit Committee Handbook*. 5th ed. Hoboken, NJ: Wiley, 2010.

Burke, Frank M., Dan M. Guy, and Kay W. Tatum. *Audit Committees: A Guide for Directors, Management, and Consultants*. 6th ed. Chicago, IL: CCH, 2009.

Cascarino, Richard E. *Corporate Fraud and Internal Control: A Framework for Prevention*. Hoboken, NJ: Wiley, 2013.

Cascarino, Richard E., and Sandy van Esch. *Internal Auditing: An Integrated Approach*. 2nd ed. Lansdowne, South Africa: Juta Academic Publishers, 2006.

Moeller, Robert. *Brink's Modern Internal Auditing*. 7th ed. Hoboken, NJ: Wiley, 2009.

Ruppel, Warren. *Not-for-Profit Audit Committee Best Practices*. Hoboken, NJ: Wiley, 2005.

Articles:

Collier, Paul Arnold. "Audit committees in major UK companies." *Managerial Auditing Journal* 8:3 (1993): 25–30.

Goodwin, Jenny. "The relationship between the audit committee and the internal audit function: Evidence from Australia and New Zealand." *International Journal of Auditing* 7:3 (November 2003): 263–278. Online at: dx.doi.org/10.1046/j.1099-1123.2003.00074.x

Reports:

Australian National Audit Office. "Public sector audit committees." Canberra, Australia: Australian National Audit Office, 2005.

Blue Ribbon Committee on Improving the Effectiveness of Corporate Audit Committees. "Report and recommendations of the blue ribbon committee on improving the effectiveness of corporate audit committees." New York: New York Stock Exchange and National Association of Securities Dealers, 1999.

European Corporate Governance Institute (ECGI). "Institutional position paper: a benchmark for audit committees." November 2002. Online at: www.ecgi.org/codes/documents/auditcom_final_paper.pdf

Institute of Internal Auditors. "Chief audit executive (CAE) reporting lines." Practice Advisory 1110-2. December 2002.

Institute of Internal Auditors. "Relationship with the audit committee." Practice Advisory 2060-2. December 2002.

Institute of Internal Auditors. "A Global Summary of the Common Body of Knowledge 2006." Online at: www.theiia.org/research/common-body-of-knowledge/

Websites:

Audit Committee Effectiveness Center: www.aicpa.org/ForThePublic/AuditCommitteeEffectiveness/Pages/ACEC.aspx

Securities and Exchange Commission (SEC; US): www.sec.gov

See Also:

★ Aligning the Internal Audit Function with Strategic Objectives (pp. 280–282)
★ Internal Audit and Partnering with Senior Management (pp. 368–371)
★ New Assurance Challenges Facing Chief Audit Executives (pp. 378–381)
★ Optimizing Internal Audit (pp. 382–384)
✔ The Chief Audit Executive's (CAE) Roles and Responsibilities (p. 1025)

NOTES

1 AICPA. "Consideration of fraud in a financial statement audit." 2002. Online at: www.aicpa.org/Storage/Resources/Standards/DownloadableDocuments/AU-00316.PDF

2 Available from the Institute of Internal Auditors: www.theiia.org

3 See www.theboardinstitute.com/web/products.asp?f=prod_acix

4 Online at: www.ecgi.org/codes/documents/auditcom_final_paper.pdf

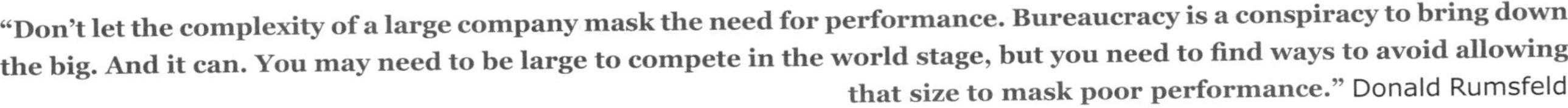

"Don't let the complexity of a large company mask the need for performance. Bureaucracy is a conspiracy to bring down the big. And it can. You may need to be large to compete in the world stage, but you need to find ways to avoid allowing that size to mask poor performance." Donald Rumsfeld

  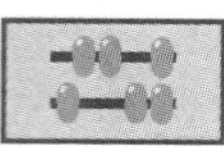      

New Assurance Challenges Facing Chief Audit Executives by Simon D'Arcy

EXECUTIVE SUMMARY

- Internal audit's *raison d'être* is to provide assurance on the effectiveness of the management and control of significant risks.
- Assurance can only ever be reasonable but not absolute—continuing corporate failure due to inadequate risk management and control challenges the value of such reasonable assurance.
- Chief audit executives can use objective criteria to demonstrate the integrity of their reasonable assurance propositions.
- Objective criteria include completeness, frequency, future orientation, explicitness, objectivity, and subject matter knowledge.
- A key challenge for CAEs is that of a shift of mindset away from just doing audits, to auditing actually providing assurance of demonstrable integrity.

INTRODUCTION

Looking back over the last 15 to 20 years, it does seem that at one time the biggest challenge facing the profession of internal auditing was whether the unique scope and contribution of internal audit was clearly defined, understood, or indeed actually needed. Much of the thought leadership around internal auditing in recent years has focused on this challenge. Two publications by PricewaterhouseCoopers in 2007,[1] and a heads of internal audit summit "The Future of Internal Auditing Starts Here" in May 2008[2] jointly facilitated by the Institute of Internal Auditors and Deloitte, have all concluded that internal audit's primary role is clearly to provide assurance on the effectiveness of risk management. In fact, in many organizations internal audit already clearly does this, as demonstrated in Protiviti's June 2007 publication *Internal Auditing Around the World*.[3] It is clear—and has been since Turnbull (1999),[4] if not before—that boards have a duty to get themselves assured on the effectiveness of their systems of internal control. There is no doubt that chief audit executives see that their raison d'être is to provide such assurance, and many will claim, with some justification, that they have provided and will continue to provide this assurance. Therefore, on the face of it, CAEs have responded to their most fundamental challenge.

THE PROBLEM WITH ASSURANCE

If Turnbull (1999) marks the turning point in corporate governance, it has nevertheless not marked a turning point in the steady stream of corporate failures and disasters, which are often due to ineffective risk management and control. The role of internal audit in these scenarios has been, if not quite exonerated, then at least found not liable, by virtue of one of the basic precepts of internal audit assurance—that it can only ever be reasonable and not absolute.

However, with the market turmoil of 2007 and 2008, the steady stream of failures has become a torrent of biblical proportions—initially, at the time of writing (September 2008), sweeping away the foundations of some major global financial institutions and likely to spread to other sectors as systemic market and recessionary risks crystallize. Accompanying the unfolding disasters is a damning commentary from governments and media on the hopelessly inadequate risk assessment and management capability of those corporates. The spotlight has been on the managers of risk and the attitude of senior executives to the assessment and management of risk. However, it will not be long before the spotlight moves toward the assurers of the effectiveness of risk management, and whether those assurers were in any way culpable. Rightly or wrongly, many will assume that reasonable assurance from internal audit should have identified and reported on the inadequacies of the risk management process, or at least been capable of doing so.

There is now a new challenge facing CAEs—that they are able to demonstrate that their assurance propositions have integrity and can withstand scrutiny against some key criteria. Internal audit assurance involves judgment, and there is an inherent imperfection in a process that relies on judgment. However, there is a difference between an omission or oversight based on accepted fallibility, and one where the scope of assurance was too narrow, where assurance conclusions lacked clarity, or were delivered too infrequently, or where work undertaken lacked sufficient knowledge or objectivity. Assurance delivered on the basis of a flawed proposition is indeed unreasonable assurance.

Therefore, in rising to meet that challenge, CAEs have been aspiring to create assurance propositions that are:

- Complete: They cover all significant risks.
- Frequent: They provide assurance with sufficient frequency.
- Explicit: They give assurance outcomes that are clear and unambiguous.
- Future-oriented: They offer assurance that controls will continue to be effective in the future, not just that they have been effective in the past.
- Objective: They provide objective assurance based on sound knowledge.

DEMONSTRATING THE INTEGRITY OF ASSURANCE IN A POST-CREDIT-CRUNCH WORLD

Most CAEs I have spoken with on the topic are in agreement that the above are valid criteria against which to assess assurance to demonstrate that the assurance given has integrity. However, there is no formulaic result or correct answer that the assessment should derive. Some CAEs are quite clear that their current risk-based methodologies score quite favorably in the assessment. The following is an amalgam of my own thoughts, assessments, and actual solutions, developed across four financial services organizations in the past decade in trying to respond to the challenge.

Completeness

First, were all significant risks in scope for my internal audit function? How sympathetic would or should a stakeholder be if the explanation was "sorry, out of scope" for not providing any assurance coverage on a significant risk area where a major issue had arisen. The default position is for "everything" to be in scope, because that is where assurance adds the most value. However, my experience is that "everything" means different things to different people, and it still leads to mismatches between expected assurance coverage and actual audit coverage. The cry of "where were the auditors?" when something goes wrong is less rhetorical and more actual than you might imagine. It served my function to define "everything" up front, rather than have to explain omissions retrospectively. This is becoming even more sensible in an environment where

"Increasingly, boards are turning to the profession for assurance." Mervyn King

many point to the least tangible risk areas, such as strategy, sustainability, and culture, as those where assurance is most needed. (In fact, many respected observers are pointing to poor culture and behavior as being what has led to the economic meltdown, rather than policy or process failure.) If something is going to be agreed as out of scope, it is better to be in a position to have clearly defined and agreed it, even if by doing so you are reducing the value of your assurance proposition.

The best method I have found for creating an assurance universe, and to use as a basis for an assurance contract with the organization, is to list the significant risks (there are normally around 20, and such a list is often referred to as a risk map or significant risk register) as recognized and agreed by the board. What is clear is that the significant risk register must include all financial, strategic, and operational risks as a minimum, including liquidity and sustainability risks. The internal audit profession is now turning its attention to the new paradigm risks that have been made painfully clear by the credit crunch—systemic/globalization risk, behavioral risks, and supply chain risks.

Frequency

The Combined Code on Corporate Governance, which sets the rules for FTSE-listed companies and is also recognized as a benchmark by nonlisted and public-sector companies in the United Kingdom, implies a minimum annual assessment of the effectiveness of internal control (as a proxy for the effectiveness of management of significant risks).

However, a once-a-year assessment—even if it is about all the risks—does not appear to be frequent enough. The organizations for which I have worked have generally used a very compelling risk-based approach that prioritizes the assurance requirement over three years. But with this scenario it seemed to me that even a once-a-year assessment can only cover one-third of the assurance requirement (accepting that it would always include the highest-priority areas). I have posed the frequency question many times to senior managers, board members, and audit committee chairs. Their answer tends to be in the negative—i.e., it would be unreasonable that a major risk management breakdown should go unnoticed by internal audit until it was too late because the CAE's view of that risk was out of date, because it had not been looked at for six months or more, and was not due to be looked at again for another six months or more.

In fact, the best frequency would be if CAEs were in a position to provide a complete opinion all of the time. Logistical and practical constraints make this impossible. However, I have been able to produce more frequent assessments by focusing on each of the risk categories for which assurance is required and creating a strategy for delivering the outputs that I need so that I can stand in front of an audit committee once a quarter and deliver conclusions that have demonstrable integrity. Such strategies comprise combinations of continuous assessment techniques, ongoing reviews, and revisions of conclusions previously arrived at, as well as baseline assessments.

REVIEWS AND ASSESSMENTS

Baseline reviews are undertaken where management of the risk is relatively stable. These are time-framed, in-depth reviews of established controls and processes. The conclusions from such reviews may have a long shelf life and, if stability continues, may only need a light refresh to remain valid.

Continuous assessments involve regular or continuous reviews of a range of information and activity that indicate whether controls are operating as intended. They are used where conclusions have previously been established but more certainty is required to ensure that those conclusions remain valid between baseline reviews. They include a review of the output of other risk and control functions—for example, compliance.

Ongoing reviews are used where projects and other business initiatives may bring changes to the risk and control framework and reduce the value of reviewing preexisting processes and controls, or where control environments are unstable/-immature and action is being undertaken to establish or remediate controls.

Orientation

In thinking about frequency challenge, I also started to think about the orientation of assurance. By orientation, I mean whether the assurance is just focused retrospectively, on things that have happened in the past, or whether it can and should look to the future. The Combined Code implies that the annual assessment will be a retrospective view of the previous year, much like the external auditor's opinion on the financial statements. However, in much the same way as external auditors consider the going concern aspects of firms, it seemed to me that my conclusions should have some element of future proofing.

Again, I considered the value of assurance that was anchored in the past (especially when it could refer to an event as long as 364 days in the past). If a risk had already crystallized, any assurance was old news and irrelevant. If controls were effective, for how long would they continue to be effective? I felt that my assurance would be more reasonable if I could "future proof" it.

But how much future proofing can and should be given? I achieved this by attaching a shelf life to quarterly conclusions. This is a concept where I vary how long my assurance conclusions are likely to remain valid, depending on certain broad criteria. For example, if the control environment is either currently unstable or will be subject to some major change in the near future, the validity of any conclusions will be short-lived. If the area is stable and likely to remain so, then a long shelf life can be given—and easily refreshed using the continuous assessment technique. In the organizations where I have employed this approach, in any set of quarterly conclusions the shelf lives given have varied considerably across risk categories. In fact, the more I have used this approach, the more I find that the fact that an explicit view on shelf life has been given has become as important as the actual length of time which is stated.

Figure 1. The assurance spectrum

Assurance is unreasonable
Key risks clearly understood, but other assurance providers involved are creating potential for confusion
Assurance is reasonable
Degree to which all significant risks are clearly understood, defined and within scope for internal audit assurance
Lack of absolute understanding and clarity, or some key risks clearly out of scope
Assumption that all key risks are understood, but no rigor around definitions
All key risks are clearly understood and defined and clearly *all* within scope

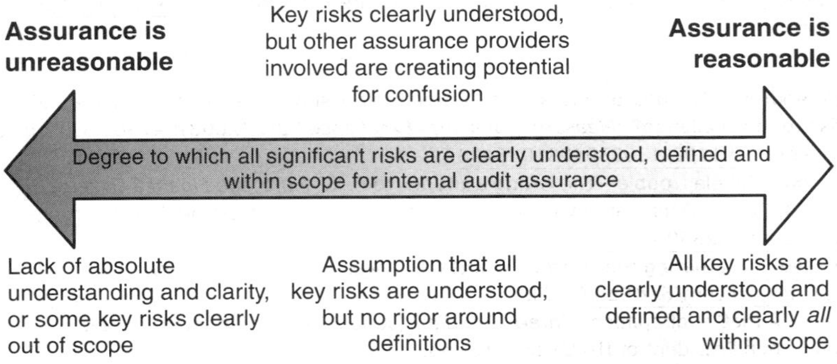

"External audit doesn't give you the sort of review and assurance over risk and controls across the spectrum of financial and non-financial aspects of the organization but a good internal auditor does." Lord Smith of Kelvin

Explicitness

The requirement (by boards) for CAEs to give opinions on the effectiveness of the system of internal control and risk management is one of the biggest areas of debate and challenge facing the profession at the moment. Because of the legal implications of opinions, many CAEs will not give them, and will only report issues as they arise. Some CAEs who are prepared to give opinions do so without much thought of the consequences, or do so in the vein of "everything is effective apart from the following issues."

Setting aside the legal status argument, in my experience such approaches are potentially flawed. The default position of the recipients of assurance is one of assuming that all other controls and risk management activities across the enterprise are effective and will continue to be so, unless they have specifically been told otherwise. Unless that was truly the intended message, the assurance that is being provided is misleading. That is why I have worked on providing separate conclusions (as opposed to opinions, to avoid the legal connotation) for each significant risk category (and sometimes at a risk subcategory level) each quarter. My preference has been to go for a binary conclusion, where "this risk is effectively managed" is signaled by a green symbol, and "this risk is not effectively managed" is represented by a red one.

For a "green" conclusion nothing further is required in the way of explanation other than an indicator of the breadth and depth of coverage used to reach the conclusion. For a "red" conclusion the list of supporting issues, as well as the reliability indicator, are described.

My experience is that the binary approach is a step too far for some, so I have also employed a three-level and a four-level approach, where the conclusions range from "well controlled," through "acceptable level of control" and "controls require improvement," to "insufficient control." The point is that it is the explicitness of the conclusion (at the level of significant risk) and the reliability indicator which provide the assurance that is intended, rather than the summary of issues reported. The approach encourages much greater challenge and scrutiny—but I have found that to be a good thing.

Objectivity and Subject Matter Expertise

These are not new concepts or challenges for CAEs, but the challenge is to rethink them in the framework of the new assurance paradigm. Many cite independence of opinion as an end in itself, but it is only valuable if it enhances objectivity. After all, in any walk of life, not just in internal audit, we tend to be more convinced by the conclusion of someone who has no vested interest in what that conclusion is. Similarly, we tend to be more convinced by a conclusion if it is given by someone who really knows the subject to which it relates. Therefore, regardless of the completeness, frequency, future orientation, or explicitness of a conclusion, it can only provide reasonable assurance if we have confidence in the objectivity and expertise in the subject matter of the person giving it. Therein lies the challenge, as sometimes one element can only increase at the expense of another. In meeting this challenge, I have found that it is the recognition of the dynamic relationship between objectivity and subject matter expertise which allows dynamic management of it.

CONCLUSION

In common with many disciplines, the challenge for CAEs is not one of technique or technical development, but one of focus. In many ways, the biggest challenge is one of a shift of mindset away from planning to deliver some audits, toward planning to deliver an assurance outcome of demonstrable integrity. However, I believe it is a challenge that must be met, so that assurers have a stronger chance of helping their organizations to avoid corporate calamity due to risk management and control failure.

MAKING IT HAPPEN

- It is most important that you have a solid anchor or hook on which to hang your assurance. Ideally this should be the board-defined risk exposures. If your organization does not have these, help your organization to define them.
- It will take several quarters to build rhythm and momentum, and up to 18 months to achieve a baseline assurance for all of the risks of equivalent requisite quality.
- If you already know something, and are confident in that knowledge, do not waste valuable resources on proving something you already know. Reliable knowledge, however gained, contributes to your assurance.
- If you set off down this path, there will be many naysayers. They will challenge whether you can realistically deliver all the work that is necessary, claiming that you can only scratch the surface. Stay focused. The best way to convince naysayers is with the outputs and outcomes. The number of audit man-days has always been, and always will be, an input measure, and is no guide to whether good, bad, or indifferent assurance is produced.
- Less—in terms of number of issues—is definitely more. The number of audit issues in any one organization should genuinely reflect the competence of risk management and not the number of auditors
- You will need to spend as much—if not more—time converting your own people to the cause. Old habits die hard. The only way to do this is to be persistent and unwavering in your assurance strategy. Be prepared to repeat... and repeat and repeat.
- Make use of early converts and use them shamelessly to help spread the message.

MORE INFO

Periodicals:

Internal Auditing, published monthly by the Chartered Institute of Internal Auditors: www.iia.org.uk/en/Publications/IA_and_BR_Magazine

Internal Auditor, published monthly by the Institute of Internal Auditors: www.theiia.org/intauditor

Articles:

Chambers, Andrew. "The board's black hole—Filling their assurance vacuum: Can internal audit rise to the challenge?" *Measuring Business Excellence* 12:1 (2008): 47–63. Online at: dx.doi.org/10.1108/13683040810864387

D'Arcy, Simon. "Bubble trouble—The wrong attitudes to risk." *Mortgage Finance Gazette* (February 4, 2009). Online at: www.mfgonline.co.uk/article/Bubble-trouble-the-wrong-attitudes-to-risk-228895.html

Perry, Michelle. "Weathering the storm." *Financial Services Review* (May 2008): 10–12. Online at: tinyurl.com/6zzt9pb [PDF].

Piper, Arthur. "A matter of opinion." *Internal Auditor* (June 2007). Interview with Alec Richmond, then President of IIA UK and Ireland.

"Internal audit could be well placed to provide continuous, 360° independent assurance; but significant changes to the internal audit paradigm will be needed." Andrew Chambers

Report:

Turnbull, N. "Internal control: Guidance for directors on the Combined Code." Institute of Chartered Accountants in England and Wales, September 1999.

See Also:

★ Aligning the Internal Audit Function with Strategic Objectives (pp. 280–282)
★ Internal Audit and Partnering with Senior Management (pp. 368–371)
★ The Internal Audit Role—Is There an Expectation Gap in Your Organization? (pp. 372–374)
★ Managing the Relationships between Audit Committees and the CAE (pp. 375–377)
★ Optimizing Internal Audit (pp. 382–384)
✔ The Chief Audit Executive's (CAE) Roles and Responsibilities (p. 1025)

NOTES

1 PricewaterhouseCoopers (PwC). "Internal audit 2012: A study examining the future of internal auditing and the potential decline of a controls-centric approach." 2007; also PwC. "State of the internal audit profession study: Pressures build for continual focus on risk." 2007. Both downloadable from www.pwc.com (search on titles).

2 Institute of Internal Auditors (UK and Ireland) in association with Deloitte. "Towards a blueprint for the internal audit profession." London: IIA, 2008. Online from: www.iia.org.uk.

3 Protiviti, *Internal Auditing Around the World*. Four volumes published between 2005 and 2008 with profiles of internal audit functions at leading international organizations. The series tells the stories of 16 successful internal audit functions and examines common denominators that separate these leaders from their peers. Available from the Protiviti website: www.knowledgeleader.com.

4 "Internal control: Guidance for directors on the Combined Code" (the Turnbull Guidance) was originally published by the Institute of Chartered Accountants in England and Wales in 1999 and was followed by a number of subsequent revisions.

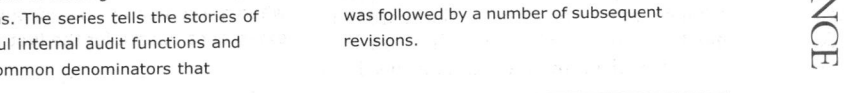

Optimizing Internal Audit by Andrew Chambers

EXECUTIVE SUMMARY

To optimize an internal audit function it is necessary to:

- conform with the International Professional Practices Framework of the global Institute of Internal Auditors;
- define the role, responsibilities, and authority of the internal audit function within a formal charter approved by the board;
- report to the board;
- embrace both assurance and consulting roles within the internal audit mission;
- function independently;
- ensure that no business areas are "off-limits" to internal audit;
- plan future audit engagements based on the chief audit executive's risk assessment;
- be committed to continuous improvement of the internal audit function.

INTRODUCTION

Internal auditing is defined by The Institute of Internal Auditors (IIA) as follows:

"Internal auditing is an independent, objective assurance and consulting activity designed to add value and improve an organization's operations. It helps an organization accomplish its objectives by bringing a systematic, disciplined approach to evaluate and improve the effectiveness of risk management, control, and governance processes."[1]

It is widely accepted that whether or not the staff of an internal audit function are affiliated to The IIA, if the internal auditing corresponds to the above definition, best-value internal auditing will only result when generally accepted internal auditing standards are applied. Internal auditing should be a valued part of the total assurance process. To be so it requires independence from the activities it audits and it needs to report independently to all those who rely on the assurance that internal audit provides.

Today, internal audit is a service for management and also for those, such as boards and audit committees, charged with governance. Particular internal audit functions may also have certain obligations to report to outside parties, such as regulators. It is important that the roles, responsibilities, and authority of internal audit are clearly set out and supported within the organization.

ESSENTIAL PREREQUISITES FOR INTERNAL AUDITING

Clear ground rules must be kept to if internal audit is to add best value to both its assurance and consulting roles. In any entity, these should be set out in the internal audit charter, which must be approved by the board or by the board's audit committee on behalf of the board. The most senior level that relies on the assurance given by internal audit needs to be confident that internal audit is not subordinating its judgment on professional matters to that of anyone else. Usually, at its most senior level internal audit reports to the audit committee of the board. Compromised professional judgment may occur with respect to:

- determining the planned programme of audits;
- accessing information and personnel necessary to properly conduct an audit;
- deciding the content of internal audit reports.

While it may appear that the chief audit executive is reporting directly to the audit committee, as indeed should be so, that reporting is of little value if it is in effect censored by senior management before it reaches the audit committee.

Internal audit is both an audit *for* management and also an audit *of* management *for* the board through the board's audit committee. If internal audit is compromised professionally, then it is essential that those who rely on the assurance that internal audit gives are fully cognizant of this. An audit committee needs to have time alone with the chief audit executive, with other executives not being in attendance; this can take place in a 15-minute session at the start of each audit committee meeting. Audit committees should also be involved in advance in decisions relating to the appointment, reappointment, dismissal, and remuneration of heads of internal audit.

Organizationally it is preferable that the internal audit function does not belong to the finance/accounting function of the organization as this makes it harder for internal audit to audit financial and accounting matters with sufficient independence and objectivity. It also makes it more difficult for internal audit to be welcomed as having a valuable contribution to make when it audits the operational areas of the business. Ideally, internal audit should report directly to the chief executive or, alternatively, to someone, or to a committee, outside of the main functional areas of the business.

"The chief audit executive must report to a level within the organization that allows the internal audit activity to fulfill its responsibilities. The chief audit executive must confirm to the board, at least annually, the organizational independence of the internal audit activity."[2]

THE SCOPE OF INTERNAL AUDIT

Contemporary internal auditing provides assurance to management and to the board, and also offers consulting services. The nature of both these services should be set out in the internal audit charter. The two services overlap: an assurance audit is likely to lead to advice on making improvements; consulting work may reveal issues that have to be taken up by internal audit in the context of its assurance role. Of the two, assurance is the core role, but some would argue that not to offer consulting services would now be inconsistent with professional internal auditing standards and would miss an opportunity to add value.

There should be no no-go areas for internal audit assurance as this limits the assurance that internal audit is able to provide; where there are no-go areas (i.e. restrictions of scope) the implications need to be clearly understood by those who rely on the assurance that internal audit gives.

CASE STUDY 1

Management and internal audit of a multinational company knew about an overstatement of oil reserves for some two years before the board and the board's audit committee learnt about it. Executive directors are said to have met before board meetings to agree a common line to be taken at the board. Reports from the chief audit executive passed across the desk of the chief financial officer before going to the audit committee. The chief executive, director of exploration, and chief financial officer left the company; when the company next appointed a new chief audit executive, the company sought an external candidate for the first time.

"Objectivity requires internal auditors not to subordinate their judgment on audit matters to others."
IIA, Glossary to *Standards*

     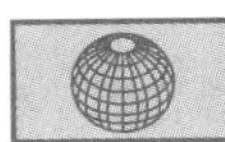   

CASE STUDY 2

The independent chairman of the board of a bank fired the bank's chief executive. The inside story was that the in-house chief audit executive used his direct access to the chair of the audit committee to contact that chair, by phone, between audit committee meetings, to discuss his concerns about apparent misconduct by the chief executive.

The chair of the audit committee, which comprised exclusively independent directors, convened a special meeting of the committee to follow this up. No executives other than the chief audit executive, who was invited to attend part of the meeting, knew that it was taking place. At the meeting the audit committee asked internal audit to investigate the matter further and report the findings directly to the committee. The chief audit executive timed the audit fieldwork to coincide with the annual vacation of the chief executive. The internal auditors gathered evidence which showed that the chief executive was using company resources for his personal benefit. Hence, when the chief executive returned from vacation, the chairman of the board dismissed him.

Had the chairman of the board not been independent, it would have been harder for the audit committee to deal with this matter effectively. His independence meant that the chairman the audit committee was able to keep him "in the loop" throughout, without risk that the confidentiality of the enquiry would be jeopardized.

Had internal audit been outsourced to an external service provider, it might have been less likely to learn about the alleged misconduct by the chief executive. However, internal audit is often identified as a point where concerned employees may blow the whistle, and this can be so whether or not internal audit is in-house.

Unlimited scope for internal audit includes the authority to audit across the operational areas of the business, not just within accounting and finance, and at all levels. An emerging issue is whether internal audit is able to provide assurance to boards themselves that the policies of boards are being implemented by management and that there are no banana skins round the corner, unknown to the board, on which the company may slip in the future.

Consulting services by internal auditors may include the provision of counsel and advice, of facilitation (such as facilitating control self-assessment workshops of managers and staff), or of training services. Internal auditors avoid assuming any management responsibilities as part of their consulting services, neither would they take on responsibility for designing processes except in an advisory capacity. One reason is that internal auditors need to be independent of management processes in order to be able to audit those processes objectively.

Internal auditors will undertake consulting work only when both internal audit and the client consider this to be justified. On the other hand, the management of a business activity should not be allowed to prevent an assurance audit from taking place.

"The chief audit executive should consider accepting proposed consulting engagements based on the engagement's potential to improve management of risks, add value, and improve the organization's operations. Accepted engagements must be included in the plan."[3]

More and more heads of internal audit are being asked not just to report the results of individual audits but also to provide *overall assurance opinions*, annually or more frequently, to top management and to boards or their audit committees. This makes it more important that internal audit optimizes the utilization of its scarce internal audit resources—in order to maximize the reliability of the overall opinion that internal audit gives.

Internal audit should plan its program of audits annually, based on a risk assessment which makes use of inputs from management and from the board or the board's audit committee. Internal audit should map its plan of audits to management's own risk map or risk register. But a proportion of internal audit time should be set aside to "look round the corners" that top management are not looking around in case there are major unnoticed or concealed risks. Not all critical risks may be on top management's radar screen, and so value is added when internal audit spends a proportion of its available time auditing in areas of the business that are not perceived to carry significant risks.

While the future plan of audits will be determined annually, the internal audit function should have a longer perspective on audit coverage that takes into account audit work done over previous years and earmarked to be done over the next three years or so. The chief audit executive should consider the extent to which work done in earlier years can be utilized in coming to the overall assurance opinion.

PROFESSIONAL BODIES AND SUPPORT

The internal auditing profession is organized globally, as is appropriate for a function that so often operates transnationally. The IIA, established in the United States in 1941 and headquartered in Florida, now has many members outside of North America, belonging to 250 chapters and affiliated institutes in 165 countries. Membership has grown from 100,000 in 2004 to over 160,000 in 2008, of whom about 75,000 are fully professionally qualified certified internal auditors (CIAs). The IIA also offers the following specialist qualifications:

- Certification in Control Self-Assessment (CCSA);
- Certified Government Auditing Professional (CGAP);
- Certified Financial Services Auditor (CFSA).

Exams for The IIA's professional certifications can be sat at 90 sites throughout the world and in 18 languages. They can be taken at times of the candidate's choosing, rather than at two set dates during the calendar year. If a candidate fails an exam, he or she may retake the exam when at least 90 days have elapsed.

CASE STUDY 3

Following a fatal, high-profile explosion at one of its oil refineries and a number of other environmental failures, the board of a multinational oil company commissioned an enquiry by an outside panel. It must have appeared to the board that the board's policy that the company should be a green and safe oil multinational was not being implemented by management. The board agreed to the panel's recommendation that the panel should appoint an external expert to provide independent assurance to the board on health and safety matters for at least five years.

Two questions arise from this. First, whether (and if not, why not) the board had been receiving sufficient internal assurance that the policies of the board were being implemented by management; and second, the extent to which internal audit could be relied on to provide the board with that assurance. The panel's solution addressed the board's needs for assurance only in the area of health and safety, and was after the failures had occurred.

"The internal audit activity must be independent, and internal auditors must be objective in performing their work."
IIA Standard 1100, Independence and Objectivity

All members of The IIA commit to observe a common *Code of Ethics*, which includes an obligation to apply the *Standards* of The IIA.[4] There are approved translations of the *Standards* in 32 languages. The global Association of Chartered Certified Accountants (ACCA) has recently endorsed The IIA's *Standards* as applicable to ACCA members working as internal auditors, and the 2009 version of the United Kingdom's HM Treasury *Government Internal Audit Standards* is modeled on the IIA's *Standards*. The International Professional Practices Framework of The IIA, which includes the *Standards* as well as the *Code of Ethics*, practice advisories and practice guides, was very significantly revised, with effect from January 1, 2009. Thereafter, the intention is to issue any necessary revisions with effect from January 1 of each year.

QUALITY ASSURANCE ASSESSMENTS AND INTERNAL AUDIT MATURITY FRAMEWORKS

An effective opportunity to ensure optimum quality internal auditing is to be found in the quality assurance requirements of the *Standards* of The IIA. These require that there should be annual internal assessments of each internal audit function, and independent, external quality assessments at least once every five years. The benchmark to be used is the *Standards* of The IIA. These Standards represent the approach to internal auditing that should be followed if an organization is to obtain optimum value from its investment in internal audit. Internal audit maturity frameworks are now being applied to assess the quality of internal audit functions.[5]

MAKING IT HAPPEN

Key guidance to get best value from your internal audit function:

1 Develop a charter for your internal audit function, approved by the board or by your audit committee of the board.
2 Staff your internal audit function with professionally qualified people and those in the process of becoming qualified.
3 Require adherence to relevant internal auditing standards.
4 Ensure a scope for internal audit that includes assurance and consulting work.
5 Don't ever ask your internal audit function to subordinate its judgment on professional matters to anyone else.
6 Benchmark your internal audit function against others.
7 Take seriously the need for both internal and external quality assurance assessments of your internal audit function.
8 Support your internal auditors and ensure that they are properly resourced.

MORE INFO

Websites:

AuditNet, a US information and resources site developed for the benefit of the internal audit profession by Jim Kaplan. There are a number of discrete areas on AuditNet. The IIA now hosts this site, which has links to and from its own: www.auditnet.org

The Institute of Internal Auditors: www.theiia.org

The IIA's Florida-based website is a fund of information. It carries the internal auditing *Standards* and *Code of Ethics* as well as, for members, the rest of the International Professional Practices Framework. Also on this site is the IIA's excellent bookstore on internal auditing.

The IIA Inc.'s Research Foundation has sponsored the development of an Internal Auditing Capability Maturity Model (IA-CMM), published late 2008. Lead researcher and author is Elizabeth (Libby) MacRae.

The IIA runs the Global Audit Information Network (GAIN), a very effective and economic online benchmarking service for internal audit functions. More information at: www.theiia.org/guidance/benchmarking/gain

United Kingdom HM Treasury website: www.hm-treasury.gov.uk. This has a wealth of guidance on internal auditing including:

"The Orange Book"—Management of Risk: Principles and Concepts: www.hm-treasury.gov.uk/media/C/6/1104_orange_book.pdf

Internal Audit Quality Assessment Framework, including the Treasury's own internal audit maturity model: ww.hm-treasury.gov.uk/psr_governance_risk_iaqaf.htm

Government Internal Audit Standards: www.hm-treasury.gov.uk/psr_governance_gia_guidance.htm

See Also:

★ Best Practices in Risk-Based Internal Auditing (pp. 303–305)
★ Internal Audit and Partnering with Senior Management (pp. 368–371)
★ New Assurance Challenges Facing Chief Audit Executives (pp. 378–381)
✔ Defining Corporate Governance: Its Aims, Goals, and Responsibilities (p. 1115)
✔ Establishing a Framework for Assessing Risk (p. 1028)
✔ Understanding Internal Audits (p. 1057)

NOTES

1 Institute of Internal Auditors (IIA). *International Standards for the Professional Practice of Internal Auditing* ("*Standards*"). Altamonte Springs, FL: IIA, 2010. Can be downloaded from www.theiia.org, along with the *Code of Ethics*, Practice advisories and Position papers. See "Websites" in "More Info."

2 IIA (2009). Standard 1110: Organizational Independence.

3 IIA. Standard 2010.C1.

4 See note 1.

5 For example, the UK HM Treasury's *Internal Audit Quality Assessment Framework*, which includes its internal audit maturity model (see "Websites" in "More Info"); or the IIA Inc. Research Foundation's Internal Auditing Capability Maturity Model (IA-CMM), authored by Elizabeth MacRae, 2009, www.theiia.org/bookstore/product/internal-audit-capability-model-iacm-for-the-public-sector-1422.cfm

"Is the internal audit function robust enough to challenge senior management? Clearly if the internal control function is too weak to effectively challenge those responsible for determining the organisation's operations, it has little value in its role of risk control." John Tiner

  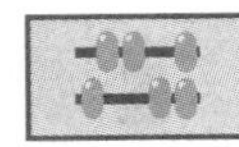   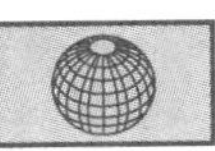   

Origins and Rationale for IFRS Convergence

by Peter Walton

EXECUTIVE SUMMARY

- Worldwide convergence on international standards for financial reporting will make investment and financial reporting more efficient.
- Investors gain access to more investment opportunities and the cost of capital comes down.
- As more countries use International Financial Reporting Standards (IFRS), so international groups can use them for subsidiary reporting and group reporting.
- The International Accounting Standards Committee, the international standard-setter, came into existence in 1973 as an initiative by the accounting profession to address the emerging needs of cross-border business.
- The standard-setter negotiated a role with the international co-ordinator of stock exchange regulators as a supplier of rules for secondary listings.
- The International Accounting Standards Board, the successor body, was created in 2000 at the time when the European Union announced it would adopt IFRS for listed companies.
- IFRS are now mandatory or permitted in more than 100 countries. Japan, India, Canada, Brazil, and South Korea are set to adopt IFRS in 2011.
- Companies using IFRS can list in the United States without preparing a costly reconciliation of their numbers to US GAAP.

INTRODUCTION

How did an internal phone call in a Sydney hotel in 1972 lead 40 years later to a worldwide movement that is changing financial reporting radically and opening up international investment?

Thanks to that conversation, companies can more and more easily access different stock markets, and investors can step across national and cultural boundaries. Investment should be getting more efficient. Since 2001, International Financial Reporting Standards (IFRS) have been set in London by the International Accounting Standards Board (IASB), a privately financed independent body. Their standards are used for listed companies within the European Union and in many other places. In 2011 China, Japan, India, Brazil, and South Korea will start using them. Even the United States is considering abandoning its rules in favor of the international ones.

WHY CONVERGENCE IS NECESSARY

Evidently, having different national accounting systems is costly for companies and investors. Companies have to keep duplicate accounting systems, and investors are wary about buying shares of companies whose accounts they do not understand. The problem arises because accounting regulation has developed over a couple of centuries in national economies whose needs have differed from each other, and whose ways of regulating people's activities have also differed. What people are looking for from accounting is often different.

Much accounting regulation is contingent: you get an accounting failure, then you get rules to shut the stable door; so, for example, the Enron debacle was followed by the Sarbanes–Oxley Act. This has been going on ever since there were accounting rules. The first government requirements were developed because of a spate of bankruptcies in Paris in the seventeenth century. Consequently, while much of the basic methodology (double entry bookkeeping, balance sheet, etc.) is the same everywhere, the details can differ—especially when it comes to the more complex situations where there is no obvious best solution.

This has a number of consequences, which in turn bring costs. Internally within a multinational group there is usually a network of national subsidiaries (e.g. Nestlé has more than a thousand) spread across the world. They have to report nationally using their national GAAP (Generally Accepted Accounting Principles) and also have to report to the parent, which has to prepare consolidated statements using parent company GAAP. This means that either the subsidiary has dual accounting systems, or the parent has to maintain a special team to adjust the accounts of subsidiaries to parent GAAP. This is costly, and it also means that it is not that easy to transfer accounting staff around the world because of the different local requirements, and it is more expensive to train them.

The group consolidated financial statements are then used to communicate to present and potential shareholders. If the company is listed on several stock exchanges, this means the possibility of having to provide information adjusted to the requirements of the individual foreign stock exchanges—as in the case of the SEC reconciliation to US GAAP. Investors are not comfortable with financial statements that are not prepared under the GAAP they are used to. Consequently they either do not invest, or they will require a higher risk premium to do so.

This situation has the effect of limiting the extent to which international capital markets are truly international. A company may choose not to list in a major market because of the reporting costs, and therefore cuts itself off from investors based there who for legal, cultural, and other reasons will not invest outside that market. Equally there is a cost for investors because their choice is restricted. The US investor cannot directly compare Whirlpool with Electrolux or Siemens. If they could directly compare all washing machine manufacturers around the globe, they could choose the most efficient, and global wealth would increase.

THE DEVELOPMENT OF GLOBAL STANDARDS

The 1972 phone call that launched what are now the International Financial Reporting Standards, or IFRS, was made by Douglas Morpeth, then a partner in the international audit firm Touche Ross (now Deloitte) and also president of the Institute of Chartered Accountants in England and Wales, to Henry Benson, a partner in Coopers & Lybrand (now part of PricewaterhouseCoopers). They were at a conference of the international accounting profession. Benson had just made a presentation about the future international organization of the profession. Morpeth asked why Benson's committee had not also suggested setting up an international standard-setter.

They called a meeting with representatives of the US and Canadian professional bodies, and by June the next year the board of the International Accounting Standards Committee (IASC), comprising representatives of nine national professional bodies, was holding its first meeting in London.

The initiative should be seen in context: international trade started to grow significantly from the 1960s, and by the early 1970s was starting to register as an issue that needed to be addressed. People were staring to transact more frequently across borders and would need a common accounting language, or at least Morpeth and Benson thought so. The second current was the development of standard-setters. The present US standard-setter, the Financial Accounting Standards Board (FASB) also started work in 1973. The United Kingdom's first standard-setter started to appear in 1969. Douglas Morpeth was deputy chairman of the Accounting Standards Committee as the UK body was eventually called. He thought that the United Kingdom's new standards could be usefully recycled for international use.

Benson was the first chairman of the IASC. It was a very small organization with a single employee based in London and a voluntary chairman and board members supported by professional accounting associations. After the initial enthusiasm for doing something international, two problems emerged. It became clear that the national bodies were doing very little about getting International Accounting Standards (IAS) adopted in their home countries, so no one was actually using these standards. Second, as standards were being developed, individuals were reluctant to see their national practices banned or ignored, and so IAS were written that included options within them. Two companies could adopt radically different stances on an issue and both be in compliance with the same standard.

By the 1980s the IASC's standards were being voluntarily adopted by multinationals in countries such as Switzerland, France, and Italy (e.g. Nestlé, Roche, Aérospatiale, Cap Gemini) to make up for a lack of detailed rules for consolidated financial statements. They were also being used as a model in developing countries that were members of the British Commonwealth to build on to the model they had inherited from the British Empire. Outside that use, they were much cited in debates about standards, but very rarely directly applied. When they were used voluntarily by individual companies, often those companies followed some but not all of the standards.

USE IN INTERNATIONAL CAPITAL MARKETS

However, change was on its way. From 1985 a new secretary general, David Cairns, set about transforming the situation. He initiated an agreement with the International Organization of Securities Commissions (IOSCO), a body that links national stock exchange regulators, for the IASC to supply standards to be used in conjunction with secondary listings. At the time, most stock exchanges required foreign issuers either to provide financial

CASE STUDY

Cadbury Changes to IFRS from UK GAAP

In common with all companies listed on EU stock exchanges, Cadbury PLC (at the time Cadbury Schweppes PLC) officially switched to IFRS in 2005, as required by the EU IAS Regulation. In practice, the real transition moment was the beginning the 2004 financial year: IFRS require that a company provides previous-year comparative figures with the annual financial statements. Consequently, when reporting the 2005 results, the company had also to provide 2004 figures according to IFRS. However, the company had also had to report 2004 under local GAAP (in Cadbury's case, UK GAAP), and IFRS 1, the standard dealing with transition, requires that a company also provide a reconciliation between the local GAAP figures for 2004 and the IFRS figures for 2004. From an investor's perspective, therefore, every company provides a statement comparing its pretransition figures with the same transactions reported under IFRS.

Cadbury is also listed in the US and therefore is registered with the Securities and Exchange Commission. Consequently, at that time it was also obliged to provide a reconciliation of its annual earnings and its equity to US GAAP. This means that, for 2004, an investor could observe the earnings and net assets of Cadbury under three different sets of GAAP: UK GAAP, IFRS, and US GAAP. The figures show that—despite the fact that all three sets of accounting rules belong to the same underlying tradition of Anglo-Saxon accounting, with financial reporting oriented toward informing investors—there still remain significant differences of measurement at a detailed level. This illustrates how difficult it is to compare the results of companies that are using different comprehensive bases of accounting, and why investors and international companies are keen to move to a different global standard.

If we take equity—the net worth of the group after deducting all liabilities from assets—the Cadbury figures at the end of 2004 were:

	£ million
UK GAAP	3,088
IFRS	2,300
US GAAP	3,998

There is a presentational difference in that the US definition of "equity" at the time excluded minority interests. For comparative purposes I have added these to the US GAAP number in the above table.

It is not particularly productive to make a detailed analysis of why the differences occur. Basically, they reflect different ways of accounting for business combinations that had occurred in the past, different treatment of pension liabilities, and the significantly different treatment of deferred tax in the United Kingdom from that under IFRS and US GAAP. There is a detailed analysis in the notes to the 2005 Cadbury (Cadbury Schweppes) annual report.

If we take net earnings, the numbers are:

	£ million
UK GAAP	453
IFRS	547
US GAAP	484

We can see that in 2003 investors had two sets of figures to choose from, while in 2004 the convergence initiative meant that in the transitional phase they had three different measures of the same performance. However, in 2007, when the SEC removed the US GAAP reconciliation requirement, they would have come down to a single view of performance which was comparable to that used in 100 countries.

It should be emphasized that, of course, the company's cash flows do not change with the different accounting bases: what drives the differences is different timing assumptions, different measurement rules for some transactions, and different allocations across time periods.

You can only know absolutely how much profit a company has made when it has stopped trading and all its assets and liabilities have been liquidated. The only profit that is irrefutable is the lifetime's net increase or net decrease in cash.

This is not much help for investors, and financial reporting is a means of estimating what part of the lifetime profit has been earned in a particular year, in order to help investors decide whether to buy, sell, or hold the company's securities. However, the annual profit is only an *estimate*, it is not a fact. All estimates are based on assumptions—change the assumptions and you have a different profit.

So none of the three sets of figures Cadbury published for 2004 is "correct" or "incorrect"—they are all justifiable estimates. It is not surprising that investors ask for a single agreed accounting standard.

statements according to local generally accepted accounting principles (GAAP) or to provide reconciliations to them. IOSCO's idea was that all stock exchanges would sign up to a single set of listing requirements for foreign issuers, so dramatically cutting the costs of a secondary listing.

At the same time Cairns set out to widen the funding base of the body so that he could expand its work, and to try to involve national standard-setters as well as professional bodies. The idea that the accounting profession should set its own standards was disappearing and standards were increasingly being set by dedicated independent committees. He agreed with IOSCO a program to improve International Accounting Standards by removing options and also by extending the range.

The road proved to be rocky, and took more than ten years. Cairns resigned in 1994, to be replaced by Bryan Carsberg, an accounting practitioner turned academic turned government regulator (he had been director-general of fair trading in the United Kingdom). Under Carsberg the program was finally completed, including the difficult standard on financial instruments, IAS 39. A strategy committee was also established to recommend how the future standard-setter should be organized.

The year 2000 was pivotal. In May IOSCO voted to approve the body of International Accounting Standards isssued by the IASC (if with some reservations). In June, the European Commission announced that it was going to propose legislation to require the use of the standards by EU listed companies from 2005, and in July the international accounting profession, meeting in Edinburgh, agreed to relinquish its control of the IASC and let the IASB be set up in its place.

The IASB is a small committee of professional standard-setters. It has a large technical team, based in London still, and is funded through voluntary contributions from companies, audit firms, and various institutions, both national and international. It adopted the predecessor body's standards, but used a different name (IFRS instead of IAS) for its own standards. IFRS is also the generic term for all the standards together with the interpretations issued by the IFRS Interpretations Committee .

CONVERGENCE ON A WORLDWIDE STANDARD

Where the IASC was part of a world of "harmonization"—or movement toward each other—the IASB is firmly committed "to develop, in the public interest, a single set of high quality, understandable and enforceable global accounting standards" and "to bring about convergence of national accounting standards and IFRSs to high quality solutions" (*Preface to IFRS*, London: IASC Foundation). Though it has not focused exclusively on the United States, the IASB's main driver is convergence with US GAAP. It entered into an agreement with the FASB in 2002 to pursue convergence through a joint program of removing differences and developing new standards together.

This program yielded a big prize in 2007. The Securities and Exchange Commission decided that it would recognize financial statements prepared under IFRS as issued by the IASB as equivalent to US GAAP. Until then, foreign registrants with the SEC were obliged to file annually either a set of accounts using US GAAP, or a reconciliation of annual earnings and equity at balance sheet date with how they would have been measured under US GAAP. This was a big burden to companies listed on the New York Stock Exchange or NASDAQ and a major disincentive to foreign companies to list there. In 2007 the chief financial officer of AXA told the SEC at a round table that the company budgeted $20 million a year to produce the reconciliation. Another part of the cost is that the companies end up publishing two, or even three, sets of figures (see the Cadbury case study) and then having to discuss with analysts and journalists which is the "correct" profit.

The removal of the reconciliation requirement means that, for example, European companies that are using IFRS can simply file with the SEC the same accounts that they file with their primary stock exchange. Of course the SEC has other requirements that still have to be complied with, including management's discussion and analysis of results. However, companies no longer have to be able to restate their figures to US GAAP, nor retain teams to monitor US GAAP.

CONCLUSION

Convergence on IFRS is taking us to a bright new world where investors can indeed take their pick from around the globe, and where companies maintain a single accounting basis throughout their network. IFRS are already either compulsory or permitted for listed companies in more than 100 countries around the world. When the next wave of adopters joins in 2011, a large slice of the world economy will be IFRS conversant.

It will take time for investors to become confident about reading IFRS accounts—although that happened quickly within the European Union. But multinational companies should quickly reap the benefits of having uniform systems across the globe and will be able to exploit the opportunities of being listed on several stock exchanges at much lower cost.

MAKING IT HAPPEN

- Using IFRS at group level is mandatory in many countries, but is voluntary in some. It is often voluntary at subsidiary level: both parent and subsidiaries need to choose this option to access the benefits.
- Using IFRS makes access to capital markets outside the country where the group has its primary listing much easier and cheaper. In what markets would there be special benefits for your company? Remember that a secondary listing is not just about access to foreign investors, it is about credibility and flexibility in that market.
- Are your group accounting and internal audit professionals able to move easily from one foreign subsidiary to another? Using IFRS would facilitate their work and potentially improve internal control.
- Do professional fund managers and analysts that you deal with understand IFRS? Talk to them about whether they are IFRS literate and ask if they see benefits in switching.
- What do your group auditors think? The large international firms are fully geared up for IFRS. They will help you switch.

MORE INFO

Books:

Camfferman, Kees, and Stephen A. Zeff. *Financial Reporting and Global Capital Markets: A History of the International Accounting Standards Committee, 1973–2000*. Oxford: Oxford University Press, 2007.

Canadian Institute of Chartered Accountants. *The CICA's Guide to IFRS in Canada*. Toronto, ON: CICA, 2009.

Walton, Peter. *An Executive's Guide for Moving from US GAAP to IFRS*. New York: Business Expert Press, 2009.

"As long as there are rich people in the world, they will be desirous of distinguishing themselves from the poor."

Jean-Jacques Rousseau

Articles:

Soderstrom, Naomi S., and Kevin Jialin Sun. "IFRS adoption and accounting quality: A review." *European Accounting Review* 16:4 (December 2007): 675–702. Online at: dx.doi.org/10.1080/09638180701706732

Tokar, Mary. "Convergence and the implementation of a single set of global standards: The real-life challenge." *Accounting in Europe* 2 (2005): 47–68. Online at: dx.doi.org/10.1080/09638180500379079

Reports:

Institute of Chartered Accountants in England and Wales. "EU implementation of IFRS and the Fair Value Directive. A report for the European Commission." London: ICAEW, 2007. Online at: tinyurl.com/y92mjyb

US Securities and Exchange Commission. "Roadmap for the potential use of financial statements prepared in accordance with International Financial Reporting Standards by US issuers." SEC Release 33-8982, November 14, 2008. Online at: www.sec.gov/spotlight/ifrsroadmap.htm

Websites:

European Financial Reporting Advisory Group, the advisory body on IFRS for the European Commission: www.efrag.org

Financial Accounting Standards Board, the US standard-setter: www.fasb.org

IAS Plus, an IFRS information site run by Deloitte: www.iasplus.com

IFRS help site by the Canadian Institute of Chartered Accountants: www.cica.ca/ifrs

IFRS resources provided by the American Institute of Certified Public Accountants: www.ifrs.com

IFRS News, a monthly newsletter on the development of global standards: www.ifrsnews.net

International Accounting Standards Board, the international standard-setter: www.iasb.org

International Organization of Securities Commissions, the international body for stock exchange regulators: www.iosco.org

US Securities and Exchange Commission: www.sec.gov

See Also:

★ How to Implement a Standard Chart of Accounts Effectively (pp. 355–357)
★ Understanding the Requirements for Preparing IFRS Financial Statements (pp. 423–424)
✔ International Financial Reporting Standards (IFRS): The Basics (p. 1039)
✔ Key Accounting Standards and Organizations (p. 1040)
✔ The Ten Accounting Principles (p. 1055)

"Wealth is not without its advantages and the case to the contrary, although it has often been made, has never proved widely persuasive." J. K. Galbraith

     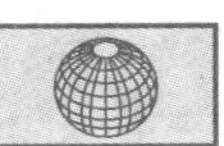   

Performance Reporting under IFRS by Peter Casson

EXECUTIVE SUMMARY

- International Accounting Standard 1 (revised), "Presentation of financial statements," requires companies to report their performance in a statement of comprehensive income.
- The International Accounting Standards Board (IASB) and the US Financial Accounting Standards Board (FASB) have agreed to converge their financial reporting standards.
- As part of the convergence, the IASB and FASB are developing a new standard that is likely to affect the way in which performance is reported in the future.

INTRODUCTION

Financial statements prepared under International Financial Reporting Standards (IFRS) include a statement of comprehensive income which, together with associated notes, report a company's performance for the accounting period. The International Accounting Standards Board (IASB), an independent body, sets the IFRS. The IASB took over responsibility for setting international accounting standards from the International Accounting Standards Committee (IASC), which issued International Accounting Standards (IAS). The IASB adopted the then existing IAS when it took over from the IASC, and the acronym IFRS is now used to include both IFRS and IAS, as well as the interpretations developed by the International Financial Reporting Interpretations Committee or the former Standing Interpretations Committee.

The presentation of a company's financial performance under IFRS is dealt with in IAS 1 (revised) "Presentation of financial statements." Revisions to the standard in 2007, which are in effect for accounting periods beginning on or after January 1, 2009, include the requirement for reporting entities to present a statement of comprehensive income.

The development of IFRS is shaped by an agreement reached between the IASB and the US Financial Accounting Standards Board (FASB) to make their existing financial reporting standards compatible and to coordinate work programs. The IASB and FASB are collaborating on a project entitled "Financial statement presentation," which may lead to further changes in the way entities report performance.

This article describes the essential features of reporting performance under IAS 1 (revised), possible future changes to performance reporting standards, and non-IFRS performance measures.

REPORTING PERFORMANCE UNDER IAS 1

IAS 1 (revised) "Presentation of financial statements" sets out the basis for the presentation of financial statements so as to achieve comparability of a company's financial statements over time and across the financial statements of different companies.

The revised standard, issued in 2007, requires a "statement of comprehensive income," where only an income statement was previously required. This change increases the comparability with the US standard FAS 130 "Comprehensive income." Comprehensive is defined in FAS 130 as "the change in equity [net assets] of a business enterprise during a period from transactions and other events and circumstances from nonowner sources. It includes all changes in equity during a period except those resulting from investments by owners and distributions to owners."

Comprehensive income is more inclusive than profit or loss for a period because, although a company is generally required to recognize all income and expenses in the period in profit or loss, some IFRSs either require or permit otherwise. Items that should/may be excluded from profit or loss include: (1) correction of errors from prior periods; (2) changes in accounting policies; (3) revaluation surpluses; (4) gains and losses arising on the translation of the financial statements of a foreign operation; and (5) gains and losses on remeasuring available-for-sale financial assets. Such items, which are excluded from profit or loss, represent components of other comprehensive income as they result in a change in equity.

In looking at the reporting of performance under IFRS it is useful to consider: The general features of reporting under IFRS; the presentation of comprehensive income; the way in which expenses may be analyzed. It is also useful to look at the specific issues related to discontinued operations and exceptional items.

General Features of Financial Reports under IFRS

IAS 1 (revised) identifies a set of general features for the reporting of financial performance. The first requirement is the fair presentation of a company's financial performance. This requires that the effects of a company's transactions and other events are faithfully represented in its statement of comprehensive income. It is generally presumed that a company will achieve this through the application of IFRSs. However, in some rare instances, it is necessary to depart from IFRSs in order to achieve a fair presentation. Other general features identified in IAS 1 (revised) are:

- Going concern: A company should prepare its statement of comprehensive income on the assumption that it will continue its operations into the indefinite future.
- Accrual basis of accounting: A company should include income and expenses when they meet definition and recognition criteria.
- Materiality and aggregation: A company should present each material class of item separately.
- Offsetting: A company cannot usually offset items of income and expense.
- Frequency of reporting: A company should usually publish its financial statements at least annually.
- Comparative information: A company should disclose comparative information for the previous period.
- Consistency of presentation: A company is required to present and classify items in its statement of comprehensive income on a consistent basis from one period to the next.

Presentation of Comprehensive Income

Companies are required to present a statement of all income and expenses recognized in an accounting period. This may be reported either in a single statement of comprehensive income or in two statements—an income statement showing the components of the profit or loss for the period, and a statement of comprehensive income that includes the components of other comprehensive income.

IAS 1 (revised) requires that the following 10 categories should, as a minimum, be presented in the statement of comprehensive income:

- Revenue.
- Finance costs.
- Share of the profit or loss of joint ventures and associates, i.e., companies over which the reporting company exercises significant influence but which are not subsidiaries or joint ventures.
- Tax expense.
- The post-tax profit or loss on discontinued operations, together with the post-tax gain or loss on the disposal of the assets of the discontinued operations.
- Profit or loss.

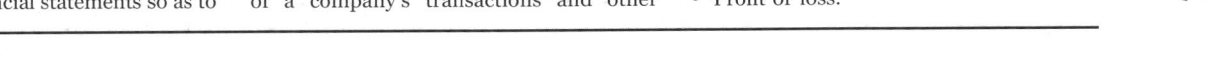

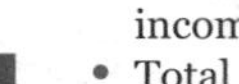

- Each component of other comprehensive income.
- Total comprehensive income.

Where a reporting company is a parent company presenting a consolidated statement of comprehensive income, it is necessary to show the allocation of:

- Profit or loss for the period attributable to: Holders of the stock of the parent company; and minority interests, i.e., holders of the subsidiary companies' common stock other than the stock held directly, or indirectly, by the parent company.
- Total comprehensive income for the period attributable to: Stockholders of the parent company; and minority interests.

Analysis of Expenses

A company is required to present an analysis of its expenses. The analysis may take one of two forms:

- The "nature of expense" method requires the company to classify expenses according to their nature—for example, expense groups such as raw materials and consumables, depreciation, employment costs, and advertising costs.
- The "function of expense" or "cost of sales" method requires the company to aggregate expenses according to their function—for example, cost of sales, distribution costs, and administrative expenses.

Management is required to select the method which, in its view, is most reliable and relevant. Where a company uses the "function of expense" method, it must provide additional information on the nature of the expense.

IAS 1 (revised), as noted above, requires companies to distinguish between continuing and discontinued operations in its reporting of performance. A discontinued operation is a major part of the company (e.g., line of business or geographical area of operation) that has either been disposed of or is held for sale.

When items of income or expense are material, a company is required to disclose their nature and amounts separately. These include: Write-downs of inventories and of property, plant, and equipment; restructuring costs; disposals of items of property, plant, and equipment; disposals of investments; litigation settlements.

PERFORMANCE REPORTING UNDER IFRS IN THE FUTURE

The IASB and the FASB agreed in 2004 to conduct a joint project on the presentation of financial statements with a view to developing a standard on the organization and presentation of information in such statements. As part of this project, the IASB and FASB issued a joint discussion paper, "Preliminary views on financial statement presentation," in 2008.[1]

In the discussion paper, the IASB and FASB propose a classification of items within a statement of comprehensive income. This classification first distinguishes between continuing and discontinued operations, and then further classifies continuing operations into business and financing, with further subclassifications of business and financing. As a result, the statement of comprehensive income would present the following components of comprehensive income:

Business:

- Operating income and expenses;
- Investment income and expenses.

Financing:

- Financing asset income;
- Financing liability expenses;
- Income taxes on continuing operations (business and financing);
- Discontinued operations (net of tax);
- Other comprehensive income.

The statement would also include a subtotal for profit or loss and a total for comprehensive income for the period. Under the proposals, all companies would be required to present a single statement of comprehensive income.

ALTERNATIVE PERFORMANCE MEASURES

Companies frequently report additional performance measures to those required under IFRS. Such additional measures may be designed to reflect the particular circumstances of the company and/or special features of the period being reported. In some cases these alternative performance measures are derived directly from a company's audited financial statements. This includes such measures as EBIT (earnings before interest and tax) and EBITDA (earnings before interest, tax, depreciation, and amortization). Sometimes the measures require adjustments to the figures reported under IFRS, such as "non-IFRS income" and "non-IFRS earnings per share." While some companies define and explain the alternative performance measures they use, others do not.

There are two explanations for the publication of alternative performance measures. The first is that company managers are providing additional information in order to reduce information asymmetry. For example, accounting information is adjusted for items that are regarded as transitory. The alternative explanation is that managers report these numbers with the intention of misleading readers of financial reports. Regulators have therefore attempted to address potential abuse. For example, the Committee of European Securities Regulators (CESR) issued recommendations on the use of alternative performance measures in 2005.

CONCLUSION

IAS 1 (revised) requires companies to present a statement of comprehensive income which includes the profit or loss for the period together with other components of comprehensive income. The IASB assumes that compliance with the provisions of the standard should ensure that companies provide users of financial reports with key information that informs economic decisions.

MAKING IT HAPPEN

- The preparation of a statement of comprehensive income, together with the accompanying notes, requires compliance with IAS 1 (revised) and the application of IFRS with the overall objective of fairly representing the transactions and other events of the reporting entity.
- There may be circumstances in which a company needs to depart from IFRS in order to provide a fair representation.
- Users of financial statements should be aware of the accounting standards, and of any departures from standards, in their analysis of the statement of comprehensive income.

MORE INFO

Book:

Ernst & Young. *International GAAP® 2009*. 2 vols. Chichester, UK: Wiley, 2009. Online at: www.wiley.com/legacy/igaap09

Websites:

Deloitte—IAS Plus: www.iasplus.com

International Accounting Standards Board (IASB): www.iasb.org

NOTE

1 FASB/IASB, "Discussion paper, preliminary views on financial statement presentation," October 16, 2008. Online at: www.fasb.org/draft/index.shtml.

"There are three ways by which an individual can get wealth—by work, by gift, and by theft. And, clearly, the reasons why the workers get so little is that the beggars and thieves get so much." Henry George

Principles versus Rules in Financial Supervision—Is There One Superior Approach? by Marc Quintyn

EXECUTIVE SUMMARY

- Financial liberalization, which started in the 1970s, has altered the nature of financial operations dramatically. In contrast with the pre-1970s, often called the period of financial repression, good financial institution governance is now critical for the soundness of the individual financial institution, and, by extension, the stability of a country's financial system.
- In response to these deep and far-reaching changes in the financial sector, financial regulation and supervision has become much more important than ever before, and the nature of its business has been changing in equally dramatic ways.
- Supervisors were likened for the longest time to compliance, or box-ticking officers. Now, in this governance-driven financial environment, they have become "governance supervisors," monitoring the operations of the financial institutions on behalf of the diffused and ill-informed deposit-holders of these institutions.
- Since the start of this transformation of the supervisory approaches, debates have been conducted about the optimal way to supervise the financial systems. Some jurisdictions believe in a principles-based approach, while others swear by a rules-based approach.
- The discussion is about guiding, or keeping in check, financial institutions through broad-based principles versus well-defined, specific rules. Practice shows that life is too complex for any of these two extremes alone. Both systems have their pros and cons, and best practice seems to go in the direction of a supervisory approach that offers a balance of principles, supported by guidelines and rules. In the aftermath of a crisis, all sides call for more rules; in quiet times, all sides think that they can steer the course with principles. As normal times inherently carry the seeds of a crisis within them, any supervisory system should balance rules and principles.

INTRODUCTION

The Challenging Nature of Financial Supervision

Two things can be stated with certainty about financial sector supervision. First, that few professions have changed so dramatically in recent years, in form, approach, scope, and substance. Second, that the task of supervisors, when compared to several other domains of public policy, has become extremely complex, and that no end is in sight with regard to this process. These fundamental changes are taking place in response to the equally dramatic changes that we are witnessing in the sectors they are mandated to oversee.

Financial Liberalization

It all started with financial liberalization, which took hold in the 1970s. Between World War II and the 1970s, all financial systems around the globe were heavily regulated, or mainly in government hands. It had become common to describe the government's approach to handling the system as "financial repression." From the mid-1970s on, first domestically, and subsequently internationally, liberalization triggered many changes that profoundly altered the face of the financial system and the nature of its operations. Financial liberalization, in turn, unleashed competitive forces, first within the banking systems, subsequently within other subsectors, and finally among all of them, leading to a blurring of boundaries among previously clearly delineated subsectors, such as banking, securities markets, and insurance. Fierce competition pressurized financial institutions to take on more risks to outpace competitors and ensure lasting profitability. Major advances in information and communication technologies further propelled this process forward—provisionally, until a few years ago when the system collapsed under the weight of too many incorrectly assessed risks and too much leverage.

Adequate risk management requires high-quality governance of financial institutions in order to preserve financial sector stability in this new environment. In sharp contrast with the financial repression period—when financial sector behavior was largely prescribed, and financial institution governance, therefore, was left with only a few degrees of freedom—financial institution governance has become a crucial variable in guaranteeing the success of these liberalized and globalized financial systems.

Reorientation of Financial Supervisors' Work

Such dramatic changes in the way the financial sector operates have required major adjustments in the supervisor's regulatory and supervisory frameworks, and in the ways they enter into dialogue with the supervised entities.[2] Thus, supervisors had to metamorphose from compliance, or box-ticking, officers in the old, repressed systems, to what we would call now "governance" supervisors. They needed to replace their reactive approach with forward-looking, proactive ways of doing business with financial institutions. Under this new paradigm, the task of the supervisor is mainly to monitor and guide financial institutions to implement comprehensive risk management and internal control frameworks suitable for their particular institutional risk profiles, subject to prudential standards.

This view of regulation and supervision is closely aligned with Dewatripont and Tirole's (1994) "representation hypothesis" of regulation. Prudential regulation "...is primarily motivated by the need to represent the small depositors and to bring about an appropriate corporate governance for banks" (p. 35). Managers of financial institutions have a fiduciary responsibility towards their shareholders, but the feature that distinguishes financial institutions from the rest of the corporate sector in the economy is that they also have a very large and diffuse group of stakeholders (or debtholders), many of them not well-informed about their financial institution. So, the above view sees the supervisor as performing the role of one important stakeholder in the financial institutions' corporate governance, representing the set of diffuse stakeholders, i.e., the depositors. From this follows that bank regulation and supervision have become part of the overall corporate governance regime of financial institutions.

In such a framework, financial institution governance consists of two parts: The regulators ensure debt governance, and shareholders ensure equity governance. As a result, bank managers have to serve two masters, the shareholders and the regulators, the latter representing the bulk of the uninformed stakeholders. These governance arrangements thus induce, or force, management to internalize the welfare of all stakeholders, not just shareholders. In recent years, this role has gained even more prominence because financial liberalization has also led to a "privatization of risk," whereby savers are increasingly dependent on financial markets to determine

  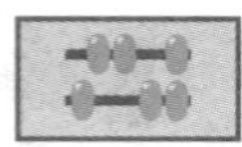   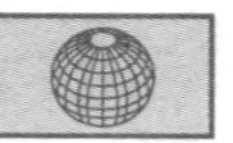   

their future financial security. This development requires more attention from the supervisors to risks that customers take upon themselves when confronted with an opaque financial system.

An Ongoing Process

So, there is broad agreement on the rationale—financial regulation and supervision are needed—and on the objectives—soundness of the individual institutions to preserve financial sector stability. But how about the best approach to get from starting point to objective? This is where most of the debate has taken place in recent years, and is most likely to continue for several years, as the discussions in the aftermath of the 2007–08 financial crisis are amply demonstrating. As the debate about the best supervisory approaches continues, discussions are frequently presented in the form of dichotomies such as "principles-based versus rules-based supervision."

This debate is about the best approach for ongoing, day-to-day supervision of financial institutions. Typically, "either/or" discussions attract a lot of attention and often have a tendency to misrepresent the extreme concepts. We will therefore present the origins of the debate, clarify the concepts and review their merits, and see how close or how far we are from best practices in financial supervision.

PRINCIPLES-BASED VERSUS RULES-BASED SUPERVISION

Financial liberalization has put the onus of preserving financial institution soundness, and by extension financial system stability, on the governance of the financial institutions. A financial world where corporate governance has been given a much greater responsibility than before, for innovation, progress, and risk management, is inconsistent with a box-ticking supervisory approach. Supervisors need to be "governance supervisors," which means that they monitor financial institution governance, and intervene where necessary to keep it within the agreed framework. In this context, greater emphasis on "principles" than on "rules" is a natural and consistent transformation.

The Financial Services Authority (FSA), the United Kingdom's unified supervisor since 1997, has advertised itself most explicitly as a "principles-based" supervisor. According to the British unified supervisor, a principles-based regulatory regime specifies desired outcomes and allows financial institutions to chart their own paths to those results. Thus, the main features of such a supervisory regime can be summarized as follows.

- The regulator defines a set of principles (11 in the case of the FSA—see Box 1) regarding the conduct of a financial institution's business. These principles are general by nature, and set normative goals with respect to, for instance, integrity, adequacy of financial resources, and proper standards of market conduct.
- By definition, these principles are outcomes-oriented. They are meant to leave the supervised institution a lot of freedom to achieve the outcomes by the ways that it deems most adequate.

It should not come as a surprise that principles-based supervision is being promoted by a UK-based supervisor. Historically, there was no legal basis for the activities of the Bank of England (the supervisor until 1997), either in regard to its central bank or supervisory functions. For the longest time, the British banking system was managed as a small gentlemen's club through the use of "moral suasion." The system perfectly matched the needs of the City of London and the British authorities, and moral suasion was considered by both sides as "best practice" to guide and supervise the system. In that regard, this system of supervision was uniquely British and has never been replicated elsewhere.

Significant changes in the institutional composition of London's financial markets in a more recent period, integration in the European financial markets, as well as a number of financial scandals have made this approach gradually obsolete, and have led to a legal formalization of the British system. Nonetheless, the roots have never entirely disappeared, and have resurfaced under the form of a preference for "principles" to guide the financial system, rather than a strictly rules-based system. The rest of the world seems more critical, or even skeptical, towards this British love for principles. So, let us look at the advantages of both approaches in the current context.

Principles-Based Supervision

Principles-based supervision leaves bank managers great freedom to pursue the outcomes set by the supervisors in ways that they deem most suitable, given the realities of their own institution. Interference from supervisors is minimal. Rules, on the other hand, tend to divert managers' attention from the big picture by keeping them focused on details and on compliance, rather than on the spirit of the principle.

Principles leave the markets in general a lot of freedom to be creative and innovative, as long as they respect the boundaries set by the principles. Strict rules tend to kill initiative, creativity, and innovation.

Principles open the door to a productive dialogue between supervisor and supervised, leading to better mutual understanding (this is also part of the spirit of Pillar 2 under Basel II). Too much reliance on rules tends to keep alive the image of the supervisor as the policeman, associated with the compliance officer from the earlier days.

Financial systems are nowadays so complex that all-encompassing principles work better than rules. It is simply impossible to have rules to govern each and every activity of a financial institution.

Rules-Based Supervision

- Rules provide clarity and certainty for financial institution managers. Principles often lack these features, and, as a result, may yield opposite results from what they intended. Indeed, if uncertainly with respect to the interpretation of the principle prevails, the supervised manager may err on the conservative side and actually interpret the principle as a rule. Such behavior would defeat the purpose of the principles.
- Rules provide transparency for bank managers and ensure more fairness. They know exactly what they can expect from the supervisors. Principles are open for interpretation, and uncertainty. Lack of transparency can even lead to obstructing a level playing field.
- Rules are more operational than principles. Principles need to be supported by guidelines or rules to become operational.
- The financial system is so complex—and becoming more complex every day—that rules or guidelines are needed in support of the broad principles, to explain the principles or direct their implementation.

Towards a Principles-cum-Rules System

Reliance on supervisory principles has a lot of appeal in our modern, governance-driven financial industry. However, putting the advantages and disadvantages of both approaches side by side leads us fairly easily to the conclusion that this discussion of principles versus rules is a false discussion. Neither approach alone would be superior and effective, and best practice would probably be a supervisory system that promulgates a number of principles that are supported by a set of prudential standards or rules. In fact, the FSA, for all

"Purchasing power is a license to purchase power." Raoul Vaneigem

  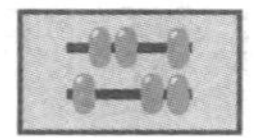      

the talk about principles-based supervision, is quick to state that its 11 principles are backed up by a 8,500-page rulebook. And the rule book is growing in the wake of the 2007–08 crisis.

Thus, the best way to design supervision of the financial system is to provide financial institution governance with the right incentives by setting out a number of principles, but to back these principles with a set of prudential rules and standards, and guidelines to further align managers' and supervisors' incentive structures. The current financial crisis, in particular, has shown that the financial system cannot survive on principles alone, without rules, which sometimes will take the form of guidelines, and sometimes need to be prescriptive. Without rules and standards, the incentives of financial institution managers will never be aligned with those of the supervisors. This seems to be the nature of the game in the financial system.

A very illustrative example of aligning incentives through rules where principles fall short, is the generalized call, in the wake of the 2007–08 financial crisis, for forms of dynamic (or countercyclical) provisioning mechanisms. Most countries' supervisory frameworks impose provisioning rules in case assets become non-performing. These provisions need to be formed at the time the asset becomes nonperforming, i.e., when the economy goes into a downturn and pressure on bank capital increases (i.e., capital shortages occur). The idea behind countercyclical provisioning is that (part of the) provisions be set aside in the good times, when the loans are made. This exercises a dampening effect on the bank's profitability in the short run, and sounds, therefore, counterintuitive. However, it forces bank managers to align their incentives with those of the supervisors who protect the banks' stakeholders. Spain is one of the few countries that went into the 2007–08 financial crisis with a version of such a system in place, and most analysts agree that it has protected the Spanish banking system compared to many other countries.

Now, part of the confusion in the principles versus rules discussion also stems from the fact that many commentators still see rules as the pre-liberalization instrument. Under the financial repression epoch, rules prescribed and governed all sides of the operation of financial institutions, such as price-setting, credit allocation, and the like. When we think of rules nowadays, we have in mind prudential rules—rules that guide the behavior of the financial institutions. They are sometimes prescriptive (risk-based capital ratios, or limits on off-balance sheet activities), but more often serve as guidelines for prudent bank behavior (such as rules about connected lending, exposure to a single borrower, foreign exposure limits, loan classification rules, and loan provisioning rules). This type of prudential rule is perfectly consistent with the establishment of governing principles.

So a further convergence toward a system that sets out a number of overriding principles that are supported by rules and guidelines seems to go in the direction of a best practice for financial sector supervision. The transition to such a balanced supervisory approach needs to be supported by some important changes in the governance of supervisors and supervised institutions as well. In general, as already mentioned, the dialogue between supervisor and supervised institution is critical. More dialogue leads to better mutual understanding of each other's motives and incentives. For supervisors, this transition also implies more attention to accountability and transparency in their own governance. A system that is based, to some extent, on principles gives a great deal of power to the supervisor. At the end of the day, the supervisor decides whether the institutions act in the spirit of the principle. To avoid the use of dual standards, and therefore to avoid undermining a level playing field among financial institutions, supervisors will benefit from accountability arrangements whereby the supervisor can explain to all stakeholders (government, supervised entities, public at large) why they took the decisions that they took.

THE FSA's 11 PRINCIPLES

1 A firm must conduct its business with integrity.
2 A firm must conduct its business with due skill, care, and diligence.
3 A firm must take reasonable care to organize and control its affairs responsibly and effectively with adequate risk management systems.
4 A firm must maintain adequate financial resources.
5 A firm must observe proper standards of market conduct.
6 A firm must pay due regard to the interest of its customers and treat them fairly.
7 A firm must pay due regard to the information needs of its clients, and communicate information to them in a way which is clear, fair, and not misleading.
8 A firm must manage conflicts of interest fairly, both between itself and its customers, and between a customer and a client.
9 A firm must take reasonable care to ensure the suitability of its advice, and of discretionary decisions for any customer who is entitled to rely on its judgment.
10 A firm must arrange adequate protection for its client's assets when it is responsible for them.
11 A firm must deal with its regulators in an open and cooperative way, and must disclose to the FSA appropriately anything relating to the firm of which the FSA would reasonably expect notice.

Source: Financial Services Authority

MORE INFO

Book:

Dewatripont, Mathias, and Jean Tirole. *The Prudential Regulation of Banks*. Cambridge, MA: MIT Press, 1994.

Article:

Geneva Reports on the World Economy. "The fundamental principles of financial regulation." Preliminary conference draft, 2009.

NOTES

1 Geneva Reports on the World Economy (2009).
2 The oversight of the financial system consists of two elements: Regulation and supervision. Both functions might be performed by one and the same person, but they are different—respectively, rule-setting and rule-implementation and enforcement. Even within the financial system, there are differences in emphasis. For instance, in the securities area, the term "regulator" is used more frequently than "supervisor," because in their tasks, the regulatory aspect dominates. In this article, we prefer to use the word "supervisor," mainly for the sake of conciseness. However, when we refer to the regulatory function specifically, we will use that term.

"Nothing is more admirable than the fortitude with which millionaires tolerate the disadvantages of their wealth."

Rex Stout

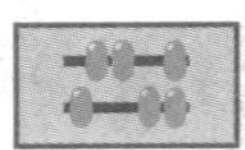

Procedures for Reporting Financial Risk in Islamic Finance by Daud Vicary Abdullah and Ramesh Pillai

EXECUTIVE SUMMARY

- Uncertainty is a defining feature of the economic environment. Economic agents' perceptions of risk, together with their willingness and ability to bear it, fundamentally shape decisions, transactions, and market prices. Well-considered decisions should be based on information that helps to highlight existing risks and uncertainties. An important component of the information system of an organization or economy is financial reporting, through which an enterprise conveys information about its financial performance and condition to external users, often identified with its actual and potential claimants. It stands to reason, therefore, that financial reporting should provide a good sense of the impact of those risks and uncertainties on measures of valuation, income, and cash flows.
- It is important to reconcile the perspectives of accounting standard-setters on the one hand, and prudential authorities on the other, on what information should be reported, and on how it should be portrayed. The final goal is a financial reporting system that is consistent, as far as possible, with sound risk management and management practices and that can serve as a basis for well-informed decisions by outside investors as well as prudential authorities.
- Outside investors, be they equity or debt holders, would normally require certain information about the financial performance of a firm so as to guide their decisions. First, they would surely wish to form a view about the firm's past and current profitability, solvency, and liquidity at a given point in time. Second, they would probably also like to develop a picture of the risk profile of those attributes over time and, hence, of their potential future evolution. Third, they might additionally wish to gain a sense of how reliable or accurate those measures are. Combined, these three elements would provide the raw material to inform views about expected returns properly adjusted for risk and for the inevitable uncertainties that surround measurement. These three types of information correspond to the key categories into which the ideal set can be divided—namely, first movement, risk, and measurement error—and they are equally applicable to financial reporting in an Islamic finance environment.

INTRODUCTION

The key elements of Islamic finance can be summarized as follows.

- Materiality and validity of transactions: there is no profit sharing without risk taking, and earning profit is legitimized by engaging in economic venture. Money is not a commodity but a medium of exchange, a store of value, and a unit of measurement.
- Mutuality of risk sharing: clearly defined risk and profit sharing characteristics serve as an additional built-in mechanism. There are clearly laid out terms and conditions.
- Avoidance of *riba* (interest), *maysir* (gambling), and *gharar* (uncertainty).

The key elements of Islamic financial risk can be summarized as follows.

- The reporting of financial risk in an Islamic financial institution (IFI) requires greater transparency and disclosure than its conventional counterpart.
- This is particularly true with respect to additional *shariah* governance and some risk areas that are unique to Islamic finance.
- IFIs have greater fiduciary duties and responsibility to their stakeholders than conventional institutions.
- The additional duties and responsibilities of IFIs are overseen by the IFI's *shariah* board.

First-movement information describes income, the balance sheet, and cash flows at a point in time. It is the type of information with the longest tradition by far in accounting.

Risk information is fundamentally forward-looking. Future profits, future cash flows, and future valuations are intrinsically uncertain. Risk information is designed to capture the prospective range of outcomes for the variables of profit as measured at a particular point in time.

Measurement error information designates the margin of error or uncertainty that surrounds the measurement of the variables of profit, including those that quantify risk. The need for this type of information arises whenever these variables have to be estimated. For instance, measurement error would be zero for first-movement information concerning items that were valued at observable market prices for which a deep and liquid market existed. However, it would be positive if, say, such items were marked to model and/or traded in illiquid markets, since a number of assumptions would need to be made to arrive at such estimates.

There has been a wide array of change and development in Islamic finance in recent years. The Accounting and Auditing Organization for Islamic Financial Institutions (AAOIFI) has tackled several of the pertinent issues in its Financial Accounting Standards (FAS). In particular, FAS 1 relates to general presentation and disclosure in the financial statements of Islamic banks and financial institutions. FAS 5 relates to the disclosure of bases for profit allocation between owners' equity and investment account holders. FAS 17 concerns investment. FAS 22 and FAS 23 deal with segment reporting and consolidation, respectively. AAOIFI Governance Standards 1–6 also provide relevant guidance. In particular, Governance Standard 6, Principles of Governance Section 7, gives guidance in respect of risk management.

Understanding Islamic Banking Risk

IFIs are exposed to all the risks that a conventional one is. However, there are some fundamental differences, particularly in the aspect of *shariah* compliance, where noncompliance can lead to reputational risk and worse.

Typical banking risk exposure includes the following:

- financial: balance sheet, capital adequacy, credit, liquidity
- operational: fraud, product, business services, system failure, delivery, and process management
- business: country, reputational, regulatory, legal, macropolicy
- event: political, banking crisis, contagion.

BASIC RISK ANALYSIS

Ratios and analytics are in a constant state of evolution in order to reflect the growing challenges of Islamic finance and the constant stream of new products. In particular, the convergence of international

"Only through international recognition and consistent application of these (AAOIFI) standards will the Islamic banking and finance industry realize the full benefits of accurate and transparent financial reporting."
Mohamad Nedal Alchaar

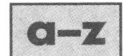

supervisory standards, initiated by the Islamic Financial Services Board (IFSB) since its inauguration in 2002, have contributed to this developing landscape. Typical ratios relate to liquidity, capital adequacy, insider and connected financing, financing portfolio quality, large exposures, and foreign exchange positions.

Peer group benchmarking is a relevant measurement criterion. Here, the behavior of an individual institution can be measured against peer–group trends and industry norms. Significant areas such as profitability, product risk, the structure of the balance sheet, and capital adequacy come to mind. Any significant deviations of the individual institution from what is considered to be the norm must be investigated and understood, as they may well represent an early warning for negative trends in both the IFI and the industry.

What's Different in an IFI?

Islamic contracts and the allocation and sharing of risk. The analysis described above should also include the nature of the Islamic contracts included in the balance sheet and a basic understanding of how the risk is allocated or shared. Therefore a fundamental understanding of the IFI's balance sheet is required.

Liabilities. These include equity capital, reserves, investment accounts (*mudarabah* and *musharakah*) and demand deposits (*amanah*). Money is deposited in investment accounts in the full knowledge that the deposit will be invested in a risk-bearing project, where the profit will be divided between the institution and the depositor on a prearranged profit-sharing ratio. The depositor is also exposed to the risk of loss if the projects invested in do not perform. In many ways these types of deposit have a similarity with an equity investment in the bank, and it is this lack of clarity between shareholders and investors/depositors that can lead to a perception of increased riskiness. IFSB and AAOIFI guidelines have provided significant help in clarifying this issue.

Assets. These include short-term trade finance (*murabahah* and *salam*), medium–term financing (*ijara* , *istisna*, etc.), long-term partnerships (*musharakah*) and fee-based services (*kifala*, etc.).

These asset and liability contracts carried in the balance sheet of an Islamic financial intermediary give a clear indication of two fundamental differences between Islamic financial intermediaries and their conventional counterparts. First, the relationship between the depositors and the bank is based on profit and loss sharing principles; and second, the asset side of the bank may include "risky" assets such as *mudarabah* and *musharakah* that a conventional bank may not carry.

KEY ELEMENTS OF GOOD CORPORATE GOVERNANCE

Good corporate governance is defined by the set of relationships between the institution's senior management, its board, its shareholders, and other stakeholders.

- Corporate strategy defines how success can be measured.
- Responsibilities include assignment and enforcement.
- Strong financial risk management should be independent of the business, with good internal control and separation of duties.
- Good values and a code of conduct should be well articulated and maintained, especially in the area of related parties.
- Proper incentives must be consistent with objectives, performance, and values.
- The roles of stakeholders must be clearly set out.

The Roles of Stakeholders

- Regulators monitor the statutory environment and help to create an enabling environment.
- *Shariah* boards protect the rights of all stakeholders in accordance with the principles of *shariah.*
- The board of directors sets the direction of the bank and ensures its soundness.
- The executive management executes the direction of the board and has sufficient competence and knowledge to manage the financial risks.
- The board audit committee and internal audit are logical extensions of the board's risk management function. They assist executive management in identifying and managing risk areas.
- External auditors are responsible for validating the results and providing assurance that appropriate governance processes are in place.
- Market participants should accept responsibility for their own investment decisions. They therefore need transparent disclosure of information from financial institutions.
- Shareholders can appoint officers in charge of the governance process, subject to appropriate screening on related party transactions.

THE ROLE OF *SHARIAH*

Shariah boards are unique to IFIs. They have a responsibility to monitor the activities of the financial institution and to ensure compliance with *shariah* principles. As such, the *shariah* board acts as a governance body to protect the rights of the stakeholders in the IFI.

In some jurisdictions, national *shariah* boards have been formed, which work closely with regulators and supervisors in protecting the rights of all investors.

TRANSPARENCY AND DISCLOSURE

Practices in IFIs have improved significantly in recent years, but there is still room for improvement in a number of areas.

- Quantitative methods for the measurement of risk still need improvement. AAOIFI is driving changes in this area.
- The decisions and methodology of the *shariah* boards should be disclosed more publicly. This will enhance the credibility of IFIs and also help to educate the public on the *shariah* decision-making process.
- There needs to be a clear demarcation between equity and depositors' funds.
- The financial information infrastructure requires constant improvement to ensure that a "virtuous cycle" of information continually forces practitioners to adopt sound corporate governance practices.
- Standardized reporting practices throughout IFIs would significantly assist in improving the collectability and analysis of data from them.

MAKING IT HAPPEN

Good financial risk management is about changing behaviors and attitudes. Boards and executive management are responsible for setting the implementation process, and regulators are responsible for creating a conducive environment. For example:

- the board must set the direction
- regulators must ensure a supportive environment that encourages transparency and good market discipline, thereby creating a virtuous cycle
- the market must value good financial discipline and risk management and must reward compliant companies accordingly
- all stakeholders must recognize their responsibilities.

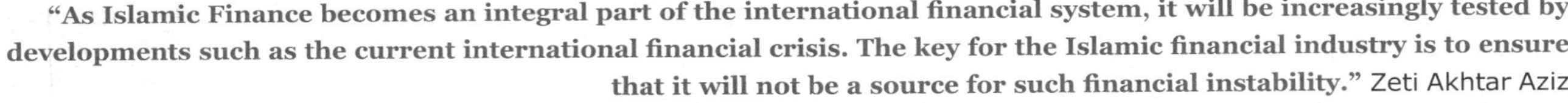

"As Islamic Finance becomes an integral part of the international financial system, it will be increasingly tested by developments such as the current international financial crisis. The key for the Islamic financial industry is to ensure that it will not be a source for such financial instability." Zeti Akhtar Aziz

CONCLUSION

There are many similarities between conventional and Islamic risk management, as well as some significant differences, which have been highlighted above. The risk management process itself in an IFI does not differ much from conventional banking practices. However, it is the analysis and the identification of the risk environment that differ.

The balance sheet of the IFI needs to be structured in a way that will allow the easy identification of risk, particularly in the area of sources of funding and in the application of those funds for financing purposes.

The role of the *shariah* board is significant in protecting the rights of all stakeholders and ensuring that the business of the IFI is conducted in accordance with the principles of *shariah*.

MORE INFO

Books:

Greuning, Hennie Van, and Sonja Brajovic Bratanovic. *Analysing and Managing Banking Risk: A Framework for Assessing Corporate Governance and Financial Risk Management.* Washington, DC: World Bank, 2000.

Karim, Rifaat Ahmed Abdel, and Simon Archer (eds). *Islamic Finance: The Regulatory Challenge*. Singapore: Wiley, 2007. See in particular Sundararajan, V. "Risk characteristics of Islamic products: Implications for risk measurement and supervision," pp. 40–68.

Article:

Grais, Wafiq, and Zamir Iqbal. "Corporate governance challenges of Islamic financial Institutions." Paper presented at the Seventh Harvard University Forum on Islamic Finance, 2006.

Websites:

Accounting and Auditing Organization for Islamic Financial Institutions (AAOIFI): www.aaoifi.com

Islamic Financial Services Board (IFSB): www.ifsb.org

Professional Risk Managers' International Association (PRMIA): www.prmia.org

See Also:

★ Identifying the Main Regulatory Challenges for Islamic Finance (pp. 358–360)
★ Islamic Modes of Finance and the Role of *Sukuk* (pp. 520–521)
✔ Business Ethics in Islamic Finance (p. 1109)
✔ Key Islamic Banking Instruments and How They Work (p. 1010)
✔ Key Principles of Islamic Finance (p. 1011)
✔ An Overview of *Shariah*-Compliant Funds (p. 1083)
✔ The Role of the *Shariah* Advisory Board in Islamic Finance (p. 1015)
An Introduction to Islamic Finance Theory and Practice (p. 1380)

"Not evil, but good, has come to the race from the accumulation of wealth by those who have the ability and energy that produce it." Andrew Carnegie

  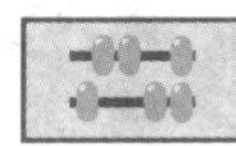      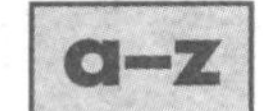

Pros and Cons of Using External Auditors for Internal Auditing and Other Services

by Curtis C. Verschoor

EXECUTIVE SUMMARY

- The advantages of engaging an external audit firm for nonaudit services.
- Regulatory bars to audit firms providing nonaudit services for their clients.
- Threats to professionalism identified in the code of ethics of the International Federation of Accountants (IFAC).
- A proposal to enhance the quality of external audit firms in Europe by limiting the services provided.
- Use of the client's external audit firm for internal auditing.
- Advantages and disadvantages of alternative staffing models for internal auditing.

INTRODUCTION

For many decades, independent auditing firms have employed the strategy of achieving growth in size and, more importantly, profitability, by expanding the scope and range of services they offered to new and existing clients. In addition to conducting audits of the effectiveness of internal controls over financial reporting as well as financial statements and expressing their opinion thereon, firms in the public accounting industry have offered tax consulting and compliance services and also consulting services that are largely related to information systems and other administrative matters not involving strategic decisions by management. Consulting services were limited to administrative and procedural areas of client operations rather than more strategic areas due to regulatory and professional ethics rules that barred a firm's participation in the client's decision-making. Thus, firms tended to provide consulting services that involved issues of technology systems, risk management, and security. Over the years, performance evaluations of the partners in many of the major firms have included an emphasis on the individual's ability to garner greater fees from existing and new clients. Selling additional services has been viewed as more important to career success in a firm than having an exceptional knowledge of accounting.

The boom in the use of computer systems that began in the 1950s gave rise to a substantial need for expertise in information technology that was required to design and install new systems and maintain existing ones. Public accounting firms participated greatly in providing these services and found the business highly lucrative. In a speech made in December 2003, Douglas R. Carmichael, chief auditor of the Public Company Accounting Oversight Board (PCAOB), commented on the reduced emphasis which auditing was receiving as a result and stated that some firms "sought to capitalize on this position of trust earned as auditors and transfer that stature to other services. At times it seemed the only criteria for these other services was whether they made money" (Carmichael, 2003).

There has always been a huge difference between the growth prospects and profitability of these nonaudit services and those of traditional auditing. Traditional auditing has always been viewed by many as largely a commodity that was required for regulatory purposes, and so fees were subject to downward pressure by management. Consequently, the growth of nonaudit services triggered a number of high-level struggles for power and control of the management of several of the major public accounting firms. The entrenched hierarchy of audit partners who were traditionally in charge of running the firm clashed with the younger nonaudit partners who were newly responsible for bringing high profits to the firm. Most of the nonaudit partners had not completed the legal requirements to perform auditing. As a result, many of the large firms established separate entities based on the consulting division that existed within the firms. These entities were later either sold to existing firms or spun off as independent entities. Some of these businesses have been very successful.

Most notable of the independent entities perhaps is Accenture plc, which began life as the business and technology consulting division of Arthur Andersen LLP. Accenture is listed on the New York Stock Exchange and had fiscal August 2011 revenues of US$25.5 billion. It calls itself a global management consulting, technology services, and outsourcing company, and currently employs more than 223,000 people serving clients in industries in more than 120 countries around the world.

Traditional auditing has always been viewed by many as largely a commodity that was required for regulatory purposes.

ADVANTAGES OF ENGAGING AN EXTERNAL AUDIT FIRM FOR NONAUDIT SERVICES

There are several benefits to utilizing an independent auditing firm for a number of nonaudit ervices. Such firms develop expertise in some business areas and industries that other types of consultants cannot match. Some firms are well known for their ability to advise on how to manage operations to minimize the burdens of taxation. Others develop tax protocols to accomplish delays or avoid the incidence of taxation. Another benefit is that public accounting firms are subject to rules of professional ethics, and a number of these are intended to protect the interests of clients.

The argument has been advanced that the major firms in the public accounting industry are better able to attract the highest quality of personnel, at least at the lower entry levels. This conclusion has been disputed by some thought leaders, at least regarding industrial companies of comparably large size and prominence, which are believed to be able to compete effectively for talented employees and motivate their superior performance.

Another factor to be considered is the relative amount of education and training provided to employees of public accounting firms and industrial companies. Auditors and management accountants who hold professional accreditations are required to continue their education on a regular basis. These requirements are undoubtedly enforced more stringently for independent auditors than for others. Larger corporate entities are finding that investment in continuing education for their accounting and financial employees does bring returns. Thus, some of the perceived benefits of using an external service provider because it might offer superior quality may be diminishing in importance.

To consider engaging the services of the same public accounting firm that a company utilizes for its audit of financial statements for internal auditing and other services adds complexity to the decision-making process. In this case, there are

"Zingerman's 3 Steps to Great Service: 1. Figure out what the customer wants. 2. Get it for them: accurately, politely, and enthusiastically. 3. Go the extra mile." Ari Weinzweig

ethical and sometimes regulatory considerations in addition to the usual criteria for the selection of a vendor to provide services.

The advantages to the client of using the same firm that does the audit include the fact that within the firm considerable knowledge already exists about the client, its systems and personnel, and the industry in which it operates. Thus, the firm does not need to spend time and bill the client for familiarization or "training" efforts. The service provider may also have developed considerable experience of dealing with challenges unique to the client's industry and can bring industry best practices to benefit its client's operations and systems. Conversely, some clients have avoided the use of accounting firms that have other clients in the same industry to avoid the possibility of losing valuable information to a competitor.

There are important cost and other benefits to be gained from the use of a company's audit firm for tax-compliance activities, such as the preparation of its annual income tax return. As part of every audit, the audit firm must be familiar with details of the company's relationship with the tax authorities. Additionally, informal consulting on industry-specific tax issues may take place during either the review of the fairness of the presentation of the provision for taxes in the financial statements or in the preparation of tax returns itself.

Representation by the client's auditing firm in matters coming before the tax authorities, however, could well involve adopting an advocacy position that would compromise the independence of the audit firm. It is interesting to note that there is no specific bar to an independent audit firm providing tax services to an audit client in the provisions of the US Sarbanes–Oxley Act of 2002. Prohibited services are discussed in the next section.

REGULATORY BARS TO AUDIT FIRMS PERFORMING NONAUDIT SERVICES FOR CLIENTS

The Sarbanes–Oxley Act of 2002 (see pp. 29–39 for additional discussion of the provisions of this statute) lists a number of nonaudit services that auditors of public companies whose securities are traded in the United States are precluded from performing for their audit clients. These services include:

- *Bookkeeping or other services related to the accounting records or financial statements of the audit client.* It is a conflict of interest for auditors to be responsible for both preparing financial statements and also providing an independent opinion on their fair presentation. This prohibition has been a long-standing rule of the US Securities and Exchange Commission and has been extended to audit firms in other jurisdictions if they audit a company that is traded in US markets.
- *Design and implementation of financial information systems.* These services are deemed to represent management prerogatives and involve internal control systems, so an expression of an audit opinion on financial statements that utilize the results of such systems would appear to lack independence.
- *Appraisal or valuation services, fairness opinions, or contribution-in-kind reports.* These services have been deemed to be outside the scope of the practice of auditing.
- *Actuarial services.* These services are used to determine information contained in the financial statements, so an expression of an audit opinion on financial statements that utilize the results of such services would appear to lack independence.
- *Internal audit outsourcing services.* These services relate at least in part to evaluating the effectiveness of a client's system of internal control. A conflict of interest would arise if the same audit firm both functioned as an element of management's internal control system and also relied on that system in connection with its independent audit or expressed an opinion on the effectiveness of the system. Auditing one's own work is obviously a conflict of interest. The use of external auditors to perform internal auditing is covered in greater depth later in this chapter.
- *Management functions or human resources.* These services have been deemed outside the scope of the practice of auditing and inconsistent with the required principles of independence.
- *Broker or dealer, investment adviser, or investment banking services.* These services involve advocacy and have been deemed outside the scope of the practice of auditing and inconsistent with the required principles of independence.
- *Legal services and expert services unrelated to the audit.* These services have been deemed outside the scope of the practice of auditing and inconsistent with the required principles of independence.

THREATS TO PROFESSIONALISM IDENTIFIED IN THE IFAC CODE OF ETHICS

Guidance governing the practices of all professional auditors, both internal and external, is provided on a global basis by the International Federation of Accountants (IFAC) (see IFAC, 2010). Through its independent standard-setting boards, IFAC develops and encourages the adoption by local professional bodies of international standards on ethics, auditing and assurance, education, and public sector accounting standards. These local bodies create and enforce specific standards governing the practice of various classes of professional accountants, including external and internal auditors.

The IFAC code of ethics sets forth five fundamental principles of professionalism. They are integrity, objectivity, professional competence and due care, confidentiality, and professional behavior. The circumstances in which professional accountants, such as internal and external auditors, operate may create specific threats to compliance with these fundamental principles. The threats that most affect internal and external auditing include:

- *Self-interest threat.* The threat that a financial or other interest will inappropriately influence the professional accountant's judgment or behavior.
- *Self-review threat.* The threat that a professional accountant will not appropriately evaluate the results of a previous judgment made or service performed by the professional accountant, or by another individual within the professional accountant's firm or employing organization, on which the accountant will rely when forming a judgment as part of providing a current service.
- *Advocacy threat.* The threat that a professional accountant will promote a client's or employer's position to the point that the professional accountant's objectivity is compromised.
- *Familiarity threat.* The threat that due to a long or close relationship with a client or employer, a professional accountant will be too sympathetic to their interests or too accepting of their work.

The Independence section of the IESBA Code of Conduct discusses specifics of the application of these concepts to the provision of internal auditing services to audit clients. The Code states that "a firm's personnel shall not assume a management responsibility when providing internal audit services to an audit client."

Paragraph 290.197 of the Code contains examples of internal audit services that involve assuming management responsibilities. These include:

- (a) Setting internal audit policies or the strategic direction of internal audit activities;

"There are three categories of things: fragile things that break, like the financial system; robust things that don't break easily but don't improve, like the Brooklyn Bridge; and my new category, 'antifragile' things that gain strength from stressors and get stronger from failure, like evolution." Nassim Nicholas Taleb

- (b) Directing and taking responsibility for the actions of the entity's internal audit employees;
- (c) Deciding which recommendations resulting from internal audit activities shall be implemented;
- (d) Reporting the results of the internal audit activities to those charged with governance on behalf of management;
- (e) Performing procedures that form part of the internal control, such as reviewing and approving changes to employee data access privileges;
- (f) Taking responsibility for designing, implementing and maintaining internal control;
- (g) Performing outsourced internal audit services, comprising all or a substantial portion of the internal audit function, where the firm is responsible for determining the scope of the internal audit work and may have responsibility for one or more of the matters noted above.

Paragraph 290.198 contains guidance to enable a firm to avoid assuming a management responsibility. The firm shall only provide internal audit services to an audit client if it is satisfied that:

- (a) The client designates an appropriate and competent resource, preferably within senior management, to be responsible at all times for internal audit activities and to acknowledge responsibility for designing, implementing, and maintaining internal control;
- (b) The client's management or those charged with governance reviews, assesses and approves the scope, risk and frequency of the internal audit services;
- (c) The client's management evaluates the adequacy of the internal audit services and the findings resulting from their performance;
- (d) The client's management evaluates and determines which recommendations resulting from internal audit services to implement and manages the implementation process; and
- (e) The client's management reports to those charged with governance the significant findings and recommendations resulting from the internal audit services.

PROPOSAL TO ENHANCE EXTERNAL AUDIT FIRM QUALITY IN EUROPE BY LIMITING SERVICES PROVIDED

On November 30, 2011, the European Commission (EC) issued a proposal to significantly alter the auditing industry as a result of the considerable shortcomings highlighted by the financial crisis of 2008. Among other provisions, its press release states that "Audit firms will be prohibited from providing non-audit services to their audit clients. In addition, large audit firms will be obliged to separate audit activities from non-audit activities in order to avoid all risks of conflict of interest" (EC, 2011).

On the very same day, the Federation of European Accountants (Fédération des Experts Comptables Européens (FEE)), the organization representing 45 institutes of professional accountants and auditors from 33 European countries, issued a strongly critical rebuttal of the EC proposal. The FEE's press release states: "The proposals relating to the creation of audit-only firms, as well as the overly restrictive rules on limiting nonaudit services, will severely limit the ability of the auditor to provide services that rely on the depth and breadth of expertise that stakeholders demand, especially in complex businesses" (FEE, 2011).

Augmenting the EC proposal to strengthen independence by limiting the scope of services provided by external auditors, EC Internal Markets Commissioner Michel Barnier stated: "The crisis has tarnished this image (of auditors) by highlighting certain conflicts of interest. Today, independence must be visible, obvious. You can't at the same time cumulate the functions of audit, internal audit and strategic consulting" (Institute of Chartered Accountants of England and Wales (ICAEW), 2011). The response by the ICAEW was: "We are always open to ideas to improve the independence of auditors but do not agree with the assumption that audit can only be performed objectively if there is no business or other relationship. It adds to the value of an audit and costs can be minimised if the auditor's knowledge can be continually improved by enabling multidisciplinary skills to be applied by practice always, of course, with a consideration of the threats and safeguards of such engagements" (ICAEW, 2011).

USE OF THE CLIENT'S EXTERNAL AUDIT FIRM FOR INTERNAL AUDITING

An organization's decision whether to outsource part or all of its internal auditing function to an external service provider has been a debated issue for many years. The subject of the sourcing of internal auditing is discussed later in this chapter. Use of the same firm for internal auditing that performs the external audit leads to additional issues, including a lack of independence. In the 1990s, Arthur Andersen was the primary advocate of the idea that independent audit firms should be able to provide "extended auditing services"—i.e. internal auditing—to their clients. One of Andersen's clients that had totally outsourced its internal auditing to the Andersen firm was Enron Corporation. It is widely believed that one of the primary contributing factors to Andersen's audit failure in the Enron case was the fact that it received such large fees for its consulting and internal auditing services and had apparently failed to concentrate sufficient attention on its responsibilities for the auditing of the financial statements.

Basic to consideration of the benefits of utilizing the services of an external provider for internal auditing is the realization that internal auditing differs in several meaningful respects from an audit of financial statements provided by an independent firm. The major focus and approach of external auditors involves the expression of an independent opinion on the client's financial statements for the benefit of external parties. External auditors base their audit plans on prescribed auditing standards that are the same for all companies in all industries as well as not-for-profit organizations.

Internal auditors have a broader mission that may have differing goals in each organization. In general, internal auditing is an independent, objective assurance and consulting activity designed to add value to and improve an organization's operations (IIA, 2011). Internal audit work is intended to benefit the organization itself rather than an external audience. The mandate for the existence of the internal auditing function is unique to the needs of each organization and is set forth in a written charter that should be approved by the organization's board of directors or equivalent governing body. In addition to evaluating the quality of policies and procedures, internal auditors are expected to make recommendations for improvements to those policies and procedures, especially in the areas of risk management, controls, and governance.

The practice of independent auditing is subject to regulatory oversight by governmental bodies in most jurisdictions of the world. Companies are required by law to obtain audits of their financial statements. In contrast, although internal auditors have a global professional organization, the Institute of Internal Auditors, that provides guidance, the use of its standards is voluntary (IIA, 2011). In fact there are few mandatory requirements for a company to have any internal auditing, although in the United States the New York Stock Exchange rules require listed companies to have an internal auditing function—albeit those

"Having been here before and lost ... I've got to tell you, winning is really a lot better than losing. Really a lot better."

Kate Winslet

  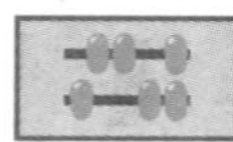      

requirements have little specificity. Another country, Israel, does have a legal mandate for internal auditing.

Mirroring the fact that the objectives of internal and external auditing are not the same, the reports of each differ markedly. The report of an independent audit on financial statements is brief, standardized, limited to a pass or fail opinion, and intended for an audience external to the entity. Comments concerning the possibilities of enhanced reporting by independent auditors were requested in a PCAOB concept release issued in June 2011 (PCAOB, 2011). In September of that year the Center for Audit Quality (CAQ) published the results of a series of stakeholder roundtable discussions on changes to the auditor's reporting model and the role of the auditor (CAQ, 2011). The International Auditing and Assurance Standards Board also issued a consultation paper in May 2011 titled "Enhancing the value of auditor reporting: Exploring options for change" (IFAC, 2010).

In contrast to the standardized reports issued by independent auditors, internal audit reports are, or at least should be, tailor-made to fit the circumstances of each engagement. They should contain much more detail that is intended to inform a knowledgeable audience within the organization. Internal audit reports typically include a detailed description of findings, their impact, and perhaps most importantly a recommended solution. Some internal audit reports also include an opinion or rating of the process that was reviewed.

In summary, a key consideration for evaluating the use of an independent audit firm to provide internal auditing services is whether that firm has a group that specializes in internal auditing. To ask external auditors whose training and experience deals with financial statements to change their perspective and then perform internal auditing runs the risk that the mindset of the external auditor might lead him or her to concentrate too heavily on evaluating the fairness of financial presentation rather than the broader mission of internal auditing. Internal auditors should have a wider outlook and be concerned with evaluating the efficiency and effectiveness of the systems and functions they review, not just the reliability of the financial information.

PROS AND CONS OF ALTERNATIVE STAFFING MODELS FOR INTERNAL AUDITING

There are four ways of staffing an internal audit function:

- by having a totally in-house team dedicated to internal auditing;
- with an in-house internal auditing team supplemented by rotational staffing from elsewhere in the organization;
- with an in-house internal auditing team augmented by cosourcing from an external service provider;
- by total outsourcing to an external service provider.

Dedicated In-House Team

Advantages of using only a dedicated team of in-house auditors to perform internal auditing include the benefits of having a reservoir of knowledge about the company that an outsider would have difficulty obtaining or would be costly to have an outsider acquire. Nuances concerning the organization's culture and strategies and how best to recommend changes in practices and achieve other results are more likely to reside with insiders than with externally contracted personnel.

A major advantage of this staffing model is that (except when key staff leave the organization) all of the personal development and experience in dealing with the challenges of the organization stay within it, rather than going to an outside group. Perhaps the most beneficial aspect of staffing completely internally is that employees should build up a loyalty and vested interest in the success of the organization. Outsiders are less likely to look on their experience with the organization as providing a long-term career opportunity. Another benefit of total in-house staffing is the avoidance of the cost of the external service provider's overhead burden.

The major disadvantage of the totally in-house staffing model is that the team may not always have all of the requisite competencies, skill sets, and expertise. Long-term career opportunities for specialized types of auditors are very difficult to provide. Another disadvantage arises if the internal audit function requires significant travel. As noted earlier, the argument that external service providers are more easily able to attract superior talent has been disputed.

In-House Team Augmented by Rotational Staffing

This method of staffing is reported to be quite popular, especially in large organizations. A cadre of experienced management-level internal auditors provides continuity and experience, and they can explain internal auditing to newcomers from other areas of the organization. Persons in other functions or business units have the opportunity to gain, in a short-term assignment, considerable valuable and broad-based knowledge of various operating aspects of the organization that deal with issues in which internal auditing has expertise. Experience in internal auditing may provide the high-level exposure that can prove to be very desirable to the organization as a development process for persons with high potential. The organization also benefits from having employees scattered in various roles throughout the organization who have had hands-on experience dealing with internal auditing issues such as risk management, controls, and governance.

In-House Team Augmented by Cosourcing

Cosourcing involves the utilization of external service firms to provide internal auditing expertise and skills that may be too expensive to maintain in-house. Cosourcing may also be helpful in organizations with operations in widely dispersed locations or where knowledge of the local language, business environment, culture, and customs, or any other specialized technical skills, is required. Some specialized audit skills may be too costly to maintain in-house. Cosourcing may also result in the ability to choose the service provider who can bring the most benefit at the least cost.

There is no single or best answer to the question when or whether an outside auditing or other financial services provider should be employed. Hearsay evidence indicates rather widespread satisfaction with the cosourcing alternative.

Total Outsourcing to an External Service Provider

Complete outsourcing to an external service provider, with only high-level management of the internal auditing function remaining as an internal responsibility, may prove beneficial for certain types of companies. These include smaller organizations, those with widely geographically dispersed entities in many countries, or organizations that require specific technical expertise which is not economically feasible to maintain in-house. Outsourcing also results in the perception, at least, of greater independence from management. A downside to total outsourcing is the need for the client to assume the cost of the outside service provider's overhead burden and profit.

With respect to sourcing the internal auditing function, the global professional internal auditing organization, the IIA (2009, 2011), believes that:

- the oversight and responsibility for establishing the scope and evaluating the performance of internal auditing cannot be outsourced;
- the audit committee of the board of directors (or equivalent governing body)

"Common Sense and Education: The more you think you have of one, the less you think you need of the other."
Tom Heehler

        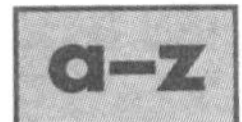

and senior management should have functional responsibility for internal auditing;

- the internal auditing function should be managed within the organization by a chief audit executive who is accountable to the organization's board of directors (or equivalent body) and its chief executive officer.

An outsource advisory consulting firm has published a checklist of ten practical insights for organizations contemplating expanding an existing or creating a new outsourcing relationship (Business Finance 2012). They are:

1. Decide on "black box" vs. "white box" outsourcing.
2. Determine the evaluation approach upfront.
3. Control the agenda.
4. Get the provider's "A" team.
5. Model real-world transition costs.
6. Encourage innovation that benefits the buyer.
7. Plan for a challenging transition.
8. Develop meaningful Service Level Agreements.
9. Prepare for negotiations.
10. Remember that the right answer might be to not outsource (see Borowski, 2012).

SUMMARY

There is no single or best answer to the question when or whether an outside auditing or other financial services provider should be employed. Hearsay evidence indicates rather widespread satisfaction with the cosourcing alternative for internal auditing. Users report that the ability to engage skills which it is not economically feasible to maintain internally is a big plus point.

The selection of a professional firm to perform services requires greater scrutiny than is necessary for selection of other vendors, as indicated below.

- Ascertain that each firm being considered for employment has the specialized staff with the knowledge and experience in your industry to effectively implement its proposal to service your needs. Not all firms perform every service equally well.
- Carefully design the objectives of both limited-term projects and longer-term assignments.
- Provide executive-level monitoring as well as general oversight during the engagement to assure accomplishment of the planned objectives within the predetermined cost parameters.
- Evaluate the effectiveness of the engagement at its conclusion or renewal point.
- Maintain awareness of possible regulatory changes that may affect the financial services industry, particularly external audit firms.
- Consider all long-term as well as immediate aspects of employing an outside contractor rather than staffing a project or function internally.

MORE INFO

Books:

Institute of Internal Auditors (IIA). *International Professional Practices Framework (IPPF)*. 2011 edition. Altamonte Springs, FL: IIA Research Foundation, 2011. Online at: tinyurl.com/79nzmne

International Federation of Accountants (IFAC). *2010 Handbook of the Code of Ethics for Professional Accountants*. 2010 edition. New York: IFAC, 2010. Online at: tinyurl.com/83oh6fb

Articles and Reports:

Borowski, David. "2012 outsourcing checklist." *Business Finance* (January 17, 2012). Online at: businessfinancemag.com/article/2012-outsourcing-checklist-0117

Carmichael, D. R. "Professionalism is primary." Speech delivered to AICPA National Conference, December 12, 2003. Online at: tinyurl.com/7gw3bjs

Center for Audit Quality (CAQ). "Observations on the evolving role of the auditor: A summary of stakeholder discussions." Washington, DC: CAQ, 2011. Online at: tinyurl.com/8y8ujnr

European Commission (EC). "Restoring confidence in financial statements: The European Commission aims at a higher quality, dynamic and open audit market." Press release, November 30, 2011. Online at: tinyurl.com/6v7u87r

Fédération des Experts Comptables Européens (FEE). "FEE initial views on European Commission proposals on audit policy." Press release, November 30, 2011. Online at: www.fee.be/publications/default.asp?library_ref=4&content_ref=1456

Institute of Chartered Accountants of England and Wales (ICAEW). "Key themes being set by governments and regulators." In "The future of audit," London: ICAEW, 2011. Online at: tinyurl.com/bngpef8

Institute of Internal Auditors (IIA). "IIA position paper: The role of internal auditing in resourcing the internal audit activity." Altamonte Springs, FL: IIA, January 2009. Online at: tinyurl.com/7mdgpu3

International Federation of Accountants (IFAC). "Enhancing the value of auditor reporting: Exploring options for change." International Auditing and Assurance Standards Board (IAASB) Consultation paper, May 2011. Online at: tinyurl.com/7hy3u5l

Public Company Accounting Oversight Board (PCAOB). "PCAOB issues concept release on auditor's reporting model." Press release, June 21, 2011. Online at: tinyurl.com/6dcm3zn

Public Company Accounting Oversight Board (PCAOB). "Concept release on possible revisions to PCAOB standards related to reports on audited financial statements and related amendments to PCAOB standards." PCAOB release no. 2011-003, June 21, 2011. Online at: pcaobus.org/Rules/Rulemaking/Docket034/Concept_Release.pdf

Websites:

American Institute of Certified Public Accountants (AICPA): www.aicpa.org
Fédération des Experts Comptables Européens (FEE): www.fee.be
Institute of Chartered Accountants of England and Wales (ICAEW): www.icaew.com
Institute of Internal Auditors (IIA): www.theiia.org
International Federation of Accountants (IFAC): www.ifac.org
Public Company Accounting Oversight Board (PCAOB; US): www.pcaobus.org

"I'm educated enough to talk myself out of any plan. To deconstruct any fantasy. Explain away any goal. I'm so smart I can negate any dream." Chuck Palahniuk

  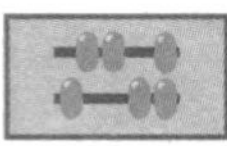      

Sarbanes–Oxley After Nearly 10 Years

by Curtis C. Verschoor

EXECUTIVE SUMMARY

- The Enron and WorldCom frauds led to the US Congress to enact the Sarbanes–Oxley Act of 2002 (SOX), which covers public corporations and their independent auditors.
- Before SOX, regulation of the auditing industry was largely carried out by the industry and by auditors themselves.
- This chapter discusses the costs and benefits of the provisions set out in the 11 titles, or sections, of the Act.
- On the whole, the legislation is viewed as having been successful. The most negative comments relate to the costs of compliance with Section 404(b), which requires the independent auditor to express an opinion on the client's internal controls over financial reporting.

INTRODUCTION

Two massive financial statement frauds were uncovered within months of each other in 2001–02: Enron and WorldCom. They capped a string of similar earlier fraud cases and became the trigger for the US Congress to overwhelmingly pass in July 2002 the most far-reaching legislation affecting public corporations and their independent auditors since the 1930s. Reflecting the diversity of subject matter covered, the Sarbanes–Oxley Act of 2002 (SOX) was known as the Public Company Accounting Reform and Investor Protection Act in the US Senate and the Corporate and Auditing Accountability and Responsibility Act in the US House of Representatives. Some of the various titles of the Act also had additional descriptive names.

The many provisions of SOX apply to all companies that are publicly traded in markets in the United States regardless of their legal domicile or country of origin. Implementing various aspects of the legislation that affect companies headquartered in other countries has been slower than the progress in the United States. This has been particularly true in countries that have a less robust regulatory environment than that existing in the United States.

The main thrusts of SOX (as well as of this chapter) involve three areas:

- a total revision of the regulatory framework for the public accounting and auditing profession;
- assignment of new responsibilities to senior management of public companies and to their boards of directors, particularly the audit committee;
- other miscellaneous provisions.

Perhaps independent auditors are the group that has been affected most significantly by SOX. Since auditing became a distinct occupation many hundreds of years ago, auditors have functioned largely as self-regulating professionals. Previous to SOX, important decisions—including setting the bar for entry into practice, promulgating the auditing standards auditors should use, determining the quality of performance in using those standards, and disciplining those who failed to practice properly in accordance with the standards—were tasks largely or exclusively performed by the auditing industry and auditors themselves.

Although sentiment for a total repeal or significant overhaul of at least some of the provisions of SOX has lingered for years, most unbiased observers believe that, on the whole, the legislation has been successful in most areas. The most negative commentary about SOX has arisen because of the costs of compliance with the provisions of Section 404(b), which requires a company's independent auditor to express an opinion on the adequacy of their client's internal controls over financial reporting. Another SOX provision that was designed to protect employee whistleblowers from retaliation in cases of financial fraud has not resulted in success.

The Act contains 11 titles, or sections, that set out specific mandates and requirements for financial reporting. The costs and benefits of the various provisions of SOX are discussed title by title more fully below.

DISCUSSION OF THE PROVISIONS OF THE SARBANES–OXLEY ACT BY TITLE

Title I: The Public Company Accounting Oversight Board

Title I establishes the Public Company Accounting Oversight Board (PCAOB) to provide independent oversight of public accounting firms that provide audit services. The functions of the PCAOB include registering auditors on a global basis to audit corporations publicly traded in the United States, setting auditing standards that registered firms must use, inspecting firms' audit performance and the effectiveness of their quality controls, and disciplining those whose performance is substandard.

These provisions totally changed the governance of the independent public accounting and auditing industry. Whereas previous to SOX the audit occupation was largely self-regulating, SOX created the PCAOB to provide guidance and to oversee the performance of audits of companies that are publicly traded in the United States. The PCAOB is an independent agency under the general oversight of the US Securities and Exchange Commission (SEC).

Since the responsibilities of the PCAOB involve only audits of publicly held companies, the setting of standards for and peer review of the performance of audits of private and nonprofit organizations remain with the American Institute of Certified Public Accountants (AICPA).

In terms of auditing standard-setting, the PCAOB in 2003 adopted the existing AICPA audit standards and concentrated its efforts on a standard for the newly required audit of effectiveness of internal control over financial reporting. Auditing Standard No. 2, "An audit of internal control over financial reporting performed in conjunction with an audit of financial statements," was issued by the PCAOB and approved by the SEC in June 2004. It was applicable to only the largest corporations. Although there had been public hearings and much public commentary, it was shortly assailed by corporations as requiring too much effort and resulting in high cost on the part of both clients and auditors.

Because of the volume of the outcry, the PCAOB held more public hearings, requested more public commentary, and totally changed its approach to the subject. The new Auditing Standard No. 5, "An audit of internal control over financial reporting that is integrated with an audit of financial statements," was approved by the SEC in July 2007 and has remained in place thereafter with only limited complaints. The cost of an independent opinion on internal control over financial reporting for smaller companies remained an issue until the SEC in 2010 permanently exempted smaller public companies from the internal control audit requirement. This subject is also discussed below under Title IV of the Act.

Through the end of 2011, the PCAOB has issued, and the SEC has approved, 10

  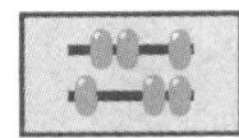      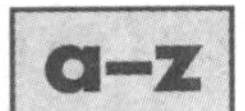

additional auditing standards, eight of them in 2010. These cover a multitude of subjects, including such important topics as audit quality, evidence, planning, materiality, and various aspects of risk. The PCAOB has also issued eight "staff audit practice alerts" covering emerging and topical issues. During this same period from 2003 to the end of 2011, the AICPA has issued 24 auditing standards applicable to audits of nonpublic and not-for-profit entities. There appears to be no plan to converge the differences between the two groups of standards. Both the PCAOB and AICPA continue to issue guidance on ethics and independence.

In terms of inspection of audit firm quality, the PCAOB's own evaluation of its success is less satisfactory. The PCAOB issued a report on June 30, 2011 titled: "Updated information on PCAOB international inspections" (PCAOB, 2011). It attached a list of more than 300 companies traded in the United States that are audited by non-US firms (mostly affiliates of the Big Four US firms) where the PCAOB had been denied access to conduct inspections. The companies are based in certain European countries and in China, including Hong Kong.

The most recent overall PCAOB report concerning the quality of audit firm performance found in firm inspections was published in September 2010 (Goelzer, 2010). Covering aspects of PCAOB inspections conducted during the 2007 through 2009 inspection cycle, acting chair Daniel L. Goelzer noted that the inspection findings "underscore the need for auditors to be diligent in assessing and responding to emerging areas of risk when economic and business conditions change." In other words, the PCAOB report indicated that improvement was required.

Specific inspection observations in the report were instances where auditors appeared not to have complied with PCAOB auditing standards in areas such as fair-value measurements, impairment of goodwill, indefinite-life intangible assets, and other long-lived assets, allowance for loan losses, off-balance sheet structures, revenue recognition, inventory, and income taxes. The report also noted that the "deficiencies identified by inspectors in their reviews of issuer audits suggest that firms should continue to focus on making improvements to their quality control systems."

It should be noted that, although some portions of the inspection reports issued on individual firm audit performance are made public, specifics of noted deficiencies are required to be kept confidential. This protects the firm when litigation is under way or threatened.

In a speech on June 2, 2011, "Rethinking the relevance, credibility, and transparency of audits", PCAOB Chairman James R. Doty gave another evaluation of the effectiveness of the PCAOB inspection process:

"The PCAOB has now conducted annual inspections of the largest audit firms for eight years. Our inspectors have reviewed more than 2,800 engagements of such firms and discovered and analyzed hundreds of cases involving what they determined to be audit failures. We have conducted more than 1,500 inspections of smaller domestic firms and of non-US firms. These include multiple inspections of hundreds of those firms. And our inspectors have identified hundreds more cases involving what they determined to be audit failures." (Doty, 2011).

In other words, there appears to be a great number of instances where auditing firms need to improve their performance in audits of public companies.

This title of the Act also directs the SEC to study the adoption of a more principles-based approach to accounting standard-setting in the United States. The report resulting from this requirement concluded that principles-based standards, if properly implemented, would result in more transparent information being provided to investors while continuing to hold management and auditors responsible for publishing financial information that conforms to the objectives of the accounting standards. The subject of whether the SEC will allow or even mandate that companies traded publicly in the United States adopt international accounting standards (IFRS) rather than US generally accepted accounting principles (GAAP) is still under development in late 2011. Efforts to converge the content of US GAAP and IFRS have been under way for several years. In November 2011 the SEC issued a staff paper, "Work plan for the consideration of incorporating international financial reporting standards into the financial reporting system for US issuers: An analysis of IFRS in practice" (SEC, 2011c). Another staff paper (SEC, 2011b) described potential alternatives as to the future involvement of the Financial Accounting Standards Board (FASB) in determining US accounting standards.

The PCAOB has also been involved with the SEC, the US General Accountability Office (GAO), and other groups formed to study various other issues involving public companies and auditors that were mandated by SOX. These topics are covered later in this chapter.

Title II: Auditor Independence

This title of SOX limits the types of non-audit services that an auditor of a public company's financial statements can provide. Audit firms had found that providing consulting services to their clients was more profitable than performing audits, which were viewed as a commodity. In 1999, the AICPA published a practice aid titled: *Making Audits Pay: Leveraging the Audit into Consulting Services* (Ramos and Delahanty, 1999).

This was an indication that the major firms thought of themselves as multiservice firms rather than just accountants and auditors. This attitude led observers to question the independence of the audit process.

There was at least the appearance of a conflict of interest when an audit firm gave a clean opinion on financial statements that were based in part at least on advice provided by the same firm as a consultant. Further, one of the driving forces leading to the enactment of SOX was Arthur Andersen's apparent loss of independence for audit purposes because it provided almost all of the internal auditing for Enron Corporation on basically an outsourcing basis. Andersen also provided significant amounts of very profitable consulting services on accounting matters to Enron. Aspects of the range of services provided by the auditor of financial statements and their advantages and disadvantages are discussed in "Pros and cons of using external auditors for internal auditing and other services"(pp. 121–131).

Additional requirements in this title of SOX include mandatory advance approval by the audit committee of all non-audit services performed by the firm auditing the financial statements. Also required are structured reports to the audit committee by the auditor about key aspects of the audit. These include a comparison of alternatives to critical accounting policies that a client has chosen. SOX also codified into law certain practices previously introduced by the SEC Practice Section of the AICPA (superseded in January 2004) including the rotation of audit partners after five years of continuous service to a client and requiring a period of time to elapse before a senior-level auditor can be employed by a client. The results of implementing SOX provisions in this area are generally believed to continue to be beneficial.

Title III: Corporate Responsibility

The provisions of SOX on corporate responsibility strengthen the understanding of all concerned as to who bears primary responsibility for the content of periodic financial reports. Both the chief executive and chief financial officers of public

"Contentment is too bland; worry is more stimulating. We don't say 'She was gripped by contentment.' The good news, though, is that worriers tend to be the smartest, most creative people we've got. It takes a lot of imagination to dream up all these worries." Edward M. Hallowell

companies must take individual responsibility and certify the accuracy and completeness of their company's financial reports on a quarterly basis. SOX also requires these individuals to certify as to the completeness and effectiveness of internal controls over disclosures of material financial and other information. The disclosure assertions are separate and distinct from the assertions on the effectiveness of internal controls. The disclosure control requirements have resulted in the formation of formal compliance activities—usually in the form of a standing staff committee that is specifically focused on periodic public disclosures. These requirements are generally believed to continue to be beneficial, although some critics believe that the benefits do not exceed the costs of compliance.

A significant SOX provision also requires audit committees and not management to be directly in charge of important relationships concerning specific matters regarding the audit engagement. Specifically, SOX requires the audit committee, in its capacity as a committee of the board of directors, to be directly responsible for the appointment, compensation, and oversight of the work of any public accounting firm that is employed by the company. An increased engagement by audit committees has been widely viewed as an important improvement in the quality of corporate governance.

Provisions in this title also require officers receiving bonuses or other compensation to repay those funds if the payments were based on information that turned out later to be false. SOX also prohibits insider trading during pension fund blackout periods. An SEC (2003a) report required by SOX analyzed enforcement actions over the past five years by the SEC that have included proceedings to obtain civil penalties or disgorgements. The objective of the study was to develop methods to more efficiently, effectively, and fairly provide restitution to injured investors and to improve the collection rates for civil penalties and disgorgement.

Title IV: Enhanced Financial Disclosures

This area of SOX requires public companies to make more specific disclosures of the details of off-balance sheet transactions as well as loans and other matters involving directors and officers. A member of the audit committee must qualify as a financial expert and be so designated. This title also includes the now infamous Section 404, which requires both a management assessment of and the independent auditor's opinion on the effectiveness of internal controls over financial reporting. As noted, this requirement is in addition to the disclosure control declaration discussed previously.

As described earlier in this chapter, the requirements of Section 404 have been the focus of the loudest and most persistent critics of SOX. Particularly distasteful to many was the realization that the immediate effect of SOX was to give audit firms the opportunity to greatly increase the amount of services provided and the corresponding fees they were able to charge to large, publicly held clients. Observers also criticized SOX's emphasis only on internal controls over financial reporting, rather than on internal controls in general. Observers believe that this limitation was at the behest of the independent auditors. The most important outcome of legislation passed after the savings and loan crisis was the need for concern about all aspects of control, not just financial reporting to the public.

At least five factors have muted, but not eliminated, the pressures for modification or total repeal of these SOX requirements, which are considered the most onerous in the entire law. They are:

- the savings since 2007 resulting from the less onerous provisions of PCAOB Auditing Standard No. 5 as compared with those of Auditing Standard No. 2;
- cost reductions made possible by management guidance issued in June 2007 by the SEC;
- elimination of the need for an independent auditor's opinion on management's assessment process for internal control over financial reporting;
- the exclusion of smaller public companies from obtaining an independent auditor's opinion on internal controls over financial reporting;
- the effects of other cost-reduction efforts by both clients and auditors.

Auditing Standard No. 5 also defines a "material weakness" in internal control.

Provisions in this title of SOX also require public companies to disclose whether or not they have adopted a code of ethics applicable to their senior financial officers.

As all companies have done so, this area has been welcomed as a favorable outcome of the enactment of SOX that has increased investor trust. Another provision in this title requires public companies to disclose on a "rapid and current basis" any material changes in their financial condition or operations. This general disclosure requirement may have received little notice or emphasis on implementation because of the preoccupation of the SEC with other matters. It is also implicit in other SEC requirements.

Title V: Analyst Conflicts of Interest

Provisions in this title of SOX do not affect auditors, but rather deal primarily with the conduct of securities analysts who previously had recommended to members of the public that they purchase securities, when actually those recommendations were based on the fact that the analyst's employer was being compensated for marketing to the public those same securities products, which sets up an obvious conflict of interest. This title also contains requirements for public disclosure of any knowable conflicts of interest. These provisions have been well accepted and are believed to have contributed to increased confidence of investors in the structure of the financial marketplace.

Title VI: Commission Resources and Authority

This section also deals with financial industry professionals, not auditors. It sets forth authority for the SEC to bar individuals from positions in the industry. Its purpose is to build public confidence in securities analysts and others. The title also lists the sources of funding for the SEC, which prior to the enactment of SOX had been a contributing factor to the scandals that occurred.

Title VII: Studies and Reports

This title directs the Comptroller General of the United States, who heads the US Government Accountability Office (GAO), and the SEC to perform various studies and report the results to Congress and the public. Topics studied include the effects of consolidating public accounting firms, the role of credit rating agencies in the operation of securities markets, securities violations and enforcement actions, and whether investment banks assisted companies, as was alleged with Enron to manipulate their financial reports. Studies analyzed the extent of off-balance sheet information and whether rotation of audit firms should be mandatory.

The SEC (2003b) report on the study of credit rating agencies outlined the proper role of such agencies in the securities markets. The Dodd–Frank Wall Street Reform and Consumer Protection Act of 2010 (US Government, 2010) mandated further study of the specific issue of reliance on credit ratings, since the regulation of the credit rating industry by the SEC had not been completely implemented. The resulting July 2011 report outlined needed amendments to several rules and regulations in order to eliminate existing legislative mandates for reliance on credit ratings (SEC, 2011c).

     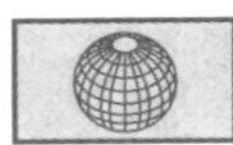   

In September 2011, the SEC issued its first annual "Summary report of commission staff's examination of each nationally recognized statistical rating organization" (SEC, 2011d). The report concluded that the SEC staff examiners had many findings and observations and made corresponding recommendations for improvements.

The Dodd–Frank Act enhanced the SEC's oversight responsibilities of the activities of nationally recognized credit rating agencies.

Another 2003 SEC report required by SOX Section 703 studied the number of securities professionals practicing before the SEC who: have aided and abetted a violation of the Federal securities laws but who have not been sanctioned, disciplined, or otherwise penalized as a primary violator in any administrative action or civil proceeding; and have been primary violators of the Federal securities laws between 1998 and 2001. An additional 2003 report in SOX Section 704 analyzed enforcement actions over the previous five years by the SEC involving violations of reporting requirements imposed under the securities laws, and restatements of financial statements. The objective of the study was to identify areas of reporting that are most susceptible to fraud, inappropriate manipulation, or inappropriate earnings management.

A SOX study of the pros and cons of audit firm rotation was required to be completed by the GAO by mid-2003, yet the subject was still under active discussion eight years later. In the same June 2, 2011, speech by PCAOB chairman Doty referred to earlier in this chapter, he stated that the 2003 report: "...noted that the SEC and the Board would need several years to evaluate whether the Sarbanes–Oxley reforms—including audit partner rotation—were sufficient, or whether further independence measures are necessary to protect investors." (Doty, 2011.)

Doty went on, in 2011, to commit the PCAOB to further examine the issue of auditor long-term tenure with "rigorous analysis and the weight of evidence in support and against."

Title VIII: Corporate and Criminal Fraud Accountability

This title is also referred to as the "Corporate and criminal fraud accountability Act of 2002." It sets forth the criminal penalties of fines and imprisonment that shall be assessed against violators of the securities laws as well as those who interfere with investigations. Its provisions increase the time for bringing legal claims of securities fraud. This title was also designed to provide employment protection against retaliation for employee whistleblowers who come forward to report fraud information about their employer.

The whistleblowing aspects of SOX have been singularly unable to provide employment security as employers have been largely successful in challenging almost all of the claims made under these provisions. Claimants must meet a very high burden of proof in order to plead their case. Administration of this aspect of SOX is with the Department of Labor, not the SEC. To remedy these inadequacies, the Dodd–Frank Act contains provisions that broaden the protections for whistleblowers provided under SOX.

The Dodd–Frank Act contains provisions that allow the SEC to pay substantial cash bounties to whistleblowers who provide information about securities frauds. The new authority granted by the Act is broad and comprehensive and is believed to be widely used, although no overall reports have yet been made. Awards to whistleblowers can range from 10% to 30% of the amount of monetary sanctions in cases over US$1 million, including penalties and interest as well as disgorgement of ill-gotten gains. Information provided to the SEC must be "original" and derived from the whistleblower's independent knowledge or analysis and not be known to the SEC from any other source. Final rules governing details of the operating methods of the SEC Office of the Whistleblower became effective in August 2011.

Title IX. White Collar Crime Penalty Enhancement

These provisions increased the criminal penalties that should be assessed for securities law and other violations under the US Federal Sentencing Guidelines. For example, imprisonment for wire fraud (fraud committed via wire, radio, or television) is increased from five years to 20 years. Conspiracy is to be treated the same as the act. A special provision adds penalties dealing with corporate reports. A false certification that a periodic report did comply with SEC rules when in fact it did not is punishable by a fine of up to US$1,000,000, imprisonment for 10 years, or both.

Title X. Corporate Tax Returns

This title merely requires the CEO to sign a public company's tax returns.

Title XI. Corporate Fraud Accountability

Provisions under this title state that securities fraud and tampering with records necessary in an investigation are criminal offenses and identify appropriate penalties. They also give the SEC the ability to "freeze" or temporarily stop the execution of transactions deemed to be large or unusual. This title also gives the SEC the power to ban any individual from future service as an officer or director of a public corporation.

SUMMARY

The Sarbanes–Oxley Act of 2002 has achieved most of the objectives set for it in providing both improved confidence in the financial marketplace and stronger investor rights. Most observers of governance would conclude that public company audit committees have accepted their increased burdens well and generally performed appropriately. As noted in this chapter, there is concern that the performance of independent auditors still needs improvement, and this is one area of SOX that is being worked on.

SOX has been criticized, perhaps unjustly, because it did not prevent the global financial crisis of 2007–09. However, that catastrophe is believed to have been caused primarily by failures in the banking system and its regulation, with only minor blame apportionable to audit failures or failures of disclosure. Some blame for the crisis has been placed at the door of the SEC for inadequate regulation of securities rating agencies, but this task was not given

MORE INFO

Book:

Ramos, Michael J., and Linda C. Delahanty. *Making Audits Pay: Leveraging the Audit into Consulting Services*. American Institute of Certified Public Accountants (AICPA) Practice Aid Series. New York: AICPA, 1999.

Articles:

Goelzer, Daniel L. "PCAOB board issues report on inspection observations of auditing during the economic crisis." Press release. September 29, 2010. Online at: tinyurl.com/8ywlqmm

Doty, James R. "Rethinking the relevance, credibility, and transparency of audits." Speech at SEC and Financial Reporting Institute 30th Annual Conference, Pasadena, CA, June 2, 2011. Online at: tinyurl.com/3dns5eo

Nowland, John, and Andreas Simon. "The effect of a change in analyst composition on analyst forecast accuracy: Evidence from U.S. cross-listings." *Journal of International Accounting Research* 9:1 (Spring 2010): 23–38. Online at: dx.doi.org/10.2308/jiar.2010.9.1.23

"We don't get a chance to do that many things, and every one should be really excellent. Because this is our life."
Steve Jobs

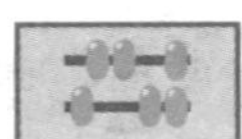

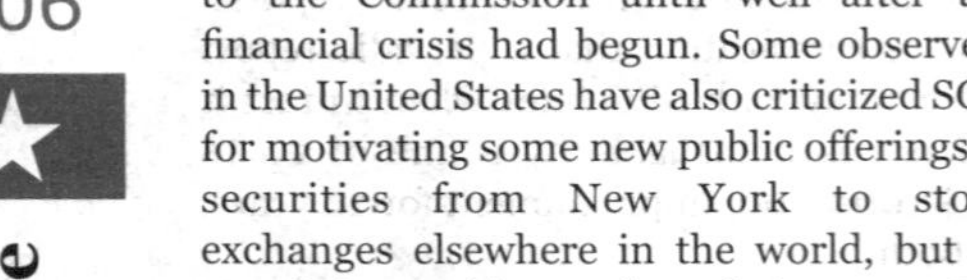

to the Commission until well after the financial crisis had begun. Some observers in the United States have also criticized SOX for motivating some new public offerings of securities from New York to stock exchanges elsewhere in the world, but as noted above, this may be only hearsay. One country's loss is another's gain.

Several studies of the cost of compliance with SOX were completed in the first few years of its existence. Particular focus has been directed to the high costs incurred by companies and the larger audit fees resulting from the audit of internal control over financial reporting. An SEC (2011a) staff study required by the Dodd–Frank Act analyzed this subject in companies with securities traded in the public markets with a market float between US$75 and $250 million. It found that:

- the costs of Section 404(b) have declined since the SEC first implemented the requirements of Section 404, particularly in response to the 2007 reforms;
- investors generally view the auditor's attestation on internal controls over financial reporting as beneficial;
- financial reporting is more reliable when the auditor is involved with internal control over financial reporting assessments;
- there is no conclusive evidence linking the requirements of Section 404(b) to listing decisions of the studied range of issuers.

Various other research studies have also examined and documented some of the benefits that have flowed from SOX. A study by Nowland and Simon (2010) showed that foreign firms cross-listed in the United States and thus subject to SOX became significantly more transparent in their dealings with share-owners than a sample of comparable firms not subject to SOX. The researchers defined transparency in terms of the dispersion and accuracy of securities analysts' forecasts of earnings. Several other studies found that internal controls have improved in companies subsequent to SOX implementation procedures. One researcher believes that these stronger controls have resulted in lower costs of capital to issuers.

Reports:

Public Company Accounting Oversight Board (PCAOB). "Updated information on PCAOB international inspections." June 30, 2011. Online at: tinyurl.com/7t9hqok

Securities and Exchange Commission (SEC). "Report pursuant to Section 308(c) of the Sarbanes Oxley Act of 2002." January 2003a. Online at: www.sec.gov/news/studies/sox308creport.pdf

Securities and Exchange Commission (SEC). "Report on the role and function of credit rating agencies in the operation of the securities markets." January 2003b. Online at: www.sec.gov/news/studies/credratingreport0103.pdf

Securities and Exchange Commission (SEC). "Study and recommendations on Section 404(b) of the Sarbanes-Oxley Act of 2002 for issuers with public float between $75 and $250 million." April 2011a. Online at: www.sec.gov/news/studies/2011/404bfloat-study.pdf

Securities and Exchange Commission (SEC). "Work plan for the consideration of incorporating international financial reporting standards into the financial reporting system for U.S. issuers: Exploring a possible method of incorporation." May 26, 2011b. Online at: tinyurl.com/3wkej8m [PDF].

Securities and Exchange Commission (SEC). "Report on review of reliance on credit ratings." July 2011c. Online at: www.sec.gov/news/studies/2011/939astudy.pdf

Securities and Exchange Commission (SEC). "2011 summary report of Commission staff's examinations of each nationally recognized statistical rating organization." September 2011d. Online at: tinyurl.com/7e3f2y2 [PDF].

Securities and Exchange Commission (SEC). "Work plan for the consideration of incorporating international financial reporting standards into the financial reporting system for US issuers: An analysis of IFRS in practice." November 16, 2011c. Online at: tinyurl.com/7s3k477 [PDF].

US Government. "H. R. 4173: Dodd-Frank Wall Street reform and consumer protection act." 2010. Online at: tinyurl.com/7nhkvgq [PDF].

Websites:

Addison-Hewitt Associates guide to the Sarbanes–Oxley Act: www.soxlaw.com
Commodity Futures Trading Commission (CFTC; US): www.cftc.gov
CFTC information on implementing the Dodd–Frank Act: www.cftc.gov/LawRegulation/DoddFrankAct/index.htm
CFTC information on whistleblowing: www.cftc.gov/ConsumerProtection/WhistleblowerInformation/index.htm
General Accountability Office (GAO; US): www. gao.gov
Public Company Accounting Oversight Board (PCAOB; US): www.pcaobus.org
PCAOB auditing standards: pcaobus.org/Standards/Auditing/Pages/default.aspx
PCAOB guidance, including staff audit practice alerts: pcaobus.org/Standards/Pages/Guidance.aspx
Securities and Exchange Commission (SEC; US): www.sec.gov
SEC information on implementing the Dodd–Frank Act: www.sec.gov/spotlight/dodd-frank.shtml
SEC Office of the Whistleblower: www.sec.gov/whistleblower

See Also:

★ The Effect of SOX on Internal Control, Risk Management, and Corporate Governance Best Practice (pp. 333–335)
✔ Sarbanes–Oxley: Its Development and Aims (p. 1052)
The Smartest Guys in the Room: The Amazing Rise and Scandalous Fall of Enron (p. 1416)

"The average individual innovator is having a smaller and smaller impact ... I've noticed that Nobel prizewinners are getting older. That's a sure sign it's taking longer to innovate." Ben Jones

  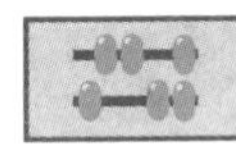      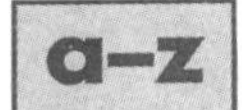

Starting a Successful Internal Audit Function to Meet Present and Future Demands by Jeffrey Ridley

EXECUTIVE SUMMARY

- Starting an internal audit function requires a clear and inspiring vision to provide the right direction for its success.
- The services provided by the internal audit role must add value and meet the needs of all its customers, at every level in the organization. This demands a wealth of knowledge and experience of governance, risk management and control processes in the function.
- The internal audit charter approved at board level must state the professional standards expected from all staff in the function.
- Internal auditors in the function should be trained to ask the right questions and advise on the impact of present and future change at all levels in the organization, from strategic to operational.
- Quality of performance in the function and its continuous improvement requires a total commitment, measured and reported at board level through key performance indicators, and feedback from its customers.
- The function should contribute to implementation of quality policies in the organization it serves by using its own experience of achieving performance quality.

INTRODUCTION

In 1998 on the occasion of the fifty-year celebration of the establishment of the Institute of Internal Auditors (IIA)'s five chapters in the United Kingdom, I wrote:[1]

"We need to be seen as innovators in the world of regulation, control and auditing. Creativity, innovation and experimentation are now key to our professional success. They must be the vision of all internal auditing functions. This means improving old and developing new products and services for delighted customers, with a focus on their objectives. This means being at the leading edge in all the markets in which we sell our internal auditing services. This means beating our competitors and knowing who these are. This means having the imagination, and foresight into what our organizations will require from us, not just in the year 2000, but also in 2005 and beyond.

In this 50th year celebration of our national institute's past and present team-work, all IIA-UK [and Ireland] members should continue to set their sights on being inventors of an improved and new internal auditing, to delight all their customers ... and increase its status as an international profession."

Establishing a successful internal audit function requires more than just support and resources approved at board and senior management levels; or an external requirement by government and regulators; or encouragement by external auditors. These are all important drivers and influences for creating the function and setting the boundaries in which it will operate and provide services. But the present and future demands of a successful function require a clear and inspiring vision for the direction of its services, which can only be provided by those who work in the function. It demands their knowledge and experience of risk management, control, and governance processes; their professionalism; their imagination, innovation, and creativity to manage change in what is and will be required from their services. All these attributes are needed if these service providers are to delight all their customers by the quality of their performance. They are needed whether internal auditing is resourced by staff in-house, outsourced, or co-sourced.

CLEAR AND INSPIRING VISION

A vision statement is key to the mission of any organization or function. In 1991 Richard Whitely wrote some inspirational words on vision statements:[2]

- A good vision leads to competitive advantage.
- One way to define vision is ... a vivid picture of an ambitious, desirable state that is connected to the customer and better in some important way than the current state.
- How does this vision represent the interests of our customers and values that are important to us?
- A vision has two vital functions, and they're more important today than ever before. One is to serve as a source of inspiration. The other is to guide decision making, aligning all the organization's parts so that they work together.
- If your vision is not an impetus to excellence, then it has failed.
- When a company clearly declares what it stands for and its people share this vision, a powerful network is created—people seeking related goals.
- Constantly communicate your vision for your organization to those who work with you and for you. Don't let a day go by without talking about it.

This advice has not dated. It can be seen in many vision statements used by organizations today and will be tomorrow. An inspirational vision for internal auditing in an organization can have a significant impact on those who provide and receive the service. It should be aligned with its organization's vision, creating direction for all its resources, promotion, planning, engagements, and reporting. From the vision should flow the strategic mission of the internal audit role and its business plan, which will set the scene for the resources needed for its achievement. Following the creation of an internal auditing vision statement, all internal auditing staff and senior management should be involved in its development. Seek total organization commitment and board approval for its direction. That direction will set the scene for the services it will provide.

KNOWLEDGE AND EXPERIENCE OF GOVERNANCE, RISK MANAGEMENT AND CONTROL PROCESSES

No internal audit function can be successful unless it is expert in the principles and practices of management, governance, risk management and control in the sector in which it works and across the supply chains developed by its organization. This expertise demands not only knowledge of what these processes require but also an understanding of the principles on which they are based, experience of how they operate at all levels within an organization, and how they are reported to all stakeholders. This expertise has to be at the management level of internal auditing and with all internal auditors.

Successful organizations assess and manage their economic, environmental, and social risks, mitigating these through appropriate strategies and controls. Successful internal audit functions focus on this corporate social responsibility and its "triple bottom line"[3] in all their engagements—across the entire range of an organization's strategies, policies, processes, and reporting. In many organizations internal auditing

"A team approach to managing knowledge needed for professional internal auditing is essential when planning its services..." *Cutting Edge Internal Auditing*

  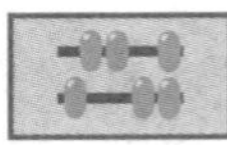   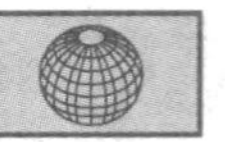   

is seen as a facilitator in the assessment and management processes addressing these risks. To be successful today, the planning of internal audit engagements and the conducting of assurance and consulting reviews must always be linked to risks and controls in an organization's "triple bottom line."

In 1991, the US Committee of Sponsoring Organizations (COSO) published its integrated control framework exposure draft. This became its risk and control guidance for management and auditors worldwide, published in 1992.[4] Its five integrated elements of "*control environment, risk assessment, control activities, monitoring, and information and communications*" are basic requirements in all risk and control processes. It defines control as a process "designed to provide reasonable assurance regarding the achievement of [effectiveness and efficiency of operations] objectives." Importance of the COSO control elements and key concepts is significant for the mitigation of risks. These have been adopted as best practices by many regulators and organizations. Their importance is even more evident today as organizations embed risk management in their processes, from strategy setting to the achievement of objectives at every level in every operation.

In 2004[5] COSO further developed its framework into an Enterprise Risk Management (ERM) model providing further guidance for the management of risk and control across all levels of an organization. Based on its 1992 control framework, this model demonstrates the importance of embedding each of the 1992 integrated framework elements in the strategic, operations, reporting, and compliance decision-making processes across the whole enterprise. Understanding the description of each of the elements in the ERM model is a good test for management and all auditors in any organization. Such understanding is essential for internal audit success.

The IIA Inc. (2006),[6] in its overview of organizational governance, discusses the internal auditors' role, recommending that "they act as catalysts for change, advising or advocating improvements to enhance the organization's governance structure and practices." Possible steps for the internal auditor to be successful in an organization's governance processes are seen as [*my comments in brackets*]:

1 Review all the relevant internal and external audit policies, codes, and charter provisions, pertaining to organizational governance. [*Look for the key words and phrases about governance.*]
2 Discuss organizational governance with executive management or members of the board. The objective of these discussions is to ensure internal auditors have a clear understanding of the governance structure and processes from the perspective of those responsible for them, as well as the maturity of these processes. [*In these discussions relate direction and control in the organization to the achievement of its vision, mission, and key objectives.*]
3 Discuss options for expanding the role of internal auditors in organizational governance with the board chair, board committee chairs, and executive managers. These discussions could involve explaining the potential actions internal auditors could take and the resources required, as well as the possibility of an assurance gap between the board's assurance requirements and the organization's practices, if internal auditors did not assist in this area. Ensure the internal audit charter is consistent with the expanded role being considered. [*Consider providing education programs on governance for all board, management, and employee training programs.*]
4 Discuss organizational governance topics with other key stakeholders including external auditors and employees of the organization's departments such as legal, public affairs corporate secretary office, compliance, and regulatory affairs. During these discussions, explore their current and future activities as well as how an expanded internal audit role could coordinate with their activities. [*This should also be in every internal audit, not only in the organization but also across all its external relationships.*]
5 Develop a broad framework of the organization's governance structure by identifying potential areas of weakness and concern. [*A real opportunity to be creative in thinking and design.*]
6 Draft a multi-year plan to develop the internal audit role in organization governance areas methodically [*Another opportunity to be creative.*]
7 Perform a pilot audit in one of the areas noted above. Select a single, well-defined, manageable topic and assess the adequacy of the design and execution of the activities related to the topic. Performing a pilot audit will allow the internal auditor a chance to gauge the organization's response to his or her

CASE STUDY

Scope and Types of Work in Successful Internal Audit Functions[11]

The scope of internal auditing covers all the activities of an organization, without regard for internal boundaries or geographical restrictions. It encompasses the adequacy and effectiveness of governance, risk management, and internal control processes in identifying and responding to all the risks facing the organization. The following are examples of the different types of work that internal audit may undertake:

- giving assurance to the board that the organization's risks have been properly identified and managed in accordance with the approved risk appetite;
- reviewing the activities undertaken by management to implement the ethical policy across the whole organization;
- giving assurance that business continuity and disaster recovery planning, including for mission-critical information systems, are adequate given the risks facing the organization and the risk appetite;
- giving assurance that the purchase process includes adequate controls to ensure agreed levels of competitiveness, cost savings, and quality performance;
- assisting the management team in evaluating the actual return on investments over a given period of time;
- carrying out an internal audit to verify an organization's compliance with labor laws and regulations;
- giving assurance that measures are properly designed and working effectively to address health, safety, and environmental risks on industrial sites;
- verifying that all purchase and sales contracts comply with the organization's policies;
- giving an opinion on the efficiency and effectiveness of the customer complaints process;
- providing advice to management on the design and implementation of risk management processes.

Consider

- How many of these examples of types of work exist in your internal audit function?
- Have you promoted all of these services in your internal audit charter?

"If governance in an organization is defined As direction and control then to be at the cutting edge today internal auditing must be involved with both, either independently or in partnership with management."

Cutting Edge Internal Auditing

expanded role and learn how to coordinate more effectively with other stakeholders. [*This should only be the start. It should lead the internal auditor along many paths in many different dimensions.*]

Note how these recommendations link in to the guidance for success in this article.

PROFESSIONALISM

Professional attributes and performance requirements for internal auditing are clearly set out in the IIA's International Standards for Professional Practice of Internal Auditing [7]. These *Standards* and their supporting guidelines have been continuously developed internationally since the 1970s. They represent and are recognised as "best practice" internal auditing and will continue to be revised by international teams to reflect both the needs of internal auditors and the organizations in which they provide their services. All internal auditing charters should require the internal audit role to comply with these standards: not all do! Yet every board would expect its external auditors to comply with developed international standards for external auditing. Why should internal auditing be different?

The *Standards* set out requirements and guidance for internal auditing attributes and performance of work. All are based on defined principles of *Integrity, Objectivity, Confidentiality*, and *Competency* in its *International Code of Ethics*, first published in 1968 and since revised to meet current and future internal auditing needs for all its members and those who have achieved the status of its qualification *Certified Internal Auditor*.[8]

MANAGING CHANGE

All operations in an organization have a past, a present, and a future. This must be recognized in the planning of all internal auditing services and in each of its engagements. What has happened before and what is happening today will influence what will happen in the future. What happens in the future will also be influenced by more change, not only in the organization but also externally, by many of its stakeholders and events beyond its control. Every test and observation in an internal audit engagement needs to be considered in this scenario of past, present, and future change. Future change is change that can be forecast during the engagement, and change that might be hinted at by events leading to "beyond the horizon." Beyond the horizon is not always an easy prediction to make, but it should be attempted by the internal auditor studying events and issues surrounding the operations being reviewed, and in discussion with board members and management at all levels.

Figure 1. Cutting-edge internal auditing framework

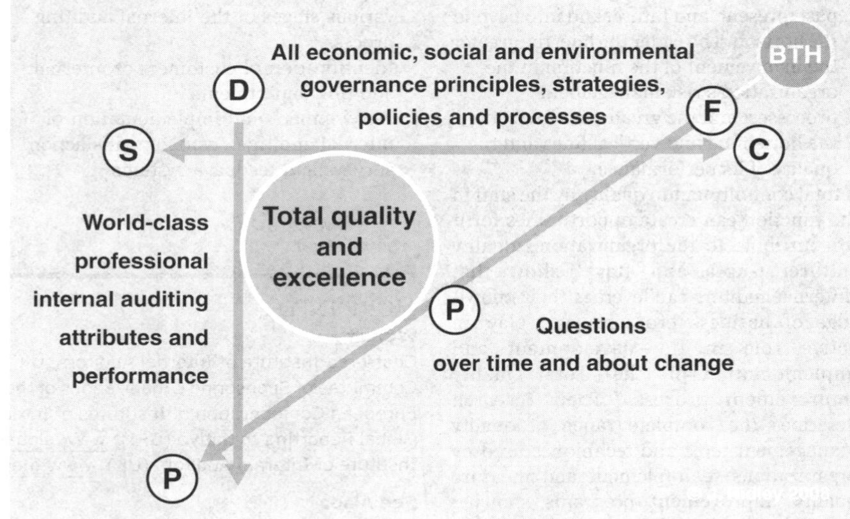

QUALITY OF PERFORMANCE

To be successful an internal audit function must have a total commitment to the quality of its performance and continuous improvement. This is a requirement of the IIA *Standards*. Such commitment will be strongly influenced by its collective knowledge, experience of governance, risk management and control; its professionalism of service; and its ability to question change in the past, present, and future. This can be seen in the cutting-edge internal auditing framework in the figure, developed within the chapters of my book *Cutting Edge Internal Auditing*.[9]

In Figure 1, each of the directional lines demonstrates an importance in the management of internal audit. Each touches and influences the quality of performance in an internal audit function:

- The horizontal line represents the level of knowledge and experience of risk management, control, and governance in the function across the organization's supply chains—supplier through operations to customers, related today to economic, social, and environmental issues and risks. The wider the line the better the service provided by the function and greater the impact on the vertical and diagonal lines and the quality of its performance.
- The vertical line represents the compliance of the function with The IIA International Standards. The deeper the line, the better the compliance and greater the impact on the horizontal and diagonal lines and the quality of its performance.

MAKING IT HAPPEN

Starting a successful internal auditing function requires a chief audit executive who is experienced in the implementation of professional internal auditing processes and has a full understanding of the principles and practices of management, government, risk management and control. That experience and knowledge must be used to educate the board and senior management in the role that internal auditing should assume to add best value to the organization. That role should be written into a charter, approved at board level, showing its purpose, authority, and responsibility. Once established, the internal auditing function should:

- create an inspiring vision linked to its aimed success;
- develop a plan to achieve its vision, focused on adding value;
- employ and train competent qualified professional staff;
- focus all its engagements on changes in the past, present, future and beyond the horizon;
- report its findings on a timely basis to appropriate management and the board;
- continuously measure and improve the quality of its services and delight its customers.

"...quality schemes and governance each strengthen the other in all supply chains, internal and external."
Cutting Edge Internal Auditing

  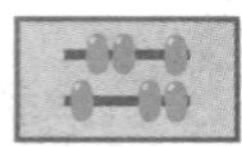      

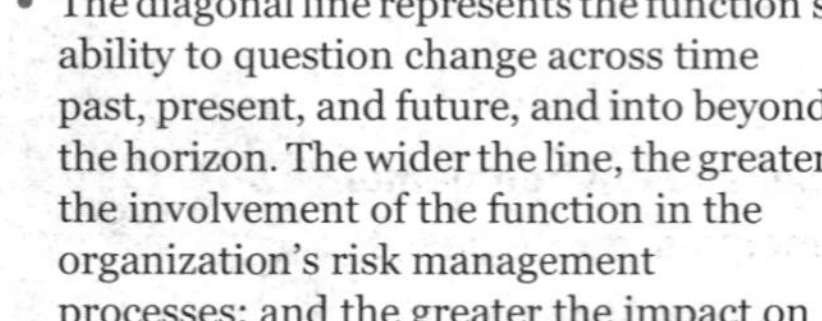

- The diagonal line represents the function's ability to question change across time past, present, and future, and into beyond the horizon. The wider the line, the greater the involvement of the function in the organization's risk management processes; and the greater the impact on the horizontal and vertical lines and the quality of its performance.

A total commitment to quality by the staff in the function can create opportunities for it to contribute to the organization's quality culture. Gupta and Ray[10] show that "internal auditors can leverage their knowledge of business processes and play an active role in the development and implementation of [the] Total Quality Improvement process." Their research describes the complete range of quality management tools and techniques used by organizations to implement and measure quality improvement programs showing how a knowledge of these and experience in their use can improve an internal audit activity's services and processes. Their research identifies seven steps (Table 4-22, p. 104) to be undertaken to implement Total Quality Improvement in internal auditing:

1 Development of Mission and Vision Statements and establishing internal audit department objectives.
2 Establishment and implementation of performance measures for various stages of the internal auditing process.
3 Identification of customers of internal auditing departments.
4 Development and implementation of internal auditing customer satisfaction surveys and feedback systems.
5 Benchmarking with other internal auditing departments.
6 Introspective self-analysis.
7 TQM training and education of the internal auditing staff.

Note how these steps have been woven into the guidance in this article for establishing a successful internal audit function to meet present and future needs for all its customers.

MORE INFO

Websites:

Chartered Institute of Internal Auditors (UK and Ireland): www.iia.org.uk
Committee of Sponsoring Organizations of the Treadway Commission (COSO): www.coso.org
European Confederation of Institutes of Internal Auditing (ECIIA): www.eciia.org
Global Reporting Initiative (GRI): www.globalreporting.org
Institute of Internal Auditors (UK): www.theiia.org

See Also:

★ Best Practices in Corporate Social Responsibility (pp. 636–639)
★ Best Practices in Risk-Based Internal Auditing (pp. 303–305)
★ Incorporating Operational and Performance Auditing into Compliance and Financial Auditing (pp. 365–367)
★ Internal Audit and Partnering with Senior Management (pp. 368–371)
★ New Assurance Challenges Facing Chief Audit Executives (pp. 378–381)
★ Optimizing Internal Audit (pp. 382–384)
✔ The IIA Code of Ethics (p. 1030)

NOTES

1 Ridley, J. "IIA—UK celebrates 50th." *Internal Auditing* (March 1998): 12.
2 Whiteley, Richard C. *The Customer-Driven Company: Moving from Talk to Action*. London: Basic Books, 1991, pp. 21, 26–28, 32, 37.
3 *Sustainability Reporting Guidelines* 2000–2006.
4 Committee of Sponsoring Organizations. *Internal Control—Integrated Control Framework*. New York: American Institute of Certified Public Accountants, 1992.
5 Committee of Sponsoring Organizations. Enterprise Risk Management - Integrated Framework, New York: American Institute of Certified Public Accountants, 2004.
6 *Organizational Governance: Guidance for Internal Auditors*. Altamonte Springs, FL: Institute of Internal Auditors, 2006.
7 The Institute of Internal Auditors (The IIA), *International Standards for the Professional Practice of Internal Auditing*, Altamonte Springs, FL: 2009.
8 See the IIA website (www.theiia.org) for details of this and other internal auditing qualifications.
9 Ridley, Jeffrey. *Cutting Edge Internal Auditing*. Chichester, UK: Wiley, 2008.
10 Gupta, Parveen P., and Manash R. Ray. *Total Quality Improvement Process and the Internal Audit Function*. Altamonte Springs, FL: IIA Research Foundation, 1995.
11 *Internal Auditing in Europe—Position Paper*. Brussels: European Confederation of Institutes of Internal Auditors, 2005.

"Without an appropriate vision, a transformation effort can easily dissolve into a list of confusing, incompatible and time-consuming projects that go in the wrong direction or nowhere at all." Bob Guccione

  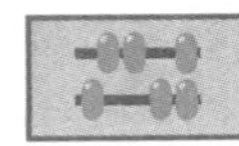   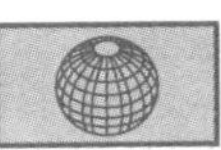   

Threats to Auditor Independence and Possible Remedies by Gilad Livne

EXECUTIVE SUMMARY

- A description of the nature of the client–auditor relationship, together with a brief historical perspective.
- How impaired auditor independence can cause significant losses to various parties, such as shareholders and lenders.
- The potential benefits when auditor independence is strong.
- A discussion of some of the main threats to independence, followed by the possible remedies and their limitations.

INTRODUCTION

The external auditor is nominated to carry out audit work on behalf of the audited company's shareholders. Being a proxy for the shareholders fundamentally requires the external auditor to be independent of the audited firm's managers. Auditing standards require independence both in mind and in appearance. Independence implies the ability and willingness of the auditor to identify a range of deficiencies during the audit process and then to challenge the audited firm on these findings. Such deficiencies include matters regarding internal control, the accounting policies adopted, and absent or misleading reporting.

In practice, the external auditor's various interactions with the audited firm are conducted through and with the client's top management. Inevitably, this gives rise to a "special" relationship between managers of the audited firm and the auditor. This special relationship typically starts with the nomination process—often the client's management suggests that a particular audit firm should be nominated[1]—and continues along several dimensions: fees are paid to the auditor by the audited firm, not directly by shareholders. During the audit process, management is responsible for providing answers to the auditor concerning matters about which it knows more, and so auditor must rely on (often self-serving) managers. In preparing the annual report, accounting and reporting issues are effectively jointly decided by management and the auditor, even though, strictly speaking, the preparation of the accounts is the responsibility of the managers. It is therefore quite sensible to ask if auditor independence, both in mind and appearance, can be maintained given this nature of the relationship. In other words, it is important to identify the threats to auditor independence in light of this special relationship.

This is not an abstract exercise. The recent financial crisis has brought the question of auditor independence to the fore. It has put auditors under a public magnifying glass, with some commentators questioning the integrity of external auditors and their complicity in producing what may be misleading reports (for example, in the case of Lehman Brothers' reporting of transactions in certain loans, known as Repo 105). Before this crisis, the accounting scandals of the early 2000s, including Enron, WorldCom, and Parmalat, led to a comprehensive rethink of matters relating to auditor independence in the United States and indeed around the world. Legislation followed—most prominently in the United States, with the Sarbanes–Oxley Act (henceforth SOX) of 2002 imposing various restrictions on the external auditors.

It is worth remembering that blaming compromised auditor independence for accounting scandals is not a recent phenomenon.[2] An early example, from 1938, is the case of McKesson & Robbins, where the firm Price, Waterhouse & Co. failed to verify the existence of inventory. The bankruptcy of Westec in 1965 raised concerns, many years before Enron, that the provision of nonaudit services compromised auditor independence. Not surprisingly, some commentators have suggested that auditors do not serve as the protectors of shareholders' and lenders' interests (e.g. Carey, 1967). These and other failures have prompted a wave of litigation against auditors, with large sums awarded to plaintiffs and paid by auditors.

These auditing failures and the large losses inflicted on shareholders, lenders, and employees demonstrate that impaired auditor independence can lead to grave consequences. However, it is not sufficient to focus on the adverse effects of compromised independence. It is also important to highlight the possible *advantages* of maintaining a high degree of auditor independence. This is the subject of the next section.

Independence of Mind vs Independence in Appearance

It is common to speak of these two types of auditor independence, but what is the difference? A clear distinction may be hard to make, as the two overlap and interact. Nevertheless, independence of mind is a desirable psychological–behavioral trait in an auditor. He or she should be objective and free from bias. He/she should be willing to challenge clients and maintain a good degree of skepticism coupled with an inquisitive mind-set. Being knowledgeable also increases the auditor's ability to challenge managers on their reporting decisions. This highlights the important role education and training can play.

Independence in appearance is about avoiding relationships or circumstances that can threaten, or may be seen to threaten, the willingness or ability to scrutinize and criticize managers. For example, having a managerial or advisory role in the client firm can impair the auditor's objectivity and hence his or her ability to carry out an effective audit on behalf of shareholders. Having connections through family ties is another example.

It should be made clear, however, that appearing to be independent is not sufficient. What truly is required is the independence of mind.

THE BENEFITS OF EMPLOYING INDEPENDENT AUDITORS

In many countries an external audit of the annual accounts is required by law. For example, in the European Union, the Fourth (1978) and Seventh Council Directives (1983) require that the annual accounts or consolidated accounts be audited by one or more persons entitled to carry out such audits of companies traded on a stock exchange within the EU.[3] This is a costly requirement for audit clients and their shareholders, and, more broadly, to society, as resources currently devoted to the audit task (inclusive of the cost of external and internal auditors, as well as the cost of regulation and enforcement) could be employed, perhaps more productively, elsewhere in the economy. It therefore begs the question what benefits can be ascribed to external audits performed by independent auditors. A somewhat deeper, and more difficult, question is whether these benefits exceed their cost.

To place these questions in context, it is important first to recognize the need to supply reliable and relevant information to investors. Financial information can be regarded as the oil that runs modern capital markets—securities markets in particular. Information of high quality enables investors to make efficient investment decisions, as investment money can be directed where it is most productive. While investors often act for profit-making purposes, society at large can benefit when money is invested where it is needed most (and hence where the returns are the highest).

However, if the provisions for financial information remain unchecked, there is a good chance that the providers of such information will use it opportunistically and/or in a misleading manner to generate private gains. For example, managers could create a false impression of a good financial performance to reward themselves with higher bonuses. The result will be a waste of scarce resources, missed growth opportunities, and ultimately the collapse of capital markets when trust in financial disclosure is lost. Independent external auditors help to produce investment-relevant and reliable information that enables investors to make sound economic decisions. This is because they verify the information provided in the financial statements (for example, the existence of inventory and cash balances). They also pass judgment on the accounting policies adopted by client firms. Their expertise and knowledge assist clients in selecting and implementing adequate measurement and reporting procedures demanded by third parties. This is called the *information role* of independent auditors, and it is linked to the trust with which investors and creditors can treat the audited financial statements.

This role and its benefits are widely recognized by investors and regulators. In the United States, SOX has as one of its main objectives to improve auditor independence because it should lead to a reduced cost of capital. Academic research has provided some evidence that is consistent with this argument.[4] And although some argue that SOX has been costly to implement but has had only limited impact, Amir, Guan, and Livne (2010) show that that auditor independence has increased following SOX and that auditor independence does reduce the cost of borrowing.

Independent auditors also help in monitoring the financial affairs of client firms. Through their tests and examinations of internal procedures, the external auditors learn how the client firm is carrying out its various transactions. At a very basic level they can thus identify causes of inefficiency, waste, and leakage. Reporting these to the audit committee and top managers provides an opportunity to improve financial performance. Moreover, the independent external auditor's scrutiny enhances the likelihood that fraud and embezzlement will be detected. This is called the *monitoring role* of independent auditors. Shareholders and lenders alike therefore benefit from strong monitoring by independent auditors because it safeguards the client's assets.[5]

In summary, the collective presence of independent auditors in the economy is capable of increasing the trust of investors in capital markets. This is because they can rely on the financial information provided by audited firms, as well as rest assured that the firms' financial affairs are conducted efficiently and honestly. In turn, such an economy can perform better because its securities markets attract capital and efficiently direct valuable resources to the most beneficial uses.

THE VARIOUS THREATS TO AUDITOR INDEPENDENCE

There are a number of threats to auditor independence. In my discussion of these threats I make reference not only to several professional and regulatory pronouncements, but also more broadly to points raised by various commentators and academics. It should also be noted that different professional and regulatory organizations have a somewhat different view of the potency of such threats. This is the case because different countries have different legal and commercial systems that are embedded in broader cultural and societal contexts. As a matter of convenience, however, I will refer mainly to the ethical framework adopted recently by the United Kingdom's Auditing Practices Board (APB).[6] The threats listed below and discussed in the following sections may, thus, not be exhaustive.

- The appointment and termination processes.
- Self-interest.
- Familiarity and complacency.
- Social bonding.
- Economic bonds.
- Management and employment.
- Litigation.

The Appointment and Termination Processes

Although the external auditor is employed for the benefit of shareholders, the appointment and dismissal processes are quite removed from shareholders. Management is responsible for suggesting the external auditor and rarely offers a choice to shareholders. As a rotation of audit firms is relatively infrequent—a periodic rotation is currently not required by law in most countries—the typical scenario is that the renewal of the incumbent auditor's term is brought to the annual general meeting (AGM) for approval by shareholders. In practice there is little that shareholders can do except vote against a nomination or renewal. In other words, the nomination and appointment mechanism does not allow for competing proposals to be brought directly before shareholders. The result is that the incumbent auditor is at the mercy of the client's managers as to the renewal process. Moreover, there are no direct channels between auditors and shareholders through which competing auditors can make a case for appointment. Thus, the special auditor–client relationship is off to a problematic start: the nominated auditor "owes it" to the client's managers and is under threat of dismissal by managers.

Occasionally auditors are rotated, on a voluntary basis. Academic evidence suggests that many voluntary rotations take place because the incumbent auditor is too independent for managers' taste (see, for example, DeFond and Subramanyam, 1998; and Lennox, 2000). The new auditor is likely selected by the client's management in an opportunistic fashion in that the new auditor is more likely to accommodate clients' wishes than the incumbent auditor. Since managers have almost exclusive control of this process, shareholders seem unable to influence the decision in a way that would ensure auditor independence. The result can be the nomination of a new and less-independent auditor.

Self-Interest

The presence of financial interest of the auditor in the audited firm can impair objectiveness, and hence independence. Consider an auditor who is also a shareholder. The (independent) auditor's duty is to ensure that financial performance is accurately reported, even if this implies reporting poor performance. However, as a shareholder, the auditor may prefer that bad news is withheld, at least until the auditor-shareholder can sell his/her position. Similar arguments hold for an auditor-lender (for example, through the holding of corporate bonds).[7]

As a second example of a self-interest threat to independence, consider the case where the external auditor carries out some nonaudit work for the client. This is quite a common situation. The auditor therefore may need to scrutinize and evaluate the nonaudit work carried out by colleagues in the audit firm. Many auditors may be quite reluctant to confront their colleagues and would have the self-interest to minimize any exposure that could risk his audit firm's reputation.

  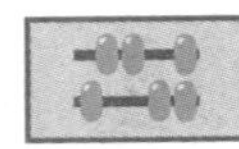      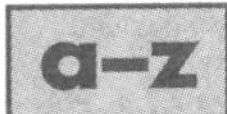

Familiarity and Complacency

Familiarity can blunt the skepticism that is expected of the auditor. This may be because the auditor develops a degree of overconfidence in his or her knowledge of the client firm. It may be that the repetitive nature of a long-term engagement between the auditor and his/her client leads to complacency and, consequently, to the underweighting of warning signs. Some commentators speak of the need for "fresh" eyes and mind that lead to a better scrutiny of the client.

Yet familiarity also has a positive aspect as it implies a better understanding of the client and helps the auditor to perform better. Research on auditor tenure suggests that, as the audit–client relationship lengthens, audit quality improves.

Social Bonding

Long-term audit engagements bring the external auditor and members of the client firm's management team closely together. It is not unusual for friendships to form in the workplace. Moreover, to the extent that a client's managers nominate auditors from their own circle of friends, the likelihood of objectivity on the part of the auditor decreases. This "self-serving" bias is grounded in psychology theory and arises when, as a consequence of close relationships, one cannot separate one's own interests from those of others.

It is not entirely clear, however, how powerful this threat is. Auditors need to follow certain professional and ethical norms, and they are bound by social norms. Moreover, concerns about reputation may be quite powerful and sufficient to rein in such a threat, even if only at the subconscious level.

The Economic Bond

Auditors' livelihoods depend on the fees they generate from audit and nonaudit services. Auditors thus have an inherent incentive to keep the client—that is, the audited firm's managers—"happy." Failure to do so can cost them the client and the loss of a long stream of future income. This economic bond is regarded by many as perhaps the greatest threat to auditor independence.

Nonaudit services have attracted the harshest criticism. These include consulting services such as corporate finance advisory, investment advisory or management, valuation services, and IT consulting and implementation services. Typically, fees for nonaudit services represent a very lucrative source of income. Some commentators have raised concern that in order to be awarded nonaudit service contracts, auditors may compromise their audit work.

Even in the absence of nonaudit services, the fundamental problem remains. While in the past audit work was relatively limited in scope, following SOX external auditors now need to audit internal control systems. As a result, there has been a sharp increase in audit fees. At the same time, SOX and similar regulations in many other countries have restricted the ability of external auditors to provide nonaudit services.[8]

These facts are also reflected in the data. Table 1 shows that average total fees (audit and nonaudit) have increased steadily since 2003, when many of the SOX requirements came into effect. Moreover, while nonaudit fees have declined sharply, audit fees have significantly increased. Importantly, these trends appear for both large and small auditors. Hence, an economic bond can still arise in the post-SOX era, though more so with respect to audit fees.

Management and Employment

The auditor and the audited firm must be different entities, as an effective and objective audit clearly requires such a separation. For this reason, US regulation explicitly prohibits the provision of nonaudit services that involve activities which otherwise should be performed by the client's management and personnel (i.e. management roles).

Matters become somewhat more complex when a previous auditor is hired by the client firm to perform a management role. One concern is that the members of the audit team will be reluctant to criticize a former colleague, perhaps because of social bonding. A second concern is that the ex-auditor, having acquired knowledge of the audit process and its weaknesses, may be able to take advantage and "game" the new auditor to the benefit of the client (and now the new employer). In the United States, therefore, there is a requirement of a one-year cooling-off period. In the United Kingdom, APB Ethical Standard 2 requires a two-year cooling-off period.

Litigation

Sometimes disputes between client and auditor end up in legal action or, short of that, a threat to take matters to the courts. In such a case auditor independence is perceived to be impaired.

The ability of the auditor to judge matters on an objective basis irrespective of allegations of deficiencies in the audit procedures and conclusions comes under threat in these circumstances. By the same token, when the auditor sues the client, the natural presumption is that objectivity is lost. The US ethical rules require the audit firm to assess whether independence is impaired. In the United Kingdom ethical standards are stricter and require the auditor to resign.

Litigation by shareholders, for example through "class action," typically targets not only the client and its management, but all too often the external auditor. The threat to the client–auditor relationship is less clear here. It is possible that the auditor would take a more "aggressive" approach to the audit to reduce potential damages that might be awarded by a court. To the extent that this creates bias in judgment, independence is impaired.

It is also interesting to note differences in legal systems. In the United States, civil litigation as well as criminal litigation is possible and there is no cap on the amount of damages that can be awarded. In the United Kingdom the legal environment changed with the new Companies Act 2006. Criminal charges can be brought against auditors, although in these cases the penalties do not include prison sentences. Perhaps more importantly, auditors and clients can for the first time enter into a "liability-limitation agreement" that caps the amount an auditor would need to pay in compensation. On one hand, this should encourage auditors to avoid a box-ticking mentality and rely more on their professional judgment as the fear of financial losses recedes. On the other hand, with the lowered threat of litigation, auditors may feel that the penalty for "collaboration" with clients is less costly. If the latter holds, auditor independence is likely to suffer.

Occasionally, the audit firm helps a client to defend itself against a legal dispute or with respect to regulatory inquiry or investigation. ASB Ethical Standard 1 (revised) calls this an "advocacy threat" because the auditor needs to defend the client. The standard states that, as a result, the audit firm effectively assumes a role very similar to a management role. This, in turn, threatens the auditor's objectivity and independence.

MEASURES TO THWART THE THREATS TO AUDITOR INDEPENDENCE

It is doubtful that the threats to auditor independence can be thwarted entirely. Arguably, some can be contained, but ultimately it is a matter of the incentives that auditors have to maintain objectivity and of their willingness to stand up to clients.

Regulators all over the world have for many years tried to find solutions through legislation. In addition, some other remedies may be available from other sources. The discussion in this section is not meant to be exhaustive of the full range of possible solutions and their effectiveness but, rather,

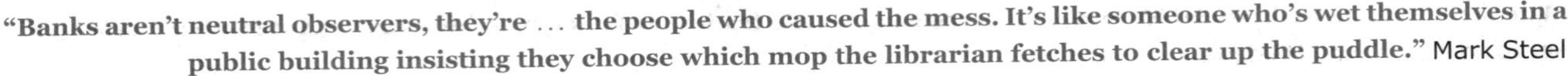

  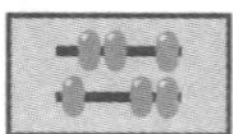   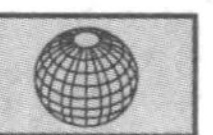   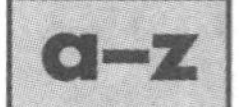

Table 1. Average audit and nonaudit fees (US dollars) earned by Big Four and non-Big Four auditors in the United States during 2000–09.* (*Source*: Audit Analytics)

	2000	2001	2002	2003	2004	2005	2006	2007	2008	2009
Overall										
Total fees	1,330,292	1,240,280	894,348	842,561	1,181,108	1,226,629	1,309,223	1,327,210	1,378,652	1,351,729
Audit fees	414,876	405,472	442,310	511,669	853,722	949,328	1,043,746	1,046,198	1,104,626	1,082,009
Nonaudit fees	915,416	834,808	452,009	330,892	327,387	277,301	265,477	281,012	274,026	269,721
Number of observations	5,648	7,784	13,343	15,284	14,180	14,014	13,892	13,548	12,804	11,815
Big Four auditors†										
Total fees	1,658,027	1,582,697	1,245,717	1,228,660	1,796,259	1,950,704	2,191,428	2,309,410	2,407,913	2,307,484
Audit fees	506,958	507,378	608,674	740,242	1,293,586	1,504,478	1,738,797	1,808,029	1,918,416	1,837,057
Nonaudit fees	1,151,070	1,075,320	637,044	488,418	502,674	446,225	452,631	501,381	489,497	470,427
Number of observations	4,442	6,044	9,308	10,140	8,985	8,349	7,801	7,287	6,874	6,503
Non-Big Four auditors										
Total fees	123,162	115,513	83,706	81,471	117,174	159,497	179,347	184,056	185,543	181,685
Audit fees	75,716	70,734	58,540	61,099	92,955	131,154	153,565	159,525	161,290	157,671
Nonaudit fees	47,447	44,780	25,167	20,373	24,219	28,342	25,782	24,530	24,253	24,014
Number of observations	1,206	1,840	4,035	5,144	5,195	5,665	6,091	6,261	5,930	5,312

* I thank Angela Pettinicchio for helping me to compile this table.

† Deloitte & Touche, Ernst & Young, KPMG, PricewaterhouseCoopers (PwC), and, prior to 2002, Arthur Andersen.

to highlight what may be considered the most notable ones. These include:

- modifying the selection process;
- limiting nonaudit services;
- rules making rotation mandatory;
- better disclosure;
- reliance on market forces;
- adoption of good corporate governance mechanisms.

These will be briefly discussed in turn.

Modifying the Selection Process

In most developed countries auditors are selected by the management of the client firm (and are nominally approved by shareholders), which makes auditors more answerable to management than to shareholders, whom they purport to represent. Shifting the balance of power to shareholders is possible by allowing them to directly nominate and appoint, or renew the appointment of, the external auditor. Some experimental evidence suggests that this will lead to greater auditor independence (Mayhew and Pike, 2004). It may be that having a regulatory oversight for the nomination process could also help, although this may fall short of requiring shareholders to take control over the process. In Korea auditors are nominated by the authorities in cases where there is a suspicion of earnings manipulations. Evidence presented by Kim and Yi (2009) suggests that these "designated" auditors are more independent than auditors selected by client firms. SOX has taken an intermediate approach whereby audit committees, not managers, are now responsible for the nomination process. This can be effective only to the extent that the audit committees themselves are sufficiently independent.

Limitation of Nonaudit Services

With the enactment of SOX in 2002, the United States took a strong opposing stand to nonaudit fees, regarding these as among the most serious threats to independence. At the same time, and as Table 1 shows, auditors are now required under this Act to audit the internal control systems and procedures of a client firm. The decline in nonaudit fees has been compensated for by an increase in audit fees, a category that now includes fees paid for the audit of the internal control systems. Table 1 even suggests that auditors now generate greater fees than before SOX.

CASE STUDY

Waste Management Inc.—A Study in Compromised Auditor Independence

Following the collapse of Enron, many have blamed nonaudit fees for distorting auditors' incentives toward collusion with managers and sacrifice of independence in favor of keeping lucrative nonaudit fees. But a few years prior to Enron another scandal was exposed—the scandal of Waste Management (WM). Studying this scandal from SEC filing[9] reveals a number of problems related to compromised auditor independence that were a result of several threats discussed in this chapter. Perhaps a faster regulatory reaction to the WM scandal could have circumvented the fall of Enron.

In February 1998, WM announced that it was restating its financial statements for the five-year period 1992 through 1996 and the first three quarters of 1997. This restatement was the largest in the SEC's history at that time. In the restatement, WM admitted that through 1996 it had materially overstated its reported pretax earnings by US$1.43 billion and that it had understated certain elements of its tax expense by US$178 million. In most instances the company had improperly deferred recognition of current operating expenses to future periods in order to inflate its current period income. The company admitted that it had misstated its expenses relating to, among other things, depreciation of vehicles, equipment, and containers, capitalized interest, asset impairments, and purchase accounting related to environmental remediation reserves.

In analyzing what the contributing factors might have been, the SEC pointed out some telling shortcomings of the client's relationship with the auditor, Arthur Andersen. Among these were:

- Capping audit fees for a number of years. Between 1991 and 1997 total audit fees were US$7.5 million.
- At the same time, the auditor billed WM US$11.8 million in nonaudit fees. In addition, Andersen Consulting billed the company US$6 million in other fees.
- Andersen served as WM's auditor since before WM became a public company in 1971.
- Andersen regarded WM as a "crown jewel" client.
- Until 1997, every chief financial officer and chief accounting officer in WM's history as a public company had previously worked as an auditor at Andersen.
- During the 1990s, approximately 14 former Andersen employees worked for WM, most often in key financial and accounting positions.

"For the first time in financial history, machines can execute trades far faster than humans can intervene. That gap is set to widen." Andy Haldane

     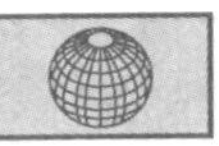  

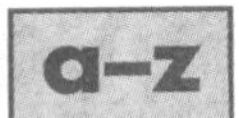

Nonaudit Services Prohibited under SOX[10]

Section 201(a) of SOX makes it unlawful for the external auditors to provide for the client, contemporaneously with the audit, any nonaudit services, including those in the following nine categories:

- bookkeeping or other services related to the client's accounting records or financial statements;
- design and implementation of financial information systems;
- appraisal or valuation services, fairness opinions, or contribution-in-kind reports;
- actuarial services;
- internal audit outsourcing services;
- management functions or human resources;
- broker or dealer, investment adviser, or investment banking services;
- legal services and expert services unrelated to the audit;
- any other service that the Public Companies Accounting Oversight Board determines, by regulation, is impermissible.

The principles governing these rules of independence with respect to services provided by auditors are largely predicated on three basic principles, violations of which would impair the auditor's independence: an auditor cannot function in the role of management; an auditor cannot audit his or her own work; and an auditor cannot serve in an advocacy role for his or her client.

Nonetheless, the provision of tax services is allowed to the extent that the service has been preapproved by the client's audit committee, bearing in mind the risk of impaired independence.

In light of these facts, it is therefore reasonable to ask whether the Act has been successful in lessening the economic dependence of auditors on clients' fees. While the nature of the fees has changed in the United States, the fundamental problem of auditors receiving their pay from the very entity which they should scrutinize is still the same.

It is interesting to note that not all countries have adopted the same approach, which suggests that some legislators do not believe in the effectiveness of this solution. Nevertheless, the requirement for an audit of the internal control systems may carry the side benefit of enabling, perhaps even forcing, the auditor to better understand the audited firm. Thus, any client-specific knowledge lost as a result of the restrictions imposed on nonaudit services may have been replenished through a more encompassing audit task.

Academic research into the effects of the economic bond has not yielded clear-cut findings, although there are a few studies that fail to implicate the economic bond as a cause of poor reporting (e.g. Ashbaugh, LaFond, and Mayhew, 2003; Chung and Kallapur, 2003; Larcker and Richardson, 2004; and Ruddock, Taylor, and Taylor, 2006).

One solution may be to make all fees paid to auditors, at least in part, contingent on future performance. For example, fees would become fully payable if subsequent to the release of audited accounts there is no restatement or regulatory investigation.

Mandatory Rotation Rules

In many countries it is now required that the leading audit partner is replaced periodically. For example, in the United States and United Kingdom the requirement is that the leading partner cannot serve in this role for more than five years. The underlying assumption is that a new partner would bring in a "fresh look," being free from familiarity and complacency threats. However, the fundamental problem of the economic bond is largely unaffected by this requirement (the fee is unlikely to change with a new partner). It may also be argued that such a change involves some setting-up costs and the loss of client-specific knowledge, which can weaken independence.

Some countries require, or are considering the requirement for, a mandatory rotation rule for the entire audit firm. It is not clear if this is a good solution, as the loss of client-specific knowledge would be larger with audit firm rotations than with partner rotation. Furthermore, ruling out long-term relationships implies a shorter fee stream for auditors which, in turn, may reduce their incentive to acquire client-specific knowledge and make them more vulnerable to independence problems.

Unfortunately, there is little empirical evidence on these issues. Academic research (e.g. Myers, Myers, and Omer, 2003) has found some evidence that audit quality improves with auditor tenure, indicating the benefits of client-specific knowledge that is acquired over the years. Such benefits may outweigh the risks of familiarity and complacency threats.

Better Disclosure

The famous maxim that sunlight is the best disinfector may apply here as well. Specifically, in many countries publicly listed firms are now required to provide disclosures of fees paid to the external auditor. Moreover, such disclosures should distinguish between audit and nonaudit fees. This information enables shareholders and potential investors to assess the degree to which economic dependence is a threat. Academic research also seems to indicate that investors use this information: where the disclosed economic bond is low, the cost of capital is low.[11]

Nevertheless, this disclosure does not go far enough in many countries. In particular, there is no widespread requirement for or practice of disclosing the names of the leading partners who sign the audit opinion. This leads to reduced accountability because shareholders and investors cannot easily assess a partner's quality.

Market Forces

In a market populated by several auditors, reputation concerns may be a powerful force. Loss of reputation can easily lead to the demise of an audit firm, as was witnessed with Arthur Andersen in the Enron debacle. Free-market enthusiasts therefore may argue that there is only limited scope for regulation. This is doubtful, because in the absence of regulation the market can engage in a "race to the bottom" through tacit collusion and no fear of penalties.

The other market force that can enhance auditor independence is litigation by shareholders of the external auditor. Fear of the cost of litigation may discipline auditors and force them to adhere to high audit standards to avoid such litigation in the first place, or to reduce its impact once litigation is under way.

Yet it is not clear how powerful this force is. Auditors can pass on to clients the cost of damages they have to pay, as long as these are not colossal and as long as the client is still financially viable. More importantly, economic theory tells us that auditors will weigh the likely benefits of pleasing clients against the probable cost of litigation. It is not clear, therefore, that the balance will always be on the side of litigation.

Corporate Governance Mechanisms

The adoption of good corporate governance mechanisms by a client firm can help to increase auditor independence by reducing the scope for conflict between auditors and managers. For example, employing proper compensation schemes that reduce incentives to manage earnings will reduce the incentive to compromise auditor independence. SOX has taken an important step in this direction by threatening to impose criminal charges against managers who provide misleading information to auditors.

In addition, setting in place a strong and independent audit committee overseeing the auditor nomination process can help to reduce independence problems. Following the nomination, ensuring that the external auditor can meet and communicate with the members of the audit committee directly, without manager intervention or oversight, can further lift obstacles to independence.

However, many firms are effectively controlled by powerful CEOs who select members of the board that are loyal to him

  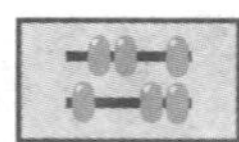      

or her. In such an environment, the threat to auditor independence may be quite significant.

Monitoring the Auditors

Auditors scrutinize their clients, but who monitors the auditors, and is it effective? Both in the United Kingdom and United States regulation now requires that auditors' work is examined by professional and independent bodies. This is done as part of an overall effort to increase independence through the threat of enforcement action. In the United Kingdom this is carried out by the Audit Inspection Unit (AIU), which is part of the Professional Oversight Board (POB; an arm of the Financial Reporting Council). In the United States the task is delegated to the Public Companies Accounting Oversight Board (PCAOB).

One of the declared aims of the AIU is to provide "monitoring of the quality of the auditing function in relation to economically significant entities."[12] The AIU tends to focus on large auditors and specific areas of concern. For example, the work plan for 2010/11 states that "The AIU will monitor and report on the quality of audits, based on the reviews of some 100 audits, of which the majority will relate to the largest audit firms, focusing on areas relating to segmental reporting, revenue recognition and fraud, and will continue to focus on going concern, fair value accounting estimates, asset impairments and compliance with ethical standards."[13]

In the United States the PCAOB replaces a peer-review function that was performed by members of the American Institute of Certified Public Accountants (AICPA). The PCAOB's mission is "to oversee the audits of public companies in order to protect the interests of investors and further the public interest in the preparation of informative, accurate and *independent* audit reports" (emphasis added).[14] The AICPA reviews were conducted by practicing auditors. The PCAOB's reviews are conducted by independent professionals. DeFond (2010) argues that this represents a trade-off between industry expertise (under the AICPA) and independence of the review process (under the PCAOB). It is not clear therefore that the PCAOB is more effective in increasing independence and, in turn, audit quality. There is not much evidence on this issue, but a recent paper by Lennox and Pittman (2010) fails to establish that the new review process is informative with respect to audit quality.

SUMMARY

Maintaining auditor independence has benefits, while violating auditor independence carries some costs. In this chapter I described these benefits and costs. I then highlighted several main threats to auditor independence. I also reviewed possible solutions and critically assessed them. The main conclusion is that, notwithstanding the adoption of some of these solutions by new regulations, many of the threats to auditor independence are still very potent.

Based on the above analysis, I would recommend the following measures that I believe can most effectively enhance auditor independence.

- Shift the auditor nomination process to a panel of members of audit committees and major shareholders. An independent audit committee should have the expertise and inside knowledge required to find a good match with the external auditor. A panel that also includes shareholders is more likely to make informed decisions that are in the interest of shareholders. In a company with a dispersed shareholding, it will make sense to ask major shareholders to participate, as their motivation is stronger.
- Increase the financial and criminal penalties for managers who sign misleading reports. SOX has already done this, but it is not a universally accepted approach. The threat of individual persecution will increase managers' incentives to cooperate with external auditors. This, in turn, would reduce conflicts and threats of dismissal.
- Require disclosure of audit and nonaudit fees as well as the identities of signing partners. Currently, this is not required everywhere. Disclosure enhances investors' ability to judge whether independence is at risk. Furthermore, disclosure should be required of the number of hours worked, and billed, by the external auditor to further help third parties to assess audit quality.
- Make fees partially contingent on whether or not published accounts are subsequently corrected. This will provide a more direct link between audit quality and pay and will reduce litigation cost at the same time. Like managerial compensation, which is often linked to performance, auditors will have stronger incentives to exert the right amount of effort and not succumb to pressure by clients.

MORE INFO

Book:

Carey, J. L. "The new pressures on the CPA." In *Symposium for Educators*. Washington, DC: Ernst & Ernst, 1967; pp. 11–22.

Articles:

Amir, Eli, Yanling Guan, and Gilad Livne. "Auditor independence and the cost of capital before and after Sarbanes–Oxley: The case of newly issued public debt." *European Accounting Review* 19:4 (2010): 633–664. Online at: dx.doi.org/10.1080/09638180903503986

Ashbaugh, Hollis, Ryan LaFond, and Brian W. Mayhew. "Do non-audit services compromise auditor independence? Further evidence." *Accounting Review* 78:3 (July 2003): 611–639. Online at: dx.doi.org/10.2308/accr.2003.78.3.611

Brandon, Duane M., Aaron D. Crabtree, and John J. Maher. "Non-audit fees, auditor independence, and bond ratings." *Auditing: A Journal of Practice and Theory* 23:2 (September 2004): 89–103. Online at: dx.doi.org/10.2308/aud.2004.23.2.89

Chung, Hyeesoo, and Sanjay Kallapur. "Client importance, non-audit services and abnormal accruals." *Accounting Review* 78:4 (October 2003): 931–955. Online at: dx.doi.org/10.2308/accr.2003.78.4.931

DeFond, Mark L. "How should the auditors be audited? Comparing the PCAOB Inspections with the AICPA Peer Reviews." *Journal of Accounting and Economics* 49:1–2 (February 2010): 104–108. Online at: dx.doi.org/10.1016/j.jacceco.2009.04.003

DeFond, Mark L., and K. R. Subramanyam. "Auditor changes and discretionary accruals." *Journal of Accounting and Economics* 25:1 (February 26, 1998): 35–67. Online at: dx.doi.org/10.1016/S0165-4101(98)00018-4

Dhaliwal, Dan S., Cristi A. Gleason, Shane Heitzman, and Kevin D. Melendrez. "Auditor fees and cost of debt." *Journal of Accounting, Auditing and Finance* 23:1 (January 2008): 1–22. Online at: dx.doi.org/10.1177/0148558X0802300103

Europa. "Fourth Directive: Annual accounts of companies with limited liability." Fourth Council Directive 78/660/EEC. July 25, 1978. Online at: tinyurl.com/896ky8x

Europa. "Seventh Directive: Consolidated accounts of companies with limited liability." Seventh Council Directive 83/349/EEC. June 13, 1983. Online at: tinyurl.com/7a2twu6

Khurana, Inder K., and K. K. Raman. "Do investors care about the auditor's economic dependence on the client?" *Contemporary Accounting Research* 23:4 (Winter 2006): 977–1016. Online at: dx.doi.org/10.1506/D171-8534-4458-K037

"Sometimes the biggest gain in productive energy will come from cleaning the cobwebs, dealing with old business, and clearing the desks—cutting loose debris that's impeding forward motion." David Allen

     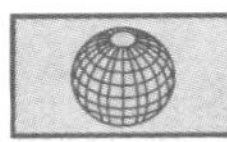   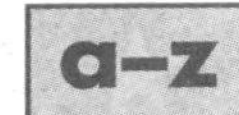

Kim, Jeon-Bon, and Cheong H. Yi. "Does auditor designation by the regulatory authority improve audit quality? Evidence from Korea." *Journal of Accounting and Public Policy* 28:3 (May–June 2009): 207–230. Online at: dx.doi.org/10.1016/j.jaccpubpol.2009.04.006

Larcker, David F., and Scott A. Richardson. "Fees paid to audit firms, accrual choices, and corporate governance." *Journal of Accounting Research* 42:3 (June 2004): 625–658. Online at: dx.doi.org/10.1111/j.1475-679X.2004.t01-1-00143.x

Lennox, Clive. "Do companies successfully engage in opinion shopping? Evidence from the UK." *Journal of Accounting and Economics* 29:3 (June 2000): 321–337. Online at: dx.doi.org/10.1016/S0165-4101(00)00025-2

Lennox, Clive, and Jeffrey Pittman. "Auditing the auditors: Evidence on the recent reforms to the external monitoring of audit firms." *Journal of Accounting and Economics* 49:1–2 (February 2010): 84–103. Online at: dx.doi.org/10.1016/j.jacceco.2009.04.002

Mayhew, Brian W., and Joel E. Pike. "Does investor selection of auditors enhance auditor independence?" *Accounting Review* 79:3 (July 2004): 797–822. Online at: dx.doi.org/10.2308/accr.2004.79.3.797

Myers, James N., Linda A. Myers, and Thomas C. Omer. "Exploring the term of the auditor–client relationship and the quality of earnings: A case for mandatory auditor rotation?" *Accounting Review* 78:3 (July 2003): 779–800. Online at: dx.doi.org/10.2308/accr.2003.78.3.779

Ruddock, Caitlin, Sarah J. Taylor, and Stephen L. Taylor. "Non-audit services and earnings conservatism: Is auditor independence impaired?" *Contemporary Accounting Research* 23:3 (Fall 2006): 701–746. Online at: dx.doi.org/10.1506/6AE8-75YW-8NVW-V8GK

Zeff, Stephen A. "How the U.S. accounting profession got where it is today: Part I." *Accounting Horizons* 17:3 (September 2003): 189–205. Online at: dx.doi.org/10.2308/acch.2003.17.3.189

Reports:

Auditing Practices Board. "Ethical standards." Online at: www.frc.org.uk/apb/publications/ethical.cfm

Websites:

Auditing Practices Board (APB; UK): www.frc.org.uk/apb

Audit Inspection Unit (AIU; UK): www.frc.org.uk/pob/audit

Professional Oversight Board (POB; UK): www.frc.org.uk/pob

Public Company Accounting Oversight Board (PCAOB; US): pcaobus.org

See Also:

★ Cultural Changes in External Auditing (pp. 327–332)

★ Optimizing Internal Audit (pp. 382–384)

✔ Independence of the Internal Audit Function (p. 1031)

NOTES

1 In the United States the audit committee and board of directors are now responsible for selecting the external auditor. Nevertheless, powerful CEOs can influence the selection process, especially when the directors are not independent.

2 In the following brief historical review of scandals in the United States I draw on Zeff (2003).

3 In the United States this requirement was first introduced by the New York Stock Exchange in 1933. Requiring that certified public accountants (CPAs) carry out the audit became statutory in the Securities Exchange Acts of 1933 and 1934, following the financial crisis in 1929–33. Interestingly, many of the firms listed on the Exchange audited their statements voluntarily (Zeff, 2003) prior to these requirements.

4 See, for example, Brandon, Crabtree, and Maher (2004); Khurana and Raman (2006); Dhaliwal *et al.* (2008).

5 This, in turn, can further reduce the cost of capital (Amir, Guan, and Livne, 2010).

6 In particular, APB Ethical Standard 1 (revised December 2010).

7 Such financial interest is disallowed in most countries. Nevertheless, from a theoretical point of view, allowing the auditor to be a shareholder in the audited firm may better align his interest with that of other shareholders. This may carry the benefit that the auditor-shareholder is incentivized to perform the audit task diligently.

8 Arguably, the restrictions in the United States are the harshest. In the United Kingdom nonaudit services are not prohibited. The UK Corporate Governance Code requires audit committees to develop the company's policy on the engagement of the external auditor to supply nonaudit services. Ethical Standard 5 of the UK Auditing Practices Board requires the external auditor to assess the extent to which the provision of nonaudit services results in conflict of interest.

9 US Securities and Exchange Commission. "Litigation release no. 17039/June 19, 2001. Accounting and auditing enforcement release no. 1410/June 19, 2001." Online at: www.sec.gov/litigation/litreleases/lr17039.htm

10 Modified from Securities and Exchange Commission. "17 CFR parts 210, 240, 249 and 274 . . . Strengthening the Commission's requirements regarding auditor independence." Modified March 27, 2003. Online at: www.sec.gov/rules/final/33-8183.htm

11 See, for example, Brandon, Crabtree, and Maher (2004) and Amir, Guan, and Livne (2010) for the link between economic bond and the cost of debt.

12 Professional Oversight Board: www.frc.org.uk/pob

13 Financial Reporting Council. "Plan 2010/11." June 2010. Online at: tinyurl.com/7x4do9r [PDF].

14 PCAOB web page "Mission, structure and history": pcaobus.org/About/History/Pages/default.aspx

     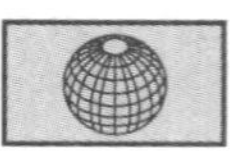   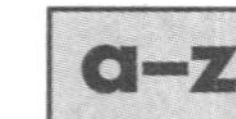

Total Quality Management and Internal Auditing by Jeffrey Ridley

EXECUTIVE SUMMARY

- The concept of total quality management (TQM) requires a total commitment by everyone in an organization to a vision of quality and continuous improvement, controlled and measured in all its practices, products, and services it provides to its customers.
- The concept of TQM requires the same commitment, controls, and measures by the suppliers of products and services to the organization.
- This vision of total quality by suppliers and to customers applies to both internal and external suppliers and customers.
- TQM is an important contributor to good corporate governance practices.
- The profession of internal auditing requires, in its code of ethics, all internal auditors to achieve high standards of quality and to implement continuous improvement in all the practices, products, and services they provide to their customers.
- Internal auditing can and should contribute to an organization's TQM policies and programs in the best practices of its independent and objective assurance, consultancy, and teaching roles.

INTRODUCTION

The 1980s and 1990s saw a worldwide increase in the teaching and implementation of quality schemes. Most of these programs focused on economics and customer satisfaction, with controlled processes, key performance indicators, and feedback mechanisms. All involved a need for continuous improvement. All required total commitment. Many evolved from existing quality control and assurance functions, and many were new, established because of regulatory, competitive, or cost pressures.

During this period "quality objectives" in business and public-sector organizations moved into all levels of direction and management decision-making. Strategic plans embraced the need for quality and customer satisfaction, *if not delight*. Directors of quality appeared on many boards. The results could be seen in a growth of quality cultures and quality system standards, fuelled by many governments and consultants. Competitive national and international quality awards were created to stimulate the development of these cultures. These awards still attract many organizations to quality self-assessment programs and external quality audits across all sectors.

TQM becomes embedded in an organization when quality programs are created by a "total commitment" to quality in all strategies, structures, and systems. Quality gurus across the world have created exciting quality principles, motivating many organizations to adopt TQM practices. These often bring significant benefits, not just for the organization, but also for its customers, suppliers, employees, and all other stakeholders. Best-practice internal auditing achieves high levels of quality in all its services and reviews quality achievements by the organization in all its planning and engagements.

CLEAR AND INSPIRING TOTAL QUALITY PRINCIPLES AND STANDARDS

The following five key quality principles underlie all TQM practices. They exist in all cutting-edge internal auditing practices. One of the most important principles is the achievement of quality and customer satisfaction with that quality across all supply chains, internal and external to the organization; this is essential for all of the principles.

1 Customer focus
   - All customers are different, but their satisfaction is paramount.
   - Focus on both internal and external customers, primary and secondary.
   - View all customers as partners in your supply chains.
   - Understand all your customers' needs.
   - Aim for customer delight at all times, not just satisfaction.
   - Ignore customer complaints at your peril.

2 Management leadership
   - Organize for quality.
   - Establish a clear and motivating vision that is understood by everyone.
   - Identify your key success factors and build these into a clear mission statement.
   - Provide the right structures, methods, and resources for quality achievement.
   - Communicate well at all levels, both in clarity and timeliness.
   - Give high visibility to your quality policy.

3 Teamwork
   - Recognize and encourage the power of teams.
   - Develop teams across the whole supply chain, internal and external.
   - Interlock all teams at operational, functional, and cross-functional levels.
   - Reinforce and reward teams for success.
   - Teach teams to focus on your vision and mission statements.
   - Delegate responsibility for action to teams.

4 Measurement
   - If it cannot be measured, it cannot be improved.
   - Measure by statistics—do not inspect.
   - Establish measures with high visibility in all processes, across all supply chains.
   - Relate all measures to your vision and mission statements.
   - Focus measures on customers, both internal and external.
   - Take prompt corrective action on all measurements.

5 Total commitment to continuous improvement
   - Look for problems, develop solutions, and train.
   - Create a learning organization with a constant commitment to improve.
   - Encourage a constant and continuous search for excellence.
   - Be creative—look for paradigm shifts.
   - Benchmark, internally and externally.
   - Verify the success of change.

Oakland (1989) describes quality chain theory (now referred to by many as supply chain theory) as a continuous chain of meeting customer requirements across processes, both external and internal to the organization:

"Throughout and beyond all organizations, whether they are manufacturing concerns, banks, retail stores, universities, or hotels, there is a series of quality chains which may be broken at any point by any one person or piece of equipment not meeting the requirements of the customer, internal or external."

An understanding of my following definition of quality in the supply chain is fundamental to the achievement of quality: "**TQM** is all the internal and external **chains of supplier, process and customer**, directed by **quality strategies** and **policies, managed**through **total commitment**to **quality principles** and **measured** by the achievement of quality

"...total commitment to quality aims and customer satisfaction in any organization (and in any internal audit activity) is essential for its success." Jeffrey Ridley, *Cutting Edge Internal Auditing* (2008)

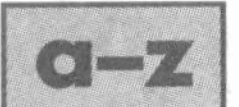

key performance indicators and **continuous improvement** to **satisfy customer needs**."

Note the emphasis on the words in **bold**.

Oakland (2001) defines quality as "simply meeting the customer requirements." But it is more than this, as explained in his book. It is about customer "satisfaction in ownership." It is about a consistency in meeting customer requirements that moves quality "to a different plane of satisfaction—delighting the customer and maintaining customer loyalty." In his thoughts on the pursuit of quality today in the global market place, he emphasizes how important this approach is:

"The complexity of today's supply chains requires a rigorous approach to quality management that integrates quality assurance, quality control and quality improvement. Quality is not just an issue for the quality department or quality management. It has a major strategic significance in delivering superior business results and enhancing shareholder value."

There can be very few internal auditors, if any, who would disagree with this statement in their pursuit of added value in the services they provide. Today, quality is still a driver of continuous improvement in products and services in many, if not all, organizations, of whatever size. The pursuit of quality is often driven by competition, but also by its association with trust and the need for long-term success—attributes that are necessary for all professional internal auditing. The framework in Figure 1 shows how TQM is embedded in an organization, from quality policy to a commitment to world-class status, across all supply chains, inside and across an organization, from suppliers (internal and external) to customers (internal and external).

Use this framework to assess your own organization's commitment to quality. It can be applied in all organizations, however small or large, and to units within organizations, including internal auditing.

ISO 9000 and TQM

There have been many debates over the years as to whether a quality system registered to ISO 9000 is TQM. Those who agree that it is usually base their opinion on the detailed requirements of ISO 9000 and supporting 1994 guidelines (9004-1). These guidelines did not form part of the registration process. However, they were advisory for the development of a quality system and clearly written in a TQM context, requiring quality systems to meet and satisfy the needs and expectations of both customer and organization:

- *The customer's needs and expectations*: For the customer, there is a need for confidence in the ability of the organization to deliver the desired quality, as well as in the consistent maintenance of that quality.
- *The organization's needs and interests*: For the organization, there is a business need to attain and to maintain the desired quality at an optimum cost; the fulfilment of this aspect is related to the planned and efficient utilization of the technological, human, and material resources available to the organization.

Those who did not agree at the time usually based their opinion on the detailed documentation required for registration of a quality system and the compliance nature of quality auditing. Many also believed that there was not sufficient focus on customer satisfaction and continuous improvement in ISO 9000 at that time, even though both were referred to in the guidelines. This debate was reflected in the revisions to ISO 9000:1994, which consolidated the family of ISO 9000 standards into four primary standards (9000, 9001, 9004, and 10011 ("Guidelines for auditing quality systems")). The introduction to the final draft of ISO 9000:2000 gave "customer needs" as the main force driving the revision. It also introduced revised guidelines ISO 9004:2000, developed to be consistent with the new ISO 9001:2000. Today, a further revised ISO 9001:2008 more clearly addresses the quality management system requirements for an organization to demonstrate its capability to meet customer requirements, and a revised ISO 9004:2009 provides a wider focus on quality management, based on eight quality management principles: customer focus, leadership, involvement of people, process approach, system approach to management, continual improvement, factual approach to decision making, and mutually beneficial supplier relationships. The ISO 9000 series of standards, with its quality principles, guidelines, and required auditing of quality

Figure 1. TQM framework: total commitment across the supply chain. (*Source*: Ridley, 2008)

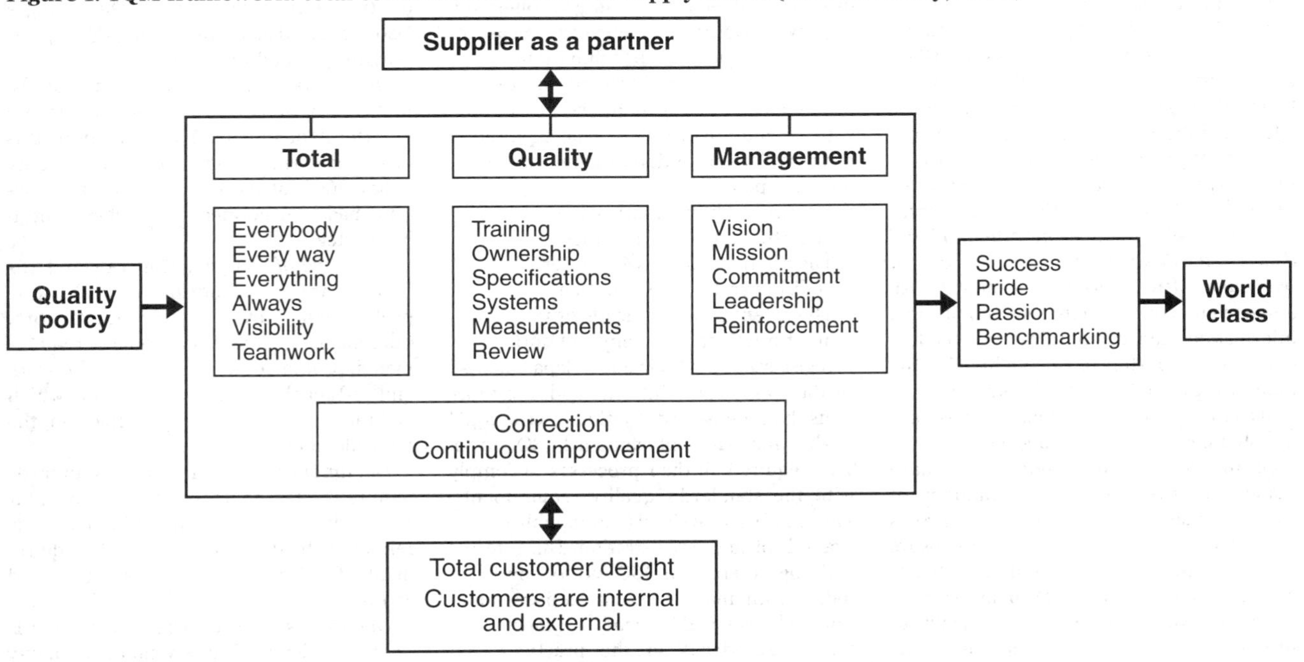

"Continuous improvement is probably the most powerful concept to guide management."
John S. Oakland, *Total Organizational Excellence* (2001)

  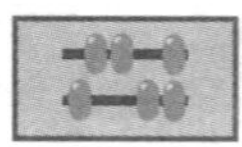   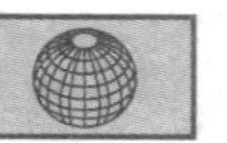   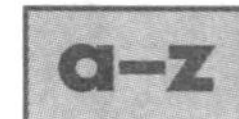

management systems, is now fully supportive of TQM.

TOTAL QUALITY IN GOVERNANCE, RISK MANAGEMENT, AND CONTROL PROCESSES

The achievement of economic success for an organization will always depend on the quality of its products and services and how well it is governed by direction and control. Bain and Band (1996) recognized that economic success is part of good governance:

"Companies and other enterprises with a professional and positive attitude to governance are stronger and have a greater record of achievement. In fact, some company directors... suggest that there is an important direct relationship between a country's corporate governance system and its economic success."

Sir Adrian Cadbury, in his foreword to Davies (1999), also links governance to effectiveness:

"The essential point is that good governance is an aid to effectiveness. It is not there to shackle enterprise, but to harness it in the achievement of its goals."

OECD (2004), in its principles of corporate governance, recognizes the importance of high standards of quality in all management practices in an organization, including flows of information, accounting, auditing, and all communications:

"V. *Disclosure and Transparency* B. Information should be prepared and disclosed in accordance with high quality standards of accounting and financial and non-financial disclosure."

The Committee of Sponsoring Organizations of the Treadway Commission (COSO) is dedicated to improving the quality of financial reporting through business ethics, effective internal controls, and corporate governance. In its latest report, *Guidance on Monitoring Internal Control Systems* (2009), it *'...presents the fundamental principles of effective monitoring and develops the linkage to the COSO integrated framework'* (the control environment, risk assessment, control activities, monitoring, information, and communication): reinforcing the importance of quality in the monitoring of all aspects of internal control:

"Over the past decade, organizations have invested heavily in improving the quality of their internal control systems. They have made the investment for a number of reasons, notably: (1) good internal control is good business—it helps organizations ensure that operating, financial and compliance objectives are met, and (2) many organizations are required to report on the quality of internal control over financial reporting, compelling them to develop specific support for their certifications and assertions."

Monitoring the quality of internal control systems as part of good governance should always include benchmarking to the TQM principles and standards mentioned earlier.

TQM IN INTERNAL AUDITING

Quality assurance in internal auditing performance has always been part of professional guidance by the Institute of Internal Auditors (IIA). In 1978, its standards for the then professional practice of internal auditing recognized the importance of this, recommending four steps to achieving quality in internal auditing work: *due professional care*, *supervision*, *internal reviews*, and *external reviews*. These will always be a fundamental part of any quality assurance framework in internal auditing, reinforced by the mandatory quality assurance and continuous improvement requirements in the IIA's current "international professional practices framework" (2011) for professional internal auditing.

The IIA and the Chartered Institute of Internal Auditors, United Kingdom and Ireland (IIA UK and Ireland) published statements on internal auditing and TQM in the early 1990s—quality assurance in internal auditing is not new. In 1993 the IIA interviewed a number of North American organizations that were using TQM to improve internal auditing processes as well as a means of contributing to the improvement of control environments, risk assessment, control activities, and monitoring. Internal auditing benefits from involvement in TQM were seen at that time to come from improved training, teamwork, measurement techniques, and benchmarking.

The IIA UK and Ireland started its professional briefing notes series in 1992 with a definition of TQM and an exploration of the following options for internal auditors to explore:

- Internal auditing appraisal of departmental TQM activities.
- The relationship between internal auditing and quality auditing.
- The extent to which heads of internal audit might seek to gain ISO 9000 registration for their audit departments.

In the 1990s some internal auditing functions had registered to the international quality management standard ISO 9000. This required all their processes to comply with the standard's quality requirements. The IIA UK and Ireland (1993) published an example of such a registration. This internal auditing interest in ISO 9000 continues today, with many internal auditing functions choosing this road to meet high quality standards in the practices and services they provide in their organizations. The IIA Research Foundation (1996) published an analysis of internal auditing registrations to ISO 9000, identifying the following reasons for registration:

Procedural
- need to update procedures;
- need to improve procedures;
- need to motivate internal auditing staff to comply with procedures;
- need for more uniform procedures.

Strategic
- requirement by an organization to pursue ISO 9000;
- requirement by an organization to demonstrate quality in services provided.

Organizational
- need to change the structure of global/national service;
- need to improve supervision;
- to improve team-building.

Marketing
- part of a program to market-test the internal auditing service in competition with other bids;
- part of a program to market internal auditing services within the organization.

The same research showed that benefits gained from registration were as listed below. These were mainly in the quality vision and mission, which required management leadership, teamwork, and good communication to mould existing internal auditing practices into compliance with ISO 9000 quality requirements. The changes also required training and writing, or rewriting, of audit procedures.

Quality policy: Like the IIA standards, ISO 9000 requires a declaration of purpose in respect of quality. For ISO 9000, this takes the form of publication of a quality policy. Each of the internal auditing functions had incorporated such a statement in its charter.

Standard of conduct: The IIA standards require internal auditors to take due professional care in their audit work. Compliance with ISO 9000 quality requirements promoted diligence in audit work and established an environment which embraced many of the principles in the IIA code of ethics.

Documentation: The IIA standards require written policies and procedures for all audit work. Such evidence was reinforced by the ISO 9000 quality requirements for controlled documentation and records.

Quality assurance: The IIA standards require evidence of supervision and quality

"The principle is that quality is about achieving sustainable results that 'delight' customers."
Chartered Institute of Internal Auditors—UK and Ireland, "Quality assurance and improvement programme" (2007)

assurance in all audit work. The ISO 9000 quality assurance and quality audit requirements provided a framework for the supervision and management of all internal auditing practices.

Mandatory quality assurance requirements are essential for all professions. In its latest statement on quality assurance and improvement programs for internal auditing, the IIA UK and Ireland (2007) states:

"Just like any other professionals, internal auditors are responsible for delivering to their customers and stakeholders a reliable service that meets their existing professional standards. To achieve this day-in and day-out, heads of internal audit should develop and maintain a Quality Assurance and Improvement Programme."

IIA UK and Ireland (2007) introduces and discusses its own quality management principles for internal auditing:

- customer (increasingly stakeholder) focus;
- leadership;
- people;
- processes and systems;
- fact-based decision-making;
- continuous or continual learning;
- partnerships, particularly with suppliers.

Compare these with the TQM principles and standards mentioned earlier.

CONTRIBUTION OF INTERNAL AUDITING TO TQM

Gupta and Ray (1995), in their research into total quality and internal auditing, also saw internal auditors as "quality champions":

"Internal auditors, by virtue of their role, are in a unique position to lead and proactively support the quality movement in their organizations. The internal auditing function does not need to be a bystander and wait to get on the quality bandwagon only when someone else in the organization sounds the quality horn. If the internal auditing function so desires there is ample opportunity to lead and support the total quality movement in an organization."

Such a championing role should never be far from any internal audit engagement—be it assurance, consulting, or teaching.

Whatever the role internal auditing follows to implement TQM principles in its own function, it is clear that the challenge of quality cannot be left out of audit planning and risk assessment in those systems and functions which it reviews in others. All internal audit engagements should:

- provide advice on all quality programs in their organization;
- link all quality policy requirements to risk management;
- benchmark TQM principles to all governance practices.

CASE STUDY

Internal Auditing in 1975, Today and Tomorrow[1]

In 1975, at my inaugural address as president of the then United Kingdom Chapter of the Institute of Internal Auditors, Inc., I said the following:

"We live in times of high economic risk and important social and business decisions. Every day we are reminded at work, in newspapers and by television of the opportunities that can be taken to develop ourselves and the profession we have chosen. The apparent insoluble problems of the present economic situation; the controversial discussions caused by exposure drafts and new accounting practices; involvement in the European Community; a new awareness of social responsibilities; higher health and safety standards; the now clearly recognised need for more efficient manpower planning and training; the urgency of energy saving; the complexity of advanced computer technology are all changes that management cannot ignore, and neither can we as internal auditors. To be successful we must be sensitive to the problems of each day. All can have an impact on our professional activities far beyond the changes we may foresee at the present time."

I have repeated this many times since as a commentary on the environment in which internal auditing operates across all sectors, both nationally and internationally. It is still a challenging statement, requiring a high level of quality in all internal auditing activities. Consider the quality needs of your customers for each of these challenges and how they are being managed. Measure the quality of your own internal auditing and how it meets these challenges. That is what TQM is all about.

MAKING IT HAPPEN

- Starting a TQM program requires an inspiring vision that will motivate everyone to a commitment to "total quality" in all processes and services which they provide.
- Define and agree what you mean by "quality" in relation to yourselves, your customers, and all your stakeholders.
- Publish a quality policy that requires continuous assurance of its implementation and effectiveness.
- Establish quality systems for all your processes.
- Respond *immediately* to customer and stakeholder complaints.
- Agree your key quality performance indicators and measure against these on a regular basis; publish the results to all your staff, customers, and stakeholders.
- Implement internal quality auditing and independent external quality assessment.
- Reward success in implementing or raising quality.
- Correct all failures so that they do not happen again.
- Aim to be *right first time*.
- Continuously improve—quality is a journey, not a destination.

MORE INFO

Books:

Bain, Neville, and David Band. *Winning Ways through Corporate Governance*. London, UK: Macmillan Business, 1996.

Davies, Adrian. *A Strategic Approach to Corporate Governance*. Aldershot, UK: Gower, 1999.

Oakland, John S. *Total Organizational Excellence: Achieving World-Class Performance*. Oxford, UK: Butterworth-Heinemann, 2001.

Oakland, John S. *Total Quality Management*. Oxford, UK: Butterworth-Heinemann, 1989.

Ridley, Jeffrey. *Cutting Edge Internal Auditing*. Chichester, UK: Wiley, 2008.

Reports:

Chartered Institute of Internal Auditors (UK and Ireland). "Total quality management: The implications for internal audit departments, PBN 1." IIA UK and Ireland, 1992.

Chartered Institute of Internal Auditors (UK and Ireland). "A quality system manual for internal auditing." IIA UK and Ireland, 1993.

Chartered Institute of Internal Auditors (UK and Ireland). "Quality assurance and improvement programme." IIA UK and Ireland, 2007. [Available to members only].

Committee of Sponsoring Organizations of the Treadway Commission (COSO). "Internal control—Integrated framework." AICPA, 1992.

"Their [internal audit] mission will be one of quality service to the organization to help management attain its goal of Total Quality Management." Institute of Internal Auditors Inc. *Internal Auditing in a Total Quality Environment: A Reference Manual* (1992)

COSO. "Guidance on monitoring internal control systems." 3 vols. AICPA, 2009.

Gupta, Parveen P., and Manash R. Ray. "Total quality improvement process and the internal auditing function." IIA Research Foundation, 1995.

Institute of Internal Auditors (IIA). "Internal auditing in a total quality environment: A reference manual." 1993.

Institute of Internal Auditors (IIA). "International Professional Practices Framework (IPPF)." 2011.

IIA UK and Ireland, *see* Chartered Institute of Internal Auditors (UK and Ireland).

International Organization for Standardization (ISO). "ISO 9000 series." Geneva: ISO, 2010.

Oakland, John S., and Mike Turner. "Global sourcing and outsourcing and the pursuit of quality: Dream or nightmare? Three ways for companies to improve." Oakland Consulting, 2008. Online at: www.oaklandconsulting.com

Organisation for Economic Co-operation and Development (OECD). "Principles of corporate governance." 2004.

Ridley, Jeffrey, and Krystyna Stephens. "International quality standards: Implications for internal auditing." IIA Research Foundation, 1996.

Websites:

Chartered Institute of Internal Auditors (UK and Ireland): www.iia.org.uk

Committee of Sponsoring Organizations of the Treadway Commission (COSO): www.coso.org

Institute of Internal Auditors (IIA): www.theiia.org

International Organization for Standardization (ISO): www.iso.org

NOTE

1 Taken from Ridley (2008).

"Someone will always be getting richer faster than you. This is not a tragedy." Charlie E. Munger

  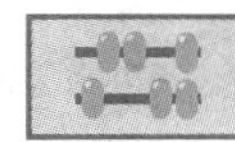   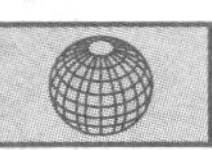   

Understanding the Requirements for Preparing IFRS Financial Statements by Véronique Weets

EXECUTIVE SUMMARY

- Financial statements made according to International Financial Reporting Standards (IFRS) have to comply with 37 standards and 26 interpretations.
- The standards are principle-based.
- An important qualitative aim of IFRS is to achieve comparability.
- Under IFRS, a complete set of financial statements comprises statements of: financial position; comprehensive income; changes in equity for the period; and cash flows. Accompanying notes should summarize significant accounting policies and provide other explanatory information.
- IFRS guidelines are primarily oriented towards the statement of financial position (formerly called the balance sheet). Those preparing financial statements should start from the definitions of the elements of the statement of financial position and the statement of comprehensive income and check whether the elements meet the recognition criteria.
- A number of different measurement bases are used to determine the monetary thresholds at which the elements of financial statements must be disclosed and appear in the statement of financial position and the statement of other comprehensive income.

INTRODUCTION

International Financial Reporting Standards (IFRS), drawn up and published by the International Accounting Standards Board (IASB), are rapidly becoming the most globally applied set of accounting standards. Approximately 9,000 public companies in the European Union had transferred to IFRS reporting as of 2005. Russia, China, Canada, Japan, Australia, and many other countries, including those in the Middle East, are adopting IFRS or have plans to converge their national standards with IFRS. There is therefore a growing need for a better understanding of these standards.

Since its inception in 1973 as the International Accounting Standards Committee, the IASB, as it became in 2001, has issued almost 3,000 pages of standards (excluding superseded ones) along with their interpretations. These treat various topics from first-time application of IFRS to property, plant and equipment, financial instruments, mineral resources, income taxes, and so on. At this moment financial statements prepared under IFRS have to comply with 38 standards and 27 interpretations. Many topics have not yet been covered, so the IASB is continuously improving the current standards and publishing new standards. The Board's current project timetable plans the publication of 16 new consultation documents and 25 final pronouncements between now and 2011. These will include two discussion papers, 14 exposure drafts, 22 final IFRS and one final guidance document. As a result, people involved with application of the standards will be obliged to invest considerable time in keeping their knowledge up to date.

BASIC PRINCIPLES

Because IFRS are a principle-based set of standards, the IASB avoids setting benchmarks to determine the appropriate accounting treatment. For example, unlike in *SFAS 13—Leases*, the US standard applying to lease arrangements, the equivalent IASB standard, *IAS 17—Leases*, sets no benchmarks to determine whether a lease is a finance lease or an operating lease. The person responsible for preparing a financial statement is thus required to use his judgment to give a faithful representation of the situation that is in accordance with the substance of the transaction and economic reality and not merely with its legal form.

Alongside that, great importance is given to the overall comparability of financial statements, both in a single period (across entities) and from period to period (within the same entity). This means that accounting policies should be applied consistently, and benchmarking within industries is encouraged. Furthermore, comparative information is required for at least the preceding accounting period. Financial statements should be prepared at least annually.

The general features of IFRS financial statements (fair representation and compliance with IFRS, along with a going-concern, accrual basis of accounting, materiality and aggregation, offsetting, frequency of reporting, the provision of comparative information, and consistency of presentation) are described in *IAS 1—Presentation of Financial Statements* (revised in 2007). The qualitative characteristics of financial statements (relevance, faithful representation, comparability, verifiability, timeliness, and understandability) are dealt with in the *Conceptual Framework for Financial Reporting* (a discussion paper to improve the framework, published in 2008).

PRESENTATION AND DISCLOSURE

The purpose of IFRS financial statements is to provide information about the reporting entity that is useful to all stakeholders of the entity. The IASB considers capital providers to be the primary users of financial statements as they provide risk capital. The IASB believes that the provision of financial statements that meet the needs of this special interest group will also meet the needs of a broad range of other users.

In order to fulfil this objective, financial statements have to provide information about an entity's assets, liabilities, equity, income and expenses (including gains and losses), contributions by and distributions to shareholders, and cash flows. Therefore a complete set of IFRS financial statements comprises:

- A statement of the financial position (formerly called the balance sheet) that presents the assets, liabilities, and equity of the entity. Although there are some minimum requirements, the entity has to use its judgment to decide on what additional items it should include depending on the nature of the business. In most cases entities will present current and non-current assets and current and non-current liabilities as separate classifications.
- A statement of comprehensive income that includes all non-owner changes in equity. Comprehensive income consists of profit or loss for the period and other comprehensive income, i.e. gains and losses that are not presented in profit or loss (for example, exchange differences on translating foreign operations, available-for-sale financial assets, cash flow hedges, gains on property revaluation, actuarial gains and losses on defined benefit pension plans, share of other comprehensive income of associates).
- A statement of changes in equity in which total comprehensive income for the period, effects of retrospective applications or restatements, and transactions with owners in their capacity as owners are presented.
- A statement of cash flows for the period, making a distinction between cash flows from operating, financing, and investing activities.

"**Before, you could look at accounting standards every 10 years, now something happens every month.**" Stig Enevoldson

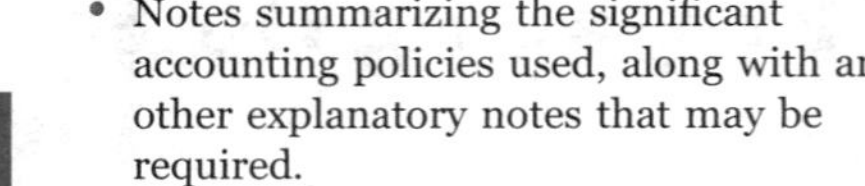

- Notes summarizing the significant accounting policies used, along with any other explanatory notes that may be required.

RECOGNITION AND MEASUREMENT

IFRS financial statements are oriented towards statement of financial position. Most of the current standards address elements that are recognized in the statement of financial position; next to that there are some standards on disclosures (segment reporting, related parties, financial instruments), and only one about the statement of other comprehensive income (IAS 18—Revenue). For most transactions those preparing statements start from the definitions and recognition criteria of items to be included in the statement of financial position and derive the elements of profit or loss from the changes in assets and liabilities.

- An asset is defined as a resource controlled by the entity as a result of past events and from which future economic benefits are expected to flow to the entity.
- A liability is a present obligation of the entity arising from past events, the settlement of which is expected to result in an outflow from the entity of resources embodying economic benefits.
- Equity is the residual interest in the assets of the entity after all its liabilities have been deducted.

Items that meet the definition of an element should be recognized if it is probable that any future economic benefit associated with the item will flow to or from the entity and the item has a cost or value that can be reliably measured.

Measurement of the elements of the statement of financial position depends on the specific guidelines for the element. Measurement methods include: historical cost, current cost, realizable (settlement) value, present value, and fair value. The newer standards often use fair value (the amount for which an asset could be exchanged, or a liability settled, between knowledgeable, willing parties in an arm's length transaction) as a basis for measurement of, for example, financial instruments, investment property, net assets of an acquiree in a business combination, and so on. But for most entities the most important part of their statement of financial position (property, plant and equipment, intangibles, inventories, receivables, trade payables, ordinary bank loans) is still measured at a value that relates to the historical cost. Often more than one measurement basis is used (for example inventories are measured at the lower of cost and net realizable value). Past entry price (cost), accumulated past entry price, allocated past entry price, amortized past price, combined past price, current exit price, value in use, future net exit price, and most likely future amount are all measurement bases used to measure the elements of an IFRS statement of financial position.

CONCLUSION

At the moment IFRS consist of 38 standards and 27 interpretations, which will be subject to significant changes in the near future. Understanding financial statements made in compliance with IFRS therefore imposes a large expenditure of effort in keeping up to date with these accounting changes.

Being principle-based and oriented towards the statement of financial position, deciding on the appropriate accounting treatment in accordance with IFRS means that preparers of such statements analyze whether elements meet the definition of an asset or a liability and then test whether the recognition criteria are met. A long list of measurement bases is currently used to determine the monetary threshold above which an element should be included in the statement of financial position.

Although the use of fair value as a measurement base has increased over the last years, for most companies it is not the most important measurement base.

In order to inform the users of financial statements about their financial position, financial performance, and changes in their financial position, entities have to prepare a statement of financial position, a statement of comprehensive income, a statement of changes in equity, and a statement of cash flows, along with notes explaining the significant accounting policies that have been used. The preparation and presentation of the financial statements is oriented towards capital providers since the IASB believes that by meeting their financial information needs, statements prepared for these users will also meet the information needs of other users, such as employees, banks, suppliers, and governments.

MAKING IT HAPPEN

Preparing IFRS financial statements requires a change in mindset toward principle-based thinking from a statement of financial position perspective. This means that the standards give clear principles for the elements that have to be recognized in the statement of financial position; changes in the value of these elements, or elements that do not meet the definition of such elements, are recognized in the statement of other comprehensive income. In addition to the need to familiarize oneself with the requirements imposed by IFRS, the preparation of high-quality financial statements in accordance with the standards requires further effort to keep up to date with modifications and new standards. The nature of the disclosures required under IFRS calls for the involvement of all departments in a company: the human resource department has to provide information about employee benefits (pensions, option plans, bonuses), engineers and technical people have to give information allowing estimation of the useful life of property, plant, and equipment, the sales department must give information on sales terms and conditions, and lawyers may be needed to provide estimations so that obligations can be measured.

In order to achieve that goal the following questions are key:

- Are key managers aware of the initial and subsequent costs and effort necessary to be fully up to date with IFRS guidelines?
- Do you have the support and commitment of other departments?
- Are changes needed in your financial reporting information systems?
- Do you have an adequate reporting pack to receive timely and correct information from associates, subsidiaries, joint ventures, etc.?
- Are you supported by valuation experts for the measurement of pensions, financial instruments, share option plans, etc.?

MORE INFO

Books:

IASCF. *International Financial Reporting Standards (IFRSs)*. London: IASCF Publications, 2009.

Alfredson, Keith, Ken Leo, Ruth Picker, Paul Praeter, Jenny Redford, and Victoria Wise. *Applying International Financial Reporting Standards*. Enhanced ed. Milton, Australia: Wiley, 2007.

Websites:

The International Accounting Standards Board (IASB) website gives access to all the IASB's standards and interpretations: www.iasb.org

Deloitte's site IAS Plus has daily updates on what is happening in the IFRS world and information on almost all IASB standards: www.iasplus.com

"The extent to which companies had to use fair value is a myth." David Cairns

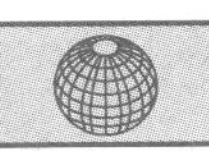

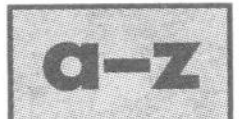

Viewpoint: Warwick Commission Highlights the Local and Political Dimensions of Global Financial Reform by Leonard Seabrooke

INTRODUCTION

Leonard Seabrooke is a professor at the International Center for Business and Politics of the Copenhagen Business School and also professor of international political economy and director of the Centre for the Study of Globalisation and Regionalisation at the University of Warwick. His publications include *The Social Sources of Financial Power* and *US Power in International Finance*, and he has coedited *Everyday Politics of the World Economy* (with John M. Hobson), *Global Standards of Market Civilization* (with Brett Bowden), and *The Politics of Housing Booms and Busts* (with Herman M. Schwartz). Professor Seabrooke is coeditor of the international journal the *Review of International Political Economy*. He was also the director of studies of the Warwick Commission on International Financial Reform.

As director of the Warwick University Centre for the Study of Globalisation and Regionalisation (CSGR), you were closely involved with the Warwick Commission on International Financial Reform. Can you tell us what effect that report has had since it was published in November 2009, and then summarize the main findings of the Commission?

The Commission and its report reflect the University of Warwick's commitment to being involved in important international policy debates. We have a particular interest in highlighting the impact that rigorous scholarly analysis can have on policy thinking. The Commission's chair was Avinash Persaud, who brought a bag of ideas and a bundle of energy to the project. The Commission comprised world-class political scientists and economists, who met at Warwick, Berlin, and Ottawa over nine months to discuss the political economy of international financial reform. I certainly feel that the argument we ended up with was very different from our opening positions—which was a sign that there was some real learning going on. Avi, I, and the commissioners are all proud of the findings published in the report and think that they highlight not only how some key problems should be addressed, but also that we have to recognize that financial systems are political—they are linked to the welfare system and the economy as a whole and are, therefore, of great political interest.

There is plenty of anecdotal evidence that the main findings of the report have found their way into mainstream thinking by regulators, politicians, and financial market practitioners. Given the nature of the report and its far-reaching conclusions, I hope that it will inform thinking long after the most acute effects of the crisis have passed. It bears fundamentally on the key question: What is a financial system for? In other words, who does it serve, and what is its purpose?

Financial markets are highly complex, and it is all too easy for well-intentioned initiatives aimed at implementing macro-prudential regulation to have unintended consequences. To quote from Lord Adair Turner's introduction to the Commission's report:

"[The Report's] focus on the credit cycle as the key driver of financial and macro-economic instability is correct and crucial, and the Report rightly identifies the danger that apparently sophisticated risk management and regulatory techniques, seeking to draw inference from observed market prices for assets and risks, can themselves generate instability of asset prices, of maturity transformation, and of credit extension."

Lord Turner (chair of the UK Financial Services Authority) goes on to praise the way that the report draws a strong distinction between macro-prudential and micro-prudential regulation. Armed with this distinction, the Commission argues that if the regulatory focus is all at the macro level it will miss the point, and that micro-prudential regulation is an equally essential part of the mix. We also argue strongly that the current focus on global regulation—understandably inspired by the desire to avoid regulatory arbitrage by financial service players (where they simply move their operations to the regulatory environment with the lightest touch)—misses the importance of local regulatory responsibilities and initiatives at the national level. The subtitle of our report is "In praise of unlevel playing fields," and this side of the argument has yet to be fully taken on board in present regulatory discussions in the European Union and the United States.

One of the big questions for regulators to decide is whether to focus on instruments or on behaviors. My view, and that of the Commission, is that the right target is behaviors.

The ratings agencies clearly had a role in the crisis. What is your opinion of how they should be treated going forward?

The power of the major ratings agencies, such as Standard & Poor's and Moody's, has not gone away since the crisis, despite the outcry against them from politicians or their conspicuous errors in classifying subprime-backed securitized products as triple A. The knee-jerk reaction from both European politicians and the European Commission was initially to threaten to extend regulatory control over the ratings agencies. Many people have discussed various solutions to how they should be regulated, including very innovative proposals from Jacques Delpla, the French economist, and others that would require strong political backing. But perhaps the moment for such change has already passed. The sovereign debt crisis has moved us in a direction that has taken the debate on a different course from talking serious regulation of the ratings agencies. European politicians and regulators are now all too aware that when it comes to eurozone economies that are not doing so well, they have no real mechanism as yet that bears on this problem other than to urge prudence on national governments.

"It is inconceivable that anyone will divulge a truly effective get-rich scheme for the price of a book. There is ample opportunity to use wealth in this world, and neither I nor my friends, nor anyone else I have ever met, has so much of it that they are interested in putting themselves at a disadvantage by sharing their secrets." Victor Niederhoffer

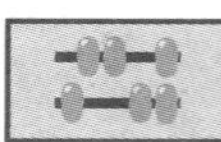

This leads to massive inefficiencies. The case of Greece gives us a very clear example. When that country's crisis was winding up, it struck me that the sums it was originally asking for to keep the vultures at bay were not vast. They were directly comparable to the US$15 billion that the three EU countries involved had put up to bail out Fortis. So on the one hand we had prompt action to rescue a failing private institution by just three members of the eurozone, while on the other we had inaction on the part of the whole European Union to bail out Greece at a time when all that the markets needed was a sign that the European Union would stand behind Greek debt.

What the incident showed very clearly was that, although the European Union is a political entity centered on Belgium, it is also an economic entity centered on Germany. When the economic and political centers of the European Union come into conflict, the economic center wins hands down. A colleague of mine on the Commission, Eleni Tsingou, who is also a research fellow at the CSGR, points out that what this highlights is a profound difference in Europe between countries that make things and those that do not. The European Union is a political project, and when things get tough the level of industry inside a country becomes extremely important. This in turn leads on to the question of what one does when it becomes clear that some of the countries within the European Union are to all intents and purposes emerging markets. In a crisis, an emerging market country would normally devalue its currency and look to export its way out of its difficulties. With the weaker EU countries that option is not available. The euro actually favors the heavily industrialized countries in general and Germany in particular, since it helps them to export. But that is achieved at the expense of countries like Greece and Spain. As a regulator trying to make sense of systemic risk, you cannot ignore macro factors like this.

You have written and spoken on Europe and Asia's involvement in the US subprime debt saga. Can you summarize your views on this?

I will start with the prime mortgage market rather than the subprime mortgage market. If you trace the money from overseas that went directly to Fannie Mae, Freddie Mac, and Ginnie Mae, the three state-sponsored entities responsible for securitizing debt in the US mortgage market, the main flows came from China and Japan. The amount of money coming from Asia into the prime securitization market in the United States can be read directly from the US Treasury funds data. These show that by June 2008 Ginnie Mae got US$369 billion from China and US$121 billion from Japan. The next biggest inflow, US$38 billion, came from Switzerland. Although we are talking about public–private hybrids here, this was in essence a state-to-state system. At the turn of the century nine-tenths of all the securitization was done by Fannie Mae and Freddie Mac, so it is not surprising that when they really starting investing in mortgage-backed securities, China and Japan thought Fannie and Freddie would be bailed out.

Another point to bear in mind is that, despite the subprime fiasco, the United States is primarily a prime mortgage market, whereas the United Kingdom and Scandinavia—if we use the same basic classifications—are really subprime mortgage markets. This is because the usual definition of subprime is that you are spending more than 34% of your post-tax income servicing your mortgage. In the United States this is high, whereas in the United Kingdom and Scandinavia it is common practice. In fact most Anglophone countries, including Ireland, are subprime in that sense.

In the United States the prime mortgage market grew very strongly through the 1990s. However, as more liquidity poured into the country and access to credit became increasingly easy, the market extended down into the subprime arena and many players began to compete aggressively for market share in what was a new space in the US mortgage market. What should have happened to counteract this is that Fannie and Freddie should have moved to properly redefine the criteria for prime lending. They did not do so. Another factor was that there was no real wage increase through this credit boom period, so the boom pushed household credit levels across the United States toward a level comparable to the norm in Anglophone countries.

In 2002 you got a real change of behavior in Fannie Mae and Freddie Mac, with a much greater willingness to concentrate on what we would consider the monied middle classes. The US Home Mortgage Disclosure Act of 1975 makes it very easy to see who is applying for loans and not getting them. This is all tied up with race politics, which is a hot topic in the United States when it comes to housing finance and legislation to address racial discrimination. It quickly became clear around 2004 that working-class African Americans and Latinos were increasingly not able to secure prime loans and had to accept subprime deals, with much heavier interest. This alone did not lead to the bust, but the structuring of securitized debts led to the panic and freeze that we saw in the financial markets in 2008.

All this does not mean that Fannie Mae and Freddie Mac should not play a role. By the end of 2008 Freddie Mac had delinquent loans (where the householder is three months or more behind with their payments) amounting to 1.8% in the prime market. Fannie Mae's equivalent delinquency level was 2.1%. However, in the subprime category delinquency rates were well above 19% for both institutions.

The interesting point here is that a regulator should conclude from this that it is impossible to get rid of Fannie and Freddie from the US housing system. Their founding charter is to bring a balance of opportunity across the races, and they are there to assist the housing sector to provide housing for ordinary Americans. Despite the crash and the huge debts of both companies, it remains a system that works. If these two institutions had recalibrated the meaning of prime debt and the growth of nonbank financial intermediaries had been curbed, the number of people forced to accept subprime loans at high interest rates would have been sharply reduced. Nor would we have seen such a wide difference in delinquency rates between prime and subprime. That in turn would have had a very beneficial knock-on effect in the financial service sector's innovations around residential mortgage-backed securities, collateralized debt obligations (CDOs), CDO squared, and so on.

Again, this speaks of micro-prudential regulatory steps that were never taken. Had they been, they would have had profound implications for the way the financial crash might have played out.

A standard part of the consensus analysis today of the financial crash is that the overready availability of cheap liquidity from abroad contributed hugely to the inflation of the US housing bubble. To what extent was this avoidable in your view?

It is very interesting to see the extent of what looks like hedge fund money coming into the subprime asset-backed securities (ABS) market from June 2008, which was very late in the development of the crisis. For example, some US$164 billion was invested in US ABS products from the Cayman Islands, one of the world's leading offshore domiciles for hedge funds. The United Kingdom was next at US$44.6 billion, though much of that was institutional investments. The Germans, Irish, and French were next at US$31 billion, US$28 billion, and US$24 billion, respectively. All this money was clearly chasing the

"Someday I want to be rich. Some people get so rich they lose all respect for humanity. That's how rich I want to be."
Rita Rudner

  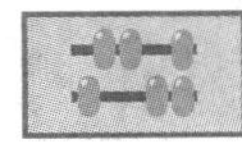      

high yields associated with subprime ABS. As we now know, those yields were illusory, but it is clear that the hot money coming into the subprime market was from Europe.

The safe money coming into the prime ABS market came from East Asia. So Europe was right in there inflating the US subprime ABS bubble, and that money was being driven, quite simply, by greed. The East Asian money was betting on the state-sponsored entities, with the assurance of a US government bailout if things went wrong. There is nothing wrong with East Asian money going into Fannie Mae and Freddie Mac. That money increases home ownership, and from the standpoint of Japan and China that is a logical long-term play. Not only do they find a home for their export-driven balance of payment surpluses, but new homeowners can be expected to go to Walmart to purchase a wide range of goods for their homes, from consumer electronics to fabrics, and that plays well for the export markets in these two countries.

Clearly, lending on housing is a very political issue in the United States. One of the groups I have studied is the National Community Reinvestment Coalition (NCRC). In January 2009 the NCRC made an official complaint against Standard and Poor's for its involvement in restructuring subprime debt on the basis of race. Their argument was that these products have had an adverse effect on African Americans and Latinos, and that the regulator had enough data available to see the damage coming. This is going to be a very interesting judgment. At the time of writing no judgment had been given, but it has the potential to be very far-reaching.

What essentially happened to regulation in the United States from the 1980s until the crash was that regulation was becoming more and more permissive, and most of the regulatory effort was focused on the banking sector via Basel I. The thrust there was the self-modeling of risk and the need to ensure that banks had enough capital to buffer them against a downturn. From the late 1990s the regulatory effort moved out to securities and, again, became much more permissive. The amount of innovation that went on was viewed as beneficial, but the innovation was clearly on a scale so large that the regulatory authorities simply lost track of what was happening.

The Warwick Commission Report laid great stress on the idea of capture, that is to say, the capture of the regulatory authorities by the sector they were supposed to be regulating. We looked in some detail at how the regulators lost their autonomy and authority, and how the market, rather than the regulator, was in the driving seat.

This phenomenon of capture carries through into the Warwick Commission's emphasis on the importance of host regulation over home regulation when it comes to regulating cross-border entities ("home" here refers to the country where the institution concerned has its headquarters). The key here is that the regulator is not distant from the market. Host regulators have a much better grasp of what is going on in their economy than a home regulator based, in some cases, on a different continent.

Going down this road also takes us into the area of considering the right size of a financial services entity. As we are now seeing from the way the banking crisis is transforming into a sovereign debt crisis, a financial system can become a threat to the sovereign entity. The Irish government, in particular, was guaranteeing a far larger volume of bank deposits than the country's GDP could cover.

Another interesting and rather neglected area which regulators are going to have to think about is the relationship between welfare systems and financial systems. I have done quite a bit of work in this area. Of course the "financialization" of the economies has extended credit to groups that previously did not have access to credit. The right-wing reaction is to blame crises on groups that have been newly included in this way, claiming that they are riskier and therefore have added more volatility to the financial system. In fact most of the volatility comes from the top end, where the instruments are made, not from the bottom end, where people are aspiring to own their home or buy a car, etc. As we have become more financialized the sensible thing to do is to have clear guidelines and regulations on access to credit. Of course those who are high risk should not be given soft loans. But it is also hard to chirp on about austerity and cut welfare during a period in which more people need it (readers really should really see Mark Blyth's view on austerity given in the references below). One of the things that the Warwick Commission Report does is to be quite blunt about the impact politics can have on financial systems, and regulators need to take cognizance of this. People with high expectations of what can be achieved through regulation also need to keep in mind the political context that shapes what the regulators can do. The next few years are going to be a very interesting demonstration of precisely these points.

MORE INFO

Books:

Abdelal, Rawi. *Capital Rules: The Construction of Global Finance*. Cambridge, MA: Harvard University Press, 2007.

Helleiner, Eric, Stefano Pagliari, and Hubert Zimmermann (eds). *Global Finance in Crisis: The Politics of International Regulatory Change*. Warwick Studies in Globalisation. Abingdon, UK: Routledge, 2010.

Seabrooke, Leonard. *The Social Sources of Financial Power: Domestic Legitimacy and International Financial Orders*. Ithaca, NY: Cornell University Press, 2006.

Sharman, J. C. *Havens in a Storm: The Struggle for Global Tax Regulation*. Ithaca, NY: Cornell University Press, 2006.

Article:

Seabrooke, Leonard, and Eleni Tsingou. "Responding to the global credit crisis: The politics of financial reform." *British Journal of Politics and International Relations* 12:2 (May 2010): 313–323. Online at: dx.doi.org/10.1111/j.1467-856X.2010.00409.x

Report:

Warwick Commission. "The Warwick Commission on international financial reform: In praise of unlevel playing fields." Coventry, UK: University of Warwick, November 2009. Online at: www2.warwick.ac.uk/research/warwickcommission

Video:

Posner, Joe (dir). *Austerity*. Watson Institute for International Studies, Brown University, September 2010. Presented by faculty fellow Mark Blyth. Online at: www.watsoninstitute.org/news_detail.cfm?id=1388

See Also:

★ Credit Ratings (pp. 478–480)

★ How Much Independence for Supervisors in Financial Market Regulation? (pp. 351–354)

★ Principles versus Rules in Financial Supervision—Is There One Superior Approach? (pp. 391–393)

★ Why Organizations Need to be Regulated—Lessons from History (pp. 437–439)

"Human beings were held accountable long before there were corporate bureaucracies. If the knight didn't deliver, the king cut off his head." Alvin Toffler

  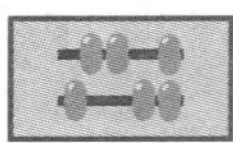   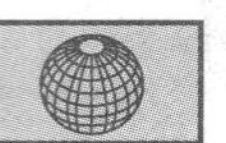   

What Are the Leading Causes of Financial Restatements? by Todd DeZoort

EXECUTIVE SUMMARY

- Financial restatements are serious corporate reporting failures that have the potential to undermine stakeholder confidence and decisions.
- The quality of corporate governance, risk management, and compliance systems is critical in controlling financial restatement risk within organizations.
- The number of financial restatements increased consistently after the Sarbanes–Oxley Act until 2007, when the number and magnitude of restatements started to decrease.
- The research literature in accounting and finance provides useful evidence about the leading causes of financial restatements, including accounting complexity, transaction complexity, human error, and fraud.
- The effects of restatements are widespread and contingent on the cause of the restatement. Possible restatement effects include negative market reactions, reduced credit access, and turnover within management and the board of directors.

INTRODUCTION

Both the International Accounting Standards Board (IASB) and the Financial Accounting Standards Board (FASB) in the United States highlight the importance of "reliability" as a primary qualitative characteristic necessary to make accounting information useful to users making economic judgments and decisions. Reliability in this context refers to a quality of financial reporting that makes it a verifiable, faithful representation of transactions and events that have occurred within an organization.[1]

Financial restatements represent reporting failures where companies admit that previous financial representations are not reliable. Such reporting failures have various potential causes and effects that can undermine company health and raise questions about the expertise and integrity of individuals that affect reporting, operations, and compliance. In the post-Sarbanes–Oxley era, financial report users (for example, investors, creditors, analysts) have seen an explosion in the number of restatements, giving rise to questions about why so many companies find it difficult to produce accurate information.

UNDERSTANDING FINANCIAL RESTATEMENT TRENDS

Companies face daunting challenges when compiling financial reports that users rely on when making economic decisions. For example, managers preparing financial reports work in highly competitive business environments where they face: complex business transactions; the need to comply with complex accounting rules, regulations, and laws; pressure to control reporting and compliance costs; and powerful incentives to report results in the best possible light. Given the diversity and magnitude of these challenges, huge emphasis has been placed on the importance of quality governance, risk assessment, and compliance (GRC) systems to help companies achieve their objectives and ensure accountability among key players in the financial reporting process.

Financial restatements must be made when financial GRC systems fail and companies file annual or quarterly reports that are not in conformity with generally accepted accounting principles (GAAP). Companies filing misstated financial statements must restate and correct previous reported results. For example, US public companies that file inaccurate reports are required to provide a formal restatement announcement in 8-K filings with the Securities and Exchange Commission (SEC).[2] Further, the SEC highlights that "the restatement process, which may take longer than 12 months, imposes significant costs on investors as well as preparers. During that process, companies often go into a 'dark period' and issue very little financial information to the public."[3] Some companies attempt to avoid alarming users by providing "stealth restatements" that are disclosed in quarterly or annual reports without formally filing an 8-K.

Although restatement numbers in the United States increased prior to 2000, the passage of the Sarbanes–Oxley Act of 2002 (SOX) prompted a dramatic increase in the number of financial statements filed each year. The Act (for example, Section 404 on internal controls) created significant focus on the quality of financial governance by management, audit committees, internal auditors, and external auditors.

Interestingly, Figure 1 indicates that the number of financial restatements in the United States dropped in 2007 for the first time since the passage of the SOX, although over 1,200 restatements were still filed. The recent decrease in number of restatements has been accompanied by recent decreases in the average number of issues per restatement and the average income effect. For example, Table 1 reveals that the average income decrease per restatement in 2005 was over $21.3 million; in 2006 the average income decrease was $17.8 million. In 2007, the average income decrease dropped to only $3.6 million.

These trends raise questions about whether financial reporting is actually improving or whether regulators are simply becoming more lenient in their approach.

CAUSES AND EFFECTS OF RESTATEMENTS

The causes of financial restatements vary considerably across cases. However, the accounting research literature (for example, Plumlee and Yohn, 2008; Scholz, 2008) and existing restatements highlight a number of potential causes of restatements, including:

Figure 1. Number of restatements in the United States 2001–07. (*Source*: Audit Analytics, 2008)

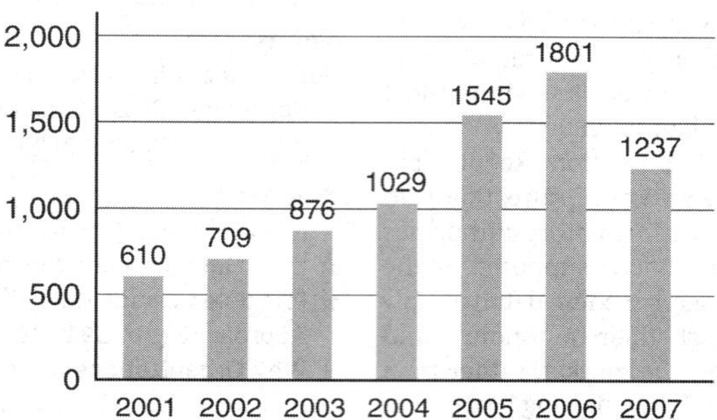

"Failure is simply the opportunity to begin again, this time more intelligently." Henry Ford

Table 1. Restatement characteristics. (*Source*: Audit Analytics, 2008)

	Average income effect	Average number of issues	Average restatement period
2005	–$21.33 million	2.41	746 days
2006	–$17.81 million	1.97	710 days
2007	–$3.64 million	1.87	643 days

- Complexity of accounting standards and/or transactions. Although there is a growing push to emphasize principles-based standards, companies in the United States still face demands related to rules from an array of authoritative bodies. GAAP involve hundreds of rules provided by IASB for most countries and FASB in the United States.
- Weak financial governance and controls. Contemporary corporate governance frameworks highlight the importance of management, the board of directors/audit committee, internal auditors, and external auditors in ensuring financial reporting reliability. Weak governance and internal controls over financial reporting increase the likelihood of financial reporting failure and restatement.
- Increased auditor and audit committee conservatism. The SOX created a number of new demands on auditors and audit committees. Increased regulation, scrutiny, and legal exposure for auditors and audit committees increase their motivation to be conservative and revisit management's judgments when evaluating financial reporting and specific accounting issues.
- Broad application of materiality. The SEC Advisory Committee on Improvements in Financial Reporting expressed concern that restatements result from overly strict materiality assessments where restatements occur to correct misstatements that investors might not find important.
- Earnings management. Management faces tremendous pressure to meet or beat expectations established by various groups (for example, analysts, directors). GAAP provide a great deal of opportunity for earnings management (for example, in areas related to depreciation, reserves, asset valuation) that is subject to abuse that can lead to restatement.
- Lack of transparency. In complex reporting environments, companies often fail to provide disclosures that are complete and understandable in compliance with GAAP. For example, footnotes that fail to provide clear, sufficient descriptions of company activities and policies undermine financial reporting reliability.
- Fraud. The largest frauds are due to financial reporting schemes where individuals intentionally misstate companies' financial statements.

Plumlee and Yohn (2008) conducted an empirical study of over 3,700 restatements during the period 2003–06, to identify the leading causes of financial restatements. They classified restatement causes as due to either a basic company error, an intentional manipulation, a transaction complexity, or some characteristic of an accounting standard. Their results revealed that over half of the restatements analyzed during the four-year period were due to "basic internal company errors" rather than to the complexity of the transaction or accounting standard.[4]

A closer look at prominent causes of restatements reveals a wide variety of accounting problems, including (but certainly not limited to) expense recognition, revenue recognition, misclassification in financial statements (for example, cash flows), executive compensation (for example, stock options), valuation of estimates (for example, liabilities, reserves), and business combinations (for example, mergers, acquisitions) and reorganizations.

While not necessarily causal, the research literature also provides evidence that highlights a variety of factors that are associated with financial restatements. Research indicates a positive link between short-term

CASE STUDY

Safety-Kleen Corporation

Safety-Kleen is a North American waste management company that issued a major financial restatement in 2001. In 2000, the company's board of directors initiated an investigation of possible accounting fraud within the company. The next year, Safety-Kleen restated (reduced) previously reported net income by $534 million for the period 1997–99.[7] The restatement issues included:

- Improper revenue recognition involving contingent contract claims, property sales, and other contingent revenue.
- Inappropriate recognition of gain on derivatives transactions. Safety-Kleen management violated GAAP by inappropriately using cash generated by derivatives transactions to increase interest income and to reduce interest and other operating expenses.
- Inappropriate capitalization and deferral of operating expenses, including capitalizing payroll expenses related to marketing and start-up activities, software development and implementation costs, and repair and maintenance expenses for company trucks.
- Inappropriate reserve and accrual accounting. Company management increased earnings by reducing certain reserve account balances without sufficient justification. It also reversed certain payroll expense accruals that had been made to account for bonuses that were paid.

In the week surrounding the announcement of Safety-Kleen's investigation, the company's stock price dropped over 70% and its auditor, PricewaterhouseCoopers, withdrew its financial statement audit reports for the previous three years. The company also saw analysts' company recommendations downgraded and its credit ratings reduced and eventually removed by some agencies. Safety-Kleen filed for Chapter 11 (reorganization) bankruptcy in 2000, and underwent a formal SEC investigation and ruling, and several class action lawsuits from external stakeholders.

MAKING IT HAPPEN

Managing the risk of financial restatements requires strong commitment to a long-term focus on financial reporting governance and internal controls. These processes should prioritize active involvement among a variety of internal and external stakeholder groups that collaborate to address key questions in the area. For example:

- Is financial restatement risk evaluated formally within the company? If so, who is involved in the risk assessment? Explicit periodic restatement risk assessment should include the audit committee, management, internal audit, and external audit.
- What are the key financial restatement risks within the company and industry? Does the organization have a plan for managing the consequences of financial restatements if they occur?
- Are cutting-edge GRC frameworks and practices being implemented around a culture of integrity and expertise to ensure that the design and operation of internal controls over financial reporting are effective?

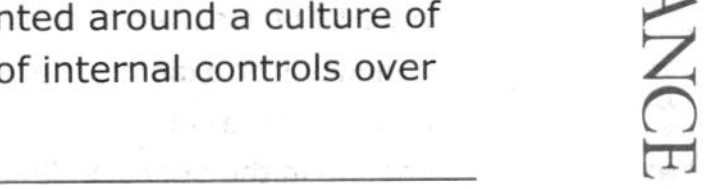

incentive compensation (for example, bonuses, stock options) for officers and audit committee members and the likelihood of restatements.[5] Such findings raise critical questions about the use and nature of incentive compensation for management and directors to motivate behavior in the interests of shareholders.

The effects of financial restatements are difficult to pinpoint precisely given the difficulty in controlling for other events (for example, company, industry) that affect companies during the period when restatements occur. However, the research literature provides some overall insights into the types of effects that restatements can have. For example, investors react negatively when their companies announce financial restatements. Studies consistently show a negative market reaction around restatement dates, although evidence suggests that the strength of the reaction depends on a variety of factors (for example, restatement cause, issue).[6] Further, market reactions appear to be less severe in the post-SOX era than they were pre-SOX, suggesting that markets have become more "comfortable" with the restatement environment.

Beyond capital market responses, restatements have the potential to affect companies' efforts to secure credit, with evidence suggesting that restatements are associated with higher interest rates and stricter borrowing terms for restating companies.[8] The research literature also links restatements (and restatement effect on income) to turnover in top management and the board of directors. For example, Srinivasan (2005) finds a positive relation between the magnitude of income-reducing annual restatements and the likelihood of independent director turnover.

CONCLUSION

Financial restatements are reporting failures that have a variety of potential causes and effects on markets, organizations, and individuals. Though the number of restatements has been declining in recent years after steady growth post-SOX, a number of events create questions about what the number and nature of restatements will look like in the future. For example, the SEC's Advisory Committee on Improvements to Financial Reporting developed recommendations to consider alternative approaches to assessing materiality to reduce the number of "unnecessary" restatements that investors do not seem to care about. Alternatively, the impending shift to International Financial Reporting Standards in the United States will likely provoke a new wave of restatements because of confusion and abuse related to the transition from the current rules-based approach to accounting and reporting using a more principles-based approach. Ultimately, stakeholders interested in minimizing financial restatement risk need to invest heavily in GRC frameworks that prioritize financial reporting reliability.

MORE INFO

Articles:

Archambeault, D. S., F. T. DeZoort, and D. R. Hermanson. "Audit committee incentive compensation and accounting." *Contemporary Accounting Research* 25:4 (2008): 965–992.

Graham, J. R., S. Li, and J. Qiu. "Corporate misreporting and bank loan contracting." *Journal of Financial Economics* 89:1 (2008): 44–61.

Srinivasan, S. "Consequences of financial reporting failure for outside directors: Evidence from accounting restatements and audit committee members." *Journal of Accounting Research* 43:2 (2005): 291–334.

Reports:

Audit Analytics. "Financial restatements: A seven year comparison." February 2008. For purchase online at: www.auditanalytics.com

Audit Analytics. "Financial restatements and market reactions." March 2008. For purchase online at: www.auditanalytics.com

Glass, Lewis & Co. "Restatements: out of sight, out of mind." May 30, 2008. Available from Glass, Lewis & Co. by subscription from: www.glasslewis.com

Government Accountability Office. "Financial restatements: Update of public company trends, market impacts, and regulatory enforcement activities." 2007. Online at: www.gao.gov/new.items/d06678.pdf

Plumlee, M., and T. L. Yohn. "An analysis of the underlying causes of restatements." Working paper, 2008. Online by search at: www.ssrn.com

Scholz, S. "The changing nature and consequences of public company financial restatements 1997–2006. Department of the Treasury, 2008. Online at: www.imanet.org/pdf/USTR.PDF

Securities and Exchange Commission. "Final report of the Advisory Committee on Improvements to Financial Reporting to the United States Securities and Exchange Commission." 2008.

See Also:

★ The Effect of SOX on Internal Control, Risk Management, and Corporate Governance Best Practice (pp. 333–335)
★ Understanding the Requirements for Preparing IFRS Financial Statements (pp. 423–424)
✔ International Financial Reporting Standards (IFRS): The Basics (p. 1039)
✔ Key Accounting Standards and Organizations (p. 1040)
✔ Sarbanes–Oxley: Its Development and Aims (p. 1052)
✔ Understanding the Key Components of GAAP: The Continuing Concern Concept (p. 1059)
Financial Accounting and Reporting (p. 1356)

NOTES

1 Financial Accounting Standards Board. FASB Concepts Statement No. 2, "Qualitative characteristics of accounting information," May 1980.

2 The SEC requires companies to file form 8-K to report the occurrence of material events and changes (for example, bankruptcy, change in control of the company, change of audit firm, change in the board of directors).

3 SEC Advisory Committee on Improvements to Financial Reporting. *Final Report of the Advisory Committee on Improvements to Financial Reporting to the United States Securities and Exchange Commission*, August 1, 2008, p. 6.

4 Plumlee, M., and T. L. Yohn. "An analysis of the underlying causes of restatements." Working paper, March 1, 2008.

5 Archambeault *et. al.* (2008).

6 Bhattacharyya, A. "Time for us to consider restatements." *Business Standard (New Delhi)* (February 25, 2008).

7 United States General Accounting Office (GAO). *Financial Statement Restatements: Trends, Market Impacts, Regulatory Responses, and Remaining Challenges*. Washington, DC: GAO, October 2002.

8 Graham *et al.* (2008).

"Risk comes from not knowing what you're doing." Warren Buffett

  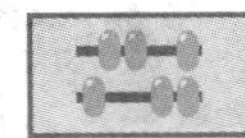      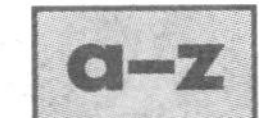

What Is the Range of the Internal Auditor's Work?

by Andrew Cox

EXECUTIVE SUMMARY

The range and type of the internal auditor's work depend on a number of factors:

- The mandate for internal audit contained in the internal audit charter.
- What the audit committee and management want internal audit to do.
- To whom the chief audit executive (head of internal audit) reports.
- The capability and skills of the internal auditors.
- Any legislative or regulatory requirements of internal audit.

But it's a bit like Forrest Gump when he said "Life is like a box of chocolates—you never know what you're gonna get." Internal auditing is a bit like that box of chocolates as the range and quality of the services are variable—and, indeed, often you really don't know what you're going to get.

INTRODUCTION

Internal auditing is an evolving profession. It has been around for a very long time, probably since the pharaohs in Egypt. But it wasn't until 1947—when the foremost professional body for internal auditing, the Institute of Internal Auditors (IIA), was formed—that internal auditing was set on its path to emerging as a profession.

Subsequently, professional standards and a code of ethics for internal auditing have been established, and in 1974 professional certification for internal auditing was created, with the designation Certified Internal Auditor. Over that time, the scope of internal auditing has changed significantly.

THE EVOLUTION OF INTERNAL AUDITING

The evolution of how internal audit determined what it would audit can be tracked in Table 1.

Nowadays, Table 2 could be the best representation.

In the future Table 3 would be more accurate.

The point is this: The range of an internal auditor's work will generally be related to where the he or she is currently placed in regard to these three evolutionary phases of the internal audit continuum. As we move into the more difficult methods of operating an internal audit function, the complexity of internal audit work increases, and the capability and skills of the internal auditor need to be greater. Many internal auditors are still in the early evolutionary phases of internal auditing, because the future is seen as too difficult and daunting.

WHAT DO THE STANDARDS SAY?

The internal auditing standards we will consider here are those issued by the Institute of Internal Auditors (IIA, 2007). The internationally accepted definition of internal auditing issued by the IIA is:

"Internal auditing is an independent, objective assurance and consulting activity designed to add value and improve an organization's operations. It helps an organization accomplish its objectives by bringing a systematic, disciplined approach to evaluate and improve the effectiveness of risk management, control, and governance processes."

This was a step up from the previous definition, which concentrated on assurance. This definition expanded the role of internal audit to encompass consulting services. To understand the difference between assurance services and consulting services, we need a couple of definitions:

Assurance: An objective examination of the evidence for the purpose of providing an independent assessment of risk management, control, or governance processes for an organization. Examples may include financial, performance, compliance, system security, and due diligence engagements.

Table 2. The evolution of internal auditing—1990s–2008

Now (1990s–2008)	Advantages	Disadvantages
Areas for internal audit identified on a functional, cross-organizational, and strategic basis—may use the organization's risk register.	Well known to internal auditors.	Can be challenging.
Discussed with senior management—additional internal audit areas may be added.	Done in consultation with the business.	Time-consuming.
Set of risk factors applied, input into a model, and prioritized based on risk rankings.	Broader scope that considers business risks.	May not be timely, relevant, or responsive.
3-year strategic internal audit plan based on risk rankings.	Facilitates integration of internal audit, risk management, and strategic planning.	
Annual internal audit plan based on available resources.		
Presented to the audit committee.	Requires strong understanding of the business.	

Table 1. The evolution of internal auditing—up to the 1990s

Then (up to the 1990s)	Advantages	Disadvantages
Areas for internal audit identified on a functional basis from historic information.	Often cyclical (every year).	Done in isolation of the business.
Set of one-dimensional risk factors applied (high, moderate, low).	Well known to internal auditors.	Time-consuming.
		Focus on functional areas.
Input into a model and prioritization based on risk rankings.	Safe approach.	
3- or 5-year strategic internal audit plan based on risk rankings.		May not be timely, relevant, or responsive.
Annual internal audit plan based on available resources.		Correlation between risk rankings and internal audit plan often weak. Assumed a static organization.
Presented to the audit committee (but not always).		

"The internal audit function needs to change from the department of 'No' to the department of 'Did you know?'"

Linda Bardo Nicholls

  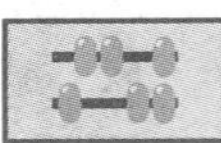   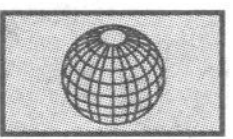   

Table 3. The evolution of internal auditing—2008 onward

Future (2008 onward)	Advantages	Disadvantages
Areas for internal audit identified on a functional, cross-organizational, and strategic basis using the organization's risk register and other relevant information.	Done in consultation with the business.	Requires strong commitment from senior management.
Develop base audit plan.	Timely, relevant, and responsive.	Requires discipline to ensure that the internal audit consultation process is effective.
Discuss with senior management, including facilitated workshops—additional audit areas may be added.	Broader scope taking into account business risks.	May not be well known to internal auditors.
Develop annual or longer-term assurance plan.	Facilitates integration of internal audit, risk management, and strategic planning.	
Develop flexible, rolling internal audit consulting plan to provide timely, relevant, and responsive services. Present to audit committee.		

Consulting: Advisory and related client service activities, the nature and scope of which are agreed with the client, and which are intended to add value and improve an organization's governance, risk management, and control processes without the internal auditor assuming management responsibility. Examples include counsel, advice, facilitation, and training.

It should be noted that the definitions of internal auditing and the standards focus on risk management, control, and governance:

Risk management: Internal audit should assist the organization by identifying and evaluating significant exposures to risk and contributing to the improvement of risk management and control systems.

Control: Internal audit should assist the organization in maintaining effective controls by evaluating their effectiveness and efficiency and by promoting continuous improvement.

Governance: Internal audit should assess and make appropriate recommendations for improving the governance process in its accomplishment of the following objectives:

- Promoting appropriate ethics and values within the organization.
- Ensuring effective organizational performance management and accountability.
- Effectively communicating risk and control information to appropriate areas of the organization.
- Effectively coordinating the activities and communicating information among the board, external and internal auditors, and management.

WHAT TYPE OF WORK?

So, what should be the range and type of work carried out by internal audit for an organization? The IIA believes that the work and methods of internal audit should encompass:

- Conducting enterprise risk assessment.
- Utilizing risk and control self-assessment.
- Using internal control processes based on COSO (Committee of Sponsoring Organizations) guidelines.
- Partnering with management.
- Integrating corporate governance into practice.
- Increasing staff performance.
- Communicating more effectively.
- Developing staff, both personally and professionally.
- Using technology to increase staff efficiency.
- Establishing an assurance function.
- Providing consulting services.
- Conducting audits in emerging areas.
- Utilizing performance measures.

This leads to the types of internal audit provided by the internal audit function, which may include some or all of the following:

Compliance audit: The review of both financial and operating controls and transactions to see how they conform with established laws, standards, regulations, and procedures.

Financial audit: The examination of the financial records and reports of a company to verify that the figures in the financial reports are relevant, accurate, and complete. The general focus is on making sure that all assets and liabilities are properly recorded on the balance sheet, and that the statement of income and expenses is correct.

Information technology (IT) audit: A review of the controls within an entity's technology infrastructure. These reviews are typically performed in conjunction with a financial statement audit, internal audit review, or other form of attestation engagement.

On-demand audit: A request for an internal audit initiated by the board, audit committee, or management in response to their particular concerns, and which has not been scheduled in the internal audit plan of work. It may also be known as a management-initiated review.

Operational audit: Sometimes called program or performance audits, these examine the use of resources to evaluate whether those resources are being used in the most efficient and effective way to fulfill an organization's objectives. An operational audit may include elements of a compliance audit, a financial audit, and an information systems audit. This term is mainly used in the private sector.

Performance audit: The independent and systematic examination of the

CASE STUDY

Designing a Comprehensive Internal Audit Plan

A large public-sector organization with a significant commitment to internal auditing provided sufficient funds to resource an internal audit function of 25,000 audit hours each year. The audit committee wanted an annual internal audit plan of work that provided assurance and examined how well the organization was operating, but which was also responsive to the changing needs and risks of the organization. The risk-based annual internal audit plan of work to achieve this designed by the chief audit executive is summarized in Table 4.

Rather than have a static annual internal audit plan, the plan shown in the table was designed to cover an 18-month period with a refresher every six months so that workflows could be smoothed and work allocated to internal auditors continuously. The plan encompassed the following areas:

- Cyclical 12 months scheduled: For high-risk areas worthy of annual internal audit attention.
- Rolling 6 months scheduled: Higher-risk areas scheduled for periodic or one-off internal audits.
- Rolling 3 months reserve: Areas held in reserve in case of postponement or cancellation of other internal audits.
- Rolling 3 months unassigned: Reserved for on-demand internal audits initiated by management for emerging business issues and risks.

"**Internal auditors should be out there winning friends and influencing people.**" David Lawler

  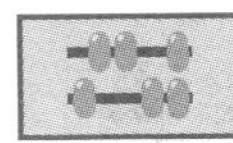      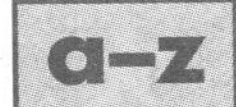

management of an organization, program, or function for the purpose of identifying whether the management is being carried out in an efficient and effective manner, and whether management practices promote improvement. This term is mainly used in the public sector, and a performance audit may be the same as or similar to an operational audit.

Quality audit: The systematic examination and evaluation of all activities related to the quality of a product or service, to determine the suitability and effectiveness of the activities to meet quality goals.

Value for money (VFM) audit: An examination of how resources are allocated and utilized. The audit is concerned with interrelated concepts of efficiency, effectiveness, economy, and organizational outcomes. VFM audits are more common in the public sector than the private sector since the profit criterion is lacking in the public sector, and they may be the same as or similar to a performance audit.

WHAT INFLUENCES THE TYPE OF WORK?

The range and type of the internal auditor's work depend on a number of factors:

The mandate for internal audit contained in the internal audit charter: This is what the audit committee and the organization want internal audit to do. Although ideally this should include both assurance services and consulting services, it is true to say that some audit committees and management believe that internal audit should not stray from its roots of providing assurance, so in some organizations the internal audit charter has focused only on the provision of assurance services. This attitude peaked following the corporate collapses of the 1990s. However, more enlightened audit committees and management of today seek a more comprehensive internal auditing service for the organization. This has the potential to add a lot of value, rather than just reporting what is wrong in compliance and financial areas.

To whom the chief audit executive reports to: The chief audit executive should report to the audit committee functionally and for operations, and to the chief executive officer for administration. Where a chief audit executive may have other reporting arrangements—for example to a chief executive officer for operations and administration, or worse, to a chief financial officer—there is a risk that internal audit may lose a measure of its independence. This has a potential to impact negatively on the range and type of work to be performed by internal audit.

The capability and skills of the internal auditors: As the work of internal audit moves toward more difficult methods of operating, the complexity of internal audit work increases. This means that the capability and skills of the internal auditor need to be greater, and many internal auditors see this as a quantum leap so great that they prefer to remain comfortable where they are.

Any legislative or regulatory requirements of internal audit: The work of internal audit will nearly always have a role to provide assurance of legislative and regulatory compliance; this is an important role that should never be forgotten.

Table 4. The chief audit executive's risk-based annual internal audit plan

Audit type	Cyclical 12 months scheduled hours	Rolling 6 months scheduled hours	Rolling 3 months reserve hours	Rolling 3 months unassigned hours	Annual total hours
Compliance	6,000	0	0	0	6,000
Assurance Consulting	0	0	0	0	
Financial	750	2,500	1,000	500	5,000
Assurance Consulting	250	0	0	0	
IT	3,000	0	0	0	6,000
Assurance Consulting	3,000	0	0	0	
Performance	0	0	0	0	5,000
Assurance Consulting	500	2,500	1,000	1,000	
Internal audit planning	500	0	0	0	500
Audit monitor and follow-up	500	0	0	0	500
Audit committee	500	0	0	0	500
External audit coordination	1,500	0	0	0	1,500
					25,000

CONCLUSION

The range and type of the internal auditor's work depend on a number of factors:

- The mandate for internal audit contained in the internal audit charter.
- What the audit committee wants internal audit to do, and how enlightened it is.
- What management wants internal audit to do.
- To whom the chief audit executive (head of internal audit) reports.
- The capability and skills of the internal auditors.
- Any legislative or regulatory requirements of internal audit.

MAKING IT HAPPEN

Chief audit executives should look to his or her audit committee and management for guidance on the range and type of work to be performed by the internal audit function. However, the chief audit executive, as an internal audit professional, should be using his or her knowledge and experience to identify and influence the formulation of a risk-based internal audit plan of work that best provides for the needs of the organization. This is likely to be a blended plan of internal audit work that encompasses both assurance services and consulting services:

Assurance Services

- Part of the overall internal audit plan of work.
- Annual or longer-term focus.
- Risk-based.
- May include cyclical internal audits of higher-risk areas.
- Need to consider legislative and regulatory requirements.
- Need to consider external audit to avoid duplication of audit effort.
- Estimated hours for audit topics assessed from previous internal audits (structured gut feel).
- Focus on compliance, financial issues and risks, financial controls, and IT reviews.

Consulting Services

- Part of the overall internal audit plan of work.
- Flexible, rolling focus—rather than fixed in time.
- Risk-based and customer-focused.
- If limited previous data are available, estimate hours needed for internal audit topics on the basis of the best available information and past experience (unstructured gut feel).
- Focus on current and emerging business issues and risks, and system under development reviews.

"Internal audit needs to have the right direction, the right people, and to be properly equipped." Bruce Turner

  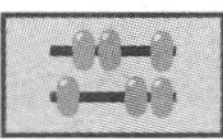      

MORE INFO

Books:

Picket, K. H. Spencer. *Audit Planning: A Risk-Based Approach*. Hoboken, NJ: Wiley, 2006.

Reding, Kurt F., Paul J. Sobel, Urton L. Anderson, Michael J. Head, *et al*. *Internal Auditing: Assurance and Consulting Services*. 2nd ed. Altamonte Springs, FL: IIA Research Foundation, 2009.

Sawyer, Lawrence B., Mortimer A. Dittenhofer, and James H. Scheiner. *Sawyer's Internal Auditing: The Practice of Modern Internal Auditing.* 5th ed. Altamonte Springs, FL: Institute of Internal Auditors, 2003.

Reports:

Australian National Audit Office. "Public sector audit committees: Having the right people is the key." Better Practice Guide. February 2005. Online at: tinyurl.com/6eezvzf [zipped PDFs].

Australian National Audit Office. "Public sector internal audit: An investment in assurance and business improvement." Better Practice Guide. September 2007. Online at: www.anao.gov.au/uploads/documents/Public_Sector_Internal_Audit.pdf

Standards:

Institute of Internal Auditors. "International standards for the professional practice of internal auditing." October 2010. Online at: www.theiia.org/guidance/standards-and-guidance/ippf/standards

Website:

Institute of Internal Auditors: www.theiia.org

See Also:

★ Has Financial Reporting Impacted on Internal Auditing Negatively? (pp. 338–341)
★ How Can Internal Audit Report Effectively to Its Stakeholders? (pp. 342–345)
★ Incorporating Operational and Performance Auditing into Compliance and Financial Auditing (pp. 365–367)
★ Managing the Relationships between Audit Committees and the CAE (pp. 375–377)
★ New Assurance Challenges Facing Chief Audit Executives (pp. 378–381)
★ Optimizing Internal Audit (pp. 382–384)
✔ The Key Components of an Audit Report (p. 1042)
✔ Understanding Internal Audits (p. 1057)

"The worker is the slave of the capitalist society, the female worker is the slave of that slave." James Connolly

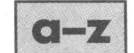

Viewpoint: Why Accounting Needs To Be More Business-Centric by Andrew Howie

INTRODUCTION

Andrew Howie is the managing partner of Grant Thornton in Scotland and has been with the firm since 2005. During his career with Grant Thornton he has worked within Assurance and now heads up the Audit practice. Andrew acts for some of the largest privately held business in Scotland and his client base covers a wide variety of sectors including property and construction, food and drink, and AIM. Since joining the firm, he's also been responsible for business development in Scotland.

A frequent criticism of the International Financial Reporting Standards (IFRS) approach to accounting standards is that it is too theoretical. What is your view?

There is no doubt that the thrust of IFRS is complicating accounting for companies and making it more complex and more detailed. For the ordinary man in the street, it is making company accounts less easy to understand. The bottom line is that it is costing businesses more money to produce accounts than it used to, and this additional spend is not necessarily generating more clarity. So why are we doing it? This question is very difficult to answer and it is one we hear a lot from clients.

For some of the large, complex businesses there are arguments that IFRS will help such businesses to achieve greater clarity in their financial reporting. There are arguments too that it will force them to provide more disclosure, which might aid the more sophisticated user of accounts. But for smaller, mid- market quoted companies it could be argued that IFRS does not really add anything to the financial statements.

Moreover, the scope and reach of IFRS are being extended. The project has now been going for some time, and when it started it was applicable only to companies listed on the main market of the London Stock Exchange. Then, in 2007, it was extended to companies listed on the Alternative Investment Market (AIM). The next proposal is to implement a more watered-down version of IFRS for all UK companies apart from the very smallest entities. This is likely to become mandatory within the next two to three years and will generate costs for businesses that in the current economic climate they will definitely not wish to bear.

What is involved for the ordinary company in moving to IFRS?

Effectively, you need to convert your accounts to IFRS as a one-off exercise. For typical businesses around the world—those which make up the vast mass of global businesses—this will simply create a cost burden. It is hard to argue that they will derive any business advantage or insights into their business from the exercise.

The one thing that can be said in favor of the global IFRS project is that if you look at it from the perspective of prospective lenders to businesses, one global set of accounting standards that everybody adheres to has to be considered a good thing. One cannot really argue against this. You want to be able to read a set of accounts without having to conduct a tedious exercise to convert from UK Generally Accepted Accounting Principles (GAAP) to US GAAP or Chinese GAAP.

The reality, though, is that any funder who is looking at investing in a company will not just look at a set of accounts. They will want to do proper due diligence on the company. They will want to understand what drives the business. There are a whole set of factors that will determine and shape the lending decision. So while one global set of standards will bring comparability between accounts and between companies in different jurisdictions, it cannot be the be all and end all for end-users, be they funders or shareholders.

Moreover, the direction taken by the standard-setting process is not going to give us one harmonious set of standards, even in the United Kingdom. Instead we are going to end up with a three-tier approach. At the very bottom we will continue to have UK GAAP for the smallest companies. Everyone in the middle will be under the watered-down version of IFRS, and the more complex and larger entities will conform to full IFRS. So, somewhat ironically, even at the end of this massive project you will not have direct comparability across all companies in the United Kingdom.

Of course, that is an impossible target anyway since you cannot compare a small company, or even a mid-market company, with a multinational bank or major oil company. Advancing on the former with principles derived from a massive theoretical exercise in accounting principles focused on the largest companies is unlikely to be particularly helpful.

Clearly some IFRS rules take one more deeply into contentious accounting theory than others. Fair-value accounting falls under this heading. What is your view?

Fair-value accounting plays a major role in IFRS. It is particularly important for financial instruments and it is a specialist topic. Two IFRS standards in particular come to mind here: IFRS 3 on acquisition accounting, and IFRS 7 on accounting for financial instruments. Without going into too much detail, IFRS 3 undoubtedly makes acquisition accounting more challenging. Under UK GAAP, if you pay £10 million for a business that you are acquiring and it has tangible assets, such as machinery and debtors, worth £4 million, then you allocate the remaining £6 million to goodwill and that is where it stays until it is amortized on an annual basis. IFRS 3 wants a great deal more analysis of that £6 million. It drives you to consider whether the £6 million is all goodwill, or whether it actually relates to other types of intangible assets, such as trademarks, brand value, and customer relationships. These things would not have been registered on the balance sheet pre-IFRS.

Now the first thing that has to be said is that this is quite a difficult exercise to achieve. Where an asset has a ready market, the price can be determined with relative ease. However, the recognition and measurement of intangible assets have always been one of the difficult areas of IFRS 3 to apply in practice. Valuation

  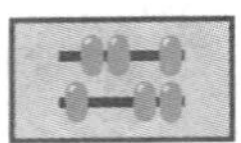      

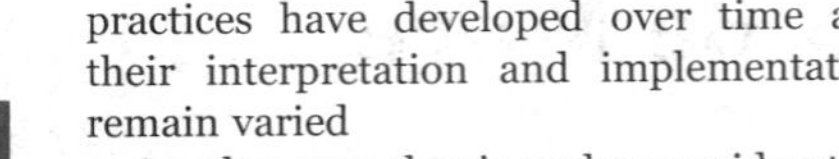

practices have developed over time and their interpretation and implementation remain varied

Another area that is under consideration at present is how companies should account for leases. There is an exposure draft out at present that is likely to be a precursor to the standard itself. This suggests that all leases should go on the balance sheet. Today, if we as a firm leased an office building, we would simply show the rental value each year through the profit and loss account. That is a simple concept and presents no conceptual problems. It costs you x to rent your building and you show x as a cost. Everyone understands that. What the exposure draft wants to happen is for the lease itself to be shown as an asset on the balance sheet, together with a liability for the totality of the lease payments for the period of the lease.

Let us say that a business takes a three-year lease on a building. How is that an asset for the business? Not many businesses would see a short-term property lease as an asset—or even a 20-year lease for that matter. Yet the thrust of IFRS is to "look through" a transaction to the philosophical substance of the transaction, and if your "look through" focuses on usage as the key factor, then whether you lease or own the building becomes irrelevant. You have the right to use it—therefore it is an asset.

However, this line of argument generates a confusion since one normally thinks of an asset as something that could, in the final analysis, be sold to realize cash. If you owned the building and the company was pressed for cash, you could do a sale and lease-back deal and realize cash that way. The building would be a real asset and could generate real cash. If you leased the building, there is the possibility that you might be able to vacate the building and "sell"—i.e. sublet the lease—but your lease may not give you that option. And yet the building is still there on your balance sheet as an "asset."

From a value investor's perspective this is an asset that they would mentally have to strip out of the accounts to get a more accurate picture of the "true" assets of the business. So this is an example of where a theoretical approach that aims to "look through" concepts to some supposed underlying reality can run into serious difficulties. What the exposure draft is recommending in effect pumps up both the assets and the liabilities on the balance sheet. This approach appears to fly in the face of what readers of accounts expect—namely, that an asset should have value. It looks certain that the exposure draft will progress through to a standard with this approach still firmly enshrined in it.

What is also interesting is that the present and upcoming generation of accounting students are all being taught under IFRS, which has simply become the way things are done. Arguably this is driving something of a wedge between the accountancy and audit professions and the business community they are there to serve. The people I speak to most about IFRS are finance directors and main board directors of companies, and they are almost unanimous in thinking that IFRS is only adding complexity to financial reporting. David Tweedie, the recently retired chair of the International Accounting Standards Board, said of IFRS 7 (on the disclosure of financial instruments) that if anyone thinks they understand IFRS 7 that simply means that they have not read it properly. That just about sums it up for me. If you are a global bank like HSBC, then perhaps a standard that goes into huge levels of complexity on how you should disclose your financial derivatives might have some relevance, but for others IFRS 7 is a sledgehammer to crack a nut.

These objections to the general thrust of the international accounting standards project are very widely felt across the business community. Do you have any belief that these objections will eventually cause a rethink of the whole project?

It is difficult to see that happening. The whole IFRS project has a particular thrust and direction that it has maintained consistently since its inception.

MORE INFO

Books:

Branson, Richard. *Screw Business as Usual*. London: Virgin, 2011.
Caan, James. *Start Your Business in 7 Days*. London: Portfolio Penguin, 2012.
Guillebeau, Chris. *The $100 Startup: Fire Your Boss, Do What You Love and Work Better to Live More*. London: Macmillan, 2012.
Patterson, Scott. *Dark Pools: High-Speed Traders, A.I. Bandits, and the Threat to the Global Financial System*. New York: Crown Business, 2012.
Wasmund, Sháá. *Stop Talking, Start Doing: A Kick in the Pants in Six Parts*. Chichester, UK: Capstone, 2011.

See Also:

★ Origins and Rationale for IFRS Convergence (pp. 385–388)
★ Viewpoint: Accounting for Value: Why the Accountancy Bodies Are Losing Their Way in the Standard-Setting Process (pp. 277–279)
✔ International Financial Reporting Standards (IFRS): The Basics (p. 1039)
Professional Services (pp. 1639–1641)

  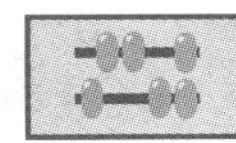   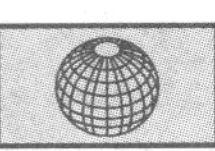   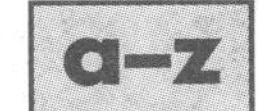

Why Organizations Need to be Regulated—Lessons from History by Bridget Hutter

EXECUTIVE SUMMARY

- Organizations both create and manage risk on a global scale, but their capacities to manage risk vary enormously.
- Since the origins of crises in organizations are well documented, anticipating risks and preparing for their control have become an essential part of risk regulation regimes.
- Regulation, which is often formulated in response to a crisis, targets the risks that organizations can pose to the stability of the macroeconomy, to fair competition, and to consumer protection.
- Typically regulation is state-based, but there has been a move to include transnational organizations.
- Regulation is about managing risk, not elimination of the underlying activities.

INTRODUCTION

As far back as the Middle Ages, history provides plenty of lessons on the effects of the failure of financial institutions, and of consumer ignorance being exploited through mis-selling. As financial products have become more complex there have been growing opportunities for the sale of inappropriate securities, pension plans, and mortgages, and of high and opaque charges for financial products and services. Arguably, regulation has become imperative today, given the increasingly transnational nature of financial markets. Another factor is the growth of large multinational organizations, now possibly more powerful than some nations. They pose particular risk and regulatory problems because they can both create and manage risks, sometimes on a global scale. Crises can have catastrophic effects nationally and internationally. Anticipating risks and organizing for their control have thus become an integral part of risk regulation regimes, which aim to influence the risk management practices of organizations. Their objectives are to make sure that organizations give high priority to risk management, to shape motives and preferences, and to influence organizations' objectives and practices accordingly.

ORGANIZATIONS AND RISKS

The capacities of financial organizations to identify and manage risks vary according to many factors. Financial organizations are often reliant on risk modeling, which itself relies on the availability of good quality data. But the past is not always a good predictor of the future (particularly where data are drawn from a period of benign economic conditions), and data may be incomplete, poorly collated, and historically limited. Moreover, staff will vary in their ability to interpret these data. Organizations need to be open to identifying new risks and understanding that circumstances and personnel change, and these may well change the risks an organization faces. Stress testing—assessing the potential impact of alternative scenarios—can usefully supplement risk modeling by introducing risks that may not be evident from past data. Organizations tend to run these stress tests by assuming that the shocks are specific to them rather than system-wide, and they find it difficult to translate the results into positive action. They may fail to recognize that specific shocks can generate contagion and other externalities. These are some of the lessons of 2007, when liquidity dried up across the financial system. Risk modeling had been undertaken in a period of economic optimism and firms overestimated their ability to identify and control the risks associated with the innovative new products they were developing.

The routines and practices of different groups and people within the organization also require consideration. For example, risk-taking may be made to seem normal, or it may be unwittingly incentivized, as in the Barings and Société Générale cases. Or organizations may deny the severity of a risk and thus inhibit their ability to deal with

CASE STUDY

UK Financial Services Legislation

The Financial Services and Markets Act 2000 brought about a major reorganization of regulation in the United Kingdom. It exemplifies many of the key reasons for regulating financial organizations. For example:

- It was a reaction to regulatory problems caused by crises that suggested an apparent inability of current regulatory regimes to cope. An underlying objective was to restore confidence to the regulatory system following a series of unrelated financial embarrassments, such as BCCI, Barings, and pension mis-selling.
- It aimed to simplify a diverse, complex, and fragmented regulatory system that had evolved piecemeal over time and was inefficient and costly. The Act amalgamated nine regulatory agencies, which employed over 2,000 staff and regulated many thousand authorized firms and registered individuals, into one organization, the Financial Services Authority.
- It responded to changes in the regulatory environment, namely a changing industry and a "global" world. Integrated regulation was seen as a response to a financial world marked by diversification, increased complexity, and new management approaches.
- Financial services are important to the economy, and the Act was designed to maintain confidence in this sector. There was a belief that supervision was essential to the competitiveness of the financial sector, both domestically and internationally.
- In addition to improving consumer protection, the new regulator was mandated to raise the financial capability of the consumer through information disclosure.

New legislation in 2013 will implement a revised institutional structure for financial services regulation in the UK:

- Again, this is a reaction to crisis.
- It is based on three-way split between the prudential regulation and supervision of banks and insurance companies; the retail and wholesale conduct of business regulation and supervision of all financial institutions; and a macro-prudential authority to identify and respond to systemic risks.
- This reflects a number of drivers, including the global regulatory shift to a much greater emphasis on system-wide financial stability.
- It also reflects domestic political considerations in re-arranging the "failed" institutional structure put in place by a previous government.

"AIG has 125,000 employees. Basically, 80 of them tanked the firm." Jeremy Siegel

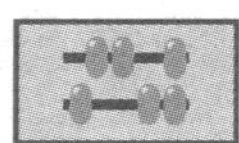

underlying problems. This is typically done by blaming individuals or part of an organization for something that is much more systemic and dangerous. Again, the Barings case is illustrative—the rogue trader was blamed and the responsibility of the organization in permitting and supporting his risky activities were initially ignored. Remuneration incentives based on short-term sales performance are an integral part of the rogue traders' stories. The 2007–09 crisis has continued to demonstrate that the excessive risk-taking such bonuses can incentivize has not led to organizations learning lessons.

The organizational origins of crises are well documented. In 1984 Charles Perrow coined the term "normal accidents" to emphasize the inevitability of something going wrong.[1] He focused on complex systems where the interaction of unexpected multiple failures can lead to catastrophe, this being most likely where the system is tightly coupled and has no slack to cope with such eventualities. Opinions differ about organizations' ability to prevent and contain risks, but most agree that large, complex, transnational organizations give rise to distinctive difficulties of risk detection, proof, responsibility, and power. This is well exemplified by the cases of AIG and UBS in 2008, where varying risk management practices in different parts of their transnational organizations led to financial crisis. One commentator remarked "AIG has 125,000 employees. Basically, 80 of them tanked the firm."[2]

RISK REGULATION

The rationales for regulating financial organizations focus on three main areas: the risk they can pose to the stability of the macroeconomy, fair competition, and consumer protection. Safeguarding the stability of the broader financial system means that concern is usually focused on risks that might arise following the failure of a financial institution. Of particular concern are the contagion effects on confidence in other financial firms, disruption to the functioning of financial markets, and the difficulties faced by customers in transferring their business to other firms. Competitive concerns focus on providing a level playing field for entry to markets and also the negative impacts that may follow for consumers. There are wider concerns about the imbalance of power arising from the asymmetry of information between firms and consumers. As a result, consumers may not have the information or understanding they need to protect themselves when choosing financial products and services. In some jurisdictions there may be a requirement to guarantee the availability of a quality product at a fair price, or even to supply a basic financial product to the entire population.

Risk regulation is often a reaction to crisis. Crises and disasters can give a major impetus to new regulations, increased supervision, and more intense monitoring, as we have seen in the wake of the Wall Street crash, the East Asian financial crisis, Barings, and the world financial crisis of 2007–09. Operating at state level, or that of business organizations, insurers, and professional bodies, regulatory reorganizations try to avoid repetition of the original incident. How suitable such reorganizations are may sometimes be questioned. There may be overcompensation and amplification of reactions that may in themselves be risky and become the source of new risks.

The classic definition of regulation views it as the use of the law to constrain and organize economic activity. The emphasis is on rules enacted by the state, backed by sanctions which are typically administrative/criminal, and are usually accompanied by the creation of administrative agencies to implement the rules. Increasingly, the concept of regulation has embraced governmental and nongovernmental sources, so financial risks and their management may involve numerous "regulatory" organizations. These include, for example, state risk regulation regimes, multinational businesses, trade organizations, and transnational regulators. Hybrid forms of regulation have emerged that involve a mix of state and corporate regulatory efforts. A notable example would be enforced self-regulation, involving a mix of state and corporate regulatory efforts. Simply put, the government lays down broad standards which companies are then expected to meet. This requires companies to develop risk management systems to secure and monitor compliance. Where compliance is not being achieved, companies are expected to have procedures in place to deal with noncompliance. Regulatory officials oversee this process. They undertake monitoring themselves and can impose public sanctions for noncompliance. An example of this is principles-based regulation, whereby a regulator sets the high-level outcomes and leaves firms (plus a potential role for trade bodies in setting codes, etc.) flexibility in how to achieve those outcomes.

It is important to understand that regulation is about the management of risk and not the elimination of the underlying activities. It tries to be enabling and to balance risk against other factors, such as costs, competitive position, and innovation. It does so in the interests of markets, firms, shareholders, and consumers, as well as national economies and the global economy. These entities may not always share common objectives. Decisions need to be made about how much uncertainty is acceptable and what levels of risk are tolerable. Making these decisions involves a complex process of risk assessment and risk management whereby risks are identified, estimated, and evaluated; decisions are then made about what to do about the risks. This process is itself fraught with many risks for both regulators and the regulated. For example, regulatory and financial organizations face the risk of either not regulating serious problems or overregulating for small risks. Organizations' risk appetites might incline state regulators to be risk-averse and businesses to be more inclined to risk-taking. At the micro level, neither may be able to identify and control risks sufficiently.

The enforcement of regulation is crucial, but the tensions and ambiguities surrounding regulation are often reflected in the sanctioning system, where most fines are smaller than the profits made by breaching the regulations, which therefore may not

MAKING IT HAPPEN

There are three main lessons here for organizations:

- The first is the importance that needs to be attached to the setting out by their boards and senior management of a clear risk policy and to making sure that this is fully embedded in the controls and culture of the organization.
- The second is the importance of taking a wider view of risk management, embracing alternative scenarios and the possibility of system-wide shocks.
- The third is taking responsibility for the risks these pose.

For the authorities, the challenges include:

- Working together effectively on a global scale.
- Introducing proportionate responses to financial crises.
- Finding a way to translate global risks into the regulation of both individual organizations and the global financial system.

"Regulation is about managing risk, not elimination of the underlying activities." Bridget Hutter

  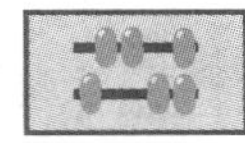      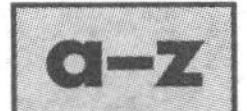

constitute a deterrent to risk-taking. The main deterrent may be the stigma attaching to being caught and sanctioned, but the evidence that these have any significant effect is contradictory.

CONCLUSION

History teaches us that organizational risk will always be present, not least because of the difficult problem of balancing risks and risk management against other organizational objectives. Organizations vary widely in their ability and willingness to manage risk, and increasingly their failures have had global impact. Traditional arguments for regulation have been reinforced by the failures of corporate governance and risk management that were brought into stark relief by the financial crisis beginning in mid-2007. These arguments include the global and interlocking nature of the financial system, the importance of recognizing the impact of system-wide shocks on individual firms, and the need for organizations to understand the risks they pose. Ideally, regulation is a cooperative effort involving the state, individual organizations, and other influential players such as insurance companies, industry associations, and consumer groups. Increasingly, this needs to involve transnational collaboration.

MORE INFO

Books:

Hutter, Bridget. *Anticipating Risks and Organising Risk Regulation*. Cambridge, UK: Cambridge University Press, 2010.

Schneiberg, Marc, and Tim Bartley. "Regulating or redesigning finance? Market architectures, normal accidents, and dilemmas of regulatory reform." In Lounsbury, Michael, and Paul M. Hirsch (eds). *Markets on Trial: The Economic Sociology of the US Financial Crisis: Part A*. Research in the Sociology of Organizations Series, Volume 30. Bingley, UK: Emerald, 2010; pp. 281–307.

Sparrow, Malcolm K. *The Character of Harms: Operational Challenges in Control.* New York: Cambridge University Press, 2008.

Taleb, Nassim Nicholas. *The Black Swan: The Impact of the Highly Improbable*. London: Penguin Books, 2008.

Article:

MacKenzie, Donald. "The credit crisis as a problem in the sociology of knowledge." *American Journal of Sociology* 116:6 (May 2011): 1778–1841.

Report:

UBS. "Shareholder report on UBS's write-downs." Zurich: UBS, April 18, 2008. Online at: www.ubs.com/1/g/investors/share_information/shareholderreport.html

Websites:

Centre for Analysis of Risk and Regulation, London School of Economics and Political Science: www.lse.ac.uk/collections/CARR

Risk Management and Decision Processes Center, Wharton School, University of Pennsylvania: grace.wharton.upenn.edu/risk

See Also:

★ How Much Independence for Supervisors in Financial Market Regulation? (pp. 351–354)
★ Identifying the Main Regulatory Challenges for Islamic Finance (pp. 358–360)
★ Rules versus Discretion in Supervisory Interventions in Financial Institutions (pp. 239–241)
✔ The EU Regulatory Regime (p. 1029)
✔ Principles of Financial Services Regulation (p. 1048)
✔ Stress Testing and Scenario Analysis for Keeping Up with Regulation (p. 1054)

NOTES

1 Perrow, Charles. *Normal Accidents: Living With High-risk Technologies*. New York: Basic Books, 1984.

2 Knowledge@Wharton. "Lesson one: What really lies behind the financial crisis?" Article discussing Professor Jeremy Siegel's ideas, January 21, 2009. Online at: knowledge.wharton.upenn.edu/article.cfm?articleid=2148

World-Class Internal Audit by Robin Pritchard

EXECUTIVE SUMMARY

- To be able to contribute and add value, internal audit must have the full backing of the board based on a sound understanding of what the service should deliver.
- There is a need for internal audit to ensure that it is in touch with the highest-profile control and risk environment within the organization and its relationship to industry and world events.
- Internal audit planning must be focused so that reporting is timely and properly directed toward critical organizational and business issues.
- To be regarded as world class, internal audit has to have the capability, skills, and confidence to influence the provision of assurance within the context of the increasing call for independent assurance from stakeholders.

THE AWARENESS DILEMMA

The world in which we live and work today has the most complex, diverse, and challenging demographics ever known to man. Not only have we developed an appetite for travel, trade, and communication across all boundaries, but the technological advancement, awareness of the dimensions of security, and the conflicts arising from political direction and change represent a demanding challenge for everyone. This encompasses both issues that are recognized as traditional risks to governance processes across all sectors of the economy and new threats that provide a constant and changing challenge to management to deliver on corporate objectives. A well-known Chinese proverb advises: "If you must play, decide on three things first: the rules of the game, the stakes, and the time to quit."

If in addition we map across this landscape the impact of the global financial crisis and the subsequent recession—which may yet in 2011 bring still further turmoil to financial markets, particularly in the eurozone—we have an environment in which world-class internal auditors can demonstrate the worth of their profession because, put simply, management cannot deal with the implications for their organization alone.

There is an increasing call for assurance that organizational expectations will be achieved, and, although this has historically reflected a financial focus, there is emerging evidence that a wider view is now much more appropriate to deal with the issues being faced by organizations. Interestingly, this voice does not come only from executive management but increasingly from stakeholders, who will, one assumes, expect nonexecutive directors to fulfil their responsibilities and provide protection of wider interests beyond share value or a balanced budget.

Clearly, there are many forms of assurance by which the board and executive management can be informed, either through the governance process or independently from external sources; however, an intrinsic aspect of the assurance framework must be a potentially enhanced role for internal audit. If organizations choose to use the independence of the internal auditor as the primary vehicle that informs the governance process, to satisfy national or global governance reporting requirements, then there is a significant challenge for internal audit to respond to the elevated transparency of an assurance agenda.

CASE STUDY: PART 1

Following a tender exercise in which providers of outsourced internal audit services were invited to provide a professional view of the need for internal audit services for the United Kingdom's National Patients Safety Agency (NPSA), KPMG was appointed on a three-year contract.

The distinguishing elements of KPMG's tender reflected a significantly better understanding of the NPSA's strategic objectives and the risks associated with the delivery of services within the anticipated agenda of cuts in public-sector expenditure following the UK general election in May 2010. The proposed plan contained a full reflection of the operational activity of the Agency, with a reduced but appropriate degree of attention to key financial controls.

Additionally, KPMG proposed a 40% reduction in the days to be committed to internal audit, a higher skill mix than other providers, a significant commitment to the contract from the partner/manager team, and a clear understanding of the *International Professional Practices Framework (IPPF)* issued by the Institute of Internal Auditors (2009).

THE DEFINITION OF INTERNAL AUDIT

The Institute of Internal Auditors (IIA) has some 170,000 members, many of whom would pledge recognition of a global standard through their own professional bodies, but the number who do so is manifestly dwarfed by those who would claim to be an internal auditor but pay no regard to standards issued by the IIA, and this would include many who hold a professional accounting qualification. It is no wonder, therefore, that organizations have vastly different views on what constitutes internal audit, let alone something that reflects a world-class standard.

The definitive guidance for the delivery of internal audit is now widely recognized to be that published by the IIA and consisting of the International Standards for the Professional Practice of Internal Auditing and the Code of Ethics, supported by other advice relating to best professional practice. A significant part of this advice supports the definition of internal audit contained in the IPPF:

"Internal auditing is an independent, objective assurance and consulting activity designed to add value and improve an organization's operations. It helps an organization accomplish its objectives by bringing a systematic, disciplined approach to evaluate and improve the effectiveness of risk management, control, and governance processes."[1]

While it is true that this is now widely regarded as a modern view of the profession, there remain two distinct issues:

- The permutations as to how to implement such a broad statement are endless, and as a result the manner in which internal audit is delivered, even by members of the professional body, varies both by organization and within an organization, resulting in the possibility that internal audit may not ask the "polite but nevertheless unwanted questions."[2]
- The extent to which the definition is recognized and adopted by the spectrum of interested people who presume to be internal auditors and by bodies involved in the provision or receipt of internal audit is unknown.

The task, therefore, of defining what world-class internal audit looks like presents a near-impossible challenge, as it reflects both the need to adopt the professional guidance and yet still satisfy the requirements of the host organization, no matter whether or not these are compatible.

As a client, the issue of assessing whether a world-class internal audit has been received by either the audit committee or the auditee is therefore probably more easily addressed in terms of recognizing

"We are responsible for actions performed in response to circumstances for which we are not responsible."
Allan Massie

what it feels like not to receive a world-class service than it is to satisfy a precise definition of what should be expected. Performance problems reflecting a lack of recognition of the client organization and its objectives, poor communication, untimely reporting, and recommendations that are detached from the risk profile or appetite of the organization are familiar indicators of poor-quality delivery. My assertion would be that there is significant tolerance of "uninspiring" internal audit between the two extremes.

Another issue that may also not help in recognizing world-class internal audit is that the guidance contained in the IPPF, its standards and the definition, is largely focused at a practitioner level, whereas the response to the issues contained in the introduction to the present article reflect the need for internal audit to engage at a strategic level, locked into the corporate objectives of the organization, mindful of the risk environment in which it operates, and confident of delivering both assurance and consultancy advice within the agenda of the board and executive team.

In this respect I would encourage the professional body and other parties to elevate the definition to a level that prescribes for the boardroom the contribution that internal audit should make in terms of supporting the governance statements in the annual report and financial accounts by drawing a specific link between a chief audit executive's annual internal audit report, the audit committee's annual report, and the governance statement.

CRITICAL COMPONENTS

I believe therefore that world-class internal audit comprises three critical components: *perception*, *people*, and *professionalism*. If all three are effectively engaged and integrated into a unified product that is recognized and understood throughout the organization, then there is a realistic chance that a service that reflects "world-class" accreditation will be received.

Perception concerns an awareness of the role that world-class internal audit should play in good governance and the responsibilities of each of the players within the governance agenda—particularly the board in complying with appropriate legislation and regulatory standards, but also executive management and all assurance providers. Underpinning this awareness is recognition of their responsibility to stakeholders for the delivery of expectations that satisfy the nature of the interest.

The *people* dimension represents a need for each of the participants to fulfil their role to the best of their ability, with particular emphasis on the internal auditor not only to deliver a world-class service on a consistent basis, but also to facilitate a better understanding of the role of internal audit in helping organizations to achieve high standards of governance and the role of internal audit within that agenda.

Professionalism is a fundamental aspect of the delivery of world-class internal audit, as it places a responsibility on the internal auditor, whether a member of the professional body itself or otherwise, to adhere to the expectations of the IPPF. The backcloth to this statement is a commitment to the full definition of internal audit and the focus of its operational scope throughout the organization. It may be beneficial for the whole profession to reflect on the fact that financial impact is for the most part a consequence of every other aspect of organizational activity and should possibly demand less attention than strategic, operational, or administrative risk features.

The combination of these three components is critical if world-class internal audit status is to be achieved. However, it is essential that we recognize that a universal model is unlikely to emerge and therefore it is for each organization to define in precise terms its expectations with regard to its understanding of the role of internal audit, the skill set, experience, and qualities it requires in terms of staffing its internal audit service, and the professionalism that it expects from it not only in terms of standards but also in terms of personal commitment to the Code of Ethics.

This may appear to be an oversimplification of the complexity of delivering a world-class internal audit service. Indeed, my personal experience would show that there are more organizations that fail to achieve such a standard than there are that approach anything like a world-class service. In reality, this may be a consequence of a lack of understanding of the role and a failure to commit sufficient resources to the service, thereby resulting in talented and career-minded individuals choosing other professions, including management consultancy—a service that is often confused quite appropriately with internal audit, given current definitions of internal audit that pursue an interest in both assurance and consultancy services.

Boards or audit committees may acquire independent and expert opinion to help them to decide on the nature of the internal audit service that would benefit them, its makeup, and the level of investment that may be required. There is value here in recalling the words of Donald Rumsfeld in 2002 concerning the "things we know we don't know,"[3] which represents the knowledge dilemma, and some assurance that internal audit is focusing on the most appropriate areas in the most effective manner is invaluable.

CASE STUDY: PART 2

One outcome of the British government's comprehensive spending review (CSR) in 2010 was the abolition of the NPSA. Its three core departments were to be dispersed to other agencies or government departments, with a combination of significant reductions in staff costs and other expenditure, as well as an emphasis for one department's future being dependent on becoming self-financing. This was all to be achieved within the current financial year.

The immediate reaction of KPMG was to propose to the NPSA's audit and risk committee (ARC) that the internal audit plan, which had been accepted in a refined form following the award of the contract, should now be restructured to focus on the new risk profile of the NPSA, the critical aspects of which were now aimed at delivery of an effective closure in line with government instructions.

The KPMG recommendations that were endorsed by the ARC retained delivery of assurance relating to key financial controls but now also provided for a "watchdog" role over adherence to the closure program and additional attention to human resources, IT, and security of information and assets. It was envisaged that this would allow the board, on the recommendation of the ARC, to deliver a clean governance statement in the annual report.

INTERNAL AUDIT REPORTING

A critical aspect of a movement to give greater status to the internal audit function would be the recognition of the meaning of two particular standards within the IPPF.

IPPF Internal Audit Standard 2050 defines the need for the chief audit executive (CAE) to take into account the sources of assurance that are available within the organization. This places a clear responsibility on the CAE to be aware of the risk profile of the organization, the significant control measures that are in place, and their vulnerabilities as well as the gaps in control that remain or are being addressed. This represents a massive agenda for the CAE, and it is therefore incumbent on the CAE to seek to rely on other forms of assurance with expertise beyond his or her own capability, while recognizing that trust must also be placed in the professionalism of each of these sources. Where there is doubt, inevitably the CAE should seek to recruit sufficient skills to provide assurance in his or her own name.

  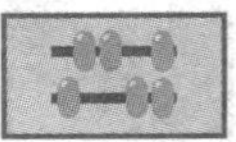      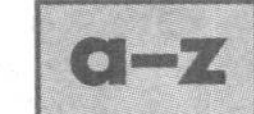

IPPF Internal Audit Standard 2060 requires the CAE to ensure that effective action is taken to report these concerns to the appropriate level, with further standards supporting the reporting of such findings outside of the organization in circumstances where the organization is not recognizing and not acting upon knowledge that will impact on the delivery of corporate objectives in a material manner. Clearly, operating in this manner places a significant strategic level of responsibility on the CAE; however, this has a direct correlation with the need to staff internal audit with competent professionals who can deliver on this world-class agenda. I believe that this would be a very pertinent development given the alignment of assurance to the needs of the stakeholder.

GOVERNANCE REPORTING

The essence of good governance lies in ensuring that the board not only sets the strategic direction for the organization, but that it also receives information that allows it to review progress toward the achievement of corporate objectives and key operational objectives. Alignment of the framework of appropriately focused internal audit reporting through the audit committee would provide independent and trusted assistance in fulfilling this role.

While recognizing the commercial sensitivities of reporting on significant risks and weaknesses, transparent reporting within governance statements is an essential aspect of satisfying stakeholder information needs.

With the knowledge provided by a CAE's report that properly reflected risk at a strategic level, it would be inappropriate for the board to fail to comment on significant weaknesses and remedial action at an appropriate time in the annual reporting cycle.

Additionally, if greater understanding of the role of internal audit were achieved through this link, wider appreciation of the benefit that can be received from internal audit would be realized. A consequence of this may even be that fewer organizations would choose to declare that the need for internal audit had been considered but the organization had chosen not to engage a service at this time, as can currently occur within governance compliance regulations. This would be even more unlikely to occur if a recognition of the availability of an off-the-shelf internal audit service, through outsourcing, was more directly advertised to board directors, and particularly to the nonexecutive directors, by the plethora of outsourced providers that now exists.

In this respect it is certainly good advice that the essential characteristics of a *curriculum vitae* for a nonexecutive member of an audit committee should include "Commonsense, diligence, [and] an attitude of constructive scepticism."[4]

It cannot be a surprise to find that—given the circumstances of each organization, the

CASE STUDY: PART 3

The ARC was concerned regarding progress against the plans for closure of NPSA by the end of the current financial year and that there were therefore emerging governance risks. This concern had arisen mostly as a result of some slippage in the receipt of instructions from the government regarding preferences and future funding.

KPMG was then requested to increase its involvement and to introduce a consultancy element to its plan with a view to providing additional business management skills to support each department to further define, finalize, and risk-assess the closure programs that would enable the board to deliver on its responsibilities, while also delivering a clean governance statement.

MAKING IT HAPPEN

There can be little argument with a statement that if the organization's board does not understand the benefits that can be derived from an effective internal audit service, it runs a risk that things can happen that are beyond its sphere of control. It is also evident that if internal audit does not understand the environment in which the organization operates, it cannot justify a claim to be contributing to the achievement of corporate objectives. Without such understanding it is equally true that recommendations to the organization for improvement are unlikely to be couched in a value-added, strategic, or operational context, and therefore any concept of partnering with senior management or the board would be difficult to demonstrate.

There are therefore a number of steps that can be taken to ensure that internal audit works for you.

- Understand what internal audit can do and promote the role positively throughout the organization.
- Define what independent assurance would be useful regarding the likelihood of achieving corporate objectives.
- Ensure that the internal audit charter supports this perception and that plans are appropriately focused on key residual risks and those areas of highest control risk.
- Invest in internal audit staff either in-house or through outsourcing or co-sourcing to ensure that internal audit has the capability to deliver assurance at the correct level.
- Ensure that internal audit, and therefore the audit committee, are supported by effective risk intelligence that provides a continuous feed of relevant information about potential threats to the achievement of objectives.
- Devise and deliver a formal structure and mechanism for communication regarding assurance that provides for a transparent review of matters that are likely to impact on the achievement of corporate objectives or result in negative opinions in governance statements.
- Periodically obtain independent professional advice on the quality of delivery of internal audit to ensure that it consistently achieves a world-class service that adds value to the organization.

It is the stakeholder agenda that should drive this momentum; the emergence of control and risk issues, necessitating additional cost and investment in recovery operations such as those arising from the BP Deepwater Horizon or Toyota incidents and subsequent stakeholder concern and litigation that have particularly manifested themselves in terms of reputational risk and loss of share value, should in all organizations raise significant assurance questions for the Board. From where can greater assurance be gained over the successful delivery of our operations? The answer must reflect strengthening the call from the board for openness regarding significant risk exposures and weaknesses, transparency in governance statements, enhancement of the role of non-executive directors and rising demand for an effective internal audit service that delivers independent assurance regarding the effectiveness of risk management, governance and control.

It is for the internal audit profession however to rise to this challenge and demonstrate its worth through the delivery of a service that is recognized as world class and which adds value, by making a significant contribution to the achievement of corporate objectives.

"The salvation of mankind lies only in making everything the concern of all." Aleksander Solzhenitsyn

interests of those responsible for its governance, and the number of professional disciplines and personal visions that proclaim to represent "internal audit"—the delivery of internal audit reflects a spectrum of varied activity. This ranges from the purely financial focus now regarded by most commentators to be traditional, historic by nature, and of limited value, to that which is best described as risk-intelligent and is able to make a positive and demonstrable contribution to the achievement of corporate and operational objectives. In this sense, it has a clear understanding of how it adds real value to the organization.

MORE INFO

Books:

Chambers, Andrew. *Tolley's Internal Auditor's Handbook*. 2nd ed. Edinburgh, UK: LexisNexis Butterworths, 2009.

Crane, Andrew, and Dirk Matten. *Business Ethics*. 3rd ed. Oxford, UK: Oxford University Press, 2010.

Institute of Internal Auditors (IIA). *International Professional Practices Framework (IPPF)*. Altamonte Springs, FL: IIA Research Foundation, 2009.

Pickett, K. H. Spencer. *The Essential Handbook of Internal Auditing*. Chichester, UK: Wiley, 2005.

Poole-Robb, Stuart, and Alan Bailey. *Risky Business: Corruption, Fraud, Terrorism and Other Threats to Global Business*. Rev. ed. London: Kogan Page, 2003.

Swanson, Dan. *Swanson on Internal Auditing: Raising the Bar*. Ely, UK: IT Governance Publishing, 2010.

Verschoor, Curtis C. *Audit Committee Essentials*. Hoboken, NJ: Wiley, 2008.

Report:

British Petroleum (BP). "Deepwater Horizon accident investigation report." September 8, 2010. Online at: tinyurl.com/36lcn49 [PDF].

Websites:

Birmingham City University Business School: www.bcu.ac.uk/audit

Institute of Internal Auditors (IIA): www.theiia.org

KPMG: www.kpmg.co.uk

Ra Business Services: www.rabizservs.co.uk

  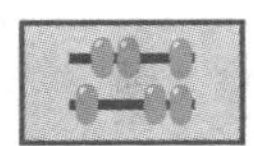      

The Ability of Ratings to Predict the Performance of Exchange-Traded Funds

by Gerasimos G. Rompotis

EXECUTIVE SUMMARY

- Rating of the past performance of securities is considered crucial by investors when they make investment decisions.
- Several rating methods are used in the financial literature and by the investing community to rate the performance of securities.
- Performance is considered to be in some way predictable, and prediction is based on past performance.
- This article empirically assesses the rating of exchange-traded funds (ETFs) and prediction of their performance.
- The methods examined are the Morningstar rating process, the excess return, the Sharpe ratio, and the Treynor ratio.
- The empirical results reveal a high consistency among the rating methods and a sufficient level of predictability of ETF performance.
- ETF performance is persistent over the short term.

INTRODUCTION

Exchange-traded funds, or ETFs, are a relatively new investment product, but they are very important for both institutional and retail investors. ETFs are hybrids of ordinary corporate stocks and open-ended mutual funds which invest in baskets of shares that closely replicate the performance and risk levels of specific broad sector and international indexes. As such, ETFs offer investors a considerable level of risk diversification with just a single transaction. The risk of investing in ETFs can be moderated by choosing non-equity investments such as corporate bonds or treasury bonds, both of which are less risky choices than the most common equity-linked ETFs. Also, fixed-income ETFs, which usually carry low risk, are available for investors along with commodity and real estate ETFs.

ETFs are cheap investment tools because their administrative costs are low. This is reflected in low expense ratios due to their passive investment character, which requires managers simply to follow the tracking indexes and not to develop complicated and high-cost investment strategies. Nevertheless, it should be borne in mind that extremely frequent trading can offset the benefits of low expense ratios. The level of ETF expense ratios varies. In particular, ETFs that track broadly diversified indexes have the lowest expenses, followed by those that track sector indexes and others which invest in international indexes. Beyond managerial costs, ETFs pay commission to brokerage companies.

ETFs provide significant trading flexibility since they offer continuous pricing and the ability to trade throughout the day, unlike most mutual funds, which are traded at the end of the day. Furthermore, ETFs offer opportunities for the implementation of both passive and active trading strategies. The most common investment strategy in ETFs is the passive buy-and-hold strategy, the return of which depends exclusively on market performance. Also, ETFs allow active intraday trading and enable investors to buy and sell, in essence, all of the securities that make up an entire market with a single trade. They therefore provide the flexibility to get into or out of a position at any time throughout the day.

Another significant element of ETFs is the potential for high tax efficiency that they offer, since they tend to generate fewer capital gains than traditional mutual funds. The tax efficiency of ETFs arises from their discrete "in kind" creation/redemption process. ETFs are created in block-sized units of 25,000, 50,000, or 100,000 shares by large investors and institutions. The creator of an ETF purchases and deposits with a trustee a portfolio of stocks that approximates the composition of a specific index. In return for this deposit, the creator receives a fixed number of ETF shares, all of which are then usually traded on a secondary exchange market. The redemption of ETFs follows the reverse direction. Buying and selling of ETF shares usually takes place among shareholders and, as a result, there is no need for the ETF to sell its assets to meet redemptions. This advantageous feature of ETFs restricts the realization of taxable capital gains.

The trading price of ETFs usually deviates from their corresponding net asset value, providing arbitrage opportunities for big investors. If the value of the underlying portfolio of stocks is greater than the ETF price, the institutional investor will redeem the low-priced units of ETF by receiving the high-priced securities. In contrast, if the value of the underlying stocks is lower than the ETF price, the investor will exchange the low-priced securities for a newly created unit of the ETF.

Finally, ETFs are characterized by large liquidity, which contributes to easy and rapid trading near their fair market value and to the narrowness of bid/ask spreads and volatility. The liquidity of an ETF is not related to its daily trading volume but rather to the liquidity of the stocks contained in the index. The high liquidity of ETFs is achieved due to the ability of market-makers, which are usually large brokerage houses, to create and redeem shares of ETFs perpetually in response to market demand.

Because of their success, ETFs have begun to attract significant interest in the finance literature. An issue that so far has not been thoroughly examined is the rating of ETF performance and the ability of ratings to predict future performance. Nevertheless, several companies provide ranking services. The most popular is Morningstar, Inc., which rates ETFs on a scale of one to five stars according to past performance. Here we provide an introduction to ETF performance rating by investigating whether ratings are indicative of future returns. We do so using a sample of 50 Barclays iShares.

PERFORMANCE RATING

Morningstar

We first rate the performance of ETFs by using the Morningstar star rating. We calculate the "Morningstar" return, which is adjusted for expenses such as management fees, 12b-1 fees (annual marketing or distribution fees charged by some mutual funds), custodian fees, and other costs that are deducted from the assets of ETFs. Then we divide average excess return by either the average excess return or the average risk-free rate. The risk-free rate is used when the average excess return is negative or lower than the average risk-free rate. Morningstar return is expressed by the following formula:

$$\text{Morningstar return} = \frac{(\text{Expense and load-adjusted return of ETF} - \text{Treasury bill})}{\max[(\text{Average sample return} - \text{Treasury bill}), \text{Treasury bill}]}$$

The risk-free return is used in the dominator of the equation in cases where the

"**ETFs might well be considered the leading financial innovation of the past Decade**" Elisabeth Hehn

     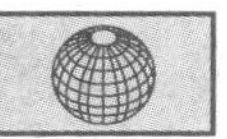   

Table 1. Consistency in performance rating

Estimated model	Alpha	t-test	Beta	t-test	R^2	F-stat
Morningstar return= $\alpha_0 + \beta$ (Excess return) + u	0.270	1.360	0.910*	15.206	0.828	231.23*
Morningstar return= $\alpha_0 + \beta$ (Sharpe ratio) + u	0.210	1.193	0.930*	17.530	0.865	307.29*
Morningstar return= $\alpha_0 + \beta$ (Treynor ratio) + u	0.240	1.279	0.920*	16.263	0.846	264.50*
Excess return= $\alpha_0 + \beta$ (Sharpe ratio) + u	0.090	0.773	0.970*	27.644	0.941	764.18*
Excess return= $\alpha_0 + \beta$ (Treynor ratio) + u	0.030	0.444	0.990*	48.621	0.980	2364.06*
Sharpe ratio= $\alpha_0 + \beta$ (Treynor ratio) + u	0.120	0.895	0.960*	23.753	0.922	564.24*

* Indicates statistical significance at the 1% level.

Table 2. Correlation coefficients between performance ratings

	Morningstar	Excess	Sharpe	Treynor
Morningstar	1.000	0.910	0.930	0.920
Excess	0.910	1.000	0.970	0.990
Sharpe	0.930	0.970	1.000	0.960
Treynor	0.920	0.990	0.960	1.000

Table 3. Regression results in predicting performance

Variables	δ_0	δ_4 (4-star)	δ_3 (3-star)	δ_2 (2-star)	δ_1 (1-star)	R^2	F-stat
Morningstar return	0.525	−0.147	−0.846	−0.913	−0.438	0.200	1.510
Excess return	0.060	−0.016	−0.032	−0.036	−0.028	0.196	2.874
Sharpe ratio	0.044	−0.006	−0.011	−0.022	−0.011	0.142	2.041
Treynor ratio	0.061	−0.018	−0.033	−0.038	−0.029	0.201	2.957

Table 4. Regression results in performance persistence

Period	Alpha	t-test	Beta	t-test	R^2	F-stat
Dependent variable: Morningstar return						
2001–02	–9.305*	–7.359	0.744*	3.447	0.198	11.883*
2002–03	0.009	0.056	0.001	0.060	0.000	0.011
2003–04	0.000	0.000	0.853**	2.141	0.217	13.318*
2004–05	–0.044	–0.115	0.065	0.207	0.226	6.699*
2005–06	–0.009	–0.051	–0.145**	–2.447	0.176	3.127**
2006–07	–0.487	–0.723	0.077	0.107	0.154	4.187**
Dependent variable: Excess return						
2001–02	–0.058*	–3.288	0.296*	3.302	0.185	10.904*
2002–03	0.103*	7.968	–0.247***	–1.956	0.168	4.636**
2003–04	–0.004	–0.257	0.538*	4.748	0.320	22.542*
2004–05	–0.009	–1.048	0.530*	2.927	0.242	15.319*
2005–06	0.059*	4.616	–0.044	–0.190	0.291	6.006*
2006–07	–0.017	–1.221	0.588*	2.940	0.153	8.645*
Dependent variable: Sharpe ratio						
2001–02	–0.034*	–6.139	0.266*	2.936	0.078	4.596**
2002–03	0.124*	13.624	0.377**	2.022	0.168	4.089**
2003–04	0.007	0.299	0.547**	2.392	0.248	15.851*
2004–05	0.005	0.524	0.280***	2.010	0.077	4.039***
2005–06	0.068*	3.317	–0.557*	–4.344	0.367	6.095*
2006–07	–0.006	–0.501	0.298***	1.867	0.068	3.486***
Dependent variable: Treynor ratio						
2001–02	–0.059*	–8.282	0.302*	3.367	0.191	11.334*
2002–03	0.108*	4.990	–0.197	–0.698	0.141	3.783**
2003–04	–0.007	–0.520	0.565*	5.222	0.362	27.274*
2004–05	–0.009	–1.045	0.529*	2.929	0.243	15.406*
2005–06	0.060*	4.526	–0.031	–0.136	0.300	6.275*
2006–07	–0.017	–1.229	0.584*	2.972	0.155	8.831*

* Statistically significant at the 1% level. **Statistically significant at the 5% level. ***Statistically significant at the 10% level.

average excess return of ETFs is negative or very low.

We then calculate "Morningstar" risk by summing up all the negative average daily excess returns of each ETF and dividing by the number of days in the assessing time period. Morningstar risk is represented by the following equation:

$$\text{Morningstar risk} = \frac{\text{Average underperformance of ETF}}{\text{Average underperformance of sample}}$$

Finally, the ETF's star rating is calculated by subtracting its Morningstar risk from its Morningstar return. Afterwards, we classify ETFs in five classes, each of which includes 10 ETFs.

Morningstar, Inc., adjusts the returns of funds for expenses such as management fees, 12b-1 fees, custodian fees, and other costs that are deducted from the assets of funds. Return is also adjusted for front-end and deferred loads. However, here we do not need to adjust for expenses and loads because we start out by calculating returns with expense-free net asset values, meaning that we can then treat ETFs as no-load funds and removing the need to adjust for loads.

Excess Return, Sharpe Ratio, and Treynor Ratio

The second performance measure we consider is the average daily excess return of ETFs, which is simply calculated by subtracting a fund's risk-free performance from its return. The third performance measure is the Sharpe ratio. Sharpe ratio is calculated by dividing the average daily excess return of ETFs by the standard deviation of daily excess returns. The last performance measure is the Treynor ratio. This is computed by dividing the average daily excess return of ETFs by their systematic risk. Systematic risk is estimated by the single index market model, where the daily excess return of each ETF is regressed on the excess return of its benchmark.

PERFORMANCE PREDICTION

We examine predictability following regression analysis, represented by the next equation:

$$P_i = \delta_0 + \delta_4 D4_i + \delta_3 D3_i + \delta_2 D2_i + \delta_1 D1_i + u$$

where P_i is the out-of-sample performance of ETFs. Performance is, successively, the Morningstar return, the excess return, the Sharpe ratio, and the Treynor ratio. The control factors of the model are four variables symbolized as D4, D3, D2, and D1, representing the ETFs that receive four, three, two, and one stars, respectively. The class of top-performing ETFs that are assigned five stars is represented by the δ_0 coefficient. This class is the reference group, and hence deltas account for the difference between the top-performing ETFs and other classes.

To estimate the model represented by this equation, we first compute all the performance measures of ETFs in a specific year between 2001 and 2006 and rank them in five classes in descending order. Then, we calculate each of the four types of performance for the subsequent period (2002–07, 2003–07, 2004–07, 2005–07, 2006–07, and 2007). The predictive ability of the model is confirmed when, first, δ estimates are negative and statistically significant and, second, when deltas become more negative as we move from δ_4 to δ_1.

It has been shown in the literature that there is a positive correlation between fund flows and persistence of performance (e.g. Wermers, 2003). Given that investors tend to put more money in mutual funds or ETFs that receive high grades from Morningstar or other agencies, we assume that this new money pushes up prices and returns and therefore that there should be a meaningful relationship between ratings and future performance.

PERFORMANCE PERSISTENCE

We examine persistence by applying simple regression analysis—specifically, cross-sectional regression of ETFs' performance in a given year on their performance in the previous year. The beta coefficient of the model is the indicator of persistence. Positive and significant betas imply persistence, and evidence of persistence strengthens as beta approaches unity. Significant negative beta values reflect inversions of ETF performance, while insignificant betas imply unsystematic variation of performance.

This study is presented in the next section.

CONCLUSION

We have investigated the ability of ETF performance ratings to predict the future performance of these funds. We ranked ETFs using the overall Morningstar star rating methodology along with three alternative performance measures: the excess return, the Sharpe ratio, and the Treynor ratio.

First, the results reveal a high level of consistency among the four types of performance measure. In other words, all assign similar ratings to ETFs without significant deviations among them. Going further, regression analysis showed that the performance of ETFs is sufficiently predictable. More specifically, the results show that the highly graded ETFs perform well through time, while low-rated ETFs deliver consistently poor performance. In addition, it was found that there is no significant difference between ETFs assigned five and four stars, respectively.

CASE STUDY

Barclays iShares

Here we will empirically examine the rating and predictability of ETF performance using a sample of 50 Barclays Global Investors iShares during the period 2001–07. Of this sample, 27 ETFs track domestic broad market or sector indexes (20 and 7 ETFs, respectively), while the other 23 ETFs track the country indexes of Morgan Stanley or other international indexes (21 and 2 ETFs, respectively).

The average estimates of the four performance measures are as follows. The average Morningstar performance is negative and equal to −0.496. The average excess return and Sharpe and Treynor ratios are 0.017, 0.013, and 0.017, respectively.

We evaluate the consistency among the ratings by applying a simple cross-sectional model. Specifically, we regress the rating of ETFs according to method *i* to the rating of ETFs according to method *j*. More specifically, we regress the rankings of ETFs (i.e. rankings 1, 2, 3, 4, and 5) and not the actual estimates derived by the Morningstar rating method on the rankings derived by excess return. We repeat the regression for all the pairs of methods used to evaluate the performance of ETFs. The measure of consistency is the beta of the model. Positive beta estimates indicate consistency among ratings. Negative or statistically insignificant betas indicate inconsistency among the ratings. Alternatively, we assess consistency by calculating the correlation coefficients among the rankings obtained using the four methods.

The results, presented in Table 1, reveal high consistency among the performance measures. All betas are positive and significant and approach unity, ranging from 0.910 for the regression between Morningstar and excess return ratings to 0.990 for the pairing of excess return and Treynor ratio. This means that the best performing ETFs receive five stars almost consistently regardless of the rating method. This is also the case for ETFs in the other four classes. Table 2 presents the correlation coefficients among the rankings given by the four methods. Correlation coefficients are all greater than 0.900 and approximate unity, confirming the high consistency among the ranking results. Overall, the results reveal that there is no best method for the rating of ETF performance, and therefore investors (could) consult various alternative methods to make their investment choices based on the available information.

The regression results for performance prediction are reported in Table 3. To begin with, the average δ_0 estimates are positive for each performance measure. Second, the average δ_4, δ_3, δ_2, and δ_1 estimates are all negative. Informationally, the majority of individual $\delta_0$in the individual regressions performed for each year of the period are positive and statistically significant, while the majority of δ_4 to δ_1 estimates are negative. Considering the significance of the δ_4 to δ_1 estimates, the results of individual regressions indicate that there is no significant difference between the ETFs included in classes 5 and 4, while there is a definite difference between the top-performing ETFs and medium and low-performing ETFs.

The results are interpreted as follows: First, the positive δ_0 estimates indicate that the top-rated ETFs display a constant behavior through time. In other words, an ETF that performs well now is likely to perform well in the future. Second, there is no significant difference in the performance of the top-rated and second-rank ETFs. Third, there is evidence that the performance of the medium- and low-rated ETFs is sufficiently predictable, the performance of both these groups being inferior to that of the highly rated ETFs.

The sufficient predictability of ETF returns on the basis of rating in a specific year or period revealed by the results indicates that institutional and retail investors should take into consideration the published ratings of ETFs when they assess their investment choices. However, investors should always bear in mind that returns are not guaranteed and markets can move both up and down. Therefore, ratings are useful but should not be the only criterion in choosing among the bulk of ETFs. Other features, such as risk and expenses, should also be taken into consideration by investors.

Regression results for performance persistence are presented in Table 4. Regarding Morningstar, beta estimates provide evidence for short-term persistence in ETF performance during the periods 2001–02 and 2003–04 but a reversal for the period 2005–06. Beta estimates for the first two periods are positive and significant, while the beta for the third mentioned period is significantly negative. Considering excess return and Treynor ratio, the results indicate short-term persistence in the periods 2001–02, 2003–04, 2004–05, and 2006–07. The excess return results indicate a reversal of performance during the period 2002–03. With respect to Sharpe ratio, the results reveal performance persistence for all the sub-periods except 2005–06, when performance reversed.

Overall, the beta estimates provide sound evidence for persistence patterns in ETF performance at the short-term level. These findings boost the results obtained for the

     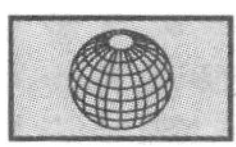   

Considering the predictive ability of each performance measure, the results show that the Treynor ratio produces the most significant results—specifically, it has better predictive ability than the other performance measures. The Morningstar rating has less predictive ability than Treynor ratio and excess return while it is essentially equivalent to Sharpe ratio. Finally, the results provide strong evidence for persistence in the performance of ETFs, at least in the short term.

predictability of ETF performance. In other words, persistence may be explained by the performance of either the top or the bottom-rated ETFs. Combining the predictability and persistence of performance, investors may find profitable opportunities by investing in ETFs.

MAKING IT HAPPEN

- ETFs provide investors with a large range of investment choices covering a variety of domestic, regional, international, and global markets. In addition, ETFs are invested in stocks, bonds, commodities, currencies, and fixed-income products.
- The assets of ETFs have shown continuous worldwide growth after their introduction on Amex in 1993.
- ETFs are preferable for both retail and institutional investors due to their trading convenience, low cost, tax efficiency, risk diversification, and portfolio transparency.
- Information on ETF profiles, management, trading processes, return, risk, holdings, and characteristics can be found from a range of sources.
- Investors should consider both the rating of an ETF's past performance and the past performance itself. However, they should bear in mind that past performance does not guarantee future returns.
- Investors should select an ETF after assessing their own investment profile and evaluating both returns and risks.

MORE INFO

Articles:

Blake, Christopher R., and Matthew R. Morey. "Morningstar ratings and mutual fund performance." *Journal of Financial and Quantitative Analysis* 35:3 (September 2000): 451–483. Online at: dx.doi.org/10.2307/2676213

Blume, Marshall E. "An anatomy of Morningstar ratings." *Financial Analysts Journal* 54:2 (March/April 1998): 19–27. Online at: dx.doi.org/10.2469/faj.v54.n2.2162

Khorana, Ajay, and Edward Nelling. "The determinants and predictive ability of mutual fund ratings." *Journal of Investing* 7:3 (Fall 1998): 61–66. Online at: dx.doi.org/10.3905/joi.1998.408470

Reports:

Sharpe, William F. "Morningstar's risk-adjusted ratings." Working paper. January 1998. Online at: www.stanford.edu/~wfsharpe/art/msrar/msrar.htm

Wermers, Russ. "Is money really 'smart'? New evidence on the relation between mutual fund flows, manager behavior, and performance persistence." Working paper. November 2003. Online at: ssrn.com/abstract=414420

Websites:

Morningstar: www.morningstar.com

NASDAQ: www.nasdaq.com

Seeking Alpha's ETF sector page: www.etfinvestor.com

See Also:

★ The Impact of Index Trackers on Shareholders and Stock Volatility (pp. 496–498)
★ Understanding the Role of Diversification (pp. 617–618)
✔ Mean–Variance Optimization: A Primer (p. 1076)
✔ Stock Markets: Their Structure and Function (p. 1091)
✔ Structured Investment Vehicles (p. 1092)
✔ Understanding Price Volatility (p. 1103)

"The indefatigable pursuit of an unattainable perfection . . . is what alone gives a meaning to our life on this unavailing star." Logan Pearsall Smith

  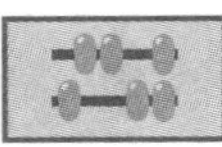      

Acquiring a Secondary Listing, or Cross-Listing by Meziane Lasfer

EXECUTIVE SUMMARY

- Over the last three decades an increasing number of companies have sourced their equity capital in foreign countries by listing their stock abroad.
- This strategy of parallel listing on both domestic and foreign stock exchanges, referred to as "cross-listing," is used by companies from both developed and emerging markets.
- In 2008, for example, 121 companies from BRIC countries (Brazil (7), Russia (24), India (24), and China (66)) were listed on the London Stock Exchange Alternative Investment Market (LSE-AIM), an equivalent to NASDAQ in the United States.
- Although the major stock markets for cross-listing are in the United States (NYSE and NASDAQ) and London (LSE and LSE-AIM), with a 43% market share in 2007, firms are also likely to cross-list in other markets of the world, such as the Singapore, Euronext, Hong Kong, and Mexico stock exchanges.
- According to the Bank of New York Mellon, during the first half of 2008 more than $2.4 trillion of depository receipts (DRs) traded on US and non-US markets and exchanges, up 85% from the previous year.

INTRODUCTION

Cross-listing is controversial and raises a number of academic and practitioner questions, particularly: Why and how does a firm cross-list, and does cross-listing create additional value for existing stockholders? The purpose of this article is to discuss the institutional framework of cross-listing, the classification of depository receipts (DRs), the types of DR available in the United States, the reasons why companies list abroad (by contrasting the advantages and disadvantages of raising equity capital in foreign markets), and the cross-listing process.

INSTITUTIONAL BACKGROUND

Companies cross-list by issuing depository receipts. These are certificates that are first issued by the company to a bank in a foreign country, which in turn issues the certificates to investors in that country. Indirectly, DRs represent ownership of home market shares in the overseas corporation. The underlying shares remain in custody in the home country, and DRs effectively convey ownership of those shares. DRs are quoted and normally pay dividends in the foreign country's currency (for example, US dollars or euros). DRs can be established either for existing shares that are already trading, or as part of a global offering of new shares. Each DR normally represents some multiple of the underlying share. This multiple allows the DR to possess a price per share that is appropriate for the foreign market, and the arbitrage normally keeps foreign and local prices of any given share the same after adjustment for transfer costs. DRs can be exchanged for the underlying foreign shares, and vice versa.

CLASSIFICATIONS OF DEPOSITORY RECEIPTS

There are a number of classifications of depository receipts, two of which are:

- Trading location: Global depositary receipts (GDRs) are certificates traded outside the United States; American depositary receipts (ADRs) are certificates traded in the United States and denominated in US dollars.
- Sponsorship: A sponsored ADR is created at the request of a foreign firm that wants its shares to be traded in the United States. In this case, the firm applies to the Securities and Exchange Commission (SEC) and to a US bank for registration and issuance. In contrast, an unsponsored ADR occurs when a US security firm initiates the creation of an ADR. Such an ADR would be unsponsored, but the SEC still requires all new ADRs to be approved by the firm itself.

TYPES OF LISTING

In the United States there are four types of depositary receipt: Levels 1 and 2 apply to cases where the DR is created using existing equity; Levels 3 and 4 apply to cases where new equity is issued, such as an initial public offering (IPO).

Level 1 is the least costly, as the DRs are traded over the counter in the United States, in the pink sheet market. There is little additional disclosure requirement, apart from the translation of the home country's financial statements into English. On average, about 56% of the approximately 1,500 DR programs are classified as Level 1.

Level 2 is relatively more costly. The DRs are traded on the NYSE, NASDAQ, and AMEX exchanges, with greater cost as the initial fee can exceed US$1 million. A cross-listed firm must also reconcile to US GAAP, report quarterly, and meet the listing requirements of the US exchange on which it trades.

Level 3 is similar to Level 2 for existing quoted companies, except that it applies to IPOs; the firm raises new equity capital in a public offering and trades on the NYSE, NASDAQ, or AMEX. A company must meet full SEC disclosure requirements, comply with US GAAP, report quarterly, and meet the listing requirements of the exchange.

Level 4, now referred to as 144A, applies to firms that raise new equity capital through a private placement. The securities are not registered for sale to the public; rather, investors follow a buy and hold strategy. Firms that use this method are exempt from disclosure requirements of a new equity issue in the United States, such as the SEC disclosure and the US GAAP. In April 1990 the SEC approved Rule 144A, which permits qualified institutional buyers to trade privately placed securities without SEC registration. These securities are traded on a screen-based automated trading system known as PORTAL, established to create a liquid secondary market for those private placements.

In other countries, the requirements depend mainly on the type of markets in which the company is going to be cross-listed. For example, requirements to list on the London Stock Exchange Official List are more extensive than those for the Alternative Investment Market.

The choice between listing in the United States (ADR) and in other markets through GDR depends on a number of factors. In particular, companies are likely to prefer listing in the United States through ADRs only if their objective has a powerful appeal to US retail investors and they are able to cover the significant cost of Sarbanes–Oxley compliance and major exposure to liability for management and board of directors. ADRs are also useful if they can benefit by selling new shares at a premium. Cross-listing through GDR may be cheaper and quicker, and could achieve the same purpose with fewer downsides. For example, cross-listing in the London Stock Exchange involves two main rounds, where the firm receives comments from the UK Listing Authority (UKLA) in about two weeks. Furthermore, since July 2005, the UKLA no longer requires 25% of GDR issues to be distributed to European investors.

"There has long prevailed a conventional wisdom rationalizing why firms pursue overseas listings." Karolyi, 2006

As an alternative to depository receipts, companies can have "Euroequity public issue." Under this method, instead of listing a share on the home market and then cross-listing, shares are issued simultaneously in multiple markets. The term Euroequity has nothing to do with Europe per se. Euroequity public issue simply refers to equity issues that are sold globally. Often these are used for very large equity issues, and different tranches are sold in different markets.

WHY DO COMPANIES CROSS-LIST?

In general, companies cross-list when the size of their financial needs exceeds their domestic market capacity. There is a limited liquidity in the domestic market, and the price of stock may be more attractive in a foreign market, especially if there is market segmentation and DRs offer diversification benefits to investors. The existing domestic investors also benefit, since cross-listing is likely to mitigate the agency conflicts with their managers. A company becomes more visible internationally, and the share prices are likely to be more efficient (known as price discovery), because trading happens in two or more markets and more financial analysts follow the cross-listing. However, some costs make cross-listing less attractive. This section provides a summary of the benefits and costs of cross-listing.

Benefits of Cross-Listing

The most widely cited benefit is the reduction in the cost of capital. Cross-listing is likely to reduce the cost of capital, because in close domestic markets the efficient frontier is determined only by the set of domestic assets. Therefore, the equity cost of capital depends on the risk premium of the domestic market portfolio. However, if the firm is cross-listed it can reach foreign investors who will be able to invest in both foreign and domestic firms, and the market risk premium will be lower because the level of diversification that investors can attain in an open capital market is far greater. As a result, a cross-listed firm's cost of capital will be lower. Karolyi (1998) reports that the cost of capital of UK cross-listed firms in the United States decreases by 2.64%, from 15.56% before to 12.91% after cross-listing. The market reaction is also positive when the firm announces the decision to list abroad.

However, it is not clear whether the market reacts positively because of the decrease in the cost of capital or whether it is driven by one or more of the additional benefits of cross-listing. These are:

- Improved liquidity of existing shares and broadening of the stockholder base, with, as a result, a reduced probability of takeovers.
- Establishment of a secondary market for shares used in acquisitions.
- An increase in the firm's visibility and political acceptability to its customers, suppliers, creditors, and host governments.
- Creation of a secondary market for shares that can be used to compensate local management and employees in a foreign subsidiary.

MAKING IT HAPPEN

Over the last few years, an increasing number of firms have listed their shares in foreign markets. The decision to cross-list is strategic and involves the following issues:

- Where to cross-list: Companies can go to the United States and issue American depository receipts (ADRs), or to other non-US stock exchanges by issuing global depository receipts (GDRs).
- The choice of a particular market depends on a number of factors. In particular, the firm needs to know whether its stock is attractive to US investors, and whether it can comply with all the requirements of listing, including stronger information disclosure, before it issues ADRs.
- A firm also needs to understand the reasons for cross-listing before issuing depository receipts. The most fundamental is often financing needs, and the inability of the firm to cover this from the domestic market.
- In general, cross-listing leads to an increase in share prices on the announcement date. Such market reactions are likely to be driven by a number of factors, including a reduction in the cost of capital, a wider geographical range of stockholders, an increase in visibility and financial analysts' coverage, and the adoption of stricter corporate governance codes.

MORE INFO

Articles:

Baker, H. Kent, John R. Nofsinger, and Daniel G. Weaver. "International cross-listing and visibility." *Journal of Financial and Quantitative Analysis* 37:3 (September 2002): 495–521. Online at: dx.doi.org/10.2307/3594990

Coffee, John C., Jr. "Racing towards the top? The impact of cross-listings and stock market competition on international corporate governance." *Columbia Law Review* 102:7 (November 2002): 1757–1831.

Dobbs, Richard, and Marc H. Goedhart. "Why cross-listing shares doesn't create value." *The McKinsey Quarterly* (November 2008). Online at: tinyurl.com/6xonzo

Doidge, Craig, G. Andrew Karolyi, and René M. Stulz. "Why are foreign firms listed in the U.S. worth more?" *Journal of Financial Economics* 71:2 (February 2004): 205–238. Online at: dx.doi.org/10.1016/S0304-405X(03)00183-1

Doidge, Craig, G. Andrew Karolyi, and René M. Stulz. "Has New York become less competitive in global markets? Evaluating foreign listing choices over time." Working paper 2007-03-012, Fisher College of Business, Ohio State University, 2007. Online at: www.cob.ohio-state.edu/fin/dice/papers/2007/2007-9.pdf

Karolyi, G. Andrew. "Why do companies list their shares abroad? A survey of the evidence and its managerial implications." *Financial Markets, Institutions and Instruments* 7:1 (February 1998): 1–60. Online at: dx.doi.org/10.1111/1468-0416.00018

Karolyi, G. Andrew. "The world of cross-listing and cross-listings of the world: Challenging conventional wisdom." *Review of Finance* 10:1 (January 2006): 99–152. Online at: dx.doi.org/10.1007/s10679-006-6980-8

Korczak, Adiana, and Meziane A. Lasfer. "Does cross listing mitigate insider trading?" Working paper, Cass Business School, City University, London, 2009.

Leuz, Christian. "Cross listing, bonding and firms' reporting incentives: A discussion of Lang, Raedy and Wilson (2006)." *Journal of Accounting and Economics* 42:1–2 (October 2006): 285–299. Online at: dx.doi.org/10.1016/j.jacceco.2006.04.003

Leuz, Christian. "Was the Sarbanes–Oxley Act of 2002 really this costly? A discussion of evidence from event returns and going-private decisions." *Journal of Accounting and Economics* 44:1–2 (September 2007): 146–165. Online at: dx.doi.org/10.1016/j.jacceco.2007.06.001

Licht, A. N. "Cross-listing and corporate governance: Bonding or avoiding?" *Chicago Journal of International Law* 4 (Spring 2003): 141–164. Online at: cjil.uchicago.edu/past-issues/spr03.html

"A fundamental benefit of cross-listing is the enhancement of investor protection." Lasfer, 2009

- The recently developed bonding hypothesis, which suggests that managers will adhere to stricter regulatory regimes when their firm is cross-listed, because they will face the regulation and corporate governance codes of their home country as well as the foreign market.

Costs of Cross-Listing

The positive market reaction to cross-listing could also reflect the trade-off between the benefits of cross-listing discussed above and some potential costs, namely disclosure costs. In cross-listing and selling equity abroad, a firm faces two barriers: an increased commitment to full disclosure and a continuing investor relations program. Non-US firms must think twice before cross-listing in the United States. Not only can the disclosure requirements be onerous, but timely quarterly information is also required by US regulators and investors. Costs are likely to be higher for firms that have been accustomed to revealing far less information.

Pagano, Marco, Ailsa A. Roell, and Josef Zechner. "The geography of equity listing: Why do companies list abroad?" *Journal of Finance* 57:6 (December 2002): 2651–2694. Online at: dx.doi.org/10.1111/1540-6261.00509

Sarkissian, Sergei, and Michael J. Schill. "The overseas listing decision: New evidence of proximity preference." *Review of Financial Studies* 17:3 (Fall 2004): 769–810. Online at: dx.doi.org/10.1093/rfs/hhg048

Websites:

Bank of New York Mellon press releases 2008: www.bnymellon.com/pressreleases/2008/pr071408b.html

Crosslisting.com: www.crosslisting.com

London Stock Exchange: www.londonstockexchange.com

Open University learning module on cross-listing: openlearn.open.ac.uk/mod/oucontent/view.php?id=397385&direct=1

US Securities and Exchange Commission: www.sec.gov

See Also:

★ The Cost of Going Public: Why IPOs Are Typically Underpriced (pp. 475–477)
★ Financial Steps in an IPO for a Small or Medium-Size Enterprise (pp. 487–489)
★ IPOs in Emerging Markets (pp. 514–516)
★ Price Discovery in IPOs (pp. 557–559)
✔ Merchant Banks: Their Structure and Function (p. 1012)
✔ Raising Capital by Issuing Shares (p. 1087)
✔ Stock Markets: Their Structure and Function (p. 1091)

     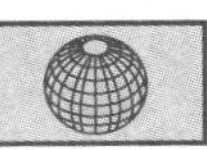   

Assessing Venture Capital Funding for Small and Medium-Sized Enterprises

by Alain Fayolle and Joseph LiPuma

EXECUTIVE SUMMARY

- Entrepreneurs and small and medium-sized enterprise (SME) managers capitalize their firms with debt equity investments, or a combination of both.
- Equity investments such as venture capital can erode executive control but can enable access to the investor's knowledge, advice, and networks.
- Venture capital can be provided by business angels, independent venture capital firms (IVCs[1]), corporations, or universities.
- The sources' differing investment objectives, backgrounds, and control mechanisms deliver varying levels of added value to the SME.
- Companies seeking venture capital should select investors whose objectives, potential to add value, and expectations of control mesh most closely with those of the entrepreneur.

INTRODUCTION

Entrepreneurs and SME managers face two key choices when financing their ventures: debt or equity. Debt in the form of personal loans (including credit cards) and bank loans, key sources for most nascent ventures, gives efficient incentives for managers to exert effort and allow entrepreneurs to maintain control. The availability and utility of debt vary significantly with economic conditions, which, in turn, will have an impact on the supply and cost of capital. To a lesser extent, entrepreneurs rely on equity financing,[2] in which parties external to a venture obtain partial ownership (and control) in exchange for financial capital, thus diluting managers' incentives to expend effort. Equity financing is particularly important for high-growth ventures, since the amount of debt financing available may not permit sufficiently rapid growth in volatile industries (for example, technology). Objectives and incentives that are well aligned between investor and manager are the most efficient and facilitate additional value for the venture.

VENTURE CAPITAL

Venture capital (VC) refers to independently managed, dedicated pools of capital which the providers channel into equity or equity-linked investments in privately held, high-growth companies.[3] Worldwide, more than $30 billion is invested annually as venture capital,[4] with the most intensive use in the United States, Europe, and Israel (with $28 billion, $6 billion, and $.7 billion invested respectively in 2007).[5] Venture capital represents a bundle of productive, value-adding resources, comprising the human capital (knowledge and experience) and social capital (network) of the venture capitalist—who oversees the investment—in addition to the financial capital. The value and productivity of these nonfinancial aspects of VC can be significant, influencing a venture's offering, geographic diversity, and growth. Venture capitalists can help to professionalize a new venture through representation on the board of directors, executive recruiting, or by exerting rights of control (over, for example, cash flow and liquidation) in exchange for capital. Despite modest levels of investment,[6] venture capital-backed companies[7] accounted for over ten million jobs and $1.8 trillion in revenue in the United States in 2003[8]—approximately one-sixth of GDP.

Venture capital can come from business angels, independent VC firms (IVCs), corporate venture capital (CVC) programs, and universities. The different ways in which these are funded, investments are managed, and partners are compensated (see Table 1[9]) result in varying allocations of control rights between the investor and the venture. Angel investors, for example, rarely require representation on corporate boards, whereas IVCs generally do seek directorships. Investment objectives influence the nature of companies in which VCs invest and, correspondingly, the value they are able to add. Independent VC firms invest solely for financial reasons and may best add value to SMEs by helping them to recruit key executives or access additional capital. Corporations that provide CVC often invest for strategic reasons, frequently in ventures with complementary offerings. These corporations are generally multinational, enabling them to add more value in the development of foreign networks of customers, suppliers, and partners. However, CVC investors generally do not invest in early-stage ventures, usually waiting until an IVC invests before committing their resources.

SELECTING THE RIGHT TYPE OF VC

Though only a small percentage of companies receive venture capital,[10] those that do can usually choose its source and should therefore select investors whose objectives, added-value potential, and expectations of control are most in accord with those of the business owner. Since the process of pitching ventures to investors and negotiating terms can be time-consuming, especially for SMEs and young ventures, it is crucial to establish your objectives and target VC sources early on. This may also help to avoid later

Table 1. Characteristics of the different providers of venture capital

	Angel	*IVC*	*CVC*	*UVC*
Typical background	Ex-entrepreneur	Ex-entrepreneur or financial	Large, tech-savvy multinational	Patent holder
Motivation	Financial and "giving back"	Financial	Strategic and financial	Commercialize patents
Fund source	Self	Limited partners	Corporate	University, government
Investment method	Direct	Direct	Direct and indirect	Direct and indirect
General partner compensation	Gain from exit or early buyout	Percentage of valuation increase	Salary plus bonus	Salary plus bonus
Average invested per venture	~$10,000[a]	~$8 million[b]	~$4.5 million[c]	< $250,000[d]

[a] Allen, Kathleen A. *Launching New Ventures: An Entrepreneurial Approach.* Boston, MA: Houghton Mifflin Company, 2006.

[b] PricewaterhouseCoopers/National Venture Capital Association. "MoneyTree™ report." Data: Thomson Reuters.

[c] *Ibid.*

[d] Miles, Morgan P., John B. White, and Eve White. "University sponsored venture capital: An exploratory study." *Journal of Business and Entrepreneurship* 13:1 (2001): 129–134.

"The creation of new ventures is the economic engine that drives regional and international economies."
Harry J. Sapienza

  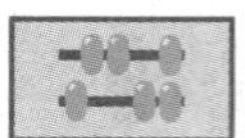      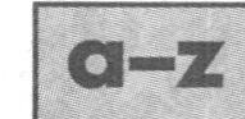

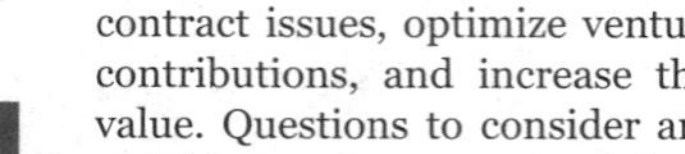

contract issues, optimize venture capitalist contributions, and increase the venture's value. Questions to consider are:

What stage are we at? At the seed or startup stage, angel financing is best because it comes with fewer strings attached and is easier to "buy out." Angel investors are good stewards and may take active, informal roles in the company. Corporations generally do not invest at early stages, so IVC is most likely at the next stage, with CVC most used in expansion stages.

How big a VC provider do you need? While this answer often depends on capital needs, prestigious or "big name" IVC providers bring broad and helpful networks, in addition to status, that can help when exiting via a public offering or acquisition. However, prominent VCs often require more control over cash flow, voting, board representation, and liquidation. Such rights are often contingent on observable performance measures. If the venture does badly, VCs obtain more control, whereas if the venture does well, VCs relinquish most control and liquidation rights.

Do I need a specialized VC provider with specific industry knowledge and contacts? Industry specialization helps VC firms to develop skills for vetting and selecting investments, and for developing relevant industry knowledge and networks. Generalist firms are able to thrive and grow as industries evolve and ebb, and they have cross-industry experience and networks that may benefit nascent ventures.

How much capital do we need, and what do we need the funds for? If funds are needed for initial technology development, CVC, with the associated corporate technology knowledge, may provide access to technical skills. In addition to supplying capital of their own, IVCs are good at helping companies in which they invest to obtain access to other funds because of their legitimacy and the networks they have.

Are we planning to enter foreign markets? The VC industry is globalizing,[11] and since VC providers tend to invest in ventures that are geographically proximate, there is limited foreign investment. In addition, some VC providers tend to eschew investments in internationalized ventures, since they cannot easily monitor their activities. CVC associated with a multinational enterprise may provide foreign market knowledge and assist in market penetration, and permit access to foreign customers, suppliers, and partners who can help to monitor the internationalized venture.

How vulnerable is my intellectual property? Working with a VC provider requires an exchange of detailed information about development projects, product specifications, and marketing plans. Corporations often invest for strategic reasons based on industry or market congruity with new ventures. Such congruity suggests that the investor could easily appropriate the intellectual property of the SME. Research suggests that receiving investments from multiple corporations may limit that risk.

CONCLUSION

SMEs and young ventures that receive capital investments can often choose their source. The boundary-spanning role of investors, as both advisers and links to external networks, places VCs in a unique position to add value to a venture. The potential for investors to aid in the growth and development of such ventures demands that entrepreneurs and SME managers make their choice in a considered manner that is consistent with their overall strategy. Careful consideration of investor types can lead to an efficient selection process that provides value throughout the life of the venture.

CASE STUDY

Tessera Enterprise Systems

Tessera Enterprise Systems, a custom software developer, was founded in Boston in 1995 by an executive team that had previously worked together for three years. Tessera's target market included some of the largest American retail and financial companies, such as Eddie Bauer and Charles Schwab. The founders provided initial funding for the venture, but after one year it was decided that venture capital was required to expand the company. Tessera, however, secured an investment offer from Greylock Management, a prominent Boston-based IVC. Greylock's status added legitimacy to the fledgling venture, permitting it to obtain contracts with target companies such as Charles Schwab, Eddie Bauer, and other prominent clients. Subsequent expansion and third-stage funding from two other prominent IVCs solidified Tessera in the market and led to a corporate expansion to San Francisco. At the same time, Tessera considered establishing an office in Switzerland to serve potential European clients. One of the VC providers likened internationalization to loading an airplane with stacks of cash and opening the doors while flying over the Atlantic.

Tessera nevertheless pursued its foreign market entry strategy and, while it slowly obtained some European contracts, it did so without the involvement or aid of its IVC investors. Had Tessera sought investment from a technology corporation such as Oracle (on whose products its offerings were often based), it might have been better able to leverage its investor's networks and knowledge to the benefit of its foreign business. A modest capital round was provided by IVCs and a private investor in preparation for an exit. Tessera, originally planning on a public offering and broad foreign expansion, was acquired in 2001 by iXL, an Atlanta-based internet services provider company with offices in San Francisco and London.

MAKING IT HAPPEN

Since VC has the potential to change the nature of resources in an SME so dramatically, entrepreneurs must approach it with a strategic view of how it may best add value, and source it accordingly. At the same time as they assess their financial capital needs, SME managers should do the following:

- Carefully consider the type of advice, information, and network access you want from an investor in the light of current needs and strategic direction.
- Identify VC providers that have great reputations for providing value in a manner consistent with your willingness to cede some control.
- Ask others who have undertaken VC-backed ventures about their experience with investors—both IVC and CVC—and the success and problems they encountered.
- Identify companies that had exits—IPOs and acquisitions—most consistent with your goals and ask about their investors.

"**. . . entrepreneurs do not stop soliciting interest from venture capitalists after receiving one offer, but rather attempt to establish a market for their companies' shares.**" Gordon Smith

MORE INFO

Books:

Gompers, Paul A., and Josh Lerner. *The Venture Capital Cycle*. Cambridge, MA: MIT Press, 1999.

Maula, M., and G. C. Murray. "Corporate venture capital and the creation of US public companies: The impact of sources of venture capital on the performance of portfolio companies." In Michael A. Hitt, Raphael Amit, Charles E. Lucier, and Robert D. Nixon (eds). *Creating Value: Winners in the New Business Environment*. Oxford: Blackwell Publishing, 2002.

McNally, Kevin. *Corporate Venture Capital: Bridging the Equity Gap in the Small Business Sector*. London: Routledge, 1997.

Articles:

Maula, Markku V. J., Erkko Autio, and Gordon C. Murray. "Corporate venture capitalists and independent venture capitalists: What do they know, who do they know and should entrepreneurs care?" *Venture Capital* 7:1 (January 2005): 3–21. Online at: dx.doi.org/10.1080/1369106042000316332

Sapienza, Harry J., Allen C. Amason, and Sophie Manigart. "The level and nature of venture capitalist involvement in their portfolio companies: A study of three European countries." *Managerial Finance* 20:1 (1994): 3–17. Online at: dx.doi.org/10.1108/eb018456

Smith, Gordon. "How early stage entrepreneurs evaluate venture capitalists." *Journal of Private Equity* 4:2 (Spring 2001): 33–45. Online at: dx.doi.org/10.3905/jpe.2001.319981

Van Osnabrugge, Mark, and Robert J. Robinson. "The influence of a venture capitalist's source of funds." *Venture Capital* 3:1 (January 2001): 25–39. Online at: dx.doi.org/10.1080/13691060117288

Websites:

National Venture Capital Association (NVCA): www.nvca.org

European Private Equity and Venture Capital Association (EVCA): www.evca.eu

See Also:

★ Sources of Venture Capital (pp. 601–603)
★ Understanding Equity Capital in Small and Medium-Sized Enterprises (pp. 607–610)
✔ Dealing with Venture Capital Companies (p. 1067)
✔ Investors and the Capital Structure (p. 1120)
✔ Options for Raising Finance (p. 1081)
✔ Raising Capital through Private and Public Equity (p. 1088)

NOTES

1 We wish to emphasize that the acronym "IVC" here refers to formal venture capital investments by independent firms specialized for this purpose. Other literature uses "IVC" to refer to informal venture capital investments.

2 For example, in the United States fewer than 7% of companies obtain outside equity financing, whereas 45% take on outside debt (Robb, Alicia, and David T. Robinson. "The capital structure decisions of new firms: Second in a series of reports using data from the Kauffman firm survey." Kansas City, MO: Kauffman Foundation, 2008). New Zealand businesses are almost six times more likely to seek additional debt financing than equity financing (www.stats.govt.nz), whereas nearly 20 times more Canadian companies sought debt financing than equity financing (www.sme-fdi.gc.ca).

3 Gompers and Lerner (1999).

4 Ernst & Young. "Transition: Global venture capital insights report 2006."

5 PricewaterhouseCoopers/National Venture Capital Association. "MoneyTree™ report." Online at: www.pwcmoneytree.com/MTPublic/ns/index.jsp. Data: Thomas Reuters (accessed March 5, 2009); www.evca.com; and www.investinisrael.gov.il respectively.

6 From 1999 to 2002, less than 0.5% of GDP was invested via venture capital in the United States (OECD report).

7 This includes those that are now public companies, such as Intel, Microsoft, eBay, and Home Depot.

8 Global Insight. "Venture impact 2004: Venture capital benefits to the U.S. economy." June 2004. Online at: www.ihsglobalinsight.com/publicDownload/genericContent/07-20-04_fullstudy.pdf

9 Note that this table is based on examples from the United States. In Europe, for example, research institutes often take the place of universities in conducting research and formulating approaches to the commercialization of intellectual property.

10 For example, in the United States fewer than 0.1% of all companies founded in the 1990s received venture capital (authors' analysis of US data from the NVCA). In Europe, the probability of receiving VC is approximately 0.07% (Achtmann, Eric. "Getting a view of VC in Europe... from the centre." 4th Annual MIT VCPI Conference, Cambridge, MA, December 1, 2001).

11 See, for example: Hall, G., and C. Tu. "Venture capitalists and the decision to invest overseas." *Venture Capital* 5:2 (2003): 181–190; and Manigart, S., *et al.* "Human capital and the internationalization of venture capital firms." *International Entrepreneurship and Management Journal* 3:1 (2007): 1–125.

"Failure is more frequently from want of energy than want of capital." Daniel Webster

  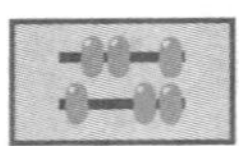      

Asset Allocation Methodologies by Tom Coyne

EXECUTIVE SUMMARY

- Asset allocation is both a process and a collection of methodologies that are intended to help a decision-maker to achieve a set of investment objectives by dividing scarce resources between different alternatives.
- Theory assumes that asset allocations are made in the face of risk, where the full range of possible future outcomes and their associated probabilities are known. In the real world this is rarely the case, and decisions must be made in the face of uncertainty.
- The appropriate asset allocation methodology to use, in part, depends on an investor's belief in the efficacy of forecasting. Assuming you believe that forecasting accuracy beyond luck is possible, there remains an inescapable trade-off between a forecasting model's fidelity to historical data and its robustness to uncertainty. Confidence in prediction also increases when models based on different methodologies reach similar conclusions. In fact, averaging the results of these models has been shown to raise forecast accuracy.
- The traditional methodology for asset allocation problems is mean–variance optimization (MVO), which is an application of linear programming that seeks to maximize the return for any given level of risk. However, MVO has many limitations, including high sensitivity to input estimation error and difficulty in handling realistic multiyear, multiobjective problems.
- Alternative techniques include equal weighting, risk budgeting, scenario-based approaches, and stochastic optimization. The choice of which to use fundamentally depends on your belief in the predictability of future levels of risk and return.
- Although they are improving, all quantitative approaches to asset allocation still suffer from various limitations. For that reason, relatively passive risk management approaches such as diversification and automatic rebalancing occasionally need to be complemented by active hedging measures, such as going to cash or buying options.

INTRODUCTION

Everyone has financial goals they want to achieve, whether it is accumulating a target amount of money before retirement, ensuring that a pension fund can provide promised incomes to retirees, or, in a different context, achieving an increase in corporate cash flow. Inevitably, we do not have unlimited resources available to achieve these goals. We often face not only financial constraints, but also shortages of information, time, and cognitive capacity. In many cases, we also face additional constraints on how we can employ available resources to achieve our goals (for example, limits to the maximum amount of funds that can be invested in one area, or the maximum acceptable probability of a result below some threshold).

Broadly, these are all asset allocation problems. We solve them every day using a variety of methodologies. Many of these are nonquantitative, such as dividing resources equally between options, using a rule of thumb that has worked in the past, or copying what others are doing. However, in cases where the stakes are high, the allocation problem is complicated, and/or our choice has to be justified to others, we often employ quantitative methodologies to help us identify, understand, and explain the potential consequences of different decision options. This article considers a typical asset allocation problem: how to allocate one's financial assets across a range of investment options in order to achieve a long-term goal, subject to a set of constraints.

THE CORE CHALLENGE: DECISION MAKING UNDER UNCERTAINTY

All investment asset allocation methodologies start with two core assumptions. First, that a range of different scenarios could occur in the future. Second, that investment alternatives are available whose performance will vary depending on the scenario that eventually develops. A critical issue is the extent to which a decision-maker believes it is possible to accurately predict future outcomes. Traditional finance theory, which is widely used in the investment management industry, assumes that both the full range of possible outcomes and their associated probabilities are known to the decision-maker. This is the classic problem of making decisions in the face of risk.

However, when you dig a bit deeper, you find that this approach is based on some questionable assumptions. The obvious question is: how can a decision-maker know the full range of possible future outcomes and their associated probabilities? One explanation is that they understand the workings of the process that produces future outcomes. In physical systems, and even in simple social systems, this may be true. But this is likely not to be the case when it comes to investment outcomes. Financial markets are complex adaptive systems, filled with positive feedback loops and nonlinear effects caused by the interaction of competing strategies (for example, value, momentum, and passive approaches) and underlying decisions made by people with imperfect information and limited cognitive capacities who are often pressed for time, affected by emotions, and subject to the influence of other people. An investor can never fully understand the way this system produces outcomes.

Even without such causal understanding, an investor could still believe that the range of possible future outcomes can be described mathematically, based on an analysis of past outcomes. For example, you could use historical data to construct a statistical distribution to describe the range of possible future outcomes, or devise a formula for projecting a time series into the future. The validity of both these approaches rests on two further assumptions. The first is that the historical data used to construct the distribution or time-series algorithm contain sufficient information to capture the full range of possible future outcomes. The second is that the unknown underlying process that generates the historical data will remain constant, or only change slowly over time. Over the past decade, we have seen repeated evidence that in financial markets these two assumptions are not true, for example in the meltdown of the Long Term Capital Management hedge fund in 1998, the crash of the technology stock bubble in 2001, and the worldwide financial market panic in 2008. In these cases, models based on historical data failed to identify the full range of possible outcomes, or to accurately assess the probability of the possible outcomes they identified. People will live with the consequences of these failures for years.

This is not to say that skilled forecasters do not exist, however. They certainly do. Unfortunately, it is usually easier to identify them with the benefit of hindsight (which also helps to distinguish between skill and luck) than it is to pick them in advance.

This discussion leads to an important conclusion. In the real world, asset allocators must make decisions not in the face of *risk*, but rather under conditions of true *uncertainty*, in which neither the full range of possible future outcomes nor their associated probabilities are fully known in advance. This has two critical implications. First, there is an inescapable trade-off between any forecasting model's fidelity to historical data and its

"A goal without a plan is just a wish." Antoine de Saint-Exupéry

     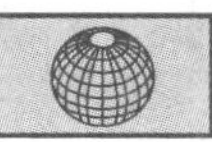   

robustness to uncertainty. The more carefully a model is backtested and tightly calibrated to accurately reproduce *past* outcomes, the less likely it is to accurately predict the future behavior of a complex adaptive system. Second, confidence in a forecast increases only when models based on differing methodologies (for example, causal, statistical, time-series, and judgmental forecasts) reach similar conclusions, and/or when their individual forecasts are combined to reduce the impact of their individual errors. In short, decision-making under uncertainty is much harder than decision-making under risk.

Asset Allocation: A Simple Example

Let us now move on to a more concrete, yet still simple, example to illustrate some key issues that underlie the most common asset allocation methodology in use today. Our quantitative data and results are summarized in the following table:

	Asset A	Asset B
Year 1 return	1%	3%
Year 2 return	5%	7%
Year 3 return	9%	20%
Year 4 return	5%	–5%
Year 5 return	1%	8%
Sample arithmetic mean	4.2%	6.6%
Standard error of the mean	1.5%	4.1%
Sample geometric mean	4.1%	6.3%
Sample standard deviation	3.3%	9.1%
Covariance of A and B	0.12%	
Correlation of A and B	0.41	
Asset weight	40%	60%
Expected arithmetic annual portfolio return	5.6%	
Expected portfolio standard deviation	6.1%	
Expected geometric annual portfolio return	4.9%	

Our portfolio comprises two assets, for which we have five years of historical data. In line with industry norms, we will treat each data point as an independent sample (i.e. we will assume that no momentum or mean-reversion processes are at work in our data series) drawn from a distribution which includes the full range of results that could be produced by the unknown return-generating process. As you can see, the sample mean (i.e. arithmetic average) annual return is 4.2% for Asset A and 6.6% for Asset B. So it is clear that Asset B should produce higher returns, right? Wrong. The next line of the table shows the standard error for our estimate of the mean. The standard error is equal to the sample standard deviation (which we'll discuss below) divided by the square root of the number of data points used in the estimate (in our case, there are five). Assuming that the data come from a normal distribution (that is, one in the shape of the bell curve), there is a 67% chance that the true mean will lie within plus or minus one standard error of our sample mean, and a 95% chance that it will lie within two standard errors. In our example, the short data history, along with the relatively high standard deviation of Asset B's returns, means that the standard errors are high relative to the sample means, and we really can't be completely sure that Asset A has a higher expected return than Asset B. In fact, we'd need a lot more data to increase our confidence about this conclusion. Assuming no change in the size of the standard deviations, the size of the standard error of the mean declines very slowly as the length of the historical data sample is increased—the square root of 5 is about 2.2; of 10, about 3.2; and of 20, about 4.5. Cutting the standard error in half—that is, doubling the accuracy of your estimate of the true mean—requires about a fourfold increase in the length of the data series. Considering that 20 years is about the limit of the available data series for many asset classes, you can see how this can create problems when it comes to generating asset allocation results in which you can have a high degree of confidence.

The next line in the table, the sample geometric mean, highlights another issue: As long as there is any variability in returns, the average return in a given year is not the same as the actual compound return that would be earned by an investor who held an asset for the full five years. In fact, the realized return—that is, the geometric mean—will be lower, and can quickly be approximated by subtracting twice the standard deviation squared from the arithmetic mean. In summary, the higher the variability of returns, the larger the gap will be between the arithmetic and the geometric mean.

The following line in the table shows the sample standard deviation of returns for Assets A and B. This measures the extent to which they are dispersed around the sample mean. In many asset allocation analyses, the standard deviation (also known as volatility) is used as a proxy for risk. Common sense tells you that the correspondence between standard deviation and most investors' understanding of risk is rough at best. Most investors find variability on the downside much less attractive than variability on the upside—and they like uncertainty even less than risk, which they can, or think that they can, measure. Also, when it comes to the distribution of returns, it is not just the average and standard deviation that are of interest to investors. Whether the distribution is Gaussian (normal)—that is, it has the typical bell curve shape—is also important. Distributions that are slightly tilted toward positive returns (as is the case with Assets A and B) are preferable to ones that are negatively skewed. Skewness should also affect preference for distributions with a higher percentage of extreme returns than the normal distribution (i.e. ones with high kurtosis). Preference for higher kurtosis should rise as skewness becomes more positive, and fall as it becomes more negative (i.e. as the probability of large negative returns rises). In fact, in our example, Asset B has positive skewness and higher than normal kurtosis (compared to Asset A's lower than normal kurtosis). Hence, some investors might be willing to trade off higher positive skewness and kurtosis against higher standard deviation in their assessment of the overall riskiness of Asset B. This might be particularly true when, as in the case of some hedge fund strategies, the expected returns on an investment have a distribution that is far from normal. However, many asset allocation methodologies still do not take these trade-offs into account, because they either assume that the returns on assets are normally distributed, or they assume that investors only have preferences concerning standard deviation, and not skewness or kurtosis.

Covariance and correlation

Covariance and correlation are two ways of measuring the relationship between the time series of returns on two or more assets. Covariance is found by multiplying each year's return for Asset A by the return for Asset B, calculating the average result, and subtracting from this the product of the average return for Asset A and by the average return for Asset B—or, more pithily, it is the average of the products less the product of the averages. Correlation standardizes the covariance by dividing it by the product of the standard deviation of Asset A's returns, multiplied by the standard deviation of Asset B's returns. Correlation takes a value between minus one (for returns that move in exactly opposite directions) and plus one (for returns that move exactly together). In theory, a correlation close to zero implies no relationship between the returns on the two sets of returns. Unfortunately, most people forget that correlation only measures the strength of the *linear* relationship between variables; if this relationship is *nonlinear*, the correlation coefficient will also be deceptively close to zero. Finally, covariance and correlation measure the average relationship between two return series; however, their relationship under extreme conditions (i.e. in the tails of the two return distributions) may differ from this average. This was another lesson taught by the events of 2008.

Forming a Portfolio

Let us now combine Asset A and Asset B into a portfolio in which the first has a 40% weight and the second has a 60% weight. The second-to-last row of our table shows the expected arithmetic portfolio return of 5.6% per year. This is simply the weighted average of each asset's expected return. The calculation of the expected standard deviation of the portfolio is more complicated, but it highlights the mathematical logic of diversification. The portfolio standard deviation equals the square root of the portfolio variance. The latter is calculated as follows: [(Asset A weight squared multiplied by Asset A standard deviation squared) plus (Asset B weight squared multiplied by Asset B standard deviation squared) plus (two times Asset A weight multiplied by Asset B weight times the covariance of A and B)]. As you can see, the portfolio standard deviation is 6.1%, which is less than 6.8%—the weighted average of Asset A's and Asset B's standard deviations. The cause of this result is the relatively low covariance between A's returns and B's returns (or alternatively, their relatively low correlation of 0.41). The fact that their respective returns apparently move in less than perfect lockstep with each other reduces the overall expected variability of the portfolio return. However, this encouraging conclusion is subject to two critical caveats. First, it assumes the absence of a nonlinear relationship between A's returns and B's returns that has not been picked up by the correlation estimate. Second, it assumes that the underlying factors giving rise to the correlation of 0.41 will remain unchanged in the future. In practice, however, this is not the case, and correlations tend to be unstable over time. For example, in 2008, investors discovered that despite relatively low estimated correlations between their historical returns, many asset classes shared a nonlinear exposure to a market liquidity risk factor. When liquidity fell sharply, correlations rose rapidly and undermined many of the expected benefits from portfolio diversification.

Expected Portfolio Returns

The last line in our table is an estimate of the geometric or compound average rate of return that an investor might be expected to actually realize on this portfolio over a multiyear period, assuming that we have accurately estimated the underlying means, standard deviations, and correlations and that they remain stable over time (all questionable assumptions, as we have noted). As you can see, it is less than the expected arithmetic annual return. Unfortunately, too many asset allocation analyses make the mistake of assuming that the arithmetic average return will be earned over time, rather than the geometric return. In the example we have used, for an initial investment of $1,000,000 and a 20-year holding period, this difference in returns results in terminal wealth that is lower by $370,358, or 12.5%, than the use of the arithmetic average would have led us to expect. This is not a trivial difference.

ASSET ALLOCATION: ADVANCED TECHNIQUES

The basic methodology we have just outlined can be used to calculate asset weights that maximize expected portfolio return for any given constraint on portfolio standard deviation (or other measure of risk, such as value-at-risk). Conversely, this approach can be used to minimize one or more portfolio risk measures for any given level of target portfolio return. These are all variants of the asset allocation methodology known as mean–variance optimization (MVO), which is an application of linear programming (for example, as found in the SOLVER function in an Excel spreadsheet). Although MVO is by far the most commonly used asset allocation methodology, it is, as we have shown, subject to many limitations.

Fortunately, there are techniques that can be used to overcome some, if not all, of the problems highlighted in our example. We will start with alternatives to the MVO methodology, and then look at alternative means of managing errors in the estimation of future asset class returns, standard deviations, covariances, and other model inputs.

Alternative Approaches to Portfolio Construction

The simplest alternative to MVO is to allocate an equal amount of money to each investment option. Known as the $1/n$ approach, this has been shown to be surprisingly effective, particularly when asset classes are broadly defined to minimize correlations (for example, a single domestic equities asset class rather than three highly related ones, including small-, mid-, and large-cap equities). Fundamentally, equal weighting is based on the assumption that no asset allocation model inputs (i.e. returns, standard deviations, and correlations) can be accurately forecast in a complex adaptive system.

Another relatively simple asset allocation methodology starts from the premise that, at least in the past, different investment options perform relatively better under different economic scenarios or regimes. For example, domestic and foreign government bonds and gold have, in the past, performed relatively well during periods of high uncertainty (for example, the 1998 Russian debt crisis and the more recent subprime credit crisis). Similarly, history has shown that inflation-indexed bonds, commodities, and commercial property have performed relatively well when inflation is high, whereas equities deliver their best performance under more normal conditions. Different approaches can be used to translate these observations into actual asset allocations. For example, you could divide your funds between the three scenarios in line with your subjective forecast of the probability of each of them occurring over a specified time horizon, and then equally divide the money allocated to each scenario between the asset classes that perform best under it.

When it comes to more quantitative asset allocation methodologies, research has shown that—at least in the past—some variables have proven easier to predict and are more stable over time than others. Specifically, relative asset class riskiness (as measured by standard deviation) has been much more stable over time than relative asset class returns. A belief that relative riskiness will remain stable in the future leads to a second alternative to MVO: risk budgeting. This involves allocating different amounts of money to each investment option, with the goal of equalizing their contribution to total portfolio risk, which can be defined using either standard deviation or one or more downside risk measures (for example, drawdown, shortfall, semi-standard deviation). However, as was demonstrated by the ineffective performance of many banks' value-at-risk models during 2008, the effectiveness of risk budgeting depends on the accuracy of the underlying assumptions it uses. For example, rapidly changing correlations and volatility, along with illiquid markets, can and did result in actual risk positions that were very different from those originally budgeted.

The most sophisticated approaches to complicated multiyear asset allocation problems use more advanced methodologies. For example, rather than a one-period MVO model, multiperiod regime-switching models can be used to replicate the way real economies and financial markets can shift between periods of inflation, deflation, and normal growth (or, alternatively, high and low volatility). These models typically

"Prediction is very difficult, especially about the future." Niels Bohr

  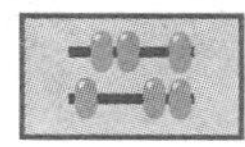      

incorporate different asset return, standard deviation, and correlation assumptions under each regime. However, they are also subject to estimation errors not only in the assumptions used in each regime, but also in the assumptions made about regime continuation and transition probabilities, for which historical data and theoretical models are quite limited.

Rebalancing Strategies

Multiperiod asset allocation models can also incorporate a range of different rebalancing strategies that manage risk by adjusting asset weights over time (for example, based on annual rebalancing, or maximum allowable deviations from target weights). When it comes to identifying the best asset allocation solution for a given problem, these models typically incorporate sophisticated evolutionary search techniques. These start with a candidate solution (for example, an integrated asset allocation and rebalancing strategy), and then run repeated model simulations to assess the probability that they will achieve the investor's specified objectives. An evolutionary technique (for example, genetic algorithms or simulated annealing) is then used to identify another potential solution, and the process is repeated until a stopping point is reached (which is usually based on the failure to find a better solution after a certain number of candidates have been tested or a maximum time limit is reached). Strictly speaking, the best solutions found using evolutionary search techniques are not *optimal* (in the sense that the word is used in the MVO approach)—meaning a unique solution that is, subject to the limits of the methodology, believed to be better than all other possible solutions. In the case of computationally hard problems, such as multiperiod, multiobjective asset allocation, it is not possible to evaluate all possible solutions exhaustively. Instead, much as for real life decision-makers, stochastic search models aim to find solutions that are robust—ones that have a high probability of achieving an investor's objectives under a wide range of possible future conditions.

ESTIMATING ASSET ALLOCATION INPUTS

A number of different techniques are also used to improve the estimates of future asset class returns, standard deviations, correlations, and other inputs that are used by various asset allocation methodologies. Of these variables, future returns are the hardest to predict. One approach to improving return forecasts is to use a model containing a small number of common factors to estimate future returns on a larger number of asset classes. In some models, these factors are economic and financial variables, such as the market/book ratio, industrial production, or the difference between long- and short-term interest rates. Perhaps the best known factor model is the CAPM (capital asset pricing model). This is based on the assumption that, in equilibrium, the return on an asset will be equal to the risk-free rate of interest, plus a risk premium that is proportional to the asset's riskiness relative to the overall market portfolio. Although they simplify the estimation of asset returns, factor models also have some limitations, including the need to forecast the variables they use accurately and their assumption that markets are usually in a state of equilibrium.

The latter assumption lies at the heart of another approach to return estimation, known as the Black–Litterman (BL) model. Assuming that markets are in equilibrium enables one to use current asset class market capitalizations to infer expectations of future returns. BL then combines these with an investor's own subjective views (in a consistent manner) to arrive at a final return estimate. More broadly, BL is an example of a so-called shrinkage estimation technique, whereby more extreme estimates (for example, the highest and lowest expected returns) are shrunk toward a more central value (for example, the average return forecast across all asset classes, or BL's equilibrium market implied returns). At a still higher level, shrinkage is but one version of model averaging, which has been shown to increase forecast accuracy in multiple domains. An example of this could be return estimates that are based on the combination of historical data and the outputs from a forecasting model.

When it comes to improving estimates of standard deviation (volatility) and correlations, one finds similar techniques employed, including factor and shrinkage models. In addition, a number of traditional (for example, moving averages and exponential smoothing) and advanced (for example, GARCH and neural network models) time-series forecasting techniques have been used as investors search for better ways to forecast volatility, correlations, and more complicated relationships between the returns on different assets. Finally,

MAKING IT HAPPEN

- Using broadly defined asset classes minimizes correlations and creates more robust solutions by reducing the sensitivity of results to deviations from assumptions about future asset class returns, which are the most difficult to forecast.
- Equal dollar weighting should be the default asset allocation, as it assumes that all prediction is impossible.
- However, there is considerable evidence that the relative riskiness of different asset classes is reasonably stable over time and therefore predictable. This makes it possible to move beyond equal weighting and to use risk budgeting. There is also evidence that different asset classes perform better under different economic conditions, such as high inflation or high uncertainty. This makes it possible to use scenario-based weighting.
- Techniques such as mean–variance optimization and stochastic search are more problematic, because they depend on the accurate prediction of future returns. Although new approaches can help to minimize estimation errors, they cannot eliminate them or change the human behavior that gives rise to bubbles and crashes. For that reason, all asset allocation approaches require not only good quantitative analysis, but also good judgment and continued risk monitoring, even after the initial asset allocation plan is implemented.

MORE INFO

Books:

Asset Allocation:

Bernstein, William. *The Intelligent Asset Allocator: How to Build Your Portfolio to Maximize Returns and Minimize Risk*. New York: McGraw-Hill, 2001.

Darst, David M. *The Art of Asset Allocation: Principles and Investment Strategies for Any Market*. 2nd ed. New York: McGraw-Hill, 2008.

Fabozzi, Frank J., Petter N. Kolm, Dessislava A. Pachamanova, and Sergio M. Focardi. *Robust Portfolio Optimization and Management*. Hoboken, NJ: Wiley, 2007.

Ferri, Richard A. *All About Asset Allocation: The Easy Way to Get Started*. New York: McGraw-Hill, 2006.

"A man who does not think and plan long ahead will find trouble right at his door." Confucius

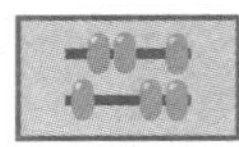

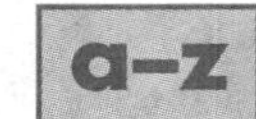

copula functions have been employed with varying degrees of success to model nonlinear dependencies between different return series.

CONCLUSION

In summary, although they are improving and becoming more robust to uncertainty than in the past, almost all quantitative approaches to asset allocation still suffer from various limitations. In a complex adaptive system this seems unavoidable, since their evolutionary processes make accurate forecasting extremely difficult using existing techniques. This argues strongly for averaging the outputs of different methodologies as the best way to make asset allocation decisions in the face of uncertainty. Moreover, these same evolutionary processes can sometimes give rise to substantial asset class over- or undervaluation that is outside the input assumptions used in the asset allocation process. Given this, relatively passive risk management approaches such as diversification and rebalancing occasionally need to be complemented with active hedging measures such as going to cash or buying options. The effective implementation of this process will require not only paying ongoing attention to asset class valuations, but also a shift in focus from external performance metrics to achieving the long-term portfolio return required to reach one's goals. When your objective is to outperform your peers or an external benchmark, it is tempting to stay too long in overvalued asset classes, as many investors painfully learned in 2001 and again in 2008.

Gibson, Roger C. *Asset Allocation: Balancing Financial Risk*. New York: McGraw-Hill, 2000.

Michaud, Richard O., and Robert O. Michaud. *Efficient Asset Management: A Practical Guide to Stock Portfolio Optimization and Asset Allocation*. 2nd ed. New York: Oxford University Press, 2008.

Swensen, David F. *Pioneering Portfolio Management: An Unconventional Approach to Institutional Investment*. New York: Free Press, 2009.

Forecasting:

Mlodinow, Leonard. *The Drunkard's Walk: How Randomness Rules Our Lives*. New York: Pantheon Books, 2008.

Osband, Kent. *Iceberg Risk: An Adventure in Portfolio Theory*. New York: Texere, 2002.

Rebonato, Riccardo. *Plight of the Fortune Tellers: Why We Need to Manage Financial Risk Differently*. Princeton, NJ: Princeton University Press, 2007.

Taleb, Nassim Nicholas. *The Black Swan: The Impact of the Highly Improbable*. New York: Random House, 2007.

Articles:

There are many academic papers on asset allocation and portfolio construction methodologies. The best single source is www.ssrn.com. SSRN is also a good source for papers on markets as complex adaptive systems by authors including Andrew Lo, Blake LeBaron, Cars H. Hommes, and J. Doyne Farmer.

Websites:

In addition to web-based tools based on mean–variance optimization, there are many vendors of more sophisticated asset allocation software. All of the following employ advanced techniques beyond simple MVO:

AlternativeSoft: www.alternativesoft.com
EnCorr: tinyurl.com/6lemmun
New Frontier Asset Allocation Suite: www.newfrontieradvisors.com
SmartFolio: www.smartfolio.com
Windham Financial Planner: www.windhamcapital.com

See Also:

★ The Role of Commodities in an Institutional Portfolio (pp. 585–588)
★ Understanding the Role of Diversification (pp. 617–618)
Harry Markowitz (p. 1292)
William F. Sharpe (p. 1309)
Portfolio Selection: Efficient Diversification of Investments (p. 1408)
Portfolio Theory and Capital Markets (p. 1409)

"It is a bad plan that admits of no modification." Publilius Syrus

  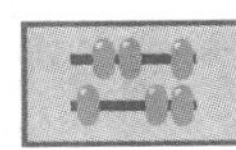   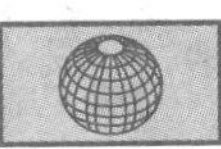   

Viewpoint: Bias-Free Investing Offers the Best Hope for Pension Funds by Yves Choueifaty

INTRODUCTION

Yves Choueifaty built TOBAM in 2006, when he was managing director, head of Lehman Brothers's quantitative asset management business in Europe. He was also previously head of Lehman Brothers Asset Management France. Prior to joining Lehman Brothers, he was CEO of Credit Lyonnais Asset Management (CLAM), with assets under management of €70 billion. Mr Choueifaty graduated in 1992 from ENSAE in statistics, actuarial studies, finance, and artificial intelligence.

TOBAM, formerly part of the Quantitative Asset Management Group inside Lehman Brothers Asset Management Europe, specializes in a maximum diversification approach that attempts to avoid what you term "speculation." How is this approach relevant to pension funds, for example, as they try to build returns to fund their future liabilities?

Let us define the word "speculation." It comes from the Latin *speculare*, which means to be able to see. To speculate you need to take a view on the future and you need to build a portfolio that expresses that view. What we saw happening up to the global crash in 2008 (which I got to view first hand at Lehman Brothers) was a tremendous interest from pension funds in tracking cap-weighted benchmarks. By 2007 there had been a long-running bull market and cap-weighted benchmarks were very heavy bets on the sectors that had outperformed through the bull market years. Then came the crash and the benchmarks lost 30–40% of their value as the sectors that had been doing well, such as finance, failed. That experience created a great deal of interest in alternative approaches to cap-weighted benchmark-tracking portfolios. As a result, funds focused on building portfolios based on low-volatility stocks got a great deal of attention. Here, however, you need to be careful about definitions. If you are talking about low volatility, are you talking about a portfolio with a heavy bias to low-volatility stocks, or are you talking about a portfolio designed to have low volatility, but which does not express a view that market conditions will favor low volatility stocks?

TOBAM's approach is to avoid all possible biases by building the most diversified portfolio possible. This brings us to the question, what exactly is diversification? It is one of the most used terms in investing. Everyone employs it, but it is not well defined. We have an approach to this at TOBAM which we have patented. A simple way of defining it is to say that if you have a universe of just two different, noncorrelated stocks, stock A and stock B, if you combine 80% of stock B with 20% of stock A, that will always result in a portfolio with volatility that is lower than 80% of the volatility of stock A plus 20% of the volatility of stock B. It is simply a mathematical fact that if you combine a set of noncorrelated assets in a proportionate way, the volatility will always be lower than if you combine the risks of the assets. If, with a larger universe, you go for the ratio of the weighted average of the volatilities divided by the volatility of the portfolio as a whole (TOBAM's diversification ratio), you have a portfolio with some very interesting mathematical properties.

To make this clear, imagine again that there are only two stocks, A and B, and that A has a volatility of 30%, while B has a volatility of 15%. Let us say that there is a 60% correlation between them. Then if you work out the largest diversification ratio it will be one-third A combined with two-thirds B, and this will give you a diversified portfolio. The same is true if you have a universe of three stocks, A, B, and C, where A and B have a correlation of 95% (making them almost identical) and C has a correlation of just 5% with the other two (which means that events that impact A and B have very little impact on C). If you maximize the diversification ratio here you have a portfolio that consists of 26% A and 26% of B, with 48% of C. That represents a highly diversified portfolio of the universe of the three stocks, A, B, and C. At no point here are you making any speculative assumptions about the kinds of returns that you will get from A, B, or C.

It follows that this approach could not be more different from that of a value "buy and hold" manager, who would spend a lot of time getting to know the companies A, B, and C, and would try to form a view of their relative probabilities of success in the market based on their current product portfolio, their research and development pipeline, and their acquisition strategies, for example. When you have built the most diversified portfolio available to you, as a quantitative manager with a maximum diversification strategy your job is done. You have absolutely no way of extrapolating from that portfolio to make any kind of prediction about the potential relative success or failure of A, B, and C as companies. What you do have is a great deal of statistical evidence that shows that taken over a medium- to long-term period—which is precisely the kind of time frame that concerns pension funds—a maximally diversified portfolio delivers greater returns than portfolios with a built-in bias. There is, however, no "proof" that this fund will be the least volatile that you could construct. All we are saying is that it is the most diversified fund that you can construct.

So what is the value of constructing the most diversified portfolio?

You have to ask yourself why anyone wants to invest in equities, which are demonstrably, over time, a relatively high-risk asset class. The only reason is that you believe that there is a premium to be had from investing in equities. This is the only reason why many pension funds, for example, risk putting a sizable proportion of their holdings into equities. They believe that equities will outperform other less risky asset classes over time and they want to capture that outperformance. Let us call that the theoretical risk premium associated with equities. So what is the ideal way of consistently capturing that risk premium over time? What the history of investing in equities has shown is that although you might be right some of the time in betting on a particular concentration of risk—say the financial sector—you will be wrong-footed and will lose substantially at other

"More money is probably lost by people who attempt to invest their money conservatively and sanely, but ignorantly, than is lost by those who enter into frank speculations." John Moody

times. Because no one has a crystal ball that will allow them to move with precision and grace from one well-performing concentrated risk to the next well-performing concentrated risk—darting from one to the other before a pull-back in your present allocation wipes out most or all of your gains—it follows that your best defense and your best offense are to have your portfolio maximally diversified across all sources of risk.

What you find, in reality, is that every time there is a concentration of risk in a portfolio toward one sector or one type of stock, be it low-volatility stocks, low-cap stocks, or whatever, what you really have is a "pollution" of the risk premium, since you are taking an implied bet that a particular subset of stocks will outperform the rest. This is a mathematical fact. We have not tinkered around with the numbers and come up with something that is empirically true but which no one quite understands. There is no "black box" here that proves true in practice but is opaque to theory. This is pure mathematics.

Contrast this with a fund that passively tracks a cap-weighted index such as the UK equity market cap-weighted index. In the 1970s this was completely biased toward consumer discretionaries at the worst possible moment. In the 1980s it was completely biased toward oil stocks at the worst possible moment. In the late 1990s it was completely biased toward technology stocks, and in 2000 we had the dot.com crash. In the run-up to 2008 the index was heavily biased toward financial stocks, and we all know what happened next. This is what happens, time after time, when you rely on a cap-weighted index as your benchmark, which is what pension funds have been doing since the 1960s. You are driving using the rear view mirror. These concentrations or weightings in the index build up through periods of prosperity and are at their height just before they crash. Following them makes no sense unless you think you can exit gracefully each time just before the crash. History shows that there are very few, if any, active managers who are that nimble.

So you have launched a series of funds that avoid the problem of market timing?

Exactly. We have launched a series of "anti-benchmark" funds. The approach is equally well suited to any universe of stocks, be it European equities, US equities, emerging market equities, or global equities. So we have funds in all these spaces, and in total we have in excess of US$2.5 billion in assets under management. The entire basis of our approach is our contention that higher returns over time result from the better capturing of the risk premia associated with equities, and that maximum diversification is the best way of capturing that premium.

A corollary of this is that it is plain that investors who want to capture the equity risk premium efficiently should avoid unrewarded risk. Concentrated risk, by definition, is time-dependent in that any returns that result from investing in such a risk vanish when the underlying causes of the excess returns being generated from that risk vanish. In the absence of perfect market timing—something that no one has yet mastered—by definition concentrated risk does not reward investors over time. The period when it outperforms is more than offset by long periods when it underperforms. As the most diversified portfolio that it is possible to construct, the anti-benchmark portfolio is not further diversifiable, and thus it can be defined as the real neutral risk allocator.

Since market cap-weighted indices are representative of a market, it is understandable that these benchmarks are widely accepted by investors as measuring market performance. What is more than questionable is their efficiency in terms of risk–return. As we have said, as a cap-weighted index develops over time, successful stocks or sources of risk (sectors) become overrepresented and create an imbalance, so that a handful of factors come to dominate the index. This maximizes the impact of volatility (price changes) and creates costly implicit bets, which generally do not pay off.

By way of contrast, using the TOBAM diversification ratio no bias accrues in the portfolio toward high- or low-volatility stocks. So, unlike with a low-volatility approach, you are not cutting out the possibility of exposing the fund to superior performance coming from growth, which is typically associated with higher-volatility stocks. In other words, there will be some high-volatility stocks in the portfolio as part of the diversification strategy. But you are limiting risk at the same time because the emphasis is not on picking high-volatility stocks but on diversification. Moreover, the benefits of diversification have the great pedigree of being theoretically grounded in accordance with Markowitz's portfolio management theory, which is the most accepted mathematical theory on finance you can find. Hence the diversification ratio captures growth but limits risk. That is a very appealing feature for institutional investors.

Another way of characterizing what TOBAM does is to see that what most portfolio managers do is to try to take advantage of market inefficiencies. Stock A or stock B is underpriced in their view because the market has not yet grasped and put an appropriate value on stock A's potential to capture additional market share, for example. This is what value investing is all about. In contrast, I actually believe that markets are really quite efficient, and efficient markets are not forecastable (by definition you cannot see in advance what is not yet priced into an efficient market). If markets are really not forecastable, then the only solution you are left with is diversification. The only bet I have, at the end of the day, is that there really is an equity premium.

There has been a great deal of pondering over the ethics of fund management. How does your approach fit into this debate?

Let me tell a personal story here. My father is a surgeon in Beirut and I grew up in a war-torn city where being a surgeon had a tremendous and obvious social benefit. I was very attracted in my university years by mathematics and fund management, but that left me with a dilemma. What was there about fund management that was socially useful, in the same way that being a surgeon made my father valuable to society? I came up with some answers. A fund manager's role is to be the link between savings and labor, and his job is to reinvest savings into the economy via labor. If you are an equity manager, the real source of return is the skills of the employees of the companies you have invested in. They generate the risk premium (the return of the undiversifiable portfolio). Your skills, if you want to express views, biases, and bets, simply pollute that risk premium. What you want to do is to extract the pure risk premium—and that is the one that is least polluted by bets—which turns out to be a consequence of the most diversified portfolio.

My second formulation is to tackle the assumption that core equity managers are there to build alpha (outperformance). That is totally wrong in my view. The original reason for which clients buy any particular fund is because they believe that there is an equity risk premium. If the client stops believing that, then they should buy something entirely different, so, again, your job as a fund manager is to give your client the undiluted risk premium. The job of a core equity manager is not to be a speculator, it is to present a fully diversified portfolio that will allow the risk premium to come through as purely as possible. This then makes it possible for pension funds to have a reasonable chance of building up sufficient assets to cater for their members in old age and so on. That, ultimately, is where the social usefulness lies and, again, it all depends on presenting as nearly as possible the undiluted risk premium. That is it, in a nutshell.

MORE INFO

Articles:

Arnott, Robert D., Jason Hsu, and Philip Moore. "Fundamental indexation." *Financial Analysts Journal* 61:2 (March/April 2005): 83–99. Online at: dx.doi.org/10.2469/faj.v61.n2.2718

Choueifaty, Yves, and Yves Coignard. "Toward maximum diversification." *Journal of Portfolio Management* 35:1 (Fall 2008): 40–51. Online at: dx.doi.org/10.3905/jpm.2008.35.1.40

Choueifaty, Yves, Tristan Froidure, and Julien Reynier. "Properties of the most diversified portfolio." Working Paper. July 2011. Online at: dx.doi.org/10.2139/ssrn.1895459

Haugen, Robert A., and Nardin L. Baker. "The efficient market inefficiency of capitalization-weighted stock portfolios." *Journal of Portfolio Management* 17:3 (Spring 1991): 35–40. Online at: dx.doi.org/10.3905/jpm.1991.409335

Markowitz, Harry. "Portfolio selection." *Journal of Finance* 7:1 (March 1952): 77–91. Online at: www.jstor.org/stable/2975974

Sharpe, William F. "Capital asset prices with and without negative holdings." Nobel Prize Lecture. December 7, 1990. Online at: tinyurl.com/b7narar

Website:

TOBAM: www.tobam.fr

See Also:

★ Asset Allocation Methodologies (pp. 454–458)
★ The Case for SMART Rebalancing (pp. 471–474)
★ Understanding the Role of Diversification (pp. 617–618)
★ Viewpoint: Understanding the Risks in Liability-Driven Investment (LDI) for Pension Funds (pp. 614–616)

"We must not allow ourselves to be at the mercy of the forces around us, but try to lead them." Fons Trompenaars

  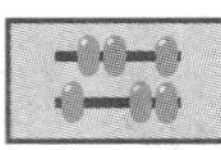   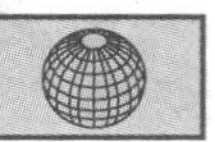   

Viewpoint: Capturing the Equity Premium

by Erik Gosule

INTRODUCTION

Erik Gosule is a director, and head of Client Solutions and Investment Strategy at PanAgora Asset Management. As such, he is responsible for assisting in the development and implementation of investment strategies across the firm, including customized solutions that combine multiple investment capabilities designed to meet clients' specific needs. Prior to joining PanAgora, Mr Gosule worked at the D. E. Shaw Group, where he was most recently a member of their Institutional Asset Management team, focused on systematic equity strategies. Prior to joining D. E. Shaw, Mr Gosule held investment oriented roles at Putnam Investments and Fidelity Investments.

The level of volatility in the markets through 2011 and 2012 has caused many institutional clients and high net worth individuals to become more interested in investment strategies that, at the very least, give them a smoother passage. Can you explain your concept of a portfolio based on risk parity, or the equal weighting of risk?

Investors' fear of heightened volatility and lower returns has led to increased interest in more efficient approaches to capturing equity risk premium, including strategies that target low-volatility stocks. An increasing number of academic studies show that stocks whose share price is more or less stable, or whose price varies significantly less than stocks that are down one minute and up the next, generate a better return over the long term (say, upwards of three years). To many investors this is somewhat counterintuitive since the established view is that there is no reward without risk. Looking at it from this perspective, when you select stocks to create a low-volatility portfolio you are selecting stocks that are likely to have lower returns. However, the real question is whether you are getting compensated for the risk that you take.

It remains to be seen whether the outperformance of lower-volatility stocks will persist. However, at a minimum we believe that many low-volatility approaches suffer from a dilemma similar to that which plagues cap-weighted equity indices—in particular, risk concentration which you may not be compensated for in the long run. As a result, we believe that an approach that balances risk across the most important dimensions within an equity portfolio is a more efficient way to capture equity risk premia, as it results in a truly diversified portfolio solution. The question to ask is simple: do you want to make a bet that low-volatility names persistently outperform on a risk-adjusted basis over time because they offer something unique and are thus unlikely to see their advantage arbitraged away? Or is the objective to truly capture equity risk premia in an efficient manner so as to stabilize returns and minimize downside while still capturing most of the market's upside when things are going well?

Our research has shown that most approaches to portfolio construction result in concentrated risk exposures. By tilting portfolios toward a particular risk concentration, such as lower-volatility names, or to a particularly sector or country (as is the case in cap-weighted indices), you risk embedding a fairly large and persistent bias into your portfolio. If the bias works, fine, you do well. But to the best of my knowledge no one has a crystal ball, and as a result no one gets it right all the time. Our research has shown that a portfolio that exhibits a balanced risk allocation and limits concentrated risk exposures does better over time than a portfolio with inbuilt bias.

This is one of the reasons why the big institutions, such as the large pension funds, are increasingly considering alternatives to portfolios that track the traditional cap-weighted benchmarks. If you take the FTSE 100, for example, financial and oil stocks have a very large presence, and as a result these two sectors have a large influence on the index's performance. Investors who allocate to funds that are proxies of the FTSE benchmark are essentially expressing a view that these two sectors are likely to outperform other sectors on a risk-adjusted basis over time, regardless of where we are in the business cycle or prevailing economic conditions.

To many investors, it has become clear that this kind of approach is not paying off, particularly over the last few years, so people are looking for alternatives. But many of these alternatives suffer from the same problem. An obvious alternative is a diversified risk portfolio—one that balances the most important foreseeable risks. If you think about this, there are multiple dimensions on which you would want to balance risks. When you do this, what you find is that you create a fund that is less likely to suffer large drawdowns (sharp or sustained downward movement in market prices) and that leads to better risk-adjusted returns over time.

The goal of this kind of approach to investing is to efficiently capture equity risk premia by dampening volatility and mitigating drawdowns while still participating in the market's upside. It is distinguished from minimum-variance and other low-volatility approaches, which, as I previously mentioned, may tend to experience greater risk concentrations, or biases, that result from their tendency to focus on low-volatility stocks. Once again, biases may be fine when they lead to outperformance, but they are also subject to bubbles and underperformance, and when the bubble bursts you may realize significant drawdowns (losses).

When using a balanced approach to better diversify a portfolio's risk exposures, such as that which is deployed in PanAgora's diversified risk equity strategies, we are not solely concerned about solving for low volatility; rather, we are simply determining the most important dimensions of risk and balancing our exposures across these dimensions to achieve true diversification. Technology stocks, for example have significantly more volatility relative to industrial stocks, so the risk contribution of an allocation to technology stocks is meaningfully higher than a similar capital allocation to the industrial sector, all else equal. What you want to do is to balance your risk allocation across as many dimensions as possible, targeting those dimensions that really matter. We have seen this lead to smaller drawdowns when the market goes against you and better returns in the medium to longer term. We find it to be a very robust strategy. When we look into portfolios constructed across sectors and across countries, a balanced risk portfolio outperforms on all these dimensions.

How willing are pension funds to allocate part of their portfolio to this kind of investment strategy?

For years now institutional investors have been anchored to cap-weighted benchmarks, and that may have served them well in the bull markets. However, after investors experienced the precipitous fall of cap-weighted equity indices in 2008, and subsequent regime shifts that seem to have occurred with increasing frequency over the past several years (an effect known as "risk-on/risk-off" trading), the door opened for alternative approaches to equity investing.

We have seen an array of strategies in the aftermath of the global crash of 2008, including the shift in interest toward lower-volatility approaches such as minimum variance and other strategies that target lower-volatility stocks. These approaches are intuitively appealing since by definition low-volatility stocks tend to be more stable, defensive stocks, and when institutions are experiencing large drawdowns they may tend to favor such strategies. That is understandable.

However, to say that low-volatility stocks are going to persistently outperform other stocks over the long term may be unreasonable, and there is always the possibility that the bulk of institutional money heading into low-volatility strategies is moving too late. Although volatility does play a role in the allocation decisions within a diversified risk portfolio, it is only one of many elements considered in the process. Focusing on low volatility alone may result in some very significant risk concentrations, such as material country or sector imbalances.

Gradually, with a great deal of educational effort, pension funds are starting to see the merits of a diversified, balanced risk approach. In some instances, the allocations that these plans make can be quite significant; however, on balance many investors begin with a modest allocation which they are likely to scale up over time. When allocating to alternative beta strategies as a whole, investors often consider appointing two or three managers using different alternative beta approaches to run a segment of their portfolio. In these instances, our diversified risk approach is often complementary to these other approaches, including minimum-variance and other defensive strategies.

In addition, the strategy is very scalable, and what funds want above all else is to capture the equity premium without having to suffer really uncomfortable levels of volatility. PanAgora's diversified risk equity strategies provide a robust solution to this objective. What we are definitely seeing is that, while it is early days for the entire pension fund universe to move, there are now a lot more conversations about alternatives to cap-weighted benchmarks, and the velocity of conversations about alternatives is picking up.

Our argument is that if you are going to move from a cap- weighted index, which is biased toward a handful of companies and a couple of sectors and/or countries that have outperformed in the recent past, the last thing you should be doing is moving to another strategy that has a strong bias toward this or that sector or type of stock (small-cap, mid-cap or large-cap, for example). What you should be thinking about is a fund that avoids bias as much as possible and tries to collect the pure equity premium. Of course, if you do not believe that there is such a thing as an equity premium—in other words, that equities will outperform cash over time—then you should not be in any equity strategy at all, except perhaps tactically in certain circumstances.

To the extent that an investor wishes to express a particular tactical view with respect to the likely relative performance of a particular attribute (i.e. low volatility), we believe that applying an approach which balances risk exposures to express or target a particular attribute will achieve the desired result with better diversification. Our research has shown that when targeting specific attributes, such as lower volatility or higher dividend yield and quality, an approach based on risk parity generates higher risk-adjusted returns relative to other approaches.

However we caution that tactically targeting specific attributes may be speculative investing in its purest form, and it is debatable whether pension funds have ever had much success long term pursuing such strategies. The "right" biases change continuously over time, and it is an excellent investor indeed that can time the markets accurately enough to switch from one bias to the next at just the right moment.

From what you are saying it sounds as if risk parity, or a balanced weighting of risk in a portfolio, is a passive strategy.

I like to think of risk parity as being the ultimate passive equity investment strategy. It is an agnostic approach that essentially expresses no implied view that one particular attribute is likely to outperform another on a risk-adjusted basis because the approach mitigates such risk concentration within the portfolio. To invest in a cap-weighted fund or other portfolios built using processes that result in some form of risk concentration generally implies that one believes that certain sectors, countries, or other such concentrations will outperform on a risk-adjusted basis. They may, but then again they may not. Or they may perform for a while, then cause the fund to experience a drawdown that more than wipes out that performance.

From this standpoint, investing in a cap-weighted index—even in a passive index tracking fund—is somewhat akin to investing with an active manager. With an active manager, you are betting on his selection of market bias. With a cap-weighted index tracker, you are betting on the inherent bias in the index. To the extent that a fund wishes to express a view that low-volatility strategies will outperform—because it believes that there is a strong possibility that recent volatility is going to persist and damage performance—we would still argue that applying an approach based on risk parity to target low-volatility stocks will generate better risk-adjusted returns.

As an example, during the dot.com crash, which ran from April 2000 to the end of September 2002, the cap-weighted index fell by some 45%. Our diversified risk portfolio fell by just 16%. This makes it a great deal easier for a diversified risk portfolio to recover from a downturn. The October 2008–April 2009 global financial crash saw the cap-weighted index drop by almost 48%. This time around diversified risk portfolios suffered as well, since the crash was all-encompassing, but they fell by just 41%. Applying the diversified risk process to a portfolio that was targeting lower-volatility stocks would have further mitigated drawdowns during these periods.

However, a characteristic that distinguishes the approach from other low-volatility strategies is that, in addition to mitigating downside and reducing volatility in difficult periods, an approach based on risk parity often participates in the market's upside during periods of strong performance. As markets recovered in the latter half of 2009, the diversified risk strategy

  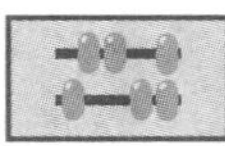      

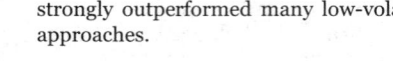

strongly outperformed many low-volatility approaches.

It sounds simple, balancing out risk, but in practice it looks like being a very complicated exercise, since when you balance risk in one direction you find you are increasing it in another.

It is not a simple exercise. As you say, balancing one dimension can have knock-on effects on other risk dimensions. It has taken us a very significant investment of time and skill to solve the problems associated with viable risk balancing. You have to consider all the trade-offs that are relevant to do this. In addition, you have to put a significant amount of resources into the effort. It is not easy for any fund management house to simply shift from what they may be doing today—whether it is offering a low-volatility fund or a long short strategy—and produce a risk parity fund that is actually going to do what it says on the tin.

So you would say that the Sharpe ratio, a measure of return per unit of absolute risk, is more important as a performance measure for your strategy than any attempt to provide a tracking error against a benchmark?

Exactly. We believe that the most efficient capture of the equity risk premium is what we are after. The Sharpe ratio is indicative of the amount of return (in excess of the risk-free rate) that an investor receives for each incremental unit of risk they take on. Our back-testing of the diversified risk approach shows a greater than 100% improvement in the Sharpe ratio by comparison with cap-weighted funds over time, and we have seen similar relative results since launching our first non-US diversified risk strategy.

We have found the diversified risk approach to be quite robust. Our research shows that the approach adds value in every region and virtually every sector. The one area that we have discovered where a risk parity approach struggles to outperform a cap-weighted index is in the technology sector. Within this sector much of the performance is heavily concentrated in a handful of stocks, with Apple and Google dominating for example. A few stocks driving the whole of a sector can be very good for the sector for a while, but when they run out of steam it can have a profound effect on the whole sector.

Interestingly, our findings show that the diversified risk approach is a good strategy even where you are trying to construct a portfolio that is tilted toward exposures which are intended to generate higher returns because balanced risk exposure is something that adds value to almost any portfolio that benefits from diversification. You can balance risk across and within many dimensions. When constructing a risk parity portfolio, you begin by identifying the various risk dimensions, then you solve for the weight that achieves the risk exposure you want for the strategy. It is important to realize that this is a very systematic approach and the portfolio will always maintain a balanced risk allocation. Once the selection is made, we continuously monitor portfolios to ensure that the risks remain balanced and that a portfolio is not wandering away from the key parameters over time. What this means is that if there are external shocks to the market, or if the business cycle changes, the portfolio should be able to weather the storm.

In contrast, if you are in a cap-weighted fund, you will be in more cyclical stocks, and when the business cycle changes your fund will lose performance. With a minimum-variance approach, for example, the reverse is true and you will be too defensively positioned if the business cycle moves into a more positive phase.

In conclusion, there are clearly far-reaching events that can happen that are going to cause a shock regardless, and there are circumstances in which no equity portfolio can outperform. However, a risk parity approach is clearly better at capturing the equity premium over a wide range of conditions.

MORE INFO

Books:

Grinold, Richard C., and Ronald N. Kahn. *Active Portfolio Management: A Quantitative Approach for Providing Superior Returns and Controlling Risk*. 2nd ed. New York: McGraw-Hill, 1999.

Mackay, Charles. *Extraordinary Popular Delusions and the Madness of Crowds*. 1841. Online at: www.gutenberg.org/ebooks/24518

Qian, Edward E., Ronald H. Hua, and Eric H. Sorensen. *Quantitative Equity Portfolio Management: Modern Techniques and Applications*. Boca Raton, FL: Chapman & Hall/CRC, 2007.

Shiller, Robert. *Irrational Exuberance*. 2nd ed. New York: Broadway Books, 2006.

See Also:

★ Asset Allocation Methodologies (pp. 454–458)
★ Passive Portfolio Management and Fixed-Income Investing (pp. 549–552)
★ Viewpoint: Bias-Free Investing Offers the Best Hope for Pension Funds (pp. 459–461)
⇄ Sharpe Ratio (p. 1253)

"Nothing is more admirable than the fortitude with which millionaires tolerate the disadvantages of their wealth."
Rex Stout

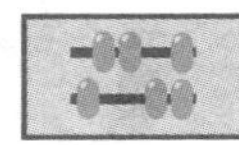

Carrying Out Due Diligence on Hedge Funds

by Amarendra Swarup

EXECUTIVE SUMMARY

- Due diligence should be the cornerstone of any hedge fund investment program.
- Hedge funds are a complex and volatile asset class, and poor selection will greatly increase the chances of fraud and poor performance.
- Due diligence is about identifying the best hedge fund manager for your investment goals and risk appetite.
- Due diligence is proactive risk management that seeks to generate superior returns while minimizing risk.
- Performance alone is meaningless.
- You need to understand how and why a hedge fund makes money.
- Dig deep and understand all the risks in all possible markets.
- If in the slightest doubt about a fund, just walk away.

INTRODUCTION

Hedge funds have often been cited as valuable additions to any institutional portfolio, thanks to their typically uncorrelated returns to traditional asset classes over the long term, and superior risk-adjusted returns. However, they are also a complex and volatile asset class, and since their ascent onto the investment podium, both institutional and private investors have found themselves burned at regular intervals by embarrassing and costly blow-ups. The oft-cited collapse of Long-Term Capital Management in 1998 and Amaranth Advisers in 2006, the litany of hedge fund managers wrong-footed by the credit crunch, and, most recently, the uncovering of the US$50 billion Ponzi scheme run by Bernie Madoff are but some of the stark reminders of the minefield investors navigate in their quest for absolute and consistent returns.

The reason is simple: Today's increasingly complex asset markets make it more difficult than ever for investors to peer under the bonnet and select the best hedge funds. Many make the naïve decision to invest based solely on a strong track record, little realizing that the simple effort of conducting a thorough investigation into the fund prior to investment can often save them considerable financial pain in the future.

Due diligence is the most important aspect of investing in hedge funds, and often also the most ignored part. It's a bizarre oversight—most people would not buy a house without learning first about the area, local schools, and amenities, conducting structural surveys, investigating the state of the housing market, and so on. Yet when most institutional investors allocate to hedge funds, the lack of simple questions as to honesty, competence, and future potential reduces most investments to the ignoble status of a crapshoot.

DUE DILIGENCE: A DEFINITION

Due diligence is the process of identifying the best hedge fund manager for your investment goals and thereafter continually reevaluating them at regular intervals to ensure that they continue to meet your requirements. In doing so, it looks across the entire gamut of the fund—its investment strategy, performance, personnel, legal structure, risk management, documentation, operational infrastructure, service providers, counterparties, and client base. In essence, it is a proactive risk management approach that successfully balances the twin goals of any investment: generating superior returns while minimizing risk.

Looking at past performance alone is often meaningless in the hedge fund world. Performance tells you nothing about the underlying strategy, its advantages and disadvantages, management's skill, the use of leverage, the impact of different market conditions, and so on. Further, selection bias means that most investors will naturally gravitate toward those strategies and funds that have performed well in the past. Any successful hedge fund strategy will seek in principle to deliver targeted returns within the confines of some defined risk constraints. Yet, while quantitative measures such as volatility capture the riskiness of performance, it does not tell investors how robust the fund's underlying risk management is and how it may react to leaner times in the future.

In contrast, careful due diligence provides a valuable insight into the quality of the fund's strategy, personnel, systems, and, vitally, their risk management. Investors know what to expect in good and bad times, and are able to approach their investment in a rational manner without worrying over every inevitable jitter.

The questions you ask are driven ultimately by your investment goals and the constraints on your balance sheet, such as your investment horizon and the need to maintain an optimal liquidity profile commensurate with your cash flow requirements. While no two investors are likely to have the same set of questions, there are fundamental areas that any proper due diligence process needs to cover.

INVESTMENT STRATEGY

There are over 8,000 hedge funds today, and most claim to have a unique edge over the rest. Further, they are scattered among a myriad of strategies and substrategies—all with very different risk and return profiles that profit during varying market conditions. For example, long/short equity funds are very liquid and target absolute performance irrespective of stock market direction, by going both long and short shares. In contrast, event-driven strategies are more catalyst-driven, focusing on changing corporate structures, mergers and acquisitions, and distressed investing. Arbitrage funds might exploit perceived pricing anomalies to eke out small, steady gains, while strong commodity, currency, and interest rate trends could be harvested by momentum-driven strategies such as those used by CTAs (commodity trading advisers) and global funds. There is no shortage of managers playing across different financial instruments, different sectors, and different geographies—all with their own unique traits, opportunities, and risks.

It's a daunting prospect for any investor looking to pick the right funds, and the two key questions in any due diligence process are:

- How does the fund make its money?
- Why does the fund make its money?

It may seem almost facile, but true outperformance and differentiation from the crowd comes from identifying trading talent and potential, and knowing how to time those investments.

To answer the first question, you need to understand and document the hedge fund's basic investment strategy and trading style. What markets does the manager operate in, and what instruments are used? What are the potential returns, and what is the downside if someone makes the wrong call? What is the outlook given today's markets?

"Performance alone is meaningless."

Finding a strategy that matches your investment needs and risk appetite is important. Changing market conditions favor different instruments and strategies. For example, CTAs invest in listed financial and commodity markets as well as in currency markets through options and futures, giving them a wide and often highly liquid market. They are highly directional as they pick trends in momentum-driven markets, and can also lose significantly when these suddenly reverse.

The strategy also needs to sit well within your broader portfolio and balance sheet. For example, despite their volatility, CTAs can be a valuable addition to a broadly diversified portfolio, providing stability and an often rare stream of positive returns at times of negative market stress. Equally, if a company is involved in the energy sector, it is unlikely to want to invest in a long/short equity hedge fund specializing in natural resources.

MORE QUESTIONS TO ASK

The first hurdle crossed, we come on to a more troubling question—what edge does the manager have, if any? Manager selection will contribute far more to your portfolio's performance than broad strategy allocation. True talent lies not in doubling your money in a bull market but in consistently growing it in all markets—good and bad. And ultimately, that's what you're paying those hefty fees for.

Two managers operating the same strategy may look ostensibly the same in terms of style and performance. But one may simply be lucky—a beta jockey riding some market wave for all it's worth, with an inevitable and costly crash looming somewhere on the horizon—while the other may be genuinely skilled, capable of producing consistently good returns irrespective of the wider market (or "alpha" in hedge fund parlance).

How do you tell the difference? The answers are all hidden within their portfolios and in how they generate and implement their ideas.

- Who are the people? A veteran manager who has proven his ability to make consistent money in many different environments is often preferable to the newbie who's churned out spectacular returns using an otherwise unfamiliar strategy for the last couple of years.
- Where do the ideas come from? A manager who grabs ideas off golfing buddies and follows the herd means that you could find yourself in the same position as many others, greatly increasing the chances of large losses in stressed situations.
- Are the people who developed the strategies and models still there? Or is the fund now relying solely on a mysterious oracle for guidance? Models may work fantastically, but they all have limitations—and inevitably stop working without constant research.
- How is the investment process implemented? Ideas need to be robustly examined and debated to ensure not only that the potential rewards are worth the risk, but that the downside is amenable. They also need to be compared to what's already there—a portfolio with 20 great pharmaceutical stocks probably doesn't need a twenty-first.
- How have they performed? Were all their returns based on a couple of great trades, or do they consistently make money on the majority? Astoundingly good performance may be just as suspicious as bad performance.
- What's the capacity of the strategy? Every strategy has an optimal size beyond which returns will begin to suffer as the market gets too crowded. Some strategies, such as global macro, invest around the world across many asset classes—their limitations are likely in the billions. Others, such as those investing in niche emerging markets, may find the constraints considerably tighter.
- Is the manager a jack of all trades? The best managers are those who stick to what they know. Sticking your finger into every pie that comes by is likely to become very messy—both for managers and their investors.
- What happens when the markets turn? Does the trading strategy have the ability to adapt? Knowing how the fund might perform when the environment suddenly changes is vital. Every strategy will inevitably make losses, but the extent, duration, and how the manager bounces back says a lot about their skill. But going down in the past whenever the broader market does is a worrying sign—that's not what you signed up for, and perhaps that perceived skill was just an extended lucky run at the roulette wheel.

RISK MANAGEMENT

Implicit in the answers to the last two questions is the quality of risk management at the hedge fund. A dynamic risk-monitoring process aimed at reviewing positions and reallocating precious capital is the key to ensuring that portfolios are nimble and always a step ahead of any downturn. The more comprehensive the risk process, the more comfortable you can feel about your assets.

Most importantly, the risk management needs to be independent, with the right of veto. A fund where management can choose to overrule or ignore risk warnings is one that's not worth investing in, no matter how good the returns are. Once past that, there are innumerable other questions regarding the strength of the control framework around the compelling investment strategy that is presented to you.

- How are positions and exposures sized? Are there any limits? It's a simple question, but many an eager manager has been caught out by betting the bank on a guaranteed winner—right up to the point where they failed.
- How is risk actually measured? Volatility is one measure, value-at-risk another, stress tests a third. Does the manager attempt to capture the unique risks within the investment strategy and actively watch out for them?
- What are the fund's exposures on the long and short sides? An equity long/short with mostly long positions and token shorts is likely to be a closet long-only fund, looking to make a bit extra from fees by masquerading as a hedge fund, and unlikely to do well in a downturn.
- How large is the leverage? Are there limits, and is it secured on a long-term basis? Some strategies, such as arbitrage, need leverage, but in a downturn this can quickly magnify losses. Equally, with too much leverage, returns could be due to leveraging substandard returns rather than any genuine talent.
- What about noninvestment risks such as liquidity? Are there plans in place if this suddenly dries up? If positions need to be liquidated quickly, this may impact the fund adversely and significantly, as shown by the experience of hedge funds trading asset-backed securities during the recent credit crunch.
- What about counterparties with whom the fund trades or relies on for derivative contracts? Are there safeguards against defaults, and are contracts watertight?

FINAL HURDLES

Assuming that these questions are all answered to your satisfaction, the due diligence can move on to more mundane but equally important topics, such as the fund's operational infrastructure and checking the legalese in the fund prospectus. Many a brilliant fund manager has been undone by a sloppy pricing process and poor systems, and many a fraud has been perpetrated on an unsuspecting investor who didn't check the clauses in the contract until after they had signed.

"The lack of simple questions as to honesty, competence and future potential can reduce most investments to the ignoble status of a crapshoot."

  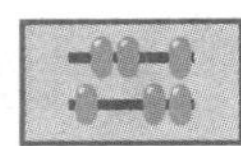   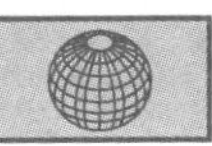   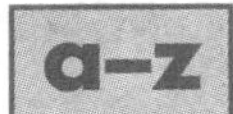

- Are the fund managers invested in the fund themselves? Nothing brings manager and client together as close as knowing you're both rowing the same boat.
- How long have the people been there? Having staff on a revolving door policy is likely to cause instability and poor performance.
- What are the fees? Talented managers have their price but, no matter how brilliant, there is always a point where you may feel that what you pay to access their skill is simply too high to justify. Moreover, if you're handing over enough cash, you may well be able to negotiate more advantageous fees.
- How long will your money be locked up for, and how quickly can you get it back? It is important that the liquidity offered by the fund is consonant with your own circumstances and investment horizons. Equally, the liquidity of the investments made by the manager needs to match or be better than that offered to investors. Otherwise, there may be problems if the fund hits a lean patch and everyone rushes for the exits—as happened with many hedge funds in 2008.
- Does the manager have reliable references who can tell you honestly about their past experiences? Ultimately, you have to trust the people you hand your money over to.
- Visit their offices. See how they work and interact. Try out some of their systems for yourself.

Potentially, there are hundreds of minor questions. The selection—in both qualitative and quantitative terms—of a successful fleet of hedge fund managers is an exhausting process, at the heart of which is an attempt to best capture trading talent. And even when complete, it's an exercise that is worth repeating every year for every hedge fund you choose to invest in.

CONCLUSION

The ultimate aim of the due diligence process is to convince you that the fund you select is genuinely suited to your investment needs. If there is any niggling doubt, the answer is simple: No matter how good it may seem in other respects, walk away.

The catastrophic demise of Amaranth is a case in point. Amaranth performed in stellar fashion for several years, and its reputation as a stable multi-strategy fund with attractive risk-adjusted returns attracted many institutional investors.

Yet its collapse in September 2006 was not the result of some unavoidable fraud. Rather, the warning signs were there for those investors who chose to look, particularly in the last year or two. Amaranth began to unilaterally change its liquidity terms to make it harder for investors to exit quickly, adopted a burdensome fee structure that passed expenses through to the investor, and morphed into a complex corporate structure which included self-administration.

Strong performances throughout the summer of 2005 flagged a rapidly increasing exposure to volatile energy markets such as natural gas futures. The size of this grew to the extent that to all intents and purposes, Amaranth effectively became the market.

Trapped eventually in a liquidity vice of its own making, its failure serves as a salient example of how active due diligence can avoid these market events. The management of Amaranth was always forthcoming in explaining strategies and exposures, and investors received exposure information continuously through the website and monthly letters. Thorough due diligence would have identified the problems, as well as revealed style drift, operational changes, and inadequate risk systems, all failing to control concentration of exposures and an ever increasing value-at-risk.

It's a powerful lesson. The hedge fund industry thrives because of the freedom offered by the lack of constraints on its activities. However, this freedom is also a double-edged sword that can make the allocation of assets to hedge funds a hazardous exercise.

A thorough due diligence process offers the best chance of avoiding fraud and incompetence, while identifying the best hedge fund managers for your investment goals. Properly carried out, due diligence gives a high probability that the managers you choose will live up to your investment goals and provide a bulwark against the inevitable downturn.

MORE INFO

Websites:

Alternative Investment Management Association (AIMA): www.aima.org
Chartered Alternative Investment Analyst (CAIA) Association: www.caia.org

See Also:

★ Funds of Hedge Funds versus Single-Manager Funds (pp. 490–491)
★ Understanding the Role of Diversification (pp. 617–618)
✔ Derivatives Markets: Their Structure and Function (p. 1007)
✔ Fund of Hedge Funds: Understanding the Risks and Returns (p. 1071)
✔ Hedge Funds: Understanding the Risks and Returns (p. 1072)
George Soros (p. 1312)
Absolute Returns: The Risk and Opportunities of Hedge Fund Investing (p. 1326)

"If there is any niggling doubt, the answer is simple: no matter how good it may seem, walk away."

  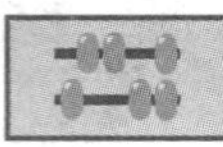   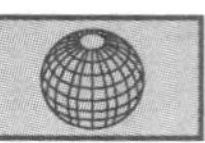   

Carrying Out Due Diligence on Private Equity Funds by Rainer Ender

EXECUTIVE SUMMARY

- Private equity fund due diligence is the first step in an investment process. The goal of due diligence is to identify the risk–return profile of a fund offer.
- A well-structured due diligence process contains a top-down macro and a bottom-up manager analysis, allowing the investor to filter the most promising funds.
- A consistent framework for fund and fund-manager assessment is essential. This assessment must address quantitative and qualitative aspects, and focus on the manager's "ingredients for success."
- At first sight, fund offerings may appear attractive from a pure return perspective. It is crucial that the investment has an attractive risk–return balance.

INTRODUCTION

The term "due diligence" covers a broad range of different due diligence types. These can be grouped into three major types; financial, legal/tax, and business due diligence. The goal of this article is to shed light on business due diligence for investing in private equity funds. Due diligence is commonly defined as "the process of investigation and evaluation, performed by investors, into the details of a potential investment, such as an examination of operations and management, the verification of material facts."[1] "It is a requirement for prudent investors and the basis for better investment decisions."[2] Private equity fund evaluation faces specific challenges; the private character of the industry makes it inherently difficult to obtain the relevant information; furthermore, the investment decision reflects a commitment to a fund manager to finance future investments rather than a straightforward purchase of specific assets. Therefore, common evaluation techniques used to assess public equity investments are not appropriate within the private equity asset class.

The private equity market has enjoyed extraordinary growth rates in the past, and private equity investments showed strong returns, supported by a booming economy and an expanding debt market. The current financial crisis will have a significant impact on the private equity market; a shake-out of fund managers is to be expected over the coming years. Managers who can demonstrate how they created value in the past, beyond just benefiting from favorable market developments, and who are able to make a compelling case for future value creation will continue to raise capital successfully.

Before investing in a private equity fund, an investor should have sufficient comfort regarding:

- Strategy perspective: the investment strategy of the fund.
- Return perspective: evidence that the manager stands out compared to his/her peer group.
- Risk perspective: assurance that risk is mitigated to the level required by the investor.

The relative youth of the private equity industry, data paucity, as well as benchmarking difficulties within and across asset classes are just a few elements that indicate why the investor has to rely on qualitative aspects and judgment during the due diligence process of private equity funds.

STRUCTURAL SET-UP OF A DUE DILIGENCE PROCESS

The Overall Framework

A solid due diligence framework contains a top-down review as a first step. This review must assess the attractiveness of the various private equity sub-segments and regions. The assessment includes various evaluation criteria, such as investment opportunities in the segment, capital demand and supply, the quality of the fund manager universe, entry and exit prices, and the future development potential of the sub-segments. Furthermore, it is important that the investment strategy of a fund manager is not only attractive on a stand-alone basis, but also within the overall context of the investor's total portfolio.

Generating a complete overview of the relevant fund manager universe is the

Figure 1. Example of a proven due diligence process structure

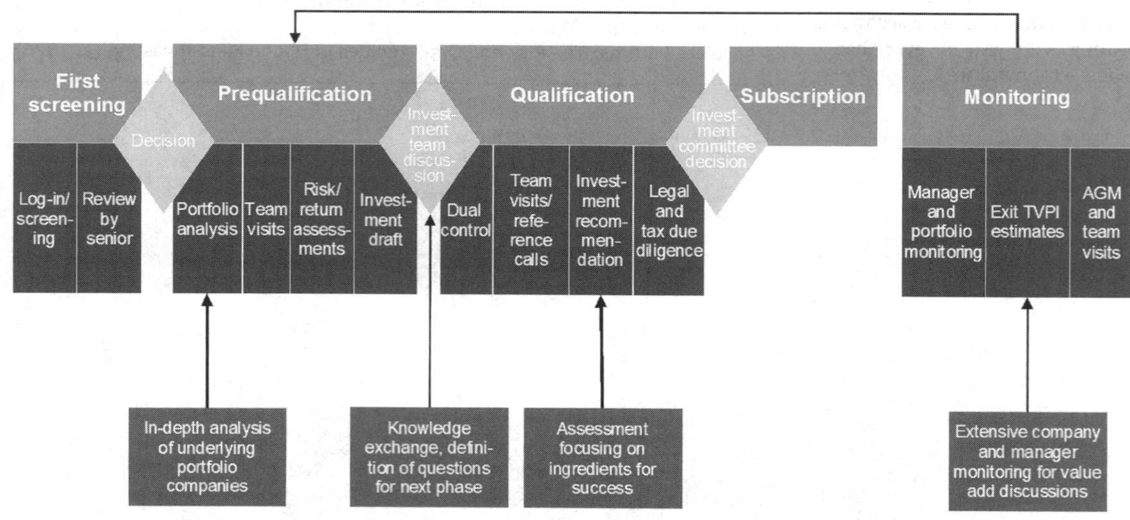

"You can eat an elephant one bit at a time." Mary Kay Ash

second step. Worldwide, there are about 3,000 private equity fund managers to be considered, making the creation of this overview a very demanding task. It is crucial not to assess the managers who provide you with their fund offering passively, but proactively to benchmark all relevant fund managers for a proper peer-group comparison.

The third step of the framework is to ensure that risks related to the potential commitment are mitigated through an in-depth due diligence process. For all identified issues, due diligence steps must be taken in order to clarify the situation. An investment should only be considered if a sufficient level of comfort is achieved on all issues.

Example of a Due Diligence Process

A clear, well-structured due diligence process, which is tailored to the context of the fund manager, with concrete steps and tools, is an important prerequisite for a comprehensive and consistent fund-manager evaluation. Below, we describe a process structure that is the result of continuous improvements over the past 25 years.

The first screening of the fund offering addresses the track record, strategy, team, and fit with the portfolio. This analysis can be performed by junior professionals, but it is important to have an experienced senior professional reviewing the screening and taking the final decision whether to conduct further due diligence. This ensures that the senior has the full picture of the deal flow and the market dynamics.

The prequalification phase starts with a detailed portfolio analysis of all past investments made by the fund manager. Interactions with the fund manager are used to clarify the impact on the value contribution of the manager to past and future investments. Putting these insights into a structured risk–return framework (see next section detailed below), combined with peer-group benchmarking, allows the identification of fund offerings with a promising risk–return potential. It is beneficial broadly to discuss fund offerings within the investment team to identify critical aspects, residual risks, and external referencing possibilities. This knowledge exchange defines questions for the qualification phase.

The qualification phase is divided into four steps:

1 Dual control: the project worker starts working with an independent devil's advocate. The goal of this step is to identify all potential weaknesses that could be discovered by a pair of fresh eyes, and to ensure the quality of the process. It also helps specify further tailored action steps that need to be addressed, and to clarify open issues.
2 The second step is to review the fund manager's governance structures and processes, with the goal of identifying operational and team dynamic risks.
3 The third step is the verification of the self-assessment through third-party referencing. Well-prepared reference calls with past and present key people

Table 1. Framework for a manager evaluation addressing risk and return aspects with a scoring system

Return assessment criteria	*Score*	*Risk assessment criteria*	*Score*
Historical performance • Quality of past performance • Aggregate deal performance over time	X.XX	**Historical performance** • Quality of past performance • Deal by deal volatility	X.XX
Deal sourcing • Quality of deal flow • Involvement in deal origination	X.XX	**Operations/team risk** • Governance structure • Process quality	X.XX
Value creation • Operational competence • Level of active involvement in deals	X.XX	**Investment strategy risk** • Investment discipline • General risk elements	X.XX
Exit capacity • Track based on many deals vs. single hit • Corporate buyers network	X.XX	**Aggregate company financing risk** • Milestone vs. upfront financing • Quality of syndication partners	X.XX
Portfolio return considerations • Common characteristics of individual companies supporting return potential	X.XX	**Portfolio return considerations** • Common characteristics of individual companies supporting risk potential	X.XX
Total return score	**X.XX**	**Total return score**	**X.XX**

CASE STUDY

Fund Due Diligence for the MCAP Fund[3]

MCAP is a newly formed, European, first-time fund manager launching a €250 million fund specialized in development capital and small buyout investments in a single industry. The key person for the fund has deep industry experience. He successfully founded and grew a company operationally superior to more mature, competitive companies. Subsequently, the company was acquired by an international corporation, where he then became the CEO. After stepping down, he formed MCAP. Besides him, there are two other partners who also left their high caliber jobs to launch MCAP. The additional team members previously worked together in various positions; however, none of them has a track record as an investment professional.

A standard due diligence process focused mainly on the historic performance of the fund would pass on this fund after the first screening. The risk–return framework has a different approach:

- The industry targeted by the fund is not covered by existing fund managers. The industry appears to be attractive for backing small, flexible, and dynamic companies with high technological and operational excellence. MCAP could, therefore, be a promising complementary investment.
- The fund manager's ingredients for success from a deal-sourcing and value-creation perspective are in place through the extensive networks of MCAP's partners, and their in-depth industry expertise. Exit capability has only been proven in the sale to the international corporation; there is neither a proven track record, nor an established competitor. Nevertheless, the risk–return assessment framework can be applied to benchmark this new fund against other funds with a single industry focus. Reference calls are important sources for validating the reputation and the competency of MCP's team.
- Risk mitigation for the investor is the most challenging aspect of the due diligence in this case. The management firm is in formation, and the concept is to operate like an industry holding company, managing five investments with deep operational involvement. It is evident that the fund operation will be loss-making, and that the partners are pre-financing this initiative substantially. They are well aligned with the investors in the fund. Close interaction with the manager, and legal terms allowing intervention by investors, should MCAP drift off course, are prerequisites for reaching the level of comfort needed to make a fund commitment.

"How you start is important, but it is how you finish that counts. In the race for success, speed is less important than stamina. The sticker outlasts the sprinter." Bertie Charles Forbes

from underlying companies are an extremely helpful resource for verifying your current impression of the fund manager. Reference calls provide the opportunity to check the contribution of the fund manager to the value creation and the investment sourcing. If external referencing confirms the current assessment and does not lead to new questions, the investment opportunity fulfils all three evaluation levels: appealing strategy, return potential, and controlled risk.

4 The last step is the legal and tax due diligence.

The investment decision and subscription: having a formalized investment approval mechanism, for example through an investment committee, rounds off the due diligence process, which, as a last step, includes the subscription process to the fund.

Thorough monitoring must be put in place once a long-term investment is made. Monitoring is needed to ensure that active measures can be taken where needed, in order to maximize value for the investor. Monitoring is also an integral part of the due diligence for the investment decision regarding the fund manager's next fund (typically after three to four years). Due diligence represents a deep monitoring effort on prior fund investments.

Risk–Return Framework

A clear fund-manager evaluation framework provides consistency among different manager evaluations, and allows for proper benchmarking of managers within a specific peer group. A scoring system that is appropriate for the qualitative and quantitative analyses on a fund manager has proven useful. By constantly applying the system, the scoring becomes well calibrated. Furthermore, it allows for best-practice manager benchmarking across geographies and segments. Due to the qualitative nature of private equity, the focus of the assessment must be on the "ingredients for success" within the future competitive landscape.

In order to enable the ranking of fund managers within a peer group, a quantitative benchmarking that looks at the return and risk aspects helps to put the full due diligence findings into an aggregate picture. We have applied the following framework during the past decade.

CONCLUSION

Private equity fund due diligence is a work-intensive undertaking. It requires a clear top-down assessment of investment segments and geographies that, based on fundamental drivers, appear attractive for investment. For the bottom-up fund manager evaluation, a proper due diligence process with clear milestones must be established. This process must be supported by tools that allow a structured assessment of a fund offering, and ensure comparability of different funds. When working in a broad team, special attention is also needed to make certain that all professionals apply the same framework, and that evaluations by different people lead to comparable results.

Finally, it must be emphasized that, while there appear to be many promising investment opportunities, the most important element for due diligence is to identify the risk behind each opportunity.

MAKING IT HAPPEN

The foundation of a successful due diligence process is a structured process, a proven evaluation framework, and an experienced team. Some valuable aspects are:

- In-depth knowledge of past fund investments, their business and investment performance, and the fund manager's value creation is crucial for the evaluation and the understanding of a private equity fund's offering.
- Broad sharing of the investment project work among all investment team members ensures the quality of the due diligence process, and a consistent investment philosophy across the firm.
- Well-prepared reference calls provide an excellent perspective on how a fund manager creates value.
- An experienced senior professional acting as devil's advocate on an investment project provides valuable, internal challenging and risk mitigation.

MORE INFO

Books:

Mayer, Thomas, and Pierre-Yves Mathonet. *Beyond the J-Curve: Managing a Portfolio of Venture Capital and Private Equity Funds*. Chichester, UK: Wiley, 2005.

Probitas Partners. *The Guide to Private Equity Investment Due Diligence*. London: PEI Media, 2005.

Report:

Kreuter, Bernd, and Oliver Gottschalg. "Quantitative private equity fund due diligence: Possible selection criteria and their efficiency." Working paper. November 7, 2006. Online at: ssrn.com/abstract=942991

See Also:

★ Carrying Out Due Diligence on Hedge Funds (pp. 465–467)
★ Due Diligence Requirements in Financial Transactions (pp. 727–729)

NOTES

1 Sood, Varun. "Investment strategies in private equity." *Journal of Private Equity* 6:3 (Summer 2003): 45–47. Online at: dx.doi.org/10.3905/jpe.2003.320050

2 Mayer and Mathonet, 2005.

3 Fictitious fund example, based on actual cases.

"**Perseverance may be just as important as speed in the battle for the future.**" Gary Hamel

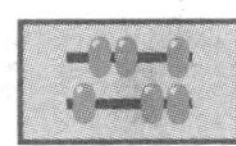

The Case for SMART Rebalancing

by Arun Muralidhar and Sanjay Muralidhar

EXECUTIVE SUMMARY

- Once investment managers establish a long-term strategic allocation or benchmark, fund managers must decide how to manage the fund's ongoing allocation.
- Daily market movements can result in constant drifts of actual portfolio allocations from the strategic benchmark.
- Traditionally, experts advised "static rebalancing" wherein simple rules bring the allocations back to the benchmark if some allocation limit is breached or some calendar date is reached.
- Static rebalancing strategies are risky, as the investors take an implicit bet to be either long or short an asset without really focusing on the view on the markets.
- While static rebalancing is often better than drift, this article describes how SMART (Systematic Management of Assets using a Rules-based Technique) can be a better tool for investors.
- By using market factors and managing allocations proactively within rebalancing ranges (i.e., no change in overall policy), investors can improve performance and risk management.
- SMART rebalancing is essential for good governance.

BACKGROUND

Every fund manager has to deal with a vexing issue—namely, how to manage the rebalancing process as the returns from this activity impact the total portfolio performance. There is a wealth of information on these strategies, and many papers have been written on this topic.[1] Nersesian (2006) does an excellent job of introducing a process to help determine the ideal rebalancing policy and examine the considerations in selecting the appropriate approach. Most rebalancing policies (periodic, range, or threshold) first focus on minimizing the tracking error or absolute standard deviation of the portfolio as the key measure of risk (either directly or by targeting the highest Sharpe ratio), and then attempt to manage the trade-off relative to the transactions costs that more frequent rebalancing generates.[2]

Many portfolio managers manage their asset allocation decisions by adopting a rebalancing policy which typically involves returning the asset allocation to the target allocation or strategic asset allocation (SAA) at calendar intervals (monthly, quarterly, or annually). Alternatively, portfolio managers may use a "range-based" approach whereby the trigger points or ranges are typically 3–5% from the target, based on the volatility of asset classes. Variations of this approach rebalance to somewhere within these allocation ranges or use periodic cash flows to move the asset allocation of the various assets closer to what a rebalancing action would attempt to do. Often these approaches are a move toward a practical maintenance of the strategic weights, trading off between managing transactions costs and tracking error relative to the benchmark. These approaches can be called "static rebalancing" because the limits are set. However, the portfolio still drifts within the bands, as most policies are silent about what actions staff should take within the bands. This is demonstrated in Figure 1.

THE ALLURE OF REBALANCING

Rebalancing is attractive because it is simple to understand and to execute, is explicit and transparent, allowing portfolio managers to put in place the exact policy to be followed and be assured that it is being followed, and avoids the appearance of "do-nothing" or "buy-and-hold." Furthermore, discipline provides a decision regime that can be modeled to quantify the historical risk and return profile. Finally, most analyses suggest that a rebalancing policy is better than doing nothing (or letting the portfolio drift), and that has been good enough for most investors.

THE PROBLEM WITH STATIC REBALANCING

Despite the low tracking error relative to their benchmarks, static rebalancing policies can be problematic owing to the large absolute and relative drawdowns (or declines in the value of the fund). Therefore, when US and European equity declined dramatically from 2000 to early 2003, rebalancing would have done little to reduce the pain of the portfolio and would have caused the rebalanced portfolio to plummet as well. While static rebalancing is attractive in up markets, the analogy in down markets would be to tying your leg to the anchor of a sinking ship.

The larger questions that this article addresses in the new rebalancing paradigm are:

- What are the appropriate performance and risk measures in determining the best asset allocation approach? Additional risk measures like the drawdown in the portfolio (maximum decline in the absolute or relative value of the fund), and success ratio (number of months that you outperform the benchmark) are utilized as these better capture the concept of practical portfolio management risk as opposed to standard deviation. After all, a low tracking error relative to a benchmark may be worthless

Figure 1. The implicit bet in traditional rebalancing policies

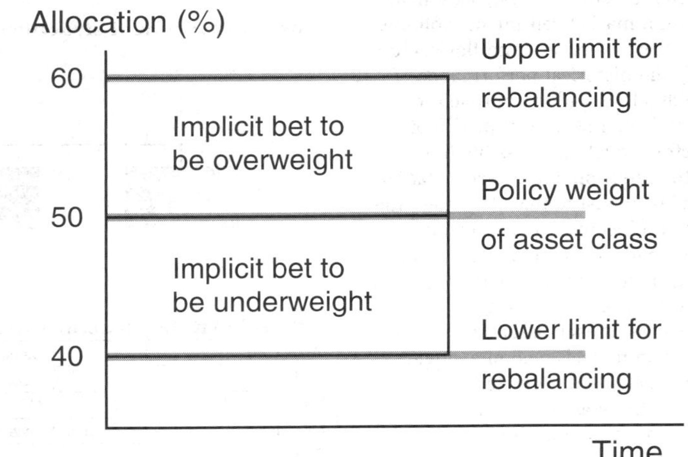

        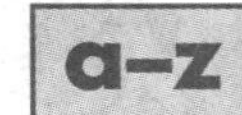

if the fund is bankrupted by a large drawdown in absolute value.

- Is there a better way to manage asset allocation decisions than static rebalancing?
- Can other approaches preserve the advantages that rebalancing policies have, namely the ability to have explicit, transparent, and disciplined asset allocation decisions?

INFORMED OR SMART REBALANCING

The more sensible way to make asset allocation decisions is by a process called "informed rebalancing." Informed rebalancing is simply about making asset allocation decisions among the various assets in a portfolio to take advantage of the higher returns in the attractive assets, while underweighting the less attractive assets commensurately. The case for informed rebalancing was made very successfully in Muralidhar (2007), though McCalla (1997) had hinted at a somewhat different approach. This is done by identifying the factors that affect which assets in your portfolio will perform well and which will perform poorly during any given regime/cycle/period. This approach, therefore, involves the following steps:

- Identify all the asset allocation decisions being made in the portfolio.
- Develop investment rules to guide the desired asset allocation tilts in the portfolio. These rules will define the assets that should be overweighted or underweighted relative to the target allocation based upon the levels of certain market or economic factors, typically sources from finance or academic journals. These factors will be measures of valuation (whether an asset class is over- or undervalued), economic activity (different economic conditions favor different asset classes), seasonality, momentum, market sentiment (volume, volatility, risk aversion, fund flows, etc.).
- Quantify the historical performance of such an asset allocation approach to understand the risk/return profile of each factor model and possibly fine-tuning the selection of the various factor-based rules to ensure that they meet the investment objectives or constraints.
- Combine many such factor-based rules into a diversified strategy that provides a net indication of the relative attractiveness of each asset class so that risks of making decisions on a single economic factor are mitigated.
- Implement these asset allocation recommendations in a disciplined way (just as one would with static

CASE STUDY

Analysis of Buy-and-Hold, Static Rebalancing and SMART Rebalancing

A simple case study indicates how a hypothetical portfolio, highlighted in Figure 2, could be managed using such investment rules. We assume a simple portfolio with a strategic investment in four core assets: US Equity (benchmarked to the S&P 500), International Equity (benchmarked to the MSCI EAFE Index), US Fixed Income (benchmarked to the Lehman Brothers Composite Index) and Commodities (benchmarked to the Goldman Sachs Commodity Index). Rules are developed for each set of assets using multiple factors and are combined to create a diversified strategy to manage the allocation across these assets. The performance of this informed rebalancing portfolio is compared with a simple buy-and-hold option and a quarterly rebalanced portfolio. The portfolio target assets and allocation are shown in Table 1.

Further, this analysis was backtested over the period from January 1990 through October 2008, so that it covers a few different market regimes, the technology boom of the late 1990s, the subsequent correction of the early 2000s, the subsequent bull market post-2003, and the more recent decline through 2008. We include transactions costs of 20 bps round trip for all assets, though actual experience suggests much lower costs are incurred.

The performance analysis is restricted to a few key metrics in Table 2 in order to facilitate this discussion, but these results are confirmed over a broader set of risk and return parameters.

As indicated in Table 2, the range rebalancing alternative represents a meaningful improvement over the buy-and-hold strategy and is consistent with most prevailing studies. However, when compared with SMART rebalancing, the only advantage of range rebalancing is a slightly lower standard deviation. However, the lower standard deviation, which is what most professionals use as a proxy for risk, comes at the expense of a 0.5% lower annualized return and therefore a return/risk ratio of 0.67 versus 0.79 for the SMART rebalancing! Notice, though, that this performance and risk advantage comes with very narrow ranges around the strategic asset allocations and hence with ±5% ranges which are more typical, the excess returns and risk management advantages will be much more significant.

More important, in reviewing alternative risk and quality of returns measures—namely *maximum drawdown*, *success ratio*, and *confidence in skill*—the results are more compelling. *Maximum drawdown* measures the maximum decline in the portfolio value during the historical period—to many a more important measure of risk as it is a better indicator of the fund's solvency. This statistic is humorously referred to as the "yield to fire," as it measures how much and for how long one can lose money before being fired or bankrupt. The *success ratio* represents the percentage of months that the portfolio outperformed its benchmark (or a comparable passive portfolio with the target allocations held constant), and the *confidence in skill* is a statistical measure of confidence one could have that these returns were the product of skill as opposed to luck.[3] On all these measures, SMART rebalancing performed much better than the other approaches. While past returns are no guarantee of future returns, essentially SMART rebalancing has the ability to take corrective action to asset allocation within the policy ranges and prevent bad asset allocation decisions from impacting performance and thereby risk.

Figure 2. Investment structure of hypothetical US pension fund

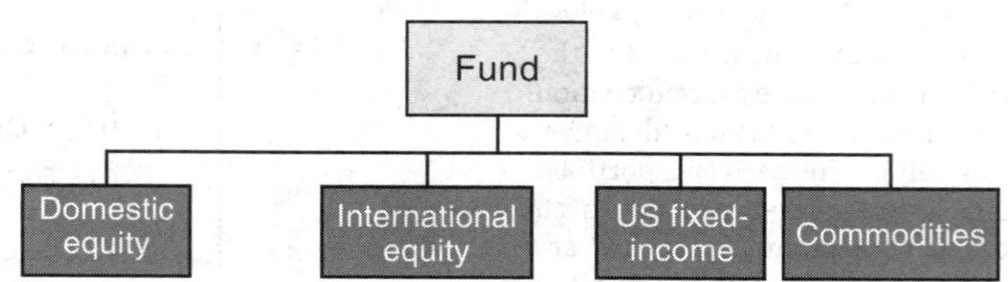

Table 1. Portfolio structure and target allocation

Asset Class	*Benchmark*	*Asset Target Allocation*	*Range*
US Equity	S&P500	31%	2.86%
International Equity	MSCI EAFE	30%	2.92%
Fixed Income	Lehman Brothers US Composite	33%	2.80%
Commodities	GSCI	6%	1.50%

"I am extraordinarily patient, provided I get my own way in the end." Margaret, Baroness Thatcher

  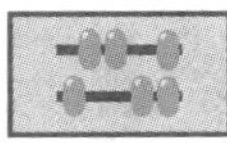   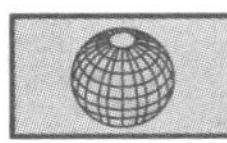   

Table 2. Comparing return and risk of informed rebalancing versus buy-and-hold and quarterly rebalancing

	Buy-and-hold	*Range rebalancing*	*SMART rebalancing*
Annualized return	6.2%	6.4%	6.9%
Standard deviation	9.3%	8.6%	8.7%
Return/risk ratio	0.67	0.75	0.79
Maximum drawdown	**−31.9%**	**−33.1%**	−31.7%
Success ratio	51.8%	51.1%	55.3%
Confidence in skill	**31.1%**	**18.7%**	99.9%

rebalancing). There are a number of ways to carry out such implementation that will be discussed separately.

For simplicity, we term this rules-based systematic approach as SMART rebalancing (systematic management of assets using a rules-based technique).

ADVANTAGES OF SMART REBALANCING

The SAA is normally derived from one of two types of optimization. The first method models assets and liabilities (ALM) to find the long-term asset allocation that has the best chance of meeting the liability (in the case of an individual, this would be the desired retirement income) requirement. The second method uses a mean-variance approach that makes assumptions of future asset returns and risk (often based upon historical performance) and finds an "efficient frontier" asset allocation with the highest return for an acceptable level of risk or the least risk for a given required return.

The attendant shortcomings of these optimizations aside—the most glaring being the need for an assumption of expected return/risk—this allocation is to be interpreted as the target allocation that over a very long period offers the best chance of meeting the fund objectives expressed in return/risk or funding terms. There is nothing in these mean-variance optimizations that reacts to market conditions in intervening periods. Again, to use a sailing analogy, naïve rebalancing is like setting the rudder in the direction of the destination without adjusting for wind direction, tides, or choppy seas, and without considering potentially faster ways of reaching the destination with less risk of drowning. SMART rebalancing, on the other hand, would involve making the appropriate adjustments.

Most importantly, as modern portfolio theory has taught us, the assets included in this portfolio are ideally uncorrelated with each other (or at least have low correlation). The logical extension of this assumption of low correlation is that in any given period (whether determined by market regimes, economic cycles, or calendar periods), some of these assets will perform better than others in the portfolio, and some will outperform their expected returns, while others will underperform these expectations. The static rebalancing approach to asset allocation assumes (or hopes) that these pluses and minuses will even out over time and should not be a concern in the ongoing asset allocation decisions. Moreover, there are many ongoing asset allocations that are necessary as a result of cash flows generated by the portfolio by way of dividends, coupon payments, and contributions, and disbursements to meet ongoing obligations.

SMART rebalancing takes the view that low correlation alone demands that responsible asset managers make asset allocation decisions to position their portfolio for these regimes/cycles/market conditions best and, by doing this well and systematically, can greatly improve the return per unit of risk. After all, most investors expect the same process from their external asset managers/mutual fund managers, and it is logical to demand this same responsibility, process, and governance at one decision level up from the portfolio's managers.

Markets are dynamic and asset returns are going up or down daily, resulting in new changes in the weights of assets changing each day. Many investors feel that if they do not take an explicit decision about an asset weight, they do not have a bet on the markets. However, quite the opposite is true! When applied to the decision on assets that have drifted in allocation above the long-term strategic weight because of strong recent performance, to not rebalance implies a view that this asset will continue to outperform. Similarly, triggering an automatic rebalancing decision to reduce (or increase) the weight on an asset back to its benchmark weight at the end of the quarter because a particular day has been reached, implies a view that this asset will do worse (or better) than other assets. Otherwise, to make such a decision would seem somewhat contradictory. In addition, a rebalancing decision makes the assumption that the benchmark

MAKING IT HAPPEN

The key to this approach is that while it does involve a little more work than implementing (or recommending) a rebalancing policy, it has similar advantages.

- Simplicity. Once the rules are articulated (and typically these are either explained by fundamental arguments, well-researched trends or common intuition) they can be easily followed and implemented. This simplicity also allows investors to track a few key factors consistently and act on them with confidence.
- *Explicitness and transparency.* By definition, this approach requires a clear definition of the market factors (signals) that will be followed, how these will be used to make asset allocation decisions for the fund, and the policy controls operating on this decision-making process (frequency, asset bandwidths, etc.). Investors then will be able to analyze and vet these decisions thoroughly prior to approving them. This then allows them to execute what is now a disciplined and systematic set of decisions.
- *Superiority.* This approach is superior to the static/naïve rebalancing approaches because it recognizes the limitations of the SAA, makes implicit decisions explicit (what gets monitored gets managed), and operates in the area where the SAA is of limited value. Further, it is both responsible and responsive to current information, which is always more relevant and up-to-date than that used as an input for the SAA decision. Implementation of SMART rebalancing is very similar to static rebalancing and would be implemented in exactly the same way that a current rebalancing program would. In our experience, both programs are easily implemented using futures contracts, so this performance is very easy to achieve and hence does not have any impact on the rest of the portfolio.

MORE INFO

Book:

Muralidhar, Arun. *Innovations in Pension Fund Management*. Stanford, CA: Stanford University Press, 2001.

Articles:

Arnott, Robert D., and Robert M. Lovell, Jr. "Rebalancing: Why? When? How often?" *Journal of Investing* 2:1 (Spring 1993): 5–10. Online at: dx.doi.org/10.3905/joi.2.1.5

allocation is the most desirable at all times (under all market conditions), and hence managing back to this asset allocation is best for the portfolio regardless of current market conditions. So, all asset managers must realize that every decision—whether to overweight, underweight, or continue to allow assets to drift—is an active decision, whether it is made explicitly or implicitly. In short, all these approaches are tactical in nature, even though they are not labeled as such and are often even cloaked as just the opposite!

CONCLUSION

This article has described how the SMART rebalancing approach can meaningfully improve the performance of the investment portfolio. All decisions to change the asset allocation—whether to let the portfolio drift or rebalance on some static policy or to make informed rebalancing decisions—are active asset allocation decisions. Therefore, it is best to make such decisions in an explicit, disciplined, and informed manner by using the various measures that one should constantly be tracking for other investment decisions (economic, valuation, momentum, and market factors). In the current return environment, every bit of performance is needed to meet investment objectives. SMART rebalancing has the advantage of working on the entire asset base, with the added benefit that it can be implemented in addition to other things that may be done in the portfolio.

Arnott, Robert D., and Lisa M. Plaxco. "Rebalancing a global policy benchmark." *Journal of Portfolio Management* 28:2 (Winter 2002): 9–22. Online at: dx.doi.org/10.3905/jpm.2002.319828

Bernstein, William J. "Case studies in rebalancing." *Efficient Frontier* (Fall 2000). Online at: www.efficientfrontier.com/ef/100/rebal100.htm

Buetow, Gerald W., Jr, Ronald Sellers, Donald Trotter, Elaine Hunter, *et al.* "The benefits of rebalancing." *Journal of Portfolio Management* 28:2 (Winter 2002): 23–32. Online at: dx.doi.org/10.3905/jpm.2002.319829

Graham, Benjamin, and David Dodd. "Investment link tutorial: Asset allocation." *Just for Funds* blog (May 26, 2007).

Leland, Hayne E. "Optimal asset rebalancing in the presence of transactions." Working paper. August 23, 1996. Online at: ssrn.com/abstract=1060

Masters, Seth J. "Rules for rebalancing." *Financial Planning* (December 2002): 89–93.

McCalla, Douglas. "Enhancing the efficient frontier with portfolio rebalancing." *Journal of Pension Plan Investing* 1:4 (Spring 1997): 16–32.

Muralidhar, Sanjay. "A new paradigm for rebalancing." *The Monitor* 22:2 (March/April 2007): 12–16. Online at: tinyurl.com/6caxvkr [PDF].

Nersesian, John. "Active portfolio rebalancing: A disciplined approach to keeping clients on track." *The Monitor* 21:1 (January/February 2006): 9–15. Online at: www.imca.org/cms_images/file_545.pdf

Website:

Mcube Investment Technologies: www.mcubeit.com/books_articles.html

See Also:

★ Asset Allocation Methodologies (pp. 454–458)
✔ Mean-Variance Optimization: A Primer (p. 1076)
✔ Understanding Asset-Liability Management (Full Balance Sheet Approach) (p. 996)
✔ Understanding Portfolio Analysis (p. 1102)
Harry Markowitz (p. 1292)
William F. Sharpe (p. 1309)
Portfolio Selection: Efficient Diversification of Investments (p. 1408)
Portfolio Theory and Capital Markets (p. 1409)

NOTES

1 See, for example, Arnott and Lovell (1993), Arnott and Plaxco (2002), Bernstein (2000), Buetow *et al.* (2002), Masters (2002), and Leland (1996).

2 Leland (1996).

3 Muralidhar (2001), ch. 9.

"There are no secrets to success: don't waste time looking for them. Success is the result of perfection, hard work, learning from failure, loyalty to those for whom you work, and persistence." Colin Powell

The Cost of Going Public: Why IPOs Are Typically Underpriced by Lena Booth

EXECUTIVE SUMMARY

- The underpricing of initial public offerings (IPOs) is an indirect cost of going public that is borne by the issuing firm. Its magnitude varies across IPOs with different issue characteristics, allocation mechanisms, underwriter reputations, and general financial market conditions.
- Commonly used share allocation methods in IPOs are auction, fixed price, and book-building. Book-building is the most popular method, and it allows smaller, less known companies to go public.
- IPOs are underpriced to signal issue quality, mitigate adverse selection problems, reward investors for truthfully revealing information, lessen underwriters' potential legal liabilities, allow underwriters to curry favor with their clients, promote ownership dispersion for liquidity and control, and attract media attention/publicity.
- Issuing firms can attempt to reduce underpricing by engaging reputable underwriters and auditors, having frequent disclosures, waiting until they possess desirable characteristics, and/or using the auction method if they are of high quality.

INTRODUCTION

When firms go public, they incur direct and indirect costs associated with the initial public offering (IPO) process. Direct costs are fairly predictable—they include registration, underwriting, and attorney and auditing fees. The indirect cost, commonly known as IPO underpricing, is one of the most perplexing puzzles in finance. It is observed in almost every financial market in the world and across all procedures of share allocation. IPOs are, on average, underpriced by 18–20% in the United States. During the hot issue period, underpricing was much higher, as many of the IPO firms did not have strong financials or growth potential and simply rode the wave to go public. In countries where regulations and restrictions are imposed in the IPO market, underpricing is higher as well.

WHAT IS IPO UNDERPRICING?

Underpricing refers to the price run up of the IPO on the first day of trading. It is also known as the initial return or first-day return of the IPO.

$$\text{Underpricing} = \frac{(\text{First-day closing price} - \text{Offer price})}{\text{Offer price}} \times 100\%$$

The first-day closing price represents what the investors are willing to pay for the firm's shares. If the offer price is lower than the first-day closing price, the IPO is said to be underpriced and money is left on the table for new investors. Since existing shareholders settle for a lower offer price/proceeds than what they could have got, money left on the table represents the wealth transfer from existing shareholders to new shareholders.

$$\text{Money left on the table} = (\text{First-day closing price} - \text{Offer price}) \times \text{Number of shares}$$

On average, the amount of money left on the table is about twice the amount of direct underwriting fees, and for many IPO firms it can equal several years of operating profit.

Although most IPOs are underpriced, the level of underpricing varies across IPOs with different issue characteristics, allocation mechanisms, underwriter reputation, and general financial market conditions. For example, the level of underpricing is reduced for larger IPOs, those underwritten by prestigious investment banks, firms with a longer operating history or more experienced insiders on the board, and those which intend to use the proceeds to repay debt. On the other hand, technology firms, firms backed by venture capital, firms with negative earnings prior to the IPO, or firms that went public during a bull market experience greater underpricing.

SHARE ALLOCATION IN IPOS

IPO underpricing happens regardless of whether issuers use the auction, the fixed-price, or the book-building method to go public. In the auction method, investors submit their desired price and quantity bids. The offer price that will allow the firm to sell all its shares is determined after bids are submitted, and hence incorporates the demand for the shares. A maximum price is usually chosen as well, so that unrealistic bids (bids well over the clearing price) can be eliminated. This is done to prevent investors from placing very high bids to ensure that they are allocated shares. Shares are then allocated, on a pro rata basis, to all the investors who placed bids between these two prices. In a uniform price auction, all the investors receiving shares will pay the same market clearing price. In the less common discriminatory price auction, investors pay the prices they bid for.

In a fixed-price offer, the issuer and the underwriter jointly determine the offer price, and investors place orders for shares at this price. If the issue is oversubscribed, shares are either allocated through lottery or on a pro rata basis.

In the book-building method, the underwriter promotes the IPO by disseminating information about the issuing firm via road shows. They gather indications of interest by soliciting from potential investors their desired prices and quantities for the issue. The underwriter then uses this information to determine the final offer price. Under this method the underwriter has complete discretion on the allocation of new shares.

Of the three allocation mechanisms, evidence has shown that IPOs under the auction method show the lowest average underpricing. However, firms that choose the auction method sometimes fail to go public because bids for their shares are insufficient. This problem is especially common for smaller, less known companies, which require substantial information production and dissemination by the underwriters. For these firms, the book-building method might be the only option that will allow them to go public. It is therefore not surprising to see the book-building method, a method that is used predominantly in the United States, gaining popularity around the world.

WHY ARE IPOS UNDERPRICED?

IPO underpricing continues to be a global phenomenon despite a vast amount of research that attempts to explain it. Theories based on information asymmetry suggest that high-quality issuers deliberately underprice their IPOs to signal their quality to outside investors, hoping that it will be too costly for low-quality issuers to mimic. Underpricing also helps to overcome adverse selection problems. Since uninformed investors tend to get a higher allocation of overpriced shares, they will stop participating in IPOs if issues are not, on average, underpriced. In the book-building framework, the theory of partial adjustment suggests that investment banks only partially adjust IPO offer prices upward when they receive positive information about the value of the issue. They purposely leave money on the table to

"Great investment opportunities come around when excellent companies are surrounded by unusual circumstances that cause the stock to be misappraised." Warren Buffett

  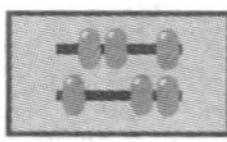      

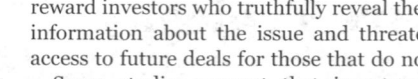

reward investors who truthfully reveal their information about the issue and threaten access to future deals for those that do not.

Some studies suggest that investment banks underprice IPOs to protect their reputation. When new issues are priced lower than they should be, investment bankers reduce their legal liability by lowering the chance of price declines. There is also evidence that greater underpricing leads to more aftermarket trading volume, which increases the revenue of investment bankers when they subsequently become the market-makers for these IPO firms. Investment bankers also benefit from underpricing because it allows them to curry favor with their clients in exchange for their loyalty and continued business. These explanations do not make it clear why issuing firms approve underpricing as it only benefits the investment banks.

There are explanations of underpricing that are based on information production and ownership dispersion which will benefit the issuing firms. If issuing firms want to have a more dispersed ownership, they need to underprice their IPOs so that more investors will be induced to produce information about the issue and subsequently buy the shares. Dispersed ownership increases liquidity and aftermarket trading, and also helps existing owners to retain control of their firms. These explanations predict a positive relationship between underpricing and aftermarket liquidity. However, there is also an explanation that predicts an inverse relationship between these two variables. When aftermarket trading for an IPO is expected to be thin, investors face higher aftermarket trading costs associated with asymmetric information; thus, they demand a higher level of underpricing to compensate them for the liquidity risk.

It has also been argued that underpricing is a substitute for marketing expenditure. Hugely underpriced IPOs tend to receive a disproportionate amount of media attention and publicity. Research shows that an extra dollar left on the table reduces other marketing expenditure by about the same amount. Higher underpricing also attracts more analyst coverage post IPO.

CONCLUSION

Underpricing comes at the expense of the original owners and venture capitalists of the issuing firm. However, these insiders typically do not strongly oppose or even attempt to avoid it, because they generally do not sell their shares until about six months later, after the lockup period expires. To them, underpricing creates excitement that could help create sustain-

CASE STUDY

The Google IPO

Google, the world's most widely used search engine, filed for an IPO in April 2004. Founded in 1998 by Sergey Brin and Larry Page, Google grew rapidly in the internet space, due mainly to its superior search technology. With a core business in selling search-based advertising, by 2004 Google had shown impressive sales growth and handsome profit margins. According to its filing, Google generated US$961.9 million of revenue and US$106.5 million of net profit in 2003. It had been profitable since 2001.

Google decided to use the auction method to go public, a deviation from the book-building method that is primarily used in the United States. According to Brin and Page, an auction would provide a fair process for all investors and help to determine the share price that reflected a fair market valuation of Google. They believed that auction mitigates problems associated with unreasonable speculation, which can result in boom–bust cycles that may hurt investors in the long run. They also wanted their shares to be within reach for any investors, unlike book-built IPOs, which are available only to those who have special relationships with the underwriters. The lead underwriters of the Google IPO, Morgan Stanley and Credit Suisse First Boston, helped to decide on a preliminary price range of US$108 to US$135 a share. That range was later revised to US$85–95, and the number of shares offered was reduced after it became apparent that the IPO wasn't as popular as expected.

Google successfully went public on August 19, 2004, at US$85 per share, selling 19.6 million shares. The first-day closing price was US$100.34, resulting in an underpricing of 18.05% and US$300.7 million left on the table. The underpricing of 18% was about average compared to other US IPOs but low relative to other internet IPOs, especially those that went public during the bubble period of 1999–2000. Google managed to go public using the auction method because it waited six years until it was well established, became a household name, and had a record of positive earnings.

However, many industry watchers felt that Google did not fare well in its IPO because it chose the auction method. It started as a hot IPO, yet had to reduce its filing price range due to insufficient demand at the higher price range that was originally proposed. Some attributed the low demand to lack of participation by institutional investors. Others claimed that Google was sabotaged by investment bankers, who prevented their clients from bidding because it had chosen a method that offered them little benefit. Could Google have got a higher offer price and larger issue proceeds if it had used the book-building method? It is a question we cannot answer but which will leave us wondering for a long time.

MAKING IT HAPPEN

Although underpricing may be inevitable due to certain risk and liquidity constraints, there are ways in which issuing firms can reduce it if they want to. Here are some suggestions:

- *Engage reputable underwriters and auditors*: Prestigious underwriters use their reputation capital to certify the value of the firm and reduce investor uncertainty about the value of the issue, and that consequently lowers the level of underpricing. Reputable auditors are better able to certify the accuracy of the financials and reduce uncertainty as well. From a partial adjustment perspective, prestigious underwriters are expected to have more future deals to compensate investors. They do not have to pre-commit a large underpricing for each issue and thus are expected to underprice less.
- *Frequent disclosure*: Issuing firms can also reduce underpricing by voluntarily and frequently disclosing information about themselves in the press, provided that the quiet period rule is not violated. Frequent disclosures reduce asymmetric information, and hence lower the information production costs incurred by investors.
- *Issuer characteristics*: IPO underpricing is lower with certain issuing firm characteristics. If issuing firms can wait until they are larger in size, have a longer operating history, and possess a record of positive earnings before going public, they are likely to reduce the level of underpricing. Underpricing can also be reduced if there are more experienced insiders sitting on the board of the issuing firm.
- *Use the auction method if feasible*: As noted above, many explanations of underpricing were derived from the book-building framework. To reduce underpricing, issuers in IPO markets in which the auction mechanism is available might want to go public that way. However, the auction method works only if the issuing firm is a superior quality firm that has high investor awareness. Also, if the issuing firm is concerned more about factors other

able interest in the firm's shares, thus keeping demand strong until they are ready to sell. Additionally, insiders are so contented with their new-found wealth that they do not mind leaving some money on the table for new investors. Underpricing is simply viewed as an inevitable cost of going public.

than underpricing—for example, price stabilization and post-IPO analyst coverage provided by investment banks—book-building may be a better choice.

- might want to go public that way. However, the auction method works only if the issuing firm is a superior quality firm that has high investor awareness. Also, if the issuing firm is concerned more about factors other than underpricing—for example, price stabilization and post-IPO analyst coverage provided by investment banks—book-building may be a better choice.

MORE INFO

Book:

Jenkinson, Tim, and Alexander Ljungqvist. *Going Public: The Theory and Evidence on How Companies Raise Equity Finance*. 2nd ed. Oxford: Oxford University Press, 2001.

Articles:

Derrien, François, and Kent L. Womack. "Auctions vs. book-building and the control of underpricing in hot IPO markets." *Review of Financial Studies* 16:1 (Spring 2003): 31–61. Online at: dx.doi.org/10.1093/rfs/16.1.31

Ritter, Jay R., and Ivo Welch. "A review of IPO activity, pricing, and allocations." *Journal of Finance* 57:4 (August 2002): 1795–1828. Online at: dx.doi.org/10.1111/1540-6261.00478

Websites:

IPO data—Jay R. Ritter's page of IPO links: bear.cba.ufl.edu/ritter/ipodata.htm

IPOresources.org: www.iporesources.org

See Also:

★ Acquiring a Secondary Listing, or Cross-Listing (pp. 448–450)
★ IPOs in Emerging Markets (pp. 514–516)
★ Price Discovery in IPOs (pp. 557–559)
✔ Conflicting Interests: The Agency Issue (p. 1110)
✔ Merchant Banks: Their Structure and Function (p. 1012)
✔ Raising Capital by Issuing Shares (p. 1087)
✔ Stock Markets: Their Structure and Function (p. 1091)
✔ Understanding Capital Markets, Structure and Function (p. 1099)
Banking and Financial Services (pp. 1612–1614)

Credit Ratings by David Wyss

EXECUTIVE SUMMARY

- A credit rating is an opinion from a credit rating agency about the creditworthiness of an issuer or the credit quality of a particular debt instrument.
- Primarily, the rating opinion considers how likely the issuer of the debt instrument is to meet its stated obligations, and whether investors will receive the payments they were promised.
- A failure to meet such payments may be considered a default.

INTRODUCTION

There are three major international rating agencies in the United States: Standard & Poor's Ratings Services (a unit of The McGraw-Hill Companies), Moody's Investors Service, and Fitch Ratings (a unit of Fimalac SA). In addition, there are many regional and niche rating agencies that tend to specialize in a geographical region or industry. The major agencies state that their opinions of the credit quality of securities are based on established, consistently applied, and transparent ratings criteria. Although the agencies use different criteria, definitions, and rating scales, they each state a view on the probability that an entity or security will default. Some rating agencies also assess the potential for recovery—how likely the investors are to recoup their investment in the event of default.

Issuers of most fixed-income securities issued in world financial markets request and receive a credit rating from a rating agency. Although credit rating evaluations are not always required, they may increase the marketability of a debt instrument by providing investors with an independent opinion about the instrument's relative credit quality.

WHY DO CORPORATIONS REQUEST A CREDIT RATING?

A credit rating opinion is often required by investors before they purchase securities. Many investors want to see an established opinion about the credit quality of a security that is not from the issuer or underwriter. In addition, some funds have made it a requirement for their investment guidelines or as part of what they have promised their investors. Issuers who are not well known or who are trying to sell into international markets may benefit from a rating from a recognized rating agency.

The rating provides market participants with an opinion on the credit quality of a particular investment. Ratings from the major credit rating agencies have a strong track record, as reported in their default and transition studies. Over the long run, securities with a higher credit rating have consistently had lower default rates than securities with lower ratings. Ratings are just opinions, however, and there have been certain periods when highly rated securities in a specific sector ultimately performed worse than other securities rated in the same category. Accordingly, ratings do not remove the need for the investor to understand what he or she is buying.

The Standard & Poor's rating scale is a simple and easy-to-understand shorthand for its credit opinions. A more detailed analysis is typically available from Standard & Poor's, including the rationale behind the rating opinion. Investors are encouraged to read the detailed analysis carefully to understand why an agency assigned a particular rating.

Having a rating may be useful even if a corporation elects to raise money privately rather than through a public bond issue. Obtaining a rating may make it easier for a company to seek funding from a private lender or bank. Although not every company needs a credit rating, most medium-sized or larger firms find it useful.

HOW A RATING IS ASSIGNED

Credit rating agencies assign ratings to issuers, including corporations and governments, of debt securities, as well as to individual issues such as bonds, notes, commercial paper, and structured finance instruments. The agencies rate an issuer by analyzing the borrower's ability and willingness to repay its obligations in accordance with their terms. The agency's analysts consider a broad range of business and financial risks that may interfere with prompt and full payment.

Most rating agencies use a mix of quantitative and qualitative analysis. Typically, analysts who consider qualitative factors contact management at the firm being rated to obtain additional information that may help them to arrive at an informed opinion. In some cases, they will ask for information that is not available to the general public, such as details of business plans, strategies, and forecasts. Agencies generally also examine the company's audited financial reports to analyze credit strengths and weaknesses.

A rating can apply to an individual issue, although the issuer may also be assigned an underlying rating based on its overall financial strength. An individual issue is usually given an evaluation based on information provided by the issuer or obtained from other reliable sources. Key considerations include:

- the issue's legal structure, including terms and conditions;
- the seniority of the issue relative to the other debt of the issuer;
- the existence of external support or credit enhancements, such as letters of credit, guarantees, insurance, and collateral—which are protections that are designed to limit the potential credit risk.

When an issuer requests a rating, it generally supplies the rating agency with its audited financial statements. In most cases, the rating agency will also meet with the issuer to discuss any questions that the agency may have and to learn about any business plans or other factors considered to be important. Frequent issuers will often have a longer-term contractual relationship with the rating agency that may include rating all new debt issues.

Credit ratings from the major rating agencies are normally paid for by the issuer of the securities, and are made public immediately thereafter, although in some cases issuers or investors may request a "private" rating on a security. When ratings are requested by parties other than the issuer, and without direct access to the issuer for questioning, they are usually marked as "public information" or given similar subscripting by the rating agency. The issuer-pays model has two hallmarks: First, the major rating agencies make ratings public (and if they didn't, *that* news would quickly become public), so it is hard to get investors to pay for what they can get for free on the news. Second, issuing a rating often involves access to the company's confidential data, which is not permissible under a subscriber-pays model.

In some circumstances, most agencies will rate some securities without any consultation with the issuing firm. In these cases the ratings are based only on public data, and are normally indicated as such.

Ratings are generally published at the time they are issued. However, sometimes a private rating may be issued for an individual investor or group of investors, usually for a security that is not intended for

  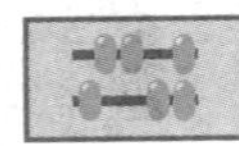   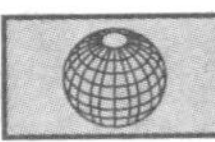  

public trading. Many firms want a confidential rating for management purposes and as a second opinion on the credit quality of a loan.

Ratings are not static, and rating opinions can change (or transition) if the credit quality changes in ways that were not expected at the time the security was issued. Ratings may be reviewed and updated on a regular basis, or when a significant change occurs in the performance of the issuer, the markets, or the economy. The acquisition or divestiture of a company, a political threat to (or from) the government, or erosion in the economy or credit markets can cause a rating to be adjusted. Normally, warning of a likely change is provided through an "outlook" or "credit watch" that states the direction in which a rating may move. However, sometimes a sudden deterioration may force a shift in a rating with little warning.

RATING SCALE

Each credit rating agency uses its own criteria and methodology to evaluate creditworthiness. The process may be predominantly quantitative or qualitative, but is usually a blend of the two. Once an agency completes the analysis, it issues a rating based on its own scale. Ratings are typically expressed as a grade, such as AAA, BB, or CC, with AAA (or equivalent) denoting the strongest and D (or its equivalent) the weakest (i.e. that a default has already occurred). Note that the rating scale for short-term instruments such as commercial paper is different from the long-term scale. For example, at S&P the top long-term rating is AAA, while the highest short-term credit rating is A-1 + . D stands for default in both scales.

Although a rating scale is relatively straightforward, the assumptions, considerations, and judgments behind the opinions can be complex. Most agencies explain their rationale in published documents that may be read by investors. Among others, the risk factors include the financial performance of the firm, the characteristics of the economy and industry it operates, and the quality of its management. Standard & Poor's credit ratings strive to be forward-looking, focusing not just on the past but also on the likely future state of the industry and the firm.

Standard & Poor's ratings are intended to be consistent across all issuers and debt instruments. Over the very long term, all instruments with the same (say, A) rating are expected to have similar default experience. However, the short-term behavior of these instruments may be very different. Different industries respond differently to economic and credit cycles.

Credit ratings are not exact measures of the default probability of an issue or issuer, but an opinion about relative credit risk. In assigning ratings, agencies rank relative credit risk from strongest to weakest, based on relative creditworthiness and credit quality within the rated universe. Actual default probabilities may change over time.

RECOVERY

Some credit rating agencies incorporate the potential for recovery into their opinions, while others may give a recovery rating that is separate from the credit rating. Recovery prospects after default are an important component in evaluating credit quality, particularly in evaluating more risky debt issues.

ISLAMIC CREDIT

Mounting demand for *shariah*-compliant financial products and services has fueled the rapid expansion of the Islamic banking industry. More and more banking clients are choosing to invest in a broadening range of Islamic financial instruments (IFI) through long-established banks in the Gulf Cooperation Council (GCC) and Malaysia. The model has spread beyond the Gulf to the Maghreb and Muslim Asia, as well as to Muslims in predominantly non-Muslim countries in the West, Asia, and Africa.

Demand for *shariah*-compliant instruments has risen sharply as a result of strong economic growth within the Islamic world and the large surpluses of the oil-producing countries. The volume of *shariah*-compliant instruments outstanding is estimated at over $500 billion, with *sukuk* (an Islamic financial certificate) issuance reaching $100 billion. Islamic banks have focused on the retail segment in the Arab world and Malaysia but are expanding to other countries. North Africa has been a recent region of strong growth, with Tunisia and Morocco authorizing Islamic banks for the first time in 2007. The central bank of Morocco became a shareholder in the International Financial Services Board (based in Malaysia), which serves as a transnational regulatory body to harmonize regulation and supervision for Islamic banks.

Islamic securities such as *sukuk* are rated by agencies employing the same fundamental analysis as are used for rating other issues. The rating provided does not, however, express an opinion regarding the *shariah* compliance of any Islamic financing instrument, institution, or debt issue. It is the responsibility of the *shariah* board of the originating institution to rule on compliance with Islamic law. The agency rates the security based on its analysis of the willingness and ability of the issuer to make the agreed payments, as specified in the security.

RATINGS AND INVESTMENT

Although credit quality is an important element in an investment decision, it is not the only or even the most important element. Ratings opinions are not investment recommendations. In making any investment, the investor should consider the trade-off between risk and reward. Credit quality is only a partial measure of one of those trade-offs.

A security's price is generally one of the most important considerations for an investor. If the price is low enough, almost any investment becomes desirable; if the price is too high, any investment becomes unattractive. The price determines the long-run return on the investment, assuming that it pays as scheduled.

As a minimum, three other factors besides price and credit quality should be considered. First, what is the downside risk or likely recovery if the security defaults? Second, what is the liquidity of the investment—how easy is it to sell if it must be disposed of before its maturity date, and how responsive is pricing to changes in interest rates or the market environment?

An important issue for investors buying outside their home country is the potential for exchange rate change or government interference with the ability to collect payment. Fortunately, foreign exchange controls have become very rare outside of a few very weak emerging economies, but foreign exchange risk is very real. The US dollar/euro exchange rate went up 20% in early 2008 and then down 20% over the next three months.

MAKING IT HAPPEN

- Ratings can be obtained from a variety of agencies. Consider who will be your likely investors before deciding to go with a global or a local rating agency.
- Have your financial and business plans in order and fully audited by a reputable firm before trying to get a rating.
- Ratings are opinions about credit risk, and not investment advice or opinions on pricing.
- Work with your banker on determining which agency to use and whether a rating is desirable.

"Risk comes from not knowing what you are doing." Warren Buffett

        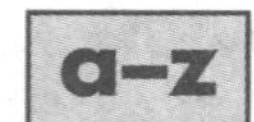

CONCLUSION

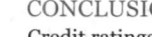

Credit ratings may be used by investors and other market participants in making investment and business decisions that are aligned with their risk tolerance or credit risk guidelines. Credit ratings are opinions about the perceived credit risk of a particular debt issue. In general, the greater the credit risk, the higher the return investors may expect for assuming that risk. For that reason, credit ratings may be useful for both issuers and investors when a debt issue is first issued in the primary markets and continues to be so for investors who trade securities in secondary markets.

MORE INFO

Books:

Duffie, Darrell, and Kenneth Singleton. *Credit Risk: Pricing, Measurement, and Management*. Princeton, NJ: Princeton University Press, 2003.

Fuchita, Yasuyuki, and Robert E. Litan (eds). *Financial Gatekeepers: Can They Protect Investors?* Baltimore, MD: Brookings Institution, 2006.

Langohr, Herwig M., and Patricia T. Langohr. *The Rating Agencies and Their Credit Ratings: What They Are, How They Work, and Why They Are Relevant*. Chichester, UK: Wiley, 2008.

Levich, Richard M., Giovanni Majnoni, and Carmen Reinhart (eds). *Ratings, Rating Agencies and the Global Financial System*. Norwell, MA: Kluwer Academic, 2002.

Article:

Cantor, Richard. "An introduction to recent research on credit ratings." *Journal of Banking and Finance* 28:11 (November 2004): 2565–2573. Online at: dx.doi.org/10.1016/j.jbankfin.2004.06.002

Websites:

The main sources of information on ratings are the websites of the three major rating agencies: www.moodys.com, www.standardandpoors.com, and www.fitchratings.com. A good discussion of ratings trends is found in the "Guide to credit rating essentials" produced by Standard & Poor's (2008, 20 pages): tinyurl.com/3942qmn [PDF].

See Also:

★ Investing in Structured Finance Products in the Debt Money Markets (pp. 510–513)
★ Minimizing Credit Risk (pp. 540–542)
✔ The Bond Market: Its Structure and Function (p. 1064)
✔ How to Manage Your Credit Rating (p. 973)
✔ How to Use Credit Rating Agencies (p. 1073)

"You can't manage what you don't measure." W. Edwards Deming (probably apocryphal)

  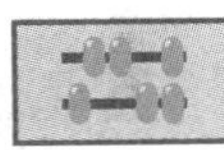      

Ethical Funds and Socially Responsible Investment: An Overview by Chendi Zhang

EXECUTIVE SUMMARY

- Ethical funds, also known as socially responsible investment (SRI) funds, have experienced rapid growth around the world. Issues such as global warming, corporate governance, and community involvement have gained significant attention from governments and investors.
- Maximization of stockholder value often conflicts with the interests of other stakeholders in a firm. Corporate social responsibility (CSR) plays a role in reducing the costs of such conflicts.
- Empirical research shows that the following components of CSR are associated with higher stockholder value: good corporate governance, sound environmental standards, and care of stakeholder relations.
- Existing studies hint, but do not unequivocally demonstrate, that SRI investors are willing to accept suboptimal financial performance to pursue social or ethical objectives.
- Given the growing social awareness of investors and the increasingly positive regulatory environment, we expect SRI to continue its growth and relative importance as an asset class.

THE RISE OF SRI

Ethical funds, often also called socially responsible investment (SRI) funds, integrate environmental, social, and governance (ESG) considerations, or purely ethical issues, into investment decision-making. SRI has experienced a phenomenal growth around the world. According to the Social Investment Forum, the professionally managed assets of SRI portfolios in the United States, including retail and, more importantly, institutional funds (for example, pension funds, insurance funds, and separate accounts), reached US$2.7 trillion in 2007, or approximately 11% of total assets under management in that country. The European SRI market is also growing rapidly. In 2007, SRI assets in Europe amounted to €2.7 trillion, representing 17% of European funds under management (European Social Investment Forum).

Although ethical investing has ancient origins that were based on religious traditions, modern SRI is based more on the varying personal, ethical, and social convictions of individual investors. Issues such as environmental protection, human rights, and labor relations have become common in the SRI investment screening process. In recent years, a series of corporate scandals has turned corporate governance and responsibility into another focal point of SRI investors. Hence, criteria such as transparency, governance, and sustainability have emerged as essential in SRI screening.

Over the past decade, a number of national governments in Europe have passed a series of regulations on social and environmental investments and savings. For instance, the United Kingdom was the first country to regulate the disclosure of the social, environmental, and ethical investment policies of pension funds and charities. The Amendment to the 1995 Pensions Act requires the trustees of occupational pension funds to disclose in the Statement of Investment Principles "the extent (if at all) to which social, environmental and ethical considerations are taken into account in the selection, retention and realization of investments." This has contributed considerably to the growth of the SRI industry.

SHOULD COMPANIES BE SOCIALLY RESPONSIBLE?

Finance textbooks tell us companies should maximize the value of their stockholders' equity. In other words, a company's only responsibility is a financial one. In recent years, corporate social responsibility has become a focal point of policymakers (and the public), who demand that corporations assume responsibility toward society, the environment, or stakeholders in general. SRI investors thus aim to promote socially and environmentally sound corporate behavior. They avoid companies that produce goods which may cause health hazards or exploit employees (negative screening), whether in developed or developing countries. They select companies with sound social and environmental records, and with good corporate governance (positive screening). In general, SRI investors expect companies to focus on social welfare in addition to maximizing value.

At the heart of the SRI movement is a fundamental question: Is a firm's aim to maximize *stockholder* value or *social* value (where social value is defined as the sum of the values generated for all stakeholders)? Classical economics (for example, Adam Smith's "invisible hand" and the social welfare theorems) states that there is no conflict between the two goals: In competitive and complete markets, when all firms maximize their own profits (value), resource allocation is optimal and social welfare is maximized. However, modern economic theory also tells us that in some circumstances, namely when some of the assumptions of the welfare theorems do not hold, profit-maximizing behavior does not necessarily imply social welfare-maximizing outcomes. One of such circumstances is the existence of externalities that arise when the costs and benefits of an agent's action are affected by the actions of other (external) agents in the economy. Jensen (2001) gives a simple example of externalities, where a fishery's catch is impaired by the pollution of an upstream chemical plant.[1] When the chemical plant maximizes its profit by increasing pollution (as the costs of pollution are not borne by the chemical plant), the fishery downstream suffers through catching fewer fish and social welfare—which in this case is equal to the sum of the profits of the two stakeholders—is not maximized.

In practice, the maximization of stockholder value often conflicts with the social welfare criterion represented by the interests of all stakeholders of a firm, including employees, customers, local communities, the environment, and so forth. By maximizing stockholder value, firms may not take care of the interests of other stakeholders. Economic solutions to the externality problem are based on the principle of internalizing externalities, for example, by imposing regulations (such as quotas, or taxes on pollution) and creating a market for externalities (such as the trading of pollution permits). Furthermore, in continental European corporate governance regimes, a stakeholder approach is more common than in Anglo-Saxon countries.

STOCKHOLDER VALUE VERSUS STAKEHOLDER VALUE

One of the main arguments in favor of CSR and the stakeholder model is that it is consistent with stockholder value maximization. For instance, by anticipating and minimizing the potential conflicts between corporations and society, CSR plays a role

"The social responsibility of business is to increase its profits." Milton Friedman

  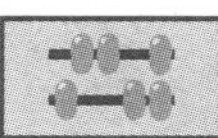      

in reducing the cost of conflicts. CSR may soften competition in product markets and lead to higher firm value, signal a firm's product quality and improve reputation, and help to attract motivated employees.

Critics of stakeholder value maximization argue that CSR, and the stakeholder theory, have problems in terms of accountability and managerial incentivization. According to the stockholder value concept, managers are expected to invest in a project if its expected return exceeds the cost of capital. In the stakeholder value story, managers are asked to balance the interests of all stakeholders to the point that aggregate welfare is maximized. Still, the stakeholder theory does not define how to aggregate welfare and how to make the trade-off between stakeholders. If the social value of firms can be maximized, society will by definition benefit. However, the question is whether this goal is achievable and how economic efficiency and managerial incentives are affected by the maximization of stakeholder value (including social and environmental value).

Furthermore, CSR and the stakeholder model are also subject to Friedman's (1962)[2] arguments: Companies should only care about profits and, therefore, their stockholders, while governments deal with the provision of public goods and the existence of externalities. If CSR lowers firms' profits due to compromises with stakeholders, firms should not implement CSR strategies as it is more efficient if they charge lower prices and allow consumers to make their own charitable contributions based on personal social and ethical values. This critique also has important implications for SRI: If SRI underperforms conventional portfolios, it would be more efficient for SRI investors to invest in better-performing conventional funds and use part of the returns to comply with their personal convictions by donating money to good causes.

PORTFOLIO CONSTRAINTS AND MARKET (IN)EFFICIENCIES

SRI applies various screening processes to retain stocks complying with specific CSR criteria on social, corporate governance, environmental, and ethical issues, which imposes a constraint on the investment universe available to non-SRI investors. SRI screens may therefore limit the diversification possibilities, and consequently shift the mean–variance frontier toward less favorable risk–return tradeoffs than those of conventional portfolios. In addition, believers in the efficient market hypothesis argue that it is impossible for SRI funds to outperform their conventional peers. Screening portfolios based on public information such as CSR issues cannot generate abnormal returns.

However, it is also possible that SRI screening processes generate value-relevant information which is otherwise not available to investors. This may help fund managers to select securities and consequently generate better risk-adjusted returns than conventional mutual funds. In this case, investors may do (financially) well while doing (social) good, i.e. investors earn positive risk-adjusted returns while at the same time contributing to a good cause. For instance, empirical research on CSR shows that portfolios constructed with reference to corporate governance, environmental, and social criteria may outperform their benchmarks.

A key assumption underlying the above hypothesis is that the stock markets misprice information on CSR in the short run. For instance, they may undervalue the costs of litigation that may have to be met by socially irresponsible corporations, while socially responsible firms may be better protected against such costs. As a result, SRI may outperform conventional funds in

CASE STUDY

Calvert Social Investment Fund

Calvert is one of the largest families of SRI mutual funds in the United States. Social investment research analysts at Calvert examine corporate performance in the following broad areas, in addition to financial criteria:

- Governance and ethics: Including disclosure of policies and procedures, board independence and diversity, executive compensation, and attention to stakeholder concerns.
- Workplace: Including labor diversity, labor relations, and employee health and safety. Calvert monitors the quality of policies and programs, compliance with national laws and regulations, and proactive management initiatives.
- Environment: Focusing on corporate environmental performance, responsiveness to incidents, and compliance with environmental regulations.
- Product safety and impact: Selecting companies that produce safe products and services, in accordance with federal consumer product safety guidelines.
- International operations and human rights: Avoiding investment in companies that have a record of serious and persistent human rights problems or that directly support governments that systematically deny human rights.
- Indigenous peoples' rights: Avoiding companies that have a pattern and practice of violating the rights of indigenous peoples around the world.
- Community relations: Investing in companies that have built solid relationships with the local communities in which they operate.

MAKING IT HAPPEN

In order for CSR/SRI to become a workable concept, the following key issues of performance yardsticks should be considered:

- Do you adopt the stockholder value maximization criterion or the stakeholder value maximization criterion? Even if you opt for the stockholder value criterion, it is important to consider the welfare of all stakeholders (employees, community, environment, etc.) as firm behavior induces important externalities. The long-run market value of a firm cannot be maximized if any important stakeholders are mistreated.
- Is corporate social/environmental performance measurable? A lack of precisely formulated corporate goals and measures in respect of CSR/SRI may destroy firm value in the long run. The long-run value of a firm remains the single most important performance measure for management. Maximizing long-run firm value is consistent with maximizing social welfare.
- Are you seeking a competitive advantage for your company by implementing CSR/SRI strategies? Empirical research shows that the following components of CSR are associated with higher stockholder value: good corporate governance, sound environmental standards, and care of stakeholder relations.
- Are investors willing to pay a price for CSR/SRI? If SRI underperforms conventional funds, it could be more efficient for SRI investors to invest in better-performing conventional funds and use part of the returns to comply with their personal convictions by donating money to good causes.

"An inconvenient truth: global warming." Al Gore

the long run. This outperformance hypothesis is also at odds with the efficient market hypothesis. If SRI screening processes do generate value-relevant information, conventional portfolio managers could easily replicate the screens, and the performance edge of SRI over conventional investments should then diminish.

The question as to whether SRI creates stockholder value is ultimately an empirical one. Empirical findings on the performance of SRI are mixed. Although there is little evidence that the average performance of SRI funds in the United States and the United Kingdom is different from that of conventional funds, SRI funds in many continental European and Asia-Pacific countries underperform their benchmarks.[3] Existing studies hint, but do not unequivocally support, that investors are willing to accept suboptimal financial performance if their personal values on social responsibility are satisfied.

CONCLUSION

SRI has experienced rapid growth around the world, reflecting investors' increasing awareness of social, environmental, and governance issues. In recent years issues such as global warming, the Kyoto Protocol, corporate governance, and community investing have gained significant attention from governments and investors around the world. In addition, governments in Western countries have taken many regulatory initiatives to stimulate SRI. Given the growing social awareness of investors and the increasingly positive regulatory environment, we expect SRI to continue its growth and relative importance as an asset class.

MORE INFO

Book:

UNEP Finance Initiative. *Values to Value: A Global Dialogue on Sustainable Finance*. United Nations Environment Programme, 2004.

Article:

Renneboog, Luc, Jenke Ter Horst, and Chendi Zhang. "Socially responsible investments: Institutional aspects, performance, and investor behavior." *Journal of Banking and Finance* 32:9 (September 2008): 1723–1742. Online at: dx.doi.org/10.1016/j.jbankfin.2007.12.039

Websites:

Association for Sustainable and Responsible Investment in Asia: www.asria.org
European Social Investment Forum (Eurosif): www.eurosif.org
Social Investment Forum: www.socialinvest.org

See Also:

★ Best Practices in Corporate Social Responsibility (pp. 636–639)
★ Business Ethics (pp. 1829–1830)
★ CSR: More than PR, Pursuing Competitive Advantage in the Long Run (pp. 664–666)
★ The Impact of Climate Change on Business (pp. 875–877)
✔ Business Ethics in Islamic Finance (p. 1109)
✔ Corporate Governance and Its Interpretations (p. 1111)
✔ The Efficient Market Hypothesis (p. 1068)
✔ The Triple Bottom Line (p. 1125)
Muhammad Yunus (p. 1319)
Banker to the Poor: The Story of the Grameen Bank (p. 1334)

NOTES

1 Jensen, Michael C. "Value maximization, stakeholder theory, and the corporate objective function." *Journal of Applied Corporate Finance* 14:3 (Fall 2001): 8–21. Online at: dx.doi.org/10.1111/j.1745-6622.2001.tb00434.x

2 Friedman, Milton. *Capitalism and Freedom*. 40th anniversary ed. Chicago, IL: University of Chicago Press, 2002.

3 Renneboog, Luc, Jenke Ter Horst, and Chendi Zhang. "The price of ethics and stakeholder governance: The performance of socially responsible mutual funds." *Journal of Corporate Finance* 14:3 (June 2008): 302–322. Online at: dx.doi.org/10.1016/j.jcorpfin.2008.03.009

"Social business will be a new kind of business introduced in the market place with the objective of making a difference in the world." Muhammad Yunus

  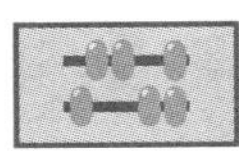   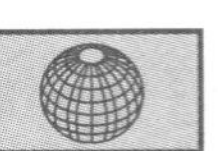   

Viewpoint: Fast Finance to Slow Finance

by Gervais Williams

INTRODUCTION

Gervais Williams is managing director of Miton Group plc, and co-manages Miton's UK Smaller Companies Fund with Martin Turner. He has been an equity portfolio manager since 1985. His career includes five years with Throgmorton Investment Management (later part of the Framlington Group), three years with Thornton Investment Management (part of Dresdner Bank), and 17 years with Gartmore Group Ltd, where he was head of UK Small Companies, investing in UK smaller companies and Irish equities. He won Investor of the Year as awarded by Grant Thornton at their Quoted Company Awards in both 2009 and 2010. He has sat on two DTI committees in the quoted small-cap sector, is a member of the AIM Advisory Council, and has joined the board of the Quoted Companies Alliance.

CHANGING INVESTMENT STRATEGIES

Stock markets are all about change. Share prices move instantaneously to reflect the latest results or the utterances from world leaders. Traders sit ready to invest or disinvest huge capital sums at any moment. In the City, most assume that successful investors need to be major players with aggressive and sophisticated strategies. But could it be the case that clients might be better advised to do the opposite in the future? That investors might do a lot better in the coming years by pulling back and adopting a "slow" strategy? Idealistic claptrap? No, the evidence is overwhelming.

The key point is that the financial world today is not "normal." For decades after the Second World War, the financial world made up just a modest part of the UK economy. Yes, stock markets moved up and down. But successful investors made good money for their clients in completely different ways to those which dominate currently.

THE CASE FOR SLOW FINANCE

Historically, stock-market investors have made their best returns from backing individual companies over long time periods. Investing in successful companies which generate decent profits, and grow their market positions progressively over many years. Profit is really important in this context, because profitable companies generate extra cash internally every year. It is this cash flow that is so important. A strong management team is well placed to ensure that their cash flow is wisely allocated. If appropriate, that cash flow can actively fund development of the business for many years, almost irrespective of economic fluctuations. And cash invested well can start a positive feedback cycle, enhancing corporate returns and boosting the internal cash generation of the business still further. Alternatively, many successful quoted companies can afford to pay out a proportion of their internally generated cash to shareholders in the form of dividends. For shareholders, this is seen as a stream of gradually increasing dividends. And it is the progressive flow that delivers the premium investment returns.[1]

Long-term investors make the best returns when they hold shares in a company that pays good and growing dividends, where annual income rises each year.[2] Over time, the share price of the quoted company is dragged up by that rising income, almost irrespective of the underlying movement of the stock market. But the investment magic comes for those who reinvest their dividend payments back into the shares of the business, because each year dividend income increases, not only due to the increased dividend component, but also to reflect the fact that the number of shares held has increased after the dividend reinvestment. This gives a multiplier effect, and over time can contribute to very strong investment returns. It's a process called compounding.[3]

Compounding is one of the ways to make highly attractive investment returns. This is why stock market returns over the very long term are so good. Investing just £1 in the equivalent of the FTSE 100 in 1900 would have compounded up to an investment sum valued at over £20,000 today.[4] However, if the same investor had only invested in the stocks with above-average dividend yields in the FTSE 100, and had rebalanced their investments each year back into those stocks with higher dividend yields, then the same £1 would have compounded to over £100,000 today. Some difference!

Given that dividend compounding is so successful, the question has to be asked why the investment world has abandoned this proven strategy over the last couple of decades. Why has the City become so dominated by short-term trading, rather than seeking out those companies that will pay good and growing dividends? Some blame the deregulation of the City with the Big Bang in 1986 for the culture change. Others highlight the "Loadsamoney" froth in the 1980s, as house prices and share prices rallied hard at the start of the rot. But in fact both of these explanations are too parochial. This cultural change is part of a global trend.

THE GROWTH OF DEBT RELATIVE TO GDP

The chart below shows US debt as a proportion of the size of the economy as a whole. Debt in the economy was broadly stable from the 1940s through to around 1985, but thereafter it took off. Similar charts apply to almost all other major economies outside the United States, with the possible exception of Japan. The key change has been the greater availability of debt.

Changes of this magnitude don't come around very often. Credit booms did occur prior to 1985, but they usually didn't last long. Credit booms tend to drive up asset prices, causing greater speculative activity. However, this normally drives up inflationary pressures, causing central banks to take action and local interest rates to rise, ultimately undermining the credit boom.

THE REASONS BEHIND THE LATEST CREDIT BOOM

So, if credit booms don't last long normally, how come the world has been in a global credit boom for over 25 years?

The reason it has been different this time is related to growing imports of cheaper traded goods from overseas. As the credit

"As a general rule in financial matters, things take longer to happen than you would expect but when they do start to move they happen more quickly." Hamish McRae

boom boosted economic activity and local inflationary pressures, the effects were progressively offset by the growing tide of cheaper goods coming in from low-cost producers elsewhere. This led to reported inflation remaining at apparently low levels. With interest rates staying at low levels, the credit boom persisted and persisted.

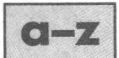

The effects of the credit boom are all around us. Prior to 2008, the price of many assets had risen and risen. Think of property prices, housing, equities, bonds, and many commodities like oil.

Investor behavior changes during credit booms. The best returns are often found in buying and selling assets for a profit. In fact, capital gains are all the larger for those who employ debt. Average UK house prices have risen almost five-fold since 1985.[5] But those who bought with a 90% mortgage have seen the value of their deposit rise approximately 50-fold. It pays to be speculative during credit booms.

Over the last quarter of a century, the persistence of the global credit boom has progressively favored those employing transaction strategies over the more traditional methods. Over time, this has been reflected in a cultural shift in the financial sector—and after 25 years that change has been profound. Essentially, the financial markets are now dominated by those employing transactional strategies. The financial world is a very long way from normality.

INVESTMENT STRATEGIES IN THE POST-CREDIT-BOOM WORLD

Slow Finance outlines the scale of the sea change that is coming; the transition from a position where many funds are potentially over-optimized for credit-boom conditions, to a period when many funds will have reallocated their capital to strategies that are better suited to a post-credit-boom world.

Already, the first glimpses of that change are evident. During the credit boom, dividends were largely ignored other than by income funds. However, a broader range of investors has now become more favorably inclined towards stocks that pay good and growing dividends.[6] And although many investors continue to follow transactional strategies, overall trading volumes in the City have moderated. This is early evidence that a change in the financial culture is beginning.

Interestingly, this change begins to take us towards some investment strategies that were in place prior to the credit boom—a time when the best returns were made by selecting those companies that grew their dividends at the most sustained rate. As highlighted previously, the step-up in overall return through following such a strategy is quite remarkable.

Slow Finance also highlights a second strategy that was widely adopted prior to the credit boom. In the past there was a willingness to invest in any of the companies quoted on the stock market. However, during the credit boom this attitude has changed. The major stock-market indices have typically risen by double-digit percentages each year. Professional fund managers have sometimes struggled to keep ahead or indeed keep up with the rise in the indices. Progressively, this has been reflected in a trend where the fund manager has focused more closely on identifying the stocks in the index that are best placed to outperform. And because those which are expected to underperform can sometimes have a nasty habit of surprising on the upside, most fund managers have become accustomed to holding these in lesser weightings. All this adds up to disproportionate interest in a small universe of stocks within the major indices, as opposed to a wider universe of all quoted companies.[7]

All this has been justified by the notion of globalization. Larger companies were better placed to participate in the globalization trend. This fitted well with the growing inclination towards more transaction strategies. At a trading level, it is easy to deal in the shares of large companies in large lot sizes and, naturally, rather more difficult in smaller companies.

The bottom line is that most portfolios have become dominated by index stocks which only represent about a quarter of the total number of listed companies. However, as we move beyond the credit boom, we can anticipate that investors will begin to widen their portfolios to include many more companies that are outside the large stock-market indices. It makes sense in so many ways.

The key advantage of smallness is that activities carried out by smaller productive units can grow in spite of a sluggish economic background. In simple terms, it's easier to double in scale if you are small than if you are large. It doesn't make it easy, but it is easier. For this reason, the indices of smaller companies tend to outperform the indices of larger companies. In the United Kingdom, the data stretch back to 1955. If you invested just £1 in the FTSE All Share Index, heavily weighted into larger companies, you would have made £620 on your initial investment. The dividend income on the share has risen over the years, and reinvesting that income in more shares that grow their income explains the reason for the sizable increase in the value of the investment.

However, if the same £1 had been invested only in quoted companies that were amongst the smallest 10% of stocks, then your investment would have grown to £3,248. If the same £1 had been invested in

Figure 1. US Credit market debt 1929–2011 as percentage of nominal US GDP. (*Source*: Developed from data sources including Morgan Stanley Research, International Monetary Fund, and Bloomberg [1960 onwards])

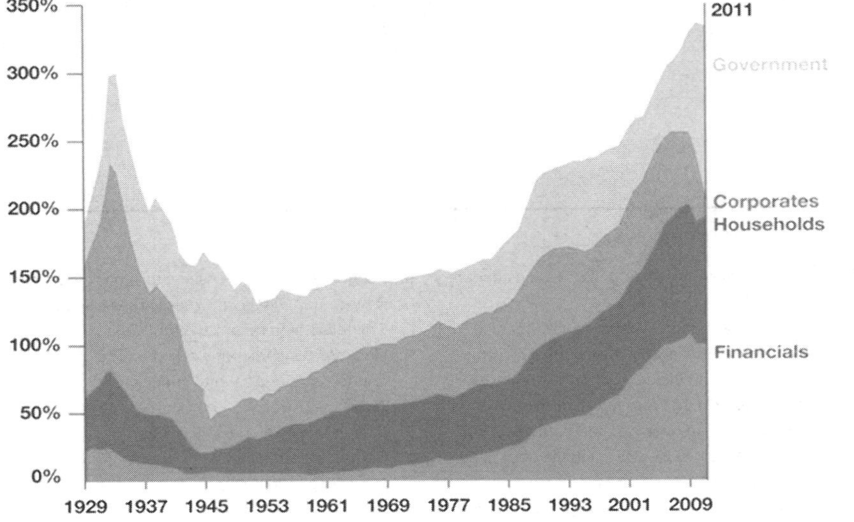

"The mechanics of running a business are really not very complicated, when you get down to essentials. You have to make some stuff and sell it to somebody for more than it cost you. That's about all there is to it, except for a few million details." John L. McCaffrey

  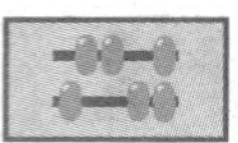      

the smallest 2% of companies by market capitalization, then the overall return would have been £7,393.[8]

CONCLUSION

In a world of austerity, most assume that stock-market returns in future will be somewhat less than those attained in a world fuelled by credit. Given that background, fund managers will need to work harder to deliver returns that are attractive to clients. Following the distortions to investment strategies caused by the credit boom, most portfolios appear poorly positioned. Given the urgent need to maximize returns, fund managers will need to consider modifying their behavior to give them a better chance at success.

First, investors are already stepping back toward strategies focusing on companies with good and growing dividends. This could become a mainstream strategy in place of the transaction strategies that came to dominate the investment world during the credit boom. Second, we can expect investors to widen their portfolios to include smaller quoted businesses. Over the longer term, they tend to outperform anyway. And given their small scale, those which grow strongly can outperform strongly too.

MORE INFO

Books:

Graham, Benjamin. *The Intelligent Investor.* 4th ed. New York: Harper and Row, 1972.

Mauldin, John, and Jonathan Tepper. *Endgame: The End of the Debt Supercycle and How It Changes Everything*. Hoboken, NJ: Wiley, 2011.

Reinhart, Carmen M., and Kenneth S. Rogoff. *This Time is Different: Eight Centuries of Financial Folly.* Princeton, NJ: Princeton University Press, 2009.

Articles:

Black, Fisher. "The dividend puzzle." *Journal of Portfolio Management* 2:2 (Winter 1976): 5–8. Online at: dx.doi.org/10.3905/jpm.1976.408558

Blackwell, David. "Desire for dividends outweighs capital growth." *Financial Times* (May 18, 2011). Online at: tinyurl.com/ccffpgg

Citibank Investment Research and Analysis. "The law of large numbers." June 30, 2008.

Miller, Merton H., and Franco Modigliani. "Dividend policy, growth, and the valuation of shares." *Journal of Business* 34:4 (October 1961): 411–433. Online at: www.jstor.org/stable/2351143

See Also:

★ Asset Allocation Methodologies (pp. 454–458)
★ Viewpoint: Bias-Free Investing Offers the Best Hope for Pension Funds (pp. 459–461)
★ Viewpoint: Why Mathematical Investing Beats Active Investment Managers Over the Medium Term (pp. 629–630)
★ Viewpoint: Why Quantitative Investing Can Do Well in Turbulent Markets (pp. 631–633)

NOTES

1. Chapter 5 of *Slow Finance* details why the focus shifted away from solid dividend payers in the boom years, based on the assumption that retained cash would allow companies to grow faster.
2. "Credit Suisse global investment returns sourcebook 2011," p. 46, "Cumulative return from low and high yielders within the top 100 stocks 1900–2010." This chart compares the performance of low and high yielders over more than 100 years.
3. "The power of compounding" illustration appears on p. 81 of *Slow Finance*.
4. "Credit Suisse global investment returns sourcebook 2011," p. 46, "Cumulative return from low and high yielders within the top 100 stocks 1900–2010." This chart compares the performance of an average market index (1900 £1 invested, 2010 £23,335; high yielders 1900 £1 invested, 2010 £100,160).
5. Nationwide House Price Index. Average prices: Q1 1985, £33,200; Q1 2012, £162,722.
6. Redgrave, James. "Pensions turn back to stocks for income." *Financial Times* (August 5, 2012). Online at: tinyurl.com/bv9ffn7
7. Fidelity. "Benchmarking and the road to unconstrained." White paper. January 2012.
8. "Credit Suisse global investment returns sourcebook 2011," cited in *Slow Finance*, p. 124.

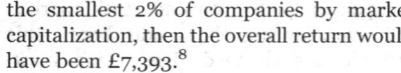

"Common sense is a very tricky instrument; it is as deceptive as it is indispensable." Susanne K. Langer

  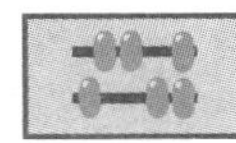      

Financial Steps in an IPO for a Small or Medium-Size Enterprise by Hung-Gay Fung

EXECUTIVE SUMMARY

- The firm forms an underwriting syndicate by selecting a lead underwriter and co-managers. Typically, for small and medium-sized firms underwriters charge a fee of 7% of the issue value. In the United States, a firm registers with the Securities and Exchange Commission (SEC) for the IPO issue, and when it has received approval it distributes a preliminary prospectus, known as a "red herring," to the public.
- The firm has to select an exchange on which to list its stock.
- The firm and the underwriter arrange road shows to promote the issue and to find out more about market demand; later this will provide useful information for setting the offer price and determining how many shares should be issued.
- After the IPO trading, the lead underwriter provides market research on the issue and other relevant information.

WHY AN IPO?

An initial public offering (IPO) of stocks is a share offering to the public by a small or medium-sized enterprise (SME) undertaken to raise additional cash for future growth or to enable existing stockholders to cash out by selling part of their holdings. Among other things, a successful IPO will provide a company with an objective valuation of its stock, create a good public image of the company—thus lowering its cost of borrowing—and provide it with a pool of publicly owned shares for future acquisitions of other companies. However, there are also drawbacks to being a public company, such as loss of freedom (including costly disclosure requirements and close monitoring by the public and government) and, if a takeover is threatened, potential loss of control.

TYPES OF IPO

There are many types of IPO, illustrating the different management and owner compensation contracts in firms.

- The plain vanilla IPO is undertaken by a privately held company, mostly owned by management, who want to secure additional funding and determine the company's fair market value.
- A venture capital-backed IPO refers to a company in which management has sold its shares to one or more groups of private investors in return for funding and advice. This provides an effective incentive scheme for venture capitalists to implement their exit strategy after they have successfully transformed a firm in which they invested so that it is financially viable in the market.
- In a reverse-leveraged buyout, the proceeds of the IPO are used to pay off the debt accumulated when a company was privatized after a previous listing on an exchange. This process enables owners who own majority shares to privatize their publicly trading firms, which are undervalued in the market, thus realizing financial gains after the public was informed of the high intrinsic value of the private firm.
- A spin-off IPO denotes the process whereby a large company carves out a stand-alone subsidiary and sells it to the public. A spin-off may also offer owners of the parent firm and hedge funds the opportunity to capitalize mispricing in both the subsidiary and parent if the market is not efficient enough. An interesting example in the United States was the spin-off of uBid by Creative Computers in 1998, which enabled arbitragers to capitalize the mispricing between the two listed companies.

THE IPO PROCESS

Overview

The first task of management is to select the underwriters who will be responsible for the new issue. This is done roughly three months before the IPO date. The underwriters provide the issuing firm with procedural and financial advice. Later they will buy the stock and then sell it to the public. The company, with the aid of lawyers, accountants, and underwriters, submits a registration statement to a regulatory body (such as the Securities and Exchange Commission (SEC) in the United States) for approval of the public offering. The registration statement is a detailed document about the company's history, business, and future plans. Specifically, the SEC requires information on the details of the company (form S-1), its financial history (form S-2), and expected cash flows (form S-3). The company must be able to back up the information provided to the SEC.

In the United States, about six weeks prior to the IPO issue the SEC reviews and approves the content of the disclosure to the public; this becomes the preliminary prospectus and is also called the "red herring." In December 2006, the SEC set new rules on what information must be included about a public company's executive compensation, including the level of executive pay, the benchmark used, and what quantitative or qualitative methods are employed in determining that pay.[1] The prospectus is a legal document describing the securities to be offered to participants and buyers. It is advised on and distributed by the underwriters, and provides information such as the types of stock to be issued, biographies of officers and directors with detailed information about their compensation, any litigation in place, and any other material information.

After publication of the prospectus the company, with the help of the underwriting syndicate, prepares for roadshows to meet potential investors—primarily institutional investors in major cities like New York, San Francisco, Boston, Chicago, and Los Angeles. Roadshows may sometimes be arranged for overseas investors. After the SEC approves registration of the IPO, the underwriters and the company will agree on the amount and price of the issue. On the day prior to the IPO issue the exact price of the shares to be issued is announced by the underwriter. After the IPO, the lead underwriter provides stock liquidity and research coverage.

The IPO date is followed by a "lockup" period, the duration of which varies across different issues and markets, but is in the region of 180 days for a typical issue. After this "insiders," who include the underwriters, are allowed to sell their shares. Insiders may or may not hold on to stock they own, depending on their motives and objectives. However, the lockup period appears to exert no control on those who bought shares at the market-offered IPO price, although there are regulatory restrictions on the types of clients to whom the firm can sell stock.

Selection of Underwriters

The board of a firm planning to launch an IPO will first meet with potential candidates for underwriters among investment banks and then select the lead underwriter. The choice of underwriter is based on criteria that include: a preliminary valuation of the

"The economic depression that struck Europe in the fourteenth century was followed ultimately by economic and technological recovery. But the depression we have moved into will have no end. We can anticipate centuries of decline and exhaustion." Jean Gimpel

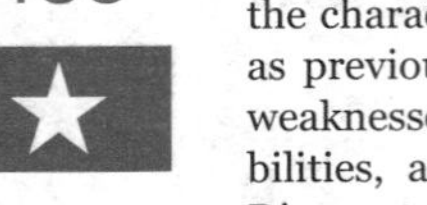

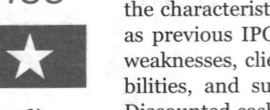

firm based on its financial information; and the characteristics of the underwriter, such as previous IPO experience, strengths and weaknesses, client network, research capabilities, and support for post-IPO issues. Discounted cash flow analysis and earnings multiples (such as the price/earnings ratio) are typically used to come up with the preliminary value of the company.

Citigroup was ranked first among underwriters in 2007, arranging $617.6 billion of offerings, and JPMorgan Chase was second with $554.1 billion. Deutsche Bank was ranked third and Merrill fourth in underwriting volume.[2] Citigroup has been top of the list for the past eight years. As a result of the global recession that began in 2008 the underwriting volume has declined, while fees have increased.

Types of Underwriting

The management of the IPO firm selects the underwriters and decides on the type of underwriting it wants. There are two types of underwriting: *firm commitment*, and *best efforts*. If the underwriter enters a firm commitment with the company, the underwriter is confident about the issue and is willing to buy all the shares if there is insufficient demand. In a firm commitment offering, the underwriters will buy the IPO shares at a discount in the range 3.5–7.0% and then sell them on to the public at the full offer price.

In a best efforts case, the investment bank will only do as much as it reasonably can to sell the shares and will return unsold equity to the firm. This practice is common for less liquid securities. However, if there is excess demand, the bank will ask for a "greenshoe" option, allowing it to buy additional stock from the IPO firm. Typically, a lead underwriter asks other investment banks to form an underwriting syndicate to take care of the IPO issue before final approval by the SEC. The syndicate serves to expand the marketing of the company's stock issue and to reduce the overall risk of the lead bank. The syndicate members are involved in the underwriting either through a commitment to sell the shares or just in marketing of the shares.

Underwriters may face legal consequences if a new issue goes wrong. Therefore, they have to present accurate and fair facts about the firm to investors, because otherwise they may be sued for misrepresentation, or for failing to carry out due diligence. Some underwriters may allocate stocks of popular new issues to their important corporate clients; this is known as "spinning," and is deemed to be unethical and illegal.

Underwriters charge different spreads, and domestic and overseas spreads may differ. The average underwriting fee (spread) runs between about 3.3% and 7% in the United Kingdom and the United States (Brealey, Myers, and Allen, 2008).

Selection of an Exchange

Different exchanges have different listing requirements. In general, they require minimum levels of pretax income, net tangible assets, and number of stockholders. For example, a New York Stock Exchange listing requires an income of either US$2.5 million before federal income taxes for the most recent year or US$2 million pretax for the each of the preceding two years. The firm must have been profitable in the two years before a listing.

The NASDAQ (National Association of Securities Dealers Automated Quotations), the largest electronic screen-based equity securities trading market in the United States, has lower listing requirements than the NYSE. Other markets, such as the NASDAQ Small Cap Market and the American Stock Exchange, offer even lower listing requirements (www.inc.com/guides/finance/20713.html). Thus, an IPO firm needs to assess its own strengths and weaknesses in order to pick the right exchange on which to list its shares.

A firm also needs to select a trading symbol for use on the exchange. For example, Microsoft trades as MSFT. A fee, which varies for each exchange, has to be paid for the services provided.

Subscription Procedure

IPO shares are distributed in different ways to investors. One approach is an open auction, where investors are invited to submit bids stating the number of shares they wish to purchase and the price they will pay for them. The highest bidders get the securities. The Google IPO of US$1.7 billion in 2004 and the Morningstar IPO of US$140 million in 2005 used this open auction method.

The bookbuilding method is the most commonly used in the United States today and is gaining popularity and dominance across the globe (Degeorge, Derrien, and Womack, 2007). During the roadshows, the investment banker asks institutional investors and individual clients about their intention to buy the shares. Each bid indicates the number to be purchased, and may include a limiting price. Such information is recorded in a "book," from which the name bookbuilding is derived. These indications of interest provide valuable information, because all bids are compiled to ascertain the market demand for the security. Although these bid indications are not binding, the investment banker can utilize the information to set the final offer price, which is made known on the day before the actual issue (Cornelli and Goldreich, 2003).

The appeal of the bookbuilding method, despite its higher underwriting costs, is that investment banks provide better promotion and research coverage of the IPO than other IPO issuing procedures. Thus, the networking of the bank with clients helps to enhance the image of the issuing firm. Chief financial officers appear to prefer this approach to IPOs despite the higher cost.

IPO COST AND PRICING

Underpricing

Besides the substantial underwriting cost and direct costs of lawyers, printers, accountants, etc., the IPO firm has to bear notional losses due to the underpricing of the issue—i.e., the IPO price is less than the true price of the stock. If the offering price is less than the true value of the issue, original stockholders effectively provide a bargain to the new investors. The finance literature shows that investors that buy at the issue price on average realize high returns (for example, 18%) over the following days. This high return from underpricing is common across the world—especially in China, which provides the highest return of 257% (Loughran, Ritter, and Rydqvist, 1994).

Underpricing, which is most likely to be seen with the bookbuilding method, can be justified as follows. First, a low offer price makes it probable that shares will later be traded at a higher price in the market, thus enhancing the firm's ability to raise capital in future. That is, underpricing ensures that the IPO is successful and that those who want to buy the issue will follow the same underwriter among those in the market.

MAKING IT HAPPEN

- An IPO is a time-consuming process.
- The success of an IPO depends on the successful selling of the firm to the investment banks, to the regulator, to the analysts, and to the public.
- During the six-month IPO process the firm's operations need to be on autopilot cruise control as management will be totally tied up during this time.

"We have gone from boom to bust faster than at any time since the oil shock. When you screech to a halt like that, it feels like getting thrown through the windshield." Stephen S. Roach

  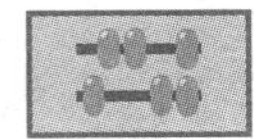      

Second, it is a way to avoid the winner's curse—the feeling of investors that they have paid too much. Simply, underpricing makes it more likely that an IPO will be successful. It appears that stockholders of the IPO firm focus more on likely gains in wealth from later stock price increases than on any short-term loss from underpricing (Loughran and Ritter, 2002).

New Price and Stock Issue

Suppose that an IPO firm has 10 million shares with a current valuation of $100 million, that it wants to raise $70 million for the issue, and that it has to pay $4.9 million for the direct cost of issuance, which is in general about 7% of the issue value (Hansen, 2001). The post-issue price, P_{new}, which includes underpricing, and the number of new shares to be issued, N, will be determined simultaneously. That is, the dollar amount of the new issue will cover the fund required and the direct cost to be paid, while the augmented value of the firm will include the old and new assets of the firm. P_{new} and N can be determined as follows:

$$P_{new} \times N = \$70,000,000 \text{ (new fund)} + \$4,900,000 \text{ (issue cost)} \quad (1)$$

$$(10,000,000 + N) \times P_{new} = \$100,000,000 \text{ (old assets)} + \$70,000,000 \text{ (new assets)} \quad (2)$$

Solving these two equations (1) – (2) yields the new price of the IPO, P_{new} = $9.51. The number of new shares to be issued, N = 7,875,920.

MORE INFO

Books:

Brealey, Richard A., Stewart C. Myers, and Franklin Allen. *Principles of Corporate Finance*. 10th ed. Boston, MA: McGraw-Hill, 2010.

Killian, Linda, Kathleen Smith, and William Smith. *IPOs for Everyone: The 12 Secrets of Investing in IPOs*. Hoboken, NJ: Wiley, 2001.

Articles:

Cornelli, Francesca, and David Goldreich. "Bookbuilding: How informative is the order book?" *Journal of Finance* 58:4 (August 2003): 1415–1443. Online at: dx.doi.org/10.1111/1540-6261.00572

Degeorge, François, François Derrien, and Kent L. Womack. "Analyst hype in IPOs: Explaining the popularity of bookbuilding." *Review of Financial Studies* 20:4 (July 2007): 1021–1058. Online at: dx.doi.org/10.1093/rfs/hhm010

Hansen, Robert S. "Do investment banks compete in IPOs? The advent of the '7% plus contract.'" *Journal of Financial Economics* 59:3 (March 2001): 313–346. Online at: dx.doi.org/10.1016/S0304-405X(00)00089-1

Loughran, Tim, Jay R. Ritter, and Kristian Rydqvist. "Initial public offerings: International insights." *Pacific-Basin Finance Journal* 2:2–3 (1994): 165–199. Online at: dx.doi.org/10.1016/0927-538X(94)90016-7

Loughran, Tim, and Jay R. Ritter. "Why don't issuers get upset about leaving money on the table in IPOs?" *Review of Financial Studies* 15:2 (Spring 2002): 413–444. Online at: dx.doi.org/10.1093/rfs/15.2.413

Websites:

Hoover's IPO Central: www.hoovers.com/global/ipoc
Inc. magazine articles on IPOs: www.inc.com/guides/finance/20713.html
Investopedia IPO definition: www.investopedia.com/terms/i/ipo.asp

See Also:

★ Corporate Finance for SMEs (pp. 33–35)
★ The Cost of Going Public: Why IPOs Are Typically Underpriced (pp. 475–477)
★ IPOs in Emerging Markets (pp. 514–516)
★ Price Discovery in IPOs (pp. 557–559)
✔ Merchant Banks: Their Structure and Function (p. 1012)
✔ Raising Capital by Issuing Shares (p. 1087)
✔ Stock Markets: Their Structure and Function (p. 1091)

NOTES

1 See *Wall Street Journal* (December 8, 2008).

2 See *International Herald Tribune* (January 1, 2008).

  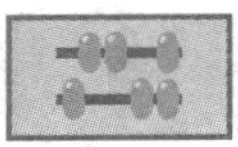      

Funds of Hedge Funds versus Single-Manager Funds by Steve Wallace

EXECUTIVE SUMMARY

- The process you undertake when selecting a FoHF is very different to that when selecting a portfolio of single managers.
- A decision on which to use, FoHF or single manager, is generally dependent on two primary factors: the monetary size of your investment allocation, and the resources at your disposal.
- The extra fee layer imposed when utilizing a FoHF structure is, in general, to pay for the resources used to source and select managers in addition to providing the investment vehicle.
- It is important to get a match between the mandate you have and that on which the FoHF is based.
- There are a number of factors that need to be considered in addition to those mentioned above when deciding whether to use a FoHF or collection of single managers; it is not a black and white decision.

INTRODUCTION

Funds of hedge funds (FoHFs) have caused heated debate over the years no matter which side of the fence you are on. The main issue this debate revolves around has two parts:

- *Fees*—that is, fees charged at the underlying manager level and then again at the FoHF level.
- *Control*: Accepting that you don't have the internal expertise and must pass control of the underlying fund selection to a FoHF manager can be difficult for some. They would rather have control even though they may not achieve the result they hoped for rather than hand over control for a result that isn't of their own making—regardless of the outcome.

The first step in choosing between FoHF or single manager should be to look inside the firm for the knowledge, expertise, and experience required to source and select the underlying managers. In this article I will be looking at elements of the decision to invest either in a basket of single managers or in a FoHF product.

A DEFINITION

A FoHF, as the name implies is a fund which invests in a collection of hedge funds. The collection of funds is constructed in an effort to provide risk/return characteristics that achieve its mandate. Before I go any further it should be noted that a FoHF does not only apply to hedge funds; it is a portfolio construction process that is also utilized by long-only products, i.e. FoFs (funds of funds).

The basic premise of a FoHF is that a portfolio can be constructed in such a way as to generate a rate of return with lower volatility than may otherwise be the case if the investor constructed the portfolio himself, dependent of course on the investor (as I will discuss in the next section). As such, the FoHF manager is saying that it has the ability to source, research, and select funds which, when brought together to form a portfolio, can satisfy the investor's investment mandate while reducing volatility.

Probably the two most often mentioned risks that a FoHF aims to reduce are manager risk and downside risk, which are in any event inextricably linked. Manager risk is reduced by the simple fact that more than one is involved in the product, thereby reducing the risk to that element of your portfolio which a single manager could bring. In other words, purely by having more managers in your portfolio you reduce the risk to your portfolio of any one of them failing, whether this be operationally, performance-wise, or in terms of strategy. The other primary risk that FoHFs aim to reduce is downside risk; arguably, one of the main benefits of a FoHF is not that it will "shoot the lights out" in terms of performance but that it will manage the downside risk.

INVESTOR TYPES

Generally investors have certain characteristics that will encourage them to opt for a FoHF rather than a single manager, and vice versa. Of course, in addition to this are emotive factors related to fear, control, and, perhaps, misplaced confidence in one's abilities.

Generally speaking, the greater the monetary value of the portfolio, the more likely an investor will go down the single-manager route. However, this leaves out one crucial element: the ability to select managers and construct a portfolio using a blend of managers to achieve a return target while minimizing risk.

Looking at Figure 1 we can draw certain conclusions as to the likelihood that—or more importantly whether—an investor should favor a FoHF strategy or a single-manager strategy when allocating to hedge funds.

The *x*-axis represents the ability of the investor to source and select individual managers. The "source" part is an important element as there are literally thousands of different funds that one can invest in, but the ability to get hold of a list of funds that you wish to consider further is an important part of the process and one that should not be taken for granted. The "select" element ties in the research part of the process as well. This is where you have managed to acquire a list of appropriate funds and are able to research them to the level of a hedge fund research professional. I use the prefix "hedge fund" in front of "research professional" as the kind of due diligence one applies to hedge funds, whatever the strategy, is very different to that required for long-only funds.

I have labeled the *y*-axis as the monetary size of the investment that the investor is seeking to allocate to hedge funds. The smaller this is, the less likely you will be able both to invest in the number of single managers necessary to satisfy diversification needs and meet minimum investment requirements.

Obviously, the descriptions of each of the four boxes illustrated in the diagram above are not mutually exclusive—there will be overlap, and other components will come

Figure 1. Factors influencing choice between FoHF and single-manager strategies

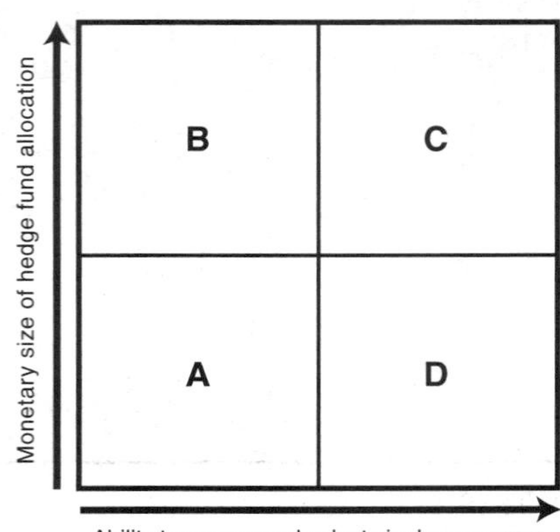

"First learn the meaning of what you say, and then speak." Epictetus

     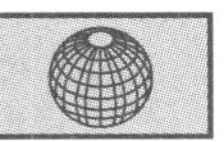   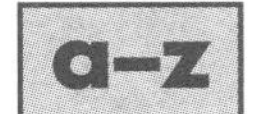

into the decision; I have taken two of the primary drivers purely to discuss.

A: This is where not only is the size of the allocation to hedge funds low, but the investor also may not have sufficient ability to source and select single managers.

B: This is where problems can occur: the size of the allocation is high, so on first inspection the situation lends itself to a selection of single managers. However, on the *x*-axis the ability to source and select managers remains relatively low. Therefore, investors who fall into this box should really look to increase their expertise before allocating to single managers.

C: This area of the diagram clearly is where the single-manager route makes sense. Here a large allocation of funds is matched by a strong ability to source and select single hedge fund managers.

D: This area represents the investor who may have a strong ability as per C above to build a portfolio of single-manager hedge funds to satisfy allocation requirements but who may not have the funds needed to satisfy the minimum investment requirements of certain funds, which will limit his choice.

ADVANTAGES AND DISADVANTAGES

Below I have listed some of the main advantages and disadvantages of each option when allocating to hedge funds. Note that this is by no means an exhaustive list.

FoHFs

Advantages

- Professionally selected underlying hedge fund managers.
- Reduced volatility.
- Manager diversification.
- Ease of access.
- Low minimum investment requirements (i.e. to invest in one FoHF the minimum investment would in most cases be less than the aggregate minimum investments of say 20 single-manager funds).
- Ability to negotiate fees.

Disadvantages

- Not bespoke.
- May not fit within the overall portfolio as well as specifically selected single managers.
- Additional layer of fees means the performance return needed to break even is higher. However, it should be noted that the investor is getting something for this extra fee level in terms of expertise at manager selection, provision of the FoHF structure, and so on. What value this translates to is dependent on the investor's situation.

Single managers

Advantages

- Bespoke portfolio.
- Ability to dovetail the hedge fund allocation into the overall portfolio.
- Transparency of the overall portfolio.

Disadvantages

- Cost of human intellectual property required to build a professional portfolio of single managers.
- Investment required to ensure an appropriately diversified hedge fund portfolio.
- Overconfidence in one's own ability, or that of one's team, to select single managers.
- Potential for large losses by any one manager to significantly and negatively impact your portfolio if not constructed properly.

MAKING IT HAPPEN

One of the points that is often made concerns a FoHF's ability to invest in up and coming hedge funds that will generate significant returns as they grow from start-up. This comes back to ability as not all FoHFs are in a position, from the standpoint of expertise and knowledge, to invest in emerging hedge funds as this calls for a much more complicated due diligence process.

If you are a novice to hedge funds, the risk to the value of one's portfolio by investing in such funds, whether they are single managers or a FoHF, is high. It should also be noted that if you do decide to access hedge funds via a FoHF this absolutely does *not* mean that you can abdicate responsibility completely. There is a whole other area of FoHF due diligence that comes into play here.

The best way to proceed is to go back to first principles—i.e. to ask yourself what was the rationale for investing in hedge funds in the first instance.

Once you have that in place, you can ask yourself the next question: What is the best way for me to access hedge fund investment opportunities? This is linked with the question whether you have the knowledge required either to invest in a FoHF or to put together a portfolio of single-manager hedge funds. If you don't, there are a number of ways of gaining that knowledge or gaining access to it, whether it is by educating yourself by going through the Chartered Alternative Investment Analyst program, discussion with peers, use of hedge fund advisory consultants, or other means.

That will then guide you in the choice between the single-manager and FoHF paths, although, as mentioned earlier, if you have the experience to construct a portfolio utilizing single-manager hedge funds but not enough funds to gain diversification benefits, it would be foolhardy to invest in single managers.

MORE INFO

Books:

Anson, Mark J. P. *Handbook of Alternative Assets*. 2nd ed. Hoboken, NJ: Wiley, 2006.
Ineichen, Alexander M. *Asymmetric Returns: The Future of Active Asset Management*. Hoboken, NJ: Wiley, 2007.
Jones, Chris. *Hedge Funds of Funds: A Guide for Investors*. Chichester, UK: Wiley, 2007.
Lhabitant, François-Serge. *Handbook of Hedge Funds*. Chichester, UK: Wiley, 2006.

Websites:

Alternative Investment Management Association (AIMA): www.aima.org
Chartered Alternative Investment Analyst (CAIA) Association: www.caia.org
EDHEC-Risk Institute: www.edhec-risk.com
Hedge Fund Matrix: www.hedgefundmatrix.com
Hedge Fund Standards Board: www.hfsb.org

See Also:

★ Carrying Out Due Diligence on Hedge Funds (pp. 465–467)
★ Understanding the Role of Diversification (pp. 617–618)
✔ Fund of Hedge Funds: Understanding the Risks and Returns (p. 1071)
✔ Hedge Funds: Understanding the Risks and Returns (p. 1072)
George Soros (p. 1312)
Absolute Returns: The Risk and Opportunities of Hedge Fund Investing (p. 1326)

"**Once you decide to work for yourself, you never go back to work for somebody else.**" Sir Alan, Lord Sugar

Viewpoint: Green Investing—Looking beyond the Financial Metrics by Stéphane Voisin

INTRODUCTION

Stéphane Voisin is head of Sustainability Research and Responsible Investment at CA Cheuvreux. He also teaches sustainable finance at Paris Dauphine University and chairs the scientific committees of Good Planet. Stephane is a board member of Eurosif, the FIR, and Agrisud. Prior to joining CA Cheuvreux in 2005 to start and develop the Sustainability Research service, he was a vice-president at JP Morgan, at Paribas in London, and at Barclays and Natwest. Stéphane Voisin has authorised a number of Sustainability Research reports and articles from both equity markets and sustainability perspectives. He contributed to the "Finance and sustainable developments" Europlace work published by Economia ed.

THE ECONOMIC VALUE OF CORPORATE SOCIAL RESPONSIBILITY (CSR)

We are a research department, working in financial research and within financial research. Our day-to-day job is to serve responsible investors, helping to provide them with the environmental, social, and governance (ESG) views on companies so that they can make better and more-informed choices about where to invest. Having said this, we are different to a ratings agency such as MSCI in that we do not look directly at a company's corporate social responsibility (CSR) performance. That is not our main interest. Our focus is on how the performance of companies, viewed in the widest context, can create or destroy value for shareholders.

In other words, one of our primary concerns is to try to demonstrate the economic value of CSR. In doing this, we look at all kinds of issues and we try to adopt a methodology that enables us to look at the social and environmental impact that an organization is having. Do they value diversity, for example? Will any externalities they might have translate into a negative financial impact for the business? We look at restructuring issues, and at corporate-governance issues. We have a thematic approach in our analysis as well as a sector approach, but the key is that we are very systematic with every company that we cover. Our commitment is to look at all the major ESG issues that can potentially impact a sector as well as the companies in that sector. We do this not merely through an analysis of the company's environmental impacts, but also with a careful regard to the work done by mainstream analysts who are wholly concerned with a company's profit and growth potential. Our analysts work very closely with us.

Our role in all this is to prove the economic business case of sustainability. This is key, since it means that our starting point is not the environment or the social case, which would be the natural starting point for an environmental non-governmental organization—such as Greenpeace or the World Wildlife Fund (WWF)—or a major charity. Our starting point is the business strategy of the company, which is much more akin to the starting point for a mainstream investment analyst. What we are looking at is the sustainability of that strategy, considered in the wider ESG context, and that is what is different from the concerns of a mainstream analyst. They look specifically at market potential and profit potential, at product pipelines, R&D capabilities, "protective moats" and so on, all the things that mainstream analysts look at to determine the appeal of a particular company and its potential for generating returns for investors. What we add is the wider vision, which looks at what is sustainable and what is not sustainable in the company's business case. We also look very closely at the business-reporting practices of the company. Is it delivering the appropriate indicators that enable you to see whether or not its practices and plans will be sustainable or harmful over the medium to longer term?

To achieve our goals, we need to contextualize the CSR strategy of the company. Our concern is always forward-looking, not backward-looking. We are not concerned with the company's profit performance in the past but with what it is currently doing and plans to do—for example in terms of human capital management, and in terms of its environmental impact. This is a major difference between ourselves and the ratings agencies, which are very focused on profit performance, liquidity, and so on. If you look at the analysis provided by a ratings agency, all their analysis is in relative terms: this quarter relative to that quarter, this year compared to last year, and so on. However, if you want to translate the impact of a company's CSR approach into pounds, or euros, or dollars you have to work in absolute terms, not in relative terms. What counts is the value they are actually creating, not how they compare to other companies. This is characteristic of our work. So we are not able to provide relevant conclusions for investors with respect to "best-in-class" judgments. What we do aim to do is to provide a very good view of the systemic issues that add value. This is not necessarily the same as talking about the way in which a company can outperform or add alpha, but it sheds important light on the company. As such, it adds value to an investor's understanding of the company and improves their ability to assess the risk profile of that organization.

From a very simple fundamental position, it is plain that financial indicators alone—this month's profit over last month's, for example—cannot capture the risk profile implied in the process of a company fulfilling its business potential. We have had a series of crises recently which prove the truth of this in spades. BP's Deep Water Horizon oil leak in the Gulf of Mexico is one obvious example. Nothing in BP's accounts showed that this was a possibility. The point is that to be in a position where you can take a holistic view of a company and its risk profile over time, you need to take into account both financial and nonfinancial information. This is why the kind of research that we do suits the needs of bond investors even more than equity investors. Clearly, equity investors are opportunity-seekers looking for the potential for outperformance. Bond investors, by way of contrast, are fundamentally risk-averse. They have entered into a transaction that offers them their money back plus interest if they hold to maturity. This can involve a five to seven-year time horizon or, more recently, even a 10-year time horizon on a corporate bond, so ESG issues and their potential impact are very important.

THE CARBON DISCLOSURE PROJECT (CDP)

Credit Agricole Cheuvreux has prepared two reports—the Carbon Disclosure Project (CDP) in 2009 and 2010. The CDP holds the largest collection globally of self-reported climate-change data. Its mission is to transform the way the world does business to prevent dangerous climate change, since climate change poses a very

"If investing is entertaining, if you're having fun, you're probably not making any money. Good investing is boring."
George Soros

obvious and significant risk to enterprises in every sector, as well as to society as a whole. The CDP works to incentivize as many companies as possible across the world's largest economies to measure and disclose greenhouse-gas emissions, climate-change strategies, and water strategies. Its vision is a world where capital is efficiently allocated to create long-term prosperity rather than short-term gain at the expense of the environment. These objectives are, of course, in alignment with our own methodology for calculating the ESG impact of a company's business strategy.

As well as working with thousands of companies, the CDP works with 655 institutional investors responsible for some US$78 trillion in assets to help reveal the risks in their investment portfolio. It also looks at how over 50 large purchasing organizations such as Dell, Pepsi Cola, and Walmart use its global CDP system to mitigate environmental risks in its supply chain.

Our latest report for the CDP came at a time when there was a clear lack of momentum on climate-change policies and a falling off in media interest in covering climate-change issues. This made—and continues to make—the work of the CDP even more important, since self-reporting by companies has to make up for the lack of regulatory pressure. In our view, the CDP is not just another initiative. It ranks along with the International Panel on Climate Change and the Stern Review of the Economics of Climate Change, since it represents the business sector's response to both scientific knowledge about climate change and the resulting threat to the economy. It paves the way for a low-carbon economy and gives investors and other stakeholders the tools to assess whether or not we are on track to meet this challenge.

At the EU level, as Connie Hedegaard, the European Commissioner for Climate Action said in the foreword to the 2010 report, the CDP complements the EU's Emissions Trading Scheme (ETS), since it encourages companies to take steps towards managing and reporting on their carbon emissions. More than 60% of European companies participating in the CDP are not covered by the EU ETS, so their participation considerably extends the degree to which European companies are showing an awareness of risks that go beyond simply market risks. It is very significant that by comparison with other regions, more than twice as many European firms have their emissions data independently verified.

Investors and shareholders have a crucial role to play in keeping up the pressure on companies to broaden their reporting of non-financial risk, particularly as happened after the Copenhagen Summit and the Durban Summits failed to provide real certainty on any post-Kyoto international framework for regulating greenhouse-gas emissions. Durban introduced the promise of a legal framework to be agreed no later than 2015, and it remains to be seen how much things are moved forward by the November 26 Climate Change Summit in Doha, Qatar. In the interim, it is up to companies, spurred on by investor interest, to increase the level of transparency in reporting on ESG risks generally. What we found was that the response rate to the CDP questionnaire on carbon emissions was at a very high level, namely 84% for the Europe 300 Index. This compared to a 70% response rate for the US S&P 500 and 41% for the Japan 500. The 2010 response rate represented a 2% improvement on the previous year and was in fact slightly better than reported if you take into account M&A activity through the year, such as the Cadbury takeover by Kraft Foods. Some 50% of European companies responding to the CDP questionnaire looked for external verification of their emissions data, providing investors with a higher level of assurance regarding those data.

What we found particularly interesting was that some 83% of companies across all sectors saw regulatory opportunities emerging from climate-change policies, including market opportunities for companies who are selling products and services that help their clients to reduce their emissions. An instance here is the fact that new generations of products developed by capital goods companies are some 12 to 15% more energy-efficient, and this will impact future emissions reductions in sectors such as the transportation, power, construction, and industrial markets.

What we also found though, in analyzing the CDP data, was that according to the disclosed carbon-reduction commitments within the European 300 Index of leading companies, the reductions are too low to enable the European Union to reach the EU ETS goal of cutting emissions by 80 to 95% by 2050. The EU ETS has set itself the goal of reducing emissions by 1.9% each year, on average, through the period from 2013 to 2020. What we found was that according to the CDP data, while the utilities sector is delivering a cut of 2.1% on average per year, the materials and energy sectors are delivering cuts of 0.8% and 0.4%, respectively. This falls short of the EU target levels and shows that there is still much more that needs to be done. Again, investor pressure for more transparency and disclosure, and then for companies to manage down their risk profiles actively, have the potential to have major impacts on improving Europe's emissions-reduction efforts.

MORE INFO

Website:

Carbon Disclosure Project: www.cdproject.net

See Also:

★ Ethical Funds and Socially Responsible Investment: An Overview (pp. 481–483)
★ Viewpoint: Outperformance through Ethical Lending (pp. 546–548)
★ Viewpoint: Principles for Responsible Investment—Looking Beyond the Financial Metrics (pp. 560–562)

        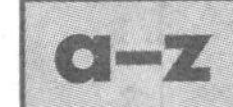

How and When to Use Nonrecourse Financing

by Thomas McKaig

EXECUTIVE SUMMARY

- Nonrecourse financing is debt where the loan is completely secured by collateral, which is often real estate. In case of default, the borrower is not liable because the lender is limited to collateral pledged for that loan—the lender has "no recourse" to the borrower's other assets.
- Nonrecourse financing is typically found in infrastructure projects such as the construction of toll roads and bridges. In this case, the borrower (a large construction company) is under no obligation to make payments on the loan if the revenue generated from the project on completion (the bridge or the toll road when built) is insufficient to cover the principal and interest payments on that loan.
- Although the benefits of such financing are obvious (the borrower is not using its balance sheet for the loan and can therefore undertake more leveraged projects than it could otherwise), such financing comes at a cost. Lenders often seek other credit guarantees and will almost certainly charge more for the loan than with more traditional, recourse financing.
- Nonrecourse financing does not mean "no risk," and some companies may undertake projects that have a riskier profile than they should otherwise assume, as will be shown in a case study.

INTRODUCTION

When companies are negotiating loans from lenders, there are many clauses that are important points for negotiation over and above the amount of the loan and interest charged. These items can include assignment of the loan (on the part of either the borrower or the lender), future fund advances, and prepayment capability. Another key clause is the nonrecourse clause, under which the lender agrees not to hold the borrower (the company) liable in the event of default on the loan.

Typically, therefore, nonrecourse financing is different from personal loans, such as mortgage loans, where the lender holds the borrower personally responsible for the sum borrowed if the value of the item being financed (the house) is insufficient to repay the total amount of the loan. Such loans are often called *recourse loans*. On the corporate side, most small business start-up loans are recourse loans—if the business fails, the owner is still liable to repay the loan amount in full.

Not all nonrecourse financing is the same—the phrase itself is very broad. Nonrecourse clauses in loan agreements, for example, may state the specific conditions under which the lender will not hold the borrower personally liable in the event of default. If these conditions are not met, then the borrower becomes liable. Such financing is sometimes referred to as *limited-recourse financing*.

It is also important to remember that, while nonrecourse loans relieve the borrower of corporate liability, they do not release whatever property is used as collateral for the loan—the lender still has an interest in the property as security for the loan.

Nonrecourse financing is the norm in the world of project financing for major projects that are government or quasi-government sponsored (infrastructure projects such as toll roads, hospitals, or power generating plants). It is so much a part of project financing that many textbook definitions of "project finance" specify that it is a key component: a project is financed based on, and secured by, the project itself, with the lender being repaid out of the project's cash flow, rather than the project being secured by the general assets or creditworthiness (the balance sheets) of the sponsors (the engineering companies, the construction companies, or even the government bodies) of an infrastructure project. In most of these cases, the companies undertaking the project are either not sufficiently creditworthy, or else unwilling to assume the high debt loads associated with traditional financing for large, multibillion dollar projects. Nonrecourse financing is also the norm in the commercial real estate world

CASE STUDY

Nonrecourse Does Not Mean No Risk

The early 1990s were a tough time for real estate investments in North America and throughout much of the world. But it was preceded by many profitable years of highly speculative construction and development of office buildings and retail facilities. This long building boom also encouraged all parties in the development process to stretch themselves and become more exposed to the overall project, which everyone agreed could only increase in value. Lenders soon became co-owners of projects. Developers, who used to sell a project on completion, wished to keep a portion of the development for themselves, and tenants wondered why they should pay rent when they could explore co-ownership arrangements.

Consider the example of a mid-size real estate asset management firm that became tired of managing the assets of others, and wanted a piece of the pie for themselves. Their plan was to obtain a nonrecourse loan for the construction of a major shopping mall. The real estate company would make money during the construction process (as construction managers) from ongoing mall management and from a small equity stake in the mall, which the managers would keep for themselves. And with a nonrecourse loan, the real estate firm wouldn't be liable for interest payments if things went badly. It was a "no lose" situation.

However, no liability is not the same as having no exposure. The real estate manager, aided by the thought that nonrecourse meant no possibility of loss, staked all of the firm's time and effort on this one project, rather than diversifying among many real estate holdings, as other managers had done. When the lender eventually took over the half-finished project, it was true that the real estate manager had no further financial liability for this project. However, because the lender stopped the project, the construction fees to the manager stopped, their own minority equity stake shrank to zero, and they didn't survive long enough to benefit from the ongoing mall management contract. The project was eventually completed many years later, but neither the original lender nor the real estate asset manager remained in business to enjoy the eventual profit.

Costs

In any negotiation—especially a loan negotiation—no concession, such as a nonrecourse clause, comes for free. In many cases, the lender may seek to mitigate its increased risk from writing a nonrecourse loan by seeking additional guarantees or warranties from the

for the construction of major projects such as office buildings or shopping malls.

The benefits of nonrecourse financing to the borrower are obvious. Borrowers are able to enter into agreements that they could not afford under traditional financing methods. Project financing deals are also highly leveraged, allowing borrowers (more accurately called "the sponsoring parties" to the agreement) to put fewer of their own funds at risk. Furthermore, depending on the structure of the loan agreement, borrowers may not be required to report any of the project debt on their balance sheet.

A large firm undertaking a project may use nonrecourse debt as a way of limiting its risk exposure by effectively isolating a new project. For example, a large university might use nonrecourse financing to fund the construction of a new building because the institution as a whole would not want to put its balance sheet at risk to fund the construction of one building.

However, some dangers accompany this increased exposure to risk. "Non-recourse" is not a synonym for "no downside risk," though some companies may come to believe that. The Case Study illustrates some of the dangers when companies forget about increased risk exposure.

CONCLUSION

There are some real advantages to nonrecourse financing for the borrower. In some cases, such as large project financing agreements, it allows projects to be completed that might not otherwise have broken ground if more traditional financing methods were used. But, as the economists say, there is no such thing as a free lunch. Be sure to take into account the costs of this financing before rushing into a nonrecourse deal.

borrower, from other parties that are part of the project finance group, or even from third parties such as governments or quasi-governmental agencies. Such "credit enhancement" can produce an end result where the borrower ends up with exposure that is very similar to a recourse loan. In still other cases, additional equity has to be pledged by the borrower to cover the lender's risk. Once again, if the borrower is pledging assets worth 110% or more of the loan amount, it is wise to question what you have to gain from having a nonrecourse loan.

Borrowers also pay for the nonrecourse clause in a loan agreement. This can either come about in the form of higher interest rates for the loan, or higher up-front financing costs and fees to arrange the loan, or both. Nonrecourse financing may also result in a shorter list of lenders (and therefore a less competitive and higher-priced marketplace) than recourse loans. The final cost comes from the greater amount of time needed to both negotiate and, ultimately, structure a nonrecourse financing agreement. Legal costs and time costs associated with these more complex financing arrangements must be considered in the overall financing equation. Selling property that is encumbered by a nonrecourse loan will often give rise to a more complex tax situation (depending on the country the company is operating in), which is another factor to consider.

MAKING IT HAPPEN

- In any loan negotiation ask yourself, "Can I afford to have nonrecourse financing?"
- When any loan is coming up for renewal, ask yourself if nonrecourse financing is appropriate for your firm.
- When circumstances at your firm change (for example, if your balance sheet strengthens), examine the appropriateness of nonrecourse financing.
- Also consider the appropriateness of nonrecourse financing when circumstances in the world change (for example, the credit market is looser/tighter, or a project is nearing completion so its risk profile changes) and you are renegotiating a loan.
- Government-backed programs can often stand between a lender and a firm, offering nonrecourse loans to the firm but providing a government guarantee if things go wrong, thereby offering a service to the lender as well. These programs vary by country and usually apply to specific, targeted industries—small business, agriculture, or protected industries. Check what programs apply to your firm, both now and in the future.

MORE INFO

Books:

Liaw, K. Thomas. *The Business of Investment Banking*. New York: Wiley, 1999.

Ling, David C., and Wayne R. Archer. *Real Estate Principles: A Value Approach*. 2nd ed. New York: McGraw-Hill, 2006.

Slee, Robert T. *Private Capital Markets: Valuation, Capitalization, and Transfer of Private Business Interests*. Hoboken, NJ: Wiley, 2004.

Tjia, John. *Building Financial Models: A Guide to Creating and Interpreting Financial Statements*. New York: McGraw-Hill, 2004.

Websites:

Collaboratory for Research on Global Projects at Stanford University: crgp.stanford.edu

International Project Finance Association (IPFA): www.ipfa.org

National Council for Public–Private Partnerships (NCPPP): ncppp.org

Project Finance Magazine: www.projectfinancemagazine.com

Project Finance Portal, Harvard Business School: www.people.hbs.edu/besty/projfinportal

Public Financial Management blog, International Monetary Fund: blog-pfm.imf.org/pfmblog/2008/02/a-primer-on-pub.html

Urban Land Institute (ULI): www.uli.org

See Also:

★ Capital Budgeting: The Dominance of Net Present Value (pp. 20–23)
★ Corporate Finance for SMEs (pp. 33–35)
✔ Assessing Cash Flow and Bank Lending Requirements (p. 964)
✔ Options for Raising Finance (p. 1081)
✔ An Overview of Loan Agreements (p. 1082)
✔ Retail Banks: Their Structure and Function (p. 1014)
✔ Steps for Obtaining Bank Financing (p. 1090)

"Some people have so much respect for their superiors they have none left for themselves." Peter McArthur

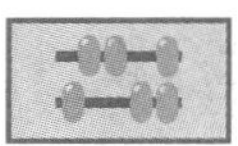

The Impact of Index Trackers on Shareholders and Stock Volatility by Martin Gold

EXECUTIVE SUMMARY

- Indexes and index-tracking strategies are an increasingly important feature of the contemporary investment environment.
- Index tracking has become a risk-averse strategy for institutional investors, and its popularity has grown strongly, especially within developed capital markets where it is considered difficult to outperform the market reliably.
- Indexes (and indexed portfolios) are actively managed instruments which are constructed according to objective criteria. Their performance typically depends on the market capitalization (size) of stocks.
- Index membership literally confers "investment grade" on firms because numerous managed funds are benchmarked to, or directly invested in, these stocks. Index membership also increases institutional investor ownership levels, trading liquidity, and research coverage by market analysts.
- Index changes can have dramatic effects on stock prices and trading volumes, especially over the short to medium term; longer-term effects remain unclear.

INTRODUCTION

Stock indexing, where investment portfolios mimic or replicate market indexes, has profound implications for both firms and investors. The practice stems from theoretical research which suggests that markets are informationally efficient. Since security prices generally reflect all public information, there is no point in employing active fund management and paying for investment research if there is no prospect of reliably beating the market. Whether or not you believe that beating the market is achievable—and this remains a perennial debate within academic and practitioner circles—the reality is that institutional investors make portfolio allocations with close reference to market indexes. The essential issue for investors and financial managers, therefore, is to be aware of how indexes are managed and to understand the implications for stocks arising from index tracking.

WHAT IS THE "MARKET"? A PRIMER ON INDEXES

This is a seemingly innocuous question, but one that is seldom asked by investors, financial managers, and consumers alike, although they closely scrutinize the fortunes of the Dow Jones in New York or the FTSE100 in London. These important yardsticks affect decision-making in financial markets and also in the real economy. Every day trillions of dollars in capital expenditure/project evaluation, risk modeling, and executive remuneration are all directly linked by market indexes. Investment managers also frequently use index derivatives as a simple and efficient alternative to buying and selling physical constituents.

In financial literature and everyday usage, indexes are given the status and importance of scientific instruments although they are far from being the precise or universal constants which exist in fields such as engineering or physics. A market index simply measures the performance of a basket of securities that is constructed in accordance with the index publisher's methodology. Consequently, an index is a "branded" measure of market performance, where the "market" is whatever the publisher deems it to be.

Although index publishers operate in a competitive marketplace, their index construction methodologies are often similar. Commonly, indexes are weighted according to market value (or capitalization) of their constituent stocks. This weighting scheme is generally regarded as the most accurate reflection of the economic outcomes experienced by all investors in a stock market. This means that once the firms are selected as being representative of the industries in the stock market covered, index performance is calculated using a sum of the individual stocks' returns weighted according to their size. For example, a stock which has a 5% return and represents 10% of the market capitalization will generate 0.5% of the index return for the period. Other schemes which can be used are equally weighted (where each stock has the same weight and performance contribution to the index return) or price weighted (where higher-priced stocks of have a larger index impact, and vice versa).

Although the performance of competing market indexes may appear to be correlated, these outcomes can mask significant differences in the index construction methodologies used. For example, although the S&P500 Index and the Dow Jones Industrial Average may show similar performance for the US stock market, the former is a capitalization-weighted, broad market index comprising 500 constituents, while the latter is a price-weighted index covering only 30 stocks.

Indexes are typically rebalanced periodically to reflect changes to the stock market and corporate actions which can affect constituent firms (known as "index events"). For example, if an index constituent is acquired by another firm, it will be removed from the index and replaced with a new constituent. The index publisher may review the composition of the index to make sure it remains representative of the market it covers. Indexes are also subject to ad hoc changes arising from market events: for example, when a firm goes into bankruptcy.

In the early 2000s, most global index publishers introduced a "free float" calculation methodology. This reduces a stock's weighting in an index (and therefore its contribution to the market's performance) where the availability (or "float") of securities is restricted due to cross-holdings (a corporation's holdings of another company's stock), or untraded ownership stakes held by governments or founders. The adoption of a free float methodology (originally used by the International Finance Corporation for the calculation of its emerging markets indexes in the 1990s) was in part precipitated by the dot com market crash. At that time, many new issues were being included in indexes at their full market capitalization, despite the reality that sometimes less than 20% of the issued shares were actually available to investors for trading in the market.

HISTORY AND RATIONALE FOR INDEXING-TRACKING STRATEGIES

Since the late 1960s, researchers have been examining the performance of professional fund managers using risk-adjusted measures, and they have found that the majority have not outperformed the market averages, even before management fees are taken into account.[1] This empirical literature, known as the "active versus passive debate" in academic and practitioner circles, provides persuasive evidence of the concept of market informational efficiency. The consensus emerging from this work provides an important validation of orthodox

"A man who trims himself to suit everybody will soon whittle himself away." Charles M. Schwab

economic theory, which asserts that financial markets generally function rationally and that security prices reflect fair value.

These research findings also spawned the development of so-called passive or index-tracking strategies in the 1970s. The first index-tracking strategy was created in 1971 by Wells Fargo (now Barclays Global Investors) for a single pension sponsor (Samsonite) and used an equally weighted portfolio. In 1973, it created a comingled fund for its trust department clients which tracked the S&P500 Index. In 1976, the Vanguard Group launched the first US index mutual fund (the Vanguard S&P500 Index Fund). Today there are numerous indexes and index-tracking products, covering stock markets, industry sectors, hedge funds, and commodities. According to Standard & Poor's, US$4.85 trillion was benchmarked to its US indexes at December 31, 2007: This figure includes US$1.5 trillion directly indexed to the S&P500.

The prudent investment standards which govern many pension funds and institutional investors in Anglo-Saxon economies have, since the late 1980s, largely endorsed the benefits (broad diversification with lower operating costs) of investment indexation compared to active portfolio management. In fact, the general intellectual acceptance of market efficiency has effectively reversed the traditional onus on pension fund trustees and other financial fiduciaries to employ active portfolio management strategies that seek to outperform the market while minimizing risks to capital.

Although index publishers disclaim indexes as being measures of investment merit, market pundits and academic researchers have paid surprisingly little attention to the suitability of market indexes for investment purposes, concerning themselves instead with tests of market efficiency. It is also important to note that indexes are themselves actively managed instruments: Index tracking is therefore not a passive, "buy-and-hold" investment strategy, familiar to most personal investors.

MARKET IMPACTS: PRICE AND VOLUME EFFECTS OF INDEX CHANGES

Although indexes have evolved as market measures, they form the underlying basis for index-tracking strategies whose portfolios are managed mechanistically using either full replication (where all constituents are held in their index proportions) or partial replication (a subset of stocks) techniques. Index-tracking strategies are compelled to alter portfolio holdings in accordance with changes announced by index publishers. Significant trading costs (as distinct from operating costs such as brokerage and taxes)—also known as market impact or frictions—can also arise from constituent changes when index funds (and many funds have active managers who also track market benchmarks for active portfolios) rebalance their portfolios.

Because index-tracking strategies involve no judgment or market timing, unlike active portfolio management disciplines, their transactions are price-insensitive. Thus, the growth in the scale of indexed portfolio assets has brought opportunities for arbitrageurs to profit from the potential volatility and liquidity imbalances which are caused by index reconstitution events. For example, arbitrageurs may purchase (or sell) securities due to be included in (or removed from) the index prior to the date of the index event. Index-tracking funds are compelled to buy (or sell) "at any cost" to rebalance their portfolios to the revised index composition.

The direct implications of index reconstitution events have been examined in the academic literature since the mid-1980s. In 1986, Harvard economist Andre Shleifer highlighted the price and volume effects' implications for stocks in the S&P500 Index.[2] He concluded that index tracking created downward sloping demand curves due to the price inelasticity of demand created for these stocks. Several subsequent studies in the United States and the United Kingdom have also documented significant price and volume effects for stocks added and deleted from stock market indexes. Other research, however, has found that prices subsequently reverse over longer time horizons. These findings do not acknowledge the costs of price volatility experienced by investors.

In response to the practical concerns of clients and stakeholders, index publishers announce index changes in advance of the actual index reconstitution events. This has had the effect of bringing forward the volatility associated with these changes from the actual index event date.

CONCLUSION

Indexes are an essential tool for measuring financial market performance characteristics. Because there has been a dramatic increase in the scale of funds that directly

CASE STUDY

News Corporation's Inclusion in the S&P500 Index

News Corporation is an integrated and diversified media company with assets of approximately US$62 billion as at September 30, 2008. The company has global operations but earns the bulk of its income in the United States. In April 2004, its chairman and CEO Rupert Murdoch announced that the company was seeking shareholder approval to consolidate the ownership of its Australian businesses and to move the company's legal domicile from Australia to the US state of Delaware.

In explaining the change of domicile to shareholders, the directors highlighted the important benefits that were expected to accrue from inclusion of the company in the leading US equity benchmarks, especially the S&P500 Index. They noted that this would:

- correct the "under investment" by US institutions, which only held approximately 52% of its shares compared to peer firms such as Disney (72%), Time Warner (78%), and Viacom (87%);
- increase demand from US institutions that were currently prevented from buying non-US stocks;
- increase trading in the company's shares, which should narrow the gap between the prices of its voting common stock and nonvoting common stock;
- lower the costs of raising equity in a deeper market: the S&P500 Index's total market capitalization exceeded US$10 trillion, 20 times larger than the Australian market benchmark, the S&P/ASX 200 Index.

On November 3, 2004, the company announced that its reincorporation had received court approval and that the New York Stock Exchange would become its primary listing. On November 17, 2004, Standard & Poor's preannounced that News Corporation would be included in the S&P500 index (at the close of trading on December 17, 2004) and that the stock would be removed from its Australian indexes in three additional equal installments. On the date of News Corporation's reincorporation announcement, and on the days it was phased out of the Australian market benchmark, over 195 million shares worth approximately AU$4.6 billion were traded on the Australian Stock Exchange—approximately one-third of this turnover occurring on the day of the reincorporation announcement alone. Since changing its domicile, the company has raised US$5.15 billion in debt securities and started a US$6 billion stock repurchase program.

  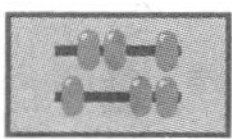      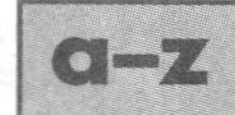

track market indexes and relative performance monitoring by actively managed portfolios, gaining and maintaining membership of an "index club" is a critically important goal for financial executives.

Compared to nonconstituents, firms included in market indexes have the potential for preferential access to capital, significantly greater research coverage in the investment community, and trading liquidity. Index inclusion can increase demand and stock prices. On the downside, firms excluded from indexes typically lose institutional ownership and can experience considerable price declines in their stocks especially in the short term. The case study shows how the phenomenon of index events creates substantial stock turnover and volatility, despite the reality that no significant changes have occurred in a company's business operations.

MAKING IT HAPPEN

- Be index-aware: Membership of the "index club" is important because it confers higher demand for stocks and trading liquidity arising from institutional ownership.
- Find out which stock market indexes cover your firm or your market. What are the inclusion and exclusion criteria used by the publishers, and how is your firm classified in terms of its market value and industry representation? Even if your stock is not included in a broad market index, it may be a potential constituent in an industry-specific or customized index.
- Financial managers need to make sure that index publishers are well informed about their business operations and ownership structures. They should also be aware that index publishers are generally reluctant to delete firms from indexes because this creates excessive index turnover.
- Given that indexes are generally market capitalization-weighted, are profitable merger and takeover opportunities available which will increase the equity base (and thus index size) of the firm?

MORE INFO

Books:

Ali, Paul, Geof Stapledon, and Martin Gold. *Corporate Governance and Investment Fiduciaries*. Pyrmont, Australia: Lawbook, 2003.

Levy, Haim, and Thierry Post. *Investments*. Harlow, UK: FT Prentice Hall, 2005.

Malkiel, Burton G. *A Random Walk Down Wall Street: The Time-Tested Strategy for Successful Investing*. 9th ed. New York: WW Norton & Co., 2007.

Report:

Gold, Martin. "Fiduciary finance and the pricing of financial claims: A conceptual approach to investment." PhD thesis, University of Wollongong, 2007.

Websites:

FTSE Group/Financial Times indices: www.ftse.com/Indices

Morgan Stanley Capital International indexes: www.msci.com

Standard & Poor's indexes: www.sandp.com

See Also:

★ The Role of Institutional Investors in Corporate Financing (pp. 589–592)

✔ The Efficient Market Hypothesis (p. 1068)

✔ Investors and the Capital Structure (p. 1120)

✔ Stock Markets: Their Structure and Function (p. 1091)

✔ Understanding Price Volatility (p. 1103)

✔ What Is Benchmarking? (p. 1184)

Burton Malkiel (p. 1291)

A Random Walk Down Wall Street: The Time-Tested Strategy for Successful Investing (p. 1412)

NOTES

1 For a review of this literature and the debate, see Gold (2007).

2 Shleifer, Andrei. "Do demand curves for stocks slope down?" *Journal of Finance* 41:3 (July 1986): 579–590. Online at: www.jstor.org/stable/2328486

"**Pedantry is the dotage of knowledge.**" Holbrook Jackson

  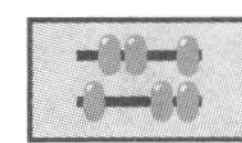      

Viewpoint: Inverse Stagflation and the Global Economy: When Real Assets and Paper Assets Part Company by Renée Haugerud

INTRODUCTION

Renee Haugerud is the founder, chief investment officer, and managing principal of Galtere, a registered investment adviser that manages approximately US$1 billion across several commodity-focused products. During her 30-year investment career she has acquired expertise across all asset classes in posts throughout the world. She began her tenure in financial markets by trading cash commodity markets in the United States and Canada for Cargill and Continental Grain. Her interest in the relationship between financial markets and geopolitics led to her first international post in Geneva, Switzerland, where she ultimately served as Cargill's foreign exchange trading manager. During her 13 years at Cargill she developed expertise in a wide range of securities and finally became vice president/structural trading manager at corporate headquarters in Minneapolis. Following Cargill, she managed proprietary trading desks at institutions including NatWest Markets in Hong Kong and Hunter Douglas in the United States. Haugerud's insight into how global markets are affected by the psychology and relationships of macroeconomic trends makes her a sought-after speaker and panelist at global investment events. She is active in the community of women and business leaders and is an active advocate for numerous global education initiatives. Haugerud received her BS degree with honors in forest resource management from the University of Montana in 1980.

As a commodities specialist for more than 30 years, what is your view of how the commodities market fared through the 2008 global recession, and how do you anticipate commodities doing from now through 2011?

I think that to understand what is happening in commodities now, one needs to look back to a position that is almost the exact mirror image, or inverse, of the period we are now going through. In the period from 1978 to 1983, commodities—what we term "real assets," the tangibles that are bought and sold, from coffee to metals—crashed in price at the same time as paper assets (by which I mean stocks and bonds) were rising. In other words, you had deflation in real asset prices and inflation in paper asset prices. This was the period which devastated the grain farms in the US Midwest, for example, with the price of wheat crashing.

Over the next few decades commodities regained their pricing momentum and caught up with paper assets. By 2007 both commodities and real asset values were booming. Then we had the crash, and there is now a very clear decoupling starting to happen once again between real assets and paper assets. This time round real assets are rising in value, but after the mini-bull market in 2009 the price of paper assets is falling. We believe that this demonstrates that under certain economic conditions you can have both very significant asset deflation and asset inflation present in the economy at the same time. We call this set of conditions "inverse stagflation."

We see low monetary inflation for a few years, but in real assets—chiefly in agricultural commodities and farmland—we expect inflation to be quite sharp. At the same time paper assets (stocks and bonds) will experience sharp deflation. This dynamic is part of a structural shift away from the dominant regime of the last 30 years, during which paper assets outperformed real assets by a factor of five.

How does the theory of inverse stagflation translate into meaningful judgments concerning asset allocation?

Taking inverse stagflation as an investment theme, we distinguish three main threads that guide our thinking. We anticipate a structural rise in the pricing of real assets, which should outperform other asset classes through the next decade and beyond. We expect to see a marked overall decline in global equity indices as the value of stocks at the major exchanges falls, and we think that fixed-income markets, which consist of various-duration government bonds and investment-grade corporate bonds, will be trapped in a narrow trading range with low to very low yields.

A key part of understanding what is driving this new dynamic hinges on grasping the fact that global growth is no longer being driven solely by consumption patterns in developed nations. The entry on to the stage of emerging market consumers is absolutely key. As emerging economies consume—rather than export—their way to growth, an inevitable corollary of this is that their diet changes.

The average emerging economy diet starts to be more protein-rich. As people eat more meat, the need for grain rises sharply. For example, the Cornell University *Journal of Environmental Development and Sustainability* points out that it takes eight grain calories to produce one calorie of protein. So when a country starts to eat more meat, that drives an accompanying escalation in demand for grain, which can be expected to create upward pricing pressure on global grain stocks.

So if we look at how this will play out, today if you chart the S&P 500 against the price of corn and the price of gold, taking 1980 prices as your base of 100, you have a very significant pricing gap between paper and real assets. Gold and corn overlap each other, but the S&P is way higher at 1,000, as against approaching 200 for gold and corn. We expect this to potentially reverse some time between 2013 and 2014, with the S&P falling to around 300 and corn going through 400, with gold not far behind. It is hard to overemphasize what a major structural shift this projection envisages.

A second important point, to set alongside the impact of diet changes in emerging economies, is water scarcity. At present this is hardly priced into soft assets at all, but it is going to be a major driver of price. The

UN Food and Agriculture Organization points out that it takes between 10,000 and 13,000 liters of water to produce 1 kilogram of beef, while a kilogram of wheat or rice takes just 1–4 liters. One effect of this is that global water consumption is doubling every 20 years.

Then there is the impact of biofuel production to be considered. The US Department of Agriculture estimated that demand for corn for ethanol would approach 4.5 billion bushels in the 2010 growing season, compared to 1.2 billion bushels seven years ago. In 2011 some 30% of the entire US corn crop will be used for ethanol, according to the US Energy Information Administration. Demand on this scale drives pricing.

Do you see inflationary pressures putting continuing upward pressure on real assets, such as equities and commodities, despite the overcapacity in the US and in Europe generally?

We agree that overcapacity will have a deflationary impact on paper assets and will certainly push down hard on any tendency toward inflation in factory output prices or in stocks. Capacity utilization in the United States hit a low of 68.3% during the recent crisis and has not yet risen back to 75%. The output gap will hold down wage inflation, which in turn should help producers to absorb, for a while at least, rising commodity supply costs. However, this dynamic will squeeze profit margins and depress equities as the developed markets settle into much lower trend growth.

Against this scenario we view global equities as the most overinvested, overvalued asset class, and the asset class most likely to fall around the world in the event of another shakeout of markets. We may not see another rerun of the 40% loss of value in equity markets that characterized 2008, but we expect equity indices to underperform other assets, trending downwards for the next five to ten years. At the same time, as commodity inflation takes hold, the ongoing erosion of earnings is likely to be exacerbated, which in turn would provoke a sharper downturn in equities.

It is important to note that the inverse stagflation hypothesis includes a focus on range-bound fixed-income markets in developed economies. Remember that stagflation in the 1970s was particularly painful because the environment of stagnating growth was accompanied by high inflation, which in turn led to extremely high interest rates, which made money very expensive for companies and hindered economic activity still further. We are in a different world today, with no real expectation of a sharp hike in interest rates in the foreseeable future.

Deflationary pressures, including overcapacity, should control any inflationary tendencies prompted by even sustained quantitative easing. So there should not be the same pressure on the US Federal Reserve for rate hikes as there was 30 years ago.

It is, of course, possible that certain supply shocks will intermittently drive up commodity prices, but the most probable scenario is that structural price inflation in grains and soft commodities will be demand-led. This is not something that central banks can or should seek to control, so there is not the same pressure on the Fed to act.

Of course, sustained quantitative easing does drive future inflation expectations, and that in turn generally leads to a steepening of the yield curve for longer-duration bonds. Such steepening did occur early in 2010, with the front-end rates staying anchored to the Fed's low-rates policy and 10-year yields rising. However, the market soon realized that the newly created liquidity was not reaching the consumer, so long-term rates came back into line. The yield curve is now in a bull flattening period that we expect to continue in the near term, creating the reverse conditions to what one would expect on the assumption of future inflation. In this context it is worth noting that despite the extraordinary measures taken by the Fed to increase liquidity, the velocity of money has dropped significantly.

In fact much of the stimulus provided in the United States since 2008 remains barricaded behind the banks, which are deleveraging and bolstering their balance sheets rather than lending. The banks are purchasing large quantities of Treasuries, which again helps to hold down long-term rates (since there is plenty of demand). Household savings, too, are on the increase as the US consumer switches from spending to saving, and much of this money also winds up in Treasuries, helping to flatten the back end of the US curve.

In the "real commodities" universe, precious metals have been hitting record highs. Do you expect that boom to run and run?

I am still bullish on gold in the medium term, though metals generally have reached fair value. We have seen astonishing performance from silver, and those who like silver say that there is more to come there, but gold has special characteristics since it is three things rather than one. It is a currency, a commodity, and a store of value, and each of these characteristics plays semi-independently. We are in a broad-based global currency revaluation with a great deal of competitive devaluation going on, so that makes gold behave as an appreciating currency. If a number of global currencies (excluding the US dollar) all devalue together, then they should go up against the dollar and gold will rise on dollar weakness. This game probably still has a long way to run, so that trend can be expected to continue to play for gold. As a store of value it attracts investment flows, and this is accounting for a larger share of the flows into gold than industrial or jewelry demand.

But currency plays are also as interesting right now as gold. Most of my career, for example, I have been either a strong buyer or a seller of the Japanese yen. I think we could be at the very beginning of a structural revaluation in the Japanese market. Some of their equities are finally trading at what amounts to a decent value and the markets are responding by driving up the yen, despite the Japanese government's commitment to weaken it. However, all this pales by comparison with the shift we are predicting from a three decade-long spree for paper assets to a long-running real commodities boom. GDP growth is switching from export-related GDP growth to consumptive GDP, and that switch impacts prices rapidly and dramatically across a whole range of soft commodities, from staples to protein.

One of our underlying premises is that in the long term this switch will play extremely well for developing economies, which are the world's primary sources of soft commodities. Brazil and Argentina will do very well. Today, economic thinking in Brazil is still trapped by its boom and bust cycles and periods of high inflation. The authorities there are not thinking in terms of an asset regime change from paper to commodities, or what that could mean for them. Brazil is the repository of everything that is bullish, from coffee to land, sugar, and ethanol. Plus they have cheap hydroelectric power and plenty of water and they are now a politically stable economy with high real interest rates at a time when there are negative real interest rates throughout the developed economies. The way to exploit this is to short the US dollar through investment in industrial foodstuffs. We see that as an excellent investment play for the medium term.

To sum up, it seems likely that the next 12 months will see that the long-promised shift in investor preference from equity investments to real assets, which has been churning since 2007, will really start to gather momentum. There is a great deal of vested interest favoring equity investment,

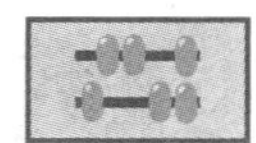

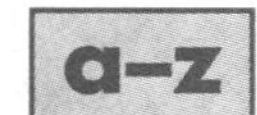

so we expect a real seesaw struggle for power between equities and real assets, with bonds functioning as the pivot-point between the two.

We expect bonds to remain range-bound and to continue to attract investment flows even during periods of turbulence. After 2011 the case for real assets should be pretty unstoppable and the "new power" in investing will have come into its own. Just as significant shifts below the Earth's surface can provoke violent upheavals that in turn form new land masses, we believe that this periodic market volatility heralds the creation of a fresh investment landscape in which real assets will reign as the dominant investment class.

MORE INFO

Reports:

Aguilar, Luis A. "Requiring that derivatives be centrally cleared is the centerpiece of reform." Statement at SEC open meeting. US Securities and Exchange Commission, December 15, 2010. Online at: www.sec.gov/news/speech/2010/spch121510laa.htm

Büyükşahin, Bahattin, Michael S. Haigh, Jeffrey H. Harris, James A. Overdahl, *et al.* "Fundamentals, trader activity and derivatives pricing." US Commodity Futures Trading Commission, December 4, 2008. Online at: tinyurl.com/6caepgl [PDF].

Website:

US Commodity Futures Trading Commission: www.cftc.gov

See Also:

★ Mixflation (pp. 215–218)

★ The Role of Commodities in an Institutional Portfolio (pp. 585–588)

✔ Trading in Commodities: Why and How (p. 1093)

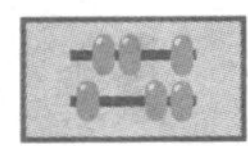

Investing Cash: Back to Basics by Mark Camp and Emma Du Haney

EXECUTIVE SUMMARY

- Have regard to risk and security when deciding where to invest.
- A guarantee is only as good as the giver. There is no such thing as an absolute guarantee.
- When investing cash:
  - use internal resources if there is a fully functioning professional treasury;
  - use your clearing bank or custodian;
  - use a specialized investment manager;
  - use suitable pooled funds (money market funds), perhaps through a treasury portal.
- Money market funds offer different yields and returns. Before investing, prioritize between yield, security, and liquidity, and carry out detailed due diligence.
- Simplicity and transparency are key factors.
- The current crisis has highlighted the importance of liquidity and credit.

LESSONS FROM RECENT EXPERIENCE IN FINANCIAL MARKETS

It has become crystal clear that cash must be treated as a separate asset class. This means taking care when considering how, and with whom, cash should be held and invested.

It is equally clear that risk is a very relevant factor for cash. Institutional investors have discovered in the past year that so-called safe cash investments have not been as secure as they thought. For many years, investors have ignored the fundamental principle that extra yield is associated with extra risk. It is now clear that the especially attractive rates paid by Icelandic banks came with significant additional risk.

In times of plenty we tend to overlook or downplay risks and concentrate on the rewards. All we tend to think about is who is top of the league table so that I can maximize my interest income. What can be all too easily forgotten is that the return *of* your money is always more important than the return *on* your money.

A flight to quality, or perceived safety, can quickly become an unstoppable tsunami that can take the good with the bad; witness the ever-lengthening queue outside Northern Rock (a British bank) last September, and the subsequent effect on confidence in all British banks. Everyone now wants a guarantee, and an absolutely safe investment.

What does "guarantee" itself mean? We now know that it is only as good as the counterparty that gives it. Having to worry about counterparty risk is something most of us thought was the thankless and purely box-ticking task of compliance officers, or the credit committee. Now we know better. It must be stressed that it is very unusual for an institutional investor to receive a specific guarantee on a cash placement, except to the extent that a bank, or investment product, receives overt support from a relevant authority that one trusts.

What no one wants to say is that, ultimately, there is no absolute guarantee. This may seem more obvious now, after a year in which we have seen that AAA credit ratings do not guarantee security, and that even a government guarantee is only as good as the economic strength of the country that gives it.

The whole financial world is built on confidence, and if that is fatally cracked then the whole pack of cards can come down, with disastrous economic consequences for us all. That is why all the major governments and central banks, in both West and East, finally acted as decisively as they did toward the end of 2008, coughing up some US$6.75 trillion to save the world. This is equivalent to some 10% of the entire US$65 trillion global economy (CIA World Factbook 2007), and has been used to recapitalize banks, buy up toxic assets (including subprime-related assets), make loans to financial institutions, and give state guarantees to get the wholesale markets moving again. Even with the size of this unprecedented rescue, risks remain in the financial system according to a recent Bank of England financial stability report.

SO WHAT CHOICES DOES A TREASURER HAVE WHEN INVESTING CASH?

Very large treasury operations. The very largest holders of cash can afford to run a well-resourced internal treasury, including a fully functioning cash desk. Aside from the major banks, however, such entities are few in number, as you have to be investing very large amounts on a daily basis to do this properly.

Treasuries with small or intermittent balances. At the other end of the scale, if one has cash balances that arise only intermittently, or if they are less than US$1.5 million, leaving them with your main clearing bank(s) (having done appropriate due diligence and negotiated the best available rates) is probably the best approach.

Netting and pooling are a must. It is assumed that any treasurer will have already maximized any pooling, netting, and aggregating possibilities, across currencies if necessary, as these always offer the best value operationally and economically—and usually in terms of security too.

For treasuries in the middle ground the main strategic options are as follows.

1. Utilize Internal Resources

This has been an attractive option in the past, often because it is considered a low-cost option. But what are the risks involved with this approach? Even if one hires a good cash specialist, where is the backup if he or she falls under the proverbial bus? Where is the backup for the credit specialist? It is no longer good enough to rely solely on the credit rating agencies, or review the agreed counterparty list once a year. Instrument and counterparty credit ratings are just one of the guides to utilize, and they can, and should, be challenged from time to time. Certainly, just calling your friendly money broker from time to time for advice cannot now be considered best practice.

2. Outsource to a Specialist Provider/-Treasury Portal

The bank. The first option is to see what your clearing bank, or custodian (if relevant), can provide, especially if cash can be automatically swept on a daily basis. The problem here is risk concentration with just one, or only a handful, of counterparties. A good example of this type of situation is a hedge fund with a single prime broker. Not only does the fund have a serious risk with the prime broker as the derivative counterparty, but the cash margin/collateral would typically be held with the same party, doubling the counterparty risk. Before the Bear Stearns and Lehman Brothers troubles, the main global prime brokers were considered too big to fail; this is not the position now.

Investment manager. If an institution has large and relatively stable cash balances to invest, then an investment manager can

"Successful investing is anticipating the anticipations of others." John Maynard Keynes be approached to run a segregated cash mandate. The advantage of this approach is that you get to choose the investment manager, and you can also specify the investment parameters and benchmark, and in that way control risk. Invested cash should also be held with a third-party custodian, thus ring-fencing the assets from the investment manager. The downside is that it is a relatively cumbersome and expensive process to set up in the first place, and it is not very flexible. A serious bespoke cash investment manager will usually require a large minimum investment balance (US$150 million plus), and/or minimum fees. Frequent redemption, or movements generally in the mandate, will not be welcomed, as they can materially affect investment strategy and performance. Such arrangements best suit long-term investment cash, and not volatile cash investment.

Pooled funds. Money market funds have been invaluable to many corporate and institutional treasurers in recent years; freeing them from the task of spreading their funds around the various banks. However, money market funds come in many guises, and, as some investors have found to their cost, some of these funds have invested in assets that have proved to be far from low risk.

Treasury portals. Use of portals is extensive in the United States, and brings operational efficiencies if one is a multi-fund user. Such portals are now available in Europe.

MONEY MARKET FUNDS

Let's remind ourselves why money market funds became so attractive. They now account for some 40%, or US$4 trillion, of all cash held in the United States. This reflects a 25% rate of growth over the last 12 months, as investors have generally seen SEC registered (Rule 2a-7) money market funds as a safe haven, in spite of a few funds exhibiting obvious stress that has required promoter support, and the well-publicized failure of both "The Reserve" and the "Lehman Funds." However, what this overall growth disguises is a clear move by US institutional investors away from traditional so-called "prime" funds, to US Treasury and government-backed security money market funds, even though the yields on such funds are very low, and even went negative for a short period.

This trend has been much less noticeable with European-domiciled money market funds, although there are now a small number of euro-denominated government securities, and one sterling government fund that has been recently launched. Demand for these new funds has largely been from European subsidiaries of US multinationals, and it remains to be seen whether such funds catch on with European institutional investors.

European money market funds now account for some €420bn (US$500 billion) equivalent in the three main currencies, and this includes around £100bn (US$145bn) plus of sterling funds.[1] The last decade has seen a very rapid growth for such funds, and although there are recent signs that growth has checked among institutional investors, it seems that high net worth investors are now taking up any slack as they move out of enhanced funds that have contracted sharply or been closed down.

However, Not All Cash Funds Are the Same

Typically, "liquidity" or "treasury-style" funds are managed to a short-dated benchmark such as 7-day Libid (London Interbank bid rate). They offer daily liquidity, carry AAA ratings, and have a constant net asset value (or stable pricing). First of all, they offer diversification—by issuer, instrument, and maturity—and to a greater degree than most institutions could achieve on their own.

Other variants of money market funds, often called cash plus or enhanced cash funds, would typically be managed to 3-month Libor (London Interbank offered rate) or similar, have two-day or longer settlement, and a variable net asset value (i.e. daily market pricing). Such funds can carry an AAA rating, but often they are lower rated. Their attraction is that they should carry a higher yield or return, because they can invest further out along the money market curve (given different benchmark and settlement requirements), and can invest in a wider range of credit instruments, including derivatives and asset-backed paper. All this depends on the extent to which they are "enhanced."

It may seem obvious now, but going forward investors will need to decide what their priorities are from an investment perspective. Security, liquidity, and yield should all be part and parcel of a money market fund, but there has to be a trade-off between yield and the first two. With the credit ratings agencies somewhat discredited, it is all the more important to seek out a professional manager who has the resources to carry out detailed credit analysis on names and instruments.

It is also worth confirming that an offshore fund is run under the IMMFA (Institutional Money Market Funds Association) Code of Practice, as this is a useful "kite mark" to have. IMMFA currently has over 20 active members, and reads like a Who's Who for the money market fund industry.

Going forward, simplicity is also going to be key. Historically, floating-rate instruments, asset-backed securities, medium-term notes and repos may have seemed ideally suited to a money market portfolio. That has proved costly for some, particularly as far as liquidity is concerned. For a pure liquidity fund, the only really acceptable instruments are deposits with reputable counterparties, certificates of deposits (CDs) issued by solid bank names, and short-dated government issued debt. Conventional floating-rate notes or CDs may play a part in some funds, but for those with liquidity as priority, the poor secondary market in these instruments needs to be factored in. The commercial paper market, meanwhile, has all but dried up, removing it as an investible option for many funds.

CURRENT ISSUES IN THE CASH WORLD

Finally, a few comments about the current state of the interbank markets. Liquidity has become a huge issue amid the ongoing financial crisis. Even instruments such as CDs with well-rated banks, which would normally be completely liquid, have become difficult to trade—indeed, the market has even been shut at times. In the United States, the Federal Reserve has recently announced that it is now giving Rule 2a-7 (treasury-style) money market funds access to the Fed window to provide them with liquidity to meet outflows, especially if these are abnormally large. The Bank of England is now committed to providing a similar facility and the European Central Bank may do something similar. A further plan to support funds is to set up a deposit insurance scheme for retail investors similar to that for bank deposits.

As a defensive move, in late September 2008 most funds increased their overnight liquidity (in sterling it was probably in the region of £20–30 billion, or US$30–45 billion), and this dislocated the interbank markets even more, exacerbating the gap between overnight rates and Libor rates. However, this exercise came at a cost to performance, especially for those funds with a higher proportion of less liquid securities like floating-rate notes and commercial paper, whose managers' therefore felt that the funds they managed had to hold an even greater proportion in overnight investments, at a time when overnight rates were collapsing.

Sterling and Euro money market funds generally seem to have weathered the storm for now, but of late the disparity between different fund performances has been much

"If investing is entertaining, if you're having fun, you're probably not making any money. Good investing is boring." George Soros

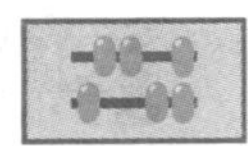

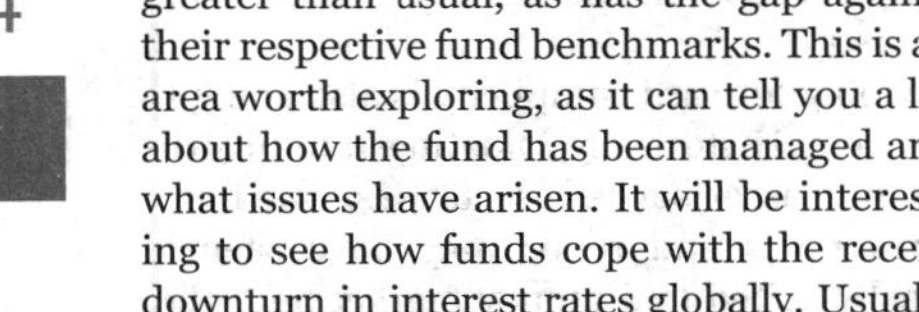

greater than usual, as has the gap against their respective fund benchmarks. This is an area worth exploring, as it can tell you a lot about how the fund has been managed and what issues have arisen. It will be interesting to see how funds cope with the recent downturn in interest rates globally. Usually funds are at their most competitive when interest rates are falling.

It is clear that Regulators both in the US and Europe will be reviewing whether, and how, money market funds should be specifically regulated. Watch this space, but in the meantime expect funds to be much more conservatively managed and operated.

MAKING IT HAPPEN

- It is important to have a clear strategy and credit procedures.
- The days of do it yourself are probably numbered, unless you can gear up to run a fully functioning, professional cash desk.
- Your bank, custodian, or financial adviser should be the first port of call.
- Longer term cash can always be placed in a segregated mandate with a specialist cash investment manager.
- There is now a viable choice of pooled funds, as long as you do the appropriate due diligence and get comfortable with the fund and the provider's credentials.
- Treasury-style money market funds can provide professional cash management at low cost with a smoothed return, and give the operational flexibility that is essential for working cash balances. Portals can offer operational advantages for the multi-fund user.
- You do have a choice, and best practice demands careful consideration of all the available options.

MORE INFO

Book:

Corporate and Institutional Money Market Funds in Europe. 4th ed. London: Treasury Today, 2008.

Articles:

Treasury Management International (tmi). Issue no. 167 (July/August 2008), "Seeking investment returns." Online at: tinyurl.com/6xltcbr

Websites:

Association of Corporate Treasurers (ACT): www.treasurers.org
Fitch Ratings: www.fitchratings.com
Institutional Money Market Funds Association (IMMFA): www.immfa.org
Treasury Management International (tmi) online: www.treasury-management.com
Treasury Today, publisher and provider of treasury info: www.treasurytoday.com

See Also:

★ Managing Counterparty Credit Risk (pp. 71–73)
★ Minimizing Credit Risk (pp. 540–542)
✔ Managing Your Credit Risk (p. 981)
✔ Money Markets: Their Structure and Function (p. 1078)
Peter L. Bernstein (p. 1271)

"Rule No.1: Never lose money. Rule No.2: Never forget rule No.1." Warren Buffett

  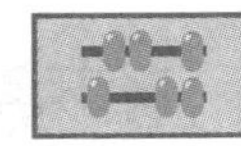      

Viewpoint: Investing in a Volatile Environment: A Black Swan Perspective by Javier Estrada

INTRODUCTION

Javier Estrada, who is professor of financial management at Barcelona-based IESE Business School, was a tennis coach in his native Argentina before moving to live and work in Spain in 1993. He set the cat among the pigeons in global investment circles with his ground-breaking research, "Black swans and market timing: How not to generate alpha," which conclusively revealed that investors who seek to time the market are unlikely to reap rewards. His research focuses on risk, portfolio management , investment strategies, emerging markets , and insider trading. The founding editor of *Emerging Markets Review*, he holds visiting professorships in Scandinavia and Latin America. As wealth management adviser at Sports Global Consulting, Estrada advises professional sports-players on their investments. His favorite football team is Club Atlético River Plate. A fan of hard-rock bands, including Queen, Kansas, and Led Zeppelin, he plays electric guitar in his spare time. His first degree, a BA in economics, was from the National University of La Plata in Buenos Aires, and he also holds MSc and PhD degrees from the University of Illinois at Urbana-Champaign.

HEALTHY EATING AND INVESTING

We all know that eating properly is essential for our health. Most of us are aware that certain types of food are good for us while others are best avoided. We are also aware of the trade-off between the desirable long-term goal of being fit and healthy and the pain associated with denying ourselves foods that we really like. We also know that patience and discipline are required.

What does healthy eating have to do with investing, you may well ask? Arguably, there are plenty of similarities. Anyone who has gone into a bookstore in search of a book on healthy eating will have been confronted by rows and rows of books, each outlining a different miracle diet.

Anyone looking for a book on investing has a similar experience. Shelf after shelf bulges with books outlining "high-return, low-risk" strategies. Each gives the impression that all we need do is to follow the indicated path to instant riches. If only life were as easy! If it was, I would not be writing these lines and you would not be reading them—we would probably both be enjoying the Caribbean sun.

A BALANCED DIET

Most of us recognize that eating healthily is going to require a long-term commitment and the making of certain sacrifices (we must kiss goodbye to all those tasty 600-calorie blueberry muffins), and that there is no such thing as a painless shortcut. The same applies to investing.

In reality, the only way to generate high long-term investment returns is to endure some risks in the short term, with the associated pain that comes from sleepless nights as our portfolio value bounces about. There is no such thing as a "high-return, low-risk" strategy. Sadly, the same "no pain, no gain" rule applies both to eating and to investing.

And yet, when it comes to investing, many investors are seduced by "get rich quick" schemes. They often get blinded by the lights of easy money and delude themselves into thinking that gain can be achieved without pain.

For the purpose of this article, I would like to group the investment strategies people are offered into two types: in one group are the "exciting" active investment strategies, which usually promise high returns but claim to achieve them with little or no risk; in the second group are the more boring and conservative passive strategies, which usually promise no gain without pain.

The two approaches can be evaluated from several standpoints, not all of which lead us to the same conclusions. I will evaluate them here through the prism of my own recent research into the so-called "black swans" in financial markets.

BLACK SWANS

A black swan is an event that has three main attributes: First, it is an outlier, lying outside the realm of regular expectations because nothing in the past can convincingly point to its occurrence; second, it carries an extreme impact; and third, despite being an outlier, plausible explanations for its occurrence can be found after the fact, thus giving it the appearance of being both explainable and predictable. In summary, a black swan has three characteristics: rarity, extreme impact, and retrospective predictability.

The black swan perspective of investing is based on three main ideas. The first is that an extremely small number of trading days have a disproportionate impact on long-term investment performance—this is an empirical fact. The second is that, although being invested on the good days and not invested on the bad days would yield extraordinary returns, investors are extremely unlikely to get the timing right. And third, because attempts to time the market are doomed to fail in the long term (in fact, their main consequence is likely to be higher transaction costs), investors are better off holding a properly diversified investment portfolio for the long term.

A PATH TO POVERTY?

Curiously, this is exactly the same recommendation that is put forward by advocates of the efficient market theory of investment. However, the black swan perspective assumes neither market efficiency nor normally distributed returns. Instead, it argues that return distributions have very fat tails and are therefore far from being normal. It also argues that mistakenly assuming that returns are normally distributed can lead to a massive destruction of wealth, as it leads investors to underestimate risk substantially.

Let's first examine the facts. My own research (Estrada, 2008) reveals that a tiny number of days can have an exceptional impact on long-term portfolio performance.

Across 15 developed markets, being out of the market on the ten days when the biggest stock market rallies occurred would have resulted in portfolios being 51% less valuable than if the money had been passively invested. Not being invested in these markets during their ten worst days would have resulted in portfolios being 150% more valuable than a passive investment would have been.

Given that these ten days represent less than 0.1% of the days in the average developed market I considered, the conclusion is obvious: A negligible proportion of days determines a massive creation or destruction of wealth, and the odds of successfully and consistently predicting the right days to be in and out of the market are nil.

In emerging markets, a tiny number of days have an even bigger impact on portfolio performance. My own research (Estrada, 2009) reveals that across 16 emerging markets, missing the ten best days would have resulted in portfolios being 69% less valuable than if the money had been passively invested. Not being invested on the ten worst ten days would have resulted in portfolios being 337% more valuable than a passive investment would have been. Given that ten days represent 0.15% of the days in the average emerging market I considered, the conclusion is again stark: The probability of successfully and consistently getting the timing right is negligible.

At times of high stock market volatility, like those we experienced during 2008, investors are often tempted to try and take advantage of large daily swings. In such turbulent times many investors attempt to capture outsized returns by frequently jumping in and out of the market, or from one market to another. But investors who engage in this sort of active trading, particularly in a volatile environment, are largely relying on luck rather than on a sound financial strategy.

Investors should bear in mind that the odds are heavily stacked against them; they should also remember that, while the additional transaction costs of their active trading strategy are certain, outsized returns are, at best, a hope.

I run a program on portfolio management for individuals (as opposed to institutions) that aims to give unsophisticated investors some basic tools with which to manage their savings. In this program I tell participants about the two "sad truths" of financial markets. I call them sad truths because these are two statements that most investors would prefer were false. Unfortunately, however, both are true.

PATIENCE IS A VIRTUE

The first statement is that the higher the required return, the greater must be the exposure to risk. The second is that the higher the exposure to risk, the longer must be the investment horizon. Deep inside, participants know that these statements are true, but a part of each of them would prefer to go on believing in painless shortcuts.

In the program, I also tell participants that they should stop focusing on forecasting. I give them many reasons why they should forget about trying to second-guess the market, which stock to buy or sell, or which currency is going to appreciate. I give them plenty of reasons why they should start focusing on asset allocation instead. As with the "sad truths," they instinctively know this advice to be right, but more often than not their next question is whether I think the dollar is going to appreciate or the market is going to fall. Oh, well...

Some investors may well question the wisdom of being passively invested in an environment such as that in 2008, when markets displayed exceptional levels of volatility and were apparently going nowhere but down. But hindsight is 20:20. It is very easy to say now that we should have cashed out at the beginning of 2008, but it did not look that obvious at the time. Trends, in fact, are not obvious until they are well in place. Black swans are unpredictable, and we only know when one has hit us after the event.

As mentioned at the beginning, eating healthily and investing have much in common; in both, the long-term goal is desirable, but the "getting there" is the problem. Most investors know what they have to do along the way; most know that pain is a part of the process; most know that patience and discipline are essential; and yet most are tempted into shortcuts ("miracle diets" or "high-return, low-risk" strategies), even though they probably recognize that these may ultimately be dead ends. When it comes down to healthy eating or investing, there is simply no gain without pain.

Black swans do exist, both in the natural world and in the financial markets. Those in nature are just a curiosity, but those in financial markets have critical implications for investor behavior. Volatile markets invite investors to engage in a losing game. And yet, at the end of the day, black swans render market timing a goose chase.

MORE INFO

Books:

Estrada, Javier. *Finance in a Nutshell: A No-nonsense Companion to the Tools and Techniques of Finance*. Harlow, UK: FT Prentice Hall, 2005.

Mandelbrot, Benoit B., and Richard L. Hudson. *The (Mis)Behavior of Markets. A Fractal View of Risk, Ruin and Reward*. London: Profile Books, 2005.

Taleb, Nassim Nicholas. *The Black Swan. The Impact of the Highly Improbable*. New York: Random House, 2007.

Articles:

Estrada, Javier. "Black swans and market timing: How not to generate alpha." *Journal of Investing* 17:3 (Fall 2008): 20–34. Online at: dx.doi.org/10.3905/joi.2008.710917

Estrada, Javier. "Black swans in emerging markets." *Journal of Investing* 18:2 (Summer 2009): 50–56. Online at: dx.doi.org/10.3905/joi.2009.18.2.050

See Also:

★ Asset Allocation Methodologies (pp. 454–458)
★ Viewpoint: Only White Swans on the Road to Revulsion (pp. 222–223)
✔ The Efficient Market Hypothesis (p. 1068)
✔ Mean–Variance Optimization: A Primer (p. 1076)
✔ Stock Markets: Their Structure and Function (p. 1091)
✔ Understanding Price Volatility (p. 1103)
The Black Swan: The Impact of the Highly Improbable (p. 1335)

"Our life is frittered away by detail ... Simplify, simplify." Henry David Thoreau

  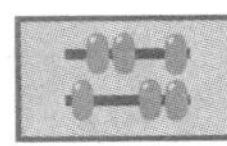      

Viewpoint: Investing in Corporate Debt in Difficult Market Conditions by Robert Marquardt

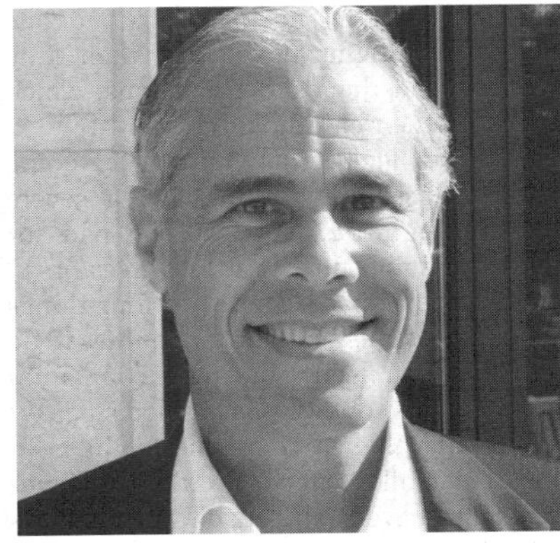

INTRODUCTION

Robert Marquardt is founder, chairman, and co-head of investment management at Signet Group, responsible for overall portfolio management and for development of the group's investment strategy. He is a member of Signet's investment committee and leads the group's top-down process of identifying investment opportunities while focusing on the most pertinent investment risks; he is also intimately involved in hedge fund due diligence. Marquardt has two decades of experience with alternative investments. Before founding Signet in 1993, he was an independent investment manager based in Luxembourg (1990–93). This followed a successful career as a credit analyst and lending officer with Chase Manhattan Bank (1979–90) in London and Bahrain, and in Luxembourg, where he was the director in charge of private banking.

We had a tumultuous last half of 2011, with the European sovereign debt crisis dominating markets. How did this impact corporate borrowing in the high-yield corporate bond market?

The first week of December 2011, leading up to the heads of government meeting on the Eurozone on December 9, may have been an inflection point as far as the European sovereign debt crisis is concerned. The markets by then were already pricing in the very substantial probability of Europe slipping into recession in 2012, along with the deflationary impact that this could be expected to have.

The head of the European Central Bank (ECB), Mario Draghi, who succeeded Jean-Claude Trichet in October 2011, is very experienced and he is a realist. He will know that while the ECB puts a huge premium on price stability, the possibility of a deflationary environment taking hold cannot be ruled out if Europe slides into a severe recession. This perception is likely to shape ECB policy, and whatever the ECB chooses to do will clearly have a huge impact on the European sovereign debt question. Already we have seen the ECB moving to grant three-year loans to banks at 1%. This has been taken up on a huge scale by European banks and has gone a long way to relieve liquidity pressures in the interbank markets.

The way both hedge funds and traditional long-only managers are playing this current period of deep uncertainty has been to move as much as possible into cash. The hedge funds have gone largely to cash, and even large private clients have sold out of assets and moved to cash. It follows from this that there is a huge war chest out there on the sidelines waiting to participate as the markets start to move in a positive direction. This adds greatly to the volatility that we are seeing in markets, with 200–300 point daily swings occurring as a matter of course as risk-on, risk-off trading rules.

At the same time, we saw fewer companies launching new bonds at the back end of 2011, which is understandable given the heightened levels of uncertainty in the markets.

Along with the downward pressure on markets, there have been several surprise upward spikes of activity. Market sentiment was so bearish through the last quarter of 2011 that reactive bounces were bound to occur. All it takes is a single "event," such as a positive statement from a senior European politician, to move markets upward, while the least negative news sends them downward once again. One of the reasons for this extreme volatility, of course, is precisely the fact that liquidity has withdrawn from the markets as people moved to cash. In low-volume, low-liquidity trading conditions, minor selling and buying moves markets in an amplified fashion.

To what extent does the present situation parallel the onset of the crash in 2008?

Though there are similarities between the present situation and the onset of the crisis in 2008, there are some major differences as well. Where you had the subprime crisis fueling the downturn in 2008, we now have the sovereign debt crisis. In 2008 there was almost no liquidity in the markets. Everyone wanted to sell and no one wanted to be a buyer. Today there is a growing lack of liquidity in the market, but it is being caused by the fact that everyone has moved to cash and is sitting on the sidelines, waiting for the fog to clear. The big advantage we have now, as opposed to back in 2008, is that stocks and high-yield bonds are now priced correctly. Bond managers feel this as much as equity managers.

High-yield bonds that were at par, or 100%, are now trading at 67–72% of their par value. If you add to this the fact that interest rates are up at 9% to 12% on corporate debt, that gives the opportunity for a tremendous upside for bond investors.

The statistics show that bonds tend to get pulled back to par value over time. Obviously the closer a bond gets to maturity, the less reason anyone has to discount it, so corporate bond investors can look forward to both a capital gain and a coupon return that is way above anything that can be earned in the risk-free or low-risk space.

How difficult has it been to shape investment strategies over this period?

There is an interesting observation one can make that demonstrates how difficult investing has been over the last quarter. Hedge funds approach investing in a different way from a long-only institutional manager, and this is just as true for high-yield bond investing as it is for equity investing. Basically, as the name suggests, hedge funds like to hedge out risk. So if you go long on one bond, you will look to find another bond with similar characteristics that you can go short on. Typically, hedge fund managers make money on their long trades, not on their short trades. However, and this is the point of my digression, through the back end of 2011 hedge fund managers have primarily made money from shorting, not from going long. Bearish sentiment has ruled and the strong market

"**Drive-in banks were established so most of the cars today could see their real owners.**" E. Joseph Cossman

movements have been downward. Consequently, hedge fund managers have made a lot of money on their short trades over the last six months. They continue to be somewhat uncomfortable at the idea of being net long in any position, and one sees them bringing down both their long positions and their short positions, which bumps up their cash holdings.

It seems likely that Europe is going to experience either a mild or a severe recession in 2012. This will be bad for equities and may further attract investors to the high-yield space. There are four things that you need, historically, for equities to do well. First, you need value in the companies you pick. This condition is fulfilled since we have great value in companies right now. They have all cleaned up their balance sheets and have been actively cutting costs and deleveraging since 2008.

Second, you need expanding liquidity in markets so that assets can be bid up, and we have already pointed out that liquidity is drying up. The remaining two things you need are profit growth and falling interest rates. There is very little sign of profit growth out there, and we have base rates that are as close to zero as they can get—and they are static rather than falling. So three out of our four necessary conditions are not working for equities right now.

Of course, stock-picking asset managers are finding stocks very cheap in today's markets and are getting quite excited. However, if we go into a recession, things that look cheap now may quickly start to look expensive if the companies concerned run into difficulties. It follows from this that in a recessionary environment, where you cannot expect real growth for at least five years, bonds look a great deal more rewarding than equities.

What do hedge funds bring to investing in corporate bonds that, say, is different to a traditional fund manager?

I would say that hedge funds are more conservative than bond fund managers and they are real specialists in credit. They read everything that a company puts out and which is available on that company. They read the debentures, they talk to the CEO, and then if they do take a long position in a corporate bond, they will hedge that out with a short position elsewhere.

The big difference between a stock and a bond is that a bond-holder does not particularly care whether or not a company is increasing its profit or has strong growth potential—which are both things that an equity manager would be very positive about. So a flat to low-growth market is not a disincentive for a bond-holder if the company's fundamentals remain strong. What a bond-holder wants is certainty that they are going to get paid back and that the company has the strength to continue to pay the coupon.

The other great thing about bonds is that you are guaranteed to have some corporate events that act as a catalyst for profit. Bonds mature, and that is a big corporate event. Or the company might go for a debt-for-debt or debt-for-equity swap that gives you the chance to realize a capital gain. There is always something, from time to time, that will drive a transaction. Then there is the fact, as we have said, that many corporate bonds are trading below their par value (the price paid when the bond is held to maturity) and can be expected to head back to full value. An equity, by way of contrast, can be thought of as a perpetual call option taken on future profitability. That might happen, or it might not. With a bond, maturity must happen if the company survives, so you have more certainty. You also have a much better chance of recovering, say, 70% of your capital if the company fails. Moreover, many of the new bonds coming to market are fully secured against the company's assets, so bond-holders both get a double-digit coupon and security, making bonds very attractive.

To what extent are pension funds now looking at corporate bonds as a way of improving returns?

There are obvious attractions for pension funds in the corporate bond market. Today they are making somewhere from 0% to −3% on their equity portfolios. By way of contrast, there are a number of high-yield bond managers who are looking at returning 15–20% for 2012. It is not always this attractive. There are years when high-yield managers make very little or no money. However, when you can get a coupon of 7% a year, and where corporate bonds with, say, two and a half years to maturity are being sold at 70 pence in the pound, the returns on high-yield look very good indeed.

However, to be successful in this space you have to take a really forensic approach to analyzing and scrutinizing corporate balance sheets. Equity managers are very focused on the company's growth potential and the growth opportunities around it. The bond manager simply wants to ensure that he or she gets paid back. This means that they are looking for different things when they analyze a company. Like any creditor, they are interested in the underlying strength of the company, but their focus is on durability. They are much less likely than equity managers to be seduced by promises of growth.

Of course, it helps if, as a credit investor, you focus on those parts of the economy that are doing well, versus those such as finance, housing, and central and local government, where a great deal of deleveraging (the paying down of debt) will continue through 2012.

This difference between the performances of the various sectors is completely masked if you look only at the overall GDP growth figure for a country. So there will be opportunities for good stock-pickers throughout 2012, but we much prefer the debt markets, where returns are much more predictable.

What of emerging markets?

Emerging markets present a very different picture. They will continue to generate growth, and they are currently outgrowing the advanced markets by between 3% and 4% a year. Moreover, their interest rates are falling, which is good for both equities and corporate bonds. Investors in these markets, though, would be wise to hedge out the currency risk because you can expect emerging market currencies to fall against sterling, the euro, and the dollar as their interest rates fall. By the end of 2011 this change in the relative values of emerging and advanced market currencies had not yet started to show itself, but these dynamics can be expected to unfold through 2012.

We see the Asian corporate bond markets being very strong for the next five to six years. So from a fixed-income perspective, with these markets now about three times larger than they were a few years ago, Asia is a very good place to be. Another dynamic that is playing out in the Asian corporate bond market is that European banks have been lending to Asian companies over the last decade and, with these banks now deleveraging, those loans are not being renewed on maturity. So a good proportion of those loans to strong Asian companies are now being renewed in the bond market and hedge funds are getting involved. Hedge funds really do help companies in this kind of situation. They understand the company's capital structure and will come in and take properly structured debt. Durations have come right down, however.

As far as the G4 countries (India, Brazil, Japan, and Germany) are concerned, I think we have five to seven difficult "muddle-through" years ahead of us. The pricing of G4 corporate debt in the markets now reflects this with high yields and attractive pricing, but the underlying dynamics in the Asian markets are much more attractive.

"Today, there are three kinds of people: the haves, the have-nots, and the have-not-paid-for-what-they-haves."
Earl Wilson

  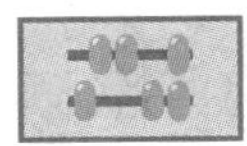      

What of country demographics?

There is no doubt that the demographic trends in some countries are pretty terrifying. We have both Japan and China, for example, with 35% of the population over the age of 60 and another 15% approaching 60. All these people want their pension entitlements, and these are being paid for by the remaining 50% of the population, who do not have a prayer of getting the same entitlements when they reach 60.

Another dynamic with the Japanese population is that women of childbearing age make up only 19% of the population, which, in demographic terms is right on the border of population collapse. Nothing here bodes well for growth or for excess liquidity in markets. If you look at this from an investment perspective, with nothing supporting a growth story, why would you want to be in equities in these markets? You can count the number of really successful long–short equity managers in Japanese and Chinese stocks on the fingers of one hand. That is not an environment that is conducive to making money in equities. Bonds, however, are a different story since many of the companies there are durable. They might not grow, but they are holding their own.

MORE INFO

Books:

Ahamed, Liaquat. *Lords of Finance: The Bankers Who Broke the World*. New York: Penguin, 2009.

Biggs, Barton. *A Hedge Fund Tale of Reach and Grasp . . . Or What's a Heaven For?* Hoboken, NJ: Wiley, 2011.

Bruner, Robert F., and Sean D. Carr. *The Panic of 1907: Lessons Learned from the Market's Perfect Storm*. Hoboken, NJ: Wiley, 2009.

Lewis, Michael. *The Big Short: Inside the Doomsday Machine*. New York: WW Norton, 2010.

Lewis, Michael. *Boomerang, The Meltdown Tour.* London: Penguin, 2011.

McDonald, Lawrence G., and Patrick Robinson. *A Colossal Failure of Common Sense: The Inside Story of the Collapse of Lehman Brothers*. New York: Crown Business, 2009.

Sampson, Anthony. *The Money Lenders: Bankers in a Dangerous World*. London, UK: Hodder & Stoughton, 1981.

See Also:

★ Viewpoint: The Corporate Bond Markets in 2012 and Beyond (pp. 151–153)

★ Viewpoint: Reflections on the Fixed-Income Market in Difficult Times (pp. 573–575)

✔ The Bond Market: Its Structure and Function (p. 1064)

✔ Trading in Corporate Bonds: Why and How (p. 1094)

i Bonds/Fixed Income (pp. 1675–1677)

Investing in Structured Finance Products in the Debt Money Markets by Moorad Choudhry

EXECUTIVE SUMMARY

- A number of structured finance investment products are available in money markets that offer investment options for cash-rich investors.
- Products include asset-backed commercial paper, total return swaps, and collateralized committed repo liquidity lines.
- The returns available for cash-rich investors differ according to asset credit quality, with higher yields on lower-rated assets.
- Returns also differ by product type.
- Investors should assess the liquidity of an instrument type as well as its credit risk.

INTRODUCTION

The application of synthetic securitization and structured finance techniques in debt capital markets has made a range of asset classes available to investors who would not otherwise have access to them. Thus banks, fund managers, and cash-rich corporate institutions can choose from a wide variety of investment options for their funds. This article introduces a sample of money market products that present alternatives for the investment of surplus funds. In each case we consider the basic product structure, and we look at the different yields across products.

The global credit and liquidity crunch in 2007–08 resulted in a widespread "flight-to-quality" as investors became excessively risk-averse. Yield spreads widened considerably and certain asset classes and products were no longer viable. We review here only instruments that remain practical products for both investors and borrowers. The products considered are:

- Asset-backed commercial paper;
- Total return swap funding, or synthetic repo;
- Collateralized committed repo liquidity lines.

ASSET-BACKED COMMERCIAL PAPER

The application of securitization technology in the money markets has led to the growth of short-term instruments backed by the cash flows from other assets, known as "asset-backed commercial paper" (ABCP). Securitization is the practice of using the cash flows from a specified asset, such as residential mortgages, car loans, or commercial bank loans as backing for an issue of bonds. In the case of ABCP the assets are funded in the commercial paper market. The assets themselves are transferred from the original owner (the "originator") to a specially created legal entity known as a "special purpose vehicle" (SPV), so as to make them separate and bankruptcy-remote from the originator. In the meantime, the originator is able to benefit from capital market financing charged at a lower rate of interest than that earned by the originator on its assets.

Figure 1 illustrates a generic securitization transaction for the debt capital markets, issuing asset-backed securities (ABS). The originator has set up the SPV, which then buys the assets from it. The SPV funds itself in the debt capital markets by issuing ABS.

Generally securitization is used as a funding instrument by companies for three main reasons: It offers lower-cost funding than traditional bank loan or bond financing; it is a mechanism by which assets such as corporate loans or mortgages can be removed from the balance sheet, thus transferring the default risk associated with those assets to investors; and it increases a borrower's funding options. For investors it offers a class of assets that would not otherwise be available to them directly, thus widening their return options and potentially diversifying the sources of risk in their portfolio. Equally, issuing ABCP enables an originator to benefit from money market financing that it might otherwise not have access to, perhaps because its credit rating is not sufficiently strong.

When entering into securitization, an entity may issue term securities against assets into the public or private market, or it may issue commercial paper via a special purpose legal entity known as a "conduit." These conduits are usually sponsored by commercial banks. ABCP trades as a money market discount instrument. Investors purchase it from a number of ABCP dealers who work on behalf of the conduit. The return available on ABCP is a function of the credit rating of the issuer, which is dependent on the credit quality of the underlying assets. Conduits often pay a fee to be backed by a line of credit, known as a "liquidity line," which is supplied by a bank. The credit quality and standing of the liquidity bank also drive the credit rating of the conduit.

The assets that can be funded via a conduit program are many and varied; to date they have included:

- trade receivables and equipment lease receivables;
- credit card receivables;
- auto loans and leases;
- corporate loans, franchise loans, and mortgage loans;
- real-estate leases;
- investment grade-rated structured finance bonds, such as asset-backed securities (ABS).

Figure 2 illustrates a typical conduit structure for ABCP issued to the US and European commercial paper markets. (The difference in yields available on ABCP rated A1/P1 compared to bank-issued commercial paper of the same rating is illustrated in Table 2. The higher yield on ABCP reflects

Figure 1. Securitization structure

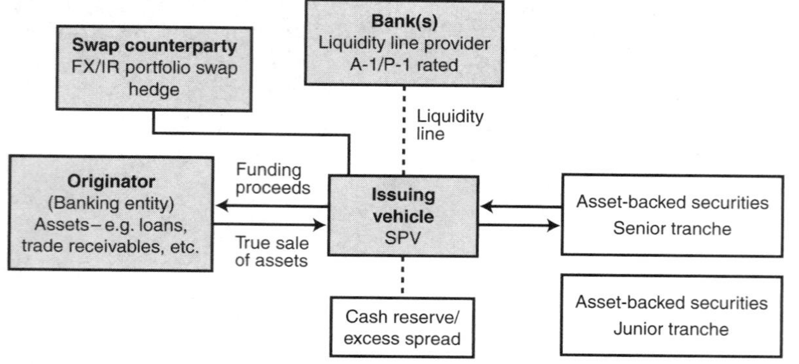

"**Business is not financial science, it's about trading... buying and selling. It's about creating a product or service so good that people will pay for it.**" Anita Roddick

     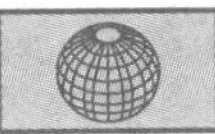   

Figure 2. Typical conduit structure for ABCP issuance

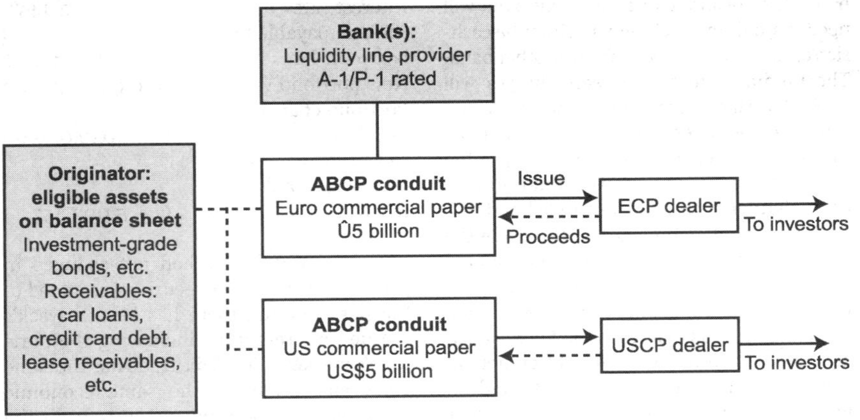

investor perception of the higher associated credit risk.)

REPO AND SYNTHETIC REPO

A repo is a transaction in which one party sells securities to another, and at the same time and as part of the same transaction commits to repurchase those securities on a specified date at a specified price. The seller delivers securities and receives cash from the buyer. The cash is supplied at a predetermined rate of interest—the repo rate—which remains constant during the term of the trade. On maturity, the original seller receives back collateral of equivalent type and quality, and returns the cash plus repo interest. Although legal title to the securities is transferred, the seller retains both the economic benefits and the market risk of owning them. This means that the seller will suffer loss if the market value of the collatôÙeral drops during the term of the repo, as the seller retains beneficial ownership of the collateral. The buyer in a repo is not affected in profit/loss account terms if the value of the collateral drops.

The repo market is a vital element of the global capital and money markets. The market experienced substantial growth during the 1990s and is now estimated to account for up to 50% of daily settlement activity in non-US government bonds worldwide; this is a phenomenal figure. Repo, from "sale and *repurchase agreement*," is closely linked to other segments of the debt and equity markets. From its use as a financing instrument for market-makers to its use in the open market operations of central banks, and its place between the bond markets and the money markets, it integrates the various disparate elements of the marketplace and allows the raising of corporate finance across all sectors.

Across the world, including financial centers in the North American, European, and Asia-Pacific region, repo is a well-established investment product, utilized by fund managers, hedge funds, corporate treasuries, and local authorities. The practicality and simplicity of repo means that it can be taken up even in capital markets that are still at an emerging stage as well as by a wide range of participants.

What we have described is in effect a secured loan, but one with added flexibility for use in a variety of applications. Market participants enter into a classic repo because they wish to invest cash, for which the transaction is deemed to be *cash-driven*, or because they wish to finance the purchase of a bond or equity that they have bought. Alternatively, they may wish to borrow a stock that they have sold short, which is known as a "reverse repo." However the reverse repo trader is also lending cash. So the trade might be cash-driven or *stock-driven*. The first and most important thing to state is that repo is a secured loan of cash, and it is categorized as a money market yield instrument. Note that every repo is also a reverse repo, depending on which counterparty viewpoint one looks at the transaction from.

Repo market-makers, which include the large money-center banks, make two-way prices in repo in the major currencies. This means they will trade both repo and reverse repo, lending and borrowing cash, against either receiving or supplying collateral, according to customer need. A generic type of collateral, such as government bonds, is known as "general collateral" and refers to a trade in which any specific bond that fits the general collateral type can be supplied as collateral.

Repo is traded under a standard legal agreement termed the Global Master Repurchase Agreement (GMRA). Such an agreement executed once between two parties governs all subsequent trades between them.

Plain Vanilla Repo

Let us say that the two parties to a repo trade are Bank A, the seller of securities, and Bank (or corporate entity) B, which is the buyer of securities. On the trade date the two banks enter into an agreement whereby on a set date, the "value" or "settlement" date, Bank A will sell to Bank B a nominal amount of securities in exchange for cash. The price received for the securities is the market price of the stock on the value date. The agreement also demands that on the termination date Bank B will sell identical stock back to Bank A at the previously agreed price; consequently, Bank B will have its cash returned with interest at the agreed repo rate.

The basic mechanism is illustrated in Figure 3.

Synthetic Repo Via the Total Return Swap

Synthetic repo, undertaken for the purposes of funding a portfolio or investing against a credit-linked instrument, is common in the market. The repo is in the form of a total return swap (TRS), which is classified as a credit derivative; however, when traded for funding or stock borrowing purposes it is identical in economic terms to a classic repo.

Figure 3. Classic repo transaction for 100-worth of collateral stock

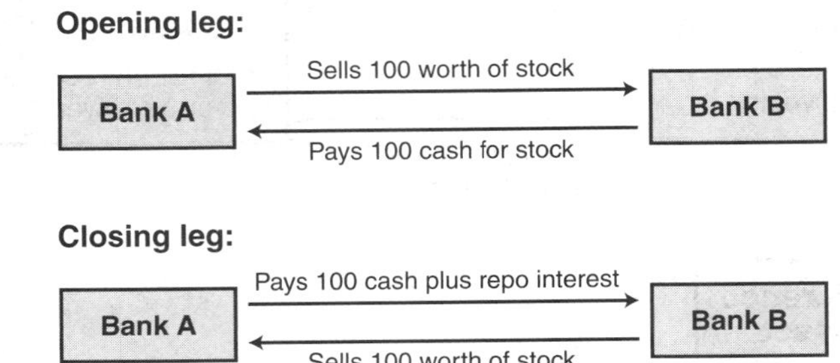

  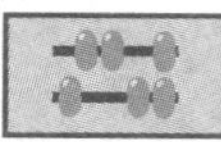 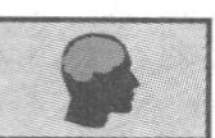     

A TRS has similarities to an interest rate swap in that it consists of two payment legs, one the "total return" and the other an interest payment linked to Libor. As a credit derivative, a TRS enables a market participant to access the total return on an asset such as a bond without actually buying it. The return is in the form of the bond's coupon and any capital appreciation during the term of the trade. For an existing investor that is already holding a bond, entering into a TRS enables it to transfer the credit risk associated with the bond to the TRS counterparty.

TRS contracts are used in a variety of applications by banks, and are discussed in detail by Choudhry (2004). When used for funding purposes, a TRS is more akin to a synthetic repo contract. To illustrate this application, we describe here the use of a TRS to fund a portfolio of bonds, as a substitute for a repo trade. This is shown at Figure 4, where counterparty A is the investor lending funds and receiving a Libor-based return. The counterparty to the trade is investing cash against a credit-linked return, which, depending on the credit quality of the linked assets, may be substantially above Libor.

Consider a bank that has a portfolio of assets on its balance sheet for which it needs to obtain funding. These assets are investment grade-rated structured finance bonds such as credit card ABS and investment grade-rated convertible bonds. In the repo market, it is able to fund these at Libor plus 200 basis points. That is, it can repo the bonds out to a bank or non-bank financial counterparty, and will pay Libor plus 200 bps on the funds it receives.

Assume that for operational reasons the bank cannot fund these assets using repo. Instead it can fund them using a basket TRS contract, provided that a suitable counterparty can be found. Under this contract, the portfolio of assets is "swapped" out to the TRS counterparty, and cash is received from the counterparty. The assets are therefore sold off the balance sheet to the counterparty, which may be a corporate treasury or an investment bank. The corporate or investment bank will need to fund this itself—it will either be cash-rich or have a line of credit from another bank. The funding rate the investor charges will depend to a large extent on the rate at which it can fund the assets itself. Assume that the TRS rate charged is Libor plus 220 bps—the higher rate reflecting the lower liquidity in the basket TRS market for non-vanilla bonds.

Assume that at the start of the trade the portfolio consists of five euro-denominated ABS bonds. The parties enter into a three-month TRS, with a one-week interest rate reset. This means that the basket is revalued at one-week intervals. The difference in value from the last valuation is paid (if higher) or received (if lower) by the lender to the borrowing bank; in return the borrowing bank also pays one-week interest on the funds it received at the start of the trade. The bonds in the reference basket can be returned, added to, or substituted. So if any stocks have been sold or bought, they can be removed or added to the basket on the reset date.

Example of a TRS

Table 1 shows a portfolio of five securities that were invested in via a TRS trade between a bank and a non-bank, cash-rich financial institution, which is the investor. The trade terms are shown below.

Trade date	January 8, 2009
Value date	January 12, 2009
Maturity date	April 13, 2009
Rate reset	January 19, 2009
Interest rate	2.445% (one-week euro Libor fix of 2.225% plus 220 bps)
Market value of reference basket	€100,002,300.00

At the start of the trade, the bonds in the basket are swapped out to the lender, who pays the market value for them. On the first reset date, the portfolio is revalued and the following calculations are confirmed:

Old portfolio value	€100,002,300.00
Interest rate	2.445%
Interest payable by borrower bank	€47,542.76
New portfolio value	€105,052,300.00
Portfolio change in value	€ + 5,050,000.00
Net payment: borrowing bank receives	€ + 5,002,457.24

The existing bonds had not changed in price; however, a new security was added to the portfolio and there has been a week's accrued interest, thus increasing the portfolio's market value. This trade has the same goals and produced the same economic effect as a classic repo transaction on the same basket of bonds. The investor is lending three-month floating money, and is receiving a higher return than from the repo market in the same securities. The cash flows are shown in Table 1.

START OF LOAN	
Portfolio additions	€0.00
Loan amount	€100,002,300.00
Interest rate (Libor + 220 bps)	2.445000%
Roll-over PAYMENTS	
Interest	
Rate	2.445000%
Principle	€100,002,300.00
Interest payable	€ + 47,542.76
Performance	
Portfolio additions	€5,000,000.00
Accrued interest	€50,000.00
Price movements	€0.00
New portfolio value	€105,052,300.00
Old portfolio value	€100,002,300.00
Performance payment	€ + 5,050,000.00
Net payment	
Borrower receives from bank/investor	€ + 5,002,457.24
NEW LOAN	
New loan amount	€105,052,300.00
New interest rate	1-week euro Libor + 220

Figure 4. Total return swap as a synthetic repo

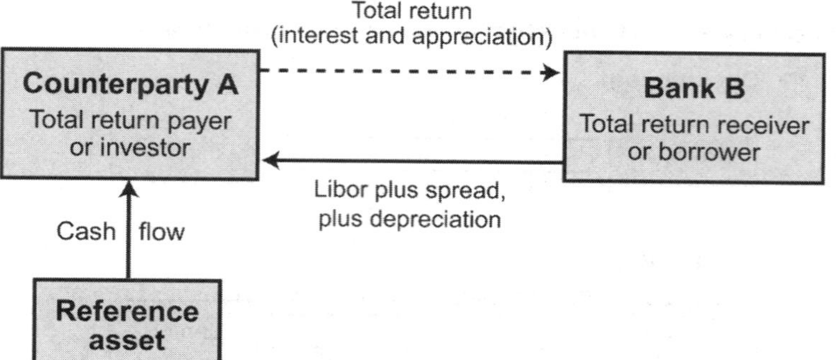

COMMITTED LIQUIDITY LINE FUNDING

The standard bank liquidity line is a standing credit facility set up for a borrower that may be drawn on at any time. Lines are usually reviewed on an annual basis, so they represent a maximum 364-day facility. A

"What is high finance? It's knowing the difference between one and ten, multiplying, subtracting and adding. You just add noughts. It's no more than that." John Bentley

Table 1. TRS trade ticket, showing portfolio value at start of trade, interest cash flows, and value at end of trade

TRS TICKET					
1-week euro Libor	2.225%				
Name	**Currency**	**Nominal**	**Price**	**Accrued**	**Consideration**
ABCTelecoms 6.25%	Euro	15,000,000	98.00	0.000000	14,700,000.00
SAD Bros 7.50%	Euro	12,000,000	105.00	0.000000	12,600,000.00
DTI 5.875%	Euro	37,000,000	108.79	0.000000	40,252,300.00
Bigenddi 8.25%	Euro	15,000,000	78.00	0.000000	11,700,000.00
BanglaBeat plc 9%	Euro	50,000,000	41.50	0.000000	20,750,000.00
Jackfruit Funding ABS	Euro	5,000,000	100.00	0.000000	5,000,000.00
(addition to basket at roll-over)					
			Portfolio value at start:		**100,002,300.00**
			Portfolio value at rollover:		**105,002,300.00**

Table 2. US dollar lending rates against different instrument types, January 2009. (*Source*: Bloomberg; market counterparties)

Instrument	1-month	3-month	1-year
Bank commercial paper			
A1-P1	0.50%	0.95%	
A2-P2	1.95%	3.56%	
Asset-backed commercial paper			
A1-P1	0.75%	1.30%	
Repo			
US Treasury	0.25%	0.30%	
AAA MBS*	0.85%	2.35%	
Total return swap			
AAA MBS*	0.95%	2.50%	
Liquidity line†			
A1 borrower			
Standing fee	20 bps		
Borrowing fee	Libor 100 bps		
A2 borrower			
Standing fee			50 bps
Borrowing fee			Libor 220 bps

* Triple-A rated mortgage-backed securities. † This is a one-year committed liquidity line, drawn against investment grade-rated collateral.

structure offered by banks to clients that desire longer-term funding is the "evergreen" committed line, which is in theory a 364-day tenor but which is formally "renewed" on a daily basis. This enables the borrower to view the line as longer-dated funding because it is always 364 days away from maturity. Liquidity credit facilities attract a Basel regulatory capital weighting if they are committed to the client. It is common for any borrowings on the line to be collateralized. This turns the liquidity into a committed repo line.

A liquidity facility is an avenue for a bank to invest surplus cash and carries two charges:

- the standing charge, usually calculated as a fixed fee in basis points and payable monthly or quarterly in advance;
- the actual borrowing cost (an interest rate charge) when the line is drawn on.

The standing fee is a function of the credit quality of the borrower. A recent development, widely used by ABCP vehicles, has been the replacement of part or all of the liquidity line with a "committed repo" facility (or committed TRS facility), which carries with it a lower fee and thus saves on costs. Under the committed repo a bank will undertake to provide a repo funding facility using the vehicle's assets as collateral. Thus, in the event that commercial paper cannot be repaid, the vehicle will repo out its assets to the repo provider, enabling it to meet maturing commercial paper obligations.

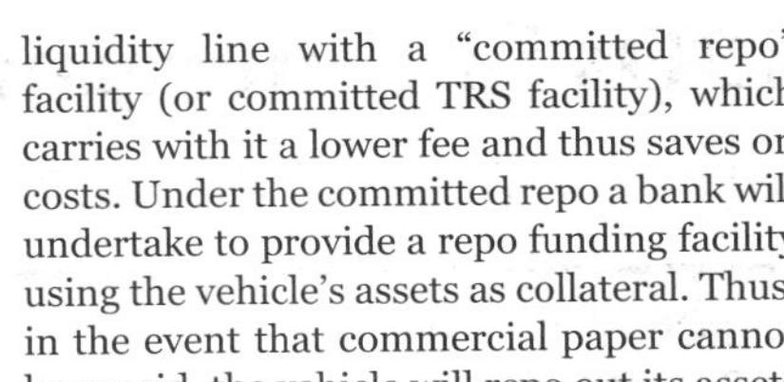

YIELD MATRIX

The different products available in money markets mean that there is a range of risk-reward profiles for investors to consider. Table 2 illustrates the variation in yields available in US dollars during January 2009. Investors expect a different return profile for different credit ratings, with higher yields on lower-rated assets. This is confirmed in Table 2. The rates in the table also confirm that returns differ for different instrument types, with a greater yield offered by TRS funding of AAA-rated structured finance securities than by repo of the same collateral.

Structured finance instruments are an alternative investment option for cash-rich long-only investors in the money markets, and in certain cases they can offer a higher return for the same theoretical credit risk. This often reflects liquidity factors, which should be factored into any investment analysis.

MAKING IT HAPPEN

Commercial and retail banks all have dedicated repo, commercial paper, and corporate banking desks that provide investment products for other banks as well as cash-rich investors. Investors may contact their correspondent bank in the first instance.

Those wishing to invest in structured finance instruments should consider the following:

- Their risk/reward profile, from both a credit-rating perspective and a value-at-risk perspective.
- The exposure to underlying assets, and how the value of their investment changes with changes in value of the underlying assets.
- The range of yields available, and why identically rated assets should have different credit spreads.
- Reviews of yields, such as those published by Bloomberg.

MORE INFO

Books:

Choudhry, Moorad. *Structured Credit Products: Credit Derivatives & Synthetic Securitisation*. Singapore: Wiley, 2004.

Choudhry, Moorad. *Bank Asset and Liability Management: Strategy, Trading, Analysis*. Singapore: Wiley, 2007.

"The social object of skilled investment should be to defeat the dark forces of time and ignorance which envelope our future." John Maynard Keynes

IPOs in Emerging Markets

by Janusz Brzeszczynski

EXECUTIVE SUMMARY

- IPO activity in emerging markets depends strongly on the macroeconomic environment, business cycles, and stock market phases.
- The number of IPOs increases during bull markets and decreases during bear markets.
- Companies launching IPOs during bull markets can count on raising more capital than if they go public in a bear market.
- There is usually a time lag of about a year between changes in stock market index returns and the subsequently observed IPO activity.

INTRODUCTION

An initial public offering (IPO) is the sale of a company's shares to the public for the first time, leading to a stock exchange listing. This process is known also as a public offering, or "going public."

The main reason for IPOs is the need for fresh capital to finance various business activities, such as the development of new products or expansion into new markets. Most IPOs are launched by relatively small but dynamic companies, which grow too fast to be financed only in traditional ways such as by bank loans. Nevertheless, many big privately owned companies also decide to become publicly traded.

Decisions about an IPO are predominantly based on the actual capital requirements and the expansion plans of the management, but the timing of the IPO is very strongly determined by the current macroeconomic environment, business cycles, and stock market phases.

IPOs are considered to be risky for both the issuers and the investors. The issuers may miscalculate the value of the company and choose the wrong time to go public. In this event, the amount of capital raised from the IPO will be less than expected, and control of the company may be lost by diluting the shares of previous stockholders in the new ownership structure after the IPO. However, when an IPO is successful, a company can raise more capital than anticipated, and the original stockholders may still be able to control the company.

As for the risks faced by the investors, first, they may make errors in assessing the company value, and second, it is very difficult to predict how the share price will behave once the company is listed on the stock exchange. Investors normally have access only to limited historical data, which makes the valuation and the appraisal of the firm's financial situation rather difficult. Moreover, the majority of IPOs are companies that are experiencing a transitory growth stage. This creates even more uncertainty about their value in the future. Last but not least, the stock market before and after an IPO may behave in an erratic way and exhibit high volatility, which in a short period of time may lead to either unexpected profits or unexpected losses.

INITIAL PUBLIC OFFERINGS

The main advantage of an IPO is that the company is not obliged to return the capital raised from the investors. The downside is that new stockholders are entitled to a share of future profits (usually in the form of a dividend). The stockholdings of the existing owners will be diluted in the new ownership structure, and in many cases they may even lose control over the company. However, they expect their shares to become more valuable after the IPO, when the company should be able to generate higher profits from the capital raised in the IPO process.

In an IPO the issuers are usually assisted by underwriting firms, such as investment banks, which help to decide on the best offer price and the timing of the offer. They also deal with the legal aspects of the entire process. Furthermore, the underwriter approaches investors with offers to sell the shares of the IPO company.

The sale of shares in an IPO may take place using different methods. These are: Dutch auction, firm commitment, best efforts, bought deal, or self distribution of stock. When the IPO is successful and the underwriters sell the shares, they are rewarded by a commission calculated as a certain percentage of the value of the shares issued and sold.

The number of new IPOs in any market always depends on business cycles. One of the best examples is the dot-com bubble in the United States during the 1990s, when share prices were rising sharply and many young companies from the high-tech sector were seeking capital through IPOs. After the companies were listed on the stock market, their share prices skyrocketed—and continued to do so until the bubble burst.

The value of the IPO of a company is usually relatively high in comparison to alternative methods of financing such as bank loans. The largest IPOs in history so far have been: Industrial & Commercial Bank of China ($21.6 billion) in 2006; NTT Mobile Communications ($18.4 billion) in 1998; Visa Inc. ($17.9 billion) in 2008; and AT&T Wireless ($10.6 billion) in 2000.

Pricing of Public Offers

In order to sell a large number of new shares and raise significant amounts of capital, an IPO has to offer investors a strong incentive to buy. That is why most IPOs tend to be underpriced. On one hand, a consequence of this is that investors who buy the shares at the offering price can earn substantial returns, and this tends to happen over a relatively short period of time. On the other hand, when an IPO is severely underpriced the result may be what is known as "money left on the table." This term is used to describe the situation when the company experiences a relative loss of capital, i.e. the loss of money that could have been raised from the market in an IPO if the shares had been offered and sold at a higher price.

If the shares are overpriced, the underwriters may not be able to sell all of them. They then face the problem of acquiring the shares themselves—which is even more troublesome when the current market price is lower than the issuing price.

The public offering price (POP) is the price at which IPOs are offered to the public by an underwriter. Several factors affect this price, including data about a company's financial situation (past, current, and forecasted), macroeconomic conditions and stock market trends (current and predicted), as well as information about investor confidence.

A preliminary registration statement filed with the securities commission, which describes a new IPO, is called a "red herring." It does not include the price or issue size and it may be updated many times before it becomes the final prospectus. The process of soliciting orders to buy an IPO before its registration is approved by the securities commission is known as "gun jumping." An advertisement published by the underwriters giving information about the details of an IPO is called a "tombstone." The first recommendation issued by an underwriter for an IPO is known as the "booster shot." Its aim is to promote the new shares of the IPO company and to increase the chance of its successful sale to the public. The underwriters cannot, however, promote the IPO during the "quiet period," which is the period of time following the filing with the securities commission and before the registration statement. The term "quiet period" refers also to a certain number of days after an IPO is listed on the stock market, during which the company and those underwriters directly engaged in the IPO are not allowed to issue any financial forecasts or recommendations for the company concerned.

IPOs in Emerging Markets

In many emerging markets the term "going public" may seem confusing. In countries that did not have free-market economies in the past, and where government ownership was dominant over private ownership, most companies that launched IPOs were in fact privatized, because they were sold by the government to *private* investors through the stock market. Hence, they were in fact going private rather than going public.

A problem in emerging market financial systems is that many small, young private firms that have good investment opportunities can show little evidence of past business and financial performance. They therefore face serious problems when they want to attract external finance for new ventures. This is because in these countries either firm financing is intermediated or the capital markets are underdeveloped. Furthermore, in many emerging markets the legal and regulatory environment is rather weak, and financial intermediaries tend to give priority to large companies that have a relevant track record and own a certain value of physical assets which can be used as collateral for loans. There is also a danger that intermediaries may favor firms controlled by politicians. In emerging markets, the development of public equity markets has been found to be beneficial for the financial systems. It is believed that public capital markets are more immune to the influence of politicians and other lobbying groups.

The development of capital markets in emerging market countries, combined with their dynamic macroeconomic growth in recent years, has triggered IPO activity on their stock exchanges. However, it is worth distinguishing between the various sources of capital that are being invested in IPOs. In many emerging markets the limited availability of capital has been a major problem. Even though the economic growth of emerging countries in recent years has helped in the accumulation of capital from domestic sources, much of the capital invested in IPOs has its origin in developed countries. An important role here is played by venture capital companies, which often use an IPO as their exit strategy. However, the activity of venture capital funds may differ from country to country—it is, for example, traditionally higher in Asian markets and lower in the emerging market countries in Europe.

A typical IPO process in an emerging market starts when a company enters a high growth phase and the management decides that there is a momentum in the firm's life during which a relatively large amount of new capital can be raised for further expansion. It is then that the shares can be sold via an IPO at prices that result in high multiples of the most commonly used financial ratios, such as price/earnings ratio (P/E), or price/book value ratio (P/BV). Other typical reasons why companies decide to become public in emerging markets and launch an IPO are easier access to capital in the future, increased liquidity of their shares, and, last but not least, visibility and prestige when they are listed on the stock market.

The number of IPOs in emerging markets is variable over time and depends on many key factors, among which the macroeconomic environment and the rate of growth of the economy are the dominant ones. There is evidence to show that IPO activity in emerging markets is related to phases of the stock market, which in turn are connected to business cycles. Bull and bear market periods always depend on the macroeconomic indicators and the prospects of economic growth.

Figure 1. New IPOs versus stock market returns in Poland in the period 1997–08. (*Source*: Warsaw Stock Exchange and author's calculations. The data exclude the NewConnect market segment)

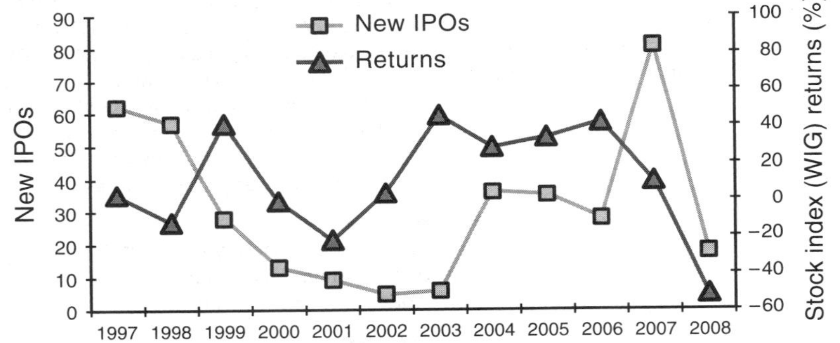

CASE STUDY

IPOs in the Emerging Market in Poland

Figure 1 shows the number of new IPOs and the main stock market index (WIG) returns for the Polish stock market over a period of 12 years from 1997 to 2008. An important feature of this graph is the one-year shift of new IPOs relative to the situation in the stock market, where the pattern of volatility of index returns clearly leads the IPO activity. The correlation coefficient between those two variables is only 0.0244 (2.44%) when IPOs and stock market index returns are analyzed simultaneously, but increases to as high as 0.5683 (56.83%) when the WIG returns are lagged by one year.

Following the period 2003–2006, during which the WIG index increased at an annual rate of nearly 40%, in 2007 the number of new IPOs jumped to 81 from an annual average of less than seven in 2001–2003 and 33 in 2004–2006. When global stock markets collapsed in 2007 and continued to seek new bottoms in 2008 (events that were reflected in the returns of the Polish market index WIG), the number of new IPOs in 2008 fell more than fourfold to less than 20 from the peak of just over 80 the year before.

This finding shows that decisions about IPOs are strictly dependent on stock market phases and that IPOs tend to increase when share prices are rising and to decrease when they fall. The relationship is not simultaneous, with some lagged effect being observed that may be linked to the length of time decision-makers need to assess the profitability of a new IPO, given the financial environment and predictions of how much capital can be raised from the stock market at current prices.

  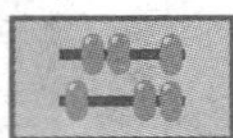      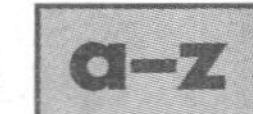

Macroeconomic activity also affects the degree of underpricing of IPOs. Although this effect tends to be more significant in emerging market countries than in developed economies, it is in fact always time-varying in its nature, and depends periodically on macroeconomic conditions. Nevertheless, there are cases in which the underpricing was so severe that the share price on the first day of listing reached a level more than 100% higher than the offer price in the IPO—in well-established markets the underpricing is typically below 20%.

CONCLUSION

The number of IPOs in emerging markets and the profitability of the public offers are related to macroeconomic conditions (both global and local), business cycles, and stock market activity. In most emerging market countries there is a time lag between movements of the stock market index and decisions to launch new IPOs.

The correct timing of an IPO is very important for a company that plans a public offering. An IPO may raise different amounts of capital from investors depending on whether stock markets are in a bull or a bear phase.

MAKING IT HAPPEN

- Emerging markets are not immune to trends in global financial markets. Hence, it is important for company executives who plan IPOs in these countries to have a good understanding of the global macroeconomic environment and of the financial linkages with developed countries.
- There are research institutes that sell forecasts of future macroeconomic trends and predictions of stock market performance. Forecasts of the world economy are also offered by such institutions as the World Bank, the International Monetary Fund, and the United Nations, as well as by central banks and the finance ministries of individual countries.
- Any decision to launch an IPO should be very carefully analyzed using not only past financial data for the company, but also macroeconomic forecasts. These may provide valuable information about future economic growth, which is likely to impact stock market activity and share prices directly.
- Timing an IPO correctly may lead to substantial gains if the IPO shares sell at a high price. Poor timing may result in the loss of capital if stock market prices are too low.

MORE INFO

Articles:

Beck, Thorsten, Asli Demirgüç-Kunt, and Vojislav Maksimovic. "Financial and legal constraints to firm growth: Does firm size matter?" *Journal of Finance* 60:1 (February 2005): 137–177. Online at: 10.1111/j.1540-6261.2005.00727.x

La Porta, Rafael, Florencio Lopez-de-Silanes, and Guillermo Zamarippa. "Related lending." *Quarterly Journal of Economics* 118:1 (February 2003): 231–268. Online at: dx.doi.org/10.1162/00335530360535199

Rajan, Raghuram G., and Luigi Zingales. "The great reversals: The politics of financial development in the 20th century." *Journal of Financial Economics* 69:1 (July 2003): 5–50. Online at: dx.doi.org/10.1016/S0304-405X(03)00125-9

Shleifer, Andrei, Rafael La Porta, Florencio Lopez-de-Silanes, and Robert W. Vishny. "Legal determinants of external finance." *Journal of Finance* 52:3 (July 1997): 1131–1150. Online at: www.afajof.org/journal/jstabstract.asp?ref=11724

Websites:

International Monetary Fund (IMF): www.imf.org
United Nations: www.un.org
World Bank: www.worldbank.org

See Also:

★ Corporate Governance in Transitional Countries—Shareholders or Stakeholders? (pp. 658–660)
★ The Cost of Going Public: Why IPOs Are Typically Underpriced (pp. 475–477)
★ Price Discovery in IPOs (pp. 557–559)
✔ Key Principles of Islamic Finance (p. 1011)
✔ Raising Capital by Issuing Shares (p. 1087)
✔ Stock Markets: Their Structure and Function (p. 1091)
✔ Understanding Capital Markets, Structure and Function (p. 1099)

Islamic Microfinance: Fulfilling Social and Developmental Expectations by Mehmet Asutay

EXECUTIVE SUMMARY

- Islamic banking and finance (IBF) is a value-oriented ethical proposition; the principles of IBF can be located in the principles and norms of Islamic moral economy (IME), which aims at human-centered economic development as opposed to the financialization of the economy.
- Social responsibility is an essential part of IBF; however, IBF institutions have been criticized for their social failure.
- Microfinance is a novel method for human-oriented economic development and a capacity-building tool, which easily fits into the IBF paradigm through social responsibility.
- The financial instruments of IBF and IME institutions can provide an important base for the development and progress of Islamic microfinance (IMF), which fulfills the aspirations of developing communities in an Islamic way.
- A number of IBF institutions have demonstrated success in IMF, particularly by overcoming the burden of interest on the poor and expanding the asset base.

RATIONALIZING ISLAMIC MICROFINANCE THROUGH ESSENTIALIZING THE ISLAMIC MORAL ECONOMY

Islamic banking and finance (IBF) has become a mainstream financing method utilized by Islamic, as well as conventional, banking and financial institutions all over the world. Recently, however, IBF has been criticized for its social failure, in the sense that its operations are not different from the existing conventional tools minus the interest. An essential nature of this criticism is related to the foundational axioms and principles of IME which, as a worldview, is based on the authentic principles of Islam. Thus, IME is an authentic response to the failure of economic developmentalism in the Muslim world in constructing a human-centered development. In this attempt, IBF was considered as the financing and operational tool of the new paradigm, and consequently it is expected to fulfill the expectations and aspirational paradigm of IME.

The foundational principles and axioms of IME aimed at revealing the principles behind IBF through an ethical worldview are:

- vertical ethicality in terms of individuals as the creature of God being equal (*tawhid*);
- social justice and beneficence (*adalah* and *ihsan*) in terms of horizontal ethicality;
- growth in harmony (*tazkiyah*);
- allowing the social (individual and society) and natural environment to reach to and sustain its perfection (*rububiyah*);
- voluntary action but also compulsory action (*fard*) in serving the social interest;
- individuals, being the vicegerent of God on Earth (*khalifah*), are expected to fulfill and act according to these principles in their economic and financial behavior.

These foundational principles are justified by a particular methodological understanding; the *maqasid al-shariah* (objectives of *shariah*) are interpreted as human well-being, which, in this context, is achieved through a socially operating moral economy in an Islamic framework that is expected to produce a socially and economic-financially optimum solution in overcoming the socio-economic problems of a society.

ETHICAL OBJECTIVE FUNCTIONS OF ISLAMIC FINANCE

As part of this ethical economic paradigm, IBF is expected to operate within such an objective function and framework to establish the optimality between financial operations and social objectives (as a morally identified objective function). To operationalize the ethical objective in IBF, further principles are developed through the ontological sources of Islam. These principles, which aim to promote an ethical and socially oriented way of "doing finance," are as follows.

- Prohibition of interest (or *riba*) with the objective of providing a stable and socially efficient economic environment.
- Prohibition of fixed return on nominal transactions, with the objective of creating productive economic activity or asset-based financing over the debt-based system.
- In this moral economy, money does not have any inherent value in itself and therefore it cannot be created through the credit system.
- The principle of profit and loss sharing, and hence risk sharing, is the essential axis around which economic and business activity takes place. This prevents the capital owner from shifting the entire risk on to the borrower, and hence it aims to establish a just balance between effort and return, and between effort and capital. This axiom identifies the essential nature of Islamic microfinance.
- An important consequence of the profit/loss sharing principle is the participatory nature of economic and business activity, as IBF instruments, capital, and labor merge to establish partnerships through their individual contributions which, as a principle, constitutes the fundamental nature of microfinance.
- By essentializing productive economic and business activity, uncertainty, speculation, and gambling are also prohibited, with the same rationale of emphasizing asset-based productive economic activity.

As can be seen, each of these principles, together with the above-mentioned axioms, provide rationale as to why microfinancing is an essential part of IME and, hence, IBF. The following description of IBF in terms of institutional and operational features provides further rationale as to why microfinance is inherently Islamic in its nature (Khan, 2007).

- It is a form of community banking aiming at serving communities, not markets;
- It offers responsible finance, as it runs systematic checks on finance providers and restrains consumer indebtedness; it also offers ethical investments and corporate social responsibility (CSR) initiatives;
- It represents an alternative paradigm in terms of stability by linking financial services to the productive, real economy; it provides a moral compass for capitalism;
- It fulfills aspirations in the sense that it widens the ownership base of society and offers success with authenticity.

As these principles indicate, IBF should serve social interests (for example, through

"The general who wins a battle makes many calculations . . . ere the battle is fought. The general who loses a battle makes but few calculations beforehand. Thus do many calculations lead to victory, and few to defeat." Sun Tzu

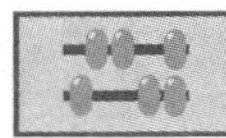

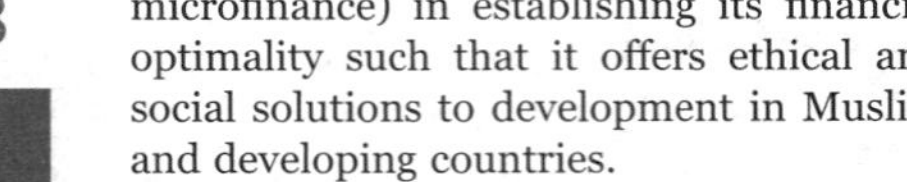

microfinance) in establishing its financial optimality such that it offers ethical and social solutions to development in Muslim and developing countries.

While IBF has been criticized for not fulfilling these principles in its current practice due to its adoption of a commercial banking structure, it can be seen that it has the potential to respond to the social objective, which is an inherent function of Islamic finance.

In helping IBF to demonstrate its original ethical and social nature, new methods of financing can be developed to appeal to their commercial nature as well. Since, by definition, IBF institutions are nevertheless expected to contribute to social development, they have to move to the third institutionalization stage (the first stage was social banking in the 1960s, followed by commercial banking as the second institutional phase from the mid-1970s until now), in which society and capacity building-oriented institutions, such as microfinancing and social banking, should run alongside the commercial banks. This fulfills the social and ethical expectations as identified by IME, but also responds to the development needs of the societies in which they are operating.

ISLAMIC MICROFINANCE

Microfinance has become a critical tool in tackling poverty and aiding development through building the capacity for the poor to enjoy greater self-sufficiency and sustainability, granting them access to financial services and conceptualizing the poor individual as someone with innate entrepreneurial abilities who can generate jobs, income, and wealth if given access to credit. Through microfinance, the poor are given the opportunity to become stakeholders in the economy; therefore, enabled and functioning individuals will be the outcome. Due to this objective function of microfinance, as a development tool it has enjoyed some success. Consequently, a number of conventional financial institutions and banks now offer microfinance in supporting business ideas from small projects to housing projects.

Despite its success, microfinance has been criticized from an Islamic perspective for getting people into debt due to its fixed interest charges. If a project does not yield the expected returns in conventional financing, difficulties can ensue for the borrower. IBF, thus, offers a more viable solution as a value-oriented financial proposition as part of the IME. Thus, typical IBF instruments, such as *musharakah* and *mudarabah* (based on profit/loss sharing), or institutions such as IBF, but also *waqfs* (pious foundations), are rather appropriate as providers of microfinance. IMF fits into the asset-based economic paradigm and equity objective of IME as well as fulfilling all other expectations. Thus, there is compatibility and complementarity between the objectives and operational mechanism of microfinance and of IBF.

Despite having similar objectives, IBFs have not fully appreciated microfinance, which is also a commercially viable undertaking. However, in recent years there has been movement in this direction, as the successful implementation of IMF has shown in countries such as Bangladesh, Indonesia, Yemen, and Syria. In Bangladesh, however, the direct involvement and success of the Bangladeshi Islamic Bank as a banking institution is an important experiment.

IBF instruments can provide an additional opportunity for microfinance to flourish by giving the entrepreneurial poor access to finance in an alternative and dynamic manner. The contractual nature of such products is consistent with the financing nature of microfinance. Table 1 provides further details of IBF instruments and their degree of compatibility with microfinancing.

Other financing methods have also been proposed, such as the *wakalah* model and special purpose vehicle (SPV). It is suggested that SPV can be used by banks for the financing of microfinance projects, which can be a subsidiary of the sponsoring firm or may be an independent SPV. Dusuki (2008: 61) highlights the features and the procedures of using SPV for Islamic microfinance as follows: "(i) the Islamic bank mobilizes various sources of funds with specific microfinance objectives; (ii) the Islamic bank creates a bankruptcy-remote SPV; (iii) the bank allocates a certain amount of funds and passes it to the SPV;

Table 1. Instruments of financing in Islamic microfinance. (Source: Obaidullah and Khan, 2008: 21)

Instrument	*Suitable for*	*Cost of capital*	*Risk to borrower*	*Risk to institution*	*Remarks*
Mudarabah/ Musharakah	Fixed assets, working capital (declining form suitable for housing and equipment finance)	Very high	Low	Very high	Costs of loan administration and monitoring are high, given the complexity of the repayment schedule and lack of proper accounting. Perceived to be ideal, but not popular in practice.
Ijarah	Fixed assets	Moderate	High	Moderate	Costs of loan administration and monitoring are low, given the simple repayment schedule that allows flexibility and customization based on client preferences. Popular among IMFs and has potential for easy adaptation in conventional microfinance.
Murabahah	Fixed assets, working capital	Moderate	High	Moderate	Costs of loan administration and monitoring are low, given the simple repayment schedule; the multiplicity of transactions in working capital financing can push up costs. Highly popular in practice, notwithstanding popular perception of it being a close substitute of *riba*-based lending.
Qard	All purposes	Very low	Very low	Moderate	Charity-based, usually combined with voluntarism. Low overheads. Popular because it is perceived to be the purest form of financing.
Salam	Working capital	High	High	High	Back-to-back nature creates risk of lack of double coincidence. Untried.
Istisna'a	Fixed assets	High	High	High	Back-to-back nature creates risk of lack of double coincidence. Untried.
Istijrar	Working capital	Moderate	Moderate	Moderate	Ideal for micro-repetitive transactions. Its complexity is not easily understood by parties, hence it is not a popular mechanism.

  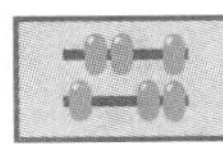      

(iv) the funds are then channeled to various clients depending on needs and demand. For example, *zakah* funds may only be allocated to poor clients for consumption purposes and capacity-building initiatives, while other types of funds can be used to finance their productive economic activities." The selective nature of expenditures and investments, for instance from *zakah* funds, under such an arrangement, can overcome the fundamental problems of microfinance, as this would render financial accessibility for the poor for their consumption but also help them to engage in capacity-building projects with the objective of productive economic activity and job creation.

In addition to mainly commercial microfinance instruments, Wilson (2007) proposes that nonbanking institutions conduct microfinancing by using the *wakalah* model through the collection of *zakah* (compulsory alms giving for those whose wealth is beyond the established threshold) and *waqf* (religious charitable foundation) funds. The *wakalah* agency model combines certain features of a credit union through financial management with the capital provided by a donor agency; in this case it can be a *zakah* fund or a *waqf*. The use of a *zakah* fund or *waqf* under such an arrangement would work in the same manner as described above.

It should be noted that *waqf*, as private nonbanking institutions, were used extensively throughout Muslim history to provide welfare services to the poor. Therefore, there is clear justification for their revitalization in modern times to fund microfinance projects aimed at self-sufficiency and a sustainable economic life for the poor. Furthermore, *zakah* have great potential in creating funds for development purposes. However, due to the absence of clear and transparent management structures in most Muslim societies, *zakah* funds are disbursed to individual causes with no questioning of their wider sustainability and social objectives. Thus, IMF can be an excellent solution for the collection and management of *zakah* funds for the alleviation of poverty. Other forms of private charitable giving such as *sadaqah* (voluntary alms), *hiba* (donations), and *tabarru* (financial contributions), can form additional funding opportunities for IMF through nonbanking microfinance institutions.

In addition to these instruments for raising funds for IMF, deposit-type banking instruments such as *wadiah*, *qard al-hasan*, and *mudarabah*, in the form of savings, current, and time deposits, respectively, can be used to raise funds for Islamic microfinance institutions. In deciding on the appropriate instrument to deploy, IMF programs have to consider the relevant costs, benefits, trade-offs, and nature of the instruments, as set out in Table 1.

In addition to the implicit administration costs of IMF projects, potential risk areas have to be taken into account by both the program and the borrower(s). The instrument selection process is dependent on the nature of the client and the project proposed. For instance, if the client is already in business and has a progressive attitude and good business record, then the *musharakah*, *mudarabah*, and *murabahah* models of financial instruments, which involve various degrees of profit/loss sharing, would be appropriate. In addition, new clients who do not have any credit or track record could be financed by the *qard al-hasan* type of soft loans, which do not have any financing or risk implications.

In the banking-oriented IMF, management of risk by the institution also becomes an important aspect of the process—based on the guarantee (or *kafalah*) and collateral (*daman*). The former is used as an alternative risk management tool for default and delinquency in the case of financing individual microfinance arrangements, while mutual *kafalah* is commonly used by IMF institutions in the case of group financing. It should be noted that *daman* in terms of physical assets as collateral is not extensively used in managing risk by IMF institutions.

Another aspect of risk management is the protection of borrowers against potential risks, for which micro-*takaful* (in the form of mutual guarantee) is proposed as a solution, though this has yet to be developed as a fully fledged instrument. In reality, however, largely informal methods are used for the protection of borrowers or members. These often take the form of short-term emergency funds in the case of hardship and difficulties. In some cases IMF institutions have managed to raise insurance funds from contributions to cover clients against any form of adversity they may face.

As regards Islamic microfinance providers, in addition to formal IMF institutions large numbers of informal microfinance institutions, member-based organizations, and nongovernmental organizations are active in delivering IMF-related services in different parts of the developing world.

CONCLUSION

A financial system should be able to provide financing to different segments of a given society such that, in addition to financial and economic objectives, social objectives may be served. Since social objectives are an essential part of the IME, it is imperative for IBF to fulfill such objectives alongside their business interests. As a social and moral method of financing, IBF, therefore, should contribute directly to economic and social development. This can become possible through social banking and microfinance, though it should be recalled that the initial experience of IBF in the early 1960s in Egypt was a social bank that was microfinancing-oriented.

Due to the complementarity between IBF and microfinance, there is a need to see further and proactive involvement of IBF and nonbanking Islamic institutions to provide IMF.

By using the essential methods and instruments outlined here, authentic models of IMF can be developed that will ensure the proactive development and efficient running of microfinancing, so that self-sustaining and human-centered development, aimed at helping poor individuals and entrepreneurs who are excluded from economic and financial life, can be achieved as expected by IME by also creating social capital.

MORE INFO

Articles:

Dusuki, Asyraf Wadji. "Banking for the poor: The role of Islamic banking in microfinance initiatives." *Humanomics* 24:1 (2008): 49–66. Online at: dx.doi.org/10.1108/08288660810851469

Wilson, Rodney. "Making development assistance sustainable through Islamic microfinance." *IIUM Journal of Economics and Management* 15:2 (2007): 197–217. Online at: www.iium.edu.my/enmjournal/152art3.pdf

Reports:

Khan, Iqbal. "Islamic finance: Relevance and growth in the modern financial age." Presentation to the Islamic Finance Seminar organized by the Harvard Islamic Finance Project, London School of Economics, UK, February 1, 2007.

Obaidullah, Mohammed, and Tariqullah Khan. "Islamic microfinance development: Challenges and initiatives." Policy Dialogue Paper no. 2. Islamic Research and Training Institute, 2008. Online at: ssrn.com/abstract=1506073

"What is really desired, under the name of riches, is essentially, power over men ... this power ... is in direct proportion to the poverty of the men over whom it is exercised, and in inverse proportion to the number of persons who are as rich as ourselves." John Ruskin

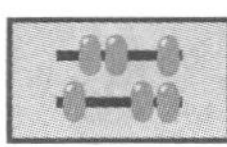

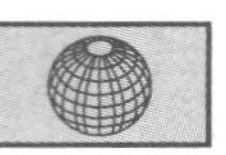

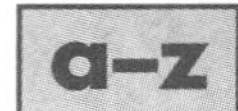

Islamic Modes of Finance and the Role of *Sukuk* by Abdel-Rahman Yousri Ahmad

EXECUTIVE SUMMARY

- Islamic finance modes are based on profit/loss sharing because of *riba* (interest) prohibition.
- *Murabaha* has been responsible since the 1970s for the employment of about 80–90% of Islamic banks' resources. The bank provides commodities on a "cost plus profit" price formula to customers who pay back their debt in installments.
- *Ijara* ranks next in importance after *murabaha* and implies a promise by the bank (lessor) to gift or sell the leased asset at a nominal price to the lessee by the end of the leasing period.
- *Diminishing musharaka* is a new product whereby the bank provides capital to a customer or partner whose share in partnership is increased gradually by repaying the principal in installments, plus a share of the realized profits to the bank.
- *Salam* entitles instant cash to a bank customer against its commitment to deliver prescribed commodities at a future date. *Parallel salam*, on the other hand, is practiced by banks to hedge their *salam* operations.
- In *istisna* the bank finances the manufacturing of a commodity for a customer who pays its price in installments. It is practiced mostly in Gulf countries.
- Islamic financial institutions, in the form of the limited liability joint stock company, rely totally on "ordinary shares" for raising their capital.
- *Multiple-party mudaraba* has enabled Islamic banks to work as partner/investor on a profit/loss basis for large numbers of capital owners whose deposits take the form of investment accounts.
- Islamic financial institutions have recently extended their activities in capital markets, and *sukuk* (Islamic bonds) are playing an important role in mobilizing resources.
- Because of *riba* prohibition, securitization (for *sukuk* purposes) should neither include *murabaha*, *istisna*, and *salam* assets, which are debt arrangements, nor allow for guaranteed regular payment to *sukuk* holders. Yet although *sukuk* experience, has been successful in terms of resources mobilized, it shows deviation from these rules.
- If *sukuk* do not maintain strict *shariah* rules they are bound to be confused with conventional bonds.

INTRODUCTION

Broadly speaking, Islamic modes of finance can be divided into two types: either they provide direct finance as capital funds through partnership (*musharaka* and *mudaraba*), or they provide indirect finance through leasing (*ijara*) and sale contracts (*murabaha*, *bai ajil*, *salam*, and *istisna*). All modes are based on the principle of *riba* (interest) prohibition, and all seek to maintain Islamic business ethics (freedom and leniency of transactions, recognition of and regard for private property, and justice).

MODES OF FINANCE

Musharaka

Musharaka (partnership) is practiced by Islamic banks either on a "permanent" or on a "diminishing" basis. In both cases capital is provided by the bank in return for a share in the realized profit (or the loss, if a loss occurred). In *diminishing musharaka*, which is a new Islamic product, the bank is entitled to receive, in addition to its share in realized profits, an extra payment that is specifically assigned for the purpose of reducing its share in the company's capital until this is fully paid off by the partner. Diminishing *musharaka* has mostly been used to finance small and medium-size enterprises, but it has also been employed in the financing of several big projects in some Arab Gulf countries (Kuwait, Bahrain, and Emirates).

Murabaha

Among all the modes of Islamic finance, *murabaha* has played the most important role. Banks' annual reports reveal that since the 1970s *murabaha* has been steadily responsible for the employment of about 80–90% of Islamic banks' resources. *Murabaha* in traditional *fiqh* (Islamic jurisprudence) is a spot sale contract where the price is based on a cost plus profit margin formula. The contract has been modified to include *bai ajil* (deferred payment sale) and renamed as "*Murabaha* to the Order of the Purchaser." According to the new contract, the bank's customer orders the purchase of a prescribed commodity that is available in the domestic or the foreign market. If the customer's creditability is satisfactory, the bank buys the commodity, adding its markup to the market price. The bank accepts payment for the commodity in installments, which normally stretch over one year or more. When *murabaha* purchase is made by means of importation from foreign markets, letters of credit and foreign conventional banks are involved, and necessary *shariah* precautions are taken to avoid payment of "interest" at any step.

Murabaha, which has established a flexible mechanism for extending interest-free trade credit on short- and medium-term bases to households and firms, has also played a significant role in financing small and microenterprises (for example Faisal Bank's Um Dorman branch in Sudan). Banking risk involved in *murabaha* operations is significantly reduced by customers undertaking to fulfill the contract once the commodity is purchased and by collaterals in the form of mortgage rights given to the bank over the purchased commodity until its price is fully paid.

The practice of *murabaha* has been the subject of criticism. It is held against Islamic banks that they are frequently guided by prevailing interest rates in determining their profit margin (markup) when they should instead consider market conditions for deferred payment sale, as intended in *shariah*. Also, (for instance in Pakistan) banks have sometimes not acted as purchasers and have merely financed customers in equivalent cash to the ordered commodity price plus markup. In this case the markup charged by the bank above the commodity price is no different from interest, which is prohibited.

Salam

Salam is the sale of a prescribed commodity for deferred delivery in exchange for immediate and full payment of its price. *Salam* is permissible in *shariah* to meet the instant cash needs of a seller who undertakes the future delivery of the commodity. *Salam* sale is absolutely forbidden in currencies, gold, silver, and all quasi-money assets, since gain in this exchange is *riba*. The objects of *salam* are commodities (or services) that are normally available in the market and can be specifically defined in terms of quantity, and quality. The exact date and place of delivery must be specified in the contract to avoid any problem. Thus,

"**Opportunities pass by as the passing of the clouds, thus seize the opportunities of goodness.**" Imam Ali ibn Abi Taleb

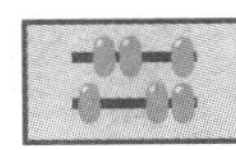

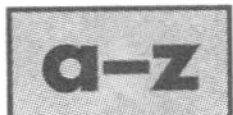

banking finance is extended to firms or individuals against their commitment to deliver commodities at future dates.

To hedge the *salam* operation banks also practice *parallel salam*. This involves making counter deals with other parties whereby they obtain immediate cash payments against a commitment to deliver commodities of similar quantity and quality to those in the *salam* contracts at some future date. Islamic banks in Pakistan, Sudan, and in some Arab Gulf countries have practiced *salam* transactions.

Istisna

Istisna is a manufacturing contract, treated in traditional *fiqh* as a special sale contract. A household that wishes to build a house, or a firm that needs to construct a building, or to manufacture equipment with particular specifications, would approach the bank for this purpose. The bank has to estimate the economic viability of the operation and the creditability of the customer. If the response is favorable, an *istisna* contract will be signed between the two parties. The customer submits a down payment and undertakes to pay the remaining part of the manufacturing price, as mutually agreed with the bank, in installments over a given period of time. The Islamic bank would then sign a *parallel istisna* contract whereby it extends finance to a firm that agrees to manufacture the requested object according to specification and to deliver it at an agreed future date. Islamic banks in the Arab Gulf countries have used this type of contract successfully to finance big operations, particularly in the construction sector and infrequently in the industrial sector.

Ijara Muntahia Bittamleek

Ijara muntahia bittamleek (lease ending with ownership) ranks next in importance after *murabaha* as an employment mode. The Islamic bank purchases *real assets* for leasing as requested and specified by its customers. The bank (lessor) and the client (lessee) will mutually agree on the leasing period, rent, and terms of payment. Maintenance and insurance of the leased asset are the bank's responsibility, whereas the lessee has to bear the running costs as well as any repair costs in the case of misuse. As *shariah* does not allow for the combination of leasing and ownership in one single contract, *ijara muntahia bittamleek* implies a promise on the part of one party—namely the bank—to gift or to sell the leased asset at a nominal price to the lessee by the end of the leasing term. *Ijara muntahia bittamleek* has opened the door for successful leasing activities by the Islamic banks, particularly in the housing sector. *Ijara* of houses gives the bank the advantage of keeping the title of property until the end of the leasing period, and gives the lessee the benefit of subleasing rights.

THE DEVELOPMENT OF *SUKUK*

Of growing importance, particularly in the last decade, has been the development of *sukuk* (Islamic bonds). *Sukuk* arose as a natural response to the remarkable growth of Islamic financial services and allowed Islamic banks, companies, and sovereigns to raise *shariah*-compliant funds through the market. It is this development in fact which has led to the growth of an Islamic capital market, though trade in shares of Islamic banks, *takaful* companies (or companies whose activities comply with *shariah*) is always feasible.

According to the Accounting and Auditing Organization for Islamic Financial Institutions' (AAIOFI) definition of investment *sukuk* (*Shariah* Standard 17), there are 14 possible forms that these can take. However, *sukuk* development meant approval of securitization within Islamic finance. Within the *shariah* framework the scope of assets that can be pooled, designated, and packaged for securitization is comparatively limited. The *ijara* contract has been widely accepted by *fuqaha* (Muslim jurists) for securitization, since *sukuk* will rightly be backed by physical assets and financial rights over usufruct. Contracts such as *murabaha*, *istisna*, or *salam* cannot be securitized because they are *debt arrangements*. According to *shariah*, debt-based contracts cannot be traded in secondary markets, If this is done it would typically mean trade in money and involvement in *riba*. Yet, the decision of the Organization of the Islamic Conference's Fiqh Academy (Number 5, Fourth Annual Plenary Session, Jeddah, 1988) opened the door for assets in the form of money or debt (for instance, *istisna* and *murabaha*) to be exceptionally securitized if mixed in "minor proportion" with physical assets (*ijara*).

Under *shariah* principles of interest prohibition and profit/loss sharing, no guarantee can be given in respect of either regular payment to *sukuk* holders or redemption of the *sukuk*'s face value. This goes against conventional market practices. Payments to *sukuk* holders should be made from the *actual or realized* cash flow of the investment that is based on the assets in the underlying pool. However, guarantees of performance, collateralization attached to *sukuk*, and their rating by conventional standards (Fitch or Standard & Poor's) imply the existence of mechanisms that secure a regular known flow of income to *sukuk* and redemption of their full face value. For example, in the Islamic Development Bank (IDB) *sukuk* issue of US$400 million in 2003, returns were calculated on a fixed-rate basis of 3.635% per annum until their full redemption in 2008. The same principle applies to all the *sukuk* issued by sovereigns, and Salman Syed Ali (2005) observes that "rents payable to *sukuk* holders are not necessarily generated from the use of *sukuk* assets but from general revenues and other earnings of the state enterprise."

All this throws doubt on the genuine submission of *sukuk* to the principle of profit/loss sharing. Besides, the exception made for possible securitization of *murabaha* and *istisna* assets in "minor proportion" with *ijara* assets has been widely extended. As in the case of IDB's US$400 million *sukuk* of 2003, the "minor proportion" of *murabaha* and *istisna* assets reached 49% of total tangible assets. More serious in this case is that under exceptional circumstances the composition of *ijara* assets can fall temporarily under 51%, but not to a minimum of 25%, of the total pool of assets!

In practice, therefore, the gap between Islamic *sukuk* and conventional bonds has narrowed considerably. In future issues, *sukuk* should stick strictly to *shariah* rules if they are not to be confused in the markets with conventional bonds.

MORE INFO

Articles:

Ali, Salman Syed. "Islamic capital market products: Developments and challenges." Jeddah: IRTI, Islamic Development Bank, Occasional Paper No. 9, 2005 . Online at: www.irtipms.org/PubDetE.asp?pub=213

Reports:

Accounting and Auditing Organization for Islamic Financial Institutions (AAOIFI). "Shari'a standards," 2008. Online at: www.aaoifi.com/keypublications.html

Islamic Fiqh Academy of the Organization of Islamic Countries. "Resolutions and recommendations of the council of the Islamic Fiqh Academy 1985–2000." Jeddah: IRTI, Islamic Development Bank, 2000. Online at: www.irtipms.org/PubDetE.asp?pub=73

  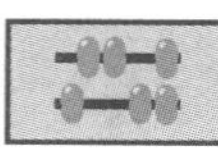      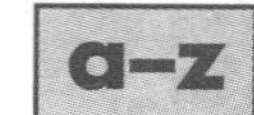

Issuing Corporate Debt by Steven Lowe

EXECUTIVE SUMMARY

- The Nobel Prize-winning Modigliani and Miller theorem that capital structure does not matter does not reflect the inefficiencies of the real world.
- Taxes, default costs, agency costs, equity dilution issues, credit rationing, and stockholder/debtholder tensions all impact the economists' perfect market.
- Divergent goals between debt and equity holders lead to a number of behaviors, such as decision risk shifting, underinvestment, and asset stripping, which can skew the financing decision. Debt covenants exist to even out the risk/reward structures between debt and equity holders.
- Current economic theory suggests that an optimal capital structure that balances the risk of bankruptcy with the tax savings of debt issuance does exist, although it can be a struggle for individual corporations to hit this target amid the constantly changing influences of the modern operating environment.

INTRODUCTION

The existence and determination of the optimal capital structure is an ongoing topic of research in corporate finance. In a perfect market setting, with no frictions, Modigliani and Miller's seminal research in 1958 suggested that the market value of a firm is independent of its capital structure. In other words, capital structure does not matter.

Miller (1991) explained the intuition for this with a simple analogy: "Think of the firm as a gigantic tub of whole milk. The farmer can sell the whole milk as it is. Or he can separate out the cream, and sell it at a considerably higher price than the whole milk would bring." He continued: "The Modigliani–Miller proposition says that if there were no costs of separation (and, of course, no government dairy support program), the cream plus the skim milk would bring the same price as the whole milk." The essence of the argument is that increasing the amount of debt (cream) lowers the value of outstanding equity (skim milk)—selling off safe cash flows to debtholders leaves the firm with more lower-valued equity, keeping the total value of the firm unchanged. Put differently, any gain from using more of what might seem to be cheaper debt is offset by the higher cost of now riskier equity. Hence, given a fixed amount of total capital, the allocation of capital between debt and equity is irrelevant because the weighted average of the two costs of capital to the firm is the same for all possible combinations of the two.

Of course, corporations do not operate in a perfect world, and few if any companies are 100% debt financed. Since Modigliani and Miller's Nobel Prize-winning paper, a host of possible explanations for the relevance of particular financial structures has emerged, centering around the impact of taxes, the costs of default, agency costs, equity dilution, and credit rationing, as well as the differing goals of management and sponsors. Modigliani and Miller have also suggested that firms maintain a reserve borrowing capacity to allow for economic uncertainty. We will look at each of these potential inefficiencies in turn.

IMPACT OF TAXES

Of the most obvious violations of Modigliani and Miller's assumptions are corporate taxes and the tax deductibility of interest payments. Usually, interest payments made to debtholders are deducted from corporate profits before they are taxed. Consequently, the corporate tax saved acts as a subsidy on interest payments. For example, if the tax rate is 34%, then for every dollar paid in interest payments 34 cents of corporate taxes are avoided by the company (although those receiving the interest must pay tax on their interest income). In contrast, if income is paid out as dividends to stockholders, that income is taxed twice, once at the corporate level via corporate taxes, and again as an income tax on the equity holder. Hence, any corporation seeking to minimize its taxes and maximize the revenues available to investors should finance itself entirely with debt.

In a 1977 article, "Determinants of corporate borrowing," Myers showed that considering corporate taxes in isolation does not reflect real world economic interactions. Transferring interest payments to individual bondholders to avoid corporate taxes does not make investors any better off if they then have to pay higher personal taxes on that interest income than the corporation and investors would have owed had the corporation not used debt. Miller argued that because tax rates on capital gains have often been lower than tax rates on individuals' dividend and interest income, the firm might lower the total tax bill paid by the corporation and investor combined by not issuing debt at all. Moreover, taxes owed on capital gains can be deferred until the realization of those gains, further lowering the effective tax rate on capital gains. Because of this interaction, there is an optimal level of debt (less than the 100% suggested above) for corporations as a whole.

DEFAULT COSTS

Costs associated with financial distress and, more obviously, bankruptcy also keep firms from issuing large levels of debt compared to their level of underlying equity finance. These costs can take two forms, being either explicit or implicit. Explicit default costs include the payments made to lawyers, accountants, and other professional advisers in the case of bankruptcy and liquidation, or filing for Chapter 11 protection. These costs can represent a significant portion of total corporate assets, which are lost to investors in the case of bankruptcy. Corporations also need to consider the indirect costs of financial distress that occur as a company moves closer to default and bankruptcy. These can include higher costs from suppliers which fear that the company might not pay its future bills, and the loss of customers who want stable and long-term relationships with their suppliers and counterparties.

Clearly, investors would prefer that firms stay out of default or financial distress so that these costs, both explicit and implicit, are not incurred. However, as a corporation takes on more and more debt, the probability of bankruptcy increases. Hence, the marginal benefit of further increases in debt declines as debt increases. At the same time, the marginal cost increases, so that a firm that is optimizing its overall value will focus on this trade-off when choosing how much debt and how much equity to use for financing. These costs are one of the factors that restrain firms from maintaining very high levels of debt, and are why different industries, with different earnings volatility, can support different levels of debt.

AGENCY COSTS

The decision to issue corporate debt arises from the conflict between competing sources of finance offered by the debt and equity markets. There are large differences between a firm that is 100% owner managed and one in which the equity is owned by external stockholders or a mix of the managers and outside stockholders. With external stockholders, the managers act as

"An appropriate capital structure is a critical decision for any business organization." Roy L. Simerly and Mingfang Li

  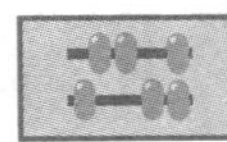      

agent for the ultimate owners. Although these agents should run the firm to maximize its value, they may not be perfect agents for the equity owners as they may make some decisions to further their own interests ahead of the ultimate owners. Agents could award themselves excess pay or benefits, or indulge in empire-building to increase their own reputations. They may even favor the security of the debtholders rather than the returns of the stockholders. The impact of these agency costs can affect the distribution of financing for a corporate.

CREDIT RATIONING

Traditional economics argues from the standpoint that markets are efficient (as we have seen with Modigliani and Miller's contribution). In 1981 Joseph Stiglitz and Andrew Weiss suggested that markets are only efficient under exceptional circumstances. To reduce potential losses, lenders without perfect knowledge of their counterparties have an incentive not only to charge higher rates to high-risk lenders, but also to ration the provision of credit to them as well. The concern for the lender is that, as it raises the rate of interest charged for its loans, only those firms which are most desperate for finance will take the loans, and these are precisely the corporations that are most likely to go into bankruptcy. If bankruptcy occurs, the corporation is able to walk away from its debt and the lending institution underwrites the cost of failure. This suggests that if a firm is able to obtain a large amount of loan financing, it has a large incentive to undertake higher-risk projects because the risk is asymmetric.

Typically, credit rationing will most often happen with smaller and younger corporations, which are more likely to be owned by their founders, rather than to firms that have a track record or some existing external investors. It is with these owner–managed firms that the risk of imperfect knowledge creates most tension between equity and debt holders. Not only is it likely that the manager/owner of a firm has superior information on his business, but he can also adjust his managerial or investment strategy after concluding a debt contract. Only corporations with riskier projects would be ready to take high interest rate loans, so raising the interest rate without credit rationing would increase the proportion of risky borrowers and reduce the overall profitability of the lender.

EQUITY DILUTION

Myers and Majluf (1984) produced research suggesting that owner-managers use external financing (debt or equity) only when there is insufficient internal financing (i.e. their own money) available for new projects. Indeed, they go as far as to suggest that managers prefer to issue debt over equity. The idea behind this theory is that managers often believe they have a better idea of the true worth of their corporation than potential outside bond or equity investors. Since potential investors cannot adequately value stock, it would generally be sold at a price below the price the managers think appropriate. Rather than sell stock too cheaply, therefore, managers who need external financing will prefer to issue debt. It can be argued that in issuing equity to outside investors, owner–managers might think that the firm is overvalued and that the current owners are taking advantage of this overvaluation. This reinforces the view that debt is likely to be preferred over equity in smaller, private companies.

DIFFERING GOALS OF FINANCIAL SPONSORS

The idea of bondholder and stockholder conflict is widely accepted as a key determinant of financial policy. Bondholders and stockholders often have competing aims and attitudes to risk-taking behavior. Even in highly profitable corporations, stockholders bear most of the investment costs but share the benefits with bondholders. Consequently, bondholders typically value a risk-averse strategy as that will increase the chances of getting all their investment back. Stockholders, on the other hand, are willing to take on riskier projects. If the risky projects succeed, they will get all the profit themselves, whereas if the projects fail the risk is shared with the bondholders.

Another area where these divergent goals are clearly demonstrated is with the problem of underinvestment in times of financial difficulty. Stockholders have little incentive to invest in new projects as corporate default approaches, because the funds they contribute to the enterprise will benefit bondholders and other creditors in the event of default; this is the so-called debt overhang problem. Even if the bondholders would be better off with the investment, equity holders will be unwilling to pay for them. Alternatively, as corporate default approaches, equity stockholders will be willing to invest all their current investment in a very risky project with high potential returns. If the project fails, the bondholders will lose more, but the stockholders can be no worse off because their claims were worthless anyway. If, however, the project succeeds, the stockholders will be the major beneficiaries.

Finally, and perhaps most obviously, stockholders could just pay out all of the firm's assets as dividends to themselves, leaving an empty shell for the bondholders to claim when the firm is then unable to

MAKING IT HAPPEN

- Economic theory can only help so much in deciding the optimal financing structure for a corporation.
- Modigliani and Miller's seminal work in 1958 suggested that it did not matter whether a corporation was debt or equity financed, but the perfect assumptions on which their theorem rested have proved an unrealistic fit to corporate experience of the real world. Here taxes, the fear of bankruptcy, and the divergent aims of bond and stockholders, particularly in times of financial distress, far outweigh the pull of economic theory.
- The ideal mix of financing for an individual corporation is almost impossible to find because of near constantly shifting debt and equity market sentiment in response to perceived risk and return, and the competitive environment of an individual corporation.
- However, a corporation can benchmark its financing structure against its competitors, similar industries, and the advice of consultants and investors.

MORE INFO

Books:

Chew, Donald H., Jr. *The New Corporate Finance: Where Theory Meets Practice*. 3rd ed. New York: McGraw-Hill, 2001.

Jaffee, D. M. *Credit Rationing and the Credit Loan Market*. New York: Wiley, 1971.

Articles:

Allen, Franklin, and Douglas Gale. "Optimal security design." *Review of Financial Studies* 1:3 (Fall 1988): 229–263. Online at: dx.doi.org/10.1093/rfs/1.3.229

Donaldson, Gordon. "Financial goals: Management vs stakeholders." *Harvard Business Review* (May–June 1963): 116–129.

"The Modern Theory of capital structure began with the celebrated paper of Modigliani and Miller (1958)." Wikipedia

repay its debt. In an effort to prevent this, most debt issues or bank lending will have covenants attached to prevent the equity holders stripping assets, and hence security, away from the corporation that takes on the debt financing. These covenants exist to restrict stockholders' freedom of action, and to try to even out the risk/reward structures between debt and equity holders. However, bond contracts cannot prevent all eventualities.

All of these strategies—risk shifting, underinvestment, paying out large dividends—are more likely the more indebted is the firm. Stockholders may adopt policies that benefit themselves at the expense of the bondholders, and the incentive to do this is strongest when it is not clear that the firm will have sufficient cash flow to cover its debt payments.

Potential lenders know this and limit the debt they extend accordingly. Similarly, corporate managers who want to attract lenders and debt funding have to judge how much debt is suitable for a company in a particular industry and state of growth. Young firms in high-growth industries, for example, tend to use less debt, and firms in stable industries with large quantities of fixed assets tend to use more debt.

CONCLUSION

Current economic theory, based on many of the ideas discussed above, suggests that an optimal capital structure exists that balances the risk of bankruptcy with the tax savings of debt. Once established, this capital structure should provide greater returns to stockholders than they would receive from an all-equity firm. However, the complexities of the competitive environment and the huge diversity of corporations and their competitive environments all affect an individual corporation's optimal capital structure.

Hackbarth, Dirk. "Determinants of corporate borrowing: A behavioral perspective." Paper presented at 14th Annual Utah Winter Finance Conference, February 5–7, 2004.

Harris, Milton, and Artur Raviv. "The theory of capital structure." *Journal of Finance* 46:1 (March 1991): 297–355. Online at: www.afajof.org/journal/jstabstract.asp?ref=11098

Jensen, Michael C., and William H. Meckling. "Theory of the firm: Managerial behavior, agency costs and ownership structure." *Journal of Financial Economics* 3:4 (October 1976): 305–360. Online at: dx.doi.org/10.1016/0304-405X(76)90026-X

Miller, Merton H. "Debt and taxes." *Journal of Finance* 32:2 (May 1977): 261–275. Online at: www.afajof.org/journal/jstabstract.asp?ref=9267

Miller, Merton H. "Leverage." *Journal of Finance* 46:2 (June 1991): 479–488. Online at: www.afajof.org/journal/jstabstract.asp?ref=11111

Modigliani, Franco, and Merton H. Miller. "The cost of capital, corporation finance and the theory of investment." *American Economic Review* 48:3 (June 1958): 261–297. Online at: www.jstor.org/stable/info/1809766

Myers, Stewart C. "Determinants of corporate borrowing." *Journal of Financial Economics* 5:2 (November 1977): 147–175. Online at: dx.doi.org/10.1016/0304-405X(77)90015-0

Myers, Stewart C. "The capital structure puzzle." *Journal of Finance* 39:3 (July 1984): 575–592. Online at: www.afajof.org/journal/jstabstract.asp?ref=10308

Myers, Stewart C., and Nicholas S. Majluf. "Corporate financing and investment decisions when firms have information that investors do not have." *Journal of Financial Economics* 13:2 (June 1984): 187–221. Online at: dx.doi.org/10.1016/0304-405X(84)90023-0

Simerly, Roy L., and Mingfang Li. "Re-thinking the capital structure decision: Translating research into practical solutions." *B>Quest* (2002). Online at: www.westga.edu/~bquest/2002/rethinking.htm

Stiglitz, Joseph E. "On the irrelevance of corporate financial policy." *American Economic Review* 64:6 (December 1974): 851–866. Online at: www.jstor.org/stable/1815238

Stiglitz, Joseph E, and Andrew Weiss. "Credit rationing in markets with imperfect information." *American Economic Review* 71:3 (June 1981): 393–410. Online at: www.jstor.org/stable/1802787

Website:

Wikipedia article on capital structure: en.wikipedia.org/wiki/Capital_structure

See Also:

★ Capital Structure: A Strategy that Makes Sense (pp. 710–714)
★ Capital Structure: Implications (pp. 715–718)
★ Capital Structure: Perspectives (pp. 24–27)
★ Everything You Need to Know About Benchmarking (pp. 850–853)
★ Optimizing the Capital Structure: Finding the Right Balance between Debt and Equity (pp. 543–545)
✔ The Efficient Market Hypothesis (p. 1068)
✔ Investors and the Capital Structure (p. 1120)
✔ Understanding Capital Structure Theory: Modigliani and Miller (p. 997)
Franco Modigliani (p. 1296)
Merton Miller (p. 1294)

"We know very little about capital structure [but] capital structure changes convey information to investors."
Stewart C. Myers

     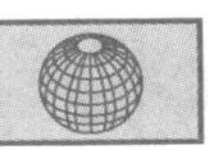   

Managing Activist Investors and Fund Managers by Leslie L. Kossoff

EXECUTIVE SUMMARY

- Organizations not previously of interest to activist investors or hedge funds should prepare to be targeted.
- Be proactive in understanding why investors become agitators, and address their concerns before they escalate.
- Organizational governance—particularly the combined chairman/CEO position—and financial management will be the easiest targets for activists.
- Activists often succeed because they communicate better than management—particularly to tagalong investors who become part of the proxy fight.
- Unlocking stockholder value and simultaneously developing and executing on a long-term strategy will give activists less reason to agitate and less success with tagalongs; executive management will then have a less volatile financial landscape within which to work.

INTRODUCTION

Whether or not your organization has been a target in the past for activist investors and fund managers, you have to plan on it becoming a fact of life from now on—things have changed.

It used to be that only a few organizations were hit by activist investor activity. From the almost prophetic, and beautifully constructed, Benjamin Graham move on Northern Pipeline in 1951, to Carl Icahn's dramatic moves on Yahoo! during the "Microhoo" (Microsoft–Yahoo!) debacle of 2008, activist investors were a rarity—something other organizations had to deal with. A problem for the really Big Boys. Not everyone else. Not you.

Not any longer.

Whether or not you have any known activist investors currently rearing their heads, you'll have to plan for when they show up—because they will. If you work it right, proactively, as well as when the activism hits, you'll manage your way through those very choppy waters and find a safe haven at the end.

WHY INVESTORS BECOME ACTIVIST

Historically, the reason that most activist investors became active was because they saw something wrong with the way things were being managed. The value of the company was not fully represented in the share value. Management was taking the organization in a direction—usually with a direct correlation to falling share value or dividends—that was making the investors unhappy.

But those reasons are historical, and they were retrospective. One of the big changes is that now investors become activists *proactively*. They see things on the horizon that they don't like, and they act accordingly. Not only may they not be happy with what has happened in the past, they're also not happy about what they see coming next.

For management, that is a wake-up call in the best possible way. It puts the onus on you to look at those components of your business that might lead investors to become activist—and take action accordingly. Because if they're seeing something they don't like, either they need to understand why it is the right thing for the business to do, or you need to take a different, objective, look at what they're not liking so that you can determine the relative merit of what they see.

Also, by looking at the organization the way the activists do, you will see other weaknesses—in everything from your strategy, to your operations, to your financial management—that might be the next focus of their attention. You don't want that; you want to make the fix before they ever have the chance to raise their voices.

TOO GOOD AN OPPORTUNITY TO MISS

And then there are those activist investors who get in because they see something that your company has to offer that is just too good an opportunity to miss. It may be because they have a history of being activist and simply see a new opportunity on which to bring their activist skills and financial acumen to bear. Or it may be because your company is such a good target for some other opportunity which you're not considering (like M&A) that they want to get in and make fast money. Whatever the reason, they'll find a way.

Activist investors have a profile. They are identifiable, as is their methodology. Part of that methodology is to get others who own shares in your company to tag along. In most cases, they can't pull off what they want on their own. They need proxy votes. That being the case, they're making a case to their counterparts that you have to counter in its entirety.

Activist investors identify where your organization is exposed. That's where their opportunities lie. Then, once they've got a handle on where, from their perspective, you're going wrong, their next move is to start communicating that shortfall to others they can bring on board. They create the tagalongs. Tagalongs start out knowing nothing more than what they are told. Many of them, on seeing where the activists are going, will become involved in finding out information for themselves—but those tend to be the larger investors who already have analysts working your organization or your sector anyway. If the activists can get enough small investors involved and on side, they'll win.

On your side is that if you can identify those activist investors and fund managers with large stockholdings in your firm, you will be able, with a high sense of assurance, to begin figuring out what their strategy will be. Track their track record.

Then, if you've done your homework and figured out where your exposure lies, you'll be able to address those problems before the activists can take the initiative. You will also be in a stronger position to tell all your investors—especially those proxy candidates—exactly what you're doing, and why the management is on top of the problems and opportunities that everything from economic conditions to global competition are throwing your way.

Activists can't win if management is doing its job—and well.

THE EASY TARGETS

There are some problems which organizations create for themselves that are easy pickings for the activists—and provide some of the highest exposure for management. Now and going forward, corporate governance is the easiest target that activist investors will be able to find.

Since the Sarbanes–Oxley Act of 2002, the question of whether the same person can be both chairman and chief executive officer, and still ensure that the organization is safe for its stockholders, is—and will continue to be—the easiest target of all. It doesn't matter in which country the

"In preparing for battle I have always found that plans are useless, but planning is indispensible."
Dwight David Eisenhower

  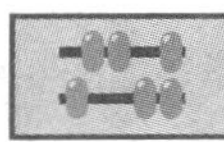      

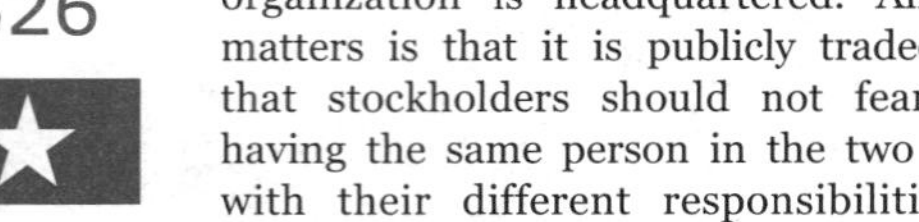

organization is headquartered. All that matters is that it is publicly traded and that stockholders should not fear that having the same person in the two roles, with their different responsibilities, is creating an increase in risk.

Activist investors and fund managers are looking for situations where the board is perceived as being entrenched. Unfortunately, even if having the same person as your chairman and CEO is the best thing that's happened to your organization in years, from an outside perspective it looks like cronyism on the board. This is a situation that many will associate with lack of transparency and with untrustworthy and inadequately considered decisions.

That puts the onus on the chief executive and the board, *in toto*, to ensure that stockholders see a level of transparency in governance that goes beyond what existed before. Transparency of voting structures—and even a periodic, situational decision to rescue him or herself by the chairman/chief executive—will go far to calm what could otherwise give rise to very contentious criticisms of the board and how the company is managed at the top.

Issues surrounding everything from operational decisions to, most particularly, executive compensation and bonuses will also be fodder for the activists, both now and in the future. The tolerance for perceived cronyism and mismanagement is lower than ever—and is likely to stay that way.

In effect, just as politicians have to deal with a 24-hour news cycle, so too do corporate executives. There is no rest and no hiding from activists once they decide they want to engage.

AVOIDING THE ACTIVISTS' GLARE

A clear-cut corporate strategy for addressing stockholder concerns will do more to avoid the possibility of successful activism than anything else.

First, the stockholders need to see, on an ongoing basis, that the company is dedicated to unlocking stockholder value; that it is committed to finding new ways to make their investment pay off for them—now and in the future.

That is achieved by ensuring that the long-term strategic objectives that are set are not only well communicated, but are also fully executed to the stockholders' satisfaction. By setting and delivering on those long-term objectives, executive management can build long-term investor trust and commitment, leading to a much less volatile financial landscape for the companies operations.

And, finally, it's all about communication. Activists become activists—particularly the successful ones—by doing a better job of getting their message across to stockholders than corporate management does. By working diligently to ensure that stockholders not only have the information they need, but never feel that anything is being withheld from them, the chances of activists getting involved and their capability to bring in others can be severely reduced.

Ultimately it's all about good management, and about thinking like an activist before they can make their arguments stick. By being proactive and objective about the company—and then doing the right things—you'll stop the activists getting a toehold. More importantly, they'll have no reason to try to do so.

CASE STUDY

Microsoft/Yahoo!

It was bad enough for Yahoo! when Microsoft decided to make an unsolicited offer for its takeover. Initially offering $31 per share—a 62% premium over the then share price—Microsoft had decided to expand its internet presence through a big acquisition. This was even though Microsoft, at number three in the search engine business, with Yahoo! in second place, had little or no chance of coming close to the big beast, Google, for the advertising revenues that were there to be had.

When Carl Icahn decided to get into the fray, however, all the rules changed. Buying 5% of Yahoo!, Icahn started actively lobbying for the so-called Microhoo (or Micro-Hoo) deal to go through. He wanted those premiums—especially when Microsoft upped its offer price to $33 per share.

But Jerry Yang, Yahoo!'s chief executive, and Roy Bostock, its nonexecutive chairman, didn't want to sell—at least not at that price. They had other plans, with and without Google. As a result a three-way fight started, but after a while it wasn't altogether clear who was on whose side—especially because so much of the fight was conducted using the business media.

The proxy fight was about to begin. Icahn was fighting to remove all the current members of Yahoo!'s board, including Yang, and to replace them with a new set chosen by him. But at that point Microsoft decided that neither was it willing to pay the price Yahoo! was asking, nor was it comfortable doing a deal with Icahn tacitly setting the terms. The fight to create Microhoo was over before it began.

That was in 2008.

For Icahn, holding 5% and looking for a way to ensure his shares would gain value in the future, he had to create an alternate win and he did so. His initial demands and wins were changes to the board of directors and a new CEO. The Yahoo! board expanded from 10 seats to 11, with one current board member stepping down, and three new board members—one of which was to be Icahn, the other two selected from his list of alternates to be added. Carol Bartz became CEO in 2009 and one of her first deals was an alliance collaborating on Microsoft's search engine, Bing.

On the face of it, Icahn was right. The Microsoft deal was the best deal going. Now, the question is how long Icahn continues to support Bartz in her new strategic direction for the company.

MAKING IT HAPPEN

- Before the activists get the chance, take an objective look at where the business is exposed, and then take action to correct those deficiencies.
- Identify activist investors who already own shares in the company, then research how, and on what particular issues, they have agitated in the past.
- Be proactive in taking steps to address the activists' issues—from leveraging, to corporate governance, management structure, strategy execution, and more—to reduce the activists' opportunities to act.
- Recognize that activism is now future-oriented—not just retrospective and based on the board's previous decisions. Make sure that forward planning and the ability to execute and deliver are sound.
- Message well and continuously to your stockholders, so that it is the company's message that gets the most traction—not that of the activists.

"Hindsight is good, foresight is better; but second sight is best of all." Evan Esar

  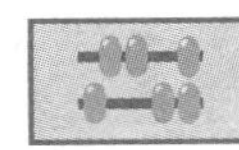   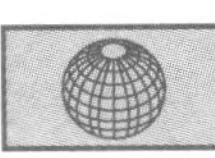   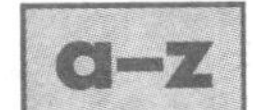

Managing *Shariah*-Compliant Portfolios: The Challenges, the Process, and the Opportunities

by John Sandwick

EXECUTIVE SUMMARY

- There is US$2.5 trillion or more in managed Muslim wealth worldwide, almost none managed according to the simple rules of *shariah*. Like everyone else, Muslim savers want professional investment management, but with *shariah*-compliant investments.
- About US$30 billion total assets are managed in fewer than 100 *shariah*-compliant funds that meet professional standards and are primarily composed of money market and equity funds. This is a less than optimal universe but sufficient for Islamic wealth and asset management.
- The overall goal is to produce a business model that follows the prudent-man rules of full liquidity from a transparent asset base through defined risk and reward profiles across income, balanced, and growth strategies that are feasible using the existing universe of Islamic funds.
- Modern portfolio theory can be applied to Islamic investing to achieve the same levels of sophistication and returns as conventional allocations. There is no need to introduce exotic or illiquid securities to achieve the standard investment objectives *shariah*-compliant investors.
- Banks and asset managers everywhere can offer *shariah*-compliant investment management now. The total potential size of the Islamic wealth management market is at least US$1 trillion, and growing.

INTRODUCTION

It is still puzzling to understand why something as straightforward as Islamic wealth and asset management has eluded the professional classes to date. At the time of writing, only one single major global money center bank, and paltry few independent asset managers, had constructed credible service offerings for Muslim clients who wish to enjoy *shariah*-compliant investing along with professional investment management.[1]

This seems counterintuitive in a time when all banks are seeking to bolster their off-balance-sheet revenue with business lines that involve small capital inputs and manageable regulatory environments. It also does not match what is obviously an important new area of business development in the asset management industry, matching new supply with an apparently large demand.

SHARIAH-COMPLIANT TOOTHPASTE

Recently reported in the *New York Times*[2] was an illustration of the lengths to which marketing specialists will go to reach the market of Muslims conscious of their spiritual identity. Colgate Palmolive and Unilever, for example, have launched new lines of shampoo and toothpaste that have been approved as *halal* and acceptable to Muslims (in these cases shampoo without pork fat derivatives and toothpaste without alcohol). Nokia has lines of mobile phones that specifically cater to the interests of Muslims. There are many other examples. One marketing specialist has remarked that ignoring this vast potential market is akin to ignoring the potential of China in the early 1990s. Another said that focusing on the individual needs of Muslims is the next big thing in marketing.

Anyone who spends any time in a predominantly Muslim country can witness the proximity of spirituality to daily life among the majority of adherents of the faith. Whether in Almaty or Riyadh, Kuala Lumpur or Karachi, there are hundreds of millions of Muslims who profess a faith that fills all aspects of their personal lives. And they have a very high savings rate.

Not wanting to sound crass, it is therefore very puzzling that global consumer product companies try to achieve market penetration with *halal* toothpaste, but that global—and even most regional—banks don't offer *shariah*-compliant investing. There is a gap, a very big divide, between the consumer products now offered to Muslims and what they evidently desire for allocation of their long-term savings. Islam matters to hundreds of millions of people, and it is not a trivial matter to them, whether in consuming food or in making investment decisions.

HISTORY OF ISLAMIC WEALTH AND ASSET MANAGEMENT

Prior to the financial crisis there were some dedicated efforts in this area. Wealth management units at Citi Private Banking and Merrill Lynch were relatively advanced in creating global platforms for Islamic asset management. Citi made the greatest advances, with real-world allocations that were being tested against the bank's own conventional portfolios. Merrill Lynch, while further behind, was compiling a dataset of the world's known *shariah*-compliant funds for an open architecture offering that would involve best-of-class portfolio allocations.

Both these units, unfortunately, were disbanded. Citibank's well-known travails caused the bank to end efforts toward a global platform for Islamic asset management, while Merrill Lynch teams were in place right up to and through the early days of its takeover by Bank of America, but were then disbanded. Since then neither has progressed in this sector, perhaps due to other priorities rebuilding bank balance sheets.

A third bank, HSBC Amanah Private Banking, made more progress than the others—mainly from Dubai. There a highly professional effort led to the establishment of fully *shariah*-compliant allocations for private clients, using some innovative techniques to overcome certain allocation hurdles (in particular for fixed-income allocations). However, before the crisis this service featured high minimum balances for new clients, usually above US$3 million. Further, the unit saw the typical staff changes that were common everywhere during the financial crisis, impeding the unit's progress toward more encompassing client generation. Today, under new staff, the unit is again offering investment across the full spectrum of asset classes. However, the growth of assets under management has not been stellar, and the unit does not seem to be advertising its existence widely to the broader market.

There are some other notable efforts to consider. The Family Office in Bahrain has for several years offered a fund product that encompasses all conventional asset classes (cash, fixed-income, equities, and alternative investments), but distribution and widespread allocations of this one-for-all product have not been excessively large.[3]

The new management team at Faisal Private Bank in Geneva, Switzerland, is said to soon be offering Islamic wealth management for individual customers, although the date of this service's launch is still unknown and the bank itself is recovering from zealous but failed investments in speculative real estate. It is said that the only truly dedicated Islamic wealth management unit in the world, with both size and experience, belongs to the family office of a well-known royal family in the lower Gulf region. However, its existence is not generally public knowledge, and even less is known about its allocations and track record.

When one considers that the worldwide managed wealth owned by Muslims is at least $2.5 trillion, and perhaps well above $3 trillion,[4] one has to ask why so little is available in the Islamic wealth and asset management space.

FOUNDATION WORK: A CONCEPTUAL FRAMEWORK

This section attempts to discuss the barriers to creating credible, professional *shariah*-compliant portfolios, and what steps can be taken to deliver this service to a wide audience of Muslims (and, in fact, non-Muslims, as *shariah* compliance equals social responsibility for many persons) who care about Islamic investing. It draws on earlier works by this author, in particular "Islamic wealth management" in the *Chancellor Guide to Shari'a & Legal Aspects of Islamic Finance*, and "Islamic wealth management" in the *Global Islamic Finance Report*.[5] The first of these articles presented the conceptual framework of Islamic wealth and asset management. It pointed out that wealth management is generally a term that describes the management of savings for individuals on a planned, professional basis, and asset management as being essentially the same activity but for institutional investors such as pension funds and endowments.

The article then described the traditional, industry-wide practice of establishing first the client's objectives, whether they were the head of a household or a pension fund, using standard measurements of current wealth, current and projected income, current and projected spending, and end-term valuation objectives. By laying these out in formulas that are well known in the industry (aka financial planning), one can determine the rates of return required to achieve specific savings goals, and then model portfolio allocations that have the potential to achieve those goals.

The article also described the process of allocation, rebalancing, reporting, and maintaining or altering investment strategies over time. It is centered on modern portfolio theory and its derivative conclusions, where one seeks optimal allocations based on expected return and the expected risk of a diversified pool of assets.

The most important conclusion of the article was that none of the steps in conventional wealth and asset management have any spiritual component, and instead are grounded in decades of scientific-type inquiry and testing, from which the modern industry was born. The lessons of wealth and asset management apply equally to people of all faiths. Only security selection causes Islamic wealth and asset management to differ from its conventional cousin.

FOUNDATION WORK: THE UNIVERSE OF *SHARIAH*-COMPLIANT ASSETS

After establishing the conceptual framework of Islamic wealth and asset management in the first article, the second article mentioned above took a more practical approach. It featured the results of an extensive survey of the *shariah*-compliant fund universe, starting with a total observed universe of more than 830 investment vehicles that were both Islamic and investment funds.

The survey continued with the typical filtering and sorting common among large asset management businesses that allow for open architecture investment, similar to what is done at, for example, Credit Suisse Fund Lab. There, third-party fund providers are invited to submit their funds for examination and possible adoption on to the bank's fund platform, which itself serves as the approved list for investment allocation decisions among the bank's many different asset management vehicles. Obtaining a position on such an approved list can mean many millions of dollars of new assets under management (AUM) for any fund, so knowing these criteria and meeting them is the goal of many fund managers worldwide.

Filtering and sorting are common practices on all mutual fund platforms, and include criteria of the number of years the fund has been actively managed (usually five years or more is required), the fund's AUM (often the minimum is set at US$100 million), and other important metrics, such as whether the fund can be internationally cleared and settled, has frequent and transparent reporting, and is relatively liquid (often such platforms require no more than monthly redemption rights).

These criteria were used to reduce the Islamic fund universe to a minimum subset that would meet standard professional requirements. However, it also added a criterion for *shariah* acceptance, i.e. whether the fund under examination had a *fatwa* with one or more signatures from about a dozen widely known and respected *shariah* scholars.

Using conventional criteria plus the *shariah* qualifying criterion, the number of funds was reduced to a minuscule 15 or so, too few to produce model portfolios that are fully allocated across all asset classes. To increase that number, the criteria were relaxed somewhat, with AUM limited to US$25 million or more and years in market at two years or more. Holding all other criteria constant, the universe of acceptable funds increased to just under 100, with almost US$30 billion total AUM, a subset deemed sufficient to achieve professional-standard allocations, as is displayed in Table 1.

The second article concluded by stating that this subset of funds can be used to professionally allocate investment funds owned by Muslims who want *shariah*-compliant investing, and that although shortcuts were made to achieve this subset, the overall environment existed where Islamic wealth and asset management could be professionally and responsibly achieved.

ISLAMIC MODEL PORTFOLIOS: REAL-WORLD ALLOCATIONS

Now we want to explore the next logical step: what happens over time when you

Table 1. The immaturity of the Islamic mutual fund market. (*Source*: Private research, Thom Polson[6])

Fund category	Number of funds	Assets under management	% of AUM
Money market	15	$9,785,093,000	33%
Sukuk	3	$118,740,000	0%
Equities	60	$11,851,334,000	40%
Real estate	5	$887,250,000	3%
Commodities	8	$5,935,261,000	20%
Portfolio strategy	8	$1,220,672,000	4%
Totals	**99**	**$29,798,349,350**	**100%**

"People would rather earn 60 grand in an area where their neighbours earn 40, than earn 80 in an area where their neighbours earn a hundred." John Lanchester

combine the existing universe of qualified Islamic mutual funds into a professional allocation for an institutional or individual client? In this regard, work has been done by this author and some others, although nothing approaching the parallel work that has been done to construct efficient portfolios in the conventional asset management space. Nevertheless, the preliminary results are very encouraging.

We start by taking a dataset for the years 2006, 2007, and 2008. This dataset represents a period that straddles the last days of the booming markets before the crisis and the first years of the crisis itself, so that the performance of an Islamic portfolio can be observed in both parts of the economic cycle. We have the benefit of data that truly represent the extremes of boom and bust, since what we experienced in the last few years was without precedent in modern times.

The underlying work on this dataset was performed in the last months of 2008 and the first two months of 2009. More up-to-date datasets need to be assembled to observe the performance of the portfolios in question in the post-crisis years. But it is presumed that after reading this article there will be some investment professionals who are eager to pursue further analysis of the conclusions presented here.

The dataset collected for this work represented the then-known and observable universe of Islamic investment products. The primary sources were Bloomberg, Reuters, and, importantly, Eurekahedge, although in some cases data were collected directly from fund managers themselves.

At that time the total universe represented approximately 600 funds, which have since increased by several hundred more. The same criteria explained above were used to filter and sort these funds, including years of performance history, minimum AUM, international clearing and settlement, and acceptable *fatwa*.

The data, however, also included funds with redemption rights up to three months, as it is common in the industry to permit a minority of assets in a client portfolio that do not enjoy more immediate liquidity. Some will argue that this alone causes the resulting portfolios to be unacceptable under conventional prudent-man rules common in most jurisdictions ("prudent man" refers to the appropriateness of any asset purchased for a customer, where the manager must judge whether such an asset is prudent given the underlying client's tolerance for risk and desire for reward).

However, we witnessed some very imprudent investing in the period 2003 through 2007 by some of the most respected names in wealth and asset management. What many considered prudent then would be rejected as extremely risky today. It is commonly known that one wellknown second-tier Swiss bank, for example, allocated fully 50% of all client funds into hedge funds and funds of hedge funds at the peak of the boom. When one considers the oversized fees earned by the manager of these products, one has to ask whether those allocations were made for the benefit of the clients or the bank.

Further, some industry analysts claim that as much as 25% of all hedge fund assets are still highly illiquid, and may remain illiquid for years to come.7 It is common knowledge that many hedge funds in the period up to the crash were heavily allocated into obscure assets that immediately went out of favor when the markets dropped, and have not yet returned to favor. Today there is still an unknown volume of assets in the hedge fund industry that may not see anywhere near their original valuations or liquidity for years to come.

Another phenomenon of the 2003–2007 boom was the proliferation of derivative-based structured products. It is well known that these products saw billions in sales, heavily favored in private client accounts but also present in institutional and treasury portfolios. Again, these products are among the most profitable (for banks) ever created by the banking industry, and were overwhelmingly sold through any and all channels. Today we can consider a great many of them useless to the average investor. Their appropriateness was in question at the time of sale, and remains equally dubious today. Many structured products suffered either total illiquidity or dramatic declines in valuation because of their derivative roots. The highly popular capital-guaranteed versions did indeed provide capital guarantees (unless, of course, they were guaranteed by Lehman Brothers, which many were), but at a high cost to the investor. They were virtually without value for anyone who tried to redeem them prior to expiration, which in many cases is years in the future.

So, when considering prudent-man regulations and Islamic mutual funds with only US$25 million AUM and a track record of less than five years, one has to argue over where there may or may not be substantial risk. Like their conventional cousins, most of the *shariah*-compliant funds in our qualifying subset suffered substantial losses, but also like their conventional cousins they rebounded with the markets as the crisis faded.

MODEL PORTFOLIOS AND INVESTMENT STRATEGIES

At this point it is important to remember that the disciplined, scientific-based process of asset allocation in the wealth and asset management industry begins with the creation of model portfolios, each representing the standard risk and reward appetites of common individual and institutional clients. It is not by mistake that the most common and universal investment strategies are income, balanced, and growth, as these three strategies encompass the investment goals and risk-aversion of nearly all investors. These strategies apply to everyone because we know that there is nothing spiritual about risk-aversion or appetite for reward.

An income strategy would, as the name implies, provide a high degree of cash yields. At the same time, capital preservation is an overwhelming objective, so income portfolios are always the least risky of the three main strategies. At the other end of the scale is the growth strategy, which also as the name implies tries to achieve growth of assets while sacrificing immediate cash gains. This is the most risky of the three main strategies.

In the conventional investment industry an income portfolio would allocate a large majority to guaranteed, fixed-income securities such as bonds, bond funds, and money market funds. Only a minority would be allocated into higher-risk investments such as real estate funds, equities, equity funds, commodities, foreign exchange trading, or hedge funds. The opposite is true for growth investing. In between is the widely accepted balanced strategy, which attempts to achieve both income and growth strategies in a balanced fashion. A balanced portfolio will have a lower percentage of cash (money market) and bond investments than income, but more than growth, along with larger amounts of more risky assets than income, and less than growth.

In fact, the balanced strategy is perhaps the most widely used template for investing anywhere, whether for Chilean pension funds, the California Endowment, Asian sovereign wealth funds, or Dutch family offices. Of course the actual percentages will vary, but not to a great degree. You will never see any prominent institutional investor heavily invested in stocks only. In sophisticated institutional portfolios one will rarely see any structured products at all. Hedge funds were increasingly visible in large institutional accounts for much of the past decade, but their growth has stalled parallel to the often dismal performance of hedge funds during the recent crisis.

"A society which reverences the attainment of riches as the supreme felicity will naturally be disposed to regard the poor as damned . . . if only to justify itself for making their life a hell." Richard Tawney

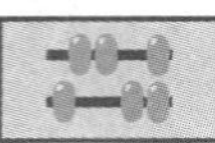

Among all managed accounts of all kinds worldwide, perhaps as much as 50% is allocated to the generically named fixed-income category. This includes the overwhelming majority of that 50% in the form of bonds and bond funds, including bonds of all types (sovereign, emerging market, high-grade corporate, junk, and asset-backed, plus many more). If Islamic wealth management is essentially no different from conventional wealth management—except for security selection—then one can conclude that *shariah*-compliant fixed-income should play an equally important role in Islamic wealth and asset management.

Interestingly, on a global basis it is clear that alternative investments play a relatively small role, yet have gained a disproportionate amount of media attention compared to their more boring cousins. Alternative investments feature as one of four main asset classes—cash, fixed-income, and equities being the other three. But they have rarely (with the exception of the Swiss bank mentioned above) been given more than 15% allocation in professionally managed portfolios.

Alternative investments include all hedge funds, whether or not they are delivered in a fund-of-funds structure. Also included are commodity funds, real estate funds, foreign exchange investing, and, importantly, any and all forms of venture capital (sometimes called private equity). By their nature alternative investments are high-risk and nearly always relatively illiquid, and therefore deservedly constitute the smallest portion of a professionally managed portfolio.

ASSET ALLOCATION FOR AN ISLAMIC MODEL PORTFOLIO

Money Market (Cash) Funds, 3%

Our subset of qualified *shariah*-compliant mutual funds constituted funds from all asset categories. In the cash (money market) segment we chose one of many available *murabahah* funds, such funds being invested according to *shariah* in short-term, low-risk trade finance transactions with very high-quality counterparty guarantees and producing returns equal to their conventional cousins.

Equity Funds, 35%

In the equities section we chose funds with a clear bias and overweight on emerging markets. And why not? Looking back at other allocations prior to the financial crisis, we see that many managers were also overweight in emerging markets or some other form of equity investing that had equivalent performance (and risk).

Here the selection of funds was relatively easy, as qualified Islamic equity funds by far outnumber the funds available in any other asset category. *Shariah*-compliant equity funds are no mystery: fund managers simply take the shares traded on one or many exchanges, filter them through conventional services such as the Dow Jones Islamic Market Index (DJIM), and then choose among the qualifying equities for their trading positions. The filters used by the DJIM are nearly identical to those used by the FTSE Shariah Global Equity Index or the MSCI Barra Global Islamic Index (and for all three the various subindices as well) and exclude the typical *haram* (forbidden) companies (alcohol, gaming, financials, etc.) and overleveraged companies (typically where debt comprises 33% or more of the balance sheet, or similar formula).

Alternative Investment Funds, 20%

For our alternative investment allocations we encountered some difficulties. We are trained to accept assets such as hedge funds, forex funds, real estate funds, and the like in our conventional allocations, and there we have no shyness about buying them preleveraged—i.e. where the fund manager has taken leveraged positions, sometimes to the extreme, in order to amplify his or her results (and greatly increase risks). However, in *shariah*-compliant investing such leverage is forbidden. That makes conventional-style hedge funds pretty much out of the question. It also makes most real estate funds far from acceptable, as well as nearly all foreign exchange trading, an asset category that is often heavily leveraged.

So what is left for alternative investments? We did find several real estate funds that met our criteria, one from HSBC Amanah that has since gone into lockup, another from Oasis in South Africa, and our favorite, a global real estate fund from Emirates NBD.

The second security in our model portfolio's alternative category was more difficult. We did find four *shariah*-compliant mutual funds on the Newedge platform, all sharing a single, respectable *fatwa*. But we soon discovered that one of them—from Old Mutual—had gone into liquidation, and information on the other three was difficult to obtain. Since those early allocation days we have not heard again about any of these *shariah*-compliant hedge funds and assume that they have all been shut down.

We also considered inserting structured products into this category. Structured products are based on derivatives, but as anyone from Deutsche Bank Private Banking will tell you, they can also be whipped into *shariah*-compliant versions of almost every flavor imaginable. Indeed, all major banks sold large volumes of these unusual products to thousands of investors throughout Arabia for several years. They were apparently most successful in their capital-guaranteed variety, where the investor is under the impression that he or she has no principal risk (forgetting, of course, the time value of money and opportunity cost, let alone inflation, all of which conspire to make these far from optimal investments).

The excessive fees built into almost all structured products are what finally forced us to abandon this as an acceptable asset for our model portfolio. The big banks had various levels of embedded fees, but we learned that some of them were charging as much as 10% at the time of purchase, a front-end load that's among the highest we have seen anywhere. It is hard to imagine the utility of these very expensive investments, let alone the ethical considerations of the banks that sold them.

Finally we lighted on a less than perfect solution for the second security in our alternative investments category: the NCB Capital AlManara High Growth fund of funds. In reality this fund goes into and out of other equity funds managed by NCB Capital, with the remaining balance in cash. Sometimes the cash portion is up to 70% or even more as the manager attempts to capture alpha in an active management style.

Technically this selection could well have been included in the equities section of our allocation, but in fact there were good arguments against putting it there. However, we felt that the fund was sufficiently "alternative" to merit inclusion in the alternative investment section of our Islamic model portfolio.

It is to be noted here that our selection process did not include any exchange-traded funds (ETF) or private equity funds. With regard to ETFs, there are still very few and—while we appreciate their utility in any portfolio and presumed lower trading and management costs— there were just not a sufficient number available that met our criteria for time in market. Future model portfolios would likely include one or more of the now widely available Islamic ETFs.

Private equity, a classic alternative investment, was also deliberately left out. In the conventional asset space there are almost no private equity (or venture capital) funds with any liquidity whatsoever. A hallmark of prudent-man investing—required by regulators everywhere—is the maintenance of a vast majority of a client's assets in liquid investments. Our Islamic

"I finally know what distinguishes man from the other beasts: financial worries." Jules Renard

model portfolio, therefore, would have none of this asset.

Fixed-Income Funds, 42%

I have saved the most problematic asset class, fixed-income, until last. Here we ran into serious difficulties, as in 2006 there were no *sukuk* funds that met even the minimum size or time-in-market criteria. Fixed-income comprises no less than 42% of our total allocation, so you can imagine our urgent need to find an honest proxy for the fixed-income section of the model.

Here we decided simply to insert the weighted performance of a basket of qualifying *sukuk* (i.e. investment-grade *sukuk* that had been previously issued and presumably would have been included in any professionally managed *sukuk* fund had one actually existed), less what we considered accurate fund management fees and costs, for the period January 2006 through September 2007. Thereafter we used the monthly performance of the *sukuk* fund from Jadwa Investment Co. in Riyadh, Saudi Arabia, to complete our three-year dataset. Since this model was created we have seen other *sukuk* funds appear, including what is now believed to be the biggest among them, a *sukuk* fund from the Qatar Islamic Bank in London.

PERFORMANCE OF THE MODEL ISLAMIC PORTFOLIO

We distilled the then-available data to create a single balanced allocation comprising diversified assets, and then ran our initial allocations through portfolio optimization software. Not surprisingly, the optimization exercise didn't alter our initial allocations by much, with, for example, the cash (money market) component falling from 5% to 2%, and the fixed-income component falling from 45% to 42%. We did, unfortunately, get an increased allocation in alternative investments. While we believe this was suboptimal, we ran the datasets anyway to find out the results.

The final optimized portfolio was then back-tested. In other words, we used the static subset of funds in our optimized portfolio as the base as of December 31, 2008, and then looked backward for the three previous calendar years to determine how well our Islamic balanced portfolio did in terms of performance.

The results were stunning, to say the least.

As indicated in Figure 1, the Islamic balanced strategy model portfolio ended the three-year period with a positive 15.3% performance. In comparison, a hypothetical and purely imaginary benchmark created from major investible indexes to somewhat reflect conventional balanced investing had a negative 8.4% performance in the same three years.

The difference is a startling 24 percentage points (Figure 1 and Table 2). Further measurements include those listed in Table 3.

The reference benchmark was simply weighted as follows: 50% Dow Jones Commercial Bond Index, five-year, investment-grade; 35% S&P 500; and 15% NASDAQ. Why this benchmark? Though far from perfect, it does in fact strikingly resemble conventional US dollar balanced strategy portfolios common in Western private banking. Of course, a true benchmark would have included far more indices tracking precisely the style of investing in our Islamic balanced portfolio, but we strongly believe that the final results would not have been greatly different.

SUMMARY RESULTS AND CONCLUSION

We have shown here that by reducing certain criteria in filtering and sorting third-party mutual funds to create a subset of professionally acceptable funds, and then allocating funds within that subset in a style replicating conventional balanced investing, we can in fact perform Islamic wealth and asset management. The performance results are superb, far beyond even our own initial estimations.

Figure 1. US dollar balance portfolio investing vs benchmark, 2006 through 2008

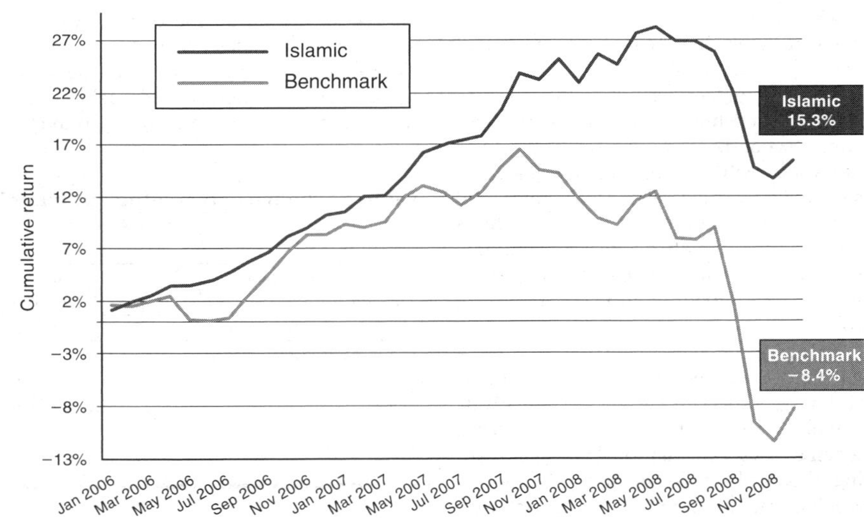

Table 2. Time-lapsed Islamic model portfolio. (*Source*: Encore Management, Geneva, 2009 Study)

	Jan	*Feb*	*Mar*	*Apr*	*May*	*Jun*	*Jul*	*Aug*	*Sep*	*Oct*	*Nov*	*Dec*	*Annual*
Islamic													
2008	−2.25	2.67	−0.97	2.98	0.67	−1.44	0.04	−1.06	−3.83	−7.25	−1.08	1.65	−9.89
2007	0.42	1.45	0.09	1.81	2.20	0.79	0.44	0.39	2.54	3.47	−0.51	1.95	15.05
2006	1.14	0.77	0.68	0.90	0.01	0.49	0.71	1.09	0.85	1.43	0.85	1.24	10.15
Benchmark													
2008	−2.48	−1.84	−0.73	2.53	0.83	−4.65	−0.07	1.13	−7.55	−11.11	−1.78	3.15	−22.56
2007	0.98	−0.26	0.46	2.44	1.10	−0.63	−1.23	1.28	2.30	1.77	−1.97	−0.34	5.89
2006	1.61	−0.06	0.49	0.41	−2.20	−0.16	0.31	2.16	1.92	2.16	1.57	0.10	8.30

"As long as there are rich people in the world, they will be desirous of distinguishing themselves from the poor."
Jean-Jacques Rousseau

  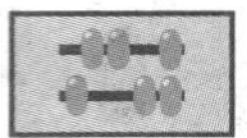      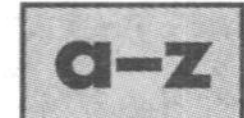

Table 3. Portfolio summary statistics

	Islamic	Benchmark
Annualized return	5.1%	− 2.8%
Annualized standard deviation	6.8%	9.8%
% of positive months	78%	56%
Sharpe ratio (4.0%)	0.16	−0.69
Correlation to Islamic	1.00	0.85
Return since inception	15.31%	− 8.37%

Why is this? Because:

- performance of the cash and fixed-income portions of our allocations fairly equaled their non-*shariah*-compliant conventional allocations, as did our alternative investments;
- Islamic investing completely avoided financial shares, meaning the dramatic drop in valuations of Western banking institutions during the financial crisis did not have nearly the effect on *shariah*-compliant investing that it did on conventional investing;
- Islamic investing had a heavier weighting in emerging-market shares, where there was in fact a dramatic drop in valuations during the crisis, but a sharp rebound afterward;
- Islamic investing avoided companies that were heavily indebted.

Of course further work can be done to make the benchmark above more precisely equal to our Islamic investment strategy, but there will still be massive losses in shares of over-leveraged companies and financial institutions. It is this author's opinion that no matter how a conventional benchmark is constructed, the outperformance of *shariah*-compliant investing will survive.

By any professional banker's measure, a 24 percentage point outperformance is stunning, especially when two relatively similar investment styles are compared together. Every conventional manager reading this will challenge and criticize the results, but if so, then we ask that they perform similar tests and provide the results. In our minds Islamic wealth and asset management of the kind described above gives investors real-world alternatives, without fee-heavy structured products, illiquid and opaque hedge funds, and hard-to-understand or inappropriate alternative investments such as private equity.

There will no doubt be plenty of critics of this approach to *shariah*-compliant investing. Chief among the skeptics will be those that say the results were compromised from the beginning because the filtering and sorting criteria were lowered. Some will argue that a mutual fund with less than $100 million AUM and less than a five-year track record is simply unacceptable.

To those critics this author will simply point to the many inappropriate and otherwise ineligible investment products that were thrown into client accounts over most of the last decade by some of the most respected names in wealth and asset management. Every banker reading these pages knows precisely what is discussed here.

I will not overemphasize the billions of dollars in client money placed into Madoff hedge funds, collateralized debt obligations backed by subprime mortgages, disreputable private equity funds, or overpriced structured products that eventually blew up with the collapse of AIG, Bear Stearns, and Lehman Brothers. Risk is in the process of being redefined and remeasured everywhere after some very shocking and disturbing allocation decisions in the past decade, so critics should be ready to provide more than just a critique of the criteria used to select our *shariah*-compliant subset of mutual funds.

Now we have time to reflect on what risk is and how to avoid it. To this author, the risk of a fund having only a two-year track record and less than $100 million AUM is really not in the same league at all as subprime collateralized debt obligations, structured derivative products, and private equity, of which very large volumes were sold to long-term conservative investors worldwide. In fact, one can say that greatly expanding the number of *shariah*-compliant mutual funds and their volume of AUM is not only an important goal in the Islamic banking community, but also a tremendous opportunity. One only has to compare what is currently available within the *shariah*-compliant space with what would be available if the Islamic mutual funds industry had matured.

Consider Table 4. In the "Should be" column we derive the estimated minimum amount of *shariah*-compliant assets that could have been invested in Islamic mutual funds had there been a broader, deeper, and more focused attempt to deliver these investment securities to Muslim investors. Compare that to what is actually invested in *shariah*-compliant funds, the "Actual" column. The gaps are enormous in every category.

We conclude that there is barely more than 10% of minimum market penetration today. Entrepreneurial spirits in major banks and mutual funds companies should see this for what it is—an opportunity to create and manage many more *shariah*-compliant funds, and profit from greater volumes of business in serving the interests of Muslim investors worldwide.

Table 4. The path to an efficient Islamic mutual fund market

Asset category	Actual AUM[8]	Capgemini allocation[9]	"Should be"[10] Islamic Funds AUM
Alternative investments	$7.1 billion	7%	$17.5 billion
Real estate	$0.89 billion	15%	$37.5 billion
Cash & deposits (*murabahah*)	$9.79 billion	20%	$50 billion
Fixed-income (*sukuk* funds)	$0.118 billion	30%	$75 billion
Equities	$11.8 billion	28%	$70 billion
Total	$29.8 billion	100%	$250 billion

MORE INFO

Books:

Sandwick, John A. "Islamic wealth management." In H. Dar and U. Moghul (eds). *The Chancellor Guide to the Legal and Shari'a Aspects of Islamic Finance*. London: Chancellor Publications, 2009a; pp. 105–126.

Sandwick, John A. "Islamic asset management: A review of the industry." In H. Dar and T. Azami (eds). *2010 Global Islamic Finance Report*. London: BMB Islamic UK, 2010a; pp. 71–78.

Articles:

Sandwick, John A. "If there's a will, there's a way." *Islamic Banking and Finance* 9 (May 2006a): 10–12.

Sandwick, John A. "Islamic wealth management." *Business Islamica* (November 2006b): 24–28.

Sandwick, John A. "Divergence of views, divergence of allocation." *Islamic Banking and Finance* 17 (June 2008): 19–21.

"It has been said that the love of money is the root of all evil. The want of money is so quite as truly." Samuel Butler

     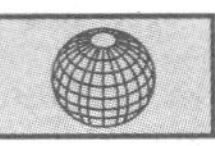   

Sandwick, John A. "Islamic asset management: Myth or reality?" *NewHorizon* 172 (July–September 2009b): 28–30.

Sandwick, John A. "Islamic asset management—Asia vs Arabia." *Islamic Finance News* 7:11 (March 17, 2010b): 12–13.

Sandwick, John A. "Where did all the money go? Private equity, investment banking and asset management in Arabia." *Business Islamica* (June 2010c). Online at: www.islamica-me.com/article.asp?cntnt=463

Website:

Additional resources on Islamic banking and wealth management may be found at the author's website: www.sandwick.ch/ResourcesPublication.html

See Also:

★ Asset Allocation Methodologies (pp. 454–458)
✔ Islamic Equity Funds (p. 1009)
✔ Key Principles of Islamic Finance (p. 1011)
✔ Possibilities for *Shariah*-Compliant Derivatives (p. 1013)

NOTES

1 The author apologizes for the fact that this article ignores the very substantial and real progress made in Malaysia in providing real-world solutions for Muslims seeking *shariah*-compliant investment management for their savings. No slight is intended. This article refers essentially to the rest of the world, where almost no progress has been made in developing and delivering credible Islamic wealth and asset management solutions.

2 "Advertisers seek to speak to Muslim consumers." *New York Times* (August 11, 2010).

3 For more information, see www.familyshariahfund.com

4 See Sandwick, 2009a.

5 Sandwick, 2009a; Sandwick, 2010a.

6 Chart first published in Sandwick, 2010a.

7 Interview with Jack Schwager, author of *Market Wizards* and *New Market Wizards*, February 2009.

8 Chart first published in Sandwick, 2010a.

9 See Capgemini *World Wealth Report 2010*, with projections for asset allocation by category. Online at: www.us.capgemini.com/worldwealthreport2010

10 "Should be" is based on a projection of 40% of the estimated minimum $2.5 trillion global Muslim managed wealth invested according to *shariah*, and 25% of that amount invested in *shariah*-compliant mutual funds (Sandwick, 2010a).

"As recently as the 1970s, the idea that the point of life was to get rich and that governments existed to facilitate this would have been ridiculed: not only by capitalism's traditional critics but also by many of its staunchest defenders."

Tony Judt

  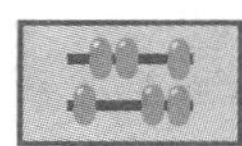      

Measuring Company Exposure to Country Risk by Aswath Damodaran

EXECUTIVE SUMMARY

- Following the piece on "Measuring Country Risk" (pp. xxx–xxx), we focus on a related question: Once we have estimated a country risk premium, how do we evaluate a company's exposure to country risk?
- In the process, we will argue that a company's exposure to country risk should not be determined by where it is incorporated and traded.
- By that measure, neither Coca-Cola nor Nestlé are exposed to country risk. Exposure to country risk should come from a company's operations, making country risk a critical component of the valuation of almost every large multinational corporation.

INTRODUCTION

If we accept the proposition of country risk, the next question that we have to address relates to the exposure of individual companies to country risk. Should all companies in a country with substantial country risk be equally exposed to country risk? While intuition suggests that they should not, we will begin by looking at standard approaches that assume that they are. We will follow up by scaling country risk exposure to established risk parameters such as betas (β), and complete the discussion with an argument that individual companies should be evaluated for exposure to country risk.

THE BLUDGEON APPROACH

The simplest assumption to make when dealing with country risk, and the one that is most often made, is that all companies in a market are equally exposed to country risk. The cost of equity for a firm in a market with country risk can then be written as:

$$\text{Cost of equity} = \text{Risk-free rate} + \beta\,(\text{Mature market premium}) + \text{Country risk premium}$$

Thus, for Brazil, where we have estimated a country risk premium of 4.43% from the melded approach, each company in the market will have an additional country risk premium of 4.43% added to its expected returns. For instance, the costs of equity for Embraer, an aerospace company listed in Brazil, with a beta[1] of 1.07 and Embratel, a Brazilian telecommunications company, with a beta of 0.80, in US dollar terms would be:

$$\text{Cost of equity for Embraer} = 3.80\% + 1.07(4.79\%) + 4.43\% = 13.35\%$$

$$\text{Cost of equity for Embratel} = 3.80\% + 0.80(4.79\%) + 4.43\% = 12.06\%$$

Note that the risk-free rate that we use is the US treasury bond rate (3.80%), and that the 4.79% figure is the equity risk premium for a mature equity market (estimated from historical data in the US market). It is also worth noting that analysts estimating the cost of equity for Brazilian companies, in US dollar terms, often use the Brazilian ten-year dollar-denominated rate as the risk-free rate. This is dangerous, since it is often also accompanied with a higher risk premium, and ends up double counting risk.

THE BETA APPROACH

For those investors who are uncomfortable with the notion that all companies in a market are equally exposed to country risk, a fairly simple alternative is to assume that a company's exposure to country risk is proportional to its exposure to all other market risk, which is measured by the beta. Thus, the cost of equity for a firm in an emerging market can be written as follows:

$$\text{Cost of equity} = \text{Risk-free rate} + \beta\,(\text{Mature market premium} + \text{Country risk premium})$$

In practical terms, scaling the country risk premium to the beta of a stock implies that stocks with betas above 1.00 will be more exposed to country risk than stocks with a beta below 1.00. For Embraer, with a beta of 1.07, this would lead to a dollar cost of equity estimate of:

$$\text{Cost of equity for Embraer} = 3.80\% + 1.07(4.79\% + 4.43\%) = 13.67\%$$

For Embratel, with its lower beta of 0.80, the cost of equity is:

$$\text{Cost of equity for Embratel} = 3.80\% + 0.80(4.79\% + 4.43\%) = 11.18\%$$

The advantage of using betas is that they are easily available for most firms. The disadvantage is that while betas measure overall exposure to macroeconomic risk, they may not be good measures of country risk.

THE LAMBDA APPROACH

The most general, and our preferred, approach is to allow for each company to have an exposure to country risk that is different from its exposure to all other market risk. For lack of a better term, let us term the measure of a company's exposure to country risk to be lambda (λ). Like a beta, a lambda will be scaled around 1.00, with a lambda of 1.00 indicating a company with average exposure to country risk and a lambda above or below 1.00 indicating above or below average exposure to country risk. The cost of equity for a firm in an emerging market can then be written as:

$$\text{Expected return} = R_f + \beta\,(\text{Mature market equity risk premium}) + \lambda(\text{Country risk premium})$$

Note that this approach essentially converts our expected return model to a two-factor model, with the second factor being country risk, with λ measuring exposure to country risk.

Determinants of Lambda

Most investors would accept the general proposition that different companies in a market should have different exposures to country risk. But what are the determinants of this exposure? We would expect at least three factors (and perhaps more) to play a role.

1 *Revenue source*: The first and most obvious determinant is how much of the revenues a firm derives from the country in question. A company that derives 30% of its revenues from Brazil should be less exposed to Brazilian country risk than a company that derives 70% of its revenues from Brazil. Note, though, that this then opens up the possibility that a company can be exposed to the risk in many countries. Thus, the company that derives only 30% of its revenues from Brazil may derive its remaining revenues from Argentina and Venezuela, exposing it to country risk in those countries. Extending this argument to multinationals, we would argue that companies like Coca-Cola and Nestlé can have substantial exposure to country risk because so much of their revenues comes from emerging markets.

2 *Production facilities*: A company can be exposed to country risk, even if it derives

"**Every man will speak of the fair as his own market has gone in it.**" Laurence Sterne

no revenues from that country, if its production facilities are in that country. After all, political and economic turmoil in the country can throw off production schedules and affect the company's profits. Companies that can move their production facilities elsewhere can spread their risk across several countries, but the problem is exaggerated for those companies that cannot move their production facilities. Consider the case of mining companies. An African gold mining company may export all of its production but it will face substantial country risk exposure because its mines are not movable.

3 *Risk management products*: Companies that would otherwise be exposed to substantial country risk may be able to reduce this exposure by buying insurance against specific (unpleasant) contingencies and by using derivatives. A company that uses risk management products should have a lower exposure to country risk–a lower lambda–than an otherwise similar company that does not use these products.

Ideally, we would like companies to be forthcoming about all three of these factors in their financial statements.

Measuring Lambda

The simplest measure of lambda is based entirely on revenues. In the last section, we argued that a company that derives a smaller proportion of its revenues from a market should be less exposed to country risk. Given the constraint that the average lambda across all stocks has to be 1.0 (someone has to bear the country risk!), we cannot use the percentage of revenues that a company gets from a market as lambda. We can, however, scale this measure by dividing it by the percentage of revenues that the average company in the market gets from the country to derive a lambda.

$$\frac{(\lambda_j - \text{\% of revenue in country}_{\text{Company}})}{\text{\% of revenue in country}_{\text{Average company in market}}}$$

Consider the two large and widely followed Brazilian companies–Embraer, an aerospace company that manufactures and sells aircraft to many of the world's leading airlines, and Embratel, the Brazilian telecommunications giant. In 2002, Embraer generated only 3% of its revenues in Brazil, whereas the average company in the market obtained 85% of its revenues in Brazil.[2] Using the measure suggested above, the lambda for Embraer would be:

$$\lambda_{\text{Embraer}} = \frac{3\%}{85\%} = 0.04$$

In contrast, Embratel generated 95% of its revenues from Brazil, giving it a lambda of

$$\lambda_{\text{Embratel}} = \frac{95\%}{85\%} = 1.12$$

Following up, Embratel is far more exposed to country risk than Embraer and will have a much higher cost of equity.

The second measure draws on the stock prices of a company and how they move in relation to movements in country risk. Bonds issued by countries offer a simple and updated measure of country risk; as investor assessments of country risk become more optimistic, bonds issued by that country go up in price, just as they go down when investors become more pessimistic. A regression of the returns on a stock against the returns on a country bond should therefore yield a measure of lambda in the slope coefficient. Applying this approach to Embraer and Embratel, we regressed monthly stock returns on the two stocks against monthly returns on the ten-year dollar-denominated Brazilian government bond and arrived at the following results:

$$\text{Return}_{\text{Embraer}} = 0.0195 + 0.2681\ \text{Return}_{\text{Brazil dollar–bond}}$$

$$\text{Return}_{\text{Embratel}} = -0.0308 + 2.0030\ \text{Return}_{\text{Brazil dollar–bond}}$$

Based upon these regressions, Embraer has a lambda of 0.27 and Embratel has a lambda of 2.00. The resulting dollar costs of equity for the two firms, using a mature market equity risk premium of 4.79% and a country equity risk premium of 4.43% for Brazil are:

$$\text{Cost of equity for Embraer} = 3.80\% + 1.07\ (4.79\%) + 0.27\ (4.43\%) = 10.12\%$$

$$\text{Cost of equity for Embratel} = 3.80\% + 0.80\ (4.79\%) + 2.00\ (4.43\%) = 16.49\%$$

What are the limitations of this approach? The lambdas estimated from these regressions are likely to have large standard errors; the standard error in the lambda estimate of Embratel is 0.35. It also requires that the country have bonds that are liquid and widely traded, preferably in a more stable currency (dollar or euro).

Risk Exposure in Many Countries

The discussion of lambdas in the last section should highlight a fact that is often lost in valuation. The exposure to country risk, whether it is measured in revenues, earnings, or stock prices, does not come from where a company is incorporated but from its operations. There are US companies that are more exposed to Brazilian country risk than is Embraer. In fact, companies like Nestlé, Coca-Cola, and Gillette have built much of their success on expansion into emerging markets. While this expansion has provided them with growth opportunities, it has also left them exposed to country risk in multiple countries.

In practical terms, what does this imply? When estimating the costs of equity and capital for these companies and others like them, we will need to incorporate an extra premium for country risk. Thus, the net effect on value from their growth strategies will depend upon whether the growth effect (from expanding into emerging markets) exceeds the risk effect. We can adapt the measures suggested above to estimate the risk exposure to different countries for an individual company.

We can break down a company's revenue by country and use the percentage of revenues that the company gets from each emerging market as a basis for estimating lambda in that market. While the percentage of revenues itself can be used as a lambda, a more precise estimate would scale this to the percentage of revenues that the average company in that market gets in the country.

If companies break earnings down by country, these numbers can be used to estimate lambdas. The peril with this approach is that the reported earnings often reflect accounting allocation decisions and differences in tax rates across countries.

If a company is exposed to only a few emerging markets on a large scale, we can regress the company's stock price against

MORE INFO

Book:

Falaschetti, Dominic, and Michael Annin Ibbotson (eds). *Stocks, Bonds, Bills and Inflation*. Chicago, IL: Ibbotson Associates, 1999.

Articles:

Booth, Laurence. "Estimating the equity risk premium and equity costs: New ways of looking at old data." *Journal of Applied Corporate Finance* 12:1 (Spring 1999): 100–112. Online at: dx.doi.org/10.1111/j.1745-6622.1999.tb00665.x

Chan, K. C., G. Andrew Karolyi, and René M. Stulz. "Global financial markets and the risk premium on US equity." *Journal of Financial Economics* 32:2 (October 1992): 137–167. Online at: dx.doi.org/10.1016/0304-405X(92)90016-Q

the country bond returns from those markets to get country-specific lambdas.

CONCLUSION

A key issue, when estimating costs of equity and capital for emerging market companies relates to how this country risk premium should be reflected in the costs of equities of individual companies in that country. While the standard approaches add the country risk premium as a constant to the cost of equity of every company in that market, we argue for a more nuanced approach where a company's exposure to country risk is measured with a lambda. This lambda can be estimated either by looking at how much of a company's revenues or earnings come from the country—the greater the percentage, the greater the lambda—or by regressing a company's stock returns against country bond returns—the greater the sensitivity, the higher the lambda. If we accept this view of the world, the costs of equity for multinationals that have significant operations in emerging markets will have to be adjusted to reflect their exposure to risk in these markets.

Damodaran, Aswath. "Country risk and company exposure: Theory and practice." *Journal of Applied Finance* 13:2 (Fall/Winter 2003): 64–78.

Godfrey, Stephen, and Ramon Espinosa. "A practical approach to calculating the cost of equity for investments in emerging markets." *Journal of Applied Corporate Finance* 9:3 (Fall 1996): 80–90. Online at: dx.doi.org/10.1111/j.1745-6622.1996.tb00300.x

Indro, Daniel C., and Wayne Y. Lee. "Biases in arithmetic and geometric averages as estimates of long-run expected returns and risk premium." *Financial Management* 26:4 (Winter 1997): 81–90. Online at: www.jstor.org/stable/3666130

Stulz, René M. "Globalization, corporate finance, and the cost of capital." *Journal of Applied Corporate Finance* 12:3 (Fall 1999): 8–25. Online at: dx.doi.org/10.1111/j.1745-6622.1999.tb00027.x

Report:

Damodaran, Aswath. "Measuring company risk exposure to country risk: Theory and practice." September 2003. Online at: www.stern.nyu.edu/~adamodar/pdfiles/papers/CountryRisk.pdf

See Also:

★ Credit Ratings (pp. 478–480)
★ Measuring Country Risk (pp. 537–539)
★ Public–Private Partnerships in Emerging Markets (pp. 563–566)
★ Using Structured Products to Manage Liabilities (pp. 115–117)
✔ Derivatives Markets: Their Structure and Function (p. 1007)
✔ Understanding the Components of an Insurance Contract (p. 1021)
✔ Understanding the Relationship between the Discount Rate and Risk (p. 1001)

NOTES

1 We used a bottom-up beta for Embraer, based upon an unlevered beta of 0.95 (estimated using aerospace companies listed globally) and Embraer's debt-to-equity ratio of 19.01%. For more on the rationale for bottom-up betas, read the companion paper on estimating risk parameters, "Measuring Country Risk" (pp. xxx–xxx).

2 To use this approach, we need to estimate the percentage of revenues both for the firm in question and for the average firm in the market. While the former may be simple to obtain, estimating the latter can be a time-consuming exercise. One simple solution is to use data that are publicly available on how much of a country's gross domestic product comes from exports. According to the World Bank data in this table, Brazil got 23.2% of its GDP from exports in 2008. If we assume that this is an approximation of export revenues for the average firm, the average firm can be assumed to generate 76.8% of its revenues domestically. Using this value would yield slightly higher betas for both Embraer and Embratel.

"A spirit of national masochism prevails, encouraged by an effete corps of impudent snobs who characterize themselves as intellectuals." Spiro Agnew

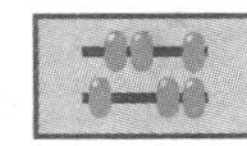

Measuring Country Risk by Aswath Damodaran

EXECUTIVE SUMMARY

- As companies and investors globalize and financial markets expand around the world, we are increasingly faced with estimation questions about the risk associated with this globalization.
- When investors invest in Petrobras, Gazprom, and China Power, they may be rewarded with higher returns, but they are also exposed to additional risk.
- When US and European multinationals push for growth in Asia and Latin America, they are clearly exposed to the political and economic turmoil that often characterize these markets.
- In practical terms, how, if at all, should we adjust for this additional risk? We review the discussion on country risk premiums and how to estimate them.

INTRODUCTION

Two key questions must be addressed when investing in emerging markets in Asia, Latin America, and Eastern Europe. The first relates to whether we should impose an additional risk premium when valuing equities in these markets. As we will see, the answer will depend upon whether we view markets to be open or segmented and whether we believe the risk can be diversified away. The second question relates to estimating an equity risk premium for emerging markets.

SHOULD THERE BE A COUNTRY RISK PREMIUM?

Is there more risk in investing in Malaysian or Brazilian equities than there is in investing in equities in the United States? Of course! But that does not automatically imply that there should be an additional risk premium charged when investing in those markets. Two arguments are generally used against adding an additional premium.

Country risk can be diversified away: If the additional risk of investing in Malaysia or Brazil can be diversified away, then there should be no additional risk premium charged. But for country risk to be diversifiable, two conditions must be met:

1 The marginal investors—i.e., active investors who hold large positions in the stock—have to be globally diversified. If the marginal investors are either unable or unwilling to invest globally, companies will have to diversify their operations across countries, which is a much more difficult and expensive exercise.

2 All or much of country risk should be country-specific. In other words, there should be low correlation across markets. If the returns across countries are positively correlated, country risk has a market risk component, is not diversifiable, and can command a premium. Whereas studies in the 1970s indicated low or no correlation across markets, increasing diversification on the part of both investors and companies has increased the correlation numbers. This is borne out by the speed with which troubles in one market can spread to a market with which it has little or no obvious relationship—say Brazil—and this contagion effect seems to become stronger during crises.

Given that both conditions are difficult to meet, we believe that on this basis, country risk should command a risk premium.

The expected cash flows for country risk can be adjusted: This second argument used against adjusting for country risk is that it is easier and more accurate to adjust the expected cash flows for the risk. However, adjusting the cash flows to reflect expectations about dire scenarios, such as nationalization or an economic meltdown, is not risk adjustment. Making the risk adjustment to cash flows requires the same analysis that we will employ to estimate the risk adjustment to discount rates.

ESTIMATING A COUNTRY RISK PREMIUM

If country risk is not diversifiable, either because the marginal investor is not globally diversified or because the risk is correlated across markets, we are left with the task of measuring country risk and estimating country risk premiums. In this section, we will consider two approaches that can be used to estimate country risk premiums. One approach builds on historical risk premiums and can be viewed as the *historical risk premium plus approach*. In the other approach, we estimate the equity risk premium by looking at how the market prices stocks and expected cash flows—this is the *implied premium approach*.

Historical Premium Plus

Most practitioners, when estimating risk premiums in the United States, look at the past. Consequently, we look at what we would have earned as investors by investing in equities as opposed to investing in riskless investments. With emerging markets, we will almost never have access to as much historical data as we do in the United States. If we combine this with the high volatility in stock returns in such markets, the conclusion is that historical risk premiums can be computed for these markets, but they will be useless because of the large standard errors in the estimates. Consequently, many analysts build their equity risk premium estimates for emerging markets from mature market historical risk premiums.

$$\text{Equity risk premium}_{\text{Emerging market}} = \text{Equity risk premium}_{\text{Mature market}} + \text{Country risk premium}$$

To estimate the base premium for a mature equity market, we will make the argument that the US equity market is a mature market and that there is sufficient historical data in the United States to make a reasonable estimate of the risk premium. Using the historical data for the United States, we estimate the geometric average premium earned by stocks over treasury bonds of 4.79% between 1928 and 2007. To estimate the country risk premium, we can use one of three approaches:

Country Bond Default Spreads

One of the simplest and most easily accessible country risk measures is the rating assigned to a country's debt by a ratings agency (S&P, Moody's, and IBCA all rate countries). These ratings measure default risk (rather than equity risk), but they are affected by many of the factors that drive equity risk—the stability of a country's currency, its budget and trade balances and its political stability for instance.[1] The other advantage of ratings is that they can be used to estimate default spreads over a riskless rate. For instance, Brazil was rated Ba1 in September 2008 by Moody's and the ten-year Brazilian ten-year dollar-denominated bond was priced to yield 5.95%, 2.15% more than the interest rate (3.80%) on a ten-year US treasury bond at the same time.[2] Analysts who use default spreads as measures of country risk typically add them on to the cost of both equity and debt of every company traded in that country. If we assume that the total equity risk premium for the United States and other mature equity markets is 4.79%, the risk premium for Brazil would be 6.94%.[3]

Relative Standard Deviation

There are some analysts who believe that the equity risk premiums of markets should reflect the differences in equity risk, as

"Change is an attitude of mind and the place to start is within ourselves." John Harvey-Jones measured by the volatilities of equities in these markets. A conventional measure of equity risk is the standard deviation in stock prices; higher standard deviations are generally associated with more risk. If we scale the standard deviation of one market against another, we obtain a measure of relative risk.

$$\text{Relative standard deviation}_{\text{Country X}} = \frac{\text{Standard deviation}_{\text{Country X}}}{\text{Standard deviation}_{\text{US}}}$$

This relative standard deviation when multiplied by the premium used for US stocks should yield a measure of the total risk premium for any market.

$$\text{Equity risk premium}_{\text{Country X}} = \text{Risk premium}_{\text{US}} \times \text{Relative standard deviation}_{\text{Country X}}$$

Assume, for the moment, that we are using a mature market premium for the United States of 4.79%. The annualized standard deviation in the S&P 500 between 2006 and 2008, using weekly returns, was 15.27%, whereas the standard deviation in the Bovespa (the Brazilian equity index) over the same period was 25.83%.[4] Using these values, the estimate of a total risk premium for Brazil would be as follows:

$$\text{Equity risk premium}_{\text{Brazil}} = 4.79\% \times \frac{25.83\%}{15.27\%} = 8.10\%$$

The country risk premium can be isolated as follows:

$$\text{Country risk premium}_{\text{Brazil}} = 8.10\% - 4.79\% = 3.31\%$$

While this approach has intuitive appeal, there are problems with comparing standard deviations computed in markets with widely different market structures and liquidity. There are very risky emerging markets that have low standard deviations for their equity markets because the markets are illiquid. This approach will understate the equity risk premiums in those markets.

Default Spreads and Relative Standard Deviations

The country default spreads that come with country ratings provide an important first step, but still only measure the premium for default risk. Intuitively, we would expect the country equity risk premium to be larger than the country default risk spread. To address the issue of how much higher, we look at the volatility of the equity market in a country relative to the volatility of the bond market used to estimate the spread. This yields the following estimate for the country equity risk premium.

$$\text{Country risk premium} = \text{Country default spread} \times \frac{\sigma\ \text{Equity}}{\sigma\ \text{Country bond}}$$

To illustrate, consider again the case of Brazil. As noted earlier, the default spread on the Brazilian dollar-denominated bond in September 2008 was 2.15%, and the annualized standard deviation in the Brazilian equity index over the previous year was 25.83%. Using two years of weekly returns, the annualized standard deviation in the Brazilian dollar-denominated ten-year bond was 12.55%.[5] The resulting country equity risk premium for Brazil is as follows:

$$\text{Additional equity risk premium}_{\text{Brazil}} = 2.15\% \times \frac{25.83\%}{12.55\%} = 4.43\%$$

Unlike the equity standard deviation approach, this premium is in addition to a mature market equity risk premium. Note that this country risk premium will increase if the country rating drops or if the relative volatility of the equity market increases. It is also in addition to the equity risk premium for a mature market. Thus, the total equity risk premium for Brazil using this approach and a 4.79% premium for the United States would be 9.22%.

Both this approach and the previous one use the standard deviation in equity of a market to make a judgment about country risk premium, but they measure it relative to different bases. This approach uses the country bond as a base, whereas the previous one uses the standard deviation in the US market. It also assumes that investors are more likely to choose between Brazilian government bonds and Brazilian equity, whereas the previous approach assumes that the choice is across equity markets.

Implied Equity Premiums

There is an alternative approach to estimating risk premiums that does not require historical data or corrections for country risk but does assume that the market, overall, is correctly priced. Consider, for instance, a very simple valuation model for stocks:

$$\text{Value} = \frac{\text{Expected dividends next period}}{(\text{Required return on equity} - \text{Expected growth rate})}$$

This is essentially the present value of dividends growing at a constant rate. Three of the four inputs in this model can be obtained externally—the current level of the market (value), the expected dividends next period, and the expected growth rate in earnings and dividends in the long term. The only "unknown" is then the required return on equity; when we solve for it, we get an implied expected return on stocks. Subtracting out the risk-free rate will yield an implied equity risk premium. We can extend the model to allow for dividends to grow at high rates, at least for short periods.

The advantage of the implied premium approach is that it is market-driven and current, and it does not require any historical data. Thus, it can be used to estimate implied equity premiums in any market. For instance, the equity risk premium for the Brazilian equity market on September 9, 2008, was estimated from the following inputs. The index (Bovespa) was at 48,345 and the current cash flow yield on the index was 5.41%. Earnings in companies in the index are expected to grow 9% (in US dollar terms) over the next five years, and 3.8% thereafter. These inputs yield a required return on equity of 10.78%, which when compared to the treasury bond rate of 3.80% on that day results in an implied equity premium of 6.98%. For simplicity, we have used nominal dollar expected growth rates[6] and treasury bond rates, but this analysis could have been done entirely in the local currency. We can decompose this number into a mature market equity risk premium and a country-specific equity risk premium by comparing it to the implied equity risk premium for a mature equity market (the United States, for instance).

- Implied equity premium for Brazil (see above) = 6.98%.
- Implied equity premium for the United States in September 2008 = 4.54%.
- Country specific equity risk premium for Brazil = 2.44%.

This approach can yield numbers very different from the other approaches,

MORE INFO

Book:

Falaschetti, Dominic, and Michael Annin Ibbotson (eds). *Stocks, Bonds, Bills and Inflation*. Chicago, IL: Ibbotson Associates, 1999.

Articles:

Booth, Laurence. "Estimating the equity risk premium and equity costs: New ways of looking at old data." *Journal of Applied Corporate Finance* 12:1 (Spring 1999): 100–112. Online at: dx.doi.org/10.1111/j.1745-6622.1999.tb00665.x

"Forget about winning and losing; forget about pride and pain. Let your opponent graze your skin and you smash into his flesh; let him smash into your flesh and you fracture his bones; let him fracture your bones and you take his life. Do not be concerned with escaping safely - lay your life before him." Bruce Lee

     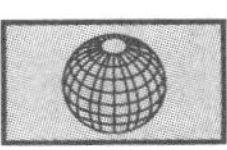   

because they reflect market prices (and views) today.

CONCLUSION

As companies expand operations into emerging markets and investors search for investment opportunities in Asia and Latin America, they are also increasingly exposed to additional risk in these countries. While it is true that globally diversified investors can eliminate some country risk by diversifying across equities in many countries, the increasing correlation across markets suggests that country risk cannot be entirely diversified away. To estimate the country risk premium, we considered three measures: the default spread on a government bond issued by that country, a premium obtained by scaling up the equity risk premium in the United States by the volatility of the country equity market relative to the US equity market, and a melded premium where the default spread on the country bond is adjusted for the higher volatility of the equity market. We also estimated an implied equity premium from stock prices and expected cash flows.

Chan, K. C., G. Andrew Karolyi, and René M. Stulz. "Global financial markets and the risk premium on US equity." *Journal of Financial Economics* 32:2 (October 1992): 137–167. Online at: dx.doi.org/10.1016/0304-405X(92)90016-Q

Indro, D. C., and W. Y. Lee. "Biases in arithmetic and geometric averages as estimates of long-run expected returns and risk premium." *Financial Management* 26:4 (Winter 1997): 81–90. Online at: www.jstor.org/stable/3666130

Report:

Damodaran, Aswath. "Equity risk premiums (ERP): Determinants, estimation and implications." October 2008. Online at: www.stern.nyu.edu/~adamodar/pdfiles/papers/ERPfull.pdf

See Also:

★ Credit Ratings (pp. 478–480)
★ Measuring Company Exposure to Country Risk (pp. 534–536)
★ Political Risk: Countering the Impact on Your Business (pp. 902–904)
★ Public–Private Partnerships in Emerging Markets (pp. 563–566)
★ Understanding the Role of Diversification (pp. 617–618)
✔ How to Use Credit Rating Agencies (p. 1073)
✔ Understanding the Relationship between the Discount Rate and Risk (p. 1001)
Prince Al-Walid bin Talal (p. 1268)

NOTES

1 The process by which country ratings are obtained is explained on the S&P website at www2.standardandpoors.com/aboutcreditratings

2 These yields were as of January 1, 2008. While this is a market rate and reflects current expectations, country bond spreads are extremely volatile and can shift significantly from day to day. To counter this volatility, the default spread can be normalized by averaging the spread over time or by using the average default spread for all countries with the same rating as Brazil in early 2008.

3 If a country has a sovereign rating and no dollar-denominated bonds, we can use a typical spread based upon the rating as the default spread for the country. These numbers are available on my website at www.damodaran.com

4 If the dependence on historical volatility is troubling, the options market can be used to get implied volatilities for both the US market (about 20%) and for the Bovespa (about 38%).

5 Both standard deviations are computed on returns: returns on the equity index and returns on the ten-year bond.

6 The input that is most difficult to estimate for emerging markets is a long-term expected growth rate. For Brazilian stocks, I used the average consensus estimate of growth in earnings for the largest Brazilian companies which have ADRs listed on them. This estimate may be biased as a consequence.

"You cannot control what happens to you, but you can control your attitude toward what happens to you, and in that, you will be mastering change rather than allowing it to master you." Brian Tracy

  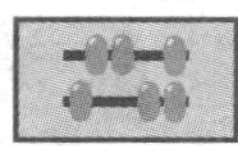   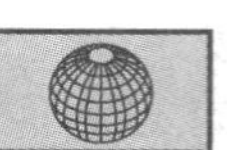   

Minimizing Credit Risk by Frank J. Fabozzi

EXECUTIVE SUMMARY

- Credit risk encompasses credit default risk, credit spread risk, and downgrade risk.
- Market participants typically gauge credit default risk in terms of the credit rating assigned by rating agencies.
- Factors that are considered in the evaluation of a corporate borrower's creditworthiness are: the quality of management; the ability of the borrower to satisfy the debt obligation; the level of seniority and the collateral available in a bankruptcy proceeding; and covenants.
- Credit risk transfer vehicles allow the redistribution of credit risk.
- Securitization is a credit risk transfer vehicle for corporations that is accomplished by selling a pool of loans or receivables to a third-party entity.
- Credit derivatives are a form of credit risk transfer vehicle.

INTRODUCTION

Financial corporations and investors face several types of risk. One major risk is credit risk. Despite the fact that market participants typically refer to "credit risk" as if it is one-dimensional, there are actually three forms of this risk: credit default risk, credit spread risk, and downgrade risk.

Credit default risk is the risk that the issuer will fail to satisfy the terms of the obligation with respect to the timely payment of interest and repayment of the amount borrowed. This form of credit risk covers counterparty risk in a trade or derivative transaction where the counterparty fails to satisfy its obligation. To gauge credit default risk, investors typically rely on credit ratings. A *credit rating* is a formal opinion given by a company referred to as a *rating agency* of the credit default risk faced by investing in a particular issue of debt securities. For long-term debt obligations, a credit rating is a forward-looking assessment of the probability of default and the relative magnitude of the loss should a default occur. For short-term debt obligations, a credit rating is a forward-looking assessment of the probability of default. The nationally recognized rating agencies include Moody's Investors Service, Standard & Poor's, and Fitch Ratings.

Credit spread risk is the loss or underperformance of an issue or issues due to an increase in the credit spread. The credit spread is the compensation sought by investors for accepting the credit default risk of an issue or issuer. The credit spread varies with market conditions and the credit rating of the issue or issuer. On the issuer side, credit spread risk is the risk that an issuer's credit spread will increase when it must come to market to offer bonds, resulting in a higher funding cost.

Downgrade risk is the risk that an issue or issuer will be downgraded, resulting in an increase in the credit spread demanded by the market. Hence, downgrade risk is related to credit spread risk. Occasionally, the ability of an issuer to make interest and principal payments diminishes seriously and unexpectedly because of an unforeseen event. This can include any number of idiosyncratic events that are specific to the corporation or to an industry, including a natural or industrial accident, a regulatory change, a takeover or corporate restructuring, or corporate fraud. This risk is referred to generically as *event risk* and will result in a downgrading of the issuer by the rating agencies.

FACTORS CONSIDERED IN ASSESSING CREDIT DEFAULT RISK

The most obvious way to protect against credit risk is to analyze the creditworthiness of the borrower. In performing such an analysis, credit analysts evaluate the factors that affect the business risk of a borrower. These factors can be classified into four general categories—the quality of the borrower; the ability of the borrower to satisfy the debt obligation; the level of seniority and the collateral available in a bankruptcy proceeding; and restrictions imposed on the borrower.

In the case of a corporation, the quality of the borrower involves assessing the firm's business strategies and management policies. More specifically, a credit analyst will study the corporation's strategic plan, accounting control systems, and financial philosophy regarding the use of debt. In assigning a credit rating, Moody's states:

"Although difficult to quantify, management quality is one of the most important factors supporting an issuer's credit strength. When the unexpected occurs, it is a management's ability to react appropriately that will sustain the company's performance."[1]

The ability of the borrower to meet its obligations begins with the analysis of the borrower's financial statements. Commonly used measures of liquidity and debt coverage combined with estimates of future cash flows are calculated and investigated if there are concerns. In addition, the analysis considers industry trends, the borrower's basic operating and competitive position, sources of liquidity (backup lines of credit), and, if applicable, the regulatory environment. An investigation of industry trends aids a credit analyst in assessing the vulnerability of the firm to economic cycles, the barriers to entry, and the exposure of the company to technological changes. An investigation of the borrower's various lines of business aids the credit analyst in assessing the firm's basic operating position.

A credit analyst will look at the position as a creditor in the case of a bankruptcy. The US Bankruptcy Act comprises 15 chapters, each covering a particular type of bankruptcy. Of particular interest here are Chapter 7, which deals with the liquidation of a company, and Chapter 11, which deals with the reorganization of a company. When a company is liquidated, creditors receive distributions based on the *absolute priority rule* to the extent that assets are available. The absolute priority rule is the principle that senior creditors are paid in full before junior creditors are paid anything. For secured creditors and unsecured creditors, the absolute priority rule guarantees their seniority to equity holders. However, in the case of a reorganization, the absolute priority rule rarely holds because in practice unsecured creditors do in fact typically receive distributions for the entire amount of their claim and common stockholders may receive something, while secured creditors may receive only a portion of their claim. The reason is that a reorganization requires the approval of all the parties. Consequently, secured creditors are willing to negotiate with both unsecured creditors and stockholders in order to obtain approval of the plan of reorganization.

The restrictions imposed on the borrower (management) that are part of the terms and conditions of the lending or bond agreement are called *covenants*. Covenants deal with limitations and restrictions on the borrower's activities. Affirmative covenants call on the debtor to make promises to do certain things. Negative covenants are those that require the borrower not to take certain actions. A violation of any covenant may provide a meaningful early warning alarm, enabling lenders to take positive and

"Great uncertainty about the values of financial assets, particularly more complex and opaque assets, has made investors extremely reluctant to bear credit risk." Ben Bernanke

  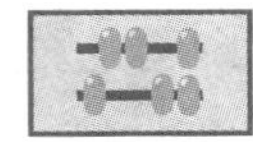   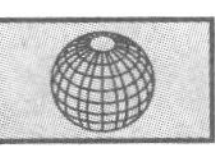   

corrective action before the situation deteriorates further. Covenants play an important part in minimizing risk to creditors.

CREDIT RISK TRANSFER VEHICLES

There are various ways that investors, particularly institutional investors, can reduce their exposure to credit risk. These arrangements are referred to as *credit transfer vehicles*. It should be borne in mind that an institutional investor may not necessarily want to eliminate credit risk but may want to control it or have an efficient means by which to reduce it. The increasing number of credit risk transfer vehicles has made it easier for financial institutions to reallocate large amounts of credit risk to the nonfinancial sector of the capital markets.

For a bank, the most obvious way to transfer the credit risk of a loan it has originated is to sell it to another party. The bank management's concern when it sells corporate loans is the potential impairment of its relationship with the corporate borrower. This concern is overcome with the use of *syndicated loans*, because banks in the syndicate may sell their loan shares in the secondary market by means of either an *assignment* or a *participation*. With an assignment, a syndicated loan requires the approval of the obligor; that is not the case with a participation since the payments by the borrower are merely passed through to the purchaser, and therefore the obligor need not know about the sale.

Two credit risk vehicles that have increased in importance since the 1990s are securitization and credit derivatives. It is important to note that the pricing of these credit risk transfer instruments is not an easy task. Pricing becomes even more complicated for lower-quality borrowers and for credits that are backed by a pool of lower-quality assets, as recent events in the capital markets have demonstrated.

SECURITIZATION

Securitization involves the pooling of loans and/or receivables and selling that pool of assets to a third-party, a special purpose vehicle (SPV). By doing so, the risks associated with that pool of assets, such as credit risk, are transferred to the SPV. In turn, the SPV obtains the funds to acquire the pool of assets by selling securities. When the pool of assets consists of consumer receivables or mortgage loans, the securities issued are referred to as *asset-backed securities*. When the asset pool consists of corporate loans, the securities issued are called *collateralized loan obligations*.

A major reason why a financial or nonfinancial corporation uses securitization as a fund-raising vehicle is that it may allow a lower funding cost than issuing secured debt. However, another important reason is that securitization is a risk management tool. Although the entity employing securitization retains some of the credit risk associated with the pool of loans (referred to as retained interest), the majority of the credit risk is transferred to the holders of the securities issued by the SPV.

CREDIT DERIVATIVES

A financial derivative is a contract designed to transfer some form of risk between two or more parties efficiently. When a financial derivative allows the transfer of credit exposure of an underlying asset or assets between two parties, it is referred to as a *credit derivative*. More specifically, credit derivatives allow investors either to acquire or to reduce credit risk exposure. Many institutional investors have portfolios that are highly sensitive to changes in the credit spread between a default-free asset and a credit-risky asset, and credit derivatives are an efficient way to manage this exposure. Conversely, other institutional investors may use credit derivatives to target specific credit exposures as a way to enhance portfolio returns. Consequently, the ability to transfer credit risk and return provides a tool for institutional–investors; the potential to improve performance. Moreover, corporate treasurers can use credit derivatives to transfer the risk associated with an increase in credit spreads (i.e., credit spread risk).

Credit derivatives include credit default swaps, asset swaps, total return swaps, credit linked notes, credit spread options, and credit spread forwards. In addition, there are index-type or basket credit products that are sponsored by banks that link the payoff to the investor to a portfolio of credits. Credit derivatives are over-the-counter instruments and are therefore not traded on an organized exchange. Hence, credit derivatives expose an investor to counterparty risk, and this has been the major concern in recent years in view of the credit problems of large banks and dealer firms who are the counterparties.

Credit derivatives also permit banks to transfer credit risk without the need to transfer assets physically. For example, in a collateral loan obligation, a bank can sell a pool of corporate loans to a special purpose vehicle (SPV) in order to reduce its exposure to the corporate borrowers. Alternatively, it can transfer the credit risk exposure by buying credit protection for the same pool of corporate loans. In this case, the transaction is referred to as a *synthetic collateralized loan obligation*.

CASE STUDY

A *credit-linked note* (CLN) is a security, usually issued by an investment-grade-rated corporation, that has an interest payment and fixed maturity structure similar to a standard bond. In contrast to a standard bond, the performance of the CLN is linked to the performance of a specified underlying asset or assets as well as that of the issuing entity. There are different ways that a CLN can be credit linked, and we will describe one case here.

British Telecom issued on December 15, 2000, a CLN with a coupon rate of 8.125% maturing on December 15, 2010. The terms of this CLN stated that the coupon rate would increase by 25 basis points for each one-notch rating downgrade of British Telecom below A–/A3 suffered during the life of the CLN. The coupon rate would decrease by 25 basis points for each rating upgrade, with a minimum coupon set at 8.125%. In other words, this CLN allows investors to make a credit play based on this issuer's credit rating. In fact, in May 2003, British Telecom was downgraded by one rating notch and the coupon rate was increased to 8.375%.

MAKING IT HAPPEN

Controlling credit risk requires not just an understanding of what credit risk is and the factors that affect a borrower's credit rating but other important implementation issues. These include:

- establishing the credit risk exposure that a corporation or institutional investor is willing to accept;
- quantifying the credit risk by using the latest quantitative tools in the field of credit risk modeling;
- understanding the various credit risk transfer vehicles that can be employed to control credit risk;
- evaluating the merits of different credit risk transfer vehicles to determine which are the most appropriate for altering credit risk exposure.

"I am far more interested in avoiding risk than I am in capturing every opportunity. My philosophy says that loss of opportunity is preferable to loss of capital." Joseph DiNapoli

An understanding of credit derivatives is critical even for those who do not want to use them. As Alan Greenspan, then the Chairman of the Federal Reserve Board, in a speech on September 25, 2002, stated: "The growing prominence of the market for credit derivatives is attributable not only to its ability to disperse risk but also to the information it contributes to enhanced risk management by banks and other financial intermediaries. Credit default swaps, for example, are priced to reflect the probability of net loss from the default of an ever broadening array of borrowers, both financial and non-financial."[2]

CONCLUSION

While market participants typically think of credit risk in terms of the failure of a borrower to make timely interest and principal payments on a debt obligation, this is only one form of credit risk: credit default risk. The other types of credit risk are credit spread risk and downgrade risk. When evaluating the credit default risk of a borrower, credit analysts look at the quality of the borrower, the ability of the borrower to satisfy the debt obligation, the level of seniority and the collateral available in a bankruptcy proceeding, and covenants. Credit risk transfer vehicles include securitization and credit derivatives. Credit derivatives include credit default swaps, asset swaps, total return swaps, credit linked notes, credit spread options, credit spread forwards, and baskets or indexes of credits.

MORE INFO

Books:

Anson, Mark J. P., Frank J. Fabozzi, Moorad Choudhry, and Ren-Raw Chen. *Credit Derivatives: Instruments, Pricing, and Applications.* Hoboken, NJ: Wiley, 2004.

Fabozzi, Frank J., Moorad Choudhry, and Steven V. Mann. *Measuring and Controlling Interest Rate and Credit Risk*. 2nd ed. Hoboken, NJ: Wiley, 2003.

Articles:

Fabozzi, Frank J., and Moorad Choudhry. "Originating collateralized debt obligations for balance sheet management." *Journal of Structured Finance* 9:3 (Fall 2003): 32–52. Online at: dx.doi.org/10.3905/jsf.2003.320318

Fabozzi, Frank J., Henry A. Davis, and Moorad Choudhry, "Credit-linked notes: A product primer." *Journal of Structured Finance* 12:4 (Winter 2007): 67–77. Online at: dx.doi.org/10.3905/jsf.12.4.67

Lucas, Douglas J., Laurie S. Goodman, and Frank J. Fabozzi. "Collateralized debt obligations and credit risk transfer." *Journal of Financial Transformation* 20 (2007): 47–59. Online at: tinyurl.com/24t4qbd [PDF].

Websites:

DefaultRisk.Com—for credit risk modeling and measurement: www.defaultrisk.com

Vinod Kothari's credit derivatives website: www.credit-deriv.com

See Also:

★ Credit Ratings (pp. 478–480)

★ Securitization: Understanding the Risks and Rewards (pp. 598–600)

✔ Derivatives Markets: Their Structure and Function (p. 1007)

✔ Hedging Credit Risk—Case Study and Strategies (p. 969)

✔ Managing Your Credit Risk (p. 981)

NOTES

1 Moody's Investor Service. "Industrial company rating methodology." *Global Credit Research* (July 2008): 6.

2 Speech titled "World Finance and Risk Management," at Lancaster House, London, United Kingdom.

"Through the fat years, the bankers were always right there by our side. But in bad times they backed off in a hurry."
Lee Iacocca

  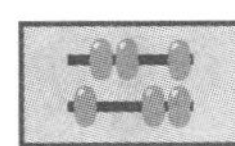      

Optimizing the Capital Structure: Finding the Right Balance between Debt and Equity by Meziane Lasfer

EXECUTIVE SUMMARY

- Just over 50 years ago Miller and Modigliani (1958) showed that under a certain set of conditions—namely perfect capital markets with no taxes and agency conflicts—a firm's capital structure is irrelevant to its valuation.
- Their results are controversial and have raised a large number of questions from academics and practitioners.
- This article summarizes the main issues underlying the choice by firms of an appropriate capital structure, taking into account their specific fundamentals as well as macroeconomic factors.
- It presents the benefits and costs of borrowing, describes how to assess these to arrive at the basic trade-off between debt and equity, and examines conditions under which debt becomes irrelevant.

TYPES OF FINANCING

There are three financing methods that companies can use: debt, equity, and hybrid securities. This categorization is based on the main characteristics of the securities.

Debt Financing

Debt financing ranges from simple bank debt to commercial paper and corporate bonds. It is a contractual arrangement between a company and an investor, whereby the company pays a predetermined claim (or interest) that is not a function of its operating performance, but which is treated in accounting standards as an expense for tax purposes and is therefore tax-deductible. The debt has a fixed life and has a priority claim on cash flows in both operating periods and bankruptcy. This is because interest is paid before the claims to equity holders, and, if the company defaults on interest payments, it will be declared bankrupt, its assets will be sold, and the amount owed to debt holders will be paid before any payments are made to equity holders.

Equity Financing

Equity financing includes owners' equity, venture capital (equity capital provided to a private firm in exchange for a share ownership of the firm), common equity, and warrants (the right to buy a share of stock in a company at a fixed price during the life of the warrant). Unlike debt, it is permanent in the company, its claim is residual and does not create a tax advantage from its payments as dividends are paid after interest and tax, it does not have priority in bankruptcy, and it provides management control for the owner.

Hybrid Securities

Hybrid securities are securities that share some characteristics with both debt and equity and include, for example, convertible securities (defined as debt that can be converted into equity at a prespecified date and conversion rate), preferred stock, and option-linked bonds.

THE IRRELEVANCE PROPOSITION

In 1958 Modigliani and Miller demonstrated that, under a certain set of assumptions, the choice between any of these securities (referred to as capital structure or leverage) is not relevant to a company's valuation. The assumptions include: no taxes, no costs of financial distress, perfect capital markets, no interest rate differentials, no agency costs (rationality), and no transaction costs. These assumptions are, in fact, the main drivers of capital structure and gave rise to the trade-off theory of leverage.

THE TRADE-OFF OF DEBT

In this so-called Miller–Modigliani framework, firms choose their optimal level of leverage by weighing the following benefits and costs of debt financing.

Benefits of Debt

There are two main advantages of debt financing: taxation, and added discipline.

Taxation: Since the interest on debt is paid before taxation, whereas dividends paid to equity holders are usually paid from profit after tax, the cost of debt is substantially less than the cost of equity. This tax-deductibility of interest makes debt financing attractive. Suppose that the debt of a company is $100 million and the interest rate is 10%. Every year the company pays interest of $10 million. Suppose that the corporation tax rate is 30%. If the company does not pay tax, its interest will be $10 million and the cost of debt will be 10%. However, if the company is able to deduct the tax on this $10 million from its corporation tax payment, then the company saves $10 million × 30% = $3 million in tax payments per year, making the effective interest payment only $7 million. If the debt is permanent, every year the company will have a $3 million tax saving, referred to as a tax shield. We can compute the present value (PV) by discounting annual value by the cost of debt, as follows:

$$\text{PV of tax shield} = \frac{k_d \times D \times t_c}{k_d} = D \times t_c$$

where k_d is the cost of debt, D is the amount of debt, and the product of k_d and D gives the amount of the interest charge. t_c is the corporation tax rate. We simplify the ratio by k_d to obtain the present value of the tax shield as the product of the amount of debt and the corporation tax rate. Thus, the value of a company that is financed with debt and equity (such a company is referred to "levered") should be equal to its value if it is financed only with equity plus the present value of the tax shield. We can write this value as:

$$\text{Value of levered firm with debt } D = \text{Value of nonlevered firm} + D \times t_c$$

These arguments suggest that the after-tax cost of debt can be computed as 10% × (1 − 30%) = 7%.

Added discipline: In practice, the managers are not the owners of the company. This so-called separation of managers and stockholders raises the possibility that managers may prefer to maximize their own wealth rather that of the stockholders. This is referred to as the agency conflict. In general, debt may make managers more disciplined because debt requires a fixed payment of interest, and defaulting on such payments will lead a company to bankruptcy.

Costs of Debt

Debt has a number of disadvantages, including a higher probability of bankruptcy, an increase in the agency conflicts between managers and bondholders, loss of future financial flexibility, and the cost of information asymmetry.

Expected bankruptcy cost. Given that debt holders can declare a company bankrupt if it defaults on its interest payment, companies that have a high level of debt are likely to have a high probability of facing such a default. This probability is also

"Smaller companies with significant growth opportunities should make limited use of debt to preserve their continuing ability to undertake positive-NPV projects." Graham and Harvey (2002)

  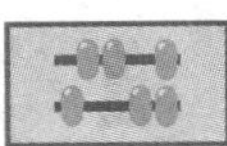      

increased when a company is operating in a high business risk environment. Debt financing creates financial risk. Thus, companies that have high business risk should not increase their risk of default by taking on a high financial risk through their use of debt. Evidence indicates that much of the loss of value occurs not in the liquidation process but in the stage of financial distress, when the firm is struggling to pay its bills (including interest), even though it may not go on to be liquidated.

Agency costs: These costs arise when a company borrows funds and the managers use the funds to finance alternative, usually more risky, activities than those specified in the borrowing contract to generate higher returns to stockholders. The greater the separation between managers and lenders, the higher the agency costs.

Loss of future financing flexibility: When a firm increases its debt substantially, it faces difficulties raising additional debt. Companies that can forecast their future financing needs accurately can plan their financing better and may not raise additional funds randomly. In general, the greater the uncertainty about future financing needs, the higher the costs.

Information asymmetry: When companies do not disclose information to the market, their information asymmetry will be high, resulting in a higher cost of debt financing.

Redeployable assets of debt: Lenders require some sort of security when they fund a company. This security is referred to as collateral. Lenders accept assets that can be resold or redeployed into other activities, such as property (real estate), as collateral. In general, the lower the value of the redeployable assets of debt, the higher are the costs.

FINANCING CHOICES AND A FIRM'S LIFE CYCLE

Although companies may prefer to use internal financing to minimize the issuance (transaction) costs, the trend in financing depends critically on the firm's life cycle.

Start-ups are small, privately owned companies. They are likely to be financed by owners' funds and bank borrowings. Their funding needs are high, but their ability to raise external funding is limited because they do not have sufficient assets to offer as security to finance providers. They will try to seek private equity funding. Their long-term leverage is likely to be low as they are mainly financed with short-term debt.

Expanding companies are those that have succeeded in attracting customers and establishing a presence in the market. They are likely to be financed by private equity and/or venture capital in addition to owners' equity and bank debt. Their level of debt is low and they have more short-term than long-term debt in their capital structure.

High-growth companies are likely to be publicly traded, with rapidly growing revenues. They will issue equity in the form of common stock, warrants, and other equity options, and probably convertible debt. They are likely to have a moderate leverage.

Mature companies are likely to finance their activities by internal financing, debt, and equity. Their leverage is likely to be relatively high but will depend on the costs and benefits of debt and their fundamental factors, such as business risk and taxation.

CONCLUSION

This article discussed the different financing methods companies can use and then argued that their choice depends on the costs and benefits of debt financing and the

MAKING IT HAPPEN

The choice of financing is strategic and involves the following issues:

- Both low- and high-debt financing are suboptimal. Companies should aim for the most advantageous level of debt financing, whereby the costs are minimized and the benefits are maximized.
- The costs of debt include a greater probability of bankruptcy, an increase in the agency conflicts between managers and bondholders, a loss of future financial flexibility (including the availability of collateral assets), and information asymmetry costs.
- The benefits relate mainly to tax shields and the added discipline to mitigate the agency conflicts between stockholders and managers.
- This equilibrium applies primarily to mature companies. Start-ups and growth companies are likely to have lower leverage as their borrowing capacity is low. It also applies to companies that normally pay dividends and do not accumulate cash for reinvestment in order to avoid the need to raise external financing.
- The recent financial crisis has highlighted another issue in debt financing, namely liquidity. Leverage concepts were developed mainly in times when debt financing was fully available. In the current credit crisis this is no longer the case. Companies therefore now have to pay an extra liquidity cost to raise additional capital. The question is whether this is a temporary situation or a permanent one, in which case debt will become more costly and leverage will be lower than in the past.
- Another challenge of debt financing relates to the ethics of the use of excessive debt financing, particularly by financial institutions. Pettifor (2006) was able to foresee the current crisis, tracing debt financing back to early times and arguing that religions are against debt because it results in usury. She provides interesting arguments, challenging the whole structure of debt financing, payment of interest, and interest tax deductibility. Possibly a new structure of debt that is linked to the profitability of assets and incurs no interest will emerge from the current crisis.

MORE INFO

Books:

Damodaran, Aswath. *Applied Corporate Finance: A User's Manual*. 2nd ed. Hoboken, NJ: Wiley, 2006.

Pettifor, Ann. *The Coming First World Debt Crisis*. Basingstoke, UK: Palgrave Macmillan, 2006.

Articles:

Graham, John R., and Campbell R. Harvey. "How do CFOs make capital budgeting and capital structure decisions?" *Journal of Applied Corporate Finance* 15:1 (Spring 2002): 8–23. Online at: dx.doi.org/10.1111/j.1745-6622.2002.tb00337.x

Lasfer, Meziane A. "Agency costs, taxes and debt: The UK evidence." *European Financial Management* 1:3 (November 1995): 265–285. Online at: dx.doi.org/10.1111/j.1468-036X.1995.tb00020.x

Modigliani, Franco, and Merton H. Miller. "The cost of capital, corporation finance and the theory of investment." *American Economic Review* 48:3 (June 1958): 261–297. Online at: www.jstor.org/stable/info/1809766

"The motivation for debt finance appears to be driven by the resolution of the agency conflicts and, in the long-run, by tax savings" Lasfer (1995)

  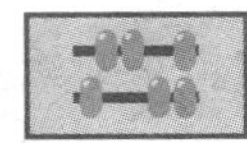   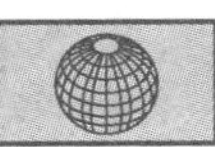   

firm's life cycle. For example, whereas start-up companies are likely to be financed with private personal funds, making their leverage low, mature companies tend to have high leverage because they are able to mitigate the costs of debt and gain from the tax benefits. In addition to these factors, in practice firms may choose their financing mix by mimicking comparable firms, or they may adopt the average level of debt of all the companies in their industry. These methods are not highly recommendable as they may result in a suboptimal choice. In other cases they follow a financing hierarchy, where retained earnings are the preferred option, followed by external financing in the form of debt, and then equity. This preference is driven by the transaction and monitoring costs.

Websites:

About.com article "Debt financing—Pros and cons": entrepreneurs.about.com/od/financing/a/debtfinancing.htm

Answers.com article "Debt financing": www.answers.com/topic/debt-financing

Washington State University teaching module "Financing sources for ICTs: Debt finance": cbdd.wsu.edu/kewlcontent/cdoutput/TR505r/page31.htm

See Also:

★ Capital Structure: A Strategy that Makes Sense (pp. 710–714)
★ Capital Structure: Implications (pp. 715–718)
★ Capital Structure: Perspectives (pp. 24–27)
✔ Conflicting Interests: The Agency Issue (p. 1110)
✔ Investors and the Capital Structure (p. 1120)
✔ Understanding and Using Leverage Ratios (p. 1097)
✔ Understanding Capital Markets, Structure and Function (p. 1099)
✔ Understanding Capital Structure Theory: Modigliani and Miller (p. 997)
Franco Modigliani (p. 1296)
Merton Miller (p. 1294)

"I'm concerned that some of the basic but important fundamentals of investing are being lost on investors. Or, even worse, simply ignored. Unless investors truly understand both the opportunities and the risks of today's market, too many may fall victim to their own wishful thinking." Arthur Levitt, Jr

  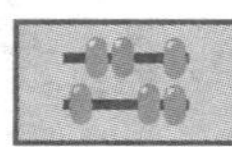      

Viewpoint: Outperformance through Ethical Lending by Dan Hird

INTRODUCTION

Dan Hird is head of corporate finance at Triodos Bank and has more than 20 years experience as a lead adviser. Since joining Triodos four years ago, he has built a corporate finance team at the bank that has completed 12 capital-raising transactions over the last two years for clients in the social and environmental sectors. Hird is a chartered accountant and spent seven years with KPMG Corporate Finance before establishing his own corporate finance business. He also has operational experience and spent six years as finance director in two medium-sized private companies in the retail and manufacturing sectors.

Triodos has a unique position in banking. Can you explain what it is that is so different about your approach?

Triodos was founded in 1980 as one of the world's first explicitly ethical banks. We have our head office in the Netherlands and branches in Spain, Germany, Belgium, and the United Kingdom. Our objective from the outset was to make money a force for good. This means that we only lend to clients who can demonstrate that they have both a strong track record and that their main aim is beneficial to either society or the environment. This positions us differently from, say, the Co-operative Bank, which will lend to any company so long as it is not actively breaching one of the Co-op's ethical criteria, such as being involved in the transfer of armaments to oppressive regimes. That is what we term a negative criterion. We apply a positive criterion whereby you have to be actively involved in doing good in some demonstrable way, not just not doing harm.

We have found that this philosophy resonates well with a number of banks, and this led us to found the Global Alliance for Banking Values. There are currently 21 banks in the Alliance, and the return on assets generated by those banks is better than the mainstream banking sector. The reason for this probably has a lot to do with the way mainstream banks suffered through excessive risk-taking during the run-up to the 2008 crash. If you have a sustainable philosophy, then much of what mainstream investment banks were doing through the boom years wouldn't wash and you wouldn't get involved in it.

Now there is pressure on companies across all sectors, not just the financial sector, to clean up their act and to put a lot back into the community or the environment, and what the Global Alliance shows is that putting the trust back into banking pays. This is not just about returns to shareholders, but about giving back in the wider context. For some companies this kind of activity is undoubtedly driven by public relations or marketing, but with our clients a focus on sustainability and social and environmental reinvestment tends to be at the very heart of what they do. Typically, they are into activities such as organic farming, fair trade, renewable power, social enterprise, or something along those lines. In other words, the core part of their mission aligns with that of Triodos. Moreover, what we aim to do is to show that our approach to banking is sustainable and works financially, that it generates good returns for us and our investors at a lower level of risk. As long as we keep doing this, we believe that we can pull mainstream banking a bit more in our direction, which would be good for everyone.

How does your model generate outperformance?

Well, take our banking model for example. In the United Kingdom we have two operations, deposit-taking and lending on the one hand, and corporate finance on the other, where we raise equity and bond instruments for clients. As far as lending is concerned, we lend out some 85% of the deposits that we take in, which gives us a far superior capital ratio to even that demanded by the new Basel III capital adequacy requirements. In many ways this is the tried and tested model of banking, where you retain 15% of all deposits as reserve capital.

The corporate finance side of our business is different as it is an advisory business which we have developed to suit the needs of our clients, many of which are charities and social enterprises. If we take a large charity as an example, it might consider raising a bond—say £5 million to £10 million (which is large for the social market)—from investors. The charity will be expected to offer at least 4% interest on the bond to make sure that it is an attractive commercial offering, but it is also giving the investor the chance to do some good with their capital.

What we see then is that a group of investors might be prepared to take a slightly subcommercial yield in return for the knowledge that their money is achieving a definite social good. On these grounds we may well be able to find sufficient investors who would be getting around 1% less yield on their money than they would get from a listed bond issued by, say, Tesco Bank or Royal Bank of Scotland. A typical duration of an unlisted social bond might be five years. Core investors tend to be charitable trusts and other institutional social investors, many of whom look to recycle their funds back into the social market; hence, they would typically look at a fixed-yield bond for no more than five years and would expect to hold that bond to maturity.

There is really no significant secondary market to speak of at this level, although there has been a matched bargain market—where a broker sets out to match a willing buyer and a willing seller—run by Brewin Dolphin, the wealth manager. Experience has shown that there is no more than about 1–2% liquidity in these kinds of bonds because the vast majority of investors fully expect to hold the bond through to term. Of course, a 4% yield is on the low side (compared to listed corporate bonds), but a large charity with a strong balance sheet and good membership income could attract interest from investors at this level. A smaller social entity with a higher risk profile (perhaps issuing a bond to finance a payment-by-results contract) might have to pay anything up to 10–12% to get its bond issue away. We see it as our job to structure

"To be extraordinarily happy and to have no concern for money drives some people nuts." Danny Baker

the bond so that it matches the perceived risk profile of the client and so that it is sufficiently attractive to investors.

Before anyone invests in a bond issued by a charity they expect to see an investment memorandum. We would approve and sponsor this for our client using our Financial Services Authority (FSA) authorization. In the document we would explain what the charity does, its aims and objectives, explain where it gets its commercial and noncommercial income (grants, donations, legacies) from, and so on. We would also list other sources of income, such as income from charity shops, centers of disability, and any government contracts it might have. Just as with a commercial bond, the key issue for investors is how the charity will redeem the bond at the end of the term.

Corporate bond issuance usually starts at around the £100 million mark, and that is on the low side. How is it possible to issue bonds of just £5 million or so for social entities and charities?

This is very much ground-breaking work. Most of our clients have never issued bonds before, so this is new for them. If you take the example of a large charity with, say, £50 million of net assets and stable sources of income, and that charity has never issued a bond and has never borrowed, there is the basis of a strong investment proposition since the charity is unencumbered by legacy debt. Plus you have to take into account the fact that many social investors have earmarked a portion of their potential portfolio for ethical investing. They want to see some positive social impact resulting from their investment, and the charity's purposes will in all probability be a very good fit for their goals and intentions. There is a question of appropriateness of scale, and with that sort of balance sheet raising a £5 million to £10 million five-year bond should be achievable.

At the same time, it is important to remember that this is not a gift that investors are making. We have to assume that they are looking at social investment as a commercial proposition and are looking at the blended financial and social return on their money that the investment is going to bring. One of the questions that will be uppermost for them will be about the charity's ability to redeem the bond. If the charity is simply hoping to redeem the bond through a new debt issuance in five years, that is a rather weak proposition. The market may well have changed and become a lot less liquid by the time the bond needs to be redeemed, and investors will take that risk into account. So it is much better to be able to point to a clear bond redemption strategy that could be supported by an income stream, be it from government grants, earnings from the charity's investments or commercial activities, or one that can be assumed with reasonable confidence from a track record of successful fund-raising.

How many successful bond issuances for social entities and charities have there been so far?

This is a very new area. I joined the bank three years ago with the brief to bring a corporate finance department into existence through this kind of issuance. Already, however, we have some real successes we can point to, and other social banks are also going down this road. At present we are doing a major bond issuance for Golden Lane Housing (GLH), a subsidiary of Mencap. GLH's mission is to support people with learning difficulties to become more independent through the provision of their own home. Its property acquisition model involved borrowing 70% of the capital required through a commercial bank loan plus a 30% grant from the local authority involved or from a primary care trust. Now that the grant element of its funding has become restricted as a result of public spending cuts, GLH came to us and asked if we could help. We are working with it on a £10 million bond which will be used to fund 100% of the cost of new freehold properties. The cost of the bond for GLH will be 4%, which is roughly the same as the previous blended cost of bank and grant capital.

During 2012 we also issued bonds for two other charitable clients—Greater Merseyside Connexions Partnership (£1.5 million) and St Mungo's (£0.9 million). Both of these bonds were at the higher-risk, higher-yield end of the spectrum as they were raised in order to finance specific payment-by-results contracts. Another social intermediary, Investing for Good, recently raised a £2 million bond for Scope, which I believe was their first bond issuance. Our bond for GLH is on target for launch in February 2013, and it will probably quickly become the largest charity bond issued to date in the United Kingdom. We are seeing quite a good appetite among investors for that particular bond. Right now this is very much an emerging market, and you have to remember that there are not many FSA-authorized social banks like us, so I think development of the market will be quite slow and steady.

One of our biggest assets is our investor base, which we can offer to our clients. This includes the mainstream institutions, such as family trusts and large charitable trusts, which have a need to invest their income ethically. We also have strong relationships within the wealth advisory community and private banks that are also interested in social investment. These organizations act for high net worth individuals, and a number of those clients want to feel that their investments are doing some good in the world, but they also want to see their capital preserved. The opportunity to buy a charity bond makes sense from the standpoint of a low-risk return that is at least above inflation, and it fulfills their stated aim of making an investment that is beneficial to society.

We have seen corporate bond investing made available to the general public through exchange-traded funds, so will we see retail investors having the chance to participate in charity and social entity bonds? It sounds like something that would appeal to the public.

The holy grail, of course, is to bring social investment into the mainstream and make it available to the general public. However, this does depend very much on the risk profile of a particular bond as it would clearly be irresponsible to market higher-risk unlisted bond instruments to investors who are not capable of understanding the risks involved. If, however, we are talking about a solid, asset-backed bond proposition issued by a large, household name charity with a real interest in building a new retail supporter base, then it should be possible to access the retail investment market. For the charity, this would not only have the advantage of raising more capital, but it could also increase general awareness of the charity, which of course would appeal to our clients. In that kind of instance we might set the minimum subscription at around £500, which would give a large number of retail investors the chance to participate. For higher-risk bonds focused on institutional investors and high net worth individuals, the minimum subscription may be £10,000–£50,000, which is well out of the reach of most retail investors.

You would have to take into consideration the charity's earnings profile. If, for example, it was being government-funded on a payment-by-results contract, that would be a risky proposition, since the charity only gets paid if it delivers the positive outcomes set out in the contract. That kind of proposition is clearly not suited to retail investors and we would set the entry subscription at a level that would only be of interest to sophisticated investors.

We recently issued a secured bond for River Cottage for just £600,000. The minimum subscription per investor on this five-year bond was £25,000, and with a yield of 7% the bond was fully placed within a couple of weeks. The transaction completed at the end of November 2012 and was in the form of a private placement where the participants were independent financial advisers (IFAs) and one or two high net worth individuals who were already known to us. Although River Cottage is a growing privately owned business, it has an extremely strong brand and the bond was backed by a secondary charge over freehold property, so 7% was seen as an attractive yield for investors.

Another interesting deal that we worked on last year was Bristol Together. This was a really interesting start-up social enterprise where Triodos worked closely with a social entrepreneur, Paul Harrod, to raise start-up capital through a social bond issue. The business proposition is that Bristol Together purchases derelict freehold properties around Bristol and refurbishes them. The key social angle is that the refurbishment contracts are placed with local social enterprises that employ young ex-offenders and give them an opportunity to develop construction and work-readiness skills. A key success factor is the recruitment of an experienced project manager who is skilled in all the construction trades, can manage the youths, and brings the refurbishments to completion on schedule and within budget.

This is quite a simple idea, and the original capital is constantly recycled because it is either in the bank or is invested in freehold property, with profits on sale of the properties covering overheads and bond interest. For this deal we have raised £1.6 million of social bonds with a yield of just 3%. This may appear to be a very low rate of return, but it is a project with very high social impact (reducing reoffending, given disadvantaged young people a chance in life, etc.) that appeals to a number of social investors in its own right, and it can be perceived as low risk because the bond is secured on freehold property. We don't normally get involved in start-ups because they are just too challenging to be commercially viable, but we made an exception on this occasion because we could see a scale-up opportunity if the start-up phase proved successful.

The original idea came from Paul Harrod, who approached us directly. Paul has shown great personal commitment to this business and remains CEO of Bristol Together. The business won Social Enterprise of the Year 2012, which was tremendous. We started Bristol Together by doing a round of funding to prove the concept, and with this we were able to buy three properties and refurbish them. They were sold at a profit, and we then raised a further £1 million after the initial proof of concept project. The business now has £1.6 million of capital, which is enough to refurbish five or six properties around Bristol at any one time. We are now engaged in rolling the concept out to the Midlands area through a larger concept called Midlands Together, for which we will be raising £5 million through a bond issue later this year. Both Bristol Together and Midlands Together are community interest companies (CICs), which tells investors that the social mission of these businesses is the most important factor for the management teams.

In conclusion, sustainable banking is not just about not doing unethical things or about having a strong capital ratio. At the heart of it is a commitment to transparency and sustainability, so that other people can see what it is that you do, see that it works socially and financially, and be inspired by it. We believe that if other banks and financial institutions had adopted a sustainable approach to using money, it is highly unlikely that they would ever have ended up in the mess that some of the largest banks in the world found themselves in when the tide went out in the great crash of 2008.

MORE INFO

Books:

Chapman, Peter. *Jungle Capitalists: A Story of Globalisation, Greed and Revolution*. Edinburgh, UK: Canongate Books, 2007.

Frank, Thomas. *Pity the Billionaire: The Hard-Times Swindle and the Unlikely Comeback of the Right*. New York: Picador, 2012.

Gilding, Paul. *The Great Disruption: Why the Climate Crisis Will Bring On the End of Shopping and the Birth of a New World* (also subtitled *How the Climate Crisis Will Change Everything (For the Better)*). New York: Bloomsbury, 2011.

Articles:

Charities Aid Foundation. "Funding good outcomes—Using social investment to support payment by results." September 2012. Online at: tinyurl.com/d9clha9

St Mungo's. "Street Impact designed to help rough sleepers rebuild their lives." December 14, 2012. Online: tinyurl.com/a3btz9r

Websites:

Bristol Together: www.bristoltogether.info
Global Alliance for Banking Values: www.gabv.org
Greater Merseyside Connexions Partnership: www.connexionslive.com
Mencap: www.mencap.org.uk
River Cottage: www.rivercottage.net
Triodos Bank on corporate finance: tinyurl.com/ck7cqlp

See Also:

★ Ethical Funds and Socially Responsible Investment: An Overview (pp. 481–483)
★ Viewpoint: Green Investing—Looking beyond the Financial Metrics (pp. 492–493)
★ Viewpoint: Principles for Responsible Investment—Looking Beyond the Financial Metrics (pp. 560–562)
Banking and Financial Services (pp. 1612–1614)

"**Money turns out to be whatever we agree it to be. It is a collective work of the imagination.**" Simon Carr

  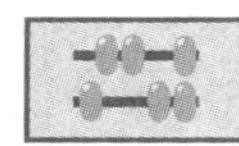      

Passive Portfolio Management and Fixed-Income Investing by Andrew Ainsworth

EXECUTIVE SUMMARY

- Fixed-income securities are an important asset class that adds considerable diversification benefits to a portfolio.
- The passive strategy known as stratified sampling allows investors to achieve benchmark returns while controlling risk and transaction costs.
- This approach can be utilized in a tactical asset-allocation strategy, as it allows for relatively quick changes in portfolio allocations.
- Stratified sampling allows for active bets to be integrated into the portfolio by tilting weights in response to forecasted returns.
- The use of back-testing will ensure that actual outcomes align with expectations by adequately controlling benchmark risks.

INTRODUCTION

An allocation of investment to fixed-income assets is an important component of any diversified investment strategy. The fixed-income asset class comprises a variety of debt instruments that include government bonds, corporate bonds, municipal bonds, mortgage-backed securities, inflation-indexed debt, and convertible bonds, among others. With such a large number of securities available from which to construct a portfolio, this article reviews the stratified sampling method of replicating the returns of a benchmark portfolio in fixed-income securities. This method is of use to investors who are undertaking both active and passive portfolio management approaches.

Figure 1 shows the daily total returns of the S&P 500 and the MSCI World equity indices as well as fixed-income indices covering a broad-based global benchmark, global high yield, and world corporate debt between February 2002 and February 2012. The impact of the financial crisis is clearly evident in the figure. Interestingly, an investment made in February 2002 in either of the fixed-income indices would be worth more today than either of the equity benchmarks. In terms of risk, the standard deviation of monthly returns is considerably higher for the two equity indices—around 16%. The global broad-based index and the world corporate index have values of 6–7%. An important benefit of including fixed income in a portfolio is the diversification benefit. The correlation coefficients between the five indices are given in Table 1. The global high-yield index is more highly correlated with the equity indices than the other fixed-income indices. Either way, it is clear that fixed income should be included in a diversified portfolio.

RISKS OF INVESTING IN FIXED INCOME

Despite the lower standard deviation of returns, the recent events of the financial crisis have shown that significant risks are involved in investing in fixed-income securities. As with any financial security, expected returns will vary with risk. Before constructing a portfolio of fixed-income securities, it is important to understand the risks that an investor faces when investing in such securities.

- *Interest rate risk*. There is an inverse relationship between the level of interest rates and bond prices. However, the prices of some bonds are more sensitive to changes in interest rates and are therefore exposed to greater interest rate risk. Reinvestment risk is also related to interest rate risk, as coupon payments received are reinvested at an uncertain interest rate.
- *Credit risk*. This is the risk that the issuer of a bond may not make periodic coupon payments or pay back the full amount of principal at maturity. Credit rating agencies (Standard & Poor's, Moody's, and Fitch IBCA) provide ratings on the creditworthiness of bond issuers. These credit ratings allow investors to differentiate between bonds on the basis of the rating agencies' assessments that an issuer will default and not meet its obligations.
- *Liquidity risk*. This represents the chance that you will not be able to trade the desired quantity of a specific security when you want to trade. Bonds that are more liquid are cheaper to trade. A prime example of liquidity risk is that which occurred in certain collateralized debt obligations and mortgage-backed securities during the financial crisis.
- *Inflation risk*. The chance that inflation will erode the value of investments.
- *Sovereign risk*. This is related to credit risk as it represents the chance that a foreign government will not repay its debts. As the recent sovereign debt crisis has highlighted, it is an important

Figure 1. Total returns of selected fixed-income and equity indices (US$), 2002–12. For key to fund names, see Table 1. (*Source*: Datastream)

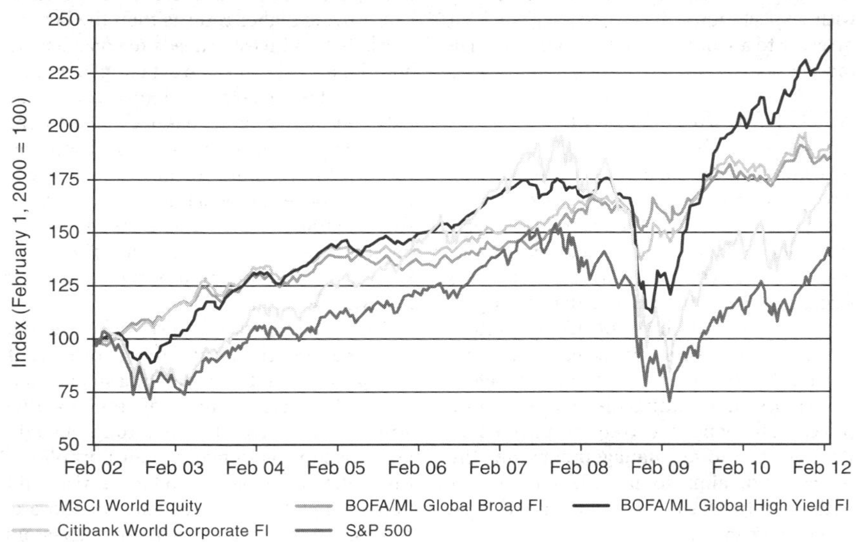

"Risk varies inversely with knowledge." Anonymous

Table 1. Correlation coefficients of monthly returns for the indexes in Figure 1, February 2002 to February 2011. (*Source*: Datastream)

	MSCI World Equity	*S&P 500*	*BOFA/ML Global Broad FI*	*BOFA/ML Global High Yield FI*	*Citibank World Corporate FI*
MSCI World Equity	1.000	0.973	0.264	0.755	0.466
S&P 500	0.973	1.000	0.166	0.705	0.357
BOFA/ML Global Broad FI	0.264	0.166	1.000	0.346	0.877
BOFA/ML Global High Yield FI	0.755	0.705	0.346	1.000	0.622
Citibank World Corporate FI	0.466	0.357	0.877	0.622	1.000

BOFA/ML: Bank of America Merrill Lynch; FI: fixed income

consideration for investors in Portugal, Ireland, Greece, and Spain.

- *Currency risk.* This represents the risk that a domestic investor may purchase a bond that is denominated in a foreign currency. A domestic investor faces uncertainty about the domestic currency value of the coupons and the principal paid in foreign currency.
- *Call risk.* Certain bonds may allow the issuer to call the issue before maturity. This adversely impacts the investor as it introduces uncertainty as to the stream of future cash flows and limits the price appreciation of the security. Generally, these bonds are called when interest rates are low, creating reinvestment risk. Prepayment risk affects mortgage-backed securities and is related to call risk. It reflects the uncertainty surrounding the timing of cash flows to the holders of securitized loans that depend on the mortgage repayments of mortgage holders.

In order to realize a return that is in line with expectations, it is necessary for an investor to adequately monitor and manage these risks.

ACTIVE VERSUS PASSIVE MANAGEMENT

Investors in fixed-income assets essentially have two choices as to how to construct their portfolio. First, active management attempts to outperform a selected benchmark index, such as the Barclays Capital US Aggregate Bond Index. In order to outperform the index, an investor needs to either exercise superior security selection or time the market by entering the market before prices rise and exiting the market before prices fall (ignoring coupon payments). Passive portfolio management, on the other hand, aims to provide an investor with a return that matches a selected benchmark index.

There is continued debate in both the industry and academic literature on whether active portfolio management is superior to passive portfolio management. The findings from the most recent academic studies show that in some instances active funds outperform passive funds. However, the fees charged by active funds are higher and they generally erode the additional return they provide. Chen, Ferson, and Peters (2010) show that, after controlling for timing ability, funds outperform benchmarks before fees and costs, but underperform when fees and costs are taken into account. Boney, Comer, and Kelly (2009) find perverse market timing ability for high-quality corporate bond funds. An earlier study by Blake, Elton, and Gruber (1993) found that active funds that performed well in the past did not exhibit continued outperformance in the future. However, there is recent evidence from Huij and Derwall (2008) that past performance predicts future performance.

Thus, the jury is still out on whether an active or passive approach to bond portfolio management is preferable. Active strategies can provide higher returns than the benchmark, but an investor needs to consider the additional risks they are taking and any additional fees charged. All in all, the choice between active and passive investment styles in fixed-income assets is based on the investor's ability to provide consistent returns above the benchmark after fees. If they are unable to do this, then adopting a passive approach that seeks to provide returns consistent with a benchmark index is a wise decision.

Active managers may also make use of a passive approach for a number of reasons. If they believe that the underlying signals that drive the performance of their active strategy are currently not strong enough, an alternative is to match their portfolio to the index to avoid introducing risk and potentially letting performance deteriorate. A passive approach is also of use if investors are engaging in tactical asset allocation. By building a portfolio that replicates the benchmark return without the need to hold all the constituents of the index, investors can be nimble in response to changes in forecasts of returns across asset classes. Enhanced indexing is another benefit, as it allows for an additional return pickup if an investor has some information about future returns that would allow them to slightly outperform the benchmark.

Finally, an important question to be addressed is whether the investor has the skill in a specific area to undertake active management. Consider an investor who specializes in European corporate debt. It may be prudent for investments in other sectors, such as US mortgage-backed securities, to be based on a passive approach rather than actively trading in mortgage-backed securities and attempting to outperform the benchmark.

CHOOSING A BENCHMARK INDEX

The first decision an investor should make is what benchmark they should target. There are a vast number of fixed-income benchmarks to choose from: Barclays Capital, Merrill Lynch, JP Morgan, and other investment banks all offer benchmark bond indices for investors to track and benchmark their performance against. These bond indices can track the performance of the global bond market, or focus on different sectors of the bond market: US Treasury, corporate, mortgage-backed securities, municipal, inflation-indexed, high-yield, Eurodollar, etc. They can also focus on different geographical areas, such as the United States, Asia, or Europe, and their specific sectors.

The primary concern regarding choice of index is to select a benchmark that has the desired risk and return profile of the investor. For example, investing in emerging market high-yield debt is going to be considerably more risky than investing in US Treasury securities (ignoring currency risk). Certain benchmarks can be selected to avoid exposure to certain risks altogether. For example, if a US investor does not want to be exposed to currency risk in their fixed-income portfolio, they should choose a US bond index. Similarly, if an investor wanted to remove inflation risk, they should select an inflation-indexed benchmark that invests only in inflation-protected securities, such as Treasury Inflation-Protected Securities (TIPS). The nature of the liabilities will also impact the choice of benchmark and could well indicate that a passive approach is unsuitable. Instead, a liabilities-based strategy such as cash flow matching would be more appropriate.

PORTFOLIO CONSTRUCTION

A number of different methods for constructing passive bond portfolios exist: tracking error minimization, factor-based replication, and derivatives-based approaches (see references in the More Info section for a more detailed discussion). One relatively straightforward method of building a portfolio designed to achieve benchmark returns is to use a stratified sampling (or cell-matching) technique. This method allows an investor to control the risk factors which they deem most important in determining returns in the bond market. This approach can be used irrespective of the scale of the portfolio and is flexible enough to be incorporated into an active portfolio management process.

After targeting a benchmark index, an investor then chooses risk factors that they think are important in determining benchmark returns. For example, an investor might choose duration (a measure of interest rate risk), credit ratings, and call risk as being important determinants of bond returns. The investor would then divide the benchmark into a number of different cells based on these three factors. If they partition the index into short, medium, and long duration; AA and above, BBB+ to AA–, and BBB and below; and callable and noncallable debt, they would get a total of $3 \times 3 \times 2 = 18$ cells. The investor then determines the percentage of market value that is contained in each cell. They would then purchase at least one bond from each cell, allocating their capital in proportion to the index weights.

One benefit of this approach is that it allows the investor to incorporate subjective forecasts in their portfolio. They can adjust the weight in each cell, relative to the benchmark index, if they believe that certain factors will provide outperformance. For example, if an investor thinks that interest rates are likely to decrease, then long-duration bond prices will increase by a greater amount than short-duration bonds. As a result, they could take an overweight position in the long-duration cells, compared to the benchmark weights, and an underweight position in the short-duration cells. They may also be underweight the callable bond cells, relative to the benchmark weights, to minimize the adverse impact of bonds being called when interest rates fall.

An important step in forming a passive portfolio is to undertake back-testing of the portfolio based on the choice of cells. This will ensure that unwanted results from omitting an important risk factor do not occur. It will also allow for a better understanding of the trade-off between achieving benchmark returns and minimizing the number of bonds held in the portfolio.

CASE STUDY

Let us consider the Barclays Capital US Aggregate Bond Index. The index has more than 8,000 constituents, which is clearly too many bonds to hold in a portfolio. First and foremost, a substantial number of these bond issues would be illiquid and very expensive to trade in. By using stratified sampling, it is possible to achieve benchmark returns without holding a large number of bonds in the portfolio.

An investor may decide that maturity and credit risk are the three important risks that they need to take into account. The benchmark can be divided based on the time until maturity of the bonds—short, medium, and long; and credit ratings—AAA, AA, A, and BBB. The investor would obtain a grid like the one in Table 2, with a total of 12 cells.

In this instance, the simplest approach would be to choose 12 bonds and allocate the portfolio investments in proportion to the market value weights in each cell for the index. With only 12 bonds in the portfolio, additional diversification benefits may accrue by including several bonds from within each cell. As mentioned above, a back-testing approach would shed light on what might be a reasonable number of bonds to include in the portfolio. The investor may also want to partition the index based on the various sectors of the market—Treasury, government-related, corporate, and securitized—to increase the number of cells from which to choose bonds.

Table 2. Credit rating

Maturity	BBB	A	AA	AAA
Short	1%	8%	9%	18%
Medium	3%	6%	12%	14%
Long	2%	4%	7%	16%

ADVANTAGES AND DISADVANTAGES OF STRATIFIED SAMPLING APPROACH

What are the advantages of pursuing a stratified sampling approach to passive portfolio construction? First, it is straightforward and easy to understand. It matches the risk profile of the index, and therefore the return generated. By reducing the number of bonds in the portfolio and selecting the liquid bonds in each cell, transaction costs can also be reduced. From an asset allocation perspective, the use of stratified sampling makes it relatively easy to adjust holdings in response to changes in forecasted returns. The stratified sampling approach also avoids problems associated with statistical models that rely on historical correlations. After the financial crisis it is clear that these correlations are not always stable. In addition, bonds mature and exit the benchmark index (unlike the case of equity securities), and it can be difficult to estimate correlations on a security that has just been issued.

One disadvantage of the stratified sampling approach is that the investor has discretion as to the number and type of risk factors to focus on, and the number of partitions to divide the index into. Investors face the risk that an omitted risk factor may be a significant driver of index performance. As mentioned above, back-testing of various combinations of risk factors and partition size will alleviate concerns. There is a trade-off between the number of cells chosen and the costs associated with the strategy. An increase in the number of cells will improve the ability of the portfolio to match the index more closely; however, transaction costs

MAKING IT HAPPEN

- Pick an appropriate benchmark and identify the risk–return profile that you are targeting.
- Assess whether you have the skills to undertake active management in a given sector of the bond market.
- Determine the risk factors that you consider important in determining the returns of the benchmark index.
- Undertake back-testing of the stratified sampling approach. Compare different combinations of risks (interest rate, credit risk, etc) and assess the performance of the strategy based on the number of cells chosen.
- Monitor your portfolio and rebalance regularly as the index weights in each cell will change over time.

are likely to rise. An additional consideration for investors is that passive strategies need to be monitored and rebalanced regularly so that the actual return does not deviate from the benchmark.

CONCLUSION

Fixed-income assets represent an important component of a diversified investment portfolio. Although debate on the relative merits of active versus passive portfolio management in fixed-income securities has not reached a resolution, indexing can play a significant role in an investment portfolio. Stratified sampling is a method of achieving benchmark risk and return while reducing transaction costs. It can also be incorporated into a tactical asset allocation process, as it allows investors to be more nimble in altering their portfolios. A further benefit of the stratified sampling approach to index replication is that it allows for active bets to be easily incorporated by altering weights in each cell relative to the benchmark weight. Investors using a stratified sampling approach should undertake back-testing to ensure that actual outcomes align with expectations.

MORE INFO

Books:

Fabozzi, Frank J. *Bond Markets, Analysis, and Strategies*. 7th ed. Boston, MA: Pearson, 2009.

Martellini, Lionel, Philippe Priaulet, and Stéphane Priaulet. *Fixed-Income Securities: Valuation, Risk Management and Portfolio Strategies*. Chichester, UK: Wiley, 2003.

Articles:

Blake, Christopher R., Edwin J. Elton, and Martin J. Gruber. "The performance of bond mutual funds." *Journal of Business* 66:3 (July 1993): 371–403. Online at: www.jstor.org/stable/2353206

Boney, Vaneesha, George Comer, and Lynne Kelly. "Timing the investment grade securities market: Evidence from high quality bond funds." *Journal of Empirical Finance* 16:1 (January 2009): 55–69. Online at: dx.doi.org/10.1016/j.jempfin.2008.06.005

Chen, Yong, Wayne Ferson, and Helen Peters. "Measuring the timing ability and performance of bond mutual funds." *Journal of Financial Economics* 98:1 (October 2010): 72–89. Online at: dx.doi.org/10.1016/j.jfineco.2010.05.009

Huij, Joop, and Jeroen Derwall. "'Hot hands' in bond funds." *Journal of Banking and Finance* 32:4 (April 2008): 559–572. Online at: dx.doi.org/10.1016/j.jbankfin.2007.04.023

Websites:

The Index Investor: www.indexinvestor.com

Investing in Bonds: www.investinginbonds.com

See Also:

★ Asset Allocation Methodologies (pp. 454–458)
★ The Case for SMART Rebalancing (pp. 471–474)
★ The Impact of Index Trackers on Shareholders and Stock Volatility (pp. 496–498)
★ Understanding the Role of Diversification (pp. 617–618)
✔ The Bond Market: Its Structure and Function (p. 1064)
✔ Trading in Corporate Bonds: Why and How (p. 1094)
✔ Trading in Government Bonds: Why and How (p. 1096)

"What good is money if you can't inspire terror in your fellow man?" Matt Groening

The Performance of Socially Responsible Mutual Funds by Luc Renneboog

EXECUTIVE SUMMARY

Socially responsible investment funds employ negative and positive screens to select firms for their portfolios. These screens are based on environmental, social, or ethical criteria.

Trade-off: SRI funds could perform better than conventional ones as SRI funds comprise more carefully and actively selected firms. However, SRI funds could perform worse as the screening reduces the diversification potential which comes at a cost.

SRI performance measurement should involve an asset pricing model that captures investment styles. The Fama–French–Carhart model includes the market, firm size, growth opportunities, and share price momentum. In addition, the performance of SRI funds should be compared with the performance of conventional (non-SRI) funds.

Recent research shows that the performance SRI funds around the world is below the expected performance (measured by, for instance, the Fama–French–Carhart model). Furthermore, SRI funds do not outperform their conventional counterparts.

INTRODUCTION

Over the past decade, socially responsible investment (SRI), frequently also called ethical investment or sustainable investment, has grown rapidly around the world. SRI is a process that integrates social, environmental, and ethical considerations into investment decision making. Unlike conventional types of investment, SRI funds apply a set of investment screens to select or exclude assets based on ecological, social, corporate governance, or ethical criteria, and SRI often engages in the local communities and in shareholder activism to further corporate strategies towards the above aims.

WHAT TYPE OF INVESTMENT SCREENS DO SRI FUNDS EMPLOY?

Table 1 presents a summary of the SRI screens used by ethical funds around the world. Usually, SRI mutual funds apply a combination of the various types of screens. 64% of all socially screened mutual funds in the United States use more than five screens, while 18% of SRI funds use only one social screen (Renneboog, Ter Horst, and Zhang, 2008a). These screens can be broadly classified into two groups: negative screens and positive ones.

Negative Screens

The oldest and most basic SRI strategy is based on negative screening. These filters refer to the practice that specific stocks or industries are excluded from SRI portfolios based on social, environmental, and ethical criteria. A typical negative screen can be applied on an initial asset pool such as the S&P 500 stocks from which the alcohol, tobacco, gambling and defense industries, or companies with poor performance in labor relations or environmental protection, are excluded. Other negative screens may include irresponsible foreign operations, pornography, abortion, poor workplace conditions, violation of human rights, and animal testing. After performing a negative SRI screening, portfolios are created via a financial and quantitative selection. Some SRI funds only exclude companies from the investment universe when these firms' revenues derived from "asocial or unethical" sectors exceed a specific threshold, whereas other SRI funds also apply negative screens to a company's branches or suppliers. A small number of SRI funds use screens based on traditional ideological or religious convictions: for instance, they exclude investments in firms producing pork products, in financial institutions paying interest on savings, and in insurance companies insuring unmarried people.

Positive Screens

SRI portfolios are nowadays also based on positive screens, which in practice boils down to selecting shares that meet superior corporate social responsibility (CSR) standards. The most common positive screens focus on corporate governance, labor relations, the environment, sustainability of investments, and the stimulation of cultural diversity. Positive screens are also frequently used to select companies with a good record concerning renewable energy usage or community involvement. The use of positive screens is often combined with a "best in class" approach. Firms are ranked within each industry or market sector according to CSR criteria. Subsequently, only those firms in each industry which pass a minimum threshold are selected.

Combining Negative and Positive Screens

Negative and positive screens are often referred to as the first and second generation of SRI screens respectively. The third generation of screens refers to an integrated approach of selecting companies based on the economic, environmental, and social criteria comprised by both negative and positive screens. This approach is often called "sustainability" or "triple bottom line" (on account of its focus on people, planet and profit).

Shareholder Activism

The fourth generation of ethical funds combines the sustainable investing approach (third generation) with shareholder activism. In this case, portfolio managers or the companies specialized in granting ethical labels attempt to influence the company's actions through direct dialogue with the management or by the use of voting rights at Annual General Meetings.

DOING WELL BY DOING GOOD?

The fact that SRI funds apply screens that limit the full diversification potential may shift the mean-variance frontier towards less favorable risk–return tradeoffs than those of conventional portfolios. For instance, excluding part of the stock market (firms producing alcohol, tobacco, pornography) may negatively influence the risk–return tradeoffs of SRI funds. By this logic, SRI funds are expected to generate a weaker performance than conventional funds for two reasons. First, SRI funds underinvest in financially attractive investment opportunities, as some of these opportunities are excluded from the investment universe because they do not contribute sufficiently to the SRI objectives of the fund. Second, more intense screening intensity further reduces the investment universe, which may further weaken performance.

However, there are two arguments supporting the alternative hypothesis that states that SRI funds outperform conventional funds. First, sound social and environmental performance signals high managerial quality, which translates into favorable financial performance. Second, social, ethical, and environmental screening may reduce the high costs that emerge during corporate social crises or environmental disasters. If financial markets tend to undervalue such costs, portfolios based on corporate governance, social, or environmental criteria may outperform their benchmarks.

"The life of money-making is one undertaken under compulsion, and wealth is evidently not the good we are seeking; for it is merely useful and for the sake of something else." Aristotle

Table 1. SRI screens. (*Source*: Renneboog, Ter Horst, and Zhang, 2008b)

Screens	*Definitions*	*Pos. or Neg. screen*
Tobacco	Avoid manufacturers of tobacco products.	–
Alcohol	Avoid firms that produce/market alcoholic beverages.	–
Gambling	Avoid casinos and suppliers of gambling equipment.	–
Defense/weapons	Avoid firms producing weapons.	–
Nuclear power	Avoid manufacturers of nuclear reactors and firms operating nuclear power plants.	–
Irresponsible foreign operations	Avoid firms with investments in firms located in oppressive regimes such as Burma or China, or firms that mistreat the indigenous peoples of developing countries.	–
Pornography/Adult entertainment	Avoid publishers of pornographic magazines; production studios that produce offensive video and audio tapes; companies that are major sponsors of graphic sex and violence on television.	–
Abortion/Birth control	Avoid providers of abortion; manufacturers of abortion drugs and birth control products; insurance companies that pay for elective abortions.	–
Labor relations and workplace conditions	Seek firms with strong union relationships, employee empowerment, and/or e mployee profit sharing.Avoid firms exploiting their workforce and sweatshops.	+–
Environment	Seek firms with proactive involvement in recycling, waste reduction, and environmental cleanup.Avoid firms producing toxic products, and contributing to global warming .	+–
Corporate governance	Seek companies demonstrating "best practices" related to board independence and elections, auditor independence, executive compensation, expensing of options, voting rights and/or other governance issues.Avoid firms with antitrust violations, consumer fraud, and marketing scandals.	+–
Business practice	Seek companies committed to sustainability through investments in R&D, quality assurance, and product safety.	+
Employment diversity	Seek firms pursuing an active policy related to the employment of minorities, women, gays/lesbians, and/or disabled persons who ought to be r epresented amongst senior management.	+
Human rights	Seek firms promoting human rights standards.Avoid firms which are complicit in human rights violations.	+–
Animal testing	Seek firms promoting the respectful treatment of animals.Avoid firms with animal testing and firms producing hunting/trapping equipment or using animals in end products.	+–
Renewable energy	Seek firms producing power derived from renewable energy sources.	+
Biotechnology	Seek firms that support sustainable agriculture, biodiversity, local farmers, and industrial applications of biotechnology.Avoid firms involved in the promotion or development of genetic engineering for agricultural applications.	+–
Community involvement	Seek firms with proactive investments in the local community by sponsoring charitable donations, employee volunteerism, and/or housing and educational programs.	+
Shareholder activism	The SRI funds that attempt to influence company actions through direct dialogue with management and/or voting at Annual General Meetings.	+
Unmarried	Avoid insurance companies that give coverage to unmarried couples.	–
Healthcare/ Pharmaceuticals	Avoid healthcare industries (used by funds targeting the "Christian Scientist" religious group).	–
Interest-based financial institutions	Avoid financial institutions that derive a significant portion of their income from interest earnings on loans or fixed-income securities (used by funds managed according to Islamic principles).	–
Pork producers	Avoid companies that derive a significant portion of their income from the manufacturing or marketing of pork products (used by funds managed according to Islamic principles).	–

HOW TO MEASURE THE PERFORMANCE OF SRI FUNDS

The performance of ethical (versus conventional) funds is measured by time-series returns of an equally weighted portfolio of funds. One can evaluate the performance of the fund portfolios on a country basis from a local investor perspective: The country portfolios of mutual funds are in local currency, evaluated against local benchmark factors while using local risk-free interest rates. Alternatively, one can assess fund performance from the perspective of an international investor by using international indices as benchmarks.

A first performance measurement method is based on the capital asset pricing model (CAPM):

$$r_t - r_{f,t} = \alpha_1 + \beta_{MKT}(r_t^m - r_{f,t}) + \epsilon_t$$

where r_t is the return on an equally weighted portfolio of funds in month t, $r_{f,t}$ is the return on a local risk-free deposit (i.e. the one-month treasury bill rate or the interbank interest rate), r_t^m is the return of a local equity market index, β_{MKT} is the factor loading on the market portfolio, and ϵ_t stands for the idiosyncratic return. α_1 is Jensen's alpha; if alpha is positive, the funds do better than anticipated, whereas a negative alpha indicates underperformance.

A more robust evaluation method consists of the four-factor model, which includes the market, size, book-to-market, and momentum factors (this is also called the Fama–French–Carhart model). This model controls for the impact of investment styles on performance:

"Invest with your brain and heart. Invest for our planet... The Funds give investors the ability to unite their financial goals with environmental progress." Sierra Club Funds prospectus

Table 2. SRI fund performance around the world. (*Source*: Renneboog, Ter Horst, and Zhang, 2008a)

		α_4
Europe		
Belgium	SRI	−5.26
Conventional		−0.78
Difference		−4.48
France	SRI	−5.96*
Conventional		−1.87
Difference		−4.08*
Germany	SRI	−0.62
Conventional		−1.35
Difference		0.73
Ireland	SRI	−6.14*
Conventional		0.55
Difference		−6.69*
Italy	SRI	−2.82
Conventional		0.86
Difference		−3.69
Luxembourg	SRI	−3.34
Conventional		0.11
Difference		−3.45
Netherlands	SRI	−4.10**
Conventional		−2.59*
Difference		−1.50
Norway	SRI	−4.20
Conventional		−1.12
Difference		−3.09
Sweden	SRI	−6.46*
Conventional		0.51
Difference		−6.97**
Switzerland	SRI	−3.01
Conventional		−0.91
Difference		−2.10
United Kingdom	SRI	−2.22*
Conventional		−1.14
Difference		−1.08
North America		
United States	SRI	−3.37*
Conventional		−2.48*
Difference		−0.89
Canada	SRI	−5.35*
Conventional		−2.24*
Difference		−3.11
Asia-Pacific		
Australia	SRI	−2.59
Conventional		−0.38
Difference		−2.21
Japan	SRI	−5.03*
Conventional		0.81
Difference		−5.84*
Malaysia	SRI	−2.99*
Conventional		0.44
Difference		−3.43
Singapore	SRI	−5.71
Conventional		0.95
Difference		−6.66

* Statistical significance

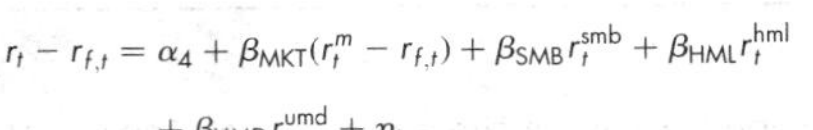

$$r_t - r_{f,t} = \alpha_4 + \beta_{\text{MKT}}(r_t^m - r_{f,t}) + \beta_{\text{SMB}} r_t^{\text{smb}} + \beta_{\text{HML}} r_t^{\text{hml}} + \beta_{\text{UMD}} r_t^{\text{umd}} + \eta_t$$

where r_t^{smb}, r_t^{hml}, and r_t^{umd} are the small-versus-big (SMB), high-minus-low (HML) and momentum (UMD) factors, β_{MKT}, β_{SMB}, β_{HML}, and β_{UMD} are the factor loadings on the four factors, and η_t stands for the idiosyncratic return. α_4 is the four-factor-adjusted return of ethical fund portfolios; if this alpha is positive, the funds do better than anticipated by this asset pricing model, whereas a negative alpha indicates underperformance.

More complex asset pricing models that allow for time-varying risk loadings can be implemented, but these are beyond the scope of this article.

Do SRI Funds Outperform?

- Performance measure 1: Is the alpha of the above asset pricing model positive? (Do SRI funds perform better than anticipated by a general asset pricing model that controls for the conventional investment styles?).
- Performance measure 2: Is the alpha of SRI funds higher than the alpha of conventional funds? (Do SRI funds outperform the reference group of conventional, non-SRI, funds?).

THE SRI RETURNS

For all SRI around the world over the period 1992–2003 (see More Info), some striking results are obtained. SRI funds in all countries on average underperform the stock market index, and SRI funds in all countries on average underperform conventional (non-SRI) funds.

Table 2 shows that:

- α_4 is negative for the SRI funds in all countries. Thus, SRI funds underperform the benchmarks: the market, size, book-to-market, and momentum factors (although it should be noted that some negative returns are not statistically different from zero).
- The conventional funds do not succeed in outperforming the market. The reason is simple: Active funds usually do not succeed in consistently beating the market.
- SRI funds on average underperform conventional funds.

CONCLUSION

Ethical, social, environmental, or governance considerations influence the stock prices, and investors pay a price for the use of SRI screening by funds. The main reason why SRI investors may be willing to pay such a price for ethics or social responsibility is based on aversion to corporate behavior which is deemed unethical or asocial. Investors of SRI funds may thus explicitly deviate from the economically rational goal of wealth-maximization by pursuing social objectives. SRI funds in many European, North-American and Asia-Pacific countries strongly underperform domestic benchmark portfolios (such as the Fama–French–Carhart factors). When comparing the alphas of the SRI funds with those of matched conventional funds, the SRI returns are lower than those of conventional funds, but there is little statistically significant evidence that SRI funds underperform their conventional counterparts in most countries (exceptions being France, Ireland, Sweden, and Japan).

CASE STUDY

In relation to the ethical fund of a major Dutch insurance company, we use the independent services of the Ethical Investment Research Service (EIRIS) to screen the suitability of shares for ethical investment. Shares are also screened by our in-house ethical research team.

Examples of the type of companies not suitable for ethical investment include companies that:

- provide animal testing services or which manufacture or sell animal tested cosmetics or pharmaceuticals;
- have any involvement in intensive farming and that operate abattoirs or slaughterhouse facilities;
- are producers or retailers of meat, poultry, fish, dairy products, or slaughterhouse byproducts;
- manufacture armaments, nuclear weapons, or associated strategic products;
- provide critical services to, or are owners or operators of, nuclear power facilities;
- provide adult entertainment services.

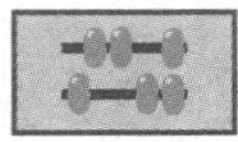

MAKING IT HAPPEN

- Decide whether you are an ethical investor: Do you care about the environment, the social responsibility of firms, human rights, or other social responsibility issues?
- If yes, are you willing to accept a return from an SRI fund that is less than that of conventional (non-SRI) funds?
- If yes, choose the type of fund by reading about the SRI of the fund. Select the screens that you deem most important—for instance, investment in producers of alternative
- energy; investment in firms with good human rights record in the developed and developing world; no investment in weapons manufacturers.
- energy; investment in firms with a good human rights record in the developed and developing world; no investment in weapons manufacturers.
- Choose the investment style of the fund: Do they use negative screens or a best-of-class approach on firms that pass the SRI filters?
- Compare the management and load fees of the selected SRI funds.

MORE INFO

Books:

Schepers, Donald. *Socially Responsible Investing*. London: Routledge, 2009.

Vogel, David. *The Market for Virtue: The Potential and Limits of Corporate Social Responsibility*. Washington, DC: Brookings Institution Press, 2006.

Articles:

Renneboog, Luc, Jenke ter Horst, and Chendi Zhang. "The price of ethics and stakeholder governance: The performance of socially responsible mutual funds." *Journal of Corporate Finance* 14:3 (June 2008a): 302–322. Online at: dx.doi.org/10.1016/j.jcorpfin.2008.03.009

Renneboog, Luc, Jenke ter Horst, and Chendi Zhang. "Socially responsible investments: Institutional aspects, performance, and investor behavior." *Journal of Banking and Finance* 32:9 (September 2008b): 1723–1742. Online at: dx.doi.org/10.1016/j.jbankfin.2007.12.039

Report:

Renneboog, Luc, Jenke ter Horst, and Chendi Zhang. "Is ethical money financially smart?" Finance working paper 117/2006. European Corporate Governance Institute, February 2006. Online at: ssrn.com/abstract=887162

Websites:

Social Investment Forum: www.socialinvest.org

Sustainable Investment Research International (SiRi): www.siricompany.com

See Also:

★ The Ability of Ratings to Predict the Performance of Exchange-Traded Funds (pp. 444–447)
★ Business Ethics (pp. 1829–1830)
★ CSR: More than PR, Pursuing Competitive Advantage in the Long Run (pp. 664–666)
★ Ethical Funds and Socially Responsible Investment: An Overview (pp. 481–483)
★ Understanding the Role of Diversification (pp. 617–618)
✔ Defining Corporate Governance: Its Aims, Goals, and Responsibilities (p. 1115)
✔ The Triple Bottom Line (p. 1125)
Ernst Friedrich Schumacher (p. 1307)
Muhammad Yunus (p. 1319)

"Our joint objective is that bankers should become uniformly acceptable as wise counsellors and friends of the community as a whole and not merely as associates of particular sections of society." Indira Gandhi

Price Discovery in IPOs by Jos van Bommel

EXECUTIVE SUMMARY

- When a company goes public, the issuer's intermediating investment bank (aka the underwriter, bookrunner, or lead manager) expends efforts and resources to discover the price at which the firm's shares can be sold.
- Buy-side clients also expend effort and resources to value the firm. The market price will be a weighted average of the many resulting value *estimates*.
- To discover the price at which the issue can be sold, the issuer helps buy-side clients with their analysis by providing a prospectus and meeting with their analysts during road show meetings.
- To extract newly produced information from the market, the issuing team asks selected buy-side clients for their indications of their interest.
- Investment banks compensate buy-side clients for their costly analysis by setting the price at a discount from the expected market price.
- In addition, investment banks allocate more shares to those buy-side clients who are more helpful in the price discovery exercise. Because of the repeated interaction between banks and their clients, free riding is curtailed, and price discovery is optimized.

PRICE DISCOVERY

The most important, yet most difficult, part of the initial public offering (IPO) process is setting the offer price. In an IPO, the issuer, aided by an intermediating investment bank, plans to sell a relatively large number of shares of common stock in which there is at that point no market. However, they know that soon after the IPO process the secondary market will impute all the information in the market in an efficient manner. Investors who believe the price to be too high will sell; investors who believe the price to be too low will buy. The key outcome of this competitive trading is the *market price* of the stock.

Naturally, the issuing team (the issuer and its investment bank would like to know the market price in advance. If they had a crystal ball, they would set the price at a small discount (say 3%) to the future market price, so as to generate sufficient interest from buy-side clients, and place the issue. In fact this is exactly what issuers do when they sell securities which already have a market price. Unfortunately, there is no secondary market for IPO shares, and neither are there crystal balls.

To estimate the market price as best as they can, issuers and their advisers conduct a costly analysis to estimate the value of the firm. We call this process *price discovery*.

Note that not only do the issuer and its investment bank analyze the firm. Prospective investors also conduct costly analysis to predict the future market price. Naturally, a good estimate of the future market price gives them a substantial advantage in their dealings with the issuer: If they have strong indications that the offer price is set too high, they stay away from the offering. If they believe the price to be below the future market price, they sign up for IPO shares enthusiastically.

ENTERPRISE VALUATION

There are two main methods to estimate the market value of the firm: multiple analysis, and discounted cash flow (DCF) analysis.

Multiple Analysis

When employing the multiple method, analysts gather performance measures of the firm. A popular measure is *earnings* or *net income*. They multiply these performance measures with *multiples*. The appropriate multiple for a firm's earnings is the *price–earnings ratio*, or P/E. The multiples are obtained from similar firms, (so-called *proxies*, or *pure-plays*). For example, if listed paper manufacturers trade at an average P/E of 9, and we want to estimate the value of an unlisted paper company that recently reported a net income of $1 million, we would estimate the market price to be $9 million. Because this single estimate is bound to be imprecise, analysts collect *many* performance measures so as to get *many* estimates. Popular accounting performance measures are earnings, sales, operating income (EBIT), and cash flow (EBITDA). Apart from these, analysts use industry-specific performance measures such as passenger miles (for airlines), overnight stays (for hotels), or page visits (for internet companies). By employing more and more multiples, analysts aim to arrive at an ever more precise estimate of the market price.

Discounted Cash Flow Analysis

A more fundamental valuation method is discounted cash flow analysis. In an efficient market, securities should be worth the present value of the future cash payments that accrue to the shareholders. Since cash today is always more valuable than cash tomorrow, investors discount projected future cash flows at the opportunity cost of capital. For example, if investors want to value a one-year promissory note of $100, and the one-year interest rate is 10%, they conclude that the note is worth $100/1.10 = $90.91. If future cash flows are uncertain (risky), investors use a higher discount rate (see p. 896 to see how the discount rate depends on risk).

Apart from deciding on an appropriate discount rate, investment analysts forecast the company's *free cash flows*, which are defined as the cash generated by operations less the cash dedicated to new investments. Often, young companies do not distribute cash flows to their financiers, but instead solicit cash from the financial markets. In fact, this is an important reason for doing an IPO in the first place. Naturally, the investments are expected to add to the future cash flows. Hence, analysts often predict negative free cash flows early in life, but expect them to become positive as the firm matures.

Forecasting a firm's free cash flows is difficult. To obtain reasonable conjectures, analysts make a *model* to project the revenues, expenses, and investments. Analysts' models can be very sophisticated. They analyze the products or services that the company provides, conduct industry analysis to gauge where the company stands vis-à-vis its competitors, consult market forecasts (of the firm's products and production costs), interview the firm's executives and other employees (as far as this is allowed by the laws that govern financial markets), and conduct sensitivity analysis.

Whatever method investment analysts use to estimate the market value of as yet untraded securities, valuing financial securities is a task that requires skill and effort.

ESTIMATES ARE OFTEN WRONG

Being an investment analyst does not just require hard work, it is also a risky job. After all, despite our best efforts, estimates often turn out to be wrong. That is the nature of *estimates*.

Each valuation is different. Analysts use different multiples, different proxies, and give different weights to individual multiple estimates. DCF valuations are highly sensitive to the many assumptions incorporated into a model, and to the discount rate used to arrive at a present value. Clearly, if we have many independent estimates, the highest estimate is likely to be too high and the lowest estimate is probably too low. If we assume that the estimates are unbiased, the true market value will lie somewhere in the middle.

Hence, there are two ways to engage in price discovery. The first is to help analysts

     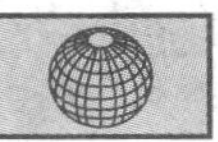   

to make more precise estimates. To do this, the issuer and its intermediaries (investment bank, auditor, legal advisers) provide buy-side analysts with a detailed prospectus, which explains the structure of the issue (for example, how many shares are sold), describes the company's business, and presents recent financial performance. In addition, they invite analysts to information sessions on the firm's products and managers. During such road-show presentations, the company presents its business plan, its managers, and its products to prospective investors. An important part of the road-show meetings is the question and answer session, during which analysts can pepper the issuing team with questions so as to fine-tune their models and estimates.

The second way to improve the price discovery is to involve more buy-side clients and more analysts. A statistical property called the *law of large numbers* says that if we have more estimates, the average of these will be closer to the true value. The problem, however, is that if we invite too many prospective investors, it will adversely affect the incentives to produce information.

SOUNDING OUT THE MARKET

When buy-side clients have done their analysis and have become "informed," issuers will find it easier to sell them their securities. However, there are still important differences in opinion among clients. Extracting these opinions is not an easy task. Clearly, buy-side clients will be reluctant to part with their hard-earned information. Nevertheless, issuers can *sound out the market* by individually targeting large and well-informed buy-side clients. They do this by ringing them up, and asking them for their opinions and indications of interest. The investment bank writes down indicative orders in a book of orders. This exercise is called *book-building*. Indicative orders can take three main forms. First there are *strike orders*, which indicate a demand that is independent of the price. Second, there are *limit orders*, such as "I sign up for 150,000 shares as long as the price is not higher than $10." Finally, there are *step* orders, which are combinations of several limit orders. For example, "If the price is set at $9 or below, we want 130,000 shares; if it is set at $10 or less, we want 80,000 shares; and if you set it higher, we don't want any shares."

After one or two weeks of making phone calls, the bookrunner will have compiled a book of orders, which forms a downward sloping demand curve (see Figure 1). Naturally, this demand curve represents very valuable information for the price discovery process.

SETTING THE PRICE

One would think that the issuing team can now simply set the price so that demand equals supply. If all orders were genuine, this would be the optimal strategy. However, the new shareholders would feel fooled if, after expending significant efforts to analyze the firm, they received no surplus in return. To reward large and sophisticated buy-side clients for their analysis of the firm, investment banks set the offer price at a discount from the expected market price. Historically, the average discount, which translates into an average *initial return* (the return from the offer price to the market price) has been around 15%. Initial returns have been extensively studied. Average discounts differ between countries and time periods. All studies, however, find that smaller and more difficult to value IPO firms tend to be discounted more, which is consistent with the "compensation for analysis efforts" story.

The promise of a discount can be made credible because of the investment bank's reputation and its repeated interaction with the market's buy-side. For example, because Fidelity knows that Goldman Sachs will price IPO shares at a reasonable discount, they are willing to expend effort to analyze the IPO firm.

The problem with setting the offer price at a discount is that it attracts "free riders." It seems that investors who simply signed up for all IPOs would, on average, make a profit because of the discount. For this reason, investment banks only invite large and sophisticated investors to submit orders in the book. From experience and repeated interaction, investment bankers know whose indicative orders are most informative. Still, even among the invited bidders there is a temptation to overbid. Because they know that the shares will be set at a discount, buy-side clients want to bid for as many shares as possible. In other words, even the orders of the repeat clients may not be entirely genuine. An important task for the investment bank is to distinguish the *real* demand from the *book* demand (Figure 1). They can never do this perfectly, but, through skill and judgment, experienced bookrunners can assess the seriousness of book orders. So, after closing the book, the issuer compiles the book demand curve, gauges where the real demand is, and then sets the price at a small discount.

The price is set during the *pricing meeting*, which typically takes place on the evening before the actual floatation. During the pricing meeting the issue is officially underwritten, so that the bookrunner becomes legally liable for placing the shares. By scheduling this important meeting shortly before the actual selling day, the bookrunner reduces the risk of being stuck with IPO shares on its books. In the example of Figure 1, the issuers may set the price at $9.50, so as to place all the shares, and leave some money on the table for the buy side analysts.

Figure 1. Example of an order book. During book-building, the lead manager calls up prospective buy-side clients and asks them for indicative orders. This results in an aggregate demand curve. However, the bookrunner knows that not all indications of interest are equally sincere, and he or she has to gauge what the *real demand* is—i.e. the demand that is not due to strategic overbidding (due to anticipated rationing). Notice that the real demand is invisible. Investment bankers use their experience and judgment to estimate it

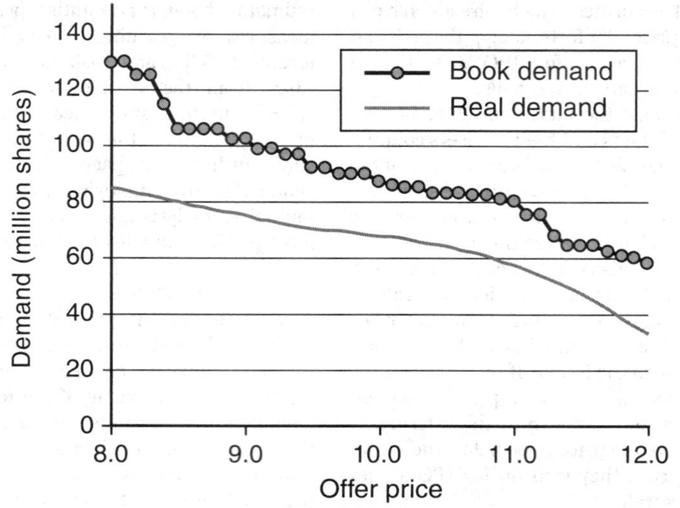

"I sincerely believe that banking establishments are more dangerous than standing armies, and that the principle of spending money to be paid by posterity, under the name of funding, is but swindling futurity on a large scale."
Thomas Jefferson

ALLOCATING THE SHARES

As mentioned, the IPO process is a repeated game for buy-side clients and investment banks. Both parties to the price discovery process develop long-term relationships. Investment bankers know which buy-side analysts provide the most accurate indications of interest, and reward them with higher allocations. One way to gauge the quality of the buy-side analysts is to monitor their order submission strategy and their trading behavior after the IPO. Strike orders may indicate poor analysis, while limit or step orders are better signals for price discovery. If a client often asks for large allocations, but then quickly sells ("flips") its shares in the secondary market, this is an indication of poor analysis. Orders that are submitted in the early stage of the book-building indicate confidence and informed decision-making. Hence, it is not surprising that we see that clients who put in limit or step orders early, and do not flip their shares in the secondary market, receive higher allocations on average.

THE OVER-ALLOTMENT OPTION

Almost all IPOs have an *over-allotment option*, also known as a *greenshoe*, named after the company that first used this mechanism. The over-allotment option gives the bookrunner the right to buy a specified number of additional shares from the issuer and sell them on to the buy-side. Or, they have the right to *over-allocate*. Typically, the option is for 15% of the offering size. In practice, the underwriter always over-allocates, so that after the offering the bank is technically "short": they have sold shares they do not yet own. The bookrunner will exercise the over-allotment option if the price in secondary market trading increases beyond the offering price, which is usually the case. If, however, the price in the secondary market comes under pressure (i.e. there is a lot of flipping), the underwriter buys back the shares in the open market.

This is sometimes referred to as *price support* or *price stabilization*. The over-allotment option is therefore a clever way to adjust the supply of shares to the uncertain demand for shares. By keeping track of flippers, bookrunners can monitor buy-side clients and gauge their quality for the price discovery process.

BOOK-BUILDING VERSUS AUCTIONS

The book-building mechanism has become the standard way of selling shares in initial public offerings. The characteristic difference from other IPO mechanisms is the close and personal interaction between relatively few players on both sides of the transaction. These cozy relationships, and the subsequent preferential allocations, sometimes make small investors, issuers, and regulators uneasy about the book-building mechanism. Naturally there is the chance that investment banks and buy-side clients collude to set the offer price low and share the profits of large initial returns. Although there certainly have been instances of doubtful allocations of conspicuously underpriced shares, the book-building mechanism has survived and is widely accepted. The key advantage is that it results in more *information production*.

An obvious alternative to book-building is the auction. Due to its fair and transparent nature, the auction mechanism has been used in several countries, including the United Kingdom, Denmark, and France. However, evidence shows that they are less effective in achieving a high price and a liquid aftermarket. Empirical studies have found that book-built IPOs have, on average, lower initial returns, especially if they were floated by prestigious investment banks.

The Google IPO and a stylized example (see Case Studies) further illustrate how targeted information exchange between relatively few informed players may be more effective for price discovery than an impersonal auction.

CASE STUDIES

The Google IPO

When Google went public in August 2004, it announced upfront that the price would be determined by a competitive Dutch auction in which everybody could participate on equal terms. Large and small investors were invited to submit their limit and step orders through the internet. The price would be set at the point where the 19.6 million shares could be sold. Large institutional investors openly grumbled and complained about the "cheap" way in which Google was selling its shares, saying that they would not bother to get out of bed for an auction.

The result was that, due to the lack of a targeted information exchange, the market price was not fully discovered. The auctioneers set the offer price at $85. When secondary market trading began, the price shot to above $100 within days, and above $200 within months, which suggested that Google did not get the full value for its shares. Many industry watchers (and the author of this article) believe that if Google had opted for a standard book building method, its shares may have fetched a higher price in the primary market.

Illustration of Targeted Information Exchange

Imagine that you receive a surprise inheritance from a distant uncle. The inheritance is a trunk full of foreign coins. Most are post-war coins from various countries, but your seven-year-old son has spotted some gold, silver, and very ancient coins. You are not much of a coin collector and are strapped for cash, so you decide to sell the coins. To do this you go to a coin collectors' fair. At the fair there is an auction session where you can put your coins up for sale. Alternatively, you can approach the three largest collectors, let each have a close look at your collection, explain your situation, and ask them for their offer. If your collection is difficult to value (as a company is), the second route may well get you a higher price.

MORE INFO

Books:

Draho, Jason. *The IPO Decision: Why and How Companies Go Public*. Cheltenham, UK: Edward Elgar Publishing, 2006.

Gregoriou, Greg N. *Initial Public Offerings: An International Perspective*. Oxford: Butterworth-Heinemann, 2006.

Article:

Benveniste, Lawrence M., and Walid Y. Busaba. "Bookbuilding versus fixed price: An analysis of competing strategies for marketing IPOs." *Journal of Financial and Quantitative Analysis* 32:4 (1997): 383–403. Online at: dx.doi.org/10.2307/2331230

Websites:

IPO Financial Network (IPOfn) news, analysis, and resources: www.ipofinancial.com

IPO Monitor—Coverage of IPOs and secondary equity offerings: www.ipomonitor.com

IPO Renaissance Capital—research and investment management services on newly public companies: www.ipohome.com

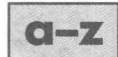

Viewpoint: Principles for Responsible Investment—Looking Beyond the Financial Metrics by James Gifford

INTRODUCTION

James Gifford is executive director of the PRI initiative and has been guiding the initiative since its inception in 2003. He worked with UNEP FI and the UN Global Compact, leading the PRI drafting process, and after the launch of the PRI secretariat in 2006 became its first executive director. He has a PhD from the Faculty of Economics and Business at the University of Sydney on the effectiveness of shareholder engagement in improving corporate environmental, social, and corporate governance performance, and a background in IT and environmental protection. In 2010 Gifford was named by the World Economic Forum as one of 200 Young Global Leaders.

What were the origins of the United Nations-backed Principles for Responsible Investment (PRI) initiative?

The PRI initiative is a network of international investors that work together to put the six Principles for Responsible Investment into practice. The PRI came out of two UN agencies: the UN Environment Programme Finance Initiative (UNEP FI) and the UN Global Compact (UNGC). UNEP FI works with banks, insurance companies, and asset managers on environmental, social, and corporate governance (ESG) issues, while the Global Compact encourages organizations to sign up to a set of 10 principles. The Global Compact is the United Nations' key initiative on corporate responsibility. In late 2003 we started thinking about ways to enable the UN to work more closely with the investment sector, and pension funds in particular, to deliver a more sustainable economy. Our team at UNEP FI proposed the development of a set of principles focused on what it would take to create a business case for mainstream pension funds and asset managers to engage with sustainability issues via ESG integration and active ownership.

In 2005, the UN Secretary-General Kofi Annan wrote to 20 of the world's largest pension funds, inviting them to UN headquarters in New York to commit to developing a set of responsible investment principles. The drafting process took place over 11 days of meetings with investors and experts, and the initial six principles were launched with some fanfare at the New York Stock Exchange in April 2006. Within a year of the launch, about 50 investor organizations had signed up.

Today there are more than 1,100 signatories, representing about US$32 trillion of assets under management, or about 15% of total global capital. Interest in becoming a signatory extends beyond the United States and Europe. We have tremendous support, for example, in Brazil, where more than half the total funds under management in that country have signed up. In Korea the National Pension Service, the fourth largest pension fund in the world, is a signatory, and they are showing real leadership in Asia. Similarly, in South Africa, GEPF, the government employees pension fund, has been a champion in that market. Australia is also very strong, with our signatories managing half of the funds under management in that country, including the majority of its superannuation funds. China, India, the Middle East, and Spanish-speaking Latin America, however, are in early stages of awareness of these issues.

Sustainability has a range of meanings. How should investors relate to the PRI initiative?

Responsible investment today is very different from the earlier movement of ethical investing and it is not focused on restricting the range of potential investments based on absolute criteria. The PRI started from the premise of engaging mainstream investors and investment processes. Telling investors they should restrict themselves to an approved list was never going to resonate with fund managers whose priorities are to achieve their benchmark returns. If we wanted to engage mainstream investors on ESG issues, it had to be entirely aligned with their fiduciary duties and, therefore, had to focus on the business case.

The PRI initiative takes a twofold approach. First, we encourage investors to look at ESG issues from a risk and opportunity perspective. The world is changing very fast. There are hugely important megatrends going on around environmental shifts, societal developments, and changes in regulatory frameworks and governance; all of these present challenges for investors and fund managers. Traditional fund managers have measured success in terms of a very narrow and short-term set of metrics, and it is clear that there are real risks with that approach. Mainstream investment is increasingly embracing the view that you need a much broader understanding of future value drivers and that traditional narrow financial metrics simply represent the tip of the iceberg, and a deeper analysis of ESG issues can help to work out what might be under the water.

Investors should therefore look at a broad range of ESG issues when evaluating and valuing companies. This does not mean that you need some kind of exclusion filter, but rather that you should look at issues such as a company's environmental performance and its relationship with its community, and how these may affect its future business. To understand the potential impact of ESG issues on shareholder value you only have to look at examples like Lonmin in South Africa, with its labor issues, which have led to a dramatic destruction of shareholder value. Similarly, it was relatively well known in the industry that BP's US division was not managing safety issues as well as its peers prior to Macondo. Massey Energy in the United States also had a poor safety record that led to a dramatic loss of shareholder value.

It is a relatively straightforward argument to make to investors that the companies that are going to prosper over the long term are those that manage ESG issues better than their peers. We encourage our signatories to consider these issues deeply when they make investment decisions. For example, when you assess two mining companies with similar fundamentals, a review of their respective ESG performance can help to reveal which one may offer the better long-term prospect and lower risk.

What is becoming clearer to investors is that ESG issues can have very material consequences, and investors have not traditionally paid attention to these issues, which could drive, or destroy, value for shareholders in the future.

Where does shareholder and investor stewardship fit into this?

The Principles themselves (see panel) were originally designed to provide a framework around which to build an active community of investors sharing best practices and, ultimately, pooling resources and influence to seek improvements in the ESG performance of investee companies. It was felt that this community would only develop, and the initiative would only fulfill its potential, if the Principles were backed by a dedicated secretariat tasked to promote them, build the community, and coordinate investor collaboration. As soon as the Principles were launched, a secretariat was established and got to work, with the strong support of the UN partner agencies.

Stewardship is the second pillar of mainstream responsible investment, and active ownership is reflected in Principle 2. The PRI urge investors to take their stewardship responsibilities seriously. They are part owners, after all, and that comes with responsibilities. If not, who will hold management to account? If capitalism is to function and flourish, it needs responsibility and accountability across the whole agency chain, from company employees right through to the owners of companies and their customers and beneficiaries. It requires monitoring and the necessary information flows to make stewardship possible. When responsible investors look carefully at the behavior of the companies they are holding in their portfolios, they will press companies that are not managing their ESG risks appropriately to do so. Investors need to engage the companies they hold in dialog, and they need to vote at annual general meetings in an informed way. They also need to vote against management when they feel that the company is on the wrong track, and they need to encourage management generally to be more long-term in its thinking. We do a lot of work with our signatories to encourage the companies in their portfolios to be world-class in their approach to ESG issues.

Transparency is another principle enshrined in the PRI. It goes hand-in-hand with stewardship, and investors should ensure that they are getting sufficient information from management to have a clear and appropriate view of the business.

How does the PRI initiative ensure that its signatories are accountable?

The PRI has an annual reporting and assessment process that is mandatory for all investor signatories to complete. We have compiled good statistics on what our signatories are doing with respect to implementing responsible investment, and it is fair to say that there has been increased activity with respect to responsible investment.

The PRI clearinghouse remains one of the most important strategic priorities for the initiative. Its role is to stimulate collaboration among large investors with companies on their ESG performance. Using a private online forum, investors post proposals for collaboration with peers to seek changes in company behavior, public policies, or systemic conditions, or they simply discuss issues of concern. The clearinghouse lowers the barriers of entry to active ownership and offers leverage to single institutions that may have a "good point" that others may not have identified. The tool, starting as a simple online bulletin board, has become an active hub of investor collaboration hosted on a searchable IT platform and supported by a number of dedicated staff. The PRI secretariat also works with signatories to come up with new ideas for collaboration and ensures that they are framed in ways that are likely to gain as much support as possible from peers.

The clearinghouse is one of the most active areas of signatory participation, and more than 350 signatories have joined in collaborations.

How well do companies respond to shareholder concerns?

There are generally a number of dialogs taking place, and sometimes the companies respond well to shareholder concerns and sometimes they don't. In the United States it is common practice for investors to file shareholder resolutions when they feel they are not getting the response they need from companies or the attention of their boards. In other countries shareholder resolutions tend to be seen as very confrontational.

Disclosure on ESG issues, which is at the heart of Principle 3, is key to much of what we do, so naturally there is an emphasis on encouraging companies (via their owners) to improve ESG disclosure. Principle 6 focuses on disclosure from the investor side, and encourages signatories to communicate with clients, customers, and beneficiaries about ESG issues and their approaches to PRI implementation. This includes determining the impact the PRI make on their investment processes and, ultimately, investee companies.

A lot of the work done in the clearinghouse revolves around finding ways to encourage companies to produce systematic disclosures about their business operations that are compliant with recognized frameworks, such as the Global Reporting Initiative or the Global Compact's Communication on Progress.

One of the successes of the PRI is that we have been able to bring investors together globally to address collective action issues. Before the PRI, there was no global forum capable of bringing investors together to address these problems across a full range of ESG issues. As well as engaging with corporations and industry sectors, our signatories engage with governments on specific issues. Investors can encourage and lobby for appropriate policies, and they can drive voluntary initiatives within the corporate and investment sectors.

The Extractive Industries Transparency Initiative, for example, is an initiative that has been driven both by the UK and other governments, investors, and Transparency International, the world's leading nongovernmental anticorruption agency. This leverages the power of investors to push governments to sign up to the UN Global Compact and to implement reporting requirements that encourage greater transparency on issues such as facilitation payments and royalty payments.

What our reporting and analysis shows beyond doubt is that the companies that create the most value are those that deliver on these wider objectives. There is a very strong connection between creating financial value for shareholders and creating products and services that people want, make their lives better, and are aligned with what society wants. That alignment between financial prosperity and the interests of society as a whole converges over the longer term. If you take a pension or superannuation fund, its obligations to its members extend over a two- to four-decade time frame, so it has a natural interest in wanting to be part of a long-term productive enterprise that is delivering value to society. This is at the heart of the culture that the PRI initiative is trying to generate: encouraging investors to invest in productive enterprises that deliver real value to society is the classic win–win over the long term.

Appendix: the UN Principles for Responsible Investment (PRI)

As institutional investors, we have a duty to act in the best long-term interests of our beneficiaries. In this fiduciary role, we believe that environmental, social, and corporate governance (ESG) issues can affect the performance of investment portfolios (to varying degrees across companies, sectors, regions, asset classes and through time). We also recognize that applying these Principles may better align investors with broader objectives of society. Therefore, where consistent with our fiduciary responsibilities, we commit to the following:

Principle 1. We will incorporate ESG issues into investment analysis and decision-making processes.
Possible actions:
- Address ESG issues in investment policy statements.
- Support development of ESG-related tools, metrics, and analyses.
- Assess the capabilities of internal investment managers to incorporate ESG issues.
- Assess the capabilities of external investment managers to incorporate ESG issues.
- Ask investment service providers (such as financial analysts, consultants, brokers, research firms, or rating companies) to integrate ESG factors into evolving research and analysis.
- Encourage academic and other research on this theme.
- Advocate ESG training for investment professionals.

Principle 2. We will be active owners and incorporate ESG issues into our ownership policies and practices.
Possible actions:
- Develop and disclose an active ownership policy consistent with the Principles.
- Exercise voting rights or monitor compliance with voting policy (if outsourced).
- Develop an engagement capability (either directly or through outsourcing).
- Participate in the development of policy, regulation, and standard-setting (such as promoting and protecting shareholder rights).
- File shareholder resolutions consistent with long-term ESG considerations.
- Engage with companies on ESG issues.
- Participate in collaborative engagement initiatives.
- Ask investment managers to undertake and report on ESG-related engagement.

Principle 3. We will seek appropriate disclosure on ESG issues by the entities in which we invest.
Possible actions:
- Ask for standardized reporting on ESG issues (using tools such as the Global Reporting Initiative).
- Ask for ESG issues to be integrated within annual financial reports.
- Ask for information from companies regarding adoption of/adherence to relevant norms, standards, codes of conduct, or international initiatives (such as the UN Global Compact).
- Support shareholder initiatives and resolutions promoting ESG disclosure.

Principle 4. We will promote acceptance and implementation of the Principles within the investment industry.
Possible actions:
- Include Principles-related requirements in requests for proposals (RFPs).
- Align investment mandates, monitoring procedures, performance indicators, and incentive structures accordingly (for example, ensure that investment management processes reflect long-term time horizons when appropriate).
- Communicate ESG expectations to investment service providers.
- Revisit relationships with service providers that fail to meet ESG expectations.
- Support the development of tools for benchmarking ESG integration.
- Support regulatory or policy developments that enable implementation of the Principles.

Principle 5. We will work together to enhance our effectiveness in implementing the Principles.
Possible actions:
- Support/participate in networks and information platforms to share tools, pool resources, and make use of investor reporting as a source of learning.
- Collectively address relevant emerging issues.
- Develop or support appropriate collaborative initiatives.

Principle 6. We will each report on our activities and progress toward implementing the Principles.
Possible actions:
- Disclose how ESG issues are integrated within investment practices.
- Disclose active ownership activities (voting, engagement, and/or policy dialog).
- Disclose what is required from service providers in relation to the Principles.
- Communicate with beneficiaries about ESG issues and the Principles.
- Report on progress and/or achievements relating to the Principles using a "comply or explain" approach.
- Seek to determine the impact of the Principles.
- Make use of reporting to raise awareness among a broader group of stakeholders.

MORE INFO

Websites:

Extractive Industries Transparency Initiative (EITI): eiti.org
Principles for Responsible Investment (PRI): www.unpri.org
Transparency International: www.transparency.org
United Nations Environment Programme Finance Initiative (UNEP FI): www.unepfi.org
United Nations Global Compact (UNGC): www.unglobalcompact.org
United Nations Global Compact "Progress & Disclosure" section—includes page on the annual Communication on Progress (COP) reporting: www.unglobalcompact.org/COP/

See Also:

★ Ethical Funds and Socially Responsible Investment: An Overview (pp. 481–483)
★ Viewpoint: Green Investing—Looking beyond the Financial Metrics (pp. 492–493)
★ Viewpoint: Outperformance through Ethical Lending (pp. 546–548)

"Those who invest only to get rich will fail. Those who invest to help others will probably succeed." Art Fry

  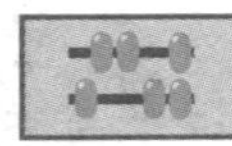      

Public–Private Partnerships in Emerging Markets

by Peter Koveos and Pierre Yourougou

EXECUTIVE SUMMARY

- A public–private partnership (PPP) is an "arrangement in which the private sector supplies infrastructure assets and services traditionally provided by governments."
- The public and private sectors have different goals and organizational philosophies and cultures. Reconciling these differences requires a strong commitment, and a clear vision regarding expectations and outcomes.
- The essence of PPP is risk allocation—whether these operations add value depends primarily on how risk is identified, managed, and priced.
- In emerging markets, international partners must address not only the project risk and country risk, but also the risks posed by the lack of local managerial skills, inadequacy of institutions, corruption, lack of transparency, and others.
- Project financing can be used for PPP projects, thus clarifying a key element of the partnership financing structure.
- One of the most significant and interesting global economic developments of the past few years is the emergence of Africa as a competitive region for business.
- The Bujagali Hydropower Project represents the largest mobilization of private financing for a power project in Africa.

INTRODUCTION

Given the poor state of public-sector resources around the world, made even worse by the global financial crisis, governments have been seeking to enhance resources by attracting private sector participation. Such participation may be somewhat unstructured, or more formal. The public–private partnership (PPP) is one of the formal approaches to cooperation. PPP, in various forms, is not a new construct. The current frailties of the global economy have forced governments to reduce costs and limit risks. This paper examines the nature of PPP, and describes some of the advantages and disadvantages of PPP. The discussion then focuses on the viability of PPP in emerging markets in general, and African countries in particular. A case study, Bujagali Hydropower Project in Uganda, illustrates many of the major concepts discussed throughout this paper.

DEFINITIONS/NATURE OF PPP

There are many definitions of PPP. Most versions of PPP are very similar, although the degree of control shared by the partners, and several other characteristics of the partnership may receive different emphasis from definition to definition. Thus, PPP is an "arrangement in which the private sector supplies infrastructure assets and services traditionally provided by governments" (Michel, 2008). Other terms for PPP include: PPI (private participation in infrastructure); PSP (private sector participation); in the UK, the term used is PFI (private finance initiative); in Australia, the reference is to PFP (privately financed projects); and P3 is commonly used in the US (see Yescombe, 2007). Other variants include the build–transfer–lease (BTL) and build–own–operate–transfer (BOOT) options. In some cases, two or more of the above terms can be used in combination. For example, project financing can be used for PPP projects, thus clarifying a key element of the partnership, financing. Project financing schemes may involve a variety of instruments such as the special-purpose vehicle (SPV), a legal entity with its own assets and obligations. Creation of this joint venture among project sponsors enables the flow of funds. An SPV is a highly leveraged company, with typically limited-recourse debt and limited equity participation. PPP can indeed be very complicated, and requires thorough analysis of associated terms and conditions.

PPP: SOME ADVANTAGES AND DISADVANTAGES

PPP is part of the recent movement of "new public management." PPP is a means through which the two sectors can become interdependent. Managers in each sector must independently answer some basic questions: Why are we participating in this partnership? Where are we going to operate? Who are our partners? How are we going to proceed? What is our exit strategy?

Specific benefits for the public sector include:

- reduces project costs and time, while enhancing its overall efficiency and effectiveness;
- enables access to and learning from private sector resources, technology, and managerial skills;
- credit enhancement and, consequently, access to long-term financing;
- shifts risk to the private sector;
- pursues an integrated approach to project completion;
- involves participation from various partners, and may legitimize the project in the eyes of the citizenry, and other stakeholders;
- PPP may provide greater economic benefits than other forms of cooperation,

Figure 1. Bujagali project simplified stockholding structure

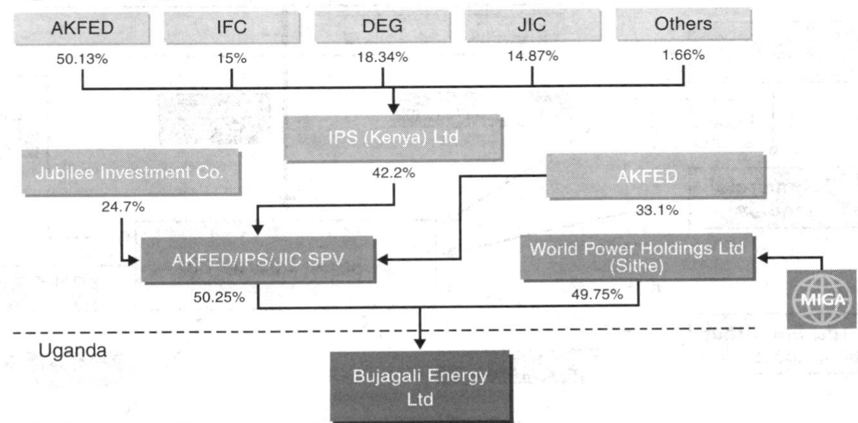

Data adapted from Bujagali Energy Limited for the Private Power Generation (Bujagali) project. "Project appraisal document." World Bank/IFC/MIGA Report No. 3 842 1 –UG, pages 68 and 72

"Anybody who said that brands were irrelevant in the 1980s will be singing the blues in the next millennium."
Michael Ovitz

such as public sector procurement. These extra benefits are usually referred to as value for money (VfM).

For the private sector participant, the analysis is based on the profitability of the project in terms of dollars and cents, and is usually more objective than that conducted by the public sector. Participation in a given project can be analyzed using standard finance tools. These projects usually involve a great deal of risk, but government backing and involvement of international financial institutions help mitigate risks. The limits of risk–return trade-offs, and the ensuing risk allocation, are even more crucial factors leading to project assessment. A great deal of emphasis is placed on risk management, including the formulation of an exit strategy.

PPP also involves potential disadvantages. PPP entails considerable agency costs, as it must be thoroughly cultivated and managed in terms of planning, monitoring, and acceptance of loss of some control. Private and public sectors often have different goals, and organizational philosophies and cultures. Reconciling these differences in order to bring about the desired project results requires a strong commitment, and a clear vision regarding expectations and outcomes.

Figure 2. Bujagali project financing plan

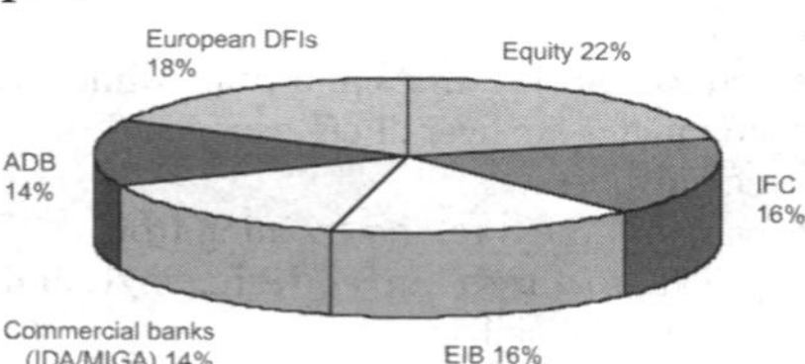

Data adapted from Bujagali Energy Limited for the Private Power Generation (Bujagali) project. "Project appraisal document." World Bank/IFC/MIGA Report No. 3 842 1 –UG, page 16

The above are especially relevant to public authorities in emerging markets. As emerging markets are so diverse, the analysis must be adjusted to fit the particular country's environment.

EMERGING MARKETS

The term "emerging market" is used to describe countries whose economies are undergoing a significant transition through a series of reforms.

For a private sector firm, operating in an emerging market can be an attractive prospect leading to profit generation, increased market share, and access to growing markets. The firm's ability to access this opportunity depends on how risk is identified, managed, and priced. Business risks exist in every country. Operating in emerging markets, however, may make these risks even more prevalent. The potential risks include:

- Political risk, defined as a change in government policy that affects foreign companies, is often associated with weak political, legal, and institutional infrastructures. To manage political risk, foreign organizations must be familiar with the political landscape, and learn how to operate in an uncertain and different environment. Property rights, a staple of Western economic institutions, can often be easily undermined. The heavy hand of government can also interfere with a firm's plans and desired outcomes.
- Economic risk. In general, emerging markets exhibit a higher degree of volatility than that shown by developed economies. Even assessing the state of the economy in many of these markets is challenging, as the "official statistics" may not be accurate. Partners, then, must rely on their own analysis of future market conditions for their services.
- Financial risk, stemming from a country's financial system weakness, may impact on the value of the currency and, subsequently, the company's bottom line.
- Other risks. The country's immature economic infrastructure is vulnerable to a number of disruptions. International partners must address risks posed by the lack of local managerial skills, inadequacy of institutions, corruption, lack of transparency, social issues, income inequalities, pollution, and other elements in the operating environment.

AFRICA

One of the most significant and interesting global economic developments of the past few years is the emergence of Africa as a competitive region for business. Africa is

Figure 3. Project contractual arrangements

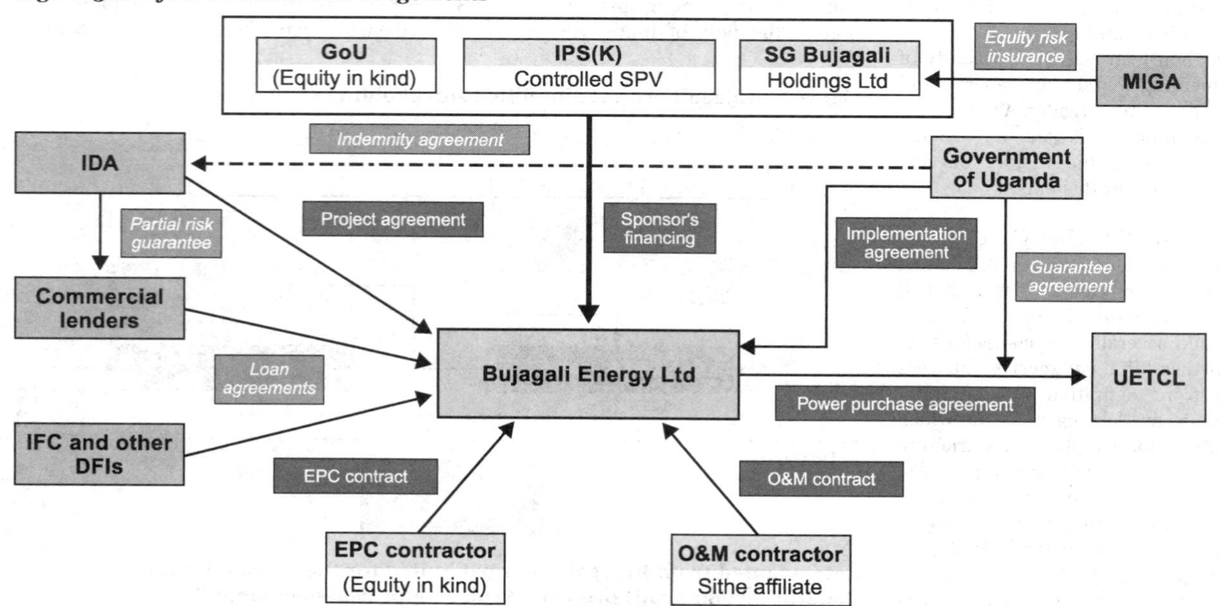

Data adapted from "Project appraisal document" World Bank/IFC/MIGA Report No. 38421–UG, page 21

CASE STUDY

Bujagali Hydropower Project, Uganda

The Bujagali Project is a private power generation project. The 250 MW run-of-the-river hydro-electric power plant, comprised of five 50 MW turbines, was completed in June 2012. The project is located on the Victoria–Nile on Dumbbell Island, Jinja, Uganda, and it achieved its financial closing in December 2007. Bujagali is the first independent power project (IPP) in Uganda, and the largest mobilization of private financing for a power project in Africa. It was named "Africa Power Deal of the Year 2007" by *Project Finance* magazine. Bujagali is a good example of how various international financial institutions can work together with private sector project sponsors to address their financing and risk mitigation concerns, and meet the client country's economic objectives.

Rationale for PPP

According to the World Bank, the severe shortage of electricity in Uganda contributed to a decline in GDP growth to around 5% in 2005/06. Bujagali is an essential part of Uganda's energy-sector strategy to provide a sustainable and affordable source of electricity. The government of Uganda lacks, however, the necessary technical expertise and financing to complete the project on its own. Private sector participation was sought to fill the gap.

Project Partners

The Bujagali project has been described as a global story for bringing together partners from 37 countries. It is a public–private partnership between the private sector project sponsors represented by Bujagali Energy Ltd (BEL), the government of Uganda, including the Ministry of Energy and Mineral Development (MEMD) and Uganda Electricity Transmission Company Ltd (UETCL), multilateral and bilateral development financial institutions,[1] and commercial lenders, including Absa Capital (South Africa) and Standard Chartered Bank (UK). BEL, a special-purpose company (SPC), is incorporated in Uganda, and is privately owned by Industrial Promotion Services (Kenya) Ltd (IPS (K)), the industrial development arm of the Aga Khan Fund for Economic Development (AKFED) and SG Bujagali Holdings Ltd (Mauritius), an affiliate of US-based Sithe Global Power LLC. The sponsors were selected through international competitive bidding procedures.

Project Description

The Bujagali project is developed, financed, constructed, and maintained by BEL on a BOOT basis. BEL also manages the construction of the Interconnection Project on behalf of UECTL, which will own and operate the project. The Interconnection Project involves the construction of about 100 km of high-voltage electrical transmission line to interconnect the power generation facility (the Bujagali project) to the national electric grid. Structured as IPP, BEL will sell the electricity to UETCL, Uganda's national transmission company, under a 30-year power purchase agreement (PPA).

Financing

Finance for the project is structured as an integrated package for both the power plant and transmission components. The total cost for the integrated projects, about US$900 million, is mobilized on a limited-recourse basis, through equity and debt in the ratio of 22:78. The government of Uganda provided an in-kind equity contribution of US$20 million. The equity financing is shared by the sponsors, IPS (K) and SG Bujagali Holdings Ltd, on a pro rata basis. The equity structure of BEL is complex. Figure 1 provides a simplified description.

The debt is being financed by loans from the group of lenders, the World Bank group providing a far more substantial amount of US$360 million (US$130 million loan from IFC, US$115 million partial-risk guarantee from International Development Association to commercial lenders, and US$115 investment guarantee from Multilateral Investment Guarantee (MIGA) to cover the equity position of SG Bujagali Holding Ltd). The project financing plan is described in Figure 2.

Contractual Arrangements and Risk-Sharing Mechanism

Contractual agreements define the transactions and allocation of the commercial, technical, and political risks among the partners.
The contractual structure of the Bujagali project is consistent with industry practice for limited-recourse project finance transactions (see Figure 3). The project implementation agreement (IA), also called the concession agreement, signed between the government of Uganda and BEL on December 13, 2005, defines the terms of the concession the government grants to BEL to design, finance, own, operate, and maintain the project. Under the 30-year PPA, BEL agrees to sell exclusively to UETCL all the production, and UETCL agrees to purchase the contracted capacity (i.e., 250 MW), with the government guaranteeing the UETCL's payment obligations. In addition to the IA and PPA, BEL signed a fixed-price, date certain, turnkey engineering, procurement, and construction (EPC) contract with Salini Costruttori SpA (Italy), and Alsthom Power Hydraulique (France), and an operation and maintenance (O&M) agreement with affiliates of Sithe Global. The EPC contract requires the power plant to be commissioned within 44 months. The EPC contractors were selected through competitive bidding, in accordance with the EIB procurement rules. The O&M agreement reflects BEL's commitments under the PPA.

The contractual structure ensured that the project-related risks, including completion and operation, were borne by the project sponsors and commercial lenders. However, these risks were mitigated by contracts and various insurance arrangements. The risks related to supply/input (hydrology risk), market, political, and natural forces were borne by the government of Uganda under the government guarantee and implementation agreements. The participation of the IFC and the guarantees provided by the World Bank group (IDA and MIGA) are critical in mitigating the completion risk, and to provide Uganda with access to long-maturity commercial loans in favorable terms.

Reaction to the Project

A project as large in impact and scope as Bujagali is bound to generate considerable reaction and skepticism. Indeed, critics point out that construction proceeded prior to resolving a number of important issues regarding the impact of the project. Questions are still being asked about the cost of the project and its true impact on the Ugandan economy, lack of resolution of compensation and resettlement challenges, hydrological and climate risks, the project's cumulative impact, and the consultation process.

Although some of these questions may never be completely answered, the Bujagali story should serve as a lesson for future PPP projects.

"As the retail trade consolidates, it will look more and more at big fresh brands that are constantly innovating."
Niall Fitzgerald

the fastest reformer in terms of easing business entry. It is now easier for private foreign firms to do business in Africa, due to recently simplified business regulations, strengthened property rights, eased tax burdens, increased access to credit, and other economic reforms. African countries are diverse with respect to their politics and economics. The risks of doing business may vary in their nature and intensity from country to country. These risks may emanate from the region's poverty, numerous conflicts, corruption, and health problems, or from the lack of adequate infrastructure. Risks also present opportunities—for example, infrastructure projects are often open to foreign participation. Moreover, many risks can be mitigated through bilateral official insurers (for example, OPIC), multilateral insurers (for example, MIGA) and private risk insurers (for example, AIG). Africa has provided the stage for PPP in such sectors as utilities, energy, minerals, health, tourism, and others.

CONCLUSION

Globalization has led to the emergence of new economies. With scarce resources, the public sector in many economies needs private sector partners. PPP is a unique opportunity for the two diverse sectors to learn how to work together. For the public sector, shifting risks and securing financing are important benefits. For the private sector, the environment represents an opportunity to add value to the organization, and act in a socially responsible manner. PPP involves complicated arrangements that require a great deal of expertise and flexibility. The essence of PPP is risk allocation—preparation, and proper risk management and pricing are a must.

Contract arrangements are very complex. For PPP to be successful, the contract must be well-designed to provide the private provider with compatible incentives and the public authority with monitoring mechanisms, and to channel private-profit-motivated objectives to attain the government's broader social objectives.

Bujagali's total impact is envisioned to be far wider than radically upgrading the country's electricity production capacity. It is also expected to revamp Uganda's social, environmental, economic, and education infrastructure. These additional effects make the Bujagali project, and PPPs in general, valuable contributors to a region's business, economic, and social development.

NOTES

1 The institutions include the African Development Bank (ADB), European Investment Bank (EIB), the World Bank Group, Agence Française de Développement (AFD), Proparco, Netherlands Development Finance Company (FMO), Kreditanstalt für Wiederaufbau (KfW), and Deutsche Investitions und Entwicklungsgesellschaft (DEG).

MAKING IT HAPPEN

- Conduct a readiness analysis of your organization.
- Know exactly what you want and expect.
- Know what the various partners want and expect.
- Work to build trust among partners.
- Put together a solid risk management process, with clear accountability and understanding of the risks faced, how they are allocated, and how risk is to be priced.
- Be as specific as possible about your role and responsibilities.
- Familiarize yourself with the nature and operations of international financial institutions and agencies, such as the World Bank, its affiliated agencies (IFC, IDA, MIGA), and other cooperating organizations.
- Make sure you do a feasibility study and conduct due diligence.
- Go slow! Learning about PPP is important. Existing relationships could serve as an easier first step.
- Decide on what valuation techniques would be appropriate (for example, internal rate of return, net present value, adjusted present value, and real options).
- Analyze all possible scenarios.
- Review and revise as appropriate.
- Work towards a sustainable relationship, but have an exit strategy.

MORE INFO

Books:

Akintoye, Akintola, Matthias Beck, and Cliff Hardcastle. *Public–Private Partnerships: Managing Risks and Opportunities*. Malden, MA: Blackwell Science, 2003.

Asian Development Bank (ADB). *Public-Private Partnership Handbook*. Manila: ADB, 2008. Online at: tinyurl.com/blbwxwv

Grimsey, Darrin, and Mervyn Lewis. *Public Private Partnerships: The Worldwide Revolution in Infrastructure Provision and Project Finance*. Northampton, MA: Edward Elgar, 2007.

Mobius, J. Mark. *Mobius on Emerging Markets*. New York: Irwin Professional, 1996.

Osborne, Stephen P. (ed). *Public–Private Partnerships: Theory and Practice in International Perspective*. London: Routledge, 2000.

Yescombe, E. R. *Public–Private Partnerships: Principles of Policy and Finance*. Oxford: Elsevier, 2007.

Article:

Michel, François. "A primer on public–private partnerships." Public Financial Management Blog (February 22, 2008). Online at: blog-pfm.imf.org/pfmblog/2008/02/a-primer-on-pub.html

Reports:

Economist Intelligence Unit. "Operating risk in emerging markets." London: Economist Intelligence Unit, 2006. Online at: graphics.eiu.com/files/ad_pdfs/eiu_Operating_Risk_wp.pdf

Kennedy, Robert E. "Project valuation in emerging markets." Boston, MA: Harvard Business School, May 14, 2002. Available from: hbsp.harvard.edu

Websites:

Bujagali Hydropower Project: www.bujagali-energy.com

World Bank on Bujagali: tinyurl.com/ml7zfq3

See Also:

★ Measuring Company Exposure to Country Risk (pp. 534–536)
★ Measuring Country Risk (pp. 537–539)
★ Middle East and North Africa Region: Financial Sector and Integration (pp. 211–214)
★ Political Risk: Countering the Impact on Your Business (pp. 902–904)
Energy (pp. 1624–1626)
Mining (pp. 1637–1638)

"For lots of big companies, their brand is worth so much to them that they can't endanger their reputation for being a quality company without really endangering their business performance." Clare Short

  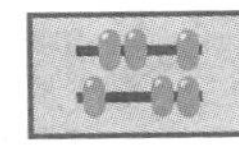   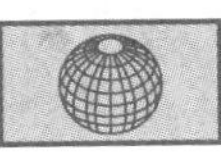   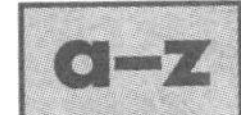

Raising Capital in Global Financial Markets

by Reena Aggarwal

EXECUTIVE SUMMARY

The major changes occurring in the capital-raising process in global financial markets are being impacted by:

- New regions and countries emerging as financial powers.
- The growth of alternative investments as an asset class.
- The role of sovereign wealth funds.
- The globalization and consolidation of stock exchanges.

INTRODUCTION

During the last decade global financial markets have grown tremendously, becoming large and liquid, and with substantial depth. At the same time demand for capital has increased significantly, with capital markets continuing to play a dominant role in the allocation of capital. However, some major shifts are occurring in the roles of suppliers and users of capital. These shifts became even more apparent during the recent financial crisis. This chapter focuses on four such shifts that impact both global firms that are looking to raise funds and institutional investors that are suppliers of the capital. The four areas that are accounting for the major shifts are: the emergence of new countries and regions as financial powers; the growth of alternative investments as an asset class; the role of sovereign wealth funds as a source of capital; and the globalization and consolidation of stock exchanges.

The recent global financial crisis has clearly highlighted the challenges that companies worldwide face in raising capital. Either funding is simply not available or the cost has gone up considerably. The combination of the global economic slowdown and challenges in raising funds in the capital markets has meant that companies are cutting costs, capital investments, and jobs. The financial markets and financial institutions collapsed in a variety of ways, and this has resulted in structural and regulatory changes that will impact the raising of capital in global financial markets.

EMERGING FINANCIAL POWERS

Historically, New York, London, and Tokyo have been the global financial centers, but now a number of new regions and countries are catching up and emerging as dominant players. During the period May 2007 to May 2008, the *McKinsey Quarterly* reports that 35 European companies, including Air France, Bayer, British Airways, and Fiat, delisted from the New York Stock Exchange as it became easier to delist.[1] European markets have integrated and the euro has proven itself to be a strong currency, and the region has increased its market share in this decade. At the same time, the BRIC countries (Brazil, Russia, India, and China) have become new economic powers as their economies have grown at rates that are much higher than those of developed countries. As seen in Figure 1, BRIC's equity markets have also outperformed Europe and the United States since 2003. This growth has resulted in the formation of large companies that are competing globally and have a need for large amounts of global capital. Private wealth in these countries has grown, and this also becomes a source of capital.

Figure 1. Market Capitalization Weighted Index, base values at 100, since 1998. (*Source:* MSCI)

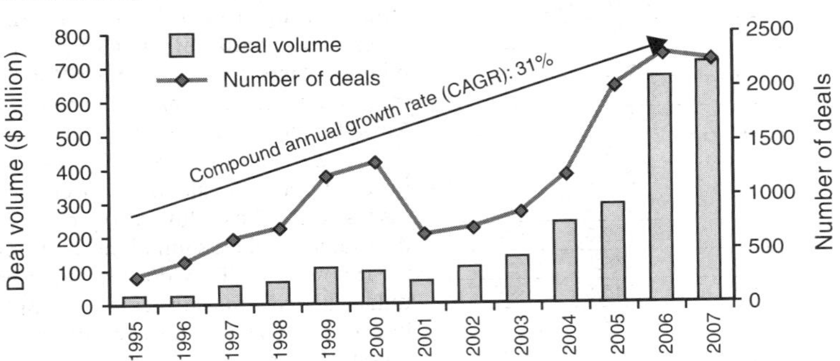

For a period of time oil-exporting countries benefited tremendously from the high oil prices. These countries or regions, which include Indonesia, the Middle East, Nigeria, Norway, Russia, and Venezuela, became the world's largest source of global capital flows. The *McKinsey Quarterly* estimates that in 2008 \$5 trillion of petrodollars went to foreign assets. It is estimated that even with oil averaging \$50/barrel, net capital outflows of \$7.4 trillion a year through 2013 from the oil-exporting countries is likely to occur. The future of the wealth from some of these countries will depend on oil prices.[2]

GROWTH OF ALTERNATIVE INVESTMENTS

During the last decade alternative investments have attracted a significant portion of allocation by institutional investors. Within alternative investments, private equity has become a major source of funds for small and large companies, for firms seeking buyout financing, and for firms in distress. The ten largest private equity firms ranked by amount of capital raised for direct private equity investment between 2003 and 2008 are shown in Table 1. Private equity is an investment in the assets of a company in which the equity does not trade in the public markets. Therefore, investment in private equity requires a long-term approach. Institutional investors such as pension funds and endowments are major investors in private equity, and private equity has become accepted as a distinct asset class. During the last decade there was considerable allocation by institutions into this asset class; however the current economic crisis brought their capital-raising activities to a halt.

Table 1. Largest private equity firms by capital raised for direct private equity investment between 2003 and 2008. (*Source: Private Equity International*, May 2009)

Firm	*Assets (US$ billion)*
Texas Pacific Group	52.35
Goldman Sachs Principal Investment Area	48.99
Carlyle Group	47.73
Kohlberg Kravis Roberts	40.46
Apollo Global Management	35.18
Bain Capital	34.95
CVC Capital Partners	33.73
Blackstone Group	30.80
Warburg Pincus	23.00
Apax Partners	21.33

The funds differ in their investment philosophy. For example, the Blackstone Group was founded in 1985, went public in 2007, and is listed on the New York Stock Exchange. It is diversified into several lines of business, including corporate private equity, real estate, hedge funds, credit, and advisory. In contrast, Apax Partners is a "pure play" global private equity firm that focuses only on specific sectors. Until recently, private equity activity was focused on investing in the United States and Europe, but now there is an increased focus on the emerging markets of Asia-Pacific as a destination for private equity funds. There has been a significant rise in the amount of private equity investment flowing to China, Singapore, South Korea, and India. Private equity will continue to become a major source of capital for companies around the world. In addition to private equity, alternative investments also include hedge funds, commodities, real estate, and venture capital.

SOVEREIGN WEALTH FUNDS AS A SOURCE OF CAPITAL

Another newcomer on the global financial scene is sovereign wealth funds (SWFs). SWFs are government investment funds that invest in foreign companies in order to earn profits and increase the wealth of the state. These funds have existed for a long time, but the increase in their scope and magnitude has recently made them a major financial player. The source of funding for SWFs varies from export revenues to foreign exchange reserves. In early 2008 the assets under control by SWFs were estimated to be $3 trillion and expected to rise to $10 trillion by 2012. In comparison, assets managed by institutional investors like pension funds and endowments amount to $53 trillion. The assets of SWFs are expected to grow at a tremendous rate and become a major provider of funding for companies in both developed and developing markets.[3,4]

Some of these funds have already taken significant positions in several foreign companies. As shown in Table 2, the largest sovereign fund is the Abu Dhabi Investment Authority, the investment arm of Abu Dhabi, with a size of $627 billion. The size of the fund grew due to the sharp rise in oil prices in early 2008. The fund made an investment of $7.5 billion in Citigroup, has a 4.5% ownership in the home builder Toll Brothers, and also has positions in companies such as EFG Hermes, one of the leading investment banks in the Arab world, and Banque de Tunisie et des Emirats, a Tunisian bank.[5] Similarly, China Investment Corporation is estimated to have $288.8 billion funded by foreign exchange reserves in China. The fund has large positions in the private equity firm Blackstone Group ($3 billion) and in the investment bank Morgan Stanley ($5 billion). There are other large SWFs based in Norway, Saudi Arabia, Singapore, and Kuwait, among other countries.

The growth and size of these funds have attracted considerable attention and discussion. These funds typically make decisions based on sound long-term investment strategies. They do not use leverage, unlike hedge fund strategies. Overall, the impact of SWFs is positive in that they invest the resources of the country effi-

Table 2. Top ten sovereign wealth funds by assets under management. (*Source*: Sovereign Wealth Fund Institute, October 2009)

Country	Sovereign wealth fund	Assets ($ billion)
UAE—Abu Dhabi	Abu Dhabi Investment Authority	627
Norway	Government Pension Fund—Global	445
Saudi Arabia	SAMA Foreign Holdings	431
China	SAFE Investment Company	347.1
China	China Investment Corporation	288.8
Singapore	Government of Singapore Investment Corporation	247.5
Kuwait	Kuwait Investment Authority	202.8
Russia	National Welfare Fund	178.5
China	National Social Security Fund	146.5
China—Hong Kong	Hong Kong Monetary Authority Investment Portfolio	139.7

MORE INFO

Books:

Harris, Larry. *Trading and Exchanges: Market Microstructure for Practitioners*. Oxford: Oxford University Press, 2003.

Ineichen, Alexander M. *Absolute Returns: The Risk and Opportunities of Hedge Fund Investing*. Hoboken, NJ: Wiley, 2003.

Article:

Fenn, George W., Nellie Liang, and Stephen Prowse. "The private equity market: An overview." *Financial Markets, Institutions and Instruments* 6:4 (November 1997): 1–106. Online at: dx.doi.org/10.1111/1468-0416.00012

Report:

World Economic Forum. *Globalization of Alternative Investments Working Papers Volume 1: The Global Economic Impact of Private Equity Report 2008*. Geneva and New York: World Economic Forum, 2008. Online at: www.weforum.org/pdf/cgi/pe/Full_Report.pdf

Websites:

Dow Jones LP Source Galantes. Contact information and investment strategies for US and international VC and PE firms, leveraged buyout firms, leveraged lenders, mezzanine investors, turnaround investment firms, and international PE investors: www.dowjones.com/privatemarkets/gal.asp

Private Equity Analyst (Dow Jones). News and profiles on VC and PE firms and companies involved in alternative investment programs: www.fis.dowjones.com/products/pe.html

Private Equity Hub (Thomson Reuters). Create customized search query to locate PE, VC, buyout, and M&A firms: thomsonreuters.com/products_services/media/media_products/professional_publishing/deals/pehub

Sovereign Wealth Fund Institute. Studies SWFs and their impact on global economics, politics, financial markets, trade, and public policy. Provides specialized services to corporations, funds, and governments: www.swfinstitute.org

See Also:

★ Optimizing the Capital Structure: Finding the Right Balance between Debt and Equity (pp. 543–545)
★ The Role of Institutional Investors in Corporate Financing (pp. 589–592)
✔ Options for Raising Finance (p. 1081)
✔ Raising Capital through Private and Public Equity (p. 1088)
Prince Al-Walid bin Talal (p. 1268)

ciently. Their investments have also been particularly welcomed in companies such as Citigroup, Morgan Stanley, and Barclays, as other sources of capital were unavailable to these companies. For the future, there is concern in some circles whether these funds will simply be financial investment vehicles or if they will take an activist role in companies with the objective of gaining political clout for their countries. There is also concern about the lack of transparency and regulation of SWFs.

GLOBALIZATION OF STOCK EXCHANGES[6]

Stock exchanges play a critical role in the capital-raising process. The total market capitalization of all publicly traded companies in the world was US$51.2 trillion in January 2007 and rose as high as US$57.5 trillion in May 2008 before dropping below US$28.7 trillion in February 2009.[7] However, exchanges across the world have transformed through major structural changes in the last few years. Starting with the demutualization of the Stockholm Stock Exchange in 1993, the number of financial exchanges that have adopted a for-profit, publicly listed organizational form has grown steadily. This trend can be seen both in stock exchanges in different countries and in financial exchanges that trade different types of securities. This rapid organizational transformation of exchanges from member-owned mutual companies to joint-stock companies is unparalleled, and this process is the manifestation of a number of innovations and deregulatory events that have occurred in the last decade. This for-profit structure has allowed exchanges to raise capital and invest in technology that is essential in order to compete. Exchanges as public companies have needed to increase market share and develop additional sources of revenue. There has been considerable consolidation among the large global exchanges. The New York Stock Exchange acquired Euronext, forming NYSE Euronext; Nasdaq gained control of OMX; and the Chicago Mercantile Exchange merged with its rival, the Chicago Board of Trade.

The globalization of stock exchanges beyond the authority of a single national regulator has meant a rethinking of the regulatory framework. It can be argued that regulatory policy rarely leads but more often follows market innovations. As such, the challenge for regulators will be to develop regulatory programs that respond to globalized markets.[8] National regulators are moving in the direction of increased coordination and convergence of regulation along mutually acceptable principles. IOSCO, the international organization of securities regulators, has played a key role in promoting greater cooperation and the development of commonly acceptable regulatory principles. The financial crisis of 2008 has again emphasized the need for global coordination in an environment where capital has no national boundary. The global consolidation of some of the largest exchanges has been beneficial both for companies raising capital and for investors/traders. This consolidation has made it easier for companies worldwide to raise large sums of capital through public offerings and cheaper for market participants to conduct transactions in deep liquid markets. In addition to public capital, there has been a tremendous increase in the use of private capital.

CONCLUSION

A number of important changes are taking place in global financial markets that need to be monitored carefully. There has been a considerable shift in the regional concentration of wealth. In addition to the traditional public capital markets, recent years have seen the emergence of private equity and sovereign wealth funds as major players in financial markets. Stock exchanges have transformed to become global entities. These changes have impacted the landscape of global financial markets.

NOTES

1 R. Dobbs and M. H. Goedhart, "Why cross-listing shares doesn't create value." *McKinsey Quarterly* November 2008. Online from www.mckinseyquarterly.com.

2 S. Lund and C. Roxburgh, "The new financial power brokers: Crisis update." *McKinsey Quarterly* September 2009. web.rollins.edu/~tlairson/ipe/financialpower.pdf.

3 Simon Johnson, "Straight talk: Emerging markets emerge." *Finance and Development* (IMF) 45:3 (September 2008). Online: www.imf.org/external/pubs/ft/fandd/2008/09/pdf/straight.pdf.

4 R. M. Kimmitt, "Public footprints in private markets: Sovereign wealth funds and the world economy." *Foreign Affairs* 87:1 (January/February 2008). Available by payment from www.foreignaffairs.com/issues/2008/87/1.

5 L. Thomas, Jr, "Cash-rich, publicity-shy, Abu Dhabi fund draws scrutiny." *New York Times* February 28, 2008.

6 R. Aggarwal and S. Dahiya, "Demutualization and public offerings of financial exchanges." *Journal of Applied Corporate Finance* 18:3 (2006): 96–106.

7 World Federation of Exchanges, available at www.world-exchanges.org/statistics/ytd-monthly.

8 R. Aggarwal, A. Ferrell, and J. Katz, "U.S. securities regulation in a world of global exchanges." Chapter 7 in S. Shojai (ed.), *World of Exchanges: Adapting to a New Environment*. London: Euromoney Books, 2007.

"Never give in, never give in, never, never, never, never—in nothing, great or small, large or petty—never give in except to convictions of honour and good sense." Sir Winston Churchill

Raising Capital in the United Kingdom

by Lauren Mills

EXECUTIVE SUMMARY

- It has never been harder to raise capital. The credit crunch means banks are even less willing to lend money to small and medium-sized enterprizes (SMEs). So raising capital is likely to be more time-consuming and costly than before. It is therefore vital you know how much money you need, and what you need it for, before approaching potential backers.
- A lot will depend on whether you are funding a start-up, buying an asset, seeking growth finance, or looking for an exit.
- Whatever stage you are at, you must have a business plan, strong management, and good growth prospects—or potential backers are unlikely to be interested.

INTRODUCTION

Raising capital to grow a business has never been more challenging or time-consuming. While there are still many sources of finance, ranging from government and EU grants, to bank loans, private equity, angel investors, or a stock market flotation, some will be easier to come by than others in the post-credit crunch climate. One of the biggest problems will be deciding which route is best for you.

Before weighing up the pros and cons of each, carry out a ruthless analysis of your business. Start by asking yourself some elementary questions. Do you have strong management in place? Do you have a business plan? Do you know what you need to do to move your business to the next stage? This may sound somewhat elementary, but it is surprising how many companies keep drifting in one direction without knowing whether this is the best route to pursue, or whether the best captain is at the helm.

It is therefore essential to have a clear idea of what you want to achieve and how you are going to achieve it before approaching potential financiers.

GRANTS

In January 2009, the United Kingdom's Business Secretary, Lord Mandelson, announced a new package of financial measures to help businesses with short-term funding issues weather the economic downturn. Help is also available for companies looking to finance the next stage of growth.

The support package consists of loan guarantees and a new Enterprise Fund. It is intended to help companies which are struggling to obtain finance for working capital and investment.

The Government measures include:

- A £10 billion Working Capital Scheme, securing up to £20 billion of short-term bank lending to companies with a turnover of up to £500 million.
- An Enterprise Finance Guarantee Scheme, securing up to £1.3 billion of additional bank loans to small firms with a turnover of up to £25 million.
- A £75 million Capital for Enterprise Fund (£50 million from government, plus £25 million from banks) to invest in small businesses which need equity.

The Working Capital Scheme is a direct response to the constraint on bank lending to ordinary-risk businesses with a turnover of up to £500 million a year. The Government has agreed to provide banks with guarantees for 50% of the risk on existing and new working capital portfolios worth up to £20 billion as part of the scheme.

The Government guarantee will free up capital, which the banks must use for new lending as a condition of this scheme. This is lending that would otherwise not have been provided, the UK Government has claimed. The first £1 billion guarantee tranche of the scheme is expected to be available in March 2009.

The Enterprise Finance Guarantee is intended to help smaller, credit-worthy companies which might otherwise fail to access the finance they need for working capital or investment finance due to strict lending conditions.

The Government will provide £1 billion worth of guarantees to support £1.3 billion of bank lending to smaller firms with an annual turnover of up to £25 million, which are looking for loans of up to £1 million for a period of up to 10 years.

The guarantee, available through high street banks, will apply to loans and can also be used to convert existing overdrafts into loans to enable businesses to free up their current overdraft facilities to meet working capital requirements.

To help businesses raise new long-term finance, the UK Government is also offering to invest in viable companies which have high levels of existing debt through the new Capital for Enterprise Fund.

The Government also provides a range of financial support to businesses—including loans and loan guarantees, grants, and equity—through various "Solutions for Business" products.

To find out more about what is on offer, the best starting point is your local Business Link. This is the Government's business advice network, which offers an abundance of information online, over the telephone, or via face-to-face meetings with an adviser.

A new "one-stop shop," easy-to-use web portal has been launched on the Business Link website to direct companies to the most appropriate form of support, and help them assess their eligibility for the various schemes.

There is also a Grant for Business Investment (GBI), which provides capital to support business investment or job creation projects and is part of the Government's Solutions for Business portfolio. The idea is to help businesses grow, become more efficient, modernize, and diversify.

A grant under GBI is for the acquisition of key assets such as buildings, machinery, and equipment, and to help create new jobs or safeguard existing ones. Grants start at a minimum of £10,000 and there is no maximum limit. The final amount will depend on the size and location of the business, and the size and quality of the project. It is also worth bearing in mind that businesses applying for this grant will be assessed according to the level of skills they require within their workforce, and their anticipated productivity improvement. So companies must be clear about what they hope to achieve before applying.

In Scotland, this is called the Grant for Regional Selective Assistance (RSA). Information about this can be found on the Scottish Business Grants website.

In Northern Ireland, it is called the Enterprise NI Loan Fund (ENILF). Information is available on the Enterprise NI website.

Remember, there is a limited pot of cash available, so competition for grant funding is extremely fierce. Furthermore, the application process is often long-winded and arduous. Applicants must complete detailed application forms. They must also demonstrate how they will satisfy the funding conditions and requirements of any one

  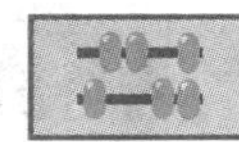      

scheme. It is essential that you understand the Government's economic objectives in providing grants and tailor your application to meet them.

BANK LOANS

Individuals looking for start-up capital, or small firms seeking finance to pay for assets such as computer equipment, machinery, or cars, could look to their bank or building society for the cash. But lending criteria are far tougher now than before the credit crunch hit.

The advantage of a bank loan—if you can get one—is that it will be for a fixed sum, over a fixed period of time, so you know how much you need to pay back and for how long. In theory, this should make it relatively easy to manage your budgets. And while you will have to pay interest on bank or building society loans, you will not be obliged to hand over a percentage of your profits or a share of your company.

Even before the global financial meltdown there were drawbacks:

- The banks impose strict terms and conditions on most loans. In some cases they may even insist you offer some sort of security. So you may be required to secure the loan against the assets of your business or even your home.
- Bank loans are not very flexible, so you may find yourself paying interest on funds you are not using. You will also have to make regular repayments, which may make it hard to manage cash flow if your customers are not paying their bills on time.

If you feel a bank loan could cover your business needs, then remember to research the market carefully.

A good place to start is the website Money Supermarket, which offers information on business current accounts—which will give you an idea of which banks to approach.

The Institute of Chartered Accountants in England and Wales (ICAEW) reckons nine out of 10 SMEs are likely to be contacted by their banks to discuss the terms of their overdrafts by the end of 2009.

Clive Lewis, SME expert at ICAEW, believes businesses should explore a range of financing alternatives and use "appropriate funding." This, he says, could include asset finance, factoring, hire purchase, invoice discounting, leasing, and equity finance.

Lewis warns of even tougher times ahead. He advises business owners to seek advice on alternatives to bank finance, because there is an estimated £800 billion funding gap between deposits and lending in the United Kingdom. This is because savings levels have dropped off and cheap foreign capital from the wholesale markets has dried up.

PRIVATE EQUITY OR VENTURE CAPITAL

Private equity firms and venture capitalists are still looking to invest in businesses with strong management and good growth prospects. However, they are more likely to invest in companies they have already backed than take on new risk in the current economic climate.

It is worth remembering that private equity investors tend to invest in a business for the medium term, rather than the longer term. In practice this often means from three to five years, although they may invest for far longer or much shorter periods of time.

Unlike lenders, they tend not to have rights to interest or to be repaid at a particular date. But they will want a share of the ownership and in some instances may demand an element of control of the business. They often insist that a non-executive is appointed to the board. This is not necessarily a bad thing. If you do your homework and bring in an external investor with experience in your sector, then you could be adding another dimension to your business by beefing up senior management expertise. And this can be invaluable in terms of brainstorming for new ideas.

Venture capital or private equity financing tends to be best suited to businesses gearing up for a flotation or trade sale—both of which will be hard to achieve while stock markets remain volatile and credit is hard to come by. This is because the investor will need to be able to realize a return for the investment via a well-thought-out exit strategy.

Before approaching potential private equity investors, it is essential to ask yourself how credible your management is. Do you have a solid track record? And do you have the communications skills necessary to sell your story effectively? You will need a strong product or service. And you must be able to show that you can deliver year-on-year growth to realistic targets. Ultimately, you must still be highly ambitious and driven to attract interest from private equity backers.

Once you have completed a serious analysis of your business and its prospects, you must draw up a detailed business plan. It should be written in plain English, without jargon or fluff—private equity professionals have a nose for sniffing out sound ideas from speculative pipe dreams.

The main advantage of private equity financing is that the investor will have a vested interest in your business's success. These types of investors are also often prepared to offer follow-up funding as the business grows.

BUSINESS ANGELS

Business angels are high net worth individuals who invest on their own, or as part of a syndicate, in high-growth businesses. In addition to money, they often make their own skills, experience, and contacts available to the companies they invest in. According to the British Business Angels Association (BBAA), angel investors rarely have a connection with a company before they invest in it. However, they are more than likely to have experience of its industry or sector, so could bring invaluable experience to the table.

The BBAA believes business angels are "an important but still under-utilized" source of money for new and growing businesses.

Typically, business angels invest between £10,000 and £750,000 in an investment, making them an attractive alternative for smaller firms looking to raise smaller sums.

Before investing, business angels will check out factors ranging from management expertise and track record, to a company's competitive edge and compatibility between the management, the business plan, and the business angel's skills and investment preferences.

A good starting point for further information is the BBAA's website.

STOCK MARKET FLOTATION

The number of companies seeking a stock market flotation has plummeted in the wake of the credit crunch. In the first half of 2008, only 333 companies sought to raise finance through an initial public offering (IPO), compared to 702 companies in the same period a year earlier.

Given the turbulent state of the world's equity markets, it is unlikely that IPOs will regain their status as a popular route to new finance in the foreseeable future.

A stock market flotation involves selling shares in your business on one of the stock markets. There are three markets in the United Kingdom. The London Stock Exchange Main Market is mostly populated with larger companies. However, the Alternative Investment Market (AIM) and the PLUS market are both aimed at smaller companies.

If an IPO is a realistic option for your business, it is important to remember it is not an exit—it is the beginning of the next stage of growth. Companies considering a stock market flotation must have strong management, a healthy track record, and excellent growth prospects.

        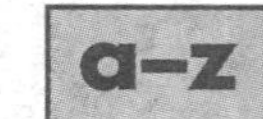

Traditionally, the main advantage of a stock market flotation is ready access to funds. Flotation may also add to your company's credibility and raise its profile. It also provides an opportunity for business owners and other investors, such as private equity backers, to realize their investment. Having your own traded shares may also help you grow your business because you can offer shares as well as cash in any potential takeover bids.

There are disadvantages, however. Costs associated with floating a business can be substantial. There will be higher ongoing professional fees, as you will need advisers to help you comply with the added regulatory burden that floating a business can bring. You will also have to consider the interests of shareholders when running the company—and there will be times when their objectives will differ from yours.

Choosing the right market is vital. London's Main Market is the most stringently regulated and is only suitable for the largest companies. A minimum of 25% of the company's equity must be traded, to ensure liquidity, and companies must have been trading for at least three years. While the main market gives access to the widest possible audience of potential investors, it comes at a price. Professional fees and costs are far higher than for AIM or PLUS.

In contrast to the main market, AIM does not require a company to have a trading record. And while it is part of the London Stock Exchange, it offers a more flexible regulatory environment and is less expensive. There is no minimum percentage of shares that has to be traded, yet AIM-listed companies attract a wide range of investors, including institutional backers. AIM offers tax breaks and incentives for owner–managers, and is a very liquid market. A nominated adviser is required at all times.

PLUS is aimed at smaller companies seeking to raise up to £10 million. While it is regulated, the rules are not as stringent as those of AIM or the Main Market. While the costs associated with floating and running a company on the PLUS market are lower than its larger rivals, the pool of investors is not as deep and is mainly restricted to private investors.

If you think your company is ready for a stock market flotation, then remember that preparing for a float is a challenging and expensive process. It can take months to organize. For businesses that have not been part of a regulated industry before, it can be a cultural shock.

CONCLUSION

Choosing the right type of finance for your business is incredibly important. You must have a thorough understanding of what stage your business is at and what you need the money for before you pursue any one of the options. A lot will depend on whether you are funding a start-up, buying an asset, seeking growth finance, or looking for an exit.

MORE INFO

Websites:

British Business Angels Association: www.bbaa.org.uk
Business Link: www.businesslink.gov.uk/realhelp/finance
Enterprise NI Loan Fund: www.enterpriseni.com/Content.aspx?nSectionId=8&nSubSectionId=84
Money Supermarket: www.moneysupermarket.com
Scottish Business Grants: www.scottishbusinessgrants.gov.uk/rsa/208.html

See Also:

★ Sources of Venture Capital (pp. 601–603)
★ Understanding Equity Capital in Small and Medium-Sized Enterprises (pp. 607–610)
✔ Dealing with Venture Capital Companies (p. 1067)
✔ Options for Raising Finance (p. 1081)
✔ Raising Capital by Issuing Bonds (p. 1086)
✔ Raising Capital by Issuing Shares (p. 1087)
✔ Raising Capital through Private and Public Equity (p. 1088)
✔ Understanding Capital Markets, Structure and Function (p. 1099)

"Miracles can be made, but only by sweating." Giovanni Agnelli

  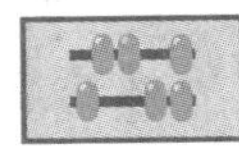   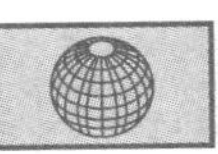   

Viewpoint: Reflections on the Fixed-Income Market in Difficult Times by Rod Davidson

INTRODUCTION

Rod Davidson, head of the fixed-income team at Alliance Trust Asset Management, has been managing money, teams, and businesses in the global fixed-income arena for more than 20 years. Prior to joining Alliance Trust Asset Management he held similar posts at Scottish Widows Investment Partnership, Aberdeen Asset Management, and Murray Johnstone. He specializes in managing global bond and currency portfolios and has responsibility at Alliance Trust Asset Management for macroeconomic research, duration strategy, and currency strategy.

What are the primary risks ahead for developed market economies?

For the United Kingdom, our forecast for GDP expansion is positive for 18 months and beyond. However, the global economy has now worked its way through the first phase of the recovery process and there are an increasing number of worrying signs that the rate of growth is slackening off. The fiscal deficit burdens of Western economies, allied to record levels of government debt, have created headwinds that are being exacerbated by weak housing and labor markets and a depressed consumer market.

One consequence of this is that it has created sustained anxiety among investors. The way this plays is that, despite the scale of government debt issuance and the historically low yields, there has been no shortage of investors in the major government bonds as people and institutions seek shelter for their assets in low-risk government debt.

As a result of this dynamic, strong demand and the very low short-term rates, yields have been able to edge down markedly from March through to September 2010 for UK, US, and German bonds. Even in Japan, where the yield on 10-year government bonds is extremely low at just over 1%, there is strong demand since they have a negative core inflation rate of –1%.

The negative economic signs, however, are a cause for concern. There are clearly real concerns about the sharp deterioration of the US housing market that was experienced by the end of the third quarter of 2010. Earlier, in the second half of 2009 and the spring of 2010, the US housing market benefited from an attractive tax credit. Initially this boosted sales to first-time home buyers, but it was extended to include existing homeowners who were buying.

The downside of this stimulus was always that it might simply bring forward sales that were going to happen anyway, creating a dearth of sales when the tax credit was withdrawn, and this is now happening. It is difficult to see how the housing market in the United States can recover until the economy is able to create large numbers of new jobs. The picture ahead, for some time to come, looks like being dominated by weak demand stemming from weak consumer confidence and weak consumer spending.

This throws the burden for global growth on to China, which needs to deliver a relatively healthy rate of growth at around 8% or higher to help the global economy to recover. Today, policy-makers in China are wrestling with measures to cool a developing bubble in the Chinese housing market, while at the same time seeking to maintain growth in fixed-asset investment. The strategy for doing this has been to shift the focus of infrastructure investment toward the central and western regions of the country, where development needs and opportunities remain high.

There are significant imbalances within the Chinese economy that need to be addressed, however. Developing economies with a major export-generated surplus tend to be characterized by a disproportionate share of GDP coming from infrastructure investment rather than from consumer spending. China's infrastructure spend accounts for 45% of GDP, three times more than the equivalent spend in the United States, which is just over 15% of GDP. Longer term, there is a very pressing need to see the GDP share of household consumption rise markedly.

Could you explain the major issues that are impacting the fixed-income market at present, particularly the longer-term market for government bonds in developed markets and what this tells us about investors' views of the global economy?

The fixed-income market is generating a lot of interest at present. The daily movement in the 10-year gilt yield is high, and since the introduction of quantitative easing in the United States the path of yields in the United Kingdom has been in an upward direction. The recent move has been quite extreme. The volume of interest in the market began to fade as we headed toward December 2010, when the yield was around 3.60%. Thereafter it kept going higher to around 3.85% by February 2011. In itself this simply reflected the concern for the inflation picture in the United Kingdom, and it is directly linked to the fact that the money markets are pricing in an anticipated, regular 0.25% rate hike by the Bank of England every quarter for the foreseeable future. In other words, the markets expected overnight rates for the end of December 2013 to be around 3.5%.

To our way of thinking, that kind of expectation is extreme, and 10-year yields are very probably close to a near-term peak. There is probably too much pessimism feeding into the market right now since the recovery in the United Kingdom does not appear to be strong enough to warrant such a prolonged tightening phase. One or two short-rate moves upward are possible, but that would be it for the medium term.

Another feature is that the yield curve, which maps the yield from short-duration bonds through to long-duration bonds, is pretty steep right now. If you take one-month US Treasury bonds, on October 27, 2010, they were just 0.13, with one-year rates at 0.23. That gives you a very gentle slope for the start of the curve, with the front end really nailed in place. But then it rises sharply to 2.75 for the 10-year rate and to 3.72 for the 20-year rate. That creates the steepness.

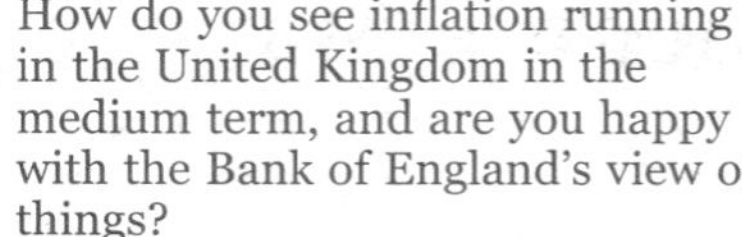

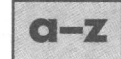

How do you see inflation running in the United Kingdom in the medium term, and are you happy with the Bank of England's view of things?

One has to remember that the governor of the Bank of England, Mervyn King, has to speak for everyone on the Monetary Policy Committee, including the hawks. Currently retail price index inflation looks high, but if one follows the capitalization-adjusted rate in the United Kingdom it is much closer to the 2% level. So the Bank of England needs to analyze the type of inflation we are enduring and the extent to which the UK economy could survive during a tightening phase that aimed to drive inflation down sharply. The Bank could drive inflation down to the 2% band, but this could well push the economy back into recession—which would not be the game plan.

By February 2011, the Bank was expecting the year-on-year inflation number to fall over the next three months, unless the impact of the VAT rise turned out to be stronger than anticipated or commodities took another surge upward.

How does all this play in the bond markets?

We are now at the point where we are looking for a flattening of the yield curve, probably out beyond 2011. Strategically, this leads us to adjust the duration of our portfolio. Our fund has been running sub-five year duration on average, which is below the industry average, and has been overweight on high-yield corporate bonds and underweight on investment-grade. We would probably look to neutralize our underweight position and increase our interest rate duration again.

The corporate bond benchmark runs from five to 15 years as the "sweet spot" for which corporates like to issue debt (i.e. their debt will mature in, say, seven years, or 10 years, or 15 years, at which point they are committed to repaying the bond in full). For most fixed-income funds that focus on the corporate bond market, their benchmark duration will be 6.25 years. This is possible because, of course, corporate bonds are not all held to maturity and there is a lot of buying and selling of bonds during the life of the bond. This provides the opportunity to construct a total portfolio position, lengthening or shortening your exposure to duration. We are happy to extend our duration; the average fund has a duration of about seven years, and ours usually has one of 6.25, but we have been down around a five-year duration average since we saw yields rising across the curve, so we were hedging out some of that risk. Much of that movement has taken place, so we are prepared to move our duration back to what for us is a more normal average duration of 6.25.

Shortening the average duration of the portfolio that you are holding lessens your exposure to long-term risk, and primarily to long-term inflation risk. It also, of course, by definition reduces your exposure to economic risk since the longer you hold the bond, the longer you bear the risk of the company collapsing before the maturity date. That collapse might be idiosyncratic to the company, or it might reflect a major downturn in the economy which cripples many companies, including many of those in your portfolio. Therefore it follows that you can lessen this basket of risks by moving more defensively to a shorter-duration portfolio, which we have done. That move also says something about the extent of the uncertainty that we see over the future direction of the economy.

As I have said, we think that the underlying strength of the economy is not sufficient to warrant short rates moving higher on a sustained path. One or two quarterly rises should be enough to take the sting out of the position without killing the economy. Of course, the steepness in today's yield curve is really caused by the Federal Reserve's "loose for longer" policy, with excessively low short-term rates. In reality, 10-year rates have themselves been trading at historic lows for developed market sovereign bonds outside of Japan, but if you squash the front end—i.e. squash the short-duration part of the curve virtually to the x-axis—that forces even a 4% 20-year rate to generate a steep curve.

We have three specific trades on to take advantage of this situation. We have a two-to-five "flattener" (where we short two-year bonds and go long on five-year bonds) in Germany and the United States. We also have a 10-to-30 flattener in Germany (shorting 10-year and going long on 30-year). We think that 10-year yields have reached an attractive entry point, so for the next 12 months the game is going to be the shape of the curve as much as directional interest rate movements. The point is that different parts of the yield curve move at different points in the cycle; they have been very steep, and we expect them to flatten.

We still expect risk assets and credit to do very well for the rest of 2011. A lot of corporates are cash-rich, with not that many opportunities for capital expenditure, so they are deleveraging the balance sheet. With financial stocks, deleveraging and reregulation is still going on, and that is good news for bondholders. There are parts of the market we are cautious of and avoid; some things are priced into the market (such as the anticipated rate hike that we have already discussed), but other things are not priced in, and you have to be able to differentiate—and not rush in where there are unpriced risks.

High-yield bonds have performed very well, but risk–reward has now moved more toward investment-grade opportunities. You are not getting sufficient premium on riskier bonds now, plus you are paying a high price. Defaults are going to be very low, but that is already reflected in the price. A number of funds have increased their exposure to high-yield bonds. Several new fixed-income funds launched through 2009 and 2010, and these typically had an allocation to high-yield of around 30%.

What is new issuance like in the corporate debt market?

By early 2011 we were seeing reasonable issuance in the United States, but considerably less in the United Kingdom and Europe. However, we expect that to build, and we are factoring that in to how we view our holdings. In terms of fund size, we are at the lower end of managed units, so our typical deal size is between £1 million and £5 million of debt. Market liquidity is not great beyond £10 million on an average deal. We have a target size of about £1 billion at most for our fund, because of the trading issues in the market at the moment.

It is important to realize that there is a wave of refinancing to come in the high-yield space over the next 18 months, and that will put some pressure on issuance. There is also the matter of "call dates," which give the company the right to call the bond and refinance it at a cheaper rate if they see the opportunity. If the bonds have call dates, you lose some of that high yield anyway once it is refinanced at cheaper levels. If they are called, by definition you cannot hold the bond to maturity and you might not get the price that you expected. The call might be at 103 when the bonds are trading at 109, which would generate a six-point loss on what you were expecting.

None of this makes the high-yield market bad, but money coming into this space now is "late money" and the rewards have largely gone. Another key point is that if there is limited liquidity in the investment-grade corporate market, there is almost no liquidity at all in the high-yield space, so holding to maturity is the de facto position.

Where do you stand on the inflation/deflation debate?

You have two things going on in the market right now. On the one hand, the Obama Administration and the Federal Reserve have decided to target reflation full-on through a package of measures that include, on the monetary side of the equation, an extension of the quantitative easing program, and on the fiscal side a rolling-over of the Bush-era tax cuts. QE2, the second round of quantitative easing, involves the Federal Reserve buying an extra US$650 billion of treasuries by the end of June 2011, with the aim of fostering maximum employment and price stability. The extension of the tax cuts could add at least 0.5% to the forecast GDP numbers next year, which may shorten the odds for an official rate hike at some stage in 2011.

Whether we get inflation or deflation is ultimately in the hands of the monetary authorities. If they tighten at the wrong time, they could push the global economy back into recession. But there is growth, so at some point they have to take the free money out of the system. There is no right or wrong here; it is a finely balanced act, and what is right today might not be the right thing in three months time.

The US Administration—and indeed, the United States in general—is firmly fixated on the mistakes of the Great Depression of the 1930s. No modern US president wants to be the person who took the decisions that plunged the United States back into a deflationary depression. So they are going to swing the bat regardless, and will do everything they can to prevent a double-dip recession. This is giving a very positive tone to the bond markets.

The second thing that is going on is that in the United Kingdom inflation continues to remain stubbornly at 3%. Most of the bad news from the UK spending review and its austerity measures is now filtering through the system. So, moving into 2011, and if UK GDP growth does not turn negative, the bond markets will focus much more closely on the risk of inflation moving outside the Bank of England's preset target. This means that the market is likely to start pricing in the threat of a rate increase and, as I have said, we now expect UK 10-year yields to move higher.

Moreover, there are already very strong indications that soft commodities, i.e. food prices, are on the march upward. On top of this, in the United Kingdom we had a VAT hike in January. All of this means that inflation will inevitably remain sticky for quite a bit of 2011.

YOU HAVE DURATION AS ONE OF YOUR DEFENSIVE TOOLS. WHAT ELSE IS THERE?

Our position is simply to keep the great majority of the Alliance Trust Monthly Income Bond Fund in corporate bonds—approximately 97% of it at the moment—since even with some defaults we can see the returns on corporate bonds comfortably exceeding the returns on gilts.

Funds that run global fixed-income portfolios will have US treasuries as one of their largest components, and the problem with this is that yields from treasuries have been rather unattractive for some time. Moreover, you would have to have concerns about inflation, looking out three or four years, with the United States maintaining its fiscal expansionary stance. Another factor is that if the US economy sees further deterioration in growth, which is currently weak, that will put the dollar under even more pressure.

The dollar is currently being hammered by the deliberate competitive devaluation of a number of countries against it, and that devaluation is inflationary in nature. This would make a global fixed-asset portfolio manager want to reduce the normal share of US treasuries in the portfolio to an underweight position. However, we would put the chances of a slide back into a double-dip global recession at no higher than a 25% right now, and if that should happen we are well positioned to move quickly to adjust our portfolio.

MORE INFO

Books:

Fabozzi, Frank J. (ed). *The Handbook of Fixed Income Securities*. 7th ed. New York: McGraw-Hill, 2005.

Lewis, Michael. *The Big Short: Inside the Doomsday Machine*. New York: WW Norton & Co., 2010.

Mackay, Charles. *Extraordinary Popular Delusions and the Madness of Crowds*. 1841. Online at: www.gutenberg.org/ebooks/24518

Porter, Michael E. *Competitive Strategy: Techniques for Analyzing Industries and Competitors*. New York: Free Press, 1998.

Smith, Adam. *An Inquiry Into the Nature and Causes of the Wealth of Nations*. Hollywood, FL: Simon & Brown, 2011.

See Also:

★ Viewpoint: The Challenges to Slow Growth in the Advanced Economies Just Keep Coming (pp. 147–148)

★ Viewpoint: Steering Between Deflation and Inflation—A Troubled Road for Developed Economies (pp. 604–606)

✔ The Bond Market: Its Structure and Function (p. 1064)

✔ Trading in Corporate Bonds: Why and How (p. 1094)

✔ Trading in Government Bonds: Why and How (p. 1096)

"I have no interest in celebrities. If all the superrich disappeared, the world economy would not even notice. The superrich are irrelevant to the economy." Peter F. Drucker

  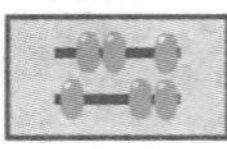      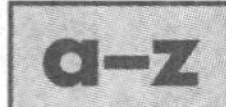

Rigidity in Microfinancing: Can One Size Fit All?

by Dean Karlan and Sendhil Mullainathan

EXECUTIVE SUMMARY

- Despite rapid growth in outreach, microfinance providers often have yet to reach a large proportion of the market of poor households.
- One explanation may be that microfinance practitioners have been slow to implement innovations to the standard lending methodologies.
- By tailoring products to clients' needs and repayment capacity, flexible microfinance has the potential to reach many more clients at lower cost. This can be proven with randomized evaluations of flexible lending contracts.
- Further work is needed to understand how this will impact on clients.

INTRODUCTION

In the span of a single decade microfinance has gone from being virtually unknown—to bankers, to development workers, and, most of all, to the poor—to being a household word. Ask anyone today to describe microfinance and most likely you will get a common answer: "That's when banks lend to groups of poor women to start little businesses." Much of this increase in awareness is thanks to the tireless work of industry advocates who have traveled the world convincing development organizations and funders that microfinance offers the best hope for large numbers of poor families to move out of poverty.

Practitioners, broadly speaking, have been offered three choices:

1 Grameen Bank-style solidarity lending, with 12-month loans offered to groups of five poor women;
2 FINCA-style village banking, with a four-month loan divided among a larger group of about 30 poor women; or
3 ACCION-style individual lending to the moderately poor.

On most other features, these options are strikingly similar. All three target entrepreneurs with capital for sewing machines, chickens, tortilla presses, and the like. And all emphasize operational efficiency through product standardization, and good repayment through frequent regular payments that start shortly after the loans are disbursed. Here we discuss ideas that can be seen as "tweaks" to the above standard models. These tweaks increase the flexibility with an aim to improving the quality of the service received by the client.

LENDING FLEXIBILITY

Problems with the Standard Model

Looking back on the evolution of microfinance one begins to wonder if perhaps its advocates might have been too successful in their messaging. By sticking to this script, the industry may have stifled creativity and individualism in the development of financial services for the poor. Consider the repayment schedule adopted with near universality for group-lending clients: weekly payments that start only one or two weeks after disbursement of the loan. This despite the fact that microfinance institution (MFI) managers are well aware that most of their clients' enterprises will not start generating returns so rapidly.

Why is this important? Being poor is not just about having too little income—it is about having an insecure income. The income of the poor can vary dramatically from day to day, month to month, season to season. The poor have good weeks and bad weeks. But microloans, like all loans with fixed repayments, are made on the basis of the borrower's ability to repay in their *worst week*. Otherwise they would end up in arrears at some point during the loan cycle. This rigidity has several ramifications. First, by basing borrowers' repayment capacity on bad weeks, instead of average weeks, it greatly limits the size of the loans the poor can borrow. If I earn 50 rupees some weeks and 550 rupees other weeks, my debt capacity is not based on my average income of 300 rupees but on the 50 rupees that I can afford to pay in the bad weeks. As a result, borrowers with variable income and little recourse outside of money lenders to smooth that variability will be given a debt capacity that is much lower than ideal.

Second, it may screen out many potential borrowers entirely: for example, any entrepreneur who pictures a week in which she might have slow sales or a household emergency. Or existing clients may leave because they experience too many "close calls" and then drop out to avoid going into default. Incidentally, these should be the bank's best customers—they are clients of such strong integrity that they refuse to borrow for fear of defaulting! Third, it precludes potential innovations like bullet loans for agriculture (a bullet loans is a loan where payment of the entire principal of the loan, and sometimes the principal and interest, is or are due at the end of the loan term).

These limitations help to explain why, despite years of growth, MFIs still fulfill only a small fraction of the financial needs of the poor. This year the Microcredit Summit Campaign has reported that its members reach a total of 150 million borrowers (Daley-Harris, 2009). This is a stunning achievement, and yet only a dent in the estimated two billion households that lack access to financial services. The need to identify ways to reach this market with appropriate financial services cannot be ignored.

How to Be Flexible: Some Suggestions

How can we practically implement flexibility in the current structure of microfinance? A full portfolio of flexible financial products has yet to be developed, but there are some promising ideas. We give three examples, each highlighting a different element of flexibility. First, we observe that flexibility can be *prebuilt* into the contract. For example, in India the monsoon is a difficult time for everyone. Contracts could reflect this by reducing payments during this period in a prespecified manner. Similarly, dairy farmers face two months a year without milk. Again, the contract could prespecify a smaller loan payment during this period. Prespecification of flexibility has many benefits. Notably, clients are not led to believe that they can negotiate down other payments. The flexibility is not after-the-fact. It is actually a "rigid" flexibility, with tightly delineated rules. As a result, it also eases technological and logistical concerns of management information systems, cash management, and loan officer fraud.

Second, one could provide a less rigid flexibility by prespecifying a number of low payment periods, but not their timing. For example, one could give clients several tokens and tell them that each token can count for one weekly payment. In this way, the client agrees to a slightly higher payment each week in return for getting a few difficult weeks—of their own choosing—off. Again, the creation of a token ought to ease the logistical problems of MIS, cash management, and fraud. Yet it still provides the borrower with a great deal of flexibility.

Finally, consider an MFI that feels that its borrowers could handle 2,000-rupee

"The people who get on in this world are the people who get up and look for the circumstances they want, and, if they can't find them, make them." George Bernard Shaw

larger loans than they currently receive. Should it just increase the initial loan size? What if instead it told all borrowers that they would be eligible for a second 2,000-rupee loan at any point during the cycle? This second loan might actually help the client more than simply increasing the initial loan by 2,000 rupees since it gives the client a safety valve in case of emergencies.

Why Have People Been Afraid of Flexibility?

Fixed-debt contracts may be problematic, but there are sensible reasons for using them. First, a flexible payment stream may generate many operational headaches. For instance, portfolio monitoring requires clear information on default status. It may be difficult (or impossible) to distinguish between someone exercising their flexibility and someone who is intending to default further. The faster lenders deal with default, it is often believed, the better they are able to recover the loans. Furthermore, depending on how the flexibility is structured, it could cause confusion in the field. It is easier to train staff to collect equal and constant weekly payments. The flexibility should be such that staff can easily understand and implement it.

Second, cash management problems may arise. If clients experience correlated shocks (for example floods or droughts), they may (should!) use the flexibility to help smooth out those shocks. This has implications for the lender if it is seeing a shortfall in repayment at the exact moments it wants to have more cash on hand to lend to individuals. Third, flexibility may put the lender at risk of loan officer fraud. The loan officer, for instance, could claim that the client exercised her "flexibility" when in fact she repaid. (As noted above, this can be mitigated by prespecifying the payment schedule: if the client is expected to pay 50 rupees in a given week, the MIS will raise a flag if any other payment is recorded.)

Last, varying contracts might weaken the repayment discipline of borrowers. Some argue that the key difference between debt programs and savings programs is that debt provides a commitment to make weekly payments, whereas with savings there is no such commitment. Thus, this is one reason why rotating savings and credit associations (ROSCAs) and chit funds exist, to provide individuals with a commitment to save. If the debt requirement allows some flexibility, some fear that this will erode the repayment discipline. Borrowers may forget which weeks to pay and which not, or find it hard to turn on and off the habit of putting money aside to pay the loan. Either way, the fear is that having a few weeks off will lead to lower repayment when the payments are required.

These costs of flexible contracts are often better articulated than the benefits. Yet qualitatively the benefits could be huge. Will these products work? Will operational hurdles prevent them from working? Will they erode repayment discipline and increase default? Or will they allow for much larger loan sizes and greater client income growth? We simply do not know. A common retort is that borrowers can use other sources of income or debt to fill in the gaps. This misses the basic point about the financial policy for the poor: these alternatives either do not exist or are very expensive. Why cede this important and potentially lucrative financial service without ever testing the water? There is only one way to know if microfinance can be more flexible: by testing. As with any new idea, there is no way to know how well it works without careful experimentation. As we note above, the point is not that flexibility will impose no costs on the organization. Flexible products may be trickier to implement, or they might have ambiguous effects, like increasing portfolio-at-risk while increasing profitability. The challenge for MFIs is to find those aspects of flexibility which can expand their reach and impact without hampering continued growth.

To examine these theories in a practical way, at Innovations for Poverty Action (IPA) we use randomized control trials to test new products and services for the poor. To determine whether the benefits of a new idea outweigh its costs we measure its impact, benchmarked against the traditional methodology.

FLEXIBILITY WORKS: SOME EXAMPLES

Group versus Individual Liability

For years a central part of the conventional wisdom of microfinance was that microfinance worked because of group liability: banks could safely lend to poor borrowers with no collateral because they would guarantee each others' loans. True, repayment rates among microfinance clients have been impressive. But, like the inflexible repayment schedules, there may be costs as well as benefits: How many potential clients might be deterred by the group-liability contract? How many don't borrow because they don't want to be responsible for other people's loans? We used a randomized control trial to measure the effects. Working with a rural bank in the Philippines, Giné and Karlan (2008) randomly selected groups of their microfinance clients to switch from group liability to individual liability, with all other aspects of the loan contract remaining constant. Following up three years later, the authors found no increase in default among individual-liability clients. On the other hand more clients had joined the individual-liability groups, suggesting that on average clients much prefer individual liability. In an expansion of that study, the authors tested with new clients by randomly marketing in some villages individual-liability loans, and in other villages group-liability loans. Again, there was no difference in default. The bank officers were much less willing to make individual liability loans, suggesting that the flexibility was perceived as too much for their staff, and they restricted the supply of credit. Whether it was right or not we cannot tell, since we do not know whether those not approved for loans would have defaulted or not.

Repayment Frequency

In another study that tested one of the key assumptions of microfinance contracts, Field and Pande (2007) experimented with altering the frequency of payments, from weekly to monthly. After one year, they found no change in default. This simple test has vast implications: if clients can meet far less often with no effect on repayment, MFIs can drastically reduce their staff costs. Those savings can be passed along to clients, potentially making credit more affordable to the poor. And more clients may join if there's less of a burden on their own time. Naturally, more time may yield different results, and proper testing and patience can help us to learn the answer to these important questions.

EVALUATING FLEXIBLE CONTRACTS

This same type of analysis can be applied to carefully examine the flexible lending contracts we describe above. In each case a (randomly selected) group receiving the innovation would be compared to clients offered only the traditional contract. The analysis can go much beyond simply "does it work?" The treatment and control groups can be evaluated on any number of dimensions: repayment, client retention, MFI profitability, etc. For example, flexibility might actually *save* on loan officer time. If every monsoon we know that clients have a tough time paying, might it not be more cost-effective to have lower or less frequent payments during that period rather than use valuable loan officer time to chase down "delinquent" clients?

Further, flexible contracts may greatly increase the impact of the loan. Clients with rigid contracts may take actions which reduce the return on their investments.

  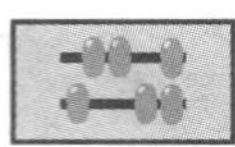      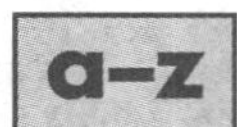

Owners of milk animals may underfeed during difficult times. Asset owners may sell off (productive) assets to repay debts. Freedom from Hunger, through its MAHP program, is helping the MFIs CARD, CRECER, and Bandhan to offer emergency health loans to their clients. It would be useful to evaluate this type of product to determine whether it is able to prevent the destruction of this value. Potentially, such a product could be as useful as the initial loan itself. Or if clients can't handle the additional debt burden, it could have negative spillovers, destabilizing their borrowing groups. If the impact is positive, however, the increased income from retaining productive assets could allow the MFI to further increase loan size.

CONCLUSION

Rigorous evaluations will become only more important as new technologies are developed to improve the efficiency and scale of microbanking. These same technologies, such as handheld computers for loan officers, have the potential to greatly increase the flexibility offered to clients—by making on-the-spot credit decisions, or handling variable repayment amounts, for example. We have focused here on one issue in particular: the flexibility or rigidity of debt products; but with the deployment of any new technology we are faced with the same unknown: how well does it work? The goal of our research around the world, as with the Innovations for Poverty Action, the Financial Access Initiative, and the Massachusetts Institute of Technology Abdul Latif Jameel Poverty Action Lab, is to bring about consensus about the circumstances under which different products and features and services are optimal for clients and institutions. Related work will shed more light on other important aspects of flexibility, including loan tenure, loan size, group size, and guarantee requirements.

MORE INFO

Article:

Field, Erica, and Rohini Pande. "Repayment frequency and default in micro-finance: Evidence from India." *Journal of the European Economic Association* 6:2–3 (April–May 2008): 501–509. Online at: ksghome.harvard.edu/~rpande/papers/repayfreqjeea_1107.pdf

Reports:

Daley-Harris, Sam. "State of the Microcredit Summit Campaign report 2009." Washington, DC: Microcredit Summit Campaign, 2009. Online at: www.microcreditsummit.org/uploads/socrs/SOCR2009_English.pdf

Giné, Xavier, and Dean S. Karlan. "Group versus individual liability: Long term evidence from Philippine microcredit lending groups." Working paper. May 2009. Online at: karlan.yale.edu/p/GroupversusIndividual-May2009.pdf

Websites:

Innovations for Poverty Action (IPA): poverty-action.org
Financial Access Initiative (FAI): financialaccess.org
Abdul Latif Jameel Poverty Action Lab: www.povertyactionlab.com

See Also:

✔ Steps for Obtaining Bank Financing (p. 1090)
Muhammad Yunus (p. 1319)
Banker to the Poor: The Story of the Grameen Bank (p. 1334)

"I wish to preach, not the doctrine of ignoble ease, but the doctrine of the strenuous life, the life of toil and effort, of labor and strife." Theodore Roosevelt

  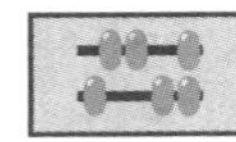   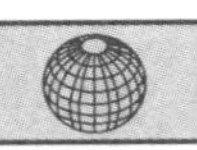   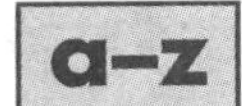

Risk Management Revisited by Duncan Hughes

EXECUTIVE SUMMARY

- Traditional risk management techniques have failed the asset management industry in recent years as portfolios have been unable to deliver sustainable returns throughout the economic cycle.
- The world, and consequently the factors affecting investment portfolios, has shown itself to be more complex and therefore less predictable than has been assumed to date, and particularly with regard to the impact of human behavior on investment returns.
- The requirement for contingency planning for risks that we cannot know about ex ante requires a sea change in the industry's approach to risk management.
- Effective liquidity planning and protection of portfolios against clear secular risks, such as inflation, must form a core part of a robust risk management approach.

INTRODUCTION

Risk management has taken centre stage in many commercial organizations in recent years, but it is in the financial services industry that it has assumed the greatest prominence, particularly since the subprime crisis and the ensuing credit crunch of the late "noughties." Major banks and asset management firms now boast a chief risk officer (CRO) sitting alongside the chief financial officer (CFO) and other executives on the main board. While this innovation could be viewed as rather shutting the stable door after the horse has bolted, it nonetheless demonstrates a renewed commitment to risk management, which has traditionally been viewed as a synonym for "business prevention." This previous sentiment was clearly demonstrated in an infamous incident involving the then CEO of the Halifax Bank of Scotland Group (HBOS)—who was also the deputy chairman of the United Kingdom's Financial Services Authority (FSA) before he was forced to resign—who fired the group's risk manager at the height of the subprime boom in 2005 for challenging the bank's cavalier approach to risk management.[1,2]

The focus on overhauling risk management in financial services gained considerable impetus from the publication of official critical reviews, such as the Turner Review[3] by the FSA, which, although primarily concentrating on the banking sector, nonetheless calls into question the fundamental tenets on which risk analysis in the asset management industry have been traditionally based. While those of us who have lived through a series of greed/fear cycles in financial markets over the last 25 years or so may be forgiven for cynically anticipating that any new prudent risk management measures will quickly be discarded if and when markets begin to rally, it is likely that the subprime crisis and its aftermath will result in a lasting philosophical change in the risk management paradigms employed by asset managers.

The statistically convenient and mathematically elegant models previously used in risk modeling must give way to more heuristic and empirically effective approaches to analysis that reflect the realities of the world of investment and are better able to allow for the idiosyncratic and, at least partially, stochastic behavior of financial markets. Economics is a social, not a pure, science, unlike pure mathematics or physics, and consequently cannot be modeled in the same way. The effect of collective human behavior that influences all economic indicators is exacerbated in financial markets, which are more strongly and immediately influenced by the emotions of greed and fear. Any analysis of risk that does not encompass the impact of human behavior in financial markets (or "behavioral finance" as it is generally called) is probably dangerously incomplete.

THE TRADITIONAL APPROACH TO RISK MANAGEMENT—A CRITIQUE

Underlying Statistical Framework

The basic tenets underlying the risk management policies and techniques that are generally employed in financial markets make perfect theoretical sense. Risk is usually equated to volatility, the idea being that the greater the variance an investment exhibits from an expected or mean return, the greater is its risk. Similarly, the idea of portfolio diversification resonates with most of us given our mothers' advice not to put all our eggs in one basket. Although the mathematics and statistical techniques required for optimal portfolio construction look impressively complex, it has become clear that these techniques, and the models on which they are based, have been ineffective in protecting investors from the risks that they faced.

The devil, as ever, is in the detail. In order to get to the root of the problem, we must first critically evaluate the statistical models that underlie risk analysis. First, let us examine the measure of volatility that is generally used, i.e. standard deviation. Standard deviation purports to provide us with a measure of how much a variable—for our purposes, the value of an investment—will vary from its mean, or expected, value, μ. From standard deviation, σ, we can readily calculate "confidence intervals," which are a measure of the probability of the actual outcome falling within a given tolerance of the expected value. Thus, for a risk tolerance of one standard deviation, we are "confident" that the actual outcome will fall within the given range 68% of the time. If we have less risk tolerance, we might insist that the actual outcomes fall within a given range 95% or 99% of the time (roughly corresponding to two and three standard deviations, respectively; see Figure 1). So far, so good: we can prescribe the level of risk that we want to assume and select investments that meet the required statistical criteria.

The problem is, however, that standard deviation does *not* at all adequately describe the possible actual outcomes of financial markets. Technically, standard deviation is the second moment of a probability density function (where the mean, or expected, return is the first moment). There are, however, two further moments of probability density functions (moments could be seen as being analogous to the four dimensions of space and time), these being skewness and kurtosis (Figures 2 and 3).

Different financial markets exhibit different, but not generally neutral, levels of skewness and kurtosis. Most notably, many financial markets have probability density functions with "fat tails" (technically, leptokurtosis). Crucially, this implies that financial markets have many more extreme outcomes than that predicted by the use of standard deviation alone and the underlying assumption of the normal distribution that a two-moment model dictates (indeed the normal distribution is expressed in statistical shorthand as $N(\mu,\sigma^2)$ where μ represents the distribution's mean, expected value, and σ represents its standard deviation). Some markets tend to exhibit skewness, where either more of the actual observed outcomes fall above (positive skewness) or below (negative skewness) the expected return. A notable example of this phenomenon is senior credit instruments, which deliver an actual return that is more often higher than the expected return due to their generally extremely low incidence of default. The key here is that the use of standard deviation alone has the *hidden assumption* of zero

"Everyone believes in the (normal) law of errors: the mathematicians, because they think it is an experimental fact, and the experimenters, because they suppose it is a theorem of mathematics." Gabriel Lippman

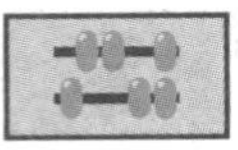

Figure 1. Standard Normal distribution and 95% confidence interval

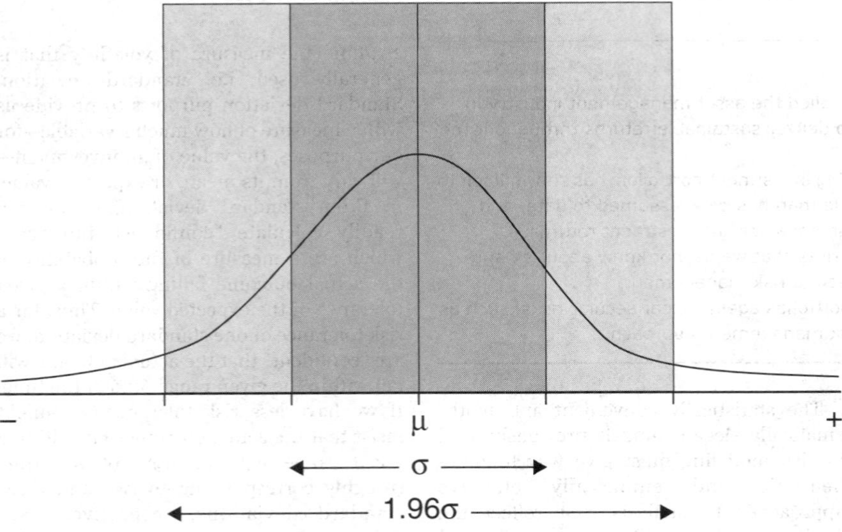

Figure 2. Third moment: skewness

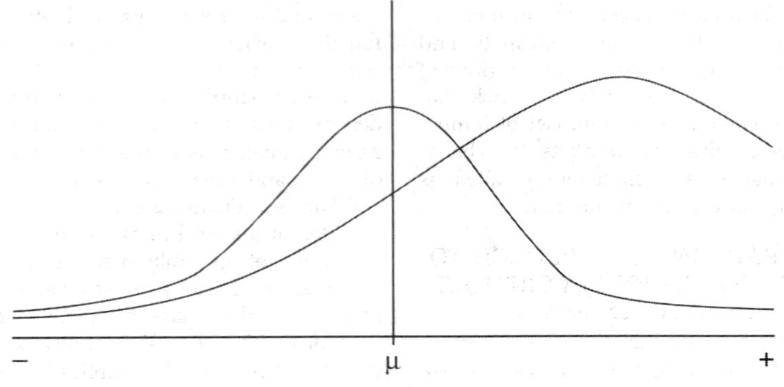

Figure 3. Fourth moment: kurtosis

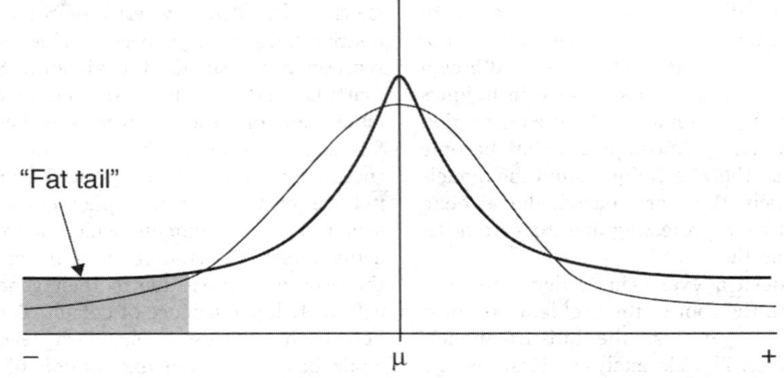

skewness and neutral kurtosis (technically, mesokurtosis) in the expected distribution of actual returns.

If we now turn to the question of portfolio diversification, the key underlying statistic here is correlation, which is the degree to which one variable, or investment for our purposes, moves in line with another investment. In forming a portfolio, optimization techniques minimize the degree of intra-portfolio correlation given the constraint of a given number of investments. Modern portfolio theory tells us that we should have as many different investments in our portfolio as possible, since each additional investment will increase the robustness of the portfolio through increased diversification. The apogee, according to modern portfolio theory, is the "market portfolio," which contains every conceivable asset, since we should seek to squeeze every last drop of correlation benefit from the available asset pool.

$$\rho X, Y = \frac{\text{cov}(X, Y)}{\sigma X \sigma Y}$$

This states that the correlation of investments *X* and *Y* is the quotient of the covariance between the returns of *X* and *Y* over the sum of the standard deviations of *X* and *Y* individually.

From this formula we can once again see the specter of standard deviation at the feast. As before, this condemns the correlation coefficient, *ρ*, to being a two-dimensional (or, strictly, two-moment) measure, ignoring the real-life facets of skewness and kurtosis in investment returns. The implication is that the benefits hoped for from diversification may be severely undermined.

None of the above is beyond the grasp of most market practitioners (skewness is, after all, nothing more than a description of the position of the mode relative to the mean in a probability function), so the question is, why have financial markets persisted with the use of these models, particularly when they have consistently proved themselves to be inadequate? The answer may lie in the sheer convenience of standard deviation-based measures: everyone can understand the idea of standard deviation and the confidence intervals that can be derived from the normal distribution which it describes. However, the fact remains that models which "stop" at the second moment of standard deviation, ignoring the third and fourth moments of skewness and kurtosis, are as limited as a description of our physical world would be if we tried to describe it using only length and breadth and ignored the dimensions of height and time.

"Risk comes from not knowing what you're doing." Warren Buffett

        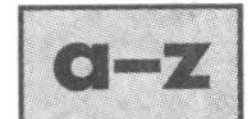

Although it is unclear what should replace this framework in the analysis of financial markets (and it clearly needs to be replaced), it is nonetheless imperative that the assumptions described above, which implicitly underlie any analysis carried out using it, must be recognized. The over-reliance and overconfidence in these models has, I believe, been a significant factor in the general empirically disappointing performance of asset portfolios, particularly in their inability to weather the all-too-frequent financial storms to which they are subjected.

Information and Other Issues

In addition to the inappropriateness of the statistical models on which investment analysis has been based to date, the received wisdom of risk management has also included other flaws and oversimplifications. One clear, and frankly gross, oversimplification is the assumption that risk is somehow homogenous and that, for example, equity investments relating to firms in Argentina or Sri Lanka can be analyzed using the same type of framework as for those stocks included in the S&P 500 index of the largest publicly quoted firms in the United States. One of the principal reasons why this approach is asinine is that the cohort of investors interested in various securities markets are different, both in their behavior and in their investment horizons and objectives. Similarly, the use of standardized techniques for the analysis of "alternative" investments such as private equity and hedge funds is fatuous at best, but more likely extremely dangerous.

Other issues include myopia, which has been proposed as an explanation for the historical outperformance of equities over bonds,[4] but which more generally manifests itself in a lack of focus on the "big picture." Asset managers are overwhelmed by information presented to them 24/7 by a plethora of sources such as CNN, Bloomberg News, broker research, and daily newspapers. This information overload can dangerously obscure the secular themes which generally represent the greatest knowable (and therefore manageable) risks to an asset portfolio over the intended investment horizon. Depending on a particular portfolio's objectives, these themes might include those shown in Table 1.

Table 1. Secular themes as sources of long-term portfolio risk

Secular Theme	Implication	Risk
Aging of G7 population	Lower demand for equities	Equity markets become moribund
Polarization of wealth	Lower consumer spending	Economic growth falters
Domination of "big oil"	Higher oil prices	Inflation
Global population explosion	Food shortages	Inflation
Globalization	Greater competition	Reduction of "lives" of businesses
Environmental concern	Higher cost of doing business	Inflation Lower equity returns

NEW DIRECTIONS IN RISK MANAGEMENT

Decomposition of Risk

A first step in the robust analysis of the risk of an investment is to break down the risks into sensible (and honest) categories. Particularly in the ambit of asset management—where investments are considered within the context of an overall portfolio, and an important consequent dynamic is their behavior with respect to the other constituents—homogeneous factors (such as the securities market and liquidity) need to be separately identified from heterogeneous factors (such as branding and management). As will be discussed subsequently, we also need to build in tolerance for those risk factors that cannot be known at a given point in time, but which may become important or dominant.

Behavioral Finance

From an academic perspective, the worlds of psychology and financial economics definitively came together in a meaningful way in 1979 with the publication of Kahneman and Tversky's seminal paper on "prospect theory,"[5] which introduced empirical evidence that a subject's attitude to loss is very different to that toward a similar gain (essentially, that subjects felt a loss considerably more than they felt a gain). This contradicts the standard utility theory assumption that underlies expected behavior in microeconomics and it is therefore an important refinement. This differential is illustrated by the asymmetric value function shown in Figure 4.

Figure 4. An asymmetric value function

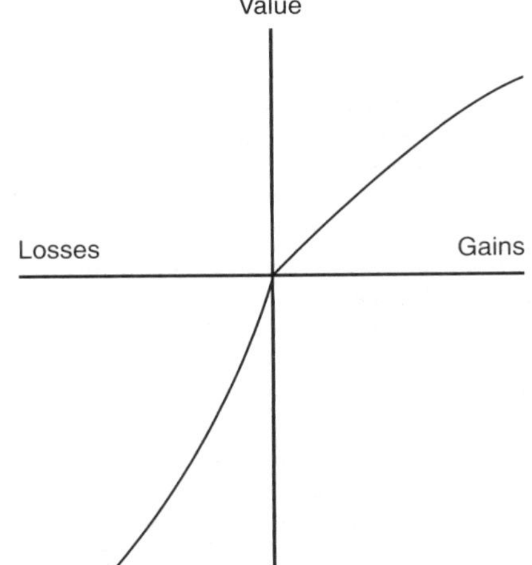

To emphasize the point, the value function relating to financial markets differs from the utility function that is generally used in microeconomics in two ways: first, the function is asymmetric, i.e. the behavior exhibited with regard to a gain (being "risk-aversion," i.e. preferring a definite gain) is different to that exhibited for a loss (being "loss-aversion," i.e. preferring to take risk to avoid a loss). Second, the value function described above illustrates far more extreme reactions to losses or gains than that exhibited by standard utility functions—particularly with regard to losses, where there is no tolerance for a small loss and experiments have shown that subjects will risk suffering a significantly larger loss to avoid a definite smaller loss. Further groundbreaking empirical research was carried out by De Bondt and Thaler[6] in 1985, which clearly demonstrated that investors and traders overreact to both good and bad news.

Bringing these discoveries back to our probability distributions from the first section, we can see a psychological rationale for the "missing" third and fourth moments of the probability distribution observed in financial markets. These are shown in Figure 5.

Behavioral finance is a burgeoning field and deserves fuller treatment than that provided here. Table 3 provides a brief summary of some important concepts that go beyond the familiar "greed and fear" paradigm.

In summary, these phenomena cannot be ignored when considering the behavior of financial markets. A logical consequence of all of these differing, and often conflicting, individual behaviors is that the aggregate behavior of the market may well just be too complex to model at all accurately.

For an interesting (and more complete) treatment of behavioral finance, see Shiller (2004).[8]

Epistemology

Although all aspects of epistemology—broadly speaking the study of knowledge and the justification of beliefs—are of interest (particularly when considered in conjunction with the psychological phenomena discussed above), from the

Figure 5. Behavioral impact on market returns profile

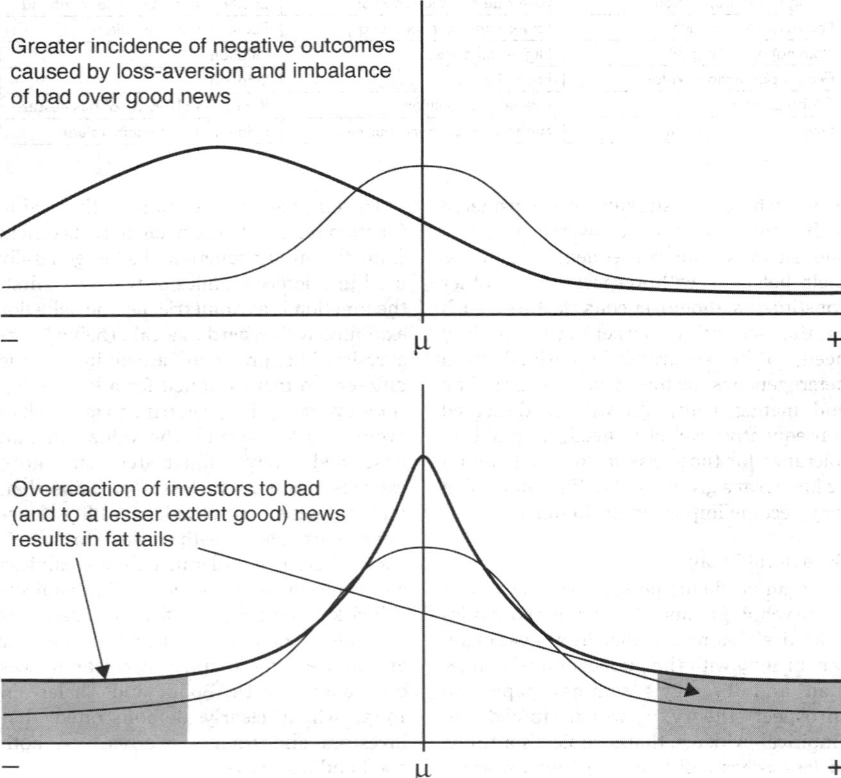
Greater incidence of negative outcomes caused by loss-aversion and imbalance of bad over good news
–
μ
+
Overreaction of investors to bad (and to a lesser extent good) news results in fat tails
–
μ
+

Table 3. Major theoretical frameworks in behavioral finance

Theory	*Concept*	*Implication*
Prospect theory	Subjects have a different approach to managing gains than to managing losses	Negative skewing of investment return profile
Allais paradox	Subjects react inconsistently with standard utility theory when presented with option of certainty	Overvaluation of certainty with respect to standard utility theory
Framing	Subjects make different decisions with regard to the same choice depending how the choices are framed	Unpredictability of investor behavior because dependent on each subject's (different) perspective
Anchoring	Subjects base their investment decisions on a fixed reference point, e.g. a previous valuation of a property	Unpredictability of investor behavior because dependent on each subject's (different) reference point
Regret theory	Subjects avoid selling stocks to crystallize a loss	Negative skewing of investment return profile
Wishful thinking bias	Exaggeration of probability of success	Positive skewing of investment return profile
Mental compartments	Individual investors compartmentalize their portfolios into a "risk-averse" part and a "risk-seeking" part. Particularly important where investors have already made (large) gains, q.v. Brian Hunter at Amaranth.[7]	Difficult to predict overall investor behavior because dependent on the compartmentalization approach of each
Representativeness heuristic	Subjects see patterns in random data (e.g. "head and shoulders," etc.)	Groups of market participants "herd" into positions when they "see" these patterns, distorting market returns
Disjunction effect	Subject's inability to make a decision without historical information	Overreliance on historical data

perspective of financial markets it is the scope and limitations of knowledge that are of most interest.

The key issue is that there are events that will occur in the future that we *cannot* know about now. These "black swans," as Nassim Taleb famously describes them,[9] can be as devastating as they are unpredictable. From the perspective of our models of potential outcomes, the most important facets of this phenomenon are as follows.

- The incidence of extreme, unpredictable outcomes is *far* higher than forecast by the normal distribution of returns described above (some of the dramatic events in a short period in 2010–11 are listed below). Thus, the probability density function that we face is more leptokurtic, i.e. has "fatter tails."
- Empirically, more unanticipated bad events are reported than good—e.g. natural and anthropic disasters.[10]
- The probability of these events is rarely, if ever, factored into asset prices and risk models, despite their frequency and consequential impact.

The limitations of knowledge extend not only to what we can know, because situations are too difficult to model and, therefore, to predict (e.g. climate change, the Russian crop fires of 2010, the devastation of Queensland in late 2010/early 2011, the causes and effects of the strife in the Arab world in early 2011, the Christchurch earthquake of February 2011, and the Japanese earthquake and ensuing tsunami of March 2011). They also affect us at the micro level, in terms of what we are not told: even the largest shareholders in publicly quoted companies can only "see through a glass darkly" into the machinations of corporations through the dimly lit and narrow apertures of shareholders' meetings and infrequent meetings with senior managers. From this perspective, private equity investment is actually less risky, or at least less opaque, since investors usually insist on having a seat on the board of the company in question.

The overwhelming point is that we think that we know more about the future than we actually do—that is, we are consistently overconfident in our predictions of the future and systematically underestimate what can go wrong and by how much it can go wrong.

FACING UNCERTAINTY AND UNKNOWNS IN THE REAL WORLD

In 2002, the US Secretary of Defense, Donald Rumsfeld, gave one of the most abstruse press conferences in the history of the English language, during which he created his now infamous paradigm of "known knowns," "known unknowns,"

"To a man with only a hammer in his toolkit, every problem looks like a nail." Abraham Maslow

CASE STUDY

Toyota Motor Corporation

In the analysis of any individual investment, the main challenge for asset managers is to establish an effective paradigm for risk analysis. Whilst some risks will be specific to the company or issuing entity to which a security relates, others will be extraneous to it, and may be common to a number of assets in a portfolio.

A key point here is that, even in this simple analysis, there is a lot of uncertainty. Although we know that sales of Toyota cars will probably fall if the oil price rises, standard supply and demand analysis may be inadequate and actual demand may well be subject to critical thresholds (e.g. oil at US$200 per barrel, or where it costs a US consumer $100 to fill his or her Toyota with gasoline) as well as other factors. The accelerator pedal issues faced in 2009, which tarnished Toyota's previously premium brand, could not have been known by asset managers who invested in 2008. The risk faced by investors is broadened purely through the membership of Toyota in the Nikkei 225 index, which is a proxy for the Japanese equity market and, more generally, the Japanese economy. Consequently, a natural disaster, such as the earthquake and tsunami of March 2011, that affects Japan will adversely affect an investment in Toyota, irrespective of that event's actual impact on Toyota's business.

It should be clear from this short case study that the risks faced by investors in Toyota cannot sensibly be summarized in one number (e.g. standard deviation)—and, indeed, that not all of the risks can easily be expressed numerically. The dangers are oversimplification, standardization of analysis, and consequent overconfidence. This is particularly so where investors rely on the perceived safety of a firm with a large capitalization that is quoted on a major stock exchange, which, although generally helpful from a liquidity perspective (actually one of the main benefits), is no panacea, and is no substitute for doing one's own research (q.v. Enron, WorldCom).

What we should really be worried about is the risk of loss in a given investment, not necessarily increased volatility (indeed, holders of options warmly welcome increased volatility since it increases their asset's value). Thus, avoiding bad situations in the first place is probably the most effective risk management tool of all. Warren Buffett's approach as a "value" investor has ensured that he has avoided such market collapses as the technology bust of 2001, since the valuations of such stocks were too high for him to consider investment.

Table 2. Examples of risks faced by investors in Toyota

Factor	Example Risks
Automobile manufacture	Oil price increase reduces demand Subject to discretionary spending by consumers Low-cost competition
Japanese equity	Share price falls along with Japanese/global market Lower demand from aging population
Brand	Strong brand undermined by accelerator pedal issues
Management	Traditional Japanese management structure and philosophy could make firm vulnerable to competition from firms that outsource manufacturing

and "unknown unknowns." Although it confused the world at that time, it nonetheless creates a useful framework for the analysis of knowledge and the risks that we face. To his three categories I would add the additional class of "unknown knowns," so that our knowledge of the world and its risks is broken down as in Table 4.

An honest appraisal of the risks that we face and an acknowledgement that there are risks that we cannot know about ex ante is the first step to better risk management. An important factor in our favor when managing risk is that the *symptoms* of risk (i.e. how any risk affects the value of our portfolio) are far less numerous than the *causes*. This is particularly helpful when trying to deal with the "unknown" risks that we face. In fact, if we look at the examples of known and unknown risks detailed in Table 4 and their potential mitigators and hedges, we can see that the action to be taken is very similar in nature. This is shown in Table 5.

In summary, we should be allowing for more risk than that which currently is clearly predictable. The $64,000 question is, of course, how much more liquidity, inflation hedging, etc., should we be incorporating into our risk management program? Since every portfolio (and its underlying liabilities) is different, it is impossible to generalize. However, in setting the quantum of the portfolio's contingent risk protection and other risk management measures, the following issues must be addressed:

- How can the concentration of risk be reduced?
- How much loss can the asset portfolio bear?
- How likely is it that the portfolio will be able to recover from a significant loss?
- What is the investment horizon (i.e. how long does the portfolio have to recover any losses)?

Table 4. Risk categories by "knowability"

Category	Meaning	Examples
Known known	Risks we know about now and can predict and quantify with reasonable accuracy now	Current volatility Short-term inflation Secular demographic factors Expected default rates
Known unknown	Risks we know about now, but cannot predict the timing of and/or quantify accurately now	Firm/industry demise Long-term inflation Changes in consumer tastes Actual default rates
Unknown known	Risks we forgot we knew about	Universal banking[11] Portfolio correlations in bear markets
Unknown unknown	Risks we cannot know about now	9/11 terrorist atrocity Madoff fraud Arab uprisings 2011

Table 5. Categories of risk and hedging strategies

Risk	Category(ies)	Mitigator(s)/Hedge(s)
Current volatility	Instrument-specific	Diversification
Short-term inflation	Inflation	Commodity hedging
Secular demographic factors	Inflation	Commodity hedging
Expected default rates	Instrument-specific	Diversification
Firm/industry demise	Instrument-specific	Diversification
Long-term inflation	Inflation	Commodity hedging
Changes in consumer tastes	Instrument-specific	Diversification
Actual default rates	Instrument-specific	Diversification
Universal banking[12]	Liquidity	Liquidity planning
9/11 terrorist atrocity	Liquidity Inflation	Liquidity planning Commodity hedging
Madoff fraud	Instrument-specific	Diversification
Arab uprisings 2011	Inflation	Commodity hedging

  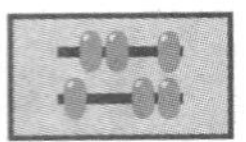      

CONCLUSION

The reality of investment risk in asset management (and other spheres of finance) has proved itself to be more complex and far less prescriptive than the implicit description of risk in the models that were originally conceived by the pioneers of modern portfolio theory. Unfortunately, no clear alternative to the intuitively appealing models centering on standard deviation, confidence intervals, and correlations is immediately apparent, but to continue to rely too heavily on these models in their current form, knowing what we now know about the nature of the modern world and the empirical behavior of investors, is negligently dangerous.

Going forward, knowing more about individual investments and their potential pitfalls, rather than relying on blind diversification, is a good first step. A good second step is greater humility in admitting to ourselves that there are some things we do not know and others that we simply cannot know at any given point. Making additional allowances for these "unknowns" (which will inevitably cause a drag on portfolio returns in the short run) is probably the greatest Rubicon that the asset management industry needs to cross.

MAKING IT HAPPEN

- Understand as much as you can about each investment in your portfolio, but accept that you cannot know everything.
- Understand the known and potential liquidity requirements of your portfolio's liabilities and how these relate to the liquidity of the portfolio's assets.
- Try not to make rash decisions: if you have made considered investment choices for the long term, don't be panicked into changing them when short-term crises arise (which they will).
- Don't rely on numbers alone: any statistics should only support a robust investment proposition that has intuitive as well as logical appeal.

MORE INFO

Books:

Gardner, Dan. *Risk: The Science and Politics of Fear.* London: Virgin Books, 2008.

Shiller, Robert J. *Market Volatility.* Cambridge, MA: MIT Press, 1989.

Taleb, Nassim Nicholas. *Fooled by Randomness: The Hidden Role of Chance in Life and in the Markets.* New York: Texere, 2004.

Report:

Sewell, Martin. "Behavioural finance." Working paper. April 2010. Online at: www.behaviouralfinance.net/behavioural-finance.pdf

Websites:

CFA Institute publications: www.cfapubs.org

EDHEC-Risk Institute: www.edhec-risk.com

NOTES

1 news.bbc.co.uk/1/hi/business/7883409.stm

2 tinyurl.com/b25pre

3 Financial Services Authority. "The Turner review: A regulatory response to the global banking crisis." March 2009. Online at: www.fsa.gov.uk/pubs/other/turner_review.pdf

4 Benartzi, Shlomo, and Richard H. Thaler. "Myopic loss aversion and the equity premium puzzle." *Quarterly Journal of Economics* 110:1 (February 1995): 73–92. Online at: dx.doi.org/10.2307/2118511

5 Kahneman, Daniel, and Amos Tversky. "Prospect theory: An analysis of decisions under risk." *Econometrica* 47:2 (March 1979): 263–292. Online at: www.jstor.org/stable/1914185

6 De Bondt, Werner F. M., and Richard Thaler. "Does the stock market overreact?" *Journal of Finance* 40:3 (July 1985): 793–805. Online at: www.jstor.org/stable/2327804

7 The case of Brian Hunter at Amaranth during 2005 and 2006 is interesting. Having made a reported US$75–100 million bonus in the previous trading year, the compartmentalization theory would suggest that the excessive risk-seeking behavior exhibited by him in the subsequent trading year (which resulted in losses of Biblical proportions) was due to Hunter having "money in the bank" which he felt he could afford to gamble with.

8 Shiller, Robert J. "Radical financial innovation." Cowles Foundation Discussion Paper No. 1461. April 2004. Online at: ssrn.com/abstract=537402

9 Taleb, Nassim Nicholas. *The Black Swan: The Impact of the Highly Improbable*. New York: Random House, 2007.

10 Whether this high incidence is "real" or perceived is largely irrelevant; even if the media industry biases reported news to bad events in order to sell more newspapers, the effect on sentiment is the same. The effect of this is that our probability density function is negatively skewed.

11 Universal banking is a business model whereby investment banking and deposit-taking activities are combined one organization. Universal banking was effectively declared illegal in the United States in 1933 (the Glass–Steagall Act, 1933) following the Wall Street crash of 1929, the failure of around 10,000 banks, and the ensuing Great Depression. The Gramm–Leach–Bliley Act, 1999 (GLB), repealed those parts of the Glass–Steagall act that prevented universal banking. GLB was widely blamed for exacerbating the financial crisis of the late noughties. Paul Krugman, the Nobel prize-winning economist, was quoted in the *New York Times* (March 2008) as saying that Senator Phil Gramm was second only to Alan Greenspan (who pumped unprecedented and, perhaps, unnecessary liquidity into the US financial system) in terms of responsibility for causing the crisis.

12 *Ibid.*

"If you are not happy while getting rich, chances are that you will not be happy when you do get rich." Robert Kiyosaki

  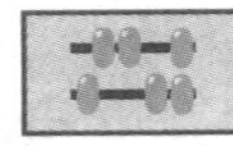      

The Role of Commodities in an Institutional Portfolio by Keith Black and Satya Kumar

EXECUTIVE SUMMARY

- Institutional investors, including public and corporate pension plans, endowments, and foundations, are rapidly increasing the portion of their assets allocated to commodity investments.
- Investments in commodity futures may improve the reward-to-risk ratio for investment portfolios, as the low correlation between commodity futures and equity and fixed-income investments reduces portfolio volatility.
- Over long periods of time, investments in commodity futures have a risk–return profile similar to that of stocks, which means that there can be substantial gains or losses in any given month or year.
- Commodity futures have a positive correlation with inflation, which can be attractive for pension plans that are required to pay inflation-adjusted benefits to their beneficiaries.
- The best way for institutional investors to access the commodity markets is by identifying skilled and active managers in the futures markets. Investing in commodity index funds, physical commodities, or equity securities are suboptimal solutions.

THE CASE FOR COMMODITIES

The case for commodities is based largely on their historical tendency to offer returns that exhibit a low correlation with those of stock and bond market indices. Although commodities may be volatile, their low correlation with traditional investments can result in a significant diversification benefit. Table 1 shows the correlation between two commodity indices—the Standard & Poor's GSCI (S&P GSCI) and the Dow Jones–AIG Commodity Index (DJ-AIG)—and traditional investments and inflation indices since 1991. Over the last 18 years, a small allocation to investments in commodity futures would have substantially reduced portfolio volatility.

Table 1. Correlation matrix for two commodity indices with traditional investments and inflation indices, January 1991 to September 2008

Correlation with	S&P GSCI	DJ-AIG
DJ Wilshire 5000 Index	0.04	0.10
Lehman Aggregate Bond Index	0.03	0.02
Consumer Price Index (CPI)	0.18	0.15
Treasury Inflation-Protected Securities (TIPS)	0.16	0.17

Historically, investments in commodity futures have offered their strongest returns during times of below-average returns from traditional stock and bond market investments. Figure 1 shows the performance of commodity futures sorted by the return of the Wilshire 5000 stock market index during the period.

From 1991 to the third quarter of 2008, the Wilshire 5000 index declined by an average of −8.2% during the 20% of calendar quarters with the largest stock market declines. During these quarters of sharp stock price corrections, the S&P GSCI averaged a total return of 4.0%, while the Dow Jones–AIG Commodity Index returned 2.1%. In the second quintile, in calendar quarters when the stock market return was 0.0%, commodity indices earned their highest returns, at 6.1% and 4.8%. Each commodity index experienced its largest gains during times of below-average stock market returns. Conversely, the only periods in which the commodity indices consistently experienced losses were those in which the stock market indices posted their largest gains.

Figure 2 tells a similar story, comparing the returns of commodity indices with those of the Lehman Brothers Aggregate Bond Market Index. In the 20% worst quarters for bond markets, the Lehman Aggregate returned −1.0% and inflation-linked bonds (TIPS) fell by 0.6%. During these quarters of weak bond markets, the commodity indices offered their highest returns: 5.4% for the S&P GSCI, and 3.5% for the DJ-AIG.

Historically, commodities have served in a defensive role, as commodities have earned their highest return in times of weak stock and bond prices. Should these correlations persist in the future, a small allocation to commodities may serve to reduce portfolio risk by increasing returns in times of falling stock and bond prices.

COMMODITY FUTURES INDICES

The two most commonly used commodity futures indices are the S&P GSCI and the Dow Jones–AIG Commodity Index. Table 2 shows the allocation of each index to various commodity markets. Note that the energy markets represent 76% of the GSCI. In contrast, the DJ-AIG index intentionally limits exposure to any single sector to around 33%. Investors may prefer the DJ-AIG index to gain a potential improvement in the risk–reward tradeoff, as the overweight given to energy commodities in the GSCI has historically resulted in higher volatility without a corresponding boost in returns. Since 1991, the GSCI has earned an average total return of 7.1% with a standard deviation (volatility) of 18.4%, while the DJ-AIG averaged an annual return of 8.1% with a lower standard deviation of 12.3%. Earlier, Table 1 showed that the two commodity indices share similar correlations with traditional stock and bond investments and inflation.

The total return to a commodity futures index consists of three components: spot return, roll return, and yield. The spot return is the return to an investment in physical commodities. The roll return is

Figure 1. Performance of commodity futures sorted by return of Wilshire 5000 Stock Market Index, 1991 to third quarter of 2008

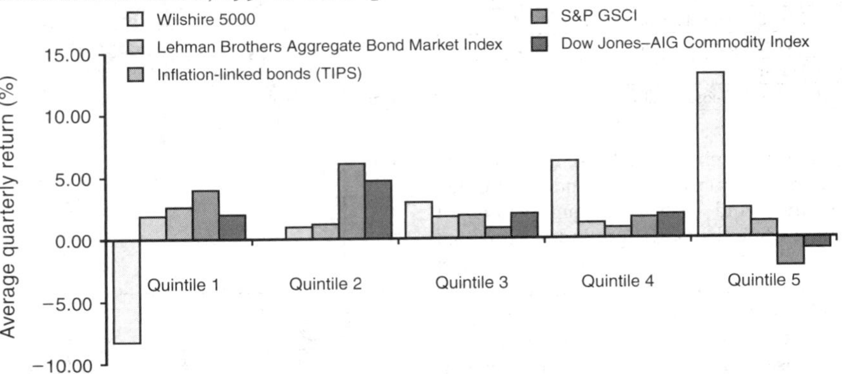

"To gain that which is worth having, it may be necessary to lose everything else." Bernadette Devlin

Figure 2. Comparison of commodity index returns with returns of Lehman Brothers Aggregate Bond Market Index

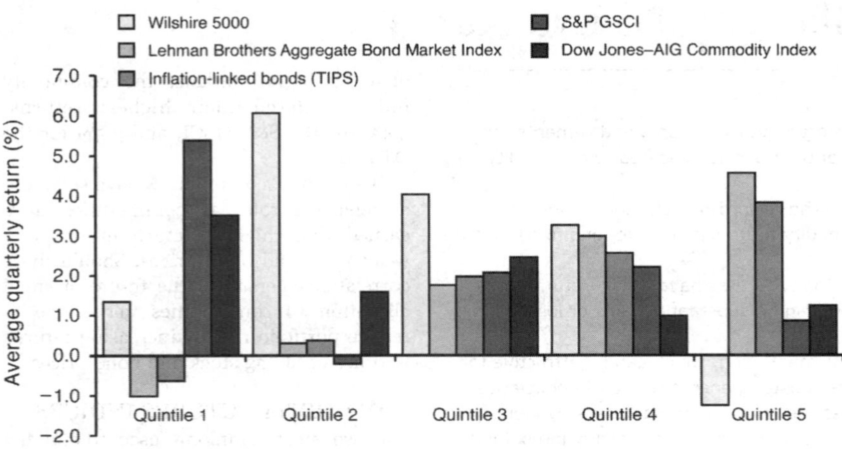

Table 2. Composition (%) of S&P GSCI and DJ-AIG indices as of September 30, 2008

Commodity sector	*S&P GSCI*	*DJ-AIG*
Energy	76.0	35.1
Precious metals	2.2	10.2
Industrial metals	6.2	17.8
Agriculture	12.0	28.4
Livestock	3.6	8.5

earned in the process of passively trading (rolling) futures contracts as they mature and must be replaced. The yield is the interest earned on a short-term fixed-income investment that is pledged to the futures exchange in order to maintain the collateral required to back the futures investments. Table 3 breaks down the total returns from spot, roll, and yield.

Figures 3 and 4 show some interesting characteristics of the returns on owning

Table 3. Decomposition of S&P GSCI returns, 1970 to September 2008

	Annualized return (%)
S&P GSCI Total Return Index	11.8
S&P GSCI Total Return Index	4.8
S&P GSCI Spot Return Index	5.3
Roll return	0.5
Three-month Treasury Bill yield	5.6

physical commodities. Most notably, spot commodity markets have underperformed inflation and cash over long periods of time: while the GSCI spot index earned an annual return of 4.8% since 1970, cash returned 5.6% and the US Consumer Price Index (CPI) increased by 4.6% per year over the same period. Commodity price increases have not exceeded the rate of inflation over long periods of time. As new natural resources are discovered, production technologies improve, and research advances in areas such as crop engineering and alternative energy, commodity prices tend to decline in real (after-inflation) terms.

How, then, could commodities futures have offered a total return since 1970 rivaling that of equities if the ownership of physical commodities does not offer a return that exceeds inflation? The answer is in the roll return and the collateral yield, as shown in Figure 3. (The roll return is approximated by the difference between the excess return and the spot return of the GSCI.) The roll return and collateral yield can only be earned when investing in commodity futures. The return on commodity futures investments, then, has significantly exceeded that of a direct investment in physical commodities over the last 37 years. An extended discussion of roll yield, and the relationship to contango and backwardation term structures in the futures markets, can be found in Black and Kumar (2008).

Figure 3. Ratio of cumulative wealth normalized to cash, 1970 to September 2008

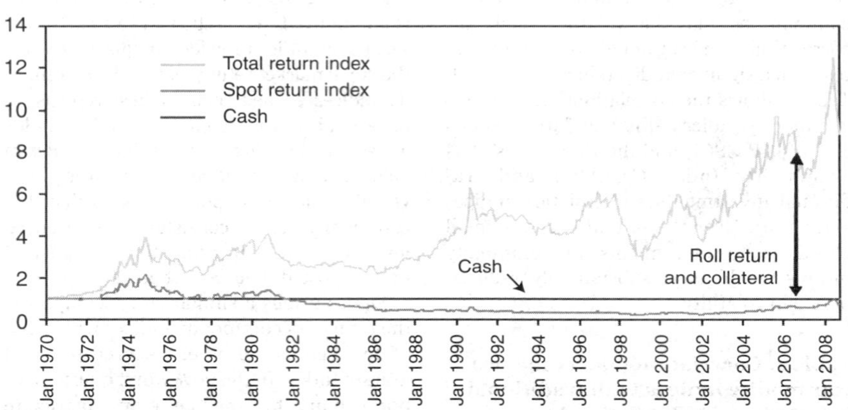

Figure 4. Ratio of cumulative wealth of spot returns normalized to cash, 1970 to September

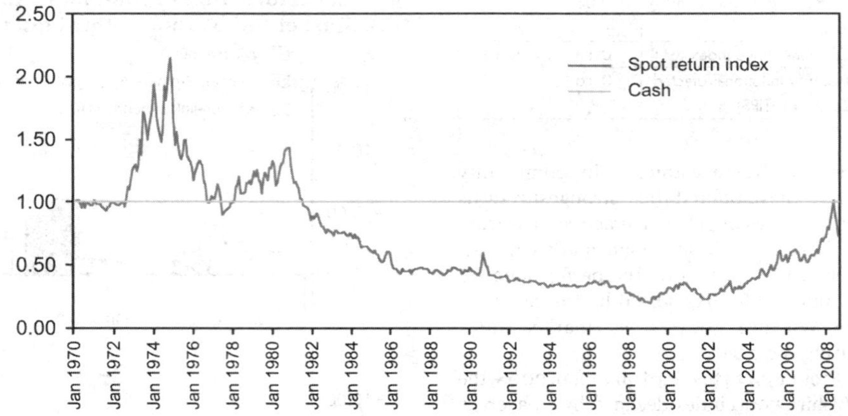

  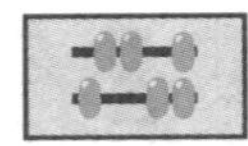      

Not every investor will choose to make use of commodities in their portfolio. It can be difficult to value commodities, as their characteristics don't neatly follow classical valuation models. Commodities do not generate a cash flow, so they can't be valued using discounted cash flow methodologies. Because commodities have a near-zero correlation to equity indices, their beta is also near zero, which disallows use of the capital asset pricing model. Variables such as political strife and weather can have a significant impact on both long- and short-run commodity prices. These exogenous variables are extremely difficult to predict, and they create systemic risks that are not priced in traditional return forecasting models.

ACTIVELY MANAGED COMMODITY FUNDS

Active management has a number of advantages over allocating assets to a commodity index fund. There are several ways in which an active commodity manager can add value relative to an investment in a commodity index. Should a manager demonstrate skill in these areas, an allocation to its managed commodity product can be supported.

First, an active commodity manager should have an intimate understanding of the shape of the futures curves in a variety of commodity markets. Commodity index funds require that investors hold long positions in the near-dated contract, regardless of the shape of the futures curve and the size of the positive or negative roll yield. Active managers, however, have significant flexibility in their selection of contract. For example, although the front-month contracts in a given market may be priced to result in roll losses, later-dated contracts, perhaps at a 12-month maturity, may be priced in such a way that investors may earn a profit from the roll. This flexibility can significantly increase the potential for a return from the futures roll. In a case where the entire futures curve for a given commodity is in contango, causing negative roll yields, an active manager may choose to reduce or eliminate exposure to that commodity. Commodity index programs also have a stated timing when they are required to roll from the front month to the later-dated futures contract. When managers follow a mechanical strategy, such as rolling 20% of their position in each of the fifth through ninth business days of the calendar month, other traders in the market become aware of the roll requirement and change their prices to maximize the market impact of that trading program. Active managers will choose to roll their positions at a date other than that of the index rolls, which can significantly reduce the market impact of their trading.

Second, commodity index investors are required to hold a certain portion of their assets in each futures market, regardless of the fundamental drivers of the spot commodity price. Active commodity managers should be able to show skill in their analysis of the supply and demand dynamics in each market. Ideally, the active manager will implement a long position only in markets where demand is likely to grow faster than supply, while avoiding or selling short in markets with less favorable supply–demand dynamics. While index investors only take

CASE STUDY

Commodity Stocks versus Commodity Futures

Some investors have chosen to implement their views on commodity prices by investing in equity securities. The prices of these stocks may be somewhat correlated with those of commodity futures. Metals firms include, for example, Alcoa, and Anglo American, while agricultural firms include Archer Daniels Midland. In the energy sector, stocks such as Exxon-Mobil, Chevron, and ConocoPhillips may be used as a proxy for crude oil. These three companies alone make up 4.6% of the market capitalization of the Wilshire 5000 index. The energy sector as a whole comprises 11% of the US stock market, and another 4% is made up by metals, food, chemicals, and other materials companies. Given that most investors already have a large allocation in equity securities, an additional allocation to commodity-linked equities may not be the best way to express a view on commodity prices.

As an example, consider that the price of a stock is the product of the earnings per share (EPS) and the stock's price/earnings multiple (P/E). When commodity firms have not hedged their output in the futures market, the profits of a firm (i.e. EPS) will be highly correlated with the prices of the commodities it produces. These profits give the firm a desirable commodity market exposure (beta), such that this portion of the stock price is responsive to changes in commodity prices. However, each firm also has a P/E ratio, which can vary with the level of the stock market. This introduces a potentially undesirable stock market beta into the commodity portfolio. This sensitivity to stock prices is unwelcome, as a key reason for investing in commodities is to experience returns that are uncorrelated with those of equity markets. In fact, commodity stocks are likely to underperform commodity futures during times of high inflation. When inflation and commodity prices are rising, stock prices are typically declining. Should the price/earnings ratio of commodity stocks decline in a bear market, the investor may not realize the anticipated benefit of the commodity firm's profits in terms of stock price appreciation. Commodity futures are a more direct way to earn the diversifying benefits of commodity investments without increasing the stock market risk of the overall portfolio.

In the first quarter of 2008, energy stocks and commodity futures indices moved in opposite directions. Even though oil prices were increasing (commodity beta) and commodity futures indices rose as much as 18% in the quarter, the stock market was decidedly negative. Energy stocks fell 8% during the quarter, as the US stock market declined nearly 10% in the quarter. While energy stocks had a higher return than the broader market, there remained a large gap between the performance of commodity stocks and commodity futures.

Though energy, metals and agricultural commodities are well represented in the futures markets, there are other commodities for which futures markets do not currently exist. Markets such as those for water, coal, steel, chemicals, and renewable energy can only be accessed by investors through equity securities. Firms that produce capital goods needed for exploration and production, or to maintain ownership, of commodities in these sectors represent a relatively small part of the equity market, and futures contracts are not available. Although investment in commodities through stocks in the energy, metals, and agricultural sector is not advocated, investors who desire exposure to these other commodity markets may do so using stocks.

MAKING IT HAPPEN

- Examine your investment portfolio to determine the potential value added by an allocation to commodity futures investments.
- Should you determine that commodities would improve the risk–return tradeoff of your portfolio, begin your search for an actively managed portfolio that can add value above an index fund investment.

"The aim of science is not to open the door to infinite wisdom, but to set a limit to infinite error." Bertolt Brecht

  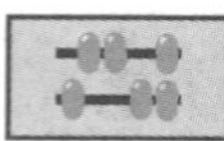      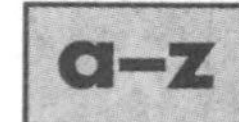

long positions in commodity markets, active managers may choose to take no position or a short (negative) position in commodity markets where their analysis predicts a low probability of price increases.

Given the significant opportunities to enhance the returns from spot returns and roll investments in the futures markets, active managers who show skill in these areas may be viewed as an attractive investment opportunity. While active managers may choose to maintain significant short positions in certain commodity markets, funds that maintain a long bias in each of the major market sectors, including energy, metals, and agriculture maximize the diversification effect of the commodities investment. For commodities to play their role as a portfolio diversifier, the fund needs to maintain long positions during times of commodity price increases.

CONCLUSION

Over the last 18 years, commodities have served as an excellent portfolio diversifier. Because of the historical tendency for commodity futures to have a high correlation with inflation, they typically offer higher returns than stocks, bonds, and even Treasury Inflation-Protected Securities during times of market stress. Commodities tend to be a defensive asset class and, as such, tend to underperform during bullish equity markets. Should these trends continue, investors can reduce their portfolio risk by allocating a small portion of their portfolio to commodity futures.

MORE INFO

Books:

Fabozzi, Frank J., Roland Füss, and Dieter G. Kaiser (eds). *The Handbook of Commodity Investing*. Hoboken, NJ: Wiley, 2008.

Till, Hilary, and Joseph Eagleeye (eds). *Intelligent Commodity Investing: New Strategies and Practical Insights for Informed Decision Making*. London: Risk Books, 2007.

Articles:

Erb, Claude B., and Campbell R. Harvey. "The strategic and tactical value of commodity futures." *Financial Analysts Journal* 62:2 (March/April 2006): 69–97. Online at: dx.doi.org/10.2469/faj.v62.n2.4084

Gorton, Gary B., and K. Geert Rouwenhorst. "Facts and fantasies about commodity futures." *Financial Analysts Journal* 62:2 (March/April 2006): 47–68. Online at: dx.doi.org/10.2469/faj.v62.n2.4083

Journal of Indexes. November/December 2008. issue, "Inside commodities." Online at: tinyurl.com/6jjrspe

Reports:

Black, Keith. "The role of institutional investors in rising commodity prices." Ennis Knupp & Associates, June 2008. Online at: tinyurl.com/5uc9xjv [PDF].

Black, Keith, and Satya Kumar. "The role of commodities and timberland in an institutional portfolio." Ennis Knupp & Associates, February 2008. Online at: tinyurl.com/6cewjk3

Websites:

Dow Jones–AIG Commodity Indexes: www.djindexes.com/aig

Standard & Poor's: www.standardandpoors.com

See Also:

★ Asset Allocation Methodologies (pp. 454–458)
★ The Impact of Index Trackers on Shareholders and Stock Volatility (pp. 496–498)
★ The Role of Institutional Investors in Corporate Financing (pp. 589–592)
★ Understanding the Role of Diversification (pp. 617–618)
✔ Mean–Variance Optimization: A Primer (p. 1076)
✔ Swaps, Options, and Futures: What They Are and Their Function (p. 988)
✔ Trading in Commodities: Why and How (p. 1093)
Portfolio Selection: Efficient Diversification of Investments (p. 1408)
Mining (pp. 1637–1638)
Oil and Gas (pp. 1638–1639)

"The essence of science; ask an impertinent question, and you are on the way to a pertinent answer." Jacob Bronowski

  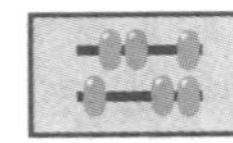      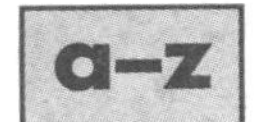

The Role of Institutional Investors in Corporate Financing by Hao Jiang

EXECUTIVE SUMMARY

- Institutional investors have become increasingly important in global capital markets.
- In equity markets, institutional investors tend to prefer liquid stocks with larger market capitalization, higher turnover, and higher price levels.
- Institutional investors particularly favor stocks in popular equity indexes, giving them higher valuations because their performance is typically benchmarked against those indexes.
- In bond markets that are mainly populated by institutional investors, there is a clear clientele effect.
- Private equity funds are an important source of capital for entrepreneurial firms.

INTRODUCTION

Institutional investors have become increasingly important in global capital markets. As of the end of December 2007, total assets under management by major global institutional investors reached US$81.90 trillion. In particular, mutual funds, pension funds, and insurance companies managed US$26.2, 28.2, and 19.9 trillion of assets, respectively, while assets managed by nontraditional managers such as hedge funds, sovereign funds, and private equity funds experienced dramatic growth, reaching US$2.3, 3.3, and 2.0 trillion in 2007 (Figure 1). In comparison, the world equity markets amounted to US$60.8 trillion, and the aggregate value of corporate bonds outstanding in the United States, the largest corporate bond market, was US$5.8 trillion in 2007. Clearly, for any successful corporate managers who raise capital to finance their future growth, it is crucial to understand such institutionalization in the global fund markets.

MAJOR INSTITUTIONAL PLAYERS

Institutional investors are a heterogeneous group of investors that populate the global capital markets. Based on their legal type, institutional investors can be broadly classified into mutual funds, pension funds, insurance companies, sovereign funds, hedge funds, and private equity funds.

A mutual fund is an investment vehicle that buys a portfolio of securities selected by a professional investment adviser to meet a specified financial goal (investment objective). Between 2000 and 2007, the total net assets of mutual funds grew from US$6.96 to 12.02 trillion in the United States, from US$3.29 to 8.98 trillion in Europe, from US$1.13 to 3.67 trillion in Asia-Pacific, and from US$16.92 to 95.22 billion in Africa (Figure 2).

A pension fund is a pool of assets forming an independent legal entity that are bought with the contributions to a pension plan for the exclusive purpose of financing pension plan benefits. Table 1 lists the world's 20 largest pension funds as ranked by *Pensions & Investments*. Insurance companies and banks are also important types of institutional investor that constitute the traditional asset managers.

Paralleling the growth of traditional institutions is the universe of nontraditional institutional investors. Among them, a sovereign wealth fund (SWF) is a state-owned investment fund composed of financial assets such as stocks, bonds, real estate, or other financial instruments funded by foreign exchange assets. Table 2 shows the top sovereign wealth funds across the world.

A hedge fund is an unregulated pool of money managed by an investment advisor, the hedge fund manager, who typically has the right to have short positions, to borrow, and to make extensive use of derivatives. Hedge fund managers receive both fixed and performance fees. Table 3 shows the top ten hedge funds based on assets under management ranked by Institutional Investor in 2007.

A private equity fund is a pooled investment vehicle which invests its money in equity securities of companies that have not "gone public" (i.e. are not listed on a public exchange). Private equity funds are typically limited partnerships with a fixed term of ten years (often with

Figure 1. Assets under management by different types of institutional investors in 2007. (*Source*: International Financial Services London)

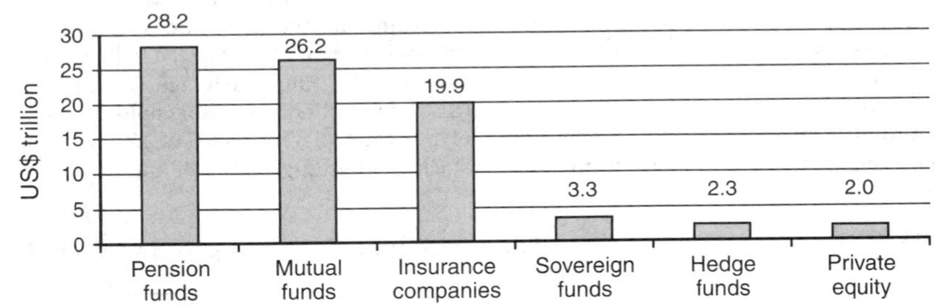

Figure 2. Total net assets of mutual funds around the world. (Source: *2008 Investment Company Fact Book*, Washington, DC: Investment Company Institute, 2008)

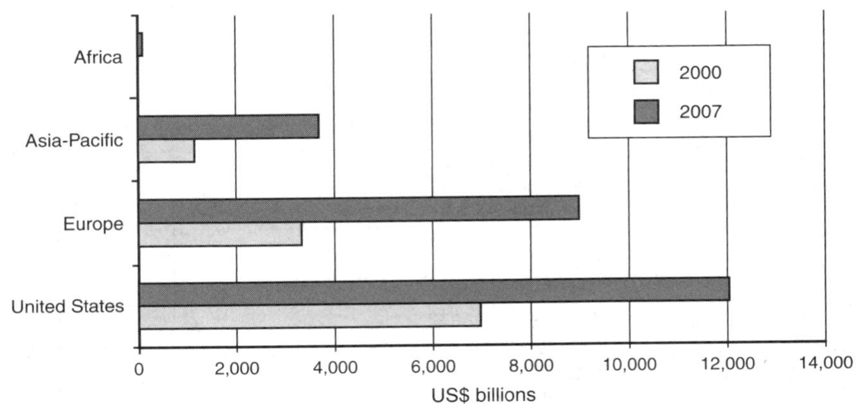

"The growing importance of the institutional sector will continue to have a profound impact on the structure of financial markets." Organization for Economic Co-Operation and Development

  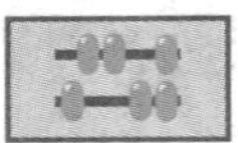   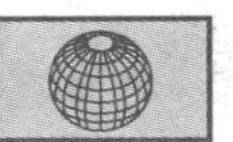   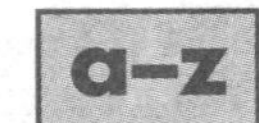

Table 1. The world's top 20 pension funds based on total assets. (*Source: Pensions & Investments*; Watson Wyatt, 2006)

Rank	Fund	Country	Assets (US$ million)
1	Government Pension Investment	Japan	870,587
2	Government Pension	Norway	235,849
3	ABP	Netherlands	226,974
4	National Pension	Korea	214,184
5	California Public Employees	US	195,978
6	Pension Fund Association	Japan	183,352
7	Federal Retirement Thrift	US	167,165
8	Local Government Officials	Japan	137,153
9	California State Teachers	US	133,988
10	New York State Common	US	131,861
11	GEPF	South Africa	124,167
12	Postal Savings Fund	Taiwan	117,265
13	Florida State Board	US	114,935
14	General Motors	US	114,271
15	New York City Retirement	US	105,860
16	Ontario Teachers	Canada	99,490
17	Texas Teachers	US	94,384
18	New York State Teachers	US	87,353
19	Public Schools Employees	Japan	85,224
20	PGGM	Netherlands	84,986

annual extensions). At inception, institutional investors such as pension funds and endowments (limited partners) commit a certain amount of capital to private equity funds, which are run by the general partners. Table 4 is a list of the ten largest private equity firms in the world as ranked by Private Equity International in 2008.

THE ROLE OF INSTITUTIONAL INVESTORS IN CORPORATE FINANCING

Institutional investors supply capital for firms seeking to raise finance from both publicly traded securities markets and from the private domain.

Institutional Investors as Holders of Publicly Traded Securities

Given their large portfolio size, institutional investors naturally become dominant holders of publicly traded securities. According to the 13F filings that institutional investors are required to lodge with the Securities and Exchange Commission (SEC), institutional investors hold over 68% of the total market value of US common stocks. According to the "Flow of Funds" data provided by the Federal Reserve, institutional investors hold approximately 86% of corporate bonds in the US corporate bond markets. Therefore, their investment behavior will have a significant influence on the pricing of these securities. For corporate managers who raise money from capital markets, it is important to understand the demand structure of institutional investors for publicly traded securities.

Despite their apparent heterogeneity, institutional investors share common characteristics because of the legal environment that they face as fiduciaries, and because of the demand for liquidity resulting from the large sizes of their portfolios and the need to reduce transaction costs. As a group, institutional investors exhibit preferences for certain stock characteristics in their equity portfolio. In particular, they tend to prefer stocks with larger market capitalization, higher turnover ratios, and higher levels of price. In other words, institutional investors are willing to pay a higher premium for stocks with these characteristics.[1]

Because most institutional investors benchmark their performance against certain indices, they naturally exhibit preferences for stocks in popular equity indexes. In the US market, when stocks are included into the S&P500 Index, the most prevalent equity index, the prices of those stocks tend to experience a 2–3% increase over a short period of time.

Firms with access to the corporate bond market tend to issue bonds as a means of debt financing. Based on the credit quality of the issue, corporate bonds can be

Table 2. The world's largest sovereign wealth funds. (Ranking by Sovereign Wealth Fund Institute, 2008)

Country	Fund	Assets (US$ billion)	Inception	Origin
UAE: Abu Dhabi	Abu Dhabi Investment Authority	875	1976	Oil
Saudi Arabia	SAMA Foreign Holdings	433.0	n/a	Oil
Singapore	Government of Singapore Investment Corporation	330	1981	Noncommodity
China	SAFE Investment Company	311.6		Noncommodity
Norway	Government Pension Fund–Global	301	1990	Oil
Kuwait	Kuwait Investment Authority	264.4	1953	Oil
China	China Investment Corporation	200	2007	Noncommodity
Russia	National Welfare Fund	189.7	2008	Oil
China: Hong Kong	Hong Kong Monetary Authority Investment Portfolio	173	1998	Noncommodity
Singapore	Temasek Holdings	134	1974	Noncommodity
UAE: Dubai	Investment Corporation of Dubai	82	2006	Oil
China	National Social Security Fund	74	2000	Noncommodity
Qatar	Qatar Investment Authority	60	2003	Oil
Libya	Libyan Investment Authority	50	2006	Oil
Algeria	Revenue Regulation Fund	47	2000	Oil
Australia	Australian Future Fund	43.8	2004	Noncommodity
US: Alaska	Alaska Permanent Fund	39.8	1976	Oil
Kazakhstan	Kazakhstan National Fund	38	2000	Oil
Ireland	National Pensions Reserve Fund	30.8	2001	Noncommodity
South Korea	Korea Investment Corporation	30	2005	Noncommodity
Brunei	Brunei Investment Agency	30	1983	Oil

"Worldwide, mutual fund assets reach $26 trillion." 2008 Investment Company Fact Book

  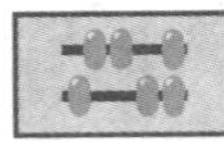      

Table 3. The world's top ten hedge funds. (Ranking by Institutional Investor, 2007)

Rank	Fund	Location	Firm capital (US$ million)
1	JP Morgan Asset Management	New York, NY	44,700
2	Bridgewater Associates	Westport, CT	36,000
3	Farallon Capital Management	San Francisco, CA	36,000
4	Renaissance Technologies Corp.	East Setauket, NY	33,300
5	Och-Ziff Capital Management Group	New York, NY	33,200
6	DE Shaw Group	New York, NY	32,240
7	Goldman Sachs Asset Management	New York, NY	29,206
8	Paulson & Co	New York, NY	28,979
9	Barclays Global Investors	London, UK	26,227
10	GLG Partners	London, UK	23,900

Table 4. The world's ten largest private equity firms. (Ranking by Private Equity International, 2008)

Rank	Firm	Headquarters	Capital raised 2003–2008
1	The Carlyle Group	Washington, DC	52
2	Goldman Sachs Principal Investment Area	New York, NY	49.05
3	Texas Pacific Group	Fort Worth, TX	48.75
4	Kohlberg Kravis Roberts	New York, NY	39.67
5	CVC Capital Partners	London, UK	36.84
6	Apollo Management	New York, NY	32.82
7	Bain Capital	Boston, MA	31.71
8	Permira	London, UK	25.43
9	Apax Partners	London, UK	25.23
10	The Blackstone Group	New York, NY	23.3

classified into investment-grade and non-investment-grade (high-yield or junk bonds, which are rated Ba and below by Moody's, or BB and below by Standard & Poor's). For corporate bond issuers, it is important to recognize the tendency of different classes of corporate bonds to attract different types of institutional investor—namely the clientele effect—in corporate bond markets.

Institutional investors generally place restrictions on investing in noninvestment-grade bonds. For example, the National Association of Insurance Commissioners (NAIC) imposes on insurance companies an upper limit of 20% of their assets for investment in high-yield bonds. Pension funds often impose limits on the value of a portfolio that can be invested in high-yield bonds. US investment-grade bond mutual funds place a limit of 5% of assets for investments in junk bonds and must sell any security if it falls below a B rating. However, there are institutional investors that specialize in junk bonds such as hedge funds with strategies in distressed assets and high-yield bond mutual funds. A recent study shows that when a bond receives a downgrade from investment to speculative grade there is a persistent price decline of 2%, whereas similar downgrades that do not cross the junk bond threshold do not experience such persistent price drops. This result suggests the importance of investor clientele for the pricing of corporate bonds.[2]

Institutional Investors as Fund Intermediaries for Private Firms

For entrepreneurial firms at the early stage of their life cycle, private equity funds comprise an important source of financing. Two primary categories of private equity funds are venture capital funds and leveraged buyout funds. In particular, venture capital funds provide equity capital for firms that are not yet profitable and lack tangible assets. Typically, such venture capital funds are active investors and play a primary role in shaping the top management team of the companies in which they invest.

Unlike venture capital funds that invest in young, fast-growing private companies, leveraged buyout funds invest in established companies and facilitate the process of purchasing an entire company or a controlling part of the stock of a company involving large amounts of debt—a "leveraged buyout." During the past two decades, both types of private equity funds have played an increasingly important role in corporate financing.

CONCLUSION

The dramatic expansion of institutional investors in global capital markets demonstrates the changing savings pattern of households in the global economy. As such, corporate managers who wish to

CASE STUDY

Hedge Funds and the Turmoil of the Convertible Bonds Market

Convertible bonds, which give holders an option to exchange the bonds for a specified number of shares of common stocks, are an importance source of capital for many firms. Among various reasons, managers favor convertible bonds because they are less costly than a direct share issuance, and because firms to which straight debt and equity are not available can still raise money in the convertible bond market. SEC Rule 144A, effective in 1990, allows firms to issue securities to qualified institutional buyers (QIBs) without having to register these securities. This regulation significantly accelerates the capital-raising process from more than one month in the public market to one or two days in the 144A market from announcement to closing. As a result, nearly all convertible bonds in recent years have been issued via the 144A market.

According to the SDC Global New Issues database, convertible bond issuance amounted to $50.2 billion in 2006, increasing more than sixfold from $7.8 billion in 1992. It is generally believed that hedge funds that conduct convertible arbitrage are the major players in the convertible bond markets, purchasing more than 70% of convertible bonds in the primary market.

In late 2004 and early 2005, large institutional investors in convertible hedge funds, unimpressed with the performance of hedge funds in 2004, started to withdraw capital from those funds. To meet investor redemptions, hedge funds sold convertible bonds, causing their prices to fall relative to their fundamental values, which in turn lowered the returns on convertible hedge funds. From January to May of 2005, the Credit Suisse/Tremont Convertible Arbitrage Hedge Fund Index decreased by 7.2%.[3] The lower returns on convertible hedge funds triggered further investor redemptions and more selling of convertible bonds, forming a vicious cycle. The price of convertible bonds dropped significantly below fundamental values. The maximum discount of convertible bonds was 2.7% in May 2005.[4] A gradual price recovery took place in 2006.

"Private Equity funds have grown from a tiny part of the financial market in the early 1980s to an important global force today." Michael Jensen

raise funds to finance the growth of their firms must understand such institutionalization in the global fund markets. In equity markets, institutional investors tend to prefer liquid stocks with larger market capitalization, higher turnover, and higher price levels. Because the performance of institutional investors is typically benchmarked against certain indexes, stocks in popular equity indexes are particularly favored by institutional investors and are thus priced at a higher valuation ratio. In bond markets that are mainly populated by institutional investors, there is a clear clientele effect. Banks, insurance companies, pension funds, and investment-grade bond mutual funds place severe restrictions on the holdings of high-yield bonds, whereas hedge funds and high-yield bond mutual funds provide capital for high-yield issuers. Lastly, private equity funds are an important source of capital for entrepreneurial firms.

MAKING IT HAPPEN

Institutional investors have dominated global capital markets. As a result, the assets under their management constitute an important source of capital for corporate managers.

- To attract institutional investors in equity markets, liquidity of shares is a major consideration. In particular, larger market capitalization, higher turnover, and higher price levels are important in attracting institutional holdings. Index membership is a strong sweetener.
- In bond markets, investment-grade bonds have a broader institutional investor base, whereas the issuance of high-yield bonds relies on capital providers such as specialized bond mutual funds and hedge funds.
- For entrepreneurial firms that seek both capital and strategic support, private equity funds appear to be increasingly important.

MORE INFO

Books:

Davis, E. Philip, and Benn Steil. *Institutional Investors*. Cambridge, MA: MIT Press, 2004.

Jaeger, Robert A. *All About Hedge Funds: The Easy Way to Get Started*. New York: McGraw-Hill, 2003.

Pozen, Robert C. *The Mutual Fund Business*. 2nd ed. Boston, MA: Houghton Mifflin, 2002.

Pratt's Guide to Private Equity & Venture Capital Sources. New York: Thomson Reuters, 2008.

Websites:

Dow Jones LP Source Galantes: www.dowjones.com/privatemarkets/gal.asp
Institutional Investor: www.institutionalinvestor.com
Investment Company Institute (ICI): www.ici.org
Pensions & Investments: www.pionline.com
Preqin: www.preqin.com
Private Equity International (PEI): www.peimedia.com
Sovereign Wealth Fund Institute: www.swfinstitute.org
Watson Wyatt: www.watsonwyatt.com

See Also:

★ Funds of Hedge Funds versus Single-Manager Funds (pp. 490–491)
★ The Impact of Index Trackers on Shareholders and Stock Volatility (pp. 496–498)
★ Valuing Pension Fund Liabilities on the Balance Sheet (pp. 122–124)
✔ Fund of Hedge Funds: Understanding the Risks and Returns (p. 1071)
✔ Hedge Funds: Understanding the Risks and Returns (p. 1072)
Warren Buffett (p. 1273)
Insurance (pp. 1633–1635)

NOTES

1 Gompers, P. A., and A. Metrick. "Institutional investors and equity prices." *Quarterly Journal of Economics* 116 (2001): 229–259.

2 Da, Z., and P. Gao. "Clientele change, persistent liquidity shock, and bond return reversal after rating downgrades." Working paper, University of Notre Dame, IN. Online at: ssrn.com/abstract=1280834

3 Based on the author's calculations.

4 Mitchell, M., Pedersen, L. H., and T. Pulvino. "Slow moving capital." *American Economic Review* 97:2 (2007): 215–220.

  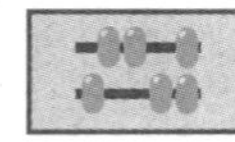      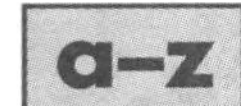

The Role of Short Sellers in the Marketplace by Raj Gupta

EXECUTIVE SUMMARY

- This article examines the role of short-sellers in the marketplace. The process of short-selling involves three major participant groups: the lenders, the agent intermediaries, and the borrowers.
- First, the history of short-selling is discussed briefly. This includes the enactment of the Securities Exchange Act of 1934, the adoption of the uptick rule following concentrated short-selling in 1937, and the relaxation of that rule in 2007.
- Next, the short-sale process is discussed. Five categories of short positions are identified. These categories include general collateral, reduced rebate, reduced rebate and fail, fail only, and buy-in.
- Third, the borrowers are identified and their activities are discussed. These borrowers include hedge funds, mutual funds, ETF counterparties, and option market-makers.
- Fourth, the lenders are identified and their motivations for lending are discussed. The primary lenders include mutual funds and pension funds.
- Fifth, historical statistics on the universe of lendable securities and the percentage of loaned equities are presented. A dramatic increase in the level of loaned securities is observed for the period 2006 to the second quarter of 2008 followed by significant declines in the third and fourth quarters of 2008. Since then, the level of loaned securities has gradually increased by 12%.
- Finally a brief review of the academic literature on short-selling is conducted.

INTRODUCTION

The term "short-selling" or "shorting" is used to describe the process of selling financial instruments (such as equities or futures) that the seller or holder does not actually own but borrows from various sources. If the value of the instrument declines, the short-seller can repurchase the instrument at a lower price and cover the loan. Short-sellers have long played the crucial role of price discovery in financial markets. If short-selling were not allowed, traders with negative views of certain stocks would at best avoid those stocks. However, short-selling allows them to generate returns based on their views if they are correct, hence making short-selling an important aspect in price discovery. Companies in certain countries where short-selling is not allowed may also list on the exchanges of countries where it is allowed. After the crash of 1929, the US Congress created the Securities and Exchange Commission (SEC) by enacting the Securities Exchange Act of 1934. Following an inquiry into the effects of concentrated short-selling during the market break of 1937, the SEC adopted Rule 10a-1. Rule 10a-1(a)(1) stated that, subject to certain exceptions, a listed security may be sold short:

- at a price above the price at which the immediately preceding sale was effected ("plus tick"); or
- at the last sale price if it is higher than the last different price ("zero-plus tick").

This implied that short sales were not permitted on minus ticks or zero-minus ticks, subject to narrow exceptions. The operation of these provisions was commonly described as the "tick test." Both the New York Stock Exchange (NYSE) and the American Stock Exchange (Amex) had elected to use the prices of trades on their own floors for the tick test. In 2007, the Commission voted to adopt amendments to Rule 10a-1 and Regulation SHO that removed Rule 10a-1 as well as any short sale price test of any self-regulatory organization (SRO). In addition, the amendments prohibited any SRO from having a price test. The amendments included a technical amendment to Rule 200(g) of Regulation SHO that removed the "short-exempt" marking requirement of that rule.

On July 15, 2008, the SEC issued an emergency order related to short-selling securities of 19 substantial financial firms,[1] which took effect July 21, 2008. This order stated that any person executing a short sale in the publicly traded securities of 19 financial firms, using the means or instrumentalities of interstate commerce, must borrow or arrange to borrow the security or otherwise have the security available to borrow in its inventory prior to executing the short sale. On September 19, 2008, the SEC, acting in concert with the UK Financial Services Authority, took temporary emergency action[2] to prohibit short-selling in 799 financial companies to protect the integrity and quality of the securities market and strengthen investor confidence. This ban was lifted on October 8, 2008.

In this article we will examine the role of short-sellers. The profile of short-sellers includes hedge funds and other speculators, proprietary desks of bank holding companies, options market-makers, and, in recent years, mutual funds that execute 1Xo/Xo strategies. We will discuss the academic literature on short sales, illustrate the short-sale process, examine the role of various participants in the process including lenders such as mutual funds and pension funds, agent intermediaries such as prime brokers, and borrowers such as hedge funds, mutual funds, and options market-makers, and we will present statistics on the universe of lendable and loaned securities. We find that the level of securities loaned versus the total universe of lendable securities increased dramatically during the period 2006 to the second quarter of 2008, followed by significant declines in the third and fourth quarters of 2008.

THE SHORT-SALE PROCESS

There are generally three groups of players in the short-sale process. The groups are securities lenders, securities borrowers (short-sellers), and agent intermediaries.

Securities lenders: Securities lenders are institutions with securities portfolios of sufficient size to make securities lending worthwhile. Generally these institutions include mutual funds, insurance companies, pension funds, and endowments. The lending activities of these groups are discussed in greater detail later.

Securities borrowers: Securities borrowers are institutions that engage in short-selling either as part of their trading strategies or to hedge their risk exposures. These institutions include hedge funds, mutual funds, ETF counterparties, and option market-makers. We will examine these groups in detail in the next section.

Agent intermediaries: Agent Intermediaries are institutions that facilitate the lending and borrowing of securities. These institutions may include custodian banks, broker-dealers, and/or prime brokers. We will examine the functions of these groups later.

The process illustrated in Figure 1 works well if there are plenty of shares available to

"I wonder how anyone can have the face to condemn others when he reflects upon his own thoughts."
W. Somerset Maugham

Figure 1. The short-sale process

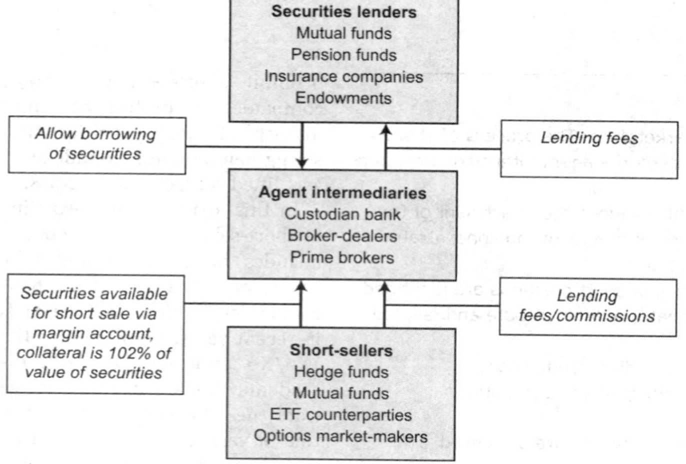

borrow. However, one must consider another possibility: What if shares desired for borrowing purposes are unavailable? Several academic articles have examined impediments to the short-selling process. Evans, Geczy, Musto, and Reed (2009) group short positions from an unnamed options market-maker into five categories: general collateral, reduced rebate, reduced rebate and fail, fail only, and buy-in. These categories as defined in their database as follows:

- *General collateral* indicates that a stock has been loaned at the normal rebate rate, i.e. the stock is easy to borrow.
- *Reduced rebate* indicates that the rebate rate is below the general collateral rate, i.e. the stock is special.
- *Reduced rebate and fail* indicates that some shares have been borrowed at a reduced rebate and that the market-maker failed to deliver some shares that were sold short.
- *Fail only* indicates that the market-maker failed to deliver any of the shares in this short position.
- *Buy-in* indicates that the counterparty of the short-sale transaction is forcing delivery on some or all of the shares in the short position.

One would expect a significant majority of short positions to fall into the general collateral category. More than 90% of the short positions in the database used by Evans *et al.* (2009) fell into that category.

THE KEY SHORT-SELLERS

In this section we will examine the key short-sellers. While certain participants may engage in short-selling by virtue of their trading strategy, others may engage in short sales to hedge their risk exposures (see Figure 1 for an illustration of the short-sale process). We will examine in detail each of these groups below.

Hedge Funds and Other Speculators

Several hedge fund strategies employ shorting stocks as part of their strategy. In the case of convertible arbitrage, the arbitrageur generally takes long positions in convertible bonds and sells short the underlying stock. In the case of equity strategies, managers may use fundamental or quantitative analysis to sell stocks short. Long/short equity strategies generally comprise the bulk of the hedge fund universe both in terms of assets under management as well as number of funds. In the case of merger arbitrage, managers sell short the acquiring company, while short-biased strategies engage in short-selling of seemingly overvalued stocks.

Bank Holding Companies

Prior to the recent requests by Goldman Sachs and Morgan Stanley to change their status to bank holding companies, investment banks borrowed stock for their proprietary trading desks.[3] However, these and other banks will continue to borrow stock for their proprietary trading desks and other functions.

Short and Ultra-Short Exchange-Traded Funds

In recent years, several exchange-traded funds have been established that offer either the inverse or twice the inverse of the returns on a certain index. These exchange-traded funds are generally referred to as short-ETF or ultra-short ETF. The funds generally achieve their short exposure using derivatives such as swaps. Although these funds generally do not short underlying stocks, they retain the ability to do so if necessary.

ETF Counterparties

One of the primary instruments that the short- and ultra-short exchange-traded funds described in the previous section use to achieve their exposures is swaps. The counterparty in the swap transaction may choose to hedge its exposures by shorting stocks.

Mutual Funds

In recent years several firms have launched 1X0/X0-type funds. Generally, the equities owned by the fund equal 1X0% of its net asset value, while the equities shorted equal X0% of the fund's net asset value. Although the vast majority of 1X0/X0-type funds are offered through separate accounts, there are several mutual funds that are available to the public.

Option Market-Makers

Options market-makers short-sell securities on a regular basis for hedging purposes. They are, however, exempt from locating shares before short-selling.

THE KEY EQUITY LENDERS

In this section we will examine the key lenders. These institutional lenders include mutual funds, pension funds, insurance companies, and endowments (see Figure 1 for an illustration of the short-sale process). Generally, the lending activities take place through an intermediary agent such as a custodian bank or broker-dealer. These intermediary agents pool securities from various lenders who are unable to lend securities directly. Most broker-dealers combine their security-lending activities with their prime-brokerage operations. We will examine each of these groups next.

Mutual Funds

The US mutual fund industry managed around US$12 trillion in assets as of year-end 2007. Stock mutual funds accounted for 54% of the total mutual fund industry. In light of the actions of the SEC relating to the banning of short sales on the securities of 799 financial firms, two major mutual funds, Vanguard Group Inc. and State Street Corp., imposed additional restrictions that halted the lending of their shares.[4] However, lending fees received by mutual funds can be substantial and permanent restrictions may impact revenues.

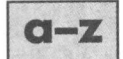

Pension Funds

Equities form a major component in the asset allocation of defined contribution (DC) plans. According to Pensions & Investment online,[5] more than 50% of assets in corporate DC plans are allocated to equities, while significant percentages are allocated by public and union DC plans as well. Defined benefit plans have a significant percentage of assets allocated to equities as well. Pension funds participate significantly in the equity-lending market.

The reasons for lending securities include not only the offsetting of custody and administrative costs but also the generation of revenue. The infrastructure to support securities lending varies from lender to lender. Lenders sometimes impose credit restrictions. As noted earlier, certain lenders imposed restrictions on borrowing activities in light of the SEC rules prohibiting short-selling.

SUMMARY DATA ON SHORT SALES

In previous sections we examined the various aspects of the short-sale process and the key players. In this section we will look at the data on short sales. Figure 2 presents statistics on total lendable equities worldwide. The data were obtained from the Risk Management Association.[6]

Figure 2. Universe of lendable (left axis) versus loaned (right axis) equities worldwide

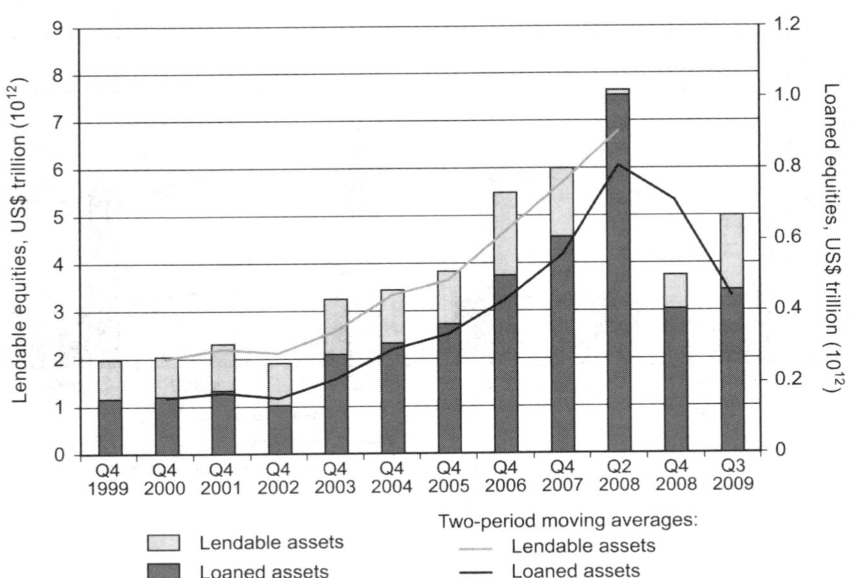

The universe of lendable equities (or lendable assets, represented on the left axis in Figure 2) denotes the total dollar value of equities available for lending worldwide. These include North American, European, and Pacific-rim equities (including Australia) along with other equities not included in the aforementioned categories. The figures are reported as aggregate assets without consideration of client- or bank-imposed guidelines. The universe of loaned assets (right axis in Figure 2) represents the total dollar value of equities loaned worldwide.

One of the interesting aspects is the growth in the universe of lendable assets from around US$2 trillion in 1999 to more than US$7 trillion at the end of the second quarter of 2008. Expectedly, the universe shrank between 2001 and 2002 and then experienced a steady increase.

The level of loaned assets worldwide has followed a similar pattern. However, the level of loaned assets experienced a dramatic increase, from less than US$600 billion at the end of 2006 to over US$1 trillion at the end of the second quarter of 2008. The numbers definitively capture the sentiments of short-sellers leading up to the third and fourth quarters of 2008.

The significant increases in the levels of loaned equities in the years 2006–2008 suggest a negative outlook on the stock market on the part of certain traders. In fact, the first signs of the subprime debacle can be traced back to early 2007. Stock prices of bond insurers such as Ambac and MBIA recorded their all-time highs in early 2007 before declining precipitously to 15-year lows in 2008, losing more than 90% of their value. The stock prices of erstwhile investment banks such as Bear Stearns and Lehman Brothers also followed similar patterns before the former merged with JP Morgan and the latter filed for bankruptcy. Further, Fannie Mae, Freddie Mac, American International Group (AIG), Merrill Lynch, Citigroup, Wachovia, and American Express among many others also witnessed precipitous declines in the value of their equities. These numbers, as well as media reports, suggest that short-biased traders such as certain hedge funds correctly predicted the decline of these companies, thus generating enormous capital appreciation for their investors (such as pension funds, endowments, and foundations). The two-period moving average lines show this more explicitly.

In Figure 3 we explore levels of lendable assets for North America, Europe, and the Pacific Rim. Not surprisingly, North American and European equities represent a significant portion of the total dollar value of lendable equities worldwide. In Figure 4 we explore levels of loaned assets for the same regions. Again, the total dollar value of loaned North American and European equities represents a significant portion of the universe.

By the end of 2008 the level of loaned equities dropped to around 408 billion dollars, a fall of almost 60%. Numerous factors contributed to this decline, including the meltdown of equity markets, the ban on short-selling of financial stocks, and the self-imposed restrictions on stock lending by various financial institutions. It is also interesting to note that the levels of loaned assets have gradually increased to around 458 billion dollars as of the third quarter 2009, an increase of around 12%.

LITERATURE REVIEW

A plethora of academic articles have examined various aspects of short-selling. In this section we will examine some of these articles and their contribution to the literature.

Seneca (1967) examined the net effects of large short positions using data between 1946 and 1965 and found that short sales acted as a predictor of stock prices. Baron and McDonald (1973) explored the risk–return patterns of reported short positions. Using data from the NYSE over the period 1961–1966, they found that stocks with more idiosyncratic risk had higher short interest. Brent, Morse, and Stice (1990) examined the increase in short interest over the period 1974–1986. They found that stocks with convertible securities, options, and high betas tended to have more shares held short. Further, Figlewski and Webb (1993) examined the effects of options on

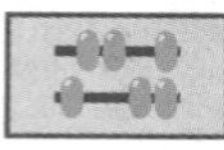

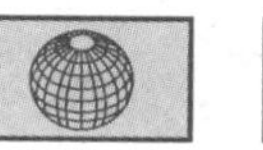

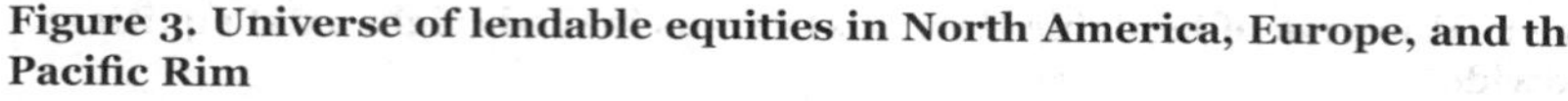

Figure 3. Universe of lendable equities in North America, Europe, and the Pacific Rim

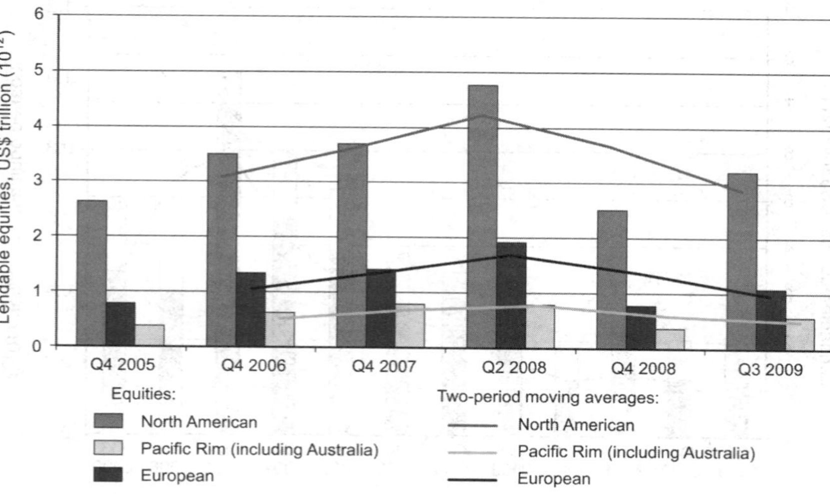

Figure 4. Universe of loaned equities in North America, Europe, and the Pacific Rim

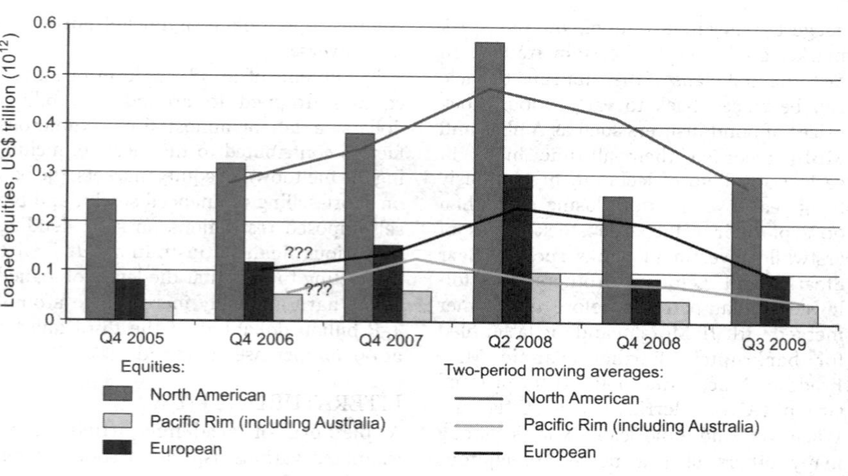

short sales. Using data from the Center for Research in Security Prices (CRSP) and Interactive Data Corp. (IDC) over the period 1969–1985, they found that options facilitated short-selling.

More recently Geczy, Musto, and Reed (2002) have examined short-selling costs and constraints. Using data from an unnamed custodian bank over the period 1998–1999, they found that short-selling frictions appear strongest in merger arbitrage. Bris, Goetzmann, and Zhu (2007) investigated the relation between short sales and market efficiency in world markets. Using data from various investment banks[7] over the period 1990–2001, they found that markets where short-selling is prohibited display significantly less negative skewness. Boehmer, Jones, and Zhang (2008) considered whether short-sellers are informed. Using data from CRSP and the NYSE over the period 2000–2004, they found that short-sellers are well informed and contribute to efficient stock prices. Diether, Lee, and Werner (2008) studied the trading strategies used by short-sellers. Using data from various exchanges for 2005, they found that short-sellers in both NYSE and NASDAQ stocks increased their short-selling activity after periods of positive returns. Finally Evans, Geczy, Musto, and Reed (2009) explored whether options market competition tends to oligopoly as stocks become difficult to short. Using data from a large options market-maker over the period 1998–1999, they found that market-makers profit when they fail to deliver stock.

CONCLUSION

In this article we examined the role of short-sellers in the marketplace. We showed that the process of short-selling involves three major participant groups: the lenders, the agent intermediaries, and the borrowers. We discussed the history of short-selling, including the enactment of the Securities Exchange Act of 1934, the adoption of the uptick rule in 1937, and the relaxation of that rule in 2007. We then discussed the short-sale process and identified five categories of short positions. Further, we discussed the profile of borrowers and lenders and provided historical statistics on the percentage of lendable securities and loaned equities. We observed a dramatic increase in the level of loaned securities between 2006 and the second quarter of 2008, followed by a dramatic decline by the fourth quarter of 2008. Finally, we presented a brief review of the academic literature on short-selling.

MORE INFO

Articles:

Boehmer, Ekkehart, Charles M. Jones, and Xiaoyan Zhang. "Which shorts are informed?" *Journal of Finance* 63:2 (April 2008): 491–527. Online at: dx.doi.org/10.1111/j.1540-6261.2008.01324.x

Brent, Averil, Dale Morse and E. Kay Stice. "Short interest: Explanations and tests." *Journal of Financial and Quantitative Analysis* 25:2 (June 1990): 273–289. Online at: dx.doi.org/10.2307/2330829

Bris, Arturo, William N. Goetzmann, and Ning Zhu. "Efficiency and the bear: Short sales and markets around the world." *Journal of Finance* 62:3 (June 2007): 1029–1079. Online at: dx.doi.org/10.1111/j.1540-6261.2007.01230.x

Diether, Karl B., Kuan-Hui Lee, and Ingrid M. Werner. "Short-sale strategies and return predictability." *Review of Financial Studies* 22:2 (February 2009): 575–607. Online at: dx.doi.org/10.1093/rfs/hhn047

Evans, Richard B., Christopher C. Geczy, David K. Musto, and Adam V. Reed. "Failure is an option: Impediments to short selling and options prices." *Review of Financial Studies* 22:5 (May 2009): 1955–1980. Online at: dx.doi.org/10.1093/rfs/hhm083

"To accuse is so easy that it is infamous to do so where proof is impossible." Zoë Akins

  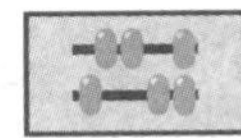      

Figlewski, Stephen, and Gwendolyn P. Webb. "Options, short sales, and market completeness." *Journal of Finance* 48:2 (June 1993): 761–777. Online at: www.jstor.org/stable/2328923

Geczy, Christopher C., David K. Musto, and Adam V. Reed. "Stocks are special too: An analysis of the equity lending market." *Journal of Financial Economics* 66:2–3 (November–December 2002): 241–269. Online at: dx.doi.org/10.1016/S0304-405X(02)00225-8

McDonald, John G., and Donald C. Baron. "Risk and return on short positions in common stocks." *Journal of Finance* 28:1 (March 1973): 97–107. Online at: www.jstor.org/stable/2978171

Seneca, Joseph J. "Short interest: Bearish or bullish." *Journal of Finance* 22:1 (March 1967): 67–70. Online at: www.jstor.org/stable/2977301

Websites:

Australian Securities Lending Association (ASLA): www.asla.com.au
High short interest stocks: www.highshortinterest.com
International Securities Lending Association (ISLA): www.isla.co.uk
NASDAQ short interest: www.nasdaqtrader.com/asp/short_interest.asp
Pan Asia Securities Lending Association (PASLA): www.paslaonline.com
Risk Management Association (RMA): www.rmahq.org/RMA
Securities Industry and Financial Markets Association (SIFMA): www.sifma.org
ShortSqueeze.com: www.shortsqueeze.com

See Also:

✔ Hedging Credit Risk—Case Study and Strategies (p. 969)
✔ Hedging Foreign Exchange Risk—Case Studies and Strategies (p. 970)
✔ Hedging Interest Rate Risk—Case Study and Strategies (p. 971)
✔ Swaps, Options, and Futures: What They Are and Their Function (p. 988)
✔ Trading in Equities on Stock Exchanges (p. 1095)
George Soros (p. 1312)
The Alchemy of Finance: Reading the Mind of the Market (p. 1330)

NOTES

1 These companies include BNP Paribas Securities Corp. (BNPQF or BNPQY), Bank of America Corporation (BAC), Barclays PLC (BCS), Citigroup Inc. (C), Credit Suisse Group (CS), Daiwa Securities Group Inc. (DSECY), Deutsche Bank Group AG (DB), Allianz SE (AZ), Goldman Sachs Group Inc. (GS), Royal Bank ADS (RBS), HSBC Holdings PLC ADS (HBC and HSI), JPMorgan Chase & Co., (JPM), Lehman Brothers Holdings Inc. (LEH), Merrill Lynch & Co., Inc. (MER), Mizuho Financial Group, Inc. (MFG), Morgan Stanley (MS), UBS AG (UBS), Freddie Mac (FRE), and Fannie Mae (FNM).

2 For more information see www.sec.gov/news/press/2008/2008-211.htm

3 The US House of Representatives on December 11, 2009, passed a 1,279-page Bank Reform bill (Financial Stability Improvement Act of 2009) that seeks to prohibit proprietary trading if it puts the firm's safety and soundness at risk. See "Winners and losers in the Bank Reform bill." *Wall Street Journal* "Dear Journal" blog (December 11, 2009). Online at: tinyurl.com/6f89h7c. To become law, the bill would have to pass the Senate, which would be a tall order.

4 See "2 mutual fund firms act to halt short sales." *Boston Globe* (September 23, 2008). Online at: tinyurl.com/4yze4w

5 For more information see www.pionline.com

6 For more information see www.rmahq.org/RMA

7 The term "investment bank" ceased to exist in 2008 when the last two remaining investment banks, Goldman Sachs and Morgan Stanley, asked the Federal Reserve to be converted to bank holding companies following the failures of Bear Stearns and Lehman Brothers and the announcement of the merger of Merrill Lynch with Bank of America.

"Wealth is not without its advantages and the case to the contrary, although it has often been made, has never proved widely persuasive." J. K. Galbraith

  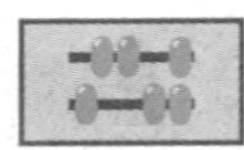      

Securitization: Understanding the Risks and Rewards by Tarun Sabarwal

EXECUTIVE SUMMARY

Securitization creates value for organizations, investors, and consumers:

- It separates the funding of receivables from their origination and servicing, and allows origination and servicing revenues to grow without additional balance sheet financing.
- It provides cash flow and balance sheet management benefits.
- It allows for targeted asset liquidation, improvements in asset liquidity, and access to capital markets at rates different from enterprise credit ratings.
- The flexibility in transforming risks permits mutually beneficial matches in targeted market opportunities, both for organizations and investors.
- Deeper capital markets allow for price discovery of illiquid assets, greater access to funds for new firms and consumers, and greater financial innovation.

Securitization creates risks of moral hazard and lack of transparency:

- Separation of funding from origination can create moral hazard, generating higher-than-expected risks and leading to conflicts between investors, firm shareholders, and firm creditors.
- Complexity of structural transformations creates lack of transparency, which, in turn, can lead to greater illiquidity and possible market failure. These effects are worse in globally inter-connected markets.

INTRODUCTION

In broad terms, securitization can be viewed as pooling receivables and selling claims to these receivables in capital markets. For example, a mortgage lender may pool together thousands of mortgages and sell claims on mortgage receivables to investors. Historically, the first securitizations in the 1970s in the United States were those of pools of mortgages. With the success of mortgage-backed securities, other groups of receivables were securitized as well, including auto loan receivables, credit card receivables, and home equity receivables.

Although a majority of securitizations are of receivables on consumer debt[1] (whether mortgage or nonmortgage), in principle, any cash flow receivable can potentially be securitized. There are several so-called "exotic" securitizations—for example, securitization of mutual fund fees, movie revenues, tobacco settlement fees, and even music royalties. Moreover, student loans, manufactured housing loans, equipment leases, and commercial mortgages are also securitized.

SECURITIZATION BASICS

Securitized products have some common characteristics.[2] They typically involve an originator of receivables who forms a pool of receivables that is then sold to a special-purpose entity. This entity in turn issues securities backed by a beneficial interest in the receivables. For a successful securitization, it is important to understand this process in detail.

The originator of receivables identifies a pool of receivables to be securitized. For example, a mortgage lender identifies which loans will form a particular pool for a securitization. As borrower and loan characteristics affect receivables and losses on a loan, the credit quality of the receivable pool is affected by its loan quality.

The originator transfers the receivable pool to a special-purpose entity (SPE), typically a type of trust. Accounting rules govern the balance sheet treatment of such a transfer. For example, if this transfer is classified as a sale, an originator can remove these receivables from its balance sheet, but in the case of a financing, it cannot do so. Moreover, for a transfer of receivables to be a true sale, the ownership of these assets should be separated from the transferor to the extent that in the case of the transferor's bankruptcy, the transferor's creditors should not be able to access these receivables and jeopardize the beneficial interest of the investors in the securities.[3]

The SPE issues securities backed by the collateral of receivables in the pool. Different securities (or tranches) issued on the same collateral pool may have very different risk characteristics, depending on how pool receivables are allocated to securities and depending on credit enhancements. For example, a *senior* tranche may have first access to pool receivables as compared to a *junior* or *subordinate* tranche, and therefore, the *senior* tranche would have a relatively lower risk. Similarly, a credit enhancement, such as third-party insurance of promised cash flows, lowers the credit risk of the security. Therefore, depending on the structure of the transaction, securities issued on the same collateral pool may carry different credit ratings. Over time, securitization structures have evolved in complex ways to take advantage of diverse demands by investors.[4]

The differential risks of these securities may change over the life of the securities. For example, credit risk for issued securities depends on the performance of the underlying collateral pool and on credit enhancements, both of which may vary over time. Important factors affecting pool performance include a lender's underwriting criteria (such as credit score of the borrower, credit history, down payment, loan-to-value ratio, and debt service coverage ratio), economic variables (such as unemployment, economic slowdown, and bankruptcies), and loan seasoning (payment patterns over the age of loans). Credit enhancements affect credit risk by providing more or less protection to promised cash flows for a security. Additional protection can help a security to achieve a higher credit rating, lower protection can help to create new securities with differently desired risks, and these differential protections can help to place a security on more attractive terms. Violation of credit enhancements can trigger an "early amortization" event, which starts prepayments on securities using available SPE resources.

Therefore, pool performance evaluation, security cash flow allocation, and servicing of receivables continue on an ongoing basis. In particular, bond rating agencies assign a credit rating to each security issued by the SPE, and they evaluate this rating periodically. Moreover, for publicly issued securities, periodic financial reports are filed with regulatory agencies. The originator of receivables typically continues to service the receivables (i.e., collect payments on the receivables, manage delinquent accounts, and so on) for a fee.

BENEFITS OF SECURITIZATION

An important idea behind securitization is that it separates the funding of receivables from their origination and servicing. Such a separation can provide cash flow and balance sheet management benefits, structural flexibility benefits, and deeper capital markets.

Cash flow and balance sheet benefits are available to the originator mainly because selling loans in capital markets allows a

"Greed is all right ... Greed is healthy. You can be greedy and still feel good about yourself." Ivan Boesky

  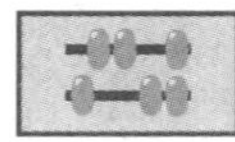      

lender to raise funds to originate more loans, which can again be securitized. As the originator typically continues to service the securitized receivables, revenue from origination and servicing activities continues to grow. Moreover, as securitized assets can typically be removed from the balance sheet, the net balance sheet effect is zero. In this sense, securitization improves revenues without additional balance sheet financing. A securitization can also improve balance sheet liquidity by converting long-term and illiquid receivables into funds that can be used for additional value-generating investments. A securitization can also help to manage any mismatch between assets and liabilities. Finally, to the extent allowable, selective securitizations of receivables can allow for regulatory capital arbitrage.

Structural benefits from securitization arise from the flexibility available in transforming cash flows and risks of the collateral pool into those of the securities issued on the pool. For example, creative use of credit enhancements allows relatively poor-quality receivables, such as subprime loans, to be transformed into some tranches of high credit quality and other tranches of low credit quality. Similarly, it is possible to carve out long-term, nonrevolving securities from short-term, revolving credit card receivables.

Structural flexibility allows originators and investors to tailor securitizations to their needs. Originators can sell particular assets with greater liquidity if these assets can be transformed creatively into securities desired by investors. Similarly, investors with particular needs may have more choices if different originators innovate to serve their needs.

In principle, deeper capital markets may arise from improved cash flows, better balance sheet management, and greater structural flexibility. A securitization of high-quality assets may allow a relatively young firm or a firm with a low credit rating to access capital market funds at lower cost than would otherwise be available. Securitization may facilitate market price discovery of illiquid assets. It allows for the sale of precisely identified assets to be independent of the asset owner's financial condition. It allows greater financial innovation and better matching of sellers and buyers, and it may allow for deeper debt market penetration by opening newer lending markets, such as subprime lending.

RISKS OF SECURITIZATION

While the unique characteristics of securitizations are capable of providing benefits, they create additional risks as well.

When standard cash flow risks[5] are combined with the separation of funding of receivables from their origination and servicing, this may produce unintended consequences. For example, if repayment behavior is significantly worse than expected, investors may be concerned about moral hazard; that is, receivables in the collateral pool were "cherry-picked," and investors may require additional support for the securities. In extreme circumstances, investors may require the originator to provide an explicit guarantee or to take back poorly performing collateral (sometimes termed moral recourse). As the collateral pool is off the originator's balance sheet, recognizing poorly performing assets jeopardizes the originator's financial condition, and such actions will be resisted by the originator's stockholders and bondholders. Similarly, if the originator is in a poor financial condition, its creditors might consider going after assets that are securitized and off the originator's balance sheet. This can jeopardize investor claims on the collateral pool and question the legitimacy of the bankruptcy-remoteness of the SPE. Moreover, a narrow focus on origination can create an incentive to over-originate (or overextend) loans to marginally less creditworthy borrowers.

The structural flexibility in transforming collateral pool characteristics into very different security characteristics, while arguably a great benefit of securitization, also has the potential to create great risks.

The more complex the structure, the greater is lack of transparency, and the harder it is to analyze and forecast security performance. For example, consider long-term securities collateralized by short-term credit card receivables. These are naturally exposed to amortization risk due to a mismatch between cash flow receipts on the receivables and cash flow payments on the securities.[6] Add to this a senior-subordinated security structure. Now add third-party insurance, and finally add subprime credit card receivables, which, because of their recent issue, come with greater uncertainty about their performance. The riskiness of securities based on such structural transformations depends in a complex manner on many factors, and a reliable evaluation of that risk may be very hard to obtain, if it can be obtained at all.

CASE STUDY

The growth of subprime lending in the United States started around the mid-1990s. A subprime borrower typically has some combination of a blemished credit history, a relatively short credit history, poorly documented income prospects, and an uncertain repayment ability.

Before the 1990s, subprime borrowers typically found it hard to qualify for bank loans. During the second half of the 1990s, in the face of relatively low interest rates, investors were more willing to seek opportunities with higher yields that came with a greater, but manageable, degree of risk.

Securitization of consumer debt receivables helped to connect these two sides, with finance companies serving as intermediaries. Improvements in credit reporting and statistical analyses facilitated the development of risk-scoring models to lend profitably to subprime borrowers. Credit enhancements and structured tranches created securities that addressed investor needs.

The success of initial securitizations fueled rapid growth in securitizations. Debt markets deepened to provide loans to subprime borrowers, finance companies found an attractive source of new financing, and could continue to increase revenues from profitable origination and servicing fees, investors found securities with desirable characteristics, rating agencies generated additional fees, and third-party insurers generated additional premiums.

In a span of about ten years, concerns started to arise as securitized products became exceedingly complex, with the introduction of collateralized debt obligations (CDOs), and of CDOs of CDOs, or "CDO-squared;" lending started to look indiscriminate, with concerns about real estate appraisals, and about lack of adequately documented repayment ability; and real estate prices appeared to defy historical trends. As the US economy slowed and house prices lowered, and as delinquencies and foreclosures on subprime debt rose, the value of securities backed by subprime receivables deteriorated. The complexity and opaqueness of the securitization structures exacerbated the problem by making it virtually impossible to put a reliable value on these securities. This led to a crisis of confidence that paralyzed trade in some of these securities. Markdowns in the value of such securities started to hemorrhage balance sheets of security holders, especially some hedge funds, and led to widespread turmoil on Wall Street, including casualties of large investment banks such as Bears Stearns and Lehman Brothers in 2008.

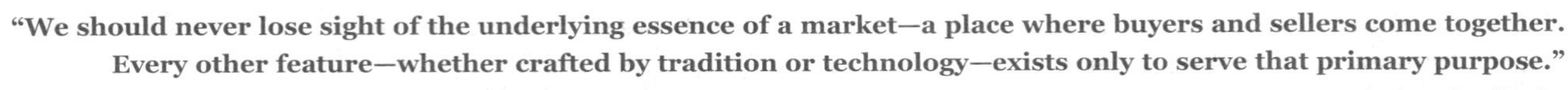

"We should never lose sight of the underlying essence of a market—a place where buyers and sellers come together.
Every other feature—whether crafted by tradition or technology—exists only to serve that primary purpose."
Arthur Levitt, Jr.

  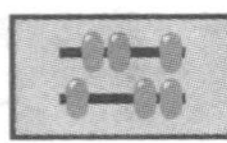   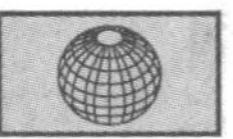   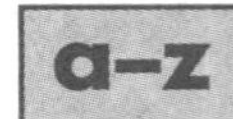

Lack of transparency is made worse when the collateral pool in a securitization has opaque or otherwise hard-to-value assets. As, in principle, any receivable can be securitized, a security that was created as a result of securitization can be used further in a new collateral pool to issue new securities. As the initial security is hard to analyze, when several such securities are pooled together and then tranched off again,[7] it is not surprising that there are cases where a final security is inscrutable, even with the most sophisticated analysis.

A complex security, by and of itself, is not an insurmountable obstacle to reap the rewards of securitization. But in uncertain times, complexity combined with lack of transparency may throw wrenches in the wheels of smoothly operating markets. In other words, if reliable information is unavailable, market participants may be unwilling to pay high prices for securities that may turn out to be bad investments, and this can lead to a crisis of confidence severe enough that trade in particular securities grinds to a halt. Moreover, interconnected debtors and creditors may serve to exacerbate such a problem by extending it to other securities. Such a dynamic has been mentioned as a core problem resulting in global credit market disruptions that started in the United States in 2007.

CONCLUSION

No doubt, securitization presents new developments and exciting opportunities. Securitization allows for more precise targeting of asset liquidation. It can create value for originators and investors. It can deepen capital markets, thereby providing funds for new borrowers and new businesses. And it can improve market price discovery for illiquid assets.

When a securitization gets beyond the analytical apparatus of market participants, however, it is capable of destroying value. The potential harm is greater in globally interconnected markets.

MAKING IT HAPPEN

Executives may find it useful to keep in mind the following key ingredients to a successful securitization.

- Characteristics of assets to be securitized should be documented well and identified clearly.
- Transfer of assets to a SPE to form a collateral pool should be a true, bankruptcy-remote sale.
- The transformation of collateral pool risks into security risks should be simple enough to provide clear and robust analysis of the dependence of security risks on collateral performance.
- Processes for servicing, and for ongoing monitoring of collateral and security performance, should be well-defined, with some evidence of success under reliability testing.
- Using collateral, securities, and structures with an established history or clear evidence of success provides greater liquidity in security trading, and more reliable analysis of collateral performance.
- Using opaque and exotic structures requires considerable expertise and comes with greater risks.

MORE INFO

Book:

Fabozzi, Frank (ed). *The Handbook of Fixed Income Securities*. 7th ed. New York: McGraw Hill, 2006.

Reports:

The Bond Market Association and the American Securitization Forum. "An analysis and description of pricing and information sources in the securitized and structured finance markets." October 2006. Online at: tinyurl.com/38s5g6n [PDF].

European Securitisation Forum. "ESF securitisation data report." Online at www.europeansecuritisation.com/dynamic.aspx?id=194

Websites:

The American Securitization Forum: www.americansecuritization.com
The European Securitisation Forum: www.europeansecuritisation.com
The Securities Industry and Financial Markets Association: www.sifma.org

See Also:

★ How to Assess a Company's Global Treasury Needs and Objectives Successfully (pp. 50–52)
★ Investing in Structured Finance Products in the Debt Money Markets (pp. 510–513)
★ Minimizing Credit Risk (pp. 540–542)
✔ Derivatives Markets: Their Structure and Function (p. 1007)
✔ Measuring Liquidity (p. 983)
✔ Understanding Capital Markets, Structure and Function (p. 1099)
✔ Understanding Debt Cover (p. 1100)

NOTES

1 Consumer debt is used here in a broad sense, including secured debt (such as home mortgages, auto loans, manufactured home loans, and so on) and unsecured debt (such as credit cards, student loans, and so on).

2 Although the principles outlined here apply to all securitizations, for concreteness, specifics are presented for consumer receivable securitizations.

3 This feature is sometimes termed bankruptcy-remoteness.

4 For additional details on some common securitization structures, see Sabarwal, T. "Common structures of asset-backed securities and their risks." *Corporate Ownership and Control* 4:1 (2006): 258–265.

5 Such risks include underwriting risk, interest rate risk, default risk, prepayment risk, and market risk.

6 This is usually addressed by having a *revolving* period and an *accumulation* period when cash flow receipts are kept aside for use later in making promised payments on the securities.

7 Collateralized debt obligations (CDOs) typically have such a structure.

"There is no human feeling to the US securities markets and sometimes no discernible evidence of human intelligence either. But they work." Robert J. Eaton

  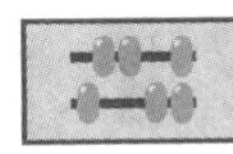      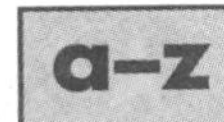

Sources of Venture Capital

by Lawrence Brotzge

EXECUTIVE SUMMARY

- Sources of capital depend on whether it is an early-stage company or a rapidly expanding business that is seeking significant financing.
- Angel investors rather than venture capital funds usually provide seed capital for new companies.
- Use your network to get connected with sources of venture funding, and know your audience before you meet with them.
- Venture capitalists look for high rates of return and have a relatively short time horizon.
- These investors will assist the entrepreneurs with many aspects of their business besides capital.

INTRODUCTION

There are many sources of venture capital. They include:

- friends and family;
- individual angel investors or angel investor groups;
- early-stage venture capital funds (VCs);
- expansion-stage and later-stage VC funds;
- community-based venture funds; these are often run by development agencies, which are usually funded or subsidized by local government funds designed to stimulate business growth.

This article answers a number of questions about obtaining venture capital. When is it appropriate to seek venture funding rather than bank financing? How do you go about finding these funding sources? How do they differ, and what drives their investment decisions? Entrepreneurs and their management team need to understand the role of these investors, what expectations they will have for return on their investment, and over what time frame they will expect to earn those returns.

EARLY-STAGE COMPANIES

Companies are usually started by a single entrepreneur or a small group of entrepreneurs. These founders frequently work for no pay, a situation that is referred to as "sweat equity."[1] The initial cash needed is likely to be provided by the founders, but may be supplemented by money from friends and family members who have a variety of reasons to want to be a part of what the founders are doing. This type of funding is sometimes referred to as "seed capital."[2] The founders may also seek bank financing, but if the bank is willing to extend credit it will probably be based on their personal assets or borrowing capacity. Banks rarely lend to companies that do not have a track record of revenues and profits.

Venture capitalists generally expect to see that the founders have put in a combination of sweat equity and personal cash, and they prefer to see that they have raised some money from friends and family. After exhausting these sources, entrepreneurs may think it is time to approach VCs to raise the funds they need to grow their business. In fact, although VCs did invest smaller amounts in the 1970s and 1980s, they are now much larger funds and tend only to invest when companies need multiple millions. As this transition was taking place, angel investors began to fill the gap between friends and family and VCs.

ANGEL INVESTORS

Typically, angel investors are thought of as wealthy financiers who want to fund startup companies that have a change-the-world idea or invention. They do usually have some wealth, but it is not necessarily the case that they are extremely rich. Successful business men and women may be sought out by entrepreneurs for their particular expertise. These individuals may not have previously thought of themselves as angels, but they may become interested in the business and impressed by the entrepreneurs and decide to invest. On the other hand there are those who regularly look for such opportunities. Angels generally invest in companies in their local area so they can keep an eye on their money.

Beginning in the mid-1990s, angel investors began to realize that there were some disadvantages to being a lone investor. For example, it is unlikely that one or even a couple of people possess all the knowledge necessary to make wise investments. They may have knowledge of many aspects of the business they are considering, but they are not likely to understand everything about the business and how to structure the investment. Additionally, a single investor would have to put a fairly large sum in a single company to have any real say in the business. A group of angels is more likely to have a breadth of knowledge and, by pooling their funds, an impact on the company. Angel investment groups have been forming over the past 10 to 15 years, and there are now several hundred such groups in the United States and Canada.

A 2008 study of US angel investing[3] showed that in 2007 some $26 billion was invested in over 57,000 entrepreneurial ventures and that the number of active investors totaled almost 260,000. It can readily be seen that individual angel investors still make up the lion's share of investors, which creates a challenge for those entrepreneurs trying to connect with them.

Finding angels requires networking. Ask attorneys and accountants, especially those who frequently work with and specialize in startup companies. If your business is technical in nature, you might contact universities, and you should certainly try to make contact with current and retired executives who come from industries related to yours.

VENTURE FUNDS

Some VCs focus on investing in particular industry sectors, or geographies, or stages of a company's life. Some may restrict their investments to local businesses. Some will fund early-stage companies, but others may only entertain investments in what are known as expansion-stage and later-stage companies.

The definition of an early-stage business can vary widely and is not easily defined in terms of revenues. If, for example, it is a service business or software company, it may not require a lot of investment for the company to achieve positive cash flows. At the other extreme, a life sciences business (biotech, pharmaceutical, and medical devices), which involves substantial research and regulatory approval, may be years from any real revenues and will need significant funding along the way. As a general rule, before a company is ready for VC funding a number of events will have taken place, such as completion of proof of concept, development of prototype products, beta testing of the product or service, and, finally, generation of revenues. However, certain types of businesses—most notably life sciences or other large technical projects—require such large amounts of capital that they are well beyond

"Angel investment groups have been forming over the past 10 to 15 years, and there are now several hundred groups in the United States and Canada."

  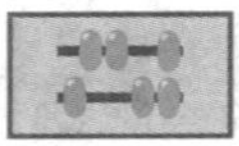      

the capacity of angels. These businesses tend only to be funded by the VC specialists. But for many new businesses there is an overlap between angels and "early-stage" VCs, and it is not uncommon that the two groups will coinvest.

What constitutes expansion- and later-stage companies? Expansion-stage companies have customers and proven revenue, and there are good reasons to believe that they are positioned to grow very rapidly, at rates of 30–100% annually. And later-stage companies already have substantial revenues, so the next round of financing is meant to grow the company to a critical mass and attract public financing, or result in a merger or acquisition by another company. In both situations it is likely that this will provide liquidity and at least a partial exit for founders and investors. Many young companies never get to the point of seeking expansion or later-stage VC funding, not because they fail, but rather because they determine that an earlier merger or acquisition makes more sense for both founders and investors.

WHAT VENTURE CAPITALISTS LOOK FOR

It makes little difference if it is an angel investor or an early-stage VC, they expect to see a business plan with a detailed description of the business model, marketing plans, competition, etc. This includes financial statements showing past results and a forecast for the next three to five years. Considerable emphasis will be placed on the cash flow forecast, as cash flow is a primary concern with any relatively new business. Investors will want to know how their investment will be put to use—often referred to as "use of proceeds." They tend to look unfavorably on large portions of their funds being used for accrued and unpaid expenses, particularly founders' salaries, or to pay down accounts payable. The prospective investors will perform considerable due diligence, which will include such areas as product reviews; speaking with customers, vendors and distributors; and examining any patent filings and pending legal matters. Primary among their assessments will be evaluating the management team.

The review performed by expansion-stage and later-stage VCs does not differ much from that outlined above; however, their investigations will look more closely at areas such as market conditions. Since at this point the business has a proven market for its product or services, it is far easier to assess future growth projections than when the company was just entering the market. Thus, a reasonably accurate assessment can be made of how fast the business can be scaled up and its ultimate potential. VCs will also reevaluate the company's management. Often the skills needed to launch a business differ from those required to grow it.

All venture investors have one question in common: When will they see a return on their investment? In other words, when will there be a liquidity event—a sale of the company or a public offering of the stock? This is called the exit strategy.[4] Venture capital is not generally meant to be long-term in nature. Most funding assumes that there will be an exit in three to seven years.

RETURN ON INVESTMENT SOUGHT BY VENTURE CAPITALISTS

The earlier in a business's life cycle the investment is made, the greater the risk. Thus, the higher the potential return on investment the venture capitalist will seek. Because there is a risk of total loss on at least some their investments, VCs must be able to see the potential for significant returns on each new investment. This means either quick returns or, if the time frame will be longer, large multiples of their investment. So company founders should not be surprised to learn that venture capitalists would like the opportunity to earn 10 or even 25 times their investment. That means that most venture investors have little interest in businesses that do not have excellent growth and profit prospects.

The terms of the investment will include the financial structure and the "pre-money value,"[5] which is the value placed on the business before the new investors put their cash into the company. Thus, pre-money value is the amount assigned to all investors who have invested in the equity of the company thus far. This determines what percentage the new investor will own. If the pre-money value is $3 million and $1 million is newly invested by VCs, they own 25% of the company.

There are also many considerations as to what security the venture investors will own. They usually require a form of a security that is "senior" to the equity held by founders and small investors. This provides legal protection and authority, even though they may be minority investors (in terms of their ownership share of the company). The instrument often used for this purpose is preferred stock, with a variety of provisions attached that allow some level of control over major business decisions.

For the venture investors to have an opportunity to earn handsome returns on their investment, they focus not only on the pre-money valuation, but also on how many future rounds of fundraising the company might need as it grows. Even if future investments are made on the basis of an increased valuation, the additional capital will dilute prior investors' ownership stake. So while the need for additional funding may be a good indication that the company is growing and needs more working capital to expand, that must translate to a much

CASE STUDY

Example of the Actual Results of an Early-Stage VC

The investors put in $120 million between 1998 and 2002, which is a typical funding period. This was invested in 31 companies and—although the fund has not yet exited all of these companies—reported results to date, plus a reasonable projection of ultimate exits, show these results:

Number of companies	*Exit as a multiple of the amount invested*
6	0
6	Less than 1 ×
7	Less than 1 ×
5	2 × to 3 ×
3	5 × to 10 ×
2	5 × to 10 ×
1	50 × plus
31	Average: 3.3 ×

The internal rate of return (IRR) to the investors will be about 23% on an annualized basis. This table illustrates how results vary by investment, indicates the degree of risk, and demonstrates why the VC must have the potential (often unrealized) to earn very large returns on each investment. In this case, without the three deals that produced very large returns, the overall results would not have been very attractive.

"Often the skills needed to launch a business differ from those required to grow it."

higher ultimate liquidation value if each investor group is to see healthy returns on the capital they put at risk. Historically, venture capital internal rates of return (IRR)[6] have averaged between 20% and 30%.

THE ROLE OF VENTURE CAPITALISTS AFTER THEY INVEST

Venture investors are not passive financiers; rather, they foster growth in companies by becoming actively involved with the management team, and in developing strategic and operational plans, marketing plans, etc. They will hold one or more positions on the company's board of directors. VCs see themselves as entrepreneurs first and financiers second.

MAKING IT HAPPEN

Companies will encounter lots of competition when seeking venture funding. So be sure to take the right steps to increase your company's chances of success:

- *Where should I be looking for investors?* Be certain to look for help from local organizations that foster new business development in your area, such as local development agencies and funds established to encourage innovation and new technologies, and universities.
- *How do I get connected to the right funding sources?* Talk to all your contacts, ask lots of questions, and remember that it is far better to arrive at a source via a referral.
- *How do I prepare to meet with prospective investors?* Consider getting someone to coach your management team, prepare a first-class, focused business plan, understand your cash flow, and prepare realistic financial projections.
- *What should I know about my audience?* They will be assessing the management team as much as the business. VCs do not invest in businesses that do not have significant growth potential, but you must be realistic and prepared to defend your numbers. They will also be interested in knowing that there are multiple exit strategies.
- *How do I sell our management team?* Show the investors that you are the right people to run the business, and address areas where you need to add missing skills. Remember that founders may not be the best people to run the company, and consider supplementing the team with an advisory board, or ask the VC to assist in identifying advisers.

MORE INFO

Book:

Van Osnabrugge, Mark, and Robert J. Robinson. *Angel Investing: Matching Startup Funds with Startup Companies—A Guide for Entrepreneurs, Individual Investors, and Venture Capitalists*. San Francisco, CA: Jossey-Bass, 2000.

Websites:

Angel Capital Association (North America's professional alliance of angel groups): www.angelcapitalassociation.org

Center for Venture Research, Whittemore School of Business and Economics, University of New Hampshire: wsbe.unh.edu/cvr

Kauffman Foundation: www.kauffman.org

National Venture Capital Association: www.nvca.org

See Also:

★ Assessing Venture Capital Funding for Small and Medium-Sized Enterprises (pp. 451–452)
★ Valuing Start-Ups (pp. 769–771)
✔ Dealing with Venture Capital Companies (p. 1067)
✔ Investors and the Capital Structure (p. 1120)
✔ Managing Working Capital (p. 980)
✔ Options for Raising Finance (p. 1081)
✔ Using Mezzanine Financing (p. 1105)
Prince Al-Walid bin Talal (p. 1268)

NOTES

1 See "Sweat equity" at www.businessfinance.com/sweat-equity.htm

2 See "Seed capital" at www.businessfinance.com/seed-capital.htm

3 Center for Venture Research. "The angel investor market in 2007: Mixed signs of growth." Online at: wsbe.unh.edu/files/2007_Analysis_Report_0.pdf

4 See "Exit strategy: Business plan basics" at www.bizplanit.com/vplan/exit/basics.html

5 See "The pre-money value of a pre-revenue startup" at www.matr.net/article-25906.html

6 For a basic explanation of IRR and a downloadable spreadsheet example, see www.solutionmatrix.com/internal-rate-of-return.html

"Historically, venture capital internal rates of return (IRR) have averaged between 20% and 30%."

  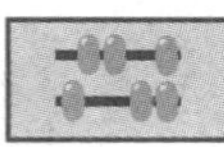      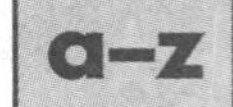

Viewpoint: Steering Between Deflation and Inflation—A Troubled Road for Developed Economies by Neil Williams

INTRODUCTION

Neil Williams is responsible for global economic research at Hermes Fund Managers and Hermes Asset Management. He has more than 20 years' experience of providing economic analysis and he generates investment strategy ideas for the fixed-income team. He adopts a top-down approach involving macro and market analysis to identify interest rate, credit value, and sovereign default risk. He began his career in 1987 at the Confederation of British Industry (CBI), becoming its youngest-ever head of economic policy. He went on to hold a number of senior positions at investment banks, including director of bond research at UBS, head of research at Sumitomo International, global head of emerging markets research at PaineWebber International, and, before joining Hermes, head of sovereign research and strategy at Mizuho International, the London-based securities arm of one of Japan's largest banking groups.

You have said in your regular monthly briefings that bonds are no longer the low-risk security that they were deemed to be through the crash of 2007–08. Can you describe what the macroeconomic forces are that are driving up risks in the bond markets and how they might affect corporates that want to raise money through bond issues?

The primary view that seems to be dominating the developed economies as we go into the last quarter of 2010 is that central banks and governments should play a "loose for longer" game, which means avoiding raising interest rates and avoiding tightening fiscal policy. Their motive for staying loose is to fight deflationary pressures in the economy. No one wants to see another major economy going down the route that took Japan into its two lost decades. I certainly place myself in the "loose for longer" camp. It definitely seems the right thing to do, and the wider market expectation is that central bank interest rates will generally be on hold until somewhere around 2012.

Before taking up the position of chief economist with Hermes I was chief economist at the Japanese securities house Mizuho International, so I am very familiar with the horrors of prolonged deflation. Very few options are available to the authorities once you have persistent deflation. It is a psychological mind set where people expect wages to chase prices downward and they become accustomed to seeing their pay packets gradually diminishing. Because prices are falling as well as pay the situation is bearable, but energy seems to seep out of the economy, leaving it stagnant.

One of the biggest risks we see is that although "loose for longer" becomes the main policy elsewhere, the eurozone is meantime going full tilt for fiscal tightening and austerity. That, of course, works directly against attempts to avoid deflation. There is no choice for the eurozone, given the sovereign debt crises that have rocked it and the scale of the fiscal deficits that are being run up, but it puts the eurozone on a course that skates frighteningly close to the Japanese position. The United Kingdom is running the same risk voluntarily. There is less burning urgency to dash for fiscal austerity right now as far as the United Kingdom is concerned, but this is what is being embraced.

My worry is that in the West we have not even begun to understand deflation. At Hermes we have a chart of the implied price deflator in the nonfinancial corporate sector of the United States that runs from 1960 to 2010. That chart has dipped to around 3% below zero and is in the same territory on the chart as our graph of deflationary pressures on Japanese GDP. That is a concern. At the very least it shows the strength of the deflationary pressures that are already making themselves felt in the US economy. We think that the US payrolls report, which indicates the number of jobs in the US economy, has been overestimated, and there could be a more than 800,000 net overestimation of payrolls since January 2009, which indicates a very soft labor market indeed. The fact that this is the backdrop for a scenario in which firms are already losing their pricing power, with a growing gap between prices paid and prices received, suggests a dislocation vis-à-vis the relatively robust earnings reports in the United States for the first half of 2010. It seems more than probable that these "robust earnings" owe more to cost control than to price increases, which makes one question the sustainability of the recent pace of job gains in the United States. We anticipate a very reasonable possibility of payrolls being revised downwards, probably in the annual benchmark review in February 2011.

The bottom line is that, despite all the quantitative easing the US Federal Reserve has gone in for (which is to say, printing money and buying government debt with it, which ultimately pumps more money into the economy and is therefore generally inflationary in impact), prices are actually falling in the nonfinancial corporate sector in the United States. That should be ringing alarm bells, and it is one of the factors that we think will stop the Fed from raising rates meaningfully right through 2011. In fact after the February 2011 downward revision of payrolls (assuming that this happens) we are likely to see the Fed going in for a second tranche of full-blown quantitative easing, with the outright purchase of Treasuries. Hawks in the Fed, such as Federal Reserve Bank of St Louis president James Bullard, are already warning that there is a 50–50 chance that quantitative easing will need to be revived.

The "loose for longer" approach also, of course, has risks. How would you characterize these?

Clearly, one of the risks in prioritizing reflationary policies and going for quantitative easing and fiscal stimulus is that you store up deficit problems for later, and these can be on a grand scale. There is no doubt

"If you can count your money, you don't have a billion dollars." J. Paul Getty

that repairing the dysfunctional balance sheets of the consumer sector and the financial sector through 2007 to 2009 had a massive impact. The fiscal expansion was on a such a scale—as it had to be—that it is the balance sheets of the governments involved that now need repair.

However, the task of repairing those balance sheets was put on hold due to the fragility of growth in the various economies. That growth is still as fragile. We have seen a bounce off the bottom for manufacturing in the Group of Seven (G7) countries and for GDP growth in these countries, but there is still a lot of ground to be made up. This is why the European Union's decision to go for fiscal tightening right now puts it on such a dangerous road. If you are trying to reduce the volume of spare capacity in the economy, making it tougher for businesses to operate and for consumers to spend is not going to help. Spare capacity holds down wages and prices and creates severe deflationary pressures. The problem the authorities have, however, is that their debt to GDP ratios are still worsening, which generates tremendous pressures for "something to be done." Even with swingeing budget cuts, for example, the UK Treasury still expects the United Kingdom's net debt to GDP ratio to lift above 70% by 2013/14. The Bank for International Settlements (BIS) has warned that the interest payments alone on UK debt, which currently stand at 5% of GDP (which, interestingly, is the same percentage as Japan's), could rise to 30% of GDP by 2040 unless the United Kingdom gets a grip of its debt problem.

The most obvious way of addressing the deficits would be for governments to "pass the parcel" back to the private sector through either rapid tax rises or big cuts in public spending, or both. The downside is that with taxes you are taking money out of the consumer's pocket at the very time when you are hoping to see more spending to drive more growth, and with public sector cuts you are deflating the economy or, at the very least, not driving growth. This is where Europe is taking such a big economic risk.

However, even where governments are able to focus more freely on fiscal repair, a quick "fiscal fix" looks unlikely. There are three reasons for this. First, there is not enough growth in the various economies for governments to take risks. The G7 economies are only just out of GDP recession, and there are plenty of cautionary signs. The US National Bureau of Economic Research has only just confirmed the trough of the US business cycle. This is probably because calling the bottom is particularly hard due to the persistently high unemployment in that country. In the eurozone, interestingly, we have a convergence of the various economies, but not in the direction that the European Union would like. Our analysis shows that the big economies are converging on the uninspired performance of the austerity-hit smaller economies.

What all this adds up to is that "double dips" for some or all G7 economies remain eminently possible. It took six months for China, buoyed by its own massive fiscal stimulus, to support recoveries elsewhere, and these recoveries are already stalling. What is more worrying is that this stalling was taking place even before the global stimuli to the various economies were lifted. With growth in China slowing, activity levels in the G5 countries (Brazil, China, India, Mexico, and South Africa) could feasibly fall again before Christmas 2010. The impact of all of this could be to keep the yields on long-duration bonds down, further flattening the long end of yield curves and also depressing mortgage rates.

On the fiscal side it is already clear that the United States is headed in a different direction to Europe. Instead of austerity, President Barack Obama will try to keep fiscal policy as expansionary as possible. On the downside, from December 2010 the US consumer faces the combined roll-off or wind-down of the 2001–03 years of the Bush era and the US$787 billion "Obama 1" tax cuts and benefit extensions of February 2009. However, the fragility of growth in the United States could well see the cuts and benefits under "Obama 1" extended for lower- and middle-income earners. High earners in the United States account for 5% of the population but about half of the Federal income-tax take, so extending help to low- and middle-income earners is relatively painless politically.

It is worth remembering, too, that only half of "Obama 1" has been allocated up to this point in time (September 2010), suggesting that a further gross stimulus of up to 3.6% of GDP, or US$530 billion, could yet follow in 2011. On top of this, we may well see an "Obama II" stimulus program. This could be rolled out as an emergency measure without a Senate super-majority (the majority necessary in normal circumstances for a measure of this nature to be carried).

The example that all Western fiscal authorities are desperate to avoid following is that of Japan. What do you make of Japan's current position, and are you hopeful that it could yet beat deflation in the near future?

We saw a rally in Japanese government bonds (JGBs) on the back of the decision to intervene to weaken the yen in mid-September 2010. This was the first time the government had done so for six years. However, this looks likely to be a short-lived affair, and the enduring macroeconomic conditions of a slowing economy, persistent deflation, weaker political control, and the chance of a further policy loosening (more quantitative easing) should all prevent JGBs from straying far from their cyclical lows. Japan's problem is that its debt is about to exceed 200% of GDP. The International Monetary Fund is predicting that debt to reach 246% of GDP by 2014! However, there are worrying signs, such as slowing consumption and the fact that the coincident indicator index (a ragbag of various activity indicators used in Japan to identify economic turning points), is now peaking some 20% short of its precrisis levels. The economy generally is stuttering and the stubbornly high yen is hurting exports, so some further quantitative easing may well be on the cards, despite the world-record deficit that Japan is currently running.

You are quite fond of a chart you call a "misery index." Can you explain this chart?

The traditional MI, or misery index, is a method of proxying economic hardship by adding together unemployment and inflation rates. Our misery index at Hermes is a bit different. It is the sum of (1) the divergence in absolute terms of a country's consumer price index (CPI) from its long-run average, which for the eurozone has been 2.25% since Maastricht in 1991, and (2) the divergence between the full-year unemployment rate and its previous five-year rolling average. Higher numbers reflect greater misery. Unsurprisingly, those countries currently undergoing strict austerity regimes are the most miserable on the index. The worrying fact is that our MI shows that far from the zone's biggest economies pulling the rest out of the doldrums, the opposite is happening. Germany, France, and Italy, though starting from a less miserable position, look set to see their position on the index deteriorate through 2011 as the effects of their own fiscal squeezes come through. In other words, the strong eurozone countries are actually converging on the rather more desperate position of the weaker countries. This is the very opposite of the "leveling up" that the European Union wanted.

To conclude, we see all the signs being in place for another round of quantitative easing by spring 2011, which, somewhat spookily, could give us a rerun of the start of 2009, with surplus cash in the economy

giving a boost to both government bond and equities markets: a "sweet spot" for markets. A scenario where central banks are injecting money into the economy at very low interest rates is what helped the stock market to bounce in March 2009. Longer term, inflation will doubtless come back to bite us, making indexed-linked bonds attractive. There are pockets of inflation around. Meanwhile, however, "loose for longer" will be an indispensable condition for us all if we are to avoid "a Japan."

MORE INFO

Reports:

Williams, Neil. "Ahead of the curve, May 2010: Will central banks fall behind the curve?" London: Hermes Fund Managers, May 11, 2010. Online at: tinyurl.com/2ud3wh4

Williams, Neil. "Economic outlook, Q3 2010: Avoiding 'a Japan'." London: Hermes Fund Managers, June 9, 2010. Online at: tinyurl.com/3x5vsld

Williams, Neil. "Ahead of the curve, July 2010: The UK's fiscal gamble." London: Hermes Fund Managers, July 9, 2010. Online at: tinyurl.com/33yq7gd

Williams, Neil. "Ahead of the curve, August 2010: The eurozone's misery." London: Hermes Fund Managers, August 4, 2010. Online at: tinyurl.com/37fs367

Williams, Neil. "Economic outlook, Q4 2010: There's no quick fix." London: Hermes Fund Managers, September 3, 2010. Online at: tinyurl.com/37dl4wl

See Also:

★ The Globalization of Inflation (pp. 184–186)
★ Why Printing Money Sometimes Works for Central Banks (pp. 267–268)
✔ The Bond Market: Its Structure and Function (p. 1064)
✔ Trading in Government Bonds: Why and How (p. 1096)
Japan (pp. 1518–1520)

Understanding Equity Capital in Small and Medium-Sized Enterprises by Siri Terjesen

EXECUTIVE SUMMARY

- Equity capital or financing is funding raised by a business in exchange for a share of the ownership.
- Equity financing enables firms to obtain money without incurring debt, or without needing to repay a specific amount of money at a particular time.
- There are four stages of equity investment: seed, early-stage, expansion, and late-stage financing.
- Equity capital sources differ in terms of timing, amount provided, type of firm funded, extent of due diligence, contract type, expectations of timing and payback, and monitoring of business decisions.

INTRODUCTION

Entrepreneurs may require both debt and equity financing, and often start their firms by financing growth through equity. Equity capital is money invested in the venture with no legal obligation on the entrepreneur to repay the principal amount or to pay interest on it; however, it requires sharing the ownership and profits with the funding source, and possibly also paying dividends to equity investors.

After value has been built, entrepreneurs may consider debt financing, which involves a payback of the funds (with interest) for use of the money. In short, debt places a burden of repayment and interest on the entrepreneur, whereas equity capital forces the entrepreneur to relinquish some degree of ownership and control.

The stages of equity financing are depicted in Figure 1. In the first stage, known as the seed stage, entrepreneurs tend to raise capital from their own savings, though they may also seek informal investment from family, friends, business angels, and public sources. Entrepreneurs may then choose to pursue formal equity capital through rounds of early-stage, expansion, and late-stage financing. This may be followed by an initial public offering (IPO) and, finally, raising of finance from public markets and banks. Summary details of the financing stages are as follows:

- Seed financing is the initial funding to develop a business concept, for example by expenditure on research, product development, and initial marketing to reach early-adopter customers. Companies that receive seed funding may be in the process of incorporation, or may have been in operation for a while.
- Early-stage financing is sought by companies that have completed the product/service development stage and test marketing but require additional financing to expand.
- Expansion financing is provided when the company is poised to grow rapidly. The funds may be used to increase production capacity, marketing, or product development, and/or provide additional working capital.
- Late-stage funding refers to pre-IPO investments to strengthen a company's positioning and to gain endorsements from top venture capital (VC) firms as the company prepares to list.

At any stage, equity investment can come from informal or formal sources. However, it is more usual to access informal sources in the seed and early stages, and formal sources in the expansion and late stages.

Figure 1. The stages of equity financing

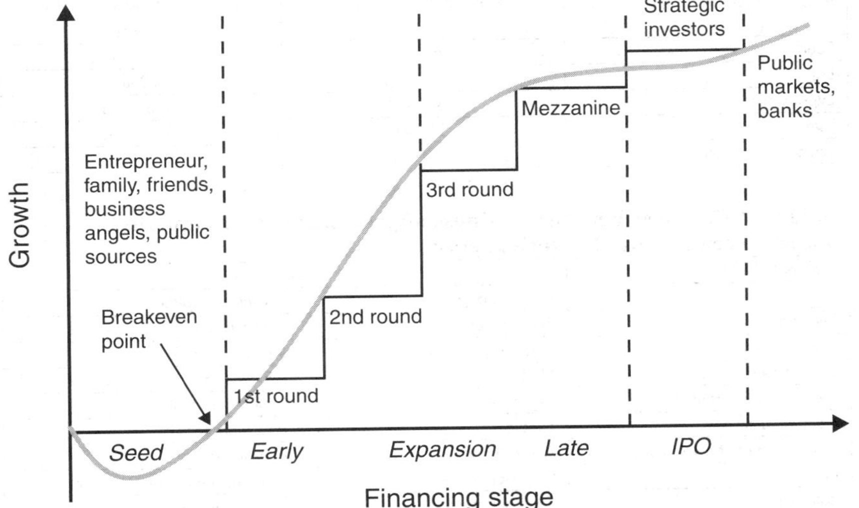

INFORMAL EQUITY SOURCES

Informal and Angel Investment

Informal investment refers to equity provided by individuals. In addition to accessing their own savings and those of family, friends, and even neighbors, entrepreneurs seek informal "angel" investors who provide financial capital as well as business expertise for running a company.

As shown in Figure 2, the rates of informal investment vary dramatically around the world, from a high of 13% in Uganda to a low of 0.5% in Japan. Business owners are approximately four times more likely to make informal investments than are non business-owners (Bygrave and Hunt, 2005). As can be seen in the figure, many informal investors have experience as owners/managers of their own businesses.

Although the profile of angel investors varies, in developed economies, angels tend to have entrepreneurship experience, be retired from their own firm or a corporation, and have net incomes in excess of US$100,000 a year. Most angels invest in companies within a two-hour traveling distance of their home, and therefore the informal investment market is geographically diverse. On average, the angel capital market is approximately ten times the size of the formal venture capital market. Indeed, small firms are eight times more likely to raise finance from business angels than from formal institutions.

Business angels tend not to have any previous relationship with the entrepreneur, and are often more objective. Angel investors can be passive (backing the judgment of others) or active (hands-on,

  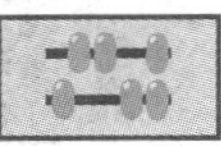      

Figure 2. Rates of informal investment around the world. (*Source*: Global Entrepreneurship Monitor data)

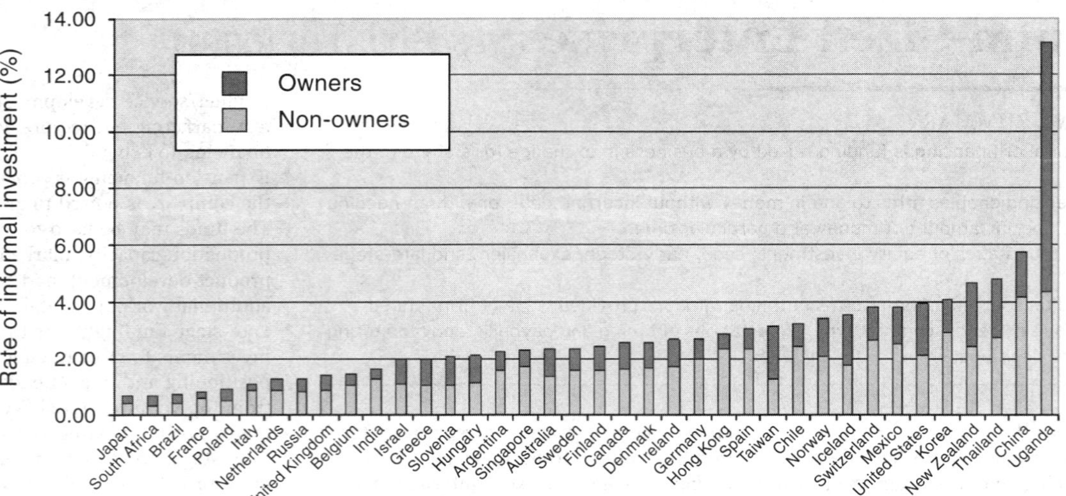

with advice or direct management input to help the business to establish itself). Angels tend to invest as individuals or as part of a larger group, and generally as a part-time interest rather than as a full-time job (as is the case of venture capitalists). In addition to financial goals, informal investors often seek other, nonfinancial returns, among them the creation of jobs in areas of high unemployment, development of technology for social needs (for example, medical or energy), local revitalization, provision of assistance to indigenous peoples, and just personal satisfaction from the assistance they give to entrepreneurs.

Business angels prefer to fund high-risk entrepreneurial firms in their earliest stages. They fill the so-called equity gap by making their investments in precisely those areas where institutional venture capital providers are reluctant to invest. Angels may also prefer to fund the smaller amounts (within the equity gap) that are needed to launch new ventures, and they invest in almost all industry sectors. Angels tend to be more flexible in their financial decisions, and also tend to have different criteria, longer investment horizons ("patient" money), shorter investment processes, and lower targeted rates of return than venture capitalists. Business angel funding can make a firm more attractive for other sources of finance. However, business angels are less likely to make follow-on investments in the same firm.

FORMAL EQUITY SOURCES

Venture Capital

Venture capitalists can be a valuable and powerful source of equity funding for new ventures, providing, in addition to capital, help with a full range of financial services for new or growing ventures. These include market research, strategy, management consulting, contacts with prospective customers/suppliers/others, assistance in negotiation and with management and accounting controls, employee recruitment, risk management, and counseling on regulations. Venture capitalists tend to have ambitious expectations for both the return on and the increase in their investment, as shown in Table 1.

The process of seeking venture capital financing includes the following four stages:

- Initial screening to assess the firm's ability to meet the VC's particular requirements.
- Detailed reading of the business plan.
- Verbal presentation to the venture capitalist.
- Final evaluation, including visiting suppliers, customers, consultants, and others; the venture capitalist then makes a final decision.

This four-step process screens out approximately 98% of all venture plans, with the remaining 2% receiving some degree of financial backing. Venture capitalists reach a go/no-go decision in an average of 6 minutes on the basis of the initial screening, and in less than 21 minutes on the basis of an overall proposal evaluation. The main factors in their decision are the firm's expected long-term growth and profitability,

Table 1. Typical returns on investment (ROI) and increase on initial investment sought by venture capitalists. (*Source*: Terjesen and Frederick, 2007)

Stage of business	*Expected annual ROI (%)*	*Expected increase on initial investment*
Seed	60 +	10–15 times
Early	40–60	6–12 times
Expansion	30–50	4–8 times
Late	25–40	3–6 times
Turnaround situation	50 +	8–15 times

Table 2. Differences between business angels and venture capitalists. (*Source*: Terjesen and Frederick, 2007)

Differential factor	*Investor type*	
	Business angel	*Venture capitalist*
Personal	Entrepreneurs	Investors
Firms funded	Small, early-stage	Large, mature
Due diligence done	Minimal	Extensive
Location of investment	Of concern	Not important
Contract used	Simple	Comprehensive
Monitoring after investment	Active, hands-on	Strategic
Exiting the firm	Of lesser concern	Highly important
Rate of return	Of lesser concern	Highly important

"**Remember this, Griffin. The revolution eats its own. Capitalism re-creates itself.**" Mordecai Richler

although an entrepreneur's background and characteristics are also taken into account.

Venture capitalists tend to agree on an exit strategy at the time of investment, with the following five main mechanisms:

- Trade sale to another company.
- Repurchase of the venture capital shares by the investee company.
- Refinancing or purchase of the venture capital equity by a longer-term investment institution.
- Stock market listing.
- Involuntary exit.

Table 2 summarizes the differences between business angels and venture capitalists.

Initial Public Offering

As the firm grows, managers may consider an initial public offering (IPO), which is when a company's shares are first sold to the public. An IPO is often the first time people outside the company have the opportunity to buy its shares; hence, IPOs are referred to as "going public" or "floating" the company. An IPO has advantages and disadvantages. The advantages are:

- *Amount and efficiency of capital raised*: Selling shares is one of the fastest ways to raise large sums of capital in a short period of time.
- *Liquidity*: A public market provides liquidity for owners, who can readily sell their shares.
- *Value*: The market puts a value on the company's shares, which in turn allows a value to be placed on the company.
- *Image*: Publicly traded companies are often perceived to be stronger by suppliers, financiers, and customers.

However, an IPO also has several disadvantages:

- *Cost*: IPO expenses are significantly higher than for other sources of capital due to fees for accounting, legal services, prospectus printing and distribution, and the cost of underwriting the shares. The cost can easily exceed $1 million.
- *Disclosure*: An IPO requires detailed public disclosure of company affairs, but new firms may prefer to keep this information private. Furthermore, the paperwork involved in meeting regulation requirements and providing regular information about performance may drain large amounts of management time, energy, and money that could be better invested in opportunities for company growth.
- *Stockholder pressure*: Stockholders are interested in a strong performance record on earnings and dividends, and so may put pressure on managers to focus on short-term performance. If managers do this, it can be at the expense of long-term growth and improvement.

The advantages and disadvantages of IPO funding are summarized in Table 3.

Should a firm decide to pursue an IPO, it is important that it be aware of laws with respect to securities and investments, which vary across countries but include the following common elements.

Table 3. Advantages and disadvantages of IPO funding. (*Source*: Terjesen and Frederick, 2007)

Advantages	*Disadvantages*
Stronger capital base	Pressure for short-term growth
Improves other financing prospects	Disclosure and confidentiality
Better placed to make acquisitions	Costs—initial and ongoing
Diversification of ownership	Restrictions on management
Increased executive compensation	Loss of personal benefits
Increased company and personal prestige	Trading restrictions

CASE STUDY

An Angel in England

Anita Roddick started her own business, The Body Shop, creating and selling beauty products. Roddick was keen to open a second shop in Chichester, but the bank turned down her request for a loan. In desperation, Roddick asked her friend Aidre, who was helping to manage the first store, for help. Aidre had a boyfriend named Ian Bentham McGlinn, who had some spare cash from operating a local garage. Scottish born McGlinn offered Roddick £4,000 in 1976 in return for 50% equity in the business. Anita accepted the offer but wrote to her husband Gordon (who was on a two-year hike in South America) to inform him of the offer. Gordon wrote back suggesting that she "not do it, not give away half the company," but it was too late.

With his equity investment, McGlinn became a business angel and sat on the board of The Body Shop, resigning just before it was floated on the stock market in 1984. At the time of the flotation McGlinn was worth £4 million, but he avoided the press by taking a holiday in Portugal. By 1991, McGlinn's 52 million shares were worth £150 million, though his dividends were worth only £638,000 annually. The Roddicks and McGlinn together owned 56% of The Body Shop, preventing a takeover. In 1996, McGlinn sold 3.5% of the business for £12 million. When L'Oréal took over The Body Shop in 2006, McGlinn's 22% stake was worth £137 million. As of 2007, Ian McGlinn was ranked no. 28 on the *Sunday Times* Rich List, with an estimated worth of £146 million.

MAKING IT HAPPEN

When approaching venture capitalists, entrepreneurs must remember that VCs are inundated with potential business opportunities. It is therefore advisable to keep the following in mind.

Do

- Prepare all your materials before soliciting firms.
- Send a business plan and a covering letter first.
- Contact several firms with this material.
- Keep phone conversations brief—prepare a one-minute and a three-minute pitch.
- Remain positive and enthusiastic about your company and its product or service.
- Know your minimum deal and walk away if necessary.
- Negotiate a deal you can live with.
- Investigate the venture capitalist's previous deals and current portfolio structure.

Don't

- Don't expect a response.
- Don't dodge questions.
- Don't give vague answers. Know what you can and cannot disclose before you start talking, so that you do not stumble over awkward questions.
- Don't switch off—be an active listener as you will always learn something.
- Don't hide significant problems.
- Don't expect immediate decisions.
- Don't become fixated on pricing.
- Don't embellish facts or projections.

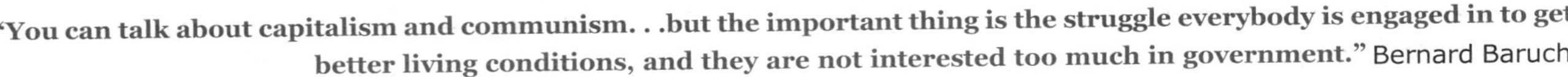

"You can talk about capitalism and communism. . .but the important thing is the struggle everybody is engaged in to get better living conditions, and they are not interested too much in government." Bernard Baruch

     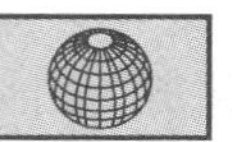   

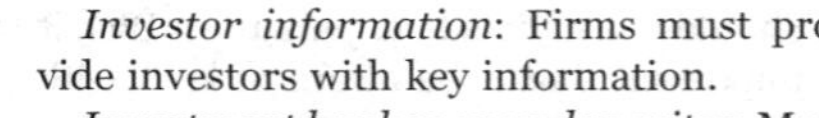

Investor information: Firms must provide investors with key information.

Investment banker or underwriter: Most firms select a lead investment banker to sell the new shares, usually at fees of about 7% of the issue value.

Ownership structure: The shares sold in the IPO are designated as primary shares, which are new shares, and secondary shares, which were previously owned by existing stockholders, usually the founders and managers of the firm. The size of the new issue relative to the existing shares and their distribution change the ownership structure. The IPO often results in moving from management by firm founders toward professional management of the firm. The IPO generally occurs when the founder's entrepreneurial activities are coming to an end, but often he or she will play a role in the future of the company.

Lockup provisions: When going public, IPOs almost always commit to a lockup period, whereby insiders (major stockholders, directors, and senior officers) are prohibited from selling shares without the written permission of the lead underwriter until a certain amount of time has passed. On average, the waiting time is 180 days. These lockup provisions control the supply of shares sold during the period after the IPO by insiders or existing stockholders who might have inside knowledge and, thus, unfair advantage.

Presence of venture capitalists: Many firms may be financed by VCs, who take an ownership position and have partial control over the entrepreneurs. The IPO may change this control as the VC distributes the shares to their limited partners. The use of an IPO may be a cheaper form of financing than that provided by VCs, and will certainly provide liquidity to the existing pre-IPO stockholders.

Issue size: With the fixed costs of an IPO to create a liquid market, the number of new shares in the IPO should be large enough to provide sufficient liquidity, but small enough so that the issuing firm does not raise more cash than it can profitably use.

Mechanisms for pricing IPOs: IPOs may be priced through auctions, fixed-price offers, or book-building. In auctions, the market-clearing price is determined after bids are submitted. In a fixed-price offer, the price is set prior to the allocation. If there is excess demand, shares are rationed on a pro rata or lottery basis. In book-building, the investment bankers canvas potential buyers and then set an offer price. Book-building is now the predominant mechanism by which IPO shares are sold around the world.

When considering an IPO, managers should ask the following questions:

- Can the company run without you while you are managing the IPO process? The work leading up to a public offering is time-intensive and can deflect your focus away from everyday operations, ultimately hurting the business. If the company lacks a strong management team, it can be helpful to appoint an interim CFO with experience of taking companies, preferably small, through the rigors of going public.
- Can you get to a market capitalization of $100 million within three years of going public? The value of a public company is a multiple of what it earns. If the result isn't near $100 million, staying private may be best. This number is a good indicator because it is the level of earnings at which the company can attract brokers and investors.
- Are you building a company with high gross and operating margins? High margins are important because they keep companies out of the volume game. For a company to reach critical mass in earnings with low margins, it must generate enormous sales growth.
- Can your business deliver double-digit sales and earnings growth? The competition among public companies, mutual funds, and other investment networks is fierce. Investors won't look twice at a company that doesn't grow fast enough to warrant the use of their time and money.
- Are you building a family business? If the succession plan for the business is set in stone to be passed on to the kids, public may not be the right route. Families measure the success of a business generation by generation. Money movers are interested in the quarter-to-quarter progress.
- Can the business be built inexpensively? The main reason companies go public is to raise initial funds for major growth. As a result, sales and growth need to reflect the use of the first round of financing. If another round of financing is needed to achieve the original plan, investors may look elsewhere.

Prospectus: If a company is raising capital by offering its shares to the public for the first time, it will issue a disclosure document called a prospectus. The prospectus is a formal written offer to sell shares and provides an investor with the information necessary to make an informed decision. All negative information must be clearly highlighted and explained. Some of the specific detailed information that must be presented includes: the history and nature of the company, its capital structure, a description of any material contracts, a description of the securities that are being registered, the salaries of major officers and directors and the price paid for any security holdings they may have, underwriting arrangements, an estimate of and planned use for the net proceeds to be raised, audited financial statements, and information about the competition with an estimate of the probability that the firm will survive.

MORE INFO

Books:

Cendrowski, Harry, James P. Martin, Louis W. Petro, and Adam A. Wadecki. *Private Equity: History, Governance, and Operations*. Hoboken, NJ: Wiley, 2008.

Gadiesh, Orit, and Hugh MacArthur. *Lessons from Private Equity Any Company Can Use*. Cambridge, MA: Harvard Business School Press, 2008.

Terjesen, Siri, and Howard Frederick. *Sources of Funding for Australia's Entrepreneurs*. Raleigh, NC: Lulu, 2007.

Report:

Bygrave, William D., with Stephen A. Hunt. "Global entrepreneurship monitor 2004 financing report." Babson College and London Business School, 2005.

Websites:

Global Entrepreneurship Monitor (GEM) data: www.gemconsortium.org

US Small Business Administration on equity financing: www.sba.gov/services/financialassistance/basics/financing

See Also:

★ Capital Structure: A Strategy that Makes Sense (pp. 710–714)
★ Optimizing the Capital Structure: Finding the Right Balance between Debt and Equity (pp. 543–545)
★ Sources of Venture Capital (pp. 601–603)
✔ Investors and the Capital Structure (p. 1120)

"The twentieth-century struggle between capitalism and socialism is, at an ideological level, a fight about the content of progress." John Berger

  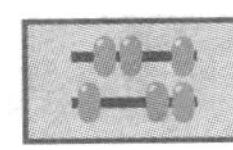      

Viewpoint: Understanding the Risks and Opportunities in Recession-Hit Markets

by Keith Guthrie

INTRODUCTION

Keith Guthrie is chief investment officer at Cardano, where he heads the investment team responsible for investment strategy, portfolio construction, and manager selection for pension fund clients. From 2002 to 2007 he worked as an investment manager at GAM, responsible for US$6 billion in arbitrage related fund-of-hedge fund strategies and US$500 million in multiasset-class portfolios. He started his career in the corporate actuarial department of the First Rand group. In 1999 he became head of long-only manager research and an investment committee member at RMB International, a subsidiary of First Rand. He joined Cardano in January 2008. Guthrie graduated from the University of Witwatersrand with a BSc in statistics and actuarial science and BSc (hons) in actuarial science. He qualified as an actuary in 1997.

Cardano is risk advisor to the majority of Dutch pension funds, as well as providing asset management services. From your perspective, how do you evaluate the risks and opportunities associated with extraordinary levels of market volatility?

The last quarter of 2011 was an extraordinary period of market volatility. However, the standpoint for addressing this is the same as in more stable periods. You are always looking to see how you can improve the value of a pension fund's assets relative to its liabilities. For many funds, the temptation is to look only at the impact of volatility on the assets, but you need to look constantly at both sides of the balance sheet. When you do this it naturally leads you to want to manage all dimensions of risk, including inflation, interest, currency, and equity risk.

The essence of solvency for a fund is to improve the asset to liability position, and this means hedging out any risks that you do not actively want to take while being practical about the costs—about the affordability of the risk-reduction exercises. If there are risks that you can hedge cost-effectively as the trustees of a fund, you should take that opportunity, targeting beneficial risk–reward opportunities wherever they may lie. This is not a single-dimensional play. It is multifaceted, particularly as no one knows how the economy is going to unfold. You have to devise strategies that prepare you for many different eventualities and outcomes. If we go into a happy world with strong growth, you want positions that do well in that environment, while if we go into a double-dip recession, you need strategies that perform there too. If you can achieve this even in a very modest way, the fund should outperform liabilities over the long term.

You act for both Netherlands-based and UK pension funds. Do they differ greatly in their approach to risk and asset management?

Dutch pension funds tend to divide the risk mandate from the investment mandate and give each to a separate organization to manage, whereas in the United Kingdom investment and risk are more often seen as two sides of the same coin. In the United Kingdom the trustees have an investment advisor who advises them on the overall investment strategy, and the trustees then appoint different fund managers to carry out the various parts of the strategy. They will have a fixed-income manager and possibly a different global equities manager, and so on. In the Netherlands the legislation encourages trustees to have several advisors to look at risks and strategic asset allocation, and then to appoint fiduciary managers who execute the strategic allocation. The risk managers have nothing to do with execution and the investment managers are chosen according to the fixed asset allocation recommended by the risk manager.

Cardano's approach in the United Kingdom starts from a different position to both of those. We start by assuming that the neutral position for a fund is to hedge out all its liability risks and not to invest in any risk assets. Since for most funds that ideal position will not generate sufficient returns to cover the liabilities, you then have to do research on economic scenarios to find a broad set of acceptable risk–reward opportunities. Then you have to figure out how you are going to build a balanced portfolio which will pay off across multiple economic scenarios. When you have done all of this, you then figure out your asset allocation using the opportunities you have identified. In the UK scenario, in other words, we do not adopt fixed asset allocations, such as *x*% in equities, *x*% in alternative assets, *x*% in bonds. We go for dynamic asset allocations that we judge to have a good chance of working across various economic scenarios.

So risk is assumed because the fund needs to achieve excess returns to be in a position to meet its liabilities, and the advisor's job is to achieve a balance between assets and liabilities while assuming as little risk as possible?

Exactly. The dilemma most funds face is that they are running large deficits with respect to the benefits they are eventually going to have to pay out. This is compounded by the fact that scheme sponsors—the companies behind the schemes—vary in the strength of their covenant. In the United Kingdom the regulator works hard to ensure that trustees are at arm's length from the sponsor and that the issue of the strength of the sponsor's covenant is hard fought over. Against that background, if a scheme has a sizable deficit and cannot afford to take massive risks to improve that—risks that the regulator would not want it to take anyway—our approach is to look to hedge the risks it is already exposed to and to be very targeted and clear about the risks it is actually actively assuming.

You need to be very clear about why you are taking a particular risk and about the returns that you expect to get from assuming that risk. With this approach we have found that it is possible to achieve the

same aggregate level of returns from a long-term investment strategy for perhaps half or quarter of the risks that are usually assumed in long-term investment strategies.

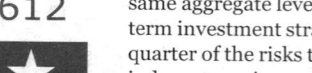

We particularly look to avoid big drawdowns. If you have a strong risk management strategy with no big drawdowns, your returns compound much better. For example, if you have a volatile strategy in which you lose 30% of a particular investment allocation when the market moves against you, you have to make 45% back simply to put yourself back on track. That is very difficult to do.

This is not a theoretical point. Most pension funds in the United Kingdom saw their solvency rate decline by 20% in the period from October to December 2011. That is horrendous to claw back. Funds have seen both sides of their balance sheet—assets and liabilities—move against them. They have liability values linked to fixed-income yield levels, and with long-term rates pushing down that has moved against them, while equity markets have had tremendous volatility.

Funds have considerable sensitivity to interest rate movements. If you look at the duration element—the length of time the fund is invested in a particular asset—a typical pension fund's duration across all its assets probably averages out to around four years. Their liabilities, on the other hand, are probably 30 years or more, so the vast majority of schemes are nowhere near fully hedged against interest rate risk. Movements in the interest rate of 10-year gilts impacts the value of their liabilities directly since it lowers the discount rate for liabilities, pushing them up. At the same time as they have seen swings against them of 15% on interest rate movements, they are very exposed to falling values in equities.

The interest rate is a particularly sensitive issue. Many schemes will look back over recent history and say that interest rates have averaged 5% to 7% over the last decade, so they will assume a mean-reversion to this rate. They will look at the yields they can hedge their liabilities at and will form a view that current yields are abnormally low. They would be correct if we lived in a world where normal growth rates could be expected to return imminently. However, the current global economic climate is being driven by massive deleveraging in advanced markets at the level of both governments and consumers. In that environment, yields are obviously going to be much lower than historically, so low yields are not an unreasonable value to which to hedge liabilities.

There is an argument which says that schemes do not need to worry about the impact of the discount rate on their liabilities, because if the asset returns are high enough the scheme will be all right. However, this assumes that there is no correlation between growth rates and the returns that you will see from asset classes. Clearly this is wrong. In a low-growth world you cannot expect magnificent stock-picking to deliver you high levels of returns on large equity portfolios. It just won't happen. So you need to be consistent in your treatment of both sides of your balance sheet. If you are hedging liabilities for a low-yield environment, you have to expect to treat assets similarly.

Taking this view, the deficits of many schemes look to be impossible to resolve unless the scheme sponsor provides a great deal more money.

Indeed, this is why so many defined-benefit schemes are closing to new members and closing to further accruals. Companies are shifting to defined contribution schemes that shift the entire funding risk to the employee. Moreover, there is as yet no decent education policy by government to help people to see how important it is to maintain a similar rate of funding for defined-contribution schemes. What we are seeing is defined-benefit schemes that cost employers—say, 15% to 25% of salary—closing and employees moving to defined-contribution schemes where employers might give 5% of salary. At that level of funding the final pension will be nowhere near adequate. What we can already say with confidence is that no subsequent generation will ever have it as good as the baby-boomer generation. That was unsustainable and is now gone. The huge unfairness in this is that the baby-boomers will get the benefit of the younger members' contributions to the pension funds, but younger members will never see equivalent benefits. This intragenerational unfairness is something that Cardano thinks a lot about, and we are looking to try to redefine pension schemes to be less unfair.

What impact do you think the eurozone crisis is going to have on pension funding?

We have seen some violent mood swings in the markets. On the one hand there is considerable relief that the politicians at last seem to realize the seriousness of the issue. What is going on in the markets right now, and will continue into 2012, is a very fast pace of deleveraging of European banks. We had penciled in a probability of 55% that there will be a mild recession in Europe early in 2012, and this was complemented by a probability of 45% that we would experience a severe recession in Europe. The probability of a severe recession has now moved up to north of 65%.

One of the problems is that European banks and governments need to roll over something like €3 trillion of debt through 2012. Italy alone, between the government and its banking system, needs to roll over around €1 trillion of debt in a market that we can all see has no appetite for even a fraction of that debt load. The debt figures for Spain are not far behind this.

At the same time, governments are saying that European banks need to strengthen their capital buffers by raising their Tier 1 capital to 9%. When this was costed by marking government debt to market in September 2011, the estimate was that eurozone banks would have to raise €106 billion in new capital. Banks have two ways of raising this money. They can do new rights issues, or they can cut lending—particularly the more capital-heavy lines of lending—and this will cut the amount of capital they need to hold in reserve. Today, the equity values of the major eurozone banks are so far below book value that no bank wants to dilute their shareholders through a rights issue. They would much rather improve their capital ratios by shrinking their balance sheets and moving out of risky loans with high capital requirements. The upshot of this is that we are already seeing the onset of a major credit crunch in Europe. If one bank alone was going through this exercise it would not have much impact, but when every major bank in the eurozone starts to do it you get a tremendous credit crunch. So we will see increased levels of bankruptcy because companies do not have access to debt to manage their cash flows.

Add a credit crunch to the sovereign debt crisis and the outlook becomes rather bleak. If, Europe-wide, we go into a 2% shrinkage of GDP through 2012, that will create strong deflationary pressures. This is a very dangerous time in the European sovereign debt crisis. The coming credit crunch and massive deleveraging is going to hammer growth at the same time as the markets are becoming unwilling to fund more debt from either European states or eurozone banks.

One clear solution—and it is something that everyone apart from the European Central Bank (ECB) and the Germans want to see happen—is for the ECB to come in and backstop the system. However, it will take a tremendous about-face to get the politicians out of the corner they have painted themselves into.

One solution would be for the politicians to take a significant portion of the €400 billion European Financial Stability Fund

(EFSF) and inject it into the banking and financial systems across Europe. This would give bank bond-holders some confidence that there is enough equity in banks for them to survive a pretty severe recession, and that in turn would take a good part of the heat out of the present situation. This would entail forcing haircuts on bank equity-holders and Tier 1 subordinate lenders, who, after all, are just one step up from holders of the organization's common stock. This was all supposed to be risk capital anyway, so it is fair to call on it. That would create sufficient confidence to halt the current deleveraging of the eurozone banks.

The remainder of the EFSF capital needs to be used to restructure the insolvent European peripheral countries by allowing them to default. It seems obvious that if you let governments default, their national banks then have no option but to default with them since they hold so much national government debt. It seems clear that the IMF will be a major part of the final answer since the IMF has considerable experience in managing sovereign restructurings. Restructurings are painful but not impossible. You give the government enough funding to maintain a reasonable level of social services and you recapitalize the banking system so that finance and the economy keep on operating

Recapitalizing the European banking system and restructuring the peripheral countries will absorb all the remaining capital in the EFSF. This would then leave the question of funding the larger Spanish and Italian bond markets. At present we are rather critical of the ECB's philosophy of supplying unlimited liquidity to the European banks and doing very little to help sovereign states with their funding costs. The sovereign debt crisis could be solved by the ECB buying unlimited quantities of Spanish and Italian debt if, for example, the market rates drifted above 5%.

If all this was done, it should be enough to get markets half-way confident again. However, it is a more radical solution than the longer-term Maastricht Treaty revisions that are currently being mooted.

The likely endgame in Europe will be the ECB dropping its resistance to quantitative easing and buying Italian and Spanish debt. We expect to see a lot of debt monetization in what used to be called the hard currencies, namely the euro, the dollar, and sterling. Against this wave, emerging market currencies will have little option but to appreciate in value in the long term, but before then they could come under pressure if a global double-dip recession happens. There has been much bad lending and poor investment in China, so a slowdown there or even a hard landing is not out of the question either. China may well come through the current turmoil in good order, but the markets are in a mood to look for negatives and people are focusing much more on potential downsides than on optimistic scenarios.

From the perspective of fund managers it matters hugely how the European sovereign crisis plays out. If we avoid an Armageddon scenario—with the total break-up of the eurozone and a reversion to national currencies, which will have catastrophic implications for European economies—it seems clear that there will be plenty of opportunities to buy into European distressed debt through 2012. Banks are going to continue to delever, and some of them are going to be forced to sell assets at a big discount to fair value. So there are some upside opportunities even in a fairly bleak environment.

Pension funds that manage their activities carefully will be able to ride through this period to calmer waters on the other side. After all, the one thing they really have going for them—provided that they don't have big losses in the short term—is time. They can afford to take the long view.

MORE INFO

Books:

Einhorn, David. *Fooling Some of the People All of the Time: A Long Short (and Now Complete) Story*. Updated ed. Hoboken, NJ: Wiley, 2011.

Kahneman, Daniel. *Thinking, Fast and Slow*. New York: Farrar, Straus and Giroux, 2011.

Kindleberger, Charles P., and Robert Z. Aliber. *Manias, Panics, and Crashes: A History of Financial Crises*. 6th ed. Basingstoke, UK: Palgrave Macmillan 2011.

Reinhart, Carmen M., and Kenneth S. Rogoff. *This Time is Different: Eight Centuries of Financial Folly*. Princeton, NJ: Princeton University Press, 2009.

Wiseman, Richard. *59 Seconds: Think a Little, Change a Lot*. New York: Knopf, 2009.

See Also:

★ Asset Liability Management for Pension Funds (pp. 13–15)

★ Viewpoint: Investing in a Volatile Environment: A Black Swan Perspective (pp. 505–506)

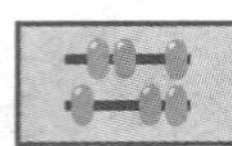

Viewpoint: Understanding the Risks in Liability-Driven Investment (LDI) for Pension Funds

by Marcus Mollan

INTRODUCTION

Marcus Mollan is head of strategy in the Pension Solutions Group at Legal & General Investment Management (LGIM), one of the leading managers in the field of liability-driven investment, with more than £90 billion in derivatives under management. His role is to design and implement risk management solutions, involving both derivatives and physical assets, for pension schemes and other institutional investors.

Legal & General Investment Management was one of the first organizations to offer LDI to final salary pension schemes as a way for both trustees and the sponsoring employer to manage risk. How useful is LDI today?

As the name suggests, liability-driven investment (LDI) for pension funds is a way of matching the timeframes of the benefits that a fund expects to pay out, with the maturity date of its assets. The idea is to take risk out of the scheme by locking in a guaranteed return that will mature when the fund needs it. However, there are risks in LDI itself that scheme trustees and sponsors need to consider. In particular, inflation is a key topic for the trustees and sponsoring employers of defined-benefit pension schemes in the United Kingdom. This is because around 70%–80% of the liabilities of most schemes are inflation-linked. Since 1997, when the UK government introduced mandatory indexation for final salary pensions, trustees and sponsoring employers have had to take into account the fact that most scheme benefits have to increase in line with inflation, although this inflation protection is typically capped at a maximum of 5% per annum.

As a result of this inflation cap, UK pension scheme trustees and sponsoring employers are particularly concerned about the risk of a scenario where long-term inflation remains consistently above the Bank of England's 2% target, yet below the cap of 5%. With recent inflation levels being recorded at around these levels, there has been discussion about how risk reduction can be achieved using LDI techniques.

At first glance it may appear that a deflationary scenario would benefit pension schemes; however, unfortunately this also tends to be an adverse scenario. This is because most schemes have a "floor" in place, which means that pension benefits do not decrease year-on-year, irrespective of how deflationary the real economy becomes. If we have a negative inflation rate, pensions are still paid out at a flat rate, while inflation-linked assets may suffer. So trustees have to manage the risks in both directions—inflationary and deflationary.

In taking risk off the table for a pension scheme, there is always a cost. How do you evaluate cost against benefit in complex circumstances?

The answer depends on your risk tolerance. However, many trustees and sponsoring employers have decided that the price they have to pay to reduce or remove inflation risk is a price worth paying for the increased certainty that it brings.

Most commonly, the way that inflation risk protection is achieved in an LDI strategy is through the use of retail price index (RPI) swaps, which are over-the-counter derivatives negotiated with an investment bank. With an RPI swap, the pension scheme pays a fixed rate of interest to the bank each year, and in return it receives a rate of payment equal to the level of the RPI in that year.

At end 2010, a 20-year RPI swap cost 3.60%. This means that to get inflation protection over a 20-year period a pension scheme would need to pay an annual rate of 3.60% to the bank with which it transacts. This RPI swap price can be seen as an estimate of the market's view of what the average inflation rate is likely to be over the next 20-year period. The rate for a 10-year RPI swap was 3.25%, and for a five-year RPI swap it was 3.05%. These rates are notably above the Bank of England's inflation target of 2%; however, it is important to note that the Bank of England targets inflation as measured by the consumer price index (CPI) rather than the RPI, and there are subtle differences between these inflation measures. Historically, pension benefits have been linked to the RPI, not the CPI, but impending legislation is likely to change some benefits to a CPI basis, which will weaken the protection afforded to pensioners by the statutory indexation of pension funds. At present, however, there is no market in physical or derivative assets linked to the CPI.

We have very good historical statistics on CPI versus RPI, and they show that although about 80% of the time the RPI is higher than the CPI, for 20% of the time this is reversed. On average, the RPI is about 0.7% per annum higher than the CPI, which suggests that the Bank of England's implicit long-term RPI target is around 2.7%. If you apply this to the current 20-year RPI swap market, what it tells you is that, to remove inflation risk, a pension scheme would need to pay a rate which assumes that the Bank of England will miss its inflation target by around 90 basis points on average over the long term. Given recent (and longer-term) experience of inflation overshooting, this may not be an unreasonable price to pay for the greater certainty that results from removing inflation risk.

Is the cost of shifting to an LDI strategy too high at the present time given how low bond yields are?

In addition to index-linked bonds, typical LDI strategies also use nominal bonds (such as UK gilts) or interest rate swaps. It is true that the yields which are effectively being locked into today by entering into these instruments are low by long-term historic standards. However, by the standards of the last five years they are very close to average. Therefore, the big question for trustees is: are we in a new environment where yields are going to stay low for years to come (in which case it may be a good time to

"The old foundations of success are gone . . . The world's wealthiest man, Bill Gates, owns nothing tangible: no land, no gold or oil, no factories . . . For the first time in history the world's wealthiest man owns only knowledge." Lester Thurow

introduce an LDI strategy), or is this a temporary phase? It is a difficult question. What we can say is that nominal interest rate expectations have changed quite significantly. These have been coming down for an extended period, and certainly the base rate in the United Kingdom does not look to be going anywhere any time soon. Schemes that have already embarked on hedging are taking the view that there may still be a risk of further falls in longer-dated bond yields. In particular, long-dated yields would probably go down further if we went into any kind of mildly deflationary scenario.

What are the major risks in LDI for schemes?

One of the biggest risks is that the Bank of England might decide to loosen its inflation target and, instead of 2%, decide to shoot for, say, 3.5%. In fact, the reality of recent years is that the Bank of England has overshot its inflation target far more often than it has undershot it, and we have had persistent, rather sticky inflation in the United Kingdom.

One of the issues with the RPI swap market is whether the price is a genuine reflection of inflation expectations, or whether the price is distorted by the fact that demand for inflation-hedging instruments exceeds current supply. There is no doubt that UK pension schemes are the main buyers of RPI swaps. There is some £1 trillion of defined-benefit liabilities in the total UK private-sector pensions market and only a limited supply of inflation-linked instruments. If you look at the government index-linked gilts market, for example, there is a maximum of £250 billion available there, which still leaves three-quarters of that £1 trillion uncovered as far as hedging is concerned. In terms of new issues of index-linked gilts, the government does not plan to issue more than around £30 billion to £40 billion of index-linked gilts a year, so that again leaves a huge shortfall that can only be covered by the swaps market. It is theoretically possible for UK pension schemes to look at foreign index-linked gilts as an alternative, but sovereign risk aside, the behavior of inflation in other markets is only poorly correlated to inflation in the United Kingdom. Inflation can often be a currency-specific issue. You can see this from the fact that UK inflation has been much stickier than in other markets during the past year or so, demonstrating that the relationship with other markets is not great.

Another alternative for schemes is to use equities as a hedge against inflation. This is not exactly a good derisking strategy if you regard equities as a higher-risk asset class than bonds, but it remains true that equities have been, historically, a good hedge against inflation. While this is not true of the last 10 years, where they have basically moved sideways, the strategy has proven successful over the longer term. In the same way, property is sometimes seen as a good hedge against inflation. Pension schemes have been attracted to properties with long-term inflation-linked leases and tenants with good covenants. This gives them a stable tenant with an asset duration that matches their liabilities and with a lease that rises in parallel with inflation. Infrastructure investments also often have inflation-linked elements. Again, however, supply—by comparison with the huge scale of UK pension fund liabilities—is very limited, and even more so post the credit crunch.

What is the cumulative effect of relatively small changes in inflation on a scheme's liabilities?

It is helpful to look at the present value, or PV, of a scheme's liabilities, and examine how sensitive this is to changes in inflation expectations. A common measure used here is the IE01, which is the change in PV that arises from a one basis point per annum change (0.01% p.a.) in inflation expectations. For a typical scheme, with a 0.01% increase in inflation expectations, you get 15 to 20 times this change in the PV of the liabilities. So if you have a 1% change in inflation expectations, you could easily get a 20% change in the value of a scheme's liabilities, depending on the scheme's maturity. Taken in the round for the entire £1 trillion liabilities of UK pension schemes, that would amount to £200 billion. This is a huge amount of volatility for schemes to put up with, so you can see why there is a considerable appetite for LDI, even at current yields, to derisk the impact of inflation.

This change, of course, feeds through to scheme funding levels and through into company accounts, which means that finance directors of UK companies will go to considerable lengths to prevent volatility on this scale from affecting their company accounts. If you were a finance director or a trustee board and you could not decide whether yields were going to go up or down, you would still want to hedge, because it removes some of the liability risk that the scheme faces. The only scenario where you would absolutely not want to hedge would be if yields were far too low and you were quite confident that they would increase significantly.

One alternative for schemes that believe yields may be currently too low is to do partial hedging. Some schemes, for example, may hedge around 25% of all their liabilities. Others would target the parts of their liability profile which they believe can be hedged at better value. If clients are particularly worried about future inflation, for example, they would hedge out their inflation exposure in their liabilities, but not necessarily the interest rate exposure. Other clients may take a view on the shape of the yield curve, looking from short-end rates to long-end rates, and choose to hedge the liabilities that sit on the parts of the curve that look more attractive.

On the positive side, when expectations about inflation are rising, this is also an environment where people can start to expect increases in bond and swap yields. As these increase, this increases the discount rate for liabilities applied by the scheme actuary, so it reduces scheme liabilities. (Discounting £1 million by 4% gives you a smaller remaining sum than discounting it by 3%.) However, if bond or swap yields increase more slowly than inflation expectations, it creates a problem. The "real yield" is the difference between the discount rate and the inflation expectation. If bond or swap yields increase more slowly than inflation expectations, the real yield will go down, and this will drive scheme liabilities up.

The difficulty with fully protecting a scheme against inflation by using a traditional instrument such as index-linked gilts is that the scheme ends up having money tied up in these physical index-linked gilts, and that money then cannot be put into other asset classes such as equities. This is another benefit of the swaps market. Since swaps do not require a payment upfront, they enable a scheme to invest in the equity markets and to use derivatives to get inflation protection on top. With this in mind, one new instrument which has been widely used over the last few years is the gilt total return swap. This instrument enables a scheme to enter into a contract with a bank to pay a short-term rate of an instrument such as Libor (or a rate close to it) in return for receiving the total return on a notional portfolio of gilts or index-linked gilts. In that way, a client entering into a one-year total return swap at the moment would pay around 1% (the current Libor rate) and would receive back from the bank any change in the capital value of the gilts plus any coupons paid by the gilts over the period. The return on the total return swap, therefore, closely replicates the overall total return that the client would have got if they had physically held the gilts over the period. Again, no payment is required upfront—the

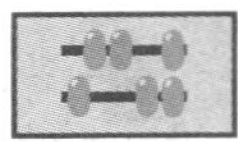

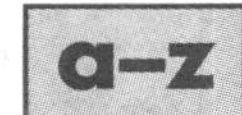

cash flow takes place only at the end of the contract.

However, like other swap contracts, a total return swap must be fully collateralized on a daily basis, so the scheme will need to set aside some assets to back its swap positions.

Just like any other investment strategy, the decision on the extent of LDI that a scheme should implement has to be made in the context of all the other investment strategy decisions that the scheme is making. Ultimately, the decision will be driven by the trustees' tolerance for risk, their views, the views of their advisors, and the relative attractiveness of different instruments and asset classes.

MORE INFO

Books:

Brealey, Richard A., Stewart C. Myers, and Franklin Allen. *Principles of Corporate Finance*. 11th ed. New York: McGraw-Hill, 2013.

Hull, John C. *Options, Futures, and Other Derivatives*. 8th ed. Upper Saddle River, NJ: Pearson, 2011.

Lewis, Michael. *Liar's Poker: Rising Through the Wreckage on Wall Street*. New York: WW Norton, 2010.

See Also:

★ Asset Liability Management for Pension Funds (pp. 13–15)
★ How to Manage Pension Costs (pp. 56–58)
★ Pension Schemes: A Unique and Unintended Basket of Risks on the Balance Sheet (pp. 87–90)
★ Valuing Pension Fund Liabilities on the Balance Sheet (pp. 122–124)

"The millionaires are a product of natural selection . . . the naturally selected agents of society for certain work. They get high wages and live in luxury, but the bargain is a good one for society." William Graham Sumner

  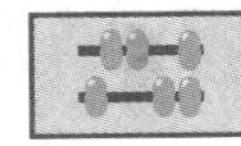      

Understanding the Role of Diversification by Guofu Zhou

EXECUTIVE SUMMARY

- Diversification is a way to reduce risk by investing in a variety of assets or business ventures.
- Systematic risk is not diversifiable, while idiosyncratic risk can be reduced or even eliminated.
- Portfolio diversification depends on risk-aversion and time horizon, and the portfolio mix must be rebalanced periodically.
- Overdiversification/"diworsification" can occur under certain conditions. Business diversification relies on endogenous opportunities, whose value depends on how flexibilities such as timing and expansion options are managed.

INTRODUCTION

To diversify is to do things with variety in order to improve well-being. Diversification is thus a common and fundamental concept in both daily life and business. However, the practice is primarily known as a way of reducing risk by investing in a variety of assets or business ventures. Buying one utility stock in the East coast and one in the West will minimize local shocks, while maintaining roughly the same return as buying either of the two alone. A shop at a resort selling both umbrellas and sunglasses clearly will have a less variable income whether a sunny or a rainy day comes up.

To obtain the optimal strategy of diversification, the risk must be defined and the associated investment opportunities modeled. In addition, the utility or investor's risk tolerance and investment horizon must be specified. In terms of asset allocation and portfolio choice, the risk is usually defined as the standard deviation of the portfolio return. This measures the variability of the return relative to the expected value of the return. Given a fixed level of expected return, the strategy that generates the minimum variance is preferred. To achieve this, the optimal diversification among the assets will usually be required. The risk tolerance of an investor determines the trade-off between return and risk, as well as the level of risk to take.

MODERN PORTFOLIO THEORY

Without a formal framework, *naive diversification* calls for an allocation of an equal amount of money across N assets, and thus it is also known as the $1/N$ rule. This rule goes back to as early as the fourth century, when Rabbi Issac bar Aha suggested: "One should always divide his wealth into three parts: a third in land, a third in merchandise, and a third ready to hand." Naive diversification is clearly not optimal in general. For example, when investing in a money market and a stock index, few investors will allocate 50% to the money market.

In 1951 Markowitz published his famous portfolio theory, which provides the optimal portfolio weights on a given N risky assets (stocks) once the expected returns, covariances, and variances of the assets are given, along with the investor's risk tolerance, in a quadratic utility function. The resulting optimal portfolio is a full diversification with money invested in all of the risky assets. The benefits of diversification depend more on how the assets perform relative to one another than on the number of assets you want to invest. The more the assets do not behave alike—that is, the lower the correlations among them—the more the risk can be minimized by holding the right mix of them.

The optimal portfolio is not risk-free. It is simply the one that has the minimum risk among all possible portfolios of the assets for a given a level of expected return. For any asset, one can decompose its total risk into two components, systematic/market-wide risk and idiosyncratic risk. The optimal portfolio has only market risk, because idiosyncratic risk is diversified away. As a result, there is no point in taking any idiosyncratic risk. But market risk is unavoidable. Intuitively, the return on a suitable portfolio of all stocks in the market has only the market risk, and will not be affected by bad news from some companies, which is likely be offset by good news from others. However, a war, a national disaster, or a global crisis will likely affect the entire portfolio in one direction.

With leverage, the optimal portfolio can theoretically be designed to obtain any desired level of expected return by taking certain necessary risk. The greater the desired expected return on the optimal portfolio, the higher is the risk. Without borrowing and short selling, the diversified portfolio must have an expected return between the highest and the lowest of the asset expected returns. However, the risk is often much smaller than the lowest risk of all the assets.

An efficient portfolio is one that offers either the highest expected return for a given level of risk or the lowest level of risk for a given expected return. The efficient frontier represents that set of portfolios that has the maximum expected return for every given level of risk. No portfolio on the efficient frontier is any better than another. Depending on the investor's risk tolerance, the investor chooses theoretically one, and only one, efficient portfolio on the frontier.

The investment opportunity set is static in the mean–variance framework underlying the Markowitz portfolio theory. As investment opportunities change over time, many argue for *time diversification*—that

CASE STUDY

A Stock Investment

Consider an investment in General Motors, or IBM, or the diversified S&P500 Index for 50 years from 1957 to 2007. Examined at a monthly frequency, and based on all the 50 years of data, the estimated expected return on the three assets are 1.12%, 0.84%, and 0.69% per month, and the estimated monthly standard deviations are 7.01%, 7.59%, and 4.13%, respectively. IBM has the highest expected return, with return per unit of risk of 0.16. Although the market has the estimated lowest expected return, its return per unit of risk is higher, 0.17. On the risk-adjusted basis, the market is the best of the three.

In practice, good firms like IBM are not easy to identify ex ante. If one randomly picks a single stock, the average expected return is almost the market return but with much higher risk. The same is true if one randomly chooses a small group of stocks. In fact, back in 1957, IBM, GM, and Eastman Kodak were all blue chip stocks in the famous Dow Jones Index. Eastman Kodak has long gone from the index, and GM it seems is on the verge of being the next to go, with its value drops of more than 75% up to October, 2008. In addition, many firms have gone bankrupt, merged, or been bought over the years. Hence it is important to hold a diversified portfolio and to manage it over time.

"Don't put all your eggs in one basket." William II of England

  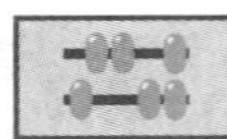      

the risk of stocks diminishes with the length of the investment horizon. While this is debatable, the benefit of diversification across assets, and much of the mean–variance theory, carry through into dynamic portfolio choice models with changing investment opportunities. However, due to incomplete information (such as parameter and model uncertainties), trading costs (such as learning and transaction costs), labor income, and solvency conditions, it can be optimal theoretically to *under-diversify*—to not invest in all assets. Diversification purely for the sake of diversification can cause unnecessary diversification or *overdiversification*, to end up *diworsification* i.e. worsening off from bad diversification.

BUSINESS DIVERSIFICATION: REAL OPTIONS

With competition, the margin of any business diminishes over time. It is therefore vital for a company to make constant innovations and take on good growth opportunities. All of these activities are closely related to diversification. To enhance existing businesses, a company can diversify geographically in its production and R&D, and diversify vertically to take on more of the functions of the businesses previously run by others. While this increases efficiency and reliability, it also increases the risk exposure of the existing business. A company can, however, diversify horizontally by making new products and opening new markets.

Business diversification is, however, much more complex than stock investment diversification. First, the diversification possibilities are not obvious and have to be studied and developed with resources. Second, the risk and return on a new business are endogenously determined by how it is managed. Third, the benefits of diversification may not show up at the start. This is because existing businesses can be weakened when both management and financial resources are switched to diversification. Also, the new business will typically experience higher risk since the firm's management has less experience in running it.

Business diversification is almost always sequential. For any project, there are usually many embedded options, such as when to start, whether to expand, and how to switch. Optimal exercise of the options can enhance the value significantly, and so they should be analyzed carefully. Various risk management practices in a company can also be viewed as diversification whereby, to reduce risk, investments are made in financial assets or derivatives to offset the occasional negative payoffs of businesses. However, business diversification can be counterproductive if funds are inefficiently allocated across divisions, if division managers are self-interested, or if the conglomerates, created through mergers of already inefficient firms perhaps, remain inefficient. In addition, diversification typically provides consistent performance with less upside surprises. Academic research finds a *diversification discount*—that a diversified firm usually trades at a discount relative to a comparable matched portfolio of single-segment firms.

CONCLUSION

For asset investments, diversification is an effective tool in reducing the risk of investments in stocks, bonds, and other securities. Utilizing the correlation structure among the assets, idiosyncratic risk can be reduced or even eliminated. For businesses, diversification is a strategic decision. It is vital for a firm's long-term value creation to identify and manage growth opportunities. Diversification is an important way to manage these opportunities well, reducing risk and ensuring success.

MAKING IT HAPPEN

For asset investments, while money managers can apply modern portfolio theory to diversify the risk with a desired level of return, individual investors can make use of the theory indirectly by investing in portfolios managed by the money managers. In practice this can be done via mutual funds and exchange traded funds. Large and wealthy investors can diversify even more with alternative asset classes such as hedge funds, collectibles (like art works), and exotic investment vehicles sold by large banks. They can diversify over various investment styles, managers, and brokerage accounts. For businesses, diversification means putting managerial and financial resources from your primary business into other opportunities. A small investment in strategic planning and diversification can pay off handsomely later. Vertical diversification may be the first to be started, though horizontal vehicles can be pursued at the same time. Diversification can increase the risk of the existing business but reduce the total risk exposure of the firm. However, the various flexibility options in diversification, such as timing and switching, must be valued carefully and managed efficiently to obtain the maximum diversification benefit.

MORE INFO

Books:

Bodie, Zvi, Alex Kane, and Alan J. Marcus. *Investments*. 8th ed. New York: McGraw-Hill, 2009.

Campbell, John Y., and Luis M. Viceira. *Strategic Asset Allocation*. Oxford: Oxford University Press, 2002.

Markowitz, Harry M. *Portfolio Selection: Efficient Diversification of Investments*. Hoboken, NJ: Wiley, 1991.

Reports:

Liu, Hong. "Portfolio insurance and underdiversification." Working paper. November 29, 2008. Online at: ssrn.com/abstract=932581

Tu, Jun, and Guofu Zhou. "Being naive about naive diversification: Can investment theory be consistently useful?" Working paper. .July 2008. Online at: ssrn.com/abstract=1099293

Website:

Guofu Zhou's references on diversification: tinyurl.com/5rwk2kw [PDF].

See Also:

★ Asset Allocation Methodologies (pp. 454–458)
★ Carrying Out Due Diligence on Hedge Funds (pp. 465–467)
★ Measuring Country Risk (pp. 537–539)
★ The Performance of Socially Responsible Mutual Funds (pp. 553–556)
✔ Fund of Hedge Funds: Understanding the Risks and Returns (p. 1071)
✔ Hedge Funds: Understanding the Risks and Returns (p. 1072)
Portfolio Selection: Efficient Diversification of Investments (p. 1408)
Stocks for the Long Run: The Definitive Guide to Financial Market Returns and Long-Term Investment Strategies (p. 1418)

"Diversification: the only free lunch on Wall Street." Anonymous

  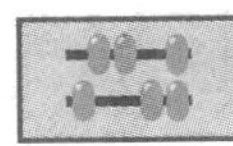   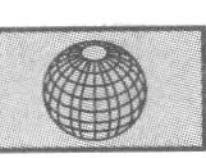   

Understanding the True Cost of Issuing Convertible Debt and Other Equity-Linked Financing by Roger Lister

EXECUTIVE SUMMARY

- Convertible securities (CSs) combine debt and equity. In option terms, CSs are a call option on a specified number of shares whose exercise price is the debt claim forgone in exchange for the shares. CSs are also like a stock with a put option whose exercise price is the market value of the convertible.
- Some critics insist that CSs are uneconomic because they address several habitats of investors at the same time. Others say that they comprise flexible, non-dilutive, easily executed, and cheap finance, which appeals to many professional investors including hedge funds.
- The basic formula defines the cost of CSs but ignores tax and dividends. The formula produces a weighted average of the cost of the debt and the cost of a call option on the issuer's shares.
- Management's task is to measure the cost of CSs with the formula while allowing for the real world influences that the basic model ignores.
- Cost-influencing factors include dividends, tax, and resolution of agency costs.

INTRODUCTION

Convertible securities (CSs) and other equity-linked instruments combine debt and equity. Depending on the terms and the issuer's future performance, CSs can range from almost pure equity to an option-free bond. In option terms, a CS can be viewed in two ways. It amounts to a straight bond with a call option on a specified number of shares. It is also effectively a share with a put option whose exercise price is the market value of the convertible.

Some iconoclasts persistently argue that CSs and other equity-linked instruments are essentially uneconomic. Classically championed by Tony Merrett and Allen Sykes, critics maintain that by jointly approaching the equity and fixed interest markets a company must offer costly conversion rights to attract the equity investor while giving virtually the same rights to the fixed interest investor who values them less. Likewise, issuers must give fixed interest investors an acceptable income. In short, CSs contradict the advantage of specialization whereby capital-raising is tailored to habitats of investors. The iconoclasts invoke studies like Ammann, Fehr, and Seiz (2006) to the effect that negative equity returns follow the announcement and issue of CS.

Loss of interest on the part of one habitat can lead to greater interest from the other. The mini-boom in convertibles in the spring of 2009 occurred as the reduced value of the equity element led to higher yields becoming available to investors interested in debt. At the same time some straight equity investors crossed over into convertibles attracted by the combination of yield and equity option.

A counterargument is that CSs are flexible, non-dilutive, easily executed, and cheap finance. CSs appeal to professional investors, including hedge funds which exploit arbitrage opportunities.

Rating agencies such as Fitch see sense in both viewpoints and hold that the desirability of CSs depends more strongly than other sources of finance on individual corporate circumstances and market context. Fitch (2006) concludes:

"Issuers must find continuing compelling reasons for such issuance...The lower costs of such issuance compared with the cost of issuing equity are certainly supportive, as are the gradual standardisation, transparency and consistency of documentation, market practice and the activities of the agencies. On the other hand, issuers and their advisers must always strive to satisfy several constituencies, including regulators, legal and tax authorities, the agencies and finally, investors. Investor appetite underpinned the buoyant corporate activity of recent years. However, that appetite arose in an environment of low interest rates that will not persist indefinitely."

What is the true cost of CSs? Definition is less difficult than measurement. Having defined the parameters and influences on cost, management must frankly ask whether their measurements are so unreliable as to make them a dubious basis for decision-taking. Of course this applies across financial management, but it is particularly acute for the cost of capital.

THE COST FORMULA

The cost of a CS is a weighted average of the cost of its debt element and the cost of a call option on the issuer's shares, since the investor in a CS is a lender and the holder of a call option on the value of the firm. The difference between a conversion right and a regular call option is that a CS holder gets new shares upon exercise. It follows that if the price at which the CS holder is entitled to shares is below market price, then the value of all corporate equity, including the convertor's, is diluted. This explains why a convertible warrant is worth less than a straight call option on the company's shares whose exercise leaves existing equity intact.

The market will discount each element to the present using appropriate required rates of return. The cost of CS is an average of the rates weighted by each element's share of total market value.

The starting point is the textbook formula (see, for example, Copeland, Weston and Shastri, 2004, Chapter 15) which can be summarized as follows.

These are the essential terms: k_{cv} is the cost of convertible debt; B is the value of debt element; W is the value of equity element, being the value of a call option on the company's shares; $B + W$ is the value of the convertible security; k_b is the required rate of return on debt; and k_c is the required rate of return on a call option on the company's shares. See below.

Using the capital asset pricing model,

$$k_c = R_f + [E(R_m) - R_f]\beta_c$$

where k_c is the required rate of return on a call option on the company's shares with the same maturity as the CS; R_f is the risk-free rate of return for a bond with the same maturity as the CS; $E(R_m)$ is the expected rate of return on a portfolio comprising all the shares in the market; β_c is the systematic risk of the call option expressing its correlation with the market. β_c is computed by reference to the β of an underlying share of the company adjusted to option using the Black–Scholes option pricing programme:

$$k_{cv} = k_b\left(\frac{B}{B+W}\right) + k_c\left(\frac{W}{B+W}\right)$$

The basic Black–Scholes option pricing scheme assumes that the issuer pays neither

"You can't run with the hare and ride with the hounds." English proverb

dividends nor tax (see, for example, Berk and DeMarzo, 2007, Chapters 21, 22, 23; Brealey and Myers, 2007, Part 6; and packages like the London Business School's).

FACTORS INFLUENCING COST

In the real world, dividends, tax, and mitigation of agency costs influence the cost of a CS.

Dividends: If a company pays dividends then the value of the call option C changes. A call option on a dividend-paying share suffers, since a cash dividend liquidates some corporate value and the proceeds go to shareholders but not option holders. The larger the dividends, the more the option suffers. Option holders who try to anticipate this by early exercise gain dividends but lose interest on the exercise price.

Options on dividend-paying stocks with assumed-continuous or, more realistically, discrete dividends can now be valued (Chandrasekhar and Gukhal, 2004), but only with protracted and complex mathematics beyond the present scope.

Tax: The impact of tax on cost is unique for every issuer, holder, and regime. Tax impinges on C, the value of the call, on β, its systematic risk and on k_b, the cost of debt. The impact in any particular case depends on:

- the issuer and holder's tax regime;
- interacting intra-group regimes;
- corporate, inter-corporate, and personal taxes at critical decision points;
- the taxable status of issuer, holder, and associates;
- how issuer and holder prioritize tax allowances.

Some aspects of recent relevant tax regulations for the United Kingdom are illustrative. The issue price is split between debt and equity. The debt element is valued by discounting comparable straight debt at the interest rate that would have been payable had the security contained no equity conversion feature. The difference between this value and the issue price of the security is treated as being either an equity instrument or an embedded derivative, according to whether the company can only issue shares or whether it has the discretion to pay cash. In the former case the conversion right is treated as an equity issue and is disregarded for tax. In the latter case it is in principle taxable as an embedded derivative. If so, a chargeable gain or allowable loss will arise when the company pays cash to the holders. The gain or loss is determined by a formula based on the difference between the book value of the equity element and the amount paid.

Any difference between the deemed issue price of the debt element and the amount payable on its redemption is amortized and is tax-deductible over the life of the security.

A company can get a high and timely tax deduction by paying high interest on a CS with a short life. This reduces k_b, the cost of debt. However if CS holders are taxable, their personal tax may negate the deduction: if debt is tax-inefficient relative to equity, such investors will require compensation by way of a higher return.

Furthermore tax benefits may be truncated by bankruptcy, voluntary conversion by bondholders, or a company decision to force conversion. If cross-border jurisdiction is involved it becomes necessary to examine how CSs would be categorized under relevant tax treaties, EC directives, and double taxation resulting from any inconsistent classification.

Mitigation of agency costs: Agency costs are costs of conflict among different classes of investor and between managers and investors. They reflect opportunities for equity to exploit debt and for managers to invest sloppily, forgo good investments, shirk, and enjoy perks. Endangered parties impose monitoring costs on the shareholders. If the endangered party is a lender, then the cost of debt rises. With CSs an equity sweetener reduces the monitoring costs by aligning the interests of debt and equity.

CSs can reduce the managerial incentive to overinvest in poor, low-return projects. For example, consider the second of two interdependent risky investments, which is only beneficial if the first succeeds. Either finance can be borrowed at the outset for both projects or CSs can be issued that will be sufficient for the first project while providing enough for the second on conversion. If all goes well, the second project will be duly financed by conversion. If the first project fails, the value of the CS will fall, nobody will convert, and management will be able to repurchase the debt at its low value in the open market. Indeed Mayers (2003) has observed a correlation between conversion and spates of corporate investment. If all had been borrowed upfront and if the first project failed, management might be tempted to invest the unused borrowings in easy, unprofitable projects.

A TREND AND ITS REVERSAL

A suitably selected trend illustrates in combination a number of the factors discussed. Such was the boom of 2003 (*Economist*, 2003) and the subsequent fall.

The factors that prompted the surge in the early 2000s to issuance to a near-historic high are concerned with cost, capital structure, value, financial mobility, and market context:

- The market had no appetite for equity, and at the same time companies were suffering from unpalatable gearing levels. CSs with a low coupon provided financial mobility and some reassurance to anxious investors and garnered tax advantage.
- Hedge funds were attracted to CSs because they perceived a bargain insofar as the issue price underestimated the volatility of the equity, which meant that the call option, C in the basic formula, was undervalued.
- Hedge funds bought the convertible, sold the debt, and kept the undervalued call option. They then sold shares short to exploit underestimated volatility.

A reversal of the trend came when

- the volatility of equities declined;

Figure 1. Annual global convertible issuance, data through March 10, 2004. (*Source*: Standard & Poor's Global Fixed Income Research, Thomson Financial)

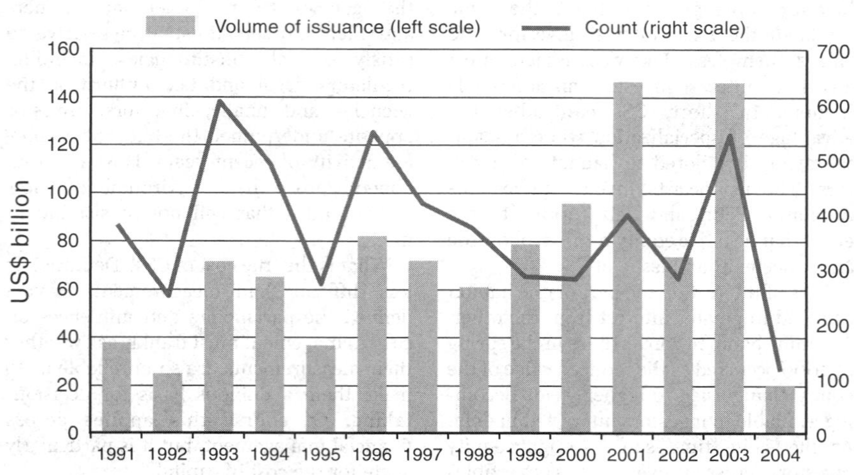

- companies grew wise to the excessive cost of CSs that they were suffering;
- for tax reasons dividends increased, and this hurt short sellers who had to pay the dividends to their purchaser.

The above trend and its reversal illustrate an underlying decision process. An issue of convertibles may be based on perceived market opportunity as above. Alternatively it may be a reaction against the relative costs of issuing straight equity or straight debt. Onerous regulation may further militate against either or both straight instruments.

MAKING IT HAPPEN

The decision to issue CSs follows the answers to a series of questions.

- Is there presently a "hot convertible debt window" in the market or are there contraindications?
- Do the causes of the window or the contraindications apply to us?
- What is our debt capacity? If we are near its limits will CSs bust us or will they enable us to stretch our borrowing?
- Can we tailor CSs to our real investment needs? Can we at the same time mitigate agency costs?
- What tax-planning opportunities do CSs offer? Should we prioritize other tax benefits?
- Measurement of the parameters of the cost of capital is notoriously difficult. How reliable are our estimates? For example, how stable is our beta and how reliable is our estimate of volatility?

MORE INFO

Books:

Berk, Jonathan, and Peter DeMarzo. *Corporate Finance*. Boston, MA: Pearson Addison Wesley, 2007.

Bhattacharya, Mihir. "Convertible securities and their valuation." In Frank J. Fabozzi (ed). *The Handbook of Fixed Income Securities*. New York: McGraw-Hill, 2005; 1393–1442.

Brealey, Richard A., Stewart C. Myers, and Franklin Allen. *Principles of Corporate Finance*. 10th ed. Boston, MA: McGraw-Hill, 2010.

Copeland, Thomas, Fred Weston, and Kuldeep Shastri. *Financial Theory and Corporate Policy*. 4th ed. Boston, MA: Addison-Wesley, 2004.

Tuckman, Bruce. *Fixed Income Securities: Tools for Today's Market*. 2nd ed. Hoboken, NJ: Wiley, 2002.

Articles:

Ammann, Manuel, Martin Fehr, and Ralf Seiz. "New evidence on the announcement effect of convertible and exchangeable bonds." *Journal of Multinational Financial Management* 16:1 (February 2006): 43–63. Online at: dx.doi.org/10.1016/j.mulfin.2005.03.001

Asquith, Paul. "Convertible bonds are not called late." *Journal of Finance* 50:4 (September 1995): 1275–1289. Online at: www.afajof.org/journal/jstabstract.asp?ref=11557

Campbell, Cynthia J., Louis H. Ederington, and Prashant Vankudre. "Tax shields, sample selection bias, and the information content of conversion-forcing bond calls." *Journal of Finance* 46:4 (September 1991): 1291–1324. Online at: www.afajof.org/journal/jstabstract.asp?ref=11156

Economist. "Convertible bombs." November 14, 2002. Online at: www.economist.com/finance/displaystory.cfm?story_id=E1_TQQGNJJ

Economist. "Options and opportunities." July 17, 2003. Online at: www.economist.com/finance/displaystory.cfm?story_id=E1_TJNSDRJ

Fitch Ratings. "Guide to hybrid securities." 2006. Online at: www.gtnews.com/feature/138_2.cfm

Laurent, Sandra. "Convertible debt and preference share financing: An empirical study." Working paper, 2005. Online at: ssrn.com/abstract=668364

Gukhal, Chandrasekhar Reddy . "The compound option approach to American options on jump-diffusions." *Journal of Economic Dynamics and Control* 28:10 (September 2004): 2055–2074. Online at: dx.doi.org/10.1016/j.jedc.2003.06.002

See Also:

★ The Role of Short Sellers in the Marketplace (pp. 593–597)
✔ Hedge Funds: Understanding the Risks and Returns (p. 1072)
✔ Raising Capital by Issuing Shares (p. 1087)
✔ Swaps, Options, and Futures: What They Are and Their Function (p. 988)
✔ Understanding Price Volatility (p. 1103)

Venture Capital Funds as an Alternative Class of Investment by Michael D. McKenzie and Bill Janeway

EXECUTIVE SUMMARY

- Venture capital funds became prominent during the dot.com/telecom boom period, which has distorted investors' perceptions of this class of asset.
- Venture funds are extremely risky and illiquid, and the evidence suggests that the average fund does not outperform public equity. Further, their supposed diversification benefits are most likely overstated.
- The funds that do well are typically large, run by managers who are very experienced, and most of the alpha comes from only a handful of projects that generate large payoffs.
- The future direction of the venture industry is toward funding large-scale projects, which are typically not a good fit of the venture capital funding model. Thus, potential investors need to be very cautious when considering this type of investment.

AN INTRODUCTION TO VENTURE CAPITAL

The modern venture capital industry began after the Second World War, when the first venture funds were created to commercialize technology that had been developed during the war.[1] A formal trade association was created in 1974 with the formation in the United States of the National Venture Capital Association (NVCA). However, venture capital was still a relatively small and esoteric investment sector, with fewer than 100 firms and less than US$500 million under management.

The mid-1990s, however, saw a remarkable change as an unprecedented volume of funds flowed into the venture capital industry on the back of the dot.com/telecom boom. This resulted in the industry becoming one of the largest asset categories in the alternative investments industry. Figure 1 presents the total capital under management for US venture funds, and the phenomenal growth rate of 45% in 1998, 58% in 1999, and 54% in 2000 is vividly illustrated. The bursting of the internet bubble, however, put an end to this meteoric rise, and the recent trend has been one of consolidation across the industry. In 2009, there were 794 venture capital firms in existence managing US$179.4 billion across 1,188 funds.

As professional venture capital evolved, it adopted the limited partnership form, which was designed (1) to protect passive sources of funds from losing more than the portion of their committed capital actually drawn down and invested, and (2) to reward the active venture managers with compensation contingent on investment success. The central character in a venture fund is the general partner (GP), who establishes a fund by seeking a financial commitment from various investors, who are referred to as limited partners (LPs). The GP's compensation takes the form of a management fee, defined as a percentage (typically 2% of committed capital), and a "carried interest" in the profits of the fund (typically 20%). Note that, at this stage, LPs are only required to commit to the fund (typically for a period of 10 years) and no money is actually invested. The year in which the fund is established is referred to as the fund vintage year, and funds typically range in size from as little as US$10 million to more than US$1 billion.

Having established the fund, the GP will then set about identifying suitable investment opportunities. Venture opportunities may be as early in their process of generation as a sole entrepreneur with an idea, or they may be as mature as a well-established organization seeking growth capital. This process of identifying opportunities is the primary role of the GP and, anecdotally, for every 100 opportunities, only 10 will be given serious consideration, and then only one investment will be made.[2]

Historically, venture capital investing in the United States has been concentrated in the information and communications technology (ICT) and the life sciences/healthcare sectors. Nowadays, venture funds invest in a wide variety of industries: for example, in 2009 the sectors most favored were biotechnology (20% of venture capital investments), software (18%), medical devices and equipment (14%), industrial/energy (13%), media and entertainment (7%), and IT services (6%).[3] A fund may choose to specialize in a particular sector, or, alternatively, it may be a general venture fund that has no restrictions on the scope of its investment activities. It is interesting to note that specialist venture funds have been found to outperform general venture funds, which is to be expected given that, unlike traditional fund managers, GPs typically engage in direct oversight of companies in which they invest. Consequently, industrial knowledge and relevant contacts are of paramount importance to successful venture investing.

Venture funds may also invest at various stages in the development of the company. For example, "seed funding" is provided to an entrepreneur to prove a concept (9% of venture capital investments in 2009 were to pure start-ups); "early-stage funding" is provided to companies which have products that are in testing or pilot production

Figure 1. Capital under management for US venture funds. (*Source*: NVCA, 2010, p. 10.)

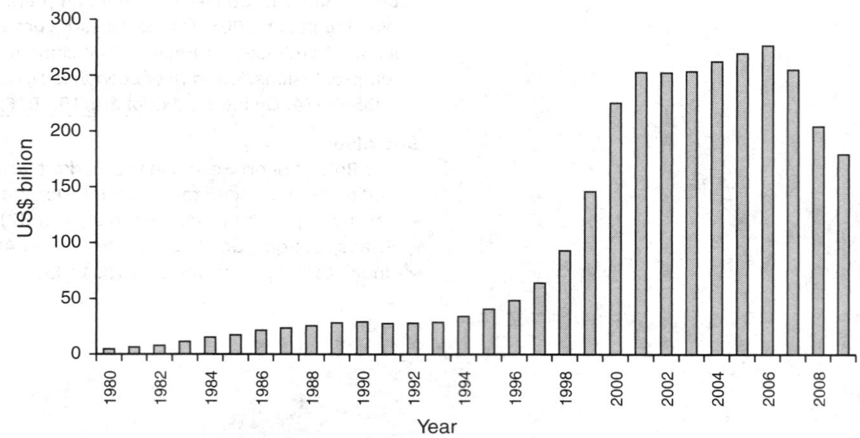

"It is easier for a camel to go through the eye of a needle, than for a rich man to enter into the kingdom of God."
New Testament

(26% of venture capital investments in 2009); "expansion funding" is where working capital is provided to a company, which may or may not be profitable, for the purposes of expansion (31% of investments in 2009); and "later-stage funding," where capital is provided to a company that has established itself in the market, is typically cash-flow positive (but not necessarily profitable), and is growing at a consistent rate (33% of investments in 2009). As a general rule, the latter stages of investment are lower risk and so have lower expected returns. While some funds may choose to specialize in funding particular stages of financing, others may have no preference.

It is worth noting that, much like other segments of the fund management industry, venture capital funds-of-funds also exist. These funds-of-funds seek to lessen the risk from this type of investment by diversifying across a number of venture capital funds.

Venture capital funds typically have a stipulated "investment period"—usually four to five years—during which full management fees are paid, with these fees generally reducing after the investment period has elapsed. Whenever an investment decision is made, the GP will draw down the needed funds from the capital committed by the LPs. There is no requirement that all of the committed funds be called over the life of the fund—if suitable investments cannot be identified, the GP will not invest. However, a venture capitalist who is unable to find suitable investments is unlikely to raise a subsequent fund.

The return to the LPs from their investment in the venture fund comes in the form of periodic distributions. These distributions are the result of the GP creating liquidity in their investments either through outright sale of the investee company or through a successful initial public offering (IPO). In the former case, the distribution may take the form of either cash or liquid securities (if the acquiring company used such securities as the medium for the transaction). In the latter case, shares of the investee company are typically distributed to the limited partners, although the timing and number of distributions will necessarily reflect the liquidity and performance of the shares.

THE PERFORMANCE OF VENTURE CAPITAL FUNDS

One key generalized fact about the performance of venture funds is that venture investing is a high-risk activity. As a general rule, only one in six companies ever goes public and one in three is acquired.[4] Thus, GPs expect only a small number of their investments to generate a return, while the majority will fail.

To understand why such a large number of investments fail, consider a simple example of the venture investment process (Table 1). Assume that there are eight different facets of the venture investment process that go together to produce a successful investment. Further, assume that the GP involved with the company has a good track record, such that it has an 80% probability of achieving success against each of these facets, or criteria. Probability theory tells us that there is only a 17% chance of success, and if we reduce three of the probabilities to 50%, the combined chance of success falls to only 4%. Of course, the real world is far more complex than depicted in this simple example, but the point remains.

The high probability of failure in any individual investment explains why successful venture capital funds tend to be heavily capitalized. In simple terms, it is necessary to have sufficient capital to invest in a variety of different projects such that, on average, at least some of them will succeed and the gains from the few winners will exceed the losses from the losers. By way of example, the American Research and Development Corporation initially invested US$70,000 in Digital and received a distribution of US$355 million following its IPO in 1968. This equates to an annualized rate of return in excess of 100% per year and accounted for half of the company's profits over its 26-year life.

This is not to say that a "shot gun" approach to venture investing works best—in fact, quite the opposite is true, as there is a high degree of persistence in venture fund returns (unlike almost every other class of managed fund). This means that managers who do well in the past will most likely continue to do well as they are better networked and more knowledgeable about the segment of the market they operate in.

A controversial question is whether venture investments provide a level of performance that justifies their risk and illiquidity. A general index of performance for the venture capital investment industry is provided by Sand Hill Econometrics (Figure 2). The incredible performance of the venture industry during the dot.com/telecom boom is clearly evident in the data, as is the subsequent bursting of the bubble. For the purpose of comparison, the S&P 500 as well as the Nasdaq indexes are also included.[5] Across the entire period over which the index is available, the average annualized return for the index over the period December 1991 to March 2010 is 20.3%, while the return to the S&P 500 was only 6.8% and 10.7% for the Nasdaq, respectively.

As noted earlier, funds in the venture industry are extremely heterogeneous. Rather than looking at industry-wide

Table 1. The probability that a venture investment will be successful. (*Source*: Zider, 1998)

Individual event	*Probability*
1. Company has sufficient capital	80%
2. Management has sufficient skills	80%
3. Product development proceeds as planned	80%
4. Input sourcing proceeds as planned	80%
5. No change in market competition	80%
6. Demand is forecast correctly	80%
7. Pricing is forecast correctly	80%
8. Patents are issued and enforceable	80%
Combined probability of success	**17%**

Figure 2. Venture capital, S&P 500 and Nasdaq indexes. (*Source*: Sand Hill Econometrics and Datastream. The Sand Hill All Industries index is presented)

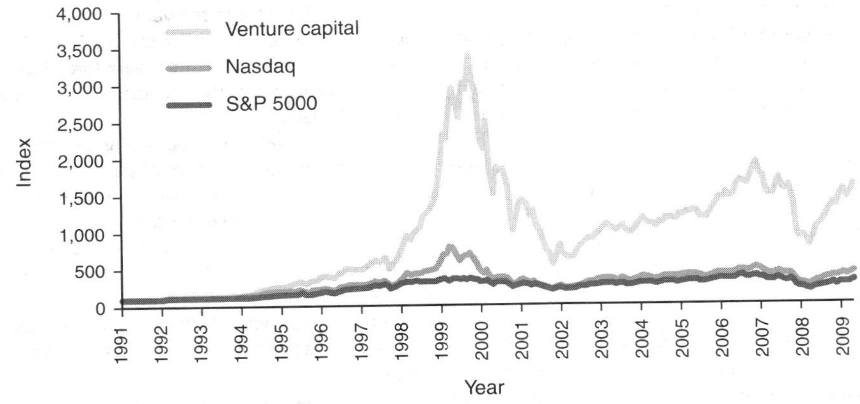

  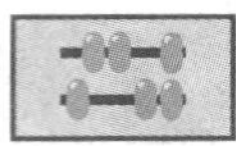   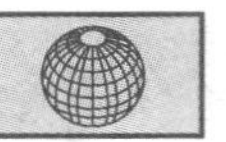   

measures of performance, a more satisfactory approach is to examine the performance of individual funds. The most commonly used database for this purpose is provided by Thomson Venture Economics, which has data for individual funds. Although the early literature on this issue generally found that venture funds outperform public equity, the Thomson database has inherent problems when used to benchmark performance that stem from self-reporting of the data and survivorship bias. After correcting for sample bias and accounting values, the average fund performance was found to change from over- to underperformance of −3.83% per year with respect to the S&P 500.[6]

GPs prefer to exit an investment through an IPO, as exit valuations for listed companies are higher than those of buyouts. For example, a US$1 investment in a firm that goes public was found to provide an average cash return of US$1.95 beyond the initial investment, while an acquisition yields a cash return of only 40 cents.[7] In fact, Metrick (2007, p. 100) goes so far as to argue:

"Without a doubt, the most important driver of VC investment is the existence of a lucrative market to exit these investments. ... The most profitable exits are achieved through initial public offerings."

This is an interesting point as, if the conditions in the IPO market exert an influence on venture fund performance, public and private equity returns may not be independent. This is potentially an important issue, as summarized by Gompers and Lerner (2004, p. 354), who state:

"... many institutions ... have increased their allocation to venture capital ... in the belief that the returns of these funds are largely uncorrelated with the public markets."

The available empirical evidence on this issue does find evidence of the existence of such a relationship. In the last 30 years, for example, the median venture fund produced an internal rate of return (IRR) of 76% when the IPO market was hot (i.e. during the 1983 Q4, 1986 Q3, 1993 Q4, 1996 Q2 and 2000 Q1 periods), which is substantially higher than the median return in a neutral (24%) and poor (9%) IPO market.[8] Thus, clear evidence of a link between the public equity market and the performance of venture funds is found, which suggests that the diversification benefits of this class of alternative investment may be significantly overstated.

THE VENTURE CAPITAL INDUSTRY: LOOKING FORWARD

To understand the future of the venture capital industry and where the profitable investment opportunities are to be found, one needs to gain an appreciation of which sectors the venture capital industry serves well and those it does not.

The history of venture investing suggests that venture capitalists have *successfully* invested in a narrow band of the spectrum of technological innovation—more specifically, ICT and biotechnology. The latter, however, comes with a caveat as biotechnology is arguably a failure when measured by cash generation (Pisano, 2006, p. 117):

"[F]rom 1975 to 2004 ... [w]hile revenues have grown exponentially ..., profit levels essentially hover close to zero throughout the life of the industry. Furthermore, the picture becomes even worse if we take the largest and most profitable firm, Amgen, out of the sample. Without Amgen the industry has sustained heavy losses throughout its history.... [T]he analysis includes no privately held firms, almost all of which lose money. Therefore, the data presented here are just for the most profitable part of the industry...."

Venture capitalists, however, have been notably *unsuccessful* in materials science and other "high-tech" areas. The key difference is that in the case of ICT, the US Department of Defense funded the enabling science, from semiconductor physics through computational logic, and also supported movement down the operational learning curve to reliable and efficient manufacturing both as an investor and as a customer. Similarly, the National Institutes of Health have funded the research base for the biotechnology industry. The search for relevant, commercially attractive applications of novel materials, however, is a very extended process, as demonstrated by the history of engineered polymers ("plastics"): commercial success was the result of billions of dollars and decades of experimentation on the part of DuPont and General Electric.

These observations do not bode well for the industry, as venture investments in the energy, nanotechnology, and green-technology sectors are likely to be the most common type of opportunity presented to investors in the future. These investments will be seeking considerable capital funding (investments are likely to be measured in billions rather than millions of dollars), with promises of big returns. Unfortunately, none are a good fit to the venture capital funding model since the science is immature, the exposure to competitive commodity pricing pressure from conventional energy sources is acute, and the capital required for economically meaningful deployment is massive.

Venture capitalists can play a useful role in funding distributed research and development for established companies and launching lightweight web start-ups. However, the industry is still considerably overcapitalized for these purposes, even taking into account the recent fall in funds under management (see Figure 1), which means that many funds will simply not be able to access the right type of investments.

CONCLUSION

The venture capital industry initially focused on exploiting technologies that had been fostered by government funding of basic science and engineering in the ICT and biotechnology sectors. Its success was amplified by the dot.com/telecom bubble of the late 1990s, which led to a considerable sum of investment funds being diverted into the industry in a very short time. The maturation of the ICT sector, however, means that there are only a limited amount of good ideas available to invest in at any given time, effectively forcing many GPs to

MAKING IT HAPPEN

A potential investor in the venture sector is likely to be overwhelmed by the substantial number of funds available to choose from. To be successful, the investor must choose wisely, and the foundation of a successful foray into venture fund investing relies on understanding the key components that go into making a successful venture capital firm. Specifically, successful GPs:

- tend to specialize in a particular segment of the investment universe;
- have a good track record of past successes;
- run large funds that allow them to gain exposure to a range of opportunities, in the expectation that many will fail;
- focus on distributed research and development for big start-up companies and launching lightweight web start-ups, which are the types of investments best suited to venture investing.

Without these elements in place, an investor is likely to lock his or her money up for a considerable period of time and at the end of it all receive a return that is akin to that of public equity.

"Not evil, but good, has come to the race from the accumulation of wealth by those who have the ability and energy that produce it." Andrew Carnegie

invest in projects that are not well suited to the venture model.

Thus, the potential venture fund investor needs to tread carefully. Venture fund returns are highly positively skewed, as the industry is dominated by a small number of well-connected and highly experienced GPs who consistently outperform the rest of the industry. To invest outside of this select group means that you are likely to find your money tied to a fund whose performance is, at best, more in keeping with that of public equity.

MORE INFO

Books:

Gompers, Paul, and Josh Lerner. *The Venture Capital Cycle*. 2nd ed. Cambridge, MA: MIT Press, 2004.

Metrick, Andrew. *Venture Capital and the Finance of Innovation*. Hoboken, NJ: Wiley, 2007.

National Venture Capital Association (NVCA). *2010 NVCA Yearbook*. Arlington, VA: NVCA, 2010. Online at: tinyurl.com/5wkwz9o

Pisano, Gary P. *Science Business: The Promise, the Reality, and the Future of Biotech*. Cambridge, MA: Harvard Business School Press, 2006.

Article:

Zider, Bob. "How venture capital works. The discipline of innovation." *Harvard Business Review* 76:6 (November–December 1998): 131–139. Online at: hbr.org/1998/11/how-venture-capital-works/ar/1

Websites:

National Venture Capital Association (NVCA): www.nvca.org

Sand Hill Econometrics: www.sandhillecon.com

Thomson Venture Economics: www.alacrastore.com/research/thomson-financial-venture-economics

NOTES

1 American Research and Development Corporation and J.H. Whitney & Company were both founded in 1946 and were the first modern venture capital funds (the latter is still active in the industry). Prior to this, wealthy individuals and family trusts were the main source of this type of development capital.

2 NVCA, 2010, p. 7.

3 NVCA, 2010, p. 12.

4 NVCA, 2010, p. 8.

5 Note that both the S&P 500 and the Nasdaq have been reindexed to start at a value of 100, the same starting value as the Sand Hill index.

6 See Phalippou, Ludovic, and Oliver Gottschalg. "The performance of private equity funds." *Review of Financial Studies* 22:4 (April 2009): 1747–1776. Online at: dx.doi.org/10.1093/rfs/hhn014

7 See Ross, Peter W., and Susan Isenstein. *Exiting Venture Capital Investments*. Wellesley Hills, MA: Venture Economics, 1988.

8 See McKenzie, Michael D., and William H. Janeway. "Venture capital funds and the public equity market." *Accounting & Finance* (forthcoming). Online at: dx.doi.org/10.1111/j.1467-629X.2010.00373.x

  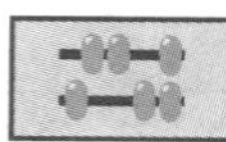   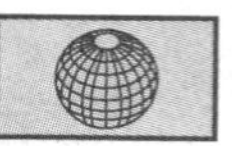   

WACC versus APV Valuation: Financial Policy and the Discount Rate by Antoine Hyafil

EXECUTIVE SUMMARY

The article uses a simple numerical example to illustrate that:

- Weighted average cost of capital (WACC) and adjusted present value (APV) valuation yield identical results in the (hypothetical) situation when expected cash flows are constant over time;
- The equivalence depends crucially on using the right discount rates;
- Such discount rates are different when the debt is constant over time, or when it is only expected to be constant over time;
- The equivalence between WACC and APV disappears in the more realistic situation when expected cash flows are nonconstant, unless the financial structure remains stable;
- The formula most often used by practitioners to relate the beta of equity and the beta of the assets of a corporation is inconsistent with WACC valuation.

INTRODUCTION

Franco Modigliani and Merton Miller's (1958) Propositions I and II have generated two valuation methodologies, hereafter referred to as WACC (weighted average cost of capital) and APV (adjusted present value) valuation. Briefly, Proposition I states that the value of a firm does not depend on its capital structure, and Proposition II states that a firm's value depends on three things: the required rate of return on its assets; its cost of debt; and its debt/equity ratio. Both valuation methodologies are equivalent provided that the discount rates are chosen appropriately and consistent assumptions are made regarding the corporation's financial policy. They are not equivalent otherwise, and both may lead to inappropriate valuation if used with insufficient care.

Modigliani and Miller's (MM) Proposition II addresses the relationship between the cost of equity of a levered firm and the cost of equity of its unlevered equivalent. Whenever financial markets are frictionless, such a relationship reflects an equilibrium generated by investors' arbitrage activities. A consequence is that, in the absence of market imperfections, neither the value nor the cost of capital of a corporation vary with its financial structure: the value of the firm is equal to the present value of the free cash flows, discounted at a constant weighted average cost of capital.

Conversely, as emphasized in many ways by contemporary corporate finance, when imperfections exist a firm's financial structure may impact its valuation. The most familiar imperfection is the tax advantage of debt implied by the tax deductibility of interest. MM Proposition I shows that the value of a levered firm is equal to the present value of the free cash flows discounted at the unlevered cost of capital, plus the present value of the tax savings. This is the basis for APV valuation. WACC valuation remains valid if an adjustment is made for a world where borrowing has a tax advantage; the value is equal to the present value of the free cash flows discounted at a weighted average cost of capital, with the latter now incorporating the impact of the tax shield:

$$\text{WACC} = \text{Cost of debt} \times w(1-t) + \text{Cost of equity} \times (1-w)$$

where w is the ratio, D/EV, of debt to enterprise value, and t is the tax rate.

The WACC and the APV approaches are equivalent to the extent that the return requirements used for discounting reflect the arbitrage-implied structure of return requirements. However, practitioners using both methodologies usually arrive at different valuations. This article shows that such differences are the consequence of different implicit assumptions regarding the firm's debt policy, and it attempts to draw conclusions on the methodological precautions that must be taken. An example will illustrate this.

VALUATION WITH CONSTANT FREE CASH FLOWS: A COMPUTATIONAL EXAMPLE

Base Case: Debt Level Is Fixed over Time

Consider a company with capital employed (CE) of 270, earnings before interest and taxes (EBIT) of 66, and beta (β_u) of the assets = 1.00; initial debt (D), with a beta (β_d) of 0.3, is set at 77.81, and the tax rate, t, is 1/3. We shall assume that the capital asset pricing model applies, with risk-free rate, R_f, = 5.7% and market risk premium, R_p, = 6.0%. As a consequence, the required return on assets, COE_u, is 11.7%, and the cost of debt, COD, is 7.5%. (COE_u is the cost of *unlevered* equity, i.e. the return shareholders would require if the assets were 100% equity financed.)

We shall start by assuming an expected growth rate of 0% and that debt remains constant over time at 77.81.

Table 1 shows that APV valuation yields an enterprise value (EV) of 402.30, and therefore a market value of equity (MVE) of 323.60. With free cash flows to the firm (FCFFs) discounted at COE_u, and tax

Table 1. Adjusted present value (APV) valuation

	Today	Year 1	Year 2	Year 3	Residual value
Growth		0%	0%	0%	0%
EBIT		66.00	66.00	66.00	66.00
Tax (33%)		22.00	22.00	22.00	22.00
Net operating profit after tax		44.00	44.00	44.00	44.00
Variation in capital employed		–	–	–	–
Free cash flows to the firm (FCFF)		44.00	44.00	44.00	44.00
Discount factor @ COE_u (11.70%)		0.90	0.80	0.72	0.72
DCFF @ COE_u		39.39	35.27	31.57	269.84
Market value of assets	376.07	376.07	376.07	376.07	
Debt	78.71	78.71	78.71	78.71	
Interest @ COD (7.50%)		5.90	5.90	5.90	5.90
Tax savings @ tax rate (33.33%)		1.97	1.97	1.97	1.97
Discount rate		7.50%	7.50%	7.50%	7.50%
Discount factor		0.93	0.87	0.80	0.80
Present value of each annual tax savings		1.83	1.70	1.58	21.12
Present value of all annual tax savings	26.24	26.24	26.24	26.24	
Enterprise value (EV)	402.30	402.30	402.30	402.30	
Debt	78.71	78.71	78.71	78.71	
Market value of equity (MVE)	323.60	323.60	323.60	323.60	

"Many believe that adjusted present value is a more flexible way of approaching valuation than traditional discounted cash flow models." Aswath Damodaran

Table 2. Weighted average cost of capital (WACC) valuation

	Today	Year 1	Year 2	Year 3	Residual value
Growth		0%	0%	0%	0%
FCFF		44.00	44.00	44.00	44.00
WACC		10.94%	10.94%	10.94%	10.94%
Discount factor @ WACC		0.90	0.81	0.73	0.73
DCFF @ WACC		39.66	35.75	32.23	294.66
Enterprise value (EV)	402.30	402.30	402.30	402.30	
Debt	78.71	78.71	78.71	78.71	
Market value of equity (MVE)	323.60	323.60	323.60	323.60	

savings (TS) discounted at COD, the terminal value of the FCFFs equals $FCFF_4/COE_u$ and the terminal value of the tax savings equals TS_4/COD. Note that using COD to discount the tax savings does not imply that the latter are assumed to be riskless, but, as in Modigliani and Miller's seminal paper, they are assumed to carry the same risk as the debt itself.

Table 2 shows that WACC valuation yields the same result as APV, with FCFF now discounted at WACC = 10.9370% and residual value at the end of the third year equaling $FCFF_4/WACC$. The WACC computation, and therefore the equivalence between the two methodologies, depends critically on the cost of equity (COE) being consistent with the arbitrage-implied structure of return requirements. In the case of debt remaining constant over time, the classical formulae used by practitioners applies:

$$COE = R_f + \beta_e \times R_p$$

and

$$\beta_e = \beta_u[1 + (1-t) \times D/EV]$$

with computation of D/EV based on the debt of 77.81 and the enterprise value of 402.30 implied by the APV valuation. The latter formula is the one that prevails in a Modigliani–Miller setting in a world *with* taxes. In this case β_e =1.1135 and COE = 12.3810%.

Modified Case: Debt Varies with the Value of the Assets

Impact on the Discount Rates

Continue to assume an expected growth of 0%, but now replace the assumption that the firm will maintain a fixed debt level equal to 77.81 over time by the assumption that it will maintain a constant proportion of debt to enterprise value (D/EV) equal to 20%, whatever the actual deviation from expected growth. The consequences are as follows:

- Tax savings beyond year 1 are now a function of the actual debt levels realized in the future, which are themselves a function of the actual free cash flows. This implies that tax savings beyond year 1 have the same probability distribution, and therefore the same risk, as the value of the assets. As a consequence, from year 2 onwards an APV valuation now needs to discount them at the rate COE_u, which reflects the risk of the assets, rather than at the cost of debt, COD.
- Equity is no longer partially protected in a downturn by a fixed level of the tax shield, since the latter adjusts to the lower value of the assets; it benefits more than before in an upturn, but, given investors' risk-aversion, this does not compensate. As a result, equity holders now require a higher return, COE.

The latter can be derived using the following formulae:

$$COE = R_f + \beta_e \times R_p$$

and

$$\beta_e = \beta_u(1 + D/EV)$$

with computation of D/EV based on the target D/EV ratio of 20%. In this case β_e = 1.1709 and COE = 12.7256%. Note that the formula for the β_e computation is no longer the same as before but is now identical to the one which would prevail in a Modigliani–Miller setting in a world *without* taxes.

Impact on Valuation

Table 3 shows APV valuation. Applying the D/EV target ratio of 20% yields D = 77.81 *as before*. Enterprise value (EV) is 393.54, and market value of equity (MVE) is 314.83, lower than when debt is assumed to remain constant whatever happens, even though *expected* debt is assumed to remain constant. FCFFs and the terminal value of the FCFFs, discounted at COE_u, yield the same value as before, but tax savings (TS), as well as the terminal value of the tax savings (equal to TS_4/COE_u), are now discounted at COD for one year only and at COE_u thereafter, which yields a lower overall value of the tax savings.

Table 4 shows that WACC valuation yields the same result as APV, with FCFF

Table 3. Adjusted present value (APV) valuation

	Today	Year 1	Year 2	Year 3	Residual value
FCFF		44.00	44.00	44.00	44.00
Discount factor @ COE_u (11.70%)		0.90	0.80	0.72	0.72
DCFF @ COE_u		39.39	35.27	31.57	269.84
Market value of assets	376.07	376.07	376.07	376.07	
Debt	78.71	78.71	78.71	78.71	
Interest @ COD (7.50%)		5.90	5.90	5.90	5.90
Tax savings @ tax rate (33.33%)		1.97	1.97	1.97	1.97
Discount rate		7.50%	11.70%	11.70%	11.70%
Discount factor		0.93	0.83	0.75	0.75
Present value of each annual tax savings		1.83	1.64	1.47	12.54
Present value of all annual tax savings	17.48	17.48	17.48	17.48	
Enterprise value (EV)	393.54	393.54	393.54	393.54	
Debt	78.71	78.71	78.71	78.71	
Market value of equity (MVE)	314.83	314.83	314.83	314.83	

Table 4. Weighted average cost of capital (WACC) valuation

	Today	Year 1	Year 2	Year 3	Residual value
FCFF		44.00	44.00	44.00	44.00
WACC		11.18%	11.18%	11.18%	11.18%
Discount factor @ WACC		0.90	0.81	0.73	0.73
DCFF @ WACC		39.58	35.60	32.02	286.36
Enterprise value (EV)	393.54	393.54	393.54	393.54	
Debt	78.71	78.71	78.71	78.71	
Market value of equity (MVE)	314.83	314.83	314.83	314.83	

"APV always works when WACC does—and sometimes when WACC doesn't." Timothy A. Luehrman

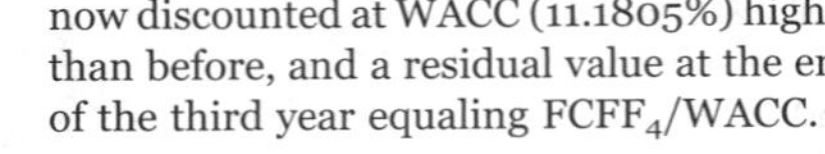

now discounted at WACC (11.1805%) higher than before, and a residual value at the end of the third year equaling $FCFF_4$/WACC.

VALUATION WHEN CASH FLOWS VARY OVER TIME

Introducing a non-zero growth rate adds to the complexity: WACC and APV valuation continue to yield the same outcome under a financial policy of a constant proportion of debt; they do *not* yield the same outcome under a policy of a constant level of debt, since such a debt level is now *expected* to be a variable proportion of the enterprise value.

- If we assume a D/EV of 20%, a 3% perpetual yearly growth of the free cash flows increases debt capacity from 77.81 to 87.77; both APV and WACC valuations yield an enterprise value (EV) = 438.85.
- On the other hand, fixed debt of 77.81 with a 3% growth of the free cash flows yields EV = 451.56 with WACC valuation, but EV = 456.51 with APV valuation. The latter correctly reflects the evolution of the financial structure over time, while the former contradictorily assumes that financial structure remains constant.

CONCLUSION

Practitioners often compute the equity beta of an unlisted corporation from the asset betas for comparable listed peers, using the formula which includes tax savings, and then discount the free cash flows at the cost of capital, thereby making the implicit assumption that the financial structure will remain constant. The latter assumption is inconsistent with the beta computation. If the financial structure is expected to remain constant, the beta computation should not incorporate tax savings into the formula. If debt is expected not to increase with the enterprise value but to remain stable or decrease over time, WACC valuation is not appropriate.

APV valuation on the other hand will always give the correct value, to the extent that the asset beta has been computed correctly and tax savings are discounted at the proper rate. In particular, and contrary to popular belief, using the formula which incorporates the tax shield when applying APV and discounting tax savings at the cost of debt *does not overestimate* the value as long as the debt level is expected to remain constant. In the case of leveraged finance, where debt levels are scheduled to decrease through time, it overestimates the beta, and therefore *underestimates* the value. From a purely methodological point of view, approaches that apply APV using the levered formula for the asset beta and cost of unlevered equity to discount tax savings are therefore overly conservative.

MAKING IT HAPPEN

- The emphasis in this article on methodological rigor may seem excessive to practitioners, given the uncertainty about many other parameters; however, in our eyes this does not justify using a wrong methodology unknowingly.
- Practitioners willing to make the methodological effort should be careful in their computation of the asset beta when using APV in leveraged finance situations.
- Computing industry beta by unleveraging peer corporations' equity beta first implies assessing, for each corporation, whether its financial policy is closer to (1) maintaining a stable target debt to enterprise value ratio or (2) maintaining a stable debt level.
- The same applies when computing the asset beta from the firm's equity beta prior to a leveraged recapitalization.
- The unlevered beta formula crucially depends on the above assumption, and may therefore vary from one peer corporation to another.
- When industry betas have been carefully computed as above, discount the tax savings at the (pretax) cost of debt.
- Do not forget to take into account the expected costs in case of default to balance the positive valuation impact of the tax savings.

MORE INFO

Books:

Note that books on this subject usually relate asset beta to equity beta using the formula that incorporates tax savings. They do not point out that this is only valid when financial structure is assumed to be constant through time.

Articles:

Harris, R. S., and J. J. Pringle. "Risk-adjusted discount rates—Extensions from the average-risk case." *Journal of Financial Research* 8 (Fall 1985): 237–244.

Miles, James A., and John R. Ezzell. "The weighted average cost of capital, perfect capital market and project life: A clarification." *Journal of Financial and Quantitative Analysis* 15:3 (September 1980): 719–730. Online at: dx.doi.org/10.2307/2330405

Modigliani, Franco, and Merton H. Miller. "The cost of capital, corporation finance and the theory of investment." *American Economic Review* 48:3 (June 1958): 261–297. Online at: www.jstor.org/stable/info/1809766

See Also:

✔ Estimating Enterprise Value with the Weighted Average Cost of Capital (p. 967)
✔ Understanding Capital Structure Theory: Modigliani and Miller (p. 997)
✔ Understanding the Weighted Average Cost of Capital (WACC) (p. 1002)
Weighted Average Cost of Capital (pp. 1260–1261)
Valuation: Measuring and Managing the Value of Companies (p. 1429)

"Nothing is more admirable than the fortitude with which millionaires tolerate the disadvantages of their wealth."
Rex Stout

  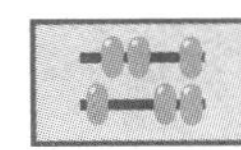   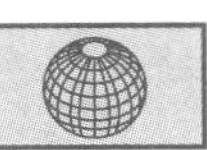   

Viewpoint: Why Mathematical Investing Beats Active Investment Managers Over the Medium Term

by David Schofield

INTRODUCTION

David Schofield is president of the international division of INTECH. He holds an joint honors MA in French and German from Oxford University. Formerly he was European business head of Janus Capital Group and before that he had 15 years in investment banking with Salomon Brothers, Lehman Brothers, and UBS, in New York, London, and Frankfurt.

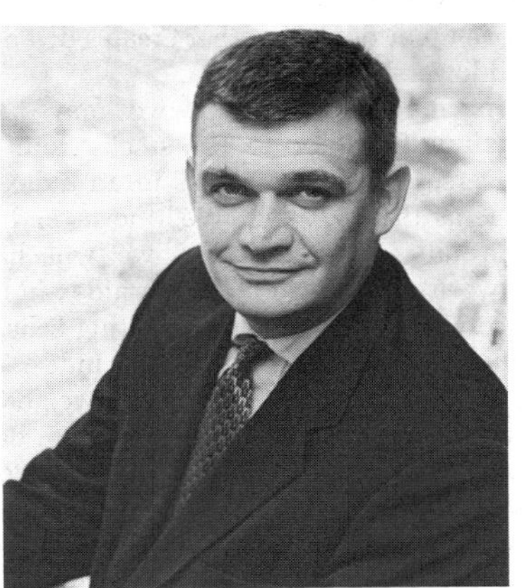

INTECH founder Bob Fernholz, a former professor of mathematics at Princeton University, was responsible for originating stochastic portfolio theory in the early 1980s. Can you explain what it is and what it has to offer as an investment methodology?

Stochastic portfolio theory is based on Bob Fernholz's discovery that, by analyzing only the volatility of stocks and how they move relative to one another, you can create an investment portfolio, or series of portfolios, capable of delivering results in excess of a particular stock market index while retaining index-like levels of risk. In plain words, using Fernholz's techniques we can build portfolios with cautious, middle-of-the-road, or more aggressive return targets and outperform a particular target index by 2–3% for the cautious portfolio, 2.5–3.5% for the middle-of-the-road portfolio, and by around 4% for the higher-returns portfolio.

If we take the cautious portfolio with its return of 2–3% above the market index, that might not sound like much. However, any fund that targets a large capitalization market such as the S&P 500 and which consistently manages to beat the S&P average by just 2% every quarter, year in and year out, will rapidly rise up the performance league table. In contrast, value managers who pick stocks for their clients' portfolios based on fundamental values will have very good years where they are way ahead of the benchmark, but they will also have very poor quarterly results when the market swings against them and will underperform significantly at such times. When you average out their underperforming years and their overperforming years, most active managers fail to even match the index, let alone outperform it.

At the same time, if you can consistently generate even 2% outperformance over the benchmark, and assuming that you are investing for the long term, the magic of compound interest means that your 2% is going to get more and more significant. Einstein famously said that he recognized no force in the universe stronger than the magic of compound interest. If you invest £1 million at 8% for 30 years, with the interest being reinvested each year, you end up with £10 million at the end of the period. If you generated 1% more return, you would end up with £13 million. Two per cent additional return would give you £17 million.

Unfortunately, by the same token, losses work very heavily against the investor. If the value of your portfolio drops by 50%, you have to generate a 100% return on that remaining 50% just to get back to where you started—a tall order if you were initially targeting an overall 8% return on your starting value each year! What this demonstrates is that avoiding the big dips in a market, the big blow-ups, is more than half the battle in successful investing. The impact of losses is what drags back active management performance over the medium to longer term.

How is stochastic portfolio management different from traditional quantitative (quant) funds with their emphasis on the mathematical modeling of performance?

What makes our entire approach different from the normal quantitative investment fund is that we do not go in for statistical arbitrage, pairing long and short stocks or groups of stocks. We only take long positions, never short positions, and we absolutely do not pick stocks for the portfolio based on any fundamental values, or on an analysis of any company's balance sheet, cash flow statements, or whatever. We never open a balance sheet to analyze the contents, and we never visit a company or talk to its CEO or board.

Our analysis is based simply on the historical volatility of the stock price, and for this we use a four-year data set of the company's price performance. This gives us an estimate for the volatility of that particular stock. Typically, stocks in the large indexes such as the S&P have an annual volatility of around 20 to 40%.

At the same time, to mitigate risk, we look for stocks that do not correlate highly with each other—in other words they do not, or tend not to, move up or down in tandem. When we have the stocks picked, which is all done automatically, our model will come up with the ideal relative weightings for all the stocks in the portfolio to achieve the specified level of return. This weighting is revised weekly on a rolling three-month horizon of prices.

In general terms, we are looking for stocks with high volatility, since the higher the volatility, the easier it is for us to generate outperformance. In fund manager terms, we look to go overweight in the portfolio with those stocks that currently have a high volatility and underweight on stocks with a low volatility. Each week we then conduct a rebalancing exercise. What this does is to take into account the impact of the week's price performance on both our volatility analysis and on our overweight and underweight positions. Those stocks which rose in value during the week will exceed their portfolio weightings, and we will sell as much of them as we need to in order to rebalance back to the same weighting as we started with. Similarly, stocks that have underperformed through the week will be underweight, so we will go into the market and buy additional units of those stocks to maintain our original weightings. This buying and selling crystallizes the value generated by the model and constitutes our outperformance.

At the same time, by definition, by using this approach you are buying low and selling high, which is good investment practice. The importance of taking corre-

"Someday I want to be rich. Some people get so rich they lose all respect for humanity. That's how rich I want to be."

Rita Rudner

lation between stocks into account in the model is that it generates a lower risk profile. If we simply locked in all the more volatile stocks without taking the correlations between stocks into account, the risk in the portfolio would rocket up. Picking stocks with low correlations that do not all move up or down together creates diversity and lowers the risk.

In any one portfolio we may have anything from 300 to 400 stocks from the universe of possible stocks in an index as large as the S&P 500. We'll never end up with all 500 stocks, but we will have between 40% and 90% of the index in our portfolio. However, our weighting scheme will be very different from the index. We have manager oversight of the weighting scheme to make sure that the system does not produce an obviously erroneous weighting, but the manager's job is not to second-guess the weighting scheme. A huge number of calculations are involved in working through the practicalities of stock picking and portfolio weighting, which makes it a very intensive computing task. The human eye simply applies an experience check to the outcome to see that there is nothing in the results that flies in the face of common sense.

This investment technique aims to generate outperformance relative to the benchmark that is appropriate for that particular portfolio. Does it follow then that such a fund is very limited in its ability to protect a client's capital in a falling market?

That is correct. We are a relative performance fund, which means relative to the benchmark. If the market as a whole falls 30% and we aim to beat the benchmark by 2%, we will have done our job if the fund performance comes in at −28%.

However, it is important to realize what this means in the overall context of asset allocation strategies. The fund managers who place a portion of their assets with us have already gone through an asset allocation strategy exercise. They have decided how much of their overall fund they want to put into equities, how much into fixed income, how much into cash, and so on. We will be a part of their asset allocation strategy. This strategy setting by the client is the appropriate place for decisions about how defensive the client's fund should be and how much should be invested in this or that asset class given the client's view of prevailing economic conditions. If we started to change our strategy in a falling market in order to become more defensive, and to, say, hold more of the fund in cash, we would be second-guessing the client's asset allocation strategy. That is not what they have given us a mandate to do. They expect us to perform as a relative returns fund and not to suddenly change our strategy and do something very different to "protect" our performance. It is very important not to confuse a relative return fund with an absolute return fund that has a mission to try to beat the market under all conditions. If an equity market drops by 30%, there is nowhere to hide, and the only way not to have your performance follow the market down is to exit the market in a timely fashion and hold cash. Again, that is not the mandate of a relative return fund. Trying to implement a market-timing strategy is widely recognized to be about the riskiest approach to investing! Very few people get it right, and no one gets it right consistently.

Does this mean, then, that whereas in an active fund where all the managers will be experiencing considerable stress when markets are plunging, a team that is using stochastic portfolio construction techniques will be conducting business as usual?

Absolutely. Our job is the same irrespective of what the market is doing. Our efforts are focused not on finding undervalued stocks in order to exploit a short-lived pricing situation, but on research around stochastic modeling and on new product generation. Bringing a new product to market, which, for us, means applying our model to a new universe of stocks, is a very time-consuming exercise. The INTECH Global Equities fund was launched six years ago, and the preparation for that took more than three years. The European equities fund was launched 18 months ago and it took two years running simulations, building portfolios, and back-testing the model against historic pricing data to achieve the right level of confidence that the system could achieve similarly consistent results across a broad range of market conditions.

To understand the performance goals of stochastic portfolio theory it is important to stay focused on the fact that the whole point is to beat the market while generating very low risk. A traditional fundamental investor who succeeds in finding underpriced value across a number of assets can generate spectacular levels of return for a time if economic conditions favor the stocks he or she has picked. But if you analyze the risk in the portfolio over time it will be high. So that is a high-risk, high-returns strategy. We follow a low-risk strategy with a very specific goal of beating the appropriate benchmark by a specific modest amount.

The measure of risk we use is called the information ratio. This has the amount you beat the market by as the numerator and the tracking error of the portfolio as the denominator. The closer the information ratio for a fund approaches one, the lower the risk. In the industry an information ratio of 0.3 is regarded as very good—more than acceptable. We strive for an information ratio of between 0.7% and 1.0%. The most aggressive of our funds, the US Growth Portfolio, targets a return of 4% over benchmark. It has been analyzed over an 18-year time frame and has generated an information ratio of very close to one over that entire period, which is a very good indicator of the strength of the model.

What market conditions do you think make your approach look less attractive?

In a large index such as the S&P, which is weighted towards large-cap stocks, when markets are rising strongly active managers who tend to be overweight in such stocks will have very strong performances. Similarly, if market conditions favor smaller-cap stocks, the active funds that specialize in small-cap stocks will outperform. Our fund will continue to generate its targeted level of performance, and that will not look as attractive, moment by moment, as the outperformance that some managers are generating. However, a mathematical, relative return fund is designed to be consistent across market conditions over time, and this is where our outperformance shows up. Institutional investors will make their own asset allocation decisions based on the characteristics of the various funds and asset classes. The job of stochastic portfolio theory is to generate consistency, which then makes the asset allocation task that much easier.

MORE INFO

See Also:

★ Viewpoint: Why Quantitative Investing Can Do Well in Turbulent Markets (pp. 631–633)
Quantitative Methods (p. 1244)
My Life as a Quant (p. 1401)

"Part of the loot went for gambling, part for horses, and part for women. The rest I spent foolishly." George Raft

Viewpoint: Why Quantitative Investing Can Do Well in Turbulent Markets by Janet Campagna

INTRODUCTION

Janet Campagna is the CEO of QS Investors, a 100% employee-owned, majority woman-owned investment management company based in New York and founded in 2010. Prior to founding QS Investors, Janet was a managing director at Deutsche Asset Management serving as the global head of quantitative strategies and a member of the global operating committee. She was a principal at Barclays Global Investors from 1994–99 and from 1989–94 an associate at First Quadrant and director of asset allocation research. She is a board member of the Mott Haven Academy in the South Bronx, a charter school for at-risk students in the foster care and child welfare system, and a member of the MFE Steering Committee for the Haas Business School, UC Berkeley. Janet has a BS from Northeastern University, an MS from California Institute of Technology, and a PhD from the University of California, Irvine, in 1990.

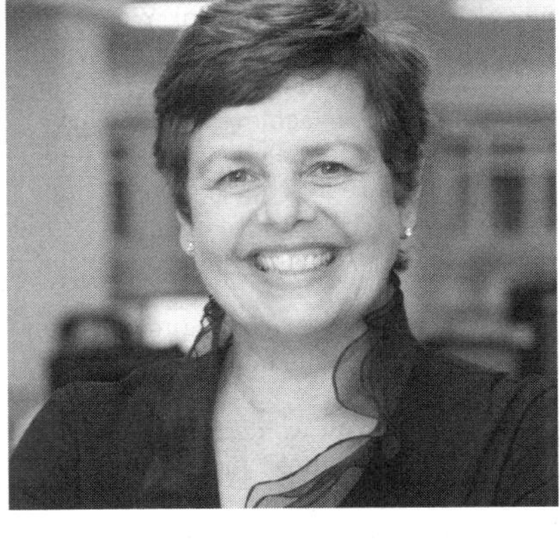

In general, the reputation of quant managers took a hammering as a result of the crash. The media pretty much blamed quants as one of the causes of the crash and certainly highlighted the losses of high-profile investment bank quant funds through the downturn. Do you feel that was unfair to mathematical investing?

Although there is no doubt that a number of quantitative funds turned in results through the crash that would not have pleased investors, there is a mistaken impression in the media—and to a lesser extent perhaps among some investors—that all quant funds are the same, and that therefore it makes sense to talk about "quants" in general terms. This paints all quants with the same brush. In reality, there are many different ways of using mathematical techniques to generate alpha, and different funds take very different approaches. Recent academic research shows that the correlation among different quant fund managers is actually substantially less than the correlation between traditional, long-only active investment managers, particularly during market crises. That, by itself, should suggest that generalizations about quants are not going to be particularly helpful, accurate, or even interesting.

What is certainly true, however, is that there is a very strong demand from the investor community for transparency. Not everyone has the background to understand the mathematics, but they expect a sensible layperson's guide to what it is that we are doing, and we are very happy to provide this. In our case, at QS Investors, we are particularly keen to do so since we believe we are taking an approach that enables our models to be very responsive to changing market conditions and to changing investor attitudes in the market over time. Our results show that incorporating these dynamics generates an enhanced performance over time.

What we have in common with many quant managers is that our approach is a relative returns one, which means that our funds will try to beat the appropriate benchmark for the universe of stocks that we are targeting by a specific amount. There are quant funds that offer an absolute return strategy—one that focuses on capital preservation under all market conditions—but that is not the role of a relative return fund.

We offer various levels of outperformance and construct portfolios that are designed to produce a risk–reward outcome that is commensurate with the target benchmark for that specific portfolio with its risk and return objectives. This gives both our institutional clients and wealth management clients the opportunity to select one or more of our funds to match what they are trying to achieve with whatever portion of their overall funds they assign to us.

This is actually a very important point to get across. We are not in the business of second-guessing the client's portfolio allocation strategy. They will have already decided how they want to allocate their portfolio across a range of asset classes, and we will get a chunk of the monies that they have decided to invest in equities. Our job is to attempt to fulfill our performance goals while staying within the risk parameters that we have set up for that particular client's portfolio. If they have decided to invest in, say, our global equity fund for a 3–4% outperformance target, we will have done our job if we beat the global index by 3–4%. If the whole market is down 10%, we will still aim to be around 4% better than that, so our portfolio will be down only 6%. But we won't suddenly try to outperform the market by 14% to give an absolute return of 4%.

"Doing well" means, in our terms, achieving the goals we set out to achieve. A number of our funds achieved exactly this through the downturn of 2008 and turned in performances that beat their benchmark indexes by 3% to 4%. Investors appreciate and put a high premium on consistency of performance over time.

How do you manage to take "views" of the market into account without compromising the mathematical approach by adding subjective opinions to the mix?

One of the most interesting things about our quantitative strategies is that we use statistical techniques to determine where in the market cycle we are at any time. Note that these are statistical techniques, not opinions. When you have a view on where in the market cycle you are, that helps you to understand which of the insights you have into the market are the most important at any moment. The kinds of things we look at when picking stocks for the portfolio are valuation information, sentiment information, and information on growth, but we determine how important each of these is through another layer in the model which looks at what is going on in the market. Is it, for example, a period of fear, of greed, or of glamor? Is there likely to be a junk rally? We have had this additional dynamic layer in the model for the last five years and it has helped us to navigate through multiple phases in the market cycle, including junk rallies, the liquidity crunch, and the banking crisis. It has also enabled us to show very good results through the financial crisis.

"Short of genius, a rich man cannot imagine poverty." Charles Pierre Péguy

Investors expect consistency, discipline, transparency, daily liquidity, and strong risk management. Our risk management is very mathematically driven, but the management team brings decades of market experience to the process and the model is never simply on cruise control. We monitor the results very carefully. We try to measure risk continuously, and we look across some 15 risk measures to achieve this. You have to monitor risk, note the changes, and understand what is driving those changes. Understanding your risk model and how it works is very different from blindly following a model.

However, the way we bring management team judgment to the table is very different from the way a traditional, long-only management team would set about things. We do not want those judgments coming in the form of emotional reactions to what happened yesterday. Our judgments are all about what goes into the model at the front end, and the judgments are made well ahead of time.

For example, in the run-up to the crash, with markets showing an almost continuous rise, volatility reached very low levels. There were any number of headlines in the press about "the death of volatility." Quant models, including ours, derived assumptions about low volatility from their analysis of data. However, we absolutely did not believe that markets were on an everlasting upward path with consequent low volatility as an enduring feature. It was clear to us that there would be some sort of crash and that volatility would return with a vengeance. So we built and tested a model that would be much more sensitive to conditions of high volatility than the low-volatility model we were using. As soon as market conditions changed, we made the judgment to take the high-volatility model off the shelf and swap it in for the low-volatility model. We had already fully tested and validated it and it was good to go. That is how we use human judgment to steer the process. It is not about saying "I don't like IBM today, I think I'll sell . . ."

What questions are you asking yourselves as a management team when you monitor the way your portfolios are tracking?

There are three things that go through our minds all the time, irrespective of whether the model strategy seems to be working or not. We watch to see if we are correctly capturing risk and alpha (outperformance), and we look to see if we are well positioned with respect to what the market is doing. We are also constantly doing research both to improve our forecasts and to find ways in which market factors might be shifting and changing. If we have an insight about how alpha could be captured, that insight does not take the form of a buy or sell judgment on a particular stock. It comes as an algorithm that we want to model and test.

As an example, one of our researchers raised a question in a recent meeting as to whether, given the patterns in the currency market, various hedged positions would continue to work. In a traditional, long-only fund that might lead to a decision to intervene directly to change the hedged positions. With us, what we look at is whether there is any forecasting information in that insight. If there is information, then we would incorporate it into a strategy. We would want to develop a modeling factor from it that would track patterns of over- or underperformance across the currency markets. Then we would test the performance of that new formula and decide whether or not to include it in the model on the basis of the test results.

What makes our approach very computationally intensive is that we look at a large number of factors for each stock in a large portfolio of stocks. We're looking at all the stocks in that universe, and we look at how the price of each of these stocks is moving relative to other stocks. Then there are those 15 dimensions of risk that I mentioned which we monitor on a weekly basis. When any of these look out of whack, we investigate it to see where any of our portfolios are vulnerable.

You have given one example, with the low-volatility/high-volatility mode, of how you might make a judgment call. Is this just a special instance of a constant process of recalibrating your models to achieve a better fit with reality?

You have to evolve in this business, and fine-tuning models is part of evolving. But if you are just reactive because you find that your model is underperforming due to some specific set of events that just happened, you end up chasing what happened yesterday and you cannot possibly perform well tomorrow. Our mantra is to be responsive, not reactive. It is necessary to challenge and question assumptions all the time, including our own "wisdom." We schedule regular strategy meetings to question and challenge our present strategies. We bring people in to these meetings who do not work on a particular strategy and ask them to try to tear the strategy apart, to find weaknesses in it. It is important to stress that we are investors first and foremost, and quant is just our way of thinking more effectively about the market. We are always asking when we would expect a particular risk model to overestimate or underestimate risk—and "when" here refers to particular states of the market. This is why the ability to incorporate views into the strategy is so important for us.

With a long-only investment strategy, we would be looking constantly to see if we are overweight, underweight, or level relative to the cap index. We want to be in securities that are relatively undervalued and not in securities that are overvalued. However, there are market conditions where stock valuations have little traction with the market. This is why we look at sentiment as well. If fear is driving the market, a valuations-weighted model will not have much bearing on what is happening, so the model will downgrade valuation and increase the weighting given to sentiment. Another dimension might be growth orientation.

We have a lot of respect for fundamental long-only analysts and investment managers and we take advantage of the information available out there from analysts. However, we do this with a very systematic structure and we look to strip the emotion out of it. This is one of the reasons why we do not do the things that fundamental managers do. We do not go and visit companies or pore over their balance sheets. I have never looked a CEO in the eye to see if a company strategy makes sense. Instead we look purely at the numbers, at relative yields, earnings-to-book price ratios, and the speed with which prices are changing. We can do this across a number of factors, over thousands and thousands of stocks, and we can track how these securities are likely to move relative to each other. This is hugely computationally intensive and it simply could not have been done a decade ago. We also work to understand what sort of exposures to systematic risk we have in our portfolios. When we add value to a portfolio, it is this analytical work that generates the value, the alpha. Because this is a mathematical process, it has a discipline and a transparency to it, and these qualities get lost in the talk about all quant funds being alike.

To provide some examples, in our US equities portfolios we run a market-neutral strategy where we are 100% short and 100% long. That portfolio returned 8% above the benchmark in 2008, when quant funds were supposedly doing terribly. With our global strategy we were up 4% versus the benchmark in 2007, and we outperformed again through 2008 purely using quant techniques. When the market is very nervous, and is characterized by oscillations between risk-on and risk-off trades, taking the market environment and investor sentiment into our modeling processes via our views approach helps us to navigate in what would otherwise be treacherous conditions.

However, if the markets move into economic Armageddon territory, then, of course, we are in the same boat as everyone else. Current market conditions throughout the developed world are tough. Growth rates are slow. Countries have ageing populations, with the associated growing public-sector costs, which pushes up deficits. Healthcare and pension costs are on unsustainable trajectories. There are lots of macro issues. From a quant point of view, you just have to figure out how you model these effects on a shorter-term, tactical basis. So far, quant funds seem to me to be doing a pretty good job.

MORE INFO

Books:

Drobny, Steven. *The Invisible Hands: Hedge Funds Off the Record—Rethinking Real Money*. Hoboken, NJ: Wiley, 2010.

Ferguson, Niall. *The Ascent of Money: A Financial History of the World*. New York: Penguin, 2008.

Joni, Saj-Nicole, and Damon Beyer. *The Right Fight: How Great Leaders Use Healthy Conflict to Drive Performance, Innovation, and Value*. New York: Harper Business, 2010.

McDonald, Larry, with Patrick Robinson. *A Colossal Failure of Common Sense: The Incredible Inside Story of the Collapse of Lehman Brothers*. London: Ebury Press, 2009.

Ramachandran, V. S., and Sandra Blakeslee. *Phantoms in the Brain: Human Nature and the Architecture of the Mind*. London: Fourth Estate, 1999.

Surowiecki, James. *The Wisdom of Crowds: Why the Many are Smarter than the Few*. New York: Abacus, 2005.

See Also:

★ Viewpoint: Why Mathematical Investing Beats Active Investment Managers Over the Medium Term (pp. 629–630)

Quantitative Methods (p. 1244)

My Life as a Quant (p. 1401)

  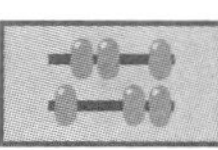      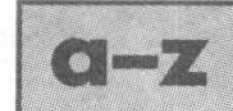

Balancing Senior Management Compensation Arrangements with Shareholders' Interests

by Henrik Cronqvist

EXECUTIVE SUMMARY

- Appropriately designed executive compensation schemes can add substantial value for the firm's shareholders.
- Base salaries should be competitive with those awarded by similar-sized firms in the industry in order to attract and retain superior top-executive talent.
- Most perquisite-type compensation is now outdated, fails to align manager–shareholder interests in any obvious way, and should be avoided.
- Annual cash bonuses should be based on measures that can't be easily manipulated through accounting practices adopted by management.
- Long-term, equity-based compensation in the form of stock options or grants is the most effective way to harmonize the interests of senior management and shareholders.
- It is important to anticipate increased disclosure and scrutiny of executive compensation structures by the media when a particular compensation structure is being designed.

INTRODUCTION

The board of directors, and specifically the compensation committee (or remuneration committee), has the challenging task of designing a compensation structure for the chief executive officer (CEO) and other senior managers that balances their interests with those of the shareholders. The general idea is to make an executive's pay sensitive to the value created for the firm's shareholders. In this way, everyone shares the common goal of maximizing shareholder value.

Corporate executives can in principle be compensated in three different ways:

- base salary and perquisites, or "perks";
- annual cash bonus;
- shares.

No one form will perfectly align the interests of senior management and shareholders. The task of designing a value-adding compensation structure is therefore about identifying the mix between these different forms of compensation that best incentivizes senior management to create value for the shareholders.

DESIGNING A VALUE-ADDING COMPENSATION STRUCTURE

The base salary is the starting point for the compensation package and is commonly set through benchmarking based on a survey of similar-sized firms in the company's industry. Because of risk aversion, most executives will not accept a purely performance-based pay package. Though not sensitive to company performance, the base salary can still play a key role in attracting and retaining superior managerial talent.

Perks such as country club membership and private use of a corporate aircraft used to be common. There is, however, a trend towards the use of fewer perks, mainly because of increased disclosure and scrutiny by media and "watch-dog" groups.[1] For example, in an article with the headline "Only the little people pay for lawn care," columnist Gretchen Morgenson of the *New York Times* wrote that Donald J. Tyson, the former CEO of Tyson Foods, received $84,000 in compensation for "lawn maintenance costs" during 1997–2001.[2] Though the perk was an insignificant portion of his pay during this period, the public's perception of its size can be much more significant than its monetary value. Perks perceived as excessive can cause customer resentment and, as a result, adversely affect both brand and shareholder value.

In contrast to base salary and perks, annual cash bonuses are conditional on short-term financial or nonfinancial goals being met by the firm or individual senior managers. Executives' bonuses, other than for the CEO should be based on their particular business unit's performance, though a part may be based on overall firm performance or cooperation among executives managing different business units.[3] Nonfinancial targets can include successfully launching a new product line, meeting a certain customer satisfaction level, or appointing a new chief financial officer (CFO). These objectives should be specific, attainable, and measurable in the short run. Examples of financial performance targets are earnings per share (EPS), earnings before interest, taxes, depreciation, and amortization (EBITDA), and economic value added (EVA). Regardless of which measure is chosen, a particular threshold has to be attained before a minimum bonus is paid. If the performance is above that threshold, the bonus should increase in increments up to a prespecified maximum. One advantage of annual cash bonuses is that they are one-time compensation for past, realized performance—unlike base salary raises, which are permanent.

Using accounting-based performance targets, such as EBITDA, carries two potential risks. First, short-term performance measures can result in myopic behavior by management: For example, managers trading off short-term earnings growth at the expense of creating shareholder value through valuable R&D projects. Second, accounting-based measures can lead to earnings management, and in the extreme case even manipulation, in order to boost current earnings.

Equity-based compensation, in the form of options or stock, can be used to circumvent some of the problems with short-term, accounting-based cash bonuses. Stock options are the most common form of long-term incentive pay. These allow the executive to purchase a certain number of shares at a prespecified exercise price, commonly the stock price on the day of the option grant, and with a specific period length, often 10 years.

To see how stock options can consolidate manager and shareholder interests, suppose that the stock price at the time of a grant of 250,000 options to a CEO is $50. If the stock price doubles over a couple of years, the CEO will make a profit of $12.5 million (250,000 shares × ($100 − $50)). In contrast, suppose that the stock price declines to $25. Then the options are said to be "underwater" and worth nothing, but the CEO does not lose any money. If the CEO creates value for the shareholder by taking actions that result in the stock price going up, he or she will be rewarded with a slice of that value added. Granted stock options commonly vest (reach a point where they cannot be taken away) over time according to a schedule, or after the firm meets certain performance targets. Executives cannot exercise options before they have vested.

One problem with stock options is that they reward executives even if the reason for the firm's stock price increase is completely beyond their control. Suppose that the world market price of oil increases

  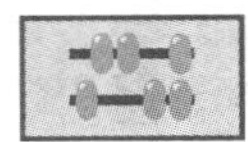      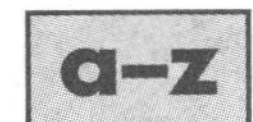

significantly; the stock prices of oil companies increase too, but for reasons that have no relation to anything an oil executive may have done. One potential solution is to benchmark the exercise price of executive stock options to the overall stock market or to a portfolio of firms in the firm's industry—i.e. oil companies in this example. In practice, however, such indexed executive stock options are extremely rare.

Another form of equity-based compensation is stock grants. One argument in favor of stock grants is that options provide executives with an asymmetric incentive because their value goes to zero if the stock price falls below the exercise price; the value of a stock grant does not go to zero. Restricted stock is a form of stock grant that involves common stock of the firm, but with the condition that a certain period of time, for example 10 years, has to pass or a target has to be met before the executive can sell the shares. Performance shares are another form of stock grant. These consist of common stock granted to an executive provided that specific firm performance targets, for example EPS, are met. The performance shares become more valuable if the stock price goes up after the grant is made.

In addition to the three forms of compensation discussed above, severance pay packages, also referred to as "golden parachutes," are also common. There are several reasons why appropriately designed severance pay for a firm's CEO can be in the interests of value-maximizing shareholders. First, shareholders want to avoid a situation in which a CEO is resisting a value-enhancing takeover of the firm because the executive's job will then be eliminated. A golden parachute can provide an incentive for a CEO to step down rather than trying to fight a takeover threat. Second, the severance pay can compensate the CEO for signing a restrictive and lengthy noncompete contract with the firm. Such a contract can be in the interest of value-maximizing shareholders, especially in R&D-intensive industries, because it prevents the individual who knows the most about the corporation's business practices from sharing them with the competition.

CONCLUSION

The design of an executive compensation structure is crucial when providing managerial incentives to create shareholder value, but in practice it is a very challenging task. Management compensation should be sensitive to a firm's performance, should reward superior current performance, and should provide incentives for similar strong results in the future. At the same time, it should prevent the firm from paying a premium for poor performance. Because compensation of senior management in public firms is subject to increased disclosure requirements and scrutiny by media and various interest groups, public perception of what constitutes "reasonable" pay is another important factor to consider.

CASE STUDY

Equity-Based Compensation at Disney

Based on his 1989 employment agreement with the Walt Disney Company, CEO Michael Eisner was granted millions of stock options as part of his compensation package. If shareholder value could be created through Eisner's actions, then he would be rewarded with a slice of that value added. Billions of dollars of shareholder value was indeed created: The stock price doubled between 1992 and 1998. Eisner's base salary was $750,000 in 1998, and his cash bonus was $5 million, based on an EPS growth target. He also exercised previously granted and vested stock options and realized a total profit of about $570 million. Since Eisner was a central to the creation of over $10 billion of shareholder value, it makes sense that he should have been rewarded appropriately.

But this compensation structure can be questioned. Was more than half a billion dollars in rewards really necessary to create a strong incentive for Eisner? Was such compensation "reasonable" from the perspective of the public, in particular the ordinary working person who is also a Disney customer?

The problem is that Disney's stock performed much less impressively from the late 1990s until Eisner resigned in 2005, to the extent that, from 1998 to 2001, more than half of the shareholder value created before 1998 was lost. In 2001 Eisner received $1 million in base salary but no cash bonus because he did not meet the short-term accounting performance targets. Nor did he exercise any stock options.

Stock option grants may incentivize a CEO to create shareholder value, but this case also emphasizes potential problems associated with them of which boards have to be aware. In particular, option grants can result in mega-payoffs that can be next to impossible to explain to the public. Also, there is nothing shareholders can do once stock options are granted, even if most or all of the previously created value is subsequently destroyed during the tenure of the very same CEO.

MAKING IT HAPPEN

A review of the compensation structure for senior management should focus on the following:

- How can the interests of senior management and shareholders be harmonized? Annual cash bonuses make executives focus on year-to-year performance targets. Grants of options and restricted stock provide long-term incentives to create shareholder value.
- What are the advantages of stock grants over options? Because options, unlike restricted stock grants, reward superior performance but do not penalize poor performance, they can result in excessive risk-taking.
- What can be done to avoid a debate about excessive CEO pay? Perks that do not align manager and shareholder interests should not be provided. The board also has to consider the likelihood of mega-payoffs from the proposed compensation scheme.

NOTES

1 An example is CIO-AFL's Executive PayWatch, www.aflcio.org/corporatewatch/paywatch

2 Morgenson, Gretchen. "Only the little people pay for lawn care." *New York Times* (May 1, 2005). Online at: www.nytimes.com/2005/05/01/business/yourmoney/01gret.html

3 For example, Citigroup recently announced that a part of senior managers' bonuses will be determined by how well they interact with other executives during meetings of a division's management committee. See the *Financial Times* (October 14, 2008).

"When you hire people that are smarter than you are, you prove you are smarter than they are." R. H. Grant

  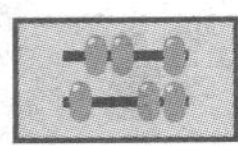      
a–z

Best Practices in Corporate Social Responsibility

by Alison Kemper and Roger Martin

EXECUTIVE SUMMARY

- Business leaders throughout the world are under increasing pressure to make socially responsible decisions even as they comply with legal requirements and generate sufficient profits.
- Corporate social responsibility (CSR) decisions demand new skills: managers must understand not only the responsibilities demanded of all firms, but also the opportunities they introduce.
- While the marketplace does not reward all good deeds, thoughtful strategies can increase the likelihood that firms increase their value while creating positive outcomes for society.
- In this essay, we review the complexity of the issue, the opportunities CSR presents, and one approach to identifying CSR opportunities.

MANAGING IN COMPLEXITY—CIVIL VS STRATEGIC

As business has become increasingly global, the values and principles that guide managers are no longer local. Raw materials from Canada and Indonesia are transformed by manufacturers in India and Brazil under contract to firms in the United States and Germany. Social activists, investors, accountants, workers, politicians, environmentalists, regulators, and customers in each and every location work to influence management's decisions. Normal business practices in one location can be objectionable to customers and investors in other areas, while labor and environmental principles in one region appear to be protectionist to businesses in other regions.[1] Companies would like to do the right thing but seldom have reliable means to choose a direction or level of investment.

For most companies, CSR presents complex problems and great opportunities. CSR allows companies to engage in sophisticated nonmarket strategies that can influence customers, regulators, and employees. It also can reveal firm weaknesses. There are no global laws. There is no single right way. Firms must distinguish the legitimate demands of multiple governments, assess the claims of diverse groups, and identify the significant problems they can best resolve.

WHAT WORKS?

Many researchers have looked for the elusive factor that will turn a firm's good deeds into profits, searching in vain for missing magic. The right answer to the question "Does doing result in doing well?" is "It depends." Firms that select a specific type of social or environmental opportunity consistent with their identity and strategy will reap rewards. Firms which make choices based on the most recent request for help or on a particular manager's enthusiasm will likely not.

The most critical factors in the success of any firm's CSR strategy are not about CSR. A successful CSR strategy builds on basics. First, a firm must be viable in order to create an effective, valuable approach to society and the environment. It is unlikely that a good CSR strategy will reverse bad business decisions. Second, firms must meet their legal and regulatory commitments. Compliance is essential. Enron's ethics policies were widely admired, but the company was nevertheless in violation of the law. Third, firms must meet basic expectations of their industry and the communities in which they operate. A company known for spilling toxic effluent is unlikely to make gains from sponsoring a children's sports team. This sequence of responsibility is illustrated in the CSR value curve IBM has described (Figure 1).

IBM recommends that firms ask their employees, suppliers, and customers what kind of CSR strategy would be optimal. Engagement with these groups helps

Figure 1. CSR value curve. (*Source*: IBM Institute for Business Value)

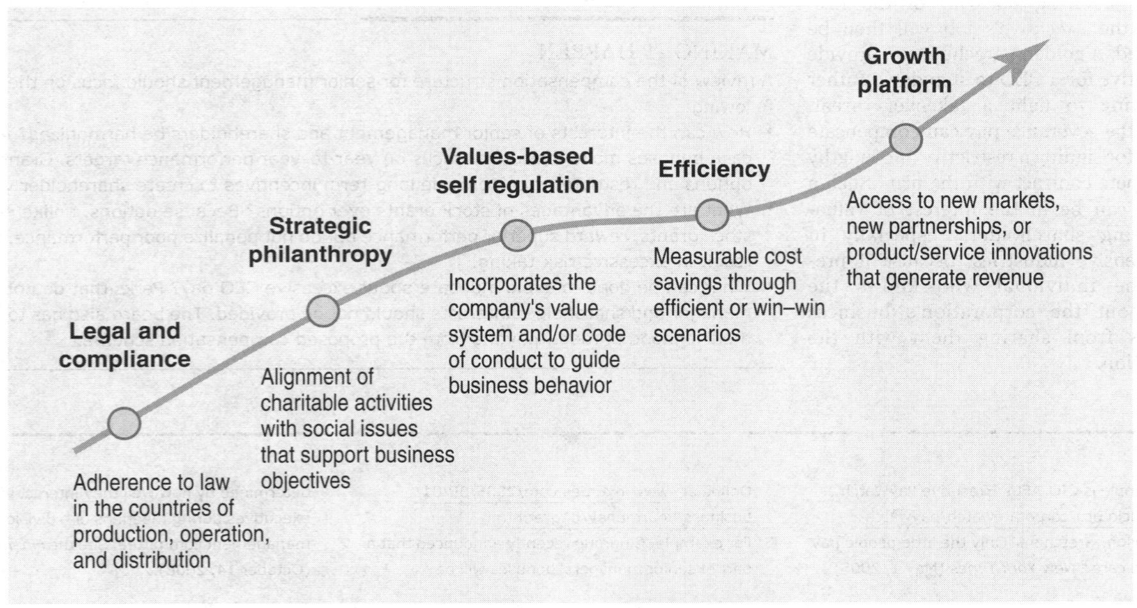
Growth platform
Access to new markets, new partnerships, or product/service innovations that generate revenue
Efficiency
Measurable cost savings through efficient or win–win scenarios
Values-based self regulation
Incorporates the company's value system and/or code of conduct to guide business behavior
Strategic philanthropy
Alignment of charitable activities with social issues that support business objectives
Legal and compliance
Adherence to law in the countries of production, operation, and distribution

"I used to play football . . . you always know the score. Now, we are ice-skating, . . . [with] a bunch of judges shouting out scores." Robert Nardelli

  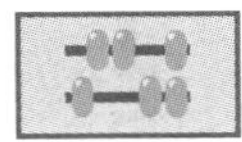      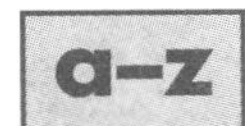

Figure 2. The virtue matrix

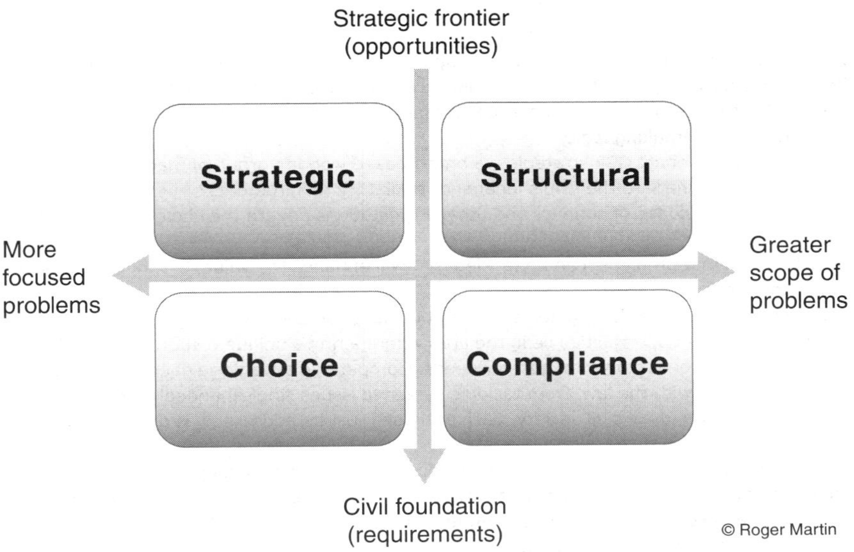

managers identify their best strategies in many settings. The IBM report suggests that consulting these groups will also help identify good CSR strategies. This is consistent with recent economic theory that makes the case for strategic approaches not only to financial gains, but also to social output.[2]

Meeting the demands of disparate social agents disperses the energy and creativity of the firm. Deliberate, strategic choices maximize social effectiveness and firm opportunities.

THE ROLE OF FINANCIAL FIRMS

Financial institutions can choose to play another, powerful role: increasingly often, they determine whether new initiatives carry more social and environmental risks than potential economic benefits.[3] Good analysts will be able to see the ways in which future growth prospects are enhanced or reduced by the social and environmental characteristics of the firms and projects they finance.

Financial analysts and investors now recognize that a firm's ability to work with indigenous people and their property rights is critical to the success of new mineral extraction projects. Corporate finance professionals in companies like Procter & Gamble know that their sustainability principles must be factored into their investment decisions and growth forecasts.[4]

The special role of the financial industry is apparent in the appearance of two CSR codes focused solely on finance. *The Equator Principles* and *Principles for Responsible Investment* both offer guidance to finance professionals who are faced with projects of great potential value and risk. Financial professionals who identify a broader set of risks and rewards will be more effective.

How Would *You* Have Responded?

Imagine that on September 1, 2007 you were one of the following:

- A financial analyst in New York focusing on the global toy industry;
- A banker reviewing loan applications for coating process machinery in Shanghai;
- Plant manager of a coating factory in Guanyao;
- Chief of manufacturing export regulations in Beijing;
- Regional manager of Toys"R"Us retail operations in California;
- Global brand manager of Thomas & Friends Wooden Railway Toys;
- Research director at Al Tawfeek, a leading provider of *shariah*-compliant investment funds.

From the perspective of the person whose position is most similar to yours, first list the strategic opportunities and risks you see in the situation you face. Then consider these issues:

1 What do governments require? Do you need to ensure that these requirements are being met?

CASE STUDY

Thomas the Tank Engine Runs Off the Rails

The spring of 2007 was promising for the global toy industry. In early June 2007, RC2 (RCRC), the manufacturer of Thomas & Friends Wooden Railway Toys, was trading at over $45 per share, the highest level it had ever reached. Mattel's stock also reached historic highs in spring 2007. In May, a trade journal announced that "China's coatings industry is benefiting from the country's thriving consumer goods market, to which it supplies almost 4.5 M tonnes/y of paint... In the electronic and computerized toys segment, coatings suppliers will be hoping to tap the country's 290 M children."[5] Painted toys were a key segment of China's manufacturing sector, and the global demand for colorful, inexpensive toys seemed insatiable.

In 2007, China's manufacturers accounted for approximately 80% of the world market for toys and employed more than 4 million workers.[6] Their business depended on the tight ties in the value chain: the links between consumers, the brands, and their personalities, the toy company giants, the Hong Kong brokers, and the Chinese manufacturers were close and profitable.

Everything changed in mid-June, when RC2 recalled 1.5 million Thomas toys that had been sprayed with lead paint.[8] RC2's share price dipped below $40 on the news. The markets began to discount other toy companies: Mattel dropped from $28 to $26 in June, and eventually to $22. Hasbro went from historic highs of $32 in June 2007 to $28 for the remainder of 2007.

The toys were pulled from shelves throughout Asia, the European Union, Canada, and Australia as well. It was not the first such recall: Of the 24 US recalls earlier in 2007, all were of Chinese manufacture. Once lead had been found in the paint on RC2's Thomas trains, parents, politicians, and retailers began to search through the toy aisles for more. By early August, they had found it. Mattel recalled two batches of toys costing in excess of $30 million.

Chinese and US officials battled over the issue: were there enough safeguards on Chinese exports? Which government was at fault?

The Hong Kong industrialists were devastated. Companies were banned from exporting goods. One toy manufacturer, Cheung Shue Hung, committed suicide.[9] The industry was in disarray from shop floors in Guanyao to retail shelves in Toronto.

Good intentions had failed. In spite of all the safeguards, millions of lead-contaminated toys were sold to families around the world. Toy companies lost millions of dollars of capitalization. Cheung was dead. It was time to move up from good intentions to effective action.

"It is to the advantage of the firm to act in a strategic manner... a strategic focus increases the firm's social output."
Husted Corregan and Salazar

2 What do consumers and other groups expect of businesses in this situation? Does your work meet their expectations?
3 Where are the opportunities for a single firm or brand to gain advantage over its competitors? Can you identify and harness them?
4 Where is there no likelihood of profit but a great likelihood of harm? Is this impossible to resolve by firms that must make profits? Can your organization contribute to a resolution?
5 From your professional standpoint, do you support a market solution based on competitive dynamics? Do you think that voluntary industry codes will work?

Would you support increased regulation? What are the issues here? Why did the Chinese toy debacle happen? Why did the incentives allow this to happen repeatedly? What can prevent its recurrence?

MAKING IT HAPPEN

The Virtue Matrix[10] as an Action Framework

By distinguishing four types of "virtue," companies can approach CSR effectively. When a firm recognizes the specific type of social activity demanded, it can respond optimally. Roger Martin's "virtue matrix" maps out these four kinds of virtue, each of which demands a different decision-making logic.

To identify and enact CSR strategies, a broad-based working group of managers can ask:

- *Compliance:* What are the firm's legal and regulatory requirements?
- *Choice:* Which codes of conduct and other expectations govern the choices of business in this context?
- *Strategic:* What problems can be tackled that will enhance the value, brand, or profits of a specific firm?
- *Structural:* What are the problems that no business can solve alone?

The best business opportunities lie in the area where a firm's unique resources and skills match social and environmental gaps or needs. Competitive advantage does not emerge from compliance with the law, from tackling systemic issues single-handedly, or from meeting the demands of civil society. Each of those must be addressed as distinct ways of doing good.

This need not be a mysterious process. Mapping the demands and opportunities requires environment scanning and research, capacities that businesses use daily. IBM suggests asking employees and suppliers to make recommendations. For most firms, there are likely to be many more opportunities to do good than there is capacity

Having gathered a planning team and a list of options, a firm might then match each idea to a quadrant in the virtue matrix and assign a priority

- Compliance issues are the most straightforward: Noncompliance is too risky for most businesses.
- Choice issues are more complex. What are the social norms? Are there any rankings or indices that give firms information about their competitive position with regard to the issues? What kind of identity does the firm wish to project? What can it afford?
- Structural issues demand the alignment of firms, governments, industries, and/or civil groupings. Each structural problem identified demands the formation of a working group or coalition. A firm can then ask if the potential benefit to a resolution warrants participation in such a group.
- Finally, strategic opportunities can be evaluated for their potential benefit to the reputation, position, or profits of a firm. Their implementation can be assessed through the same processes as are used for other business strategies.

By categorizing each type of CSR, a firm can make better decisions.

MORE INFO

Books:

Crane, Andrew, Abagail McWilliams, Dirk Matten, Jeremy Moon, *et al.* (eds). *The Oxford Handbook of Corporate Social Responsibility*. Oxford: Oxford University Press, 2008.

Kline, John M. *Ethics for International Business: Decision Making in a Global Political Economy*. London: Routledge, 2005.

Prahalad, C. K., Michael E. Porter, and Charles Handy (eds). *Harvard Business Review on Corporate Responsibility*. Boston, MA: Harvard Business School Press, 2003.

Vogel, David. *The Market for Virtue: The Potential and Limits of Corporate Social Responsibility*. Washington, DC: Brookings Institution, 2005.

Websites:

Global organizations

International Finance Corporation on sustainability: www.ifc.org/sustainability

Organisation for Economic Co-operation and Development (OECD): www.oecd.org

United Nations. See especially the United Nations Global Compact, starting here: www.un.org/partners

United Nations Conference on Trade and Development (UNCTAD); search on "ISAR" to find the webpages of the Intergovernmental Working Group of Experts on International Standards of Accounting and Reporting: www.unctad.org

World Bank. The bank's website has many useful resources, including CSR links and

"Sustainability is a business strategy at P&G... integrated into day-to-day business decisions... an important part of how P&G is designed to grow." A. G. Lafley

information on the Inclusive and Sustainable Business Program and Business Fighting Corruption. Search from the home page: www.worldbank.org

Accounting and reporting standards

AA1000: www.accountability.org/standards/

Global Reporting Initiative: www.globalreporting.org

ISO 14000: tinyurl.com/23tamv

Social Accountability 8000 (SA8000): tinyurl.com/4xhlv95

Other sources

Business for Social Responsibility (BSR): www.bsr.org

Equator Principles, a benchmark for the financial industry to manage social and environmental issues in project financing: www.equator-principles.com

Ethical Corporation: www.ethicalcorp.com

Global Reporting Initiative (GRI): www.globalreporting.org

Industry Canada: www.ic.gc.ca

Principles for Responsible Investment (PRI), a UN-based initiative which provides a framework to integrate responsible investment into mainstream decision-making: www.unpri.org

Forum for Sustainable and Responsible Investment (US SIF): ussif.org

Wikipedia on CSR: en.wikipedia.org/wiki/Corporate_social_responsibility

World Business Council on Sustainable Development (WBCSD): www.wbcsd.org

See Also:

★ Business Ethics (pp. 645–647)

★ Corporate Responsibility in a Global World: Marrying Investment in Human Capital with Focus on Costs (pp. 661–663)

★ CSR: More than PR, Pursuing Competitive Advantage in the Long Run (pp. 664–666)

★ Ethical Funds and Socially Responsible Investment: An Overview (pp. 481–483)

★ The Impact of Climate Change on Business (pp. 875–877)

★ Starting a Successful Internal Audit Function to Meet Present and Future Demands (pp. 407–410)

✔ Business Ethics in Islamic Finance (p. 1109)

✔ Creating a Sustainable Development Policy (p. 1113)

✔ The Triple Bottom Line (p. 1125)

NOTES

1 Kline (2005).

2 Husted, B. W., and Jose De Jesus Salazar. "Taking Friedman seriously: Maximizing profits and social performance." *Journal of Management Studies* 43:1 (January 2006): 75–91. Online at: dx.doi.org/10.1111/j.1467-6486.2006.00583.x

3 See the Equator Principles: www.equator-principles.com

4 Procter & Gamble. "P&G 2007 global sustainability report." Online at: tinyurl.com/n7csrg [PDF].

5 "China has enormous potential in paint and coatings for cars, electronics and computerized toys." *ICIS Chemical Business* (May 21, 2007). Online at: tinyurl.com/3qn4qhk

6 Chen, Shu-Ching Jean. "Trapped in the Chinese toy closet." Forbes.com (August 21, 2007). Online at: tinyurl.com/3jg3va5

7 Dee, Jonathan. "A toy maker's conscience." *New York Times* (December 23, 2007): magazine section. Online at: tinyurl.com/2499y4

8 Chen, Shu-Ching Jean. "Subcontractor at heart of Fisher-Price toy recall is apparent suicide." Forbes.com (August 13, 2007). Online at: tinyurl.com/44lumrb

9 *Ibid.* 2007.

10 Martin, Roger L. "The virtue matrix: Calculating the return on corporate responsibility." *Harvard Business Review* 80:3 (March 2002): 68–75. Online at: tinyurl.com/43lgcvx

"I'll tell you what leadership is. It's persuasion and conciliation, and education, and patience." Dwight David Eisenhower

  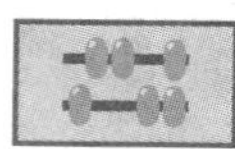      

Best Practices in Investment Governance for Pension Funds by Roger Urwin

EXECUTIVE SUMMARY

- This article demonstrates the influence of governance by institutional fund asset owners on their performance.
- Using examples from across the whole spectrum of institutional funds by type and geography, we illustrate the principles and practice of good governance.
- A number of lessons can be learned from our examples, and we boil these down to a set of 12 findings about global best practice.
- We suggest best-practice models for funds that employ significant investment staff and a separate model for those funds whose decision-taking is done by boards and investment committees.
- We conclude that funds tend to perform better when they correctly assess their governance and determine their investment strategy commensurate with their capabilities. Although there are ways to adapt the governance budget over time, with implications for likely investment performance and pay-offs, there is currently an unpreparedness in the industry to consider in-house resources as anything other than highly visible "costs," whereas external spending on managers and transactions costs tend to be seen as "performance benefits." This has always seemed like a case of tortured logic and a false economy.
- It is only at the high end of this spectrum that we see funds succeeding with the challenges of running complex multi-asset and multi-manager program.

INTRODUCTION

There is increasing evidence to support a link between superior investment performance and an institutional investor's strong governance. Recent research conducted jointly by the author and Gordon Clark of Oxford University, entitled "Best-practice investment management: Lessons for asset owners," further clarified this link and identified 12 best-practice factors as being indicative of future success in meeting institutional goals.

The research focused on 10 of the top institutional funds around the world. All had made the move up from being seen as 'good' in their field to something close to 'great' by committing passion and excellence to their mission through their governance structure. If there is one marker of this excellence, it seems to lie in having a strong investment leader or CIO on the staff, but sadly most funds don't take this step.

Many pension funds are beginning to realize that their governance arrangement should be a top priority, not only through responsibility to literally billions of individuals, but also because it creates an opportunity for wealth creation. At the same time, it is important to point out that while strong governance (with "governance" defined quite broadly as *all the resources applied to investment decision-making*) is hugely important in institutional investment, it is a very difficult area to get right, with only the most conscientious and gifted succeeding in all areas. Among this number are some prominent institutional investment funds that made the right sort of strides with their governance arrangements and have successfully shown the world that very good performance can come from those strides.

For a long time governance has been seen simply as a constraint. Funds have learned to simply get by without being adequately resourced. However, the investment world has now changed irrevocably, and the last 10 years have added more complexity than any period in history. Greater regulation, product proliferation, and much competition for effective investment strategies and products have complicated the sorts of decisions that funds have to face. Among the critical issues to be faced are: how much risk, what types of risk, what types of return (absolute or relative); what types of strategy (mainstream or alternatives), beta or alpha. But, stepping back, the managers of institutional funds must first deal with a higher-level question: how much time and resource should be committed to governance, and how should this effort be organized?

According to our research, only a minority of pension funds worldwide have investment strategies and governance arrangements that are aligned. The research shows that the more common misalignment is to be overambitious in their investment structures, introducing too much complexity for their governance to cope with.

THREE TYPES OF GOVERNANCE

As a simple step, we consider three types of governance arrangements (grouped by the size of their governance budget) and then suggest investment arrangements that are aligned and can be implemented with confidence and good outcomes. Governance budget is defined as a combination of time, expertise, and organizational effectiveness of the decision-makers.

Limited governance budget: The *cost minimizer*—compatible with the lowest governance resources—is a set of arrangements that manage down all costs and focus on easily available investment returns. Being the least sophisticated investment strategy, it would have only bonds and equities and use mainly passive managers.

Mid-range governance budget: The *diversity seeker*—with greater governance available, the fund can pursue more value creation opportunities. The focus would be mainly on improving market exposure diversity outside equities and bonds. Generally these arrangements would again not contain large exposures to active management, simply because alpha is the hardest part of the investment spectrum to create value from.

Advanced governance budget: The *diversity and skill exploiter*—with very strong governance, the arrangements would major on diversification, but also include a significant amount of risk in active manager structures. There is greater emphasis on identifying manager skill opportunities, including ones where the market return and the active manager return are difficult to separate, as is the case with many absolute return products.

We acknowledge that in practice funds may not find it easy to position themselves this way. Most have taken their different investment strategy routes by reference to a peer group mentality that has established one institutional norm, rather than by reference to governance budgets. This needs to change, and indeed there are some positive signs that this is occurring.

Research Findings on the Relation between Governance and Fund Performance

One of these is the growing body of research showing a clear link between superior performance and strong governance, particularly among larger funds. It is perhaps not surprising that the best-governed funds tend to perform better than averagely governed funds. While quantitative data on the precise size of the "bad–good governance gap" is relatively scarce, in the *Ambachtsheer Letter* of June 2006,

"Here lies one who knew how to get around him men who were cleverer than himself." Andrew Carnegie

Keith Ambachtsheer uses estimates from his database research that the gap has been worth 1–2% of additional return per annum.[1]

We have also recently undertaken our own research (in combination with Oxford University) into actual practice at top funds around the world. The research, entitled "Best-practice investment management: lessons for asset owners,"[2] involved case studies on 10 funds across the world that were cherry-picked for their exceptional reputation and strong sustained performance. The 10 comprise six pension funds, two endowments, and two sovereign funds, located in North America (five funds), Europe (three funds) and Asia–Pacific (two funds), and they are all large in terms of assets, ranging from around US$5 billion to well over US$50 billion.

The study identified five main areas of critical significance to institutional funds where these funds excel, namely: risk management; time–horizon focus on the long term; innovative capabilities; clarity of mission; and effective management of external fund managers and other agents. However, even these funds with exceptionally strong governance capabilities find it difficult to overcome certain constraints. The research shows that the most common constraints are inherited regulations and systems of control, and the competing claims of multiple stakeholders. In addition, it shows that there is an unpreparedness in the industry to consider in-house resources as anything other than highly visible "costs," whereas external spending on managers and transactions costs tend to be seen as "performance benefits." This has always seemed like an extreme case of tortured logic.

The central finding of the research was in isolating 12 best-practice factors as being indicative of future success in meeting institutional goals. Six of these are assessed as being within the reach of most institutional funds, and are called "core attributes;" they are: mission clarity; effective focusing of time; investment committee leadership; strong beliefs; risk budgeting framework; and a fit-for-purpose manager line-up.

Six further global best-practice factors were isolated in the research and described as requiring significant resources, including an executive team, usually with a CIO. The research suggests that these "exceptional attributes" are not easy for most funds to achieve. They are: a highly competent investment executive; high-level board competencies; supportive compensation; real-time decision-making; the ability to exploit competitive advantage; and learning organization.

In terms of structure, leading funds tend to split the key functions between a board, which governs, and an executive, which implements and manages. The board also appoints and supervises the CIO. In terms of people, the CIO will tend to have a very high degree of investment expertise and be supported by strong researchers. Process-wise, leading funds are extremely skilled at maximizing any sustainable comparative advantage they have over competing funds, and tend to have impressively efficient decision-making structures.

Aside from societal responsibility, the potential return advantage should be a strong motivator among pension funds to

MAKING IT HAPPEN

The 12 governance factors associated with organizational effectiveness are:

Core Attributes

- mission clarity
- effective focusing of time
- investment committee leadership
- strong beliefs
- a risk budgeting framework
- fit-for-purpose manager line-up

Exceptional Attributes

- highly competent investment executive
- high-level board competencies
- supportive compensation
- real-time decision-making
- ability to exploit competitive advantage
- a learning organization

The six exceptional best-practice attributes differentiate what one might call the "great" funds from the rest.

- **Investment executive**: The merits of separating governance into a governing function, which sets the framework, monitors, and controls, and an executive function, which makes the decisions within the given framework and implements them cannot be understated. Not only does this improve efficiency and accountability, but it also allows for the concentration of investment expertise within the executive function. Best-practice funds adopt a clear separation of governing and executive functions, with a strong culture of accountability. Furthermore, the executive function has a high level of investment competency, enabling the funds to implement and monitor complex investment arrangements.
- **Board selection and competence**: Sound investment competencies are also observed at the board level of best-practice funds. Board members ideally have strong numeric skills and the ability to think logically within a probability-based domain, such skills enabling the board to function effectively in its long-horizon mission.
- **Supportive compensation**: Leading funds address this at both the board and executive level, with some success at using compensation to attract appropriate skills and align actions to the goals of the fund. Current practice among funds in general appears to result in significantly more being paid to external agents. There is scope to address this imbalance through greater use of internal resources—an approach that is becoming more widely adopted.
- **Competitive advantage**: Investment is a highly competitive activity, and, for funds to succeed, they need to be aware of their competitive advantages and disadvantages and adapt their decision-making accordingly. Much of their competitive advantage will be built on a sound belief structure, but will also maximize their own particular areas of competence. It is equally important that funds should be aware of areas where they have no expertise, and seek to limit their strategy accordingly.
- **Real-time decisions**: Most funds are geared toward making decisions around a calendar-based series of meetings. Best-practice funds, however, tend to have processes in place that enable decisions to be taken as and when necessary, based on investment market conditions. Making such a change from calendar to real-time focus involves more delegation and a clear definition of responsibilities.
- **Learning organization**: Best-practice funds tend to be innovative. To be successful they need to operate in a culture that learns from experience. They also need to be willing to challenge conventional wisdom and deal enthusiastically with change.

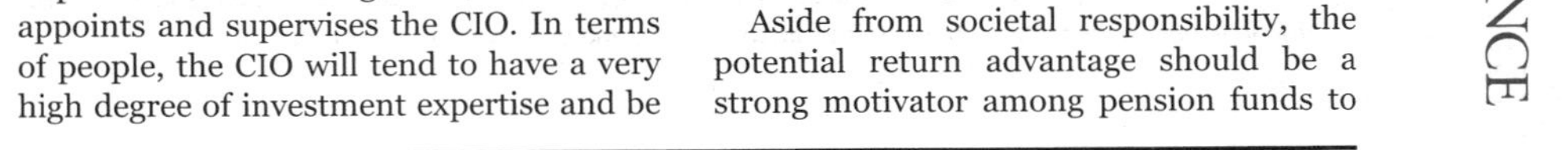

  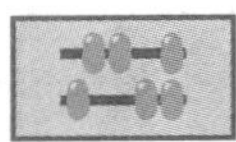   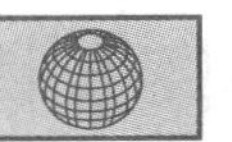   

improve governance and then align it with investment strategy. However, it is clear that for many funds the "governance gap"—insufficient governance for the complexity of the investment strategy pursued—is widening because a lack of focus on these core attributes coincides with the greater complexity of prime investment opportunities. Some investors will see merit in improving their governance arrangements by increasing the time they spend on investment issues, adding expertise, and rethinking their organizational structures. However, it is unrealistic to suppose that all pension funds can improve their arrangements to such an extent that they become high-governance funds.

As such, governance is likely to become one of the bigger polarizing factors among pension funds, which would indeed be a welcome development.

To conclude, I find strong evidence that investment success and value creation are driven by the quality of the decision-making involved. It follows that there should be a much stronger link between governance and investment strategy. The potential to destroy value through unsuitable investment strategies can be significantly reduced if pension fund trustees are honest with themselves about their governance capabilities in the first instance. And if funds can start to treat governance as a variable and not a constraint, and make some moves in the direction of best practice, things could look altogether brighter for their considerable numbers of stakeholders. We are living in a period of extreme investment conditions. Such times reinforce the idea that we should give more attention to the governance factor.

MORE INFO

Articles:

Ambachtsheer, Keith. "How much is good governance worth?" *Ambachtsheer Letter* 245 (June 2006). Online at: www.kpa-advisory.com/ambachtsheer.htm

Ambachtsheer, Keith, Ronald Capelle, and Tom Scheibelhut. "Improving pension fund performance." *Financial Analysts Journal* (November/December 1998): 15–21.

Reports:

Clark, Gordon L., and Roger Urwin. "Best-practice investment management: Lessons for asset owners from the Oxford–Watson Wyatt project on governance." White paper, October 2007.

Watson Wyatt and Oxford University. "Best-practice investment governance: 'Good to great' opportunities. Case study research by Watson Wyatt and Oxford University on governance and investment capabilities." Slide-show presentation.

See Also:

★ Best Practices in Risk-Based Internal Auditing (pp. 303–305)
★ Boardroom Roles (pp. 643–644)
★ Internal Audit and Partnering with Senior Management (pp. 368–371)
✔ Corporate Governance and Its Interpretations (p. 1111)
✔ Directors' Duties: A Primer (p. 1117)

NOTES

1 See "How much is good governance worth?" *The Ambachtsheer Letter* (June 2006). For additional evidence in this area, see Ambachtsheer, Capelle, and Scheibelhut (1998).

2 Clark and Urwin (2007).

"Most people in big companies are administered, not led. They are treated as personnel, not people." Robert Townsend

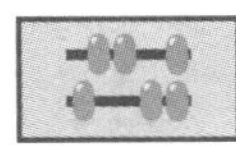

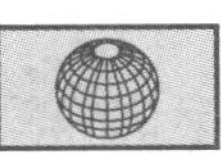

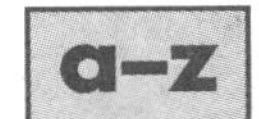

Boardroom Roles by Sir Adrian Cadbury

EXECUTIVE SUMMARY

- The role of the board is to direct, not to manage.
- Balance of board membership and choice of individuals are key.
- Chairmen are responsible for the effectiveness of their boards.
- Nonexecutive directors have a particular contribution to make to the work of a board.
- Board committees are important structurally and for the tasks they undertake.
- Executive directors should be appointed solely for the value they can add to the board.
- Board members have different roles; what matters is how they combine to form the board team.

THE ROLE OF THE BOARD

The crispest definition of a board's role is Sir John Harvey-Jones's: *"to create tomorrow's company out of today's."* Boards are in place to direct and control, not to manage. Boards have the task of defining the purpose of their enterprises and of agreeing the strategy for achieving that purpose. They are responsible for appointing chief executives to turn strategic plans into action, for supporting and counseling them in so doing, and if necessary for replacing them. Above all, boards are there to provide leadership, and it is in that context that the roles of board members need to be considered.

BOARD COMPOSITION

A single board at the head of a company is the commonest form of board structure. Unitary boards of this nature are made up of executive and nonexecutive or outside directors. Two-tier boards separate these two kinds of director, and their structure is covered briefly in the next section. Given that both executive and outside directors sit on unitary boards, the first issue is the balance between them. In the United States the chief executive is often the only executive on the board, and is usually its chairman as well. Fifteen years ago the ratio on UK boards was around two-thirds executive directors and one-third outside directors. This has now moved through parity to the position where outside directors are in the majority.

The Combined Code on Corporate Governance,[1] in provision A.3.2, states: *"Except for smaller companies, at least half the board, excluding the chairman, should comprise non-executive directors determined by the board to be independent. A smaller company should have at least two independent non-executive directors."* The issue of independence is dealt with under the heading of the Role of Non-Executive Directors.

In addition to the question of balance, there is the question of size. There is a clear move to smaller boards, both in Britain and the United States. Martin Lipton and Jay W. Lorsch, in their "Modest proposal for improved corporate governance" (*Business Lawyer* vol. 48, no. 1, Nov. 1992), recommend a maximum board size of ten and favor eight or nine. The argument for smaller boards is that they enable all the directors to get to know each other and to contribute effectively in board discussions, thus arriving at a true consensus. The crucial point is that boards are teams and provide collective leadership. So the balance of membership and choice of individuals are key to forming the team.

TWO-TIER BOARDS

These boards are constituted of a supervisory board whose members are all nonexecutive and a management board made up of executive directors. The management board is responsible for strategy as well as for running the business. The supervisory board appoints and can dismiss the management board, and no one can be on both boards. The legal responsibilities of the two boards and of their directors are different, whereas with a unitary board all directors have the same legal duties however the board is structured.

Since supervisory boards may have employee members, this raises the question of their role on boards.[2] My own view is that employees can most effectively participate at levels below the board, where the decisions are taken that affect them most directly and to which they can contribute knowledgeably.

THE CHAIRMAN'S ROLE

Chairmen are responsible for the effectiveness of their boards. This responsibility rests with chairmen whatever their other duties. It leads on to the point that all companies are different and the issues they face are constantly changing. Individual boards have to follow accepted board principles, but in ways which meet their particular circumstances. It is chairmen who have the responsibility of ensuring that the make-up of their boards is appropriate for the challenges ahead. Similarly, it is chairmen who have the task of welding their directors into an effective team. Effective boards are not brought into being simply by sitting competent individuals around a board table. Creating effective boards requires effort by their members, but above all coaching and leadership by their chairmen. This is an argument for chairmen not also being chief executives.

Chairmen are responsible for the running of their boards. Their responsibilities include the agenda, the provision of adequate and timely information to all directors, and the actual conduct of board meetings. They are also, provided they are not chief executives, responsible for putting in place a means by which their boards can evaluate their own performance.

Where chairmen are also chief executives, their duties in relation to their boards remain the same, but the senior independent nonexecutive director would be responsible for the appraisal of the chief executive and for the review of the board's performance.

ROLE OF NONEXECUTIVE DIRECTORS

All directors are equal in that they all carry the same legal responsibilities. Outside or nonexecutive directors are in that sense no different from their executive colleagues. They do, however, have particular contributions to make to their boards by virtue of standing further back from the business. One is in reviewing the performance of the chief executive and of the executive team; clearly the outside directors are the only board members in a position to do this objectively.

Another is in relation to potential conflicts of interest, such as those between the interests of the executives and those of the shareholders. Examples are directors' pay, dividends versus re-investment, and whether top appointments should be made from within or from outside the company. Decisions on these matters are ultimately decisions of the whole board, but the outside directors are well-placed to give a lead over where the best interests of the company—to which all directors owe their duty—lie.

Outside directors bring with them their experience in fields which are different from those of the executive directors, and this external experience is of particular value in the formulation of strategy. The potential advantage which the unitary board has over the two-tier board is that it provides the

"No other area offers richer opportunities for successful innovation than the unexpected success." Peter F. Drucker

opportunity to combine, in the same body, the depth of knowledge of the business of the executives with the breadth of knowledge of the outside directors. Once again, it is up to chairmen to make the most of these different viewpoints by the way they structure board debates.

The role of outside directors in helping to resolve conflicts of interest does not imply that they have higher ethical standards than their executive colleagues. The difference is simply that they can judge these matters more objectively because their interests are less directly involved. Not all nonexecutive directors are considered independent. The Combined Code, provision A.3.1, states: *"The board should identify in the annual report each non-executive director it considers to be independent. The board should determine whether the director is independent in character and judgement and whether there are relationships or circumstances which are likely to affect, or could appear to affect, the director's judgement."* Nonexecutive directors who do not meet these tests may be valued board members in their own right, but they cannot be classed as independent.

Another provision of the Combined Code, A.3.3, requires that boards *"Should appoint one of the independent non-executive directors to be the senior independent director. The senior independent director should be available to shareholders if they have concerns which contact through the normal channels of chairman, chief executive or finance director has failed to resolve or for which such contact is inappropriate."*

ROLE OF BOARD COMMITTEES

As the responsibilities of directors have become more demanding, boards have increasingly formed committees to deal with some of their more detailed work. The Combined Code requires all quoted companies to establish audit and remuneration committees and, unless they have a small board, nomination committees. These committees strengthen the position of the nonexecutive directors, of whom they are made up, and are important for the work they do. The essential point is that they are committees of the board. It is the board which appoints them, sets their terms of reference, and turns their recommendations into decisions.

ROLE OF EXECUTIVE DIRECTORS

The duties of executive directors are the same as those of the nonexecutive directors. They are as responsible for the monitoring task of the board as the nonexecutive directors, who in turn are as responsible for the strategy and leadership of the company as the executives. This means that executive directors have to take their executive hats off on entering the boardroom and put on their directorial ones. They should only be appointed for the contribution they can make to the board, and they are there to further the company's interests, not those of their function or department. It is not an easy transition to make, and executive directors can be helped to adopt their new governance role through appropriate training or through a nonexecutive directorship elsewhere.

ROLE OF THE COMPANY SECRETARY

Chairmen and board members should be able to look to the company secretary for impartial and professional guidance on their responsibilities, and all directors should have access to the advice and services of a company secretary, who is responsible for ensuring that board procedures are followed.

CONCLUSION

Although board members have different roles, what counts is the way those roles are combined in the board team. This is why board selection is so fundamental. Directors should only be appointed for the value they can add to their boards. All directors should have terms of office to enable renewal to take place, although I am personally against rigid rules tying retirement to age or length of board service, preferring to rely on the judgement of boards and their shareholders.

The search for nonexecutive directors should be purposeful, with the aim of filling gaps in the experience and backgrounds of the existing directors, and their selection should involve the board as a whole. Chairmen, however, have a particular responsibility for the choice of board members since it is they who have to turn them into an effective team.

MORE INFO

Books:

Carver, John. *John Carver on Board Leadership*. San Francisco, CA: Jossey-Bass, 2002.

Charkham, Jonathan. *Keeping Better Company: Corporate Governance Ten Years On*. 2nd ed. Oxford: Oxford University Press, 2005.

Harvey-Jones, John. *Making It Happen: Reflections on Leadership*. London: Profile Books, 2003.

See Also:

★ Identifying the Right Nonexecutive Director (pp. 682–684)
★ Viewpoint: Lessons from the Credit Crisis: Governing Financial Institutions (pp. 694–695)
✔ The Board's Role in Executive Compensation (p. 1108)
✔ Creating Executive Compensation (p. 1114)
✔ Directors' Duties: A Primer (p. 1117)
✔ Regulatory Responsibilities of Executive and Nonexecutive Directors: An International Overview (p. 1121)
Arnold, Lord Weinstock (p. 1317)

NOTES

1 The Combined Code on Corporate Governance was published by the London Stock Exchange in July 2003; it includes Guidance on Internal Control and on Audit Committees and Suggestions for Good Practice from the Higgs Report. Companies listed on the London Stock Exchange are required to disclose how far they comply with the Code as a condition of listing. The latest version was published in June 2008 by the Financial Reporting Council, which is now responsible for the Combined Code, but it does not include the Turnbull and Smith guidance.

2 Although the supervisory boards of German companies above a certain size include employee members, Dutch supervisory boards, for example, do not.

"I get many invitations but I only join the boards of companies where I admire the management and believe in the company." Jill Ker Conway

Business Ethics by Sue Newell

EXECUTIVE SUMMARY

- Business ethics focuses on identifying the moral standards of right and wrong as they apply to behavior within and across business institutions and other related organizations.
- Corporations sometimes behave unethically, having a harmful effect on people or the environment.
- Unethical behavior is typically not caused by a single "bad apple," but is a result of complex interactions between individuals, groups, and organizational cultures.
- Ethical behavior can be defined either as behavior that maximizes happiness and minimizes harm or as behavior that is motivated by principles of duty.
- While behaving unethically may have some short-term benefit for a company, in the long term it will harm stakeholder support.
- Long-term sustainability comes from concentrating on the *triple bottom line*: that is, social, environmental, and financial performance (Elkington, 1998).

INTRODUCTION

Look in the newspaper on virtually any day of the week and you will find at least one business scandal in which a corporation appears to have violated the rules or standards of behavior generally accepted by society. Company finances have been manipulated in order to show a better balance sheet than actually exists, toxic waste has been allowed to flow into a river, bribes have been paid to secure a business deal, child labor has been used to assemble a product, discriminatory practices have prevented the employment or promotion of members of a particular group. When businesses behave unethically, they act in ways that have a harmful effect on others and in ways that are morally unacceptable to the larger community. This is very serious because corporate power and impact are increasing as corporations become larger (indeed, global) and as profit-making concerns take over functions that were once publicly controlled, such as the railroads, water utilities, and healthcare. Increasingly, it is the private sector that determines the quality of the air we breathe, the water we drink, our standard of living, and even where we live and how easily we can move around.

COMMON ETHICAL PROBLEMS WITHIN CORPORATIONS

Given the increasing social impact of business, business ethics has emerged as a discrete subject over the last 20 years. Business ethics is concerned with exploring the moral principles by which we can evaluate business organizations in relation to their impact on people and the environment. Trevino and Nelson (2004) categorize four types of ethical problems that are commonly found in business organizations.

First are the *human resource problems*: These relate to the equitable and just treatment of current and potential employees. Unethical behavior here involves treating people unfairly because of their gender, sexuality, skin color, religion, ethnic background, and so on.

Second are ethical problems arising from *conflicts of interest*, when particular individuals or organizations are given special treatment because of some personal relationship with the individual or group making a decision. A company might get a lucrative contract, for example, because a bribe was paid to the management team of the contracting organization, not because of the quality of its proposal.

Third are ethical problems that involve *customer confidence*. Corporations sometimes behave in ways that show a lack of respect for customers or a lack of concern with public safety. Examples here include advertisements that lie (or at least conceal the truth) about particular goods or services, and the sale of products, such as drugs, where a company conceals or obfuscates negative data about safety and/or efficacy.

Finally, there are ethical problems surrounding the *use of corporate resources* by employees who make private phone calls at work, submit false expense claims, take company stationery home, etc.

The financial scandals that have rocked the corporate world in recent years (Enron, WorldCom, Parmalat, Lehman Brothers, for example) have involved a number of these different ethical issues. In these cases, senior managers have engaged in improper bookkeeping, making companies look more financially profitable than they actually are. As a consequence the stockholder value of the company increases, and anyone with stock profits directly. Among those profiting will be those making the decisions to manipulate the accounts—and so there is a conflict of interest. However, the fallout from the downfall of these companies affects stockholders, employees, and society at large negatively, with innocent people losing their retirement reserves and/or savings, and employees losing their jobs.

Another category can be added to this list—ethical problems surrounding the *use of the world's environmental resources*. Many organizations have externalized the costs associated with their negative impact on the environment, whether in relation to their own operations to produce goods and services, or in terms of the use and later the disposal of the goods that they have sold. Externalizing means that organizations do not themselves pay for the environmental costs that they create. For example, carbon dioxide emissions, a by-product of energy use for all kinds of organizations, are now recognized as contributing to global warming; computer equipment contains toxic waste that pollutes the land where it is dumped; and packaging of all kinds, including plastic bags that are handed out by supermarkets, are creating mounting problems as local authorities run out of landfill sites. Increasingly, ethical business is seen to require that a business takes into account and offsets its "environmental footprint" so that it engages in sustainable activity. Sustainability broadly means that a business meets the needs of the present without compromising the ability of future generations to meet their needs.

ACCOUNTING FOR ETHICAL AND UNETHICAL BEHAVIOR

While it may be very easy to identify and blame an individual or small group of individuals, to see these individuals as the perpetrators of an unethical act—the "bad apple"—and hold them responsible for the harm caused, is an oversimplification. Most accounts of unethical behavior that are restricted to the level of the individual are inadequate. Despite popular belief, decisions harmful to others or the environment that are made within organizations are not typically the result of an isolated, immoral individual seeking to gain personally. Although an individual's level of moral maturity or the locus of control (for example, the degree to which they perceive they control their behaviors and actions) are factors, we also need to explore the decision-making context—the group dynamics and the organizational practices and procedures—to understand why an unethical decision was made.

Group dynamics influence the decision-making process. A particularly important group-level influence is *groupthink*, a phenomenon identified by Irving Janis (1982) in his research on US foreign policy groups. The research demonstrates the presence of strong pressures towards conformity in these groups: individual members suspend their own critical judgment and right to question, with the result that they make bad and/or immoral decisions. Janis defines groupthink as "the psychological drive for consensus at any cost that suppresses dissent and appraisal of alternatives in cohesive decision-making groups."

The degree to which decisions are ethical is also influenced by organizational culture or climate. Organizational ethical climates can differ; some are more egoistic, others are more benevolent, still others are highly principled, and these contexts can shape a manager's ethical decision-making. Smith and Johnson (1996) identify three general approaches that organizations take to corporate responsibility:

- **Social obligation**: The corporation does only what is legally required.
- **Social responsiveness**: The corporation responds to pressure from different stakeholder groups.
- **Social responsibility**: The corporation has an agenda of proactively trying to improve society.

In a company in which the dominant approach to business ethics is social obligation, it is likely to be difficult to justify a decision based on ethical criteria; morally irresponsible behavior may be condoned as long as it does not break the law. Legal loopholes, for example, may be exploited in such a company if these can benefit the company in the short term, even if they might have a negative influence on others in society.

ETHICAL DILEMMAS

Sometimes it is clear that a business has behaved unethically—for example, where a drug is sold illegally, the company accounts have been falsely presented, or where client funds have been embezzled. Of more interest, and much more common, are situations that pose an ethical dilemma—situations that present a conflict between right and wrong or between values and obligations—so that a choice is necessary. For example, a corporation may want to build a new factory on a previously undeveloped and popular tourist site in a location where there is large-scale unemployment among the local population. Here we have a conflict between the benefits of wealth and job creation in a location in which these are crucial and the cost of spoiling some naturally beautiful countryside. Philosophers have attempted to develop prescriptive theories providing universal laws that enable us to differentiate between right and wrong, and good and bad, in these situations.

PRESCRIPTIVE ETHICAL THEORIES

Essentially there are two schools of thought. The consequentialists argue that behavior is ethical if it maximizes the common good (happiness) and minimizes harm. The opposing nonconsequentialists argue that behavior is ethical if it is motivated by a sense of duty or a set of moral principles about human conduct—regardless of the consequences of the action.

Consequentialist Accounts of Ethical Behavior

Philosophers who adopt the consequentialist approach (sometimes also referred to as utilitarianism) consider that behavior can be judged ethical if it has been enacted in order to maximize human happiness and minimize harm. Jeremy Bentham (1748–1832) and John Stuart Mill (1806–73) are two of the best-known early proponents of this view. Importantly it is the common good, not personal happiness, that is the arbiter of right and wrong. Indeed, we are required to sacrifice our personal happiness if doing so enhances the total sum of happiness. For someone faced with a decision choice, the ethical action is the one that achieves the greatest good for the greatest number of people after weighing the impact on those involved. Common criticisms of this approach are that it is impossible to measure happiness adequately and that it essentially condones injustice if this is to the benefit of the majority.

Nonconsequentialist Accounts of Ethical Behavior

Philosophers who adopt a nonconsequentialist approach (also referred to as deontological theory) argue that behavior can be judged as ethical if it is based on a sense of duty and carried out in accordance with defined principles. Immanuel Kant (1724–1804), for example, articulated the principle of *respect for persons*, which states that people should never be treated as a means to an end, but always as an end in themselves; leading to the easy to remember maxim – do as you would be done by. The idea here is that we can establish moral judgments that are true because they can be based on the unique human ability to reason. One common criticism of this approach is that it is impossible to agree on the basic ethical principles of duty or their relative weighting in order to direct choices when multiple ethical principles are called into question at the same time, or when decisions cut across cultures with different ethical principles.

WHY BEHAVING ETHICALLY IS IMPORTANT FOR BUSINESS

Choosing to be ethical can involve short-term disadvantages for a corporation. Yet in the long term it is clear that behaving ethically is the key to sustainable development. When you're faced with an ethical dilemma in which the immoral choice looks appealing, ask yourself three questions:

1 **What will happen when (not if) the action is discovered?** Increasingly, the behavior of corporations is under scrutiny from their various stakeholders—customers, suppliers, stockholders, employees, competitors, regulators, environmental groups, and the general public. People are less willing

MAKING IT HAPPEN

While the two approaches to evaluating behavior described above are clearly different, they can be integrated to create a checklist that will help an individual or group make sound ethical decisions.

- Gather the facts: What is the problem, and what are the potential solutions?
- Define the ethical issues. This is a step that is often neglected, so that the ethical dilemmas raised by a particular decision are never even considered.
- Identify the various stakeholders involved.
- Think through the consequences of each solution: What happiness or harm will be caused?
- Identify the obligations and rights of those potentially affected: What is my duty here? Can I uphold my duty to avoid doing harm and make reasonable efforts toward that end?
- Check your gut feeling.

The last step is crucial. Those involved need to ask themselves what they would feel like if friends or family found out they had been involved in making a particular corporate decision, whether personally or collectively.

to keep quiet when they feel an injustice has been done, and the internet and other media give them the means to make their concerns very public, reaching a global audience. Corporations that behave unethically are unlikely to get away with it, and the impact when they are discovered can be catastrophic. This leads to the second question.

2 **Is the decision really in the long-term interests of the corporation?** Many financial services companies in the United Kingdom generated short-term profits in the 1990s by miss selling personal pensions to people who would have been better off staying in their company's pension plan. However, in the long term these companies have suffered by having to repay this money and pay penalties. Most significantly, the practice has eroded public confidence. The same is true of many banks and mortgage brokers in the first part of the 21st century when they sold mortgages to individuals who could not afford to repay their debts. The eventual result was that large numbers defaulted, causing a meltdown in the global financial system beginning in 2008.

3 **Will organizations that behave unethically attract the employees they need?** Corporations that harm society or the environment are actually harming their own employees, including those who are making the decisions. For example, corporations that pour toxins into the air are polluting the air their employees' families breathe. Ultimately, a business relies on its human resources. If a company cannot attract high-quality people because it has a poor public image based on previous unethical behavior, it will certainly flounder.

Behaving ethically is clearly key to the long-term sustainability of any business. Focusing on the triple bottom line—the social and environmental as well as the economic impact of a company—provides the basis for sound stakeholder relationships that can sustain a business into the future.

MORE INFO

Books:

Elkington, John. *Cannibals with Forks: The Triple Bottom Line of 21st Century Business*. Gabriola Island, BC: New Society Publishers, 1998.

Janis, Irving L. *Groupthink: Psychological Studies of Policy Decisions and Fiascoes*. 2nd ed. Boston, MA: Houghton Mifflin College, 1982.

Smith, Ken G., and Phil Johnson. *Business Ethics and Business Behaviour*. Boston, MA: International Thomson Business Press, 1996.

Trevino, Linda K., and Katherine A. Nelson. *Managing Business Ethics: Straight Talk About How to Do It Right*. New York: Wiley, 2004.

Velasquez, M. *Business Ethics: Concepts and Cases*. 6th ed. Upper Saddle River, NJ: Prentice Hall, 2006.

Websites:

Aspen Institute: www.aspeninstitute.org
Bentley University Center for Business Ethics: www.bentley.edu/cbe/about
Business in Society Gateway: www.businessinsociety.eu
Institute of Business Ethics: www.ibe.org.uk
International Business Ethics Institute: www.business-ethics.org

See Also:

★ Best Practices in Corporate Social Responsibility (pp. 636–639)
★ CSR: More than PR, Pursuing Competitive Advantage in the Long Run (pp. 664–666)
★ Ethical Funds and Socially Responsible Investment: An Overview (pp. 481–483)
★ The Impact of Climate Change on Business (pp. 875–877)
✔ Business Ethics in Islamic Finance (p. 1109)
✔ The Triple Bottom Line (p. 1125)
Ernst Friedrich Schumacher (p. 1307)

  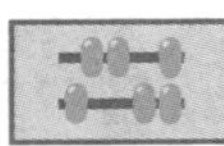   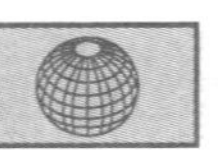   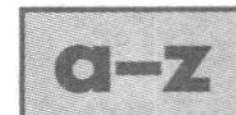

Viewpoint: The Companies Bill, 2012, and its Impact on the Future of Corporate Social Responsibility in India by Sudhir Singh Dungarpur

INTRODUCTION

Sudhir Singh Dungarpur is partner and head of the development sector practice at KPMG in India. He has over 18 years' global experience working in both start-ups and large multinational corporations in the areas of technology, education, and consulting. Sudhir's strength lies in developing new businesses and he has successfully built new divisions and businesses in highly competitive environments. Building strong relationships and networks, a clear control on market dynamics, and creating the best teams has ensured that Sudhir has delivered consistent results in growth, revenue, operational performance, and profitability.

BACKGROUND TO THE INDIA COMPANIES BILL, 2012

The peril of socio-economic inequality has become an urgent priority in India, especially over the last decade. Inequalities vary from region to region, between rural and urban populations, between social and ethnic groups, and most obviously between the rich and the poor. It is in recognition of these challenges that the Indian government has repeatedly articulated its commitment towards "inclusive growth." There has also been a widespread recognition that critical to the push towards "inclusive growth" is the participation of a wide range of stakeholders in designing, financing, implementing, and evaluating development interventions.

With the Companies Bill, 2012, passed in the Lok Sabha in December 2012, discussions on its impact on corporate India have been gathering steam. The Companies Bill states that companies with a specified net worth, or turnover, or net profit during any financial year shall constitute a Corporate Social Responsibility Committee of the board of the company, and, accordingly decide the strategy and spend on corporate social responsibility (CSR) activities.

In this article, I outline the opportunities for CSR in India and the priorities on which companies should focus in the new regulatory regime. Companies should view this as an opportunity to expand their scope and reach towards society at large, by transforming themselves into model corporate citizens. This may very well be achieved through a strategic approach towards CSR and by incorporating rigorous standards of effectiveness in the projects funded as part of its CSR interventions.

CORPORATES AND INCLUSIVE GROWTH

India ranked a lowly 134 out of 187 countries in the UN Human Development Index 2011, with 30% of its population estimated to be living below the poverty line. Over the last decade therefore addressing socio-economic inequality has become an urgent priority in India. In its endeavor to counter this inequality among citizens of the country, the Indian government has initiated various social-sector schemes in education, public health, food security, and livelihood support in order to reach out to the poorest of the poor and facilitate their socio-economic development. At the same time, there has been a widespread recognition that critical to the push towards "inclusive growth" is the participation of a wide range of stakeholders in designing, financing, implementing, and evaluating development interventions.

The society looks at the corporation as a social organ for wealth creation. Peter F. Drucker had in the 1950s eloquently said that "even the most private of business enterprise is an organ of society and serves a social function ... the very nature of the modern business enterprise imposes responsibilities on the manager ... it can no longer be based on the assumptions that the self-interest of the owner of property will lead to public good, or that the self-interest and public good can be kept apart and be considered to have nothing to do with the other."

There is a growing consensus that companies are expected to contribute to the welfare of the society in which they operate and wherefrom they draw their resources to generate profits. To meet its goal of inclusive growth, the Indian government has mandated CSR for all companies, including the private sector, through a statutory provision in the Companies Bill, 2012. This is a significant step by the government, given that in most developed economies there are hardly any jurisdictions mandating an allocation towards CSR. By and large, it is a voluntary initiative by the corporate sector. And while in countries like Denmark, Sweden, and France reporting on CSR practices is mandatory, investing in CSR is not.

INDIA'S COMPANIES BILL, 2012 AND THE EMPHASIS ON CSR

Section 135 of the Companies Bill, 2012 mandates that companies having net worth of INR 500 crore (circa US$100million) or more, or turnover of INR 1000 crore (circa US$200million) or more, or a net profit of INR 5 crore (circa US$1million) or more during any financial year shall constitute a Corporate Social Responsibility Committee of the board constituted of three or more directors, out of which at least one director shall be an independent director. This section also directs the committee to:

- formulate a CSR policy;
- allocate funds;
- monitor the progress of the CSR activities.

The Companies Bill, 2012, further directs companies to ensure the expenditure of at least 2% of the average net profit made during the three financial years immediately preceding the current year, or to specify the reasons for not spending the amount as part of the board's report to the financial statement.

The Bill therefore attempts to make CSR a sustained and systematic activity by:

- mandating the presence of an independent director, thereby encouraging companies to bring in people with specific social-sector expertise and an objective outlook;

"Leaders are almost like midwives of ideas. They really understand what is going on. You know when you come to them with an idea, they aren't going to just say, 'Well, that's nice, and maybe we can use that.'" Warren Bennis

- formulating a comprehensive CSR policy as a strategic engagement, and not an episodic charitable activity;
- encouraging companies not only to allocate funds for CSR, but also to monitor (and evaluate) progress and outcomes.

IMPLICATIONS FOR COMPANIES

The new CSR model has moved away from simple social concerns to a model in which generating value for both the society and for the companies go hand in hand. Currently, barring a few notable exceptions, CSR largely comprises voluntary initiatives by companies. One has to recognize that companies have to worry about their bottom line and, therefore, they may not see this as an obligation. The Companies Bill provides an opportunity for companies to develop social businesses and to integrate responsible business activities by making use of 2% of their profits. However, in establishing a sustainable CSR architecture, there are many issues that need to be considered. Three critical ones are set out below.

- **Identifying Opportunities for Investing in Strategic CSR**: In the emerging regulatory regime, companies must make the transition from voluntary, sporadic, CSR activities to a strategic CSR roadmap. The Companies Bill identifies a number of areas (mostly on the lines of the Millennium Development Goals (MDGs) and supporting local projects and contributions to relief funds) from which companies can choose. At the same time, companies must ensure that CSR is strategic—that the CSR activities selected are aligned with the corporation's core competencies and businesses. This will require professionals, internal and external, who can design programs that have a long-term vision, are mutually beneficial for the company and the local community in which it operates, and are in tune with the country's priority for inclusive growth.
- **Delivery Mechanisms for CSR: Broadly**, companies can be guided by the provisions in the bill, which allow CSR spending as per the priorities that are in line with the MDGs. At the same time, companies also need to determine how CSR is best done. Is CSR to be undertaken through activities managed directly by the company (employee engagement or a corporate foundation), or through supporting non-government organizations (NGOs), and promising development interventions? The Companies Bill propels macro-level CSR to become a core business function that is central to the corporation's overall strategy and success. At the micro level, companies will need to formulate a robust governance structure for their CSR programs.
- **Making Visible Impact by Doing "Good"**: It is clear that companies that take up CSR activities will do so with a dual objective—that of doing good to the society at large, while at the same time gaining visibility for the impact it achieves. Critical to this is the ability to monitor and measure outputs and outcomes of development projects. As for any business investment, monitoring the accountability and performance of CSR activities is the key. For example when building a classroom in a village school, one should assess whether the investment has translated into an increase in enrolment and an improvement in learning. Also, without a robust monitoring system it will be difficult to ascertain where further investments are needed, whether there is value for money, and value-creation for the communities supported, and, most importantly whether the 2% hard-earned contribution is leading to the larger inclusive development agenda of the nation.

IMPACT MEASUREMENT: NEW PARADIGMS

Today, those investing in India's development sector are under increasing pressure to demonstrate the social impact created through their activities, in a language easily understood by different groups of stakeholders. This applies to companies as they seek to create value through their CSR activities, while seeking to report the impact they create accurately. All around us, we are constantly seeing traditional social-impact methodologies being challenged, as greater emphasis is placed by decision-makers on showing value-for-money and understanding "return on spend" in monetary terms.

For companies, this implies measuring and reporting "return on investment," an idiom that appeals to the judgment of corporate boardrooms. In this context, the impact-measurement tools used must be innovative, combining rigor with smart reporting. I believe that the important characteristics of an impact-measurement tool should be the following:

- a tool that monetizes social, environmental, and financial outcomes of a development-sector project or program, organization, or even a policy, through a combination of Return on Investment (ROI), Cost-Benefit Analysis (CBA), Opportunity Cost Analysis, and so on;
- a participatory tool, and it uses financial proxies to uncover the value of all outcomes, including those that do not have direct market values, and which are often left out of traditional impact assessments;
- a tool that goes beyond a quantitative indicator and gives a narrative—of how a project, program, organization, or policy creates and destroys values in the course of implementing a development project. Further, it must explore the processes and mechanisms by which it attempts to create an impact, thereby yielding lessons for both internal and external stakeholders.

Using impact-measurement tools that bring together the characteristics outlined above requires commitment towards measurement and reporting. Companies must recognize the benefits that accrue from the use of a robust and comprehensive measurement framework. Some of these are as follows:

- Gaining a clear understanding of the wider impact: Impact measurement can help understand and account for the wider impact of the work being done as a result of the CSR spend by the company. It further fine-tunes understanding of the potential and actual impacts.
- Clear communication of impact: Impact measurement can help to communicate to the stakeholders the value created by time and money invested in the development of interventions in a consistent, robust, and rigorous way (this may be to board members, shareholders, funders, or beneficiaries). It will show others how valuable the interventions are.
- Refinements and improvements: Impact measurement can reveal potential refinements and improvements to enable the company to take informed decisions and support better design, planning, and implementation.
- Informed decision-making: An impact measurement analysis can provide a strong basis for internal and external stakeholders to make decisions regarding funding, thus assisting them to recognize impact in a language that they understand.
- Stronger partnerships with stakeholders: Impact measurement can help to develop a strong ongoing relationship and dialogue with stakeholders, particularly beneficiaries. Using impact measurement shows beneficiaries that their needs and concerns are being addressed.

- Profile raising: Using impact measurement can provide a differentiator for an organization trying to raise itself above its competitors.
- Risk management: All of the above factors ultimately support good risk-management practices.

CONCLUSION

It is advisable that companies view this new regulatory regime not as a constraint, but as an opportunity to expand their scope and reach by transforming themselves into model corporate citizens. This can be achieved through a strategic approach towards CSR and by incorporating rigorous standards of effectiveness in the projects funded as part of its CSR interventions. Evaluating CSR programs using rigorous impact-measurement tools can bring a lot of value to companies. It provides a solid foundation with which to communicate simply and effectively CSR results to the board and to other stakeholders. Ultimately, to be ahead in the game, companies must not only engage in strategic CSR, but they must also demonstrate how their investments are creating sustainable value for the society at large.

MORE INFO

Book:

Drucker, Peter F. The Practice of Management. New York: Harper, 1954.

Websites:

India Companies Bill, 2012: www.mca.gov.in/Ministry/pdf/The_Companies_Bill_2012.pdf
UN Human Development Index: hdr.undp.org/en/statistics/hdi/
UN Millennium Development Goals: www.un.org/millenniumgoals/

See Also:

★ CSR: More than PR, Pursuing Competitive Advantage in the Long Run (pp. 664–666)
★ Viewpoint: The CFO and the Sustainable Corporation (pp. 719–720)
★ Viewpoint: Embedding CSR and Sustainability in Corporate Culture: The Boots Experience (pp. 671–672)
★ Viewpoint: The Growth of Sustainability Reporting (pp. 680–681)
India (pp. 1505–1507)

"Capitalism is at its liberating best in a noncapitalist environment. The crypto-businessman is the true revolutionary in a Communist country." Eric Hoffer

  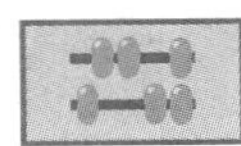      

Viewpoint: The "Comply or Explain" Approach to Improving Standards of Corporate Governance

by Sir Christopher Hogg

INTRODUCTION

Sir Christopher Hogg was chairman of the Financial Reporting Council from January 1, 2006, to May 1, 2010. He began his career in industry with Courtaulds in 1968, going on to become chief executive in 1979, executive chairman from 1980, and nonexecutive chairman from 1991 to 1996. He was a nonexecutive director and subsequently chairman of Reuters Group (1984–2004), SmithKline Beecham and then GlaxoSmithKline (1993–2004), and Allied Domecq (1995–2002). He was a non-executive director of Air Liquide SA from 2000 to 2005.

Sir Christopher was a member of the Department of Industry's Industrial Development Advisory Board from 1976 to 1980 and a nonexecutive director of the Bank of England from March 1992 to 1996. He was nonexecutive chairman of the National Theatre from 1995 to 2004 and a trustee of the Ford Foundation from 1987 to 1999.

Sir Christopher is a graduate of Oxford and Harvard and saw active service with the Parachute Regiment in Cyprus and Suez on National Service. Before his career in industry he worked for three years in corporate financein the City and two years in thepublic sector.

This article sets out the rationale for and benefits of the "comply or explain" principle by reference to experience in the United Kingdom and identifies some of the factors that influence its effectiveness.

THE RATIONALE FOR "COMPLY OR EXPLAIN"

In 1992, in response to a series of corporate scandals, the United Kingdom introduced what is believed to be the first code setting out best practice in corporate governance. Known as the Cadbury Code, it introduced a new regulatory concept known as "comply or explain," under which companies have the option either to follow thebest practicesor to explain to their shareholders why they considered that they were not appropriate in the company's particular circumstances. Although the Cadbury Code has now been superseded by the UK Corporate Governance Code (which in turn was titled until a review in 2009 as the Combined Code), the "comply or explain" mechanism remains an important part of the system of corporate governancein the United Kingdom.

The "comply or explain" mechanism has also been adopted more widely—particularly, but not only, in other European countries—and in 2006 was enshrined in a European Union Directive. The directive requires all companies listed on EU-regulated markets to comply with the relevant corporate governance code or explain why they have not. While the precise content of these codes varies from country to country, they all address issues such as the role, composition, and effectiveness of the board and its committees, the remuneration of executive directors, risk management and internal control, and communication with shareholders.

There are three primary reasons why the "comply or explain" approach is considered to be more appropriate for addressing most governance issues than more traditional forms of regulation:

- It leaves decisions about the appropriateness of a company's governance arrangements in the hands of its management and shareholders. In most cases the primary purpose of good governance is to protect the long-term interests of the company and its owners, so it is right that collectively they should decide how to achieve that objective. In certain companies or sectors there may also be public interest considerations, in which case the arguments for a more traditional approach to regulation may be stronger.
- While it encourages companies to follow accepted best practice, it recognizes that in certain circumstances it may be appropriate for them to achieve good governance by other means. To be effective, good governance needs to be implemented in a way that fits the culture and organization of the individual company; these can vary enormously between companies depending on factors such as size, ownership structure, and the complexity of the business model. In general, one size does not fit all.
- By allowing a degree of flexibility, it enables codes to set more demanding standards. It can be more aspirational than legislation. Regulation tends to be written in terms of the minimum necessary requirements in order not to impose unjustified or disproportionate burdens on those being regulated. In contrast, a "comply or explain" code can set out market-leading practices and encourage the rest to aspire to the standards of the best.
- Codes can also be more easily adapted than regulation to take account of developments inbest practiceand encourage good practice relating to "softer" issues for which it would be inappropriate to prescribe minimum requirements in law, such as training and support for directors.

THE RELATIONSHIP BETWEEN CODES AND REGULATION

Corporate governance codes that operate on the basis of "comply or explain" are sometimes characterized as self-regulation. This is inaccurate. These codes are simply one part of a more comprehensive regulatory framework.

In most countries the basic responsibilities of company boards and individual directors are set out in regulation, which will also include sanctions where those responsibilities are not met. In the United Kingdom, for example, the Companies Act 2006 sets out the duties of directors, which include the duty to promote the success of the company, to exercise independent judgement, to avoid conflicts of interest, and to exercise reasonable care, skill, and diligence.

"**Consensus is the negation of leadership.**" Margaret, Baroness Thatcher

  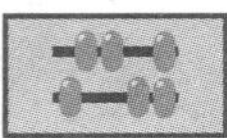      

There will be times when the boundary between codes and regulation is moved. For example, this happened in the United Kingdom in 2002 when regulations were introduced that required companies to report on their remuneration policy and the remuneration of individual directors. Before 2002 these matters had been dealt with through the UK Corporate Governance Code. And, as noted above, for sectors where the public interest is important, the balance between codes and regulation is likely to be more heavily weighted toward the latter. In the United Kingdom, sectors such as financial services, public utilities, and the media are all subject to sector-specific regulation in addition to general-company law.

Regulatory underpinning is also essential for "comply or explain" to operate effectively. If shareholders are to be able effectively to hold boards to account, they need both the information and rights to enable them to do so.

Shareholders need to have appropriate and relevant *information* to enable them to make a judgment on the governance practices of the companies in which they invest. Therefore, under the listing rules of the main market of the London Stock Exchange, companies are required to report on the extent to which they have followed the UK Corporate Governance Code, including by reporting on their internal controls, the work of the audit and remuneration committees, and a number of other activities.

Under UK company law, shareholders have comparatively extensive *rights*, including the rights to appoint and dismiss individual directors, to vote on the company's remuneration policy, and, in certain circumstances, to call an extraordinary general meetingof the company. This means that—provided they have the requisite information—shareholders in effect have sufficient rights to make them a force to be reckoned with. However, everything depends on proper reporting.

DOES "COMPLY OR EXPLAIN" WORK?

"Comply or explain" is probably not appropriate in all markets. As well as the legal framework, and in particular the rights available to shareholders, there are other factors that impact its effectiveness. For example, there may be a need for greater intervention by regulators in markets where most companies have a dominant shareholder in order to protect the interest ofminority shareholders. Conversely, in markets where share ownership is highly dispersed it can be difficult for individual investors to make their voices heard in the absence of influential institutions or collective action.

However, in markets where the right conditions are in place, such as the United Kingdom, it does appear that "comply or explain" has been successful in raising overall standards of corporate governance. That was the opinion of the majority of both companies and investors in the United Kingdom who responded to a consultation held by the Financial Reporting Council(FRC) in the first half of 2009, and similar results have been reported in surveys ofpension funds andi nvestment managers carried out by their representative bodies. Other, separate data show that the rate of compliance with the best practicesset out in the UK Corporate Governance Code has consistently risen over time, with compliance rates for the most of these practices now being greater than 90%.

CHALLENGES TO "COMPLY OR EXPLAIN"

Clearly, "comply or explain" was not sufficient to prevent the problems which led to the global crash of 2008. These were more deep-seated issues that had to do with regulatory matters such as the mispricing of risks by banks. The UK Code has clear limitations in dealing with complex investment behaviors, but then the same applies to regulation. There is a recognition that the quality of corporate governance ultimately depends on behavior, not process, with the result that there is a limit to the extent to which anyregulatory framework can deliver good governance.

That is not to say that the system is working perfectly. When the FRC carried out its earlier review of the Combined Code in 2007 , it found that investors remained concerned by what they considered to be the poor quality of explanations and other disclosures provided by some companies. For their part, companies complained about what they perceived to be the "box-ticking" approach taken by some investors and voting advisory services. What they meant by this was that some investors did not give adequate attention to the statedreasons why a company had chosen not to comply with the UK Corporate Governance Code, but automatically opposed any deviation from the Code.

The review also highlighted some structural features that can undermine "comply or explain" and make it more difficult for constructive engagement to take place. One such feature is the bunching of annual general meetings. As most companies' financial years end in December or March, the majority of AGMs are concentrated into a very short period: more than 300 UK-listed companies held their AGMs during a five-week period in April–May 2007. Investors and voting service agencies have finite resources, and at peak periods such as this it is not realistic to expect them to be able to give each company's corporate governance arrangements the level of consideration that companies understandably believe they deserve.

One of the main challenges to a system that relies on constructive engagement for its effectiveness is the changing nature of the investor base. In the United Kingdom most engagement has traditionally been led by UKpension fundsandinsurance companies. When the first UK Code was published in 1992, these institutions owned more than 50% of the London market; by 2006 this had fallen to just over 25%. During that period there has been a significant increase in overseas investors, who now own over 40% of the London market, as well as the emergence of different types of investor, such as hedge funds. Ensuring that "comply or explain" remains effective despite these changes will be one of the main challenges in the future.

To be fully effective, "comply or explain" also requires both sides to be willing to engage when necessary. The discussions with company chairmen carried out as part of the 2007 FRC review identified a number of potential benefits from engagement, including developing a relationship that might encourage investors to take a long-term view, and getting an investor's view on the strategy and quality of the management team.

While some companies reported that they had been able to develop constructive relationships with their major shareholders, there was also a lot of frustration with how engagement worked in practice. This frustration was shared by many active investors, some of whom also commented on the variable quality of reporting on corporate governance matters.

Many leading institutions have chosen to engage actively in the belief that doing so can add to the value of their investment. For a variety of reasons—such as their choice of investment strategy, constraints on resources, or skepticism about the value of engagement and governance—others have not. In addition, the market share of those institutions that have traditionally taken the lead in engagement (UK insurance companies and pension funds) has declined in recent years as they have diversified their investments and other UK and foreign investors have increased their holdings.

Given the highly dispersed ownership of many listed companies, it is understandable

  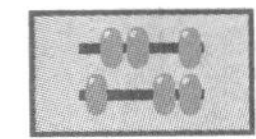      

that some investors may have concluded that resources devoted to engagement have little return in terms of direct influence on the board. But it also seems likely that, looking at the cumulative impact of investor engagement, the whole may be greater than the sum of the parts by making specific interventions more effective and because of the message this then sends to the market as a whole.

CONCLUSIONS

Both companies and investors have expressed reservations about the way in which "comply or explain" works in practice, and it is clear that more needs to be done to encourage all parties to apply it in the intended manner. These issues are addressed in the final report of the FRC's 2009 review of the Combined Code.

The FRC shares the market's view that the flexible "soft law" approach remains the most appropriate way of raising standards of corporate governance in listed companies. But the continuing credibility of this approach depends on a consensus that the contents of the Code are conducive to best practice, and on companies and investors acting in the spirit, not just the letter, of the Code and "comply or explain."

In particular it is of critical importance that there are sufficient institutional investors willing and able to engage actively with the companies in which they invest. This cannot be taken for granted—dispersed ownership, the declining market shareof UK insurance companies and pension funds, and resource constraints are all potential obstacles to achieving this objective. In their turn, companies must be willing to welcome communication with their shareholders as an opportunity to obtain an informed external perspective on their performance.

In summary, one can say that:

- The UK Corporate Governance Code and its predecessors have contributed to clear improvements in governance standards since the first code was introduced in 1992.
- While there are differing views about the extent to which the perceived shortcomings in governance in the banking sector are replicated in the listed sector as a whole, many consider at least some of them to be specific to that sector.
- There is a recognition that the quality of corporate governance ultimately depends on behavior, not process, with the result that there is a limit to the extent to which any regulatory frame workc an deliver good governance.
- Market participants have expressed a strong preference for retaining the current approach of "soft law" underpinned by some regulation, rather than moving to one that is more reliant on legislation and regulation. It is seen as better able to react to developments inbest practice; also, because it can take into account the different circumstances in which companies operate, it can set higher standards to which they are encouraged to aspire.

MORE INFO

Reports:

Financial Reporting Council. "Revisions to the UK Corporate Governance Code (formerly the Combined Code)." May 2010. Online at:tinyurl.com/2wyqq7m

Financial Reporting Council. "The UK Corporate Governance Code." June 2010. Online at:tinyurl.com/33eulsh

Sants, Hector. "Do regulators have a role to play in judging culture and ethics?" Speech given at the Chartered Institute of Securities and Investments Conference, London, June 17, 2010. Online at:tinyurl.com/369s2ry

See Also:

★ Viewpoint:Lessons from the Credit Crisis: Governing Financial Institutions (pp. 694–695)
★ Viewpoint:Mobilizing the Power of Pension Funds to Transform Corporate Behavior (pp. 698–700)
✔ Corporate Governance and Its Interpretations (p. 1111)
✔ Defining Corporate Governance: Its Aims, Goals, and Responsibilities (p. 1115)

  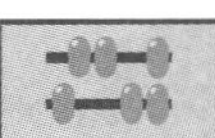     

Corporate Board Structures by Vidhan Goyal

EXECUTIVE SUMMARY

- Firms choose their board structures based on a value-maximizing process.
- Large and outsider-dominated boards are optimal for complex firms (such as large firms, firms with multiple business segments, and complex operational and financial structures). Conversely, small and insider-dominated boards are optimal for small, young, and high-growth firms.
- CEOs who also hold the title of chairman appear to have greater influence on the board. In firms with combined titles, boards do not dismiss poorly performing CEOs at the same rate as they do in firms with CEO and chairman titles vested in different individuals.
- Politically connected directors add substantial value to the firms. They matter more in firms in which politics plays an important role, such as firms where sales to government, exports, and lobbying are greater.
- Women in the boardroom have a positive impact on how firms are governed. Women have fewer attendance problems, and they improve the attendance behavior of male directors.

INTRODUCTION

The job of the board is to control the managerial succession process (involving hiring, assessing, promoting, and if required, dismissing the CEO), and to provide high-level counsel to top management.

There is a widespread skepticism of the effectiveness of boards. Recent accounting scandals at firms such as Enron, WorldCom, and Parmalat have resulted in intense scrutiny of the function of boards. Critics point out that corporate boards have failed primarily because of poor board structures. Top management and board members are tied together though a web of personal and business connections, compromising a board's ability to monitor firms. Michael Jensen puts it more bluntly by stating that, in large US corporations, "even the outside directors basically see themselves as employees of the CEO... And this means that, in American companies, the CEO effectively has no boss."[1]

Many scholars, regulators, legislators, and investors are, therefore, calling for a reform of corporate boards. The codes of conduct for good corporate governance frequently recommend that boards should be small, and comprised largely of independent directors.[2] TIAA-CREF, one of the largest pension funds, will only invest in firms that have boards consisting of a majority of outside directors. CalPERS, another large pension fund, recommends that the CEO should be the only inside director on the board. The Sarbanes-Oxley Act of 2002 mandates that audit committees of boards should consist entirely of outside directors. The stock exchanges, such as the NYSE and the NASDAQ, require listed firms to use a majority of outside directors. These intense institutional, regulatory, and legislative pressures are indeed working. YiLin Wu, for example, shows that after firms are publicly named for poor governance by CalPERS, the number of inside board members declines, and board sizes shrink.[3] Governance activists have also been calling for boards to elect their directors annually, to separate the CEO and chairman positions, and for greater diversity on boards.

This article reviews the literature that inquires into whether differences in board structures affects the way in which boards conduct themselves, and whether boards affect firm performance. Board sizes and board compositions differ across firms. Many firms continue to operate with large boards and boards with high insider representation. Boards are often elected on staggered terms, and it is common in large corporations to have the CEO and chairman positions vested in the same individual. If these board structures are suboptimal, as the critics of existing board structures claim, they why do they persist? Should we compel all firms to conform to a single model of board structure?

The emerging academic evidence suggests that the conventional wisdom on board structures is misguided. Recent work suggests that boards are organized according to a value-maximizing calculus. This work carefully highlights the tradeoffs associated with different board structures, and shows that the observable variation in board structures reflects careful attention to these tradeoffs. Firms choose the board structures that suit their circumstances.

CAUSES AND CONSEQUENCES OF BOARD STRUCTURES

Board Size

It is often asserted that small boards are more effective than large boards. For example, Martin Lipton and Jay Lorsch argue that, "[W]hen a board has more than 10 members it becomes more difficult for them all to express their ideas and opinions."[4] Michael Jensen takes up this theme, and conjectures that "keeping boards small can help improve their performance. When boards get beyond seven or eight people they are less likely to function effectively and are easier for the CEO to control."[5] These conjectures are supported by David Yermack, who finds that smaller boards are associated with higher firm value.[6]

A careful examination of the forces affecting board structures reveals that firms face a tradeoff in determining board sizes. As boards become larger, the directors collectively possess more information that is important for both monitoring and advisory functions. Each prospective director brings additional information to the board. Consequently, larger boards have more aggregate information about product markets, technology, regulation, financing choices, and mergers and acquisition opportunities.

However, the costs of decision-making increase as boards become large, because of higher coordination costs and the free-rider problems associated with larger boards. With an increase in board size, each member considers its influence on board decisions to be of lesser significance. This reduces the director's incentives to incur the private costs of acquiring information and actively monitoring top management. In other words, the decision to add a new member to the board is determined by a tradeoff between the additional information that a prospective director brings to the board against the increased coordination costs and free-rider problems.

Large firms with more diverse operations find the additional information that a prospective director brings more valuable. Large firms and those with more complex operations have a higher volume of activity and larger information requirements. These firms frequently engage in mergers and acquisitions, and more often use sophisticated financing techniques. Thus, large firms benefit from the specialized information that new board members bring to the firm.

On the other hand, young, fast-growing firms with lots of intangible assets should optimally keep their boards small. A primary reason is that large information differences exist among managers and outside directors in young and high-growth firms. These information differences

     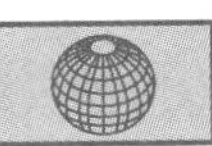   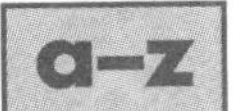

increase monitoring costs. By keeping their boards small, firms ensure that board members will have sufficient private interest to bear the high costs of monitoring. In addition, young and high-growth firms will find the slow and deliberate decision-making associated with large boards more costly. Young and high-growth firms, particularly those operating in more volatile environments, face rapid technological changes and unstable market shares. Smaller boards are likely to be more nimble, providing these firms with the flexibility to react quickly.

The empirical evidence is consistent with these predictions. Kenneth Lehn, Sukesh Patro, and Mengxin Zhao examined a sample of 81 firms that survived over the period 1935–2000, and show that "two variables, firm size and growth opportunities, explain a large amount of cross-sectional and inter-temporal variation in the size and composition of boards."[7] Audra Boone, Laura Field, Jonathan Karpoff, and Charu Raheja studied the development of corporate boards during the first 10 years after a firm's initial public offering.[8] They found that as firms become larger, older, and start to add more segments, boards become larger. Conversely, boards become smaller as a firm's environment becomes noisier, as R&D expenditures increase, and as growth opportunities become more abundant.

Recent work by Jeffrey Coles, Naveen Daniel and Lalitha Naveen showed that firm value is increasing in board size in firms with greater advising needs (such as large firms, diversified firms, and high debt firms).[9] Their evidence suggests that certain classes of firms actually benefit from larger boards, contrary to the calls from governance activists requiring all boards to reduce their sizes.

Board Composition

Typically, boards of directors can be divided into two groups—inside directors (management), or outside directors (non-management). Inside directors are full-time employees of the firm, while outside directors are not employed by the firm. Often, outside directors are taken to be independent, but sometimes they are not because of business or personal relationships with the firm or the CEO. On average, outside directors make up about 55–60% of the total directors of large US firms. This proportion has increased in the last decade, particularly for listed firms, since the enactment of the Sarbanes-Oxley Act of 2002, which led to an increase in the number of outside directors on US firms.

Conventional wisdom suggests that outsider-dominated boards are more effective boards. Following up on this conventional wisdom, there is a general push from institutional investors, regulators, and legislators towards more independent boards. Martin Lipton and Jay Lorsch suggested that there be at least two independent directors for every affiliated director. Michael Jensen goes even further and writes that, "it is almost impossible for those who report directly to the CEO to participate openly and critically in effective evaluation and monitoring of the CEO . . . , the only inside board member should be the CEO." A large number of codes of conduct for good governance put forth by various countries recommend firms to have a majority of independent directors on their boards.

Similar to our discussion of board sizes, a serious consideration of tradeoffs reveals that firms choose the board composition that is optimal for their circumstances. Independent-outsider-dominated boards serve important advisory and monitoring functions. CEOs of large firms, firms with diverse operations, and firms with complex operating and financing structures have greater need for advice. These firms benefit more from the specialized expertise outside directors bring to the firm. At the same time, small, young, high-growth firms will find it optimal to have fewer outside directors. The reason is that information problems are relatively more severe in small and high-growth firms. Outside board members find it relatively costly to obtain information that is relevant for monitoring and advisory functions. These information differences also slow down decision-making associated with outsider-dominated boards in small, young, high-growth firms.

The available evidence suggests that, indeed, outside directors are effective monitors. Michael Weisbach finds that in firms with outsider-dominated boards, poorly performing CEOs are removed at a relatively higher frequency compared to that in firms with insider-dominated boards.[10] However, the size of these effects remains controversial.

The research cited earlier also finds systematic cross-sectional variation in board independence. Large firms, firms with diversified operations, and high-debt firms have more independent boards. Small, young, and high-growth firms have boards that consist largely of insiders.[11]

Classified Boards

Boards also differ in the terms they offer to their directors. A majority of US firms have classified boards, which stagger the annual election of director slates. With classified boards, directors are grouped into distinct classes (typically three), with a single class of directors standing for re-election each year. Thus, in classified boards, directors serve for three-year terms. In firms with a single class of directors, directors are elected for one-year terms. Almost 60% of major US firms have classified boards.

Many scholars criticize classified board structures for their anti-takeover properties. Paul Gompers, Joy Ishii, and Andrew Metrick suggest that board classification is "one of the few provisions that clearly retains some deterrent value in modern takeover battles."[12] Similarly, Lucian Bebchuk and Alma Cohen criticize board classification by arguing that it raises the expected costs of bidders contemplating a hostile change-in-control bid.[13] They argue that by insulating management from takeovers, classified boards entrench management, and, consequently, reduce shareholder wealth.

On the other side of the debate, several commentators point out the advantages of classified boards. By providing multi-year terms, classified boards increase board stability and board independence. If directors are elected to multi-year terms, they will have greater incentives to invest in the information required to monitor managers actively, and to provide advice and guidance to top managers. John Wilcox argued that classified boards increase board stability, and enhance director independence by insulating directors from outside pressures.[14] Thomas Bates, David Becher, and Michael Lemmon argued that in takeover situations, board classification can facilitate bargaining for a greater share of transaction surplus.[15]

The costs and benefits of classified boards are likely to vary across firms. Seoungpil Ahn, Vidhan Goyal, and Keshab Shrestha argued that staggered terms are likely to be most useful when firms have greater advising needs, and outside directors can more effectively monitor managers.[16] Advising needs are often greater in firms with a greater scope and complexity of operations. These firms are more likely to benefit from classified boards. Classified boards tend to be less useful, even value-destroying, in firms where monitoring managers by outside directors is particularly difficult. Outsider-controlled boards are generally less effective in monitoring firms that are relatively opaque (firms with high R&D intensity or with lots of intangible assets). Staggering the terms of these insider-controlled boards would further entrench management, and it is optimal

"On the face of it, shareholder value is the dumbest idea in the world. Shareholder value is a result, not a strategy . . . Your main constituencies are your employees, your customers and your products." Jack Welch

for these firms to have a single class of directors.

These views continue to remain controversial. It is unclear whether classified boards actually reduce the likelihood of a firm becoming a takeover target, as recent research by Thomas Bates, David Becher, and Michael Lemmon showed that takeover targets with a classified board are acquired at an equivalent rate to targets with a single class of directors. Moreover, target firms with classified boards do obtain a larger proportional share of the total value gains in merger and acquisition transactions.

Research by Seoungpil Ahn, Vidhan Goyal, and Keshab Shrestha showed that certain classes of firms actually benefit from board classification, as their market value is higher when they adopt classified boards. In particular, firms with greater advising needs (large and more complex operations) and low monitoring costs (low R&D intensity) have higher market value when they adopt classified boards.

OTHER BOARD ATTRIBUTES

CEO-Chairman Duality

In a large fraction of major US firms, CEOs also hold the title of chairman of the board. Many commentators have called for a prohibition of the CEO serving as chairman, based on the argument that this structure gives CEOs greater control at the expense of other board members. Michael Jensen argued that "the function of the chairman is to run board meetings and oversee the process of hiring, firing, evaluating, and compensating the CEO. Clearly, the CEO cannot perform this function apart from his or her personal interest ... for the board to be effective, it is important to separate the CEO and chairman positions."

Indeed, CEOs who also hold the chairman title have greater power. For example, Vidhan Goyal and Chul Park found that in firms with combined titles, boards do not dismiss poorly performing CEOs at the same rate compared to firms where the CEO and chairman titles are vested in different individuals.[17] Overall, the evidence in the literature confirms that combined titles provide CEOs with greater influence in the firm. There is little evidence, however, that combining or separating CEO and chairman titles leads to any appreciable differences in corporate performance.[18]

Politically Connected Boards

Boards can also add value through the connections they provide with politicians. Anup Agarwal and Charles Knoeber showed that firms in which politics matter more tend to have a larger number of political directors.[19] These politically experienced directors are more common in firms where sales to government, exports, and lobbying are greater. Similarly, firms that are exposed to costly environmental regulation appoint more directors with backgrounds in law. Firms also respond to changes in regulation by adjusting board composition. In the 1990s, as retail competition in electricity became an increasingly political issue, outside directors with political backgrounds increased in number and importance on the boards of US electric utilities.

Politically connected boards add substantial value to the firms. The stock prices of firms nominating politically connected directors to their boards increase on the announcement dates of such nominations. Research by Eitan Goldman, Jörg Rocholl, and Jongil So showed that in the 2000 presidential election in the US, companies with political connections to the Republican Party increased in value upon the Republican win, while companies with connections to the Democratic Party suffered a drop in value.[20] If politically connected boards add value in countries with strong legal systems, as has been shown in the existing research, the added value of politically connected directors would be even larger in other countries with relatively weak legal systems.

Women in the Boardroom

Boards worldwide are under increasing pressure to choose female directors. Renée Adams and Daniel Ferreira confronted the issue of whether women directors affect the functioning of boards.[21] The evidence suggests that women have fewer attendance problems than men. In fact, having women directors on boards improves the attendance behavior of male directors. Boards with greater gender diversity meet more often, and offer more performance-based pay to board members. Overall, women have a positive impact on how boards are governed.

CONCLUSION

In the last 10 years, boards have become more independent and diligent. Contributing to this change is the increased pressure from institutional investors, greater regulation, litigation threats from shareholders, and new exchange requirements regarding the composition of boards. Data show that the proportion of outside directors on boards is now larger than in previous decades. Importantly, outside directors nominated to boards since 2000 are relatively more independent, more of them have financial acumen, and more of them are women. The increasing independence of boards has changed the way boards operate.

MAKING IT HAPPEN

- Large, multidivisional firms should optimally choose bigger and more independent boards. Small, young, fast-growing firms should optimally choose smaller boards.
- Large and multidivisional firms, where boards have a greater number of outside directors, should consider staggering the election of directors. By contrast, small, young, fast-growing firms should consider electing their directors every year.
- The titles of CEO and chairman should be vested in different individuals.
- Politically experienced directors add substantial value in firms that sell to the government, or those which are exposed to costly regulation. Women on boards positively affect the governance of firms. Boards with more women meet more often and offer more performance-based pay to board members.

MORE INFO

Books:

Harvard Business Review on Corporate Governance. Boston, MA: Harvard Business School Press, 2000.

Macey, Jonathan R. *Corporate Governance: Promises Kept, Promises Broken*. Princeton, NJ: Princeton University Press, 2008.

Monks, Robert A. G., and Nell Minow. *Corporate Governance*. Chichester, UK: Wiley, 2008.

Articles:

Ahn, S., V. K. Goyal, and K. Shrestha. "The differential effects of classified boards on firm value." Working paper, National University of Singapore, HKUST, and Nanyang Technological University, 2009.

Boone, A. L., L. C. Field, J. M. Karpoff, and C. G. Raheja. "The determinants of corporate board size and composition: An empirical analysis." *Journal of Financial Economics* 85 (2007): 66–101.

"In order for an ideal to become a reality, there must be a person, a personality to translate it." Jesse Jackson

A direct impact of this can be seen in the shortening of CEO tenure in the last decade, compared to earlier periods.

Overall, the academic evidence suggests that a "one size fits all" approach to board structures is misguided. A large part of variation in board structures can be explained by underlying firm characteristics suggesting that there is an underlying economic logic at work in determining these structures. Greater regulation on board structures may force firms towards an inefficient board structure, imposing heavy deadweight costs on firm and their shareholders.

Coles, J. L., N. D. Daniel, and L. Naveen. "Boards: Does one size fit all?" *Journal of Financial Economics* 87 (2008): 329–356.

Goyal, V. K., and C. W. Park. "Board leadership structure and CEO turnover." *Journal of Corporate Finance* 8 (2002): 49–66.

Jensen, M. C. "The modern industrial revolution, exit and the failure of internal control systems." *Journal of Finance* 48 (1993): 831–880.

Lehn, K., S. Patro, and M. Zhao. "Determinants of the size and structure of corporate boards: 1935–2000." *Financial Management* 38:4 (Winter 2009): 747–780.

Website:

European Corporate Governance Initiative (ECGI): www.ecgi.org

See Also:

★ Boardroom Roles (pp. 643–644)
★ Identifying the Right Nonexecutive Director (pp. 682–684)
✔ The Board's Role in Executive Compensation (p. 1108)
✔ Defining Corporate Governance: Its Aims, Goals, and Responsibilities (p. 1115)
✔ Regulatory Responsibilities of Executive and Nonexecutive Directors: An International Overview (p. 1121)
✔ Selecting the Board and Evaluation Process (p. 1123)

NOTES

1 "US corporate governance: Accomplishments and failings: A discussion with Michael Jensen and Robert Monks." *Journal of Applied Corporate Finance* 20:1 (Winter 2008): 28–46. Online at: dx.doi.org/10.1111/j.1745-6622.2008.00167.x

2 The codes of conduct for good governance can be accessed from the homepage of the European Corporate Governance Institute (www.ecgi.org).

3 Wu, YiLin. "The impact of public opinion on board structure changes, director career progression, and CEO turnover: Evidence from CalPERS' corporate governance program." *Journal of Corporate Finance* 10:1 (January 2004): 199–227. Online at: dx.doi.org/10.1016/S0929-1199(03)00024-5

4 Lipton, Martin, and Jay W. Lorsch. "A modest proposal for improved corporate governance." *Business Lawyer* 48 (1992): 59–77.

5 Jensen, Michael C. "The modern industrial revolution, exit and the failure of internal control systems." *Journal of Finance* 48:3 (July 1993): 831–880. Online at www.jstor.org/stable/2329018

6 Yermack, David. "Higher market valuation of companies with a small board of directors." *Journal of Financial Economics* 40:2 (February 1996): 185–211. Online at: dx.doi.org/10.1016/0304-405X(95)00844-5

7 Lehn, Kenneth M., Sukesh Patro, and Mengxin Zhao. "Determinants of the size and structure of corporate boards: 1935–2000." *Financial Management* 38:4 (Winter 2009): 747–780. Online at: dx.doi.org/10.1111/j.1755-053X.2009.01055.x

8 Boone, Audra L., Laura Casares Field, Jonathan M. Karpoffc, and Charu G. Rahejad. "The determinants of corporate board size and composition: An empirical analysis." *Journal of Financial Economics*. 85:1 (July 2007): 66–101. Online at: dx.doi.org/10.1016/j.jfineco.2006.05.004

9 Coles, Jeffrey L., Naveen D. Daniel, and Lalitha Naveen. "Boards: Does one size fit all?" *Journal of Financial Economics* 87:2 (February 2008): 329–356. Online at: dx.doi.org/10.1016/j.jfineco.2006.08.008

10 Weisbach, Michael S. "Outside directors and CEO turnover." *Journal of Financial Economics* 20 (January–March 1988): 431–460. Online at: dx.doi.org/10.1016/0304-405X(88)90053-0

11 See Boone *et al*. (2007), Coles *et al*. (2008), and Lehn *et al*. (2009).

12 Gompers, Paul, Joy Ishii, and Andrew Metrick. "Corporate governance and equity prices." *Quarterly Journal of Economics* 118:1 (February 2003): 107–155. Online at: dx.doi.org/10.1162/00335530360535162

13 Bebchuk, Lucian A., and Alma Cohen. "The costs of entrenched boards." *Journal of Financial Economics* 78:2 (November 2005): 409–433. Online at: dx.doi.org/10.1016/j.jfineco.2004.12.006

14 Wilcox, J. C. "Two cheers for staggered boards." *Corporate Governance Advisor* 10 (2002): 1–5.

15 Bates, Thomas W., David A. Becher, and Michael L. Lemmon. "Board classification and managerial entrenchment: Evidence from the market for corporate control." *Journal of Financial Economics* 87:3 (March 2008): 656–677. Online at: dx.doi.org/10.1016/j.jfineco.2007.03.007

16 Ahn, Seoungpil, Vidhan K. Goyal, and Keshab Shrestha. "The differential effects of classified boards on firm value." Working paper, National University of Singapore, HKUST, and Nanyang Technological University, 2009. Online at: papers.ssrn.com/sol3/papers.cfm?abstract_id=1265078

17 Goyal, Vidhan K., and Chul W. Park. "Board leadership structure and CEO turnover." *Journal of Corporate Finance* 8:1 (January 2002): 49–66. Online at: dx.doi.org/10.1016/S0929-1199(01)00028-1

18 See Brickley, James A., Jeffrey L. Coles, and Gregg Jarrell. "Leadership structure: Separating the CEO and chairman of the board." *Journal of Corporate Finance* 3:3 (June 1997): 189–220. Online at: dx.doi.org/10.1016/S0929-1199(96)00013-2

19 Agarwal, Anup, and Charles R. Knoeber. "Do some outside directors play a political role?" *Journal of Law and Economics* 44:1 (April 2001): 179–198. Online at: www.jstor.org/stable/10.1086/320271

20 Goldman, Eitan, Jörg Rocholl, and Jongil So. "Do politically connected boards affect firm value?" *Review of Financial Studies* 22:6 (June 2009): 2331–2360. Online at: dx.doi.org/10.1093/rfs/hhn088

21 Adams, Renee B., and Daniel Ferreira. "Women in the boardroom and their impact on governance and performance." Working paper, University of Queensland, London School of Economics, CEPR, and ECGI. 2008. Online at: papers.ssrn.com/sol3/papers.cfm?abstract_id=1107721

"Leadership comes through respect, and a large part of respect is liking someone." Carol Leonard

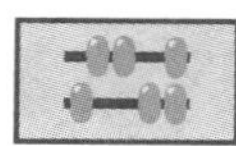

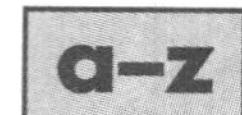

Corporate Governance in Transitional Countries—Shareholders or Stakeholders?

by Irena Jindrichovska

EXECUTIVE SUMMARY

Corporate governance is primarily understood as a set of rules through which corporations are governed. What are the implications of corporate governance and rules of corporate management for the role of business in society? What is the position of transitional countries in today's system? Can a new approach to corporate governance create some new opportunities for sustainable development? What are the changes of corporate governance in transitional countries?

- Understanding corporate governance.
- Corporate governance in the narrow and broad senses.
- The case of the Postal and Investment Bank in Prague—culture changes and conflicts.
- Shareholders, stakeholders, and the problem of short-termism.

INTRODUCTION

Changes in the global environment, society, and business environment, and even recent issues closely connected with the credit crunch have an impact on countries in transition. Transitional economies represented new markets for global companies in the 1990s, and the early years of the 21st century.

However, transition is not so straightforward. From the standpoint of global corporations, it is not just about the acquisition of new markets and a relatively cheap and qualified workforce. Global companies need to export and institutionalize new corporate governance measures.

UNDERSTANDING CORPORATE GOVERNANCE

Corporate governance "is the way in which are companies directed and controlled" (source: *Cadbury Report*, 1992). Over the years, corporate governance has become a much broader issue and includes other aspects of a corporation's management. Many authors also include the broader role of business in society and do not limit their view solely to shareholders' interests. Moreover, shareholders' interests are difficult to administer and enforce because of dispersed ownership and the increasing role of institutional investors in wealth management.

CORPORATE GOVERNANCE IN THE NARROW AND BROAD SENSES

Narrow Sense

"Corporate governance is concerned with ensuring the firm is run in the interests of shareholders" (Allen, 2005, p. 164).

This view is concerned with value maximization for shareholders, and the underlying principle of the "invisible hand" coined by Adam Smith.

Companies must comply with certain rules and regulations and adhere to the directions agreed by the board of directors. They institutionalize and adhere to rules of executive compensation, and are monitored by financial institutions and banks. Company executives and managers on lower levels comply with set rules. This system should ensure that the gap between shareholders and managers is bridged (Jensen and Meckling, 1976) and that managers act in the interest of shareholders.

This principle (running the company in the interest of shareholders) is inherent in the legal systems of Anglo-Saxon countries, and law and regulations play a major role in corporate governance and the enforcement measures of the corporate world. However, there are differences between UK and US-based corporate governance. In the UK, the Cadbury Code interpretation, "comply or explain" is used, and rules are not strictly enforced but principles need to be respected. In the US, corporate governance is rules-driven. This creates a danger that the law must be broken down into rules and regulations for each company, so that companies are able to comply with them. Each measure is administered by a particular set of forms and reports. The danger is that the basic principles can become lost in this jungle of administrative forms, and that companies end up complying only with forms, and that may lead to a simple box-ticking approach. This would effectively mean that the original purpose is lost.

As we witnessed in the early years of the 21st century, this simplified approach and focus on shareholders does not work. Recent faults in the system only confirm that formal adherence to regulations without principles and a broader understanding of the context do not work.

Broad Sense

"Corporate governance is concerned with ensuring that firms are run in such a way that society's resources are used efficiently" (Allen, 2005, p. 165).

The Anglo-Saxon model is just one of those that is globally used. However, in other parts of the world, the functioning of companies has evolved from different societal principles.

With broader objectives, corporate governance does not concentrate solely on companies and their owners, but takes into consideration a broader spectrum of stakeholders (for example, shareholders, employees, government, environment, and local community). The objective is that everybody can potentially be better off by using resources accountably and in a reasonable manner. An often-used example

CASE STUDY

The Case of the Postal and Investment Bank in Prague—Culture Changes and Conflicts

Prior to the changes that started in the 1990s, local control systems existed in transitional countries. However, the actual reality following these system changes is more complex, namely that there is a conflict with the traditional corporate governance that is now being implemented by new owners, such as international investors focusing on value for shareholders. The case of the Investment and Postal Bank of Prague illustrates several clashes between the different cultures, and the different perceptions of goals between a Czech bank and a global (in this case, Japanese) investor.

The Investment and Postal Bank of Prague (IPB) was established in 1990 as a then-new Czechoslovak bank, and it rapidly gained its market share. The bank's management had two strategies remaining from its origins—a strategy of business development, and a strategy of ownership by its own management. The first strategy led to success in retail banking. At the same time, however, the credit expansion in the risky environment of a transforming economy, and the conflict of interest within IPB led to a crisis. The bank acted simultaneously as a creditor and an owner (through its subsidiaries) of a vast industrial empire.

In 1996, IPB had problems as an increasing proportion of bad debts in its portfolio began to appear. IPB was under pressure because of capital inadequacy, and faced a potential insolvency problem. While the bank itself did not perceive any problems, as it felt it had sufficient deposits from individuals, it was alleged in the press that Coopers & Lybrand, its auditors, were requesting additional provisions to cover bad debts for year-end 1996. The bank rejected Coopers & Lybrand and brought in Ernst and Young, who carried out a new audit for year-end 1996. The subsequent accounts for IPB for 1996 showed the bank earning a profit. Audit company, KPMG, was also asked to tender for the same audit, but according to one of its partners, "in the time that we were given, we refused to do it," (PBJ, 2001). Although the new auditor, in 1997, approved the 1996 annual report, it required the bank to increase its share capital by CZK11 billion (about US$550 million). Furthermore, one of the extraordinary audits for 1997 showed that the value of the bank was negative. IPB managed to postpone the day when the problems would become apparent, all within the current legal framework. However, it was clear that the majority of these problems had already started in 1996 (Nollen et al., 2005).

The Czech state sold its minority share in IPB to Nomura in 1998 in the hope that a strategic partner would be found that could help to improve IPB's capital adequacy situation by injecting CZK6 billion (about US$300 million). Initially, the public perceived Nomura's entry as a positive signal and the bank's deposits increased. Nomura, however, did not act as a strategic partner. Instead, it concentrated on selling off significant stakes in Czech industrial companies, which were held in portfolios of investment funds owned and managed by IPB.

The situation of the bank did not improve and it gradually started losing credibility. IPB ran into even more dramatic problems in February 2000, when many creditors started withdrawing short-term deposits. The Czech central bank (CNB) had to impose forced administration. The situation was finally resolved by selling IPB to another Czech commercial bank CSOB (Ceskoslovenska Obchodni Banka), which was one of the four original Czech banks that had carried over from the previous system (CNB, 2000c).

This case shows the conflict between the traditional (but in the Czech Republic still "new") Anglo-Saxon approach, which strives mainly to increase value for shareholders, and the continental approach, with its roots in a broader stakeholder mentality, coming from the German tradition. The actions of the bank were in accordance with existing rules of law, but were they in accordance with good governance?

in this context can be pollution. If firms took a broader view on corporate governance, they would change their behavior and produce a socially acceptable level of pollution. "In general, although it may not be possible to reach efficiency, it may be possible to achieve a better allocation of resources" (Allen, 2005, p. 165). Modern companies now introduce new concepts that are approaching this broader view. These concepts started in the 1990s with the notion of the triple bottom line by J. Elkingdon (1998), which requires that companies now care for broader issues, and, furthermore, that their reports will detail their approach to economic, social, and environmental issues. This leads to broader issues of sustainability and corporate social responsibility (see also Sawitz and Weber, 2006).

In certain European countries (such as France and Germany), Japan, and more recently in India, the broader approach is stressed, and companies in these countries do not to take the creation of shareholders' value as their major goal.

Again, the operationalization of goals may be a different issue and is practiced differently in companies. Many companies now produce reports on sustainability or corporate responsibility in line with their global reporting initiative (GRI). For example, German and French companies have recently focused on employees but not on all aspects of the sustainability movement.

SHAREHOLDERS, STAKEHOLDERS, AND THE PROBLEM OF SHORT-TERMISM

Anglo-Saxon companies concentrate primarily on increasing value for shareholders. The management of these companies has strong incentives to act in the interests of their shareholders. In these cases, management behavior is often prone to short-termism and tends to ignore the long-term goals of social responsibility and development. Corporate governance as interpreted by such tradition is not the same globally. European and Asian companies do not have this unique goal of creating value for shareholders, and devote some energy to other aspects, such as ecology and social responsibility.

Again, depending on which country we have in mind, the relevant tradition applies. Some countries were very much knowledge-based. Should global companies be in the forefront of this initiative? Should there be any room for governments? What are the best practices? What are the needs of transitional economies? One of the needs of companies in transitional economies is frequently trying to gain new capital for future development, and, furthermore, to gain capital and funding through their more-capitalized Anglo-Saxon peers. Companies in transitional countries are being listed on foreign exchanges, where rules and regulations, and demands for documentation, are much more stringent. This also requires a large amount of effort in putting the case together, as well as convincing the authorities that the accounting system and internal rules of corporate governance of a company from a transitional country

MAKING IT HAPPEN

The rules of corporate governance need to be taken in the context of the whole society.

- For Anglo-Saxon corporate governance please see the example of BT at www.btplc.com/societyandenvironment
- For alternative corporate governance, please see the example of Toyota at www.toyota-industries.com/corporateinfo/governance

Obviously, these are examples of big companies, and it remains to be seen whether similar practices can be cost-efficient in smaller and medium-sized corporations.

MORE INFO

Books:

Claessens, S. "Corporate governance and development." In *Focus 1: Corporate Governance and Development*. Washington, DC: World Bank, 2003.

Elkington, J. *Cannibals with Forks: The Triple Bottom Line of 21st Century Business*. Gabriola Island, Canada: New Society Publishers, 1998.

Savitz, Andrew W., and Karl Weber. *The Triple Bottom Line: How Today's Best-Run Companies Are Achieving Economic, Social, and Environmental Success—and How You Can Too*. San Francisco, CA: Jossey-Bass, 2006.

"Charisma becomes the undoing of leaders. It makes them inflexible, convinced of their own infallibility, unable to change." Peter F. Drucker

comply with the requirements of the British or American stock exchanges. The costs of compliance with stock-exchange rules are huge, and many companies incur these costs to demonstrate that they have good corporate governance and attract investors because of the perceived lower risk.

CONCLUSION

Can transitional economies bring something new to developed economies apart from new markets and new business opportunities? In view of corporate governance in the broad sense, such companies can also be a good opportunity to create new governance rules and practices, and not to slip into the simple box-ticking trap. On the contrary, corporate managers can make significant steps towards care for the environment and long-term sustainability, increasing the (positive) role of business in society.

Articles:

Allen, F. "Corporate governance in emerging economies." *Oxford Review of Economic Policy* 21:2 (2005): 164–177.

Jensen, Michael C., and William H. Meckling. "Theory of the firm: Managerial behavior, agency costs, and capital structure." *Journal of Financial Economics* 3:4 (1976): 305–560. Online at: dx.doi.org/10.1016/0304-405X(76)90026-X

Kreuzbergová, E. "Banking socialism in transition: The experience of the Czech Republic." *Global Business and Economics Review* 8:1/2 (2006): 161–177.

La Porta, Rafael, Florencio Lopez-De-Silanes, and Andrei Shleifer. "Corporate ownership around the world." *Journal of Finance* 54:2 (1999): 471–517.

La Porta, Rafael, Florencio Lopez-de-Silanes, Andrei Shleifer, and Robert Vishny. "Investor protection and corporate governance." *Journal of Financial Economics* 58:1–2 (2000): 3–27. Online at: dx.doi.org/10.1016/S0304-405X(00)00065-9

Nollen, S., Z. Kudrna, and R. Pazdernik. "The troubled transition of Czech banks to competitive markets." *Post-Communist Economies* 17:3 (2005): 363–380. Online at: dx.doi.org/10.1080/14631370500204396

Report:

Committee on the Financial Aspects of Corporate Governance. "Report of the Committee on the Financial Aspects of Corporate Governance" (Cadbury Report). London: Gee, December 1, 1992. Online at: www.ecgi.org/codes/documents/cadbury.pdf

Websites:

European Corporate Governance Institute (ECGI): www.ecgi.org
Global Corporate Governance Forum: www.gcgf.org
Global Reporting Initiative: www.globalreporting.org
World Bank Corporate Governance Reports: rru.worldbank.org/Toolkits/CorporateGovernance

See Also:

★ How to Manage Emerging Market Risks with Third Party Insurance (pp. 866–868)
★ IPOs in Emerging Markets (pp. 514–516)
★ Middle East and North Africa Region: Financial Sector and Integration (pp. 211–214)
★ Political Risk: Countering the Impact on Your Business (pp. 902–904)
★ Public–Private Partnerships in Emerging Markets (pp. 563–566)
✔ Corporate Governance and Its Interpretations (p. 1111)
✔ Corporate Governance Practices in Private Equity-Owned Firms (p. 1112)
✔ Defining Corporate Governance: Its Aims, Goals, and Responsibilities (p. 1115)

"The market is a mechanism for sorting the efficient from the inefficient, it is not a substitute for responsibility."
Charles Handy

  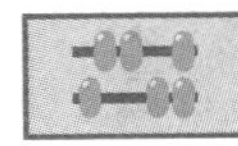      

Corporate Responsibility in a Global World: Marrying Investment in Human Capital with Focus on Costs by Angela Baron

EXECUTIVE SUMMARY

- A human capital approach to the management of people shifts the emphasis of people management from minimization of cost to maximization of return on investment.
- Human capital is an important element of intellectual capital, and hence the market value of an organization.
- The importance of human capital has increased as the shift to knowledge-based work and a knowledge-based economy has accelerated.
- Human capital management combines information on the value and contribution of people with management processes, to direct their efforts and behavior.
- Human capital information can be collected on a number of levels, all of which have value to the organization.
- At its highest level, human capital information can produce meaningful insights to enhance business decision-making, or assist the achievement of strategic objectives.

INTRODUCTION

Love it or loathe it, the term human capital has entered the HR vocabulary for keeps. The term is much criticized for implying that people can be subjected to the same rules as more traditional forms of capital, regardless of personal aspirations and objectives. Yet the same grounds for criticism are also the impetus for a fundamental shift in organizational thinking in terms of the people employed. Organizations that adopt a human capital approach to the management of their workforce immediately shift that workforce from the cost to the asset side of the balance sheet. People become assets to be invested in, and from which a return that can be maximized is expected, as opposed to a set of costs to be kept to a minimum.

Immediately the focus of people is asset-based, the organization needs to rethink a whole set of assumptions and people-management actions. When organizations treat people as costs, they assume:

- that people need to be incentivized to work harder;
- that people should be bought in with the highest possible value for the lowest possible cost;
- that it is only worth investing in training if there is an immediate need;
- that the removal of people from the organization is primarily a cost decision.

When people are assets, organizations assume:

- people will work better when they have interesting and challenging work to do;
- people work harder when they are motivated and committed to their work, experiencing high levels of satisfaction;
- people should be brought into the organization on the basis of their potential to develop and grow;
- investment in training and skills is worthwhile, if there is likely to be a return on that investment in the medium to long term;
- when people leave the organization, there are knowledge retention and capacity issues to be considered and managed.

This, therefore, has given rise to a whole new set of rules about how we recruit, develop, and finally exit people from the organization.

A DEFINITION OF HUMAN CAPITAL

There have been many definitions of human capital over the years. However, there now seems to be general agreement that human capital is the knowledge, skills, abilities, and capacity to develop and innovate possessed by people in an organization. It is an aspect of intellectual capital—the stocks and flows of knowledge available to an organization—and is associated with the concepts of social capital—the knowledge derived from relationships within and outside the organization—and organizational capital, the institutionalized knowledge possessed by an organization which is stored in databases, manuals, etc. It hence contributes to the market value of an organization through its contribution to intellectual value, which also accounts for the value of brand and reputation. Our research at the Chartered Institute & Personnel (and Development) (CIPD) has resulted in the following definition of human capital (Figure 1), viewed as an element of intangible value, and it is this definition that has shaped our work to date.

Human capital management is important because it enables organizations to make more productive use of people through measurements, analysis, and evaluation rather than guesswork. It provides guidance on the development of HR and business strategies which enable improvements in levels of business performance, and higher levels of engagement to be achieved by such means as better selection, training, and leadership. It encourages the initiation of processes for the assessment and satisfaction of future people requirements. It provides the basis for developing policies and practices which enhance the inherent capacities of people—their contributions, potential, and employability—by providing learning, and continuous development opportunities. It also shapes the way in which people share and apply their knowl-

Figure 1. Human capital as an intangible asset

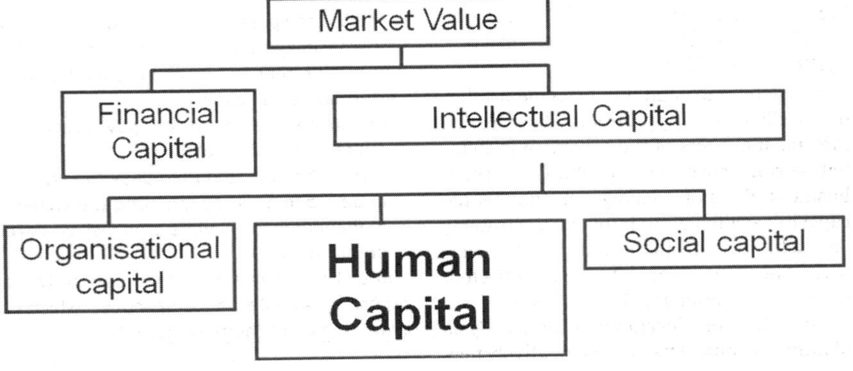

"The most effective leader is the one who satisfies the psychological needs of his followers." David Ogilvy

Table 1. Levels of human capital data collection and analysis

	Level		
	Basic	**Intermediate**	**Higher**
Action	Collect basic input data e.g. absence, employee turnover Identify useful data already available, such as data from pay reviews, performance management, job evaluation, training, the recruitment process Use this data to communicate essential information to managers about absence, turnover, or accident levels, compared by department look for trends or patterns in the data, and investigate their causes	Design data collection for specific human capital needs. For example, conduct an employee attitude survey to measure satisfaction, or follow up on training activity to monitor implementation and use Use this data to inform the design and implementation of people-management policies and processes Look for correlations between data, for example, whether high levels of job satisfaction occur when certain HR practices are in place, such as performance management, career management, or flexible working Communicate the value of processes to line managers, and identify specific actions to improve people management	Identify key performance indicators relating to the business strategy, and design and implement data collection processes to measure against them Feed both quantitative and qualitative information into an analysis model, such as a balanced scorecard Provide managers with indicators on a range of measures designed to inform them on performance and progress in their department Accompany this with specific actions to be taken, informed by the resulting human capital data Interpret and communicate data in ways that will be meaningful to a range of audiences
Outcome	Measures of efficiency and effectiveness Basic information for managers on headcount, make-up of the workforce, and so on Identification of any action that might be needed as a result of these measures, for example to reduce accident rates, to improve the diversity profile of the workforce, or to reduce absence	Measures of process Information to help design the HR model that is most likely to contribute to performance Communication to managers, not just how to implement processes but with accompanying information on why they are important, and what they can achieve	Identification of the drivers of business performance Information that will enable better-informed decision-making, both internally on the management of people, and externally on the progress with regard to strategy

edge. Therefore, if human capital management processes are aligned with business processes, it can ensure that the effort and behavior of people are focused on the things that are important for the business, and the achievement of strategic objectives.

The impact human capital can have on markets is huge. In advanced economies, the only distinctive asset which cannot be imitated easily is the skills, talent, and know-how of people. The 1999 Competitiveness White Paper, "Building the Knowledge-Driven Economy," published by Peter Mandelson while UK Secretary of State for Trade and Industry, argued that "...we will only compete successfully in the future if we create an economy that is genuinely knowledge-driven." It is no accident, therefore, that interest in human capital, how to measure it, and how to manage it has increased as the knowledge-intensive sector of the economy has expanded.

WHAT INFORMATION SHOULD BE COLLECTED TO INFORM HUMAN CAPITAL MANAGEMENT?

Effective human capital management relies on credible and appropriate data, which informs managers of the drivers of individual performance, and enables informed business decision-making on the people capacity available to implement strategy, and achieve strategic objectives. There are several levels at which data can be collected, which are described in Table 1 below.

The collection, development, and analysis of human capital data is still a relatively new process for the majority of organizations. Most of those making systematic efforts to collect information to describe the contribution of people are using existing data, often collected for another purpose. So, for example, most organizations collect data on

CASE STUDY
Nationwide Building Society

Nationwide has been investigating the links between employee commitment, customer commitment, and business performance for some years. Its objectives were to:

- establish the key drivers of customer commitment;
- measure the impact of improved employee commitment on customer commitment, and business performance;
- identify activities that can be undertaken, at corporate and local levels, to leverage this knowledge, and bring about business improvements.

It collected data from four main sources:

- HR data: from PeopleSoft;
- employee opinion data: from the "Viewpoint" survey;
- customer satisfaction and commitment data: from the "Member Perception" questionnaire;
- business performance data: from the Operational Sales database.

Analysis revealed that employee commitment and length of service were the most critical factors driving customer commitment and sales. Further modeling demonstrated that areas generating the best performance were also those with the highest average length of service.

It was then possible to investigate further the drivers of employee commitment, and means of increasing employee tenure. Five key drivers were found to have the most effect on employee retention, which in turn affect positively customer satisfaction and business performance, as follows:

- employees' perceptions of pay levels;
- average age of employees;
- levels of resource during peak times;
- understanding and promoting the values of Nationwide;
- management behaviors emphasized in Nationwide's organizational development program, PRIDE.

(*Note*: The full version of this case study is available in the CIPD guide, "Human capital reporting: An internal perspective," which can be downloaded from www.cipd.co.uk/humancapital.)

"Managers have been brought up on a diet of power, divide and rule. they have been pre-occupied with authority, rather than making small things happen." Charles Handy

absence, retention, training provision, pay, health, and safety (i.e. the number of accidents). This is the basic level of data, and can be very useful in terms of identifying patterns, or trends, and informing management action. It can also be important for informing external stakeholders about their commitment and understanding of factors which might impact on future performance, such as retention of key staff, and management of risk.

However, higher levels of data are more likely to be of use to the investment community, particularly data likely to provide insight into the drivers of business performance. It is these factors which can enable informed decision-making, both assessing the impact of cost, and the return on investment in people. Although many organizations are making huge progress in this area, it represents a significant investment in terms of time and effort.

CONCLUSION

Good managers have always known instinctively that better managed people perform better and contribute to high performance outcomes. However, human capital literature now contains both theory and evidence to prove this, as well as a number of frameworks which can assist managers in developing information and insight to inform their business decision-making. This does not mean ignoring the cost implications of employing people. It does, however, mean that these cost implications can be considered and assessed in the context of the investment opportunities that people present and the role they play in achieving strategic business objectives.

MORE INFO

Books:

Baron, Angela, and Michael Armstrong. *Human Capital Management: Achieving Added Value through People*. London: Kogan Page, 2007.

Kinnie, Nicholas, Juani Swart, Mark Lund, Shad Morris, *et al. Managing People and Knowledge in Professional Service Firms*. London: CIPD, 2006.

Article:

Kinnie, Nicholas, and Juani Swart. "The alchemists." *People Management* 12:7 (April 6, 2006): 42–45.

Websites:

Chartered Institute of Personnel and Development, section on human capital: www.cipd.co.uk/humancapital

Human Capital Management magazine: www.humancapitalmanagement.org

Institute for Employment Studies: www.employment-studies.co.uk

PricewaterhouseCoopers: www.pwc.com

Society for Human Resource Management: www.shrm.org

See Also:

★ Allocating Corporate Capital Fairly (pp. 11–12)
★ CSR: More than PR, Pursuing Competitive Advantage in the Long Run (pp. 664–666)
★ Managing Retirement Costs (pp. 77–79)
★ Profitability Analysis Using Activity-Based Costing (pp. 908–910)
✔ Creating a Sustainable Development Policy (p. 1113)
✔ Understanding the Financial Aspects of Employing People (p. 1183)
Gary Becker (p. 1270)

"You just have to be the kind of guy to get people to do things." Donald J. Trump

  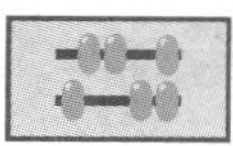   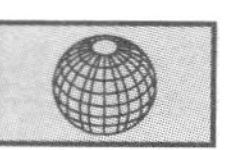   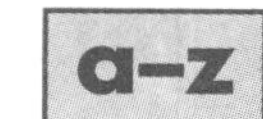

CSR: More than PR, Pursuing Competitive Advantage in the Long Run by John Surdyk

EXECUTIVE SUMMARY

- Consumers increasingly expect companies to act in "responsible" ways.
- Because of their scale and reach, companies have unusual opportunities to address social concerns in innovative and productive ways.
- Evidence suggests that corporate social responsibility (CSR) practices produce long-term benefits with financial performance gains.
- Advancing CSR is made easier with modern risk management tools, reporting guidelines, and committed leadership and employees.

THE EMERGENCE OF CORPORATE SOCIAL RESPONSIBILITY

Global greenhouse gas emissions continue to rise. Diseases wreak havoc across entire continents. An entire host of seemingly intractable issues confront governments throughout the world, which are sometimes unable to effect positive changes. With the emergence of companies as some of the most powerful institutions for innovation and social change, more shareholders, regulators, customers, and corporate partners are increasingly interested in understanding the impact of these organizations' regular activities upon the community and its natural resources. With the world's largest 800 nonfinancial companies accounting for as much economic output as the world's poorest 144 countries, the importance of these organizations in addressing trade imbalances, income inequality, resource degradation, and other issues is clear. While companies are not tasked with the responsibilities of governments, their scale and their ability to influence these issues necessitate their involvement and create opportunities for forward-looking organizations to exercise great leadership.

In public opinion surveys, consumers admit that they prefer to buy products and services from companies they feel are socially responsible (72%) and that they sell shares of those companies they feel don't pass muster (27%). Challenging Nobel laureate Milton Friedman's notion that companies' only responsibility is to make profit, executives are increasingly seeking ways to combine economic gain with social well-being in ways that will produce more customer loyalty, better relationships with regulators, and a host of other advantages. CSR practices may, in fact, prove pivotal to the success of a company.

Sometimes described simply as "doing well by doing good," corporate social responsibility initiatives gained traction in the 1990s as consumer interest in management practices erupted in the wake of several substantial incidences of executive malfeasance and of escalating environmental challenges. While originally focused on environmental factors, CSR reports increasingly include social measures. Likewise, company leaders today express interest in business models that weave together explicit goals for profit, environmental performance, and social factors, at the same time recognizing that these efforts will likely yield no short-term financial benefits but rather long-term performance improvements.

A CLOUDY CONCEPT BEGINS TO CRYSTALLIZE

The phrase "corporate social responsibility" (CSR) describes both:

- A social movement;
- A collection of specific management practices and initiatives.

Business leaders, government professionals, and others use these principles and tools to assess and report on organizations' impact on society.

Globally, CSR is an evolving concept without a clear definition, yet it describes a set of corporate obligations and practices somewhere on the spectrum between traditional charitable giving on the one hand and merely strict compliance with laws on the other.

While operating definitions remain elusive, the term "CSR" generally refers to a company's efforts to include social and environmental concerns explicitly in its decision-making along with a commitment to increasing the organization's positive impact on society. Beneath these efforts is a realization that improved CSR reporting and better risk-management systems generally promote the transparency and accountability essential to good company governance and improved financial performance. These systems, in effect, enable a company to anticipate and respond to opportunities when it senses that society's expectations aren't being met by its performance.

BENEFITS FROM CSR

The benefits of corporate social performance reporting spread over an entire organization.

Areas of greatest gain for a company's market value, operational efficiency, access to capital, and brand value typically come from:

- Establishing ethics, values and principles for the organization;
- Improving environmental processes or reducing environmental impact;
- Improving workplace conditions.

Other efforts, such as better governance measures, also tend to yield positive benefits for companies.

MAKING CSR REAL

Traditional rhetoric about "private versus public" responsibilities is diminishing while companies operate more and more with an understanding of an acknowledged (if tacit) role to play in society. In the United States many people feel companies should be doing more to improve society through changing their business practices.

Table 1. Benefits of CSR

Business Area	Reduce Costs	Create Value
License to Operate	More favorable government relations; reduced shareholder activism; reduced risk of lawsuits	Increased community support for the company's operations ("a bank account of goodwill")
Reputational Capital	Reduced negative consumer activism/boycotts; positive media coverage/"free advertising"; positive "word-of-mouth" advertising	Increased customer attraction; increased customer retention
Human Resources	Increased employee retention and morale	Enhanced recruitment; increased productivity
Finance		Social screens and investment funds are attracted to companies perceived as good social performers

"Society never advances. It recedes as fast on one side as it gains on the other. Society acquires new arts, and loses old instincts." Ralph Waldo Emerson

  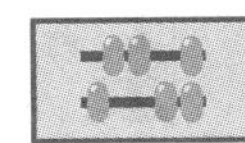   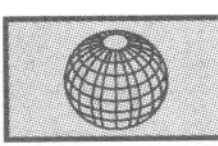   

Although implementing CSR initiatives in modern companies is a daunting prospect because of their increasingly complex and global operations, many CSR management frameworks have moved onto the international stage. Approximately 400 companies—including many of the world's largest—use all or some of the Global Reporting Initiative (GRI), and combined environmental and social reports are increasingly common alongside companies' regular sustainability reports. Launched in 1997 by the Coalition of Environmentally Responsible Economies, the GRI report contains 50 core environmental, social, and economic indicators for a broad range of companies. It also offers additional modules with distinct metrics for companies, depending on their industry sector and operations. The price range for producing a report spans from $100,000 for a basic GRI to more than $3 million for complex organizations like Shell.

Other major initiatives and reporting standards provide helpful guidance and principles; among them are:

- The United Nations Global Compact;
- Global Environmental Management Initiative;
- International Standards Organization guidelines (for example, ISO14000).

The continued growth of the socially responsible investment movement, especially in the United States and Europe, is stimulating companies' adoption of GRI and other instruments. In the United States alone, capital available to socially responsible companies reached $2.29 trillion in 2005.

CHALLENGES TO CSR

The majority of corporations in the world do not produce any reports on their CSR practices. Executives often cite several concerns, including:

- Fear that they may undertake a CSR program while competitors do not, meaning they incur expenses and refocus management talent that may put them at a competitive disadvantage.
- No feeling of urgency to act on many societal issues.
- No accepted standard of what type of information should be reported or at what depth.
- Concern that if they only achieve goals they largely establish for themselves, they may appear only half-heartedly committed—or they may even open themselves to lawsuits.
- Trouble identifying stakeholders, meaning the audience for their reports may be ambiguous, which may, in turn, undermine the quality of the reporting generally.
- Belief that traditional philanthropy fulfils an organization's commitment to society.
- Reporting on the entire scope of a company's impact on society and the environment is increasingly complex.

Recognizing "that one size does not fit all," more companies are exercising greater discretion in reporting initiatives to highlight key information for their sector or the parts of the world in which they operate.

CASE STUDY

Beginning with $1,000 in a garage in 1990, Greg Erickson founded a new energy bar company, Clif Bars, Inc., in Berkeley, California. Committed to exercising environmental stewardship, Greg made expensive investments in organic ingredients and renewable energy while pursuing progressive employment practices such as six-month sabbaticals for employees. Refusing acquisition overtures from other companies, Clif Bars' commitments to corporate responsibility laid a strong, long-term foundation for the growing $100 + million company and its meteoric rise against titans like Kellogg and Quaker Oats.

HOW TO GET STARTED

These principles must be grounded in an organization for CSR management frameworks to yield their maximum benefit.

- Ensure long-term organizational commitment by involving the top leadership *and* the employees.

MAKING IT HAPPEN

There is no consensus among government bodies, companies, or consumers about what precisely constitutes a definition—or even a consistent set of management topics—under the umbrella of corporate social responsibility. Several intergovernmental bodies, company federations, and nonprofits have advanced competing definitions. Among the most influential are:

- *World Bank*. "Corporate Social Responsibility, or CSR, is the commitment of business to contribute to sustainable economic development, working with employees, their families, the local community, and society at large to improve their quality of life, in ways that are both good for business and good for development."
- *World Economic Forum*. "Corporate Citizenship can be defined as the contribution a company makes to society through its core business activities, its social investment and philanthropy programs, and its engagement in public policy. The manner in which a company manages its economic, social, and environmental relationships, as well as those with different stakeholders, in particular shareholders, employees, customers, business partners, governments, and communities, determine its impact."
- *Business for Social Responsibility*. "CSR is operating a business in a manner that
- meets or exceeds the ethical, legal, commercial, and public expectations that society has of business. CSR is seen by leadership companies as more than a collection of discrete practices and occasional gestures, or initiatives motivated by marketing, public relations, or other business benefits. Rather, it is viewed as a comprehensive set of policies, practices, and programs that are integrated throughout business operations, and decision-making processes that are supported and rewarded by top management."
- *Center for Corporate Citizenship at Boston College*. "Corporate Citizenship refers to the way a company integrates basic social values with everyday business practices, operations, and policies. A corporate citizenship company understands that its own success is intertwined with societal health and well-being. Therefore, it takes into account its impact on all stakeholders, including employees, customers, communities, suppliers, and the natural environment."
- *International Business Leaders Forum*. "Corporate Social Responsibility means open and transparent business practices that are based on ethical values and respect for employees, communities, and the environment. It is designed to deliver sustainable value to society at large as well as to shareholders."
- *United Nations*. While not advocating a particular definition of corporate social responsibility, the United Nations uses the term "global corporate citizenship" to describe international companies' obligations to respect human rights, improve labor conditions, and protect the environment. The UN Research Institute for Sustainable Development, which follows academic work in this area, typically concentrates on ethical issues and principles guiding how a company's management engages stakeholders.

"Corporate courage is usually no greater than personal courage." Edward Teller

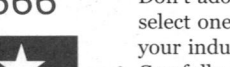

- Don't adopt every reporting system: select one that makes the most sense for your industry and scale.
- Carefully identify stakeholders to help develop feedback loops so you can adjust your course.
- Consider benchmarking against peer companies.
- Communicate your results widely.
- Don't be afraid to revise standards or develop new metrics of your own.

CONCLUSION

Evidence is mounting that CSR provides tangible benefits and lasting competitive advantage to organizations. While difficult to implement, corporate social responsibility practices and frameworks provide companies with a chance to influence the rules of competition positively while playing a crucial—and increasingly expected—role in the world.

FUN FACTS

The Institute of Business Ethics published a study of FTSE 250 companies, providing evidence that those with an ethical code in place for over five years generated greater economic value and market value than their peers over the period 1997–2000.

For 79% of fund managers and analysts surveyed in 2003, the management of social and environmental risks has a positive impact on a company's market value in the long term.

MORE INFO

Book:

United Nations Conference on Trade and Development. *Disclosure of the Impact of Corporations on Society: Current Trends and Issues*. New York: United Nations, 2004. Online at: www.unctad.org/en/docs/iteteb20037_en.pdf

Websites:

Business for Social Responsibility: www.bsr.org
CSR Network: www.csrnetwork.com
Ethical Corp: www.ethicalcorp.com
SustainAbility: www.sustainability.com
World Business Council for Sustainable Development: www.wbcsd.org

See Also:

★ Best Practices in Corporate Social Responsibility (pp. 636–639)
★ Business Ethics (pp. 645–647)
★ Corporate Responsibility in a Global World: Marrying Investment in Human Capital with Focus on Costs (p. 661)
★ Ethical Funds and Socially Responsible Investment: An Overview (pp. 481–483)
✔ Creating a Sustainable Development Policy (p. 1113)
✔ The Triple Bottom Line (p. 1125)
Ernst Friedrich Schumacher (p. 1307)

"Business doesn't have to choose ... between economic success and ethical responsibility, between satisfying the customer and meeting the demands of other stakeholders ... we don't have to make a choice between profits and principles." Jeroen Van der Vee

  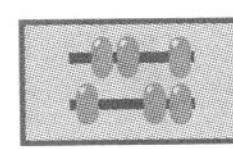   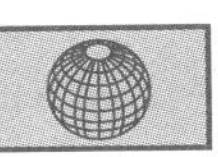   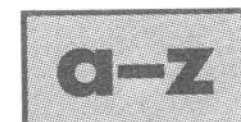

Dividend Policy: Maximizing Shareholder Value

by Harold Bierman, Jr

EXECUTIVE SUMMARY

- Dividend policy (or distribution policy) distributes some amount of cash (possibly zero) to its investors.
- Retained earnings is a very tax efficient (zero dividend) policy.
- If cash is to be distributed, with most tax systems and taxed investors, share repurchase is the preferred method.
- The choice of method is important on several different dimensions.

INTRODUCTION

The amount of dividends can affect stock prices. Barsky and De Long (1993) stated: "... changes in current and expected future dividends can account for the bulk of long-run stock price fluctuations, although much less so for short-term price movements."[1]

The title of this paper could be "Distribution Policy," since dividends are not the only way of implementing a policy aimed at financially rewarding a firm's stockholders. The various methods of distributing cash (or not distributing cash), listed in order of preference order from an economic–finance perspective of maximizing shareholder wealth, are:

- retained earnings;
- share repurchase;
- sale of firm (or part of a firm);
- LBOs (buyouts);
- cash dividends with a dividend reinvestment plans (DRIP);
- cash dividends.

RETENTION: TAX DEFERRAL

It has been proven that, with enough assumptions, dividend policy is not relevant to the valuation of the common stock equity of a firm. However, the proof assumes zero investor taxes; thus it does not apply to a real-world situation in which such taxes exist. With income taxes, an investor benefits from being able to defer the payment of taxes as well as from the fact that some types of income (capital gains) for individuals may be taxed at lower rates than other types of income (dividends).

If a company retains $100, earns 0.10 in one period, and then pays a dividend of $110, the investor taxed at a rate of 0.40 will net: $110 × (1 – 0.4) = $66.

If the same company had paid a dividend of $100 and if the investor also could earn 0.10 before tax and 0.06 after tax on the $60 after tax proceeds, the investor receiving the $100 dividend ($60 after tax) would have after one period: 60 × 1.06 = $63.60.

The investor is better off by $2.40 with the one-period delay in cash distribution. The investor "defers" $40 of taxes that earn 0.10, or $4. The $4 is taxed ($1.60) and the investor is better off by $2.40.

If desired, one could compute the return necessary for the firm to justify retention. It would be equal to the after-tax return (0.06) available in the market to the investor. Thus, if the corporation could earn 0.06 and then pay a dividend, the investor would net: $100 × 1.06 × (1 – 0.4) = $63.60. This is the same as the investor would net with an immediate cash dividend.

If the planning horizon is n periods instead of one period, then 0.06 still measures the return that the firm must earn to justify retention. If the earning opportunities available to the corporation are greater than 0.06, retention is more desirable than an immediate dividend.

If the planning horizon is n periods, the dollar advantage of tax deferral increases. For example, if the firm can earn 0.10 and the time horizon is 20 years with retention and then a tax rate of 0.40, the investor has:

$$\$100 \times 1.10^{20} \times (1-0.4) = \$100 \times 6.73 \times 0.6 = \$404$$

With an immediate $100 cash dividend and the investment of $60 by the stockholder to earn 0.06 after tax for 20 years, the investor would have:

$$\$60 \times 1.06^{20} = \$60 \times 3.207 = \$192$$

With a planning horizon of 20 years, the advantage of tax deferral is $212 for the retention of the $100 earnings. There will be 19 other years between now and the end of the 20 years that will generate comparable tax deferral savings (although of decreasing amounts).

CAPITAL GAINS

To this point, we have assumed that all income is taxed at one rate. Now we assume that a capital gains tax rate of 0.20 applies to capital gains income. This assumes that retention of earnings leads to stock price increases and that these increases can be realized by investors as capital gains.

Returning to the 20-year horizon, with retention and then capital gains taxation of 0.20, the investor would have:

$$\$100 \times 1.10^{20} \times (1-0.20) = \$100 \times 6.73 \times 0.80 = \$538$$

The cash dividend and an after-tax earning rate of 0.06 again leads to a value of $192 after 20 years.

The net advantage of retention is $538 – $192 = $346. Capital gains taxation increases the value of retention from the $212 obtained above to $346.

Again, if we considered the tax consequences of the dividend decision for all subsequent years, the value of the difference would be even larger. Tax deferral and capital gains are two powerful factors that must be considered in deciding a distribution policy.

SHARE REPURCHASE

A number of explanations of the motivation behind share repurchase (where a company buys its own stock) have been suggested. It has been argued, for example, that firms buy back their own shares to have them available to acquire other companies or to fulfill the obligations of stock option plans. Unquestionably, some repurchasing has been done for these reasons. Income tax considerations may make it possible for firms to acquire other companies more cheaply for stock than for cash, and the use of stock options and restricted stock as forms of executive compensation have been widespread. However, the growth of share repurchasing cannot be explained by merger and stock option plans. There is no essential reason why firms should use repurchased shares for these purposes, rather than newly issued shares.

Corporations also repurchase shares with the intention of retiring them, or at least holding them indefinitely in the treasury. It has been suggested that firms with excessive liquid assets have one or more of the following motives to repurchase shares:

- repurchasing shares is the best investment that can be made with these assets;
- repurchasing shares has beneficial leverage effects;
- repurchasing shares, rather than paying dividends, has a significant tax advantage for stockholders.

Is a firm's purchase of its own common stock an investment? There are authors who think so: "The repurchase of its own stock

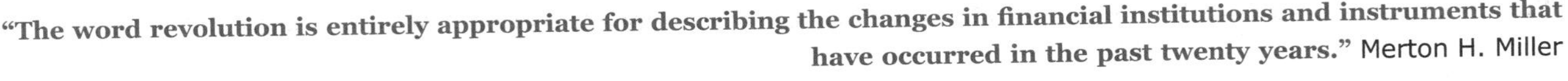
"The word revolution is entirely appropriate for describing the changes in financial institutions and instruments that have occurred in the past twenty years." Merton H. Miller

by a company is an investment decision—plain and simple."[2]

Share Repurchasing as an Investment

Share repurchasing does not possess the same general characteristics as other acts of investment by a firm—for instance, purchasing plant and equipment. Normal investments increase the size of the firm and do not decrease the stockholders' equity balance. A firm's repurchase of its own common stock, on the other hand, reduces the size of the enterprise. Specifically, the cash balance is decreased and the stockholders' equity balance is reduced. In short, repurchasing shares has few characteristics which identify it as a normal investment.

While share repurchasing is clearly not an investment by the firm, there is a change in the relative proportions of ownership if some stockholders sell their shares and some do not sell. The investors who do not sell are implicitly making an investment compared with the investors who do sell. Also, investors not selling make an investment in the firm compared with what would have happened if they had received a cash dividend.

Even though share repurchasing is not an investment, it may be the best use of corporate cash from the point of view of the present investors. This may be the case if the present stock price is below the intrinsic value of the shares.

Taxes and Share Repurchasing

The tax laws can provide powerful incentives for firms with excess liquid assets to repurchase shares rather than pay dividends. The tax code may lead individuals to prefer capital gains to ordinary income, assuming that the top marginal rate of taxation on ordinary income is higher than the rate on capital gains.

Consider now a corporation with excess cash that it desires to pay out to stockholders in the form that will be most attractive from its shareholders' point of view. If it distributes the assets as dividends, they will represent ordinary income to shareholders, and will be taxed accordingly. If, on the other hand, the corporation buys back shares, the tax basis of the stock will be regarded as a return to the shareholders' capital and will not be taxed at all, while that portion of the return which is taxed—i.e., the capital gain—will be subject to a lower rate than ordinary income. In addition, the investor who merely wants to reinvest and does not sell is not taxed at all.

Abby Cohen (1994) captures the essence of this thought:[3] "First, shareholders are not thrilled by the prospect of double taxation on cash dividends. Many prefer that corporations 'pay out' the cash indirectly to shareholders in the form of share repurchases, rather than in the form of cash dividends."

Given these incentives for returning cash to stockholders by repurchasing shares, a relevant question would seem to be: Why, if the tax law is as described, do firms pay dividends? One important answer is that many stockholders do not pay tax on the dividends they receive (for example, Cornell University and low-income retirees). A second reason (related to the first) is that the receipt of cash dividends to low-tax investors reduces the transaction costs for those investors who need cash. But even if one were to accept the above explanations, the basic question still remains. Why do firms pay dividends to investors who are taxed at high ordinary income tax rates?

Example

A firm has 100,000 shares outstanding and $100,000 available for distribution. Should it pay a dividend or repurchase shares? Assume that the personal tax rate is 0.36 and the capital gains tax rate is 0.20. The initial stock price is $20. Assume that the tax basis is also $20. There is an investor who owns 1,000 shares. With a $1,000 cash dividend for this investor we have:

Dividend	
Cash received	$1,000
Tax (0.36)	$360
Net	$640

If the company acquires 100,000/20 = 5,000 shares and the investor tenders 0.05 of the 1,000 shares held, we have:

Stock repurchase	
Cash received (50 × $20)	$1,000
Tax	$0
Net	$1,000

There is a $360 cash flow advantage for share repurchase compared to a cash dividend.

With a zero tax basis and a 0.20 tax rate, we have for the share repurchase:

Stock repurchase	
Cash received	$1,000
Tax (0.20)	$200
Net	$800

Not selling, the investor's percentage ownership goes up from 0.01 to 0.0105 (that is, 1,000/95,000). The investor has a choice of receiving cash (selling some stock) or increasing the relative investment in the firm.

When capital gains and ordinary income have different tax treatment, the value of the firm's stock is influenced by the form of its cash distribution. In addition, with share repurchase and a positive-tax basis, part of the cash distribution is not taxed. There are three factors at work that cause the buying back of shares to be more profitable than dividend payments (from the stockholders' point of view) under any reasonable set of assumptions that includes taxation of income. For one thing, part of the distribution under the share-repurchasing arrangement is considered a return of capital and is not taxed. Secondly, that part of the distribution subject to tax (i.e., the capital gain) is generally taxed at a lower rate than ordinary income. Finally, the investor can avoid all taxes by not selling.

Stock Option Plans

Share repurchase programs by corporations enhance the value of stock options compared to cash dividends by forcing the stock price up relative to a cash dividend of equal dollar amount (the number of shares outstanding is reduced). The stock price effect is not a real advantage to the investor, but it is an advantage to the holders of stock options.

For example, suppose a firm has one million shares outstanding selling at $40 per share. The value of the stock equity is $40 million. If it pays a $4 million cash dividend, the value of the stock equity will be $36 million. Then, as a result of the cash dividend:

Stock price per share	$36
Cash received	$4
Total value to investor per share	$40

The investor is indifferent to the share repurchase and dividends (with zero taxes), but the holder of the stock options prefers the share repurchase.

The firm could buy 100,000 shares with the $4 million. The value of the firm after purchase will be $36 million, and the stock price per share will be $40 (that is, $36,000,000/900,000 = $40). The investor is indifferent to share repurchase and cash dividend (with no taxes), but the holder of a stock option prefers the $40 market price with share repurchase to the $36 price with cash dividends.

The stock price after one year is interesting. Assume that the stock equity is again $40 million (the firm made earnings of $4 million during the year).

Having paid a $4 million dividend last year, the stock value per share would be $40. If the firm had repurchased 100,000 shares instead of a dividend, the stock value per share would be $40,000,000/900,000 = $44.44.

"Special or Extra Dividends have been used by some firms to distribute excess cash." Merton H. Miller

  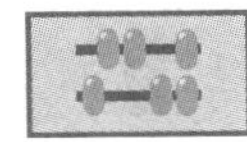      

A share repurchase program, all things equal, will result in an increasing stock price through time compared to the price with dividends being paid. With a stock option contract (not adjusted for share repurchases) the increase in stock price resulting from a share repurchase strategy rather than a cash dividend is valuable for the holder of the stock option.

Of course, the owner of an exercisable option can convert it to stock and receive any dividend that is paid. This will require a cash outlay equal to the option's exercise price. Also, the cash dividend is taxed. With the stock repurchase by the firm and the owner not exercising the option, the tax on the cash dividend is avoided and the cash outlay of the option's exercise price is delayed.

A Flexible Dividend

One tax advantage of stock repurchase in lieu of cash dividends is that investors who do not want to convert their investments into cash do not sell their stock back to the corporation. By not selling, they avoid realization of the capital gain and do not have any taxation on the increment to the value of their wealth (they also avoid transaction costs).

The investors who want to receive cash sell a portion of their holdings, and even though they pay tax on the gain, it is apt to be less than if the cash distribution were taxed as ordinary income. By using stock repurchase as the means of the cash distribution, the company tends to direct the cash to those investors who want the cash and bypass the investors who do not need cash at the present time. Also, the tax consequences are favorable for investors.

THE SIGNALING EFFECT OF REPURCHASE

Would management be more likely to launch a share repurchase program if the firm's stock is overvalued or undervalued? While many companies implement share repurchase programs irrespective of whether the stock price is too low or too high, there is evidence that firms are more likely to buy stock that is undervalued by the market. Thus, some investors will consider the start of a stock buyback program as a signal that management thinks the stock is undervalued. Two studies that find evidence supporting this signaling effect are Dann (1981) and Vermaelen (1981).

Investors Like Dividends

The attitude of investors is an important factor to be considered. Consistently increasing dividends are generally welcomed by investors as indicators of profitability and safety. Uncertainty is increased by lack of dividends or dividends that fluctuate widely. Grigoli (1986) agrees with this conclusion: "Because investors value stable dividends, it may not be in a corporation's best interests to raise dividends to unsustainable levels."[4]

Dividends are thought to have an information content; that is, an increase in dividends means that the board of directors expects the firm to do well in the future. This "signaling effect" might favorably affect the firm's common stock price. On the other hand, if income expectations do not justify the optimism, the indication of a more positive future than is justified by the facts is not likely to lead to a favorable outcome.

Since trust officers can only invest in securities with a consistent dividend history, firms like to establish a history of dividends so that they can make the "trust legal list." This consideration sometimes leads to the payment of cash dividends before the firm would otherwise start paying a dividend.

Another important reason for the payment of dividends is that a wide range of investors need the dividends for consumption purposes. Although such investors could sell a portion of their holdings, this latter transaction has relatively high processing costs compared with cashing a dividend check. The presence of investors desiring cash for consumption makes it difficult to change the current dividend policy. One group of investors may benefit from a change in dividend policy, but another group may be harmed. Although we see that income taxes paid by investors tend to make a retention policy more desirable than cash dividends, the presence in the real world of zero tax and low tax investors needing cash dictates that we consider each situation individually and be flexible in arriving at a dividend policy.

There are stockholders who desire cash. A dividend supplies cash without the investor incurring brokerage expense. If cash is retained by the corporation, the stockholders wanting liquidity will have to sell a fraction of their holdings to obtain cash, and this process will result in brokerage fees. Retired individuals living off their dividends and tax-free universities are apt to prefer dividend-paying corporations to corporations retaining income. While a 100% earnings payout cash dividend has the advantage of giving cash to those investors who desire cash, the policy also results in cash being given to those investors who do not desire cash, and who must incur brokerage fees to reinvest the dividends, and who pay taxes.

Dividend Changes and Signaling

A study by Liu, Szewczyk, and Zantout (2008) shows that "there is no compelling evidence of a post-dividend-reduction or post-dividend-omission price drift" (p. 987).

Assume that a firm's stock is fairly priced. Let us assume that this firm's management thinks that if dividends are increased, the market will conclude that this is a favorable signal and the stock price will increase significantly. If the stock was fairly priced to begin with, the stock price after the dividend increase will be too high. This means that with no other changes, the new stockholders will earn less than the firm's required return on stock. Thus, if a stock is fairly priced initially, an increase in dividends that leads to an unjustifiable stock price is not desirable since it leads to investor returns that are less than those required by the new stockholders.

CONCLUSION

If investors in a high tax bracket expect the price of a stock to increase because of improved earnings (and a higher level of future dividends), they will be willing to pay more for a stock knowing that if their expectations are realized the stock can be sold and be taxed at the relatively lower capital gains tax rate. Whereas the lower capital gains tax rate tends to increase the value of a share of stock, we have shown that another powerful factor arises from the ability of the stockholder to defer paying taxes if the corporation retains income

CASE STUDY

Microsoft (2003–2004)

In 2003, the US tax rates on dividends and capital gains were reduced to a maximum rate of 0.15. Microsoft had over US$40 billion in cash.

In January 2003, Microsoft issued its first cash dividend of US$0.02 per quarter. Some investors thought the dividend too low. Others thought the company should have repurchased more shares rather than pay a cash dividend. In July 2004, the company announced a special US$3 cash dividend. With almost 11 billion shares outstanding, this dividend would require a cash outlay of US$33 billion.

"A corporation may want to choose its dividend policy under the assumption that changes in dividend policy will have no permanent effect on its stock price." Fisher Black and Myron Scholes

  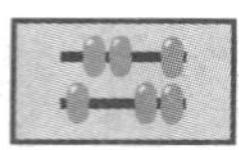      

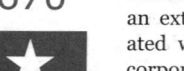

rather than paying dividends. Tax deferral is an extremely important advantage associated with the retention of earnings by a corporation.

The present tax law allows deferral of tax payment (or complete avoidance) on capital gains, and recognized gains may be taxed at a lower rate than ordinary income. Dividend policies of firms have relevance for public policy in the areas of taxation of both corporations and individuals. As corporate managers adjust their decision-making to include the tax law considerations, the makers of public policy must decide whether the results are beneficial to society.

It is not being argued that all firms should discontinue dividend payments. There is a place for a variety of payout policies, but there is a high cost to investors for all firms attempting to cater to the dividend and reinvestment preferences of an average investor. However, it is entirely appropriate that not all corporations appeal to all investors and that corporations design their common stock (and other securities) in the same way they design their consumer products. A corporation should have a financial personality resulting from its various financial policies (especially capital structure and dividend policies) that is attractive to a given group of investors, and is inappropriate for other groups. Corporate securities should have clienteles.

Define the price (and value) of a share of common stock as being equal to the present value of the next dividend (assumed to be declared and paid one period from now) and the price of the share at the time the dividend is paid. If we keep repeating the substitution process, we find that the value of the firm is equal to the present value of all future dividends, where the word "dividend" is used to include all cash distributions made from the firm to its investors. We replace the price at each future moment in time by the dividends that causes the stock to have value.

A board of directors acting in the interests of the stockholders of a corporation sets the dividend policy of a firm. The ability of an investor to defer income taxes as a result of the company retaining earnings is an important consideration. In addition, the distinction between ordinary income and capital gains for purposes of income taxation by the federal government accentuates the importance of investors knowing the dividend policy of the firm whose stock they are considering purchasing or have already purchased. In turn, this means that the corporation (and its board) has a responsibility to announce its dividend policy and to attempt to be consistent in its policy, changing only when its economic situation changes significantly. In the particular situation in which a firm is expanding its investments rapidly and is financing this expansion by issuing securities to its stockholders, the payment of cash dividends is especially vulnerable to criticism.

MORE INFO

Book:

Bierman, Harold, Jr. *Increasing Shareholder Value: Distribution Policy, A Corporate Finance Challenge*. Norwell, MA: Kluwer Academic Publishers, 2001.

Articles:

Barsky, Robert B., and J. Bradford De Long. "Why does the stock market fluctuate?" *Quarterly Journal of Economics* 108:2 (May 1993): 291–311.

Black, Fisher. "The dividend puzzle." *Journal of Portfolio Management* (Winter 1976): 5–8.

Dann, Larry Y. "Common stock repurchases: An analysis of returns to bondholders and stockholders." *Journal of Financial Economics* 9:2 (June 1981): 113–38.

Liu, Y., H. Szewczyk, and Z. Zantout. "Under-reaction to dividend reductions and omissions." *Journal of Finance* 63:2 (April 2008): 987–1020.

Miller, Merton H., and Franco Modigliani. "Dividend policy, growth, and the valuation of shares." *Journal of Business* 34:4 (Jan 1961): 411–433.

Rundell, C. A. "From the thoughtful businessman." *Harvard Business Review* 43:6 (November–December, 1965): 39.

Vermaelen, Theo. "Common stock repurchase and market signaling." *Journal of Financial Economics* 9:2 (June 1981): 139–83.

Reports:

Cohen, Abby Joseph. "No problem with dividend growths." Goldman Sachs Portfolio Strategy, August 12, 1994, p. 1.

Grigoli, Carmine J. "The great corporate de-financing." Merrill Lynch, March 1986, p. 5.

See Also:

★ Managing 21st Century Finances (pp. 66–67)
★ Reinvesting in the Company versus Rewarding Investors with Distributions (pp. 701–702)
✔ Calculating Total Shareholder Return (p. 1066)
✔ An Overview of Stockholders' Agreements (p. 1084)
✔ Setting Up a Dividend Policy (p. 987)
✔ Using Multistage Dividend Discount Models (p. 1106)
✔ Using Shareholder Value Analysis (p. 1107)
Jack Welch (p. 1318)

NOTES

1 Barsky and De Long (1993).
2 Rundell (1965), p. 39.
3 Cohen (1994), p. 1.
4 Grigoli (1986), p. 5.

"They seldom pretend to understand anything of the business of the company...but receive contentedly such half yearly or yearly dividends, as the directors think proper to make them." Adam Smith

  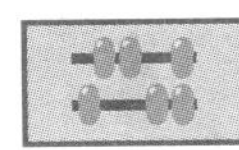   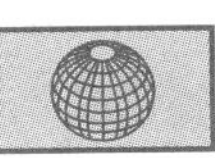   

Viewpoint: Embedding CSR and Sustainability in Corporate Culture: The Boots Experience

by Richard Ellis

INTRODUCTION

Richard Ellis, Director of corporate social responsibility (CSR) at Alliance Boots Group, has spent the past 30 years working for a range of companies on all aspects of the CSR agenda. The early part of his career was spent in banking, before he became involved in CSR after the inner city riots of the early 1980s. After this involvement he held CSR-related positions at HSBC, TSB, and British Aerospace, and ran his own CSR consultancy for five years. In 2003 he joined Boots and became responsible for all of the company's CSR activities. Following the merger between Boots and Alliance UniChem and the subsequent private equity buyout, he was appointed to his current role.

When did Boots UK first start to take sustainability seriously as a concept?

We can almost go back to 1849 on this. One of the first slogans Boots had was "Cheap medicines for poor people," and part of ensuring medicines remained cheap was getting people to bring back their used glass medicine bottles, so that they could be washed and refilled. This approach helped to make medicines available to more people than ever before, so in terms of sustainability and repackaging, this has been a fundamental part of our approach to business from the outset. Before Boots was founded, the only people who could afford pharmaceutical medicines were the rich, so recycling as a way of keeping costs down was very much part of the DNA of the business.

In a similar way—although we are only now starting to see hybrid and electric vehicles coming into mainstream use—Boots had electric vehicles on-site back in 1914. The warehouse used electrically powered vehicles to move supplies around the central warehouse complex in Nottingham.

What is clear then is that sustainability is something that is part of Boots UK's social legacy and heritage, so it has always been integral to our business.

Your title, Director of CSR, seems to hark back to the 1980s. Many companies today favor a title with "sustainability" in it to describe your position. Are you comfortable putting CSR at the center of things?

CSR predates "green issues" and "sustainability" by a few decades, but we should not get too hung up on the wording. What this is all about is the way businesses behave and think.

Alliance Boots has developed into a leading international, pharmacy-led health and beauty group, and so to maintain stability and continuity we have retained our traditional job titles. Everyone across the group, wherever they work, knows what CSR means and if you change the title you run the risk of confusing people. An academic might want to split hairs over how much of my job is related to traditional CSR and how much is sustainability, but my job has not changed. I am doing the same things now as I have been doing for the past decade.

How does the CSR report rank, in terms of importance, by comparison with the financial report and accounts?

Our CSR Report is very much on an equal footing with our Annual Report. There is a section on CSR in the Annual Report and also a dedicated CSR Report, which we produce annually. By having two separate reports it helps Alliance Boots to demonstrate how important CSR issues remain to us.

I work very closely with the finance team at Alliance Boots. Our rigorous data-gathering process supports and verifies our CSR programs, so that everyone—from board members to employees, to customers and suppliers—can have complete confidence in the CSR claims we make. In each business unit there is a CSR champion who organizes the collection of all the metrics from the various sources in that business. This is captured by the finance team and then approved by our Financial Director.

This means that when I present the results of our CSR initiatives to the board, the information has the same focus on assigning monetary outcomes to processes that the board would get from the Annual Report. When I talk about our road transport initiatives, for example, I can not only say that we had a reduction of over 1.8 million kilometers and approximately 1,800 tons of carbon dioxide from deliveries between our Boots UK central warehouses and stores compared to the previous year, I can say that we have also saved from the reduced fuel costs.

Individual examples like this are very strong, but the importance of presenting information with a solid financial dimension to it is clear for me. There are too many people working in sustainability functions in big organizations who are highly focused on saving the planet but who have no real grasp of how to communicate the importance of what they are doing in a language to which board members can easily relate. If you just talk in sustainability terms, say, x percentage of waste saved, you run into what I call the "So what?" question. You need to present in a way that shows how what you are doing matters in financial terms. So to use another example, I can say that with the initiatives that we undertook to improve our Christmas packaging from a sustainability point of view, we reduced the volume of waste substantially. We not only reduced the number of plastic bags used, we adapted some of the plastic packaging that holds items in place. This has clearly made the packaging more sustainable, but a hard-headed person might still say, "So what?" So we need to go further and say that for Christmas 2011 we reduced the weight of packaging used by 12% compared to 2010. We saved 230 tons of plastic packaging which saved on production costs.

How do you set your sustainability targets, given the scale of your organization?

The way we approach targets falls into two categories. We have long-term aspirational

"Corporate bodies are more corrupt and profligate than individuals because they have more power to do mischief and are less amenable to disgrace or punishment. They feel neither shame, remorse, gratitude, nor goodwill." William Hazlitt

targets, such as our goals for reducing our carbon footprint by 80% by 2050, and we have short-term aims and ambitions, such as three-year targets around reducing packaging, reducing waste, and so on.

But as an international group, we have to set targets that are realistic for our different businesses across more then 25 countries. For example, Germany has a very developed infrastructure for recycling and they have had punitive landfill taxes for the last 50 years, so we have zero waste to landfill in Germany. However, in Russia there is a less-developed recycling infrastructure and a completely different cultural and philosophical approach to the whole concept of waste. So if you set a target of, say, reducing waste by 80% in three years as an edict across all business units, the Germans would laugh and say we were there 10 years ago, while the Russians would laugh and say "impossible!" What we have done is to adjust our targets to meet the practical realities of each region, and work towards our goals in the most practical way possible across regions that might not currently be very sympathetic to sustainability.

If you take a hypothetical product launch, in the past a director in charge of a new product might want to make their reputation with their work, so typically they would do a major rebranding exercise. This would involve new counters in the stores and the re-launch would make or break reputations. Whether a success or not, they probably would not be around to pick up the pieces from a sustainability point of view. Today at Alliance Boots, if a new director wants to put a new counter in a store, then every element of that counter has to be designed in such a way that allows it to be reused or recycled. It has to have detachable lights, internal dividers that can be reused, and so on. This is a small change in philosophy but a simple one which allows us to get to a wider end-goal. The point is that sustainability does not possess a silver-bullet type solution. You cannot get there with one shot, but by accumulating multiple smaller wins.

In our view, the people who are best placed to define where sustainability gains can be made are likely to be the people who own the processes in the businesses. They can see what needs to be done to make their element of the overall business more sustainable. Those engaged in developing cosmetics, for example, are best placed to see where plant ingredients could be used instead of mineral ingredients. So you need to push the sustainability project out to the businesses and employees to gain maximum traction.

Do you find it difficult to keep up the momentum for sustainable initiatives during a major economic downturn?

For companies that have not really discovered or properly come to grips with the sustainability agenda there is a perception that during difficult economic times, sustainability programs are a drain upon scarce resources, and constitute a cost rather than a benefit.

For us, what helps us most to overcome any pull in this direction is the fact that we are able to prove and verify the benefits to the business that our CSR initiatives have. In fact, when you are saving the company significant sums then the importance of sustainability initiatives is even greater in tough economic times.

It was not always easy to integrate the finance function into our sustainability reporting but having operated this way for four years, it now works very successfully.

We also know that CSR is of huge importance to our employees—it helps to increase satisfaction levels and lowers employee turnover, so it is important that we ensure continued momentum.

The fact that we have been able to influence others with our enthusiasm for this agenda also helps. Kohlberg Kravis Roberts (KKR) embraced this agenda as well and were one of the first private equity (PE) companies to produce a CSR report. PE houses are used to evaluating and managing their investments in a particular way, and with our CSR numbers being validated by the finance function, KKR can see real value in what we are doing.

Companies looking at the cost of making changes to move to a more sustainable agenda need to be aware of these positive benefits and they need to create targets around them so that they can achieve real financial benefits, as well as lower their emissions and improve their public standing as good corporate citizens.

MORE INFO

Books:

Hoskins, Tony. Corporate Social Responsibility Handbook: Making CSR and Narrative Reporting Work for Your Business. London: ICSA Publishing, 2012.

May, Brendan. How to Make Your Organisation a Recognised Sustainability Champion. Oxford: Dō Sustainability, 2012. Order from: tinyurl.com/ok7njy2

See Also:

★ Best Practices in Corporate Social Responsibility (pp. 636–639)
★ CSR: More than PR, Pursuing Competitive Advantage in the Long Run (pp. 664–666)
★ Viewpoint: The Companies Bill, 2012, and its Impact on the Future of Corporate Social Responsibility in India (pp. 648–650)
★ Viewpoint: The Growth of Sustainability Reporting (pp. 680–681)
✔ Creating a Sustainable Development Policy (p. 1113)

"In essence leadership appears to be the art of getting others to want to do something you are convinced should be done." Vance Packard

  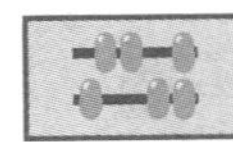      

Executive Rewards: Ensuring That Financial Rewards Match Performance by Shaun Tyson

EXECUTIVE SUMMARY

- Executive pay is used to attract and retain executives, and to drive performance.
- Business strategy objectives are cascaded down the organization and used as performance targets for the variable element in the reward package, in order to provide a clear line of sight.
- Reward packages for executive pay include base pay, short-term incentives, benefits, long-term incentives, and perks. Base pay is determined by the market rate in similar organizations.
- Variable pay incentives usually take the form of an annual bonus scheme, or, in the case of long-term incentives, deferred bonus and/or stock option plans.
- Reward packages are decided by remuneration committees as an important aspect of good corporate governance; the decisions are made by nonexecutive directors, with transparent reporting in annual reports. In the United Kingdom stockholders vote on the report.

INTRODUCTION

Effective management of executive rewards resides at the heart of a network of pressures and issues of central relevance to the management of organizational performance. These pressures can be represented diagrammatically to show how stockholder interests and corporate governance issues impact on business performance, objective setting, the motivation of executives, and the position of the organization as an employer in specific labor markets; and how all of these are affected by corporate values/culture and vision (Figure 1).

However, the economic events of 2008 have reminded us all that these issues are conditioned by the broader economic climate in which corporations operate, where survival is more risky and uncertain. The recession which began with a massive banking crisis and near financial collapse, has affected the UK especially, because of the reliance on the financial sector revenues, and the significance of the City of London to the UK economy. Recovery and emergence from recession began in the US, Germany, Japan and other major economies however, in 2009. One of the consequences of the recession has been a search for more international regulation of the financial sector, in particular control over rewards associated with risk taking. The topic of executive rewards must be seen as a dynamic field, and this caveat informs all that follows. Nevertheless, there are systematic and enduring influences in the linkages between reward and performance.

We will examine rewards to show the major impact of reward policies and practices on organizational performance. This article takes rewards from the organizational perspective, and the starting point is an examination of the significance of corporate values, vision, and the culture of rewards.

CORPORATE VALUES/CULTURE/VISION

Corporate values and vision statements are an explicit expression of the formal values and vision of the organization, including the sometimes implicitly preferred behaviors and attitudes of managers in their leadership roles. These values may be published but, if not explicitly stated, will still emerge in the actions of senior managers and the founders. The objectives of a reward policy can be summarized as:

- Building stockholder value (or sustaining value for the citizen in the public sector).
- Being competitive in the recruitment of executives.
- Motivating and retaining executives.
- Being cost-effective.
- Being seen as fair by employees.
- Providing a degree of security for employees.

How these objectives are interpreted in any organization is contingent on that organization's values and the nature of its objectives—for example, profit maximization, market share, and service provision.

A number of authors have suggested that there are specific best practices to drive a philosophy of rewards that will support the corporate vision. For example *The New Pay*, by Schuster and Zingheim (1996), was a reward ideology that emphasized the strategic role of rewards and the supremacy of the marketplace. Key features of *The New Pay* were:

- Emphasis on external market-sensitive pay rather than annual increases.
- Risk-sharing partnership with employees rather than entitlements.
- Variable, performance-based pay.
- Flexibility in pay systems.
- Lateral promotions rather than career paths.
- Employability, not job security.

Later, the same authors argued that there are general reward principles that include aligning rewards with business goals; extending the "line of sight" of all employees to see the relationship between individual performance, corporate performance, and their rewards; and recognizing the market value of the individual with base pay, while

Figure 1. Reward at the centre of internal and external pressures

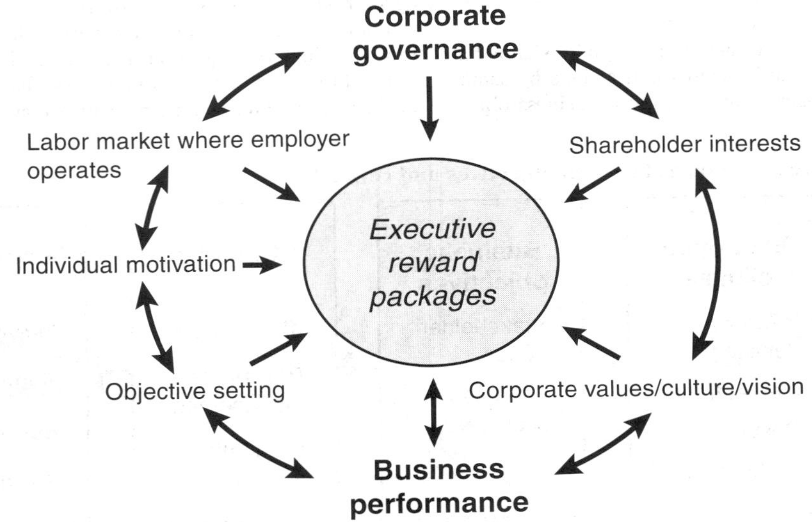

"The top 20% must be loved, nurtured and rewarded in the soul and wallet because they are the ones who make magic happen." General Electric

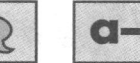

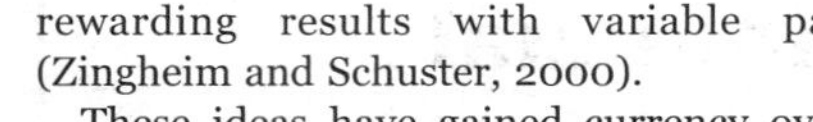

rewarding results with variable pay (Zingheim and Schuster, 2000).

These ideas have gained currency over the last 20 years. Even though the economic storm now raging across the globe challenges some of this received wisdom, the ideas remain consistent with the prevailing concepts of market capitalism.

RELATING BUSINESS PERFORMANCE TO REWARDS

According to economic logic, there is a clear and consequential relationship, or line of sight, between the economic climate, the organization's performance, and the rewards provided (Figure 2).

Certain linkages, such as that between strategies and accountabilities, are critical. The diagram demonstrates the importance of line of sight. There is also the question of how quickly strategies, accountabilities, and rewards can adapt in response to changes in the economic climate.

Objective Setting and Targets

Objectives are normally "cascaded" down from the business strategy—each business unit or department having agreed short-term (next year) and longer-term (three to five year) plans. Objectives are usually both financial and qualitative. Financial objectives are typically total stockholder returns (TSR) and return on capital employed (ROCE). Budget targets are also often used, as well as share price. In remuneration planning, the performance objectives should be measured, and they should be designed to drive the business forward: "Paying for value creation is the most reliable way of generating it" (Credit Suisse First Boston). Targets are usually discussed and agreed at the annual performance review.

The Reward Package

Reward packages are pay policies aimed at achieving behaviors and actions by senior managers that accomplish business objectives. A package consists of base pay, short-term incentives, benefits, long-term incentives, and perks (perquisites). Base pay is decided by reference to pay rates in comparable organizations (see below), and usually according to internal relativities decided by the job evaluation scheme in use.

The decision of where to be in the market is a matter for corporate policy (for example, at the market median, or the upper quartile rate), reflecting labor market pressures and attraction and retention strategies. Short-term incentives are usually annual bonus schemes. Long-term incentive plans (LTIPs) use stock options and/or bonuses, merit pay, company-wide share plans, and the like.

Benefits include pensions to which the employer makes a contribution, private health plans, life insurance, and similar personal benefits. Perks are fringe benefits such as status cars, concierge services, use of company accommodation, etc. In most countries such perks are taxable as benefits in kind, although the package as a whole should be constructed to be as tax-effective as possible. Benefits may be flexible, so that individuals can choose a mix of benefits and perks within the agreed total value package. In some organizations there will also be the opportunity to sacrifice a proportion of salary for benefits.

Reward specialists structure executive reward packages taking into account the proportion of the base pay to variable pay available in the bonus opportunities, and typically they seek to balance the various elements in the package to drive the performance (both short and long term) required to achieve corporate objectives. The trend is toward variable pay based on performance being a high proportion of the total reward package, especially as managers become more senior. In this way senior managers take a larger risk with their rewards, since variable rewards are related more directly to the performance of the business in market conditions, which may vary for any number of reasons. Irrespective of these market conditions, directors and senior managers are accountable for profit, cost, and market share objectives.

LTIPs are normally constructed using bonus and stock option plans. Stock options give the right to purchase a defined quantity of stock at a stipulated price over a given period, according to predetermined eligibility requirements. There may be stock appreciation rights—the share award is triggered by increases in the share price, at a time chosen by the executive in the time period allowed.

Stock options have been popular as a way to retain key executives, to provide them with a stake in the company, and, at a time when share prices were rising, the opportunity to acquire real wealth. The change from a bull to a bear market has diminished enthusiasm for stock option schemes because the schemes depend on rising share prices so that executives can gain in wealth either by owning an appreciating asset, or by selling the shares and realizing the difference between the stipulated price (the strike price) and the enhanced market price.

Various performance conditions may be attached to the granting of a stock option or bonus. These include improvements in TSR, ROCE, EPS, and EBITDA (earnings before interest, taxation, depreciation, and amortization), usually in the corporate figures produced for the annual accounts. Table 1 is example from BP in 2007 to show how the package works.

There is an annual bonus scheme. Performance measures and targets were set at the beginning of the year. Bonus opportunities were: on target (120%), and maximum (150%), of salary. The remuneration committee can, in exceptional circumstances, increase these payments, or reduce them to zero if appropriate. Targets for 2007 and 2008 were: half of the bonus is based on financial measures (EBITDA, ROCE, and cash flow), the other half on

Figure 2. Linkages between objectives and rewards

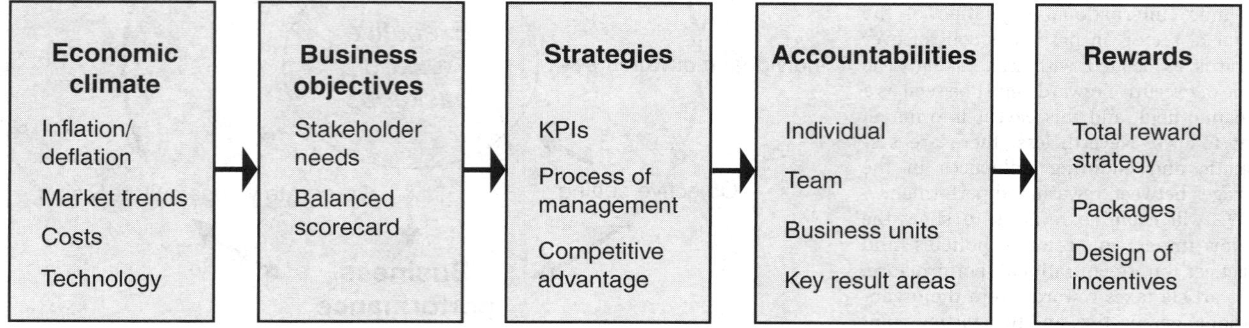

  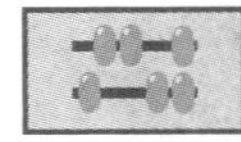      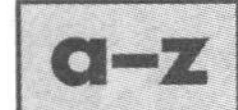

Table 1. Example of a reward package: BP executive directors as at December 2007. (*Source*: IDS *Executive Compensation Review* 326 (April 2008): 12)

	Salary p.a.	*Annual bonus*	*Benefits*	*Performance shares*	*Total*
Chief executive	£877,000	£1,262,000	£14,000	Zero vested	£2,153,000
Chief finance officer	£591,755	£781,117	£5,036	Zero vested	£1,377,908

nonfinancial measures and individual performance. Nonfinancial targets were safety and people (including values and culture); individual performance targets were results and leadership.

The LTIP had three elements: shares, stock options, and cash; up to 5.5 times salary could be awarded in performance shares. Performance measured in TSR was compared to other oil companies. Although in this particular case shares were not vested (i.e. not passed into the ownership of the executives for 2007, due to operational problems that affected performance compared to other oil companies), high performance in previous years had resulted in substantial numbers of shares being vested. This demonstrates how the package reflects performance.

CORPORATE GOVERNANCE ISSUES

Reward for Failure

Much attention has been paid to excessive pay increases and bonuses for senior executives, especially where these appear to be awarded regardless of the corporate performance achieved.

Criticism of directors for receiving massive bonus and termination payments typically happens when there seems to be an element of reward for failure. UK directors in the FTSE 100 companies are paid more than in the rest of the FTSE companies, but they do not receive the massive sums seen in Fortune 500 companies in the United States. There is a tradition of higher rewards in financial services. A big bonus culture existed in financial services among those dealing in the markets, as well as in the boardroom. Whether this was a cause of the recession is not yet clear, but it may have increased the propensity of managers and traders to take higher risks.

Although executive pay increases have tended to be modest, as with other workers during the recession, in 2009, CEO's in the UK and in the USA were receiving base pay increases and bonus payments in some industry sectors. In the UK, CEO's of larger companies saw bonus payments cut by around a third, down to around £500,000, according to IDS. In February 2009 President Obama stated he would cap bank executives' pay at $500,000, and forbid bonuses to banks which had received Government aid.

In the UK and USA, public outrage at the idea that those Banks which had received bail outs from the State should pay bonuses prompted a response from politicians. The view that there was a link between reward structure and the acceptance of excessive risk which had produced the financial crisis, was widely held. The UK's Financial Services Authority launched a new Code for Pay and Reward to be effective from January 2010, providing advice on how to mitigate risk, when awarding bonuses. This favours deferred bonus payments, with performance and claw back provisions attached.

Stockholder activism among both institutional stockholders, such as the Association of British Insurers, and small stockholder groups means that stockholders are likely to be consulted before new schemes are introduced. The court of public opinion is assisted by a vigilant press and the transparency rules. Accounting rules are now generally applied that require the cost of stock options and LTIPs to be fully expensed in the accounts. Increased volatility in share prices and the massive fall from the last quarter of 2008 onward have made stock options much less attractive, so there is less likelihood of big payouts at a later time when the executive cashes in the shares.

Base pay and total rewards are typically decided according to the market capitalization, the total number of employees, and the financial turnover of a business with respect to its industry comparators, but they are also, of course, contractually negotiated. Pressure from institutional investors and the press/media has created interest among the general public in this area, fueled by a number of high-profile cases where corporate failure has not been reflected in reductions in bonus or reward. As a consequence, director-level rewards are now very highly regulated and scrutinized compared to other employee groups.

Remuneration Committees

There is a convergence in corporate governance arrangements, based on the principles of transparency, the need to justify pay awards, the independent judgments of a remuneration committee, an accent on the process rather than on the content of rewards, and compliance with the rules as a condition of being listed on the appropriate stock exchange. Some of these principles were found in the original voluntary rules of the stock exchanges (for example in the Combined Code of the London Stock Exchange). Statutory provision has reinforced these rules—Directors' Remuneration Report Regulations 2002 (UK), Sarbanes–Oxley 2002 (US), SEC rules (US), NRE Act 2001 (France), and in Germany, the Cromme Code (2002). The UK regulations of 2002 require listed companies to have a remuneration committee of independent (nonexecutive) directors, which must produce and publish a report as part of the annual company report. This must include a statement of reward policy, the role of the remuneration

MAKING IT HAPPEN

- Effective reward policies for senior managers and directors can only be created if there is a clear line of sight between their performance goals and the business objectives. This requires:
    - strategic planning and accurate budgeting;
    - clear accountabilities, cascaded down the business;
    - realistic, measurable, demanding performance targets for the short and long term.
- Job evaluation techniques such as the Hay system can help to review accountabilities systematically.
- Base pay should be decided from market data on rates, with comparator organizations in the same industry sector that have similar market capitalization and employee numbers.
- Variable pay is used to recognize and drive performance. Short-term performance will need bonus schemes to be designed with annual performance targets, and there are design decisions to be made about whether there should be a threshold performance level, any weighting on particular targets, etc. Bonus is normally a percentage of base pay (typically 20%–40%). Long-term incentives might include a deferred bonus paid out after two or three years, with further performance conditions attached, and/or stock option schemes.
- Decisions on rewards are made by remuneration committees for director-level pay in quoted companies, with annual public reporting and stockholder involvement.

"The idea that Wall Street banks should give themselves $18 billion worth of bonuses is the height of irresponsibility. It is shameful." Barack Obama

committee, proposals for directors' pay going forward, and must include a graph showing comparisons in terms of TSR with a named broad equity index over the previous five years, stating the reasons for selecting the index. Stockholders must be given the opportunity to vote on the remuneration committee report at the AGM. The stockholders' vote is not binding, but it would be unusual for a company and CEO to implement a pay award to the directors if this was voted down.

MORE INFO

Articles:

Balkin, David B., and Lius R. Gomez-Mejia. "Matching compensation and organizational strategies." *Strategic Management Journal* 11:2 (February 1990): 153–169. Online at: dx.doi.org/10.1002/smj.4250110207

Cascio, Wayne F., and Peter Cappelli. "Lessons from the financial services crisis." *HR Magazine* 54:1 (2009): 46–50. Online at: tinyurl.com/3ogadg5

Websites:

Hay Group global management consulting: www.haygroup.com
Mercer HR and finance consultancy: www.mercer.com
Thomson/Sweet & Maxwell Incomes Data Services (IDS): www.incomesdata.co.uk
Towers Watson global professional services: www.towerswatson.com

See Also:

★ Balancing Senior Management Compensation Arrangements with Shareholders' Interests (pp. 634–635)
★ Corporate Board Structures (pp. 654–657)
★ Creating Value with EVA (pp. 814–816)
★ Employee Stock Options (pp. 835–836)
✔ Assessing Business Performance (p. 1144)
✔ The Board's Role in Executive Compensation (p. 1108)
✔ Creating Executive Compensation (p. 1114)
Jack Welch (p. 1318)

"The FSA is determined that banks' remuneration policies should be consistent with and promote, effective risk management." FSA Chief Executive

  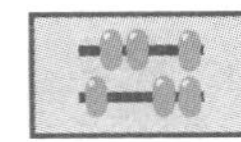   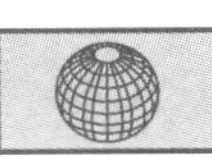   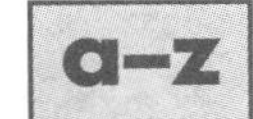

Financial Reporting: Conveying the Message Down the Line by Leslie L. Kossoff

EXECUTIVE SUMMARY

- Finance department participation must be cross-organizational to ensure the financial health and welfare of the enterprise.
- Financial data should be better shared, and finance personnel become more involved, at all levels of the organization.
- Middle management presents the greatest barrier to finance messaging. To overcome this, finance must present data sharing as a verifiable win to them.
- Integrating into ad-hoc or lean-team initiatives provides finance personnel with the opportunity to become friendly advisers to the organization as a whole.

INTRODUCTION

Of all the functions in an enterprise that cannot, indeed *must not*, be the province of the function itself is finance. In fact, the more finance is separated from the rest of the organization's thinking and operations, the greater the risk for the enterprise and its stakeholders.

Finance people not only know the numbers behind what's going on, they also know why those numbers exist. From greasing the wheels to get things done, to putting the brake on projects that carry too high a financial risk, finance knows the answers—and acts on them.

The problem is that when you ask those in other parts of the organization what finance does, what you'll hear will likely be either resounding silence from a lack of knowledge, a description of some of its most basic tasks, or a stream of complaints about the problems and obstacles that finance causes.

Yet, in best of breed organizations, finance is there as much to help the body of the organization as it is to ensure the strategic and tactical financial health and welfare of the enterprise. The beauty of the function is that it can be as overarching and as specific as necessary—simultaneously and serially. The data are there to be used to help, not hurt, or obstruct. So are the people.

Until that word gets out, however, finance will be at best a boring function left to others or, at worst, seen as an enemy within the enterprise.

That's why finance has to change its image across all divisions, directorates, departments, and levels. Finance has to become an organizational player.

REDEFINING THE ROLE OF FINANCE

The problem with becoming a player is that, first, you have to want to play. That is very often the prime difficulty for the people who work in finance. Starting at the highest level and systematically working down through the enterprise, finance people must become some of the most familiar—and welcome—faces in the organization.

And so, as with every other successful organizational initiative, it starts at the top. The CEO and CFO have to agree that more financial information will be shared throughout the enterprise. They have to discuss with the senior executive team which information should be shared, when, and with whom. That means safety checks and limits on what information is given to whom—because the given is that someone, somehow, is going to give the game away outside the enterprise. As a result, damage control measures must be put in place before information is shared.

The chances are that these measures and limits are already in place. The chances are even higher that comparatively few executives or managers have accessed the information available to them. Even if they have, it probably hasn't been adequately communicated (if it was communicated at all), or they didn't know what to do with it once it was in their hands.

That is where finance's role changes from a service that is perceived to be "outside" and auditing in nature (for which read obstructive), to the organization's most involved, friendly adviser.

The goal, of course, is to turn every employee into a mini-CFO in their own job within their own department. From senior manager to frontline employee, everyone needs to understand where the organization stands financially, why, and, most importantly, how their particular job or functional area is contributing to that state of affairs. Good or bad.

BUILDING SUPPORT AMONG MIDDLE MANAGEMENT

The biggest challenge is to involve middle management positively in the process—and it's a big challenge.

Executives understand the need for financial data. The senior team will be onside as you look at how you are going to inculcate financial thinking into the larger organization.

Middle management, on the other hand, will either see the offer of financial advice and guidance as a potential threat, or as a weapon they can use at some later date against some other part of the organization. Even though they never touch a banknote, the more they see in their spreadsheet coffers, the more they believe they can manipulate the rest of the organization into doing things the way they want. Budgeting, to middle management, is empire building. It's fiefdoms. It's silos.

Enter finance. With all the good intentions in the world, your people will be facing an audience who, at least in part, are frightened that seeing your faces means the end of the world as they've known it. Fear will be the prevailing—if hidden—emotion.

It gets worse. As you bring financial knowledge to the lower levels of the enterprise, middle management will become even more frightened at the prospect of their power base being dissolved.

This means that finance has to develop a strategy to make not just knowing, but also sharing, financial information a benefit to the middle management group as well as to their employees. The good news is that, because they believe information is power, if you position what you're offering as something that will enable them to improve their position in the organization, you will achieve at least a first-level sell. They'll be open to what you have to offer.

From there, use what you're providing to make them shine. To help them succeed. To make them open to your next step—bringing finance to the front line in every department.

Because the real goal—the thing that will make the biggest change, both in the way that finance is seen and in the extent to which smart financial thinking becomes standard operating procedure in the organization—is when you start working with the lower levels. Then, just watch what happens. Even the middle managers will join in and see the win at that point.

CREATING THE WIN

At the middle and lower levels of the organization, employees know that there are financial underpinnings to what they are doing, but they have little to no idea what

"Even if your idea is worth stealing, the hard part is implementing the idea, not coming up with it." Guy Kawasaki

those underpinnings are. What they do know is that they are, all too often, told that the company can't afford what would, from the employees' perspective, make all the difference in the world.

By bringing financial knowledge to all levels of the enterprise, finance breaks the existing mold. Suddenly the mystery behind the decisions is gone. The veil has been lifted and everyone knows and understands things in the same way.

Employees gain a new respect for how the finances of the company act as a driver for overall success. They begin to understand that there are financial implications in every action they make and decision they take. There is, suddenly, a direct, causal correlation between what they are doing and how it is impacting the organization, positively or negatively.

That is your chance. The more you position finance as a friendly adviser to departments and workgroups at all levels, the faster the decisions will improve across the organization. Employees at every level will know exactly what's in it for them to participate positively.

Moreover, if there are teams of any kind—from ad-hoc groups to an ongoing lean initiative—the more both they and finance will shine.

Teams are formed to generate options, recommendations, and, in some cases, decisions to move the organization from where it is to where senior executives want it to go. Unfortunately, those teams rarely have a full understanding of the financial foundations or consequences of the recommendations they make.

Too often, that results in finance having to come in after the fact and, like the villain of the piece, tell the teams they can't go forward with their ideas because they are not financially viable. Finance becomes, once again, the bad guy.

Instead, by insinuating finance into every existing and forming team in the enterprise, senior management is assured—from the get-go—that they won't have to be concerned about what the recommendations are going to cost. Instead, they'll be presented with recommendations that have annual costs, with detail on the associated savings, avoidances, and return on investment, that each recommendation brings.

Sweet.

Even better, as the organization gets smarter at using financial data at all levels, the enterprise can start moving toward stretch goals—those infamous goals so typical of best of breed organizations. That's when, even though management knows what its budget is for any fiscal year, their greater goal is not to meet budget, but to meet and exceed productivity and output targets, while returning anywhere from 10 to 15% of the annual budget back to the organization.

Really sweet.

But that can only happen if finance has developed a system for working with the rest of the enterprise. And that means taking it back to basics.

BUILDING THE FRIENDLY ADVISER

Every employee in the finance function needs to practice relationship building with the rest of the enterprise. Finance personnel must become the first choice go-to guys as everyone, from senior executives to middle managers to line level employees, looks at what's next.

The challenge for you and your personnel will be learning a new language to explain what, to you, is self-evident.

People in the body of the organization don't know how elegant the finance function is. They don't understand that the data are there to provide answers which are simultaneously overarching and exquisitely specific, strategic, and tactical.

They don't know what you do. That puts the onus on you not only to determine what information is shared, but also how best to share it. This is a learning process for everyone—both those within the finance function and those they will be assisting.

Be clear on what you want to achieve as you take employees at all levels through the learning process. Be prepared to explain things that you don't think need explanation. They do. Moreover, those to whom you're providing guidance probably won't ask for the explanations they need, if only because they're concerned that they might not look as clever as they would like. Take it for granted that your audience knows less than they admit—even when asked directly.

CASE STUDY

Sony Electronics

When one of Sony Electronics' technology divisions decided it was time to look at cost reductions, senior management at one of the US plants decided it was make-or-break time. They had to show headquarters in Japan what they could do.

Adopting and adapting the Sony Six Sigma management system for a Western audience, they immediately brought finance in as a centerpiece of the initiative. The process and results were:

- Management at all levels, from manufacturing floor supervisors to external sales managers to R&D directors, were briefed and briefed again on how the financials fit into the initiative—and, by extension, into every decision they were to make.
- Dedicated finance representatives worked with management and teams to ensure that the decisions being made were financially sound, simultaneously dovetailing with and enhancing decisions made across the enterprise.
- Finance team members became operations specialists and, for the first time, fully understood the organization they were supporting.
- External contracts were both expanded and discarded, based on verifiable financial data.
- Within four months, overall productivity increased in the double digits, with a corresponding reduction in operating costs.
- For the first time in the plant's history, management returned budget to headquarters at the end of the fiscal year.

MAKING IT HAPPEN

- The CEO and CFO, with executive management, put together a plan for sharing financial data across the organization.
- Data protection and damage control plans are put into place, in case any financial data are released without permission.
- Finance personnel are trained to become participants in educating and supporting the organization to use financial data to make better decisions.
- Middle management is co-opted to incorporate financial data and finance department support in all planning and decision-making.
- Teams (ad-hoc, lean, departmental, etc.) are assigned dedicated finance representatives to assist in using financial data for sound decision-making.

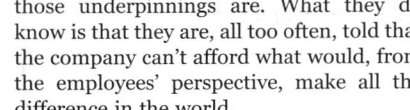

"High achievement always takes place in the framework of high expectation." Jack Kinder

  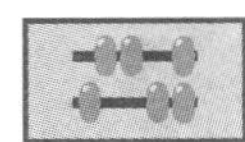      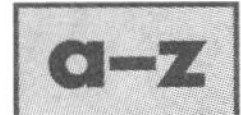

Be gentle but firm. You're giving them the ability to succeed in ways that transcend anything they've achieved before. Not only will they have answers, they will also have financially sound solutions, which can lead to quantum leaps in everything from productivity to profits.

They will finally know what you yourself know about the job you do—that it's one of the most exciting and satisfying functions out there. Especially when everyone is involved.

MORE INFO

Books:

Creelman, James. *Creating a World-Class Finance Function: Five Core Capabilities That Generate Added Business Value*. London: Business Intelligence, 2005.

Donegan, Michael C. *Growth and Profitability: Optimizing the Finance Function for Small and Emerging Businesses*. Hoboken, NJ: Wiley, 2002.

Articles:

Desai, Mihir A. "The finance function in a global corporation." *Harvard Business Review* 86:7/8 (2008). Online at: tinyurl.com/3rosetz

Pohl, Herbert. "Building a competitive finance function: An executive roundtable." *McKinsey Quarterly* (December 2007). Online at: www.nemrod-partners.com/Building.pdf

Report:

IBM Global Business Services. "Balancing risk and performance with an integrated finance organization: The global CFO study 2008." 2008. Online at: tinyurl.com/43tcl99

Website:

CFO.com news and insight for financial executives: www.cfo.com

See Also:

★ Accounting for Business Combinations in Accordance with International Financial Reporting Standards (IFRS) Requirements (pp. 706–707)
★ Engaging Senior Management in Internal Control (pp. 336–337)
✔ International Financial Reporting Standards (IFRS): The Basics (p. 1039)
✔ Key Accounting Standards and Organizations (p. 1040)

  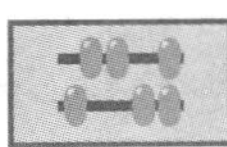   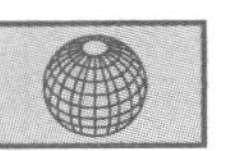   

Viewpoint: The Growth of Sustainability Reporting by Wim Bartels

INTRODUCTION

Wim Bartels has been global head of KPMG's Sustainability Services Network since October 2007. He studied business economics and accountancy at Amsterdam's Vrije Universiteit before qualifying as a chartered accountant in 1993. He has worked as an auditor and forensic accountant. In 2001 he became a KPMG partner, taking overall responsibility for the group's sustainability services, including the provision of sustainability assurance services to multinational businesses such as BASF, DSM, Heineken, KLM, Philips and Rabobank. Wim is closely involved with initiatives including the UN's Global Reporting Initiative and AccountAbility. In his spare time Wim sings and plays trumpet in a band that performs cover versions of 1970s and 1980s hits, for charitable causes. He is also involved in a foundation that supports children in Tanzania.

SUSTAINABILITY REPORTING

Social and environmental reporting has come a long way in the past decade. However it still has a long way to go.

Back in the 1990s, when sustainability reporting was still in its infancy, it was often seen to be used by corporates as a form of window-dressing or "greenwash."

Responsibility for corporate social responsibility reporting was often handed to the communications department. In many cases, corporates were perceived to embark on the journey for largely cosmetic reasons—whereas their intentions may already have been different. In the wake of reputational disasters like the Brent Spar, the production of glossy corporate social responsibility (CSR) reports was seen as the perfect antidote to interfering non-government organizations (NGOs) and socio-environmental campaigners.

Today, all that has changed. Companies have now widely recognized that, in order to give themselves a long-term future, they are going to have to become more serious, accountable and transparent where sustainability is concerned.

This implies first of all a different way of structuring it and a proper approach to embedding it within the corporate management systems. Businesses are also recognizing that they will need a properly thought-out strategy to address pressing global issues such as global warming, resource depletion and demographic change—and find ways to accurately reflect such a strategy in their reporting.

For their part, investors are demanding greater access to transparent, accountable, robust, reliable, and comparable data from companies about their "nonfinancial" performance. And this is not just out of altruism or personal ethical curiosity; it is because asset managers increasingly believe that having such knowledge will enable them to make better investment decisions and achieve superior returns for their own clients. This means that the nonfinancial information has effectively become as important as financial information.

MOVING UP THE CORPORATE AGENDA

Recent research by KPMG Global Sustainability Services confirmed that sustainability reporting is moving up the corporate agenda and is now mainstream.

The report, which assessed the sustainability reports of 2,200 companies across 22 countries worldwide, found that far from being put together for appearances' sake, these are now regarded as an internal management tool that enables companies to prioritize issues likely to contribute to their long-term success.

For a growing band of larger, quoted companies worldwide, sustainability reporting has become a core part of their strategy development processes and business reporting cycles. The KPMG International Survey of Corporate Responsibility Reporting, published in October 2008, found that that 80% of Global Fortune 250 (G250) companies now disclose their sustainability performance in "sustainability" or "corporate responsibility" reports, a jump from 50% in 2005.

Reporting also increased on a national level, and a further rise is expected. Among the hundred largest companies by revenue in 22 countries worldwide (N100 companies), only 45% are reporting their own sustainability performance, albeit with marked variations between countries. Mexico was lowest at 18%, while Japan and the UK ranked highest, both scoring over 85%.

NO ROOM FOR COMPLACENCY

Encouragingly, the 2008 survey also revealed that growing numbers of companies worldwide base their sustainability reports on GRI guidelines, which significantly boosts the value of what they are doing, since it contributes significantly to the professionalism and comparability of corporate responsibility reporting.

However, the report also revealed that there is little room for complacency. A surprisingly large proportion of the world's largest companies (25%) still think they can manage perfectly well without any sustainability strategy. And the report also identified some surprising weaknesses where reporting on sustainability practices within the supply chain are concerned. This was especially true among the N100 companies. Also only few companies surveyed were making an explicit link between risk management and CSR within their reports. An insufficient number alluded to the business risk of climate change in their sustainability reports, while a disappointing proportion provided data on the size of their carbon footprints.

However, the main findings of the triannual survey were positive. Sustainability is moving up the corporate agenda, and responsibility for it is moving away from the corporate communications department—where it was often considered more in presentational than in material terms—and closer to the chief executive. Nowadays, it is often the responsibility of a CSR officer or sustainability manager who, though unlikely to be a member of the main board, tend to report directly to an executive board member.

Also, more than half of the G250 have disclosed business opportunities and/or the financial value of corporate responsibility. This value could be in terms of bottom line savings due to efficiency or risk aversion, or top line growth due to new innovations in products and services as a direct response to social or environmental challenges.

Corporate structures clearly play a big role in how CSR issues are handled within an organization. One of the dangers of having responsibility for CSR set too low down within an organization, or apart from normal business line reporting and management, is that it falls between two stools and therefore gets ignored.

This was recently highlighted by Michael Dell, founder, chairman, and chief executive of the Dell, Inc, who admitted on a visit to London that his company was having difficulties persuading its corporate customers to pay a tiny margin for energy-efficient personal computers, servers, and other hardware. Chief technology officers, said Dell, are reluctant to pay the premium for these pieces of kit, largely because energy does not come under their budget. As a result, they don't personally believe that they have anything to gain from paying a premium for equipment that would reduce corporate energy use. Instead, they think they have something to lose.

FINANCIAL IMPACT OF NONFINANCIAL ISSUES

To avoid this sort of situation arising, I believe the ultimate responsibility for sustainability reporting ought, in future, to rest with the chief financial officer (CFO). The so-called "nonfinancial issues" often have a financial impact, and since CFOs have profound experience of managing risk and installing good internal controls, they are well-placed to take this under their belts too. If CSR reporting and control were to become their responsibility, I think that it could play a major part in changing corporate behavior.

Overnight, the CFO would become less obsessed with financial performance and more open to the significance of other types of performance. They are already used to gathering and assembling accurate performance data from all levels within their companies. They are also used to questioning and auditing this data to ensure its veracity.

CFOs also produce timely and accurate performance information, according to a strict reporting cycle. Given this experience, why shouldn't they take responsibility for ensuring their companies produce accurate and timely nonfinancial data too?

There are, of course, psychological and practical barriers. For a start, finance directors do not yet necessarily know how to integrate nonfinancial indicators into their model. This can be overcome if they think about sustainability reporting as a means of reporting on risk factors that drive the company's full performance (for example, the level of carbon emissions, safety at work or diversity).

The perfect situation for me would be for nonfinancial standards to be seamlessly integrated into both internal and external assessments of a company's performance.

At a practical level, the CFO would need to get connected with those who have access to nonfinancial information, such as HSE professionals and HR staff and persuade them to become part of the company's financial planning and control cycle.

Some CFOs remain prejudiced against, or even dismissive of, nonfinancial indicators. However, they are increasingly aware that corporate social responsibility can have a major impact on a company's finance, such as its stock market valuation. In the end, I believe they will accept the need to measure corporate performance in a holistic way, not just through a narrow financial angle.

This process has, to an extent, already started, through projects like the Enhanced Analytics Initiative. Established by a group of prominent European institutional investors in 2004, this project aims to persuade sell-side analysts that they should take greater cognizance of a company's nonfinancial performance when assessing its overall performance.

The credit crunch is a turning point here. The positive side of what occurred between August 2007 and October 2008 is that lessons will be learned. The unprecedented downfall of so many once-revered banks and other financial institutions across Europe and the United States, in the autumn of 2008, provided an illustration that an extremely single-minded focus on financial indicators—short-term profits growth; earnings before interest, taxes, depreciation and amortization; earnings per share, and return on investment—can be a recipe for disaster.

If a bank is managed using only such measurements, it makes it near impossible for it to be managed responsibly. During 2002–08, banks' and investors' obsession with financial performance prompted many banks to take extraordinary risks, that can be seen as socially irresponsible, without considering whether their actions could risk their own futures or even the destruction of the entire financial system.

While greater commitment to CSR would not necessarily have prevented the banks from collapsing in the way that they did, it might at least have reduced the carnage and the costs that have had to be borne by taxpayers.

The experience of mutually owned banks such as Rabobank (based in the Netherlands) and the Cooperative Bank (based in Manchester, UK) demonstrates that when a bank's top management thinks beyond narrow financial parameters, and considers other measures to be of equal importance, it is more likely to survive and prosper in the long term. It is perhaps telling that, whereas it might have been mocked at the height of the credit bubble, Rabobank is today seen as one of the strongest and well-managed banks around. Admittedly, being a mutual is a different position to being a listed bank, since its management is under no pressure to maximize profits every quarter.

With the credit crunch behind us, CSR is likely to become even more critical to how companies are perceived and rated by investors. A growing numbers of organizations, even listed ones, will start to think along similar lines to banks like Rabobank.

Once shareholders become convinced that it makes more sense to invest in organizations that want to secure themselves a long-term future, rather than in the ones that are designed to maximize short-term profits but are at risk of going bust at any time, then this battle will have been won.

MORE INFO

Article:

Becchetti, Leonardo, and Rocco Ciciretti. "Corporate responsibility and stock market performance." Centre for International Studies on Economic Growth Research Paper Series. Working paper no. 79. March 2006.

Reports:

KPMG and SustainAbility. "Count me in—the readers' take on sustainability reporting." 2008.

United Nations Environment Programme Finance Initiative Asset Management Working Group and Mercer. "Demystifying responsible investment performance: A review of key academic and broker research on ESG factors." October 2007.

Website:

A sustainability report of a bank currently seen as well-managed and strong: www.annualreportsrabobank.com/annual_report_2008/

"The first lesson is: To hell with centralized strategic planning. If you don't have a good leader, it's all nothing; it's just a bunch of papers flying around." Robert Townsend

Identifying the Right Nonexecutive Director

by Terry Carroll

EXECUTIVE SUMMARY

- In the past, some have seen NED posts as a sinecure.
- Risk, diligence, and compliance factors may have changed this.
- Companies and prospective NEDs need the role to be seen as more professional.
- Remuneration for the right NED should reflect the increased "risk premium."
- NEDs should protect all stakeholders and apply sound corporate governance.
- Independence is paramount.
- Governance regulations and best practice continue to evolve.
- Successive Companies Acts have growing impact and change demands.
- The "right" NED needs wider skills and relevant business and sector experience.
- A range of sources exists, but thorough evaluation and selection are required.
- The quantity of candidates may reduce but the quality should increase.

INTRODUCTION

The "Credit Crunch" has thrown up many challenges and controversies. The extraordinary losses at Société Générale were reminiscent of the Barings debacle. The unaccountable losses suffered by many banks, especially in America, also beg serious questions about nonexecutive directors (NEDs). Never have times been tougher, or the challenges greater—and not just for banks but for all companies. Never has there been a clearer need for the right NEDs.

This article examines the challenges for all companies from a British perspective and suggests some key characteristics that are needed in the "right" NED. It also looks at wider aspects of the role, and where and how suitable candidates may be found.

GOVERNANCE AND MORE GOVERNANCE

On March 22, 2007, Naguib Kheraj resigned as finance director of Barclays, quoted by *Accountancy Age* as being "sick of compliance." As an executive director he was required to understand the same governance and regulatory matters as a NED.

In the past, some saw the role of NED as a sinecure. Now they may be rethinking that jaundiced view, as the toll of legislation, regulation, compliance, and the globalized economy increase the risk for those who occupy the role. There may still be some who approach the task altruistically, but, in general, to attract the best this increased risk should be reflected in higher remuneration.

Whether or not reward and recognition have been motivators in the past, the growing risk, diligence, and compliance factors may now be more important considerations in the mind of a prospective NED.

THE ROLE OF THE NED

In its simplest terms, the NED is there to protect the interests of the owners of the business. But now, major considerations such as health and safety, derivatives, new legislation concerning companies and employment, and risk management have added immeasurably to the potential legal and practical consequences for a NED—and, correspondingly, to the risks. These are in addition to the economic and commercial challenges that may have been the greatest for years.

To the layperson, the remuneration a NED receives may seem generous. Often it is the FTSE100 companies that hit the headlines in this respect. Not far below this level, NED packages are much more modest, and, although the scale and complexity may not be as vast as for big companies, the weight of regulation and compliance is similar.

The 2003 Higgs Review[1] drew on many of the strands of corporate governance that had been developing since the Cadbury Report in 1992.[2] It created a wholesome debate about the composition and responsibilities of the board. NEDs are now expected to play a more active role in the corporation, while being required to maintain their independence.

Two days a month is a reasonable expectation for a NED, whose day rate may be equal to that of a management consultant. But how can any diligent person be expected to perform their board and committee duties, spend time in the company, *and* keep up to date with information that, if ignored or overlooked, may land them in court, in two days per month?

COMBINED CODE OF CORPORATE GOVERNANCE

Every company needs NEDs, but not all can afford them. The law is pretty much the same for most companies; governance and guidance vary little except for small companies and quoted companies. It would do no harm for more companies to embrace the standards of the Combined Code,[3] whether or not they are required to. It would improve any company and is a useful starting point to guide any prospective NED.

RISK AND REWARD

"For some, the burden of being a NED in a public company is too onerous in terms of time and the potential financial or reputational risk. A point of inflexion is reached when good candidates say "no thanks." In this increasingly litigious world, NEDs should be adequately rewarded for their effort in proportion to the risks they run."

Virginia Bottomley, Head of Practice at Odgers Ray & Berndtson

As the demands and the potential exposure grow, so there is a commensurate increase in the risk factor. Ignorance or incompetence is no excuse; insurance and indemnity only go so far. Remuneration should increase to recognize the risk factor and reward the professional.

While NEDs are not responsible for, or engaged in, the day-to-day management, they are nevertheless subject to legal duties and responsibilities similar to those of the executives and are similarly liable for dismissal. Furthermore, it is also recommended that their remuneration should *not* be a significant proportion of their overall income.

So, will we see the emergence of the "professional" NED? A growing number are striking a balance between number of appointments and diligence. Enlightened companies encourage executive directors to accept NED appointments elsewhere to widen their perspective and personal development.

EVOLUTION OF THE ROLE

According to the Higgs Review, NEDs should:

- contribute to and constructively challenge the development of company strategy;
- scrutinize management performance;
- satisfy themselves that financial information is accurate and ensure that robust risk management is in place;
- meet at least once a year without the chairman or executive directors;
- be prepared to attend AGMs and discuss issues relating to their roles;

"A leader is a man who has the ability to get other people to do what they don't want to do and like it." Harry S. Truman

- have a greater exposure to major shareholders.

If only it was that simple. And according to Higgs, 60% of NEDs are still recruited with no formal process.

NEDs are, however, increasingly being sourced through search and selection. Since Higgs, diversity has been a more significant factor. Many would-be NEDs may prefer to go into private companies, where there are fewer governance requirements and financial rewards can still be attractive. Also, government and public bodies have opened themselves to advertised selection, but the fees they offer are much lower or even zero.

Executive secondment and private companies are a good proving ground. There is still, however, an apparent shortage of suitably qualified NED candidates. Organizations such as Directorbank (www.directorbank.com) have attempted to address this challenge.

The best boards should provide the newly recruited NED with a formal induction and an ongoing training program, whatever the degree of experience. Key aspects would include strategy, governance and regulation, and, of course, an introduction to the company itself, and its key people, products, and services.

This still leaves the onus on the individual to keep up to date and prepare diligently. Some take the view that this would require up to 30 days a year.

KEY ISSUES

According to Ernst & Young's annual survey in 2006, ("Concerns that keep Non-Executives awake at night"; *E&Y Newsletter*, June 2006) NEDs now spend up to 40% of their time on governance. The matters that most preoccupy them are:

- understanding a new sector;
- audit and finance;
- overseas knowledge;
- technology and security;
- remuneration policy in the company as a whole;
- the company's reputational risk.

Furthermore, a MORI poll cited in the same survey suggested that people were less likely to accept a NED appointment, and much less likely to accept an appointment as chair of the audit committee, than a year before.

INDEPENDENCE

Best practice and regulation dictate the need for independence. It's not just about individual thinking, because teamwork between the NEDs and with the executive is highly desirable. Share options as incentives for NEDs are, however, actively discouraged for quoted companies, and performance-related rewards should be geared to the share price rather than profits or sales.

The NED is required to judge and act in the best interests of the shareholders, yet, ironically, this begins with having the company's best interests at heart. Those who seek personal reward or recognition as a result of their directorship may not instinctively make impartial judgments where the company's interests should prevail.

Above all, integrity, teamwork, and trust across the board are paramount. Consensus is ideal, with a vote hardly ever needed. Consequently, these qualities matter most of all in the selection of the chairman of the board or audit committee.

THE EFFECTS OF THE 2006 COMPANIES ACT

The Companies Act 2006 came into effect in the United Kingdom in October 2008. While it codified the guidance and requirements from many sources, ultimately it made the duties even more significant and onerous. Alongside this, you have the extension of the crime of "corporate manslaughter" to the company itself, thereby effectively doubling the directors' liability.

The Act clearly sets out the seven general duties of directors:

1. A duty to act in accordance with the company's constitution, and to use powers only for the purposes for which they were conferred.
2. A duty to promote the success of the company for the benefit of its members. In doing this the directors are required to take account of:
    - the likely long-term consequences of their decisions;
    - the interests of the company's employees;
    - the need to foster the company's business relationships with suppliers, customers, and others;
    - the impact of the company's operations on the community and the environment;
    - the desirability of maintaining a reputation for high standards of business conduct;
    - the need to act fairly as between members of the company.
3. A duty to exercise independent judgment.
4. A duty to exercise reasonable care, skill, and diligence.
5. A duty to avoid conflicts of interest.
6. A duty not to accept benefits from third parties.
7. A duty to declare to the company's other directors any interest a director has in a proposed transaction or arrangement with the company.

It is likely that the new provisions will cause the greatest difficulty for directors who sit on more than one board. The Act introduces a new statutory right of shareholders to sue directors, in the company's name, to recover on the company's behalf loss it has suffered as a result of the directors' negligence, default, breach of duty, or breach of trust.

The new statutory right, or "derivative action," will undoubtedly make it easier for shareholders to take directors to court. Considerable concern has been expressed that this, taken together with the statutory statement of duties—particularly the detailed list of factors to which directors are to have regard—will lead to significant risks for directors.

Even if directors are able to obtain indemnity or insurance, the above requirements not only codify the requirements of best practice or regulation from a number of different sources, they also increase individual risks and exposure significantly.

One might wonder why anyone would want to be a nonexecutive director. The risks, responsibilities, and liabilities have increased considerably, as has the amount of knowledge and understanding now required of them.

Nevertheless, there will always be a supply of would-be NEDs, and not just for the money. We shall inevitably see the growth of the profession of director, which the United Kingdom's Institute of Directors has done much to foster, through collectivization and training. There will always be some people who either wish to carry their executive experience into semi-retirement or have the personal and professional qualities to perform the role. In addition, there is a ready supply from the executive ranks of other companies.

SO HOW DO YOU FIND AND IDENTIFY THE RIGHT NEDS?

First, all companies of a certain size should encourage their executive directors to seek a NED appointment elsewhere as part of their personal development. This opportunity not only helps them grow as individuals and executives, it also gives them an acute insight into what is required of those fulfilling such roles.

While it is not beyond the whit of a chairman to seek out people with directly relevant sectoral experience and/or skills, there is no reason why this process should be any different from that of selecting executives. Search consultants have been playing an increasing role in identifying and selecting suitable candidates, but ultimately it is for the board to apply an appropriate

and objective recruitment and selection process for the right candidate.

It has been too often said in the past that there aren't enough good and suitable candidates. Certainly, not only the diligent governance requirements, but also the personal qualities needed, justify significant expense and a rigorous process of selection.

Ultimately, the fundamental role of NEDs is to protect the interests of the owners of the business. They need to be dispassionate, courageous, and of the highest integrity. The remuneration may not always have compensated for the potential corporate and personal risks, but maybe this is because they weren't always recognized either. Now the British Government and others are ensuring that these considerations are paramount.

ESSENTIAL CHARACTERISTICS

Ideally, a prospective NED should have experience relevant to the business or to the sector in which it operates. However, alongside this goes a set of professional skills. If you can identify the core executive roles, it would be ideal to have an equivalent "shadow" on the board. This is most evident in the case of the finance director. A senior professional from another company, or maybe a retired executive director, can be a coach, mentor, and sounding board.

Above all, the board needs to be capable of acting as a team—NEDs and executives together, comprehensive and all-embracing; neither shy of their collective responsibility to the shareholders, nor of their commitment to the long-term success of the enterprise.

Executive directors may be rigorously reviewed and vetted for their relevant skills; but those required of the NED go one step beyond. If the post ever was a sinecure, it should be no longer. Not only the future of the company, but that of a country's economy and wider reputation lie in the hands of this new generation. The chairman and his colleagues may realize that they are protecting interests beyond their own and those of the owners in having a thorough, objective, and professional identification and selection process for their new NED colleagues.

STILL INTERESTED?

The growth of regulation and the duties of governance may drive some prospective NEDs away. If Naguib Kheraj found life too onerous as an executive director, what might many who contemplate putting themselves forward as candidates for a nonexecutive directorship think? Others, increasingly professional, may be drawn by the challenge, complexity, and variety, together with the intellectual and increasingly appropriate financial reward for a job diligently and well done.

MORE INFO

Website:

Directorbank, for executive and non-executive recruitment: www.directorbank.com

See Also:

★ Boardroom Roles (pp. 643–644)
★ Corporate Board Structures (pp. 654–657)
✔ The Board's Role in Executive Compensation (p. 1108)
✔ Defining Corporate Governance: Its Aims, Goals, and Responsibilities (p. 1115)
✔ Regulatory Responsibilities of Executive and Nonexecutive Directors: An International Overview (p. 1121)
✔ Selecting the Board and Evaluation Process (p. 1123)
Alan Greenspan (p. 1286)

NOTES

1 Higgs, Derek. *Review of the Role and Effectiveness of Non-Executive Directors*. London: The Stationery Office, 2003.

2 *Report of the Committee on the Financial Aspects of Corporate Governance*. "The Cadbury Report." London: Gee, 1992.

3 Financial Reporting Council (FRC). *The Combined Code on Corporate Governance*. London: FRC, 2008.

"At a rehearsal I let the orchestra play as they like. At the concert I make them play as I like." Sir Thomas Beecham, Bt

  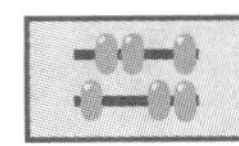   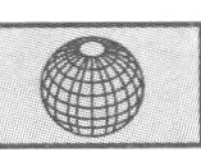   

Improving Corporate Profitability Through Accountability

by Marc J. Epstein and Priscilla Wisner

EXECUTIVE SUMMARY

- Traditional measures of performance are of limited use to modern businesses, being rooted in evaluating past performance. They are a poor guide to true value, often missing the key factors that promote long-term worth.
- It is essential to include the leading financial and nonfinancial indicators of performance that drive long-term value. This provides broader and more sophisticated information that highlights future trends.
- Effectively managing and communicating a broader set of performance measures reduces uncertainty, ensures better relationships with stockholders and analysts, and enables improved financial performance.
- Full accountability and disclosure, combined with improved measures and new systems to drive the process throughout the organization, create greater value for stakeholders, promoting future success.

INTRODUCTION

Improved governance requires the right employees, the right culture and values, and the right systems, information, and decision-making. Unfortunately, most organizations are attempting to steer their information-age businesses using industrial-age measurements. Managers have struggled for decades with accounting systems that fail to measure many of the variables that drive long-term value. The historical lagging indicators of performance that are commonly used by accountants are of limited value in determining the value of businesses for external stakeholders, and are of little use in guiding the business internally. Financial data on profitability and return on investment are valuable measures of corporate performance, but they are lagging indicators that measure past performance. A broader set of financial measures is necessary (for example, measurement of intangible assets such as intellectual capital and research-and-development value), in addition to an expanded set relating to customers, internal processes, and organizational measures.

The metrics must include the *leading* financial and nonfinancial indicators of performance that are the drivers and predictors of future financial performance. For example, fines and penalties may be a leading indicator of corporate reputation, employee turnover is a leading measure of future recruitment and training costs, and product quality is a leading measure of customer satisfaction, which in turn is a leading measure of market share. Each of these factors (reputation, employee-related costs, customer satisfaction, and market share) impacts financial performance.

IMPROVED INTERNAL AND EXTERNAL REPORTING

Just as companies expand their performance measurement parameters, they must also expand their performance reporting models. Employees, stockholders, financial analysts, activists, customers, suppliers, government regulators, and others increasingly demand detailed information about corporate activities, and the internet has made the dissemination of that information easier and faster. No longer can managers claim they don't have the information. The data are easy to collect, and it's essential to have broader and more forward-looking information to effectively manage the diverse issues that managers now confront daily. Managers should collect this broader array of information on activities and impacts both inside and outside the company, and select a set of data to provide adequate disclosure to their various stakeholders. External stakeholders need a broader set of information to effectively evaluate corporate performance, and voluntary disclosure of this information is critical for corporate accountability. This accountability, both inside and outside the company, through an effective corporate communications strategy, is an essential element of effective and responsible corporate governance.

Proactively managing external disclosures should be a fundamental part of

MAKING IT HAPPEN

The rewards from building the accountable organization are much like those from building the quality organization—the more committed the managers and workers and the better integrated the concept with company line operations, the greater the benefit. As a first step, managers must build accountable systems and practices within the company. Then they can build bridges to the outside. As they move toward full accountability—well-governed, measured, managed, and publicly responsive—they will position themselves to reap many benefits:

- Executing strategy: the accountable organization articulates each strategy and tactic with specific measures that align direction in ways that broader objectives cannot. The hard measures then give managers objective feedback on what the strategy execution is achieving.
- Improving decision-making: the accountable organization generates a wealth of information on performance, which in turn informs decision-making through facts, not intuition. People inside and outside the company can make more effective decisions to further company strategy and goals.
- Empowering people: the accountable organization thins the ranks of middle managers that distil and convey information and empowers decision-making authority to the front lines. As management articulates what it wants with concrete quantitative measures, workers have clear guidance of goals and objectives and how they relate to strategy.
- Accelerating learning: the accountable organization installs feedback systems that yield rapid-fire learning from people both across and outside the company. The company with the most feedback loops—internal and external—is the most successful.
- Communicating the story: the accountable organization delivers its story of value with credible financial and nonfinancial numbers. As senior managers report more numbers externally, exposing performance transparently, stockholders and analysts have less reason to undervalue their stock.
- Inspiring loyalty: the accountable organization markets its value on a basis of reliable performance measures. The no-smoke-and-mirrors approach spurs cooperation and inspires the loyalty of investors, customers, suppliers, employees, business partners, and communities.

"Good men prefer to be accountable." Michael Owen Edwardes

corporate communications strategy. By externally disclosing a more comprehensive set of measures, company executives are seizing the initiative to describe the company's strategy, set expectations, increase transparency, and ensure goal alignment between the company and a broad set of stakeholders. Disclosing performance measures allows investors and other stakeholders to view the company through the eyes of management. A clear, comprehensive communications strategy is highly valued by stockholders and analysts alike.

CONCLUSION

Once a company has decided to improve corporate governance, measure a broader set of indicators of past and future success, and report internally and externally, managers must develop systems to drive these decisions through the organization. Leading companies are developing integrated, closed-loop planning, budgeting, and feedback systems to help align strategy implementation with corporate performance. While leadership at the top is critical, buy-in at the shop floor level is essential for the success of any system implementation. Metrics must be linked to strategy and must be consistent throughout the organization. Companies are increasingly stating desires to become more customer focused or more socially responsible, yet many are still basing employee rewards on meeting revenue and profit goals. If companies expect employees to be more customer focused or more socially or environmentally responsible, part of overall performance evaluations and rewards should be on the basis of customer focus or social responsibility.

Accountable managers encourage not only continuous judgment, but continuous improvement. They insist that everyone in the organization participate in decision-making. They implement a culture of constant learning and insist on building learning organizations. Accountable managers communicate constantly, setting a tone of forthright feedback and transparency.

Full accountability comes only when a company combines a strong governance structure, improved and broad measurement of relevant performance impacts, timely and full internal and external reporting, and comprehensive management systems to drive the accountability model throughout the organization. By combining these elements companies are creating value for the stakeholders whose support they need in order to prosper—customers, investors, employees, suppliers, communities, the public, regulators, and other government officials.

CASE STUDY

The Campbell Soup Company has continually improved corporate governance.

Changes undertaken in the early 1990s required a majority of directors to come from outside the organization. All directors must stand for election every year and must own at least 6,000 shares of stock within three years of election. Among other provisions, interlocking directorships are not allowed and insiders are banned from certain key committees. In 1995, the board began a rotating yearly performance evaluation of directors, board committees, and the board as a whole. In 2000, the board approved a new director compensation program to closely link director compensation to the creation of stockholder value; only 20% is paid in cash (tied to attendance at meetings). The full set of Campbell Soup's governance standards and current performance review are disclosed in the annual proxy statement to stockholders.

The Cooperative Bank, based in the United Kingdom and with 4,000 employees, has won numerous awards for the high degree of transparency and accountability the company has exhibited. The bank has identified six partners in its quest for corporate value: stockholders, customers, staff and their families, suppliers, national and international societies, and past and future generations of cooperators. The company surveys all stakeholder groups to determine the critical elements in creating value for each, and performance targets are set on the basis of this information. In 2003, 70 targets were established in three principal areas: delivering value, social responsibility, and ecological sustainability. The Cooperative Bank 2004 Sustainability Report states that 33 targets were fully achieved, acceptable progress was made on 22, and 15 were not achieved. The bank reports progress on each target, providing data and management commentary, and establishes targets for the coming year.

MORE INFO

Books:

Epstein, Marc J., and Bill Birchard. *Counting What Counts: Turning Corporate Accountability to Competitive Advantage*. Cambridge, MA: Perseus, 2000.

Epstein, Marc J., and K. O. Hanson (eds). *The Accountable Corporation*. Westport, CT: Praeger Publications, 2006.

Monks, Robert A. G. *The Emperor's Nightingale: Restoring the Integrity of the Corporation in the Age of Shareholder Activism*. Cambridge, MA: Perseus, 1999.

Ward, Ralph D. *Improving Corporate Boards: The Boardroom Insider Guidebook*. New York: Wiley, 2000.

Articles:

Botosan, Christine. "Disclosure level and the cost of equity capital." *Accounting Review* 72:3 (July 1997): 323–349.

Epstein, Marc J., and Krishna Palepu. "What financial analysts want." *Strategic Finance* (April 1999): 48–52.

Healy, Paul, Amy Hutton, and Krishna Palepu. "Stock performance and intermediation changes surrounding sustained increases in disclosure." *Contemporary Accounting Research* 16:3 (Fall 1999): 485–520.

Hutton, Amy. "Beyond financial reporting—An integrated approach to corporate disclosure." *Journal of Applied Corporate Finance* 16:4 (Fall 2004): 8–16.

Sengupta, Partha. "Corporate disclosure quality and the cost of debt." *Accounting Review* 73:4 (October 1998): 459–474.

Report:

Engen, Travis, and Samuel DiPiazza. "Beyond reporting: Creating business value and accountability." World Business Council on Sustainable Development, June 2005. Online at: tinyurl.com/45ye76z

See Also:

★ Engaging Senior Management in Internal Control (pp. 336–337)
★ Incorporating Operational and Performance Auditing into Compliance and Financial Auditing (pp. 365–367)
★ Internal Audit and Partnering with Senior Management (pp. 368–371)
★ Starting a Successful Internal Audit Function to Meet Present and Future Demands (pp. 407–410)
✔ Corporate Governance and Its Interpretations (p. 1111)
✔ Understanding Internal Audits (p. 1057)

"We are responsible for actions performed in response to circumstances for which we are not responsible."
Allan Massie

  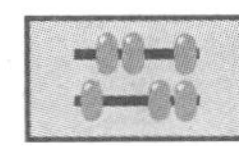      

Internal Auditing's Contribution to Sustainability by Jeffrey Ridley

EXECUTIVE SUMMARY

- Start with an understanding of, and an internationally recognized and accepted definition of, sustainability in your organization.
- Relate this definition to your organization's vision statement, strategies, and key objectives.
- Relate this definition to your terms of reference for internal auditing. Sustainability should be there as part of your role to provide assurance in the management of risk and controls.
- In today's and tomorrow's internal auditing engagements, the sustainability of your organization and of the planet should always be among your assurance objectives.
- If your terms of reference include assurance of governance in your organization, you have a much wider contribution to make in sustainability programs at board level.
- Whatever your internal auditing assurance role is in sustainability, you have the challenge and opportunities to develop this into consultancy and teaching roles covering all aspects of sustainability, at all levels in your organization.
- Contributing to the sustainability of your organization is the pinnacle of added value from your best-practice internal auditing services.

INTRODUCTION

Sustainability programs have three aims: people, planet, and profit. Few organizations today, across all sectors, will be without some form of sustainable development program—be it for altruistic reasons, required by regulation, or to stay at the cutting edge in their competitive market places. There can also be strong economic, environmental, and social reasons for marketing sustainable products and services: for reputational reasons and to control energy costs, or, even more importantly, to attract and keep both staff and investment.

Sustainability means more than just the economic, environmental, and social challenges an organization faces in its everyday and future operations: it means the ethics in these operations, touching on all the lives of those in the organization, its stakeholders, and the planet. The objectives of all sustainable development programs must be measured, and the results reported in and outside the organization. Stakeholders and society need to be assured independently that such measures are recorded accurately and in timely fashion before being reported. There are opportunities for internal auditing to contribute its independent and objective assurance services as an auditor as well as a consultant and teacher. Such a contribution can take best-practice internal auditing to a high level of added value.

WHAT IS SUSTAINABILITY?

Most governments and many organizations now define sustainability widely to include current and future issues and possible events that can impact an organization's resources and stakeholders at community, national, and global levels. The Global Reporting Initiative's (GRI) 2002 "Sustainability reporting guidelines" defined corporate social responsibility (CSR) as part of sustainability, and sustainability as "one of the three ideas that are playing a pivotal role in shaping how business and other organizations operate in the 21st century." The other two ideas stated by GRI are accountability and governance. Linking sustainability into accountability and governance is an important statement for internal auditors in their assurance role. Sustainability programs should be a part of every organization's governance structure and practices in all sectors—private, public, and voluntary. This is now recognized globally. The now well-known GRI "triple bottom line" reporting of economic, social, and environmental performance has been adopted by many organizations as part of their annual reporting to stakeholders. The European Commission and national governments in Europe, if not the world, have been and are continuing to recommend triple bottom line reporting of performance. In some countries and for some companies this is now a legal/regulatory requirement.

Standards and awards for sustainable programs exist at national and international levels. At international level there are sustainability management and leadership standards for environmental, social, and risk (ISO 14000, 26000, and 31000, respectively), human rights (SA 8000; see SAI, 2008), ethics (GoodCorporation, 2010), and corporate responsibility and sustainable development (the AA1000 series published by AccountAbility). One example of national awards is the UK Business in the Community annual awards for corporate responsibility run in association with the *Financial Times* newspaper. These recognize and celebrate companies that have a presence in the United Kingdom and which have shown innovation, creativity, and a sustained commitment to corporate responsibility.

The United Nations Global Compact (UNGC) in its recent research "A new era of sustainability" (Lacy *et al.*, 2010) continues the reinforcement of economic, environmental, and social reporting with its definition of sustainability:

"Throughout this report, we use the term 'sustainability' to encompass environmental, social and corporate governance issues, as embodied in the United Nations Global Compact's Ten Principles. These ten principles [cover] areas of human rights, labour, the environment and anti-corruption..."

Consider how the following ten principles, published by the UNGC in 2004, are embedded in your own organization's strategies and operations and, more importantly, how they are audited.

Human Rights

- *Principle 1*: Businesses should support and respect the protection of internationally proclaimed human rights.
- *Principle 2*: They should make sure that they are not complicit in human rights abuses.

Labor Standards

- *Principle 3*: Businesses should uphold the freedom of association and the effective recognition of the right to collective bargaining.
- *Principle 4*: The elimination of all forms of forced and compulsory labor.
- *Principle 5*: The effective abolition of child labor.
- *Principle 6*: The elimination of discrimination in respect of employment and occupation.

Environment

- *Principle 7*: Businesses should support a precautionary approach to environmental challenges.
- *Principle 8*: They should undertake initiatives to promote greater environmental responsibility.

  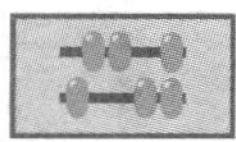 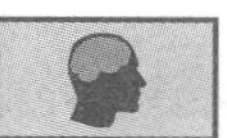  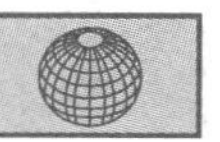   

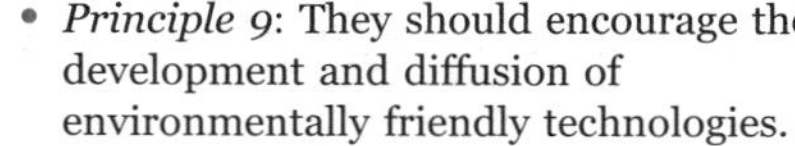

- *Principle 9*: They should encourage the development and diffusion of environmentally friendly technologies.

Anticorruption

- *Principle 10*: Businesses should work against corruption in all its forms, including extortion and bribery.

This wide definition of sustainability recognizes and reinforces the importance of an organization's sustainable strategy as being part of the ethical way it conducts its business. Questions every board and internal auditor should ask are listed in the next section.

The answers will always lead sustainability risk assessments to controls, challenges, weaknesses, strengths, and improvements. The questions in the box are a benchmark for those every internal auditor should seek to answer.

HOW GOOD IS YOUR SUSTAINABILITY CONDUCT?

Is it:

- required by your regulators?
- led from the top—by style and values?
- embedded in all strategies, plans, and operations?
- seen in all structures and systems?
- communicated internally to everyone—staff and visitors?
- communicated externally to all stakeholders?
- known across all supply chains?
- included in all review processes?
- independently monitored?

Does it:

- create or reduce wealth?
- improve or reduce the quality of performance?
- increase or decrease the efficiency and effectiveness of all staff?
- increase or decrease customers' satisfaction?
- improve or lower the organization's reputation in society?
- increase or decrease competitive edge?
- consider or ignore all stakeholders' needs?
- encourage or discourage good behavior?

Do you have:

- a formal and published code of conduct?
- a procedure for dealing with all irregularities?
- a whistleblowing procedure?
- practical ethics training for all your staff?
- environmental, health, and safety policies?
- environmental, social, and ethical accounting, auditing, and reporting?

Source: Ridley (2008).

SUSTAINABILITY IN GOVERNANCE, RISK MANAGEMENT, AND CONTROL PROCESSES

In all economic, environmental, and social sustainability programs the Cadbury (1992) corporate governance principles of *openness*, *integrity*, and *accountability* should be seen and practiced. The linking of sustainability programs into corporate governance by the UNGC is essential if the challenges of sustainability are to be addressed successfully across the world. The UNGC research highlights today's need "to embed environmental, social and corporate governance issues within core business" and "environmental, social and governance issues should be fully integrated into the strategy and operations of a company" (Lacy *et al.*, 2010). There is already evidence that these questions are being addressed and answered by law and regulation in many countries. For example, in the United Kingdom the Companies Act 2006 (Sect. 417) now requires publicly quoted companies to report annually on economic, environmental, and social issues raised by their operations, stating how these are being addressed strategically and how they are managed, measured, and monitored in every operation. Many organizations now do publish statements internally and externally on sustainability programs as a part of their good corporate governance, risk management, and control practices.

In 1992 the Commission of Sponsoring Organizations of the Treadway Commission (COSO) published its now internationally well-known integrated pyramid framework for internal control, which uses the following components:

- control environment;
- risk assessment;
- control activities;
- information and communication;
- monitoring.

This was followed in 2004 by a publication on enterprise risk management (ERM), defining this as "a process, effected by the entity's board of directors, management, and other personnel, applied in a strategy setting and across the enterprise, designed to identify potential events that may affect the entity, and manage risk to be within the risk appetite, to provide reasonable assurance regarding the achievement of objectives." ERM is now a process that must consider sustainability as a "potential event" in all its assessments of risk. It is considered to be the best guidance for risk management in organizations. The 2004 publication has been followed by other COSO statements on ERM, the latest being "Strengthening enterprise risk management for strategic advantage" in 2009.

Currently, the formality of risk management has been addressed by the Association of Certified and Chartered Accountants in its recent analysis of the elements of good risk management (Davies, Moxey, and Welch, 2010). This lists the essential requirement for "an independent assurance function that gives objective assurance, to the board or the nonexecutive directors." An internal audit function that complies with the Institute of Internal Auditor's *International Professional Practices Framework* (IIA, 2011), with its defined "systematic, disciplined approach" to assurance, is in an ideal position to review and report on sustainability risks.

CASE STUDY

What the AA1000 Series Means for Internal Auditors[1]

Internal auditors may find the AA1000 series standards formulated by AccountAbility useful when they are providing assurance or consulting services in the field of sustainability (i.e. ethics and corporate social responsibility). It is the managers of the organization who are responsible for establishing and implementing policies in this area. However, internal auditors may be in a position to facilitate their work by telling them about the AA1000 series and, in particular, the "AccountAbility principles standard" and the "Stakeholder engagement standard." As AccountAbility has designed AA1000 Assurance Standard (AA1000 AS (2008)) for external assurance providers, it is likely that internal auditors will never use it in full. However, the standard itself and its supporting guidance can assist internal auditors in conducting their own internal audit engagements in the area of sustainability. The IIA (2011) standards require internal auditors to establish criteria against which to evaluate the subject matter of the engagement. The AA1000 AS and its guidance are a good source of criteria for the area of sustainability. If the organization has engaged external providers to give assurance on sustainability reporting, the internal audit function will wish to coordinate and liaise with those providers. It will be useful to understand one of the principal standards that they may be following. Given that the AA1000 AS follows processes similar to those of the ISO standards, this area may provide a learning and development opportunity for internal auditors who are interested in sustainability and in working as external assurance providers.

"If it is not right, don't do it; if it is not true, don't say it." John A. Byrne

  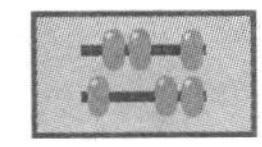      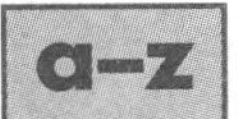

SUSTAINABILITY IS AN IMPORTANT FOCUS FOR PROFESSIONAL INTERNAL AUDITING

The IIA's first statement on the responsibilities of the internal auditor in 1947 described internal auditing as an "independent appraisal activity within an organization for the review of the accounting, financial, and other operations as a basis for protective and constructive service to management" (Brink, 1977). The objectives of internal auditing were stated as being:

"...to assist management in achieving the most efficient administration of the operations of the organization. The total objective has two major phases, as follows:

1 The protection of the interests of the organization, including the pointing out of existing deficiencies to provide a basis for appropriate corrective action.
2 The furtherance of the interests of the organization, including the recommendation of changes for the improvement of the various phases of operations."

These objectives have formed the foundation for all subsequent developments of internal auditing as it has changed from a service to a recognized international profession. Later, in 1981, the "service to management" was changed to "service to the organization," recognizing a changing role of reporting to the board as well as to management, and also a widening scope of assurance covering stakeholder influences and needs in the achievement of an organization's objectives. The IIA's national institute, the Chartered Institute of Internal Auditors, United Kingdom and Ireland (IIA UK and Ireland), published guidance on corporate social responsibility (CSR) auditing for internal auditors in the 1990s and early 2000s. In 2003 it published a statement discussing emerging social responsibility issues such as trust, materiality, and brand and the role of internal auditing (IIA UK and Ireland, 2003b):

"The internal auditor is a vital conduit to the creation of trust. The internal auditor is already contributing to a number of CSR and sustainability issues by keeping management informed on aspects of operational and compliance issues, which is part of their core function, as well as brand management audits and through participation in the stakeholder dialogue process. Also, the increasing importance of CSR and sustainability and its impact on risk management brings additional challenges involving the control environment, including the provision and installation of effective management and reporting systems, which will provide clarity and transparency, and therefore trust."

And:

"The internal auditor... has a key role to play in determining the materiality of the content of the CSR and sustainability report. This is a responsibility that can only increase with the burgeoning of CSR and sustainability reports, both in volume and size of content."

The services provided by many of today's professional internal auditors have developed into a wide scope of assurance, consulting, and teaching. There is clearly evidence in the past and today that internal auditing as a profession is being guided into being involved in the visions for sustainability programs—guided by, for example, the IIA to include this involvement in its annual planning and engagements into governance, risk management, and control implementation. Yet these internal auditing services are not evident in all organizations today, and they vary across those organizations where internal auditing has established a presence in sustainability. However, this involvement will grow in the future, both in practice and through the continuous development and improvement of internal auditing professional practices, fueled by board needs and regulation.

The IIA Research Foundation has promoted and sponsored international research into the internal auditing role in governance, risk management, and control, including their influence and impact on sustainability. Its research paper "Sustainability and internal auditing" (published in book form as Niewlands, 2006) develops *a* model of internal auditing relevant to sustainability in emerging markets. In a case study developed by the research, internal auditors are declared to have the following opportunities to demonstrate added value to their sustainable organization. The roles that auditors can play include:

- assisting in the design/implementation of the sustainability management system;
- assisting in creating sustainability awareness or training employees;
- performing audits of limited scope requested by top management;
- performing supply chain audits;
- performing compliance audits;
- advising on the appointment of outside assessors;
- coordinating audit activities by external assessors.

The IIA, in its latest statements on CSR and internal auditing, "Evaluating corporate social responsibility/sustainable development" (2010b), brings together and updates its past guidance for internal auditors in adding value to sustainability strategies in their organizations. In the introduction it emphasizes that:

"Internal auditors should understand the risks and controls related to CSR objectives. Where appropriate, the CAE [chief audit executive] should plan to audit, facilitate control self-assessments, verify results, and consult on the various subjects. Internal auditors should maintain the skills and knowledge necessary to understand and evaluate the governance, risks, and controls of CSR strategies."

This guide introduces two approaches to auditing sustainability—auditing by (CSR) element and auditing by stakeholder group. Elements are listed and discussed as: governance, ethics, environment, transparency, health, safety, security, human rights, work conditions, and community investment. Stakeholders are listed and discussed as: employees and their families, environment, customers, suppliers, communities, shareholders, and investors. Both approaches can be as separate engagements or as part of a functional/system engagement. When sustainability audit plans are developed, it suggests that the following questions should always be asked and developed into a program of assurance to be reported at board level. · How well is CSR information communicated across the organization and its supply chains?

- Which CSR reporting standards have been adopted?
- How are CSR strategies and priorities established/communicated?
- Are organizational CSR responsibilities documented for all elements?
- Is the organization signatory to any CSR standards of performance?

In my book *Cutting Edge Internal Auditing* (Ridley, 2008), I develop the following *principium* for all internal auditors at the cutting edge of their profession:

"Internal auditing has a responsibility to contribute to the processes of assessing reputation risks and advising at all levels in their organizations on how reputation can be managed and enhanced through good corporate responsibility practices."

This statement is based on many years of research and observation of best-practice internal auditing. Sustainability should always be the foundation of every internal audit engagement.

Writing on the social responsibility audit in the 1970s, John Humble (1973) cited Peter Drucker's key areas in which an organization must set objectives as:

- business(es);
- profitability;
- innovation;
- market standing;
- productivity;

"Green is the first socio-political movement in which every single leader and spokesperson is filthy rich." Julie Burchill

  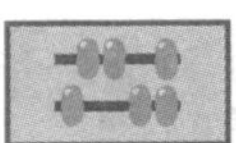      

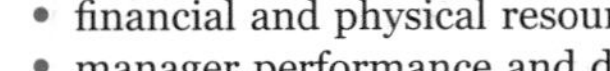

- financial and physical resources;
- manager performance and development;
- worker performance and attitude;
- public (though Humble preferred "social") responsibility.

Little has changed! All of these areas are a part of every organization's objectives today and require independent assurance. Humble viewed the challenge of social responsibility at that time as follows: "... one of the critical and difficult management tasks is balancing these objectives at any time, taking into consideration the changing requirements of stockholders, employees, customers and society generally." He went on to define social responsibility as one of the key areas of the business, one that is "typically concerned with the external environment problems of pollution, community and consumer relations, and the internal environment problems of working conditions, minority groups, education and training."

Chambers and Rand (2010) recommend the following environmental control objectives as those which require assurance by internal audit.

- Provision of an authorized and documented policy on environment issues as a framework for responsibly conducting related business activities.
- Minimization of the impact of the organization's activities on the environment.
- Ensuring that the organization's products are environmentally friendly.
- Ensuring that waste is minimized and properly disposed of.
- Avoidance of pollution and environmental contamination.
- The assessment, on an ongoing basis, of the environmental impacts of business operations and defining the requirements to be adhered to.
- Ensuring that alternative and potentially environmentally friendly processes and technologies are considered and implemented where justified.
- Minimization or avoidance of the use of scarce materials and non-renewable energy sources.
- Ensuring that harmful or hazardous materials and waste products are safely and responsibly transported and disposed of.
- Ensuring that all environmental legislation and regulations are fully complied with.
- Avoidance of adverse impacts on the organization's reputation and image.
- Ensuring that environmental issues are subject to monitoring and management.

MAKING IT HAPPEN

A Model of the Relevance of Sustainability to Internal Auditing

A model by Niewlands (2006) includes the following assurance, consulting, and teaching roles:

- Assistance in the design/implementation of the sustainability management system.
- Assistance in creating sustainability awareness or in training employees.
- Performing limited-scope audits requested by top management.
- Performing supply chain audits.
- Performing compliance audits.
- Advising on the appointment of outside assessors.
- Coordination of audit activities by external assessors.

Each of these actions can lead to one or more engagements in the internal auditing risk-based planning.

MORE INFO

Books:

Brink, Victor Z. *Foundations for Unlimited Horizons: The Institute of Internal Auditors 1941–1976*. Altamonte Springs, FL: IIA, 1977.

Chambers, Andrew, and Graham Rand. *Operational Auditing Handbook: Auditing Business and IT Processes*. 2nd ed. Chichester, UK: Wiley, 2010.

Humble, John William. *Social Responsibility Audit*. London, UK: Foundation for Business Responsibilities, 1973.

IIA. *International Professional Practices Framework (IPPF)*. Altamonte Springs, FL: IIA Research Foundation, 2011.

Nieuwlands, Hans. *Sustainability and Internal Auditing*. Altamonte Springs, FL: IIA Research Foundation, 2006.

Ridley, Jeffrey. *Cutting Edge Internal Auditing*. Chichester, UK: Wiley, 2008.

Reports:

Committee on the Financial Aspects of Corporate Governance. "Report of the Committee on the Financial Aspects of Corporate Governance" (Cadbury Report). London: Gee, December 1, 1992. Online at: www.ecgi.org/codes/documents/cadbury.pdf

Chartered Institute of Internal Auditors (IIA UK and Ireland). "Sustainability, environmental and social responsibility assurance." 2002.

Chartered Institute of Internal Auditors. "Professional issues bulletin ethical and social; auditing and reporting—The challenge for the internal auditor." 2003a.

Chartered Institute of Internal Auditors. "Emerging corporate social responsibility issues: Trust, materiality and brand." 2003b.

Chartered Institute of Internal Auditors. "IIA risk based internal auditing tool." February 2006.

Chartered Institute of Internal Auditors. "Sustainability and the AA1000 series." 2009.

Committee of Sponsoring Organizations of the Treadway Commission (COSO). "Internal control—Integrated framework." AICPA, 1992.

COSO. "Enterprise risk management—Integrated framework." 2004. Online at: www.coso.org/ERM-IntegratedFramework.htm

COSO. Guidance on Monitoring Internal Control Systems. 3 vols. New York: AICPA, 2009a.

COSO. "Strengthening enterprise risk management for strategic advantage." Thought paper. COSO, 2009b. Online at: www.coso.org/guidance.htm

COSO. "Effective enterprise risk management oversight: The role of the board of directors." Thought paper. COSO, 2009c. Online at: tinyurl.com/69q5hnu [PDF].

Davies, J., P. Moxey, and I. Welch. "Risk and reward: Tempering the pursuit of profit." Association of Chartered and Certified Accountants (ACCA), June 2010.

Global Reporting Initiative (GRI). "Sustainability reporting guidelines." G2 guidelines. 2002.

GoodCorporation. "The GoodCorporation Standard." Revised July 2010. 2010. Online at: www.goodcorporation.com/good-corporation-standard.php

Institute of Internal Auditors (IIA). "Evaluating corporate social responsibility/sustainable development." IPPF practice guide. February 2010b. Online at: tinyurl.com/6hd66n9

IIA UK and Ireland *see* Chartered Institute of Internal Auditors.

International Organization for Standardization (ISO). "ISO 14000 Environmental management." 2004, 2007. Online at: tinyurl.com/68chdow

        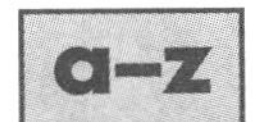

CONCLUSION

The importance of all aspects of sustainability in organizations as part of risk management will continue to drive a need for assurance that the issue of sustainability is being addressed and controlled economically, effectively, and efficiently. Risk management, control, and independent monitoring are key to the successful implementation of all sustainability strategies. There is evidence in the past and today that professional internal auditing is being guided, is involved in, and is contributing to sustainability visions and programs at national and international levels. In practice that contribution will grow in the future through the continuous development of internal auditing professionalism and from the needs of the organizations in which internal auditors work. Sustainability strategies, programs, and reporting should always be a part of the scope and planning of all internal audit engagements.

ISO. "ISO 31000:2009 Risk management." 2009. Online at: www.iso.org/iso/catalogue_detail.htm?csnumber=43170

ISO. "ISO 26000:2010 Guidance on social responsibility." 2010. Online at: www.iso.org/iso/catalogue_detail?csnumber=42546

Lacy, Peter, Tim Cooper, Rob Hayward, and Lisa Neuberger. "A new era of sustainability: UN Global Compact–Accenture CEO study 2010." Accenture, June 2010. Online at: tinyurl.com/2fk4x38 [PDF].

Organisation for Economic Co-operation and Development (OECD). "OECD guidelines for multinational enterprises." 2008.

Social Accountability International (SAI). "Social accountability 8000." SAI Standard SA8000. 2008. Online at: tinyurl.com/6x44g3f

United Nations Global Compact (UNGC). "The ten principles." 2004. Online at: www.unglobalcompact.org/aboutthegc/thetenprinciples

World Business Council For Sustainable Development (WBCSD). "Vision 2050: The new agenda for business." WBCSD report. 2010. Online at: tinyurl.com/6yf2ryw

Standards:

AccountAbility. "AA1000 series of standards." 2008. Online at: www.accountability.org/standards/

Websites:

AccountAbility: www.accountability.org
Business in the Community: www.bitc.org.uk
Chartered Institute of Internal Auditors: www.iia.org.uk
Committee of Sponsoring Organizations of the Treadway Commission (COSO): www.coso.org
European Confederation of Institutes of Internal Auditing (ECIIA): www.eciia.org
Global Reporting Initiative (GRI): www.globalreporting.org
GoodCorporation: www.goodcorporation.com
International Organization for Standardization (ISO): www.iso.org
Institute of Internal Auditors (IIA): www.theiia.org
Organisation for Economic Co-operation and Development (OECD): www.oecd.org
Social Accountability International: www.sa-intl.org
United Nations Global Compact: www.unglobalcompact.org
World Business Council for Sustainable Development: www.wbcsd.org

See Also:

★ Aligning the Internal Audit Function with Strategic Objectives (pp. 280–282)
★ New Assurance Challenges Facing Chief Audit Executives (pp. 378–381)
★ Starting a Successful Internal Audit Function to Meet Present and Future Demands (pp. 407–410)
★ Viewpoint: The Growth of Sustainability Reporting (pp. 680–681)
✔ Creating a Sustainable Development Policy (p. 1113)

NOTE

1 Reprinted with permission from the IIA UK and Ireland (2009).

"The trouble with a free market economy is that it requires so many policemen to make it work." Dean Acheson

  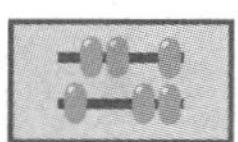      

Viewpoint: Ladies in Waiting by Tim Hindle

INTRODUCTION

Tim Hindle is a freelance writer and editor. Educated at Worcester College, Oxford, and Heriot-Watt University, Edinburgh, he was a research analyst in the City of London before joining *The Banker* magazine as deputy editor. He subsequently wrote for *The Economist* for many years, acting as finance editor in the 1980s before taking on the new role of management editor.

He launched EuroBusiness magazine in the early 1990s, and then re-launched the Institute of Directors' magazine, Director, later that decade. He has written a number of books. The Essential Manager's Manual, published by Dorling Kindersley, was a worldwide bestseller. His latest book, Guide to Management Ideas and Gurus, was published in 2008 to widespread acclaim. Hindle has also written extensively about Turkey. His wife is Turkish and he has visited the country over 100 times in the past 35 years. During that time he has seen the country grow from an underdeveloped agricultural economy into a thriving European neighbor, a vital geopolitical bridge between Christian and Muslim nations.

TRADERS AND GENDER

There are too few women in key jobs in the financial sector. Promoting them is not just a matter of fairness; it's a matter of prudent regulation.

Remember *Liar's Poker*, Michael Lewis's best-selling tale of his life as a Salomon Brothers' bond trader in the 1980s? It is a story of how macho traders on Wall Street fleeced innocents on the high street, including front-line mortgage lenders like the Savings & Loan Associations. The book's most memorable line—"If he could make millions of dollars come out of those phones, he became that most revered of all species: A Big Swinging Dick"—epitomized the financiers' *modus operandi* at the time.

Twenty years on, little has changed. The ethos of Wall Street-type firms is still male, rude, and ruthless. If anything, it has become worse. In the 1980s the commanding positions in these firms were taken mostly by graduate investment bankers. But in recent years the biggest profit-makers have been the traders of both old- and new-fangled securities. Traders tend to be rough and ready, and to have a limited interest in the world outside their dealing rooms. Their rewards and their status have risen to reflect their growing contribution to their employers' profits.

Traders, however, have shown that, uncontrolled, they can be lethal. At very short notice, they can throw banks into deep trouble. Nick Leeson, who brought down Barings in the 1990s, was a trader. His story was published as a book (and made into a film) under the title *Rogue Trader*. Jerome Kerviel, a Frenchman whose wildly spiraling deals at the beginning of 2008 lost US$7 billion for a much bigger bank, Société Générale, was also a trader.

These two rogues had other things in common. In the first place, both were young (in their twenties at the time) and male. And both came from humble backgrounds: Leeson's father was a plasterer; Kerviel's mother was a hairdresser. They had had little money of their own before billions of dollars of other people's was thrust into their care.

NO PLACE FOR WOMEN

As yet, few women have made their mark in this particular world. While they have made great strides in entering the lower echelons of financial services firms, women in the industry have largely been excluded from its trading rooms and its corridors of power. Where women have reached high levels it has usually been in "softer" areas, including fund management, public affairs, or as a general counsel. At the time of writing, Goldman Sachs has only three women on its management committee of 29. Credit Suisse has none.

What's more, the few women who really make breakthroughs seem to fall (or be felled) at the final hurdle. In 2007 Zoe Cruz, who started her banking career as a trader with Morgan Stanley, was fired just as she was about to take over as boss of the whole organization. The following year, Sally Krawcheck was eased out of Citigroup after being effectively demoted from the job of CFO.

Meanwhile, the bank that made the most creditable attempts to promote women, Lehman Brothers, is no more. Its much vaunted scheme to persuade female alumni to return after some years of absence evaporated when the bank went bust. At the same time, the Lehman Brothers Centre for Women in Business at the London Business School has, perhaps unsurprisingly, dropped the bank's name from its title.

I believe promoting more women on Wall Street and in the City of London is part of the solution to the world's financial ills, helping to ensure that banks and other institutions resist the urge to pursue suicidal strategies.

What the financial services industry needs is not just re-regulation in the place of deregulation, but more women in the place of men. It is not merely a matter of fairness. There is growing evidence that women are better suited to the work.

Writing in the *Financial Times* in April 2008, John Coates, a research fellow at Cambridge University who also once worked as a trader in New York, claimed that "as levels of testosterone rise, effective risk-taking gradually turns into dangerous behavior... testosterone is likely to rise in a bull market, increase risk and exaggerate the rally." On average, men produce 40-60 times more testosterone than women. And young men, who are a majority in most trading rooms, produce much more than older men.

Coates then pointed to another hormone, cortisol—the so-called "stress hormone" — as having a similar effect, but in the opposite direction. "Chronic cortisol exposure," he wrote, "promotes feelings of anxiety... and a tendency to find danger where none exists. Cortisol is likely to rise in a crash, make traders dramatically and perhaps irrationally risk-averse, and exaggerate the sell-off."

And guess what? Cortisol production is dampened under stress by yet another hormone, oxytocin, which is produced in far larger quantities in women than it is in men. Which explains the very different reactions of the two sexes to stress. Men tend towards the "fight or flight" option, both of them choices which leave them fending for themselves.

Women, on the other hand, tend towards each other. They seek the comfort and

"The final test of a leader is that he leaves behind him in other men the conviction and the will to carry on."
Walter Lippmann

        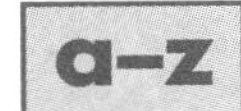

strength that comes from being part of a group. Hence, so the argument goes, if trading floors were run by women rather than men, market booms and busts would be far less extreme.

MALE PREJUDICE AND FEMALE RESIGNATION

Why then are there so few women in high places in the industry? Based on the endocrinal evidence, the market's invisible hand should be firmly pushing them forward.

The answer is a mix of male prejudice and female resignation. Women naturally opt out of an arena where the ultimate accolade is to become a "big swinging dick." They say that exclusion from the industry's male-dominated informal networks is one of the main reasons why so few of them reach the top rungs of the corporate ladder. Jock talk and late-night boozing oil the wheels of progress in many corporations, not just those in finance. A trip round the City of London's bars after 7pm any weekday provides ample evidence. The general increase in heavy female drinking in recent years may, in part, be a sad reflection of women's attempts to climb these particular corporate ladders on men's terms.

Katherine Bucknell, an author and the wife of a one-time top investment banker, recently wrote: "The size of a banker's pile of money is like the size of anything else in a macho environment: you need the biggest one to show that you are good at what you do. The pile does not necessarily reflect personal greed, it reflects the need to be the best banker." Women tend to find reward in things that lie beyond size—be it of paychecks, bonuses, air-miles, or just the working day.

At the same time, the male tribe which lucratively occupies the financial services high ground has successfully excluded them. The people who make the decisions as to who does what jobs within large organizations—essentially old, white men—are (unconsciously and unavoidably) biased in favor of their own kind (as are all such small groups in power). The ability of unconscious bias to distort management decisions in this way is now undeniable.

Women (who, of course, have their own biases) believe that organizations are biased against them. A survey undertaken by the publication*Financial News*in September 2008, found that 60% of a sample of 1,350 women in financial services firms in the City of London (one-third of them in investment banks) believed that their gender made it harder for them to succeed.

Women complain that they are in a Catch-22 situation. While several studies show that those who actively promote their own interests are seen as aggressive, uncooperative, and selfish (Zoe Cruz was known as the "Cruz missile"), a similar number of studies show that when women don't promote their own interests they don't get anywhere.

A recent report by management consultants McKinsey quotes Julie Daum, a headhunter who specializes in recruiting company board directors. She said that senior women on boards still lose out by not speaking up: "They hang back if they think that they have nothing new to say or that their ideas fall short of profound." Men don't worry so much about profundity. And they see people who do as weak and indecisive—i.e., not fit to run large financial institutions.

There are areas of life where male dominance makes sense. Women are unlikely ever to play rugby for the New Zealand All-Blacks or American football for the New York Giants. We need take no action to rectify these imbalances.

But with financial services it is different. The continuing absence of women at the top of the industry really does matter. The links between the rational and emotional parts of the brain are greater in women than they are in men. When emotions are high, as when markets are dramatically rising or dramatically falling, women are able to keep in closer touch with their intelligence. Testosterone and cortisol are less likely to get in the way.

BREAKING THE BARRIER

The only country that has managed to break the barrier that is preventing women from rising to levels where they can influence key decisions is Norway. And it achieved that by legislation. In 2003 it passed a law decreeing that by 2008 40% of the directors of all quoted companies should be women.

From all accounts, the Norwegian experiment has been a great success despite widespread initial skepticism. It may be a coincidence, but Norwegian banks have been less scathed by the global financial crisis than banks in many other countries.

Now countries like Spain and the Netherlands are considering taking similar steps, and others should quickly follow suit. For promoting women is now not just about sexual equality, it is about prudent regulation. We need many more women in high places in the financial services industry well before the next time hormonal madness hits the markets.

MORE INFO

Books:

Bazerman, Max B., and Don A. Moore.*Judgment in Managerial Decision Making.* Hoboken, NJ: Wiley, 2009.

Lewis, Michael. *Liar's Poker.* London: Hodder Paperbacks, 2006.

Thomson, Peninah, and Jacey Graham. *A Woman's Place is in the Boardroom*. Basingstoke, UK: Palgrave Macmillan, 2005.

Articles:

Barsh, Joanna, Susie Cranston, and Rebecca Craske. "Centered leadership: How talented women thrive." *McKinsey Quarterly*(September 2008). Online at: tinyurl.com/5kg77q

Coates, John. "Traders should track their hormones." *Financial Times*(April 14, 2008). Online at: tinyurl.com/3ubaqbs

Economist. "Helping women get to the top." July 23, 2005. Online at: www.economist.com/node/4198363?story_id=E1_QTJRPGP

Fabrikant, Geraldine. "When Citi lost Sallie." *New York Times*(November 15, 2008). Online at: www.nytimes.com/2008/11/16/business/16sallie.html

Report:

Catalyst. "The connection between women board directors and women corporate officers." July 2008.

See Also:

★ Corporate Board Structures (pp. 654–657)

✔ Understanding the Financial Aspects of Employing People (p. 1183)

"Few trends could so thoroughly undermine the very foundations of our free society as the acceptance by corporate officials of a social responsibility other than to make as much money for their stockholders as possible." Milton Friedman

  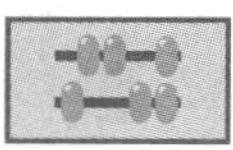      

Viewpoint: Lessons from the Credit Crisis: Governing Financial Institutions by Jay W. Lorsch

INTRODUCTION

Jay W. Lorsch is an internationally recognized expert in boards and corporate governance. Here he argues that the lack of experienced bankers on bank boards was a major contributor to the 2008 financial crisis. He believes that the "independence" criteria played a big part in banks' preference for nonbankers as nonexecutives, and must now be reconsidered. Lorsch also argues that US companies should keep the roles of chairman and CEO separate as is the case in the United Kingdom.

Lorsch is Louis Kirstein professor of human relations at Harvard Business School and chairman of the school's global corporate governance initiative. He has taught in all of HBS's educational programs. As a consultant, Lorsch's clients have included Citicorp, Deloitte & Touche, DLA Piper Rudnick, Goldman Sachs, Tyco International, and Shire Pharmaceuticals.

Lorsch graduated from Antioch College in 1955. He has an MSc in business from Columbia University and a doctorate in business administration from HBS. From 1956 to 1959, he served as a lieutenant in the US Army Finance Corp. He is also a fellow of the American Academy of Arts & Sciences.

THE CRISIS AND FINANCIAL INSTITUTIONS

In the many commentaries about the credit crisis, blame has been placed squarely on the management of the failed financial institutions. While these leaders certainly bear some responsibility, the boards of directors to whom they report should not be let off the hook so easily. After all, boards are ultimately responsible for the performance of their companies.

In this essay I explore the lessons we should draw from these failures about the role of boards in overseeing complex financial institutions. I do so with two caveats. First, boards are not the only governance body that has failed. Government regulators, credit rating agencies, and accounting firms, among others, must also bear some of the responsibility. Second, knowing how boards of directors failed must largely be a matter of informed speculation on my part, since in the current legal environment the board members directly involved are not willing to talk about what went wrong. I say "informed speculation" because I have had the opportunity to consult for boards of such firms in more halcyon times.

BOARDROOM REALITIES

While boards on both sides of the Atlantic are the ultimate legal authority in corporations, their ability actually to carry out this duty is constrained by several realities. The central factor among these is what directors know and understand about their companies' plans, activities, and results.

To an extent, such knowledge can be affected by the number of times the directors meet. The less time directors spend in discussions together and with management, the less informed they may be.

However, a cursory examination of proxy statements reveals that, in 2007, the boards of the large Wall Street institutions did meet much more often than the average American company's board—on average 10 times a year for the Wall Street firms, and six times for the typical company. Even more impressively, the audit committees of these financial institutions met an average of 11 times during 2007. All of this I believe is evidence that these directors were spending time trying to understand the complexity of their companies.

However, what directors understand about these institutions is obviously the result of more than just how much time they spend together. Another significant factor can be the depth of knowledge directors bring to the boardroom about financial markets, products, and institutions from prior career experience. Unfortunately, current rules and best practices make such transfer of knowledge unlikely. The emphasis in selecting board members in the United States is on finding individuals who are "independent."

This generally means selecting directors who have no current or recent experience working for the company, its competitors or clients. The underlying idea is to create boards whose members have no conflicts of interest. While this is an understandable and worthy goal, a significant result is that most boards of financial institutions in the United States have few nonmanagement directors with prior experience in that industry.

Again, looking at the boards of the 12 largest Wall Street firms, each has at most two independent directors with prior financial experience. The other independent directors, experienced and accomplished as they may be in other industries and professions, start with a sizeable handicap.

Whether independent or not, and whether they have a prior experience of financial organizations, board members must rely on their management as the most important source of information about future plans and current company activities, risks, and results. There is no other way for directors to understand what is happening in their companies.

Trying to understand the debacles in these financial firms from outside the boardroom, it is not clear whether management understood the problems that their companies faced and chose to withhold this knowledge from the board, or else whether the top management itself did not understand the situation. However, it really doesn't matter, because either way the directors, even those few who might have had deep knowledge of financial issues, were unaware of the storm that was about to break upon them.

The fact that these boards were unaware of the catastrophe that struck their companies until after it had occurred points to the fact that boards need knowledge for two reasons.

One is to understand and make judgments about how well their company has been performing, to look in the rear view mirror. Their failure in this regard is what many observers are most likely to criticize.

However, I believe that their more serious sin occurred many years earlier, as they approved (or should have approved) the strategic plans for their company. It was

"A company is an organic, living, breathing thing, not just an income sheet and balance sheet. You have to lead it with that in mind." Carly Fiorina

  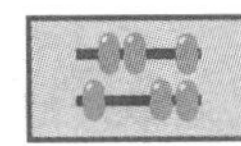      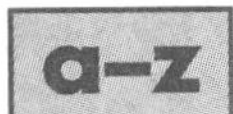

at this stage that they allowed their managements to set off in new directions, which eventually did so much damage to the companies and the wider economy. My hunch is that the reception for these innovative new "products," if they were presented to the board by management, was as enthusiastic among the directors as it was among the managers proposing them.

With so little financial knowledge among the board members, my hunch is that they were reluctant or unable to raise any doubts about management's "exciting" new ideas. At least this is too often the case in boards with which I am familiar. Further, it is unlikely that the directors understood the necessity to create monitoring systems, which would keep them aware of any new risks associated with the new-fangled innovations.

It may be unfair or even unreasonable to expect directors to have been able to predict or anticipate the failures in the financial system, when top executives, regulators, and academic experts with much greater knowledge were unable to do so.

Yet, I cannot ignore the fact that the boards of these institutions have a legal and moral obligation for the health of their company, including its equity value for shareholders, and the safety of investor assets entrusted to the company. While it is unhelpful to cast blame on these boards, I do want to consider what they can do going forward to prevent future calamities.

LOOKING TO THE FUTURE

Over the past two decades there have been plenty of ideas about boardroom best practices, including that they should have a preponderance of independent directors, the requisite committees, discussions among independent directors without management present, and board approval of strategic plans. While these innovations have been helpful to many boards, they did not go far enough to prevent the crisis that hit and, in some cases, nearly destroyed their companies.

Even assiduously adopting all these practices does not go far enough to prevent a recurrence of such problems, unless the independent directors have the information and knowledge to assess plans and results intelligently. Thus, I believe that attention needs to be focused primarily on solving this part of the problem.

I would start by requiring the boards of financial companies to have more independent directors who have deep knowledge and experience of the world of financial markets and institutions. I have in mind a principle similar to that used in the Sarbanes–Oxley Act's definition of the competence required for members of audit committees.

Based on my own experience, I believe it is possible to find directors who meet both the test of independence and have deep financial understanding. Finding such individuals requires dropping the assumption that the best directors for these financial firms are prestigious CEOs or other comparable high-status individuals. It will also require corporate governance committees and any consultants they choose to use to search more carefully for candidates who meet both criteria.

Second, these boards should adopt an idea first proposed in 1972 by the late Justice Arthur Goldberg, who was on the board of Trans World Airlines. He asked that the board create a small staff to support it with analysis and interpretation of data. This proposal was rejected at the time, but I believe it is an idea whose time has come for complex financial institutions.

There is simply too much complicated data about performance and risks for independent directors to understand, even if boards do meet monthly and consist of more members with deep financial expertise. I envision a relatively small "staff" of young professionals with the relevant expertise.

Third, I believe that these boards should recognize that their company's complexity requires them to have a chair who is not the CEO. While this idea is widely accepted in the United Kingdom and the rest of Europe, there is resistance to it in the United States.

However, it seems clear that boards which are meeting almost monthly, and which face such complicated issues, need a leader who has no other obligations within the company.

Some may see this proposal as a reheating of an old campaign from corporate governance reformers. However, I would remind the reader that I was one of the originators of the concept of a lead director, as an alternative to a separate chair for US boards. I am proposing the idea of a separate chair because I truly believe it is relevant for the boards of these complex financial institutions.

In doing so, I recognize that one requirement for its successful implementation is a very clear and explicit definition of the chair's job. It should be to lead the board in its oversight duties. This includes assuring that the board has appropriate membership and committees, the right agendas, sufficient information, and overseeing the board's staff proposed above, as well as presiding at board meetings. What the chair's job must not entail is being a personal "boss" of the CEO, or usurping the board's duties in this regard.

While I do not believe that these changes alone will prevent a repetition of the failures of so many financial institutions, I do believe that, along with improved regulatory oversight, they should vastly improve the odds that boards can be the guardians of their companies that society has the right to expect.

MORE INFO

Books:

Carter, Colin B., and Jay W. Lorsch. *Back to the Drawing Board: Designing Corporate Boards for a Complex World*. Cambridge, MA: Harvard Business School Press, 2003.

Lawrence, Paul R., and Jay W. Lorsch. *Organization and Environment: Managing Differentiation and Integration*. Cambridge, MA: Harvard Business School Press, 1967.

Lorsch, Jay W., and Elizabeth McIver. *Pawns or Potentates: The Reality of America's Corporate Boards*. Cambridge, MA: Harvard Business School Press, 1989.

Lorsch, Jay W., and Thomas J. Tierney. *Aligning the Stars: How to Succeed when Professionals Drive Results*. Cambridge, MA: Harvard Business School Press, 2002.

See Also:

★ Boardroom Roles (pp. 643–644)
★ Identifying the Right Nonexecutive Director (pp. 682–684)
★ Rules versus Discretion in Supervisory Interventions in Financial Institutions (pp. 239–241)
✔ Defining Corporate Governance: Its Aims, Goals, and Responsibilities (p. 1115)
✔ Principles of Financial Services Regulation (p. 1048)
✔ Selecting the Board and Evaluation Process (p. 1123)
Irrational Exuberance (p. 1385)

"The hierarchical manager of yesterday ran the Industrial Age company with Yes Sir! Yes Sir ... When you're running an Information Age company, you've got to allow a lot of dissent." Bill Campbell

Viewpoint: Leveraging Influence to Impact Climate-Change Policy by Mark Kenber

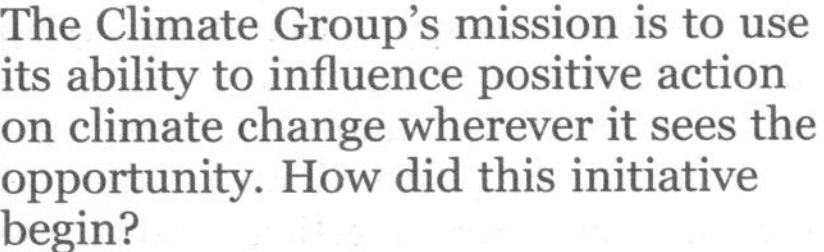

INTRODUCTION

Mark Kenber is CEO of international NGO The Climate Group. He has worked on climate change for fifteen years and is an expert on international climate policy. Before becoming CEO, he was The Climate Group's deputy CEO (2010) and international policy director (2004–10). Mark advised former UK Prime Minister Tony Blair in the joint policy initiative Breaking the Climate Deadlock. He is also a carbon markets expert and cofounded the Voluntary Carbon Standard (VCS), now the most popular kitemark for the US$400 million voluntary market. He continues to be involved as deputy chair of the VCS Association. Prior to joining The Climate Group, Mark worked for WWF and Fundacion Natura, Ecuador's largest environmental organization. Mark currently sits on the Climate Change Advisory Council at Zurich Insurance (since 2009), BP's targetneutral Assurance and Advisory Panel (since 2007), the Climate Policy Editorial Advisory Board (since 2005), and the Institutional Investors Group on Climate Change Steering Committee (since 2005). Mark has a degree in economics and an MPhil in development studies.

The Climate Group's mission is to use its ability to influence positive action on climate change wherever it sees the opportunity. How did this initiative begin?

In mid-2003 Michael Northrop, Program Director at Rockefeller Brothers Fund, was concerned that the United States had pulled out of Kyoto. He wanted to ensure that not everyone in the United States got tarred with the same brush, and to show that there was real concern in the United States about the potential adverse impacts of climate change. However, he also saw clearly that for US companies to participate positively in actions to alleviate climate change, the fundamental thrust had to switch from one that viewed climate-change initiatives as a cost burden on companies to one that saw it as an opportunity. As a result, The Climate Group was launched in April 2004 with the simple mission to change the perception of climate change from burden-sharing to opportunity. The key to doing this was—and continues to be—our ability to demonstrate in project after project that specific climate-change initiatives bring real benefits to the participating parties. One of our earliest initiatives was the C40 Network, a network of 40 of the world's most populous cities, all committed to pushing through initiatives to lower their carbon footprint as cities and to look at ways of making their cities run more efficiently by utilizing and disseminating best practice between themselves.

The C40 Network became independent and now runs its own affairs, but it all began when Ken Livingston was the Mayor of London, about the time of the G8 meeting in 2005. We worked with the office of the Mayor of London to produce an initial C20 group of global cities, but it grew very rapidly from there. Now, despite the name, which has stuck, the C40 Network has around 60 city members that exchange best practice and support each other. That is a pretty fair indication of the kind of project that The Climate Group has been active in promoting. Our aim is always to find interaction points where a combination of our own network of members and interested parties, and our combined skills can have the biggest impact in promoting action on climate change.

The C40 Network was a very impressive initiative. What were the others?

We created the Verified Carbon Standard (VCS). This too, is now a fully independent organization on whose board I sit. VCS was founded to provide a robust quality-assurance standard that various projects could use to quantify greenhouse gas (GHG) emissions. The program is still evolving to meet the needs of the market, but its mission is to provide a trusted, robust, and user-friendly way of bringing quality assurance to voluntary carbon markets. It aims to pioneer innovative rules and tools that open up new avenues for carbon crediting and that will allow businesses, not-for-profit organizations, and government entities to engage in very specific, measurable climate action.

The aim too, is to share knowledge and to encourage the uptake of best practice in carbon markets, so that markets develop along coherent and compatible lines, even as top-down regulations are being developed.

Another major project of ours, one that is still very much in play, is the light-emitting diodes (LED) street-lighting scheme. The LED street-lighting campaign started when we realized that while consumers were taking up LED lighting and enjoying very substantial savings, as well as lowering the overall carbon footprint of their homes, this was simply not the case in many public spaces. Street lighting, which can be very successfully addressed with LED lighting, was simply being ignored and the opportunity was not being adopted. So we formed a working party to look at the barriers to take-up and to look at how we could overcome such barriers as there were out there. The opportunities were huge, and ranged from Sydney, to Central Park in New York, to Calcutta. We looked to see if we could come up with a model that would enable 15 pilot projects in 12 major cities to be scaled up their take-up.

The first problem any city fathers face is that initially it costs more, since the upfront costs for LED lighting are higher than for a sodium bulb, for example. But what we sought to impress upon city authorities was that you get the costs back over two to three years, and you make very substantial savings on your power usage, and you enjoy a significant lowering of your carbon footprint. Another problem that we faced, straight away, was that the quality of a light bulb has for decades now been measured by the amount of electricity it consumes. So we expect a 40W bulb to be dimmer (that is, of a lower quality) than a 100W bulb. Moreover, if you measure yellow light instead of white light, more often than not the instruments that you are using are not suited to giving you an accurate view of the quality of the light output of the yellow LED. The way in which we addressed this issue in Calcutta, for example, was first to have a pilot scheme of 150 LED street lights and then to do surveys of the views of women and children who were using an LED-lit park. What emerged was that they felt significantly safer with the LED lighting. That was very interesting.

"Conservation is business too." Gaston Vizcarra

Calcutta is now negotiating a loan to scale-up its project from 150 LED bulbs to 15,000 bulbs, and Sydney has committed itself to full LED street lighting. To summarize this project, our undertaking of pilot studies allowed city authorities to see in a tangible way the realities and the benefits of LED lighting. This now has some momentum of its own, so we are not planning and do not intend to do any more pilot studies. What we do now is to help a few states to prepare their tenders for LED street lighting, but we feel quite confident that we have done our bit in terms of demonstrating and catalyzing the potential out there.

One still meets global-warming skeptics out there, including some scientists. They are headed in a diametrically opposed direction to your initiatives. What do you say to them?

We are aware that a "rubbishing-climate-change" lobby exists. I have been in debates with exponents of this view over the years, but in reality theirs is not a serious voice. The overwhelming scientific and anecdotal evidence points to the fact that climate change is happening and happening because of our industrialization. What we try to emphasize, however, is that irrespective of whether you are a believer or a skeptic on climate change, the opportunities that come from shifting to a more carbon-conscious framework have a positive internal rate of return, with or without climate change. A lot of the things that have been done, such as the LED-lighting initiative are good in and of themselves. The LED bulbs simply produce a better quality of light and are more power-efficient. A shopkeeper in Calcutta, for example, told us that switching from the old sodium lights to LEDs made his products look fresher to potential purchasers, so he sold more! The fact is that there is a whole range of things that it is absolutely important to do, including transitioning from an oil-based economy, even if the whole climate-change issue was proved to have been misconceived. A lot of what we do concerning low-carbon solutions have very positive immediate returns, create profits by doing things more efficiently, and lead to a better life. The climate-change argument is not necessary to make this worthwhile. There are other projects, of course—such as carbon capture and storage—that cost a huge amount of money to implement and you need to have a broad consensus on the importance of introducing fairly dramatic measures to combat climate change if you are going to get these projects to happen. Our role, however, is not to argue with the skeptics. We focus on categorizing the many opportunities that do exist.

What we have seen, without a shadow of doubt, is that if you look at climate-related insurance claims in the 1980s and compare them to recent levels of claims, it is clear that climate-related claims have gone up six-fold in three decades. Then there is the drought effect in many countries that has been predicted as one of the consequences of global warming. Drought cost 1% of US GDP through 2012, and those sorts of things are pretty consistent with what the theory of global warming says we should expect. The overall pattern is very conformant with what the Intergovernmental Panel on Climate Change's (IPCC) climate-change model says should happen.

However, if you just take it down to common sense and look at it from the positive side, every additional dollar invested in clean energy can generate three dollars in future fuel savings by 2050, so there are a lot of areas where carbon reduction makes real economic sense, whatever your views on climate change. A householder with a well-insulated house, for example, has a more comfortable house and one that costs less to heat, and in a world where energy bills are going up year on year, that matters. There are numerous examples of this at city and at state level. If you live in Beijing, for example, and have to put up with particulate matter that is 40 times higher than the World Health Organization recommends it is palpably clear that there would be strong collateral benefits to reducing the city's level of carbon pollution.

How do you go about giving structure to your work when it is so project-based?

We split our work into two parts. The first part involves the strategic communications dimension. This looks at the way you can change the mindset of political and business decision-makers on issues such as giving leadership on low-carbon initiatives, on renewables, and on investment programs. Already it is clear that companies that take a leadership position on green strategies are more successful than their peers. A study by the Harvard Business Review showed this quite clearly. We now have just over 40 corporate members of The Climate Group and 60 state and regional members. We also work with a number of cities and we have other institutional partners, ranging from The World Bank to the European Climate Community. There is a whole range of organizations that we work with to identify blockages and barriers to low-carbon initiatives and to see where there are significant low-carbon opportunities that are not being taken up. Then, the second part of our work kicks in and we form a project that helps to overcome those barriers and blockages.

For example, it is clear that there are significant barriers still in the way of a wider take-up of electric vehicles. So we are looking into the feasibility of fleet-goods owners forming a procurement alliance to bring down the cost of electric vehicles to their members. Another factor here is looking at predictable short routes, so there is no anxiety about power running down and no range anxiety. The fleet charges up at the depot, so there are no refueling issues associated with the absence of recharging stations for electric vehicles. The aim is to choose the battles that we fight fairly carefully and to bring our network of partners together to help identify opportunities and problems. It is a very pragmatic approach and has real successes to point show.

What else are you working on now that holds out significant promise?

We are currently looking at the policy barriers to using IT to accelerate and scale-up energy efficiency and clean energy. We are looking, for example, at the way cities and corporates procure their energy solutions and at the way they use IT to run sustainable-energy partnerships. Right now we are pretty well-known in the climate-change space and in the subset of the corporate community that is already well-engaged with sustainability issues. However, the challenge is to build recognition beyond this space. That is true not just for us, but for many climate-change organizations who are looking at how to resonate outside their established niche. Our solution is to seek continuously to partner with organizations that are not yet part of the climate-change space. There actually is a tremendous willingness by people who are not committed climate-change activists to get involved. The Climate Group hosts Climate Week NYC every year, which is a series of events, and in 2012 it was astonishing to see how many sectors and communities—from farmers' organizations to veterans' groups, to bankers and electricity companies—were involved. They were motivated by a very wide spectrum of reasons, and it is very encouraging to see just how much energy and willingness there is out there, waiting to be tapped.

MORE INFO

Websites:

The Climate Group: www.theclimategroup.org

Verified Carbon Standard (VCS): www.v-c-s.org

See Also:

★ Climate Change and Insurance (pp. 149–150)

★ The Impact of Climate Change on Business (pp. 875–877)

"Study how a society uses its land, and you can come to pretty reliable conclusions as to what its future will be."
Ernst Friedrich Schumacher

  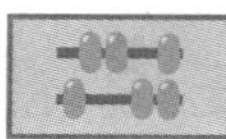      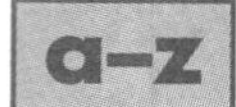

Viewpoint: Mobilizing the Power of Pension Funds to Transform Corporate Behavior by Catherine Howarth

INTRODUCTION

Catherine Howarth has been chief executive of FairPensions since July 2008. Established in 2005, FairPensions is the United Kingdom's only charity that is devoted to campaigning for responsible investment in the pensions industry. It aims to mobilize the financial power of pension investments to improve corporate behavior. Howarth was previously employed at London Citizens. During seven years there she developed a high-profile campaign for a London living wage, successfully influencing a broad cross-section of stakeholders, including companies, investors, public bodies, and politicians. Previously she was senior researcher at the New Policy Institute, London. Howarth has a first-class BA in modern history from Oxford University and an MSc in industrial relations from the London School of Economics. She is a member-nominated trustee at the Pensions Trust and a member of the Pensions Trust's investment committee.

Can you tell me why FairPensions was started, how it was started, and what its goals are?

FairPensions owes its origins to the pioneering campaign by students and university staff to influence the investment strategy of the Universities Superannuation Scheme (USS) in the 1990s. Campaigners pressed the fund's trustees to invest more ethically and responsibly. The USS didn't go as far as introducing ethically based screening, but it did adopt a robust, responsible investment strategy that committed it to active engagement with companies in its portfolio around environmental, social, and governance risks. That success helped to raise awareness of responsible investment across the pensions industry and encouraged a group of civil society leaders from trade unions, NGOs, etc., to establish FairPensions in 2005. The focus remains on ensuring that major pension providers use their financial clout to encourage more responsible corporate behavior. Another goal is to ensure that pension funds and institutional investors are better attuned to the views, interests, and beliefs of their ultimate beneficiaries.

On the subject of climate change, can you outline the resolutions that FairPensions introduced at the 2010 annual general meetings of Shell and BP?

The resolutions were, effectively, a request to the companies to report to shareholders about the environmental, social, and financial risks associated with their operations in the Canadian tar sands. These controversial projects are hugely environmentally destructive, not least in being one of the most carbon-intensive forms of oil production. Our point was—setting aside concerns about local environmental destruction—that the level of carbon which is built into these long-term investments could put these projects at serious financial risk.

What level of support did you get from pension funds?

The resolutions were supported by some of the largest pension funds in the world, including the likes of CalPERS, CalSTRS, and the New York State Common Retirement Fund. In the case of BP, more than one in seven investors rejected the management's recommendation to vote against the resolution. At Shell, more than 10% of investors refused to side with management's recommendation. Sadly, support from institutional investors in the United Kingdom was weak. The best we got were abstentions from F&C and Aviva. Everyone else supported the oil companies' managements' views that they were handling the risks well. Five days after the BP vote the explosion in the Gulf of Mexico suggested that BP management, at least, was not fully on top of the types of risk that we flagged up with our resolution.

Were you surprised that the best you got from UK investors was an abstention?

I was not particularly surprised, but I am enormously concerned on behalf of pension fund members. The episode demonstrated that UK pension funds and their fund managers are timid compared to overseas investors when it comes to robustly demanding that corporate management take the longer-term view. You have to question whether that attitude by professional investors is sufficient to protect their customers' long-term financial interests.

Is one reason that the likes of CalPERS and the Norwegian Government Pension Fund Global perform much better in this regard that they handle asset management inhouse, as opposed to outsourcing it?

If asset management is done inhouse, it's much easier to align the investment team's interests with those of the fund's long-term beneficiaries. Plenty of European funds have adopted this model, including the Swedish national pension funds AP 1 through 7, the Dutch pension giant ABP, the Universities Superannuation Scheme, and the BT pension fund.

In the intermediated model, however, there tends to be a greater conflict of interest between the short-term views and tight horizons of the external fund managers—whose bonuses are paid on an annual cycle, and whose performance is measured on short-term trajectories—and the long-term beneficiaries of pension funds.

There are also questions about the value for money offered by the fund management industry. This is of particular public concern in the United Kingdom, where we have one of the least generous systems of state pension provision in Europe. To ensure that Britons have anything approaching a decent standard of living in retirement, more needs to be done to educate the public about how the fund management sector works and how well it serves its customers.

What part, if any, do you think fund managers played in stoking up the global financial crisis?

In October 2010 there was an article in the *Financial Times*'s fund management section in which the European Commission accused the asset management industry of having played a key part in causing the credit crisis.[1] The fund management sector itself is in denial about this. It seems that fund managers have forgotten about their encouragement of behaviors and business practices in the banking sector which fueled short-term profitability but in the long term saw players like Northern Rock self-destruct. What worries me is that the fund management industry seems incapable of learning anything from the episode. If they won't face

"**Too many people are on boards because they want to have nice-looking visiting cards.**" Utz Felcht

  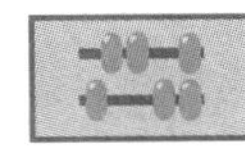      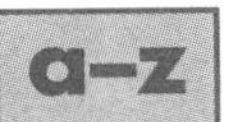

up to past failures, can we expect them to be properly alert to future risks?

In the United Kingdom and the United States, shareholders are expected to act as policemen, to rein in corporate excess on governments' behalves. But the European Union generally doesn't, believing government and regulator interventions are necessary. Which view of the world does FairPensions subscribe to?

If you look at fund managers' voting behavior in the run-up to the financial crisis, it's impossible to describe them as having acted as a brake on risk-taking. Rather, many were actively encouraging risk-taking to boost short-term returns. There was a fascinating recent interview with Tesco chief executive Sir Terry Leahy in the *Sunday Times* in which he criticized the fund management industry for forcing business leaders like himself to take a short-term perspective.[2] His view, as someone who has slowly built Tesco into a world-leading retailer, is that institutional investors have been more of a hindrance than a help to Tesco management.

Can we rely on asset managers to exert downward pressure on corporate pay, given that they probably also have a vested interest in seeing inflation-busting settlements, since these make their own remuneration appear more palatable?

Shareholders have a direct financial interest in pay restraint. Interestingly, Goldman Sachs's most profitable quarter in the past three years was the one in which it exercised the most pay restraint. But the fund management industry is not genuinely committed to the idea of pay restraint. It's also wrong to assume that giving more powers to shareholders will automatically lead to better-managed companies. What has to change is the way in which fund-management companies themselves are incentivized.

There have been suggestions that the United Kingdom's new "Stewardship Code" is really window-dressing designed to pre-empt further EU regulation of corporate governance. Do you think there's any truth in this?

We very much welcome the Stewardship Code and see it as a step in the right direction.[3] However, we do all need to check the extent to which fund manager signatories are walking the talk on voting and engagement. Too many still blindly vote with management. One of the things that we at FairPensions are pushing for is mandatory voting disclosure: we're not saying that institutional investors have to vote, merely that they should disclose how they vote.

Wouldn't annual general meetings have greater credibility as forums for shareholder democracy if institutional investors bothered to turn up and speak? When fund managers seek to influence corporate behavior, they always seem to do it behind closed doors? Don't we need more transparency and accountability?

Yes, institutional investors ought to be making their presence felt at AGMs. Unfortunately, the "behind closed doors engagement strategy" is the model that's being promoted by the Stewardship Code. It has its place. But it is also very important for major shareholders to be more publicly robust with companies.

Asset managers argue that turning up at AGMs would make their services more expensive; they would have to charge more for managing the money because of the cost of sending representatives to the meetings, etc.

Yes, but I don't see how they can claim to be looking after investors' interests if they won't even go to companies' AGMs once a year!

If you were to reinvent pension fund investment practice from scratch, what kind of model would you advocate?

I would like to see a system that is less obsessed with short-term gains and more interested in companies' long-term income-generating qualities; a system in which pension funds work alongside corporate management to encourage and enable corporations to take a sustainable longer-term view. There are certainly alternative financial models that better align the interests of fund managers with the ultimate owners of the assets.

Colin Melvin, chief executive of Hermes Equity Ownership Services, has suggested that there are ways of rewarding asset managers for performance over the long term . . .

Colin has talked a lot about longer-term mandates, but I don't see them as the whole answer. One reason that Hermes is ahead of the pack where recognition of longer-term risks is concerned is that it is wholly owned by the BT pension fund. It would be great if we could see a similar alignment of interests at other fund management companies.

Do you think that pension funds ought to be putting a smaller portion of their portfolios into equities and more into bonds—and perhaps more into "alternative" asset classes?

The big pension funds are currently switching into bonds in a big way. However, this may well turn out to be the next big wave of risk. It has been suggested that there may be a bond bubble. Bonds could be very risky if inflation takes off. And while it looks like there is deflationary pressure now, with quantitative easing and ultra-low interest rates, inflation may be just around the corner. In fact, inflation is running well above the 2% rate that is supposedly the target for the Bank of England.

MORE INFO

Books:

Blackburn, Robin. *Banking on Death or Investing in Life: The History and Future of Pensions*. London: Verso, 2002.

Davis, Stephen, Jon Lukomnik, and David Pitt-Watson. *The New Capitalists: How Citizen Investors Are Reshaping the Corporate Agenda*. Boston, MA: Harvard Business School Press, 2006.

Drucker, Peter F. *The Unseen Revolution: How Pension Fund Socialism Came to America*. New York: Harper & Row, 1976.

Peston, Robert.*Who Runs Britain? ... and Who's to Blame for the Economic Mess We're In*. London: Hodder, 2008.

Ruskin, John. *Unto This Last: Four essays on the First Principles of Political Economy*. London: Pallas Athene, 2010.

See Also:

★ CSR: More than PR, Pursuing Competitive Advantage in the Long Run (pp. 664–666)
★ Ethical Funds and Socially Responsible Investment: An Overview (pp. 481–483)
★ Managing Activist Investors and Fund Managers (pp. 525–526)

NOTES

1 Grene, Sophia. "Asset chiefs fear EU's activities tax." *Financial Times*(October 24, 2010). Online at: tinyurl.com/cko2rtd

2 "Investors must behave like owners and look to the longer term." *Sunday Times* (September 26, 2010).

3 Financial Reporting Council. "The UK stewardship code." July 2010. Online at: tinyurl.com/d2wvovq [PDF].

"The way management treats their associates is exactly how the associates will then treat the customers." Sam M. Walton

  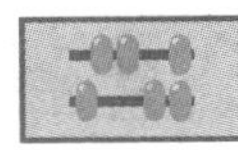      

Reinvesting in the Company versus Rewarding Investors with Distributions by Ruth Bender

EXECUTIVE SUMMARY

- Dividend payouts will always depend on having sufficient retained profits and cash.
- Companies should invest in growth if doing so will generate a return above the cost of capital, as this will increase stockholder value. If there are no value-enhancing investments, surplus cash should be returned to stockholders.
- Stockholder expectations will drive dividend policy, and changes to that policy should be signaled clearly to investors.

INTRODUCTION

Stockholders gain value from their investments in two ways—either by receiving dividends or by realizing a capital gain. Dividend policy is determined directly by a company's board, which has to decide whether to make a payout or to reinvest.

Although many factors underlie the dividend decision, there is one basic rule: If there are investment opportunities where the expected return exceeds the company's cost of capital, value will be created by making the investment and it should be done. If there are insufficient value-creating opportunities, the surplus cash should be distributed to stockholders.

Therefore, the question to ask when considering reinvestment versus distribution to investors should be: Will this create stockholder value?

DIVIDEND POLICY

Companies that pay dividends try to increase the absolute level of dividend each year in order to meet investor expectations.

Two numbers are relevant to understanding dividend policy: The level of the annual dividend (which may in practice be paid in quarterly or semi-annual installments), and the dividend payout ratio (the dividend for the year as a percentage of after-tax income). Stockholders are concerned with the absolute level of dividend they receive, but will also have an eye on the dividend payout ratio.

If the payout ratio is kept constant, then, as profits grow, the absolute level of dividend will become progressively larger. However, volatility in profits would mean volatility in payouts, and this is unsatisfactory to investors. Accordingly, most companies have a more flexible attitude to the payout ratio, aiming to smooth the distribution, increasing dividends annually but not exactly in line with the change in profits.[1] This is particularly relevant in cyclical industries, where a progressive dividend implies a changing payout ratio over the cycle.

DRIVERS OF DIVIDEND POLICY

Two fundamentals underlie a company's ability to pay dividends to its stockholders—is there enough cash, and are there enough profits?

The issue of cash is a universal one: if a company does not have sufficient liquidity to manage its operations in the way it needs to, it would be foolish to deplete cash resources by making payouts. As to whether there are sufficient profits, this is often a legal issue, and so specific to a particular jurisdiction. However, a general rule is that dividends should only be paid out of realized retained profits.

Moving beyond these fundamentals, a key issue for management to consider is the business of the company. Companies in different industries, or at different stages of their life cycle, have different cash needs and investment opportunities, and these will drive dividend policy.

Investors in an early-stage business have different expectations from those investing in a mature business. The early-stage business has low (if any) profits but high growth potential, and the investor will be seeking a capital gain. That gain will come from growing the business, which is likely to involve considerable investment along the way. So for these types of business, paying a dividend would reduce the growth potential; investors would not, therefore, expect a high payout.

In a mature company there are fewer investment opportunities and so less growth is expected. To obtain the required returns, stockholders will expect a large dividend. Indeed, if a company with no clear investment opportunities were to retain profits rather than paying them out as dividends, stockholders could rightly query the executives' motives in doing so as this is not a value-creating strategy.

In determining their dividend policy, boards also need to ensure that the capital structure of the business is sound. Because debt is a cheaper form of finance than equity, companies generally want a proportion of their finance to be debt. However, too much debt will drive a business to bankruptcy. Accordingly, the dividend decision has to be consistent with the financing policy—a riskier business will have more equity in its capital structure, and it is unlikely that a company that is equity-financed would pay out a large dividend. Table 1 illustrates this.

For an early-stage operation there is no point in paying a dividend, as this would deplete the company's much needed cash resources, and the only source of replacement funds would be the same stockholders that are receiving the dividend. However, as the business gains the traction to use more debt-based instruments, a higher payout to stockholders can be made. For declining business there will be few, if any, value-enhancing investment opportunities, so the dividend payout should be as great as cash flow allows, probably paying out previously retained profits.

A further consideration in deciding dividend policy is the tax situation of the company and its investors. In many jurisdictions, investors are taxed more highly on dividends than on capital gains, which means that they might prefer to receive value by selling their shares in the market at a time of their choosing (or selling them to the company in a buyback) rather than taking this highly taxed income. Also, in some jurisdictions companies can face a tax penalty for paying dividends.

Table 1. Financing and dividend policy over the business life cycle. (*Source*: Bender and Ward, 2009)

	Stage of life cycle			
	Launch	Growth	Maturity	Decline
Capital required to support value-enhancing growth	Very high	High	Medium	Negative
Main source of finance for the business	Equity (venture capital)	Equity	Equity and debt	Debt
Dividend policy	Nil	Nil or low	Substantial	100% payout

THE IMPACT OF CHANGING DIVIDEND POLICY

A strong influence on how much dividend a company pays out is the level of dividends in previous years. Stockholders prefer a predictable and sustainable dividend strategy, and companies have particular clienteles of investors with different requirements for distributions. Investors who want their value creation to come from capital gains tend not to invest too much in high-yielding shares. Similarly, those who need a stream of income from dividends seek out companies that will provide this.

Given that the dividend decision is made by balancing the company's cash needs and its investment needs, significant changes in a company's level of dividend could be seen as good or bad by the investment community; it depends on the story that the company is telling, and whether the markets believe it. Table 2 illustrates this.

If the dividend on a high-yielding stock were to be cut without this being properly signaled, the income-seeking stockholders might be obliged to sell shares in order to make good the shortfall in the inflows they were expecting. And if a growth stock were suddenly to start paying a dividend, this might be unwelcome (for example, for tax reasons) to its particular stockholder constituency, who again might become sellers. So an unexpected change in dividend policy can lead, in the short term, to the share price falling because there are too many sellers.

BUYBACKS AS AN ALTERNATIVE TO CASH DIVIDENDS

Companies that do not want to commit to a regular dividend, or those making one-off large distributions to stockholders (for example, the proceeds of a major disposal), may do so by way of a share buyback rather than a dividend. For tax purposes, the proceeds of a buyback are often treated as capital rather than income, which favors some investors. Another advantage to investors is that, depending on how the transaction is structured, they can choose whether or not to sell their shares to the company, giving them more flexibility in managing their investment. And, from the company's point of view, the buyback does not create expectations in the same way that a regularly increasing dividend does.

However, buybacks are not permitted in all jurisdictions. Also, these programs are more expensive for companies to administer than are dividends.

Table 2. What might a change in dividend signal?

	Increase dividend	Reduce dividend
Interpreted as good news	Company is prospering and throwing off cash	A change of strategy means that the directors see more profitable investment opportunities and future profitable growth
Interpreted as bad news	Directors have run out of investment ideas for profitable growth	Falls in profits and cash flow have led to the need to preserve cash

CONCLUSION

Ultimately, all the profits a business creates will be paid out to its stockholders; dividends are just a payment on account to those that currently own its stock. The board has a practical decision to make: Whether to make that payment now, or to retain the money and put it to use by reinvesting in the business.

In addition to the availability of cash and profits to support the dividend, other factors to influence the board's decision should include the company's investment opportunities and stockholder expectations.

Investors value stability in dividend policy, and an increasing payout.

CASE STUDY

Microsoft[2]

Microsoft, one of the largest and most profitable companies in the world, has a somewhat unusual track record on distributions. Although enormously cash-generative, until 2003 the company had never paid out a dividend to its stockholders, though it had returned money to them through buybacks. (In 2003 the tax treatment of US dividends was eased, although the company stated that this was a coincidence.) A quarterly dividend is now paid, which has grown steadily each year.

In 2004 Microsoft announced its quarterly dividend (US$0.08), and also a special one-off dividend of US$3 per share, plus plans for a buyback program of up to US$30 billion.

At the time, Steve Ballmer, the CEO, explained the distributions as follows:

"We are confident in our long-term ability to grow revenue, profits and shareholder value ... We will continue to make major investments across all our businesses, and maintain our position as a leading innovator in the industry, but we can now also provide up to $75 billion in total value to shareholders over the next four years."

In this way the payout was clearly signaled as a growth story, with excess cash rather than a lack of managerial ideas for the future.

Bringing the story up to date, in September 2008, following its abortive bid for Yahoo!, Microsoft announced a US$0.02 increase in its quarterly dividend (to US$0.13), and a new US$40 billion share repurchase program, to expire in 2013. (And this at a time when most companies were preserving cash because of the credit crunch.) The company stated that it had returned more than US$115 billion to stockholders via dividends and buybacks in the last five years and that the new buyback program reflected its confidence in Microsoft's long-term growth. This return of equity to stockholders may be funded by bringing debt into the capital structure.

MAKING IT HAPPEN

In setting dividend policy, the board should consider several key factors. For example:

- What are the current investment opportunities (organic and by acquisition) available to the business, and are they likely to change in the next few years?
- What is the current cash position? Do we have sufficient cash for our needs in the foreseeable future? Are we holding too much cash? How accurately can we forecast this?
- Legally, are there any restraints on paying out a dividend this year?
- If we change our dividend policy, how will the markets react?

NOTES

1 Lintner, J. "Distribution of incomes of corporations among dividends, retained earnings, and taxes." *American Economic Review* 46 (1956): 97–113.

2 *Source*: www.microsoft.com

"If a business does well, the stock eventually follows." Warren Buffett

Role of Internal Auditing at Board Committee Level

by Sridhar Ramamoorti

EXECUTIVE SUMMARY

- Boards of directors and their committees, despite receiving extremely summarized and condensed information, now have a well-established responsibility for managing the overall organizational risk.
- The effective management of risk is a prerequisite for ensuring good corporate governance.
- Because governance seems to be so intertwined with risk, one strategy might be to leverage the internal audit function to work with different board committees and provide risk-relevant information.
- The independent audit committee fulfills a vital role in corporate governance. The audit committee can be a critical component in ensuring quality reporting and controls, as well as the proper identification and management of risk.
- A summary of internal audit-audit committee interactions is provided through the perspective of *20 Questions Directors Should Ask of Internal Audit*
- The internal audit function has long been serving as the "eyes and ears" as well as the "arms and legs" of the audit committee of the board.
- Internal audit role plays a critical role in keeping the audit committee abreast of the latest developments and goings-on of the company, and without such assistance, the audit committee cannot realistically fulfill its risk oversight responsibilities.

INTRODUCTION

In the aftermath of the Wall Street financial crisis, one of the major areas that has been identified as needing improvement is corporate governance. Boards of directors and their committees, despite receiving extremely summarized and condensed information, now have a well-established responsibility for managing the overall organizational risk (Kolb and Schwartz, 2010). A critically important element that was lacking before and during the financial crisis was relevant risk intelligence—most boards were caught offguard and were truly surprised by the turn of events. Recent guidance from the Information Systems Audit and Control Association (ISACA, 2010) highlights the importance of risk monitoring by noting that "better monitoring means fewer surprises."

The effective management of risk is a prerequisite for ensuring good corporate governance. Organizations exist to achieve their goals and objectives; however, because these goals and objectives have to be achieved in the context or environment of risk, they are not always assured (McNamee and Selim, 1998). Although the practice of risk management, on an enterprise-wide basis, is fundamentally the responsibility of executive management, the internal auditing function is typically charged with examining and reporting on risk exposures, as well as on the quality of the organization's risk management efforts. The board has oversight responsibility with respect to management and, by extension, has responsibility for both effective risk management and governance.

It is evident that organizations worldwide need to strengthen their governance mechanisms. Nevertheless, placing the governance burden in its entirety on the board of directors is an unrealistic position to advocate, given the infrequency of meetings and their limited knowledge of business operations on a day-to-day basis. Because governance seems to be so intertwined with risk, one strategy might be to leverage the internal audit function to work with different board committees and provide risk-relevant information. In this article we will focus on the internal audit function supporting the audit committee with respect to enterprise risk management.

INTERNAL AUDIT–AUDIT COMMITTEE INTERACTIONS

Treating the internal audit function as one of the cornerstones of corporate governance, Swanson (2010) says that "internal auditing can provide strategic, operational and tactical value to an organization's operations." He proceeds to emphasize that audit committee members should not only empower the internal audit function by providing it with resources and encouraging it to take on a leadership role, but that they should also actively oversee its performance. To help formulate the right perspective and ensure that these interactions are ideal, he usefully refers to a publication by the Canadian Institute of Chartered Accountants, *20 Questions Directors Should Ask of Internal Audit* (Fraser and Lindsay, 2008). It is worthwhile to excerpt these 20 questions across six categories, *viz.*

1 *Internal audit's role and mandate*
 a Should we have an internal audit function?
 b What should our internal audit function do?
 c What should be the mandate of the internal audit function?
2 *Internal audit relationships*
 a What is the relationship between internal auditing and the audit committee?
 b To whom does internal auditing report administratively?
3 *Internal audit resources*
 a How is the internal audit function staffed?
 b How does internal auditing get and maintain the expertise it needs to conduct its assignments?
 c Are the activities of internal auditing appropriately coordinated with those of the external auditors?
4 *Internal audit process*
 a How is the internal audit plan developed?
 b What does the internal audit plan not cover?
 c How are internal audit findings reported?
 d How are corporate mangers required to respond to internal audit findings and recommendations?
 e What services does internal audit provide in connection with fraud?
 f How do you assess the effectiveness of your internal audit function?
5 *Closing questions*
 a Does internal auditing have sufficient resources?
 b Does the internal audit function get appropriate support from the CEO and senior management team?
 c **Are you satisfied that this organization has adequate internal controls over its major risks?**
 d Are there any other matters that you wish to bring to the audit committee's attention?
 e Are there other ways in which internal auditing and the audit committees could support each other?
6 *Audit committee overall assessment*
 a Are we (the audit committee) satisfied with our internal audit function?

(Item 5(c) above has been bolded to indicate that in a very significant way enterprise risk management does pertain to the audit

"Along with senior management, corporate boards have primary responsibility for managing the risk of the firm."
Kolb and Schwartz (2010)

committee, and this is the focus of the next section of this article).

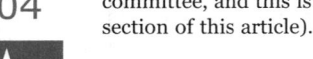

ENTERPRISE RISK MANAGEMENT

Risk is best considered at the portfolio, aggregate, or organization- or enterprise-wide level. Enterprise risk management (ERM) is a process-driven methodology combined with tools that enable senior management to visualize, assess, and manage significant risks that may adversely impact the attainment of key organizational objectives (see COSO, 2004). ERM risks can be categorized as follows.

- *Strategic*: affects the achievement of strategic goals and objectives.
- *Compliance*: affects compliance with federal, state, and local laws, rules and regulations.
- *Reputational*: affects public perception and reputation, including employee morale.
- *Financial*: affects assets, technology, financial reporting, and auditing.
- *Operational*: affects ongoing management processes and procedures.

As noted above, it makes sense for the internal audit function be viewed as the ideal group within an organization to work on ERM issues that are pertinent to each of the committees of the board. The International Professional Practices Framework (IPPF) issued by the Institute of Internal Auditors (IIA, 2011a) supports such an arrangement.

The IPPF Standard 2120 (see below) can be interpreted as follows.

- Implementation of this standard helps assess whether risk management processes are effective and encapsulates the internal auditor's assessment of:
  - whether organizational objectives support and align with the organization's mission; whether significant risks are identified and assessed;
  - whether appropriate risk responses are selected that align risks with the organization's risk appetite; and
  - whether relevant risk information is captured and communicated in a timely manner across the organization, enabling staff, management, and the board to carry out their responsibilities.
- The internal audit activity may gather the information to support this assessment during multiple assurance and/or consulting engagements. The results of these engagements, when viewed together, provide an understanding of the organization's risk management processes and their effectiveness.
- Risk management processes are monitored through ongoing management activities, separate evaluations, or both (see also COSO, 2009).

All that is needed is a requirement that the internal audit function considers direct reporting to different board committees—the governance, nominating, compensation, and audit committees—in their review of risk management efforts undertaken, their effectiveness, and any significant residual exposures.

APPLICABLE PROFESSIONAL STANDARDS

2120 Risk Management

The internal audit activity must evaluate the effectiveness and contribute to the improvement of risk management processes.

2120.A1 The internal audit activity must evaluate risk exposures relating to the organization's governance, operations, and information systems regarding the:

- Reliability and integrity of financial and operational information;
- Effectiveness and efficiency of operations and programs;
- Safeguarding of assets;
- and Compliance with laws, regulations, policies, procedures, and contracts.

2120.A2 The internal audit activity must evaluate the potential for the occurrence of fraud and how the organization manages fraud risk.

2120.C1 During consulting engagements, internal auditors must address risk consistent with the engagement's objectives and be alert to the existence of other significant risks.

2120.C2 Internal auditors must incorporate knowledge of risks gained from consulting engagements into their evaluation of the organization's risk management processes.

2120.C3 When assisting management in establishing or improving risk management processes, internal auditors must refrain from assuming any management responsibility by actually managing risks.

Source: IIA, 2011b.

BOARD COMMUNICATIONS

Board Communications

Although internal audit work plans and programs may be conducted at a detailed level, most board members are unlikely to appreciate the results and findings of assurance engagements at that level of granularity. They would like for internal audit to aggregate their findings and recommendations and present them in a "big picture" fashion. In other words, the chief audit executive (CAE) must consciously work at making board briefings relevant to their corporate governance mandate. Key audit risks may be highlighted in this connection, keeping in mind the level of communications that are appropriate when dealing with board committees (Orsini, 2004).

Some of these risks, as highlighted by Orsini (2004), are outlined below.

- *Risk of missing the big picture*: Organization-wide governance and enterprise-wide risk management necessarily involve looking at risk at an aggregate, macro-level, so that the organizational (risk) profile assessed and opined upon is comprehensive and strategic.
- *Risk of missing the dynamics of change*: The auditors use a maturity-capability model and factor in the current stage of development in the executive management agenda. For instance, it would be helpful for them to use a control baselining methodology in order to track effectively any changes in people, processes, and technology, as well as the overall risk profile (see COSO, 2009).
- *Risk of subjective second-guessing of management*: Audit assessments are based on formal analyses and typically eschew opinions, hearsay, rumor, etc., that are "notoriously unreliable." However, where there exists an "execution capability" concern based on track record, it may be appropriate to drive outcomes and accountability by making critical assessments of management integrity and leadership.
- *Risk of providing insightful but not actionable intelligence*: Audit assessments of (governance) risk exposures should not merely be insightful, but meaningful, practical, and actionable. Thus, if the organization lacks the means to respond effectively or in a timely fashion because it lacks the tools, or because the solutions are simply too costly or would take too long to implement, it is imprudent for the internal auditor to raise the issue (as an extension of the idea of second-guessing management).

ASSISTING THE AUDIT COMMITTEE: A BROAD MANDATE AND MYRIAD OPPORTUNITIES FOR INTERNAL AUDIT

The report of the National Association of Corporate Directors' Blue Ribbon Commission on Audit Committees (NACD, 2000) provided the following rationale for why corporations need audit committees:

"The independent audit committee fulfills a vital role in corporate governance. The audit committee can be a critical component in ensuring quality reporting and

"The risk oversight function of the board of directors continues to take center stage... The reputational damage to boards of companies that fail to properly manage risk is a major threat." Law firm Wachtell, Lipton, Rosen & Katz in a 2010 report

  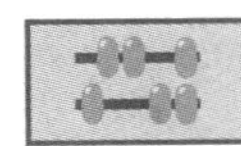      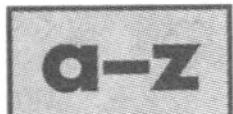

controls, as well as the proper identification and management of risk."

Internal auditing can not only play a critical role in helping establish and define appropriate risk oversight expectations, but also identify the source(s) of information and associated monitoring processes to meet these expectations. Clearly, the audit committee of the board must be the conduit for such information.

Bromark and Hoffman (1992) note that the role of the audit committee is expanding because of the need to meet the challenges of constantly changing business conditions. They highlight the following primary responsibilities of the audit committee:

- assisting the board to fulfill its oversight responsibilities as they relate to the financial reporting process and the internal structure;
- maintaining, by way of regularly scheduled meetings, direct lines of communication between the board, financial management, the independent accountant, and internal audit.

Additional responsibilities quoted in Braiotta *et al.* (2010) include the following:

- reviewing corporate policies related to compliance with laws and regulations, ethics, conflict of interests, and the investigation of misconduct and fraud;
- conducting periodic reviews of current pending litigation of regulatory proceedings bearing on corporate governance in which the corporation is a party;
- coordinating annual reviews of compliance with corporate governance policies through internal audit or the company's independent accountants;
- performing or supervising special investigations;
- reviewing executive expenses;
- reviewing policies on sensitive payments;
- reviewing past or proposed transactions between the corporation and members of management; · reviewing the corporation's benefits programs;
- assessing the performance of financial management.

The internal audit function has long been serving as the "eyes and ears" as well as the "arms and legs" of the audit committee of the board. In the context of the above detailed list of responsibilities of the audit committee, it is evident that the internal audit role plays a critical role in keeping the audit committee abreast of the latest developments and goings on of the company.

CONCLUSION

Audit committees have typically been viewed as the group within the board structure with responsibility for risk oversight. As such, they end up relying to a large extent on the internal audit function to assure them about management's effectiveness in assessing, measuring, and responding to the array of risks that affect the organization. Although internal audit must undertake certain types of assurance engagements in this connection, establish safeguards to preserve independence and objectivity in other circumstances, and eschew taking on those activities that would compromise its independence and objectivity, it is clear that it does have a substantive role to play with respect to ERM. Without such involvement, it would simply not be possible for the audit committee to discharge its own ERM oversight function effectively.

MORE INFO

Books:

Braiotta, Louis, Jr, R. Trent Gazzaway, Robert Colson, and Sridhar Ramamoorti. *The Audit Committee Handbook*. 5th ed. Hoboken, NJ: Wiley, 2010.

Information Systems Audit and Control Association (ISACA). *Monitoring Internal Control Systems and IT: A Primer for Business Executives, Managers and Auditors on How to Embrace and Advance Best Practices*. Rolling Meadows, IL: ISACA, 2010.

Institute of Internal Auditors (IIA). *International Professional Practices Framework*. Altamonte Springs, FL: IIA Research Foundation, 2011a.

Kolb, Robert W., and Donald Schwartz (eds). *Corporate Boards: Managers of Risk, Sources of Risk*. Chichester, UK: Wiley, 2010.

McNamee, David, and Georges M. Selim. *Risk Management: Changing the Internal Auditor's Paradigm.* Altamonte Springs, FL: Institute of Internal Auditors Research Foundation, 1998.

National Association of Corporate Directors (NACD). *Report of the NACD Blue Ribbon Commission on Audit Committees*. Washington, DC: NACD, 2000.

Swanson, Dan. *Swanson on Internal Auditing: Raising the Bar.* Ely, UK: IT Governance Publishing, 2010.

Articles:

Bromark, Ray, and Ralph Hoffman. "An audit committee for dynamic times." *Directors and Boards* 16:3 (Spring 1992). Online at: tinyurl.com/65txg4o

Orsini, Basil. "Auditing governance: The Canadian government offers an audit tool for addressing the risks in implementing management reform." *Internal Auditor* (June 2004). Online at: tinyurl.com/6xaagbv

Reports:

Committee of Sponsoring Organizations of the Treadway Commission (COSO). "Enterprise risk management—Integrated framework." September 2004.

Committee of Sponsoring Organizations of the Treadway Commission (COSO). "Guidance on monitoring internal control systems." February 2009.

Fraser, John, and Hugh Lindsay. "20 questions directors should ask about internal audit." 2nd ed. Canadian Institute of Chartered Accountants, 2008. Online at: www.theiia.org/download.cfm?file=2927 [PDF].

Standards:

IIA. "International standards for the professional practice of internal auditing (Standards)." Rev. ed. Altamonte Springs, FL: IIA, 2011b. Online at: tinyurl.com/42kad8u

See Also:

★ Engaging Senior Management in Internal Control (pp. 336–337)
★ Internal Audit and Partnering with Senior Management (pp. 368–371)

"The audit committee can be a critical component in ensuring quality reporting and controls, as well as the proper identification and management of risk." NACD Blue Ribbon Commission on Audit Committees, 2000

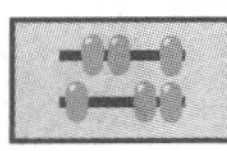

Accounting for Business Combinations in Accordance with International Financial Reporting Standards (IFRS) Requirements

by Shân Kennedy

EXECUTIVE SUMMARY

The International Accounting Standards Board (IASB) has introduced requirements in the last few years to make those involved in business combinations more accountable for the transactions that have taken place. In particular:

- All business combinations must now be accounted for using the acquisition accounting method.
- The intangible assets arising from a business combination must be identified and recognized separately from purchased goodwill.
- Purchased goodwill is no longer permitted to be amortized; instead, it must be tested for impairment each year.

INTRODUCTION

The accounting for business combinations under IFRS is governed by four key standards:

- IFRS 3, Business Combinations;
- IAS (International Accounting Standards) 27, Consolidated Financial Statements;
- IAS 36, Impairment of Assets;
- IAS 38, Intangible Assets.

IFRS 3 sets out the requirements to be followed in accounting for a business combination. Its introduction in 2004 represented a substantial change from the standard it superseded, IAS 22. IFRS 3 signaled the end of the benign method of accounting for business combinations known as "merger accounting." Instead, all business combinations must be accounted for using the acquisition accounting method. This requires that both acquirer and acquiree are identified for each transaction, that a fair value exercise is performed on the acquiree's assets and liabilities, and that purchased goodwill arising from the transaction is capitalized in the balance sheet.

A further consequence of the introduction of IFRS 3 is that intangible assets must be recognized separately from purchased goodwill instead of being subsumed within purchased goodwill. Purchased goodwill itself is not amortized, but must be reviewed for impairment annually. The performance of the impairment review is covered by IAS 36, Impairment of Assets, and the identification and recognition of intangible assets is covered by IAS 38, Intangible Assets.

The tightening up of business combination accounting was noted by accountants PricewaterhouseCoopers: "The acquisition process will need to become more rigorous, from planning to execution."[1]

The following steps are involved in accounting for a business combination under IFRS 3:

- identification of the acquirer and the acquiree;
- performance of a fair value exercise on the acquiree's assets and liabilities;
- identification and measurement of the fair value of the intangible assets arising;
- measurement of the amount of any non-controlling interest in the acquiree;
- measurement of the amount of goodwill arising from the transaction.

A revised version of IFRS 3 was issued by the IASB in January 2008, and its requirements will be mandatory for accounting periods from July 2009 onward. While the revision is quite comprehensive, it does not change the overall approach set out above. The revision is part of the Convergence Program underway between the IASB and the Financial Accounting Standards Board (FASB), aimed at reducing the number of differences between IFRS requirements and US Generally Accepted Accounting Principles (US GAAP). In addition to tightening up certain areas, the revision developed the previous IFRS 3 by:

- providing additional guidance regarding the recognition and fair value measurement of the acquiree's assets and liabilities;
- changing the requirements for measuring goodwill and the remaining noncontrolling interest when less than a 100% stake in the acquiree is purchased or when an increase in an existing stake is involved.

IDENTIFICATION OF ACQUIRER AND ACQUIREE

IAS 27 demands that the acquirer in a business combination be identified as the party that gains control, with control being defined as "the power to govern the financial and operating policies of an entity so as to benefit from its activities." Control is presumed to exist if one entity owns more than 50% of the voting power of the other, unless it can be demonstrated that this voting power does not constitute control. Conversely, control can be seen to exist when one entity owns less than 50% of the voting rights in the other but controls it through some other means, such as a shareholder agreement. This situation was seen when ABN AMRO was acquired by the Royal Bank of Scotland (RBS)—RBS owns only 38% of the issued share capital of ABN AMRO but is able to control it through a consortium agreement with the other owners, Fortis and Santander. Thus, RBS consolidates ABN AMRO in its financial statements.

Other guidance provided in IAS 27 for identifying the acquirer includes that, generally, the acquirer is:

- larger than the acquiree;
- the party issuing equity or paying cash as consideration;
- the party that has more seats on the board of directors of the combined entity.

IFRS 3 does, however, also deal with reverse acquisitions in which smaller companies acquire larger ones through the issue of significant amounts of equity.

FAIR VALUE EXERCISE ON THE ACQUIREE'S ASSETS AND LIABILITIES

Consistent with any acquisition accounting exercise, IFRS 3 requires that the acquired assets and liabilities are recognized initially at fair value in the consolidated financial statements of the combined entity. The standard provides some clarification regarding identification of these assets and liabilities. For instance, IFRS 3 prohibits the setting up of acquisition reorganization provisions since these are not liabilities of the acquirer at the acquisition date. Prior to IFRS 3, acquiring companies often set up substantial acquisition reorganization provisions. Costs, such as those relating to redundancy and factory closures, were charged to these provisions post acquisition rather than to the profit and loss account. Now, such costs must be charged to the profit and loss account of the combined entity post acquisition.

"When you sell 30% of a business, it is like taking two limbs off a body—it's not surprising there is a negative effect on the rest of the business." Sir Clive Thompson

IDENTIFICATION AND MEASUREMENT OF THE INTANGIBLE ASSETS ARISING FROM A COMBINATION

IAS 38 defines an intangible asset as "identifiable" if it can be separated from the entity—i.e. can be leased or sold separately from the entity—or if it is secured legally. By defining identifiability in terms of separability as well as legal security, the number of potentially recognizable intangible assets increases. For instance, software technology may not be legally protected by a patent, but this does not prevent it from being licensed or sold to a third party. Consequently, if a software company is acquired, those intangible assets that may be recognized include both patent protected and unprotected software. Since IFRS 3 assumes that the fair value of intangible assets arising from an acquisition can be measured reliably, if in existence such assets must be recognized in the fair value balance sheet.

It is the broadening of the net of intangible assets to include those that are not secured legally, together with the assumption that all identifiable intangible assets arising from a business combination can be measured reliably, that has greatly increased the number of intangible assets recognised separately from goodwill following a business combination.

IFRS 3 clarifies that certain intangible assets might be recognized in the consolidated financial statements but are not recognized in the financial statements of the acquiree. Thus, internally developed brands and customer relationship assets of the acquiree would not be recognized as intangible assets in the financial statements of the acquiree, because the cost of their development would be recorded as an expense. However, provided they satisfy the IAS 38 requirement to be identifiable intangible assets—i.e. if they are intangible, identifiable, controlled by the entity, and expected to give rise to future economic benefits—they are recognized in the consolidated financial statements.

Potentially, a very large number of intangible assets might need to be valued for balance sheet recognition purposes. IAS 38, however, allows the preparer of accounts to combine certain complementary intangible assets as a composite intangible asset—a brand—if the fair values of the underlying component intangible assets cannot be determined reliably or if they have similar useful lives. In practice, this concession is often used to reduce the number of intangible assets that need to be valued following a business combination. A proposed amendment to IAS 38 suggests that the concession could be extended to complementary assets other than brands.

An example of the increased number of intangible assets recognized following business combinations can be seen in the results of Yell Group plc (see Table 1).

Table 1. Analysis of intangible assets in Yell Group financial statements March 2008

Contracts	£47m
Non-compete agreements	£6m
Customer lists	£366m
Brand names	£856m
Software costs	£44m
Total identifiable intangible assets	£1,319m
Goodwill	£3,899m

In contrast, the Yell Group financial statements for March 2005—the last before transition to IFRS—show a goodwill balance of £1,635 million and no identifiable intangible assets.

Neither IFRS 3 nor IAS 38 provides any substantive guidance on determining the fair value of intangible assets. Instead, best practice has developed in the marketplace and tends to be driven by the auditors of the accounts. Many intangible asset valuation consultancies have commented on the difficulty of valuing these intangible assets. One such consultancy, Brand Finance, notes in its website literature: "In many instances the valuation of such assets is a complex undertaking" and "it will be important to demonstrate that best practice techniques are being applied."

In January 2009, the International Valuation Standards Council (IVSC) issued two Exposure Drafts on the valuation of intangible assets generally and on the valuation of intangible assets for IFRS reporting purposes. These set out the key valuation methods that are used and address some of the more complex issues that can arise. They follow their issue, in July 2007, of a Discussion Paper on the topic of the valuation of intangible assets for IFRS reporting purposes.

In response to the IVSC's Discussion Paper, the International Actuarial Association noted: "We support the issuance of guidance on valuation of intangible assets for IFRS reporting purposes."

MEASURING THE AMOUNT OF ANY NON-CONTROLLING INTEREST IN THE ACQUIREE

If, as a result of a business combination, the acquirer owns less than 100% of the acquiree, there is a remaining non-controlling interest, previously known as a minority interest, in the acquiree to be recognized. Accounting for this non-controlling interest has changed following the recent revision to IFRS 3. Previously, the non-controlling interest had to be measured at its proportionate share of the identifiable net assets, i.e. excluding its goodwill. The revision introduced the option to measure the non-controlling interest at its fair value and thus include its goodwill. Several commentators were concerned about the difficulty of measuring this fair value, especially where the acquiree company's shares were unlisted, and for this reason the option to measure at fair value was not made mandatory. Under US GAAP, however, the non-controlling interest must be measured at fair value—no option is permitted. This represents a continuing difference between IFRS and US GAAP requirements.

MEASURING THE GOODWILL ARISING FROM A BUSINESS COMBINATION

The revised IFRS 3 requires that goodwill is measured as the following:

The sum of:

- the fair value of the consideration paid;
- the amount of any non-controlling interest measured as described above;
- the fair value of any previously held non-controlling interest in the acquiree;

Less:

- the net sum of the acquisition date assets acquired and liabilities assumed, measured as required by IFRS 3.

It is important to note that goodwill itself is not measured at fair value—it is the residual amount that results from applying the calculation above. As a result of the option with respect to measurement of any non-controlling interest, the amount measured for goodwill may or may not include goodwill in such non-controlling interest.

NOTE

1 *Source*: PricewaterhouseCoopers. "Acquisitions: Accounting and transparency under IFRS 3." April 2004. Online at: www.pwc.com/fi/fin/ifrs/pwc_acq_acc_transp_ifrs3.pdf

Acquisition Integration: How to Do It Successfully by David Sadtler

EXECUTIVE SUMMARY

- Successful integration of an acquisition by the acquiring company is often the most important determinant of the overall success of the acquisition process.
- Gaining financial control of the acquired company and tight cash management are essential from the start.
- Integrating management processes and systems can be difficult and time-consuming, but it is essential if the newly acquired management team is to be involved and empowered.
- Use all available sources of information to make key management appointments as quickly as possible.
- Ensure that the key drivers of value creation are known to all involved in the project, and that the process of searching, negotiating, and integrating reflects the most important of them.
- Move as quickly as possible when integrating.

INTRODUCTION

Acquisitions of any size are a major undertaking for both the acquirer and the target. Substantial returns—in particular returns in excess of the cost of capital employed in the entire initiative—are required not only to create stockholder value, but also to justify the enormous investment of managerial time and effort that goes into a takeover. Many acquisitions succeed. Indeed, many corporate acquirers do a large number of deals and become really good at it. Making money through acquisition, for them, is a key skill to be nourished and developed. But, as repeated studies have demonstrated all too well, many acquisitions—according to some, the vast majority—fail to justify the investment involved.

The success or otherwise of acquisitions is a much studied field, and we can therefore readily identify the principle causes of failure and disappointment.[1] Among them are the payment of excessive prices, missing problems during the due diligence phase, and even the use of faulty financial logic. But perhaps the biggest contributor to the failure of acquisitions is inadequate attention to the process of integrating the newly acquired business.

MAJOR CAUSES OF FAILURE

- Paying too much—especially likely in an auction.
- Targeting the wrong company because the value creation logic is inadequate.
- Power struggles among top management and disagreement about who is to be the boss.
- Cultural obstacles, especially in cross-border deals.
- Incompatibility of IT systems.
- Applying obsolete strategic rationales such as sector diversification, vertical integration, financial synergy, and gap-filling.
- Resistance by regulatory authorities and pressure groups.
- Use of faulty financial logic—i.e. getting the numbers wrong.
- Sloppy due diligence.
- Poorly planned and executed acquisition integration.

Successful integration requires that four tasks be done well. The more attention and skill that is marshaled for this purpose, the better the result is likely to be. The four tasks are: assuming financial control, integrating processes and systems, making key managerial appointments, and ensuring that the value creation logic for the acquisition drives the whole process. Inattention to any of them can cause big trouble.

THE FOUR KEY TASKS OF SUCCESSFUL INTEGRATION

1. Assume Financial Control

Serious acquirers know that it is essential to assume immediate control over financial performance and cash management. In some cases, the target may have been left vulnerable to acquisition by poor financial management. Such businesses will need special attention in this area.

This phase involves steps such as installing corporate financial reporting procedures and clarifying expenditure-level authority. In some cases it may also involve more frequent reporting of critical cash flow components, until the required systems are bedded in and the management team of the acquired business becomes familiar with what is expected of it. For example, weekly sales figures may temporarily require early scrutiny to ensure that commercial performance has not deteriorated owing to the demands of the acquisition experience. This phase lends itself to detailed checklists and procedures, constructed with expert help and developed and honed through corporate experience.

2. Integrate Processes and Systems

If the newly acquired business is to play its part in the larger organization, its principal managerial processes—business planning, budgeting, capital expenditure approval, and human resource management—must be integrated with those of the acquirer, so that the target can begin to function as part of the larger whole as quickly as possible. The sooner operational managers can become familiar and comfortable with the new process requirements, the better able they will be to concentrate their efforts on securing competitive advantage and on realizing the benefits expected from the combination of the two organizations.

A major and sometimes seemingly overwhelming aspect of this phase of integration is that of bringing together IT systems. In recent years the IT structures of large organizations have become more all-embracing and, in the case of so-called enterprise systems, may even constitute the digital backbone of the entire business. In such circumstances the criticality of ensuring that the target's systems are quickly and effectively integrated with those of the acquirer is obvious. But sometimes the process is simply too difficult. A number of mergers and acquisitions in the so-called bancassurance sector have floundered because of IT integration problems. The prime rationale for such mergers is usually that of cross-selling—selling the products of the acquirer to the customers of the acquired company and vice versa. This is a difficult goal to achieve at the best of times, and one that is critically dependent on the effective interfacing of the merging organizations' IT systems. When this does not happen, the merger is bound to be a financial disappointment.

3. Make Key Appointments

The aim here is to do the best possible job in the shortest possible time by putting the right people in charge of the newly acquired business and moving aside those who have not made the cut. Some will say it is not possible for corporate overseers to know which managers are best for the key jobs until they have been observed in action for some time. The existing management team—the same people who perhaps failed

"**With the catching end the pleasures of the chase.**" Abraham Lincoln

to perform well enough to keep their business independent—may thus be left in place.

Typically, the most demanding step in this phase is the decision about who is to run the new business. Who is to be the boss? All possible sources of information about prospective candidates must be pressed into service. Managers who have experienced prior dealings with the candidate should be interviewed, the directors of the acquired business surveyed, and even individual performance reviews scrutinized. Getting this right is perhaps the most important task of all. If the right candidate is appointed, delays and failures in other areas are more likely to be remedied to everyone's satisfaction. But the wrong appointment can result in long-lasting problems and disappointment.

The object must be to find the right trade-off between speed and the effectiveness of the managerial appointment process. This may mean acting with less certainty, as opposed to delaying the decision until everyone is completely satisfied with the selection.

4. Ensure the Primacy of Value Creation

Most of all, acquirers must be crystal clear about the value creation rationale for the acquisition, and they must ensure that this thinking drives the entire acquisition process, including that of integration. All involved in the acquisition—analysts, negotiators, professional advisers, the top management of the acquiring company, and those who will be responsible for integration—must be clear about how the acquisition is to make money for the stockholders of the acquirer, and must be constantly reminded of this throughout the process.

The value creation rationale is first proposed, clarified, agreed, and approved when acquisition criteria are developed and target candidates are identified. The thinking behind how the combination with the prospective target is to enhance competitive advantage and thus generate superior returns must be clear. That rationale should drive the contract-negotiating process and the due diligence work which backs it up, so that the important drivers of value creation continue to be reflected along the way.

Finally, the small number (perhaps only two or three) of initiatives that will create the value must be given the highest priority when it comes to integrating the new business. The sooner these initiatives are successfully completed, the greater the payoff, owing to the greater present value of the cash flows achieved.

OTHER FACTORS THAT CONTRIBUTE TO SUCCESS

Finally, a comment about speed. There is widespread agreement among serial acquirers that moving as quickly as possible is best. It may be tempting to keep the pressure off the acquired organization, at least temporarily, because they have been through a demanding and possibly anxious time. But momentum can be lost, benefits delayed, and the acquired management team even led to believe that the acquirers are less than serious about achieving the projected financial benefit. Speed is best.

One major UK retailer got this one wrong. To its credit, it was quite clear about its value creation rationale for the acquisition, which was that of implementing its proven EPOS (electronic point of sale) systems in the acquired company. It saw from its observation of the company—and confirmed this during the diligence process—that introducing its technology would impart major operational benefit to the target company. Inventories would be reduced, stockouts would decline, and overall customer satisfaction would increase. But it delayed implementation, reasoning that steps to integrate the target into its organization and enabling the new employees to become comfortable in their new surroundings were necessary for good morale. Sensing a lack of commitment to change, the acquired company's supply chain and IT specialists took the initiative to bolster their systems and make it hard for any subsequent changeover—along with the potential for staff reductions in the process. Operational integration was delayed for over a year and the financial benefits suffered accordingly. The corporate development director, who had been the project manager for the acquisition, commented that this was the biggest mistake in the entire process and that it would never happen again.

In larger organizations, and especially those that regard acquisitions as a key source of future growth and competitive advantage, specialists are often developed to perform the tasks of integration. Dedicated teams can reduce the possibility of delays of the kind described above. Smaller companies, and those with less experience, may not have the luxury of maintaining a dedicated staff, but if deals become a way of life, it is probably advisable that a specialized group be formed to capture the company's experience and institutionalize emerging best practice.

CONCLUSION

Integration is a tough and demanding job, but one that frequently spells the difference between success and failure in an acquisition. The task must be treated as one of the highest priority and responsibility apportioned to the people best suited to doing it. If this is done, and if the four tasks enumerated above are handled quickly and effectively, the chances of financial, strategic, and operational success will be that much higher.

MAKING IT HAPPEN

- Design the entire acquisition process to focus on the key drivers of value creation, and ensure that the integration process deals with each as a high priority.
- Prepare a complete plan to action the four key areas—financial control, the introduction of new processes and systems, key appointments, and the pursuit of value creation—as soon as ownership changes hands.
- Develop a cadre of specialists to speed the acquisition process so that operational managers can focus on the business itself.
- Don't delay. Move fast.

MORE INFO

Books:

Galpin, Timothy J., and Mark Herndon. *The Complete Guide to Mergers and Acquisitions: Process Tools to Support M&A Integration at Every Level*. San Francisco, CA: Jossey-Bass, 2007.

Sadtler, David, David Smith, and Andrew Campbell. *Smarter Acquisitions: Ten Steps to Successful Deals*. Harlow, UK: Pearson Education, 2008.

NOTE

1 The major causes of acquisition failure are dealt with at some length in Sadtler *et al.* (2008).

  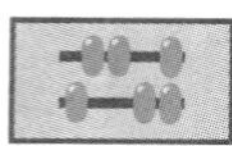      

Capital Structure: A Strategy that Makes Sense by John C. Groth

EXECUTIVE SUMMARY

- Perfect capital markets prescribe an optimal capital structure.
- Imperfect capital markets, the seasonal and cyclical aspects of an economy, and the variability of market conditions argue that a company should have a target capital structure and an operating capital structure range.
- Managers should be sensitive to changes in the business risk of a company, as these alter the optimal capital structure.
- Maintaining good debt capacity makes sense and may favorably influence stock price.
- Using bad debt capacity does not make sense from the viewpoint of stockholders and primary creditors.
- Projects with good economic returns restore debt capacity and reduce the debt/equity (D/E) ratio. Bad projects that do not have attractive economic returns will have an adverse effect on capital structure, increase the D/E ratio, and eventually decrease the optimal D/E ratio.
- Managers may adjust capital structure quickly or gradually. Whether quickly or gradually hinges on a variety of factors.
- Capital structure is important for privately held firms.
- Stock repurchase programs call for sensitivity and possible adjustment of debt capital so that one attains and/or preserves the desired capital structure.
- Leveraged buyouts often distort capital structure. The decision to accept abnormal capital structures originates with those promoting the buyout and their perceptions about gains relative to personal capital at risk.
- Issues related to control may influence the choice of capital structure.

INTRODUCTION

Perfect capital markets enjoy an array of assumptions, including no cost to bankruptcy, infinitely divisible financial assets and liabilities, no transaction costs, etc. Pursuing a selected optimal capital structure would allow minute adjustments, the issuance or redemption of small amounts of capital, and other conveniences. We would simply strive for the optimal debt/equity ratio depicted in Figure 1. Indeed, in this unreal world one would keep all the equity for control and to maximize wealth—and employ massive amounts of debt.[1]

Imperfect Capital Markets

The rudeness of imperfect markets prompts us to adopt a reasonable strategy that allows one to benefit from the tenets of capital structure theory while respecting the reality of markets and economies. Imperfect capital markets, bankruptcy costs, and that a company with financial flexibility may have attractive opportunities during periods of adverse market conditions argue for a strategy for the management of capital structure. Additionally, capital market participants may value a company with the financial flexibility that would allow it to pursue opportunities even (or especially) during periods of high market stress. A company with financial flexibility may find bargains during periods of distress.

In this article we first address background issues. Then we will move to recommendations. We will see that the suggested strategy does not seek to have the theoretical optimal debt/equity (D/E) ratio.

Good and Bad Debt Capacity

A company that has a less than optimal D/E ratio has unused good capacity. Normally a company with "good" debt capacity can borrow quickly on favorable terms to pursue an attractive opportunity. Thus, it can obtain capital quickly without the delays or possible undesirability of an equity offering.

Exceeding the optimal D/E ratio results in the company using "bad" debt capacity. History tells us that it is possible to do stupid things. Occasionally, we also see agents taking actions that promote their own interests, rather than acting in a way that benefits owners and creditors. Bad debt capacity adversely affects the weighted cost of capital, limits flexibility, and decreases stock price.

ISSUES AND STRATEGY

Interrelationships

The *expected* streams of cash flows that originate in the business or operating side of a company service the sources of capital, including short-term liabilities such as accounts payable. Choices on the asset side of the company, and how successfully the company operates assets and interacts with the markets for goods and services, precipitate effects on the financing side of the company.

Although EBITDDA (earnings before interest, taxes, depreciation, depletion, and amortization) is not necessarily a cash flow in a period of time, for reasons explained in my article "Accounting and Economics—Critical Perspectives" (see qfinance.com), let us for simplicity assume that it *is* a cash flow. Those who have provided financing for the company have a keen interest in the level of expected cash flows, and the timing and the uncertainty of those cash flows. Hence, what the company chooses to do (its investments) and how well it employs those assets to generate cash flows (production, sales, collections, etc.) influence the business risk of the company.

The business risk, and factors such as tax rules and rates, influence the optimal financing for the company and, in turn, the financial risk of the company. Let us share some summary comments.

MANAGING AND ADJUSTING CAPITAL STRUCTURE

The company might select a gradual, a lumpy, or a quick process for adjusting capital structure. For discussion, we will assume that the company has the ratio D/E = C in Figure 1, a level which is less than the optimal D/E = O. Its WCOC is higher than it need be, and the value of the company and equity are lower than they could be.

We will examine different ways of altering the D/E ratio. Our discussion will explain ways to either increase or decrease the D/E ratio to show how different variables influence the ratio. Later we will suggest how this sample company might move towards the optimal point. Shortly we will explain why normally we probably *don't* want to move to the optimal point.

Possible Gradual Process Steps

To move the D/E ratio to the left (which is not our objective for the company in Figure 1), do one or more of the following:

- If a dividend-paying company, have a payout ratio of less than 100%. To adjust the payout ratio, one can increase dividends at a slower rate than the growth in earnings.
- Pay off some of the principal of the debt using cash flow from operations and/or from the sale of assets.
- Do both.

"Whenever I think about the budgetary problems, I think about the problems of Errol Flynn... reconciling net income with gross habits." Malcolm Rifkind

  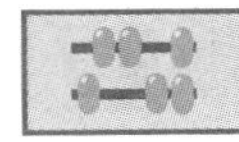      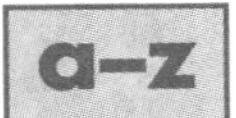

Figure 1. Adjusting capital structure

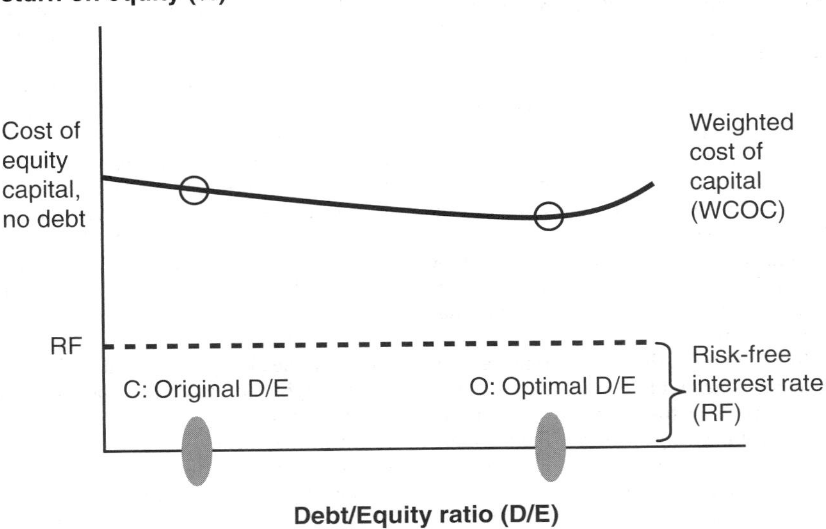

To move the D/E to the right, towards the optimal ratio:

- Increase the payout ratio.
- Delay, if without penalty and with explanation to the market, the retirement of principal on debt.[2]

The Lumpy Approach

The borrowing of chunks of money for corporate use, such as capital projects, will result in a jump to the right in the D/E ratio. Employed wisely in projects that have good economic results, the freshly raised capital generates fresh additions to equity. The D/E gradually moves back to the left.

The Quick Process

Adjusting capital structure quickly is relatively easy if the company has less than the optimal amount of debt and wants to increase its D/E ratio. The tactic calls for arrangement for, and announcement of, the borrowing of the appropriate amount of money for the purpose of using the proceeds to repurchase some of its stock *to adjust the capital structure to an optimal level.* Explaining the purpose for the borrowing gives notice to all stockholders and offers a positive reason for stock repurchase, thus avoiding arguments of possible negative signaling associated with stock repurchase.

To increase the D/E ratio quickly, one might borrow a chunk of capital (again with explanation to the market) and declare a special cash dividend. This approach requires careful consideration of tax preferences of the stockholders in tax environments where dividends are taxed at a high rate.

As part of an acquisition strategy—though not as a reason for acquisition—the company might acquire another company that has too much debt. The combined companies could have a capital structure closer to the optimum. This is shown as follows. If the acquiring company has a less than optimal D/E ratio, its stock price will be depressed. If the acquired company has a D/E ratio greater than the optimal, its stock price will also be depressed. A combination of two companies with the "correct" proportions will result in an increase in value traceable to the movement towards a more optimal capital structure.

This improvement in stock value could be realized *without the acquisition* by just adjusting the capital structure of both companies. We mention this only because capital structure considerations and adjustments are sometimes important in acquisitions.

If a company has more than the optimal amount of debt, adjusting capital structure may not be as easy, or at least not as advisable, under certain market conditions. Even if capital markets are in turmoil, some theorists will argue for the following approach: announce the issuance of common stock, with the proceeds dedicated to retiring some debt. The market's knowledge of this act of moving towards the optimal debt ratio should favorably affect the price of the stock.

Practitioners might suggest that such a change could have adverse effects if the company is under duress or when markets are in tumult. Some would argue that the funds realized from the equity offering make this a poor strategy. Instead, the company should ride out the bad times or bad markets and make adjustments to its capital structure at a later date.

ISSUES CONCERNING CONTROL

A company may alter its capital structure for reasons of control. Equity holders—except for certain classes of stock found in some markets—have voting rights. Assume that some current equity holders value control. We will term these the "control group." The nature and manner of altering the capital structure may influence control in one or more ways:

- The company repurchases some of its stock. Repurchased shares, or "treasury stock," do not confer voting rights. Those in the control group do not sell any stock. The control group now has a larger percentage of ownership. The D/E moves to the right.
- The company issues new stock with a rights offering. The D/E moves to the left. Members of the control group exercise their rights and buy the shares. If not all other stockholders exercise their rights, one or both of the following may occur:
  - Some do not exercise rights at all: the control group's proportion of ownership increases.
  - Some sell rights to others, who exercise the rights and buy stock, leading to dispersion of stockholder ownership. Dispersion of ownership may increase the effective control of the control group, even with the exercise of all rights.[3]

OTHER ISSUES

Risk Preferences and the Choice of D/E Ratio

Recall a fundamental principle of the valuation of risky assets. *Markets* value assets, not management or the board of directors. The implications of this fundamental principle are straightforward—and important. *Do what the markets like.* The risk preferences of market participants, rather than the personal preferences of management, should guide decisions and influence the choice of capital structure. Select a target capital structure based on market inputs.

Capital Structure and Privately or Closely Held Organizations

Decisions and strategies for privately/closely held taxable companies rest on the same principles. However, the tax scenario for the corporation as well as its tax position with respect to the other taxable entities owned by the same people—and the resultant consolidated tax position—may suggest different strategies.

For example, owners with deep pockets who are willing and ready to provide infusions of equity in bad times may argue for a more aggressive D/E ratio for the company in the hope of garnering greater tax benefits. Additionally, different risk preferences influence choice. If one "owns the store" and *currently* has no concern about market valuation, the choice of capital structure will anchor to personal tax circumstance and risk preferences. The issues are complex and very sensitive to the particular consolidated tax position, as well as to personal risk preferences and attitudes towards debt.

Agency Costs

Investors should guard against a form of management agency costs, namely, the use of bad debt capacity to further management's objectives and interests at the expense of stockholders, and possibly creditors. For example, management may employ excessive debt to protect against takeover, and thus preserve its position. In another example, a management might use excess debt rather than raise equity, because raising equity would dilute its equity position, including the proportion of votes it controls—which is important in preserving board/management control. This dilution could occur for one or both of the following reasons: managers own the stock but are not willing to purchase the correct proportions of the new equity; ownership of stock is dispersed in a way such that newly issued shares are held by those who are less supportive of management.

A RECOMMENDATION FOR CAPITAL STRUCTURE STRATEGY

Transaction costs associated with the issuance of securities, changes in economic and market conditions, the "lumpiness" of capital investments, and the arrival of misfortune despite the best planning, the potential for unexpected opportunities, as well as other factors prompt us to suggest a particular strategy for capital structure.

Strategy

Pursue a capital structure that garners a substantial portion of the benefits of an optimal capital structure. Preserve flexibility for the company. Explain the strategy to the markets. Hope—and we think it will—that markets value the strategy.

In my article "Capital Structure: Perspectives," Table 1 depicts the behavior of the weighted cost of capital as one alters the D/E ratio. A substantial proportion of the decline in the WCOC occurs with the first increments of debt. The decline in the WCOC becomes less with increasing increments of debt as one moves towards the optimal D/E. Figure 2 depicts this relationship. Note the portion of the curve marked as "Shallow portion" and on the vertical axis the indication of the WCOC for the two marked points.

Suppose the company operates with a D/E ratio in the shallow range. The "Possible price of flexibility" in Figure 2—the maximum possible difference in WCOC over this range—represents the maximum costs of operating in this range rather than at the optimal D/E.

In Figure 2, let the asterisk represent the company's current D/E ratio, and recall that with this ratio the company has unused good debt capacity. Consider the flexibility offered by the shallow range, illustrated by the following example.

Markets are in turmoil. The company recognizes an opportunity. The good debt capacity allows it to borrow money quickly to pursue the opportunity. The borrowing moves the asterisk to the right by a chunk, but not past the optimal D/E ratio. The good economic results of the project generate equity and move the D/E back to the left, restoring the good debt capacity. This occurs because good projects increase the value of equity (and we measure D/E in market values), and such projects generate returns to equity. As the company generates cash flow, it may also pay off principal on the debt, accelerating the movement of the D/E to the left.

The Value of Flexibility

Investors may value flexibility. We suspect that both equity and debt holders do place value on flexibility, especially in the recent years of turmoil in capital markets. To the extent that investors value flexibility, the company may not actually pay the price in terms of WCOC. In fact, the company and its investors may benefit. Figure 3 depicts possible relationships, showing the optimal D/E in terms of theory, and the optimum that exists if investors value flexibility.

In these figures I have plotted stock price versus D/E.[4] Figure 3 shows the stock price maximized for the optimal D/E ratio according to theory. If investors do indeed value the flexibility we describe, the stock price might be higher if the company pursued a capital structure that moved about in the shallow portion of the curve, resulting in the "Optimal practice" in Figure 3. This scheme results in a stock price that is maximized with less than the "Optimal theory" D/E ratio. The heavy dotted curve for stock price intentionally has a slightly higher maximum stock price—a speculation on our part. We caution that many theorists would not agree with this conclusion. On the other hand, a number of practitioners as well as investors might find the assertion reasonable.

CONCLUSION, IDEAS, AND ACTIONS

Theory is important. Common sense is powerful. Strategy benefits from theory and common sense. The time horizon for strategy depends on a variety of factors,

Figure 2. Capital structure versus WCOC

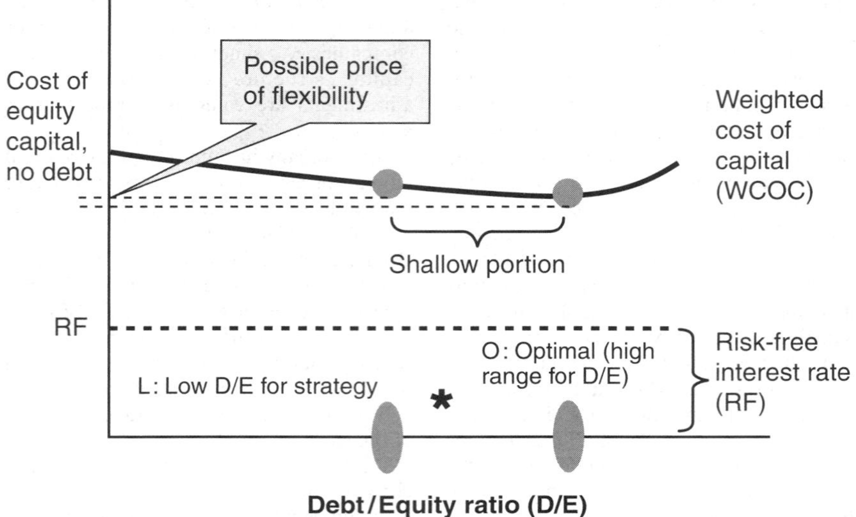

"Markets operate under uncertainty. It is therefore crucial to market performance that participants manage their risks properly... the answer, as it always has been... less debt, more equity, and hence a larger buffer against adversity."
Alan Greenspan

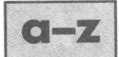

Figure 3. Flexible capital structure and value

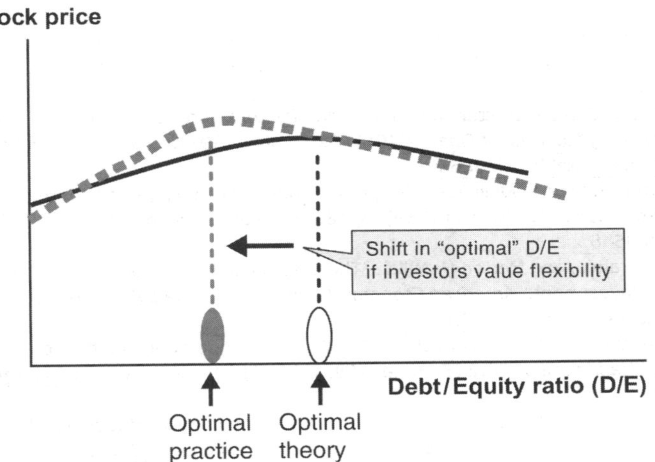

including the dynamics of the social, political, economic, and technology environments. Tactics should be consistent with short-term success and long-term opportunities.

Here are some suggestions that might fare well in dynamic environments and prepare you to survive on a favorable basis in periods of high economic uncertainty and market turmoil.

- Estimate your current optimal capital structure.
- Many (all) economies enjoy/suffer the effects of cycles. When times are good, and as the tide moves to flood, pay down some debt. Move to the left on the shallow portion of the capital structure curve, rather than remain in the region of theoretical optimal debt. Increasing good unused debt capacity not only helps in survival, but also may allow for harvesting opportunities when the falling tides have carried others to peril.
- Operate in the shallow part of the WCOC curve. Leave a reasonable chunk of unused debt capacity, enough to allow rapid financing of unusual opportunities.
- Compare the current D/E to the target D/E and the shallow curve range for the D/E. If it lies within the shallow curve range, you don't need major adjustments now. Continue to track and anticipate how the company will "walk about" in the shallow curve range.
- If the company is outside the shallow curve range, decide on the strategy to move to the target range. The choice of how to move to a more optimal debt/equity ratio hinges on a number of factors, including the expected internally generated cash flows, the expected internal generation of equity, the principal repayment/refunding schedule, cash flow relative to capital investments, dividend policies, and external market conditions.
- Compare the business risk of actions you anticipate taking with your current business. Recognize and react to a change in the business risk of the company. If the business risk of the company increases/decreases as a result of good investment choices that are of higher risk, adjust financial risk by decreasing/increasing the target debt/equity ratio.
- If you currently have significant unused good debt capacity, recognize that this good debt capacity is of potential interest to a company seeking acquisitions. The buying company can use your unused good capacity as a way of financing the acquisition, or to move the combined company capital structure to a more favorable range.
- Changing from the use of bad debt capacity might involve one or several different actions, including the acquisition of a company that has unused good capacity. Do not buy a company for this reason alone! However, recognize this potential effect in acquisition strategies.
- Evaluate whether control issues are important or even dominant; control is often a concern for private or closely held companies. We assert that, for public companies, efforts by management to protect management's position and issues of control should rarely if ever determine the correct course of action.
- Decide on a strategy for capital structure that is consistent with the corporate strategy.
- Communicate your capital structure target and strategy to markets. Separately from the choice of D/E and the strategy, effective communication reduces the uncertainty in investors' minds. Here is a sample statement:
  - "Given our intended investments, likely market conditions, and the tax environment, our target D/E is about 25%. To allow us to take advantage of favorable opportunities during different phases of economic cycles, we will typically maintain a working D/E capital structure. in the 15% to 25% range."
  - "This strategy allows us to employ good debt capacity to obtain funds quickly to pursue attractive opportunities, regardless of economic conditions and capital market circumstances"
  - "We feel that investors value a flexible financing policy that allows their company to maintain choice of action and to avoid ever being forced to take particular actions."
- Behave consistently with your strategy. Demonstrated behavior builds and sustains credibility. Increased credibility reduces investor uncertainty and enhances stock prices.
- Remember that an increase/decrease in the corporate tax rate increases/decreases the value of using debt. Changes in tax rates should prompt a review and adjustment of capital structure.

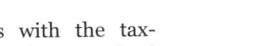

SUMMARY

The prudent use of debt in financing *if interest is tax-deductible* offers the prospect of increasing firm value.

Issues of control also influence the use of debt versus equity.[5] For publicly owned companies, managers might, inappropriately, use too much debt as a means of perpetuating management's control or to promote management's interests. Making D/E choices to perpetuate control is defensible (although perhaps not wise) to maintain control of private and/or family-owned firms.

Perfect capital markets with the tax-deductibility of interest argue for an optimal debt/equity ratio. The presence of imperfect capital markets, seasonal and cyclical business cycles, a change in the nature and risks of investments, and human behavior suggest a strategy for the management of capital structure.

Finance the company in the shallow segment of the weighted cost of capital

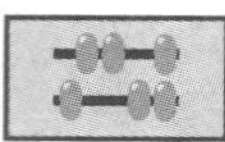

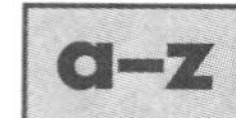

curve. Leave some unused good debt capacity to allow the company to pursue opportunities even if capital market conditions are unfavorable, or to use as an emergency reserve. The emergency reserve concept rests on the common sense perspective that a company should never be forced into a course of action—but should be able to *choose* to follow a course of action.

Operate with a debt/equity ratio that is lower than the optimal ratio. This posture provides flexibility, allows practical management in raising capital, and keeps the company away from the steeply increasing WCOC that occurs above the optimal D/E. This position of creditworthiness allows one to raise a chunk of capital from debt to fund an opportunity independent of the conditions in capital markets.

Investing the raised capital in good investments will generate cash flow and increase the equity base, with a resultant decrease in the D/E ratio, moving it back to the left. Good projects that are managed well restore good debt capacity and will allow one to repeat the process in future periods.

In summary: capital structure makes a difference in an environment in which interest is tax-deductible.

MORE INFO

Articles:

Groth, John C., and Ronald C. Anderson. "Capital structure: Perspectives for managers." *Management Decision* 35:7 (1997): 552–561. Online at: dx.doi.org/10.1108/00251749710170529

Israel, Ronan. "Capital structure and the market for corporate control: The defensive role of debt financing." *Journal of Finance* 46:4 (September 1991): 1391–1409. Online at: www.jstor.org/stable/2328863

Miller, Merton H. "The Modigliani–Miller propositions after thirty years." *Journal of Applied Corporate Finance* 2:1 (Spring 1989): 6–18. Online at: dx.doi.org/10.1111/j.1745-6622.1989.tb00548.x

Modigliani, Franco, and Merton H. Miller. "The cost of capital, corporation finance, and the theory of investment." *American Economic Review* 48:3 (June 1958): 261–297. Online at: www.jstor.org/stable/1809766

Prezas, Alexandros P. "Effects of debt on the degrees of operating and financial leverage." *Financial Management* 16:2 (Summer 1987): 39–44. Online at: www.jstor.org/stable/3666002

Prezas, Alexandros P. "Interactions of the firm's real and financial decisions." *Applied Economics* 20:4 (April 1988): 551–560. Online at: dx.doi.org/10.1080/00036848800000064

See Also:

★ Capital Structure: Implications (pp. 715–718)
★ Capital Structure: Perspectives (pp. 24–27)
★ Corporate Finance for SMEs (pp. 33–35)
★ Optimizing the Capital Structure: Finding the Right Balance between Debt and Equity (pp. 543–545)
✔ Investors and the Capital Structure (p. 1120)
✔ Understanding Capital Structure Theory: Modigliani and Miller (p. 997)
Franco Modigliani (p. 1296)
Merton Miller (p. 1294)

NOTES

1 Since in perfect capital markets one has no costs and bankruptcy has no undesirable consequences.

2 We want the market to understand that the delay in repayment of principal is part of altering the capital structure—to avoid any perception that the company is unable to make the payments of principal. This delay approach is only to avoid debt issuance costs for fresh debt.

3 Depending on circumstances, the structuring of the rights offering can almost certainly ensure that some shareholders not in the control group do not exercise their rights.

4 In many presentations and discussions the plot/discussion is total firm value versus D/E.

5 Managers and boards of directors that make capital structure decisions to protect their position or influence their rewards generate agency costs borne by stockholders and, in some circumstances, also by creditors.

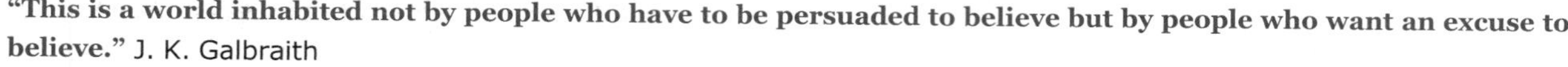
"This is a world inhabited not by people who have to be persuaded to believe but by people who want an excuse to believe." J. K. Galbraith

Capital Structure: Implications by John C. Groth

EXECUTIVE SUMMARY

- Reducing the weighted cost of capital increases the net economic returns, and adds to company value.
- Place the company in a position that it can choose what it wants to do, rather than have circumstances force it to take a course of action.
- The use of too little debt (L) results in a lower stock price, and too much debt (M) also lowers the stock price.
- The more uncertain an environment, the greater the importance of the choice of and the strategy for managing capital structure.
- If a company's business risk is very sensitive to economic cycles, a company should manage its debt/equity (D/E) ratio across the cycle.
- Knowledge of capital structure theory and practice is important in stock repurchase programs, mergers and acquisitions, divestitures, leveraged buyouts, and strategies aimed at defeating takeover.

INTRODUCTION

A tax environment that allows for the deduction of interest charges, but not the deduction of dividends, results in an optimal capital structure for a company. The optimal structure results in a lower weighted cost of capital (WCOC) for reasons examined in the article, "Capital Structure: Perspectives." This article examines the implications of capital structure, and some of the key factors that influence capital structure.

KEY IMPLICATION: WCOC AND VALUE

Recognizing the behavior of the WCOC when there are changes in the D/E ratio, we now review how the correct capital structure ultimately adds benefits in terms of economic margins and resultant value.

Figure 1 illustrates the origin of value, and the significance of lowering the WCOC that results from selecting the optimal D/E ratio for a company. Recall that value arises from earning a net economic return that exceeds the cost of capital. For example, the net present value of a project represents the dollar value of having earned economic returns in excess of the cost of capital while the capital is in a project.

In Figure 1, with no debt the economic returns are labeled NER @ D/E = 0. Moving down the WCOC curve in the diagram increases the net economic returns, with attendant increases in value. The WCOC is for projects that do not alter the business risk of the firm.

Figure 2 graphically illustrates the impact of capital structure on stock price, keeping in mind that as we go from no debt to an increasing D/E we are reducing the number of shares. The use of too little debt (L) results in a lower stock price, and too much debt (M) also lowers the stock price.

Moving from L to the optimal level is quite easy. Borrow money and buy back some shares. Moving from M back to the optimal level is, in theory, equally easy, but in practice may face challenges depending on market conditions. Capital structure strategy is discussed in the article, "Capital Structure: A Strategy that Makes Sense."

Figure 1. WCOC and net economic returns as D/E ratio varies

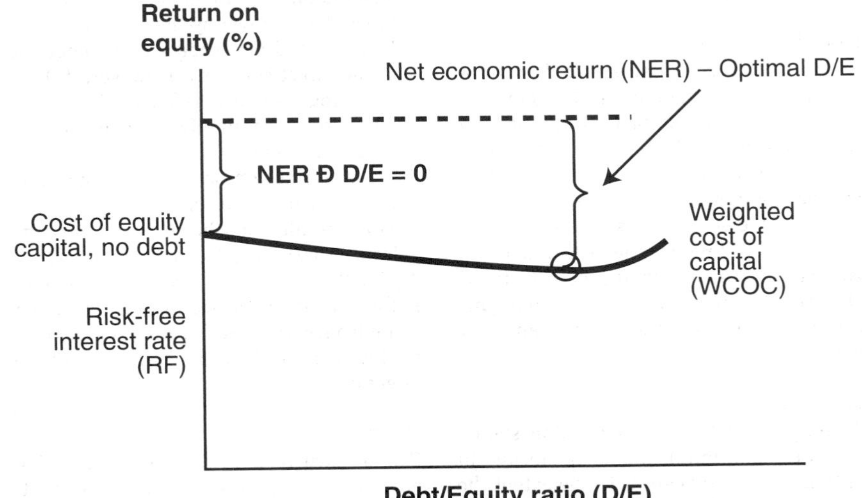

The Core Implication

Reducing the weighted cost of capital increases the net economic returns, and adds to company value. Remember that the relationship between WCOC and value is non-linear, making the choice and management of D/E particularly important.[1]

OTHER IMPLICATIONS

Capital structure has numerous additional implications, including the following.

Business Risk Change and Capital Structure

- Recall that business risk is the risk associated with the asset side and operations of the company. The greater the business risk of the company, the higher the cost of equity, and the lower the optimal debt/equity ratio. Changes in business risk stem from one or more of the following:
- Changes in market conditions: For example, an increase in competition, trends in consumer preferences, greater uncertainty about the costs of inputs, political risk, and other forces over which a company normally has no or little control;
- Changes in how things are done: for example, management of the operating cycle, decisions on working capital, cost control, efficiency of operations, effectiveness of product design, marketing.
- Changes in what is done: for example, the markets pursued, and the investments made to support those choices.

Investments and Optimal Structure

The interrelationships between capital structure, assets, and a dynamic environment have implications in terms of risk, value, choice, strategy, and actions. For example, if a company changes the nature or structure of its assets by investing in projects of greater risk than its current risk, and/or if external changes and trends in markets alter the business risk of the company, then the optimal capital structure changes.[2]

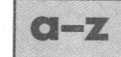

Figure 2. Capital structure and stock price

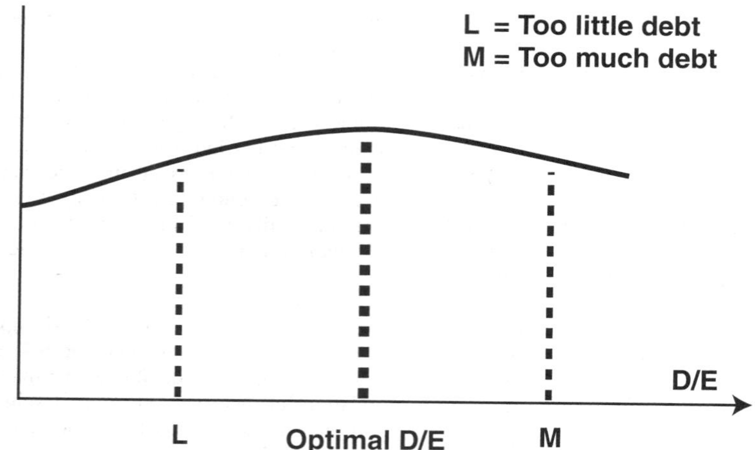

Effects of Financial Risk on Business Risk

In imperfect markets, excess financial risk resulting from the financing of the firm may affect the business risk of the company.[3] This crossover or feedback effect alters the risk on the operating side of the company. Developments in the economy, and the automotive industry in the fall of 2008 are an examples. A company offers a 100,000-mile warranty on its cars, but customers feel that high financial risk might result in the company going bankrupt. Hence, the high perceived financial risk of the company by customers affects purchase decisions, and the perceived value of the warranty in their purchase decision. In reality, the asset side and finance side of a company are not independent.

Cyclical Business

The choice of capital structure has an impact on alternatives, decisions, and strategy—especially across economic cycles. In a cyclical business, the patterns and magnitudes of expected cash generation from the business, or "asset side," of the company are subject to the influence of the economy, an influence over which a company has no control. In this scenario, the business risk of the company changes as it lives through the ebbs and flows in the economy.

The sensitivity of companies to a cyclical economy varies. A company may adjust its asset structure and operations in anticipation of, or in response to swings in the economy. However, other than adding liquidity in anticipation of a deteriorating economy, major changes in other assets are often costly, or not practical. [4]Some companies may also try to insulate the adverse effects of the cycle on the business risk of company with other strategies, such as in-house finance companies to support credit sales.[5]

A change in the business risk (BR) alters the optimal capital structure of the company. An increase (decrease) in BR decreases (increases) the optimal D/E. A significant sensitivity to the business cycle has important implications.[6] A company will survive (or perish), or have opportunities (or miss opportunities), according to its strategy and financial position at a point in time.

Place the company in a position that it can choose what it wants to do–rather than have circumstances force it to take a course of action.[7]

The implication is that a company that generates cash flow in a cyclical pattern should reduce its debt during periods of high cash generation, moving its D/E to the lower D/E limit of the target capital structure, consistent with the discussion in the article, "Capital Structure: A Strategy that Makes Sense."

Stock Repurchase

Knowledge of capital structure theory and practice is important in stock repurchase programs. If the company does not issue new common stock—for example, issuing stock for an acquisition, or as a result of the exercise of options—the repurchase of a company's own stock is a reduction in equity that will reduce the D/E ratio of the company. To maintain the desired target D/E ratio, a repurchase of stock will require a corresponding reduction in the company's debt.

Acquisitions

A company making an acquisition should consider the implications in terms of optimal capital structure. To the extent the business risk of the target and acquiring companies differ, the optimal D/E ratios for the target and acquiring companies differ. One may adjust to the desired post-acquisition target D/E, coincident with the acquisition and attendant financing arrangements. Additional issues are important, including the following.

Independent of any operational or "synergistic effects" that may result from a merger, a pure financial merger benefit may exist. Lewellen (1971) offered astute arguments addressing this issue. Essentially, one can demonstrate that the mere combination of firms may offer financial benefit. The combined cash flows of the two companies may result in lower risks to creditors, with this reduction stemming from a co-insurance effect.

Capital structure opportunities may also exist if the target company does not have an optimal capital structure. These particular benefits differ from the pure financial rationale, and their realization is not dependent on the acquisition. If the current management of the target company has ignored the prescriptions of capital structure theory, the acquiring company may benefit by adjusting the capital structure concurrently with the acquisition. In a merger, "good" or "bad" debt capacity in the target or acquiring firms has practical implications.[8] Returning to Figure 2, we can consider two scenarios:

- Assume the target company has too little debt, shown by the D/E of L. The target company has unused good-debt capacity, and also a share price that is lower than the optimal level. The acquiring company can use this unused good-debt capacity to help finance the acquisition, and, at the same time, realize the increment in share price represented by the change from the D/E of L to the optimal D/E.
- Assume the target company has too much debt, shown by the D/E of M. Unused good-debt capacity does not exist in the target company. However, if the acquiring company "refinances" the acquisition and, in effect, moves the acquired company to the optimal D/E, the acquiring company realizes the value represented by the share-price gain that would result from the company moving from M D/E back to the optimal D/E.

Again, the gains for these scenarios have nothing to do with acquisition itself, but result from correcting the mistakes made by management in the capital structure of the target company.

Divestments

Capital structure in the divesting of a portion of the company is important. Separate from the appropriateness of the

  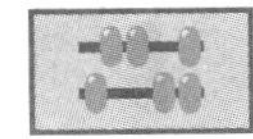      

divestment, casting off the new company with the optimal D/E ratio will maximize the value realized.

Tax Issues

Assuming interest is tax-deductible, uncertainty about future tax rates and other changes in taxes do influence capital structure decisions. If one knew the effective dates of new tax rates, or thought tax rates would increase (decrease) in the future, one would consider altering the target D/E ratio. Recall that the higher the tax rate, the lower the after-tax cost of debt—if the company has sufficient pretax income to allow the interest deduction.

Implications for capital structure would exist if dividends also became deductible. If the tax-rate effect was the same for dividends or interest deductions, under some circumstances an optimal D/E would no longer exist, as debt offers no advantage over equity. If interest and dividend payments were both deductible, but the tax rate applicable to these deductions varied, an optimal D/E would remain.[9]

In many tax environments, a company may carry back or forward certain tax variables, and realize tax effects in previous or future periods. This results in timing the realization of tax benefits, and thus affects the present value of the tax treatment. In addition, tax issues can be very important in an acquisition, especially if certain tax options will expire at a point in time. In some tax environments and circumstances, an acquisition with attendant changes in capital structure might allow realization of a tax benefit, or at least preserve it for a future period.

Other Implications

Strategies aimed at defeating a potential takeover have, some assert, included exceeding the optimal amount of debt to make the company an unattractive target. Following this practice is inappropriate, and generally not aligned with shareholder interests. However, the observation reflects that a management might understand and employ capital structure theory to promote management's rather than shareholder interests.

In a leveraged buyout (LBO), equity participants often intentionally ignore the guidelines of capital structure in an attempt to maximize personal wealth. For example, in an LBO those with an equity position attempt to maximize personal return on equity. Consequently, over the shorter term, they allow the company to greatly exceed the optimal D/E ratio, as they seek to maximize the future value of equity interest, rather than a current share price. With this approach, the plan is that, over time, the company can pay down debt, and attain an optimal D/E ratio. Then those with the equity interest take the company public with a stock issue, and the pricing of the equity issue reflects the now-optimal D/E ratio.

CONCLUSION

The fact that interest is tax-deductible in many economies is an argument for the use of some debt in financing a company. The right combination of debt and equity results in a capital structure that reduces the weighted cost of capital. The lower weighted cost of capital results in a higher net economic margin—the difference between the economic return on a project and the weighted cost of capital.

The expected benefit of the tax deduction flows to shareholders, who bear the added financial risk associated with the debt. As long as shareholders view the expected value of the tax benefits as attractive compared to the added financial risk, then they welcome the use of debt.

A dynamic environment complicates decisions. Understanding core issues allows one to make/manage prudent actions in a dynamic environment. In particular, we should recognize that although a company should have a target capital structure, its management must remain sensitive to internal changes as well as changes in the markets and economies, and pursue a strategy that "makes sense." For example, if a company alters its business risk, it should adjust its debt/equity ratio. Similarly, if management perceives greater/less risk in the external environment, it should decrease/increase the debt/equity ratio.

In the end, we see the need for a keen awareness of circumstance and future possibility, coupled with an understanding of fundamental concepts better equip us to make judgments—and then take actions that add value.

MAKING IT HAPPEN

The implications of capital structure theory are many. We have shared some of the most important. In summary:

- Recognize that changes in what you do, and how you do it (markets pursued, capital investments) influence the capital structure decision, and the management of capital structure.
- Changing the business risk of a company changes its optimal capital structure.
- Changing the capital structure of a company will change its risk, and its value.
- Reducing unnecessary business risk (see "Risk: Perspectives and Common Sense Rules for Survival") allows one to derive greater benefits from capital structure since one will enjoy a higher optimal debt/equity ratio.
- The interrelationships between capital structure, assets, and a dynamic environment have implications in terms of risk, value, choice, strategy, and actions.
- The nature of liabilities in terms of maturity, variable versus fixed interest rate, principal repayment schedules, restrictive covenant of debt, etc., influence the optimal capital structure.
- Reduce uncertainty in investors' minds by adopting and disclosing an optimal target D/E ratio. Provide a simple explanation of the logic for the company's target D/E ratio, and the strategy the company will follow. The article, "Capital Structure: A Strategy That Makes Sense," focuses on issues in capital structure, and strategy.
- If a company's business risk is very sensitive to economic cycles, a company should manage and adjust its D/E across the cycle. Reducing the D/E ratio during periods of robust economic activity and high cash generation restores debt capacity to sustain and support the pursuit of opportunities during downturns in the economy.

MORE INFO

Articles:

Israel, Ronan. "Capital structure and the market for corporate control: The defensive role of debt financing." *Journal of Finance* 46:4 (September 1991): 1391–1409. Online at: www.jstor.org/stable/2328863

Lewellen, Wilbur G. "A pure financial rationale for the conglomerate merger." *Journal of Finance* 26:2 (May 1971): 521–537. Online at: www.jstor.org/stable/2326063

Prezas, Alexandros P. "Effects of debt on the degrees of operating and financial leverage." *Financial Management* 16:2 (Summer 1987): 39–44. Online at: www.jstor.org/stable/3666002

"Wealth consists not in having great possessions, but in having few wants." Epicurus, 341–270 BC, ancient Greek philosopher

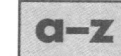

Prezas, Alexandros P. "Interactions of the firm's real and financial decisions." *Applied Economics* 20:4 (April 1988): 551–560. Online at: dx.doi.org/10.1080/00036848800000064

Website:

Basic Modigliani–Miller theorem: en.wikipedia.org/wiki/Modigliani-Miller_theorem

See Also:

★ Capital Structure: A Strategy that Makes Sense (pp. 710–714)
★ Capital Structure: Perspectives (pp. 24–27)
★ Issuing Corporate Debt (pp. 522–524)
★ Optimizing the Capital Structure: Finding the Right Balance between Debt and Equity (pp. 543–545)
✔ Investors and the Capital Structure (p. 1120)
✔ Structuring M&A Deals and Tax Planning (p. 1135)
✔ Understanding Capital Structure Theory: Modigliani and Miller (p. 997)
✔ Understanding the Weighted Average Cost of Capital (WACC) (p. 1002)

NOTES

1 As addressed in the article, "Risk—Perspectives and Common Sense Rules for Survival."
2 If investing in projects with a risk different from the company's normal investment, one must be careful to adjust the cost of capital used in project evaluation.
3 For example, perfect capital markets assume no cost to bankruptcy—clearly not the case for shareholders, creditors, customers, the economy, and society.
4 A company might also seek to mitigate or hedge certain risks that influence the asset side of the company.
5 Some companies sales and operations are quite sensitive to interest rates, and the availability of credit to their customers. Some suggest one strategy (we do not): have an in-house finance company to finance sales to customers; engage in actions to offset the interest-rate risk in the finance company; and then attempt to reduce the impact on sales of economic and consumer credit conditions by offering customers cut-rate financing. Remember that an in-house finance company does not make the risk go away, but rather parks the risk in a different place. This doesn't sound like a good idea. For example, if in the business of making and selling appliances, focusing on making and selling appliances sounds like the correct strategy. If one wants to be in consumer credit or speculate on interest rates, then do that elsewhere.
6 Theorists might argue that capital markets anticipate potential changes in the economy, and recognize that some companies are more sensitive to economy-wide swings than are other companies. Consequently, some argue these "variances in business risk" across time are recognized, and already captured in the market-derived estimates of an optimal D/E and attendant WCOC.
7 See the article, "Risk—Perspectives and Common Sense Rules for Survival."
8 A discussion of good and bad capacity appears in the article, "Capital Structure: A Strategy that Makes Sense."
9 The issues and arguments concerning these issues are beyond the scope of this article. For example, whether a company would or would not pay a cash dividend would influence the decisions. Issues to do with control might also be an argument for debt rather than equity. For example, if a company issues equity, those with control dilute their ownership unless they invest at least proportionately in the new equity issue.

"I just made a smart deal for myself. This is America. This isn't the Soviet Union. It's the supply-and-demand of the marketplace." Michael Ovitz

Viewpoint: The CFO and the Sustainable Corporation

by Ravi Nedungadi

INTRODUCTION

Ravi Nedungadi, President and group CFO of United Breweries Group, has steered the India-based brewing and aviation group through a number of major acquisitions. He is proud to have resisted the hard-sell tactics from investment bankers to get into exotic derivatives before their valuations tumbled. He was the youngest student ever to qualify in the final of the chartered accountancy exam at the age of 20. Early positions at industrial companies were followed by a move to UB Group in 1990 as corporate treasurer. Two years later, Nedungadi transferred to London as finance director of the group's international businesses. Appointed president and group CFO in 1998, he has led the way to sharpening the group's focus on areas of core competence and global reach. Under his leadership the market capitalization of the three principal group companies has grown to US$7.7 billion, up from US$145 million three years earlier. He has many awards, including the Udyog Ratan Award, CNBC TV18's CFO of the Year M&A (2006), the CNBC Award for India's best CFO in the FMCG & Retail Sector (2007), and the IMA Award for CFO of the year (2007). He lives in Bangalore, India, with his wife and two children.

SUCCESS FOR CFOS

Success means different things to different CFOs. This is because the solutions finance directors come up with are largely determined by the strategic goals of their organization, and the particular challenges of the sector and markets in which they operate.

In our own case, managing rapid growth in India's burgeoning economy over the past two decades has given our finance function some sharp lessons and made us acutely aware of the importance of remaining focused on customer satisfaction.

In the light of the spectacular implosions of some previously highly respected institutions in the banking sector and elsewhere over the course of 2008 and 2009, the importance of putting customer satisfaction—rather than the pursuit of short-term profits—at the center of the organization's business processes has been highlighted in the most dramatic way.

When our organization first began to develop an international dimension 20 years ago, it was a conglomerate. One of my first lessons was the importance of achieving a sharp focus for management and strategic thinking, since it is next to impossible to devise a coherent group-wide strategy for a conglomerate. The importance of thinking about what was core and what was noncore, and deciding where your strengths as an organization lie, were very obvious in that sort of structure.

After I became group CFO, we set about selling off noncore assets and focusing on two very clear business lines: alcoholic beverages and Kingfisher Airlines. Both are positioned in the consumer arena.

There were two major lessons from these changes. The first concerns the importance of establishing and maintaining strong brands. The second is that you will get the behavior you reward.

Regulators around the world are now taking on board the fact that what undoubtedly helped to create last year's banking disasters was a reward structure based on a very short-term and partial view of profits. If you reward exuberant greed, you get exuberant greed.

REWARDING BEHAVIORS

Ten years ago, we found that some of our drinks businesses had a long history of being focused on volumes. What mattered above all else was how many millions of liters we could ship; we lost sight of the costs of producing, selling, and shipping the product. The reward matrix and definitions of success were all about volume. The irony was that, as you competed for more and more volume, you inevitably slipped down the market to where margins were increasingly thinner, as that is where the large volumes are to be had.

So the reward matrix entrenched management behavior that was actually destroying economic value rather than creating it, since it was geared to tying up more and more resources in less and less profitable market segments.

Now the metric that really matters to me is economic value-added. It is not rocket science. It is about knowing what it costs you to make something and get it to market and knowing that you are achieving the appropriate returns to justify that effort. Our solution—one that I commend to others—is to analyze and completely recast our reward matrix to bring them into line with our strategy, which is to seek to grow margins in core markets.

We gave a tremendous degree of autonomy to senior management in our various business units, but the reward structure emphasized economic value-added, and it is focused on long-term performance over three to five years with an emphasis on driving margin improvements.

If you are aiming at the consumer market, it is impossible to overestimate the importance of establishing a strong brand. In an emerging market such as India, it is the difference between success and failure. The Indian market has been characterized by 50 years of deprivation and, as the country's economy has been growing strongly, there is a huge appetite for new experiences and for a bit of what one might call "conspicuous consumption." The pent-up demand in the young, relatively well-paid professional and semi-professional workforce is massive. But this does not mean you can take the consumer for granted.

You have to challenge your assumptions and quality standards continuously. When we chose to launch a new airline, a winning play for us was to recognize that we were not seeking to create just another transportation company. It was not going to be about volumes and filling seats. It had to be about the quality of the passenger experience from the moment they arrive at the kurbside of the airport to when they leave the airport at their destination.

None of this is about short-term thinking or short-term profits. If you look at the era of exuberant greed that characterized Wall Street for most of the last decade, you will look in vain for anything resembling a long-term strategy. The key desire was to make as much money in as short a time as possible. The client's best interests were assumed to be served by chasing the upward spiral as

"Dividing an elephant in half does not produce two elephants." Peter Senge

hard as one could. So questions about the levels of risk that clients, and ultimately the organizations themselves, were being subjected to, vanished from the radar.

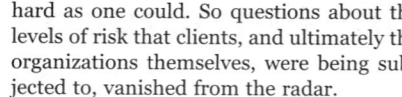

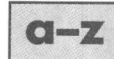

RESISTING WALL STREET'S SALESMEN

People just forgot that a two decades long bull run has to end some time. In fact, one heard plenty of arguments to the effect that we had reached a point where valuations, whether of property or stocks and shares, could only ever go up. In the sheer testosterone rush of being in the thick of it all, people forgot about fundamentals.

If one looks at the CDS swaps market, I heard a count recently that put the value outstanding for global CDSs at 12 times the global economic output in 2007. That kind of figure is just nonsense.

As a CFO I was contacted again and again by bankers before the crash. All of them had a similar story to tell. I was shown complex derivatives products that we were told were guaranteed to turn our treasury function into a massive profit center for the company. However, we have always taken a very prudent view of the treasury function. For us, it is essentially a defensive function, hedging us against interest rate and currency risks. That is what a properly run treasury function is supposed to do and we resisted all the instruments the bankers tried to sell us.

In retrospect, it turns out that those instruments were devised by professors of mathematics who had no idea of the real economy and were being sold by sales people who had no grasp of what they were selling.

We avoided falling into this trap not because we "saw through" the products, but because we recognized that we did not understand them. We took the decision many years ago that we would only do what we understood as an organization, and that we would look at everything else only in so far as it was necessary defensively.

So we budget for a particular exchange rate, and we hedge our position to make sure we achieve that rate, but we certainly do not look to turn a profit out of derivatives and hedge mechanisms. We look at our hedging efforts as insurance. This, in my view, is very much what the CFO should be about, preventing the organization, whatever it is, from getting into territory that management does not understand.

This does not necessarily mean being passive. We have done more acquisitions in the last 10 years than many companies around the world. I am completely supportive of the idea that a company should grow through acquisition when it sees the right opportunities. However, you have to follow the discipline of knowing why you are doing it and that your operations people are fully committed to delivering measurable results from the acquisition.

The moment an acquisition is something that some external M&A team has dreamed up for you and talked you into is the moment that you risk destroying value in your organization.

M&A THAT PAYS

When we bought our biggest competitor in the Indian drinks business for one and a half times our market capitalization at the time, it was a tremendously large venture for us. But we knew why we were doing it and what we needed to do to make it work. As a result, the acquisition delivered unprecedented returns and allowed us to grow our market capitalization 10 times in a few years.

But not every acquisition is going to be easy and, where there is a real cultural divide, it will almost certainly prove difficult. Before making acquisitions, my advice to CFOs is to devote plenty of time to understanding the target before pulling the trigger. Thereafter, once you have ensured that the right structures are in place, you should resist the temptation to swamp the acquired business with your own people. Their main role should be the temporary one of ensuring that all the reporting and other systems are what you want them to be.

What attracted us to the Scotch whisky group Whyte & Mackay, which we acquired for £600 million in May 2007, was that it gave us an opportunity to bring our brand creation strength to bear on an organization that was strongly focused on bulk Scotch. Whyte & Mackay is today selling far more branded whisky than it did in the last several years combined. The moral of the story is—know where you are strong and where you can bring your strengths to bear.

Governance in India and other emerging economies will be hugely helped by the global adoption of International Financial Reporting Standards. One of the really good things about IFRS is that it moves away from an accounting perspective based on following formal rules, which companies then "game," to prioritizing substance over form.

Of course, IFRS has its problems. Among other things, mark-to-market accounting has been criticized as having contributed to the credit crunch. There is no doubt that mark-to-market in mayhem conditions is really mark-to-meltdown, and that helps no one. But the enduring strength of IFRS is that is that it can and does constantly push one to look for substance over form, and that has to be a good thing.

Markets across the emerging economies are increasingly rewarding transparency and coherence. As companies perceive this, they will move to bring their practices in line with what the market is rewarding. When I started my career, corporate governance in India did not really exist. However, for some time now, audit committees in India have been taking it very seriously indeed.

One example is one of India's larger IT companies, which recently tried to do a related-party transaction without transparency. The institutional shareholders strongly resisted, forcing the company to reverse its stand. In the process, the company lost nearly 60 % of its market capitalization over a matter of a few days. If the markets are going to punish senior management misbehavior like this, then inappropriate or idiosyncratic management behavior that is not designed to enhance shareholder value will disappear.

MORE INFO

Books:

Bernstein, Peter L. *Against the Gods: The Remarkable Story of Risk*. Chichester, UK: Wiley, 1998.
Bossidy, Larry, and Ram Charan. *Confronting Reality: Doing What Matters to Get Things Right*. London: Crown Business, 2004.
Charan, Ram. *Profitable Growth Is Everyone's Business: 10 Tools You Can Use on Monday Morning*. London: Crown Business, 2004.
Huntsman, Jon M. *Winners Never Cheat: Everyday Values We Learned As Children*. Philadelphia, PA: Wharton School Publishing, 2005.
Middleton, Julia. *Beyond Authority: Leadership in a Changing World*. Basingstoke, UK: Palgrave Macmillan, 2007.
Taleb, Nassim Nicholas. *Fooled by Randomness: The Hidden Role of Chance in Life and in the Markets*. 2nd ed. London: Random House, 2008.

See Also:

★ Creating Value with EVA (pp. 814–816)
★ Dangers of Corporate Derivative Transactions (pp. 36–38)
★ Viewpoint: India Today and Tomorrow (pp. 884–886)
✔ Acquiring a Company (p. 1128)
India (p. 1505)

"Leadership that's reliant on mergers and acquisitions is dangerous leadership." John Varley

  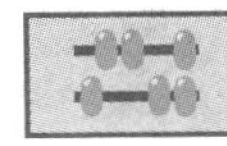   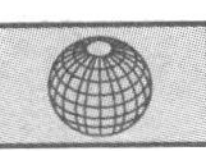   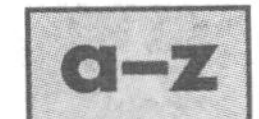

Coping with Equity Market Reactions to M&A Transactions by Scott Moeller

EXECUTIVE SUMMARY

- Overall, stock returns to acquirers tend to be negative or insignificant—in contrast to target companies, where stockholders can benefit greatly.
- Companies that believe they may be targets can influence the value of an ultimate acquisition through the design of defensive techniques and by how they react to bids when they occur. Similarly, acquirers can influence the target share prices through their actions prior to the bid.
- Most acquirers are overconfident in their ability to conduct acquisitions successfully.
- Careful planning, including a robust internal and external communications plan, is required to mitigate the impact on equity markets of acquirers.
- Many factors influence equity market reactions to an M&A bid, including how friendly or hostile the bid is, the financing structure of the bid, the relative size of the two companies, and whether the transaction is a merger or an acquisition.
- Deals conducted in the most recent merger wave appear to have taken some of these issues into account and show better relative performance (relative to the market) than deals conducted in the 1980s and 1990s.

INTRODUCTION

It would be nice if the markets were to react consistently in response to the announcement of M&A deals. But they don't. At least not always. But you can depend on one thing: In the short run, shareholders of target companies benefit more than those of the acquiring company.

It is important to know how to cope with the likely equity market reaction to the announcement of a deal. First of all, you need to understand what those likely reactions will be ... and then to work out whether there is anything that can be done to influence the market. Bidders can mitigate the likely negative market reaction to their share price, and targets may be able to provoke even higher bids.

This article discusses public companies only—as these are naturally the only ones with an "equity market reaction." However, one can properly extrapolate their experience to private companies as well. While most advisers and principals in privately held companies take into account the experience of publicly held companies, the reaction of the equity markets regarding the bidder's share price is not dependent on whether the target is public or private. Either way, the shareholder value of bidders declines, on average, following the announcement of a large acquisition.

"Most mergers fail. If that's not a bona fide fact, plenty of smart people think it is. McKinsey & Company says it's true. Harvard, too. Booz Allen & Hamilton, KPMG, A.T. Kearney—the list goes on. If a deal enriches an acquirer's shareholders, the statistics say, it is probably an accident."
New York Times, February 28, 2008

EQUITY MARKET REACTIONS FOR TARGETS

Relatively few deals make money for the bidding company's shareholders. The market rather consistently shows that bidding companies lose money for their shareholders, or at best break even around the time of the announcement of a takeover, whereas target companies attract offer premiums that typically range from 20% to 40%. Stock prices often rise above the offer price if a competing bidder is anticipated.

These returns are relatively consistent in the United States and the United Kingdom, with the data for other countries less clear but indicating similar results. When the bidder and target returns are combined, the overall shareholder wealth effects are typically found to be insignificant over the short term and positive over the longer term.

In the absence of a competing bid, when a takeover is announced the target company's stock price typically rises to a level *below* the offer price, but slowly rises to approach the bid price as time approaches the closing date when the final deal is consummated, which for most deals is 3–6 months after the announcement date (Figure 1). This is because there is some risk that the deal will not go through or will be repriced (usually lower) because of negative information that the bidder finds while conducting due diligence on the target (see "Due Diligence Requirements in Financial Transactions" for a discussion of the best ways to conduct due diligence in M&A deals).

INFLUENCING TARGET COMPANY STOCK PRICES

The target company itself can have an influence on the potential price offered in a number of ways:

- By having a strong defense in place to protect the company from an unsolicited takeover bid. Such defenses can include so-called poison pills (including underfunded pension plans), shares owned by insiders or in friendly hands, golden and silver parachutes not just for senior management but for a wider group of employees (often called "tin parachutes"), and a history of successfully fending off hostile bidders. Research has shown that these defenses, especially poison pills, do result in higher premiums for target companies.
- Most of these defenses are put in place to make it more difficult (that is, expensive), but not impossible, to be purchased. For example, Mellon Bank put in place tin

Figure 1. Movement of target company share price

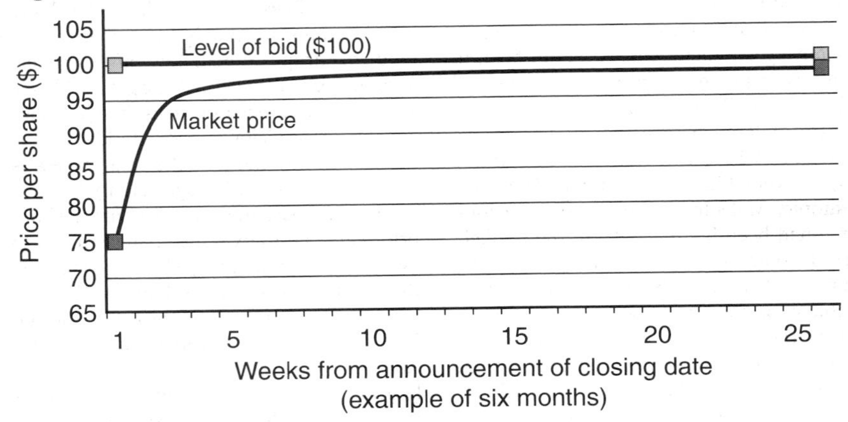

"Equity markets will respond to the announcement of a deal and often NOT the way management expects."

  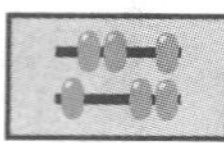   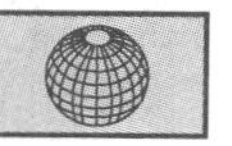   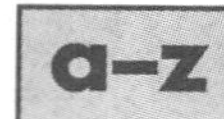

parachutes for all its employees following an unsuccessful hostile bid by the Bank of New York in 1998; when later, in 2006, a friendly deal was proposed and accepted by Mellon Bank, the senior managers and employees were requested to waive their golden, silver, and tin parachute rights in order to put them on an equal footing with the Bank of New York employees, who had no such employment provisions.

- By letting the market know that a high threshold premium value will be required for any unsolicited bid before the board of directors will recommend it to the shareholders. Yahoo! used this technique when it successfully fended off an unwelcome bid from Microsoft in early 2008 that had a 62% premium associated with it (a so-called "bear hug" offer, which designates an offer above the typical premium range of 20–40%).
- By encouraging competing bids. By opening up the purchase of the company to an auction, the directors admit that the company is for sale and will likely lose its independence, but that they are actively seeking the highest possible price. After Morrisons, the supermarket chain in the United Kingdom, made a formal offer to purchase Safeway for £2.4 billion in January 2003, an auction for Safeway ensued with competing bids from Asda (controlled by Wal-Mart) and J. Sainsbury. There was a feeding frenzy that included Tesco, retail magnate Sir Philip Green, and venture capitalists Kohlberg Kravis Roberts. The price that Morrisons ultimately paid for Safeway was £3.0 billion.

Bidders can also influence the target company's share price, naturally wanting to keep the price of the target down. The most common technique is to conduct a "street sweep," whereby the target company's shares (or a controlling interest in the target) are purchased in a blitzkrieg that gives the market and the target's management no time to react before the takeover is effectively complete. This is very difficult to conduct in practice, and is most successful when a small number of shareholders control a large percentage of the target's shares or where the bidder already has a large ownership in the target. Thus, for example, Malcolm Glazer, who for a long time had been holding 28% of the publicly listed football club Manchester United, purchased a similarly sized holding from Cubic Expression in May 2004, and thus in one purchase came to control the club.

Many bidders, when purchasing their toeholds in potential targets, will publicly announce that they have no interest "at this time" in making a bid for the entire company, maintaining that their holding is a financial interest only "because the shares represent an attractive investment." This was the position declared by Malcolm Glazer in the Manchester United case from the time he first disclosed a 3% ownership in the club in March 2003 up until the time he bought the shares that gave him control in 2005. In his case, the market expected a bid for the entire company, but his public position nevertheless may have lowered the price he ultimately had to pay for that controlling interest.

In all of these situations, it must be noted that proper legal advice must be taken in order not to fall foul of the many regulations and laws that prohibit market manipulation.

EQUITY MARKET REACTIONS FOR BIDDERS

The shareholders of acquiring companies are not as fortunate as those of the targets. On average, their shares decline in value around the time the company announces its intention to take over another company. Thus, in the example above, when Morrisons launched its surprise bid for Safeway (at a 30.3% premium to the prior day's close), its shares declined 14.3%, and when J. Sainsbury entered with its competing bid, its own share price declined on the day by 3.5%. The shareholders of neither bidder benefited, in distinct contrast to Safeway's shareholders.

Because of the relative consistency over time of stock market movements in response to deal announcements, the market will assume that future deals will do the same, including that only 30-40% of all deals are successful, that mid- and long-term shareholder wealth declines by 10-35%, and that the share prices for acquirers and targets move within certain ranges (on average) around the announcement day. Merger arbitrageurs—whether in hedge funds or investment banks—take large positions knowing that bidders' share prices tend to drop immediately after a deal announcement and that targets will see share price appreciation. This then becomes a virtuous (or vicious, for the bidder) cycle, where the movement in the share prices is magnified by this arbitrage activity.

In many cases these movements in share price can lead to extreme changes in share ownership. For example, when the Deutsche Börse (the largest stock exchange at the time in mainland Europe) made a bid for the London Stock Exchange in 2004, the Anglo-American arbitrageurs rapidly became the largest group of shareholders, displacing the long-term German shareholders, whose ownership was reduced to only a third. It was these arbitrageurs who forced the Deutsche Börse CEO to drop the bid in March 2005, leading to a 30% price rise in the Deutsche Börse shares as it became less and less likely that the deal would succeed.

As with the Deutsche Börse CEO who didn't anticipate this change, most managers seem to be oblivious to facts which appear to be obvious to those outside the company. A DLA Piper survey in 2006 showed that 81% of corporate respondents rated their M&A experience as fairly or highly successful, and over 90% of venture capitalists felt the same, yet we know that 60–70% of all deals fail.

INFLUENCING THE STOCK PRICE OF THE BIDDER

In most M&A situations, the bidder controls the timing of when the bid is publicized. The notable exception to this is when there is a market leak, but even in these situations the leak either happens early in the negotiations when it is easier to deny to the press that any deal is pending (as the negotiations have not progressed sufficiently far for a deal to be in place) or late enough in the proceedings that an emergency communication plan should already be in place for just such a situation.

The announcement event is therefore not a surprise to the bidder. Through proper planning and the use of external advisers (including investment banks, but also specialist public relations firms), positive spin on the deal can be delivered to the market: Benefits to all stakeholders are emphasized; new markets are announced; product innovations are forecast. Support from clients, suppliers, and even outside parties (such as local government) can be rallied. Potential problems will have been anticipated, and strategies to neutralize these will have been developed and disclosed.

Nevertheless, to paraphrase Robert Burns, "The best laid plans of mice and men / Go oft awry." In M&A deals, there are ultimately just too many individuals involved and there is just so much that can go wrong that much often does. Therefore, the press turns negative, equity analysts forecast too much dilution of earnings, cash flow declines, and clients, suppliers, employees, and even managers become very worried about their positions—and naturally assume the worst.

Thus the acquirer must have a very robust communications plan at the ready. Not every contingency will be anticipated, but many can be. Most important is to have teams in place to be able to respond quickly to any false rumors and to replace

"Shareholders of acquirers tend to lose money; target company shareholders almost always gain."

immediately any such gossip with fact. The company needs to stay in control—as best it can—during the entire deal process. The most effective way to do this is to have a continuous stream of positive stories prepared for periodic, if not even daily, release. Constant communication with the staff of both bidder and target can go a long way towards allaying anxiety and even panic.

One must remember that those who can benefit from the flip side will be acting accordingly as well: these include competitors who see opportunities to grab market share and even valued staff, and trading arbitrageurs who have made bets in the market that the share price will fall. These arbitrageurs certainly have been very successful in pushing down the price of acquirers in many deals, as in the above example where the Deutsche Börse was forced to drop its bid for the London Stock Exchange.

OTHER FACTORS AFFECTING EQUITY VALUES

The above discussion "averages" the results for many companies. Individual deals and individual companies will show different results and provide different returns over time from these averages, and takeover and defensive tactics will also need to be customized for each situation.

There are also other factors that will impact on the equity markets for both the target and bidder's share price. When cash is used to finance the deal instead of issuing more shares, the returns to the bidder are usually higher. In countries such as the United States, where tender offers (often hostile) are common, these do better than friendly mergers. The smaller the target is in relation to the acquirer, the more likely it is that the bidder's share price will not decline relative to the market.

There are also differences in short- and long-term shareholder value effects. This article has looked principally at the short-term effects around the time of deal announcement, but if a longer-term perspective is taken (more than six months), then the negative returns to the bidder are reduced, although still typically remaining negative. Also, one can look at the combined returns when the bidder and target are taken together over the longer term: in this case as noted earlier, history shows that the overall shareholder wealth effects are typically positive.

CONCLUSION

Despite the doom and gloom of the analyses that have looked at the success of companies that merge or acquire, there is some hope: Several recent studies (from Towers Perrin/Cass Business School, McKinsey, and KPMG) have shown that acquiring companies since 2003 are doing better with their deals. Not much, but at least measurably so. Some of the suggestions we've made in this article have been recently more widely adopted by the market. There *is* more focus on careful deal selection and corporate governance. Post-merger integration *is* receiving attention even before the deal closes, and sometimes even before announcement. There is hope—and evidence—with some of these recent studies that perhaps equity markets may start to award an equity premium to companies that acquire well.

MAKING IT HAPPEN

The Key Factors

- Understand that the premium offered to the target is only one aspect of the deal's success, and that it is often overshadowed by other factors, especially people issues.
- Formulate a plan for addressing surprises. Try to identify all the ways that the deal could fail ... and then look for still more ways it could go wrong.
- Do not be overconfident in your ability to integrate an acquisition successfully. Prior experience is helpful, but not sufficient. Each deal is different.
- Proper legal advice should always be taken.
- Plan for a dynamic deal process where changes will need to be made to the acquisition strategy.
- Incorporate a robust communications plan into any deal.

MORE INFO

Books:

Gaughan, Patrick A. *Mergers, Acquisitions, and Corporate Restructurings*. 4th ed. Hoboken, NJ: Wiley, 2007.

Moeller, Scott, and Chris Brady. *Intelligent M&A: Navigating the Mergers and Acquisitions Minefield*. Chichester, UK: Wiley, 2007.

Sudarsanam, Sudi. *Creating Value from Mergers and Acquisition: The Challenges*. Harlow, UK: FT Prentice Hall, 2003.

See Also:

★ Acquisition Integration: How to Do It Successfully (pp. 708–709)
★ Mergers and Acquisitions: Today's Catalyst Is Working Capital (pp. 763–765)
✔ Achieving Success in International Acquisitions (p. 1127)
✔ Acquisition Accounting (p. 1129)
✔ Calculating a Company's Net Worth (p. 1065)
✔ Planning the Acquisition Process (p. 1132)
✔ Structuring M&A Deals and Tax Planning (p. 1135)
✔ Using IRR for M&A Financing (p. 1137)
✔ Using the Market-Value Method for Acquisitions (p. 1139)

        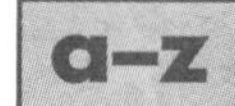

Cultural Alignment and Risk Management: Developing the Right Culture

by R. Brayton Bowen

EXECUTIVE SUMMARY

- Organization culture may vary in definition from country to country, but it is essentially the sum total of the behaviors and styles of the people who drive the system.
- Organizations that properly align organization culture with business goals and objectives can realize up to 40% improvement in performance compared to peer and competitor organizations.
- Generally, 80% of acquisitions and mergers fail to perform to management's expectations, in most instances, because of a failure to understand and manage organization culture.
- Organizational members have an innate knowledge of what is and is not working within the culture of the organization and, therefore, must be engaged in the process of building the right culture.
- Culture changes within an organization require total mastery of the change management process.
- Organization culture ultimately impacts the financial performance and long-term success of an enterprise.

INTRODUCTION

The goal was to beat Microsoft at its own game. After rebuffing a takeover attempt by the giant corporation, Novell Nouveau went on an acquisition binge of its own. The strategy was to acquire a premier word-processing company that could rival Microsoft, and Microsoft's "Microsoft Word" in particular. So, in 1994, Raymond Noorda, CEO for the then second-largest software company, acquired WordPerfect Corp. for US$1.4 billion in stock. Novell was to become a "software powerhouse," delivering "stand-alone, software suites, groupware, and network applications that were to define new capabilities for information systems," according to WordPerfect's leading executive. Two years later, WordPerfect was sold for less than one-seventh of its original purchase price. The reason for the failed strategy: "The cultures were very, very different," as reported by Novell's successor CEO, Robert Frankenberg (*The Wall Street Journal*, 1996).

Taking the role of the dominator, management of Novell Nouveau assumed their ways and methods to be superior to those of WordPerfect. They eliminated the sales force, assuming the Novell Nouveau organization could assume the sales and marketing function, and went on to make a host of other mistakes. Indeed, their experience was similar to those of the majority of acquiring firms. Generally, 80% of acquisitions and mergers fail to perform to management's expectations, and the overarching factor in most instances is a failure to understand and manage organization culture.

ALIGNING ORGANIZATION CULTURES

What Is Culture?

Culture can be thought of as the organizational context in which behaviors can be characterized and assessed. It is the environmental code that prompts people to act in certain ways to "fit in" at different levels and perform in "expected" ways. For example, customers entering a fine dining establishment understand they are expected to dress appropriately, deport themselves in a dignified manner, wait to be seated at an assigned table, and ultimately, pay a high price for the experience. Yet, there are usually no formal rules that are posted stating how guests are supposed to dress or how they are to behave. Once seated at their table with friends or other guests, they can adjust their behaviors to a more relaxed and interactive mode. This analogy equates to organizational cultures, wherein the overarching culture may prompt people to act one way, whereas once they settle into their own departments or business units, their behavior may change somewhat from the corporate norm. Bringing about change on an organization-wide basis requires considerable understanding of what is needed and why; and it requires superior change-management ability.

Elements of organization culture include: How people work together; how responsible they feel for the success of the enterprise; how ethically they behave; how people behave toward customers; how they feel about the quality of the company's goods and services; how prideful they feel about the mission of the enterprise; and ultimately, how fulfilled people feel in having a say in the business or making a difference in people's lives as a result of the work they perform. In the end, highly constructive and productive cultures lead to optimum outcomes.

Why Change?

More corporations are coming to appreciate that relationship marketing is leading to increased sales, as compared to transactional marketing. To effect a shift of such magnitude requires a carefully planned migration of both structural and cultural change. Companies such as Globus, the German based hypermarket; DM-Drogeriemarkt, a retail chemist; Southwest Airlines and Lufthansa, both commercial airline companies; and Ikea, the Swedish multinational home furnishing retailer—all have created cultural environments that have enabled them to be enormously profitable compared to their industry counterparts. In each of these organizations, employees work as teams. Management provides prescriptive guidance rather than restrictive direction. Employees are entrusted to do the right thing and encouraged to be the best at what they do, namely, providing customers not only with quality goods and services but also with great customer experiences.

Up to 40% improvement in performance can be achieved by changing organization culture. According to Stanford Business School professor, Jeffery Pfeffer, providing training, status equalization, employment stability, and strong recognition and reward programs can propel any number of organizations to enviable levels of success.

To remain viable and competitive, even service sector entities, for example utilities, financial institutions, and government services, are recognizing the need to shift from transaction-based systems to ones that are more relationship-focused. Such changes require enormous changes in organization culture, as well as in supporting structures, i.e., operational, technological, and policy structures. Because "structure follows strategy," it is virtually impossible to make shifts in organizational culture unless changes in structure occur, as well, to support such seismic shifts.

When Is Change Necessary?

Nowhere is the need for cultural alignment more evident than in the case of acquisitions

"When you are through changing, you are through." Percy Barnevik and mergers. What usually happens is that the acquiring entity assumes its culture to be superior to that of the entity being acquired, as in the case of Novell Nouveau cited earlier. Rather than identifying and optimizing the most constructive aspects of the acquired organization's culture, the culture of the acquirer subsumes the culture of the acquired organization. Consequently, the outcome is not unlike that of Novell Nouveau's in acquiring WordPerfect. Equally, compelling circumstances exist when organizations are pummeled by downturns in the economy or paradigm shifts in industry standards and/or customer preferences. Organizational transformations are required to jumpstart the business concept or power-charge employees, propelling them in a new direction. Out of the ashes of the past must arise a new phoenix, if the organization is to transform itself into a vital resource for meeting, if not exceeding, customer needs and marketplace demands. Today, Starbucks, the international brand, roaster, and specialty coffee retailer, which operates in 43 countries with approximately 15,000 stores, is being assailed by competitors offering cheaper alternative products. Under Howard Schultz, returning to the company as chairman and CEO, the company is adopting a turnaround strategy of providing customers not only with the distinctive Starbucks "experience," and innovations, but also, a can-do employee attitude. "Welcome to Starbucks! What can I get started for you?" is the greeting welcoming every customer. While it is still early in the game, the emphasis is on reigniting the emotional attachment customers have had in the past with the product and the people who are the face of the company.

Similarly, when organizations determine that their focus must shift from product sales to customer satisfaction and retention, a significant change in organization culture is required. Employees need to be trained and empowered to improve the quality of goods and services, solve problems, and earn the respect and, ultimately, the loyalty of their customers. For example, in 1993, when CEO Louis Gerstner took the reins of IBM, the company had just lost US$8 billion. His challenge was to transform IBM from a stodgy, centralized, mainframe computer company, where customers were expected to come to "Big Blue" and turf wars among departments abounded, to a fast-paced, customer-focused, well-oiled machine, where employees were expected to work as a team to meet and exceed the needs of their customers. In *Who Says Elephants Can't Dance*, Gerstner wrote, "Culture isn't just one aspect of the game. It *is* the game. In the end, an organization is nothing more than the collective capacity of its people to create value."

As organizations continue to grow globally, it becomes a virtual impossibility for management to be ever-present, critically focused on day-to-day operations. Instead, organization cultures must be designed that are conducive to teamwork, self-direction, ethical decision-making, and the achievement of outstanding results. Team members throughout the organizational system must share a vision and a passion that can only come from an organization culture that is carefully designed and ardently nurtured.

A MODEL FOR THE IDEAL CULTURE

Organizational Awareness

Ask any employee about his or her organizational culture, and chances are the words chosen to describe the environment will range from "political," "highly competitive," "collaborative," and "team-like" to "stressful," "mission driven," even "rewarding." The collective wisdom of organizational members represents a sort of meta-knowledge about the behaviors exhibited as a result of the cultural context in which they function. These descriptors, in essence, paint a picture of how functional or dysfunctional an organization's culture is and, in turn, how successful or unsuccessful the organization is as a whole in the way it operates. Moreover, it is this collective conscience, or meta-knowledge, that contains the answers as to how the organizational culture could and should be ideally.

Dimensions of Culture

Various models exist for assessing the culture of an organization. Perhaps the most widely used survey instruments have been developed by Human Synergistics International. Their Organizational Culture Inventory®, for example, measures 12 thinking and behavioral styles, which make up three groupings, termed the "constructive," "passive-aggressive," and "passive-defensive" styles. An "ideal" culture is "constructive" when the dominant organizational styles are "self-actualizing," "achieving," "humanistic and encouraging," and "affiliative." Summary results from completed assessments enable organizations to understand how their cultures operate and where improvements can be made to improve outcomes in a variety of areas, including employee/labor relations, customer relations, organizational performance, and profitability.

Blueprint for Change

The benefit of using such assessments as described above is that organizational leadership is better able to target areas for change. Knowing how the present organizational culture impacts on performance, and where enhancements can be made to improve performance can form the basis of a master plan, or blueprint for change. Moreover, by tapping into the collective conscience of the organization and enlisting the involvement of organizational members, leadership can manage the change process more effectively—simply put, it becomes a holistic process or a "bottoms-up-top-down" approach. In the end, the change effort is sustainable, because all organizational members understand what is needed and how to make it happen—more importantly, they become collaborators in the change process rather than victims or passive spectators. Any number of corporations, including American Eagle Outfitters,

MAKING IT HAPPEN

Culture change requires a strategic perspective on why culture is important to the organization, and how it will make a significant difference in the strategic positioning and success of an enterprise. The process begins with articulation of the vision and mission of the organization. To achieve optimum performance, the culture of the organization needs to be aligned with the vision, mission, and strategic goals and objectives of the organization. The behaviors of senior leadership must model the new standard, and the change and implementation process must begin with senior leadership.

- Conduct a system-wide assessment of the organization's current culture.
- Determine where change is necessary and why.
- Profile the desired culture of the organization, ensuring that the targeted profile will bring out the best in the organization.
- Engage organizational members in the processes of assessing the current culture, profiling the desired culture, and implementing needed change.
- Incorporate the desired behavioral styles into the performance-planning and management process for both individual members, and the business as a whole.
- Continue to assess progress versus plan. Be certain to obtain feedback from key stakeholders such as customers, vendors, and investors, and make adjustments as needed to improve results.

"Change is the process by which the future invades our lives." Alvin Toffler

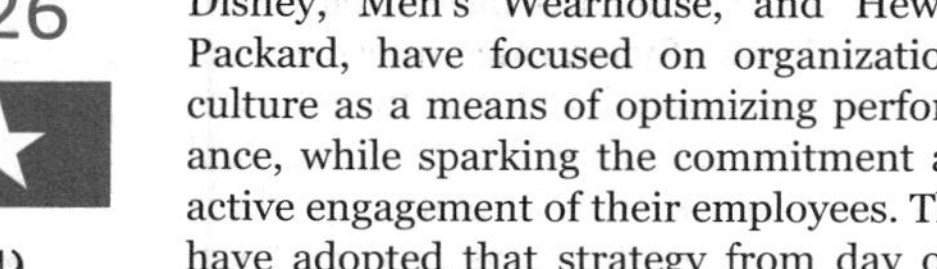

Disney, Men's Wearhouse, and Hewlett Packard, have focused on organizational culture as a means of optimizing performance, while sparking the commitment and active engagement of their employees. They have adopted that strategy from day one, and it has been the foundation for success.

Further Implications

In addition to profiling the culture of an organization, management can extend the evaluative process to assessing the individual behavioral styles of organizational members. Consistent with the notion that "a chain is only as strong as its weakest link," the behavior of every member of the organizational "chain" must be aligned with the desired profile of the organization's ideal culture to ensure optimum results. Further, individual performance plans should be honed to include the behavioral norms expected of organizational members, and periodic reviews conducted to help determine how well behaviors are aligned, and where improvement in individual behavioral styles is needed.

CONCLUSION

In a global economy that is becoming more complex and conflicted, there is little room for error, and even less room for guesswork. Organizational culture is as critical an element in managing a business as information technology, or financial controls. Indeed, it is more elusive but equally powerful to ensuring the success of an enterprise. The experience of Novell Nouveau and WordPerfect proves how costly the neglect of organizational culture can be to the financial performance of a business. By way of contrast, those organizations that consciously tend to the process of building the right organizational culture have reaped rewards well beyond those achieved by their peer and competitor organizations.

MORE INFO

Books:

Bowen, R. Brayton. *Recognizing and Rewarding Employees*. New York: McGraw-Hill, 2000.

Cameron, Kim S., and Robert E. Quinn. *Diagnosing and Changing Organizational Culture: Based on the Competing Values Framework*. San Francisco, CA: Jossey-Bass, 2005.

Driskill, Gerald W., and Angela Laird Brenton. *Organizational Culture in Action: A Cultural Analysis Workbook*. Thousand Oaks, CA: Sage Publications, 2005.

Gerstner, Louis V. *Who Says Elephants Can't Dance: Leading a Great Enterprise Through Dramatic Change*. New York: HarperCollins, 2002.

Hennig-Thurau, Thorsten, and Ursula Hansen (eds). *Relationship Marketing: Gaining Competitive Advantage Through Customer Satisfaction and Customer Retention*. New York: McGraw-Hill/Irwin, 2000.

Pfeffer, Jeffrey. *The Human Equation: Building Profits by Putting People First*. Boston, MA: Harvard Business School Press, 1998.

Schein, Edgar H. *Organizational Culture and Leadership*. 3rd ed. San Francisco, CA: Jossey-Bass, 2004.

Articles:

Barriere, Michael T., Betty R. Anson, Robin S. Ording, and Evelyn Rogers. "Culture transformation in a health care organization: A process for building adaptive capabilities through leadership development." *Consulting Psychology Journal: Practice and Research* 54:2 (Spring 2002): 116–130. Online at: tinyurl.com/6y4tn8g

Clark, Don. "Novell Nouveau: Software firm fights to remake business after ill-fated merger." *Wall Street Journal (Midwest ed)* 76:62 (January 12, 1996): A1, A6.

Singh, Kavita. "Predicting organizational commitment through organization culture: A study of automobile industry in India." *Journal of Business Economics and Management* 8:1 (2007): 29–37. Online at: dx.doi.org/10.1080/16111699.2007.9636149

Websites:

The Howland Group: www.howlandgroup.com

Human Synergistics International: www.humansynergistics.com

See Also:

★ Acquisition Integration: How to Do It Successfully (pp. 708–709)

★ Merger Integration and Transition Management: A New Slant for Finance Executives (pp. 756–758)

✔ Assessing Business Performance (p. 1144)

✔ Planning the Acquisition Process (p. 1132)

  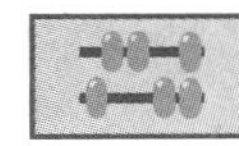      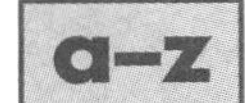

Due Diligence Requirements in Financial Transactions by Scott Moeller

EXECUTIVE SUMMARY

- There is an urgency for companies to conduct intensive due diligence in financial deals, both before announcement (when it should be easy to call off the deal) and after.
- Traditional due diligence merely verifies the history of the target and projects the future based on that history; correctly applied due diligence digs much deeper and provides insight into the future value of the target across a wide variety of factors.
- Although due diligence does enable prospective acquirers to find potential black holes, the aim of due diligence should be this and more, including looking for opportunities to realize future prospects for the enlarged corporation through leveraging of the acquiring and the acquired firms' resources and capabilities, identification of synergistic benefits, and post-merger integration planning.
- Due diligence should start from the inception of a deal.
- Areas to probe include finance, management, employees, IT, legal, risk management systems, culture, innovation, and even ethics.
- Critical to the success of the due diligence process is the identification of the necessary information required, where it can best be sourced, and who is best qualified to review and interpret the data.
- Requesting too much information is just as dangerous as requesting too little. Having the wrong people looking at the data is also hazardous.

INTRODUCTION

This is not your father's due diligence.

Due diligence is one of the two most critical elements in the success of a mergers and acquisitions (M&A) transaction (the other being the proper execution of the integration process), according to a survey conducted in 2006 by the Economist Intelligence Unit (EIU) and Accenture. Due diligence was considered to be of greater importance than target selection, negotiation, pricing the deal, and the development of the company's overall M&A strategy.

But not even a decade ago, when due diligence was conducted in financial transactions, the focus was almost always limited to financial factors, pending law suits, and information technology (IT) systems. Today, those areas remain important, but they must be supplemented during the due diligence process by attention to the assessment of other factors: management and employees (and not just their contracts, but how good they actually are in their jobs), commercial operations (products, marketing, strategy, and competition—both existing and potential), and corporate culture (can the companies actually work together when they're merged?). But even these areas are now mainstream when due diligence is conducted. Newer areas of due diligence are developing rapidly: risk management, innovation, and ethical (including corporate social responsibility) due diligence.

The 2006 EIU/Accenture survey also found that although due diligence is considered as a top challenge by 23% of CEOs in making domestic acquisitions, this rises to 41% in the much more complex cross-border transactions, which make up the majority of financial transactions, even in today's depressed markets.

ORGANIZING FOR DUE DILIGENCE

It's a two-way street: Buyers must understand what they are buying; and targets must understand who's pursuing them and whether they should accept an offer.

To be successfully conducted, due diligence must have senior management involvement and control, often assisted by outside experts such as management consulting firms, accountants, investment banks, and maybe even specialist investigation firms.

To quote from a PricewaterhouseCoopers report issued in late 2002: "We always have to make decisions based on imperfect information. But the more information you have and the more you transform that into what we call knowledge, the more likely you are to be successful."

That said, there is only a certain amount that can be handled by the number of people involved, the time restrictions under which they are working, and the quality and variety of resources available to them. Moreover, there is the danger of being overloaded by too much information if those involved do not have good management and analytical methods they can deploy.

By and large, it is not the quantity of information that matters so much as its quality and how it is used. Although diligence may not be cheap (as a result of fees charged for often highly complex work by professional services firms), the alternative of litigation or the destruction of stockholder value (as a consequence of having been "penny wise and pound foolish" in the execution of the due diligence process) may prove far more costly in the long run.

THE DUE DILIGENCE PROCESS

Although due diligence may be only one part of an acquisition or investment exercise, in many ways it is by far the most significant aspect of the M&A process. Done properly, acquirers should be better able to control the risks inherent in any deal, while simultaneously contributing to the ultimate effective management of the target and the realization of the goals of the acquisition.

As an instrument through which to reveal and remedy potential sources of risk, due diligence—by confirming the expectations of the buyer and the understanding of the seller—enables firms to formulate remedies and solutions to enable a deal to proceed. In many ways, due diligence lends comfort to an acquirer's senior management, the board, and ultimately the stockholders, who should all insist on a rigorous due diligence process, which provides them with relative (though not absolute) assurance that the deal is sensible, and that they have uncovered any problems pertaining to it that may derail matters in the future.

Ideally, due diligence should start during the conception phase of the deal, and initially it can use publicly available information. It should then continue throughout the merger process as further proprietary information becomes available. Full use of the due diligence information collected would mean that it is not just used to make a go/no-go decision about whether the acquisition should proceed and to determine the terms of the deal, but that the findings from due diligence should also be incorporated in the planning for the postmerger integration.

Clearly it is easier to obtain high-quality data if the deal is friendly; in unfriendly deals due diligence may never progress further than publicly available data. This lack of access to internal information has scuppered many a deal—for example, the takeover attempt by Sir Philip Green of Marks & Spencer in 2004.

"Know thy enemy and know thyself; in a hundred battles you will never be in peril." Sun Tzu

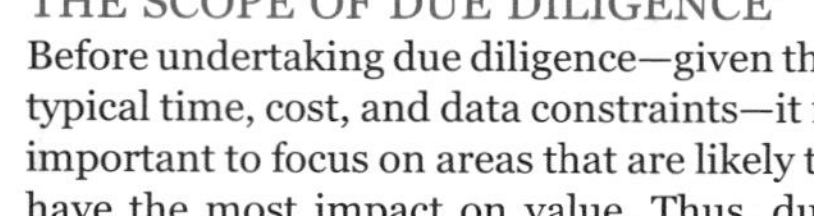

THE SCOPE OF DUE DILIGENCE[1]

Before undertaking due diligence—given the typical time, cost, and data constraints—it is important to focus on areas that are likely to have the most impact on value. Thus, due diligence should be tailored to:

- the type of transaction
- the motivation for doing the deal
- plans for the target once acquired
- the impact on the existing operations of the acquirer.

Some basic questions to ask include:

- Is the acquirer a strategic or a financial buyer?
- How fully integrated will the target be once acquired, and in what time frame?
- Is the whole company being acquired?
- Does the target represent new product lines, marketing channels, or geographic territories, or is there overlap with the acquirer's existing operations?
- Will certain functional operations of the target be eliminated?
- Will the IT systems of the target be retained?
- How will the rating agencies respond to the transaction?

TYPES OF DUE DILIGENCE INFORMATION

Each industry has its own special due diligence requirements. For example, an insurance company will need a review of major policies, actuarial assumptions, and sales practices, whereas the purchase of a bank would require a review of its marking policies and risk management systems.

As noted above, one starts with external sources. Although these rarely provide a sufficient overview of an organization at the level required to obtain a proper understanding, secondary sources do equip management with valuable information, allowing them to strategize and develop honed, and more focused, questions for their further internal due diligence on the prospective acquisition.

In spite of the centrality of financial, legal, cultural, and other areas of due diligence, examples abound of transactions that were completed without effective due diligence being done through lack of time, or because management was overconfident in its ability to understand the target, resulting in devastating losses of stockholder value.

Financial Due Diligence

Financial due diligence enables companies to obtain a view of an organization's historical profits, which can then be used as a canvas on which to paint a picture of the company's financial future. Developed around an array of building blocks—including auditing and verifying financial results on which an offer is based, identifying deal breakers, reviewing forecasts and budgets, pinpointing areas where warranties or indemnities may be needed, and providing confidence in the underlying performance, and therefore future profits, of a company—financial due diligence allows the bidder to make the proper offer for the target, or perhaps uncover reasons for not proceeding with the deal.

Legal Due Diligence

As companies expand into hitherto commercially less experienced parts of the world in search of new markets and products (such as China, Vietnam, or certain countries in the Middle East and Africa), the requirement to conduct effective and sufficient legal due diligence work can prove more trying, and in certain cases near impossible. Nevertheless, the need to check title over assets that are being sold, and to ensure that the entity being acquired is legitimate and free of any contractual or legal obstacles which might derail the M&A process, will undoubtedly remain pivotal to the due diligence process no matter where the target resides. Governmental regulatory concerns, such as monopolies, employment law, taxes, etc., will also be investigated as part of the legal due diligence.

Commercial Due Diligence

Given that companies are bought not for their past performance but for their ability to generate profits in the future, acquirers must use commercial due diligence to obtain an objective view of a company's markets, prospects, and competitive position. As noted by Towers Perrin in a discussion of operational due diligence, there is a "need to look at all the relevant sources of value to avoid unpleasant surprises."[2] This means a deeper query into certain operations that heavily determine a target's ultimate value to the acquirer—i.e. growth opportunities and resulting future income.

Whether obtained to reduce risk associated with the transaction, to help with the company valuation, or to plan for post-merger integration, commercial due diligence enables acquirers to examine a target's markets and performance—identifying strengths, weaknesses, opportunities, and threats. Focused on the likely strategic position of the combined entity, commercial due diligence, by reviewing the drivers that underpin forecasts and business plans, concentrates on the ability of the target's businesses to achieve the projected sales and profitability growth post acquisition.

Despite the seemingly obvious pivotal benefits that commercial due diligence can bring to acquiring organizations, *Competitive Intelligence Magazine* reported in 2003 that "only 10% of respondents to an Accenture survey of M&A practitioners said that their due diligence process included four or more sources from outside the company."

Innovation Due Diligence

Linked closely to commercial risk but meriting special attention is the due diligence of the research and development (R&D) process. This is more than just an analysis of intellectual property rights. Many nonindustrial companies may not have explicit R&D groups, but still remain

---

CASE STUDY

Failure in Due Diligence: VeriSign's Purchase of Jamba

In June 2004, VeriSign acquired privately held Berlin-based Jamba for US$273 million. VeriSign was an internet infrastructure services company which provided the services that enabled over 3,000 enterprises and 500,000 websites to operate. Through its domain name registry it managed over 50 million digital identities in more than 350 languages. Revenues exceeded US$1 billion dollars in the previous year. VeriSign had extensive experience with acquisitions, having made 17 acquisitions prior to Jamba, including four that were valued at more than this particular purchase.

Jamba had millions of subscribers and was the leading provider of mobile content delivery services in Europe. It was best known for the Crazy Frog character used in the most successful ring tone of all time.

But, beneath the surface, trouble was brewing that could easily have been uncovered by even the most rudimentary due diligence: complaints to regulators had noted that Jamster, the UK and US rebranding of Jamba, was targeting children, despite the fact that Jamster's mobile content services were intended for adult customers only. Perhaps more disturbingly, only days before the acquisition VeriSign discovered that a significant portion of Jamba's profits came from the distribution of adult content in Germany—despite a VeriSign policy of not supporting adult or pornographic companies. There were backlashes in Germany over other issues and Jamba was forced to make a declaration of discontinuance regarding many of its contracts. Other legal actions were pending in Germany and the United States.

Unsurprisingly, Jamba's revenues peaked early the following year.

  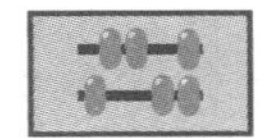      

dependent on the development of intellectual property to maintain their business growth. It must be understood how this is encouraged.

Management Due Diligence

Naturally, acquirers need to perform discrete investigations in order to evaluate both the competence of the target's management and the quality of their past performances, and to ensure that the management of the target and acquirer are compatible. One would think that this would be recognized by any acquirer today, but one acquisition team recently told us that their senior management felt confident enough in their own ability to conduct their management due diligence that they could do this "over a cup of tea," basically, by eyeing the management team from across the table. Nevertheless, in the rush to do deals in the peak merger year of 2007, many of the largest deals properly included extensive management surveys, including 360 degree appraisals, psychometrics, and even investigative reporting.

Cultural Due Diligence

Since one of the more difficult areas for integrating two companies concerns combining their corporate cultures, due care needs to be applied to ensure cultural fit. Indeed, cultural fit is so important that 85% of underperforming acquisitions blame different management attitudes and culture for the poor performance of the combined entities, as reported at a conference in 2006 by Towers Perrin and Cass Business School. Thus, by assessing soft factors such as a company's leadership style, corporate behavior, and even dress code, an acquirer may be able to build an accurate picture of a target's values, attitudes, and beliefs, and so determine if there will be a good cultural fit within their own organizational structure.

Ethical Due Diligence

There is an emerging area, best described as ethical due diligence, that overlaps in many ways with management and cultural due diligence but is not to be confused with legal due diligence. The most obvious requirement of ethical due diligence is to determine whether management have engaged in unethical professional acts (as defined, usually, by the ethical standards of the acquiring company), but it also necessarily includes assessment of the corporate social responsibility activities of the company.

CASE STUDY

No Cultural Fit for Sony in the Movie Industry

In 1988, Sony (a Japanese electronics manufacturer) acquired Columbia Pictures (an American moviemaker) for US$3.4 billion. With cultures that could scarcely have been more different, the acquisition—which involved little consideration of cultural fit between the two entities—failed to live up to commercial expectations, with Sony famously writing down US$2.7 billion on the deal by 1994.

Risk Management Due Diligence

It is critical to understand how the target reports and monitors its inherent business risks. The events in financial and real estate markets in the past several years highlight the need to check carefully not just all risk management systems, but also the *culture* of risk in a company.

CONCLUSION

According to the EIU/Accenture survey, only 18% of executives were highly confident that their company had carried out satisfactory due diligence. This is probably due to the lack of attention given to this critical aspect of a deal, or to the view that it is merely a box-ticking exercise conducted by outside advisers.

In short, the probing of a wide variety of due diligence areas should provide a counterbalance to the short-termism of traditionally limited financial and legal due diligence, helping acquirers to understand how markets and competitive environments will affect their purchase, and confirming that the opportunity is a sensible one to undertake from a commercial and strategic perspective, especially in cross-border deals.

MAKING IT HAPPEN

Key factors in conducting informative and timely due diligence are:

- Identifying the critical areas to probe: financial, legal, business, cultural, management, ethical, risk management, etc.
- Identifying the most important information to collect in those areas, as there is never enough time to look at everything in as much detail as one might want.
- Identifying the right sources for the desired information.
- Identifying the right people to review the data: this should include those who know most about that area and also those who will be managing the business post acquisition.

Due diligence should not be a mere confirmation of the facts. Bridging the strategic review and completion phases of any merger or acquisition exercise, the due diligence process allows prospective acquirers to understand as much as possible about the target company, and to make sure that what it believes is being purchased is actually what is being purchased. The due diligence process digs deeper *before* the point of no return in consummating a deal.

MORE INFO

Books:

Howson, Peter. *Due Diligence: The Critical Stage in Mergers and Acquisitions*. Aldershot, UK: Gower Publishing, 2003.

Moeller, Scott, and Chris Brady. *Intelligent M&A: Navigating the Mergers and Acquisitions Minefield*. Chichester, UK: Wiley, 2007.

Sudarsanam, Sudi. *Creating Value from Mergers and Acquisition: The Challenges*. Harlow, UK: Pearson Education, 2003.

Article:

May, Michael, Patricia Anslinger, and Justin Jenk. "Avoiding the perils of traditional due diligence." *Outlook Journal* (July 2002). Online at: tinyurl.com/67mh4cj [PDF].

Website:

Intelligent Mergers—Scott Moeller's blog: intelligentmergers.com

NOTES

1 Adapted from Fell, Bruce D. "Operational due diligence for value." *Emphasis* (2006/3): 6–9. Online at: tinyurl.com/d7w36t

2 *Ibid.*

"Few things are impossible to diligence and skill." Samuel Johnson

  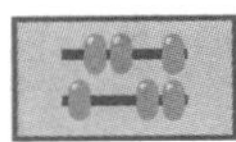      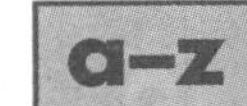

Going Private: Public-to-Private Leveraged Buyouts by Luc Renneboog

EXECUTIVE SUMMARY

- Listed firms go private through a leveraged buyout (LBO)—for example, a management buyout or an institutional buyout).
- Reasons for going private are the value of the tax shield, increased incentives for management through equity ownership, to reduce cash flows, to avoid the direct and indirect costs of maintaining a listing, or as an anti-takeover device.
- At announcement of the LBO of a listed firm, the premium (the offer price relative to the pre-buyout share price) amounts to about 40% and abnormal returns to about 25%.
- Good candidates for LBOs have stable cash flows, low and predictable capital investment needs, a liquid balance sheet with collateralizable assets, an established market position, and are in a recession-proof industry.

INTRODUCTION

When a listed company is acquired and subsequently delisted, the transaction is referred to as a public-to-private or going-private transaction. As most such transactions are financed by substantial borrowing, which is used to repurchase most of the outstanding equity, they are called leveraged buyouts (LBOs). An overview of the different types of LBO is given in Table 1. Four categories are generally recognized: management buyouts (MBOs), management buyins (MBIs), buyin management buyouts (BIMBOs), and institutional buyouts (IBOs).

Table 1. Summary definitions of types of public-to-private transaction

Term	Definition
LBO	*Leveraged buyout.* Acquisition in which a nonstrategic bidder acquires a listed or non-listed company utilizing funds containing a proportion of debt that is substantially above the industry average. If the acquired company is listed, it is subsequently delisted (in a going-private or public-to-private transaction)
MBO	*Management buyout.* An LBO in which the target firm's management bids for control of the firm, often supported by a third-party private equity investor
MBI	*Management buyin.* An LBO in which an outside management team (often backed by a third-party private equity investor) acquires a company and replaces the incumbent management team
BIMBO	*Buyin management buyout.* An LBO in which the bidding team comprises members of the incumbent management team and externally hired managers, often alongside a third-party private equity investor
IBO	*Institutional buyout.* An LBO in which an institutional investor or private equity house acquires a company. Incumbent management can be retained and may be rewarded with equity participation
Reverse LBO	A transaction in which a firm that was previously taken private reobtains public status through a secondary initial public offering (SIPO)

WHY DO LISTED FIRMS GO PRIVATE?

Reduction of Stockholder-Related Agency Costs

The central dilemma of principal-agent models is how to get the manager (the agent) to act in the best interests of the stockholders (the principals) when the agent has interests that diverge from those of the principals and an informational advantage.

- The *incentive realignment* hypothesis states that the gains in stockholder wealth that arise from going private are a result of providing more rewards for managers (through an increased ownership stake) that induce them to act in line with the interests of investors. Furthermore, in the case of an institutional buyout, the concentration of ownership leads to improved monitoring of management.
- The *free cash flow* hypothesis suggests that the expected stock returns follow from debt-induced mechanisms that force managers to pay out free cash flows. Free cash flow is the cash flow in excess of that required to fund all projects that have positive net present value (NPV) when discounted at the appropriate cost of capital. The high leverage does not allow managers to grow the firm beyond its optimal size (so-called "empire building") and at the expense of value creation.

Tax Benefits

The substantial increase in cash flow creates a major tax shield, which increases the pre-transaction (or pre-recapitalization) value. After the buyout, firms pay almost no tax for a period of at least five years. Consequently, the (new) stockholders gain, but the government loses out.

Reduction of Transaction Costs

The cost of maintaining a stock exchange listing is very high. Although the direct costs (fees paid to the stock exchange) are relatively small, the indirect costs of being listed are substantial (for example the cost of complying with corporate governance/-transparency regulations, which requires larger accounting/legal departments, the cost of investor relations managers, and the cost of management time in general, etc.). For a medium-sized listed company these indirect costs are estimated at US$750,000–1,500,000 annually. The going-private transaction eliminates many of the transaction costs.

Wealth Transfers from Bondholders to Stockholders

Gains in stockholder wealth that arise from going private result from the expropriation of value belonging to pre-transaction bondholders. There are three mechanisms through which a firm can transfer wealth from bondholders to stockholders: an unexpected increase in the asset risk (the asset substitution risk); large increases in dividends; or an unexpected issue of debt of higher or equal seniority, or of shorter maturity. In a going-private transaction, the last mechanism in particular can lead to substantial expropriation of bondholder wealth if protective covenants are not in place.

Defense Against Takeover

Afraid of losing their jobs if a hostile suitor takes control, the management may decide to take the company private. Thus, an MBO is the ultimate defensive measure against a hostile stockholder or tender offer.

Undervaluation

As a firm is a portfolio of projects, there may be asymmetric information between the management and outsiders concerning the maximum value that can be realized with the assets in place. If management believes that the share price is undervalued in relation to the firm's true potential, they may privatize the firm through an MBO. Alternatively, if an external party believes that it is able to generate more value with

"We feel unloved. The lack of investor appetite for small company shares... is one of the main reasons for going private." Bill Ainscough

  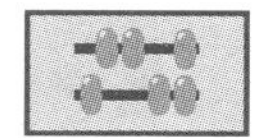      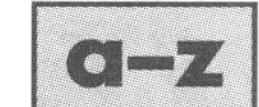

the assets of the firm, the firm may be taken over by means of an IBO or MBI.

HOW HIGH ARE THE PREMIUMS PAID IN LBOS

The premiums (relative to the pre-transaction share price) are in line with those on ordinary takeover transactions: Over last 25 years they have been in the range 35% to 45%. The cumulative average abnormal returns (CAARs) calculated over two months around the event date (the announcement of the going-public transaction) average around 25%, which is similar to those of ordinary takeover transactions. The abnormal returns are equal to the realized returns corrected for the market movement (the return of the market index) and the riskiness of the firm (the beta).

THE PHASES OF THE BUYOUT PROCESS

Figure 1 shows the structure of the buyout process, the main research questions for each phase of the process, and their explanations. The first phase (Intent) consists of the identification of good LBO candidates; the second phase (Impact) comprises the actual LBO and an analysis of the expected returns; the third phase (Process) consists of the value creation while the firm is privately listed; and the fourth phase (Duration) concerns the duration of the private phase until the main shareholder exits through an IPO or trade sale. At every phase, eight main hypotheses or triggers can be examined: realignment of incentives, acquisition of control, reduction of free cash flow, wealth transfers from various stakeholders, tax benefits, a reduction of transaction costs, the importance of takeover defense mechanisms, and undervaluation of the target firm.

What makes firms good buyout candidates? The "Intent" phase encompasses the characteristics of firms prior to their decision to go private and compares these characteristics to those of firms which remain publicly listed. Out of the eight value drivers (mentioned above) to go public in the United States, the reduction in taxation resulting from the tax shield is the main one. Thus, firms with a high tax bill may consider going private with a lot of leverage *provided that* a stable cash flow stream enables the firm to service the debt. In addition, firms with substantial free cash flow (excess cash) that could lead to value-destroying investments have also been shown to be prime candidates for a public-to-private transaction. In the United States, decisions to go private in the 1980s were frequently motivated by anti-takeover defense strategies.

Figure 1. Phases and hypotheses of going private

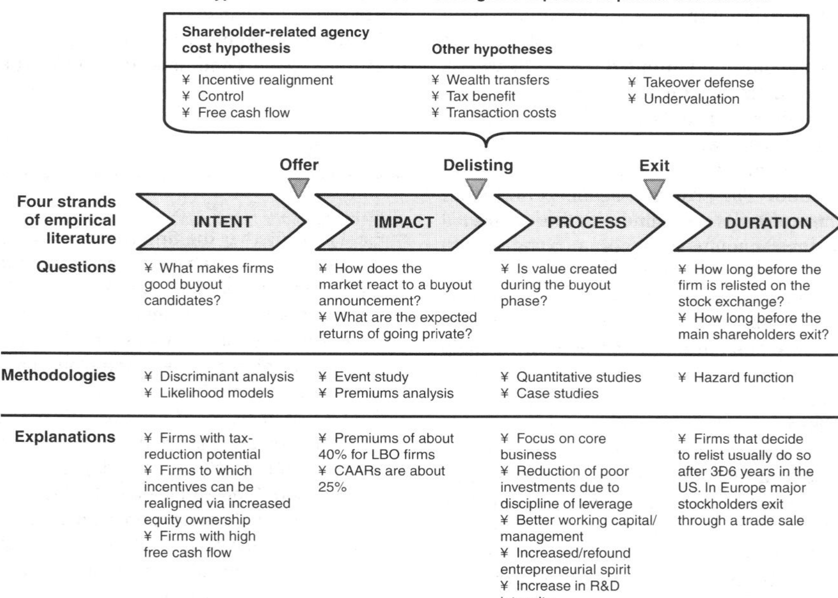

How does the market react to a buyout? The *impact* of an LBO offer can be estimated by analyzing the immediate stock price reaction or the premiums paid to pre-transaction stockholders. The CAARs and premiums reflect the expected value creation when the firm becomes privately held. They are larger at the announcement for firms in which pre-transaction managers hold small equity stakes, which implies that the buyout may induce a realignment of incentives. Furthermore, the fact that the buyout will reduce large free cash flows triggers positive share price returns. Also,

CASE STUDY

Safeway and Kroger

One of the key characteristics of going private through an LBO is the high-leverage structure that results. Nevertheless, the discipline of high leverage can also be induced by a leveraged recapitalization without privatization. Denis (1994) investigated the difference between the two approaches by contrasting two grocery store firms—Kroger, which undertook a recapitalization, and Safeway, which took the LBO route. The higher leverage and the pressure to generate cash led to a performance increase at Kroger, but the performance improvement at Safeway was significantly higher. Why should this have been so?

- Top managers at Safeway put part of their wealth at stake and hold substantial equity stakes (amounting to a total of about 20%) such that every managerial decision has a significant direct impact on their wealth. In addition, management is even more directed towards a focus on value as its bonuses are linked to the market value of assets and managers receive stock options.
- There is a major external stockholder (the private equity firm Kohlberg Kravis Roberts, or KKR) that monitors the firm closely and ensures that management does not maximize its private benefits at the expense of other stockholders and the firm itself.
- Safeway restructured the board to consist of management and representatives of KKR, who provided expertise on corporate restructuring.
- Safeway restructured its operations more drastically than Kroger, closing stores that did not generate sufficient operational cash flows. It also cut back on discretionary expenses, such as advertising and maintenance, to meet its short-term debt obligations, and it cut non-core business.
- Safeway removed leverage-induced cash flow streams as fast as possible through asset sales in order to increase capital expenditures.

"The public company with dispersed ownership suffers from too high a degree of managerial discretion resulting from a lack of monitoring." Renneboog and Simons (2005)

  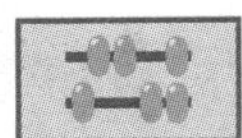      

for firms paying a large amount of tax, the buyout announcement leads to positive abnormal returns. Finally, bondholder wealth transfers appear to exist but are playing only a very limited role in the wealth gains of pre-buyout stockholders.

Is value created during the private phase? Once a company is privatized, what post-buyout processes lead to more wealth creation? The post-transaction performance improvements are in line with those expected at the announcement of a going-private transaction. The causes of the performance and efficiency improvements are primarily the organizational structure of the LBO (high leverage and strong (managerial) ownership concentration). In the private phase, a firm's productivity increases due to a focused strategy and the avoidance of excess growth. Post-buyout performance improvements arise from an improved quality of the R&D function and intensified venturing activities. This revamped entrepreneurial spirit follows from reduced stockholder-related agency costs. Also typical of firms that go private is a significant improvement in the management of working capital.

How long is it before a firm is relisted on the stock exchange? An investor may decide to end a company's private status through an exit via a SIPO (secondary initial public offering, or reverse LBO). Especially in the United States, some firms seem to use the organizational form of a privatization transaction as a temporary shock therapy to enable them to restructure efficiently, while others view the LBO as a sustainable and superior organizational form. Firms that do a reverse LBO have usually been private for three to six years. In Europe, major stockholders usually do not exit via a SIPO but perform a trade sale. The longevity of private ownership and its determinants are studied in the literature on *duration*.

CONCLUSION

Firms that undergo leveraged (management) buyouts have significant advantages over publicly listed firms. First, the high leverage creates value through the tax shield. Second, the management is incentivized to focus on value creation because it (co-) owns the firm (in the case of a MBO/MBI) or because strict monitoring of the incumbent management is induced by the major stockholders (in the case of an IBO). The organizational structure reduces the firm's free cash flow such that money is not squandered by investing in negative-NPV projects. The private status of the firm requires little information disclosure compared to a listed firm, which allows the firm to avoid expenses related to compliance with the regulations on corporate governance/transparency.

It should be emphasized that not every firm is a good candidate for LBO. The requirements are: stable cash flows, low and predictable capital investment needs, a liquid balance sheet with collateralizable assets, an established market position, and being in a recession-proof industry.

MAKING IT HAPPEN

- Establish whether the firm is a suitable candidate for privatization via an LBO:
  - Does it have a stable stream of operational cash flows that is sufficient to service the post-transaction debt even in a recession?
  - Does it have a large debt cushion, and liquid and collateralizable assets?
  - Does it have, and will it be able to maintain, a stable market share?
  - Is the economic value of the plant, property, and equipment high, and is future capital expenditure modest?
- Contact an investment bank or LBO specialist (private equity group) to write a prospectus that contains the valuation of the company and maps the risks.
- Take on bank debt (issue bonds) to finance the deal and buy out the pre-transaction stockholders (and bondholders). This results in a small equity stake and a capital structure that has 70–80% of debt on total assets.
- Once it has been privatized, restructure the firm (for example through asset sales), focus on the core business, improve the efficiency of its operations, and increase the efficiency of working capital management.

MORE INFO

Books:

Amihud, Yakov (ed). *Leveraged Management Buyouts: Causes and Consequences*. Washington, DC: Beard Books, 2002.

Wright, Mike, and Hans Bruining (eds). *Private Equity and Management Buy-Outs*. Cheltenham, UK: Edward Elgar, 2008.

Articles:

Denis, David J. "Organizational form and the consequences of highly leveraged transactions: Kroger's recapitalization and Safeway's LBO." *Journal of Financial Economics* 36:2 (October 1994): 193–224. Online at: dx.doi.org/10.1016/0304-405X(94)90024-8

Renneboog, Luc, Tomas Simons, and Mike Wright. "Why do public firms go private in the UK? The impact of private equity investors, incentive realignment and undervaluation." *Journal of Corporate Finance* 13:4 (September 2007): 591–628. Online at: dx.doi.org/10.1016/j.jcorpfin.2007.04.005

Simons, Tomas, and Luc Renneboog. "Public-to-private transactions: LBOs, MBOs, MBIs and IBOs." Working paper no. 94/2005, European Corporate Governance Institute, August 2005. Online at: ssrn.com/abstract=796047

Wright, Mike, Luc Renneboog, Tomas Simons, and Louise Scholes. "Leveraged buyouts in the UK and continental Europe: Retrospect and prospect." *Journal of Applied Corporate Finance* 18:3 (Summer 2006): 38–55. Online at: dx.doi.org/10.1111/j.1745-6622.2006.00097.x

Websites:

The MBO Guide: www.mboguide.co.uk

Nottingham University Centre for Management Buy-Out Research: www.nottingham.ac.uk/business/cmbor

See Also:

★ Comparing Net Present Value and Internal Rate of Return (pp. 30–32)
✔ Corporate Governance Practices in Private Equity-Owned Firms (p. 1112)
✔ Raising Capital through Private and Public Equity (p. 1088)
✔ Understanding Anti-Takeover Strategies (p. 1136)

"Financial distress represents a forced exit: over the last 20 years, 12% of the 12,267 UK buyouts entered protection from creditors." Renneboog *et al.* (2006)

  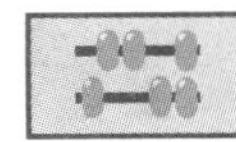      

Grow Globally: The New Altitude of Cross-Border M&A by Mona Pearl

EXECUTIVE SUMMARY

- Three out of five cross-border M&A deals do not live up to expectations, mainly due to culture clash, poor due diligence, and contrasting management styles.
- With the growing trend of cross-border transactions, post M&A failure can be eliminated with systematic M&A due-diligence.
- While most firms focus on fundamental "hard" challenges such as infrastructure, EBIDTA, ROI, and more, 80% of the risks associated with international M&A derive from "soft" challenges such as cultural integration.
- The skills required to negotiate successfully in one's own country do not necessarily translate to success abroad. The key is to identify which skills cross over, which skills require retooling, and which skills are simply missing from the toolbox.
- Knowledge and understanding of the business operations and finance of the target company, no matter how in-depth, will not compensate for lack of cultural understanding in the negotiating process.
- Successful negotiations only occur when both sides understand and trust each other and are willing and able to engage in a process of meaningful information exchange. Therefore, getting the right advisory team to help with focal points and issues in different regions of the world is crucial.
- From the very first stages of negotiation, and certainly before a letter of intent has been entered into, the parties in a cross-border transaction must think carefully about their legal assumptions and question whether they apply before coming to the negotiating table.
- Following basic guidelines will help prevent late-stage cultural problems from derailing an otherwise sound international M&A transaction.

INTRODUCTION

Companies choose to undertake a merger or acquisition (M&A) for a variety of strategic reasons: to access new markets and expand their global footprint, obtain new technology, new brands, complementary products, access to experienced management, or to remove a competitor or potential competitor. Over the past decade, M&A activity has increased substantially as this route is a natural progression for businesses that are gaining experience and confidence abroad.

The global crisis did further fuel the M&A frenzy as sellers are generally more distressed and, therefore, more inclined to consider this route. Also, there is less competition from buyers in the seller's home country, and, most importantly, prices have fallen to attractive levels.

However, the picture isn't as rosy as we may wish to see. Rise up, stretch, and rub the green dollar signs from your eyes. Three out of five deals do not live up to expectations, mainly due to culture clash, poor due diligence, misalignment of strategic goals with the market reality, and contrasting management styles, but also to a myriad of other pitfalls.

This article serves as a focal point for businesses planning to enter into the world of M&A, as well as a troubleshooting guide for the ones already working in that space who are having difficulties. *Success* is considered to mean a post-M&A integration of both companies where they continue to do well by capitalizing on growth while pursuing as well as adapting the goals they planned to pursue at the outset. Successful companies integrate M&A with a strategy that starts with due diligence and continues through negotiations to a post-integration phase that has been investigated and planned ahead.

So, how should companies avoid the hasty pre-deal planning that turns so many of today's M&A transactions into disasters?

STRATEGIC ALIGNMENT

For some, the world is flat; others say it is a bumpy and curved world. Whatever the terrain, there is one major change that companies are having an extremely hard time planning for: designing a new kind of global strategy which focuses on the ability to change in almost a moment's notice, and still maintain the action plan as an integrated unit. Sounds like a contradiction? Maybe, but it is the new reality as events in the world force companies to redefine the meaning of strategic planning, and therefore, the way companies should see the global playground.

For many companies, cross-border M&A is a new altitude they need to manage. Like high-altitude climbing differs from many other pursuits because of the constant threat of danger and potential death, so do many successful leaders in national markets feel about global markets; the potential risk, the daunting idea of failure, and the unknowns. The difference is that elite high-altitude climbers mentally prepare for the climb while maintaining an effective focus on the mountain. They keep their eyes open, looking up, reaching the new altitude. They know they need to acquire new skills to reach the top.

DUE DILIGENCE

Start With the End Game in Mind

Pursuing expansion and growth in the global market requires a whole new realm of due diligence and risk assessment, or should we relate to it as opportunity assessment? That's proving to be a significant obstacle for most businesses. Acquiring or merging with a foreign company is much more than a business deal based primarily on the numbers. In fact, the numbers are generally known well in advance and rarely become deal-breakers later in the game. Rather, the critical issues in the due diligence phase (though it does include some aspects of valuation) are strategic and cultural in nature. Success in this area requires dealing effectively with differences in corporate culture, maintaining the loyalty of the employees, stakeholders, and customers of a foreign company, and gaining an understanding of that company's human and business values.

While most firms focus on fundamental "hard" challenges such as infrastructure, EBIDTA, ROI, and more, 80% of the risks associated with international M&A derive from "soft" challenges such as cultural integration. Understanding a corporate culture along with the culture of a country or region play a crucial role in determining the long-term success of an M&A deal.

As we face a higher volume, a greater degree of complexity, more competition, and change that transcends borders, industries, and disciplines, companies will need a new kind of expertise to thrive in the new reality. How will you fill the gap? More people, different people, or a different way to operate?

Today, most companies are operating in a manual-like, old-fashioned way: follow the crowd, neglecting to align company capability with target market. The degree and complexity has never been greater, and it is going to grow, so how about simplifying your approach and

"This extraordinary arrogance that change must start at the top is a way of guaranteeing that change will not happen in most companies." Gary Hamel

  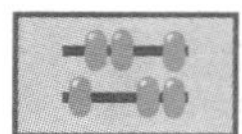      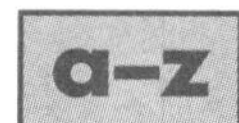

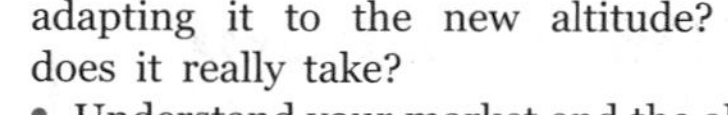

adapting it to the new altitude? What does it really take?

- Understand your market and the altitude of your customer, decision makers, and other crucial factors.
- Know how to attach the importance of global strategic planning to some of the converging factors that are going on.
- Deal with disruptions in the business level: how do you plan to utilize them and pull them through?
- Are you going to engage in "trendjacking"? Either create your own trend and deliver on it or trendjack an existing one? Do you know enough?

Due diligence on a global scale requires a company to go beyond traditional M&A work and consider variables that may be unfamiliar to most companies and business people. It means obtaining relevant, detailed information and advice concerning the political, national, corporate, and human culture of the target company, as well as the ability to interpret the relevance of this information to their business operations. This means using a holistic approach that can be painful at times. The information, sometimes imperceptible for some, for others are very clear; but it requires careful interpretation if it is to be transformed into a road map.

This is an area where doing things the way you are used to just may not work. There is a need to operate and think different than in-country. Ignoring or misunderstanding these issues can leave a company's M&A initiative dead in the water.

Start Looking in the Right Places

Contracts, labor and employment law, profits, EBIDTA, and potential ROI may be obvious matters, but these considerations represent just the tip of the iceberg—the visible tip. Underneath the water and hidden from view is where real danger lurks. For example, there are a myriad of less well known social norms, including methods of communication, chains of command, power relations, ethics, and pace of life, to name just a few. In many countries it's important to understand seniority and to whom questions must be addressed. With so much at stake, it's worth the investment of resources to prepare, train, and develop those who will be conducting the due diligence abroad as well as making sure that they will ask the right questions and look for the answers in the right places. Better still, engage an expert to help anticipate probable issues so that preparations are completed properly and surprises are eliminated.

Cultural Due Diligence

While all M&A require bridging the differences between corporate cultures, this exercise becomes even more daunting when you add in the effects of national cultural differences, distance, and language barriers.

In many cross-border M&A deals, the effort involved in cultural integration proves more difficult and just takes longer than expected. Part of the problem stems from the strictures of "political correctness," which discourage any overt references to national differences out of a fear of creating offense. Other problems arise from a lack of understanding of the basic rules that govern how business is conducted in different cultures. For example, when working with Japanese colleagues, anyone who fails to understand the importance of maintaining the appearance of harmony and agreement (even when neither actually exists) risks creating serious discomfort among coworkers or causing offense at meetings with behavior that would otherwise be viewed as perfectly acceptable.

Factor In

Too often, the real difficulties and challenges of M&A surface months after deals are signed. Then the tough questions-that should have been addressed in the front-end due diligence process-start flowing. For example:

- How will this newly acquired enterprise be integrated into the existing company?
- Will it operate independently or as a division?
- How will the integration be made as smooth and seamless as possible?
- How will the acquiring company deal with duplicate departments, systems, and vendors?
- How will the new business be operated the day after that deal was sealed?
- Will this organizational structure produce loyalty?
- Will the employees and managers stay?
- What will the local reaction be to any proposed changes?
- What is the new competitive landscape?
- Determine how the target company operates in a broader, human-capital sense.
- How will its customers and employees view a foreign company moving on to their turf?
- What is the work ethic of the employees?
- How is productivity viewed, measured, and maintained?
- What is the management style in the country, region, and of the company?
- Which are the company's main competitors?
- How stable is the political environment?
- Last but not least: are there any FCPA issues that may arise as a result of the above points of reference?

The answers to these questions and many others come from gathering the right information through due-diligence in a cultural context, and having a strategic plan, i.e. how will the company operate in the new structure from day one? Companies need to look internally at their strengths and weaknesses in relation to their action plan. That means evaluating corporate resources, manpower, internal knowledge, and their own culture (perception, loyalty, motivation) before determining whether expansion opportunities are viable and warrant penetration into new markets.

NEGOTIATION

The Importance of Cultural Tune In

Beware: the skills required to negotiate successfully in your own country do not necessarily translate to success abroad. In fact, past strengths can be future weaknesses on the international stage. The key is to identify which skills cross over, which skills require retooling, and which skills are simply missing from the toolbox. Most importantly, business people should never assume that knowledge and understanding of the business operations and finance of the target company, no matter how in-depth, will compensate for lack of cultural understanding in the negotiating process. It won't. Cultural awareness is no longer a nice skill to have; it's essential for success overseas.

For example, negotiation, as it is understood in the United States, is the process by which interested parties resolve disputes, agree on courses of action, bargain for an individual or collective advantage, and attempt to fashion outcomes that serve mutual interests. Internationally, however, negotiating has much more to do with understanding people and their customs and developing relationships. Unfortunately, many US executives are unfamiliar with this dance and mistakenly launch directly into the technical phase of negotiations. Such short-circuiting of the negotiating process will lead to frustration, disappointment, squandered resources, and lost opportunities.

The Art of Negotiating Across Borders

After months of preparation to enter the global marketplace—including extensive market analysis, identification of a target market, numerous product modifications, and the development of an elaborate market entry strategy—it's finally time to seal the deal! But not so fast. Sealing that deal successfully will require tremendous finesse in terms of international negotiation skills. The fact is

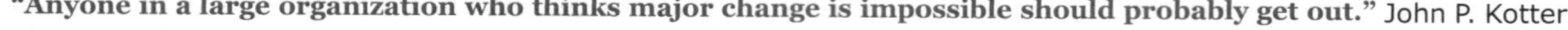

  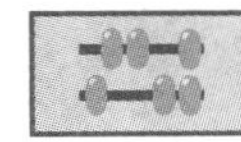      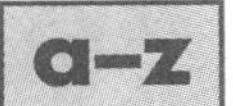

that cross-cultural negotiations can make or break even the most carefully executed global expansion efforts. Not to mention, for example, that both Asian and European countries have, as a matter of survival, developed expertise in negotiating in an international marketplace and are light-years ahead of the United States in this proficiency.

Be Aware of Differing Legal Frameworks and Assumptions

In significant cross-border transactions, the parties will almost always be assisted by legal counsel who can help their clients with negotiations. These advisors can be invaluable, as they bring experience, as well as specific legal knowledge, to the negotiating table.

That said, it is important for a business person to understand his or her own relationship with the foreign legal framework and to constantly question the assumptions at work. Although we tend not to think about it, we carry our legal culture with us. In other words, while most sophisticated business people understand that laws and accounting rules may vary in foreign countries, they tend not to focus on the fact that the legal assumptions underlying transaction negotiations also vary. The result is that even when assisted by top legal counsel, business people may not be able to use them effectively because they do not question their underlying assumptions about the legal framework.

This can best be illustrated by example. In the United States, one of the basic assumptions that business people bring to the negotiating table is that "freedom of contract" prevails. In other words, by and large they assume that if the two parties willingly agree to certain terms and conditions, they can be enforced. It is therefore an unpleasant surprise for the US business person when he or she finds that certain agreements entered into are unenforceable—even if the other party wants the agreements enforced as well. In specific instances, legal counsel will advise on the applicable law, but by that point the business person may have lost negotiating power on the issue involved. Having gotten the foreign party to agree to a particular issue after long negotiations, they must now throw out their agreement and start from scratch!

In emerging markets, increasing wages and social benefit obligations may not be deal breakers, but it is critical that these and other human capital costs be included and played under several scenarios for a number of years if a buyer is to get a more realistic picture of a target company's value and of future integration issues. The lack of transparency combined with the greater overlap between political, regulatory, and economic policies in emerging markets adds to the nature of unpredictability, and therefore requires more due diligence, data points, and sensitivity to cultural nuances.

The more a country falls into the category of emerging market, the more likely it is that political red tape will slow the pace of progress, as well as labor laws that may vary from one jurisdiction to another. Other issues may include the limit on the number of foreign nationals that can be brought in to assume key responsibilities, and there is of course the issue of local employee loyalty and how to maintain it. US firms face the Sarbanes–Oxley issue, since most companies in the emerging markets are not obliged to comply with that regulation.

All of this means that from the very first stages of negotiation, and certainly before a letter of intent has been entered into, the parties in a cross-border transaction must think carefully about their legal assumptions and question whether they apply before coming to the negotiating table. Legal counsel can certainly assist in this endeavor, but it is up to the business person to raise the issues in a timely manner. Such successful negotiations only occur when both sides understand and trust each other and are willing and able to engage in a process of meaningful information exchange. Although it may sound simple, it isn't.

POST-MERGER INTEGRATION: CAN IT BE DONE?

Most international deals fall through in the later, integrative stages of a merger or acquisition. Initial price negotiations, while certainly important, are rarely, if ever, the primary reason for failure. More often than not, it is the *cultural* evaluation of a target company that creates problems. Will its employees remain loyal? What motivates them? How about the customers? How will these issues affect operations and the business's chances of future success?

A well planned post-M&A integration enables:

- companies to achieve business objectives;
- the business to grow more rapidly.

Failure at this stage causes:

- lost customers;
- lost employees;
- lost focus on the core business;
- damaged image in the marketplace;
- reluctance to undertake future M&A deals.

Years ago Michael Porter argued that most cross-border ventures were bound to fail mainly due to cultural issues. To emphasize the cultural effect, Prof. Geert Hofstede says that culture is more often a source of conflict than of synergy. Cultural differences are a nuisance at best and often a disaster. Integrating after an acquisition is hard, and is the reason that failure is common. This is especially true since it involves emotional and personal factors that are embedded in one's cultural background and beliefs. The facts of the matter are that:

- Two years after an acquisition, the vast majority of acquisitions fail to meet pre-acquisition objectives.
- Three years after an acquisition, a mere 12% of companies grow more quickly than they did before.

Unsurprisingly, it has become a widely accepted belief that the rate of success in the post-merger phase remains poor because of the difficulties of culturally integrating the two companies involved. Constrained by the limited time in which it has to obtain results and by lack of planning, the acquiring company seeks to imprint its own culture on the acquired company. It seems as if the challenging issues come as a surprise, rather than being addressed during the due diligence stage.

AVOID CULTURAL PITFALLS AND SEAL THE DEAL

Here are additional basic guidelines to help prevent late-stage cultural problems from derailing an otherwise sound cross-border initiative:

- *Practice cultural due diligence.* Determine how the target company operates in a broader, human-capital sense. How will customers and employees view a foreign company moving on to their turf?
- *Align internal and external teams* in order to preserve continuity and create a healthy foundation for collaboration.
- *Make a strong commitment.* Peter Drucker once said that "Unless commitment is made, there are only promises and hopes... but no plans." Management must be on-board one hundred per cent—on both sides! Developing an international market requires enormous energy, knowledge, managerial buy-in, and an understanding of business practices in other countries. Few, if any, companies have the resources to go it alone. They'll need a global lens and the assistance of people experienced in global business transactions.
- *Be humble.* The brash, pushy approach of the rugged American business person doesn't cut it in the global arena. Successful international business leaders possess a quiet, respectful humility combined with a passion for learning, understanding, and even practicing how people in other cultures live, work, and like to be rewarded. Customers in different countries have unique ways of relating to products and services. Their lifestyles vary greatly, along with their

     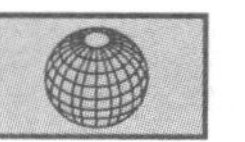   

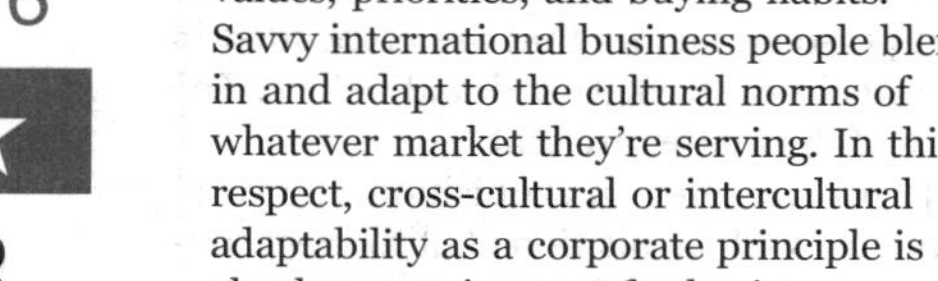

values, priorities, and buying habits. Savvy international business people blend in and adapt to the cultural norms of whatever market they're serving. In this respect, cross-cultural or intercultural adaptability as a corporate principle is an absolute requirement for business survival and long-term profitability.

- *Educate your people on cross-cultural communication.* Research shows that communication between culturally different organizations is often plagued by prejudice and stereotyping on the part of the acquiring company's managers. Poor or insensitive communication between managers and the target company's employees can absolutely derail an international venture's chances of success. On the other hand, with proper cross-cultural training, these problems can be minimized or prevented altogether.
- *Get help.* Seek guidance from an experienced, hands-on international business expert—someone who thoroughly understands how to do business internationally and in that specific region. Such a professional should be keenly sensitive to the national and corporate cultures of both the client and target countries. For example, what does it mean when foreign business executives go quiet at a key meeting? Are they in agreement? Disagreement? Feeling insulted? Or just trying to hide their laughter? How does the country's ethical system differ from your own country's? Is corruption rampant? Will you be competing with businesses owned by relatives of the country's president? (Good luck—you'll need it!) Although there are no guarantees in any business venture, the right international business expert can make a dramatic difference to one's ultimate success.

CONCLUSION: WALK THE WALK, TALK THE TALK

So you identified the target to acquire, and your corporate development person and CPA made sure the numbers work. Then your attorneys made sure you comply with the legal guidelines, and your tech people figured a way to integrate the systems. Most chances are that the major hurtles are still to come. Cultural disconnects are among the leading causes of failed M&A, which then leads to major losses and can be one fundamental that can make or break the deal. How does a company determine what's important/material? A company needs to understand the business strategy and how to run it in the target country; how the strategy is implemented and how its key stakeholders are related to the strategy–customers and markets, products, vendors, employees (operational, technical/engineering, etc).

Don't neglect to ask the right questions, do research, gather data, and analyze information carefully in order to establish a specific strategy and a comprehensive plan for international expansion and integration. Neglecting these is why more than half of global M&A ventures end in failure, squandering valuable resources.

Companies need to be prepared, ready, and willing to get in the game wherever opportunity presents itself around the world. Once you are there, get in tune with the culture. Be ready to learn, be willing to observe, and be accepting of new ways of conducting business. Inevitably, this new dynamic will put certain companies up against companies from other nations with far more international experience. But that's no reason to hold back. As you gain experience and master the ability to analyze, assess, evaluate, understand, and negotiate with other cultures, you too will become a fierce competitor in the world marketplace.

Penetrating, developing, and operating in international markets require an entrepreneurial philosophy and drive—the same kind of philosophy and drive behind every successful startup business. Companies must develop highly flexible business models that enable them to respond to new opportunities and threats. A new process for planning and continuous assessment, to include new tools and an elevated approach, will be necessary for success in the global arena.

When trying to reach a higher altitude, you need different equipment with you to better navigate, view, and move forward. Also, not everybody can operate at a different altitude. From the lowest place in the world to some with the highest elevation, people react in different ways: hypoxia, fainting, blood pressure, and so on. It also takes time to acclimate, and again, people need different timeframes. So, when we apply this logic to the business world, companies need to prepare for this new altitude: make sure the company has the necessary resources to make it; practice and train while being nimble and flexible.

MORE INFO

Books:

Buono, Anthony F., and James L. Bowditch. *The Human Side of Mergers and Acquisitions. Managing Collisions Between People, Cultures and Organizations*. London: Jossey-Bass, 1989.

Hofstede, Geert. *Culture's Consequences: International Differences in Work-Related Values*. Beverly Hills, CA: Sage, 1980.

Marks, Kenneth H., Robert T. Slee, Christian W. Blees, and Michael R. Nall. *Middle Market M & A: Handbook for Investment Banking and Business Consulting*. Hoboken, NJ: Wiley, 2012.

Pearl, Mona. *Grow Globally: Opportunities for Your Middle Market Company Around the World.* Hoboken, NJ: Wiley, 2011.

Rosenbloum, Arthur H. *Due Diligence for Global Deal Making: The Definitive Guide to Cross-Border Mergers and Acquisitions, Joint Ventures, Financings, and Strategic Alliances*. Princeton, NJ: Bloomberg Press, 2002.

Articles:

Brannen, Mary Yoko, and Mark F. Peterson. "Merging without alienating: interventions promoting cross-cultural organizational integration and their limitations." *Journal of International Business Studies* 40:3 (April 2009): 468–489. Online at: dx.doi.org/10.1057/jibs.2008.80

Capron, Laurence, and Nathalie Pistre. "When do acquirers earn abnormal returns?" *Strategic Management Journal* 23:9 (September 2008): 781–795. Online at: dx.doi.org/10.1002/smj.262

Porter, Michael E. "From competitive advantage to corporate strategy." *Harvard Business Review* 65:3 (May 1987): 43–59. Online at: tinyurl.com/434jzzl

Websites:

Geert Hofstede Cultural Dimensions: www.geert-hofstede.com

Association for Corporate Growth (ACG): www.acg.org

ISI Emerging Markets DealWatch: www.securities.com/dw

See Also:

★ Acquisition Integration: How to Do It Successfully (pp. 708–709)

★ Cultural Alignment and Risk Management: Developing the Right Culture (pp. 724–726)

★ Maximizing a New Strategic Alliance (pp. 749–750)

★ Mergers and Acquisitions: Patterns, Motives, and Strategic Fit (pp. 759–762)

★ Why Mergers Fail and How to Prevent It (pp. 772–773)

✔ The Rationale for an Acquisition (p. 1134)

"Blameless people are always the most exasperating." George Eliot

  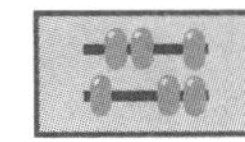     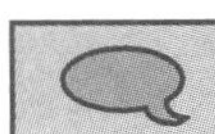 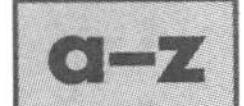

How to Set the Hurdle Rate for Capital Investments by Jon Tucker

EXECUTIVE SUMMARY

- There exists a wide range of approaches to setting the hurdle rate for capital investments.
- It is essential that we do not set the hurdle rate too high, thereby foregoing valuable investment opportunities, or too low, thereby destroying value for shareholders.
- While academics tend to advocate a series of, at times, complex adjustments, most CFOs settle for a relatively simple approach, and allow for complexity instead in their cash flow projections.
- The most common approach is to employ a CAPM-based equity cost as an input to a WACC calculation.
- A company-wide hurdle rate is typically employed by companies, although adjustments are made for projects of atypical risk.

INTRODUCTION

Chief financial officers are charged with the task of maximizing shareholder wealth. They do this by pursuing two key goals: Maximizing the stream of future cash flows, and minimizing the company's cost of capital. Cognizant of the separation theorem, we tend to separate one goal from the other. However, both are of strategic importance—a healthy stream of cash flows can actually destroy value (and hence reduce shareholder wealth) if the company suffers from a high cost of capital. In a very real sense, then, a company's cost of capital represents an important "hurdle," which its portfolio of projects must exceed in order to create wealth for shareholders. Clearly, the cost of capital, as implied by the company's financing mix, is a good starting point when arriving at the hurdle rate for capital investment appraisal (capital budgeting), but the way in which the company arrives at this cost of capital, and the adjustments made thereafter to arrive at the hurdle rate, warrant further explanation.

HURDLE RATE: A DEFINITION

The hurdle rate is the required rate of return on investment appraisal, above which an investment project is worth pursuing. We know when computing a project's net present value (NPV) that if the discount rate exceeds the project's internal rate of return (IRR), then we should not proceed with the project. The starting point for the hurdle rate is, then, the company's cost of capital, to which a company may then decide to make some adjustment for that project's specific risk, perhaps adding a risk premium. The difficulty for practitioners is that there exists a wide variation of approaches to arriving at the hurdle rate—even academics cannot agree on the best way forward.

Some examples of the difficulties involved are: How do we arrive at the cost of equity capital? How do we arrive at the cost of debt and other financing components? Do we employ the weighted average cost of capital (WACC), or some other metric, to arrive at the cost of capital? If we do employ the WACC, how do we weight the cost of each financing component? What additional adjustment do we make for risk? We will tackle each of these issues in turn, and explore the broad alternative approaches available to the CFO.

THE COST OF EQUITY

There are a variety of ways in which CFOs tend to compute the cost of equity capital. The most prominent and widely employed approach is the capital asset pricing model (CAPM):[1]

$$r_e = r_f + \beta(r_m - r_f)$$

where:
r_e = the expected cost of equity capital for a company;
r_f = the risk-free rate of return;
β = the share beta;
r_m = the return on the market portfolio;
$r_m - r_f$ = the expected premium offered by the market portfolio over and above the risk-free rate.

However, we encounter a number of difficulties with this approach in a practical setting. Which risk-free rate should be employed—a three-month Treasury bill rate, or a long-term government bond rate? Most academics would suggest the latter, although in practice, the three-month rate is often employed. Should CFOs compute their own beta coefficient, or employ a beta computed by data agencies such as Bloomberg? This is a matter of personal choice, although in practice most companies probably employ an externally published source. What equity risk premium should be employed, and is it realistic in terms of expectations? We could apply an average historical risk premium here, or even estimate the rate implied by current asset prices. Further, if we compute our own average historical premium figure, then applying the geometric average premium is probably the best approach. Each of these issues could warrant a chapter to itself—in the real world, CFOs arrive at a CAPM-based equity cost of capital after much debate within the company, and consultation with their external corporate advisers (such as investment banks). Academics have extended the CAPM to a multi-factor framework to better capture equity risk, adding size and book-to-market factors, although in practice it is unlikely that companies employ such models extensively.

An alternative approach is to employ an earnings model to arrive at the cost of equity capital, that is, to compute the price-to-earnings (PE) ratio (or earnings yield) for a company. This is a relatively simple procedure, given the wide availability of PE ratios, and the broad understanding and use of asset yields in the financial media, although it is most appropriately employed for non-growth companies. The cost of equity, then, is equal to the inverse of the PE ratio:

$$r_e = \frac{E}{P}$$

where:
r_e = the company's cost of equity capital;
E = the company's earnings;
P = the company's share price.

A further alternative is to arrive at the cost of equity capital by means of a simple dividend model. When we rearrange the dividend model, the cost of equity capital equals the expected dividend yield (D_1/P_0) plus the constant compound growth rate of dividends, the latter often based on past trends as a proxy for growth expectations:

$$r_e = \frac{D_1}{P_0} + g$$

where:
r_e = the company's cost of equity capital;
D_1 = the dividend in year 1;
P_0 = the company's share price in year 0;
g = the growth rate of dividends.

In the real world, CFOs should probably compute a cost of equity using all three approaches, benchmark their rate with other companies in their industry (which

"It is extremely important that you show some insensitivity to your past in order to show the proper respect for the future." Roberto Goizueta

are likely to have similar betas, business models, and enjoy similar access to financial markets), and only then settle on a suitable figure. In the case of pure equity-financed companies, the cost of equity capital is, by definition, the pivotal figure in arriving at the hurdle rate.

THE COST OF DEBT

A minority of companies set their overall cost of capital at the cost of debt. However, even the cost of debt presents a number of interesting issues to the CFO. First, do we employ the historical cost of debt, or the more meaningful expected cost of debt? Do we look at the cost of total debt, thereby including the cost of short-term debt, or do we focus upon the cost of long-term debt? Regardless of these variations, we certainly need to take into account the tax advantage to debt arising from the deductibility of debt interest payments (whereas equity enjoys no such advantage). Even here, we face an added complication—do we apply a tax advantage based upon statutory corporate tax rates, or marginal rates? Many CFOs will, in practice, employ a long-term debt rate, expressed after tax, based on the marginal corporate tax rate. Further, for the purposes of economic consistency, debt should also include lease obligations. If a company is bond-financed, and there is an active market for those bonds, then the yield to maturity is the appropriate rate, whereas with non-traded debt (such as bank loans) the stated interest rate is the appropriate rate.

CASE STUDY

Determining the Hurdle Rate for a Food Retailer

Company X plc is a FTSE 100 food and drug retailer, listed on the UK stock exchange. The market value of its capital structure components is £12 billion for equity, and £8 billion for debt. The β computed by a reputable data agency is 0.9. The UK 3-month Treasury bill rate is 4.5%, and you estimate that the market tends to pay a premium over and above this rate, of 4.7%. The UK corporate tax rate is 30%, and the rate paid by the company on its 10-year bonds is 5.5%.

We start by computing X plc's cost of equity capital:

$$r_e = r_f + \beta(r_m - r_f)$$
$$= 4.5\% + 0.9(4.7\%) = 8.73\%$$

We then compute the proportions of debt and equity in the company's capital structure:

$$\frac{D}{D+E} = 40\% \text{ and } \frac{D}{D+E} = 60\%$$

We can then compute its weighted average cost of capital:

$$\text{WACC} = \left(\frac{D}{D+E}\right) r_d(1 - T_c) + \left(\frac{E}{D+E}\right) r_e$$
$$= 40\% \times 5.5\% \times (1-0.30) + 60\% \times 8.73\% = 6.78\%$$

Company X plc applies a hurdle rate of 6.78% to projects of average risk, but adds a margin for projects of higher risk such as an investment in a new product line (+5%) or a company acquisition (+10%).

THE WEIGHTED AVERAGE COST OF CAPITAL

The WACC is simply the average discount rate applied by the debt-holders and equity-holders of the company to its future cash flows. Discounting the stream of a project's future cash flows by the WACC gives us the capitalized value of that project, whereas so doing for the company's total cash flows gives us the capitalized value of the entire company.

We compute the WACC as follows:

$$\text{WACC} = \left(\frac{D}{D+E}\right) r_d(1 - T_c) + \left(\frac{E}{D+E}\right) r_e$$

where:
WACC = the weighted average cost of capital;
D = the market value of debt;
E = the market value of equity;
r_d = the company's cost of debt capital;
r_e = the company's cost of equity capital;
T_c = the corporate tax rate.

The WACC for a company, then, is simply the cost of the company's financing components (r_d and r_e), weighted by the proportion of those components in the company's capital structure ($D/(D + E)$ and $E/(D + E)$, respectively). We can easily extend this expression for additional forms of financing by weighting them by their proportion in the company's capital structure. The correct approach to weighting here is to compute the market value of each component as a proportion of the total market value of all claims against the company. Note that the cost of debt is effectively reduced by virtue of the fact that there is a tax advantage to debt, as discussed earlier, hence the cost is not r_d but $r_d\ (1 - T_c)$. This merely reflects the calculation of the corporate tax liability after debt interest costs have been deducted. Employing the WACC as the basis for the hurdle rate makes intuitive sense, as the company must ensure that it is exceeding, on average, the average rate of return required by all of its claimholders. If it is not, then it is destroying value for shareholders.

DEALING WITH RISK

As a general rule, the company should consider investing in projects that generate returns which are higher than the company's hurdle rate. Further, the hurdle rate should be higher for riskier projects than for safer projects.

How do we adjust for risk then? We could adjust the hurdle rate for numerous project characteristics, including: The size of the project, the division within which the project is located, whether the project will be at home or overseas, whether the project is new or existing, and so on. The simplest approach is to apply a company-wide cost of capital as the hurdle rate. The dangers of this approach, however, are that the project under consideration may be more or less risky than the "average" risk of the company's portfolio of investment projects. Large projects are often scrutinized more carefully than smaller projects, given their more material impact on the company's cash flows, and a premium for risk is added to the cost of capital figure to arrive at an appropriate hurdle rate. Most companies add a premium over and above the domestic project hurdle rate for foreign investments. New projects are more risky than existing projects, and should therefore reflect a premium over and above the observed earnings yield of an existing project investment. Ventures such as mergers are more risky still, and thus their returns should exceed a much higher hurdle rate before being sanctioned. Some companies employ a sliding scale of discount rates, depending on a project's nature—discount rates increase as we move from equipment upgrading, through expansion of existing business lines, through new project investments, to more speculative projects.[2]

"The inevitability of gradualness." Sidney Webb (Lord Passfield)

In the real world, some practitioners argue that we cannot expect the hurdle rate to "take all of the strain" when adjusting for risk. Instead, many argue that the project cash flows themselves should be adjusted for risk to achieve a more realistic estimation of a project's IRR or NPV. Project risk will have a differential impact on the range of cash inflows and outflows and, therefore, a risk-adjusted hurdle rate does not always adequately deal with risk—it can be too blunt an instrument. A carefully computed hurdle rate, in conjunction with risk-adjusted cash flows, and a comprehensive scenario analysis, might be the best way forward, taking care not to double-count risk in the process.

However, presuming that we do indeed employ a hurdle rate which captures risk in some objective and appropriate manner, one way of assuring a more robust approach to capital investment appraisal is to accept only those projects with the highest IRRs, that is, those that exceed the hurdle rate by the highest margin. This may be necessary for most companies in the real world, anyway, in the presence of limited investment funds, and capital rationing.

FREQUENCY OF REVISION

Given the real-world complexity and strategic sensitivity of the hurdle rate figure, it is likely that most companies do not revise the rate on a very frequent basis, often maintaining the same figure for months, or even as long as a year. Events which may encourage CFOs to take another look at the company-wide hurdle rate might include changes in the returns required by investors (such as interest-rate changes), the consideration of major projects, and the prospect of corporate restructuring. Major corporate restructuring has an impact not only on the profile of future cash flows, but also on the returns required by both existing and new claimholders in relation to those cash flows. Given the strategic importance of the hurdle rate, it is typically decided at the level of the board of directors, who take the advice of the CFO, and his/her advisers (consultants, bankers, and so on).

CONCLUSION

In the real world, most practitioners have little appetite for adjusting the hurdle rate for the multitude of factors advocated so fervently by academics. Excepting the all-equity financed case, company CFOs should typically pursue a CAPM-based weighted average cost of capital, and then make sensible and consistent risk adjustments to determine project hurdle rates. All capital structure components should be expressed at market values, and all costs should be forward looking. A company-wide hurdle rate is probably adequate for many investment projects, although the figure should always be reviewed when dealing with more material, large-scale projects, or indeed corporate restructuring.

MORE INFO

Book:

Bierman, Harold, Jr., and Seymour Smidt. *The Capital Budgeting Decision: Economic Analysis of Investment Projects*. 9th ed. New York: Routledge, 2006.

Articles:

Bruner, Robert F., Kenneth M. Eades, Robert S. Harris, and Robert C. Higgins. "Best practices in estimating the cost of capital: Survey and synthesis." *Financial Practice and Education* 8:1 (Spring/Summer 1998): 13–28.

McLaney, Edward, John Pointon, Melanie Thomas, and Jon Tucker. "Practitioners' perspectives on the cost of capital." *European Journal of Finance* 10:2 (April 2004): 123–138. Online at: dx.doi.org/10.1080/1351847032000137401

See Also:

★ Allocating Corporate Capital Fairly (pp. 11–12)
★ Capital Budgeting: The Dominance of Net Present Value (pp. 20–23)
★ Optimizing the Capital Structure: Finding the Right Balance between Debt and Equity (pp. 543–545)
✔ Appraising Investment Opportunities (p. 1143)
✔ Understanding the Cost of Capital and the Hurdle Rate (p. 1000)
✔ Understanding the Relationship between the Discount Rate and Risk (p. 1001)
✔ Understanding the Weighted Average Cost of Capital (WACC) (p. 1002)
Capital Asset Pricing Model (pp. 1201–1202)

NOTES

1 See Sharpe, William F. "Capital asset prices: A theory of market equilibrium under conditions of risk." *Journal of Finance* 19:3 (September 1964): 425–442. Online at: www.jstor.org/stable/2977928; and Lintner, John. "The valuation of risk assets and the selection of risk investments in stock portfolios and capital budgets." *Review of Economics and Statistics* 47:1 (February 1965): 13–37. Online at: www.jstor.org/stable/1924119

2 A useful discussion of the cost of capital, and how we deal with risk, can be found in Brealey, Richard A., Stewart C. Myers, and Franklin Allen. *Principles of Corporate Finance*. New York: McGraw Hill/Irwin, 2008; 239–240.

"Change means movement. Movement means friction." Saul Alinsky

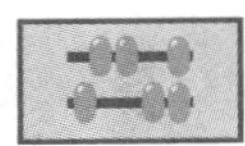

Identifying and Minimizing the Strategic Risks from M&A by Peter Howson

EXECUTIVE SUMMARY

- The high failure rate of acquisitions can be mitigated considerably by dealing with the strategic risks that are present at every stage of the acquisition process.
- It is best to start with a well-developed business strategy, a clear idea of the place of mergers and acquisitions (M&A) in this strategy, and an acquisition target that furthers strategic aims.
- Before embarking on negotiations, acquirers should avoid the risk of overpaying by setting a price above which they will not go.
- Before negotiating the final details, due diligence should be used as a final confirmation of the strategy and the target's fit.
- The most important thing is to make sure that the post acquisition plan is put together early and in as much detail as possible. Acquirers need to add value, and they can only do this if they are clearly focused on the sources of extra value and how to realize them right from the very start.

INTRODUCTION

M&A is extremely risky. Studies carried out over the last 30 years suggest that the failure rate is above 50% and probably close to 75%. However, by identifying and acting to minimize the strategic risks early on in the process, the rewards can be spectacular.

There are four stages in the M&A process:

- acquisition strategy
- due diligence
- negotiation
- post-acquisition integration.

Strategic risks are present in each.

Acquisition Strategy

M&A is glamorous. Market analysts see M&A as a sign of a dynamic management and mark up share prices accordingly. For management, M&A can be a means of bolstering short-term performance and/or masking underlying problems. It is hardly surprising that the failure rate is so high when the mystique of M&A encourages acquirers to rush into acquisitions.

M&A Is a Strategic Tool

This brings us to the first strategic risk—a failure to recognize that M&A is a strategic weapon. Strategy is all about giving customers what they want, and to do it better or more cheaply than anyone else. It is about competitive advantage gained through superior capabilities and resources. M&A should fit into this framework.

Given the high risk of failure, acquirers should ask themselves if acquisition is the best means of achieving aims. There will generally be a tradeoff between risk and time. Acquisition is the highest-risk route to corporate development, but it is often the quickest. Acquisition should be examined alongside all the other options—organic development, joint venture, merger, etc.

Is the Timing Right?

Implementation is the key to successful strategy and this is the clue to the next strategic risk—is this the right time to be acquiring? Getting the transaction done and integrating it afterwards will take up a disproportionate amount of time, resource, and expertise. This means making sure that there is:

- a strong base business (if existing operations are struggling, acquisitions will only add to the problems);
- the resources to add value (where there are insufficient resources to manage an acquisition, the chances of adding value are slim).

Select the Right Target

The next risk may sound obvious, but one of the biggest ever M&A disasters stemmed in part from selecting the wrong target. In 1991 AT&T, the US telecommunications company, bought NCR for $7.48 billion. AT&T was implementing a so called "3Cs strategy" where communications, computers, and consumer electronics were expected to coalesce into a new market. It bought NCR to provide a capability in computers. But NCR was not a computer company. Its core business was in retail transaction processing and banking systems, and it happened also to manufacture a range of "me too" personal computers. While this may be an extreme example, it is not uncommon for buyers to misunderstand the target company's capabilities.

Due Diligence

The strategic risks in due diligence all stem from making the focus of due diligence too narrow.

The success of any acquisition depends on buyers creating value. Due diligence presents a potential buyer with the access and information it needs to confirm that a transaction can be a long-term success. This means using due diligence not just as an input to the sale and purchase agreement but, more importantly, also to confirm both the robustness of synergy assumptions and their deliverability. As people will deliver the extra value, buyers should also make sure that due diligence covers cultural and people issues.

Negotiation

In negotiation, the strategic risk is overpaying. Buyers are almost certainly going to have to pay a premium for the control of a company. The challenge is to make sure that the synergies are big enough to cover both the premium and the deal costs. Work out a price in advance and, as it is all too easy to get carried away, always set a maximum walk-away price before negotiations begin.

Post-Acquisition Integration

The major cause of acquisition failure is poor integration. Integration is poorly carried out because it gets forgotten. Doing the deal may be sexy, but integration is where the real money is made or lost. The strategic risks stem from not starting work on the integration plan early enough in the process. As integration is central to valuation, the integration plan must be put together well before negotiations begin, and the other golden rules of acquisition integration also demand an early plan:

- Integrate quickly to minimize uncertainty. In particular, integration changes related to personnel need to be made as soon as possible; early communication is paramount; and there should be early victories to demonstrate progress.
- Do not neglect the soft issues. The culture of a company is the set of assumptions, beliefs, and accepted rules of conduct that define the way things are done. These are never written down, and most people in an organization would be hard

"The benefits of many mergers have been lost during the integration phase." Richard Corzone

        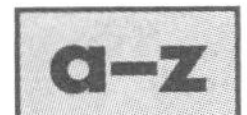

CASE STUDY

In 1996, Federal-Mogul, a US auto parts company, appointed a new Chairman and Chief Executive, Dick Snell, whose view was that in the automotive industry, a firm must be big.

Automobile makers were focusing on assembly, branding, and marketing, and were encouraging parts manufacturers to play a bigger role in the design and development of components. They were also encouraging the larger suppliers to supply modules and systems rather than components.

Federal-Mogul's "growth by acquisition" strategy had the simple aim of increasing sales from $2 billion to $10 billion in six years. The company already made gaskets and seals, but not enough to market a full engine or transmission-sealing package. Federal-Mogul also made engine bearings, but did not have the ability to market the bearings as a system complete with pistons, piston rings, connecting rods, and cylinder liners.

Federal-Mogul first bought T&N Plc (in 1997), a supplier of engine and transmission products and Europe's leading supplier of gaskets. With sales of $3 billion, T&N was bigger than Federal-Mogul itself. Soon after (in 1998), Federal-Mogul paid $720 million for privately held Fel-Pro Inc., of Skokie, IL. Fel-Pro was a leading brand of replacement sealing products. Following these two acquisitions, Federal-Mogul had a $1 billion global sealing business and the basis for providing an integrated engine package. Later that year, Federal-Mogul went on to buy Cooper Automotive for $1.9 billion. Cooper added three completely new product areas (see Table 1).

Table 1. Federal-Mogul's acquisitions

	Existing operations (as of 1996)	1997: T&N acquisition	1998: Fel-Pro acquisition	1998: Cooper Automotive acquisition
Engine and transmission				
Engine Bearings	X	X		
Pistons and piston rings		X		
Seals	X	X	X	
Camshafts	X	X		
Other				
Lighting	X			
Fuel pumps	X			
Friction (brake and clutch pads)		X		
Powdered metals		X		
Ignition				X
Chassis				X
Wiper blades				X

In July 1998, Federal-Mogul's share price was $72. By September 2001 it was $1. On October 1, 2001, the company filed under Chapter 11 of the US Bankruptcy Code. What went wrong?

Overambitious Strategy

Following the Fel-Pro acquisition, the logical thing would have been to continue building the engine and transmissions business. Instead, Federal-Mogul kept its electrical businesses and the friction businesses acquired with T&N, and went on to add three entirely new product ranges. Focusing only on revenue and growth rarely, if ever, produces a strong organization and financial results over the long term.

Problems Picked Up in Due Diligence Not Acted On

T&N had at one time manufactured building products containing asbestos, and for years it paid out an increasing number of compensation claims for asbestos-related diseases. Following the takeover, the number of asbestos claims against T&N and its former subsidiaries exploded. In October 2001 there were 365,000 asbestos claims pending. By the end of 2001, Federal Mogul had paid out $1 billion in claims.

While Federal-Mogul was aware of the asbestos issue, Federal-Mogul leaders did minimal due diligence, failed to appreciate just how serious it was, and believed that, because it operated in the United States, it would be able to manage the litigation better.

Poor Integration

Federal-Mogul paid a high price for T&N and the other big acquisitions, promised too much, and failed to deliver. Federal-Mogul leadership repeatedly promised the market that integration would bring tens of millions of dollars worth of synergies. In fact, according to a stockholder class action, the company's integration activities destroyed the acquired businesses. The class action claimed that, "After an acquisition, the Company would slash sales staff at the acquired company, close manufacturing and warehouse facilities, reduce investment in research and development, reduce customer service and implement aggressive sales practices."

Federal-Mogul's management lacked an understanding of how international businesses operate. It was obsessed with the Detroit Big Three and dismissive of the other vehicle assemblers, yet the strategic logic of acquiring parts manufacturers should be to broaden geographic reach and bring closer relationships with vehicle assemblers.

Federal-Mogul management also failed to appreciate that the rest of the world was not like the United States and, in particular, that Europe was not like a group of US states. Federal-Mogul centralized all its operations, including customer service. When Federal-Mogul moved aftermarket operations to the United States, it was surprised that its telecom ordering system did not recognize overseas telephone numbers. In contrast, T&N had given a great deal of autonomy to its regions.

Finally, Federal-Mogul lost key staff by insisting that anyone who stayed had to move to Detroit. Most former T&N leaders opted to take the money. While it is not impossible to buy a company larger than yourself, it is difficult to manage something the size of T&N without retaining most of the management team—and T&N was actually quite good at managing asbestos claims.

Federal-Mogul emerged from Chapter 11 bankruptcy on December 27, 2007 after a financial reorganization designed to protect it from asbestos claims.

"The big danger in mega-mergers is that they are seen as a mating of dinosaurs." Peter Bonfield

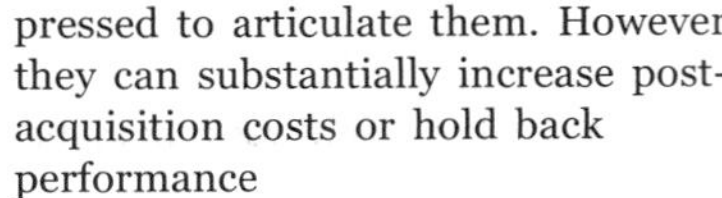

pressed to articulate them. However, they can substantially increase post-acquisition costs or hold back performance

- Manage properly. Buyers should appoint an integration manager. Like any other big project, acquisitions need one person to be accountable for the project's success.

MAKING IT HAPPEN

- Think of M&A as a means to gain competitive advantage rather than short-term improvements in financials.
- M&A is the most risky form of corporate development, so be sure to consider alternatives such as organic growth or joint ventures.
- M&A will divert resources from the existing business, so make sure it is strong before embarking on acquisitions.
- Be sure to understand the target company—what it does, how it operates, how it makes money—and be able to articulate why it fits the strategy.
- Do not neglect soft issues like management and culture. Do not assume that "they are just like us," because they won't be.
- Prepare a detailed integration plan in advance.
- Keep the due diligence scope wide. Always use it to confirm the sources of added value identified and quantified in the integration plan.
- Never be lured into overpaying. Set a clear walk-away price and do not exceed it.
- Once the deal is done, communicate immediately, clearly, consistently, and abundantly to everyone concerned. Do not forget external parties, above all customers.
- Implement changes quickly and smoothly and do not underestimate the size of the task.

MORE INFO

Books:

Camp, Jim. *Start with NO: The Negotiating Tools that the Pros Don't Want You to Know*. New York: Crown Business, 2002.

Carey, Dennis, *et al*. *Harvard Business Review on Mergers and Acquisitions*. Boston, MA: Harvard Business School, 2001.

Cleary, Patrick J. *The Negotiation Handbook*. Armonk, NY: ME Sharpe, 2001.

Freund, James C. *Smart Negotiating: How to Make Good Deals in the Real World*. New York: Fireside, 1993.

Howson, Peter. *Due Diligence: The Critical Stage in Acquisitions and Mergers*. Aldershot, UK: Gower Publishing, 2003.

Howson, Peter. *Commercial Due Diligence: The Key to Understanding Value in an Acquisition*. Aldershot, UK: Gower Publishing, 2006.

Howson, Peter. *Checklists for Due Diligence*. Aldershot, UK: Gower Publishing, 2008.

Howson, Peter, with Denzil Rankine. *Acquisition Essentials*. London: Pearson Education, 2005.

Hubbard, Nancy. *Acquisition: Strategy and Implementation*. Basingstoke, UK: Palgrave Macmillan, 1999.

Hunt, J. W., S. Lees, J. J. Grumbar, and P. D. Vivian. *Acquisitions: The Human Factor*. London: London Business School and Egon Zehnder International, 1987.

Lajoux, Alexandra Reed, and Charles Elson. *The Art of M&A Due Diligence: Navigating Critical Steps and Uncovering Crucial Data*. New York: McGraw-Hill, 2000.

Rankine, Denzil. *Why Acquisitions Fail: Practical Advice for Making Acquisitions Succeed*. London: Pearson Education, 2001.

Article:

Davy, Jeanette A., Angelo Kinicki, John Kilroy, and Christine Scheck. "After the merger: Dealing with people's uncertainty." *Training and Development Journal* 42 (November 1988): 57–61.

Report:

KPMG. "Unlocking shareholder value: Keys to success." London: KPMG, 1999. Online at: tinyurl.com/3yn35rz [PDF].

Websites:

Commercial due diligence—AMR International: www.amrinternational.com

Financial due diligence—BDO Stoy Hayward: www.bdo.co.uk

See Also:

★ Acquisition Integration: How to Do It Successfully (pp. 708–709)
★ Cultural Alignment and Risk Management: Developing the Right Culture (pp. 724–726)
★ Due Diligence Requirements in Financial Transactions (pp. 727–729)
★ Merger Integration and Transition Management: A New Slant for Finance Executives (pp. 756–758)
★ Mergers and Acquisitions: Today's Catalyst Is Working Capital (pp. 763–765)
✔ Assessing Business Performance (p. 1144)
✔ Planning the Acquisition Process (p. 1132)

"The role of takeovers is to improve unsatisfactory companies and to allow healthy companies to grow strategically by acquisitions." James Goldsmith

  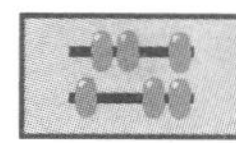      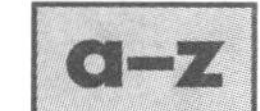

Leveraged Buyouts: What, Why, When, and How

by Scott S. Johnson

EXECUTIVE SUMMARY

- A leveraged buyout (LBO) is the acquisition of a company financed by debt.
- The use of debt multiplies both the potential return and risk.
- LBOs require active and liquid credit markets.
- Stable, mature businesses with predictable—and ideally recurring—revenues are generally the best LBO targets.
- LBO returns are maximized by buying low and selling high, properly capitalizing the buyout, and maximizing profitable and high-quality growth during the hold period.

WHAT

A leveraged buyout (LBO) is the acquisition of a company financed by debt. It is not unlike the typical purchase of a residence where the majority of financing is derived from a mortgage, and the balance from cash (equity) contributed by the buyer.

The use of debt in an LBO leverages the equity return, providing the equity holder with the possibility of higher returns at the cost of higher risk. Debt levels have averaged 72% of total capital from 1996 to 2008, according to Standard & Poor's. Debt levels vary due to numerous factors, including the vibrancy of credit markets, the ability of the company to support debt, and the strategy of the given LBO.

Although select transactions that could be considered LBOs occurred prior to the 1980s, this acquisition strategy grew in popularity in the 1980s when ample debt financing became available, in particular with the rise of the sub-investment grade, or "junk" debt market. Over the past decade, the strategy has seen even more activity with more than US$100 billion raised by private equity funds. Buyouts have, in fact, become a material element in mergers and acquisitions. From 2004 to 2008, US buyout volume was US$1 trillion, according to Standard & Poor's, though activity has of course significantly decreased with the recession of the world's economies and credit markets.

LBOs can involve the acquisition of an entire company or a division of a company. In some cases, management, usually with the financial backing and transactional expertise of a private equity group, buys out its own entity, which is then more specifically referred to as a management buyout (MBO). Yet another permutation is leveraged recapitalization, whereby some equity plus debt are used to provide liquidity to shareholders, either to buy their shares outright, or provide cash to them (not unlike a residential mortgage refinancing).

WHY

Although the leveraged buyout entails risk, given the challenges of servicing debt, significant returns are possible without the need for material growth.

Furthermore, the need to generate sufficient cash flow for debt service imposes discipline. Companies that, pre-LBO, were inefficient, or overloaded with expenses are forced to streamline their operations and cost structure to succeed. At the same time, the need to service debt can generate short-term decision-making that may not always be in the best long-term interest of the business. However, the World Economic Forum's "Global impact of private equity report 2009"[1] estimated that the extra productivity from 1,400 private equity transactions of US manufacturing concerns raised output by US$4 billion, to US$15 billion per year from 1980 to 2005 (expressed in inflation-adjusted 2007 dollars).

WHEN

LBOs are most commonly considered when a candidate company can support the required leverage, and credit markets can provide such leverage.

Good LBO candidates operate in relatively stable businesses with consistent business models. These are generally mature companies with positive cash flow, and an established operating and profitability history. Earlier-stage companies, or those that require continued cash investments to achieve their objectives are generally not good candidates.

Furthermore, companies with a cyclical business, or those materially exposed to major exogenous risks such as technological obsolescence or fashion risk, are also less-optimal buyout candidates. Explicitly recurring revenue businesses (i.e., contractual) or implicit (for example, regularly

CASE STUDY

How Debt Can Magnify Both Returns and Risk

Let's take a company with US$10 in profit and assume it is acquired for 6x profit, or US$60. In the LBO of this company, US$40 of the purchase price is financed with debt and US$20 is an equity investment, so equity is one-third of the total capital. In the unleveraged scenario, US$60 of equity—100% of the consideration—is used to acquire the company.

If the company is sold at the end of five years, and profits have grown at a compound annual growth rate of 10% to US$16 (a cumulative growth of 60%), and the purchase price multiple remains 6x, the business is sold for US$97. In the unleveraged scenario, the annual return is equal to the profit growth, i.e., 10% per annum and 60% on a cumulative basis.

On the other hand, the LBO equity return is much higher. In the LBO, the company sale price value (its enterprise value, or EV) is still US$97. Of the US$97, the first US$40 is returned to the debt holders to pay off their principal, leaving US$57 for the equity. Unlike the unleveraged case, where the sale price is 60% greater than the investment, here the US$57 is 183% greater than the US$20 investment.

The annual return in the LBO is more than double the unleveraged deal: 23% vs. 10% (See Figure 1). Please note that this scenario is an oversimplification, with numerous factors such as transaction costs, working capital, and annual cash flow generation excluded (even when those factors are included, the LBO continues to outperform the unleveraged deal approximately 2:1).

Our case study also illustrates the risks of the leveraged buyout strategy. Without any interest expense or debt principal due, the unleveraged company in our simplified example can weather substantial declines in operating profit, and still maintain positive cash flow. Conversely, if the leveraged company sees a decline of profits of just 25%, its profits after interest expense fall three times that level, or 75%. If the leveraged company had material levels of capital expenditures, or debt principal repayments (which are both post-tax items), it may not be able to service its cash needs. The likely result would be a cash squeeze, which would have negative or potentially disastrous implications (See Figure 2).

"Leverage is a very sharp, double-edged sword." Richard Bernstein

Figure 1. Case study: Sample LBO vs all equity acquisition

	LBO	All equity
Initial acquisition		
Profit	$10	
Multiple	6.0 ×	
Value	$60	
Capitalization		
Debt	4.0 ×	0.00 ×
	$40.0	$0.0
Equity	2.0 ×	6.00 ×
	$20.0	$60.0
Return after year-5 sale		
Value	$96.63	
Less: debt	($40.00)	$0.0
Equity value	$56.63	$96.63
Annual return	23.1%	10.0%
Return on capital	1.8 ×	0.6 ×
Profit after five years:		
Annual growth	10.0%	
Cumulative growth	161.1%	
Year-5 profit	$16.11	
Year-5 sale price:		
Year-5 profit	$16.11	
times multiple of	6.0 ×	
gives sale price	$96.63	

Note: Excludes transaction and closing fees and assumes no principal amortization or cash generated.

repurchased consumables) are good targets. Sectors that often exhibit these characteristics and have yielded successful buyouts include consumer, business services, defense, and media.

HOW

LBO returns can be generated from five factors as follows:

1 **Buying low**. The lower the entry valuation level, the greater margin of safety provided for investors. Furthermore, a company acquired at a lower valuation will require less debt to achieve the optimal debt-to-capital mix. On the other hand, higher quality and larger companies often have greater growth prospects, are generally more stable, and thus usually sell for higher valuations. When valuations are high, buyers take the risk that even if the business is properly capitalized and shows good growth, exit valuation levels could be lower and will not be sufficient to generate an acceptable return. While careful analysis can help determine if the steps below are to be a success, entry valuation is critical, as it is a factor that is controllable at the beginning of the LBO.

2 **Maximizing equity returns by minimizing equity investment to prudent levels**. An LBO investor must first decide the maximum leverage the business can support, and then try to finance the deal to that level, but not more. In strong credit markets, LBO investors should resist the temptation to overleverage their portfolio companies. In weak credit markets, investors need to ensure that, at lower debt levels, they can still achieve their minimum return hurdles (often accomplished by "buying lower").What is the appropriate debt level? This clearly varies. Two helpful benchmarks to consider are the overall leverage, and the ability of the company to support its debt, and other obligations. Debt levels are often measured as a multiple of earnings before interest, taxes, depreciation, and amortization (EBITDA), a simplified proxy for cash flow. Debt-to-EBITDA levels for buyouts have historically varied by year, largely as a function of the state of the debt markets. In 2007, average debt to EBITDA was 6.0x, but fell to 4.8x in 2008, and averaged as low as 3.5x in 2001, according to Standard & Poor's.LBO investors will also be concerned with their buyout's ability to service its debt. The fixed-charge covenant ratio (FCCR) is a common measure used to measure debt service levels. The FCCR is the ratio of a company's cash flow to its fixed charges, which typically include taxes, interest, capital expenditures, and debt principal payments. Lenders often seek minimum FCCR levels of 1.10–1.35x.Debt levels also vary due to the structure of the debt offered. In larger transactions, publicly traded bonds, which can form the bulk of the financing, do not typically carry principal amortization, allowing for greater debt capacity. In smaller transactions, debt is typically provided in two tranches: senior debt, typically from banks, and "mezzanine debt," which is subordinate to the senior debt and carries higher rates of interest and sometimes includes equity participation in the form of warrants. Senior debt in such structures often includes principal amortization, which can impose material burdens on a company.Thus, the financing structure makes a material difference in the level of debt a company can support. In particular, debt capital structures that have less (or no) principal amortization are more conducive to higher debt levels, as the total debt servicing costs are much lower (especially when it is considered that debt principal repayments are post-tax obligations).Debt levels are also a function of the strategy of the buyout group. Some groups tend to use comparatively less debt, so they have "dry powder" to more easily execute add-on acquisitions and weather shortfalls.

3 **Maximizing quality organic growth before exit**. Generally, the more growth that occurs during the holding period, the more valuable the company will be at exit. However, a company must be careful to focus on generating "good" revenue. While "good" revenue may vary

Figure 2. Case study: Effect of profit decline

	LBO	All equity
Base profit	$10.00	
Decline in profit	25%	
New profit	$7.50	
Interest	$5.00	$0.00
Profit after interest	$2.50	$7.50
Decline in profit after interest	-75.0%	-25.0%
Debt	$40.00	
Interest rate	12.5%	
Interest expense	$5.00	

MAKING IT HAPPEN

- Do your diligence. While confirmatory diligence to verify financial and operating assumptions is critical, exploratory diligence is often not given enough focus. The buyout investor should, in particular, understand the sustainability of a company's competitive advantages, and make sure they understand not just the recent history of a company's sector, but the sector's outlook, and what underlying threats may exist to that sector.
- Debt structure. While the price of debt is critical, equally if not more important are the terms of that debt. Key areas worth considering include the maturity date of the debt, the level of principal amortization, if any, and how a given lender may act as a partner (especially if results are poor, and covenants are violated).
- "Skin in the game." While a buyout investor can provide management equity upside, through the use of stock options, having a management team invest their own cash in the deal—putting "skin in the game"—confirms management's confidence in the opportunity, and binds them to both the upside and downside.

"When things go wrong you have to pass the blame along the line, like pass-the-parcel, till the music stops."
Tom Stoppard

from company to company, it generally entails business that preserves or bolsters a company's competitive advantages and margins, does not create unnecessarily high customer concentration, is ideally of a recurring nature, still yields a good return on investment net of capital expenditures and working capital requirements, and is the type of business that would appeal to a potential buyer.To achieve these goals, the buyout group relies on its partnership with management.Furthermore, the buyout investor must carefully use the correct management incentives to generate the desired results. These programs usually revolve around the use of longer-term equity incentives that help shape management's overall motivation, and minimize short-term decision-making. For a typical buyout CEO, the annual compensation will be lower than a corporate position, but if the buyout is successful, the payout can be much higher than what would have been possible as a corporate employee.

4 **Making profitable add-on acquisitions or divestitures as appropriate**. Buyout investors may seek to grow a business through acquisition, or sell off divisions as appropriate. The buyout investor must carefully weigh the return on capital that will be generated by incremental investment, as well as the cash that could be generated from a divestiture, which would likely be used to deleverage the business.

5 **Selling high**. After an investment holding period of typically three to seven years, a buyout firm will seek to exit its investment, so that the proceeds may be returned to its own investors. If growth has been positive and consistent, and industry trends and valuation levels are favorable, the buyout firm should achieve a good return on its investment. However, the reality is that valuation levels years after a deal is consummated are well outside of the control of the buyout firm, so having a flexible timetable, entering the deal at a reasonable valuation level, improving the performance of the company during the holding period, and appropriately capitalizing the company are essential to executing a profitable LBO.

MORE INFO

Report:

Standard and Poor's. "A guide to the loan market." September 2011. Online at: www.lcdcomps.com/d/pdf/LoanMarketguide.pdf

Websites:

Association for Corporate Growth (ACG), the predominant industry association for the middle market buyout industry: www.acg.org

The Deal, magazine and online resource: www.thedeal.com

The Private Equity Analyst, a periodical published by Dow Jones: www.dowjones.com/privatemarkets/pea.asp

Private Equity Growth Capital Council (PEGCC): www.pegcc.org

See Also:

★ Going Private: Public-to-Private Leveraged Buyouts (pp. 730–732)
★ MBOs: A High-Octane and Life-Changing Mode of Business (pp. 754–755)
✔ Corporate Governance Practices in Private Equity-Owned Firms (p. 1112)
✔ Management Buyouts (p. 1131)
✔ Understanding and Using Leverage Ratios (p. 1097)

NOTE

1 www.weforum.org/pdf/cgi/pe/Full_Report2.pdf, p. 44.

Maximize the Selling Price of Your Business

by Frederick Lipman

EXECUTIVE SUMMARY

- Plan the sale of your business several years ahead.
- Choose the right time to sell your business.
- Obtain a professional valuation of your business and then seek to maximize it.
- Use an investment banker with experience in your industry.
- Target your marketing to potential buyers.
- Conduct an auction.
- Identify impediments to the sale of your business and work to eliminate them.

INTRODUCTION

Many business owners make the mistake of thinking that it is simple to sell their business at a good price. The reality is that selling a business is a complicated process that requires advance planning many years prior to the sale target date in order to maximize the sale price. The advance planning steps are covered in detail in the author's book entitled *Valuing Your Business: Strategies to Maximize the Sale Price* (Wiley, 2005).

The purpose of this article is to discuss some of the most important best practices which can assist the business owner in maximizing the ultimate sale price.

TAKE ADVANTAGE OF BENEFICIAL FLUCTUATIONS IN THE VALUE OF YOUR BUSINESS

It is important to understand the primary drivers of the valuation of your business and to time the sale process to coincide with a period of high valuations. We can divide the valuation drivers into two categories: macro factors such as the state of the economy and your industry, and micro factors which relate to the peculiar aspects of your business such as revenues, business prospects, etc. For example, no matter how well your business was performing in 2009 (the micro factors), this was a bad year to sell your business because of the macro economic factors affecting the entire economy, and very few sales were consummated.

A key to maximizing the sale price is to sell at a time when there is the maximum number of potential buyers. It is important to time the sale so that there are financial buyers available to compete with any strategic buyers. Financial buyers are most likely to be available when the banks and other financial institutions from which they borrow have the most generous lending terms and afford them the largest amount of leverage in making the purchase. If there are a significant number of potential financial and strategic buyers, this will enable you to conduct an auction, which typically will give you the highest possible sale price, as discussed below.

Every business owner should obtain a valuation of their business by a competent professional appraiser even though they have no current plans to sell the business. A well documented appraisal report will help identify the primary macro as well as micro factors affecting the valuation of your business. Such a report will enable the entrepreneur to concentrate on the micro factors such as revenues, EPITDA, business prospects, etc., while waiting for the macro valuation factors to be favorable.

For example, a valuation report may indicate that one particular line of business has a much higher multiplier of value than a second line of business. The entrepreneur might therefore focus more attention and funding on the first line of business in order to maximize the valuation at such time as the macro economic factors became favorable.

USE A QUALIFIED INVESTMENT BANKER TO HELP SELL YOUR BUSINESS

An entrepreneur can sell their own business without an investment banker, just as they could sell their own house without a real estate agent. However, while some businesses can be sold without an investment banker at reasonable valuations, most entrepreneurs do not have the background or experience to properly market the business, locate potential buyers, and negotiate deal terms.

The advantages of using an investment banker are as follows:

- An investment banker experienced in your industry has a greater knowledge of potential buyers for your business than you do.
- Even if you know one obvious buyer for your business, an investment banker may be able to find one or more other prospects, thereby enabling an auction to occur.
- The investment banker can help screen your potential buyers and prevent you from wasting your time on financially unqualified buyers.
- An experienced investment banker can assist in negotiating the sale, smoothing rough spots, and protecting you from unrealistic demands.

A qualified investment banker should be able to add more value to the transaction than the small percentage that they charge as a fee. Structure the fee arrangement with the investment banker to align their interest with yours, such as a higher percentage for sale prices beyond your expectations. It is important that you use an attorney specializing in mergers and acquisitions to negotiate the agreement with the investment banker.

Some investment bankers will not handle smaller businesses and business brokers typically charge very high fees as a percentage of the purchase price if the business is extremely small, such as businesses worth less than $1 million or even $5 million. With these smaller businesses, it may be worthwhile for the owner to try to sell the business before engaging a business broker. Alternatively some lawyers or accountants can sometimes provide all the necessary professional advice, perhaps with a low up-front but incentivized fee structure.

CREATE A MARKETING BROCHURE APPEALING TO POTENTIAL BUYERS

A qualified investment banker will assist the company in creating a marketing brochure. Even if no investment banker is retained, it is extremely important that the owner create a marketing brochure. No entrepreneur would attempt to sell a specific product or service without good marketing material. Likewise, no business should be offered to potential buyers without a well prepared marketing brochure.

The effective marketing of your business requires you to understand the thinking of potential buyers and characteristics they would find appealing. You must learn to think like a buyer. Many business owners are abysmally ignorant of their competitive position in their own industry. Yet this is very important to buyers and a key to effectively marketing to them.

During the years prior to your sale target date, you must learn as much as possible about the competitors in your industry—both their strengths and their weaknesses. Potential buyers would expect you to understand your strengths and weaknesses

"When you sell 30% of a business, it is like taking two limbs off a body—it's not surprising there is a negative effect on the rest of the business." Sir Clive Thompson

vis-à-vis your competition. Therefore, it is essential that you become more knowledgeable about your competition.

You must also become an expert about your markets and customers. Do you have a special niche in the marketplace? Is your market growing, flat, or declining? If one of the latter two, what are you doing in order to diversify your markets?

A useful step is to try to prepare a marketing brochure five years prior to your sale target date. See where the weaknesses are in the description of your business. A good marketing brochure will require several months to prepare. You will need the help of your accountant, attorneys, and your investment banker, if any. The marketing brochure should emphasize favorable valuation factors including customer relationships and market identification. Your competitive strengths should be carefully noted and explained.

The marketing brochure should contain financial information about the results of your operation which would reflect how they would look in the hands of the potential buyer. For example, if substantial savings to the buyer are possible, these savings should be added to your earnings as pro forma calculations.

The following table presents some of the specific factors which will increase your valuation and some of the factors that will decrease your valuation:

Factors Increasing Valuation	Factors Decreasing Valuation
1. Strong customer relationships at all levels.	1. Weak customer relationships and frequent turnover.
2. Proprietary products or services.	2. Lack of proprietary products or services.
3. No single customer accounts for more than 5% of revenues or profits.	3. A single customer accounts for over 15% of revenues or profits.
4. Strong management team (important mainly to financial buyers).	4. A weak management team (so-called one-man-show syndrome).
5. Excellent employee turnover and relations.	5. Poor employee turnover and relations.
6. Consistent revenue and earnings trends.	6. Inconsistent revenue and earnings trends.
7. Plant and equipment in good repair.	7. Plant or equipment has been neglected and requires significant repairs.
8. Intellectual property assets which are legally protected.	8. Lack of legally protected intellectual property assets.

During the years prior to the sale target date, grow your business in a manner to eliminate these weaknesses and improve your strengths. The maximization of the ultimate sale price depends upon how successful you are. Your goal should be to persuade the buyer that your business is properly managed, and well positioned for long term competitive success.

CONDUCT AN AUCTION

It is generally agreed that an auction produces the highest price for a business. Generally, you need two or more bidders to conduct an auction. However, an auction can be conducted with only one bidder if the auction is a closed auction, that is, no one knows who else is bidding.

To induce potential buyers to bid at an auction of your business, you must assure them that you do intend to sell and that the auction will be conducted fairly.

If you have not made a decision whether or not you really want to sell your business, you will not be able to hold an auction effectively. Likewise, if you favor one bidder over another and want to give your favored bidder the last bid, it is unlikely that you will be able to induce other potential buyers to participate in the auction.

The most suitable businesses for an auction are businesses with good financial results and a strategic market position. If neither of these characteristics is present, the auction may not be as successful but should still be considered if there are competing buyers.

The auction must be conducted by a person in whom bidders have confidence and pursuant to written rules and procedures that are uniformly applied to all bidders. Your investment banker or attorney can fulfill this role.

Bidders are generally turned off by open auctions—in other words, auctions where their bids are disclosed to all other bidders—and by auctions in which there are innumerable rounds of bidding.

Auctions can also be classified as controlled auctions and uncontrolled auctions. In a controlled auction, the company initiates contact only with selected buyers, whereas in an uncontrolled auction (also sometimes called an open auction) there is no limit on the number of potential bidders. Uncontrolled auctions potentially attract the largest number of buyers, but may be highly disruptive to the company and its employees. Many companies prefer a controlled auction which is less disruptive.

To induce bidders to participate in your auction, bids should be submitted in writing and maintained in confidence. Cutoff dates for bids should be advertised and adhered to.

It is preferable from the seller's point of view to have at least two rounds of bidding, with the second round of bidding confined to the highest two bidders. If there are more than four bidders, you may wish a third round of bidding.

It is essential that you provide all bidders with the same agreement of sale form, which will be prepared by your counsel. Each bidder should be requested to state any changes in the agreement of sale form when submitting his or her bid. In determining the highest bidder, the legal terms must be considered along with the price. You should also check any laws which may be applicable to your auction to be certain that you have complied.

ELIMINATE DEAL KILLERS AND OTHER SALE IMPEDIMENTS

During the advance planning stages it is important to eliminate deal killers and other sale impediments. The following are a few examples of sale impediments:

- environmental liabilities;
- litigation liabilities;
- tax liabilities resulting from misclassification of employees as independent contractors;
- unfunded pension obligations and multiemployer pension plan liabilities;
- product warranty obligations of unreasonable scope or length.

If you expect to sell your business within a year or two, you should carefully consider the effect on the sale of entering into long-term contracts that will have to be assumed by the buyer. For example, a five-year contract tying you to a particular supplier may make your business less valuable to a potential buyer. Likewise, committing your company to purchase very expensive equipment shortly before the sale could also reduce the value of your business to a potential buyer and impede the sale.

The lack of audited or auditable financial statements can be a serious impediment to a sale. Public companies in particular may need audited financial statements of your business for a number of years in order to consummate a sale if your business is viewed as a significant subsidiary under financial tests prescribed by the US Securities and Exchange Commission.

Your assets should be made transferable to the extent possible without the consent of a third party. For example, most leases are typically not transferable without the consent of the landlord and most licenses for intellectual property are typically not transferable without the consent of the licensor. During the advance planning period it is important to negotiate changes to these limitations on transferability with landlords and licensors.

"Unless the company becomes obsessed with constant change for the better, gradual change for the worse usually goes unnoticed." Vineet Nayar

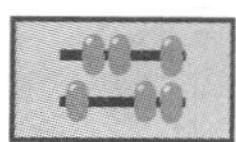

Finally, and most importantly, align the interests of your key employees with your own by creating incentives for them in the event of a sale. Nothing is more disruptive to a sale than having key employees leave during the sale process because they are concerned about their personal futures. Key sales employees should be required to agree to not solicit your customers if they do leave your employment. You want all of your key employees to be motivated to help and not hinder the sale process.

MORE INFO

Book:

Lipman, Frederick D. *Valuing Your Business: Strategies to Maximize the Sale Price*. Hoboken, NJ: Wiley, 2005.

See Also:

★ Maximizing Value when Selling a Business (pp. 751–753)
✔ M&A Regulations: A Global Overview (p. 1130)
✔ Planning the Disposal Process (p. 1133)
✔ The Rationale for an Acquisition (p. 1134)

"So many companies adhere to the Zimbabwe school of change management—altering course only after ruin, by coup d'etat." Simon Caulkin

  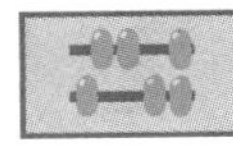    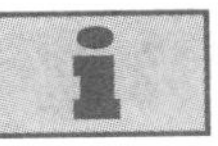 

Maximizing a New Strategic Alliance by Peter Killing

EXECUTIVE SUMMARY

- Over 60,000 strategic alliances have been formed in the past decade. About half were joint ventures. Only 40% meet or exceed their partners' expectations.
- To be successful with strategic alliances you must be clear about your objectives, get the alliance design right, and manage the alliance effectively after it is formed.
- There is an important difference between shallow and deep alliances, and you should know which type you need and why.
- Alliance success depends in large part on skilled managers who are good with people, have a high tolerance for ambiguity and conflict, and are patient yet persistent.
- The clearest sign of alliance success is growing trust between the partners.

INTRODUCTION

More than 60,000 strategic alliances were formed in the 1990s. About half of these were joint ventures. The other 50% were nonequity arrangements such as technology licensing agreements, joint marketing arrangements, and joint research or development projects. Most of these alliances were international, so it's no surprise to learn that the world's largest multinationals are heavy alliance users: IBM (254 alliances), General Motors (138), Mitsubishi (233), Toshiba (147), Philips (207), and Siemens (200) are just some examples.

Clearly the ability to create and manage strategic alliances is an important skill for most management teams. If you cannot make effective use of alliances in today's world, you will be at a serious competitive disadvantage.

GETTING IT RIGHT

A 1999 study by Andersen Consulting indicates that only 40% of alliances achieve or exceed the initial expectations of their partners, which suggests there's a lot of room for improvement. One of the reasons for the relatively low success rate is that there are many different aspects of the design and management of alliances that you need to get right, from clearly understanding your objectives, to managing the alliance after it is formed. They can be grouped into three sequential steps:

- **Clarify objectives.** What do we need and for how long? Is an alliance the best way to get what we need?
- **Design the alliance.** What type of alliance should we create? What should our role be?
- **Manage after the deal is done.** How do we effectively manage the alliance? Can we build trust?

Clarify Objectives and the Need for the Alliance

The first challenge is to be clear about what your company needs to fulfil its strategy, which may be different from what others in your industry need. The second challenge is to decide whether an alliance is the best way to get what you need. Three common reasons for forming alliances are:

- **To enter new markets.** One of the classic purposes of joint ventures is to enter foreign markets. Typically the foreign company finds the local market attractive but does not feel confident enough to enter without local knowledge, and so takes a local partner. In some countries the government insists on such a relationship. In China, for example, joint ventures between foreigners and local companies are prevalent. Often, as foreign companies gain confidence in their ability to operate locally, they end the joint venture by buying out their local partner and creating a wholly-owned subsidiary. In this case the alliance is a step on the road to something else.
- **To create new technology and set industry standards.** In technology-intensive industries like computing and telecommunications, companies often use alliances to attempt to create a new technology that will become the industry standard. An example is Symbian, a joint venture formed in 1998 by Psion, Ericsson, Nokia, and Motorola. Symbian's objective is to create an operating system for wireless devices to exchange information efficiently. Microsoft has also shown an interest in this area and has considered building its own alliance around its CE operating system with partners including NTT DoCoMo and British Telecom. The competition has shifted from company versus company to alliance versus alliance.
- **To shape consolidation.** In consolidating industries such as airlines, telecoms, and the automotive industry, alliances are often formed between companies that fear they are too small to continue independently (and that do not want to be taken over) and those that intend to play a dominant role in the consolidation. The alliance between Fiat and GM was formed for precisely this reason. This deal involves cross-ownership holdings between the two companies, two 50–50 joint ventures, and a variety of smaller cooperative arrangements. Fiat also had an option to sell itself to GM (before agreeing a "divorce" worth $2 billion in 2005). The immediate motives behind such alliances are to gain economies of scale and global reach, to eliminate excess capacity, and to keep the smaller company out of the hands of predators.

Why Use an Alliance?

Alliances are often the least-preferred choice of the companies that enter them. Many companies would rather enter a new market themselves, or perhaps make an acquisition. GM, for example, would probably have preferred to buy Fiat, but the company was not for sale. Alliances are often seen as difficult to manage, ambiguous in terms of control and decision-making (and as a result slow moving), and requiring an extraordinary amount of management time and attention.

The usual motives, positive and negative, for proceeding with an alliance are:

Positive

- to harness the partner's energy and knowledge;
- to set an industry standard by involving partners;
- to learn something;
- to gain economies of scale or global reach;
- to reduce risk;
- to gain speed.

Negative

- government insists on alliance;
- acquisitions are too expensive or not available;
- it's the only financially affordable alternative;
- the company fears being acquired;
- an alliance will prevent a competitor's acquisition of, or alliance with, the partner;
- closing the business is too expensive; an alliance provides a more graceful exit.

You should be clear on your own motives as well as your partner's. There are no data on this issue, but alliances formed for positive motives may have a higher success rate.

Design the Alliance

There are many types of alliance. The simplest are straightforward license agreements and shared marketing deals; the

"You should never underestimate the challenge of operating a multicultural business... As businesses are being intimately linked in the global economy, and as they partner with competitors... we become more and more reliant on each other." William T. Esrey

        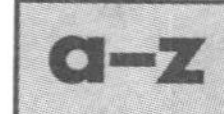

most complex are multipart arrangements such as cross-ownership positions, joint ventures, and cooperative projects between partners. Faced with an abundance of choice, managers entering an alliance need to make a key decision: whether they want a shallow alliance or a deep alliance.

Shallow Alliances—Traveling Light

A shallow alliance might be thought of as a flirtation—a low-commitment alliance that doesn't have a lot of resources devoted to it and that can be broken on short notice. As an example, think of current airline alliances such as the Star and One World alliances, which seem to feature new partners every month. Or consider Cisco and its internet-related businesses. Cisco often cannot judge if a young company's fledgling technology will prove to be important a year later. The shallow alliance solution is to buy 10% of the company's stock in a friendly transaction and get a seat on the board and an option to buy the remainder of the equity. The assigned board member can then assess the company's management, its market prospects, and its technology. If it looks good, they buy the rest of the company. If not, they leave. Shallow alliances thus create options for companies in fast-changing industries in which the way ahead is not clear. The alliances are not usually intended to be permanent.

Deep Alliances—Commitment

At the other end of the spectrum are deep alliances involving high levels of financial and managerial commitment by the partners. Deep alliances feature many links between the partners, usually including one or more seats on the board of directors, cross-ownership positions, at least two or three joint ventures, and many less formal but important cooperative projects. Deep alliances are generally slower-moving than shallow alliances, more difficult to manage, and more difficult to end. The benefits of success can be high, but so can the costs of failure. Deep alliances are not for the timid.

Manage After the Deal Is Done

Once you've formed an alliance, you'll sooner or later discover that you have brought together partners with different ways of doing things and somewhat different objectives, priorities, and performance standards. These differences make the management of alliances a difficult task. The single most important thing you can do to maximize the probability of success is to assign some of your very best people to work on it. "Best" means managers with excellent people skills, cross-cultural sensitivity, and a tolerance for ambiguity and frustration. Alliance managers need to be patient, yet persistent.

Six months into the life of your alliance you should look closely at the relationship between the partners. Is trust starting to develop? If not, why not? Where are the trouble spots? Many texts advise that when choosing a partner you should choose someone you trust. This is difficult to do unless you have worked together before. The real question is whether or not you can develop trust over time. The best predictor of the future performance of any alliance is the current level of trust between the partners.

Finally, don't assume that the alliance is done when the deal is signed. This is just the beginning. Be flexible and open to change and learning. There will be plenty of opportunity for both.

MAKING IT HAPPEN

Strategic alliances are increasingly popular, even necessary; however they are often a high-risk strategy. It is worth viewing the alliance in three distinct phases:

- **Before the deal is struck:** The vital period when goals are considered, resources prepared, and partners considered. Internal agreement on the goals, strategy, and resources to be used is important, as is choosing the right partner and evaluating them thoroughly through due diligence.
- **Negotiating the deal:** The terms of the agreement and, significantly, the expectations of each partner and the *spirit* of the agreement, will be decisive in determining the effectiveness of the alliance.
- **Post-agreement management:** Successful agreements are those that are consistently and attentively resourced, managed, and valued. If they are not, they are unlikely to survive normal commercial pressures.

Some key questions to consider include:

- Have you formally assessed the aims and benefits of the strategic alliance?
- How does the alliance fit with your overall commercial strategy?
- Who needs to be informed of the alliance—and when?
- Have you sought the advice of professional advisers?
- Have you taken time to understand the target and the commercial implications?
- To what extent should the alliance be integrated into your existing business? Who will lead this?
- Do you have a fully costed and resourced plan for managing the alliance? What are the targets and success criteria for the alliance?

MORE INFO

Books:

Cauley de la Sierra, M. *Managing Global Alliances: Key Steps for Successful Collaboration*. Reading, MA: Addison-Wesley, 1995.

Doz, Yves L., and Gary Hamel. *Alliance Advantage: The Art of Creating Value through Partnering*. Cambridge, MA: Harvard Business School Press, 1998.

Lewis, Jordan D. *Trusted Partners: How Companies Build Mutual Trust and Win Together*. New York: Free Press, 2000.

Website:

Alliance Strategy offers resources and readings on alliance strategy and management. It is maintained by Ben Gomes-Casseres, author of *The Alliance Revolution*: www.alliancestrategy.com

See Also:

★ Due Diligence Requirements in Financial Transactions (pp. 727–729)
★ Why Mergers Fail and How to Prevent It (pp. 772–773)
✔ Assessing Economies of Scale in Business (p. 1145)
✔ M&A Regulations: A Global Overview (p. 1130)
✔ Structuring and Negotiating Joint Ventures (p. 1175)
✔ Structuring M&A Deals and Tax Planning (p. 1135)

"We are always willing to be trade partners, but never trade patsies." Ronald Reagan

  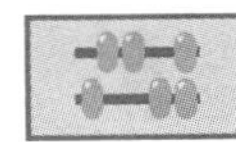      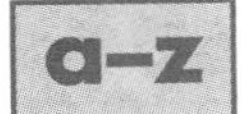

Maximizing Value when Selling a Business by John Gilligan

EXECUTIVE SUMMARY

- *Advisers advise, principals decide*. Advisers may not understand industry-specific risks and are therefore badly placed to make judgments on some risk issues. Be prepared to debate with your own advisers and to overrule them if your knowledge is superior, no matter how much they are being paid.
- *Don't buy a dog and bark yourself*. Corporate sales are complex and risky. Appoint experienced advisers and get them to manage the process under your control.
- *Information*. The importance of information cannot be overemphasized. Buyers are motivated by fear and greed: The quality, tone, and flow of information critically impact both motives.
- *Valuation*. Agree what the walkaway price is with your advisers before starting a process, review it constantly, and be prepared to walk away if necessary.
- *Competitive tension*. The best deals are achieved where more than one buyer with cash (but not an uncontrollable host) wants to purchase a business. Use this rivalry to maximize the bids received and to eliminate risks that might prevent the buyer from delivering the deal.
- *Blunderbuss versus rifle shot*. Most businesses have a limited target population of buyers who may pay a strategic premium. The approach when marketing needs to favor those most likely to pay the best price.
- *Financial bidders are active*. In the past 20 years more businesses worldwide have probably been sold to private equity firms than any other type of acquirer. Use them to create competitive tension.
- *Auctions have to be managed*. Theory and practice suggest that many tactics in auctions are counterintuitive. Think through what you are going to do and clearly communicate it to potential purchasers.
- *Say nothing*. There are always matters that are uncertain in any deal. Staff are always unsettled by uncertainty. It is best to say nothing at all to them, but if you do decide to explain what is happening, you must be completely honest. But remember, any ambiguity is interpreted negatively.
- *Only the fittest survive*. Transactions are long and often tedious. Do not let boredom, fatigue, or lack of patience deflect you from your final goal, especially when the winning line is near.
- *The one that got away*. The world is full of people who nearly did the best deal ever. To achieve success, you need to give and take; it is not a war, it is a negotiation.

INTRODUCTION

All corporations seem complex to those looking in from the outside. The cocktail of relationships, contracts, and assets coming together to generate value is different in every company, and the process of realizing the value embedded in that cocktail requires planning, foresight, and pragmatic judgment. Failure to sell a business that has been publicly put up for sale can destroy huge amounts of value. Each situation is unique and no text can provide a comprehensive guide, any more than you could write the complete guide to sailing in all weathers. This article will deal with general principles and strategies, not technical details. Furthermore, it will address the question of *how* to sell a business, not *why* you should sell a business.

ADVISERS—WHAT THEY DO, WHAT THEY DON'T DO

It would be perverse not to believe that corporate finance advice is valuable. Here is one casual, empirical data point that supports this view: Private equity firms, many themselves ex-corporate financiers, and whose core business is buying and selling companies, almost always use advisers. The question is not *whether* to appoint advisers; it is what should they be tasked with doing, and what is the limit of their role. Their role is not to make decisions. They are there to limit the number of decisions the vendor has to make regarding the key commercial factors that make deals happen. Good advisers should be prepared to debate decisions and use their experience to guide their clients toward the paths of least resistance. However, only the owners can make the final decisions.

Having described what advisers don't do, the natural question is: So what *do* they do? The answer to this is—pretty much everything except making the final commercial decisions. Expect advisers to prepare, collate, and analyze data that will be presented to potential purchasers. They should project manage every aspect of the sale process, providing a clear and coherent strategy to achieve a successful outcome with an acceptable level of risk. This is the necessary skill set of any adviser and it enables the company to concentrate on delivering to its customers, not preparing itself for sale. As the saying goes, "Don't buy a dog and bark yourself."

The added value in corporate finance comes in three ways. First is the ephemeral thing called judgment. As one partner of a major British practice used to describe it, having a good "bullshit detector" helps. Second is the ability to take the burden away from the client. Advisers should do all the heavy lifting, leaving their clients to concentrate on the business itself and the key decisions. Finally, and of crucial importance in many deals, advisers need to be able to access the right people in the right places who may wish to acquire the business.

INFORMATION—WHAT YOU SAY, AND HOW YOU SAY IT

In 2001 three US economists, Akerlof, Steiglitz, and Spencer shared the Nobel Prize in economics. Their body of work deals with an area formally known as "information asymmetry," or more colloquially: What do you do when I know things you don't know? This section tries to answer a simple question: If a purchaser can't tell a good car from a bad car, how can a seller get a premium for a good car? The same problem arises when you are selling a company, only more so. Companies are the most complex things that are traded, and selling one may transfer all the future and historical risks and rewards to the new owner. If you cannot persuade the new owner that the net value of those risks and rewards is quantifiable and positive, you won't sell the business. This is one of the commonest areas in which transactions fail. A failure to think through the strategy of managing and transmitting information results in transactions falling apart further down the line, as purchasers narrow the information asymmetry in due diligence and find that what they were told originally is not what they found to be true subsequently.

There are a number of ways to deal with information asymmetry. The simplest and crudest solution is to ignore the issue entirely. Provide limited data and tell purchasers to rely on their own judgment. In essence, this is what happens in an unsolicited hostile takeover, and may well

"It's far better to buy a wonderful company at a fair price than a fair company at a wonderful price." Warren Buffett

Figure 1. Typical business sale process

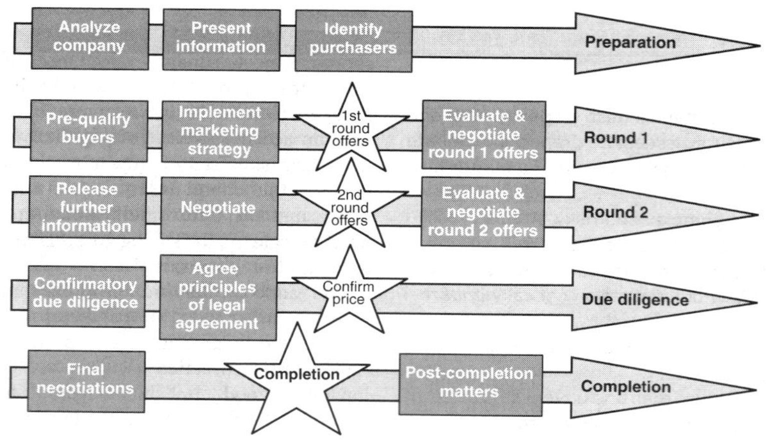

be the reason that so many hostile approaches subsequently turn out to be failures.

To bridge the asymmetry you can either transmit information (under a suitable confidentiality agreement) or agree to take residual risks away from the purchaser by, for example, giving warranties. At the extremes, the negotiating positions are either: "We will give you access to do whatever due diligence you like, but we are not warranting anything," or "We will warrant that the information we give to you is materially correct, but you are not getting any more access than that." The approach to this question needs to be decided early on since it flows through the entire transaction approach and materially influences the form of legal agreement that will emerge at the end of the process. It is also important to communicate your approach to purchasers clearly and consistently. If you do not, they will impose their view on you and purchasers will seek both a belt and suspenders: full access, and full warranties.

VALUATION … IS IN THE EYE OF THE BEHOLDER

In theory, the value of any asset is the present value of its future cash flows. To maximize value, you need to show the maximum future cash flow and the minimum cost of capital. This leads to the infamous "hockey stick" projections—projections that reverse a declining trend and rise thereafter. These are fed into a spreadsheet and out pops a valuation. The danger of believing your own propaganda is that you set unrealistic targets. You must aim high, but not every attempt can be a world record.

In addition to DCF (discounted cash flow) valuations, advisers should prepare a variety of analyses. Comparable transactions that have occurred recently and analysis of comparable quoted companies valuations are the most frequently seen.

Another way to discover what advisers think your business is really worth is to look at where their fee proposal starts to generate significant uplift. Where fees are correlated to value, you can often work out the implicit valuation of any adviser from their fee proposal.

It is frequently contended that the most important output of the theoretical valuation process is not the maximum number calculated, but that it validates a "walkaway" price—the price at which the vendor will simply stop the process and refuse to sell. This number needs to be at the forefront of your mind in any negotiation. It also needs to be refreshed periodically if the prospects for the business or its markets change materially.

It is also important to remember that all these analyses are simply checking out the potential valuation. To actually achieve a transaction at a particular valuation, you normally need competitive tension or a compelling strategic premium.

COMPETITIVE TENSION—CREATING FEAR, ENCOURAGING GREED

Once you have surveyed the landscape, the task is to identify and communicate with those purchasers most likely to place a valuation on the business that they can afford to pay and which exceeds the walkaway price. When considering the number of parties to approach to create a market, again there are two extremes: blunderbuss or rifle shot.

The blunderbuss approach says that since you never know who might be looking for a business like yours, you should maximize the probability of hitting the target by firing as widely as possible. The downside is that circulating information widely makes a confidential process most unlikely.

The rifle shot approach targets a limited number of buyers, maximizing the probability of reaching those specific purchasers wishing to acquire the business. You risk missing a purchaser that you don't know of, but the process can be managed much more efficiently in a small and tightly controlled market.

Whichever approach is used, maximum tension requires only a few, well-funded potential purchasers to emerge from the initial marketing. There is not much to gain from an auction with seven purchasers compared to an auction with six, but it is much harder to efficiently manage a large number of parties. The number of parties taken into the final process needs to be consistent with the information strategy adopted. It's no use offering open access with no warranties to a large number of bidders; it is unmanageable in practice.

The special case of a market with one buyer presents different challenges. Here there are different ways to motivate a deal. In a market of one, you have to adopt either the "takeaway sale," or enter a courtship.

The takeaway sale is a tactic used by realtors and used car salesmen across the globe. You quickly show your wares and then you rapidly remove them. The message is clear: It is a once in a lifetime opportunity to buy this house/car/company, and it won't come again; act quickly. This is a risky approach. If the purchaser doesn't believe you, your negotiating position can be seriously undermined if they react with a studied show of indifference to the opportunity presented. However when it does work, it can produce spectacular results because a strategic premium is paid by the purchaser.

Courtship is subtler and has its own risks and rewards. It involves exploring possibilities and exchanging information and plans to build a consensus on the way forward and what that means in terms of valuation. When the logic of bringing two companies together is compelling, two questions often arise: First, which is the diner and which is the dinner? Second, even if the cake is bigger, you still have to negotiate how it is going to be shared. A courtship strategy requires a significant investment of senior management time and emotion.

The biggest risk in a failed courtship is, as we all know, the effect of a broken heart. The impact on corporations of a failed courtship should not be underestimated: It can paralyze a corporation just as surely as

"Before everything else, getting ready is the secret of success." Henry Ford

it can turn a teenager into a gibbering wreck.

FINANCIAL PURCHASERS—ELEPHANTS OR DUNG BEETLES

Financial buyers come in many forms and provide liquidity to many different markets. The private equity (PE) industry contains both large strategic purchasers (elephants) and opportunists, who seek to snap up companies when no strategic purchaser emerges (dung beetles). Whichever strategy they are pursuing, and despite being much misunderstood and maligned, over the past 20 years financial purchasers have acquired more companies than trade acquirers. Any vendor who does not consider the PE market as a potential purchaser may be missing, at a minimum, a valuable source of competitive tension, and possibly the optimal purchaser.

AUCTIONS—THEORY AND PRACTICE

In a traditional, so-called English auction, bidding stops when the last but one bidder drops out. The vendor receives fractionally more than the second highest bidder was willing to pay. There are various ways to attempt to capture the value that the highest bidder might have paid. For example, a reverse auction (also known as a Dutch or clock auction) operates by the price declining until it is accepted by a bidder. This results in the so-called winner's curse—the only thing that the purchaser knows for certain is that they paid more than anyone else would have.

A counterintuitive solution to the problem was proposed by US economist William Vickrey. In a Vickrey auction, sealed bids are received and the asset is sold to the highest bidder, but at the price bid by the second highest bidder. This system ensures that each bidder bids their own true valuation, rather than speculating on the possible bids of other parties. The theoretical underpinnings are outside the scope of this chapter, but Vickrey was (jointly) awarded the 1996 Nobel Prize in economics for his work in this area.

Information from the first round of bids can be used to intensify informed competitive tension in subsequent rounds. For example, in a group of four second-round bidders, all the bidders might be informed of the value of the third highest bid received in round one. This tells the two highest bidders that they were one of two, but not who was highest. It tells the third highest bidder that they were third, and similarly tells the fourth highest that they are playing catch-up. The information provided by the first-round bids gives each party a clear steer on their position in the process and a strong guide regarding the landscape of the bids.

In practice much of auction theory is of only partial relevance to any corporate sale because the theory is predicated on the assumption that completion of the transaction occurs simultaneously with acceptance of the bid. In practice, of course, there is usually confirmatory due diligence and negotiation of legal agreements to follow.

DEFENDING THE PRICE

Whereas the auction process is designed to drive up the price, the period between accepting an offer and completion is usually defensive. The purchaser may try to find a justification to "chip" the price, and will rarely give any credit for positive variances against any plans they have relied on in the bid. The standard negotiating position of any purchaser when faced with positive information is, "We anticipated improvements in our original bid."

Negative variances are rarely anticipated in a bid and often result in variations to the terms of the indicative offer. Be aware that the legal status of an indicative offer varies from country to country. Whereas most UK and US acquirers view indicative offers relatively lightly, many non-Anglo-Saxon countries view the making of any offer, however qualified it may be, as significant and, in some jurisdictions, potentially legally binding. It helps to understand this when judging both the offers received and the ability to meet any timetable that you might have set for purchasers.

A contract race may alleviate exposure to price chipping, but it requires purchasers to risk paying significant fees in pursuit of a transaction that they have (on average) around a 50% possibility of completing. They may not wish to play that game. Furthermore, the process may increase acquisition risk for the purchaser due to the uncertainty caused to the business, resulting in a reduced final price.

The ability to defend the price depends on the relationship between the purchasers' and vendors' teams, and the effective implementation of the information strategy agreed at the start of the process. If the "hockey stick" projections are not being met, expect a conversation about price to occur.

DEALING WITH STAFF

Companies are possibly the only assets you can sell where the value of the asset is dependent on the goodwill of the people employed in the business. It is extremely difficult to maintain complete secrecy in any transaction. The requirement to collate information not routinely produced often causes questions to be asked. Similarly, e-mails and telephone calls from unfamiliar advisers may trigger suspicion. Uncertainty invariably causes discontent, and transactions involve great uncertainties. Against this background, it is generally advisable to say nothing to staff unless required to do so. Any ambiguous information is often interpreted negatively, causing even more speculation and disruption. The alternative is to communicate honestly, including all the unknowns and uncertainties, giving legitimacy to the speculation but fanning the uncertainty.

Once a deal is certain, communication with staff must form a key part of the post-transaction integration plan.

MAKING IT HAPPEN

Any transaction involves extensive amounts of work and lengthy negotiations peppered with key decisions. There are periods of little apparent activity followed by periods characterized by long meetings that often drag into the night. Transactions are done by people, not by processes, and it is of utmost importance that the key decision-makers do not let boredom, frustration, or fatigue cloud their judgment. Many deals have failed because the principals or their advisers could not keep their head when the finish line was in sight.

Risks often seem more significant when you stare at them for too long. At the end of any transaction there are often negotiations regarding matters that no senior manager would normally consider material. Principals need to use commercial judgment to cut through any of these issues that are holding up a deal.

Finally, the world of mergers and acquisitions (M&A) is full of people who nearly did the best deal ever. M&A is often spoken about using the language of conflict, with winners and losers. In fact, it is about negotiation, a process that requires give and take. There is no point in beating your "opponent" at the negotiating table if all you end up with is a large bill for an aborted transaction.

"In modern business it is not the crook who is to be feared most, it is the honest man who doesn't know what he is doing." William Wordsworth

  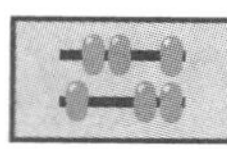      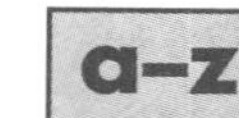

MBOs: A High-Octane and Life-Changing Mode of Business by Andy Nash

EXECUTIVE SUMMARY

This article is aimed at prospective managers of a management buy-out (MBO).

- MBOs are inherently risky, with a relatively high failure rate.
- It's the leverage in the deal structure that makes success so rewarding. Unfortunately leverage works just as impressively in reverse!
- Every year around 600 deals will be completed, and every year broadly that number will reach the exit stage. Unfortunately, one of the most common "exits" over the last 20 years has been receivership!
- Research, good advice, and planning will increase your chances of success
- You can increase your chances of success by knowing what the common elephant traps are.
- Setting out on an MBO without the best advice and support you can muster is akin to walking blindfold through a minefield. You have been warned!

MBOS: THE BEAST EXPLAINED

MBOs—shorthand for MBIs, BIMBOs, IBOs and the like, as well as management buy-outs—make or lose fortunes for the risk-takers because of the leverage involved. Leverage is the fulcrum on which these deals seesaw between success and failure. Every venture capitalist's portfolio has a range of leveraged companies, and average returns to their investors are determined by the balance between their star investments and those which stagnate or go bust. Leverage is a business school type word—my eldest daughter would probably say it was cool! If your company were an automobile, leveraging it would be like filling the trunk with high explosive and then driving off on a long journey with your fingers crossed.

Management buy-outs and buy-ins are a high-octane part of the business world. Since 2001, the most common exit from MBOs/MBIs hasn't been flotation, or even trade sales, but receivership. It is a high-risk/reward arena. Metaphorically, an MBO/MBI is like fitting an eight-liter V12 engine into an aged VW Beetle and expecting it to perform much better than before.

I've worked with twelve MBOs since 1991 in a variety of roles: as chairman, executive director, nonexecutive director, and as a personal coach to a managing director. The experience has varied greatly: from staggering success to the verge of financial oblivion—and fortunately back again. The deals have ranged across very different markets: from the sophisticated world of global drug discovery in mythical Tintagel to heavy-metal bashing (dustcarts) in the West Midlands of England, and from the rarefied academia of international publishing to horticulture in the Welsh valleys. The deals have been backed by many different venture capitalists and financed by UK and international banks.

I have been very fortunate to have seen many MBOs through the prism of management. There are many good books written by academics and professionals that describe the process, structure, and chronology of an MBO. It is important that you understand these topics; however, it's crucial that you also understand other aspects: where the main elephant traps are; what the key success factors are likely to be; and how an MBO's chances of success can be maximized.

After 12 deals I have no idea what constitutes "best practice" because I've discovered that every MBO is unique. I have reflected long and hard on the lessons I've learned on these deals over 18 years, and they are set out below.

MBOS: THE MAIN LESSONS I HAVE LEARNED

1. Do an MBO with your eyes wide open

Conducting an MBO is extremely demanding. The demands on you, your colleagues, and your family and friends will be severe. And this is just to complete the deal. After completion, the difficulties and pressures are unlikely to abate. The risks are significant, even for a well-managed and successful business. You can materially reduce the odds against you by understanding the lessons learned by those who have gone before you.

For a manager, an MBO/MBI is a life-changing experience.

2. Ensure that you are an effective team

A talented group of individuals isn't enough! You must be a team. I don't need to amplify this—any senior manager will understand the difference. If there are fault lines within management, they will be exposed.

You should make any changes that may be needed before you set out on the deal—or at worst during the deal. Afterwards is far more difficult, and it might be too late.

3. Don't overpay—Work to a realistic business plan

There is an inevitable conflict between preparing a plan which, on the one hand, is achievable, and, on the other, is capable of supporting a price high enough to ensure that you can buy your target company. You need to strike the right balance—but this is easier said than done.

It is said that it is better to overpay for the right business than underpay for the wrong one. The thrust of this must be right; however, if you knowingly overpay, with the purchase price predicated on optimistic numbers, you will almost certainly regret it. In any business, performance will deviate from budget or plan. In a highly leveraged business, the margin of underperformance that can be accommodated is relatively small. Some excellent businesses have failed in this way. There was nothing wrong with the company, its management, or its prospects. Its financing structure simply couldn't withstand an unforeseen financial shock.

4. Choose advisors and backers you feel comfortable with

There is no shortage of accountants, legal firms, bankers, and private equity houses that will have an appetite for a good deal. It is, however, important that you feel very comfortable with your advisors and backers.

Your respective commercial and career prospects will be in each other's hands. There must therefore be openness, trust, and mutual respect. This is obviously a totally personal and intangible matter. It may well be that you need to kiss a lot of frogs before you find your prince.

5. Do your deal on a contingent basis

This might be stating the obvious, but some management teams have been caught out in this area. Provided that you are well advised, it is usually possible to ensure that you are not exposed, or left holding the baby, if the deal falls over and fails to complete.

At the right time in the process, advisors are quite adept at securing some degree of cost underwriting from the vendor. These break-fee arrangements are useful in that

"The new environment dictates two rules: first, everything happens faster; second, anything that can be done will be done, if not by you, then by someone else, somewhere." Andrew S. Grove

they tend to provide some security and incentive to see a deal through.

6. Your strategy must be capable of being understood and implemented

Warren Buffett says that if a plan can't fit on a side of A4 it can't be understood. Given that 80% of strategy is about implementation, what he's probably referring to is the difficulties businesses have of actually achieving their objectives if there are not absolute clarity and understanding of strategy throughout the company.

Put another way, if you can't explain your strategy during an elevator ride (i.e. in 20 seconds), you probably can't explain it at all.

7. Take heed of the due diligence report

You will meet many managers who have been scarred by the due diligence process. While due diligence is in many ways akin to a lifebuoy for the backers, it nonetheless shines a torch of some intensity into every corner of your business. Recognize that any management team's first instinct when faced with criticism is to deny it. Make sure it isn't you who is in denial.

Further, task a member of the management team with analyzing the due diligence report, and draw up a list of points to be addressed post completion.

8. Your board must be effective

As Patrick Dunne of 3i Group wrote: "Bad boards destroy value." Directors must be individually and severally effective. The nonexecutive directors must add value and fit in as part of the team. An annual board calendar should be prepared and adhered to. Board papers should be circulated at least three working days before meetings and must contain information, not data. Really important performance indicators (e.g. cash forecasts and covenants) should be graphed so that they can easily be understood. The board agenda should focus on key issues and decision-making and not allow endless waffle or a mere exchange of information. Research shows conclusively that the most effective board meetings last between two and three hours. Communications between the board and fund providers must also be frequent, candid, and well-managed.

9. Incentivize your important managers

Businesses are run by people. Retaining all of the potentially very valuable sweet equity amongst just the top team can be divisive. It may create an us-and-them mentality, which can be very counterproductive. Consider incentivizing managers who are significant in the running of the business. Some companies have incentivized all employees, which is said to have had a very positive effect on the company's performance.

10. If it goes wrong, act fast and get outside help

Many MBOs/MBIs experience a drift from plan which invokes a recovery situation. If a company drifts from plan, remedial action must be taken very fast. If analysis indicates that this is not a one-off but a recurring problem, then your survival is at stake. Recognize this and act accordingly. Frequently, the skills needed to reduce costs and generate cash are not available in the management team. You can train a rabbit to climb trees, but it's better to hire a squirrel! There are experienced individuals who specialize in these situations. You should consider getting them on board to help you negotiate the choppy waters ahead.

11. The exit: Seize the moment

It is highly unlikely that there will ever be a perfect time to exit. Inevitably, there will always be some clouds in view: a potential loss of a contract, a delisting, significant price increases in raw materials, etc. However, if you have the opportunity to unload your trunk load of high-explosive (debt) and it is within the time frame originally envisaged, then you will be well-advised to take it. In short, *carpe diem*.

12. Be true to yourselves and the company

There will be several occasions when you face a moral maze. Whichever way you turn, someone stands to lose. Advice may conflict, and you will be subjected to the most passionate advocacy from parties with different objectives. This is especially likely if you require a second, or third, round of fund-raising. In these situations, do the right thing for the business as invariably this will, over differing timescales, benefit just about everyone involved with the company. Again, easier said than done, but it's the best compass. A great example is that of one serial entrepreneur I know: when trading was tough in the early stage of an MBO, he had a choice: pay the wages or pay the VAT. He got it right—he paid his employees!

MORE INFO

See Also:

★ Executive Rewards: Ensuring That Financial Rewards Match Performance (pp. 673–676)
★ Going Private: Public-to-Private Leveraged Buyouts (pp. 730–732)
★ Leveraged Buyouts: What, Why, When, and How (pp. 743–745)
★ Sources of Venture Capital (pp. 601–603)
✔ Dealing with Venture Capital Companies (p. 1067)
✔ Management Buyouts (pp. 1754–1755)
✔ Planning the Disposal Process (p. 1133)
✔ Understanding and Using Leverage Ratios (p. 1097)
Valuation: Measuring and Managing the Value of Companies (p. 1429)

"The incremental approach to change is effective when what you want is more of what you've already got."
Richard Pascale

  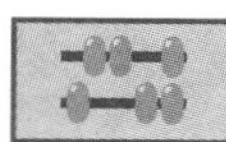      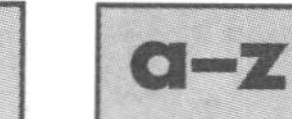

Merger Integration and Transition Management: A New Slant for Finance Executives by Price Pritchett

EXECUTIVE SUMMARY

- Negotiating a good deal is a dangerous act if management isn't solidly prepared to make the deal work.
- Mergers are a fast-growth strategy—and they require fast management.
- The pre-close period is the staging platform for effective integration.
- A merger is always based on a financial proposition, but success invariably rests on the human proposition.

INTRODUCTION

Merger success—defined as value creation—depends heavily on how well conceived the deal was to begin with. But a good outcome is even more dependent on having a well-designed and carefully implemented integration strategy. To put it simply, no deal is a good deal if management can't make it work. Studies over the past several decades prove, however, that far too often companies lack the ability to design and execute a viable integration plan. Over half of all mergers end up as disappointments or outright failures that destroy shareholder value.

Many things contribute to the high casualty rate, but the myriad risk factors can be greatly reduced and in some cases eliminated. The odds of success dramatically improve when management adheres to some fundamental rules for effective integration.

Nevertheless, merger and acquisition (M&A) remains a high stakes game that is undertaken in pursuit of uncommon growth. As such, it calls for uncommon management.

TRANSITION MANAGEMENT SHOULD BEGIN EARLY

The merger transition period starts long before the deal gets final approval and actually closes. Weeks and months can pass as negotiations, due diligence, and the regulatory approval process proceed. Problems, however, don't wait around on management to close the deal. As soon as people pick up the scent that their company is in play, they begin to think and act differently. Their attitudinal shifts and behavior changes create leadership challenges that are unique to mergers. This explains why status quo management stops working.

The troublesome organizational dynamics that kick into gear need immediate attention, so transition management and integration planning should begin at least as soon as the deal becomes public knowledge. The pre-close period is a crucial phase. It's the mobilization zone for merger success where you set the stage for an informed, well- executed integration.

Particularly during the pre-close period, there are far more questions than answers, so the major workforce issue that needs to be addressed is *uncertainty*. People in leadership roles will need the merger management skills necessary to:

- navigate uncertainty and prepare for change;
- deal with people's negativity and resistance;
- keep employees engaged and retain talent;
- protect productivity and client relations.

A lot of damage can occur even before the deal papers are signed if managers at all levels don't respond appropriately to the new organizational dynamics.

Figure 1. Integration framework for the CME–CBOT merger

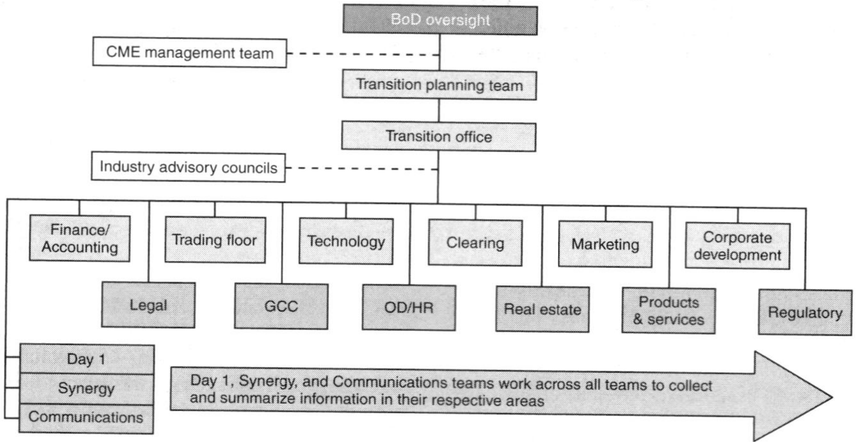

GOVERNANCE OF THE INTEGRATION PROCESS

The transition management infrastructure should be set up, staffed, and functioning prior to the closing date. One person—a credible, experienced senior manager—should be appointed as integration manager with responsibility for overseeing integration planning and implementation. This position provides a single point of accountability for integration success. Given the unique demands of the job, the integration manager needs to possess a high energy level, strong sense of urgency, tolerance for ambiguity, and strong project management skills. The role also calls for in-depth knowledge of the business, good communication skills, plus the ability to create structure and process.

Typically a project management office is established to support the integration manager in running the integration effort. This will consist of a small group of people who meet daily, or at least weekly, to facilitate work streams, set priorities, coordinate schedules, etc., to ensure that the project runs in a disciplined manner.

An executive oversight body ordinarily serves as a steering committee. Members of this group (some drawn from the acquired company) might include the CEO, president, legal counsel, CFO, a senior level human resources executive, a senior communications officer, plus the integration manager. The steering committee designs the high-level merger integration strategy, sets timelines, and decides on synergy targets. Additionally, this group removes roadblocks, resolves sensitive merger issues, and serves as the final sign-off authority on expenditures and key staffing decisions.

"Things will probably come out all right, but sometimes it takes strong nerves just to watch." Hedley Donovan

  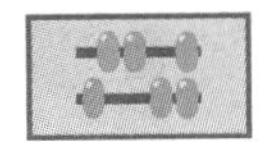      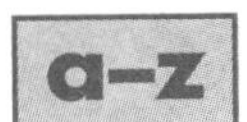

A number of merger integration teams should be formed to conduct the analysis and integration planning for combining the various functional areas. Also, additional teams usually are needed to address cross-functional issues or company-wide matters such as communications, culture integration, etc.

In small mergers with limited staff, integration planning and execution is ordinarily handled by the managers who are accountable for the various functional areas. But even in small deals the integration should be conducted with strict project management discipline and a single person in charge as integration manager.

Of course, legal restrictions or the realities of competition can limit merging companies' ability to plan and organize prior to finalizing the deal. But preparation pays huge dividends, so management should make maximum use of the pre-close period.

Day 1—that point on the calendar when the merger goes live—is a day of reckoning. The acquirer's "opening moves" reveal the quality of pre-close planning and make a defining statement about management's ability to execute. Day 1 activities also are scrutinized for what they might imply about the future, so what's said and done should be carefully orchestrated to manage people's expectations appropriately.

FIVE GROUND RULES FOR EFFECTIVE INTEGRATION

There are two sides to the merger integration coin: project management and people management. Project management deals with the *mechanics*—that is, the administrative, operational, and technical matters involved in consolidating two organizations. People management deals with the so-called *soft stuff*, the highly-charged political, cultural, and personal issues that surface during a merger. It's generally agreed that "the soft stuff is the hard stuff," meaning that people management is more difficult than project management in mergers and acquisitions.

Actually, both aspects of integration management are complicated. But the following ground rules can help the merger process go smoothly and greatly improve the odds of success.

1. Remember—the first word in merger is "me"

Employees, first and foremost, are concerned about themselves. The question they want answered is "How will I personally be affected by the merger?" Until the individual gets answers to the "me issues," you're going to have only half an employee even though you're paying full salary. People can adjust to tremendous amounts of change, and they can deal with disappointment, but they hate to be left hanging in the wind wondering how they'll be affected in the shakeout. Provide closure as soon as possible.

2. Tighten up the integration time-frame

The longer you take to integrate, the closer you live to the edge. You are in a race—a race against the organizational problems and risk factors that are generic to mergers . . . a race against competitors who are building counterstrategies . . . and a race against the merger critics who would love to see you fail. The integration period is a destabilized, perilous time, and speed is your friend. As the saying goes, "Skate fast over thin ice."

3. Promise problems

Mergers are designed to strengthen organizations, but invariably things get worse before they get better. You need to predict this. And you should explain why it happens. Otherwise, the merger critics will point to the normal side effects of change as proof that the deal was ill-advised or that it is being poorly executed. You can preempt the critics, protect management's credibility, and actually make the merger less stressful by straightforwardly telling people what to expect.

4. Educate your workforce on how to perform during the merger

The integration period is a time of ambiguity, instability, and stress. It's not business-as-usual. Train your managers in

CASE STUDY

Merger of Chicago Mercantile Exchange with Chicago Board of Trade

CME and CBOT competed against each other for more than a century, first in agricultural commodities and later in futures and options trading. By acquiring CBOT Holdings for roughly US$8 billion, CME created a combined company valued at approximately US$25 billion. The merger produced the world's largest financial exchange with a market reach that encircles the globe.

The diagram below shows the integration management framework that was designed to transition the two firms into a single organization.

CME invested substantial time and money in laying the groundwork for effective integration. For example, managers in both companies were given briefings on best practices in mergers. Also, a day-long kickoff meeting for integration team leaders was designed to:

- work through the team charters;
- review regulatory guidelines on information sharing;
- provide an orientation regarding the integration planning approach, rules of engagement, expectations, etc.;
- define the scope and boundaries for each planning work stream;
- share information about each other's business;
- begin building cross-company relationships.

Overall, the CME–CBOT merger followed a disciplined integration process and adhered to an urgent timeline for completion.

MAKING IT HAPPEN

Integration planning and execution typically take shape through a financial lens, and appropriately so. The problem with this, however, is that many of the heavy-duty merger success factors revolve around the "soft stuff," which doesn't lend itself readily to hard financial metrics in the *predictive* sense. Of course, *after the fact*, the costs of poorly handling these people management issues may be obvious and easily calculated.

- Financial executives, perhaps even more than the people in human resources, should be champions for an integration effort that respects the influence and monetary impact of cultural, political, and personal issues.
- Calculate the potential costs associated with *not* managing the "soft stuff" effectively. Studies prove that people/cultural issues can wreck a deal.
- Culture problems are conveniently blamed when mergers go bad, but usually executives give culture little more than lip-service during integration. Treat culture as a make-or-break issue from the beginning, and make the investment of money and true expertise needed to deal appropriately with cultural differences.
- Engineer some "early wins." Defuse the critics and resistors by showcasing evidence that the merger is rapidly bringing benefits.

"Trying to squash a rumor is like trying to unring a bell." Shana Alexander

the unique challenges of mergers, and provide guidance on how to lead during large-scale change. Give all employees an orientation on the basics of being acquired and merged—explain how organizations are affected, the difficulties that can be expected, how people react, and how they personally can have a positive influence on the merger process. If you fail to tell the workforce what's coming, or if you don't coach them on how you want them to handle it, why should you expect people to perform the way you'd like?

5. Communicate, communicate, communicate

People crave information and answers. If your communication efforts fail to satisfy their curiosity, the rumor mill will fill the void. Remember, "The more unpleasant the message, the more effort should go into communicating it." But give it to people straight—the good, the bad, and the ugly. Don't shave the truth, and don't slip into a propaganda mode with too much "happy talk" about the merger. Communication problems spawn all kinds of additional problems, so feed a steady stream of accurate and helpful information to all key stakeholders.

CONCLUSION

Mergers represent unconventional growth, and they produce a highly predictable set of "growing pains." But while all mergers are alike in this regard, every merger is different in that each brings its own idiosyncratic problems, which may be very unpredictable.

There's no excuse for failing to prepare merging organizations for the generic challenges. And, for that matter, management also should "expect the unexpected" and be fully prepared to improvise. If people have been trained properly, and if the appropriate transition management infrastructure is in place, the integration effort should succeed in spite of the inevitable surprises.

MORE INFO

Books:

Pritchett, Price. *The Employee Guide to Mergers and Acquisitions.* Dallas, TX: Pritchett, 1986.

Pritchett, Price. *Making Mergers Work: A Guide to Managing Mergers and Acquisitions.* New York: McGraw-Hill, 1987.

Pritchett, Price. *The Employee Handbook for Shaping Corporate Culture: The Mission Critical Approach to Culture Integration and Culture Change*. Dallas, TX: Pritchett, 2002.

Pritchett, Price. *The Unfolding: A Handbook for Living Strong, Being Effective, and Knowing Happiness During Uncertain Times*. Dallas, TX: Pritchett, 2006.

Pritchett, Price. *Deep Strengths: Getting to the Heart of High Performance*. New York: McGraw-Hill, 2008.

Pritchett, Price, Donald Robinson, and Russell Clarkson. *After the Merger: The Authoritative Guide for Integration Success*. 2nd ed. New York: McGraw-Hill, 1997.

Websites:

Association for Corporate Growth (ACG): www.acg.org
Mergers Unleashed: www.mergersunleashed.com
The Deal: www.thedeal.com

See Also:

★ Acquisition Integration: How to Do It Successfully (pp. 708–709)
★ Cultural Alignment and Risk Management: Developing the Right Culture (pp. 724–726)
★ Mergers and Acquisitions: Patterns, Motives, and Strategic Fit (pp. 759–762)
★ Mergers and Acquisitions: Today's Catalyst Is Working Capital (pp. 763–765)
✔ Assessing Business Performance (p. 1144)
✔ Planning the Acquisition Process (p. 1132)

"Speak the truth, but leave immediately after." Slovenian proverb

  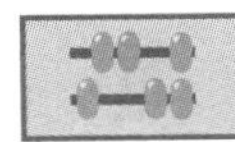   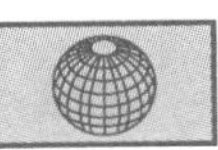   

Mergers and Acquisitions: Patterns, Motives, and Strategic Fit by Siri Terjesen

EXECUTIVE SUMMARY

- Mergers and acquisitions (M&A) are two broad types of restructuring through which managers seek economies of scale, enhanced market visibility, and other efficiencies.
- A merger occurs when two companies decide to combine their assets and liabilities into one entity, or when one company purchases another.
- An acquisition describes one company's purchase of another—for example, the absorption of a smaller target firm into a larger acquiring firm.
- The nature and scope of M&A activity has changed over time, with a growing trend to cross-border transactions.
- M&As are motivated by the expectation of financially rewarding synergies in terms of reduced fixed costs, increased market share, cross-sales, economies of scale, lower taxes, and more efficient resource distribution.
- At the individual level, executives may pursue M&As because of psychological drivers such as empire-building, hubris, fear, and mimicry.
- There are five broad types of strategic fit: overcapacity, geographic roll-up, product or market extension, research and development, and industry convergence.
- M&A execution can be hampered by incompatible corporate cultures, with failure to achieve synergies, high executive turnover, and too much focus on integration at the expense of customers.
- Before the deal, managers should formulate a clear and convincing strategy, preassess the deal, undertake extensive due diligence, formulate a workable plan, and communicate to internal and external stakeholders.
- After the deal, managers should establish leadership, manage culture and respect employees, explore new growth opportunities, exploit early wins, and focus on the customer.

INTRODUCTION

Mergers and acquisitions are two broad types of restructuring through which managers seek economies of scale, enhanced market visibility, and other efficiencies. A merger occurs when two companies decide to combine their assets and liabilities into one entity, or when one company purchases another. The term is often used to describe a merger of equals, such as that of Daimler-Benz and Chrysler, which was renamed DaimlerChrysler (see case study). The term "acquisition" simply refers to one company's purchase of another—as when a smaller target firm is bought and absorbed into a larger acquiring firm.

PATTERNS

The worldwide M&A market topped US$4.3 trillion and over 40,000 deals in 2007. Figure 1 depicts the growth of M&A activity, quarter by quarter, over the last five years.

The nature and scope of M&A activity has changed substantially over time. In the United States, the Great Merger Movement (1895 to 1905) was characterized by mergers across small firms with little market share, resulting in companies such as DuPont, Nabisco, and General Electric.

More recently, globalization has increased the market for cross-border M&As. In 2007 cross-border transactions were worth US$2.1 trillion, up from US$256 billion in 1996. Transnational M&As have seen annual increases of as much as 300% in China, 68% in India, 58% in Europe, and 21% in Japan.[1] The regional share of today's M&A market is shown in Figure 2.

MOTIVES

Mergers and acquisitions are often motivated by company performance, but can also be linked to executive decision-makers' empire-building, hubris, fear, and tendency to copy other firms.

The dominant rationale used to explain M&A activity is that acquiring firms seek improved financial performance through synergies that enhance revenues and lower costs. The two companies are expected to achieve cost savings that offset any decline in revenues. Then Hewlett-Packard CEO Carly Fiorina justified the merger with Compaq at a launch effort on September 3, 2001: "This is a decisive move that accelerates our strategy and positions us to win by offering even greater value to our customers and partners. In addition to the clear strategic benefits of combining two highly complementary organizations and product families, we can create substantial shareowner value through significant cost-structure improvements and access to new growth opportunities."[2]

The formula for the minimum value of the synergies required to protect the acquiring firm's stockholder value (i.e. to avoid dilution in earnings per share) is:

$$\frac{(\text{Pre}-\text{M\&A value of both firms}+\text{Synergies})}{\text{Post}-\text{M\&A firm number of shares}}=\text{Pre}-\text{M\&A firm stock price}$$

Managers may be motivated by the potential for the following synergies:

- Reduced fixed costs: Duplicate departments and operations are removed, staff often made redundant, and typically the former CEO also leaves.

Figure 1. Global M&A activity 2002–07. (*Source*: Thomson Financial, Bain & Company analysis)

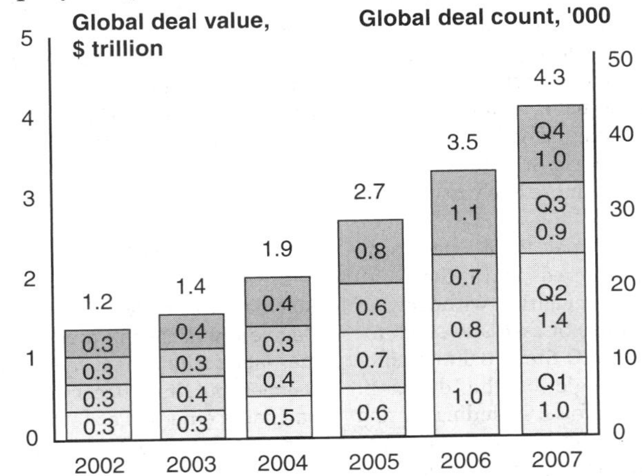

"...we can create substantial shareowner value through significant cost-structure improvements and access to new growth opportunities." Carly Fiorina

  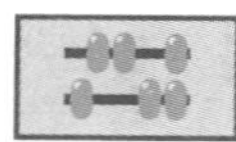      

- Increased market share: The new larger company has increased market share and, potentially, greater market power to set prices.
- Cross-sales: The new larger company will be able to cross-sell one firm's products to the other firm's customers, and vice versa.
- Greater economies of scale: Greater size enables better negotiations with suppliers over bulk buying.
- Lower taxes: In some countries, a company that acquires a loss-making firm can use the target's loss to reduce liability.
- More efficient resource distribution: A larger company can pool scarce resources, or might distribute the technological know-how of one company, reducing information asymmetries.

At the individual decision-making level, M&A activity is also linked to the following:

- Empire-building: M&As may result from glory-seeking, as managers believe bigger is better and seek to create a large firm quickly via acquisition, rather than through the generally slower process of organic growth. In some firms, executive compensation is linked to total profits rather than profit per share, creating an incentive to merge/acquire to create a firm with higher total profits. Furthermore, executives often receive bonuses for completing mergers and acquisitions, regardless of the resulting impact on share price.
- Hubris: Public awards and increasing praise may lead an executive to overestimate his or her ability to add value to firms. CEOs who are publicly praised in the popular press tend to pay 4.8% more for target firms. Hubris can also lead executives to fall in love with the deal, lose objectivity, and overestimate expected synergies.
- Fear: Managers' fear of an uncertain environment, particularly in terms of globalization and technological development, may lead them to believe they have little choice but to acquire if they are to avoid being acquired.
- Mimicry: If leading firms in their industry have merged or acquired others, executives may be more likely to consider the strategy.

Executives may overpay for a target firm. Microsoft has acquired more than 128 companies, but recently withdrew a US$44.6 billion offer of cash and stock for Yahoo. Microsoft CEO Steve Ballmer commented on the logic of the decision: "Despite our best efforts, including raising our bid by roughly $5 billion, Yahoo! has not moved toward accepting our offer. After

Figure 2. Global M&A market 2007—share by region. (*Source*: Thomson Financial)

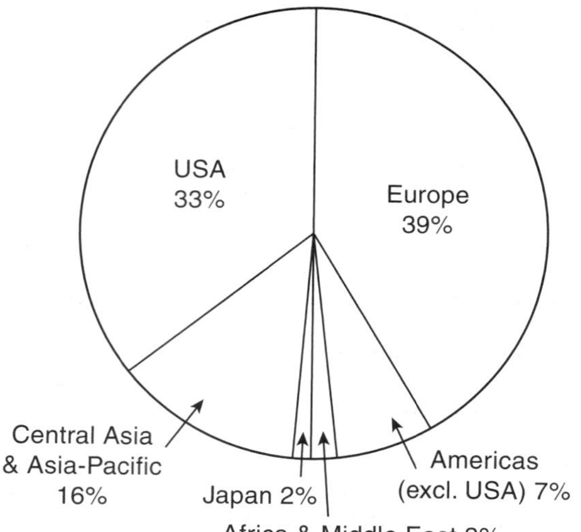

CASE STUDY

The Failed Merger of DaimlerChrysler

Germany's Daimler and the United States' Chrysler merged in 1988, creating the world's largest commercial auto manufacturer. At the time of the merger, Daimler's CEO claimed that the merger of a luxury car maker (Daimler) with a mass-market brand (Chrysler) would become the world's most profitable auto manufacturer due to new economies of scale and scope across brands, product niches, manufacturing expertise, and distribution networks. For example, it was hoped Daimler's high-end manufacturing expertise and worldwide network would help to distribute Chrysler products and compete successfully against increasingly strong Asian competitors, especially Toyota and Honda. However, at the time, not all executives were positive. One DaimlerChrysler executive was quoted as saying, "It is unthinkable for a Chrysler car to be built in a Mercedes-Benz factory, and for as long as I'm responsible for the Mercedes-Benz brand, only over my dead body will a Mercedes be built in a Chrysler factory."[6]

By the end of 2003 DaimlerChrysler's market capitalization was just US$38 billion, significantly lower than the pre-merger US$47 billion in 1998. Despite product costs, DaimlerChrysler was unable to realize expected synergies. Furthermore, many competitors followed Chrysler's lead, introducing minivans, pickup trucks, and SUVs that eroded Chrysler's formerly attractive market share. Further barriers to success came with management and national cultural differences: Daimler's mostly German management used approaches that did not go down well with Chrysler managers. By early 2003 most of Chrysler's top executive team had left the firm.

Seven years after the merger the picture became more positive, with Chrysler contributing one-third of the company's earnings in the first half of 2005. Dieter Zetsche was promoted to chairman of DaimlerChrysler's board. By August, market capitalization reached US$54 billion and worldwide sales of the newly launched Mercedes were up 9%. Still, the American market proved difficult, with the three major American auto manufacturers experiencing significantly declining sales. Meanwhile, Toyota and Honda sales were up 16% and 10% respectively, gaining in the upscale market DaimlerChrysler had hoped to dominate.

In the summer of 2006, DaimlerChrysler sought to make a positive out of a negative in its US television advertisements, with Zetsche presented as an amusing cultural misfit to America. Still the company faced high labor and health care costs and soaring fuel costs. By April 2007, DaimlerChrysler confirmed that buyers were being sought, as German investors declared "this marriage made in heaven turned out to be a complete failure." In fact, some suggested that Daimler could itself become a takeover target if it did not sell Chrysler. By May, DaimlerChrysler had paid Cerberus Capital Management, a private equity investment firm, US$650 million to end its exposure to health care and other costs as well as to ongoing operational losses.

"...for as long as I'm responsible for the Mercedes-Benz brand, only over my dead body will a Mercedes be built in a Chrysler factory." DaimlerChrysler executive

  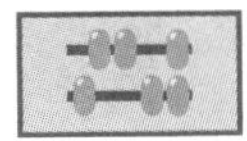      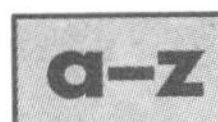

careful consideration, we believe the economics demanded by Yahoo! do not make sense for us, and it is in the best interests of Microsoft stockholders, employees, and other stakeholders to withdraw our proposal."[3]

STRATEGIC FIT

Regardless of their category or structure, all M&As share the common goal that the value of the combined companies will be greater than the sum of the two parts. M&A success depends on the ability to achieve strategic fit. Harvard Professor Joseph Bower identifies five broad types of strategic fit, based on the relationship between the two companies and the synergies sought: overcapacity M&A, geographic roll-up M&A, product or market extension M&A, M&A as R&D, and industry convergence M&A.[4]

Overcapacity M&A

In this horizontal M&A, the two companies often competed directly, with similar product lines and markets. The new combined entity is expected to leverage synergies related to overcapacity by rationalizing operations (for example, shutting factories). This often one-time M&A can be especially difficult to execute as both companies' management groups are inclined to fight for control.

Geographic Roll-Up M&A

In a geographic roll-up the new entity seeks geographic expansion, but often keeps operating units local. For example, Banc One purchased many local banks across the United States in the 1980s. Banc One was, in turn, acquired by JPMorgan Chase & Co. in 2004.

Product or Market Extension M&A

Market-based roll-up focuses on extending a product line or international coverage. Often the two companies sell similar products but in different markets, or different products in similar markets. Brands are often a key motivation. Philip Morris purchased Kraft for US$12.9 billion—four times its book value. Philip Morris CEO Hamish Marshall justified the premium: "The future of consumer marketing belongs to companies with the strongest brands."[5]

M&A as R&D

A fourth type of strategic fit is research and development. Companies may acquire or merge with others to access technologies. Microsoft has aggressively pursued this strategy, acquiring smaller, entrepreneurial firms such as Forethought, which had presentation software that would eventually be known as PowerPoint.

Industry Convergence M&A

Finally, the new entity may be motivated by a "bet" that a new industry is emerging and the desire to have a position in this industry. For example, Viacom purchased Paramount and Blockbuster in the expectation that integrated media firms controlling both content and distribution were the wave of the future.

CONCLUSION

Mergers and acquisitions can be accretive in that they increase financial performance, or dilutive in the reverse case, where a

MAKING IT HAPPEN

Despite the grim statistics, several companies are skilled M&A executors. For example, General Electric has integrated as many as 534 companies over a six-year period, and Kellogg's delivered a 25% return to stockholders after purchasing Keebler.[7] The following are key steps to facilitating a successful process before and after a merger:

Before the Merger

1. Begin by formulating a clear and convincing strategy. Strategists must first develop a compelling and sustainable strategy. Key questions include: What is your firm's strategy? What role does the M&A play in this strategy? What is the vision of the strategy of the new entity?

2. Preassess the deal. Prior to signing a memo of understanding, managers should examine operational and management issues and risks. Seek answers to the following questions: Is this the right target? What is the compelling logic behind this deal? What is the value? How would we communicate this value to the board of directors and other key stakeholders? What will our strategy be for bidding and negotiations? How much are we willing to spend? If we are successful, how can we accelerate integration?

3. Do your due diligence. Executives must acquire and analyze as much information as possible about potential synergies. In addition to managers across key functional areas in the firm, outside experts can be brought in to help appraise answers in the preassessment, and especially to challenge assumptions, by asking questions such as:
Are our estimates of future growth and profitability rates reliable? Are there aspects of the company history/culture or of the environment (for example, legal, cultural, political, economic) that should be taken into account?

4. Devise a workable plan. Formulate plans that take into account some of the following: What is our new entity's organizational structure? Who is in charge? What products will be taken forward? How will we manage company accounts? What IT systems will we use?

5. Communicate. M&A transactions tend to be viewed favorably when executives can convincingly discuss integration plans, both internally and externally. Managers should be prepared to answer the questions identified above, as well as: How can we prepare our people psychologically for the deal? What value will be created? What are the priorities for integration? What are the primary risks? How will progress be measured? How will we address any surprises?

After the Deal

6. Establish leadership. The new entity will require the quick identification and buy-in of managers, especially at top and middle levels. Ask: Who will lead the new entity? Do we have buy-in and support from the right people?

7. Manage the culture and respect the employees of the merged/acquired company. An atmosphere of respect and tolerance can aid the speed and ease of integration. Executives should formulate plans that address the following concerns: How can we encourage the best and brightest employees to stay on in the new entity? How can we build loyalty and buy-in?

8. Explore new growth opportunities. Long-run performance is linked to identifying and acting on both internal and external growth opportunities. Managers should seek out any untapped growth opportunities in the new entity.

9. Exploit early wins. To build momentum, the new entity should actively seek early wins and communicate these. To identify them, consider whether there early wins in sales, knowledge management, or the work environment.

10. Focus on the customer. To survive, firms must create value for customers. Managers must continue to ask: Are we at risk of losing customers? Are our salespeople informed about the new entity? Can our salespeople get our customers excited about the new entity?

"After careful consideration, we believe the economics demanded by Yahoo! do not make sense for us. . ."
Steve Ballmer, Chief Executive Officer, Microsoft

measure such as earnings per share (EPS) actually falls. It is a fact that 70% of mergers and acquisitions actually destroy value.

In implementation, M&As typically face the following critical issues:

- Incompatible corporate cultures: The cultures of the two companies may be inconsistent, resulting in resources being diverted away from the focal synergies.
- Business as usual: The target company may allow redundant staff and overlapping operations to continue, thwarting efficiency.
- High executive turnover: The target company may lose critical top management team leadership. A recent study reports that target companies lose 21% of their executives each year for at least ten years following an acquisition (twice the turnover experienced in nonmerged firms).
- Neglect business at hand: A recent McKinsey study reported that too many companies focus on integration and cost cutting, and neglect the daily business at hand and customers.

MORE INFO

Books:

Bruner, Robert F. *Deals from Hell: M&A Lessons That Rise Above the Ashes*. Hoboken, NJ: Wiley, 2005.

Galpin, Timothy J., and Mark Herndon. *The Complete Guide to Mergers and Acquisitions: Process Tools to Support M&A Integration at Every Level*. San Francisco, CA: Jossey-Bass, 2007.

Miller, Edwin L. *Mergers and Acquisitions: A Step-by-Step Legal and Practical Guide*. Hoboken, NJ: Wiley, 2008.

Sadtler, David, David Smith, and Andrew Campbell. *Smarter Acquisitions: Ten Steps to Successful Deals*. Harlow, UK: Pearson Education, 2008.

Websites:

Google Scholar articles—search on terms "mergers and acquisitions" or "M&A": scholar.google.com

Yahoo! Finance M&A news: finance.yahoo.com/news/category-m-a/

See Also:

★ Acquisition Integration: How to Do It Successfully (pp. 708–709)
★ Mergers and Acquisitions: Today's Catalyst Is Working Capital (pp. 763–765)
★ Why Mergers Fail and How to Prevent It (pp. 772–773)
✔ Acquiring a Company (p. 1128)
✔ M&A Regulations: A Global Overview (p. 1130)
✔ Planning the Acquisition Process (p. 1132)
✔ The Rationale for an Acquisition (p. 1134)
✔ Structuring M&A Deals and Tax Planning (p. 1135)

NOTES

1 Firstbrook, Caroline. "Transnational mergers and acquisitions: How to beat the odds of disaster." *Journal of Business Strategy* 28:1 (2007): 53–56. Online at: dx.doi.org/10.1108/02756660710723215

2 Quoted on ThinkExist.com: thinkexist.com/quotation/this_is_a_decisive_move_that_accelerates_our/346964.html

3 Smalley, Tim. "Microsoft withdraws from Yahoo! acquisition." *Bit-tech.net* (May 5, 2008). Online at: tinyurl.com/3wu9t2e

4 Bower, Joseph. L. "Not all M&As are alike—and that matters." *Harvard Business Review* 79:3 (March 2001): 92–101. Online at: tinyurl.com/3bbl38u

5 Biggar, J. M., and E. Selame. "Building brand assets." *Chief Executive* 78 (1992): 36–39. Cited in Bahadir, S. Cem, Sundar G. Bharadwaj, and Rajendra K. Srivastava. "Financial value of brands in mergers and acquisitions: Is value in the eye of the beholder?" *Journal of Marketing* 72:6 (November 2008): 147–154.

6 Waller, David. *Wheels on Fire: The Amazing Inside Story of the Daimler–Chrysler Merger*. London: Hodder & Stoughton, 2001; p. 243.

7 Perry, Jeffrey S., and Thomas J. Herd. "Mergers and acquisitions: Reducing M&A risk through improved due diligence." *Strategy and Leadership* 32:2 (2004): 12–19.

"Some M&As can be quite profitable, for example, Kellogg's acquisition of Keebler delivered a 25% return to the shareholders."

  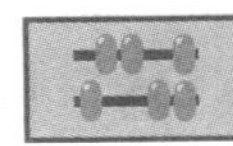   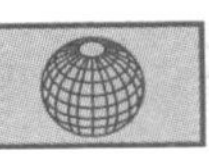   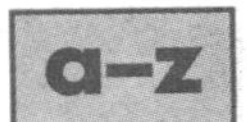

Mergers and Acquisitions: Today's Catalyst Is Working Capital by James S. Sagner

EXECUTIVE SUMMARY

- In developed economies M&As are now used to acquire balance sheet assets, particularly cash hoards and other working capital; previously, M&A was oriented to strategic diversification or integration.
- Although the volume of deals is down due to global economic conditions, the premiums paid for companies remain robust.
- Acquirers appear to understand the risk inherent in these transactions, including the threat of investigation by US, EU, and Japanese regulators.
- Until the recent problems with lines of credit provided by banks, many companies held excessive amounts of liquidity, making them vulnerable to unfriendly takeovers.
- Various consulting companies have international practices in working capital management, including advising on mergers and assisting management to achieve efficiencies after the deal is completed.
- Global M&A looks for the following characteristics: a high current assets-to-revenue relationship; a holding of cash that is not likely to be applied to business operations; and a proven income stream that should provide adequate cash flow to pay down borrowings used to provide financing for an acquisition.

INTRODUCTION

Merger and acquisition (M&A) activities in developed countries once focused on strategic transactions for diversification or for vertical or horizontal integration. While that continues to be the situation in the developing economies, the M&A game in the United States, Western Europe, and Japan is often either to gain balance sheet assets, particularly hoards of underperforming cash, or to improve the acquired company's working capital management. It's a complete revolution in the way companies and investment bankers look at candidates for M&A. What's going on?

CHANGES IN THE M&A LANDSCAPE

M&A transactions for all of 2012 declined about 10% from 2011 to US$2.2 trillion, the same level as 2010. CFOs have been holding more than US$3.5 trillion in cash while delaying deals for most of 2012, as EU countries slid into recession and developing economies such as China and India experienced lower growth.[1] However, improving economic prospects and the need to manage costs and reduce competition led to several recently announced deals, including the merger of AMR (parent of American Airlines) and US Airways, and the acquisition of HJ Heinz by Berkshire Hathaway and the Brazilian firm 3G Capital Management (for US$28 billion).

Prior to the recession that began in 2008, the global annual appetite for M&A was nearly US$4 trillion. The premiums being paid for companies continues to remain strong, with the Heinz deal at 19% above the publicly traded stock price as compared to pre-recession deals averaging about 25% above the share price.[2] The weak US dollar has brought several foreign buyers to the United States in the search for access to attractive markets and technologies.

Some of the past M&A hype has been tempered by a better understanding of the risk of these transactions, as documented by such publications as *BusinessWeek*[3] and as experienced in the loss of value to investors.[4] The lure of expanding markets, product lines, technologies, and customer bases drove much of M&A through the last three decades of the 20th century. Many of these hopes turned out to be illusory as mergers underperformed or failed due to incompatibilities between the marketing, production, engineering, financial, and systems functions of the participants.

Some mergers came under investigation by one or more US regulatory agencies, and were delayed, rejected, or abandoned. For example, the Federal Trade Commission has acted against "threats" of raised concentration in markets for frozen pizza, carburetor kits, urological catheters, and casket parts. The Justice Department hit mergers threatening to raise concentration in markets for frozen dessert pies, artificial Christmas trees, vandal-resistant plumbing fixtures used in prisons, local towel rental services, drapery hardware, and commercial trash hauling in Dallas.[5] The European Commission has been even more rigorous in its merger reviews than the two US agencies.

Research by Towers Perrin and the Cass Business School finds that the most recent era of M&A deals has created value, rather than led to its destruction as in earlier periods.[6] The emphasis has switched to the execution of the deal and a focus on improved financial performance.

Although strategic expansion will continue to be of interest despite the threat of antitrust review, future M&A practice will likely focus on two completely different attractions that avoid the regulators' microscope:

- underused liquidity on balance sheets, offering opportunities for the acquirer to redeploy cash in productive activities;
- inefficient working capital management, leading to opportunities to improve the utilization of current assets and liabilities.

UNDERUSED LIQUIDITY

Recent studies illustrate the predicament that many businesses currently face: too much money on balance sheets and too few attractive capital investments. This situation has been developing for at least a half dozen years; for example, the Association for Financial Professionals (AFP) conducted a study reported in 2007 that 36% of respondents held larger amounts of short-term investments than six months earlier.[7]

As of early 2013, the typical public company had a weighted average cost of capital of just over 10%; see Table for the calculation. A company with cash or near-cash investments can only earn about 1% pre-tax on these assets at the current rates available,[8] or about $\frac{3}{4}$% (75 basis points) after tax, assuming some holdings of medium-term investments. Thus, companies holding cash incur a direct *loss* of more than 9% on that asset without receiving any possible strategic gain. Acquirers of these cash hoards can use these funds to pay down debt, acquire stock in the open market, increase dividends, or expand business operations. In fact M&A deals are often financed by loans made against the

Table 1. Illustration of cost-of-capital calculation

	Balance sheet portion	After-tax costs	Weighted component costs
Debt	40%	0.056*	0.022
Equity	60%	0.140**	0.084
	100%		0.106

* Pre-tax 8% less corporate tax rate.

** 12% growth + 2% dividend.

"Happiness is a positive cash flow." Fred Adler

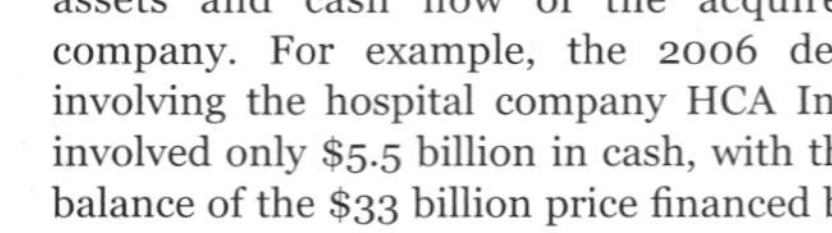

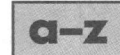

assets and cash flow of the acquired company. For example, the 2006 deal involving the hospital company HCA Inc. involved only $5.5 billion in cash, with the balance of the $33 billion price financed by the cash and future income of HCA.

INEFFICIENT WORKING CAPITAL MANAGEMENT

Working capital (WC) is defined as current assets less current liabilities; in this section we will focus on current assets other than cash. In the last four decades of the previous century, the percentage of WC as a percentage of sales declined by three-fourths.[9] Although this represents a significant improvement in the management of these balance sheet accounts, estimates are that the total of excess WC may still exceed $900 billion, up one-third since 2005.[10]

There are merger opportunities in acquiring companies with excess WC and managing these accounts so that it approaches as close to zero as possible. The concept of WC as a hindrance to financial performance is a complete change in attitude from the conventional wisdom before the turn of the 21st century. However, WC has never contributed to a company's profits; instead, it just sits on the balance sheet awaiting disposition. The Checklist box gives some ideas for working capital management.

Various consulting companies have developed international practices in working capital management, including advising on mergers and assisting management to achieve efficiencies once the deal has been completed. For example, REI is a US-based advisory services organization that has developed a global brand in WC services. REI has enabled clients in more than 60 countries to free up tens of billions of US dollars through optimization of working capital in the last 10 years alone. FTI Consulting offers an array of services designed to help companies address critical issues and improve performance prior to engaging advisory services for acquisitions, divestitures, and recapitalizations. There are several other firms that support M&A analyses while assisting the new management to squeeze efficiencies out of the current asset and/or current liability portions of the balance sheet.

CHECKLIST OF WORKING CAPITAL IDEAS

Accounts Receivable

The credit and collection process, no matter how aggressive, inevitably results in some uncollectable amounts. When faced with the cost of the credit review process, bad debt expenses, and the cost of credit and collections, some businesses outsource their collection activities to a factor. Factors purchase or lend money on accounts receivable based on an evaluation of the creditworthiness of prospective customers of the business calculated as a discount from the sale amount, usually about 3 to 4%. That is, the factor will receive the entire sales amount, the selling company having received 96 to 97% at the time that the buyer was accepted by the factor.

Receivables Collateralization

In collateralization, a receivables package is offered as a security to investors. The critical element is a periodic, predictable flow of cash in payment of debts, such as credit cards, automobile loans, equipment leases, healthcare receivables, health club fees, and airline ticket receivables.

The market for public collateralizations is in the hundreds of billions of dollars, which has driven the required interest return to investors to become competitive with bank lending arrangements. Initial costs are higher than bank loans because the services of several professionals are required: attorneys; commercial and/or investment bankers; accountants; rating agencies (when ratings are required); and income servicers. However, the advantage of receivables collateralization is substantial—the transformation of receivables into cash.

Inventory

Just-in-time (JIT) requires that required materials be in the place of manufacture or assembly at the appropriate time to minimize excess inventory and to reduce wastage and expense. JIT succeeds when there are: a limited number of transactions; few "disturbances" due to unscheduled downtime, depending instead on periodic maintenance; the grouping of production processes to reduce the movement of work-in-process; and a significant focus on quality control (QC). QC minimizes downtime and the holding of buffer or safety stock to replace defective materials.

In traditional JIT, the company owns the inventory of components and parts, assuring access as the next production operation begins. JIT as currently practiced places the materials at the manufacturing or assembly site, but title remains with the vendor until production begins. This relationship requires suppliers to optimize the stock of inventory, holding only those items that have been specified or are known to be required based on a statistical analysis of purchasing history. Both the provider and the user of materials are forced to develop a strong partnering attitude and minimize the adversarial stance often observed between purchasing counterparties.

Accounts Payable

Inefficient payables pervade US business. Invoices presented for payment should be matched against purchase orders and receiving reports to determine that the vendor has met the terms and conditions of the order, and that materials were received in good condition and in the correct amount. In practice, invoices are often paid without ascertaining that all requirements have been met. In about one-third of all payables situations, no purchase order was ever issued, nor was there a contract or other written agreement as to price or specifications.

A substantial number of companies have inadequate policies regarding appropriate purchasing and accounts payables practices. For example:

- Should the payment be released on the due date or some specified number of days after the due date?
- Are all cash discounts to be taken, or only those that provide a stipulated discount?
- Can the requesting business unit choose the supplier, or does purchasing have the authority to select vendors so as to maximize volume pricing?
- Has purchasing determined that approved vendors are legitimate businesses, with a suitable record of providing goods and services to the business community?

LET'S LOOK AT A DEAL

The $90 billion hostile takeover by Pfizer of Warner-Lambert (Warner), completed in 2000, was hyped as a traditional horizontal integration of two powerful pharmaceutical companies. Clearly, Pfizer was acquiring a significant asset in Lipitor, Warner's cholesterol-lowering drug, and established cost savings through headcount reductions. Stock analysts even made statements to the effect that the deal was strictly "...for strategic reasons—for Lipitor, for the therapeutic enhancements Warner-Lambert brings, and for the sheer marketing clout..."[11]

However, the merger was motivated in large part by financial considerations. In 1999 Warner reported cash and short-term investments of $1.943 billion, equivalent to 17.0% of total assets of $11.442 billion, versus 13.8% for the industry. Pfizer was buying the cash hoard, which was $360 million more than the rest of the industry required for the assets carried. Pfizer was also buying an excellent balance sheet, including a current ratio of 1.5 times and current assets as a percentage of sales of 44.0%. And Warner earned $2.441 billion before taxes in 1999,

  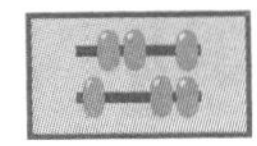      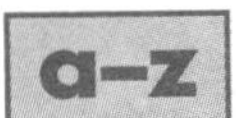

a very healthy 18.9% of sales versus 9.6% for the industry.

TIPS FOR CFOS ON FUTURE M&A DEALS

The flood of US dollars in foreign ownership continues to grow due to the persistent balance of payments deficits in the United States. Global investors looking for properties will be looking at public companies with the following characteristics:

- a high current assets-to-revenue relationship, particularly where the current ratio exceeds the average for the industry;
- a cash (and near-cash) hoard that is not likely to be applied to business operations and is unlikely to be used for dividends or stock repurchases;
- a proven income stream that should provide adequate cash flow to pay down borrowings used to provide partial financing for an acquisition.

Furthermore, there is a trend toward M&A that is not strategic within an industry, meaning that a hostile or friendly approach can come from anywhere at any time.

Too many companies hoard cash while waiting for capital projects with superior returns. In fact, those opportunities may never appear. Financial analysts are beginning to recognize that worthwhile capital investments are unusual and are likely to be short-lived. In other words, the reality of international competition shortens any competitive advantage a company may gain, unless protected by patents or other exclusive arrangements. To quote a leading finance text:

"It is a basic principle of economics that positive NPV [net present value] investments will be rare in a highly competitive environment. Therefore, proposals that appear to show significant value in the face of stiff competition are particularly troublesome, and the likely reaction of the competition to any innovations must be closely examined."[12]

Savvy outsiders can analyze the financial statements of targeted companies and, with the help of their investment bankers, take friendly or hostile action to seize a financially inefficient business.

MORE INFO

See Also:

★ Acquisition Integration: How to Do It Successfully (pp. 708–709)
★ Coping with Equity Market Reactions to M&A Transactions (pp. 721–723)
✔ Achieving Success in International Acquisitions (p. 1127)
✔ Acquiring a Company (p. 1128)
✔ Acquisition Accounting (p. 1129)
✔ Planning the Acquisition Process (p. 1132)
✔ Structuring M&A Deals and Tax Planning (p. 1135)
✔ Using IRR for M&A Financing (p. 1137)
✔ Using the Market-Value Method for Acquisitions (p. 1139)

NOTES

An earlier version of this article appeared as "Why working capital drives M&A today." *Journal of Corporate Accounting & Finance* 18:2 (2007): 41–45. Used by permission of John Wiley & Sons, Inc.

1 Kirchfeld, Aaron, and Serena Saitto. "Fourth-quarter M&A surge spurs optimism after 2012 deals decline." *Bloomberg.com* (December 27, 2012). Online at: tinyurl.com/ahbsn4m

2 Data from June 2008; see "M&A premiums up despite slowdown" at www.businessweek.com/investing/insights/blog/archives/2008/06/despite_the_ma.html

3 David Henry. "Mergers: Why most big deals don't pay off." *BusinessWeek* (October 14, 2002). Online at: www.businessweek.com/magazine/content/02_41/b3803001.htm

4 According to *BusinessWeek*, 61% of acquirers in a merger destroyed their stockholders' wealth (*ibid.*).

5 These situations were noted by Frederick M. Rowe on pp. 1512–13 of "The decline of antitrust and the delusions of models: The Faustian pact of law and economics." *Georgetown Law Journal* 72:5 (1984): 1511–1570. For a review of American antitrust policy, see James S. Sagner. "Antitrust as frontier justice: Is it time to retire the sheriff?" *Business and Society Review* 111 (March 2006): 37–54.

6 At www.innovations-report.com/html/reports/economy_finances/report-112476.html (June 17, 2008). Towers Perrin is a global consulting firm that specializes in human capital strategy, program design and management, and risk and capital management.

7 AFP in conjunction with Citigroup. *2007 AFP liquidity survey: Report of survey results.* Online at: www.afponline.org/pub/pdf/Liquidity_2007.pdf

8 Commercial paper rates for up to 120 days were 2.50% in mid-June 2008 according to the *Wall Street Journal* (rates are from June 10, 2008, as quoted on page C10). Early 2013 rates are about one-tenth of that paid in 2008 (about 25 basis points).

9 Standard and Poor's *Financial Analyst's Handbook*, 2002.

10 Banham, Russ. "Too much of a good thing." *CFO Europe* (July/August 2012). Online at: tinyurl.com/cg9gpdm

11 Comment by Martyn Postle, Cambridge Pharma Consultancy (UK), reported in David Shook. "Pfizer-Warner: One drug merger that might just deliver." *BusinessWeek* (May 17, 2000). Online at: www.businessweek.com/investor/content/eemi/emi0517a.html

12 Ross, Stephen A., Randolph W. Westerfield, and Bradford D. Jordan. *Essentials of Corporate Finance*. 5th ed. Boston, MA: McGraw-Hill/Irwin, 2007, p. 275.

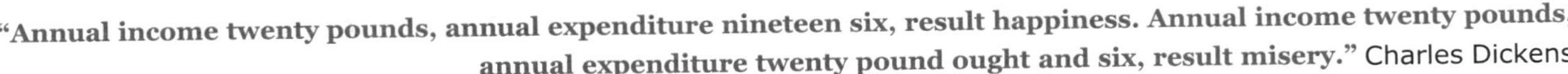

"Annual income twenty pounds, annual expenditure nineteen six, result happiness. Annual income twenty pounds, annual expenditure twenty pound ought and six, result misery." Charles Dickens

  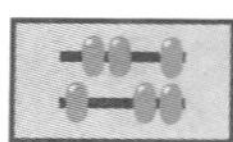      

The Missing Metrics: Managing the Cost of Complexity

by John L. Mariotti

EXECUTIVE SUMMARY

- Despite the best efforts in many areas, the accounting and finance systems currently in use overlook the costs of complexity.
- The costs are hidden in the operating statements of a company until the period-end results show the adverse effects.
- It is time to recognize that these costs exist, identify them, and develop new metrics in the place of those that are missing.
- The responsibility for new metrics should begin with boards of directors and senior (C-suite) executives, and also fall upon public accounting firms and the regulations they observe.

INTRODUCTION

Accounting systems have come a long way in the past decades. Activity-based costing revealed where costs were being incurred and what was driving them. The blizzard of regulations following the debacles involving Enron, WorldCom, and others led to the passage of the Sarbanes–Oxley Act (in the United States). The most recent financial crisis spawned the US Dodd-Frank Wall Street Reform and Consumer Protection Act, which will undoubtedly lead to many more new regulations.

These burdensome new laws impose some necessary discipline on finance and accounting, but fail to deal with a huge, unmeasured, and unmanaged area—the costs of complexity. When I began studying this area in earnest about a decade ago, I discovered just how far-reaching the negative impact of complexity has grown, and how much it has gone unnoticed. Certainly there is discussion of complexity, but following all the talk, there is very little organized action.

As far back as 2001, Oracle CEO Larry Ellison described a "War on Complexity" in computer software. There were simply too many systems that were not integrated, and others that were very difficult to integrate. This fragmentation of systems caused huge complexity, duplication of effort, and waste (which Ellison's Oracle Corporation hoped to solve).

In 2006–08 there was another flurry of reports and articles from major consultancies (Bain, McKinsey) and university publications (Wharton, Harvard). More recently, IBM's May 2010 report described a comprehensive survey of 1500 CEOs, which confirmed the breadth, depth, and magnitude of the risks of complexity and how dangerous it is to business around the world. And yet, words have not been converted into action effectively, and complexity management continues to be situational and far from fully effective. A great opportunity still awaits global business.

VARIETY CAN ADD VALUE—IF MANAGED PROPERLY

On the other hand, there are instances when complexity—properly managed—can be a source of great competitive advantage. Structure, systems, and processes must be carefully designed to minimize transaction cost and complexity. One example of the productive use of complexity is the web retailer Amazon, whose breadth of offering is extensive, thus making it a "one-stop shopping" site for millions. While Amazon's distribution system is always at risk of being overburdened by complexity, its front end handles the huge variety of goods seamlessly.

Similarly, US sandwich seller Subway assembles sandwiches to order from about 30 containers of meat, cheese, and vegetables, using just a half-dozen varieties of bread. It can make millions of sandwich (and salad) combinations, to customer preferences, with minimal waste. There are many other examples like these two. All depend on the right systemic design to keep complexity from growing out of control, causing waste and inefficiency.

COMPLEXITY COSTS ARE HIDDEN

When I first began to research why complexity costs remained unmeasured in nearly all companies, I discovered that it was because these costs are, by their nature, hidden in accounting systems. To bring this problem into perspective, let's consider how complexity occurs and what kinds of waste it causes. It will become apparent why financial systems simply "overlook" complexity's costs until the end-of-period reporting shows the detrimental effects.

There is no doubt that complexity's effects are readily apparent in month-end, quarter-end, and year-end results, where they adversely affect both the income statement and the balance sheet. Unfortunately, the only place where they are visible is on the bottom line, or on a few lines of the balance sheet. Even then, there's no indication of how these costs were incurred, or what might have been done to manage them.

SEEKING HIGH GROWTH IN LOW GROWTH MARKETS

Much of the complexity that goes unmeasured and unmanaged is created with the best of intentions, in search of revenue growth. Many wealthy developed countries (the United States, most of Europe, Japan, etc.) are growing very slowly, both in population and in their economies. When companies seek growth in these mature markets, they usually resort to proliferation, which leads to complexity. The gain in revenue is redistributed across a broader range of products and services, with only modest increases in total. The many resulting new products, customers, markets, and suppliers add much more in complexity costs than in profit. As rapidly growing economies like China slow, even slightly, complexity costs will start to impact them as well.

Mergers and acquisitions are another source of complexity. If either of the two combined companies is already burdened with complexity, this will transfer to the merger. If both are thus burdened, real trouble is likely. Simply combining the "DNA" of two companies is a daunting task without struggling under a burden of being "infected" with complexities of two different "strains." There are issues of product and customer overlap, duplications of organization and facility, systems redundancies, and large cultural conflicts that must be sorted out. This is perhaps one of the main reasons why mergers seldom lead to long-term growth in shareholder value.

Less developed countries are typically growing at much higher rates (China, India, Brazil, etc.). Emerging consumer societies and favorable balances of trade fuel their economic growth. There's a different complexity problem here: most of these countries save more and spend less—both as consumers and as governments. Further, these countries are less familiar to sellers who operate in developed countries, and therefore marketing and operating mistakes are made. These mistakes also lead to proliferation, often due to errors in targeting or serving the desired markets and customers.

"Not everything that counts can be counted; not everything that can be counted counts." Albert Einstein

PROFITS ARE PROPORTIONAL TO REVENUES; COSTS ARE PROPORTIONAL TO TRANSACTIONS

Thus, either approach to growth adds to complexity, but for different reasons, and in different ways. Profits are derived from increased revenues, but costs are incurred from increased transactions. Therein lies the root of the problem. A few simple reports can expose the problem, but more sophisticated solutions are needed later. Starting with the simpler metrics is advisable. (More on "simplicity" later).

First, calculate sales per customer, per product, per location, etc., and track the trends. They are typically declining, indicating more transactions for less revenue. Next, sort the annual sales, profits, etc., for customers and products, in descending order of value, and compute a cumulative column. Now look at the bottom of the list. There is always page after page of "losers" with few sales and low or negative profits. These are candidates for a major "house-cleaning."

Few accounting systems calculate a couple of simple, yet important, measures. What is the cost to process a customer order from "end to end"—from receipt of the order until the payment is in the bank? Few, if any, companies know the answer to this question. One US study, performed by Sterling Commerce, calculated it at about $50. Consider the following quick calculation to show how complexity adds cost and waste.

Average companies make about 5% net profit (after tax) on sales revenue. That means they must get $20 of sales to make $1 of net profit. If processing an order costs $50, they must get a $1,000 order to earn the equivalent of what it costs to process the order. If that type of customer orders every week, $50,000 worth of annual sales is barely generating net profit that equals the cost of processing the orders.

This dramatically illustrates how customer orders that are small and frequent can add complexity cost, and yet this cost can remain undetected as a drain on profit. A similar comparison could be made for the cost to process purchase orders, or the expense to set up and maintain documentation for a product or service. Nowhere are these costs gathered—or managed. Most companies have a few departments that perform these functions. Therefore, totaling those departmental expenses and dividing that sum by the total number of orders processed will yield an approximation of how much each order costs to process. Yet, few or no companies do this calculation or consider its impact.

Complexity costs are also insidious because most of them are hidden in "catch-all" accounts such as variances, allowances and deductions, premium freight, need for overtime labor, scrap and rework, closeout pricing, and so forth. Extra effort is needed to reveal the origin of such entries (more on that later). First, let's consider a simple example of how easily complexity can occur and grow.

A SIMPLE EXAMPLE: ONE WHITE COFFEE MUG

Imagine a product: a coffee mug offered in one style, color, size, and type of packaging. It is sourced from one supplier, packaged and stocked in one location, and offered for sale to one customer. If the mug's total landed cost is $1 and it sells for $2, this yields a 50% gross profit margin.

Because the mug is successful, the company has decided to expand the line to four styles, four colors, two sizes, and two package options. There are now 64 different mug variations, which lead to increased complexity in forecasting, buying, controlling, and managing raw materials, inventory, etc. The "standard cost," however, is still computed in the same way as before, which yields apparently accurate results: cost = $1 (assuming a good job of purchase negotiation), price = $2, and gross profit margin = 50%. *But something is wrong.* Intuitively, you know that there are complexity costs that the old metrics don't capture—at least, not assigned to the product line. The true profitability is not the same as before.

Expand the product line again: Purchase from two suppliers, package and stock in three locations, and sell into (just) three different countries. Assuming there are no differences in purchase cost or productivity, the standard cost, price, and gross profit margin remain the same. But now, the combinations and permutations have grown to over a thousand, and the company must take into account different marketing materials, purchasing errors (due to forecast errors and demand volatility), and more. Now the profitability is clearly lower.

On top of all this, there are color mixes and assortments of the product that vary according to market, customer, production plant, distribution center, and country. Consequently the warehouse begins to fill up with products in the wrong colors or styles, wrong package sizes, etc. Something must be done with these oddments, so they are repacked (at a cost variance) and sold at discounts (at a price variance), and new replacements are flown in (at huge freight expense variances) to meet customer service needs. More of the profits disappear into those "catch-all" accounts.

Complexity creates noticeable increases in overhead and administrative expenses; impacts the reserve available for inventory obsolescence; or incurs additional labor to rework, repack, and remark inventory. Few, if any, of these costs impact the standard cost of sales and the standard gross margin. Thus, the product still appears to be nicely profitable, and the complexity costs remain hidden in undifferentiated accounts—or result in "non-recurring charges," which, mysteriously, seem to "recur" from time to time. At the end of accounting periods, the true costs hit with full impact, in many cases wiping out all profit.

A COMPLEXITY CRISIS CALLS FOR METRICS

I call this sequence of events "a complexity crisis." The finance and accounting metrics, intended to help track the results of the company do so—eventually. Unfortunately, the waste from complexity remains unmanaged and the missing metrics do not reveal the problems until after the fact. Complexity strikes like a robber. The money is gone. Clues to the crime are few, and the perpetrators plead innocence. Only a knowledgeable accountant, with help from supply chain or marketing staff can unearth the clues and track the waste back to its root causes.

The solution for this is evident: to devise and implement the "missing metrics." Many of these are easy to create; some are already in use. In other instances they will require whole new initiatives. If new metrics were in place and tracked regularly, such losses would be found much sooner. Then corrective actions could be started sooner as well. Major public accounting companies could help by sanctioning such metrics, to provide some uniformity. Unfortunately, thus far, they have been unresponsive to those needs.

Typical Missing Metrics

- Sales per product stock keeping unit (SKU);
- Sales per product category;
- Sales per customer;
- Sales per location;
- Sales per employee (hourly, including full-time equivalent, salaried, and total);
- Sales per part number (components, materials, work in process, and finished goods (FG)).
- Gross profit per product SKU;
- Gross profit per product category;
- Gross profit per customer;
- Gross profit per location.
- Purchases per vendor;
- Purchases per commodity type;
- Production (output value) per person-hour (or equivalent measure of labor input);
- Total number of SKUs by division or business unit and company total;
- Number of SKUs added and dropped during the last time period (quarterly, semiannually or annually).

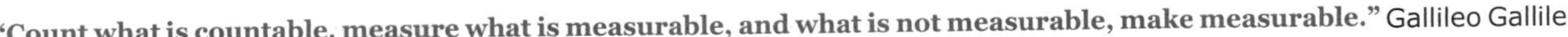

- Cost to process a customer order (end to end);
- Cost to process a purchase order (end to end);
- Cost to set up and maintain a product SKU;
- Cost to serve by customer (including freight, handling, and order processing costs).

Within "catchall accounts" like Deductions and Allowances, Variances, and Writeoffs for Obsolescence, add subcategories to segregate entries by major customers (or groups), products (or categories), and locations (divisions).

- Expenses per product line or category;
- Expenses per customer, and/or by customer type/category;
- Expenses per location;
- Percentage of sales per product line or category;
- Percentage of sales per customer, and customer type or category.

PLUS A TOTALLY NEW METRIC—THE COMPLEXITY FACTOR (CF)

Obviously, there is a common overall purpose among these metrics. Remember that the objective of new metrics is to reveal where the costs of complexity are hiding and are wasting time and money. Choose among those, or devise your own that measure similar complexity-related outcomes. Finally, an overall Complexity Factor can be calculated by means of the following formula (where "locations" are meaningful facilities and "countries" are places where legal entities exist):

$$\frac{\text{(No. of suppliers + No. of customers + No. of employees)} \times \text{No. of FG SKUs} \times \text{No. of markets served} \times \text{No. of locations} \times \text{No. of countries}}{\text{Total annual sales revenue (in the company currency of choice)}}$$

The resultant number provides a "benchmark," called a Complexity Factor (CF), for the business (or subunit) whose data were used to calculate it. Obviously, a CF can be calculated for each business unit, division, geographical unit, etc. *and* for the entire company.

While this may seem like a large number of new metrics, the data to compile them should already exist. Different parts of the business should use and manage CFs based on various metrics that are relevant to their activities. Not all parts need use all metrics.

Some much simpler solutions have been developed in two different continents: Simpler in the United Kingdom, and Simpler Business Institute in Australia. Each offers a range of solutions that focus on simplicity instead of complexity. Whichever direction you choose to manage complexity will use largely similar approached and metrics—find where the complexity resides, how much it costs, and then drive it out and manage it. Complexity is like weeds in a garden. Removing it once is insufficient. It comes back. It must be constantly measured and managed.

When more sophisticated, analytical solutions are needed, new ones have been developed by Emcien, which analyses and optimizes complex patterns/assortments, and by Ontonix, which also measures risk. As complexity grows, an organization can be overwhelmed by it, and lose control of the company. This is a catastrophic failure and must be avoided at all costs. The OntoNet™ system analyses complexity in terms of risk and the fragility of an entity, and can be applied for a wide range of situations. This kind of solution is the ultimate "insurance policy missing metric"—complexity risk.

WHAT GETS MEASURED, GETS MANAGED; WHAT DOESN'T, DOESN'T

The mere presence of metrics doesn't mean management will do anything different. On the other hand, the absence of metrics virtually assures that nothing will be done. The old line "What gets measured, gets managed," is true. The opposite, "If you can't—or don't—measure it, you can't—or don't—manage it," is also likely to be true.

Measurement alone doesn't solve any problems. It merely points to the effects of those problems. To manage them requires a series of steps. First, use Pareto's Principle (the 80-20 rule). Sort products and customers in descending order of annual revenues and profits, and carefully analyze the bottom of the list. Most of these are "losers" with a few strategically important "potential winners" scattered about. Getting rid of the losers is imperative.

Upgrading some "losers" into "winners" (top 20%) is possible, but for most, it is impractical. In the middle group careful analysis helps choose potential winners for upgrading and imminent losers downgrading and removal. When more powerful tools are needed, the newly devised, more-powerful tools and systems (Emcien, Ontonix) can help greatly in sorting, selection, and optimization of complex situations.

THE TIME FOR NEW METRICS IS NOW

Now is the time for boards of directors, senior management, and accounting and finance organizations around the globe to recognize the huge cost of complexity and how poorly measured and managed it is.

The waste of time and money due to "missing metrics" and the failure to track and manage complexity are immense, costing companies around the globe billions in profits. Now is the time to stop that waste in its tracks—by installing those "missing metrics" —and then acting on the new information and knowledge they provide.

MORE INFO

Books:

George, Michael L., and Stephen A. Wilson. *Conquering Complexity in Your Business*. New York: McGraw-Hill, 2004.

Mariotti, John. *The Complexity Crisis: Why Too Many Products, Markets, and Customers Are Crippling Your Company—And What to Do About It*. Avon, MA: Adams Media, 2008.

Articles:

Berlind, David. "Oracle: Misquoted, misunderstood." *ZDnet Tech Update* (September 6, 2001). Online at: tinyurl.com/3usfr6a

Gottfredson, Mark, and Keith Aspinall. "Innovation versus complexity: What is too much of a good thing?" *Harvard Business Review* 83:11 (November 2005): 62–71. Online at: tinyurl.com/3lkanaw

Reports:

George Group and Knowledge@Wharton. "Unraveling complexity in products and services." Special report, 2006. Online at: tinyurl.com/3u4lrke

IBM Global Business Services. "Capitalizing on complexity: Insights from the chief executive officer study." May 2010. Online at: tinyurl.com/cxm32k5 [PDF].

Website:

Emcien, optimization tools for complex solutions: www.emcien.com
Ontonix, complexity and risk management tools: www.ontonix.com
Simpler: www.simpler.com
Simpler Business Institute: www.simplerbusiness.com

"When you can measure what you are speaking about, and express it in numbers, you know something about it; but when you cannot measure it, when you cannot express it in numbers, your knowledge is of a meager and unsatisfactory kind." William Thompson, Lord Kelvin

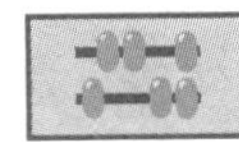

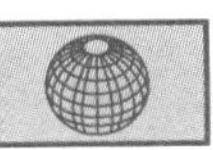

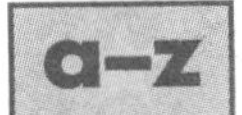

Valuing Start-Ups by Aswath Damodaran

EXECUTIVE SUMMARY

- Young and start-up companies pose the most problems in valuation, for a variety of reasons.
- Start-ups have a limited history, are generally not publicly traded, and often don't survive to become successful commercial enterprises.
- Faced with daunting estimation challenges, analysts often fall back on simplistic forecasts of revenues and earnings, coupled with high discount rates, to capture the high failure rate.
- In this article I suggest that traditional valuation models can be used to yield better estimates of the value of these firms.

INTRODUCTION

Although the fundamentals of valuation are straightforward, the challenges in valuing companies shift as they move through their life cycle: from the initial idea and start-up business, often privately owned, to young growth companies, either public or on the verge of going public, to mature companies with diverse products and serving different markets, and finally to companies in decline, marking time until they disappear. At each stage we may be called on to estimate the same inputs—cash flows, growth rates, and discount rates—but with varying amounts of information and different degrees of precision.

DETERMINANTS OF VALUE

If we accept the premise that the value of a business is the present value of the expected cash flows from its assets, there are four broad questions that we need to answer in order to value any business:

1. What are the cash flows generated by existing assets?

If a firm has significant investments that it has already made, the first inputs into valuation are the cash flows from these existing assets. In practical terms, this requires estimates of: how much the firm generated in earnings and cash flows from these assets in the most recent period; how much growth (if any) is expected in these earnings/cash flows over time; and how long the assets will continue to generate cash flows.

2. How much value will be added by future investments?

For some companies, the bulk of the value will be derived from investments they are expected to make in the future. To estimate the value added by these investments, you have to make judgments on both the magnitude of these new investments relative to the earnings from existing assets; and the quality of the new investments, measured in terms of excess returns, i.e. the returns the firm makes on the investments over and above the cost of funding them.

3. How risky are the cash flows, and what are the consequences for discount rates?

Neither the cash flows from existing assets nor the cash flows from growth investments are guaranteed. When valuing these cash flows, we have to consider risk somewhere, and the discount rate is usually the vehicle we use. Higher discount rates are used to discount riskier cash flows, and thus give them a lower value than more predictable cash flows.

4. When will the firm become mature?

The question of when a firm is mature (i.e. when the growth in earnings/cash flows is sustainable forever) is relevant because it determines the length of the high-growth period and the value we attach to the firm at the end of the period (the terminal value). It is a question that may be easy to answer for a few firms, including larger and more stable firms that are either already mature businesses or close to it, and firms that derive their growth from a single competitive advantage with an expiration date (for instance, a patent).

A framework for valuing any business that takes into account these four considerations is shown in Figure 1.

Figure 1. The fundamental questions in valuation

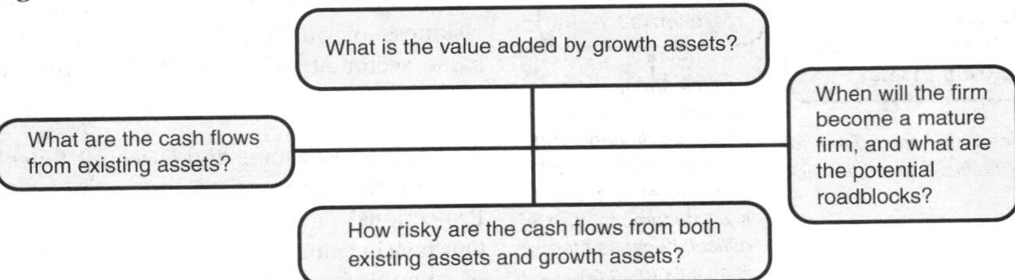

Although these questions may not change as we value individual firms, the ease with which we can answer them may change, not only as we look across firms at a point in time, but also across time—even for the same firm.

VALUING YOUNG COMPANIES

Every business starts with an idea stimulated by a market need that an entrepreneur sees (or thinks that he or she sees) and a way of filling that need. Although many ideas go nowhere, some individuals take the next step of investing in the idea.

The capital to finance the project usually comes from personal funds (from savings, friends, and family), and if things work out as planned the result is a commercial product or service. If the product or service finds a ready market, the business will usually need more capital, and the providers of this are often venture capitalists, who provide funds in return for a share of the equity in the business. Building on the most optimistic assumptions, success for the investors in the business may ultimately be manifested as a public offering to the market or sale to a larger entity.

ESTIMATION ISSUES

At each stage in the process we need estimates of value. At the idea stage, the value may never be put down on paper, but it is the potential of realizing this value that induces the entrepreneur to invest time and money in developing the idea. At subsequent stages of the capital-raising process, valuations become more important because they determine what share of ownership the entrepreneur will have to give up in return for external funding. At the time of the public offering, the valuation is key to determining the offering price.

From the template for valuation that we developed in the last section, it is easy to see why young companies also pose the most daunting challenges. There are few or no existing assets, and almost all of the value is based on the expectations of future growth. The current financial statements of the firm provide no clues about the potential margins and returns that may be generated in the future, and there are few historical data that can be used to develop risk measures.

To complete our consideration of estimation problems, we should remember that many young firms do not make it to the stable growth stage. Estimating when this will happen for firms that do survive is difficult. In addition, these firms are often dependent on one or a few key people for their success, and losing them can have a significant effect on value.

Figure 2 summarizes these valuation challenges.

Given these problems, it is not surprising that analysts often fall back on simplistic measures of value, guesstimates, or on rules of thumb to value young companies. In the process, though, they risk making serious valuation errors.

MEETING THE ESTIMATION CHALLENGE

Given the challenges we face in estimating cash flows and discount rates for the purpose of valuing young companies, it should come as no surprise that many analysts use shortcuts, such as applying multiples to expected future earnings or revenues, to obtain dubious estimates of value. We believe that staying within the valuation framework and making the best estimates of cash flows is still the best approach.

CASH FLOWS AND GROWTH RATES

For many young companies, the biggest challenge in estimating future cash flows is that there is no historical base of any substance to build on. However, we can still estimate expected cash flows using one of two approaches:

Top-Down Approach

In this approach, we begin with the potential market for the firm's products and services and work backwards:

- Estimate the share of this market which the firm hopes to gain in the future and how quickly it can reach this share; this gives expected revenues in future years.
- Make a judgment on the profit margins the firm should see once it attains the targeted market share; this provides the earnings that it hopes to generate each period.
- Finally, evaluate what the firm needs to invest to accomplish this objective; this represents the capital that it has to reinvest in the business, which is a cash drain each year.

Generally, as the firm's revenues grow and it moves toward the target margins, we should expect to see losses in the earlier years become profits in the later ones. With high growth, it is entirely possible that cash flows will stay negative even after profits turn the corner, since the growth will require substantial reinvestment. As growth subsides in the later years, the reinvestment will also decline and cash flows will become positive.

The key to succeeding with this approach is getting the potential market share and target margin right, and making realistic assumptions about reinvestment needs.

Bottom-Up Approach

For those who believe that the top-down approach is too ambitious, the alternative is to start with what the young company can generate as output, given its resource constraints, and make estimates of the revenues and profits that will be generated as a consequence. This is more akin to a capital budgeting exercise than to a valuation, and the valuation will depend on the quality of the forecasts of earnings and cash flows.

The projected earnings and cash flows from both approaches are dependent on the promoters of the company not only being able to come up with a product or service that meets a need, but also that they can adapt to unexpected circumstances at the same time as delivering their forecast results.

DISCOUNT RATES

The absence of historical data on stock prices and earnings makes it difficult, but not impossible, to analyze the risk of young companies. To make realistic estimates of discount rates, we need to be able to do the following:

Assess Risk from the Right Viewpoint

The risk in an investment can vary, depending on the point of view that we bring to the assessment.

- For the founder/owner who has his or her entire wealth invested in the private business, all risk that the firm is exposed to is relevant risk.
- For a venture capitalist who takes a stake in this private business as part of a portfolio of many such investments, there is a diversification effect, where some of the risk will be averaged out in the portfolio.
- For an investor in a public market, the focus will narrow even more, to only the risk that cannot be diversified away in a portfolio.

As a general rule, the discount rates we obtain using conventional risk and return models, which are built for the last setting, will understate the risk (and discount rates) for young companies, which are usually privately held.

Focus on the Business/Sector, Not on the Company

Since young firms have little operating history and are generally not publicly traded, it is pointless trying to estimate risk parameters by looking at the firm's history. We can get a much better handle on risk by looking at the sector or business of which the firm is a part and evaluating the riskiness of publicly traded firms in the same sector at different stages in the life cycle.

Adjust Risk Measures and Discount Rates as the Firm Matures (At Least in the Projections)

Our task in valuation is not to assess the risk of a young firm today, but to evaluate how

Figure 2. Estimation issues for young and start-up companies

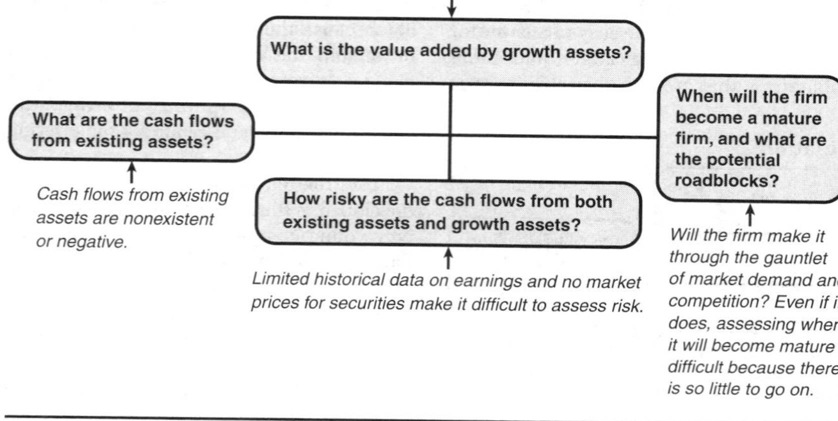

that risk will change as the firm matures. In other words, as revenues grow and margins move toward target levels, the risk that we assess in a company and the discount rates we use should change consistently: lower growth generally should be coupled with lower risk and discount rates.

TERMINAL VALUE

In most discounted cash flow valuations, it is the terminal value that delivers the biggest portion of the value. With young firms this will be doubly so, partly because the cash flows in the early years are often negative and partly because the anticipated growth will increase the size of the firm over time.

Consider Scaling Effects and Competition

When firms are young, revenue growth rates can be very high, reflecting the fact that the revenues being grown are small. As revenues grow, the growth rate will slow, and assessing how quickly this will happen becomes a key part of valuing young companies. In general, the speed with which revenue growth will decelerate as firms get larger will depend on the size of the overall market and the intensity of competition. In smaller markets, and with more intense competition, revenue growth will decline much more quickly and stable growth will approach sooner.

Change the Firm's Characteristics to Reflect Growth

As a firm moves from start-up to stable growth, it is not just the growth rate that changes, but the other characteristics of the firm as well. In addition to the discount rate adjustments we mentioned in the last section, mature firms will also tend to reinvest less and have lower excess returns than younger firms.

Consider the Possibility That the Firm Will Not Make It

Most young firms do not make it to become mature firms. To get realistic estimates of value for young firms, we should consider the likelihood that they will not make it through the life cycle, either because key employees leave or because of capital constraints.

CONCLUSION

It is far more difficult to estimate the value of a young company than a mature company. There is little history to draw on and the firm's survival is often open to question. However, that should not lead us to abandon valuation fundamentals or to adopt fresh paradigms. With a little persistence, we can still estimate the value of young companies. These values may not be precise, but the lack of precision reflects real uncertainty about the future of these companies.

MAKING IT HAPPEN

To value young growth companies:

- Assess the potential market and the company's likely market share (if successful).
- Estimate what the company has to do (in terms of operations and investments) to get to this market share.
- Estimate the cash flows based on these assessments.
- Evaluate the risk in the investments and also how it will change as the company goes through the growth cycle, and convert the risk into discount rates.
- Value the business and the various equity stakes in that business.

MORE INFO

Books:

Damodaran, Aswath. *The Dark Side of Valuation; Valuing Old Tech, New Tech, and New Economy Companies*. Upper Saddle River, NJ: Prentice Hall, 2001.

Gompers, Paul, and Josh Lerner. *The Venture Capital Cycle.* 2nd ed. Cambridge, MA: MIT Press, 2006.

Metrick, Andrew. *Venture Capital and the Finance of Innovation*. Hoboken, NJ: Wiley, 2007.

Guidelines:

Multiple authors. "International private equity and venture capital valuation guidelines." October 2006. Online from: www.privateequityvaluation.com

Website:

Damodaran Online: www.damodaran.com

See Also:

★ Comparing Net Present Value and Internal Rate of Return (pp. 30–32)
★ Understanding the Role of Diversification (pp. 617–618)
✔ Assessing Cash Flow and Bank Lending Requirements (p. 964)
✔ Basic Steps for Starting a Business (p. 1147)
✔ Preparing a Cash Flow Forecast (p. 986)
✔ Understanding the Relationship between the Discount Rate and Risk (p. 1001)
Jean-Baptiste Say (p. 1305)

"The future is already upon us, it is just unevenly distributed." William Gibson

  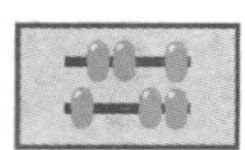   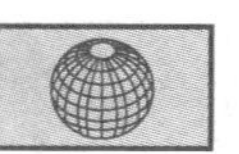   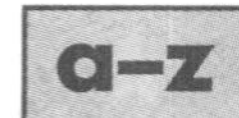

Why Mergers Fail and How to Prevent It

by Susan Cartwright

EXECUTIVE SUMMARY

- Mergers and acquisitions (M&A) are increasing in frequency, yet at least half fail to meet financial expectations.
- The United States and the United Kingdom continue to dominate M&A activity. As the number of cross-border deals increases, however, many other national players are entering the field, further highlighting the issue of cultural compatibility.
- Financial and strategic factors alone are insufficient to explain the high rate of failure; greater account needs to be taken of human factors.
- The successful management of integrating people and their organizational cultures is the key to achieving desired M&A outcomes.

INTRODUCTION

The incidence of M&A has continued to increase significantly during the last decade, both domestically and internationally. The sectors most affected by M&A activity have been service- and knowledge-based industries such as banking, insurance, pharmaceuticals, and leisure. Although M&A is a popular means of increasing or protecting market share, the strategy does not always deliver what is expected in terms of increased profitability or economies of scale. While the motives for merger can variously be described as practical, psychological, or opportunist, the objective of all related M&A is to achieve synergy, or what is commonly referred to as the 2 + 2 = 5 effect. However, as many organizations learn to their cost, the mere recognition of potential synergy is no guarantee that the combination will actually realize that potential.

MERGER FAILURE RATES

The burning question remains—why do so many mergers fail to live up to stockholder expectations? In the short term, many seemingly successful acquisitions look good, but disappointing productivity levels are often masked by one-time cost savings, asset disposals, or astute tax maneuvers that inflate balance-sheet figures during the first few years.

Merger gains are notoriously difficult to assess. There are problems in selecting appropriate indices to make any assessment, as well as difficulties in deciding on a suitable measurement period. Typically, the criteria selected by analysts are:

- profit-to-earning ratios;
- stock-price fluctuations;
- managerial assessments.

Irrespective of the evaluation method selected, the evidence on M&A performance is consistent in suggesting that a high proportion of M&As are financially unsuccessful. US sources place merger failure rates as high as 80%, with evidence indicating that around half of mergers fail to meet financial expectations. A much-cited McKinsey study presents evidence that most organizations would have received a better return on their investment if they had merely banked their money instead of buying another company. Consequently, many commentators have concluded that the true beneficiaries from M&A activity are those who sell their shares when deals are announced, and the marriage brokers—the bankers, lawyers, and accountants—who arrange, advise, and execute the deals.

TRADITIONAL REASONS FOR MERGER FAILURE

M&A is still regarded by many decision makers as an exclusively rational, financial, and strategic activity, and not as a human collaboration. Financial and strategic considerations, along with price and availability, therefore dominate target selection, overriding the soft issues such as people and cultural fit. Explanations of merger failure or underperformance tend to focus on reexamining the factors that prompted the initial selection decision, for example:

- payment of an overinflated price for the acquired company;
- poor strategic fit;
- failure to achieve potential economies of scale because of financial mismanagement or incompetence;
- sudden and unpredicted changes in market conditions.

This ground has been well trodden, yet the rate of merger, acquisition, and joint-venture success has improved little. Clearly these factors may contribute to disappointing M&A outcomes, but this conventional wisdom only partly explains what goes wrong in M&A management.

THE FORGOTTEN FACTOR IN M&A

The false distinction that has developed between hard and soft merger issues has been extremely unhelpful in extending our understanding of merger failure, as it separates the impact of the merger on the individual from its financial impact on the organization. Successful M&A outcomes are linked closely to the extent to which management is able to integrate members of organizations and their cultures, and sensitively address and minimize individuals' concerns.

Because they represent sudden and major change, mergers generate considerable uncertainty and feelings of powerlessness. This can lead to reduced morale, job and career dissatisfaction, and employee stress. Rather than increased profitability, mergers have become associated with a range of negative behavioral outcomes such as:

- acts of sabotage and petty theft;
- increased staff turnover, with rates as high as 60% reported;
- increased sickness and absenteeism.

Ironically, this occurs at the very time when organizations need and expect greater employee loyalty, flexibility, cooperation, and productivity.

PEOPLE FACTORS ASSOCIATED WITH M&A FAILURE

Studies like the one conducted by the Chartered Management Institute in the UK have identified a variety of people factors associated with unsuccessful M&A. These include:

- underestimating the difficulties of merging two cultures;
- underestimating the problem of skills transfer;
- demotivation of employees;
- departure of key people;
- expenditure of too much energy on doing the deal at the expense of postmerger planning;
- lack of clear responsibilities, leading to postmerger conflicts;
- too narrow a focus on internal issues to the neglect of the customers and the external environment;
- insufficient research about the merger partner or acquired organization.

DIFFERENCES BETWEEN MERGERS AND ACQUISITIONS

In terms of employee response, whether the transaction is described as a merger or an acquisition, the event will trigger uncer-

"The system of private property is the most important guarantee of freedom, not only for those who own property, but scarcely less for those who do not." Friedrich August von Hayek

  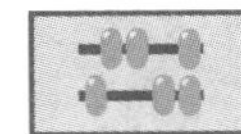   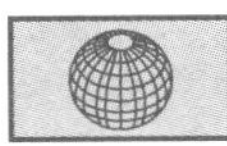   

tainty and fears of job losses. However, there are important differences. In an acquisition, power is substantially assumed by the new parent. Change is usually swift and often brutal as the acquirer imposes its own control systems and financial restraints. Parties to a merger are likely to be more evenly matched in terms of size, and the power and cultural dynamics of the combination are more ambiguous. Integration is a more drawn-out process.

This has implications for the individual. During an acquisition there is often more overt conflict and resistance, and a sense of powerlessness. In mergers, however, because of the prolonged period between the initial announcement and actual integration, uncertainty and anxiety continue for a much longer time as the organization remains in a state of limbo.

CULTURAL COMPATIBILITY

The process of merger is often likened to marriage. In the same way that clashes of personality and misunderstanding lead to difficulties in personal relationships, differences in organizational cultures, communication problems, and mistaken assumptions lead to conflicts in organizational partnerships.

Mergers are rarely a marriage of equals, and it's still the case that most acquirers or dominant merger partners pursue a strategy of cultural absorption; the acquired company or smaller merger partner is expected to assimilate and adopt the culture of the other. Whether the outcome is successful depends on the willingness of organizational members to surrender their own culture, and at the same time perceive that the other culture is attractive and therefore worth adopting.

Cultural similarity may make absorption easier than when the two cultures are very different, yet the process of due diligence rarely extends to evaluating the degree of cultural fit. Furthermore, few organizations bother to try to understand the cultural values and strengths of the acquiring workforce or their merger partners in order to inform and guide the way in which they should go about introducing change.

CONCLUSION

Despite thorough pre-merger procedures, mergers continue to fall far short of financial expectations. The single biggest cause of this failure rate is poor integration following the acquisition. The identification of the target company, the subsequent and often drawn-out negotiations, and attending to the myriad of financial, technical, and legal details are all exhausting activities. Once the target company has been acquired, little energy or motivation is left to plan and implement the integration of the people and cultures following the merger. It seems nonsensical to waste all the resources and energy that have gone into the merger through inadequate planning of the integration stage of the process, yet all too often organizations do just that. Without a properly planned integration process or its effective implementation, mergers will not be able to achieve the full potential of the acquisition.

CASE STUDY

Paul Hodder was involved as director of human resource management in the formation of Aon Risk Services, a merger of four rather different retail-insurance-broking and risk-management companies. A major theme of their integration process was the formation of a series of task groups to review and identify best practice. Another part involved an organization-wide training program to provide individuals with life skills to help them initiate and cope with change, to improve teamwork, and to develop support networks. Enthusiasm for the program provided several hundred change champions to lead change projects and assume support and mentoring roles. Good communication of early wins and successes has reassured organizational members that the changes are working and are beneficial.

MAKING IT HAPPEN

Making a good organizational marriage currently seems to be a matter of chance and luck. This needs to change so that there is a greater awareness of the people issues involved, and consequently a more informed integration strategy. Some basic guidelines for more effective management include:

- extension of the due diligence process to incorporate issues of cultural fit;
- greater involvement of human resource professionals;
- the conducting of culture audits before the introduction of change management initiatives;
- increased communication and involvement of employees at all levels in the integration process;
- the introduction of mechanisms to monitor employee stress levels;
- fair and objective reselection processes and role allocation;
- providing management with the skills and training to sensitively handle M&A issues such as insecurity and job loss;
- creating a superordinate goal which will unify work efforts.

MORE INFO

Books:

Cartwright, Susan, and Cary L. Cooper. *Managing Mergers, Acquisitions and Strategic Alliances*. 2nd ed. Woburn, MA: Butterworth-Heinemann, 1996.

Cooper, Cary L., and Alan Gregory (eds). *Advances in Mergers and Acquisitions*. Vol. 1. New York: JAI Press, 2000.

Stahl, Gunter, and Mark E. Mendenhall (eds). *Mergers and Acquisitions*. Stanford, CA: Stanford University Press, 2005.

See Also:

★ Acquisition Integration: How to Do It Successfully (pp. 708–709)
★ Cultural Alignment and Risk Management: Developing the Right Culture (pp. 724–726)
★ Maximizing a New Strategic Alliance (pp. 749–750)
★ Merger Integration and Transition Management: A New Slant for Finance Executives (pp. 756–758)
★ Mergers and Acquisitions: Patterns, Motives, and Strategic Fit (pp. 759–762)
✔ Assessing Economies of Scale in Business (p. 1145)
✔ The Rationale for an Acquisition (p. 1134)
John D. Rockefeller (p. 1301)

"I skate to where the puck is going to be, not to where it has been." Wayne Gretzky

Aligning Structure with Strategy: Recalibrating for Improved Performance and Increased Profitability

by R. Brayton Bowen

EXECUTIVE SUMMARY

- Aligning organizational structure with corporate strategy requires financial "rethinking."
- In difficult economic times, it is not unusual for organizational leaders to demand across-the-board cuts of some arbitrary percentage to achieve bottom-line results.
- Unfortunately, that approach often cuts into the "muscle" of critical functions that are vital to the successful performance of the enterprise and its future viability.
- As an alternative, activity-based cost accounting quantifies the cost of specific work activities throughout organizational systems.
- This approach to redesign helps the organization recalibrate how and where work can be better aligned with corporate direction.
- The enterprise can achieve not only better organizational performance with this method, but also bottom-line efficiencies that improve financial results.

INTRODUCTION

Phlebotomy—the ancient practice of bloodletting—seemed logical when medical science centered on the belief that four humors made up the human body: yellow bile, black bile, phlegm, and blood. It was thought at the time that an ailing person could be brought to good health by vomiting, purging, starving, and bloodletting. Unfortunately, in the latter instance, any number of the sick bled to death! By today's medical standards, the practice is considered quackery. Now when a patient is ill, the condition is diagnosed extensively until the source of the problem is identified. If an operation is required, the repair is made with surgical precision.

Oddly enough, phlebotomy continues to be practiced on the body "corporate" in any number of organizations, where the four key elements are considered to be: capital, equipment, product (services), and people. A poor-performing organization, like an ailing patient in ancient times, is "bled" of its people resource. If the economy turns down, more blood is let, until the enterprise either recovers, or dies. In rough economic times, it is not unusual for organizational leaders to demand across-the-board cuts of some arbitrary percentage to achieve bottom-line results—not unlike phlebotomy, where cuts were made on almost all parts of the body. Unfortunately, that approach often cuts into the "muscle" of critical functions that are vital to the successful performance of the enterprise, and its future viability. And, the reality is that once an organization goes through a major bloodletting, a.k.a., "downsizing," "rightsizing," or "rationalizing," management will resort to doing it again and again. Invariably, the organization fails to achieve its performance objectives, and the scars of phlebotomy serve only to remind the employees who remain that they too may be the subjects of such savagery in the future. Trimming excess resource is certainly necessary from time to time, but keeping trim and fit on a regular basis should be the norm.

DESIGNING FROM THE OUTSIDE IN

Why Are We in Business?

Ask anyone why he or she is in business, and the answer ultimately is "to make money." Certainly, that should be the final result, but the mission is "to serve customers," and the outcome should be "customer satisfaction." Without customers, there is no business. Consequently, the design of an organization must be built from the outside in. In other words, it must begin with the end-customer in mind. Adrian Slywotzky makes the point in

WHAT IS THE "ESSENCE" OF THE BUSINESS?

Continuous realignment requires the ongoing process of taking time out of the design, fabrication, and delivery cycles. Time savings equal cost savings. Increasing the value proposition for customers and shareholders requires the ongoing process of assessing the cost of doing business, as well as the return on investment. But, downsizing structure for the sole purpose of reducing cost, in and of itself, is not a sustainable strategy. Form must follow function. Structure must follow strategy. Consequently, any restructuring must begin with outcomes in mind, and the quintessential outcome in business is the value proposition for the customer. So, recognizing that businesses change constantly, how does one go about the process of continuous realignment? Rather than across-the-board cutting—like phlebotomy—consider the alternative: activity-based costing, more commonly referred to as "ABC" accounting. This approach more accurately assigns value to discrete activities, business functions, cross-organizational processes, and, ultimately, specific products and services. It even identifies the cost of what is not being done, like "waiting for instructions" or "idling in traffic." Indeed, it is a process that encourages long-range thinking and strategic decision-making rather than short-term, knee jerk reacting.

STRUCTURAL REDESIGN

Begin with Outcomes in Mind

Establish expectations from the outset by beginning with the outcomes to be realized, for example: The proposed redesign will be aligned with the organization's vision, mission, values, and major strategies;

- The overall design will enhance the value proposition for the customer;
- Opportunities for income generation will be identified, and a more effective allocation of resources will be proposed according to the income opportunities identified;
- The new structure will be at least 80% aligned with the primary, value-adding initiatives of the organization;
- Organizational members will be empowered to work in self-directed work teams to enhance the exchange of diverse opinions and the sharing of ideas and solutions;
- The number of organizational levels will be reduced to facilitate the rapid transference of information;
- Quality assurance and continuous improvement will be built into the collective cognition and processes of the new organizational design.

Of course, one of the expected outcomes might be a targeted reduction in the cost of people resources; but even if it is not a stated outcome, typically an organization will realize a 10% reduction in the cost of human resources as a result of more efficient and effective organizational design.

Once outcomes have been established, the next step is to identify all work activities.

"The introduction of a new grammar, not just new words, is the key to organizational transformation."
Michael D. McMaster

  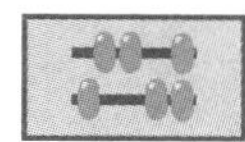   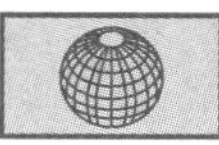   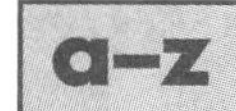

TAKING STOCK OF WORK ACTIVITIES AND THEIR IMPORTANCE

Taking stock requires identification of every work activity performed throughout the organizational system. For example, in the area of finance (partial list):

- Accounts payable;
- Accounts receivable;
- General accounting.

In the area of manufacturing (partial list):

- Requisitioning materials;
- Assembling parts;
- Testing finished products.

The next step is to identify those activities that are "primary," i.e., value-adding and essential to the organization's primary mission; and those that are "secondary," albeit important, but, nevertheless, ancillary to the core mission of the organization. Hence, for a marketing firm, an example of a primary activity would be "advertising layout," while an example of a secondary activity would be "accounting." (If an enterprise is in the business of advertising, it is not in the business of accounting; therefore, accounting is a secondary activity.) In the final stage of design, it is important to retain 80–90% of the primary activities for the integrity of the organization. Only the most important support activities should be retained, roughly 10–20%. The remaining support activities would be targeted for outsourcing and/or elimination. In this way, the essence of the organization is preserved and, indeed, strengthened.

THE PROCESS OF REDESIGNING

To ensure acceptance of proposed changes in the new structure and enhance the effectiveness of the design itself, utilization of a cross-organizational/cross-functional design team is recommended. Using the inventory of activities suggested above, the design team proceeds with surveying the organization to determine what activities are being performed by people throughout the organizational system, as well as the amount of time expended in performing each activity. This survey feedback is integrated with a reporting system that contains a comprehensive listing of all positions, and the payroll associated with each person. The process is also effective in capturing non-productive time. Once data collection is complete, and the data are integrated with the payroll reporting system, reports can be generated that allow the design team to assess what work is being done currently, where it is being done, who is doing it, and what the associated costs are. Armed with this knowledge, the design team can go on to look at design alternatives that better align with the outcomes expressed at the outset of the process.

SAMPLE REPORTS

Data can be arrayed in several formats to provide the right information to facilitate the redesign process for the team.

The Activity Cost by Function report (Table 1) allows team members to see the actual cost of each function within the organization. The High to Low Activity Cost report (Table 2) gives an instant snapshot of where the organization is spending its money. In the example shown, 80% of the payroll cost is being expended on 27% of the total activities performed within the system. And, finally, Table 3, identifying Primary and Support work, provides a ready assessment of how aligned organizational activities are with the primary mission, vision, and strategies of the organization. Ideally, primary activities account for 80–90% of all the activities in the organization. Typically, at the start of a redesign process, it is not unusual to see only 55–65% alignment. The difference between the actual and ideal allocation constitutes the "gap" in alignment that then has to be addressed in the redesign process.

CONTINUOUS REDESIGN

Building quality into the system means incorporating the ability of organizational members to redesign continuously—taking time and cost out of organizational processes, while imbedding flexibility and resiliency into the fabric of the corporate being. Embracing this competency and cultivating its continuous application can potentially stave off the need for major restructuring in the event of severe economic downturns, or increased competitive forces in the marketplace. Indeed, as many times as GE's Appliance Division faced

Table 1. Activity costs by function

Code	Activity description	Cost US$ (000)	Cost %	FTE	Avg. time
0400	**Finance**	**238.3**	**16.1**	**12.36**	**26.3**
0401	Accounting	88.9	6.0	5.02	15.2
0249	Accounting – general	7.7	0.5	0.35	5.8
0250	Accounting – revenue	4.3	0.3	0.10	5.0

Table 2. Activity costs—High to low

Code	Activity description	Cost US$ (000)	Cost %	Cumulative %	FTE people	Avg. time
0001	Managing	179.8	12.1	12.1	2.55	14.2
0356	Marketing	75.1	5.1	37.3	2.20	44.0
0534	Customer service	68.0	4.6	41.9	4.38	24.3
	...	...	...	...	...	...
	# OF ACTIVITIES: 29	**1,186.2**			**46.44**	

27% of 109 activities cost 80% of payroll

Table 3. Activity costs by primary and support designation

Code	Activity Description	Cost US$(000)	Cost %	FTE	Avg. Time
0100	**Primary Work**	**606.6**	**40.9**	**24.63**	**58.6**
0315	Product development	161.2	10.9	6.20	36.5
0356	Marketing	75.1	5.1	2.20	44.0
	...	...	...	...	...
0200	**Support Work**	**876.6**	**59.1**	**32.97**	**55.9**
0249	Accounting – general	7.7	0.5	0.35	5.8
0250	Accounting – revenue	4.3	0.3	0.10	5.0
	...	...	...	...	...

MAKING IT HAPPEN

Aligning organizational structure with strategic goals and objectives requires intelligent planning and detailed analysis. The benefits of an ABC approach to organizational design far exceed those realized as a result of executive fiats or corporate bloodletting. The following steps are needed to ensure optimum results:

- Determine the desired outcomes of any restructuring – begin with the end in mind.
- Plan to design from the outside-in, by identifying customer needs and expectations.
- Assemble a cross-organizational and cross-functional team to conduct the analysis and propose structural change.

"Most of our organization tends to be arranged on the assumption that people cannot be trusted ... that sort of attitude creates a paraphernalia of systems, checkers, and checkers checking checkers—expensive and deadening."

Charles Handy

  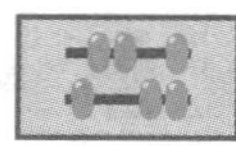      

potential closing, continuous reengineering and structural redesign prevented the threat from ever being realized.

CONCLUSION

In a global economy flexibility, adaptability, and quick response times are critical attributes for any organization that wishes to compete in today's competitive environment. Traditional accounting methods and other management metrics fail to capture the true cost of organizational processes, "hidden work," and even "non-work." Activity-based cost accounting provides a level of accountability and transparency that is not achievable with more traditional systems. Moreover, the team-based approach suggested here not only builds relationships among organizational members and understanding throughout the organizational system, it also facilitates the management of change, as design team participants prepare themselves for the implementation of changes in organizational structure they have designed. And, finally, this approach allows for continuous and systematic analysis of the organization and its processes to ensure the ongoing alignment of organizational structure with the strategic goals and desired outcomes of the enterprise.

- Identify and catalog the unique work activities that exist throughout the organizational system.
- Conduct a comprehensive analysis of the work that is being done, capturing cost, people units, and time quantities.
- Compare the feedback with personnel data, specifically pay and hours worked.
- Generate meaningful management reports that will allow intelligent analysis by the team.
- Train the team in organizational design concepts that will result in a more horizontal organization and self-direction.
- Secure management approval of the changes and encourage continued analysis of organizational processes and related structures.

MORE INFO

Books:

Kaplan, R. S., and W. Bruns. *Accounting and Management: A Field Study Perspective*. Boston, MA: Harvard Business School Press, 1987.

Ostroff, F. *The Horizontal Organization: What the Organization of the Future Actually Looks Like and How It Delivers Value to Customers*. Oxford: Oxford University Press, 1999.

Pfeffer, J. *The Human Equation: Building Profits by Putting People First*. Boston, MA: Harvard Business School Press, 1998.

Slywotzky, A. J., and D. J. Morrison. *The Profit Zone: How Strategic Business Design Will Lead You to Tomorrow's Profits*. New York: Times Books, 1997.

Websites:

BNET, the go-to-place for management: www.bnet.com

The Howland Group, Inc.: www.howlandgroup.com

See Also:

★ Capital Structure: A Strategy that Makes Sense (pp. 710–714)

★ Using Financial Analysis to Evaluate Strategy (pp. 949–951)

Corporate-Level Strategy: Creating Value in the Multibusiness Company (p. 1345)

Corporate Strategy: An Analytic Approach to Business Policy for Growth and Expansion (p. 1346)

"The first steps to becoming a really great manager are simply common sense; but common sense is not very common."
Gerald M. Blair

  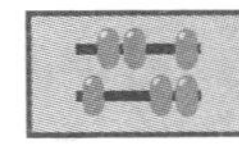   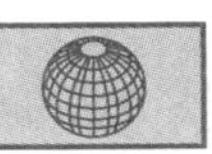   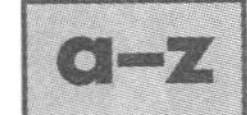

An Approach to Understanding Reputation Risk in Financial Services by Philip Whittingham

EXECUTIVE SUMMARY

- What we mean by reputational risk, why reputation risk is important in financial services, and how it is related to other risks faced by financial services businesses.
- The regulatory drivers that are increasing the pressure on financial services firms to manage reputation risk.
- Some practical suggestions on how reputation risk can be usefully incorporated in the risk management cycle and processes in a financial services business.

INTRODUCTION

The Oxford English Dictionary 2010 defines reputation as "the beliefs or opinions that are generally held about someone or something." If we follow that definition, reputational risk must be the potential for loss or damage that occurs to an organization through an adverse impact on its reputation. In other words, something must happen that causes people to doubt previously held beliefs. We assume, of course, that these are "good" beliefs that are being damaged.

Why are these beliefs so important? Well, think about what happens when you move to a new area. Typically you will ask your neighbors if they can recommend a "good" doctor, or dentist, or place to eat, and so on. The same applies to financial services. Our buying decisions—such as our choice to take out an insurance policy or take a mortgage—are very influenced by a number of factors that include price and perception of quality or brand. Indeed, we might pay more for a product which we perceive to provide greater value (as car manufacturers established a lpong while ago). This is why television and media adverts for financial services products are typically geared at building a perception of trust and stability, rather than focusing on the purely financial benefits and product features. Firms invest a lot in building these public profiles and in establishing a reputation to support the profile through the appropriate customer service.

So, how does this link to reputational risk? Let us consider two possible scenarios.

- A well known high-street bank is subject to rumors about its financial security. What happens? There is a sudden increase in customers transferring their accounts or business relationships elsewhere.
- A well-known insurer receives publicity that it is disputing claims. What happens? It loses potential customers.

Are these realistic scenarios? Well, a little research will quickly show that they are indeed based in reality. What they both have in common, though, is that although there is loss, it is not a "typical" loss for the business. Retail banks typically are used to sustaining loss through the credit default of a customer, while insurers (particularly personal lines insurers) are used to losing customers primarily on price.[1] However, in both scenarios a contributory driver or factor in the loss of client trust and declining business volume as a result is loss of reputation.

CAUSES OF LOSS DUE TO REPUTATION RISK

One of the great debates around reputational risk is whether it is a risk in itself or whether it is an outcome or a consequence of other risks. The latter is easy to explain if we consider the following scenarios.

- Because of a breakdown in claims processing (perhaps due to a systems failure), there is a delay in paying claims. This could lead to reputational damage—possibly arising out of unwanted press coverage—leading to loss of business, whether new or existing.
- Rumors concerning the financial strength of a bank, perhaps following losses in its investment banking division, result in customers closing their deposit accounts.

In both these cases the underlying cause of loss is an operational (or other) risk event. However, along with a direct financial impact—for example, the cost of rectifying the system failure in the first case—there is also a reputational impact, which typically comes in the form of loss of business. It is driven by the adverse publicity that arises from the operational (or other) failure.

So, for this author, reputational risk is primarily an unintended outcome that is derived from the actualization of other risk types. In other words, it might be deemed to be a "consequential" risk rather than a primary risk. However, while this may be the view on which this chapter is based, there are other aspects that must be considered, including the multiplier effect that reputational risk can have. For example, consider the situation where a bank is rumored to have liquidity problems. Customers start to lose confidence and withdraw their funds, further exacerbating the liquidity problems. This in turn causes further withdrawals by customers who were not initially nervous but now are as a result of the publicity that is starting to emerge. This is an example of what could be termed the "reputational multiplier" effect.

The existence of this multiplier has been examined in a number of studies, one of the first being that by Cummins, Lewis, and Wei (2006), who identified the impact on stock price as being larger than the underlying loss of value because of the reputational multiplier. Further analysis was undertaken by Micocci *et al.* (2008), who examined the impact of operational risk events on reputation through a study of stock price movements following large (in excess of US$20 million) operational risk events. The study, drawing on very well known operational risk losses in the financial services sector (such as the US$9 billion loss of Banco National in South America due to credit fraud in 1995, and the US$2.6 billion loss at Sumitomo Corporation due to unauthorized trading activity in 1996) found significant downward movement in the share price, particularly in the month after the reported losses.

RISK TAXONOMY AND REPUTATION RISK

Over the last five or so years, financial services organizations have had to develop a more rigorous taxonomy of risk and a more clearly defined universe of risks. This is essential since the regulators have been asking not just what risks are faced by the organization, but what risks capital is held for. To answer this seemingly simple question requires a firm to define classes of risk very clearly and to make these known throughout the organization so that they can be treated in line with risk management objectives.

Much of the focus to date has been on defining operational risk and, in particular, defining the treatment for so-called "boundary events."[2] However, what firms have perhaps not been as robust in doing is articulating where reputational risk sits in their risk taxonomy, how it should be classified, and whether it is a primary risk, a consequential risk, or just an outcome.

"Innovation is trying to figure out a way to do something better than it s ever been done before."
David Neeleman

Clearly, given the increasing need to discuss the topic, there is a benefit in agreeing how reputational risk should be described and articulated up front so that all key stakeholders within the firm understand it in the same way. Managing the understanding for those outside the company is more challenging but should not be ignored, and there are plenty of disclosure opportunities for firms to get their message across.

REGULATORY DRIVERS FOR REPUTATION RISK MANAGEMENT

As risk managers, we do not wish to suggest that risk management frameworks are implemented just to satisfy regulatory expectations. Nonetheless, financial services is an increasingly heavily regulated sector and we cannot ignore the importance of regulation. What is interesting is that the regulators have identified reputation risk as something that requires addressing. Why might that be? To a great extent the driver comes from the overarching regulatory goals of consumer confidence and financial stability. If firms are seen—or in the particular case of reputation risk, perceived—to be failing, then consumers may lose confidence in the financial market and even in the regulator as well. This is exactly the risk that the regulator has been set up to avoid, and avoiding it is also in the regulator's self-interest. As such, there is increasing regulatory guidance as to what should be done. In other words, even if financial services firms themselves did not recognize the importance of reputational risk, the regulator's own interests mean that it cannot be ignored.

Perhaps the most recent example of the expectation is set out in the Solvency II directive and its related guidance. Solvency II is the new set of regulations for the European insurance industry that comes into force in 2013.

Solvency II, Article 44, level 2, guidance states that the risk management system should be extended to include reputation risk. This is defined as "the risk of potential loss to an undertaking through deterioration of its reputation or standing due to a negative perception of the undertaking's image among customers, counterparties, shareholders and/or supervisory authorities. To that extent it may be regarded as less of a separate risk, than one consequent on the overall conduct of an undertaking." The guidance goes on to state that "The administrative, management or supervisory body of the undertaking should be aware of potential reputational risks it is exposed to and the correlation with all other material risks" and that "the undertaking should pay great attention to understanding and recognizing key values affecting reputation, considering expectations of the stakeholders and sensitivity of the marketplace."

Furthermore, there is a requirement for firms to consider the impact of reputation risk in their Pillar 2 "Own risk and solvency assessment" (ORSA), where the regulators state: "The following risks are examples of risks not considered in the standard formula, but which should be considered in the ORSA, if they are material for the undertaking:
1 Liquidity risk;
2 Reputational risk;
3 Strategic risk."

THE RISK MANAGEMENT CYCLE AND REPUTATION RISK

Risk Governance

Who owns or is responsible for managing reputational risk? Although we are all familiar with the work of the marketing and public relations function in assisting with the building of a brand, the reality is that it is not solely responsible. In some senses it is all of the business that is responsible, from the board and CEO down. Indeed, we all know from our experience of being a customer that any interaction with an institution leaves an impression that can shape our view of its reputation—be it the receptionist, a salesman, or other.

Indeed, a clear example of this can be seen in the HSBC's published corporate governance approach, where it states that "safeguarding [HSBC's] reputation . . . is the responsibility of every member of staff." To ensure that this is understood throughout the organization, HSBC trains directors on appointment in reputational matters, and reputation risks are considered at a number of levels including:

- the board;
- the group management board;
- risk management meetings;
- subsidiary company boards;
- board committees;
- senior management.

Because reputation risk is so important, we cannot leave its management to chance. There need to be clear guidelines as to who is responsible for managing that risk (or rather outcome). It may appear obvious that a process owner is responsible. For example, if poor claims service can lead to loss of reputation, then surely the head of claims should be responsible for managing that risk? This may be the case, but in fact there are a number of stakeholders with whom reputation can be lost.

Therefore, one easy way to look at the governance around reputational risk is to do a mapping of stakeholders with whom we might lose reputation (clients, rating agencies, etc.) and to work out who has the primary responsibility for the management of these relationships and the associated reputational risks. Key here is to document and communicate those responsibilities in the same way that it is for other risk types (in terms of reference, for example). A possible mapping of some of the responsibilities in an insurance company is set out in the breakout box.

The roles of the second and third lines of defense in the management of reputational risk (being independent risk oversight and assurance, respectively) are no different. However, it is possible, given the challenging nature of the risk, that the risk function may be called on to provide more coaching, guidance, and advice than with other risks.

Risk Culture

Establishing the governance around reputational risk is, however, only part of the equation. As with all things in risk management, the processes, structures, and risk management tools are only as good as the culture that supports them. Reputational risk is quite esoteric, and the role of culture and its place in terms of people and firms doing the "right thing" is therefore of even greater importance.

Stronger risk cultures propagate themselves better and communicate better, which as we have seen is essential for the management of reputational risk. Firms with a good risk culture understand the consequences for their reputation of good and bad behaviors and do not tolerate mistakes that involve lapses in integrity or which knowingly put the firm's reputation at risk.

A good risk culture reinforces good behaviors, and vice versa. It helps firms to avoid risks for which no returns are expected and ultimately to attract clients who want to avoid surprises in their business dealings and want to trust and believe in the organizations with which they contract.

While the topic of culture is not the subject of this chapter, it is fair to say that strong cultures begin at the very outset, with the HR process of hiring, and continue into compensating people for the right behaviors—and not just for maximizing profit. In firms that take risk management seriously, this should include rewarding people in accordance with how their behavior protects brand and reputation.

Risk Identification and Assessment

In order to successfully manage reputational risk, we need to have a process for its identification. This process needs to be a

"Like snowflakes falling one after another finally create an avalanche, human thoughts amass to create breakthroughs for the benefit of humankind." Abdallah S. Jum'ah

dynamic one that looks at existing risks but which also considers new, emerging risks. Causes of reputational damage may vary over time. For example, with more trends driven by the green agenda, firms now have to demonstrate greater corporate social responsibility than they might have 20 years ago. Those firms that are not perceived to be good corporate citizens, or "green," might increasingly see their reputation damaged. In fact this is explicitly addressed as a reputational risk impact by the HSBC when it considers "environmental, social and governance" risks and their link to reputation.

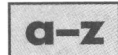

As such, the identification of reputational risk is an ongoing task. Typically, firms consider this at two levels.

- *Level 1*: Within core business processes, when the question has to be asked about any major decision whether there is a potential reputational impact of implementing it; an example might be moving a call center offshore.
- *Level 2*: Within the risk management processes that are overlaid to give further assurance that risks are being treated correctly. Within these, there are two tools that stand out for consideration: stress-testing and the risk register. Internal capital models used by firms, on the other hand, are not as useful since it is hard to quantify the risk in a way that lends itself to modeling.

Thus, two key tools for identification and assessment are emerging around reputational risk. The first is the risk register, a tool that has been around for a while now. The second is a specific form of stress-testing known as reverse stress-testing.

Risk Registers

Risk registers have become a standard tool for risk identification and quantification in the financial services industry. Typically, these involve scoring risks on a predefined matrix of impact and probability. In the past the outcomes have been measured in terms of financial impact. However, there is an increasing trend to use the risk register as a device for the quantification of potential reputational impact. This is done by extending the impact matrix to include a range of reputational impact outcomes that can occur either alongside or instead of the financial impacts. These might range from an incident that is known and communicated internally through to things that lead to national press coverage, or perhaps even rating agency action. The purpose is to help firms to understand the range of outcomes that are possible, not just the financial impacts. This can then drive appropriate risk treatment.

Reverse Stress-Tests

The purpose of the reverse stress-test (which is mandated by regulators in Europe but is also gaining wider traction with other regulators worldwide, for example in Bermuda) is different from that of most stress-tests. Most stress-testing work considers an event and looks at the impact of that event on the business and the achievability of the business plan. Typically the outcome is couched in financial terms (for example impact on earnings, impact on capital held, and sometimes impact on liquidity).

The reverse stress-test is different because it works back from the failure. In other words, we know the outcome of the stress-test (failure), but we do not necessarily know what causes it. In the most extreme cases, reputational risk can lead to business failure. Indeed, it is difficult to overestimate the importance of perception in business. The financial crisis in 2007–08 showed us just how the views of stakeholders—ranging from customers, the rating agencies, through regulators, governments, and others—could adversely affect the future of once seemingly sound institutions.

Therefore, it does not take a big leap to establish that once we have realized that a primary cause of failure can be loss of reputation, we should undertake scenario analysis to understand how this might manifest itself.

Risk Treatment and Response

What is the appropriate treatment for reputational risk? Clearly, a number of the controls in place for the management of reputational risk are also those linked to the underlying risk (certainly in the case of operational risk). So, we have controls to prevent IT downtime, and through that reduced likelihood of IT downtime we are mitigating our reputational risk.

However, it is not straightforward as that. If we consider the situation where we do have IT downtime (resulting from fire, for example), the typical response is to implement a business continuity plan that gets the business up and running again. However, another reputational risk mitigant could be a communication to key stakeholders that says: "Yes, there is a problem, but it is under control." Even more importantly, there should be agreement on what the message should be. It would be less than ideal for the CEO to be communicating one message to a journalist in a telephone call while a preapproved press release tells a different story.

In the days of the Internet, Twitter, and other social media, bad news moves very quickly and therefore firms need to have a defined response plan depending on the nature and level of the "bad news" that they need to manage against. Furthermore, firms need to accept that they will often be defending themselves against stories that might not be 100% accurate but are spreading nonetheless. Experience is increasingly showing that, unless the story is just not true, the best defense is an honest one that accepts what has happened, apologizes for it, and articulates what is being done to control it. Indeed, a rule of thumb should be to be fast, to be honest, and to be complete in one's response rather than drip-feeding incremental responses.

In fact, this is where, again, a use can be found for reverse stress-testing, since the typical approach will look at what contingency plans are in place and what management actions might control how the scenario develops. A good analysis of reputational risk will allow firms to develop communications and crisis management plans, along with other, more scenario-specific tools of mitigation.

The other question we should consider is whether a firm should hold capital as a mitigant for reputational risk. In the main, firms are not going down this route.

MAKING IT HAPPEN

- Review the existing risk taxonomy and risk universe. How is reputational risk defined? Is its relationship with other risks clearly set out? Does this cascade through the organization in all risk management decisions?
- Review the ownership of reputational risk. Is it clear who is responsible for managing the reputation of the business with key stakeholders?
- Review the risk management cycle for reputational risk. Are the controls that are in place adequate for the management of the reputational dimension of the risks as well as the financial dimensions? Is there a coordinated communication strategy for the management of reputational risk?
- Review the existing approach to stress-testing. Are there stress-tests in place, particularly reverse stress-tests that really help the organization to examine the potential reputational downsides, including those that might lead to business failure?
- Review the existing risk culture in the firm to determine whether it supports the establishment of an effective risk management process for reputational risk.

However, the study by Micocci *et al.* (2008) suggests that, at a 99.9% confidence level, the reputational value-at-risk (VaR) is 1.08% of shareholder's value (for a monthly event window). Given the increasingly numerate analysis of reputational risk impacts, it seems likely that at some point in the future firms may be pressed to hold capital by the regulators, notwithstanding the controls the firm puts in place to avoid consequential losses.

Risk Reporting

Given the nature of reputational risk, much of the risk reporting that might take place around it could be linked to other types of risk—using primarily the same indicators that tell the firm if there is an emerging operational risk issue. However, of equal importance is reporting on the status of the contingency and communication plans. So, in the same way that business continuity plan testing would be reported, consideration should be given to the reporting of weaknesses in reputational risk management contingency plans.

MAPPING THE OWNERSHIP OF REPUTATION RISK

Clearly identifying who "owns" a risk is good practice, and the same applies to the reputational dimension of risk. Some examples of the stakeholders with whom we might need to manage the risk and the relevant internal owner are set out below for the example of an insurance company:

- *Customers*—All those who interact with customers, but primarily underwriters, direct sales forces, and claims handlers. As such, the allocation might require identification down to the business process level.
- *Employees*—Human resources and line management.
- *Investors*—The senior management team and often a dedicated investor relations team.
- *Regulators*—Those handling compliance, but also senior management who will encounter regulators frequently. *Rating agencies*—The senior management team.

As with any risk, it is important to recognize that risk ownership does not mean exclusivity, in the sense that all employees in an organization should be aware of their role in the management of risk and their responsibilities. However, we do need to recognize that there are some with a more defined accountability.

REVERSE STRESS-TESTS AND REPUTATION RISK

Reverse stress-tests are a relatively new idea, but they have quickly gained traction with financial services regulators and are now enshrined in local regulation in a number of territories and are also addressed in emerging regulation such as Solvency II.

They are known as reverse stress-tests since, unlike with most stress tests, we start with an outcome and work back, rather than starting with a cause or an event to understand the outcome. With the reverse stress-test, that outcome is failure of the business.

The value of performing a reverse stress-test is in what the process can tell the firm. So, if we consider a firm, failure could arise for a number of reasons, including a loss of capital. This might arise out of a single catastrophic event. It could arise from a liquidity failure. The latter could be caused by a single event, but if we look back at the earlier case study of Northern Rock, we can see that the problem might be exacerbated by reputational issues.

Equally, there might be other losses that are small but which cause key stakeholders to lose confidence, resulting perhaps in loss of capital support, a drop in share price, or loss of business that means that the firm's income is not sufficient to support the business plan.

It is in these latter circumstances that the consideration of reputational risk really comes to the fore. Take a small insurance company which tells its shareholders that it is writing two or three lines of business. For speculative reasons it decides to write a small amount of a fourth line of business because it has been offered what it regards as an attractive opportunity. If there is a loss on this business and the shareholders regard the loss as surprising and unexpected, they might not unreasonably lose confidence on the grounds that they are worried about what else there is in the firm's business activities that they do not know about. It is not inconceivable that in some circumstances this might lead to failure. This is an example of when reputational risk as an outcome (or consequential risk) is actually the most significant element.

A robust reverse stress-testing process that starts with the outcome of failure before examining the scenarios that might cause this and how they manifest themselves will almost certainly include a reputational dimension.

CONCLUSION

So, what have we learnt? Reputational risk is in fact the flip side of one of the most important commodities in the business world today—brand, and the perception that comes with it. To build a brand can take many years, but it can be lost very quickly as a consequence of mismanaging the reputational elements of an event that might arise out of an operational, liquidity, or other risk.

While most firms will probably have arrived at this conclusion themselves, financial services businesses are also being driven by a regulatory agenda that requires regulators to implement a supervision regime which engenders public confidence in the stability of the financial system itself. This is driving regulation to push firms to implement ways of managing reputational risk.

As such, even though we might regard reputational risk as an outcome of other risks, we should not simply assume that the risk management processes that are in place for those risks are adequate to manage reputational risk also. Firms need to consciously take action to ensure that their risk management processes are adequate for the management of reputational risk.

MORE INFO

Book:

Bruni, Franco, and David T. Llewellyn (eds). *The Failure of Northern Rock: A Multi-Dimensional Case Study*. Vienna: SUERF, 2009. Online at: www.suerf.org/download/studies/study20091.pdf

Articles:

Cummins, J. David, Christopher M. Lewis, and Ran Wei. "The market value impact of operational loss events for US banks and insurers." *Journal of Banking and Finance* 30:10 (October 2006): 2605–2634. Online at: dx.doi.org/10.1016/j.jbankfin.2005.09.015

The Economist. "Lessons of the fall: How a financial darling fell from grace, and why regulators didn't catch it." October 18, 2007. Online at: www.economist.com/node/9988865

Squires, Tris. "Banking on a reputation." *Financial Risks Today* (June 2, 2011). Online at: www.financialriskstoday.com/reputation_june.php

Thirwell, John. "Managing reputation risk—our 'purest' treasure." *Mutally Yours* (May 2011). Online at: www.johnthirlwell.co.uk/Purest_treasure_030511.pdf

Reports:

Kaiser, Thomas. "Nowhere to hide: Reputational risk management." *Frontiers in Finance* (December 2009): 18–21. Online at: www.frontiersinfinance.com/15108.htm

Micocci, Marco, Giovanni Masala, Giuseppina Cannas, and Giovanna Flore. "Reputational effects of operational risk events for financial institutions." Paper presented to the 18th International AFIR Colloquium, Rome, October 2, 2008. Online at: tinyurl.com/3w2y6rx [PDF].

Websites:

European Commission on Solvency II: tinyurl.com/2usz3wb

HSBC on reputational and operational risks: www.hsbc.com/1/2/investor-relations/governance/risks

See Also:

★ The CEO's Role in Reputation Management (pp. 797–800)

★ The Cost of Reputation: The Impact of Events on a Company's Financial Performance (pp. 808–811)

★ How Firms Should Fight Rumors (pp. 861–865)

★ Smart Use of Reputation Capital: How to Benefit from Different Reputation Investment Strategies (pp. 933–938)

Banking and Financial Services (pp. 1612–1614)

NOTES

1 For the more "typical" losses, the bank or insurance company had a profit opportunity that justified taking the risk. This is different from reputational risk, where there are no expected revenues/opportunities associated with taking the risk and incurring losses.

2 Boundary events are where an operational failure leads to an increase in an event that primarily arises out of another risk category. For example, a bank customer may default and the loss is made larger because the bank had exceeded its guidelines on lending to that customer.

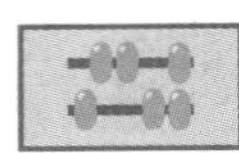

Viewpoint: Balancing Control with Dynamic Flexibility in Large Multinationals—The View from the Finance Function by Toby Willson

INTRODUCTION

Toby Willson was appointed finance director of Microsoft UK in July 2008. In this role he is responsible for all finance and accounting operations in Microsoft's UK subsidiary and is a member of the subsidiary leadership team. He has performed a number of finance roles within Microsoft UK, including those of financial controller and manager of the business control team. During the previous three years he has been based in Amsterdam performing the role of finance director Netherlands, and most recently he has spent six months as acting controller Western Europe. Prior to joining Microsoft he worked for Xerox and Centerprise International. Wilson has an economics degree and is a member of the Chartered Institute of Management Accountants.

How is it possible for a financial director of a large global company such as Microsoft, with a very diverse range of products, to keep control of all the elements required to deliver a balanced view of the risks and opportunities facing the organization? Particularly when the field in which you operate is so dynamic and so susceptible to new, game-changing technologies.

That is a question with a very broad reach, so let's take it in parts. There are three key operating principles in Microsoft that we all work with. The first of these is the scorecard. This is a set of 25 metrics that are essential both for Microsoft at a global level and for each particular subsidiary.

Before we go into the detail here, it is important to state that these metrics are not fixed for all time. They can be reset by the board each year, with some metrics being dropped and others added, as experience and the changing dynamic of the business dictate. What is key, though, is that there are never more than 25 metrics. If some new metric is added, another has to be dropped. The metrics range from key revenue drivers for this financial year, through customer and partner loyalty statistics, innovation, how we are perceived in the media, to internal people metrics.

Next, we have a shared "dashboard" with just eight core metrics. This lets us see at a glance how we are performing in the market against our key competitors in our mainstream product areas. It shows where we need to maintain or earn additional market share. These are quite broad-brush metrics, generating basic numbers such as the volume of Windows server licenses shipped versus the total shipment figures for the server market. This kind of figure shows us instantly if we are holding our own in that space.

By comparison, the 25 metrics on the first scorecard are more targeted and refined for certain incubation projects and for aspects of emerging technology, such as cloud computing. You mentioned game-changing innovation. Cloud computing certainly fits into that category. It is expected to take off this year, 2010, and to become an increasingly large part of Microsoft's business in 2011. For this reason we are keeping a very close eye on the total number of cloud computing seats that customers are buying. It is a targeted metric that is quite crucial for the future success of our company. Other examples of technology metrics that are crucial for us are search engine revenues and the growth in usage of search engines.

Apart from this, we have the usual metrics that are common to all organizations, such as revenue and profit and loss, and these constitute the third operating principle, or axis, for us.

So, to recap, the three core operating principles are defined by the scorecard, the shared dashboard, and the standard financial metrics. The idea is to ensure that you are getting a green light on all three of these core operating dimensions. If you are not, then you need to work out with your leadership team the actions that are necessary to get you back into the green!

In a nutshell, that is how we stay tightly focused. Microsoft is an incredibly complex company, with many different revenue streams. However, if we take the consumer space for example, with our Xbox console and Kinect shipments I have this as a separate breakout metric because the consumer space is a vital component of our strategy. Kinect, I should explain, is Microsoft's new controller-free technology that allows the viewer to interact directly with the game and the Xbox.

How does Microsoft move from the national and subsidiary level to the global level when it comes to getting a view on how the business is doing as a whole? How do you ensure that relevant detail is not lost in the consolidation process?

The key here is that every country and region has the same core operating principles that I have just described. This gives you a standard platform for comparison and for benchmarking best practice across your various subsidiaries. That in turn gives you huge management benefits. We revisit our 25 metrics, as I said, each year and we look very hard at how our priorities are changing as our marketplace changes. However, if you look at the metrics in general, it is hard to see how you could steer the ship if you dropped any section. Customer and partner loyalty metrics are obviously vitally important to any business that sells things. The metrics concerning your own people are equally fundamental, as is the issue of how your company is perceived in the media.

Again, there are the big revenue-driving items that have to be measured and that are highlighted as key to the current year's business performance. On top of this, in the IT industry in particular, with its fast pace of change, you have to have a space for emerging products and future areas so that you have a very clear sense what you are going to be betting the business on for the future.

For every metric that we deploy, there is someone at a senior level who owns that particular metric and who drives it. Nobody tries to own all 25 metrics personally, so that spreads the burden very efficiently,

"You can only raise individual performance by elevating that of the entire system." W. Edwards Deming

although it is the responsibility of everyone in the subsidiary to execute against them. At a country level these give the finance director and the general manager for the country an "at-a-glance" view of how their particular business is doing, and how the global business is doing. This helps you to stay focused—and that is incredibly important, since over the last decade we have had to deal with much higher levels of complexity in terms of both our own product portfolio and the environment in which we operate.

Regulatory pressures have intensified. We have had the introduction in the United States of Sarbanes–Oxley, and since then more legislation on anticorruption. I now get asked a great deal by investors and analysts about business continuity as a key issue. They want to see very robust business continuity plans. On this theme it was interesting that during the course of winter 2009/10, with deep snow on the ground, the business park that is home to our UK headquarters ran out of salt. No one was able to get into the office for days. To make matters worse we were in the middle of setting our second-half forecasts and proposed plan for the following year.

However, we were all able to link up from home remotely and my team was able to complete the task as if they were in the office. We would not have been able to do that five years ago. It was absolutely amazing to see that we could all work remotely together on a project as complicated as this without being face to face at any point. Another recent example, of course, was the ash cloud from the Icelandic volcano which knocked out air travel. We shifted many meetings that would have been face-to-face to video conferencing, and that worked very well. So far our business continuity plans have been able to deal with these disruptions.

At the same time as we are coping with regulation there is a constant pressure on the finance director and his team to gain an ever deeper understanding of our products and markets. My job is to focus on helping the company to increase shareholder value. This means that my role has shifted over time from being primarily concerned with being the custodian of the numbers, to embracing an ever-larger business partnership role, ensuring that the numbers are shared and understood by every corner of the business in a very open way.

It is important to realize that this is a fundamental shift in the role of the chief financial officer (CFO). Instead of being the one with the numbers, who people have to go to in order to discover *x* or *y*, people in the business groups now have those numbers as a matter of course. The new role for the CFO in this context is to become a facilitator of the discussion, since everyone already has the numbers.

Microsoft has had a very successful track record so far in betting large sums of R&D spend on what it believes to be innovative products that the market is going to want. What are the challenges in allocating R&D spend?

The business groups within the company that are making the investment in R&D have a strategic plan, with annual milestones and targets. These metrics in turn get cascaded into the Microsoft scorecard. As long as the business group is meeting its targets, that gives its members a high degree of confidence that the strategic plans associated with their previous and present R&D spends have got the right kind of traction and are generating the right kinds of return.

You are right to highlight the fact that in this industry the entry stakes to get into particular market segments can be extremely high. When we entered the console market with the Xbox, our goal was to be number one in that market—and it looks like we are now shaping up to be the number one in that market, especially in the United Kingdom. But the primary investment was very substantial. We have invested heavily in search technology as well, and we are now seeing some market gains for our search technology.

These are areas that the company has decided that we need to play in, so the numbers that reflect market share and market growth are key indicators for us. The current estimate for the total value of the UK search engine market is annual revenues of around £3.0 billion (US$4.8 billion). The console market, which includes games plus keyboards and other peripherals, is even larger. These are very large numbers and they are still growing rapidly, so gaining market share is vital for the future success of Microsoft.

Things move incredibly rapidly in this market. When we launched the computer game Halo, it became the fastest-selling entertainment product ever. When we launched Windows 7, our new operating system, the launch was huge. In June 2010 sales already exceeded 150 million licenses. Many areas of our business are not "slow and steady," and in those fast-changing segments you need to plan and forecast for big movements.

What do you think is changing, not just for Microsoft, but across the board, for finance directors as far as the pressures on them and the areas they need to focus on are concerned?

Apart from ever increasing regulatory pressure, it comes down to people, organization, and capability. There is a huge need in modern companies for softer skills, particularly in the finance function. You need people with a business brain and with people management skills, and you get that by developing and building proper career paths for your people. Succession planning is huge for us, as is inculcating the skills that you need to progress in the finance function as a whole right across Microsoft.

This last is a key point and is specific to us. Most people in the finance function do not sit in the finance area. They are out sitting side by side with the management teams heading up the various business areas. This enables them to keep me abreast of exactly how we are doing in all those areas. They enable the finance function to be very tightly integrated with the business as a whole, and so each of them plays a very key role. Having the right people bench to replace them as they move on to other roles (some in the business they support) is therefore crucial for the future evolution and success of the finance team.

This structure means that when I sit down with our general managerI can give him a very accurate perspective on where there are risks and performance issues right across our business in the United Kingdom.

Another point—and this is a general one across most modern international companies—is that the workforce is becoming a lot more mobile. You need to be opening the way for your team to be taking jobs overseas and to be moving on to bigger, more demanding jobs elsewhere in the global organization.

From your perspective at the heart of the UK and global IT industry, what do you see as the big "game-changing" emerging technologies?

Without a doubt the biggest emerging thing for us right now is cloud computing. It is the biggest transition in computing since the invention of the internet. We are currently spending about 70% of our R&D on cloud products, and that is due to go up to 90% shortly. That should show that we are taking the cloud very seriously indeed. The benefits for the company are huge. Because the cloud is all about being able to make services available from a large, centralized source, it means that our clients will in future be able to be on the latest version of our operating systems or applications with no deployment or rollout within their organization.

When you consider the scale of the effort required from an organization to push through a major upgrade across its IT platform, the idea of rendering all that

  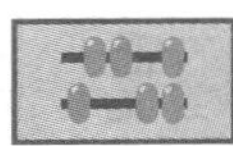   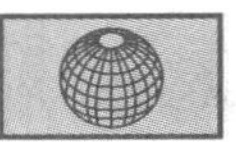   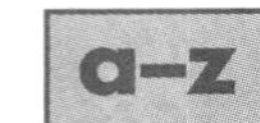

expenditure of resource and effort unnecessary has huge implications for companies. Then there is the fact that the cloud favors pay-per-use. This means that companies with huge peaks and troughs in their business cycle do not need to invest heavily in an IT platform that is sufficient for their absolute peak but which sits idle most of the time. Pay-per-use achieves an exact match between demand and supply, which is a tremendously efficient way of using resources.

The ultimate investment burden for the IT infrastructure then sits where it can best be borne—with an infrastructure provider that is the equivalent of a utility company. Its investment cost is then spread across thousands of subscriber companies on a pay-per-use basis. It is a model that will completely transform IT as we know it, both for business and, ultimately, for the consumer.

The move to the cloud will be gradual over the next 12 months, but things could then move forward very rapidly after that. We are not quite sure how fast things will swing in this direction, but we are quite certain that it will happen. As our CEO, Steve Bulmer, noted in a recent presentation, the industry as a whole is already spending some US$3.3 trillion on the cloud. We do not see it necessarily replacing our traditional IT business completely, at least not for the near future, but it will be a very important additional or alternative revenue stream.

The "super users" in a company will still have laptops and desktop computers, but many organizations have a range of other users to whom they would like to offer facilities such as e-mail, and these additional services are ideally suited to be delivered from the cloud on a per-use basis.

The final thing I would point to as a huge emerging change is virtual interaction. We are already seeing it with our Kinect product, where the technology on the console replaces any handheld input device. Basically the system "sees" what you are doing with your body and interprets that interaction according to the context. So you could turn pages with a flick of your hand, push and pull things on and off screen, tunnel into data; here, the possibilities of using movement metaphors are really starting to expand beyond gaming and into the realm of mainstream business activities.

These are all dynamic "bleeding edge" technologies, and trying to put revenue numbers to them is very challenging. I would say that we have very conservative target numbers associated with these technologies at present, and things are likely to move forward far faster than our targets suggest. It is a very exciting place to be right now.

MORE INFO

Books:

Bossidy, Larry, and Ram Charan.*Execution: The Discipline of Getting Things Done*. New York: Crown Business, 2002.

Buckingham, Marcus, and Curt Coffman. *First, Break All the Rules: What the World's Greatest Managers Do Differently*. New York: Simon & Schuster, 1999.

Hope, Jeremy. *Reinventing the CFO: How Financial Managers Can Transform Their Roles and Add Greater Value*. Boston, MA: Harvard Business School Publishing, 2006.

Semler, Ricardo. *The Seven-Day Weekend: Changing the Way Work Works*. London: Century, 2003.

See Also:

★ Aligning Structure with Strategy: Recalibrating for Improved Performance and Increased Profitability (pp. 774–776)
★ Everything You Need to Know About Benchmarking (pp. 850–853)
★ Multinationality and Financial Performance (pp. 900–901)
✔ Assessing Business Performance (p. 1144)
✔ Understanding Key Performance Indicators (p. 1180)
✔ What Is Benchmarking? (p. 1184)
🌐 Information Technology (pp. 1632–1633)

"Some companies inadvertently or knowingly have overinternationalized so that a negative effect on performance is seen." Farok Contractor

  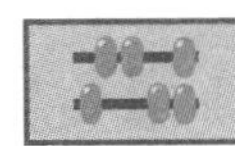   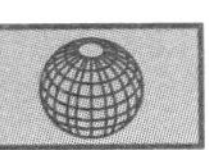   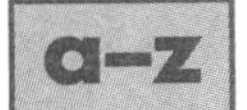

Building Potential Catastrophe Management into a Strategic Risk Framework by Duncan Martin

EXECUTIVE SUMMARY

- Most organizations recognize the need for a strategic risk framework. Such a framework typically identifies and analyzes the key strategic risks faced by the organization, such as competitive, regulatory, technological, demographic, and environmental changes.
- If adopted at the highest level, an effective framework will drive resource allocation and, consequently, the ability of the organization to achieve its goals.
- Many organizations fail to integrate the potential impact of catastrophes into their framework. Despite investing considerable time and energy into a risk management framework, this failure can result in large, unexpected losses. For example, a business might foresee, and mitigate, the entry of a new competitor but be caught off guard by a major flood that causes equal disruption and loss in value.
- To avoid being blindsided in this way, best-practice risk management builds catastrophe risk management into the same framework as strategic (and other) risks. With resources directed at those risks that pose the greatest threat, the full spectrum of risks is measured and managed consistently, thereby underpinning long-run organizational success.

DEFINITIONS

What is catastrophic risk? In brief, catastrophic risk is: "stuff happens." More precisely, it is the risk of extreme damage and loss of life from a natural or human cause. Some unexpected, perhaps unexpectable, event occurs. Half a world away from its source in southern China, SARS kills 38 people in Toronto; a nuclear reactor at Chernobyl is driven into a state its designers never even imagined even as its operators disable critical safety features, and it explodes; events in the Middle East cause Britons to blow themselves up on the London Underground.

Strategic risk is also stuff happening, but from a business point of view. An ailing computer manufacturer trounces established consumer electronics firms by producing the killer portable music device, and then follows up with a mobile phone that is both revolutionary and beautiful; tiny car firms constrained by postwar, small island scarcity eliminate waste by worshipping quality, end up reinventing the entire manufacturing process, and brutally upend incumbents; Wall Street's best and brightest simulate endless market disruption scenarios except the one that finally happens—no bids and no offers. Result: total paralysis.

Beyond strategic and catastrophe risk, financial and operational risk are equally necessary if less glamorous parts of a fully functional risk framework. Only through the consistent identification, measurement, and management of the full spectrum of risks can an organization be sure that it meets its objectives successfully.

CORE CONCEPTS

More formally, there are four core concepts in risk: frequency, severity, correlation, and uncertainty.

An event is frequent if it occurs often. Most catastrophes are, mercifully, infrequent. Historically, there is a severe earthquake (seven or greater on the Richter scale) about once every 25 years in California. Hence, the frequency of big earthquakes in California is 1/25, or about 4% each year.

An event is severe if it causes a lot of damage. For example, according to the US Geological Survey, between 1900 and 2005 China experienced 13 earthquakes that in total killed an estimated 800,000 people. The average severity was 61,000 deaths.

Most people's perception of risk focuses on events that are low-frequency and high-severity, such as severe earthquakes, aircraft crashes, and accidents at nuclear power plants. Strategic risk also focuses on such low-frequency/high-severity changes, such as disruptive technologies or new entrants. However, a fuller notion of risk includes two additional concepts: correlation and uncertainty.

Events are correlated if they tend to happen at the same time and place. For example, the flooding of New Orleans in 2005 was caused by a hurricane; the 1906 earthquake in San Francisco also caused an enormous fire.

Estimates of frequency, severity, and correlation are just that: estimates. They are usually based on past experience and, as investors know well, past performance offers no guarantee of what will happen in the future. Similarly, the probabilities, severities, and correlations of events in the future cannot be extrapolated with certainty from history: They are uncertain.

The rarer and more extreme the event, the greater the uncertainty. For example, according to the US National Oceanic and Atmospheric Administration, in the 105 years between 1900 and 2004 there were 25 severe (category four and five) hurricanes in the United States. At the end of 2004, you would have estimated the frequency of a severe hurricane at 25/105 or about 24% per year, but there were four severe hurricanes in 2005 alone. Recalculating the frequency at the end of 2005, you would end up with about 27% per year (29/106). That's a large difference, and would have a material impact on preparations.

Which estimate is correct? Neither, and both: Uncertainty prohibits "correctness." Uncertainty is the essence of risk, and coping with it is the essence of risk management.

Both catastrophic and strategic risk management are thus predicting and managing the consequences of rare, severe, and potentially correlated events under great uncertainty.

THINK, PLAN, DO

Integrating catastrophe risk into strategic risk management requires a common conceptual framework. Best-practice risk management is—always and everywhere—a three-step process: Think, plan, do (Figure 1).

Figure 1. Think, plan, do

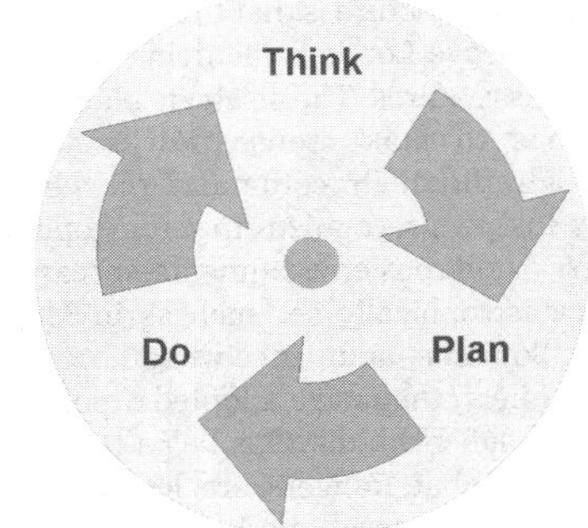

Think

Thinking comes first. Before being able to manage risk, risk managers must know how much is acceptable to their organization, and at what stage to cut any losses.

This risk appetite is not self-evident. It is a philosophical choice, an issue of comfort with the frequency, severity, and correlation

of and uncertainty around potential events. Different individuals and organizations have different preferences.

Some people enjoy mountain climbing. They are comfortable with the knowledge that they're holding on to a small crack in a wet rock face with their fingertips and it's a long way down. Others prefer gardening, their feet firmly planted on the ground, their fingertips on their secateurs and not far from a cup of coffee. Similarly, some organizations aspire to blue chip, triple-A solidity, others to the rough and tumble of start-ups and venture capital, with the added drama of the San Andreas fault under their feet.

For strategic risk, managers attempt to simplify risk appetite down to how much money an organization is prepared to lose before it cuts its losses and changes objectives. For catastrophes, it is the frequency with which a certain event results in death—the frequency and severity of fatal terrorist attacks in London for example. In some cases, it is defined externally. For example, on oil rigs in the North Sea it is defined through legislation. Events that cause death more often than once in 10,000 years are not tolerable and rig operators must mitigate the risk of any event with worse odds than this.

Plan

Planning is next. There are two parts: a strategic plan that matches resources and risks; and a tactical plan that assesses all the major risks identified and details the response to each one.

The first part is the big picture risk appetite. If, for example, an organization decides that the frequency, severity, and uncertainty of flooding in London are too great, the big picture is that the organization needs to leave London, incurring whatever costs this requires. The strategic big picture also has to make sense. For example, although the high command of the US Army Rangers recognizes that they operate in very dangerous environments—occasionally catastrophically so, such as in Mogadishu, Somalia—and hence will on occasion lose soldiers, they have adopted a policy of "no man left behind." This helps to ensure that in combat Rangers are less likely to surrender or retreat, perhaps as a result winning the day. Consequently, governments spend a lot on flood defences, and armies spend a lot on search and rescue capabilities.

The next stage is detailed tactical planning. First, identify all the risks, strategic and catastrophic, financial and operational—all the things that might go wrong. Then, assess and compare them to see which are the most likely and the most damaging. Finally, figure out what to do, who's going to do it, and how much that's going to cost.

Many firms create business continuity plans on this basis. California's statewide disaster planning process is an excellent template for responding to catastrophes, because there's plenty of opportunity to practice: All manner of major incidents there—earthquakes, tsunamis, floods, wildfires, landslides, oil spills—occur relatively frequently. State law specifies the extent of mutual aid obligations between local communities and requires each to appoint a state-certified emergency manager. Emergency managers create a detailed disaster-management and recovery plan for their local community, reflecting local issues and needs. These plans are audited by state inspectors and rolled up into a statewide plan. To obtain the necessary resources, the plan is input to the state budgeting process.

Risk aversion does not necessarily make you safer. Many people or communities express a low risk appetite but baulk at the expense of reducing their risk to match their risk appetite. They don't put their money where their mouth is; instead they simply hope that the rare event doesn't happen. However, in the end, even rare events do occur. The results of mismatching risk appetite and resources were devastatingly demonstrated recently as Katrina drowned New Orleans.

Conversely, a large risk appetite is not the same thing as recklessness. Technology venture capital firms quite deliberately "bet the farm" on a few firms in narrow technology domains that they believe will be highly disruptive and hence profitable. This is high risk for sure, but the extensive deliberation and diligence of the investment and management processes mitigate the risk.

Do

Doing is a combination of activities. Before an event, *doing* means being prepared. This consists of acquiring and positioning the appropriate equipment, communications systems, and budget; recruiting, training, and rehearsing response teams; and ensuring that both the public and the response teams know what to do and what not to do. A contingency plan that is not tested is likely to fail.

After an event, *doing* means keeping your wits about you while implementing your plan, managing the inevitable unexpected events that crop up, and, to the extent possible, collecting data on the experience.

Once the epidemic has broken out or the earthquake has hit, the key is not to panic. Colin Sharples, a former acrobatic pilot and now the head of training and industry affairs at a British airline, observes that instinctively "your mind freezes for about ten seconds in an emergency. Then it reboots." Frozen individuals cannot help themselves or others. To counter this instinct, pilots are required go through a continuous and demanding training program in a flight simulator which "covers all known scenarios, with the more critical ones, for example engine fires, covered every six months. Pilots who do not pass the test have to retrain."

Most organizations operating in environments where catastrophes are possible have similar training programs, albeit usually without the fancy simulation hardware. In addition to providing direct experience of extreme conditions, such training also increases skill levels to the point where difficult activities become routine, even reflexive. Together, the experience and the training allow team members to create some "breathing space" with respect to the immediate danger. This breathing space ensures that

CASE STUDY

Morgan Stanley was until recently a leading American investment bank. Investment banking is not for the fainthearted since it involves taking very large financial risks. Consequently, Morgan Stanley invested very large amounts in financial risk management. In general, this worked well and the firm was mostly profitable through the 1990s.

Managing financial risk is merely par for the course for investment banks. One thing that set Morgan Stanley apart from its peers was its assessment of catastrophe risk at one of its major operational hubs, the World Trade Center (WTC) in downtown New York. The corporate security manager, a decorated former soldier named Rick Rescorla, predicted the 1993 WTC bombing and had been able to convince the firm that such an attack would happen again; the firm had committed to move out at the end of its lease in 2006. On September 11, 2001, Morgan Stanley had 3,700 employees in the WTC. All but six—one of them Rescorla—got out alive, a direct result of constant practice and calm execution.

The integration of catastrophe risk into the strategic risk framework of the firm saved many lives. Few cases are this dramatic, but the point is the same: Risks are risks, regardless of source. The way we label them is entirely arbitrary. If, because of that labeling, we fail to treat all risks consistently, the consequences can be serious.

  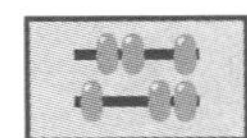   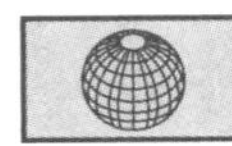   

team members can play their part and in addition preserve some spare mental capacity to cope with unexpected events.

The importance of this "breathing space" reflex reflects a truth about many extreme situations: They don't usually start out that way, but a "chain of misfortune" builds up where one bad thing builds on another and the situation turns from bad to critical to catastrophic. First, something bad happens. For example, first a patient reports with novel symptoms and doesn't respond to treatment. Then they die . . . then one of their caregivers dies too. Then one of their relatives ends up in hospital with the same symptoms . . . and so on. A team with "breathing space" can interrupt this chain by solving the problems at source as they arise, allowing them no time to compound. In this case, a suspicious (and perhaps even paranoid) infectious disease consultant (the best kind) might isolate the patient and implement strict patient/physician contact precautions before the infection was able to spread.

For most organizations, the critical learning point is not to create a continuity or contingency plan and then let it sit on a shelf. A plan that gathers dust is a dead plan—only living plans can save lives.

CLOSE THE LOOP

When the *doing* is over and the situation has returned to normal, risk managers must close the loop and return to *thinking*. The group has to ask itself: "So, how did it go?" Using information collected centrally and participants' own experience, each part of the plan is evaluated against its original intention. This debrief can be formal or informal, depending on what works best. Sometimes it might even be public, such as the Cullen inquiry into the disastrous Piper Alpha North Sea oil platform fire in 1989 that cost 165 lives.

Where performance was bad, the group must question whether the cause was local: training, procedures, and equipment; or strategic: the situation was riskier than the organization wants to tolerate, or is able to afford. These conclusions feed into the next round of *thinking* and *planning*.

PITFALLS

The main pitfall in the integration of catastrophe risk into strategic risk management is an insufficiently holistic process. Usually, this stems from the separation of strategy development, risk management, and, in many cases, insurance. In many organizations strategy development is the sexiest assignment and is jealously guarded by its departmental owners. As a result, sometimes strategic plans can be insufficiently informed by risk assessment. Since they tend to communicate in jargon and equations, risk management departments often do not help themselves. Sometimes, insurance is not a component of the risk management scheme; it is part of the finance area, and an obscure part at that. As a result, decisions on which risks to cover and to what degree may be taken without consideration of the organization's overall risk appetite. This lack of integration of the risk assessment process can ultimately lead to inconsistent treatment of risks and misallocation of scarce resources.

MAKING IT HAPPEN

In terms of implementation, there are five key principles.

- First, integration must be top down. Only senior management can both view the full holistic picture and require compliance further down.
- Second, the integration has to be genuinely "lived" by the senior managers. If employees feel that integration is merely lip service, they will not participate and the experiment will fail.
- Third, since risk appetites tend to be low with respect to very severe events, the resultant scarcity of events may drive hubris: Since it hasn't happened for a while, it probably won't or can't happen again. In industrial settings, researchers have observed that the odds of a serious accident increase with the time elapsed since the last one. Avoiding this complacency is critical.
- Fourth is the balance between sounding the alarm and having people respond. The more often an alarm sounds, the more likely it is that individuals will assume it's just a drill, or faulty, and tune it out, but if an alarm never sounds, no one will know what to do.
- Finally, many risk issues are amenable to sophisticated mathematical and computational treatments. There is a temptation to assume that just because a risk is measured, it is managed. It isn't.

MORE INFO

Books:

Abraham, Thomas. *Twenty-first Century Plague: The Story of SARS*. Baltimore, MD: Johns Hopkins University Press, 2005.

Cullen, Lord W. Douglas. *The Public Inquiry into the Piper Alpha Disaster.* London: The Stationery Office, 1990.

Junger, Sebastian. *The Perfect Storm: A True Story of Men Against the Sea.* London: HarperCollins, 2007.

Perrow, Charles. *Normal Accidents: Living with High-Risk Technologies.* Princeton, NJ: Princeton University Press, 1999.

Pyne, Stephen. *Year of the Fires: The Story of the Great Fires of 1910*. London: Penguin, 2002.

Singer, P. W. *Corporate Warriors: The Rise of the Privatized Military Industry*. Ithaca, NY: Cornell University Press, 2004.

Article:

Stewart, James B. "The real heroes are dead." *The New Yorker* February 11, 2002. Online: www.rickrescorla.com/All%20The%20Heros%20Are%20Dead.htm.

Websites:

California Governor's Office of Emergency Services: www.oes.ca.gov

Federal Emergency Management Agency: www.fema.gov

London Resilience: www.londonprepared.gov.uk

See Also:

★ Political Risk: Countering the Impact on Your Business (pp. 902–904)
✔ Creating a Risk Register (p. 1156)
✔ Establishing a Framework for Assessing Risk (p. 1028)
✔ Insuring Against Business Interruption (p. 1161)
✔ Understanding and Calculating Probable Maximum Loss (PML) (p. 1019)
Mastering Risk, Volume 1: Concepts (p. 1393)

"Frightened, nervous managers use thick, convoluted planning books and busy slides filled with everything they've known since childhood." Jack Welch

  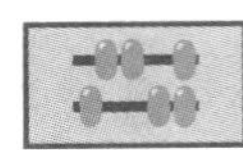      

Business Continuity Management: How to Prepare for the Worst by Andrew Hiles

EXECUTIVE SUMMARY

- No organization is immune from disaster.
- Business continuity management (BCM) is an integral part of corporate governance.
- A business continuity plan (BCP) can protect your brand, reputation and market share.
- The prerequisite discipline of risk and impact assessment reveals critical dependencies and threats to them, enabling preventative measures to be taken.
- Risk and impact assessment identifies and prioritizes mission-critical activities and the timeframe in which they must be resumed; it can also provide new risk insights to improve your business performance.

INTRODUCTION

Over five years even a well-managed organization has an 80% chance of suffering an event that damages its profits by 20%.[1]

The cause could be equipment downtime, failure of utilities or supply chain, terrorism, fire, flood, explosion, or adverse weather. Whatever the cause, without a business continuity plan (BCP), the result is the same: damage to reputation, brand, competitive position, and market share. Sometimes this damage, and subsequent losses, are severe enough to lead to permanent closure.

Yet such loss can be minimized, or even avoided, by implementing a business continuity management (BCM) system which includes developing a BCP.

Quite simply, those organizations that have a BCP tend to survive a major adverse incident, while those without a BCP tend to fail.

WHAT IS BCM?

According to one definition, BCM is: a "holistic management process that identifies potential impacts that threaten an organisation and provides a framework for building resilience and the capability for an effective response which safeguards the interests of its key stakeholders, reputation, brand and value creating activities."[2]

Information and communications technology (ICT) disaster recovery is an important and integral part of BCM—but only one part. BCM covers all mission-critical activities (MCAs)—operations, manufacturing, sales, logistics, HR, finance, etc.—not just the technology.

THE BC PROJECT

BCM starts as a project, but, once the BCP has been developed, audited and exercised, it becomes an ongoing program needing regular maintenance and exercise.

The project activities are illustrated in Figure 1.

Figure 1. BCP project structure

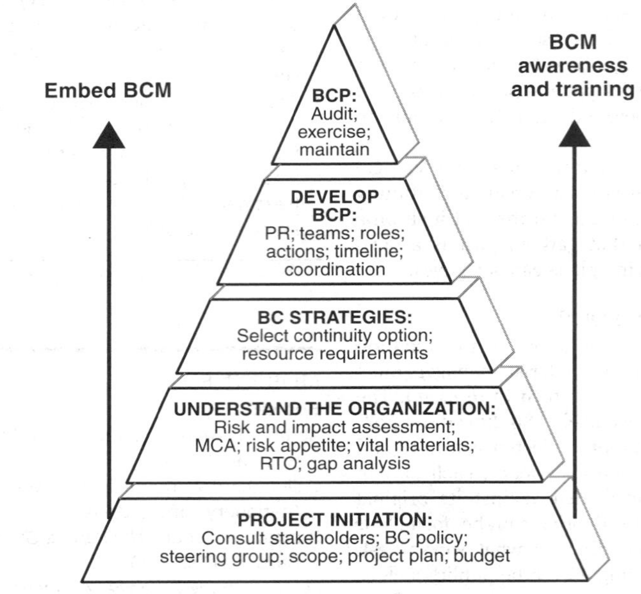

CASE STUDY

Buncefield

Buncefield Oil Storage Terminal supplied fuel to London Heathrow from pipelines transporting fuel from the north of England. It was owned by Hertfordshire Oil Storage Ltd, a joint venture between Total and Texaco. Other businesses were attracted to the site—Marylands Industrial Park—because of its low cost.

Around 06:00 hours on Sunday, December 11, 2005, an explosion occurred, measuring 2.4 on the Richter scale; it was heard as far away as France and the Netherlands.

The Buncefield incident was the biggest explosion, and the accompanying fire was the biggest fire, in peacetime Europe. Twenty-five different fire services tackled the blaze with 600 fire fighters.

The explosion and subsequent fire:

- destroyed some 5% of UK petrol stocks and destroyed 20 fuel tanks;
- injured 200 people; 2,000 were evacuated;
- damaged more than 300 houses and required 10 buildings to be demolished;
- caused all the schools in the county to be closed;
- cost local businesses and local authorities £1 billion: it impacted 600 businesses and prevented 25,000 staff from getting to work;
- disrupted global air traffic schedules and local transport;

MAKING IT HAPPEN

Phase One

The BC project should start with a clear understanding of the needs of the stakeholders and the support of the board. BC policy needs to be set.

A high-level steering group needs to be set up to decide priorities and define the scope of the project. For instance, is the objective to be "business as usual"—or will it just cover the 20% of goods or services that

"Just because the river is quiet does not mean the crocodiles have left." Malay proverb

generates 80% of the profits? Will it cover all customers, or just the most important ones? Does it embrace all locations, or just head office? How far does it go down into the supply chain? Will it cover only local disasters, or is it to cope with wide area disasters—hurricanes, major floods, etc.?

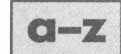

Next, a project plan should be developed, identifying the milestones and deliverables of the project. These include:

- risk and impact assessment;
- agreeing BC strategies;
- developing the BCP and implementing contingency arrangements;
- audit and exercising the BCP.

A budget can be established for Phase One from a knowledge of how many sites are to be covered, how many people are to be interviewed, how many processes are to be included at each site, and an assessment of time for research and report-writing.

Risk and impact assessment can be broken down into subactivities:

- identification of assets and threats to them;
- weighting threats for probability and impact (in cash and non-cash terms);
- identification of MCAs and their dependencies;
- establishing the recovery time objective (RTO) for each (the maximum acceptable period of service outage);
- establishing the recovery point objective (RPO) for each (the time-stamp to which data and transactions have to be recovered);
- identifying the resources needed for recovery and the timeframe in which they are required;
- identifying any gaps between the RTO, RPO, and actual capability (for example, the IT backup method may not permit recovery within the RTO);
- establishing the organization's appetite for risk;
- making recommendations for risk management and mitigation;
- making recommendations to close any gaps revealed.

The risk and impact assessment is usually conducted by analysis of building plans and operational layouts; review of reports on audit, health, safety, and environmental and operational incidents; interview of key personnel; and physical inspection.

Once these activities have been completed, possible contingency arrangements can be considered. The instinctive reaction is to replicate existing capability—but there may be more cost-effective options.

Holding buffer stock could cover equipment downtime. Increased resilience and "hardening" of facilities may reduce risk to an acceptable level. Items or services could be bought in, rather than undertaken in-house. Contracts could be placed with commercial BC service vendors for standby IT, telecommunications, and work area recovery requirements.

- caused businesses to suffer disruption of supply;
- caused many organizations to invoke their BC plans;
- made big retailers reassess their supply chain issues;
- forced companies to make public statements to protect their share value;
- created major environmental impact from millions of gallons of burning oil, which required more than three million gallons of contaminated firewater with up to 40 different contaminants to be disposed of; it took 500 tankers five weeks to move it.

Other impacts were equally devastating:

- By January 10, 2006, data recovery and communications restoration was still ongoing.
- By January 11, 2006, 75 businesses employing 5,000 people were still unable to use their premises.
- Insurance cover was inadequate to cover losses.
- In August 2006, 2,700 claimants sued for a billion pounds in a case that will cost £61 million.
- Supermarket chain Sainsbury's closed three stores damaged by fire.
- Brewers Scottish & Newcastle lost £10 million of stock.
- Retailer Marks & Spencer closed a food depot, disrupting deliveries to retail outlets.
- Fujifilm, 3Com Corporation, and Alcom buildings were damaged.
- Andromeda Logistics' distribution centre was evacuated: operations resumed on December 12 from their alternative distribution center.
- Shares in British Petroleum, a bystander, briefly dived.
- ASOS (As Seen On Screen), an online fashion retailer, lost its new warehouse with £5.5 million stock (19,000 orders were refunded).
- British Airport Authority rationed aviation fuel at Heathrow: airlines diverted to other European airports to refuel.
- Broadcasts on BBC radio and television news urged motorists to avoid panic buying of fuel.
- The HQ of XL Video, a video producer for trade shows, events, television, and concerts suffered structural damage. They had 12 projects to load on the Monday morning. Their BCP diverted projects: all shows were shipped on December 12.
- IT outsourcing company Northgate Information Solutions Ltd had backups ready for collection at 07:00 hours daily, but the fire happened at 06:00. Local tax payments went uncollected, and billing information for utility companies was lost.

Hertfordshire County Council's crisis management plan worked: it had been used at the two rail incidents at Potters Bar and Hatfield and been thoroughly tested in October 2005.

The risk and impact assessment then forms the basis for a cost–benefit analysis of the contingency options and allows a BC strategy to be recommended and agreed.

This report, incorporating the findings and recommendations from the risk and impact assessment, forms a natural closure to Phase One. Usually there is a natural break while recommendations are considered and the budget for Phase Two is agreed.

Phase Two

Once the BC strategy has been agreed, the BC plan can be started, bearing in mind what constraints may be placed on your organization by emergency services, public authorities, regulators, and landlords and other occupants (if you occupy a building with more than one tenant).

Incident and emergency management plans (for instance, evacuation, fire, bomb threat, etc.) need to be consistent with the BCP, and there needs to be escalation processes from them into the BCP. Triggers should also be identified for escalation from customer complaints, failure of service-level agreements, problem and incident management processes, etc., into the BC process.

The BC organization may not necessarily mirror the normal organization—for instance, multidisciplined teams may be appropriate—and the BC manager or coordinator may not usually hold the level of authority they are accorded under disaster invocation.

Typically the board will be separated in two: one to manage the ongoing business, the other to deal with the disaster situation. The emergency, crisis or business continuity management team (BCMT) will include board-level decision-makers. These include members from business and support units, and the BC manager (effectively the project manager for recovery) will report to them.

Business and support unit teams, including ICT, will report on recovery progress and seek clarification, information, and support from the BC manager. The BC manager will resolve any priority clashes

  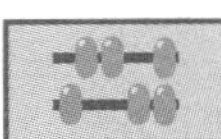      

within their authority and refer others to the BCMT.

Table 1 is a partial example of a BC organization. Additional BC teams will be created as necessary to cover each MCA, business or support unit. The overview at Table 1 needs to be amplified by detailed action plans covering each BC team.

The BCP coordinator is not necessarily the same person who will be BC manager once the BCP is completed. The BCP coordinator's role is to ensure that all BCPs are completed consistently and comprehensively.

The BCPs should not be scenario-based, since the disaster is unlikely to fit neatly into any scenario envisaged. Instead, they should be based on a worst-case scenario: total loss of MCAs. However, if they are developed in a modular fashion, only that part which is relevant need be invoked if a lesser disaster happens.

The BCP coordinator will draft a BCP for the BCMT and for their BC activities, including BCP invocation procedure, and will provide advice and guidance to the business and support unit BC coordinators.

Next, a template BCP should be developed that can be used for each team. Once they have had training, BCP development coordinators for each business and support unit complete these. A support program can be created for their guidance as they develop their BCPs.

Each BCP should spell out assumptions so they may be challenged (for example, an assumption that more than one site will not suffer a disaster at the same time; or that skilled people will be available post-disaster).

The minimum content should include:

- prioritized MCAs and a credible action plan for their recovery within RTO and RPO;
- lists of team members, alternates, roles, and contacts;
- resource requirements and when and how they are to be obtained;
- contact details of internal and external contacts;
- information on relevant contracts and insurance;
- reporting requirements;
- instructions on handling the media;
- any useful supporting information (such as damage assessment forms; maps and information about alternate sites; detailed technical recovery procedures).

Once the BCPs have been developed they can be audited, reviewing each BCP for comprehensiveness, clarity, and accuracy. This also ensures that interrelationships between BCPs are reflected in the counterparty BCP.

Rigorous exercises probe BCP effectiveness under different disaster scenarios and provide realistic training for BC team members.

Lessons from BC audit and tests should be incorporated into the BCPs. Where this has not yet been done, a list should be provided at the beginning of the BCP stating what weaknesses were found to exist; who is responsible for rectifying them; and the timeframe for doing so.

The BCP may take many forms: hard copy; handheld devices; memory sticks, etc. Whatever the format, it should be kept secure, and steps should be taken to ensure that only the current version can be held.

Partial example of a BC organization

BC Management team	IT team	Base site recovery team
Leader: BC management team leader Alternate	*Leader:* TBD Alternate: TBD	*Leader:* TBD Alternate: TBD
Members: CFO Alternate COO Alternate PRO Alternate Marketing director Alternate Estates manager Alternate: TBD Admin support: TBD	*Members:* Applications manager Alternate PC servers/LAN manager Alternate Data/voice communications manager Alternate: TBD Admin support: TBD	*Members:* Office services manager Alternate PC servers/LAN Alternate: TBD Data/voice communications Alternate: TBD Damage assessment/salvage Alternate Loss adjuster: TBD Admin support: TBD
Reports: BC manager Alternate	*Roles:* Recovery of all platforms, systems applications and data at standby site: TBD Data/voice communications recovery at standby site: TBD	*Roles:* Damage assessment, limitation and salvage Recovery at base site Recovery of operational capability at base site IT, data/voice communications recovery at base site
Roles: Consider group (corporate) impacts. Manage recovery. Coordinate all team action. Consider safety and security and environmental issues. Decide on priorities. Reassure media and authorities.		

TBD – to be determined

CONCLUSION

Wise executives have long known the importance of risk and impact assessment and the need for contingency planning. With today's threats, this has never been more important. Buncefield proved the need to:

- develop a BCP to protect reputation, brand, and share value and market share;
- communicate to key stakeholders;
- communicate to emergency services and staff;
- keep investors and customers informed;
- have alternative sites for operations and for a control center;
- read and understand the emergency plans of the local authorities;
- ensure that key standby resources are in place, such as information (status, contacts); accommodation (operations and work area); and reserves (stock, spare equipment, etc.).

Buncefield cost local businesses £70 million, much of it uninsured. It is imperative to check insurance cover. The impact of a major disaster could last for months, or even years.

"Chance favors the prepared mind." Louis Pasteur

MORE INFO

Books:

Hiles, Andrew. *Business Continuity: Best Practices—World-class Continuity Management*. Brookfield, CT: Rothstein Associates, 2007.

Hiles, Andrew. *The Definitive Handbook of Business Continuity Management*. 2nd ed. Chichester, UK: Wiley, 2007.

Hiles, Andrew N. *Enterprise Risk Assessment and Business Impact Analysis: Best Practices*. Brookfield, CT: Rothstein Associates, 2002.

Von Roessing, Rolf. *Auditing Business Continuity—Global Best Practices*. Brookfield, CT: Rothstein Associates, 2002.

Websites:

Association of Contingency Planners: www.acp-international.com
Business Continuity Institute: www.thebci.org
Continuity Central: www.continuitycentral.com
Disaster Recovery Institute International: www.drii.org

Standards:

BS 25999 Business Continuity Management (UK)
HB 221 Business Continuity Management (Australia)
NFPA 1600 Emergency Management and Business Continuity (USA)

See Also:

✔ Applying Stress-Testing to Business Continuity Management (p. 1141)
✔ Applying Stress-Testing to Operational Risk Exposure (p. 1142)
✔ Establishing a Framework for Assessing Risk (p. 1028)
✔ Understanding Continuity Insurance (p. 1177)
✔ Understanding Crisis Management (p. 1178)
Mastering Risk, Volume 1: Concepts (p. 1393)

GLOSSARY

BC: Business continuity
BCM: Business continuity management
BCP: Business continuity plan
BIA: Business impact assessment
DRP: A plan for the continuity or recovery of information and communications technology (ICT)
MCA: Mission-critical activities
Risk appetite: The level of loss that an organization is prepared to tolerate
RTO: Recovery time objective
RPO: Recovery point objective (of data or transactions)

NOTES

1 Oxford Metrica, www.oxfordmetrica.com

2 British Standards Institute/Business Continuity Institute Publicly Available Specification 56.

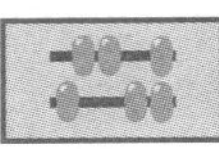

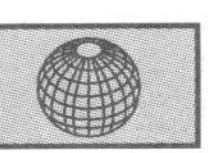

The Case for Continuous Auditing of Management Information Systems by Robert E. Davis

EXECUTIVE SUMMARY

- Managers should concentrate on making business decisions based on management information systems that reduce the risk of inappropriate responses to the entity's environment.
- Since management is responsible for the entity's controls, it should have the means to determine, on an ongoing basis, whether selected controls are operating as designed.
- Continuous auditing is an uninterrupted monitoring approach that allows IT auditors to examine controls on an ongoing basis and to gather selective audit evidence through the computer for timely opinions.

INTRODUCTION

Management information systems represent the aggregation of personnel, computer hardware and software, and associated policies and procedures, allowing data processing to generate information that can be used for decision-making. Corporations typically have management information systems with specific objectives designed to comply with external and internal business requirements. In this context, management information systems can exist at three configuration levels: decision support systems, expert systems, and continuous monitoring systems. Through an understanding of the development and deployment of these technologies, a case can be made for the continuous auditing of management information systems.

Considering the impact on decision processes, automated management information systems necessitate a higher degree of reliability and integrity than other information technology deployments. This is a result of the common need to extract system-generated information as opposed to manually created information to aid in making business decisions. Hence, corporate auditors need to convey timely opinions on both the quality of management information systems and the information produced by management information systems utilizing continuous assurance techniques. On the benefit side, employing continuous auditing can reduce the risk of management initiating inappropriate actions based on faulty logic and/or data.

DECISION SUPPORT SYSTEMS AS AN AID TO ENTERPRISE GOVERNANCE

Control systems can be categorized as being either technical systems or decision systems. Classically, corporate technical systems represent specialized configurations that support business units in achieving objectives, whereas decision systems represent information systems, or analytic models, designed to effectively aid managers and professionals in decision-making. Nonetheless, assistance for the decision-making process may be contained in a technology-based decision support system (DSS).

Interpretatively, a technology-based information system represents an architectural component that collects data, processes transactions, and communicates operational results, while an analytical model is a set of relationships with variable continua of:

- complexity, from one variable to many;
- uncertainty, from deterministic to probabilistic;
- time, from static to dynamic.

Thus, through proper system or model construction, an entity-centric DSS is deployed to enable the evaluation of alternative courses of action and efficient choice from the presented options to achieve the defined business objective.

Optimizing IT Assistance for Making Decisions

Reliable decision support systems should provide accurate and complete disclosure of available options, while maintaining the confidentiality and integrity required to enable effective responses. The "quality of management" depends heavily on having managers evaluate alternatives and select from the available options as many correct responses as possible. To ensure managerial quality, most managers are under observation for situational responses that impact the entity. Therefore, the ratio of decisional hits to misses must weigh favorably in the direction of hits for a manager to retain his status within most organizational formations. In other words, a regular pattern of failure to make appropriate decisions usually disqualifies an employee from retaining directional authority within an entity.

Generally, supporting decisions with software and hardware is wholly inadequate if there is no clear idea about the kinds of decisions that need to be made. Enterprise governance involves different types of decisions. The first type, *routine decisions*, is commonly treated within the entity's framework of policies and procedures. The second type, *nonroutine decisions*, typically requires one-time or nonrepetitive solutions based on environmental considerations. The third type, *nonroutine motley decisions*, is generally ill-structured and complex, arising from one-of-a-kind situations, and for an optimal response relies on scientific assessment. Nevertheless, decision techniques have become largely synonymous with quantitative approaches or mathematical analysis, which are well suited to IT processes. Some types of the latter are financial and statistical analysis that, depending on the circumstances, may be addressed through game theory, linear programming, simulation, and operations research.

At a minimum, governance decision support systems should include word processing, database, spreadsheet, and modeling capabilities. Of these, modeling is crucial to reducing uncertainty in the response to circumstances requiring a decision. Rudimentarily, a model comprises variables and objectives, where the structure must reflect the purpose for which it is constructed.

The variables in a quantitative model constitute a mathematical description of the relation between elements that can be classified as decision, intermediate, or output variables. The decision variables are usually controlled by the decision-maker and vary with the alternative selected. Intermediate variables link decisions to outcomes, thus functioning as consolidation variables. Output variables measure decision performance, and are referred to as "attributes."

Right-Sizing the Governance Model

Many types of detail variables can be associated with a mathematical model. Binary variables are employed for "go" and "no-go" decisions. Discrete variables are utilized for any of a finite number of values. Questions of "which" and "when" are represented as specific discrete values. Such data need not be continuous; however, continuous variables present an infinite number of possible values, and all the

"A rock pile ceases to be a rock pile the moment a single man contemplates it bearing within him the image of a cathedral." Antoine de Saint-Exupéry

values will lie within a specific range. Among the other characteristics of detail variables, they can be random variables that model uncertainty and are expressed as probabilities. They can also be exogenous variables, ones that are external to the model and cannot be influenced by decision-makers.

DSS models are abstractions that operate as substitutes for the actual circumstances under evaluation. A model-driven DSS emphasizes access to and manipulation of statistical, financial, optimization, or simulation archetypes. Consequently, a model-driven DSS utilizes data and parameters provided by users to assist decision-makers in analyzing a situation; however, they are not necessarily data-intensive.

The construction of a DSS model for governance includes: making a large number of assumptions about the nature of the environment in which the entity's programs, systems, processes, activities and/or tasks operate; selecting the operating characteristics of components; and making paradigm suppositions about the way animate and/or inanimate objects are likely to behave. A model is ready for use by management when it matches the set of objectives and attributes that require analytical consideration.

The value of information assets is continuously increasing in this information age due to their integration into decision-making processes. Governance decisions are highly visible, often offer immediate results, tend to be goal-focused, and are directive. Although there are various techniques that can be applied to types of governance decisions, the final outcome is a matter of judgment. Normally, IT processes can be adapted to support judgmental decisions through the utilization of engineered business processes.

To ensure robustness for the intended application, DSS models must pass three tests: relevance, accuracy, and aggregation. Relevance is measured by the alignment of the defined condition to possible problem solutions. Accuracy can vary depending on the decision that is being made. Aggregation permits the grouping of a number of individual quantities into a larger quantity.

Impact of Decision Support Systems

Decision-making is the process of evaluating alternatives and choosing from among them. Information may drive leadership; however, data accuracy and completeness are prerequisites to ensuring that appropriate decisions are made. A DSS commonly assists middle-level and upper-level managers in long-term, non-routine, and often unstructured decision-making. Typically, the deployed system contains at least one decision model, and it is usually interactive, dedicated, and time-shared—although it need not be real-time. Thus, a DSS should be viewed as an aid to decision-making rather than simply the automation of decision processes. Managers should concentrate on making professional governance decisions based on a DSS that reduces the potential for inappropriate responses to the entity's environment.

CASE STUDY

In this information age the value of information assets is continuously increasing due to their integration into decision-making processes. Assistance in the decision-making process may be contained in an IT DSS. Thus, utilizable decision support information should provide accurate and complete disclosure of available data while maintaining the expected confidentiality and integrity.

Technology deployment and associated management information systems can provide a competitive advantage as well as increased control requirements. Considering the adamant demands for continuous process improvements, a focus on overall information protection and security delivery value in terms of enabled services has become the managerial norm. Information security service management is a set of processes that enable and potentially optimize IT security services for an entity to satisfy business requirements, while simultaneously providing strategic and tactical management of the IT security infrastructure. In this context, information security service level management should be considered a quality of service administration that makes demonstrable contributions to process improvement.

Noncompliance risks are an irrefutable fact, where the consequences range from significant financial penalties to the threat of damage to an entity's reputation. Fielding an appropriate response to a security incident is typically a crucial business requirement. To enable effective management, a security MIS should correlate data to intended usage to determine the repercussions of a security failure. Considering that the primary contingency management objective is to provide solutions through an understanding of risk, an adequate response to an IT security incident depends on timely, reliable information to assess the risks and subsequently apply resources.

Auditors are indirectly, if not directly, an entity control mechanism which assures that mandated compliance expectations are adequately addressed by management. Amplifying the criticality of information security is the number of laws related to the protection of information assets and regulations that impact compliance expectations. In one form or another, assuring compliance serves as a significant information security audit objective for most entities which can best be served through continuous auditing of information security incidents. Therefore, an auditor should continuously audit whether effective procedures for the protection of information assets are implemented to manage and maintain the confidentiality and integrity of information throughout the information lifecycle.

EXPERT SYSTEMS AS AN AID TO COMPLIANCE

Technology is an ever-changing tool driven by compliance requirements as well as entity-centric requirements to satisfy market demands. For compliance requirements, IT deployments tend to be reactionary rather than a continuous, proactive process. Consequently, IT compliance efforts are typically lacking in constancy and conformity. To combat this tendency, IT planners should focus design and transition efforts on three time frames that meet entity needs: the current state, the near-term state, and the long-term state of compliance requirements. Within this context, expert systems can be an invaluable tool for implementing mandates that satisfy immediate needs and simultaneously position the entity to meet the next potential compliance issue effectively.

Expert System Development Activities

IT usually pervades all organizational formations that are pursuing effective and efficient processing in response to compliance requirements, thus facilitating better decision-making through various information delivery mechanisms and offering opportunities for business model development that may lead to value creation as well as competitive advantage. To construct an expert compliance system a knowledge engineer—performing a function similar to a system or business analyst—is typically needed. A designated knowledge engineer is responsible for defining issues in manageable terms, soliciting the knowledge, skills, and abilities of experts, and translating these talents into electronically encoded formats.

The development of an expert system is usually a four-step process. It starts with the knowledge engineer gaining an understanding of a particular judgment issue. This is followed by the acquisition of the thought processes of experts in solving the issue. Next, if a shell program is not available, a computer model is programmed to reproduce the thought processes that have been adopted for defined situations. Finally, the system is tested and certified to ensure that the resulting decisions are appropriate and usable. These steps are commonly known as knowledge representation, knowledge acquisition, computational modeling, and model validation.

Populating the Expert System

A knowledge engineer can obtain knowledge in several ways. One option is to go through textbooks and professional journals to extract definitions, axioms, and rules that apply to the issue. This type of knowledge acquisition is especially useful for teaching and reference situations because the question–response paths are direct. However, the way in which questions are posed to the expert system can lead to misleading results. Another method of acquiring knowledge is to ask human experts to explain their thought processes and ways of solving problem scenarios; this is sometimes referred to as verbal protocol analysis. Last, a human expert can enhance the information obtained from literary resources and will often bring unpublished knowledge, gained through experience, to the decision process paths. This combinational knowledge makes human-based expert systems a valuable technology.

To incorporate human expert knowledge into a technology-based expert system, the right individuals must be identified and selected. Specialists tend to be trained in rather narrow domains and are best at solving problems within their defined realms of expertise. Assuming that experts do exist and are willing to participate, good experts are those who are able to solve particular types of problem scenarios that few others can solve with the same efficiency and/or effectiveness. Additionally, considerable time can be saved in developing an expert compliance system if the knowledge engineer has experience in the area that is being modeled.

After experts have been selected, the knowledge engineer must take the expert knowledge and transform it into a computational model. However, issues may arise because an expert discovers that he or she is unable to describe how a situation is resolved. Typically, this is due to the way they may operate at a subconscious level while performing some tasks to address a scenario. In view of the possibility that undefined steps may generate misaligned logic paths in the inference engine, it is common for interdisciplinary teams of specialists to work together to formulate deductive reasoning processes for defined problems.

To assist in assessing decisional acumen, most managers are under observation for situational responses that may impact the entity. The reliability of business-related information used in making decisions is therefore critical. During the final stage of preparation for deployment, an expert system has to be validated to ascertain the reliability and scope of its decisional processes. In the model validation step a knowledge engineer and/or IT assurance professional identifies errors, omissions, and mistakes in the knowledge base. Furthermore, since the constructed system is designed to simulate an expert's decision-making process, it should be tested against the opinions of subject matter experts. Finally, if the system is later updated to keep the knowledge base current, reevaluation of the model is necessary to ensure its continued decisional reliability.

Impact of Expert Systems

From a technical perspective, the typical expert system can be divided into two essential parts: the knowledge base, and the inference engine. The knowledge base contains the body of knowledge, or set of facts and relationships, obtained in the knowledge acquisition phase. The rules associated with a knowledge base tend to be heuristic and take the form of conditional statements, whereas the inference engine is a collection of computer routines that control the system paths through the knowledge base to enable recommendations. In addition, the inference engine serves as a bridge between the knowledge base and the user.

Methodologically, for expert systems the knowledge engineer defines the ambit of issues that the system will address. A logic path that is too broad may result in a system that is too difficult to manage and it may cause a system crash. Contrastingly, the knowledge engineer must be careful not to limit an issue overly because a logic path that is too narrow will produce a system so rudimentary that the results will be worthless.

CONTINUOUS MONITORING SYSTEMS AS A RISK MANAGEMENT AID

A management information system is often deployed to permit performance monitoring to assess compliance with adopted standards and enable corrective actions and/or process improvements to an entity's control systems. A generally accepted key element that enables the risks inherent in many control systems to be successfully managed is the ability to monitor processes independently and continuously as close to the execution point as possible. Yet, analytic technologies capable of continuous monitoring are typically lacking in management information system deployments. Therefore, a continuous monitoring system that is conjointly implemented within management information systems can enhance the detection of variance as well as improve compliance verification and exception reporting systems.

"Monitoring encompasses the tracking of individual processes, so that information on their state can be easily seen, and statistics on the performance of one or more processes can be provided." From Wikipedia entry, "Business process management."

Foundations for Managing Processes

Prespecified and routine decisions, which form the policies and procedures that are typically documented by an entity, are designed to provide time for managers to address non-routine activities and consider improvements to the currently deployed control processes by removing them from the more mundane aspects of day-to-day operations. However, process monitoring is required to ensure that expected outcomes are achieved for assigned functional responsibilities and that irregular activities are detected on a timely basis.

Conceptually, continuous monitoring systems generally consist of three levels: data provisioning, information management, and information presentation. Data provisioning is enabled by the collection and storage of specified items in an assigned location. Information management utilizes the combination of knowledge of IT

MAKING IT HAPPEN

- Survey the deployment of computerized management information systems.
- Acquire support for the investigation of continuous auditing options.
- Assess the risk of inappropriate decision-making based on unreliable and inaccurate information.
- Present a transparent case for establishing continuous auditing of high-risk management information systems.
- If necessary, confer with the IT department to establish service-level agreements for continuous auditing systems.

"Ultimately, the job of the manager is to get ordinary people to create extraordinary results." Christopher Bartlett

architecture, analytic knowledge, and collected data to assess processing. Information presentation provides results from the conditions that are being monitored.

To enable effective deployment, the three levels of continuous monitoring must operate harmoniously. The data provisioning level supplies raw data for analysis after the collection process has been completed. These collected data can be extracted from processed and formatted output that is produced by defined processes and/or through direct data access. The extracted data are commonly stored in a data repository and/or retained in original form. However, certain data may also need to be stored at the information management level. This includes information about the structure of the systems that are being monitored as well as analytic definitions, such as conditional statements. Analysis of the data is performed using various tools, and the output is sent to the presentation level for evaluation by designated users.

Path to Continuous Monitoring

According to the Institute of Internal Auditors (2005), "Continuous monitoring of controls is a process that management puts in place to ensure that its policies and procedures are adhered to, and that business processes are operating effectively." Though manual performance monitoring may suffice in low-technology situations, in most high-technology environments automated controls become a necessary part of the IT architecture for ensuring information reliability and integrity. As suggested by John Verver (2003), the technology underpinnings to enable an effective continuous monitoring strategy should include several key components: independence from the system that processes the data; the ability to compare data and information across multiple platforms; the ability to process large volumes of data; and prompt notification to management of items that represent control exceptions.

To ensure effective continuous monitoring, adequate segregation of functions must be sustained. Continuous monitoring and segregation of functions are not new control concepts. Yet technological integration issues can be a barrier to implementing continuous monitoring systems that are independent of operational processes and capable of easy configuration for specific risk tolerance requirements. Procedurally, achieving appropriate functional independence in an automated system necessitates defining IT and operational user work units with consideration of the control context. As a result, when properly implemented, the segregation of functions assures that organizational responsibilities do not impinge on the independence or corrupt the integrity of information system assets while data on individual processes are being tracked and collected.

Continuous monitoring allows management to have greater insight into the entity's current state of compliance. Typically, for IT, continuous monitoring involves ongoing automated testing of selected data within a given process area against a suite of control protocols. Management can utilize this information to set or reset process guidelines, rules, and tests via applied analytics that identify performance gaps or unusual events that may suggest control failures. This type of continuous monitoring can exist in IT hardware, firmware, or software that is enabled to observe and record automated activities. Therefore, automated continuous monitoring provides a timely feedback mechanism for management to ensure that configuration items and controls are operating as designed and that data are processed appropriately.

IMPACT OF CONTINUOUS MONITORING

Since management is responsible for the entity's controls, they should have the means to determine, on an ongoing basis, whether selected controls are operating as designed. Continuous monitoring typically addresses management's responsibility to assess the adequacy and effectiveness of controls in a timely manner. It enhances managerial capabilities and entity-level controls, while striving to facilitate the maintenance of acceptable performance levels. Furthermore, with the ability to identify and correct control problems on a timely basis, automated continuous monitoring enriches an entity's compliance program. Nonetheless, the key to a successful deployment of automated continuous monitoring is process ownership by personnel who are assigned responsibility for responding to reported exception conditions.

SUMMARY

Continuous auditing is an uninterrupted monitoring approach that allows IT auditors to examine controls on an ongoing basis and to gather selective audit evidence through the computer. Theoretically, in some environments it should be possible to significantly shorten the audit reporting time frame to render nearly instantaneous or truly continuous assurance. In particular, continuous assurance is well suited for use in high-risk, high-volume, paperless environments. As a technique, continuous auditing is designed to enable IT auditors to report on subject matter within a much shorter time frame than under other audit models. As a process, continuous auditing can be employed to enable timely reporting by IT auditors through continuous testing.

MORE INFO

Books:

Akerkar, Rajendra, and Priti Sajja. *Knowledge-Based Systems*. Sudbury, MA: Jones & Bartlett, 2009.

Davis, Robert E. *Assuring IT Legal Compliance*. Los Gatos, CA: Smashwords, 2011.

Higson, Andrew. "Effective financial reporting and auditing: Importance and limitations." In *QFINANCE: The Ultimate Resource*. 3rd ed. London: Bloomsbury, 2012; pp. 338–340. Online at: tinyurl.com/6mw6qe6

Laudon, Ken, and Jane Laudon. *Management Information Systems*. 11th ed. Upper Saddle River, NJ: Prentice Hall, 2009.

Mainardi, Robert L. *Harnessing the Power of Continuous Auditing: Developing and Implementing a Practical Methodology*. Hoboken, NJ: Wiley, 2011.

O'Brien, James, and George Marakas. *Management Information Systems*. 9th ed. New York: McGraw-Hill, 2008.

Seref, Michelle M. H., Ravindra A. Ahuja, and Wayne L. Winston. *Developing Spreadsheet-Based Decision Support Systems*. Charlestown, MA: Dynamic Ideas. 2007.

Article:

Verver, John. "Risk management and continuous monitoring." *AuditNet* (March 2003). Online at: tinyurl.com/6vmqu4p [PDF].

Report:

Institute of Internal Auditors. "Continuous auditing: Implications for assurance, monitoring, and risk assessment." White paper. 2005. Online at: tinyurl.com/cheh2wn [PDF].

Websites:

Information Systems Audit and Control Association (ISACA): www.isaca.org

Institute of Internal Auditors (IIA): www.theiia.org

International Federation of Accountants (IFAC): www.ifac.org

See Also:

★ Continuous Auditing: Putting Theory into Practice (pp. 319–324)

★ Reducing Costs and Improving Efficiency with New Management Information Systems (pp. 921–923)

✔ Auditing Information Technology and Information Systems (p. 1023)

"We must dare to think unthinkable thoughts. We must learn to explore all the options and possibilities that confront us in a complex and rapidly changing world. We must learn to welcome and not fear the voices of dissent."

J. William Fulbright

  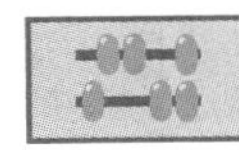   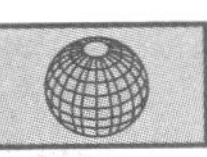   

The CEO's Role in Reputation Management

by Leslie Gaines-Ross

EXECUTIVE SUMMARY

- The importance of the CEO in the reputation management of his or her company.
- Why the CEO's role is of paramount importance for the reputation of the enterprise.
- How the CEO can manage reputation.
- The rising focus on corporate reputation in an age of unprecedented reputation risk and the CEO's increased responsibility as steward of this reputation.
- Five recommendations for CEOs who recognize their accountability in safeguarding their firm's reputation. Each is based on extensive research conducted by the author over the course of two decades.

INTRODUCTION

"Our reputation is more important than the last hundred million dollars." Rupert Murdoch, Chairman and CEO of News Corporation

Corporate reputation matters more than ever, as Rupert Murdoch would be the first to admit today. An increasingly complex business environment, marked by higher standards of corporate governance, citizen journalism, a more cynical public, and emerging special interest groups, places ever more pressure on leadership to protect corporate reputations. In fact, after financial risk, loss of reputation is the biggest risk cited by corporate board members in a recent study by accounting consultancy EisnerAmper LLC (2011). Even annual reports are recognizing the magnitude of reputation as a factor in business health; companies such as Goldman Sachs and AIG are now reporting "adverse publicity" as a risk factor in their 10-K filings.

One statistic often gets the attention of chairmen and CEOs. More than four in 10 of the world's most respected companies lost reputational status in *Fortune*'s World's Most Admired Companies survey 2011. This is the "stumble rate" that we at Weber Shandwick study closely, which is based on the performance of companies that lose their no. 1 most admired status in their respective industries. As Virgin Atlantic founding CEO Richard Branson confirms about the loss of reputation: "Your reputation is all you have in life—your personal reputation and the reputation of your brand. And if you do anything that damages that reputation, you can destroy your company … and it's going to be very difficult for that brand to ever recover."

Not surprisingly, 100% of CEOs report that they think frequently about their company's reputation (Gaines-Ross, *CEO Capital*, 2003), and almost six in 10 believe their company's reputation to be under threat. CEOs have taken the reins as guardians of reputation for their organizations. They know that, ultimately, they will earn credit when their companies are doing well, and get all the blame when reputation is in jeopardy. Executive recruiter Korn/Ferry has quantified this sense of CEO responsibility. In a survey of global executives, the CEO was cited most often as the person directly responsible for risk management (Korn/Ferry Institute, 2010). Similarly, Weber Shandwick's "Safeguarding reputation" study with KRC Research found that 60% of senior global business executives blame the CEO when companies lose reputation after a crisis. The proverbial buck stops with the CEO.

Before recommending different ways that CEOs must take responsibility for any reputational risk that their companies face, one thing cannot be overstated enough—that reputational risks are often the result of ethical lapses in the culture or leadership of an organization. The CEO has tremendous influence on setting the tone and, consequently, the destiny of the company. Recognition of how leadership behavior and actions are perceived has a disproportionate effect, both positive and negative, on how employees behave.

So, what can a chief executive do to manage his or her company's reputation? Based on numerous studies of reputational best practices and years of monitoring global corporate leadership, five ways are recommended that CEOs can follow when seeking to safeguard their company's most valuable intangible and competitive asset.

MONITOR, MONITOR, MONITOR

Executives who systematically examine the ways risks silently emerge and proliferate can foresee and prepare for reputation threats more effectively. CEOs need to know the risks that lurk around corners. Without a rigorous risk assessment process, the CEO can be caught unprepared for addressing a reputational threat. The CEO must not only ensure that his or her team is monitoring for danger, but also grant sufficient resources for the structuring of these systems.

Importantly, reputation monitoring should be broad and deep, not only keeping a watchful eye on competitors, regulators, vendors, NGOs, and the major media, but also scrutinizing all information sources to understand the business environment. Also key is the development of systems that can connect the dots between seemingly innocuous and unrelated issues that can converge and erupt into reputational threats or even crises.

One example of a successful monitoring system comes from a document services firm listed on Fortune 500. The entire board of directors is held responsible for risk management. More than 60 risk categories are assigned to an "owner" within the company's executive ranks, who then reports on that risk to a committee on the board. Committees are developed based on expertise and experience among the directors. The head of enterprise risk management at the company was quoted as saying: "Directors have told me that if you join a board today and you're not doing risk, you're crazy … when directors come on board, they come by my office and ask for the latest copy of the risks."

Over the years, CEOs have been adding chief risk officers to their executive teams. Responsible for leading risk management practices, this burgeoning executive position has grown 140% according to data from Liberum Research (Nash, 2008). In some companies, these risk or compliance officers report to the board. CEOs should recognize that managing risk is not just about compliance with regulations, but also about ensuring that all employees and activities related to the company are doing the "right thing" at all times.

Companies are also using "reputation dashboards" to monitor traditional and online media for reputation threats. Services from companies such as Nielsen BuzzMetrics, Radian6, Biz360, evolve24, and Cymfony can identify issues of concern from millions of blogs and other social media. In addition, there are online sites where employees can post opinions about their workplaces and reveal festering problems that deserve greater attention. Although it is best to hear about these issues directly, such "smoke signals" can be addressed before it is too late if a CEO or his

"Every week, an astonishing number of internet start-ups get established, without objection from initial venture capital … They think everything is up for grabs … all the rules are to be changed." William (Walid) Mougayar

or her team is vigilantly monitoring. The Internet is especially important to monitor, as the Weber Shandwick/KRC Research (2006) "Safeguarding reputation" study found that online sources often contain distress signals that should concern companies. Measurement systems can also come in the form of ongoing surveys of customers, employees, and other stakeholders.

Some risk managers engage in the study of "near misses," calculating the chances that something will go wrong. Nuclear power and aviation companies are big fans of this practice. NASA, for example, used to put the chance of any shuttle mission ending in disaster at 1 in 89. The concept of assessing a company's near misses is appealing for reputation management. If a company regularly tabulates and reviews its near misses, it might be able to prepare for improbable events and develop strategies for when a crisis arises. Hospital professionals have been known to meet monthly to review near misses where things could have gone much worse for patients or other members of their medical facilities. The regular discussion among hospital staff sensitizes them to how human error can raise the daily risks they face, and makes them more alert to problems that might surface. If more companies engaged in regular near-miss reviews, we might have fewer reputation scars and slower CEO turnover.

It is the responsibility of CEOs to place reputation monitoring front and center on their strategic agendas, as well as to provide the resources described here, enabling their companies to track, report on, and prepare for potential threats.

KEEP YOUR DOOR OPEN

Monitoring systems are not enough without CEO leadership that listens and is open to different points of view. It is critical for a successful reputation steward to be known as someone who will listen and listens first. British Petroleum's (BP) 2005 refinery explosion in Texas City was partly attributed to poor internal communication channels that allowed safety procedures to weaken. As one Texas City refinery employee told a *Fortune*reporter: "The values are real, but they haven't been aligned with our business practices in the field. A scream at our level is, if anything, a whisper at their level" (Schwartz, 2006).

One way to keep the door open is to request data on a company's problems within a certain period of their occurrence. The chairman and CEO of a Fortune 200 company did exactly that. He received red transparent folders of "situation alerts" for any issue his company faced within 24 hours of it transpiring. Everything from employee injury to a competitor's price change was reported in these folders. The CEO ensured that he had a handle on large and small issues that could topple his company's well-led organization.

CEOs, like presidents and prime ministers, are often isolated. They become siloed and lose track of the context in which their business is operating. Anita Dunn, former US White House communications director, described to a meeting of communications officers in 2011 what the world looked like when she departed. Dunn recalled how reading the news on one's smartphone eliminated all context on how the general public outside the capital was actually absorbing the news. She noted that capturing the news of the day on a small screen without seeing or hearing what else was making headlines and what other stories were rising to the top led to extreme "tunnel vision." Dunn said that she has since implored her communications colleagues at the White House to make it their business to abandon smartphone myopia and get the full screen, the full view, of the pulse of average citizens with all the context it deserves. Like presidents, CEOs must force themselves to move outside their limited boundaries and immerse themselves in the daily workings of their employees, customers, and publics to stay truly informed of potential reputational issues.

Another way to demonstrate openness to what is working and not working in a company is to tear down the walls. Some CEOs work out of cubicles or have glass doors or walls to their offices. They model their offices as newsrooms where there are no hushed sounds but where everyone is in the thick of the hustle and bustle. Without hearing what others are saying and seeing what others are doing, CEOs can easily lose their reputational touch points. Other CEOs make the point that reputation management is their job by seating their communications executives nearby on the same floor. These types of symbolic actions signal that reputation is always on the mind of the CEO, that communications inside and outside the organization are mission-critical, and that all ears and eyes are open to the company's reputational well-being.

Other CEOs have been known to "walk the halls," hold town hall meetings with employees, travel to customers, and solicit feedback from stakeholders via email. As Xerox's ex-CEO Anne Mulcahy noted, "My title should be Chief Communication Officer, because that's really what I do. When I became CEO, I spent the first 90 days on planes traveling to various offices and listening to anyone who had a perspective on what was wrong with the company. If you spend as much time listening as talking, that's time well spent."

Visibility is important, as is the ability to demonstrate that the door is open. CEOs who publicly disclose solutions to problems they've uncovered with the help of employees, customers, and others who speak up signal the value they place on collective vigilance against reputation risk.

LEARN FROM EVERY CRISIS

Once a reputational crisis has been successfully dealt with, leaders should step back and start asking questions. By studying one's own mistakes and those of others, companies can avoid repeating or encountering even larger problems that may lie ahead.

Some CEOs request a "root-cause analysis" to determine how the company got itself into a quandary in the first place. This type of analysis enables companies to direct corrective measures at the underlying causes of a problem, rather than merely addressing symptoms or repairing damage.

Other institutions apply similar investigative principles to minimize the recurrence of problems in the longer term. For example, the US Army conducts "after-action reviews" to study errors in judgment after battles have concluded. Increasingly, CEOs are establishing task forces to identify

MAKING IT HAPPEN

There are many other ways in which today's chief executive can help to burnish the reputation of his or her company, but those outlined in this chapter are critical in demonstrating the character of the organization, its high ethical standards, its transparency in doing the right thing day in and day out, and the rewards of foresight and preparation. The most important advice to impart is that reputation is more important than ever, and it will continue to become increasingly complex as ever more social networks emerge and reputation activists are emboldened. In the end, preparation is key, and the CEO's role will continue to be paramount. As *Fortune*'s editor Geoff Colvin said, "We've long heard that reputation is the new currency of corporate success, and 'reputation economy' became a fashionable word a few years ago. The News Corp. affair may be looked back on as the moment that companies broadly became believers."

problems that have led to issues that jeopardize their company's reputation. In the engineering profession, it is becoming more prevalent for senior management to form quality audit teams that assess completed projects and prepare "lessons learned" memos which are disseminated to all engineers at the company working on similar projects. By sharing these lessons with a cadre of employees, a consensus for change can develop. Just as companies form audit committees, so too should there be reputation committees, focusing on past missteps and how to avoid them in the future.

And not only is it important to learn from mistakes, but companies should also catalog what they did right when a problem arose. After all, it is easier for employees to accept change if they are presented with positive as well as negative information. One rule that CEOs shouldn't forget is to celebrate and commend people when things go right. Reputation management sometimes comes down to one-to-one or one-to-many communications by the CEO.

SOCIALIZE THE CEO AND PREPARE

Julian Assange's release of confidential embassy cables on WikiLeaks is one of the better known examples of how an individual or small group can inflict reputation damage on an institution. One of two world-class companies in a Weber Shandwick/Forbes Insights (2011) study cited WikiLeaks' confidential releases as increasing the level of online anxiety about reputation threats among global senior officers. As reputation insurgency intensifies over the Internet, it will be increasingly important for corporate leaders to consider adopting the tactics, if not the tools, of their online critics.

Chief executives—though not many—have started to expand their use of and participation on the Internet to enhance their companies' reputations. Some CEOs blog, tweet, maintain a Facebook page, or communicate using videos on their corporate websites. Examples of social CEOs include Marriott International's Bill Marriott, Best Buy's Brian Dunn, and Virgin Group's Richard Branson. Even President Barack Obama has personally started tweeting. As of Father's Day 2011, when he reflected on his paternal role, any message on the @BarackObama Twitter account signed "-BO" will be written by the President himself, rather than a staffer.

However, not enough CEOs are becoming digitally "social." Research conducted by Weber Shandwick (2009) found that only 36% of major corporate CEOs communicate through company websites or social media channels in any way. And when these CEOs do venture beyond traditional communication vehicles, the largest proportion go social by posting messages on their company websites (28%) or are featured in videos or podcasts (18%). Instead of using the latest media to convey their messages, CEOs of major companies choose traditional methods; during the same year 93% were quoted in the business press, delivered keynote speeches, or participated in business school forums.

CEOs could take note of the example set by Domino's Pizza US president J. Patrick Doyle. When faced with declining sales after an employee posted a video on YouTube of a colleague defacing food as it was being prepared, Doyle chose the same medium to address the issue. Within two days of the original video's release, Doyle posted a company apology on YouTube and outlined steps he was taking to safeguard Domino's products. His quick response and chosen venue became a bigger story than the original, unappetizing video.

Obviously, traditional forms of communication are also important, so executives should get inline by getting comfortable using all media assets when devising reputation communication strategies. Not only do a company's stakeholders want to read CEO opinions in the *Financial Times*, they also expect to see them online, in the "social" ways that are especially compelling today. Critical to this multimedia solution is a preparedness strategy. How can the senior executive and his or her team effectively respond to reputational threats? At Weber Shandwick, we recommend a new media drill called FireBell (Weber Shandwick, 2010), which simulates the company's response to corporate crises such as reputational attacks on Twitter, product recalls, or leaked documents. Preparedness comes from having diverse systems at the ready, executive knowhow before the crisis happens, and knowing how to execute the systems when the need arises.

IF A CRISIS HITS, ADDRESS IT HEAD ON

As I have devoted an entire book to the topic of reputation recovery (Gaines-Ross, *Corporate Reputation*, 2008), it would be remiss of me not to offer a few words of advice on the CEO's critical role in times of crisis.

Corporate chieftains should be prepared to act quickly, decisively, and transparently when navigating reputation upheaval. Strategic advisors Rory Knight and Deborah Pretty of Oxford Metrica have explored the relationship between leadership and reputation recovery. In their research, they found that "honesty, transparency and effective communication have a clear and fundamental financial value ... Management must respond honestly and rapidly in a non-defensive way." (Knight and Pretty, 2001). As this chapter was being written, UK Prime Minister David Cameron was returning to the city from his vacation in Italy to head up an emergency meeting on the London riots which have upended the country and damaged the city's reputation. This quick action demonstrated the importance of managing a reputational crisis and taking charge.

First and foremost, CEOs should be accountable for defusing a reputational crisis. A straightforward apology approach has been adopted by several corporate leaders over recent years, and has been quite effective. In fact, research from Stanford's Graduate School of Business has found that higher share prices generally follow corporate apologies within one year.

Apologies should be sincere and honest, with care given to choosing the appropriate channel for this important moment. For example, an email to employees can be less effective than a form of communication that allows them to see and hear the emotion behind genuine regret. Goldman Sachs' CEO sent a voicemail to employees worldwide encouraging them to maintain their focus when civil fraud charges were brought

MORE INFO

Books:

Gaines-Ross, Leslie. *CEO Capital: A Guide to Building CEO Reputation and Company Success*. Hoboken, NJ: Wiley, 2003.

Gaines-Ross, Leslie. *Corporate Reputation: 12 Steps to Safeguarding and Recovering Reputation*. Hoboken, NJ: Wiley, 2008.

Articles:

Colvin, Geoff. "Behind the Murdoch scandal? Scandalous governance." *Fortune* 164:3 (August 15, 2011).

Eccles, Robert G., Scott C. Newquist, and Roland Schatz. "Reputation and its risks." *Harvard Business Review* (February 2007). Online at: hbr.org/2007/02/reputation-and-its-risks/ar/1

Favaro, Ken, Per-Ola Karlsson, and Gary L. Neilson. "CEO succession 2010: The four types of CEOs." *Strategy+Business* 63 (Summer 2011). Online at: tinyurl.com/3l5eqbt [PDF].

"The substitution of monetary values for all other values is pushing society toward a dangerous disequilibrium."

George Soros

by the US Securities and Exchange Commission against the company in 2010. Harris Interactive's Reputation Quotient survey of US consumers demonstrates the value of honesty, as it found that communicating from the top, from where communications often originate with accurateness, sincerity, and consistency, correlates highly with corporate reputation. (Harris Interactive, 2011).

CEOs should also swiftly announce specific actions that their company will take to fix the problem when their corporate reputation is at risk. Indeed, 76% of global executives cite this solution as the best way to start reputation recovery after a crisis, according to the "Safeguarding reputation" study by Weber Shandwick. And when answering questions about a corporate problem, admitting what is still unknown is acceptable in the early stages of a company's recovery phase. The important thing is to demonstrate that the company's leadership, particularly the CEO, is taking the appropriate steps to get to the root cause of the problem, and then fix it.

And finally, it is the CEO's role to communicate tirelessly during reputation renewal. Employees, customers, the financial community, and other stakeholders regain confidence after uncertain times when provided with consistent communications. In the aftermath of Hurricane Katrina, an energy company faced the daunting task of evacuating employees who were separated from their families and relocating the company's headquarters. The CEO frequently emailed employees, launched a special website, printed all his communications for line and remote workers, and visited field operations. He shared his compassion and concern on a regular basis and received attention from the national media for his hands-on approach to the crisis.

Gaines-Ross, Leslie. "Reputation warfare." *Harvard Business Review* 88:12 (2010): 70–76. Online at: tinyurl.com/3ckwlxl [PDF].

Gaines-Ross, Leslie. "Reputation stumble rate still high." *ReputationXchange* (April 29, 2011). Online at: tinyurl.com/3b9n3hb

Korn/Ferry Institute. "Korn/Ferry survey notes that risk management is an increasing priority for corporations." *Korn/Ferry Institute website* (August 11, 2010). Online at: tinyurl.com/2com94h

Krakovsky, Marina. "Admitting missteps may boost stock prices." *Stanford Graduate School of Business Research News* (August 2004). Online at: tinyurl.com/6ks48bq

Lafley, A. G. "What only the CEO can do." *Harvard Business Review* (May 2009). Online at: hbr.org/2009/05/what-only-the-ceo-can-do/ar/1

Nash, Jeff. "Risk climbs to top of corporate to-do list." *Financial Week* (April 28, 2008). Online at: tinyurl.com/3o2g43j

Schwartz, Nelson. "Can BP bounce back?" *Fortune* (October 31, 2006). Online at: tinyurl.com/3ctdzv3

Reports:

EisnerAmper. "Concerns about risks confronting boards. Second annual board of directors survey 2011." 2011. Online at: tinyurl.com/3c3q65m [PDF].

Harris Interactive. "The 2011 Harris Interactive annual RQ summary report." April 2011. Online at: tinyurl.com/3dh8uww [PDF].

Knight, Rory F., and Deborah J. Pretty. "Reputation and value: The case of corporate catastrophes." Oxford Metrica, 2001. Online at: tinyurl.com/2b6e4em [PDF].

Weber Shandwick. "Socializing your CEO: From (un)social to social." 2009. Online at: tinyurl.com/5rzs9cf

Weber Shandwick. "Meet FireBell: Weber Shandwick's social crisis simulator." 2010. Online at: www.webershandwick.com/firebell

Weber Shandwick and Forbes Insights. "Socializing your brand: A brand's guide to sociability." October 2011.

Weber Shandwick and KRC Research. "Safeguarding reputation" survey. 2006. Executive summaries online at: tinyurl.com/44u5wld

Websites:

Ethics Resource Center: www.ethics.org

Fortune world's most admired companies 2011: money.cnn.com/magazines/fortune/mostadmired/2011/

Online Reputation Management—Risky Business: Reputations Online, presenting research by Weber Shandwick in cooperation with the Economist Intelligence Unit: www.online-reputations.com

Reputation Institute: www.reputationinstitute.com

ReputationXchange, the author's blog: reputationxchange.com

See Also:

★ The Cost of Reputation: The Impact of Events on a Company's Financial Performance (pp. 808–811)

★ Crisis Management and Strategies for Dealing with Crisis (pp. 817–820)

★ How Firms Should Fight Rumors (pp. 861–865)

★ Managing Reputational Risk: Business Journalism (pp. 893–896)

★ Smart Use of Reputation Capital: How to Benefit from Different Reputation Investment Strategies (pp. 933–938)

"Running a media brand is about harnessing the value of people . . . journalists, DJs, editors—all of them are the brand." Vijay Solanki

  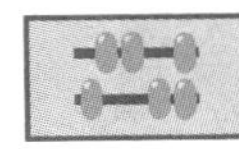   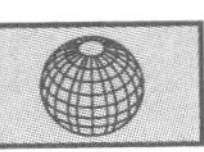   

Viewpoint: CEOs Should Refresh Their Finance Skills by Theo Vermaelen

INTRODUCTION

Theo Vermaelen is the Schroders professor of international finance and asset management at INSEAD, Fontainebleau, where he teaches Corporate Financial Strategy in Global Markets. He is a graduate of the Department of Applied Economics at the Catholic University of Leuven and obtained an MBA and PhD in finance from the Graduate School of Business, University of Chicago. He has taught at the University of British Columbia, the Catholic University of Leuven, the London Business School, UCLA, and the University of Chicago. Vermaelen has published articles on corporate finance and investment in leading academic journals, including the *Journal of Finance*, the *Journal of Financial Economics*and the *Journal of Banking and Finance*. He is coeditor of the *Journal of Empirical Finance*and associate editor of the *Journal of Corporate Finance*and the *European Financial Review*. He is also a consultant to various corporations and government agencies and program director of the Amsterdam Institute of Finance.

FINANCE COURSES TODAY

The CEO of a major consulting firm recently gave a speech at INSEAD in which he argued that the financial crisis has shown that finance professors should no longer teach the concept of maximization of shareholder value. When I asked him afterwards how he could say such a thing, considering that the shareholders of Lehman Brothers lost all their money, he replied that "they were maximizing profits to maximize their bonuses."

This exchange convinced me that there is a lot of ignorance and confusion about what is taught and what should be taught in finance courses. In this case, the consulting firm boss seemed to have confused profits and the pursuit of bonuses with shareholder-value maximization. Ignorance can only be defeated by education. Many CEOs of major companies have completely forgotten what they were taught in MBA programs, which is an argument for sending them back to school. Actually, shareholders should insist that money spent on CEO training should at least be partially devoted to acquiring financial knowledge. Currently, I have the impression that CEOs prefer to attend leadership courses where they are taught how to manage people, rather than how to forecast cash flows and value their businesses.

THE BASIC MESSAGE SHOULD BE THAT MAXIMIZING SHAREHOLDER VALUE IS NOT THE SAME AS MAXIMIZING PROFITS OR THE STOCK PRICE

Shareholder value is defined as the present value of future expected cash flows, from now until infinity. These cash flows are discounted at a rate that reflects the risks to these cash flows. Managers should be taught to build a spreadsheet that incorporates the relevant cash flows and risks. Subsequently, they should try to execute the strategy implied by the spreadsheet. Clearly, this is not the same thing as maximizing short-term objectives such as profits or earnings per share. For example, a private banker who sells a bad product to his clients may see bank profits rise as a result of the fees, but the value of his business will go down if, as a result of that sale, the client leaves the bank. In other words, the banker should consider the present value of all expected cash flows from his client.

If the market is efficient, maximizing the stock price would be the same as maximizing shareholder value. In this case the stock price reflects the strategy reflected in the spreadsheet, and then there is no difference between long-term and short-term shareholder value. However, if the market is not efficient, stocks could be overvalued or undervalued relative to the predictions of the spreadsheet. What most managers will do, and should do, is to ignore these deviations and focus on implementing the strategy. Occasionally, they may want to buy back stock if the shares seem undervalued and to issue new shares when they seem overvalued. In that case, the objective is to maximize long-term shareholder value to the existing shareholders.

Alternatively, the CEO may be encouraged to revise his forecasts as a result of "messages from the market." For example, a sharp fall in the share price may make a CEO think about whether his strategic plans should be revised to reflect the new information revealed through stock price movements. In that case the stock price and shareholder value may converge again.

One fundamental risk of focusing on the spreadsheet and ignoring market movements is the risk of a takeover bid that is below the value reflected in the spreadsheet. Typically, takeover bids require the bidder to pay a premium of 30–40% above market prices. If the stock is trading at such a large discount from fundamental value, an argument can be made that one should make sure that takeover bids are avoided. This can be done by implementing various preemptive takeover defenses, with the risk that these measures allow value-destroying managers to retain their jobs. Alternatively, the company can try to "signal" that it is undervalued.

Based on empirical studies, the most convincing signaling mechanism is the buyback tender offer. In such an offer the company offers to buy back its own shares at a significant premium (more than 20%) above the market price. If the management owns a significant fraction of the shares and commits itself not to tender its shares, managers will incur a significant personal wealth loss if the tender price is above the fair value of the stock. This potential cost of "lying" makes the signal credible.

CORPORATE GOVERNANCE IS CRUCIAL

A typical corporate finance textbook teaches students how to maximize shareholder value. However, the fact remains that managers, like anyone else, maximize their own personal happiness subject to constraints. This agency problem can only be resolved by appropriate corporate governance, i.e. by providing the right carrots and sticks to ensure that the donkey walks. One thing we learned from the financial crisis is the importance of good governance and the

"These capitalists generally act harmoniously and in concert to fleece the people." Abraham Lincoln

  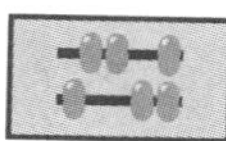      

alignment of incentive mechanisms with long-term shareholder value. Obviously, everyone likes to blame bankers' bonuses tied to short-term profits, but agency costs also lie behind the sovereign debt crisis—i.e. the lack of concern of managers (politicians) for shareholders (the taxpayers).

I always give the example to students of a company that gives away its goods and services for free and where the CEO issues equity and borrows money to finance the investments. Moreover, the CEO can force shareholders to put up equity when necessary. The debt holders know this and are therefore willing to lend money at low interest rates to the company. At the same time, the CEO stays in power because not only shareholders, but also customers and workers, have voting rights.

When I ask students whether they know of such a company, many immediately recognize it as the government. They also realize that such poor governance systems are not sustainable as eventually shareholders will no longer be able to finance the company. This in turn will make lenders reluctant to lend, in which case we all end up like Greece.

So I believe that a significant part of corporate finance courses should be devoted to corporate governance: how to compensate managers so that they care about shareholder value, not short-term profits. Another matter that they should address is the performance of boards—in particular how to trade off the so-called objectivity of external directors against their relatively poor knowledge of the business operations.

SOMETHING THAT PROMISES A HIGHER RETURN IS PROBABLY MORE RISKY

When an Icelandic bank pays a higher return on deposits than a Dutch bank, the investors have to realize that such a difference in returns is likely to reflect higher risks. When a complicated financial instrument receives an A credit rating but promises a higher yield than a simple product that also has an A rating, then one has to expect that at least one of the ratings is probably incorrect. The basic idea of efficient markets cannot be repeated often enough: in a competitive world all assets are priced correctly. The only way to beat the market is to have access to superior information. Unless you are a company insider, you should choose your investments on the basis of your tolerance for risk, your tax situation, and your consumption preferences. But, as an outsider, it is difficult to make the case that an investment is "cheap" or "expensive." If something is cheap, buyers will drive up the price, so that the expected rate of return (adjusted for risk) is the same for all assets.

Of course, CEOs can argue that they know their company better than the market and can occasionally observe mispricing. And indeed there is a fair amount of research that suggests that managers are able to time the market: companies tend to issue shares when they are overvalued and buy them back when they are cheap, and the market does not fully understand this.

MARKET EFFICIENCY DOES NOT MEAN PERFECT FORESIGHT

The efficient market hypothesis (EMH) invariably comes under fire whenever stocks go up a lot and then fall a lot, such as during the Internet bubble and the recent real estate bubble. The EMH argues that asset prices at time *t* reflect all publicly available information at time *t*. As new information becomes available, it is normal that stock prices adjust to this information—and sometimes quite substantially. The EMH does not predict these unexpected events. It also does not predict stable or steadily rising prices. Volatility as a result of changing expectations is a sign of efficiency.

During the Internet bubble investors overstated the extent to which the benefits from the Internet could be captured by shareholders. It turned out that most of the benefits went to consumers. Once this became increasingly clear after March 2000, technology stocks collapsed. This collapse did not lead to a banking crisis as banks were not lending to Internet companies. Most Internet companies financed their investments by issuing equity. Banks were lending to old-economy stocks, which did relatively well when the Internet bubble collapsed. What was different about the recent crisis was that here the driving force was the spectacular rise in the US real estate market from 2002 to 2007, which of course exposed the financial sector. Real estate prices are different from stock prices in that you can't short real estate, so efficient pricing is more difficult to guarantee. So, if we have learned anything, it is that if you want to have an efficient market in the pricing of a particular asset, you should make it easy to short, so that undeserved bubbles get deflated sooner. Of course, this is exactly the opposite of the conclusions of many politicians who see short-sellers of, for example, Greek bonds as evildoers.

DEBT IS NOT CHEAPER THAN EQUITY

The directors of banks should be reminded of the basic Miller–Modigliani theorems, in particular the proposition that if you borrow money and the cost of debt is lower than the return on assets, your return on equity will go up. But this is not creating value for your shareholders, as the remaining equity will become riskier. So the weighted average cost of capital will not fall if you borrow more money.

Bank CEOs seem to have failed to grasp this basic idea. If they had, why do they persist with setting return-on-equity targets, and why are they so strongly opposed to regulatory requirements that they should issue more equity? It is true that, once you incorporate the fact that interest is tax-deductible, shareholder value increases as leverage increases, but then you should also introduce the other market imperfections—i.e. the cost of financial distress. Setting return-on-equity targets encourages borrowing without consideration of these costs of financial distress.

The problem with the banking sector is that regulators set the capital structure, in the same way that the government sets the speed limit. Like a car driver who drives as fast as is legally permitted, bankers try to reach the government-recommended leverage without asking whether this limit corresponds to shareholder-value maximization.

SUMMARY

Although I cannot really argue that taking such a course will prevent the next crisis, it seems to me that having a bit more finance training cannot hurt when the next crisis happens.

MORE INFO

Book:

Smith, N. Craig, and Gilbert Lenssen (eds). *Mainstreaming Corporate Responsibility.* Chichester, UK: Wiley, 2009.

See Also:

★ Viewpoint: Poverty of Thinking in University Economics and Accountancy Departments (pp. 905–907)
★ Viewpoint: Urgent Need to Retool Business Faculties with Financial Historians and Eject the Financial Engineers (pp. 943–944)
★ Viewpoint: Why Management Development Is a Challenge for Both Business Schools and Client Organizations (pp. 954–956)

"We must not allow ourselves to be at the mercy of the forces around us, but try to lead them." Fons Trompenaars

  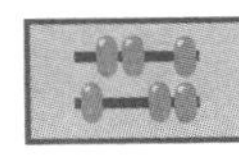   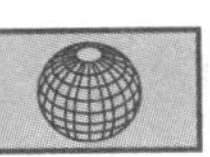   

Viewpoint: Challenges in Management Skills Development by Simon Earp and Eddie Cochrane

INTRODUCTION

Simon Earp is director of corporate development and director of the University of Edinburgh Business School's part-time MBA program. He has a BSc Dip. Marketing and obtained his management science degree at Warwick University. In addition to running several TCS programs he has overall responsibility for TCS programs throughout the university. Prior to becoming Director of Corporate Engagement and Marketing he was a marketing lecturer in the department. His research interests include relationship marketing, customer service, marketing strategy, and marketing information systems.

Eddie Cochrane is executive development manager at the University of Edinburgh Business School. Currently studying for a PhD in the area of emotional management, he holds the British Psychological Society Certificate of Competence in Occupational Testing (Level A & B). He delivers and manages external executive programs to corporate clients, with recent clients including RBS, NPower, BP, and Nucleus. He has featured regularly in the UK press, most recently for his work on emotional engagement in organizations. He also has responsibility for the design and delivery of leadership and management skills throughout the various MBA programs. He has 15 years' experience in HR Management where he managed a variety of HR teams in both the private and public sectors.

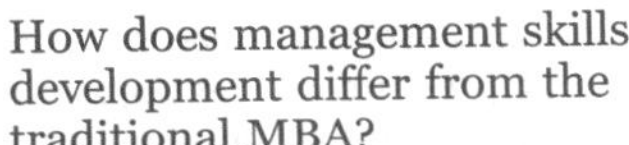

How does management skills development differ from the traditional MBA?

In our opinion and practice there is a marked difference between the goals of a full-time MBA program and those of a management development program. Many people taking a full-time MBA do so in order to make a sea change in their career path. They use it to reorientate their career and their skill sets. So they will use it to change industry sectors, for example, or to move from a specialist to a general management role. The implications are that the skills and training that they are looking for from the MBA are not skills that they currently possess to a significant degree. They are looking to move outside their existing career trajectory, or of the view of management that is provided by their current organization.

They are investing a very significant sum—usually upward of US$36,000 plus the salary they are foregoing, plus their living costs for the year—in order to step off their current career path and branch out afresh. When you total all that it is without doubt one of the most significant investments, apart, say, from buying a home, that most of them will make in their lives.

By contrast, people doing a part-time MBA program are generally doing so to accelerate their career inside their existing organization. In many instances they will be at least partially sponsored by their organization, and much of the project work that they undertake in the course of their MBA may well address real issues and challenges in the parent organization. In our experience, about two-thirds of students on our part-time program will have some form of sponsorship from their organization, which will be somewhere on a sliding scale from around 15% sponsorship to the company picking up 100% of the fees.

Management development is a very different affair altogether. With management development you are looking at a program that is instigated by an organization, and whose content is worked out by the business school in close cooperation with the organization. Inevitably, for an organization to be willing to invest in a management development program there will be an identified development need inside the organization. This may come about as the result of some fundamental change that the organization is going through, or recognition of the need for a development program may have come about through an internal staff appraisal process. Alternatively, as we will see, it can also be that new developments in management science, such as the development of emotional intelligence and the realization of the benefits that flow from training in emotional intelligence, create a requirement for the development of a program for that organization.

However, the trend in the market for management development—for the last five years at least, and continuing into the present—is that most interventions are not to teach or develop generic skills but to fulfill a development need that is tailored specifically to that organization and where it is at that particular point in time. We use the word "intervention" advisedly here, for a management development program, as we have described it, is very much an intervention in an organization with the aim of achieving specific goals. These are crafted, tailored interventions with measurable outcomes.

From time to time we do see opportunities for syndicated consortia programs, where two or more organizations with common requirements get together to share the costs and benefits of a management development program. For example, one management development program that we are working on involves four organizations, all with a similar need for executive coaching, and we are putting together a program that will go across all four organizations. At present each of the organizations involved is talking about putting 20 of their executives through the course, so that brings the unit cost of course development down considerably for each of

  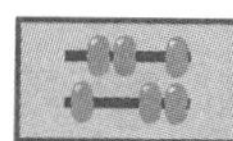      

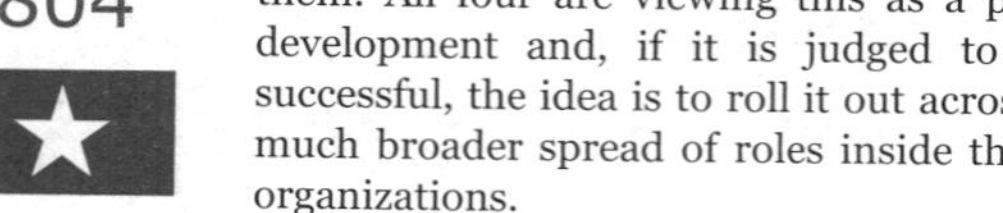

them. All four are viewing this as a pilot development and, if it is judged to be successful, the idea is to roll it out across a much broader spread of roles inside those organizations.

How do consortia programs like this, and management development interventions in general, come about? Does it require active selling into the private and public sector by business schools, or do organizations signal a requirement by contacting a business school?

This question goes to the heart of the relationship between a business school and its network of connections in the private and public sectors. In the case of the four-organization consortium project, this was initiated by the network of contacts that the client organizations were involved with. One of them discovered that they had a common requirement with a counterparty, and the idea spread by network effect. In general, though, the instigation is often a phone call from an organization to discuss a potential training issue that they have identified.

What we bring to the discussion is deep experience of helping organizations to identify and articulate the nature of the training challenge that they are facing and the ability to develop a bespoke course to meet that requirement. This is very different from taking down an off-the-shelf, generic set of courseware aimed at executives. We start by analyzing what is happening in the organization rather than saying to the organization: "Here are five topics that are generally covered in management development courses." The investigation is at the heart of the process.

Of course, there are classic management competencies that need to be present in the skill sets of executives from middle management upward, irrespective of what type of organization they are working for. So the course will be a combination of interventions aimed squarely at the management problem the organization is facing, combined with approaches designed to sharpen the skill sets that are most appropriate to that problem. Typical competencies that people look for in managers include persuasiveness, creativity, emotional intelligence, and leadership.

What you are not trying to do is to take a middle-of-the-road executive and turn him or her into an Alan Sugar or a Richard Branson. There are, in fact, very few truly inspirational leaders heading up major organizations. It is much more common to find that they are headed by good, very capable, competent leaders rather than by great inspirational figures. The implication then is that for people who already have the right aptitude in a sufficient degree you can, through a training intervention in terms of specific management development, turn them into very good, capable, successful leaders. A very few individuals will make the leap from there to being truly inspirational figures who can transform the fortunes of their organization, but that is a one-in-a-hundred occurrence. The intervention is more than justified, in terms of payback to the organization, at a much lower level of success than that! You cannot manufacture a Richard Branson, so there is no point in a business school trying to achieve this. But you can learn lessons from it. You can analyze and explain some of their behaviors and choices. The Bill Gates and Steve Jobs of the business world are transformative figures and they inspire very illuminating instances of inspirational management practice in their organizations. Those practices add to the repertoire of options available to management generally and, in some instances, challenge and improve or transform existing practice. All these are lessons that business schools absorb and incorporate into management intervention techniques.

One of the enduring focuses in management theory is the study of how management impacts and leads. In some of the courses we have put together we have had senior military figures come in and speak of how things are done in the army, navy, or airforce, which always generates very interesting debates and discussions. There are obvious differences between the military and a private- or public-sector organization, but there are lessons and parallels that can be drawn. The fundamental difference is that there is an acceptance by military personnel of the authority embedded in the military structure.

In contrast, the extent of a particular manager's authority is always being defined and redefined by daily practice inside their organization. This is where the concept of emotional intelligence comes into play, and this is an area that we have particularly focused on in our interventions. What we are trying to do here is to help executives to be aware of how their behavior impacts those around them and generates a range of likely outcomes. This is true both of their subordinates and of those above them in the organization. We see emotional intelligence as being one of the most important areas of development in management practice in the decades ahead, particularly as organizations become more dispersed and more flexible, and where partnerships and alliances with other organizations become an increasingly important feature of how many organizations seek to attain their strategic goals.

In analyzing an organization's management development requirements, what are you looking for?

Bespoke management development is very driven by the needs of the organization and will vary hugely from instance to instance. An organization might be looking for functional, technical skills—such as skills in international marketing which it does not yet have in sufficient depth because it plans to extend export sales. It might want competencies in supply-side development to improve its procurement capabilities and supplier sourcing and management. There is no one-size-fits-all solution. The course, the nature of the intervention, that we propose has to come out of a full analysis of the organization's challenge and the probable solutions.

What has the demand for management development been like during the global downturn since 2008? Has there been a pickup in demand now that growth appears to be returning?

The state of the economy in 2008–09 meant that companies were first and foremost looking to cut costs and conserve cash. This clearly put pressure on development and training budgets, but at the same time there was a widespread recognition across both the private and the public sectors that simply stopping management development would be intensely short-sighted. Even in the depths of a global recession, organizations need to manage their talent pool so that they are in reasonable shape when the economy picks up.

What we found was some slowness in demand in the early months of the recession, but developing the management cadre that you have is now very much back on the agenda. Demand for open enrollment programs, such as executive MBAs, is now extremely buoyant, and we saw an increase in applications in 2010 of around 26% compared to 2009, and that trend continued into 2011. Demand from the corporate market for management development interventions has been more mixed, but it too is recovering. We are also seeing a good recovery in international demand. Many of the requests that we receive for proposals for management development come from outside the United Kingdom.

You have been focusing on emotional intelligence as a key component of your approach to management development. How responsive are companies to this as a key factor?

The intelligent management of emotions, both your own and of those around you, is part of what makes for success at the personal and organizational level. Many

"The trouble with organizing a thing is that pretty soon folks get to paying more attention to the organization than to what they're organized for." Laura Ingalls Wilder

  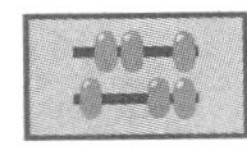      

organizations today are involved with doing "engagement" work, by which is meant engagement with staff, with stakeholders, with suppliers, and with clients. It is fundamental to both understanding and managing the key relationships that the organization has with those around it and contributes to both operational efficiency and reputational enhancement.

When you approach the subject of emotional intelligence in the context of an engagement exercise it becomes very easy for organizations to grasp the importance of the topic. Engagement, after all, is an emotive word and it is impossible to gauge the engagement of staff with the company, for example, without measuring the emotional dimension. So then the question becomes whether an intervention based on issues of emotional intelligence is of benefit. That is part of a larger question about what it is that is causing the organization pain—what the nature of the problem is. If the issues involved are not issues of leadership, why spend money on leadership training? If the issues are not about team cohesion, why spend money on team training? If the issue is one of engagement, then you need to look at emotional intelligence.

Our approach uses some proprietary data analysis techniques that enable us to look at large volumes of emails and conversations or interviews with employees or whichever group the engagement exercise is targeting, to pick out the key emotions contained in the language, and then to relate those emotions directly to the key issues. If there is stress in the relationship, the analysis picks up the stress and shows what people are annoyed or stressed about. The analysis we carry out will show an organization, for example, what are the five things that people in the organization are most negative about. These five things then become amenable to interventions to address and change them, and they are highlighted as issues that are clearly worth spending money on—even if there are 20 other issues that are more interesting and seductive and which an organization might have been tempted to address instead. It allows management, in other words, to focus an intervention precisely on those areas that are of most concern in the context of engagement.

How receptive have companies been to the idea of interventions based on emotional intelligence?

We have found that there are two types of organizations that are interested in emotional intelligence as a major theme. The first are vibrant, growing companies that want to do things that will help them in their growth period. The second class of organizations are those with some clear crisis. For example, one of the leading banks was not dealing with customer complaints properly and was fined very substantially by the regulator. It needed to find out what was going wrong and what needed to be done to correct that. Emotional intelligence analysis played a key part in identifying staff attitudes and in helping the bank to focus on what needed to be addressed and changed. Emotional intelligence addresses motivation—the factors that align staff with the goals of the organization—and brings a sharper focus to areas of excessive stress. Stress in the workplace leads directly to higher rates of staff illness and absenteeism and to high staff turnover, all of which damage the organization's capacity to deliver on its goals.

MORE INFO

See Also:

★ Viewpoint: Urgent Need to Retool Business Faculties with Financial Historians and Eject the Financial Engineers (pp. 943–944)

★ Viewpoint: Why Management Development Is a Challenge for Both Business Schools and Client Organizations (pp. 954–956)

The Portable MBA in Finance and Accounting (p. 1407)

"America's business problem is that it is entering the twenty-first century with companies designed during the nineteenth century to work well in the twentieth." Michael Hammer

  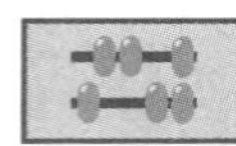      

Viewpoint: The Changing Role of the CFO

by Thibault de Tersant

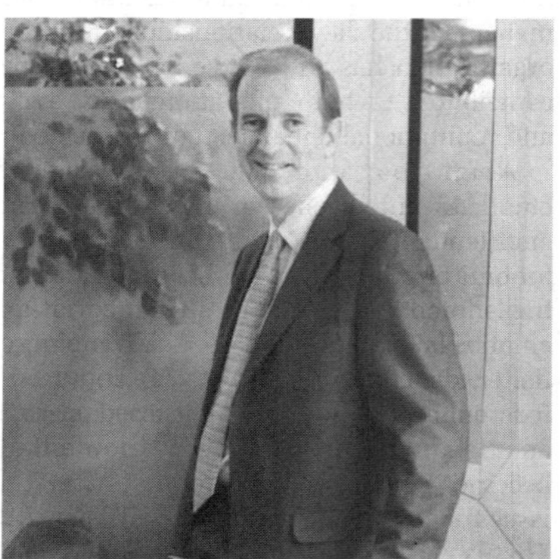

INTRODUCTION

Thibault de Tersant has been executive vice president and CFO of Dassault Systèmes since joining the company in 1988 and was appointed senior executive vice-president in 2006. He is responsible for finance, investor relations, legal affairs, sales business administration, information technology, and internal controls for the company. He was elected to the board of the company in 1993 and currently holds directorships of various subsidiaries. He is also responsible for mergers and acquisitions and has conducted more than 20 successful acquisitions totaling around $2 billion over the last ten years. He oversaw Dassault Systèmes' successful initial public offering on the Paris and Nasdaq stock exchanges in 1996, as well as a secondary offering in 1997. Prior to joining the company, he served as a finance executive in export financing at Dassault Aviation from 1983 until 1988. The recipient of France's prestigious Chief Financial Officer of the Year award in 2002, de Tersant is a graduate of the ESSEC Business School and of the Institut d'Etudes Politiques de Paris.

How has the role of the CFO changed over the last decade?

There is no doubt that it has changed a great deal. In part this is because topics that were not particularly to the fore a decade ago, such as compliance, have now come more and more within the scope of the CFO's responsibilities. This is part of the general change that has seen the CFO becoming responsible for far more than the accuracy of the numbers. It is about implementing an industrial, robust process for financial information for the company, together with a high level of risk assessment. It is the CFO's role, working with the board, to see that risk mitigation is carried through diligently. Circumstances have forced CFOs to develop the skills required to meet these new challenges, which is why I say that the CFO of today is very different from the CFO of 20 years ago. He or she is required to have a much more sophisticated understanding of many areas of the business and its operations. A deep understanding of the business and its strategy is vital for them to perform their role.

It is important too, to realize that the necessity for risk mitigation, combined with the increasing sophistication of accounting rules, has had a profound influence on how companies organize themselves and conduct their business.

CFOs are a lot more involved these days in investor relations. Is this a good use of their time?

Investors are looking for CFOs who not only understand the strategy of the company, but who can also demonstrate to them how, in pragmatic terms, that strategy is likely to impact on future revenue streams. This is why CFOs find themselves more and more responsible for investor intelligence relationships, which means keeping investors informed about matters that could impact the company's present and future plans and performance, as well as keeping them abreast of those plans, as appropriate. It is also why the CFO has had to develop the requisite skills to be able to represent the company message. He or she has to be articulate. At the same time, many CFOs undoubtedly find it a struggle to make time for all the investor roadshows and conferences plus face to face exchanges with financial analysts, as well as keeping abreast of their other mainstream corporate responsibilities. Today the investor relations department more often than not reports to the CFO rather than to the CEO.

Where does information technology sit these days? Should it report to the finance director?

Information technology is now such an integral part of business that the budget associated with IT tends to be one of the larger budgets. For this reason IT will often report to the CFO. Another reason is that IT is increasingly seen as a strategic asset. It is not just about buying an agreed number of boxes. For this reason, where IT sits and who it reports to will often depend on the ability of the CFO to grasp new technology and to understand how advances in technology play to the strategic goals of the company. In a software company such as ours, where IT is fundamental to what we do, it is not surprising for IT to report to the finance department.

In virtually all industry sectors business is becoming increasingly more complex. How is a CFO to stay on top of a growing number of specialist areas?

The solution to budgeting for complex areas and complex activities is the tried and trusted one of breaking the business down into lines of business and business units. No one can be master of all things at the global level. Instead of trying to control every single action and put a figure on it, the CFO has to work off business models. To do this, he or she has to allow the people in charge of each line of business to shape their operations, but they need a clear sense of the corporate goals they have to achieve. They need to understand the internal pricing rules very well so that they know what they have to reach in terms of cash flow and margins.

What this means is that the CFO role is now much more about setting the benchmarks and running iterations on the business models, so that the overall targets the board has set for the company can be achieved.

To accomplish this you have to have business models that accurately render the real processes of the company and you have to have a model for the life cycle management of projects. At the beginning of any project it is not for the CFO to decide if that particular project has a chance of succeeding. The CFO's role is to determine, once the project is in train, whether it is actually succeeding in reality or not.

Has the relationship between the CFO and the CEO changed over the last decade?

The CFO provides an essential service to the CEO. The relationship between the two has to be one where there is real mutual confidence and trust. The CFO introduces a frame, an environment inside which the company can operate. To do this you need deep intelligence of the business strategy, and discussions between the CFO and the CEO allow the CFO to assess whether the

"They have not any difficulties on the way up because they fly, but they have many when they reach the summit." Niccolò Machiavelli

company strategy can indeed be fulfilled. It is the CFO's role to forecast evolving company activities in an accurate way so that the organization is not surprised by anything that happens. Once projects are launched it is usually very costly if they fail, so the implications need to be thought through. At the same time, the CFO has to be able to trust the CEO to take the corporate mission—i.e. the formulation and execution of the company's strategy—forward, while the CEO has to back the CFO completely on compliance issues.

This can be seen particularly clearly in the case of acquisitions. There is a tremendous amount of work for the finance function in any acquisition. The company is generally committed to achieving synergies across a range of heads, from margin targets to market activities. Once you have announced your aims and objectives in making the acquisition, you have to achieve these aims or the market will punish the company through the share price. What is also clear on acquisitions is that the CFO has to be able to tolerate a reasonable level of risk. If you are too conservative as a CFO, you will end up killing a number of transactions that might well be very good for the organization. This can really stifle the development of a company. It follows from this that risk management has become a highly critical area for a CFO, and risk management skills are now absolutely essential if the CFO is to be a major contributor to the company's prosperity.

At the same time, risk management is still a developing area and it is still more of an art than a science. You need deep skills and a very thorough understanding of your market as well as a very clear sense of the strong points of your organization. You also need to be able to form a clear view of what is missing from the mix and how gaps can be filled. You have to be very closely associated with the development of the business.

What do you regard as the critical areas to be watched in the ongoing running of the business?

For me as the CFO of a software products company, one of the key areas is pricing and discounts. You need to develop a clear sense of the value that your product provides to the customer, and you need to be able to put a price on that value which corresponds to something that the customer feels is right. This forces you to understand not only your company's product offerings, but also how the customer is going to be using a product in their business to add value, and what exactly is the nature of that value that they are generating. For example, is it saving them production time by comparison with alternative approaches? Does it enable them to get their product to market more rapidly—and if so, what does that mean in terms of increased returns for them? When you understand this, you then need to look at the channels and means available to you to deliver that product to the customer. Is it to be through outright purchase? Through renewable licenses? Through the traditional software approach of a license purchase followed by annual maintenance fees? Through a rental "software as a service" model?

Revenue recognition has become very sophisticated, and it is up to the CFO to ensure that the transactions done by the company are in fact transactions that you will be able to recognize in revenue within an acceptable time frame. It is all too easy for companies to get involved in transactions where revenue recognition will be delayed by a number of years. Therefore the way transactions are structured has become a key part of delivering results for a company and enabling it to meet its goals.

One of the major advantages of the rental model, for example, is that it "locks in" a specific, predictable revenue stream for the organization and gives the company a good measure of predictability on future revenues.

As a CFO you also have to understand the nature of the life cycle of the products in your organization's portfolio. In our case, a product will generate revenues for approximately a decade, which means we aim to make a very substantial improvement to the product at least every seven years.

One of the things the CFO has to be able to provide for an organization is accurate forecasting of revenues and costs. Strong revenue recognition really is part of the CFO's mission. This is not about the arithmetical addition of figures coming back from field operations. This is where the CFO's deep understanding of the business really comes into play. You have to understand what the deeper significance is of the numbers on the screen or the printed page, what the trends are that lie behind the numbers. In a multinational operation this requires an even greater level of skill.

How much can the CFO do to mitigate price volatility, whether in currency movements or the price of inputs?

Currency risks have become one of the headaches of the CFO as globalization has increased. Today you have to understand hedging, and you have to understand too that the best hedges are natural ones. If, for example, you move your cost base to where you make your revenues, you remove what would otherwise be an exposure. In our case, opening up offices in the United States and making acquisitions where we have a number of key clients was absolutely critical in mitigating dollar/euro swings. The treasury function in any large company is now a much more important function. Today, credit risk management has become a very deep skill, and there is a real art to it. As a CFO, though, you need to have a clear sense of what risks you should *not* be allowing your organization to take. For example, we had any number of salesmen trying to sell us derivatives products, but we took an extremely conservative line. We did not look to turn our treasury function into a profit center by taking on risk that was not central to our business. As a CFO you have to be prudent, with an eye to the longer game. It is not just this year's results that matter, but where the organization will be in three to five years time. In today's markets, if you are not looking at least three years ahead, you are really flying blind.

MORE INFO

See Also:

★ Advantages of Finance Best Practice Networks (pp. 8–10)
★ Managing Activist Investors and Fund Managers (pp. 525–526)
★ Managing 21st Century Finances (pp. 66–67)
★ To Hedge or Not to Hedge (pp. 104–106)
★ Viewpoint: The CFO and the Sustainable Corporation (pp. 719–720)
★ Viewpoint: The Evolving Role of the CFO (pp. 854–855)

The Cost of Reputation: The Impact of Events on a Company's Financial Performance by Daniel Diermeier

EXECUTIVE SUMMARY

- Reputational crises have a significant impact on a company's valuation.
- They can be triggered by any business activity and do not necessarily reflect lapses in a company's ethics or integrity.
- Both the frequency and the magnitude of such events is increasing.
- The underlying factors that drive these developments are likely to increase in importance.
- Since reputational risk cannot be hedged or "outsourced," companies need to develop effective reputation management capabilities.
- Such capabilities consist of an integrated reputation management system and its core components: (1) mindset, (2) processes, and (3) values and culture.
- A reputation management process consists of a decision-making system and an intelligence system.

INTRODUCTION

CEOs and board members routinely list reputation as one the company's most valuable assets. Yet every month a new reputational disaster makes the headlines, destroying shareholder value and trust with customers and other stakeholders. During the last year, leading companies such as Toyota, Goldman Sachs, BP, Johnson & Johnson, and HP battled severe reputational crises. In all cases, financial markets punished the companies, leading to a severe and sustained erosion of their market values. In many cases, reputational damage is followed by lawsuits, public hearings, investigations, and regulatory actions.

In contrast to the scandals related to Enron, WorldCom, and Arthur Andersen a decade earlier, these crises are not limited to a specific domain (accounting practices and standards, especially with "new economy" firms) or caused by a dramatic increase in blatantly unethical or illegal activities. Rather, the involved companies were all category leaders, some with iconic status in their respective industries, and the issues involved ranged from quality and safety to disclosure and (alleged) executive misconduct.

The increase in the frequency and impact of reputational issues suggests that more fundamental shifts are occurring in the business environment and that companies are unprepared for dealing with them. What companies lack is an effective reputation management capability in the presence of increasing reputational risk. Too often, reputation management is considered a (sub)function of corporate communication and isolated from business decisions. Rather, companies need to adopt a strategic approach that treats reputational challenges as understandable and even predictable. As a result, companies should manage their reputation like any other major business challenge: based on principled leadership and supported by sophisticated processes and capabilities that are integrated with the company's business strategy and culture.

THE COST OF REPUTATIONAL CRISES

Severe erosion of shareholder value is common during reputational crises. During its recent crisis triggered by the sudden acceleration issue, Toyota's stock price dropped by as much as 24%, wiping out about US$33 billion in shareholder value, close to the total market value of Time Warner. In its battle with the US government in the aftermath of the 2008–09 financial crisis, Goldman Sachs lost US$24 billion of its market capitalization, a 26% drop in share price that exceeded the entire value of American Express. During the BP oil spill disaster in the Gulf of Mexico, BP's stock was almost cut in half, the equivalent of about US$90 billion in shareholder value, more than the market value of Procter & Gamble.

In some cases the drop in stock value is temporary, in other cases permanent. Much depends on how the companies handle the aftermath of crisis and commit to fixing the underlying business issue rather than engaging in shallow PR exercises. Toyota, for example, commenced a global quality improvement initiative that involved cultural and process changes at every level of the company.

THE PROBLEM OF MEASUREMENT

In general, the impact of reputational events is difficult to quantify. Many existing studies point to a correlation between superior corporate reputations and financial performance. In most studies, corporate reputation is measured using lists from Fortune's Most Admired Companies[1]. There are various problems with this approach.

First, there is little change in the list membership. This may constitute evidence that reputation is persistent, but may also point to a metric that is too coarse to detect changes in a company's reputation on a smaller timescale, by region or product. Second, both inclusion in the list of most-admired companies and superior financial performance may be consequences of an underlying third characteristic that drives them both, such as "good management.

Studies that show the positive impact of reputation at the more general, macro-level are of limited use to managers as they typically fail to identify underlying factors driving a company's reputation. Given the difficulty with such macro-level studies, a better understanding of the processes that shape perceptions at the micro-level is desirable.

REPUTATION AS A BANK ACCOUNT

One common view of reputation is that it serves as a "trust bank account" or "buffer." The idea is that, through their actions, companies make "deposits" into a "trust account" that generates goodwill with their various stakeholders and constituencies. In case of a crisis, companies then are able to make a "withdrawal" from this bank account that helps to at least partially isolate them from the impact.

There is some evidence for this claim in the context of corporate social responsibility (CSR). Recent research suggests that in the case of a product recalls, for example, companies with high CSR ratings lose on average US$600 million less in firm market value than companies with low ratings. However, other evidence suggests that, in a crisis context, previous "good deeds" are swamped by current actions (good or bad). Trust, it seems, can't easily be deposited; it must be earned.

PERCEPTION DRIVERS

To understand these processes in more detail, a rigorous approach using controlled experiments is helpful. The approach is similar to the market research studies that are conducted when companies design or evaluate brands. In such studies, subjects read vignettes of fictitious newspaper articles that describe a crisis. For example, a food manufacturer may be accused of using a potentially harmful food additive in order to increase the shelf life of its

"Organizational values always derive from individual values—especially those of the founding fathers and of the very top executives." S. K. Chakraborty

products, or the company may be involved in a nasty sexual harassment lawsuit. In addition to this background information, subjects are also provided with the fictitious company's responses, which range from engaged and caring to dismissive.

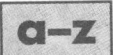

While a "trust bank account" (here measured by past good deeds) does have some effect, companies' current actions have a greater effect on shaping attitudes toward the company in question, as well as apparently unrelated issues such as the aesthetic evaluation of logos or product design.

Even more strikingly, when subjects were asked to evaluate the taste of a product (e.g. bottled water) from a company with a low "trust bank account," they rated the taste lower and drank less water. Corporate executives are only partially aware of these effects. When asked to predict how public attitudes would be affected by these same scenarios, corporate executives correctly predicted that an engaged response would be viewed more favorably than a defensive response, but they were overly optimistic about the public's ability to refrain from forming opinions when the company offered "no comment."

In sum, corporate reputation strategies have direct and measurable effects on the evaluation of core brand attributes. They can affect overall customer perceptions, evaluation of corporate logos, and even opinions of product taste and levels of consumption. Corporate executives are largely unaware of such effects.

REPUTATION AS A CURRENCY

These findings can be reconciled if we think of reputation less as a bank account and more as a currency. Currencies act as multiplies (not "linearly" as the bank account suggests). That is, if a currency is strong, purchasing power increases for all sorts of goods.

So, what does this mean in the context of reputation? The idea is that the same statement carries more weight and has more impact if it comes from a company with a good reputation. Or alternatively, a company with a strong reputation will need to do less than a company with a weak reputation to achieve the same effect.

Some evidence from the 2011 Edelman Trust Barometer[2]supports this intuition (Table 1).

In case of "low trust" we find the well-known negativity bias. A negative message has roughly four times as much impact as a positive message. But, strikingly, the situation is reversed in the "high trust" case, where a negative message has only half as much impact as a positive one. So, by

Table 1. Effect of company trust. (*Source*: 2011 Edelman Trust Barometer)

Company trust	Will believe negative information if hearing it 1–2 times	Will believe positive information if hearing it 1–2 times
High	25%	51%
Low	57%	15%

moving from a high to a low trust "currency" a company gets an eight-fold increase of positive information impact—not bad.

Still, these results are to be treated with some caution. Ideally, one would want to replicate this behavior in a controlled laboratory setting. Yet this phenomenon would explain the "Teflon" characteristic of some companies, such as Apple, as witnessed in the limited impact of recent issues such as the dropped calls/antenna problem in the iPhone 4 on Apple's reputation. Surveys consistently put the high-tech industry at the top of the list of most-trusted industries.

REPUTATION MANAGEMENT CAPABILITIES

The difficulty in exactly quantifying the impact of reputational events implies that reputational risk cannot easily be hedged or insured against. It therefore must be managed. This means that companies need to build reputation management capabilities appropriate to their level of risk.

A company's reputation needs to be managed *actively*. Good business practices and ethical conduct are necessary, but they alone are not sufficient for successful reputation management. That responsibility should lie with business leaders. It should not be delegated to specialists such as lawyers or public relations experts, even though such experts play a valuable role in the reputation management process. Integration with business practices is necessary as reputational challenges arise out of a specific business context. In many cases, the most effective way to manage reputational risk is to improve the capabilities of business leaders (supported by well-designed processes) rather than adding another corporate layer.

Reputational challenges can arise from any area of day-to-day decision making, but executives tend to make decisions without consideration for the reputational impact. The key skill for business leaders is the ability to maintain an external perspective throughout decision-making processes and incorporate this perspective into the design of business decisions, e.g. the launch of a new product and its market-entry strategy. Companies need to understand that their decisions are creating a record today that will serve as the basis for their story tomorrow. Assessing reputational risk requires anticipating what a reputational crisis would look like and then taking proactive steps to prevent and prepare.

During a reputational crisis, the spotlight will not only be on the company's *current*actions, such as how the CEO answers questions and what the company will do to fix the problem, but also on its *past*actions. Reporters will ask when the company first knew about the problem, or why management didn't do more to fix it. The thought process behind each past decision can be brought out into the public arena and questioned. These past actions and decisions are now part of the record and cannot be changed. Even actions that looked reasonable at the time may wither under scrutiny from a hostile audience in a crisis context after any negative consequences come to light.

After the Gulf of Mexico oil spill, every minute decision that BP made concerning its safety processes took on disproportionate significance, leading to severe criticism of the company. And when Toyota had to recall its cars, commentators quickly alleged that its aggressive growth strategy had sacrificed quality and safety.

An easy way to improve decision making is the *Wall Street Journal*test, which suggests that decision makers should ask themselves whether they would be proud if a decision were *accurately* reported on the front page of the *Wall Street Journal*. This test evocatively captures the idea that a decision may look different once it comes under public scrutiny.

Such approaches help to transition from a crisis management mindset to a risk management one. Taking reputational risk seriously does not necessarily mean refraining from giving the green light to decisions that carry some reputational risk. Rather, the goal of proactive reputation management is to identify possible risks and mitigate them through *current*actions to reach an acceptable balance level of risk and control.

REPUTATION MANAGEMENT PROCESSES

Who should own reputation management? Many executives answer: everyone. That sounds reasonable enough, but it is easy for things that are owned by everybody to actually be owned by nobody. Questions about decision rights, reporting, and accountability still need to be answered.

Many board members agree that the ultimate accountability for reputation man-

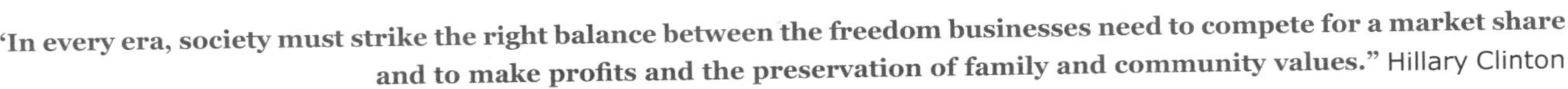

agement processes needs to be located at a level of the organization whose job description is the long-term viability of the company: the board. One reason why the board is a good choice is that it can keep management's incentives for short-term solutions in check. By setting clear guidelines and emphasizing the need to safeguard reputational equity, the board can help management avoid short-sighted cost-cutting mistakes.

But the board's role is to oversee and supervise; it is not to manage the company. So, where should reputation management reside within a company's decision-making structure? A common response is that it belongs on the agenda of senior management, including the CEO. The reason that reputation management belongs on the CEO's agenda is not only that reputational risk is one of the main risks facing the company, but also that the company's reputation is one of the few sources of sustained competitive advantage. Companies with stellar reputations can charge premiums and are difficult to imitate.

One of the CEO's main tasks is to integrate reputation management into the operational processes of the business. One approach to accomplishing this task has been to create a separate corporate function: a chief reputation officer (CRO) or chief reputational risk officer (CRRO). This approach works only if the position carries weight and if the company can avoid creating yet another corporate officer with little budget and less influence. The danger in this approach is that it could create additional barriers to the integration of reputation management and business strategy, and actually hurt the process rather than help it.

An alternative is the creation of a corporate reputation council (CRC). This is a cross-functional unit composed of senior executives with actual decision-making authority. The actual composition of the council needs to mirror the organizational structure of the company. For example, a matrix organization based on global territory and product lines would have representatives from both the major territories and the business lines. In addition, the main corporate functions (marketing, finance, supply chain, HR, communication, legal, government relations, and so on) need to be represented, as reputational problems are almost always multidimensional. The decision structure must be designed to handle the complexity of such issues.

It is critical that the CRC mirrors the actual operating structure of the business. One of the reasons that Toyota was slow in responding to the 2010 sudden acceleration crisis was the lack of a truly global decision-making structure. While Toyota's economic fortunes were heavily dependent on robust US sales, decision making was largely centered in Japan, with little input from the United States. Similarly, BP lacked a strong presence in the US regulatory and political environment, despite the fact that BP's US oil and gas assets represented more than one-quarter of the group's total annual production.

Good governance and decision-making structures are necessary for effective reputation management, but these alone are not sufficient. Here is why:

- Reputation consists of the perceptions of customers and other constituencies.
- In many cases, these perceptions are derived not from actual experience with the company or a deep knowledge of any given issue, but from an ever-changing mixture of opinion and information driven by the media, peer-to-peer websites, and various influencers ranging from experts to advocacy groups.
- Proactive reputation management requires companies to identify issues early, connect them with business strategy, develop prevention and preparation strategies, and implement possible changes in business practices in advance of an issue's gaining momentum.

This sequence can break down at various points. Executives may not realize the importance of reputation management for business success, governance structures may be lacking, or incentive structures may reward short-term vision. But companies may also fail to adopt effective strategies simply because they are unaware of the imminent danger. In other words, even perfectly designed governance and decision-making structures will be ineffective if they lack critical intelligence: decisions are then made in the dark.

This is the business case for investing in intelligence capabilities. Because reputation is driven by many ever-changing actors, the strategic landscape is frequently diffuse and unclear. Because successful reputational strategies need to be designed before a crisis occurs, simply surveying customers, investors, or other business partners will not do. Once customers or investors start to worry, it is too late—the deck is already stacked against the company. Therefore, in many cases, traditional business research tools such as surveys and focus groups can only measure the damage rather than prevent it in the first place. Proactive reputation management is impossible without good intelligence.

The governance structure needs to be closely connected with the intelligence function. This means that the CRC should provide strategic direction to the intelligence function and receive actionable intelligence that is directly connected to the corporate strategy. The intelligence function provides the core capabilities of issue identification, evaluation, and monitoring. The goal is both to function as an early warning system and to be able to assess the impact of corporate actions through a feedback mechanism. Without an intelligence function, the CRC will be operating in the dark and making decisions based on intuition rather than data. A company's intelligence function may range from informal monitoring of various media sources and proactive stakeholder outreach to the creation of a fully developed internal intelligence capability with its own staff and budget.

Intelligence functions are not only important for management. Given the critical role of the board as guardian of a

CASE STUDY

Bausch & Lomb

Markets do not always properly adjust to reputational risk. One such example is Bausch & Lomb, a producer of soft contact lenses and lens care products. On April 10, 2006, the US Centers for Disease Control and Prevention linked a surge in potentially blinding fungal infections with Bausch & Lomb's new ReNu contact lens solution. As a result, Bausch & Lomb's stock price dropped from a closing price of US$57.67 on Friday, April 7, to US$45.61 on Wednesday, April 12. The company was heavily criticized for its handling of the crisis and the depressed stock price persisted. Bausch & Lomb subsequently experienced accounting restatements and was acquired by the private equity firm Warburg Pincus.

Remarkably, the link between the infections and ReNu, however, had been uncovered almost two months earlier, on February 22, in a public announcement by Singapore's Ministry of Health. (Bausch & Lomb subsequently withdrew the ReNu solution from its markets in Singapore and Hong Kong). The government announcement had been reported in the region's major newspapers, but had not been covered in the United States. Bausch & Lomb's stock lost a mere 3% from a closing price of US$71.51 on February 21 to US$69.40 on February 23, and quickly recovered. In other words, financial markets ignored the early warning signs.

company's reputation, it is surprising and worrisome that most corporate boards are not supported by a separate intelligence function. Such a function is ideally provided by a third party, not by company staff. Much of the critical reputational intelligence is external to the company, and it may lead board members to ask more probing questions of management.

In summary, a strategic mindset needs to be supported by effective processes. First, companies must develop a proper governance structure that should mirror the company's organizational structure. A cross-functional council is preferable to a separate corporate function unless that function is endowed with sufficient influence and resources. Second, companies need an intelligence capability. In contrast to other corporate capabilities, an intelligence system is not optional; it is essential. Reputational challenges can emerge from anywhere in the company's operations or external business environment. The lack of intelligence capabilities means that the company acts in the dark and loses its ability to manage emerging issues proactively.

THE ROLE OF PEOPLE

Business leaders also need to understand that even the most advanced reputation management system is implemented by people. They need to assess the situation, evaluate risks, and then make appropriate decisions. Getting this right requires not only a strategic mindset but also values and culture in order to provide guidance to individuals. We cannot expect each employee of a company to correctly assess the reputational risk of an issue, but we can expect him or her to raise a red flag when something does not "look right."

Acting as corporate steward does not only mean doing right by customers, employees, and suppliers. It requires the ability to *think strategically*. This implies, on the one hand, viewing reputational decisions not solely as PR issues, but as decisions that are tightly connected to the company's strategy, its core competencies and values, and its distinctive position in the marketplace. On the other hand, it requires the ability to view even a familiar business decision from the point of view of people who are not specialists, but still may have strong opinions on an issue. More often than not, these opinions are not just driven by cool reason, but involve powerful emotions and passionate views of what is right or wrong behavior.

A strategic mindset also requires *situational awareness*. Reputation is essentially public. It is driven by third parties who have their own agenda. Understanding and anticipating the motivations and capabilities of these actors is essential for situational awareness. But reputational challenges are not simply the consequence of wrong decisions, accidents, or bad luck; they are frequently created by activists, interest groups, and public actors, with the goal of forcing changes in business practices through "private politics." Activists are competitors for the company's reputation. They need to be treated as seriously as competitors in the marketplace.

The last component of a strategic mindset is to avoid the *expert trap*. Becoming an expert means learning to see the world in a particular way. A doctor learns to identify symptoms and decide on a diagnosis, a poker player learns to identify "tells" of opponents that provide critical information on the strength of their hand, and a music enthusiast can pick a favorite pianist from dozens of recordings of the same piece. Acquiring and using expertise in a coordinated fashion is, of course, tremendously valuable and is at the root of the efficient organization of business processes. But, in the context of reputational challenges, it can lead us astray.

When a company collapses as a result of an earnings restatement, a trained accountant may focus on the fact that no accounting rules were violated, while everybody else will be affected by images of crying employees leaving their office for the last time. A safety engineer will point to his company's industry-leading safety standards and may be bewildered when the media focuses on one specific victim. A loan officer may view missed mortgage payments as lost revenue, while the borrower may experience them as the fear of losing the family home. The difficulty lies in the public nature of reputational challenges where company actions are evaluated by non-experts through the filter of the media. This requires decision makers to set aside their expertise and see the situation from the point of view of laypeople in a heightened emotional state.

In summary, reputation management is not a corporate function, but a capability. It requires the right mindset integrated with the company's strategy, guided by its culture and values, and supported by carefully designed governance and intelligence processes. Developing this capability is as demanding and as challenging as developing customer focus or the ability to execute. Today's companies need to embrace this challenge.

MORE INFO

Book:

Diermeier, Daniel. *Reputation Rules: Strategies for Building Your Company's Most Valuable Asset*. New York: McGraw-Hill, 2011.

Articles:

Minor, Dylan. "CSR as reputation insurance: Theory and evidence." Working paper. Kellogg School of Management, 2010.

Roberts, Peter W., and Grahame R. Dowling. "Corporate reputation and sustained superior financial performance." *Strategic Management Journal* 23:12 (December 2002): 1077-1093. Online at: dx.doi.org/10.1002/smj.274

Uhlmann, Eric Luis, George E. Newman, Victoria Medvec, Adam Galinsky, and Daniel Diermeier. "The sound of silence: Corporate crisis communication and its effects on consumer attitudes and behavior." Working paper. Kellogg School of Management, 2010. Online at: tinyurl.com/3n89y65 [PDF].

See Also:

★ An Approach to Understanding Reputation Risk in Financial Services (pp. 777–781)
★ The CEO's Role in Reputation Management (pp. 797–800)
★ Engaging Your Stakeholders: How To Make Allies of Investors and Activists (pp. 837–840)
★ Managing Reputational Risk: Business Journalism (pp. 893–896)
★ Viewpoint: The Importance of Trust—In Everything (pp. 878–880)

NOTES

1 Fortune's Most Admired Companies: money.cnn.com/magazines/fortune/mostadmired

2 2011 Edelman Trust Barometer: www.edelman.com/trust/2011/

"There's no such thing as information overload—only filter failure." Clay Shirky

  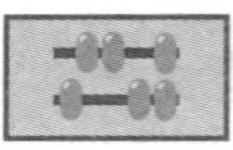      

Countering Supply Chain Risk by Vinod Lall

EXECUTIVE SUMMARY

- Business strategies such as outsourcing, lean manufacturing , and just-in-time lead to efficiency gains but at the same time expose the supply chain to higher risks.
- There are different sources of risk in a modern supply chain. Recognizing and appropriately managing these risks is necessary for a glitch-free functioning of the supply chain.
- Supply chain risk management strategies must be holistic and integrated with the whole supply chain environment.
- Firms must have dedicated budget line items for supply chain risk management activities.
- Failure mode effects analysis (FMEA) can be used to assess supply chain risks.

INTRODUCTION

In March 2000, a fire at a Philips semiconductor factory damaged some components used to make chips for mobile phones. Ericsson and Nokia—two of Philips' major customers—responded to the event in very different ways. Ericsson decided to let the delay take its own course, while supply chain managers at Nokia monitored the situation closely and developed contingency plans. By the time Philips discovered that the fire had contaminated a large area that would disrupt production for months, Nokia had already lined up alternative suppliers for the chips. Ericsson used Philips as a sole supplier and faced a severe shortage of chips, leading to delay in product launch and huge losses to its mobile phone division.

Today's global supply chains are complex and lean while efficiently delivering products and services to the marketplace. These supply chains involve a rigid set of transactions and decisions that span over longer distances and more time zones with very little slack built into them. As a result they are susceptible to several types of risk. These risks include operational risk due to demand variability, supply fluctuations and disruption risk due to natural disasters, terrorist attacks, pandemics, and breaches in data security. Such risks disrupt or slow the flow of material, information, and cash, and put billions of dollars at stake due to stock market capitalization, failed product launches, and the possibility of bankruptcies. In the above example, Ericsson lost 400 million euros after the Philips semiconductor plant caught fire; another example occurred when Apple lost many customer orders during a supply shortage of memory chips after an earthquake in Taiwan in 1999. Supply chain executives and managers must visualize and have a clear understanding of these risks along the entire supply chain, starting from the sourcing of raw materials to the delivery of the final product or service to the consumer. Once these risks are identified, they need to be scored on the likelihood of occurrence, and their impact must be quantified. Resources must then be used to mitigate or eliminate elements of high risk.

TYPES OF SUPPLY CHAIN RISK

Supply chain risks can be classified into different types depending on their origin. These include supply risk, demand risk, internal risk, and external environment risk.

Supply risk: These are the risks on the supply/inbound side of the supply chain. Supply risk may be defined as the possibility of disruptions of product availability from the supplier or disruptions in the process of transportation from the supplier, to the customer. A supplier may be unavailable to complete an order for a number of reasons, including problems sourcing necessary raw materials, low process yield due to increased scrap, equipment failure, damaged facilities, or the need to ration its limited product among several customers. Transportation disruptions occur while products are in transit and add to the delivery lead time. They may be caused by delays in customs clearance at borders, or problems with the mode of transportation, such as the grounding of air traffic.

Demand risk : Demand risk is the downstream equivalent of supply risk and is present on the demand/outbound side of the supply chain. It may be due to an unexpected increase or decrease in customer demand that leads to a mismatch between the firm's forecast and actual demand. Increase in customer demand leads to depletion of safety stocks, resulting in stock-outs, back orders, and the need to expedite. A fall in customer demand leads to increased costs of holding inventory and, inevitably, price reductions. Other sources of demand risk are dependence on a single customer, customer solvency, and failure of the distribution logistics service provider.

Internal risk: This is the risk associated with events that are related to internal operations of the firm. Examples include fire or chemical spillage leading to plant closure, labor strikes, quality problems, and shortage of employees.

External environment risk: These risk elements are external to and uncontrollable from the firm's perspective. Examples include blockades of ports or depots, natural disasters such as earthquakes, hurricanes or cyclones, war, terrorist activity, and financial factors such as exchange rates and market pressures. These events disrupt the flow of material and may lead to plant shutdown, shortage of high-demand items, and price increases.

STRATEGIES FOR SUPPLY CHAIN RISK MANAGEMENT

Strategies for managing risk must be a part of supply chain management and must include processes to reduce supply chain risks that at the same time increase resilience and efficiency. Firms typically use basic strategies of risk-bearing, risk avoidance or risk mitigation, and risk transference to another party. The goal of risk-bearing is to reduce the potential damage caused by the materialization of a risk, and to be successful requires that early warning systems be installed along the supply chain. The main goal of risk avoidance is to reduce the probability of occurrence of a risk by being proactive, while under risk transfer the potential impact of risk is transferred to another organization such as an insurance company.

MITIGATING SUPPLY CHAIN RISKS

A firm could use strategic and tactical plans under four basic approaches to mitigate the impact of supply chain risks. These approaches include supply management, demand management, product management, and information management. The task of managing supply chain risk is difficult as approaches that mitigate one risk element can end up exacerbating another. Also, actions taken by one partner in the supply chain can increase the risk for another partner.

Supply Management

Supply risks can be reduced by building a web of internal and external sources. Strategically, firms should focus their core competencies on new products and ideas and the engineering necessary to reduce time-to-market. They should continue to manufacture strategic, high-value, long-life products that have relatively low demand volatility while outsourcing non-strategic,

"Educated risks are the key to success." William Olsten

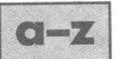

low-value manufacturing and logistics services. It is important to be very selective in building a strong web of vendors and closely managing the vendor network. For each new product, the firm must capitalize on the varying expertise of its vendor network and use expected time-to-market, quality level and price to select a vendor from the network.

Tactical plans under supply management focus mostly on supplier selection and supplier order allocation. For this, firms should develop a profile of their supply bases to get a more complete picture of the supply side of the chain. This profile should include a wide range of supplier information including the total number of suppliers, the location and diversity of suppliers, and flexibility in the volume and variety of supplier capacities. Analysis of these data will help firms identify vulnerabilities in their supply chains so they can strategize, create contingency plans, conduct trade-off analysis of issues such as single sourcing, and, if needed, identify and line up backup sources.

Demand Management

Strategic plans under demand management focus on product pricing, while tactical plans are used to shift demand across time, across markets, and across products. One product pricing strategy is called the "price-postponement strategy," whereby the firm decides on the quantity of the order in the first period and then determines the price in the second period after observing updated information about demand. Shifting demand across time is known as "revenue management" or "yield management," whereby firms usually set higher prices during peak seasons to shift demand to off-peak seasons. One technique for shifting demand across markets is called "solo-rollover by market;" this involves selling new products in different markets with time delays, leading to non-overlapping selling seasons. To shift demand across products, firms use pricing and promotion techniques to entice customers to switch products or brands.

As with the supply side, firms must also develop a profile of the demand side to analyze the outbound side of the supply chain. Analysis of the demand side will identify dangers such as those associated with overreliance on a single distribution center to serve a large market, or the risks of having a highly concentrated customer base.

Supply Chain Reserves Management

Firms can deal with supply chain risks by holding reserves of inventory and capacity in the supply chain. Managers must decide carefully on the optimal location and size of these reserves as an undisciplined approach may lead to increased costs and hurt the bottom line.

Product Management

Firms can look at their internal networks and develop a profile of their products, processes, and services. Analysis of data in this profile can help to determine if there is a good mix of products and services and if there are risks in processes such as those used for fulfilling orders.

Information Management

Information technology tools can be used to understand and manage risk better by providing visibility into planned events and warnings for unplanned events in the entire supply chain. Firms must manufacture low-risk products first and use improved forecasts to produce the riskiest products very close to the selling season. This requires the use of reliable data and better forecasting methods. Key members in the supply chain must have easy and timely access to accurate information on such measures as inventory, demand, forecasts, production and shipment plans, work in process, process yields, capacities, backlogs, etc. This offers more opportunities to all parties to respond quickly to sudden changes in the supply chain and requires the implementation of information technology solutions that interface business data and processes end to end.

The collaborative planning, forecasting, and replenishment (CPFR) model is often used to induce collaboration and coordination through information sharing between supply chain partners such as retailers and manufacturers. Under CPFR, the manufacturer generates an initial demand forecast based on market intelligence on products, and the retailer creates its initial demand forecast based on customer response to pricing and promotion decisions. Both parties share their initial demand forecasts and reconcile the differences to obtain a common forecast. Once both parties agree on the common forecast, the manufacturer develops a production plan and the retailer develops a replenishment plan.

CONCLUSION

The pursuit of new markets for products and of new sources for components is making supply chains longer and more complex. With this expansion comes increased risk, which may result in disruptions to the supply chain. These disruptions may be unexpected and statistically rare, but they must be understood, identified, and managed.

MAKING IT HAPPEN

It is critical to have an easy-to-use tool to identify and manage supply chain risk. FMEA is a well-documented and proven risk management tool that is used to evaluate the risk of failures in product and process designs. It can be used to evaluate supply chain risk using the following process steps:

- **Step 1**. Identify the categories of supply chain risk.
- **Step 2**. Identify potential risks in each category.
- **Step 3**. Use a rating scale of 1–5 to rate the opportunity, probability, and severity for each risk. The opportunity score for a risk is the frequency with which it occurs. One-time risk events receive an opportunity score of 1, while commonly occurring risk events are assigned an opportunity score of 5. The probability score is the score for the expected likelihood that a risk event will actually happen, so high probability scores are used when the probability of a risk event occurring is large. The severity score indicates the level of impact if the risk materializes. Low-risk events cause a minimum impact on the supply chain and receive a low severity score. Risk events that have a significant impact on the supply chain in terms of cost, time, and quality are assigned a high severity score.
- **Step 4**. For each potential risk, calculate the risk priority number (RPN) as RPN = opportunity × probability × severity.
- **Step 5**. Use Pareto analysis to analyze risks by RPN. Pareto analysis is a formal technique used where many possible courses of action are competing for the attention of the problem-solver. The problem-solver estimates the benefit delivered by each action and then selects the most effective action.
- **Step 6**. Develop action plans to mitigate risks with high RPN.
- **Step 7**. Use another cycle of FMEA to reassess the risks.

"Great successes never come without risks." Flavius Josephus

  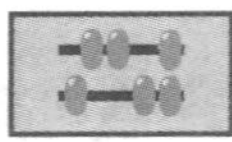      

Creating Value with EVA by S. David Young

EXECUTIVE SUMMARY

- Economic value added (EVA) can serve as the cornerstone of a value-based management system.[1]
- EVA is more than a performance metric. It also represents a mindset that focuses management attention on the value-creation imperative.
- EVA is profit as economists think about profit. It differs from the conventional accounting-based approach in that it imposes charges for the use of all capital, including equity.
- The value of the firm equals capital employed, plus the present value of future EVAs. By motivating managers to increase future EVA, companies can promote value-creating behavior.
- When managers are evaluated and paid on the basis of EVA, they have stronger incentives to improve operational and capital efficiency, dispose of unprofitable business, achieve more optimal capital structures, and invest in value-creating projects.

INTRODUCTION

The value-based management movement is based on two assumptions. The first is that the main aim of any business in a market economy is to maximize shareholder value. The second is that markets are too competitive for companies to create such value by accident. They must plan for it. And that means having the right culture, systems, and processes in place so managers make decisions in ways that deliver better returns to shareholders.

At the very least, corporate functions must be informed by value-based thinking—planning, capital allocation, operating budgets, performance measurement, incentive compensation, and corporate communication. EVA is a tool for achieving this. EVA is a measure of performance, but its uses extend further. When implemented properly, and especially if tied to management compensation, it is a powerful way to promote shareholder value.

EVA: A DEFINITION

EVA is a measure of profit. Not the accounting profit we are accustomed to seeing in a corporate income statement, but profit as economists define it. Both are measured net of operating expenses; they differ only in the treatment of capital costs. While income statements recognize only the interest paid to bankers and bondholders, EVA recognizes all capital costs, including the opportunity cost of shareholder funds.

The difference between accounting profit and economic profit can be seen in Figure 1. On the left side is profit as it appears on the typical income statement, where EBIT is earnings before interest and tax (a popular term for pre-tax operating income), I is interest expense, T is income taxes, and IC is invested capital. Net income is simply operating income, with interest and taxes removed. Note that the only capital cost included in the profit measure is interest expense (the amount of debt multiplied by the interest rate).

Figure 1. Accounting profit (EBIT) versus economic profit (EVA)

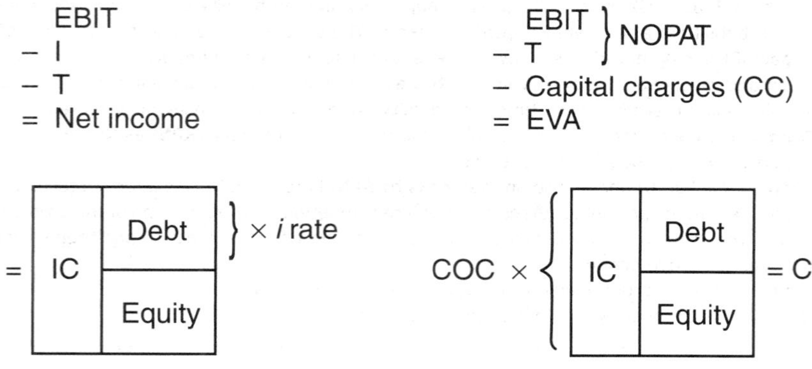

EVA, or economic profit, also starts with EBIT. Income taxes are subtracted to produce net operating profit after tax, or NOPAT. But instead of subtracting interest, EVA charges for the use of *all* capital, including equity finance. While accounting profit charges only for the cost of debt, capital charges for the calculation of EVA equal the product of invested capital and the cost of capital (COC). The cost of capital, popularly known as the weighted-average cost of capital (WACC), is a function of the cost of debt and equity weighted for their relative proportions in the company's capital structure.

Economic profit is based on an idea generated by the English economist Alfred Marshall in the late 19th century: for investors to earn true economic profits, sales must be sufficient to cover all costs, including operating expenses (such as labor and materials) and capital charges. Such economic profits are the basis of value creation. Indeed, as management guru Peter Drucker has written, "EVA is based on something we have known for a long time: what we generally call profits, the money left to service equity, is usually not profit at all. Until a business returns a profit that is greater than its cost of capital, it operates at a loss."[2]

It can be mathematically proven that the worth of a business must equal invested capital—the sum of fixed assets, cash, and working capital—plus the present (or discounted) value of future EVA. Value determined in this way is mathematically equivalent to the value estimates produced by discounted cash flow models. The upshot: as capital market expectations of corporate EVA increase, so do share prices. Companies can thus use EVA targets to motivate managers to deliver the financial results that capital markets want. This approach is especially useful for executives one or two levels below top management, managers who have little direct influence over share price and for whom stock options are less effective.

EVA-DRIVEN COMPANIES AND FINANCIAL PERFORMANCE

So, what exactly have EVA companies done to improve financial performance and deliver superior returns to shareholders? The clues can be seen in the definition of EVA. EVA equals after-tax operating profit minus capital costs, with capital costs equal to invested capital multiplied by the WACC.[3] However, EVA can be expressed in a different, yet equivalent, way.

"Annual income twenty pounds, annual expenditure nineteen nineteen six, result happiness. Annual income twenty pounds, annual expenditure twenty pounds ought and six, result misery." Charles Dickens

When operating profit is divided by invested capital, it yields a measure called return on invested capital (ROIC). The difference between ROIC and WACC, multiplied by capital employed, equals EVA:

EVA = (ROIC – WACC) x Capital employed

Holding other variables constant, EVA increases when ROIC increases; when WACC decreases; when capital employed increases (assuming profitable growth); or when capital employed decreases (in the case of money-losing assets). Evidence from EVA adopters shows several ways to achieve improvements:

- Increasing asset turnover. For example, EVA companies are more likely to drive reductions in inventory and speed up the collection of receivables.
- Repairing assets. Many companies discover that managers on EVA incentive plans are inclined to overhaul existing assets rather than request capital to buy new ones. Also, when additional capacity is required, managers are more likely to acquire used assets.
- Structuring deals that require less capital. For example, Armstrong, an American plastics and floor products company, had always insisted on a controlling stake in any acquisition. After adopting EVA, the company began to define the minimum amount of capital it could put into a deal and still get what it wanted.
- Disposing of unprofitable businesses. Well-managed companies have always done this, but EVA-driven bonus plans create a sense of urgency to use assets more efficiently by, for example, shedding chronic money-losing operations.
- Increasing debt financing. Senior managers tend to "underlever" their businesses, which means they rely too much on equity finance and not enough on debt. As a result, companies fail to take advantage of valuation tax shields that can increase after-tax cash flows to capital providers. EVA changes such behavior because, when managers are charged for capital, they have powerful incentives to design capital structures that minimize the cost of capital. For the underlevered company, this means taking on debt, which is precisely what many companies have done after adopting EVA.
- Investing in profitable growth. The net present value (NPV) of future cash flows for a proposed capital investment is mathematically equivalent to the present value of incremental EVAs. Therefore, future EVA will increase to the extent that investments are made in projects with positive NPV. However, because the short-term effect of investment may be to cause EVA to decline, companies must take special care to ensure that senior managers have long-term incentives to create value. This need explains, in part, why companies continue to rely on stock options. Equity participation, if structured properly, provides incentives for managers to seek out investments that will boost EVA in the future even if short-term results are compromised.

The first three of the above actions increase EVA through improvements in ROIC. Disposing of unprofitable businesses increases EVA, provided that improvements in the spread between ROIC and WACC more than compensate for the reduction in invested capital. Increasing financial leverage increases EVA by reducing the WACC, assuming that the company is underlevered when it begins taking on more debt. Investing is profitable, and increases EVA, as long as the ROIC for new investments exceeds the WACC.

EVA AND MANAGERIAL COMPENSATION

Although EVA is a potentially powerful tool for creating value-creating incentives, there are some limitations and drawbacks to its use. For example, capital charges might compel managers to forgo potentially value-creating projects out of fear that short-term EVA will suffer. Simply put, because EVA is a single-period measure of performance, managers with EVA-linked bonuses may willingly sacrifice long-term competitiveness in the interests of pursuing short-term

CASE STUDY

SPX—Corporate Transformation through EVA

SPX is a large US auto parts and industrial products company. It was a chronic underperformer in the early 1990s, with low profits and a languishing share price. After a change of CEO in 1995, the company adopted EVA as the centerpiece of its change program. By the end of the following year a dramatic improvement in performance was evident.

After adopting EVA, SPX engaged in a broad range of actions, all with one overriding purpose: the creation of shareholder value. For example:

- In the first year after adopting EVA, inventories were cut by 15%, despite higher sales.
- SPX's portfolio of businesses underwent important changes. Several business units were sold, not because they were unprofitable but because strategic reviews revealed that the businesses were worth more to other companies. Meanwhile, several key value-enhancing acquisitions were made.
- Divisions were consolidated for greater operating efficiency. Substantial cost savings were realized.
- Several finance-based initiatives were undertaken. For example, the quarterly dividend was eliminated in favor of stock repurchases, a more tax-efficient way of returning cash to shareholders.

The above actions were neither unusual nor dramatic. Any good executive knows what they are. What makes this company's experience so instructive is that it was able to create a business culture that put value creation at the center of all key management processes and systems. Most critically, senior management bonuses were linked to EVA improvement. It's this link that provided managers with the incentive to aggressively pursue value-creating initiatives. Perhaps the key issue in any business is not whether its managers are capable of creating value, but whether they are motivated to do so.

MAKING IT HAPPEN

Because EVA is really about changing behavior and attitudes, the implementation process must begin with the board and the CEO. However, the CFO's advice and counsel will carry a lot of weight on several key implementation issues. For example,

- How will EVA be calculated? Some companies choose to make adjustments to the standard EVA measure. Finance professionals must decide which adjustments, if any, are appropriate for their own business.
- Are changes needed to the company's accounting and IT systems? Often, significant upgrades are needed to deliver divisional EVA figures in a timely fashion.
- How far down the organizational hierarchy will EVA be calculated? The rule of thumb in most companies is to limit EVA to large business units. Of course, EVA can be calculated at lower levels, but the measurement process will likely be compromised by the arbitrary nature of

"I just never got involved with the cash flow thing. My attitude was creativity will see me through." Adrienne Landau

  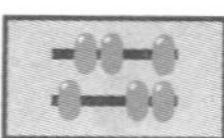      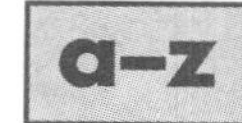

targets. Another potential drawback is found in attempts to bring EVA into levels of the firm below the level of strategic business units. Inevitably, contentious and arbitrary cost allocations and transfer prices are required to calculate EVA. In such cases, even the most ardent proponents of EVA have found that performance indicators that represent components or predictors of EVA are more appropriate than EVA itself for incentivizing behaviour.

CONCLUSION

Great business leaders, past and present, have always known about EVA without calling it that. EVA reveals to the rest of us the insights the best business managers have always had at a deep intuitive level. To make the most of this powerful tool for value creation, managers should know that EVA is much more than a measurement system. It's also an instrument for changing managerial behavior. Implementing value-based principles requires acceptance and understanding among all managers, who not only must appreciate why value creation is so important but also must grasp the fundamental concepts underlying value creation. One of the great virtues of EVA is that it makes sound finance theory accessible, so that operating managers, including those with no background or experience in accounting or finance, can incorporate insights from these disciplines into the way they run their businesses.

transfer pricing and overhead allocation practices. Instead, companies tend to rely on other key performance indicators.

- Which managers will have bonuses linked to EVA? Most users limit EVA-linked bonuses to senior managers for the same reasons noted above (i.e., the difficulty of calculating EVA below the level of strategic business units).
- Who will need training in EVA and how will the training needs be executed? Anyone whose performance evaluation or pay is affected in any way by EVA needs to understand the measure—how it's constructed and the steps they can take to improve it.

MORE INFO

Books:

Koller, Tim, Marc Goedhart, and David Wessels. *Valuation: Measuring and Managing the Value of Companies*. 5th ed. Hoboken, NJ: Wiley, 2010.

Martin, John D., and William J. Petty. *Value Based Management*. Boston, MA: Harvard Business School Press, 2000.

Young, S. David, and Stephen F. O'Byrne. *EVA and Value Based Management: A Practical Guide to Implementation*. New York: McGraw-Hill, 2001.

Website:

Value-Based Management: www.valuebasedmanagement.net/methods_eva.html

See Also:

★ Capital Budgeting: The Dominance of Net Present Value (pp. 20–23)
★ Comparing Net Present Value and Internal Rate of Return (pp. 30–32)
★ Multinationality and Financial Performance (pp. 900–901)
★ Why EVA Is the Best Measurement Tool for Creating Shareholder Value (pp. 952–953)
★ Viewpoint: The CFO and the Sustainable Corporation (pp. 719–720)
✔ Managing the Time Value of Money (p. 979)
✔ Understanding the Weighted Average Cost of Capital (WACC) (p. 1002)
The EVA Challenge: Implementing Value-Added Change in an Organization (p. 1351)

NOTES

1 EVA is a registered trademark of Stern Stewart & Company.

2 Drucker, Peter. *Classic Drucker*. Boston, MA: Harvard Business School Press, 2008; p. 107.

3 Some companies prefer to calculate EVA on a pre-tax basis, especially for division performance measurement.

"Forecasting by bureaucrats tends to be used for anxiety relief rather than for adequate policy making."
Nassim Nicholas Taleb

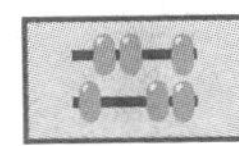

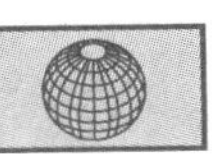

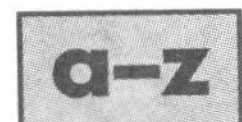

Crisis Management and Strategies for Dealing with Crisis by Jon White

EXECUTIVE SUMMARY

- Crises and their characteristics—what distinguishes crises from disasters, emergencies, and other exceptional situations.
- Crisis management—phases in crisis management, and the requirements in each phase for effective management.
- Techniques for anticipating crises, and preparations for dealing with them.
- The benefits to be gained by routine management from paying attention to crisis management.
- The demands made on management at times of crisis and the importance of psychological preparation.
- Practical conclusions.

INTRODUCTION: CRISES AND THEIR CHARACTERISTICS

The term "crisis" is much used in the media coverage of events, in public discussion, and by organization leaders describing the situations that they face and try to manage. The consequences of failure to manage these situations may prove more or less damaging to their organizations. However, not all situations that are described as crises should be labeled as such, and it is important to distinguish real crises from other situations as a first step toward managing them as effectively as possible.

Before looking at the characteristics of crisis situations, we will examine a situation—the Deepwater Horizon oil spill in the Gulf of Mexico—that was recognized at the time as a crisis for the organization involved to draw out the features that define it as a crisis.

DISTINGUISHING CRISES

In the academic literature on crisis management, crises are distinguished from other serious situations faced by organizations by a number of defining features.

Level of Threat

First, a crisis has to be serious in its consequences, involving loss of life, or threat to life, and serious injury or the possibility of serious injury, to numbers of people. It will also involve actual or possible damage to property. The first defining feature of crisis is the *level of threat* involved. The threat may also extend to the organization's existence, vital interests, or "raison d'être."

How an organization responds to a crisis will have an impact on its reputation, which is an aggregation of perceptions of its performance. Failure to perform to expectations at a time of crisis will result in damage to a company's reputation, which in some cases will be terminal.

There are also well-documented examples of corporate performance at times of crisis that enhance an organization's reputation. An example is the performance of Swissair (the airline went bankrupt in 2002) at the time of the crash of one of its aircraft off Nova Scotia, Canada, in 1998, a crash in which all 229 people on board the aircraft died. The airline's competent and sensitive handling of its obligations to those affected by the crash protected, maintained, and enhanced the airline's reputation.

Time Pressure

A second defining feature of crisis is *time pressure*. Threat or damage must be dealt with as soon as possible to minimize their consequences—whether these are further loss of life, threat to life, or damage to property. A good example here is the Japanese response to continuing threats of radiation leakage from the Fukushima nuclear plant damaged in the tsunami which followed an earthquake off Japan in March 2011.

Stress

A third defining feature of crisis is *stress*, as experienced by the decision-makers who have to deal with the situation. In crisis, their response will be marked by surprise, uncertainty, and flawed decision-making. In many crisis situations, the observation will be made that decision-makers are "out of position"—not where they need to be to deal with the situation as it develops.

Crises are unexpected, unforeseen events, which distinguishes them from disasters. Disasters, although serious in their consequences and sharing characteristics with crises, can be anticipated and plans made for dealing with them. For example, countries that experience earthquakes can prepare to respond to them when they occur, and take steps to minimize their consequences, by setting up early warning systems and buildings that can withstand earthquake damage.

Crisis management depends on classifying events or situations that will constitute crises for any organization. They will pose threats to life and property, and to the existence and reputation of the organization. They will need to be dealt with quickly to minimize their consequences, and they will make difficult demands on decision-makers and others who have to deal with them.

The Deepwater Horizon Incident as an Example of a Crisis

The BP case shows all these characteristics—the accident killed numbers of employees, damaged equipment, and created a huge oil spill that impacted the environment, the communities around the Gulf, and the livelihoods of their inhabitants. The company's vital interests—its reputation and ability to operate in deepwater environments in the United States and worldwide—were called into question, as were the abilities of the managers who tried to deal with the accident and the oil discharge and their consequences.

In addition, the crisis was played out in public, against sustained questioning and criticism from government, the media, the public, and investors in the company.

Categories of Corporate Crisis

The Deepwater Horizon incident was a "perfect storm" of a crisis. At end of the film *The Perfect Storm*, the fishing boat that is trying to ride through the storm is overwhelmed by the sea. How can organizations save themselves from being overwhelmed by such "storms"? They need first of all to understand what they may be up against, by trying to understand what, for them, will constitute crises so that they can prepare for them.

Lerbinger (1997) has outlined a number of broad categories of corporate crises.

- *Crises involving technology*: In a world that is increasingly dependent on technology, when technology fails the consequences may be catastrophic. Examples of these crises are provided by the difficulties at the Fukushima nuclear plant in 2011 following the earthquake and tsunami in Japan, and the Bhopal

"You never want a serious crisis to go to waste. And what I mean by that is [don't pass up] an opportunity to do things you think you could not do before." Rahm Emanuel

     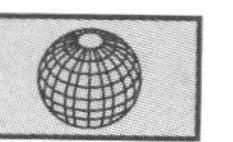   

industrial accident in 1984 when gas released from a Union Carbide plant in Bhopal, India, caused many fatalities.

- *Crises arising from confrontation*: These are caused when groups confront corporations or other authorities and criticize their actions, or go to more extreme lengths to express their opposition or discontent. An example of this is provided by the action of animal rights pressure groups in mounting strong, or even violent, opposition to companies that make use of animals in product testing or research.
- *Crises caused by malevolence*: These are crises caused by the malevolent actions of individuals or groups, such as terrorist groups placing bombs in unlikely locations to bring about maximum disruption of business and everyday life. The 7/7 attacks on London's transportation systems—the subway and buses on 7 July, 2005—are an example of a crisis created by malevolence.
- *Crises of management failure*: These are crises caused by management groups within the organization failing to carry out their responsibilities. Arguments have been made that the so-called financial crisis of recent years could be attributed to failure on the part of managers of financial institutions to manage the risks that their organizations were taking.
- *Crises involving other threats to the organization*: Examples include unexpected takeover bids.

CRISIS MANAGEMENT

How can the unexpected be prepared for and managed? How can the manager plan for that which cannot be planned for? How much attention should be given to planning for events or situations which may never happen? These are practical and difficult questions for managers thinking about crisis management to address.

Crisis management can be approached in terms of three phases of crisis management, and the requirements for managing each phase can be explored. Crisis management involves:

- crisis planning;
- crisis management—management of the crisis when it occurs;
- managing the aftermath of a crisis.

Crisis Planning

With hindsight, it is easy to ask whether or not an organization in crisis did enough to plan for the situation that arose. Questions along these lines were asked about BP's preparations for the oil spill which occurred in the Gulf of Mexico.

Crisis planning is an exercise in thinking the unthinkable—what, given the organization's interests, operations, plans, and links to groups such as suppliers, the community, and interest groups, could possibly go wrong for the organization? This exercise is one that should involve the most senior managers of the organization, and it may be difficult to get their attention and time for this—some will feel that they need not concern themselves with events that are unlikely to happen.

The exercise will typically generate a list of between 20 or 30 events and situations, which can be categorized and judged in terms of their likelihood of occurrence and impact. They may be placed on a scale of severity, ranging from crises (events or situations that affect the central interests or existence of the organization, involve threats to life and property, and require prompt action), disasters (similar, but more predictable), emergencies (less threatening situations, predictable, but still requiring prompt action), and exceptions to routine operations (predictable, requiring prompt remedial action). When events and situations have been categorized, plans can be made to deal with each category.

Crises require specific plans, which set out the situations that the organization has identified as crises. The plans set out arrangements for mobilizing the organization—identifying its senior managers and others who will be involved in managing the crisis situation. Crisis management requires two management teams—one to make decisions regarding the organization's response to the crisis, the other to implement the decisions made by this group and ensure that the organization deals with the demands of the situation. Arrangements have to be made for these two teams to work alongside each other, from facilities suitable for their work and with sufficient communication links between the teams, to the rest of the organization and to the outside world.

Crisis plans will identify roles in crisis management and the individuals who are to carry them out, and will set out arrangements for filling these roles over periods of time.

Communication at a time of crisis needs special attention. Will the communication links required be in place and sufficient? Who are the groups of people with whom the organization will need to communicate? What can and should be said at the outset in any crisis situation to groups such as the affected stakeholder groups (for example, the relatives of any employees injured in a crisis situation), or the media?

Some of this material can and should be prepared before any crisis situation develops. This can be incorporated into website content, into specific websites prepared for opening to the public at time of crisis, or into sections of already accessible websites.

A recent development in crisis communication has been to take into account the part played by the social media, allowing for stakeholder and public comment on the crisis situation as it develops. Planning for crisis communication now requires planning for possible developments in the discussion of crisis situations on such media, where the organization needs to decide what its approach to these channels will be before the crisis situation develops.

Once developed, crisis plans have to be tested, rehearsed through simulations, and kept up to date. It is particularly important to keep up to date the information about individuals who are nominated to play specific roles. All details of the plan can be tested against experience from simulations,

MAKING IT HAPPEN

- The reality of the modern world is that there are endless possibilities for things to go badly wrong for organizations, large and small. They confront scarcity of resources, political uncertainty, heavy social expectations, competition, and potential for conflict.
- It is essential that management groups prepare for difficult situations. These will be defined organization by organization, depending on their interests, their relationships, and their prospects.
- Preparation must be thorough and undertaken by the most senior and responsible managers in the organization, since they have the authority to see that the preparations made will be followed through.
- Crisis management depends on management accepting the necessity of preparation for potential crisis. This means lifting attention from the immediate, the short term, and day-to-day practical concerns to look to the future, and to anticipate disruption.
- The phase of crisis planning lays the basis for all the work that will be done in managing a crisis, and this depends on a commitment of effort by senior management.
- The other essential of crisis management is the psychological preparation of managers for the demands it will make of them. This adds to management capability and is a grounding for management in the modern world.

"Humankind cannot bear very much reality." T. S. Eliot

where situations similar to those foreseen in the planning phase are presented to the organization to test the response of crisis management teams and the organization itself.

Managing the Crisis Itself

Despite the importance of planning, during a time of crisis the plans that have been developed may not fit the actual crisis situation. The situation may differ from any that was considered in the planning phase, or the crisis may overturn key features of existing plans. For example, the plans may call for the use of specific facilities from which the crisis is to be managed, but the actual crisis may involve the destruction of facilities intended for this use. Back-up plans should be in place, but there may be a need for improvisation at a time when the quality of decision-making is degraded by time pressure and stress.

Crisis management under these conditions is improved by preparation—although managers do not have specific preparation, they are prepared for stress and the difficulties of decision-making under stressful conditions. A characteristic of decision-making under these conditions is "group think." This is a term developed by the psychologist Irving Janis in the early 1970s to explain faulty group decision-making. In this, groups rely on their own resources and focus on group interests rather than on information from outside that might contradict prevailing views within the group. Group think can be avoided by ensuring an adequate flow of information to decision-making groups, which in turn requires sufficient communication links for these groups.

Organizations that face the possibility of demanding crisis situations need, where resources allow, to have in place advisors who at a time of crisis can monitor, comment on, and raise questions about the quality of decision-making and the need for additional information to inform decisions.

Managing the Aftermath of Crisis

After the immediate crisis situation has been brought under control—for example, after BP finally capped the well in the Gulf of Mexico—organizations have to manage the aftermath. This may involve correcting practices that led to the crisis, compensating those who have been affected, and reestablishing external confidence in the organization. Managing the aftermath requires longer-term effort, and will also involve communicating with important groups that changes have been made and that management will avoid similar situations in future. A primary interest here may be in repairing damage to reputation, as in BP's case. Exxon's experience with the Alaskan oil spill from the Exxon Valdez shows how the task of restoring reputation continues long after the crisis.

TECHNIQUES FOR ANTICIPATING CRISES, AND PREPARATIONS FOR DEALING WITH THEM

Senior managers can call on the advice of specialist groups to help them to anticipate crisis situations. These will include management consultants skilled in futures research, scenario planning, and risk assessment; internal and external groups that take a strategic perspective on the organization's interests; and specialists such as public relations and public affairs practitioners. These practitioners have expertise in dealing with issues and crisis management, communication during a crisis, and reputation management.

The techniques such advisors will draw on include the following.

- *Futures research*, which makes use of techniques such as scenario planning—a planning approach that looks into the future in a disciplined way, creating and examining plausible scenarios—or Delphi studies. The latter work through a series of rounds of questions to experts on likely developments and possible risks. Questioning is pursued with, and summarized to, the group of experts until consensus, or consensus on differences of opinion, is reached. The results of Delphi studies can be used to inform decision-making.
- *Risk assessments*, which weigh the likelihood of events or situations developing and their possible impacts, and making judgments on threats and vulnerability. A specialization in risk assessment relates to reputation risk assessment—what could happen to seriously damage the organization's reputation, and what steps should be taken to avoid damage to reputation.
- *Issues management*, where topics of concern to particular groups are identified and tracked through environmental scanning and monitoring. Involved here may be social research, analysis of traditional and social media content, and close attention to the concerns of special interest groups.

BENEFITS FOR ROUTINE MANAGEMENT OF ATTENTION TO CRISIS MANAGEMENT

Advisors on crisis management, whether internal or external to the organization, will encounter scepticism from management regarding the time, effort, and resources to be committed to crisis management. Too often, organizations have to experience a crisis situation before they will take the task of crisis management seriously—and for some this will be too late.

A benefit of attention to crisis management that may be overlooked is that it improves routine management. By asking at the planning stage what could go wrong, current practices and processes can be reexamined from this perspective. Improvements can be made that will avoid problems, as well as improve management perspectives, skills, and decision-making.

THE IMPORTANCE OF PSYCHOLOGICAL PREPARATION

Attention to crisis management, to crisis planning, and to rehearsal of the response to potential crisis situations also improves management capability. Management is essentially an attempt to bring order to the work of groups of people and to the use of resources to achieve objectives. Crisis situations disrupt the existing order—sometimes catastrophically (think for example of the 9/11 terrorist attacks in New York in 2001, or the Japanese earthquake and tsunami in 2011)—and make exceptional demands on decision-makers. Managers and decision-makers, prepared through training for these situations, will still find them very difficult to deal with, but they will feel psychologically prepared for them. After BP's experience in the Gulf of Mexico, the company's CEO Tony Hayward told a BBC documentary program that he had felt ill-prepared for the demands of the situation.

Training for crisis management involves the following.

- Working through simulations. Simulations set up situations as realistically as possible, through the use of real-time but simulated developments, actors, and creation of pressure on decision-makers. They allow decision-makers, working through developed plans, to see how the plans—and they themselves—perform against the demands of the simulated situation.
- Preparation for the communication requirements of crisis situations. Who will speak for the organization, what will they be able to say, and how will they cope with media interest in crisis situations? The training here will be very specific—how can individual managers be prepared for the encounter with the media? How should they present themselves, what should they be prepared to say and where, and how should they be prepared for the approaches to questioning that will be taken by the media?

"The average individual innovator is having a smaller and smaller impact ... I've noticed that Nobel prizewinners are getting older. That's a sure sign it's taking longer to innovate." Ben Jones

MORE INFO

Books:

Griffin, A. *New Strategies for Reputation Management: Gaining Control of Issues, Crises & Corporate Social Responsibility*. London: Kogan Page, 2007.

Griffin, A., M. Regester, T. Johnson, and J. Larkin. *Risk Issues and Crisis Management in Public Relations: A Casebook of Best Practice*. 4th ed. London: Kogan Page, 2008.

Janis, I. *Group Think*. 2nd ed. Boston, MA: Houghton Mifflin, 1982.

Larkin, J. *Strategic Reputation Risk Management*. Basingstoke, UK: Palgrave Macmillan, 2002.

Lerbinger, Otto. *The Crisis Manager: Facing Risk and Responsibility*. Oxford, UK: Routledge Communication Series, 1997. (To be republished 2012.)

Movie:

Petersen, Wolfgang (dir). *The Perfect Storm*. Warner Bros, 2000.

See Also:

✔ Understanding Crisis Management (p. 1178)

"Leadership used to be about ideas, setting an example and doing the right thing. Today, if you make enough money for the firm (and are not currently an ax murderer) you will be promoted into a position of influence." Greg Smith

  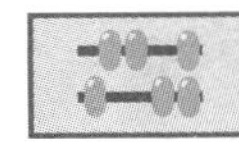   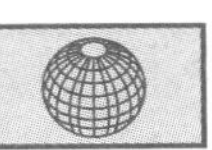   

Digital Reputation Management by Shireen Smith

EXECUTIVE SUMMARY

- The impact of Web 2.0 and social media.
- Managing reputations: proactively and reactively.
- Gauging the company's online presence.
- Handling negative content.
- Search engine optimization, forums, defamation.
- Anonymity, enforcement, litigation and jurisdiction.
- Monitoring conversations, and engagement.
- Putting in place a strategy.

INTRODUCTION

The changes happening in the world with the arrival of social media are having a far-reaching impact on the ways we do business, communicate with one another, and engage with our customers. The impact of social media as a communication channel is apparent when we compare it to earlier developments in society (Table 1).

Table 1. Growth of media formats

Medium	Time taken to reach 50 million users[1]
Radio	38 years
Television	13 years
Internet	4 years
iPod	3 years
Facebook	200 million in 1 year

Yet we are still at an early stage of this revolution in society. In the early days of the Internet, when websites and email addresses were uncommon, we gradually began to see what were then odd-looking address details appearing on people's business cards and letterheads. Nowadays, any business without a blog, Facebook page, and Twitter account is behind the times, and people are increasingly putting their Twitter handles and other social media address details on their business cards.

Key in this new age of instant global communications, where the influence and reach of word of mouth is growing, is effective management of your business reputation. To grow and prosper, companies need to build reputational capital among all stakeholders. Although a company has many different stakeholders, each one reacting to a specific facet of its business (as employee, supplier, financial investor, or client), in fact they are all sensitive to the company's ability to meet the expectations of all its stakeholders.

As there is a link between reputation and share performance, companies are very sensitive about their reputation nowadays and appreciate the need to manage their visibility and actions to maximize reputational capital. How quickly trust in an organization can be lost is evident from the damage to Ratner when its CEO called the jewelry which the company sold "crap" in 1991. After this, and a subsequent comment that Ratner's earrings were "cheaper than an M&S prawn sandwich but probably wouldn't last as long," the value of the business dropped by £500 million, as the share price went from £4 to 10 pence.

Reputation is a judgment from the market that needs to be preserved. Changes in reputation affect all stakeholders. Monitoring reputation is designed to ensure that the behavior and performance of the business consistently meet or exceed expectations. With the growing importance of social media, companies are extending their monitoring to include online discussions.

WEB 2.0

As participation in social media platforms such as Facebook, LinkedIn, Twitter, and blogging increases, it becomes necessary to know what is being said about you in order to protect reputation. Whether a company is a web-based business or a bricks and mortar one, it needs to understand that conversations about it will take place online regardless of whether or not it takes part in them.

It's hard to remember a time when only those with specialized skills could post content online. Yet it was only a few years ago that the development of blogging platforms, enabled by Web 2.0 technologies, made it possible for those without specialist web skills to freely communicate online. It is not an exaggeration to say that this change has revolutionized society. The fact that so many people are engaging in discussions on the Web, and are commenting on blogs, forums, and social media sites—sometimes anonymously—is one reason that companies need to keep up with these trends and monitor the digital space.

What makes comments a matter of serious concern is that they can be instantly and indefinitely accessible to millions of people around the world. If a consumer is dissatisfied with a product or service, Web 2.0 makes it possible for them to broadcast their disappointment worldwide. This takes on more sinister significance, as what may have originally been a grumble down the pub heard by a handful of people is captured and remains there for everyone to see, possibly for years.

Even if the original site where the adverse comment was posted has disappeared, the comment may remain cached in a search engine or appear on other websites or blogs. Indeed, it matters a lot on what type of site comments appear. The important point is that whether there is any truth to online smears is immaterial. Once a smear is on the Internet, it's in the public sphere, where it stays. Therefore, as people react more and more to names and reputations, to rumors and word of mouth, and given that so many conversations are taking place online, management of digital word of mouth is more necessary than on any other medium. Being able to respond quickly and appropriately to whatever is discovered is one of the fundamental pillars of online reputation management.

MANAGING REPUTATION

There are two ways in which a company's reputation may need to be defended: proactively, or reactively. The best policy is to be proactive and put in place a plan for how the organization will address its reputation management, including its reaction to disaster. The company should be properly prepared in case it is affected by a situation that calls for a fast reaction.

Such situations sometimes arise due to the company's own strategy going awry, as in the case of a campaign by CE Europe to promote its *Resident Evil* video game, which led users to believe that their mobile phones had been infected by the "T-Virus," resulting in panicked telephone calls to antivirus providers.

Proactive reputation management involves taking steps to prepare for deliberate or accidental damage to the good name of the business. Reactive reputation defense is when you've suffered damage and need to put it right after the event.

There are many threats online; however, social media and conversations are the greatest threats to a company's reputation and should be managed proactively at the earliest opportunity.

"To be extraordinarily happy and to have no concern for money drives some people nuts." Danny Baker

        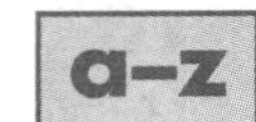

GAUGING THE COMPANY'S ONLINE PRESENCE

Google accounts for 50% of all Internet searches. Many Google searchers reportedly never look beyond the first 10 links. For businesses and individuals worldwide, this means that their most visible reputation is dictated by 10 blue links and a few lines of text.

If your business is "ABCFashion" and your potential customers are searching for information about you, their first impression is most likely influenced not by your official website, but by the information that comes up when they conduct a Google search. The first or second link might be to the official "ABCFashion.com" site. But what if among the other search results in the top 10 there is one featuring links to a disgruntled review of one of the company's brands, a forum thread entitled "ABCFashion has its clothes manufactured by a company using child slave labor—boycott them," or even a dedicated complaints blog called BoycottABCFashion.com!

It is immaterial whether the comments on the negative sites are inaccurate. The problem is that just like in the offline world, first impressions count. No matter how good your official website, those negative sites are going to sit in the minds of your potential customers and contacts, and will raise doubts. The potential customer could pass over your organization and seek out a company with a more favorable online presence.

There are established ways in which a positive identity for the business may be created and a prominent online presence cultivated. Being active on Twitter—a high-ranking site on Google—is an important way to manage the company's reputation, while also helping it to occupy one of the first 10 links on Google. A good online presence reduces the likelihood of isolated incidents rising to the first page of Google.

NEGATIVE CONTENT

If there is negative content found about the company, what can be done? People's first instinct is to want to do everything they can to get the negative content removed. After all, if someone spray-painted something about your business on the wall of your shop, you would want it removed as quickly as possible. Unfortunately, when it comes to online content, having items deleted is not always straightforward. On many occasions, efforts to force people to remove online comment have backfired.

A "softly softly" approach generally achieves a better outcome online than heavy-handedly removing negative content. You could respond by putting across your side in a constructive and positive way.

Examples of mistakes by others include that made by AOL Time Warner when it sent cease and desist letters to a number of Harry Potter fan pages prior to the completion of the official website. This led to considerable animosity in the online community. In response, an alliance of UK fan site owners devoted substantial efforts to alerting the public to what they considered to be the "despicable" actions of AOL Time Warner.

PAGERANK

PageRank is a measurement of the value of a webpage used by Google to order search results. Hundreds of factors contribute, but one of the key elements is the number and quality of other websites that link to a page.

SEARCH ENGINE OPTIMIZATION (SEO)

SEO has its place in online reputation management, as it's aimed at increasing your website's performance in the "organic" search results (that is, the results that appear in a search engine because that search engine considers your site to be relevant to the surfer's search terms). It doesn't take long to realize that if your content appears in front of buyers at the time they're searching for products or services, your reputation could benefit by the exposure. Using SEO to build up a strong online presence is an effective way to prevent problems by ensuring that websites with favorable mentions of your company, not negative sites, are the ones that customers see when they search for your product or service. The goal is to make negative content less likely to become prominent, pushing it out of top search results with your own material.

Occasionally, it might be appropriate to engage the services of an SEO company to manipulate the search results with the aim of eliminating negative content. It's important to be clear whether SEO is the correct strategy for *reacting* to negative content, though. For example, if an adverse comment is on a site with a high Google PageRank score (such as the BBC or other news organization), it's not really feasible for SEO to displace that site from the first page of Google. Other strategies would be more effective, and valuable time could be lost by implementing SEO as the solution.

A page with damaging content and a low PageRank score might still appear in normal search results despite an otherwise low ranking. For example, it is possible to appear *above* normal results on page one by using paid advertisements on the company's name for Google's AdWords service. Google's policy on keyword and trademark use has been the subject of a string of legal cases. Discussing these is outside the scope of this article beyond mentioning that it is possible for objectionable content to be promoted with sponsored links.

Even if you decide that SEO is an appropriate way to respond to negative content, it's important to select a company carefully. Certain SEO approaches offer benefits in the short term, that can lead to a website being penalized by search engines later. This would work against long-term goals, as well as potentially impacting adversely on the company's reputation.

Given that many websites are frequented by tens or hundreds of thousands of users irrespective of your SEO efforts (for example, popular discussion forums), SEO is often not appropriate if you discover the existence of adverse comments.

When responding to negative comments, it is important to know what to ignore, and how to deal with the rest. Ignoring a bad review is generally not advisable, but attracting attention or alienating prospective customers with an inappropriate official response is also undesirable. A typical reaction from companies that find negative material online is to try to have it removed by contacting the owner of the website, directory, or forum. The circumstances when it is acceptable to request Google directly to remove content from its index are rare.

FORUMS

Forum operators are unlikely to be amenable to requests for the removal of poor reviews. The Electronic Commerce Regulations[2] provide some immunity for them and for website hosts, which they lose in certain circumstances, such as when they have been alerted to contentious content on their site. So, for a request for removal to be persuasive, the offending content will likely need to be clearly defamatory or otherwise against the law.

Often, in practice, the only available recourse is to respond to the forum comment. But beware of posting official comments which come close to marketing. They will not be well received, and will often be prohibited by the forum's terms of use.

On the other hand, posting unofficial positive comments using false identities (often referred to as "astroturfing") is one of 31 items in a nonexhaustive list of practices banned outright by the Consumer Protection from Unfair Trading Regulations 2008,[3] and which can attract investigation, prosecution, and a fine. Quite apart from such regulations, responding under false identities could have other adverse consequences. Social media communities value transparency, openness, and engagement,

"What humans want is not just happiness ... if that were all people were interested in, we should have been extinguished a long time ago." Martin Seligman

so the company's reputation management efforts are likely to be better received if negative feedback is dealt with in a transparent and nondefensive manner.

Legal professionals who understand branding and reputation management are unlikely to be defamation or litigation lawyers. Yet many litigation law firms brand themselves as reputation management experts on the Web. Litigators are in reality ill-equipped to advise a company's PR or other department on reputation management because the advice should rarely be to take legal action.

DEFAMATION

Many comments that people make, and which could be extremely damaging to a brand, may well not amount to libel. Even if comments are defamatory, whether or not you should resort to litigation is a matter to consider carefully. Reasons not to do so are provided by the number of high-profile instances where a legal or heavy-handed approach online has backfired.

WHO IS RESPONSIBLE, AND WHERE ARE THEY BASED?

More recently, in May 2011, the use of injunctions to gag the press led to a "Streisand effect" for the litigant footballer who sought an injunction to prevent the publication of details of his alleged affair. Perhaps predictably, this led to increased media and public interest as more and more people on Twitter took to naming him, in contravention of the terms of the injunction.

Aside from showing how legal action to suppress information can have undesirable consequences, these examples illustrate that, although litigation specialists are key in securing an outcome once a strategy has been decided on, a different type of expertise is relevant when coming to that decision. Litigators, though experts in their field, are inappropriate managers of corporate reputation.

LITIGATION AND JURISDICTION

Two important issues when considering litigation are the enforceability of orders against defendants in jurisdictions beyond the reach of English courts, and whether it will be possible to identify those responsible for posting material online.

Despite the existence of what was initially billed as a "super injunction" to prevent the footballer's identity being revealed, the terms of the injunction were widely breached by Twitter users. Twitter is based in the United States, and the order being enforced was granted by a UK court. Under such circumstances, the subject of an order will not necessarily feel obliged to comply, and due to the global nature of the Internet, an injunction is rendered ineffective.

That is not to say that a UK business cannot take legal action in these circumstances. In contrast to the footballer case, a group of councillors in South Tyneside successfully obtained an order *from a US court* forcing Twitter to disclose contact details and IP addresses of users allegedly responsible for libelous messages by suing in the US courts.

It is worth noting that even where details of the email or user account are disclosed, further information may be necessary to identify the person who is physically in control of that account. This means that sometimes there may be no recourse if there is no authentic name or email address to trace the identity of the person behind the pseudonym or anonymous comment.

A user's IP address does not necessarily identify them. IP addresses are often not fixed, and might be reassigned from one Internet connection to another quite regularly. Also, IP addresses are tied to Internet connections rather than to individuals. The same IP address might be shared between a number of devices and a number of different people. In the case of a wireless network, an unscrupulous next-door neighbor might be hijacking the Internet connection.

So, this is another complex issue to address when deciding what action to take—whether the result will lead to successful identification, and whether the court orders obtained will be enforceable.

SOCIAL MEDIA SITES

For businesses, six important services are:

- Facebook.com
- LinkedIn.com
- Twitter.com
- Quora.com
- Foursquare.com
- Ecademy.com

ENGAGING IN ONLINE CONVERSATIONS

Web 2.0 has spawned social media platforms and online conversations. An effective reputation management program should involve "engagement"—i.e., participating in conversations—alongside monitoring. There is much discussion among social media enthusiasts about the importance and meaning of "engagement." Given the strength of opinion among vociferous sections of the online community about what is "proper engagement," some methods of managing reputation on social media platforms could themselves create a reputational risk.

Understanding the issues before settling your social media strategy, using Twitter, or outsourcing your tweeting, makes sense. It helps to consider in advance what the company will use a platform for. A clear plan of action should be implemented. If the intention is to send out corporate news predominantly via Twitter, the company should be aware that people speak disparagingly of those who "broadcast" promotional messages about their business without listening to what anyone else is saying.

Building some engagement into the plan could considerably enhance how others experience the company.

Therefore, on a day-to-day level, protecting a company's reputation requires active communication and participation in conversations with consumers and others.

CASE STUDY

The Streisand Effect

The seminal example of this concerned the publication online of a photograph of Barbara Streisand's residence. On hearing that her villa was pictured on the Internet, Streisand began legal proceedings to have it removed, with disastrous consequences. Rather than having her privacy respected by suppressing the photograph, the action attracted an enormous amount of attention from website operators and eventually the media. The exposure gained would have been difficult to replicate had her intention been to publicize the image rather than hide it.

This episode brought into Internet vocabulary the term *Streisand effect*, which is now synonymous with any action designed to suppress material online but which has the unintended consequence of amplifying it.

Since then, there have been a number of incidences of this phenomenon, such as the Trafigura scandal. There, an injunction brought to prevent publication of a question asked in the UK Parliament triggered media interest, bolstering public awareness of the report about Trafigura's dumping of toxic waste in the Ivory Coast. This caused far more serious damage to Trafigura's reputation than might have otherwise occurred. Certainly the legal action did nothing to help.

"The danger is not an ever-expanding socialist state, per Hayek's road to serfdom, but of a move to economic feudalism, in which a small set of wealthy masters dominate markets and the state and subvert or outsmart efforts to regulate their behavior or rein them in." Richard B. Freeman

  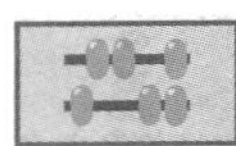      

Many large organizations are using Twitter as a customer service platform, as it is the first place where disgruntled consumers voice their dissatisfaction about a company. By actively listening for negative comments, a company can do a lot to listen, learn, and limit damage to its reputation.

Dell is a good example of a company that had a very poor online customer feedback record but transformed itself by, among other things, creating a number of different Twitter profiles to handle customer service and market its offers. Subsequently, Dell announced that its Twitter strategy had resulted in US$3 million of revenue over two years.

Interestingly, Dell's Twitter accounts, like @DellOutlet, encourage discussion and can be used to provide direct and responsive advice to customers online—for example, where they have difficulties using a website. This approach helped Dell to build a strong community of customer advocates and to quickly respond to community concerns.

Engagement does not come easily to many organizations, especially large ones with different departments that are responsible for distinct aspects of a company's operations. A new dynamic comes into play when the organization is unable to *control* messages about its brand and instead has to *respond to* whatever messages consumers choose to communicate (such as on forums). Corporate reputation boils down to consumer trust, and trust is difficult to control.

MONITORING CONVERSATIONS

The sheer volume of information makes it difficult to keep track of online comments and to identify which are significant. Therefore, choosing tools appropriate to the size and type of organization is critical, as is the decision about which keywords to monitor.

The development of an emotional commitment to companies by their consumers is now a critical business success issue. Companies may aim to build up this kind of commitment by being part of trusted organizations, trying to create a brand that stands for more than the product or service, or by associating themselves with popular causes, such as green policies.

Employees' and other stakeholders' reputations also have a strong impact on the company's reputation. The degree to which their personal name affects the company name depends on how well known they are, and what role they occupy in the business.

The reputational risks that can impact on stakeholders of a business include incidents like unethical employee behavior, suppliers' business practices, involvement in unpopular conduct (such as that which harms the environment or the safety or security of citizens), having sexist, racist, or similar policies, or backing unpopular causes.

PUTTING A STRATEGY IN PLACE

When a company is considering its approach to online reputation management, it is worth bearing in mind the six pillars of global reputation (according to Fombrun, Gardberg, and Server, 2000):[4]

- emotional appeal (trust, admiration, and respect);
- products and services (quality, innovativeness, value for money, etc.);
- vision and leadership;
- workplace quality (well-managed, appealing workplace, employee talent);
- financial performance;
- social responsibility.

Monitoring online reputation is not simply a case of watching out for mentions of the corporate name on Twitter or other platforms. It is also necessary for the company to avoid reputational damage in the myriad other ways in which its reputation could suffer, such as being associated with the wrong partners (those whose activities become embarrassing), having the wrong employees, or backing the wrong causes.

Once such risks to the corporate reputation have been identified, representative keywords should be selected so that the company receives an early alert to possible problems. If the company markets a variety of products or services, it will want to track mentions of the different brand names; it may also want to be alerted when directors and other senior figures in the organization are discussed; it will also likely be interested in what its competitors are doing.

A number of keywords will need to be monitored. In a large company, different departments may have different risk areas which they will want to address by monitoring their own individual keywords.

The most effective reputation management strategy will monitor all six pillars of global reputation mentioned earlier. Successful strategies for the management of reputation risks rely not only on vigilance and staying informed, but also on a readiness to respond quickly and effectively to problems as and when they arise.

Putting a plan of action and an effective team together for online communication is key to success. It is much less possible to control how consumers perceive the business, and all manner of unpredictable events can happen. An effective strategy is to bring together an interdisciplinary team drawing on the skills of various functions within the company which may need to be involved, including the marketing, IT, PR, and legal departments.

Such a team, once put together, should designate responsibilities so that it is ready and able to make swift decisions in a crisis. Only then does the organization give itself a good chance to react instantly to whatever happens, and to develop the know-how to deal with any scenario that arises. With this structure in place, the company will be able to engage with potential and actual consumers while accessing the knowledge and skills of whichever department needs to be involved on a particular question.

Taking a purely legal approach may sometimes be appropriate, as where there is clear defamation. At other times, a cease and desist letter may have its place, and recovery of a domain name may avoid unnecessary expense and aggravation. Other types of response may suggest themselves in some cases. Knowing when to ignore a disgruntled consumer will also be important—it can take a lot of energy to maintain anger, so will it simply burn out?

A well-led team with clear lines of responsibility delegated to members helps the organization to negotiate its way in social media. This may explain why there are so many general counsels on Twitter, and why in-house lawyers tend to be streets ahead of commercial lawyers in private practice when it comes to understanding the risks new media influences represent for corporate reputations.

FREE AND PAID REPUTATION MANAGEMENT TOOLS

Many of the reputation-monitoring tools on the market are designed to measure sentiment following marketing initiatives. A key consideration in effective monitoring is establishing a process for easy access and review of online material, bearing in mind that the volume of discussion to be monitored could be vast. Collecting the

MAKING IT HAPPEN

- Word of mouth on social media presents unique challenges.
- Reputation impacts on share price and the company's stakeholders.
- Businesses need to be alert to online conversations, even if they do not operate online.
- Freely available tools allow you to monitor reputation in-house.
- Bringing together an interdisciplinary team for online communication is helpful.

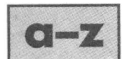

data can be quite straightforward, but making them manageable is another issue altogether. A *dashboard* is the popular approach to dealing with this, and involves constructing an interface that presents new data in one place, and in an accessible way.

The keywords to track should be words or phrases of interest which are not too general. The aim is to flag up interesting material without being overloaded with irrelevant chatter.

There are many paid reputation-monitoring services on offer, with a variety of price plans. Deciding which to select depends on whether the number of keywords to be tracked will increase the charges. If so, the paid services can become prohibitively expensive. Any business with a broad product range, and keywords such as those representing the names of directors, heads of departments, suppliers, investors, marketing campaigns, clients, and competitors, will find it sensible to carry out some in-house monitoring using free tools, even when a paid service is used as well. The company will then be able to monitor more terms, which is desirable for effective reputation monitoring.

Drawing on a selection of the many free tools, such as Google Alerts,[5] it is possible to put together your own monitoring platform and bring the results together in RSS feeds, which can be fed into a dashboard using something like Google Reader. This results in a single webpage that pulls together recent mentions of your keywords from a wide variety of sources for easy access.

However, ensuring that a wide net is cast, so that relevant content is collected from a broad cross section of the web, can be time-consuming to set up, as can arranging this information into an easily digestible format. The optimum combination of paid or free tools will also depend on the keywords chosen and the reasons for monitoring.

CONCLUSION

It is realistic to expect that, of the hundreds of millions of people online, some will occasionally have a negative comment about the company. It is also useful to know that when something plays out on the social media, it can erupt in a matter of hours. Reaction time can be critical. Therefore, any strategic plan should enable even a large organization to react very rapidly. Situations can creep up on a business all too quickly. Something trivial or which starts off in a minor way can escalate rapidly and catch people and organizations unawares.

Hopefully this article has explained why online conversations pose a unique threat to reputation, and highlighted some of the challenges, both in determining what to monitor, and in limiting the possible impact on stakeholders.

MORE INFO

Books:

Beal, Andy, and Judy Strauss. *Radically Transparent: Monitoring and Managing Reputations Online*. Indianapolis, IN: Wiley, 2008.

Brown. Rob. *How to Build Your Reputation*. Penryn, UK: Ecademy Press, 2007. Includes a valuable foreword by Sir Digby Jones explaining the critical importance of reputation to businesses.

Websites:

Azrights IP Brands blog: ip-brands.com/blog

Distilled blog: www.distilled.net/blog

Mashable, an independent news site covering digital culture, social media, and technology: mashable.com

See Also:

★ Digital Strategies for Enhancing Reputation (pp. 826–831)

NOTES

1 blog.facebook.com/blog.php?post=72353897130;www.un.org/cyberschoolbus/briefing/technology/tech.pdf

2 ss.17–19 Electronic Commerce (EC Directive) Regulations 2002.

3 These are listed in Schedule 1 to the Consumer Protection from Unfair Trading Regulations 2008.

4 Fombrun, Charles J., Naomi A. Gardberg, and Joy M. Sever. "The reputation quotient: A multi-stakeholder measure of corporate reputation." *Journal of Brand Management* 7:4 (2000): 241–255.

5 Find out more about Google Alerts at www.google.com/alerts

"It's not what you say, it's what people hear." Frank Luntz

Digital Strategies for Enhancing Reputation

by Paul A. Argenti and Georgia Aarons

EXECUTIVE SUMMARY

- This chapter provides an overview on the changing environment for business and the impact recent scandals have had on the public's trust in corporations.
- Understanding the potential value of reputation is a competitive advantage, and knowledge of the potential value of reputation and specific messages can drive communication strategy. Reputation must be measured and managed.
- With the rise of social media, reputation management is more challenging than ever, but those companies that embrace change have an opportunity to reposition themselves.

INTRODUCTION: THE WORLD WE LIVE IN

TMI. Of all the acronyms to enter the hallowed pages of the *Oxford English Dictionary* in 2011, this one may be the most apt in describing the world we now live in. Of the thousands of media impressions each of us faces on a daily basis, it seems that many relate to leaked information and corporate scandal, be it investment guru Warren Buffett's involvement in an insider trading deal, the *News of the World* phone-hacking scandal, or the most illicit, US Congressman Anthony Weiner's sweatpants[1]—TMI, or too much information, indeed.

These headlines underscore a central irony of today's environment: never has trust in business been lower, yet never has it been more important. Beginning most notably in 2001 with the infamous dissolution of Enron, corporate scandals have become ubiquitous in recent years, and trust in business institutions has subsequently dropped. In the 2011 Edelman Trust Barometer, only 46% of Americans and 44% of Britons polled said that they trusted business to do what's right; despite this decline, respondents ranked "transparent and honest business practices" as the second most important factor influencing corporate reputation.[2]

This rise in public scrutiny correlates strongly with the emergence of new digital communications platforms and their widespread adoption. An ever-growing list of interactive tools has given stakeholders the ability to communicate with one another, to disseminate messaging, and, ultimately, to threaten companies' increasingly vulnerable reputations. A third of the world's population uses these tools, or more than two billion people.[3] Where before, messages were created by executives to meet the needs of particular groups, information can now be shared and interpreted by billions of people. For the first time in marketing history, consumers are as influenced by their peers as by the company behind the message.[4] The result is that companies have never been less in control of their messaging. This uneasy reality requires business leaders worldwide to redefine their strategies and brands in the context of these new platforms, and to find a way to use them to their advantage.

This chapter provides an overview of the current business environment and the reputational challenges that have emerged with the growth of digital channels. We will take a closer look at reputation and how it relates to identity, brand, and image, and more importantly, examine why reputation matters. Finally, we will outline the strategies and tactics needed to regain control by exploiting new channels.

TODAY'S BUSINESS ENVIRONMENT

Over the course of the last decade, a number of factors came together to catalyze a massive change in the way business is conducted around the world: a decline in trust following the wake of corporate scandals and a turbulent economy; intense public scrutiny of business; disillusionment over excessive executive pay; the growth of digital communications platforms; and the impact of an interwoven "global village."

Corporate Scandal and Credit Crisis Lead to Decline in Trust

Although corporate malfeasance was by no means unheard of in the twentieth century, a stream of scandals began in 2001 that rattled the public's trust in business. Enron was the first major headline; its fraudulent accounting practices were exposed to an already skeptical public, which was still recovering from the bursting dot.com bubble. One could argue that after 2001 the landscape went from bad to worse: in 2002, approximately 81% of surveyed investors "did not have much confidence in those running Big Business."[5] This grim statistic set the tone for what would become a common theme for corporate leaders: the decline in their credibility in the face of increased scrutiny by diverse stakeholder groups.

That many of these scandals occurred during or because of the worst economic recession since the Second World War only exacerbated the existing slide in trust. Beginning in 2007, the global credit crisis shook trust in the financial services industry to its core across all stakeholder groups. One of the major sources of public skepticism about business was compensation within the very institutions that had caused the economic downturn. It seemed that executives were rewarded for failure: the top execs of the seven major financial firms that either collapsed, were sold at low prices, or received taxpayer-funded bailouts were each paid a total of US$464 million in performance pay since 2005, according to an analysis by the *New York Times*. Those same firms lost more than US$107 billion between 2007 and 2009.[6] In total, Wall Street paid over US$144 billion in bonuses at a time when unemployment skyrocketed across the United States and Europe.[7]

Shareholder Activism

Alongside this alarming disparity grew shareholder activism. In fact, activist shareholders had been a driving force in modern investor relations for some time, since corporate scandals, including Enron, Tyco International, and ImClone Systems, Inc., became commonplace in the early 2000s. As financial malfeasance permeated the corporate world, activist investors popped up in droves. When asked what they considered to be the main driver of shareholder activism, 94% of surveyed investor relations professionals cited corporate scandals.[8] With the credit crisis and worldwide attention focused on executive compensation policies, executives found themselves fielding aggressive advances from shareholders demanding increased transparency. One of the most outspoken was Carl Icahn, who in 2007 was responsible for forcing behemoth Time Warner to restructure four of its divisions and create a share repurchase program.[9] Icahn's website, www.icahnreport.com, has since become a platform for "comment on the desultory state of corporate governance in America."[10]

Rise of Digital Communications Platforms

Icahn's blog—his personal loudspeaker to likeminded investors—illustrates a critical

"As computing and the internet become more ubiquitous over the coming decades and offline and online worlds blur, the very notion of being addicted to digital connectivity will seem as absurd and laughable as being addicted to electricity." Rhodri Marsden

point: while the rising distrust of companies and their leaders may not have been so detrimental on its own, it took place in tandem with another trend, namely the emergence and adoption of new digital communications platforms.

Before the digital explosion at the turn of the twenty-first century, corporations' reputations were shaped by one-dimensional messaging that was pushed down the corporate ladder and disseminated without discussion. But, with an ever-growing list of new tools, stakeholders—companies' employees, customers, or shareholders like Icahn—were suddenly empowered to talk back. Social communities and blogs gave stakeholders the ability to disseminate their own messaging about an organization, and to share and build communities around that information. The rise in corporate scandals and credit crisis, combined with the emergence of these new channels, created a perfect storm that radically altered the business landscape.

The Global Village

This storm occurred on a global level: technology strengthened communication channels around the world to produce what Canadian philosopher Marshall McLuhan foresaw decades ago—the creation of a world so interwoven by shared knowledge that it becomes a "global village."[11] This trend has had a monumental impact on trust in business, particularly over the last decade.

Through the Internet, people have discovered and invented new ways to share relevant knowledge with blinding speed. The data are staggering: by the end of 2010, nearly 80% of the world's population had a mobile cellular phone subscription, and more than 30% regularly used the Internet.[12] As of late 2010, Technorati tracked more than 150 million blogs.[13] Collectively, we created nearly 300 billion gigabytes of information last year.[14] These numbers translate into communications issues that simply didn't exist in the corporate world 10 years ago. The current global connectivity accentuates the volume at which negative feelings can be heard, and makes it difficult for companies to prevent negative—and positive—news from reaching people. Data suggest that these numbers will only continue to increase as consumers assume further control of corporate reputations and communicate with each other in real time, 24/7.

To summarize, the variables that traditionally acted as catalysts in reputational crises have mutated and multiplied exponentially in the face of all the factors discussed above: a decline in trust, a turbulent economy, diverse stakeholder groups' growing influence, the emergence and speed of propagation of digital communications platforms, and an increasingly global marketplace. An understanding of reputation and why reputation matters is more important now than ever.

ENHANCING STRATEGY THROUGH REPUTATION MANAGEMENT

In the changed environment for business, corporate reputation has gained visibility and importance in the eyes of many constituencies. Reputation is now an integral driver in a company's success and credibility, but many managers who have not thought about corporate reputation continue to underestimate its value. This error is partly due to a lack of understanding about what corporate identity, brand, image, and reputation are all about, and what they can do for a business. Skeptics should understand that an inappropriate identity can be as damaging to a firm as poor financial performance. Individuals are seeking trust and transparency, and if perceptions about a company fail to mesh with reality, constituents will take their money elsewhere.

What are Identity, Brand, Image, and Reputation?

A company's *identity* is the actual manifestation of the company's reality as conveyed through the organization's name, logo, motto, products, services, building, stationery, uniforms, and all other tangible pieces of evidence created by the organization and communicated to a variety of constituencies. Constituencies then form perceptions based on the messages that companies send in these tangible forms. If the images accurately reflect an organization's reality, the identity program is a success. If the perceptions differ dramatically from the reality, then either the strategy is ineffective, or the corporation's understanding of itself needs to be modified.

Because identity is the only part of reputation management that an organization can actually create and control, it is critical that it is strategically shaped. One of the key factors that contributes to a successful corporate identity is a careful *brand*: a name or logo that differentiates the goods and services of one seller from those of its competitors. Branding is much more complex and nuanced than a swoosh or a pair of golden arches, however. A brand can provoke an emotional reaction from the consumer; a brand is a promise that sets an expectation of an experience. As marketing expert Kevin Keller explains, "the power of a brand lies in the minds of consumers."[15] A company's value can be considerately influenced by the success of its corporate branding strategy. Coca-Cola, for instance, has a value that far exceeds its total tangible assets because of its strong brand name.

An organization's *image* is a function of how constituencies perceive the organization, based on all the messages it sends out through names, logo, and self-presentation. It is the organization as seen from the viewpoint of its constituencies. But image is in the eye of the beholder: depending on the vantage point of a particular constituency, a company can have many different images. For example, employees will perceive their company's image differently than customers. Even customers who have never interacted with a product will have preconceived notions (just because you've never eaten a McDonald's hamburger doesn't mean you don't have certain perceptions about the company and the product). Large, diversified companies may also struggle to define their images. What is the image for a company as large as Tata, or one as diverse as General Electric?

Reputation is the sum of *all* of an organization's constituencies' perceptions. It differs from image in that it is built gradually, and is therefore not simply a perception in any moment of time. It differs from identity because it is a product of both internal and external constituencies, whereas identity is constructed by the company itself. A strong reputation has important strategic implications for a company, as we shall see.

Why Reputation Matters

The importance of reputation is evidenced by several prominent surveys and rankings that seek to identify the best and worst among them: *Fortune*'s "Most Admired" list, *BusinessWeek* and Interbrand's "Best Global Brands" ranking, and the Reputation Institute's Global RepTrak Pulse studies. These highly publicized rankings are evidence of what many business leaders already know: that companies with strong reputations have financial and competitive advantages and experience greater stability.

Reputation is a source of tangible economic value. According to the 2008 Hill and Knowlton Corporate Reputation Watch, more than 90% of analysts agree that if a company fails to look after the reputational aspects of its performance, it will ultimately suffer financially.[16] Reputation does indeed correlate with higher market valuation and stock price, and with less stock price volatility. A comprehensive study by the Munich-based Market-Based Management Institute compared the reputation and stock-market performance

"Confidence is what you have before you understand the problem." Woody Allen

  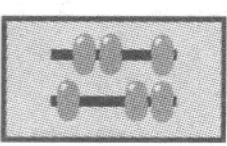   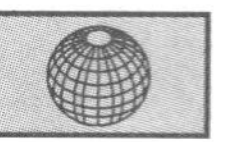   

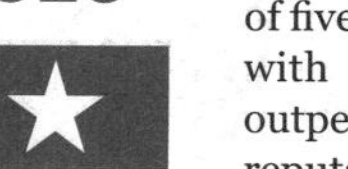

of 60 blue-chip companies over the course of five years. The 25% (Top25) of companies with the best reputations considerably outperformed the companies with poorer reputations and, compared to price movements on the DAX 30 in general, the Top25 returned greater yield with lower risk.[17]

The less tangible entities of a strong reputation can also result in competitive advantage. Companies with strong reputations attract and retain the best talent, as well as loyal customers and business partners, all of which contribute positively to growth and success. Reputation "calls attention to a company's attractive features and widens the options available to its managers; for instance, whether to charge higher or lower prices for products and services, or to implement innovative programs."[18] Companies whose corporate communications promote sincerity and accuracy have greater operating leverage and the power to buck negative trends in the economy and in their respective industries. Being able to weather a corporate crisis is a particularly valuable position in an age of skepticism and mistrust, where information travels at lightning speed.

Against the backdrop of the current business environment, organizations are increasingly appreciating the financial and competitive advantages of a strong reputation. How does an organization know where it stands? How does it build trust? Since reputation is formed by the perceptions of all of their constituencies, companies must first uncover what those perceptions are and then choose their reputation strategy accordingly.

Measuring and Managing Reputation

You can't manage what you don't measure. This adage rings especially true when looking at corporate reputation. In assessing its reputation, an organization must examine the perceptions of *all* of its constituencies. Only when perceptions and identity are in alignment will a strong reputation result.

Many consulting firms, like the Reputation Institute (RI), have developed diagnostics for helping companies conduct this research. Nearly all of these tools require constituency research. The RI's RepTrak Alignment Monitor, for example, conducts extensive internal analysis of employee alignment. Such tools exist because companies run into trouble when they do not practice the values that they promote internally. Walmart is perhaps one of the best examples of a company that has frequently been entangled in contradictions between the values it espouses and its employees' perceptions. The company, which defines its three basic beliefs and values to be respect for the individual, service to its customers, and striving for excellence,[19] has been embroiled in a constant stream of lawsuits, including what would have been the largest employment discrimination class action in US history. However, Walmart has made significant attempts to close the gap that exists between its identity and image in other areas of its business, as we shall later discuss.

Customer perceptions of an organization must also align with identity, vision, and values. On Valentine's Day, 2007, JetBlue learned not only what can happen when this is *not* the case, but also how reputation can be restored by taking bold steps. Since it was founded, in 1999, JetBlue had prided itself on an almost cult-like following amongst its loyal customers. But on February 14, 2007, the airline faced a reputational crisis that put customer loyalty to the test: during a particularly nasty nor'easter, the airline had an operational meltdown that resulted from a combination of bad luck, flawed decision-making, and multiple systematic failures. The airline canceled more than 1,000 flights, incurring millions of dollars in losses and tarnishing its sterling reputation among customers who were stranded at its hub, JFK Airport. Yet, after a publicity nightmare and an enquiry from Congress, CEO and founder David Neeleman was inspired to search for inventive solutions to win back his constituents' loyalty. Some of those solutions, like the industry's first ever customer bill of rights, were groundbreaking, and helped JetBlue to regain, if not exceed, its reputational standing in the eyes of its customers.[20]

The Impact of Corporate Social Responsibility on Reputation

Today, reputational risk transcends simply staying out of trouble; rather, stakeholders are far more proactive in seeking out information about companies, and corporate social responsibility (CSR) now plays a larger role in forming these groups' perceptions. Study after study demonstrates that "good corporate citizenship" directly correlates with the strength of a company's reputation and its bottom line.

Consumers are increasingly preoccupied with the values and reputations of the companies with which they interact: the 2010 Cone Cause Evolution Study, for example, reveals that 83% of Americans want more of the products, services, and retailers they use to support causes. 85% of consumers have a more positive image of a product or company when it supports a cause they care about, and 90% of consumers want companies to communicate to them the ways in which they are supporting causes.[21] Strategically directed CSR programs can be key vehicles for the creation of competitive advantage.

When a company understands what each of its constituencies is concerned about, what matters to them, and what they already think about the company, it is well positioned to structure the right kinds of CSR programs. Walmart is an example of a company that has made significant progress in enhancing its corporate reputation by focusing its CSR efforts on one of the key issues which its constituents have most publicly been concerned about—environmental sustainability. In 2005, Walmart hired a sustainability and energy think-tank to conduct an efficiency overhaul and audit, and then outlined three clear environmental goals: to be supplied entirely by renewable energy, to create zero waste, and to sell products that sustain resources and the environment. The implementation of the plan cost Walmart more than US$500 million, but by talking the talk in its logistics, operations, and sales practices, the retailer has hugely enhanced its perceived environmental impact. In the 2010 *Newsweek* Green Rankings, a ranking of the top 100 global companies based on their environmental impact, green policies and performance, and reputation, Walmart ranked 39th, up from 59th the year before.[22]

To summarize, CSR programs can greatly contribute to a company's reputational capital and provide a distinct competitive advantage in an environment where constituencies increasingly expect responsible and accountable behavior, along with profit. To respond to this demand, executives must manage and measure stakeholders' perceptions, and implement new and creative ways to position themselves.

REPUTATION MANAGEMENT IN A SOCIAL MEDIA WORLD

Thus far, we have examined the modern business environment in the context of the profound changes that have redefined the way companies interact with their stakeholders, especially in terms of the two-way conversations facilitated by digital communications platforms. Using examples set by industry leaders, we will now look at strategies and tactics that exploit these platforms and allow companies to regain the control ceded to stakeholders. Those that have embraced social media have successfully adapted to the new environment. Just as digital platforms spawn reputational crises, so too can they solve them.

From Monolog to Dialog

As digital communications have evolved, stakeholders have gained enormous influence in shaping corporate messaging. Whereas corporate communications professionals formerly fed their messaging to stakeholders in a one-way conversation, they now find themselves at the mercy of the people they once controlled, and their organizations' reputations hang in the balance. Those companies that not only embrace this two-way dialog but also recognize that it serves as a source for ideas, opinions, and competitive intelligence will be best positioned.

Dell is an excellent example of a company that has embraced social media as a means of enhancing conversations with the stakeholders it cares most about. Dell learned early on to embrace rather than ignore. Back in 2005, the computer manufacturer's reputation was thrown for a loop when an irate blogger named Jeff Jarvis lambasted the company for poor customer service ("Dell Hell," he called it). Within hours, hordes of customers who were in agreement with Jarvis's claims posted comments on his blog and their own, creating a maelstrom of negative publicity. The company struggled for months as a result of failing to address the criticism, but in July 2006 it launched its own blog, where executives could fat last join the conversation. The blog allowed customers to comment freely on this and later crises, and in February 2007 Michael Dell launched IdeaStorm, a permanent forum in which customers could give the company advice. Metrics showed that the company's customer-service rating rose significantly immediately afterwards.[23] In fact, Dell's communications team estimates that since Dell began using social media, negative comments about the company have gone down by 30%.[24]

Focus on Structure

Dell executives recognized that, in order to remain competitive, they needed to rethink the way they positioned themselves internally to have a positive impact externally. By 2009, IdeaStorm employed a chief blogger and a team of 42 people who worked hand in hand with the broader corporate communications function. Dell evolved its organizational structure to meet changing stakeholder demands, integrating an entirely new division within its communications function and giving it visibility within the company.

This is a critical lesson: at world-class companies, digital communications has morphed from a backroom tactical department to a strategic liaison between an organization and its many stakeholder groups. HP, as well, employed a digital communications team to facilitate conversations between its constituents during a period of incredible change, its 2002 merger with Compaq. Recognizing the challenges behind aligning different cultures and information management systems, HP executives developed @HP, a business-to-employee portal that acted as a gateway to the merging HP and Compaq intranets. The platform served as the infrastructure to communicate messages to all 88,000 plus employees around the globe, and ensured that the right messages were delivered to the right internal audiences. The intranet embodied the new corporate culture.

Focus on Values

As mentioned earlier, the level of concern about corporate responsibility and trust has increased dramatically in recent years, and has been amplified by the ability of digital platforms to democratize access to information. Stakeholders are increasingly demanding value for their money when purchasing goods and services, and are also expecting to see a strong set of values in the companies with which they do business. Once again, companies, like Walmart, that embrace digital tools to engage individual stakeholder groups in the context of their corporate responsibility efforts will prosper over those that run away.

CEO Howard Schultz of Starbucks incorporated an innovative crowdsourcing strategy into his plan to transform the coffee retailer, following years of overexpansion and sliding stock prices. Schultz's challenge was to "rekindle an emotional attachment with customers," and in 2009, the brand created www.mystarbucksidea.com, a forum where customers could literally submit ideas on how to make the brand better. The ideas were categorized, and users could then vote on which they thought should be implemented. Schultz also invested heavily in Starbucks' "shared planet" campaign, which marketed the company's dedication to being "bigger than coffee." Whether these crowdsourcing and CSR initiatives can be directly related to a bump in stock price is difficult to prove, but Starbuck's popularity, at least, has grown in the three years since these programs were implemented: in 2010, Starbucks reported record fiscal revenue of US$10.7 billion.[25,26]

Communicate Online Or Others Will Do It For You

In today's environment, you don't have to search too hard to find stories of corporate giants felled by lone bloggers, or more intimate disasters of celebrities and politicians whose online behavior led to their public demise. The lesson seems to be: tell your story online or have it told for you. In the age of social media, no amount of avoidance can keep crises at bay. The access to information online is staggering, and succumbing to the temptation of sweeping dirty secrets under the rug may come back to haunt an organization's reputation.

During a crisis, the best approach is to provide stakeholders with facts directly on the company's own domain, whether a corporate website, blog, or official Twitter account. Taco Bell's "real beef" campaign is a recent example of how a company can preempt a reputational disaster by acknowledging the truth and then communicating it online. When a lawsuit was announced charging that Taco Bell's taco filling was not 100% real beef, the company realized that the allegations would spread like wildfire online, and it mounted an immediate and aggressive campaign to address the claims. The corporate website had a link on the homepage to a newly created "About our seasoned beef" page with interactive videos, press releases, and statements, and a link to its signature taco meat recipe, which boldly acknowledged the additives in its taco filling. Taco Bell President Greg Creed posted videos on YouTube and messages on Facebook. He then began an online and print advertising campaign, announcing: "Thank you for suing us. Here's the truth about our seasoned beef." Under the gathering storm of public interest, the lawsuit was dropped.[27]

MAKING IT HAPPEN

- Today's manager has to grow and protect value in an extraordinary global economic environment. To do this, reputation must be proactively measured and managed.
- Don't forget that corporate reputations are determined by how well a corporate brand is crafted and conveyed to the public; brand, image and identity are all critical components of shaping your organization's reputation.
- Embracing social media can help today's leaders develop new ways to communicate and engage with key constituents. If you don't communicate online, someone else will do it for you. Be proactive. Fortune favors the bold.

"Entrepreneurs must love what they do to such a degree that doing it is worth sacrifice and, at times, pain. But doing anything else, we think, would be unimaginable." Howard Schultz

Opportunity to Reposition and Redevelop

Just as many reputational crises spawn from digital platforms, so too can they be managed when the Web is used effectively to regain control. As best-in-class companies demonstrate, harnessing social media actually strengthens relationships and communication. Corporate blogs, for example, open the lines of communication between company leaders and their stakeholders, as we have seen with the examples of Dell and Starbucks. The CEO blog, in particular, is a trend that allows executives to communicate directly with their customers. Twitter is yet another tool that connects brands with their consumers, which can be especially effective during emergencies. Delta Airlines, for instance, learned a thing or two from competitors like JetBlue, and now has a dedicated customer service team that rebooks stranded passengers during storms and other operational crises through Twitter.[28]

When companies empower communities with collaborative skills and tools, they have an enormous opportunity. Facilitating, instead of closing, dialogs with key constituents allows organizations to address emerging problems early. During the 2008–09 recession, Ford Motor Company took advantage of its website and social media platforms to launch live conversations among suppliers, dealers, and customers. These were designed to bring Ford's bright performance—bright compared with the looming bankruptcies and bailouts involving rivals GM and Chrysler—to everyone's attention.

Ford recognized that monitoring influential digital channels, embracing transparency, identifying affected audiences, and customizing communications for each are all critical strategies for survival in what is a new and revolutionary environment.

CONCLUSION

In the complex modern business environment, organizations' reputations are vulnerable to an increasingly skeptical public and the immeasurable unknowns brought to bear by digital communications platforms. Crises that affect companies today are born of things that didn't exist 10 or even five years ago: a Congressman's misguided photo on Twitter, a British spy identified by his wife on Facebook, or Time Warner kowtowing to a lone blogger. These are unimaginable circumstances for the business environment of years ago, when information was fed to constituencies in one-way monologs.

The two-way dialog benefits both ends of the conversation, and best-in-class companies have already moved from adoption to anticipation. Brands are starting to catch up with their consumers, and they are increasingly trying to become proactive about understanding how consumers spend time online and where they're going next. Companies have also been establishing sophisticated guidelines and protocols for internal social media usage, and many institutions, like Wall Street investment banks, are starting to allow their employees to set up social media accounts specifically to communicate with clients. Over time, the best companies will learn to have better conversations with their constituents through social media engagement. The net result will be trust, loyalty, and more business.

MORE INFO

Books:

Argenti, Paul A., and Courtney M. Barnes. *Digital Strategies for Powerful Corporate Communications*. New York: McGraw-Hill, 2009.

Keller, Kevin. *Strategic Brand Management*. 3rd ed. Upper Saddle River, NJ: Prentice Hall, 2008.

Aaker, David A. *Building Strong Brands*. New York: Free Press, 1996.

Article:

Argenti, Paul A., James Lytton-Hitchens, and Richard Verity. "The good, the bad and the trustworthy." *Strategy + Business* (November 23, 2010). Online at: www.strategy-business.com/article/10401?gko=4adb7

Website:

2011 Edelman Trust Barometer: www.edelman.com/trust/2011/

See Also:

★ Digital Reputation Management (pp. 821–825)

NOTES

1 Adams, Richard. "Anthony Weiner photo scandal—As it happened." *Guardian* (June 6, 2011). Online at: tinyurl.com/5spkys3

2 2011 Edelman Trust Barometer: www.edelman.com/trust/2011/

3 Internet World Stats: Usage and Population Statistics: www.internetworldstats.com/stats.htm

4 Bernoff, Josh. "Introducing peer influence analysis: 500 billion peer impressions per year." Forrester blog (April 20, 2010). Online at: tinyurl.com/y3ko8of

5 Vickers, Marcia, Mike McNamee, Peter Coy, David Henry, *et al*. "The betrayed investor." *BusinessWeek* (February 25, 2002): 105. Online at: tinyurl.com/44o2t93

6 Morgenson, Gretchen. "After huge losses, a move to reclaim executives' pay." *New York Times* (February 21, 2009). Online at: www.nytimes.com/2009/02/22/business/22pay.html

7 Rappaport, Liz, Aaron Luchetti, Stephen Grocer. "Wall Street pay: A record $144 billion." *Wall Street Journal* (October 11, 2010). Online at: tinyurl.com/2cowbqu

8 National Investor Relations Institute. "NIRI activist investor survey—Engage for success." August 27, 2007.

9 Levingston, Steven. "Icahn, Time Warner end fight." *Washington Post* (February 18, 2006): D1. Online at: tinyurl.com/ybnb24

10 Wikipedia on Carl Icahn: en.wikipedia.org/wiki/Carl_Icahn

11 McLuhan, Marshall, and Bruce R. Powers. *The Global Village: Transformations in World Life and Media in the 21st Century*. New York: Oxford University Press, 1989.

12 International Telecommunication Union Statistics: www.itu.int/ITU-D/ict/statistics/

13 Technorati: technorati.com

14 Hilbert, Martin, and Priscila Lopez. "The world's technological capacity to store, communicate, and compute information." *Science* 332:6025 (April 1, 2011): 60–65. Online at: dx.doi.org/10.1126/science.1200970

15 Keller, Kevin Lane. *Strategic Brand Management*. 3rd ed. Upper Saddle River, NJ: Prentice-Hall, 2008.

16 Hill and Knowlton. "Reputation and the war for talent: Corporate reputation watch 2008." Online at: www2.hillandknowlton.com/crw/

17 "How a good name influences performance on the stock market." July 4, 2011. Online at: www.ketchum.com/Reputation_Capital

18 Aaker, David A. *Building Strong Brands*. New York: Free Press, 1996; p. 51.

19 Walmart's 3 basic beliefs and values: walmartstores.com/aboutus/321.aspx

20 Lee, Jennifer 8. "JetBlue flight snarls continue." *New York Times* (February 16, 2007): 7. Online at: www.nytimes.com/2007/02/16/nyregion/16airport.html

21 Cone. "2010 cause evolution study." Online at: www.coneinc.com/news/request.php?id=3350

22 Newsweek Green Rankings 2010: tinyurl.com/3ovelmo

23 Customer Engagement Strategies. "Dell social media snapshot." Online at: tinyurl.com/3ryadvm

24 Odden, Lee. "Dell social media interview with Richard Binhammer." *TopRank* (December 2008). Online at: tinyurl.com/5lkn2g

25 Adamy, Janet. "At Starbucks, a tall order for new cuts, store closures." *Wall Street Journal* (January 29, 2009). Online at: online.wsj.com/article/SB123317714771825681.html

26 Miller, Claire Cain. "A changed Starbucks. A changed CEO." *New York Times* (March 12, 2011). Online at: www.nytimes.com/2011/03/13/business/13coffee.html

27 Jones, Ashby. "'A calculated risk': Taco Bell presses the '88 percent real' campaign." *Wall Street Journal*blog (February 28, 2011). Online at: tinyurl.com/67248b5

28 Eckhouse, John. "How Delta used Twitter to help passengers during a storm." *The Realtime Report* (January 26, 2011). Online at: tinyurl.com/67ynzwk

"The pleasure we found in working together made us exceptionally patient; it is much easier to strive for perfection when you are never bored." Daniel Kahneman

  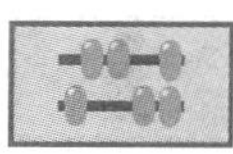      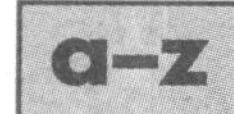

Electronic Invoicing in the European Union

by Hansjörg Nymphius

EXECUTIVE SUMMARY

This article examines the following issues:

- The EU Expert Group on e-invoicing and the European framework.
- The goals—more effective value chains and streamlined information flows.
- The current state of e-invoicing.
- EDI as a precursor to e-invoicing.
- Growth in the supplier market.
- Issues with current models of e-invoicing.

INTRODUCTION

Europe is entering a crucial stage in the development of electronic invoicing. The European Commission (EC) has made the development of e-invoicing an objective in both the 2002 and the 2005 eEurope Action Plans.[1]

The invoice, just to summarize, consists of an itemized account of goods shipped, services performed or work done, an amount expended or owed, and a demand for payment. It may contain a range of other administrative or logistics information, and usually will state applicable taxes payable. It is the crucial link, or perhaps the pivot, between the physical and financial supply chains and, accordingly, has been described as the "queen" of commercial documents. It is important to note that in traditional invoicing all these features are derived from a single paper document, often with the word "invoice" on it.[2]

Two years ago the EC formed an Expert Group on e-invoicing with the aim of establishing a Europe-wide framework that allows for the standardized exchange of e-invoices by all market participants, particularly those involved in purchase and supply. Studies indicate that implementing electronic invoicing on a Europe-wide basis could reduce supply-chain costs by €243 billion, by streamlining business processes and driving innovation.

The Expert Group initiative emerged from the EC's "Broad-Based Innovation Strategy," launched in September 2006, which recognized that "Europe cannot compete unless it becomes more inventive, reacts better to consumer needs and preferences, and innovates more." This in turn goes back to the Lisbon Treaty, which aims to enhance the efficiency of Europe through installing innovation at all levels and by implementing modern democratic institutions. "E-government, or the ready availability of government services over the internet, including online payment and online invoicing—which equates to e-invoicing—is seen as a natural part of this progression. The Lisbon Treaty aims to make Europe the most competitive and dynamic knowledge-based economy in the world by 2010."

In recognizing and reacting to the competitive challenge facing Europe, two aspects emerge as the basis for improving European competitiveness in a global economy: Efficiency and certainty. More efficient value chains reduce cost; improving the certainty of the environment in which they operate makes them more competitive.

Streamlining the flow of information in any value chain will reduce inefficiencies, improve certainty, and reduce costs. As Europe moves to adopt the Single Euro Payments Area (SEPA), it is logical that this is linked to the business processes that settle a vast majority of business-to-business (B2B) and business-to-government payments. SEPA is expected to contribute significantly to the Lisbon agenda.

Electronic invoicing involves the replacement of manual paper-based routines with new integrated systems and processes. Expected benefits include the creation of integrated supply chains which are more cost-effective, less error-prone, faster, and simpler to manage. Other benefits include improved customer care (typically, as the joint EBA/Innopay report, "E-invoicing 2008," points out, nearly half of customer queries relate to invoicing) as well as improved risk management. Cross-selling and up-selling opportunities can also enabled through electronic invoicing, the report notes.

The outlook for these developments is promising despite obvious barriers to initial adoption. The European Banking Association (EBA), as a force for collaboration in the European payments industry over many years, is strongly committed to working with all stakeholders to identify practical solutions and to working closely within the European Electronic Invoicing Framework (EEIF) as it develops.

Today e-invoicing in Europe across all organizations, from government to the private sector, has a relatively low penetration, just as in North America and the Asia–Pacific region. There were some 28 billion invoices (paper and electronic) in 2006 in Europe. Approximately 50% of these invoices were B2B and the remaining 50% were business-to-consumer (B2C). However, the growth in e-invoicing is rapid, as would be expected from a low base, and annual rates of growth of 60%–100% are mentioned, with some markets growing at an even faster rate. So far the various country-specific e-invoicing initiatives amount to between 2% and 3% of the total invoices issued, with the total number of e-invoices issued in Europe being around 490 million in 2006 and, when the statistics have been finalized, are expected to be around 710 million for 2007. The leaders are the Nordic countries and Switzerland, with adoption rates of around 10% in B2B invoicing. The Swedish government, for example, decided that all government agencies had to be capable of handling invoices electronically by July 2008, a move that is expected to generate savings of around €400 million over the next five years.

EDI AS A PRECURSOR TO E-INVOICING

Electronic data interchange (EDI) was a precursor to e-invoicing. EDI is a standard for the dematerialization of trade-related documents between trading partners, and invoices are a part of this standardization effort. However, in some countries, even an EDI electronic invoice requires a paper summary to meet national legislation requirements. So far, EDI adoption around the world has largely happened with large companies with well-defined supply chains.

There are a number of studies which show that it costs between four and 70 euros to process a paper invoice, with cross-border invoicing being the most expensive. This estimate includes the cost of handling and receiving the invoice, matching against orders and deliveries, and approving payment. Accounts payable automation can significantly reduce the cost of handling these inbound invoices. There have also been successful total invoice management

"Targets make organisations stupid. Because they are a simplistic response to a complex issue, they have unintended and unwelcome consequences … so every target generates others to counter the perverse effects of the first one."
Simon Caulkin

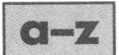

initiatives, with suppliers becoming outsource providers of both accounts payable and accounts receivable functions. Scanning, optical character recognition, and data mapping techniques support the dematerialization of paper documentation across parties.

Online banking is a major driver for the adoption of e-invoicing around the world. Countries with high rates of online banking adoption also show high e-invoicing adoption rates. Large companies have adopted EDI. However, online banking has appealed strongly to medium-sized firms, who often use their bank's e-invoicing offerings to pay clients.

We are also witnessing many government initiatives to promote e-invoicing. The European Commission website, ec.europa.eu, lists a number of examples, including an interesting one in Slovenia which has the potential to involve neighboring countries.

The business of service providers in the e-invoicing market is to add value to invoice senders and/or invoice receivers. Such value-added services can be categorized from exchange and conversion services (mainly focused on creation of an exchange network) to complete sourcing of accounts payable or accounts receivable management services. In Europe, there are a large number of service providers and service solutions with a huge variety of product features and business models. This, in part, is a reflection of the variety of countries, languages, commercial practices, service concepts, legal environments, and implementations of relevant EU directives. Many of the generic models are similar to practices carried out in North America and elsewhere.

GROWTH IN THE E-INVOICING SUPPLIER MARKET

The overall number of service providers involved in the e-invoicing market has grown from 160 in 2006 to 260 in 2007. Some commentators suggest a continued growth in the number of service providers, whilst others are expecting a major consolidation. Critical mass for an e-invoicing service provider is believed to be around 1.5 million invoices per year. The e-invoicing sector is worth around €1 billion per year.[3]

A number of banks have entered the market, competing directly to offer a bundle of supply chain services, typically to large corporations. There are collective schemes with a community of banks cooperating to provide a service based on a common set of rules, standards, and agreed terminology.

A key functionality to these service models and providers is the ability to exchange electronic documents between a sender and a receiver. There are four models for this exchange:

1 **Bilateral model**: Buyers and sellers in a one-to-one relationship.
2 **Three-party model**: Senders and receivers are connected to a single central hub. This model's limitation is that senders and receivers can only reach other senders or receivers attached to that hub. So one sender committed to e-invoicing might have to become a member of multiple hubs. To solve this "limited reach" problem in the three-party model, the concept of "roaming" has been introduced.
3 **Roaming Model**: Emerging model which looks to a "hub of hubs," or a network of hub-to-hub connections to provide real cross-border reach.
4 **Four-party model**: Senders and receivers of invoices are supported by their own consolidator service provider (for the sender) and aggregator service provider (for the receiver). A network usually based on open standards provides connectivity and the facilities for the secure, trusted exchange of invoices and/or other business documents. In the four-party model, the consolidator and aggregator roles are often two different service providers.

BARRIERS TO E-INVOICING

As the EEI Expert Group's interim report on e-invoicing points out, while the current legislative environment across Europe has a foundation that underpins the integrity and authenticity of an e-invoice, and that will serve for a Europe-wide e-invoicing solution, there are legislative hurdles. E-invoicing lies at the crossroads of several areas of legislation, including VAT, accounting, payment, authentication, company transparency, and data retention. There are complexities for both supplier and buyer, and for service providers.

Securing European compliance for an e-invoicing solution is complicated. VAT issues will require unanimity from member states, and requirements on archiving and other processes will also take time to resolve.

The operational barriers to e-invoicing largely depend on trust and technical interoperability issues. In some respects, e-invoicing suffers from the fact that some believe that it will progress more easily once we have a universally open, fully secure, and interoperable internet-based B2B network across Europe. In reality, this is likely to be challenging and a pragmatic approach may yield better and faster results, based on emerging "best practice" models.

The EU informal Task Force report noted that standardization of e-invoices is currently fragmented, with many specifications in use both in the EU and abroad. Further standardization work is required. There is a strong school of thought that recommends that any solution should be global, not simply an EU solution. Steps are being taken to get the major international standards-setting bodies, such as the UN's CEFACT and the ISO's Technical Committee on Financial Services, to work together for the development and delivery of an international e-invoicing standard.

Others argue that the absence of a global standard is not as big an inhibitor as many believe. The history of XML has shown that it is possible for standards to be communicated and managed through a variety of technical means, including translation services working on an "any format in, any format out" basis.

Overall, most view the absence of a uniform global standard for e-invoicing as not being a "showstopper." However, any improvements in this direction will certainly help market development in the long run.

ISSUES WITH BUSINESS AND COOPERATION MODELS

End-users and businesses tend to be reluctant to choose a particular model or solution, because often that model only addresses one subset of their requirements and solves only one particular issue. Many experts feel that the current industrial structure has too many players, excessive market fragmentation, and a lack of interoperability. The current collaboration model between the various stakeholders is felt to be inadequate, and there is evidence of a degree of contention/defensiveness for market positions. More clarity is needed on an agreed definition of the cooperative versus competitive space. The prize in terms of market expansion from the creation of a platform for appropriate and targeted collaboration, for example in the area of interoperability, could be very large indeed.

MORE INFO

Reports:

de Boer, Tonnis, *et al*. "E-invoicing 2008: European market description and analysis." Euro Banking Association/Innopay, February 2008. Online at: www.abe-eba.eu/Repository.aspx?ID=54942e07-ad65-4dc4-920e-09c7cce51497

Koch, Bruno. "E-invoicing and EBPP: European market overview." Billentis, February 2009. Online at: www.billentis.com/ebilling_e-invoicing_European_Market_Overview_2009.pdf

See Also:

★ Cash Flow Best Practice for Small and Medium-Sized Enterprises (pp. 28–29)
★ Payment Factories: How to Streamline Financial Flows (pp. 85–86)
★ The Payment Services Directive: A Crucial Step Toward Payment Harmonization Across the EU (pp. 229–231)
✔ Building an Efficient Credit and Collection Accounts System (p. 1148)
✔ Building an Electronic Invoicing System (p. 1149)
✔ Efficient Invoicing Procedures (p. 1158)
✔ The EU Regulatory Regime (p. 1029)

NOTES

1 eEurope 2005: An Information Society for All: ec.europa.eu/information_society/eeurope/2005/index_en.htm

2 de Boer, Tonnis, *et al*. (2008).

3 Figures cited from a speech by Bruno Koch, a recognised authority on e-invoicing; see www.billentis.com

"If you don't do it excellently, don't do it at all. Because if it's not excellent, it won't be profitable or fun, and if you're not in business for fun or profit, what the hell are you doing there?" Robert Townsend

Employee Stock Options by Peter Casson

EXECUTIVE SUMMARY

- Employee stock options are call options on the employer company's common stock, and are usually not transferable.
- Most employee stock options have a vesting period, during which the holder is not unconditionally entitled to the option, with options vesting at the end of the period if performance conditions are met.
- Employee stock options may be used by companies to recruit, retain, and provide incentives to employees and executives. Companies with weak cash flows that cannot afford to pay employees the market rate entirely in cash may use stock options in lieu of cash.
- Companies may use employee stock options to capture tax or accounting benefits associated with them.

INTRODUCTION

Employee stock options are a component of the compensation package of many employees and executives. As well as providing a mechanism for linking pay with the performance of the company's stock price, stock options can facilitate the recruitment and retention of employees. The effectiveness of stock option compensation derives from the basic characteristics of options and from particular features found in many employee stock options. This article describes the essential features of employee stock options and explores the ways in which they are used by companies.

CHARACTERISTICS OF EMPLOYEE STOCK OPTIONS

Employee stock options are call options granted by an employer on the company's common stock. Call options are contracts that give holders the right, but not the obligation, to acquire stock at a specified price (the exercise price), either on a specified date or over a specified period. The fair value of a call option has two components. The first, known as intrinsic value, is the amount that the holder would receive were the option to be exercised today. This amount, which cannot be negative, is the greater of zero and the difference between the fair value of the underlying stock and the exercise price of the option. The second, known as time value, is the difference between the fair value and the intrinsic value of the option.

The fair value of a call option on a company's common stock is sensitive to changes in:

- The fair value of the underlying stock—the value of the option rises with increases in the fair value of the stock.
- The expected volatility of the returns on the underlying stock—the value of the option increases with increases in expected volatility.
- The risk-free rate of interest—the value of the option increases with increases in the risk-free rate.
- The time until the option expires—the value of the option decreases as time to expiry decreases.
- The dividends expected to be paid on the underlying stock over the life of the option—the value of the option decreases with increases in the expected dividend payments.

Stock options granted to employees usually have an exercise price equal to the fair value of the underlying stock on the date the option is granted, and have a life of seven to ten years. Stock options generally have additional features that affect their fair value. First, there is usually an initial period, often three years, after the grant of the option (the vesting period), during which the employee is not unconditionally entitled to the option. Rather, the employee's entitlement to the option at the end of the vesting period only comes about if performance conditions are met. The performance condition for employees is usually to remain in the employment of the grantor company during the vesting period. Options, especially those granted to senior executives, may have additional performance conditions relating to company and/or personal performance. Second, once vested, options are usually forfeited if the employee leaves the grantor company. However, it is usual for employees to be able to exercise options within a period, often 90 days, after leaving the company. The forfeiture provision normally means that employees are forced into an early exercise of in-the-money options. Third, employee stock options are usually nontransferable, which means the employees can only realize value by exercising the option and selling the stock. In so doing, they forego the time value of the option.

WHY COMPANIES USE EMPLOYEE SHARE OPTIONS

Companies grant stock options to attract, retain, and motivate employees and executives. In addition, start-up companies and companies with weak cash flows may grant stock options to compensate for the below-market cash wages that they can afford. Finally, options may be granted to capture taxation and/or accounting benefits.

Stock options attract employees and executives for the following reasons. First, individuals whose abilities match the needs of the company may be attracted by stock options because they believe that their abilities will improve company performance and that this will be reflected in an enhanced stock price. Second, the offer of stock options may attract those employees who are most optimistic about the company's future prospects. Their optimism may lead them to overvalue the options, so reducing the company's overall employment costs. Finally, stock options may attract relatively less risk-averse employees who meet the needs of the company.

Employee stock options can be used as a way to increase employee retention. The vesting conditions usually found in the options encourage employees to remain with the company until the options become exercisable. In addition, employees will forego the time value of vested options if they are forced into early exercise by leaving the company. Finally, as employees build up a portfolio of options over time, it becomes more costly for a competitor to attract the company's employees, as the competitor may have to compensate them for the value foregone from forfeiting unvested options or from suboptimally exercising options.

Holders of employee stock options have an incentive to act in a way that increases the value of the options. The fair value of employee stock options is, as described above, sensitive to the company's stock price, the expected volatility of the stock, and the dividends expected to be paid on the stock during the life of the options. Employees may act, through enhanced performance, to increase company performance, and that in turn may be reflected in the stock price. Although grants of stock options to CEOs and senior executives may be effective in increasing company performance, the incentive effects of grants to other employees are questionable, as there are significant free-rider problems. The other incentive effects are confined to options held by senior executives, especially CEOs. Senior executives holding stock options may make riskier

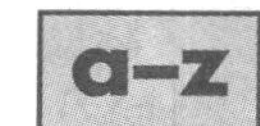

investment decisions and/or increase the company's leverage with a view to increasing the expected stock volatility. Stock options may also reduce the dividend on the company's stock.

Stock options may be used by start-up companies and companies experiencing cash constraints. Here employees may sacrifice part of their cash compensation in exchange for stock options. Although financial institutions are usually seen to be in a better position than employees to bear the risks associated with lending, employees may be willing to do so because: (1) options attract risk-seeking individuals, who, if the company fails, will move to another company; (2) they possess superior knowledge and so perceive the risk differently to financial institutions; or (3) they do not understand the risks.

Companies may use stock option compensation because of preferential tax policies, although this depends on the tax regime of the country in which the employee and the company are resident. Stock option compensation may, depending on the jurisdiction, be taxed at the time of grant, or at the time the option is exercised, or when the stock acquired on the exercise of the option is subsequently sold. Employees may be charged either to income tax or to capital gains tax on their stock option compensation. Finally, stock option compensation by the company may or may not be tax-deductible. A country's tax regime may offer favorable tax treatment to stock option schemes that have particular features. In such cases, the provisions of the tax regime may shape the option schemes that companies use.

Stock option compensation may also be used because of the way it is accounted for in company financial statements. The accounting treatment of stock options was seen in the past to be advantageous when stock options were recorded at their intrinsic value at the time of grant. As options are usually granted with an exercise price equal to the fair value of the stock on the date of grant, the intrinsic value of the option is zero. This meant that there was no charge against income. However, both international and US accounting standards now require companies to charge the fair value of stock options, as measured at the time of grant, against income.

CONCLUSION

The structure of employee stock options facilitates their use by companies to attract, retain, and motivate employees and executives. In particular, the vesting provisions provide incentives for employees to remain with the company. Employee stock options have a role in aligning employees' and executives' interests with those of stockholders. Performance conditions attached to the vesting of some stock options may also align the objectives of employees with those of the company. The structure of stock options may be shaped to take advantage of tax and/or accounting rules.

CASE STUDY

BG Group plc[1]

BG Group plc is a UK-listed company engaged in the discovery, extraction, transmission, distribution, and supply of natural gas. BG has about 5,000 employees, more than 60% of whom are located outside the United Kingdom. The company operates two stock option schemes, a company share option scheme (CSOS) and a sharesave scheme. The CSOS is open to UK and overseas employees above a certain grade. The number of CSOS options granted to individuals depends on their past performance and their expected contribution to the company. The CSOS scheme aims to "drive real earnings growth over the long term." Options granted under this scheme, which have an exercise price equal to the fair value of the company's shares at the time of grant, have a vesting period of three years, and vested options may be exercised at any time until the tenth anniversary of the grant. Options vest to the extent that there has been real growth in earnings per share (EPS) over the vesting period. All the options will vest if EPS growth over the vesting period is at least 30% more than growth in the retail prices index (excluding mortgage payments) (RPIX), and half the options will vest if EPS growth is at least 15% more than RPIX growth.

The sharesave scheme, which is approved by the UK tax authority, allows eligible employees to acquire shares in the company using the proceeds of a tax-exempt monthly savings plan. BG Group uses the scheme as a way of encouraging share ownership in the company.

MAKING IT HAPPEN

The decision to establish stock options schemes usually rests with the board of directors, and it may require stockholder approval. In designing a scheme it is necessary to consider:

- Why the company wants an employee stock option scheme.
- Which employees should be included within the scheme.
- The characteristics of the stock options. This includes consideration of the exercise price, the vesting period (if any), vesting conditions, the forfeiting of vested options if the employee leaves the company, and the life of the option.
- The tax and accounting implications of the scheme.

MORE INFO

Book:

Wheeler, Peter R. *Stock Options + Grants: The Executive's Guide to Equity Compensation*. Sunnyvale, CA: AdviserPress, 2004.

Article:

Hall, B. R. "Six challenges in designing equity-based pay." *Journal of Applied Corporate Finance* 15:3 (2003): 49–70.

Website:

National Center for Employee Ownership (NCEO): www.nceo.org

See Also:

★ Balancing Senior Management Compensation Arrangements with Shareholders' Interests (pp. 634–635)
★ Executive Rewards: Ensuring That Financial Rewards Match Performance (pp. 673–676)
✔ Assessing Business Performance (p. 1144)
✔ The Board's Role in Executive Compensation (p. 1108)
✔ Creating Executive Compensation (p. 1114)

NOTES

1 Information from BG Group plc Annual Report 2007.

Engaging Your Stakeholders: How To Make Allies of Investors and Activists by Peter Firestein

EXECUTIVE SUMMARY

- The cultures of corporate managers and investors are vastly different, requiring managers to learn the language of investors to derive fair value in financial markets.
- Systematic research by companies into the perceptions of investors is essential in converting market skeptics into supporters.
- Insularity is the enemy of good decision-making. The airing of diverse perspectives provides the best protection against a management's own excesses.
- The sustainability of an enterprise requires its alignment with the society in which it functions.
- A company's reputation depends on the narrative that it creates through its actions and its communications.
- A company's reputation depends ultimately on its values.

INTRODUCTION

No company exists without the consent of widely diverse groups of individuals and organizations. These range from customers to investors to social and civic groups—in fact, to the entire society that surrounds the corporation. It is a mistake—sometimes a fatal one—when any company takes the position that it is free to ignore those who have an interest in its financial health or the impact of its operations. But if the company chooses to take these relationships seriously and implements objective strategies to accommodate the interests of those who consider themselves part of its orbit, it maximizes the chance that it will survive crises and achieve long-term sustainability as a healthy and productive enterprise.

LIVING IN PEACE WITH THE ARBITERS OF VALUE: YOUR SHAREHOLDERS

The Yin–Yang of Companies and Capital Markets

There isn't a company anywhere that is free of dissonance with its shareholders and analysts. That's the nature of life in the equities markets. The market always wants more information, and the company wants the market to be satisfied with the information that it is comfortable giving. Although corporate managers and investors can hardly expect to agree on everything, the distance between them is unnecessary and costly to both.

No management of a public company, regardless of the strength of its financial performance, can consider itself successful without growth in the equity price. Many factors can conspire to prevent price and performance from matching up, including investors' macroeconomic expectations and their view of industry prospects.

But the real disconnect between company managements and equity investors lies in the two groups' wildly divergent cultures. You could say that managers are from Mars and investors from Venus. While both may be reasonable and rational, they often approach a single company with profoundly different ideas on how to create value from its assets.

CEOs often feel victimized by what they see as the refusal of investors and the financial media to accept their views of their own companies. After all, who knows the company better than those who run it? They often remark that the investors who feel so free to offer their criticism couldn't run a public company for one single day. And the investors would agree, but that's not the point. The differences between them are more profound.

Managers go to the office every day with highly evolved ideas about how to create value in the companies they lead. Their professional lives involve the development of strategy, the execution of business plans, allocation of capital, forecasting of product cycles, divining what the competition is up to, and engaging in dozens of other disciplines for which their boards, investors, and employees hold them responsible. Investors, on the other hand, operate in great part from objective valuation models. They can take a more or less mechanical view of the company's past financial performance and, having listened to management's plans and guidance, extrapolate the past into the future. They assess the company's announced strategy and try to read current management's ability to execute it. In many ways, the two groups speak a different language.

Complicating the issue is the absence of serious consideration of investor relations in business education. Despite the fact that investors' understanding of a company is one of the most important factors in determining its market value—and therefore the personal wealth of its managers—the investor relations enterprise has often been regarded as a side issue in the development of capital. "Value paradox" is the term I have coined to describe the weird dynamic by which a company's well-being is determined by investors who seldom come near the company, never sit in on its strategy sessions, and carry on only intermittent communication with those who do.

Giving Investors the Tools to Make Judgments

Investors care about few things more than a company's level of financial disclosure. Whether management breaks out its results by product, by specific geographic areas, by business unit, or by other categories is of crucial importance for at least two major reasons.

- First is the information itself. Investors must justify to their own managements and clients their decisions to buy or sell a stock. The level of confidence they have in their future ability to explain their actions—whether the stock price rises or falls—vastly affects their willingness to invest.
- The second reason a company's level of disclosure receives so much attention has to do with what that disclosure says about the seriousness with which management regards investors. Other factors being equal, investors will commit to a company whose management they believe will not only tell them the truth, but will also give them the best sense of the business. After all, the investor's ability to succeed in his or her profession depends on the ability to read the company, and you can't read a company whose management you can't trust. So, it is management's obligation not only to run the company well, but also to be believable. One of the most profound difficulties in this relationship lies in the fact that management can only demonstrate past performance, whereas investors only care about the future.

So, how do you turn your skeptics in the market into supporters?

You begin by making yourself predictable. The strongest rhetorical structure through which CEOs can speak to investors is one in which they show that a plan set forth a year ago (or two years or six months

  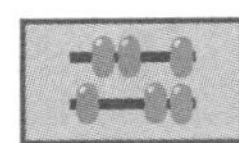      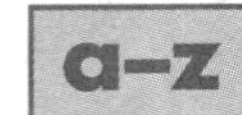

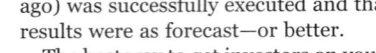

ago) was successfully executed and that the results were as forecast—or better.

The best way to get investors on your side is to educate them about the company. Make them experts. With all the technology available, and the sophistication of current valuation models, it is remarkable how well investors still respond to a manager's personal generosity in communicating about the company.

There is almost always a tug-of-war in management's mind about how much information to release. First of all, managers must consider that any information offered to investors may become available to the competition. You can't swear an investor to secrecy, so there is a powerful impulse to withhold information—sometimes to ridiculous degrees.

On the other hand, the availability of information about the company can be a powerful force in raising share value. Managements must consider how much the unnecessary restriction of information is costing them. They can go a long way toward resolving this dilemma by convening regularly to identify the information that must be ring-fenced for competitive reasons. Companies that are realistic about this understand that the criticality of specific information is always changing. Making these regular reassessments allows them to free up information that could contribute to investors' understanding of the business and therefore, potentially, to pay more for the shares.

Diversity of Perspectives as a Safety Net

Avoid the echo chamber. There is a structural trap into which many management teams fall in which they discuss the value proposition and strategies of the company only among themselves without the moderating benefit of external points of view. I believe that many of the decisions by pharmaceutical companies to withhold information on the side effects of drugs resulted from a damaging level of insularity. Managers should understand the importance of allowing the terms by which informed outsiders judge the company to inform their internal discussions.

When applied to capital markets, this principle means that managers must learn to speak the investors' language—to know which parts of the investment story hold value for them, and which do not. The company may be very proud of a technology it has developed, for example. It may believe that its superior design and engineering prove that it will succeed against competitors in the future. But investors may resist paying the company simply for being smart. They are likely to demand information about how the company will monetize its technology. No matter how brilliant it is, they may consider a technology to be a misguided R&D investment and an example of poor management if there isn't a clear payoff.

The Perception Study

Perhaps the best way to go about developing the market intelligence that would avoid such pitfalls lies in what is known in the investor relations world as a "perception study." This is an intelligence-development resource whereby a company authorizes a consultant to act as an intermediary with investors in carrying on discussions about the means by which they judge its share value. These conversations are confidential and candid in a way that would not be possible for the company itself.

The findings of a perception study can be both surprising and highly nuanced. Depending, of course, on the talents of the consultant, company management may learn that specific changes in its disclosure practices will give investors an improved perspective, and therefore the comfort to increase their commitment to the company's shares.

A perception study can impact more than a company's communications practices. Management may be able to identify in investor comments possible changes in strategy that are both reasonable to carry out and capable of bringing investors to a higher estimate of the company's future earnings potential.

A deliberate program of gathering investor intelligence over an extended period of time—say, two years—not only delivers critical market intelligence, but it can also educate management instincts to the extent that executives find themselves capable of anticipating market reaction to strategies and initiatives they have not yet announced—or even decided on. Such instincts can be developed to the point of enabling management to forecast market reaction to M&A transactions which it may only be considering.

While the perception study's purpose is to collect intelligence on investor attitudes toward the corporation, it also provides a meaningful tool of outward communication in demonstrating the company's sensitivity to market attitudes. After all, no investor will be interested in holding a stock unless he or she believes that someone else will come along in the future to pay a higher price. Clear evidence that management is working to achieve this often provides current investors with an additional source of confidence in the company.

The Strange Brew of Numbers and Psychology

The management of a publicly traded company must understand that, although conversations with investors and analysts focus primarily on financial performance figures and descriptions of strategy, investors' private considerations involve much more nuanced and subjective matters. Their observations go to such a personal level as interpreting managers' body language when they speak, assessing their apparent degree of confidence, and, most of all, noting the consistency of what they say over time.

Investors also care a great deal about "bench strength," that is, the talent just below top management that runs business divisions and makes day-to-day decisions. They need to get to know such people through investor conferences which the company may attend or sponsor, or through the participation of these second-tier managers in meetings that corporate leaders undertake from time to time in making "roadshow" trips to visit investors.

CASE STUDY

Chiquita Brands

Management must establish a process of collecting views from throughout the company. Then it must relinquish control. Chiquita Brands, famous for its bananas, sought a number of years ago to transcend a reputation developed over many decades for exerting excessive power over workers in its Central American plantations.

Among many initiatives, the company drafted a set of corporate values at its headquarters in the American Midwest, then sent the list out for review and suggestions to its employees who work the plantations.

The document returned to headquarters with a surprising addition. The Latin American workers had found a big gap: headquarters' list of values failed to mention the importance of family. Seeing the revised list, the management team at headquarters—whose families were also central to their lives—realized for the first time that for a company's values to be legitimate they had to encompass all important features of the lives both of senior executives in glass towers and of those who cultivated the bananas in the field. And that's how commitment to a discrete and unique set of values came to be achieved in a widely diverse corporation.

"Capitalism depends on people keeping their promises to one another, often over very long periods of time. "
William Davies

  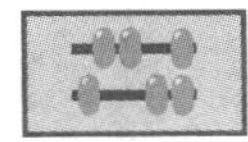      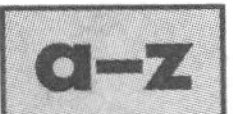

Considerations of the talent pool come into play particularly when, as is often the case in these days of rapid turnover, investors concern themselves with a company's leadership succession plan. Is there talent within the organization to replace the current chief? And would that new leader be able to continue to replenish the ranks of management?

In the end, making allies of investors means building their confidence in the company by helping them to understand it in their own terms rather than exclusively in the light in which management wishes it to be seen.

THE VALUE PARADOX

The relationship between public companies and investors can be described as a "value paradox." Corporate managers must be administrators, creative strategists, shrewd allocators of capital, and savvy about both customer psychology and industry competition. Investors, on the other hand, are analysts of financial data and, to a considerable extent, psychologists in their assessments of management's abilities and candor. Investors can dissolve the relationship with the company at any moment by selling their stock. Company managements have no such freedom. It is therefore critical that they *learn the language* of investors as a way of keeping them and attracting new ones to maximize market value.

TRANSPARENCY AS A MATTER OF SURVIVAL

The defining reality of the information age is that transparency is no longer a choice. If you don't offer it to the world, the world will impose it on you anyway. Every corporate action, therefore, requires thought along two independent tracks. The first, of course, centers on the value of the action itself. How does it support the company's overall value proposition? The second—equally important and often missed—involves a careful assessment of how the action will play out with the company's various constituencies. Will investors attribute the same value to the action as management? Will resistance among social constituencies divert the company in ways that compromise its original intended value? No conceived action has value until it is accompanied by a strategy to explain and defend it.

MAKING ALLIES OF SOCIAL STAKEHOLDERS

In the age of the Internet and 24-hour cable news, it has become virtually impossible for a company to hide anything at all. The age of the fortress corporation—when companies had the ability to act almost exclusively in their own interests and control the information that circulated about them among the public—ended when it became possible for dissident employees and bloggers everywhere to communicate at the push of a computer button. And they not only began to communicate, they quickly became able to organize opposition to a company with surprising ease.

Because of the reputation risk the information age has brought upon us, the influence of investors has been matched by that of nonfinancial stakeholders. These may include governments, regulators, communities in which a company operates, the media that speak to those communities, and activist groups with interests in the environment, human rights, and labor. To an increasing extent, the "buzz" about a company can determine its destiny. So it is nothing more than sensible management these days to assume that any company will run into trouble some day—whether it deserves to or not.

The Time to Prepare for Crisis Is Now

The time to prepare for a crisis is five years before it occurs. Crises seldom approach slowly over the horizon. Most often, they explode in front of corporate headquarters without advance notice. It is the CEO's job to prepare for crisis every day that he or she holds the position. The least of this obligation is to organize the preparation, and continual updating, of a crisis action plan. So, when a significant adverse event occurs, everyone who is involved in the corporation's defense will immediately know his or her specific duties and lines of communication.

Far more challenging is the design and execution of strategies that will attract the support of critical stakeholder groups, which, in a crisis, can make the difference between life and death for a company. Their support often means that the company is more likely than otherwise to receive the benefit of the doubt when things go wrong—when a product is shown to be dangerous to the public, when an environmental mishap occurs, or if it turns out that workers have been mistreated.

When a pipeline bursts, or a product turns out suddenly to be harmful to customers, or improper marketing practices are publicly disclosed, there is a short period of time—often called the "golden hour"—before the press stakes its claim to the event and when the company is able to tell its story, establish the initiative, declare empathy for any victims, and demonstrate that it is the solution, not the problem.

If the company has already established a reputation of trust with influential individuals and organizations, it will find allies in its time of need to resist the impulse on the part of the press, politicians, and the public to assign blame. It is those politicians, in particular, whose carefully developed support may turn critical at a moment when the company's future may hang in the balance.

How does the company establish this support?

A company that wishes to protect itself from a future crisis must undertake two initiatives that are distinct but deeply connected with each other.

- It must vigorously pursue the development of relationships with crucial stakeholders in government and among regulators, the media, and activist groups who may place themselves in opposition to the company.
- And it must base these relationships on a clear and candid narrative about itself founded on legitimate and clearly defined values. The company should demonstrate day after day, and year after year, that its values are aligned with those of the society around it. This is not easy to do; and it is impossible to fake.

The Communication of Convergence

One of the most creative initiatives a management can take to defend itself against unknown future crises is to engage those groups with whom there is friction and little or no communication. A simple invitation to talk extended to an opposition group can result in a dialog that grows over time. The content of the dialog matters less than the simple fact that it happens. Eventually, both sides become committed to the communication process and develop an interest in seeing it succeed.

One of the results of this "communication of convergence" is that the two sides will begin to develop a shared vocabulary around contentious issues. Over time, the company may begin to hear its own phrases and manner of describing the problem echoed not only by its interlocutors on the other side, but also by that part of the public that adheres to opposing opinions.

The requirement for entering into such a dialog is the willingness to commit to a mutual vulnerability. You can't ask for an engagement by the other side that you yourself do not offer. So, your dialog will also evolve as a result of this interchange.

While the benefits of this process are great, their achievement requires commitment on the part of a senior executive not only to the idea, but also to the task of convincing dissenting voices within the organization that the idea is a good one. The rewards, however, are worth the trouble.

  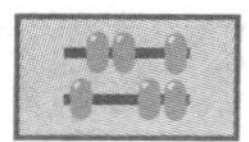      

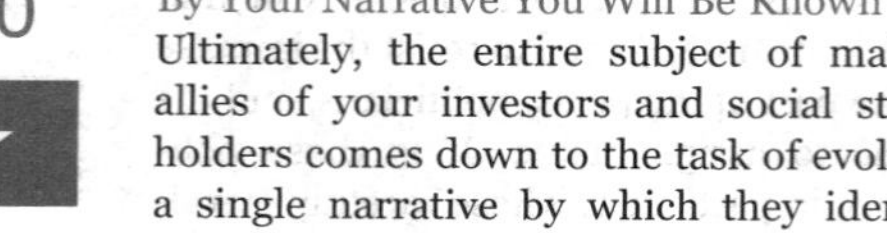

By Your Narrative You Will Be Known

Ultimately, the entire subject of making allies of your investors and social stakeholders comes down to the task of evolving a single narrative by which they identify you.

Coca-Cola's narrative is not "We quench your thirst." Water does that. Coca-Cola's narrative is "We bring the world together."

Like any company, Coca-Cola has to support its narrative in its public actions. So, when social activists and some elements in the international media took note that Coca-Cola was diverting water from parched villages in India to make its soft drinks, it made little difference that the company had a legal contract that allowed it to do so. The company had to take whatever steps necessary to dispel the notion that it was exercising its power for commercial purposes at the expense of powerless people. That's how Coca-Cola—reluctantly at first, but later with great creative energy—became a leader in developing technology to support sustainable water supplies.

It Is All About Your Values

If the requirement for a good reputation is to align with the social norms of the community around you, that community will be asking one question: What are your values? And developing a solid set of values—values that mean something—may be the hardest part of building a strong reputation.

The moral tone of an organization—whether it is a small office or a global enterprise that involves hundreds of thousands of employees—comes from the top, from the single leader. But the great paradox in the matter of corporate values is that, although the leader must lead, he does not create the company's values on his own. The walls of corporate cafeterias everywhere are adorned with lists of corporate values, and they're worth about as much as the attention they are paid by those rushing through their meals. You can mandate strategy, investment, and standards of all kinds. But you can't mandate values. They must come from everywhere within an organization. That's the only way to obtain commitment.

A solid and legitimate set of values not only increases the likelihood that conduct throughout the organization will limit risk, but it also provides a foundation for all important relationships. Values are the language of association—and therefore of survival.

THE VALUES-BASED ENTERPRISE

Corporate survival in a world where there are few secrets requires alignment of the enterprise with the norms of the society that surrounds it. Companies will always be defined by the narratives which their actions project. So, achieving the most secure levels of sustainability requires that a company create for itself a deliberate narrative based on an observant understanding of its constituencies. The core of this narrative will always be the fundamental values the company is seen to hold. To maximize the chance of companywide commitment to a set of values, they must be derived from a conversation that includes the whole organization. Values cannot be mandated from above.

MAKING IT HAPPEN

- The cultures of corporate managers and professional investors are far different from each other. It is management's obligation to understand how investors assign value to the company and to address them in terms that give the company the best chance to achieve the highest reasonable valuation.
- In the information age, managers must assume that virtually everything they do will eventually come to public light. Transparency is no longer an option, it is imposed. So managers must understand the "optics" of their actions and know that any business planning process must include a strategy for communicating it to financial markets and the public. If you can't explain it openly, you probably shouldn't do it.
- Long-term sustainability requires alignment of a company's values with its social context. A corporate leader must implement a systematic review of his or her company's standing among its social constituency and invest in senior personnel to assess how the company's practices and policies match up with public norms and expectations.

MORE INFO

Books:

Bennis, Warren G., and Burt Nanus. *Leaders: Strategies for Taking Charge*. 2nd ed. New York: HarperBusiness, 2003.

Dowling, Grahame. *Creating Corporate Reputations: Identity Image and Performance*. Oxford: Oxford University Press, 2001.

Firestein, Peter. *Crisis of Character: Building Corporate Reputation in the Age of Skepticism*. New York: Sterling Publishing, 2009.

Fombrun, Charles J. *Reputation: Realizing Value from the Corporate Image*. Boston, MA: Harvard Business School Press, 1996.

Gaines-Ross, Leslie. *CEO Capital: A Guide to Building CEO Reputation and Company Success*. Hoboken, NJ: Wiley, 2003.

Gardner, Howard. *Changing Minds: The Art and Science of Changing Our Own and Other People's Minds*. Boston, MA: Harvard Business School Press, 2006.

Joiner, Bill, and Stephen Josephs. *Leadership Agility: Five Levels of Mastery for Anticipating and Initiating Change*. San Francisco, CA: Jossey-Bass, 2006.

Larkin, Judy. *Strategic Reputation Risk Management*. Basingstoke, UK: Palgrave Macmillan, 2003. Peters, Glen. *Waltzing with the Raptors: A Practical Roadmap to Protecting Your Company's Reputation*. New York: Wiley, 1999.

Article:

Firestein, Peter. "The investor valuation analysis/open perception study." Online at: tinyurl.com/5uvqf7l [PDF].

Websites:

Author's website: www.firesteinco.com

Author's blog: www.peterfiresteinblog.com

See Also:

★ Digital Strategies for Enhancing Reputation (pp. 826–831)

"In some situations, doing nothing—forever—is the right response ... Sometimes, not trying to fix something is precisely what's needed to fix it." Peter Bregman

  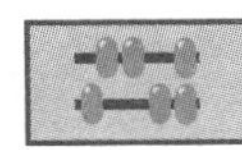      

Enhance Competitive Performance via Critical Key Performance Indicators (KPIs) by Zahirul Hoque

EXECUTIVE SUMMARY

- Measuring performance is a fundamental part of every organization, whether it is run by a private sector or a government sector.
- Performance measures are used to evaluate organizational as well as managerial performance.
- A key performance indicator (KPI) is a quantitative value that can be scaled and used for performance evaluation.
- Organizations should use both financial and nonfinancial KPIs when measuring employee as well as firm performance.
- KPIs should be aligned with business strategy, work environment, and employee incentives.
- Too many KPIs should be avoided, to maximize their usage by employees in their day-to-day operations.
- "It is much more difficult to measure nonperformance than performance."

INTRODUCTION

Measuring performance is a fundamental part of every organization, whether it is run by a private sector or a government sector. A performance measurement system (PMS) highlights whether the organization is on track to achieve its desired goals. Performance measures are primarily used to evaluate organizational, as well as employee performance. A PMS develops key performance indicators (KPIs), or metrics, depending on the nature and activities of the organization. KPIs can serve as the cornerstone of an organization's employee incentive schemes. KPIs are used as guidelines and incentives to facilitate the coordination of managers and business unit goals, with those of the overall corporation goals, that is, they encourage goal congruency. Through these metrics, the organization communicates how it wishes the employees to behave, and how this behavior will be judged and evaluated. Effective organizational managers rely on KPIs to set direction, make strategic decisions, and achieved desired goals.[1]

It has been suggested that, in today's competitive and global financial crisis environments, organizations need to be masters at anticipating customers' needs, devising radical new product and service offerings, and rapidly deploying new production technologies into operating and service delivery processes.[2] For several decades, performance measurement has been used as an internal informational tool to evaluate business units' operations, and make program and budgetary decisions.

PMS AND KPIS: DEFINITIONS

A PMS typically comprises systematic methods of setting business goals, together with periodic feedback reports that indicate progress against those goals.[3] Within a PMS, an organization develops some key performance metrics or indicators. A KPI can be defined as "a quantitative value that can be scaled and used for purposes of comparison."[4] There is also the view that KPIs are quantifiable performance measurements used to define success factors, and measure progress toward the achievement of business goals."[5] The PMS literature classifies performance measures into two major groups: financial and non-financial. Financial measures may include return on investment (ROI), earnings per share (EPS), revenue (sales) growth, profit margin, etc. Non-financial measures may include customer satisfaction, employee satisfaction, production efficiency, quality, customer services, etc.

BALANCED SCORECARD MEASURES

In today's competitive environment, one that encompasses fierce global competition, advancing technology, and increased customer awareness, traditional KPIs such as ROI and EPS can be inadequate for a business organization. Traditional KPIs. although they can aid in detecting weaknesses with respect to the use, or non-use of individual investment or assets, and focus management's attention upon earning the best profit possible on the capital available, tend to avoid isolating individual business units, in that it may not be reasonable to expect the same ROI for each unit. If the unit sells its respective products in markets that differ widely, with respect to product development, competition, and customer demand, lack of agreement on the optimum rate of return might discourage managers who believe the rate is set at an unfair level.

For the sake of making the current period performance measure look good, be it ROI or EPS, managers may be influenced to make decisions that are not in the best long-run interests of the firm. A major concern with traditional KPIs is that these performance metrics focus on results largely internal to the firm. During the last decade, there has been an overemphasis on the use of financial KPIs to measure firm performance. This has resulted in organizations losing sight of important indicators which measure levels of customer satisfaction, process flexibility, or adaptation in response to changing needs. A strategy which concentrates on financial criteria is too closely related to short-term profit maximization. Broader measures such as customer-based measures, product and process measures, and continual improvement and innovation measures, enable the organization to establish longer-term improvements which further effective competition.

Further, the imperative for improved performance measures cannot be ignored with today's worldwide competition and advancing technologies. Once new technologies are introduced, major organization changes are required, as the interaction between people and technology is essential to ensure business processes become more and more effective, and, therefore, performance measures which focus only on financial criteria will not reflect the new technological and competitive environments. New performance measures, if devised strategically, will profoundly influence business performance. Thus, more attention also needs to be placed on generating suitable non- financial performance measures to be a successful competitor, given today's global financial crisis. Significant attention is now being given by academics and managers to building a more extensive and linked set of measures for appraising and directing corporate and divisional performance, influenced largely by Kaplan and Norton's notion of the "balanced scorecard."

The balanced scorecard approach focuses on both financial and non-financial measures. The financial measures indicate if improvements in financial performance resulted from sacrificing investments in new products, or on-time delivery. The balanced scorecard includes financial measures that tell the results of actions already taken. Kaplan and Norton suggest that financial measures should not be

"**Measurement matters: If you can't measure, you can't manage it.**" Robert S. Kaplan and David P. Norton

eliminated altogether, because a well-designed financial performance measurement system can actually enhance, rather than inhibit an organization's management program. The balanced scorecard supplements the financial measures with operational measures on customer satisfaction, internal processes, and the firm's innovation and improvement activities. Kaplan and Norton's balanced scorecard comprises the following four dimensions:

- Financial—applying appropriate financial performance measures to ascertain whether the company is profitable.
- Customer—assessing customer satisfaction (the customer perspective). In a competitive market, customers must be content, or market share will drop. Customers care about price, faster and reliable deliveries, design, quality, and level of services.
- Internal business processes—tracking inter-organizational indicators to determine whether the business units are efficiently using resources, and ascertaining competitive performance in developing "next generation" products.
- Learning and growth dimension—this measures such things as training and development, information systems, employee satisfaction, employee productivity, etc.

Kaplan and Norton suggest that the use of the balanced scorecard may motivate breakthrough improvements in critical activity areas such as products, processes, customers, and market developments. They further suggest that, while traditional

Table 1. KPIs in a PMS within a manufacturing setting

Perspective	KPIs
Financial	Operating income Sales growth Return on investment Earnings per share
Customer	Market share Customer response time On-time delivery Number of customer complaints Number of warranty claims Customer satisfaction survey Sales return due to poor quality
Internal business processes	Material efficiency variance Labor efficiency Ratio of good output to total output at each production process Rate of material scrap loss Number of new patents Number of new product launches
Employee learning and growth	Employee satisfaction survey Employee education and training Employee health and safety

Table 2. KPIs of Omega

Major strategic focus	KPIs
Customer focus	% Customer satisfaction % Compliance with verbal service-request response times Number of water supply interruptions per 1,000 properties Number of planned water supply interruptions per 1,000 properties Number of unplanned water supply interruptions per 1,000 properties % of water and wastewater service interruptions within 5 hours Number of customer complaints per 1,000 properties Number of water quality complaints per 1,000 properties Number of odor complaints per 1,000 properties % of meters installed within 14 days from date of payment
Chosen employer	% lost working days Training expenditure versus total operating expenditure (%)
Environmental sustainability	% tests meeting WWTP EPA license criteria Quantity of treated water supplied per property, not seasonally adjusted Number of uncontained wastewater spills % of wastewater spilt per wastewater treated % effluent reused
Commercial sustainability	Combined operating costs per property % expended of revenue-funded capital expenditure Water and wastewater renewals expenditure as a percentage of current replacement cost of system assets % unaccounted water Operating profit Return on turnover (net profit after tax/sales) Return on net operating assets (EBIT/total net assets) Debt-equity ratio (total interest-bearing debt/total equity) Total financial distribution to council (as a % of post-tax profits)
Quality water service provision	% tests meeting NHMRC (1996) bacteria criteria % tests meeting NHMRC (1996) chemical criteria Water main breaks per 100km of water main Sewer chokes per 100km of wastewater main Wastewater main (gravity and pressure) breaks per 100km of main
Accountability	% Compliance with wastewater spillage procedure (ensures spillages are properly reported and remedied) Maintenance of ISO 9000 and 14000 third-party certification

CASE STUDY

Aligning KPIs and Strategy[6]

Omega is a water utility company that provides five core services to its customers, namely bulk water supply, water purification, reticulation of water and wastewater treatment, and wastewater disposal. On average, Omega provides services to more than 157,000 residential properties. In July 2003, Omega introduced a multidimensional PMS to improve accountability, and to communicate to organizational members the objectives and targets of the entity. As shown in Table 2, Omega developed a total of 33 KPIs for each of its six major activities. Table 2 shows this new KPI system, which, consistent with the balanced scorecard, combines a series of non-financial and financial KPIs. According to Omega's senior management, one of the advantages of adopting a multidimensional PMS is that it gives a better indication to employees of the long-term organizational priorities. It also helps to communicate any crisis to all of Omega's divisions, which was important to ensure that any impact is minimized. Each KPI is tailored, not to a division but to one of the five major activities of Omega, consistent with its attempts to become more outcome-focused. For instance, the percentage of lost working days or absentees is aimed at measuring Omega's ability to be a chosen employer. Similarly, the return on net operating assets is a new KPI, which is used to measure the commercial sustainability of Omega. In setting the KPIs, Omega employees suggested that it was common when the information was available to benchmark against other water entities, to ensure that the divisions are providing a service at a similar standard as their private and public counterparts, so that they are not seen to be performing poorly when the contractual period ends. Some of Omega's subdivisions also suggested that this had put the division under pressure to improve its performance.

"In all businesses, there is a constant tension between profit, growth, and control." Robert Simon

financial measures report on what happened in the last period without indicating how managers can improve performance in the next, the balanced scorecard functions as the cornerstone of a company's current and future success.

Table 1 provides examples of widely used KPIs within a PMS in a manufacturing setting.

CONCLUSION

An English-born American communications executive, who was president and CEO of ITT, suggests that, "the best way to inspire people to superior performance is to convince them by everything you do and by your everyday attitude that you are wholeheartedly supporting them."[7] This short article suggests that measuring performance is important for all businesses. However, it is much more difficult to develop KPIs for each area of performance within the organization which can be measured effectively. Effective KPIs are those that enhance business performance in all areas of businesses—financial and non-financial. Harold Green remarks: "Performance stands out like a ton of diamonds. Non-performance can always be explained away." KPIs need to be developed to fit to the business process flow, and focus attention on the critical success factors of the business.

MAKING IT HAPPEN

Developing KPIs is a critical decision-making process for any organization. Effective KPIs are those that help the organization to achieve its desired outcomes. Performance indicators must advocate the firm's internal and external environment. However, for many firms the difficulty is that there are too many KPIs, ones that are outmoded, and that are not harmonious. KPIs should observe changes in the market environment, determine and assess progress towards business strategies and goals, and affirm achievement of performance goals. This is elaborated in turn. Robert Simon at Harvard University developed three tests to assess whether a measure or metric is suitable to support a performance goal.

1 Does the KPI align with business strategy?
2 Can it measured effectively (that is, metrics should be objective, complete and responsive)?
3 Is the measure linked to economic value?[8]

According to Robert Simon (2000, p.239): "To be effective as communication devices, managers must use measures to focus attention. As you all know, what gets measured gets managed."

Linking KPIs to Business Strategy and Competitive Environments

Strategy plays an important role in the choice of KPIs, and effective KPIs must be able to assess the organization's progress on strategic priorities. Business strategy has been broadly conceptualized as a continuum spectrum between two extreme orientations: at one extreme, prospector or differentiator firms; and at the other end, defender or cost-leader firms. However, some business units may stand between both defenders and prospectors, which are often refereed to as "analyzers."[9]

As defender or cost leaders focus on searching for new ways to reduce production and distribution costs, to cut marketing expenses, and to improve product quality, short-term, retrospective financial and efficiency indices (for example, cost control, internal business processes, quality and efficiency, operating profit, cash flow from operations, return on investment, etc) are relatively informative KPIs of performance. In contrast, as prospectors or differentiators compete in a broad product market domain by introducing new products and developing new markets, KPIs for focuses such as these would necessarily come from knowing what the customer wants, the level of staff involvement in creativity, and the ability of the organization to produce and market new products. Hence, a greater usage of non-financial KPIs (for example, new product development, market share, and customer satisfaction), as opposed to short-term financial indicators, would be prominent in this type of firm.

Analyzer strategies combine both defender and prospector strategies. As a result, an analyzer firm's organizational problem is how to accommodate both stable and dynamic areas of operations. The first concentrates on being efficient, and the second concentrates on watching its competitors closely, so as to determine the possibility of introducing new products or services as rapidly as possible. In relation to the first area, analyzers may tend to emphasize stability, defense of the firm's position in the market, and to earn the best profit possible. The key rationale being that too many firms are able to provide the same product at the same price, hence the incentive to increase sales, or the profit margin, is to ensure its internal processes are acting as efficiently and cost-effectively as possible. As a result, analyzers may place emphasis on short-term, financial KPIs. The second area focuses on new market opportunities by developing new brands in response to emerging environmental trends. Consequently, the level of uncertainty would be high in organizations pursuing analyzer strategy. Consistent with this strategic position, analyzers are also likely to rely more on non-financial KPIs. Thus, since analyzers operate in two combined market areas, these firms would then be more prone to incorporate a much broader range of KPIs, such as that required by the balanced scorecard. It is felt that for analyzers, four dimensions of the balanced scorecard, as outlined above, can be regarded as meeting organizational performance measurement requirements, as they provide useful insights into the firm's performance evaluation paradox in one report. In conclusion, different types of strategy will require different types of PMS and KPIs, and an appropriate fit between PMS and strategy is likely to enhance a firm's performance.

Aligning KPIs and Incentives

Are KPIs linked to employee incentives? If KPIs are not linked to employee incentive schemes they tend to be overlooked by employees and therefore they are likely to result in no desired outcomes. KPIs must be aligned with employees' individual goals and job descriptions. As a rule of thumb, Robert Simon suggested a maximum of 10 KPIs for each individual; otherwise individuals may suffer from information overload. With a reasonable number of KPIs, at the individual level, employees use KPIs to track their performance against agreed targets.

  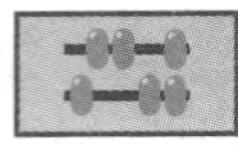      

Further, when developing KPIs for individuals, financial indicators should integrate nonfinancial or operational indicators on customer satisfaction, internal processes and the firm's innovation and improvement activities.

Implementation of KPIs

Organizations also need to place greater emphasis on implementation issues when designing and implementing a PMS, and relevant KPIs. A recent study in Australia identified several factors (such as top management support, adequate technology, greater employee involvement in the design stage, adequate staff training and education, and linking PMS and KPIs with other financial control models) that impact on the successful implementation of a new PMS.[10]

MORE INFO

Books:

Hoque, Z. *Handbook of Cost and Management Accounting*. London: Spiramus, 2005.

Hoque, Z. *Strategic Management Accounting: Concepts, Processes and Issues*. 2nd ed. Sydney, Audtralia: Pearson Education, 2003.

Johnson, H. T., and R. S. Kaplan. *Relevance Lost, the Rise and Fall of Management Accounting*. Boston, MA: Harvard Business School Press, 1987.

Kaplan, R. S., and D. P. Norton. *The Balanced Scorecard: Translating Strategy into Action*. Boston, MA: Harvard Business School Press, 1996.

Lynch, R. L., and K. F. Cross. *Measure Up!* Cambridge, MA: Blackwell Publishers, 1991.

Niven, P. R. *Balanced Scorecard Step by Step: Maximizing Performance and Maintaining Results*. New York: Wiley, 2000.

Simon, R. *Performance Measurement & Control Systems for Implementing Strategy*. Upper Saddle River, NJ: Prentice Hall, 2000.

Articles:

Ittner, C. D., D. F. Larcker, and M. V. Rajan. "The choice of performance measures in annual bonus contracts." *The Accounting Review* 72:2 (1997): 231–255.

Kaplan, R. S., and D. P. Norton. "The balanced scorecard—Measures that drive performance." *Harvard Business Review* (January–February 1992): 71–79.

Kaplan, R. S., and D. P. Norton. "Putting the balanced scorecard to work." *Harvard Business Review* (September–October 1993): 134–147.

Nanni, A. J. Jr, J. R. Dixon, and T. E. Vollmann. "Integrated performance measurement: Management accounting to support the new manufacturing realities." *Journal of Management Accounting Research* 4 (1992): 1–19.

Websites:

Website of Better Management: www.bettermanagement.com

Website of the Balanced Scorecard Institute: www.balancedscorecard.org

See Also:

★ Multidimensional Performance Measurement Using the Balanced Scorecard (pp. 897–899)

★ Navigating a Liquidity Crisis Effectively (pp. 82–84)

✔ Assessing Business Performance (p. 1144)

✔ Understanding Key Performance Indicators (p. 1180)

✔ Understanding the Balance Sheet (p. 999)

NOTES

1 Simon (2000), p.3.

2 Kaplan and Norton (1996).

3 Simon (2000), p.7.

4 *Ibid*., p.234.

5 See www.bettermanagement.com/topic/subject.aspx?f=11&s=704, accessed on February 11, 2009.

6 Based on Moll, J. and Z. Hoque. "New organizational forms and accounting innovation: The specifier/provider model in the Australian public sector." *Journal of Accounting & Organizational Change* 4:3 (2008): 243–269.

7 See www.thinkexist.com/English/Author/x/Author_3037_1.htm, accessed on February 19, 2009.

8 For further details, refer to Simon (2000), pp.234–238.

9 Miles, R.E. and Snow, C.G. *Organizational Strategy, Structure, and Process*. New York: McGraw Hill.

10 Hoque, Z. and C. Adams. *Measuring Public Sector Performance: A Study of Australian Government Departments*. Melbourne: CPA Australia, 2008.

"Biopiracy is the Columbian discovery 500 years after Columbus." Vandana Shiva

  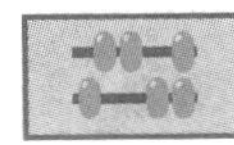   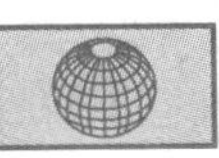   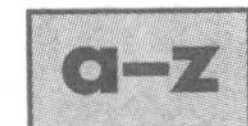

Essentials for Export Success: Understanding How Risks and Relationships Lead to Rewards

by Paul Beretz

EXECUTIVE SUMMARY

- The global business environment can present opportunities for rewards for the exporter if international risk attributes can be determined and mitigated.
- Exporters who want to succeed should be able to identify and evaluate their "IQ" (international qualities).
- The risk elements of country, currency, and culture can significantly impact global business transactions.
- Relationship-building and the ability to sustain those relationships are necessary qualities for reaping rewards.

INTRODUCTION

More and more, companies located throughout the world are recognizing that the way to sustain long-term growth is not by continuing to emphasize local, in-country markets. Whether it be for better or worse, global business is a factor that can provide businesses with the opportunity to consider new and challenging markets. In 2008, we saw that severe credit and financial issues could spread quickly, and that no part of the world was immune. Therefore, an understanding of the key risk factors that can lead to rewards is essential.

How should a business assess world markets? One initial approach for exporters is to determine their "IQ," or international qualities, before either entering or expanding their overseas markets.

RATING YOUR COMPANY'S "IQ"

The "IQ" test shown in Figure 1 will address your company's readiness to compete in the global marketplace. For each question, give your company a letter grade (A–F, or U for "Unknown") and state the reason(s) for your grade. Grade A = 90–100%, B = 80–89%, and so on.

Figure 1. The "IQ" test

"IQ" question	Grade	Reason
What percentage of your revenues do you expect from the country(ies) you will be exporting to?		
What do you expect as your market share and industry ranking in that/those country(ies)?		
Will you establish direct sales relationships with your major customers?		
Will you ever expect to be considered a company that is "part" of the country you are exporting to?		
Have you analyzed all the cultural, currency, and country issues you will encounter in exporting to a particular country?		
What is your knowledge of the market for your product in a given country?		
What is your knowledge of the economic structure and the current state of the economy in a new country?		
Have you analyzed the legal system in a new country for the legality of your contracts or relationships? Can you cancel a relationship with a distributor or an agent if necessary? Is your documentation of sale legally binding?		
Once the sale is made, and payment is not forthcoming, what are your options in achieving payment? Practically, culturally, and legally, what are the norms?		

RISKS FACING THE EXPORTER

An exporter will face many risks once the decision to sell in overseas markets is made. Key risk areas, in particular, are known as the "three Cs"—country, currency, and culture.

Country Risk

Figure 2 outlines the dimensions of country risk when goods or services are sold globally. Exporters may wish to use the chart to classify the major risk issues and attributes of each risk by country.

Theses are the questions to ask when determining the dimensions of country risk:

- What currency will you be selling in? Is the decision a competitive one? Are you equipped internally to deal in multicurrencies?
- Do you know the laws in specific countries? (For example, a joint venture in China must balance imports with exports, or else it could be barred by the government from obtaining hard currency.)
- What is the recent political history (that could influence the availability of funds or internal stability)? This will include government takeover of properties, whether with or without compensation, operational restrictions, or damage to property or personnel.
- What is the current economic environment in the country? Have there been local currency devaluations recently?
- Have there been border disputes that could escalate military readiness and therefore impact the availability of hard currency, both within the country's borders and as funds leaving the country? If the exporter's customer base is expanding through direct investment abroad, will there be access to the invested capital and will earnings be able to be repatriated? This could impact cash flow and the ability to meet its trade obligations.

Currency Risk

Exporters have to consider selling in foreign currencies to offshore customers. In this competitive environment, an exporter needs flexibility in determining the currency that is billed to the customer. In a volatile global economy, however, billing a buyer in a currency that differs from the seller's own currency can be fraught with risk: When

"It is simply too easily forgotten that when it comes to economic activities, one of the greatest virtues a country or community can have is a culture of tolerance." Thomas Friedman

Figure 2. Dimensions of country risk

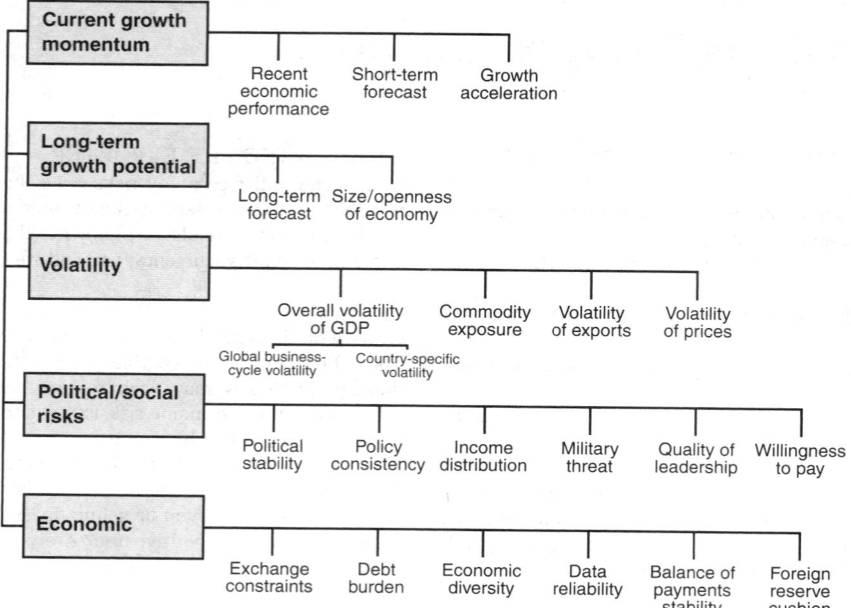

payment is due, has the value of the currency fallen in value against the seller's currency?

One approach for the exporter is to deal in the foreign exchange (FX) market, which is an enormous, sophisticated, and efficient global communications system operating around the clock to enable international transactions. Large commercial banks are the dominant players in the FX market, serving as intermediaries between supply and demand; corporations are the principal end-users. FX transactions are speculative by nature and thus can be volatile, thereby increasing risk.

Three basic transactions for managing FX risk are *spot transactions*, *forward transactions* and *options*. *Spot transactions* are purchases or sales of foreign currency for "immediate" delivery. *Forward transactions* carry a specified price and stipulated future value date for the exchange of currencies. They are used most often to cover future foreign currency payables and anticipated receipts. *Options* are a more suitable tool for "hedging" risk when a foreign customer's commitment is not firm. Buyers pay a premium for the option to exchange foreign currency at a predetermined rate ("strike price"). Options are bought and sold on the "exchange-traded" (less flexible, less expensive) and "over the counter" (more flexible, more expensive) markets, and they allow buyers to take advantage of favorable changes in currency rates while guarding against adverse changes.

The prudent financial manager recognizes that currency risk is a major factor in the export decision.

Culture Risk

The proactive, truly globally oriented exporter living in today's competitive marketplace understands that business decision making is a form of art as much as a science. All the evaluation tools available cannot take the place of experience. It is essential to possess a fundamental, analytical approach to the export selling process. The "art" form of today's global business process includes an understanding of how the cultures and negotiation processes of different countries become part of the arsenal of tools in making an intelligent decision. How the culture of each country or region impacts the risk is material to the ultimate business decision.

A lack of awareness—whether it be intentional or not—can impact the business relationship, impede the negotiations, and end the opportunity to complete the business transaction. Does the exporter understand customs and practices regarding whether or not to shake hands and what clothes to wear? Does the exporter know about presenting business cards (in different languages)—and not writing on the card? Mistakes that involve eating and drinking have been known to end a business opportunity; many Westerners do not know that in certain Chinese provinces the act of putting chopsticks in a rice bowl means "death" to the person on the other side of the table. In many world cultures, the customer expects the eldest representative of the exporter to be involved in negotiations (such elders are known as the "gray-haired gods"), even if this person is not the most astute.

HOW RELATIONSHIPS CAN LEAD TO REWARDS FOR THE EXPORTER

Awareness, attitude, and anticipation are crucial. In the global business environment, the observant exporter should know how to watch and listen, rather than expect the transaction to happen "now." Relationship building is not only critical with offshore customers, but also imperative with a company's own "internal" customer—the branch office or agent in that country of business. Many exporters demonstrate hubris in their belief that how they do business in their own country is how it is best to do business in the country of the potential importer.

The proactive, successful exporter desiring to succeed in other lands will study behavior, learn about verbal and nonverbal differences that exist, and often will use a "go-between" in order to create the desired relationship. The person who is the intermediary may be one's own country manager; or it could be a banker, business owner, or government employee in a key position in the country who understands how to help achieve the connection between

CASE STUDIES

Country Risk

A large forest products company based in the United States had solid business relations with five distributors located in a Latin American country. These distributors, in total, owed US$10 million to the exporter, all within payment terms. When the central bank of the country froze all payments leaving the country, the government bank instructed all vendors selling into the country that they would have to wait five years for any repayment of debt. The country manager of the forest products company, who had developed excellent relations with several key executives at the central bank over the years, was able to discount the US$10 million debt with a global bank located outside the country. The result? The exporter was paid 95 cents on the dollar within 60 days. In addition, future sales were paid through an escrow account with the same bank. What is the moral of the story? Even though the five customers were well financed and deemed extremely creditworthy, a country calamity impacted their ability to process business normally. Without the relationship the forest products country manager had developed, the exporter would have had to wait five years for payment.

"When tolerance is the norm, everyone flourishes—because tolerance breeds trust, and trust is the foundation of innovation and entrepreneurship." Thomas Friedman

the two parties. Any person-to-person relationship, especially in the business world, has a better chance of succeeding when trust is both understood and established. This need for relationship means that a feeling of complete trust and confidence must exist, not only that the other party will not take advantage of them, but also that they can presume upon the indulgence of the other.

Trust, as part of relationship-building, is paramount in much of the negotiating process. In China, *guanxi* literally means "relationships" and is understood as the network of relationships among various parties that cooperate together and support one another. In Japan, *shokaijo* can mean a letter of introduction, indicating that the status of the exporter is confirmed with the Japanese customer or contact, as opposed to a "cold" call. It provides more of a "guarantee" that the exporter is connected to the business process in Japan. *Jeito* (in Brazil) is the way a businessperson, though local contacts and experiences, is given the chance to succeed.

CONCLUSION

The exporter needs to evaluate their "IQ." Once that process is completed, the exporter should identify the critical risk factors of country, currency, and culture with the business transaction. Woven into these risk factors are the attributes of relationships. By carefully evaluating the risks and ensuing relationships, an exporter can reap rewards.

Currency Risk

Tyco International, Ltd., based in Bermuda, with headquarter operations in Princeton, NJ, US, is a maker of safety, industrial, and construction products. According to a *Wall Street Journal* article of November 12, 2008 ("Tyco warns currencies, costs will hit earnings"), the company said that in September and October 2008, it saw about a 20% devaluation in currencies of foreign countries where the company did business. The chief executive estimated that these exchange rate fluctuations could reduce fiscal revenue in 2009 by about $2 billion and reduce annual earnings by about 38 cents a share. Tyco generates about 50% of its revenue abroad.

Culture Risk

A large chemical company had been negotiating a licensing agreement with a Middle-Eastern country for close to a year. As the final meeting was drawing to a close, a junior member of the exporter's team asked the customer's executives present at the meeting if everything was "OK" and, at the same time, made the standard Western gesture meaning the same thing.

In the customer's culture this hand signal was an insulting and vulgar sign, so the customer took offense and walked out of the meeting. It took numerous apologies from the exporter and another six months to restore the relationship before the transaction was eventually consummated.

MAKING IT HAPPEN

To understand how to navigate both the risks and the relationships to reap the rewards, the exporter should:

- Be proactive in determining the ("IQ") international qualities of their own organization.
- Evaluate the risk dimensions of the particular country (or countries) where they want to do business.
- Know enough about how to assess currency risks to know when to call the experts.
- Study, study, and study some more the cultural mores of the countries in which they do business.
- Observe, listen, and learn from their mistakes.

MORE INFO

Books:

Coface *The Handbook of Country Risk 2009–2010*. 11th ed. London: GMB Publishing Ltd., 2009.

Morrison, Terri, Wayne A. Conaway, and Joseph J. Douress. *Dun & Bradstreet's Guide to Doing Business Around the World*. Paramus, NJ: Prentice Hall, 2000.

Websites:

Country risk—Investopedia: www.investopedia.com/terms/c/countryrisk.asp
Culture risk—Wise GEEK: www.wisegeek.com/what-is-a-faux-pas.htm
Currency risk—Investopedia: www.investopedia.com/terms/c/currencyrisk.asp
FCIB (an association of executives in finance, credit and international business): www.fcibglobal.com
International Education Systems: www.marybosrock.com/faux_pas.html

See Also:

★ Measuring Company Exposure to Country Risk (pp. 534–536)
★ Measuring Country Risk (pp. 537–539)
★ Political Risk: Countering the Impact on Your Business (pp. 902–904)
★ To Hedge or Not to Hedge (pp. 104–106)

"The policy of being too cautious is the greatest risk of all." Jawaharlal Nehru

  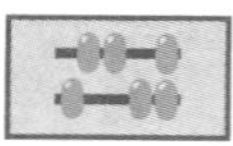      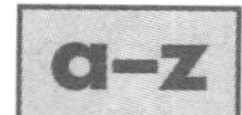

Viewpoint: Every Company Is a Media Company

by Richard Sambrook

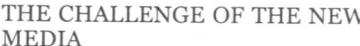

INTRODUCTION

Richard Sambrook was an influential and senior BBC executive and leading manager of its news services before joining the Edelman public relations company in 2010. Born in 1956, he was educated at Maidstone Technical High School, the University of Reading (where he gained a BA in English), and Birkbeck College, University of London. He joined BBC Radio News as a subeditor in 1980. He was a BBC journalist and news executive, becoming successively director of BBC Sport, BBC News, and, latterly, director of the BBC World Service and Global News. During this time he was responsible for merging radio and television news, as well as domestic and World Service news-gathering, resulting in the world's largest broadcast news operation. He oversaw a major restructuring of the World Service and the opening of Arabic and Persian television, as well as of commercial interactive services.

THE CHALLENGE OF THE NEW MEDIA

Every company is a media company, no matter what its business or activity. I believe that engagement with the internet is critical to the company that wants to ensure that its message is heard. Equally, a company must be alert to comments on its products, brands, or personnel on the web so that it can produce its responses as quickly as the bloggers produce theirs.

To achieve such a role, a company must undergo a cultural change. This involves two key strategic attitudes. First, it must gear itself to the transparency of the new media. Second, it needs to remove hierarchies from its own media and communications structures.

The need to be transparent is based on the fact that readers are now much better informed about a company's activities across its various organizations due to the amount of information in circulation on the web. Information is not so easily lost in one remote newspaper or media outlet, as it used to be, because of the activities of websurfers and search engines. Indeed, I would go so far as to say that there is always someone out there who is much better informed about a story than the journalist. The advent of communications technology like the internet, which is so widely available, means that commercial organizations, like the media themselves, need to have greater respect than ever for the consumers of information.

I believe that the speed and efficiency of the technology is a catalyst for corporate change. This produces great challenges for big organizations, which, because they're big and unwieldy, take time to get themselves together. If there's some allegation somewhere out there on Twitter, which for some reason is getting picked up and circulated, you haven't got two days to go into a corporate meeting to sort out your response; you've got an hour or two at most. Big organizations struggle with being able to respond that dynamically. They need to find a way of doing it, and they need to have people who understand this new environment, who are empowered to do that.

A rumor can gather momentum with great speed on the web, especially if it is championed by a skillful blogger or commentator. It was Churchill who said that "A lie gets halfway around the world before the truth has a chance to get its pants on."

I believe that slicker and more efficient processes for preparing responses to a journalist's critique of a company are critical. The old and laborious top-down processes will be too cumbersome to reverse the momentum of criticism. Communications functions need to be shaken up, ensuring swifter communication between the company's knowledge centers and its media and news dissemination functions. Senior management needs to understand new communications technology. Managers need to be aware not only of the information that is in circulation, but also of the company's own communications strategy and media. The media-orientated company is very inclusive, unhierarchical, and engaged. New communications technologies are also highly challenging to the stratified institution that puts media into a discrete department that does not adequately communicate with hands-on management and staff.

I would argue that the same media that have the scope to damage a company through reputational loss also present the company with some extraordinary opportunities. It can, for example, have its own journalists who blog on the web to enhance the company's presence. Companies can also launch their own television channels to compete with independent stations. Finally, they may wish over time to link up with other companies across many sectors to launch an entirely separate corporate internet, a most radical and speculative proposal!

THE INTERNET

I am convinced that the value of the internet as a showcase for your company cannot be exaggerated. There is an increasing appetite among companies to tell their own stories and have direct access to their consumers, stakeholders, and suppliers as well. They are beginning to recognize that the means to do this can be their own website or television channel; it can be through social media, on Twitter or Facebook, or whatever else; they're beginning to recognize the effectiveness of direct communication with the public, and of being able to inform those conversations, and there is huge potential in all of that.

The web presents a company with a forum that is not controlled by a media company on which to present its point of view and inform the wider debate. It is no longer dependent on journalists and commentators, who may have their established prejudices. The internet allows the company to go direct to the audience, rather than through a mediated channel. It represents a remarkable shift. They don't have to go to a magazine and argue to get a little paragraph on page 7 any more. They can do it themselves, and go direct to the public in a rather sophisticated media sense, which is far more powerful. In terms of telling their own story, they can be very effective. You'd hope that responsible organizations do it with integrity and values and so on, and I think the vast majority of them will do so.

There is no doubt that the use of journalists sponsored by a company to

"There are three secrets to managing. The first secret is have patience. The second is be patient. And the third most important secret is patience." Chuck Tanner

blog about it is now a widespread practice among more savvy corporations. I advise companies using this technique to make sure that they are transparent and open about the provenance of the information retailed by the journalist. The company that is shown to be deceiving the wider media will instantly lose face. Indeed, independent journalists, alert as they now are to the extensive use of sponsored bloggers, will assume that the opaque and untransparent company has something to hide that is to its detriment. The key to corporate blogging is transparency. If someone gets a journalist who pretends to be independent when they're not, that's just going to lead to problems because they will be found out, which is a very stupid thing to do. If they're transparent about it, it's just another conversation that's out there, and people can take it or leave it, and make up their own minds about it.

Technology is moving very quickly and I advise corporates reviewing their media strategies to think beyond blogging. A blog is a rather static way of doing it now, and it's much more about Twitter and other media forms. These conversations are much faster, much more dynamic, and you have to be in there. Someone can put something up on Twitter and it'll spread out, so you need to be back in there within an hour or two saying well, actually, here's another point of view.

While corporates are exploring the latest forms of media and communications, I have observed that some have gone one step further and are discussing the possibility of creating an entirely separate internet structure. This would deal with the vexed issue of payment for access to websites. The new structure would run in parallel to the "public web" and users would be required to pay to enter this "private web." Corporates would collect a subscription and would reserve their most exclusive information for the pay-to-use web. There are a number of suggestions by big corporates and others that they could build a parallel internet, a commercial internet. You'd have to pay for this, there would be different terms of access.

I would observe that this raises the question about the free flow of information. A philosophical debate is starting about whether it is right that the internet is free to all forever—or, actually, should you get more if you're prepared to pay, or get something different if you're prepared to pay?

Companies is every field are under growing pressure to make money out of the web as more users turn away from traditional media and seek their information on the internet and in new media. It is not obvious that subscriptions are the answer. Newspapers have to find a viable business model, so it's perfectly reasonable to look at subscription. Content is not free and it's got to be paid for, whether through advertising or subscriptions or something else. I don't think it'll work because you are sacrificing about 80% of your traffic—the casual grazers, who come through Google and just want to look at whatever they've searched for—for the 20% who are brand loyalists.

I am concerned that you're going to shut out the people who just casually come across the site, because actually they don't spend very long there; they're not very loyal, and they're not looking at the ads. So, we'll sacrifice all of them, and we'll get more value out of the people who actually want what our product is producing, and are prepared to subscribe to it.

I accept that there may be an economic case for such an approach. But I am concerned that you're starting to build up walls, so you're not part of the public realm and the public debate on the web. Articles start not to show up on Google, or if they do show up people can't look at them without having to decide whether they want to take out a subscription; you start to shut off your content, and the debate around your content, into a smaller and smaller sub-community. Meanwhile the whole public realm is going on outside, and it becomes different.

CONCLUSION

The state-of-the-art company has always placed communications at the top of its list of priorities. But now the effort required to monitor and maximize the power of communications has increased as technology moves forward at breakneck speed. This means that more money needs to be spent on keeping up with the latest and most sophisticated media.

Although there is a cost, there is also an opportunity. As the latest media offer companies greater and more free exposure, many argue that companies have no choice but to follow where the new media lead. Every company needs to be a media company, and those that duck the choice will be made to rue their decision. The internet is an unforgiving institution.

MORE INFO

Books:

Gillin, Paul. *The New Influencers: A Marketer's Guide to the New Social Media*. Sanger, CA: Quill Driver Books/Word Dancer Press, 2007.

Gillmor, Dan. *We the Media: Grassroots Journalism By the People, For the People*. Sebastopol, CA: O'Reilly Media, 2004.

Kovach, Bill, and Tom Rosenstiel. *The Elements of Journalism: What Newspeople Should Know and the Public Should Expect*. New York: Three Rivers Press, 2001.

Tapscott, Don. *Grown Up Digital: How the Net Generation is Changing Your World*. New York: McGraw-Hill, 2009.

See Also:

Wikinomics: How Mass Collaboration Changes Everything (p. 1437)
Media (pp. 1877–1878)

"Good management to Wall Street means nothing more than a company with three consecutive quarters of rising earnings. Make it four quarters and you have great management." Ralph Wanger

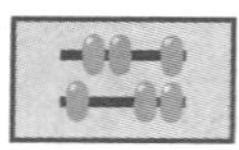

Everything You Need to Know About Benchmarking

by Robin Mann

EXECUTIVE SUMMARY

- Benchmarking is much more than a comparison of performance.
- Benchmarking focuses on learning from the experience of others and can be defined as "identifying, adapting, and implementing the practices that produce the best performance results."
- Benchmarking is a powerful method for breakthrough thinking, innovation, and improvement, and for delivering exceptional bottom-line results.
- New benchmarking methodologies aim to ensure that benchmarking projects result in major benefits, both financial and nonfinancial.
- New tools available on the internet make benchmarking easier.

INTRODUCTION

Organizations are constantly looking for new ways and methodologies to improve their performance and gain a competitive advantage. As they seek improvements to their own business processes, many organizations recognize the importance of learning from best practices that have been achieved by other organizations. By removing the need to reinvent the wheel and providing the potential to adopt proven practices, benchmarking has become an important methodology for providing a fast track to achieving organizational excellence.

TYPES OF BENCHMARKING

It is useful to distinguish between the main types of benchmarking.

First, there is *informal benchmarking*. This is a type of benchmarking that most of us do unconsciously at work and in our home life. We constantly compare and learn from the behavior and practices of others—whether it is how to use a software program, cook a better meal, or play our favorite sport. In the context of work, most learning from informal benchmarking comes from the following:

- Talking to colleagues and learning from their experience (coffee breaks and team meetings are a great place to network and learn from others);
- Consulting with experts (for example, business consultants who have experience of implementing a particular process or activity in many business environments);
- Networking with people from other organizations at conferences, seminars, and internet forums;
- Websites, online databases, and publications that share benchmarking information provide quick and easy ways to learn of best practices and benchmarks.

Second, there is *formal benchmarking*, of which there are two types: performance benchmarking, and best practice benchmarking.

Performance Benchmarking

Performance benchmarking describes the comparison of performance data obtained by studying similar processes or activities. Comparisons of performance may be undertaken between companies, or internally within an organization. It is useful for identifying strengths and opportunities for improvement. Performance benchmarking may involve the comparison of financial measures (such as expenditure, cost of labor, cost of buildings/equipment, cost of energy, adherence to budget, cash flow, revenue collected) or nonfinancial measures (such as absenteeism, staff turnover, the percentage of administrative staff to front-line staff, budget processing time, complaints, environmental impact, or call centre performance).

Most people equate benchmarking to performance benchmarking. This is unfortunate, because performance benchmarking on its own is of limited use. Too often performance benchmarking data are collected (often at significant cost) and no further action is taken after the data have been obtained. While performance benchmarking enables a performance gap to be identified, it does not provide the idea, best practice, or solution as to how performance can be improved and the gap closed.

Best Practice Benchmarking

Best practice benchmarking describes the comparison of performance data obtained by studying similar processes or activities *and identifying, adapting, and implementing the practices that produced the best performance results*. Best practice benchmarking is the most powerful type of benchmarking. It is used for learning from the experience of others and achieving breakthrough improvements in performance. Best practice benchmarking focuses on "action"—i.e. doing something with the comparison data and learning why other organizations are achieving higher levels of performance.

Best practice benchmarking projects typically take from two to four months to identify best practices. The practices then need to be adapted and implemented. The time taken for the whole project varies depending on the project's scope and importance, and on the resources used. Projects are usually resource-intensive (in terms of the project team's time), and so care needs to be taken that they focus on issues of high strategic importance that will deliver major bottom-line benefits.

POPULARITY OF BENCHMARKING

Research by the Centre for Organisational Excellence Research (COER), on behalf of the Global Benchmarking Network, identified the popularity of benchmarking in comparison to other business improvement tools.[1] This research was based on a survey that was completed by over 450 companies from more than 20 countries.

Figure 1 shows the results in terms of the popularity of 20 business improvement tools. *Mission and vision statements* and *Customer (client) surveys* were the most popular (used by 77% of organizations), followed by *Strengths, weaknesses, opportunities, and threats* (72%), and *Informal benchmarking* (68%). *Performance benchmarking* was used by 49% and *Best practice benchmarking* by 39%.

WHAT IS THE PAYBACK FROM BENCHMARKING

This depends on the type of benchmarking used. For informal or performance benchmarking it is difficult to assess as these types of benchmarking are focused on organizational learning and/or better decision-making, and usually the benefits are not quantified by organizations that employ these techniques. However, it can be assumed that these methods, and benchmarking in general, are very important if an organization wishes to compete nationally and internationally—it makes sense for an organization to have management processes and systems of a similar or better standard than competitors. Certainly, business excellence models, which are used in over 80 countries to encourage

"Fools say 'Learn from your mistakes.' I prefer to learn from the mistakes of others." Otto von Bismarck

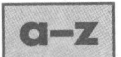

Figure 1. Use of business improvement tools worldwide. (From study by COER, 2008[2])

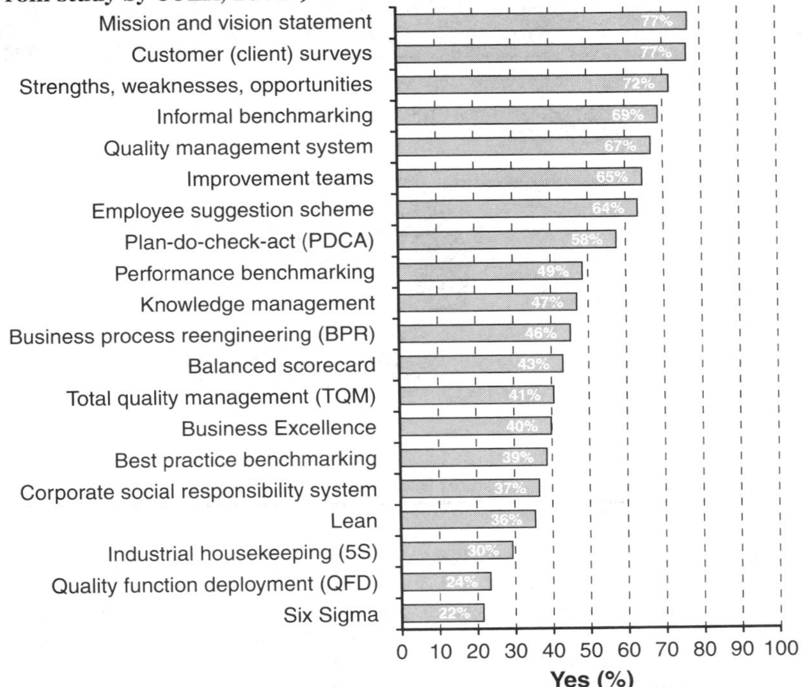

companies to apply the principles of business excellence, have as a core element the need for organizations to benchmark, identify performance gaps, and learn from others. The most popular business excellence models are the Baldrige Criteria for Performance Excellence (developed in the United States), where benchmarking accounts for approximately 50% of the model score, and the European Foundation for Quality Management (EFQM) Excellence Model. For further details, see under Websites at the end of the article.

For best practice benchmarking, the payback can be calculated on a project by project basis. Payback, from a financial perspective, is likely to vary depending on the specific aims of the project. If projects are carefully selected, planned, and managed, there is no reason why major benefits (financial and nonfinancial) should not be obtained. A study of 30 organizations that used best practice benchmarking indicated an average financial return of $100,000 to $150,000 per project, with some reaping benefits of more than $1,000,000 per project.[3]

There are many case studies that focus on the success gained through benchmarking. The best known of these describe the experience of Xerox, which was the pioneer in applying benchmarking concepts (Dr Robert Camp, previously of Xerox, wrote the first book on benchmarking in 1989). It was in the late 1970s and early 1980s that Xerox, faced with ruin due to more efficient Japanese competitors, first undertook some performance benchmarking, and the findings were astonishing. The results showed that:

- Xerox's ratio of indirect to direct staff was twice that of the direct competition;
- It had nine times the number of production suppliers;
- Assembly line rejects were in the order of ten times worse;
- Defects per 100 machines were seven times worse;
- Product time to market was twice as long.

To address this crisis, Xerox developed its benchmarking approach to identify not only performance gaps but also to learn why other organizations were performing better. Much of this learning came from studying the practices of organizations from outside their industry, as this often resulted in identifying breakthrough practices. For example, Xerox benchmarked L.L. Bean, a Maine outdoor sporting goods retailer, because of their excellent warehouse procedures (which are now the standard at most companies). In total, over a period of ten years, almost 230 performance areas were benchmarked. This resulted in Xerox becoming an industry leader and recognized as world class. Xerox won the Malcolm Baldrige National Quality Award in the United States in 1989.

METHODOLOGIES FOR BEST PRACTICE BENCHMARKING

There is no single benchmarking methodology that has been universally adopted. The wide appeal and acceptance of benchmarking has led to the emergence of a range of benchmarking methodologies. TRADE is one such methodology. The TRADE

Figure 2. TRADE best practice benchmarking methodology

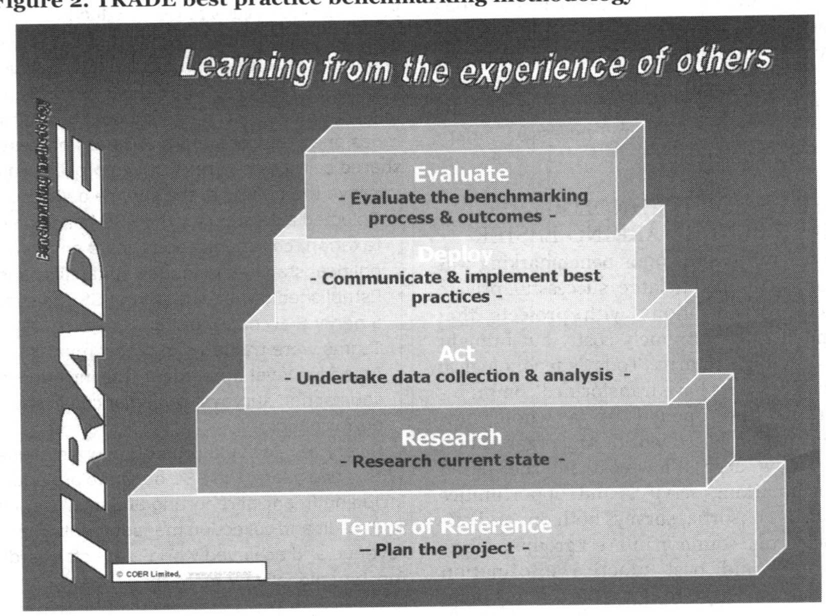

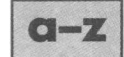

benchmarking methodology (Figure 2) focuses on the exchange (or "trade") of information and best practices to improve the performance of processes, goods and services. TRADE consists of five stages:

- **T**erms of reference: Plan the project (aims, objectives, scope, resources, cost/benefit analysis);
- **R**esearch: Research the current state/performance;
- **A**ct: Undertake data collection and analysis to compare against others;
- **D**eploy: Communicate and implement best practices;
- **E**valuate: Evaluate the benchmarking process and outcomes to ensure that the project has achieved its aims.

Benchmarking projects should be targeted at a process area or activity that will deliver the best value to an organization. The project aim can be broad, or it can be specific. The aim may relate to improving the performance of a process, activity/task, business improvement tool, equipment, strategy, or behaviour. Examples of project aims are:

- To improve a customer complaint management process to world-class standard;
- To identify and implement best practices in the application of the balanced scorecard;
- To become an industry leader in ways of providing financial information to clients;
- To develop a winning team culture;
- To reduce the time taken to recruit new staff.

Once a project aim is set, the process or activity to be studied should be broken down into its component parts and current performance measured. Benchmarking partners to learn from can then be identified for the component parts and their practices studied through surveys or site visits. An analysis is then conducted to determine which processes or activities should be adopted and, after any necessary adaptations, implemented.

THE USE OF TECHNOLOGY TO MAKE BENCHMARKING EASIER

In the 1980s and 1990s benchmarking was mainly confined to large, successful, private sector organizations with projects that tended to be extremely costly but brought in very high returns. Today's technological advancements have transformed communications and opened up a whole new information-based world. Any organization can now access low-cost internet-based benchmarking services and opportunities such as consortia, surveys both on- and off-line, virtual common interest groups such as forums, and best practice information resources. These resources are a real boon to organizations that want to access best practices and expert advice/opinion but do not have the resources for full-scale benchmarking projects.

The Business Performance Improvement Resource (BPIR; see under Websites at the end of the article) is one of the new resources that are a valuable support to benchmarking projects. The BPIR (Figure 3) is a vast knowledge repository containing databases with thousands of benchmarks, measures, best practices, benchmarking partners, case studies, and studies/trends that cover virtually every aspect of business. The resource can help to improve any business practice, from handling customer complaints, through undertaking performance appraisals, to improving strategic planning processes. PricewaterhouseCoopers summed up the potential that this new generation of tools can have. In a Trendsetter Barometer Survey,[4] it concluded that evidence suggested that users of benchmarking databases can achieve 69% faster growth and 45% greater productivity than nonusers.

Figure 3. Business Performance Improvement Resource (www.BPIR.com)

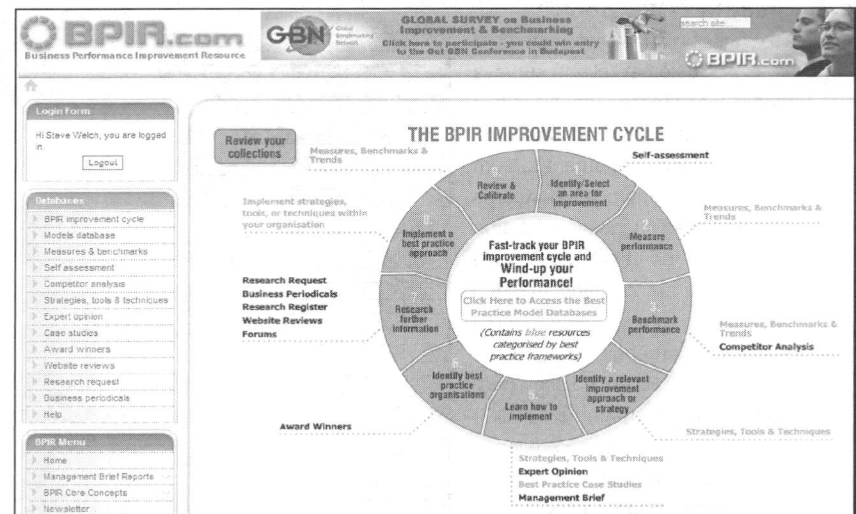

CASE STUDY

Benchmarking Leads to Cost Reduction of the Finance Function

An Australian company conducted a global benchmarking exercise on its finance function and found that it had an outdated infrastructure that cost more than 4% of company revenues to run, that staff spent more than half of their time collecting data, and that the information did not meet its global business information needs. A reengineering team redesigned the company's business processes and proposed that the company create a shared services centre (SSC) to process common transactions, drive down costs, and improve the quality of the service delivery. The company achieved the following:

- Selected a location for the SSC based on the quality/skill/cost/flexibility of the workforce, taxation, communications costs and infrastructure, real estate cost, travel accessibility, political stability, language suitability, and company infrastructure;
- Established three teams in the SSC: a supplier process team, a customer process team, and a general accounting team;
- Teams were trained and a new mind-set was developed to service the business units;
- A service level agreement was introduced and customer satisfaction surveys, employee satisfaction surveys, the balanced scorecard, and Six Sigma were used to measure performance;
- Salary reviews and promotion were aligned with performance.

Within two years, the SSC began to provide high value-added services to the business units, including financial reporting and analysis, treasury management, tax and legal consulting, and credit and collection management. The cost of running the SSC was less than 1% of sales revenue and achieved world-class standards. The SSC reduced the cost of the finance function globally by more than 50%.

"Benchmarking is the process of identifying, understanding and adapting superior practices from organizations locally and worldwide to help your organization improve its performance and achieve priority business results." Robert Camp

  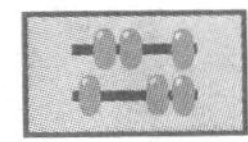      

CONCLUSION

Benchmarking is a proven, powerful tool that can facilitate improvements to efficiency by organizations, increase value added, and enable them to gain a competitive edge. The rationale underpinning benchmarking is sound, and the benchmarking concept of learning from others should be embedded throughout all improvement-focused organizations. Benchmarking projects should be linked to key organizational objectives, and support from senior management needs to be both strong and visible.

There is little doubt about the potential and versatility of benchmarking as a tool. It has been successfully applied by organizations of different sizes and in different industry sectors and has become one of the most popular management tools. However, it is thought that most organizations use performance benchmarking (comparing performance) rather than the more powerful but resource-intensive approach of best practice benchmarking (comparing and learning from others and implementing best practices). Using best practice benchmarking methodologies, such as TRADE, and website resources, such as the BPIR website, will help more organizations to reap the benefits of benchmarking.

MAKING IT HAPPEN

Benchmarking—learning from the experience of others—makes common sense. How should this technique be used to reap the most benefits? Here are some tips:

- Undertake a self-assessment (a business excellence self-assessment is best) or quality audit, or have a brainstorming meeting to identify key opportunities for improvement in your organization. For those key practices or processes that require improvement, undertake a best practice benchmarking project to seek out best practices. If you do not have the resource to do this, search for benchmarks and best practices using a literature or website search.
- Have at least one person within your organization who is trained in benchmarking and who acts as your benchmarking champion. This person can help to facilitate your benchmarking projects and/or conduct benchmarking research.
- When undertaking reviews of your organization's processes and practices, always ask the question "Is this a best practice?" If evidence is not forthcoming that it is a best practice, then it suggests that the process or practice will benefit from benchmarking.
- When undertaking benchmarking, ensure that your organization follows an internationally recognized benchmarking code of conduct.[5] A code of conduct provides ethical guidelines and protocols on the exchange of information between organizations.
- Benchmark your benchmarking process. Learn from others how to conduct benchmarking successfully, and continually strive to refine your process to achieve better outcomes.

MORE INFO

Book:

Camp, Robert C. *Benchmarking: The Search for Industry Best Practices That Lead to Superior Performance.* Portland, OR: Productivity Press, 1989.

Websites:

Baldrige National Quality Program, on the National Institute of Standards and Technology (NIST) website. A US government website that promotes the Baldrige Criteria for Performance Excellence: www.quality.nist.gov

Business Performance Improvement Resource (BPIR) has a large collection of information and resources on benchmarking and best practice: www.bpir.com

Centre for Organisational Excellence Research (COER), a New Zealand-based research and consultancy organization headed by the author. The website provides information on business excellence and TRADE benchmarking projects: www.coer.org.nz

European Foundation for Quality Management (EFQM), developers and custodians of the EFQM Excellence Model: www.efqm.org

Global Benchmarking Network (GBN) provides a listing of the main promoters/experts in benchmarking from over 20 countries: www.globalbenchmarking.org

See Also:

✔ Assessing Business Performance (p. 1144)
✔ Understanding Internal Audits (p. 1057)
✔ Understanding Strategy Maps (p. 1182)
✔ What Is Benchmarking? (p. 1184)
Michael Eugene Porter (p. 1299)
Balanced Scorecard: Translating Strategy into Action (p. 1333)

NOTES

1 Centre for Organisational Excellence Research (COER). *Report on the Global Use of Business Improvement Tools and Benchmarking* COER Report. Palmerston North, New Zealand: Massey University, November 2008. Available from: www.coer.org.nz

2 *Ibid.*

3 *Ibid.*

4 PricewaterhouseCoopers (PWC). "Fast-growth companies that benchmark grow faster, are more productive than their peers." Barometer Surveys, May 1, 2002. Online at: www.barometersurveys.com, go to "Trendsetter Barometer," and download from "Archives."

5 Global Benchmarking Network (GBN). *Benchmarking Code of Conduct.* Berlin: GBN Secretariat, 2008. Available from: www.globalbenchmarking.org/download_archive

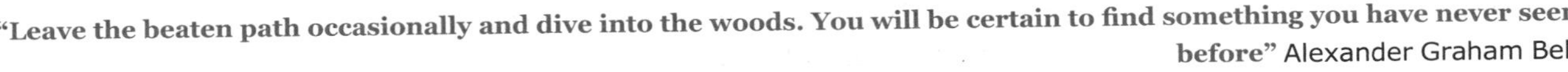
"Leave the beaten path occasionally and dive into the woods. You will be certain to find something you have never seen before" Alexander Graham Bell

  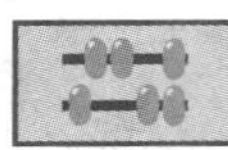   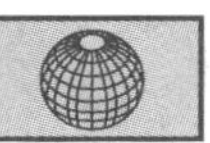   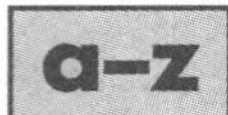

Viewpoint: The Evolving Role of the CFO

by Aldo Mareuse

INTRODUCTION

Aldo Mareuse, 44, has been chief financial officer of Orascom Telecom Holding, the Middle East's most successful mobile telecoms group since 2002. Based in Cairo, Egypt, Orascom Telecom is listed on the Cairo and London stock exchanges. Aldo Mareuse is also CFO of Weather Investment SpA, a private company that owns a majority stake in Orascom Telecom. Weather also owns Wind, Italy's third largest mobile operator, and Wind Hellas, the third largest such operator in Greece. Prior to joining Orascom Telecom, Frenchman Mareuse worked in various positions and locations for the investment bank Credit Suisse First Boston. His last role was as managing director of CSFB's investment banking division, telecommunications group, where he focused on advising telecom players in M&A, equity and debt financing. He holds an engineering degree from École Centrale de Lyon and is married with three children. When he is not traveling between Islamabad, Cairo, Rome or New York in the winter, he enjoys back country skiing in the Alps or in the Rockies, and in the summer he likes to cruise on the Mediterranean.

How has the CFO role evolved in the past five to 10 years?

The whole pace has stepped up a gear. Capital markets have evolved dramatically in the past five years and continue to evolve. As a result, the capital markets function has become much more central to the CFO role. Financings have become much more sophisticated and the products used for raising capital—including equity, debt, and a range of other instruments—have a much shorter lifetime. So the CFO has to be much more aware of his products and able to make decisions more quickly. In the old days, you could plan something six months ahead. That's no longer possible.

Has Orascom Telecom been actively raising capital in recent times?

Even though it is a private company, Weather Investments SpA is much bigger than Orascom. Like Weather, we have raised a substantial amount of debt, across the spectrum including bank debt, bonds and mezzanine finance. So we have covered the capital markets spectrum and have been extremely active in the last three to four years.

Have you found that raising capital became more difficult since the credit crisis erupted in August 2007?

Basically the market has been frozen. So it hasn't been difficult; it's been non-existent. This has meant that, in the short term, the CFO role has been much more about looking at cost reduction and free cash flow optimization, rather than the capital market activities, which have been shut down. The CFO role has become a much more inwardly focused function than a year or so ago.

How do you predict the CFO role will evolve over the next five or 10 years? Will we return to a more outward-looking function and more active in capital markets?

I don't think the capital markets will be nearly as active as they were in the period between 2003 and 2007. They're going to be much slower for a very long period of time. It's going to be much more difficult and expensive to raise finance. And the focus will be more on the cash flow a company generates, rather than raising it externally from third parties.

Will that make the CFO's job more boring and/or more difficult?

I don't know if it will become more boring, but it will certainly become more difficult. During the period of easy credit, you could simply put up your hand and five banks would come offering you whatever you wanted. It had become slightly artificial, slightly surreal. It's back to basics now.

What other factors are driving change in the way finance departments must function?

As a result of Sarbanes-Oxley, we have an odd situation where corporates are obliged to be very transparent. They have to publish earnings releases quarterly, disclose numbers every quarter, and respond openly to detailed questions from investors. Yet, the hedge funds and long-only investors who are asking these questions are under no obligation to tell you how many shares they own, or indeed if they have any at all. There's an un-level playing field in transparency. Investors want all this transparency, but they're not being transparent themselves. I always laugh when I sit down with an investor and he asks me why my profit margin fell from 43.5% to 43.2% in a given quarter; I then ask him if he holds any shares and he says, "Sorry, I can't tell you."

Do you think that ought to change?

There's so much pressure for hedge funds to be more transparent; yes, I think that this will definitely change.

How can finance managers, including CFOs, add value to their organizations and ensure standards of corporate governance are improved? What attributes do CFOs need to achieve this?

The best tools the CFO has in his armory are the financial results themselves. However, there's lots of leeway in terms of how you present these results. You can present the same set of figures to the same accountancy standards. However, one version could be made so opaque that hardly anybody understands it, and another could be written so transparently that everybody instantly understands the issues.

What's the temptation as a CFO? Is it to produce the opaque type or the transparent type?

That is a very, very important question, and I don't really have the answer. If you disclose too much, and you don't know the agenda of the investor, who is across the table from you, you could really suffer. In the past, I would always have advocated full transparency, but I've discovered that this can work against you.

Can you give me an example of how that could work against you?

Well, let's say a corporate does an attractive financing. Let's say the terms of this

"People are ambitious and unrealistic. They set targets for themselves that are higher than what you would set for them. And because they set them, they hit them." Liisa Joronen

financing are based on the share price. If you were to disclose all the terms, some investors—and particularly hedge funds—are going to play against you.

Do you mean by pushing the share price up or down?

Yes, depending on whether your financing is built on the share price going up or down. With the derivatives tools that are available now, you can do whatever you want in terms of financing. And obviously people can play against you and they don't have to tell anyone. If someone is a short-seller of your stock, he doesn't have to tell you that he's a shorter; yet, he's going to ask you exactly the same sorts of questions that a long-only investor would ask you. It can be quite frustrating.

Would you say that part of it is trying to second guess these guys whenever you're preparing how to release information to the market?

Exactly. Whenever you're preparing financial statements and other reports, it's difficult because these documents are going to be published and could be read by anybody.

What about ethical values? How do they sit in all this?

At the end of the day, what you always carry with you is your reputation. As a CFO, this is arguably the most important asset you have. Therefore, you need to maintain it at any price. Frankly speaking, I am not a big fan of all these Sarbanes-Oxley rules. I have been a board member of a company listed in the US and which has to abide by all these rules. It's a lot of paperwork; it makes a lot more money for the lawyers, but it doesn't increase transparency at all.

Did the use of "fair value" accounting exacerbate the recent financial crisis?

It definitely did. The US banks ran into trouble much faster than the European banks, because the European banks had more leeway in terms of not marking assets to market. That put the US banks in a very tight spot. I wouldn't be surprised if there are still further big blowouts among European banks. I am not sure that forcing banks to mark to market immediately is a particularly good idea. It just intensifies the nervousness and panic in the market.

Should CFOs be more cognizant of nonfinancial performance indicators, including the environmental and social impact of their business, over and above their existing focus on financial performance?

As CFOs, we are not currently equipped to do this. However, in principle, I believe that the CFO should worry more about these things. In future, companies are going to have to properly allocate resources to measure all that.

What sort of relationship should the CFO have with the CEO, other board members and with investors?

At the end of the day, the CEO and the board decide on the allocation of capital.

The allocation of capital is an easy task if you've got good tools, and the CFO is there to provide these tools, both to the board and to external investors. Obviously, reporting to the CEO, the CFO has to provide all the relevant numbers and ensure these are robust, reliable and transparent, for the benefit of the entire board as well as investors.

In terms of the training required for a CFO, the traditional route is for them to first qualify as accountants, work in private practice and then move into the industry. Is this a sensible career path?

Accountants tend to be good at recording what has happened in the past but they are generally pretty clueless when it comes to thinking about the future. In today's market, it's more important to be able to raise funds. If you're able to raise funds, you can talk to investors and you can probably also do a budget. These three functions are critically important. Because I was an investment banker at CSFB before becoming Orascom's CFO, I found it easy to do the financing part, the investor relations part, the budget part, and the treasury part. It was more of a challenge for me to do the accounting part.

What is your view of the quality of audits provided by the "big four" accountancy firms PricewaterhouseCoopers, Ernst & Young, KPMG, and Deloitte?

There is substantial room for improvement in the quality of the audit reports. They don't really understand the commercial issues. And, if you don't understand commercial issues, you don't understand risk. They're just playing by the book. They are too focused on rules, and they often don't understand the bigger picture. Accountancy firms and rating agencies need to improve their understanding of the issues before they can provide more added value. They're more into preservation, acting as a safety net to ensure companies don't do things that are completely stupid.

So what can be done to improve the quality of auditing?

I think audit firms should employ higher caliber people, which would make auditing more expensive.

But you, as a company, would be happy to pay more if you were getting better quality auditing?

If the entire industry was doing it, yes. It would enhance the quality of all companies' financials and give investors less incentive to question the figures all the time. So, at the end of the day, yes.

A few years ago there were suggestions that it was somehow inappropriate for a Cairo-based group to acquire a mobile phone company in developed countries. Does that sort of prejudice still exist?

When we bought Italy-based Wind, people were saying, "What is Italy doing? They're selling a mobile phone company to an Egyptian!" There was an assumption that we would turn up on camels wearing djellabas! Likewise, eyebrows were raised when Mittal bought Arcelor. Now, however, everybody understands that an Indian, Chinese or Asian company can manage assets in Europe or the US better than the Europeans or Americans. Whilst the credit crisis caused emerging markets to become less fashionable, in the long term, the growth is going to be these markets. Everyone understands they have disciplined management teams, who are capable of running assets anywhere in the world.

MORE INFO

Books:

Bainville, Jacques, and Hamish Miles (trans). *Napoleon*. Paperback ed. Safety Harbor, FL: Simon Publications, 2002.

Carnegie, Dale. *How to Win Friends and Influence People*. New ed. London: Vermillion, 2007.

Gallo, Max. *Louis XIV: Le Roi Soleil*. Paris: XO Editions, 2007.

Minc, Alain. *Une Histoire de France*. Paris: Éditions Grasset & Fasquelle, 2008.

See Also:

★ Viewpoint: The CFO and the Sustainable Corporation (pp. 719–720)

★ Viewpoint: The Changing Role of the CFO (pp. 806–807)

"We have a technique at Hewlett-Packard for helping managers and supervisors know their people and understand the work their people are doing ... Management by Walking About." David Packard

Fraud: Minimizing the Impact on Corporate Image

by Tim Johnson

EXECUTIVE SUMMARY

- Fraud is a threat faced by all organizations, regardless of their size or sector, that can easily plunge any organization into crisis, real or perceived.
- The key to crisis management—particularly when trust in business remains very low—is to set the agenda, communicate robustly, and not allow speculation or rumor to run rife.
- Robust communication strategies require organizations to consider their *message*, their *audience*, and the *medium* theywill use to communicate their message.
- In cases of fraud, such messages should center on *concern*, *control*, *commitment*,and *containment*.

INTRODUCTION

The threat of fraud is faced by all organizations regardless of their size or sector. From the perspective of reputation management, controlling the impact of fraud is particularly challenging for two reasons:

1 That an organization has become a victim of fraud suggests either that someone in the organization is corrupt, or that the organization and its compliance systems are vulnerable. Neither possibility inspires confidence.

2 The word "fraud" has a wide range of meanings. It can refer to a sustained, systemic failure that can bring an organization to its knees. Or it can refer to low-level compliance failure that, while regrettable, is unlikely to lead to long-lasting damage.

If fraud has been committed or is suspected, how can an organization's reputation be protected? First, we need to understand what reputation is and its importance. We also need to understand the rudiments of crisis reputation management.

REPUTATION AND WHY IT IS IMPORTANT

Reputation is hard to define. Famously, there are numerous definitions. Put simply, it is the sum total of what our stakeholders feel about a company and how they act as a result of that feeling. This sounds woolly, and indeed it is. Over the years, many attempts have been made to try and measure organizational reputation in quantifiable and, preferably, hard financial terms. Some progress has been made. But you still won't find a line on the asset—or liability—side of your balance sheet that refers to your organization's reputation.

Most practitioners and academics now accept that reputation will always be difficult to define and quantify. However, there is broad agreement that reputation is built on the trust stakeholders have in an organization, and that trust is far from woolly. On the contrary, trust brings hard commercial benefits: it helps to build strong brands, launch new products, secure licensing deals, recruit the best staff, and avoid intrusive regulation. Few would disagree that protecting that trust, and thus reputation, is critical to the business.

However, that's easier said than done because trust is a rare commodity—particularly in light of high-profile incidents, such as the rogue trading which led to the collapse of Barings Bank and, more recently, the Enron scandal. In 2006, Ipsos MORI found that only 31% of those surveyed in the United Kingdom trusted business leaders to tell the truth. This lack of trust manifests itself in many ways, including a surge in the numbers of nongovernmental organizations, a breakdown in accepted societal structures, and the growth of antiglobalization sentiment that is often fueled by an aggressive 24/7 media. Even during times of "business as usual," reputation management is not an easy business.

So what should be done to protect organizational reputation during a crisis prompted by, for example, a case of fraud?

CRISIS COMMUNICATIONS

When something goes wrong, the natural instinct is to want to fix the problem behind closed doors. This is perfectly understandable, and in an ideal world the issue would be attended to and the relevant stakeholders told about the actions taken to rectify the problem—if anyone needs to be told at all.

However, in a world of citizen journalists and social networking, even problems such as *suspected* fraud become harder to contain within an organization. News often leaks to the wider world long before the organization has found a solution. Sometimes, news can reach the outside world even before it reaches management.

In such circumstances, the key to reputation management is to be ready and willing to communicate about the problem, outlining what has happened, the extent of the situation, and, critically, what the organization is doing to put it right. The organization must establish itself as the authoritative source of information about the situation, crushing harmful speculation and robustly deflecting the vicious rumors that inevitably accompany such stories.

In developing such a communication plan, an organization needs to consider the following factors:

- *Message*: What it will say about the situation and when.
- *Audience*: Who it will say it to and in what order.
- *Medium*: The platform it will use to say it.

Each crisis situation is different, but in cases of fraud organizations should consider the following.

Key Considerations

Messaging

Fraud can be brought to an organization's attention in many ways (for example, internal audit, whistleblower, media inquiry, etc.). Regardless of how the news reaches an organization, holding messages are required immediately. These are for use until an investigation is complete.

In cases of fraud, the "4Cs" should be applied:

- *Concern* (for what's happened): The incident is being treated extremely seriously.
- *Control* (of the situation): The claim is being investigated thoroughly.
- *Containment* (of the consequences): While regrettable, this will not have a material impact on the organization.
- *Commitment* (to compliance): "If this is the first time such an allegation has been made, initiate organizational compliance procedures over and above what is required."

It is often helpful when considering how to communicate *containment* to try to contextualize the message. For example, "This allegation relates to less than 0.0001% of turnover in just one of 30 markets we operate in." However, it is important not to downplay the alleged fraud if it may materially affect the organization.

Audience

Although an organization should be prepared to use this interim messaging widely and rapidly, if news of the alleged fraud is successfully contained, it may only be

"Bad administration, to be sure, can destroy good policy; but good administration can never save bad policy." Adlai E. Stevenson

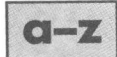

Figure 1. Stakeholder mapping—Matrix to plot which audiences should receive proactive communication in a crisis

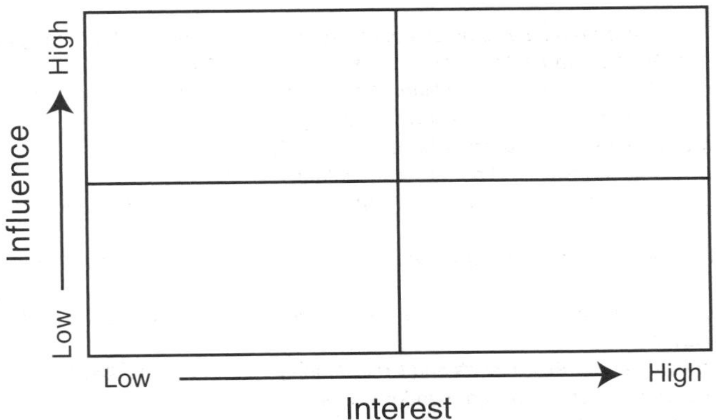

necessary to communicate it to a limited number of stakeholders.

To help identify which stakeholders should be proactively notified with these messages, an organization must consider which of its audiences have an interest in the problem (often the same as those who are affected) and those who may have some influence on its resolution. This can be plotted on a simple matrix (see figure 1).

Stakeholders in the top right-hand corner should be identified and a stepwise briefing process should be implemented. Clearly, this takes judgment and this is where external reputation management advisers can prove extremely valuable. When identifying your stakeholders, it is important to be as precise about them as possible:

- "Staff" is not a useful stakeholder category. A specific level of management in a specific department is more useful and will focus the process.
- There may be regulatory procedures to follow (for example, stock market announcements), and these must be adhered to.

Finally, it is worth noting that through an organization's ongoing "peacetime" reputation management program, solid relationships with these key stakeholders should already be in place. This is known as banking "relationship credit." The more relationship credit you have banked in peacetime, the easier it will be to draw on that credit in times of crisis, and the more forgiving stakeholders are likely to be.

Medium

Organizations should form a small senior team to manage the situation and use it to brainstorm how these messages will be delivered—for example, in person, by written letter, or via the media. However, it is important not to overcomplicate this part of the process. It is simply a case of considering those who are being notified and thinking about how they might be approached. For example, the head of a regulatory agency may appreciate it if the organization's CEO/MD delivers these messages in person.

There are three additional considerations:

- It is often useful (with legal advice) to put things in writing to stakeholders. However, always assume that whatever is written may be leaked or will be subject to compulsory disclosure in court. As a rule, an organization should not write anything that it wouldn't want to see in a newspaper or hear repeated in front of a judge.
- Putting a human face on things should never be underestimated. Even hardened regulators and authorities respond better to a one-to-one interaction than they do to a statutory written communication. An organization should consider who should make that interaction. If a minor regulatory infringement is involved, using the CEO to deliver the message is not appropriate. But if potentially it's a major issue, the chair of the board is the only appropriate person.
- Everyone will have their own agenda. The regulators and authorities may decide that they want to showcase an organization or defend any possible allegations that they were "asleep at the wheel." It can't stop the latter, but it is better that those stakeholders know your side of the story.

DRAWING A LINE UNDER THE SITUATION

Once the investigation has been completed, you should be prepared to draw a line under the situation. To some extent, doing this depends on how public the situation has become. If developments have been highly publicized and commented on by a wide range of stakeholders, then a wide-ranging outreach plan should be developed to communicate how the organization intends

CASE STUDY

Société Générale

In January 2008, French bank Société Générale, one of Europe's biggest financial services companies, revealed that it had lost €4.9 billion in an incident of fraud involving a single futures trader.

Société Générale managed the incident very well. It was required to respond quickly, and it did: Two days after suspicions were aroused concerning unusual trading activity, the bank's chairman, Daniel Bouton, informed the governor of the Bank of France and suspended the trader in question, Jérôme Kerviel. The company successfully contained the incident and did not attempt to play down its potential magnitude.

As soon as Société Générale had complied with regulatory reporting, it moved from interim messages to release its first public statement, establishing itself as the authoritative source of information. The bank successfully communicated its containment of the crisis—despite admitting that it would need significant new capital to offset the losses, it reassured the financial community that it was still on course to make a good profit. It continued to give information to the authorities before releasing a candid statement about the incident: who Kerviel was, arbitrage activities, the method behind the fraud, how it was uncovered, and measures taken since the event.

The crisis required a human face, and the frontline response came from Daniel Bouton, whose resignation as executive chairman was rejected by the board early on but who eventually stepped down to nonexecutive chairman.

At the time of writing, Jérôme Kerviel is facing charges of breach of trust, computer abuse, and falsification. He has denied any wrongdoing and claims that the bank knew of his actions but let him continue as long as he was making money. The ongoing investigation and a €4 million fine imposed by France's banking regulator clearly makes it difficult for Société Générale to draw a line under the incident. However, the bank has laid the groundwork with strong actions to back up its messages (such as internal investigations into compliance) that have demonstrated its determination to stakeholders and built trust in the process.

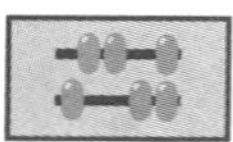

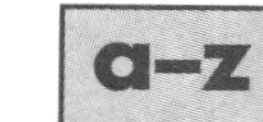

to move on. If the situation has been relatively contained, the outreach plan may be far less reaching.

Irrespective of the reach of the communications plan, some underpinning messages will be required. The 4Cs formula outlined above can be revisited and revised. And it is important that messages are backed up by action. With stakeholders now less trusting than they were, an organization needs to *show* its audience that it has moved on, not just *tell* them.

For example, if an organization says that it is committed to compliance, can it allow the person accused of fraud to stay in their position? If an organization says it is confident that the situation is now under control and cannot recur, what tangible steps or changes can it point to as evidence that it really has acted to prevent a recurrence?

The more tangible the evidence underpinning the message, the firmer and more convincing the line the organization will be able to draw under the situation.

CONCLUSION

Everyone accepts that things go wrong from time to time. What most organizations will be judged on is not that something has gone wrong, but on how they respond to the situation.

Although every situation has its own dynamics, by following some of the broad guidelines outlined above organizations that are victims of fraud will go a long way toward protecting themselves from some of the reputational fallout they may suffer. Ultimately these guidelines should also help to maintain that all-important trust from their stakeholders.

MORE INFO

Books:

Alsop, R. J. *The 18 Immutable Laws of Corporate Reputation: Creating, Protecting and Repairing Your Most Valuable Asset*. London: Kogan Page, 2006.

Doorley, J., and H. F. Garcia. *Reputation Management: The Key to Successful Corporate and Organizational Communication*. New York: Routledge, 2005.

Griffin, A. *New Strategies for Reputation Management: Gaining Control of Issues, Crises and Corporate Social Responsibility*. London: Kogan Page, 2007.

Larkin, J. *Strategic Reputation Risk Management*. Basingstoke, UK: Palgrave MacMillan, 2003.

Mitroff, I. A. *Why Some Companies Emerge Stronger and Better from a Crisis*. New York: Amacom, 2005.

O'Hanlon, Bill. *Thriving Through Crisis: Turn Tragedy and Trauma Into Growth and Change*. New York: Perigee, 2005.

Regester, M., and J. Larkin. *Risk Issues and Crisis Management in Public Relations: A Casebook of Best Practice*. 4th ed. London: Kogan Page, 2008.

Ulmer, R., T. Sellnow, and M. W. Seeger. *Effective Crisis Communication: Moving from Crisis to Opportunity*. Thousand Oaks, CA: Sage Publications, 2006.

van Reil, C. B. M., and C. J. Fombrun. *Essentials of Corporate Communication: Implementing Practices for Effective Reputation Management*. New York: Routledge, 2006.

Articles:

Ettenson, R., and J. Knowles. "Don't confuse reputation with brand." *MIT Sloan Management Review* 49:2 (2008). Online at: sloanreview.mit.edu/the-magazine/articles/2008/winter/49213.

Gardberg, N., and C. Fombrun. "The global reputation quotient project: First steps towards a cross-nationally valid measure of corporate reputation." *Corporate Reputation Review* 4:4 (2002): 303–307.

MacMillan, K., Kevin Money, Steve Downing, and Carola Hillenbrand. "Giving your organisation SPIRIT: An overview and call to action for directors on issues of corporate governance, corporate reputation and corporate responsibility." *Journal of General Management* 30:2 (2004): 15–42.

See Also:

★ CSR: More than PR, Pursuing Competitive Advantage in the Long Run (pp. 664–666)
★ How Internal Auditing Can Help with a Company's Fraud Issues (pp. 346–350)
★ What Is the Range of the Internal Auditor's Work? (pp. 431–434)
✔ Understanding Internal Audits (p. 1057)
✔ What Is Forensic Auditing? (p. 1060)

"Society has become unmanageable as a result of management." Henry Mintzberg

  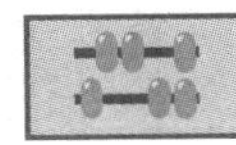   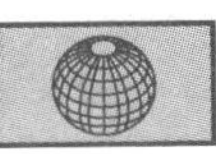   

Growing and Maximizing SME Profitability Without Compromising ROI by Neil Marriott

EXECUTIVE SUMMARY

- Small and medium-sized enterprises (SMEs) are increasingly important to long-term regional, national, and global economic prosperity.
- While growing, many SMEs encounter periods that require investment in assets and/or research and development (R&D) in advance of any resulting increase in turnover and associated profits.
- During this period, known as the "valley of death," key performance indicators such as return on investment (ROI) can be adversely impacted and limit the scope for future investment.
- To manage growth, SMEs must determine the right timing and response to customer demands.
- To recover ROI, SMEs must control costs and balance long-term prospects with short-term profitable opportunities.

INTRODUCTION

Small and medium-sized enterprises (SMEs) are, more than ever, the lifeblood of regional and national economies. The structural shift from goods to service sectors favors the creation of more small firms, where a smaller size is an economic choice for a business vehicle. This shift was exacerbated by techn ological changes such as the extensive use of microchip technology, which now makes smaller-scale production more economically viable.

SMEs can be more flexible and responsive to new market opportunities and economic recessions. In periods of high unemployment many former employees start their own enterprises, relying on their experience, education, and managerial skills. Furthermore, large firms increasingly place part of their work outside the organization—providing a further incentive for the creation of new small firms, since subcontracting and outsourcing can reduce production costs. However, as SMEs grow and develop, they face strains on their profitability that impact on a key performance indicator— return on investment (ROI). Furthermore any deterioration in ROI will compromise a firm's ability to obtain finance for further expansion.

DEFINITION OF RETURN ON INVESTMENT

Return on investment, often abbreviated to ROI, is a ratio that takes the firm's profit for a given accounting period (normally one year) and divides this by its invested capital, as measured by the balance sheet. The capital invested is calculated as stock and long-term debt. ROI is a measure that demonstrates the effectiveness of the management to use the capital available to generate profit, and hence a return for those investing in the company. The higher the ROI, the better the performance, and the happier existing investors will be. A higher ratio will also improve the company's ability to find new investors.

THE VALLEY OF DEATH

A problem occurs for SMEs during their growth and development phase, when expenditures on asset acquisition and R&D need to be funded and financing obligations must be serviced. Debt finance, in particular, adversely impacts profitability because interest payments reduce the net profit available for distribution to equity investors. This difficult period, known as the "valley of death," or "death valley curve" (see Figure 1), is experienced by all SMEs as their need for funds increases and they rack up large accumulated losses before profits from sales can be realized. SMEs that engage in technology transfer and new product development face the greatest difficulties in making it through these challenging times.

Figure 1. The valley of death. (*Source*: Osawa and Miyazaki, 2006)

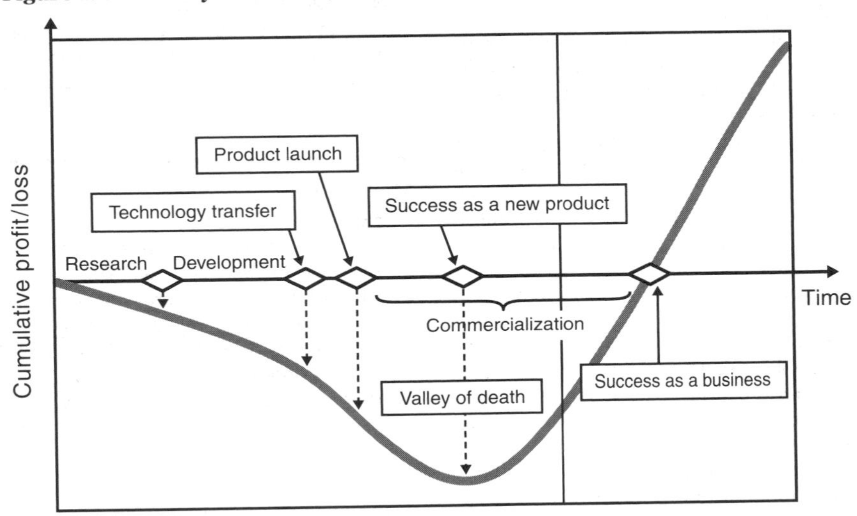

CASE STUDY

DeepStream Technologies

UK-based DeepStream Technologies was founded in May 2003 by chief executive Mark Crosier, along with ten other people. They worked unpaid for almost a year to realize their ambition for the product and the company, designing and manufacturing intelligent embedded sensors for remote service enablement in, for example, energy management and building efficiency applications.

Early in 2004, DeepStream secured a total £2.8 million (then US$5.2 million) investment, raised between Doughty Hanson Technology Ventures and the company founders. Later that year DeepStream was awarded two contracts for over US$15 million to design and supply contracts for miniaturized electronic protection modules for switchgear products. A number of business awards followed in 2005. Second tier funding was obtained in September 2006—£5 million (then US$9.5 million) from 3i, a world leader in private equity and venture capital, and a further £2.8 million (then US$5.3 million) from initial investor Doughty Hanson; additionally, they were awarded government grants of £1.5 million (US$2.9 million).

More success came when DeepStream was named a 2007 Technology Pioneer by the World Economic Forum[1] in Davos, and Mark Crosier was named Ernst & Young's Science &

GROWING AND MAXIMIZING SME PROFITABILITY WITHOUT COMPROMISING ROI

So how can SMEs grow and maximize their profitability without compromising ROI? The first rule is that growth must be carefully managed, with expansion financed through a series of stages. DeepStream had backers with deep pockets and a lot of patience. Venture capitalists are in it for the long term, but many companies are financed by debt provided by banks, who expect their interest and capital payments to be made on time, regardless of the firm's position on the death valley curve.

Instead of diving headlong into expansion at all costs, SMEs need to manage their customers' aspirations, planning where they want to be and when. In this way the size of the valley can be limited and it will be possible to return to a profitable position far sooner than would otherwise be the case. It is far better to have a series of planned growth phases between which ROI can be allowed to return to acceptable levels. This will demonstrate to potential equity investors that management is in control of the company's destiny and that it is not being controlled by any unrealistic demands from customers.

The second rule is to manage your costs, as it can be quite easy for SME managers to accept the loss-making situations that are experienced as a company expands and to lose control of expenditure. Debt blindness sets in as the figures become ever larger and managers lose sight of the original business plan.

Finally, focus on the more short-term profitable options available to the business. Long-term contracts are fine and can keep investors happy, but economic conditions may change and a bird in the hand is worth two in the bush. The contentedness of investors will quickly change if the long-term contracts fail to come to fruition because customers go bankrupt or file for administration.

NOTE

1 The World Economic Forum is an independent international organization committed to improving the state of the world by engaging leaders in partnerships to shape global, regional, and industry agendas.

Technology Entrepreneur of the Year for the United Kingdom's northern region. In July 2007 employee numbers reached 60. Further long-term contracts were obtained in 2008 and employee numbers expanded to 80, with a new production facility opened as the company announced plans to double in size by 2010.

This case study is of a company that is a huge success story, but what do the figures say about this SME during its growth and expansion phase? The large contracts, though headline-grabbing, are long term, and realized annual sales over the period 2004–07 averaged less than £0.3 million (US$0.6 million). During this time, the costs of expansion continued to rise until by March 31, 2007, the company had accumulated a total loss of £7.8 million (US$15 million). The effect on ROI was devastating, with negative returns reported, and yet the long-term prospects for the company are good, the investors are content, and the credit rating of the firm is measured as stable.

MAKING IT HAPPEN

- Control the growth of your company; don't let its growth control you.
- Who is in charge—the management or the customers? Sure you have to respond to customer needs, but they are not going to deal with the bank manager when your overdraft exceeds the agreed limit.
- Keep the costs under control and according to plan. Don't think that because you are investing in a growing company you can't keep on top of purchases and investments.
- Don't chase the end of the rainbow. Some large orders may appear very attractive and profitable in the long term, but would you really be able to cope in the meantime?
- Take smaller strides forward and allow profitability to return. Let the business catch its breath, and then take the next steps to further growth and development.

MORE INFO

Books:

Murphy, L. M., and P. L. Edwards. *Bridging the Valley of Death: Transitioning from Public to Private Sector Financing*. Golden, CO: National Renewable Energy Laboratory, 2003. Online at: www.cleanenergystates.org/CaseStudies/NREL-Bridging_the_Valley_of_Death.pdf

O'Berry, Denise. *Small Business Cash Flow: Strategies for Making Your Business a Financial Success*. Hoboken, NJ: Wiley, 2007.

Scarborough, Norman M., Douglas L. Wilson, and Thomas W. Zimmerer. *Effective Small Business Management: An Entrepreneurial Approach*. 9th ed. Upper Saddle River, NJ: Prentice Hall, 2008.

Article:

Osawa, Yoshitaka, and Kumiko Miyazaki. "An empirical analysis of the valley of death: Large-scale R&D project performance in a Japanese diversified company." *Asian Journal of Technology Innovation* 14:2 (2006): 93–116.

Websites:

European Business Angel Network (EBAN): www.eban.org
Institute for Small Business and Entrepreneurship (ISBE): www.isbe.org.uk
International Network for SMEs (INSME): www.insme.org
National Venture Capital Association (NVCA): www.nvca.org
US Small Business Administration (SBA): www.sba.gov

See Also:

★ Cash Flow Best Practice for Small and Medium-Sized Enterprises (pp. 28–29)
★ Corporate Finance for SMEs (pp. 33–35)
★ Reducing Costs and Improving Efficiency with New Management Information Systems (pp. 921–923)
✔ Invoicing and Credit Control for Small and Medium-Sized Enterprises (p. 976)
✔ Preparing a Budget (p. 985)
Return on Investment (pp. 1249–1250)

"The manager has his eye on the bottom line; the leader has his eye on the horizon." Warren Bennis

     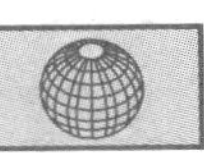   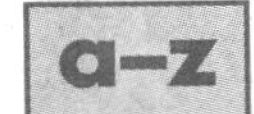

How Firms Should Fight Rumors by Andrew Hiles

EXECUTIVE SUMMARY

- What a rumor is.
- What makes a successful rumor.
- How rumors spread.
- The impact of rumor.
- Examples and case studies.
- How to fight rumors: lessons and guidelines.

INTRODUCTION: WHAT IS A RUMOR?

To understand how to fight rumors, we need first to understand what a rumor is and then how and why it circulates.

There are many definitions of "rumor," but what they have in common is that a rumor comprises unverified, unconfirmed information of uncertain origin and doubtful veracity that has got into general circulation. It may contain elements of truth as well as unfounded allegations. A rumor may be positive ("This stock is going to rocket—they've struck oil") or negative ("That restaurant serves cat as chicken"). A rumor may be substantively true, such as unconfirmed bad or good news that is being prematurely released by unofficial sources.

The scientist Robert Knapp, who helped the US Office of Strategic Services (OSS) to use rumor as a weapon in World War II, defined rumor as: "a proposition or belief of topical reference without official verification."[1]

Rumor differs from propaganda, which is an organized campaign to promote a doctrine or practice. However rumor may form part of a propaganda campaign.

WHAT MAKES A SUCCESSFUL RUMOR

The originally secret, since declassified, OSS "Doctrine re Rumors" (effectively a "How To" manual on spreading rumors)[2] described an effective rumor as being "self-propelled." It described five characteristics:

- *It is easy to remember*. It is vivid, and contains local color, concrete detail, often a slogan, and humor.
- *It follows a stereotyped plot*. It recalls the history and folklore of the target group and is an old story dressed in new clothes.
- *It reflects the momentary interests and circumstances of the target group*. It interprets some current event and fills a knowledge gap. It contains some verifiable element of fact and appears to be supported by other events or rumors.
- *It exploits the emotions and sentiments of the target group*. It provides a justification for shared, suppressed emotions and articulates them.
- *It is challenging*. It contains "inside information" that cannot be verified directly and is "neither too plausible nor too implausible."

HOW RUMORS SPREAD

The OSS manual described the qualities that make a rumor spread as being:

- Plausibility.
- Simplicity.
- Suitability for task—for example, slogan rumors can be short and simple, building on existing situations or beliefs. New "information" may need more narrative.
- Vividness.
- Suggestiveness.

The OSS "Doctrine" suggested spreading rumors by designing different, apparently independent supporting rumors in different places.

Long before the Internet, Mark Twain saw the force of rumor: "A lie can travel halfway around the world while the truth is putting on its shoes," he wrote. Sadly, the truth travels (or at least is acknowledged) somewhat more slowly, against the tide. Rumors are spread by word of mouth at informal meetings over coffee or round the water cooler (referred to as the "watercooler effect").[3] A team of scientists and mathematicians at Rochester University has come up with dynamic social impact theory[4]—a model to calculate the spread of rumor. One of the motivations for spreading rumors is the kudos which the spreader gets from apparently being on the inside—"knowledge" is power.

With the advent of social media, rumor can be spread farther, quicker, and with more devastating effect. Wikipedia lists over 300 social networking sites,[5] ranging from the well-known (Facebook, with more than 640 million subscribers; Myspace, 100 million plus; Twitter, over 175 million; LinkedIn, over 100 million) to specialist sites and blogs with a few thousand subscribers. Another source lists 750 "top" sites.[6]

Increasingly, rumors are being spread by email and SMS. Viral emails can spread globally within hours. In March 2011, an email and SMS about a nuclear radiation rain shower were reported to be spreading panic across the South East Asian region, including countries like the Philippines that are close to Japan.[7] In Kyrgyzstan, Skype groups were reportedly validating rumors of ethnic disturbances. Skype currently handles 30 million concurrent users. The threat is serious enough to have made the Securities and Exchange Board of India (SEBI) issue an advisory that said intermediaries (brokerages, etc.) must have in place an internal code of conduct; ensure that employees, temporary staff, and even voluntary workers do not circulate unverified information; restrict access to blogs, chat forums, and messenger sites; and keep logs of such blogs.[8]

DYNAMIC SOCIAL IMPACT THEORY (DSIT)

DSIT states that beliefs and attitudes are based on:

- *Strength of influential sources*: You are more likely to believe a rumor told by a friend or family member.
- *Immediacy of influence*: Rumors often take hold in close-knit, homogeneous neighborhoods and communities.
- *Number of sources*: The more people in your network there are who believe a rumor, the more likely you are to believe it.

Based on this, Brooks and DiFonzo developed the "MBN-dialogue model of rumor transmission," where the spread of rumor is based on the motivations (M) for spreading the rumor, the strength of belief (B) in the rumor, and the novelty (N) or newness of the rumor.

THE IMPACT OF RUMOR

Recent research by Convergys Corp. found that one negative customer review on YouTube, Twitter, or Facebook could cost a company up to 30 customers.[9] Negative *rumors* can hardly have less of an effect.

The impact of false rumors can seriously damage a company's health in many different ways. The most precious asset a company has is its brand value and reputation. Often this exceeds, in value, the tangible assets of the firm. Table 1 presents a 2010 valuation by Brand Finance of the top 10 brands, their brand valuations, and their credit ratings. 1

Brands and the goodwill associated with a company name have a real value—which is capable of being severely damaged by adverse rumor. As I wrote in *The Definitive*

Table 1. Brand value: Top 10 brands in 2010. (*Source*: Brand Finance[1])

Brand	Country	Brand value (US$ billion)	Credit rating
Walmart	US	41.4	AA–
Google	US	36.2	AAA–
Coca-Cola	US	34.8	AAA
IBM	US	33.7	AA–
Microsoft	US	33.6	AAA
General Electric	US	31.9	AA–
Vodafone	UK	29.0	AAA–
HSBC	UK	28.4	AAA
Hewlett-Packard	US	27.4	AA +
Toyota	Japan	27.3	AAA–

Handbook of Business Continuity Management: "That value is created by many years of advertising and good experience by the consumers of the product or service and it can be quickly eroded. When contamination of Coca-Cola was alleged in France and Belgium a few years ago, the brand value of Coca-Cola was reported to have sunk by $8 billion."[10]

Other impacts can include:

- Loss of share value.
- Loss of sales.
- Loss of customers.
- Loss of credit rating.
- Cash flow problems.
- Vulnerability to predatory and opportunist takeover.
- Loss or delay of the capability to market new products or services under the brand name (brand development/brand extension).
- Increase in public relations, advertising costs, and legal fees to counter negative rumor and recover market share.

EXAMPLES OF RUMORS

A few examples follow of rumors that have affected firms, their products and services.

- Coca-Cola has suffered continual rumors that the Coca-Cola trademark can be read as meaning "No Mohammed, No Mecca" in Arabic when it is reversed and read from right to left. The Coca-Cola website[13] dismisses this, pointing out that "The Coca-Cola trademark was created in 1886 in Atlanta, Georgia, at a time and place where there was little knowledge of Arabic." It adds that the rumor has been rejected by leading Muslim scholars, whom it quotes. Nevertheless, the rumor persists, and Coca-Cola's sales in the Middle East are negligible. The website also refutes some 27 other rumors.
- In August 2000 Procter & Gamble (P&G) lost a business-defamation lawsuit against independent distributors of Amway Corp. products, who were accused of spreading, in 1995, a voice-mail rumor linking P&G to Satanism. The rumor may have arisen because Procter & Gamble's president had discussed Satanism on the Phil Donahue program, a nationally televized talk show, some 20 years before. It was also said that a logo depicting a bearded, crescent-shaped man-in-the-moon looking over a field of 13 stars was a Satanic symbol. P&G shares fell 1 3/8 to 62 15/16 on the New York Stock Exchange. After appeal, the case was finally settled in 2007 with an award of US$19.25 million to P&G.
- In the 1980s it was rumored that Mexican employees urinated into bottles of Corona beer to be exported to the United States. The rumor was traced back to Luce & Sons, distributor of competing Heineken Beer. Corona sued and won, but reportedly spent US$500,000 in public relations and related costs to recover the damage.
- For more than 30 years a rumor has claimed that McDonald's restaurants use earthworms in their hamburgers, another that they used cow eyeballs. McDonald's countered this by stating that they met the stringent standards set by the US Food and Drug Administration and by the equivalent authority of each country in which they operated. There are more than 100 defamatory rumors circulating against McDonald's. In another case in the United Kingdom, environmental activists Helen Steel and David Morris were sued over a pamphlet against McDonald's. The case dragged on for 10 years, eventually being settled in McDonald's favor. McDonald's said that it did not plan to collect the £40,000 award. Although McDonald's won, the case generated a great deal of adverse publicity.
- In September 2004, the Kryptonite bicycle lock company suffered from an Internet rumor that some of its cycle locks could be picked with a Bic ballpoint pen. They responded by supplying more than 380,000 replacement locks to customers worldwide.

SUMMARY

Rumors can come from any direction, at any time. They are frequently a mix of fiction and fact, but they may also be unconfirmed fact that has escaped control. 360 degree environmental scanning is essential to provide an early warning. A predetermined strategy is needed to ignore or to combat them. A rebuttal needs to be quick and comprehensive.

HOW TO FIGHT RUMORS: LESSONS AND GUIDELINES

Here are a few lessons, suggestions and prompts, learned the hard way, by companies that got it wrong.

Be Prepared

- Create a bank of goodwill by acting transparently, ethically, and socially

CASE STUDY

The Qantas Crash That Never Was

On November 4, 2010, Qantas A380 flight QF32 was bound for Sydney with 433 passengers and 26 crew on board when Indonesian authorities said that there had been some sort of explosion over the island of Batam, just south of Singapore, at about 9.15 a.m. local time. Local eye witnesses found aircraft debris, and pictures on local television showed the Qantas logo on some of this.

The plane defueled and returned to Singapore's Changi Airport after the pilots were forced to shut down one engine, engine two, of its four engines. Qantas said that the airliner landed at 11.45 a.m. local time. The flight landed safely and no passengers or crew were injured.

Widespread and inaccurate rumors spread rapidly through Twitter that the plane had crashed.

Reuters reported that Qantas had told CNBC television that a plane had crashed near Singapore and that it was an Airbus A380. Kompas, a popular Indonesian newspaper, reported on its website that it was "suspected that a Qantas plane exploded in the air near Batam."

On initial rumors of a crash, Qantas shares dived 15 cents, or 3%, to AU$2.82.

On landing, a passenger twittered its safe arrival with a photograph of its damaged engine and wing and Qantas issued a press statement.

Shares recovered to AU$2.92.

"I actually think most people don't want Google to answer their questions. They want Google to tell them what they should be doing next." Eric Schmidt

responsibly. Court opinion influencers, analysts, and the media. The strength of your brand and reputation is the front line of your defence.

- The bigger they are, the harder they fall. How big are you? Who would like to see you fall? Why? What can you do to eliminate these reasons or to create a soft landing?
- Carefully analyze your product, its contents, and its packaging and promotion. What could be misinterpreted and lead to adverse rumors? In the 1960s fish fingers commonly included a deep-sea fish that was in plentiful supply. This fish was colloquially known as "rats tail." When this was brought to the notice of Birds Eye, it quickly opted to use alternative fish. Indeed, the "fish finger" has been replaced in some markets by "fish stick." Plan for the worst and hope for the best.
- Identify your partners, allies, and adversaries. How could they cause you problems? Sweatshops, child labor, unethical practices? Choose your suppliers carefully.
- Consider security: what hacking, internal emails, mail or trash-can contents could set off the rumor machine? What is kept on laptops or USB memory sticks that could be lost or stolen? Control them.
- Develop or review your crisis management and product recall plans to reflect rumor management aspects.
- Develop a rumor management plan that includes social media.
- Actively monitor social media for adverse mentions of your company as well as monitoring the traditional media.
- Don't just hear; listen! Don't go into denial: face the issues. See a rumor from the perspective of your customers. Remember the Ford Explore/Firestone issues in 2000–01 when Ford vehicles fitted with Firestone tyres were crashing. Ford insisted that it was a tyre issue. Wrong. It was a Ford issue—*they* fitted the tyres.

CASE STUDY

The Impact of Rumor: The Toyota Recalls, 2009–10[11]

In 2009, Toyota was the world's number one car manufacturer, outselling Ford and GM. Rumors spread of electronic control problems, unexpected acceleration, and other defects. From fall 2009 to spring 2010, Toyota recalled 8.5 million cars, 8 million with potential floor mat, braking, unwanted acceleration, accelerator pedal, and steering problems. The recall-affected models make up 58% of Toyota sales. During this time many other manufacturers also recalled cars, but they attracted little publicity.

By March 2010, Toyota had been unable to replicate the alleged electronics failure as the cause of the random unwanted acceleration and had rejected software failure as a cause.

Edolphus Towns, Chairman of the US Committee on Oversight and Government Reform, claimed that up to 39 crash deaths in the United States from 1990 to 2010 may have been linked to accelerator-related problems.

- Toyota shares fell 23% to US$71.78 in the three-week period to February 4, 2010—8% in a single day—and 14%, US$21 billion, in just one week. Before the final recalls, Reuters said that $30 billion had been wiped from Toyota's share value.
- A 35% drop in brand value was forecast by Brand Finance and, depending on which brand value survey is used as a base, this cost between US$9.6 and US$11.7 billion.
- On February 4, 2010, Toyota itself estimated that it would have to spend US$1.12 billion on warranty expenses and would lose as much as US$895 million in lost sales over the recall.
- The cost of a global advertising and public relations campaigns to recover Toyota's tarnished reputation and damaged market share can be roughly estimated, by comparing it with similar campaigns, at about US$300 million initially.
- Toyota closed factories in the United States.
- Toyota saw its US market share fall to 14% in January 2010—its lowest level since January 2006—from 17% for full-year 2009, putting it behind GM.
- To incentivize buyers to kick-start the relaunch is estimated to have cost US$3.1 million in the first year.
- In January 2010 Toyota enjoyed a Standard & Poor's (S&P) AAA– credit rating. Its credit rating dictates the interest rate at which it can borrow funds. Toyota Motor Corp.'s corporate credit rating was reduced by S&P to A-1 + . Moody's downgraded Toyota to AA1.
- Toyota has not put a price on productivity losses. Productivity losses caused by factory closure and lower sales may be US$800 million to US$1 billion.
- The value of used Toyotas dropped by around 10%.

In February 2011 the National Highway Traffic Safety Administration (NHTSA) and the National Aeronautics and Space Administration (NASA) report found that the most common problem was drivers hitting the accelerator when they thought they were hitting the brake. NHTSA called this "pedal misapplication." Of the 58 cases by then reported, 18 were instantly dismissed. Of the 40 cases left, 39 were held to have no cause. The rest were deemed "pedal entrapment."[12]

So, while some of the reasons for the recalls remain valid, the key rumor triggering them was simply that: a rumor.

Take Prompt Action

- Act quickly. A fire doubles in size every few minutes, and it's easier to extinguish a match than an inferno. Know the deadlines for local, national, and international trade and general press, radio, and television and prepare appropriate material in time for each news cycle. And remember, social media never sleep. A few clicks, and another million people can hear the rumor.
- Expect heavy traffic on your website. Drop images, videos, Flash, that consume bandwidth. Plan for upscaling—traffic could increase on your website, Facebook, and Twitter outlets by 1,000%. Minimize inbound traffic by using self-help and voice mail—and update information regularly and frequently.

Get—and Keep—On-Message

- Pull your advertising on any products or services that are at risk from the rumor (at least until you have a rebuttal plan). Advertise other services or products instead.
- Your spokesperson should stay calm, collected, and logical in the event of a rumor, no matter how outrageous it may be. Emotional outbursts give the impression of bluster and lack of control. BP CEO Tony Hayward's remark at the time of the BP Gulf of Mexico oil spill was a classic example. He said he wanted "to get my life back." Fisherman Mike Frenette's riposte was killing. He said: "I want mine back, too. He's ruined it."
- Choose a credible spokesperson to represent you. A PR person or the CEO are not as trusted as doctors or an employee whom the rumor target can identify with as being "someone like me."
- Try to avoid reinforcing minor rumors by repeating them in order to deny them.
- Silence is not always golden—it might be interpreted as proof of guilt. Avoid "No comment" responses. Rumors thrive on uncertainty. Remember, at least some of the rumor circulators may be trying to

     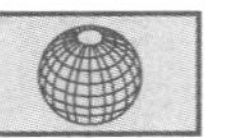   

establish the truth by circulating it for verification or rebuttal within a peer group.

- On the other hand, there may be times when ignoring a rumor—taking the moral high ground—may be appropriate, especially if the rumor is trivial.
- Pre-empt potential rumors and rebut the current rumor by publishing explanations and facts that undermine its credibility. A strong, vivid rebuttal may change public perception and actually improve a company's image. Sometimes it can be effective to take a high-profile stand, publishing a strong rebuttal that's supported by facts. Examples are the Coca-Cola[14] website and President Barack Obama's Fight the Smears website.[15]Both list false rumors, with explanations and rebuttals.
- The soccer saying "Play the man as well as the ball" holds true. Take the battle to the enemy. Attack may be a good defense. But think hard before trying to undermine accepted authorities, especially if they are respected and independent.
- Communicate, communicate, communicate. Counter the rumors with explanations and facts. Spread a tsunami of good news stories about the company. It takes three positives to overcome one negative. Consider all stakeholders, including employees and regulators.
- Use video where practicable: it has greater impact than statements.
- Make sure the entire organization is on-message: communications to customers, suppliers, employees, the public, and the media have to be consistent.
- Communicate acceptable priorities: life, health, and environmental concerns need addressing before issues of profitability and supply.

Minimize Scope for Error and Misunderstanding

- Treble-check all facts.
- Do not speculate.
- Consider cultural differences and their impact on how your advertising, packaging, and marketing slogans may be interpreted. Avoid unintentional offence and address those differences.
- In interviews, make sure that the nonverbal language matches the words. More is communicated nonverbally than verbally, and inconsistency is easy to spot. Be positive and confident—but not arrogant. Avoid negative implications. Remember that humor may be inappropriate or misinterpreted.
- Identify and actively target the likely audience(s) for the rumor.
- Don't deny the truth—it might take time, but the truth will always out. The earlier denial will come back to haunt the firm.

Protect Your Market and Share Value

- Act to protect your share price: prepare and deliver statements to stock exchanges if appropriate.

Take Responsibility

- If at fault, don't play down the impact of problems—these may be a serious matter to the customer. Avoid arrogance. Show humility and repentance. Show care, empathy, and compassion.
- Avoid the blame game. It might be a problem with your suppliers, but as far as the customer is concerned, if they buy from you, it is down to you to accept responsibility. You can sue the suppliers later.
- Never, ever, ever, lie to the media.

Make Restitution

- If at fault, make restitution—quickly. Take prompt action to remedy a product or service defect, like Kryptonite. Simply changing the product packaging may help. In 1992 Snapple, a US beverage manufacturer, was rumored to support the Klu Klux Klan (KKK) because the picture of a ship on the Snapple label was said to be a slave ship and the "K" on the label was said to indicate support for the KKK. Snapple redesigned its label to make it clear that the ship showed the Boston Tea Party and the "K" stood for "kosher pareve" (food without meat or dairy ingredients). In 1998 Wall's ice cream changed its logo when it was claimed that the original, when read upside down, was defamatory to Muslims.

Call in the Cavalry

- Let someone else defend you. Refer to respected, independent experts to refute the rumors. Toyota chose NASA.

Get It Out, Get It Over, Move On

- If there is bad news, get it out—all of it. Rumors will persist like a chronic illness if bad news drips out a drop at a time. And try to publish it at a time when more important news is making the headlines.

Be Cautious About Lawsuits

- Think carefully before taking legal action, especially if it is against a little guy and your firm is a big guy. The media love "David and Goliath" stories. Besides, legal action is expensive, time-consuming, distracting for senior management, and can create a steady, debilitating drip of news stories that reiterate the rumor as the case drags on—maybe for many years—through judicial processes that may include repeated appeals.

MORE INFO

Books:

DiFonzo, Nicholas. *The Watercooler Effect: A Psychologist Explores the Extraordinary Power of Rumors*. New York: Avery, 2008. For the psychology of rumor. (Paperback subtitled *An Indispensable Guide to Understanding and Harnessing the Power of Rumors*.)

Doorley, John, and Helio Fred Garcia. *Reputation Management: The Key to Successful Public Relations and Corporate Communication*. New York: Routledge, 2010. For responses to rumors.

Hiles, Andrew (ed). *The Definitive Handbook of Business Continuity Management*. 3rd ed. Chichester, UK: Wiley, 2010. For case studies on Toyota and BP, and detail on marketing protection.

McCusker, Gerry. *Public Relations Disasters: Talespin—Inside Stories and Lessons Learnt*. Philadelphia, PA: Kogan Page, 2006. For detail on the Procter & Gamble and BA vs Virgin rumors.

See Also:

★ Crisis Management and Strategies for Dealing with Crisis (pp. 817–819)
★ Digital Reputation Management (pp. 821–825)
★ Engaging Your Stakeholders: How To Make Allies of Investors and Activists (pp. 837–840)
★ Managing Reputational Risk: Business Journalism (pp. 893–896)

"Making rich people richer doesn't make the rest of us richer." Ha-Joon Chang

NOTES

1 Brand Finance. "Brand Finance global 500 2010." March 2010. Online at: tinyurl.com/6c5gnho
2 Knapp, Robert H. "A psychology of rumor." *Public Opinion Quarterly* 8:1 (Spring 1944): 22–37. Online at: www.jstor.org/stable/27456862. Office of Strategic Services Planning Group. "Doctrine re rumors." June 2, 1943. Online at: www.icdc.com/~paulwolf/oss/rumormanual2june1943.htm
3 DiFonzo (2008).
4 Dube, William. "Deciphering the watercooler effect." *Research at RIT*(May 2010). Online at: www.rit.edu/research/other_story.php?id=23
5 List of social networking websites from Wikipedia: en.wikipedia.org/wiki/List_of_social_networking_websites
6 List of the top 750 social networking sites and tools from e-crm: tinyurl.com/yfw9un3
7 Kumar, Manish. "Nuclear radiation rain email, SMS rumor spreads panic in Philippines, India." *ForestLaneShul* (March 15, 2011). Online at: tinyurl.com/4zhtsln
8 Raman, Kripa. "Keeping a tab on staff spreading rumours is difficult: Marketmen." *Hindu Business Line* (March 25, 2011). Online at: www.thehindubusinessline.com/markets/article1571507.ece
9 Shannon, Sarah. "One bad Twitter 'tweet' can cost 30 customers, survey shows." *Bloomberg* (November 26, 2009). Online at: tinyurl.com/ygqsul2
10 Hiles (2010), ch. 5.
11 For the full story of the Toyota recalls, see Hiles (2010), Appendix A1-AC, p. 597 ff.
12 National Highway Traffic Safety Administration (NHTSA) and National Aeronautics and Space Administration (NASA). "NHTSA–NASA study of unintended acceleration in Toyota vehicles." February 8, 2011. Online at: www.nhtsa.gov/UA
13 Coca-Cola Company—Middle East rumors: tinyurl.com/64xxrh3
14 *Ibid*.
15 Fight the Smears: www.fightthesmears.com

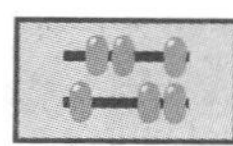

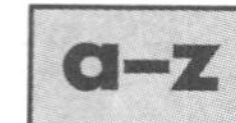

How to Manage Emerging Market Risks with Third Party Insurance by Rod Morris

EXECUTIVE SUMMARY

- Emerging markets present significant noncommercial political risks.
- Political risks can be mitigated through insurance products known as political risk insurance (PRI).
- PRI is a vehicle designed to help both equity investors and financial institutions to mitigate the losses that can result from a foreign government's substantive violation of the terms and conditions that originally attracted the foreign investment.
- More than 40 insurers, both private and public sector, offer such coverage.
- This article gives a comparative overview of the features of the public and private sector approaches.

INTRODUCTION

There are numerous issues that investors and companies must consider when contemplating an investment in a foreign country. Take for example cultural differences, the tax regime, foreign currency exchange restrictions, the regulatory and legal environment, the judicial system, and security requirements for both assets and employees. For emerging markets in particular, each of these factors can be further complicated by the potential for politically motivated interference, or changes in the government's attitude to foreign investment.

Foreign governments, especially those without an effective system of checks and balances, can create a favorable investment climate and then reverse or alter it quickly and dramatically. The results can be devastating to a foreign investor's ability to survive. A government's abrogation or unilateral alteration of an investor's licenses or agreements, new and onerous regulations or taxes, confiscation of property, and so on can happen, do happen, and will continue to happen, even if an investor hires an entire team of international and local lawyers and does everything right. None of that will matter when the local political environment takes an abrupt turn, which can happen for any number of reasons, including financial crisis, coup, or regime change. Nor will it be much use if terrorists or organized crime factions create an untenable atmosphere of insecurity.

There is also a growing trend known as "resource nationalism," in which governments have tried to grab a bigger share of the control and profits derived from diminishing supplies of, or increasing demand for (and therefore increasing prices of), their country's commodities such as tin, gold, and oil. Some governments are forcing unilateral restructuring of contracts and concessions, or even forcing a change in ownership that flips the foreign investor from a majority to minority position. The trend is particularly notable in Russia, Latin America, and Africa. Even if an investment is experiencing no problems with the sovereign government, there is no guarantee that it will be safe from interference from increasingly militant local governments, local judges interpreting local laws, or activist community organizations, which can frustrate or destroy a project just as effectively as an outright confiscation.

It is therefore essential that any potential investor makes a study of the current and likely economic and political risks of a country. Countries with developing or struggling economies and immature or undemocratic political structures can offer significant opportunities but at the same time pose significant risk. Much of that risk can be described as political, and many of these political risks can be mitigated through insurance products, known generically as PRI (political risk insurance). Assessing these risks may require some outside assistance, and there are a number of organizations that can help (see the More Info section).

WHAT IS PRI?

Political risk insurance is a broad term that includes a variety of coverage options for losses that have as their cause some kind of political motivation—whether by those in government or by others acting against it. PRI is designed to help both equity investors and financial institutions to mitigate the kinds of losses that can result from a host government's substantive violation of the terms and conditions which attracted the original investment. For equity investors, PRI can indemnify them for losses of their assets and/or interruption of their business income resulting not only from politically inspired violence, but also from the type of governmental actions that go beyond the normal, prudent, reasonable, and responsible exercise of governmental authority. For financial institutions, PRI provides the aforementioned coverage, as well as additional benefits such as the ability to increase capacity for international loans; the ability to offer clients more attractive financial terms; risk management of country, region, or sector concentrations; and protection against payment defaults by a governmental entity.

PRI products insure a wide range of risks or causes of loss, but, for the sake of simplicity, the coverage options generally fall within three broad categories: expropriation, inconvertibility, and political violence.

Expropriation (CEN)

Expropriation is the most commonly purchased political risk coverage. It is also referred to as confiscation, expropriation, and nationalization (CEN) coverage. Essentially, it insures against wrongful interference by a foreign government that deprives investors of their fundamental rights to proceeds or ownership. Such actions can include not only outright confiscation or nationalization, but also breach of contracts, abrogation of licenses, changes that result in unfairly discriminatory treatment in regulation, taxes, tariffs, and/or impairment of the ability to pass costs through to consumers. Coverage can apply to a single discrete action, such as the seizure of assets, plants, or equipment by the government, or a series of actions that ultimately make the investment no longer economically viable—usually referred to as "creeping expropriation."

Although it does not fit well within the category of expropriation, there is a related product that is referred to as "nonhonoring of a sovereign guarantee." Briefly, this protects financial institutions and exporters against a payment default guaranteed by a sovereign, sub-sovereign, or in some cases a sovereign-owned enterprise.

Inconvertibility (T&C)

Also known as transfer and convertibility (T&C) insurance, inconvertibility coverage insures earnings, return of capital, principal and interest payments, and technical assistance fees against the imposition of new currency restrictions or controls that prevent conversion from local currency to hard currency and/or the transfer and repatriation of funds. It does not protect against currency fluctuation, devaluation, or any preexisting restrictions on conversion or transfer.

"Perpetual optimism is annoying. It's a sign that you are not paying attention." Maureen Dowd

Political Violence

This coverage protects against a loss of assets or income due to events such as terrorism, sabotage, revolution, insurrection, war, civil war—essentially, any politically motivated act of violence. This coverage is a much broader protection than is normally afforded under property and casualty insurance policies, which typically exclude perils such as war, or offer very limited protection against terrorism and sabotage. *No one can afford to assume that they are immune from potential loss due to terrorism and violence.* The number of terror attacks worldwide continues to rise, and emerging markets are at greater risk than Western Europe or the United States. According to the regional breakdown shown in Table 1, there are almost 15,000 terrorist attacks per year. It is unlikely that the world will see a sudden reversal of this trend. Far from it.

Table 1. Terror attacks 2005–07. (*Source*: US National Counterterrorism Center)

Year	Africa	East Asia	Europe and Eurasia	Middle East	South Asia	Western Hemisphere	Total
2005	256	1,005	780	4,222	4,022	868	11,153
2006	422	1,036	659	7,755	3,654	826	14,352
2007	835	1,429	606	7,540	3,607	482	14,449

PRI INSURERS

A web search will produce a number of hits for both insurers and intermediaries (brokers and consultants) offering PRI products. Such a search, however, provides no clear evidence of the competence, capabilities, or financial strength of these companies. There is, nevertheless, an association of over 40 of the most reputable PRI carriers in the world, both private and public, known as the Berne Union. You can access a list of its members at www.berneunion.org.uk and be confident that you will find a responsible insurer. Although Lloyd's syndicates are not members, they are equally excellent.

PRI insurers fall into two categories: government-sponsored (public) and private. Government-sponsored programs are offered by many developed countries to encourage trade and investment in emerging markets. Such programs would include not only those sponsored by single governments (for example, EFIC of Australia, NEXI of Japan, OPIC of the United States, Sinosure of China), but also multilateral organizations (for example, ADB, the Asian Development Bank; ICIEC, of the Islamic Development Bank; and MIGA of the World Bank) that are funded and supported by multiple countries.

In general, private-market insurers such as Lloyd's, AIG, Chubb, and Zurich are unwilling to assume as much risk or offer terms, limits, or policy periods that are as expansive as the public insurers such as OPIC and MIGA. This can present significant practical problems not only for investors, but also for intermediaries such as brokers, as evidenced by the case study below.

COMPARISON OF PRI FROM PUBLIC AND PRIVATE INSURERS

A detailed comparison of the differences between individual programs is not possible here, but some general comments on some of the more significant considerations as between the private and public markets may be informative. Generalities are never quite fair, but they can provide some basic insight into what to expect when seeking cover. For government-sponsored programs, the references below are to OPIC and MIGA since they are the largest and most experienced. When referring to private insurers, the commonalities of programs from companies such as AIG, Zurich, and Lloyd's are used.

Capacity: The private market offers less per project/investment than government-sponsored programs. The capacity of private insurers has increased over the years, but it is still considerably less than MIGA's $200 million and OPIC's $250 million policy maximum, with the ability to exceed even this ceiling under extremely unusual circumstances.[2]

Term: Private insurers usually cover contracts for no longer than 15 years, whereas MIGA offers 15–20 years, and OPIC has offered 20-year contracts for a very long time.

Eligibility: Private insurers are basically unrestricted, while MIGA is restricted to insuring investors from member countries, and OPIC is restricted to investors with significant US ownership.

Rates: Private insurers price for profit, while the public market prices to be self-sustaining. Low-risk situations favor the

CASE STUDY

Sempra Energy: A Cautionary Tale

Sempra Energy, a Fortune 500 energy services holding company, successfully bid to participate in the privatization of the Argentine gas sector in the 1990s. Sempra then became interested in purchasing PRI for its investment, and hired Marsh USA Inc. to act as its broker in finding an appropriate product. Argentina's spotty and inconsistent handling of foreign investment justified the company's concern, and it believed that Marsh would survey the market and identify the best choice. Marsh chose a policy from National Union, an AIG affiliate. In January 2002, the government of Argentina was in the midst of a financial crisis that resulted in the enactment of, *inter alia*, the Emergency System Act, which converted and froze public utility tariffs in pesos rather than the agreed US dollar amounts.

Sempra filed a claim with National Union, but compensation was denied. Sempra took the denial to arbitration and lost because, in fact, National Union's contract was not sufficiently broad to provide coverage under the particularly confusing chain of facts. In its arbitral opinion, however, the panel pointed out that an OPIC policy would, in fact, have provided coverage. Considering that Marsh had selected the National Union policy over the OPIC policy, Sempra then filed suit[1] in July of 2007 in the Los Angeles Superior Court alleging that Marsh had failed "to obtain an insurance policy that provided the coverage it promised to procure for Sempra." It accused Marsh of negligence, breach of oral and written contracts, breach of fiduciary duty, and negligent misrepresentation. Sempra was awarded US$48.5 million in damages.

This case illustrates a number of lessons but, suffice to say, investors should review carefully their approach to emerging market investments: Analyze the country risk, and make an informed decision about mitigating the risk through insurance or some other approach; carefully evaluate any intermediaries; vet the reasons and justifications for PRI recommendations; and carefully evaluate the recommended product to be certain that it is sufficiently broad to cover the types of claims or problems that might arise.

Notwithstanding the events in the case study, it has to be said that private insurers can often be more flexible in terms and conditions and quicker to execute contracts, and they are not encumbered by statutes or covenants that restrict eligibility or require a lot of information. Additionally, public carriers do not like to be seen as competing with the private market. Their preference is that investors only approach them when the private market is inadequate or unavailable.

  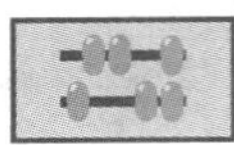      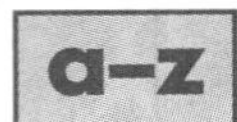

private market, but, as risk increases, any such advantage tends to disappear. Also, much more than government-sponsored insurers, private insurers increase price based on demand and their own country concentrations. OPIC's rates are based only on risk and are guaranteed for the full term of the contract.

Appetite: OPIC and MIGA are designed to be markets of last resort (i.e. an investor is expected to try the private market first), yet they may very well be the only viable or affordable market in high-risk situations—for example, Afghanistan, Pakistan, and much of Africa.

Small business: Private insurers find it difficult to make money on policies for small amounts. Government-sponsored carriers, on the other hand, assist small investors as a matter of public policy.

Financial strength: Certainly Lloyd's and all of the Berne Union insurers are A-rated or equivalent. Because it is a US government agency, OPIC is not rated, but a rating is unnecessary as it is backed by the full faith and credit of the US government.

Coverage: OPIC has a history and reputation of being a product innovator but is sometimes constrained by its authorizing statute. With respect to political violence, however, only OPIC covers losses resulting from chemical, nuclear, and biological events. In today's world, that is not an insignificant difference. OPIC is the only carrier in the world that has been offering such broad coverage, and they have been doing it for decades.

Loss avoidance: Government-sponsored insurers have the ability to bring considerable pressure to bear on foreign governments when there is advance indication of a potential problem.

Claim payment histories: For many reasons, private insurers reveal almost no information about the number, type, or amounts of paid claims, denied claims, or claim determinations that are in dispute or arbitration. The same is not true of OPIC, which is the only carrier in the world whose records are open to the public both with respect to individual claim determinations and to aggregate numbers, which convey some interesting stories and patterns.

Ease of doing business: Without question, it is easier to do business with private market insurers. Public carriers require more information, both at the time of application and throughout the term of the contract. They need additional information in order to report to their governing bodies that they are fulfilling their missions, by supporting investments which help both the country of investment as well as its people by protecting worker and human rights and the environment, while doing no harm to the US economy or jobs.

CONCLUSION

Investment in emerging markets is replete with risk. A thorough vetting should be done not only of the risk factors, but also of the tools that can be used to mitigate those risks. Political risk insurance is one of the best tools for mitigating these risks and it is available from a growing and capable population of insurers, both private and public.

MAKING IT HAPPEN

The always quotable American baseball player, Yogi Berra, said: "If you don't know where you're going, chances are you'll wind up someplace else." Without a clear perspective on the political, judicial, regulatory, and social climate for foreign investment, one can easily make a mistake. Even with full knowledge of current conditions, the climate for investment can change very quickly. It is always prudent to consider options in mitigating the substantial risks that can arise and overtake you.

- Consider the use of firms that provide expert analysis of emerging market risks.
- Compare and contrast the advantages of the private and public PRI carriers for the needs of your specific investment.
- There are many advantages to using an insurance broker but, especially for the public PRI carriers, they are not required.
- Insist that the insurance broker thoroughly explains all your options and the reasons for their recommendations to satisfy yourself that the recommendations fulfill your needs rather than theirs.
- Pick an insurer that is financially strong with a proven track record.

MORE INFO

Brokers:

Aon: www.aon.com/uk/en/risk_management/political-risk
Lloyd's: www.pri-center.com/directories/partner_specific.cfm?pgid=5&orgnum=34313
Marsh: global.marsh.com/risk/politicalRisk
Willis: www.willis.com/Client_Solutions/Services/Political_Risk

Sovereign Ratings and Other Info:

Fitch Ratings: www.fitchratings.com
IMF: www.imf.org/external/country
Moody's (registration required): www.moodys.com
S&P—Find "Sovereigns" from the home page: www.standardandpoors.com

Other Sources:

Berne Union: www.berneunion.org.uk
CountryRisk.com guide to country research on the internet: www.countryrisk.com
Economist Intelligence Unit: www.eiu.com
Eurasia Group: www.eurasiagroup.net
Global Insight: www.globalinsight.com
Oxford Analytica global strategic analysis: www.oxan.com

See Also:

★ Measuring Company Exposure to Country Risk (pp. 534–536)
★ Measuring Country Risk (pp. 537–539)
★ Political Risk: Countering the Impact on Your Business (pp. 902–904)

NOTES

1 Sempra Energy v Marsh USA Inc. et al., case no. cv07-5431 in US District Court, Central District of California.

2 Having greater limits available from one carrier is always an advantage when the alternative is to piece cover together from a number of different carriers with the potential for gaps in cover or tenor that may require yet another contract to cover the "Difference in Conditions" (DIC).

"No institution can possibly survive if it needs geniuses or supermen to manage it. It must be organized in such a way as to be able to get along under a leadership composed of average human beings." Peter F. Drucker

  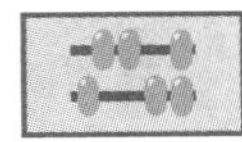      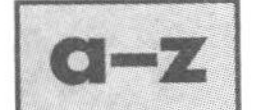

Viewpoint: Human Resources and the Crisis

by Christopher Johnson

INTRODUCTION

Christopher Johnson is a senior partner at Mercer, a leading international provider of HR and related financial advice, products, and services. He is responsible for developing Mercer's reputation for human capital services and the provision of human capital strategy, talent, and reward services in the UK market. He has been in consulting for nearly 25 years, supporting private and public-sector organizations in managing human resource issues. Before joining Mercer in 2008, he worked for the UK government's Cabinet Office, where he was responsible for employee relations and rewards across the Civil Service. Prior to that, he was with the Hay Group, Kinsley Lord, and Towers Perrin.

There are many facets to human resources (HR), but the economic context in which HR management takes place is clearly a critical determining factor. What do you make of the current business environment and its impact on corporate decision-making?

By late 2011 developed markets, particularly in Europe, were going through a time of intense political uncertainty. What emerged strongly in our conversations with clients in the second half of 2011 was their feeling of unease and frustration at the lack of political leadership in resolving the sovereign debt crisis. If you go back a few months before that, confidence about growth was an issue, but companies felt that they knew how to take investment decisions in difficult markets and they knew how to mitigate the risks of things turning out differently from whatever was envisaged in their "plan A." However, as political uncertainty has come to the fore, it has become very difficult for business to take big decisions. Merger and acquisition activity shrank through the second half of 2011 as companies opted to wait to see how things developed. Similarly, there has been a falling off in recruitment and expansionary projects of all kinds.

Companies are looking to the politicians to improve the climate for enterprise, which means tackling public debt and creating a climate for growth. Meanwhile, in developing and emerging economies there is growth, investments and being made, and talent is in short supply. Many multinationals are not investing in the developed markets, where the economic crisis has been most marked; rather, they are focused on growth markets in Asia, Africa, and eastern Europe.

The crisis is exacerbated by the fact that through the boom years many governments invested in public services and drove up public-sector debt. It is now clear that a number of governments were quite highly leveraged when the 2008 downturn took hold. Without the banking crash that followed, many of these ills might not have come home to roost, but the crash happened and getting fiscal and public sector deficits back on to an even keel is going to take hard work. This is the backdrop to what is going on internally in companies as far as recruitment, retention, and staff rewards and benefits are concerned.

Through the crash and the subsequent emergence from recession, companies were confident in their ability to navigate economic uncertainty. They were investing in their people, and that continued to drive business for HR consultancies such as ours. However, with the emergence of political uncertainty a more disabling state of affairs has arisen. Companies have to mitigate risk, and one of the most obvious ways of mitigating it is to be very cautious about investments and about increasing staff numbers. This is why many companies have loads of cash and, at the same time, are keeping people costs tightly under control.

What was your experience of corporate reactions to the downturn of 2008 and its aftermath as far as retrenchment was concerned?

A striking feature of this recession is that companies did not immediately turn to cutting jobs. On the whole they have tried to hold on to talent, recognizing that they have invested heavily in staff recruitment and development, and that these are the very people who they will need to help them to come through the contraction and the subsequent emergence into a new growth phase. Since jobs have not been cut, but companies have nevertheless been under intense pressure to reduce their cost base, we have seen a variety of methods deployed to reduce or contain staff costs. These have included pay freezes and a shift to part-time working and voluntary sabbaticals. As a consequence, over the last 12 months job creation has been at a far lower level in the economy as a whole than one might have expected from historical trends.

There is another dimension on the back of this that is very interesting. As companies have sought to utilize existing staff, rather than recruiting, to meet new demand, there has been a significant growth in the trend of retirement-age staff opting to stay on now that default retirement age has been removed. This means that the baby-boomer generation is going to be around for a good bit longer. They need to stay in work because they are living longer while trying to fund the lifestyle they are comfortable with. This in turn has a knock-on effect on jobs for younger generations since it becomes more difficult for them to find a way into the workplace if there is less movement in the upper levels of career progression.

On the macro-scale, you can see what happens when the numbers of unemployed youth climb to the proportions that have been reached in Egypt, Tunisia, and other North African and Middle Eastern countries caught up in the turmoil of the Arab Spring. It is very destabilizing to an economy to have large-scale unemployment and for the economy not to be producing jobs for new arrivals on the jobs market.

Again, on the macro-level in advanced economies we are seeing a huge disparity between the baby-boomer generation and those just arriving on the jobs market. By and large, the baby-boomers have already got relatively good pensions and quite a bit of capital, since many sold their houses at the height of the property boom. In contrast, people in their mid-20s are going to have relatively poor pensions, are having extreme difficulty getting on to the housing ladder, and have university loans to repay.

  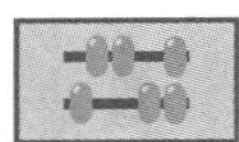      

And even when they do manage to finally buy a house, it is unlikely to appreciate in value at anything like the rate enjoyed by the baby-boomers.

So the baby-boomer generation is truly the golden generation, and we are unlikely to see its success replicated by subsequent generations. We are now into a much tougher rewards picture for entrants to the jobs market and for the generation that will follow.

At the same time, we are seeing governments forced to scale back the benefits they have become accustomed to promising their citizens. This all adds up to considerable and mounting pressure on people to work far longer for lower rewards, and that is a tough environment for corporates to operate in. Companies have an obvious need to motivate staff and to have them aligned with and committed to their goals. But this all has to take place in the context of a significantly less rewarding picture overall. In an era characterized by zero to low single-digit growth and a return to low price inflation, year-on-year salary increases are also going to be extremely modest. That, too, impacts the way companies need to think about reward structures.

What are the challenges for HR arising from removal of the default retirement age?

There is no doubt that companies need to adapt and find ways of managing a workforce that has within it a much wider age spread and a much broader range of needs than before. Again, this goes directly to the need to think more imaginatively about the range of benefits that the company wants to provide as an employer. What a young worker wants and values will be very different from the older worker. So you need to design a benefit structure that allows individuals to choose. This used to be called Flex, or flexible benefits, but Flex has become closely associated with salary sacrifice, where an employee gives up part of their salary and the employer increases the employer's contribution to the employee's pension fund or other benefits.

Another point is that flexible benefit schemes generally have been associated with the expensive IT platforms required to administer and track a large matrix of benefits across a sizable workforce. This tended to price Flex schemes out of the reach of smaller to mid-sized companies. However, the advent of cloud computing—where software can be delivered as an internet-based service by an external service provider on an inexpensive "per user" basis—is going to be incredibly helpful in bringing flexible benefit systems within the reach of companies of all sizes.

Could we see HR services themselves becoming much more of an outsourced offering for mid-range to smaller companies?

We are not seeing much demand for HR as an outsourced service to small to medium-sized enterprises as yet. This market is still very underdeveloped, but there is no doubt that industry would benefit hugely from the development of a vigorous outsourced HR market. The public sector, too, in a number of advanced economies is going to have to think much more about outsourcing HR policy advice as it seeks to get to grips with the new wave of austerity in public-sector finances.

The development of HR outsourcing in the public sector would play a very important role in disseminating best practice in HR across public sectors. It is clear that a number of leading public-sector employers have very similar staffing issues and would benefit greatly from access to good-quality HR. Best-in-class HR skills are quite rare and expensive, so outsourcing would definitely make it a lot easier to access those skills. It seems obvious that shared advice and administration of HR is going to be the only way for the public sector to go. In fact that would solve many issues in both the public and the private sectors.

With the modern emphasis on the knowledge economy and the importance of people to an organization, should HR directors expect to be full board members of plcs?

It is not a right that every HR director has simply because he or she is an HR director. It comes down to where the company places people in its priorities. At Mercer we recently did a piece of research on the FTSE top 20 companies, asking what priority they attached to people in their annual report. Our question was: Where do your people fit in when your company talks about itself? Our analysis showed that 18 of the top 20 had people as a top priority. That would argue for HR to be a main board role in those companies. But then you also have to look at the caliber of the people in the HR role. Those who can bring the people agenda within the company to life in the same way that, say, a finance director of a FTSE plc is expected to bring finance to life at the top table would be a real asset to the board, and HR directors who can do this tend to be main board members.

We are seeing a clear shift within HR to a much more analytical, data-orientated approach, and when an HR director has this in his or her armory, they are much better equipped to bring analysis and evidence to the table when talking about the organization's skills and people issues. If the HR director has the right infrastructure in place, they can then present the people agenda with the same rigor as the finance director presents the finance agenda.

At its simplest this means looking at the internal labor market in the organization, understanding those practices that are most aligned with the improvements that the organization is seeking to bring about. You need to know what to do as an organization to create high-performing talent. The relevant questions for HR are: Do we have effective career development? What is it that we do to create top performers? You find that out by analyzing your top performers and understanding what was done to enable them to achieve that potential.

Doing this requires good data analysis and processes that generate the metrics you need. Without this evidence, organizations go in for simpler, more naïve solutions, which often boils down to a focus on looking for ways to improve the organization's incentive plans. The problem with these naïve solutions is that the solution to improved performance might lie in a completely different direction—which would show up if you had the ability to analyze the relevant data.

For example, we did an exercise for a client recently that involved helping the client to improve delivery by van drivers. Workforce analytics showed that it all came down to the tenure of drivers and their supervisors. After a couple of years, the more familiar drivers were with the delivery route, the poorer was their performance—tenure was a bad thing. For supervisors tenure was a good thing because they would be more familiar with the work of a particular driver. Managing tenure, therefore, resulted in better performance.

So this was not about incentives, it was about workforce management, and this kind of example shows the power of workforce analytics in addressing specific HR management issues. It is all about how well you understand the impact of what you are doing as an organization, and without measurement you are flying blind.

How common is workplace analytics as a process in major plcs?

In the United States workplace analytics is pretty common among larger companies. In the United Kingdom most of the major plcs either already have it or are working on ways of implementing it in their organizations. Continental Europe in general is

"A good paymaster never wants workmen." Thomas Fuller

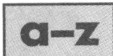

behind, with Germany as the clear exception. A number of German multinationals are doing very interesting work with workplace analytics.

This is less prevalent with mid-range companies, and is not that important at all in smaller companies which, as a general rule, are much better connected with their employees. Smaller companies have the huge advantage of being able to operate much more intuitively, and this is what the best HR practice is striving to bring to large organizations, but based on best-in-class practice rather than on the whims of a charismatic entrepreneur.

What are the top priorities today for HR directors?

HR directors are focused on three major things: first, talent, or the acquisition, development, and deployment of really good people; second, engagement, which is how the organization connects and resonates with the employee; and third, the deployment of workforce analytics, which is about generating the data that allow you to be confident that the actions you are taking are generating the results you want. All three areas are hugely important. On top of this you have to manage pay and rewards really well and you have to get the benefit structure in the organization right.

How important is it for an organization to become accredited—for example, through gaining an Investors in People accreditation?

Accreditation is important, but it is what you might think of as "table stakes." You have to do it to be in the game, but it will not be sufficient to differentiate you as an organization. The fundamental thing is how you manage your people as an organization. Being a great employer is a consequence of doing the fundamentals well, and if you do that any accreditation process should not be particularly challenging. So I see accreditation as a tactical rather than a fundamental goal. The fundamental goal for HR is being able to be confident that what you are doing creates high-performing people. Focusing on talent, engagement, and workforce analytics is the way forward there.

MORE INFO

Websites:

Investors in People standard: www.investorsinpeople.co.uk

Mercer: www.mercer.com

See Also:

✔ Understanding the Financial Aspects of Employing People (p. 1183)

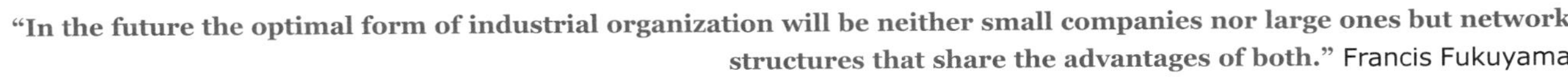

"In the future the optimal form of industrial organization will be neither small companies nor large ones but network structures that share the advantages of both." Francis Fukuyama

  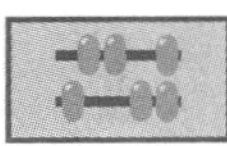      

Human Risk: How Effective Strategic Risk Management Can Identify Rogues by Thomas McKaig

EXECUTIVE SUMMARY

- Corporations and high-level risk management are built around the people in organizations—and people are fallible.
- The need to evaluate human risk is clear: Stories abound of rogue employees in large and small organizations who have destroyed their entire firm.
- At the extreme, rogue firms, such as Enron, can destroy shareholder value and employees' lives.
- Building a quality-based organization helps to drive out rogues, but that's not the only way.
- Control measures need to be in place.
- Legal measures, the spotlight of publicity, and backing up corporate policies with firm action are all effective tools.

INTRODUCTION

Best practices in strategic risk management are intended to prevent weaknesses within corporations causing damage or even pulling down the firm. However, effective strategic risk management tools and techniques became harder to implement as business operations grow, become more complex, and operate in multiple locations. The controls that might have once been deemed acceptable in keeping employees within corporations on the same page begin to be less effective in cases of corporate restructurings that split businesses into smaller business units, and where employees are prodded into making deeper contributions to the bottom line.

Technology has not necessarily been a savior in this type of situation. Although technology has provided a platform for enhancing competitive advantage for business, it has also been a tool used by smart, capable, yet ill-intentioned employees to steal and distort overall results.

In the age of managerial cutbacks and increased workloads, a lot of things can happen that go unnoticed by overburdened managers. Interview techniques intended to keep rogues out of the workplace are—in spite of all the high-end questionnaires and intensive interview techniques that may be used—oftentimes ineffective, as potential employees are extremely savvy about modern interview techniques. Players in the job market are often familiar with the drill. Job hunters pass through many revolving interview doors, allowing them to hone their skills on how to dupe the interview process. Some interviewers may be incompetent or show poor judgment. HR departments are not foolproof, and it is only realistic to accept the fact that rogues in the workplace are here to stay. HR people will sometimes catch potential wrongdoers at the gatepost through psychological tests and other forms of due diligence involving intuition and criminal checks. But don't count on it.

Newspapers are full of stories about accountants who pad the books and give kickbacks to friends and family. Unhappy workers can damage product on the assembly line. A fired employee can show up at the workplace intent on payback for the injustice he or she feels they have suffered (in the United States this is called "going postal"). A multinational manager away from the watchful eyes of the home office can withhold information and deliver selective reports. Expense accounts can be padded. Goods can be pilfered from warehouses.

Given the current economic and political shocks, the last thing a company needs is to find itself in the news on account of the excessive creativity of one or more of its employees. Managers must face the fact that rogues will enter their organizations. So the question becomes: What can be done about it before the damage is done?

Keep in mind that human risk is about more than employees stealing from a firm; it can include individuals making unsound business decisions because nobody told them otherwise. Mistakes can be just as

CASE STUDY

An Invitation to Rogue Employees

The example of a small Costa Rican bank serves to illustrate this point. At the height of the opening of Costa Rica's financial markets to foreign financial institutions in 1995 there was a rush to change operations practice. In the pre-free market era, Costa Rican banks could do as they pleased and were immune to punishment even when there were banking scandals and losses that were large for Costa Rica's fragile economy during the 1980s and 1990s. Old-style banks, accustomed to getting away with providing poor customer service and having lax internal controls, found that their business environment was changing with the pending legislative changes, set to open Costa Rica's financial markets to the world.

With poor leadership at the helm, and a lack of almost any strategic management initiative, employees were forced to take on new and undefined roles in their bank. Most of these were ill-suited to employees who were given inadequate training and guidance for their new tasks.

As part of rising to the challenge of this expected competition from foreign banks, and in light of the assumed effectiveness of recently ordered ATM machines, the bank we are considering decided that a lean and mean (and ill-informed) policy of rampant firing would be an acceptable cost-saving measure. Half of the bank's staff lost their jobs, and those who remained quickly became demoralized. The newly installed bank machines did not function properly. Friday afternoon payday waits grew to two hours from the already unacceptable 15–30 minutes.

Internal communications broke down. In place of the usual courteous conversations, vitriolic emails flew from one cubicle to the next—seeding the environment for "surprise actions" from a growing league of unhappy, overworked, and demoralized employees. With no controls in place, an inexperienced bank teller authorized a loan of $US 1 million to a long-standing customer—based solely on the fact that the teller liked the man and felt that he could be trusted with the money. For a small bank with a net worth of $US37 million, this inappropriate loan decision was the start of a string of poor management decisions that led to its implosion. Throughout this process the business culture undermined any attempts to implement benchmarking studies or best-practice management solutions. The "generous" employee was not fired and kept his duties with a severe reprimand. The future of the bank was sealed, and eventually it went down.

"However, quality leadership can also be lost through some catastrophic change." In Juran and Gryna (eds) (1988)

  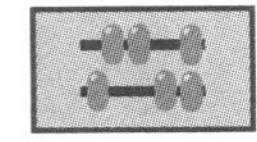    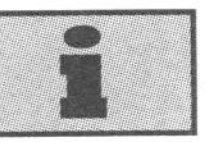  

bad as deliberate fraud, as the following case shows.

AT THE EXTREME

At the extreme end of the spectrum, there is a widespread pattern of "pushing the boundaries" of everything from accounting rules to disclosure rules for public companies, lax internal controls, managements that focus on doing deals rather than managing, outright fraud and theft, and incentive systems that reward the wrong actions.

Enron followed this pattern. The case of Enron shows how a combination of intellectual laziness and groupthink by a large number of employees, consultants, and analysts allowed a group of greedy and ambitious individuals to get away with massive fraud. Enron was not a case of one or two people at the top undertaking a complex scheme unbeknown to others, but rather a case of many individuals who knew what they were supposed to do, but didn't do it. This was a case of analysts who never really questioned how Enron made its money, of accountants who didn't ask simple questions, and of employees and board members who saw dubious things but were afraid to stand up and ask the questions they should have.

STRATEGIC RISK MANAGEMENT: A VIEW

What is risk management, and how does it apply to the actions of employees? According to Kent D. Miller, "'risk' refers to variation in corporate outcomes or performance that cannot be forecast ex ante."[1] The key element here is to recognize that there is true uncertainty about human risk, or indeed any risk. The fact that an organization has survived to today without major scandal does not guarantee that it is safe in the future.

So what to do? According to Miller, effective risk management responses frequently include avoidance (which we have noted is almost impossible with the case of human risk), control (to be addressed in a moment), and cooperation and imitation (which can be achieved through quality initiatives).

QUALITY INITIATIVES CAN HELP

An organization is only as good as its parts—in this case the human parts. One fractured link in the chain means one vulnerable corporation. The quality aspect of management can be evoked to work hand in hand with problem prevention, but it is all too often overlooked.

Typically quality applies to (but is not limited to) reducing or eliminating defects in manufactured products. Beyond this, management also needs to invoke quality principles that smooth the internal environment. When intra-corporate communication channels are damaged, the ensuing misinformation may foster rogue behavior within the organization. Many quality experts cite training, transparency, empowerment, and clear communication as vital steps in building a quality organization.

Whether dealing with production issues or those relating to customer service, quality initiatives espoused by management thinkers like Armand V. Feigenbaum, J. M. Juran, Philip B. Crosby, and Frank Gryna can help a business. Firms that include quality as a core value, and reinforce this value through everyday practice, have experienced reductions down to zero of defects on production lines, lower worker turnover, higher levels of worker empowerment through training, more worker satisfaction, greater productivity, and a positive outlook on the company. Valuing people as the key drivers of both quality and performance is important to a firm and can go a long way toward identifying rogues and frustrating their efforts.

Quality starts with managers. Being an ethical role model is a key function of any leader. And the good news is that nothing special has to be done to become such a positive model. However, when leadership falters it can open the door to a rogue hit, doing as much damage to the corporation as a rogue wave can do to a ship at sea. You have to work at good leadership.

But the emphasis on quality alone is not enough. Control mechanisms, including both financial and performance audits, are important for preventing and uncovering potential problems. The really effective tools are punishment and brandishing the legal arsenal available to the company. Such measures reassure the public. A corporation just can't hunker down to avoid embarrassment. Swift and fair measures will fill the void of those strategic management initiatives that fail to catch rogue employees and will serve as a heavy reminder to others who may be about to embark on a negative course of action.

To many, the idea of punishment seems to be a return to management's dark past in the days of command and control. This is not the case. Taking corrective action, including negative reinforcements and punishments, is a legitimate function of managers, just as much as positive reinforcements are. Corrective actions can include firings, admonishments, wage deductions, and suspension without pay. People in authority are chary about digging in their heels to fight for what is ethically and obviously right for fear of being politically incorrect, or worse, manifestly insensitive. Many in decision-making positions prefer a course of inaction because they lack the gumption required to stay the course. If a manager has documented proof (paper or electronic) of wrongdoing by an employee, and particularly in a unionized environment, there is little that a union can do to "rescue" the employee from receiving the appropriate reprimand, short of the union condoning such rogue behavior.

CONCLUSION

A manager faces many risks—from industry-wide risks such as currency and interest rate risks, to department-specific risks such as accounting and treasury risks. Most of these risks can be quantified, though we are finding out that many of the numbers assigned to these risks are little more than educated guesses. Unfortunately the identification, measurement, and quantification of human risk are difficult and challenging. In spite of our best efforts, and in spite of pundits who spout an arsenal of "proof" to the contrary, reliable numbers cannot be assigned to human risk. Nor can risk be completely eliminated from an organization. But quality initiatives and control mechanisms can go a very long way to minimize exposure.

MAKING IT HAPPEN

- Learn to live with the uncertainty of any risk, especially human risk.
- Place renewed emphasis on what is already being done, including audits (financial and performance), internal financial controls, and clear financial reporting.
- Vigilantly tweak and enforce the control mechanisms already in place. Think about expanding and/or adding controls.
- Revisit your own role as a highly visible manager. Are corporate controls short-sighted, or are they clearly structured so as to prevent deceit, fraud, and rogues from doing future damage?
- Identify high-risk areas in your firm—from inventory to treasury areas. Think about safety and security measures in addition to internal controls.

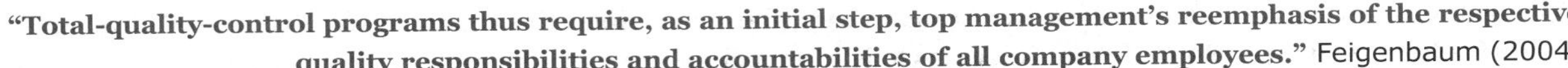
"Total-quality-control programs thus require, as an initial step, top management's reemphasis of the respective quality responsibilities and accountabilities of all company employees." Feigenbaum (2004)

MORE INFO

Books:

Crosby, Philip B. *Completeness: Quality for the 21st Century*. New York: Dutton, 1992.

Feigenbaum, Armand V. *Total Quality Control*. 4th ed. New York: McGraw-Hill, 2004.

Gryna, Frank, M. *Quality Planning & Analysis: From Product Development Through Use*. 4th ed. New York: McGraw-Hill, 2000.

Hill, Charles W. L., and Thomas McKaig. *Global Business Today*. 2nd Canadian ed. Whitby, ON: McGraw-Hill Ryerson, 2009.

Juran, J. M., and Frank M. Gryna (eds). *Juran's Quality Control Handbook*. 4th ed. New York: McGraw-Hill, 1988.

Mintzberg, Henry. *Managers Not MBAs: A Hard Look at the Soft Practice of Managing and Management Development*. San Francisco, CA: Berrett-Koehler Publishers, 2004.

Articles:

Becker, David M. "Testimony concerning new regulatory tools to control the activities of rogue individuals in the financial services industries." Given before the Subcommittee on Oversight and Investigations and the Subcommittee on Financial Institutions and Consumer Credit, US House of Representatives, March 6, 2001. Online at: www.sec.gov/news/testimony/ts042001.htm

Boak, Joshua. "Rogue trader rocks firm: Huge wheat futures loss stuns MFGlobal." *Chicago Tribune* (February 29, 2008). Online at: archives.chicagotribune.com/2008/feb/29/business/chi-fri_traderfeb29

Clark, Andrew. "From ethical champion to rogue interloper—BP's American nightmare: Accidents and allegations of market fixing destroy environmentalist image." *Guardian (London)* (November 16, 2006). Online at: www.guardian.co.uk/business/2006/nov/16/ethicalbusiness.oilandpetrol

Gunther, Will. "In the crosshairs: Limiting the impact of workplace shootings." *Risk Management* 55 (November 2008). Online at: findarticles.com/p/articles/mi_qa5332/is_11_55/ai_n31162724

Johnston, David Cay. "Staff says IRS concealed improper audits and rogue agent." *New York Times* (May 1, 1998). Online at: tinyurl.com/aqf9tr

KPMG. "An approach to mitigating rogue trading risks." KPMG LLP, 2008. Online at: www.us.kpmg.com/Rutus_Prod/Documents/12/19429NSS_RogueTrader_screen.pdf

Malakian, Anthony. "Internal controls need to be tightened." *Bank Technology News* (April 2008). Online at: www.americanbanker.com/btn_article.html?id=20080327QJ4HD229

Prince, C. J. "To catch a thief: Employee fraud hits growing businesses hardest. Here's what you can do to make sure there's not a thief among you." *Entrepreneur Magazine* (September 2007). Online at: www.entrepreneur.com/magazine/entrepreneur/2007/september/183068.html

Website:

CBC News coverage of the Conrad Black affair: www.cbc.ca/news/background/black_conrad

See Also:

★ How Internal Auditing Can Help with a Company's Fraud Issues (pp. 346–350)
★ New Assurance Challenges Facing Chief Audit Executives (pp. 377–381)
★ Risk Management: Beyond Compliance (pp. 929–932)
✔ Establishing a Framework for Assessing Risk (p. 1028)
✔ Understanding Internal Audits (p. 1057)
Mastering Risk, Volume 1: Concepts (p. 1393)

NOTE

1 Miller, Kent D. "A framework for integrated risk management in international business." *Journal of International Business Studies* 23:2 (1992): 311–331.

"The extent to which the task of the worker is adequately planned reflects the degree to which the worker is placed in a state of self-control. The plan, do, check, act cycle is often called the 'Deming cycle.'" Gryna (2000)

The Impact of Climate Change on Business

by Graham Dawson

EXECUTIVE SUMMARY

- The impact of climate change on business—or the monetary value of the costs that may be incurred by affected parties and the benefits that they may accrue—is difficult to assess with any degree of precision.
- The Stern Review and the United Nations Intergovernmental Panel on Climate Change (IPCC) have reported the results of running complex computer models that integrate climate science and economics with the aim of predicting the economic impact of climate change far into the future.
- There is no agreement concerning the appropriate discount rate or the monetary value of effects where market prices are not available.
- Uncertainty also surrounds the rate, and carbon-intensiveness, of the growth of the world economy for decades and even centuries ahead, while the hypothesis of anthropogenic climate change itself continues to be controversial.

THE GLOBAL IMPACT OF CLIMATE CHANGE ON PEOPLE

The standard approach to assessing the economic impact of climate change on business requires giving a monetary value to the costs that may be incurred by those affected and the benefits that may accrue to them.

The most comprehensive attempt to do this is the Stern Review (2007), commissioned by the UK government, which predicts severe impacts from an average global temperature rise of 2–3°C within the next 50 years or so. These impacts include an increased risk of flooding from melting glaciers, followed by disruption to water supplies, affecting up to one-sixth of the world's population, mainly in the Indian subcontinent and parts of China and South America. In higher-latitude areas, such as Northern Europe, agricultural yields may increase with a temperature increase of 2–3°C, but declining yields, especially in Africa, could leave hundreds of millions of people without sufficient food. Increased mortality from heat-related deaths and the spread of tropical diseases is predicted, although there will be fewer deaths from exposure to cold. With warming of 3–4°C, thermal expansion of the oceans is predicted to cause rising sea levels, which could lead to inundation of low-lying coastal land, displacing "tens to hundreds of millions" of people. The risks are greatest for Southeast Asia (Bangladesh and Vietnam), small islands in the Caribbean and the Pacific, and large coastal cities, such as Tokyo, New York, Cairo, and London. Extreme weather events may become more frequent.

MODELING THE COSTS OF CLIMATE CHANGE

It is easy enough to put a monetary value on some of these impacts. For example, there is a lot of expensive real estate with known market prices in major coastal cities such as London, New York, and Tokyo. Moreover, without offices or factories for people to work in, or homes for them to live in, output would fall, at least for a while. Declining crop yields (adjusted for higher prices) and also fish stocks would reduce the value of world output. Standard practice is to estimate the loss of output consequent upon people's incapacity for paid and unpaid work.

Quantifying these predicted impacts of climate change in monetary terms requires degrees of certainty and precision that may not be attainable. Both the science and the economics of climate change are subject to considerable uncertainty and are therefore deeply controversial.

The impacts of climate change on business depend on the magnitude of temperature changes associated with different concentrations of CO_2 and other greenhouse gas (GHG) emissions, according to the scientific hypothesis of anthropogenic climate change. The earliest studies of the economic impact of climate change assumed a doubling of atmospheric concentrations of CO_2 by 2050, and estimated the costs of the resulting increase in global mean surface temperature at approximately 2% of world gross domestic product (GDP).

Subsequent modeling of the economic impact of climate change has sought to integrate scientific models of the global climate and economic models of future world economic growth. The anthropogenic hypothesis holds that most of the observed rise in temperature has been caused by GHG emissions from fossil fuel use in economic activity. The future path of GHG emissions depends on the rate of growth of world economic activity and how that growth is divided between more and less carbon-intensive processes. So predicting the future path of GHG emissions, and hence the impact of climate change on business, involves modeling the rate of growth of the world economy well into the future.

The United Nations Intergovernmental Panel on Climate Change (IPCC) occupies a near-monopoly position in disseminating climate science to policy makers throughout the world. It does not predict future temperature increases and their impacts but prepares a number of illustrative outcomes, using integrated assessment models (IAM). Models of world economic growth and consequent GHG emissions are combined with climate science models, showing the links between those GHG emissions and temperature change.

The Stern Review used PAGE2002, an IAM designed by the UK government in 2000 and modified two years later. Stern claims that the overall costs and risks of business-as-usual (BAU) climate change would be equivalent to losing 5–20% of global GDP each year, "now and forever,"

CASE STUDY

What Would This Mean for Business Activity in, for example, the United States?

If predictions such as those reported by Stern prove to be accurate, business will be forced to adapt to changes in climate. Adaptation would involve a range of measures of varying cost. In the United States, temperature increases of up to 2–3°C might cause the wheat belt to shift northward into Canada; US farmers in the Midwest would have to plant new crop varieties, a fairly routine adjustment. In northern areas, winter deaths from exposure to the cold would fall and tourism might increase. Further south, the melting of snow could make the water supply to California and the Mississippi basin more erratic, causing more acute problems for agriculture. Deaths from exposure to heat and the cost of air conditioning and refrigeration would increase. At higher temperatures, southern parts of the United States would see an increased risk of extreme weather events, requiring substantial investment to defend low-lying cities, such as New Orleans and New York, from flooding.

"You cannot control what happens to you, but you can control your attitude toward what happens to you, and in that, you will be mastering change rather than allowing it to master you." Brian Tracy

but this may not be as apocalyptic as it sounds.

Stern explains the different stages by which this estimate of the economic impact of climate change was reached. The model is run to simulate a period of 200 years or more and "produces a mean warming of 3.9°C relative to pre-industrial in 2100." The first stage indicates that the costs and risks of climate change that can be quantified in terms of market values (basically, lost output) would be equivalent to losing at least 5% of global GDP each year, "now and forever."

At this point, Stern departs from most other models by adding in "non-market" impacts on the environment and human health. Nonmarket impacts are those that cannot be given a monetary value by referring to a market price (for instance, the price of land lost to coastal flooding). The costs of disease or of lost agricultural land in subsistence economies, for example, do not have a market price. Including this second stage increases the total cost from 5% to 11% of global GDP. These estimates are highly controversial. Since standard practice is to estimate health impacts in terms of lost output from incapacity to work, applying this and other techniques to estimate the cost of nonmarket impacts is subject to considerable uncertainty. It has also been argued that the degree to which both disease and casualties from natural disasters are related to income rather than environmental factors is not taken into account.

The third stage adds amplifying feedback effects, including the risk of catastrophic climate change, which increase the potential total cost from 11% to 14% of global GDP. Finally, Stern considers the view that a disproportionate burden of climate change would fall on poor regions. If this were given a stronger relative weight, the total cost of global warming could increase to "around 20%" of global GDP. Stern arrives at such a large adjustment for poor regions because he assumes that vulnerability to climate change is independent of development, but it seems more likely that such vulnerability depends on the capacity to adapt and hence on the level of development.

UNCERTAINTIES IN THE ECONOMIC VALUATION OF IMPACTS

"Now and Forever"

The phrase "now and forever" invites examination. The effects of climate change are expected to occur year by year over a very long period of time. The Stern Review calculates the present value of the costs of climate change by averaging the total costs over the number of years the model runs at a rate of discount. Nordhaus ran the Stern model to calculate the costs of climate change, including nonmarket and catastrophic impacts that take Stern's estimate up to 14% of world output, for each year the model covers. According to Nordhaus, the model projects a mean loss of only 0.4% of world output in 2060, rising to 2.9% in 2100 and 13.8% in 2200. Losses averaging about 1% over the period 2000–2100 become about 14% "now and forever" because the losses in the distant future are extremely high (and a low discount rate is used). Nordhaus argues that, "using the [Stern] *Review*'s methodology, more than half of the estimated damages now and forever' occur after the year 2800."

Discounting

For most people, $100 is worth more today than $100 next year because there is a degree of uncertainty about what might happen between now and next year; they would prefer to have $100 to spend right now to having it at some point in an uncertain future. In other words, the *present value* of that $100 payable to you in 10 years is less than $100 paid to you now. Similarly, the expected future costs, no less than the benefits, of an event or occurrence should be discounted, i.e. reduced in value, in order to estimate their present value.

Since many economic impacts of climate change are not expected to occur until decades or even centuries into the future, their occurrence is inevitably subject to a degree of uncertainty. The impacts of catastrophic climate change may never happen, so economists discount, or reduce the value of, their costs. As you add up the costs of climate change year by year, you might want to adjust downward those expected in later years—that is, you might want to *discount* them to reflect the uncertainty of their occurrence. The higher the rate at which you discount such costs, the lower will be their present value.

The discount rate used may influence the results of a model more than any other parameter or value used in the model. There is no agreement about the appropriate rate of discount to use, and Stern argues that any discount rate greater than zero unfairly devalues the interests of future generations. He sets the "pure time preference rate" at zero, on the grounds that a future generation has the same claim on our ethical attention as the current one. Based on a zero pure time preference rate, the discount rates used in Stern's running of PAGE2002 are lower than those used in most other models and do much to explain why Stern's "baseline" cost of 5% of world GDP is higher than the results of other models (typically 1–2% of world GDP). Other ethical approaches are at least as convincing. For example, agent-relative ethics holds that agents naturally value people who are linked to them by kinship or proximity above strangers who are remote in space or time. This approach implies a higher discount rate, which would reduce the loss from "business as usual" in Stern's model substantially below 5% of world GDP.

The estimate is an annual average for an indefinite future; losses are low for the first 50 years or so, and using unusually low discount rates produces a high present value for the catastrophic losses predicted for 2200 and beyond. By that time, given rates of world economic growth sufficient to cause the projected carbon emissions and climate change, it is reasonable to assume that most people will be very much better off than the current generation, although not quite as much better off as they would have been in the absence of climate change.

Scenarios of Future World Economic Growth

How much better off would these future generations be, and which groups of people would gain most? What will the world economy look like 100 years from now? Wisely, the IPCC has demurred from making any such prediction, offering instead six illustrative scenarios of possible future courses that the world economy might take. In 2007 the IPCC reported the "best estimates and likely ranges for global average surface air warming for six...

MAKING IT HAPPEN

Business may be affected by policies to mitigate climate change as much as by climate change itself. In the negotiations for the Kyoto Protocol, which seeks to establish a global framework for reductions in GHG emissions, the fossil fuel producers and users resisted aggressive reductions, while insurance companies and renewable energy producers were more favorably disposed toward them. It is not clear whether aggressive mitigation policies will survive the financial crisis of 2008, with many policy makers more concerned to reduce the effects of the expected global recession than the more distant threats posed by climate change.

emissions marker scenarios." The best estimate for the low scenario is 1.8°C, and the best estimate for the high scenario is 4.0°C. The important point here is that scenarios are descriptions of possible outcomes to which no probability can be attached. Of the six scenarios, the IPCC asserts that that: "All should be considered equally sound." If it is impossible to assess the risk of any of the associated impacts, there is radical uncertainty.

It is widely believed that the impact of an increase in global temperature of less than 2°C will be mild, and that cereal yields will actually increase in temperate regions. With a global temperature increase of 4°C, the impacts are projected to be catastrophic, with up to 80 million people exposed to malaria, and up to 300 million more affected by coastal flooding each year, with rising risks of extreme weather events. But, on the IPCC's own admission, it is impossible to say whether the impact of climate change will be mild or catastrophic.

Uncertainty in Climate Science

Uncertainty also surrounds the science of climate change. In its most recent report, the IPCC claims that there is 90% certainty that most of the increase in global mean temperature since the middle of the twentieth century has been caused by the observed increase in greenhouse gas concentrations in the atmosphere. This is actually a rather cautious and vague claim, because it is consistent with a significant role for natural causes being the reason for the rise in global temperature. In the decade since 1998 global temperature has not risen, and critics of the IPCC argue that the scientific evidence for dangerous change is far from overwhelming.

Conclusion

The impact of climate change on business, or the monetary value on the costs that may be incurred by affected parties and the benefits that they may accrue, is difficult to assess with any degree of precision.

The Stern Review and IPCC have reported the results of running complex computer models that integrate climate science and economics with the aim of predicting the economic impact of climate change into the remote future. However, there is no agreement concerning (i) the appropriate discount rate and (ii) the monetary value of effects where market values are unavailable. Uncertainty also surrounds the rate, and carbon-intensiveness, of the growth of the world economy for decades and even centuries ahead, while the hypothesis of anthropogenic climate change itself continues to be controversial.

MORE INFO

Books:

Lawson, N. *An Appeal to Reason: A Cool Look at Global Warming*. London: Duckworth, 2008.
Nordhaus, W. D. *The Challenge of Global Warming: Economic Models and Environmental Policy*. New Haven, CT: Yale University Press, 2007.
Singer, S. F., and D. T. Avery. *Unstoppable Global Warming: Every 1500 Years*. Lanham, MD: Rowman & Littlefield, 2006.
Stern, N. *The Economics of Climate Change: The Stern Review*. Cambridge, UK: Cambridge University Press, 2007.

Articles:

Beckerman, W., and C. Hepburn. "Ethics of the discount rate in the Stern Review." *World Economics* 8:1 (2007): 187–210.
Brittan, S. "On climate change and good sense." *Financial Times* (February 9, 2007).
Byatt, I., *et al*. "The Stern Review: A dual critique. Part II: Economic aspects." *World Economics* 7:4 (2006): 199–232.
Carter, R. M., et al. "The Stern Review: A dual critique. Part I: The science." *World Economics* 7:4 (2006): 167–198.
Tol, R. S. J., and G. W. Yohe. "A review of the Stern Review." *World Economics* 7:4 (2006): 233–250.

Reports:

Goklany, I. M. "Death and death rates due to extreme weather events: Global and US trends 1900–2006." In *Civil Society Report on Climate Change*. London: International Policy Press, 2007, pp. 47–60. Online at: www.csccc.info/reports/report_20.pdf
House of Lords. "The economics of climate change." HL Paper 12-1, Select Committee on Economic Affairs 2nd Report of Session 2005–06. London, 2005.
Intergovernmental Panel on Climate Change, Working Group 1: The Physical Science Basis of Climate Change, 4th Assessment Report (IPCC WG1 AR4 Report), "Summary for policymakers." IPCC Secretariat, c/o WMO, Switzerland, 2007. Online at: ipcc-wg1.ucar.edu/wg1/wg1-report.html
Reiter, P. "Human ecology and human behaviour: Climate change and health in perspective." In *Civil Society Report on Climate Change*. London: International Policy Press, 2007, pp. 21–46. Online at: www.csccc.info/reports/report_20.pdf
US Climate Change Science Program (CCSP), Annual Report to Congress. *Our Changing Planet: The US Climate Change Science Program for Fiscal Year 2009*. Online at: www.climatescience.gov/infosheets/ccsp-8

Websites:

Global and Development Environment Institute at Tufts University: www.ase.tufts.edu/gdae
Intergovernmental Panel on Climate Change (IPCC): www.ipcc.ch
Science and Environmental Policy Project: www.sepp.org
United Nations Environment Programme (UNEP) climate change pages: www.unep.org/themes/climatechange
US Climate Change Science Program (CCSP), integrating federal research on global change and climate change: www.climatescience.gov

See Also:

★ Best Practices in Corporate Social Responsibility (pp. 636–639)
★ Business Ethics (pp. 645–647)
★ Climate Change and Insurance (pp. 149–150)
★ CSR: More than PR, Pursuing Competitive Advantage in the Long Run (pp. 664–666)
★ Ethical Funds and Socially Responsible Investment: An Overview (pp. 481–483)
✔ Creating a Sustainable Development Policy (p. 1113)
✔ Managing the Time Value of Money (p. 979)
✔ The Triple Bottom Line (p. 1125)
Ernst Friedrich Schumacher (p. 1307)

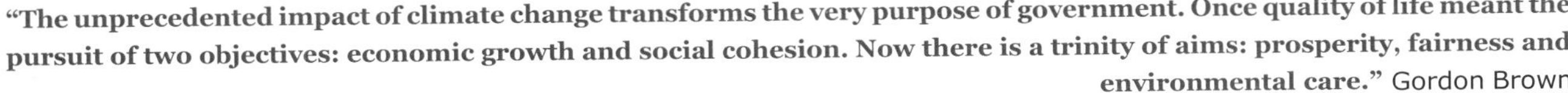
"The unprecedented impact of climate change transforms the very purpose of government. Once quality of life meant the pursuit of two objectives: economic growth and social cohesion. Now there is a trinity of aims: prosperity, fairness and environmental care." Gordon Brown

  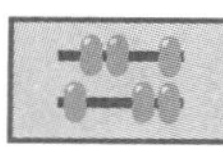      

Viewpoint: The Importance of Trust—In Everything

by Jonathan M. Karpoff

INTRODUCTION

Jonathan M. Karpoff has particular interest in what drives executives to commit corporate crimes and misdemeanors. Here, he explains how a breakdown of trust can have long-term repercussions for individual corporations and how it led to the wider financial collapse of 2008–09.

A professor of finance at the University of Washington's Michael G. Foster School of Business, Karpoff is also associate editor of a number of academic journals including the *Journal of Finance*. Karpoff won the best paper award in the CRSP Forum at the University of Chicago in both 2006 and 2008 for his research into corporate and financial scandals. Karpoff was the founding director of the University of Washington's environmental management program and was director of its CFO Forum from 2004 to 2007.

Karpoff's extra-curricular activities include rock climbing, mountaineering, and adventure skate skiing in the Cascade Mountains. He received his BA (1978) from the University of Alaska/Anchorage, and his MA (1980) and PhD (1982) degrees from UCLA.

XEROX AND OTHER EXAMPLES

Most investors had a terrible 2008. But stockholders in Xerox Corporation have had a bad *decade*. Xerox's story contains an important lesson because, in addition to a decreasing demand for copiers, its struggles have been compounded by a lack of trust in its financial reporting.

Xerox's share price was flying high until October 8, 1999, when the firm announced that its quarterly earnings would fall short of expectations. As investors soon discovered, the company's prior strong financial performance had been a mirage.

Since early 1997, managers had manipulated the books by recognizing as current revenue its customers' promises to pay on long-term equipment lease contracts. The manipulation worked for a couple of years, and the share price peaked at US$59.01 on May 3, 1999. But revenue-acceleration schemes like that at Xerox have a way of catching up with the perpetrators. Eventually, Xerox had to restate its earnings to reflect the lower revenues that it had actually received.

Xerox's financial reporting misconduct proved costly. Controlling for market movements, Xerox's market capitalization fell by a cumulated amount of US$5 billion on the days that news of its misconduct was first reported to investors. My colleagues Scott Lee, Jerry Martin, and I have determined that US$1.14 billion of this loss represents the adjustment back to Xerox's pre-inflated level—the market cap that Xerox would have attained had its books never been cooked in the first place. Another US$523 million of the loss is due to penalties imposed by the SEC and a class action lawsuit by angry investors.

But most of Xerox shareholders' loss—US$3.34 billion or 67% of the total—represents something more powerful than even the disciplinary arm of the SEC. It is the direct financial cost from the breakdown in investors' trust in the company and the transparency of its financial reports.

We all know the value of a good reputation. Indeed, as parents one of our greatest tasks is to instill in our children an appreciation for honesty and integrity. But recent research has shed new light on the role of trust and reputation in business. In many cases—as with Xerox—researchers can even put a dollar value on the loss in reputation that comes when a firm behaves badly and loses the trust of its customers, suppliers, and investors.

As I use them here, "trust" and "reputation" are not fuzzy, feel-good terms. By reputation I mean the present value of the income that accrues from repeat business on profitable terms. And repeat business comes from trust. Firms that act opportunistically undermine that trust, and face tougher terms of trade with counterparties, who learn to be wary of such opportunism.

By tougher terms of trade, I mean such things as higher borrowing costs and lower sales. In recent research, John Graham, Si Li, and Jaiping Qiu show that firms that restate earnings subsequently face greater borrowing restrictions, including higher loan rates, when seeking loans from banks. Deborah Murphy, Ronald Shrieves, and Samuel Tibbs show that firms caught in various types of misconduct, including misreporting, suffer a double whammy: they experience a higher cost of capital and they lose sales.

Xerox's experience is by no means unusual. In January, Satyam Computer Services' share price fell more than 88% in the two days after its founder and chairman, B. Ramalinga Raju, disclosed that the Hyderabad-based firm's assets had been inflated by more than US$1 billion. Parmalat, the Italian dairy company was declared bankrupt in December 2003, in the wake of revelations of financial misconduct involving its top officers. Shares in Ahold, the Dutch grocery chain, dropped two-thirds of their value upon revelation that a subsidiary's profits were overstated by US$500 million. And in 2007, Royal Dutch Shell settled investor lawsuits for US$352.6m (£178.3m) for previously inflating its oil and gas reserves by 20%.

Each of these firms reflects the pattern documented in a recent study that I conducted with Scott Lee and Jerry Martin. Using data from all firms disciplined by the US SEC for financial misrepresentation, we found that shareholders lose a tremendous amount of value when their firms are caught cooking the books.

The average firm loses 38% of its market capitalization. Even more importantly, two-thirds of this loss is from lost reputation. The lost reputation is the decrease in present value as these firms face a higher cost of capital and less attractive terms when trading with their (now) more skeptical customers and suppliers.

Stated differently, managers are putting a lot at risk when they cook the books. Financial manipulation can inflate prices over the short term. But when the manipulation is discovered, the firm loses much more than the short-term price inflation. For every dollar the stock price was artificially inflated, the firm loses this dollar plus US$3 more. Of this additional loss, most is from lost reputation (the rest is from legal pelaties.). This is the real impact of financial misrepresentation on the firm's

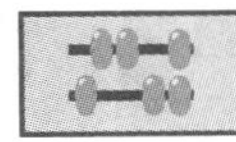

long-term operations. By cheating investors, the firm faces a higher cost of financial capital until it can reestablish trust and a new reputation for financial transparency—and that can take a very long time.

The reputational effects for managers and directors also are severe. In a related study, Lee, Martin, and I found that over 92% of executives involved in financial misrepresentations lose their jobs. Most are fired. Fully 42% are barred from serving as officers or directors, and 28% are indicted on criminal charges. Directors also have a lot of reputation at stake. Anil Shivdasani and Eliezer Fich found that directors of firms that are sued for financial misconduct become tainted. As a result, they lose 50% of their seats on other boards, on average.

TRUST MATTERS

A firm's trust and reputation are important not only for its investors. They affect the firm's relationships with all counterparties. Culinary gourmets might sneer at McDonalds's hamburgers, but those burgers sell by the millions because customers know what they will get when they walk through the golden arches. That trust from customers—and the profit stream that accrues because of it—is McDonalds's reputational capital. It is every bit as valuable as the firm's proprietary method of deep-frying French fries.

Different firms invest in, and accumulate, different levels of reputation. Johnson & Johnson, the maker of Tylenol, has a huge reputational investment in Tylenol, which it protects through elaborate quality control measures. Generic producers of acetaminophen, in contrast, have little reputational capital. Customers know this, and infer that Johnson & Johnson has much greater incentives to control the quality of its product. That is, Johnson & Johnson has more reputational capital at stake. As we see in sales figures, some people are willing to pay for the extra assurance of quality provided by the Tylenol™ brand name.

A good reputation encourages customers to buy from the firm and investors to buy the stock. But reputation is a double-edged sword, because any hint that the firm has failed to provide the expected quality imposes a large penalty. This is especially true for firms that defraud or cheat their customers or investors. Businesses that cheat their customers lose future sales. Those that cheat suppliers or employees find it difficult to keep their inventory stocked and workforce productive. And, as we have seen, those that cheat their investors by misreporting financial statements find it difficult to raise new capital.

ABSENCE OF TRUST

The importance of trust illuminates the issues at the core of the current financial crisis. Fraudsters like Bernie Madoff exploit other people's trust. What is remarkable about the Madoff experience is not only the size and devastation of his pyramid scheme, but the fact that he had acquired—and sacrificed—a huge amount of reputational capital.

Madoff's scam could be so large only because—as a highly respected member of the financial community and former chairman of NASDAQ—he had such a good reputation. Had he acted honestly, Madoff could have enjoyed a lifetime of wealth and social prestige about which most people can only dream. By perpetrating a fraud, in contrast, Madoff enjoyed years of the appearance of phenomenal success, but at a cost of all his reputational capital.

Beyond the Madoff scandal, trust—or its lack—lies at the heart of the broader financial crisis. The crisis has many causes, including overleveraged financial institutions, bad loans, a housing bubble, and interlocking credit default swaps. But what shocked central bankers around the world into pumping billions of dollars into the financial system was the specter of a massive credit crunch. And the credit crunch is, in essence, a breakdown of trust. The reason anyone lends money is the trust that they will be repaid. When such trust evaporates, so does the willingness to lend.

Trust is central to the financial crisis. The fear of a deep worldwide recession is exacerbated by the prospect of a credit freeze, which in turn results from the breakdown in trust between lenders and borrowers. Many firms were highly leveraged—indeed, the average asset-to-equity ratio of US securities broker-dealers in the middle of last year was approximately 32, an historically high ratio. European banks' leverage ratios were even higher, approaching 40. With a decrease in asset values, many financial institutions sought at once to deleverage by dumping assets and hoarding cash.

Many of these same firms' assets were of uncertain quality. Firms such as Lehman Brothers and Washington Mutual sought short-term financing to weather the storm, but potential counterparties could not determine the value of these firms' collateral, or the likelihood that they were solvent.

Both effects—high leverage and poor asset quality—eroded trust in many firms' abilities to pay off new loans. This breakdown of trust has increased the cost of private borrowing for both financial and industrial firms, increasing operational costs and dramatically slowing economic investment and growth. Trust, or its absence, continues to be at the centre of the financial crisis.

REPUTATION IS ALL

Business gurus frequently advise us to do well by treating our customers, suppliers, and investors well. This is sound advice, but its impact is limited by the absence of hard data to back it up. The paucity of data may be one reason executives frequently underestimate the importance of trust and the cost of squandering their firm's reputation with investors or customers.

There is a story, perhaps apocryphal, that years ago Ford Motor Company calculated the financial costs and benefits of reengineering the gas tank in its Pinto automobile. On paper, the costs appeared be greater

Figure 1. Xerox's cumulated market-adjusted returns from January 1997 through December 2008

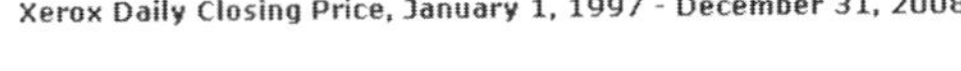

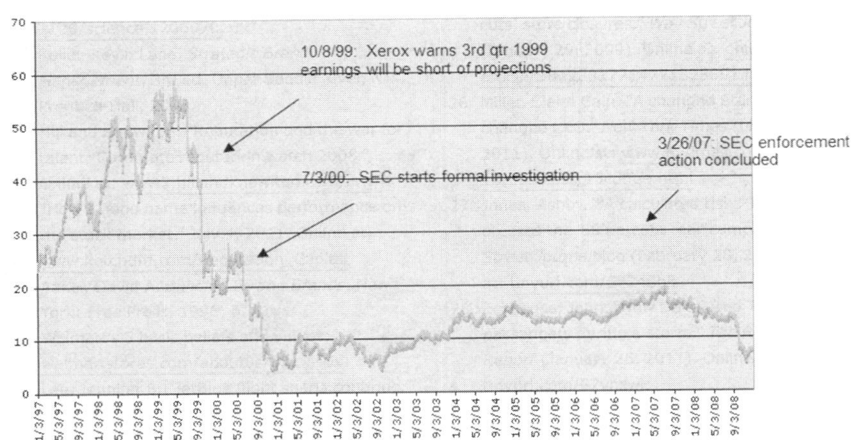

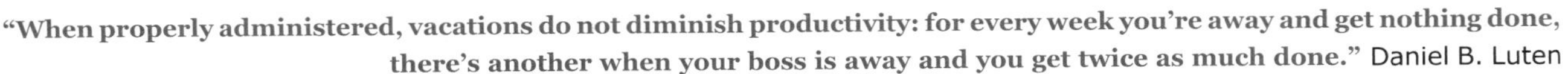

  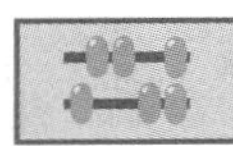      

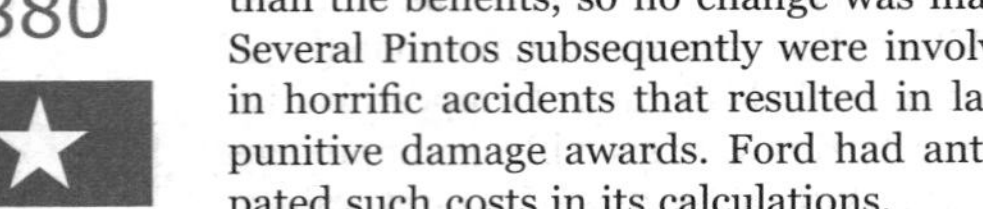

than the benefits, so no change was made. Several Pintos subsequently were involved in horrific accidents that resulted in large punitive damage awards. Ford had anticipated such costs in its calculations.

What the car company had not considered, however, was the reputational cost from having a potentially lethal car in its fleet. In researching the impact of punitive damage-seeking lawsuits, John Lott and I discovered that the direct cost of a damage award is only a small portion of the total cost to the paying company. The mere publicity of the lawsuit and the punitive award scares away customers and investors, decreasing the firm's future sales, and increasing its cost of capital.

To the extent that this story is true, Ford's Pinto experience highlights a managerial experience that is all too common: underestimating the importance of trust and the value of reputation. Events or actions that undermine trust in their firms—from accounting irregularities, to charges of fraud, to lawsuits seeking punitive awards—scare away customers, suppliers, and investors. Such events have repercussions that extend far beyond the immediate crisis because they affect counterparties' future willingness to do business with the firm.

Managing a firm's reputation—that is, building a track record that attracts customers and investors—is not simply a feel-good concept from the latest trendy management book. Rather, it is a core competency that has real and measurable impact on firm operations and value.

MORE INFO

Articles:

Alexander, Cindy R. "On the nature of the reputational penalty for corporate crime: Evidence." *Journal of Law and Economics* 42:S1 (April 1999): 489–526. Online at: dx.doi.org/10.1086/467433

Fich, Eliezer M., and Anil Shivdasani. "Financial fraud, director reputation, and shareholder wealth." *Journal of Financial Economics* 86:2 (November 2007): 306–336. Online at: dx.doi.org/10.1016/j.jfineco.2006.05.012

Graham, John R., Si Li, and Jaiping Qiu. "Corporate misreporting and bank loan contracting." *Journal of Financial Economics* 89:1 (July 2008): 44–61. Online at: dx.doi.org/10.1016/j.jfineco.2007.08.005

Karpoff, Jonathan, D. Scott Lee, and Gerald S. Martin. "The consequences to managers for financial misrepresentation." *Journal of Financial Economics* 88:2 (May 2008): 193–215. Online at: dx.doi.org/10.1016/j.jfineco.2007.06.003

Karpoff, Jonathan, D. Scott Lee, and Gerald S. Martin. "The cost to firms of cooking the books." *Journal of Financial and Quantitative Analysis* 43:3 (September 2008): 581–612. Online at: dx.doi.org/10.1017/S0022109000004221

Karpoff, Jonathan M., and John R. Lott, Jr. "The reputational penalty firms bear from committing criminal fraud." *Journal of Law and Economics* 36:2 (October 1993): 757–802. Online at: www.jstor.org/stable/725807

Karpoff, Jonathan M., and John R. Lott, Jr. "On the determinants and importance of punitive damage awards." *Journal of Law and Economics* 42:S1 (April 1999): 527–573. Online at: dx.doi.org/10.1086/467434

Murphy, Deborah L., Ronald E. Shrieves, and Samuel L. Tibbs. "Understanding the penalties associated with corporate misconduct: An empirical examination of earnings and risk." *Journal of Financial Quantitative Analysis* 44:1 (February 2009): 55–83. Online at: dx.doi.org/10.1017/S0022109009090036

See Also:

★ What Are the Leading Causes of Financial Restatements? (pp. 428–430)
✔ International Financial Reporting Standards (IFRS): The Basics (p. 1039)
✔ Key Accounting Standards and Organizations (p. 1040)
✔ The Ten Accounting Principles (p. 1055)

"Managing is getting paid for home runs someone else hits." Casey Stengel

  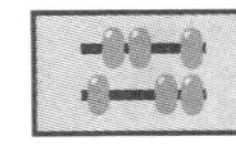      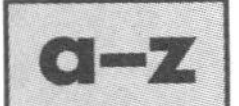

Viewpoint: In Data We Trust by Björn Bloching

INTRODUCTION

Björn Bloching is a senior partner at Roland Berger Strategy Consultants where he is responsible for global business in the areas of marketing and sales, and retail and consumer goods. Besides brand management, quantitative marketing, and sales strategies, his consulting focuses on a range of topics from creative urban development and tourism to projects involving culture, education, academia, and professional sports. Professor Bloching has dealt extensively with data and their use, including writing the book *In Data We Trust*.

BEER AND NAPPIES: HOW THE CUSTOMER DATA REVOLUTION STARTED

There were harbingers of the customer data revolution in the early 1990s—on the shelves of Wal-Mart's stores, among other places. The world's largest retailer had invested early in database systems, initially in order to optimize its logistics and warehousing. A number of anecdotes circulate about how the company's marketers had their eureka moment regarding information technology. A Wal-Mart manager told us it happened like this: a smart cookie on the board never tired of stressing that in the databases' jumble of information there were unbelievable treasures, of which no one had yet dreamed. He convinced his colleagues to set up a competition with substantial prize money. Two people in the IT department started to sift through billions of lines of receipt data, where they found surprising correlations. And what do you know? From early evening onwards, beer and nappies often ended up in the same shopping trolley. It's not hard to find the psychological triggers behind this purchase pattern. Men on their way home are not thrilled by the thought of soon having to change nappies, so they reward themselves in advance. The two IT workers had suggested placing beer offers next to the nappy shelves. Test markets showed that impulse purchases shot up. And this simple but effective marketing measure of "shelf optimization" was introduced in all stores. The beer and nappies example is now 20 years old.

Back then, only a few large corporations had the resources for data mining—in other words, the intelligent analysis of structured data sets. The technology is more democratic now. Today, any pizza delivery service can use databases to improve customer retention. The more advanced users know what their customers are willing to pay and have an approximate idea of what and how much they purchase with the competition. Google, Amazon, Apple, eBay, and Facebook have built their global business models on (customer) data. They and their all-conquering information point to where things are going in the realm of comprehensive customer knowledge and differentiated communication.

WHALES IN THE SEA OF DATA: THE AGE OF GUESSING IS OVER

The customer data revolution is part of a larger change. After the personal computer and the Internet, digitalization has now reached a third stage. Data storage is becoming ever cheaper, data processing ever faster, and the algorithmic software that analyzes the data is ever more intelligent. Information scientists have dubbed this revolution "Big Data." The data sets are growing exponentially. We are just learning how to use informational raw material in all areas of life. Data are the stepping stone to a new level of understanding; Big Data will change society, politics, and business as fundamentally as electricity and the Internet did.

Wired magazine's founder Kevin Kelly sees the Internet as a "magic window." Only little children had dreamed that such a window would ever exist. IT systems in the era of Big Data can do what IT visionaries foresaw decades ago. They can collect the knowledge of the world on a screen. They spot connections that are too complicated for people to grasp on their own. And they form models that use calculations of probability to give us a window into the future. Computers know us better than we know ourselves—or, at least, they are often more reliable than we are at saying how we will behave in certain situations. Based on our customer profile, car hire companies know how much petrol will be in the tank when we return the car. An analytically driven online retailer knows the probability of a regular customer buying something at a certain price. And the retailer will know how much has to be invested in personalized advertising in order to make the sale. Credit card companies can predict with a high degree of success which couples will divorce in the next five years.

There is no lack of data with which to measure reality, nor is there a lack of business-relevant data. The smartphone has removed the distinction between the online and offline worlds. It translates our day into a stream of data. Digital payment systems are ever more popular and bring purchases out of the anonymity of the bricks-and-mortar world. Businesses themselves leave ever more digital tracks and so become increasingly transparent in business-to-business markets. At the same time, we are learning to recognize patterns in the exabytes (that is, 10 to the power of 18 bytes) of publicly accessible data—for example in the relationships on social media, where the motto could be "show me your friends and I will tell you who you are." We can use these patterns for predictive modeling in order to calculate the probable behavior of groups and individuals. The idea might not be one we are fond of, but as consumers we are predictable. The value of data grows when they are linked up. If this happens in real time, the door to a new age of customer interaction is opened. The era of intuition is over. Not only can IBM information technology beat the human all-time champions in answering ironic, trickily formulated general knowledge questions on the cult US quiz show Jeopardy!, but when IT has access to the right customer data, it also sells better than the experience and gut instinct of marketers. And that's not someone's opinion; it is empirically provable.

SAP's CEO Jim Hagemann Snabe describes the challenge of data mining and business analytics in our age of huge quantities of data as the need to find the "needle in the haystack" in real time. A marketer who is well-versed in IT put it nicely when he said, "We have to find the whales in the sea of data." Condensed into a single word or slogan like a classic ad, it might go: "Crunch! Crack the data sets!"

Your own, and the easily available ones floating in that sea! If you don't do it, others will. Analytically driven companies know the markets they can address much better than those businesses that don't work their data sets hard; they can segment their target groups more appropriately, and they are able to interact with customers in a more personalized way as they know their customers' needs.

Data-based marketing offers businesses a wonderful opportunity to become more intelligent than the competition. In 10 years' time at most it will be seen as a matter of simple "hygiene" for customer data to be gathered and evaluated intelligently. In other words, companies without this capability will disappear from the market. And, moreover, customers can now crack the data too. Checking a price comparison app on your smartphone as you stand in front of a shelf is just the start.

THE EVIDENCE OF EVIDENCE: LOOKING INSIDE CUSTOMERS' HEADS

There has never been a more interesting time to work in marketing and sales. For the first time in the history of mass-market selling, we are able to look inside the head of each individual customer. A 360-degree view of the customer has long been a wish of sales and marketing teams, but today—if we link up data intelligently—a deep understanding of individual customers can now become real. We are no longer asking small focus groups, as traditional market research did, "What did you think of this product? Which product would you like to have?" We are finally moving from the role of the questioner to an observer's perspective. The aggregated data points allow us to measure customers' behavior and from that to draw the right conclusions about the four great marketing Ps: Product, Price, Place, and Promotion. Data-driven marketing—or data marketing for short—allows us to communicate the right offers in the right way at the right price to an individual customer at the right time. When added up, knowledge of every individual customer also means that we have a much more accurate bird's-eye perspective of the whole marketplace, including market potential and the interesting segments of the market.

The world is flat. Technology, processes, and business models are copied mercilessly. Products and services are becoming increasingly similar. The technology executives of an important car manufacturer once expressed it like this: "Today we are all the same under the bonnet." Banks and insurance companies provide white-label services. Who, in a blind tasting, will notice the difference between a market leader's jam and a discounter's own brand? If it is hard for consumers to distinguish between products, knowledge about the customer is one of the most important competitive advantages that businesses can still have. And to look at it from the other side of the coin, knowledge of what is done with our data should be part of everyone's general education.

IN DATA WE TRUST—IN A NUTSHELL

Data marketing does not make current marketing methods obsolete; rather, it harnesses them and uses analytics to develop them further. A small shopkeeper could do many things without the aid of systems that today's mass market companies are only just realizing are once again possible. For example, the shopkeeper knew his customers and could serve them personally.

He practiced customer relationship management on a scribbling pad or in his head. His friendly words for everyone were much more customer-centric than were the massive temples to shopping in the second half of the last century. As the mass markets of the Western world were slowly becoming saturated, and as societies were becoming more diverse and consumption needs ever more individual, producers and merchants started to realize that pushing an unending wave of products with ever louder traditional advertising no longer had the same impact. Companies needed to approach customers in different—and differentiated—ways.

DATA ANALYSIS OR DATA PARALYSIS? OVERCOMING THE CRM TRAUMA

In the 1980s, by which time all large companies had mainframe computers in their basements for bookkeeping and inventory purposes, US banks and airlines achieved their first successes with the newly dubbed "database marketing," soon to be called "customer relationship management" (CRM). As so often in the history of information technology, the new systems promised much and started promisingly—but the realization of plans proved difficult. Many companies burned holes in their pockets trying to get closer to customers via data. Data analysis turned into data paralysis. The disappointment was as great as the hopes had been, and CRM became a curse. At roughly the same time the so-called "New Economy" collapsed. Enter the second generation of online users. They had a built-in connection to data, while the technology start-ups had their own natural interest in using such data in competition against offline companies. Social media gave this development a turbo boost. In online worlds suddenly much was possible—20 years after the IT industry had prematurely said that new ways of working would "not be a technical problem." Companies with offline backgrounds can learn a lot about understanding customers from the digitally driven newcomers.

Even though many of the best practices come from business-to-consumer (B2C) markets, the potential in business-to-business (B2B) markets should not be neglected. There is a simple reason for this. When considering the use of data for marketing purposes, the focus is normally on consumer relationships. However, in our experience, in the B2B sector the whales of the data sea are often easier to catch. This is because the necessary data are often more readily available in companies' or public databases, and so the restrictions relating to data usage are considerably fewer and competitors are often—as far as data analysis goes—still playing in the amateur league. In many industries, competitors have not even started analyzing their data yet. The competitive advantage of B2B companies that start data crunching can thus be correspondingly high.

THE PRIVACY ISSUE

However, there is the largest challenge of all: customers have at least to tolerate data marketing and, if possible, love it. If the marketing feels like spying, then obviously the company has shot itself in the foot. The data do not belong to the marketer but to the customer, and right-thinking companies will not stray into murky legal waters even when the frontiers of the data world are not always adequately policed. There is no need for a moral appeal here. It is a matter of self-interest, because customers are more powerful than any data-protection agency.

NOBODY WANTS TO BE A NOBODY NOW: THE NEW CONSUMER CULTURE

In the coming years, a consumer culture will develop along the lines of a list of the conditions according to which most customers are willing to share data with companies. The data-marketer has to create a sufficiently transparent and safe framework. Customers have to see the value of this and consider that the use of the data is appropriate. We all know that trust is hard to gain and easy to lose, and this is particularly true for the commercial use of personal data. The companies to profit from the customer data revolution will be those that respect the rules of this new

"There is no substitute for accurate knowledge. Know yourself, know your business, know your men." Randall Jacobs

     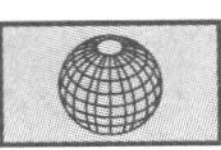   

consumer culture, build trust—and prove they deserve it.

No one today can predict where in the future consumers will draw the line regarding privacy. There will be areas where we keep an extremely close eye on the potential for our data to be misused. And there will be areas where we are more relaxed about the information we share, because the advantages far outweigh the danger of misuse.

In current discussions about data use, the skeptics and regulators set the tone of the debate. The advantages and opportunities to both providers and consumers are often neglected in these exchanges. Our book, In Data We Trust, casts a realistic eye on what is technologically possible and economically sensible regarding the commercial use of customer data. Customer trust is the necessary foundation for all of these suggestions. However, we have considerably more confidence in the competence and learning curve of users than we are in those of the loudest voices in today's data protection debates.

Most enlightened consumers share their data voluntarily and consciously—and not because they are tricked into it by loyalty card administrators or social networks. Loyalty card users—many of them signed up long before the Internet came along—receive discounts or special offers. Facebook users, often "digital natives," use a technological platform for social interactions that are important to them. Neither group is made up of sheep that need to be protected from the data wolves. They draw their own lines around public and private spheres. No one is forced to use a loyalty card or Facebook profile. Of course, there is the danger of data being misused. The wisdom of the mass of users will, in the medium term, force the provider of data-driven services to play by the users' rules. Among other things, this means clear and easily understood opt-in and opt-out functions when private data move into the public digital domain.

Skeptics and regulators are holding on to a strangely idealized image of anonymity in public space. The majority of people want to be themselves online and offline. People want to be addressed by their own name. They use the name in their passport for customer reviews. They have no problem about telling the world what their relationship status is; nor must their mobile number be as secret as MI5's.

The Internet's age of "masks" is over. No longer will people camouflage themselves like Odysseus in front of the Cyclops. Second Life—the online world where people used avatars, brands advertised on virtual billboards, and retailers had digital shops—was the Internet flop of the last decade. Today, people want to be themselves.

They want to be found. A growing group of consumers is sharing data out of conviction and with enthusiasm. The blippy.com platform provides an insight into what self-chosen transparency can look like. When a member of the community pays for a product by credit card, the social shopping platform automatically publishes the location, price, and time of the purchase. The default setting for consumption is public, as the network user's friends can benefit from this information. For marketers and sales people, it means this: enlightened consumers are open to dialog with companies. Many even actively seek dialog. Marketing and sales need to seize this chance—in order to get to know customers better. And in order to predict their consumption moods. And, ideally, in order to know their wishes before the customer even knows that he or she has them.

BUY THE BOOK

To purchase a copy of the full book *In Data We Trust: How Customer Data Is Revolutionising Our Economy*, by Björn Bloching, Lars Luck, and Thomas Ramge, published by Bloomsbury, visit www.bloomsbury.com/uk/in-data-we-trust-9781408179512/.

MORE INFO

Books:

Davenport, Thomas H., and Jeanne G. Harris. *Competing on Analytics: The New Science of Winning*. Boston, MA: Harvard Business School, 2007.

Jeffery, Mark. *Data-Driven Marketing. The 15 Metrics Everyone in Marketing Should Know*. Hoboken, NJ: Wiley, 2010.

Report:

Brynjolfsson, Erik, Lorin M. Hitt, and Heekyung Hellen Kim. "Strength in numbers: How does data-driven decision-making affect firm performance?" Sloan School of Management, April 2011. Online at: tinyurl.com/cuh3uqy [PDF].

Website:

In Data We Trust on Facebook: www.facebook.com/In.Data.We.Trust

See Also:

★ Reducing Costs and Improving Efficiency with New Management Information Systems (pp. 921–923)

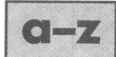

Viewpoint: India Today and Tomorrow by Rajiv Dogra

INTRODUCTION

Rajiv Dogra is a diplomat by profession, engineer by training, writer by choice and an artist by inclination. He is currently based in New Delhi and is a well-known commentator and columnist. He became a member of the Indian Diplomatic Service in 1974. During the course of a wide ranging professional career he was India's Ambassador to Italy, Romania, Moldova, Albania and San Marino . He was also India's Permanent Representative to the United Nations Agencies in Rome (FAO, WFP and IFAD), and India's last full time Consul General in Karachi. He is the author of two novels; Footprints in Foreign Sands and Almost an Ambassador. Amongst the honours received by him is an Honorary Doctorate.

A TENTATIVE POWER

India has long been the subject of many myths. The early Romans believed that this phenomenally rich country was guarded in the north by a solid wall of ivory, while Pliny the senior worried that India's huge trade surplus would bankrupt the Roman Empire. More recently, in the 18th century, India accounted for 22.6% of global trade.

Today, however, with close to 18% of the world's population, India's GDP is barely 1% of the global total. This modest rating seems natural for a country which has spent much of its independent existence in a mode of self-preservation, a principal priority for a nation that was subjugated for centuries by numerous invaders before its bloody rebirth in 1947.

It is little surprise then that apprehension defined many of India's early policies. Nonalignment was essentially an astute institutional mechanism to keep the eastern and western blocs at bay. The same wariness was responsible for an inward-looking approach to economic development, and domestic monopolies encouraged this fear of the foreign.

As a result, India was fatalistically wedded to an austere rate of growth till the early 1990s. It was content with this soul satisfying, but bare-to-the-bones performance, as long as it validated its part socialist, part capitalist, agonizingly plural, and noisily democratic experiment in nation building.

As in the past, the proudest achievement in its post independence history has been reinscribing into the national ethos the value of tolerance. Consequently, everything is possible and all avenues are open. That is why India continues to pursue a firmly secular line, adopting all religions. This spirit of accommodation also leads again and again to foreign policy choices that can best be termed as those of a soft power, not that of a smart power.

This idealism has also led India to technological choices where it has sought gain through pain by insisting on reinventing the wheel, terming that struggle "appropriate technology." It established technological and business universities to rival those in the West, and started on its own torturously slow course to enhance its technological capabilities. This set it apart from others in the region, and also paved the way for an educated, ambitious middle-class that today equally powers Silicon Valley and Bangalore's technology call centers.

In part, this self-imposed grind is a principled position—an application at all levels of its motto that truth alone should triumph, even if that truth needs to be technologically carved out by its own efforts. There is even a label for this painful quest: *swadeshi*or self-reliance.

In contrast, China has taken a different, more pragmatic route, choosing instead to harness the technological revolutions in the West for its growth. In part therefore, China's exports are intimately linked to the American economy, while Indian companies pursue patiently the domestic consumer. This same difference in approach between India and China can also be witnessed when they tackle the issue of future prosperity. China has a foreign exchange reserve of US$2 trillion and sits happily on it. India has a little over US$250 billion and worries constantly.

But managing large foreign exchange reserves is the lesser of India's worries in the coming years. There are larger, more fundamental challenges that lie ahead, and how India handles them will determine its place on the global stage. In particular, the litmus test is whether India, or rather its democracy, can deliver in a country that is largely poor, suffers a scarcity of food and water, and is governed by coalition governments whose partners often pull in different ideological directions. Can India continue to avoid a million mutinies as it sets forth on a new, faster paced agenda?

BOOM, BUST, AND PROMISE

There is no doubt that India broke out of its long self-imposed slumber in the early 1990s. Two important changes took place almost simultaneously. First, a new generation began to step into decision-making positions within the government and industry. This ambitious leadership was no longer encumbered by the neuroses of a colonial past. It was instead confident and bubbling with ideas for India's place in a new technological world. Second, the 1990s also marked the beginning of the end of a deep held suspicion about the private sector, leading to a major shift in attitude.

On a practical level, however, caution was still the watchword and its mantra make haste slowly. Reforms arrived warily and with limitations, but the doors of the Indian economy had definitely creaked open and investor confidence increased correspondingly.

Previously, Indians settled abroad remitted funds to their families back home on an as needed basis. Now, they began to park their funds in high yielding financial instruments, hoping to tap into this prosperous new India. Investments in fresh start-ups grew dramatically, and, by 2008, inward remittances to India had reached an annual figure of US$45 billion. International investors also began looking for trophy acquisitions in Indian industry, actively adding the "Indian option" to their portfolios.

In the early 2000s, as Indian software companies leveraged off their success in preparing for the feared millennium bug, it seemed that the sky was no longer the limit. Year after year, the Indian economy began posting 8–9% GDP growth. Superlatives such as *India Rising*, *India Shining*, and *Incredible India* rolled in routinely. The international media was besotted and began to laud India, regardless of its warts. For a few years, it looked as if India was truly everywhere.

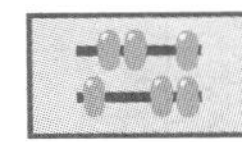

In line with this promising economic record, 2008 started magnificently with India finally within sight of double digit economic growth. At a societal level, secular India was now increasingly ambition driven rather than separated by religion. The stock market was booming and the flood of foreign capital was assuming embarrassingly large proportions.

But the turmoil in the financial markets through the year soon provided a sharp reminder that this new paradigm brought not only opportunities, but also the real risk of a sharp economic downturn. India could not avoid the debris of the Western financial meltdown and this revived the idea that perhaps India's earlier phobia of anything external was not unwarranted.

The slowdown has also brought home the growing realization that as an economic power, India has many problems in its own backyard. Ideally, the subcontinental region around India should be in intense engagement with itself—an eminently sensible approach as the alternative is strife.

Viewed dispassionately, the region shows tremendous potential. China, India, Pakistan and Bangladesh together contain a population of almost 2.8 billion people, a little over 41% of the global total. This is a formidable human resource, with history-shaping possibilities as a market. Properly harnessed, one could only imagine the boost this could give to regional industry and trade. In today's context of an increasingly globalized economy, it also represents an incredible new opportunity for the wider world.

THE GEOPOLITICAL LANDSCAPE

That's the theoretically feasible part. The reality, unfortunately, is ridden with roadblocks. India is surrounded by a number of neighbors who are unlikely to see it progress with a friendly eye. So, the illusion that it could make others in the region partners in its progress is likely to be stumped by a rude reality check.

If the European Union is the largest example of a stable economic and political union, South Asia presents the picture in reverse. From one country, it devolved into three—India, Pakistan, and Bangladesh. Economic integration may provide a useful slogan occasionally at regional meetings in South Asia, but businessmen who value their money are unlikely to take it seriously for a very long time yet.

India lives in a tough neighborhood. The countries to its west are particularly fragile. Pakistan is a failing economy, riven with terror and drugs. Under an almost constant military thumb from its inception, it is poised presently between naïve optimism and harmful self-destruction. Further up, Afghanistan is in historical hemorrhage. Every so often, it finds itself a new reason to bleed, with the Taliban providing the latest iteration of a thousand cuts.

To the south, Sri Lanka hass finally emerged from a bloody civil war. But its disparate society will take a long time to settle. To India's east, Myanmar lurches between being a forbidden state and a forbidding entity thanks to its military junta. Bangladesh has episodic experiments with democracy before a general whimsically decides that enough is enough. In the north, Nepal has transitioned quickly from a self-serving monarchy to a society dominated by stultifying Maoists, Nepal's current ideological inspiration, and its neighbor, China, is in an all weather monochromatic mode. Now, it is biding time to impose its will on the region around it and on the world as well.

By their very nature, dictatorships do not encourage the spirit of enquiry that is so essential to the evolution of a nation. Like human beings, nations must reinvent themselves constantly to succeed. But such churning is only possible in a democracy, and it seems that India may remain an isolated island of democracy in the region for some time to come.

The other reality that India must remain conscious of is the fact that its weaknesses are no longer only internal. It is true that there are plenty of internal tensions: regional disparities, social inequality, shoddy infrastructure, and poor healthcare, to name just a few of the issues that keep people angry. But the ability to shout democratically lets off some steam continually and, more recently, there is also the assurance that the idea of growth is working and is broadly inclusive.

The larger and more serious challenges for India are external. Terror, as 26/11 so shockingly reminded, remains the biggest security concern. The lack of democracy elsewhere in the region will keep adding to large-scale migration into India. Moreover, the economy will continue to be sensitive to global cues. Therefore, ignoring these external factors would be poor policy and India's greatest advances in the future are likely to come from its ability to manage them.

THE FUTURE?

In this, it should be served well by the fact that nearly 50% of India's population is below the voting age. Just as the youthful generation of the 1990s did not carry the baggage of post-colonial prejudices, the new crop of leaders do not have bitter memories of economic deprivation from the 1950s and 1960s. Instead, they have been brought up on a diet of liberalization and have seen innovation pay rich dividends. These young men and women will influence the important decisions that need to be made on transformational issues, such as development and India's place in the new world architecture.

There is no doubt that India wants to participate with greater vigor on the global stage and feels it has a justifiable claim. There is also a growing recognition by the outside world that the changed global realities necessitate that a large country like India must not remain on the sidelines. The reasons are unambiguous: it has the second largest population in the world, and is the biggest democracy which actively promotes secularism as its governing article of faith. Moreover, with its growing intellectual, economic, and technological participation in the world, it can contribute meaningfully in shaping a post- credit crunch global order.

But the passage to the global high table is not going to be smooth. Leaving aside regional prejudices, the Big Five—the United States, United Kingdom, Russian Federation, China, and France—still maintain the Security Council of the United Nations as an exclusive preserve. Not all of them retain any longer the global status they once had, and so are likely to resist any expansion till the last possible moment. India may, therefore, find itself waiting at the door-step of the UN Security Council for a long while yet.

However, it is being consulted ever more frequently on matters of global governance. Acquisitions of global industries by Indian businessmen have helped shape this new confidence in India. Its membership of G20, and an active role there, may set in motion a chain of events where India's pragmatic approach and balance could lead to it becoming a de-facto member of the world's inner councils.

This participation will bring with it greater responsibilities. The recent global financial turmoil has brought about the belated recognition that the world urgently needs a more effective regulatory system, if it is to avoid any more painful shocks of this magnitude. Here, India's record of a prudently run and mostly unscathed banking system stands out.

Over the next few decades, as its profile becomes larger and more complex, the challenges for India will multiply too. As it confronts and adapts to them it may have to make yet another transition; from moral idealism to what is practically moral. From ancient times, India has fascinated visitors by its abstraction and bewildered them with its

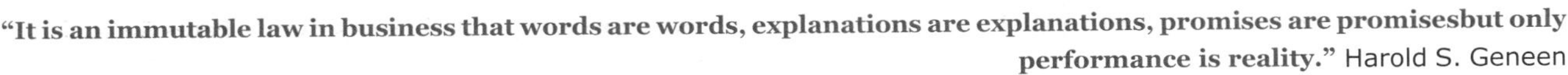
"It is an immutable law in business that words are words, explanations are explanations, promises are promisesbut only performance is reality." Harold S. Geneen

variety. Now, and increasingly in the future, outsiders will seek a more comprehensible India and one with which they can do business.

India's challenge lies in putting up that modern face.

MORE INFO

Books:

Nilekani, Nandan. *Imagining India: The Idea of a Renewed Nation*. New York: Penguin Press, 2009.

Sen, Amartya. *The Argumentative Indian: Writings on Indian History, Culture and Identity*. New York: Farrar, Straus and Giroux, 2005.

See Also:

★ Viewpoint: The Companies Bill, 2012, and its Impact on the Future of Corporate Social Responsibility in India (pp. 648–650)

India (p. 1505)

"Most of what we call management consists of making it difficult for people to get their work done." Peter F. Drucker

  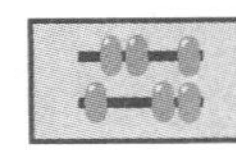      

International Arbitration: Basic Principles and Characteristics by Stavros Brekoulakis

EXECUTIVE SUMMARY

- International arbitration is a contractually based dispute resolution mechanism that offers an alternative to national courts.
- International arbitration has experienced a remarkable growth in the last three decades, due to its unique advantages over litigation.
- The advantages of arbitration include privacy and confidentiality of proceedings, procedural flexibility, and high rates of enforceability of arbitral awards.
- Despite its many advantages, there is growing concern that arbitration is becoming increasingly expensive and time-consuming. This concern, although not unfounded, is often overplayed. Ultimately, it is down to the users of arbitration to draft effective arbitration agreements and to put an effective arbitration procedure in place.
- To arrive at a successful resolution of disputes through arbitration, the parties involved should pay particular attention to the choice of arbitrators and the arbitration institution, and, most importantly, give due consideration to the drafting of the arbitration agreement.

DEFINITION AND DISTINCTIVE FEATURES OF ARBITRATION

International arbitration can be defined as a specially established mechanism for the final and binding determination of disputes concerning a contract between two or more parties that has an international element. The disputes are determined by independent arbitrators in accordance with standards and procedures chosen by the parties involved in the dispute.[1]

The distinctive feature of arbitration is that it is a *private* dispute resolution mechanism, which nevertheless provides arbitrators with *judicial* power. More specifically:

- arbitration is a private dispute resolution method, in which the arbitrators' mandate to resolve a dispute derives from a contract (i.e., an arbitration agreement or arbitration clause).
- arbitrators have the power to deliver an award that finally resolves the dispute that is binding on the parties.

The above characteristics of arbitration distinguish it from the following.

Litigation proceedings before national courts. In litigation, national courts are an expression of state power and they are bound to apply the rules and procedures of the state they are attached to. National judges owe allegiance to their state and they have limited or no discretion to deviate from the procedural codes and rules of that state. By contrast, in arbitration parties are free to determine how the proceedings are to be conducted, subject only to minimum safeguards (due process). Party autonomy is a fundamental principle in arbitration, which gives the parties the opportunity to tailor the proceedings in accordance with their commercial needs and the special characteristics of the case. Arbitrators are private judges whose mandate is determined by the arbitration agreement concluded by the parties, and who owe allegiance to the parties that have appointed them rather than to a state.

Alternative dispute resolution (ADR) methods. Despite the fact that their authority derives from a contract, arbitrators have the power to grant an award, which is a final decision that is binding on the parties. Arbitral awards are enforceable in the same way that national judgments are. Therefore, arbitration must be distinguished from other forms of ADR, such as mediation. Here, as in arbitration, a third party (mediator) is involved in the resolution of the dispute between the two commercial parties. However, the mediator has no power to impose a decision on the parties. Mediators work with the parties to resolve their dispute by an agreement; they cannot issue a binding decision. Thus, the outcome of a successful mediation is a settlement rather than an enforceable award.

DIFFERENT FORMS OF ARBITRATION

There are two basic types of arbitration: *ad hoc* and *institutional*. Parties are free to choose between these two types in their arbitration agreement. If the parties fail to specify in their agreement which type of arbitration they prefer, the arbitration will be presumed to be *ad hoc*.

Ad hoc arbitration is an arbitration that is specifically designed by the parties for a particular dispute. Here there are predetermined rules for the arbitrators to rely on when conducting the proceedings (although sometimes the United Nations Commission on International Trade Law (UNCITRAL) arbitration rules are used). Thus, it is up to the parties to determine the proceedings and to the arbitrators to fill any gaps. Ad hoc arbitration is more flexible than institutional, as the parties are completely free to adapt the proceedings to the particulars of the case. It can also be less expensive than institutional arbitration, as the parties avoid the fees of the institution and they can negotiate the fees of the arbitrators. However, for an ad hoc arbitration to work, the parties must have provided for a clear set of proceedings in advance, as there are no institutional rules to fall back on if they disagree on the arbitration process after the dispute arises.

Institutional arbitration is an arbitration that is conducted under the auspices of a particular arbitration institution and in accordance with the rules of that institution. Institutional arbitration is more popular among international parties.[2] This is because the parties feel more comfortable with experienced institutional administrators (known as "case managers") who are willing to take care of any issue that might arise during the proceedings. Parties are also attracted by the reputation and the strong brand name of many established arbitration institutions, which, as many parties believe, increases the enforceability of an arbitration award. The most popular institutions are the International Chambers of Commerce (ICC), the London Court of International Arbitration (LCIA), the American Arbitration Association (AAA), and the Stockholm Chamber of Commerce.[3]

ADVANTAGES OF INTERNATIONAL ARBITRATION

International arbitration has experienced a remarkable growth in the last three decades, and it is now perceived as the natural dispute resolution mechanism for disputes arising out of international transactions.

The remarkable growth of arbitration is due to the following advantages compared to national litigation and other ADR methods:

Privacy and confidentiality: Unlike litigation proceedings that take place in public, arbitration proceedings are private and, unless the parties agree otherwise, they remain confidential. Thus, the existence of the arbitration, the evidence and the documents exchanged in the arbitration, and the final award cannot be divulged to third parties. The duty of confidentiality is binding on the arbitrators, the parties, and their counsel, and it is considered an

"I can imagine no society which does not embody some method of arbitration." Herbert Read

  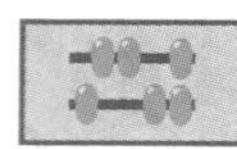      

important commercial advantage of arbitration.

The parties appoint the arbitral tribunal: Unlike litigation, where the dispute is determined by national judges appointed by the state, in arbitration the parties have the opportunity to appoint those who will decide on the dispute (i.e., the arbitrators). Usually, arbitral tribunals consist of either one arbitrator, who is chosen by both parties, or three arbitrators, where each party appoints one arbitrator and a chairman is then chosen by the two party-appointed arbitrators. The fact that the parties may participate in the constitution of the tribunal enhances their confidence in the arbitration process, as they can appoint arbitrators who are familiar with their legal or cultural background. It also gives the parties the opportunity to select arbitrators who have the expert knowledge required by the particular characteristics of the dispute. For example, an engineer or an architect is often appointed as an arbitrator to determine a complex construction dispute.

Enforceability of arbitral awards: International arbitration awards are more easily enforceable than national judgments. This is due to the 1958 New York Convention on the Recognition and Enforcement of Foreign Arbitral Awards, which has now been signed and ratified by 143 countries. The New York Convention has thus established an internationally harmonized regime for the enforcement of arbitral awards, where recognition and enforcement are only exceptionally disallowed on limited grounds. By contrast, there is no international convention that enables the enforcement of national judgments.

Procedural flexibility: Arbitration proceedings are determined by the arbitration agreement of the parties. Thus, the principle of party autonomy provides parties with considerable liberty to tailor their own dispute resolution process in accordance with their needs and the particulars of their dispute. Therefore, procedural flexibility and party autonomy make arbitration the most suitable dispute resolution mechanism for international commercial transactions.

Neutrality: Arguably this is the most attractive feature of international arbitration. Proceedings generally take place in a country with which neither party has links; the dispute is determined in accordance with transnational rules, or according to the national law of a neutral country; and arbitrators are appointed from different countries and with different nationalities. Neutrality is of utmost importance in the context of international arbitration, where each party wants to avoid a national court of its co-contractor.

AREAS OF CONCERN

Arbitration has always been considered a quicker and less expensive means of dispute resolution than national courts. Although in theory and in many cases this is still so, there is growing concern that arbitration proceedings are becoming increasingly costly and time-consuming. International arbitration is now widely perceived to be even more expensive than litigation.[4] The international arbitration community is concerned about these issues, and arbitration institutions have issued guidelines for the parties and the arbitrators to reduce the time and cost of arbitration proceedings.

Costs related to arbitration can be divided into two groups: Fees for the counsel; and arbitration costs, which include the fees of the arbitrators, the administrative fees of the institution (if the arbitration is institutional), and expenses related to the hearings (hiring the venue, translation costs, traveling costs for the witnesses, fees for the experts appointed by the tribunal, etc.).

Ultimately, arbitration is a party-led mechanism, and therefore it is up to the parties, who also are the fee payers, to take the necessary steps for the proceedings to take less time and money.

INCREASING THE CHANCES OF SUCCESSFUL ARBITRATION

Here are some of the factors that parties should consider to arrive at a successful resolution of their disputes through arbitration:

Appoint the right arbitrator: Parties should look for arbitrators who are available to embark on the proceedings quickly. Many arbitrators have a busy schedule, which inevitably will lead to delays in the hearings and the issuance of the final award. Parties are advised to do thorough research before selecting their arbitrators. Nowadays it is general practice for parties to interview potential arbitrators and gather information relating to their previous work. The number of arbitrators appointed may also impact the cost of the proceedings. A panel of three arbitrators will normally improve the quality of the award and reduce the risk of an arbitrary decision. However, three-arbitrator tribunals will generally be more expensive and time-consuming as it is more difficult to convene meetings, arrange hearings, or reach a final agreement when three arbitrators are involved.

Choose the right arbitration institution: Parties should be aware that while in ad hoc arbitrations parties may negotiate the arbitrators' fees, in institutional proceedings fees are calculated in accordance with predetermined rules. Different institutions have different methods for calculating arbitrators' fees. For example, the LCIA's rules set out a recommended range of hourly rates which may only be deviated from in exceptional circumstances, while under ICC rules the arbitrators' fees are calculated as a proportion of the sum in dispute (the so-called *ad valorem* method). Thus, parties are advised to look into the methods that different institutions use to

CASE STUDY

Ill-Drafted Arbitration Clauses Result in Further Litigation

The parties in *Lucky Goldstar v Nag Moo Kee Engineering* (High Court of Hong Kong, 1993) had included the following arbitration agreement in their contract: "Any dispute or difference arising out of this contract shall be arbitrated in a 3rd Country, under the rule of a 3rd Country and in accordance with the rules of procedure of the International Commercial Arbitration Association."

This was a "pathological" arbitration clause that made no sense, for the following reasons:

- The institution provided for in the clause, namely the "International Commercial Arbitration Association," did not exist.
- No seat of arbitration was specified; the rather ambiguous reference to "a 3rd Country" made no sense; and there was no indication which this "3rd Country" might be.

Therefore, when a dispute arose over the contract, the parties could not commence arbitration proceedings as there was no arbitration institution to which the parties could submit their dispute. Inevitably, therefore, the parties had to resort to a national court, which came up with a rather creative interpretation of the ambiguous arbitration clause in order to give effect to the parties' original intention to submit their dispute to arbitration. The High Court of Hong Kong held that since there was no "International Commercial Arbitration Association," the parties should be referred to the best-known international arbitration institution, which it judged to be the ICC.

It is, of course, fortunate in this specific case that the national court managed to give meaning to and enforce this ill-drafted arbitration agreement. However, the parties eventually lost time and money, as they had first to resort to a national court before finally starting arbitration proceedings.

"International arbitration may be defined as the substitution of many burning questions for a smoldering one."
Ambrose Bierce

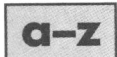

calculate arbitrators' fees before deciding which institution they should submit their dispute to.

Draft efficient arbitration clauses: Parties often focus on the substantive clauses of their contracts but pay little attention to the arbitration clauses. Arbitration clauses are usually the last provisions to be incorporated in a contract, and they are drafted without debate or much consideration of the specific needs of the particular contract. Ambiguous arbitration clauses will most likely result in lengthy litigation, causing delays and increasing the cost of the arbitration proceedings. Parties are advised to draft clear arbitration clauses that set out an effective and rapid set of arbitration proceedings (see the Making It Happen section).

Make use of technology: As mentioned above, arbitration proceedings are flexible and can be specifically designed to suit the particular case. There is no need for the hearings to be conducted in person at a particular venue. Arbitrators and parties are advised to make use of technology in order to reduce the costs of the proceedings. For example, arbitration hearings, including witness and expert examination, may be conducted via video-conference; and documents, including the submissions of the parties, may be communicated by email or other convenient means.

MAKING IT HAPPEN

Drafting Effective Arbitration Clauses

Ill-drafted arbitration clauses can prolong litigation proceedings and thwart the resolution of a dispute in a quick and efficient way. In order to draft effective arbitration clauses, parties should consider the following points carefully:

- The intention to arbitrate must be clearly and unambiguously stated in the arbitration clause. Avoid permissive language such as "parties *may* submit any dispute to arbitration."
- It should be stated clearly whether the arbitration is to be ad hoc or institutional. If the parties opt for an institutional arbitration, it is very important that unambiguous reference is made to an arbitration institution that exists (see the Case Study). If ad hoc arbitration is chosen, the seat of the arbitration must be clearly stated.
- The safest solution is for the parties to use one of the arbitration clauses recommended by well-known arbitration institutions. However, parties should not attempt to modify these set arbitration clauses, as there is a risk that the clause will be rendered unenforceable.
- Here, for example, is the arbitration clause recommended by the ICC: "All disputes arising out of or in connection with the present contract shall be finally settled under the Rules of Arbitration of the International Chamber of Commerce by one or more arbitrators appointed in accordance with the said Rules."

MORE INFO

Books:

Born, Gary. *International Arbitration and Forum Selection Agreements: Planning Drafting and Enforcing*. 2nd ed. The Hague: Kluwer Law International, 2006.

Lew, Julian D. M., Loukas A. Mistelis, and Stefan Kröll. *Comparative International Commercial Arbitration*. The Hague: Kluwer Law International, 2003.

Redfern, Alan, and Martin Hunter, with Nigel Blackaby and Constantine Partasides. *Law and Practice of International Commercial Arbitration*. 4th ed. London: Sweet & Maxwell, 2004.

Websites:

American Arbitration Association: www.adr.org

ICC Commission on Arbitration: www.iccwbo.org/policy/arbitration/id2882/index.html

London Court of International Arbitration: www.lcia-arbitration.com

School of International Arbitration, Queen Mary University of London: www.schoolofinternationalarbitration.org

United Nations Commission on International Trade Law (UNCITRAL): www.uncitral.org

See Also:

✔ Islamic Law of Contracts (p. 1167)

✔ Nonperformance and Breach of Contract (p. 1169)

✔ Practical Techniques for Commercial Mediation (p. 1172)

✔ The Principles of Litigation (p. 1173)

NOTES

1 Lew, Mistelis, and Kröll, *Comparative International Commercial Arbitration* (2003), para 1-1.

2 In a survey conducted by the School of International Arbitration, Queen Mary University of London, and PricewaterhouseCoopers, entitled "International arbitration: Corporate attitudes and practices 2006," it was found that 76% of parties prefer institutional arbitration to ad hoc arbitration. This study and a second published in 2008 are available online at: www.pwc.com/arbitrationstudy.

3 See the above study for a list of the popularity of the various arbitration institutions.

4 In the 2006 survey mentioned in note 2, it was found that 65% of respondents perceived arbitration to be more expensive than litigation.

"To give a satisfactory decision as to the truth it is necessary to be rather an arbitrator than a party to the dispute."
Aristotle

  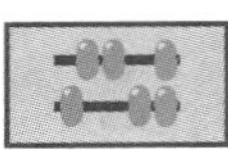   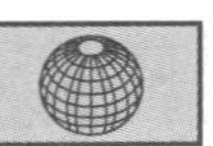   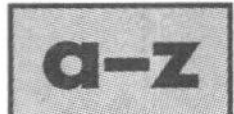

Joint Ventures: Synergies and Benefits by Siri Terjesen

EXECUTIVE SUMMARY

- A joint venture (JV) is a formal arrangement between two or more firms to create a new business for the purpose of carrying out some kind of mutually beneficial activity, often related to business expansion, especially new product and/or market development.
- An important first step is for each firm's managers to review the firm's business and corporate strategies to determine synergy with the objectives of a joint venture.
- A second key step is to assess the suitability of the potential joint venture partner(s) for fit with the firm's strategy, and compatibility during the life of the JV.
- There are four basic JV types: consolidation (deep combination of existing businesses); skills-transfer (transfer of some key skill from one partner); coordination (leveraging complementary capabilities of all partners); and new business (combining existing capabilities, not businesses, to create new growth).
- JVs can offer an array of benefits to partner firms through access to new and/or greater resources including markets, distribution networks, capacity, staff, purchasing, technology/intellectual property, and finance.
- JV risks can arise from disparate communication, culture, strategy, and resources, and result in loss of control, lower profits, conflict, and transferability of key assets.
- NUMMI is an example of a successful JV offering mutual benefits to its partners, General Motors (GM) and Toyota.
- To succeed, JV partners must mitigate potential risk factors, including poor communication, different objectives, imbalanced resources, and cultural clashes.

INTRODUCTION

A joint venture (JV) is a formal arrangement between two or more firms to create a new business for the purpose of carrying out some kind of mutually beneficial activity, often related to business expansion, especially new product and/or market development. A JV is the most popular type of contractual alliance among firms; other types include formal long-term contracts, informal alliances, and acquisitions. JVs may take the form of a corporation, limited liability company (LLC), partnership, or other structure. The 100 largest JVs worldwide account for more than US$350 billion in revenues (Bamford, Ernst & Fubini, 2008). An increasing number of JVs involve foreign partners, in part due to laws in some countries that require foreign firms to partner with local firms in order to conduct business in that country.

SYNERGY TO STRATEGY

An important first step is for management to review the firm's business and corporate strategies to determine synergy with the objectives of a joint venture. In this process, managers can apply a range of strategy methodologies such as SWOT (strengths, weaknesses, opportunities, and threats), Porter's Five Forces, stakeholder analysis, and the value chain to assess the firm's strategy and future vision. Managers may then determine that the joint venture is not the most optimal organizational form for achieving the firm's objectives, and that another form, such as a long-term contract, may offer a better strategic fit.

A second key step is to assess the suitability of the potential joint venture partner(s) for fit with the firm's strategy, and compatibility during the life of the JV. Key questions here include:

- Does the potential JV partner share the same business objectives and vision for the joint venture?
- Is the potential partner firm trustworthy and financially secure?
- Does the potential partner firm already have JV partnerships with other firms? If so, how are these performing?
- How would you rate the potential partner firm's performance in terms of production, marketing, customers, personnel, innovation, and reputation?
- What are the general strengths and weaknesses of the potential partner? How do they complement our firm?
- What benefits might the potential partner firm realize from the JV?
- What risks might we be exposing our firm to in the JV?

A joint venture should only be formed when the parties mutually agree that this form offers the best possibility of optimizing opportunities.

Thirdly, the parties set out JV terms in a written agreement which addresses structure (for example, if it should be a separate business or not), objectives, financial and other resource contributions (of each partner), including the transferability of any assets or employees to the JV, ownership of intellectual property created in the JV, management and control responsibilities and processes, sharing/re-allocation of liabilities/profits/losses, resolution of disputes, and exit strategy. Joint ventures can be flexible, covering only a limited life span or a limited scope of firm activities.

Four basic types of JVs and their respective benefits are (Bamford, Ernst & Fubini, 2004):

- Consolidation JV: value derived from deep combination of existing businesses.
- Skills-transfer JV: value derived from the transfer of some key skill from one partner to the JV (or to the other JV partner).
- Coordination JV: value derived from leveraging the complementary capabilities of all partners.
- New business JV: value derived from combining existing capabilities, not businesses, to create new growth.

JOINT VENTURE BENEFITS

Joint ventures can offer an array of benefits to partner firms through access to new and/or greater resources including markets, distribution networks, capacity, staff, purchasing, technology/intellectual property, and finance. Often, one firm supplies a key resource such as technology, while the other firm(s) might provide distribution or other assets. The following are key resources that can be shared:

Access to markets: JVs can facilitate increased access to customers. One JV partner might, for example, enable the partner to sell other goods/services to their existing customers. International JVs involve partners from different countries, and are frequently pursued to provide access to foreign markets.

Distribution networks: Similarly, JV partners may be willing to share access to distribution networks. If one partner was previously a supplier to the other, then there may be opportunities to strengthen supplier relationships.

Capacity: JV partners may take advantage of increased capacity in terms of production, as well as other economies of scale and scope.

Staff: JVs may share staff, enabling both firms to benefit from complementary, specialized staff. Staff may also transfer innovative management practices across firms.

Purchasing: As a result of their increased resource requirements, JV partners may be able to collectively benefit from better

"Competition and cooperation is the underlying principle of the growth of the world economy. Our joint venture is founded on this approach. We hope to make this project a success as a model of economic cooperation between Japan and the United States—one that contributes to the American economy." Eiji Toyoda

conditions (for example, price, quality, or timing) when purchasing.

Technology/intellectual property: As with other resources, JV partners may share technology. A JV may also enable increased research, and the development of new innovative technologies.

Finance: In a joint venture, firms also pool their financial resources, potentially eliminating the need to borrow funds or seek outside investors.

Taken together, the benefits suggest an improved competitive position for the JV, and each of the partners.

JOINT VENTURE RISKS

There are, however, a number of risks related to joint ventures that can result in loss of control, lower profits, conflict with partners, and transferability of key assets. In fact, studies in the 1980s and 1990s revealed failure rates of 49% and 47% (Bamford, Ernst, Fubini, 2004). More recent work reports failure rates varying from 2% to 90%, depending on the partners involved (see, for example, Perkins, Morck & Yeung, 2008). JV risks stem from many sources, including the following:

Communication: The firms may not communicate their objectives clearly, resulting in misunderstanding. These communication issues can be exacerbated by geographic and cultural distance among partner firms, and by the use of language such as "us versus them."

Strategy: The firms may have divergent strategies for the joint venture, and fail to reach a set of mutually agreeable objectives regarding business and exit strategies. Risks can also emerge from a lack of agreed processes regarding governance, accountability, decision-making, HR, and conflict resolution.

Imbalanced resources: The firms may bring imbalanced resources to the table, a source of great conflict. Another source of conflict may be that the JV disproportionately allocates resources among the firms. For example, one firm may find that its technology is being appropriated by another firm.

Culture: The JV partner firms may have distinct corporate (and in the case of cross-border JVs, national) cultures and management styles, resulting in poor integration and cooperation.

CONCLUSION

As the NUMMI case study illustrates, JVs offer benefits to both partners as well as other stakeholders—providing customers with more and a higher quality variety of car choices and manufacturers, with a model of labor-management relations.

CASE STUDY

NUMMI Joint Venture

Established in Fremont, California, in 1984, the New United Motor Manufacturing Inc. (NUMMI) is a joint venture between General Motors (GM) and Toyota. The NUMMI JV began as an experiment. The allure for GM was a chance to learn how to build cars, especially of a small size and high quality, using Toyota's "lean" production system. Toyota was interested in testing its production methods in an American setting. According to Eiji Toyoda, then the Chairman of Toyota Motor Company: "Competition and cooperation is the underlying principle of the growth of the world economy. Our joint venture is founded on this approach. We hope to make this project a success as a model of economic cooperation between Japan and the United States—one that contributes to the American economy." (Source: www.nummi.com/us_roots.php).

To start the joint venture, US$450 million in funding was required. GM contributed its plant in Fremont, which it had closed in 1982. Toyota provided US$100 million of start-up capital. The remaining capital was raised by NUMMI as an independent Californian corporation. The US Federal Trade Commission (FTC) approved the formation of the company for an initial 12-year period, stating that the venture would offer a wider range of automobile choices to customers. The 12-year limit was eventually lifted, and NUMMI continues to operate. Ford and Chrysler opposed the joint venture and filed an unsuccessful lawsuit to block NUMMI.

NUMMI invited former GM workers to apply for jobs, and expressed a special "need for employees willing to contribute to an atmosphere of trust and cooperation." Following a rigorous hiring assessment, the new employees attended orientation sessions about NUMMI's concept, system, principles, policy, and philosophy. Team members were introduced to NUMMI's core values, which are based on teamwork, equity, involvement, mutual trust and respect, and safety. Approximately 450 group and team leaders traveled to Toyota's Takaeoka plant in Japan to spend three weeks learning in the classroom and on the job about Toyota's production system, team building, union–management relations, and safety. NUMMI's first effort was the Chevrolet Nova, built by 700 team members in 1984. NUMMI has established a collaborative partnership with United Auto Workers (UAW) in which UAW agrees to be a cooperative and active participant in labor-management relationships, to accept Toyota's production methods, and to work to improve productivity and quality. NUMMI has been presented as a case-study model of labor-management cooperation to the International Labor Organization Conference.

NUMMI's unique corporate learning and cultural environment optimizes the best of GM, Toyota, and nearby Silicon Valley. The JV is considered to have been instrumental in introducing the Toyota production system and a team-based working environment to the US automobile industry. NUMMI remains a key source of innovative knowledge about quality, continuous improvement, and human resource management. GM and Toyota regularly send managers to visit NUMMI in order to learn lessons to be applied in their home unit's strategies.

Today, NUMMI has more than 5,440 team members, and annually produces approximately 250,000 cars and 170,000 trucks under the brands of Toyota Corolla, Toyota Tacoma, and Pontiac Vibe. More details about NUMMI can be found at www.nummi.com.

MAKING IT HAPPEN

To succeed, JV partners must mitigate several potential sources of risk: poor communication, different objectives, imbalanced resources, and cultural clashes. Firstly, JV partners must establish clear communication channels at the top of the firms involved, and also with employees whose daily work is related to the joint venture. This communication is often facilitated through regular, face-to-face meetings to establish not only the benefits from the JV, but also the risks if the JV does not work. Secondly, it is essential that partners agree on objectives and milestones. Key performance indicators (KPIs) can be established to measure performance and provide early warning guidance. Imbalanced resources, such as different levels of financing or expertise, can also lead to conflict. Finally, each firm has a unique culture, and cultural clashes in management style may become apparent. These issues may be exacerbated across foreign JV partners as a result of language and cultural differences. Flexibility and an open approach to trying to make things work are essential.

"The 100 largest JVs worldwide account for over US$350 billion in revenues." Bamford, Ernst, and Fubini, 2008

  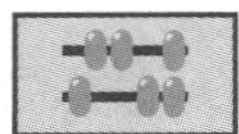      

There are, however, many risks to be considered.

Interrelationships among small and large firms are increasingly common, and offer unique benefits to each partner. For a small firm, a joint venture may offer a unique opportunity to grow quickly with other small firms, or to partner with a larger firm. Often the large partner benefits from the smaller firm's flexibility and intellectual property, while the small partner benefits from increased access to markets, reputation, and other key resources. Increasingly, JV partners of all sizes join together as a defensive response to blurring industry boundaries.

MORE INFO

Books:

Child, J., D. Faulkner, and S. Tallman. *Strategies of Cooperation: Managing Alliances, Networks, and Joint Ventures*. Oxford: Oxford University Press, 2005.

Wallace, Robert L. *Strategic Partnerships: An Entrepreneur's Guide to Joint Ventures and Alliances*. New York: Kaplan Publishing, 2004.

Articles:

Bamford, James, David Ernst, and David G. Fubini. "Launching a world-class joint venture." *Harvard Business Review* (February 2004): 90–100. Online at: hbr.harvardbusiness.org/2004/02/launching-a-world-class-joint-venture/ar/1

Perkins, Susan, Randall Morck, and Bernard Yeung. "Innocents abroad: The hazards of international joint ventures with pyramidal group firms." NBER Working Paper 13914 (April 2008). Online at: www.nber.org/papers/w13914

Steensma, H. K., J. Q. Barden, C. Dhanaraj, M. Lyles, and L. Tihanyi. "The evolution and internalization of international joint ventures in a transitioning economy." *Journal of International Business Studies* 39:3 (April 2008): 491–507. Online at: dx.doi.org/10.1057/palgrave.jibs.8400341

Website:

Google's latest joint venture news: news.google.com/news?pz=1&ned=us&hl=en&q=%22joint + venture%22

See Also:

★ Maximizing a New Strategic Alliance (pp. 749–750)
✔ Assessing Economies of Scale in Business (p. 1145)
✔ Options for Raising Finance (p. 1081)
✔ Structuring and Negotiating Joint Ventures (p. 1175)

"JVs can offer an array of benefits to partner firms through access to new and/or greater resources including markets, distribution networks, capacity, staff, purchasing, technology/intellectual property, and finance."

  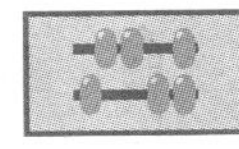      

Managing Reputational Risk: Business Journalism

by Jonathan Silberstein-Loeb

EXECUTIVE SUMMARY

- How credible commitments can help to mitigate reputational risk.
- Establishing credible commitment, and trust, requires a better understanding of the incentives of journalists, as well as the perceptions of business, both of which are explored in this chapter.
- The consequences of these differing incentives for building trust between journalists and businesses and for company strategy are explored in the final section.

INTRODUCTION

It is taken as given that journalism affects corporate reputation. To understand better how journalism about businesses is written and what can be done to contend with the reputational risk that it may present, this chapter seeks to explain how business practitioners and business journalists perceive each other and interact. It is the central argument of this chapter that establishing mechanisms for credible commitment helps to mitigate reputational risk. As there is no formal mechanism for establishing credible commitment between business representatives and business journalists, doing so depends on their respective incentives and corresponding informal constraints, such as career advancement and the loss of reputation. Insofar as journalists must have sources, and sources must communicate with their stakeholders, journalists and corporate decision-makers rely equally on each other, and therefore may be hostages of one another in instances of repeated interaction. The implicit recognition that both parties are beholden to each other may be the most effective mechanism of credible commitment. Behavior that demonstrates an awareness of this codependence helps to establish trust, which is central to effective media relations.[1] Trusting relationships facilitate an understanding of the incentives that undergird credible commitments, which helps to make them reinforcing. Recognizing the importance of credible commitments has clear consequences for the way in which companies develop communication strategies.

Much of what follows is predicated on the preliminary results of an international study of business journalism and corporate reputation that the Oxford University Centre for Corporate Reputation is conducting. This chapter relies on evidence gathered as part of this study in more than 80 informal, off-the-record interviews conducted in England with journalists from major national dailies that publish business sections and with business leaders (see Appendix 1).

APPENDIX 1

Interviewees for Oxford University Centre for Corporate Reputation study of business journalism and corporate reputation

Newspapers and journals	*Business leaders*	
Breakingviews.com	Torsten Altmann	Carol Leonard
Daily Mail	Norman Askew	David Mansfield
The Economist	John Barton	Peter Morgan
Financial Times	Alex Brog	John Peace
The Guardian	Roger Carr	Roger Parry
The Independent	Peter Cawdron	Sir Ian Prosser
The Times	Stuart Chambers	Michael Rake
Sunday Times	Doug Daft	Don Robert
Wall Street Journal Europe	Terry Duddy	Robin Saunders
	Steve Easterbrook	Oliver Stocken
	Andrew Grant	Robert Swannell
	Andy Hornby	John Tiner
	Lady Barbara Judge	David Tyler
	Frederick Kempe	Lucas Van Praag
	Roddy Kennedy	Sarah Weller
	John Kingman	Gerhard Zeiler

THE INCENTIVES OF JOURNALISTS

For Whom Do Journalists Write?

It might reasonably be expected that the audience for business journalism would affect journalists' incentives, but journalists have, at best, an imperfect impression of the reader for whom they write, or who reads their articles. "The general reader" is a phrase that journalists frequently use, but it lacks a clear definition. There is considerable difference among writers at each publication, which makes for little differentiation between publications, although the *Financial Times* is tailored toward the investment community more than the *Sunday Times*. Some business journalists claim to write for the person on the Clapham omnibus, others for the clerk in the City. The public is largely financially illiterate, and journalists are obliged to explain the basics to the general reader, but this duty does not undermine the value that business news holds for specialists. Those business professionals who read the business sections—and most do—do so less for insight than for context.

What Motivates Journalists?

Journalists' motivations affect their incentives. In a survey of American journalists that has been conducted four times over the past 30 years, Weaver and Wilhoit (1996) identified three principal functions among journalists: disseminators of information; interpreters of events; and adversaries of business and government. Throughout the survey period, the dominant professional role of journalists has been "interpretive"—that is, to provide analysis and interpretation of complex issues. Since the 1970s, it has always been the case that only a very small minority of the sample felt that the adversary role was important. The percentage of journalists surveyed who believed that it was extremely important for the mass media to "be an adversary of business by being constantly skeptical of their actions" has always been low, even in the wake of dozens of scandals involving large corporations. The percentage of journalists who believed the adversarial function to be extremely important was greatest among those working for news magazines, and least among those working for radio. Although these data pertain to American journalism, cultural similarities between Britain and the United States, and responses from journalists interviewed in London, provide reasons to suspect that a like study carried out in the United Kingdom would produce similar results.

The motivation of business journalists in part derives from the way in which they perceive the companies about which they report. Opinions vary from journalist to journalist, and journalists change their minds over time. When they believe they are on to a hot story, their approach may be adversarial; when they are covering a diary event, it may be interpretive. The journalists who were interviewed evinced as much a desire simply to "understand how the world works" as to serve an interpretive or watchdog function, although many professed themselves to be skeptical of authority. Regardless of their perceived role, most journalists interviewed believe that

"The free market doesn't exist. Every market has some rules and boundaries that restrict freedom of choice. A market looks free only because we so unconditionally accept its underlying restrictions that we fail to see them." Ha-Joon Chang

they can hold business to account when required. It is broadly the case, and common sense, that business journalists at the *Financial Times* tend to see themselves as serving more of an interpretive function, whereas journalists at *The Guardian* tend to see themselves more as watchdogs of business. Journalists at the *Daily Mail* were also more likely to think it their job to hold business to account. Journalists at other publications are either indifferent, or opinions among them vary so considerably that any characterization by publication is impossible.

How Do Journalists Interact with Business Sources?

Regulations respecting the disclosure requirements imposed on businesses significantly affect the quantity and quality of information available to journalists, but the material divulged in disclosure documents is in the public domain. Such material is unlikely to be newsworthy, especially now that the Internet makes it so easy to search for and share this information. Journalists require scoops, and for this reason, contacts are critical to all journalists, regardless of publication. How journalists develop these contacts varies according to publication, and to style of writing. Breakingviews.com and *The Economist*, for example, as well as columnists at the dailies, need not worry about quoting sources on-the-record. If discussions are *de facto* off-the-record, then journalists have an easier time getting information. The perception of a particular publication, and its perceived audience, among sources is also influential: people in the City are more likely to find time for a chat with journalists from the *Financial Times* than they are with journalists from *The Guardian*. Consequently, those journalists who see themselves as watchdogs find it more difficult to cultivate the sources they require to fulfill this function.

There is irony here that bespeaks a fundamental problem in all forms of journalism. Readers of *The Guardian*, and similar publications, are less interested than readers of the *Financial Times* in the daily operations of big business. Journalists who see themselves as adversaries of business tend to work for publications that circulate among readers with a dislike for big business, or at least only a secondary interest in it. Given their readership, adversarial journalists are therefore less likely than journalists working at business-friendly publications to contact, or be contacted by, the very people whom they seek to hold to account. Journalists waging crusades tend to operate on the margins, and to rely on workers in the third sector for information, rather than the business decision-makers, on whom journalists at business-orientated publications tend to rely. Further, publications tailored for business, such as Breakingviews.com, *The Economist*, the *Financial Times*, and the *Wall Street Journal*, have been more successful than general publications at charging for their online content, not least because the people who read these publications perceive them to be important to their careers. Publications tailored for business audiences have more resources to devote to serving a watchdog function, but perhaps less incentive to do so. The fact that News Corporation owns Dow Jones, which covers day-to-day events, enables journalists at the *Wall Street Journal Europe*, which News Corporation also owns, to devote more time to in-depth reporting, and yet comparatively few journalists at the *Wall Street Journal Europe* see themselves as watchdogs of business.

Regardless of the way in which journalists perceive their role, it is broadly the case that they are concerned to advance their careers—and obtaining scoops, or exclusive news, is an effective way for them to do so. Although journalists may obtain exclusive news either through investigation, which is typically adversarial, or through sources, which rely on relationships, in practice the two often overlap: sources provide leads, which require further investigation, which requires sources. The reality is that journalists rely on their contacts and the strength of their relationships with sources to do their jobs effectively. Whether journalists perceive their function to be interpretive or adversarial will determine the extent to which they are willing to bite the hands that feed them. In an age of WikiLeaks and whistleblowing, journalists will always find someone with a story, but those journalists with a proclivity for provocation are likely to find that their pool of contacts dries up quickly. All journalists must constantly query whether flouting or favoring their sources best serves their interests. If journalists are unwilling to cross their sources, they risk being mere conduits.

Journalists Have a Code of Behavior

To further their careers and to obtain quality contacts, journalists must maintain their credibility, which is achieved through accuracy and consistency. Relationships with sources are built up over years and are based on trust. Maintaining these relationships requires journalists to be accurate and honest. Unsurprisingly, all journalists profess to uphold these standards and to behave professionally. Assuming journalists are committed to doing their jobs well, which may be a large assumption, they will seek to obtain access to credible and authoritative sources, which typically means bypassing PR in favor of speaking directly with executives. They will also attempt to corroborate the facts of a story through a process of triangulation.

The relationship between journalist and source can be a game of cat and mouse, one of tit-for-tat, of "you scratch my back, I'll scratch yours," or a continuous negotiation. Journalists know, and business decision-makers confirm, that without prior relationships journalists will be directed first to PR, although most journalists hope to speak to C-suite executives on every story. Even then, to talk to a company that is not PR-trained is rare. Some sources are more forthcoming than others. Most of the journalists interviewed believe that external PR professionals are better sources than internal communications officers, but it is occasionally the case that company employees are especially well briefed and agency employees are uninformed. On the one hand, to the extent that journalists perceive PR to be a hindrance that must be circumvented, the presence of PR may radicalize journalists; on the other hand, if a PR professional, or any source, is discovered to have lied to a journalist, they will lose their credibility as a source. Among business journalists, there exist the "good" and "smart" PR professionals who understand this game, and the "bad" PR who "don't get it." A process of name-and-shame in newsrooms generates and promulgates a source's reputation.

THE INCENTIVES OF BUSINESS REPRESENTATIVES

Most companies proactively undertake to conduct, in conjunction with an external financial public relations agency, a series of strategic, staged formal meetings with journalists throughout the year that coincide with annual announcements. Interactions between companies and journalists more frequently take place in informal environments, which, from a corporate perspective, are less orchestrated and strategic, and which consequently have potentially greater reputational repercussions.

Willingness of Business to Engage with Journalists

Willingness to engage with the media varies, but some form of interaction is necessary and important. Saying "no comment" may make it difficult for journalists to write a story, but more often it tends to annoy them, and it rarely prevents them from writing. Few C-suite executives court business journalists, but nearly all are

"It is easier to see the joy of competition if you are the one getting the prizes." Lucy Kellaway

convinced of the importance and beneficial effects of trusting relationships. As a general rule, CEOs tend to interact more with the media than with nonexecutives. Chairpersons only get involved when there is a strategic event, such as a takeover bid or a governance issue. Much of the interaction with journalists tends to focus around the reporting of company results, but executives make efforts to have regular contact with journalists to provide background information. Much of this interaction is conducted under the guise of helping journalists to understand the business, explaining decisions made, or making sure they get the facts of the story straight.

The Importance of Trusting Relationships

Trusting relationships may help CEOs to avoid negative coverage. Creating such relationships with journalists entails interactions outside work-related environments. These informal interactions, typically conducted off the record, may be informative for journalists and executives. CEOs and other executives are convinced that even if they have lousy news to give, they receive more balanced treatment from journalists they know. A "professional relationship," according to many business leaders, helps them to promulgate messages that kill adverse rumors and gossip. Long-term relationships make journalists more receptive to the views businesses put across. It can be dangerous to court journalists, but once a trusting relationship is established, journalists will seek to maintain it through good behavior to ensure continued access to a reliable source. Developing effective relationships with journalists requires honest discussion and exchange. Trade in information does not characterize such relationships. Journalists may grant businesses favorable treatment on negative stories in exchange for off-the-record comments, but this a perilous strategy to pursue. Sustainable, effective relationships rely on a modicum of respect and quite a lot of patronizing. Trust is critical, and so is honesty.

Although personal contact creates more credible relations, evidence suggests that the Internet has made the relationship between journalists and corporations more mediated. The personal communication that previously followed the release of statements—and which allowed for clarification—has ceased, making public statements more important. The focus of media relations is now more on preparation than on relationship building. This shift also reflects the fact that traditional media are less important than they once were. Creating a case for a company that meets the needs of all its stakeholders requires waging battles on multiple fronts, and not just in the *Financial Times*. Media fragmentation also makes relationships between journalists and sources less manageable. The permanency, accessibility, and transportability of information on the Internet means that companies must have a clear message.

CREATING CREDIBLE COMMITMENTS TO MITIGATE REPUTATIONAL RISK

Journalists, whether they perceive themselves to be watchdogs or not, require information. To obtain this information, and to do their jobs effectively, journalists must gain the trust of their sources. Corporate decision-makers likewise have an incentive to gain the trust of journalists so that they may effectively communicate important information to the market. At the upper echelons of business and business journalism in London, theory and practice converge more often than not. There is an implicit recognition that both parties require each other.

Decision-makers have information at their disposal that journalists do not, and consequently they are obliged to convey this information to journalists frankly and in such a way that the journalists are satisfied that there has been full disclosure. The uneven distribution of information and the burdensome obligation of disclosure make mistrust and miscommunication likely. Journalists, by dint of their information deficit, are likely to be suspicious of their sources. Decision-makers, confronting such suspicion, are likely to be convinced that journalists are always looking for dirt. If a company is conducted in a strategically sound manner and within the law, it has little to worry about from the media. (Even if it is conducted in an unsound manner, recent history suggests that journalists may be slow to cotton on.) A consistently sound strategy achieves favorable results. Profits are facts on the ground with which it is difficult for even the most biased journalist to argue. If the business is performing poorly, it is only fair, and of service to the market, that this be reflected in the papers.

Yet, the blame game is subjective, and journalists are fallible, so it is reasonable that in the court of public opinion businesses should have advocates as they do in courts of chancery. Even the good have need of an advocate. Although the rules of the game that dictate the behavior of advocates in the court of public opinion are by necessity unwritten, and more informal than those regulations under which barristers labor, adherence to them is as necessary for the orderly distribution of justice, and flouting them is just as punishable. These are the rules that apply to the construction and maintenance of trusting relationships.

Trusting relationships diminish the prospect that rogue journalists will undeservedly lash out at corporations and their representatives. As with capital, during good times business leaders should seek to generate favorable relationships that are resistant to change during less fortuitous periods in the life of the organization. Journalists seek to build trusting relationships by obtaining a reputation for credibility, which is obtained through professionalism. Being credible does not mean being sympathetic to sources—it means being fair. For decision-makers to convey their opinions effectively to journalists, they too must be seen as being credible. The best way to achieve credibility with journalists is for business-decision makers to be open and honest. Of course, journalists may sensationalize a story to augment their own career or to sell newspapers, just as companies may employ strategies of obfuscation and spin, but for journalists opportunistic behavior undermines credibility, and for corporations spin is at best a fallible prophylactic.

A Continuous Process of Negotiation

It is useful to imagine relationships between journalists and corporate decision-makers as a continuous process of negotiation. In an insightful article, Charron (1989) observed that these relationships are "at once cooperative and fraught with conflict." The dual nature of these relationships, wrote Charron, "implies a double negotiation: over the exchange of resources, and over the rules regulating this exchange." Cooperation results from mutual interdependence of the players for resources. Each actor's dependence on the other varies according to the possibility of alternatives. A more adversarial dimension arises from attempts by either journalists or sources to manage this relationship. Charron concluded that collaboration and accommodation are the best strategies for sources, although these strategies entail risks, whereas journalists, when their interests are not directly at stake, will tend to adopt a strategy of avoidance rather than accommodation.

For many years PR professionals have known that "spin" is self-defeating. It is widely recognized that nuance, and presenting both sides of the story, is critical to maintaining the credibility of PR. In the upper echelons of PR in England these enlightened views hold sway. When possible, PR professionals ought to provide journalists with reliable information and facilitate their access to C-suite executives. All journalists recognize that sources will put their version of the story across, and they regard this as reasonable, but anything less than collaboration and accommodation is likely to incur the wrath of journalists and do a disservice to public relations. The power to improve media relations, and to augment corporate reputation, therefore lies with corporations. In the blame game, corporations are both more permanent and more manageable players than individual journalists, whose personality and practice is less readily determined or constrained. Mechanisms, such as professional codes of conduct, however fallible they may be, already exist to dissuade journalists from opportunistic behavior. Any further restrictions on journalistic activity would have an adverse effect on the social benefit they provide to the public. The onus to improve relations lies with business.

PR Should Play a Role in Strategy

Businesses ought to avoid putting those that communicate on their behalf in a position in which they are obligated to jeopardize their relationships with journalists. Instead, the PR function should play a more influential role in developing corporate strategy so that company behavior is justifiable to journalists, and so that sources are able to retain credibility with them. So long as businesses do not oblige sources to deceive journalists, media relations will be predicated on trust, which enables businesses to convey effectively the rationale behind strategic decisions.

During the past decade, there have been indications of a greater appreciation of the role and value of the PR function in management, but it is still seen by many as foremost a communications role. Corporate decision-makers are concerned about how actions will be portrayed on the cover of the *Daily Mail*, but there is little direct connection between PR and strategy. In part, this gradual increase in the managerial role of PR is due to the growing importance of investor relations. As Davis ("Public relations, business news and the reproduction of corporate elite power," 2000) has observed, publicly quoted companies periodically devote resources to government policy-making and institutional regulation, but they are more concerned with institutional shareholders and the wider business community. Such concerns translate into an emphasis on communications with investment analysts, business leaders, and business journalists.

Given the influence that the media may exercise on company reputation, executives must weigh the gains to be had from strategic actions against the losses to be expected from adverse media commentary. If the executive is convinced that the profits to be gained from a particular strategic action outweigh the potential loss to profits incurred from negative media coverage, the executive has a responsibility to carry out the action. If, however, the response of the media may be so adverse as to cause damage in excess of the benefit derived from strategic action, the executive has an equally powerful but opposite obligation to avoid the strategy, to modify it, or to explain it to the media in such a way as to limit losses when the strategy is carried out. The PR function should help in making this calculation. This is not to say that PR ought to be the conscience of the corporation; rather, PR professionals should bring to bear on the process of strategic planning the perspective and interest of different stakeholders whose support is critical to profitability.

When relationships between corporations and business journalists function effectively, they generate transparency and the amount of information about a company available to the media may consequently increase. Transparency enables the market to know what a company does, and why. All things being equal, a greater quantity of information will better ensure that market perceptions parallel corporate behavior. Transparency may compel companies to adhere to social norms and behave responsibly without sacrificing profitability. Having increased the quantity of information available to the media, and by extension to the public, corporations will have more to manage, but this outcome is conducive to the effective function of markets, which is necessary for economic growth generally and corporate growth specifically.

MAKING IT HAPPEN

- Implicit recognition that journalists and corporate decision-makers require each other leads to a credible commitment that builds trust.
- Closer cooperation between the managerial and communications functions within firms helps to facilitate trusting relationships with journalists, and consequently to mitigate reputational risk.

MORE INFO

Book:

Weaver, David H., and G. Cleveland Wilhoit. *The American Journalist in the 1990s: U.S. News People at the End of an Era*. Mawah, NJ: Lawrence Elbaum Associates, 1996.

Articles:

Charron, Jean. "Relations between journalists and public relations practitioners: Cooperation, conflict and negotiation." *Canadian Journal of Communication* 14:2 (1989): 41–54. Online at: tinyurl.com/6fg78qd [PDF].

Davis, Aeron. "Public relations, news production and changing patterns of source access in the British national media." *Media, Culture & Society* 22:1 (January 2000): 39–59. Online at: dx.doi.org/10.1177/016344300022001003

Davis, Aeron. "Public relations, business news and the reproduction of corporate elite power." *Journalism* 1:3 (December 2000): 282–304. Online at: dx.doi.org/10.1177/146488490000100301

See Also:

★ The CEO's Role in Reputation Management (pp. 797–800)
★ Digital Reputation Management (pp. 821–825)
★ Engaging Your Stakeholders: How To Make Allies of Investors and Activists (pp. 837–840)

NOTES

1 I am grateful to Dr Paolo Campana for help on this point.

"Experts say our brains need boredom so we can process thoughts and be creative. I think they're right. I've noticed that my best ideas always bubble up when the outside world fails in its primary job of frightening, wounding, or entertaining me." Scott Adams

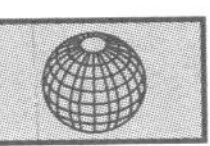

Multidimensional Performance Measurement Using the Balanced Scorecard by Priscilla Wisner

EXECUTIVE SUMMARY

- An organization's financial performance results from decisions made by its managers and employees.
- Managers and employees need operational performance metrics that are aligned with the daily decisions being made, rather than a high-level set of financial metrics that are reported on a monthly or a quarterly basis.
- The Balanced Scorecard (BSC) represents a set of financial, customer, operational, and organizational metrics that capture multidimensional aspects of performance.
- Using a BSC, top management can signal strategic objectives to managers and employees. Top management can then gather data that shows whether or not performance at the individual and the strategic business unit levels is aligned with the strategic objectives of the firm.

INTRODUCTION

For generations, many businesses have measured organizational success based on a narrow set of financial performance measures, such as operating and net profit, return on investment, and earnings per share of stock. Financial performance measures are valuable in that they capture the economic consequences of business decisions; however, they tend to be "lagging" indicators of performance that report the financial effects of operational business decisions weeks or months after the decisions have been implemented.

Organizational managers and employees typically manage their work in terms of physical flows and other nonfinancial resources. For example, sales managers focus on market size, sales volume, share of wallet, customer satisfaction, and similar measures. Production managers concentrate on production capacity, throughput time, quality, and productivity metrics. Human resource managers are responsible for hiring appropriately skilled personnel, maintaining a safe and legal workplace, and organizational development outcomes. Managers and employees throughout the organization make decisions and use resources that eventually impact the financial outcomes of the firm; to do so effectively, they need performance feedback that links the outcomes of their decisions to the strategic and financial goals of the firm. This feedback is most useful when it is a "leading" performance indicator, or one that is closely related to the work being performed. The Balanced Scorecard (BSC) was developed as a management tool to help managers better understand and link customer, operational, and organizational decisions to financial outcomes, and to the strategy of the organization.

BSC BASICS

While General Electric has been credited with developing one of the first balanced scorecard performance models,[1] the BSC concept was first described by Dr Robert Kaplan and David Norton in a series of *Harvard Business Review* articles in the early 1990s, and was subsequently expanded upon in books and articles by these and other professionals. The BSC as a management tool has gained widespread acceptance in the corporate world. In a survey of more than 700 companies operating in five continents, Bain and Company reported that 62% of the respondents used the BSC.[2]

BSC perspectives typically include financial, customer, operational (internal business processes), and organizational (learning and growth) aspects. By identifying key performance measures within each of these perspectives, top management signals strategic objectives and organizational goals to managers and employees. By receiving feedback on achieved outcomes for each of these measures, management is able to evaluate how closely performance is meeting strategic objectives.

As shown in Figure 1, the four traditional BSC perspectives are interlinked, and are linked to the overall vision and strategy of the organization. Each perspective reflects a focus area for the implementation of strategy and, therefore, for performance measurement:[3]

- Financial perspective—focuses on financial aspects of performance, and links strategic objectives with financial impacts. Balance sheet, income statement, and cash flow performance measures are often included in this dimension. Some firms include alternative measures of financial performance, such as economic value added, recycling income, and sales growth by channel.
- Customer perspective—contains measures that reflect how the firm is creating customer value. Customer satisfaction measures are typical, but leading firms will include measures such as share of mind and share of wallet, consumption per capita, customer retention, and product accessibility measures.

Figure 1. Linking of BSC perspectives

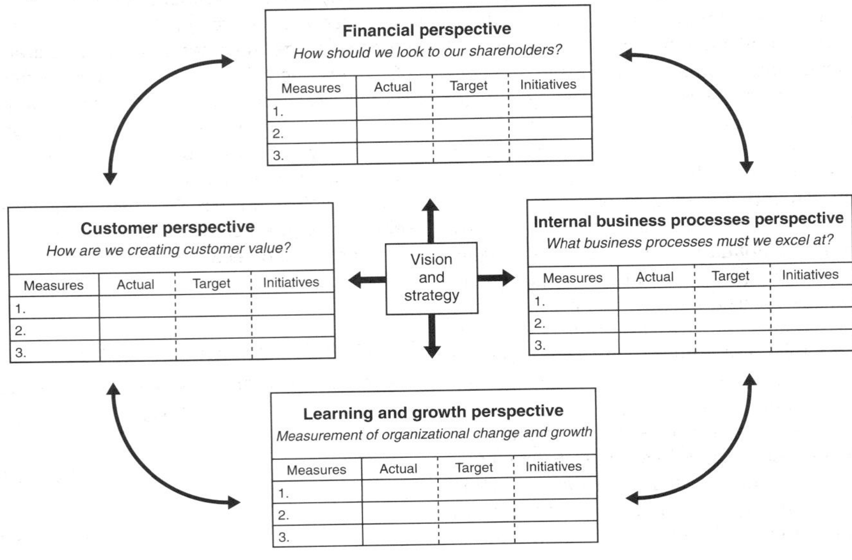

"It is sobering to reflect on the extent to which the structure of our business has been dictated by the limitations of the file folder." Michael Hammer

- Internal business processes perspective—focuses on how a company is performing through an operational lens. Internal business processes encompasses many facets of operations, including engineering design, purchasing, manufacturing, distribution, and environmental and social performance. In a customer service organization, measures might include response time, process quality, employee productivity, and bridge to sales ratios.
- Learning and growth perspective—assesses how well the organization is preparing itself and its employees for the future. This perspective often includes measures of organizational practices, employee development and satisfaction, and systems development and deployment. Aspects commonly measured in this perspective include employee turnover, diversity, promotions from within, training hours or expense by employee, innovation measures, and surveys of corporate climate.

IMPLEMENTING A BSC

The BSC is not a "one size fits all" management tool. Each BSC is unique to the strategy, objectives, and culture of the individual organization. However, the following guidelines are important to any successful BSC implementation.

Stakeholder participation in BSC development: Every top management team employing a BSC must carefully translate the organization's strategy into meaningful and actionable performance measures. This process requires the participation and input of the organizational stakeholders who are either impacted by the strategy or responsible for implementing the strategy. For example, building a set of customer-related performance measures is difficult without understanding customer needs and perceptions. Similarly, requiring a firm's workers to focus on improving quality metrics without involving these employees in discussions about quality creates a disconnect with those responsible for implementing the improvements.

Create cascaded scorecards that are organizationally appropriate: At higher levels of the organization, management will be focused on performance outcomes that reflect the overall company strategic objectives. But, a high-level scorecard would not be appropriate throughout the organization. Some firms develop scorecards at the individual employee level. For example, a high-level objective in a firm's BSC might be "increase market share." In the marketing area, this objective might be broken down into mid-level objectives, for example, "increase market share in Europe," "increase market share in Asia," or "increase market share of customers aged 18–25 years old." At the individual level, this objective could be further defined in a way that reflects the responsibilities of that marketer, such as "increase market share in France" or "increase market share in China." Alternatively, the objective might be related to a specific product or service. The goal of cascading is 1) to translate the strategic objective into specific objectives for the hundreds and thousands of employees throughout the organization that carry out the day-to-day work; and 2) to link the work of each employee and strategic business unit to the overall strategic goals of the organization by defining measures appropriate to the employee and business unit.

Define linkages between measures: Value creation in any organization is accomplished by understanding and creating synergies between the various aspects of organizational performance. Increasing sales without having the corresponding production or service capabilities will likely lead to loss of value rather than a long-term increase in value. Increasing production output at the cost of reducing product safety and reliability will negatively affect quality,

CASE STUDY
Mobil Corporation

In the early 1990s, Mobil Corporation's North America Marketing and Refining group (Mobil) implemented a strategy that resulted in an increased return on capital from 6% to 16%, and an improved operating cash flow of over $1 billion per year.[4] This dramatic improvement in financial results was achieved in just three years, and was aided by a BSC implementation to help focus and align the organization.

In 1994, Mobil began a BSC project as a means to help communicate and implement a strategic organizational change. Mobil's new strategy was twofold:

1 increase volume and revenues of premium products; and
2 reduce costs and improve value chain productivity.

Mobil began by defining its high-level financial objectives—return on capital employed and net margin—and then disaggregated these objectives into specific objectives related to its revenue growth and productivity strategies. An example of Mobil's objectives in relation to its revenue growth strategy is shown in Figure 2.

After developing the financial perspective of the BSC, Mobil's managers developed the customer, internal, and learning and growth perspectives. The customer perspective focused on customer satisfaction and dealer relationships, using specific performance measures to capture achievement on each objective. The largest set of measures were the internal business processes measures, which included new product volume and profitability, dealer quality, refinery performance, inventory management, order quality, and safety measures. In the learning and growth perspective, the firm focused on measures such as an employee climate survey, core competency achievements, and the availability of strategic information.

Each perspective contained a small set of focused and interlinked measures that were keys to achieving corporate strategy. The development of the BSC was accompanied by a realignment of organizational structures, the use and communication of the new measurement system, and linking compensation with meeting the explicit goals and objectives. The outcomes for Mobil were dramatic—surveys showed that employee awareness of strategy increased from 20% to 80%, safety and environmental statistics improved, lost yield was reduced by 70%, new products were being introduced, volume growth exceeded the industry averages by over 2% annually, cash expenses were reduced, and Mobil's relative profitability within the North American oil industry improved from last to first in class. Each of these improvements had an impact on increasing Mobil's operating cash flows and return on capital employed. The BSC helped management to communicate corporate strategy through a set of strategic objectives and specific goals, essentially aligning the organization toward a common set of objectives.

Figure 2. Revenue growth strategy

Revenue Growth → Nongasoline revenue
- Increase nongasoline revenues and margins

Premium brands revenue
- Improve volume of premium (versus industry)
- Increase percentage of premium mix

"In an industrial society which confuses work and productivity, the necessity of producing has always been an enemy of the desire to create." Raoul Vaneigem

  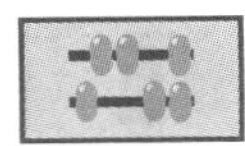      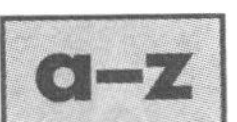

costs, and reputation. An effective BSC explicitly shows the cause and effect linkages between key performance indicators. A leading insurance company was concerned about its market stock price. By evaluating company data, company managers determined that the amount of time it took a claims adjuster to contact the customer following an accident could influence market stock price. How was this so? The study showed that the length of contact time influenced customer satisfaction, which influenced policy renewal rates, which led to revenues from premiums, which ultimately influenced operating income and stock price.

Choose a small set of focused measures: Each BSC should contain a small set of performance measures, generally with not more than 15–20 recommendations for any single BSC. Developing a limited set of measures is challenging, but forces managers to focus on the most important aspects of organizational performance. Having too many measures tends to create "noise" in the process, both for the managers and for the employees who are working toward the stated goals, leading to uncertainty about which measures are key drivers of success.

Create balance in the scorecard: To be "balanced" does not mean to be equal in all dimensions. A balanced scorecard is one that contains:

- multiple perspectives of performance;
- leading and lagging measures;
- internally focused and externally focused measures;
- short-term and long-term measures;
- quantitative and qualitative measures.

Link the BSC to employee compensation: An effective BSC sends a message to employees that "strategy is everyone's job." If this is the case, then firms need to reward employees for carrying out the strategic intent of the organization. If the objectives and measures within the BSC are aligned in such a way that value is created by carrying out these actions, then employees should be rewarded for increasing the firm's value proposition. Organizational development research has shown that linking reward systems to explicit and controllable expectations creates strong linkages between employee behaviors and the achievement of organizational goals.

CONCLUSION

The BSC is a powerful concept that enables organizational change. The BSC is not just a performance measurement tool, but a multidimensional system that requires management to define strategy in operational terms, and to understand and communicate the cause and effect relationships between the work performed at all levels of the organization and the high-level strategic goals. An effective BSC communicates strategy throughout the organization, thereby signaling to the employees what achievements are needed to implement strategy. A BSC also serves to communicate results back to management, using measures that link into specific strategic objectives. By having such a detailed map of strategic intent and accomplishments, both managers and employees can become more effective in their work.

MAKING IT HAPPEN

- Top management involvement is key—The BSC is a strategic management system that is used to change organizational culture, making strategy everyone's job. This change cannot happen without the involvement of top management.
- Translate strategy into operational terms—Strategic objectives must be linked to specific operational perspectives, objectives and indicators. In effect, the BSC "tells the story of the work."
- Link measures within and between the perspectives—All measures should lead to increasing value for the organization. Management should be able to articulate the cause and effect relationships between the measures, and the paths by which the measures link to each other and to organizational value.
- Cascade the BSC throughout the organization—BSCs can be created for each strategic business unit, for departments within each business unit, and, ultimately, for each employee. These cascaded BSCs help to define the performance objectives into meaningful metrics that link the work being performed at all levels of the organization to the strategic goals of the firm.
- Link the BSC to compensation—By rewarding employees for specific performance outcomes that are linked to strategic objectives, alignment is created between the work being done and the broader strategic goals of the firm. There is a cause and effect relationship between "what gets measured, gets managed" and "what gets rewarded, gets attention." By rewarding the specifically defined actions that create value, management is assuring that employees are focused on doing the right things.

MORE INFO

Books:

Epstein, Marc J., and Bill Birchard. *Counting What Counts: Turning Corporate Accountability to Competitive Advantage.* Reading, MA: Perseus Books, 1999.

Kaplan, Robert, and David P. Norton. *The Balanced Scorecard: Translating Strategy into Action*. Boston, MA: Harvard Business School Press, 1996.

Kaplan, Robert, and David P. Norton. *The Strategy-Focused Organization: How Balanced Scorecard Companies Thrive in the New Business Environment*. Boston, MA: Harvard Business School Press, 2001

Websites:

Balanced Scorecard Institute: balancedscorecard.org

Balanced Scorecard Report: harvardbusinessonline.hbsp.harvard.edu/b02/en/newsletters/news-bsr_home.jhtml

Management and Accounting Web: www.maaw.info

Optima Media Group Business Intelligence. See the "Performance Measurement Portfolios" for BSC information: www.business-intelligence.co.uk

NOTES

1 Hendricks, Kevin, Larry Menor, and Christine Wiedman. "The Balanced Scorecard: To adopt or not to adopt?" *Ivey Business Journal* (November/December 2004).

2 Ibid.

3 Adapted from: Kaplan, R. S., and D. P. Norton. "Using the Balanced Scorecard as a strategic management system." *Harvard Business Review* 74:1 (January–February 1996): 75–85.

4 Data from this case study was reported in: Kaplan, R. S., and D. P Norton. *The Strategy-Focused Organization*. Boston, MA: Harvard Business School Press, 2001.

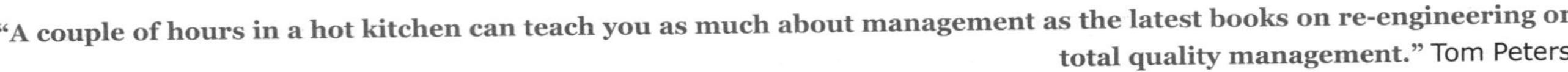
"A couple of hours in a hot kitchen can teach you as much about management as the latest books on re-engineering or total quality management." Tom Peters

  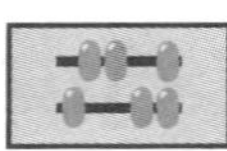      

Multinationality and Financial Performance

by Alan Rugman

EXECUTIVE SUMMARY

- Senior executives, especially finance officers, need to be aware that standardized metrics to evaluate international performance are only applicable when firms operate globally. Now that research shows that large firms actually operate regionally, it is necessary to use new regional metrics to measure performance.
- Regional variables are important new measures that supplement the traditional measures of multinationality; indeed, the regional measure is a superior measure of the financial performance of multinational enterprises (MNEs).
- There is evidence that MNEs perform in an intraregional manner, on the basis of both sales and assets; there are strong intraregional effects across all industry sectors.
- Analysis of multinationality and financial performance needs to take into account the new metrics available on regional sales and assets, and the return on foreign assets.

INTRODUCTION

Most of the world's 500 largest firms have extensive international operations; indeed, these firms average 35% of their sales in other countries. Finance officers and senior executives involved in strategic management usually assume that such firms are operating globally. This is a bad mistake, since recent academic research has demonstrated that the vast majority of the foreign sales of these firms are actually made within the firm's home region of the broad triad of the European Union, North America, and Asia–Pacific. In other words, the world's largest firms are actually operating regionally rather than globally.

The regional nature of business means that the traditional financial and accounting metrics used to evaluate international performance need to be revised. These measures assume that firms operate globally, such that financial performance can assume standardized operations across the world. (Globalization is usually defined as worldwide economic integration leading to standardization and commonality.) Instead, financial performance needs to be measured within the home region and not globally. Large firms face additional risks in expanding operations beyond their home region. Such additional risks need to be compensated by a better performance on interregional sales in contrast to the less risky intraregional sales. In this article we outline the nature of regional activity and the new regional metrics required to measure the financial performance of large firms.

THE REGIONAL DIMENSION OF MULTINATIONALITY AND PERFORMANCE

Recent empirical research has established that MNEs operate regionally rather than globally. It was shown by Rugman and Verbeke (2004) that only nine of the world's 500 largest firms operate globally, i.e. in all three regions of the broad triad of North America, Europe, and Asia–Pacific. In contrast, of the 380 firms that provide data for the year 2001 on the geographic scope of their sales, 320 average 80% of such sales in their home region. In Rugman (2005) some 60 cases were examined to establish the robust nature of this regional effect. It was also demonstrated that whenever data on assets were provided by firms these upstream production data also revealed a regional rather than a global effect. The implications are that the MNEs are more likely to source through regional clusters than through a global supply chain. However, robust testing of the asset data remains to be undertaken.

We shall now present data on both sales and assets. These data are presented for the five-year time period 2001–05. The purpose of these data will be to demonstrate that the regional effect is applicable over time and that there appears to be no trend towards globalization. Rather, these data indicate that there is a longitudinal argument that regionalization is now a stable phenomenon.

Table 1 reports data on intraregional sales and assets for the period 2001–05. This is for a set of the world's largest 500 firms. Among 500 firms, geographic sales and assets data are available for 386 firms during this period. The data are compiled from the annual reports of these publicly traded companies. These annual reports are now available on the internet under each company's name. This table updates and supplements the data for 2001 reported in Rugman and Verbeke (2004) and in Rugman (2005). In Table 2 data are reported for the ratio of regional to total sales (R/TS) and also for the ratio of regional to total assets (R/TA). In addition the table reports the conventional measure of multinationality in previous empirical research. This is (F/TS), i.e. the ratio of foreign (F) to total (T) sales. The table also reports the ratio of foreign to total assets (F/TA). For more detail, see Rugman (2007).

Table 1. Foreign and intraregional sales and assets of large firms, 2001–05

	Sales		Assets	
	F/TS (%)	R/TS (%)	F/TA (%)	R/TA (%)
2001	33.6	75.6	31.2	77.2
2002	34.9	75.8	32.1	76.9
2003	35.5	75.8	32.7	76.4
2004	35.8	75.2	33.2	76.4
2005	36.4	75.2	33.1	76.5
Average	35.2	75.7	32.5	76.7

The table reports that the average (R/TS) for the world's largest firms is 75.7%. There is almost no variation over time. Next the table reports that the average (R/TA) is 76.7%. Again, there is very little variation over time. These data suggest that the world's largest firms are slightly more regional on assets than on sales. Table 2 also reports that the average (F/T) for sales is 35.2%, while the average (F/T) for assets is 32.5%.

Table 2. Foreign and intraregional sales and assets of large firms by regional origin, 2001–05

	Sales		Assets	
	F/TS (%)	R/TS (%)	F/TA (%)	R/TA (%)
N.America	26.9	78.0	27.0	76.5
Europe	55.5	70.8	52.1	72.9
Asia	27.4	77.2	21.1	81.6
Average	35.2	75.7	32.5	76.7

CHOOSING THE CORRECT METRICS

There is an interesting variation by triad region. In Table 2 the (F/TS) for Europe is 55.5%, and for assets it is 52.1%. This partly reflects the historical lag in statistical data collection whereby the 27 member states of the European Union still record trade, foreign investment, and foreign sales data across country borders. In practice, the European Union is now an integrated internal market with common political institutions, a uniform judicial system, and one with a common currency for most of the member states. Thus scholars need to be careful in using data on (F/T), since the international aspect of both sales and assets is exaggerated for Europe. In contrast, the regional variable is stable across the three

"The evidence is that most of the world's largest firms are stay at home multinationals. The world of international business is a regional one not a global one." Alan M. Rugman

regions of the triad. The distortionary effect of Europe does not appear in the average of (R/TS) of 75.7% and (R/TA) of 76.7%. It can be concluded that the (R/T) variable is more stable and, perhaps, more reliable than the traditional (F/T) variable.

Both variables are preferable to the "scope," measure, which simply counts the number of foreign countries in which an MNE has subsidiaries. This gives only a vague indication of geographic sales (or asset) dispersion, and it is probably very misleading as it misses the magnitude of sales (or assets) across countries and triad regions. For example, for a UK firm to have a subsidiary in the United States is much more significant than for it to have 12 subsidiaries in the new member states of the European Union. Yet the scope measure would count the UK firm as 12 times more internationalized in Europe than in North America.

CONCLUSION

It has been shown here that large firms, including the vast majority of the world's multinational enterprises (MNEs), operate regionally rather than globally. The 500 largest firms average about 75% of their sales in their home region of the triad. They also have most of their assets in their home region. It is reasonable to assume that smaller firms are even less global and more local in their operations. Indeed, small firms are often associated with large MNEs in localized clusters and act as key suppliers and distributers in partnership with the MNEs. In other words, the world's largest MNEs act as strategic leaders (flagships) in determining the regional nature of business around the world.

For financial officers, the key implication of the evidence that large firms perform regionally is that new metrics are required to evaluate firm performance. It is no longer appropriate to consider the aggregate ratio of foreign to total sales since interregional sales are more risky than intraregional sales. Rather, it is necessary to use the ratio of regional to total sales. Data have been presented in this article for both types of metrics. It is apparent that the regional sales metric provides important new information to financial officers. New academic work is being undertaken to assess financial performance of large firms using the regional metric rather than the aggregate metric for multinationality. Initial results demonstrate that the financial performance of a firm is better explained by the regional metric than by the old multinationality metric. In the future, business practice and performance metrics for MNEs must be better aligned to the new academic research which has demonstrated the lack of globalization and the regional nature of business activity.

CASE STUDY

The relationship between multinationality (M) and performance (P) is a traditional topic in the areas of international business and the financing of multinational enterprises (MNEs). In this literature, *P*, as a dependent variable, is broadly determined by the degree of multinationality, *M*, where *M* is usually proxied by the ratio of foreign to total sales or assets, i.e., (*F/T*). There is either a linear, quadratic, or cubic (*S*-curve) fit, allowing for controls such as size of the firm, industry grouping, and organizational learning effect over time, etc. (see Rugman (2007)). Recently, this *M* and *P* literature has included regional aspects of (*F/T*) and performance—for example, performance now includes return on foreign assets (ROFA).

There are now better and more detailed data on the geographic dispersion of activities.

The new accounting standards affecting most of the world's MNEs now make it possible to adopt both a new dependent variable (for performance) and a new independent variable (for multinationality):

1 Performance can now capture the return on foreign assets (ROFA), not just the return on total assets (ROTA).
2 Multinationality is now available on a regional basis, i.e., the ratio of regional (R) to total (T) sales (R/T). This offers better information on the strategic performance of an MNE, in comparison to the traditional metric of the return of foreign-to total sales or assets (F/T).

Further, it is possible to calculate the performance of MNEs using Tobin's *q* as a performance measure. While this is restricted to examining the performance of the consolidated MNE, Tobin's *q* permits us to modify the accounting data reported by the firms with a stock market capitalization measure. The Tobin's *q* captures both the stock market valuation of the firm along with key elements of accounting-based rates of return. In a recent paper Tobin's *q* has been explained both by traditional (*F/T*) measures of multinationality and by the regional variable (*R/T*). These results are reported in Rugman (2007).

MAKING IT HAPPEN

Finance professionals need to keep up to date about academic research on the financial performance of multinational enterprises (MNEs). These firms disclose accounting information in their annual reports. Traditionally they disclose their degree of multinationality, usually the ratio of foreign (F) to total (T) operations. Thus it is relatively easy to calculate the F/T for sales and/or assets. The average F/T ratio is approximately 35% for sales and slightly less for assets. Large firms also disclose aspects of their financial performance, including return on assets (ROA). Academic studies traditionally examine the impact of F/T on ROA.

Recently, both variables have been modified. First, we can now assemble data on the ratio of regional (R) to total (T) operations. Most of the world's largest 500 firms have R/T ratios of over 70% for both sales and assets. Second, many large firms now report the ROFA. This allows us to calculate the performance of foreign subsidiaries. This is a finer-grained performance measure than the traditional ROA. These data showing the impact of ROFA on R/T have been reported in Rugman (2007) and by Rugman, Yip, and Jayaratne (2007).

MORE INFO

Books:

Rugman, A. M. *The Regional Multinationals: MNEs and "Global" Strategic Management*. Cambridge, UK: Cambridge University Press, 2005.

Rugman, A. M. (ed). *Regional Aspects of Multinationality and Performance*. Oxford: Elsevier, 2007.

Articles:

Rugman, A. M., and A. Verbeke. "A perspective on regional and global strategies of multinational enterprises." *Journal of International Business Studies* 35:1 (2004): 3–18.

Rugman, A. M., and A. Verbeke. "Liabilities of regional foreignness and the use of firm-level versus country-level data: A response to Dunning et al." *Journal of International Business Studies* 38:1 (2007): 200–205.

Rugman, A. M., George S. Yip, and S. Jayaratne. "A note on return on foreign assets and foreign presence for UK multinationals." *British Journal of Management* 19 (2008): 162–170.

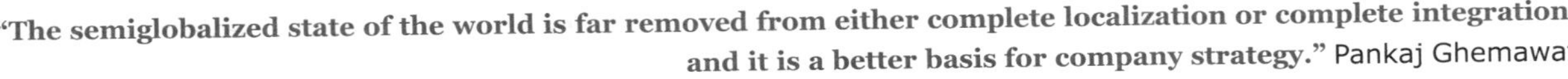

"The semiglobalized state of the world is far removed from either complete localization or complete integration, and it is a better basis for company strategy." Pankaj Ghemawat

  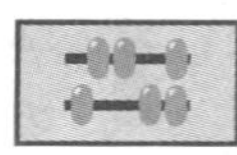      

Political Risk: Countering the Impact on Your Business by Ian Bremmer

EXECUTIVE SUMMARY

- Business decision-makers must understand the political dynamics within the emerging market countries in which they operate.
- We can measure a state's stability—the ability of its government to implement policy and enforce laws despite a shock to the system.
- Essential to managing any type of risk is the development of a detailed and effective hedging strategy.
- Companies should not accept too much risk exposure within any one country or region.
- Rules of the game can change quickly in developing countries, and the cultivation of "friends in high places" isn't always a strong enough hedge.
- Operating in some developing countries comes with reputational risks at home.
- Too many companies have historically relied for insight into local politics and culture on employees who have lived in a particular country for only a short time—or have even merely traveled there.
- Those doing business in developing states need to have credible emergency response plans in place when events outside their control shut down supply chains, prevent local workers from coming to work, or otherwise disrupt operations.
- Developing strategies to recruit and train local managers serves several useful purposes.
- Devoting a share of profits to investment in local schools and universities, infrastructure, and charities can generate stores of goodwill, which is sometimes essential for cooperation with local workers and government officials.
- In some countries, foreign companies should be wary of transferring proprietary information to local partners or developing it inside the country.
- A foreign firm must look beyond what its local competitors are capable of producing today. It must anticipate how those capabilities are likely to develop over time.
- Conditions sometimes force companies to cut their losses and head for the exit. Ensuring that process is as painless and inexpensive as possible forms a crucial part of any sound risk mitigation strategy.
- Political risk can be managed. It should not be avoided altogether.

INTRODUCTION

Over the past several years, and across a broad range of companies, corporate decision-makers seeking opportunities overseas have learned that it is not enough to have a knowledge of a foreign country's economic fundamentals. They also have to understand the forces and dynamics that shape these countries' politics. This is especially true for emerging markets, where politics matters at least as much as economic factors for market outcomes. Of course, understanding that political risk matters is one thing. Knowing how to use it is another.

STABILITY

Starting with the basics, when committing a company to risk exposure in an emerging market country, it's essential to understand how political risk impacts the underlying strength of its government. There are two key elements to consider: stability and shock. Shocks are especially tough to forecast, because there are so many different kinds and because shocks are, by definition, unpredictable. We can't know when an earthquake will strike Pakistan, an elected leader will fall gravely ill in Nigeria, or a previously unknown group will carry out a successful terrorist attack in Indonesia.

But we can take the measure of a state's stability, which is defined as a government's ability to implement policy and enforce laws despite a shock to the system. The global financial crisis, a potent shock, has inflicted heavy losses on Russia's stock market. But Prime Minister Vladimir Putin has amassed plenty of political capital over the past several years, and President Dmitry Medvedev, his handpicked successor, basks in Putin's reflected glow. Neither need fear that large numbers of Russian citizens will turn on them anytime soon. In addition, a half-decade of windfall energy profits has generated more than $500 billion in reserves, ready cash that can be used to bail out stock markets, banks, and, if necessary, an unpopular government. That's why, for the near-term, Russia will remain stable.

Pakistan is a different story. The country's newly elected government has a range of rivals and enemies. Inflation, power shortages, and a wave of suicide attacks have undermined the ruling Pakistan Peoples Party's domestic popularity. The financial crisis leaves the country at risk of debt default, forcing the government to negotiate a loan package with the International Monetary Fund that could impose austerity measures—the kind that helped topple civilian governments in Pakistan in the 1990s. The country is less stable than Russia, because it is much more vulnerable to the worst effects of shock.

President Luiz Inácio Lula da Silva has bolstered Brazil's stability over the past several years by quelling fears of left-wing populism with responsible (and predictable) macroeconomic policies. The Chinese Communist Party's ability to generate prosperity at home via three decades of successful economic liberalization has helped its leadership to build durable near-term stability.

But Nigeria's future stability remains at the mercy of President Umaru Yar'Adua's failing health, as historical tensions between northern Muslims and southern Christians combine with ongoing security challenges in the oil-rich Niger Delta region to prevent his government from building a national reputation for competence, vision, and strength. Iran's theocrats and firebrand president Mahmoud Ahmadinejad have effectively used the international conflict over the country's nuclear program to shore up support for the government in the face of high inflation and gasoline rationing. Underlying political factors in all these countries have a substantial impact on stability—and, therefore, on the country's business climate.

DIVERSIFY

Yet it is not sufficient to possess broad insights into state stability. If corporate decision-makers are to design a credible business strategy that mitigates political risk and maximizes profit opportunities, they have to look deeper at the vulnerabilities that are peculiar to each country, each province, each community. Essential to managing any type of risk is the development of a detailed and effective diversification strategy. Given the political volatility within many developing world states—countries that will generate a large share of global growth over the next several decades—this kind of strategy is especially important. Even within a country as

"As a general rule, the most successful man in life is the man who has the best information." Benjamin Disraeli

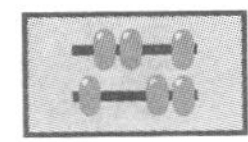

relatively stable as China, a closer look at internal political dynamics can identify various kinds of risk.

Two years ago, US officials worried publicly over a spike in sales of Russian arms to China. Dire predictions of a developing Russian–Chinese military axis became commonplace. But in 2007, sales of Russian arms to China fell by some 62%. Was it because the two governments had some sort of behind-the-scenes falling out? Did the Chinese leadership suddenly doubt the quality of Russian-made products? In reality, the arms sales slowed because China had mastered the design of many of the weapons, and Chinese companies began to produce them in sufficient quantities that demand for foreign-made weaponry fell sharply.

This is a cautionary tale, one that reminds us that any company betting heavily on long-term access to Chinese consumers (or to customers in many other developing countries) may be making a big mistake. There is plenty of money to be made in China for the next several years, but putting too many eggs in a single basket remains as risky as ever. For businesses with supply chains in China and other developing states, it's also important to build redundancies that are not overly exposed within any one region within these countries.

There are other, less obvious, components of a solid diversification strategy. Multinational companies should use all the leverage that their home governments and international institutions can provide to ensure that the governments of the countries in which they accept risk exposure protect their intellectual property rights, enforce all local laws intended to safeguard their commercial interests, and maintain open markets. Rules of the game can change quickly in developing countries, and the cultivation of "friends in high places" isn't always by itself an effective plan.

KNOW THE COUNTRY

Gaining insight into a country's political, economic, social, and cultural traditions is essential for a successful risk-mitigation strategy. Where should this insight come from? Too many companies have historically relied on employees who have lived in a particular country for only a short time—or may even have done no more than travel there. Turning to the guy who backpacked through country X during college for useful information about its politics and culture—not as rare a phenomenon as you might think—is no substitute for the knowledge that can be gained from local workers themselves and from trained political risk analysts.

DESIGN AN EMERGENCY RESPONSE

Generally speaking, emerging market countries are more vulnerable than rich world states to large-scale civil unrest, public health crises, and environmental disasters. Those doing business in developing states need credible emergency response plans in place when events outside their control shut down supply chains, prevent local workers from coming to work, or otherwise disrupt operations. Some businesses have designed technology plans that allow workers to work from home. In cases when circumstances force foreign workers to leave the country, locals should have the necessary training and skills to assume their responsibilities for an extended period. The added expense and time for training are well worth the cost. In some countries, they're essential.

INVEST IN LOCAL WORKERS

Developing strategies to recruit and train local managers serves several useful purposes. First, it gives the host country government an investment in the success of a foreign-owned business. Every job created by a foreign firm is one that local government doesn't have to create. All governments want to keep unemployment at a minimum. Second, it gives local citizens a stake in the foreign company's success and helps to build solid relationships within the community. Some multinational firms have formed mutually profitable partnerships with local colleges and universities that give companies a fertile recruiting ground and ambitious students opportunities for work.

INVEST IN THEIR COMMUNITIES

Devoting a share of profits to investment in local schools and universities, infrastructure, and charities can generate stores of goodwill, which is sometimes essential for cooperation with local workers and government officials. Yet, sensitivity to the local culture matters too. In many developing states, suspicions that Western (especially American) companies have a political or ideological agenda can undermine efforts to promote trust. Contributions to local quality of life should be seen to come without strings attached.

PROTECT INTELLECTUAL PROPERTY

In some countries, foreign companies should be wary of transferring proprietary information to local partners or developing it inside the country. Forging alliances with local partners in joint ventures often serves as an effective risk mitigation strategy, but today's partner can become tomorrow's competitor, and a foreign firm can't always count on local courts or officials to safeguard its assets. Ironically, some foreign multinationals with long-term plans to remain inside a particular emerging market country have invested in local innovation. In the process, they have given locals an incentive to press their own government for stronger legal protections for intellectual property rights. Others have pooled their lobbying efforts with both local businesses and other foreign firms. When lobbying a government, strength in numbers can make a difference.

KNOW THE LOCAL COMPETITION

Successful firms understand their comparative advantages. But a foreign company must look beyond what its local competitors are capable of producing today. It must anticipate how those capabilities are likely to develop over time. Identifying the markets in which a firm's core competencies are likely to deliver profits for the foreseeable future is essential for long-term risk-mitigation strategies.

In many emerging market countries, local companies are often better at large-scale efficient manufacturing than at designing products, marketing them, and delivering them to the customer. Knowing how quickly the local competition can climb the value chain helps with the design of an intelligent, long-term business strategy.

KNOW WHERE TO FIND THE EXITS

Many companies have made lots of money in emerging markets. But as Wall Street veterans like to say, "Don't confuse brilliance with a bull market." Some companies have gotten away with ignoring the need for solid risk-management strategies and have simply ridden the wave produced by the inevitable rise of emerging market economies.

Yet, as skepticism of globalization grows in some developing countries, as their governments respond to domestic political pressure by rewriting rules to favor local companies at the expense of their foreign competitors, and as the challenges facing multinational companies operating inside these countries become more complex, it's important to have an exit strategy. There are plenty of developing states that are now open for business and investment. They have different strengths and vulnerabilities. Too much risk exposure in any one of them can create unnecessary risks. Conditions sometimes force companies to cut their losses and head for the door. Ensuring that this process is as painless and inexpensive as possible forms a crucial part of any sound risk-mitigation strategy.

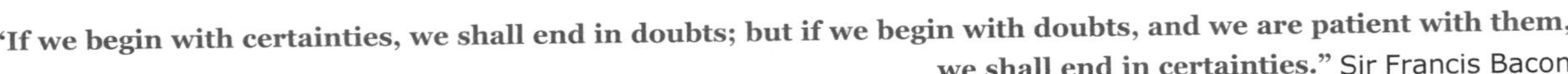

"If we begin with certainties, we shall end in doubts; but if we begin with doubts, and we are patient with them, we shall end in certainties." Sir Francis Bacon

DON'T FORGET THE POWER OF PERCEPTION

Operating in some developing countries comes with reputational risks at home. Several US companies have faced tough domestic criticism for doing business with governments that are accused of violating international labor, environmental, and human-rights standards. For a company's leadership, clearly communicating what the company will and won't do to gain market access in certain countries—and strict adherence to these standards of conduct — can help to minimize this risk.

POLITICAL RISK INSURANCE

As a last resort, a firm can purchase political risk insurance from providers like the Multilateral Investment Guarantee Agency, an arm of the World Bank, or the US government's Overseas Private Investment Corporation. But this should be a last resort strategy, because high premiums, substantial transaction and opportunity costs, and the complexities of establishing a valid claim have taught many companies that it is far more cost-effective to prevent or preempt bad outcomes than to rely heavily on plans to cope with their aftermath.

A LITTLE TOLERANCE IS A GOOD THING

It's useful to remember that having a good exit strategy does not require you to use it. Doing business in developing states comes with risk. But refusing to enter these markets or pulling out at the first sign of trouble comes with a high cost to opportunity. Foreign companies will be earning solid profits within emerging market states for many years to come. Political risk can be managed. It should not be avoided altogether.

MORE INFO

Books:

Bracken, Paul, Ian Bremmer, and David Gordon (eds). *Managing Strategic Surprise: Lessons from Risk Management and Risk Assessment*. New York: Cambridge University Press, 2008.

Howell, Llewellyn D. (ed.). *Handbook of Country and Political Risk Analysis*. 3rd ed. East Syracuse, NY: Political Risk Services Group, 2002.

Moran, Theodore H. (ed.). *Managing International Political Risk*. London: Blackwell Publishing, 1999.

Moran, Theodore H., Gerald T. West, and Keith Martin (eds). *International Political Risk Management: Meeting the Needs of the Present, Anticipating the Challenges of the Future*. Washington, DC: World Bank Publications, 2007.

Wilkin, Sam (ed.). *Country and Political Risk: Practical Insights for Global Finance.* London: Risk Books, 2004.

Articles:

Bremmer, Ian, and Fareed Zakaria. "Hedging political risk in China." *Harvard Business Review* 84:11 (2006): 22–25.

Henisz, Witold J., and Bennet A. Zelner. "Political risk management: A strategic perspective." Online at: www.management.wharton.upenn.edu/henisz/papers/hz_prm.pdf

"Insuring against political risk." *The Economist* (April 4, 2007). Online at: www.economist.com/finance/displaystory.cfm?story_id=8967224.

"Integrating political risk into enterprise risk management." Online at: www.pwc.com/extweb/pwcpublications.nsf/docid/EAB01AC994713716852570FF006868B6

Stanislav, Markus. "Corporate governance as political insurance: Firm-level institutional creation in emerging markets and beyond." *Socio-Economic Review* 6:1 (2008): 69–98.

Websites:

Eurasia Group, global political risk advisory and consulting firm: www.eurasiagroup.net

Multilateral Investment Guarantee Agency (MIGA)'s Political Risk Insurance Center: www.pri-center.com

PricewaterhouseCoopers: www.pwc.com. Enter "political risk" in search box to find articles and resources.

See Also:

★ How to Manage Emerging Market Risks with Third Party Insurance (pp. 866–868)
★ Measuring Company Exposure to Country Risk (pp. 534–536)
★ Measuring Country Risk (pp. 537–539)
★ To Hedge or Not to Hedge (pp. 104–106)

"The key to running an entrepreneurial business with feet on four continents lies in constant access to information."
Lycourgos Kyprianou

  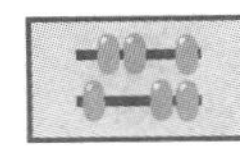      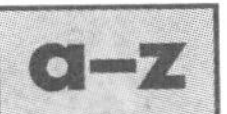

Viewpoint: Poverty of Thinking in University Economics and Accountancy Departments

by Richard Murphy

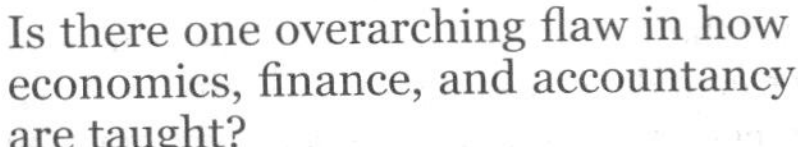

INTRODUCTION

Richard Murphy believes that the way in which accountancy and economics are currently taught is fundamentally flawed since it is based on a false premise—that markets are perfect and investors rational. A graduate in economics and accountancy from Southampton University, Murphy was articled to Peat Marwick Mitchell & Co., a forerunner of KPMG in London. Since 2003 he has been researching and campaigning on economic and taxation policy issues. He founded the Tax Justice Network and is director of Tax Research LLP, which undertakes work on taxation policy for aid agencies, unions, NGOs, and others in the United Kingdom and abroad.

Murphy has helped to reshape the debate on international tax policy, for example through the creation of country-by-country reporting. As principal researcher of the Tax Justice Network until 2009, he helped to put tax havens on the international agenda. He is a coauthor of *Tax Havens: How Globalization Really Works* (2009) and is working on a new book entitled *The Joy of Tax*.

Is there one overarching flaw in how economics, finance, and accountancy are taught?

Yes. There is a hegemony of ideas. Anyone who wants to teach economics or accountancy these days has to subscribe to neoliberal economic thinking. There was a time when you didn't have to be a mathematician to become an economist. However, that changed in the 1970s. Economics—and as a consequence accounting—moved on to a different plane, with everything becoming "rational." Everything had to be reduced to something that could be measured—and if it couldn't be measured, then it didn't really matter. A. J. Ayer's logical positivism became orthodox thinking, giving rise to a mathematically-based, value-free approach that led to some extraordinary assumptions being made.

Who else was instrumental in ensuring that this sort of thinking became mainstream?

Milton Friedman and the Chicago School came to dominate economic thinking from the 1970s. Going back a little earlier, immediately after the Second World War, Paul Samuelson built a model of what he called "Keynesian" economics around mathematical analysis. This was very useful for educationalists since it became possible to set exams with right and wrong answers, which are considerably easier to mark than answers to open-ended questions. That drove the educational agenda in a fundamentally wrong direction.

When economics is taught in this way, it's easier to exclude anyone who lacks the required technical skill and to rubbish anything that interferes with the models as "not economics." This undermines the truth and validity of the entire system.

One of the more surprising aspects of the system for teaching economics and accountancy is the navel-gazing. About one-third of research undertaken by UK accountancy faculties is into the performance of UK accountancy faculties. That is a terrible waste of resources when you think of the areas that could do with analysis and study.

Are there any pockets of resistance to the way accountancy and economics are taught?

No, this way of teaching has swept all before it, largely because it's so easy to do. The teachers do not need to be particularly well trained. In accountancy degrees, the seminars are run by pre-PhD students, many of whom are teaching accountancy to earn some extra cash merely because they happen to be competent in mathematical analysis. Very few have any experience of the world outside. They're not qualified accountants. This has led to a dumbing-down of teaching.

When and where did you study, and how do you feel you were taught?

In my first year of economics and accountancy at Southampton University in 1976 to 1979, I realized that the assumptions that underpinned the course—including that competition was "perfect" and that this would always lead to "correct" outcomes in the markets—bore no relation to reality. I had the advantage of arriving at university with some previous experience of accountancy. I started my accounting career at 17 with a summer holiday job at a local accountancy firm. Even then I realized that what was actually happening in businesses bore no relation to how the economists were describing it.

However, one positive aspect was that the teachers on the accountancy course were practitioners who had transferred into academe—the audit teacher had trained with Deloitte and had done six years in the profession. So it was a very experience-based approach. I found the economics teaching staff much more frustrating. And that was before maths was universal. I fundamentally questioned the assumptions.

One of the things I recognized as exceptionally dangerous was the discounting of future cash flows, which entered mainstream economic theory in the 1950s and became prevalent in accounting from the 1970s onwards. What I found extraordinary about this was the assumption that you could dismiss the future consequences of current behavior and appraise it only with regard to its impact on the present. Of course that drives a short-term mind-set where business pays no heed to future consequences of its actions, one where all that matters is peak performance now.

Modeling is now the bedrock for the teaching of all financial disciplines. However, future consequences are never built into the models, since they are literally "discounted," which is a very close synonym of "dismissed." Students are told that the only thing is now, that future consequences are irrelevant.

This is taught universally across all business teaching, and it does have a pervasive influence. It gave rise to the

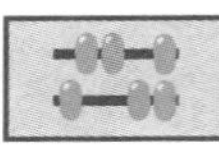

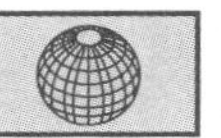

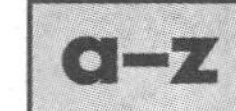

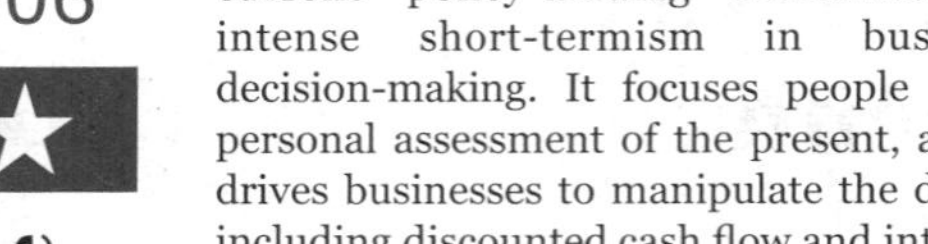

current policy-making framework of intense short-termism in business decision-making. It focuses people on a personal assessment of the present, and it drives businesses to manipulate the data—including discounted cash flow and internal rate of return—to maximize current returns.

Prem Sikka (professor of accounting at Essex University) said to me in January 2008 that the very language of accountancy militates against ethical behavior, since to classify labor and pensions as "costs" means that they are seen as a burden rather than a contribution. Do you agree with his argument?

Yes. The decision-making process has eliminated any appearance of subjective, ethical, or qualitative analysis. Everything must be boiled down to a purely quantitative analysis, so that we systematize and commodify everything. We end up with the absurd notion—related to me by the head of the Confederation of British Industry's tax committee, Philip Gillett—that "you just have to accept that a company is just a bundle of contracts." The result is environmental and social degradation, because we consider only the present. There's also a real element of dishonesty in the approach—the subjectivity is all hidden in the assumptions that are used, such as the discount rate.

Is it the accountancy profession that's forcing these views on to the colleges and universities, or is it the other way around?

The academic profession is pretty weak and highly susceptible to influence from the large firms. It has been undermined by the requirement that all accounting academics must have a PhD, which is quite a hurdle to jump and rules out a lot of talent. The net result is that most of the people teaching accountancy in the United Kingdom have never been accountants, and some don't even have an accounting qualification.

I would say that the "Big Four" accountancy firms—PwC, Deloitte, KPMG, and Ernst & Young—have exploited this. There has been an enormous shift in accountancy, which is reflected in the development of international financial reporting standards (IFRS) and the interrelationship between the International Accounting Standards Board (IASB) and academic bodies, especially in the United States.

The Big Four, led I think by PwC, saw their chance to change the very nature of accounting. They saw how what had been a very subjective subject—the "true and fair view"—could become much more "objective." So they refined what a "true and fair view" meant. Following the realization that globalization exposed them to considerable risk in the 1990s—at the time their liability to shareholders was unfathomable—they pushed through a number of changes that helped to limit their liability in the United Kingdom.

Are you suggesting that the Big Four firms sought to reshape how accountancy was practiced and taught solely to reduce their risk of being sued?

Yes. The Big Four still more or less control the professional bodies, such as the *Institute of Chartered Accountants in England and Wales (ICAEW)* and the Institute of Chartered Accountants of Scotl and (ICAS). They can influence them by threatening to take their training business elsewhere unless concessions are made. We saw pressure being brought to bear on ICAEW after ICAS offered a course to suit the Big Four and therefore secured more of their training contracts. We see the influence that the Big Four have had on changing the curriculum, moving it away from a broad-based curriculum toward specialist-based education. No university that provides an accounting degree will do so without ensuring that it meets the requirements for exemption from first-part professional accounting exams. They are basically beholden to the professional bodies, which in turn must satisfy the Big Four.

Do the Big Four firms continue to wield massive influence in the way accountancy is taught in the United Kingdom and worldwide?

Most certainly. Globalization increased their risk. They wanted to reduce their risk at a time when the quantum of their liability was uncertain: they didn't know if they would be able to convert to LLPs or what the legal environment was going to be. They believed that the best way of achieving this was to change the underlying thinking of accounting in order to objectivize the process.

There has been a fundamental shift in the nature of audit—all that now matters is whether or not something complies with IFRS. Bizarrely, that is what "true and fair" has come to mean. IFRS itself has been objectified, so we have seen a reduction in the scope of personal and professional responsibility.

IFRS decrees that the principal users of financial statements are the suppliers of capital, and that all other users will have the same needs. So annual accounts are designed with the sole purpose of giving suppliers of capital the information they need to decide whether or not to buy or sell a company's shares.

So we can't just blame the way accountancy is taught, because it's a systemic problem?

We are talking about the capture of the educational system by the commercial interests that have driven that process. So I suggest that the education has been objectified and, in the process, it has had its critical facilities lobotomized!

Didn't we see something along those lines in the film "Inside Job," which showed that academic economists had become cheerleaders for Wall Street?

Yes, and that is what I am saying has happened. Which is why someone on the staff of *Accountancy* magazine once said to me: "Richard, you are the only person within the industry who we can go to for a contrary opinion." You need to be quite brave to stick your head above the parapet and argue against the prevailing orthodoxies; you get ostracized and alienated from ever working in the profession. Before you can dare to say that the Emperor has no clothes, you need the confidence to weigh up whether you can somehow maintain yourself without the need to work in the profession again. Not many can, or are willing to, take that risk.

Given the audit failures ahead of the banking crisis, isn't there a desperate need for change?

I see very little prospect of change. The commodification of university education is increasing and, with tuition fees, the pressures will increase further. Students are going to demand an economic return on their investment—because that's what they're taught to do; this is a vicious circle, meaning they expect a guaranteed high-paying job at the end of it. That will further increase the pressure on universities to give them the qualifications demanded by potential employers.

I'm extremely worried about the future of education. Accountancy was once an academic discipline, underpinned by the teaching of ethics and philosophy. But it has become little more than a technical training course. Vast numbers of graduates have been sold short by the process. I am even wondering why they go to university at all! The capacity to question, to criticize, is being removed.

Why do you think the underpinnings of market fundamentalism are never even questioned?

Because nobody has yet come up with an alternative set of diagrams that accountancy lecturers can put on their whiteboards or in their PowerPoint presentations which they use to underpin first-year economics and

"Management today is reactive behavior. You put your hand on a hot stove and yank it off. A cat would know to do as much." W. Edwards Deming

accountancy courses. In other words, because they have a set of nice, easy-to-teach diagrams with crisscrossing supply and demand curves which prove that market profit maximization delivers optimal results for society—and this model is so ingrained in the textbooks, and the presentation so convenient, that it's going to take time to change.

In *Gulliver's Travels*, the Laputans on their floating island are terribly good at maths, science, music, and technology, but they can't actually make anything that works! Are there parallels with classical economists?

In the current hegemony, which underpins the syllabus, profit maximization is never challenged. This is farcical for two reasons. First, because maximizing profit invariably involves plundering the Earth and screwing up other people's lives. Second, because the accounting and economic definitions of profit are fundamentally different. Most people don't realize this. When accountants refer to profit in a set of accounts they are under the impression that it is the same sort of profit that economists talk about. But it isn't. They are absolutely different concepts: one is historical, the other is cash flow. But accountancy education does not even go as far as explaining that. There is a real poverty of thinking inside the system.

MORE INFO

Books:

Aldred, Jonathan. *The Skeptical Economist: Revealing the Ethics Inside Economics*. London: Earthscan, 2010.

Judt, Tony. *Ill Fares the Land: A Treatise On Our Present Discontents*. London: Allen Lane 2010.

Keen, Steve. *Debunking Economics: The Naked Emperor of the Social Sciences*. London: Zed Books, 2001.

Palan, Ronen, Richard Murphy, and Christian Chavagneux. *Tax Havens: How Globalization Really Works*. New York: Cornell University Press, 2010.

Skidelsky, Robert. *Keynes: The Return of the Master.* London: Allen Lane, 2009.

Website:

Richard Murphy's Tax Research UK blog: www.taxresearch.org.uk

See Also:

★ Viewpoint: CEOs Should Refresh Their Finance Skills (pp. 801–802)

★ Viewpoint: Urgent Need to Retool Business Faculties with Financial Historians and Eject the Financial Engineers (pp. 943–944)

★ Viewpoint: Why Management Development Is a Challenge for Both Business Schools and Client Organizations (pp. 954–956)

  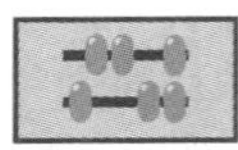   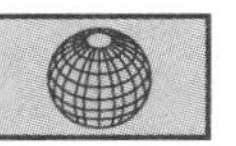   

Profitability Analysis Using Activity-Based Costing

by Priscilla Wisner

EXECUTIVE SUMMARY

- Traditional cost allocation methodologies in firms can provide misleading information about the profitability of products, product lines, customers, and markets.
- Activity-based costing (ABC) provides more meaningful information about the drivers of costs, the activities performed in a firm, and the relationship between costs and products, customers, markets, and segments.
- In addition to supplying more detailed and better cost and profitability information, an ABC analysis enables managers to evaluate processes from an activity viewpoint, leading to identification of non value-adding activities and process inefficiencies.
- ABC does not change overall profitability in a firm; it better aligns cost assignment to the *causes* of those costs.
- With better information, better decisions can be made in a firm to improve profitability—this is the power of ABC.

INTRODUCTION

Cost allocation in firms can provide misleading information about the profitability of products, product lines, customers, and markets. Traditional cost allocation practices allocate all manufacturing overhead costs using a single driver such as direct labor hours, direct labor dollars, or machine hours. Sales-related costs are typically ignored. While technically accurate, in most complex organizations a single overhead cost driver is not sufficient to accurately assign the pool of overhead costs to the products that are being produced or the customers that are being served.

Many firms—from manufacturing to medical and healthcare to banking and financial services to hospitality and not-for-profit organizations—have benefited from designing and implementing ABC allocation systems. Using ABC tools has helped these organizations to understand profitability more clearly, and has provided meaningful information about processes and costs associated with delivering goods and services. A well-designed and implemented ABC system is a powerful aid to management evaluation and decision-making, thereby improving organizational performance.

TRADITIONAL COST ALLOCATION

Factory overhead costs in a manufacturing organization are varied and complex. These costs consist of indirect labor, indirect materials, and other indirect factory support costs. Factory support personnel include process design engineers, supervisors, maintenance workers, inspectors, purchasing agents, security personnel, and administrative workers such as accountants and human resource personnel. Indirect materials are those materials that cannot be individually associated with a product—such as drill bits, shop supplies, paper goods, and maintenance supplies. Other indirect costs include utilities for the plant, depreciation of the machinery, training costs, and technology to run the production systems.

Using a traditional cost allocation methodology, factory overhead costs are allocated to products using a single driver, often direct labor hours. Sales, general, and administrative costs are typically ignored in a traditional costing methodology, since they are not part of the production process and are not considered in the cost of goods sold equation.

Overhead costs have grown substantially in the past decades, as a result of factors such as globalization, technology, product customization, security concerns, and regulatory oversight. In the past, when overhead costs were a smaller proportion of factory costs and direct labor was a larger proportion, it made sense to allocate overhead costs to products using a traditional methodology. The direct labor base was a large proportion of costs, and overhead support costs were a relatively small proportion of total costs. As shown in Figure 1, direct labor costs have declined as a percentage of total costs, while overhead costs have grown.

Figure 1. Total costs over time

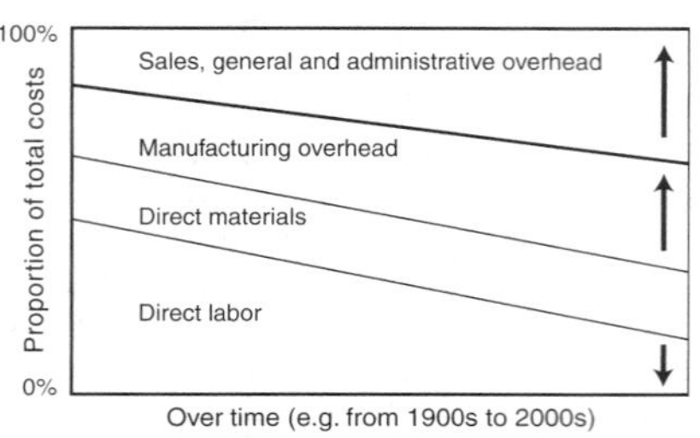

The increased complexity of manufacturing operations makes the traditional methodology obsolete. What is needed to improve the understanding of costs is, first, to associate costs with the activities that are causing the resources to be used, and then to associate these activities with the products that are being produced. This way, products that require a complex set of activities or a high-cost set of resources as part of the production process will be allocated the costs associated with these activities and resources.

IS YOUR COST ALLOCATION SYSTEM FAULTY?

There are various indicators that a cost allocation system is not providing accurate information. You need a new cost system when:

- *The volume of production increases but profitability declines.* This often happens when management cannot accurately determine the cost of activities and resources associated with production processes.
- *The product mix changes from lower- to higher-margin products, but profitability declines.* This situation indicates that the "high-margin" product was actually using more resources than it was being allocated in the cost system. As the firm makes more of this product, more resources are consumed and profitability decreases.
- *Managers do not trust the numbers from the accounting system and sometimes build their own cost systems.* Functional managers often have good process knowledge about the organization. For example, when the sales group ignores accounting information in pricing products and instead uses its own calculations, it is an indication that the accounting system is not supplying accurate information.
- *The firm produces a mix of higher-volume standardized products or services and lower-volume customized products or services, yet the cost allocation system uses a single driver to assign overhead costs to products.* A single driver ignores variation in overhead costs and variation in process activity, resulting in an average number. As complexity increases in a firm, averages distort information at a segment level.

"Because business equates success or failure with profitability, the superficial conclusion is that profit is the sole objective . . . the difficult decisions . . . are those involving the conditions under which profit may be realized."
Crawford H. Greenewalt

  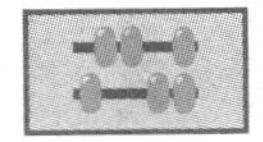      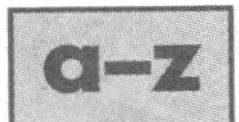

ABC: HOW IT WORKS

Consider an organization with two primary products:

- The first product is well established in the marketplace, sells in high volumes, and is made from a relatively small number of components. In sum, it is a relatively simple product to make and support. Each month, 2,500 direct labor hours are used to produce 100,000 units of this product.
- The second product is newer and sells in smaller volumes. It requires a complex series of steps to produce, with modifications to units requested by various customers. Each month, 2,500 direct labor hours are used to produce 25,000 units of this product.

Using a traditional cost allocation methodology, all overhead costs would be assigned using the number of direct labor hours used to produce each product; therefore, each product line would be assigned 50% of the overhead costs because each product line uses 2,500 direct labor hours. However, the second product is more complex to make, in that:

- more supervisory oversight is needed to ensure that the product is correctly made;
- each item has to be inspected to make sure that the modifications have been correctly done;
- the shipped batches are much smaller in size.

Each of these resources—supervision, inspection, packing, and shipping—costs money, and the need for them is increased by the second product line. An ABC allocation would more accurately associate their costs with the product lines that consumed them, thereby assigning more supervision, inspection, and pack-and-ship costs to the second product line. The data in the following example compare a traditional costing outcome with an ABC outcome for the two products.

BENEFITS OF ABC

An ABC analysis provides management with a wealth of financial and operational information. The benefits of ABC include the following:

- Costs are associated with activities that create those costs.
- Profitability can be calculated from multiple perspectives, such as product line, customer, or market.
- It provides information about "hidden" losers and winners, i.e. which product lines/customers/markets have lower profit margins than was originally thought and which give better profit margins.

Table 1. Comparison of traditional and ABC costings for the same product lines

Example:	Units	Direct labor hours	Supervision *% of effort*	Inspection *Inspect hours*	Pack & ship *# shipments*	Total overhead
Product 1	*100,000*	*2,500*	*40%*	*200*	*30*	
Product 2	*25,000*	*2,500*	*60%*	*800*	*50*	
Overhead costs by activity:			$100,000	$50,000	$40,000	$190,000

Traditional costing (single overhead cost pool)

Overhead rate (190,000 Ö Direct labor hours (5,000)) =		$38.00	
Product 1 overhead:	(2,500 direct labor hours x $38) =		$ 95.000
Product 2 overhead:	(2,500 direct labor hours x $38) =		$ 95,000
			$190,000

Activity-based costing (multiple cost pools)

Each cost pool is allocated according to the activity used by each product

	Supervision	Inspection	Pack & ship	Total overhead
Activity rate:	*Proportional allocation (% of effort)*	*$50.00 per inspection hour*	*$500.00 per shipment*	
Product 1 overhead:	$40,000	$10,000	$15,000	$ 65,000
Product 2 overhead:	$60,000	$40,000	$20,000	$125,000
				$190,000

CASE STUDY

ABC Used to Improve Processes and Evaluate Customer Profitability

Kanthal[1] is a global producer of electrical heating material and elements that are used in industries including electronics, chemical, ceramics, medical, and appliances. Headquartered in Sweden, Kanthal sells its products throughout the world. In the mid-1980s, Kanthal implemented an ABC project to help it realize its strategy for higher growth and profitability. The specific goals of the company were to:

- achieve profit objectives by division, product line, and market;
- determine order and sales support costs, so that the sales force could make better decisions about customer requests;
- increase sales without increasing overhead costs.

At the time of the initial analysis, Kanthal had about 10,000 customers and produced about 15,000 items.

The ABC analysis showed that, of Kanthal's total Swedish customer base, 30% contributed the majority of the profits, about 40% were break even, and 30% were not profitable. The analysis also showed that two of the largest customers were among the least profitable for the firm.

An activity analysis helped to focus on the root causes of the low-margin customers. These were the customers that ordered in small order sizes or in unpredictable amounts, changed their orders frequently, ordered nonstocked or customized products, required additional technical advice and support either pre- or post-sale, demanded large discounts, or were slow to pay invoices. In a culture that focuses on building sales, many firms say yes to one-off customer requests and demands; however, the additional sales volume then comes at costs that very often are not directly associated with the customer's order.

Kanthal management used the ABC information to change internal processes and also to change its relationships with customers. The firm reduced the variation in product offerings, and used distributors to stock smaller-volume items, enabling it to meet more orders from stock rather than building to order. On-line order entry systems were installed for the large customers. Some customers were given a small discount as an incentive to increase order sizes; for example, when one customer was given a 5% discount to increase order lines by 50%, profitability for that customer increased from 19% to 45%. In one division, average order size increased by over 60%, the percentage of orders fulfilled from stock increased from 36% to 63%, and profitability went from a small loss to a 9% positive margin. For the company as a whole, sales increased by 20% without a corresponding increase in employees, leading to a 45% increase in profitability.

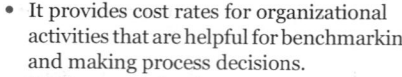

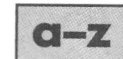

- It provides cost rates for organizational activities that are helpful for benchmarking and making process decisions.
- It aligns with business process reengineering work by helping managers to put a price tag on non value-added activities, such as waste or rework.
- Attention is focused on process costs and how they interact with profitability segments. Armed with explicit measurements of the costs of activities and processes, management can communicate that paying attention to these factors is important. In other words, what gets measured gets managed.

CONCLUSION

An ABC analysis requires an in-depth evaluation of an organization's processes and activities, which in turn enables an allocation of costs that better reflects resource usage. Conducting an ABC analysis provides financial and operational information to management that facilitates more effective decision-making, thereby leading to improved financial outcomes.

MAKING IT HAPPEN

To conduct an ABC analysis, organizational data are needed about costs incurred, work performed, and the cost objectives (for example products, customers, markets) of the analysis. An ABC analysis can be done for one department, for an entire manufacturing operation, or for the whole organization. However, it is often an advantage to start with a smaller-sized project (a single department or a plant) as the learning curve is steep.

1 Gather the cost data from the general ledger or other financial records. Segment the data into cost pools, whereby each cost pool represents a related set of costs. For example, a maintenance cost pool might consist of maintenance labor costs, supervision, tools and equipment used for maintenance, and training costs for maintenance workers.

2 Define the activities of the business (*what work is performed*), using the following framework:

- *Facility-level activities:* Those related to overall operations (for example management, human resources, security, legal).
- *Cost-object level activities:* Activities that support a product (for example design, testing, engineering), or a customer (for example order processing, shipping, technical support), or a market (for example advertising, sales support).
- *Batch-level activities:* Activities related to a batch, equally and at the same time (for example set-up, material handling, inspection).
- *Unit-level activities:* Activities performed for each unit of activity (for example direct labor).

Once the activities of work are determined, assign the resource costs to the activities.

3 Assign the activity costs to the cost objectives (product lines, customer, markets, etc.) according to the cost object's use of each activity. Determining the allocation basis requires process knowledge and transactional data; often statistical analysis can be used to verify relationships between transactions performed and costs incurred.

MORE INFO

Books:

Bleeker, Ron R., and Kenneth J. Euske (eds). *Activity-based Cost Management Design Framework: Getting It Right the First Time.* Austin, TX: Consortium of Advanced Management, International, 2004.

Cokins, Gary. *Activity-based Cost Management: An Executive's Guide.* New York: Wiley, 2001.

Kaplan, Robert S., and Steven R. Anderson. *Time-driven Activity-based Costing: A Simpler and More Powerful Path to Higher Profits.* Boston, MA: Harvard Business School Press, 2007.

Websites:

The Activity Based Costing Benchmarking Association (ABCBA) is a group of ABC practitioners who share data and best practice information: www.abcbenchmarking.com

The Consortium of Advanced Management, International (CAM-I), is an international consortium of business, government, and academic leaders who work collaboratively on cost, process, and performance management issues: www.cam-i.org

The Institute of Management Accountants (IMA) is a global organization that "provides a dynamic forum for management accounting and finance professionals to develop and advance their careers through certification, research and practice development, education, networking, and the advocacy of the highest ethical and professional practices": www.imanet.org

The International Federation of Accountants (IFAC) is a global consortium of accountants that promulgates standards and publishes articles and papers on topics of interest in the accounting and finance disciplines: www.ifac.org

The Management and Accounting Web is dedicated to education, research, and the practice of management and accounting disciplines. Contains links to dozens of management accounting and finance resources: maaw.info

See Also:

★ The Missing Metrics: Managing the Cost of Complexity (pp. 766–768)
★ Reducing Costs and Improving Efficiency by Outsourcing and Selecting Suppliers (pp. 918–920)
★ Reducing Costs and Improving Efficiency with New Management Information Systems (pp. 921–923)
★ Reducing Costs through Production and Supply Chain Management (pp. 924–926)
★ Statistical Process Control for Quality Improvement (pp. 939–942)
✔ Assessing Business Performance (p. 1144)
Activity-Based Costing (pp. 1190–1192)
Cost and Effect: Using Integrated Cost Systems to Drive Profitability and Performance (p. 1347)

NOTE

1 Data for this mini-case were reported in Robert S. Kaplan, *Kanthal (A)*, Harvard Business School Case 190-002, 1995.

"Watch the costs and the profits will take care of themselves." Andrew Carnegie

  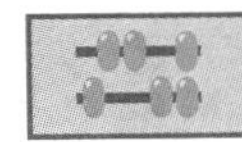   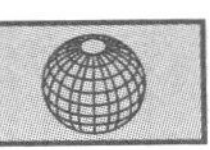   

Protecting Your Intellectual Property—Nonregistered Rights by Jeremy Phillips

EXECUTIVE SUMMARY

- Copyright, database rights, and some countries' design rights—as well as rights covering confidential information, know-how, trade names, and get-up—are intellectual property rights that do not depend on an application process that results in registration.
- If a right is not registered, third parties may find it impossible to identify either the ownership and/or the extent to which the unregistered right is protected.
- Statutory unregistered rights are generally vested with the characteristics of property and may be assigned, licensed, and used as collateral, whereas nonstatutory rights may not possess these qualities.
- The most legally and commercially significant nonregistered intellectual property right is copyright, a broad term that encompasses many different types of right. Some unregistered designs are also accorded protection.
- Rights involving confidential information and trade secrets are generally recognized, although the manner in which the law protects them may differ substantially between different jurisdictions.
- Unregistered rights in trade names and get-up, variously protected by laws of unfair competition and passing-off, serve to reinforce the registered protection provided by trademark and registered design law.

INTRODUCTION

While patents, trademarks, and some other intellectual property rights require registration following a process of application and examination or deposit, other rights (such as copyright or some design rights) automatically come into being either when a work is created or as a consequence of a relationship. Examples of the latter are the rights in confidential information that arise from the relationship of a person who communicates information to a specific person or persons, and rights in the goodwill in a trading name that result from the relationship between a trader and his customers.

Nonregistered intellectual property rights are just as important as registered rights. Examples of extremely valuable nonregistered rights include J. K. Rowling's copyright in the *Harry Potter* books and the formula for the Coca-Cola syrup. Both nonregistered and registered rights may exist together in the same object, whether serially or simultaneously. Thus an invention, which is vulnerable until the patent right is granted, is protected as a trade secret until it is disclosed to the public. Equally, a computer program that satisfies the appropriate criteria for patentability is also protected by copyright.

PROBLEMS ARISING FROM NONREGISTERED RIGHTS

Without registration, it is not easy to identify the rights holder of, in particular, a copyright work. It is dangerous to rely on information contained in a copyright notice in a published work or on a web page, since title to the copyright may have passed on more than once since the notice was originally published. Often a work is considered to be an "orphan work" if the author or copyright owner cannot be identified or traced at all. Some businesses are prepared to take the risk of using an orphan work without permission on the assumption that, if no author or copyright owner can be found, that use will remain undetected.

For practical reasons, it is not possible to provide a registration system for confidential information and technical know-how. A licensee of the use of such information may therefore unwittingly be paying for the right to use information that is already available in the public domain and which, with effort, the licensee could have found and used without payment. The party possessing such information will be reluctant to warrant its secret nature since it too has no means of verifying whether this is so.

As for trade dress (the visual appearance of a product), trade names, and logos, internet search engines have now facilitated identification of their existence and the extent and geographical scope of their use. Instances of accidental use of a trade name or trade dress that closely resembles that of a competitor have therefore fallen sharply. The same applies to unregistered designs of products whose shape is distinctive.

NONREGISTERED RIGHTS AS PROPERTY

Although details vary between different countries, copyright, database rights, and designs are generally protected by statute that specifically accords them the status of property that can be assigned, licensed, mortgaged, or left to someone in a will or on death. Rights in respect of confidential information, know-how, trade dress, get-up and the like are generally said to be *in personam*. This means that those rights can only be enforced against others when they are infringed in certain circumstances, but they do not constitute property as such. Commercial practice in most countries, however, is to treat the latter category of rights as though they were property when assigning them (whether together with the business from which they originated or separately).

Because of its variety and longevity, copyright in a single work may be simultaneously the subject of many separate property transactions. For example, the right to publish a work of fiction in book form may be assigned to A for 20 years, the right to serialize it in a newspaper may be exclusively licensed to B for six months, and the right to reproduce it in cartoon form for the full copyright term may be nonexclusively licensed to D. An option to purchase the movie rights, exercisable for 10 years, may be bought by E, and the right to produce a computer game based on it may be pledged to F as collateral for a loan which enables the copyright owner to pay for its translation into French so that it may be published in that language by G for 50 years. Since assigned rights may themselves be disposed of by the assignee, and many licenses permit the grant of sublicenses, a party that is not aware of all these transactions may struggle to establish precisely who controls which rights to a given work.

In principle, the owner of copyright, database right, or design right is the party that initially creates it. Rules which vary from country to country regulate issues relating to ownership where the creator is employed by another or is commissioned by another as an independent contractor.

COPYRIGHT, DATABASE RIGHT, AND UNREGISTERED DESIGNS

In general, copyright extends to original literary, dramatic, artistic, and musical works and movies, sound recordings, broadcasts, and transmissions, but there may be substantial national variations. Thus, some countries' copyright laws protect original perfumes, while others protect new published editions of old works and the first publication of a hitherto-unpublished work after expiry of the normal copyright

"**In a human capital-intensive environment, all you bring to the table is your own intellectual property. You will not share this precious resource with others unless you trust them to reciprocate.**" Francis Fukuyama

term. The term of protection for original authors' works generally contains a substantial *postmortem* element, while media that contain or transmit works are protected for a shorter, fixed period. Complex rules relate to normally unauthorized uses of others' works that are permitted for news reporting, criticism and review, freedom of speech, and, in some jurisdictions, transformative use that results in the creation of a substantially new work.

Where a copyright work is created by an identifiable human author, that author may be entitled to exercise moral rights in addition to normal commercial rights. Moral rights may include the right to be known as the author, the right to object to pejorative alterations, the right to decide when the work is finished, and the right to withdraw it from circulation. In addition, in some countries a nonauthor has a corresponding right not to be falsely identified as author. These rights may be commercially insignificant, but if ignored can add delay, expense, and ill-will to any commercialization of an affected work.

Database right protects compilations of data where there has been substantial investment in their creation or acquisition but that fail to satisfy the criterion of originality for copyright in an author's work. This 15-year right is provided in the national law of each European Union member state but has not yet been accepted as an international norm.

Many countries protect original or novel designs under an unregistered design right, either in place of or in addition to a regime for registration of designs. In the European Union, the harmonized national unregistered design right provides protection for three years—usually sufficient to assist a product based on a novel design concept at the earliest stages of its marketing.

RIGHTS IN CONFIDENTIAL INFORMATION AND KNOW-HOW

Depending on the jurisdiction, confidential information is generally protected by principles of civil law or by equitable rules that govern unreasonable conduct. Where the relationship of confidentiality between discloser and disclosee is contractual (as in the case of the licensing of trade secrets or technical know-how), the nature and extent of protection against wrongful use or disclosure are governed by the terms of the contract. If the confidentiality relates to personal rather than technical or commercial information, a further level of protection may be imposed by obligations to protect personal privacy under the Universal Declaration of Human Rights, the European Convention on Human Rights, or under local laws.

Where the confidentiality of information is lost through a wrongful act, the accused party may face both a claim for damages and an injunction to prevent it obtaining advantage from the fact that the information is no longer secret.

RIGHTS IN COMMERCIAL GET-UP, TRADE NAMES, AND THE LIKE

Even where no trademark right is registered, any sign, emblem, or get-up identified with one trader may not be used by another with a view to diverting custom. This is achieved by rules relating to unfair competition, or passing-off, or by statutes that prohibit specific unfair marketing practices. To invoke this protection, injured parties must generally prove that the allegedly infringing item is associated with them by their customers. Such evidence can be expensive to obtain and, where obtained by survey evidence, may be rejected as methodologically flawed.

Although this relief is invoked with decreasing frequency as the scope of registrability of trademarks widens, it remains important. It may be the only relief where, for example, the plaintiff's trade name or get-up is not registrable as a trademark, or where the activity objected to does not fall within the legal definition of trademark infringement but nonetheless interferes with the plaintiff 's trade.

HYPOTHETICAL CASE STUDY

Fancy-Fry

Calorie Corporation develops a fast-food concept that it wishes to develop as a business format franchise. Following confidential discussions with external consultants and key officers, the corporation creates a manual containing descriptions of the various concepts that will comprise the new franchise, together with sketches and guidance on operating, reordering stock, accounting, and advertising. Each element of the manual is protected by copyright as well as by confidentiality.

Calorie next produces a model for the restaurant, including furniture and design concepts, which it trials at a nearby location. Now the existence of the restaurant becomes public knowledge, though the contents of the manual do not. Members of the public give their reactions, which are favorable, to the ambience and décor, which, collectively, constitute the restaurant's get-up. The name Fancy-Fry is chosen for the concept. This cannot initially be registered as a trademark since it is descriptive of the restaurant's fare. However, the name catches on and generates goodwill among local diners.

A disgruntled ex-employee surreptitiously obtains a copy of the format manual, which he photocopies and returns. Using it, he opens up the Fancy-Free restaurant across the street from Fancy-Fry. The ambience and get-up of the two restaurants cause diners to assume that they belong to the same franchise.

Calorie can sue for injury to its confidential information, infringement of its unregistered trademark and its copyright, for misappropriation of its trade dress, and can force Fancy-Free to change or close—all without the assistance of any registered intellectual property rights.

MORE INFO

Books:

Derclaye, Estelle. *The Legal Protection of Databases: A Comparative Analysis*. Cheltenham, UK: Edward Elgar Publishing, 2008.

Milgrim, Roger M. *Milgrim on Trade Secrets*. New York: Matthew Bender, 1967. Current copies looseleaf to order with additions and revisions.

Wadlow, Christopher. *The Law of Passing Off: Unfair Competition by Misrepresentation*. 3rd ed. London: Sweet & Maxwell, 2004.

Website:

The IPKat weblog: www.ipkat.com

See Also:

★ Protecting Your Intellectual Property—Registered Rights (pp. 913–914)
★ The Value and Management of Intellectual Property, Intangible Assets, and Goodwill (pp. 118–121)
✔ Intellectual Property—Copyright (p. 1162)
✔ Intellectual Property—Patents—An International Overview (p. 1163)
✔ Intellectual Property—Registered Designs and Trademarks (p. 1164)

"**The newness of an idea matters less than its ease of use.**" Mari Matsunaga

  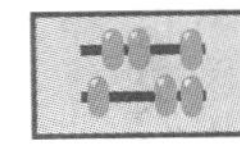      

Protecting Your Intellectual Property—Registered Rights by Jeremy Phillips

EXECUTIVE SUMMARY

- There are many types of intellectual property right, only some of which are registrable; those that are registrable have little in common other than their registrability.
- Registration of intellectual property rights provides objective and verifiable legal protection against competitors.
- Registration provides national or regional protection and can be costly, requiring careful budgeting.
- Failure to register a transaction involving an intellectual property right may have adverse legal consequences for the beneficiary of the transaction.
- Once registered, an intellectual property right is presumed to be valid until the contrary is established, thus providing a powerful strategic weapon for controlling a market.
- Registered intellectual property rights may be expensive to maintain, incurring renewal fees and, in some cases, regular policing against unauthorized use.

INTRODUCTION

Although some intellectual property rights come into existence on the creation of their subject matter, most intellectual property rights are not recognized by law until a process of registration is completed. Patents for inventions, trademarks, and some types of design are generally subject to registration systems.

Patents protect inventions that are new, nonobvious, and industrially applicable. Trademarks protect words, names, logos, product packaging, and shapes, among other things, that enable the consumer to distinguish the goods or services of one business from those of another. Designs protect the aesthetic and not totally functional elements of the shapes of manufactured products.

Registration of each of these rights enables others to ascertain: the nature of the right protected; legal entitlements of owners and users of the right; and information from which the expiry date of that right can be calculated.

Registration is not synonymous with examination: It may follow a rigorous, often interactive application procedure over a period of months or years—this is usually the case for patents and trademarks—or it may only require a deposit, as in the case of some designs.

REGISTRATION AND CERTIFICATION

Proof of registration of any interest in an intellectual property right is necessary if that interest is invoked in litigation. In patent and trademark infringement proceedings, for example, a court will accept a certificate of entitlement to that right as evidence. Registration helps a prospective licensee of a right to identify who must be approached for a license request. When a business is acquired, registration enables a due diligence search to find out which of the assets used by the target business are owned by it. Where the information recorded on the register does not accord with reality, it may be necessary to seek rectification of the register, a process that may be both slow and costly.

In some circumstances the state of the register will not accord with reality because of the length of time taken by the registry in question to record an assignment or license. Sometimes the information on the register may be up to two years out of date, or more. Local practitioners should be able to advise, in any given jurisdiction, on the state of the register.

INTERNATIONAL, REGIONAL AND NATIONAL REGISTRATION

With some exceptions, patents, trademarks, and designs are rights granted under national law; the scope of their exercise is thus coextensive with national borders. The owner of the rights must therefore factor into any business plan the identity and number of countries in which protection of the registered right is needed. More than 200 countries provide some form of intellectual property protection, but the cost of obtaining registration in each of them is often prohibitive for even the wealthiest corporations (the cost of truly international patent protection can easily exceed US$2 million, and many new products and processes incorporate several separate patentable concepts). Therefore, proprietors have to balance the cost of formalities in protecting the right against the potential value of exploiting that right in a particular country. In all cases, the intellectual property owner incurs official fees as well as those of local professional representatives. In the case of patents, further expense is incurred in searches of the patent records and technical literature to see whether an invention has been anticipated by an earlier patent, and by the cost of translating the patent into the language of each country in which protection is sought (this may exceed 85% of the total cost). For trademarks, additional expense is incurred in finding out whether the mark to be registered would be likely to cause confusion to consumers or damage an earlier mark.

The World Intellectual Property Organization (WIPO) administers facilitative systems that enable an applicant to seek registration of a patent, trademark, or design in a multiplicity of countries through a single application that is processed by WIPO and then forwarded to the granting office of each target country. These schemes (the Patent Cooperation Treaty, the Madrid System for trademarks, and the Hague scheme for designs) reduce the cost and bureaucracy of international protection but do not remove the obstacles to registration that exist at national level.

Not all registered rights are limited by national borders. As an alternative to national registration, the European Union has introduced pan-European trademark and design rights that confer protection via a single registration throughout the 27 EU member states, and the African Intellectual Property Organization offers a single patent that covers 16 francophone African nations. The European Union does not yet have a pan-European patent; the European Patent Office, which processes and examines patent applications for up to 35 European countries, is not an organ of the European Union.

CONSEQUENCES OF FAILURE TO REGISTER AN INTEREST

The initial grant of a patent, trademark, or design is automatically recorded on the register. Subsequent transactions involving these rights require registration in most countries, and this requires action on the part of the party that acquires the right or gains permission to use it.

Where registration is not effected, the purchaser of a registered right may not be able to assert its entitlement against a later purchaser of the same right from the same seller. The holder of a nonregistered right may also be penalized when suing an infringer, either through a prohibition on the recovery of damages or through a bar on the recovery of legal costs.

"Owning the intellectual property is like owning land: You need to keep investing in it again and again to get a payoff; you can't simply sit back and collect rent." Esther Dyson

STRATEGIC VALUE OF A REGISTERED RIGHT

Once an intellectual property right is registered, its strategic value to the proprietor is enormous. Because a certificate of registration is presumptive evidence of the validity of the registered right, a court will take the validity of an asserted right at face value in proceedings for its enforcement. This is particularly valuable where the proprietor of the right seeks interim relief against an allegedly infringing act, such as the manufacture, importation, or sale of an infringing product, by having that activity stopped until a full trial can take place, often more than a year later. Even if a patent is later held to be invalid, the fact that it is presumed valid until the contrary is proved can block a competitor from entering the market for the patented product for long enough to force the competitor to abandon its plans altogether. Although the patent term may for up to 20 years, most patents do not remain in force for more than half that period. Since their commercial currency may be short, even a short period of interim relief may be crucial.

The law does provide checks and balances against abuse of the power wielded by the intellectual property right's owner. For example, where an interim order prevents a competitor from performing an act which, following the full trial, turns out never to have infringed the right, the competitor may be entitled to receive compensation. Many jurisdictions also provide that the making of an unwarranted threat to commence infringement proceedings is itself a civil wrong. In most developed and developing economies, competition and antitrust rules prevent uses of intellectual property rights that are deemed to be an abuse of their proprietor's dominant position or a means of distorting the normal operation of a competitive market.

MAINTENANCE OF A REGISTERED RIGHT

Although details vary across the jurisdictions, most registered rights incur renewal fees which, if not paid, result in the lapse of the right. Some countries provide for late renewal or even the resuscitation of lapsed rights on payment of the appropriate fee, so it is prudent for any business that does not have its own in-house intellectual property administration to outsource its renewals to a specialist in the field.

Trademarks in most countries run for a 10-year period that is renewable indefinitely so long as the renewal fee is paid. In some jurisdictions, renewal is contingent on proof of use of the trademark, so the proprietor should make sure that samples proving use of the trademark in the form in which it is registered, and for the goods or services for which it is registered, are preserved. In many countries, nonuse of a registered mark for a continuous period, usually three or five years, will expose it to the risk of revocation for nonuse.

The registration of a trademark is vulnerable to "genericity," when, by virtue of the use made of the trademark by competitors or by consumers, the mark has ceased to function as a means of distinguishing the goods of one business from another and has become the name of a product itself. Trademarks such as Aspirin, Caterpillar, Hoover, Thermos, and Walkman have at times been threatened by their own popularity—in some cases losing registration in certain jurisdictions while preserving it in others.

HYPOTHETICAL CASE STUDY

Nimboshave

Nimbo Corporation devised a three-in-one product, being a combination bottle opener, corkscrew, and electric razor. Following consultation with its patent lawyer, the corporation was advised that the product as a whole was not patentable, being a combination of known parts each of which performed its normal function. However, the process of affixing the bottle opener to the outer casing of the electric shaver involved a novel technical solution that was patentable. Nimbo decided to apply for patent protection in jurisdictions in which electric razors were made or widely used but not to seek patent protection in jurisdictions in which males favored the growth of beards or those in which the consumption of alcohol was illegal.

The casing of the electric razor had to be shaped to accommodate the fixture of the corkscrew when it was not in use and to provide a comfortable grip for the corkscrew when opening bottles. This shape was not merely functional but possessed a substantial aesthetic appeal, on the basis of which it appeared to be registrable as a design in certain markets. Initially, Nimbo did not consider it worth registering a design right, but it later discovered that the cost of design registration was very small and that the nuisance effect of design registration might deter prospective competitors.

Nimbo Corporation elected to brand the product as "Nimboshave." A search of the Bulgarian register revealed that another company already held an earlier registration of the word mark Nimboshave for a conventional wet-shave apparatus. Suspecting that Nimboshave had not been used for a continuous period of more than five years, Nimbo proposed to apply to have the mark revoked to clear the way for registration of its own mark. The proprietor of the earlier mark proposed to resist this application. After a brief negotiation, Nimbo agreed not to challenge the earlier mark, took an exclusive license to use Nimboshave in Bulgaria for a trivial royalty, registered its interest as exclusive licensee of that mark, and then imported and sold Nimboshave products there.

MORE INFO

Books:

Bently, Lionel, and Brad Sherman. *Intellectual Property Law*. 3rd ed. Oxford: Oxford University Press, 2008.

Chisum, Donald. *Chisum on Patents*. New York: Matthew Bender, no date. 27 volumes, looseleaf, updated with revisions.

McCarthy, J. Thomas. *McCarthy on Trademarks and Unfair Competition*. 4th ed. New York: West Publishing, 1998–2008. Binder/looseleaf.

Websites:

United States Patent and Trademark Office: www.uspto.gov
World Intellectual Property Organization (WIPO): www.wipo.int

See Also:

★ Protecting Your Intellectual Property—Nonregistered Rights (pp. 911–912)
★ The Value and Management of Intellectual Property, Intangible Assets, and Goodwill (pp. 118–121)
✔ Intellectual Property—Copyright (p. 1162)
✔ Intellectual Property—Patents—An International Overview (p. 1163)
✔ Intellectual Property—Registered Designs and Trademarks (p. 1164)

"Both Apple and Pixar ... Their product is pure intellectual property. Bits on a disk." Steve Jobs

Real Options: Opportunity from Risk

by David Shimko

EXECUTIVE SUMMARY

Real options arise from the ability of economic agents to adjust their behavior to maximize the values of their assets or contracts.

- Common examples are the right to make, expand, contract, defer, or cancel an investment or contract.
- Value real options by considering the value of the asset or contract with and without the ability to adjust.
- In some cases, the Black–Scholes model can be used to approximate the value of real options directly.
- Real options generally increase in value as uncertainty about the future increases.
- Real options can be proprietary or shared, simple or compound, restructurable or not.
- Real options have real value; many corporate valuations cannot be explained except for the presence of real options.

WHAT IS A REAL OPTION?

The origin of the term "real option" derives from financial options. For example, the right to buy a house for a fixed period of time at a fixed price is a call option,[1] except that the underlying asset is a real asset, not a financial asset. Business people and economists discovered that many business processes involve options, and that financial mathematics can be brought to bear to value those options. Some popular examples include:

- the right to make an investment, such as the option to build a plastics plant in China;
- the right to expand or contract an investment based on changes in market conditions, such as a plant design that accommodates changes in production rates at very low cost;
- the right to defer an investment, such as the right to wait for better market conditions to develop a property;
- the right to accelerate an investment;
- the right to cancel a contract;
- the right to produce or not to produce a product, such as the right of a petroleum refinery or electricity power plant to produce or not produce fuel or power;
- the right to choose how to undertake an investment, such as a gold producer's right to choose the mining strategy that maximizes its value.

"Option" and "optimize" share the same root, the word "opt"—meaning, of course, "to choose." Therefore, the value of a real option can be thought of as the value of any right to choose, when compared with following a strategy where no such right is conferred. This suggests the mathematical relation:

Value of real option =
Value of strategy with decision rights
– Value of strategy without decision rights

In some cases, the option value may be computed directly, as shown in Example 1.

Example 1

A company has a one-year option to acquire an oil-producing property for $100 million. The present value of the drilling profits is currently estimated to be $100 million, and the oil reserves are currently being depleted at the rate of 2% per year. The present value assessment varies according to the price of oil, with a percentage volatility (standard deviation) of 15% per year. If the interest rate is 4%, what is the value of the option?

To value the option, it is helpful to see how the real option resembles a standard financial call option. The owner of an equity call option has the right to buy a stock at a predetermined price (the strike price) for a predetermined period of time. The stock pays dividends which the option holder will not receive if the option is unexercised. Stock volatility makes the option valuable—the more volatile the stock, the greater the value of deciding to buy later at a fixed price.

In the case of the oil option, the "stock value" is the present value of the profits, the "volatility" is the percentage variation in the present value, the "strike price" is the acquisition price of the property, and the "dividend" is the depletion of the oil reserve.

As a first approximation, an analyst might use the Black–Scholes formula of stock option pricing to value the real option. Using any online calculator, and the inputs below, the resulting call option value is $6.82 million.

Stock price	US$100
Dividend	2%
Exercise price	US$100
Volatility	15%
Interest rate	4%
Time	1 year

Call option value = US$6.82

Some real options fit the Black–Scholes framework nicely, but most real options have degrees of complexity that are not captured by the option pricing model.

Example 2

A developer owns a piece of land that is currently used as a parking lot. The present value of the parking lot revenues is $5 million. He can convert the land into an apartment building and net an additional $5.5 million in present value. Or he can convert the parking lot into an office building and net an additional $6 million in present value. What is the value of the property in this case?

1 US$5 million, since it currently being used as a parking lot.
2 US$11 million, since the office project is more profitable than the apartment project.
3 The value of the highest current net present value (NPV) usage of the land.
4 None of the above.

CASE STUDY

In 1998, the NYSEG's Homer City power plant, an 1,884 megawatt coal-fired plant located on the border of New York and Pennsylvania, sold for a price of $955 per kilowatt of capacity. Similar plants, Dunkirk and Huntley, sold for about a third of that price. What was the difference? Was it a problem of irrational exuberance on the part of the bidders, or was there something else going on?

It turns out that because of its location, the Homer City plant had the option of delivering power into New York, and into Pennsylvania and Ohio, giving it the opportunity to benefit from price discrepancies in the three regions. At one hour's notice, the plant could decide to sell in whichever market had the higher price. This real option owned by the NYSEG accounted for roughly two thirds of the market value of the plant. This case was analyzed by Robert Ethier.[3]

"The real options approach . . . provides important insights about businesses and strategic investment. These insights are more vital than ever, given the rapid pace of economic change." Michael Mauboussin

The answer is clearly not 1; a parking lot is worth more than the present value of its current income since it has demonstrated valuable alternative uses. Answer 2 is tempting, but it is wrong if there are any other projects more valuable. Answer 3 may be correct, but also could be incorrect because of the use of the word "current." It may have a more valuable use in the future and, under some conditions, it would be worthwhile to wait to develop the land until that possibility materializes.

The correct answer is generally 4, since the value of the land is equal to *or higher than* its current value in the highest use. The reason for this is that conditions change over time. If the property owner waits a year, they may find that residential real estate grows faster than commercial, or vice versa. At some point, however, it is optimal to make the irreversible decision as to how to convert the property. In those cases, the value of waiting is zero.

Because the property owner has the right to wait to invest, this confers additional value to investment until the moment when it is no longer optimal to wait, and the option is exercised.

PROPERTIES OF REAL OPTIONS

In many situations, increased project risk reduces project value. This is particularly true when a company has constrained capital and increased risks put the company's survival in jeopardy.

Real options have the opposite effect. Like financial options, they generally increase in value the more uncertain the values of the underlying variables. They generally increase in value the longer the time an option can be deferred. And they increase in value as the cost to exercising falls.

Real options also tend to mitigate project risk, since the project owner has the right to modify strategy midcourse. This can help avoid the worst outcomes for the project, providing a kind of operational hedge against downside risk.

VALUING REAL OPTIONS

When an option pricing formula cannot be applied, there are two other ways to value real options: One using backward induction (best for decision trees) and one using simulation (best for problems with continuous input price changes). As an example of option valuation using backward induction, consider the following game, similar to the American television show *The Price is Right*.

Backward Induction

The contestant is given $50 and has to make a decision whether to keep the $50 or pay $50 to choose one of three boxes. One box has a valuable prize worth $100, but the other two boxes have nothing. After choosing a box, the host reveals an empty box and offers the contestant a chance to switch. What is the value of the player's option to switch?

Figure 1. Decision problem summary

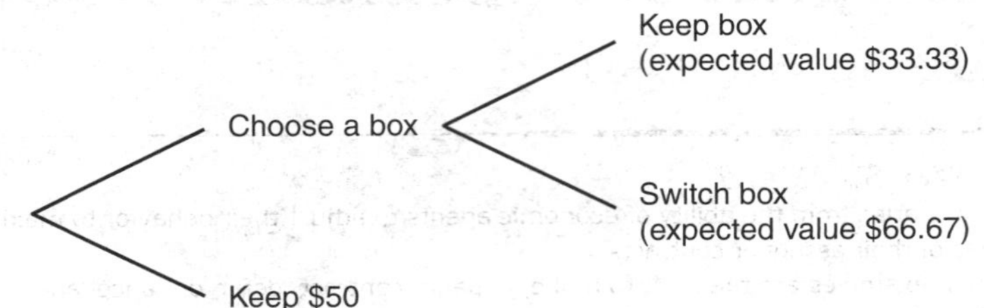

The tree in Figure 1 summarizes the decision problem.

If the contestant always keeps their box of choice, the expected value is 33.33 since there is a ã chance of getting $100. If they switch after seeing an empty box, there is a ã chance they changed an empty box for a valuable one, and a ã chance they changed a valuable box for an empty one.

Using backward induction, we confirm that switching is the best strategy, and since the value of that is greater than $50, the value of the game is $66.67. The value of the game without the right to switch is $50, since it is optimal not to play the game. Therefore, the value of the option to switch in this case is $16.67 (= 66.67 − 50).

Simulation

More generally, real options are valued using stochastic modeling and some form of optimization theory. For example, plastics can be produced from natural gas or from naphtha. To value a plant that has the option to choose its feedstock, it is necessary to simulate price fluctuations in natural gas and naphtha and determine how the company would optimize its feedstock strategy depending on the prices realized.

MAKING IT HAPPEN

- Identify an aspect of a business where managers respond differently to different market conditions. It may be evidence of the existence of a real option.
- Value the option by considering how the company behaves with and without the flexibility.
- Evaluate the cost/benefit of increases or reductions in flexibility using the same framework.
- Apply this methodology to other corporate situations, and the valuation of acquisitions and divestitures.

MORE INFO

Books:

Copeland, Tom, and Vladimir Antikarov. *Real Options, Revised Edition: A Practitioner's Guide.* New York: WW Norton, 2001.

Kodukula, Prasad, and Chandra Papudesu. *Project Valuation Using Real Options: A Practitioner's Guide*. Fort Lauderdale, FL: J. Ross Publishing, 2006.

Mun, Jonathan. *Real Options Analysis: Tools and Techniques for Valuing Strategic Investments and Decisions*. 2nd ed. New York: Wiley, 2005.

Schwartz, Eduardo S., and Lenos Trigeorgis. *Real Options and Investment Under Uncertainty: Classical Readings and Recent Contributions.* Cambridge, MA: MIT Press, 2001.

Trigeorgis, Lenos. *Real Options: Managerial Flexibility and Strategy in Resource Allocation.* Cambridge, MA: MIT Press, 1996.

Website:

Links to articles, papers, and other resources on real options: www.puc-rio.br/marco.ind/ro-links.html

See Also:

★ Comparing Net Present Value and Internal Rate of Return (pp. 30–32)
✔ Managing the Time Value of Money (p. 979)
✔ Understanding Real Options (p. 1181)

"Real options represent what is possible beyond the current business operations. Investors can ignore real options, try to find real option value for free, or consciously seek out companies that have abundant real option value."
Zeke Ashton

This problem is complex because switching is costly and cannot be accomplished instantaneously.

Clearly, there is always value in having the ability to switch feedstocks; however, that value may be very small if the costs of switching are high or the volatility of feedstock prices is low. Generally we can say that the value of the switching option is the difference in value between the plant that can switch its feedstock and the value of the plant that cannot.

NPV AND REAL OPTIONS

Many companies make avoidable NPV mistakes. According to the textbook approach, for example, a manufacturing firm should update its production methods if the present value of the benefits exceeds the present value of the costs. This is not necessarily correct. If new and better innovations are being made available over time, management may find an even better renovation alternative. If they repeatedly renovate every time they make a small gain, they will have lost the opportunity to have made a big gain on the best possible renovation.

For this reason, the NPV rule must consider the value of the option to wait to renovate. The NPV rule can be adjusted by including the lost option as a cost or by requiring the present value of benefits to exceed a predetermined multiple of the present value of the costs. This problem was first analyzed rigorously by McDonald and Siegel (1986).[2]

ADVANCED REAL OPTIONS

The options discussed so far were proprietary to a particular economic agent. In some cases, real options are shared, introducing an element of game theory into their valuation. For example, the option to enter a new market may be shared by one's competitors, and the value of the option depends on competitor strategy. Also, some options are compound rather than simple; in these cases, one exercises an option to obtain another option, which adds a layer of analytical complexity, but the financial intuition remains the same.

NOTES

1 A financial call option is the right to buy a security at a predetermined price for a predetermined time period. A put is the right to sell a security at preset terms.

2 McDonald, Robert, and Daniel Siegel. "The value of waiting to invest." *Quarterly Journal of Economics* 101:4 (1986): 707–728.

3 Ethier, Robert G. "Valuing electricity assets in deregulated markets: A real options model with mean reversion and jumps." February 1999. Viewable on the New York State Library website at www.nysl.nysed.gov

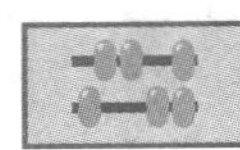

Reducing Costs and Improving Efficiency by Outsourcing and Selecting Suppliers by Paul Davies

EXECUTIVE SUMMARY

- Start outsourcing by constructing the exit clause; this will tell you and your outsource partner what you are focused on and will save you time and expense if things go wrong.
- Focus on the downsides first and understand the management changes required, the communication strategy, the training needs, and your regular engagement with the outsourcer.
- Outsourcing is a process, not an event. What and how you outsource will change over time.
- Outsource chore and focus on core. Keep value creation for your clients in-house.
- In general, outsource a process as is. Let your outsource partner reengineer processes.
- Do not manage your outsource partner; rather, monitor, review, and reassess.
- Choose a partner, not a supplier—one that you can work with through good and difficult times.
- The lowest-priced outsourcer will usually be the most expensive in the long term.
- Outsourcing can not only save money and increase efficiency, but can also reju-venate your business by refocusing your attention on what makes you great.

INTRODUCTION

As a tool for the CFO, outsourcing has an important role to play in reducing costs and improving efficiency. It is important, however, to bear in mind that in addition to the direct and indirect benefits of outsourcing, there are also direct and indirect disadvantages. Outsourcing isn't the answer on its own, and it has to be part of a holistic analysis to be successful.

START WITH THE EXIT CLAUSE

Without putting a damper on the idea, whenever you contemplate outsourcing always consider how you will exit. This may seem curious, but over the years I have found it to be absolutely essential. If outsourcing does not deliver what you expected, if your strategy changes, if the outsource partner decides on a different business model, or if the whole market turns in a different direction—all of which can happen—you need to be able to regain control of what is often a vital, if not mission-critical, process. In such circumstances, you will need to be able to take it back yourself or pass it to another outsourcing company.

Think carefully about this because what you take back won't be what you outsourced. There may well be new IT systems being used, and certainly the processes won't be as you left them. If you haven't an exit agreement, working out who owns the intellectual property underlying the new processes is very difficult and is just one example of the problems that can occur.

The moment to decide how you want to be able to exit is before it becomes a necessity and, preferably, when you are negotiating the contract. If this sounds obvious, many companies fail to do so and suffer as a result.

Understanding your exit strategy will also tell you a great deal about what you want from the outsourcing process. You may be rightly seduced by the idea of not having to spend management time on human resource back-office processing, or by the advantages of not having to worry about expense account processing. If at this same moment you think rationally about what would prompt you to exit from the contract, you will understand most clearly what your business drivers for outsourcing are. If, for example, you put in the exit clause that you have the power to terminate if the proposed savings are not realized, you know what your real objective is. It may be that you insist on a range of triggers and if, for example, you focus on service levels and your end clients' satisfaction with your overall service, you have the same knowledge about your objectives and, more importantly, so does the outsource provider.

In short, brainstorm why you might want to get out of the contract—preferably together with the company that you intend to outsource to—and you will find that not only do you have the comfort of being able to get out of the contract effectively, but that you are also much less likely to have to do so. You will have a much better sense of the advantages and disadvantages of working with your outsourcing partner—and that company will better understand you.

DISADVANTAGES AS A POINTER TO THE BENEFITS

Let us continue by considering the disadvantages of outsourcing, and, by doing so—paradoxically perhaps—you will better understand what you have to do to be successful. You will discover, despite your efforts to communicate, that your current employees do not fully understand why you are taking the outsourcing route. They will probably be fearful that their roles are next, and this can harm performance. In addition, you will lose the sense of immediate control that you had and, instead of going down to the relevant office, you have to go through a process to achieve something that was very simple. You may find that your outsource partner doesn't give you the service you thought you were buying and, without proper review processes, correcting this can waste time and effort. You may find that the insights that cross-departmental meetings and discussions bring are no longer informed by the different perspective that the outsourced department brought. Some of the drawbacks will be relatively obvious, but others will come into your perspective just at the wrong moment, such as when you can't make sense of some information just prior to a board meeting.

These disadvantages point up how your approach to outsourcing must be holistic and built on solid communications.

One area that nearly always gets less attention than it needs is training. It is a significant extra cost that rarely makes itself known until after the deal is signed off. Typically, you will focus on the training of the staff of the outsourcing company, only to discover that your own people have largely been ignored. There will have been a communication to your existing staff about what is going on, but very little to show them how to get, for example, HR support now that it has been outsourced beyond a telephone number.

To get the best out of the new arrangements, you have to train your staff how to deal with accounts payable now that it is remote. Your managers have to move beyond control and micromanagement into monitoring. That can be very difficult to achieve.

You will have noted the focus on communication—and this, as in any serious business reengineering, has to be well thought through and effective. The best way to achieve this is to ensure that there is a feedback mechanism both on the information and the quality of the way it is presented, not to say its timeliness.

"Think carefully about how you will exit because what you take back won't be what you outsourced."

Figure 1. Reasons for outsourcing—CFOs' responses. (*Source*: Computerworld and InterUnity Group, Inc.)

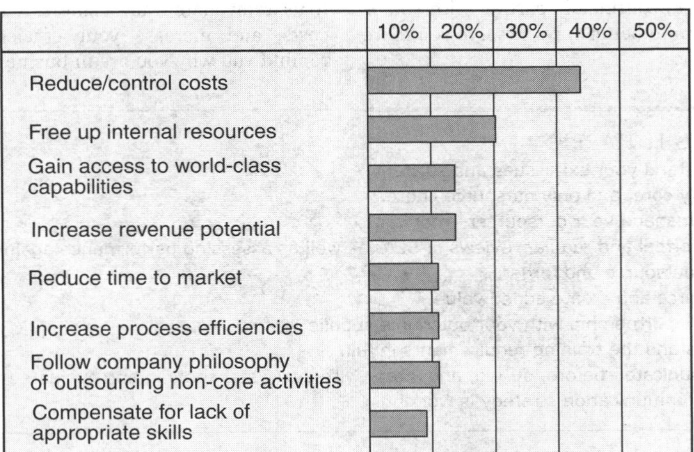

OUTSOURCING IS A PROCESS

Outsourcing is often presented as an event that you get right once. When you find that the service isn't delivering what you thought you were paying for, you will be grateful that you included in the review mechanisms not just a focus on whether the service level agreement (SLA) has been met, but a real, hard look at the SLA itself. Your review process, including market testing on a periodic basis, is more important and should be given more attention than you may at first imagine.

If you have a clear-eyed perspective on the downsides, it will help you appreciate the benefits of outsourcing. If you have outsourced a process to your outsourcing partner, the amount of management time devoted to that process can be reduced—and refocused. You can devote the time you spent agonizing over the process to instead considering the outputs and, more importantly, the outcomes. That is probably the greatest benefit of outsourcing, but you will have to train yourself and your organization to get there.

CORE AND *CHORE*

Choose carefully what you outsource. Think of core and chore. Ask yourself what the focus of your business is, what gives you competitive edge, and what gives you your unique qualities. Anything fitting that description is core to you—and should only be considered for outsourcing as a last resort.

Another way of deciding whether a process or processes can be outsourced is to ask yourself how close the process is to value creation; that is, how essential it is to your relationship with your customers. To appreciate the distinction, look at the difference between sales, which is generally very customer-focused and vital to your value proposition, and marketing, which is equally focused on your customers, but at one stage removed from value creation. You may well, for example, already use a marketing agency, which is a form of outsourcing, and you may use a logistics company to fulfill your orders. They both touch your customers, but what they do doesn't have the immediate effect of a salesperson.

That is not to say that sales cannot be outsourced, and I have seen very successful franchise arrangements, again a form of outsourcing. You just have to be pretty sure that the real value in your goods and services isn't affected by outsourcing sales.

There is a strong line of research that says that outsourcing your core business processes can be very detrimental to your business. You should analyze this carefully, with particular attention to concerns such as impacts on customer satisfaction.

Chore, on the other hand, includes all processes that make precious little difference to your effectiveness in the marketplace. By outsourcing them to a specialist company you gain from economies of scale, as the outsource company will provide the service to more than one company. To you, saving 30 seconds on processing an expense claim is probably neither here nor there. To an outsourcing company, it can mean the difference between profit and loss, with savings also passed to you.

What you will find over time is that you are presented with an incredible, shrinking core. What you initially regarded as a fundamental element in your value proposition can be broken down into smaller processes, and those from which you are not directly gaining value can be outsourced. In the IT world, for example, it is normal for programming to be outsourced. The work of system specification remained in-house, until it was realized that value creation resides in the business analysis that underpinned the specification. In turn, the business analysis was really only a service, parts of which could be outsourced, as the real value lay in understanding the client and the client's business model. It should be no surprise, then, that in the IT world major corporations keep only two things in-house: sales and strategy.

You may not choose that route for your business—and imagine the exit strategy needed if you ever brought it all back in-house. But part of your internal debate once you have started outsourcing processes has to be focused on what is next, and if there is

CASE STUDY

A property management company wanted to expand, but also wished to minimize disruption and stay in the same offices. Through our discovery phase, we identified that by outsourcing some of the chore—rent collection, invoicing, accounting—not only could they do that and save money, but they could release their experienced staff to address higher-value business opportunities. These included, for example, identifying additional properties, working more closely with their clients, and increasing the range of services.

We achieved these major aims—and reduced the cost per property managed. Over a relatively short period, what was outsourced expanded to include insurance policy processing, legal secretarial work, and, as the property development side of the business came into the picture, land development applications. From the company's retail interests, the back-office processing of accounts receivable and accounts payable was brought into the contract.

The key was the relationship between the property company and the outsourcer—and the trust that was built up—so that either side could suggest further areas for outsourcing.

Finally—and this might be an interesting challenge for CFOs—the company's CFO realized that his function, as currently understood, had almost entirely been taken over. He was faced with a dilemma. His alternative, however, was to take a more strategic role, which was what the company wanted, and he was persuaded to view the role differently and become the strategic planner rather than a deliverer of information.

"Typically, you will focus on the training of the staff of the outsourcing company, only to discover that your own people have largely been ignored."

nothing else that you want to consider outsourcing, why not?

AS IS OR REENGINEER FIRST?

Consider next the major stumbling block to decisions on outsourcing. Most internal debates, once you are persuaded that outsourcing will achieve cost savings and efficiency gains, focus on whether you should outsource your processes as is, or whether you should reengineer them first. There is no absolutely right answer, but in practice allowing a fresh pair of eyes to reengineer your processes usually produces immediate benefits. Just ensure that the contract allows you to share in your outsourcing partner's gains! The real message is that you shouldn't allow such debates to delay any decisions on outsourcing. So the best course usually is to outsource as is. You didn't reengineer your cleaning or your security before you outsourced them, and yet your outsourcing partner will have done so and provided a better service.

Choosing a company with which to outsource your processes is clearly a major decision. You should be looking for a partner. While you may think that outsourcing your cleaning will not require a solid partnership, devoting time to working with your outsourcer—in HR processes, in accounts payable and receivable, in expenses administration, in property management—is essential. If there is one rule about outsourcing, it is that you should not outsource and forget. Outsource and review; outsource and monitor; outsource and work with your outsource provider as a partner, exploring what should be outsourced next, what should come back in house, and what is needed to be even more successful.

If you do that, it becomes obvious that you need to select a company to take on your processes that you can work with as a partner, taking formal time to meet and review regularly. Selecting such a company relies on matching your company's culture, sharing an explicit set of values, and relying on their integrity and honesty. You need a company that you can say no to and one that you can discuss your exit requirements with when there is no intention of doing anything but signing the contract.

This is a challenge to your procurement department—but one that will pay real dividends. The short-term lowest price is always the most expensive route in outsourcing, because a low-price provider will usually be one that hasn't built in the time required to continually partner with you or find new and better ways to serve you more efficiently.

REJUVENATION

Outsourcing can, as one of our clients said to us, rejuvenate your business, reduce your costs, and increase your efficiency—and remind you why you are in business.

MAKING IT HAPPEN

- Understand your exit issues and strategy.
- Identify core, and only outsource chore.
- Don't manage your outsourcer—monitor.
- Have formal and regular reviews of SLAs as well as assessing performance against them.
- Don't outsource and forget.
- Outsource and create added value.
- Work in partnership with your outsource supplier.
- Understand the training requirements in full.
- Communicate—before, during, and after—with every stakeholder, and evaluate how well your communication strategy is working.

MORE INFO

Books:

Benn, I., and J. Pearcy. *Strategic Outsourcing: Exploiting the Skills of Third Parties*. London: Management Consultancies Association, 2002.

Halvey, J. K., and B. M. Melby. *Business Process Outsourcing: Process, Strategies, and Contracts*. Hoboken, NJ: Wiley, 2000.

Reports:

Syntel on service level agreements: "The keys to successful service level agreements: Effectively meeting enterprise demands." Online at: www.syntelinc.com/uploadedFiles/Syntel_SLA(1).pdf

Whitaker, Jonathan, Mayuram S. Krishnan, and Claes Fornell. "Does offshoring impact customer satisfaction?" May 2008. Online at: papers.ssrn.com/sol3/papers.cfm?abstract_id=1010457

(See also Wharton Business School for incisive research into outsourcing, including: "Globalization and Outsourcing: Integration with India and China." April 2007. Online at: www.wharton.upenn.edu/alumni/wharton125/events/finale/panels.cfm?panel=panels%5Cday1%5Csession1%5Cpanel5.xml)

Websites:

National Association of Software and Services Companies, India: www.nasscom.in
National Outsourcing Organisation, UK: www.noa.co.uk
Outsourcing Institute, USA: www.outsourcing.com
The Wharton Business School has incisive research into outsourcing. Search on "outsourcing" at: www.wharton.upenn.edu

See Also:

★ Profitability Analysis Using Activity-Based Costing (pp. 908–910)
★ Reducing Costs through Production and Supply Chain Management (pp. 924–926)
✔ Assessing Business Performance (p. 1144)
✔ Assessing Economies of Scale in Business (p. 1145)
✔ Assessing the Value of Outsourcing and Offshoring (p. 1146)
✔ Efficient Invoicing Procedures (p. 1158)
✔ Understanding Economic Efficiency Theory (p. 1126)
Cost and Effect: Using Integrated Cost Systems to Drive Profitability and Performance (p. 1347)

"You will gain from focused expertise on something that you do as part of your operations but at which they work hard to achieve greater efficiency."

  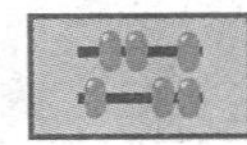      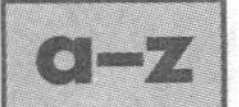

Reducing Costs and Improving Efficiency with New Management Information Systems by Beverly Goldberg

EXECUTIVE SUMMARY

- A management information system (MIS) enables businesses to provide answers to managers in search of knowledge. MIS does this by combining raw data about the organization's operations (contained in its basic information technology systems) with information gathered from employees in expert systems that reflect the organization's procedures.
- As organizations grow, MIS allows information to move between functional areas and departments instantly, reducing the need for face-to-face communications among employees, thus increasing the responsiveness of the organization.
- Putting in place the advanced technological systems needed to collect and sort data and employee information can be costly unless senior management, especially the CFO, controls the purchasing of the basic systems needed by different functional areas from the outset.
- Well-constructed and well-organized MIS can provide management with the knowledge it needs to reduce operating costs and increase profits.
- MIS can help management increase efficiency by quickly providing critical information about procedures and operations.

INTRODUCTION

Management information systems (MIS) make it possible for organizations to get the right information to the right people at the right time by enhancing the interaction between the organization's people, the data collected in its various IT systems, and the procedures it uses. It brings together the raw data collected by the various business areas of the organization, which, while useful for specific functions such as accounting, does not provide, by itself, information that can be used to make decisions. Moreover, in older companies, the systems in which the data reside may be incompatible and need to be migrated to a data warehouse (DW)[1] before they can be used. Once all the basic data are pulled together, they can be combined with information collected in more advanced systems meant to simulate human reasoning, such as expert systems[2] and decision support systems.[3] This enables the data mining (DM)[4] of all the collected information in response to the needs of management involved in operational, strategic, and tactical decision-making.

In many companies, functional/departmental systems are being replaced by enterprise-wide systems—such as enterprise resource planning (ERP), customer relationship management systems (CRM), and supply chain management (SCM)—that ease the problems that arise from having multiple, incompatible systems. Whatever move is made to modernize and simplify data collection, however, the key to using a company's systems to increase efficiency is the technical business analyst, whose job, according to a guide by the International Institute of Business Analysts, is to "collaborate with business stakeholders to build a strong relationship between the business and the technical communities when implementing a new IT-enabled business solution." In most organizations today, the person overseeing the work of the technical business analyst is the chief financial officer. In the past, when people thought about the role of CFO, they considered it primarily an accounting role. That is no longer the case. As Pfizer CFO David L. Shedlarz says, "when you take a look at a CFO's responsibility today, you also have operations planning and analysis, information technology, strategic planning, and M&A."[5]

THE COSTS ASPECT OF MIS

When it comes to costs and MIS, there are three parts to the story. The first involves the costs of MIS itself.

- **1. Adopting MIS can be costly**. Older, larger companies usually have accumulated huge amounts of data stored in various systems adopted at different times in the company's history, usually well before the idea of mining those data for decision support was a possibility. These older systems, known as legacy systems,[6] include critical historic data about finances, sales, inventory, customers, and suppliers. The problem is that these systems tend not to be compatible, often using different definitions of key concepts. When the organization needs information, the raw data in these disparate, incompatible systems need to be extracted and migrated to a database designed to organize the raw data and make them available for analysis. Building these databases is both expensive and time-consuming.
  Smaller companies, especially start-ups, can avoid this problem by adopting suites of applications for various functional areas that have been developed to be compatible. Ensuring that the heads of the business's functional areas do not purchase incompatible components simply because of their familiarity with them is critical. The CFO must work with the IT department to make sure that everyone in IT knows that they have his or her backing to refuse to support unauthorized purchases. When there is no formal IT department, the CFO should review the purchasing decisions of various departments frequently to ensure that their managers have not used discretionary funds to buy applications that are not part of the chosen suite. If the CFO can discover such purchases quickly, he can work with the CEO to stop their use before time and money is spent adopting them—and creating problems as the company expands.The second and third cost considerations show that in the long-run, the costs of *not* adopting MIS can far exceed the costs of adopting and implementing a system. The second bullet shows the ways in which MIS can lower operating costs once in use, and the third reveals the profits that MIS can help to generate.
- **2. MIS can lower operating costs in many ways**. By using MIS to share information across functional areas, redundant efforts can be eliminated. This is particularly important as a small business grows. When a company has only a few employees, it is relatively easy for them to be in contact with one another often enough to share knowledge directly. As the number of employees increases, however, and people are divided into teams or functional areas, it becomes more difficult to keep the lines of communication open and encourage the sharing of ideas. As a result, for example, the sales and marketing departments may each spend time developing descriptions of new products that

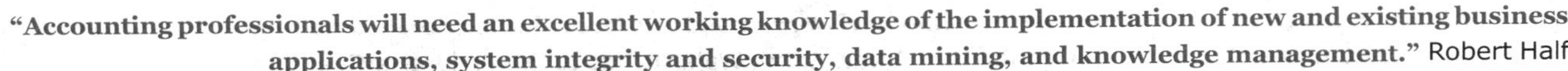
"Accounting professionals will need an excellent working knowledge of the implementation of new and existing business applications, system integrity and security, data mining, and knowledge management." Robert Half

highlight different features of the product, creating confusion that ends up with customers not understanding exactly what a product does and leading to product returns or even the loss of customers. If there was a database that contained information about all the products in development that employees were mandated to use, this kind of duplication of effort and the resulting confusion could be avoided. The same principle would apply to any two departments with overlapping functions.

- **3. MIS can increase profits**. By pulling together information, MIS can help identify ways to improve products and expand the customer base, as in the following situation: A manager in a company with a good MIS thinks that one of the components used in manufacturing scooters has been ordered with unusual frequency at certain times of the year. She can access the company's database to see if and when there might have been unusual spikes in sales of that part and find out who is doing the unusual ordering. She discovers that a spike in sales takes place in winter, a time when other components needed to manufacture that product are not usually ordered. By identifying and then calling companies that are ordering the parts out-of-season, she discovers that the product develops problems in regions where the temperature changes are often sudden and significant. After some research, the company changes the metal compound used in making the part to one that is less affected by temperature changes. This presents the company's sales force with an opportunity to reach out to all companies that use that type of component to explain the improvement made, giving them an opportunity to capture new clients and increase market share.

A ROAD TO IMPROVED EFFICIENCY

MIS provides a valuable time-saving benefit to the workforce. Employees do not have to collect data manually for filing and analysis. Instead, that information can be entered quickly and easily into a computer program. As the amount of raw data grows too large for employees to analyze, business analysts can build programs to access the data and information in response to queries by management. With faster access to needed information, managers can make better decisions about procedures, future directions, and developments by competitors, and make them more quickly. For

CASE STUDY

A Major Northeastern Music School

The music school's endowment was not sufficient to support its plans for growth, which would require, among other things, building a new dormitory. In the past, the institution had relied primarily on members of the board and the president of the college to raise funds for the endowment through personal appeals to friends and associates, but it was clear to senior management that the amount now needed was far in excess of what they could possibly raise themselves. So they decided to hire a fundraiser.

Once the fundraiser was hired, he held a number of meetings with the board, the president, the CFO, and the faculty, many of whom are world-renowned musicians. Among other things, he discovered that the faculty had not been asked to help in fundraising in the past and that there had been little effort to solicit contributions from alumni—or their parents. He also gained the agreement of the faculty to provide him with lists of potential donors.

He then turned to the head of the information technology department to ask about the data available about current students, alumni, and their parents; subscribers to the various programs that the school offered, such as operas, jazz events, and instrumental performances; and past donors to the school. He explained that he needed to combine all these data—along with the information he hoped to get from the faculty and his own extensive lists of people who supported the arts—into an integrated fundraising data program.

He suggested a fundraising program that he had worked with before. On looking into it, the information systems manager discovered that the program would not be compatible with the school's systems. When he explored other programs, he found that while some were somewhat more compatible, the difference was not great enough to force the fundraiser to adapt to a new system. Inevitably, there were going to be major legacy issues because most of the programs that needed to be integrated had been bought on a noncentralized purchasing plan over the years. It was clear that a new comprehensive database would have to built to combine the data from the student informational database, the donor database, the subscriber mailing lists, and the new lists of potential donors.

During a follow-up board meeting that included the president and the CFO, building the new database became a point of contention because of its cost, the time it would take, and the added costs of hiring additional technology staff to ensure that the normal running of the school would not be affected by the work involved. The fundraiser presented information about his past results in fundraising that convinced the CFO., after careful analysis, that the effort eventually would bring in enough to cover those costs and raise the needed funds. The CFO also warned everyone involved in the decision-making that the schedule originally proposed would have to be extended, which carried its own costs.

In one of the many follow-up meetings, the school's recruitment officer pointed out that the new database would allow for broad circulation of a newsletter that could be used to attract new students as well as for future fundraising from alumni and potential donors. The value of being able to mix and match data—such as drawing a special audience for an "opening night" performance that could be priced higher than usual because it would be followed by a reception attended by the musicians—became clear to all the players. At that point the plan was approved. The outcome was positive: The funds needed for the dormitory were raised only a few months behind the original schedule.

MAKING IT HAPPEN

Since knowledge of the business and its customers and competitors is the key to an organization's continued health, companies must keep in mind from their inception the need for access to data about every aspect of the business, its procedures, and the knowledge of its employees. The important information involved in running the business is easy to handle when the company is small and has few employees. But, with growth, the amount of data accumulated can become overwhelming and the easy, frequent communication among employees can be impaired as people are divided into teams and functional areas. Because the responsibility for accounting systems, which tend to be the first that are automated, belongs to the CFO, the responsibility for adopting other technologies tends to stay with him or her as the organization grows. This means that the CFO should take steps early on to ensure that:

- the computer systems purchased for the various areas of the business are compatible, so that the data they contain can be merged;

"A well-structured MIS allows resources to be effectively organised and provides for consistent, appropriate information system flows across the organisation." New South Wales Office of the Children's Guardian

  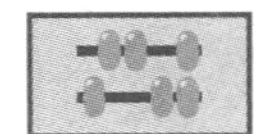      

example, MIS, drawing on past experience and knowledge gathered about competitors, can be used to predict the effect on sales if a product's price were to be altered.

In addition, MIS can help businesses to:

- enhance communication among employees;
- reduce expenses related to labor-intensive manual activities;
- reduce product development and marketing life cycles;
- increase their understanding of customers' needs;
- engage in business process reengineering;
- optimize their utilization of resources;
- identify and manage risks;
- make strategic decisions.

CONCLUSION

Preparing for the adoption of MIS when a company grows large enough to need such a system is critical to an organization's success. The CFO, who is usually the first to adopt IT systems for accounting purposes, can begin the process by careful oversight of the IT component of the business from the outset. Ensuring compatibility of the systems put in place as the organization grows—usually by adopting the right suite of applications and insisting that they are the only applications used throughout the organization—will make creation of sophisticated databases a far easier, and less costly, process. And it will facilitate eventual inclusion of programs that collect procedural and other knowledge garnered by employees.

- the company begins to collect the knowledge of its employees in forms that other people in the company can access when face-to-face communications become difficult;
- overarching MIS is developed by talented business analysts, so managers can make decisions based on a combination of the data and information about procedures gathered on various systems over time about such things as:
  a customers' needs;
  b the potential value of proposed new products;
  c the potential value of procedural innovations;
  d the risks inherent in strategic decisions.

MORE INFO

Books:

Fleisher, Craig S., and Babette E. Bensoussan. *Business and Competitive Analysis: Effective Application of New and Classic Methods*. Upper Saddle River, NJ: FT Press, 2007.

Haag, Stephen, Maeve Cummings, and Amy Phillips. *Management Information Systems for the Information Age*. 6th ed. New York: Irwin/McGraw-Hill, 2007.

Kroenke, David M. *Using MIS*. 2nd ed. Englewood Cliffs, NJ: Prentice Hall, 2008.

Kroenke, David, and Richard Hatch. *Management Information Systems*. 3rd ed. New York: McGraw Hill, 1994.

Post, Gerald V., and David L. Anderson. *Management Information Systems: Solving Business Problems with Information Technology*. 4th ed. New York: McGraw Hill, 2005.

Websites:

International Institute of Business Analysis (IIBA). Guide to the Business Analysis Body of Knowledge: www.theiiba.org/AM/Template.cfm?Section=Body_of_Knowledge

Journal of Management Information Systems: www.jmis-web.org

See Also:

★ Aligning Structure with Strategy: Recalibrating for Improved Performance and Increased Profitability (pp. 774–776)

★ Reducing Costs and Improving Efficiency by Outsourcing and Selecting Suppliers (pp. 918–920)

★ Reducing Costs through Production and Supply Chain Management (pp. 924–926)

✔ Key Components of an Optimal Enterprise Resource Planning System (p. 977)

✔ Setting Up a Key Risk Indicator (KRI) System (p. 1174)

NOTES

1 The Data Warehousing Information Center: www.dwinfocenter.org

2 Jackson, Peter. *Introduction to Expert Systems*. 3rd ed. Boston, MA: Addison Wesley, 1998.

3 Power, D. J. "A brief history of decision support systems." dssresources.com/history/dsshistory.html

4 Anon. "Data mining: What is data mining?" www.anderson.ucla.edu/faculty/jason.frand/teacher/technologies/palace/datamining.htm

5 Norton, Rob (ed). *CFO Thought Leaders: Advancing the Frontiers of Finance*. McLean, VA: Booz Allen Hamilton, 2005.

6 Zoufaly, Frederico. "Issues and challenges facing legacy systems." www.developer.com/mgmt/article.php/1492531

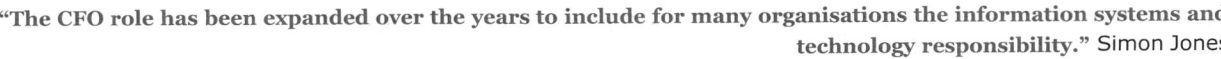

"The CFO role has been expanded over the years to include for many organisations the information systems and technology responsibility." Simon Jones

  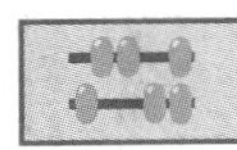      

Reducing Costs through Production and Supply Chain Management by Vinod Lall

EXECUTIVE SUMMARY

- There are numerous drivers of production and the supply chain, and there are several processes under each driver. These processes are associated with high overheads and offer opportunities for cost reduction.
- Cost reduction requires a complete knowledge and mapping of all costs, cycle times, purchases, inventories, suppliers, customers, logistics, and other service providers throughout the supply chain.
- Cost reduction in the supply chain often requires trade-off analysis amongst conflicting alternatives using the total cost approach.
- Successfully achieving supply chain cost savings requires the use of cross-functional teams with representation from marketing, design, procurement, production, distribution, and transportation employing an organized approach.

INTRODUCTION

IKEA, the Swedish home products retailer, is known for its good-quality, inexpensive products, which are typically sold at prices 30–50% below those of its competitors. While the price of products from other companies continues to rise over time, IKEA claims that its retail prices have been reduced by a total of 20% over the last four years. At IKEA, the process of cost reduction starts at product conception and continues throughout the process of design, sourcing of materials and components, production, and distribution. For example, the "Bang" mug has been redesigned many times to realize shipping cost savings. Originally, 864 mugs would fit into a pallet. After redesign a pallet held 1,280 mugs, and with a further redesign 2,024 mugs could be squeezed into a pallet, reducing shipping costs by 60%.

Organizations today are looking for opportunities to improve operational efficiencies and reduce cost without having a negative effect on customer service levels. Production and supply chain management can help to reduce costs by connecting every unit in the supply chain, fostering collaboration among supply chain partners, and offering visibility into the demand and supply side of the chain.

Production and supply chain management involves a number of drivers through which acquired raw materials are converted into finished goods for sale to customers. In turn, these drivers involve several processes that offer opportunities for cost reduction. Common drivers include procurement, design of the supply chain, inventory, transportation, warehousing, and collaboration. Cost reduction requires timely and improved decision-making for common processes under each driver.

PROCUREMENT

Procurement, also known as purchasing, is the process of acquiring raw materials, components, products, services, and other resources necessary either for the production processes themselves or for the support of production processes. Procurement processes ensure that supplies are available in the right place, in the right quantity, and at the right time. Buyers can play a major role in reducing supply chain costs by taking actions to reduce costs incurred in the flow of products from the suppliers to the ultimate customers. Some of the actions are discussed below.

Buyers must increase the flow of information throughout the supply chain, from the customer to the manufacturer and on to the supplier. This will make each entity in the chain aware of the inventory carried by the others and work towards the reduction of inventory without sacrificing customer service levels. Buyers must also take action to reduce cycle times, which will make the supply chain more responsive. To achieve a reduction in lead times, buyers must track and measure supplier lead-times, analyze trade-offs that result from lead time reduction, and then negotiate shorter lead times. Another action buyers can undertake to reduce supply chain cost is to select suppliers on the basis of their total supply chain capability and not just price, lead time, and quality levels.

DESIGN OF SUPPLY CHAIN

There are several principles under design of the supply chain that can help to reduce costs. These include component commonality, component modularity, and postponement.

Component commonality: The principle of component commonality focuses on the design and use of common components for families of products. When there are a large number of products in a supply chain, the inventory of components will naturally be large. Component commonality calls for the use of common components in a variety of products. This reduces costs not only by reducing inventory cost but also through reduced material cost, reduced production cost, and reduced product obsolescence. For example, a computer manufacturer can design common components such as memory and disk drives and use different combinations of these components to produce different finished products.

Component modularity: The principle of component modularity recommends that common subsystems be designed as modules to meet a broad range of feature requirements. This reduces the number of components that must be produced, kept in materials and repair parts inventory, and integrated into the product during the production process. This reduces procurement, manufacturing, and inventory costs, leading to a lower supply chain cost. Manufacturers of electronic products, for example, use the principle of modularity to design and assemble printers, computers, and so on.

Postponement: Postponement means delaying the bringing of products into their final form until close to the point of sale, when customer demand is known with greater accuracy. This results in a better match between supply and demand, leading to reduced costs mainly through inventory reductions. For example, a traditional garment manufacturer might dye the thread before knitting it into sweaters, whereas a garment manufacturer using postponement would postpone dying until the last point in the supply chain, when customer color preferences are known with a greater degree of certainty.

INVENTORY

Inventory resides at several locations in a supply chain, and the goal of inventory management is to reduce or eliminate inventory wherever it exists in the supply chain. This increases the velocity of movement of material through the chain, reducing the time from the point where material enters to the point of final consumption or sale. Slow movement of material leads to higher average inventories throughout the supply chain and results in higher inventory carrying costs.

"Compromise is but the sacrifice of one right or good in the hope of retaining another, too often ending in the loss of both." Tryon Edwards

Techniques that can help reduce these costs include the following.

The first technique is to use models such as vendor-managed inventory (VMI) and drop-shipments to reduce the number of locations where inventory is stored. With VMI the buyer of a product provides certain information to a vendor of that product, and the vendor takes full responsibility for maintaining an agreed level of inventory of the material, usually at the location where the buyer uses it.

Second, the same strategy should not be used to manage and control all inventory items regardless of their value. Instead, use ABC analysis (not the same as activity-based costing) to classify inventory into different classes and to maintain appropriately safe stock levels based on the class ABC analysis makes use of Pareto's Law and classifies inventory into classes A, B and C. A-class items are high in value and low in number, requiring tight control, while C-class items are low-value, high-number items that can be loosely controlled. Items classed as B include medium-value, medium-number items and typically require a blanket policy for control.

Other inventory management techniques include reducing the amount of transportation/pipeline inventory, and application of lean and just-in-time techniques to reduce or eliminate waste.

TRANSPORTATION

Transportation is used to move products from one location in the supply chain to another and is a significant component of the supply chain cost. A responsive transportation system can help to lower supply chain costs by achieving a high level of product availability at a reasonable price. A common technique for making a transportation system responsive is "cross-docking." Under cross-docking, products from a supplier are aggregated into trucks that arrive at distribution centers. At these centers the process of cross-docking means that products are exchanged between different trucks so that each truck leaving for a given retail location is loaded with products from several suppliers.

Transportation planners can reduce supply chain costs by reducing transportation costs by selecting low-cost modes of transport and using software to plan optimal routes and delivery schedules. The various modes of transport include water, rail, truck, intermodal, and air, and package carriers such as DHL, FedEx, and UPS. Having a low-cost supply chain depends closely on the selection and use of an appropriate mode of transport. Water is typically the least expensive, although slowest, whereas air is the most expensive and fastest. Transportation planners often use the approach of total cost analysis to select the best mode. This requires finding the total cost for each mode of transportation and using the mode that has the lowest total cost. The total cost is made up of, and considers, the trade-off between the cost of transport, cost of inventory at the origin, cost of inventory in the pipeline, and cost of inventory at the destination. Several companies develop and provide software that helps planners to construct transportation routes and schedules. Planners also use satellite-based global positioning systems to lower costs while still maintaining a responsive transport system.

WAREHOUSING

Warehouses are locations in the supply chain to and from which inventory is transported. Supply chain planners can help to reduce costs by making good decisions about warehousing strategies, such as the location and capacity of warehouses, and operational decisions such as the functions to be performed at the warehouse, the order-fulfilment methodology to be used, etc.

When deciding on the location of warehouses, planners use a trade-off analysis to choose between a large centralized location, which is more efficient, and multiple decentralized locations that offer a higher level of responsiveness. A number of factors including the quality, cost and availability of the workforce, tax effects, and proximity to customers are used in the analysis. Capacity decisions typically involve decisions on the need for and amount of extra capacity. Warehouses with excess capacity offer flexibility at a cost, while those with little excess capacity are more efficient. Trade-off analysis is also used to make decisions on warehouse capacity. Operational decisions deal with day-to-day processes such as stock placement, stock picking, and cycle counting. Warehouse planners use warehouse management system (WMS) software to plan and execute these processes.

COLLABORATION

Collaboration in a supply chain focuses on joint planning, coordination, and process integration between the firm and its suppliers, customers, and other partners such as the logistics providers. In addition to cost reduction, collaboration offers the advantages of business expansion to other areas, increased return on assets, improved customer service, reduced lead times, increased reliability and responsiveness to market trends, and a shorter time to market. Several options are available for achieving collaboration in a supply chain. These include:

- systems that transmit information between partners using technologies such as fax, e-mail, electronic data interchange (EDI), or extensible markup language (XML);
- systems such as electronic hubs and portals that facilitate the procurement of goods or services from electronic marketplaces, catalogs, and auctions;
- systems such as collaborative planning, forecasting and replenishment (CPFR) that permit shared collaboration rather

CASE STUDY

Transportation Analysis Pays Off for Computer Products Firm

A leading US manufacturer of computer accessories makes many products in China and then funnels them into a single distribution center on the West Coast that serves hundreds of retail clients. The company contracted with various freight services to send the products to retail customers using different modes of transportation, including small-package air, small-package ground, less-than-truckload, truckload, and heavy-weight air freight. The company wanted to have a better understanding of transportation processes and to control transportation costs. To do so, it hired the services of UPS Consulting (UPSC).

UPSC undertook a careful analysis and helped the manufacturer to reduce its domestic transportation costs by approximately 30% by the following means:

- negotiation of better rates with new freight service providers;
- setting up a returns program with a single carrier that picks up and returns the product using the most cost-effective transportation mode;
- development of a user-friendly one-page guide to carrier and mode selection that matches the weight and size of a parcel shipment with the preferred shipping method;
- helping employees to understand shipping parameters;
- establishing a compliance system that requires weekly meetings to review shipping activities and handle any special issues that arise.

  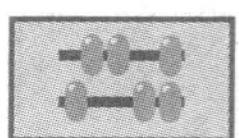      

than just a simple exchange of information amongst the supply chain partners.

The three systems identified above offer different levels of benefits and are associated with varying levels of expected costs. Organizations need to examine and quantify the benefits and costs of the alternative systems before selecting an appropriate system.

CONCLUSION

This article has explored major sources of cost savings in a production and supply chain and identified some techniques used by supply chain personnel such as buyers, inventory managers, and transportation planners. The techniques identified were discussed by grouping supply chain processes under the common supply chain drivers of procurement, design of the supply chain, inventory, transportation, warehousing, and collaboration.

MORE INFO

Books:

Chopra, Sunil, and Peter Meindl. *Supply Chain Management: Strategy, Planning & Operations*. 3rd ed. Upper Saddle River, NJ: Prentice Hall, 2006.

Jacobs, F. Robert, and Richard B. Chase. *Operations and Supply Management: The Core*. Boston, MA: McGraw-Hill/Irwin, 2008.

Websites:

Council of Supply Chain Management Professionals: cscmp.org

Supply Chain Council: www.supply-chain.org

UPS Supply Chain Solutions: www.ups-scs.com

See Also:

★ Countering Supply Chain Risk (pp. 812–813)
★ Profitability Analysis Using Activity-Based Costing (pp. 908–910)
★ Reducing Costs and Improving Efficiency by Outsourcing and Selecting Suppliers (pp. 918–920)
✔ Business Process Reengineering (p. 1150)
✔ Performing Total Cost of Ownership Analysis (p. 1170)
✔ Understanding Economic Efficiency Theory (p. 1126)
Michael Eugene Porter (p. 1299)

  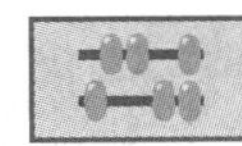   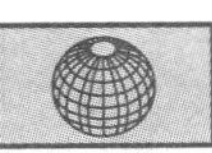   

Return on Talent by Subir Chowdhury

EXECUTIVE SUMMARY

- The performance of an organization is determined by the performance of its employees.
- Organizations must therefore measure return on talent as well as return on investment.
- Knowledge is one of the most important factors for business success. If knowledge assets are increased, related factors such as sales will also increase.
- Talent—or intellectual capital—has fast become one of the most significant areas of business activity and competition.

INTRODUCTION

The performance of an organization is entirely determined by the performance of its employees. This bold statement deserves further study. If the determinant of corporate performance is not its employees, what is? Is it strategic intent? Core competencies? Manufacturing? Is it proprietary technologies? The best equipment and laboratories? A visionary CEO? Yes, it's all of these things. And all of these things are created and constantly improved by employees. Talented employees are the agents of change. Good employees join in to help implement new initiatives. Others follow at various times, depending on when they can break the bounds of their comfort zone to enter the area of change, uncertainty, and opportunity. They fall by the wayside because they were in the wrong job.

It is broadly recognized that past performance is not a reliable indicator of potential or future success. Yet many organizations continue to use past performance to identify high-potential employees. How much true talent is overlooked by this practice? Overlooked and misplaced high-potential employees stagnate. The problem of identifying, positioning, and compensating high-potential employees spans all disciplines and levels, from the loading dock to the boardroom. Lost and underused employees represent enormous, largely unreckoned financial loss. A second problem is the difficulty of measuring the financial contribution of employees beyond global measures such as revenues per employee.

To focus a successful organization, managers must use a new tool called return on talent (ROT). Most organizations focus on return on investment (ROI), and fail to understand the key strategy of how to increase ROI by increasing ROT.

HARNESSING TALENT

ROT has the power to revolutionize business. ROT is calculated by dividing the knowledge generated and applied by the investment in talent. You need to address the dilemma of how to measure an intangible asset and how to generate high ROT value. For decades, organizations have used key metrics like ROI and ROA (return on assets) to determine value. But increasingly an effective new-economy organization will use ROT. Current business measurements merely measure the use of capital, but ROT is expressed as follows:

$$\text{ROT} = \frac{\text{Knowledge generated \& applied}}{\text{Investment in talent}}$$

If you have talented people, knowledge is just one component. The generation of knowledge is the most important thing talent can provide. Now you may realize that knowledge generated by the talent doesn't equal knowledge applied, right? And if knowledge isn't applied, the company loses most of the market value of that knowledge. Whatever knowledge a person generates in a year divided by how much is invested in that particular person is the value.

If an employee generates many innovative ideas but never implements any of them, that person fails to generate any value because the return to the company is zero. Knowledge generated does not necessarily mean knowledge applied. So value is knowledge generated *and* applied. Knowledge becomes an asset only when it's captured and used effectively; if it isn't effectively applied, it can't generate any yield or ROI. Generating a lot of knowledge within organizations doesn't add any value unless that knowledge is used in effective strategy formulation. Knowledge assets, like money or equipment, are worth cultivating only in the context of strategy. You can't define and manage intellectual assets unless you know what you are trying to do with them. This is the backbone of the knowledge economy; success in this field depends on mastery of talent, just as success in manufacturing relies on the skilful employment of plant and supply chains.

THE VALUE OF KNOWLEDGE

Return on Talent

The value of knowledge generated increases with its effective deployment. Effective knowledge generated means high ROT. It leads to a creative workforce, innovations, smooth processes, continuous product improvements, and improved communications. It helps management to be flexible, to capitalize on opportunities, and to keep pace with the changing business climate. Talented people influence those around them, and their knowledge is shared over time. Top knowledge generators should be rewarded. If managers expect top talents to achieve their maximum performance and produce maximum return, they must not place them in routine jobs.

ROT measures the payback from investment in people; it shows whether managers are hiring the right people and how effectively they use them to achieve business success. It can be a quantitative or qualitative measurement, based on management's viewpoint. Are managers getting the maximum payback on their investment? If managers want to see quantitative results, they need to put a price on knowledge generated, based on the results achieved. Talent generates knowledge, which is one of the greatest assets in the global economy. True knowledge brings creativity and innovation, and adds value to the company. Knowledge has become a key production factor, along with traditional resources such as raw materials, buildings, and machinery. Companies that measure the knowledge generated and applied by their talent can make their investments in talent more profitable. Further, companies cannot improve what they do not measure.

Effective managers use ROT measurements to make their investments in talent more profitable. ROT measurements help monitor performance, forecast opportunity, and determine the profitability of their investment in talent. To make their investment more profitable, management must constantly measure ROT, continuously improve ROT, and nurture, develop, and refresh talent.

Return on Knowledge

Return on knowledge generated and applied is more difficult to calculate and track. Knowledge creates real wealth through multiple applications, for example, repeating the same application pervasively through a corporation, or finding new applications to new situations. Knowledge applications have breadth (across organizations) and length (in time). Years may pass between the generation of knowledge and its first application, let alone subsequent applications.

"There is no such thing as great talent without great will-power." Honoré de Balzac

  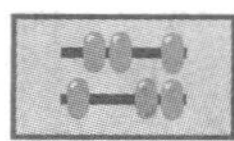      

In order to properly account for the value of knowledge generated, initial estimates need to be made and refined yearly as applications appear on the horizon and then are realized. Leading indicators of return are based on projections of the probability of each anticipated application and the monetary value of each application summed over all anticipated applications.

Forward-looking projections and backward-looking allocations are both judgments, and there's no reason to believe that one is any better than the other. Indeed, projections made while focusing on the knowledge generated may be the more reliable of the two. It is certain that the combination of early projections, after-the-fact allocations, and annual updating and tracking between knowledge generated and the first of a series of applications, greatly improves the capability to measure and link return on knowledge generated and applied, and investment in talent.

CONCLUSION

Organizations that constantly improve ROT grow at a rapid rate. Management can monitor the performances of individuals as well as teams. Knowledge is one of the most important factors for business success. If knowledge assets are increased, then all other related factors like production and sales will be automatically increased. Consequently, organizations should try to improve ROT continuously to sustain sales growth. ROT is a superb key performance indicator, and one that is set to be measured and managed in much the same way as financial issues.

MAKING IT HAPPEN

- **Build a team focused on developing talent.** To reach high ROT scores, you need a talent team. Often you find one or two good people who can generate knowledge and perhaps even apply that knowledge, but you don't have a talent team that can leverage their ideas. Most of the individual talent in a company can be innovative if the team dynamics are right. If you have a low ROT score, you may have a dysfunctional team. ROT scores are not fixed; they change over time.
- **Measure and monitor ROT.** If you are a manager who hires and invests in talent, you need to monitor ROT closely. In a company the size of General Motors or General Electric, you probably view salaries as a regular fixed cost that is standard. The portion that may vary is how much you invest in certain ideas. If you see that certain employees are not generating enough knowledge and success relative to your investment in them, that should be a big red flag because your ROT value might become negative, or much lower than your competitor's ROT value.
- **Decide how to increase ROT throughout the organization.** If you were hired to manage talent with a low ROT score (perhaps even a negative value), you need to do some things to boost the ROT fast. How do you turn around an organization and achieve higher ROT scores? You do it person by person, function by function. You have to assess the talent on your team and find out who and what is bringing the most profit to the company, who and what is winning and keeping the best customers. Your first task is to perform talent diagnostics. You might easily spend six months identifying all your talent and determining which ones you can work with to turn the company around. But usually you don't have six months to do talent diagnostics. So you need to do it faster, even in a large company. There is much to be said for focusing on quick, high-profile actions that build support and momentum behind the need to increase ROT.

Many managers assess employees' talent intuitively—they don't necessarily need a measurement tool. Every manager, however, benefits from having a tool to measure and monitor ROT. Apple soared when Steve Jobs was CEO, and faded when he left. It soared again when he returned as Apple's CEO. It doesn't mean that Jobs was a good or bad person. He was a very effective person in that environment. Many good CEOs fail in environments in which there is no structure. They go by intuition. After you identify the key talents, give them the authority and resources to boost the ROT team score. The talent diagnostic may show that in one division you have a lot of talented people, while in a different division you have very few. You have to cross functions, making sure you balance the talent according to the needs of the organization, and then challenge each talent and team to reach a financial goal.

MORE INFO

Books:

Becker, Brian E., Mark A. Huselid, and Richard W. Beatty. *The Workforce Scorecard: Managing Human Capital to Execute Strategy*. Cambridge, MA: Harvard Business School Press, 2005.

Brockbank, Wayne, and David Ulrich. *The HR Value Proposition*. Cambridge, MA: Harvard Business School Press, 2005.

Chowdhury, Subir. *The Talent Era: Achieving a High Return on Talent*. Upper Saddle River, NJ: Financial Times Prentice Hall, 2002.

Kaplan, Robert S., and David P. Norton. *Alignment: Using the Balanced Scorecard to Create Corporate Strategies*. Cambridge, MA: Harvard Business School Press, 2006.

See Also:

★ Managing Retirement Costs (pp. 77–79)

✔ Understanding the Financial Aspects of Employing People (p. 1183)

Gary Becker (p. 1270)

"All our talents increase in the using, and every faculty, both good and bad, strengthens by exercise." Anne Brontë

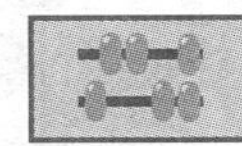

Risk Management: Beyond Compliance

by Bill Sharon

EXECUTIVE SUMMARY

- The boundaries between risk management and compliance have eroded over the past decade, to the detriment of both functions.
- The definition of risk should be expanded to include opportunities and uncertainties, not just hazards.
- The context for assessing operational risk is business strategy.
- The role of risk managers needs to expand so that they become coordinators of the risk information that is readily available in operational and business units.
- The perception of risk is dependent on one's organizational responsibilities, and the convergence of those perceptions is the central focus of the management of risk.

INTRODUCTION

Over the past decade the line between risk management and compliance has been blurred to the point where, in many organizations, it is impossible to determine if they are not one and the same. In part, this confusion between the two functions was initiated and then exacerbated by the passage of the Sarbanes–Oxley Act of 2002 and the implementation of Basel II. Both of these events consumed a great deal of resources, and many consulting firms labeled these efforts "risk management." They are, in fact, compliance requirements designed to protect stakeholders and, in the latter case, ensure the viability of the financial system. They are not designed for, and nor can their implementation achieve, the management of risk in individual companies or financial institutions.

This confusion between compliance and risk management has led to a defensive posture in dealing with the uncertainties of the competitive business environment. Risk has been confined to the analysis of what could go wrong rather than what needs to go right. Risk management organizations have become the arbiters of what constitutes risk and have assumed an adversarial relationship with business managers, particularly in capital allocation exercises. Failures and scandals are met with calls for more regulation, the implementation of regulations becomes the province of risk management organizations, and the execution of strategy (arguably the area in most need of risk management) becomes further separated from any kind of disciplined analysis.

AN EXPANDED DEFINITION OF RISK

As Peter Bernstein tells us in his book *Against the Gods: The Remarkable Story of Risk*, the word risk comes from the old Italian *risicare*, which means "to dare." Daring is the driving idea behind business, the idea that a product or a service can achieve excellence and value in the marketplace. Strategy necessarily incorporates risk from the perspective of those actions which are required for its success.

In 1996 Robert G. Eccles, a former Harvard Business School professor, and Lee Puschaver, a partner at Price Waterhouse (now PricewaterhouseCoopers), developed the concept of the "business risk continuum." They argued that organizations that were successful in managing risk were those that focused on uncertainties and opportunities as much as they did on hazards. The context for evaluating risk in this manner is business strategy. This idea—that the definition of risk should be expanded to include those actions that an organization needed to embrace to achieve its goals—was revolutionary and codified what some companies were already beginning to initiate. Unfortunately, the narrow view of risk has prevailed for the past decade, and Eccles' and Puschaver's work has essentially been ignored.

The overwhelming emphasis of most risk organizations today is on the hazard end of the scale. Dot.com, Enron, and now subprime, along with the increased focus on terrorism, cataclysmic natural disasters, and the potential for pandemic diseases, have placed most complex organizations in a defensive posture. The problem with this approach is that risk driven from the hazard perspective is experienced as overhead in the operational disciplines and business units; it's a cost of business, not an activity that enhances value or improves the possibility of success.

By expanding the definition of risk (or returning to its original meaning) companies can harness the inherent risk management abilities and information available throughout their organization and develop a predictive process to address mission-critical tasks. Understanding how risk is perceived and how people react to those perceptions is an essential step in managing the opportunities and uncertainties inherent in implementing a business strategy.

ORGANIZATIONAL ROLES AND THE PERCEPTION OF RISK

Daniel Kahneman and Amos Tversky, the authors of "Prospect Theory," conducted a variety of experiments on the perception of risk and the responses that people had to identical information presented in different contexts. Among their conclusions they determined that:

1. emotion always overrides logic in the decision-making process,
2. people suffer from cognitive dysfunction in making decisions because they never have enough information,
3. people are not risk-averse, they are loss-averse.

While these conclusions may be unsettling to those involved in quantitative risk analysis, all three are useful assumptions around which to build a proactive risk management process. Emotion is at the core of any business—the desire to produce the best product, offer the best service, and compete in the marketplace comes from passion, not analytics. Managing risk is about managing emotion, not eliminating it.

From an organizational perspective, the perception of risk is colored by one's responsibilities. In the operational environment, technologists see opportunities in deploying software and hardware. HR professionals define success as the attraction and retention of high-performance employees. In business units, opportunities require risks to be taken in order to capture market share or evolve a product line to the next level. Often these business leaders are unaware of the operational capabilities and capacities on which they must rely to achieve their goals. Operational managers often lack clarity on the business models they support. Individually, these perceptions of risk tell only part of the story and require the balance of all of the organizational perceptions in order for the cognitive dissonance to be managed and mitigated.

In this context, risk managers become coordinators of business intelligence rather than arbiters of what is and is not a risk. The management of risk is a communication

"Real commitment is rare in today's organization . . . 90% of the time what passes for commitment is compliance."
Peter Senge

process that is central to the success of the enterprise rather than an overhead process that compliance so often becomes. Participation in risk management is equivalent to participating in the development of business strategy. The desire not to lose (rather than the misguided view of being averse to "daring") is the underlying motivation for the process.

Figure 1.The risk perception continuum

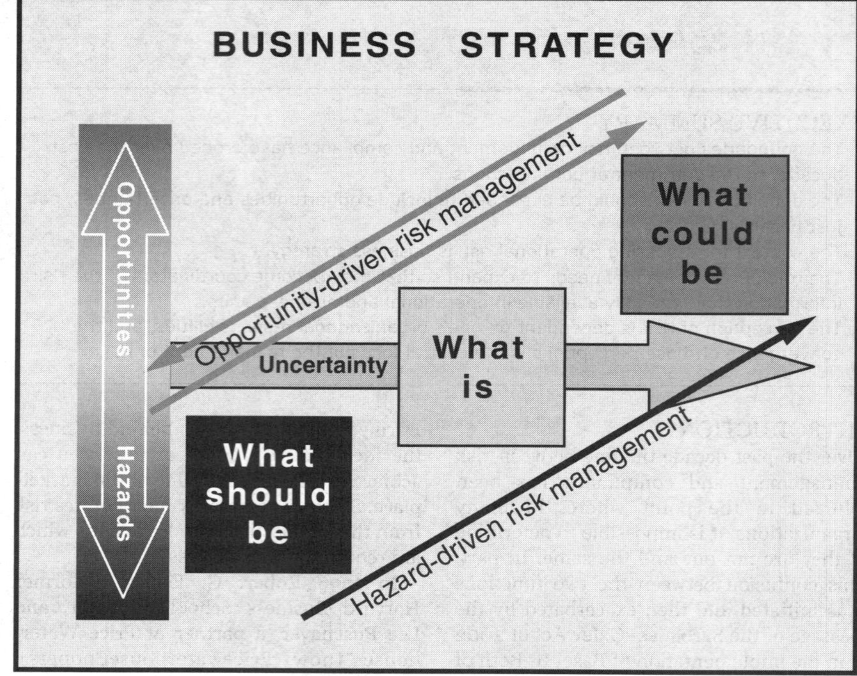

THE RISK PERCEPTION CONTINUUM

The risk perception continuum (Figure 1) summarizes the categories of risk and how they can be placed in an operational context. Using Eccles and Puschaver's concept of the three categories of risk, an organization can assign one of three different perceptions to determine the source and value of risk information:

- What Should Be is the perception of risk that comes from external standards. These are "best practices" for both operational and business managers. The measures involved determine the degree to which an organization is aligned with these practices in the context of what the organization wants to achieve. For example, alignment with "best practices" for a data center is likely to be more important for a financial institution than an advertising agency.It is tempting to place compliance functions in this area and track these issues as hazards. This is a mistake on two levels. First, the risk management process is central to the success of the organization and needs the oversight of the audit function. Putting them in the same unit creates a conflict of interest, one that is clearly identified in the Committee of Sponsoring Organization's (COSO) enterprise risk management framework. Second, compliance is a legal and regulatory function. One does not assess the risk of not complying. The primary audiences for this information are regulators and external auditors, and the ability to adhere to these requirements is really the baseline for participating in the marketplace.
- What Is comprises the uncertainty of the operating environment of the organization. This is the area where quantitative analysis and hedging are done to determine the upside and downside of a deal. It is here that both business and operational managers have the greatest impact on the management of risk, and it is here that the communication of the different perceptions of risk is most critical. The convergence of these perceptions constitutes valuable business intelligence.The classic example of managing risk in this manner is the HR hiring process. The MD of equity trading in an investment bank may have an urgent need for a large number of junior traders. The human resources department has a responsibility to ensure that the people the MD wants to hire have actually attended the universities claimed on their resumés and that they have passed a strenuous background check. The tension between these two perceptions is satisfied by the candidates signing a letter accepting their immediate dismissal should they be found to have misrepresented their qualifications. The organization embraces the risk that the contributions to the strategy will outweigh the potential for any damage that might be done during a relatively small window of time.
- What Could Be is the repository of the strategy of the organization and the perception of what risks need to be taken for it to be achieved. This perception is dynamic and responds to the demands of the marketplace, as well as the capabilities of the operating environment.

Perhaps the best known example of how strategy drives the management of risk in an organization is the behavior of the US space agency, NASA, following John F. Kennedy's announcement that there would be an American on the moon by the end of the 1960s. In recently released tapes of meetings between Kennedy and James Webb, the director of NASA, the impact of strategy on operational capabilities is well illustrated. Webb advises Kennedy of the vagaries of space and the need to expand the space program to include a number of interim steps necessary to gain a better understanding before anyone can go to the moon. Kennedy listens and then tells Webb that he doesn't care about space, he wants to get to the moon before the Russians.What's interesting about this exchange is that Kennedy was defining a strategic goal that had no near-term likelihood of being achieved. He was also using that strategic goal to redefine the risk. The technical risk was unknowable at the time, but the political risk was quantifiable. Strategy organizes the operational environment and focuses it in specific directions. It requires operational managers to converge their perceptions of risk with the goals of the organization.

Figure 1 also demonstrates the difference between driving risk management from the opportunity or strategy perspective as opposed to the hazard perspective. The latter approach tries to force standards up

  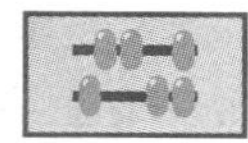    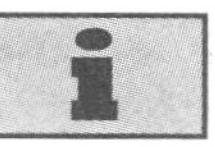  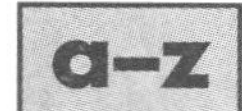

Figure 2.Converging the perceptions of risk

through the organization. Operational managers experience this as an audit process and, other than quarterly reports from the audit committee, very little of this information receives much attention from the senior executives responsible for implementing strategy.

Alternatively, risk management driven from the opportunity perspective creates a communications vehicle for the entire organization. This is a bi-directional process because, as the strategy is communicated into the operating environment, the organization responds with business intelligence.

IMPLEMENTING A RISK MANAGEMENT PROCESS

Using the organization's strategy as the context (rather than "best practices" or regulatory requirements), the first step in the process is to ask operational managers to identify the risks that must be embraced in order to achieve this strategy (operational disciplines are defined as those organizational units that do not generate income, i.e. finance, HR, IT, PR, etc.). Once identified, these activities are assessed—usually using a RAG (red, amber, green) rating—to determine the likelihood of their being achieved.

There are two important steps in this first stage of the process that are often lacking in risk management programs.

1 Operational managers are asked to predict a risk rating, usually on a quarterly basis, for the next four quarters. This provides the organization with more valuable data than point-in-time risk assessments, whose shelf-life tends to be quite short. It also provides operational managers with the ability to communicate anticipated challenges in the future and/or illustrate how current challenges will be positively addressed over time.

2 Operational managers are also asked to note whether the activities they believe must be undertaken have sufficient funding. Once this information has been collated, the organization has a map of where it is investing in managing risks central to the strategy and where it is not.

Operational managers are then asked to complete an actual vs. planned assessment at the end of each quarter. This is not an exercise to assess competency, but rather another channel for communication in the risk management process. Strategy may change, requiring a new perception of risk. Operational awareness of greater or lesser challenges may impact the original risk rating. Departures from the original assessment are expected and should be viewed as business intelligence rather than as a scoring of prescient abilities.

Once the process is established with the operational managers, the second stage of the risk management process can be implemented. Here, business managers are asked to contribute their perceptions of risk to the mission-critical operational activities that have been identified. For example, if the IT department identified the rollout of a new operating system as a risk that needed to be embraced and rated it as an amber or a red, given the exposure in maintenance and security, the business managers might rate it as a green as they have no clear knowledge of the technical issues. Differences in the perception of risk are expected and provide an opportunity to understand risk across operational and business disciplines.

The third stage (Figure 2) in the risk management process is the audit review, which not only validates the process itself, but also uses the risk assessments as a

CASE STUDY

JP Morgan—Managing the Risk of Outsourcing

The risk management process can be scaled to encompass the entire organization, a specific business unit, or a large project. A year prior to outsourcing 40% of its technology, JP Morgan initiated a predictive risk management program that converged the perceptions of technology and business managers and established an IT risk profile for each business unit.

- The IT self-assessment process was conducted quarterly on a global basis, and provided the bank with a portfolio view of IT operational risk across all business units.
- The risk profiles allowed the bank to negotiate service levels based on an understanding of where the internal IT group was supporting the business strategy and where improvements were necessary.
- The IT self-assessment process was transferred to the successful vendors and the business units continued to contribute their perceptions, resulting in a shared process between the vendors and the bank.
- Perhaps the most important result of the process was a better understanding in the business units of IT capabilities and capacities. The organization gained an understanding of the technology that provided a competitive advantage (and should therefore be retained in the bank) and of the infrastructure and shared applications that could be turned over to external vendors.

  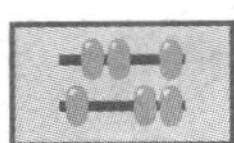      

source for audit oversight of specific operational activities. The convergence of perception between operational and business managers and the audit function provides the risk management process with the widest possible range of understanding of risks to the strategy.

Once this process is established, metrics can be applied to risk ratings, operational disciplines can be weighted in importance by business unit, and portfolio views of risk can be developed across business units.

CONCLUSION

No risk management function can ensure that negative events won't happen. The complexity of the markets and the speed of change create exposures that are difficult to predict. Managing risk as a process that engages the entire enterprise in the achievement of the business strategy does, however, create a resilient organization that can better respond to difficulties that always arise.

MAKING IT HAPPEN

The operational risk management process described in this article begins with the business strategy but ultimately engages the entire organization. Senior management needs not only to endorse the process but also to participate in and use it on a continuing basis. The early stages of the process require patience, and some care should be taken in the initial implementation.

- There is often confusion in the operational disciplines about what is a risk to the business strategy and what is a best-practice or compliance requirement. Risk managers will likely need to assist operational managers in this distinction.
- Simplicity is key in the early stages of the risk management process. Many efforts collapse under their own weight when organizations attempt to accomplish too much in a short period. Risk management is about leveraging existing expertise; complex metrics can be applied once the system is robust.
- Using the risk management process as a communication process, not only for challenges but also for capacities and creative solutions, is essential in making it a robust vehicle for the generation of business intelligence.

MORE INFO

Book:

Bernstein, Peter L. *Against the Gods, The Remarkable Story of Risk*. New York: Wiley, 1996.

Article:

Kloman, Felix. "Risk management and Monty Python, part 2." *Risk Management Reports* 32:12 (December 2005). Online at tinyurl.com/34hwowx

Report:

Puschaver, Lee, and Robert G. Eccles. "In pursuit of the upside: The new opportunity in risk management." Leading Thinking on Issues of Risk, PricewaterhouseCoopers, 1998.

Websites:

COSO (Committee of Sponsoring Organizations of the Treadway Commission): www.coso.org

Prospect theory: prospect-theory.behaviouralfinance.net and www.sjsu.edu/faculty/watkins/prospect.htm

Risk Metrics: www.riskmetrics.com

Strategic Operational Risk Management Solutions (SORMS): www.sorms.com

See Also:

★ The Effect of SOX on Internal Control, Risk Management, and Corporate Governance Best Practice (pp. 333–335)
★ A Total Balance Sheet Approach to Financial Risk (pp. 113–114)
✔ Applying Stress-Testing to Operational Risk Exposure (p. 1142)
✔ Establishing a Framework for Assessing Risk (p. 1028)
✔ Understanding and Calculating the Total Cost of Risk (p. 990)
Mastering Risk, Volume 1: Concepts (p. 1393)

"Risk occurs when you don't know what you're doing." Warren Buffett

  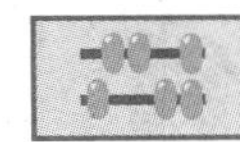   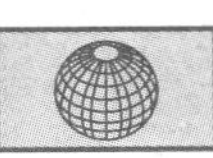   

Smart Use of Reputation Capital: How to Benefit from Different Reputation Investment Strategies

by Joachim Klewes and Robert Wreschniok

EXECUTIVE SUMMARY

- The importance of building reputation as the "social capital" of an organization, including its key components *trust* and *credibility* under societal, market, and media conditions of the 21st century.
- Four strategies for managing reputation capital used in business to increase valuable trust capital and to protect against losses, which should be mastered by every reputation manager.
- Which strategy to choose according to the type of risk, company, and/or time.
- The fact that today's management essentially consists of (communicative) dealing with crisis and change, and how leadership can contribute to an organization and its employees becoming "crisis-proof" long before a crisis occurs.

INTRODUCTION

Today, those responsible for corporate communications are facing tremendous challenges. They are forced to take ever greater risks regarding reputation, and increasingly they are compelled to use more radical methods and messages in the traditional media—above all in advertising communication. This appears to be the only way to catch the attention of consumers and stakeholders.

On the other hand, the new social media, digital networks, and blogs seem to require the exact opposite—i.e. communicating a brand in a way that will allow the brand to be cherished for its own sake. This requires a radically new way of communicating: a dialog instead of the conventional one-way communication from sender to receiver. With this new approach, the core message counts less than the interactions between consumers and a company. The consumer is able to use social media to understand and experience a company and a brand, instead of having to simply believe promises. In this new world where consumer needs are met directly with customized offers, past recipes for success no longer count. Both creativity and wastage are eliminated. Andrew Robertson, the CEO of BBDO, one of the largest global advertising agencies, used strong words to emphasize this when, years ago, Google founders Sergey Brin and Larry Page presented their new advertising concept to him: "Guys, you killed the fucking magic."

In the following article the authors highlight four different approaches—what we call "investment strategies for reputation capital"—that companies can use to boost awareness and trust at the same time.

REPUTATION AND STRATEGY

Reputation management has experienced much unrest and undergone rapid changes in recent times. A few years ago Warren Buffet was able to say that a good reputation can take 20 years to develop, but that it can be ruined in as little as five minutes. This seems strangely remote now. It might still take five minutes to ruin a reputation, but the idea that anyone might steadily work on and build a corporate reputation over a period of 20 years is rather unrealistic nowadays.

Today, anyone with access to the Internet can form and voice their opinion without depending on classical media. As a consequence, published opinion no longer equates to public opinion. Scandals appear more often and proliferate more quickly than ever before—a development that harbors major risks for companies. But it is not just the channels of communication that have changed; market conditions themselves are also different. The shift in the perceived importance of hard and soft corporate factors—a shift that now increasingly favors intangible assets—has resulted in a heightened risk to reputation.

This took on especially drastic forms during the recent financial and economic crisis. During this time many public companies were hit by a "reputation penalty," and the share prices of some of the leading global players fell as much as 50% below the company's actual market value. Furthermore, the number of companies per industry that are capable of supplying comparable products of good quality and at reasonable prices is growing explosively. Increasingly keen competition in itself can result in an impasse, since these "hard" corporate and product factors of the competing companies have in many cases become only marginally distinguishable. So intangible assets need to be stressed to express the unique selling-point (customer-centricity and satisfaction, user-friendliness, loyalty programs, etc.) to clients and shareholders.

In other words, these are hard times for "relaxed" reputation strategies, since in this dynamic environment you can no longer be sure that the strongest reputation will win in the long run. As a result, more and more companies are turning to reputation strategies whose mechanisms are comparable to those of conventional corporate strategies. Such strategies "actively influence the effects of competition and the speed of change. This lends strategy an essential effect: it shortens time." (von Oetinger, 2003).

Consequently, there are three central questions today for any strategy in the area of corporate communications. The first concerns the resources one needs to implement such a strategy, and how to use these in order to quickly achieve one's goals. The second question is how best to balance effectiveness and efficiency in the process. And last but not least, a reputation manager should aim to find the adequate ratio of reputation risks versus chances in the light of his reputation goals.

WHY REPUTATION MATTERS

Today, more and more corporate managers and their communications experts ask themselves how they can make their company the customer's first choice in its industry. Or how to make it a company whose excellent reputation precedes it. A company that is the first choice for high-worth job candidates. A company that enjoys a trust bonus from banks and investors when capital needs to be increased or an issue floated to ensure continued growth. Or a company whose advice is sought by politicians during essential legislation processes because they trust its integrity, expertise, experience, and technical competence.

Such companies are the exception, yet they do exist in most industries—much admired, sometimes marveled at, and always keenly watched. Their competitors sense that there are ways they might themselves catch up by making targeted investments in their own reputations. For reputation allows companies to generate added value through favorable exchange conditions. After all, reputation is considered to be the "social capital" of a company, or an indirect catalyst that can amplify a company's social capital.

"It's amazing how easy the Internet makes it to destroy a business without creating another one in its place."
Robert Levine

Reputation is a key corporate asset; it can be managed and accumulated, and it can be exchanged for:

- the legitimization of positions of power;
- social respect;
- a price premium for goods and services offered;
- an increased willingness by others to hold equity stakes in times of crisis;
- a willingness to invest preferably in the shares of a company.

The currency in all these exchange activities is identical for all stakeholders of a company: it is called "trust." In times of economic crisis the value of this special capital becomes especially obvious. For, as so often, the true value of something is not recognized until after it has been lost. Today we have almost forgotten what we were reading in 2008 as the real-estate and financial crisis slowly wound its way into public awareness. As early as the spring of that year, similar opinions could be found in economic commentary in the leading international press; these can best be summarized in the following statement, "When the new economic bubble burst at the beginning of the 21st century, money was burned. During the real-estate and financial crisis, not money but trust was burned." Somehow, it was a very comforting message for many readers: "No money is getting burned," the message read, "just trust. So don't worry, it can't possibly be that bad."

In October of the same year, people realized that this was not true; this was the month in which the investment bank Lehman Brothers went bust. Hardly anyone in America or Europe had been capable of imagining that such a bank, with its good name and renowned address, would simply go bankrupt. But when exactly this happened, trust was thoroughly shaken—trust not only in this individual bank, but in the whole banking system. To this day, reputation surveys show that trust still has not been completely restored. The burning of trust—or reputation capital—resulted in the greatest economic crisis of recent decades, and as a consequence, in a gigantic destruction of assets in the stock markets. Trust-engendering company reputation is now fueled primarily by factors that are defined by economic competence; in short, by an intact economic reputation. Therefore, the next economic and financial crisis will also primarily express itself as a crisis of trust.

FOUR STRATEGIES FOR MANAGING REPUTATION CAPITAL

The authors' consulting experience clearly shows them that, today, the logic and mechanisms of successfully accumulating reputation capital increasingly resemble the rules and investment strategies used in the actual economy for maximizing company assets or protecting them from losses. The growth of capital on the financial as well as on the reputation level follows very similar strategies, which can help to identify existing risks and make them calculable and manageable. Following our observations of the market, we can identify four types of reputation strategy:

- hedge strategies;
- growth strategies;
- value strategies;
- total-return strategies.

These are used in business to increase valuable trust capital and to protect against losses. Table 1 shows the differences between the four approaches and explains why not every strategy works with every company, and why organizations will choose one approach rather than another on the basis of the type of risk, the type of company, and/or time.

Hedge Strategies

Hedge strategies have a high degree of inherent risk, but in the right circumstances they are highly efficient. They focus on achieving goals in as short a time as possible. Essentially, a hedge strategy is about leveraging the use of reputation drivers by focusing communication strongly on one issue or person so that the reputation result will persist for a certain time period regardless of the company's actual situation. Hedge strategies include reputation management approaches that are very closely linked to the company strategy. This is also where the hedging takes place—provided that the business strategy works. If it works in the sense that the projected sales targets are met, or the planned market penetration or market leadership is achieved, this success will satisfy the expectations stimulated by the communications strategy. Meeting expectations is at the core of these reputation strategies, as a bet is being made that a promise made will be fulfilled. Companies and politicians use hedge strategies to establish charismatic leaders and to control high-profile topics on the public agenda in hope that this will result in short-term positive effects on their own reputation. They focus on networking with holders of institutional reputation or opinion leaders in order to accumulate—within a very short period of time—the social and cultural capital necessary for pursuing or securing their goals.

Attempts to implement hedge strategies are not only made by small companies,

Table 1. The four reputation strategies

	Hedging	*Growth*	*Value*	*Total return*
Main feature	Monothematic, proactive, target group-focused communication	Focused profile development along carefully analyzed reputation drivers and industry issues	Consciously internalized, structure-oriented reputation building	Focusing on products or services without trying to reinforce them with communication
Investment in communication	High spending for external communication—often also reach-oriented	Investment balanced between internal expenses (e.g. for analyses) and external communication	Clearly higher investment in internal process optimization and measured efforts in external communication	Communication efforts limited to a minimum
Opportunities	High-profile reputation established rapidly	Broadly hedged, well-founded reputation profile with several options available	High multiplication effect from employees and industry circles	Low degree of attention as long as company is not in public crisis
Risks	Words and deeds do not match; public criticism; expectations not met	Low degree of profile development compared to aggressive competitors	Reputation profile not supported by wide recognition	Crash in a crisis as there is no trust buffer. Internally: lack of orientation and support for corporate policy
Especially suited for	Companies in start-up phases	Companies in oligopolistic markets	B2B, hidden champions, large "middle class"	Unsuitable today
Time dimension	Short-term	Medium-term	Long-term	Long-term

"Economists arguing about the economy: they're like angry astrologers arguing about the effects of Saturn." Simon Carr

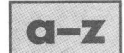

start-ups, or gamblers. Even internationally active corporations engage in risky reputation-hedging strategies, as in the context of spin-offs, M&A transactions, or even in marketing. For example, much of the automobile industry, which discovered its "green soul" a few years ago, has so far not been able to keep its promises on a large scale. The very same incongruity may be found in energy corporations which project the image of pumping solar energy instead of oil; or the biofoods industry, which has been growing at a breathtaking pace and sometimes creates the illusion of having convinced farmers in China of the benefits of this new way of farming. It does not require prophetic skills to foresee the failure of the hedge strategy in at least some of these fields.

The inherent risk of this type of strategy is exemplified by BP's "beyond petroleum" approach. Its former CEO, John Brown, developed BP's vision as the company of the future, which does business in an ecologically correct manner. In this vision, he focused on more than the short-term benefits for shareholders and drew attention to the positive effects for society. Reality, however, showed that corporate responsibility toward shareholders and long-term responsibility toward the environment and society were incompatible at BP. For example, the company communicated the message that greenhouse gases represent a danger to the planet and heavily advertised ecologically compatible energies. At the same time, nongovernmental organizations pointed out—also by means of massive internet campaigns—what the company's factual reality was, from the Prudhoe Bay scandal more than 30 years ago, to the Deepwater Horizon disaster in the Gulf of Mexico in 2010.

CASE STUDY

Walmart

Walmart, the US retail giant, attracted global attention when it changed its complete supply chain management by strategically adopting the slogan "going green," which had extensive consequences for its growth, distribution methods, and corporate identity. Walmart declared its sustainability initiative to be an integral part of its future business logic. Tyler Elm, Walmart's vice president and senior director of corporate strategy and business sustainability, put it this way: "We recognized early on that we had to look at the entire value chain. If we had focused on just our own operations, we would have limited ourselves to 10 percent of our effect on the environment and eliminated 90 percent of the opportunity that's out there." (Plambeck, 2007).

Furthermore, Walmart topped its new strategic alignment by announcing a zero-waste program. Through this, the company—which is, after all, the world's largest retail group—intends to reduce its nonrecyclable waste to nil over the medium to long term. In order to achieve this goal, which is both ambitious as well as likely to bolster the company's reputation, Walmart established 14 sustainable value networks comprising renowned experts, nonprofit organizations, and suppliers. They have been tasked with reviewing Walmart's social and environmental standards and identifying both innovations and cost savings. There is no doubt that this approach can result in great gains in reputation, as long as it is pursued with as much perseverance as Walmart devotes to it.

Growth Strategies

On the stock market, a growth strategy tries to identify, ahead of time, markets with future growth prospects. Investors thus select companies that have the highest growth potential for their portfolios. They are less concerned with individual companies, but rather with entire sectors of the economy. A similar approach is adopted by companies trying to understand how specific sector-related issues affect their reputation and that of their competitors. They assume a controlled reputational risk, which they seek to limit through analyses of reputation drivers. This process identifies the areas in which reputation management activities will in fact improve their competitive position. Siemens, for example, is representative of a company that has adopted a growth strategy. With the "Siemens answers" campaign, the company offers answers to the world's toughest questions in the fields of urbanization, climate change, and demographic change, and the company has streamlined all corporate communications around these three key themes.

Growth strategies are all about taking on a controllable reputation risk with the aim of achieving the goal in the medium term, and this is enabled by a thorough analysis at the outset. A company would therefore analyze the effects of dealing with specific industry issues (as in Siemens' three key themes) and determine the effects on itself and its competition's reputations in the opinion market. Using analyses of reputation drivers, the company will then evaluate where new strategies might have a positive effect on its reputation. Identification of reputation drivers is done through stakeholder analyses, which might be based on an opinion poll conducted among the general public or on surveys of specific acceptance markets (politicians, investors, journalists, etc.). These stakeholder surveys collect information related to numerous factors including, but not limited to, a company's trustworthiness, product and service quality, competitive positioning, responsibility, and management leadership qualities.

The impact communication has on the respective reputation drivers is reinforced by means of agenda alignment processes that focus communication on specific industry issues. It is these issues—for example, how well or badly a company tackles the CO_2 problem as a main cause of climate change—that have a crucial impact on the public perception of reputation.

Value Strategies

Value strategies are carefully planned and sustainable in nature, accepting only moderate risks when building reputation capital. An additional characteristic is the claim to long-term and sustainable goal fulfillment. Compared to the other two reputation strategies, this strategy is much more internally focused. Primary target groups are a company's own employees, followed by business partners and customers. It is by these target groups that businesses that select value investing as their reputation strategy traditionally feel more strongly held to high ethical and social standards. As Robert Bosch, the German industrialist, engineer, and inventor, once said: "It is better to lose money than trust."

"As a general rule in financial matters, things take longer to happen than you would expect but when they do start to move they happen more quickly." Hamish McRae

In its external relationships, a value strategy relies on corporate communications that always emphasize ethical actions. Communications serve primarily to improve perceptions of a company's functional performance (economic reputation) in alignment with the dimensions of its competence and economic performance. Here, however, the focus of reputation management is on minimizing the risk of internal reputation issues impinging on the area of social reputation. In other words, there is a strict focus on not accepting structures or processes within the company that might result in reports that focus on topics other than economics—such as the questioning of matters concerning integrity or of a company's social and environmental standards (social reputation). Furthermore, a value strategy relies on precautionary structural measures within the company

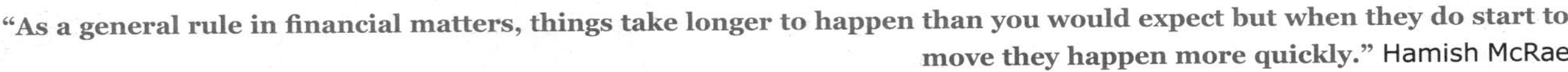

and its environment in order to proactively remove any risk of potential scandals.

Typical representatives of successful value strategies can primarily be found among industrial, raw material, and food production companies—though not, however, in retail. In analyses, their economic reputation accounts for 80–93% of their total reputation score. Many examples of value strategies can be found among small and medium-sized family businesses that enjoy an especially good reputation with experts and in specialized industries where some of these "hidden champions" can even be global market leaders without causing a big wave outside their own region.

TOTAL-RETURN STRATEGIES

Total-return strategies are particularly promising and safe. However, the low reputation risk they entail must unavoidably be paid for with a low return on reputation. This strategy has by far the lowest communication-intensity both in external and internal communications. Strictly speaking, total-return strategies tend to invoke the inertia of the "same old" proven methods, rather than being coherent, independent, and future-oriented. This is also the main difference from the value strategies mentioned above. Both are very reserved in their external communications, but in addition total-return strategies see little need to invest in internal communications. Typical statements from companies practicing a total-return approach might be as follows, "We don't need any reputation management or active internal or external communications. We have done very well without these for the last 150 years, and we will continue to do well." Or, "We invest in the quality of our products, and that is a guarantee of high customer satisfaction—which is all that matters to us." Or, "You know, we had our image with the public and in the media examined just last year, and we found that we are almost not perceived at all—and we can live with that very well."

However, such convictions are now colliding violently with the specific societal conditions and market environment of the 21st century. The major difference today is the fact that a well-differentiated media system with a logic of its own has developed that operates on the basis of market criteria and has over the past decades increasingly established itself in society. This has become obvious in the striking acceleration of the quantitative and qualitative spread of publication media that are available in ever-new forms and formats. Furthermore, the publishing of information happens in an increasingly rapid and comprehensive manner, while enjoying growing attention and penetration by the public. This degree of penetration is complemented and reinforced by the Internet, which, after all, is more than just another media channel. Today, anyone who has Internet access can form an opinion outside of the traditional channels of information and leading media.

This dual structural change in the media system—i.e. the increasing involvement of society and the growth of people's information autonomy due to the Internet—has resulted in the problem that the speed of scandal-mongering has clearly increased over the past years. The reputation losses due to scandal-mongering must be borne primarily by economic organizations and institutions—often those practicing total-return strategies, whether explicitly or implicitly. The reason for this is that, during the neoliberal 1990s, the solving of fundamental societal problems was delegated almost exclusively to the economic system. It was denied, for example, that the state had any competence for solving societal problems. And even if, due to the current economic crisis, the state is again accorded more trust, the discussion remains about whose "fault" the current economic malaise is. This has thrust into the limelight those companies which have previously been able to keep themselves out of the media—even if their product quality or other structural company processes have not deteriorated.

This calamity often hits those companies especially hard which have not been able to establish a clear profile with their stakeholder group, something that is essential in a crisis; as a consequence, they will be at the mercy of media interests or of the Internet rumor mill. Issues of good governance, or whether a company treating its employees or external stakeholder groups with social integrity, are subject to controversial discussions by the media and on social networks on the Internet—no matter whether the company concerned exerts an active influence or not. This is one of the reasons why today more and more companies in the business-to-business (B2B) sector, which have for years failed to see any reason why they should build their reputation profile for a wider public beyond their target customer group, must deal with the issue of reputation risk and return. Examples can be found among companies in the pharmaceutical and chemical industries, and also among those active exclusively in the B2B segment, as well as many small and medium-sized companies.

WHAT TO CONSIDER WHEN CHOOSING A STRATEGY

How should top managers or entrepreneurs proceed when selecting one of the four strategies described? Which strategy suits their company best? What should be taken into account here is not just the company-specific reputation risks and potentials, but also the specific media and societal

MAKING IT HAPPEN

Given the great importance of proper change management for building and keeping a good reputation, reputation managers must be capable of applying all four strategies "by heart." Today it is no longer enough to be a specialist in just one strategy. One could compare this to investment funds that combine elements from different alternative investments; similarly a reputation manager must be able to combine elements of multiple existing strategies, both simultaneously and successively.

The following checklist should help smart reputation managers to improve their own and their company's situation. The checklist is inspired by the strategies we have described and encourages finding the right combination of strategies needed to build a good reputation.

- Have you examined your competitors' reputation strategies?
- Have you presented your findings to the top management of your company?
- What can you learn from your most successful competitor?
- What are the things you don't want to learn?
- Have you identified the reputation risks and opportunities faced by your company?
- Are you monitoring these on a regular basis?
- Has your top management attended reputation management training that has alerted them to the risks, possibilities, and limits of high-quality reputation management?
- Have you documented your company's reputation strategy, and has consensus been reached among top management for the full support of this strategy?
- Are the employees and top management of your company aware of the important factors in a good reputation strategy?
- Can you describe the reputation strategy of your company in 90 seconds?

If you can answer most of these questions positively, it is likely that your company is dealing competently with the issue of selecting and applying an appropriate reputation management strategy.

"Being ambitious is like being thin. It's nice to have in your youth—but hold on to it into middle age, and you're going to end up with a sour little face on you." Julie Burchill

framework conditions of the 21st century. The causes of reputation risks lie primarily in the attention structures of the mass media and increasingly in social networks. Both these factors are essentially responsible for what will be perceived by recipients, and what may consequently represent a risk to a company's reputation.

What applies more than ever is that reputation is produced by communications—and is exposed to the permanent suspicion of having been orchestrated exactly for this reason. Therefore, active reputation management in the sense of focused risk minimization starts long before an attempt to define the media headlines. And it does so by taking stock of all processes within the company and its environment, however remote they might seem from communications, that can result in relevant perception structures and expectations within the internal and external public. They can be identified and prioritized, for example by using the issue-mapping approach—a prerequisite for being able to adjust or even eliminate them when necessary. This clearly shows that reputation management is more than just communication—it must have a sustainable effect on the reality of the company and its essential decisions. And that is exactly what lies in the hands of top management.

Excellence, backed up by sincere and reliable corporate communications, often remains the best thing companies can do for their reputation. However, attention should be paid to how these communications are delivered, since the traditional form of corporate communications as one-to-many delivery has now itself become a risk to reputation: the unidirectional type of communication can no longer do justice to today's realities of communications. This has to do with the communicative behavior of many stakeholders (such as is obvious in the social media on the Internet) and the resulting expectations that corporate communications policy faces.

This new communicative behavior promotes, for example, growing market transparency and, as explained above, an acceleration of scandal-mongering cycles, which are very difficult to control.

Continuously handling these reputation risks is essential, because the evaluation of individual facts increasingly depends on the zeitgeist; business methods which were considered completely unproblematic only a few years ago may suddenly be seen as morally wrong and worthy of being the subject of scandal-mongering. Issues such as environmental protection, diversity, equal rights, the role of taxpayers, all the way to the controversial discussion of management salaries, emerge and then disappear again.

REPUTATION MANAGEMENT IN TIMES OF RAPID CHANGE

Beyond these issues, there is another more fundamental factor that influences the success or failure of reputation management—the skill of being able to continuously manage crisis and change.

Many communications bosses view their work as ongoing crisis management. And indeed, visiting corporate offices where communications are managed in major international corporations gives the impression that nothing is as common as one crisis following another at a rapid pace.

From product recalls to compliance cases, from US class-action suits to executive misconduct, from mergers to carve-outs, from cost-savings programs to acquisitions (which, due to circumstances, may only be possible during a small window of time), from the issues that blow up almost without warning and escalate rapidly to the more ordinary malfunctions, to drastic fluctuations in share price to an impending takeover. In all these situations, the more strings that are pulled by communications bosses, the more complex, and above all the more international a company or institution is, the stronger is the impression that all that matters is being able to anticipate, prevent, manage, or document any crisis at any time. These are the critical phases during which a company will benefit from the smart use of reputation investment strategies; times during which a company's "good reputation" has to stand the test while under a magnifying glass—indeed, when this reputation may even implode instantly.

Business as usual does not seem to be possible any more—business as usual *is* crisis and change. From a reputational point of view, it is particularly internal communications that have gained tremendously in importance—especially communications about change. Due to the fact that management nowadays is less and less able to control how the organization is perceived from the outside—because organizations are becoming increasingly permeable to the outflow of information from those within them—all those in charge of communications are well advised to empower their organization's employees to act as loyal messengers.

In times of increasing contingency, during phases of disruptive change, this will not be sufficient for managing reputation sustainably. What good communications managers must be able to do in such cases goes far beyond simply providing employees with the correct messages. Instead, management and employees must be made "crisis-proof." An organization is crisis-proof, in the meaning of this article, if it experiences changes and crises as part of its normal business, and if it can see the creative aspects rather than the threats in these developments.

Of course, from a reputation point of view, leadership is a key factor in these situations. The leader must empathize, provide direction, and dispense encouragement when faced with change or crisis. However, it is equally important to listen to people in an organization in situations that are full of uncertainty, change, and crisis, and to invite them to contribute their share to managing the situation. This means that reputation managers have to act on the following points.

- First, in cooperation with other members of top management, reputation managers must develop a communicable vision of the organization's long-term targets. It does not matter whether we call this a "vision" or "target reputation." Hedge and growth reputation strategies tend to be better at this than the more "passive" strategies.
- Second, reputation managers must ensure that communication does not only work top-down, but also among employees and from employees upward—and that employees communicate well and quickly. This is not only a technology and channel management issue, but rather a question of attitude, practice, and organization. For example, reputation managers should see to it that individual organizational units have, as a rule, no more than 150 employees, because above that number self-regulation and internal communications will barely work.
- Third, reputation managers must ensure that any and all employees know that even in a crisis they are not without options to act or to participate, and that they will be treated respectfully when they do.

The result of these deliberations may be surprising. Leadership during change is, so to speak, the linchpin of reputation management—irrespective of the fundamental reputation strategy that is being pursued. In order to solve the three tasks outlined above—whether as an external or internal consultant—you primarily have to work with your management, and do so at all levels.

If reputation management under conditions of almost permanent disruption is analyzed from a perspective that extends beyond the bounds of the organization (i.e.

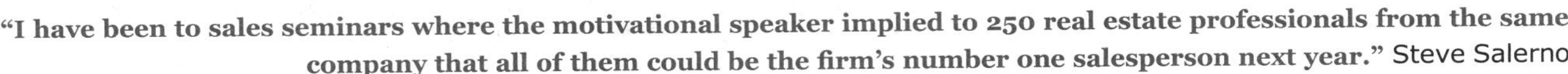
"I have been to sales seminars where the motivational speaker implied to 250 real estate professionals from the same company that all of them could be the firm's number one salesperson next year." Steve Salerno

  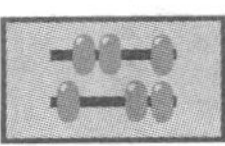      

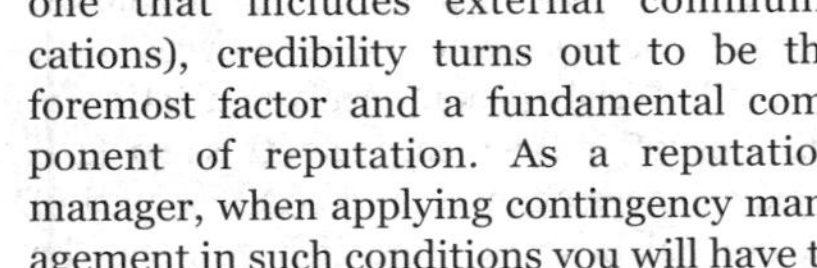

one that includes external communications), credibility turns out to be the foremost factor and a fundamental component of reputation. As a reputation manager, when applying contingency management in such conditions you will have to do the following.

- Ensure that the company is recognizable—that the public know whom they should trust. This begins with recognition, and is much more than just the faces that represent the company. (You may guess which reputation strategy will fail in this context.)
- Do everything in your power to ensure that nothing is promised which cannot be delivered. As a reputation manager, your primary task is to define the tone in which the organization represents itself externally, on all channels; in particular, on the marketing and distribution channels. This can be a challenge for old-style communications bosses.
- Ensure that the messages for and relationships with the different stakeholder groups remain more or less consistent. The challenge here is that "one-voice policies" no longer work in times of WikiLeaks and social media; nevertheless, a certain consistency across channels and stakeholder groups will be very helpful for the organization's credibility.

More than other functional experts, those in charge of communications are in a position to enable the people in organizations to handle contingency and change correctly, thus lowering risks to reputation considerably, or even making reputation sustainable.

MORE INFO

Books:

Bourdieu, Pierre. "Ökonomisches kapital, kulturelles kapital, soziales kapital." In Reinhard Kreckel (ed). *Soziale Ungleichheiten*. Göttingen, Germany: Otto Schartz & Co, 1983; pp. 183–198.

Eisenegger, Mark. *Reputation in der Mediengesellschaft: Konstitution—Issues Monitoring—Issues Management*. Wiesbaden, Germany: VS Verlag für Sozialwissenschaften, 2005.

Eisenegger, Mark, and Kurt Imhof. "The true, the good and the beautiful: Reputation management in the media society." In Ansgar Zerfass, Betteke van Ruler, and Krishnamurthy Sriramesh (eds). *Public Relations Research: European and International Perspectives and Innovations*. Wiesbaden, Germany: VS Verlag für Sozialwissenschaften, 2008; pp. 125–146.

Kim, W. Chan, and Renée Mauborgne. *Blue Ocean Strategy: How to Create Uncontested Market Space and Make Competition Irrelevant*. Boston, MA: Harvard Business School, 2005.

Klewes, Joachim, and Robert Wreschniok (eds). *Reputation Capital: Building and Maintaining Trust in the 21st Century*. Heidelberg, Germany: Springer, 2009.

Markowitz, Harry M. *Portfolio Selection: Efficient Diversification of Investments*. 2nd ed. Malden, MA: Blackwell, 1991.

von Oetinger, Bolko. "Das Wesen der Strategie." In *Das Boston Consulting Group Strategie-Buch: Die wichtigsten Managementkonzepte für die Praktiker*. Berlin, Germany: Econ Verlag, 2003.

Washington, George. *Rules of Civility and Decent Behaviour in Company and Conversation: A Book of Etiquette*. Williamsburg, VA: Beaver Press, 1971. Online at: www.history.org/almanack/life/manners/rules2.cfm

Articles:

Plambeck, Erica. "The greening of Wal-Mart's supply chain." *Supply Chain Management Review* (July/August 2007).

Schütz, Tobias, and Manfred Schwaiger. "Der einfluss der unternehmensreputation auf entscheidungen privater anleger." *Kredit und Kapital* 40:2 (2007): 189–223.

Website:

Change Centre Foundation: www.change-centre.org/foundation

European Centre for Reputation Studies: www.reputation-centre.org

See Also:

★ The CEO's Role in Reputation Management (pp. 797–800)
★ Digital Strategies for Enhancing Reputation (pp. 826–831)
★ Engaging Your Stakeholders: How To Make Allies of Investors and Activists (pp. 837–840)

"Why did the Roman Empire collapse? What is Latin for office automation?" Alan Jay Perlis

  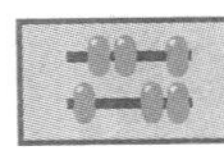   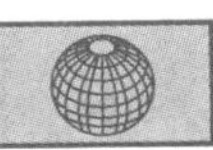   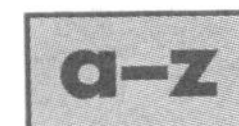

Statistical Process Control for Quality Improvement

by Priscilla Wisner

EXECUTIVE SUMMARY

- Statistical process control (SPC) is a management philosophy that relies on straightforward statistical tools to identify and solve process problems.
- By systematically identifying potential problems in process control, managers can proactively make corrections before quality outcomes suffer.
- SPC methods are useful in helping managers to measure whether their processes and products conform to design specifications, and they also help organizations to improve productivity and reduce waste.
- SPC methods are used extensively in manufacturing settings but are also relevant in the service sector.

INTRODUCTION

Statistical process control (SPC) is an optimization philosophy centered on using a variety of statistical tools to enable continuous process improvement. Closely linked to the total quality management (TQM) philosophy, SPC helps firms to improve profitability by improving process and product quality. Although initially used in manufacturing, SPC tools and methods work equally well in a service environment.

SPC methods are used extensively by organizations to enable systematic learning. Using methods developed in the 1920s by Walter Shewhart and subsequently enhanced by quality consultants William Edwards Deming and Joseph Juran, organizations are able to use a set of straightforward statistics to find out whether or not their processes conform to expectations. Furthermore, the use of SPC methods can help to identify instances of process variation that may signal a problem in the process. By identifying process variation and potential nonconformance with design expectations early in the production or service environment, managers can proactively make corrections before the process variation negatively impacts quality and customer perceptions.

AN OVERVIEW

Although SPC is enabled with statistical analysis, the management philosophy that underlies SPC is much broader than a set of statistics. To improve a process systematically, managers must first identify key processes and key variables of interest. Every organization has hundreds, if not thousands, of processes and variables that can affect product and service outcomes, and one challenge is to focus on the processes and variables that are of key concern. SPC tools can be useful in identifying areas that need attention, but managerial insight is needed to use the SPC tools strategically.

Managers can directly influence organizational performance using SPC practices. Their choice of key processes and performance variables creates a feed-forward signaling device to the organization about key performance indicators. This causes attention to be paid to these processes and variables. Feedback is then received through the SPC information, enabling evaluation of the data and an opportunity for corrective actions to be taken. Thus, SPC is not merely a set of statistical tools, but a management philosophy that helps organizations to improve performance through feed-forward and feed-back loops.

SPC TOOLS

The SPC toolkit contains a number of tools to help managers to evaluate processes. Many of the tools were first identified as essential to continuous quality improvement by Kaoru Ishikawa, a Japanese quality expert. This section describes a number of the tools that are commonly used by organizations to evaluate and improve quality performance. To learn more about how to construct each of these and other SPC tools, refer to the More Info section at the end of this article, where details and links are given.

Flowcharts

Flowcharts depict the progress of work through a series of defined steps. They can be used to communicate a process to employees who are being trained for the work, and management can use them to evaluate process flows, constraints, and gaps. The symbols used in flowcharting are standardized; some of the more commonly used are rectangles (activities and tasks), diamonds (decision points), rectangles with a wavy base (documents), cylinders (files), and arrows (linkages). The flowchart in Figure 1 demonstrates an order entry process.

Figure 1. Flowchart for an order entry process

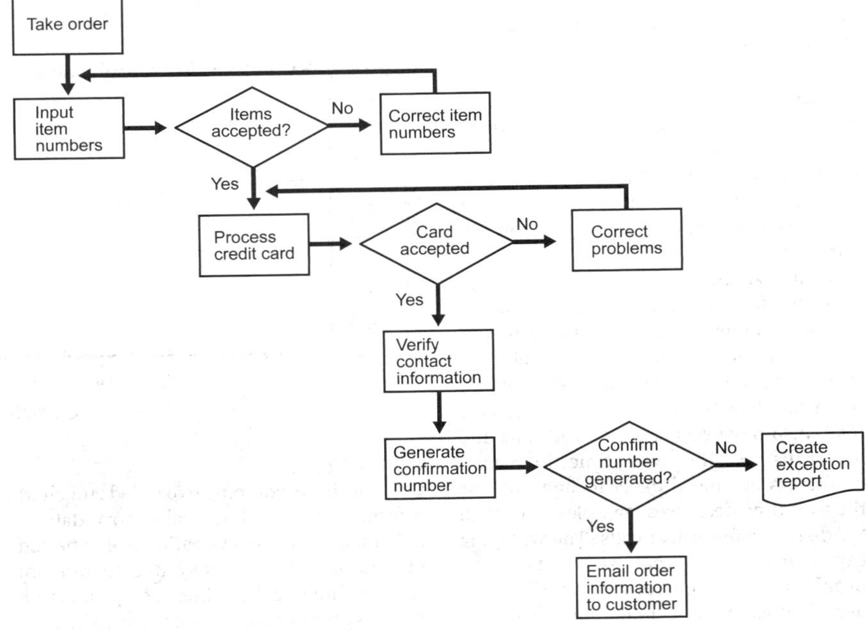

"Not everything that can be counted counts; and not everything that counts can be counted." George Gallup

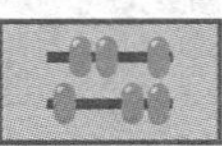

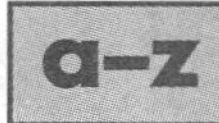

Pareto Charts

Pareto charts are graphical demonstrations of occurrences, with the most frequently occurring event to the left and less frequent occurrences to the right. Pareto charts are named after Vilfredo Pareto, an Italian economist who identified that 80% of the wealth is held by a relatively small share of the population. This has been translated into the Pareto principle, which says that about 80% of outcomes are typically created by about 20% of causes. By constructing a Pareto chart, managers can quickly see what problems are most prevalent in their organizations.

The Pareto chart in Figure 2 shows the occurrences of accidents in a manufacturing organization. 58% of the accidents in the plant are falls, followed by broken bones at 21%. The managers can see that these two types of accident are the most prevalent, and they are perhaps related.

Figure 2. Pareto chart of accidents in a manufacturing plant

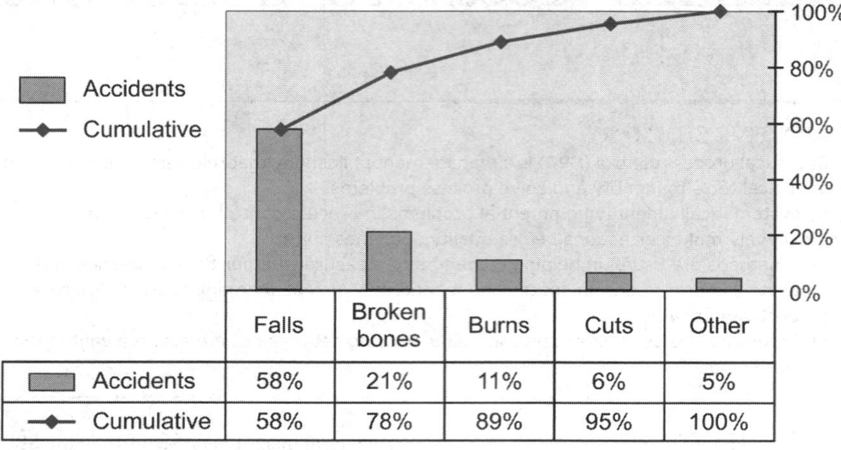

	Falls	Broken bones	Burns	Cuts	Other
Accidents	58%	21%	11%	6%	5%
Cumulative	58%	78%	89%	95%	100%

Ishikawa Cause-and-Effect or Fishbone Diagrams

These diagrams depict an array of potential causes of quality problems. The problem (the head of the fish) is displayed on the right, and the bones of the fish—representing the potential causes of the problem—are drawn to the left. Potential causes are often categorized as materials, equipment, people, environment, and management. Other categories may be included as appropriate. Useful in brainstorming the causes of problems (including potential problems) from multiple perspectives, these diagrams should include all possible reasons for a problem. When completed, further analysis is done to identify the root cause. Figure 3 is an Ishikawa diagram in an airline setting.

Figure 3. Ishikawa diagram prepared for investigation of cause(s) of delayed flight departures

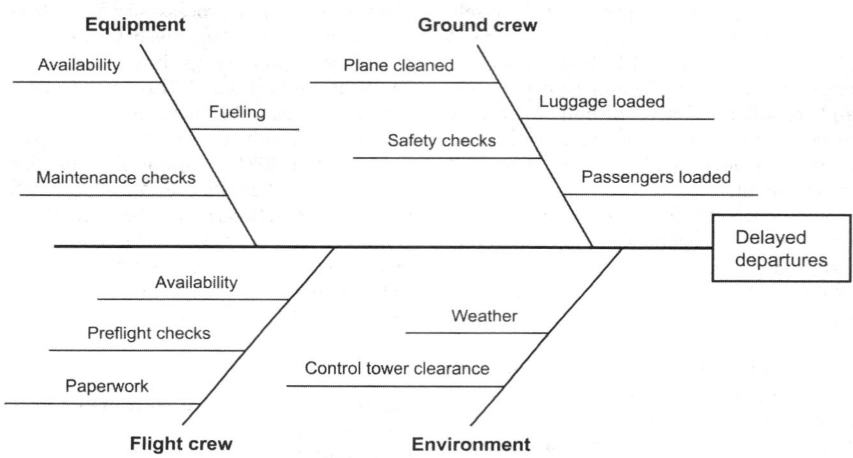

Run Charts

Run charts are graphical plots of a variable over time. These charts can be made for a single variable, but they are useful in detecting trends or relationships between variables when two are included on the same run chart.

In the example in Figure 4, the average wait time for a telephone customer service is plotted along with the number of lost calls—customers who hang up before a customer service person takes the call. As the run chart demonstrates, there is a relationship between average wait time and lost calls: as the wait time increases, customers are more likely to hang up. As the wait time decreases (samples 6 through 8), there are fewer lost calls. The widening gap between the lines shows that the problem of a customer hanging up decreases as the wait time diminishes.

Figure 4. Run chart for telephone customer service

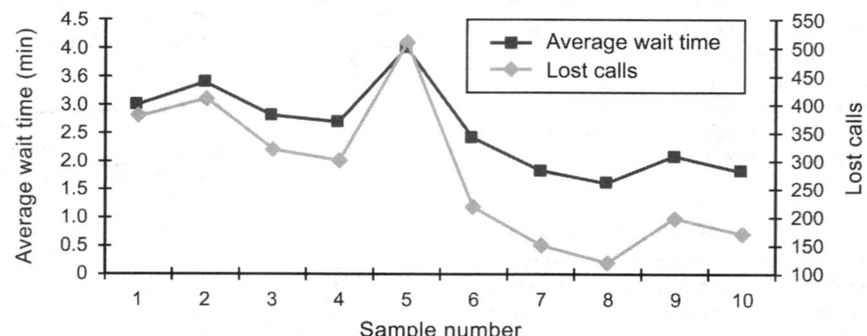

Control Charts

Control charts combine expanded run chart information with statistical control data to help identify process variation over a period of time that is not likely due to random chance. Time can be defined as a production run, a series of batches, a day's activities, or any relevant time period that captures the process being evaluated. Useful in manufacturing, administrative, and service functions, control charts provide rapid feedback on key variables of interest. Control variables of interest might include those listed in Table 1.

  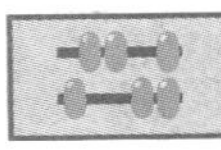      

Table 1. Examples of control variables in different business sectors

Manufacturing environment	Service environment
Liters of liquid in a container	Wait time in a bank line
Thickness of a coating	Delivery time for packages
Tension in a coil	Temperature of a restaurant entrée
Direct labor time per unit	Time lag between a customer request and a service response
Changeover time between batches	Infection rates in a medical setting
Defect rates	Loan approval time
Overhead costs	

Control charts are used to show when a process is in, or out of, statistical control. Statistical control does not imply zero variation—some degree of variation is normal and it is unrealistic to expect zero variation. However, the control chart is able to demonstrate data patterns that indicate that a process is out of control, and it is useful as a tool for making continuous improvement by reducing variability. The most commonly employed control charts are the mean chart and the range chart, often referred to as X-bar and R-charts.

The Mean Chart

The mean chart (X- bar chart) shows the variation in a process by plotting the actual mean values of a set of sample data. Each set of sample data consists of multiple observations of the process that's being evaluated. These data are plotted against the background of the mean of all the samples taken and the upper and lower control limits for the data. These limiting bounds are each three-sigma limits, meaning that almost all (99.73%) of the variation in the process is expected to fall within a six-sigma limit. Sigma, represented by the greek symbol s, is the standard deviation of a distribution.

Signals from a mean chart that a process is out of control include the following:

- Data points that fall above the upper control limit or below the lower control limit.
- Eight or more consecutive data points that fall above or below the mean line.
- Two out of three consecutive points in the lower or upper third of the chart.
- Six or more consecutive data points that trend up or down within the chart, as this indicates a trend or drift of the variation in the process.
- Fourteen or more points that alternate in an up or down direction, indicating that there may be too much variation in the process.

Figure 5 is an example of a mean control chart, constructed for a month's sample data. The chart shows that samples 2, 9, and 16 are all above the upper control limit, indicating a problem. Interestingly, each of these samples was taken on the same day of the week (each is seven days apart). Another problem highlighted by the chart is the set of daily sample means recorded after day 20. Starting on that day, a series of sample means falls below the mean for the set of data. Although these data points are all within the control limits, they indicate a potential problem in the process because more than eight consecutive points fall below the mean.

The Range Chart

The range chart (R-chart) is similar to the mean chart in having upper and lower (three-sigma) control limits, but the data plotted for each sample are now the *range* between the largest and the smallest value in the sample. By plotting the range of values, variation within each sample is more apparent.

Signals from a range chart indicating that a process is out of control are similar to those for the mean chart and include the following:

- Data points that fall above the upper control limit or below the lower control limit.
- Eight or more data points in succession that fall above or below the mean.
- Six or more consecutive data points that trend up or down, as this indicates a trend or drift of variation in the process.
- Fourteen or more points that alternate in up and down directions, indicating that there may be too much variation in the process.

Figure 5. Mean control chart for a production process (y axis represents mean values)

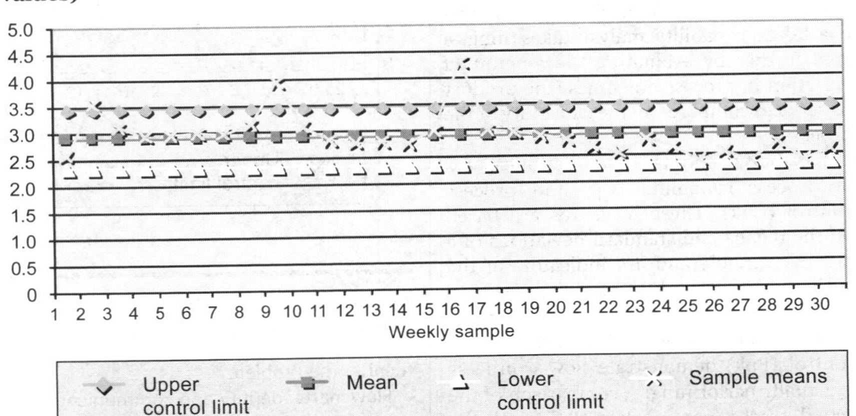

CASE STUDY

Graco Children's Products[1]

Graco Children's Products, a US manufacturer of children's equipment such as high chairs, baby swings, and car seats, set itself the goal of improving product quality in the design phase of operations. By identifying problems early in the design process, the firm expected to reap benefits in manufacturing performance, product quality, and customer satisfaction.

Using SPC tools, Graco managers were able to analyze multiple design options efficiently. For example, in the plastics injection molding area there were more than 30 variables of interest to evaluate. One analysis was done for a plastic grip handle on a child carrier seat. The handle had a problem with warping, which caused too much curvature in the part, making later assembly of the carrier seat difficult. Eight machine variables were identified as potential causes of the problem. By using SPC analysis data, Graco determined that three variables—hold time, cure time, and material temperature—significantly impacted warping. By modifying these processes, the organization was able to correct the problem and reduce associated costs. The SPC analysis also showed that cooling temperatures did not significantly impact quality outcomes, which led to a decision not to invest in expensive cooling equipment. By using SPC tools to focus attention on process variables that could be controlled in the design phase of the product, Graco managers improved process and product quality, which resulted in savings for the organization.

  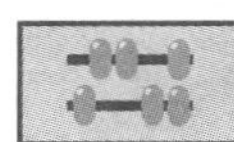      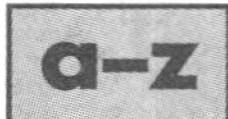

The range chart in Figure 6, which has been constructed for the same set of data as the mean chart, demonstrates that there is wide variation in the sample data. As in the mean chart, the three data points that fall outside of the upper control limit indicate a process that is not in control. The strong variability in consecutive data points also indicates potential problem in process control. As a general rule, although data points may fall within the control limits, variations from the norm can be pointers to performance problems, product returns, possible lawsuits, loss of customer loyalty, and loss of reputation. All of these risks can be costly for an organization.

Process Capability Analysis

Process capability analysis is a technique that is used to determine the ability of a process to meet product or service specifications. It is a useful tool to evaluate variation within a process and whether improvements can be made to process control. Although a process may be within control limits as determined by control chart data, capability analysis takes things a step further by evaluating the amount of variation in process outcomes (the product or service) compared to the capability of the process.

Capability analysis is based on measures of process capability (Cp) and process control (Cpk). These measures are based on the means and standard deviations of a process variable and are indicators of the aptitude, or capability, of the process to perform. Similarly, measures of actual process performance (Pp) and process control (Ppk) demonstrate how a process is actually performing. A comparison of the actual process control data (Ppk) with the process capability data (Cpk) helps managers to numerically evaluate how much variation there is in an in-control (within control limits) process, and whether modifications of the process will reduce variation. Refer to the isixsigma website for details of process capability calculations and uses.

Taguchi Loss Function

The Taguchi loss function is based on the assumption that all variation has a cost, even when the variation does not violate the data patterns defined by control charts. This concept is most useful where deviations from expectation are expected to be costly. Taguchi posited that all deviations from target values ultimately result in customer dissatisfaction. The Taguchi loss function enables organizations to calculate the financial consequence of process variability, making it useful in reaching design decisions.

CONCLUSION

Statistical process control benefits organizations by providing a systematic method for the monitoring and evaluation of process variation. Too often, managers do not notice changes and problems in processes until either the output is inspected or customers make complaints.

By proactively identifying potential process problems and using SPC tools to evaluate process outcomes and improve process control, organizations are able to direct their resources more efficiently and can focus management time and attention on the most pressing problems.

Figure 6. Range chart for same process data as in Figure 5 (y axis represents difference between largest and smallest values within a sample of data)

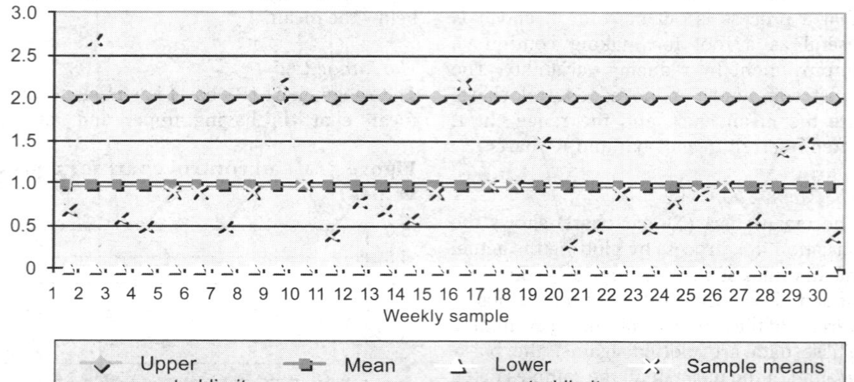

MAKING IT HAPPEN

SPC tools can be used in the following stages of process evaluation and improvement:

Identify the Problem

- Flowcharts identify and communicate information about the flow of a process, including constraints and gaps.
- Pareto analysis identifies the issues that are causing most of the problems.

Identify the Reasons for the Problem

- Use Ishikawa cause-and-effect diagrams to brainstorm the causes of a problem from a multidimensional perspective.

Analyze the Data

- Run charts show the variability in data over time and the potential relationships between multiple variables.
- Control charts identify process variation using a set of statistical tools, enabling the identification of out-of-control variation.
- Process capability analysis is used to show the amount of variation in an in-control process, and can be useful in improving a process.
- The Taguchi loss function assigns an economic value to variation, helping to make trade-off decisions in process and product design.

NOTE

1 Excerpted from Anon. "Graco uses SPC software to improve quality of products (statistical process control at Graco's Children's Products)." *IIE Solutions* (January 1, 1997).

"That action is best, which provides the greatest happiness for the greatest numbers." Francis Hutcheson

  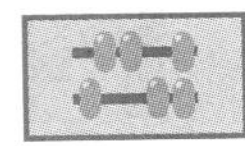   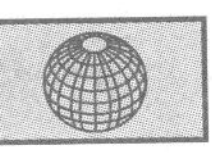   

Viewpoint: Urgent Need to Retool Business Faculties with Financial Historians and Eject the Financial Engineers by Russell Napier

INTRODUCTION

Russell Napier is an Edinburgh-based consultant for Asia-focused brokerage CLSA Asia-Pacific Markets who writes about issues impacting the global equity markets. With more than two decades in the industry, he has contributed to the development and scope of CLSA's equity research. He started his career in investment at Edinburgh-based asset managers Baillie Gifford before joining CLSA in 1995 as an Asian equity strategist based in Hong Kong. He remained in that post until 1999 and was ranked number one for Asian strategy in the *Asiamoney* and *Institutional Investor* polls from 1997 to 1999. Napier is a nonexecutive director of the Scottish Investment Trust and the Mid Wynd International Investment Trust. His book *Anatomy of a Bear* was published to critical acclaim in 2005 (an updated edition was published in 2009). He created and runs a course for finance professionals at the Edinburgh Business School called "A practical history of financial markets."

THE EMPEROR IS NAKED: THE FALLACY OF MARKET EFFICIENCY

"Only someone who has Asperger's would read a subprime mortgage bond prospectus." This is the opinion of Michael Burry, a man diagnosed with Asperger's syndrome and one of the few investors who made a fortune betting that there would be a subprime mortgage crisis. Burry is quoted in *The Big Short* by Michael Lewis, which recounts the story of how the investors who foresaw and profited from the debacle in the US mortgage market were people who just didn't fit in. Educated as a doctor, Burry saw something that the business school graduates missed. This doctor with a "disorder" saw something coming which escaped even the Nobel laureates. Michael Burry could see that the price was wrong when everybody schooled in price determination believed it to be right. Understanding why Burry sees things differently from the financially educated is the key to understanding why financial education needs root and branch reform.

Why did so few people see what was so spectacularly wrong? Did it really take a genius to recognize that lending money to people who couldn't pay it back was unwise?

Almost 200 years after the publication of Hans Christian Andersen's story "The emperor's new clothes" the world was once again full of people looking at one thing but seeing something else. The great tragedy is that these people had paid large amounts of money to be trained and educated... in order to see clothes where none existed. This tragedy, with calamitous consequences for global financial stability, continues. To understand why this is the case, and how we can stop it, we need to understand the intellectual disaster in which a characteristic that is usually associated with the physical sciences was ascribed to a sociological activity. How did we come to believe that a market is *efficient*—and how do we stop believing this?

The compost left by the decay of one idea can be the key nutrient for the growth of the next. The failed idea was that governments would be better at allocating resources than individuals. What grew out of this was the observation that the marketplace, through price determination, could allocate resources more efficiently than the government. The woeful misallocation of resources by government in the postwar era didn't exactly set a high hurdle: it was not difficult to demonstrate that the market could allocate resources more efficiently than politicians and civil servants.

The evidence of superior resource allocation was compelling, and the observation gave impetus to an ideology that opposed government interference in the economy. Through the prism of that ascendant ideology, much higher claims could be made for the market than just that it was more efficient. If the market was more efficient at allocating resources, didn't this mean that it was also "perfect"?

If so, a huge prize awaited the economists. By assuming that markets were always efficient, the "dismal science" of economics could be transformed. It could at last take its place as a true science. The uncertainty would be banished from economics and Harry Truman's one-handed economist could be born.

VEGETABLES VS MORTGAGE-BACKED SECURITIES

Anyone who has ever been to a real market will know that a market is simply a meeting of human beings—buyers and sellers—attempting to reach agreement on prices. When human beings are involved, nothing is truly efficient. It doesn't matter if the market is a local market for vegetables or a market for mortgage-backed securities.

Indeed, one could argue that a market for vegetables is likely to be much more efficient than a market for complex and opaque financial instruments. It is easy to assess the present value of a vegetable by looking at its condition and noting how this will influence its taste when it is consumed in the very near future. The present value of a mortgage-backed security, however, is dependent on future income streams that are often far in the future, and these are subject to considerable uncertainty.

While opinion on the present value of a tomato has a high likelihood of being accurate, there is much greater room for error when assessing the value of a mortgage-backed security. Even though many generations were aware of the inefficiencies, deception, and theft that occur in a vegetable market, a new generation somehow convinced itself that such uncertainties were absent from financial markets. The reason for this delusion was the normal human failing of searching for certainty in an uncertain world. More cynically, it will always be true that certainty fetches a higher price than uncertainty. By attributing features to financial markets which are not there when human beings gather to determine prices, precision could seemingly be brought to the treacherous task of forecasting.

  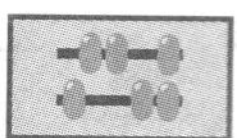   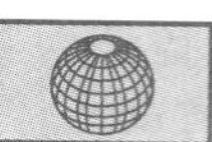   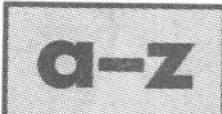

ECONOMICS: THE QUEST TO TRANSFORM A SOCIAL SCIENCE INTO A PRECISE SCIENCE

The problem that bedevils economists, formerly known as "political economists," is that they lacked fixed variables to place in their equations. This dearth of fixed variables was not surprising to those who understood that economics was a social science, but it was very frustrating for those who aspired to elevate economics to a hard science. Just one fixed variable in the equation would lift economics to this higher plain and the great triumph of explaining everything with the certainty of mathematics. So, in the pursuit of certainty, researchers mined the rich seam of financial market price data to prove the efficiency of markets, establish a fixed variable, and transform economics.

The financial market data were tortured for so long that a confession was eventually extracted. The confession was that there was nothing in the history of prices which could predict future prices. This was taken to be evidence of efficiency. The fixed variable was in place and the fun could start.

As we have since discovered, there were just a few problems with this new certainty. Perhaps not surprisingly, it increasingly emerged that the tortured data had confessed to what its torturers had wanted it to confess to. More research revealed that there were numerous "anomalies" where past prices did indeed contain information which could be used to predict future prices. Even more worryingly, it became clear that the dubious confession had been elicited in response to the wrong question.

Oscar Wilde once remarked that a cynic is "a man who knows the price of everything and the value of nothing." The economists doing the data-mining to prove efficiency didn't bother with value; in fact they didn't bother with anything apart from price. If the price, in isolation, was shown to move randomly, then this was taken as evidence that a market was efficient. One assumes they ignored the common factors that impact prices; this would have added a level of subjectivity that would have defeated the purpose of finding a scientifically provable constant variable.

Would a market that responded predictably to certain stimuli be classified as efficient? A crowd of human beings will rush predictably away from fire. The same mass of human beings will rush to pick up dollar bills falling from the sky. If the price movements can be predicted given certain stimuli, is a market efficient? If prices, when they reach certain values relative to a fundamental, are more likely to rise than fall, is the market still efficient?

Instead, a simple question was asked in isolation about prices and a whole generation—armed with economics degrees and other financial qualifications that had invariably supplied the wrong answers to the wrong questions—marched off to create a new era of certainty.

The economic rubble from that new era of certainty lies all around us. The certainty led otherwise sane people to believe that risk was inherently understandable and forecastable. It led them to believe that they were reducing risks when in fact their greater confidence meant that they were increasing risk. The greater risks that were taken on inevitably came home to roost, and the wealth destruction which ensued would have bankrupted the global financial system had governments not stepped in at the eleventh hour.

We have paid a very high price for the journey up this particular intellectual cul-de-sac. Incredibly, though, our universities continue to lead their students up the same blind alley. The same equations are being taught today as were taught before. The next generation of certain economists and financiers are entering the real world with the same unshakable belief that their equations can explain and thus manage risk. Unless this production line can be halted, the whole thing is going to happen again.

A RETURN TO THE REAL WORLD WITH FINANCIAL HISTORY

It has been said that science advances funeral by funeral, but do we really have to wait so long? Must we really wait for the death march to carry away a flawed approach to understanding that has such dangerous practical consequences? Retooling a university is clearly more difficult than retooling a factory, but we urgently need to retool our business faculties with financial historians and remove the financial engineers.

The American baseball player Lawrence Peter "Yogi" Berra got it right when he said "you can observe a lot by watching." A study of financial history tells us how the price determination mechanism works in real life. Although prices may be random in isolation, financial history shows how they are likely to behave in certain conditions. Those conditions change, and financial history also helps to explain how and why those conditions change. Observing how animals behave in relation to certain stimuli tells us a lot about how they will behave in the future when subjected to the same stimuli. Observing human beings coming together to determine prices when subjected to certain stimuli also helps to explain their future behavior.

A study of financial history is simply the study of how the world *does* work. Yet our universities insist on teaching how the world *should* work. Einstein suggested that progress would result if we asked the right question and kept going until we found the right answer. The financial engineers in our universities continue to ask the wrong questions, so their answers are useless and sadly dangerous. Financial history will provide us with the right questions, and for those who keep going it will also provide better answers. The right answers, of course, are not available. Finance is not a physical science and it does not lend itself to certain answers. It is time to live with that truth rather than perpetuate a false certainty that will once again come back to haunt us.

MORE INFO

Books:

Dimson, Elroy, Paul Marsh, and Mike Staunton. *Triumph of the Optimists: 101 Years of Global Investment Returns*. Princeton, NJ: Princeton University Press, 2002.

Friedman, Milton, and Anna Jacobson Schwartz. *A Monetary History of the United States, 1867–1960*. Princeton, NJ: Princeton University Press, 1971.

Grant, James. *Money of the Mind: Borrowing and Lending in America from the Civil War to Michael Milken*. New York: Farrar, Straus and Giroux, 1994.

Homer, Sidney, and Richard Eugene Sylla. *A History of Interest Rates*. 4th ed. Hoboken, NJ: Wiley, 2005.

Lewis, Michael. *The Big Short: Inside the Doomsday Machine*. New York: WW Norton, 2010.

Napier, Russell. *Anatomy of the Bear: Lessons From Wall Street's Four Great Bottoms*. Petersfield, UK: Harriman House, 2009.

Smith, Adam. *The Money Game*. New York: Vintage Books, 1976.

See Also:

★ Viewpoint: CEOs Should Refresh Their Finance Skills (pp. 801–802)
★ Viewpoint: Poverty of Thinking in University Economics and Accountancy Departments (pp. 905–907)
★ Viewpoint: Why Management Development Is a Challenge for Both Business Schools and Client Organizations (pp. 954–956)
The Ascent of Money: A Financial History of the World (p. 1332)
A Farewell to Alms: A Brief Economic History of the World (p. 1352)

  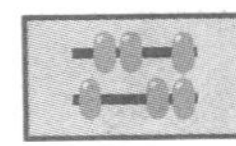      

Using Decision Analysis to Value R&D Projects

by Bert De Reyck

EXECUTIVE SUMMARY

- Valuing R&D projects is a critical component of project portfolio management.
- Traditional methods for valuing financial assets cannot be easily used for valuing R&D projects, as they are very different in nature.
- Decision analysis is widely used for valuing projects in R&D-intensive industries such as pharmaceuticals and energy.
- Using decision trees, one can determine a project's expected net present value (eNPV) and downside risk, two essential ingredients for determining whether or not to proceed with the project.

INTRODUCTION

Project portfolio management, the equivalent of financial portfolio management but focused on R&D projects rather than financial assets, often relies on decision analysis methods to value projects rather than traditional financial valuation methods such as net present value (NPV). In finance, the idea of managing portfolios of assets goes back a long time, with the first formal methods being developed in the 1950s. Simply put, assembling a portfolio of stocks, bonds, and other financial instruments balances the risk a manager is taking with any one of the investments. Over time, this same idea has also taken hold for managing a portfolio of R&D projects, where it is referred to as *project portfolio management*.

Project portfolio management considers the company's set of projects in a holistic way, providing an overview of the potential value, as well as the inherent risks of both the projects a company is currently engaged in and those it plans to initiate in the future. By means of project portfolio management, risks can be reduced through diversification of the product portfolio and value enhanced by identifying synergies between projects. Companies in the pharmaceutical and energy industries, for instance, have long recognized the value of project portfolio management, and they are using sophisticated methods and software tools to support this process.

Project portfolio management comprises the following functions:[1]

- determine a viable project mix;
- balance the portfolio;
- monitor the projects in the portfolio;
- analyze and enhance project performance;
- evaluate new opportunities against the current portfolio, taking into account capacity and funding capabilities;
- provide information and recommendations to decision-makers.

THE DIFFERENCE BETWEEN FINANCIAL AND R&D PORTFOLIO MANAGEMENT

Financial portfolios and project portfolios are very different in nature. The main characteristics of investing in financial instruments include:

Divisible investments: Financial instruments allow investment in small portions of an asset, rather than being all or nothing.

Simple interdependencies: The interrelationships between different investment opportunities can typically be captured by: The correlation between the assets' returns; and their financial value, as established by the financial markets.

Passive participation: Investing in financial instruments is typically a passive form of participation: The decision is mainly whether or not to invest, and how much.

Availability of information: Much information is available about financial assets in the form of historical performance and fundamental analyses concerning the future outlook.

Tradability: Most financial instruments are tradable assets, resulting in agreed-on valuations and opportunities to sell assets that do not fit your portfolio.

Clear objectives: The main objective is to maximize the risk–return performance of your portfolio.

Contractual clarity: Clearly defined terms exist for investing in a financial instrument, outlining the rights of the parties involved relying on established market rules.

These characteristics are not shared by a portfolio of R&D projects, which can be characterized as follows:

Discrete investments: Investments in projects are nondivisible, increasing the impact of an investment decision on your portfolio.

Complex interdependencies: Complex interdependencies and interactions exist between projects. Project outcomes are subject to synergies—for example, through the sharing of proprietary knowledge—and investment decisions may affect the options available in related projects.

Active participation: Investing in projects requires active management. Besides making a go/no-go decision and setting a budget, numerous decisions will have to be made during the project lifetime that will impact the outcome.

Lack of information: Since projects are largely unique, not much information is available on related past projects or for the prediction of future performance.

Nontradability: Projects cannot be easily sold, resulting in a lack of valuation information and lock-in situations.

Fuzzy objectives: Projects are typically governed by a multitude of objectives, both financial and nonfinancial, and typically include qualitative objectives.

Contract ambiguity: Project investments may result in disagreement concerning who is entitled to which benefit, with multiple stakeholders holding different views.

As a result, conclusions derived from finance cannot simply be transferred to other areas, nor can their methods be used without adaptation. That is why a variety of approaches have been proposed for valuing R&D projects, which is *the* central issue in managing a portfolio of R&D projects. The most commonly used is *decision analysis*, in which decision trees are used to represent the project's potential outcomes and their likelihood.

DECISION ANALYSIS: A DEFINITION

A central component in decision analysis is the concept of a decision tree. An example of a decision tree is given in Figure 1. In the figure:

- The squares, circles, and triangles represent points in time, which proceeds from left to right.
- The squares, or decision nodes, indicate decisions to be made, and the circles, or chance nodes, indicate the time when the result of an uncertain event becomes known. The triangles, or end nodes, indicate the end of the time horizon.
- The branches indicate the stage that follows, depending on which decision is made or which scenario unfolds.
- A probability is given on top of each branch that emanates from a chance node. This indicates the likelihood of that particular outcome materializing, given

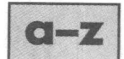

that all the preceding steps have already happened. These uncertainties are outside your control. The probabilities of all the branches emanating from a chance node sum to one.

- Below each branch that emanates from a decision or chance node a monetary value can be added to indicate the cash in- or outflows associated with that particular decision or outcome.
- To the right of the end node two numbers are shown, the upper one representing the likelihood of ending up in that particular scenario, and the lower one the cumulative monetary value.

A key insight resulting from a decision-tree analysis is the so-called *expected value*. Starting at the right of the tree and working back to the left, we perform two types of calculations:

- At each chance node (circle), we compute an expected value as the sum of the probability-weighted expected values associated with the successor nodes.
- At each decision node (square), we determine the highest expected value of the successor nodes. The branch(es) resulting in the highest expected value are indicated by "TRUE," the others by "FALSE," indicating a preferred set of actions based on maximizing the expected value of the project.

Continuing this process, we arrive at the root node of the tree with the *expected value* of the decision tree. The term "expected value" is rather confusing, however, as this value should never be *expected*. In fact, it may even be impossible to obtain, and is merely a probability- weighted average of all the potential outcomes.

USING DECISION ANALYSIS TO VALUE R&D PROJECTS

Decision trees are a natural tool to value R&D projects, as these projects typically consist of several phases. Each project phase can be associated with a stage-gate, a point at which one decides whether or not to continue with the project, depending on the results of the earlier phases and new information obtained about the future. The results of each stage can be represented by a chance node in a decision tree, with the option to abandon the project as a decision node. Other chance nodes can be added to represent possible competitor actions, legislation uncertainties, and global economic conditions. Decision nodes can be added to represent different possible actions, including the injection of more funds and resources in case of favorable developments, accelerating the project to bring forward its market launch date, etc.

Figure 1. Example of decision-tree analysis for a R&D project

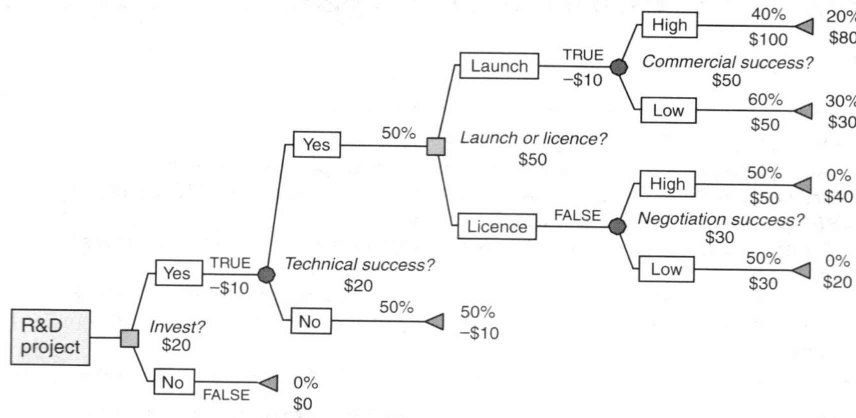

Figure 2. Decision tree for the Phytopharm project

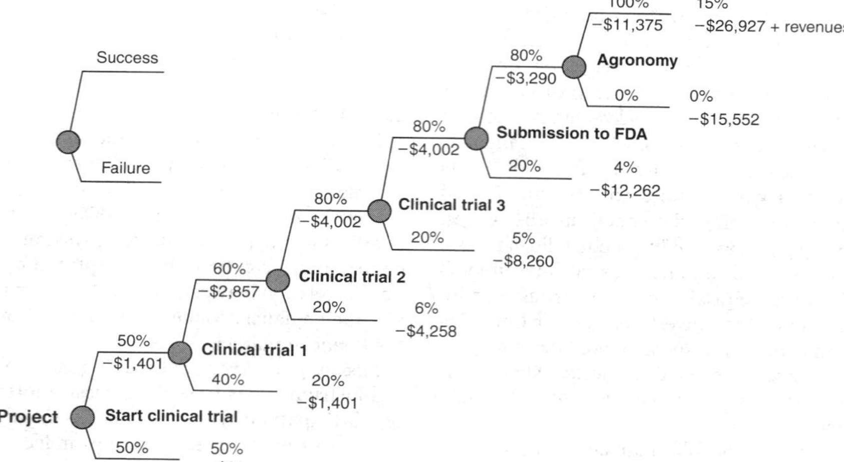

Figure 3. Example of a tornado diagram

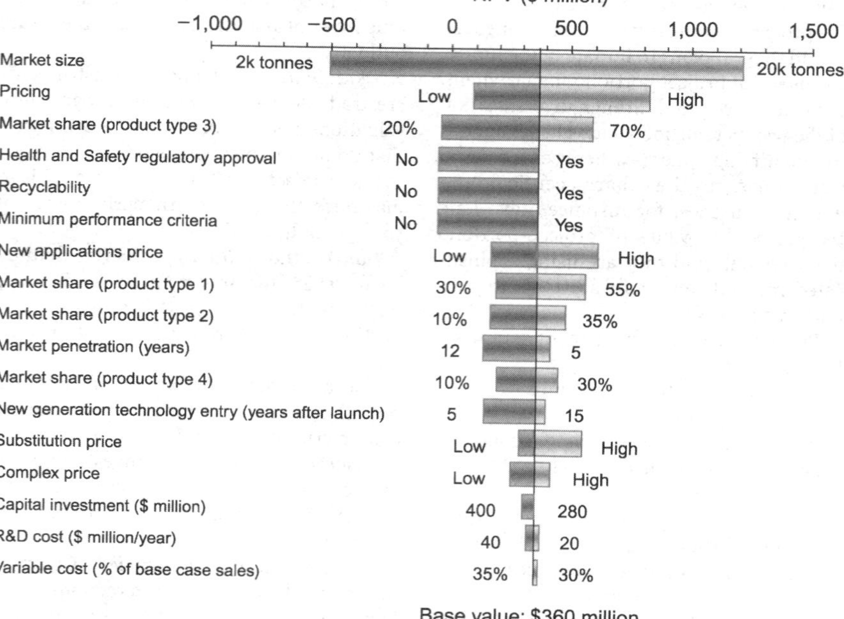

"If a man will begin with certainties, he shall end in doubts, but if he will be content to begin with doubts, he shall end in certainties." Francis Bacon

  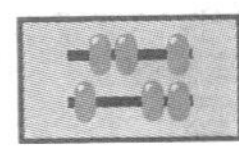   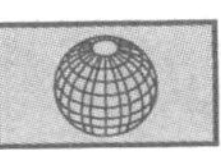   
a–z

As R&D projects typically take several years to complete, it is essential that the cash flows in the decision tree are discounted at an appropriate rate to take into account the firm's cost of capital. As each chance and decision node corresponds to a point in time, this can be accomplished by discounting each cash flow associated with a chance or decision node appropriately. When all cash flows are discounted, the expected value will then become an *expected net present value*, or eNPV.

Again, the eNPV should not be expected, but is merely a probability- weighted average of all the potential results, discounted at an appropriate cost of capital. Nevertheless, the eNPV is a crucial number, indicating the value of the project, because it considers all possible scenarios and how likely they are. In principle, if the eNPV of a project is positive, the project will add value and should be undertaken. Although for a one-time project the eNPV should not be expected, the strategy of pursuing projects with positive eNPV will, in the long run, result in the highest possible profit for your organization. If, however, the eNPV is negative, other and better uses for the required funds and resources can be found.

A second deliverable of a decision-tree analysis for R&D projects, apart from the eNPV, is the risk profile, which shows the potential outcomes and their likelihood. Of particular interest is the potential downside, the worst possible result with a nonzero likelihood. If this downside is large enough to cause potential financial distress to the company, then perhaps the project should not be pursued after all, despite a potential positive eNPV. If the worst-case scenario is very unlikely, another useful metric can be used, namely the value-at-risk (VaR). The VaR indicates the loss that could result from a project with a certain probability, for example 5%. So if the VaR of an R&D project is $10 million, this means that we estimate a 5% chance of losing $10 million or more if we pursue the project. Again, this could be a reason for rejecting a project that would otherwise be interesting (because of a positive eNPV), depending on the risk appetite and liquidity of the company.

CONCLUSION

Decision analysis and decision trees are widely used for valuing R&D projects, because they are ideally suited to deal with the phased nature of R&D investments. Traditional financial valuation methods are based on assumptions that are not realistic in a R&D environment. The key deliverables of a decision-tree analysis of a R&D project is the project's expected net present value (eNPV) and its value-at-risk (VaR), two crucial criteria when deciding whether or not to pursue a project and include it in the organization's portfolio. The general rule is that the eNPV should be positive, and the VaR not so high that it may cause financial distress in case of an unfavorable outcome.

CASE STUDY

Phytopharm plc

All of the world's leading life sciences companies use decision-analytic approaches to value their portfolio of R&D projects. In fact, many have a decision-analysis group, responsible for reviewing the R&D portfolio. They typically use a wide variety of criteria to assess R&D projects, including financial value measured by the projects' net present value, sales, and growth potential, with a special focus on potential blockbusters, pipeline balance over time and over different therapeutic areas, risk, unmet medical need, and strategic fit, expressed as a desire to build strength in certain therapy areas. An array of tools is used to support this analysis, including net present value, decision analysis, and Monte Carlo simulation.

Before a pharmaceutical drug can be approved for production and marketing, stringent scientific procedures must be followed in several stages to ensure patient safety. The drug development process is typically composed of basic research (approximately two years), pre-clinical testing (approximately three years), clinical trials (approximately six years, consisting of phases I, II, and III), followed by a review by regulatory authorities. A new pharmaceutical drug that is being investigated can fail to make it through any one of these stages due to potential harmful side effects or insufficient proof of effectiveness. On average, only one in five medicines that enters clinical trials is launched; and only 1 in 10,000 compounds in the research phase makes it to the market.

Due to the massive resources required to perform the late-stage clinical trials, smaller firms such as biotech companies or university spin-offs typically only perform the first steps of pharmaceutical research and development. If the product passes these first few stages, the product is outlicensed to partners with the financial, R&D, and marketing capabilities to further develop and launch it in the market. This was the case for Phytopharm plc, a pharmaceutical and functional food company based in Cambridgeshire, England.

Several years ago, Phytopharm acquired the exclusive license to develop and market a natural appetite suppressant derived from the *Hoodia gordonii* succulent, a cactus that grows in the Kalahari Desert. In 2004, Phytopharm's senior management was preparing to start negotiations for outlicensing this product, which had shown promise in early pre-clinical and clinical trials and successfully passed proof-of-principle. Although Phytopharm's senior management was confident that the product could be very successful, it needed a comprehensive and flexible methodology to rigorously predict and value the product's potential. A choice was made to use decision analysis as it provided transparency and flexibility, useful characteristics in a negotiation environment.

Figure 2 shows how the project was represented as a decision tree, with the different chance nodes corresponding to the different stages that had to be successfully navigated before the product could be marketed (all numbers are disguised and for illustrative purposes only). Decision nodes (not shown) could be added to represent decisions such as abandoning the development in case of unfavorable clinical trial results or commercial outlook, or choosing between different alternative technologies or markets.

In December 2004, Phytopharm licensed the product to Unilever for $40 million and an undisclosed royalty on the sales of all products containing the extract. Unfortunately, in November 2008, Unilever decided to abandon the product due to a recent clinical study that provided unsatisfactory results. This possibility was foreseen in the decision-tree analysis, and had been incorporated when calculating the project's value at the time of licensing[2].

MAKING IT HAPPEN

There are several challenges when using decision trees for valuing R&D projects. For example:

- Which discount rate should be used? Traditional finance theory suggests that a discount rate should be used that reflects the cost of capital of a typical project. The question, however, is what to do when a project is not very typical. And what if the risk changes profoundly over the life cycle of the project? These issues are currently the topic of heated debate, both in R&D organizations and business schools. Note, however, that since the

"Profits arise out of the inherent, absolute unpredictability of things." Frank Knight

possibility of failure is already explicitly included in a decision-tree analysis, this risk should not be used to further increase the discount rate used to evaluate the project. The only risk that should be considered is the nondiversifiable market risk of the project, i.e., the correlation of the project and market returns.
- When a project contains many stages, with numerous uncertainties and possible decisions, a decision tree can easily "explode" and become unwieldy. Therefore, it is recommended that before carrying out a decision-tree analysis, a sensitivity analysis is performed to determine the main causes of uncertainty, which can then be incorporated in the decision tree. A so-called tornado diagram, which visualizes the key risks in a horizontal bar chart that resembles a tornado, can be used to determine these key risks. An example is shown in Figure 3.
- The validity of any conclusions drawn from a decision analysis depends heavily on the quality of the information used in the analysis. The principle "garbage-in-garbage-out" applies in this context. A common issue that has been observed is the tendency for people to be overconfident, in the sense that we all typically underestimate the magnitude of risks that we are facing. This has led to many criticizing the value-at-risk concept for performing a financial risk assessment, as none of these models could predict the magnitude of the current financial crisis. Therefore, it is essential that sufficient attention is paid to the quality of the data used in the analysis.
- A chance node in a decision tree can distinguish several possible outcomes, but it cannot specify a continuous range of outcomes. This, of course, can be approximated by defining numerous separate outcomes, but doing this will result in the tree "exploding." A better approach is to combine decision-tree analysis with a Monte Carlo simulation, which is ideally suited for analyzing risks with a continuous range of potential outcomes.

MORE INFO

Books:

Savage, Sam L. *Decision Making with Insight*. 2nd ed. Cincinnati, OH: South-Western College Publishing, 2003.

Winston, Wayne L., and S. Christian Albright. *Practical Management Science*. 3rd ed. Cincinnati, OH: South-Western College Publishing, 2006.

Websites:

Decision Analysis Society, a subdivision of the Institute for Operations Research and Management Science (INFORMS): decision-analysis.society.informs.org

Palisade Corporation, a provider of decision-analysis software, used to create the examples in this article: www.palisade.com

Strategic Decisions Group, a strategy consulting firm specializing in decision analysis and founded by, among others, the father of decision analysis, Professor Ronald A. Howard of Stanford University: www.sdg.com

See Also:

★ Real Options: Opportunity from Risk (pp. 915–917)
★ Reinvesting in the Company versus Rewarding Investors with Distributions (pp. 701–702)
✔ Analysis Using Monte Carlo Simulation (p. 1062)
✔ Understanding Decision-Tree Analysis (p. 1179)
✔ Understanding Real Options (p. 1181)
✔ Understanding the Weighted Average Cost of Capital (WACC) (p. 1002)
Amos Tversky (p. 1316)

NOTE

1 Kendall, Gerald I., and Steven C. Rollins. *Advanced Project Portfolio Management and the PMO: Multiplying ROI at Warp Speed*. Boca Raton, FL: J. Ross Publishing, 2003.

"Chance favors only the prepared mind." Louis Pasteur

  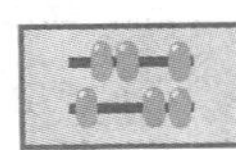   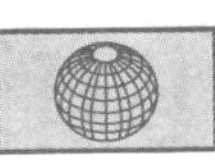   

Using Financial Analysis to Evaluate Strategy

by David Sadtler

EXECUTIVE SUMMARY

- Financial analysis is widely used to assess investment proposals, but less commonly to evaluate strategy.
- Strategy, both at business unit level (are we competing successfully?) and at the corporate level (does this portfolio of businesses make sense for the shareholders?), needs continuing evaluation.
- Business-level strategy can be judged by economic value added (EVA) analysis.
- Corporate-level strategy can be assessed by breakup analysis.
- Line managers are not necessarily motivated to do these analyses; it is thus up to others, especially the nonexecutive members of the board, to advocate them

INTRODUCTION

Many well-known tools and techniques of financial analysis are used by investors, stockbrokers, and corporate managers to assess corporate performance. Their use is particularly prevalent in mergers and acquisitions and in the analysis of capital expenditure. But how often do we say: "Let's do some financial analysis to see if this strategy is any good. Let's take a view on the corporate portfolio and the extent to which value is added by the corporate center and use financial tools to do it." In my experience, this doesn't happen much.

When companies undertake an acquisition, extensive financial analysis accompanies the investigation by managers, the proposals put to the board, and, if necessary, the story that is told to investors and the financial community. Comparisons are made with valuations of similar businesses and with transactions of a similar nature. Discounted cash flow techniques are used to assess the impact of different outcomes and the extent to which the investment is likely to recover the cost of capital employed in it. So the use of financial analysis for decision-making in the corporate environment is well known and widespread. Indeed, the essence of the core technique—present value and discounted cash flow analysis—has been around for at least 50 years. The tools are well known, credible, and widely accepted.

What about using financial analysis to assess strategy? In nearly all companies there are two levels of strategy that must be kept under constant surveillance by the custodians of stockholder investment. First, the viability of the individual businesses must be constantly examined. Are they earning satisfactory returns—or, indeed, returns in excess of the cost of capital employed in them? Second, does the corporate portfolio make sense? Would some parts of the business be better off elsewhere? There are straightforward tools to help in answering these questions and they should be regularly applied by the board of directors.

Why then does such an analysis not seem to be a widespread and regular practice? I think that the answer is pretty obvious. Top managers often do not want to admit that some parts of their business portfolio are unviable or that they are not the right owners. It's an agency problem, where management's motives diverge from the interests of the stockholders. But there are others whose job it is to question performance and to be sure that these agency problems do not stand in the way of the interests of stockholders. Nonexecutive directors on the board of directors are in this position, as are representatives of the investment community who decide on whether to advocate support for the organization. But to assess strategy—both at the corporate level and at the level of the individual business—they need suitable tools.

CORPORATE-LEVEL STRATEGY

Corporate-level strategy, as comprehensively described in the writings and teachings of the Ashridge Strategic Management Centre (see the More Info section) involves ensuring that value is added by the corporate center to each and every business unit within the portfolio. A number of useful frameworks and techniques have been available for some time to test the quality and intensity of corporate value added. Managers at both the business unit level and at the corporate center can be challenged to explain the exact nature of corporate value added (what do you do to make this business more successful and thus more valuable?). Long-term competitive performance (market share in key segments) can be used to assess the center's role in ensuring lasting commercial and financial viability. Comparison of the management structure and style with key comparator companies (especially those with more successful financial performance) can be used to assess both strengths and weaknesses in value added.

It is thus possible to take a reading on whether or not the corporate owners are doing an adequate job. The owners must address two questions: first, do we really add substantive value to each of our businesses; and, second, what businesses should we be in?

But these tests are *qualitative*. They make use of individual judgments, recollections, and viewpoints. While often pertinent and relevant, they can also be dreadfully biased. An alternative is to make the evaluation a *quantitative* one.

A straightforward financial tool is available to assess the overall success of the parenting capability of any big company, namely, breakup analysis. Breakup analysis takes an arm's length view of the market value of each of the company's businesses and compares the total of these values with corporate market capitalization, which is the value the marketplace places on the corporation as a whole. If the latter is less than the former, corporate strategy isn't working. The market is saying that the corporate center is *destroying* value. Synergies are not believed.

HOW TO DO A BREAKUP ANALYSIS

1. Subdivide the company into discrete businesses, focusing on particular customer groups and operating in identifiable industries. You will know that you are defining the business at the right level when it is easy to identify comparable companies.
2. Determine a baseline profit-after-tax figure for each business. Outside analysts will be constrained by the availability of reported information, but insiders should have all the necessary information. If profit performance has been uneven, use the budgeted figure for the coming year tempered by a judgment about how likely it is to be realized.
3. Corporate overhead costs, if allocated, should be removed from the cost basis of the individual businesses, subject to the limitation that any activities which would have to be added in were the business to be operating on its own must be accounted for. One famous Dutch electrical equipment company assesses a

"The business world worships mediocrity. Officially we revere free enterprise, initiative, and individuality. Unofficially we fear it." George Lois

  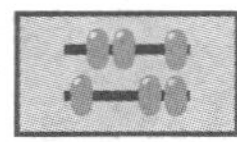      

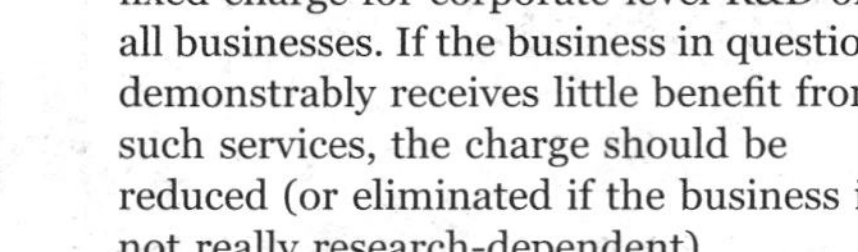

fixed charge for corporate-level R&D on all businesses. If the business in question demonstrably receives little benefit from such services, the charge should be reduced (or eliminated if the business is not really research-dependent) accordingly.

4 Identify comparable companies whose stock is publicly traded. Make a judgment about whether the business being analyzed deserves a rating below, equal to, or above that of the average of comparable companies. Decide on an earnings multiple and calculate *pro forma* market value accordingly.
5 Take note of the current market capitalization of the company as a whole. Make a judgment about whether any exceptional circumstances have caused a temporary departure from the norm. Determine a baseline market capitalization figure. For example, the sudden appearance of very bad news (like a financial scandal) concerning a key competitor can sometimes cause a selloff of major sector participants until the market's nervousness is allayed. Such an apparent "blip" must be considered.
6 Compare this latter figure with the total of the *pro forma* market values of the individual businesses and compare the two figures, after adjusting for borrowings at the corporate level.

Stockbroker analysts often perform similar analyses when judging whether a company is a plausible takeover candidate.

Perhaps the most famous example of a failed corporate-level strategy was that characterizing Imperial Chemical Industries (ICI) in the 1980s, at the time Britain's largest industrial company. ICI was a dominant player in basic chemicals, a notoriously cyclical and increasingly competitive business, where returns have often been unsatisfactory. It also owned a highly successful pharmaceuticals business which produced most of ICI's profit. Outside observers noted that an arm's length valuation of the pharmaceutical business alone was worth more than all of ICI together.[1] This is just another way of saying that the corporate-level strategy was a failure (or that the chemicals business was worth less than nothing). Had ICI's board made this calculation and honestly confronted it, it would have broken the company up itself rather than waiting for a threat from outside to necessitate it.

BUSINESS UNIT STRATEGY

Similarly, many tools and techniques are available to assess the viability of strategy at the level of each business in the corporate portfolio. Each company has its own favourite measures, against which managerial bonuses are often paid. Much attention is paid to these measures, and therefore what they are, and the objectivity with which they have been selected, is important for stockholders. Alas, there are many ways to rig the numbers to make the outcome appear satisfactory even if the reality is somewhat different.

But there is one measure that is hard to rig. Economic value added (EVA) analysis simply calculates business profitability after the imposition of a charge for the capital employed in the business. The tools for doing this are highly developed and, indeed, are championed by a number of consulting firms. The measures can be applied to any business in any company. A division earning $10 million pretax on turnover of $100 million and capital employed in the business of $60 million might, at first glance, be viewed as displaying creditable performance. But at a 35% tax rate and with a cost of capital of 12%, EVA is negative ($10 million × 65% − 0.12 × $60 million = $6.5 million − $7.2 million = − $0.7 million).

The implications of such an analysis are clear. If a business consistently demonstrates negative EVA, it is "parasitical"—eroding stockholder wealth. New investment is folly unless a fundamental game change can credibly be expected to result in positive EVA.

There is the possibility that it is not the fault of the operating management team. Some industries, in the aggregate, produce negative EVA. Airlines are the classic example. Warren Buffett recently observed that the total profitability for the entire industry since its inception has been zero. No one in their right mind would start an airline now. Since deregulation in 1978, there have been at least 100 bankruptcies in the airline businesses.[2] Management teams operating in one of these unhappy industries may actually be doing a good job on a relative basis but, alas, not for their stockholders or for the economy as a whole. How is it possible that an entire industry, perhaps with one or two exceptions, can fail to earn an "economic rent"? How can investors continue to commit capital to industries in which acceptable returns are unlikely? A number of explanations have been offered.

In developed economies major employers, with the major political pressure they can bring to bear, often prop up failing performers and keep marginal plants open, as in the car industry. Barriers to exit can be formidable, especially in industries where capital equipment is only of use in that industry and lasts a long time. Measures of profitability may be misleading. Managerial bias and incentives can prevent problems from being addressed in an objective way. Managers in unsatisfactory industries may not want to admit to the situation because it could make them look foolish—or worse, unemployable. And investors may simply be incompetent. It is not enough to suggest that they might simply buy stocks with high dividend yields on the basis of a very low valuation of assets. Any investor looking to the longer term, as most institutional investors seem to do, will eventually focus on total stockholder return. Term lenders presumably do the same. They'll want capital investment to pay out.

HOW TO CALCULATE EVA

1 The formula to calculate EVA is fairly simple. The formula is: EVA = net operating profit after taxes less the after-tax cost of capital employed.
2 The operating profit includes deductions from revenues for the cost of goods sold and for the operating expenses. Interest expense is then subtracted to cover the cost of the debt capital used, income taxes are then subtracted, and, finally, a cost for the equity capital is subtracted from the net income after tax to obtain the EVA.
3 The cost of equity capital can be derived by using any one of several approaches. Perhaps the simplest approach is to use the interest rate that a company can borrow at and then add a risk premium. The risk premium is added because investors require a higher return to invest in stock than they require for bonds. This is often called the bond yield plus risk premium approach. A typical equity risk premium is about 4%, so if a company can borrow at 10% its cost of equity capital would be 14%.
Alternatively, use the weighted average cost of capital (WACC), a figure that is often well known to big companies and available from public data sources.

Alternatively, the cause of negative EVA may simply be poor management and a consistently weak competitive position. The managers of such a business are simply not offering a product or service which pleases enough customers for the business to be viable. We call this a failed competitive strategy.

Whether the problem at business unit level is participation in a low-profit industry or a failed competitive strategy, the business does not deserve further investment. It should be liquidated in the best way possible. Such businesses are likely to display longer-term negative EVA.

  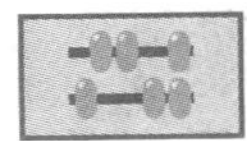      

OBJECTIONS

Understandably, there are those who resist the notion of assessing strategy at either level by means of quantitative measures and analysis. Many such arguments claim unfairness, or a lack of true comparability. We see this for example in the daily news, when head teachers complain about league tables (often, of course, because the tables give their school a low rank) because, they say, the circumstances of their school are exceptional. They may even be right. But the school's performance is still lousy.

Similarly, business people will often argue in this way against the imposition of regular objective checks.

CONCLUSION

Financial calculations of the kind described above which give a clear indication of failed strategy at either the corporate or business unit level require action.

- Failed corporate strategies call for remedies ranging from reinvigorated management to structural breakup. It is up to the board to decide on the seriousness of the problem and the nature of the appropriate remedies. Failure to take appropriate action will often result in stockholder dissatisfaction and attempts by outsiders to restructure the company.
- Failed business unit strategies likewise demand action, since continuing on this basis constitutes a *de facto* drain on capital. Obviously, this cannot continue indefinitely. Whatever the remedy, the key is a managerial realization that "business as usual" is not an option.
- This thinking and approach to analysis is simple. Good stewardship demands that these questions are raised regularly and acted on.

MORE INFO

Books:

Collis, David J., and Cynthia A. Montgomery. *Corporate Strategy: A Resource-Based Approach*. 2nd ed. Boston, MA: McGraw-Hill/Irwin, 2005.

Goold, Michael, Andrew Campbell, and Marcus Alexander. *Corporate-Level Sttrategy: Creating Value in the Multibusiness Company*. New York: Wiley, 1994.

Johnson, Gerry, Kevan Scholes, and Richard Whittington. *Exploring Corporate Strategy: Text and Cases*. 8th ed. Harlow, UK: Pearson Education, 2008.

Sadtler, David, Andrew Campbell, and Richard Koch. *Break Up! When Large Companies Are Worth More Dead Than Alive*. London: Capstone, 1997.

Stern, Joel M., John S. Shiely, and Irwin Ross. *The EVA Challenge: Implementing Value Added Change in an Organization*. New York: Wiley, 2004.

Article:

Campbell, Andrew, Michael Goold, and Marcus Alexander. "Corporate strategy: The quest for parenting advantage." *Harvard Business Review* (March–April 1995): 120–132. Online at: hbr.org/1995/03/corporate-strategy/ar/1

Websites:

Ashridge Strategic Management Centre, linked from Ashridge Business School home page: www.ashridge.org.uk

Investopedia article on EVA: www.investopedia.com/university/EVA

See Also:

★ Allocating Corporate Capital Fairly (pp. 11–12)
★ Boardroom Roles (pp. 643–644)
★ Improving Corporate Profitability Through Accountability (pp. 685–686)
Economic Value Added (p. 1222)
Corporate-Level Strategy: Creating Value in the Multibusiness Company (p. 1345)
Corporate Strategy: An Analytic Approach to Business Policy for Growth and Expansion (p. 1346)
The EVA Challenge: Implementing Value-Added Change in an Organization (p. 1351)

NOTES

1 Geoffrey Owen and Trevor Harrison. "Why ICI chose to demerge." *Harvard Business Review* (March–April 1995): 133–142.

2 Jon Bonné. "Airlines still struggle with paths to profit: After 100 years, it's no easier to get rich flying planes." msnbc.com (December 12, 2003).

"A manager is an assistant to his men." Thomas J. Watson, Sr

        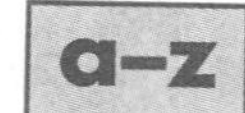

Why EVA Is the Best Measurement Tool for Creating Shareholder Value by Erik Stern

EXECUTIVE SUMMARY

- Economic value added (EVA) has transformed the corporate finance scene and business practice by transferring modern business theory from classroom to boardroom.
- Traditional metrics, with their roots in accounting, distort economic reality. For example, crucial long-term intangible investments often fall foul of traditional metrics.
- If stockholder value is the goal, then the key to any metric must be the cost of capital, or stockholders' required return.
- At its best EVA is not just a financial metric, it is a complete management system focused on value creation.
- Incentive-based EVA uniquely aligns the interests of managers, employees, and stockholders. Studies show that EVA companies, after implementation, have increased their market value over peer by some 50% over five years.
- Bold implementation of EVA signals the beginnings of transparency and accountability, though it is too often the subject of lip service. Implementing EVA half-heartedly or without incentives spells disappointment.
- A balanced scorecard demands EVA as the balancing mechanism. EVA covers everything managers can influence, and therefore all drivers of value.

INTRODUCTION

Financial measuring tools are many and varied. The media and equity analysts focus on financial accounting metrics such as sales and sales growth, margin, operating profit and operating profit growth, bottom-line earnings and its partner earnings per share (EPS), market value, return on equity, and return on assets or cash flow.

Each of these metrics is flawed. Neither sales nor operating profit accounts for the financial requirements necessary to achieve them, in terms of either annual expenses or capital invested. Bottom-line profits and EPS take no account of the fact that equity has a cost. Market value ignores the capital employed to create it—invest more, and of course market value rises, without necessarily creating value. And yet each is popular.

Why is so fundamental a series of misapprehensions so widespread? The answer lies in the past. Accounting operating profit is conservative—literally. It focuses on collateral, or at least what would be left of a company after bankruptcy. This is a more than adequate measure for a bank, but it is misleading for an investor. The theory of modern business is founded on the blindingly simple insight that business is primarily about economics, not accounting.

THE PROBLEMS WITH EXISTING CORPORATE FINANCE MEASURES

Debt-inspired measures are misleading because they *expense*—write off as expenses—aspects of business that are becoming increasingly important. Long-term intangible investments (training, brand building, and so on), in particular, create much of the value of companies today. Yet traditional accounting procedures expense these rather than treating them as investments. Additionally, investments in acquisitions (goodwill) and in restructuring (extraordinary items) are expensed. This is a mistake. A focus on value demands that long-term investments should appear on the balance sheet for the current year, taking the cost of capital into account.

Unless they take into account the cost of capital, return measures can become inflated. Furthermore, concentrating on percentages can lead to a misguided focus—for example, reducing capital investments (especially intangibles) calculated to create profits in the future.

If the hurdle rate for returns is very high, increases may discourage optimal creation of value. If the hurdle for returns is very low, increases may destroy value. If return objectives are above the required returns of investors—the right benchmark—then managers may forgo investments that create value. If returns are the objective and an increase fails to meet this required return, value destruction results.

Of other measures, cash flow will not provide the right answers in growing businesses. When Wal-Mart was growing rapidly, new stores cost more than the existing cash flow, yet no one demanded that the company stop investing and growing. Furthermore, the net present value of free cash flow emphasizes success in the terminal value of the equation rather than the horizon that managers can visualize and experience. Free cash flow, in other words, is not a flow measure.

MVA

The best measure of corporate performance is market value added (MVA), because this measure differentiates between the total market value, including debt and equity, and the total capital invested: MVA is the difference. (MVA may also be viewed as management value added—the value managers have added to a company.)

The problem is that MVA is strongly affected by stock price, which is notoriously independent of senior executives. This makes MVA less useful for encouraging the creation of value, since it has limited operational use.

THE NEED FOR A MEANINGFUL FINANCIAL MEASURE

An alternative is necessary, one that focuses on what managers can influence rather than what they cannot. The measure should differentiate between financial inputs—what enters a company over time—and outputs—the value created. Clearly our choice should not be a driver of value such as the financial accounting metrics that managers can influence. Consider instead output, on an annual basis, as operating profit after tax, with certain adjustments for intangible and other long-term investments and other accounting anomalies, and input as the annual rental charge on the total capital employed, both debt and equity. The rental charge or required return, known alternatively as the hurdle rate for investments or the weighted average cost of capital, is the true benchmark against which all investments and management should be measured. This is economic value added (EVA).

UNDERSTANDING EVA

EVA covers all that managers can influence, all drivers of value. This is seen more easily if we view EVA as the capital investment multiplied by the difference between the actual return and the required return. If we think in addition about the required return as a mix of business risk and financial risk (where financial risk, or debt level, has a potential benefit also), then we have four of the major components of market value as defined by Merton Miller and Franco Modigliani. These are:

- the cost of capital for business risk
- the amount of debt

"In our view, derivatives are financial weapons of mass destruction carrying dangers that, while latent, are potentially lethal." Warren Buffett

  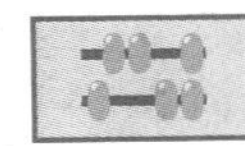      

- the current level of operating profit
- capital expenditure

The other components look at future EVA (investor expectations for future growth) in the current level of EVA—what we call FGV, or future growth value. They are the expected return on new investment, and the time horizon for excess growth in profitability or EVA. Managers can influence more or less imperfectly the debt, operating profit, capital expenditure, and future returns. They influence the horizon and business risk little, if at all.

The Value and Scope of EVA

EVA covers profit and loss and the balance sheet, differentiating intangibles and growth, and thus all factors of production. Growing or improving EVA is the goal, with historic investments viewed as sunk. Hence, managers should focus on growing when the returns are greater than the cost of capital, redeploying capital when the returns are less than the cost, and improving returns on existing capital, as well as having an optimal capital structure (debt versus equity).

If value creation is key, then EVA is the answer, and improvement of EVA is the goal. How managers achieve this or choose to accomplish this depends on what they think is success for their business. Of course the answer may depend on the state of the economy. In reality, investing and containing costs are crucial everywhere in the economic cycle. However, criticism thrives in a falling market and falters in a rising one. A falling market puts failing companies under the microscope, and a rising market forgives all but the worst performers.

In other words, containing costs increases current and near-term EVA, and is always crucial. But investing determines near-term and future EVA and is also always crucial, if the cash is available.

Performance measurement is the bedrock of business. Since people manage what they measure, EVA can form the foundation for a more transparent and accountable management system, especially when combined with powerful incentives to improve EVA at every level, in every activity, across all functions, and independent of geography. With rights to make decisions accurately allocated, a fair system of transfer pricing in place, information flowing freely, and the appropriate tools and training offered, responsibility joins transparency and accountability through robust control and performance evaluation. Pay for the right performance, and value-based management results.

Under EVA, budgeting gives way to long-term planning. Control of the ends and the means is relinquished respectively to externally and objectively determined investor expectations, and to management choice and opportunity that allow managers to bet their own success on their meeting or beating stockholder requirements.

CONCLUSION

EVA is, in short, the best measurement tool for creating stockholder value. A balanced scorecard of metrics allows for a big-picture view, but what is the balancing mechanism? If value creation over the long term is the goal (and if it isn't, stockholders should run), then EVA must be the balancing mechanism. Sales, margin, operating profit, and bottom-line profit simply fall short. Market value lacks levers. Return measures give the wrong answers. Only EVA can change companies.

Indeed, EVA correlates better with stock price than any other measure: by 50%, compared with up to 30% for other metrics. Since EVA charges for all the factors of production, continuous improvement in EVA always furnishes investors with an increase in value.

Clearly, if an organization pays lip service to EVA and blindly measures it without thinking about the behavioral consequences and the need to balance simplicity and accuracy, or else provides poorly considered or misguided incentives to create EVA, the outcome will disappoint. However, a robust system that's adhered to in times of boom and bust will provide the foundation of sound decision-making and business practices.

MAKING IT HAPPEN

- Start using EVA as the key financial measure: subtract input (annual rental charge on the total capital employed) from output (adjusted operating profit after tax).
- Employ EVA as the foundation of a more transparent, responsible, and accountable management system, with robust control and performance evaluation.
- With the right to make decisions accurately allocated, put a fair EVA-based system of transfer pricing in place.
- Couple continuous restructuring of existing businesses to milk value with cautious investment in future businesses.
- Focus managers on growing where returns exceed cost of capital, and on redeploying capital where returns are less than its cost.
- Insist on improving returns on existing capital as well as on having an optimal capital structure (debt versus equity).

MORE INFO

Books:

Bloxham, Eleanor. *Economic Value Management: Applications and Techniques*. Hoboken, NJ: Wiley, 2003.

Stern, Joel M., and John S. Shiely. *The EVA Challenge: Implementing Value-Added Change in an Organization*. New York: Wiley, 2004.

Young, David, and Stephen F. O'Byrne. *EVA and Value-Based Management: A Practical Guide To Implementation*. New York: McGraw-Hill, 2000.

Website:

A site set up by Stern Stewart, the global consulting company which pioneered the development of the EVA framework: www.eva.com

See Also:

★ Creating Value with EVA (pp. 814–816)
★ Managing 21st Century Finances (pp. 66–67)
★ The Missing Metrics: Managing the Cost of Complexity (pp. 766–768)
★ Reinvesting in the Company versus Rewarding Investors with Distributions (pp. 701–702)
✔ Assessing Business Performance (p. 1144)
✔ Calculating Total Shareholder Return (p. 1066)
✔ Managing the Time Value of Money (p. 979)
✔ Understanding the Weighted Average Cost of Capital (WACC) (p. 1002)
The EVA Challenge: Implementing Value-Added Change in an Organization (p. 1351)

"One of the soundest rules to remember when making forecasts in the field of economics is that whatever is to happen is happening already." Sylvia Porter

  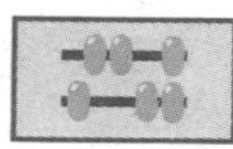   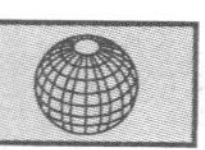   

Viewpoint: Why Management Development Is a Challenge for Both Business Schools and Client Organizations by Andrew Kakabadse

INTRODUCTION

Andrew Kakabadse is professor of international management development at Cranfield Business School. He was the H. Smith Richardson Fellow at the Center for Creative Leadership, North Carolina, in 2005–06 and is a visiting professor at the University of Ulster, Ireland, Macquarie Graduate School of Management, Australia, Thunderbird School of Global Management, Arizona, Université Panthéon-Assas (Paris II), France, and Swinburne University of Technology, Australia. His research covers boards, top teams, and the governance of governments. He has published 37 books, more than 220 articles, and 18 monographs. Kakabadse is coeditor of the *Journal of Management Development* and *Corporate Governance: The International Journal of Business in Society*. Among his most recent books are *Bilderberg People: Elite Power and Consensus in World Affairs* (with Ian Richardson and Nada Kakabadse), *Rice Wine with the Minister: Distilled Wisdom to Manage, Lead and Succeed on the Global Stage* (with Nada Kakabadse) and *Global Boards: One Desire, Many Realities* (with Nada Kakabadse).

If there are general competencies that all managers need, why are so few generic management development programs available from business schools? Why is there such a marked preference for bespoke courses?

The simple and straightforward answer is that the requirement to "skill up" a particular management cadre is almost always raised as a specific issue inside an organization and is driven by events and by the operational context of that organization. At the back of it there is always a problem that needs resolving. Every expenditure by a company or a public body needs to be justified. There is always at least an ad-hoc cost evaluation of the anticipated benefits against the probable costs. So, training initiatives at a senior level, which cost significantly in terms of time and money, have an inertial weight against them to begin with, and very few organizations are prepared to embrace the idea of generic training for senior management. They will sponsor or partly sponsor MBA candidates at lower to middle management level, but that is a different thing altogether.

This being the case, business schools have generally eschewed the idea of putting on generic management development courses, even though you could specify general management competencies that could go into such a course. Courses like that simply would not sell a sufficient number of places. As a result, management development training has evolved as a bespoke discipline geared to meet the particular challenges and problems of specific client organizations.

Is there much common material from course to course, or does everything have to be developed from scratch on each occasion?

The courses tend to have some basic elements that are common to all or to most courses, such as an introduction to leadership, or some of the psychological profiling that we use. But the challenges that the client organizations face make the courses very different from each other. There can be targeting by level, by function, and also by region or division within the organization.

Does the client organization, then, already have a clearly articulated sense of the business or operational challenge that it is facing when it seeks to enlist the help of a business school in developing a course for its management team?

It may, or it may just have a sense that its performance in particular areas is not at an optimal level, or is falling behind by comparison with the competition. Clearly, an organization that is about to undertake a major initiative or new project will be faced, fairly sharply, by the challenges associated with that venture. But even here there is usually a substantial amount of work to be done by the business school in refining the perception of the problem so that the course can be targeted more specifically. Clients will, in general, have a pretty clear sense of what is causing them pain. They have a sense of the damage that is being done or will be done to the organization through people not having sufficient competencies in particular areas.

In this sense, if one steps back and looks at the exercise as a whole, the criteria for the success or otherwise of a particular management training and development initiative are fairly sharply delineated—which is clearly a good thing, both from the client's perspective and from the standpoint of the business school.

Success means that either some area of the business or the organization that was problematic is solved and is perceived to function more smoothly, or the pain associated with getting some new project off the ground, such as a major expansion in a new region or country, is eased. The benefits in each case are palpable and are seen as justifying the intervention.

A far more difficult problem, in many instances, is not how to judge success, but how to get the client organization to open up and allow light to be shed on the real problems that they are having. You have to remember that, in most instances, the project will be initiated by a telephone call and the person making the call may be unable or unwilling to specify the problem at anything like the required level. Our first task, then, is to work at defining the problem to our own satisfaction and to the client's. Then we have to make a judgment about whether that problem is such that it can be helped significantly by our intervention. What can we do, and will what we do make a sufficient difference?

It may well turn out to be the case, when the problem is properly analyzed, that what is required is not management development training but some transformation in operational procedures which the organization may or may not be willing to make. Problem

"Nobody is sure anymore who really runs the company (not even the people who are credited with running it), but the company does run." Joseph Heller

analysis can be a very complex and demanding field. It is a field in which we have acquired a great deal of experience and skill over the years, and part of that skill is recognizing when we can usefully be part of the solution and when we probably cannot.

Is there a significant overlap between the analysis and fact finding that has to be done to specify the type of management development project that will suit a particular organization and the work that a business consultancy would undertake?

There is a great deal of overlap, but of course the aim of a business consultancy is very different. It is usually concerned with business process transformation of one sort or another. Our role is simply to understand the problem or set of challenges that is being faced and to then define what that means in terms of management competencies. However, because the starting-point is always the business as it is—with all that means in terms of internal politics and the dynamics going on inside the organization—getting to the heart of the problem can pose its own significant challenges. It may be, for example, that the processes or strategies devised at the center, at head office level, for example, are not working at a regional level for reasons that no one has clearly articulated. Getting people to speak up honestly and clearly so that we can design the appropriate course for them can be a nontrivial exercise!

The precontract phase of the relationship, then, between the business school and a prospective client will often involve multiple meetings, negotiations, and renegotiations. This whole phase—before there is an agreed contract for a management development project—may take anything from nine to 18 months.

How important is management development as a revenue stream for the business school?

The whole business of executive development is a major part of Cranfield's budget and is a very successful part of our operation. But it has not been easy to grow this side of our business to its current proportions. The market for management development is a very sophisticated one. If you look at the corporate market, a company's value proposition can differ markedly depending on where in the world it is located. In Asia, for example, the focus when it comes to defining the value proposition could be on excellent customer service and delivery. In a developed market the focus may well be on discipline on costs, given the competitive pressure on margins. So it would be a mistake for a business school to develop too generic an approach to management development.

Under tight economic conditions, for an organization to achieve its value proposition depends on the whole of the top team identifying with the proposition and pushing hard to achieve it, irrespective of how it plays in their particular locality. Client companies know this, and they are very sophisticated buyers. They are well beyond generic programs. They want fundamental skill building that will give them the capacity that makes the difference for them and will enable them to outperform the competition, or at least to bring them up to the point where they can compete against the best in their class.

Of course, we do run functional programs, such as courses on financial skills for nonfinancial managers. But these courses are aimed at middle management groups—for example, specialists in sales who have not been exposed to finance. These programs assist individuals, but they don't make the real competitive difference that companies are looking for from management development. An example of a more generic course that addresses the ability to make a real difference would be a course on strategic leadership for CEOs, or the nonexecutive course we run specifically for board members.

For a CEO-level course, what we would be looking at is a workshop approach. This might involve, say, a finance director who has been identified by the organization for the top role coming in and working through a series of problem-solving workshops around the role of the CEO and the issues the CEO faces. The content here, in other words, is the experience that goes with the role, rather than a specific competency such as leadership.

What does the business school bring to the party that the organization itself could not provide as an internal initiative in management development?

The business school, if it is a top school, will have faculty that has a history of in-depth research into management issues, and whose members have worked with CEOs from all kinds of organizations and with government officials and ministers. So there is a wealth of experience there to draw on. Plus, of course, the act of running a program like this for a number of years means that you have built up a considerable body of experience in working through issues with companies, helping them to define their problems and to propose solutions. On top of this, there is the business school's familiarity with techniques such as psychological programming, which looks at how an individual could improve him- or herself in a particular role. All this is a long way from a generic course and it is also, in general, outside the competency of organizations, which have other skills and goals.

We also bring a considered sense of the global context in which the business or organization operates. The business person, for example, who thinks that politics is a mug's game and ignores the political context of the country in which the organization operates is flying blind. A CEO who does not know how to respond to a situation of risk or bribery, or who has not considered the implications for their organization of the various antibribery acts now in force in the advanced economies, is on perilous ground. So we have workshops for CEOs, chairmen, and board members to enable them to make themselves very aware politically, with politics here having both a small "p" and a large "P."

We talk about the necessity for senior management to be at the appropriate level on all three of the "Qs"—namely IQ, EQ, and PQ—the last two referring to their emotional awareness index and political awareness index. All three are important for anyone aspiring to be an organizational strategist. This point is taken better in some countries than in others. Senior management in the United Kingdom, for example, tends not to be particularly context aware.

Many of our clients are from continental Europe. The Germans and the French are much better at realizing the need to contextualize themselves. Senior management of a German or French company going into real estate in Kuwait, for example, would read up on Islam and would do a fair amount of research on the country and region. The British would be likely to focus almost exclusively on real estate values and their probable trajectory. Sometimes that specificity of focus works well, but the risk is that you get blindsided by events that are predictable when seen in a wider context. Political risk is not the least significant of the risks that organizations run when they develop abroad.

One of the weaknesses that we see in both UK and US companies at a senior level is that in today's globalized environment senior management does not understand the movement of monies, of capital flows, around the world and the impact this can have on economies. Again, that is a contextual issue that can have a significant bearing on the success or failure of operational decisions.

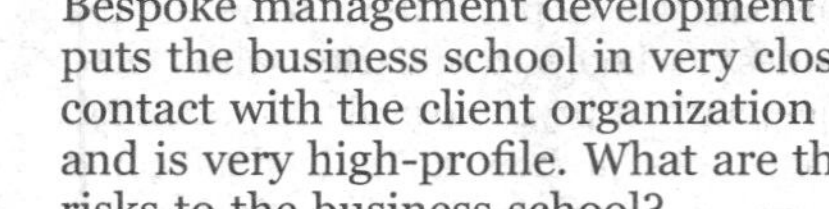

Bespoke management development puts the business school in very close contact with the client organization and is very high-profile. What are the risks to the business school?

Clearly, if you take on an assignment and the intervention is judged to have not delivered the expected value, you have failed and your reputation is at risk—not just with that organization, but with their entire network, through network effects, which are a crucial source of business for business schools.

So, if you are leading this kind of contract, there are things that you have to ensure in order for you to be able to agree to take on the project in the first place. First, you have to be confident that you have clearly defined the problem which the organization is facing, and getting to the heart of this can be a very demanding and nontrivial exercise. You can be faced with several competing, politically influenced versions of the problem from various quarters inside the organization, and you need skill and experience to cut through this to the core of the matter. It may be that things are too fluid in the organization and that there are multiple conflicting issues for which there is no immediate resolution, given the current state of affairs. All you can do then is to present matters as you see them and be prepared to walk away if things cannot be brought into focus. In other words, the business school must not be hell-bent on winning the contract at all costs. Being prepared to say that, as things stand, you cannot proceed is key. The same goes if the problem, once defined, is outside your main competencies as a business school, or does not require those competencies.

Second, you have to achieve the right time frame to deliver the course. Third, you and the client organization have to be comfortable with each other. If they recognize that your definition of their problem is right but they are not comfortable with you, that would be a very strong reason not to proceed and to pass the client on elsewhere. For all these reasons management development remains a challenging field, but it is hugely rewarding for all the parties involved.

MORE INFO

Books:

Bain, Neville, and Roger Barker. *The Effective Board: Building Individual and Board Success*. London: Kogan Page, 2010.

Galavan, Robert, John Murray, and Costas Markides. *Strategy, Innovation, and Change: Challenges for Management*. Oxford: Oxford University Press, 2008.

Gladwell, Malcolm. *Outliers: The Story of Success*. London: Penguin, 2008.

Hall, Tony, and Karen Janman. *The Leadership Illusion: The Importance of Context and Connections*. Basingstoke, UK: Palgrave Macmillan, 2010.

Paxman, Jeremy. *The Political Animal: An Anatomy*. London: Penguin. 2003.

See Also:

★ Viewpoint: CEOs Should Refresh Their Finance Skills (pp. 801–802)

★ Viewpoint: Poverty of Thinking in University Economics and Accountancy Departments (pp. 905–907)

★ Viewpoint: Urgent Need to Retool Business Faculties with Financial Historians and Eject the Financial Engineers (pp. 943–944)

"To be dilatory about giving orders, but to expect absolute punctuality, that is called being a tormentor." Confucius

  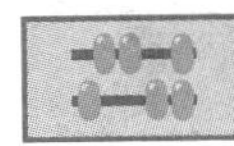   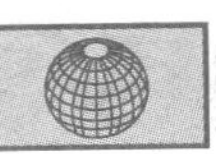   

Winning Commercial Tenders by Damian Merciar

EXECUTIVE SUMMARY

- Winning commercial tenders is a key component of success for professional services firms.
- In order to win, your firm must invest time and resources in gaining knowledge that provides a competitive edge.
- Relationships are vital: remember that you are not aiming just to win one contract, but to establish a long and mutually beneficial partnership with your client.
- Use tendering strategically; when successfully deployed, tendering can be the catalyst for developing new skills and exploring new markets.
- Understand the power and scope of your pricing principles. These can garner greater profit than simple pricing techniques and exploit market positioning for the bidder.

This chapter refers primarily to professional services firms, though the application lends itself more widely across the commercial, if not the manufacturing, sectors. The chapter will follow the headings of an appreciation of what it is that the client is after, followed by an analysis of the market and then the competition. Vendor selection will be discussed and of key consideration, the role of price in formulating a bid.

DETERMINE THE DESIRED OUTCOME

Before a vendor or bidding contractor can consider whether his or her deliverable output is aligned with the client's desired outcome, the client must fully understand what it is they want to achieve by the project. A clearly defined project will greatly assist the vendor in removing the element of second-guessing the client.

Fundamentally, the scope of a project comes down to three things:

- Understanding the client: Appreciate where the client is relative to his or her competitors, and where, with existing resources, he or she would like to be.
- A plan: To get them from their current position to where they would like to be—even if the aim of the project itself is simply to gain greater knowledge of the competitive marketplace. Such insight could be a development milestone and lay the groundwork for implementation.
- Implementation of the results: the application of the operational and strategic recommendations that arise from successful completion of a project.

Of course, the fact-finding may result in a fuller understanding of the client's environment, and so a better proposition than the client originally requested. Firms that are able to outline this additional benefit are more likely to be selected by potential clients.

ANALYZE THE CLIENT

Knowing all about the buyer is crucial—have they been in the market for this type of project before and, if so, who did they use last time? Did they act on the vendor's recommendations? Is the client easy to bid for? Are they likely to have clear expectations, or is the initial bidder selection going to be a time-wasting process because the client has left areas open to interpretation? Do you, as vendor, know how receptive the client may be to recommendations? Is there scope for the client to use your services further—for example to implement the project or to identify and develop an additional plan?

Of all these questions, this last is the most important. Time spent bidding for contracts is vital to winning new work, but time misspent in bidding for the wrong contracts can waste valuable resources and distract attention from more appropriate and winnable contracts.

ANALYZE THE COMPETITION

Develop a comprehensive database of your competitors' activities. Find out the number of bids they place and their success rates. Knowing the client and the brief, would you expect to see your company on a list of bidders? Aim for objectivity—seen through the eyes of a competitor, how would you rate your company's chances of success? Do you have employees who have worked for companies on your list of other bidders, and if so, can they be mined for tactical advantage?

If not, search through public information about the competitors you expect to be bidding against. Break down the search by industry sector and by geography. If time permits, take a calculated view and include an outlier on your shortlist: new companies come to the fore for a reason—can you spot who may be on the ascendant? Include reputation and reliability, cost, and a view on their persuasiveness as a vendor. Do you know how many clients have acted on his or her respective recommendations?

VENDOR SELECTION

Frequently, vendors are disqualified for not following the brief—the college mantra of "answer the question" applies here. *Have* you answered the question? Consider simple but decisive issues such as proofreading your document for clarity and

CASE STUDY

Niche Consultancies—Bidding to Win

A niche consultancy practice in England that specializes in business economics and management received an invitation to tender from a large national telecoms company in Europe. The client was a new one, as was the sector specialism. The time allowed to complete the project was four months, and the potential contribution to that year's fees was £500,000. The managing director was keen to win the project as it would show his company in a favorable light, add intellectual capital, and generally increase the firm's prestige. This would likely help to secure future contracts.

In this project, the relation between fixed telephony and wireless was critical to understanding the client's commercial offering. The MD set about learning all about the sector and the geography in which the telecoms company operated, and he began to put his bid calculations together. He included his best consultants and contacted external contractors to be included in the submission. After pricing for travel, hotels, and currency fluctuation, he stripped down his margin by 15% so that the bid would be seen as evidently competitive. The bid was submitted—only to fail. Genuinely disappointed, the MD requested a debriefing and was told that he had been beaten by an established competitor with greater experience of the intended project.

The client, however, had noted the professionalism of the submission and the obvious care and thought that went into it, and also was impressed by how the MD interviewed over the phone. The next year, when the same client published a follow-up invitation to tender, the MD again submitted a proposal—and won, despite this time excluding the 15% discount. The strategy of bidding carefully and thoroughly, and doing so again after a disappointment, paid off and the learning process had been worth it.

"What they fail to realize is that the quality of the implementation often depends on the quality of the plan."
Freed, Freed, and Romano

        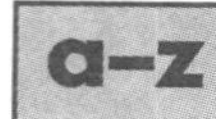

presentation. Are you going to get it done on time? Be comprehensive—do you cover everything fully in the terms of reference, expression of interest, or invitation to bid?

The qualifications of your team need to be part of how you persuade a potential client to use you. Have you got the right people, and if not, can you get them? If you can get them, does it make commercial sense to do so—how will it affect your margin? Using external contractors presents both risks and rewards: at what stage do you decide which is a risk and which an inspired choice? Is there scope for bringing in additional people or swapping people once the project is underway? Can the project be used as a testing ground for potential collaborators? Are those collaborators part of your potential future revenue stream, bringing additional contacts and likely insights with them?

Present the strengths of your team members to the vendor. Promote their relevant experience in a way that will appeal to the client. If necessary, rewrite team member's résumés, concentrating on what they can deliver—this is easier said than done, but it can be worth the time spent. Simple visual tricks, such as leading the eye with paragraph alignment, can help to highlight these skills. Remember that you may have just seconds to stand out.

PRICE CAREFULLY

This section is split into a discussion of the initially appraised price for the tender and the price that is actually submitted after careful and comprehensive consideration.

Initial Price

The bidder's initial price is likely simply to be a function of the expected benefits to the client, how long he has known the client, and the estimated likelihood of winning. In basic economic terms, this is necessary, but not sufficient, information. Your company needs to decide first on a basic pricing strategy:

- Value-based pricing: This is where the price to the client is based on an expectation of the value of the product, where the product is typically either a plan or an implementation. This is a difficult, though potentially more lucrative, approach than rate-based pricing and requires a thorough knowledge of the client's business. It also requires an understanding of how they assess their anticipated changes after completion of the project. Useful metrics for an accurate valuation could be based on increases in revenue, increased market share, a change in market position, insights gained, or likelihood of success.
- Rate-based, or per diem, pricing: More straightforward, the price here can simply be the number of consultants multiplied by their respective rates, multiplied by the number of days on the project. Expenses should be included.

Then there are strategic values to winning a tender:

- How much do you wish to work with the client? They may occupy a sector you have specifically targeted.
- Will your competence as a firm increase—for example, by broadening the experience and skills of your consultants?
- Does the project promote a new regional or national presence for your company?
- Is there scope for additional fees or continued work with the client?

Tactical values should also enter into your consideration. For instance, will the project utilize otherwise underused staff? Will it lead to more training for those engaged in consultancy? Could it increase publicity for your firm? Is your firm in a position to negotiate counter offers and to price for subsequent phases with the same client?

Submitted Price

When all these factors have been duly thought through, the bid may be put forward at a high price—we are confident of winning and can clearly show our greater added value than the competition. Or a low price—for our own internal reasons, we wish to make our presence known in this sector, and so shall view our bid as an investment contributing to the likelihood of future contracts. On the client side, typically, their return on investment will be between 5:1 and 10:1—that is, over the three years after the project or implementation they will be seeking returns between five and ten times the cost of utilizing you.

CONCLUSION: THE STRATEGIC VALUE OF WINNING, AND THE ASSOCIATED RISKS

Some of these values have already been touched on—for example, the opportunity to break into new markets and increase the capabilities of your staff. Directly aligned with these values are potential costs. Can your finances support a start on the project—how are payments to be structured? Do you accurately understand the client's requirements, and can you fulfill them? Do all parties agree on the gains from the project? Will pursuing the project result in a conflict of interest for existing clients? Is there an opportunity cost to fulfilling the project? Might it fundamentally alter the direction of your business? Does the cost of *not* pursuing the bid outweigh all the potential for a negative outcome? If the answer to this last point is yes, then go ahead and bid strategically.

MAKING IT HAPPEN

- Know your competencies, and where you fit in the market place. Are you certain you have access to the professionals needed to do the job?
- Know your competitors and what their strengths are.
- Understand the requirements of your client—*precisely what* do they want?
- Understand that bidding is both a knowledge-based affair and a tactical affair. Ensure that you know how and where to utilize this knowledge. Fully understand your pricing strategy—and make sure you are able to defend it when challenged.

MORE INFO

Books:

Freed, Richard C., Shervin Freed, and Joe Romano. *Writing Winning Business Proposals: Your Guide to Landing the Client, Making the Sale, & Persuading the Boss*. 2nd ed. New York: McGraw-Hill, 2003.

Lewis, Harold. *Bids, Tenders & Proposals: Winning Business Through Best Practice*. 2nd ed. London: Kogan Page, 2007.

Weiss, Alan. *Million Dollar Consulting: The Professional's Guide to Growing a Practice*. 3rd ed. New York: McGraw-Hill, 2003.

Articles and Guides:

Business Link. "Price your product or service." Online at: tinyurl.com/b2q7y5

Small Business Notes. "Value-based pricing." Online at: tinyurl.com/y8jcd4g

Small Business Notes. "Marketing." Online at: tinyurl.com/36s3pr6

UK Trade & Investment. "European Union external aid—Guide to winning business." Online at: tinyurl.com/d9mm9b

"A long term contract is usually established at the request of the client, not as a result of a proposal by you."
Alan Weiss (2003)

CHECKLISTS

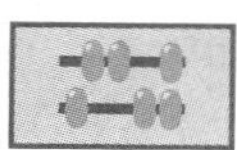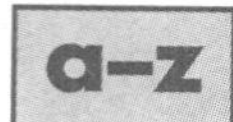

Checklists

Practical solutions for everyday questions and challenges

The Checklists provide you with a comprehensive handbook of practical answers and concepts that appear in business on a daily basis. Each entry reflects current thinking and best management practice, and is designed to give you a practical answer to your problem—fast.

The Checklists provide problem solving via the fast route and cover a variety of subjects from "Setting Up a Key Risk Indicator System" and "Structuring and Negotiating Joint Ventures" to "Understanding and Using Currency Swaps" and "Options for Raising Finance."

Each Checklist includes a definition, a useful list of dos and don'ts, advantages and disadvantages, and action pointers. More information is also included to provide the reader with the opportunity to delve deeper into the subject area.

  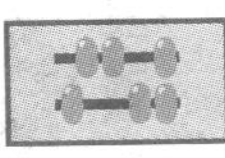   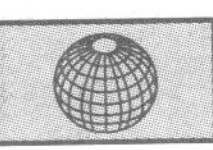   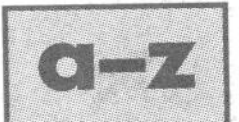

Contents

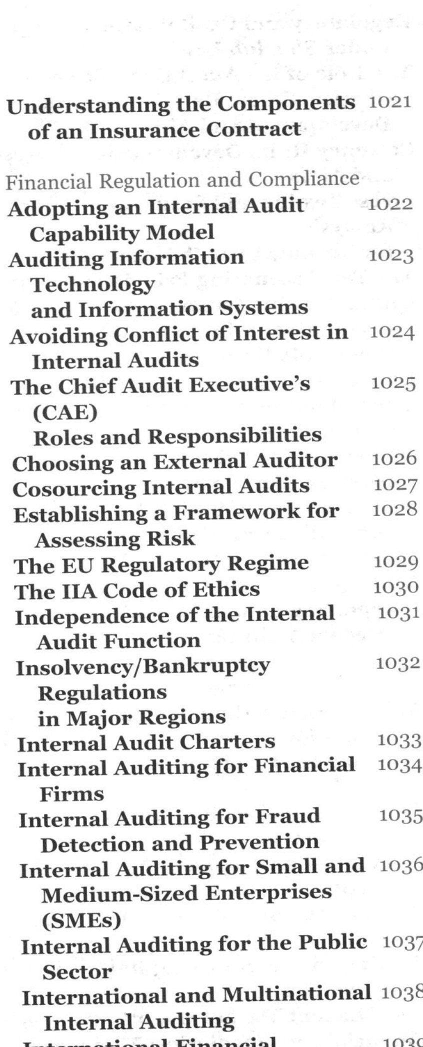

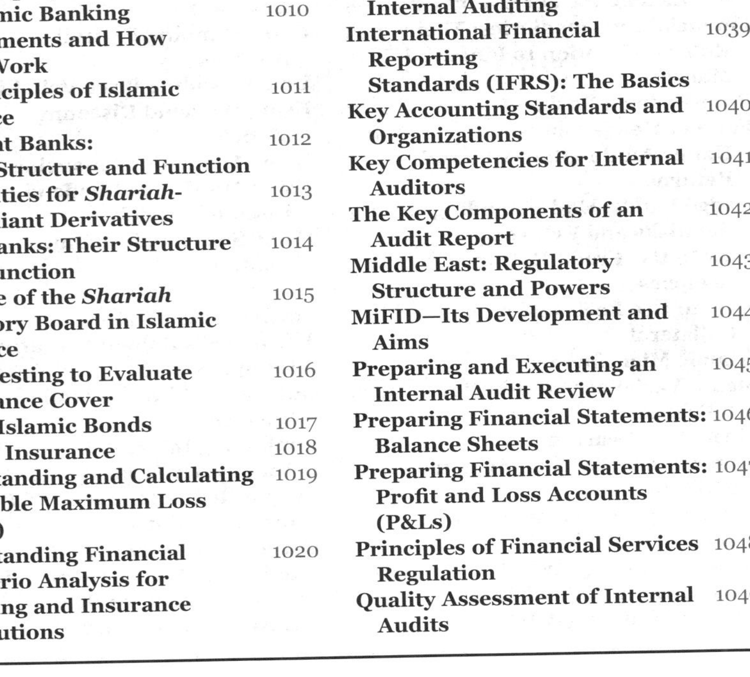

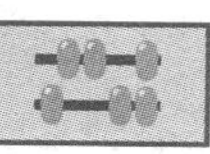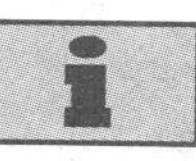

  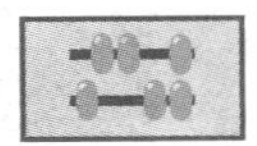      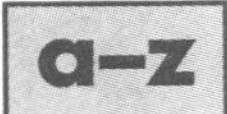

Checklists · Contents

  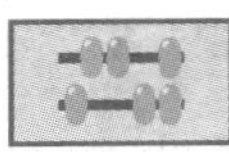      

Assessing Cash Flow and Bank Lending Requirements

DEFINITION

Lack of cash flow is a major cause of a business failing as, even though it may be turning a profit, if the money does not flow in on time the business will not be able to settle its debts. Cash flow is basically the measure of a company's financial health, showing the amount of cash generated and used by a company in any given period. Cash flow is essential to ensure solvency, as having enough cash ensures that creditors and employees can be paid on time. Banks require companies to show the difference between sales and costs within a specified period, which act as an indicator of the performance of a business better than the profit margin. Sales and costs, and therefore profits, do not necessarily coincide with their associated cash inflows and outflows. Even though a sale has been secured and goods delivered, payment may be deferred as a result of credit to the customer, yet suppliers and staff still have to be paid and cash invested in rebuilding depleted stocks. The net result is that although profits may be reported, the business may experience a short-term cash shortfall.

The main sources of cash flow into a business are receipts from sales, increases in bank loans, proceeds of share issues and asset disposals, and other income, such as interest earned. Cash outflows include payments to suppliers and staff, capital and interest repayments for loans, dividends, taxation, and capital expenditure. Cash flow planning entails forecasting and tabulating all significant cash inflows and analyzing in detail the timing of expected payments, which include suppliers, wages, other expenses, capital expenditure, loan repayments, dividends, tax, and interest payments.

A computerized cash flow model can be used to compile forecasts, assess possible funding requirements, and explore the financial consequences of other strategies. Computerized models can help prevent major planning errors, anticipate problems, and identify opportunities to improve cash flow and negotiate loans.

Banks must ensure that a business is viable, which entails asking pertinent questions. Lenders will insist on up-to-date information on the type of industry, management capabilities and experience, business plans and daily operations, key competition, and PR and marketing plans. They have to know that the business makes sense and can repay a loan, and what security is available in case of insolvency. Companies have to keep within their cash limits regardless of anticipated business. Business factoring is an alternative to bank loans—a factoring company buys your credit invoices and provides you with immediate cash in exchange for a small fee ranging between 1.5% and 5.0%. Factoring is more flexible than a bank loan.

ADVANTAGES

Ensuring good cash flow through a company helps to:

- increase sales;
- reduce direct and indirect costs and overhead expenses;
- raise additional equity;
- gain the confidence of banks and potentially secure more loans.

DISADVANTAGES

- If your profit margins are already low, you might not be able to afford bank fees.
- Banks have a tendency to increase fees and charge for late payments.

ACTION CHECKLIST

It is essential to keep track of your cash and not allow any surplus to sit idle. Accounts must be carefully monitored and cash invested to maximize returns. There are many ways to increase cash flow:

- ✔ reducing credit terms for historically slow payers;
- ✔ reviewing customer payment performance;
- ✔ becoming more selective when granting credit;
- ✔ seeking other ways to pay rather than all in one installment, such as deposits or staggered payments;
- ✔ reducing the amount of time of the credit terms;
- ✔ invoicing immediately the work has been done;
- ✔ improving collection systems for billing;
- ✔ adding late payment charges.

DOS AND DON'TS

DO

Do understand the way your company works, using a detailed analysis of banking procedure and taking into consideration:

- overdraft facilities and investment accounts;
- the number of monthly transactions;
- the number of written monthly checks;
- how customers pay you;
- the suitability of electronic banking for your business;
- cash access facilities;
- interest income;
- overall expenses and fees.

DON'T

- Don't overestimate sales forecasts.
- Don't underestimate costs.
- Don't underestimate delays in payments.
- Don't forget to check your debtors' credit histories carefully.

MORE INFO

Books:

Fight, Andrew. *Cash Flow Forecasting*. Oxford: Butterworth-Heinemann, 2006.

Mulford, Charles W., and Eugene E. Comiskey. *Creative Cash Flow Reporting and Analysis: Uncovering Sustainable Financial Performance*. Hoboken, NJ: Wiley, 2005.

Reider, Rob, and Peter B. Heyler. *Managing Cash Flow: An Operational Focus*. Hoboken, NJ: Wiley, 2003.

See Also:

★ Best Practices in Cash Flow Management and Reporting (pp. 16–19)
✔ Preparing a Cash Flow Forecast (p. 986)
✔ Retail Banks: Their Structure and Function (p. 1014)
✔ Steps for Obtaining Bank Financing (p. 1090)
Discounted Cash Flow (pp. 1217–1218)

"**The debt is like a crazy aunt we keep down in the basement. All the neighbors know she's there, but nobody wants to talk about her.**" H. Ross Perot

  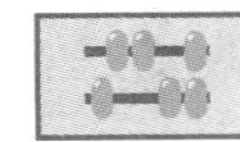      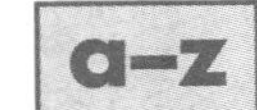

Building a Forex Plan

DEFINITION

Forex, which is short for "foreign exchange," is the largest trading market in the world, turning over on average US$4.0 trillion every day. There is no central marketplace for currency exchange, which is done over the counter. Currencies are traded on a global basis 24 hours a day, five days a week. Financial transactions involve one party purchasing a quantity of one currency in exchange for selling a quantity of another. Trading commonly occurs between large and central banks, currency speculators, corporations, governments, and other institutions. Currency prices depend on many factors, but ultimately the price depends upon supply and demand.

Forex markets react to trade levels and trends. Trade and investment flows indicate the demand for goods and services, in turn indicating demand for a country's currency to conduct trade. Trade deficits can have a negative impact on a nation's currency. A currency loses value when a country experiences rising inflation, which erodes demand for that particular currency. As a generalization, the healthier a country's economy, the better its currency will perform. Factors to look out for include economic factors, political conditions, and market psychology.

An effective and proven plan can help a company to exploit the forex currency trading system to its best potential. Customizing a forex plan in line with specific issues and needs can help to manage foreign exchange in the most cost-effective and efficient way. It is customary—and wise—to begin with a simulated forex trading account, which does not need any investment upfront but is used to train beginners in the strategies and fundamentals of forex trading.

A well-considered forex plan needs to take into account various elements. Decide whether you will hedge recorded or future assets and liabilities and how. Choose a trustworthy and competitive forex supplier. Plan the scope of activity taking into account objectives and time frames in which to achieve set goals. Make sure you schedule regular assessments of your forex business and revise any activities as needed. A forex plan should be sustainable, so aim to negotiate transactions at the most favorable prices. Keep track of your forex exposure by implementing methods for data capture. A good plan also has internal controls—consider your business processes and documentation requirements, ensure that you have strict authorization limits, and keep tasks segregated where necessary. Finally, stay familiar with accounting and reporting requirements.

A forex plan should be reviewed at every stage, from the first planning phase and throughout implementation. Senior management should sign off all decisions to ensure that risks are minimized. If the forex plan is of limited duration (for example for a specific project), then a post-implementation review is wise as it can identify areas for improvement and efficiency gains if you decide to enter the forex markets in the future.

ADVANTAGES

- When a company needs to use forex (for example, if it conducts business abroad), a strong forex plan can boost profits if transactions are conducted with care and insight. A good understanding of how to use forex transactions to advantage can also give an edge over business competitors.

DISADVANTAGES

- There is always a risk of losing money and thus profit, especially if you ignore advice and are overconfident about market conditions.

ACTION CHECKLIST

- ✔ Be as informed as you can be on how the forex currency trading system operates.
- ✔ Enroll in a reputable forex trading system course online and familiarize yourself with the forex currency market with a simulated trading account.
- ✔ Learn forex investment strategies, including the buy signals that forex charts give traders.
- ✔ Choose the amount you want to make on every forex trade before you begin trading; this is usually more than or equal to the earnings that you can afford to lose in the forex trade.
- ✔ Select your forex suppliers and counterparts.
- ✔ Negotiate forex transactions at more favorable price points.

DOS AND DON'TS

DO

- Watch charts and indicators.
- Work out how much you are willing to risk per trade.
- Review existing general ledger activity in the foreign currency accounts (gain/loss account and other comprehensive income (OCI) accounts).
- Take a sample historical review or monitor current activity to compare forex rates and forex hedge costs.

DON'T

- Don't ignore factors such as government budget deficits or surpluses, inflation levels and trends, economic growth and health, political conditions, long-term trends, technical trading considerations, and domestic, regional, and international political conditions and events.
- Don't be too greedy—don't expect too much too soon.

MORE INFO

Books:

Miner, Robert C. *High Probability Trading Strategies: Entry to Exit Tactics for the Forex, Futures, and Stock Markets*. Hoboken, NJ: Wiley, 2009.

Norris, Jay, Teresa Bell, and Al Gaskill. *Mastering the Currency Market: Forex Strategies for High- and Low-Volatility Markets*. New York: McGraw-Hill, 2010.

Ponsi, Ed. *The Ed Ponsi Forex Playbook: Strategies and Trade Set-Ups*. Hoboken, NJ: Wiley, 2010.

See Also:

✔ The Foreign Exchange Market: Its Structure and Function (p. 968)
✔ Hedging Foreign Exchange Risk—Case Studies and Strategies (p. 970)

"We all of us, rich and poor, have to live with the insecurity caused by an out of control global casino with a built-in bias towards instability. Because it is instability that makes money for the money-traders." Anita Roddick

Developing a Contingency Funding Plan

DEFINITION

A contingency fund is an amount of money that's kept in reserve for use in times when other funding resources have run out. In this way, the contingency fund can help guard against possible losses of important assets. In short, it's about sound budgeting for emergencies and the unexpected.

Historically, banks or companies have generally failed because they had no meaningful contingency plan. Indeed, banks with a sound contingency funding plan are considered much more likely to survive a funding crisis. While no retail bank actually failed during the global credit crunch of 2007–08, the British-based Northern Rock came close after fears over its liquidity caused customers to make a run on its funds and the Bank of England was forced to step in and shore up its finances. Having a credible contingency funding plan enables a bank or organization to forecast its liquidity in various worst-case scenarios.

The sensible realization that at some time in the future things might not be rosy is the first step towards setting up a contingency fund. Financial resources can run dry quickly in an emergency, forcing an organization to look elsewhere for funding. Having a contingency fund can help avoid the need to rely on other entities.

ADVANTAGES

- A contingency fund can help to relieve an organization of financial problems in times of difficulty.
- A contingency fund may even save an organization from going under.

DISADVANTAGES

- Salting away money into a contingency fund can seem like wasting money that could be used elsewhere, for example, for running the business, buying more assets, etc.
- It can be tempting to use the money in a contingency fund for other "emergencies" that are not actually defined for the use of the fund.

ACTION CHECKLIST

✔ Decide what the contingency fund will be for. Draw up a list of all possible situations where things might go wrong (worst-case scenarios) that are not covered by your insurance policies and consider under what circumstances you might need to draw on a contingency fund. This will help to define the uses for the fund. Then calculate how much it would cost in total to fund those areas of concern, and start setting aside spare cash in the contingency fund.

✔ Establish a set of rules for its use. In what circumstances will it be used? How much of the contingency fund can be used for a particular event or at one time? How long should it last? The uses of a contingency fund should be clearly defined. Veering from the rules for its use could compromise the financial health of the organization should a real need for the fund ever arise. Don't view it as a handy pot of money to dip into whenever needed.

✔ Establish a budget. Determine how much money to feed into the fund, and how often.

DOS AND DON'TS

DO

- Establish a budget.
- Decide exactly what the contingency fund will be for.
- Move money into the fund as appropriate.
- Automate saving into the fund so that it is not optional. Set up a standing order at the bank to ensure a regular transfer of money.
- Take advantage of the best savings account available so that the contingency fund earns interest while not in active use.

DON'T

- Don't ignore the rules for the use of the fund.
- Don't miss payments into the fund.
- Don't withdraw from the fund for purposes other than those for which it was set up, or before the end of a predefined period.

MORE INFO

Book:

Nissenbaum, Martin, Barbara J. Raasch, and Charles L. Ratner. *Ernst & Young's Personal Financial Planning Guide*. 5th ed. Hoboken, NJ: Wiley, 2004.

Article:

Nelson, Michael. "Establishing a capital contingency fund for utilities." *Public Works* (October 1994).

See Also:

✔ Identifying Your Continuity Needs (p. 1160)
✔ Options for Raising Finance (p. 1081)
✔ Understanding Crisis Management (p. 1178)

"A crash does not come knocking at the front door by appointment." Jim Slater

  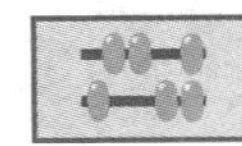      

Estimating Enterprise Value with the Weighted Average Cost of Capital

DEFINITION

Enterprise value (EV) is a fundamental metric for measuring a company's market worth and is often used in place of market capitalization. The standard formula for EV is the market capitalization *plus* debt, minority interest, and preferred shares, *minus* total cash and cash equivalents. Because enterprise value is more comprehensive than market capitalization and takes debt into account, it is considered to be a more accurate representation of a company's value and often viewed as the theoretical takeover price.

Estimating enterprise value with the weighted average cost of capital (WACC) also takes the share price into account. WACC is the rate at which a company must pay to finance its assets. It is the minimum return that a company needs to earn from its existing asset base in order to satisfy its creditors, owners, and any other of its capital providers, and to keep its stock price constant.

WACC is used to discount expected cash flows during the excess return period to arrive at the aggregate of the organization's cash flow from operations. The company's residual value is calculated by dividing the net operating profit after tax by its WACC (based on an assumed terminal growth rate of 0%). Enterprise value is the sum of cash flow from operations, the residual value, and the short-term assets.

ADVANTAGES

- Using WACC to calculate a company's enterprise value gives the most accurate figure possible for the value of a company. Some investors follow a value philosophy and look for companies that generate a lot of cash flow compared with their enterprise value. In general terms, businesses that do this are likely to require less additional reinvestment. With plenty of cash, the owners can take the profit out of the business and invest it elsewhere or pay dividends to investors.

DISADVANTAGES

- The main disadvantage is that enterprise value is not as easy to calculate as market capitalization. The latter is a simple multiplication of the number of shares by the shares' unit value, whereas enterprise value takes other, less-tangible factors into account, making the calculation more elusive.

ACTION CHECKLIST

✔ Understand the reasons why you want to value a company. Is it to buy the company or to buy the stock?

✔ Assess whether you really need very accurate figures. The enterprise value calculation will provide these, but adding in the WACC will give an even more accurate result.

DOS AND DON'TS

DO

- Use enterprise value with WACC if you are considering buying a company.

DON'T

- Don't overcomplicate your calculations if you just want a ballpark figure. In that case, use market capitalization.
- Don't add cash in to the value of a company—take it away.

MORE INFO

Books:

Koller, Tim, Marc Goedhart, and David Wessels. *Valuation: Measuring and Managing the Value of Companies*. 5th ed. Hoboken, NJ: Wiley, 2010.

Koller, Tim, Marc Goedhart, David Wessels, and Erik Benrud. *Valuation Workbook: Step-by-Step Exercises and Tests to Help You Master Valuation*. 5th ed. Hoboken, NJ: Wiley, 2011.

See Also:

✔ Obtaining an Equity Value Using the Weighted Average Cost of Capital (WACC) (p. 1080)
✔ Understanding the Weighted Average Cost of Capital (WACC) (p. 1002)
✔ Using the Market-Value Method for Acquisitions (p. 1139)
Enterprise Value (p. 1224)
Damodaran on Valuation: Security Analysis for Investment and Corporate Finance (p. 1348)

"**Accuracy, n. A certain uninteresting quality carefully excluded from human statements.**" Ambrose Bierce

The Foreign Exchange Market: Its Structure and Function

DEFINITION

The foreign exchange market, also known as the forex, FX, or currency market, involves the trading of one currency for another. Prior to 1996 the market was confined to large corporate banks and international corporations. However it has since opened up to include all traders and speculators. The average daily turnover in forex markets is US$4.0 trillion, according to the Bank of International Settlements's Triennial Survey from 2010. The market is growing rapidly as investors gain more information and develop more interest.

In trading foreign exchange, investors bet that one currency will appreciate over another; they profit when they bet correctly and collect the profit in the form of an interest rate spread when they return to the original currency. The profit margins are low compared with other fixed-income markets. Large trading volumes can, however, result in very high profits. Over half of all forex trading takes place in London and New York, with London dominating the market at 37% of all transactions. New York's market share is 18%, with Tokyo ranked third at 6%. Singapore, Switzerland, and Hong Kong are the next-largest forex markets globally with approximately 5% market share each.

One type of very short-term transaction is the *spot transaction* between two currencies, delivering over two days and using cash as opposed to a contract.

In a *forward transaction*, the money is not exchanged until an arranged date and an exchange rate is agreed in advance. The time period ranges from days to years. *Currency swaps* are a popular type of forward transaction; these involve the exchange of currency by two parties for an agreed length of time and an arrangement to swap currencies at an agreed later date. Another type is a *foreign currency future*, which is inclusive of interest. A standard contract is drawn up and a maturity date arranged. The time schedule is about three months.

In a *foreign exchange option* (FX option), the most liquid and biggest options market in the world, the owner may elect to exchange money in a designated currency for another currency at an agreed date in the future. This type of transaction depends on the availability of option contracts on an organized exchange. Otherwise, such forex deals may be carried out using an over-the-counter (OTC) contract.

ADVANTAGES

- The forex market is extremely liquid, hence its rapidly growing popularity. Currencies may be converted when bought or sold without causing too much movement in the price and keeping losses to a minimum.
- As there is no central bank, trading can take place anywhere in the world and operates on a 24-hour basis apart from weekends.
- An investor needs only small amounts of capital compared with other investments. Forex trading is outstanding in this regard.
- It is an unregulated market, meaning that there is no trade commission overseeing transactions and there are no restrictions on trade.
- In common with futures, forex is traded using a "good faith deposit" rather than a loan. The interest rate spread is an attractive advantage.

DISADVANTAGES

- The major risk is that one counterparty fails to deliver the currency involved in a very large transaction. In theory at least, such a failure could bring ruin to the forex market as a whole.
- Investors need a lot of capital to make good profits because the profit margins on small-scale trades are very low.

ACTION CHECKLIST

- ✔ Be alert for unanticipated corrections and wild fluctuations in currency exchange rates.
- ✔ Look for volatile markets that offer opportunities for quick profit.
- ✔ Watch out for lost payments, and be aware of delays in payments and money received. There may also be discrepancies between bank drafts received and the original price of the contract.
- ✔ It is wise to exit from the forex market at the point when your profit targets have been achieved as this ensures that you stay within the profit zone.

DOS AND DON'TS

DO

- Make sure when you pick a pair of currencies that you understand their relationship.
- Use a trading system that you can trust with your money.

DON'T

- Don't be greedy: take your profits at the right time.
- Don't be emotional when you trade.

MORE INFO

Books:

Archer, Michael Duane. *Getting Started in Currency Trading: Winning in Today's Market*. 4th ed. Hoboken, NJ: Wiley, 2012.

Chen, James. *Essentials of Foreign Exchange Trading*. Hoboken, NJ: Wiley, 2009.

Report:

Bank for International Settlements. "Triennial central bank survey: Report on global foreign exchange market activity in 2010." December 2010. Online at: www.bis.org/publ/rpfxf10t.htm

Website:

Forex on Top, provides a ranked list of the most visited forex websites including trading platforms: www.forexontop.com

See Also:

✔ Building a Forex Plan (p. 965)
✔ Hedging Foreign Exchange Risk—Case Studies and Strategies (p. 970)

"That realm cannot be rich whose coin is poor or base." William Cecil

  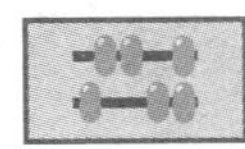   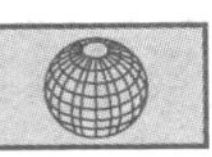   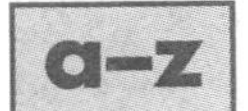

Hedging Credit Risk—Case Study and Strategies

DEFINITION

Credit risk is the uncertainty about the ability of a debtor or the counterparty in an agreement to make a payment. Strategies for managing credit risk use traditional credit analysis techniques to screen counterparties and may also take advantage of hedging via derivatives.

Corporations frequently need to estimate the likelihood of defaults, the exposure, and the severity of loss from a default event. Taking into account these factors and market-based inputs, it is possible to estimate both expected and unexpected losses across a portfolio.

Expected credit losses can be statistically estimated over a period of time. Risk-adjusted credit loss provisions can then be set and factored into pricing as part of the normal cost of doing business. Unexpected losses form the basis for the credit risk capital-allocation process.

INSTRUMENTS

There are three main structures of derivatives that enable an organization to manage credit risks more effectively.

With a credit default swap (CDS), a buyer purchases a contract and makes regular payments to a seller of credit protection. In the event of a default, the buyer receives compensation from the seller. This is commonly seen as an insurance policy for the buyer. It can, however, be used speculatively as there is no requirement for the buyer to hold any asset or have any potentially loss-making relationship with the so-called "reference entity."

Total return swaps are similar to interest rate swaps. One side makes payments based on the total return from an asset. The other makes floating or fixed payments. The notional amount of the underlying asset is the same for both parties.

A credit linked note (CLN) covers a specific credit risk. Investors receive a higher yield in return for accepting risk relating to a specific event. It provides a hedge for borrowers against an explicit risk. A CLN is created through a trust using very low-risk securities as collateral. Investors are paid a floating or fixed rate throughout the period of the note. At its completion they will either receive par or, if the reference entity has defaulted, the recovery rate value of the note.

CASE STUDY

Credit Default Swap

Although swaps can be used to hedge against any sort of credit risk, they are easiest to explain through a notional case study of an instrument such as a bond. A fund may, for example, hold $8,000,000 of Mega Car Company's five-year bond, and is concerned about the possibility of default due to market conditions arising from rising oil prices, increased government regulation on emissions, or the macroeconomic climate.

The fund decides to buy a credit default swap in a notional amount of $8,000,000 to cover the potential default value. The CDS in this case trades at 150 basis points, so the fund will pay 1.5% of $8,000,000, or $120,000 annually.

If Mega Car Company does not default, the fund will simply receive the full $8,000,000. In this case its return will not be as good as it would have been without the CDS.

On the other hand, if the corporation does default after, say, two years, the fund will receive its $8,000,000 from the seller of the CDS. It could be that the seller will take the bond or pay the difference between the recovery value and the par value of the bond.

Alternatively, Mega Car Company could make a breakthrough in low-emission technology and dramatically improve its credit profile. In that case the fund might decide to reduce its outgoings by selling the remaining period of the CDS.

ADVANTAGES

- Derivatives such as a CDS will reduce or entirely remove the risk of default.

DISADVANTAGES

- The cost of hedging will reduce the return on investment.

MORE INFO

Books:

Chacko, George, Anders Sjöman, Hideto Motohashi, and Vincent Dessain. *Credit Derivatives: A Primer on Credit Risk, Modeling, and Instruments*. Upper Saddle River, NJ: Wharton School Publishing, 2006.

Colquitt, Joetta. *Credit Risk Management: How to Avoid Lending Disasters and Maximize Earnings*. New York: McGraw-Hill, 2007.

de Servigny, Arnaud, and Olivier Renault. *The Standard & Poor's Guide to Measuring and Managing Credit Risk*. New York: McGraw-Hill, 2004.

See Also:

★ The Role of Short Sellers in the Marketplace (pp. 593–597)

✔ Managing Your Credit Risk (p. 981)

✔ Swaps, Options, and Futures: What They Are and Their Function (p. 988)

"There's only one thing to do with loose change of course. Tighten it." Flann O'Brien

        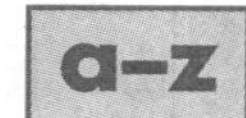

Hedging Foreign Exchange Risk—Case Studies and Strategies

DEFINITION

A company that imports raw materials, exports finished goods, or has overseas assets or subsidiaries is exposed to fluctuations in exchange rates. Adverse movements can wipe out export profits, while positive changes can increase the price of its products in the foreign market. Equally, the company could benefit from windfall profits as a result of exchange rate fluctuations.

A company trading across national borders therefore has a number of choices. It can take a chance with spot rates, buying currency when required. This leaves it totally at the mercy of exchange rates. The risk can be removed if it books a forward exchange contract that fixes the rate for the date on which it will be needed for a transaction. If the rate improves, however, the company will not be able to take advantage of the improvement.

Using a combination of flexible products allows the company to protect itself against adverse movements while still giving it the ability to profit from improvements. A wide variety of instruments are available that allow companies to pursue this strategy. Which is chosen depends partly on the level of risk and also on the ease of converting the currencies.

CASE STUDIES

The Participating Forward

This product is similar to a forward exchange contract in that it limits risk by offering a worst-case exchange rate for a transaction. If, however, there is a favorable move in exchange rates, the company can take advantage—generally with half its currency. There is usually no premium payable for this product.

Example

A company imports Cava wine from Spain to the United Kingdom. It is April, and a supplier has to be paid €4 million in October in time to catch the Christmas market.

The forward rate is 1.2100, and the company wants the certainty of a worst-case rate but doesn't want to lose out if the rate goes up. The foreign exchange broker offers a rate of 1.1800, with the option to buy half the currency on the spot market two days before completion of the transaction.

Possible Outcomes

Sterling strengthens against the euro and the rate rises to 1.2500. The customer pays £1,694,915 for the first €2,000,000 at the low rate agreed in advance and £1,600,000 for the second €2,000,000 at the spot rate. The average rate is therefore 1.2150, slightly better than the forward rate, but not as good as the spot rate.

Alternatively, the euro strengthens against sterling and the spot rate is 1.1600. The company then pays the rate of 1.1800 for the whole transaction.

The advantages of a participating forward are: a guaranteed worst-case rate; total protection against currency falls; a partial benefit from currency gains; and no premium. The disadvantages are: if the currency weakens the rate will not be as good as a forward exchange contract; and the spot rate will be better if there is a positive move in currency.

The Protection Option

With this service a company pays a premium for an option to exchange currency on a fixed forward date at a predetermined rate. If the spot rate on that date is better than the predetermined rate, the company can decide not to exercise its option to sell at the predetermined rate.

Example

A UK company is selling dresses to a customer in the United States. In six months it will receive US$4,000,000. The current forward rate for this date is 2.0000. Fearing that sterling is going to strengthen against the dollar, the company opts to buy a protection option at the forward rate.

Possible Outcomes

Sterling does strengthen against the dollar, taking the rate to 2.1500. The company then exercises its right to sell dollars at 2.0000.

The dollar strengthens against sterling. The rate is now 1.8500. The company takes the better rate on the spot market.

The advantages of the protection option are: a guaranteed worst-case rate; total protection against negative currency fluctuations; and the ability to take full advantage of positive currency movements. The disadvantage is that a premium is payable to the foreign exchange trader.

OTHER HEDGING PRODUCTS

There are many other ways for companies to hedge against currency variations using derivatives. Currency markets are extremely volatile, and it makes sense for any organization trading across national borders to protect itself from these fluctuations.

MORE INFO

Books:

Hakala, Jürgen, and Uwe Wystup (eds). *Foreign Exchange Risk: Models, Instruments and Strategies*. London: Risk Books, 2002.

Jacque, Laurent L. *Management and Control of Foreign Exchange Risk*. Norwell, MA: Kluwer Academic Publishers, 1996.

See Also:

★ Using Structured Products to Manage Liabilities (pp. 115–117)
✔ Building a Forex Plan (p. 965)
✔ The Foreign Exchange Market: Its Structure and Function (p. 968)
✔ Identifying and Managing Exposure to Interest and Exchange Rate Risks (p. 974)
✔ Understanding and Using Currency Swaps (p. 992)

"When a system of national currencies run by a central bank is transformed into a global electronic marketplace driven by currency traders, power changes hands." Walter Wriston

     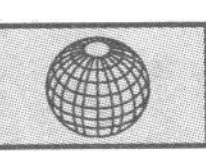   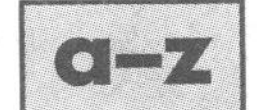

Hedging Interest Rate Risk—Case Study and Strategies

DEFINITION

Risks arise from the way the value of an investment changes with the level of interest rates. This is most clearly seen in the value of fixed-rate investments such as bonds. If interest rates rise, the opportunity cost from holding the bond falls as it becomes more advantageous to switch to other investments.

Alternatively, a company with a loan at a variable rate of interest may want to adapt its payments to avoid the risk arising from a rise in interest rates. It may also want to aid its financial planning by creating a more even pattern of repayment.

A number of instruments exist to hedge against the risks posed by changing interest rates. For a company that decides to reduce its exposure to rising interest rates associated with variable rate funding, there are two main types of derivative.

A cap will ensure that the company does not have to find more than a maximum agreed level of interest. The company will benefit if interest rate levels stay below that level. A cap is paid for up-front. A variation on this instrument is the cap and collar, whereby the company will pay the seller of the product if interest rates fall below an agreed level.

Swaps allow the company to exchange variable-rate payments for a guaranteed fixed rate. Swaps do not generally require any advance payment to the seller.

There are a huge variety of swap instruments, reflecting the international nature of the debt market. For instance, although there would be no advantage in swapping a fixed rate for another fixed rate within the same currency, as the outcome would be known, it may be desirable to swap fixed rates between two currencies. Every variable of currency, floating, and fixed exchange rate can be swapped.

CASE STUDY

Vanilla Interest Rate Swap

A company enters into a vanilla interest rate swap with a bank to reduce the risk from fluctuations on a $10 million loan it has taken out on a floating rate. The bank agrees to a fixed rate of, for example, 6% over five years, while the floating rates are based on the six-monthly Libor (London Interbank Borrowing Rate) plus 2%. If the Libor is 4% at the start of the agreement, the amount payable is 6% in both cases, although any percentage could be agreed.

If the Libor rises to 6%, the amount payable every six months would be 8% of $10 million divided by two, or $400,000. The company's agreement with the bank is for a rate of 6%, or a payment of $300,000 in this case. The company will receive the difference of $100,000 from the bank.

The amount of the loan does not change hands and the company may continue to make the variable payments. It will receive cash if interest rates rise, and pay the bank if they fall. The net effect on the company is the same as if it had taken out a fixed-rate loan. Although the obvious route would be for a company to take out a fixed-rate loan, initially this may not be available or it may be too expensive.

Moreover, because the amount of the swap is notional, it is not necessary for the company to match the whole amount of the loan or to ensure that its entire life is covered. There may well be occasions when risk managers expect interest rate rises over the short to medium term. Continuing with a swap arrangement after the rises have peaked could wipe out initial gains.

ADVANTAGES

- A swap is flexible, allowing a company to adjust its maturity, payment frequency, and principal to suit its ongoing financial arrangements.
- Interest rates can be managed independently of financing arrangements.
- There is no requirement for a payment up-front.

DISADVANTAGES

- The arrangement locks the company into a fixed rate that may not be advantageous.
- Early termination may incur a cost.
- There is a slight additional risk of failure from involving an additional financial institution in the swap arrangement.

MORE INFO

Books:

Mercurio, Fabio. *Modelling Interest Rates*. London: Risk Books, 2009.

Nawalkha, Sanjay K., Gloria M. Soto, and Natalia K. Beliaeva. *Interest Rate Risk Modeling*. Hoboken, NJ: Wiley, 2005.

See Also:

★ The Role of Short Sellers in the Marketplace (pp. 593–597)
✔ Identifying and Managing Exposure to Interest and Exchange Rate Risks (p. 974)
✔ Understanding and Using Interest Rate Swaps (p. 994)
✔ Understanding and Using the Repos Market (p. 1098)

        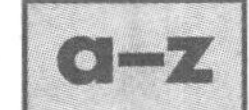

Hedging Liquidity Risk—Case Study and Strategies

DEFINITION

The concept of "liquidity risk" tends to be very loosely defined. It is used most commonly with reference to the banking and finance industry, but it is an important issue for all companies. Broadly, liquidity risk is the danger that it will be difficult or impossible for an organization to sell an asset in order to provide capital to meet short-term financial demands.

A company needs to remain solvent; the liquidity risk is in the secondary market for its assets, which may not be sellable in time to meet short-term financial commitments, or will be sold at a price considerably below the perceived current market value. The problem may arise as the result of a liquidity gap or mismatch. This means that the dates for inflow and outflow of funds do not match up, creating a shortage.

Systemic liquidity risks arise from external factors. National or international recessions and credit crunches have the largest general impact on liquidity. Capital market disruptions, however, are more common. The collapse of the Russian ruble in 1998, for instance, created a global liquidity crisis, with a capital flight to quality away from the highly speculative Russian stock market.

Generally, liquidity is abundant during times when the economy is booming. During a downturn the impact on companies may increase if they continue with strategies based on the assumption that the high liquidity will continue indefinitely.

CASE STUDY

A company has outgoings of $8,000,000 per month against income from sales of $10,000,000. It faces a number of threats to its liquidity: for example, the price of the commodity it sells has fallen by 25%, leaving its income at $7,500,000 against $8,000,000 outgoings, and it has to find a way to raise the additional $500,000.

Some major customers have axed or cut their orders, leaving the company with a surplus of products to sell on the market. It has lost $4,000,000 in "normal" monthly sales and now has to offload products it is forced to sell, below cost, at 50% of the expected price simply to pay its bills ($6,000,000 in expected sales plus $2,000,000 to meet monthly obligations of $8,000,000).

The company chose to secure its position and iron out liquidity problems in the following ways:

- It held cash to cover some of the shortfall, but it lost the potential income from this capital.
- It set up a line of credit with its bank to help cover the shortfall.
- It sold off some assets in order to meet its financial obligations. This is risky as assets that have to be sold in a hurry may not realize their book price.

All this assumes that the company assessed its liquidity risks accurately and market conditions did not change.

STRATEGIES

Threats to a company's liquidity seldom happen in isolation but are intertwined with other financial risks. If, for example, a company fails to receive a payment, it may be forced to raise cash elsewhere or default on its payments. In this scenario, credit risk and liquidity risk are linked.

The aim of a liquidity management strategy is to minimize the cost of capital, allowing efficient access to capital and money markets at competitive prices during times of "normal" activity. Concurrently, the strategy should provide high levels of liquidity during periods when the financial markets are impaired.

The latter part of the strategy is often described as "life insurance." At a simple level this can mean organizing lines of credit well in advance of market turmoil, which is the cheapest option. However, the activities of a company and the market it operates in are dynamic. There will be periods when it is cash-rich and others when it is cash-poor. As cash is the ultimate liquid asset, there will be periods when it can "self-insure" and times when it will need to approach an external source for insurance.

ACTION CHECKLIST

- ✔ Examine predicted cash flows for the company. Look for any major negatives. Their impact can be stress-tested by analyzing the effect of a default by the major parties.
- ✔ Ensure that inflows and outflows match as far as possible.
- ✔ Assess the risk profile of the company before deciding what measures to put in place. In general liquid assets have a lower rate of return.
- ✔ Start a process of scenario testing. What happens if there is a default within an income stream?
- ✔ Ensure that the impacts of rare events are tested too. They may be unusual in isolation, but the more there are, statistically the higher the probability that one will occur.

MORE INFO

Books:

Fiedler, Robert. *Liquidity Modelling*. London: Risk Books, 2011.
Matz, Leonard, and Peter Neu (eds). *Liquidity Risk Management*. Singapore: Wiley, 2007.

See Also:

★ How Taxation Impacts on Liquidity Management (pp. 48–49)
★ Navigating a Liquidity Crisis Effectively (pp. 82–84)
✔ Managing Working Capital (p. 980)
✔ Measuring Liquidity (p. 983)
Liquidity Ratio Analysis (pp. 1232–1233)

"The eighties was an era when many companies were asset rich and cash poor." Nicola Horlick

     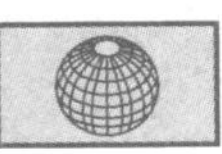   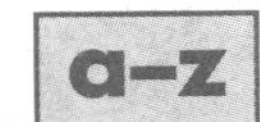

How to Manage Your Credit Rating

DEFINITION

A credit rating is an assessment of the creditworthiness of an entity such as an individual, a corporation, or even a country. Credit ratings are worked out from past financial history as well as current assets and liabilities, and are used to inform a potential lender or investor about the probability of the entity being able to pay back a loan. However, in recent years credit ratings have been used more widely. They have, for example, been used to make adjustments to insurance premiums or to establish the amount of a leasing deposit.

Credit reference agencies compile credit histories on individuals using information from sources such as electoral registers, court judgments, and lenders. Anyone applying for credit can expect to have their request recorded for the credit agencies to access and use. Financial institutions compile their own credit ratings for companies. The best known credit raters are Fitch, Moody's, and Standard & Poor's, which produce credit ratings for listed companies, banks, and even countries.

Credit reference agencies do not make the decision on whether to offer credit to would-be borrowers. It is for the lenders to reach a decision using information amassed by the credit agencies, combined with their own lending criteria and knowledge.

Having a bad credit rating limits your borrowing options. Court judgments, defaults on payments, and bankruptcy orders will all reduce your credit rating score. This applies equally to individuals and businesses. Where a credit applicant has a poor credit rating, credit may still be obtained through the subprime market, where the borrower is charged much higher rates of interest.

ADVANTAGES

Managing your credit rating can help to:

- ensure that you have access to credit in the future;
- enable you to take out a mortgage or loan;
- give you peace of mind.

DISADVANTAGES

- Repeated applications for credit (particularly unsuccessful ones) are recorded on your file.
- Repeated checks of your credit rating are recorded on your file.

ACTION CHECKLIST

- ✔ Buy access to your credit history and use it to check your credit rating.
- ✔ Make sure that any spent court judgments are recorded as such on your file.
- ✔ Ensure that any annulled or discharged bankruptcy order is recorded as such on your file.
- ✔ Keep up with all payments.

DOS AND DON'TS

DO

- Understand what your credit rating is.
- Check for errors in your credit rating, and have them amended.
- Work to make your credit history better if it has been poor in the past.
- Ask a potential lender if you fit their profile of a typical successful credit applicant as this may help you to avoid an actual credit check.
- Pay your creditors on time. If you miss a payment, inform your creditor straight away.
- Make sure you are on the electoral register.
- Make sure you complete credit card application forms correctly.
- Make your credit card, store card, loan, and mortgage repayments on time.
- Consider asking a family member or friend with a good credit rating to co-sign for a small loan or credit card. This can help your own rating.

DON'T

- Don't miss any payments.
- Don't check your credit record too often.
- Don't apply for loans too often, especially if you have a doubtful credit record.
- Don't avoid having any credit—no credit record is as bad as a poor credit record.

MORE INFO

Books:

de Servigny, Arnaud, and Olivier Renault. *The Standard & Poor's Guide to Measuring and Managing Credit Risk*. New York: McGraw-Hill, 2004.

Ong, Michael K. (ed). *Credit Ratings—Methodologies, Rationale and Default Risk*. London: Risk Books, 2002.

See Also:

★ Credit Ratings (pp. 478–480)
✔ Basic Steps for Starting a Business (p. 1147)
✔ How to Use Credit Rating Agencies (p. 1073)
✔ Managing Bankruptcy and Insolvency (p. 1168)
✔ Steps for Obtaining Bank Financing (p. 1090)

"Nowhere does history indulge in repetitions so often or so uniformly as in Wall Street." Jesse Livermore

  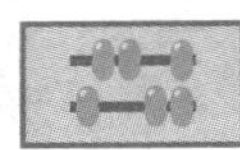      

Identifying and Managing Exposure to Interest and Exchange Rate Risks

DEFINITION

The successful management of a portfolio includes maximizing returns from shifts in exchange and interest rates, which in turn requires an appreciation of the associated exposures. Not knowing the exposure can leave the portfolio open to significant risk.

Exchange rate risk is the risk arising from a change in the price of one currency against another. Companies or institutions that trade internationally are exposed to exchange rate risk if they do not hedge their positions. There are two main risks associated with exposure to exchange rates.

- Transaction risk arises because exchange rates may change unfavorably over time. The best protection is to use forward currency contracts to hedge against such changes.
- Translation risk concerns the accounts, and the level of risk is proportional to the amount of assets held in foreign currencies. Over a period of time, changes in exchange rates will cause the accounts to become inaccurate. To avoid this, assets need to be offset by borrowings in the affected currency.

The significance of the exposure will depend on the portfolio's weightings and operations. Identifying the level of risk in the above exposures should help with selecting a suitable defense strategy.

Interest rate risk relates to changes in the floating rate. Failure to understand exposure to interest rates can lead to substantial risk. The two main areas of concern here should be borrowings and cash investments. The best way of appreciating exposure to changing interest rates is to stress-test various scenarios. How, for example, would a change in rate from 4% to 6% affect your ability to borrow?

MITIGATING THE RISK

Exchange Rate Exposure

Other than the two strategies mentioned above, good strategies for minimizing exchange rate exposure involve employing one or more of the following products.

- **Spot foreign exchange**: An obligation to buy/sell a specified quantity of currency at the current market rate to be settled in two business days.
- **Structured forwards**: Exchange forwards embedded with, generally, more than one currency option. This adaptation allows a more effective hedge and should improve the exchange rate within the client's perception of the market.
- **Currency options**: An option to the right to buy/sell a certain amount of currency at a specific exchange rate on or before a specific future date.

Interest Rate Exposure

Once identified, the risks can be minimized using the following methods:

- **Interest rate swap**: A method for changing the interest rate you earn/pay on an agreed amount for a specified time period.
- **Cross-currency swap**: An exchange of principal and interest payments in separate currencies.
- **Forward rate agreement**: Two parties fix the interest rate that will apply to a loan or deposit.
- **Interest rate caps**: The seller and borrower agree to limit the borrower's floating interest rate to a specified level for a period of time.
- **Structured swap**: An interest rate/cross-currency swap embedded with one or more derivatives. This allows the client to minimize exposure on their perception of the market.

DOS AND DON'TS

DO

- Set realistic targets.
- Stick to your strategy.
- Research best strategy and implementation.

DON'T

- Don't be overoptimistic.
- Don't alter your strategy midway.
- Don't expose yourself to excessive risk.

MORE INFO

Books:

Fornés, Gastón. *Foreign Exchange Exposure in Emerging Markets: How Companies Can Minimize It*. Basingstoke, UK: Palgrave Macmillan, 2009.

Friberg, Richard. *Exchange Rates and the Firm: Strategies to Manage Exposure and the Impact of EMU*. Basingstoke, UK: Macmillan, 1999.

See Also:

★ To Hedge or Not to Hedge (pp. 104–106)
✔ Hedging Foreign Exchange Risk—Case Studies and Strategies (p. 970)
✔ Hedging Interest Rate Risk—Case Study and Strategies (p. 971)
✔ Understanding and Using Inflation Swaps (p. 993)

ADVANTAGES

- The one key advantage to identifying exposure to interest and exchange rate fluctuations is the ability to minimize possible losses in the event that your view of the market is wrong. This approach will also minimize the chance of unexpected events disrupting the investment strategy.

DISADVANTAGES

- As with any hedge strategy, minimizing possible losses also reduces potential gains. Only those who are supremely confident in their forecasts and with a cushion to absorb losses should consider taking any extra risk to maximize returns.

ACTION CHECKLIST

✔ Plan your approach. Establish what your aims are when dealing with exchange rates/foreign currencies. Decide on your strategies for dealing with interest rate exposure. Create risk registers that set out clear procedures for dealing with risks as they arise.

✔ Calculate what losses you can afford, or what profits you need to make, and stick to them.

"**Better never means better for everyone … It always means worse, for some.**" Margaret Atwood

  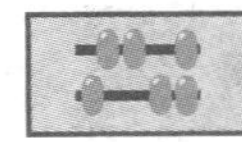      

Insuring Against Financial Loss

DEFINITION

Every business faces a unique combination of exposures. The overall impact of an incident can reach far beyond the immediate damage to property and be far more expensive and harmful to the company than the original loss.

Policies covering these areas are often grouped together as "miscellaneous financial loss" or "contingency" insurance. A combination of policies may be required to cover these consequential losses in tandem with a business continuity plan. It will be necessary for the company to weigh up the risks from self-insuring (i.e. having an emergency fund for such contingencies) or buying cover from an insurer.

CHECKLIST OF FINANCIAL RISKS THAT CAN BE COVERED

Weather

Some types of business, particularly in the construction, leisure, and agricultural sectors, may be adversely affected by unfavorable weather conditions.

Business Interruption

Interruption insurance can fill the gaps in existing policies. It can cover both the continuing and emergency costs faced by the business along with loss of income arising from an enforced shutdown.

Breakdown of Machinery

The failure of specialist machinery can lead to losses considerably greater than the cost of repair if it affects the output of the business.

Credit Insurance

Domestic and export credit risks can be covered through a commercial risks policy. This provides protection against events such as a customer becoming insolvent or defaulting on payment for a prolonged period, or a political event delaying or preventing payment.

Crime

A company can be covered against third party theft, employee dishonesty, forgery, copyright theft, and so on. Particular attention should be paid to ensuring that it is not only forced entry that is included in the policy as a larger proportion of crime is committed by insiders than by third parties.

Theft and Personal Injury

Robbery, attempted robbery, and injuries resulting from these crimes can be covered whether they occur on a company's premises, in or out of working hours, or when cash is being transported from a bank safe or from a company strong room.

Key Man Insurance

Many businesses are reliant on particular individuals. Key man cover protects against losses arising from their death or long-term illness. The types of loss that may be included are profits, the cost of hiring a replacement, and the delay before the replacement starts to make a contribution to profits.

Kidnap, Ransom, and Extortion

This type of cover is particularly relevant to companies operating in certain high-risk territories. Companies are often less than transparent about policies that include ransom insurance for fear that it will be seen to encourage kidnapping and extortion.

License Loss

Establishments such as bars, restaurants, hotels, clubs, and casinos are vulnerable to loss of license. Cover may be available against this eventuality.

Cyber Insurance

In recent years there has been an increasing risk arising from so-called "cyber crime." This includes damage from hack attacks, viruses, and defamation. These can all have an effect on profits, as well costing money to resolve and potentially causing damage to third parties.

Single Project Insurance

Sometimes a company faces a specific collection of risks arising from a single major project. A construction company, for example, that wins a government contract may face a combination of public liability, funding, and penalty risks—cover against which may be rolled into a single, limited-time policy for the duration of the project.

ADVANTAGES

- It is possible to insure against almost every eventuality and business risk.

DISADVANTAGES

- The cost of such cover would be prohibitive. A risk profile should be drawn up to analyze which areas of the balance sheet it is cost-effective and appropriate to insure.

MORE INFO

Books:

Gaughan, Patrick A. *Measuring Business Interruption Losses and Other Commercial Damages*. Hoboken, NJ: Wiley, 2003.

Hoffman, Philip T., Gilles Postel-Vinay, and Jean-Laurent Rosenthal. *Surviving Large Losses: Financial Crises, the Middle Class, and the Development of Capital Markets*. Cambridge, MA: Belknap Press, 2007.

See Also:

✔ Corporate Insurance Cover: A Primer (p. 1154)
✔ Insuring Against Business Interruption (p. 1161)
✔ Stress Testing to Evaluate Insurance Cover (p. 1016)
✔ Understanding the Components of an Insurance Contract (p. 1021)

        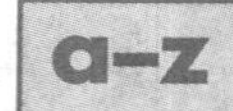

Invoicing and Credit Control for Small and Medium-Sized Enterprises

DEFINITION

Invoicing and credit control should be priorities in all businesses. Poor management of cash flow is the main reason that SMEs go under. A good credit control system is an indispensable part of any business's accounting procedures. Maintaining dependable cash flow, avoiding bad debt, and minimizing late payments are essential for survival. Therefore, while you are planning the business, prepare an invoicing and credit control system that will bring in your money on time.

- An invoice should be easy to read, clearly showing who has sent the invoice, to whom, for what, for how much, how to respond, and when to respond by. It should always be accurate in every detail, and to the penny, when quoting amounts. Inaccuracy is an excuse to query and delay payment. Always put a retention of title on your invoice, for example, "All goods are the property of EG Inc. until paid for in full."
- Put in place a detailed credit control system that allows you to identify whether an invoice has been created, sent to clients, and/or paid, or needs chasing up.
- Do credit checks on customers, especially when orders are large. Try to get them to put down a deposit as a sign of good faith. This applies particularly when you have to buy in special materials. If a customer doesn't want to put down a deposit, it may be an indication that they should be avoided. With large orders allow for "stage payments" invoicing, as large orders that are payable only at the end of the project can be ruinous to your cash flow.
- Decide on your general payment terms, including a payment date. Always have a "payable by" clause on your invoice and make sure that it is unambiguously linked to a date on the invoice. Bear in mind that new customers should be given only a short time in which to pay. Print terms clearly on the invoice and go through them with customers. It is best not to offer a discount for early payment; most people will just take advantage of it and still pay late.
- Prompt invoicing is essential—aim to send out invoices the day after the goods are delivered. Start an automatic reminder system that flags overdue invoices so that you can chase them up.

Make it a priority to set up a detailed credit control system. A good system is an essential part of any SME's accounting procedures, and getting control of your invoicing is essential if you want to succeed.

ADVANTAGES

- A detailed credit control system allows you to identify whether an invoice has been created, sent to clients, and paid, or needs chasing up.
- A good credit control system will help to maintain cash flow, avoid bad debt, and minimize late payments, contributing to the smooth running of your business.
- Staged payments on large orders can help your cash flow.

DISADVANTAGES

- Not getting paid for the work that you do, or the products that you sell, is very common. You will probably always have a few debtors.

ACTION CHECKLIST

✔ Find out whether your level of credit control is better than those of other businesses in the same sector.

✔ Ask the client to sign a purchase order, agreeing what they want, and when and how they will pay. The purchase order should also contain terms and conditions that cover areas such as modification from the original requirement, quality standards, etc.

✔ Your invoice should always be accurate in every detail and to the penny when quoting amounts. Inaccuracy gives customers an excuse to query and delay payment.

✔ Invoice promptly—aim to send out your invoice the day after delivery of the goods.

DOS AND DON'TS

DO

- On the basis of a credit check, give a customer a credit limit if necessary and do not let them exceed it.
- Follow up invoices before their due date.
- Have a no-credit or cash-only list for late-paying customers.

DON'T

- Don't think you can just "wing it"; a good credit control system is essential for survival.

MORE INFO

Books:

Bragg, Steven M. *Accounting Reference Desktop*. Hoboken, NJ: Wiley, 2002.

Shavick, Andrea. *The Cheque's in the Post: Credit Control for the Small Business*. London: Kogan Page, 1998.

Articles:

Credit Management. "Track those invoices." *Credit Management* (April 2008).

Hirst, Sue. "Business invoicing: Steps to avoid bad debts." *Flying Solo* (October 2007). Online at: tinyurl.com/3t92pxn

See Also:

★ Electronic Invoicing in the European Union (pp. 832–834)
★ How to Better Manage Your Financial Supply Chain (pp. 53–55)
✔ Building an Efficient Credit and Collection Accounts System (p. 1148)
✔ Building an Electronic Invoicing System (p. 1149)
✔ Efficient Invoicing Procedures (p. 1158)

"**Creditors have better memories than debtors.**" Benjamin Franklin

  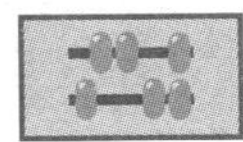   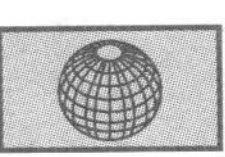   

Key Components of an Optimal Enterprise Resource Planning System

DEFINITION

ERP computerized systems integrate a company's entire business operation. Simply put, an ERP system binds together different computer systems for any large organization, with each department having its own system that communicates and shares information with the rest of the company's systems. ERP integrates all key areas, including accounting, planning, purchasing, inventory, sales, marketing, PR, finance, human resources, and any other areas of importance to a company. Installing an ERP system enables a company to monitor and manage effectively the performance level of equipment, while simultaneously increasing uptime and increasing responsiveness, thus facilitating and fulfilling customer needs as well as streamlining company performance.

Although originally developed for large companies, ERP also benefits small and medium-sized companies and those involved in service rather than manufacturing, with ERP programmers creating a new generation of software that is easier to install, more manageable, and importantly, cheaper. The new systems are more modular, allowing installation to proceed gradually as a company evolves. ERP can also be outsourced, with the ERP manufacturer supplying the technology and the support staff required. This option has proved easier and cheaper than buying and implementing a whole system in-house. Hosted ERP or web-deployed ERP enables a company to run its ERP system through a web-hosted server and access it via the internet. This allows companies to reduce their IT investment in hardware and personnel.

ERP systems have also expanded through the evolution of technology to include new functions such as linking ERP to other software systems that affect the supply chain. This allows companies to view inventory and its status as it moves through the supply chain. ERP has also been adapted to support e-commerce by making order fulfillment and distribution easier and simplifying electronic procurement.

Computer security is included within an ERP to protect against both outsider crime, such as industrial espionage, and insider crime, such as embezzlement.

ADVANTAGES

- Deploying an ERP system can improve efficiency and reduce operational costs.
- New levels of transaction visibility can be gained for all involved in a process.
- Companies can make smarter business decisions, keep up to date with customer requirements, track inventory, implement and maintain industry best practices, and forecast product demand.
- Complex computer applications can be replaced with a single, integrated system.

DISADVANTAGES

- ERP systems require the installation of new technical support and training of staff, and they are expensive.
- They desensitize operations procedures and rely on the whole system working.
- Systems can be difficult to use or too restrictive.
- The system may be overengineered relative to the actual needs of the customer, resulting in lack of personal service.

ACTION CHECKLIST

✔ Evaluate all company needs carefully and create a list of business issues that the ERP system has to address.

✔ Research potential ERP vendors by talking to other companies that have similar working requirements. Avoid choosing an ERP system vendor too quickly.

✔ Check the user-friendliness of the system.

✔ Ensure that you can customize the system to meet your requirements comprehensively.

DOS AND DON'TS

DO

- Assess plenty of systems and see how they can work for your company.
- Look at the needs of your company from every angle.
- Check that your personnel are up to the task and, if not, check that you can employ the right personnel.

DON'T

- Don't sign up to an ERP without all the facts.
- Don't expect an ERP to run the business for you without your input.
- Don't be too ambitious and believe that the system will solve any ongoing problems with communication within your company.

MORE INFO

Book:

Magal, Simha R., and Jeffrey Word. *Integrated Business Processes with ERP Systems*. Hoboken, NJ: Wiley, 2011.

Articles:

Scott, Judy E., and Lisa Kaindl. "Enhancing functionality in an enterprise software package." *Information and Management* 37:3 (April 2000): 111–122. Online at: dx.doi.org/10.1016/S0378-7206(99)00040-3

Wailgum, Thomas. "ERP definition and solutions." *CIO* (April 17, 2008). Online at: www.cio.com/article/40323

Wei, Chun-Chin, and Mao-Jiun J. Wang. "A comprehensive framework for selecting an ERP system." *International Journal of Project Management* 22:2 (February 2004): 161–169. Online at: dx.doi.org/10.1016/S0263-7863(02)00064-9

Website:

Dos and don'ts of ERP implementation: tinyurl.com/nk4rmck [via archive.org].

See Also:

★ How to Better Manage Your Financial Supply Chain (pp. 53–55)

✔ Business Process Reengineering (p. 1150)

"The biggest opportunity is harnessing our knowledge within the organisation to provide better solutions." Martin Sorrell

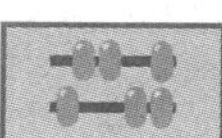

Managing Risk in Islamic Finance

DEFINITION

There are differences between Islamic finance and conventional finance, but some fundamental principles involved in managing risk apply equally to both. In particular, rigorous risk management and sound corporate governance help to ensure the safety of financial institutions in both the Islamic and non-Islamic worlds.

The key difference between Islamic finance and conventional finance is that Islamic finance involves risk sharing rather than risk transfers. Thus, all parties involved in a transaction must share the rewards and the risks equitably. Furthermore, institutions in the former category must ensure that their activities are always compliant with the restrictions imposed by *shariah* law. This is complicated by the fact that scholars can and do change their minds over what is permitted under *shariah*.

Islamic institutions are confronted with unique risks as a result of the asset and liability structures that compliance with *shariah* law imposes upon them.

Operational risk is significant for *shariah* financial institutions due to their specific contractual features.

Liquidity risk is also more complicated than in conventional finance. This is because Islamic bank funding comes from personal customer accounts, the vast majority of which are on call or very short notice. In addition, until very recently, hedging risk by using conventional methods was not in compliance with *shariah*. Furthermore, there is no central receiver and provider of liquidity to and from the Islamic financial market. Finally, and again unlike the conventional market, most debt is not tradable.

In addition, some of the tools used to manage risk in Western financial institutions either cannot be used or have limited use in the Islamic world because they contravene *shariah* law. Thus, derivatives have been few and far between in Islamic countries, despite their widespread use in the West to protect against market volatility. Islamic institutions have had limited access to derivative products, mainly because *shariah* law requires the underlying assets in any transaction to be tangible. This excludes most of the mainstream derivative instruments.

However, Islamic finance is developing apace, and products are being launched that can have useful risk management attributes and even mimic risk tools used in the West without contravening *shariah* law.

In March 2010, for example, the Bahrain-based International Islamic Financial Market, in cooperation with the International Swaps and Derivatives Association, launched the *Tahawwut* (Hedging) Master Agreement, which gives the global Islamic financial industry the ability to trade *shariah*-compliant hedging transactions such as profit-rate and currency swaps, which are estimated to represent most of the current Islamic hedging transactions.

Under *shariah* principles, the *tahawwut* or hedge must be strictly linked to underlying transactions and cannot be a transaction that has the sole purpose of making money from money. The lack of hedging products for managing risk has put many investors and institutions involved in Islamic finance at a disadvantage.

The *Tahawwut* Master Agreement should pave the way for quicker and cheaper Islamic risk management and more frequent cross-currency transactions. The contract creates a standard legal framework for over-the-counter (OTC) derivatives in the Islamic market, whereas currently contracts are arranged on an ad-hoc basis.

ADVANTAGES

- The lack of risk tools that are widely used in the West, such as derivatives, and the avoidance of certain sectors, such as banks, means that Islamic financial markets have a low correlation to other financial markets. This has provided protection from market turbulence, such as that seen during the subprime crisis.
- Many argue that the use of risk tools such as derivatives does not protect against volatility but simply increases it, while financial institutions earn vast profits through their deployment to the detriment of clients. Thus the lack of such tools in Islamic finance may benefit investors.

DISADVANTAGES

- The Islamic finance industry is governed by a patchwork of national banking regulations, its own standard-setting bodies, and scholars interpreting Islamic laws, making contracts much more complicated.
- Islamic scholars are split on the legitimacy of risk tools such as derivatives: some see them as permissible instruments to hedge risk, but others regard them as speculative transactions, which Islam forbids.
- While Islamic banks have avoided the complex instruments that were central to the credit crisis, they have still been susceptible to the downturn. Nonperforming loans and investment impairments in the region have mounted, partly due to inadequate risk-monitoring systems.

ACTION CHECKLIST

✔ Ensure that risk-management tools and systems are in place to ensure high standards of corporate governance and transparency.

✔ Establish whether compliance with *shariah* law creates unique risks, and create systems and tools that can monitor and protect against such threats.

DOS AND DON'TS

DO

- Ensure that any risk-management methods are compliant with local *shariah* rules governing finance. Rules can vary widely from one jurisdiction to another.
- Establish whether *shariah*-compliant tools for managing risk are available. The market is developing at a very rapid pace.

DON'T

- Don't ignore the fundamentals of risk management, including credit and counterparty checks.
- Don't assume that *shariah* law governing financial management is rigid. It is partly a question of interpretation, and there are usually solutions to even the most complex problems.

MORE INFO

Book:

Akkizidis, Ioannis, and Sunil Kumar Khandelwal. *Financial Risk Management for Islamic Banking and Finance*. New York: Palgrave Macmillan, 2008.

See Also:

★ Introduction to Islamic Financial Risk Management Products (pp. 59–62)
★ Risk Management of Islamic Finance Instruments (pp. 94–97)

"We are pioneers and the history of pioneers is not that good." Jeff Bezos

  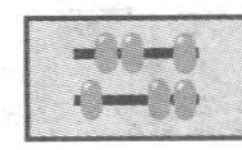   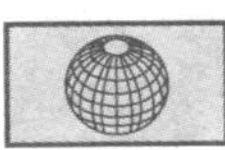   

Managing the Time Value of Money

DEFINITION

The time value of money is based on the premise that most people would choose to receive, say, $10,000 now, rather than the same sum in five years' time. Why? Firstly, because any rational person knows that the $10,000 will almost certainly buy you less in five years' time than it will today. Secondly, there is no certainty that you will actually receive the money five years from now. As the proverb says, a bird in the hand is worth two in the bush.

Businesses use time-value-of-money formulae to make rational decisions on future expectations.

Discounting allows us to understand what we would need to invest today if we wanted to receive a certain amount in the future. Compounding helps us to calculate the sum that we will receive in the future if we invest a certain amount today.

Several other equations can be used to calculate loans, mortgages, the future values of annuities, etc. These equations are frequently combined for particular uses. For example, bonds can be readily priced using these equations. A typical coupon bond is composed of two types of payment: a stream of coupon payments similar to an annuity, and a lump-sum return of capital when the bond matures—that is, a future payment. The two formulae can be combined to determine the present value of the bond.

For an annuity that makes one payment per year, there is an annual interest rate. However, the time frame in years must be converted into the number of periods consistent with the compounding frequency of the rate. For an income or payment stream with a different payment schedule, the interest rate must be converted into the relevant periodic interest rate. For example, if a mortgage requires monthly payments, the interest rate has to be divided by twelve.

The rate of return in these calculations can be either the variable solved or a predefined variable that measures a discount rate, interest, inflation, rate of return, cost of equity, cost of debt, or any number of similar concepts. The choice of the suitable rate is vital to the exercise, and the use of an incorrect discount rate will make the results worthless.

For calculations involving annuities, you must decide whether the payments are made at the end of each period (i.e. ordinary annuity) or at the beginning of each period (i.e. annuity due).

Most formulae are available on financial calculators or can be set up on a spreadsheet.

ADVANTAGES

- Time-value-of-money formulae are generally easy to understand and are widely used.
- The data used by the formulae are readily available.
- Discounting tells us what we would need to invest today if we wanted to receive a certain amount in the future.
- Compounding helps us to calculate the sum that we will receive in the future if we invest a certain amount today.

DISADVANTAGES

- It can often be difficult to identify the appropriate formula without expert help.
- The data on which the initial investment was made often change over the lifetime of the investment.

ACTION CHECKLIST

- ✔ Before you use time-value-of-money formulae, you need to understand the cash flows your business is likely to have and how your cash cycle is calculated.
- ✔ You need to understand how a business manages its working capital as a whole, focusing particularly on how debtors are managed.
- ✔ You must familiarize yourself with the way the banking system and financial markets work—what influences those markets and how a business seeks additional finance when it is required.
- ✔ You must understand what capital expenditure budgeting is and how a business decides whether or not to spend money on a particular project.

DOS AND DON'TS

DO

- Seek help in identifying an appropriate rate for your calculations.

DON'T

- Don't base your planning completely on these formulae, as the data on which the initial investment was made often change over the lifetime of the investment.

MORE INFO

Books:

Clayton, Gary E., and Christopher B. Spivey. *The Time Value of Money: Worked and Solved Problems*. Philadelphia, PA: WB Saunders, 1978.

Luecke, Richard A. *Manager's Toolkit: The 13 Skills Managers Need to Succeed*. Boston, MA: Harvard Business School Press, 2004.

Tuckman, Bruce, and Angel Serrat. *Fixed Income Securities: Tools for Today's Markets*. 3rd ed. Chichester, UK: Wiley, 2011.

Article:

Baldwin, William. "To pay or delay?" *Forbes* (June 27, 2011). Online at: tinyurl.com/3gya84h

Website:

TVM tutorial from Get Objects: tinyurl.com/ru8ed

See Also:

✔ Managing Working Capital (p. 980)

Time Value of Money (p. 1258)

"Time is an illusion. Lunchtime doubly so." Douglas Adams

        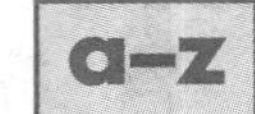

Managing Working Capital

DEFINITION

Working capital, also known as net working capital, is a measurement of a business's current assets, after subtracting its short-term liabilities, typically short term. Sometimes referred to as operating capital, it is a valuation of the assets that a business or organization has available to manage and build the business. Generally speaking, companies with higher amounts of working capital are better positioned for success because they have the liquid assets that are essential to expand their business operations when required.

Working capital refers to the cash that a business requires for its day-to-day operations—for example, to finance the conversion of raw materials into finished goods that the company can then sell for payment.

Among the most important items of working capital are levels of inventory, accounts receivable, and accounts payable. Working capital can be expressed as a positive or a negative number. When a company has more debts than current assets, it has negative working capital. When current assets outweigh debts, a company has positive working capital.

The requirement for working capital depends on the type of company. Some companies are intrinsically better off than others. Examples include retailers (which have a fast turnover of cash) and insurance companies (which receive premiums before having to settle claims).

Manufacturing companies, on the other hand, can incur considerable upfront costs for materials and labor before they receive payment. For much of the time, these companies spend more cash than they generate.

A company will try to manage cash by:

- identifying the cash balance that allows it to meet day-to-day expenses but minimizes the cost of holding cash;
- finding the level of inventory that allows for continuous production but lessens the investment in raw materials and reduces reordering costs;
- identifying the appropriate source of financing, given the cash-conversion cycle.

It may be necessary to use a bank loan or overdraft. However, inventory is preferably financed by credit arranged with the supplier.

If a company is not operating efficiently, this will show up as an increase in the working capital. This can be judged by comparing the amounts of working capital from one period to another. Slow collection and inventory turnover may signal an underlying problem in the company's operations.

ADVANTAGES

- Proper management of working capital gives a firm the assurance that it is able to continue its operations and that it has sufficient cash flow to satisfy both maturing short-term debt and upcoming operational expenses.

DISADVANTAGES

- If a company's current assets do not exceed its current liabilities, then it may run into trouble paying back creditors in the short term.
- A declining working-capital ratio over a longer time period could also be a red flag that merits further analysis. For example, it could be that the company's sales volumes are decreasing and, as a result, its accounts receivable are diminishing.

ACTION CHECKLIST

✔ Check the amount of working capital. If a company is not operating in the most efficient manner (for example slow collection), it will show up as an increase in working capital. This can be understood by comparing the working capital from one period to another. Slow collection may signal a fundamental problem in the company's management.

✔ Is your 'performance indicator' for credit control better than those of other businesses in the same sector?

✔ Invoices should always be accurate in every detail and to the penny when quoting amounts. Inaccuracy is an excuse to query and delay payment. Also aim to send out your invoice the day after delivery of the goods.

✔ Chase debtors—Money that customers still owe cannot be used meet other obligations.

DOS AND DON'TS

DO

- Check that a company has sufficient working capital, as this is an indicator of the success of the business. Lack of working capital may not only mean that a company is unable to grow, but also that it has too little cash to meet its short-term obligations.

DON'T

- Don't allow working capital to fall below the level at which the company has more debts than current assets.

MORE INFO

Books:

Berman, Karen, and Joe Knight, with John Case. *Financial Intelligence: A Manager's Guide to Knowing What the Numbers Really Mean*. Boston, MA: Harvard Business School Press, 2006.

Downes, John, and Jordan Goodman. *Finance and Investment Handbook*. 8th ed. Hauppauge, NY: Barron's Educational Series, 2010.

Articles:

García-Teruel, Pedro Juan, and Pedro Martínez-Solano. "Effects of working capital management on SME profitability." *International Journal of Managerial Finance* 3:2 (March 2007): 164–177. Online at: dx.doi.org/10.1108/17439130710738718

Tooling and Production. "Conserve working capital." June 2008. Online at: tinyurl.com/36eugve

Website:

Working capital reduction case study from Hackett Group: www.thehackettgroup.com/casestudies/cytec/

See Also:

- Working Capital (pp. 1261–1262)
- Working Capital Cycle (p. 1262)
- Working Capital Productivity (p. 1263)

"Once the what is decided the how always follows. We must not make the how an excuse for not facing and accepting the what." Pearl S. Buck

  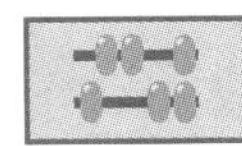   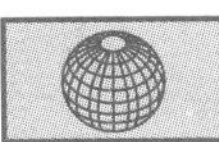   

Managing Your Credit Risk

DEFINITION

Credit risk is the risk of loss caused by a debtor defaulting on a loan or other line of credit, whether the principal, the interest, or both. The sound management of credit risk involves reining in all exposure to financial risk to within acceptable limits. A company's rate of return should always be risk-adjusted to take account of credit risk and other risks.

Good control of credit risk involves managing not only the risk associated with individual deals or transactions, but also that of an entire portfolio (i.e. ensuring that risk is both minimized and evenly spread). Banks in particular need to have a comprehensive policy in place for managing all kinds of risk—credit risk forms the most important part of any such policy. The collapse of Barings Bank in 1995 is a textbook example of what can happen when an organization lacks safeguards for managing credit risk. Loans tend to be the main source of credit risk for many banks. They are, however, exposed to other sources of credit risk, such as in the trading book, or on and off the balance sheet. For all kinds of companies credit risk also exists in other financial instruments, such as interbank or currency transactions, trade financing, equities, and derivatives.

Exposure to credit risk remains a key problem on a global basis. Companies need to learn lessons from high-profile cases such as Barings and Northern Rock. The Basel Committee drew up a set of principles to be used when evaluating a credit risk management system. Although the principles are aimed at financial institutions, they apply equally to all organizations. How a company approaches the issue will vary according to factors such as the supervisory techniques they use, whether they employ external auditors, and the size of the institution. Smaller businesses, in particular, need to ensure they have an adequate risk–return policy in place.

Firms are exposed to credit risk when, for example, they do not insist on advance payment for products or services. By billing after delivery, the company takes the risk that the customer may default on payment, leaving it out of pocket. Many companies quote payment terms of 30 days as standard, and it only takes one large defaulted payment to expose the firm to cash flow problems and possible bankruptcy.

Many firms operate a credit risk department whose role is to assess the financial health of their customers and decide whether to extend credit or not. They may use software to analyze such risks and assess how to avoid, reduce, or transfer any credit risk. Credit rating companies such as Standard & Poor's, Moody's, and Dun and Bradstreet also sell financial intelligence to firms needing external assistance in managing credit risk with their clients.

Companies can lessen their credit risk by, for example, cutting their payment terms to 15 days, limiting the amount of goods or services available on credit per transaction, or even insisting on payment up-front. Strategies such as these cut exposure to risk, but the downside is that they can affect the volume of sales and subsequent cash flow.

ADVANTAGES

- A keen awareness of credit risk that includes processes to identify, measure, monitor, and control credit risk should protect all but the smallest organizations from major problems.

DISADVANTAGES

- Small firms that have only a very few customers find it difficult to manage credit risk due to their vulnerability should a customer turn out to be a late-payer or even default on payment entirely.

ACTION CHECKLIST

Specific credit risk management practices vary among organizations according to the type and complexity of their credit activities. A comprehensive policy for managing credit risk should address the following points:

- ✔ Create an appropriate credit risk environment.
- ✔ Implement a policy that ensures the credit-granting process is sound.
- ✔ Assess the quality of your assets and determine that you have adequate provisions and reserves.
- ✔ Maintain quality procedures for credit administration, measurement, and monitoring processes.
- ✔ Ensure that you have adequate controls in place.

MORE INFO

Books:

Bluhm, Christian, Ludger Overbeck, and Christoph Wagner. *An Introduction to Credit Risk Modeling*. Financial Mathematics Series. Boca Raton, FL: Chapman & Hall/CRC, 2002.

de Servigny, Arnaud, and Olivier Renault. *The Standard & Poor's Guide to Measuring and Managing Credit Risk*. New York: McGraw-Hill, 2004.

Duffie, Darrell, and Kenneth J. Singleton. *Credit Risk: Pricing, Measurement, and Management*. Princeton Series in Finance. Princeton, NJ: Princeton University Press, 2003.

See Also:

★ Minimizing Credit Risk (pp. 540–542)
✔ Building an Efficient Credit and Collection Accounts System (p. 1148)
✔ Derivatives Markets: Their Structure and Function (p. 1007)
✔ Hedging Credit Risk—Case Study and Strategies (p. 969)

"Bankruptcy or credit default is not an issue." Bernie Ebbers

  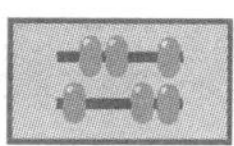      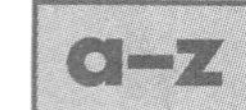

Measuring Financial Health

DEFINITION

When measuring a business's financial health we have to ask a number of questions. What is the source of its revenue? On what does it spend its income, and where? How much profit is it earning? The answer lies in a company's financial statements and by law all public companies have to make these statements freely available to everyone. Financial statements can be broken down into three parts: the profit and loss statement (also called the income statement), the balance sheet, and the cash flow forecast.

The profit-and-loss statement tells us whether the company is making a profit. It indicates how revenue (money received from the sale of products and services before expenses are taken out, also known as the "top line") is transformed into net income (the result after all revenues and expenses have been accounted for, also known as the "bottom line"). A profit and loss account covers a period of time – usually a year or part of a year.

The balance sheet is a snapshot of a business's financial health at a specific moment in time, usually at the close of an accounting period. A balance sheet shows assets, liabilities, and shareholders' equity/capital. Assets and liabilities are divided into short term and long term obligations. The balance sheet does not show the flows into and out of the accounts during the period. A balance sheet's assets should equal liabilities plus owners' equity.

The cash-flow forecast or statement identifies the sources and amounts of cash coming into and going out of a business over a given period. In an established business, an acceptable method is to combine sales revenues for the same period one year earlier with predicted growth.

To survive, the organization's total assets should be greater than its total liabilities. Current assets (such as cash, receivables, and securities) should also be able to cover current liabilities (such as payables, deferred revenue, and current-year loan and note payments). If an organization's cash and equivalents greatly exceed its current liabilities, the organization may not be putting its money to the best use.

ADVANTAGES

- Profit and loss statements track revenues and expenses, so that managers and investors can determine the operating performance of a business over a period of time.
- Balance sheets can be used to identify and analyze trends, particularly in the area of receivables and payables.
- A cash flow forecast shows where cash is employed or tied up. It is an early warning indicator when expenditures are running out of line or sales targets are not being met.

DISADVANTAGES

- Profit and loss statements do not report factors that might be highly relevant but cannot be reliably measured (for example: brand recognition and customer loyalty).
- A balance sheet shows a snapshot of a company's assets, liabilities, and shareholders' equity. It does not show the flows into and out of the accounts during the period.

ACTION CHECKLIST

✔ Use financial ratios on financial statements to evaluate the overall financial condition of the business. Financial ratios help gauge viability, liabilities, and projected future performance.

✔ Carefully analyze any profit and loss accounts for differences during the reporting period. Anomalies might be due to seasonal or other variations or may indicate deeper problems.

✔ Quantify in financial terms how decisions based on the financial statement could impact on business.

✔ Financial statements cannot resolve all grey areas. Be prepared to consult and be involved in a long and complicated process of analysis.

✔ Consult and question managers and key business stakeholders when evaluating financial statements.

DOS AND DON'TS

DO

- Make sure that you have used the financial ratios when analyzing financial statements. If in doubt, consult an expert analyst.
- Check which accounting principles were used when drawing up the accounts.

DON'T

- Don't assume that all financial statements truly reflect a company's financial position. Measuring and reporting permit considerable discretion and the opportunity to influence results.

MORE INFO

Books:

Koller, Tim, Marc Goedhart, and David Wessels. *Valuation: Measuring and Managing the Value of Companies*. 5th ed. Hoboken, NJ: Wiley, 2010.

Pereiro, Luis E. *Valuation of Companies in Emerging Markets: A Practical Approach*. Chichester, UK: Wiley, 2002.

Article:

Lewellen, Jonathan. "Predicting returns with financial ratios." *Journal of Financial Economics* 74:2 (November 2004): 209–235. Online at: dx.doi.org/10.1016/j.jfineco.2002.11.002

Websites

American Accounting Association (AAA): aaahq.org

International Federation of Accountants (IFAC): www.ifac.org

See Also:

✔ Assessing Business Performance (p. 1144)

✔ Managing Working Capital (p. 980)

✔ Understanding Key Performance Indicators (p. 1180)

✔ Understanding the Balance Sheet (p. 999)

"One can't say that figures lie. But figures, as used in financial arguments, seem to have the bad habit of expressing a small part of the truth forcibly, and neglecting the other part, as do some people we know." Fred Schwed

  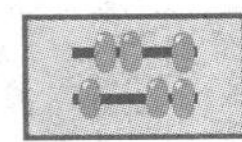      

Measuring Liquidity

DEFINITION

Liquidity refers to the ability of an asset to be easily converted to cash without bringing about a major movement in price and with the lowest loss in value. Liquidity also refers to a company's ability to meet its obligations in terms of possessing sufficient liquid assets.

Various ratios are used to measure liquidity. These include: the current ratio, which is the simplest measure and is calculated by dividing total current assets by total current liabilities; and the quick ratio, calculated by deducting inventories from current assets and then dividing by current liabilities. Although the two ratios are similar, the quick ratio provides a more accurate assessment of a business's ability to pay its current liabilities. The quick ratio cuts out all but the most liquid of current assets. Inventory is the most notable omission, because it is not as speedily convertible to cash.

For example, Table 1 using the quick ratio on the balance sheet.

Total current assets ($115,000) divided by total current liabilities ($70,000) = 1.65. Therefore, for every dollar of liabilities, the company has $1.65 in liquid assets to meet those obligations. As a general guide, companies with a quick ratio of greater than 1.0 are considered satisfactorily able to meet their short term liabilities. Liquidity is a measure of the ability of a debtor to pay their debts. It is crucial that a business has enough cash on hand to meet accounts payable, interest expenses, and other bills as and when they become due.

Table 1. Example balance sheet

Cash	$55,000	*Accounts payable*	$25,000
Equities/securities	$15,000	*Expenses (accrued)*	$20,000
Accounts receivable	$45,000	*Notes payable*	$10,000
		Debt	$15,000
Total current assets	**$115,000**	*Total current liabilities*	**$70,000**

ADVANTAGES

- The quick ratio is a reasonable marker of a business's short term liquidity. The quick ratio gauges a company's ability to meet its short term obligations with its most liquid assets. The higher the quick ratio, the better the position of the business.
- A high or increasing quick ratio usually signifies that a business is experiencing above average growth, is rapidly changing receivables into cash, and is able to cover its financial obligations.

DISADVANTAGES

- The current ratio is the simplest measure and is calculated by dividing total current assets by total current liabilities. However, the current ratio does include inventory, which is often not as swiftly redeemable for cash and is often sold on credit.
- Simple liquidity ratios do not give information about the level and timing of cash flows, which really establish a company's ability to pay liabilities when due.

ACTION CHECKLIST

- ✔ Check whether a business has a low or decreasing quick ratio. This normally suggests that the business
- ✔ is over leveraged, unable to maintain or increase its sales, settling its bills too quickly, or collecting its receivables too slowly.
- ✔ Capital requirements, which differ from industry to industry, can have an effect on quick ratios. Therefore, make liquidity comparisons among companies within the same industry.
- ✔ Take into account factors such as type of industry (long/short cycle), allowances for bad debt, and payment and collection procedures.

DOS AND DON'TS

DO

- When using liquidity ratios to compare a business with others in an industry, allow for any material differences in accounting policies between the compared company and industry norms.
- Determine whether liquidity ratios were calculated before or after adjustments were made to the balance sheet or income statement. In some cases, these adjustments can significantly affect the ratios.

DON'T

- Don't forget that, although the current ratio is the simplest measure, it does include inventory, which is often not as swiftly redeemable for cash and is often sold on credit.
- Don't forget to take into account factors such as type of industry (long/short cycle), allowances for bad debt, and payment and collection procedures.

MORE INFO

Books:

Fiedler, Robert. *Liquidity Modelling*. London: Risk Books, 2011.

Matz, Leonard, and Peter Neu (eds). *Liquidity Risk Management*. Singapore: Wiley, 2007.

International Monetary Fund (IMF). *Financial Soundness Indicators: Compilation Guide*. Washington, DC: IMF, 2006. Online at: www.imf.org/external/pubs/ft/fsi/guide/2006/

Article:

Scordis, Nicos. "The value of smoothing cash flows." *Risk Management* 55:6 (June 2008). Online at: tinyurl.com/3cgho6d

See Also:

★ How to Assess a Company's Global Treasury Needs and Objectives Successfully (pp. 50–52)
★ Navigating a Liquidity Crisis Effectively (pp. 82–84)
✔ Hedging Liquidity Risk—Case Study and Strategies (p. 972)
✔ Managing Working Capital (p. 980)

"All money nowadays seems to be produced with a homing instinct for the Treasury." Prince Philip (Duke of Edinburgh)

  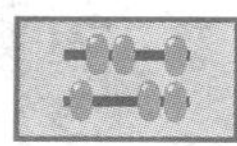      

Methods for Dealing with Inflation Risk

DEFINITION

Inflation risk can be defined as the risk that the value of physical or financial assets will be eroded by inflation. To protect against that loss, investment managers need to employ one or more of several tried and tested methods.

Investors generally choose investments that offer "insurance" against inflation risk. However, it is important to remember that the overall risk of an investment comes from all risk sources, not just the risk of inflation.

Inflation hedging, which takes into account the co-movements of inflation rates and asset returns from period to period, is one of the most commonly used methods for managing inflation risk. The less influence the rate of inflation has on the real return of an investment, the more effective the inflation hedge will be for the investment. Popular hedges against inflation include property, equities, or commodities that generally have a rising value. Studies of periods of high inflation in the 1970s and 1980s show that, in the mid-term, earnings and the dividend growth rates of equities at least kept pace with inflation.

A popular method for managing inflation risk is the use of inflation protection, which examines the inflation risk of an asset and assesses whether that asset's real return will be lower than a specific target return (such as zero) at the end of a determined investment period. One downside to using this risk metric is that it only takes into consideration the probability of negative deviations from the target return, but not the amount of them.

The third main method is the inflation swap. Here, the swap involves the use of inflation derivatives (or inflation-indexed derivatives) to transfer inflation risk from one party to another and protect against future liabilities. The derivatives used may be over-the-counter or exchange-traded derivatives.

ADVANTAGES

- Taking practical steps to deal with inflation risk minimizes both the possibility of real losses and of losses themselves should they occur.

DISADVANTAGES

- There is no guarantee that any methods used will protect completely against inflation, and there will always be a degree of risk. The real return of an investment is always uncertain, even for safe assets such as default-free zero-coupon bonds that have a maturity equal to the length of the investment period, even though the nominal cash flow is guaranteed.

ACTION CHECKLIST

✔ Check that the dividend yields and payout ratios of your chosen method are suitably high and at least in line with inflation.

✔ Assess each method thoroughly to determine which is likely to give your assets the best protection against inflation.

✔ Run full risk management scenarios that take into account all risks, not just inflation.

DOS AND DON'TS

DO

- Take into account all risk factors, not just the risk of inflation.
- Calculate the probability and amount of any shortfall when making inflation-proof investment decisions.
- Review your decisions if the global economy starts shifting unexpectedly, as you may need to adjust your portfolio for the best protection.

DON'T

- Don't assume that traditionally inflation-proof investments such as property are a safe haven. For example, during the credit crunch of 2007–08, the real value of both property and equities fell steeply while inflation rose sharply.

MORE INFO

Books:

Baumol, William J., and Alan S. Blinder. *Macroeconomics: Principles and Policy*. 12th ed. Mason, OH: South-Western Cengage Learning, 2011.

Brice, Benaben (ed). *Inflation-linked Products: A Guide for Investors and Asset & Liability Managers*. London: Risk Books, 2005.

Brigo, Damiano, and Fabio Mercurio. *Interest Rate Models—Theory and Practice, with Smile, Inflation and Credit*. 2nd ed. Berlin: Springer-Verlag, 2007.

Deacon, Mark, Andrew Derry, and Dariush Mirfendereski. *Inflation-indexed Securities: Bonds, Swaps & Other Derivatives*. 2nd ed. Chichester, UK: Wiley, 2004.

Mishkin, Frederic S. *The Economics of Money, Banking, and Financial Markets*. 10th ed. Boston, MA: Pearson, 2012.

Walmsley, Julian. *The Foreign Exchange and Money Markets Guide*. 2nd ed. Wiley Frontiers in Finance Series. New York: Wiley, 2000.

See Also:

★ The Globalization of Inflation (pp. 184–186)

✔ Hedging Interest Rate Risk—Case Study and Strategies (p. 971)

✔ Swaps, Options, and Futures: What They Are and Their Function (p. 988)

✔ Understanding and Using Inflation Swaps (p. 993)

✔ Understanding Asset–Liability Management (Full Balance Sheet Approach) (p. 996)

"**Inflation is as violent as a mugger, as frightening as an armed robber, and as deadly as a hit man.**" Ronald Reagan

  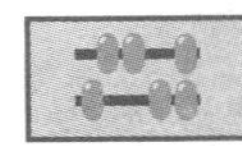   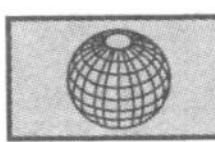   

Preparing a Budget

DEFINITION

Many businesses that are under pressure overlook budgeting, because with already tight schedules they feel they can do without extra work that may seem to be unproductive. In fact, budgeting can save time, as it helps you to prepare for the future and anticipate problems before they occur.

A budget is basically a translation of your business plan into numbers. In its simplest form, a budget is a detailed plan of future receipts and expenditure. You can use your budget to confirm the activities you have planned for the coming year. Can you afford additional staff? Do you need to expand? When should you start a new sales campaign? When are the slow periods, when making ends meet is a challenge? There are no fixed time periods for budgets, but generally they coincide with the financial year. Businesses normally divide the budget into manageable areas, for example sales, production, materials purchasing, marketing, etc.

The **sales budget** is normally calculated by multiplying the expected number of sales by the selling price of the product.

The **production budget** will be made for the proposed flow of stock, using unit numbers instead of financial figures.

The **materials purchasing budget** will use the figures proposed on the production budget to determine the amount of raw materials needed to manufacture the necessary number of units.

The **staff budget** determines how many staff you will need for the operations of the business.

The **overheads budget** can be compiled either by apportioning the overheads to each product/service or by keeping the overheads as a single budget.

The **capital expenditure** budgetcovers the purchase of land or buildings, the hire of equipment, etc.

These individual budgets all come together to create the master budget. You can use this to compare actual results with anticipated goals. If some of your expenses are higher than you expected, do you need to look for ways to cut them, or is it because business has increased? If your sales aren't on track, what has caused the difference? Use the information constructively, so that you can make adjustments immediately, if needed, and improve your next budget.

Knowing what all your business activities will cost, and when such expenses will occur, will help prevent any unexpected surprises that could lead to financial problems down the road.

ADVANTAGES

- Budgeting can help save time, because it helps you to prepare for the future and anticipate problems before they occur.
- Your budget can be used to assess whether your present profit is adequate. In a small business, the profit should be large enough to make a return on your investment and a return on your own work.
- Being aware of what business activities will cost, and when such expenses will occur, will help to prevent any unexpected surprises that could lead to financial problems down the road.

DISADVANTAGES

- Protracted budget evaluation could divert key resources away from core business activities, potentially resulting in the business overlooking valuable opportunities.
- Some numbers depend on judgments, estimates, and interpretation, because certain factors might be highly relevant but cannot be reliably measured.

ACTION CHECKLIST

- ✔ Use your budget to validate the activities you have planned for the coming year. Will you be able to afford to expand your facilities or equipment? Can you employ new staff? When would be the best time to launch a new product?
- ✔ Do you have times when sales are slow? If so, how can you meet that challenge?
- ✔ Compare your budgeted figures with your actual results. Then, ask yourself why the numbers are different. If some of your expenses are higher than you expected, do you need to look for ways to cut them, or has the volume of business increased? If your sales are not on track, what has happened to cause the difference? Use the information constructively, so that you can make adjustments immediately, if needed, and improve your next budget.

DOS AND DON'TS

DO

- Use your budget as a benchmark to check your progress toward your business goals.

DON'T

- Don't overlook budgeting. Being unaware of what all your business activities will cost, and when such expenses will arise, could lead to problems.

MORE INFO

Books:

Kemp, Sid, and Eric Dunbar. *Budgeting for Managers: A Briefcase Book.* New York: McGraw-Hill, 2003.

Longenecker, Justin C., J. William Petty, Leslie E. Palich, and Frank Hoy. *Small Business Management: Launching and Growing Entrepreneurial Ventures*. 16th ed. Mason, OH: South-Western Cengage Learning, 2011.

Article:

Adams, Paul E. "Corporation bookkeeping for your small business budgeting." *MoreBusiness.com* (April 1, 2002). Online at: tinyurl.com/95efys

Website:

Brefi Group on preparing a business plan and budget: www.brefigroup.co.uk/consultancy/business_plans.html

See Also:

★ Capital Budgeting: The Dominance of Net Present Value (pp. 20–23)
★ Managing Capital Budgets for Small and Medium-Sized Companies (pp. 68–70)
★ Viewpoint: Moving Away from Traditional Budgeting (pp. 80–81)
Management Accounts (pp. 1233–1234)

"Watch the costs and the profits will take care of themselves." Andrew Carnegie

Preparing a Cash Flow Forecast

DEFINITION

A cash flow forecast aims to predict a company's future financial liquidity over a specific period of time, using tried and tested financial models. While cash normally refers to the liquid assets in a company's bank account, the forecast usually estimates its treasury position, which is cash plus short-term investments minus short-term debt. The cash flow itself refers to the change in the cash or treasury position from one period to the next. The cash flow forecast is an important way to value assets, work out budgets, and determine appropriate capital structures. It will provide a good indicator of a company's financial health for potential investors.

Several methods are generally used to forecast cash flow—one direct, and three indirect. The direct method is most suitable for short-term forecasts of anywhere from 30 days up to a year, since it is based on actual data from which the projections are extrapolated. The data used are the company's cash receipts and disbursements (R&D). Receipts primarily include accounts from recent sales, sales of other assets, proceeds of financing, etc. Disbursements include salaries, payments for recent purchases, dividends, and debt servicing. Many of the R&D entries are based on projected future sales.

The other methods all use a company's projected income statements and balance sheets as their basis. The first method is adjusted net income (ANI), which first examines the operating income (EBIT or EBITDA), then looks at changes on the balance sheet such as receivables, payables, and inventory to forecast cash flow. The pro forma balance sheet (PBS) method looks at the projected book cash account—if the projections for all other balance sheet accounts are correct, then the cash flow will also be correct. Both these methods can be used to make short-term (up to 12 months) and long-term (multiple year) forecasts. Since they use the monthly or quarterly intervals of a company's financial plan, they must be adjusted to account for the differences between the book cash and the actual bank balance, and these may be significantly different.

The third method uses the accrual reversal method (ARM), which reverses large accruals (revenues and expenses that are recognized when they are earned or incurred, disregarding the actual receipt or dispersal of cash) and calculates the cash effects based on statistical distributions and algorithms. This allows the forecasting period to be weekly or even daily. It can also be used to extend the R&D method beyond the 30-day horizon because it eliminates the inherent cumulative errors. This is the most complicated of all methods and is best suited for medium-term forecasts.

ADVANTAGES

- Cash flow projections offer a useful indicator of a company's financial health.
- Cash flow forecasts enable you to predict the peaks and troughs in your cash balance, helping you to plan borrowings, and they tell you how much surplus cash you may have at a given time. Most banks insists on forecasts before considering a loan.

DISADVANTAGES

- A cash flow forecast never tells the whole story about a company's financial situation and should not be relied on as the sole indicator.

ACTION CHECKLIST

✔ Be realistic when inputting your estimates. An acceptable method is to combine sales revenues for the same period 12 months earlier with predicted growth.

✔ Choose suitable accounting software to help you prepare a cash flow forecast. Check that it will enable you to update your projections if there is any change in market trends or your company's fortunes. Good software simplifies planning for seasonal peaks and troughs and can also calculate for "what if" scenarios.

DOS AND DON'TS

DO

- Use the most appropriate method, depending on how long you want your forecasting horizon to be.
- Remember that a cash flow forecast can only determine the short-term sustainability of a company. The longer the forecast horizon, the higher the chance of an inaccurate projection.
- Bear in mind that the forecast is dynamic—you will need to adjust it frequently depending on business activity, payment patterns, and supplier demands.

DON'T

- Don't rely solely on a cash flow forecast to determine a company's financial stability—look at the other financial statements and forecasts, such as an income statement and a balance sheet, to see what's actually going on.
- Don't forget to incorporate warning signals into your cash flow forecast. For example, if predicted cash levels come close to your overdraft limits, this should sound an alarm and trigger action to bring cash back to an acceptable level.

MORE INFO

Books:

Coyle, Brian. *Cash Flow Forecasting and Liquidity*. London: Global Professional Publishing, 2001.

Fight, Andrew. *Cash Flow Forecasting*. Burlington, MA: Butterworth-Heinemann, 2005.

Loscalzo, William. *Cash Flow Forecasting: Guide for Accountants and Financial Managers*. Maidenhead, UK: McGraw-Hill, 1982.

See Also:

★ Best Practices in Cash Flow Management and Reporting (pp. 16–19)
★ Cash Flow Best Practice for Small and Medium-Sized Enterprises (pp. 28–29)
✔ Assessing Cash Flow and Bank Lending Requirements (p. 964)
⇄ Creating a Cash Flow Statement (p. 1210)
⇄ Discounted Cash Flow (pp. 1217–1218)

"If you're trying to create a healthy organization, one that can sustain itself over time, simply legislating and dictating behavior and outcomes doesn't work at all." Walter Wriston

  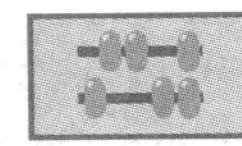      

Setting Up a Dividend Policy

DEFINITION

A dividend is a payment made to a stockholder by a company from any earned profits (i.e. not from any other surplus). Companies generally use profit for two things—to reward stockholders for investing in the company or to reinvest in the business (known as retained earnings). Most companies generally reinvest a portion of the profit and pay out the rest in dividends. From the company's perspective, the payment of dividends is the division of an asset among stockholders.

Dividends are paid out on after-tax income, although the dividends received by stockholders are usually treated as taxable income for tax purposes, depending on their country of residence. Dividends are usually settled on a cash basis, although payment often is in the form of a check. However, many companies pay dividends in the form of additional shares or offer a dividend reinvestment program that enables stockholders to use the cash dividend to buy more shares in the company.

The dividend is normally paid out as a fixed amount per share. Thus, each stockholder receives a dividend in proportion to his or her holding. Most companies pay dividends on a fixed schedule, such as quarterly, half-yearly, or annually. However, a company can declare a dividend whenever it chooses—this is usually known as a special dividend to distinguish it from the regular payouts.

When setting up your dividend policy, key decisions will be how frequently to pay out, what percentage of profit to distribute among stockholders, and whether you will offer them other options, such as stocks in lieu of cash. Once the policy is in place, it needs to be communicated clearly to all stockholders so that they know how often and in what form dividends will be distributed. Policies can always be amended. For example, if the company's profits are badly hit one year, the board may decide not to pay dividends but to reinvest all the profit in the hope of better subsequent profits.

It is usual to publish the policy as a distinct corporate document for distribution in printed form. Many companies also publish the dividend policy on their websites. Amendments to the policy should be distributed in the same way.

ADVANTAGES

- Having a clear and transparent policy is essential for attracting stockholders. They are putting trust into a company by investing in it, and the company returns that trust by being open about what investors can expect to receive in return.
- It is also important that any changes to the dividend policy, whether temporary or permanent, are communicated clearly and in a timely fashion to stockholders.

DISADVANTAGES

- The only real disadvantage of a dividend policy is that some stockholders may be exposed to double taxation. In such a situation, stock repurchases may be more efficient if the tax rate for capital gains is lower.

ACTION CHECKLIST

✔ Determine how frequently you will pay out dividends. Be realistic about this—don't announce quarterly dividends if you know the cash flow patterns mean that a payout can only be made half-yearly.

✔ Have your policy written up professionally by someone experienced in the field.

✔ Ensure that the policy document is checked for compliance with all relevant financial regulations and laws in your territory of jurisdiction.

DOS AND DON'TS

DO

- Keep the dividend policy up to date and ensure that stockholders receive regular mailings about any changes.
- Inform stockholders well in advance of each payment date what percentage of profit the payout will be.

DON'T

- Don't amend dividend policy without good reason or telling your stockholders why.

MORE INFO

Books:

Baker, H. Kent. *Dividend Policy: Its Impact on Firm Value*. Hoboken, NJ: Wiley, 2009.

Frankfurter, George M., and Bob G. Wood, with James Wansley. *Dividend Policy: Theory and Practice*. San Diego, CA: Academic Press, 2003.

Manos, Ronny. *Capital Structure and Dividend Policy: Evidence from Emerging Markets*. Saarbrücken, Germany: VDM Verlag, 2008.

See Also:

★ Dividend Policy: Maximizing Shareholder Value (pp. 667–670)

★ Reinvesting in the Company versus Rewarding Investors with Distributions (pp. 701–702)

✔ An Overview of Stockholders' Agreements (p. 1084)

✔ Using Shareholder Value Analysis (p. 1107)

Dividend Yield (p. 1219)

"They seldom pretend to understand anything of the business of the company ... but receive contentedly such half yearly or yearly dividends, as the directors think proper to make them." Adam Smith

  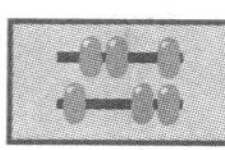   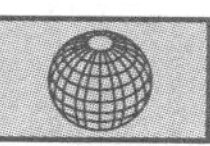   

Swaps, Options, and Futures: What They Are and Their Function

DEFINITION

A swap is a derivative in which two parties agree to exchange a set of cash flows (or leg) for another set. A notional principal amount is used to calculate each cash flow; these are rarely exchanged by the parties. A swap is usually used to hedge a risk, such as an interest-rate risk, or to speculate on a price change. It may also be used to access an underlying asset in order to earn a profit or loss from any change in price while avoiding posting the notional amount in cash or collateral.

An option is a financial instrument that gives the holder the right to engage in a future transaction on an underlying security or futures contract. The holder is under no obligation to exercise this right. There are two main types of option. A call option gives the holder the right to purchase a specified quantity of a security at a fixed price (the strike price) on or before the specified expiration date. A put option gives the holder the right to sell. If the holder chooses to exercise the option, the party who sold, or wrote, the option is obliged to fulfill the terms of the contract.

Futures are traded on a futures exchange and represent an obligation to buy or sell a specified underlying instrument on a specified date (the delivery date or final settlement date) in the future at a specified price (the futures price). The settlement price is the price of the underlying asset on the delivery date. Both parties to a futures contract are legally bound to fulfill the contract on the delivery date. If the holder of a futures position wishes to exit their obligation before the delivery date, they must offset it either by selling a long position or buying back a short position. Such an action effectively closes the futures position and its contractual obligations.

ADVANTAGES

- The use of derivatives means that some financial risks can be transferred to other parties who are more willing or better suited to take or manage those risks and can thus be a useful tool for risk management.
- Purchasing derivatives can be a safer choice if there is a possibility of a looming bear market as they are hedged, unlike equities.
- Buying now at a future price can be cheaper than buying at market price in the future, bearing in mind that the spot price could be less expensive.
- A long call option requires no obligation when it is due.

DISADVANTAGES

- If the market changes dramatically, it is possible to lose financially if the derivatives are being used as a speculative instrument.
- If you hold the put option on a derivative, you are obliged to adhere to it if the holder of the call chooses to exercise their right to sell or buy.

DOS AND DON'TS

DO

- Take time to consider which derivative is most suitable for the transaction you have in mind.
- Consult a financial intermediary or seek other expert guidance if you are unsure.

DON'T

- Don't enter into a contract that will lock you in if there's the slightest possibility that you may need to exit before its expiration date.

MORE INFO

Books:

Arditti, Fred D. *Derivatives: A Comprehensive Resource for Options, Futures, Interest Rate Swaps, and Mortgage Securities*. Boston, MA: Harvard Business School Press, 1996.

Cox, John C., and Mark Rubinstein. *Options Markets*. Englewood Cliffs, NJ: Prentice Hall, 1985.

Hull, John C. *Options, Futures, and Other Derivatives*. 8th ed. Upper Saddle River, NJ: Pearson, 2011.

Redhead, Keith. *Financial Derivatives: An Introduction to Futures, Forwards, Options and Swaps*. London: Prentice-Hall, 1996.

Articles:

Black, Fischer, and Myron Scholes. "The pricing of options and corporate liabilities." *Journal of Political Economy* 81:3 (May–June 1973): 637–654. Online at: www.jstor.org/stable/1831029

Cox, John C., Stephen A. Ross, and Mark Rubinstein. "Options pricing: A simplified approach." *Journal of Financial Economics* 7:3 (September 1979): 229–263. Online at: dx.doi.org/10.1016/0304-405X(79)90015-1

Moran, Matthew. "Stabilizing returns with derivatives." *Journal of Indexes* (4th Quarter 2002): 34–40. Online at: tinyurl.com/3rwqgqp

Schneeweis, Thomas, and Richard Spurgin. "The benefits of index option-based strategies for institutional portfolios." *Journal of Alternative Investments* 3:4 (Spring 2001): 44–52. Online at: dx.doi.org/10.3905/jai.2001.318987

See Also:

★ The Role of Short Sellers in the Marketplace (pp. 593–597)
✔ Derivatives Markets: Their Structure and Function (p. 1007)
✔ Hedge Funds: Understanding the Risks and Returns (p. 1072)
Futures, Options, and Swaps (p. 1366)
Option Volatility and Pricing: Advanced Trading Strategies and Techniques (p. 1404)

"Derivatives are financial weapons of mass destruction." Warren Buffett

  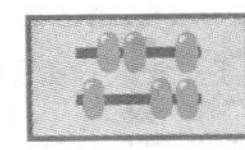      

Understanding Activity-Based Costing

DEFINITION

Activity-based costing (ABC) is a means of analyzing costs according to particular activities performed by individuals, teams, divisions, or other components of a company. These activities can be analyzed on many levels, for example, looking at a process to determine the cost of the overall process, or breaking down a process into activities to determine more precisely how resources are consumed by each identified activity of that process. Therefore ABC is a means to identify the activities that drive overall costs in a company. At an individual employee level, an ABC analysis would measure how much time an employee spends on a particular task related to providing a product or service, as part of a process to attribute employee overhead costs to that particular activity. When applied throughout an organization, ABC models can analyze and cost the activities of all processes in a company, providing a range of information to support decisions in areas such as operations, marketing, and customer support. Information derived from ABC can also help companies to quote more accurately when bidding for new business, as improved knowledge about how much each activity involved in the new business costs to provide can help companies to price jobs more efficiently.

ABC is extensively used in the manufacturing industry, but it has also proved its worth in other sectors where a sound understanding of the costs of activities required to provide a product or service is needed, such as banks and finance companies, airlines, and logistics companies. ABC has also found favor in the public sector given the increasing pressure to provide accountability for funds spent and to provide services on a cost-efficient basis.

ADVANTAGES

- Understanding your costs better helps to support better management decisions.
- ABC is relatively easy for everyone involved to understand.
- ABC can help to challenge assumptions about which activities consume most resources.
- The methodology can also support more efficient setting of quotes for new business, given the improved knowledge about the costs of all activities necessary to fulfill the requirements.

DISADVANTAGES

- Data collection and analysis can be a protracted and time-consuming process.
- The focus on cost—as opposed to value—could fail to recognize that some seemingly costly activities may act as a "loss leader" that supports other highly profitable business from the same clients.
- Maintaining an ongoing ABC system can be expensive.

ACTION CHECKLIST

- ✔ Decide the scope of the ABC program, including the areas to be included and the level of depth of the study.
- ✔ Identify the relevant processes and activities that are to be examined as part of the ABC analysis.
- ✔ Consider whether your ABC study is to be a one-off or is to be undertaken at regular intervals.
- ✔ Determine the scope of distribution of the results within the organization.

DOS AND DON'TS

DO

- Use ABC to help identify areas of inefficiency, such as services that are being provided for unattractive margins.
- Assess whether the cost of the ABC study could be offset by providing information on which customers are most profitable and whether some customers have actually detracted from profits.

DON'T

- Do not expect the adoption of an ABC study to be universally popular in your company—some managers may be concerned that their pet projects could be exposed as less profitable than previously assumed.
- Don't share ABC information with employees who may subsequently be attracted by a competitor. ABC studies require the evaluation of a wealth of operational and financial data; these data may be proprietary to the firm and therefore commercially sensitive.

MORE INFO

Books:

Cokins, Gary. *Activity-Based Cost Management: An Executive's Guide.* New York: Wiley, 2001.

Kaplan, Robert S., and Steven R. Anderson. *Time-Driven Activity-Based Costing: A Simpler and More Powerful Path to Higher Profits.* Boston, MA: Harvard Business School Publishing, 2007.

Article:

Leahy, Tad. "Where are you on the ABC learning curve?" *Business Finance* (December 1, 2004). Online at: tinyurl.com/yeqm96y

Report:

Liu, Lana Yan Jun, and Fei Pan. "Activity based costing in China: A case study of Xu Ji Electric Co. Ltd." Research executive summary series, vol. 7, iss. 13. Chartered Institute of Management Accountants, August 2011. Online at: tinyurl.com/3gng2he [PDF].

See Also:

★ The Missing Metrics: Managing the Cost of Complexity (pp. 766–768)
★ Profitability Analysis Using Activity-Based Costing (pp. 908–910)
✔ Business Process Reengineering (p. 1150)
Activity-Based Costing (pp. 1190–1192)
Cost and Effect: Using Integrated Cost Systems to Drive Profitability and Performance (p. 1347)

"Annual income twenty pounds, annual expenditure nineteen nineteen six, result happiness. Annual income twenty pounds, annual expenditure twenty pounds ought and six, result misery." Charles Dickens

Understanding and Calculating the Total Cost of Risk

DEFINITION

Risk exists virtually everywhere in business—from the obvious, easily insurable risks such as cover for property assets to more obscure, yet not insignificant, risks such as the loss of key employees to illness. However, in an effort to cover as many bases as possible, some companies channel resources into their risk management operations, potentially raising questions over whether these units are delivering good value for stakeholders in the company. The total cost of risk (TCOR) is a tool for measuring the overall costs associated with the running of the corporate risk management operation, including all insurance premiums, risk control and financing costs, administrative costs, and any self-retained losses incurred, relative to other key measures such as overall company revenues, total headcount, and its asset base. Over time, TCOR therefore provides a yardstick to assess how a company's risk-related costs are changing relative to the overall growth rate of the business. In turn, management can then explore potential ways to assess how the company's TCOR is changing relative to industry benchmarks, typically with the use of data derived from research—e.g., "physical" risk research conducted by trade groups and industry organizations. Given that the cost considerations are uppermost in the oil distribution business, yet food producers may focus more on liability insurance risks, working with these industry bodies can be the best way to obtain relevant and comparable risk-related cost data.

ADVANTAGES

- Calculating the total cost of risk can help companies to highlight inconsistencies in their approach to risk management.
- The process can also identify areas where the cost of managing a particular risk may be excessive relative to risks elsewhere, potentially leading to reallocation of some elements of the risk management budget.
- By highlighting inefficiencies in the risk management process, TCOR can also generate direct cost savings.

DISADVANTAGES

- Truly comparable TCOR data can be difficult to access, though trade bodies can help. However, prized data on direct competitors—such as a key rival also pushing into a new, high-growth market segment—are plainly sensitive and therefore not generally available.
- TCOR analysis can be mistakenly seen purely as a cost-cutting exercise.

ACTION CHECKLIST

- ✔ Use a basic framework to break down costs into component categories such as risk financing, risk administration, risk compliance costs, and self-insured losses.
- ✔ Identify existing costs for each category, expressed as a percentage of overall company revenues.
- ✔ Use any available data from industry bodies for comparison with your existing TCOR figures in each category.
- ✔ Consider possible reasons for differences between your company's numbers and industry-wide figures.
- ✔ Establish targets for each category for future years.

DOS AND DON'TS

DO

- Remember that industry benchmarks may not always be truly comparable with your company in every aspect.
- Consider whether some minor risks could be covered in-house.
- Make use of specialist software to help you arrive at decisions on issues such as risk retention, as risk management budgeting is by nature complex.

DON'T

- Don't ignore the value added by the risk management function when making budgeting decisions. This is a mistake. Risk management should not be seen purely as a cost.
- Don't expect that TCOR analysis will lead to immediate cost savings. This could lead to disappointment. Be prepared to invest in risk management tools which will deliver financial benefits over time.
- Don't see the management of risk-related costs as an issue for which all possible solutions lie within the company. Explaining your objectives and priorities to external risk management specialists and insurance brokers could be very productive.

MORE INFO

Books:

Frenkel, Michael, Ulrich Hommel, Gunter Dufey, and Markus Rudolf. *Risk Management: Challenge and Opportunity*. 2nd ed. Berlin: Springer, 2005.

Merna, Tony, and Thaisal F. Al-Fani. *Corporate Risk Management: An Organisational Perspective*. Chichester, UK: Wiley, 2008.

Report:

Green, Andrew, Randy Garber, and Jim Hanna. "The real cost of risk: Reducing cost and schedule overruns at the US Department of Defense." AT Kearney, 2010. Online at: tinyurl.com/p8s97h2

Website:

Risk and Insurance Management Society (RIMS): www.rims.org

See Also:

★ Risk Management: Beyond Compliance (pp. 929–932)
Mastering Risk, Volume 1: Concepts (p. 1393)

"Business today is about making decisions amid ambiguity." Geraldine Laybourne

  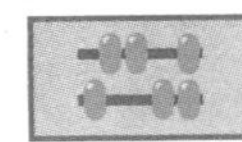   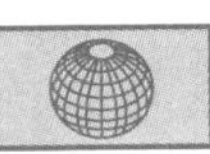   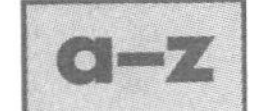

Understanding and Using Carry Trades

DEFINITION

The term "carry" refers to the practice of borrowing a low-yielding currency and lending a high-yielding currency. The trader attempts to capture the difference between the rates, which can often be substantial, depending on the amount of leverage the trader chooses to use.

Carry trading correlates with global financial and exchange rate stability. It is less commonly used when there are global liquidity shortages. The risk in carry trading is that foreign exchange rates may change unfavorably for the trader, who must then pay back a more expensive currency with a less valuable currency. Carry trades can weaken the target currency because traders sell the borrowed sum and convert it into other currencies. Historically, commercial banks exploited the carry trade by borrowing cheaper short-term funds in their domestic credit markets. They would then lend at longer maturities in the same domestic credit market by making loans to corporate or individual customers or by buying government or corporate bonds. This spread between short-term and long-term funding costs made it a very attractive way of creating credit.

In order to curtail monetary growth as inflation picked up, central banks got into the habit of raising short-term rates, but in recent years this practice of raising rates has spread from domestic banks to a broader range of international financial institutions. Two factors have helped to create this cross-currency carry trade. First has been the growing efficiency of credit markets, thanks to the development of information systems such as computer-driven trading systems with automated stop-loss options, and the diffusion of these trading techniques. Second, the improvement in macroeconomic management techniques over the last 15 years has played a major part in reducing volatility in a range of markets, and this has encouraged investors to take risks across more asset classes.

Monetary policies in the first half of the 2000s led to the yield curves in most major economies becoming flat or inverted. As a result, the scope for funding carry trades narrowed down to the Japanese yen and the Swiss franc. By early 2007, it is estimated that US$1 trillion was staked on the yen carry trade. However, Japanese inflation was much weaker in 2008, implying a possible return to deflation and meaning that the Bank of Japan will not be able to raise interest rates very much. Thus the yen will remain low yielding and will continue to be an attractive funding currency for international carry traders in the short term.

During the economic turmoil of 2008, investors became increasingly desensitized to the measures that were introduced domestically and internationally, and banks became reluctant to lend to each other. With aggressive selling in the euro/yen and sterling/yen carry trades, those in euro/dollar and sterling/dollar have come under pressure.

ADVANTAGES

- Carry trades are profitable as long as the prices of the assets that are bought rise in value or if the price of the liability (domestic currency) does not increase.
- Assets need to be highly liquid—for example quoted equities, commodities, bonds, higher-yielding currencies.

DISADVANTAGES

- The uncertainty of exchange rates makes the carry trade risky.
- A small movement in exchange rates can result in huge losses unless the money is hedged appropriately.
- In slumping economies interest rates tend to fall, which encourages lower-valued and lower-yielding currency.

ACTION CHECKLIST

✔ Ensure that there are low-yielding currencies available to be borrowed to finance the trade.

✔ Check that the current business cycle is perceived to be still in the expansion phase.

✔ Watch out for low-volatility conditions.

✔ Borrow in the low interest rate currency (yen, Swiss franc, offshore yuan).

✔ Invest in the high interest rate currency (US dollar, NZ dollar, Australian dollar, Korean won, Indian rupee).

DOS AND DON'TS

DO

- Take your cash out of the market if you can.
- Keep a careful eye on the currencies of the countries in which you are investing.

DON'T

- Don't expect a fast return on your money.
- Don't assume that the markets will recover quickly in times of economic difficulty.

MORE INFO

Book:

Maeda, Martha, and Jermaine Burrell. *The Complete Guide to Currency Trading and Investing: How to Earn High Rates of Return Safely and Take Control of Your Financial Investments*. 2nd ed. Ocala, FL: Atlantic Publishing Group, 2011.

Article:

Galati, Gabriele, Alexandra Heath, and Patrick McGuire. "Evidence of carry trade activity." *BIS Quarterly Review* (September 2007): 27–41. Online at: www.bis.org/publ/qtrpdf/r_qt0709e.pdf

Website:

Carry trade strategy example: www.fxwords.com/c/carry-trade.html

See Also:

✔ Building a Forex Plan (p. 965)
✔ The Foreign Exchange Market: Its Structure and Function (p. 968)
✔ Hedging Foreign Exchange Risk—Case Studies and Strategies (p. 970)
✔ Understanding and Using Currency Swaps (p. 992)

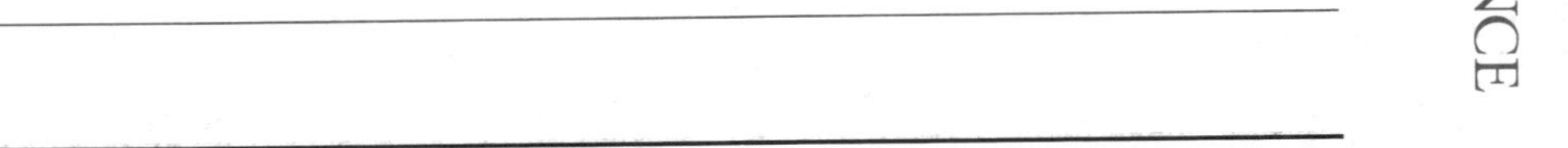

"Markets can remain irrational longer than you can remain solvent." John Maynard Keynes

        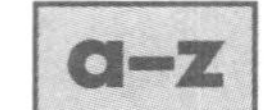

Understanding and Using Currency Swaps

DEFINITION

A currency swap is a foreign exchange transaction in which two or more parties agree to exchange a set amount of one currency for another for a specified period of time. At the end of the determined time-span, each party returns to the other the original sum swapped. Currency swaps are a useful tool for legitimately bypassing foreign exchange controls. Currency swaps are typically negotiated for any period of time up to 30 years' maturity.

Under international accounting rules, a currency swap is not considered to be a loan and therefore does not usually appear on a company balance sheet. Rather, it is accounted as a foreign exchange transaction (the short leg), with the requirement to close the swap (the far leg) being accounted as a forward contract. All cash flows associated with the swap are paid—the initial receipt/payment of loaned principal, the payment/receipt of interest (in the same currency), and the ultimate return/recovery of the principal upon maturity.

It is not uncommon for a company to shop around to reduce the amount needed to service a debt. By borrowing at a lower cost in a particular currency and then exchanging it for a debt in the currency the company really desires, both parties can improve the condition of their debt while also maximizing their cash flows.

ADVANTAGES

- The main advantage of entering into a currency swap is its flexibility—the maturity of a swap is usually negotiable for at least 10 years. Entering into a currency swap can help both parties limit or manage their exposure to fluctuations in interest rates or to obtain a lower interest rate—a foreign company is unlikely to have access to better rates than a domestic company. As companies service their swap obligations with cash flow generated in a foreign currency, they thus also reduce their exchange rate risk exposure. An additional benefit to engaging in a currency swap is the reduction of counterparty risk, as evidenced by the bid–ask spread.
- By definition currency swaps are also combined with an interest rate swap in two currencies. The terms of a swap may be drawn up to have fixed versus floating payments in different currencies beyond fixed rates.

DISADVANTAGES

- Any benefit of entering into a currency swap must be balanced against the costs of the transaction and managing risks such the pre-settlement risk and the settlement risk. However, the chief risk in engaging in a currency swap is that the other party may fail to meet its obligations either during the period of the swap or upon maturity. Should one party wish to exit the swap before maturity, the exiting party must secure the consent of its counterparty before pursuing a mutually agreed exit strategy, much as in the case of selling an exchange-traded futures or option contract before maturity. Some exit routes include the following:

a Entering into an offsetting swap. For example, the exiting party could enter into a second swap, this time receiving a fixed rate and paying a floating rate.

b Selling the swap to a third party. As swaps have a calculable value, one party may sell the contract to a third party, with the permission of the counterparty.

c Purchasing a "swaption." This allows a party to set up, but not enter into, a potentially offsetting swap at the time they execute the original swap.

MORE INFO

Books:

Hull, John C. *Options, Futures, and Other Derivatives*. 8th ed. Upper Saddle River, NJ: Pearson, 2011.

Redhead, Keith. *Financial Derivatives: An Introduction to Futures, Forwards, Options and Swaps*. London: Prentice Hall, 1996.

Walmsley, Julian. *The Foreign Exchange and Money Markets Guide*. 2nd ed. Wiley Frontiers in Finance Series. New York: Wiley, 2000.

See Also:

★ To Hedge or Not to Hedge (pp. 104–106)
★ A Total Balance Sheet Approach to Financial Risk (pp. 113–114)
✔ Building a Forex Plan (p. 965)
✔ The Foreign Exchange Market: Its Structure and Function (p. 968)
✔ Hedging Foreign Exchange Risk—Case Studies and Strategies (p. 970)

"I made my money by selling too soon." Bernard Baruch

  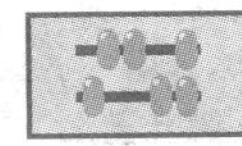   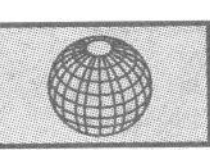   

Understanding and Using Inflation Swaps

DEFINITION

An inflation swap involves the use of inflation derivatives (or inflation-indexed derivatives) to transfer inflation risk from one party to another. The derivatives used may be over-the-counter or exchange-traded derivatives. Inflation swaps have become increasingly popular since the turn of the century as pension funds, for example, recognize the need for inflation-linked assets that match future liabilities. Conversely, borrowers such as governments or large corporations understand that inflation-linked assets or revenues can be funded by inflation-linked debt. Inflation swaps frequently include real rate swaps, such as asset swaps of inflation-indexed bonds. Inflation swaps are simply a linear form of such derivatives. Real rate swaps consist of the nominal interest swap rate minus the corresponding inflation swap.

There are three main types of inflation swap. In a standard interbank inflation-linked swap, or zero-coupon inflation-linked swap, cash flow is exchanged on the maturity date. This swap pays out the exact value of the cumulative inflation for a fixed capital sum over a determined period. This is a good option for investors, particularly pension funds, seeking an investment mix aimed at compliance with long-term, inflation-related obligations.

In a year-on-year inflation-linked swap, inflation is used on an annual basis rather than a cumulative one. This structure is suitable for investors seeking to protect cash flow. Typically, an inflation swap is priced on a zero-coupon basis, with payment exchanged upon maturity. One party pays the compound fixed rate, while the other pays the actual inflation rate for the term of the swap. In Europe, inflation swaps are typically paid on a year-on-year basis where the year-on-year rate of change of the price index is paid. In the United States, payment is more typically on a month-on-month basis, although the inflation rate used is still the year-on-year rate.

In an inflation-linked income swap two cash flows are exchanged, each of which follows the inflation index. One party pays a fixed inflation increase annually over the period of the contract. The other party pays the actual inflation over the period of the contract. The swap itself consists of a series of zero-coupon swaps.

Other traded inflation derivatives include caps, floors, and straddles, which are usually priced against year-on-year swaps. The inflation derivatives market in the United Kingdom is substantial, although the equivalent market in the eurozone is many times bigger.

ADVANTAGES

- Public authorities, and companies dealing in utilities, real estate, and distribution all benefit from high inflation as it brings bigger profits. Conversely, insurers, pension funds, and private investors fare better when inflation is low, as otherwise they face a shrinking margin. Thus, there is a potential market for selling or buying inflation. The key advantage of entering into an inflation swap is being able to hedge against future price rises or diminishing margins. By selling inflation in an inflation-linked swap, future income linked to inflation can be protected.

DISADVANTAGES

- The main disadvantage of participating in an inflation swap is the risk that inflation rates may change drastically as a result of unexpected shifts in the global economy. Such changes can expose parties to loss of profit or negative equity.

MORE INFO

Books:

Brice, Benaben (ed). *Inflation-Linked Products: A Guide for Investors and Asset and Liability Managers*. London: Risk Books, 2005.

Brigo, Damiano, and Fabio Mercurio. *Interest Rate Models—Theory and Practice, with Smile, Inflation and Credit*. 2nd ed. Berlin: Springer, 2007.

Deacon, Mark, Andrew Derry, and Dariush Mirfendereski. *Inflation-Indexed Securities: Bonds, Swaps and Other Derivatives*. 2nd ed. Wiley Finance Series. Chichester, UK: Wiley, 2004.

Hull, John C. *Options, Futures, and Other Derivatives*. 8th ed. Upper Saddle River, NJ: Pearson, 2011.

Redhead, Keith. *Financial Derivatives: An Introduction to Futures, Forwards, Options and Swaps*. London: Prentice Hall, 1996.

Walmsley, Julian. *The Foreign Exchange and Money Markets Guide*. 2nd ed. Wiley Frontiers in Finance Series. New York: Wiley, 2000.

Report:

Boscher, Erwan. "Strategies for managing inflation risk." Asset Liability Management Conference, Prague, April 27, 2007. Online at: www.soa.org/files/pd/boscher-inflation.pdf

See Also:

★ A Total Balance Sheet Approach to Financial Risk (pp. 113–114)
✔ Derivatives Markets: Their Structure and Function (p. 1007)
✔ Methods for Dealing with Inflation Risk (p. 984)
✔ Swaps, Options, and Futures: What They Are and Their Function (p. 988)
Futures, Options, and Swaps (p. 1366)

"Inflation might be called prosperity with high blood pressure." Arnold H. Glasgow

  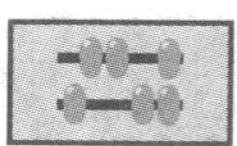   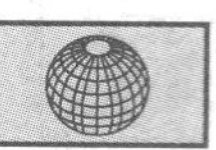   

Understanding and Using Interest Rate Swaps

DEFINITION

An interest rate swap is a popular, highly liquid derivatives instrument in which one party exchanges its stream of interest payments for another party's stream of cash flows. Interest rate swaps are used by hedgers to manage their fixed or floating assets and liabilities, and by speculators to profit from changes in interest rates.

There are various types of interest rate swap, the most common being where one party agrees to pay a fixed rate (the swap rate) to the other party, which in return pays a floating rate to the first party. The rate is usually denominated in a particular currency, which is then multiplied by a notional principal amount (for example, US$1 million). The notional amount is generally used only to calculate the size of cash flows to be exchanged. The floating rate is usually pegged to a reference rate such as the Libor, and the interest payments are settled net. When the swap is initiated, it is priced so that its net present value is zero.

Other popular swap types are fixed–fixed, floating–floating, or a combination including different currencies (interest rate swaps are often combined with currency swaps).

ADVANTAGES

- The chief advantage of an interest rate swap is that it limits a company's exposure to interest rate fluctuations, and thus reduces risk. By swapping interest rates, a firm is able to alter its interest rate exposures and bring them in line with management's appetite for interest rate risk.
- Where there is a positive quality spread differential, a further benefit is the opportunity for arbitrage. This enables each party to take advantage of the other's credit-worthiness in the swap.
- Other pluses include increasing the certainty of an issuer's future obligations, saving money should interest rates decline (here, the party paying a floating rate will be the beneficiary of a rate drop), the option of revising your debt profile to benefit from anticipated future market conditions, and reducing the amount of debt service.
- Interest rate swaps generally involve minimal cash outlay. It is usual that on a payment date only the difference between the two payment amounts is paid to the entitled, rather than an exchange of the full amount of interest.

DISADVANTAGES

- The downside to participating in an interest rate swap is the exposure to risk, typically interest rate risk and credit risk. The interest rate risk occurs when there are changes in the floating rate. In a standard fixed-for-floating swap, the party paying the floating rate benefits if rates fall but is exposed if rates rise, in a similar fashion to holding a long bond position. The credit risk remains whether the swap is in-the-money or not. If one party to the swap is in-the-money, then the risk is their exposure to the other party defaulting.

MORE INFO

Books:

Arditti, Fred D. *Derivatives: A Comprehensive Resource for Options, Futures, Interest Rate Swaps, and Mortgage Securities*. Financial Management Association Survey and Synthesis Series. Boston, MA: Harvard Business School Press, 1996.

Hull, John C. *Options, Futures, and Other Derivatives*. 8th ed. Upper Saddle River, NJ: Pearson, 2011.

Redhead, Keith. *Financial Derivatives: An Introduction to Futures, Forwards, Options and Swaps*. London: Prentice Hall, 1996.

Walmsley, Julian. *The Foreign Exchange and Money Markets Guide*. 2nd ed. Wiley Frontiers in Finance Series. New York: Wiley, 2000.

See Also:

★ A Total Balance Sheet Approach to Financial Risk (pp. 113–114)
✔ Hedging Interest Rate Risk—Case Study and Strategies (p. 971)
✔ Identifying and Managing Exposure to Interest and Exchange Rate Risks (p. 974)
✔ Swaps, Options, and Futures: What They Are and Their Function (p. 988)
✔ Understanding and Using the Repos Market (p. 1098)

     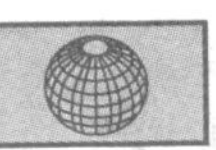   

Understanding and Using the Cash Conversion Cycle

DEFINITION

The cash conversion cycle (CCC) refers to the period of time in which a company is able to convert its resources into cash. Resources can include such factors as labor, raw materials, and utilities. This metric is used as part of working capital analysis. The cycle can, perhaps, be best defined as the time it takes to collect the cash from sales after paying for the resources purchased by the company. The cycle may consist of up to five separate stages of conversion:

- Resources into inventories
- Inventories into finished goods
- Finished goods into sales
- Sales into accounts receivable
- Receivables into cash

The cash conversion cycle uses a basic formula to calculate the time period, which is always in days, as follows:

$$\begin{aligned} \text{CCC} = {} & \text{Inventory conversion period (DIO)} \\ & + \text{Receivables conversion period (DSO)} \\ & - \text{Payables conversion period (DPO)} \end{aligned}$$

Inventory conversion period (DIO)

$$= \frac{\text{Inventory}}{\text{CGS}} \times 365$$

Receivables conversion period (DSO)

$$= \frac{\text{Receivables}}{\text{Sales}} \times 365$$

Payables conversion period (DPO)

$$= \frac{\text{Accounts payable}}{\text{CGS}} \times 365$$

where CGS is cost of goods sold, DIO is days of inventory outstanding, DSO is days of sales outstanding, and DPO is days payable outstanding.

The above formulae should be adjusted to take into account any reduction in requirements due to delaying payment for purchases. The formulae are also based on averages and do not take account of seasonality, or trends in growth, or decline of the business.

The cash conversion cycle is important for both retailers and manufacturers as it measures how quickly a company can convert sales into hard cash. Companies should aim to have the shortest possible cycle as it means capital is tied up for less time, making the bottom line stronger.

Economists cite the CCC as one the most accurate metrics for the real financial health of a company, as it is not only easy to calculate but it also reflects the dynamic situation on a day-to-day basis when you input the data.

ADVANTAGES

- In a short cash conversion cycle, capital is freed up for investment purposes or capital expenditure.

DISADVANTAGES

- In a long cash conversion cycle, capital is locked into core operations and cannot be used for anything else.

ACTION CHECKLIST

✔ Note that often both sales and purchases are made on credit rather than with cash—this difference should be accounted for when calculating the cycle. Special attention should also be given to the length of the receivables processing period: A shorter period is generally best, but in certain circumstances it can sometimes be offset by an increase in that for accounts payable by paying creditors more slowly, although this may be viewed as irresponsible.

✔ Note that the receivables days look backward (debtors arise out of sales that have already been made), whereas the inventory days look forward (inventory is held in order to meet future sales).

✔ The cash conversion cycle can be used as part of a company's strategy. For example, a firm aiming to be the lowest-price supplier on the market will probably tailor its inventory and receivables days accordingly, with tight payment times and a willingness to accept stock-outs in order to avoid holding excessive inventory. Conversely, a high-end supplier would be more likely to extend generous credit terms, and hold more lines of inventory, to reflect a business model that charges higher prices to its customers.

DOS AND DON'TS

DO

- Remember that some businesses will have a smaller CCC, such as those selling goods for cash, which therefore have no receivables, or those selling services, which therefore have no inventory.
- Remember that the cycle may be negative if a company settles with its creditors immediately after purchasing raw materials, manufacturing the goods, and selling them for cash.

DON'T

- Don't run any of the formulae without first making the specific adjustments applicable to your business.

MORE INFO

Books:

Bygrave, William, and Andrew Zacharaki. *Entrepreneurship*. 2nd ed. Hoboken, NJ: Wiley, 2010.

Hilton, Ronald W. *Managerial Accounting: Creating Value in a Dynamic Business Environment*. 9th ed. New York: McGraw-Hill, 2011.

See Also:

★ How to Better Manage Your Financial Supply Chain (pp. 53–55)
✔ Building an Efficient Credit and Collection Accounts System (p. 1148)
✔ Choosing the Right Payment Policy (p. 1151)
✔ How to Optimize Stock Control (p. 1159)

"Sex and taxes are in many ways the same. Tax does to cash what males do to genes. It dispenses assets among the population as a whole." Steve Jones

  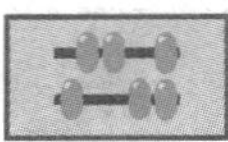      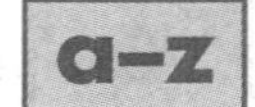

Understanding Asset–Liability Management (Full Balance Sheet Approach)

DEFINITION

Asset–liability management, or ALM, is a means of managing the risk that can arise from changes in the relationship between assets and liabilities. ALM was originally pioneered by financial institutions in the 1970s as interest rates became increasingly volatile. This volatility had dangerous implications for financial institutions. Some, for example, had sold long-term guaranteed interest contracts—some guaranteed rates of around 16% for periods up to 10 years. However, when short-term interest rates subsequently fell, these institutions, such as the Equitable in the United States, were crippled. Prior to the 1970s, interest rates in developed countries varied little and thus losses accruing from asset–liability mismatches tended to be minimal.

Following the experience of Equitable and other institutions, financial firms increasingly focused on ALM, whereby they sought to manage balance sheets in order to maintain a mix of loans and deposits consistent with the firm's goals for long-term growth and risk management. They set up ALM committees to oversee the ALM process. Today, ALM has been adopted by many corporations, as well as financial institutions. ALM now seeks to ascertain and control three types of financial risk: Interest rate risk, credit risk (the probability of default), and liquidity risk, which refers to the danger that a given security or asset cannot be traded quickly enough in the market to prevent a loss (or make a predetermined profit).

But ALM also now seeks to address other risks, such as foreign exchange risks and operational risks (covering areas such as fraud and legal risks, as well as physical or environmental risks). The techniques that are now applied by ALM practitioners have also developed, reflecting the growth of derivatives and other complex financial instruments. ALM now includes hedging, for example, whereby airlines will seek to hedge against movements in fuel prices and manufacturers will seek to mitigate the risk of fluctuations in commodity prices. Meanwhile, securitization has allowed firms to directly address asset–liability risk by removing assets or liabilities from their balance sheets.

ADVANTAGES

- ALM can help protect a financial institution or corporation against a variety of financial and nonfinancial risks.
- The mere process of identifying risks enables businesses to be better prepared to deal with these risks in the most cost-effective way.
- ALM ensures that a company's capital and assets are used in the most efficient way.
- It can be used as a strategic and business tool to improve earnings.

DISADVANTAGES

- ALM is only as good as the people on the ALM committee and the operational procedures that they follow.
- ALM can prove costly in terms of both the time required of employees and the investment required in management tools such as IT and techniques such as hedging.

ACTION CHECKLIST

- ✔ Establish an ALM committee to oversee the process.
- ✔ Ensure the committee has the necessary tools and techniques for measuring and managing rate, credit, and funding risk. This should include a computer system that enables the monitoring of funding sources and credit exposures.
- ✔ Acquire a managerial accounting system that can control the information fed into the computer system.
- ✔ Establish a reward and penalty system to manage those employees who are taking rate, credit, funding and other risks.

DOS AND DON'TS

DO

- Talk to one of the many consultancy firms that specialize in ALM, and that can advise on establishing an ALM committee and improving its performance.
- Ensure those appointed to the ALM committee have the necessary knowledge and experience to perform their tasks.
- Constantly monitor the performance of your committee.

DON'T

- Don't seek to cut costs in terms of investing in management tools and personnel.
- Don't forget that risks are constantly changing and developing. Make sure your ALM committee has the skills to deal with the latest developments.

MORE INFO

Books:

Buckley, Adrian. *Multinational Finance*. 5th ed. Harlow, UK: FT Prentice Hall, 2003.

Dermine, Jean, and Youssef F. Bissada. *Asset and Liability Management: The Banker's Guide to Value Creation and Risk Control*. 2nd ed. Harlow, UK: FT Prentice Hall, 2007.

Tilman, Leo M. (ed). *Asset Liability Management of Financial Institutions: Maximising Shareholder Value through Risk-Conscious Investing*. London: Euromoney, 2003.

Article:

Buehler, Kevin S., and Anthony M. Santomero. "How is asset and liability management changing? Insights from the McKinsey survey." *RMA Journal* 90:6 (March 2008): 44–49. Online at: tinyurl.com/owm2mdd [PDF; via archive.org].

Website:

Institute of Risk Management (IRM): www.theirm.org

See Also:

★ Asset Liability Management for Pension Funds (pp. 13–15)
★ Using Structured Products to Manage Liabilities (pp. 115–117)

"In business a reputation for keeping absolutely to the letter and spirit of an agreement, even when it is unfavorable, is the most precious of assets, although it is not entered in the balance sheet." Viscount Chandos (Oliver Lyttelton)

  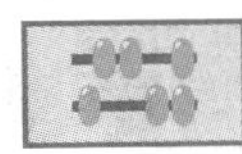   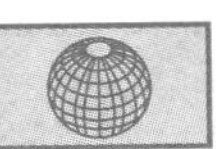   

Understanding Capital Structure Theory: Modigliani and Miller

DEFINITION

The Modigliani–Miller theorem states that, in the absence of taxes, bankruptcy costs, and asymmetric information, and in an efficient market, a company's value is unaffected by how it is financed, regardless of whether the company's capital consists of equities or debt, or a combination of these, or what the dividend policy is. The theorem is also known as the capital structure irrelevance principle.

A number of principles underlie the theorem, which holds under the assumption of both taxation and no taxation. The two most important principles are that, first, if there are no taxes, increasing leverage brings no benefits in terms of value creation, and second, that where there are taxes, such benefits, by way of an interest tax shield, accrue when leverage is introduced and/or increased.

The theorem compares two companies—one unlevered (i.e. financed purely by equity) and the other levered (i.e. financed partly by equity and partly by debt)—and states that if they are identical in every other way the value of the two companies is the same.

As an illustration of why this must be true, suppose that an investor is considering buying one of either an unlevered company or a levered company. The investor could purchase the shares of the levered company, or purchase the shares of the unlevered company and borrow an equivalent sum of money to that borrowed by the levered company. In either case, the return on investment would be identical. Thus, the price of the levered company must be the same as the price of the unlevered company minus the borrowed sum of money, which is the value of the levered company's debt. There is an implicit assumption that the investor's cost of borrowing money is the same as that of the levered company, which is not necessarily true in the presence of asymmetric information or in the absence of efficient markets. For a company that has risky debt, as the ratio of debt to equity increases the weighted average cost of capital remains constant, but there is a higher required return on equity because of the higher risk involved for equity-holders in a company with debt.

ADVANTAGES

- In practice, it's fair to say that none of the assumptions are met in the real world, but what the theorem teaches is that capital structure is important because one or more of the assumptions will be violated. By applying the theorem's equations, economists can find the determinants of optimal capital structure and see how those factors might affect optimal capital structure.

DISADVANTAGES

- Modigliani and Miller's theorem, which justifies almost unlimited financial leverage, has been used to boost economic and financial activities. However, its use also resulted in increased complexity, lack of transparency, and higher risk and uncertainty in those activities. The global financial crisis of 2008, which saw a number of highly leveraged investment banks fail, has been in part attributed to excessive leverage ratios.

MORE INFO

Books:

Brealey, Richard A., Stewart C. Myers, and Franklin Allen. *Principles of Corporate Finance*. 11th ed. New York: McGraw-Hill, 2013.

Stewart, G. Bennett. *The Quest for Value: A Guide for Senior Managers*. New York: HarperBusiness, 1991.

Articles:

Miles, James A., and John R. Ezzell. "The weighted average cost of capital, perfect capital markets, and project life: A clarification." *Journal of Financial and Quantitative Analysis* 15:3 (September 1980): 719–730. Online at: dx.doi.org/10.2307/2330405

Modigliani, Franco, and Merton H. Miller. "The cost of capital, corporation finance, and the theory of investment." *American Economic Review* 48:3 (June 1958): 261–297. Online at: www.jstor.org/stable/1809766

Modigliani, Franco, and Merton H. Miller. "Corporate income taxes and the cost of capital: A correction." *American Economic Review* 53:3 (June 1963): 433–443. Online at: www.jstor.org/stable/1809167

See Also:

★ Capital Structure: Perspectives (pp. 24–27)
★ Optimizing the Capital Structure: Finding the Right Balance between Debt and Equity (pp. 543–545)
✔ Investors and the Capital Structure (p. 1120)
Franco Modigliani (p. 1296)
Merton Miller (p. 1294)

"In companies whose wealth is intellectual capital, networks, rather than hierarchies, are the right organizational design." Thomas A. Stewart

  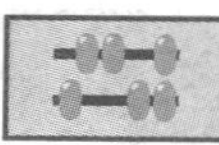      

Understanding Key Financial Terms and Statements

DEFINITION

Publicly traded companies are under an obligation to deliver regular trading updates to the market, ensuring that at all times they present a reasonable reflection of their actual trading performance. However, the terms commonly used in trading statements range from the readily understood, such as "sales" to the more complex and obscure such as "EBITA." While audited accounts are intended to ensure that the company's interim and full-year trading statements provide a truthful assessment as to how the company has fared during the specified trading period, investors frequently pay particular attention to the "outlook" or "prospects" section of a company review, on the basis that stock valuations are heavily geared to perceptions of future earnings. Given that many stocks typically trade on multiples of 10 or more of earnings, stocks are, therefore, highly sensitive to the perception of how future earnings could vary from existing market forecasts. How a company's results compare to the market's consensus expectations is usually the major driver for the stock's direction following a trading update. For example, should a company announce record results, the stock is actually likely to decline should even these results fail to match the market's even more optimistic expectations.

When reporting their performance, companies present four kinds of financial statements:

1. Balance sheet—a breakdown of the company's assets and its liabilities at a fixed date.
2. Income statement—details of how much money the company earned and what it spent during the period.
3. Cash flow statement—how cash moved in and out of the company during the period.
4. Stockholders' equity statement—a statement summarizing the opening balance, additions to and deductions from, and the closing balance of the stockholders' equity account, over a stated period.

While the purpose of each of these statements is relatively easy to understand, some of the terminology contained in company reports can be confusing without some accountancy knowledge. The following paragraphs present a small selection of examples of commonly misunderstood terms used by companies in their trading updates:

- EPS—Earnings per stock. The figure represents the company's total net income during the period, minus dividends to be paid to preferred stockholders (i.e. guaranteed dividends), divided by the number of stocks in issue. As the latter can change during the review period, many companies use a weighted average stock count figure for the review period as a whole.
- EBIT—Earnings before interest and tax. This figure represents the total income from all sources before interest payments and taxes are taken into account.
- Working capital—Trading current assets less trading current liabilities.
- Retained earnings—This figure refers to the total of net earnings—revenues after all expenses, taxes, and interest deductions—that the company has built up.
- Return on capital employed—Also known as ROCE, this is a measure of the returns that a business is achieving from the capital employed, usually expressed in percentage terms. Typically used as a guide as to how efficiently a company is using the money invested in it, ROCE can be expressed as the ratio of operating profits achieved to the total amount of operating capital invested (i.e. both equity and debt) in the business.

ADVANTAGES

- Understanding financial terms and statements helps investors to make more informed decisions.
- During extended periods of volatility in financial markets, investment news becomes mainstream news, so an understanding of the terms used becomes even more beneficial.

DISADVANTAGES

- Some of the terminology used in finance and investment can be complex.
- Detailed analysis of statements and company-specific financial number crunching requires knowledge and considerable resources, so it is best left to expert analysts.

ACTION CHECKLIST

✔ Keeping abreast of general economic and financial news can add a greater sense of perspective when looking at financial statements.

DOS AND DON'TS

DO

- Take advantage of freely available investment research when making investment decisions.
- Be prepared to contact companies' investor relations departments with any queries you may have.

DON'T

- Don't be afraid to seek advice. Attempting to study company trading statements in detail is best reserved for those with accounting expertise.
- Don't focus exclusively on one company's results without reference to factors that may be impacting on the wider industry.

MORE INFO

Book:

Becket, Michael Ivan H. *How the Stock Market Works: A Beginner's Guide to Investment.* 4th ed. London: Kogan Page, 2012.

Website:

US Securities and Exchange Commission's "Beginners' guide to financial statements": www.sec.gov/investor/pubs/begfinstmtguide.htm

See Also:

✔ Preparing Financial Statements: Balance Sheets (p. 1046)
✔ Preparing Financial Statements: Profit and Loss Accounts (P&Ls) (p. 1047)

"Market values are fixed only in part by balance sheets and income statements; much more by the hopes and fears of humanity; by greed, ambition, acts of God, invention, financial stress and strain, weather, discovery, fashion and numberless other causes impossible to be listed without omission." Gerald M. Loeb

  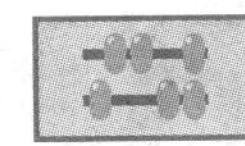   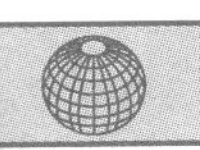   

Understanding the Balance Sheet

DEFINITION

In financial accounting, the balance sheet is one of four standard financial statements and is a summary of a company's financial position at a given point in time. The balance sheet normally is broken down into three main elements—assets, liabilities, and net equity—to show what the company owns and owes on that date. It is usual to include intangible assets such as goodwill alongside tangible assets such as property. Typically, a balance sheet is published at the end of the company's financial year when the accounts have been audited, but it may also be produced at the end of a quarter, half-year, or other specified period.

Of the three elements on the balance sheet, the assets are normally listed first, followed by any liabilities. The difference between the two is the equity, or worth, of the company. The equity may be referred to as net assets, shareholders' equity, or net worth. The equity will always equal the assets minus the liabilities, or, conversely, the assets must equal the liabilities plus the equity:

Equity = Assets − Liabilities

or

Assets = Liabilities + Equity

The balance sheet is always drawn up so that the assets are presented in one section with the liabilities and equity in the other, and they must match each other, or balance (hence the title "balance sheet"). Double-entry bookkeeping is used to record the value of each line on the balance sheet. Because a corporate balance sheet tends to be lengthy and complex, it is usually published in the company's annual report, typically with that of the previous year alongside for comparative purposes.

The International Accounting Standards Committee is responsible for drawing up guidelines for corporate balance sheets. Accounts published to this standard are usually marked as IAS compliant. There are also a number of country-specific bodies that draw up accounting guidelines, and, depending on the country where a company is based, such standards may be obligatory.

The assets on a balance sheet typically include the following items: current assets such as inventory, accounts receivable, cash and cash equivalents, and prepaid expenses; long-term assets such as property, plant and equipment; investment property such as real estate held for investment purposes; intangible assets, which includes goodwill, patents and intellectual property; and other financial assets.

The liabilities are usually items such as: accounts payable, provisions for warranties or court decisions, financial liabilities (excluding the two previous items) such as promissory notes and corporate bonds, liabilities and assets for current tax, and deferred tax liabilities and tax assets.

The last element on the balance sheet is the equity, or net worth. Theoretically, the shareholders' equity actually forms part of a company's liabilities, as the shares in fact represent monies owed to the shareholders after payment of all other liabilities. In practice, however, the liabilities on the balance sheet exclude the shareholders' equity. Thus, the equity by definition is equal to the assets minus the liabilities, i.e. the difference between the two.

On the balance sheet equity typically includes: the total number of shares authorized, issued and fully paid, and issued but not fully paid; the par value, i.e. face value, of the shares; a reconciliation of shares outstanding at the beginning and the end of the period covered by the balance sheet; a list of any rights, preferences, or restrictions of the shares; treasury shares, including those held by subsidiary or associated companies; and any shares reserved for issuance under options and contracts.

MORE INFO

Book:

Williams, Jan R., Susan F. Haka, Mark S. Bettner, and Joseph V. Carcello. *Financial and Managerial Accounting: The Basis for Business Decisions*. 16th ed. Boston, MA: McGraw-Hill/Irwin, 2011.

Websites:

American Institute of Certified Public Accountants (AICPA): www.aicpa.org
Financial Accounting Standards Board (FASB; US): www.fasb.org
IFRS Foundation and the International Accounting Standards Board (IASB): www.ifrs.org
Institute of Chartered Accountants in England and Wales (ICAEW): www.icaew.com

See Also:

★ The Missing Metrics: Managing the Cost of Complexity (pp. 766–768)
★ Understanding the Requirements for Preparing IFRS Financial Statements (pp. 423–424)
★ Valuing Pension Fund Liabilities on the Balance Sheet (pp. 122–124)
✔ Preparing Financial Statements: Balance Sheets (p. 1046)
✔ Understanding Asset–Liability Management (Full Balance Sheet Approach) (p. 996)

"It sounds extraordinary, but it's a fact that balance sheets can make fascinating reading." Mary, Lady Archer

  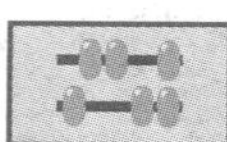      

Understanding the Cost of Capital and the Hurdle Rate

DEFINITION

The cost of capital is the rate of return that an investor expects to earn on his or her investment. If an investment is to be worthwhile, the expected return on capital must be greater than its cost. In other words, the *risk-adjusted* return on capital (that is, incorporating not just the projected returns, but the probabilities of those projections) must be higher than the cost of capital.

Cost of capital is made up of two elements: debt and equity. The cost of debt is, in the simplest terms, the amount of interest paid on the debt. The interest cost is historical, but investor expectations may also influence the actual cost (i.e. investors may accept a higher cost in the short term where the long-term gains are better). Other factors may also affect the cost of debt. The interest rate usually includes the risk-free rate plus a risk component, which takes into account the probability of default on the debt.

The cost of equity is more complex. The traditional calculation used is that of dividend capitalization, whereby the dividends per share are divided by the current market value of the stock plus the dividend growth rate. Thus, the cost of equity is equal to the compensation demanded by the market in exchange for ownership of the asset and bearing the risk of ownership.

The cost of capital is often used as the discount rate, i.e. the rate at which the projected cash flow is discounted to determine the net present value.

The weighted average cost of capital (WACC) is a method of measuring a company's cost of capital. The total capital is taken to be the value of a company's equity (if there are no outstanding warrants and options, this is equal to the company's market capitalization) plus the cost of its debt (this must be continually updated as the cost of debt changes every time there is a change in the interest rate). When calculating the WACC, the equity in the debt-to-equity ratio is the market value of all equity, rather than the shareholders' equity on the balance sheet.

The hurdle rate is the minimum rate of return, when applying a discounted cash flow analysis, that an investor requires before they commit to an investment. A company may apply it when deciding whether to undertake a project, or a bank when extending loans. It must be equal to the incremental cost of capital. It is known as the hurdle rate because the amount of return determines if the investor is "over the hurdle" and ready to invest.

ADVANTAGES

- Using a hurdle rate can help take the emotion out of making a decision on investment by focusing purely on the financial aspects. When an investment looks exciting, it can be easy to overlook the risks or a potentially poor rate of return. A risk premium can be appended to the hurdle rate if evaluation of the investment shows that specific opportunities inherently contain high levels of risk.

DISADVANTAGES

- A major downside to using a hurdle rate is that, inevitably, some profitable projects will be rejected. Additionally, if the hurdle rate is too high, a company may only favor projects that are profitable in the short term rather than taking a long-term view. Thus it can make companies seem conservative and deter them from investing in innovation where the returns are uncertain.

MORE INFO

Book:

Ross, Stephen A., Randolph W. Westerfield, and Jeffrey Jaffe. *Corporate Finance*. 10th ed. New York: McGraw-Hill/Irwin, 2012.

Articles:

Modigliani, Franco, and Merton H. Miller. "The cost of capital, corporation finance, and the theory of investment." *American Economic Review* 48:3 (June 1958): 261–297. Online at: www.jstor.org/stable/1809766

Yee, Kenton K. "Aggregation, dividend irrelevancy, and earnings-value relations." *Contemporary Accounting Research* 22:2 (Summer 2005): 453–480. Online at: dx.doi.org/10.1506/GEH4-WNJR-G58F-UM0U

See Also:

✔ Appraising Investment Opportunities (p. 1143)
✔ Assessing Cash Flow and Bank Lending Requirements (p. 964)
✔ Understanding the Relationship between the Discount Rate and Risk (p. 1001)
✔ Understanding the Weighted Average Cost of Capital (WACC) (p. 1002)
Merton Miller (p. 1294)

"Capital, technology, and ideas flow these days like quicksilver across national boundaries." Robert H. Waterman, Jr

  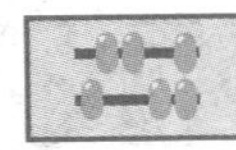    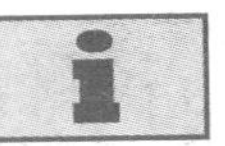  

Understanding the Relationship between the Discount Rate and Risk

DEFINITION

The discount rate is the percentage by which a discounted cash flow (DCF) valuation is reduced in each time period beyond the present. Estimating a suitable discount rate is difficult and is an uncertain part of DCF. The problems are magnified by the fact that small changes in the interest rate can cause large changes in value for the final result down the line.

The discount rate used in financial calculations is commonly taken to be equal to the cost of capital. Adjustments can be made to the discount rate to take into account associated risks for uncertain cash flows. Examples of discount rates applied to various types of companies show a wide range:

Start-up companies seeking new money	50–100%
Early start-ups	40–60%
Late start-ups	30–50%
Mature companies	0–25%

High discount rates apply to more risky companies, for a number of reasons:

- Stocks are not traded publicly, so there is a reduced market for ownership.
- The number of willing investors is limited.
- The risk that start-ups will fail is higher.
- Forecasts by the business owners may be overoptimistic.

When a business has made a profit and is deciding whether to reinvest it in the business or pass it to stockholders, it must consider the discount rate. In an ideal world, reinvestment now guarantees larger profits later, and the amount of extra profit required by stockholders in the future, so that they will agree to reinvestment now, based on the stockholder's discount rate. The capital asset pricing model (CAPM) is a way of estimating stockholders' discount rates. These rates are usually applied by businesses to their decisions on reinvestment by calculating the net present value of the decision. If a company uses the CAPM to work out the discount rate, it must first determine the equity cash flows that are subject to this rate.

The capital asset pricing model takes three variables into account when calculating a discount rate:

Risk-free rate: This is the return (as a percentage) from investing in risk-free securities, for example government bonds.

Beta: Beta is a measurement of how the stock price of a company reacts to a change in the market. A beta figure greater than 1 means that the stock price of the company changes more than the rest of the market. A beta below 1 means that the stock price is stable and does not respond wildly to changes in the market. A beta of less than zero means that the stock price moves in the opposite direction to the market, taking leveraging effects into account.

Equity market risk premium: This is the return on investment above the risk-free rate that investors require.

The discount rate is calculated as follows:

$$\text{Discountrate} = \text{Risk-free rate} + \text{Beta} \times \text{Equity market risk premium}$$

The relationship between the discount rate and risk needs to be considered when performing a DCF analysis because any adjustment of the discount rate needs to allow for risk in future cash flows, and investors need to understand the trade-off between the amount of risk and expected future returns. A higher expected return is usually accompanied by a higher risk. Risk-averse investors usually prefer to hold a risk-free asset that has an expected return that is lower than that of a risky asset. Thus the discount rate would have to rise in order to attract risk-averse investors.

ADVANTAGES

- Applying risk to discount rates gives a better understanding of risks and returns.
- Considering the risk associated with a company gives an investor a better chance of understanding the risk associated with the investment.

DISADVANTAGES

- Many low-level investors may not wish to consider the complexity of the relationship of discount rates to risk.
- Becoming too concerned about risk could mean missing out on a spectacular future return.

ACTION CHECKLIST

When considering an investment, consider the position of the company:

✔ What are the expected rates of return?

✔ What are the risks involved?

✔ Do the rates of return compensate for those risks?

DOS AND DON'TS

DO

- Ensure that the risks associated with the expected returns are taken into account and understood.
- Understand the calculations involved in determining discount rates.
- Understand the nature of the company that is seeking inward investment—i.e. its level of maturity.

DON'T

- Don't ignore the risks.

MORE INFO

Books:

Bailey, Martin J., and Michael C. Jensen. "Risk and the discount rate for public investment." In Michael C. Jensen (ed). *Studies in the Theory of Capital Markets*. New York: Praeger, 1972.

Pannell, David J., and Steven G. M. Schilizzi (eds). *Economics and the Future: Time and Discounting in Private and Public Decision Making*. Cheltenham, UK: Edward Elgar Publishing, 2006.

See Also:

★ Valuing Pension Fund Liabilities on the Balance Sheet (pp. 122–124)
✔ Preparing a Cash Flow Forecast (p. 986)
✔ Understanding the Cost of Capital and the Hurdle Rate (p. 1000)

"I am far more interested in avoiding risk than I am in capturing every opportunity. My philosophy says that loss of opportunity is preferable to loss of capital." Joseph DiNapoli

  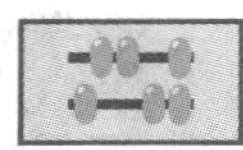      

Understanding the Weighted Average Cost of Capital (WACC)

DEFINITION

The weighted average cost of capital (WACC) measures the capital discount of a company's income and expenditure. It is a component of the formula used for calculating the expected cost of new capital and it represents the rate that a company is expected to pay to finance its assets. It is thus the minimum return that a company must earn on its existing asset base to satisfy its creditors, owners, and other providers of capital.

WACC is calculated by taking into account the relative weight of each component of a company's capital structure. The calculation usually uses the market values of the components, rather than their book values, which may differ significantly. Components may include equity (both common and preferred), debt (straight, convertible, or exchangeable), warrants, options, pension liabilities, executive stock options, and government subsidies. More exotic sources of financing, such as convertible/callable bonds or convertible preferred stock, may also be included in a WACC calculation if they are present in significant amounts as the cost of these is usually different from plain vanilla financing methods. For a company with a complex capital structure, calculating WACC can be a time-consuming exercise.

The equation used to calculate WACC uses the cost of each capital component multiplied by its proportional weight as follows:

$$WACC = E/V \times R_e + D/V \times R_d \times (1 - T_c)$$

where R_e is the cost of equity, R_d is the cost of debt, E is the market value of the firm's equity, D is the market value of the firm's debt, $V = E + D$, E/V is the percentage of financing that is equity, D/V is the percentage of financing that is debt, and T_c is the corporate tax rate.

To determine the value of each component it is assumed that the weight of a source of financing is simply its market value (rather than the book value, which may be significantly different) divided by the sum of the values of all the components. The easiest component to calculate is the market value of the equity of a publicly traded company, as this is simply the price per share multiplied by the number of outstanding shares. Likewise, the market value of preferred shares is easy to determine and is calculated by multiplying the cost per share by number of outstanding shares. The market value of a company's debt is also easy to discover if a company has publicly traded bonds. However, many companies have debt in the form of bank loans, whose market value is not easily found. However, the market value of debt is often fairly close to the book value, at least for companies that have not experienced significant changes in credit rating. Thus, calculation of WACC typically uses the book value of any debt.

On the cost side, the cost of preferred shares is calculated by dividing the periodic payment by the price of the preferred shares. The cost of ordinary shares is typically determined using the capital asset pricing model. The cost of debt is usually the yield to maturity on the company's publicly traded bonds, or the rates of interest charged by the banks on recent loans. The cost of debt can be cut further as a company can usually write off taxes on the interest it pays on the debt. Thus, the cost of debt is calculated as yield to maturity multiplied by (1 minus the tax rate).

Because governments usually allow tax to be deducted from interest, there is an inherent bias towards debt financing. However, the cost of financial distress, such as bankruptcy, tilts any bias towards equity financing. In theory, therefore, the ideal debt-to-equity ratio in a company is usually the point at which any tax benefits accrued by debt financing are outweighed by the costs of financial distress.

MORE INFO

Books:

Armitage, Seth. *The Cost of Capital: Intermediate Theory*. Cambridge, UK: Cambridge University Press, 2005.

Johnson, Hazel. *Determining Cost of Capital: The Key to Firm Value*. London: FT Prentice Hall, 1999.

Pratt, Shannon P., and Roger J. Grabowski. *Cost of Capital: Applications and Examples*. 4th ed. Hoboken, NJ: Wiley, 2010.

Website:

Formularium on WACC calculation: formularium.org/en/10.html?go=96.169

See Also:

★ WACC versus APV Valuation: Financial Policy and the Discount Rate (pp. 626–628)
✔ Estimating Enterprise Value with the Weighted Average Cost of Capital (p. 967)
✔ Obtaining an Equity Value Using the Weighted Average Cost of Capital (WACC) (p. 1080)
✔ Understanding the Cost of Capital and the Hurdle Rate (p. 1000)
Weighted Average Cost of Capital (pp. 1260–1261)

"Global democratic capitalism is as unrealizable a condition as worldwide communism." John Gray

  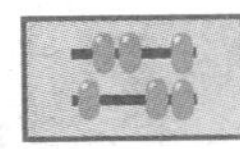      

Understanding Yield/Revenue Management

DEFINITION

Originally developed and refined in the airline industry in the 1970s, yield management ("YM" or revenue management as it is also known) is a tool that aims to capitalize on a full understanding of customer buying behavior, in order to maximize the benefit that can be derived from providing a limited-life product or service.

Sophisticated PC-based YM models harness a range of inputs to help create a pattern of projected demand, and then look to help the provider to match the demand with goods or service provision at the optimal level, using pricing as the key mechanism to help shape the demand pattern. The "perishable" element of the product or service is very important for both the buyer and the seller as it heightens the need for a transaction to be struck within a particular time frame. YM seeks to exploit the passage of time in order to maximize revenues for the provider, though this "perishability" element can, of course, be a double-edged sword in that unsold goods essentially expire with a lost opportunity cost to the seller. Yield/revenue management techniques also rely on the essentially limited supply of the product or service, and an acceptance from buyers that prices paid can vary over time and between different buyer categories. The tools are at their most valuable in situations where the fixed cost related to the provision of the perishable goods or service far outweighs any variable costs.

Through the study of consumer buyer behavior, YM can generate sales of essentially identical goods or services to different customers at different prices. A straightforward example in the sale of airline tickets would be a low fare offered to a client booking weeks in advance, with this client potentially finding him/herself sitting next to another passenger who exhibited different buying behavior, perhaps buying his/her ticket only the day before travel, thereby paying a huge premium to the early booker. YM can also discriminate on the basis of time in other ways. A supermarket, for example, could heavily discount fresh goods as they approach their "best before" dates, or could even vary the displayed price of goods on LED screens at different times of the week in an attempt to manage demand, perhaps making goods more expensive on busy Friday evenings/weekends and cheaper on quieter weekday mornings, in an effort to encourage some shoppers to adjust their shopping times.

Under some circumstances, however, there can be an ethical argument against excessive use of YM techniques. Just as price discrimination can be based on inputs such as time, prices can also be varied according to factors such as the buyer's location, financial profile and frequency of previous transactions. This could, for example, create the basis for a potential client to be quoted a higher price based on past customer buying patterns which might suggest that clients from a particular geographic location are prepared to pay more than those from elsewhere. However, this can create situations in which a relatively poor retail client who happens to reside in a particular area can be penalized. Above all, attitudes to the acceptability of some aspects of YM techniques vary between industries and countries.

ADVANTAGES

- YM helps companies to enhance revenues or profits through understanding of customers' buying behavior.
- YM models can also help companies to plan their output to capitalize on the predicted demand patterns.
- The tool can help lower the chances of "opportunity loss" for both buyers and sellers when perishable goods or services go unsold.
- YM has a long, proven track record of giving a significant marketing advantage over rivals not implementing YM method.

DISADVANTAGES

- The techniques can be inappropriate for goods or services available in virtually unlimited supply, those which are not time-sensitive or perishable in nature, or where variable costs of provision are large in relation to fixed costs.
- YM can raise ethical issues related to varying prices for the same goods or services between different customers.
- Some customers could react badly to perceived injustices related to the principle of price discrimination, potentially resulting in a public relations issue.

ACTION CHECKLIST

- ✔ Ensure you have some flexibility to respond to variations in demand.
- ✔ Assess how any segmentation within your market breaks down.
- ✔ Consider the range of input factors you would apply to your YM model, for example, advance booking discounts.
- ✔ Discuss how you will inform customers of the new pricing structures.
- ✔ Be prepared to go back and make regular adjustments to your YM system for optimization purposes.

DOS AND DON'TS

DO

- Ensure that employees are trained in the benefits of YM systems—some key insights about buyer behavior may be gleaned from employees with direct customer contact.
- Utilize information about buyer behavior patterns to help shape the development of your product offering, rather than using it purely as an input for pricing.
- Assess the potential impact of a poorly received YM system—some customers may react badly if the new charging structure is perceived to be unfair compared to legacy fixed-pricing structures.

DON'T

- Don't assume that the introduction of YM systems will be universally approved. Consider the risk of alienating long-standing core customers.
- Don't send out confusing messages to customers—it's important to understand your market segmentation.
- Don't assume that YM systems are only commercially viable for industry leaders. The potential benefits of such systems may out weigh implementation cut offs.

MORE INFO

Article:

Jarvis, Peter. "Introducing yield management into a new industry." *Journal of Revenue and Pricing Management* 1:1 (May 2002): 67–75. Online at: dx.doi.org/10.1057/palgrave.rpm.5170007

Websites:

Revenue management system providers, IDeaS: www.ideas.com; JDA Software: www.jda.com; and Revenue Management Systems: www.revenuemanagement.com

"Investing is an activity of forecasting the yield over the life of the asset; speculation is the activity of forecasting the psychology of the market." John Maynard Keynes

  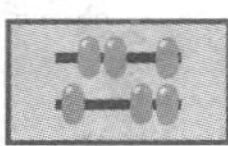      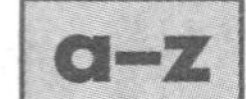

Banks "Planning for Failure"—Living Wills as Resolution and Recovery Plans

DEFINITION

The bankruptcy of investment bank Lehman Brothers in September 2008 rocked the financial markets and shook confidence in the strength of the global banking system as the credit crunch intensified. Administrators faced a gargantuan challenge in dealing with the aftermath of the failure of the fourth-largest US investment bank; at the point of its collapse, Lehman had US$613 billion in debts and US$639 billion in assets, including US$43 billion in property alone. The bankruptcy judge overseeing the case described the collapse as the "most massive cross-border insolvency in the history of the world;" globally, Lehman consisted of 3,000 legal entities and has since become the subject of 76 individual insolvency procedures. Yet administrators arrived faced with the challenge of understanding and then winding down a global business with around US$1.2 trillion of open market exposure, with risks spread across a hugely complex organizational structure.

In September 2009 the United Kingdom, which had previously stepped in to rescue banks such as Northern Rock, the Royal Bank of Scotland and Lloyds Banking Group, revealed plans, through the Financial Services Authority regulator, to oblige banks to create "resolution and recovery plans" which would give administrators a head start toward dismantling banks in the event of their bankruptcy. Although similar plans have been floated elsewhere, the UK government has been a particularly active proponent of living wills. However, it stands opposed to the forced separation of retail and investment banking activities, despite support for this separation voiced by none other than Mervyn King, governor of the Bank of England. Such a radical move would be reminiscent of the changes instigated by the imposition in the United States of the Glass–Steagall Act of 1933, which enforced the separation of banking and broking activities.

ADVANTAGES

- The creation of living wills would be of immense benefit to administrators faced with the challenge of dismantling failed institutions with complex structures.
- Moves to clarify and simplify the structure of banks could also ease the process of integrating successful banks during a merger or acquisition.
- Although some banks may be reluctant to support the move toward the creation of living wills, those majority-owned by the state may be less able to resist pressure to impose this requirement.

DISADVANTAGES

- Some institutions could resist pressure to create living wills on the grounds that their balance sheet strength makes failure highly unlikely.
- The creation and maintenance of living wills entails a resource overhead which some institutions may balk at.
- These documents would be highly sensitive and confidential in nature, with their creation potentially creating greater scope for uncertainty and instability over the strength of some banks.
- Moves toward simplified structures could also have adverse tax implications for banks that have created complex, opaque structures specifically to minimize their tax liabilities. The impact on profits could lessen their attractiveness to shareholders.

ACTION CHECKLIST

- ✔ Some banks have already created structures that could simplify administrators' tasks in the event of failure.
- ✔ For example, the HSBC has stated that each of its national units holds capital separately in its operating country, simplifying the job of regulators in dismantling the global structure should Europe's largest bank ever fail.
- ✔ Nevertheless, regulators need to address complex issues surrounding living wills for cross-border banks, such as conflicts between different insolvency procedures and "burden-sharing" between authorities should taxpayers' funds be needed to support the orderly winding down of international banks.
- ✔ Some industry figures have questioned the motivation behind the push toward living wills, with some suggesting the likelihood of a hidden agenda that is more related to preventing banks from employing tax-efficient structures, with a view to raising government income from corporation tax.

DOS AND DON'TS

DO

- Recognize the positive side of living wills; governments and regulators aim to facilitate the "orderly" failure of a bank, minimizing uncertainty and stress in the wider banking system.
- Living wills will also force banks to separate their trading and deposit-taking units. However, regulators should understand that forcing banks to hold more capital reserves, such as required by the Basel II framework, to cover risks in their trading arms could adversely impact the amount of capital available for lending by retail banks.
- As with conventional wills, banks' living wills must address the issue of how assets are to be ring-fenced and allocated in the event of the will writers' demise. In particular, they will need to address the issue of which elements of the assets are to be protected and how this should be achieved.

DON'T

- Such documents would be highly sensitive in nature, so banks would need to avoid any risk of leaks that could potentially trigger rumors and instability in the sector.
- Don't "throw the baby out with the bathwater." In proposing moves to make the structure of banks more transparent and generally less complex, governments and regulators could seriously undermine banks' present business models.

MORE INFO

Books:

Davies, Howard, and David Green. *Global Financial Regulation*. Cambridge, UK: Polity Press, 2008.

Peláez, Carlos M., and Carlos A. Peláez. *Financial Regulation after the Global Recession*. London: Palgrave MacMillan, 2009.

Articles:

The Economist. "Death warmed up: Are living wills really the answer to banks that are too big to fail?" October 1, 2009. Online at: Online at: www.economist.com/node/14558456

Miron, Jeffrey A. "Financial market reform: Why new regulations must avoid moral hazards." *Reason* (October 27, 2009). Online at: tinyurl.com/yhzdw5e

"A bank is a place that will lend you money if you can prove that you don't need it." Bob Hope

  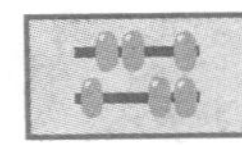      

Calculating Your Total Economic Capital

DEFINITION

Economic capital is the amount of risk capital that a company must have to cover any risks it is facing, such as operational risk, credit risk, or market risk. The amount held is that needed to ensure the business could overcome a worst-case scenario and still survive. Economic capital must be realistically estimated to manage the risks and to budget the costs of regulatory capital that needs to be maintained across the different divisions of the company. It is not the same as regulatory capital, which is a mandatory sum that a company must hold. The sum is determined by the regulators. Financial services should aspire to ensure the amount of risk capital they hold is at least equal to their economic capital.

Economic capital is calculated by determining the amount of capital that a company must have at its disposal to ensure it remains solvent over a defined period of time, taking into account the probability of any risks actually occurring. Thus, economic capital is usually calculated as the value-at-risk (VaR), where VaR is defined as the tipping point for the probability of a mark-to-market loss on the business within the predetermined time frame, assuming the markets are stable and no trading has occurred. There is no universally accepted method for calculating economic capital.

The full economic scenario (FES) method is an approach that takes into account all possible risks for a company, and is useful where the main goal is to determine the economic capital for all the combined risks. However, the FES approach does not allocate any explicit amount of economic capital to any particular risk. It is calculated by applying a set of economic scenarios to all divisions of the company, then applying assumptions for each scenario. These assumptions usually include interest, equity returns, inflation, defaults, and actual versus expected claims for various products.

ADVANTAGES

- A one year mark-to-market, stress-testing approach to calculating economic capital is probably the easiest and fastest way to quantify a company's risk exposure and achieve quantifiable business benefits.

DISADVANTAGES

- Combining results that have been derived over different time horizons, even where they have been calculated consistently, can present difficulties as it allows risks in one time frame period to be hedged against other risks in a different time frame, which may be unjustifiable.

ACTION CHECKLIST

✔ First calculate the potential losses for each risk category. The more detailed the calculation, the better, but you may find that you do not have sufficient data to do more than a simple assessment.

✔ Next determine the probability and severity of such losses. Use a VaR model for market price risks, and self-assessment for operational and strategic risk, to generate the possible losses and their distribution across the business. Allow for worst-case scenarios when determining how severe losses could be theoretically.

✔ Consider using scenario analysis to determine the risk probabilities of infrequent but severe events, as these are hard to calculate within economic capital.

DOS AND DON'TS

DO

- Remember that the use of economic capital as an internal model for capital adequacy has been driven by regulatory requirements, particularly the Solvency II proposals, which introduce a comprehensive risk management framework for defining required capital levels, and implementing procedures to identify, measure, and manage risk levels.

DON'T

- Don't forget that strategic risks are not usually calculated when determining economic capital, as it makes no sense to calculate a capital charge for this unless a suitable modeling method is used that considers the benefits of the strategic options.

MORE INFO

Books:

Porteous, Bruce T., and Tapadar Pradip. *Economic Capital and Financial Risk Management for Financial Services Firms and Conglomerates*. Basingstoke, UK: Palgrave Macmillan, 2005.

van Lelyveld, Iman (ed). *Economic Capital Modelling: Concepts, Measurement and Implementation*. London: Risk Books, 2006.

See Also:

★ Understanding the Role of Diversification (pp. 617–618)
✔ Measuring Financial Health (p. 982)
✔ Understanding Asset–Liability Management (Full Balance Sheet Approach) (p. 996)

"We have a good deal of comfort about the capital cushions at these firms at the moment." Christopher Cox

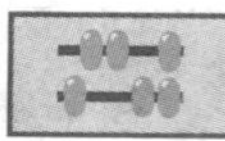

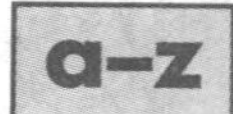

Catastrophe Bonds: What They Are and How They Function

DEFINITION

Catastrophe bonds (sometimes abbreviated to cat bonds) are fixed income securities, typically issued by insurance companies, which pay an attractive yield to investors, but with the proviso that should a specific predetermined event, such as a natural or human-inspired disaster occur, bondholders suffer the loss of their income and potentially also their capital. From the perspective of the issuer, catastrophe bonds spread at least some—but not necessarily all—of a particular risk to the buyers of the bonds, in turn helping to protect their balance sheets from some of the impact of massive payouts related to a specific risk. From the bond investors' perspective, catastrophe bonds need to pay a sufficient yield premium, or be priced at a sufficient discount, relative to conventional bonds to compensate for the risk of losing their money entirely.

Catastrophe bonds are generally issued via a special purpose vehicle (SPV) or special purpose entities (SPE), both of which are companies created purely for transactions related to the bond issue. These bonds usually achieve ratings of below investment grade, though the rating agencies will consider a range of factors including regulatory considerations and structural issues as well as the specific risks for which the bond is intended to provide cover for the issuer.

Though insurance companies are the most common issuers of catastrophe bonds, other bodies seeking protection from pre-identified risks can also make use of catastrophe bonds. For example, in 1999 Tokyo Disneyland issued cat bonds to protect itself against the risk of an earthquake (after finding cat bonds more attractive than using conventional insurance). More recently, FIFA (the Féderation Internationale de Football Association) made use of catastrophe bonds to insure itself effectively against the risk that terrorism could force the cancellation of the 2006 World Cup.

ADVANTAGES

- Cat bonds are a kind of insurance securitization which transfer risk from issuers to investors, in return for a premium yield.
- By presenting an alternative to traditional reinsurance, the development of cat bonds has forced re-insurers to become more competitive with pricing.
- These bonds can present opportunities for fixed income managers to gain a yield pickup, in return for a theoretically low risk of income and capital loss.
- Cat bonds can provide excellent diversification opportunities for bond portfolios, given that cat bonds insurance risk categorization shows little or no correlation with either equities or conventional bonds.

DISADVANTAGES

- Catastrophe bonds are available only to institutional investors.
- The market in cat bonds generally suffers from lower levels of liquidity relative to mainstream bonds.
- The dramatic recent growth in the catastrophe bond market has in turn spurred the launch of some new insurance-related businesses which could potentially undermine the long-term growth prospects of the cat bond market.

DOS AND DON'TS

DO

- Recognize that the structure of catastrophe bonds may vary considerably between different legal jurisdictions.
- Appreciate that some cat bonds may suffer from liquidity issues.

DON'T

- Don't ignore the availability of objective, independent research to help assess specific risks related to particular catastrophe bonds. A number of independent organizations exist with specific expertise in peril modeling.
- Don't invest without understanding the product. The catastrophe bond market globally has grown rapidly since the Hurricane Katrina disaster. Given the increasing sophistication of the market, professional asset managers should not invest in catastrophe bonds before seeking expert legal and insurance-related advice as to the suitability of these highly specialized securities for inclusion in their portfolios.

ACTION CHECKLIST

✔ Investors in cat bonds need to recognize that the higher returns associated with these securities come with the risk—albeit small—of losing all their money.

✔ Potential issuers of catastrophe bonds should first explore whether conventional insurance services would better meet their requirements.

✔ It is important to understand that the pricing of cat bonds is primarily related to prevailing insurance market prices and the perceived risk of the specified catastrophic loss, rather than to conventional bond pricing considerations such as inflationary or credit-quality risks.

MORE INFO

Books:

Grossi, Patricia, and Howard Kunreuther. *Catastrophe Modeling: A New Approach to Managing Risk*. New York: Springer, 2005.

Thau, Annette. *The Bond Book*. New York: McGraw-Hill, 2000.

Articles:

Moyer, Liz. "Catastrophe bonds." *Forbes* (August 31, 2005). Online at: tinyurl.com/3mq7qx7

Wickham, Chris. "New catastrophe bonds on hold pending reinsurance market hardening." *Insurance Journal* (November 24, 2008). Online at: tinyurl.com/3r4cx58

Websites:

American Insurance Association (AIA): www.aiadc.org

Milken Institute: www.milkeninstitute.org (search for "catastrophe bonds").

See Also:

★ Building Potential Catastrophe Management into a Strategic Risk Framework (pp. 785–787)
★ Climate Change and Insurance (pp. 149–150)
✔ The Bond Market: Its Structure and Function (p. 1064)
✔ Insuring Against Financial Loss (p. 975)
✔ Understanding and Calculating Probable Maximum Loss (PML) (p. 1019)

"It's time to make things ship-shape, to get rid of the debt, to get a bit of a cash box to work from, to enjoy life a bit more."
Conrad, Lord Black

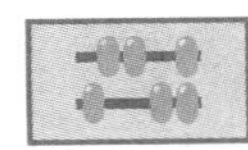

Derivatives Markets: Their Structure and Function

DEFINITION

Derivatives markets attract three main types of participants: hedgers, speculators, and arbitrageurs. Hedgers reduce the risk that they face in terms of asset prices by using futures or options markets. Speculators focus on future price movements, for which futures and options contracts provide them with extra leverage. Such investors speculate on potential gains and losses and help to make the market more liquid. Arbitrageurs, on the other hand, take advantage of price differences in different markets. For example, they use the discrepancy between cash prices and future prices to make a profit.

The derivatives market can be seen as providing a number of economic benefits. Being speculative in nature, it provides the investor with a perception of the market not only in terms of current prices, but also in terms of the future. A further function is that derivatives markets transfer risks from those who have no appetite for them to those who do. Finally, the underlying cash market enjoys higher trading volumes from more players as a result of risk mitigation.

ADVANTAGES

- The derivatives market is a thoroughly exciting one for certain types of investor. It attracts creative, educated, vibrant, and intelligent investors who make optimal use of the opportunities offered and transfer their enthusiasm to new entrants as well. This perpetuates the entrepreneurial spirit within the economy, and not only creates better and new products but also has a positive effect on the job market.
- Importantly, derivatives markets can be extremely beneficial for both individuals and the overall economy of a country. Entrepreneurial players are energized to create new businesses, products, and concomitant employment opportunities from the profits they make from the derivatives markets. In addition, derivatives markets then also increase savings and long-term investment through the risk-transferring function. In this way, participants in the market can expand the volume of their activity as a result of the wide variety of choices available.

DISADVANTAGES

- The main disadvantage of the derivatives markets arises from the lack of thorough investigation into how to use the risk transfer factor. This can result in difficulty when trying to margin transactions, or to monitor various participants' activities and tailor one's own activity accordingly.
- A lack of thorough research and sound investment may lead to investment losses for which the investor is not prepared. The risk transfer factor therefore needs to be applied in a targeted way in order to ensure that the investor does not take unnecessary risks.
- Several risks may be involved for those who are not thoroughly familiar with speculative markets. Even though risks can be transferred, remember that the derivatives market operates on a paradigm of uncertainty. An investor who is not comfortable with uncertainty in investment might be more comfortable taking on a different type of investment structure.

ACTION CHECKLIST

✔ Make sure you have thoroughly investigated your company's ability to take risks and absorb possible losses if you decide to participate in the derivatives market.

✔ You must be comfortable with a significant element of speculation.

✔ Seek advice and guidance from the relevant professional experts.

DOS AND DON'TS

DO

- Investigate your options in this market thoroughly.
- Ensure that you are fully aware of the risks you will be taking, and of what level of risk you are comfortable with.
- Make an informed choice, particularly where risk is concerned.
- Make sure that you continually review your risk level and modify it if and when necessary.

DON'T

- Don't take unnecessary risks.
- Don't forget to check regularly that you are not exceeding the risk level at which you are comfortable.
- Don't approach the derivatives market with a careless attitude. Make sure that you are always aware of trends and speculations in the market.
- Don't invest if you are not completely comfortable with participating in a speculative market.

MORE INFO

Books:

Marthinsen, John. *Risk Takers: Uses and Abuses of Financial Derivatives*. 2nd ed. Boston, MA: Prentice Hall, 2008.

McDonald, Robert L. *Derivatives Markets*. 3rd ed. Boston, MA: Pearson, 2009.

Taylor, Francesca. *Mastering Derivatives Markets: A Step-by-Step Guide to the Products, Applications and Risks*. 4th ed. Harlow, UK: FT Prentice Hall, 2011.

See Also:

★ Credit Derivatives—The Origins of the Problem (pp. 156–157)
★ Using Structured Products to Manage Liabilities (pp. 115–117)
★ Viewpoint: Staying in the Dark about Derivatives Will Bring Economic Collapse (pp. 249–250)
✔ Swaps, Options, and Futures: What They Are and Their Function (p. 988)
Banking and Financial Services (pp. 1612–1614)

"When I was young, people called me a gambler. As the scale of my operations increased I became known as a speculator. Now I am called a banker. But I have been doing the same thing all the time." Sir Ernest Cassel

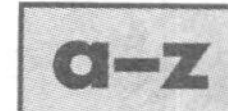

The Interbank Market: Its Structure and Function

DEFINITION

The interbank market is the market on which individual banks conduct transactions among themselves. It consists primarily of commercial and investment banks that buy and sell currencies. They are obliged to establish set rules and clearly defined lines of credit between themselves before they can trade. The interbank market has the greatest monopoly of all trading, both commercial and speculative. Members can influence supply and demand, and their trading activities can alter the exchange rates at any time. They have most power selling in the foreign currency exchange market.

These banks trade on their customers' behalf, but their other important purpose is to make profits for themselves. They have at their fingertips specialist knowledge and awareness of the market, as well as the skills required to keep an eye on the activities of their co-participants in the market.

Since the early 1980s there have been many important developments in the interbank market. The introduction of Reuters' electronic brokerage system, known as the Monitor Dealing Service, followed by its Dealing 2000-1 system in 1989, are examples. However, the market was entirely transformed by the introduction of Reuters' Dealing 2000-3 system in 1992 and the subsequent launch by FX market-making banks of the Electronic Broking Services (EBS) system, which made possible the automatic matching of quotes from dealers. Since the introduction of electronic systems, dealers have been able to conduct a number of trades simultaneously and can achieve a greater level of efficiency in doing so, along with tighter spreads and lower costs. There is a consequent greater level of transparency, and a greater number of players can now operate alongside the commercial and investment banks.

EBS and Reuters D2/Dealing 3000 are direct competitors—a trader's choice of which system they will use usually depends on the currencies they need to trade. EBS is standard for matching euros, US dollars, yen and Swiss francs with each other, whereas D2 is generally used for all other currency pairings.

ADVANTAGES

- The close interbank relationships described above are valuable in that they give all members access to the cooperating institutions within a relationship. Their combined expertise serves as a useful role model for other lenders, who are monitored by those banks. The interbank system also enables the smaller, less powerful banks to be monitored with regard to their levels of market discipline and compliance.
- Competition between the member banks ensures that there are tight spreads and fair pricing. For individual investors this is the source of their price quotes as the interbank market is dominated by larger players: customers are the large mutual and hedge funds and the big multinational corporations.
- All the member banks can see the best market rates.

DISADVANTAGES

- Smaller banks suffer restrictions in dealing with the larger banks and as a result have less favorable pricing available to them. It is even worse for individual investors, who cannot access the interbank market at all. The lowest quote that banks are able to give is between US$10 million and US$100 million. This means that individuals have to rely on online market-makers for their pricing, which may not be very competitive. Only the big players with plenty of capital really benefit from the interbank market.

ACTION CHECKLIST

✔ Do your homework diligently, accessing as much help as you can in securing as good pricing as possible.

✔ Seek the advice of a skilled financial expert.

DOS AND DON'TS

DO

- Take utmost care with your choice of interbank broker, especially for foreign exchange transactions.
- Be diligent and persevere in obtaining the best deal possible with your broker.

DON'T

- Don't rush into a transaction.
- Don't give in to persuasive selling by your broker.

MORE INFO

Book:

Boele, Georgette. *Strategic Market Analysis: EUR/USD Interbank Market as Diversified Organization*. Massapequa, NY: Alan Guinn, 2002.

See Also:

✔ The Foreign Exchange Market: Its Structure and Function (p. 968)
✔ Hedging Foreign Exchange Risk—Case Studies and Strategies (p. 970)
✔ Understanding and Using Carry Trades (p. 991)
✔ Understanding and Using Currency Swaps (p. 992)

"The derivatives genie is now well and truly out of the bottle, and these instruments will almost certainly multiply in variety and number until some event makes their toxicity clear." Warren Buffett

  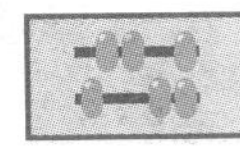      

Islamic Equity Funds

DEFINITION

Islamic equity funds (IEFs) are similar to traditional equity funds in that investors pool their funds to invest in shares. However, the main difference between IEFs and standard equity funds is that investors in IEFs earn halal profits in strict conformity with the precepts of Islamic *shariah*.

Returns are achieved largely through the capital gains earned by purchasing shares and selling them when their price increases. Profits are also achieved from the dividends distributed by the relevant companies.

Of course, these funds are not allowed to invest in certain areas. They cannot, for example, invest in companies involved in areas that are not lawful in terms of *shariah*, such as alcohol, gambling, or pornography. They also have a restricted ability to invest in areas such as financial companies and fixed-income securities, due to the *shariah* ban on usury. These funds generally avoid bonds and other interest-bearing securities, while seeking protection against inflation by making long-term equity investments.

The first IEF was the Amana Income Fund, established in June 1986 by members of the North American Islamic Trust, the historical Islamic equivalent of an American trust or endowment, serving Muslims in the United States and their institutions. The fund is still in existence today. Prior to the growth of IEFs, few investment alternatives were available to Muslim investors.

A wide variety of investment managers, including major financial institutions, now offer these funds. Examples include Citibank, Deutsche Bank, HSBC, Merrill Lynch, and UBS. Following the growth of IEFs, credible equity benchmarks have been established, including the Dow Jones Islamic Market (DJIM) index and the FTSE Global Islamic Index Series.

Fund managers can use indices, such as the DJIM index , to screen stocks. The DJIM tracks *shariah*-compliant stocks from around the world. It eliminates those that fail to meet *shariah* guidelines, including financial ratio filters.

The Islamic equity funds industry had grown to around US$20 billion in assets under management by February 2008, according to Failaka Advisors, a fund-monitoring company. Failaka Advisors said that the IEFs had grown rapidly, tripling over the previous five years, driven by Gulf Cooperation Council investors. Saudi Arabian funds and fund managers dominate the industry, accounting for nearly 75 funds out of around 300 IEFs worldwide. Bahrain has become the favored center for fund registrations in the Gulf.

ADVANTAGES

- These funds have obvious advantages to Muslims, who can invest their money safe in the knowledge that the fund will not compromise any of their religious beliefs.
- Many funds have been around for a long time and have a good track record of generating healthy returns for their investors.
- It can be argued that, over the long term, IEFs will tend to perform better than conventional funds, since the former avoid investing in heavily leveraged companies.

DISADVANTAGES

- The restricted ability of IEFs to invest in certain market sectors limits opportunities and may increase the risk of losses during economic downturns.
- Since Islamic principles preclude the use of interest-paying instruments, the IEFs do not maximize current income because reserves remain in cash.
- Most of the funds target high net-worth individuals and corporate institutions, rather than the small investor. Minimum investments range from US$50,000 to as high as US$1 million.

ACTION CHECKLIST

✔ As with traditional equity funds, the value of an IEF rises and falls as the value of the stocks in which the fund invests goes up and down. Therefore, only consider investing in an IEF if you are willing to accept the risk that you may lose money.

✔ Research sites that monitor the performance of IEFs to ascertain which fund is most likely to suit your needs and which have performed the best over a number of years. However, remember that past performance does not necessarily provide a guide to how well the fund will perform in the future.

DOS AND DON'TS

DO

- Analyze these funds in the same way as you would any other equity investment. Ask yourself whether you are looking for income or capital gain and whether you are prepared to tie up your money for a long period—most investment managers believe that anyone investing in an equity fund should be prepared to commit for at least five years.
- Ask yourself whether you are prepared to accept the risk involved in investing in equities—stocks go down as well as up.

DON'T

- Don't invest without exploring the wide range of funds on the market to find out which is best suited to your needs.
- Don't invest without consulting an independent financial adviser. However, make sure that they are truly independent and do not earn a commission by recommending clients to a certain fund.

MORE INFO

Books:

Ayub, Muhammad. *Understanding Islamic Finance*. Chichester, UK: Wiley, 2007.

Siddiqi, Adnan, and Peter Hrubi. *Islamic Investments Funds Versus Hedge Funds*. Munich, Germany: Grin Verlag, 2008.

Website:

Failaka Advisors monitor the performance of Islamic equity funds and provide a comprehensive list of Islamic funds worldwide: www.failaka.com

See Also:

★ Carrying Out Due Diligence on Private Equity Funds (pp. 468–470)
✔ Key Islamic Banking Instruments and How They Work (p. 1010)
✔ Trading in Equities on Stock Exchanges (p. 1095)

  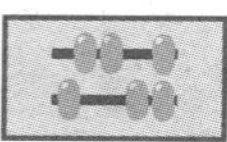      

Key Islamic Banking Instruments and How They Work

DEFINITION

The need to fully conform to *shariah* law has created both challenges and opportunities for financial institutions aiming to serve their growing Muslim client base. Requirements that money cannot be used for the purposes of making money (effectively forbidding the charging of interest), and the need for investments to deliver some form of collective or community benefit, have necessitated a high degree of innovation from Islamic financial institutions to develop a range of new products for customers seeking full compliance with *shariah* law.

Among the leading Islamic banking products are the following.

Murabaha

A kind of "cost-plus" transaction in which the bank buys the asset then immediately sells it to the customer at a pre-agreed higher price payable by installments. This price is set at a level that takes account of the time value of money until the customer's monthly payments cover the bank's selling price, less any deposit paid. This facility is often used in the way that mainstream banking customers might seek a mortgage when buying property.

Bai Salam

A kind of forward sales contract which requires the buyer to pay in advance for goods that are to be supplied later. *Bai salam* contracts are often used in manufacturing; a buyer would expect to receive a more attractive price when paying in advance with funds that can be used in the meantime by the producer.

Istisna'a

Istisna'a, another form of forward sales contract, is a longer-term financing mechanism under which a price is agreed before the asset described in the agreement is actually built. Sellers can then either create the asset themselves or subcontract, with buyers also having the option of paying the entire sum due either in advance or as installments during the manufacturing process. *Istisna'a*, meaning "asking someone to manufacture" in Arabic, is a common form of financing in the construction industry.

Ijara

A form of *shariah* law-compliant leasing involving rights over the use of an asset under which the bank buys the asset then leases it to the customer over a fixed period in return for a pre-agreed monthly price. Provisions can be made for the customer to buy the asset at the end of the agreed period. Thought needs to be given to issues such as the provision of insurance, as the asset is effectively owned by the bank during the lease period.

Mudaraba

A form of investment partnership between a bank and a business that shares the risk and losses or profits between both parties at pre-agreed levels. A *mudaraba* transaction, bringing some of the benefits of a business loan to *shariah*-compliant business customers, effectively requires the bank to take a stake in the business, with clients investing their time and expertise in running the enterprise.

ADVANTAGES

- Islamic banking instruments permit Muslims to benefit from a growing range of financial products in compliance with *shariah* law.
- Some products require a partnership between the client and the bank, encouraging both parties to take a longer-term view.
- Islamic banking dictates that transactions should serve to provide some form of benefit to the community at large, rather than setting pure profit as the aim.

DISADVANTAGES

- With some financial aspects of *shariah* law open to interpretation, some instruments may be offered by some institutions, but not by others.
- Some non-Muslim clients could find that the conditions imposed by Islamic banks prevent them from taking advantage of shorter-term opportunities.

ACTION CHECKLIST

- ✔ When entering into leasing-style arrangements, ensure that all "grey" areas are covered by the agreement, such as the insurance and maintenance costs of the asset.
- ✔ Islamic banking is by definition more stable than conventional mainstream banking in that it outlaws involvement in speculation or short-term industry "trends." However, clients must ensure that they are committed to operating within the boundaries set by *shariah* law before using Islamic banking services.

DOS AND DON'TS

DO

- Appreciate that the stability of the Islamic banking sector can come at the price of a slower pace of product innovation.
- Recognize that the rapid growth in Islamic banking globally could present an attractive source of funds for businesses prepared to make a long-term commitment to operation under *shariah* principles.

DON'T

- Don't ignore the aim of Islamic banking to bring a wider benefit to society.
- Don't see Islamic banking institutions as financial services providers for Muslims only; such banks can be valuable long-term commercial partners for a range of individuals and companies.

MORE INFO

Book:

Iqbal, Munawar. *A Guide to Islamic Finance*. London: Risk Books, 2007.

Articles:

Patel, Ebrahim. "Islamic finance: Special report." *Accountancy SA* (June 2008): 40–44. Online at: tinyurl.com/3qp8xys [PDF].

Wilson, Scott B. "Islamic finance: Origins, emergence and future title." *Illinois Business Law Journal* (September 18, 2007). Online at: tinyurl.com/3erd9k5

Website:

Institute of Islamic Banking and Insurance (IIBI): www.islamic-banking.com

"I doubt if there is any occupation which is more consistently and unfairly demeaned, degraded, denounced, and deplored than banking." William Proxmire

  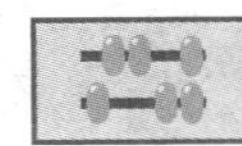      

Key Principles of Islamic Finance

DEFINITION

The principles of Islamic law derive from interpretations of two sources: the Qur'an and the Sunna. The central pillars of Islamic finance are that wealth must be generated from legitimate trade and asset-based investment, while the use of money for the purposes of making money is expressly forbidden. Crucially, the latter means that Islamic finance does not permit the charging or paying of interest (*riba*). Under Islamic principles, investment must have a social and an ethical benefit to wider society, with short-term speculative investments (known as *masir*) strictly forbidden. Islamic finance also prohibits investment in sectors classified as inappropriate on moral grounds by *shariah* law. These include industries involving alcohol, gambling, or drugs, but can extend well beyond these narrow boundaries. Each Islamic bank's adherence to the principles of *shariah* law is governed by its own *shariah* board, a body charged with the responsibility of overseeing all processes of the bank. While some aspects of *shariah* law may be subject to individual interpretation, the board also has the responsibility to decide which proposed deals are acceptable to the bank on *shariah* grounds, and which are not.

Given that Islamic finance forbids the charging of interest, banks must earn their profits through the provision of fee-based services, or through a kind of partnership with clients in which both the risk and the profits or losses are shared between the bank and the customer, according to pre-agreed conditions. Such arrangements typically allow the client to draw a salary from the business, which is then deducted from profits. *Shariah* law permits a range of leasing-style agreements under which the bank can buy an asset on behalf of a customer, then charge a regular, pre-agreed rental fee. As in mainstream Western banking, these agreements can be fixed-term operating leases or lease purchases, with the latter obliging the client to buy the asset at the end of the period, at a predetermined price. While some leasing arrangements can be relatively straightforward, others can become more complex, depending on how the asset is originally purchased by the bank. Given that Islamic finance does not permit the charging of interest, a bank originally buying the asset on the basis of a variable interest rate may seek an arrangement by which the rental charge is increased, to effectively compensate any increase that it faces in financing costs. However, some *shariah* boards may refuse to sanction such agreements, potentially leaving the bank with exposure to interest rate risk.

ADVANTAGES

- Islamic finance provides a basis for commercial transactions for followers of Islam to enter into, which would be impossible on conventional banking terms.
- The adoption of Islamic finance principles gives banks access to a substantial new customer base.
- The partnership basis on which some Islamic businesses are established with banks ensures that the bank has a direct stake in the success of the venture.
- The rejection of deals involving short-term, speculative activity encourages businesses to invest for the longer term.
- Islamic finance contracts offer flexibility in terms of the applicable legal jurisdiction.

DISADVANTAGES

- Some financial aspects of *shariah* law can be open to interpretation, with the result that some Islamic banks may agree transactions that would be rejected by other banks.
- These "grey" areas, resulting from inconsistencies in interpretation, can create more uncertainty for clients than under conventional banking arrangements.
- Some leasing arrangements can become appreciably more complicated when trying to ensure conformity to Islamic principles.
- Given that the banks are the legal owners of assets under rental or leasing agreements with clients, issues such as liability for insurance and risk can be complications.

ACTION CHECKLIST

✔ Non-Muslims should consider how Islamic finance can provide them

✔ with access to financial backing from those seeking *shariah*-compliant funds.

✔ As more institutions launch products compliant with *shariah* principles, investors should take time to assess their best choice of potential banking partners.

✔ Understand that adherence to interpretations of Islamic principles can create complications over the medium term.

DOS AND DON'TS

DO

- Recognize that the ethical considerations and long-term partnership advantages offered by Islamic finance can come with the price of greater complexity and uncertainty.
- Take professional advice as to the tax treatment of Islamic finance transactions within your particular jurisdiction.
- Appreciate that the prohibition of activities perceived as speculative could limit the business's scope to capitalize on potentially lucrative short-term opportunities.

DON'T

- Don't regard Islamic finance as purely "specialty" banking; the market is fast becoming mainstream with a rapidly expanding range of products available.
- Don't look at Islamic banking in isolation, as deals can be structured with a combination of conventional and *shariah*-compliant finance.

MORE INFO

Book:

Usmani, Muhammad Taqi. *An Introduction to Islamic Finance*. The Hague: Kluwer Law International, 2002.

Article:

Dar, Humayon A., and John R. Presley. "Islamic finance: A Western perspective." *International Journal of Islamic Financial Services* 1:1 (April 1999). Online at: www.iiibf.org/journals/journal1/art1.pdf

Websites:

International Institute of Islamic Finance Inc. (IIIF): www.iiif-inc.com

Islamic Financial Services Board (IFSB): www.ifsb.org

"It has been the bankers' destiny ... to find themselves on the dangerous edge of the world, pointing up the contradictions and cross-purposes. They are not often loved for it." Anthony Sampson

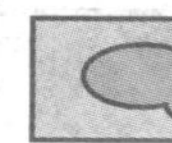

Merchant Banks: Their Structure and Function

DEFINITION

Merchant banks, also known as investment banks, offer various services in international finance and long-term loans for wealthy individuals, multinational corporations, and governments.

An investment bank is split into the so-called front, middle, and back office functions. The front office deals with investment banking and management, sales and trading, structured products, private equity investment, research, and strategy. The middle office deals with risk management, finance, and compliance. The back office deals with transactions, operations, and technology.

The main function of a merchant bank is to buy and sell financial products. They manage risk through proprietary trading, carried out by special traders who do not interface with clients. The trader manages the risk for the principal after they buy or sell a product to a client but does not hedge their total exposure. Banks also try to maximize the profitability of certain risk on their balance sheets.

Merchant banks manage debt and equity offerings. They assist companies in raising funds from the market. This can include designing instruments, pricing issues, registering offer documents, underwriting support, issue marketing, allotment and refund, and stock exchange listing. They also help in distributing securities such as equity shares, mutual fund products, debt instruments, insurance products, and fixed deposits among others. Merchant banks use a mix of institutional networks—mutual funds, foreign institutional investors, pension funds, private equity funds, and financial institutions—and retail networks, depending on how they interact with specific clients.

Merchant banks offer corporate advisory services to clients for their financial problems. Advice may be sought in such areas as determining the right debt-to-equity ratio, the gearing ratio, and the appropriate capital structure. Other areas of advice may be in areas of refinancing and seeking sources of cheaper funds, risk management, and hedging strategies. Further areas for advice are rehabilitation and turnaround management. Merchant bankers may design a revival package in conjunction with other financial institutions.

Merchant bankers assist clients with project advice, helping them from the project concept stage, through feasibility studies to examine a project's viability, to the preparation of documents such as a detailed project report.

Merchant banks arrange loan syndication for their clients. This begins with an analysis of the client's cash flow patterns, helping to determine the terms for borrowing. The merchant bank then prepares a detailed loan memorandum to be circulated to the banks and financial institutions that are to join the syndicate. Finally, the terms of lending are negotiated for the final allocation.

Merchant banks provide venture capital and mezzanine financing (a hybrid of debt and equity financing that is typically used to finance the expansion of existing companies). In this way they can help companies to finance new and innovative ventures.

Following the global financial crisis of 2008, which saw the collapse of several prominent investment banks in Europe and the United States in September of that year, the viability of using a business model that is based heavily on banks purchasing each others' debts has been severely questioned. Certainly in the United States, the view is that this business model is no longer sustainable and is unlikely to continue in the same form in the future. It remains to be seen how merchant banks will restructure in the aftermath of the financial turbulence of 2008.

ADVANTAGES

- Merchant banks perform functions that cannot be carried out by businesses on their own.
- Merchant banks have access to traders, financial institutions, and markets that companies or individuals could not possibly reach.
- By using their skills and contacts, merchant banks can get the best possible deals for their clients.

DISADVANTAGES

- Merchant banks are really only for large corporate customers, or extremely wealthy smaller businesses owned by individual clients.
- Not all deals carried out by merchant banks meet with unqualified success.
- There is always risk attached to the kinds of deal that merchant banks undertake.

ACTION CHECKLIST

✔ Shop around for a merchant bank.

✔ Understand what the bank is offering and make clear exactly what you expect it to do.

✔ Make sure that the results are fully monitored and reported back to you.

DOS AND DON'TS

DO

- Use a merchant bank with good standing and history.
- Use a merchant bank with a firm financial footing—especially in times of uncertainty about financial institutions.

DON'T

- Don't use a merchant bank if you are a small business.
- Don't use the first merchant bank you find.
- Don't go in blindly without understanding the risks involved.

MORE INFO

Books:

Chapman, Stanley. *The Rise of Merchant Banking*. Economic History Series. London: Routledge, 2005.

Young, George Kennedy. *Merchant Banking: Practice and Prospects*. 2nd ed. London: Weidenfeld & Nicholson, 1971.

See Also:

Investment Banking: Valuation, Leveraged Buyouts, and Mergers and Acquisitions (p. 1382)

Banking and Financial Services (pp. 1612–1614)

"They're just cold-blooded fish sitting at the top of some bloody great building looking at stats—and they've got handbooks." Peter de Savary

  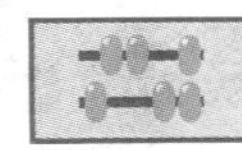      

Possibilities for *Shariah*-Compliant Derivatives

DEFINITION

The market in derivatives—financial products with characteristics and pricing based on an underlying instrument—has grown rapidly over recent decades. Derivatives can be based on financial instruments such as bonds, equities, and currencies, as well as commodities and alternative investment such as infrastructure. Derivatives allow the transfer of risk between parties, either in the form of futures, via a recognized financial exchange or, typically in the case of swaps, on an over-the-counter basis between investors.

Used correctly, derivatives such as futures and options can be used to hedge risk: for example, soft commodity derivatives can be used for a variety of beneficial purposes, such as protecting producers from adverse price declines, or enabling food processors to invest in long-term infrastructure in the knowledge that they have some protection against erratic price movements. Given that shariah stipulates the need for a wide public interest in financial dealings, compatible instruments that help to reduce uncertainty and risk are compliant with the Islamic principle of *maslahah* (public interest). However, some Islamic scholars take the view that as one party seeks to lower risk using derivatives, the counterparty is assuming risk in return for a potential reward. Therefore, given that *shariah* prohibits speculation, the compatibility and use of derivatives remains a hotly contested subject. Margin calls on futures can be a further source of controversy for some scholars, given that the party bearing an adverse price movement has to lodge money with a clearing house without any corresponding transfer of the underlying asset.

However, Islamic financial services providers can attempt to overcome many of the problematic issues surrounding conventional derivatives through the use of *shariah*-compatible transactions within specific Islamic derivatives. For example, Islamic swaps can be constructed from specific types of *murabahah* contracts traded between two parties, specifying the actual transfer of underlying assets, with the sales price paid on a specified future date (to include a premium related to the payment timeframe). Some finance providers also offer arboun, a kind of option contract normally offered in conjunction with *murabahah*. Under the latter, the provider buys the asset for the client with an agreement to sell at a particular price on a future date. Under an arboun contract, in return for a nonrefundable deposit, the investor has the option (but not the obligation) to purchase the asset at a specified price at any time until the contract matures.

ADVANTAGES

- Some *shariah* scholars believe that Islamic derivatives can play a *shariah*-compliant beneficial purpose by offering users, such as farmers, protection from adverse price movements.
- Derivatives can be used to offset risks for producers, and can therefore be used as tools in support of long-term investment plans of benefit to communities.
- *Shariah*-compliant transaction structures can be used to create synthetic derivatives that win wider acceptance over their compatibility with Islamic principles than conventional derivatives.

DISADVANTAGES

- Derivatives such as futures and options are widely used for speculative purposes—activities that can equate to gambling, and therefore run contrary to the principles of Islam.
- Most *shariah* scholars maintain that, by their very nature, derivatives—both conventional and Islamic—are priced according to assets that are not in the possession of the seller, in violation of the *hadith* principle. Most scholars therefore believe that Muslims should not trade in derivatives.
- Specialist Islamic synthetic derivatives can suffer from severe liquidity shortages, because they are unattractive to conventional investors.
- The noncompliance of conventional derivatives with *shariah* meant that some Islamic institutions were less able to employ hedging strategies to protect their interests during the global banking industry crisis in the wake of the Lehman Brothers collapse in late 2008.

ACTION CHECKLIST

- ✔ Users of futures and options seeking shariah compliance should demonstrate that their transactions constitute true hedging activities to protect against adverse price movements in assets they already own.
- ✔ The use of derivatives is more likely to gain the approval of Islamic scholars where changes in the asset value can bring some kind of benefit to both parties, rather than one party gaining while the counterparty loses (a so-called "zero-sum" situation).
- ✔ Derivative structures should be kept as simple and transparent as possible to help improve the prospects of acceptance.

DOS AND DON'TS

DO

- Remember that speculative activity and gambling of all kinds are prohibited under Islamic law.
- Acknowledge that variations of opinion exist between scholars as to the compatibility of different derivatives with Islamic principles.

DON'T

- Don't underestimate the potential complexity of derivates such as swap transactions, particularly synthetic swaps, aimed at gaining acceptance with Islamic principles.
- Don't expect the range of available Islamic derivatives to be as comprehensive as those available to conventional investors.

MORE INFO

Books:

Jobst, Andreas A. "Derivatives in Islamic finance." In Syed Salman Ali (ed). *Islamic Capital Markets: Products, Regulation and Development*. Jeddah, Saudi Arabia: Islamic Research and Training Institute, 2008; pp. 97–124.

Kamali, Mohammad Hashim. *Islamic Commercial Law: An Analysis of Futures and Options*. Cambridge, UK: Islamic Texts Society, 2001; ch. 10.

Website:

Financial Times special report on Islamic finance: www.ft.com/reports/islamic-finance-2010

See Also:

★ Risk Management of Islamic Finance Instruments (pp. 94–97)
✔ Derivatives Markets: Their Structure and Function (p. 1007)
✔ Key Principles of Islamic Finance (p. 1011)

"Like other branches of the study of society, economics remains culturally parochial, and its underlying concepts based on a few centuries of Western experience." John Gray

        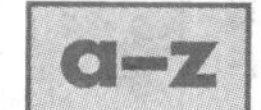

Retail Banks: Their Structure and Function

DEFINITION

Retail banks offer a range of services to individual customers and small businesses, rather than to large companies and other banks. The services can include current accounts, savings accounts, investment advice and broking, and loans and mortgages. Retail banks perform two crucial functions for customers: firstly, they enable customers to bank their money securely, access it easily, and conduct transactions; and secondly, they provide access to additional money to fund large purchases, such as buying a home. In return for holding customers' funds, which they can then invest, banks pay customers interest.

Traditionally, retail banks have provided these services directly to the customer via branches. While many still do this, retail banks now offer their services by telephone and the internet as well. Some operate solely via the internet and do not have facilities to serve customers at physical outlets. Other organizations, such as supermarkets, have now entered the banking sector and also offer a wide range of banking services.

It has become more difficult to identify the traditional retail bank—a bank that funds itself through customer deposits and lending—because retail banks now often combine retail and wholesale banking. It is therefore more relevant to today's banking structure to regard retail banking as a series of processes rather than as an institution.

The intermediation services offered by retail banks (such as looking after customers' money and making loans) and the payment services (allowing customers to make transactions using debit cards, checks, etc.) mean that they have to make funds available to customers at very short or immediate notice. This inevitably means that a retail bank has to manage the risk that more money will be requested by customers than it has available and of customers defaulting on loans. Banks do this by holding stocks of liquid assets, maintaining a cushion of capital, lending to different types of borrower, adjusting interest rates, and screening potential borrowers (credit scoring).

ADVANTAGES

- Your money is much more secure than in a box under your bed and you can buy goods, be paid, and sell things without cash changing hands.
- The bank you are familiar with and which knows you can also offer you a wide range of other services, such as mortgages and insurance. Your bank may be able to offer you competitive deals in return for your loyalty as a customer.
- Retail banks offer a variety of ways you can access your account and manage your money, most notably via internet banking. This means that you can keep a close eye on your finances and avert many potential problems.

DISADVANTAGES

- Banks are a business, and they need to make money from looking after yours. If the bank decides to apply charges to your account (within the terms of the account), you may only find out about it afterwards—for example if you accidentally go overdrawn without permission. If you disagree with a charge, you will need to contest it to recover the money.

ACTION CHECKLIST

- ✔ Think carefully about what you want from a bank account and what is important to you. For example, if you are not concerned about having face-to-face contact with your bank, an internet-only bank may suit you.
- ✔ When choosing an account, check the interest rate offered and how quickly and by what methods you can access your money.
- ✔ When looking for a current or checking account, find out what extra services the bank can offer you, such as a debit card, overdraft facility, free or cheap insurance policies, etc.
- ✔ Does the bank have local branches, or is it internet only? Are you comfortable with the ways in which you can communicate with the bank?
- ✔ Most importantly, find out what charges apply to various transactions and events, such as going overdrawn without the bank's approval.

DOS AND DON'TS

DO

- Compare different banks and their products and services.
- Look for added value, such as free insurance.
- Challenge charges you feel are unfair or wrongly applied to your account.
- Regularly review your savings accounts to make sure you continue to get the best interest rates available.

DON'T

- Don't let financial problems get out of control, and don't put off talking to your bank about them if they do.
- Don't be afraid to move to a new bank if you are not happy with your current one and if, via sound research, you have found something better. The bank you want to move to will be happy to take on the transfer arrangements for you.

MORE INFO

Books:

Casu, Barbara, Claudia Girardone, and Philip Molyneux. *Introduction to Banking*. Harlow, UK: Pearson Education, 2006.

Heffernan, Shelagh. *Modern Banking*. 2nd ed. Chichester, UK: Wiley, 2004.

Pond, Keith. *Retail Banking*. London: Global Professional Publishing, 2007.

Websites:

Bank.org.uk reviews all UK banks: www.bank.org.uk
British Bankers' Association: www.bba.org.uk
US Federal Reserve: www.federalreserve.gov
US Treasury Comptroller of the Currency: www.comptrollerofthecurrency.gov

See Also:

✔ Assessing Cash Flow and Bank Lending Requirements (p. 964)
✔ An Overview of Loan Agreements (p. 1082)
✔ Understanding Debt Cover (p. 1100)
Banking and Financial Services (pp. 1612–1614)

"I've come to the belief that banks are not in the business of banking. They're in the business of collecting fees."
Patrick C. Kelly

  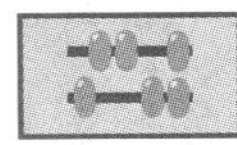   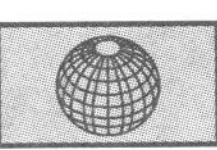   

The Role of the *Shariah* Advisory Board in Islamic Finance

DEFINITION

The *shariah* board is a key element of the structure of an Islamic financial institution, carrying the responsibility of ensuring that all products and services offered by that institution are fully compliant with the principles of *shariah* law. The role of the board also involves the reviewing and overseeing of all potential new product offerings. Additionally, the board may be called on to make a judgment on individual cases referred to it, relating to whether specific customer business requests are acceptable to the institution. Given that *shariah* law is derived from studies of both the Qur'an and the Sunna, inconsistencies can occur in the interpretations of precisely where the boundaries of compatibility lie, with the result that some *shariah* boards may deem unacceptable proposals that may be approved by other boards.

With demand for *shariah*-compliant financial services growing at a faster rate than mainstream banking, the board can play a vital role in helping to develop new procedures and products to position the institution to adapt to industry trends and customers' expectations. The board should be closely involved in overseeing *shariah*-compliant training programs for employees. Board members also participate in the preparation of an annual investors' report on the bank's balance sheet, with particular reference to its compliance with *shariah* principles.

Given the importance of the role of the *shariah* boards in ensuring the conformity of the institution's offerings, boards typically include acknowledged experts, such as contemporary Islamic scholars. It is common for such scholars to sit on the *shariah* boards of multiple institutions; some senior scholars may sit on the boards of 15 or more institutions. The activities of individual boards are supervised by an independent body, the International Association of Islamic Bankers. This association's Supreme Religious Board examines the judgments, or *fatwas*, of individual *shariah* boards to ensure conformity to *shariah* law.

ADVANTAGES

- The board's role is well defined: ensuring that the institution's activities are fully compliant with *shariah* law is its responsibility.
- Given the speed of change in the financial services industry, the board plays a vital role in advising the institution as to the feasibility of potential new products and services.
- *Shariah* audits can be undertaken in conjunction with the board to give greater reassurance to customers.

DISADVANTAGES

- *Shariah* law is highly subject to interpretation, particularly in relation to its significance in the demand-driven financial services industry.
- Inconsistencies occur between different boards in their interpretations of what is and is not permissible.
- Precedents are not binding in Islamic jurisdictions, with the result that personnel changes to a board may shift the balance of collective opinion over time.

ACTION CHECKLIST

✔ Some Islamic investors may seek reassurance that products and services which have been approved by *shariah* boards outside their own jurisdictions are truly compliant with their own *shariah*-compliant objectives.

✔ Given the complexity of some Islamic *sukuk* structures (the arrangements established to create the Islamic equivalent of a bond), it is important that *shariah* boards are given the considerable resources needed to ensure the true compliance of these instruments.

DOS AND DON'TS

DO

- Ensure that *shariah* boards have a high level of autonomy and independence, protecting them from commercial pressures.
- Do ensure *shariah* boards are well resourced to ensure full compliance with both legal and religious requirements.

DON'T

- Don't expect every board member to be an expert on every aspect of Islamic finance. While *shariah* boards require a range of members with a diverse range of religious and financial knowledge, institutions should not expect individual board members to be experts in every aspect of their wide-ranging brief. However, board members with specialized knowledge of particular aspects can work very effectively on sub-boards related to particular initiatives or projects.
- Don't overlook the need to ensure that *shariah* board members are well informed about developments and trends in the global financial marketplace.

MORE INFO

Books:

Archer, Simon, and Rifaat Ahmed Abdel Karim. *Islamic Finance: The Regulatory Challenge.* Singapore: Wiley, 2007.

El-Gamal, Mahmoud A. *Islamic Finance.* Cambridge, UK: Cambridge University Press, 2006.

Article:

El Ahmed, Waleed M. "A unified voice: The role of shariah advisory boards in Islamic finance." *Business Islamica* (October 2007). Online at: tinyurl.com/4xgxxqd

Websites:

Harvard Law School Islamic Finance Project: ifp.law.harvard.edu

Islamic Financial Services Board (IFSB): www.ifsb.org

See Also:

★ Managing *Shariah*-Compliant Portfolios: The Challenges, the Process, and the Opportunities (pp. 527–533)

★ Viewpoint: *Shariah* Law—Bringing a New Ethical Dimension to Banking (pp. 242–243)

"I've come to the belief that banks are not in the business of banking. They're in the business of collecting fees."

Patrick C. Kelly

  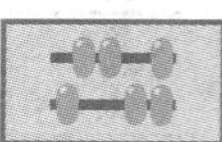   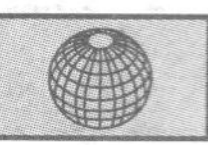   

Stress Testing to Evaluate Insurance Cover

DEFINITION

Stress testing aims to determine how well systems and procedures perform when subjected to a wide range of operational conditions. It is frequently employed to help assess performance during extreme or unexpected conditions. During stress testing, a system is subjected either to sudden extreme demands or to gradually higher loads until the point is reached when at least one element of the system stops delivering the desired level of performance. This evaluation helps companies to understand the kind of market conditions under which key elements of their businesses become vulnerable.

Although retail-focused insurance products have become more standardized in recent years, and are increasingly sold via the internet and call centers as consumers focus on price, the commercial insurance industry has retained a high level of complexity. This is largely driven by a broadening of the spectrum of risks faced by businesses in areas such as environmental protection, human resources, product safety, counterparty agreements, and technology. Given the wider range of risks that businesses face, partly as a result of tighter legislation and regulation, ensuring that the appropriate insurance is in place to provide robust protection against unexpected events has never been more important.

ADVANTAGES

- A better understanding of the risks—both systemic and non-systemic—facing a business can help in contingency planning.
- Regular stress testing can help to keep management vigilant in an environment of constantly changing business risks.
- This type of evaluation can identify multiple, seemingly minor chinks in the armor of a business that cumulatively could have a serious impact.
- What if? analysis can be useful in highlighting event risks that may not otherwise be immediately apparent.
- Robust financial protection can insulate businesses from the risk of a catastrophic event that could otherwise threaten the viability of the entity.

DISADVANTAGES

- Protracted evaluation over extended periods of time could divert key resources away from core business activities, potentially resulting in the business overlooking valuable opportunities.
- Extended periods of evaluation run the risk of "paralysis through analysis." Understanding the shortcomings of available options can be beneficial, but, taken to an extreme, it could be counterproductive.
- Under some circumstances, stress testing may even run the risk of effectively encouraging risky practices by creating a false sense of control.

ACTION CHECKLIST

✔ Encourage an environment of openness about the kinds of risk facing the business. Some risks are obvious, but more covert risks are sometimes known only to the managers of individual business units.

✔ Involve key business stakeholders in the evaluation of risks and alternative ways to protect against them.

✔ Consider how existing policies insure against multiple minor claims as well as more significant/catastrophic single incidents. Examine whether particular exclusion clauses could leave your business exposed to risks that you thought were covered.

✔ Do try to quantify in financial terms how falling foul of various risks could affect your business. Only once an actual liability figure is available can you expect an insurance provider to be able to provide a quotation to cover that risk.

✔ Be prepared to seek the advice of specialist insurance providers. The field of commercial insurance can be immensely more complex than its consumer equivalent, and risk consultants can help companies to understand and evaluate both risks and potential solutions. Industry-specific experts from specialist risk-management companies can help to devise customized solutions to protect against potential liabilities.

DOS AND DON'TS

DO

- Remember that emerging risks necessitate regular reviews of the way you protect your business.
- Involve key stakeholders in the evaluation of both risks and potential solutions.
- Consider seeking the help of specialist consultants.

DON'T

- Don't make the mistake of basing a decision purely on price. Commercial insurance is a highly complex field and insurance solutions are many and varied.
- Don't fall into the trap of thinking that insurance can cover absolutely every conceivable risk your business could face.
- Don't see the right insurance for your company as simply another expense. Securing the appropriate protection for your business can help you concentrate on doing what you do best.

MORE INFO

Book:

Overbeck, Ludger, and Gerrit Jan van den Brink. *Integrated Stress Testing for Financial Institutions*. London: Palgrave Macmillan, 2009.

Article:

Hilbers, Paul, and Matthew T. Jones. "What if . . . ?" *Finance and Development* 41:4 (December 2004): 24–27. Online at: tinyurl.com/3ncffh6 [PDF].

Websites:

Risk consultancy and management companies: Willis: www.willis.com; Towers Watson: www.towerswatson.com

Society of Actuaries (SOA; includes "Effective stress testing" presentation by Mark Chaplin, SOA Annual Meeting, Oct 2007): www.soa.org

"Politicians and policymakers became victims of a sort of Stockholm syndrome. Having been taken hostage by the bankers, they began to identify with their interests." Ruth Sunderland

  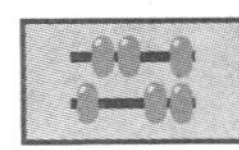      

Sukuk: Islamic Bonds

DEFINITION

Sukuk, an Arabic word meaning financial certificates, refers to the *shariah*-compliant equivalent of interest-bearing fixed-income instruments. Following the first issue around a decade ago, *sukuk* have become one of the fastest-growing areas of Islamic finance as borrowers and investors look to meet their requirements while ensuring compliance with their principles and values.

Given that the charging of interest is strictly forbidden by *shariah* law, *sukuk* securities are instruments constructed in such a way as to avoid the accrual of interest and thus be fully compliant with Islamic principles. *Sukuk*, the plural form of the Arabic word *sakk*, represent claims to the ownership of assets or a pool of underlying tangible assets, proportionate to the size of the investment. In contrast, conventional bonds are debt obligations, valued on the basis of cash flows derived from the issuer's contractual commitment according to pre-agreed dates, interest, and principal repayment. Investors in *sukuk* hold the right to both a share of revenues generated by the underlying asset and a share of any realization of the underlying *sukuk* asset. While *sukuk* bear many similarities to conventional fixed-income assets, a *sukuk* investment is founded on the part-ownership of an approved asset in return for a price which offers the investor the potential to benefit from a rise in the price of the underlying asset. The key difference between *sukuk* and conventional bonds is that *sukuk* are always asset-backed.

Since the turn of the millennium, *sukuk* have emerged as a key means for banks, sovereign borrowers, and multinational corporate borrowers to raise finance as an alternative to conventional syndicated financing, in a way fully compliant with Islamic principles.

Sukuk come in various forms, according to the issuer's requirements. They can be issued to help finance specific new projects, while asset-specific *sukuk* are often employed to sell the beneficiary right of existing assets. Quasi-government organizations can also make use of balance sheet-specific *sukuk* to raise finance for multiple projects.

Sukuk deals typically fall into four main categories: *ijarah*, *mudharabah*, *musharakah*, and *istisna'a*. *Ijarah sukuk* are commonly employed in longer-term financing, typically leasing arrangements. *Mudharabah sukuk* are often used for profit-sharing between investors and entrepreneurs in ventures. *Musharakah sukuk* are used to finance businesses on the basis of partnership contracts, and *sukuk istisna'a* are frequently used in the financing of major infrastructure projects. *Sukuk* are issued in many forms, such as *ijarah* floating-rate *sukuk*, *murabahah* fixed-rate *sukuk*, and *salam sukuk*, a form of bond which cannot be sold and must therefore be held until maturity.

ADVANTAGES

- The development of the *sukuk* market over recent years has provided opportunities for both borrowers and investors unable to access conventional bond markets due to their noncompliance with *shariah* principles.
- After dramatic growth, *sukuk* instruments are now both liquid and readily tradable.
- *Sukuk* securities are rated by mainstream credit agencies, making their risk profiles comparable with mainstream fixed-income instruments.

DISADVANTAGES

- Under certain circumstances, *sukuk* can present additional taxation or stamp duty costs for the issuer.
- Islamic law's broad exclusion of the trading of instruments at above or below par (their redeemable value on expiration of the particular issue) can severely restrict the structures available for *sukuk* issuers, although interpretations differ between countries and regions as to what is acceptable practice.

ACTION CHECKLIST

✔ *Sukuk* issuers must ensure that their securities are fully compliant with *shariah* law; otherwise they run the risk of being categorized alongside conventional interest-bearing bonds.

✔ *Sukuk* are by their very nature controversial in that some more conservative Islamic scholars believe that sukuk infringes the *riba* principle by effectively putting a time value on money. Issuers should therefore take advice from *shariah* experts on how best to avoid compromising the risk and profit/loss sharing requirements to ensure the widest possible investor base for their issues.

✔ Where the *sukuk* are a debt owed to the investor by the issuer, the investor can either hold the *sukuk* until maturity or sell the issue at par, without the option of selling on the secondary market.

DOS AND DON'TS

DO

- Expect some ongoing debate over the suitability of *sukuk* for Muslims. Despite their rapid growth over recent years, some Islamic scholars contend that *sukuk* may not be truly compliant with Islamic law, given that pricing still factors in the time value of money.
- Issuers should remember that *sukuk* investors have an inherent right to transparency in how their funds are being used and should therefore be fully prepared to keep investors informed about how the underlying assets are being employed.

DON'T

- Don't expect liquidity in the secondary *sukuk* market to be as high as that of most conventional bonds, as *sukuk* securities are typically acquired by long-term holders.
- Don't ignore the risk that the issuer could default, despite the well-intentioned principles behind *sukuk*.

MORE INFO

Book:

Nathif, Adam, and Thomas Abdulkader. *Islamic Bonds: Your Guide to Issuing, Structuring and Investing in Sukuk*. London: Euromoney Books, 2004.

Article:

Vishwanath, S. R., and Sabahuddin Azmi. "An overview of Islamic sukuk bonds." *Journal of Structured Finance* 14:4 (Winter 2009): 58–67. Online at: dx.doi.org/10.3905/JSF.2009.14.4.058

See Also:

★ Islamic Modes of Finance and the Role of *Sukuk* (pp. 520–521)

"There's a whole branch of economics devoted to proving that ... what most of us would consider humankind's cardinal virtues—love, honor, compassion—do not actually exist." Philipp Meyer

  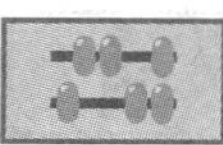      

Takaful Insurance

DEFINITION

Takaful, an Arabic word meaning "guaranteeing each other," is a form of mutual insurance that is fully compliant with shariah principles. *Takaful* works on the basis of members cooperating with and protecting each other, but it can also be used by investors seeking returns while adhering to the principles of Islamic law. Members of the *takaful* scheme pool their individual contributions together to create a pot of money which is then available to cover any subsequent loss or damage claims. Any surplus, after the costs of running the scheme, is then distributed between the *takaful* operator and members or investors on pre-agreed terms.

Conventional commercial insurance contravenes shariah law on multiple grounds, chiefly the banning of gambling (*al-maisir*), the charging of interest (*riba*) and attempting to profit from uncertainty (*al-gharar*). However, *takaful* insurance is founded on the principle of shared responsibility and has been practiced in one form or another for well over 1,000 years. As a mutual-style concept, *takaful* does not function on conventional profit-making lines, instead typically working on the basis of *mudharabah* or *wakalah*, or sometimes even a combination of the two. However, conventions and acceptable practices for *takaful* may vary widely between different countries. Today, *takaful* is most developed in Malaysia following the country's introduction of legislation in 1983.

Under *mudharabah*, the *takaful* operator collects regular installments from the *takaful* members. In keeping with the *mudharabah* principle, a contract between members specifies how any surplus gathered by the collector after any payouts is to be distributed. The contract can specify whether each member's contributions are purely to cover potential liabilities, or alternatively to include some element of investment. To ensure full *shariah* compliance, under the *tabarru* (contribution) principle, any payout is determined only after all members suffering a defined loss have been compensated. Under the *wakalah* model, *takaful* operators collect a prearranged fee in advance, in addition to a share in the profits from the investment element of the scheme. However, the *wakalah takaful* operator does not benefit from the insurance underwriting.

Variations on the above models include the *waqf* methodology, which can specify that a percentage of any surplus is to be retained by the scheme to help protect against any future loss. Or a share of any surplus may be donated to community or charity projects each year.

In response to the surge in demand for *shariah*-compliant finances services over recent years, both in traditional Muslim countries and Western nations, a number of new providers have emerged, including specialist *takaful*-only providers as well as companies offering *takaful* alongside a range of conventional insurance services.

ADVANTAGES

- *Takaful* is flexible in its range of applications, covering residences, places of business, cars, and inventory, as well as accident and life cover.
- It provides a form of financial protection for Muslims unable to access conventional insurance.

DISADVANTAGES

- While shunning conventional insurance schemes, some Muslims believe that even *takaful* is unnecessary, as it is the duty of all to help compensate others' losses.
- Some Muslims may be uncomfortable with the scope for *takaful* to be used for investment purposes on the basis that investors are effectively speculating that low accident payouts will generate a surplus or profit.

ACTION CHECKLIST

✔ Potential *takaful* operators should consider how their own resources could be put to work to ensure some kind of true competitive advantage in *takaful* provision.

✔ *Takaful* operators are likely to benefit from regular contact with *shariah* experts to ensure that the schemes remain compliant with Islamic law.

✔ Providers should seek to address the unique challenges of governance of *takaful* schemes with the establishment of a supervisory board.

DOS AND DON'TS

DO

- Be prepared for some operating differences between principle-based *takaful* theorists and those employed by *takaful* providers to operate the schemes and deal with the processing of individual claims.
- Understand that distinctions will arise between *takaful* schemes in different countries according to local attitudes and conventions.

DON'T

- Don't regard *takaful* as some kind of niche market; given the suspicion with which some consumers regard conventional financial services companies, *takaful* could be attractive as a mutual-based protection and/or investment scheme for many consumers.
- Don't think that the growth potential in *takaful* is limited to Middle Eastern or South-East Asian countries, as the scope for development in Europe and US markets is considerable.

MORE INFO

Books:

Archer, Simon, Rifaat Ahmed, Abdel Karim, and Volker Nienhaus. *Takaful Islamic Insurance: Concepts and Regulatory Issues*. Singapore: Wiley, 2009.

Jaffer, Sohail. *Islamic Insurance: Trends, Opportunities and the Future of Takaful*. London: Euromoney, 2007.

Reports:

Gosrani, Neil, Kevin Willis, and Ritesh Maheshwari. "Takaful insurance has long-term viability and benefits from expected growth, but stiff competition persists." Standard & Poor's, July 13, 2010. Online at: tinyurl.com/nh7beox [PDF].

Katsipis, Vasilis, and Yvette Essen. "Takaful poised for growth, but greater focus is required." AM Best, July 11, 2011. Online at: tinyurl.com/6byzere [PDF].

Websites:

International Cooperative and Mutual Insurance Federation (ICMIF) guide to *takaful*: www.takaful.coop

Malaysian Takaful Association (MTA): www.malaysiantakaful.com.my

"If freedom were not so economically efficient it certainly wouldn't stand a chance." Milton Friedman

Understanding and Calculating Probable Maximum Loss (PML)

DEFINITION

Probable maximum loss (PML) is a term chiefly used in the insurance industry. PML is the anticipated value of the biggest monetary loss affecting a business and/or a building that could result from a catastrophe, whether natural or otherwise, called for this purpose a "maximum credible event" (buildings are considered separately by insurers as the owner may be different from the owner(s) of any businesses contained therein). For example, the catastrophe could be a hurricane, floods, or other severe weather event, or other disaster that has a given probability of occurrence within a stated time period (such as the loss of a building and the value of the business contained therein as a result of fire). PML is usually expressed as a percentage of the total value, experienced by a structure or collection of structures when subjected to a maximum credible event. The PML is usually smaller than the maximum foreseeable loss (MFL), which assumes that all protective features fail, resulting in a complete write off. For example, in a fire this would include such things as failure of the sprinkler systems in the building. Underwriting decisions are typically influenced by the evaluation of the PML. The amount of reinsurance for a known risk is also normally based on the valuation of the PML. PML and MFL are both calculated as the percentage of a building or business that under normal conditions could be damaged or destroyed in a single event. The calculation takes into account variables such as construction of the building, susceptibility of the contents (including the value of any business), and protection measures. The MFL calculation also includes failures of key loss reduction systems in place (for example, sprinkler systems failing to activate in the case of a fire).

ADVANTAGES

- Consistent, accurate estimates of PML and MFL help to understand the extent of the risk involved, analyze the hazards and potential losses in order to manage them better, assess economic losses, determine the amount of reinsurance, and satisfy any reinsurance requirements.

DISADVANTAGES

- Calculating PML and paying for the resulting insurance may not be viable in geographic areas that are typically subject to natural disasters such as earthquakes or hurricanes. It may be cheaper, instead, to purchase business continuity insurance to cover for such losses caused by fire or other destruction.

ACTION CHECKLIST

✔ Carry out a risk assessment before calculating the PML, to reduce insurance costs. The information gleaned from this can be used to assist the insured to develop long-term strategies for risk reduction. Such strategies could include upgrading buildings and equipment, developing better operating procedures, transferring risk through insurance, and improving emergency response and business recovery plans.

DOS AND DON'TS

DO

- Take a practical and logical approach that covers all important aspects of a maximum credible event, such as damage to structures, equipment and inventory, business interruption costs, and the safety of staff.

DON'T

- Don't underestimate the potential amount of downtime your business may experience if hit by the kind of loss covered by PML.

MORE INFO

Books:

Grace, Martin Francis, Robert W. Klein, Paul R. Kleindorfer, and Michael R. Murray. *Catastrophe Insurance: Consumer Demand, Markets and Regulation*. Boston, MA: Kluwer Academic, 2003.

Grossi, Patricia, Howard Kunreuther, and Chandu C. Patel. *Catastrophe Modeling: A New Approach to Managing Risk*. New York: Springer, 2005.

Messy, Flore-Anne. *Catastrophic Risks and Insurance*. Policy Issues Series. Paris: OECD Publishing, 2005.

Article:

Woo, Gordon. "Natural catastrophe: Probable maximum loss." *British Actuarial Journal* 8:5 (December 2002): 943–959. Online at: dx.doi.org/10.1017/S1357321700004037

See Also:

★ Building Potential Catastrophe Management into a Strategic Risk Framework (pp. 785–787)
★ Business Continuity Management: How to Prepare for the Worst (pp. 788–791)
✔ Applying Stress-Testing to Business Continuity Management (p. 1141)
✔ Identifying Your Continuity Needs (p. 1160)

"The world of finance hails the invention of the wheel over and over again, often in a slightly more unstable form."
J. K. Galbraith

Understanding Financial Scenario Analysis for Banking and Insurance Institutions

DEFINITION

Scenario analysis is the process of forecasting the likely outcomes of future events by following a variety of possible scenarios. It is the formalized process of "what if" analysis that in reality has always been part of business decision-making. The objective of scenario analysis is to improve decision-making by analyzing possible outcomes and their implications.

Financial scenario analysis is thought have originated in banks and insurance companies in the 1970s and 1980s, when interest rate volatility began to constitute a threat to balance sheets. Today, financial institutions use scenario analysis in asset liability management and corporate risk management, and it remains the primary tool for analyzing interest rate risk. Businesses use scenario analysis for the analysis of a number of risks.

A financial institution may use scenario analysis to forecast what might happen to the economy by following various paths (e.g. rapid growth, slow growth, slowdown, recession), and what might happen to financial market returns, such as bonds, stocks, or cash, in each of those economic scenarios. The scenarios may have sub-scenarios, and probabilities may be assigned to each. Such analysis will help the institution to determine how to distribute its assets between asset types, and from this it can calculate a scenario-weighted expected return to help demonstrate the attractiveness of the financial environment.

A scenario is usually specified as a set of "paths" that will be determined by risk factors. Typically, in financial matters these risk factors include interest rates, exchange rates, equity prices, commodity prices, and implied volatilities. Outcomes can be modeled mathematically or statistically, and the figures can be put through a spreadsheet program or other modeling software.

Financial scenario analysis usually seeks to estimate a portfolio's value in a worst-case situation. Different reinvestment rates for expected returns which are then reinvested during the period are calculated using scenario analysis. This may be approached in many ways, but usually the standard deviation of daily or monthly returns on securities is determined, and the value of the portfolio is calculated assuming that each security has given returns two or three standard deviations above or below the average return.

Thus an analyst will have reasonable certainty that the value of a portfolio is unlikely to drop below (or increase above) a certain value during a given time period.

ADVANTAGES

- Financial scenario analysis enables a financial institution to manage its own business risk as well as its customers' portfolio risks.
- It gives a likely range of values for investments.

DISADVANTAGES

- Financial scenario analysis can be a demanding exercise that requires skill and expertise.
- As it is difficult to forecast exactly what the future holds, the actual future outcome may be entirely unexpected and not foreseen in the modeling.
- It is difficult to imagine all possible scenarios and assign probabilities to them.

ACTION CHECKLIST

- ✔ Decide on a subject for scenario planning (e.g. a range of investments).
- ✔ Decide whether to group scenarios into subsets.
- ✔ Determine the risk factors, list all scenarios, and assign probabilities.
- ✔ Decide on a step-horizon (e.g. month, quarter, year).
- ✔ Process using your chosen software.

DOS AND DON'TS

DO

- Try to define scenarios that are independent of human decisions.
- Identify which random events are most important for the company.
- Consider worst-case scenarios.

DON'T

- Don't pick events that are unimportant to the company.
- Don't be limited by the software you use.
- Don't underestimate the worst possible cases.

MORE INFO

Books:

Fahey, Liam, and Robert M. Randall (eds). *Learning from the Future: Competitive Foresight Scenarios*. New York: Wiley, 1997.

Wilson, Ian, and William K. Ralston, Jr. *The Scenario Planning Handbook: Developing Strategies in Uncertain Times*. Mason, OH: South-Western Educational Publishing, 2006.

Article:

French, Nick. "Value and worth: Scenario analysis." *Journal of Property Investment & Finance* 24:2 (2006): 176–179. Online at: dx.doi.org/10.1108/14635780610655111

See Also:

★ Using Decision Analysis to Value R&D Projects (pp. 945–948)
✔ Stress Testing and Scenario Analysis for Keeping Up with Regulation (p. 1054)
✔ Understanding Decision-Tree Analysis (p. 1179)
Scenario Analysis (p. 1252)

"A speculator is a man who observes the future, and acts before it occurs." Bernard Baruch

  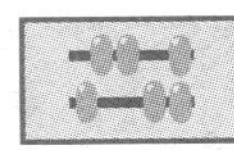   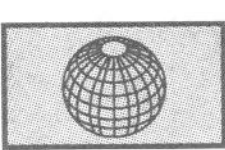   

Understanding the Components of an Insurance Contract

DEFINITION

Within all the small print that comes with any new insurance contract, there are some of the most complicated legal provisions and contractual terms that you are likely to find anywhere. The insurance industry spends millions on lawyers' fees and has teams of in-house professionals constantly updating and revising the terms of their contracts to cover every possible eventuality. It is, therefore, worthwhile being familiar with some of the main components of these contracts.

Agreement (proposal and acceptance): There can be no contract without the compliance or mutual consent of the parties. The agreement reviews the major pledges of the insurance company. It explains the dangers covered, the risks assumed, and the nature of coverage.

Utmost good faith: This requires both parties to the insurance contact to deal in good faith. In particular, it imposes on the insured a duty to disclose all relevant facts that relate to the risk to be covered.

Competent Parties: For a contract to be binding, both parties must have the legal power to sign a contract.

Declarations: These identify who or what is insured, the insured's address, the insuring company, what risks or property are covered, the amount of insurance, any applicable deductibles, the policy period, and the premium amount.

Conditions: These are the provisions, rules of conduct, duties, and obligations required for coverage. If the policy conditions are not met, the insurer can deny the claim.

Exclusions: These clauses describe property, perils, hazards, or losses arising from specific causes that are not covered by the policy.

All insurance contracts basically have the same principles and processes. They assume the risk of an event that may or may not occur, and pay the cost of it if it does.

ADVANTAGES

- Businesses can cover financial risks by taking out insurance in areas such as property, public and product liability, professional indemnity, employee benefits, employers' liability, motor, and medical expenses.
- Life insurance provides a monetary benefit to a descendant's family or other designated beneficiary, and may specifically provide income for an insured person's family or cover funeral and other final expenses.
- Life-insurance policies often allow the option of having the proceeds paid to the beneficiary either as a lump sum cash payment or as an annuity.

DISADVANTAGES

- The complexity of business insurance contracts requires expert help, which is not always unbiased.
- Cover can sometimes include remote risks that could be covered out of a specific set-aside investment fund.
- This fund could be earning income for the business and used only if the risk occurs.

ACTION CHECKLIST

- ✔ Consider how existing policies insure against multiple minor events as well as more significant/catastrophic single incidents. Examine whether particular exclusion clauses could leave your business exposed to risks you thought were covered.
- ✔ In what circumstances will the policy pay out and what risks are not covered?
- ✔ Try to quantify in financial terms how falling foul of various risks could impact on your business. Only once an actual liability figure is available can you expect an insurance provider to be able to give a quotation to cover that risk.
- ✔ Be prepared to seek the advice of specialist risk consultants. The field of commercial insurance can be far more complex than its consumer equivalent and risk consultants can help companies to understand and evaluate both risks and potential solutions.
- ✔ Consider the conditions you must meet to keep the policy valid.
- ✔ Get several quotes and at least two expert opinions.

DOS AND DON'TS

DO

- Regularly update your frameworks for assessing risks and keep your policies up to date to reflect those risks.

DON'T

- Don't make the mistake of basing a decision purely on price. Insurance is highly complex and insurance solutions are many and varied.

MORE INFO

Books:

Clarke, Malcolm A. *Law of Insurance Contracts*. 6th ed. London: Informa, 2009.

Stempel, Jeffrey W. *Stempel on Insurance Contracts*. 3rd ed. New York: Aspen Publishers, 2006.

Tarr, Julie-Anne. *Disclosure and Concealment in Consumer Insurance Contracts*. London: Cavendish, 2002.

Websites:

American Insurance Association (AIA): www.aiadc.org

Association of British Insurers (ABI): www.abi.org.uk

See Also:

✔ Corporate Insurance Cover: A Primer (p. 1154)
✔ Insuring Against Business Interruption (p. 1161)
✔ Insuring Against Financial Loss (p. 975)
✔ Stress Testing to Evaluate Insurance Cover (p. 1016)

"If you must play, decide on three things at the start: the rules of the game, the stakes, and the quitting time." Anonymous

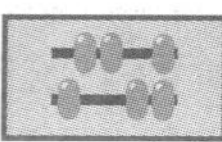

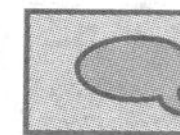

Adopting an Internal Audit Capability Model

DEFINITION

An internal audit capability model (IACM) provides a framework for assessing the quality, impact, and cost-effectiveness of an internal audit activity. It also identifies the fundamentals needed for effective internal auditing and describes the levels and stages through which internal audit activity can develop and improve processes and practices. The Institute of Internal Auditors (IIA) produced an "Internal Audit Capability Model for the Public Sector" in 2009, for example, which can be used in public-sector organizations, and others are available, with some service providers producing IACMs.

The IIA model consists of five progressive capability levels, each describing the characteristics and capabilities of an internal audit activity at that level. Implementing repeatable and sustainable processes at one level provides the foundation on which to progress to the next. The levels are as follows.

Level 1. Initial. No sustainable, repeatable capabilities; dependent on individual efforts.

Level 2. Infrastructure. Sustainable and repeatable internal audit processes.

Level 3. Integrated. Internal audit and professional practices uniformly applied.

Level 4. Managed. Internal auditing integrates information from across the organization to improve governance and risk management.

Level 5. Optimizing. Internal auditing learns from inside and outside the organization for continuous improvement.

At Level 1, the least advanced, the internal audit infrastructure and its institutional capability are undeveloped. There may be isolated single audits, but the results are dependent on the skills of individuals. Internal auditing is ad hoc and unstructured. On reaching the most advanced level, the internal audit activity is a learning organization with continuous process improvements and innovation.

ADVANTAGES

- An IACM can assist users to develop an internal audit strategic plan, as well as to develop an effective internal audit function.
- The model can be used as a self-assessment and continuous improvement tool for internal audit activities by audit committees, senior management, and legislators to evaluate the need for and the type of internal audit activity appropriate to their organization or jurisdiction. The model could also be used by national, regional, and local legislative auditors as a source of benchmarks.

DISADVANTAGES

- As with any self-assessment process, the results obtained from the model are dependent on the supply of objective and accurate information.
- An internal audit activity might, for example, assess itself at a higher capability level than actually applies because the participants are not fully aware of professional practices.
- Implementing the model can be timeconsuming and costly, particularly for a small organization.

ACTION CHECKLIST

✔ Participants in the IACM need to understand the structure and underlying principles of the capability model.

✔ The chief audit executive and the internal auditors must be committed to the exercise and its results, and should develop an action plan for improvement.

✔ Management needs to support and clarify the purpose of using the IACM, explaining how it will improve the capability of staff members and the potentially positive implications for their career development.

DOS AND DON'TS

DO

- Ensure that the team includes at least one person skilled in conducting internal or external assessments of an internal audit activity and another person who has responsibility for making improvements to the activity.
- When implementing the IACM, take into account organizational factors such as corporate governance, culture, internal control systems, and human resource capacities.
- Communicate the results by identifying strengths and areas for improvement and by formulating an action plan for the development of internal auditing.

DON'T

- Don't ignore the fact that internal auditing capabilities cannot outpace the maturity of the organization that they support. To reach the higher levels will need advanced enterprise risk management strategies and practices.

MORE INFO

Books:

Chambers, Andrew, and Graham Rand. *The Operational Auditing Handbook: Auditing Business and IT Processes*. 2nd ed. Hoboken, NJ: Wiley, 2010.

Institute of Internal Auditors Research Foundation. *Internal Audit Capability Model (IA-CM) for the Public Sector.* Altamonte Springs, FL: IIA Research Foundation, 2009.

Moeller, Robert R. *Brink's Modern Internal Auditing: A Common Body of Knowledge*. 7th ed. Hoboken, NJ: Wiley, 2009.

Swanson, Dan. *Swanson on Internal Auditing: Raising the Bar.* Cambridge, UK: IT Governance, 2010.

See Also:

★ Optimizing Internal Audit (pp. 382–384)

✔ Preparing and Executing an Internal Audit Review (p. 1045)

✔ Quality Assessment of Internal Audits (p. 1049)

"All knowledge is of itself of some value. There is nothing so minute or inconsiderable, that I would not rather know it than not." Samuel Johnson

  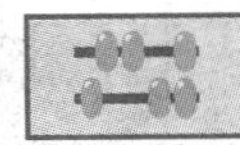   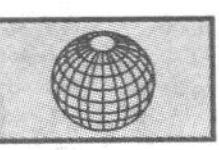   

Auditing Information Technology and Information Systems

DEFINITION

The benefits of information technology (IT) are accompanied by a need to manage the complexities, risks, and challenges that come with it. Auditing IT and information systems involves auditing an organization's hardware, software, and data organization and processing methods to ensure quality control and security. It certainly does not involve the popularly held belief that it amounts to merely counting computers. Even the smallest companies are dependent on IT systems, and in order for an organization to take full advantage of the IT system at its disposal it is vital that any system can be controlled and is reliable. Moreover, fraudsters can exploit IT systems, so it is vital these systems are secure and that safeguards have been implemented to detect and deter fraud. Data protection legislation also requires that data are secure and remain confidential. According to the Institute of Internal Auditors, some of the more obvious results of information system failures include reputational damage, placing the organization at a competitive disadvantage, and contractual noncompliance.

ADVANTAGES

- Paying attention to the challenges involved in establishing and maintaining an IT system can prevent waste of money and resources, loss of trust, and reputational damage.
- Timely involvement by internal auditors can help to assure that problems are identified and solved at an early stage.
- IT auditors can serve as a bridge between individual business units and the IT function, point out previously unidentified risks, and recommend controls for enhancing outcomes.
- An IT audit can identify IT weaknesses that could be exploited by a fraudster or which could compromise compliance with data protection laws.

DISADVANTAGES

- Carrying out an IT audit and ensuring that staff have the necessary training can be timeconsuming and costly (although not doing so can be far more costly).

ACTION CHECKLIST

- ✔ Develop an IT audit plan. This can help chief audit executives and internal auditors to understand the organization and how IT supports it, to define and understand the IT environment, to identify the role of risk assessments in determining the IT audit universe, and to formalize the annual IT audit plan.
- ✔ Develop an "audit checklist" to ensure that the auditors focus on areas and issues of concern.

DOS AND DON'TS

DO

- Make sure that your IT audit staff receive the latest technology and training, given the rapid pace of development in the IT world.
- Consider external IT auditors if the necessary skills are not available inhouse.
- Make sure that your staff are aware of all the legal requirements regarding data protection.

DON'T

- Don't carry out IT internal audits at fixed times. If staff know the timing of audits, they may adjust the way they use their IT resources, giving an inaccurate impression of their effectiveness, efficiency.

MORE INFO

Books:

Cascarino, Richard E. *Auditor's Guide to Information Systems Auditing*. Hoboken, NJ: Wiley, 2007.

Champlain, Jack J. *Auditing Information Systems*. 2nd ed. Hoboken, NJ: Wiley, 2003.

Wright, Craig, Brian Freedman, and Dale Liu. *The IT Regulatory and Standards Compliance Handbook: How to Survive an Information Systems Audit and Assessments*. Rockland, MA: Syngress Publishing, 2008.

Article:

Bayuk Jennifer. "Information systems audit: The basics." *IT World* (May 26, 2009). Online at: tinyurl.com/p3ly99

Websites:

Chartered Institute of Internal Auditors (UK and Ireland): www.iia.org.uk

Institute of Internal Auditors (IIA): www.theiia.org

See Also:

✔ Understanding Internal Audits (p. 1057)

Information Technology (pp. 1632–1633)

"For a successful technology, reality must take precedence over public relations, for Nature cannot be fooled."
Richard P. Feynman

Avoiding Conflict of Interest in Internal Audits

DEFINITION

Every year a company undergoes an external audit and will also undertake a program of internal auditing. Using external auditors to carry out internal audit work can lead to a conflict of interest. A conflict of interest may also occur when an internal auditor has a personal or professional involvement or association with the area that is subject to the audit.

There are two essential elements that apply to ensure that such conflicts of interest are avoided: independence and objectivity. *Independence*can be achieved by having an appropriate written internal audit charter that ensures the independence of auditors. The chief audit executive should report directly to the audit committee. Also, it is advisable that internal auditors do not have any operational responsibilities. The independence of an internal auditor appointed by the management of a company may be called into question if he or she is involved in reviewing the conduct of the management.

The *objectivity* element is ensured by the professionalism of the internal auditors. This is achieved by having a well-written and implemented internal audit charter. Recruiting and appointing the right internal auditor is of the essential. Maintaining good professional relations between the internal audit function and management is also extremely important. A good management team will be interested in a good audit process that will objectively highlight any positive or negative aspects of the way a company is managed. An internal auditor has a professional and ethical obligation to disclose any involvement on his or her part in an activity that could give rise to a conflict of interest.

The same firm should never be appointed to do both the internal audit and the external audit. Using different audit firms will not only avoid a conflict of interest but will provide independent opinions and reports that the management and shareholders can use to assess the business of the company.

ADVANTAGES

- Having an independent external audit helps an organization to assess the state of its business and to put in place measures to improve and develop it.
- Making sure that internal auditors are not involved in operational responsibilities avoids potential conflicts of interest.

DISADVANTAGES

- External auditors are expensive, but trying to cut costs by using the same auditors for both internal and external audits can lead to conflicts of interest and may in the end increase costs.
- In certain circumstances, a company will be required to change its external auditor after a fixed period and avoid using the same audit company for both internal and external audit work.

ACTION CHECKLIST

✔ Carefully assess your options for internal and external auditors. Obtain as much information from as many sources as you can before appointing auditors.

✔ Consider a selection bidding process and examine each bid carefully before making a decision.

DOS AND DON'TS

DO

- Establish good communication between management and auditors.
- Avoid conflicts of interest by choosing separate internal and external auditors.
- Encourage internal auditors to disclose any involvement in activities that might give rise to conflicts of interest.
- Consider reputation: a more expensive external auditor may offer better value for money in the medium to long term.

DON'T

- Don't make decisions that endanger the impartiality of an audit solely on the basis of financial considerations.
- Don't appoint internal auditors that have had management functions in the company.

MORE INFO

Books:

Gray, Iain, and Stuart Manson. *The Audit Process: Principles, Practice and Cases*. 5th ed. Andover, UK: South-Western Cengage Learning, 2011.

Pastor, Joan. *Conflict Management and Negotiation Skills for Internal Auditors*. Altamonte Springs, FL: Institute of Internal Auditors Research Foundation, 2007.

Websites:

Chartered Institute of Internal Auditors (UK and Ireland): www.iia.org.uk
Institute of Internal Auditors (IIA): www.theiia.org

See Also:

★ How Can Internal Audit Report Effectively to Its Stakeholders? (pp. 342–345)
★ Managing the Relationships between Audit Committees and the CAE (pp. 375–377)
✔ Independence of the Internal Audit Function (p. 1031)
✔ Internal Audit Charters (p. 1033)
✔ Quality Assessment of Internal Audits (p. 1049)

"God is in the details." Ludwig Mies van der Rohe

  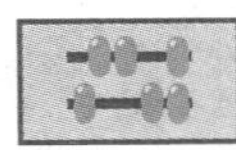      

The Chief Audit Executive's (CAE) Roles and Responsibilities

DEFINITION

The CAE has an in-depth knowledge of the business and is concerned principally with its systems for internal control and efficiency of operations, the reliability of its financial reporting, and its observance of relevant laws and regulations.

Corporate accounting scandals and the resultant outcry for transparency and honesty in reporting have led to a progressively more important role for the CAE. A CAE has two important and sometimes conflicting functions within an organization. The first is to examine and evaluate the organization's systems of internal control, as part of the requirement for stricter corporate governance. The second is to be fully cognizant of the risks, goals, policies, and processes of the organization while maintaining autonomy from management direction and control.

The CAE normally reports directly to the management and audit committee and is responsible for producing an annual assessment of the effectiveness of the organization's risk management and processes for control and governance, as set out by the board or management. Risk management deals with the way an organization sets goals, then recognizes, interprets, and reacts to risks that could affect its ability to realize those goals. Processes for control and governance deal with the effectiveness and efficiency of operations, the reliability of financial reports and conformity with appropriate rules and laws.

ADVANTAGES

- CAEs improve business organization and risk management by providing reassurance on the effectiveness and efficiency of operations, the reliability of financial reporting, and compliance with applicable laws and regulations.
- CAEs provide management with an in-depth and unbiased understanding of the risks that the organization may be facing, allowing for pre-emptive planning.
- CAEs give company officers and directors forewarning of ethical and legal issues that the organization may be facing.

DISADVANTAGES

- Although CAEs are meant to be independent and impartial, they are paid by the company and are an integral part of the company's management. This can lead to conflicts of interest.
- CAEs' judgments, estimates, and interpretations are not always objective because of their close relationships with the organizations for which they work.
- A CAE's relationship with the management of a company is generally informal and the CAE's position does not carry the power to change processes.
- Although there are international bodies such as the Institute of Internal Auditors (IIA), CAEs as a profession are unregulated.

ACTION CHECKLIST

- ✔ Has the CAE previously worked in related business fields? If so, for how long and what did they achieve?
- ✔ How good is the CAE's track record on risk assessment and planning for contingencies?
- ✔ In assessing business processes, how up-to-date is the CAE with information audit technology controls?
- ✔ To which internationally recognized standards-setting body, such as the IIA, does the CAE belong?

DOS AND DON'TS

DO

- Allow CAEs unrestricted access to information to enable them to evaluate risks, management activities, and personnel better.
- Take into account that CAEs are not responsible for carrying out company activities; their role is solely advisory.
- Consult with the CAE if there are any implications where ethical or legal issues may be involved.

DON'T

- Don't involve CAEs in decisions that might compromise their autonomy as independent internal auditors.

MORE INFO

Websites:

Deloitte articles for CAEs: tinyurl.com/62mcmv8
Institute of Internal Auditors (IIA): www.theiia.org

See Also:

★ New Assurance Challenges Facing Chief Audit Executives (pp. 378–380)
✔ Establishing a Framework for Assessing Risk (p. 1028)
✔ The Key Components of an Audit Report (p. 1042)

"I am a risk taker but only within rules. I just like the support that an organisation gives, combined with the freedom to express myself." Guy Hands

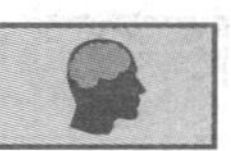

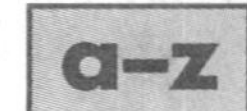

Choosing an External Auditor

DEFINITION

An external audit is an unbiased, independent review of a company's business and financial situation conducted by an external auditor. Public organizations and publicly traded firms are usually required to have an external audit conducted yearly. The firm's management is responsible for the selection and appointment of an external auditor.

There are many external audit firms to choose from. Public organizations and publicly traded firms must undergo a stringent process of appointing an external auditor that usually involves tenders and bids. The external auditors who are invited to tender are persons or companies with an in-depth knowledge of audit, finance, and management. The invitation to tender and bid must contain a clear description of the company and its audit requirements. It will explain the type of business the company undertakes, will specify what type of audit it is seeking, and should also give a clear description of the company's internal audit controls, administrative procedures, and management.

Once the bids are submitted the organization or company will start to analyze them. Certain bigger organization might put in place an evaluation committee to examine the bids and to ensure a transparent and fair selection process.

There are many factors to consider in the decision, including the auditor's reputation, past experience, and staff.

If the bids and tenders submitted are not sufficient to arrive at a decision, interviews and consultations can be organized to allow the evaluation committee to make better-informed decisions during the selection process.

Once the external auditor has been selected and appointed, the appointment is confirmed through a written agreement between the company and the external auditor. The agreement deals with the scope of the audit and its timing, cost, and standards, and it will also contain information relating to the obligations of the auditor and the support that the company will provide.

External audit regulations around the world differ. In the United States companies can use only certified public accountants to undertake their audit, while in Commonwealth countries, such as the United Kingdom, Canada, Australia, and New Zealand, the regulations demand the use of a chartered accountant.

ADVANTAGES

- An external audit helps an organization to assess the state of its business and to put in place measures to improve and develop it.
- External audits assess its risk management policies and help to deter fraud.
- Appointing the right external auditors will ensure a smooth and thorough examination of the company and a transparent and thorough audit.

DISADVANTAGES

- External auditors can be expensive. Plan your budget accordingly and make sure you negotiate a reasonable fee.
- In certain circumstances a company will be required to change its external auditor yearly or after a fixed period.

ACTION CHECKLIST

✔ Take time to recruit the best external auditors. Obtain as much information from as many sources as you can before appointing an external auditor.

✔ Consider a selection bidding process and examine each bid carefully before making a decision.

✔ Communicate clearly to your external auditors what you would like to achieve from the auditing process. Explain your business plans and aims and allow the external auditors transparency in examining documents and speaking with key staff.

DOS AND DON'TS

DO

- Establish good communication between management and external auditors.

DON'T

- Do not appoint external auditors based only on cost—consider other factors such as reputation and experience; a more expensive auditor may offer better value for money in the medium to long term.
- Do not underestimate the need for proper training of directors and employees to help them to fulfill their duties.

MORE INFO

Book:

Porter, Brenda, David J. Hatherly, and Jonathan Simon. *Principles of External Auditing*. 3rd ed. Hoboken, NJ: Wiley, 2008.

Articles:

Fan, Joseph P. H., and T. J. Wong. "Do external auditors perform a corporate governance role in emerging markets? Evidence from East Asia." *Journal of Accounting Research* 43:1 (March 2005): 35–72. Online at: dx.doi.org/10.1111/j.1475-679x.2004.00162.x

Wang, Kun, and Zahid Iqbal. "Auditor choice, retained ownership, and earnings disclosure for IPO firms: Further evidence. " *International Journal of Managerial Finance* 2:3 (2006): 220–240. Online at: dx.doi.org/10.1108/17439130610676484

See Also:

★ Contemporary Developments in International Auditing Regulation (pp. 315–318)
✔ The Chief Audit Executive's (CAE) Roles and Responsibilities (p. 1025)
✔ The Key Components of an Audit Report (p. 1042)

"Government's view of the economy could be summed up in a few short phrases: If it moves, tax it. If it keeps moving, regulate it. And if it stops moving, subsidise it." Ronald Reagan

  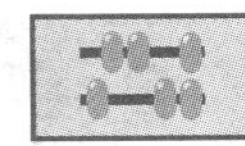      

Cosourcing Internal Audits

DEFINITION

The internal audit departments of even the largest organizations cannot afford to employ the technical and expert resources required to meet all the requirements that they are likely to encounter at all times. By using cosourcing, organizations can tap into specialized skills that are not available inhouse. Cosourcing gives organizations access to world-class, global internal audit resources and capabilities, along with access to state-of-the-art technology, and it allows for the redeployment of staff to core activities. Moreover, it can cut costs (by not employing specialist staff on a full-time basis). Recruiting internal audit staff of sufficient caliber can also be time-consuming and recruitment costs are invariably loaded upfront, while mistakes in recruitment are expensive to reverse. Buying in expertise to assist with a particular assignment can therefore be a sensible alternative.

Cosourcing has become increasingly popular as the internal auditing function develops beyond its traditional role and provides information to management to assist its decision-making, as well as protecting organizations against risk and improving control systems. Under cosourcing, a service provider is contracted to assist the inhouse team with specific projects, such as supply chain efficiency or IT risk management. Costs are partially fixed and partially variable. Cosourcing can also be useful where extra internal audit resources are required or where internal audit staff vacancies remain unfilled for a long time.

ADVANTAGES

- Gives an organization access to auditors with specialist skills.
- Enables an organization to top up its internal audit resources.
- Can provide immediate access to resources that help the company to adjust to changing business conditions.
- Can cut costs: businesses can call on skills when they need them and gain access to world-class resources without investing heavily to develop those resources inhouse.
- Exposes internal staff to alternative practices, tools, training, and processes.
- Risks reside with an inhouse manager.
- Fewer employee shortages.
- Greater knowledge of company business, objectives, risks, systems, and culture.
- Greater flexibility.
- Fewer conflicts of interest.
- More direct control over quality of work.
- Corporate knowledge is retained.
- Can provide training for future managers.
- Critical mass makes inhouse internal audit department viable and sustainable.
- Skills transfer to inhouse employees from service providers.

DISADVANTAGES

- It is not always possible to gain access to auditors specializing in a specific technical topic because they are in such high demand.
- Gaining access to a specialist auditor may be an even bigger problem if an organization is not located in a major business market.
- Service providers cost more than inhouse staff.

ACTION CHECKLIST

✔ Take time to make sure that you choose the right service provider. Some firms may be motivated by profit and seek to take on as much work as possible and get it completed as quickly as possible. Other firms are more interested in building a long-term relationship and in gaining future assignments. It is also important to look for firms with a history of success in similar assignments in your industry.

✔ Carefully assess the audit plan and staff capabilities to identify gaps that can be filled by cosourcing. The cosourcing contract should directly address the missing skills and should be for a minimum of three years to build relationships, trust, and consistency.

✔ Implement specific guidelines and procedures, including a communication plan that embraces open and honest communication with rapid resolution of problems and clarification of doubtful issues.

DOS AND DON'TS

DO

- Insist that services are provided by certified internal auditors, and for IT audits by certified information systems auditors.
- Insist that audits are conducted in accordance with the International Standards for the Professional Practice of Internal Auditing issued by the Institute of Internal Auditors.
- Require a minimum level of qualifications and experience from service providers so that you are not assigned inexperienced graduates who you end up training.
- Require CVs for the service provider staff who will do the work and do not allow them to be replaced without your written authorization.
- Provide an induction for the service provider staff.
- Establish matrices and scorecards to evaluate potential providers in terms of cultural compatibility, industry experience, and knowledge of the organization's business.
- Ensure that knowledge transfer takes place so that a department retains specialist knowledge internally for future uses of that information—for example, for revising a procedure, a policy, or a process.
- Use the organization's report format and not that of the service provider.
- Have an inhouse quality assurance process for the work and work papers, and do not just rely on the service provider's procedures.

DON'T

- Don't hire a firm simply on the basis that they offer the cheapest deal.
- Don't forget to establish monitoring procedures and means of evaluating whether the service provider has met your requirements.
- Don't forget to actively manage the service provider.

MORE INFO

Books:

Pickett, K. H. Spencer. *The Internal Auditing Handbook*. 3rd ed. Chichester, UK: Wiley, 2010.

Johnstone, Karla M., Audrey A. Gramling, and Larry E. Rittenberg. *Auditing: A Risk-Based Approach to Conducting a Quality Audit*. 9th ed. Mason, OH: Cengage, 2013.

"I come from an environment where, if you see a snake, you kill it. At General Motors, if you see a snake, the first thing you do is hire a consultant on snakes." H. Ross Perot

Establishing a Framework for Assessing Risk

DEFINITION

Instituting a framework for identifying risks (or opportunities), assessing their probability and impact, and determining which controls should be in place can be critical to achieving the company's business objectives. Identifying and proactively addressing risks and opportunities helps businesses to defend themselves. Debt rating agencies and regulators are also increasingly stipulating that companies institute risk-identifying frameworks.

Enterprise Risk Management (ERM) is a name given to the structures, methods, and procedures used by organizations to identify and combat risk. The setting up and monitoring of ERM is typically performed by management as part of its internal control activities, such as appraisals of analytical reports or management committee meetings with relevant experts to make sure that the risk-response strategy is working and that the objectives are being achieved.

Once the risks have been identified and assessed, management chooses a risk-response approach. This may include:

- Avoidance: Leave risky activities.
- Reduction: Lessen their probability or impact.
- Share or insure: Diminish risk by transferring or sharing.
- Accept: In response to a cost–benefit analysis, take no action.

The most widely used ERM frameworks are COSO (from an organization that prepares audit-related reports) and RIMS (The Risk and Insurance Management Society). Both use methods for identifying, analyzing, responding to, and scrutinizing risks or opportunities within the internal and external settings of the business.

ADVANTAGES

- ERM allows an enterprise to identify and prioritize the risks that might be facing the organization.
- An improved understanding of the risks—both systemic and non-systemic—facing businesses can help in contingency planning for when the unexpected happens.
- Robust identification of risks can protect businesses from events that might otherwise threaten the viability of the entity.

DISADVANTAGES

- Protracted risk-framework evaluation could be counterproductive if the fruitless pursuit of perfection leaves the company exposed to the very risks it hoped to avoid.
- Evaluating risks depends on judgments, estimates, and interpretation. Risks are often intangible issues that might be highly relevant but cannot be easily measured.

ACTION CHECKLIST

✔ Overcome resistance to the introduction or upgrading of risk frameworks by ensuring that the board and managers are conscious of the fact that it is in everyone's interest to be aware of business risks.

✔ Encourage an open environment when establishing a risk framework. Some risks are obvious, but stakeholders or managers of individual business sectors may sometimes know more about hidden risks.

✔ Engage key business stakeholders and managers in the evaluation of risks and when seeking the best resolutions for those risks.

DOS AND DON'TS

DO

- Regularly update risk-assessment frameworks, as these can help to keep management informed of the constantly changing business environment and its risks.
- Spell out in clear terms the risks that the organization may be facing, their probability, and their potential impact.

DON'T

- Don't take risks for granted; just because a risk has been the same in the past, there is no guarantee that it will be the same in the future. Only by fully understanding the risks and updating risk frameworks can you counteract the dangers.
- Don't get bogged down by risk frameworks. Risk is sometimes a natural and acceptable part of doing business.

MORE INFO

Books:

Baxter, Keith. *Risk Management: Fast Track to Success*. Harlow, UK: FT Prentice Hall, 2010.

Leitch, Matthew. *Intelligent Internal Control and Risk Management: Designing High-Performance Risk Control Systems*. Aldershot, UK: Gower, 2008.

Websites:

American Accounting Association (AAA): aaahq.org

Society of Actuaries (SOA): www.soa.org

See Also:

★ Quantifying Corporate Financial Risk (pp. 91–93)

✔ Creating a Risk Register (p. 1156)

✔ Setting Up a Key Risk Indicator (KRI) System (p. 1174)

✔ Understanding Internal Audits (p. 1057)

"Control and learning are deeply embedded in the specific cultural and institutional ethos of an organization." Yanni Yan

  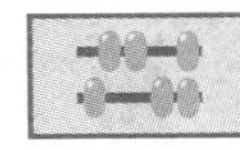      

The EU Regulatory Regime

DEFINITION

Within the EU, the approach to regulation of the markets is twofold. Member states each have their own regulatory body at national level, the role and purpose of which is to set policy, enforce applicable laws, license providers of financial services, work to prevent financial crime, and maintain confidence in the financial system. The more well-known regulatory bodies include the Financial Services Authority (United Kingdom), Autorité des Marchés Financiers (AMF) (France), Bundesanstalt für Finanzdienstleistungsaufsicht (BaFin) (Germany) and the Netherlands Authority for the Financial Markets.

There is no supranational regulatory body for the whole of the EU. Instead, markets around the EU are managed through the imposition of Directives, with which member states must comply. The European Commission launched its Financial Services Action Plan (FSAP) in 1999, which was the cornerstone of the EU's aim to create a single market for financial services, and was intended to last for six years. The FSAP consisted of 42 articles aimed at harmonizing financial services markets within the EU. The most important Directive that emerged from this action plan is the Markets in Financial Instruments Directive (MiFID), which came into effect in 2007.

During the development of the FSAP, in 2001 the EU adopted what became known as the Lamfalussy process, named after Alexandre Lamfalussy, chair of the EU advisory committee that created it. The Lamfalussy process concentrates solely on the development of financial services industry regulations for EU member states, and it has four levels, each focusing on a specific stage of the implementation of legislation.

At level one, the European Parliament and the Council of the European Union work to draft a piece of legislation, establish the core values of this law, and develop guidelines for its implementation. At level two, sector-specific committees and regulators advise on technical details for the law, which is then voted on by member state representatives. At level three, national regulators work on coordinating the new regulations with other member states. Because of the diversity of member states, laws and Directives need to be flexible as to how they are adopted in each nation, while making use of the so-called passport approach (seeSolvency II: Its Development and Aims) that ensures harmonization. Level four consists of compliance with, and enforcement of, the new rules and laws.

The adoption of MiFID has to date been the most significant piece of legislation introduced under the Lamfalussy process, which is intended to offer a number of benefits over the traditional legislative process, such as engendering a more consistent approach to interpretation, convergence of national supervisory practices, and an improved quality of financial services legislation.

Besides MiFID, there are three other Lamfalussy Directives—the Prospectus Directive, the Market Abuse Directive, and the Transparency Directive.

The Prospectus Directive requires anybody offering shares to the public in the EU to issue a prospectus that complies with the detailed rules issued by EU countries under the Directive. A key plank of the Prospectus Directive allows companies to issue a prospectus in one EU country that would cover subsequent offers of securities to the public or admission to trading throughout Europe, with minimal translation obligations.

The Market Abuse Directive introduces a common approach for preventing and detecting market abuse, and ensuring a proper flow of information to the market. New measures include the following requirements:

- issuers to keep "insider lists" of persons who have access to inside information;
- trading firms to disclose: information on deals where involved staff have any personal interest in an issuer's shares and any related derivatives; their research sources and methods, and any conflicts of interest that may impact on the impartiality of the research;
- reporting of any suspicious transactions.

The Transparency Directive is designed to enhance transparency on EU capital markets, by establishing mechanisms and minimum requirements for periodic financial reporting and on the disclosure of major stockholdings for issuers whose securities are traded on any regulated market in the EU. It also establishes disclosure requirements on an ongoing basis about issuers who trade securities on a regulated market situated, or operated within, the EU, for investors who invest in these securities.

MORE INFO

Books:

Craig, Paul, and Gráinne de Búrca (eds). *The Evolution of EU Law*. 2nd ed. Oxford: Oxford University Press, 2011

Katz, Etay (ed). *Financial Services Regulation in Europe*. 2nd ed. Oxford: Oxford University Press, 2008.

See Also:

★ The Payment Services Directive: A Crucial Step Toward Payment Harmonization Across the EU (pp. 229–231)
★ Why Organizations Need to be Regulated—Lessons from History (pp. 437–439)
✔ MiFID—Its Development and Aims (p. 1044)
✔ Solvency II: Its Development and Aims (p. 1053)

"It's a safe banking system, a sound banking system. Our regulators are on top of it. This is a very manageable situation."
Henry Paulson

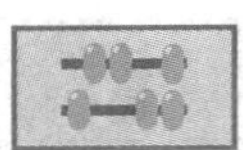

The IIA Code of Ethics

DEFINITION

Established in 1941, the Institute of Internal Auditors aims to provide global leadership for the profession. Based in Florida, the Institute is the internal auditing industry's recognized authority across the world and is keen to promote the profession through improved education. The Institute's membership base covers 165 countries, with members spread across professions such as risk management, corporate governance, information-technology auditing and education, as well as mainstream internal auditing.

The objective of the Institute's code of ethics is to create an ethical culture throughout the profession. The Institute's members aim to help organizations to achieve their objectives through disciplined and highly systematic efforts to strengthen their governance, control, and risk-management procedures. The code of ethics not only covers the core activity of internal auditing but also extends to cover principles relevant to the profession, as well as the rules of conduct to which practitioners should adhere.

ADVANTAGES

- The code of ethics helps to ensure the objectivity of internal auditors, aiming to assist them to assess all relevant factors without being unduly influenced by others or by their own interests.
- By defining the standards expected of internal auditing professionals, the code helps to reinforce the trust that forms the main foundation of the profession. The code also aims to ensure that individual internal auditors have the required competencies to cover the particular task they are expected to perform.
- The confidentiality element of the code aims to make certain that internal auditors always appreciate the value of information. It underlines their requirement to safeguard information at all times, subject only to legal or professional obligations.
- The Institute has disciplinary procedures in place for instances where members are accused of violating the code of ethics, helping to ensure that members can be trusted to act in a consistently professional manner.

DISADVANTAGES

- Ethical standards in business can vary widely from country to country. Therefore, auditing professionals in some countries may have to work harder than those in other countries to fully achieve all the standards expected of a global code of ethics.
- Cultural differences between companies could also put more pressure on internal auditors in some organizations to adhere to the consistently high standards demanded by the code.

DOS AND DON'TS

DO

- Recognize that internal auditing is a progressive profession, the development of which is driven by clients' increasingly demanding needs.
- Take advantage of the Institute's commitment to help internal auditors to achieve their full potential through training and development. For example, the Institute offers a wide range of in-house, company-specific courses.

DON'T

- Don't interpret the code of ethics as simply a list of aspirations for internal auditors. The Institute demands the highest standards of professionalism from its members.
- Don't forget that, despite the best efforts of the Institute to ensure uniformity of standards across the profession worldwide, some individuals may benefit from extra employer support in view of the variations in business ethical standards across different countries and cultures.

ACTION CHECKLIST

✔ In joining the Institute, professionals commit to the highest standards of integrity and professionalism, offering a high level of reassurance to clients.

✔ By encouraging employees to become members, companies help their internal auditors in areas such as self-development, potentially significantly increasing their long-term value to the organization.

✔ The Institute unites over 150,000 internal auditing professionals worldwide. Membership brings access to valuable resources, such as a dedicated resource library, a technical helpline and the latest published professional guidance. Access to these resources can bring significant benefits to an organization.

MORE INFO

Books:

Pickett, K. H. Spencer. *The Internal Auditor at Work: A Practical Guide to Everyday Challenges*. Hoboken, NJ: Wiley, 2004.

Root, Stephen J. *Beyond COSO: Internal Control to Enhance Corporate Governance*. Hoboken, NJ: Wiley, 2000.

Articles:

Colbert, Janet L. "New and expanded internal audit standards." *CPA Journal* (May 2002). Online at: www.nysscpa.org/cpajournal/2002/0502/features/f053402.htm

Gavin, Thomas A., Richard A. Roy, and Glenn E. Sumners. "A corporate code of conduct: The internal auditor's role." *Managerial Auditing Journal* 5:2 (1990). Online at: dx.doi.org/10.1108/02686909010138412. (Also published in *Leadership and Organization Development Journal* 11:3 (1990): 32–40. Online at: dx.doi.org/10.1108/EUM0000000001152)

Website:

Institute of Internal Auditors (IIA): www.theiia.org

See Also:

★ Business Ethics (pp. 1829–1830)
✔ Business Ethics in Islamic Finance (p. 1109)
✔ Corporate Governance and Its Interpretations (p. 1111)
✔ Understanding Internal Audits (p. 1057)

"If networks are to be more efficient . . . this will come about only on the basis of a high level of trust and the existence of shared norms of ethical behavior between network members." Francis Fukuyama

  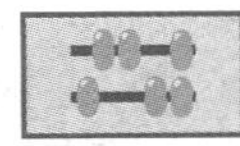      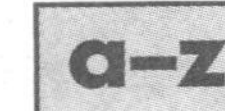

Independence of the Internal Audit Function

DEFINITION

If an internal audit is to prove effective, the auditors must have complete independence to carry out the audit as they see fit and must be free from interference by executives. However, as the Institute of Internal Auditors (IIA) points outs:[1]

"The internal auditor occupies a unique position—he or she is 'employed' by management, but is also expected to review the conduct of management. This can create significant tension since the internal auditor's 'independence' from management is necessary for the auditor to objectively assess management's actions, but the auditor's 'dependence' on management for employment is clear."

With regard to independence, the IIA adds that:[2]

"The audit charter should establish independence of the internal audit activity by the dual reporting relationship to management and the organization's most senior oversight group. Specifically, the CAE [chief audit executive] should report to executive management for assistance in establishing direction, support, and administrative interface; and typically to the audit committee for strategic direction, reinforcement, and accountability. The internal auditors should have access to records and personnel as necessary, and be allowed to employ appropriate probing techniques without impediment."

Senior management should ensure that the internal audit department does not participate in activities that may compromise, or appear to compromise, its independence. These activities may include preparing reports or records, developing procedures, or performing other operational duties that are normally reviewed by auditors. To ensure that auditors are independent, they should be given the authority to:

- access all records and staff necessary to conduct the audit;
- expect from management a formal and timely response to significant adverse audit findings through the taking of appropriate corrective action.

The IIA adds that threats to independence must be managed at the individual auditor, engagement, functional, and organizational levels.

ADVANTAGES

- Having independent auditors ensures that an objective assessment of the risks facing an organization and of the procedures in place to deal with these risks, can be carried out.
- The independence of internal auditors ensures that audits are effective in detecting and preventing fraud.
- Independence and objectivity are critical components of effective internal audit activity.

DISADVANTAGES

- There are no disadvantages of an independent internal audit function.

ACTION CHECKLIST

- ✔ Ensure that the chief audit executive (CAE) reports administratively to the chief executive officer (CEO) and not to the chief financial officer (CFO) or a similar officer who has a direct responsibility for systems being audited. Reporting to executives other than the CEO is not desirable as they can influence the internal audit work to be conducted in their area of responsibility, leading to a loss of independence by internal audit.
- ✔ The board or its audit committee should determine the CAE's performance evaluations and compensation.
- ✔ The CAE should report functionally for internal audit operations to the audit committee and for administration to the CEO.
- ✔ Ensure that the internal audit activity is free from interference in determining the scope of internal auditing, performing work, and communicating results.
- ✔ Establish the independence and the authority of internal audit staff by detailing this in a formal document such as an internal audit charter.

DOS AND DON'TS

DO

- Ensure that there is adequate consideration of audit reports.
- Ensure appropriate action on audit recommendations.
- Make sure that the CAE communicates directly with the board, has regular private meetings with the board, and habitually attends and participates in audit committee meetings.

DON'T

- Don't allow internal auditors to assume operating responsibilities.
- Don't allow internal auditors to draft procedures for, design, install, or operate systems.
- Don't let internal auditors audit activities they previously performed until a reasonable amount of time has elapsed, for example, two years.

MORE INFO

Books:

Harrer, Julie. *Internal Control Strategies: A Mid to Small Business Guide*. Hoboken, NJ: Wiley, 2008.

Johnstone, Karla M., Audrey A. Gramling, and Larry E. Rittenberg. *Auditing: A Risk-Based Approach to Conducting a Quality Audit*. 9th ed. Mason, OH: Cengage, 2013.

Moeller, Robert R. *Brink's Modern Internal Auditing: A Common Body of Knowledge*. 7th ed. Hoboken, NJ: Wiley, 2009.

Website:

Institute of Internal Auditors (IIA): www.theiia.org

See Also:

★ Optimizing Internal Audit (pp. 382–384)
✔ Avoiding Conflict of Interest in Internal Audits (p. 1024)

NOTES

1 Fraser, J., and Lindsay, H. "20 questions directors should ask aboutinternal audit." IIA Research Foundation, 2004. Online at: www.theiia.org/iia/download.cfm?file=2927 [PDF].

2 IIA. "How doesinternal auditingmaintain its independence and objectivity?" Online at: na.theiia.org/about-us/about-ia/Pages/frequently-asked-questions.aspx

"Responsibility without control is at the core of management." Paul Corrigan

  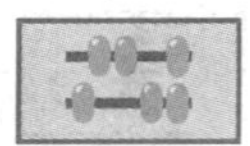      

Insolvency/Bankruptcy Regulations in Major Regions

DEFINITION

An individual or legal entity is considered insolvent if he/she/it is unable to pay debts when they are due.

Insolvency procedures differ around the world, but all of them allow debtors to find a solution to their indebtedness and protect them from creditors.

In the United Kingdom, the bankruptcy procedures available to an individual depend on the amount of money that individual owes. If the debts are less than £5,000, an administration order can be obtained. The order is issued by the local county court, which administers the debts. The effect is that the creditors cannot take any legal action against the individual. If the debts are over £5,000 but under £15,000, a debt management plan (DMP) could be suitable if the individual can pay all his/her debts within a five-year period. If an individual has assets to protect or is restricted by his/her employment from bankruptcy, has more than three creditors and debts over £15,000, and can afford to pay £200 per month, an individual voluntary arrangement (IVA) might be appropriate. This is, however, expensive.

Declaring oneself bankrupt is only suitable for someone who has no assets to worry about. Bankruptcy gives that individual the right to protect himself from a crippling level of debt. If there are any assets, they transfer to a trustee, who will administer them and pay off creditors. The debt will be written off, but control of the individual's outgoings and earnings will be in the hands of the trustee. Once declared bankrupt, an individual will find it very difficult to find credit, and his or her reputation will be tarnished.

In the United States, bankruptcy is regulated by the Bankruptcy Code, which was enacted in 1978. This is also known as Title 11 of the United States Code and is recognized as the federal law that governs all bankruptcy cases. Each US district has a bankruptcy court, which deals with the bankruptcy procedure. The court's decisions are made by a bankruptcy judge.

The purpose of bankruptcy is to obtain a bankruptcy discharge, which will release the debtor from personal liability for specific debts and prohibits any creditor from taking action to collect those debts. In the United States there are six types of bankruptcy case, which are known by the numbers of the chapters that apply to them: Chapters 7, 9, 11, 12, 13, and 15.

Chapter 7 covers liquidation, a court-supervised procedure in which a trustee is appointed to take over the assets of a debtor's estate, transform them into cash, and distribute this cash to creditors. Chapters 9 and 11 deal with reorganization, which is used by companies that intend to continue their business while repaying creditors through a court-approved reorganization plan. Chapter 9 deals with indebted municipalities. Chapters 12 and 13 cover the adjustment of debts of an individual with a regular income. The individual can keep his/her main assets, such as a house, and repay debt over a three- to five-year period. The procedure under Chapter 12 applies to farmers or fishermen. Chapter 15 deals with cross-border cases of insolvency.

ADVANTAGES

- Insolvency and bankruptcy regulations protect debtors by allowing them to schedule payment of their debt.
- The regulations prevent a company or individual from acquiring irresponsible and unlimited debt and allow creditors to take charge of the future of an indebted business.

DISADVANTAGES

- Insolvency and bankruptcy regulations are very complex.
- Specialist financial and legal advice is always required when someone is declared bankrupt or insolvent.
- Insolvency and bankruptcy should be used as a last resort and not as a shield or an escape from debt or responsibility to creditors.
- Once declared bankrupt or insolvent, an individual or entity will find it very difficult to obtain credit. Their credit record will be damaged and their credibility undermined.

DOS AND DON'TS

DO

- Carefully weigh up the implications of declaring yourself or a business bankrupt or insolvent. Understand that the consequences can be very serious. Your creditworthiness, reputation, and future can be put in jeopardy.
- Obtain relevant legal and financial advice on any decision to declare yourself bankrupt or the business insolvent.
- Research the consequences carefully before making a decision.

DON'T

- Don't underestimate the need for proper research and professional advice.
- Don't use bankruptcy and insolvency as an escape. It could influence your financial and business dealings for the rest of your life.

MORE INFO

Books:

Blum, Brian A. *Bankruptcy and Debtor/Creditor: Examples and Explanations*. 5th ed. New York: Aspen Publishers, 2010.

Israel, J. *European Cross-Border Insolvency Regulation*. Antwerp, Belgium: Intersentia Publishers, 2005.

Article:

Parker, Susan, Gary F. Peters, and Howard F. Turetsky. "Corporate governance and corporate failure: A survival analysis." *Corporate Governance* 2:2 (2002): 4–12. Online at: dx.doi.org/10.1108/14720700210430298

Websites:

American Bankruptcy Institute (ABI): www.abiworld.org

California Bankruptcy Forum: www.calbf.org

See Also:

✔ Managing Bankruptcy and Insolvency (p. 1168)

"Capitalism without bankruptcy is like Christianity without hell." Frank Borman

  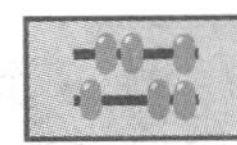      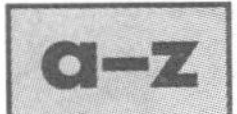

Internal Audit Charters

DEFINITION

An internal audit charter is a formal document approved by the audit committee. It should be developed by the chief audit executive and agreed at the highest level of the organization. Standards published by the Institute of Internal Auditors (IIA) require that there be an internal audit charter, but there is no fixed requirement for what it should contain. At a minimum, the IIA standards require a charter to define the purpose, authority, and responsibility of the internal audit function. A charter establishes internal audit 's position within an organization and authorizes it to access records, personnel, and physical property that are relevant to internal audit work. It can be used, for example, by an auditor when a manager in a remote part of the business questions the auditor's need to access particular documents, computer records, or personnel. A charter is particularly useful in large organizations but it is important to remember that such situations can also occur in smaller organizations.

The IIA refers to the need for a charter but does not provide specific guidance on what it should contain. IIA Standard 1000 says:[1]

"The internal audit charter is a formal document that defines the internal audit activity's purpose, authority, and responsibility. The internal audit charter establishes the internal audit activity's position within the organization, including the nature of the chief audit executive's functional reporting relationship with the board; authorizes access to records, personnel, and physical properties relevant to the performance of engagements; and defines the scope of internal audit activities. Final approval of the internal audit charter resides with the board."

ADVANTAGES

- A charter can be used in a positive fashion to describe the aims of internal audit.
- It can also be used to defend the audit against hostile managers or staff.
- A charter compels departments that need to be audited to cooperate with the auditor. Without this charter or similar authority, managers might not see the need for an audit and might refuse the auditor's requests.

DISADVANTAGES

- Such a formal document might not be necessary in a small organization.

ACTION CHECKLIST

- ✔ Develop a precise definition of internal auditing. This should be formally worded and include the objectives of the internal audit function. It may be possible to use the definition outlined by a body such as the IIA.
- ✔ Ensure that the charter makes it clear that internal audit engagements will cover the following four areas: reliability and integrity of financial and operational information; effectiveness and efficiency of operations; safeguarding of assets; and compliance with laws, regulations, and contracts.

Here is a suggested checklist for use in formulating an internal audit charter. The charter should:

- ✔ detail the purpose, authority, and responsibility of the internal audit function, together with the scope of its activities;
- ✔ establish internal audit 's position within the organization;
- ✔ define the nature of the assurance services that will be provided by internal audit;
- ✔ include a definition of internal auditing;
- ✔ define the nature of the assurance services that will be provided by internal audit;
- ✔ authorize access to records, personnel, and physical property relevant to the performance of engagements;
- ✔ specify a periodic review of internal audit performance and of the charter itself;
- ✔ be approved by the audit committee.

DOS AND DON'TS

DO

- Ensure that the role of the internal audit function is clearly set out and that it is distinguished from management's responsibilities. Management should, for example, be responsible for establishing procedures to prevent fraud, while the auditors should be responsible for establishing the effectiveness of those procedures.
- Ensure that the charter is simple and unambiguous.
- Make sure that senior management supports the charter or serious problems could ensue.
- Keep the charter short and to the point.

DON'T

- Don't forget to revisit the charter periodically to ensure that it remains relevant to the organization's needs.

MORE INFO

Books:

Moeller, Robert R. *Brink's Modern Internal Auditing: A Common Body of Knowledge*. 7th ed. Hoboken, NJ: Wiley, 2009.

Pickett, K. H. Spencer. *The Internal Auditing Handbook*. 3rd ed. Chichester, UK: Wiley, 2010.

Website:

Institute of Internal Auditors (IIA): www.theiia.org

See Also:

★ Aligning the Internal Audit Function with Strategic Objectives (pp. 280–282)
★ Starting a Successful Internal Audit Function to Meet Present and Future Demands (pp. 407–410)
✔ Avoiding Conflict of Interest in Internal Audits (p. 1024)
✔ Understanding Internal Audits (p. 1057)

NOTE

1 IIA. "1000—Purpose, authority, and responsibility." Online at: na.theiia.org/standards-guidance/mandatory-guidance/Pages/Standards.aspx

"Bad administration, to be sure, can destroy good policy; but good administration can never save bad policy."
Adlai E. Stevenson

Internal Auditing for Financial Firms

DEFINITION

In view of the recent global recession of 2009–10, when investments made by banks and financial institutions proved unsafe and almost triggered a financial meltdown that required strong input and investment by most democratic governments, the need for internationally regulated and well-audited financial institutions is greater than ever. Therefore, financial institutions have started to concentrate on rigorous internal audit processes undertaken by an internal audit team that conducts regular control self-assessments. This is a process in which management and staff analyze their roles and activities, and assess how efficient and effective their internal control procedures are.

Financial institutions should have an internal audit team that has a dual role of assessing whether the risks taken are appropriately managed and of making recommendations to consolidate the institution's controls. The internal audit team should be independent in its evaluation of the control systems within the organization.

The internal audit team must also assess and report on management's performance, analyzing and reporting on whether it has performed appropriately, effectively, and efficiently. The internal audit team needs to ensure that the financial institution has complied with all the procedures, standards, and policies imposed by the applicable laws and regulations. This is no mean task as the financial sector is complex and highly regulated.

The nature of the role means that internal auditors will not only gather and provide information, but that they will also help in the assessment and interpretation of that information as it pertains to the overall compliance and security of the organization, including the procedures that are in place to manage and control risk. The actual control of risk will in all probability be in the hands of specific risk managers, but the internal audit team will want to report on the effectiveness of the procedures involved and on executive management's relationship with the risk managers. One of the problems of the crash was the way in which the concerns of risk managers were sidelined by managements intent on boosting profits without regard, or without sufficient regard, to the risks that were being assumed.

ADVANTAGES

- Internal auditing of financial institutions improves their productivity.
- It should provide an insight into the performance of an institution and provide constructive criticism on what should be changed and how.
- It can help to prevent fraud and mismanagement.

DISADVANTAGES

- Regulations and laws are increasingly stringent and the cost of compliance is now a significant factor.
- Trained staff are required and this requires a substantial investment. An internal audit department is a pure "cost" to the company. However, not having a strong internal audit function exposes the company to fraud and to failures of control and compliance that could ultimately cost it everything—as spectacular cases such as Enron demonstrate.
- Line management can be resentful of the "braking" effect of a rigorous internal audit policy and an active internal audit department, blaming the latter for "undue caution" and for implementing time-consuming control procedures. This is a factor that requires handling by senior management.
- The internal audit function can only be as effective as it is allowed to be. It requires board-level support to be effective.

ACTION CHECKLIST

✔ Study the relevant laws carefully. Compliance with regulations for the internal audit of financial firms is closely monitored.

✔ Ensure that the board of directors has reviewed the control systems and capital assessment procedures of the bank or financial institution.

✔ Ensure that the internal auditors have examined and evaluated the effectiveness of the internal control systems.

✔ See that the internal auditors have assessed the means of safeguarding assets.

✔ Review the internal audit analysis of operational efficiency.

✔ Ensure that the members of the internal audit team have no connection or conflict of interest with the financial sector they will investigate.

DOS AND DON'TS

DO

- Appoint the best possible team of internal auditors, ensuring that they have the capability and authority required to assess the financial state of the firm.
- Provide board-level support for the function to enable it to gain access to everything it requires to fulfill its role.
- Comply with all the laws and regulations governing the assessment and operation of financial institutions.
- Ensure that the integrity of the internal audit function is maintained at all times.

DON'T

- Don't ignore any constructive criticism made by the internal audit team.
- Don't cut costs by appointing low-caliber internal auditors—it could turn out to be a very expensive economy.
- Don't appoint auditors that have connections with personnel in the departments to be examined by the internal audit function.

MORE INFO

Book:

Regulatory Compliance Associates Inc. *Bank Internal Audit: A Working Guide to Regulatory Compliance*. Austin, TX: Sheshunoff. Periodic updates via subscription.

Article:

Cahill, Edward. "Audit committee and internal audit effectiveness in a multinational bank subsidiary: A case study." *Journal of Banking Regulation* 7:1 (February 2006): 160–179. Online at: dx.doi.org/10.1057/palgrave.jbr.2340011

"If you were alive, they would give you a loan. Actually, I think if you were dead, they would still give you a loan."
Steven M. Knoebel

   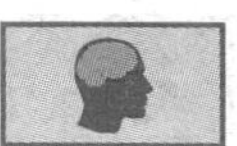     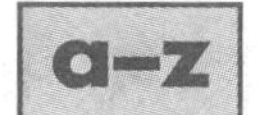

Internal Auditing for Fraud Detection and Prevention

DEFINITION

Fraud protection is a key concern for businesses, and internal audits can play a major role in both detecting and preventing fraud. According to the Institute of Internal Auditors (IIA), for example, "internal auditors support management's efforts to establish a culture that embraces ethics, honesty, and integrity" and "they assist management with the evaluation of internal controls used to detect or mitigate fraud, evaluate the organization's assessment of fraud risk, and are involved in any fraud investigations." This is because, although it is management's responsibility to design internal controls to prevent, detect, and mitigate fraud, the internal auditors are "the appropriate resource" for assessing the effectiveness of the measures that management has implemented. Consequently, the IIA says that depending on directives from management, the board, audit committee, or other governing body, internal auditors can play a variety of consulting, assurance, collaborative, advisory, oversight, and investigative roles in an organization's fraud management process. Internal auditors are well placed to deter and detect fraud because they are highly proficient in techniques used to evaluate internal controls. These skills, "coupled with their understanding of the indicators of fraud, enables them to assess an organization's fraud risks and advise management of the necessary steps to take when indicators are present," concludes the IIA.

ADVANTAGES

- As a part of their assurance activities, internal auditors watch for potential fraud risks, assess the adequacy of related controls, and make recommendations for improvement. They can help also to benchmark statistics related to the probability of occurrence and consequences of fraud.
- Internal auditors are exposed to key processes throughout the organization and have open lines of communication with the executive board and staff. They are thus able to play an important role in fraud detection.
- Since internal auditors report directly to the board or governing body, they have the independence and objectivity necessary for them to undertake investigations of a sensitive nature.

DISADVANTAGES

- Although internal auditors may have a direct role in investigating fraud, they generally lack the expertise of professionals whose primary responsibility is detecting and investigating fraud.

DOS AND DON'TS

DO

- Establish a culture of integrity, as it is a critical component of fraud control. Executive management must set the highest levels of integrity as a benchmark.
- Ensure that you comply with IIA standards on this issue. In January 2009, for example, the IIA implemented a new standard making auditing for fraud mandatory for internal auditors.
- Make sure that your internal auditors consider using technology-based audit and other data analysis techniques in line with IIA standards.

DON'T

- Don't rely solely on internal auditors to root out and deter fraud. Simple procedures such as vetting employment candidates thoroughly can be highly effective and relatively cheap ways of preventing fraud.

ACTION CHECKLIST

✔ Consult the internal auditors on methods to ensure integrity within the organization and involve them in communicating or interpreting those methods. Internal auditors can also help to develop training related to integrity policies and fraud prevention and detection.

✔ Ensure that the internal auditors have key competencies for this work through specialized training and related experiences. They can also gain certification as fraud or forensic investigators.

✔ Ensure that the chief audit executive is responsible for responding to issues raised on ethics that may lead to detection of fraud.

MORE INFO

Books:

Pickett, K. H. Spencer. *The Internal Auditing Handbook*. 3rd ed. Chichester, UK: Wiley, 2010.

Rezaee, Zabihollah, and Richard Riley. *Financial Statement Fraud: Prevention and Detection*. 2nd ed. Hoboken, NJ: Wiley, 2010.

Vona, Leonard W. *Fraud Risk Assessment: Building a Fraud Audit Program*. Hoboken, NJ: Wiley, 2008.

Reports:

Coram, Paul, Colin Ferguson, and Robyn Moroney. "The importance of internal audit in fraud detection." Paper presented at AFAANZ Conference, July 2–4, 2006, Wellington, New Zealand. Online at: tinyurl.com/6fvsvxl [PDF].

IIA. "Internal auditing and fraud." December 2009. Online at: tinyurl.com/4vsycok

Websites:

Chartered Institute of Internal Auditors (UK and Ireland): www.iia.org.uk

Institute of Internal Auditors (IIA): www.theiia.org

See Also:

★ How Internal Auditing Can Help with a Company's Fraud Issues (pp. 346–350)

★ Human Risk: How Effective Strategic Risk Management Can Identify Rogues (pp. 872–874)

✔ What Is Forensic Auditing? (p. 1060)

"Three years after our horrific financial crisis caused by financial fraud, not a single financial executive has gone to jail, and that's wrong." Craig Ferguson

        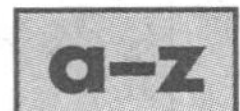

Internal Auditing for Small and Medium-Sized Enterprises (SMEs)

DEFINITION

Internal audits can have a range of functions, from determining the financial health of an organization to looking at how efficient and effective it is. Internal audits can also assess the nonfinancial areas of an entity. However, small and medium-sized enterprises (SMEs) have particular needs in terms of internal auditing. The accounts of very small businesses, for example, are less complex than those of larger organizations, and they can neither afford, nor do they probably need, the services of qualified auditing professionals.

An internal audit can vary from encompassing all areas of a business to focusing on a very narrow and specific aspect of an enterprise's operations and systems. However, performing a successful small business audit is likely to involve examining various areas, including: cash flow, accounts receivable, accounts payable, quality, human resources, procurement, payroll, IT, and profitability. Auditing these areas helps to ensure that the small business is able to meet its main goal, which is to generate a profit.

As survival is the key requirement for any SME, understanding cash flow is essential. Auditing cash flow involves examining the receipts of the business and determining the sources from which they are derived. This will highlight key factors, such as dependence on a particular source or the volatility of receipts, and will reveal how much money is flowing in and out the business. Examining the accounts receivable highlights how long money is tied up before it is released for the business, and the results may prompt a revision of credit policy. Examining accounts payable will determine how much money is owed to suppliers, and such an examination should leave the managers better positioned to control cash flow. Examining quality, which involves looking at products, marketing, advertising, and the overall image of the business, as well as human resources, will highlight any problems in these areas. Examining profit enables a business to ensure that its assets and liabilities are correctly balanced, as well as whether a business is generating sufficient profit to justify the investment that has gone into it.

ADVANTAGES

- Performing an internal audit of a SME can provide assurance that it is operating as efficiently as possible, as it will highlight any problem areas that need to be addressed.
- Internal audits can also be used in a preventive fashion. An internal auditor may, for example, spot potential problems and risks in business operations, allowing management to take preemptive action that stops the potential problem from developing.
- Carrying out an audit can deter or detect fraud and other crimes. Knowing how many computers your company owns, for example, can protect against theft. A bigger risk in a small organization is likely to be inadequate controls when people perform multiple tasks.

DISADVANTAGES

- Carrying out an internal audit can be time-consuming, diverting key staff from core activities.
- Internal audit has a cost, and the benefits must outweigh the cost.

ACTION CHECKLIST

✔ The purpose of the audit should be discussed and agreed by the SME's management. The auditor should establish the audit's scope and objectives, as agreed with the relevant managers.

✔ Establish how frequently the audit should be carried out. The riskier units of a SME should be audited more frequently than other departments. They should also be audited more intensely.

✔ Policies and procedures should focus on continuously improving how work is performed. Management should review all organizational policies and procedures on an annual basis to ensure that they reflect the changing business environment.

✔ If, as the result of an audit, a SME's net income is found to be low, corrective strategies must be implemented in the affected areas to correct the problem and restore the business to financial health.

DOS AND DON'TS

DO

- Ensure that the person carrying out the audit is given the authority to act independently and produce results without fear or favor.
- Ensure that the internal auditor is given specific reporting guidelines, a time frame, and access to all files so as to avoid conflict within departments or among superiors.

DON'T

- Don't provide any unrequested or extraneous information. If you are unsure about the information and how it may relate to the audit, but the auditor has not specifically requested it, consult with the managers responsible for the internal audit first so that a decision can be made on how to proceed.

MORE INFO

Books:

Chadwick, Leslie. *Essential Finance and Accounting for Managers*. Harlow, UK: FT Prentice Hall, 2002.

Harrer, Julie. *Internal Control Strategies: A Mid to Small Business Guide*. Hoboken, NJ: Wiley, 2008.

Henschel, Thomas. *Risk Management Practices of SMEs: Evaluating and Implementing Effective Risk Management Systems*. Berlin: Erich Schmidt Verlag, 2008.

See Also:

★ Considerations when Outsourcing Internal Audit (pp. 312–314)
✔ Cosourcing Internal Audits (p. 1027)
✔ Key Competencies for Internal Auditors (p. 1041)
✔ Understanding Internal Audits (p. 1057)

"Successful entrepreneurs judge correctly the need for change, then do something about it." James Edward, Lord Hanson

  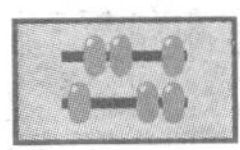      

Internal Auditing for the Public Sector

DEFINITION

Governments and government departments in democratic societies are subject to internal audit. This is essential to assess whether the departments are run efficiently and provide good value for taxpayers' money.

The UK government's internal audit standards (HM Treasury, 2011) define internal auditing as an independent, objective assurance and consulting activity designed to add value and improve an organization's operations. Its scope is to help an organization to accomplish its objectives by bringing a systematic, disciplined approach to the evaluation and improvement of the effectiveness of risk management, control, and governance processes.

Internal auditors must be independent from the public sector that they audit in order to be able to provide impartial audit review and advice. This means that the process of appointing public auditors must be well regulated and impartial. Usually this is regulated by law; however, in the public sector the appointment of internal auditors is usually a decision for management or the audit committee.

The auditing process in the public sector has a wide remit. The scope of the internal audit work will usually focus on:

- reviewing the achievement of objectives;
- making sure decisions are properly authorized;
- assuring the reliability and integrity of information;
- promoting efficiency and effectiveness;
- safeguarding assets;
- assessing compliance with laws, regulations, policies, and contracts;
- reviewing the opportunities for fraud.

ADVANTAGES

- Internal auditing of public sector organizations and government departments is a necessary process that provides an insight into how the public sector is run.
- It provides an assessment of the resource budget estimates that in turn helps a government department to meet its published aims and objectives.
- It offers consultancy advice in the form of recommendations that management are free to accept or reject.

DISADVANTAGES

- Regulations and statutes can make the internal auditing of public sector departments lengthy and complicated.
- Since many departments are concerned with vital public services, subjecting them to internal audit can be disruptive and can create difficulties with line management if the function, objectives, and ultimately the benefits of internal audit are not understood by department personnel.
- Unless the internal audit function is properly trained, with a full understanding and appreciation of the department that is being audited, its judgments will be challenged by line management. Proper training is essential.

ACTION CHECKLIST

✔ Ensure that internal auditors are appointed in full compliance with the relevant legislation.

✔ Make sure that the auditors appointed have no connection or conflict of interest with the public sector they will investigate.

DOS AND DON'TS

DO

- Set up a transparent and clear process which the public can easily consult.
- Make sure that the principles of independence of public sector auditors, propriety of auditors, and providing good value for money are achieved.
- Make sure that the internal audit process is supervised by an independent watchdog such as the Audit Commission in the United Kingdom or equivalent.

DON'T

- Don't ignore the importance of public sector auditing. It may seem expensive, but it will provide value for money in the long term.
- Don't appoint auditors that have any connection with the public sector in question; otherwise the impartiality of the audit function will be put at risk.

MORE INFO

Book:

Keating, Lori. *Performance Auditing of Public Sector Property Contracts*. Aldershot, UK: Gower Publishing, 2011.

Articles:

Broadbent, Jane, and James Guthrie. "Public sector to public services: 20 years of 'contextual' accounting research." *Accounting, Auditing and Accountability Journal* 21:2 (2008): 129–169. Online at: dx.doi.org/10.1108/09513570810854383

Parker, Lee, and Graeme Gould. "Changing public sector accountability: Critiquing new directions." *Accounting Forum* 23:2 (June 1999): 109–135.

Reports:

Chartered Institute of Public Finance and Accountancy. "Code of practice for internal audit in local government in the United Kingdom 2006." Online at: tinyurl.com/6bx4q4h [PDF].

HM Treasury. "Public sector internal audit standards." June 14, 2013. Online at: www.gov.uk/government/publications/public-sector-internal-audit-standards

Websites:

Audit Commission (UK): www.audit-commission.gov.uk

MIS Training Institute (audit and information security training): www.mistieurope.com

See Also:

★ Considerations when Outsourcing Internal Audit (pp. 312–314)
✔ Adopting an Internal Audit Capability Model (p. 1022)
✔ Cosourcing Internal Audits (p. 1027)
✔ Internal Audit Charters (p. 1033)
✔ Preparing and Executing an Internal Audit Review (p. 1045)

"Profit has to be a means to other ends rather than an end in itself." Charles Handy

  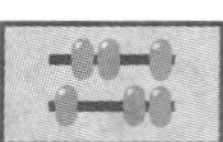      

International and Multinational Internal Auditing

DEFINITION

Internal audit activities are performed in diverse legal and cultural environments and within organizations that vary in purpose, size, and structure; and by persons within or outside the organization. These differences may affect the practice of internal auditing in each environment. Standards have been established by bodies such as the International Federation of Accountants (IFAC) to ensure that internal audits are carried out to the same high level across international boundaries. More than 100 countries have either adopted international standards on auditing (ISAs) issued by the IFAC or have declared their intent to do so in the future. ISAs, as well as international financial reporting standards (IFRSs), are endorsed by the World Bank, the International Monetary Fund, and other international institutions as the best-practice standards for corporate financial reporting.

ISAs are issued by the International Auditing and Assurance Standards Board (IAASB), an independent standard-setting body that operates under the auspices of the IFAC. The objective of the IAASB is to "serve the public interest by setting high quality auditing, assurance, quality control and related services standards and by facilitating the convergence of international and national standards, thereby enhancing the quality and uniformity of practice throughout the world and strengthening public confidence in the global auditing and assurance profession."

The growth of multinational businesses has increased pressure to harmonize international auditing standards. The auditing of multinational enterprises needs to take into account the rules in their home country, such as Sarbanes–Oxley in the United States. The internationalization of auditing has largely taken place within international audit firms. During the past few decades many local audit firms have merged into international groups.

ADVANTAGES

The benefits of international standards for auditing include the following.

- They give readers of audit reports confidence in the auditors' opinions.
- They provide greater assurance that accounting standard are being adhered to.
- They facilitate international financial comparisons.
- They assist in the flow of investment capital.
- Developing countries can use them as a basis for their own standards.

DISADVANTAGES

- Organizations have different auditing requirements, and a standardized approach may not suit every business or entity.
- It can be expensive for companies in developing countries to apply international standards, some of which may not be relevant or needed in their domicile.

ACTION CHECKLIST

- ✔ Ensure that your financial statements are prepared in line with international standards such as IFRSs.
- ✔ Make sure that you are aware of issues such as transfer pricing —the price setting for cross-border transfer of goods, services, and intangibles between associated parties. Errors in this area could result in double taxation involving foreign tax authorities.
- ✔ Intellectual property (IP) is another problematic area. The benefits of IP should lie with the owner, so it is important to establish both where the IP has been created and where it is legally owned.

DOS AND DON'TS

DO

- Be aware that tax authorities around the world are increasing their audit activities, and the need to meet international auditing standards has never been more pressing.

DON'T

- Don't forget that the responsibility for safeguarding the assets of the company and for the prevention and detection of fraud, error, and noncompliance with law or regulations continues to rest with management.

MORE INFO

Books:

Collings, Steven. *Interpretation and Application of International Standards on Auditing*. Chichester, UK: Wiley, 2011.

Dauber, Nick A., Anique Ahmed Qureshi, Marc H. Levine, and Joel G. Siegel. *The Complete Guide to Auditing Standards and Other Professional Standards for Accountants 2009*. Hoboken, NJ: Wiley, 2009.

Hayes, Rick, Roger Dassen, Arnold Schilder, and Philip Wallage. *Principles of Auditing: An Introduction to International Standards on Auditing*. 2nd ed. Harlow, UK: FT Prentice Hall, 2005.

Websites:

Chratered Institute of Internal Auditors (UK and Ireland) on international standards: tinyurl.com/5vsuhkl

International Auditing and Assurance Standards Board (IAASB): www.ifac.org/auditing-assurance

International Federation of Accountants (IFAC): www.ifac.org

See Also:

★ Origins and Rationale for IFRS Convergence (pp. 385–387)
✔ Internal Audit Charters (p. 1033)
✔ Internal Control Frameworks: COSO, CoCo, and the UK Corporate Governance Code (p. 1119)
✔ The Key Components of an Audit Report (p. 1042)

"No one can bring together a country that has 265 kinds of cheese." Charles de Gaulle

International Financial Reporting Standards (IFRS): The Basics

DEFINITION

The increasing pace of globalization over recent years has forced the pace for the adoption of truly comparable and consistent international accounting standards. A decade ago, national versions of Generally Accepted Accounting Principles (GAAP) were commonplace. Nowadays, IFRS has gained broad acceptance and is used in over 100 countries. The United States is moving towards the convergence of US GAAP and IFRS, with the present timetable indicating that the set of standards will be applied to large public companies in 2014, though some should have the option to make the move even earlier. Since early 2008, IFRS has been allowed in the United States without reconciliation for foreign private issuers. The Securities and Exchange Commission 's (SEC's) roadmap suggests that the decision over the future adoption of IFRS should be made in 2011, though the SEC has suggested that this timescale may be subject to delays.

Presently, the widespread use of US GAAP rather than IFRS can create difficulties for financial analysts, given the challenges in making financial comparisons. However, the timelines for change are far from clear. A joint initiative by the Financial Accounting Standards Board (FASB) and the International Accounting Standards Board (IASB) is aiming to converge existing standards into a single set of standards. In contrast, IFRS has been a requirement in Europe for listed companies since 2005.

In light of the increasingly international trend of IFRS, some emerging economies have been quick to adopt IFRS as their national version of GAAP.

First adopted in 2001, IFRS includes many of the International Accounting Standards (IAS) previously set by the IASB with the objective of improving the level of transparency of companies' finances. IFRS also generally includes the International Financial Reporting Interpretations Committee (IFRIC) interpretation and that of its predecessor, Standing Interpretations Committee (SIC), prior to March 2002. While the impact of the adoption of the IFRS on company accounts varies between countries, the set of standards imposes very strict disclosure requirements on companies. Intended to improve the visibility of companies' liabilities, IFRS requires the full disclosure of pension-related obligations, while executive remuneration visibility is also tackled, with IFRS dictating that stock options granted to executives must be included in the accounts. IFRS also has implications for the way companies account for their fixed assets, setting requirements over the fair value of assets. The impact of the adoption of IFRS can also have significance in areas such as merger and acquisition strategy, the provision of bank covenants, and distributions.

ADVANTAGES

- IFRS improves the level of comparability between the accounts of companies across different countries.
- The stringent disclosure requirements improve the visibility of liabilities such as future pension costs and employee stock schemes.
- The adoption of IFRS can provide greater reassurance for investors, credit rating agencies and lenders, potentially giving companies access to lower-cost capital in line with the lower risk.

DISADVANTAGES

- The adoption of IFRS can bring significant additional short-term costs to businesses, such as fees to pay specialist external accountants.
- As adjustments to comply with IFRS can make year-on-year performance comparisons difficult for investment analysts, potentially creating uncertainty and stock price volatility, companies must also devote resources to the preparation of accounts using the legacy conventions.

ACTION CHECKLIST

✔ Consider the benefits of introducing IFRS to management reporting, bringing improved quality and consistency to internal company information on which key decisions are based.

✔ Multinationals should examine the benefits of adopting IFRS throughout their organization to improve international comparability.

✔ Companies should be prepared to utilize external expertise to help with the transition to IFRS conventions.

DOS AND DON'TS

DO

- Companies adopting IFRS should budget for higher short-term costs.
- Aim to embed the principles of IFRS throughout all levels of an organization to extract maximum benefit.
- Explore the potential benefits in using XBRL (Extensible Business Reporting Language) infinancial reporting.

DON'T

- Don't see IFRS as a "threat;" it can bring long-term material benefits, such as higher investor confidence and lower-cost capital.
- Don't ignore IFRS until you are obliged to adopt it by regulators. An understanding of IFRS can help companies to prepare for its adoption, and can offer firms the flexibility to adopt IFRS at a time that works to their advantage.

MORE INFO

Articles:

Daske, Holger. "Economic benefits of adopting IFRS or US-GAAP—Have the expected cost of equity capital really decreased?" *Journal of Business Finance and Accounting* 33:3–4 (April/May 2006): 329–373. Online at: dx.doi.org/10.1111/j.1468-5957.2006.00611.x

Hail, Luzi, Holger Daske, Christian Leuz, and Rodrigo Verdi. "Mandatory IFRS reporting around the world: Early evidence on the economic consequences." *Journal of Accounting Research* 46:5 (December 2008): 1085–1142. Online at: dx.doi.org/10.1111/j.1475-679X.2008.00306.x

Websites:

American Institute of Certified Public Accountants (AICPA) on IFRS: www.ifrs.com
IFRS Foundation and International Accounting Standards Board (IASB): www.ifrs.org

"How we feel about the evolving future tells us who we are as individuals and as a civilization: Do we search for stasis—a regulated, engineered world? Or do we embrace dynamism—a world of constant creation, discovery, and competition?"

Virginia Postrel

Key Accounting Standards and Organizations

DEFINITION

Accounting standards are rules according to which accounting statements have to be prepared. They demand minimum levels of disclosure, establish fundamental principles, delineate the meanings of terms, and stipulate how numbers must be calculated. Accounting standards vary not only between countries but also between industries.

The financial situation and operations of a business are reported through accounting statements, which are generally required by law and are prepared by an enterprise to communicate its performance. The balance sheet provides information on the financial position of a business. The income statement provides information on the performance of a business. The elements of the balance sheet are assets, liabilities, and equity. The elements of the income statement are revenues, expenses, gains, losses, and other items. Collectively, the six fundamentals are referred to as the core accounts in an accounting statement.

There are no legally laid down, internationally recognized accounting standards. Generally Accepted Accounting Principles (GAAP) are sets of rules, accounting principles, and standards that are used in specific countries, regions or industries.

In March 2001, in an attempt to bring about an internationally accepted accounting standard, the International Accounting Standards Committee (IASC) Foundation was formed as a not-for-profit corporation, incorporated in the US State of Delaware. The IASC Foundation is the parent entity of the International Accounting Standards Board (IASB), an independent accounting-standards regulator based in London, United Kingdom. The IASB is responsible for developing the International Financial Reporting Standards (IFRS) and for promoting the use and application of these standards. In the global trading world, even countries that have not adopted IFRS are now attempting to converge their national standards with IFRS.

In the case of European Union (EU) members, both EU and national legislation apply and incompatible requirements may mean that reconciliations need to be made available or more than one set of accounts needs to be presented. Companies that have EU and US listings will also need to reconcile or present more than one set of accounts.

ADVANTAGES

- Financial standards protect governments, businesses and consumers alike, as they set down standardized rules of conduct, which give society financial stability and, if the rules are broken, recourse in law.
- Financial standards allow for the comparison of companies on equal terms. This gives potential investors the tools to judge and compare the viability and liabilities of companies or industries.
- Financial standards provide regulatory benchmarks for companies and individuals.
- Financial standards give governments the instruments to impose impartial taxes to pay for government services.

ACTION CHECKLIST

✔ Check which GAAP are used in the specific enterprise, business area or country in which you are interested.

✔ If in doubt, contact the authority that sets GAAP in your area of interest.

✔ Obtain as much information as you can and be ready to be involved in a long and tedious process.

✔ Seek specialist help, from different sources. Accountants, like doctors, are not infallible.

✔ Don't be afraid to ask what may seem naïve or awkward questions.

✔ Consider how different accounting standards may affect your attitude and judgment when quantifying risk.

DOS AND DON'TS

DO

- Check which accounting statements have to be prepared according to the correct GAAP norms.
- Make sure that particular accounting standards apply to the specific industry.
- When in doubt, contact the authority that sets the nationally accepted accounting principles.
- Get professional advice; "cooking the books" is not that uncommon, especially in loosely regulated countries.
- When operating in countries with unfamiliar accounting standards, get in touch with your country's consular officials, who will generally have a list of reliable local accountants.
- Carefully examine any departures from GAAP norms, as they may indicate deeper problems.

DON'T

- Don't rely on accounting standards to protect you from fraud.
- Don't be put off by the complexity of GAAP when investigating a company.
- Don't make the mistake of basing a decision purely on GAAP. Accounting standards are highly complex and require professional advice.
- Don't forget that if an enterprise is a multinational, it may have to prepare two or more reconcilements.
- Don't forget that in the case of EU members, both EU and national legislation apply.

MORE INFO

Websites:

Financial Reporting Council (UK): www.frc.org.uk

IFRS Foundation and International Accounting Standards Board (IASB): www.ifrs.org

See Also:

★ Origins and Rationale for IFRS Convergence (pp. 385–387)
✔ International Financial Reporting Standards (IFRS): The Basics (p. 1039)
✔ The Ten Accounting Principles (p. 1055)
Financial Accounting and Reporting (p. 1356)

"Important principles may and must be inflexible." Abraham Lincoln

     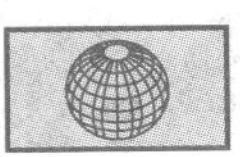   

Key Competencies for Internal Auditors

DEFINITION

Internal auditors work in many organizations in the public and private sectors. They can either be trained while working or will possess an internal audit or accountancy qualification before applying for an internal audit position. However, other qualifications can also be useful as the work is varied, challenging, and draws on a broad range of skills.

However, there is a range of key competencies that are required if internal auditors are to carry out their function effectively. These will vary depending on the seniority of the auditor. The requirement in terms of qualifications varies from country to country. In the United Kingdom, for example, an internal auditor is likely to hold the Chartered Institute of Internal Auditors Diploma in Internal Audit Practice (PIIA) or equivalent. Senior internal auditors should hold the Institute's Advanced Diploma in Internal Auditing and Management (MIIA) or equivalent.

According to the UK government,[1] an internal auditor should have the following competencies.

- Understands the principles of the identification, assessment, and management of risk, including that arising from the extended enterprise nature of organizations.
- Is able to identify and critically evaluate the elements of governance and risk management in an organization.
- Is aware of and understands the organization's risk management strategy.
- Understands the relationship of risk management to corporate governance.
- Is able to review and provide advice and recommendations on the implementation of the risk management strategy.
- Understands the organization's high-level objectives, how these are funded, and key related risks.
- Identifies and understands how operational objectives link into the higher-level objectives.
- Understands the relationship between internal audit and risk management, including the choice of roles available to internal audit depending on the risk maturity of the organization and its possible impact on corporate governance.
- Understands the specific risks related to operational activities and is able to contribute to the review of risks in operational areas.
- Is able to relate the organization's risk appetite to the appropriateness of controls and is able to undertake reviews to assess their effectiveness and report to management accordingly.
- Understands the principles of performance measurement and output targets designed to deliver objectives.

ADVANTAGES

- Possessing key competencies enables internal auditors to do their job effectively.
- Possession of these competencies helps internal audit staff to gain the confidence and respect of senior management and of other staff they come into contact with. This is important if they are to carry out their professional duties effectively.

DISADVANTAGES

- Inevitably there will be costs involved in ensuring staff have the correct training and skills.

ACTION CHECKLIST

✔ Ensure that your internal auditors have a continuing commitment to learning. Business and technology are ever-changing, as are the political and regulatory environments in which a business operates.

✔ Before developing a training and development plan, ensure that training and development are linked to the organization's goals as well as those of personnel.

DOS AND DON'TS

DO

- Assess the competency level of each internal auditor, identify the gaps that need remediation, and develop an individual development plan for each internal auditor.
- Ensure that internal audit staff have an ability to manage projects and to work on their own initiative.
- Link the key competencies required by an internal auditor with your organization's personal development and appraisal systems.
- Ensure that internal audit staff have good written and verbal communication skills and are capable of interacting with senior management.

DON'T

- Don't forget to conduct a post-audit assessment, which should look at a variety of issues, including scoring auditors against key competencies.

MORE INFO

Books:

IIA Research Foundation. *Core Competencies for Today's Internal Auditor*. Altamonte Springs, FL: IIA Research Foundation, 2010.

Moeller, Robert R. *Brink's Modern Internal Auditing: A Common Body of Knowledge*. 7th ed. Hoboken, NJ: Wiley, 2009.

Pickett, K. H. Spencer. *The Internal Auditing Handbook*. 3rd ed. Chichester, UK: Wiley, 2010.

Website:

Chartered Institute of Internal Auditors (UK and Ireland): www.iia.org.uk

See Also:

✔ Avoiding Conflict of Interest in Internal Audits (p. 1024)
✔ Establishing a Framework for Assessing Risk (p. 1028)
✔ Independence of the Internal Audit Function (p. 1031)
✔ The IIA Code of Ethics (p. 1030)
✔ Understanding Internal Audits (p. 1057)

NOTE

1 Assurance, Control and Risk Team/PSG Competency Framework Working Group. "Government internal audit competency framework." HM Treasury, March 2007. Online at: tinyurl.com/memre8l [PDF].

"**Competence, like truth, beauty, and contact lenses, is in the eye of the beholder.**" Laurence J. Peter

The Key Components of an Audit Report

DEFINITION

An audit is the examination and verification of an organization's financial statements and records. Audits provide independent and impartial opinion as to whether the information is presented objectively. Most organizations—privately held businesses, publicly owned corporations, and nonprofit organizations —have to prepare financial reports, which are audited. These reports assist owners and managers to make decisions, and help to show the company's financial status to stockholders, employees, regulators, and the public.

When reviewing an audit report on a company, key questions include: What is the source of its revenue? Where, and on what, does it spend its income? How much profit is it earning?

The answer lies in the company's financial statements, and, by law, all public companies have to make these statements freely available to everyone.

These financial statements can be broken down into two key components: the profit-and-loss statement (or income statement) and the balance sheet.

*The profit-and-loss statement*tells us whether the company is making a profit. It indicates how revenue is transformed into net income. Profit-and-loss statements cover a period of time—usually a year or part of a year.

The balance sheet is a snapshot of a business's financial health at a specific moment in time—usually the close of an accounting period. A balance sheet shows assets, liabilities, and stockholders' equity/-capital. Assets and liabilities are divided into short-term and long-term obligations. The balance sheet does not show the flows into and out of the accounts during the period. A balance sheet 's assets should equal liabilities plus owners' equity.

There are two kinds of audit: internal and external.

Internal audits ensure that the management of the business is meeting internal goals such as productivity, quality, compliance controls, consistency, and cost, as well as external goals such as customer satisfaction and market share.

External audits are carried out by outside auditors, who do not have any ties to the organization or its financial statements. The outside auditor checks the financial statements prepared by management for balance, and also to see whether the company is adhering to professional standards and Generally Accepted Accounting Principles (GAAP).

ADVANTAGES

- External audits improve understanding of underlying business trends and provide an objective opinion as to whether the information is presented fairly.
- Internal audits let managers know whether a business can expand or needs to adopt a more conservative approach. Can it deal with the normal ebbs and flows in revenue, or should it take immediate steps to bolster cash reserves ?
- Internal audits focus on processes within the business, and can identify and help to analyze trends, particularly in the area of receivables and payables, i.e. is the receivables cycle lengthening? Can receivables be collected more aggressively? Is some debt uncollectible?

DISADVANTAGES

- Results sometimes depend on the accounting methods used. Measuring and reporting give management considerable discretion and the opportunity to influence an audit's results.
- Internal audits are not always carried out rigorously and the figures may not reflect the true financial position of the company. Salaries for internal audit staff are paid for by the organization. This can lead to questions about objectivity.

ACTION CHECKLIST

✔ Carefully analyze any profit-and-loss statements for differences during the reporting period. Anomalies might be due to seasonal or other variations, or may indicate deeper problems.

✔ When reviewing internal audits, be prepared to be involved in a long and detailed process of analysis. Some areas will need clarification by experts.

✔ Check which GAAP are used in the internal audit of the business in which you are interested.

✔ Internal audits are not infallible. If you are unsure about specific areas or numbers, don't hesitate to ask for clarification.

DOS AND DON'TS

DO

- Make sure that you take the time and effort to analyze the audit. If in doubt, consult an independent auditor.
- Use your judgment when reviewing internal audits; results do not always tell the whole story.

DON'T

- Don't assume that all audits truly reflect a company's financial position; they only reflect the auditor's opinion.

MORE INFO

Books:

Cardwell, Harvey. *Principles of Audit Surveillance*. Philadelphia, PA: R. T. Edwards, 2005.

President's Council on Integrity and Efficiency, US General Accounting Office. *Financial Audit Manual*. Darby, PA: DIANE Publishing, 2000.

Wealleans, David. *The Quality Audit for ISO 9001:2000: A Practical Guide*. Burlington, VT: Gower Publishing, 2005.

Websites:

American Accounting Association (AAA): aaahq.org

Institute of Internal Auditors (IIA): www.theiia.org

See Also:

✔ Choosing an External Auditor (p. 1026)
✔ Internal Audit Charters (p. 1033)
✔ Preparing and Executing an Internal Audit Review (p. 1045)
✔ Quality Assessment of Internal Audits (p. 1049)
✔ Understanding Internal Audits (p. 1057)

"Anything that I've ever done that ended up worthwhile, initially scared me to death. You have to risk everything sometimes or you risk even more." Danny McCrossan

  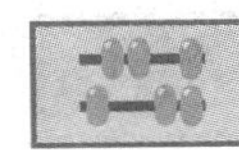   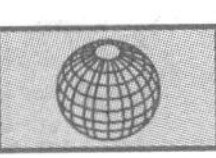   

Middle East: Regulatory Structure and Powers

DEFINITION

The Middle East region consists of Afghanistan, Bahrain, Egypt, Iran, Iraq, Israel, Jordan, Kuwait, Lebanon, Oman, Pakistan, Qatar, Saudi Arabia, Syria, United Arab Emirates (UAE), West Bank and Gaza, and Yemen. Sometimes the region is grouped with North African countries, together known as the MENA (Middle East and North Africa) region, and includes Algeria, Djibouti, Libya, Mauritania, Morocco, Somalia, Sudan, and Tunisia.

Only Saudi Arabia is part of the G20, so MENA's influence on the G20 is limited, and, critically, the influence of the G20 on MENA is also limited.

Saudi Arabia's membership of G20 means that it can carry influence in the Middle East region. King Abdullah has quietly built Saudi Arabia into a major power in the region, which gives the country the opportunity to exert power in the area, by influencing policies.

The Gulf Cooperation Council (GCC) is making progress to fit in with global frameworks, with 89% of Middle East banking assets expected to be covered by Basel II by the end of 2009. The banking sector is better developed in the Middle East than elsewhere in the MENA region.

The development of regulatory institutions in the GCC has shown marked progress, as growth in the finance sector has brought with it increased awareness of the need to keep up and, indeed, be proactive. Saudi Arabia's Capital Market Authority is one example of a new regulatory authority in the region, and Qatar is seeing the streamlining of market regulators; both are examples of the development of effective bodies. The Dubai International Financial Centre has introduced a more accessible court system, working with new regulations in English, and the Dubai Financial Services Authority issued a hedge fund code of practice at the end of 2007—the first such code to be issued by a financial market regulator.

Regulators in the region are growing in size, and strengthening their links regionally and internationally, but the picture remains mixed, with some further down the line with Basel II than others. As plans for a GCC common currency and the creation of a common GCC market seem to be making some progress, the opening of markets will mean that regulators will have to work more closely to create a common approach.

Saudi Arabia has the biggest economy in the region. In 2003 it established the Capital Market Authority, which issues rules, regulations, and instructions related to the capital markets. In Qatar, the Qatar Financial Centre Regulatory Authority was set up in 2005, and in 2004 the Central Bank of Bahrain issued its *CBB Rulebook*, with updates appearing regularly ever since. The regulatory framework for banking in the UAE stipulates that banks must have fully paid-up capital of at least AED 40 million, and must place a tenth of their net annual profits in a special reserve until the fund amounts to half the capital.

Progress has undoubtedly been made, but with freer markets and greater foreign interaction, more will be required. World Trade Organization (WTO) accession initiatives and International Monetary Fund (IMF) financial sector assessment programs will bring challenges in the future. Opening the markets to foreign capital regulators will increase risks in the sector and the region.

There is little doubt that in order to promote continuing and lasting economic growth, financial sector reform and regulation should be a high priority. Studies have shown that well-developed financial systems promote efficiency and growth owing to reduced information, transaction, and monitoring costs. A study carried out by the IMF showed that MENA countries were fairly strong in financial regulation and supervision, but there are wide variations. In those countries with the most advanced financial sectors, appropriate financial regulation and supervision was found to be an important part of development of the financial sector. In other words, better financial sector regulation promotes a more healthy financial system and economy.

MORE INFO

Books:

Middle East and Arabic Countries Banking Law Handbook. 2nd ed. Washington, DC: International Business Publications, 2006.

Ross, Tim. *Financial Services Regulation in the Middle East*. 2nd ed. Oxford: Oxford University Press, 2008.

Sabri, Nidal Rashid. *Financial Markets and Institutions in the Arab Economy*. New York: Nova Science Publishers, 2008.

Article:

Gentzoglanis, Anastassios. "Financial integration, regulation and competitiveness in Middle East and North Africa countries." *Managerial Finance* 33:7 (2007): 461–476. Online at: dx.doi.org/10.1108/03074350710753744

Website:

MENA legal news from Zawya: www.zawya.com/middle-east/legal/

See Also:

✔ Key Islamic Banking Instruments and How They Work (p. 1010)
✔ Key Principles of Islamic Finance (p. 1011)
✔ An Overview of *Shariah*-Compliant Funds (p. 1083)
✔ Regulatory and Capital Issues under *Shariah* Law (p. 1050)
✔ The Role of the *Shariah* Advisory Board in Islamic Finance (p. 1015)

"Our deepest fear is not that we are inadequate. Our deepest fear is that we are powerful beyond measure."
Marianne Williamson

  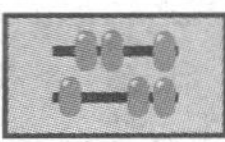      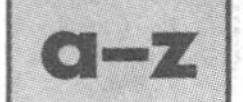

MiFID—Its Development and Aims

DEFINITION

The European Commission 's Markets in Financial Instruments Directive (MiFID, EU Directive 2004/39/EC), was implemented on November 1, 2007, replacing the Investment Services Directive, and applies to all 27 EU member states plus Iceland, Norway, and Liechtenstein. Each country must incorporate MiFID either into local law or into the rules of the local regulatory handbook, depending on how financial regulation is applied in that state.

The objective of MiFID, apart from increased harmonization, is to boost innovation and competition across the financial markets within the European Union and adjoining states, improve liquidity in the markets, and reduce costs for issuers and investors.

REGULATORY APPROACH

As the key plank of the European Commission 's Financial Services Action Plan, MiFID's 42 measures bring significant changes to how EU financial service markets operate. Whereas previous EU financial service legislation focused on "minimum harmonization and mutual recognition," MiFID's "maximum harmonization" principle places emphasis on home state supervision within a level playing field. The EU "passport" approach has been retained, but the old "concentration rule," which let member states require investment firms to route client orders through regulated markets, has been abolished.

MiFID's various articles cover almost all tradable financial products, with the exception of certain foreign exchange trades. This includes commodity and other derivatives such as freight, climate, and carbon derivatives, which were not covered by the Investment Services Directive. Any investment firm operating in Europe's financial markets is affected.

MiFID distinguishes between "investment services and activities" (core services) and "ancillary services" (non-core services). Details of these can be found in Annex 1 Sections A and B of the MiFID Level 1 Directive. A company providing core services is subject to MiFID in respect of both these and also ancillary services and can use the MiFID passport to provide them to other member states. However, a company engaged only in ancillary services is not subject to MiFID and cannot benefit from the MiFID passport.

GOOD PRACTICE

MiFID sets out various elements of good practice, such as how an investment firm should protect its customers or retain records. These apply to whatever is being traded. The following areas form the key aspects of the directive.

Authorization, Regulation, and Passporting

Companies are authorized and regulated in their "home state," typically the country in which they are registered. They can use the passport to provide services to customers in other member states.

Client Categorization and Order Handling

Companies must categorize clients as "eligible counterparties," professional clients, or retail clients (these have increasing levels of protection). Clear procedures must be in place to categorize clients and assess their suitability for each type of investment product. There are stringent requirements on the information to be collected when accepting client orders, to ensure that the company is acting in its clients' best interests, and on how orders from different clients may be aggregated. Appropriate investment advice or suggested financial transactions must be verified before being given.

Pre- and Post-Trade Transparency

Before trading, operators of continuous order-matching systems must aggregate their order information on liquid shares available at the five best price levels on the buy and sell side. The best bids and offers of market-makers must be made available for quote-driven markets. Post-trade, companies must publish the price, volume, and time of all trades in listed shares, even where conducted outside of a regulated market, unless certain requirements are met to allow for deferred publication.

Best Execution

Companies must take all reasonable steps to obtain the best possible result in the execution of a client order. This includes not just the execution price but also cost, speed, likelihood of execution, likelihood of settlement, and any other relevant factors.

Systematic Internalizers

A systematic internalizer is a company that executes orders from its clients against its own book or against orders from other clients. Under MiFID, systematic internalizers are treated as mini-exchanges and are thus subject to pre-trade and post-trade transparency requirements.

MORE INFO

Books:

Casey, Jean-Pierre, and Karel Lannoo. *The MiFID Revolution*. Cambridge, UK: Cambridge University Press, 2009.

Nelson, Paul. *Capital Markets Law and Compliance: The Implications of MiFID*. Law Practitioner Series. Cambridge, UK: Cambridge University Press, 2008.

Skinner, Chris (ed). *The Future of Investing in Europe's Markets after MiFID*. Chichester, UK: Wiley, 2007.

Websites:

European Commission on MiFID: tinyurl.com/yyulyz

MiFID resources: www.mifidirective.com

See Also:

★ Contemporary Developments in International Auditing Regulation (pp. 315–318)

✔ The EU Regulatory Regime (p. 1029)

✔ International Financial Reporting Standards (IFRS): The Basics (p. 1039)

"If you want truly to understand something, try to change it." Kurt Lewin

  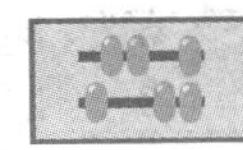      

Preparing and Executing an Internal Audit Review

DEFINITION

An internal audit review is the systematic process of analyzing a firm's business and includes planning (also called a survey or preliminary review), fieldwork, an audit report and a follow-up review. The internal audit review is conducted to assess the firm's compliance with laws and regulations, efficiency of operations (process, procedures), and progress toward key goals (including preserving and enhancing assets). The main aims of the internal audit review are to assess business operations, review progress toward business objectives, determine the reliability of financial and other operations, ensure that legal and regulatory requirements are met, identify the effectiveness of risk management activities, and deter fraud.

An internal audit review is a legal requirement for many firms, especially those which are publicly traded. Regulations such as Sarbanes–Oxley have increased the demand for internal auditors. The review is undertaken annually by appointed internal auditors. In general, an internal audit review committee is established which reports to the board of directors and the CEO. Internal auditors are hired. Currently, the internal audit profession is unregulated; however, the Institute of Internal Auditors (IIA) publishes standards and has more than 150,000 members in 165 countries.

Each firm has a unique auditing process. Auditors usually begin the planning process by gaining a detailed understanding of the firm and the objectives of the audit. Audit objectives can include: an assessment of management; verification of internal control procedures; assessment of the ability to respond to urgent market needs and events; improving risk management in the company; and assessing the skills of employees of the company and its training program.

At the fieldwork stage internal auditors examine all divisions of the firm, and across finance management, risk management, internal compliance control, and procedures and operations.

Following the fieldwork, the internal auditors prepare an initial report summarizing their findings. The draft is read by the firm's leadership (e.g. CEO, board of directors) and is then finalized.

The final step, often one year after the audit report is completed, is a follow-up review. This review involves assessing the extent to which recommendations have been implemented.

ADVANTAGES

- An internal audit helps a firm to assess the state of its business.
- Internal audit reports can lead to solid suggestions for business improvement.
- Internal auditing helps to assess risk management policies and deter fraud.

DISADVANTAGES

- Internal auditing can be an expensive process, beginning with recruiting talented internal auditors with high levels of professional experience and qualifications. A third party may provide an interim internal audit.

ACTION CHECKLIST

✔ Recruit the right individuals as internal auditors. Obtain as much information from as many sources as you can before appointing these individuals. Consider the use of a third party for an interim internal audit.

✔ Communicate your business plans and aims to auditors.

✔ Allow the auditors transparency in examining documents and speaking with key staff.

✔ Implement the suggestions made in the auditing report.

DOS AND DON'TS

DO

- Invest in internal audit technology to improve the quality of the audit process.
- Establish good communication between management and internal auditors. This helps both with the audit process and with the implementation of recommendations. Even if an internal audit review is not a requirement for your firm, consider undertaking the process to assess and improve the business.

DON'T

- Don't underestimate the need for proper training of directors and employees in order to help them to fulfill their duties.
- As directors, do not ignore the recommendations made in the final internal audit report as doing so could adversely impact your firm.

MORE INFO

Books:

Simpson, R. K. *Checklist for Developing a Specification of Internal Audit*. London: Chartered Institute of Public Finance and Accountancy, 1998.

Wade, Keith. *A Practical Approach to Internal Auditing*. Butterworth Tolley, 2004.

Articles:

Dickhart, Gary. "Risk: Key to governance." *Internal Auditor* (December 2008).

Smith, Philip. "IT skills for internal auditors." *Internal Auditor* (August 2008).

Websites:

AuditNet example of an internal audit review for a university: tinyurl.com/mwmrmt6 [via archive.org]

Chartered Institute of Internal Auditors (UK and Ireland): www.iia.org.uk

Institute of Internal Auditors (IIA): www.theiia.org

See Also:

★ Optimizing Internal Audit (pp. 382–384)

★ What Is the Range of the Internal Auditor's Work? (pp. 431–434)

✔ The Key Components of an Audit Report (p. 1042)

✔ Understanding Internal Audits (p. 1057)

"If you want truly to understand something, try to change it." Kurt Lewin

  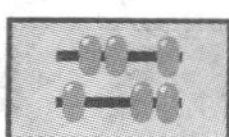      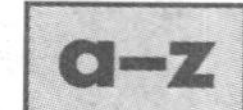

Preparing Financial Statements: Balance Sheets

DEFINITION

A balance sheet is a snapshot of a business's financial health at a specific moment in time, usually at the close of an accounting period. A balance sheet comprises assets, liabilities, and stockholders' equity/capital. Assets and liabilities are divided into short-term and long-term obligations. On a balance sheet, assets should equal liabilities plus owners' equity.

- Assets: Current assets are those that can be converted to cash in one year or less. Common current assets include cash, account receivables, inventory (products manufactured or even work in progress held for sale in the normal course of business), prepaid expenses, and investment securities. Long-term assets are assets that companies retain for an extended time, such as land, plant, and machinery. Long-term assets earn income and/or are held to manage the companies in which the investment is made. Intangible assets also come under the broad category of long-term assets. Intangible assets are those that have no physical or tangible characteristics, for example patents, trademarks, copyrights, and goodwill.
- Liabilities: Current liabilities are debts to outsiders that should be paid within one year. Some common items that fall into this category are accounts payable and accrued liabilities, such as salaries and wages that have been incurred but not yet paid. Long-term liabilities are obligations that do not have to be met within one year. These might include long-term notes, bonds, and mortgages.
- Stockholders' equity/capital: The difference between the assets and the liabilities is referred to as stockholders' equity. Equity is the amount of capital that would remain once the liabilities were satisfied.

ADVANTAGES

- A balance sheet helps managers to decide if the business is in a position to expand, if it can easily handle the normal financial ebbs and flows of revenues and expenses, or if it should take immediate steps to boost cash reserves.
- Balance sheets can identify and analyze trends, particularly in the area of receivables and payables. Is the receivables cycle lengthening? Can receivables be collected more aggressively? Is some debt un-collectable? Has the business been slowing down payables to forestall a cash shortage?

DISADVANTAGES

- A balance sheet shows a snapshot of a company's assets, liabilities and stockholders' equity at the end of the reporting period. It does not show the flows into and out of the accounts during the period.
- Some numbers depend on judgments, estimates, and interpretation. Intangible assets are factors that might be highly relevant but cannot be reliably measured.
- Financial standards are not always applied to the letter, and balance sheets may not be a true reflection of the financial position of the company.

ACTION CHECKLIST

✔ Quantify in financial terms how decisions based on the balance sheet could impact on the business.

✔ Obtain as much information as possible and compare financial ratios before committing to expensive decisions.

✔ Be prepared to be involved in a long and complicated process of analysis. Some gray areas will not be resolved by financial ratios.

DOS AND DON'TS

DO

- Involve managers and key stakeholders in the company when evaluating balance-sheet findings.
- Determine whether ratios were calculated before or after adjustments were made to the balance sheet. In many cases, these adjustments can significantly affect the ratios.

DON'T

- Don't fall into the trap of thinking that financial ratios are infallible when analyzing balance sheets using ratios; use research to confirm results.
- Don't rely on factors that cannot be reliably measured. Some numbers, such as those for intangible assets, depend on judgments, estimates, and interpretation.

MORE INFO

Websites:

HM Treasury (UK): www.hm-treasury.gov.uk
Institute of Management Accountants: www.imanet.org
US Treasury: www.treasury.gov

See Also:

★ Understanding the Requirements for Preparing IFRS Financial Statements (pp. 423–424)
✔ Assessing Business Performance (p. 1144)
✔ Understanding the Balance Sheet (p. 999)
Creating a Balance Sheet (p. 1209)
Financial Management (p. 1357)

“I set a rule that people weren't allowed to send good news unless they sent around an equal amount of bad news. We had to get a balanced picture. In fact, I kind of favored just hearing about the accounts we were losing because . . . bad news is generally more actionable than good news.” Bill Gates

        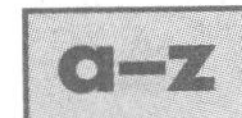

Preparing Financial Statements: Profit and Loss Accounts (P&Ls)

DEFINITION

A profit and loss account, also known as an income statement or a statement of revenue and expense, is a financial statement that indicates how revenue (money received from the sale of products and services before expenses are taken out) is transformed into net income (the result after all revenues and expenses have been accounted for). The important thing to remember about P&Ls is that they represent a period of time (usually a year or part of a year), rather than being snapshots. They should indicate to managers and investors whether a company made a profit or a loss during the period of time being reported. This contrasts with the balance sheet, which represents a single moment in time.

P&Ls can be broken into two groups: revenues and expenses. Both the revenues and expenses are recorded in the year (or other time period) that they are earned or accrued, not when the revenue is actually received or the expenses paid.

Revenues are the income the business receives in exchange for the products or services it provides. In most cases, revenues are associated with the sale of goods or services. Some of the more common sources of revenue are sales revenue, service revenue, and interest revenue.

The recorded expenses reflect the amount of resources used in earning the reported revenue. Some common examples of expenses are: salaries, research and development, bad debt, depreciation for the current year, and taxes.

For the investor, P&Ls also report earnings per share (EPS). This calculation shows how much money stockholders would receive if the company decided to distribute all of its net earnings for the period reported.

ADVANTAGES

- P&Ls should help investors and creditors to determine the past performance of the enterprise, predict future performance, and assess the enterprise's capability to generate future cash flow.
- P&Ls, along with balance sheets, are the most basic elements required by potential lenders, such as banks, investors, and vendors. Lenders will use the financial information contained in P&Ls to determine credit limits.
- P&Ls can also track dramatic increases in product returns or the cost of goods sold as a percentage of sales. They can also be used to determine income tax liability.

DISADVANTAGES

- Factors that might be highly relevant but cannot be reliably measured (for example brand recognition and customer loyalty) are not reported in P&Ls.
- Some numbers depend on the accounting methods used. The use of current costs or exit prices leaves room for manipulation. Measuring and reporting give management considerable discretion and the opportunity to influence results.
- Some numbers depend on judgments, estimates and interpretation.

ACTION CHECKLIST

✔ Use financial ratios on the P&Ls to evaluate the overall financial condition. Financial-ratio analysis will gauge viability, liabilities, and projected future performance.

✔ Carefully analyze any P&Ls for differences during the reporting period. Anomalies might be due to seasonal or other variations, or may indicate deeper problems.

✔ Consult and question managers and key business stakeholders in the evaluation process for P&Ls.

DOS AND DON'TS

DO

- Make sure that you have used the financial ratios when analyzing profit and loss accounts. If in doubt, consult an expert analyst.
- Consider seeking the help of specialist consultants.
- Check for any changes in accounting policies or anomalies that occurred during the period. Carefully examine any departures from industry norms.

DON'T

- Don't take shortcuts. Accounting can be a complicated process and remember that any undiscovered problems might cost more in the long run.
- Don't rely on accounting standards to protect you from fraud.
- Don't assume that P&Ls are a true reflection of a company's financial position. Measuring and reporting permit considerable discretion and the opportunity to influence results.

MORE INFO

Website:

American Accounting Association (AAA): aaahq.org

See Also:

✔ Preparing a Cash Flow Forecast (p. 986)
✔ Preparing Financial Statements: Balance Sheets (p. 1046)
Creating a Profit and Loss (P&L) Account (pp. 1210–1211)
Financial Management (p. 1357)

"When the facts change, I change my mind." John Maynard Keynes

  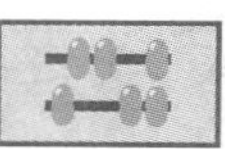   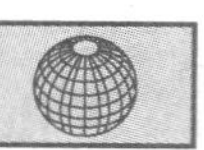   

Principles of Financial Services Regulation

DEFINITION

Financial regulations attempt to ensure that financial institutions adhere to specific requirements, restrictions, and guidelines that aim to maintain the integrity of the financial system and which may be legislated or exist as a voluntary or obligatory code of conduct.

Primarily, financial regulation should attempt to follow these three strategic principles:

1. Promote efficient, fair and orderly markets.
2. Help retail customers obtain a fair deal.
3. Improve business capability and regulatory effectiveness of the financial overseer.

A financial overseer or regulatory body usually regulates most financial services markets, exchanges, and firms in its country, setting standards that financial institutions must meet. This body can take action against companies that fail to meet those standards. For example, in the UK, the Financial Services Authority (FSA) has been the single financial services regulator since 2001. Its powers were (and are) not all encompassing, but have grown since inception. For example, mortgage business has been regulated since November 2004, and general insurance activities since January 2005.

A regulatory body typically has wide-ranging powers to make and enforce rules, and to carry out investigations in order to attain the principles of financial services regulation. The regulator will attempt to assess and monitor the risk of an activity or a firm and ascertain whether it has the potential to cause harm in one of the following areas:

- Market confidence;
- Public awareness;
- Consumers;
- Financial crime.

The regulator is charged with maintaining confidence in the financial system; maintaining and raising public understanding of the financial system; protection of consumers; preventing and/or reducing financial crime; and negating the ways in which a business could be used for financially criminal activities. A regulator's remit is broad, and as achieving one hundred percent compliance is nigh on impossible, it must prioritize its activities. Building on the three principles, a financial regulator must use its often limited resources in the most efficient and economic manner. The regulatory body typically produces regular reports on various aspects of a country's financial systems; these may result in recommendations for changes in legislation or regulations, where loopholes or faults have been shown to exist.

In terms of companies themselves, the senior management is usually responsible for the business activities and ensuring compliance with the regulations, including risk management and internal controls, such as Chinese Walls. This principle has the objective of preventing unnecessary intrusion by the regulator into the business of a firm.

Financial regulation within a country is, of course, complicated by the international overlap of financial laws and markets. Thus, each country's financial regulator must seek cooperation with those of other countries and reach joint agreement with international standards.

During the global economic turmoil of 2008, UK Prime Minister Gordon Brown appealed to world leaders to back the premise of an international supervisory body to restore order to the chaotic markets. His appeal was part of a long campaign to win support for more effective regulation of global capitalism.

Regulators must achieve all these goals while maintaining aspects of healthy competition, minimizing the cost to companies of compliance, and considering competition and innovation that can improve financial services for everyone.

MORE INFO

Books:

Hood, Christopher, Henry Rothstein, and Robert Baldwin. *The Government of Risk: Understanding Risk Regulation Regimes*. Oxford: Oxford University Press, 2004.

Mishkin, Frederic S., and Stanley G. Eakins. *Financial Markets and Institutions*. 7th ed. New York: FT Prentice Hall, 2011.

Mills, Annie. *Essential Strategies for Financial Services Compliance*. Chichester, UK: Wiley, 2008.

Websites:

Federal Financial Institutions Examination Council (FFIEC; US): www.ffiec.gov
Financial Services Authority (FSA; UK): www.fsa.gov.uk
Securities and Exchange Commission (SEC; US): www.sec.gov

See Also:

★ Why Organizations Need to be Regulated—Lessons from History (pp. 437–439)
✔ The EU Regulatory Regime (p. 1029)
✔ MiFID—Its Development and Aims (p. 1044)

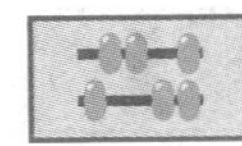

Quality Assessment of Internal Audits

DEFINITION

Most countries have established standards that aim to improve the quality of internal auditing services. In the United Kingdom, for example, HM Treasury has established the Internal Audit Quality Assessment Framework (IAQAF), a tool for evaluating the quality of the internal audit service in an organization. HM Treasury says that the IAQAF is intended to: "facilitate identification of actions for continuous improvement; facilitate evaluation of progress with improvement plans; [and] provide an approach to both internal and external quality assurance reviews which is not 'tick box' and which goes beyond compliance with the Standards alone."

Internationally, best practice as set out by the Institute of Internal Auditors (IIA) requires an independent quality assessment of the internal audit function at least once every five years. The IIA has established a program related to the quality assurance process that is known as Standard 1300. The program is designed to enable an evaluation of the internal audit activity's conformance with the Definition of Internal Auditing and the Standards, and an evaluation of whether internal auditors apply the IIA's code of ethics. There are various requirements within Standard 1300. Standard 1312, for example, requires every internal audit department to undergo an external quality assessment at least once every five years by a qualified independent reviewer from outside the organization. The IIA also offers courses which help firms to meet quality assessment standards. Studies have found that the level of use of the Standards and compliance with the Standards varies from country to country.

ADVANTAGES

- Quality assessment monitors on a continuous basis the internal audit activity of a company.
- It helps the organization to comply with the IIA's internal auditing standards and code of ethics.
- It adds value and helps to improve an organization's objectives, activities, and business.

DISADVANTAGES

- Quality assessment of internal audit involves a process within a process, and therefore extra time and expense.

ACTION CHECKLIST

✔ Keep up-to-date with the rules and regulations that govern the internal audit process.

✔ Monitor the technology that is used in internal auditing and improve it to the best of the company's ability.

✔ Employ the best consultants you can afford to evaluate your internal audit process.

✔ Establish good communications between internal auditors, the management, and the reviewers.

DOS AND DON'TS

DO

- Prepare for the quality assessment by interviewing employees, monitoring procedures, and comparing results against written policies to identify inconsistencies and opportunities for improvement.
- Ensure that employees rely on established policy and procedures rather than following their own.
- Establish processes for updating policies and procedures and develop methods to train employees when modifications require training or retraining.

DON'T

- Don't ignore the need to assess the quality of your internal audit. A badly managed internal audit can harm the business by not unearthing serious failings in procedures.
- Don't skimp on appointing the right people to review your internal audit systems and processes.

MORE INFO

Books:

Palmes, Paul C. *Process Driven Comprehensive Auditing: A New Way to Conduct ISO 9001:2008 Internal Audits*. 2nd ed. Milwaukee, WI: ASQ Quality Press, 2009.

Pastor, Joan. *Conflict Management and Negotiation Skills for Internal Auditors*. Altamonte Springs, FL: Institute of Internal Auditors Research Foundation, 2007.

Articles:

Karapetrovic, Stanislav, and Walter Willborn. "Quality assurance and effectiveness of audit systems." *International Journal of Quality and Reliability Management* 17:6 (2000): 679–703. Online at: dx.doi.org/10.1108/02656710010315256

Marais, M. "Quality assurance in internal auditing: An analysis of the standards and guidelines implemented by the Institute of Internal Auditors (IIA)." *Meditari Accountancy Research*12:2 (2004): 85–107. Online at: www.meditari.org.za/docs/2004vol2/85_107.pdf

Websites:

Chartered Institute of Internal Auditors (UK and Ireland): www.iia.org.uk

HM Treasury Internal Audit Quality Assessment Framework (IAQAF): tinyurl.com/koftqvf

Institute of Internal Auditors (IIA): www.theiia.org

See Also:

★ Optimizing Internal Audit (pp. 382–384)

✔ The Key Components of an Audit Report (p. 1042)

✔ Preparing and Executing an Internal Audit Review (p. 1045)

✔ Understanding Internal Audits (p. 1057)

"Quality control was treated as a fad here, but it's been part of the Japanese business philosophy for decades. That's why they laugh at us." Peter Senge

Regulatory and Capital Issues under *Shariah* Law

DEFINITION

Following the early development of Islamic finance in the Middle East, the growth in *shariah*-compliant financial services over the last decade has been dramatic. Local and national banks in predominately Muslim countries have sought to introduce compliant products and services to their customers. International banks also have been quick to recognize the potential in adding Islamic products to their range.

The relentless advance of *shariah*-compliant finance has generated debate on how Islamic finance should respond to developments in the international financial regulatory environment. Although at first glance amended regulatory standards and governance requirements may seem unworkable in the context of Islamic finance, in many instances, the amended standards and expectations can be easily integrated. In fact, the biggest challenge towards achieving greater compatibility between international regulatory and capital standards and Islamic finance is frequently how to change providers' attitudes to greater integration.

The Dubai Financial Services Authority provides a good example of how a new regulatory framework can be developed to be compatible with both mainstream and Islamic finance companies. Dubai, a major centre for *sukuk* investment, has created a common law-based legal system and a regulatory environment which is based on existing international structures, yet is supportive of the key aspects of Islamic finance. Given its leading position in the *sukuk* market, the Emirate also enforces high standards of disclosure and transparency.

Product and industry trade bodies have shown the value of international collaboration on regulatory progress. Given rising interest in Islamic derivative trading over recent years, the International Swaps and Derivatives Association (ISDA) has been working with the International Islamic Financial Market (IIFM) towards the goal of creating a guideline framework for the industry. The work under development is to be called the ISDA/IIFM *ta'hawwut* (hedging) master agreement and, as at January 2009, is on course to be the standard contract for international cross border Islamic derivatives transactions. However, despite the progress towards these standard contracts, the ISDA has stressed the need for individual Islamic jurisdictions to strengthen their own regulatory and legislative environments to ensure that the agreed transactions are legally enforceable. The ISDA has also highlighted that issues related to regulatory capital, and accounting policies surrounding Islamic derivatives transactions, need to be addressed by local regulators.

ADVANTAGES

- Improved regulatory and capital structures can play an important role in the ongoing success of Islamic finance.
- Increased transparency and better governance should boost the uptake of new financial products.
- Collaboration between states and organizations can result in major advances to promote the growth of Islamic finance.

DISADVANTAGES

- Conventional Western risk management often views Islamic finance as carrying very specific risks related to issues such as the lack of consistent *shariah* compatibility standards. Particular concerns have been raised over the application of the Basel II Accord/capital adequacy requirements which were originally created for mainstream Western banks, with no regard to the very specific risks faced by Islamic institutions.
- Regulatory attitudes between Western and Islamic systems can differ greatly. For example, a Western regulator may question whether a *shariah* board's role is advisory, and if it has executive powers.
- Difficulties can arise for regulators as to how to classify some Islamic financial products. For example, *musharaka* home purchase products may not be approved as a regulated mortgage product.

ACTION CHECKLIST

✔ Recognize the compatibility between many aspects of Western and Islamic systems. In other aspects, differences may not be as stark as they first appear. For example, Islamic corporate governance standards may appear weak by formal western standards, but some could argue that in practice, these are underpinned by the Islamic emphasis on integrity and sense of fair play.

✔ Appreciate that excessively tight regulatory structures could hamper the development of innovative new products.

DOS AND DON'TS

DO

- Acknowledge that improved regulatory structures can only be achieved where a supportive political backdrop for change exists.
- Consider whether Islamic product providers products could also appeal to non-Muslims.
- The increasing overlap of Western and Islamic finance could be demonstrated when a non-Muslim country eventually issues *sukuk*. Mooted for some years by the UK government, the form of any future issue could be worthy of close scrutiny as Western sovereign issuers look to tap into massive demand for *shariah*-compliant investment products.

DON'T

- Don't expect regulation to generate product innovation.
- Don't expect a true "single market" for Islamic products.

MORE INFO

Report:

Ainley, Michael, Ali Mashayekhi, Robert Hicks, Arshadur Rahman, and Ali Ravalia. "Islamic finance in the UK: Regulation and challenges." Financial Services Authority, November 2007. Online at: www.fsa.gov.uk/pubs/other/islamic_finance.pdf

Website:

Harvard Law School Islamic Finance Project: ifp.law.harvard.edu

  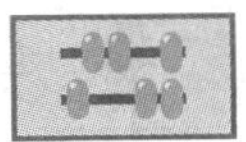      

The Role of the Audit Committee

DEFINITION

The audit committee is an operating committee that deals with financial reporting and disclosure of the financial situation of a company. Since the Sarbanes–Oxley Act of 2002, the committee's role has become essential to a company's financial wellbeing. Depending on the size of a company and whether it is private or public, the audit committee is composed of three to six members with financial, accounting, and auditing experience.

The role of an audit committee is varied. The committee reviews the internal auditors' report and makes recommendations to the board of directors based on its findings. It also reviews the chairman's statement of internal control of a company.

The audit committee performs a reporting and accounting role by overseeing external auditors, reviewing their report and management letter.

Another important role of the audit committee is to assess the risk management of a company by reporting directly to the executive board of a company on the effectiveness of the risk management arrangements and making recommendations. For this the audit committee will familiarize itself with the risk management procedures of a company, review any corporate governance statements, and assess the internal and external audit reports of the company.

Each member of the audit committee should declare any potential conflict of interest that may arise out of the business of the company. In order to be able to fulfill their role, members of the committee must have a good understanding of the company's objectives and priorities. Ideally, the members as a group should bring expertise to the audit committee in various disciplines such as finance and law and in the industry in which the company operates. They must have a clear picture of their appointment, including duration and time commitments. The members must also understand how their individual performance will be reviewed.

ADVANTAGES

- An audit committee is an oversight body that is independent of management.
- An audit committee sets standards in respect of governance, risk management, and controls.
- It performs a reporting and accounting role as well as assessing the risk management of a company.

DISADVANTAGES

- Getting the right expertise to serve on an audit committee can be difficult.
- Setting appropriate terms of reference and giving the committee sufficient authority to be effective can be problematic.
- An audit committee is another corporate overhead.

ACTION CHECKLIST

✔ An audit committee should have an independent chairman and comprise an appropriate mix of people, skills, and experience relevant to company operations. Appointees should include nonexecutive directors and independent members.

✔ The committee should have a charter (terms of reference), a code of conduct, and a register of members' interests. Institute a procedure for dealing with conflicts of interest.

✔ There should be a thorough process for appointing committee members.

✔ The full audit committee should meet regularly, with a written agenda that is distributed in advance.

✔ Agenda items should address key governance matters of the company.

✔ Written records (minutes) should be kept of audit committee meetings.

✔ Consider an evaluation process to assess the effectiveness of the audit committee.

✔ The audit committee should meet with representatives of external and internal auditors at least once a year without management being present.

✔ The audit committee should prepare an annual report for the board of directors on governance, risk management, controls, and fraud.

DOS AND DON'TS

DO

- Review the chairman's statement regarding the internal control of a company.
- Submit the internal auditors' annual report to the audit committee for their consideration.
- Review the external auditors' report and management letter.
- Implement the recommendations made by the audit committee.
- Periodically monitor reports on risks.
- Make sure that the corporate objectives of the company are mapped against risks.

DON'T

- Don't ignore the findings of the audit committee or any recommendations it may make.
- Don't make decisions solely on financial grounds that may endanger the impartiality of audit committee have regard to the reputation of the members of the audit committee and their professionalism.

MORE INFO

Books:

Ruppel, Warren. *Not-for-Profit Audit Committee Best Practices*. Hoboken, NJ: Wiley, 2006.
Verschoor, Curtis C. *Audit Committee Essentials*. Hoboken, NJ: Wiley, 2008.

Articles:

Bugalla, John, Janice Hackett, Mary Lynn McPherson, and Kristina Narvaez. "Audit committees monitor control functions, risk committees provide oversight of a strategic function." *BoardMember.com* (November 2010). Online at: tinyurl.com/cullopy
George, Nashwa. "The role of audit committees in the public sector." *CPA Journal* (August 2005). Online at: www.nysscpa.org/cpajournal/2005/805/essentials/p42.htm

See Also:

★ Managing the Relationships between Audit Committees and the CAE (pp. 375–377)
✔ The Chief Audit Executive's (CAE) Roles and Responsibilities (p. 1025)
✔ Preparing and Executing an Internal Audit Review (p. 1045)
✔ Quality Assessment of Internal Audits (p. 1049)

"Outside of traffic, there is nothing that has held this country back as much as committees." Will Rogers

Sarbanes–Oxley: Its Development and Aims

DEFINITION

The Sarbanes–Oxley Act is a US federal law that was enacted in response to several major corporate and accounting scandals, such as those affecting Enron and WorldCom, which involved large-scale internal fraud. These scandals damaged confidence in US financial markets. A variety of complex factors created the conditions and culture in which the fraudulent activities were able to flourish undetected for a number of years, including conflicts of interest and incentive compensation practices. The analysis of their complex and contentious root causes contributed to the passage of the bill in 2002. The Act was named after Senator Paul Sarbanes and Representative Michael G. Oxley. It is also known as the Public Company Accounting Reform and Investor Protection Act of 2002 and is often referred to as Sarbanes–Oxley, Sarbox, or SOX.

The act imposes high standards of accountability and transparency on the boards and management of all US publicly listed companies and public accounting firms. The legal framework established a new, quasi-public agency, the Public Company Accounting Oversight Board (PCAOB), which has responsibility for the overseeing, registration, regulation, inspection, and disciplining of accountancy companies that carry out audits of public companies.

Beside the PCAOB, Sarbox covers issues such as auditor independence, corporate governance, assessment of internal control, enhanced financial disclosure, analysts' conflicts of interest, corporate tax, and corporate fraud. There are 11 legislative sections for this purpose, known as titles, which enable the imposition of additional corporate board responsibilities as well as criminal penalties. The Securities and Exchange Commission (SEC) has the power to implement rulings on requirements to comply with Sarbanes–Oxley.

There remains much disagreement over whether Sarbox has been a useful piece of legislation. Although the Act has helped to restore public confidence in the US capital markets and has strengthened corporate accounting controls, there is also evidence to suggest that it has displaced business from the United States to the United Kingdom, where regulations for the financial sector are less overbearing. In the United Kingdom, the nonstatutory Combined Code of Corporate Governance, monitored by the Financial Services Authority, is similar to Sarbox but has a lighter touch.

As the capital markets are global, Sarbox has also affected non-US companies cross-listed in the United States. Companies based in countries with poor regulation have benefited from better credit ratings by complying with Sarbox, despite the cost. Companies in countries that have a strong regulatory regime already benefit from adequate transparency, so the cost of compliance with Sarbox is less. Either way, companies that choose to be cross-listed on other exchanges, such as the London Stock Exchange, benefit from better credit ratings anyway. Studies comparing new foreign listings on both the US and UK exchanges between 1995 and 2006 showed that Sarbox had no real impact on the listing preferences of large foreign companies for the main exchanges. However, since Sarbox was enacted there is evidence that small foreign companies choosing between Nasdaq and the London Stock Exchange's Alternative Investment Market are less likely to opt for the US listing. It is thought that this is due to the higher costs associated with compliance with Sarbox. Certainly, the Alternative Investment Market has enjoyed spectacular growth since Sarbox was enacted, and this cannot be put down to coincidence alone.

Legislation or regulation similar to Sarbanes–Oxley has been introduced in Canada, Japan, Australia, South Africa, France, Germany, and Italy, ensuring that tighter antifraud controls have been brought into play in most major markets.

MORE INFO

Books:

Anand, Sanjay. *Sarbanes–Oxley Guide for Finance and Information Technology Professionals*. 2nd ed. Hoboken, NJ: Wiley, 2006.

Bainbridge, Stephen M. *The Complete Guide to Sarbanes–Oxley: Understanding How Sarbanes–Oxley Affects Your Business*. Avon, MA: Adams Media, 2007.

Marchetti, Anne M. *Sarbanes–Oxley Ongoing Compliance Guide: Key Processes and Summary Checklists*. Hoboken, NJ: Wiley, 2007.

Website:

Guidance on Sarbanes–Oxley: www.soxlaw.com

SEC on laws that govern the securities industry: www.sec.gov/about/laws.shtml

See Also:

★ The Effect of SOX on Internal Control, Risk Management, and Corporate Governance Best Practice (pp. 333–335)

★ Has Financial Reporting Impacted on Internal Auditing Negatively? (pp. 338–340)

✔ Corporate Governance and Its Interpretations (p. 1111)

Innovation Corrupted: The Origins and Legacy of Enron's Collapse (p. 1375)

"I have come to view strong corporate governance as indispensable to resilient and vibrant capital markets. And without financial reporting premised on sound, honest numbers, capital markets will collapse upon themselves, suffocate, and die." Arthur Levitt, Jr

  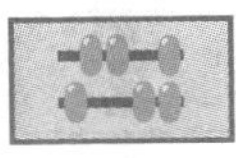   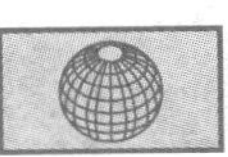   

Solvency II: Its Development and Aims

DEFINITION

Solvency II is the most up-to-date and comprehensive set of regulatory requirements for insurance companies operating within the member states of the European Union (EU). The original solvency regulations for insurers were introduced in the early 1970s and later updated under Solvency I. Since then, the principle of risk management has become an integral component of capital adequacy for insurers, and sophisticated risk management systems have been developed and implemented. The Solvency II Directive, to be introduced across the EU in 2014, replaces the existing 14 Directives and forms part of the European Commission 's Better Regulation program, which aims to simplify the regulatory environment and reduce red tape. It has been nicknamed "Basel for insurers" as it bears a number of similarities to the Basel II banking regulations.

The EU's principle of the single market drives the rationale behind Solvency II, with the aim of introducing harmonized regulations and legislation for insurance services in the member states. Currently, insurers within the EU use the "passport" system (a single license across all member states), which is based on the concept of maximum harmonization and mutual recognition. A significant number of member states have introduced national reforms where they believe that the current minimum requirements are insufficient. This has led to a patchwork of regulatory requirements across the EU, which Solvency II aims to resolve.

Solvency II is based on economic principles for the measurement of assets and liabilities. It has a very wide scope, and consists of a comprehensive risk management framework that defines the required levels of capital adequacy, outlines procedures to identify, measure and manage levels of risk, modernizes the supervisory regime, increases the international competitiveness of European insurers, extends market integration, and improves consumer protection. Insurers will have to take account of all types of risk to which they are exposed, and manage those risks more effectively. Like Basel II, the proposed Solvency II framework consists of three main pillars.

Pillar 1 consists of the quantitative requirements for increasing financial soundness. The solvency requirements for insurers will be more sophisticated, in order to guarantee that they have sufficient capital to withstand adverse events, such as acts of God or major accidents. Current EU solvency requirements only cover insurance risks; under Solvency II, insurers will have to hold capital against market risk, credit risk, and operational risk, all of which pose material threats to insurers' solvency.

Pillar 2 sets out requirements for the governance, risk management, and effective supervision of insurers. Insurers will be obliged to focus on the active identification, measurement, and management of risks, and to take into account all future developments, such as new business plans or the possibility of catastrophic events, that might affect their financial standing. Under Solvency II, insurers must use the "Own Risk and Solvency Assessment" to assess their capital needs in light of all risks. The "Supervisory Review Process" (SRP) will shift supervisors' focus from compliance monitoring and capital to evaluating insurers' risk profiles and the quality of their risk management and governance systems.

Pillar 3 focuses on disclosure and transparency requirements. Insurers will have to disclose certain information publicly. This will enforce greater market discipline, and help to ensure the stability of insurers and reinsurers. Insurance companies will also be required to report a far greater amount of information to their supervisors. Solvency II also imposes a "group supervisor" in each country that will have specific responsibilities to be exercised in close cooperation with the relevant national supervisors. The aim is to streamline supervision and ensure that groupwide risks are not overlooked. Groups should be able to operate more efficiently, while policyholders will receive a higher level of protection. Groups that are sufficiently diversified may also be allowed to reduce their capital adequacy if they meet certain conditions.

MORE INFO

Books:

Doff, Rene. *Risk Management for Insurers: Risk Control, Economic Capital and Solvency II*. London: Risk Books, 2007.

Rusalovskiy, Artem. *Challenges of Solvency II Implementation*. Saarbrücken, Germany: VDM Verlag, 2008.

Websites:

European Commission on Solvency II: tinyurl.com/2usz3wb

FSA on Solvency II: tinyurl.com/nuhngp

See Also:

★ Enterprise Risk Management and Solvency II (p. 173)

★ Solvency II—A New Regulatory Framework for the Insurance Sector (pp. 247–248)

✔ Corporate Insurance Cover: A Primer (p. 1154)

✔ The EU Regulatory Regime (p. 1029)

✔ Understanding Continuity Insurance (p. 1177)

"I have come to view strong corporate governance as indispensable to resilient and vibrant capital markets. And without financial reporting premised on sound, honest numbers, capital markets will collapse upon themselves, suffocate, and die." Arthur Levitt, Jr

  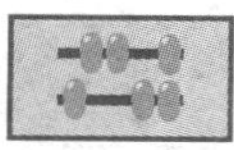      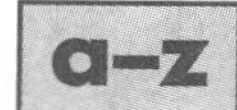

Stress Testing and Scenario Analysis for Keeping Up with Regulation

DEFINITION

Stress testing generally refers to examining how a company's finances respond to an extreme scenario. The stress-testing process is important for prudent business management, as it looks at the "what if" scenarios companies need to explore to determine their vulnerabilities. Since the early 1990s, catastrophe modeling, which is a form of scenario analysis for providing insight into the magnitude and probabilities of potential business disasters, has become increasingly sophisticated. Regulators globally are increasingly encouraging the use of stress testing to evaluate capital adequacy. As financial products, markets, and regulations become increasingly complex, the challenges for treasurers, supervisors, bankers, and regulators become ever greater in trying to keep up with the risks. Business leaders must ensure that the risk management and control framework within their businesses can keep up with changes in markets, financial instruments, business models, and regulation in order to help protect their long-term sustainability and profitability. There have been calls—likely to be heeded—for even more strengthening of regulation in areas such as off- balance sheet risk, liquidity and funding risk, and incremental trading risk.

There have also been calls for improved stress testing and scenario analysis, particularly in the wake of the 2008 banking crisis when it became clear quickly that something had gone badly wrong with the banks' stress-testing regimes. Although financial institutions monitor and forecast for various risks—operational, market, and credit, as well as sensitivity analysis —to determine how much capital they should hold, it seems that many of them ignored the risks of overextended credit in this case.

When new regulations are brought into play, financial institutions adapt themselves, but adaptation is not the only way forward. They must learn how to best use the data that they already possess to enable them to embrace regulatory change without seeing it as a burden. Although companies seek to increase reliability and profitability, and regulation can be a drain on costs, the seamless integration of risk management processes and tools—which includes stress testing and scenario analysis—should give them a competitive advantage and enable them to become more sustainable.

Ongoing business planning is dependent on accurate forecasting. Without good stress testing and scenario analysis, big corporations cannot make accurate business forecasts. One approach is to view the business from a portfolio perspective, with capital management, liquidity management, and financial performance integrated into the process. Comprehensive stress testing and scenario analysis must take into account all risk factors, including credit, market, liquidity, operational, funding, interest, foreign exchange, and trading risks. To these must be added operational risks due to inadequate systems and controls, insurance risk (including catastrophes), business risk factors (including interest rate, securitization, and residual risks), concentration risk, high-impact low-probability events, and cyclicality and capital planning.

ADVANTAGES

- Senior management needs to be involved in the development of scenarios that could affect their business and, in some cases, the economy as a whole. Accurate analysis of business strategies is critical for compliance with regulation and improving performance. When both these goals are achieved, adapting the company for regulatory compliance can be seen as an opportunity for competitive advantage.

DISADVANTAGES

- There are no real disadvantages to performing stress testing and scenario analysis. However, it can be very expensive, which may be a deterrent to using them.

ACTION CHECKLIST

✔ Include stress testing and scenario analysis in your business planning every year, or even every quarter, or more often if the situation changes enough to justify it.

✔ Investigate software options that can help predict scenario outcomes.

DOS AND DON'TS

DO

- Employ external specialists to conduct stress testing if your company is not big enough to justify an internal department for this purpose.
- Keep asking "what if?"

DON'T

- Don't ignore the need to perform these analyses.

MORE INFO

Book:

Halliman, Charles. *Business Intelligence Using Smart Techniques: Environmental Scanning Using Text Mining And Competitor Analysis Using Scenarios And Manual Simulation*. Houston, TX: Information Uncover, 2006.

Article:

de Bandt, O., C. Bruneau, and W. El Amri. "Stress testing and corporate finance." *Journal of Financial Stability*4:3 (September 2008): 258–274. Online at: dx.doi.org/10.1016/j.jfs.2008.03.001

Reports:

Brawn, David, and Alan Cathcart. "Stress testing and scenario analysis in risk management." London: Financial Services Authority. October 25, 2006.

Garcia, João. "Integrating stress tests and scenario analysis for strategic management of a financial institution." Risk Training, December 4, 2006. Online at: tinyurl.com/6ednfxw [PDF].

See Also:

★ Why Organizations Need to be Regulated—Lessons from History (pp. 437–439)
Stress Testing (p. 1255)

"I shall find a way or make one." Robert Edwin Peary

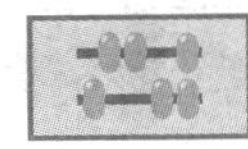

The Ten Accounting Principles

DEFINITION

The field of accounting is governed by certain general concepts. These general concepts, referred to as basic accounting principles and guidelines, are the basis for a detailed and comprehensive set of accounting rules and standards.

We can better recognize the value of Generally Accepted Accounting Principles (GAAP) if we understand the ten principles and guidelines on which they are based:

1. *Economic Entity Assumption*: For accounting purposes, a sole proprietorship and its owner are considered to be two separate entities.
2. *Monetary Unit Assumption*: For accounting purposes, economic activity is measured in US dollars.
3. *Time Period Assumption*: There is an assumption that it is possible to report the activities of a business in distinct time intervals.
4. *Cost Principle*: Cost refers to the price of a purchase when it was originally bought and, therefore, amounts on financial statements refer to historical cost.
5. *Full Disclosure Principle*: If information is vital to a lender or investor, that information should be disclosed within the financial statement or its notes.
6. *Going Concern Principle*: It is assumed that a company will continue to exist long enough to meet its objectives and obligations and that it will not shut down in the foreseeable future.
7. *Matching Principle*: This obliges companies to use the accrual basis of accounting, which requires that expenses be matched with revenues.
8. *Revenue Recognition Principle*: Under the accrual basis of accounting, revenues are recognized when a product has been sold or a service performed, regardless of when the money is actually received.
9. *Materiality*: This basic accounting principle or guideline permits an accountant to violate another accounting principle if an amount is insignificant or immaterial.
10. *Conservatism*: Where there are two acceptable alternatives for reporting an item, conservatism directs the accountant to choose the alternative that will result in less net income and/or a lower asset amount.

ADVANTAGES

- These general concepts direct the field of accounting and form the foundation on which more detailed, complicated and legalistic accounting rules are based.
- The Financial Accounting Standards Board (FASB) uses the basic accounting principles and guidelines as the starting place for its own set of accounting rules and standards, which are more detailed and comprehensive.
- If we understand the ten principles and guidelines, it is easier to comprehend GAAP.

DISADVANTAGES

- Although the basic accounting principles and guidelines form the basis for GAAP, the latter have become more complex over the years because financial transactions have become more complex and variations in reporting exist from industry to industry and from country to country.

ACTION CHECKLIST

✔ Use the ten principles and guidelines as a way to help understand the more complex GAAPs that are used in the specific enterprise, business area or country in which you are interested.

MORE INFO

Websites:

Financial Accounting Standards Board (FASB): www.fasb.org
Government Accountability Office (GAO): www.gao.gov
Principles of Accounting guide: www.principlesofaccounting.com

See Also:

✔ International Financial Reporting Standards (IFRS): The Basics (p. 1039)
✔ Key Accounting Standards and Organizations (p. 1040)
✔ Understanding the Key Components of GAAP: The Continuing Concern Concept (p. 1059)
Financial Accounting and Reporting (p. 1356)
Frank Wood's Business Accounting, Volumes 1 and 2 (p. 1363)

"We made a professional judgement about the appropriate accounting treatment that turned out to be wrong."
Joseph Berardino

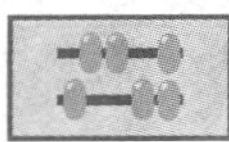

Understanding Impairment Accounting: What It Is and When It Is Used

DEFINITION

Impairment of assets is the diminishing in quality, strength, amount, or value of an asset. The term "long-lived asset" refers to such properties as a business organization's buildings, land, machinery, and equipment. These assets may be susceptible to an impairment (decline) of their value, which may be caused by factors such as poor management, new competition, and technological innovations. Impairment losses are stated in the profit-and-loss account. The impairment value is measured by comparing the value of the fixed asset or income-generating unit with its recoverable amount. The recoverable amount is the highest value that can be obtained from selling the fixed asset or income-generating unit.

As with most generally accepted accounting principles (GAAP), the definition of impairment is often in the eye of the beholder. Determining fair value has always been problematic, with different professionals arriving at different valuations. There is limited guidance as to how or when to recognize impairments, how impairments should be measured, and how impairments should be disclosed.

The impairment of assets provides investors with a way to evaluate corporate management and its decision-making track record. Investors, creditors, and financial analysts who have not kept their eye on the ball are often surprised when asset write-downs are reported.

ADVANTAGES

- Impairment charges, if applied correctly, provide investors and analysts with ways to assess company management and its decision-making track record. Managers that must write down or write off assets due to impairment have not made first-class investment choices.
- Many business failures are preceded by a decline in the impairment value of assets. Such revelations could serve as early warning signals to investors and creditors.

DISADVANTAGES

- It can be difficult to determine which measure of value should be used when assessing impairment. Options include current cost (replacement cost), current market value (selling price), net realizable value (selling price minus disposal costs), or the sum of the future net cash flows from the income-generating unit.
- There is little detailed guidance on accounting for asset impairments, when to recognize impairments, how impairments should be measured, and how impairments should be disclosed. The definition of impairment is often, therefore, just a matter of individual judgment.

ACTION CHECKLIST

✔ Study carefully the impairment of assets of any business in which you have an interest. Obtain as much information from as many different sources as possible to confirm the findings before making decisions.

✔ Check which measure of value was used when assessing impairment: Current cost (replacement cost), current market value (selling price), net realizable value (selling price minus disposal costs), or the sum of the future net cash flows from the income-generating unit.

✔ Don't take shortcuts because hidden potential write-downs may cost more in the long run.

✔ Check which GAAP are used in the specific enterprise, business area, or country in which you are interested.

DOS AND DON'TS

DO

- Make sure that you have checked the financial ratios used in the impairment analysis in detail. If in doubt, consult an expert analyst.
- Involve accountants and industry experts in your evaluation of the financial impairment of a company.
- When comparing a business's impairment valuations with other firms in an industry, allow for any material differences in accounting policies between the compared company and industry norms.

DON'T

- Don't take for granted goodwill valuations that have sometimes come from acquisitions during the "bubble" years, when companies overpaid for assets by using overpriced stock.
- Don't rely solely on ratios when making decisions. Use market research to confirm the results.
- Don't fall into the trap of thinking that financial ratios are infallible.

MORE INFO

Books:

Horngren, Charles T., Gary L. Sundem, John A. Elliott, and Donna Philbrick. *Introduction to Financial Accounting*. 10th ed. Upper Saddle River, NJ: Prentice Hall, 2010.

Nikolai, Loren A., John D. Bazley, and Jefferson P. Jones. *Intermediate Accounting*. 11th ed. Mason, OH: South-Western Cengage Learning, 2009.

Rolfe, Tom. *Financial Accounting and Tax Principles: Managerial Level*. Oxford: Butterworth-Heinemann, 2007.

Websites:

American Accounting Association (AAA): aaahq.org
Financial Accounting Standards Board (FASB): www.fasb.org
International Federation of Accountants (IFAC): www.ifac.org

See Also:

✔ Key Accounting Standards and Organizations (p. 1040)
✔ The Ten Accounting Principles (p. 1055)
✔ Understanding the Key Components of GAAP: The Continuing Concern Concept (p. 1059)

"**I just love it when people say I can't do something.**" David Andrews

  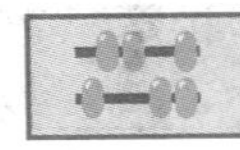      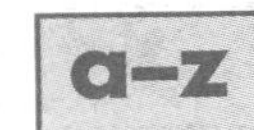

Understanding Internal Audits

DEFINITION

The Institute for Internal Auditors (IIA) defines internal auditing as "an independent, objective assurance and consulting activity designed to add value and improve an organization's operations." An internal audit "helps an organization accomplish its objectives by bringing a systematic, disciplined approach to evaluate and improve the effectiveness of risk management, control and governance processes."

The following comprise a set of guidelines for initiating an internal audit:

- Clarify guidelines and expectations with management (for example, purpose, timing, scope).
- Set up an audit committee and, with its help, develop an audit charter.
- Consider an appropriate budget and staffing model.
- Formulate reporting responsibilities for the internal audit function.
- Initiate a risk assessment, with management and audit committee involvement.
- Develop an internal audit plan in response to the risk assessment.
- Determine staffing requirements.
- Carry out the audit plan, including a monitoring and follow-up system.
- Update the risk assessment plan as circumstances change.
- Enhance and modify the audit function to meet the organization's changing needs.

If an evaluation of internal controls is to be effective, the audit function should be properly financed. When making staffing decisions, companies should look at their risk profiles. A business facing a significant number of risks or particularly complex risks will require various types of specialist expertise. A chief audit executive heads most internal audit departments, with specialist support staff.

ADVANTAGES

- Internal audits improve understanding of underlying business trends by giving independent objective financial information.
- Internal audits let managers know if a business can expand or needs to pull back, if it can deal with the normal revenue ebbs and flows, or if it should take immediate steps to boost cash reserves.
- Internal audits can identify and help to analyze trends, particularly in the areas of receivables and payables. For example, is the receivables cycle lengthening? Can receivables be collected more aggressively? Is some debt uncollectable?

DISADVANTAGES

- Results sometimes depend on the accounting methods used. Measuring and reporting give management considerable discretion and opportunity to influence results.
- Internal audits are not always rigorously carried out, and figures may not be a true reflection of the financial position of the company.
- Salaries for internal audit staff are paid for by the organization; this can lead to bias.

ACTION CHECKLIST

✔ When reviewing internal audits be prepared to be involved in a long and detailed process of analysis where some areas will need clarification by experts.

✔ Check which Generally Accepted Accounting Principles (GAAP) are used in the internal audit of the business area or country in which you have an interest.

✔ Internal audits are not infallible. If you are unsure about specific areas or numbers, don't hesitate to ask for clarification.

DOS AND DON'TS

DO

- Make sure that you take the time and effort to analyze the internal audit and, if in doubt, consult an external expert.
- Use your judgment when reviewing internal audits; numbers do not always tell the whole story.

DON'T

- Don't leave out the boring bits; number crunching is not always effortless or interesting, and often it is tempting to skip parts. Sometimes, however, the truth lies in the detail.

MORE INFO

Websites:

HM Treasury (UK): www.hm-treasury.gov.uk
Institute of Internal Auditors (IIA): www.theiia.org
US Treasury: www.treasury.gov

See Also:

★ Aligning the Internal Audit Function with Strategic Objectives (pp. 280–282)
★ Contemporary Developments in International Auditing Regulation (pp. 315–318)
★ Starting a Successful Internal Audit Function to Meet Present and Future Demands (pp. 407–410)
✔ Internal Audit Charters (p. 1033)
✔ The Key Components of an Audit Report (p. 1042)

     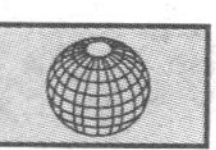   

Understanding the Internal Capital Adequacy Assessment Process (ICAAP)

DEFINITION

Under Basel II, ICAAP is a new requirement for financial institutions, requiring the following assessments:

- Pillar I minimum capital requirements;
- the extent of total stockholder funds required to meet a firm's strategy and maintain minimum capital requirements;
- ensuring that material risks of the firm are understood by its board, and that there is sufficient and appropriate risk management.

Four crucial elements in any ICAAP are:

1. assessment (identification and measurement) of the risks a bank is, or may be, exposed to;
2. application of mitigation techniques that may help to lower capital requirements;
3. stress-testing techniques;
4. role of the board of directors and management.

Pillar II requires that risks are presented to, and discussed by, the board to ensure its acceptance and understanding. Pillar II also requires a bank to maintain capital ratios and convince the regulator. Risk models and capital are only part of this. A financial institution must also consider any other internal risks that the firm may face which may result in losses such as fraud, rogue trading, or strategy failure.

The preparation of a capital plan should incorporate all risks, and requires the cooperation of, and collaboration with, the finance, treasury, business, and risk departments. Capital plans are usually based on a firm's forecasts for growth, given the maintenance of a capital ratio.

The ICAAP should be customized for each firm, taking into account the particular risks and information available. The process usually consists of the following stages:

1. Identifying risks—List all material risks, interview staff in relevant departments, and assess the probability of risks occurring.
2. Assessing capital—How much capital would a risk require?
3. Forward capital planning—Assess how the capital calculated from the capital assessment might be altered by its business plan, i.e. perform stress and scenario analyses.
4. Conclusion—What are the ranges of capital identified, and how much internal capital should a firm hold?

Managers should also consider the following risks:

- credit risk;
- market risk;
- operational risk;
- liquidity risk;
- insurance risk;
- concentration risk;
- residual risk;
- securitization risk;
- business risk;
- interest rate risk;
- pension obligation risk;
- any other risks identified.

The ICAAP typically has the following structure:

1. executive summary;
2. background of the ICAAP process;
3. statement of firm's attitude to risk;
4. business strategy;
5. risk assessment;
6. capital planning;
7. stress and scenario testing;
8. adoption of the ICAAP.

Banks tend to calculate the capital buffer they hold by simply extrapolating figures from previous events, instead of using a forecast risk profile. The ICAAP should clearly distinguish between a company's regulatory capital, its actual capital, and the capital it needs to hold for business purposes. Using a newly developed ICAAP should provide firms with the best capital buffer required, and the best level of funds from stockholders. Risks are often considered by a bank, yet are not always reflected in strategic options and capital planning. ICAAP requires stress and scenario analysis to demonstrate risks at an enterprise level.

Firm managers must show that ICAAP is an integral part of its processes and demonstrate that senior management both supports and is engaged in the ICAAP. In addition, companies need to explain in detail how they will use the ICAAP as they move forward and how key risk indicators and economic capital indicators/assumptions can be updated and presented to the board of directors when required. ICAAP is still in its early stages—companies are being encouraged to embrace the process for the sake of their business rather than for purposes of regulation. Management should understand the positive benefits and strive, through ICAAP, to make the business more efficient and less risky.

MORE INFO

Website:

Financial Services Authority on ICAAP submission: tinyurl.com/3dc76ux

See Also:

★ Why Organizations Need to be Regulated—Lessons from History (pp. 437–439)
✔ The EU Regulatory Regime (p. 1029)
✔ Principles of Financial Services Regulation (p. 1048)

"You have to put in many, many, many tiny efforts that nobody sees or appreciates before you achieve anything worthwhile." Brian Tracy

  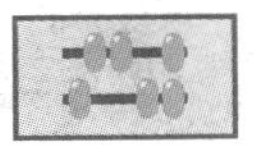   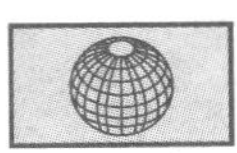   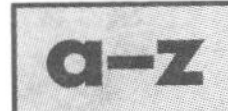

Understanding the Key Components of GAAP: The Continuing Concern Concept

DEFINITION

Generally Accepted Accounting Principles (GAAP) are not a fixed set of rules. They are guidelines or a group of objectives and concepts that have evolved on the best way to govern how financial statements are prepared and presented.

The guidelines are as follows:

- The *business entity concept* provides that the balance sheet of the business must reflect the financial position of the business alone.
- The *continuing concern concept* assumes that a business will continue to operate, unless it is known otherwise.
- The *principle of conservatism* provides that accounting for a business should be fair and that evaluations and estimates should be reasonable.
- The *objectivity principle* states that accounting will be recorded on the basis of objective evidence—that accounting entries will be based on fact and not on personal opinion or feelings.
- The *time period concept* provides that accounting takes place over specific fiscal periods of equal length.
- The *revenue recognition convention* provides that revenues are recognized at the time the transaction is completed.
- The *matching principle* states that each expense item related to revenue earned must be recorded in the same accounting period as the revenue it helped to earn.
- The *cost principle* states that accounting for purchases must be at their cost price.
- The *consistency principle* requires accountants to apply the same methods and procedures from period to period, because the readers of financial statements have the right to assume that consistency has been applied if there is no statement to the contrary.
- The *materiality principle* requires accountants to use GAAP except when to do so would be expensive or difficult, and where it makes no real difference if the rules are ignored.
- The *full disclosure principle* states that any and all information that affects the full understanding of a company's financial statements must be included with the financial statements.

GAAP compliance is vital. It helps businesses to maintain their creditability with creditors and shareholders because the principles reassure the public that a company's financial reports accurately portray its financial position.

Note that Generally Accepted Accounting Principles are known in the United Kingdom as Generally Accepted Accounting Practice.

ADVANTAGES

- These are general rules and concepts that direct the field of accounting and form the foundation on which more detailed, complicated, and legalistic accounting rules are based.
- The Financial Accounting Standards Board (FASB) uses the basic GAAP accounting principles and guidelines as the starting place for its own, more detailed and comprehensive set of accounting rules and standards.

DISADVANTAGES

- GAAP compliance poses challenges to small businesses with limited resources.
- GAAP are not strict rules. They are only guidelines or a group of objectives and concepts that have evolved on the best way to govern how financial statements are prepared and presented.
- Measuring and reporting give management considerable discretion and the opportunity to influence results. Those results sometimes depend on the accounting methods used.

ACTION CHECKLIST

✔ When reviewing audits based on GAAP, be prepared to be involved in a long and detailed analysis. Some areas will need clarification by experts.

✔ Check which GAAP are used in the internal audit of the business in which you are interested.

✔ GAAP is not infallible. If you are unsure about specific areas or numbers, ask for clarification.

✔ Don't be frightened to ask what may seem naïve or uncomfortable questions.

✔ Use the GAAP concepts and guidelines as a basis to help you understand the more complex accounting practices that are used in the specific enterprise, business area, or country in which you are interested.

DOS AND DON'TS

DO

- Make sure that you take the time and make the effort to analyze the accounts. If in doubt, consult an independent expert.

DON'T

- Don't skip the boring bits; accounting is not always simple or interesting, and often it is easier to skip parts. However, sometimes the truth lies in the detail.

MORE INFO

Books:

Bragg, Steven M. *Wiley GAAP 2012: Interpretation and Application of Generally Accepted Accounting Principles*. Hoboken, NJ: Wiley, 2011.

Epstein, Barry J., and Nadira M. Saafir. *Wiley GAAP: Practical Implementation Guide and Workbook*. Hoboken, NJ: Wiley, 2011.

PricewaterhouseCoopers. *Manual of Accounting: UK GAAP 2012*. Haywards Heath, UK: Bloomsbury Professional, 2011.

Websites:

Federal Accounting Standards Advisory Board (FASAB) Generally Accepted Accounting Principles: tinyurl.com/45xo9n6

International Accounting Standards Board (IASB): www.iasb.org

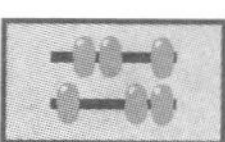

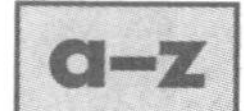

What Is Forensic Auditing?

DEFINITION

Forensic auditing is a blend of traditional accounting, auditing, and financial detective work. Technology has an increasingly important role to play, with complex data analysis techniques employed to help flag areas that warrant further investigation.

Forensic auditing offers a toolset that company managers can use to help detect and investigate various forms of white-collar financial impropriety and inappropriate or inefficient use of resources. As company structures and controls become ever more complex, so too does the scope for employees with specialized knowledge of the way control systems work to bypass them. In the past, various forms of auditing have been employed after a major control breach has come to light, but executives are now increasingly looking at forensic auditing to help identify vulnerabilities in financial control.

ADVANTAGES

- Forensic auditing strengthens control mechanisms, with the objective of protecting the business against financial crimes, be they potentially catastrophic one-off events that could threaten the viability of the business, or smaller-scale but repetitive misappropriations of company assets over a number of years.
- Forensic auditing can play an important role for companies under review by regulatory authorities and can also be invaluable to ensure regulatory compliance. For example, forensic auditing can be useful in helping companies to ensure that their anti-money laundering procedures are both effective and robust.
- Forensic auditing can help protect organizations from the long-term damage to reputation caused by the publicity associated with insider crimes. A forensic audit also provides a sound base of factual information that can be used to help resolve disputes, and can be used in court should the victim seek legal redress.
- Forensic auditing can improve efficiency by identifying areas of waste.
- Forensic auditing can help with the detection and recording of potential conflicts of interest for executives by improving transparency and probity in the way resources are used, in both private and public entities.

DISADVANTAGES

- A poorly managed forensic audit could consume excessive management time and could become an unwelcome distraction for the business.
- Forensic audits can have wide-ranging scope across the business. Under certain circumstances, the scope of the audit may need to be extended, with an increase in its budget.
- Some employees can interpret a proactive forensic audit as a slight on their integrity, rather than as a means to improve control procedures for the benefit of the business.

ACTION CHECKLIST

✔ Understand your risks, routes to their potential exploitation, and the tools available to detect abuses, fraud, or wastage.

✔ Analyze numerical data, comparing actual costs against expected costs.

✔ Investigate possible reasons for inconsistencies.

✔ Consider whether covert detection techniques might be more appropriate when investigating cases of possible fraud. Higher-profile full forensic audits can deter future fraud but could also reduce the likelihood of witnessing the culprit carrying out a fraudulent act.

✔ External auditing specialists with extensive experience of complex forensic audits can offer industry-specific experience, auditing management expertise, and advanced interviewing techniques. A combination of these external specialists and companies' internal accountants/auditors can achieve shorter audit timescales and lower levels of disruption to the business.

DOS AND DON'TS

DO

- Remember that well-resourced forensic auditing processes can help to identify misreporting at many levels of an organization.
- Bear in mind that regular proactive forensic audits can help businesses to ensure that their processes stay robust.
- Be prepared to widen the scope of a forensic audit to ensure maximum effectiveness.
- See forensic auditing as a continuous process, rather than a one-off event. On completing one audit, restarting the process could uncover something that was previously overlooked.
- Be prepared to share the findings of the forensic audit with other areas of your company, and take into account industry best practice to improve efficiency and combat fraud.

DON'T

- Don't lose sight of the objective of a forensic audit. The cost can be high, but the potential cost of not undertaking an audit and implementing its findings can be even higher.
- Don't fall into the trap of overlooking the importance of the "forensic" element of the audit. With the results of such a process deemed suitable for inclusion in legal proceedings, the high potential costs of the forensic audit process could easily be recovered from dispute resolution or higher levels of loss recovery.

MORE INFO

Book:

Cardwell, Harvey. *Principles of Audit Surveillance*. Reprise ed. Philadelphia, PA: RT Edwards, 2005.

Article:

Brannen, Laurie. "Top of mind: Is a forensic audit in your future?" *Business Finance* (June 2007). Online at: tinyurl.com/6aunj87

Website:

Institute of Forensic Accounting and Investigative Audit (IFAIA): www.ifaia.org

See Also:

★ Fraud: Minimizing the Impact on Corporate Image (pp. 856–858)
★ How Internal Auditing Can Help with a Company's Fraud Issues (pp. 346–350)
✔ Internal Auditing for Fraud Detection and Prevention (p. 1035)

"**When you consider something ideal, you lose the opportunity to improve it.**" Shoji Shiba

  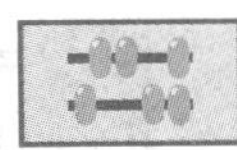      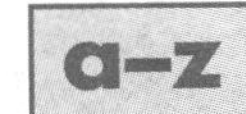

XBRL (eXtensible Business Reporting Language) and Internal Auditing

DEFINITION

XBRL (eXtensible Business Reporting Language) is a computer language for the electronic transmission of business and financial data. The goal of XBRL is to standardize the automation of business intelligence and thus create a global standard for sharing business information. XBRL uses tags to describe and identify each item of data in an electronic document. The tags allow computer programs to sort through data and analyze relationships quickly and generate output in various formats. Because the tags are standardized, analysis can be conducted across multiple documents from multiple sources, even if the text in the documents is written in different languages.

XBRL provides major benefits in the preparation, analysis, and communication of business information, and at a reduced cost. It provides standardized controls that can result in improved efficiency and effectiveness of audits. Filing financial statements in XBRL format has become a regulatory mandate for many companies in the world. In the United States, for example, the Securities and Exchange Commission ruled that as of June 2009 all public companies with more than US$5 billion in assets must report financials using XBRL. It is thus important that management and internal auditors understand the value it brings throughout the entire compliance and reporting process.

ADVANTAGES

- XBRL helps internal auditors by facilitating the migration from manual to automated processes in key activities.
- XBRL gives auditors the ability to more efficiently access and integrate data across an organization.
- XBRL allows the abstraction of business rules and controls that can be applied across a wide range of software applications.

DISADVANTAGES

- If inexperienced users create data for transmission, XBRL's complexity increases the opportunity for errors.
- Outsourcing the implementation of XBRL, as is done by many organizations, leads to increased costs. This undermines one of the main advantages of XBRL, which is to cut costs.

ACTION CHECKLIST

- ✔ Examine whether it is best to instruct your accountant, your auditor, or a specialist provider to convert your accounts to XBRL. Cost is clearly an important consideration, but the timescale may also be an issue.
- ✔ Send your report to third parties in Word or Excel format rather than as a PDF to make it easier for them to convert it to XBRL.

DOS AND DON'TS

DO

- Discuss XBRL with your audit advisers before purchasing any Word/Excel-based tagging solutions.
- Be aware that the initial setting up of XBRL can be costly. Unless a company has an automated tagging process, tagging XBRL data consumes hours of labor.
- Investigate all the numerous software products on the market for converting accounting reports to XBRL to find the one most suited to your organization.

DON'T

- Don't forget that XBRL data remain available at all times and thus require greater security to maintain their integrity.

MORE INFO

Books:

Coderre, David. *Internal Audit: Efficiency through Automation*. Hoboken, NJ: Wiley, 2009.
Deshmukh, Ashutosh. *Digital Accounting: The Effects of the Internet and ERP on Accounting*. Hershey, PA: IRM Press, 2006.
Hoffman, Charles, and Liv Apneseth Watson. *XBRL for Dummies*. Hoboken, NJ: Wiley, 2009.

Websites:

Chartered Institute of Internal Auditors (UK and Ireland): www.iia.org.uk
Institute of Internal Auditors (IIA): www.theiia.org
International Accounting Standards Board/International Financial Reporting Standards (IASB/IFRS) on XRBL: www.ifrs.org/xbrl/xbrl.htm
XBRL International: www.xbrl.org
XBRL UK: www.xbrl.org.uk

See Also:

✔ International Financial Reporting Standards (IFRS): The Basics (p. 1039)

"We live in a society exquisitely dependent on science and technology, in which hardly anyone knows anything about science and technology." Carl Sagan

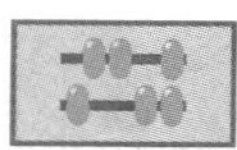

Analysis Using Monte Carlo Simulation

DEFINITION

The Monte Carlo method of simulation uses repeated random sampling to obtain results and is generally used for simulating physical and mathematical systems. It is best suited to calculations using a computer, due to the reliance on repetitive computations and its use of random (or pseudo-random) numbers. It is most often used when it is not possible to reach an exact result using a deterministic algorithm. Monte Carlo simulation is useful for modeling situations that have a good deal of uncertainty in the inputs, and this includes calculations of risks in business.

There is no single Monte Carlo method—the term covers a wide range of approaches to simulation. However, these approaches use a certain pattern in which:

1. A domain of possible inputs is defined;
2. Inputs are randomly generated from the domain;
3. Using the inputs, a deterministic computation is performed;
4. The results are aggregated from the individual computations to give a final result.

Monte Carlo simulation randomly samples inputs to produce many thousands of possible outcomes, rather than a few discrete scenarios as produced, for example, by deterministic modeling using single-point estimates. Monte Carlo results also give probabilities for different outcomes. Lay decision-makers can use Monte Carlo to determine confidence levels for a graphical representation.

In finance, Monte Carlo methods are used in the following areas:

- By financial analysts in corporate finance, project finance, and real option analysis to construct probabilistic financial models.
- To generate many possible price paths to value options on equity.
- To value bonds and bond options.
- To evaluate a portfolio.
- In personal finance planning.

Monte Carlo methods are flexible and can take many sources of uncertainty, but they may not always be appropriate. In general, the method is preferable only if there are several sources of uncertainty.

ADVANTAGES

- Using Monte Carlo simulation is quite straightforward.
- It can provide statistical sampling for numerical experiments using a computer.
- In optimization problems, Monte Carlo simulation can often reach the optimum and overcome local extremes.
- It provides approximate solutions to many mathematical problems.
- Monte Carlo analysis produces a narrower range of results than a "what if" analysis.

DISADVANTAGES

- Monte Carlo simulation is not universally accepted in simulating a system that is not in equilibrium (i.e. in a transient state).
- A large number of samples is required to reach the desired results. This can be time-consuming compared to using a spreadsheet program, such as Excel, which can generate a simple calculation fairly quickly.
- A single sample cannot be used in simulation; to obtain results there must be many samples.
- The results are only an approximation of the true value.
- Simulation results can show large variance.

ACTION CHECKLIST

✔ Consider the problem. Does it have many sources of uncertainty?

✔ Is there an analytical solution? If so, use that.

✔ Choose the software you will use for Monte Carlo simulation.

✔ Decide on the inputs and generate the results.

DOS AND DON'TS

DO

- Use Monte Carlo simulation where an analytical solution either does not exist or is too complicated.
- Use it where there are lots of uncertainties.

DON'T

- Don't use Monte Carlo simulations that might require months or years of computer time—it is not worth it.
- Don't use Monte Carlo simulations where an analytical solution exists and is simple. In this case it is easier to use the analytical solution to solve the problem.

MORE INFO

Books:

Fishman, George S. *Monte Carlo: Concepts, Algorithms, and Applications*. New York: Springer, 2003.

McLeish, Don L. *Monte Carlo Simulation and Finance*. Hoboken, NJ: Wiley, 2005.

Mooney, Christopher Z. *Monte Carlo Simulation*. Thousand Oaks, CA: Sage Publications, 1997.

Website:

Monte Carlo simulation basics from Vertex42: tinyurl.com/2l9qzf

See Also:

★ Asset Allocation Methodologies (pp. 454–458)
★ Using Decision Analysis to Value R&D Projects (pp. 945–948)
Stochastic Modeling (pp. 1254–1255)
Stress Testing (p. 1255)
Value at Risk (p. 1260)

"Make your company stock a consumer product. When consumers buy stock in your company, they'll never buy a competitive product. You've linked their Financial Future to yours." Faith Popcorn

  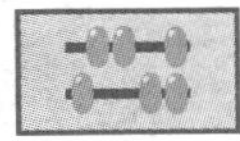      

Applying the Gordon Growth Model

DEFINITION

The Gordon growth model is a tool that is commonly used to value stocks. Originally developed by Professor Myron Gordon and also known as Gordon's growth model, the aim of the method is to value a stock or company in today's terms, using discounted cash flows to take into account the present value of future dividends.

The model requires three inputs:

- *D*: The expected level of the stock's dividend one year ahead
- *R*: The rate of return the investor is seeking
- *G*: The assumed constant rate of future dividend growth in perpetuity.

The formula is as follows:

$$\text{Gordon growth stock valuation per share} = D \div R - G$$

ADVANTAGES

- The main strength of the Gordon growth model is that the valuation calculation is easily performed using readily available or easily estimated inputs.
- The model is particularly useful among companies or industries where cash flows are typically strong and relatively stable, and where leverage patterns are also generally consistent.
- The model is widely used to provide guideline fair values in mature industries such as financial services and in large-scale real-estate ventures. The model can be particularly appropriate in the valuation of real-estate investment trusts, given the high proportion of income paid out in dividends and the trusts' strictly defined investment policies.

DISADVANTAGES

- Although the model's simplicity can be regarded as one of its major strengths, in another sense this is its major drawback, as the purely quantitative model takes no account of qualitative factors such as industry trends or management strategy. For example, even in a highly cash-generative company, near-future dividend payouts could be capped by management's strategy of retaining cash to fund a likely future investment. The simplicity of the model affords no flexibility to take into account projected changes in the rate of future dividend growth.
- The calculation relies on the assumption that future dividends will grow at a constant rate in perpetuity, taking no account of the possibility that rapid near-term growth could be offset by slower growth further into the future. This limitation makes the Gordon growth model less suitable for use in rapidly growing industries with less predictable dividend patterns, such as software or mobile telecommunications. Its use is typically more appropriate in relatively mature industries or stock-market indices where companies demonstrate more stable and predictable dividend growth patterns.

ACTION CHECKLIST

✔ The Gordon growth model is generally more effective among companies and industries where dividend payments tend to be high—ideally, close to free cash flow to equity (FCFE). FCFE is a measure of how much cash a company can afford to pay out to shareholders after allowing for factors such as debt repayments and various expenses. Consider whether the entity to be valued exhibits such high dividend payments before making use of the model.

✔ Take into account other company-specific factors before applying the model to particular stocks. For example, consider how changes to the regulatory environment could affect a company's prospects.

✔ In the case of individual company valuations, consider whether a shift in the management's geographical horizon or major investment programs could affect cash flow and future dividend patterns. Remember that the Gordon growth model does not take into account possible fluctuations in future dividend growth rates.

DOS AND DON'TS

DO

- Understand the underlying characteristics of the company, industry, or market index before deciding whether to use this model.
- If appropriate, use the model for easily calculated outline valuations.
- Consider the benefits of using other valuation tools in conjunction with or as alternatives to the Gordon growth model.

DON'T

- Don't use the model for companies, industries, or market indices where growth rates are rapid or leverage is subject to sudden swings.
- Don't make the mistake of blindly applying the model to companies in isolation.
- Don't totally ignore nonquantitative factors that could have a major bearing on future valuations.

MORE INFO

Books:

Gordon, Myron J. *The Investment, Financing, and Valuation of the Corporation*. Westport, CT: Greenwood Press, 1982.

Hitchner, James R. *Financial Valuation: Applications and Models*. 3rd ed. Hoboken, NJ: Wiley, 2011.

Articles:

Jackson, Marcus. "The Gordon growth model and the income approach to value." *Appraisal Journal* 62:1 (Spring 1994): 124–128.

Kiley, Michael T. "Stock prices and fundamentals: A macroeconomic perspective." *Journal of Business* 77:4 (October 2004): 909–936. Online at: dx.doi.org/10.1086/422629

Website:

Myron J. Gordon's homepage: www.rotman.utoronto.ca/~gordon

See Also:

✔ Using Dividend Discount Models (p. 1104)
✔ Using Multistage Dividend Discount Models (p. 1106)
Discounted Cash Flow (pp. 1217–1218)
Damodaran on Valuation: Security Analysis for Investment and Corporate Finance (p. 1348)

"People who are making decisions about the future often don't have access to some of the best ideas in the company, which may be at the periphery or at lower levels." Rosabeth Moss Kanter

The Bond Market: Its Structure and Function

DEFINITION

The bond market is the market for debt securities in the form of bonds where buyers and sellers determine their prices and therefore their accompanying interest rates. It is also known as the fixed-income or debit or credit market.

In purchasing a bond you are effectively lending money to a government, corporation, or municipality, known as the issuer, which agrees to pay you a certain rate of interest during the lifetime of the bond and repay its principal or face value when it matures or becomes due.

The international bond market is estimated to have a size of almost US$47 trillion. The US bond market is the largest in the world, with an outstanding debt of more than US$25 trillion. In 2007, the volume of trade in the US bond market was US$923 billion.

Since 2000, the international bond market has doubled in size as a result of the activity of big multinational companies. According to the International Capital Market Association, about US$10 trillion worth of bonds were outstanding in 2007.

The individual government bond markets have a high level of liquidity and considerable size—these are included in the international bond market. They are noted for their low credit risk and are unaffected by interest rates.

Trading generally takes place over the counter (known as OTC) between broker dealers and big institutions. The stock exchanges list a small number of bonds too.

The largest centralized bond market is the New York Stock Exchange (NYSE), which mainly represents corporate bonds. In contrast to this, most governments have bond markets that lack centralization, mostly due to the fact that bond issues vary widely and there is a large choice of different securities by comparison.

Most outstanding bonds are in the hands of institutions: pension funds, mutual funds, and banks. This is because individual bond issues are so specific and a large number of smaller issues lack liquidity.

The volatility of the bond market is in direct proportion to the monetary and economic policy of the country of the participant.

The main difference between corporate and government bonds is that the latter are guaranteed and thus carry a low risk of investment, albeit at a lower rate of return. Corporate bonds generally offer a higher rate of return on investment, but carry more risk—if the company fails, the bondholder risks losing their investment.

ADVANTAGES

- It is considered a wise move to invest in bonds as part of a considered diversified investment portfolio that also consists of stocks and cash. They are considered to be a relatively safe investment for increasing capital and receiving a reliable interest income. The principal and interest are set at the time the bond is purchased. If the owner collects the coupon and holds it to maturity, the market is irrelevant to final payout. As a long-term investment, bonds may be considered a wise choice—bearing in mind the disadvantages.

DISADVANTAGES

- Bonds are not advisable for short-term savings for the individual participant in the market.
- Long-term commitment is essential as the participant who cashes in before maturity is open to the risk of fluctuations in interest rates. Whenever there is an increase in interest rates, there is a corresponding decrease in the value of existing bonds. Conversely, a decrease in interest rates will correspond to a rise in the value of existing bonds. This is due to the fact that new issues pay out a lower yield. The basic concept of bond market volatility is that the value of bonds and changes in interest rates run inversely to each other.
- When interest rates drop, investors have to reinvest their interest income and return of principal at lower rates.
- The final purchasing power of an investment in bonds is reduced by a corresponding increase in inflation, which also results in higher interest rates and correspondingly lower bond prices.
- If there is a decline in the bond market as a whole, individual securities also fall in value.
- Timing is crucial: a security may in the future unexpectedly underperform relative to the market.
- A bond may perform poorly after purchase, or it may improve after you sell it.
- Corporate bonds have relatively low liquidity compared with government bonds, which usually have a short lock-in period (i.e. they can be cashed in quickly).

ACTION CHECKLIST

✔ Make sure that you can afford to invest in long-term savings before you commit yourself to taking out bonds.

✔ Have another form of savings as an emergency fund in case you meet with an unexpected financial problem in the future.

✔ Read all the available literature and take advice from an impartial financial consultant before making a final commitment.

DOS AND DON'TS

DO

- Be sure to choose a security that is approved by a financial expert.

DON'T

- Don't rush into a transaction or pay over the odds for it.

MORE INFO

Books:

Adams, Tom. *Savings Bond Advisor: How U.S. Savings Bonds Really Work—With Investment, Tax, and Estate Strategies*. 5th ed. New York: Alert Media, 2007.

Pederson, Daniel J. *Savings Bonds: When to Hold, When to Fold and Everything In-Between*. 4th ed. Detroit, MI: TSBI Publishing, 1999.

See Also:

✔ Raising Capital by Issuing Bonds (p. 1086)
✔ Trading in Corporate Bonds: Why and How (p. 1094)
✔ Trading in Government Bonds: Why and How (p. 1096)
Bond Yield (pp. 1197–1198)
Current Price of a Bond (p. 1212)

"If it is virtually impossible to make worthwhile predictions about the price movement of stocks, it is completely impossible to do so for bonds." Benjamin Graham

Calculating a Company's Net Worth

DEFINITION

The net worth of a company (sometimes referred to as its net assets) is measured by subtracting the total assets of the company from its total liabilities. Thus, net worth represents the liquidation proceeds a company would fetch if its operations were to cease immediately and the firm were sold off. For example, if a company has total assets of US$80 million and total liabilities of US$40 million, its net worth would amount to US$40 million. In this example, the company might own a factory worth US$40 million, machinery valued at US$20 million, and a fleet of vans valued at a further US$20 million. Its liabilities might consist of a loan of US$40 million used to fund the purchase of the machinery and vans. The net worth of a company is also known as the shareholders' equity.

Net worth can be easily identified by referring to the company's balance sheet, which will detail its total assets and liabilities, as well as its net worth. Of course, the balance sheet does not necessarily reflect the current market value of a firm but simply expresses the value at a particular point in time, i.e. when the balance sheet was drawn up. It is also important to remember that net worth does not take any account of how profitable the company is. It may be worth more or less if sold as a going concern.

ADVANTAGES

- It is easy to find out the net worth of a company—simply refer to its latest balance sheet.
- Net worth provides a simple and straightforward way of measuring a company's breakup value if it were to cease trading.

DISADVANTAGES

- The balance sheet does not necessarily reflect the current market value of a firm but simply expresses the value at a particular point in time, i.e. when the balance sheet was drawn up.
- It is also worth remembering that a company may have a different value if it is sold as a going concern. Net worth may underestimate or overestimate the true value of a company by a considerable extent. It does not take into account intangible assets such as goodwill, copyright, patents, and intellectual property. It also ignores how much revenue and profit (or loss) a company is generating.

ACTION CHECKLIST

✔ Obtain the company's net worth from its latest balance sheet.

✔ Obtain as much other financial information as possible, including figures for revenue and profit (or loss).

✔ Look at other indicators, such as the firm's order book, and try to assess nonfinancial factors such as goodwill and the competitiveness of the company's goods and services.

DOS AND DON'TS

DO

- Obtain an estimate of the intangible assets of a company, such as intellectual property.
- Look at other measures of corporate health, such as revenues, costs, and profits (or losses), as well as forward indicators such as order books.
- Try to obtain estimates of the current value of the company's assets and liabilities, rather than rely on figures from the balance sheets, which may be considerably out of date in volatile market conditions.

DON'T

- Don't assume that net worth provides an accurate guide to the current value of a company.

MORE INFO

Books:

Baker, H. Kent, and Gary E. Powell. *Understanding Financial Management: A Practical Guide*. Malden, MA: Blackwell Publishing, 2005.

Bandler, James. *How to Use Financial Statements: A Guide to Understanding the Numbers*. Burr Ridge, IL: Irwin, 1994.

Dickie, Robert B. *Financial Statement Analysis and Business Valuation for the Practical Lawyer*. 2nd ed. Chicago, IL: American Bar Association, 2006.

Articles:

Cummins, Jason G., Kevin A. Hassett, and Stephen D. Oliner. "Investment behavior, observable expectations, and internal funds." *American Economic Review* 96:3 (June 2006): 796–810. Online at: dx.doi.org/10.1257/aer.96.3.796

Halliwell, Leigh J. "ROE, utility, and the pricing of risk." *CAS Forum* (Spring 1999). Online at: www.casact.org/pubs/forum/99spforum/99spf071.pdf

Huberman, Gur. "Familiarity breeds investment." *Review of Financial Studies* 14:3 (Fall 2001): 659–680. Online at: dx.doi.org/10.1093/rfs/14.3.659

See Also:

★ Maximizing Value when Selling a Business (pp. 751–753)
✔ Estimating Enterprise Value with the Weighted Average Cost of Capital (p. 967)
✔ Planning the Acquisition Process (p. 1132)
✔ Planning the Disposal Process (p. 1133)
Damodaran on Valuation: Security Analysis for Investment and Corporate Finance (p. 1348)

"It is very unusual to find a company with one asset on its balance sheet that is worth £12 billion." Phil Nolan

Calculating Total Shareholder Return

DEFINITION

When assessing the performance of stocks, inexperienced investors risk falling into the trap of looking purely at stock price movements, in the process ignoring the value of dividends which may be paid. Total shareholder return (TSR) over a period is defined as the net stock price change plus the dividends paid during that period. While it is possible that a stock could deliver a negative price performance over a certain period yet still generate a positive total shareholder return should the dividend paid outweigh the stock price fall, in practice this happens only rarely. In most markets, the dividend yield indicators are low, with the result that stock prices are generally the key driver of TSR. However, the importance of the dividend component of the total return calculation is typically more significant in traditionally higher-yielding areas of the stock market such as utilities, tobacco companies, and beverage producers.

Total shareholder return over a period can be calculated as follows:

$$\text{Total shareholder return} = (\text{Stock price}_{\text{End of period}} - \text{Stock price}_{\text{Start of period}} + \text{Dividends paid}) \div \text{Stock price}_{\text{Start of period}}$$

Importantly, when calculating TSR, we must take account of only the dividends that our period of ownership of the stock entitles us to receive, so we need to take account of the stock ex-dividend date rather than the dividend payment date. It could be that we own the stock on the day when the dividend is actually payable, yet we would only be entitled to receive the dividend had we owned the stock on the ex-dividend day.

An alternative ways of thinking of total shareholder return is the internal rate of return of all cash flows paid to investors during a particular period. However, whichever method we choose to calculate total shareholder return, the result essentially represents an indication of the overall return generated for stockholders, expressed in percentage terms. In all cases, the "dividends paid" element of the calculation should also include any special cash payments returned to stockholders, as well as any stock buyback programs. The figure should also take account of any special one-off dividend payments, as well as regular dividend payouts.

ADVANTAGES

- TSR represents a readily understood figure of the overall financial benefits generated for stockholders.
- The figure can be interpreted as a measure of how the market evaluates the overall performance of a company over a specified period.
- Given that TSRs are expressed in percentage terms, the figures are readily comparable between companies in the same sector.

DISADVANTAGES

- TSRs can be calculated for publicly traded companies at the overall level, but not at a divisional level.
- The calculation is not "forward looking" in that it reflects the past overall return to shareholders, with no consideration of future returns.
- TSR is externally focused in that it reflects the market's perception of performance; it could, therefore, be adversely impacted should a share price of a fundamentally strong company suffer excessively in the short term.

ACTION CHECKLIST

- ✔ Calculate the share price change over the specified period plus any dividends paid to generate a simple TSR calculation.
- ✔ If necessary, be prepared to make adjustments for special events such as share buybacks and/or splits in stocks' prices.
- ✔ Investors can use TSR percentages to make comparisons against industry benchmarks.
- ✔ From a company perspective, remuneration packages can be linked to TSR.

DOS AND DON'TS

DO

- Consider how TSR calculations might be applied to mutual funds as well as company stocks, thus taking account of income paid out by yield-orientated funds when looking at their annual performance.
- However, remember that TSR reflects past performance rather than a perception or indication of future returns.

DON'T

- Don't forget that past performance shouldn't be taken as the best guide to future returns.
- Don't look to calculate TSR for privately held companies as the calculation requires stock price inputs.

MORE INFO

Books:

Ward, Keith. *Marketing Strategies: Turning Marketing Strategies into Shareholders Value*. Burlington, MA: Butterworth-Heinemann, 2004.

Young, David S., and Stephen F. O'Byrne. *EVA and Value Based Management*. New York: McGraw-Hill, 2000.

Articles:

Elali, Wajeeh. "Contemporaneous relationship between EVA and shareholder value." *International Journal of Business Governance and Ethics* 2:3–4 (October 2006): 237–253. Online at: dx.doi.org/10.1504/IJBGE.2006.011157

Gardner, Tim, and Eric Spielgel. "Total shareholder return: Planning a perfect future." *Public Utilities Fortnightly* 144:1 (January 2006): 45–50.

See Also:

★ Dividend Policy: Maximizing Shareholder Value (pp. 667–670)
★ Why EVA Is the Best Measurement Tool for Creating Shareholder Value (pp. 952–953)
⇄ Earnings per Share (pp. 1220–1221)
⇄ Return on Investment (pp. 1249–1250)
⇄ Return on Stockholders' Equity (pp. 1250–1251)

"My advice to this investor is the same that I give to the young investors in my classes ... Devote the same earnest attention to investing that $50,000 as you devoted to earning it." Ivan Boesky

  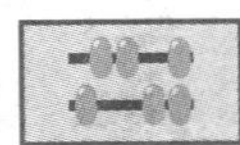   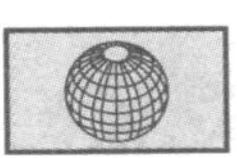   

Dealing with Venture Capital Companies

DEFINITION

Small and growing businesses seeking to finance further development, but which cannot raise the necessary funds through a bank loan or overdraft, or by an injection of further capital from the current owner, may find that venture capitalists provide the best solution to their needs. Venture capital (VC) is the term used for unsecured funding provided by specialist firms in return for a proportion of a company's shares. Venture capital investments are seen as relatively high risk for the lender because they are unsecured.

VC funds are often used in conjunction with a management buyout or buyin, in which a management team is demonstrating its commitment to a firm's success by investing their own money in the business.

Venture capital firms consider various factors before committing funds to a business. These include the track record of the business and whether the management team has a proven record of success; for this reason, VC companies generally do not consider start-ups as suitable for investment. They will seek to determine whether the management's plans for the business are credible. They will also try to determine whether a viable exit strategy can be achieved within a preferred timescale, usually within three to five years of making their investment. This could be executed via a trade sale, stock market listing, refinancing by another institution, or a repurchasing of the entire capital by management.

In return for their investment, VC firms make a number of demands, including the following:

- A high return (perhaps a compound return of 25% or more), largely generated by growth in the capital value of the business.
- Representation on the company's board.

In the past, companies have approached venture capital funds to provide seed, start-up, and expansion financing, as well as management/leveraged buyout financing. However, nowadays VC companies focus almost entirely on funding businesses that have proprietary technology or knowledge. Thus they tend to favor businesses with a product or service that offers a unique selling point or other competitive advantage.

ADVANTAGES

- VC investors put money into risky or innovative businesses and projects that might otherwise have trouble obtaining funding.
- Apart from providing funding, a VC company takes an active role in the management of a business, to which it can bring a great deal of administrative expertise and market knowledge. It may also have valuable skills and contacts, and can assist with strategy and key decision-making.
- Having invested in a project, a VC company will do all it can to ensure that it is a success.
- VC companies can also provide access to funding by other VC investors.
- Investors are often prepared to provide follow-up funding as the business grows.

DISADVANTAGES

There may be disadvantages to accepting VC investment, and the following points should be considered carefully.

- Is the VC company acting as a lead investor? If so, are there complementary or competing companies in its portfolio? Does it have experience with similar types of investment?
- Will the VC company be able to come up with extra financing if it becomes necessary?
- What type of role does it want in the management of your business?
- Can your management team live up to the conditions demanded by the VC company, and does it have complementary skills?
- If your firm reaches the deal negotiation stage with a VC investor, you will have to pay legal and accounting fees whether or not you are successful in securing funds.

DOS AND DON'TS

DO

- Seek expert legal and financial advice when negotiating any agreement with a VC company.
- Be aware of the significant time required to complete the process.
- When researching venture capitalists, go for geographic and industry specializations that complement your own.

DON'T

- Don't take on venture capital unless you are sure that you can cope mentally and physically with the provider's requirements.
- Don't forget that you will lose some of your power to make management decisions.
- Don't forget that there can be legal and regulatory issues to comply with when raising finance.

MORE INFO

Books:

Cardis, Joel, *et al*. *Venture Capital: The Definitive Guide for Entrepreneurs, Investors, and Practitioners*. New York: Wiley, 2001.

Gladstone, David, and Laura Gladstone. *Venture Capital Handbook: An Entrepreneur's Guide to Raising Venture Capital*. Upper Saddle River, NJ: Prentice Hall, 2002.

Hill, Brian E., and Dee Power. *Inside Secrets to Venture Capital*. New York: Wiley, 2001.

Article:

Iwata, Edward. "Venture capital spreads the wealth around the country." *USA Today* (March 11, 2008). Online at: tinyurl.com/yvj5n8

Websites:

British Venture Capital Association (BVCA): www.bvca.co.uk
European Private Equity & Venture Capital Association (EVCA): www.evca.eu
National Venture Capital Association (NVCA, US): www.nvca.org
vFinance directory of venture capital resources and related services: www.vfinance.com

See Also:

★ Assessing Venture Capital Funding for Small and Medium-Sized Enterprises (pp. 451–453)
★ Sources of Venture Capital (pp. 601–603)
✔ Options for Raising Finance (p. 1081)
Mastering the VC Game: A Venture Capital Insider Reveals How to Get from Start Up to IPO on Your Terms (p. 1394)

"I don't invest in anything I don't understand—it makes more sense to buy TV stations than oil wells." Oprah Winfrey

The Efficient Market Hypothesis

DEFINITION

The efficient market hypothesis (EMH) is a controversial economic theory that states that it is impossible for investors to purchase undervalued stocks or sell stocks for inflated prices because share prices always reflect all relevant information. It is therefore impossible to beat the market except by chance. According to the EMH, expert stock selection or market timing is of no value. Indeed, the only way an investor can possibly obtain higher than average returns is by purchasing riskier investments.

The EMH led to the argument that a blindfolded chimpanzee throwing darts at the *Wall Street Journal* would perform as well as highly-paid investment managers. The inevitable conclusion was that investors would be better off placing their money in broad-based index or tracker funds, which reflect the overall composition of the market and charge very low fees. These funds are known as passive funds, as opposed to actively managed funds, which aim to outperform the market by identifying undervalued stocks.

The EMH was developed by Professor Eugene Fama at the University of Chicago Business School in the 1960s. The theory was widely accepted until the 1990s, when behavioral economists began to question its validity. They argued that markets were far from perfect in terms of processing information and that other factors such as investor confidence have to be taken into account. They reasoned that it was indeed possible for investors to outperform the market by identifying undervalued stocks.

Empirical evidence can be used to support both sides of the argument. Many point to a wealth of data showing that few active managers consistently outperform the overall index. But there is other evidence that undermines the EMH. For example, it can be argued that markets do behave irrationally, with stock prices overshooting during bull markets and falling back excessively in bear markets, in the latter case allowing shrewd investors to buy undervalued stocks. There are also some investors—such as Warren Buffett—who appear able to beat the market consistently, which should not be possible if the EMH is correct.

ADVANTAGES

- If the EMH is correct there is no need for investors to pay the high fees charged by investment managers and their armies of analysts, researchers, and fund managers. They can simply put their money in tracker or index funds, which mirror the overall performance of the market.
- Investing in a tracker or index fund reduces risk since the investor is exposed to an entire market, rather than a selected number of stocks. It also eliminates the risk that a manager of an actively managed fund could simply make a mistake and invest in the wrong firm.
- Selecting passive over active fund management also means that the investor does not incur the high transaction costs resulting from the frequent trading undertaken by active managers.

DISADVANTAGES

- Actively managed funds aim to outperform the market. Thus, if an investor chooses only index funds, he will miss out on the opportunities for extra returns that an active manager can potentially generate.
- By avoiding actively managed funds, an investor will also fail to benefit from the other advantages that investing in such a fund can bring. During an economic downturn, for example, an active manager can focus on defensive stocks and sectors, which should outperform more cyclical stocks. The converse is true when the economy is performing well.

ACTION CHECKLIST

✔ Look at the performance of actively managed and passive funds to make your own assessment of the merits of the EMH.

✔ Decide whether it is worth paying the extra money required to invest in an actively managed fund compared to a passive fund.

DOS AND DON'TS

DO

- Consider investing in index or tracker funds if you believe that the EMH is true—i.e. that active managers cannot outperform the market on a sustained basis.
- Remember that if an active manager does beat the benchmark index, this may simply be due to chance rather than skill—unless, of course, the manager can outperform it consistently over a number of years.

DON'T

- Don't ignore the benefits that actively managed funds can bring in terms of risk reduction and the potential to outperform the overall market.
- Don't ignore the benefits of investing in both actively managed and passive funds.

MORE INFO

Books:

Graham, Benjamin, and David L. Dodd. *Security Analysis*. 6th ed. New York: McGraw-Hill, 2009.

Malkiel, Burton G. *A Random Walk Down Wall Street: The Time-Tested Strategy for Successful Investing*. 10th ed. New York: WW Norton & Co., 2011.

Mandelbrot, Benoit, and Richard L. Hudson. *The (Mis)behavior of Markets: A Fractal View of Risk, Ruin, and Reward*. London: Profile, 2004.

Articles:

Eom, Cheoljun, Gabjin Oh, and Woo-Sung Jung. "Relationship between efficiency and predictability in stock price change." *Physica A* 387:22 (15 September 2008): 5511–5517. Online at: dx.doi.org/10.1016/j.physa.2008.05.059

Ozdemir, Zeynel Abidin. "Efficient market hypothesis: Evidence from a small open-economy." *Applied Economics* 40:5 (March 2008): 633–641. Online at: dx.doi.org/10.1080/00036840600722315

Yen, Gili, and Cheng-few Lee. "Efficient market hypothesis (EMH): Past, present and future." *Review of Pacific Basin Financial Markets and Policies* 11:2 (June 2008): 305–329. Online at: dx.doi.org/10.1142/S0219091508001362

Website:

A personal website on the academic background to EMH: www.e-m-h.org

See Also:

✔ Understanding Price Volatility (p. 1103)

"Lethargy bordering on sloth remains the cornerstone of our investment style." Warren Buffett

  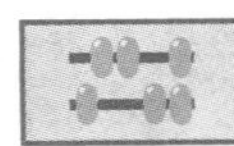      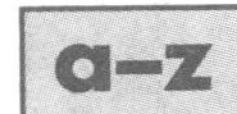

Financial Intermediaries: Their Role and Relation to Financial Markets

DEFINITION

Generally, when a company wants to enter a financial market, it uses the services of a financial intermediary rather than entering directly. In many transactions the intermediary will be the company's commercial bank, which will broker financial deals such as loans. For more complex or specialist deals a company is likely to turn to an intermediary that specializes in transactions for financial products such as mutual funds, pension funds, bonds and shares, and insurance. In such cases, the intermediary may be a fund or insurer itself.

A financial intermediary typically facilitates the channeling of funds between lenders and borrowers indirectly, in the form of a loan or a mortgage. Sometimes the intermediary may lend money directly via the financial markets. This is known as financial disintermediation.

The intermediary's role is to seek the best possible investment opportunities on behalf of its clients. The intermediary will often have contacts within its areas of expertise that would not be accessible to private individuals using a retail bank, for example. This enables the intermediary to broker the most appropriate deals for its client, which is spared the trouble of having to seek these out itself. The intermediary charges a fee to the client for its services.

ADVANTAGES

- Lending is often less risky through an intermediary, who can, for example, diversify lending, providing the company with a variety of different loan plans. If some loans then prove themselves to be unviable, they are offset by those that are sound. Experience is an important element of this. By making many and diverse loans, financial intermediaries gain experience in identifying clients who will be able to repay their loans, as well as those who will not. This reduces risk and minimizes the number of unviable loans for the client, who is spared the burden of making expensive mistakes.
- Financial intermediaries have liquidity, which means they are in a position to convert assets to money quickly. This has obvious advantages in terms of obtaining cash when it is needed. For a company this can be of crucial importance if it experiences difficulties such as temporary cash flow problems.

DISADVANTAGES

- The main disadvantage is that, on top of their fee, financial intermediaries often take a percentage of profits as part of any transaction they broker. Direct loaning can significantly increase the potential income of such a loan for the intermediary. However, the advantages outlined above significantly mitigate any such disadvantages. That is why many companies use intermediaries rather than entering the market directly.

ACTION CHECKLIST

✔ Ask around for recommendations. Your bank should have knowledge of specialist intermediaries who can cater for your needs, for example. Your accountant or lawyer may also have useful contacts.

✔ Investigate a financial intermediary thoroughly before entering into a relationship. Check that they have any necessary certification or license.

✔ You should be confident that your intermediary is a responsible and experienced broker and/or lender.

DOS AND DON'TS

DO

- Approach your decision by comparing and contrasting several choices of intermediary.
- Research your options carefully to ensure that potential intermediaries are both experienced and economically sound.
- Have interview meetings with intermediaries you are considering to ensure that you will be able to work with each other before you enter into any financial relationship.

DON'T

- Don't rush hastily into a relationship with an intermediary.
- Don't use an intermediary who cannot produce evidence of the right certification or license to practice.

MORE INFO

Books:

Harrison, Tina. *Marketing Financial Services*. 2nd ed. New York: FT Prentice Hall, 2000.
Taylor, Bernard, and Ian Morison (eds). *Driving Strategic Change in Financial Services*. Cambridge, UK: Woodhead Publishing, 1999.

See Also:

✔ Conflicting Interests: The Agency Issue (p. 1110)
✔ Structuring, Negotiating, and Drafting Agency Agreements (p. 1176)
Banking and Financial Services (pp. 1612–1614)

"A bank is a place that will lend you money if you can prove that you don't need it." Bob Hope

Franchising a Business

DEFINITION

The term "franchising" can refer to a number of different business models, including licensing, distributor, and agency arrangements. Here, however, we take it to mean "business-format franchising." The British Franchise Association defines this concept as the granting of a license by a franchisor to a franchisee that "entitles the franchisee to trade under the trademark/ trade name of the franchisor and to make use of an entire package, comprising all the elements necessary to establish a previously untrained person in the business and to run it with continual assistance on a predetermined basis."

Franchising can provide an excellent means of expanding a business rapidly and in a cost-effective manner. It can also generate a number of revenue streams for the franchisor. These include: the franchise fee; franchise royalties; equipment sales; supplies; material sales; sales of services; property rental; and rebates from vendors of equipment and supplies.

Each business outlet is owned and operated by the franchisee. However, the franchisor retains control over the way products and services are marketed and sold, and controls the quality and standards of the business. Not all businesses can be franchised, but most business concepts can be. Businesses that can be franchised tend to be unique and very new, with the potential to expand nationally or internationally, and profitable, with the ability to generate continuous and predictable profits. They tend to have a systemized business model, with efficient operating procedures that can be easily transferred from one location to another, and an easily understandable format, so that it is straightforward to train other people to manage the operation. They should also be affordable, so that a wide range of potential franchisees can be attracted.

ADVANTAGES

- It can be difficult to raise capital to expand a business. If you use franchising, the capital is provided by the franchisee.
- Franchisees tend to be highly motivated, since it is their capital that is at risk.
- Franchising allows you to expand a business very rapidly.
- Expanding the business leads to economies of scale, with benefits such as greater buying power.

DISADVANTAGES

- You need an effective marketing program and very good salespeople to develop the concept and drive sales forward once the franchise network has been established.
- You inevitably lose some control of the business unless you have a very strict operating model and the ability to oversee the way each franchisee is operating the business.
- It can be difficult to manage the business if it grows very rapidly (as is often the case with franchise networks).
- The threat of litigation between franchisor and franchisee can be high, particularly if the franchisee fails to make the profits they expected.

ACTION CHECKLIST

✔ Identify whether the business concept you are developing is suitable for a franchise arrangement.

✔ Register your trade name and trademarks with the relevant trademark office. You should also register your name and marks in all the countries or provinces where you do business or intend to do business.

✔ Open four or five business units before embarking on a national expansion. This will give you time to identify any potential pitfalls. You will also be able to gauge whether the business format can be copied from one geographic location to another.

DOS AND DON'TS

DO

- Avoid conflict and potential litigation by supporting your franchisees and ensuring that they are successful.
- Make sure you have enough staff to support the growth of your franchisees and service their needs.
- Draw up a very strict franchise agreement that allows the franchisee little latitude to vary from your system.

DON'T

- Don't ignore the importance of training. Even franchisees in a simple business model will require a very strong training program so that they are completely conversant with your systems and procedures.
- Don't think you can relax once franchisees have signed on. They will need continuous support if their business, and thus you, are to be successful.

MORE INFO

Books:

Shook, Carrie, and Robert L. Shook. *Franchising: The Business Strategy that Changed the World*. Englewood Cliffs, NJ: Prentice Hall, 1993.

Spinelli, Stephen, Jr., Robert M. Rosenberg, and Sue Birley. *Franchising: Pathway to Wealth Creation*. Upper Saddle River, NJ: FT Prentice Hall, 2004.

Tarbutton, Lloyd T. *Franchising: The How-to Book*. Englewood Cliffs, NJ: Prentice Hall, 1986.

Articles:

Kaufmann, Patrick J., and Rajiv P. Dant. "Multi-unit franchising: Growth and management issues." *Journal of Business Venturing* 11:5 (September 1996): 343–358. Online at: dx.doi.org/10.1016/0883-9026(96)00057-2

Mathewson, G. Frank, and Ralph A. Winter. "The economics of franchise contracts." *Journal of Law and Economics* 28:3 (October 1985): 503–526. Online at: dx.doi.org/10.1086/467099

See Also:

✔ Assessing Economies of Scale in Business (p. 1145)

"If we had the means to review and judge the effectiveness of operations, we could safely leave the prosecution of these operations to the men in charge of them." Alfred P. Sloan

  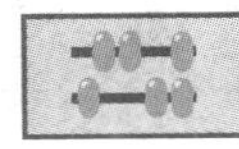    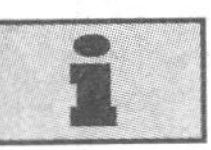  

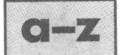

Fund of Hedge Funds: Understanding the Risks and Returns

DEFINITION

Generally, a fund of funds is a fund that invests in other funds in order to provide investors with a lower-risk product through exposure to a larger number of vehicles, often of different types and with different regional focuses.

A hedge fund of funds is one that invests in a pool of hedge funds, instead of just investing in an individual fund. It is any fund of funds that pools capital together, while employing two or more submanagers that invest in two or more funds, and which is not dictated to by the underlying investment of such funds.

Funds of funds are set up as limited partnerships, which offer advantages to the investor. Due diligence is a primary benefit, because managers can use their time and expertise to evaluate strategies and analyze individual fund performance—a task that would be a difficult undertaking for an individual investor. The fund of funds tries to avoid untoward risk because of the different investment strategies employed by the principal fund managers. Funds of funds can be invested in, for example, a venture fund, a long/short fund, a distressed fund, and/or a private equity fund. Investors assign assets to a fund of funds mainly to limit their risk to exposure.

However, funds of funds do have some disadvantages, such as the double layer of fees and the issue of transparency. When investing in a fund of funds, a backer must pay not only the fees of the pool of funds, but also the fees of the fund of funds manager. Transparency about the fund of funds manager's background and reputation, not to mention the nature of the investments made, are issues of primary importance.

ADVANTAGES

- Funds of hedge funds normally offer a lower risk than single funds, because they are invested in a wider variety of sectors, with national and international focuses.
- Because managers can devote all of their time to evaluating strategies and analyzing individual fund performance, they are more likely to achieve a better return than an individual investor.
- Because principal fund managers are specialists in their investment areas, funds of funds benefit from the different specialist investment strategies employed.

DISADVANTAGES

- When investors buy into a fund of funds, they are charged management fees twice: First by the fund of funds manager, and then by the individual fund managers.
- Funds of hedge funds are inevitably very secretive, which makes it difficult for an investor to assess the fund manager's performance on a daily basis.
- The Securities & Exchange Commission (SEC), the Financial Services Authority (FSA), and other securities supervisory bodies generally have limited powers to check on hedge fund activities.

ACTION CHECKLIST

✔ Find out what you will be paying in total fees: after you have deducted the double fees, it might prove wiser to select less risky investments.

✔ Check the long-term track record of the fund of funds: an experienced manager, who delivers a consistent (though perhaps lower) return, is probably a better bet than a new start-up. The manager's skills, background, and reputation, and the type of investments made, are very important issues.

DOS AND DON'TS

DO

- Research the different funds and their tactics, and make sure that you have analyzed your real return on investment after fees and expenses.
- Engage your lawyers and accountants in the evaluation of the risks and possible benefits of investing in funds of hedge funds.

DON'T

- Don't take your investment in funds of hedge funds for granted; market and legislative developments can mean that the playing field changes. Just because a risk, area, market, or country has been stable in the past is no guarantee that it will be the same in the future.

MORE INFO

Books:

Drobny, Steven. *Inside the House of Money: Top Hedge Fund Traders on Profiting in the Global Markets*. Hoboken, NJ: Wiley, 2006.

Jaeger, Robert A. *All About Hedge Funds: The Easy Way to Get Started*. New York: McGraw-Hill Professional, 2002.

Jaffer, Sohail. *Funds of Hedge Funds: For Professional Investors and Managers*. London: Euromoney Books, 2003.

Nicholas, Joseph G. *Hedge Fund of Funds Investing: An Investor's Guide*. New York: Bloomberg Press, 2004.

Articles:

Chen, Peng. "Hedge funds: Are they worth it?" *On Wall Street* (August 1, 2006). Online at: tinyurl.com/6j562cx

Jones, Bernard. "Hedge funding." *Investors Chronicle* (May 25, 2007). Online at: tinyurl.com/5reogza

Websites:

Financial Services Authority (FSA; UK): www.fsa.gov.uk

Hedge fund research from Morningstar: www.morningstar.com

HedgeFund.net: www.hedgefund.net

See Also:

★ Carrying Out Due Diligence on Hedge Funds (pp. 465–467)

★ Funds of Hedge Funds versus Single-Manager Funds (pp. 490–491)

★ To Hedge or Not to Hedge (pp. 104–106)

✔ Hedge Funds: Understanding the Risks and Returns (p. 1072)

Absolute Returns: The Risk and Opportunities of Hedge Fund Investing (p. 1326)

"If we had the means to review and judge the effectiveness of operations, we could safely leave the prosecution of these operations to the men in charge of them." Alfred P. Sloan

  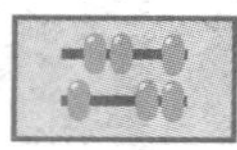     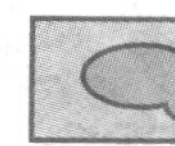 

Hedge Funds: Understanding the Risks and Returns

DEFINITION

Although hedge funds seem to have hit the headlines only recently, the first of these funds was actually started in 1949.

Hedge funds are normally run by small teams of portfolio managers, traders, and analysts, investing private pools of capital with few restrictions as to the areas in which they can speculate. Hedge funds benefit from limited regulation and are not required to make periodic reports to the Securities & Exchange Commission (SEC) under the Securities and Exchange Act of 1934. In order to be exempt from direct regulation, a hedge fund must be open to a limited number of accredited investors.

Hedge funds use a wide array of strategies, and sometimes are not "hedged" against the market at all. Many, but not all, of these funds aim to produce much higher returns than other investment vehicles, and markets with high volatility are often preferred, as they sometimes yield the highest returns (but also the greatest risks).

Hedge funds have the advantage that they can employ a large number of strategies and can invest in more areas than other investments. They may use leverage, short-selling, asset-backed lending, arbitrage, or a variety of other techniques in order to gain maximum returns for investors.

Hedge fund managers normally earn both a management fee and a performance or incentive fee. Performance fees are intended to be an inducement for the investment managers to produce the greatest returns they can. Typical fees are a management fee of 2% of the fund's net asset value per annum and a performance fee of 20% of the fund's profits. Fees are payable from the fund to the investment manager, and are taken directly from the assets that the backer holds in the fund.

A hedge fund can apply a high watermark to an investor's money, where the manager will only receive performance fees, on the invested money, when its value is greater than its previous greatest value.

ADVANTAGES

- Hedge funds can make use of a larger number of strategies and can invest in many more areas than with traditional investment products.
- Performance fees, calculated as a percentage of the fund's profits, act as an incentive for managers to perform above average.

DISADVANTAGES

- To make money and not disclose strategies, hedge funds are of necessity very secretive, with few public disclosure requirements. This makes it difficult for investors to assess how well or badly their fund managers are doing.
- Some, though not all, hedge funds borrow and speculate with (leverage) sums that are many times larger than the initial investment. This is fine when the investment works, but it can mean that the fund folds if it doesn't.
- When a hedge fund uses short selling as an investment strategy, rather than as a hedging strategy, it can experience very high losses if the market turns against it.
- The SEC and other securities regulators generally have limited ability to check routinely on hedge fund activities.

DOS AND DON'TS

DO

- Seek advice, preferably from a specialist in the industry who has some years of experience and has seen both the good and the bad.
- Involve your lawyers and accountants in the evaluation of both the risks and the potential benefits of investing in a hedge fund.

DON'T

- Don't jump or be pushed into a decision. Take time to do your research before deciding.
- Don't follow tips or the sheep—sleep on it before you make your move.

ACTION CHECKLIST

✔ Before investing in hedge funds, you should be aware of the risks as well as the rewards: Leverage amplifies profits but also losses; short selling opens up new investment opportunities; riskier investments typically provide higher returns but, as in poker, you shouldn't sit down at the table if you can't afford to lose.

✔ Qualify and quantify in financial terms how the failure of the fund could impact on your life or business.

✔ Seek the advice of specialists and always ask for a second opinion. There are over 10,000 hedge funds in existence, with close to $3 trillion in assets under management; separating the wood from the trees can be a difficult and risky process.

MORE INFO

Books:

Black, Keith H. *Managing a Hedge Fund: A Complete Guide to Trading, Business Strategies, Operations, and Regulations*. New York: McGraw-Hill Professional, 2004.

Lhabitant, François-Serge. *Handbook of Hedge Funds*. Chichester, UK: Wiley, 2006.

Nicholas, Joseph G. *Investing in Hedge Funds*. New York: Bloomberg Press, 2005.

Ridley, Matthew. *How to Invest in Hedge Funds: An Investment Professional's Guide*. London: Kogan Page, 2004.

Article:

Sender, Henny, and Javier Blas. "Hedge funds turn to gold." *Financial Times* (March 8, 2009). Online at: tinyurl.com/bux3hl

Websites:

Hedge fund database from BarclayHedge: www.barclayhedge.com

HedgeWorld: www.hedgeworld.com

See Also:

★ Carrying Out Due Diligence on Hedge Funds (pp. 465–467)

★ Funds of Hedge Funds versus Single-Manager Funds (pp. 490–491)

★ To Hedge or Not to Hedge (pp. 104–106)

✔ Fund of Hedge Funds: Understanding the Risks and Returns (p. 1071)

Absolute Returns: The Risk and Opportunities of Hedge Fund Investing (p. 1326)

"**Never invest your money in anything that eats or needs repainting.**" Billy Rose

  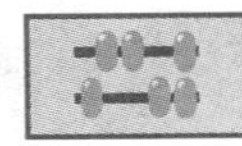      

How to Use Credit Rating Agencies

DEFINITION

A credit rating agency is a company that assigns credit ratings to issuers of debt instruments and to the debt instruments themselves. A wide variety of organizations may issue debt in the primary market and thus come under the scrutiny of the credit rating agencies. These include companies, national, and local governments, and government and semi-government entities. Their debt instruments are then traded on a secondary market. Credit rating agencies assign ratings that seek to determine how creditworthy the issuer is, i.e. to gauge the level of risk that they will be unable to repay the loan.

An entity with very strong finances will be given the highest rating, often described as AAA, while the least creditworthy will receive the lowest rating, normally D, which applies to debt that is already in arrears. An entity with low credit ratings will have to pay a premium in terms of the interest on loans in order to compensate the lender for the higher risk that the loan may not be repaid. The rating agencies constantly monitor all the instruments they rate and will issue upgrades or downgrades if an issuer's creditworthiness has changed.

Ratings are an invaluable tool for investors, providing a convenient way to identify the creditworthiness of a potential investment. Issuers use credit ratings to provide an independent analysis of their own creditworthiness, thus helping to determine the value of the instruments they issue. Government regulators and other agencies also use credit ratings to gauge the health of their financial system. Thus, regulators allow banks to use credit ratings from certain approved ratings agencies when calculating their net capital reserve requirements. Regulators could, for example, allow banks to include highly rated, liquid bonds when calculating their net capital reserve requirements.

The three largest credit rating agencies are Standard & Poor's, Moody's, and Fitch. All have come under fire as a result of the global credit crunch that developed in 2007. In July 2008, a damning report from the US Securities and Exchange Commission identified "serious shortcomings" in the rating of securities related to subprime mortgages, the products that triggered the crisis. Credit rating agencies have also come under fire for problems in structured finance products that they have rated, particularly in assigning AAA ratings to structured debt, which in a large number of cases has subsequently been downgraded or defaulted. There is thus increasing pressure to introduce greater regulation of the credit rating agencies.

ADVANTAGES

- The ratings assigned by credit rating agencies allow investors to quickly, cheaply, and conveniently identify the risk involved in buying a particular debt instrument or in developing a business relationship with a particular organization.
- The use of ratings opens capital markets to entities such as new companies.
- Credit ratings give you an insight into an entity from an independent expert analyst.

DISADVANTAGES

- The rating agencies have come under criticism as a result of the credit crunch. Many AAA-rated companies were downgraded to very low levels within a very short space of time.
- Credit rating agencies have come under fire for failing to downgrade companies quickly enough, with some companies faltering despite being assigned relatively good ratings.
- Credit rating agencies have been criticized for developing too close a relationship with the management of the companies that they rate.
- Credit rating agencies have been criticized for their role in rating structured finance products, and in particular for large losses in the collateralized debt obligation (CDO) market that occurred despite being assigned top ratings by the agencies.

ACTION CHECKLIST

✔ Look at the ratings from as many credit rating agencies as possible.

✔ Gather as much other information as you can on a potential investment or business partner.

DOS AND DON'TS

DO

- Be aware that issuers pay the rating agencies a fee. Critics say that this creates a potential conflict of interest.
- Conduct your own research as well as looking at the analysis supplied by the agencies.

DON'T

- Don't forget that the ratings agencies are not infallible.
- Don't forget that entities are subject to constant monitoring by the credit rating agencies. Ratings can and do change over time.

MORE INFO

Books:

Beder, Sharon. *Suiting Themselves: How Corporations Drive the Global Agenda*. London: Earthscan, 2005.

Brooks, Chris. *Introductory Econometrics for Finance*. 2nd ed. Cambridge, UK: Cambridge University Press, 2008.

Ganguin, Blaise, and John Bilardello. *Fundamentals of Corporate Credit Analysis*. New York: McGraw-Hill, 2005.

Articles:

Goodhart, C. A. E. "The background to the 2007 financial crisis." *International Economics and Economic Policy* 4:4 (February 2008): 331–346. Online at: dx.doi.org/10.1007/s10368-007-0098-0

Maxwell, James. "Ratings agencies eye ERM for all industries." *Financial Executive* (March 2008): 44–46. Online at: tinyurl.com/68ju22f [PDF].

Wray, L. Randall. "Lessons from the subprime meltdown." *Challenge* 51:2 (March–April 2008): 40–68. Online at: www.challengemagazine.com/extra/040_068.pdf

See Also:

★ Credit Ratings (pp. 478–480)

✔ Hedging Credit Risk—Case Study and Strategies (p. 969)

✔ How to Manage Your Credit Rating (p. 973)

✔ Managing Your Credit Risk (p. 981)

How to Use Receivables as Collateral

DEFINITION

Receivables are money owed by customers, whether they are individuals or businesses, to another entity for goods or services that have been delivered or used, but have not yet been paid for. Receivables are usually due within a short time period, which typically ranges from a few days to a year.

Accounts receivable financing is used by companies facing short-term cash flow problems, and it can take many forms. The major source of accounts receivable financing is commercial finance companies and factoring companies, as well as banks that will consider receivables as security or collateral for a business loan. Most companies operate by allowing a portion of sales to be on credit, usually to customers that are invoiced periodically, which removes the burden of physically making payments as each transaction occurs. Credit acts as an IOU for goods or services already received or rendered and is given in good faith. Collateralizing receivables is a form of secured lending that gives companies short-term financing by selling their trade receivables or pledging receivables as collateral for a loan from a lender. Until the global financial crisis of 2008, receivables were securitized as well.

Direct sale of accounts receivable is called factoring. A loan from a bank secured or collateralized against accounts receivable is known as a discount, where the borrower draws against a line of credit that is less than the full value of the trade credits. Accounts receivable financing is a flexible way of obtaining credit, and borrowers' financing costs are related directly to their business cycle. In a general assignment, all receivables can serve as collateral, with new receivables substituted for those collected. In a specific assignment, the parties involved can specify who will receive collection, whether customers will be notified of the arrangement, and which accounts are to be collateralized.

Accounts receivable factoring is different from using accounts receivable as loan collateral because you sell the receivables to a factor at a discount; the factor then collects the debt and you don't have to worry about loan repayments. Accounts receivable factoring makes up about a third of all financing secured by American companies using accounts receivable and inventory as collateral.

When a loan is obtained from a bank with receivables as collateral, there are rather more formal guidelines. Banks and finance companies insist on weekly reports on sales, collections, and ineligibility analysis, as well as internally generated financial statements with detailed accounts receivable and accounts payable information. The amount borrowed is then repaid within a specified short-term period as the receivables are collected.

ADVANTAGES

- Collateralizing receivables can provide another source of working capital, freeing up essential funds for items such as payroll and taxes.
- This form of financing can provide relief from the responsibility of collection from nonpaying and slow-paying clients.

DISADVANTAGES

- Receivables financing is often priced at spreads above the bank prime rate and is relatively expensive compared with other forms of credit, particularly factoring.
- The older the account, the less value it has.

ACTION CHECKLIST

✔ When you sell an account to an accounts receivable factoring company, try to get a personal recommendation for the company and ensure that your accounts receivable factoring agreement states the exact conditions and charges for the purchase of your accounts receivable.

✔ Check the rates carefully and find out the amount a lender is willing to advance against the value of your collateralized receivables. The borrowing base is determined by multiplying the value of the assigned collateral by a discount factor, a process known as margining.

DOS AND DON'TS

DO

- Set up an easy-to-check accounts receivable report.
- Have a system in place to assess monies owed and monies unpaid.

DON'T

- Don't wait too long to take action on debts.
- Don't fall back on sentiment and loyalty.
- Don't forget to check bank rates, loan rates, and factoring rates.
- Don't use accounts receivable factoring as a way to get ready cash.

MORE INFO

Books:

Bond, Cecil J. *Credit Management Handbook: A Complete Guide to Credit and Accounts Receivable Operations*. New York: McGraw-Hill, 1993.

Salek, John G. *Accounts Receivable Management Best Practices*. Hoboken, NJ: Wiley, 2005.

See Also:

★ Factoring and Invoice Discounting: Working Capital Management Options (pp. 39–41)
✔ Assessing Cash Flow and Bank Lending Requirements (p. 964)
✔ Options for Raising Finance (p. 1081)
✔ An Overview of Loan Agreements (p. 1082)

"Incremental change is not enough. The whole command and control tradition is being turned on its head."
Richard Pascale

     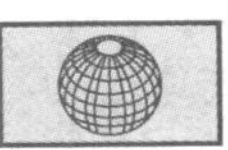   

Islamic Microfinance

DEFINITION

Islamic microfinance refers to a system of localized finance arrangements set up as an alternative source of funds for small, low-income Islamic clients. Typically, users of Islamic microfinance have little or no collateral, as they do not possess significant assets, and would therefore be excluded from other forms of financing, including Islamic bank financing. Thus, Islamic microfinance provides a means of accessing funds for those who are unlikely to qualify for other forms of finance, yet are still seeking full compliance with Islamic law and the Islamic way of life.

In essence, key Islamic microfinance contracts are based on *musharakah* and *mudarabah*, while microfinance users can also take advantage of *takaful* Islamic insurance.

Musharakah can be used either for assets or working capital. In principle it involves an equity participation in a business. The parties involved will share any profits or losses resulting from the business according to a pre-established ratio.

A *mudarabah* contract is basically a trustee financing scheme. The financier invests the funds while the other party supplies the expertise for the project. The contract requires rigorous following and transparency to ensure a fair distribution of profits.

Takaful insurance is based on the principle of shared responsibility and has been practiced in one form or another for well over 1,000 years. As a mutual-style concept, *takaful* does not function on conventional profit-making lines. It derives from the Arabic word *kafalah*, which means a joint guarantee. According to the *takaful* principle of insurance, each member of a scheme contributes to a fund that is used to help in case of need such as accidents, loss of crops, or death.

ADVANTAGES

- Islamic microfinance can play an important role in helping to address poverty in parts of the Muslim world.
- Islamic microfinance contracts can be operated individually or combined, giving greater flexibility to their application.
- Islamic microfinance contracts provide an alternative to low-income Muslim clients.
- *Musharakah* and *mudarabah* are the most approved contracts under shariah law and their application is encouraged by *shariah* scholars.
- *Takaful* is flexible in its range of applications, covering areas such as residences, places of business, cars, and inventory, as well as accident and life cover.

DISADVANTAGES

- *Mudarabah* arrangements require a high level of regulation and transparency to ensure a fair distribution of profits, so can be expensive to operate.
- Some Muslims may be uncomfortable with the scope for *takaful* to be used for investment purposes on the basis that investors are effectively speculating that low accident payouts will generate a surplus or profit.
- In general, Islamic microfinance is seen as more a social support system based on philanthropic principles rather than a business.
- Like other forms of microfinance, Islamic microfinance needs support to ensure its sustainability. Typically this support entails some form of ongoing subsidy such as a *waqf* endowment.

ACTION CHECKLIST

- ✔ Assess carefully the contracts and products offered and whether they are too expensive to operate. Often smaller-scale transactions cost more to operate, process, and regulate than larger ones.
- ✔ Investigate and understand local customs and financial practices, as these can vary widely between countries and even regions.
- ✔ Gain an understanding of local cultural attitudes to maximize the potential of microfinance; for example, some schemes have more success than others in introducing microfinance to women.
- ✔ Certain Muslim countries actively encourage Islamic microfinance. Potential users should investigate whether state support is offered to promote local microfinance schemes.

DOS AND DON'TS

DO

- Encourage communication and dialogue between shariah experts and the financiers in order to ensure that the products offered are compliant with *shariah* law.
- Understand that there will be differences between schemes in different countries according to local attitudes and conventions.
- Be realistic in assessing that Islamic microfinance has potential for growth but currently is still exercised on a very small scale.

DON'T

- Don't underestimate the help that local religious leaders can give in explaining to the local population that the financial contracts offered are *shariah*-compliant, which will increase confidence in the use of the products.
- Don't assume that limited-income clients will accept any products offered on unattractive terms; they often drive a hard bargain.

MORE INFO

Books:

Al-Harran, Saad. *An Islamic Microfinance Enterprise: The Financial Vehicle That Will Change the Face of the Islamic World*. London: Xlibris, 2008.

Nenova, Tatiana, and Cecile Thioro Niang. *Bringing Finance to Pakistan's Poor: Access to Finance for Small Enterprises and the Underserved*. New York: World Bank Publications, 2009.

Websites:

Consultative Group to Assist the Poor (CGAP): www.cgap.org
Microfinance Management Institute (MMI): www.themfmi.org

See Also:

★ Rigidity in Microfinancing: Can One Size Fit All? (pp. 576–578)

"Money is neither my god nor my devil. It is a form of energy that tends to make us more of who we already are, whethr it's greedy or loving." Dan Millman

  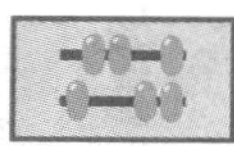      

Mean–Variance Optimization: A Primer

DEFINITION

Mean–variance optimization (MVO) is a quantitative tool used to spread investment across different assets within a portfolio by assessing the trade-off between risk and return in order to maximize the return while minimizing any risks. The concept was devised by economist Harry M. Markowitz, who developed an algorithm to calculate optimized returns over a specified period. MVO is part of Markowitz's modern portfolio theory (MPT), which assumes that investors will optimize their investment portfolios through diversifying their investments on a balanced risk–return basis. Markowitz's concept of efficiency as laid out in MVO contributed to the development of the capital asset pricing model (CAPM).

The Markowitz algorithm relies on inputting three data sets on a graph: expected return per asset, standard deviation of each asset (a metric for risk), and the correlation between the two. Together these produce what Markowitz named the "efficient frontier," or those assets expected to produce better returns than others that carry the same or fewer risks, and, conversely, a smaller risk than those expected to produce the same or a higher rate of return. Investors should ensure the three data sets, or inputs, represent their expectations of probability for the specified period, as well as include possible outcomes, each with a return per asset and probability of occurrence. The expected return, standard deviation, and correlations can then be calculated with standard statistical formulae.

ADVANTAGES

- Because MVO assumes that investors are risk-averse and will choose a less-risky investment among any assets that offer similar expected returns, it is a useful tool for identifying assets that have the most favorable risk–return profile.

DISADVANTAGES

- MVO treats return as a future expectation and uses volatility as a proxy for risk, the flaw being that volatility is a historical parameter and you cannot assume that today's prices provide an accurate forecast for the future.

ACTION CHECKLIST

- ✔ Be aware of the risks of using only historical data for your inputs—you may prefer to use your own estimates for a given asset's future performance in the specified period.
- ✔ Watch out for something called mean reversion. This occurs when an asset performs extremely well for a period and then performs spectacularly badly in the following period, or vice versa. If you have used historical data for your inputs, your outputs will indicate a strong (weak) future performance, but if mean reversion occurs, you will have results opposite to what you expected in the specified period.

DOS AND DON'TS

DO

- Make careful decisions about which data sets to use as inputs.
- Pay extra attention when calculating the expected returns, as your choices will determine the actual returns that you assign to each asset in the investment portfolio.

DON'T

- Don't assume that historical data are an accurate reflection of future performance.

MORE INFO

Book:

Markowitz, Harry M. *Portfolio Selection*. 2nd ed. Malden, MA: Blackwell Publishers, 1991.

Article:

Markowitz, Harry. "Portfolio selection." *Journal of Finance* 7:1 (March 1952): 77–91. Online at: www.jstor.org/stable/2975974

Website:

Full text of Markowitz book: cowles.econ.yale.edu/P/cm/m16

See Also:

★ Asset Allocation Methodologies (pp. 454–458)
✔ Trading in Commodities: Why and How (p. 1093)
✔ Trading in Corporate Bonds: Why and How (p. 1094)
Harry Markowitz (p. 1292)
William F. Sharpe (p. 1309)

"More money is probably lost by people who attempt to invest their money conservatively and sanely, but ignorantly, than is lost by those who enter into frank speculations." John Moody

  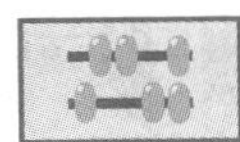   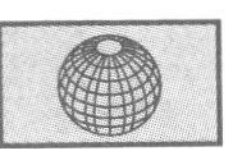   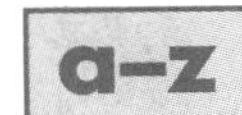

Measuring Gearing

DEFINITION

Gearing, also known as leverage, is an indicator of a company's ability to service its debt. Gearing is usually expressed as a percentage and is calculated by dividing the company's debt by its equity. Gearing shows the degree to which a firm's activities are funded by owners' funds versus creditors' funds. The higher a company's degree of leverage, the more the company is considered risky. If a company has a large amount of debt in proportion to its equity, this could be a warning that the company may have problems paying its debts in the future. As when using most ratios, an acceptable level of risk is determined through comparison with other companies in the same industry.

The three most common examples of gearing ratios are:

- The debt/equity ratio (total debt/total equity), multiplied by interest earned (earnings before interest and taxes, divided by total interest).
- The equity ratio: total equity/total assets.
- The debt ratio: total debt/total assets.

In derivatives markets, gearing compares the amount of cash spent purchasing an option or a futures contract with the actual value of the underlying position. The more highly leveraged the trading position, the bigger the risk that a minor change in market prices will totally wipe out the investment. Equally, however, a minor change in markets in the right direction could generate large profits in relation to the size of the investment.

Negative gearing is when an investor borrows to buy an asset, but the returns on the asset do not cover the interest on the loan. A negative gearing strategy works when the asset rises in value and creates enough capital gains to cover the initial investment loss. The investor must finance the shortfall until the asset is sold.

ADVANTAGES

- Gearing ratios allow potential investors to judge the viability, liabilities and likely future performance of a company or industry.
- Gearing ratios permit analysts to read between the lines of financial statements and quantify a company's strengths and weaknesses.
- Gearing ratios provide lead indications of potential problem areas and allow corrective measures to be taken.

DISADVANTAGES

- Gearing ratios may not always reflect the true nature of a company's accounts, as managers may attempt to gloss over problems.
- Gearing ratios are only predictive, based on past performance; and cannot take into account future events.
- Using gearing ratios to make comparisons between companies and industries is not always possible, due to different worldwide accounting standards.

ACTION CHECKLIST

- ✔ Obtain as much information as you can, and compare a company's ratios to those of other firms in the same industry, before committing to an expensive decision.
- ✔ Make sure that you have analyzed the gearing ratios in detail. If in doubt, consult an expert analyst.
- ✔ Be sure you thoroughly understand the ratios. Economizing by taking shortcuts or skipping details may cost more in the long run.

DOS AND DON'TS

DO

- When comparing a business's gearing ratios with its competitors, allow for any material differences in accounting policies between the compared company and industry norms.

DON'T

- Don't rely solely on gearing ratios. Use market research to confirm the results. Don't fall into the trap of thinking that gearing ratios are infallible.

MORE INFO

Books:

Chadwick, Leslie. *Essential Finance and Accounting for Managers*. Harlow, UK: Pearson Education, 2002.

Fraser-Sampson, Guy. *Private Equity as an Asset Class*. Chichester, UK: Wiley, 2007.

Myddelton, David Roderic. *Managing Business Finance*. Harlow, UK: Pearson Education, 2000.

Articles:

Calder, Stephen. "Super leverage." *Australasian Business Journal* (January 2008).

Rees, Mathew. "On leveraged buyouts." *The International Economy* (June 2008).

Website:

The Motley Fool on gearing: www.fool.co.uk/school/2005/sch050803.htm

See Also:

✔ Investors and the Capital Structure (p. 1120)
✔ Steps for Obtaining Bank Financing (p. 1090)
✔ Understanding and Using Leverage Ratios (p. 1097)
✔ Understanding Debt Cover (p. 1100)
Debt/Capital Ratio (p. 1214)

"Investing in stocks is an art, not a science, and people who've been trained to rigidly quantify everything have a big disadvantage." Peter Lynch

  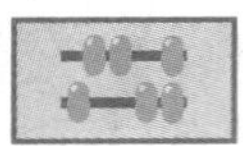      

Money Markets: Their Structure and Function

DEFINITION

Money markets are the part of the global financial market that deals with short-term lending and borrowing. They are often used as a solution to short-term cash needs by governments, large institutions, and, sometimes, individuals.

Generally, participants in the money markets are retail banks and large corporate organizations that can trade with each other using the benchmark of the London Interbank Offered Rate (Libor). This rate is generated on a daily basis through researching the interest rates at which banks are prepared to lend on unsecured assets. The money markets are considered to be quite a low-risk investment, but they do not promise particularly high gains either.

Typically, a transaction in a money market will be of very short duration and will be of a particular type of dealing called "paper." Examples of papers are treasury bills, repurchase agreements, and foreign currency swaps. The time frame of the transaction may range from one day to 13 months, and it is this short-term approach that sets money markets apart from the capital market.

Repurchase agreements, or "repos," are very short term loans, often lasting for only a day, where assets are sold to an investor with an agreement to repurchase them at a later date for a fixed price. In foreign currency swaps, currencies are swapped with an agreement to reverse the deal at a later, agreed date.

ADVANTAGES

- For an organization in need of a quick cash injection the money markets are extremely useful. They generally allow easy borrowing or lending in a low-risk environment. For example, a one-day loan where the seller can repurchase its securities for a set price at a certain time in the future is extremely safe. If we compare this transaction to those made in the unforgiving world of the stock market, where investors have no control over the future performance of their stocks, it is easy to see the appeal of money markets.

DISADVANTAGES

- Money markets are particularly low risk and therefore are not suitable for an investor looking for high returns.
- The money markets are used for short-term loans only and are not designed to achieve long-term growth of assets.
- Despite the apparent low risk of the money markets, all transactions in them must be properly assessed in the context of the global market. When the global financial markets go through one of their periodic cycles of turmoil and instability, one should always err on the side of caution with any investment.

ACTION CHECKLIST

✔ Consider your reasons for investing. Do you require a quick cash release or are you planning for the long term?

✔ What kind of investment are you looking for? Consult your financial adviser to determine what type of transaction would work best for your company.

✔ Check carefully on the financial status of the organization with which you are considering entering into a money market agreement.

DOS AND DON'TS

DO

- Research all the available fundraising options fully.
- Give yourself as comprehensive an understanding of the current financial market as you can before investing.
- Examine your motives for using the money markets as a long-term investment may make more sense.

DON'T

- Don't invest in the money markets if you are looking for a high return on your investments.
- Don't believe that because the money markets are low risk your assets are perfectly safe.

MORE INFO

Books:

Choudhry, Moorad. *Bond and Money Markets: Strategy, Trading, Analysis*. Oxford: Butterworth-Heinemann, 2003.

Choudhry, Moorad. *The Money Markets Handbook: A Practitioner's Guide*. Singapore: Wiley, 2005.

Article:

Fleming, Jeff, Chris Kirby, and Barbara Ostdiek. "Information and volatility linkages in the stock, bond, and money markets." *Journal of Financial Economics* 49:1 (July 1, 1998): 111–137. Online at: dx.doi.org/10.1016/S0304-405X(98)00019-1

Websites:

The Bank of England's framework for its operations in the sterling money markets: www.bankofengland.co.uk/markets/money

The US Federal Reserve's policy for its dollar operations: www.federalreserve.gov/monetarypolicy

See Also:

★ Investing in Structured Finance Products in the Debt Money Markets (pp. 510–513)

★ Managing Liquidity Risk in a Financial Institution: The Dangers of Short-Term Liabilities (pp. 74–76)

✔ Structured Investment Vehicles (p. 1092)

✔ Understanding and Using Currency Swaps (p. 992)

✔ Understanding and Using the Repos Market (p. 1098)

"The more volatile the market, the quicker an organization's success formula becomes obsolete." Daryl R. Conner

  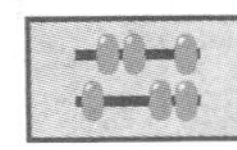      

Murabahah Sale Instruments and Their Applications

DEFINITION

Murabahah is a transaction in which a buyer purchases items at a profit margin agreed by both parties. The profit made by the seller is not regarded as a reward for the use of his or her capital, since it is not permissible to rent out money in Islam, but is instead seen as a profit on the sale of goods.

It is important to note that the profit in *murabahah* can be determined by mutual consent either in terms of a lump sum or through an agreed ratio of profit, which will be charged above the cost of the item.

All the expenses incurred by the seller in acquiring the commodity, such as freight, customs duties, and other costs, may be included in the cost price, and the markup can be applied to the aggregate cost.

Murabahah is valid only when it is possible to determine the exact cost of a commodity. If the exact cost cannot be ascertained, the commodity cannot be sold on a *murabahah* basis. In such an eventuality, the commodity must be sold on the basis of *musawamah* (bargaining), i.e. without any reference to the cost or to the profit/markup ratio. The price of the commodity in such cases shall be determined in lump sum by mutual consent.

In modern Islamic financial practice, *murabahah* has become an established mode of asset financing with an agreed and known markup. Being the most prevalent financing mechanism in Islamic finance, the *murabahah* sale instrument has provided a *shariah*-compliant alternative to interest-based financing mechanisms. The *murabahah* contract has also been applied for deposit-taking and issuance of *sukuk*.

Murabahah can be applied to large-scale projects. For example, it may be used to fund a plantation, whereby participants purchase seedlings and fertilizers and then sell these seedlings and fertilizers to the plantation operator at an agreed markup.

It can also be used to facilitate liquidity management, risk management in the Islamic financial market, and Islamic financial product offerings. For example, an Islamic bank can buy a commodity from the commodity market at the spot price and sell it to a corporate client on a deferred basis. This client can then sell the commodity back to the commodity market at the spot price for cash, returning to the bank the original sum plus an agreed markup.

ADVANTAGES

- *Murabahah* is not an interest-bearing loan, which is considered riba (excess). *Murabahah* is an acceptable form of credit sale under *shariah*. The agreement is similar in structure to a rent-to-own arrangement, with the intermediary retaining ownership of the property until the loan is paid in full.
- Because the Islamic bank that arranges a *murabahah* transaction does so as a partner, it is, in theory, concerned to ensure that the person who receives the money to make purchases is able to repay it. This should ensure that it behaves more cautiously than Western institutions, providing greater financial stability.
- Muslims can take advantage of the interest-free loans available from Western institutions if the seller decides not to charge a markup.

DISADVANTAGES

- *Murabahah* is not applicable in all cases. For example, it cannot be used when the price of the good cannot be determined.
- The agreed markup is not subject to inflation or fluctuations in the currency.

ACTION CHECKLIST

✔ Determine the markup, in the form of an absolute amount or a certain percentage of acquisition cost, and make sure that it is specified before the conclusion of the *murabahah* contract.

✔ Determine the benchmark to be used to find the agreed markup. Any mutually agreed benchmark, including but not limited to conventional financial benchmarks such as the base lending rate, may be used to determine the markup in the *murabahah* contract.

DOS AND DON'TS

DO

- Ensure that you understand the full acquisition cost, which may include direct expenses (costs incurred to enable the acquisition of goods) such as storage and delivery.
- Ensure that indirect expenses, such as staff wages and labor charges that are not part of the cost of acquisition, are not included in the acquisition cost. They are not allowed to be included.
- Note that in the contract, the asset transfer date and the title transfer date may not coincide.

DON'T

- Don't forget that whenever a purchase order involves a transaction requiring the issuance of a letter of credit, the commission for issuing the letter is not part of the acquisition cost.
- Don't forget that any additional direct expenses not specified in the agreement relating to a *murabahah* contract and incurred after the conclusion of the contract shall be borne by the customer, provided that a clause to that effect is already incorporated in the contract.

MORE INFO

Books:

Akgunduz, Ahmed (ed). *Studies in Islamic Economics: Islamic Banking and Development*. Rotterdam, Netherlands: IUR Press, 2009.

Ayub, Muhammad. *Understanding Islamic Finance*. Hoboken, NJ: Wiley, 2007.

Iqbal, Jaquir. *Islamic Financial Management*. New Delhi: Global Vision Publishing House, 2009.

See Also:

★ Procedures for Reporting Financial Risk in Islamic Finance (pp. 394–396)

✔ Key Islamic Banking Instruments and How They Work (p. 1010)

✔ Key Principles of Islamic Finance (p. 1011)

✔ An Overview of *Shariah*-Compliant Funds (p. 1083)

"We all know how the size of sums of money appear to vary in a remarkable way according as they are paid in or out."
Sir Julian Huxley

  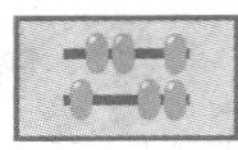      

Obtaining an Equity Value Using the Weighted Average Cost of Capital (WACC)

DEFINITION

Equity value is a market-based measure of the value of a company. In mergers and acquisitions, equity value is a more accurate measure of the value of a company than is market capitalization because equity value incorporates all equity interests in a firm. In contrast, market capitalization is calculated by multiplying the number of common shares currently outstanding by the share price.

WACC influences the calculation of equity value because the cost of financing any debt will reduce the company's nominal value. Valuation of a business using WACC means using the market value of equity, not its book value.

The example below shows how using WACC to calculate the debt value actually reduces the value of the debt and therefore reduces the company's overall equity value.

Example

Let us assume that a company has five million shares outstanding and that each share has a current market value of \$8. The market capitalization of this company is thus 5,000,000 × \$8 = \$40,000,000.

Now let us assume the company has a debt value of \$10 million and a WACC of 15%. The WACC equity value is calculated as follows:

Equity value =
Market capitalization + [Debt value × (1 − WACC)]
= \$40,000,000 + [\$10,000,000 × (1 − 0.15)]
= \$40,000,000 + \$8,500,000
= \$48,500,000

If WACC were not used in this calculation, the equity value of the company would simply be the sum of market capitalization and the debt value—that is, \$50 million.

WACC is particularly used in acquisitions or financing business operations, and is also the method used to determine the discount rate for valuing a company using the discounted cash flow method.

ADVANTAGES

- Calculating equity value using WACC takes into account the market capitalization *plus* the debt *plus* the cost of financing that debt.

DISADVANTAGES

- WACC is not easy to obtain because of the different types of data that have to be found. It is a complicated measure that requires a lot of detailed company information.

ACTION CHECKLIST

✔ A company with an investment return that is greater than its WACC is creating value. Conversely, a company with a return less than WACC is losing value and investors should look elsewhere.

✔ WACC should be recalculated annually in order to maintain correct figures.

DOS AND DON'TS

DO

- Use the market value of equity to value a business.
- Use the WACC if you are considering buying a business or if you are a value investor.

DON'T

- Don't use the book value of the equity to value a business.
- Don't invest in a company with a rate of return less than the WACC.

MORE INFO

Books:

Loos, Nicolaus. *Value Creation in Leveraged Buyouts: Analysis of Factors Driving Private Equity Investment Performance*. Wiesbaden, Germany: Deutscher Universitäts-Verlag (DUV), 2006.

Stewart, G. Bennett, III. *The Quest for Value: A Guide for Senior Managers*. 27th ed. New York: HarperCollins, 1991.

Articles:

Miles, James A., and John R. Ezzell. "The weighted average cost of capital, perfect capital markets and project life: A clarification." *Journal of Financial and Quantitative Analysis* 15:3 (September 1980): 719–730. Online at: dx.doi.org/10.2307/2330405

Yee, Kenton K. "Earnings quality and the equity risk premium: A benchmark model." *Contemporary Accounting Research* 23:3 (Fall 2006): 833–877. Online at: dx.doi.org/10.1506/8M44-W1DG-PLG4-8E0M

See Also:

✔ Calculating a Company's Net Worth (p. 1065)
✔ Estimating Enterprise Value with the Weighted Average Cost of Capital (p. 967)
✔ Understanding Capital Markets, Structure and Function (p. 1099)
✔ Understanding the Weighted Average Cost of Capital (WACC) (p. 1002)
⇄ Weighted Average Cost of Capital (pp. 1260–1261)

"The more volatile the market, the quicker an organization's success formula becomes obsolete." Daryl R. Conner

  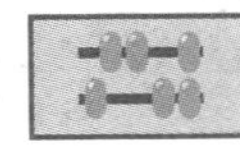      

Options for Raising Finance

DEFINITION

Funding small and medium-sized enterprises is a major part of the general business finance market. When a budding company is growing rapidly and needs to invest in capital equipment or other assets, its financial capital may be insufficient. Few emerging companies are able to finance their expansion plans from cash flow alone. Therefore, entrepreneurs need to consider raising finance from external sources. Once they have decided to raise capital, they need to consider what source and type of finance will suit their needs.

- **Venture capital**: Is intended for higher risks, such as start up situations and development capital for established companies.
- **Joint venture**: Find an individual or organization to both invest in and work with a company in its business project.
- **Limited company**: Raise capital by setting up a limited company and selling shares to investors.
- **Banks for working capital**: Short-term finance or the working capital necessary to fund the day-to-day running of the business. This can take the form of an agreed overdraft, where the interest will be calculated on your daily outstanding balance and charged on a monthly or quarterly basis.
- **Banks for medium-term loans**: A loan paid back over an agreed term (typically three to ten years), where principal and interest are paid off monthly. This type of loan is used mainly to invest in equipment, expansion, and development.
- **Banks for long-term loans**: The most common way to arrange long-term borrowing. This type of loan is normally used to purchase assets such as a business, land, buildings, plant, or machinery that can be shown to directly or indirectly add to profit over a number of years.
- **Factoring and invoice discounting**: To improve cash flow, finance can also be raised against customer debts using factoring or invoice discounting.
- **Leasing**: Provides finance for the acquisition of specific assets, such as cars, equipment, and machinery. Leasing involves a deposit and repayments over, typically, three to ten years. The financier purchases the equipment you require and then leases it to you in return for regular payments for the duration of the lease period.
- **Personal loans**: If it is impossible to arrange a loan in your business's name, you could consider arranging a personal loan. However, check that the conditions do not jeopardize control of the business and that you are very confident of being able to repay or you may lose the assets put up as collateral.
- **Family and friends**: To avoid any misunderstandings and/or resolve any dispute if things go wrong, it is imperative to make a written agreement, including the timescale and interest payments.

ADVANTAGES

- Finding the finance on the right terms allows small and medium-sized enterprises to invest in land, new capital equipment, R&D, etc. Very few emergent companies are able to finance their expansion plans from cash flow alone.
- Raising finance helps to avoid the dilution of business control or share capital.

DISADVANTAGES

- Venture capitalists normally want preference shares or loan stock in addition to their equity stake.
- Joint ventures and the setting up of limited companies can often result in the loss of control over aspects such as policy and development.
- Banks have the power to place a business into administration or bankruptcy if it defaults on debt interest or repayments.
- Borrowing from family or friends can lead to disputes or interference in the management of the venture.

ACTION CHECKLIST

- ✔ Prepare a written business plan explaining in detail your business objectives, your operating plan, projected earnings, marketing strategy, and other relevant information.
- ✔ Use the strategy laid out in the business plan to help you assess all the alternatives and then negotiate terms with several financial providers before choosing the one that suits you best.

DOS AND DON'TS

DO

- Consider what source and type of finance suits your needs. Then match the method of funding and the term of the loan to the reason for the finance.

DON'T

- Don't forget that your financing decisions may have an impact on business cash flow and taxation obligations.

MORE INFO

Books:

Burk, James E., and Richard P. Lehman. *Financing Your Small Business: From SBA Loans and Credit Cards to Common Stock and Partnership Interests*. Naperville, IL: Sourcebooks, 2006.

Lister, Kate, and Tom Harnish. *Finding Money: The Small Business Guide to Financing*. Chichester, UK: Wiley, 1995.

Timmons, Jeffry A., Stephen Spinelli, and Andrew Zacharakis. *How to Raise Capital: Techniques and Strategies for Financing and Valuing Your Small Business*. Maidenhead, UK: McGraw-Hill Professional, 2005.

Articles:

Thomas, Tony. "How to raise business finance." *NZ Business* (June 2006).

Williams, Gary. "How to balance ownership with the need to raise capital." *Deseret News* (April 20, 2008). Online at: tinyurl.com/2f7llc7

Websites:

Support for small and medium-sized enterprises: www.rba.co.uk

US Chamber of Commerce: www.uschamber.com

See Also:

★ Raising Capital in Global Financial Markets (pp. 567–569)
✔ Raising Capital by Issuing Bonds (p. 1086)
✔ Raising Capital by Issuing Shares (p. 1087)
✔ Raising Capital through Private and Public Equity (p. 1088)
✔ Using Mezzanine Financing (p. 1105)

"Wealth is not without its advantages and the case to the contrary, although it has often been made, has never proved widely persuasive." J. K. Galbraith

  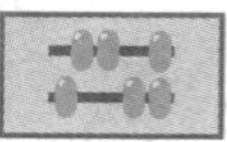      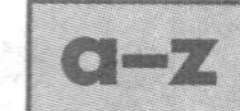

An Overview of Loan Agreements

DEFINITION

Most businesses need to borrow money, and obtaining a loan from a bank is the most usual way of financing a business. If successful in an application for a loan, an individual, partnership, or company has to enter into a loan agreement that sets out the terms on which the loan is given.

A loan agreement is entered into by the bank as lender, and by the individual, partnership, or company that borrows as borrower.

A loan agreement contains all the terms and conditions under which the lender will lend the borrower the money. It states the amount of the loan, when the amount will be lent, the tranches if the money is to be lent in amounts at different dates, the repayment schedule, the interest to be paid by the borrower, and other conditions, terms, and warranties required by the lender from the borrower.

The repayment schedule is usually very precise and will state the exact dates on which the lender expects to be paid back by the borrower. The loan agreement can contain a voluntary prepayment clause that will allow a borrower to prepay the loan in certain circumstances. It may also set out mandatory prepayment obligations that apply in certain cases—for example, if the borrower sells or lists its business, or if the business is acquired by someone else and control changes hands.

A loan agreement specifies the rate of interest, and how this will be calculated and paid by the borrower. It also deals with the consequences and penalties in the case of default on payments by the borrower.

The borrower usually has to pay the lender an arrangement fee for the loan and is also expected to pay all reasonable legal, accountancy, valuation, and due diligence costs and other fees, costs, and expenses of arranging the loan.

In general, a bank will not give a loan without obtaining security for that loan. The loan agreement will contain details of the debentures, guarantees, or charges given by the borrower as security for the loan.

The borrower will be asked to make and give certain representations and warranties in relation to its constitution and business. It will also be required to give certain covenants (promises) as to how it will conduct its business in the future.

ADVANTAGES

- A loan agreement sets out the terms and conditions upon which a bank will lend money to a borrower.
- Because it is an agreement, it can be negotiated and agreed by the two parties.
- A loan agreement protects both parties and is a legally enforceable agreement.

DISADVANTAGES

- In practice, a bank sets its own conditions for lending, and a borrower will have to comply and agree to such terms if it needs the funds.
- Negotiating a loan agreement can be complex and time-consuming. The documentation must be thoroughly understood, and if specialist legal advice is required the process may be expensive.

ACTION CHECKLIST

✔ Study a loan agreement carefully before you sign. Obtain as much information from as many sources as you can before committing to an expensive agreement.

✔ Shop around for a better deal. Go to several banks and see if there are better offers and conditions for the loan you want.

✔ Be prepared for long and complicated negotiations, which could prove time-consuming and costly.

DOS AND DON'TS

DO

- Choose your bank carefully.
- Make sure that you understand the conditions of your loan.
- Involve your solicitors in the evaluation of both the risks and benefits of entering into a loan agreement.
- Check if it's possible to negotiate the terms and conditions of the loan.
- If in trouble with repayments, tell your bank as they may be able to help in various ways, such as temporarily reducing your repayments.

DON'T

- Don't make the mistake of being attracted by a loan without understanding the implications of all the terms of the loan and the total cost to your business.
- Don't overlook the importance of negotiating warranties and indemnities that you will be able to give with confidence. If you know of anything that may go against these warranties, disclose it to the bank.
- Don't ignore the importance of telling the bank if you have problems with repayments. It might prove to your advantage.

MORE INFO

Books:

Clasen, Thomas F. (ed). *International Agency and Distribution Agreements*. Looseleaf ed. Charlottesville, VA: Lexis Law Publishing, 1991.

Singleton, Susan. *Commercial Agency Agreements: Law and Practice*. 3rd ed. Haywards Heath, UK: Bloomsbury Professional, 2010.

Websites:

About.com Business Finance: bizfinance.about.com
AllBusiness: www.allbusiness.com
National Federation of Independent Business (US): www.nfib.com
Western Economic Diversification Canada: www.wd-deo.gc.ca

See Also:

★ How and When to Use Nonrecourse Financing (pp. 494–495)
✔ Assessing Cash Flow and Bank Lending Requirements (p. 964)
✔ Retail Banks: Their Structure and Function (p. 1014)
✔ Steps for Obtaining Bank Financing (p. 1090)

"Purchasing power is a license to purchase power." Raoul Vaneigem

An Overview of *Shariah*-Compliant Funds

DEFINITION

Shariah-compliant funds are investment vehicles which are fully compliant with the principles of Islam. The funds are prohibited from making investments in industries categorized as morally deficient, such as those related to gambling or alcohol. Because Islam does not permit any form of exploitation, any kind of investment in conventional banking is outlawed. With the concept of debt also contrary to the principles of Islam, investment in highly leveraged companies is also not permitted for *shariah*-compliant funds. The exclusions extend to potential investments in other funds which offer guaranteed returns. Any use of futures and options, either by the fund managers or by companies in which the funds invest, is also likely to attract close scrutiny by the funds' supervisory *shariah* boards.

Due to the rapid growth in Islamic finance over recent years, the available range of *shariah*-compliant funds has expanded as financial services providers seek to tap into the increasing demand for investment products that respect the principles of Islam. The most common forms of *shariah*-compliant funds are described below.

Ijarah

Ijarah (also transliterated *ijara*) is a leasing-type fund that acquires assets such as real estate or equipment and then leases them out to another party in return for a regular rental payment. In all cases the fund retains ownership of the asset and must ensure that usage of the asset is at all times in accordance with Islamic principles.

Murabahah

Murabahah (or *murabaha*) is a kind of development fund that acquires assets and then sells them to a client at a predetermined price which reflects the fund's cost of acquiring the asset plus a profit margin. Sometimes described as "cost-plus" funds, *murabahah* investment vehicles do not hold long-term ownership of the assets, but instead generate a financial return from the payment obligations taken on by clients for a pre-agreed period.

Equity

Equity funds invest directly in companies through the purchase of shares. Given the difficulties involved in scrutinizing every aspect of how a company operates to verify *shariah*-compliance, this new, more progressive attitude allows investment in companies that operate in permitted industries, with the proviso that a proportion of the returns generated for the fund from any interest-bearing deposits held by the company must be donated to charity.

Commodity

Commodity funds invest in physical commodities, although speculative activities such as short selling are not permitted. However, the fund manager may make use of *istisna'a* contracts, pre-agreeing the price of goods to be manufactured and delivered at a specified future date, with the manufacturer benefiting from advance receipt of the agreed sale price. Commodity fund managers can also use *bai salam* contracts. These can be compared to conventional forward contracts, though the key *shariah*-compliant differentiator is that the seller's position is protected because payment is passed to the seller on agreement of the contract rather than on its completion. However, in return for the effective transfer of contract risk, the buyer is compensated by the fact that the agreed delivery price is set at a discount to the physical spot price.

ADVANTAGES

- *Shariah*-compliant investment funds provide a means of investing while still honoring the high morals and principles of Islam.
- *Shariah*-compliant funds promote large-scale investment along lines similar to the niche ethical funds available to Western consumers.

DISADVANTAGES

- The funds can be more expensive to develop and administer than mainstream funds due to the need for greater verification of compliance with *shariah* principles.

ACTION CHECKLIST

✔ Assess the full range of available *shariah*-compliant investment products before selecting the type you wish to use.

✔ Consider how much risk you are prepared to assume before investing.

✔ Mainstream investors may wish to consider potential investments in *shariah*-compliant funds.

DOS AND DON'TS

DO

- Compare fund management charges between different providers.
- Consider using index products such as exchange-traded funds to gain exposure to Islamic investment indices.

DON'T

- Don't feel you have to verify the compliance of a fund yourself—contact a fund provider for advice.
- Don't expect guaranteed attractive returns, even from the most ethical forms of investment.

MORE INFO

Books:

Anwar, Habiba, and Roderick Millar (eds). *Islamic Finance: A Guide for International Business and Investment*. London: GMB Publishing, 2008.

Jaffer, Sohail (ed). *Islamic Asset Management: Forming the Future for Shari'a-Compliant Investment Strategies*. London: Euromoney Books, 2004.

Vogel, Frank E., and Samuel L. Hayes, III. *Islamic Law and Finance: Religion, Risk, and Return*. The Hague: Kluwer Law International, 1998.

Articles:

Feinberg, Phyllis. "Seeking pension money: Mutual fund family follows Islamic law." *Pensions and Investments* (October 30, 2000). Online at: tinyurl.com/6zugr7a

Siddiqi, Moin A. "Growing appeal of Islamic investment funds." *Middle East* (July–August 1997).

See Also:

★ The Performance of Socially Responsible Mutual Funds (pp. 553–555)

✔ Key Islamic Banking Instruments and How They Work (p. 1010)

✔ Key Principles of Islamic Finance (p. 1011)

✔ Regulatory and Capital Issues under *Shariah* Law (p. 1050)

✔ The Role of the *Shariah* Advisory Board in Islamic Finance (p. 1015)

        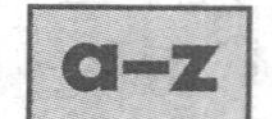

An Overview of Stockholders' Agreements

DEFINITION

The shares (or stock) issued by most limited companies are classed as "ordinary," and each share carries one vote. Majority shareholders will therefore control voting in the company. Since minority shareholders may resent not having any say in important company decisions, conflicts can arise. To minimize these, it is advisable that the shareholders sign a stockholders' agreement—which will give small shareholders a voice in these big decisions.

Stockholders' agreements are more commonly used in certain circumstances: for example, when some shareholders are not directors and thus do not have much of a role in the decisions of the board, or in the case of equal-stake joint ventures.

A stockholders' agreement will establish the constitution of the board, the number of directors, which shareholder(s) will have the right to appoint directors (and how many), and who will be the chairman of the board and have the casting vote if needed. It will also decide who will have management control and how board meetings and voting will operate.

The agreement can also establish that certain business issues will require the approval of 100% of the shares. These are usually only very important issues, such as: the company entering into a contract with directors or shareholders; the incurring of expenditure or liability over a certain predetermined value; the company giving a guarantee or taking on an encumbrance (debt) of a certain value; the sale, transfer, lease, or licensing of any of the assets of the company other than in the ordinary course of business; or the altering of any provisions of the company bylaws.

In general, a stockholders' agreement is a contract between shareholders that can stipulate more or less anything, as long as it does not contravene the law or the bylaws of the company

ADVANTAGES

- Stockholders' agreements protect minority shareholders and allow them to participate in decisions from which they might otherwise be excluded.
- Stockholders' agreements are not regulated. Shareholders have the flexibility to decide the type of contract they want.
- The stockholders' agreement can also restrict the transfer of shares and will establish pre-emption rights (the right of existing shareholders to be the first to acquire the shares of another shareholder).

DISADVANTAGES

- Assenting to a stockholders' agreement may involve extensive negotiations and require professional advice. It could be expensive to draft and put in place.

ACTION CHECKLIST

- ✔ Study any shareholder agreement carefully before signing. Be clear what you would like to achieve from it.
- ✔ Be prepared for extensive negotiations, which could prove time-consuming as well as costly.
- ✔ Economize by negotiating a reasonable rate with your legal and financial advisers, but remember that it is better to incur costs and understand the agreement you sign than to enter into an agreement that you do not understand and may not represent your interests.

DOS AND DON'TS

DO

- Involve your lawyers in the negotiation of a stockholders' agreement.
- Think carefully what you would like to achieve from it.
- If necessary, request the right to appoint a director as your representative on the board. In this way, you can influence decisions in the company at board level.

DON'T

- Don't make the mistake of entering into a stockholders' agreement that you do not understand and does not represent your interests.

MORE INFO

Books:

Wilkinson, Chris (ed). *Joint Ventures and Shareholders' Agreements*. 3rd ed. Haywards Heath, UK: Tottel Publishing, 2009.

Stedman, Graham, Janet Jones, and John Cadman. *Shareholders' Agreements*. 4th ed. Andover, UK: Sweet & Maxwell, 2003.

Articles:

Sisca, Eileen R., and Eckert Seamans. "Protect your investment with a shareholders' agreement." *Leader's Edge* 2:9 (1999): 4.

Waldman, Glenn J. "The shareholders' agreement—Don't leave your P.A. without it." *Florida Bar Journal* 71:9 (October 1997): 57. Online at: tinyurl.com/2ct3bum

Websites:

Canadian legal resources: www.canadalegal.com

Exile From the Herd: The Official Mark Jeftovic blog: www.privateworld.com

International Financial Law Review: www.iflr.com

Net Lawman legal documents (UK): www.netlawman.co.uk

See Also:

★ Reinvesting in the Company versus Rewarding Investors with Distributions (pp. 701–702)
✔ Raising Capital by Issuing Shares (p. 1087)
✔ Setting Up a Dividend Policy (p. 987)
✔ Using Dividend Discount Models (p. 1104)
✔ Using Shareholder Value Analysis (p. 1107)

"In every well-governed state wealth is a sacred thing; in democracies it is the only sacred thing." Anatole France

  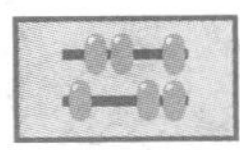      

An Overview of Tax Deeds

DEFINITION

A tax deed is usually entered into upon an acquisition of the majority shares in a company. The tax deed is concerned with the tax affairs of the business and the company acquired. Under the tax deed, the seller agrees to pay to the buyer any tax liability and charge resulting from an event occurring before the buyer acquired the company. This includes any reasonable costs and expenses which were properly incurred and payable by the company or the buyer in connection with any reasonable action to avoid or settle a tax claim or liability. In any tax deed, the sellers will seek to limit their liability in such an undertaking to a maximum agreed amount. For example, the undertaking will not be given and the seller will not be liable to the extent that any provision or reserve in respect of the liability to taxation was taken into account in the accounts of the company. Also the seller will not be made to pay if the amount has already been recovered by the buyer under the sale and purchase agreement. The tax deed will also deal with the procedure to be followed by the parties in the event of a tax claim which the seller is not aware of. The deed will also cover how the payments, if any, will be made and scheduled. The undertaking by the seller will usually be valid for a period of seven years from the date of acquisition of the company but this can vary depending upon the laws of the applicable jurisdiction.

ACTION CHECKLIST

✔ Carefully study any tax deed which you might sign. Obtain as much information from as many sources as you can before committing to expensive liabilities. Do not sign a document that you do not understand.

✔ Through your advisers try and limit your exposure of liabilities to an amount you feel comfortable with. If your company has had its tax affairs in order you do not have much to worry about.

ADVANTAGES

- A tax deed sets out the terms and conditions under which the buyer of a company will be compensated for any tax liability that he/she must pay after the acquisition as a result of an event which occurred before the date of the acquisition.
- Because a tax deed is an agreement, it can be negotiated and agreed by the two parties, the buyer and the seller.
- Tax deeds protect buyers from unnecessary and unforeseen tax liabilities they may have as a result of acquiring a company. In general, they are reasonably standard and accepted as a necessary document by the parties of an acquisition of a majority of shares in a company.

DISADVANTAGES

- Negotiating a tax deed can be complex and time consuming. It involves thorough knowledge of the documentation and requires specialist legal, accounting, and tax advice and can therefore be an expensive process.

DOS AND DON'TS

DO

- Choose your advisers carefully. Make sure that you understand the undertakings you are giving. Involve your tax advisers and accountants in the negotiation process.
- Involve your solicitors in the evaluation of both the risks and potential benefits of entering into a tax deed.
- If you know of any tax liabilities that are due before the completion of your sale, disclose them and try to sort them out with the relevant authorities.

DON'T

- Don't make the mistake of ignoring the importance of the undertakings you will give in a tax deed. They can come back to haunt you.
- Don't overlook the importance of negotiating undertakings and indemnities that you could give with confidence. Make sure that if you know of anything that may go against these warranties, you disclose them to the buyer.

MORE INFO

Books:

CCH Tax Law Editors. *US Master Sales and Use Tax Guide*. Chicago, IL: CCH, 2007.

Reuvid, Jonathan. *Mergers and Acquisitions: A Practical Guide for Private Companies and their UK and Overseas Advisers*. Philadelphia, PA: Kogan Page, 2008.

Articles:

Gustafson, Jeanne. "GenPrime signs big distribution agreement." *Journal of Business* (October 2000).

Quinn, Robert M. "Florida tax deed sales are getting risky." *Florida Bar Journal* 81:7 (July/August 2007). Online at: tinyurl.com/6kjs6fk

See Also:

★ Due Diligence Requirements in Financial Transactions (pp. 727–729)
★ How Taxation Impacts on Liquidity Management (pp. 48–49)
✔ Acquiring a Company (p. 1128)
✔ Planning the Acquisition Process (p. 1132)
✔ Structuring M&A Deals and Tax Planning (p. 1135)

"Someone will always be getting richer faster than you. This is not a tragedy." Charlie E. Munger

Raising Capital by Issuing Bonds

DEFINITION

Raising capital by issuing bonds is a popular alternative to selling shares, as it allows a company to avoid relinquishing ownership of part of the business. A bond is a loan in the form of a debt security. The authorized issuer (the borrower) owes the bondholder (the lender) a debt and has an obligation to repay the principal and the coupon (interest) on the maturity of the loan. Bonds enable the issuer to finance long-term investments with external funds.

The loan collateral may be the company's land, buildings, or other physical assets that can be sold off if the issuer defaults on repayment of the principal. In today's bond markets, however, a much wider range of assets can fulfill the function of collateral, such as receivables that produce a flow of income.

ADVANTAGES

- Taking on debt by issuing bonds is usually cheaper than either a bank overdraft or the cost of raising equity through a share issue. A major advantage is that the return on debt (interest) is tax-deductible, whereas the return on equity (dividends) is paid out of a company's profits, which are taxed before dividend payments can be made to stockholders.
- Financing by raising debt is a useful way of monitoring a corporation's overall health, as the ability to repay the debt reflects the overall financial stability of the company.
- Bonds offer a more secure return for investors—dividends are paid out purely at the discretion of the company, whereas interest on debt must be paid according to the set terms of the bond.
- Debt issuance can also be advantageous from a governance point of view. In the United States and United Kingdom, for example, creditors have no influence on the board or company policy—unlike stockholders, who often have the right to vote on policies and the appointment of directors. Financing through debt can thus be very useful for companies that do not want to relinquish control to others.

DISADVANTAGES

- The risks for bondholders rise as more debt is issued.
- The debt covenants may prove too restrictive for the company. A company that is highly leveraged is more likely to face cash flow difficulties as it has to meet the coupon payments regardless of its income. The cost of servicing the debt may rise beyond the ability to pay, either because of external events, such as falling income, or because of internal problems, such as poor company management. The company may find that it runs into solvency problems if the amount of debt becomes higher than the value of its realizable assets. Thus, the cost of debt rises as its proportion rises in relation to equity. The higher the debt-to-equity ratio, the greater the risk.
- If the company is publicly listed on a stock exchange, the risk to stockholders increases when debt is issued. This is due to the increased claims of the creditors, or bondholders, on the company's capital and earnings, which must be used to service the debt before anything else. And if the company has problems servicing the debt, stockholders risk the loss of their equity in the case of bankruptcy.

ACTION CHECKLIST

✔ *Choose the right type of debt*. For large investments, you generally have a choice of borrowing the principal from a creditor, usually a bank, or issuing bonds underwritten by the bank that can be sold to investors. If the bond can be retraded, it is beneficial for the bondholders as they can exit at the right moment, but the company still has access to the funds via new purchasers.

✔ *Choose the right interest rate*. Bonds usually have either a fixed interest rate for a specified period or a floating rate linked to an agreed index. Fixed-rate debt means that the issuer knows the exact cost across the debt's lifetime and can budget for the principal and interest payments each year. Floating-rate debt usually has a mark-up over the base rate set by the central bank in charge of the currency that is being borrowed, meaning that the issuer may have to pay more if monetary policy is tightened and interest rates rise during the period of the loan.

DOS AND DON'TS

DO

- Do a full cost analysis to determine if debt will be cheaper for the company than equity.
- Take into account that unexpected market volatility and inflation will affect the coupon level.

DON'T

- Don't issue bonds if you think that meeting regular payments to the bondholders will overstretch your cash flow.

MORE INFO

Books:

Brown, Patrick J. *An Introduction to the Bond Markets*. Hoboken. NJ: Wiley, 2006.

Choudhry, Moorad. *The Bond and Money Markets: Strategy, Trading, Analysis*. Oxford: Butterworth-Heinemann, 2003.

See Also:

✔ The Bond Market: Its Structure and Function (p. 1064)
✔ Options for Raising Finance (p. 1081)
✔ Trading in Corporate Bonds: Why and How (p. 1094)
✔ Understanding Capital Markets, Structure and Function (p. 1099)

"A nation cannot prosper long when it favors only the prosperous." Barack Obama

  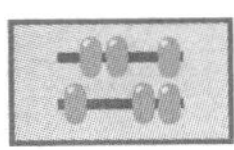      

Raising Capital by Issuing Shares

DEFINITION

A company that wants to raise capital by issuing shares has several options. If it is not yet listed on a stock exchange, the company can prepare for an initial public offering (IPO), in which it will be valued and an opening price will be set for its shares when they are released onto the market. How much finance can be raised through an IPO depends partly on the perceived value, and thus share price, of the company, and partly on how much interest there is in the shares when they are released on the market.

For a company that is already listed on an exchange, an alternative route is to launch an additional share issue (also known as a seasoned equity offering, or SEO) or a rights issue. A SEO is a new equity issue by a company following its IPO. A rights issue permits existing stockholders to purchase a designated number of new shares from a company at a specified price within a specified time. The offer may be rejected, or accepted in full or in part, by each stockholder. Rights are usually transferable, meaning that the holder can sell them on the open market. The additional shares in a rights issue are generally issued to stockholders on a pro rata basis—for example, in a two-for-five rights issue stockholders are offered two shares for every five they already hold.

Renounceable rights are rights offered by a company to existing stockholders to purchase further stock, usually at a discount. These rights have a value and can be traded. If rights are to be issued, the company has to set the price of the new shares, determine how many it will sell, and assess how the current share value will be affected as well as the effect on new and existing stockholders. Nonrenounceable rights are not transferable and cannot be bought or sold; these rights must be taken up or they will lapse.

ADVANTAGES

- For a company that has reached a certain size and has a strong reputation, an IPO can be a good route to raising a large sum of capital that will enable it to expand, or invest in assets that will enable it to grow in the future.
- The company does not need to repay this share capital, but instead agrees to distribute future profits to stockholders in return for their investment.
- Once listed, a company can periodically issue further shares via a rights issue, raising yet more capital for expansion without running up debt. Being in a position to raise capital from the stock markets, rather than privately from individual investors, is a major incentive for many companies to issue shares on an exchange.

DISADVANTAGES

- The main disadvantage of issuing shares through an IPO is that a company's owners no longer have full control of the business and become accountable to stockholders. Stockholders can block plans if they believe they pose too great a risk to their investment.
- Any issuance of further shares dilutes the holdings of existing stockholders as a proportion of the company's total shares. This can lead to dissatisfaction from minority stockholders, who have the most to lose. In some jurisdictions, such as the UK, stockholders have preemptive rights by law, which means they have the right to purchase new issuances first. In other jurisdictions, such as the US, preemptive rights must be enshrined in a company's constitution. Stockholders who do not have preemptive rights are most at risk of seeing their investment diluted.

ACTION CHECKLIST

✔ Consider whether options for raising capital other than a share issue might be more suited to your investment plans.

✔ Consult your bank and other financial advisers on the time scale for an IPO or rights issues, and on the timing of the offer.

DOS AND DON'TS

DO

- Issue a proper prospectus for your share offer.
- Keep stockholders informed about how much dividend they can expect to receive each year.

DON'T

- Don't issue shares if you are not prepared to give up a certain amount of decision-making to stockholders.

MORE INFO

Books:

Gregoriou, Greg N. *Initial Public Offerings: An International Perspective*. Amsterdam: Butterworth-Heinemann, 2006.

Temple, Peter. *First Steps in Shares*. Harlow, UK: Pearson Education, 2001.

Articles:

Goergen, Marc, Arif Khurshed, and Ram Mudambi. "The strategy of going public: How UK firms choose their listing contracts." *Journal of Business Finance and Accounting* 33:1–2 (January/March 2006): 79–101. Online at: dx.doi.org/10.1111/j.1468-5957.2006.00657.x

Loughran, Tim, and Jay R. Ritter. "Why don't issuers get upset about leaving money on the table in IPOs?" *Review of Financial Studies* 15:2 (Spring 2002): 413–444. Online at: dx.doi.org/10.1093/rfs/15.2.413

See Also:

★ Understanding Equity Capital in Small and Medium-Sized Enterprises (pp. 607–610)
✔ An Overview of Stockholders' Agreements (p. 1084)
✔ Stock Markets: Their Structure and Function (p. 1091)

"Someday I want to be rich. Some people get so rich they lose all respect for humanity. That's how rich I want to be."
Rita Rudner

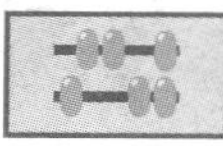

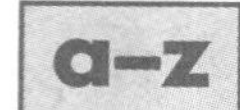

Raising Capital through Private and Public Equity

DEFINITION

Many publicly listed companies needing to raise funds for investment choose not to offer shares or issue bonds on the open markets, but instead look for capital on the private equity markets. In the former case, funding comes from a publicly listed company looking to invest in other companies that offer synergy, as well as good financial returns. In the latter, the funds come from institutional investors who invest their wealth indirectly through private equity funds—private equity being a class of assets that are not publicly traded on the exchanges. Institutional investors provide such capital with the aim of achieving risk-adjusted returns that exceed those possible on the stock markets.

In both cases, a percentage stake in the company is surrendered in exchange for the investment, and the deal usually includes one or more seats on the board of directors as well. Companies seeking equity funding may use a financial intermediary to broker the best deal for the investment.

Companies that raise investment capital in this way can usually expect to deliver a return on investment through one of the following routes: *Recapitalization*, in which the company distributes dividends or cash to its stakeholders; a *merger* or *acquisition*, in which the company may be absorbed by or merged with its public equity investor, or sold for either cash or shares in another company by its private equity backers; a *buy-out*, in which the equity investor agrees to pull out in exchange for a cash sum from the company, which thereupon regains its independence; or an *initial public offering (IPO)*, whereby company shares are offered to the public on a stock exchange, which offers the equity investor both an immediate partial cash return on its investment, in addition to a public market in which additional share issues can be placed at a later date.

ADVANTAGES

- Raising capital through equity can be a good choice for companies that are not ready for an IPO or are unwilling to finance expansion through debt.
- An equity deal means that the company has access to business experts through its investors, who can help to steer the business strategically as well as financially.

DISADVANTAGES

- Taking the equity route can lock a company into an agreement over a long time frame.
- The company may have to surrender a large stake in return for investment, possibly as much as 50%, and also provide seats on the board.
- Investors may interfere with the company's business plan and other areas of strategic importance.
- With either type of equity deal, there needs to be chemistry between the counterparties. Lack of chemistry can lead to board disagreements and other problems, souring the relationship.
- It can be difficult for a company to extricate itself from an equity investment arrangement, depending on the terms of the deal.

ACTION CHECKLIST

✔ Look for synergies if choosing the equity investment route, as the relationship with investors is likely to be more fruitful and less fraught if the counterparties feel they want the same things for the business, and can agree on essentials such as direction and strategy.

✔ Private equity firms are more likely to be concerned about the long-term relationship in terms of ultimate financial return, whereas a public equity investor may be concerned only with the bottom line.

DOS AND DON'TS

DO

- Hold talks with a range of potential investors to compare the deals on offer.
- Look at other possible financing options—an equity deal may not always be the right solution.

DON'T

- Don't enter into an equity deal if you feel pressured to give away a greater stake in the business than you want to. You may regret it later.
- Don't be afraid to bargain hard at the negotiating stage of the deal.

MORE INFO

Books:

Fraser-Sampson, Guy. *Private Equity as an Asset Class*. Chichester, UK: Wiley, 2007.

Jenkinson, Tim, and Alexander Ljungqvist. *Going Public: The Theory and Evidence on How Companies Raise Equity Finance*. 2nd ed. Oxford: Oxford University Press, 2001.

Mathonet, Pierre-Yves, and Thomas Meyer. *J-Curve Exposure: Managing a Portfolio of Venture Capital and Private Equity Funds*. Chichester, UK: Wiley, 2007.

Mavrikakis, Alexis. *Public Companies and Equity Finance 2009*. Guildford, UK: College of Law Publishing, 2009.

See Also:

✔ Options for Raising Finance (p. 1081)

✔ Raising Capital by Issuing Shares (p. 1087)

  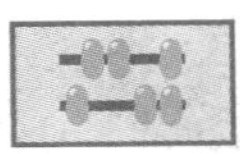      

Sovereign Wealth Funds—Investment Strategies and Objectives

DEFINITION

Sovereign wealth funds' (SWFs) investment decisions are typically made with one of two goals in mind: either the funds are seeking an attractive rate of return in purely economic terms, or they are hoping to generate strategic benefits for their country. In the former case, SWFs regularly describe themselves as passive investors in that they do not seek to influence or control the companies they invest in, sometimes preferring to avoid holding voting shares at all. In contrast to typical private equity investors, SWFs are also frequently happy to put their faith in existing company management, rather than aiming to parachute their own executives onto the board. When a SWF invests in a company for strategic benefits, commonly in sectors such as financial services or leisure, the objective is usually to gain insights into the management's operational expertise with a long-term view of helping to develop or grow a related industry in the fund's own country.

While many SWFs may emphasize that their investment strategies tend to be longer term and more "hands off" than the average private equity investor, there are signs that some SWFs are prepared to work more closely with these more active investors to help achieve their investment goals. For example, Abu Dhabi-based Mubadala's 2007 purchase of a 7.5% stake in Carlyle, and news that China Investment Corporation (CIC) had raised its stake in Blackstone to around 12.5% in late 2008, raised the prospect of further cooperation between SWFs and private equity groups.

Though many SWFs have demonstrated their willingness to hold a geographically diverse spread of assets, few have historically provided much insight into the precise investment strategies they employ to achieve their stated objectives. However, Norway's GPF-G Fund (Government Pension Fund—Global), the world's second-largest SWF (after the Abu Dhabi Investment Authority), is the notable exception, providing regular updates on its holdings and demonstrating a high level of commitment to ethical investing. Nevertheless, the SWFs' general perceived lack of investment transparency and doubts over their commitment to high standards of corporate governance standards have done little to help the image of SWFs. Though political pressure is growing in some jurisdictions for greater standards of transparency and improved disclosure from SWFs with the potential to acquire assets of significant national importance or prestige, there is evidence that many SWFs would prefer to work within more loosely worded "best practice" investment frameworks. In October 2008, the International Working Group of Sovereign Wealth Funds presented a proposed set of principles guiding the operations of SWFs to the International Monetary Fund's (IMF) policy-focused International Monetary and Financial Committee. Both the IMF and the Organisation for Economic Co-operation and Development (OECD) are set to present their own proposals in reports due in 2009.

ADVANTAGES

- The long-term and "hands-off" nature of investments by SWFs can make them attractive shareholders for some companies.
- SWFs have been a particularly valuable source of immediate capital injections into financial institutions whose balance sheets have been in urgent need of strengthening.
- High levels of investable cash give SWFs the ability to capitalize on opportunities generated by market swings, with the meaning SWFs can be a stabilizing influence during times of market volatility.

DISADVANTAGES

- Doubts persist in some quarters over the motives behind some SWFs investments, particularly those made for long-term strategic reasons.
- Political concerns are frequently raised over the prospect of key national resources falling under the control of secretive overseas investors, particularly in view of most SWFs' poor disclosure standards.

ACTION CHECKLIST

- ✔ By moving towards the adoption of best practice guidelines to be proposed by the IMF and the OECD, it should be possible to alleviate some concerns over the lack of transparency and disclosure of most SWFs.
- ✔ By taking non-voting shares only, SWFs can help to overcome objections over the motivation for some of their more politically sensitive investments.

DOS AND DON'TS

DO

- Recognize the increasing scope for private equity and SWF investors to cooperate on investment projects.
- Appreciate that the generally poor level of transparency of SWFs does little to alleviate concerns over their motives when making overseas investments.

DON'T

- Don't be afraid of improved disclosure; follow the example of Norway's pension SWF.
- Don't overlook the role of SWFs, as cash-rich, long-term investors, in helping to stabilize volatile markets and recapitalize struggling companies.

MORE INFO

Book:

Hassan, Adnan. *A Practical Guide to Sovereign Wealth Funds*. London: Euromoney Institutional Investor, 2008.

Articles:

Jen, Stephen. "Sovereign wealth funds: What they are and what's happening." *World Economics* 8:4 (2007): 1–7. Online at: tinyurl.com/77avvaw

Raphaeli, Nimrod, and Bianca Gersten. "Sovereign wealth funds: Investment vehicles for the Persian Gulf countries." *Middle East Quarterly* 15:2 (Spring 2008): 45–53. Online at: tinyurl.com/ybyjbt2

Websites:

International Working Group of Sovereign Wealth Funds: www.iwg-swf.org

Opalesque Sovereign Wealth Funds Briefing: www.opalesque.com/SWF_Briefing/

Sovereign Wealth Fund Institute: www.swfinstitute.org

Steps for Obtaining Bank Financing

DEFINITION

A major problem for both emerging and established companies is the cost of raising capital. Can the owners obtain bank financing instead of incurring dilution by giving up additional ownership in the company? An owner of a promising business may perceive itself as being creditworthy, however a bank will require "proof," for example in the form of a full quarter or year of sustained profitability, depending on the industry and levels of profitability. Decision makers at the bank will judge the company on a number of factors, including the following ratios:

- *Leverage/gearing*: to guarantee the company is sufficiently capitalized, i.e. total liabilities divided by tangible net worth.
- *Liquidity*: to guarantee sufficient working capital; measured by current ratio, i.e. current assets divided by current liabilities.
- *Debt service coverage*: to guarantee the company has sufficient operating cash flow to cover principal and interest and any capital leases.

Companies will need to present a written business plan explaining business objectives in detail, operating plans, projected earnings for the next one to five years, marketing strategy, and other relevant information. Marketing strategies must be outlined in detail to lend credence to sales projections. The first two years of projections should be detailed by month or by quarter to measure the projected performance against financial ratios. These projections should be composed of balance sheets, income statements, and cash-flow statements. The bank will also want to know:

- How much money do you need?
- How do you plan to use the money? (For example, to buy new assets, to pay off debts, or to pay operating expenses?)
- How long will it take you to repay the loan? (Use your cash flow projections to help plan the repayments.)
- What loan repayments can you afford to make without damaging the business?
- What can you offer as security for the loan? (Bankers generally require personal guarantees from the owners.)

The bank will also want to determine whether the management has the skills to run the business. Typical questions include: is the manager/owner talented enough to direct the company? Are the sales team knowledgeable about the industry and have they demonstrated successful sales growth in other companies? Does the financial officer have an in depth understanding of the financial background of the company? Do the management team get on well together and complement each other?

ADVANTAGES

- Bank financing allows the owners to keep a major interest in the company, instead of diluting interest by selling shares. Looking for bank financing will force the owners to focus on detailed projections. In order to present a written business plan, the owners must concentrate on the strategic planning that is vital to a business's survival. Building a successful relationship with the bank will help with future business expansion.

DISADVANTAGES

- Research, preparation, and presentation of the details required by the bank will take time away from the day to day functions of running the business.
- The company will be leveraged and therefore subject to detailed bank scrutiny during the period of the loan.
- An unfavorable payback period.

ACTION CHECKLIST

✔ Prepare a detailed business plan explaining objectives, operations, marketing strategy, and projected earnings for the next five years.

✔ Make sure you are not taking on too much debt. There is no sense in taking out a loan that will squeeze out your profits and bleed your business dry. Check your leverage/gearing and liquidity ratios and then capacity for debt service coverage.

✔ Prepare answers to the bank's key questions. For example, how much money do you need? How do you plan to use the money? How long will it take you to repay the loan? What will you use as security for the loan?

DOS AND DON'TS

DO

- Get expert advice when preparing your proposal. Getting a bank loan for an emerging company or even an established business is not always simple.

DON'T

- Don't go to the bank thinking that you'll get the loan just because you have a good idea. You will need to take a rigorously detailed proposal.

MORE INFO

Books:

Burk, James E., and Richard P. Lehman. *Financing Your Small Business: From SBA Loans and Credit Cards to Common Stock and Partnership Interests*. Naperville, IL: Sourcebooks, 2006.

Sisson, Robert. *Financing the Small Business: A Complete Guide to Obtaining Bank Loans and All Other Types of Financing*. Cincinnati, OH: Adams Media Corporation, 2002.

Timmons, Jeffry A., Stephen Spinelli, and Andrew Zacharakis. *How to Raise Capital: Techniques and Strategies for Financing and Valuing Your Small Business*. Maidenhead, UK: McGraw-Hill Professional, 2005.

See Also:

★ Assessing Venture Capital Funding for Small and Medium-Sized Enterprises (pp. 451–453)
✔ Assessing Cash Flow and Bank Lending Requirements (p. 964)
✔ Basic Steps for Starting a Business (p. 1147)
✔ An Overview of Loan Agreements (p. 1082)
✔ Retail Banks: Their Structure and Function (p. 1014)

"Nothing is more admirable than the fortitude with which millionaires tolerate the disadvantages of their wealth."
Rex Stout

     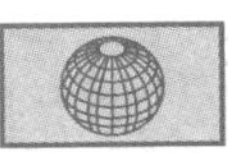   

Stock Markets: Their Structure and Function

DEFINITION

A stock market is a private or public market for the trading of stocks and shares in companies and derivatives of company stocks at an agreed price. These include securities listed on a stock exchange as well as those traded privately. A stock market is sometimes also known as an equity market.

The estimated size of the world stock market is around US$51 trillion. Even larger, it is estimated that the world derivatives market is worth about US$480 trillion face, or nominal, value; that is well over ten times the size of the whole world economy. However, the derivatives market is stated in terms of notional values and therefore cannot be directly compared to stocks, which refer to an actual value.

Stock markets specialize in bringing buyers and sellers of stocks and securities together. Famous stock exchanges include the New York Stock Exchange, the London Stock Exchange, the Deutsche Börse, and the Paris/Amsterdam Euronext.

A stock market is an important way for a company to raise money. It allows businesses to be publicly traded, or to raise extra capital for expansion by selling shares in the company in a public market. Share owners then have a share of ownership of that company. A stock market provides liquidity to give investors the chance to sell securities rapidly and easily. This makes investing in stocks attractive compared with, for example, real estate, which is less liquid.

The price of shares and other assets plays an important part in the economic activity of a country. It can influence or reflect the social mood of a country. A stock market is often taken as a primary indicator of a country's economic well-being as it enables the efficient allocation of capital. Stock prices reflect where capital is being invested, or should be. If share prices are rising, this is usually coupled with increased business investment, and vice versa. Share prices also have an influence on the wealth of households, and thus on how much they spend. Central banks watch the movement of the stock market closely and also the smooth operation of financial system functions. This was highlighted in September 2008, when stock markets plunged in response to failing financial institutions—particularly in the United States—and central banks stepped in to try to arrest the slide.

Stock exchanges act as a clearing house for each transaction made on them. This means that they guarantee payment to the seller of the security and collect and deliver the shares. In this way there is no risk to a buyer or seller of a default on the transaction.

With these activities functioning smoothly, economic growth is enhanced because lower costs and enterprise risks help to promote the production of goods and services, and employment. As such, financial systems contribute to increased prosperity.

ADVANTAGES

- Trading in stock and shares can be done rapidly and easily, making them an attractive liquid investment.
- A rising stock market helps to boost prosperity in a country and promote a confident social mood.
- Stock markets allow anyone to participate in the growth of any listed company.

DISADVANTAGES

- Share prices can change very quickly in today's electronic markets, driven by trading by very large institutions.
- A falling stock market creates an unhappy mood in a country and can lead to difficult economic times and unemployment.
- Prices of stocks and shares can fall as well as rise.

ACTION CHECKLIST

✔ Check the history of a stock market. How long ago was it established? How stable is it? How does its average performance rate compared with other exchanges?

✔ Check the risks involved in a particular stock market. Is it easy to buy and sell on your chosen stock market? What fees are involved? How well is it regulated? Some countries regulate less well than others, increasing your risk.

✔ Check how easy it is to find current prices on your chosen stock market.

DOS AND DON'TS

DO

- Understand the volatility and risk of a stock market before investing.
- Understand the risks involved. Some emerging markets have higher growth potential, but much higher risks too.
- Keep an eye on the progress of the stocks and shares you have purchased.

DON'T

- Don't rush into stock market investments.
- Don't buy when the price is high.
- Don't sell when the price is low.

MORE INFO

Books:

Becket, Michael, and Yvette Essen. *How the Stock Market Works: A Beginner's Guide to Investment*. 4th ed. London: Kogan Page, 2011.

Chapman, Colin. *How the Stock Markets Work*. 9th ed. London: Random House Business Books, 2006.

Gough, Leo. *How the Stock Market Really Works*. 5th ed. Financial Times Guides Series. Harlow, UK: FT Prentice Hall, 2011.

Websites:

Financial Times markets news: www.ft.com/markets
London Stock Exchange: www.londonstockexchange.com
New York Stock Exchange: www.nyse.com
Wall Street Journal: www.wsj.com

See Also:

✔ The Bond Market: Its Structure and Function (p. 1064)
✔ Money Markets: Their Structure and Function (p. 1078)
✔ Trading in Equities on Stock Exchanges (p. 1095)
How the Stock Market Works: A Beginner's Guide to Investment (p. 1373)
Capital Markets and Stock Markets (pp. 1689–1691)

"Money is to the fore now. It is the romance, the poetry of our age." William Dean Howells

  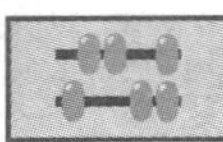      

Structured Investment Vehicles

DEFINITION

A structured investment vehicle, or SIV, is a limited-purpose operating company or "virtual bank" that undertakes arbitrage activities by purchasing mostly highly rated medium- and long-term fixed-income assets. These assets are funded though the issue of short-term, highly rated commercial paper or medium-term notes, which traditionally offer a rate close to the London Interbank Offered Rate (Libor). The SIV thus makes its profits from the spread between the short-term borrowing rate and long-term returns. A SIV has an open-ended and rollover business structure whereby it buys new assets as the old ones mature.

The costs of running a SIV are balanced by the economic returns: that is, the net spread to pay subordinated note-holder returns and the generation of management fee income. Most SIVs are administered or sponsored by banks, but a number are managed independently. The number of SIVs has proliferated in recent years and they control assets worth hundreds of billions of dollars. SIVs are generally quite opaque, invest in complex securities, and often do not need to be displayed on a bank's balance sheet.

The subprime crisis has caused a widespread liquidity crunch in the commercial paper markets and, given that SIVs rely on making their profits from the spread between the short-term borrowing rate and long-term returns, many SIVs have seen their business drastically reduced. Although the Federal Reserve and the European Central Bank have injected billions of dollars and euros into the market, a number of independent SIVs have closed, while other SIVs are being supported by their sponsoring banks.

ADVANTAGES

- SIVs offer good returns in highly liquid markets.
- Most SIVs are sponsored by banks, which back them when they have liquidity problems.

DISADVANTAGES

- Most SIVs issue a mixture of commercial paper or of medium-term notes, and their weighted-average liability to maturity is normally from four to six months, but the assets in the vehicle will have significantly longer average maturities.
- SIVs suffer from the credit risks associated with assets and hedges and the market risk linked to the cost of liquidating assets and hedges. There is the potential for defaults due to a lack of liquidity in world financial markets.
- Some of the SIV's assets may entail due diligence by potential purchasers, thus increasing the sale period for these assets.
- Losses can result from unhedged changes in currencies and interest rates.

ACTION CHECKLIST

✔ In the current illiquid market conditions, make sure that the SIV has a portfolio of highly liquid assets and less liquid, higher-yielding investments.

✔ Ensure that the SIV is exposed to a range of fixed-rate and currency assets and that the portfolio is conservatively hedged.

DOS AND DON'TS

DO

- Use the rating agencies (Moody's, Standard & Poor's, and Fitch IBCA) to check on the SIV. Whatever their faults in the past, rating agencies have tightened up their criteria and will give a good guide to the viability of a particular asset.
- Check who the principal backers are.

DON'T

- Don't forget that although many SIVs are administered or sponsored by banks, a number are managed independently, which might make them more likely to have liquidity problems.

MORE INFO

Books:

de Servigny, Arnaud, and Norbert Jobst (eds). *The Handbook of Structured Finance*. New York: McGraw-Hill, 2007.

El-Erian, Mohamed. *When Markets Collide: Investment Strategies for the Age of Global Economic Change*. New York: McGraw-Hill, 2008.

Tavakoli, Janet M. *Collateralized Debt Obligations and Structured Finance: New Developments in Cash and Synthetic Securitization*. Hoboken, NJ: Wiley, 2003.

Article:

Dolbeck, Andrew. "SIV survival: The fate of structured investment vehicles." *Weekly Corporate Growth Report* (November 5, 2007).

Websites:

Use search options on these websites to look up "structured investment vehicles."

Bank of Montreal: www.bmo.com

Citigroup: www.citi.com

See Also:

★ Credit Ratings (pp. 478–480)
★ Investing in Structured Finance Products in the Debt Money Markets (pp. 510–513)
✔ How to Use Credit Rating Agencies (p. 1073)
✔ Money Markets: Their Structure and Function (p. 1078)

"To achieve satisfactory investment results is easier than most people realize; to achieve superior results is harder than it looks." Benjamin Graham

  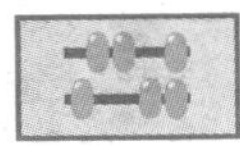      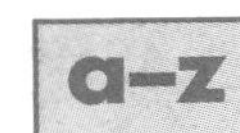

Trading in Commodities: Why and How

DEFINITION

In contrast to other kinds of investment, such as stocks or bonds, when you trade in commodities or futures you do not in fact buy or own anything. You are speculating on the future direction of the price of the commodity. The terms "commodities" and "futures" are often used to describe commodity trading or futures trading. *Commodities* are the actual physical goods, such as corn, soybeans, gold, or crude oil. *Futures* are contracts for those commodities, which are traded at a futures exchange such as the Chicago Board of Trade.

Futures are standardized contracts among buyers and sellers of commodities, specifying the amount of a commodity, grade/quality, and delivery location. Each futures exchange has producers and consumers who want to hedge their risks of future price changes. In between them are the traders, who do not actually buy and sell the physical commodities but are there to help maintain an organized market and provide liquidity. Futures markets are generally very actively traded, so typically there is a large daily price range and trading volume.

Futures contracts have now expanded beyond just physical commodities, and there are futures contracts on financial markets such as the S&P500, treasury notes, currencies, etc.

Futures markets can be traded in both up and down. If a trader expects the market to move upwards, he will make a long trade by buying a contract and leave the trade by selling a contract. Conversely, if a trader expects the market to move downwards, he will make a short trade by selling a contract and leave the trade by buying a contract. By being able to trade in both directions, traders can make a profit or loss regardless of which direction the market is moving. In order to make decisions about when to trade commodity futures, traders tend to use price-activity charts that show futures movements and which are easily understood when tackling historical and current price movements.

ADVANTAGES

- Futures markets are available with a wide variety of underlying instruments, which in turn offer a wide range of price movements and liquidity. Some are available for day-trading 24 hours per day.
- Futures markets can be day-traded without any restrictions, which makes them preferable to stock markets that have day-trading restrictions.
- Futures markets are offered with trades in currencies such as the euro to US dollar exchange rate, stock indexes such as the Dow Jones and DAX, and commodities such as gold, silver, and oil.

DISADVANTAGES

- Unforeseen events such as floods, droughts, government currency interventions, and crop reports can cause sudden and unpredictable losses.
- Risk and reward go hand in hand. It is ridiculous to expect to be able to earn above-average profits without above-average risks.

ACTION CHECKLIST

✔ Learn about and specialize in a particular commodity before you begin trading. Every commodity has different trading guidelines and a profile that includes the basics of contract specifications, market reports, and charts.

✔ Begin trading with small amounts until you learn the ropes; trades on some exchanges are available for as little as $100.

DOS AND DON'TS

DO

- Do your homework and start by trading in small amounts until you are thoroughly familiar with your chosen commodity.
- Use price-activity charts before making decisions about when to trade in futures.

DON'T

- Don't forget that, although the risks can be managed, they can never be eliminated. Keep in mind that the high returns are available only because the trader is being paid to take risk away from others.
- Don't forget that losses are part of the process and that the best traders lose money, but over time they make even more.

MORE INFO

Books:

Buckley, John (ed). *Guide to World Commodity Markets: Physical, Futures and Options Trading*. 7th ed. London: Kogan Page, 1996.

Chicago Board of Trade. *Commodity Trading Manual*. London: Lessons Professional Publishing, 1998.

Gregoriou, Greg N., Vassilios N. Karavas, François-Serge Lhabitant, and Fabrice Rouah. *Commodity Trading Advisers: Risk, Performance Analysis, and Selection*. Hoboken, NJ: Wiley, 2004.

Article:

Chong, Sidney. "Commodity investment." *Australasian Business Intelligence* (July 27, 2006).

Websites:

Commodity Futures Trading Commission (CFTC; US): www.cftc.gov

Financial Services Authority (FSA; UK): www.fsa.gov.uk

See Also:

★ The Role of Commodities in an Institutional Portfolio (pp. 585–588)

✔ Swaps, Options, and Futures: What They Are and Their Function (p. 988)

Portfolio Selection: Efficient Diversification of Investments (p. 1408)

Mining (pp. 1637–1638)

Oil and Gas (pp. 1638–1639)

"There are two sorts of forecasters. Those who don't know and those who don't know they don't know." J. K. Galbraith

Trading in Corporate Bonds: Why and How

DEFINITION

The term "corporate bond" is, from time to time, used to refer to all bonds except those issued by governments in their own currencies. However, it should actually be applied only to longer-term debt instruments that are issued by corporations.

Corporate bonds promise a higher return than some other investments, but the higher return comes at a cost. Most corporate bonds are debentures, which means that they are not secured by collateral. Investors in these bonds must take on not only the interest rate risk but also the credit risk, which is the chance that the corporate issuer will default on its debt. It is important that investors in corporate bonds know how to weigh up credit risk and its possible payoffs. Rising interest rates can reduce the value of your bond investment, and a default can almost eliminate it. The *total yield* on a bond is all gains from coupons and price appreciation, and *current yield* is that from coupon payments.

Corporate bonds are like no other bonds in that they carry an implied risk. Takeovers, corporate restructuring, and leveraged buyouts can change a corporate bond's credit rating and price. Institutional investors use credit rating agencies such as Moody's, Standard & Poor's, and Fitch IBCA to check credit risk. However, many investors also use interest-coverage ratios and capitalization ratios. The *interest-coverage ratio* tells one how much money the company generates each year to fund the annual interest on its debt. The higher the ratio the better, but a company should at least generate enough earnings to service its annual debt. The *capitalization ratio* shows the company's degree of financial leverage. The lower the capitalization ratio, the better the company's financial leverage.

There are also other risk factors. If the bond is *callable*, the company has the right to buy it back after a period of time, while the *poison pill provision* permits shareholders to buy stock at a heavily discounted price to prevent or hinder takeovers. *Putable* bonds have a feature designed to protect against interest rate fluctuations, which allows the holder to return, or "tender," the bond to the issuer at par before the bond's maturity date. With junk bonds (i.e. those rated below S&P's BBB) the risk of losing everything is high and investors should consider the diversification of a high-yield bond fund, which can support a few defaults while still giving high returns.

ADVANTAGES

- Corporate bonds offer higher yields than their treasury equivalents. If you can spot the right investment, the compounding interest over the life of the bond can be quite astounding.
- The default risk on corporate bonds can be quantified using spread analysis, which seeks to determine the difference in yield between a given corporate bond and a risk-free treasury bond of the same maturity.

DISADVANTAGES

- Corporate bonds have an implied event risk. Takeovers, corporate restructuring, and even leveraged buyouts can penalize a bond's credit rating and price.
- Rising interest rates can reduce the value of your bond investment; a default can almost eliminate it.

ACTION CHECKLIST

✔ Assess the bond's credit risk rating in lists published by Standard & Poor's, Moody's, and Fitch IBCA.

✔ Analyze the credit risk and remember that bonds may have multiple issuances; each of these issues will receive different ratings from the credit agencies due to the fact that they have different repayment structures and conditions.

DOS AND DON'TS

DO

- Use interest-coverage ratios and capitalization ratios to back up the ratings given by Standard & Poor's, Moody's, and Fitch IBCA.
- Think about investing in a high-yield bond fund, which can support a few failures yet still provide high returns.

DON'T

- Don't take on credit risk or default from a single corporate bond issue unless you are receiving enough extra yield to cover the risk.

MORE INFO

Books:

Crabbe, Leland E., and Frank J. Fabozzi. *Managing a Corporate Bond Portfolio*. New York: Wiley, 2002.

Swensen, David F. *Unconventional Success: A Fundamental Approach to Personal Investment*. New York: Simon & Schuster, 2005.

Wilson, Richard S., and Frank J. Fabozzi. *Corporate Bonds: Structures & Analysis*. New York: Wiley, 1995.

Article:

Investment Adviser. "The complete James Bond guide to investing." (May 21, 2007). Online at: tinyurl.com/64brvgj

Website:

Standard & Poor's: www.standardandpoors.com

See Also:

★ Credit Ratings (pp. 478–480)
✔ The Bond Market: Its Structure and Function (p. 1064)
✔ How to Use Credit Rating Agencies (p. 1073)
✔ Raising Capital by Issuing Bonds (p. 1086)
✔ Trading in Government Bonds: Why and How (p. 1096)

"There are two sorts of forecasters. Those who don't know and those who don't know they don't know." J. K. Galbraith

  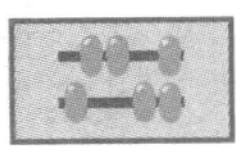      

Trading in Equities on Stock Exchanges

DEFINITION

Equity trading is the buying and selling of company stocks and shares. Stocks and shares in publicly traded companies are bought and sold through one of the major stock exchanges, which serve as managed auctions for stock. A stock exchange, share market, or bourse is a company, corporation, or mutual organization that provides facilities for stockbrokers and traders to trade stocks and other securities. Stock exchanges also provide facilities for the issue and redemption of securities, trading in other financial instruments, and the payment of income and dividends. To be traded on a stock exchange, a company has to be listed on it. Some international companies are listed on more than one exchange.

A share is one of a finite number of equal portions in the capital of a company, and a person owning shares is called a shareholder. Shares entitle the owner to a proportion of distributed, non-reinvested profits known as dividends, and to a proportion of the value of the company in the event of liquidation. Shares are classed as voting (Class A), with the right to vote on the board of directors, or non-voting (Class B). This right can often affect the value of the share.

The value of a publicly traded company is called its market capitalization. This is calculated as the number of shares outstanding (as opposed to those authorized but not necessarily issued) times the price per share. A company's market capitalization should not be confused with the fair market value of the company, as the price per share can be influenced by factors such as the volume of shares traded.

A stockbroker is a qualified and regulated professional who buys and sells shares and other securities on his or her own behalf or on behalf of investors. Equity trading can be performed by the owner of the shares or by a stockbroker authorized to buy and sell on behalf of the owner (in return for a commission). Most trading is carried out on electronic networks, which offer the advantages of up-to-the-second prices and information on the number of shares bought or sold, together with speed and a low transaction cost. The initial public offering (IPO) of stocks and shares to investors is done on the primary market and any subsequent trading is done in the secondary market.

ADVANTAGES

- Holding shares allows an investor to spread investment risk and participate in some of the world's premier companies.
- As a general rule, shares as an investment vehicle have, over the long run, outperformed all other types of investment.

DISADVANTAGES

- Share prices can be very volatile, and the value of shares depends on a number of external factors over which the investor has no control.
- Different shares can have different levels of liquidity, i.e. demand from buyers and sellers. Normally, blue-chip stocks have greater depth and liquidity. The lower the market capitalization, the lower the liquidity, which may affect the ease with which the shares can be sold. Liquidity also affects share prices because, if the shares have low liquidity, it is sometimes more difficult to convert them into cash.

ACTION CHECKLIST

- ✔ To trade shares, you must have an account with a stockbroker or a licensed intermediary (financial planner, accountant, etc.). This is to ensure that the trading environment is secure. Many new investors start using stockbrokers but others prefer to do their own research and use online brokers.
- ✔ Most brokers require you to have an account to ensure that you have the funds to cover orders. Some online brokers require you to have an account with an associated financial institution before you can begin trading.
- ✔ When placing a buy or sell order, there are two ways you can trade. Shares can be traded at *market order*, which means buying at the prevailing market price. The alternative is the *limit order*, where you set the minimum or maximum price.

DOS AND DON'TS

DO

- Research the company, and take into account any risks you feel might arise. If in doubt, use a *stop loss* to help protect your investment.

DON'T

- Don't invest on the basis of tips unless you are extremely confident of the source. More often than not, tipped shares—like tipped horses—will end up as "also-rans."

MORE INFO

Books:

Maginn, John L., Donald L. Tuttle, Jerald E. Pinto, and Dennis W. McLeavey. *Managing Investment Portfolios: A Dynamic Process*. 3rd ed. CFA Institute Investment Series. Hoboken, NJ: Wiley, 2007.

Mobius, Mark. *Equities: An Introduction to the Core Concepts*. Singapore: Wiley, 2006.

Morris, Virginia B., and Kenneth M. Morris. *Standard & Poor's Guide to Money and Investing*. New York: Lightbulb Press, 2005.

Articles:

Investment Adviser. "Worldwide equity trading portal comes to the market." November 5, 2007. Online at: tinyurl.com/698evb3

Mehta, Nina. "TradeWeb eyes equity expansion in 2008." *Traders* (December 2007). Online at: www.tradersmagazine.com/issues/20_275/100087-1.html

Websites:

E*TRADE trading (US): www.etrade.com

Interactive Investor share dealing (UK): www.iii.co.uk/sharedealing

See Also:

✔ Stock Markets: Their Structure and Function (p. 1091)
✔ Trading in Commodities: Why and How (p. 1093)
✔ Trading in Corporate Bonds: Why and How (p. 1094)
How the Stock Market Works: A Beginner's Guide to Investment (p. 1373)
Capital Markets and Stock Markets (pp. 1689–1691)

"You never need to chase a trade. The market has plenty of opportunities. The money runs out before the opportunities do." John Saleeby

Trading in Government Bonds: Why and How

DEFINITION

A government bond is a bond issued by a national government, denominated in the country's own currency. Sovereign bonds are those issued by foreign governments in their own currencies. Government bonds are usually thought of as risk-free, because even if a government has problems it can always raise taxes or simply print more money to redeem the bond. The maturities of sovereign bonds vary and will depend on the issuing government. The US government is the largest seller of government or treasury bonds in the world. Its bonds are auctioned in February and August, and have 30-year maturities.

In the *primary market*, bonds are sold in auctions. Bids are divided into competitive and noncompetitive bids. Competitive bids are restricted to primary government dealers, while noncompetitive bids are open to individual investors and small institutions.

Secondary market trading in bonds occurs in the over-the-counter (OTC) market. All US government securities are traded OTC, with the primary government securities dealers being the largest and most important market participants. In the secondary market a wide variety of investors use bonds for investing, hedging, and speculation. These investors include commercial and investment banks, insurance companies, pension funds, mutual funds, and retail investors.

While some electronic bond trading is available to retail investors, the entire bond market remains very much an OTC market. The bond market, unlike the equity markets (where electronic dealing and transparency have leveled the playing field for individual and institutional investors), lacks price transparency and liquidity, except in the case of government bonds. For the independent bond investor who would prefer to spread his or her risk and not pay the high fees for a managed fund, a good alternative is an *exchange-traded fund* or an *index bond fund*, which will track government bond indices and, given the high liquidity of these bonds, will present fewer problems than corporate bonds.

ADVANTAGES

- Price transparency and liquidity for government bonds are comparatively high, providing a safe platform for a wide range of investors to hedge and speculate. These investors include commercial and investment banks, insurance companies, pension funds, mutual funds, and retail investors.
- Government bonds are generally referred to as risk-free bonds, because governments can simply raise more taxes or print more money to pay for them.
- Government bonds are highly liquid and investors can recover some of their investment quickly if necessary.

DISADVANTAGES

- There is foreign-exchange risk for investors when the currency of the bonds in which they have invested declines in relation to their own.
- The risks of trading in government bonds stem, above all, from changes in interest rates, which can cause fluctuations in prices for bonds.
- Bond prices are influenced by economic data such as employment, income growth/decline, and consumer and industrial prices. Any information that implies rising inflation will weaken bond prices, as inflation reduces the income from a bond.

ACTION CHECKLIST

- ✔ If you are investing in sovereign funds, how safe is the government or region? Don't forget that in 1998 the Russian government defaulted on its debt.
- ✔ What are interest rates going to do? Investors who buy and sell bonds before maturity are exposed to many risks, most importantly changes in interest rates. When interest rates increase, new issues will pay a higher yield and the value of existing bonds will fall. When interest rates decline, the value of existing bonds will rise as new issues pay a lower yield.

DOS AND DON'TS

DO

- Before you buy, check how quickly you will be able to sell if necessary, and at what discount and dealing fee.

DON'T

- Don't unless you are completely confident, invest in only one type of bond. An exchange-traded fund or an index bond fund might be a much safer bet.

MORE INFO

Books:

Faerber, Esmé. *All About Bonds and Bond Mutual Funds: The Easy Way to Get Started*. 2nd ed. New York: McGraw-Hill, 1999.

Rini, William A. *Mathematics of the Securities Industry*. New York: McGraw-Hill Professional, 2003.

Wong, M. Anthony, in collaboration with Robert High. *Trading and Investing in Bond Options: Risk Management, Arbitrage, and Value Investing*. New York: Wiley, 1991.

Articles:

Pensions Management. "Comment: Investment—Getting the best from bonds." April 2008.

Rodier, Melanie. "The massive growth of electronic bond trading." *Wall Street and Technology* (April 15, 2008). Online at: www.wallstreetandtech.com/articles/207200781

Websites:

Bloomberg current government bond prices: tinyurl.com/2dbqurw

FTSE Global Bond Index Series: www.ftse.com/Indices/FTSE_Global_Bond_Index_Series

See Also:

- ✔ The Bond Market: Its Structure and Function (p. 1064)
- ✔ Trading in Commodities: Why and How (p. 1093)
- ✔ Trading in Corporate Bonds: Why and How (p. 1094)
- ✔ Trading in Equities on Stock Exchanges (p. 1095)

"The best traders have no ego. You cannot let ego get in the way of a trade that is a loser; you have to swallow your pride and get out." Tom Baldwin

  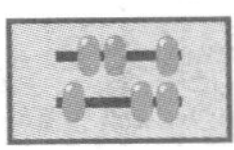      

Understanding and Using Leverage Ratios

DEFINITION

Leveraging is a way to use funds whereby most of the money is raised by borrowing rather than by stock issue (for a company) or use of capital (by an individual). At its most basic, leveraging means taking out a loan so that you can invest the money and hoping your investment makes more money than you will have to pay in interest on the loan.

The leverage ratio is used to calculate the financial leverage of a company. This information gives an insight into the company's financing methods, or it can be used to measure the company's ability to meet its financial obligations. There are a number of different ratios, but the main factors involved are debt, equity, assets, operating income, and interest expenses.

The most commonly used ratio is debt to equity (D/E, or financial leverage), which indicates how much the business relies on debt financing. In normal circumstances the typical D/E ratio is 2:1, with only one-third of the debt in the long term. A high D/E ratio might show up possible difficulty in paying interest and capital while obtaining extra funding. As an example, if a company has $10 million of debt and $20 million of equity, it has a D/E ratio of 0.5 ($10 million ÷ $20 million).

Another leveraging ratio can be used to measure the operating cost mix. This helps to indicate how any change in output may affect operating income. There are two types of operating costs: fixed and variable. The mix of these will differ depending on the company and the industry. A high operating leverage can lead to forecasting risk. For example, a tiny error made in a sales forecast could trigger far bigger errors when it comes to projecting cash flows based on those sales.

There is also interest coverage, which measures a company's margin of safety and indicates how many times the company can make its interest payments. This figure is calculated by dividing earnings prior to interest and taxes by the interest expense.

ADVANTAGES

- Leveraging means borrowing money to invest. Anyone who takes out a mortgage is effectively leveraging. By paying a deposit to obtain a loan, you can buy a home that otherwise you would not be able to afford. Although property prices can and do fall periodically, over the long term property usually increases in value. If it does, you can sell the property and make a profit on your original mortgage loan.
- Leveraging enables an individual or a company to gain access to larger capital sums to make investments, with the aim of making a profit by doing so.
- Strategies in leveraging run from basic to highly sophisticated, and the degree of risk varies in the same way. The benefits of leveraging will depend on your financial situation, your objectives, and your attitude to risk.

DISADVANTAGES

- Anything that has the potential to make money involves some risk. Gains can be better than normal; losses can be worse. A change in interest rates can have an effect on your profit too. There is a risk that your investment will not make enough profit to pay off the interest on your loan.
- You can mitigate the risks by diversifying your portfolio, thereby guarding against high losses, although this will probably limit opportunities to make spectacular gains. A fixed-rate loan can protect against a rise in interest rates.

ACTION CHECKLIST

✔ Are you comfortable borrowing money that you might struggle to pay back?

✔ Are you comfortable with high risk in your finances?

✔ Are you confident that interest rates will not rise to add further risk to your borrowings?

✔ Are you confident your investment will make more than the interest you have to pay back on your loan?

DOS AND DON'TS

DO

- Look at leveraging as a way of using other people's money (by way of a loan) to make your own investments.
- Understand how your loan works and what and when you will have to pay back.
- As much research as you can. And then more research.

DON'T

- Don't get involved with leveraging if you are uncomfortable with financial risk.
- Don't choose an investment without a full understanding of what you are investing in.

MORE INFO

Books:

Marr, Bernard. *Strategic Performance Management: Leveraging and Measuring Your Intangible Value Drivers*. Oxford: Butterworth-Heinemann, 2006.

Matthäus-Maier, Ingrid, and J. D. von Pischke (eds). *Microfinance Investment Funds: Leveraging Private Capital for Economic Growth and Poverty Reduction*. Berlin: Springer-Verlag, 2006.

Militello, Frederick C., and Michael D. Schwalberg. *Leverage Competencies: What Financial Executives Need to Lead*. Upper Saddle River, NJ: FT Prentice Hall, 2002.

See Also:

★ Going Private: Public-to-Private Leveraged Buyouts (pp. 730–732)
★ Leveraged Buyouts: What, Why, When, and How (pp. 743–745)
✔ Measuring Gearing (p. 1077)
⇄ Capitalization Ratios (pp. 1202–1203)

"A speculator is a man who observes the future, and acts before it occurs." Bernard Baruch

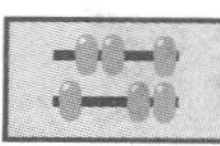

Understanding and Using the Repos Market

DEFINITION

A repo, or repurchase agreement, is an agreement between two parties whereby one party sells the other a security at a specified price with a commitment to buy the security back at a later date. A repo is economically similar to a secured loan, with the buyer receiving securities as collateral to protect against default. Virtually any security can be used as a repo: treasury and government bills, corporate and government bonds, and stocks or shares can all be used as securities to back a repo. Although the transaction is similar to a loan, it differs in that the seller repurchases the legal ownership of the securities from the buyer at the end of the agreement. Also, while the legal title to the securities passes from the seller to the buyer, coupons that are paid while the repo buyer owns the securities are normally passed directly to the repo seller.

Repos are contracts for the sale and future repurchase of a financial asset, normally treasury securities. The annualized rate of interest paid on the loan is known as the repo rate. Repos can be of any duration, but are most commonly overnight loans, or *overnight repos*. Repos longer than this are known as *term repos*. There are also *open repos*, which can be terminated by either side on a day's notice. The lender normally receives a margin on the security, meaning that it is priced below market value, typically by 2% to 5%, depending on maturity. Repos are normally not for the smaller investor: in the primary market dealers frequently transact hundreds of millions of dollars, and in the secondary market repos of one million dollars are not uncommon.

The Federal Reserve Bank also uses repos in its open-market operations as a method of fine-tuning the money supply. To expand the supply of money temporarily, the Federal Reserve arranges to buy securities from non-bank dealers, which deposit the proceeds in their commercial bank accounts, thereby adding to reserves. The repos usually last 1 to 15 days, or whatever length of time the Federal Reserve needs to make the adjustment. When it wishes to reduce the money supply, it reverses the process using a "matched sale purchase transaction": it sells securities to dealers, who either draw on bank balances directly or take out a bank loan to make the payment, thereby withdrawing reserves.

ADVANTAGES

- Repos allow investors to keep surplus funds invested without losing liquidity or incurring price risk or credit risk because the collateral is more often than not in high-class securities.
- Repos can be used for investing surplus funds in the short term, or for short-term borrowing against collateral. Corporations can use repos to help manage their liquidity and short-term financing of their inventories.

DISADVANTAGES

- Overnight changes in interest rates or currency fluctuations can affect the value of a dealer's securities holding, and a dealer who holds a large position takes a risk.
- Repos are normally not for the smaller investor: in the primary market dealers frequently transact hundreds of millions of dollars, and in the secondary market repos of one million dollars are not uncommon.
- The seller could default on his or her obligation and fail to repurchase the securities.

ACTION CHECKLIST

✔ What type of repo are you buying, and in which international market? Will risk and return be affected by currency fluctuations, credit risk, the type and liquidity of the security, or third-party involvement?

✔ Does the securities dealer have a special repo account at a clearing bank to settle his or her trades?

✔ Primary dealers must be authorized by the Federal Reserve Bank to bid on newly issued treasury securities for resale on the markets.

DOS AND DON'TS

DO

- Check on any repos in equity securities. Complications can arise sometimes because of greater complexity in the tax rules on dividends.

DON'T

- Don't fail to check on the credit risk associated with the repo, i.e. type and liquidity of security, other parties involved, etc.

MORE INFO

Books:

Fabozzi, Frank J., and Moorad Choudhry (eds). *The Handbook of European Fixed Income Securities*. Frank J. Fabozzi Series. Hoboken, NJ: Wiley, 2004.

Levinson, Marc. *Guide to Financial Markets*. 4th ed. London: Profile, 2006.

Mathieson, Donald J., and Garry J. Schinasi. *International Capital Markets: Developments, Prospects, and Key Policy Issues*. Washington, DC: International Monetary Fund, 2001.

Articles:

de Teran, Natasha. "Euribor swap a boost for repo market." *Financial News* (September 15, 2003).

Wright, Ben. "Growth of European repo market stalls." *Financial News* (March 16, 2003).

Websites:

European Central Bank (ECB): www.ecb.int

Federal Reserve (US): www.federalreserve.gov

See Also:

★ Investing in Structured Finance Products in the Debt Money Markets (pp. 510–513)

★ Managing Liquidity Risk in a Financial Institution: The Dangers of Short-Term Liabilities (pp. 74–76)

✔ Measuring Liquidity (p. 983)

✔ Money Markets: Their Structure and Function (p. 1078)

"It's not how much you earn, it's how much you owe." Ted Turner

  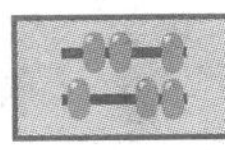   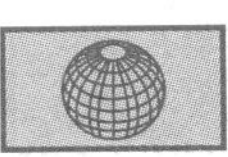   

Understanding Capital Markets, Structure and Function

DEFINITION

Capital markets provide a wide range of products and services that are related to financial investments. Capital markets include the stock market, commodities exchanges, the bond market, and just about any physical or virtual service or intermediary where debt and equity securities can be bought or sold. Their primary purpose is to raise funds and channel investors' money to areas where there is a deficit or need for investment. They play a vital role as intermediaries between governments and companies, which use them to finance a myriad of activities.

The capital markets can be broken down into the primary market, where new stocks and bonds are issued to investors, and the secondary market, where existing stocks and bonds are traded.

In the primary market, governments, companies, or public sector organizations can obtain funding through the sale of a new stock or bonds. These are normally issued through securities dealers and banks, which underwrite the offered stocks or bonds. The issuers earn a commission, which is built into the price of the security offering.

In the secondary market, stocks and shares in publicly traded companies are bought and sold through one of the major stock exchanges, which serve as managed auctions for stock. A stock exchange, share market, or bourse is a company, corporation, or mutual organization that provides facilities for stockbrokers and traders to trade stocks and other securities. Stock exchanges also provide facilities for the issue and redemption of securities, trading in other financial instruments, and the payment of income and dividends.

ADVANTAGES

- Capital markets provide the lubricant between investors and those needing to raise capital.
- Capital markets create price transparency and liquidity. They provide a safe platform for a wide range of investors —including commercial and investment banks, insurance companies, pension funds, mutual funds, and retail investors—to hedge and speculate.
- Holding different shares or bonds allows an investor to spread investment risk.
- The secondary market gives important pricing information that permits efficient use of limited capital.

DISADVANTAGES

- In capital markets, bond prices are influenced by economic data such as employment, income growth/decline, consumer prices, and industrial prices. Any information that implies rising inflation will weaken bond prices, as inflation reduces the income from a bond.
- Prices for shares in capital markets can be very volatile. Their value depends on a number of external factors over which the investor has no control.
- Different shares can have different levels of liquidity, i.e. demand from buyers and sellers.

ACTION CHECKLIST

✔ When placing a buy or sell order, there are two ways you can trade. Shares can be traded at *market order*, which means buying at the prevailing market price. The alternative is the *limit order*, in which you set the minimum or maximum price.

✔ What are interest rates going to do? Investors who buy and sell bonds before maturity are exposed to many risks, most importantly changes in interest rates. When interest rates increase, new issues will pay a higher yield and the value of existing bonds will fall. When interest rates decline, the value of existing bonds will rise as new issues pay a lower yield.

DOS AND DON'TS

DO

- Before you buy, check how quickly you will be able to sell if necessary, and at what discount and dealing fee.

DON'T

- Don't, unless you are completely confident, invest in only one type of bond or security. An exchange-traded fund or an index fund might be a much safer bet.

MORE INFO

Books:

Fabozzi, Frank J., and Franco Modigliani. *Capital Markets: Institutions and Instruments*. 4th ed. Upper Saddle River, NJ: Prentice Hall, 2008.

Maginn, John L., Donald L. Tuttle, Jerald E. Pinto, and Dennis W. McLeavey (eds). *Managing Investment Portfolios: A Dynamic Process*. 3rd ed. Hoboken, NJ: Wiley, 2007.

McInish, Thomas H. *Capital Markets: A Global Perspective*. Malden, MA: Blackwell Publishers, 2000.

Articles:

Mehta, Nina. "TradeWeb eyes equity expansion in 2008." *Traders Magazine* (December 2007). Online at: www.tradersmagazine.com/issues/20_275/100087-1.html

Rodier, Melanie. "The massive growth of electronic bond trading." *Wall Street and Technology* (April 15, 2008). Online at: www.wallstreetandtech.com/articles/207200781

Websites:

FTSE Global Bond Index: markets.ft.com/markets/overview.asp

Interactive Investor: www.iii.co.uk/sharedealing

See Also:

✔ The Bond Market: Its Structure and Function (p. 1064)
✔ Investors and the Capital Structure (p. 1120)
✔ Stock Markets: Their Structure and Function (p. 1091)
Portfolio Theory and Capital Markets (p. 1409)

"To turn $100 into $110 is work. To turn $100 million into $110 million is inevitable." Edgar Bronfman, Jr

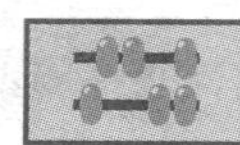

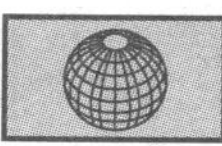

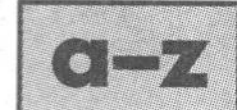

Understanding Debt Cover

DEFINITION

Debt cover is defined as the ratio of a company's total assets to its debt. It helps to assess the amount of cash flow available to meet annual interest and principal payments on a debt, including sinking fund payments. Should a company be wound up, the ratio would indicate by how much the shareholders' redemption value and prior charges and any future capital charges would be covered by the assets. This useful metric indicates how easily a company can meet its interest and principal payments from its revenues.

Debt cover is calculated by dividing a company's operating income (either EBIT or EBITDA) by the debt expenses, i.e. the interest charges. Banks typically use debt cover as an indicator for determining economic risk when making loans. Typically, a bank looks for a ratio of between 1.15 × and 1.35 × (net operating income divided by annual debt service) to be satisfied that there is sufficient cash flow available on an ongoing basis to repay the loan instalments.

However, the debt cover may sometimes be less than 1 × for a loan. This does not necessarily mean that the company is at risk of default, although it is certainly an indicator of potential financial problems ahead as it means there is, at the time of calculation, a negative cash flow. For example, a ratio of 0.9 × indicates that there is only enough net operating income to cover 90% of annual debt payments, and the company would therefore have to repay borrowings using cash or by taking out a further loan. Usually banks are unlikely to lend where there is negative cash flow, but they may decide to take the risk if the company can clearly demonstrate that this is a temporary blip.

Over a period of time the debt cover should improve as a company pays down its debts and, generally speaking, as with other metrics that measure credit risk, the higher the ratio the better as it means a lower risk of capital loss.

ADVANTAGES

- Debt cover is a useful measure of financial strength. It can indicate not only what the debt cover was at a particular point in time, but also how much it has changed since it was last evaluated. It is thus a way of assessing a company's financial quality and associated risk levels.

DISADVANTAGES

- Debt cover should never be used as the sole metric test of a company's financial soundness. Only if you have access to the current books can you know if there are otherwise unknown changes in a company's financial situation. Use other metrics in conjunction, such as the interest coverage ratio, to gain a fuller picture.

MORE INFO

Books:

Duffie, Darrell, and Kenneth J. Singleton. *Credit Risk: Pricing, Measurement, and Management*. Princeton, NJ: Princeton University Press, 2003.

Lando, David. *Credit Risk Modeling: Theory and Applications*. Princeton, NJ: Princeton University Press, 2004.

van Deventer, Donald R., and Kenji Imai. *Credit Risk Models & the Basel Accords*. Singapore: Wiley, 2003.

See Also:

★ Securitization: Understanding the Risks and Rewards (pp. 598–600)
✔ Measuring Financial Health (p. 982)
✔ Measuring Gearing (p. 1077)

"A debt may get mouldy, but it never decays." Chinua Achebe

Understanding Fixed-Charge Coverage

DEFINITION

Fixed-charge coverage is a financial ratio that is used to gauge the quality of a bond issue or the ability of a project to meet its debt repayments. It is calculated by dividing total fixed charges into the net income (or earnings before interest and tax) available for these charges. The fixed charges are gross interest, contractual payments under operating leases, and preference dividends.

Thus, a fixed-charge coverage ratio would look like this:

$$\text{Fixed-charge coverage} = \text{EBIT} + \frac{\text{Fixed charge}}{\text{Fixed charge} + \text{Interest}}$$

where EBIT is earnings before interest and tax, and the fixed charge is before tax.

Generally, the greatest fixed charge a company is likely to face is the interest on its debt. However, the fixed-charge coverage ratio assumes particular importance if the company you are evaluating spends heavily on leases, such as leases on buildings and equipment. A lease payment is effectively the same thing as a debt payment, and it should be taken just as seriously. The lower a company's net income, the greater the negative impact of the lease payments on the ratio.

Overall, the lower the ratio, the worse is the financial position of the company. Bond issues can contain covenants that set limits on how low the fixed-charge coverage ratio can fall. Such a covenant is designed to provide the lender with protection, so that the borrower's financial position will remain more or less the same as it was when the loan was made. Thus, a bond may contain a covenant that prevents the fixed-charge coverage ratio from falling below 2.

ADVANTAGES

- The fixed-charge coverage ratio is readily identifiable.
- It provides a straightforward measure of the financial health of a company.

DISADVANTAGES

- There is no standardized procedure for determining either fixed charges or the net income available for these charges.
- Other ratios may provide a better indicator of a company's financial health.

ACTION CHECKLIST

✔ Identify the fixed-charge coverage ratio from the company's accounts.

✔ If it is less than 1, speak to the company's managers immediately to ascertain how they plan to meet their fixed-cost obligations.

DOS AND DON'TS

DO

- Remember that if a company has a fixed-charge coverage of less than 1, it cannot meet its fixed obligations through earnings and thus must rely on other funds, such as extra borrowings or drawing down working capital.
- Remember that this ratio often comes into play if you have a working-capital loan; the lender will insist that a specific fixed-charge coverage ratio is maintained or your loan will be recalled.
- Remember to try to gauge the attitudes of managers toward taking on more debt as the existing debt matures.

DON'T

- Don't just rely on the fixed-charge coverage ratio. Other ratios that can be used to measure a company's ability to meet its debt obligations include the interest coverage ratio and the debt service coverage ratio.
- Don't ignore the pro forma coverage ratio. It has essentially the same components as the fixed-charge coverage ratio but is forward looking. It can tell you whether this year's earnings (if repeated) would be able to cover what must be paid in the coming year.

MORE INFO

Books:

Geddes, Ross. *Valuation and Investment Appraisal*. London: Financial World Publishing, 2002.

Holmes, Geoffrey, Alan Sugden, and Paul Gee. *Interpreting Company Reports and Accounts*. 10th ed. Harlow, UK: FT Prentice Hall, 2008.

The Ultimate Small Business Guide: A Resource for Startups and Growing Businesses. New York: Basic Books, 2003.

Article:

Goodacre, Alan. "Operating lease finance in the UK retail sector." *International Review of Retail, Distribution and Consumer Research* 13:1 (2003): 99–125. Online at: dx.doi.org/10.1080/0959396032000065373

Website:

American Bankruptcy Institute (ABI): www.abiworld.org

See Also:

✔ Assessing Cash Flow and Bank Lending Requirements (p. 964)
✔ Measuring Financial Health (p. 982)
✔ Understanding Debt Cover (p. 1100)
Interest Coverage (p. 1231)

"When the facts change, I change my mind." John Maynard Keynes

  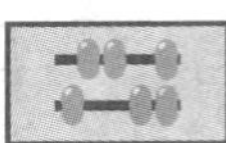      

Understanding Portfolio Analysis

DEFINITION

Portfolio analysis is a tool which helps managers assess how best to identify opportunities and to allocate resources across a set of products or businesses. The portfolio analysis framework seeks to first identify individual business units' growth cycle stages. The tool then examines these business units in the context of the overall growth of their respective industries, with a view to optimizing resources and maximizing overall portfolio performance. As an example, the technique seeks to identify resource-hungry units in sectors with the potential for dynamic growth and then shows how highly profitable cash-generative units in more mature industry sectors could be exploited to meet the resource needs of the growing businesses in such a way as to maximize overall portfolio returns. Portfolio analysis can also be used to identify business units or products that have already fulfilled their potential and could therefore be sold to free up resources for more productive investment elsewhere.

Though there are many different portfolio analysis tools, many approaches assess business units on the basis of market share and the growth rate of the industry or sector in which they operate. The technique is founded on the basis that increasing market share should generate higher earnings, while a higher rate of overall market growth typically requires higher levels of investment if the business is to capitalize on the available opportunities. Portfolio analysis also seeks to evaluate the strength of a company's competitive franchise within an industry or sector, using inputs such as its rate of change of market share, cost base, and product factors such as cost per unit and the strength of its new product pipeline. Using these inputs, portfolio analysis can help to promote success by highlighting areas with the potential to deliver the most attractive future profits, while flagging other areas with limited prospects, thus helping management to steer resources toward areas where they can best be invested.

ADVANTAGES

- Portfolio analysis simplifies complex situations and provides a valuable overview of the strengths and weaknesses of a company's mix of businesses and products.
- The technique is forward-looking and can play an important role in delivering improved returns for stockholders over the medium to long term.
- Portfolio analysis can help understanding of diversification and identify risks in a company's portfolio, for example by drawing attention to an overemphasis on particular areas.
- The technique underlines the need to understand business and product lifecycles and emphasizes the importance of achieving the breakthrough to profitability early, long before an industry or a product begins to mature.
- The analysis can help to overcome the danger that managers favor their pet projects and industries with extra resources, particularly if some inputs to analysis, such as industry growth projections, can be sourced independently.
- Portfolio analysis also encourages a view of businesses as collections of diversified cash flows and investments and so shows how corporate strategy integrates with individual business strategy at the business unit level.

DISADVANTAGES

- Portfolio analysis relies heavily on estimates of future patterns. Even a slight change in a forecast can significantly impact the results of the analysis.
- Excessively short-term use of portfolio analysis can lead to frequent and expensive switches of company resources.
- Acquiring or divesting businesses can be complex and time-consuming. One should take these costs into account before acting on marginal recommendations on portfolio changes.
- Most businesses are actually "average" but should still be kept. For example, Apple's laptop business is not growing and the market for laptops isn't growing, but it is still important to keep it in the firm.
- Market share is not the same as profitability: firms with low market share can be quite profitable (e.g. mail order catalogs).
- There may be better places to put your money than in your surplus cash cows (e.g. the open market).
- Portfolio analysis techniques do not generally consider synergies across businesses or products.

ACTION CHECKLIST

✔ Before applying portfolio analysis, managers should achieve some understanding of all business units/products and the challenges/opportunities they face.

✔ Consider using particular forms of portfolio analysis, such as the Boston Consulting matrix. This places business units into readily understandable categories (cash cow, stars, problem child, dogs) according to factors such as market share and industry growth rate.

✔ Use the technique to emphasize the goal of portfolio balance and the need to achieve a "pipeline" of future income streams, rather than relying on the hope of any single blockbuster product resulting from a R&D success.

DOS AND DON'TS

DO

- Whenever possible, include statistical inputs from external sources to avoid the risk that internal company-specific assumptions may be inaccurate.
- Be prepared to question and challenge assumptions during the process.

DON'T

- Don't rely totally on any one strategic planning technique.
- Don't plan for every conceivable eventuality as it is not practical to do this—even the best analysis can come unstuck should a highly improbable "freak" event happen. For example, as a result of the recent credit crunch, a reliance on bank finance to fund future product development costs has been a weakness against the backdrop of tighter credit conditions.

MORE INFO

Websites:

Tutor2u guide to portfolio analysis (including Boston Consulting grid and McKinsey/GE matrix): tutor2u.net/business/strategy/ge_matrix.htm

Value Based Management.net guide to McKinsey/GE matrix: www.valuebasedmanagement.net/methods_ge_mckinsey.html

"In economics, hope and faith coexist with great scientific pretension and also a deep desire for respectability."
J. K. Galbraith

  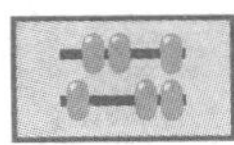      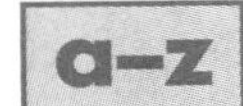

Understanding Price Volatility

DEFINITION

In a free market, prices are effectively set by the relative levels of supply and demand for the underlying asset. Thus, prices are naturally impacted by rapid changes in the levels of confidence and conviction of market participants, both over short and long terms. Though price fluctuations are part of normal free market activity, at times unexpected major events can have a significant impact on the market's confidence. During such periods, normal price movements can give way to greater price swings, as market prices gyrate according to the participants' rapidly changing view of fair value. These price swings are exacerbated in periods of sharp market declines, partly because liquidity can also fall as fewer market participants are willing to attempt to underpin tumbling markets hit by panic selling. In contrast, rising markets typically enjoy higher levels of liquidity, but can, nevertheless, also suffer from rapid price swings, although these are frequently less dramatic in nature than in sudden market slides. Nevertheless, all kinds of market uncertainty can breed volatility.

Though the general concept of volatility is widely understood, in statistical terms volatility represents the relative rate at which the price moves up or down, as defined by the daily price movement's annualized standard deviation. Thinking in terms of the "bell curve" image associated with the mention of statistical calculations, one standard deviation represents the maximum daily movement we can expect 68% of the time, while the range of two standard deviations should cover 95% of daily net changes. However, it's important to recognize that by utilizing the input of past data, we are calculating *historical volatility*. Another way of expressing volatility is *implied volatility*, which uses the prices of market instruments, such as options, to evaluate investors' forecasts of future volatility. Though the models developed for options pricing can be highly complex, it is predictable that options prices are likely to be higher at a time of greater perceived uncertainty and elevated volatility, than at other times when investors' expectations of market conditions are more benign.

ADVANTAGES

- Volatility calculations allow comparisons of market conditions during different eras.
- The pricing of derivative instruments, such as options, relies on some form of volatility variable.
- Elevated levels of market volatility can create opportunities for longer-term investors.

DISADVANTAGES

- Volatility-related calculations can be complex, particularly when related to advanced options pricing models.
- High levels of volatility can add to existing levels of market uncertainty, creating a vicious circle for inexperienced market participants.

ACTION CHECKLIST

✔ Visualize the basic "bell curve" image of past price movement outcomes to help introduce the concept of volatility to inexperienced investors.

✔ Acknowledge that volatility in itself is not a guide to market direction, as volatility can move independently of market sentiment.

✔ Consider how derivative instruments, such as options, caps, and collars, could help you towards your volatility and wider risk management objectives.

DOS AND DON'TS

DO

- Recognize the difference between historical (backward-focused) and implied volatility (based on future perceptions).
- Appreciate that volatility isn't a "bad thing" or a "good thing" as such—it's part and parcel of free markets.

DON'T

- Don't waste resources crunching the numbers manually—use spreadsheets or specialized volatility/options pricing packages for calculations.
- Don't mistake calculations based on historical data as any definitive guide to the market's future movements—more stocks can be subject to movements beyond the "predicted" standard deviations than the numbers might suggest.

MORE INFO

Books:

Knight, John, and Stephen Satchell. *Forecasting Volatility in the Financial Markets*. 3rd ed. Quantitative Finance Series. Woburn, MA: Butterworth-Heinemann, 2007.

Taylor, Stephen J. *Asset Price Dynamics, Volatility and Prediction*. Princeton, NJ: Princeton University Press, 2007.

Articles:

Garman, Mark B., and Michael J. Klass. "On the estimation of security price volatility from historical data." *Journal of Business* 53:1 (1980): 67–78. Updated version online at: tinyurl.com/28o42u [PDF].

Mazzucato, M., and W. Semmler. "The determinants of stock price volatility: An industry study." *Nonlinear Dynamics, Psychology, and Life Sciences* 6:2 (April 2002): 197–216. Online at: oro.open.ac.uk/9463

Website:

Volatility and option price calculator: www.option-price.com

See Also:

★ The Ability of Ratings to Predict the Performance of Exchange-Traded Funds (pp. 444–447)
★ The Impact of Index Trackers on Shareholders and Stock Volatility (pp. 496–498)
✔ Stock Markets: Their Structure and Function (p. 1091)
Eugene Fama (p. 1281)
How the Stock Market Works: A Beginner's Guide to Investment (p. 1373)

"In economics, hope and faith coexist with great scientific pretension and also a deep desire for respectability."
J. K. Galbraith

  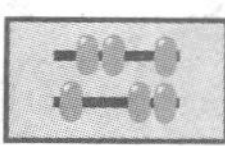      

Using Dividend Discount Models

DEFINITION

Dividend discount models are essentially tools that have been developed to value a stock on the basis of estimated future dividends, discounted to reflect their value in today's terms.

Many variations of dividend discount models exist, but their central basis is the following formula:

$$\text{Estimated valuation} = \frac{D}{(R-G)}$$

where D is present dividend per share, R is discount rate, and G is dividend growth rate.

Variations on the standard model can be used, depending on the company's stage in the growth cycle, but the common theme of dividend discount models is that the resulting estimated valuation is compared with the share's prevailing market price to determine whether the share is presently trading above or below its fair value.

ADVANTAGES

- Dividend discount models attempt to put a valuation on shares, based on forecasts of the sums to be paid out to investors. This should, in theory, provide a very solid basis to determine the share's true value in present terms.
- Dividend discount models can be of great use over the short to medium term, making use of widely available company research over timescales of up to five years.
- In stable industries, dividend discount models can still be of value over the longer term if investors are prepared to make the assumption that current dividend payout policies will remain in place.

DISADVANTAGES

- Standard dividend discount models are of no value in determining the estimated value of companies that don't pay dividends. This is typically not a problem in mature industries such as utilities and food, but the models are generally of less value in industries such as technology and mobile telecoms, where investors commonly look for share price appreciation rather than high dividend payments.
- The ability of a company to maintain a certain rate of dividend growth over the longer term can be extremely difficult to forecast accurately. Dividend discount models rely heavily on the validity of the data inputs, making them of questionable value given the challenges associated with accurately forecasting growth rates beyond five or so years.
- When used for longer-term analysis, the valuations provided by dividend discount models take no account of the possibility of a deliberate change to a company's dividend policy. This can further compromise the usefulness of dividend discount models over the longer term.

ACTION CHECKLIST

✔ Make every effort to establish the integrity and validity of the data to be input into a dividend discount model. The calculation relies on the accuracy of the source data, making the result very susceptible to inaccurate inputs.

✔ Consider using a dividend discount model as a screening tool, such that stocks that are apparently undervalued according to the model could scrutinized more closely using alternative valuation techniques.

DOS AND DON'TS

DOS

- Recognize the limitations imposed by the assumption made by standard dividend discount models that dividend growth rates will be fixed in perpetuity.
- Consider whether a multistage dividend discount model would be more appropriate. These models take account of the various stages in a company's development, from growth to maturity.

DON'TS

- Don't attempt to use standard dividend discount models for growth-orientated companies that have yet to establish dividend payouts.
- Don't invest purely on the basis of the result of a single dividend discount model calculation in isolation. Given the total reliance on the data inputs, using a wider range of valuation tools could result in better investment decisions.

MORE INFO

Books:

Correia, Carlos, David Flynn, Enrico Uliana, and Michael Wormald. *Financial Management*. 6th ed (spiral-bound). Lansdowne, South Africa: Juta, 2007.

Pinto, Jerald E., Elaine Henry, Thomas R. Robinson, and John D. Stowe. *Equity Asset Valuation*. 2nd ed. Hoboken, NJ: Wiley, 2010.

Articles:

Beneda, Nancy L. "Estimating free cash flows and valuing a growth company." *Journal of Asset Management* 4:4 (December 2003): 247–257. Online at: dx.doi.org/10.1057/palgrave.jam.2240106

Foerster, Stephen R., and Stephen G. Sapp. "The dividend discount model in the long-run: A clinical study." *Journal of Applied Finance* 15:2 (Fall/Winter 2005): 55–75. Online at: ssrn.com/abstract=869545

Report:

Harris, Robert S., Kenneth M. Eades, and Susan J. Chaplinsky. "The dividend discount model." Darden case no. UVA-F-1234. Darden Business School, University of Virginia, 1998. Online at: ssrn.com/abstract=909419

See Also:

✔ Applying the Gordon Growth Model (p. 1063)
✔ Calculating a Company's Net Worth (p. 1065)
✔ Estimating Enterprise Value with the Weighted Average Cost of Capital (p. 967)
✔ Using Multistage Dividend Discount Models (p. 1106)
Dividend Yield (p. 1219)

"I didn't understand how they were turning all this garbage into gold." Anonymous

  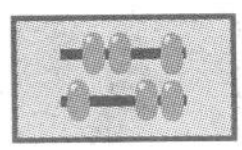   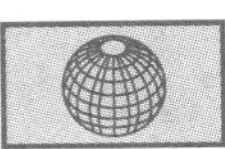   

Using Mezzanine Financing

DEFINITION

Mezzanine financing can be an ideal solution for firms looking for a quick injection of capital to grow their already successful business without giving up an interest in that business.

Mezzanine financing presents a way for publicly and privately held companies to obtain financing without ownership of the company being given up. It is a mixture of traditional debt financing and equity financing that offers the benefits of both. Mezzanine financing, like equity financing, is an unsecured debt that requires no collateral, unlike a traditional bank loan. Like debt financing, mezzanine financing is very flexible and does not necessarily involve giving up an interest in the company. Likely sources of mezzanine financing are private investors, insurance companies, mutual funds, pension funds, and banks.

Because mezzanine financing is normally provided very quickly, with little due diligence by the lender and with little or no collateral required from the borrower, this type of financing tends to be expensive, with the lender seeking a return of between 20% and 30%. Mezzanine financing also has the advantage that it is treated like equity on a company's balance sheet, which may make it easier to obtain standard bank financing.

To attract mezzanine financing, a company usually must demonstrate:

- A track record in the industry, with an established reputation and product.
- A history of profitability, or at least of breaking even.
- A viable expansion plan for the business through acquisition, broader penetration of the market, etc.
- Solid management and operations planning.
- An established business plan.

In leveraged buyouts, mezzanine capital is often used in conjunction with other securities to fund the purchase price of the company that is being acquired. Typically, mezzanine capital will be used to fill a financing gap between less expensive forms of financing (senior loans, second-lien loans, high-yield financing) and equity.

Due to the lack of valid collateral, as well as the high speed of lending, mezzanine financing is typically more difficult to obtain than a traditional bank loan or equity financing. However, the benefits are that mezzanine financiers do not normally interfere in company management and, except in the case of a default, they do not want an interest in the company. Whereas traditional equity investors may attempt to gain some level of company control, mezzanine financiers will do what they can to ensure that the debt is paid off without resorting to default.

ADVANTAGES

- Mezzanine financing often offers more flexible financing options, such as coupons and covenants that take into account the business's cash flow.
- Mezzanine financing provides business owners with the funds they may need to buy another business or to expand.
- Little or no due diligence and collateral.
- Generally no loss of ownership control.

DISADVANTAGES

- Mezzanine financing is normally aggressively priced, with lenders seeking returns of between 20% and 30%.
- Financiers can include restrictive covenants that the borrower has to endure. These can include agreements by the lender not to borrow more money or refinance senior debt from traditional loans.
- Financiers might want to have a vote on the board of directors.
- Many financial experts believe that this type of financing has aggravated the recent credit crunch.

ACTION CHECKLIST

✔ What other avenues of financing are available that would not load the company with so much debt?

✔ In return for the loan, does the company have to cede some independence to the lender?

✔ Does the loan restrict the company to spending money in certain areas?

✔ Does your company have a strong market position based on its products/technology and a market share that will allow it to repay the loan?

✔ Does your company have a focused business strategy and positive long-term development prospects?

✔ Do you have positive, stable cash flows that can be forecasted reliably?

DOS AND DON'TS

DO

- Check that the possibilities for funding from other resources have been exhausted or are insufficient.

DON'T

- Don't use mezzanine financing if there are serious underlying business problems that need to be addressed.

MORE INFO

Books:

Fabozzi, Frank J. (ed). *The Handbook of Financial Instruments*. Hoboken, NJ: Wiley, 2002.

Longenecker, Justin G., J. William Petty, Leslie E. Palich, and Carlos W. Moore. *Small Business Management: An Entrepreneurial Emphasis*. 15th ed. Mason, OH: South-Western Cengage Learning, 2010.

Vance, David E. *Raising Capital*. New York: Springer Science + Business Media, 2005.

Article:

Bean, LuAnn. "Mezzanine financing: Is it for you?" *Journal of Corporate Accounting and Finance* 19:2 (January/February 2008): 33–35. Online at: dx.doi.org/10.1002/jcaf.20370

See Also:

✔ Options for Raising Finance (p. 1081)

✔ Raising Capital by Issuing Bonds (p. 1086)

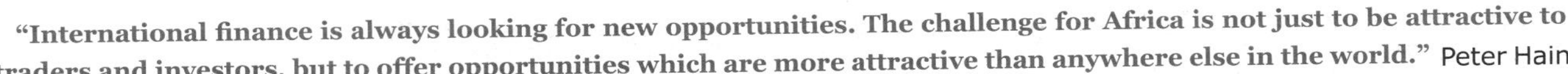

"International finance is always looking for new opportunities. The challenge for Africa is not just to be attractive to traders and investors, but to offer opportunities which are more attractive than anywhere else in the world." Peter Hain

  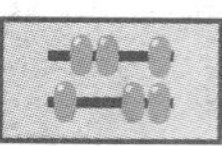   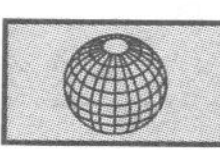   

Using Multistage Dividend Discount Models

DEFINITION

Conventional dividend discount models attempt to value a company based on projections of future dividends discounted to reflect their present value. However, the main drawback of these models is their assumption that dividends will grow in perpetuity at a constant rate that can be determined at the time of the calculation. In practice this assumption is frequently unrealistic, with companies typically undergoing different stages of growth:

- *High growth*: Fast growth is typical early in the company's development as it capitalizes on exciting opportunities in a new market segment or uses a new approach to aggressively gain a share of an existing market. With the overall market expanding, new clients may be relatively easy to attract, and revenues grow rapidly.
- *Transition*: The company's initial growth spurt slows as the "market grab" period ends. Typically, the overall market may grow at a slower pace or the market may become more competitive, reducing scope for dynamic revenue growth.
- *Maturity*: Revenue growth slows as the market moves closer to saturation. New clients become more difficult to attract and companies may have to compete more aggressively on price or service to persuade new clients to switch from a competitor.

Recognizing the different phases of the growth of companies, multistage dividend models typically focus on forecast cash flows for the high-growth and transition stages. Only when the maturity phase is reached would this approach advocate using a constant dividend growth projection, often employing the Gordon growth model to assess a company's longer-term value.

ADVANTAGES

- The multistage approach to companies' development makes intuitive sense, recognizing and addressing the limitations of fixed-growth assumptions, making it more readily applicable to a wider range of nonmature companies.
- Multistage discount dividend models are versatile and flexible, readily facilitating amendments to their data inputs.
- The model's flexibility extends to allowing us to test market assumptions by reversing the underlying calculation. For example, we can test the levels of growth at various time intervals implied by the prevailing share price.

DISADVANTAGES

- Dividend discount models of all kinds put heavy reliance on the quality and accuracy of their data inputs. Despite their perceived advantages over fixed-growth techniques such as the Gordon growth model, multistage dividend growth models remain vulnerable to relatively minor inaccuracies in source data.
- Multistage models are particularly prone to errors in calculations resulting from poor cash flow estimates during the high-growth phase of a company's development. At this relatively early stage, estimates of the constant dividend growth rate to be used in the maturity phase can be very difficult to make.
- For companies that are still in the early phases of growth, it can also be very difficult to accurately forecast the duration of the high-growth and subsequent transition stages. This may necessitate applying the models using a range of input parameters to help arrive at a more realistic valuation band.

ACTION CHECKLIST

✔ As with all dividend discount models, it is imperative to establish the integrity and validity of the input data as far as is possible. The models are totally reliant on the numbers fed into them, making the resulting estimated valuations very sensitive to inaccurate inputs.

✔ Apply the multistage dividend discount model to the company you are interested in, and also to some of its industry competitors. Companies within the same sector could highlight apparent valuation anomalies or unjustified differences in their implied growth rates.

DOS AND DON'TS

DO

- Realize that, despite their undoubted advantages over the fixed-growth approach, multistage discount models remain prone to inaccuracies from any one of a number of inputs.
- However, make maximum use of the model's flexibility to test the market's underlying assumptions. Use the model to ask questions, such as whether the implied growth phase timescales are too long or short, and whether the early growth rate forecasts are appropriate based on the present valuation.

DON'T

- Don't use the models in isolation; rather, combine the technique with other methods of valuation.
- Don't simply employ the model to test whether a stock is currently either under- or overvalued. Test your own assumptions on factors such as future growth rates and the duration of the growth cycle, performing "what if" analysis using variations on your initial input.

MORE INFO

Books:

Barker, Richard. *Determining Value: Valuation Models and Financial Statements*. Harlow, UK: Pearson Education, 2001.

Hitchner, James R. *Financial Valuation: Applications and Models*. Hoboken, NJ: Wiley, 2003.

See Also:

★ Reinvesting in the Company versus Rewarding Investors with Distributions (pp. 701–702)

✔ Applying the Gordon Growth Model (p. 1063)

✔ Calculating a Company's Net Worth (p. 1065)

✔ Using Dividend Discount Models (p. 1104)

"The world of finance hails the invention of the wheel over and over again, often in a slightly more unstable form."
J. K. Galbraith

Using Shareholder Value Analysis

DEFINITION

Shareholder value is a term that suggests that the decisive measure of a company's success is how well it enriches its shareholders. Shareholder Value Analysis (SVA) is one of a number of techniques used as substitutes for traditional business measurements. It became fashionable in the 1980s, when it was linked to Jack Welch, then CEO of General Electric.

Essentially, the idea is that shareholders' money should be used to earn a higher return than it could by investing in other assets with the same amount of risk. To calculate shareholder value, you estimate the total net worth of a company, i.e. total assets minus total liabilities, and divide this figure by the value of its shares. The result gives you the shareholder value of the company. The basic rule of SVA is that a company adds value for its shareholders only when equity returns exceed equity costs. When that value has been calculated, the company can take steps to improve its performance and also use SVA to measure the success of those actions.

Although there are some complex formulae for working out shareholder value, it can also be determined using three simpler approaches:

- Discount the expected cash flows to the present to reach an estimated economic value for the business.
- Use the appropriate cost of capital for the business to find the actual cost of investment discounted to the present.
- Work out the economic value of the business by calculating the difference between the results of the above analyses.

SVA is also known as value-based management. The principle is that the management of any company should first and foremost consider how the interests of its shareholders will be affected by any decisions it takes. This is not a new management theory; it is the legal premise upon which any publicly traded company is set up.

ADVANTAGES

- SVA holds that management should first and foremost consider the interests of shareholders in its business decisions.
- SVA takes a long-term view and is about measuring and managing cash flows over time. It provides the user with a clear understanding of value creation or degradation over time within each business unit.
- SVA offers a common approach, which is not subject to the particular accounting policies that are adopted. It is therefore globally applicable and can be used across most sectors.
- SVA forces companies to focus on the future and their customers, with specific attention to the value of future cash flows.

DISADVANTAGES

- The concentration on shareholder value does not take into account societal needs. Shareholder value financially benefits only the owners of a corporation; it does not provide a clear measure of social factors such as employment, environmental issues, or ethical business practices. Therefore, a management decision can maximize shareholder value while adversely affecting third parties, including other companies.
- It can be extremely difficult to estimate future cash flows accurately—a key component of SVA. This can lead to the use of faulty or ambiguous figures as the basis for strategic decisions.
- The development and implementation of an SVA system can be long and complex.
- Management of shareholder value requires more complete information than traditional measures and can therefore take up management time.

ACTION CHECKLIST

✔ Before adopting SVA, it is important to understand the implications it will have for your business.

✔ You should consult professional advisers, such as accountants or consultants who specialize in this area and who can inform you of what the ramifications may be.

✔ SVA is based on the principle that creation and maximization of shareholder value is the most important measure of a business's performance.

✔ All members of the organization must be committed to the principle for it to work effectively.

DOS AND DON'TS

DO

- Consult professional advisers, such as accountants or consultants who specialize in this area. The changes required to implement SVA could be costly—even more so if you find you need to reverse them.

DON'T

- Don't take on board SVA as a system unless you are positive that your overriding concern is shareholder value.

MORE INFO

Books:

Barker, Richard. *Determining Value: Valuation Models and Financial Statements*. Harlow, UK: FT Prentice Hall, 2001.

Pike, Richard, and Bill Neale. *Corporate Finance and Investment: Decisions and Strategies*. 6th ed. Harlow, UK: FT Prentice Hall, 2009.

Report:

Chartered Management Institute. "Shareholder value analysis (Checklist 160)." April 2010. Online at: tinyurl.com/3bevp2s

Websites:

American Accounting Association (AAA): aaahq.org
Institute of Internal Auditors (IIA): www.theiia.org

See Also:

★ Dividend Policy: Maximizing Shareholder Value (pp. 667–670)
★ Why EVA Is the Best Measurement Tool for Creating Shareholder Value (pp. 952–953)
✔ Calculating Total Shareholder Return (p. 1066)
Economic Value Added (p. 1222)
Jack Welch (p. 1318)

"**Companies have to be socially responsible or the shareholders pay eventually.**" Warren Shaw

  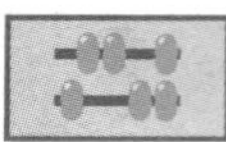      

The Board's Role in Executive Compensation

DEFINITION

Salary is just one of many elements that collectively form executive compensation. Bonuses (sometimes performance-related or even guaranteed), stocks, stock options, pension contributions, medical provisions, and even the use of chauffeured cars all contribute toward the compensation that company executives enjoy.

Setting the appropriate level of compensation for executives can be a considerable challenge for the company board. Set the level too low, and key decision-makers could be tempted away by rival firms. Set the level too high, and the board is left open to the charge that executive performance has failed to deliver value for shareholders. So, in setting compensation levels, the company must seek to attract and retain executive talent while satisfying itself that management is delivering returns appropriate for the level of investment made in the company by stockholders.

Given the scope for executive mobility between firms, the levels of executive compensation in any one firm are frequently compared with those of other companies. Cultural factors play a role in the level of executive mobility between companies and society's general acceptance of executive remuneration. In Japan, for example, executive compensation is typically a more modest multiple of average salaries than in countries such as the United States, where executive compensation, boosted dramatically by the impact of stock options, tends to tower far above the pay and benefits of the average worker.

As levels of executive compensation have risen sharply over recent years, particularly in the United States, pressure on company boards has resulted in increased use of independent parties to help set an appropriate level of remuneration. These typically take the form of a remuneration committee or an independent nonexecutive director charged with the responsibility of creating a "Chinese wall" between those deciding remuneration and those benefiting from it.

ADVANTAGES

- Linking executive pay to the achievement of clearly defined performance targets incentivizes managers while still delivering value for stockholders.
- Establishing and supporting an impartial and independent remuneration committee ensures that the board cannot be accused of "feathering their own nests" by awarding themselves excessive benefits.
- The board can delegate all responsibilities relating to pay and terms of employment for senior staff, freeing resources for other matters relating to the success of the business.

DISADVANTAGES

- The correlation between improvement in a company's overall performance and the precise contribution of any single executive can be difficult to quantify. This could result in an underperforming executive receiving excessive remuneration relative to better-performing colleagues.
- Some chief executives take the view that they should retain the power to decide the level of remuneration of senior executives, arguing that they are in a strong position to judge individual contributions.

ACTION CHECKLIST

✔ The remuneration committee should be a committee of the board composed of independent nonexecutive directors.

✔ The board must ensure that the executive remuneration committee is widely acknowedged to be truly impartial and independent. Any doubts over the committee's independence could cause damage to the firm's reputation among the investment community.

✔ The chairman of the board should ensure that the independent remuneration committee has access to external compensation expertise, such as independent benefits consultants. However, to avoid conflicts of interest, the committee should not use consultants with professional links to the board.

DOS AND DON'TS

DO

- Disclose executive remuneration, as proper reporting improves accountability. Listed companies should detail directors' compensation in the remuneration section of the company's annual report.
- Allocate space in the annual report for a statement from the remuneration committee to facilitate direct communication with stockholders on matters such as remuneration policies and service contracts.

DON'T

- Don't permit the chairman of the remuneration committee to be also the chairman of the pension fund trustees, as this could present potential conflicts of interest.
- Don't expect use of a remuneration committee to put an end to all criticism of executive pay.

MORE INFO

Books:

Ellig, Bruce R. *The Complete Guide to Executive Compensation*. 2nd ed. New York: McGraw-Hill, 2007.

Reda, James F., Stewart Reifler, and Laura G. Thatcher. *The Compensation Committee Handbook*. 3rd ed. Hoboken, NJ: Wiley, 2007.

Articles:

Bruce, Alistair, Trevor William Buck, and Brian G. M. Main. "Top executive remuneration: A view from Europe." *Journal of Management Studies* 42:7 (November 2005): 1493–1506. Online at: dx.doi.org/10.1111/j.1467-6486.2005.00553.x

Hill, Jennifer G. "Regulating executive remuneration: International developments in the post-scandal era." *European Company Law* 3:2 (2006): 64–74.

See Also:

★ Balancing Senior Management Compensation Arrangements with Shareholders' Interests (pp. 634–635)

★ Executive Rewards: Ensuring That Financial Rewards Match Performance (pp. 673–676)

✔ Creating Executive Compensation (p. 1114)

"Be content with your wages." Luke 3:14, New Testament

  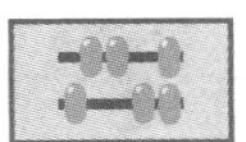      

Business Ethics in Islamic Finance

DEFINITION

The overarching principles of Islam set the operating framework for every aspect of how business is conducted in the Muslim world. While the shifting boundaries of acceptable behavior in conventional Western business are set by laws, regulations, and corporate governance guidelines, Islamic business is governed by divine principles covering values such as fairness, equality, and morality dating back more than a thousand years. More specifically, Islamic finance adopts a long-term partnership approach between businesses, often based on investors essentially taking an equity stake in businesses. *Shariah* law outlaws the charging of interest of any kind, while in the wider context the use of money to generate interest is not permitted. Speculation of any kind is also forbidden, while investments are required to deliver social benefits to the community. Islam also forbids activities in prohibited areas such as gambling or alcohol, instead specifying that *shariah*-compliant businesses should focus on legitimate trade-based activities.

The ethical standards to which Islamic businesses operate reflect the same standards and principles of the Qu'ran, which every Muslim is expected to follow in every aspect of their lives. Therefore, Islamic businesses must operate on a basis of fairness and integrity, while treating everyone equally. The need for honesty, truthfulness, and fair dealing is inherent in Islamic business, requirements which have wide-ranging implications across the full spectrum of business activities, from advertising to after-sales customer service. Islamic companies must also respect the principle of trusting others to be as good as their word. However, this puts the responsibility on businesses to cover their liabilities promptly, honoring their word with timely payment, given the exclusion of credit facilities. The emphasis on the partnership approach to business is further underlined by the need for companies to look after their investors' interests, thus protecting them whenever possible from *dharar* (any kind of harm). The "stakeholder" element of Islamic financing is reflected in the onus on working in tandem with other businesses whenever possible, while markets should generally be free and prices competitive. For example, attempting to squeeze suppliers on price would be unacceptable behavior, as would any attempt to capitalize on others' misfortune by raising selling price excessively should, for example, the supply of goods be temporarily interrupted.

ADVANTAGES

- Business ethics in Islamic finance reflect the moral principles and standards which every Muslim must follow in every aspect of their lives.
- Islamic business encourages a long-term partnership approach, based on mutual interest and a spirit of cooperation.
- Honestly, integrity, and a sense of genuine fair play are ingrained in the operating principles of Islamic business.

DISADVANTAGES

- Muslim businesses may be less able to capitalize on short-term market opportunities given that speculative activities are not permitted by Islamic ethical standards.
- Islamic business managers do not enjoy the same financial incentives which drive managers of many mainstream Western businesses, though they are motivated by moral objectives and standards.
- Given the moral and ethical goals of Islamic businesses—rather than the pursuit of pure profit—less efficient businesses (in purely financial terms) could hamper the development of newer, more entrepreneurial, customer-focused start-ups.

ACTION CHECKLIST

✔ In view of the increasing global influence of Islamic finance, companies aiming to do business with *shariah*-compliant organizations should gain some understanding of their guiding principles and ethics.

✔ Understand the importance for Islamic business of building long-term partnerships, rather than the pure pursuit of short-term profit.

✔ Compliance with Islamic principles may create complications for non-Muslims in the short term. However, it is important to understand that Islamic business aims to bring collective benefit to wider society.

DOS AND DON'TS

DO

- Recognize the importance that Islamic business ethics place on high moral values, while bringing collective benefit to the wider community, rather than the objective of making short-term profits.
- Appreciate that while high ethical standards are enshrined in the principles of Islamic businesses, the interpretation of the conformity of some financial products to *shariah* law may vary slightly between institutions.

DON'T

- Don't make the mistake of thinking that conventional Western business ethics are fully compatible with the ways of Islam: managers shouldn't enter into partnerships with Islamic businesses without first understanding and appreciating how attitudes to the pursuit of profit differ.
- Don't adopt a "pick-and-mix" approach to business ethics: the way Muslim businesses operate reflects their owners' deep-rooted attitudes, beliefs, and commitment to the principles of Islam.

MORE INFO

Books:

Ayub, Muhammad. *Understanding Islamic Finance*. Chichester, UK: Wiley, 2007.

Iqbal, Zamir, and Abbas Mirakhor. *An Introduction to Islamic Finance: Theory and Practice*. Singapore: Wiley, 2007.

Articles:

Parvez, Zahid. "Lack of business responsibility: An Islamic perspective." *International Journal of Business Governance and Ethics* 3:1 (January 2007): 42–45. Online at: dx.doi.org/10.1504/IJBGE.2007.011933

Rice, Gillian. "Islamic ethics and the implications for business." *Journal of Business Ethics* 18:4 (February 1999): 345–358. Online at: dx.doi.org/10.1023/A:1005711414306

Website:

International Institute of Islamic Business and Finance (IIBF): www.iiibf.org

"Consumerism has become a new religion, complete with its high priests at Which? and its fatwas against anyone with the temerity to try to sell anything at more than cost price ... It is a depressingly medieval outlook on economic life."

Sean O'Grady

Conflicting Interests: The Agency Issue

DEFINITION

Those running a company should be committed to delivering maximum returns to its stockholders. However, vested interests can sometimes play a role in decision making, frequently managers' personal interests. The way in which a company's stock is dispersed across various stockholder groups can also have a significant bearing on the nature of the specific corporate governance issues it faces. In many developing countries, as well as in some parts of Europe, company stock ownership can be concentrated within a relatively narrow group of investors—certainly when compared with the wider stock-ownership base that is typical in the United States. This concentration of ownership can heighten the risk that the company board is pressurized to make a particular decision—for example, by a powerful industrialist or oligarch with widespread interests and considerable influence, who attempts to steer a company's board down a particular route, potentially to the detriment of other stockholders.

Even in countries where stockholder bases are generally more diversified, conflicts of interest can still arise between company principals and boards of directors in cases where those making decisions are influenced by self-interest. Managers should in all cases inform the board of any potential conflict of interest between themselves and stockholders in advance. Stakeholders can then be made aware of the potential conflict of interest through a disclosure statement, while the board should take appropriate action to ensure that the interests of stockholders are not compromised. This could involve independent monitoring of management decision making or the insistence that the relationship behind the potential conflict of interest is severed.

ADVANTAGES

- Correctly anticipating potential conflicts of interest gives corporate governance professionals the scope to instigate procedures that will ensure probity and help to protect stockholders.
- A well-diversified stockholder base and thorough research by investment analysts into a company's decision making can help to remind managers that any actions they take to put their own interests ahead of the wider stockholder base could be exposed, making them vulnerable to removal from their positions.
- Companies seen to be operating in an inappropriate manner can rapidly lose stockholder support, exposing them to the risk of a hostile takeover. This risk can create an element of "self-policing" by managers who would otherwise be tempted to put their own interests ahead of those of the wider stockholder base.

DISADVANTAGES

- Aiming for complete protection against the impact of the agency issue is unrealistic. Steps can be taken to try to address the main risks, but in practice major stockholders may still hold considerable influence.
- Striking the balance between rewarding top-performing managers and allowing them excessive influence over their own remuneration levels can be difficult.
- Operating an effective and robust corporate governance program can be expensive, with the costs ultimately carried by the stockholders.

ACTION CHECKLIST

- ✔ The establishment of an independent remuneration committee is often an important step toward adequately rewarding top-performing executives and satisfying large institutional stockholders that the company's resources are being used appropriately.
- ✔ Aim to align executive compensation with stockholders' interests by granting managers stock options.
- ✔ Other elements of executive compensation can be linked to factors such as sales or earnings growth.
- ✔ The establishment of a management monitoring program can help to counter the risk of pressure from dominant external stockholders and protect the interests of other stockholders by scrutinizing executives' decisions.

DOS AND DON'TS

DO

- Ensure that executive remuneration is set by an independent committee with an understanding of competitors' compensation levels.
- Be prepared to permit the remuneration committee to grant stock options to managers to incentivize them to deliver maximum returns for stockholders.

DON'T

- Don't see scrutiny by external investment analysts as a threat: the greater threat to a company's stock price could come from suspicions that managers are feathering their own nests, rather than working to deliver maximum stockholder value.
- Don't skimp unnecessarily on the costs of establishing appropriate structures to oversee executive remuneration and decision making. Disquiet over the probity of decision making can trigger a loss of confidence among key institutional stockholders. In terms of executive remuneration, excessive levels could trigger a stockholder revolt, while companies that under-remunerate executives risk the upheaval of losing key talent to rivals.

MORE INFO

Books:

Sullivan, John D., Jean Rogers, Catherine Kuchta-Helbling, and Aleksandr Shkolnikov (eds). *In Search of Good Directors: A Guide to Building Corporate Governance in the 21st Century*. 3rd ed. Washington, DC: Center for International Private Enterprise, 2003.

Luo, Yadong. *Global Dimensions of Corporate Governance*. Malden, MA: Blackwell Publishing, 2007.

Organisation for Economic Co-operation and Development (OECD). *OECD Principles of Corporate Governance*. Paris: OECD, 2004. Online at: www.oecd.org/daf/corporateaffairs/principles/text

Website:

International Corporate Governance Network (ICGN): www.icgn.org

"Nobody is sure anymore who really runs the company (not even the people who are credited with running it), but the company does run." Joseph Heller

Corporate Governance and Its Interpretations

DEFINITION

Corporate governance is the system by which organizations are directed and controlled. The defects of poor corporate governance have recently been very visible in financial institutions around the world. Since the endorsement of Sarbanes–Oxley, companies have set up audit committees, added financial experts to their boards, improved financial whistle-blowing capacity, and enhanced corporate transparency in financial statements and shareholder disclosures. However, are there any benefits from all of these requirements and best practices, and do they pay any dividends?

For good corporate governance to work, open and honest communication is necessary, with transparent policies and practices, clear lines of authority, and strong internal controls and audit functions, backed by a board that can act with clear independence from management.

A board has to identify with the business and its competition, focus on strategic problems and risk management, and establish high, yet pragmatic, standards of performance. The board directs the plans of the company but does not manage the company. The board must pick first-rate people to run the business while retaining its role to confront, evaluate, and hold managers accountable.

To do this, the board must develop and approve a strategic plan, establish specific and measurable goals, establish risk parameters (which should be reviewed regularly in light of the strategic objectives), encourage and preserve open lines of communication, select competent management, measure managers' performance, and hold management responsible using compensation and continued employment.

In contrast, management has the responsibility to implement the board's strategy, risk tolerances, and policies; keep directors fully informed; deal with the day-to-day operations of the business and its staff; and operate the information systems, procedures, and reports that keep the lines of communication open.

The costs of poor corporate governance have been very evident in the present financial crisis. Firms that engage in unscrupulous and risky behavior will generally fail, while those that have enhanced corporate governance will have higher valuations, greater profitability, and better sales. The recent market turmoil suggests that buying shares in firms that score highly in corporate governance may yield positive returns.

ADVANTAGES

- Good corporate governance is part of good risk management. It brings problems and concerns to light, allowing them to be addressed promptly.
- Good corporate governance helps businesses to focus on strategic issues and risk management, and establishes realistic standards of performance.
- Decision-making is improved by thorough analysis under good corporate governance. Management is held accountable, and management compensation is linked to shareholder value.
- The board can select good managers to run the business while maintaining its role to challenge, measure, and hold managers responsible.

DISADVANTAGES

- A board that lacks independence may not be willing to address poor performance by a line of business or even hold the management accountable.
- The dual loyalty that many board members feel to the management and to the institution is normally resolved in favor of the institution.

ACTION CHECKLIST

- ✔ Risks need to be reviewed periodically in light of the strategic objectives and margins of the business.
- ✔ How strong is the audit committee, and does the audit committee charter reflect the committee's areas of competence?
- ✔ Conduct a self-assessment periodically to help match expectations and actions.
- ✔ How effective is the risk-assessment program, how successful is the internal governance control, and are managers held accountable?
- ✔ Does the board and/or audit committee receive adequate and timely information from the internal and external audit staff?
- ✔ Does the relationship between board and management reflect their independent roles?

DOS AND DON'TS

DO

- Set up an effective and independent corporate governance program.

DON'T

- Don't cut back on good corporate governance programs because of reduced margins—objective opinions may help to resolve problems.

MORE INFO

Books:

Colley, John L., Jacqueline L. Doyle, George W. Logan, and Wallace Stettinius. *What is Corporate Governance?* New York: McGraw-Hill Professional, 2005.

Mallin, Christine. *Corporate Governance*. 4th ed. Oxford: Oxford University Press, 2012.

Monks, Robert A. G., and Nell Minow. *Corporate Governance*. Malden, MA: Blackwell Publishing, 2004.

Websites:

European Corporate Governance Institute (ECGI): www.ecgi.org

Global Corporate Governance Forum (GCGF), International Finance Corporation (IFC): www.gcgf.org

International Corporate Governance Network (ICGN): www.icgn.org

See Also:

★ Improving Corporate Profitability Through Accountability (pp. 685–686)

★ Viewpoint: The "Comply or Explain" Approach to Improving Standards of Corporate Governance (pp. 651–653)

✔ Defining Corporate Governance: Its Aims, Goals, and Responsibilities (p. 1115)

Governance and Risk: An Analytical Handbook for Investors, Managers, Directors, and Stakeholders (p. 1370)

"Experience teaches you that the man who looks you straight in the eye, particularly if he adds a firm handshake, is hiding something." Clifton Fadiman

        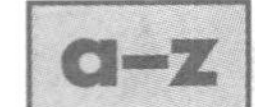

Corporate Governance Practices in Private Equity-Owned Firms

DEFINITION

The relative ease with which acquisition funds can be raised from the capital markets and global investors' push for higher rewards from specialized forms of investment have significantly raised the profile of private equity companies. As leading private equity players have capitalized on opportunities to expand their investment portfolios, their disclosure and other corporate governance responsibilities have also grown, with reforms such as the Sarbanes–Oxley Act (2002) increasing the costs associated with meeting regulatory requirements for listed companies. However, such higher costs may actually have played a role in the growth of the titans of the private equity industry. While the regulatory costs associated with the acquisition of medium-sized, medium-growth companies could lessen the attraction of these deals for smaller private equity firms, the largest private equity houses can use their fund-raising clout to capitalize on the effective regulatory economies of scale achievable through the acquisition of much larger industry players. The elimination of costs associated with regulatory requirements can also be very significant among smaller companies, such as those merged into larger entities owned by private equity firms.

There is no shortage of evidence that the combined benefits of active ownership and the improved corporate governance approach taken by private equity firms are important drivers of the success of private equity-driven deals. From a governance perspective, the representation of private equity firms at the board level is an important mechanism for improved effectiveness, while the streamlining of management structures can help to address agency issues. Private equity firms are also frequently able to call on external governance experts with experience of potential conflicts of interest at other companies in the same industry. The higher management incentives created by private equity houses can help to accelerate change by sweeping away long-standing inefficient working practices, creating an enhanced performance culture and generally improving the transparency of decision making.

ADVANTAGES

- Private equity firms can use their board-level representation to improve corporate governance standards.
- Improved governance can be an important driver of the improved financial returns resulting from private equity firms' investment in underperforming companies. Most private equity deals are also heavily levered with the view of reducing the cost of capital to enhance returns.
- The improved performance associated with better governance standards can also be implemented at the subsidiaries of a conglomerate acquired by a private equity company.

DISADVANTAGES

- Despite evidence that the involvement of private equity specialists strengthens acquired businesses and creates new jobs over the medium term, private equity companies are sometimes still regarded as "asset strippers."
- The poor perception of private equity companies among such bodies as trade unions could slow the pace of change in countries where union representation on company boards is commonplace.
- Unless they are subject to a heavily discounted valuation, smaller businesses in mature, slower-growth markets are generally unattractive to private equity companies, with the result that the private equity route to improved governance is rarely an option.

ACTION CHECKLIST

✔ Private equity firms do not regard corporate governance improvements as merely a "bolt-on" measure after the acquisition. Governance considerations should begin as early as the due diligence process, so that the benefits can be realized as early as possible.

✔ Every effort should be made to achieve consistency in corporate governance standards across a private equity firm's investment portfolio. Plainly, some acquired companies are likely to require more reform than others.

DOS AND DON'TS

DO

- Be transparent on governance issues, notably executive incentives, to help build trust and ease lingering suspicions about the motives of the private equity industry.
- Take account of cultural and social considerations when implementing change in acquired companies. It can be helpful to retain the support of the workforce when introducing structural reform to improve efficiency and raise governance standards.

DON'T

- Don't wait for regulations to be imposed on the private equity industry on issues such as accountability for decisions taken and transparency in areas such as management remuneration. The best approach is to be proactive.
- Don't overlook the need to inform all stakeholders of progress made in improvements to corporate governance structures. Investors in private equity firms, such as pension funds and sovereign wealth funds, are likely to take an active interest in reforms introduced in companies within the private equity firms' portfolios.

MORE INFO

Books:

Cendrowski, Harry, James P. Martin, Louis W. Petro, and Adam A. Wadecki. *Private Equity: History, Governance, and Operations*. Hoboken, NJ: Wiley, 2008.

O'Brien, Justin. *Private Equity, Corporate Governance and the Dynamics of Capital Market Regulation*. London: Imperial College Press, 2007.

Article:

Cumming, Douglas, Donald S. Siegel, and Mike Wright. "Private equity, leveraged buyouts, and governance." *Journal of Corporate Finance* 13:4 (September 2007): 439–460. Online at: dx.doi.org/10.1016/j.jcorpfin.2007.04.008

"As in law so in war, the longest purse finally wins." Mahatma Gandhi

  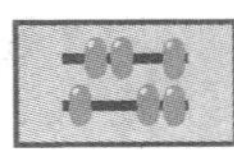      

Creating a Sustainable Development Policy

DEFINITION

The Brundtland Commission coined what has become the most often quoted definition of sustainable development as being development that "meets the needs of the present without compromising the ability of future generations to meet their own needs."

A sustainable development policy is a model of resource use that aims to meet human requirements while preserving the environment, so that these needs can be met not only in the present but also for the indefinite future. It is a means of trying to resolve the conflict between various competing goals, and it involves the simultaneous pursuit of economic prosperity, environmental quality, and social equity.

Businesses are becoming increasingly interested in sustainable development, and many companies are taking steps to ensure that they conduct themselves in a socially responsible manner. Some are even introducing codes of conduct for their suppliers, to ensure that other companies' policies or practices do not tarnish their own reputation.

The positive outcomes that can arise when businesses adopt a policy of social responsibility include:

- enhanced brand image and increased sales and customer loyalty;
- greater productivity and quality;
- improved ability to attract and retain employees;
- possible improved financial performance, with lower operating costs;
- reduced regulatory oversight;
- access to capital;
- product safety and reduced liability.

The payback to the community and the general public includes:

- improved charitable contributions;
- more employee volunteer programs;
- business involvement in community welfare, education, and employment programs;
- product safety and quality;
- greater material recycling;
- better product durability and functionality;
- greater use of renewable resources.

Whereas traditional business models were all about profit, sustainable development recognizes that without happy, healthy people to staff a business and the natural environment able to sustain those people, the supply of resources for the business is simply unsustainable over the long term. Therefore, environmental management tools—including life-cycle assessment and costing, environmental management standards, and eco-labeling—are now commonly integrated with business plans in enterprises worldwide.

ADVANTAGES

- "At the most fundamental level, the sustainability of human societies is a function of the relationship between ecosystem energy production, human energy expropriation and the ecosystem transformations that result from human withdrawals of energy and matter and additions of waste and pollution." (Freese, 1997).

DISADVANTAGES

- Although it is possible to replace some natural resources, it is unlikely that it will ever be possible to replace ecosystem benefits, such as the protection provided by the ozone layer.
- The evolutionary loss of some biodiversity is irreversible.
- The use of fossil fuels, for example, is not sustainable. But how does society plan to eliminate the use of petroleum products?
- Under sustainable development, all resources must be regulated and controlled in order to meet the needs of the present generation as well as those of all future generations. How do you plan to regulate and control the use of resources by all individuals, families, and businesses?
- Sustainable development is for rich nations. When you don't have enough to eat, you don't worry about sustainability.

ACTION CHECKLIST

✔ If you are considering integrating environmental projects with business plans, carefully study the potential business risks and obtain as much information from as many sources as you can before committing to an expensive process.

✔ Encourage an environment of openness about the kinds of risk facing the business from sustainable development policies. Some risks are obvious, but managers of individual business units may sometimes know more about hidden risks.

✔ Involve key business stakeholders in the evaluation of sustainable development and the alternative solutions.

DOS AND DON'TS

DO

- Carefully plan and implement the integration of sustainable development policies.

DON'T

- Don't make the mistake of being attracted to sustainable development policies without being sure that the conversion process has been thoroughly understood.

MORE INFO

Books:

Mawhinney, Mark. *Sustainable Development: Understanding the Green Debates*. Oxford: Blackwell Publishing, 2002.

Organisation for Economic Co-operation and Development (OECD). *Sustainable Development: Critical Issues*. Paris: OECD, 2001.

Schmandt, Jurgen, and C. H. Ward. *Sustainable Development: The Challenge of Transition*. Cambridge, UK: Cambridge University Press, 2000.

Websites:

DEFRA (UK) on sustainable development: sd.defra.gov.uk
International Institute for Sustainable Development (IISD): www.iisd.org
Sustainability links: www.dmoz.org/Science/Environment/Sustainability

See Also:

★ Internal Auditing's Contribution to Sustainability (pp. 687–691)
★ Viewpoint: The Growth of Sustainability Reporting (pp. 680–681)

"**Always do right. This will gratify some people, and astonish the rest.**" Mark Twain

  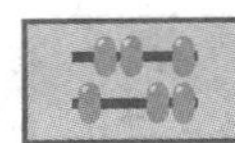      

Creating Executive Compensation

DEFINITION

The level of executive remuneration has risen sharply in many of the World's developed economies over recent decades, with the pay gap between those at the top of the corporate tree and those at the bottom growing ever wider. While this growing divide may trouble some on ideological grounds, the need to set compensation levels at the right level to attract and to retain talented executives has never been greater. Moves to link executive remuneration to performance have found increasing favor over recent years. The objective is to reward executives on the basis of their achieving predetermined measures of the success of the business. While middle-ranking managers may benefit from bonuses linked to relatively simplistic targets such as annual sales increases, the performance-related element of top executives' remuneration can often be more complex, depending on a variety of factors that include company earnings, outright share price performance, and share price performance relative to the company's peer group.

In the United States, executives can expect to benefit from a combination of salary, bonus, stock options, stock grants, and a range of long-term incentive contracts. Over recent years executives have increasingly benefited from a shift to offer stock options.

Specialist independent remuneration committees have increasingly been established by leading listed companies wishing to strike the balance between rewarding top talent and making sure that shareholders' interests are well served. This approach typically stands up well to shareholder scrutiny by distancing executives from the role of effectively setting their own levels of remuneration.

Cultural factors can also have a considerable influence over the acceptable boundaries for top-level managerial pay. Remuneration packages which aggressively leverage private-sector executive remuneration to performance have been widely accepted in countries such as the United States for several decades, though in more conservative countries such as Japan the link between pay and performance has historically been more tentative. However, recent moves by activist investors to extract better shareholder returns in Japan have seen the performance culture penetrate through to boardroom salaries. In other countries such as the United Kingdom, elements of performance-related pay have also percolated into the remuneration packages of senior public service workers as a result of the need to compete with the increasingly incentive-driven private sector for top managerial talent.

ADVANTAGES

- A balanced, well-structured executive remuneration package can help to attract and retain key decision makers.
- Transparency in executive remuneration can find favor with institutional shareholders and is an important element in sound corporate governance.
- A mix of short and long-term performance-related elements can provide further incentives for executives to deliver success. Granting longer-term share options can help to further align executives' and shareholders' interests.

DISADVANTAGES

- The perception that executives may be excessively rewarded for moderate or poor performance can be very damaging to morale among lower-ranking employees.
- Poorly conceived incentive schemes can skew performance toward particular targets that may not necessarily align with the success of the business.
- During boom years, the pay scales in remuneration structures can be equivalent to an arms race as companies compete to attract recognized industry talent. This potentially leaves companies committed to paying excessive rewards for apparent failure during leaner times.

ACTION CHECKLIST

✔ Gain a full understanding of how existing remuneration policies operate before rushing to implement changes.

✔ Study the remuneration arrangements employed by the wider market and compare those used by your own company.

✔ Consider the cultural factors within your company which could effectively limit acceptable multiples between the potential remuneration of executives and that of lower-ranking employees.

✔ Introduce some element of performance-related pay to avoid alienating key workers at lower levels of the corporate structure.

✔ Consider how the performance strength of individual executives can be judged in relation to the overall performance of the company or division.

DOS AND DON'TS

DO

- Make sure that any new proposed executive reward scheme is in keeping with the culture of the company.
- Target consistency and fairness in creative executive compensation. Inflated remuneration to tempt talent from rivals could generate ill-feeling.
- Consider the tax implications before introducing changes to remuneration policies.

DON'T

- Don't underestimate the resources needed to effectively develop and manage executive remuneration policies.
- Don't aim for a remuneration structure which incentivizes managers to shift focus to hitting short-term targets. Opportunities to deliver long-term benefits could be missed.

MORE INFO

Book:

Berger, Lance A., and Dorothy R. Berger. *The Compensation Handbook*. 5th ed. New York: McGraw-Hill, 2008.

Article:

Cahill, Miles B., and Alaina C. George. "Executive compensation incentives in a volatile market." *American Economist* 49:2 (Fall 2005): 33–43. Online at: www.jstor.org/stable/25604323

Website:

Mercer Consulting Executive Remuneration Perspective: www.mercer.com/perspective

"We're overpaying him, but he's worth it." Samuel Goldwyn

  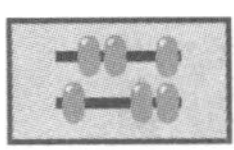      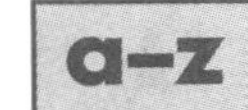

Defining Corporate Governance: Its Aims, Goals, and Responsibilities

DEFINITION

In order for a company to exist, it has to be set up and registered with the appropriate company authority. Once registered, the company is regarded as a legal person, with legal rights and obligations. A company's existence and organization are continuously scrutinized through a well-established set of rules, laws, and policies that govern the way in which the company is run and controlled. This is known as corporate governance.

Companies can be private or public. Public companies, under certain circumstances, can choose to list their shares on a stock exchange or alternative investment markets. The corporate governance rules apply to every company, whether private or public. However, the larger and more complex a company is, the more closely its decisions are scrutinized. For multinational companies corporate governance has extended internationally, with rules and regulations that cooperate at cross-border levels.

Corporate governance exists to protect the shareholders of a company. It also aims to preserve the reputation of a company and its business against any fraudulent acts committed by its directors and officers. The directors of a company must always make decisions objectively, in the best interests of the company's business and its shareholders. They have the responsibility to run the company successfully and bring in profits for the shareholders. They have to do this ethically, within the framework of laws and regulations that govern the running of a company.

Companies must file yearly accounts that are subject to public notice. Accounts and the auditing of accounts by independent auditors are important aspects of corporate governance. They ensure the smooth running of the business and its good reputation.

ADVANTAGES

- A system of corporate governance gives the shareholders confidence that a company is well monitored and that its directors are acting in the best interests of the company and its shareholders.
- Corporate governance guards against defrauding of shareholders and the company's business.

DISADVANTAGES

- The bigger the company, the more it will be scrutinized. The need to comply with numerous corporate governance requirements is expensive and can deter the directors from their main priority, which should be running the business in the best interests of the shareholders.
- Too much supervision could restrict the independence of a company in the way it runs its business.

ACTION CHECKLIST

✔ Be well informed about any corporate governance rules.

✔ Be prepared to put in place a thorough system of auditing and risk management.

DOS AND DON'TS

DO

- Obtain advice from your legal advisers and accountants regarding the best system of auditing and risk management to put in place and the consequences of a breach of the rules.

DON'T

- Don't ignore compliance with the rules of corporate governance. The consequences could be not only financial penalties for the company but also criminal responsibility for the directors.
- Don't overlook the importance of setting up proper procedures to deal with the consequences of a breach.

MORE INFO

Books:

Keasey, Kevin, Steve Thompson, and Michael Wright. *Corporate Governance: Accountability, Enterprise and International Comparisons*. Chichester, UK: Wiley, 2005.

Solomon, Jill. *Corporate Governance and Accountability*. 3rd ed. Chichester, UK: Wiley, 2010.

Article:

Lee, Soo Hee, Jonathan Michie, and Christine Oughton. "Comparative corporate governance: Beyond 'shareholder value'." *Journal of Interdisciplinary Economics* 14:2 (June 2003): 81–111.

Websites:

Corporate Board corporate governance magazine: www.corporateboard.com

Financial Reporting Council (FRC; UK): www.frc.org.uk

Institute of Chartered Accountants in England and Wales (ICAEW): www.icaew.com

Institute of Chartered Accountants in Scotland (ICAS): www.icas.org.uk

See Also:

★ Improving Corporate Profitability Through Accountability (pp. 685–686)

★ Viewpoint: The "Comply or Explain" Approach to Improving Standards of Corporate Governance (pp. 651–653)

✔ Corporate Governance and Its Interpretations (p. 1111)

✔ Directors' Duties: A Primer (p. 1117)

Governance and Risk: An Analytical Handbook for Investors, Managers, Directors, and Stakeholders (p. 1370)

"**Standards are always out of date. That's what makes them standards.**" Alan Bennett

        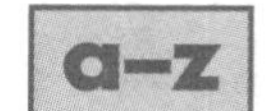

Directors' and Officers' (D&O) Liability Insurance

DEFINITION

Directors' and Officers' (D&O) insurance provides financial security for the directors and officers of a business in the event that they are sued because of their performance or actions undertaken in the course of their duties as they relate to the company.

This type of insurance is sometimes confused with errors and omissions liability insurance. Errors and omissions liability is concerned with performance failures and negligence with respect to products and services and not the performance or duties of management.

D&O insurance normally incorporates employment practices liability and sometimes fiduciary liability. This includes cover against harassment and discrimination suits, which is where there is the most risk. In the United States, employment practice suits comprise the single largest area of claim activity under D&O policies—more than 50% of D&O claims are related to employment practices.

Businesses should have D&O insurance to protect directors and officers against antitrust or unfair trade practice allegations made by stockholders, employees, clients, regulators, and competitors.

Since a director or officer can be held personally responsible for the acts of the company, most directors and officers will stipulate that they are to be protected. If they were not, their own assets would be at risk.

Banks, investors, and venture capitalists will also demand that businesses have D&O insurance as part of their conditions for funding a company.

A common misconception about D&O insurance is that it allows directors or officers to operate in areas, or be employed in acts, that they know to be incorrect. Intentional actions are not covered by D&O insurance.

Due to recent bank failures (for example, Lehman Brothers), banks and other financial institutions that are facing operational or financial challenges are now finding it difficult to obtain D&O insurance.

ADVANTAGES

- The cost of defending lawsuits might exceed the net worth of most private companies and, therefore, judgments can be financially crippling.
- D&O insurance protects the company's assets, as well as those of the company's directors and officers.
- Conflicts of interest may exist, due to the complexity of responsibilities, and companies may have a difficult time attracting qualified individuals to their boards without D&O coverage.
- Banks, investors, and venture capitalists are more willing to fund businesses that have D&O insurance.

DISADVANTAGES

- Premiums can be high, depending on the industry and the size of the risk.
- It is impossible for insurance to cover all eventualities.

ACTION CHECKLIST

✔ Analyze the risks your business may be facing, their probability, and their likely impact.

✔ Consider how existing D&O policies insure against multiple minor claims as well as more significant/catastrophic single incidents. Examine whether any particular exclusion clauses could leave your business exposed to risks you thought were covered.

✔ Try to quantify in financial terms how falling foul of various risks could affect your business. Only once an actual liability figure is available can you expect an insurance supplier to be able to provide a D&O quotation to cover that risk.

✔ Be prepared to seek the advice of specialist risk consultants. The field of commercial insurance can be far more complex than its consumer equivalent, and risk consultants can help companies to understand and evaluate both risks and potential solutions. Industry-specific experts from specialist risk-management companies can help you to devise customized solutions to protect against potential D&O liabilities.

DOS AND DON'TS

DO

- Update risk-assessment frameworks regularly, to help keep management informed of the constantly changing business environment and its hazards.

DON'T

- Don't make the mistake of basing a decision purely on price. D&O insurance is a highly complex area and insurance solutions are many and varied.

MORE INFO

Books:

Hoffman, Douglas G. *Managing Operational Risk: 20 Firmwide Best Practice Strategies*. Hoboken, NJ: Wiley, 2002.

Mathias, John H., Jr, David M. Kroeger, Matthew M. Neumeier, and Jerry J. Burgdoerfer. *Directors and Officers Liability: Prevention, Insurance, and Indemnification*. Looseleaf ed. New York: Law Journal Press, 2000.

Davisson, Michael R., Martin J. O'Leary, Eric C. Scheiner, Edward G. Smerdon, *et al*. *Directors and Officers Liability Insurance Deskbook*. 3rd ed. Chicago, IL: American Bar Association, 2011.

Websites:

American Insurance Association (AIA): www.aiadc.org
Association of British Insurers (ABI): www.abi.org.uk

See Also:

✔ Corporate Insurance Cover: A Primer (p. 1154)
✔ Directors' Duties: A Primer (p. 1117)
✔ Stress Testing to Evaluate Insurance Cover (p. 1016)
✔ Understanding the Components of an Insurance Contract (p. 1021)

"I find it rather easy to portray a businessman. Being bland, rather cruel and incompetent comes naturally to me."
John Cleese

  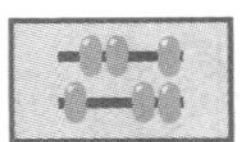   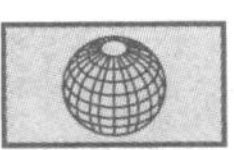   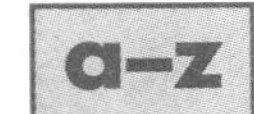

Directors' Duties: A Primer

DEFINITION

Directors have important and powerful positions in a company. The stockholders entrust them with the running of the company, and this is why the law requires directors to comply with certain duties.

Directors have a duty to act within their powers for a proper purpose, which is underlined in the bylaws of the company. They also have a duty to promote the success of the company and, in doing this, must balance the interests of the stockholders, employees, suppliers, and customers of the company. The law does not define success, but in general this is agreed to mean increasing the value of the company and its business.

The directors are required to exercise independent judgment when making their decisions. They also have a duty to exercise reasonable care, skill, and diligence in the performance of their duties. An experienced director will be expected to exercise a higher degree of care, skill, and diligence in the performance of his or her activities.

Directors have a duty to avoid conflicts of interest. What constitutes a conflict of interest is a complex issue, but in general it refers to transactions between a director and third parties, rather than between a director and the company. Directors have a duty not to accept benefits from third parties if they give rise to a conflict of interest. Benefits in this sense include money and benefits in kind, such as corporate hospitality. It is advisable to obtain specific legal advice in respect of conflicts of interest, as this subject can be quite controversial and difficult to assess.

Directors have a duty to declare any interest in proposed transactions or arrangements with the company. They must disclose any such interest to the board of directors and, in certain circumstances, obtain the approval of the stockholders. This includes transactions involving the director or any person connected with the director, such as a spouse or children, and the company.

ADVANTAGES

- Directors' duties enhance the role of a company's directors and guide their direction of the company's business.
- These duties also reduce the risk of fraud and nonperformance, in the interests of the stockholders.
- The duties give stockholders and investors the confidence to invest in companies and enable them to follow the directors in the performance of their responsibilities.

DISADVANTAGES

- Compliance with directors' duties can be expensive in terms of both time and money. It requires an active training program and professional advice.

ACTION CHECKLIST

✔ When accepting an appointment as a director of a company, make sure you understand the consequences of the appointment. Obtain specific information about the company itself and the duties imposed upon directors by the bylaws of the company, as well as the company laws in the country where the company is incorporated.

✔ If necessary, obtain legal advice regarding the consequences of your appointment, and the duties, obligations, and responsibilities you will have as a director under the law.

✔ Most jurisdictions require a transparency in any personal interest a director may have in the company, and it will oblige the director to declare any conflict of interest it may have with the business of the company.

DOS AND DON'TS

DO

- Put in place a good training program that will keep the directors up to date with their duties.
- Obtain legal and professional advice regarding any changes in the legislation governing directors' duties.

DON'T

- Don't ignore the importance of complying with directors' duties and responsibilities. Doing so could be damaging both to the directors in question and to the company.
- Don't underestimate the need for proper training of directors and professional advice to help them fulfill their duties.

MORE INFO

Books:

Loose, Peter, Michael Griffiths, and David Impey. *The Company Director: Powers, Duties and Liabilities*. 11th ed. Bristol, UK: Jordan Publishing, 2011.

Mitchell, Philip. *Tolley's Director's Duties*. Croydon, UK: Tolley Publishing, 2007.

Webster, Martin (ed). *The Director's Handbook: Your Duties, Responsibilities and Liabilities*. 3rd ed. London: Kogan Page, 2010.

Article:

Cooke, Peter. "Duties of directors in new Companies Act 2006: Legal Q&A." *Personnel Today* (May 8, 2007). Online at: tinyurl.com/3wpukru

Websites:

Institute of Directors (IoD; UK): www.iod.com

National Association of Corporate Directors (NACD; US): www.nacdonline.org

See Also:

★ Boardroom Roles (pp. 643–644)
★ Corporate Board Structures (pp. 654–657)
★ Identifying the Right Nonexecutive Director (pp. 682–684)
✔ Defining Corporate Governance: Its Aims, Goals, and Responsibilities (p. 1115)
✔ Regulatory Responsibilities of Executive and Nonexecutive Directors: An International Overview (p. 1121)

"The one predominant duty is to find one's work and do it." Charlotte Gilman

        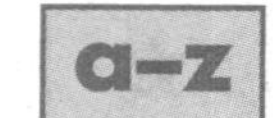

Governance Practices in Family-Owned Firms

DEFINITION

Corporate governance practices have come under greater scrutiny in recent years, particularly in the wake of the 2001 corporate debacle that was the collapse of the energy trader Enron. Even at the opposite end of the capitalization spectrum, family-owned businesses have not entirely escaped some suspicious investors' attention, leading to increased pressure for reform. Many businesses owned largely by families have responded by making the governance practices more formal, while generally increasing the transparency of their operations.

Family ownership of listed companies is commonplace, with wealthy families continuing to own large stakes in listed companies. In some European countries, powerful families effectively control their family-owned companies using voting rights that exceed their actual economic stake in the business.

Family-owned businesses benefit from a stronger personal bond between the owners and the actual business, and between the owners and employees, with the result that the family owners can be less focused on short-term earnings growth and more on long-term strategic development. However, governance structures within family businesses typically evolve with the development of the business—a process formalized in the model of family-business growth and governance developed in the late 1990s by Kelin Gersick, John Davis, Marion Hampton and Ivan Lansberg. This widely accepted model identifies three stages of transition of family businesses:

1. Founder or controlling owner stage

Management and ownership are in the hands of one individual or a couple benefiting from the input of close advisers such as accountants and legal professionals. Governance is typically informal, although the personal attitudes of the owner(s) are often reflected in the way the business operates.

2. Sibling partnership stage

With the approaching retirement of the founder(s), control passes to the next family generation. Governance is frequently complicated by the involvement of a wider base of stakeholders than at the founder stage. Some governance needs are best overseen by a board of directors or a separate advisory body.

3. Cousin consortium

Control of the business becomes further diversified as the siblings pass control of the business to their own children. Some may exit the business completely, potentially selling their stake to outsiders and conceivably diluting the family interest to the extent that the business may no longer be regarded as a family operation. In other cases, some siblings may seek to concentrate control by buying out other stakeholders. The need for an independent governance structure increases considerably.

ADVANTAGES

- Greater transparency can improve the public perception of how family-controlled businesses hope to serve the needs of all stakeholders.
- Understanding the development pattern of a business can help to identify how its governance needs are changing.
- The centralized nature of family ownership can help to keep the costs of corporate governance lower than is the case for firms with wider public share ownership.

DISADVANTAGES

- Some investors may be skeptical as to how committed family-run businesses are to equally serving the interests of all shareholders.
- Some growing family businesses can be slow to recognize the need to put in place measures to satisfy outsiders.
- Liquidity in family-owned companies is often tighter than in other companies, with some families creating legal barriers to the disposal of stock. This can lead to greater resistance to the transparency demanded by modern corporate governance standards.

ACTION CHECKLIST

✔ Family businesses should play to their greatest strength—the ability to pursue a strategy for longer-term gain.

✔ Family-owned businesses should also resist short-term industry fads and instead focus on building a long-term market presence.

✔ It is necessary to be aware of the risk that some stakeholders in family businesses might languish in the comfort zone away from mainstream shareholder pressure and instead pursue their personal goals on the business's time and at the expense of other stakeholders.

DOS AND DON'TS

DO

- Recognize how governance needs evolve over time.
- Appreciate that an external perspective can help family members better understand the need for more formal governance procedures to reassure non-family investors.
- Understand that accepting the accountability to an independent governance board can bring real advantages to the business.

DON'T

- Don't fall into the trap of thinking that corporate governance only amounts to protecting the reputation of the family.
- Don't ignore the benefits that external accountability can bring, such as an increased incentive to drive the company's strategy.

MORE INFO

Articles:

Steier, Lloyd P., James J. Chrisman, and Jess H. Chua (eds). Special issue on "Entrepreneurial management and governance in family firms." *Entrepreneurship Theory and Practice* 28:4 (June 2004): 295–411. Online at: tinyurl.com/3tujmkc

Ward, John L. "Governing family businesses." *eJournal USA* (February 2005): 38–41.

Website:

International Finance Corporation (IFC) on corporate governance: www.ifc.org/corporate-governance

See Also:

✔ Defining Corporate Governance: Its Aims, Goals, and Responsibilities (p. 1115)

"I avoided the company because I wanted the opportunity to have a track record of starting a business where you are not the boss's son." James Murdoch

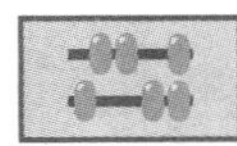

Internal Control Frameworks: COSO, CoCo, and the UK Corporate Governance Code

DEFINITION

In auditing and accounting, internal control is defined as a process that is designed to help an organization to accomplish specific goals or objectives.

Organizations can choose from a number of internal control frameworks. The "Internal control—Integrated framework" published by the Committee of Sponsoring Organizations of the Treadway Commission (COSO) is a widely used framework in the United States and around the world. It was initially published in 1992 "to address key challenges presented by an increasingly complex business environment and help organizations worldwide better assess, design, and manage internal control." The COSO framework defines internal control as a process, effected by an entity's board of directors, management, and other personnel, that is designed to provide "reasonable assurance" regarding the achievement of objectives in the following categories:

- effectiveness and efficiency of operations;
- reliability of financial reporting;
- compliance with applicable laws and regulations.

COSO describes internal control as consisting of five essential components. These components, which are subdivided into 17 factors, include:

- the control environment;
- risk assessment;
- control activities;
- information and communication;
- monitoring.

The CoCo (criteria of control) framework was first published by the Canadian Institute of Chartered Accountants in 1995. This model builds on COSO and is thought by some to be more concrete and user-friendly. CoCo describes internal control as actions that foster the best result for an organization. These actions, which contribute to the achievement of the organization's objectives, focus on:

- effectiveness and efficiency of operations;
- reliability of internal and external reporting;
- compliance with applicable laws and regulations and internal policies.

CoCo indicates that control comprises: "Those elements of an organization (including its resources, systems, processes, culture, structure, and tasks) that, taken together, support people in the achievement of the organization's objectives."

The UK Corporate Governance Code (formerly the Combined Code) was developed by the UK authorities in the early 1990s and last updated in 2010. The Code is principles-based and includes guidelines for best practice. All companies with a Premium Listing on the London Stock Exchange are required to report on how they have complied with the Code and to provide an explanation where they have not.

ADVANTAGES

- Effective internal controls provide a reasonable assurance, but not a guarantee, that an organization's objectives will be met.
- In a large organization, a focus on internal controls should encourage greater standardization of processes.
- Implementing effective internal controls does not necessarily involve extra costs.

DISADVANTAGES

- Internal control cannot ensure that objectives will be met.

ACTION CHECKLIST

✔ Check local legislation. In some countries effective internal control is mandatory, and failure to meet these requirements may result in penalties.

✔ Establish a process for reporting internal control deficiencies, with serious matters reported immediately to top administration and governing boards.

DOS AND DON'TS

DO

- Ensure that all personnel receive a clear message from top management that control responsibilities must be taken seriously.
- Ensure that internal control systems are monitored through a process that assesses the quality of the system's performance over time.
- Be aware that internal control systems change over time, and the way in which controls are applied may evolve. Ensure that new personnel are fully trained in processes and that management knows whether the internal control system continues to be relevant and able to address new risks.

DON'T

- Don't forget that there is no such thing as a perfect control system.

MORE INFO

Books:

Hall, James A. *Accounting Information Systems*. 6th ed. Mason, OH: South-Western Cengage Learning, 2008.

Leitch, Matthew. *Intelligent Internal Control and Risk Management: Designing High-Performance Risk Control Systems*. Aldershot, UK: Gower Publishing, 2008.

Reports:

Committee of Sponsoring Organizations of the Treadway Commission (COSO). "Internal control—Integrated framework." Online at: www.coso.org/IC-IntegratedFramework-summary.htm

Financial Reporting Council. "The UK corporate governance code." June 2010. Online at: www.frc.org.uk/corporate/ukcgcode.cfm

Websites:

Canadian Institute of Chartered Accountants (CICA): www.cica.ca

Committee of Sponsoring Organizations of the Treadway Commission (COSO): www.coso.org

Financial Reporting Council (FRC; UK): www.frc.org.uk

Institute of Internal Auditors (IIA): www.theiia.org

Investors and the Capital Structure

DEFINITION

A company's capital structure is determined by its long-term financing arrangements, including a combination of common stock, debentures, preferred stock, long-term debt, and retained earnings. The capital structure, which is also known as the capitalization structure, differs from the financial structure in that the latter reflects short-term liabilities and accounts payable.

To better understand the nature of a company's capital structure, it is worth considering the comparative levels of equity and debt. Companies with relatively high levels of debt are said to have higher "gearing." However, a company's gearing outlook is not always as simple as it may appear at first glance. Convertible bonds, for example, are classed as debt at the time of issue but could subsequently become equity. Conversely, preference shares are by nature equity, but they have a fixed-return element that gives them certain debt-like characteristics.

At a simplistic level, a company's choice of capital structure should have no impact on the company's total value, as represented by the sum of equity and debt. This theory is sometimes known as "capital structure irrelevance" or the "Modigliani–Miller theory." Promulgated in the 1960s by Franco Modigliani and Merton Miller, who later collected the Nobel Prize for Economics, the basis of the theory is that all investors in the company ultimately benefit from the total cash flows enjoyed by the company. Changes to the overall balance between equity and debt have no effect on the cash flows, only on how they are effectively divided up between different types of investor. However, more advanced financial models subsequently demonstrated the limitations first recognized by Modigliani and Miller: factors of relevance include the impact of taxation and agency issues, i.e. conflicts of interests between executives, equity investors, and bondholders.

ADVANTAGES

- A basic understanding of a company's capital structure, particularly its level of gearing, is a useful starting point when considering an investment in the company.
- Investors in companies with capital structures based on equity would expect to receive returns on their investment via dividends. Capital growth is also likely when the company is performing well. However, one advantage of this structure from the company's perspective is that payment of dividends is optional, giving the company the right to make no dividend payments during challenging trading periods.

DISADVANTAGES

- A company with a capital structure based largely on debt is required to pay interest to the debt holders, regardless of how the company is performing. However, there may be tax advantages associated with debt repayments.
- Careful thought needs to be given to capital-structure decisions, based on factors such as expected rate of investment return and cost of capital. Ill-judged capital-structure decisions can lead to serious financial problems.

ACTION CHECKLIST

✔ Be clear about the differences between capital structure and financial structure—terms that are often confused. Capital structure is the equity/debt balance of a company's long-term finances, whereas financial structure also includes short-term funding arrangements, as represented in the current liabilities on the company's balance sheet.

✔ Aim to understand the factors behind companies' choice of capital structure. There are many considerations behind these decisions, including cash flow projections, possible taxation benefits, funding availability, industry factors, risk considerations, and cash management.

DOS AND DON'TS

DO

- Consider the benefits of buying a combination of shares and debt when making an investment in a company. This approach would effectively lower the gearing of the investment opportunity relative to a shares-only purchase.
- Bear in mind that, while differences between rival companies' capital structures can seem significant, research based on extensions of the Modigliani–Miller theory has suggested that the benefits of adjustments to companies' capital structures are frequently limited.

DON'T

- Don't ignore a company simply because of its capital structure. An investor looking for a more highly geared proposition could buy shares in the company, then lend against them.
- Don't ignore the possible impact of agency problems when analyzing companies. Conflicts of interest can occur in many forms, even between stockholders, debt holders, and executives.

MORE INFO

Books:

Kühn, Christian. *Capital Structure Decisions in Institutional Buyouts*. Wiesbaden, Germany: DUV, 2006.

Riahi-Belkaoui, Ahmed. *Capital Structure: Determination, Evaluation, and Accounting*. Westport, CT: Quorum Books, 1999.

Articles:

Brounen, Dirk, Abe de Jong, and Kees Koedijk. "Capital structure policies in Europe: Survey evidence." *Journal of Banking and Finance* 30:5 (May 2006): 1409–1442. Online at: dx.doi.org/10.1016/j.jbankfin.2005.02.010

Talberg, Magnus, Christian Winge, Stein Frydenberg, and Sjur Westgaard. "Capital structure across industries." *International Journal of the Economics of Business* 15:2 (2008): 181–200. Online at: dx.doi.org/10.1080/13571510802134304

See Also:

★ Capital Structure: A Strategy that Makes Sense (pp. 710–714)
★ Capital Structure: Implications (pp. 715–718)
★ Capital Structure: Perspectives (pp. 24–27)
★ Optimizing the Capital Structure: Finding the Right Balance between Debt and Equity (pp. 543–545)
✔ Understanding Capital Structure Theory: Modigliani and Miller (p. 997)

"Bond investors are the vampires of the investment world. They love decay, recession—anything that leads to low inflation and the protection of the real value of their loans." Bill Gross

  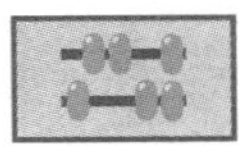      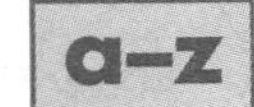

Regulatory Responsibilities of Executive and Nonexecutive Directors: An International Overview

DEFINITION

From a legal point of view, there is no difference between the executive and nonexecutive directors in terms of their responsibilities towards the company and its stockholders. It is recognized, however, that executive directors have an active role in directing the company's affairs for the benefit of, and in the best interests of, the stockholders. The executive directors—and especially the managing director—have overall responsibility for the performance of the company's business. The nonexecutive directors have a supervisory and balancing role, controlling the activities of the executive directors and the board in general.

The directors are responsible for the company's books and accounts and are responsible to stockholders and investors for the company's activities and results. They must act in good faith, in the best interests of the company's business and stockholders. Any conflict of interest with the company's business must be declared and approved by the board and, in certain circumstances, by the stockholders at a general meeting.

Directors must always act with due skill and care and must keep up to date with the needs of the company and its business. They must also consider the needs of the company's employees.

Directors have a responsibility to establish the company's objectives and policies and, once these have been established, to monitor their development and progress. They also appoint the company's senior management.

Directors have an active duty to comply with money-laundering regulations, which are now established internationally. In certain circumstances (when, for example, nonexecutive directors supply their services to the company via another business), they will have to register with certain government departments for the purposes of the money-laundering regulations.

ADVANTAGES

- Regulatory responsibilities enhance the role of a company's directors and guide their direction of the company's business.
- These responsibilities also reduce the risk of fraud and nonperformance, in the interest of the stockholders.
- The regulations give stockholders and investors the confidence to invest in companies and enable them to follow the directors in the performance of their responsibilities.

DISADVANTAGES

- Compliance with the regulatory responsibilities can be expensive in terms of both time and money. It requires an active training program and professional advice.

ACTION CHECKLIST

- ✔ Make sure that you appoint the right individuals as executive and nonexecutive directors. Executive directors will have an active role in the day-to-day running of the company while the nonexecutive will play more of a guiding role.
- ✔ Stress to your chosen appointees that all directors, executive and nonexecutive, have, in view of the law, equal duties and responsibilities.
- ✔ Establish training programmes that will allow the directors to keep up to date with any changes in the law in respect of the running of the company, their duties and responsibilities.

DOS AND DON'TS

DO

- Put in place a good training program that will keep the directors' skills up to date with their regulatory responsibilities.
- Obtain legal and professional advice regarding any changes in the legislation governing directors' responsibilities.

DON'T

- Don't ignore the importance of complying with the regulations governing directors' duties and responsibilities.
- Don't underestimate the need for proper training of directors and professional advice to help them fulfill their responsibilities.

MORE INFO

Books:

Loose, Peter, Michael Griffiths, and David Impey. *The Company Director: Powers, Duties and Liabilities*. 11th ed. Bristol, UK: Jordan Publishing, 2011.

Mitchell, Philip. *Tolley's Director's Duties*. Croydon, UK: Tolley Publishing, 2007.

Smithson, John. *The Role of the Non-executive Director in the Small to Medium Sized Business*. New York: Palgrave Macmillan, 2003.

Webster, Martin (ed). *The Director's Handbook: Your Duties, Responsibilities and Liabilities*. 3rd ed. London: Kogan Page, 2010.

Wilson, Andrew. *The Importance of Being Ethical: Business Ethics and the Non-Executive Director*. Berkhamsted, UK: Ashridge Management College, 1993.

Article:

Cooke, Peter. "Duties of directors in new Companies Act 2006: Legal Q&A." *Personnel Today* (May 8, 2007). Online at: tinyurl.com/3wpukru

Websites:

Institute of Directors (IoD; UK): www.iod.com

National Association of Corporate Directors (NACD; US): www.nacdonline.org

See Also:

★ Boardroom Roles (pp. 643–644)

★ Corporate Board Structures (pp. 654–657)

✔ Directors' Duties: A Primer (p. 1117)

"I'll keep it short and sweet. Family. Religion. Friendship. These are the three demons you must slay if you wish to succeed in business." Matt Groening

  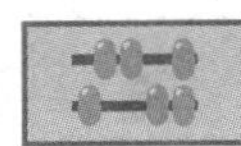      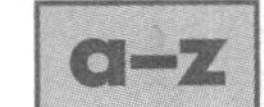

The Responsibilities of Trustees

DEFINITION

A trust or charity can be set up either to benefit particular persons or for any charitable reason. "Trustee" is the legal word that bestows on a person or institution legal title to hold property on behalf of a recipient, such as a trust or charity. Trustees are generally selected because of their personal reputation or professional status. They are given independent authority to make decisions according to their best judgment or professional criteria, and are empowered to act on behalf of the beneficiary.

The great majority of trustees serve as volunteers, and receive no payment for their work. Their responsibilities and duties are generally to:

- accept ultimate responsibility for directing the trust's affairs, and ensure that it is solvent, well run, and delivers the outcomes and benefits for which it was set up;
- ensure that the trust complies with law, and prepare reports on what it has achieved, and annual returns and accounts as required by law;
- ensure that the trust does not breach any of the requirements or rules set out in its governing document and that it remains true to its purpose and goals;
- comply with the requirements of legislation and other regulations that govern the activities of the trust;
- act with integrity, and avoid any personal conflicts of interest or misuse of funds or assets;
- ensure that the charity is and will remain solvent (duty of prudence);
- use charitable funds and assets reasonably, and only in furtherance of the trust's objectives;
- avoid undertaking activities that might place the trust's funds, assets, or reputation at any undue risk;
- use reasonable care and skill in the role of trustee, using personal skills and experience as needed to ensure that the trust is efficiently managed (duty of care);
- obtain independent professional advice on all matters where there may be material risk to the trust, or where the trustees may be in breach of their duties.

As a rule, all the trustees—acting as a team—take all decisions. However, decisions need not be unanimous, and a majority decision is sufficient unless the charity's governing document states otherwise.

Different jurisdictions regard a trustee's duties in different ways. Normally, however, the legislation follows the general body of elementary fiduciary law that is found in most common-law jurisdictions.

ADVANTAGES

- Trustees are chosen for their independence, personal repute, and professional standing.
- Most trustees serve as volunteers, receive no payment for their work, and are collaborating for altruistic reasons.
- Because of their commitment to create positive change in society, trustees should do their utmost to ensure that the charity or trust succeeds in its aims.

DISADVANTAGES

- As trustees are volunteers and receive no recompense, it may sometimes be difficult to find people with the management skills necessary to run what may be a complex organization.

ACTION CHECKLIST

- ✔ Look for an in-depth analysis of particular jurisdictional differences between countries before setting up a trust or charity and consult independent specialists in fiduciary law.
- ✔ When selecting trustees, find out what specialist skills they can bring. Most modern charities need skilled support in areas such as management, advertising, public relations, and fund raising, which are highly specialized.
- ✔ Set up a professional, formal selection procedure when looking for trustees to ensure that you have the right balance of skilled candidates.
- ✔ Seek legal advice from specialists when setting up the charters or governing documents.

DOS AND DON'TS

DO

- Spell out in clear terms the goals of the trust, their probable impact, and the effort that may be required.

DON'T

- Don't take on the job of a trustee unless you are sure that you have skills to offer and the time required to do the job properly.

MORE INFO

Books:

Claricoat, John, and Hilary Phillips. *Charity Law A to Z: Key Questions Answered*. 2nd ed. Bristol, UK: Jordan Publishing, 1998.

Gaudiani, Claire. *The Greater Good: How Philanthropy Drives the American Economy and Can Save Capitalism*. New York: Times Books/Henry Holt, 2003.

Thompson, Kenneth W. (ed). *Philanthropy: Private Means, Public Ends*. Lanham, MD: University Press of America, 1987.

Report:

Charity Commission. "The essential trustee: What you need to know." February 2008. Online at: tinyurl.com/36d93um

Websites:

American Institute of Philanthropy (AIP): www.charitywatch.org

Charity Trustee Network (CTN): www.trusteenet.org.uk

See Also:

✔ Defining Corporate Governance: Its Aims, Goals, and Responsibilities (p. 1115)
✔ Selecting the Board and Evaluation Process (p. 1123)
✔ Understanding Decision-Tree Analysis (p. 1179)

"In London, Washington, and Paris people talk of bonuses or no bonuses. In parts of Africa, South Asia, and Latin America, the struggle is for food or no food." Robert Zoellick

  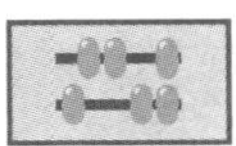   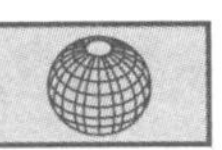   

Selecting the Board and Evaluation Process

DEFINITION

The role of a company's directors and board is to ensure the prosperity of the business and to manage the company in the best interests of its stockholders.

The law and the bylaws of a company usually establish the minimum number of directors that should be appointed to the board—from one in small companies to dozens in more complex public listed companies. They will also specify the composition of the board, in terms of executive and nonexecutive directors. There should be a minimum number of independent directors. These are people who have independence from any party with influence over the board, the company, or its business.

In general, appointing directors to the board is an objective and formal process. Following recent international scandals involving directors and a lack of control exercised by the board, the rules of corporate governance of selection and appointment of the board have been tightened. The role of the nonexecutive director has become more important than ever.

Directors are appointed by a company's stockholders or by its board. However, the dismissal of a director can only be done by the stockholders.

The appointed directors have a position of trust towards the company, its business and its stockholders. The appointment of a board involves a thorough selection process. The executive directors must have the right level of professional experience and skills to be able to run, enhance and develop the business of the company. The nonexecutive directors are not involved in the day-to-day running of the business but must be able to give enough time to the supervision and running of the board. Their role in supervising the activities of the board and executive directors has become increasingly important. Nonexecutive directors are usually businesspeople with significant experience in the running of businesses and boards.

The bylaws of a company usually require the board to appoint a chairperson. The chairperson supervises board meetings and procedures and has a casting vote in the event that the board cannot come to an agreement. (The board normally makes decisions based on a majority of votes.) This means that the chairperson's decision is final.

ADVANTAGES

- Putting in place a good selection process for directors, and selecting an appropriate board, will enhance the performance of the company.
- A well-selected board, which can work in harmony, will not only be enjoyable to work with but will also produce the most efficient results.

DISADVANTAGES

- Selecting the right board can be time consuming.
- Attracting the right directors can be expensive, because it means paying them competitive salaries.
- It is sometimes necessary to use a specialist headhunting agency to help with the selection of directors. This can be very expensive.

ACTION CHECKLIST

✔ Thoroughly research potential appointees to join the board of the company. Look at their credentials, résumé and experience, and also discuss their suitability with them. It is essential that the appointment will work in the interest of the board and the company's business overall.

✔ Highlight the implications of being a director in the company; what is expected of the individual, how the company operates, how you expect the decisions to be made.

✔ Assess how the individuals who will form part of the board will work together. Determine who would be best in an executive directorship and who would be better as a nonexecutive member. Consider if their experience is relevant in view of the aims of the company.

DOS AND DON'TS

DO

- Always select a board through a thorough process of interviews and evaluation.
- Obtain relevant information regarding the experience and skills of each member of the board before appointment.
- Research the market carefully before deciding whom to invite to be a board member.
- Make sure that each member of the board—especially the nonexecutive directors—can dedicate to the company as much time as is required.
- If necessary, be prepared to use specialist recruitment consultants, who will be able to help you find the right members of the board.

DON'T

- Don't rush into appointing someone as a member of the board on the sole basis of their reputation. A good reputation and the right credits are important, but they may not be sufficient for the needs of the company. Interview and get to know the people you will be appointing to the board.
- Don't underestimate the need for proper research and professional advice when selecting the right board.

MORE INFO

Books:

Loose, Peter, Michael Griffiths, and David Impey. *The Company Director: Powers, Duties and Liabilities*. 11th ed. Bristol, UK: Jordan Publishing, 2011.

Mitchell, Philip. *Tolley's Director's Duties*. Croydon, UK: Tolley Publishing, 2007.

Webster, Martin (ed). *The Director's Handbook: Your Duties, Responsibilities and Liabilities*. 3rd ed. London: Kogan Page, 2010.

Article:

Cooke, Peter. "Duties of directors in new Companies Act 2006: Legal Q&A." *Personnel Today* (May 8, 2007). Online at: tinyurl.com/3wpukru

Websites:

Institute of Directors (IoD; UK): www.iod.com

FT Non-Executive Directors' Club: www.non-execs.com

National Association of Corporate Directors (NACD; US): www.nacdonline.org

See Also:

★ Corporate Board Structures (pp. 654–657)

✔ Assessing Business Performance (p. 1144)

✔ The Board's Role in Executive Compensation (p. 1108)

✔ Directors' Duties: A Primer (p. 1117)

✔ Regulatory Responsibilities of Executive and Nonexecutive Directors: An International Overview (p. 1121)

"I get many invitations but I only join the boards of companies where I admire the management and believe in the company." Jill Ker Conway

        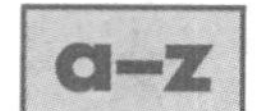

Social Return on Investment

DEFINITION

Analyzing the return on an investment in financial terms is intuitively relatively easy, yet many investments can deliver other forms of return that are more difficult to express purely in terms of money.

The social return on investment (SROI) refers to the total social, environmental, and economic value of an activity undertaken by a nonprofit organization or business. SROI has developed from both cost/benefit analysis and social accounting, though the formal concept was originated by the Roberts Enterprise Development Fund, a San Francisco-based philanthropic fund that invests in institutions and organizations working for social returns rather than purely profit.

Social return on investment aims to support a better understanding and management of the outcomes of an existing or potential project. Different individuals or bodies involved in the project, often referred to as stakeholders (for example, those managing, funding, working for, or benefiting from the activity), may place a different emphasis on the relevance of each benefit of SROI.

What sets SROI apart from conventional social accounting is that it aims to put a monetary value on the combined benefits of the activity with a view to maximizing the use of resources. For example, an SROI study could demonstrate that for every $1 invested in a particular social project, a return of $5 was achieved from sources such as healthcare benefits, reduced welfare payments, or lower delinquency rates in the local community. SROI performed retrospectively, known as evaluative SROI, assesses outcomes that have already occurred with a view to judging their overall effectiveness, whereas forecast SROI can be useful in planning terms given its aim of helping to assess the likely total future social, environmental, and economic value of a project or activity.

ADVANTAGES

- Helps to assess the total value of projects for society.
- The analysis supports a long-term view of the overall social, environmental, and economic benefits an activity can generate.
- Can be a valuable tool in promoting existing or potential projects by helping to attract new funding.
- The technique can also help those bodies funding existing projects to understand the full value of benefits delivered.
- Thorough SROI analysis can also identify possible undesirable consequences of projects, providing an early opportunity to change strategy or put in place measures to address negative outcomes.

DISADVANTAGES

- SROI is dependent on subjective considerations, so attitudes to monetary values may differ between stakeholders. Putting a monetary value on some benefits can be extremely difficult.
- Adopting an SROI approach to a project can involve significant resources, both in terms of time and level of commitment.
- Estimating the amount of time needed to implement SROI can be difficult as this depends on the availability of the required data and the skill set of those involved in the study.
- The findings of SROI can lack credibility to any parties who are opposed to the project in the first place; given its reliance on subjective inputs, opponents may see SROI as a means to justify spending on a "pet" project.

ACTION CHECKLIST

- ✔ When considering investing in a project or activity, give an overall thought to the value and implications it might have for society as a whole.
- ✔ Ensure that you are communicating effectively with all stakeholders so that they understand what you are measuring, how you are doing it, and what you are hoping to achieve.
- ✔ Make use of impact maps to foster a better understanding among stakeholders of the relationship between the availability of resources, the possible uses of those resources, and the likely results.
- ✔ Don't overstate the value of the project—attributing unrelated benefits to the project in an SROI study could undermine the whole credibility of the analysis.
- ✔ Be transparent about the assumptions you are making—SROI is not an exact science and shouldn't be portrayed as such.

DOS AND DON'TS

DO

- Plan thoroughly and understand what you aim to achieve from your study.
- Identify who all the stakeholders are and understand their goals and objectives.
- Make reasonable and balanced projections and stick to your aims and plans.
- Ensure that any judgments involved in SROI are fully documented to ensure transparency.
- Where resources permit, look to underpin the credibility of your analysis by inviting an independent third party to validate your findings.

DON'T

- Don't think of SROI as an exact science—values are subjective as different stakeholders may have different priorities in terms of outcome.
- Don't become obsessive about the ratio of "money spent versus the total value of benefits received"—rather, use SROI analysis as a basis for a better understanding of the likely outcomes of a project.
- Don't undermine the integrity of your findings by trying to put a value on unrelated outcomes that have little or nothing to do with the project.
- Don't underestimate the value of effective results reporting—present your analysis to stakeholders and encourage ongoing communication with them.

MORE INFO

Books:

Nicholls, Jeremy, Susan Mackenzie, and Alibeth Somers. *Measuring Real Value: A DIY Guide to Social Return on Investment*. London: New Economics Foundation, 2007.

Scholten, Peter, Jeremy Nicholls, Sara Olsen, and Brett Galimidi. *Social Return on Investment: A Guide to SROI Analysis*. Amstelveen, The Netherlands: Lenthe Publishers, 2006.

Websites:

ClearlySo, an online marketplace for social business and enterprise, commerce, and investment: www.clearlyso.com

Social ROI, a social entrepreneurship blog: socialroi.com

SROI Network, the social return on investment website: www.thesroinetwork.org

"Most men are individuals no longer so far as their business, its activities, or its moralities are concerned. They are not units but fractions." Woodrow T. Wilson

The Triple Bottom Line

DEFINITION

Traditional accounting models are all about profit and more profit, whereas triple bottom line accounting recognizes that, without content, healthy people to run a business, and the natural environment to sustain those people and resources the business is simply unsustainable in the long term. Triple bottom line accounting means expanding the traditional reporting framework to take into account environmental and social factors as well as financial performance.

The idea proposes that an organization's license to operate in society comes not just from rewarding shareholders through enhanced profits (the economic bottom line), but by improving its environmental and social performance. As such, it includes environmental responsibility, social awareness, and economic profitability.

The triple bottom line is sometimes referred to as "TBL" or "3BL." Triple bottom line can also be simply summarized as People, Planet and Profit:

People

People are also known as *human capital*. The people aspect means treating employees, the community, and the region in which a corporation conducts its business correctly. In this part of the TBL, business not only ensures a fair day's work for a fair day's pay but also reinvests some of its profits into the surrounding community through education, sponsorships, or donations, or helping in projects that promote the common good.

Planet

Under the planet principle, or *natural capital*, a business will endeavor to minimize its ecological impact in all areas—from obtaining raw materials, through production processes, to shipping and management. It is a "cradle to grave" attitude, and in some cases "cradle to cradle," i.e. taking responsibility for goods after they've been sold by, for example, offering a recycling or return program.

Profit

TBL is about making a principled profit, rather than earning a profit at any cost. In other words, the profit made should be in accord with the other two principles of People and Planet.

The TBL concept is important because it is not just about commerce; it is an ongoing process that helps a company to run a more sustainable and greener business and demonstrates to the community at large that the company is working not just for profit but also for the members of the community. On balance, without people and planet, there would be no profit to be made.

ADVANTAGES

- A TBL business endeavors to benefit the natural order as much as possible—or at least do no harm and curtail environmental impact.
- TBL manufacturing businesses conduct a life-cycle assessment of products to determine their true environmental cost, from the growth and harvesting of raw materials to manufacture, and then from distribution to eventual disposal by the end user.
- TBL companies make an effort to reduce their ecological footprint by vigilantly managing the consumption of energy and nonrenewables and reducing manufacturing waste, as well as rendering waste less toxic before disposing of it in a safe and legal manner.

DISADVANTAGES

- Quantifying this bottom line is a relatively new task. Therefore, it is sometimes problematic and often subjective.
- The types of problems that occur in social and environmental realms do not lend themselves to a measure that would allow for clear-cut accounting. How, in financial terms, do you measure the two factors of People and Planet?

ACTION CHECKLIST

✔ If you are considering TBL, carefully study any potential downsides and obtain as much information from as many sources as you can before committing to an expensive process.

✔ Will the TBL model suit your business, and how will you measure the People and Planet principles?

✔ Support an atmosphere of openness about the kinds of problems the business will face if it adopts TBL.

✔ Involve key local stakeholders in the evaluation of how a TBL program could benefit the local community.

DOS AND DON'TS

DO

- Involve both your accountants and lawyers in the evaluation of the risks and potential benefits of TBL.

DON'T

- Don't make the mistake of being attracted to TBL because it is politically advantageous. Implementation could be expensive and time-consuming, with potentially unpredictable results.

MORE INFO

Books:

Elkington, John. *Cannibals with Forks: The Triple Bottom Line of 21st Century Business*. Gabriola Island, BC: New Society Publishers, 1998.

Henriques, Adrian, and Julie Richardson (eds). *The Triple Bottom Line, Does It All Add Up? Assessing the Sustainability of Business and CSR*. London: Earthscan, 2004.

Savitz, Andrew W., with Karl Weber. *The Triple Bottom Line: How Today's Best-run Companies are Achieving Economic, Social, and Environmental Success—And How You Can Too*. San Francisco, CA: Jossey Bass, 2006.

Willard, Bob. *The Sustainability Advantage: Seven Business Case Benefits of a Triple Bottom Line*. Gabriola Island, BC: New Society Publishers, 2002.

Articles:

Colman, R. "Triple bottom line benefits." *CMA Management* 78:1 (2004): 3.

Henderson, Lance. "Triple bottom line: The conceptual frontier." *Bellingham Business Journal* (April 2008). Online at: tinyurl.com/2v3l2cb

Websites:

Ethical Investment Association (EIA; UK): www.ethicalinvestment.org.uk

SustainAbility: www.sustainability.com

Understanding Economic Efficiency Theory

DEFINITION

Conventional economic efficiency theory states that companies should structure their output to achieve the lowest possible cost per unit produced. Given the combination of fixed and variable costs typical in business, low levels of output are inefficient because fixed costs are shared out across a relatively small number of units. At the other extreme, although above-optimal production can, in theory, generate economies of scale, in practice this apparent benefit is often more than offset by additional costs related to the overstressing of existing systems. In the short term, the point of maximum operational efficiency is achieved at the level of output at which all available economies of scale are taken advantage of, yet short of the level at which the diseconomies of overstraining existing systems come into play. Over the longer term, however, the optimal level of productive efficiency can be raised by increasing the capacity of existing systems.

The second element of conventional economic efficiency theory relates to the way existing resources are allocated. The logic is that high levels of competition among producers should prevent them from making excessive profits by raising their selling prices to an unreasonable level above their marginal costs. At the company level, maximum allocative efficiency is achieved when the firm produces the optimal output level of a combination of goods or services to maximize the benefit to the company as a whole. The theory takes account of the fact that company resources are finite and can be used only once, with the result that using a quantity of a material for one purpose involves an opportunity cost—that is, it denies the company the chance to use the same material for another purpose. Allocative efficiency is achieved only when no other pattern of utilization of resources can deliver a better overall result in terms of the welfare of all interested parties. This point of maximum allocative efficiency, at which improvements in one aspect of usage can only be achieved at the expense of losses elsewhere, is sometimes referred to as the Pareto optimal allocation of resources.

ADVANTAGES

- The theory provides a basic framework to help understand the various factors that are associated with existing operating costs.
- An understanding of the main principles of the theory could provide scope for managers to find ways of making some elements of their business work more efficiently.

DISADVANTAGES

- The theory encourages managers to take a "static" view of their business, with no regard to the possibilities offered by innovation. The rapid pace of technological development over recent years has highlighted this shortcoming in classic economic efficiency theory.
- The focus on the lowest possible cost can give an overly simplistic representation of the way businesses operate, although the theory retains value in some low-technology, noninnovative manufacturing applications.

ACTION CHECKLIST

✔ Analyze your company's cost structure, determining which costs are fixed and which are largely variable; in practice most costs tend to be semivariable in nature.

✔ Consider the levels of production that are likely to begin to put serious strain on existing infrastructure to the point that diseconomies of scale begin to appear. It may be that lessons can be learned from the way systems performed during past periods of temporary high demand.

✔ Study how finite resources are being put to work at present. Excessive downtime of resources, including human resources, should be investigated in an effort to bolster allocative efficiency.

DOS AND DON'TS

DO

- Make use of the theory to gain a greater understanding of various cost and resource utilization patterns within companies. However, remember that an excessive focus on miniscule cost improvements could distract management from changing industry trends, potentially allowing competitors to capitalize on exciting new opportunities.
- Consider whether present resource allocation has more to do with past needs and in-house politics than present or future requirements. Remember that, as the business environment evolves, company resource allocation decisions should reflect changing demands on the business.

DON'T

- Don't use economic efficiency theory in isolation. Remember that taking a static view of your business is unlikely to be the best preparation for change.
- Don't ignore human factors when seeking greater efficiency. Demoralizing staff in the pursuit of insignificant cost savings could generate unforeseen human resource costs.
- Don't lose sight of wider opportunities to make a quantum leap in efficiency, rather than the small incremental improvements that are typically achieved using economic efficiency theory. Innovation, particularly related to technology, can deliver substantial efficiency benefits.

MORE INFO

Books:

Quinzii, Martine, and Sujaya Parthasarathy (trans). *Increasing Returns and Efficiency.* New York: Oxford University Press, 1993.

Ravenscraft, David J., and Frederic M. Scherer. *Mergers, Sell-Offs, and Economic Efficiency.* Washington, DC: Brookings Institution, 1987.

Zerbe, Richard O., Jr. *Economic Efficiency in Law and Economics*. Cheltenham, UK: Edward Elgar Publishing, 2001.

Article:

Ng, Yew-Kwang. "Increasing returns and economic organization: Introduction." *Journal of Economic Behavior & Organization* 55:2 (October 2004): 129–136. Online at: dx.doi.org/10.1016/j.jebo.2004.05.001

"When I find a short-seller, I want to tear his heart out and eat it before his eyes while he's still alive." Richard S. Fuld, Jr

  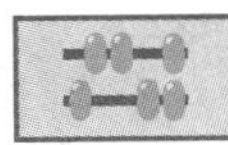      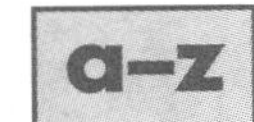

Achieving Success in International Acquisitions

DEFINITION

All too often, domestic acquisitions fail to deliver all of the stockholder value envisaged by management ahead of the deal. According to a 2003 survey by KPMG, 70% of M&A transactions failed to achieve the goals set by top management. Throw into the mix the further complications of international acquisitions, such as possible culture clashes and suspicions over the impact of foreign control, and the prospects of making a real success of an international acquisition would seem to diminish even further. However, there are several issues, such as the need to ensure effective communication and the importance of technology integration, which companies should consider ahead of an international deal, as together these could significantly increase the prospects for success.

As with domestic acquisitions, potential acquirers should fully assess the extent of the strategic fit between the companies, considering whether the businesses could be combined in such a way as to unlock sufficient benefits as a single entity. In some cases, companies that have had a long period of successful strategic partnerships can find that their existing operational familiarity can work to their advantage in a merger or acquisition. From the employees' perspective, experience of working in partnership with a potential acquirer may also allay some concerns over the risk of a serious culture clash.

Effective communication is at least as important in international acquisitions as in domestic transactions. Such communication should extend beyond the boundaries of the companies involved to include clients, suppliers, local authorities, and governments, as well as employees and investors, as a failure to communicate effectively and truthfully with any party could create suspicion over the objective of the acquisition.

While cultural factors can play an important role in the success or failure of an international acquisition, conventional practicalities of day-to-day operations of the combined entities must also be given adequate consideration. For example, a survey by PricewaterhouseCoopers in 2000 found that the integration of information systems was the biggest challenge following an acquisition, with almost three in four firms reporting problems in this area.

ADVANTAGES

- International acquisitions can improve operational efficiency (for example, through economies of scale), enabling companies to compete more effectively against the backdrop of increased globalization.
- Acquisitions can also help a company to capitalize further on an existing competitive advantage.
- International acquisitions can enable the acquirer to gain access to an existing network of clients and suppliers rapidly in a new market. Establishing an effective presence in a foreign market from scratch, by means other than an acquisition, could take many years.

DISADVANTAGES

- Most acquisitions fail to deliver all the originally projected benefits.
- Poorly managed acquisitions can create a climate of suspicion among employees of the target company, affecting morale and productivity.
- Acquisitions can involve a considerable drain on management resources and can also generate high transaction costs.

ACTION CHECKLIST

✔ Take time to identify a target company that has some strategic fit with your own organization.

✔ Consider how closely the target company should be integrated following acquisition. There is some evidence that close integration can be disadvantageous in cases where the cultural fit between companies is limited.

✔ Learn from the successes and failures of other similar cross-border acquisitions in specific industries.

DOS AND DON'TS

DO

- Take professional advice on the regulatory environment in the target market at an early stage in the process.
- Ensure that all relevant information is effectively communicated to all stakeholders before and after the acquisition.
- Utilize the experience of managers from the acquired company in the post-merger management team.

DON'T

- Don't ignore the importance of cultural factors as well as operational requirements when planning an acquisition.
- Don't underestimate the importance of due diligence, particularly in markets where business practices may be different from those in your domestic market.
- Don't change management personnel unnecessarily as this can be highly disruptive to existing operations.

MORE INFO

Books:

BenDaniel, David J., Arthur H. Rosenbloom, and James J. Hanks, Jr. *International M&A, Joint Ventures and Beyond: Doing the Deal, Workbook*. 2nd ed. Hoboken, NJ: Wiley, 2002.

Child, John, David Faulkner, and Robert Pitkethly. *The Management of International Acquisitions*. Oxford: Oxford University Press, 2001.

Articles:

Duncan, Catriona, and Monia Mtar. "Determinants of international acquisition success: Lessons from FirstGroup in North America." *European Management Journal* 24:6 (December 2006): 396–410. Online at: dx.doi.org/10.1016/j.emj.2006.08.002

Lynch, Richard. "International acquisition and other growth strategies: Some lessons from the food and drink industry." *Thunderbird International Business Review* 48:5 (September/October 2006): 605–622. Online at: dx.doi.org/10.1002/tie.20112

Website:

International Network of M&A Partners (IMAP): www.imap.com

"If you want to succeed you should strike out on new paths rather than travel the worn paths of accepted success."

Anita Roddick

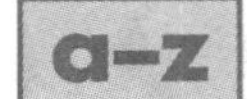

Acquiring a Company

DEFINITION

The acquisition of a company involves buying the company's shares. The expression is also used when the business of a company is acquired. In legal terms, the consequences of an acquisition of shares or an acquisition of business assets are different. One of the key differences is that an acquisition of shares involves buying the underlying business of that company, with all of its assets but also its liabilities. By acquiring the business only, the assets are transferred but in principle the liabilities are left with the seller. There are some exceptions to this rule so it is advisable to seek specific legal, financial, and commercial advice before taking any decision.

The process starts with the identification of the business to be acquired. The commercial price of the shares is linked to the value of the business of the company. Usually, negotiations will take place between the buyer and the seller, with a purchase price agreed upon. The next stage involves the investigation of the business to be acquired, a process often called due diligence. In order to reassure the seller, a confidentiality agreement should be signed to protect the seller against any leaks of sensitive company-specific information to third parties. The process involves: a legal due diligence (undertaken by the buyer's lawyers), which investigates the legal rights and obligations affecting the business of the company; a financial due diligence (undertaken by the buyer's accountants), which looks at all the financial, accounting and tax affairs of the company; and a commercial due diligence (usually undertaken by the buyer's own team), which looks mainly at the integration and practical aspects of the business following the acquisition. These final aspects could include: the integration of key members of staff in the buyer's operations; and the revision of commercial and insurance contracts to facilitate the planning of logistical aspects of the buyer's operations and to avoid any unnecessary duplication of suppliers or insurance.

Following the due diligence process, the legal documentation is drafted, agreed upon, and ultimately signed. In practice, negotiations can break down as a result of the discovery of underlying liabilities that seriously devalue the business of the seller's company. The sale and purchase agreement will incorporate certain warranties and indemnities that the seller will be required to give to the buyer. Warranties are factual statements regarding the state of the seller's business affairs, while indemnities provide the buyer with rights to obtain a certain payment in specific circumstances. Warranties can also result in a payment by the seller to the buyer, but actual proof of a loss is required before any payment is due.

ADVANTAGES

Advantages of a business-asset acquisition, rather than a share acquisition:

- An existing business can be improved by acquiring certain assets without the difficulties and costs involved in acquiring the seller's company.
- The assets will be acquired at the current market value, which will give them a high base cost in terms of capital gains tax. The purchase will, therefore, attract maximum capital allowances. The seller can obtain certain reliefs against capital gains tax.
- Overall, a less complicated and less thorough investigation is required than in a share acquisition. The latter would involve the valuation and assessment of all the existing rights and liabilities of the seller's company, including all contractual agreements.

DISADVANTAGES

- In the United Kingdom, for example, VAT is chargeable on an asset sale but not on a share sale.
- Stamp duty for an acquisition of shares is paid by the buyer. In the United Kingdom, Stamp Duty Reserve Tax is charged at a rate of 0.5% of the price of the shares, while for assets involving property Stamp Duty Land Tax must be paid at up to 4% depending on the value of the property.

ACTION CHECKLIST

- ✔ Study carefully any business you might acquire. Obtain as much information from as many sources as you can before committing to an expensive due diligence process.
- ✔ Know your market and make sure that you have analyzed the consequences for your own business of the acquisition of another business.
- ✔ Be prepared for a long and complicated due diligence process, which could prove time consuming as well as costly.
- ✔ Economize by negotiating a reasonable rate with your legal and financial advisers, but remember that it is better to incur costs by conducting a thorough investigation than to accept a level of service that may fail to reveal potentially costly liabilities.

DOS AND DON'TS

DO

- Involve your solicitors and accountants in the evaluation of both the risks and potential benefits of an acquisition, as well as the due diligence process.
- Negotiate your rates and make a contingency plan for any cost overrun.
- Plan carefully the integration of the new business within your own.

DON'T

- Don't be attracted by a business that has not been thoroughly investigated.
- Don't overlook the importance of negotiating complex warranties and indemnities that would protect you in the event that underlying liabilities are discovered.

MORE INFO

Books:

Dewhurst, John. *Buying a Company: The Keys to Successful Acquisition*. London: Bloomsbury Publishing, 1997.

Lajoux, Alexandra Reed. *The Art of M&A Integration: A Guide to Merging Resources, Processes, and Responsibilities*. New York: McGraw-Hill Professional, 2005.

Rao, P. M. *Mergers and Acquisitions of Companies*. New Delhi, India: Deep & Deep Publications, 2002.

Article:

Rowan-Robinson, Jeremy, and Norman Hutchinson. "Compensation for the compulsory acquisition of business interests: Satisfaction or sacrifice." *Journal of Property Valuation and Investment* 13:1 (1995): 44–65. Online at: dx.doi.org/10.1108/14635789510077287

"I buy when other people are selling." J. Paul Getty

  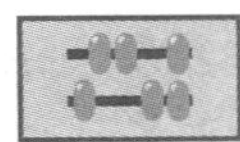      

Acquisition Accounting

DEFINITION

Acquisition accounting relates to the accounting procedure following the takeover of one company by another. The resulting entity is often known as a business combination. Exact standards may vary from one country to another so it is important to obtain professional advice on the procedures relating to acquisition accounting in the country in which the business combination will be operating. In the United Kingdom, for example, the FRS 7 standard, " Fair values in acquisition accounting," sets out the principles of accounting for a business combination under the acquisition method of accounting. In the United States, the Financial Accounting Standard Board's statement no. 141 sets out what a reporting entity should provide in its financial reports in relation to a business combination and its effects. However, there is a process of convergence taking place across the globe, led by the International Accounting Standards Board (IASB). Its standards for business combinations, IFRS 3 and IAS 27, are increasingly recognized by governments around the world.

Prior to June 2001, two accounting methods could be used when a merger or acquisition took place. They were the purchase method and the pooling of interests method. However, the purchase method is now compulsory in both the United States and the European Union, and wherever else the IFRS standard issued by the IASB is recognized. Under the purchase method, the assets and liabilities of the merged company are presented at their market values as on the date of acquisition. The acquisition must be estimated at fair value and the difference between the purchase price and the fair value should be recognized as goodwill. Under the pooling of interests method, transactions are considered as exchange of equity securities. The assets and liabilities of the two firms are combined according to their book value on the acquisition date.

ADVANTAGES

- The increasing use of the purchase method means that it is easier to compare potential acquisition targets around the world in accountancy terms at least.
- Under the purchase method, a company cannot create a restructuring provision to provide for future losses or restructuring costs as a result of an acquisition. Such costs must be treated as post acquisition costs. Consequently, it is easier to gauge the impact of restructuring costs on profits, and prevent the use of provisions to exaggerate the immediate impact of an acquisition on profits, while boosting reported profits in subsequent years.

DISADVANTAGES

- One of the main drawbacks of the purchase method is that it may overrate depreciation charges because the book value of assets used in accounting is generally lower than the fair value if the economy is experiencing relatively high inflation.
- If the amount paid for a company is greater than fair market value, the difference is reflected as goodwill. Since goodwill must be written off against future earnings, the pooling of interests method is preferable to the purchase method.

ACTION CHECKLIST

✔ Check which acquisition accounting standards apply in the country in which you are undertaking an acquisition.

✔ If you can use either the purchase method or the pooling of interests method take professional advice on which is the most advantageous.

DOS AND DON'TS

DO

- Obtain advice from legal and accounting professionals before proceeding with any acquisition.
- Remember that, the purchase method, of accounting must identify the acquirer (the entity that obtains control over the other entity).

DON'T

- Don't forget that, under the purchase method, investors are likely to disregard the impact of goodwill.
- Don't forget that, under the purchase method, the elimination of provisions creates extra visibility and helps prevent abuses.

MORE INFO

Books:

Lewis, Richard, and David Pendrill. *Advanced Financial Accounting*. London: Pearson Education, 2004.

Siegel, Joel G., Nick Dauber, and Jae K. Shim. *The Vest Pocket CPA.*. Hoboken, NJ: Wiley, 2005.

Smith, Ian. *Financial Techniques for Business Acquisitions and Disposals*. 2nd ed. Hawksmere Report Series. London: Thorogood Publishing, 1998.

Articles:

Dos Santos, Marcelo B., Vihang R. Errunza, and Darius P. Miller. "Does corporate international diversification destroy value? Evidence from cross-border mergers and acquisitions." *Journal of Banking and Finance* 32:12 (December 2008): 2716–2724. Online at: dx.doi.org/10.1016/j.jbankfin.2008.07.010

James, Kieran, Janice How, and Peter Verhoeven. "Did the goodwill accounting standard impose material economic consequences on Australian acquirers?" *Accounting and Finance* 48:4 (December 2008): 625–647. Online at: dx.doi.org/10.1111/j.1467-629X.2007.00246.x

Pasiouras, Fotios, Chrysovalantis Gaganis, and Constantin Zopounidis. "Regulations, supervision approaches and acquisition likelihood in the Asian banking industry." *Asia Pacific Financial Markets* 15:2 (June 2008): 135–154. Online at: dx.doi.org/10.1007/s10690-008-9075-z

Wesbite:

IFRS Foundation and the International Accounting Standards Board (IASB): www.ifrs.org

See Also:

✔ Structuring M&A Deals and Tax Planning (p. 1135)

✔ Using IRR for M&A Financing (p. 1137)

✔ Using the Market-Value Method for Acquisitions (p. 1139)

"Chief executives seem no more able to resist their biological urge to merge, than dogs can resist chasing rabbits."

Philip Coggan

M&A Regulations: A Global Overview

DEFINITION

Mergers and acquisitions (M&A) has become a mundane expression, used daily in the media. In order to operate successfully in a global economy, corporations have become transnational and have to perform at a multinational level. To achieve such expansion, corporations acquire other companies or merge with them. These large corporations are publicly owned, listed on stock exchanges or alternative markets around the world, and engage in M&A activities that are thoroughly regulated by governments to protect the shareholders of target companies.

The laws and regulations governing M&A are very complex and strict. High levels of expertise and specialist advice are required, and corporations use several teams of lawyers who specialize in the jurisdictions involved in M&A.

In 2003, the European Parliament published a directive that regulated the way in which securities were to be offered to the public or admitted to trading. This became known as the EU Prospective Directive. Its scope was to harmonize and homogenize capital markets within the European Union. In essence, the directive allows a company that issues shares in more than one EU member state to be governed by a single member state, rather than by each member state in which the shares are offered.

In the United States, federal securities laws and regulations are generally applicable if US investors own securities in a foreign target company. In the United States, the Securities and Exchange Commission is the body that supervises and oversees the most important participants in the securities world, such as securities exchanges, dealers, brokers, and mutual funds. Its most important role is to promote disclosure and transparency of market information by maintaining fair dealing and ensuring protection against fraud.

In Australia, the responsibility belongs to the Australian Stock Exchange and the Australian Securities and Investments Commission, while the relevant body in the United Kingdom is the London Stock Exchange.

In September 2006 the Regulations on Foreign Investors' Mergers and Acquisitions of Domestic Enterprises came into force in China, as a direct result of an increase in M&A transactions and the general opening up of the country.

Japan has recently eased regulation on foreign investment by introducing legislation that allows foreign-owned companies to invest in Japanese companies through stock-for-stock (share-for-share) exchanges with the Japanese subsidiaries of those companies.

ADVANTAGES

- M&A regulations protect shareholders and investors in the acquirer and target company.
- In general M&A regulations allow for the harmonization and homogenization of international markets and thus maintain transparency, fair dealing, and protection against fraud.

DISADVANTAGES

- M&A regulations are very complex.
- Specialist financial and legal advice is always required when participating in M&A activity.
- The cost of an acquisition is usually high, and specialist advice only adds to this cost.

ACTION CHECKLIST

✔ Recognize the complexity of M&A regulations.

✔ Seek specialist professional advice at an early stage when considering a possible M&A deal.

✔ Appreciate that while the costs of enlisting professional help to explore global M&A opportunities can be high, the long-term rewards from successful international deals can be considerably higher.

DOS AND DON'TS

DO

- Carefully balance the implications of a developing business against the advantages and disadvantages of acquiring an existing one before committing to any expense.
- Obtain relevant advice regarding the acquisition or merger.
- Research the market carefully before making a decision.

DON'T

- Don't underestimate the need for proper research and professional advice.
- Don't ignore the importance of integrating the new operations within the existing business; otherwise the consequences could be costly.
- Don't be afraid to decide against the acquisition if the signs are that it will not be a good investment.

MORE INFO

Books:

McGrath, Michael. *Practical M&A Execution and Integration: A Step by Step Guide To Successful Strategy, Risk and Integration Management*. Chichester, UK: Wiley, 2011.

Sherman, Andrew J. *Mergers and Acquisitions from A to Z*. 3rd ed. New York: AMACOM, 2011.

Report:

Khalili, Anita, Uvarshanie Nandram, Mariana Trindade, Pratik M. Patel, Roger Conner, and Jill Lewandosky. "2012 M&A outlook." Bloomberg, 2011. Online at: media.bloomberg.com/bb/avfile/ru20IiusvjMM

Websites:

Beyond the Deal: www.beyondthedeal.com

Reuters M&A news: www.reuters.com/finance/deals/mergers

See Also:

★ Due Diligence Requirements in Financial Transactions (pp. 727–729)

✔ Achieving Success in International Acquisitions (p. 1127)

✔ Acquiring a Company (p. 1128)

✔ Planning the Acquisition Process (p. 1132)

✔ The Rationale for an Acquisition (p. 1134)

"When it comes to mergers, hope triumphs over experience." Irwin Stelzer

Management Buyouts

DEFINITION

A management buyout (MBO) is the acquisition of a business by its management. The management will usually buy the target business from its parent company. The management will incorporate a new company to buy the business or shares of the target company. The transaction usually involves another party, a venture capitalist, which, together with the management, will invest in the new company. A venture capitalist is a company or fund that invests in unquoted companies. The investment usually takes the form of an equity stake.

In an MBO it is very important to establish whether the parent company, the vendor, is willing to sell. The management are usually in a very good position to buy, since they already understand the business they intend to acquire. Funding the acquisition usually requires not only the personal financial commitment of the managers but also additional funding in the shape of a loan or an equity investment.

It is essential that the management establish a coherent business plan, which will help not only in obtaining the funding required for the MBO but also in convincing the parent company that the managers are the best buyers for the business. As for investors, what they need is assurance that the business will be able to continue successfully and that it will provide them with a profitable return on their investment.

In an MBO, confidentiality while negotiations are taking place between the parent company and the management team is essential. The consequences of a leak could be damaging to the business and its staff.

ADVANTAGES

- An MBO will give the management the chance to run their business.
- The new company will have a highly motivated management team, who are not only eager to make a profit but also have a deep knowledge of the business they will be running.
- Since the management understand and have been involved in the running of the business to be acquired, the commercial due diligence that is usually undertaken when a company is acquired should be easier and less time-consuming.

DISADVANTAGES

- An MBO involves a very serious financial commitment and acceptance of risk by the management. The management will move from being employees to being owners of the business. If the business is not successful, they will feel it directly.
- Even though the commercial due diligence required could be less extensive, the legal and financial affairs of the business still need to be examined. This will involve advice and expense.
- Since acquisition by an MBO is highly leveraged (i.e. has a high proportion of debt relative to equity), this does not put the new company in the best position to compete on price.

ACTION CHECKLIST

✔ Think carefully about the business before you acquire it. Obtain as much information from as many sources as you can before committing to an expensive due diligence process.

✔ Know your market and make sure that you have analyzed the consequences of owning your own business.

✔ Be prepared for a long and complicated due diligence process, which could prove time-consuming as well as costly.

✔ Economize by negotiating a reasonable rate with your legal and financial advisers, but remember that it is better to incur costs by conducting a thorough investigation than to accept a level of service that may fail to reveal potentially costly liabilities.

✔ Always be aware of confidentiality while the MBO is being planned, as any leak can affect the confidence of the staff and affect the performance of the business.

DOS AND DON'TS

DO

- Involve your lawyers and accountants in the evaluation of both the risks and potential benefits of an MBO, as well as in the due diligence process.
- Negotiate your rates and make a contingency plan for any cost overrun.
- Draw up an accurate and achievable business plan.

DON'T

- Don't make the mistake of being attracted by the idea of owning a business without fully weighing up the risks you might be taking.
- Don't underestimate the importance of finance and the financial commitment that owning a business will entail. The risks to the owners of a business are high if the business does not perform.
- Don't forget that many of the banks that offer finance will be looking for collateral for the loan, and the managers could be required to provide personal guarantees that will affect their personal wealth if things do not work out.

MORE INFO

Books:

Sharp, Garry. *Buy Outs: A Guide for the Management Team*. London: Euromoney Institutional Investor, 2002.

Wright, Mike, and Hans Bruining. *Private Equity and Management Buy-Outs*. Cheltenham, UK: Edward Elgar Publishing, 2008.

Website:

MBO Guide: www.mboguide.co.uk

See Also:

★ Going Private: Public-to-Private Leveraged Buyouts (pp. 730–732)
★ Leveraged Buyouts: What, Why, When, and How (pp. 743–745)
★ MBOs: A High-Octane and Life-Changing Mode of Business (pp. 754–755)
ℹ Management Buyouts (pp. 1754–1755)

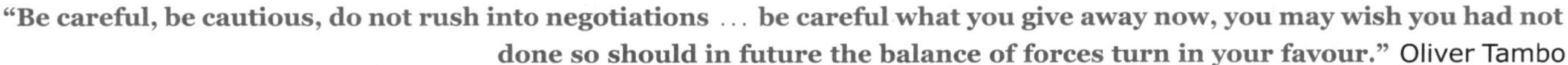

"Be careful, be cautious, do not rush into negotiations ... be careful what you give away now, you may wish you had not done so should in future the balance of forces turn in your favour." Oliver Tambo

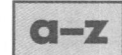

Planning the Acquisition Process

DEFINITION

After a buyer decides to acquire a business, the process starts with the search for a suitable business. The targeted business could be known to the buyer or could be a competitor of the buyer. It could also be advertised for sale in a trade journal or newspaper, or the buyer could be approached directly by the seller or its intermediary.

After finding a business, the buyer must assess its value in order to establish the best offer price. If the business to be acquired is part of a company, it will have to file yearly accounts, which are of public record.

Every business is affected by cash flow, profit and loss, and how its finances are run. The balance sheet and accounts will give a good indication of all these elements. A buyer should also look at: the overall market within which the targeted business operates; the business's performance and reputation; its competitors; and any other interested buyers. Another element to look at is the legislation in the country where the business operates. The logistics of acquiring a national business and an international business can be very different. A buyer should obtain information on the management of the targeted business. If a business is well managed, it is usually successful and well reputed. The buyer should also consider the workforce.

The buyer should consider the advantages the acquisition will have upon its own business and should start planning how it will be integrated within its own company.

In order to consider the purchase more thoroughly, more detailed investigations should be made. During this process, the buyer may well like to involve advisers who will provide a more thorough and objective valuation. However, this assistance may be expensive.

This investigation should give a buyer an idea of the value of the business and of the offer to make to the seller. The initial information will be verified by the later due diligence process, which takes place with the permission and cooperation of the seller. The buyer will approach the seller either directly or via its advisers and make an offer for the business. Negotiations on the price will usually commence, with the buyer and seller subsequently signing a document called heads of term. This will deal with the main points of the acquisition, such as price, warranties to be given by the seller and other essential conditions. The buyer and its advisers will have to sign a confidentiality agreement, which will protect the data disclosed by the seller and will give the buyer access to more detailed information from the seller's private records. The due diligence process can last a few weeks, depending on the amount and complexity of the information to be investigated. The buyer will look in detail at all the business's contracts with clients and suppliers, insurance, employees' records, any intellectual property and IT issues, and any existent litigation. A buyer should also look at the business premises, any licenses, and environmental issues. Separately, the buyer's accountants will investigate the financial details of the business. At the end of the due diligence process, the buyer will usually receive a legal due diligence report from its lawyers and a financial due diligence report from its accountants. These, together with the buyer's own commercial and business assessment, will provide a very clear picture of the business and will allow the buyer to decide whether the acquisition is worth making or not.

ADVANTAGES

A well-informed and prepared buyer:

- Will be in a better position to decide whether the target business is worth buying in the first place.
- Will be able to decide on an accurate valuation of the business and make a competitive offer price.
- Will have a thorough understanding of the business to be sold and will, therefore, be able to conduct more advantageous negotiations.
- Will be better able to help in running and integration of the business once the acquisition is made.

DISADVANTAGES

- Initial investigations and later due diligence could be costly, and may show that the business is not worth acquiring.
- An acquisition involves huge effort and a concentration of resources, which sometimes could be used to improve its own business.

ACTION CHECKLIST

- ✔ Consider carefully any business you might acquire. Obtain as much information from as many sources as you can before committing to an expensive due diligence process.
- ✔ Know your market and make sure that you have analyzed the consequences for your own business of the acquisition of another.
- ✔ Be prepared for a long and complicated due diligence process, taking time and being costly.
- ✔ Economize by negotiating a reasonable rate with your legal and financial advisers, but remember that it is better to incur costs by conducting a thorough investigation than to accept service that may fail to reveal potentially costly liabilities.

DOS AND DON'TS

DO

- Involve your solicitors and accountants in the evaluation of both the risks and potential benefits of an acquisition, as well as in the due diligence process.
- Negotiate your rates and make a contingency plan for any cost overrun.
- Plan carefully the integration of the new business within your own.

DON'T

- Don't make the mistake of being attracted by a business that has not been thoroughly investigated.
- Don't overlook the importance of negotiating complex warranties and indemnities that would protect you in the event that underlying liabilities are discovered.

MORE INFO

Book:

Dewhurst, John. *Buying a Company: The Keys to Successful Acquisition*. London: Bloomsbury Publishing, 1997.

Article:

Rowan-Robinson, Jeremy, and Norman Hutchinson. "Compensation for the compulsory acquisition of business interests: Satisfaction or sacrifice." *Journal of Property Valuation and Investment* 13:1 (1995): 44–65. Online at: dx.doi.org/10.1108/14635789510077287

"There is no resting place for an enterprise in a competitive economy." Alfred P. Sloan

  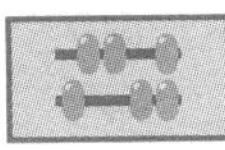   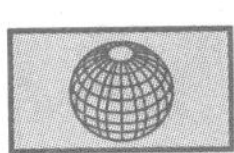   

Planning the Disposal Process

DEFINITION

The preparation for the disposal process starts after the seller has decided to sell the business. There can be several reasons why someone might want to sell his business. The business could need substantial investment, and selling a percentage of shares – and, therefore, a share in the business – would bring in the necessary finance to help develop the business overall. Lifestyle factors could also be involved: a seller may want to sell the whole of his business because of a wish to retire or to do something completely different.

Whatever the reason for the sale, preparing a business for disposal requires time and effort, and it can be expensive. In certain circumstances, a buyer may only be interested in the goodwill of the business sold and certain of its assets. A seller should be aware that such a sale would leave him with the rest of the business, including its liabilities. Usually, the best time to sell a business is when it is doing well, has a good set-up and is running smoothly, bringing in high profits, and has a successful financial and management record. Then a seller can fully capitalize on its success. In some cases, the buyer of a business is its own management team. This is known as a management buy-out (MBO).

A seller should start preparing for the sale long in advance. He or she needs to make sure that all papers, legal documents and contracts, permits for the business, and its books are in good order. He or she should involve professional advisers, legal and financial, as early as possible. Their help and advice will be required during the disposal process, but they can also provide useful tips when preparing the business for sale.

Staff knowledge of the planned sale is not necessary at this stage. Usually, managers are told because his or her cooperation is required when preparing the sale, but spreading the knowledge of the potential sale through the entire workforce could have a negative influence on the running of the business, as staff could begin to worry about work security.

With the advice of accountants, a seller should consider any tax issues that will affect a disposal, so that the tax burden is minimized. Any buyer will be interested in a well-run business with a good grip on its credit and creditors. A seller should consider renegotiating inefficient contracts with clients and utility providers and should sort out any existent and potential litigation.

ADVANTAGES

- A well-prepared seller will be in a better position to negotiate a good price for the business.
- A well-prepared seller will be in a better position to assess what warranties they will be able to give to the buyer without submitting himself or herself to unexpected risk.
- An MBO could be more advantageous for a seller, as the managers know the business inside out.

DISADVANTAGES

- The initial investigations and later due diligence process could be expensive, both financially and in terms of time, if the acquisition does not go ahead.
- Preparing for a sale will involve huge effort and a concentration of resources, which sometimes could be used to improve the business itself.
- Selling is frequently emotionally difficult on a seller.
- In an MBO, less money is usually offered for a business, because managers may not have access to good finance.

ACTION CHECKLIST

✔ Consider carefully the need to sell and why you want to sell. It may well be that the timing is not ideal and that waiting could be advantageous.

✔ Be prepared for a long and complicated due diligence process, which could prove time consuming as well as costly.

DOS AND DON'TS

DO

- Involve your solicitors and accountants in the evaluation of both the risks and potential benefits of a disposal, as well as the due diligence process.
- Negotiate your rates and make a contingency plan for any cost overrun.
- Plan carefully the tax implications of the disposal.

DON'T

- Don't make the mistake of selling at the wrong time if waiting a while could bring a higher price.
- Don't overlook the importance of mitigating your liabilities under any warranties and indemnities given to the buyer, obtaining advice, and understanding your business.

MORE INFO

Books:

Smith, Ian. *Financial Techniques for Business Acquisitions and Disposals*. 2nd ed. Hawksmere Report Series. London: Thorogood Publishing, 1998.

Steingold, Fred S. *The Complete Guide to Selling a Business*. 4th ed. Berkeley, CA: Nolo, 2012.

Articles:

Card, Jon. "Selling your business." *Growing Business*. Online at: tinyurl.com/7ymdwhw

Gole, William J., and Paul J. Hilger. "Managing corporate divestiture transactions." *Journal of Accountancy* (August 2008): 48–51. Online at: tinyurl.com/3keqrwy

See Also:

★ Maximize the Selling Price of Your Business (pp. 746–748)

★ Maximizing Value when Selling a Business (pp. 751–753)

"Inequality of knowledge is the key to a sale." Deil O. Gustafson

  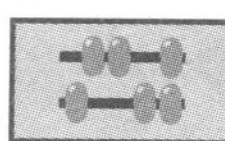 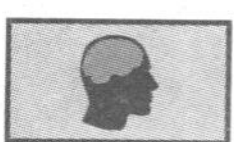     

The Rationale for an Acquisition

DEFINITION

Companies and businesses are bought and sold regularly all over the world. Acquisition is a complex and expensive process that influences both the business and financial future of the buyer. Why would a person either physical or legal decide it is time to acquire a company or business? Which factors drive its decisions and define its thought process?

A person with no experience of running a business may find it difficult to assess and scale the difficulties and risks of an acquisition. At the opposite extreme, an experienced business person may readily understand and be able to assess more clearly the reasons for an acquisition. It may be that the buyer wants to develop his existent interests and the acquired business will provide the key technology to help with the expansion of the overall operation. The business to be acquired may bring to the buyer the perfect supply chain, which otherwise will take time and expense to set up from scratch. It could well be that the workforce of the company to be acquired has such specialist skills and knowledge for these to be the main incentive for the acquisition, as an alternative to instigating a training programme for existing employees. Another reason could be that the brand and customers of the business to be purchased are of such value that they justify the acquisition rather than the time and expense of the buyer building its own.

Whatever the reasons for an acquisition, a buyer should consider the following practical suggestions.

ADVANTAGES

- Any existing, successful business will already be functioning and properly set up.
- The workforce of the business will already be in place and well organized.
- The business's marketing and contacts will be established.
- Its customer base will also be well established.
- Acquiring a well-developed business or company will make it easier to borrow money, because the company will already have a good business plan in place and will offer credibility to the lender.

DISADVANTAGES

- The acquisition of an existing company or business could have a negative effect on the business's reputation within the market if the acquisition is not done professionally, with due diligence and care.
- An acquisition can negatively influence a business's staff, who are usually excluded from any negotiations.
- The cost of an acquisition is usually high and will have to be paid all at once.
- Contracts with suppliers and contractors may have to be reassessed and renegotiated.
- Any missteps in integrating the new business can be costly.

DOS AND DON'TS

DO

- Carefully balance the implications of a developing business against the advantages and disadvantages of acquiring an existing one before committing to any expense.
- Obtain relevant advice regarding the acquisition.
- Research the market carefully before making a decision.

DON'T

- Don't rush into the unknown without a proper plan. It is easier to make a good decision in a market and area of business to which you are already accustomed.
- Don't underestimate the need for proper research and professional advice.
- Don't ignore the importance of integrating the new operations within the existent business, otherwise the consequences could be costly.
- Don't be afraid to decide against the acquisition if the signs are that it will not be a good investment. However, make sure that no commitment to buy has been made in the relevant jurisdiction.

MORE INFO

Books:

Dewhurst, John. *Buying a Company: The Keys to Successful Acquisition*. London: Bloomsbury Publishing, 1997.

Miller, Edwin *Mergers and Acquisitions: A Step-by-Step Legal and Practical Guide*. Hoboken, NJ: Wiley, 2008.

Rao, P. M. *Mergers and Acquisitions of Companies*. New Delhi, India: Deep & Deep Publications, 2002.

Article:

Rowan-Robinson, Jeremy, and Norman Hutchinson. "Compensation for the compulsory acquisition of business interests: Satisfaction or sacrifice." *Journal of Property Valuation and Investment* 13:1 (1995): 44–65. Online at: dx.doi.org/10.1108/14635789510077287

See Also:

★ Acquisition Integration: How to Do It Successfully (pp. 708–709)
✔ Achieving Success in International Acquisitions (p. 1127)
✔ Acquiring a Company (p. 1128)
✔ Planning the Acquisition Process (p. 1132)
✔ Structuring M&A Deals and Tax Planning (p. 1135)

"The big danger in mega-mergers is that they are seen as a mating of dinosaurs." Sir Peter Bonfield

  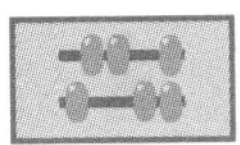      

Structuring M&A Deals and Tax Planning

DEFINITION

In planning for an acquisition, a decision needs to be made on whether the deal involves simply buying the target company's shares or actually acquiring the business itself. Though the distinction may at first glance appear to be a technicality, in practice its significance can be considerable. This is because the acquisition of shares involves buying not only the underlying business of the target company, but also its assets, both tangible and intangible, and, crucially, its liabilities. In this respect, a share-based acquisition can carry higher risk for the acquirer, potentially exposing them to the risk of unforeseen skeletons in the closet. To help compensate for the higher practical risk of the share-based acquisition, buyers can demand warranties from the seller as part of the deal.

However, in spite of the prospect of having to agree to these terms to help protect the buyer from unknown potential risks, there can be some financial advantages for the seller in a share-based transaction. Chiefly, US tax law dictates that, provided they have held the stock for a minimum of one year, selling stockholders need to pay tax only once on the deal. This is levied at personal capital gains tax rates on the difference between their original share purchase price and the agreed acquisition sale price.

Although the stock transaction route can be highly advantageous from the seller's perspective, the tax treatment of fixed assets can be disadvantageous for the buyer, who generally inherits the historically used depreciation structure. Under some specific circumstances other alternatives can apply, although the buyer nevertheless still assumes greater potential exposure to bombshells such as pension fund liabilities and product-related claims when making a share-based acquisition. However, this needs to be balanced against some of the pluses of a share-based deal from the buyer's perspective.

Structuring a deal on the basis of the transfer of the assets of a business permits a buyer to sidestep most unforeseen liabilities and also to benefit from much greater flexibility in writing off asset depreciation. The chief downside is that the seller can effectively be hit twice by tax, substantially reducing the benefit the seller enjoys after the proceeds are taxed first at the corporate level. Should the corporation then be liquidated and the proceeds shared among stockholders, these beneficiaries are then liable for tax at the personal level. Given the complexity of the issues involves, sellers should seek professional advice at an early stage when considering entering into a transaction.

ADVANTAGES

- Well-structured deals can bring many pluses for both buyer and seller, allowing both parties to adjust their market exposure to reflect changes in their business objectives or personal circumstances.
- Stock-based transactions are frequently preferred by sellers, offering attractive tax advantages to those who have held shares for longer than one year prior to the sale.
- Stock-based deals can help buyers to benefit from existing contractual arrangements.

DISADVANTAGES

- The structuring of deals and the associated negotiations are, by their very nature, complex and time-consuming, with no guarantee that a deal will ultimately result.
- An asset-based deal will typically expose the seller to two levels of taxation, corporate and personal.
- A stock-based transaction can be unattractive to a buyer given the tax treatment of fixed asset values.

ACTION CHECKLIST

- ✔ Appreciate and understand the importance of the structure of the transactions.
- ✔ Aim to find a consensus over the final structure of the deal.
- ✔ Seek up-to-date professional advice on taxation matters, as specific circumstances may alter the taxation implications for one or both sides.
- ✔ Bear in mind the importance of the after-tax numbers resulting from a proposed deal, rather than the pre-tax figure.
- ✔ Recognize that only with a comprehensive understanding of the taxation implications of the deal can realistic discussions take place to strike a deal that is acceptable to both sides.

DOS AND DON'TS

DO

- Aim to maintain cordial negotiations whenever possible.
- Seek warranties wherever appropriate when buying to guard against potentially crippling unforeseen surprises.
- Remember that sellers looking to realize the cash from the transaction at an early stage will generally be exposed to higher tax liabilities.

DON'T

- Don't skimp on the cost of professional tax advice, particularly given the substantial tax implications associated with particular deal structures.
- Don't leave involving your lawyers and accountants until the last minute, as only with informed professional advice can your options be considered objectively.
- Don't ignore the importance of effective communication with key stakeholders during the planning process.

MORE INFO

Articles:

Ayers, Benjamin C., Craig E. Lefanowicz, and John R. Robinson. "The effect of shareholder-level capital gains taxes on acquisition structure." *Accounting Review* 79:4 (October 2004): 859–887. Online at: www.jstor.org/stable/4093079

Erickson, Merle. "The effect of taxes on the structure of corporate acquisitions." *Journal of Accounting Research* 36:2 (Autumn 1998): 279–298. Online at: www.jstor.org/stable/2491478

Website:

International Network of M&A Partners (IMAP): www.imap.com

"It was as true as ... taxes. And nothing's truer than taxes." Charles Dickens

  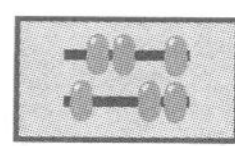      

Understanding Anti-Takeover Strategies

DEFINITION

Anti-takeover strategies come in a number of different guises. Terms such as "shark repellent" and "poison pill" are used to describe the defensive methods or tactics that companies use to attempt to prevent mergers, i.e. the joining of two or more businesses into one, or hostile takeovers, when a business is acquired against the management's or shareholders' wishes.

Anti-takeover strategies are designed to make a company unattractive to predators. They do this in the following ways:

- A shareholder rights plan or poison pill has two different strategies. The "flip-in" allows existing shareholders to purchase more shares at a discount in order to dilute the value of the shares, while the "flip-over" allows shareholders to purchase the bidder's shares at a discount.
- A provision in the company's charter or articles allows shareholders to sell their shares to the bidder for more than the market price.
- A company takes on sufficient debts to make it unattractive, as a bidder would be responsible for those debts.
- The business issues bonds that have to be redeemed at a higher price if the company is taken over.
- The company offers its employees stock options, high bonuses, and exceptional severance pay that would cost a bidder dearly.
- Staggered elections to the board of directors over a period of years can mean that a potential bidder is faced with a hostile board of directors until new elections can be held.

In some jurisdictions, such as the United Kingdom, anti-takeover strategies are illegal or some control on their use is mandated. However, in the United States, where they are legal, the recent economic decline and fear of becoming an acquisition target have renewed interest in anti-takeover strategies in all their forms.

ADVANTAGES

- Anti-takeover strategies are useful when a company feels that its stock has become undervalued and that it may become the target for a takeover.
- Anti-takeover strategies are useful when the predator company's intentions are to acquire the company and then load the company with so much debt that it is unviable.
- Short-term poison pills may help businesses through difficult financial periods when they could be vulnerable as targets.

DISADVANTAGES

- Anti-takeover strategies are sometimes used to entrench management and prevent shareholders from selling their stock and maximizing its price.
- Board members sometimes hide behind poison pills to retain their positions.

ACTION CHECKLIST

✔ Check that the use of anti-takeover strategies is legal in the country or jurisdiction in which the company is operating.

✔ Determine which method would provide the greatest protection without hurting the company's value.

✔ Avoid tying the company to stock options, high bonuses, and exceptional severance pay for employees you might later want to fire.

✔ If you are taking on debts or issuing bonds to make the company unattractive, make sure that you can service those debts even if the economy turns down.

DOS AND DON'TS

DO

- Consult with partners, directors, lawyers and accountants before initiating anti-takeover strategies.

DON'T

- Don't use anti-takeover strategies unless you are sure that they won't backfire and leave the company vulnerable.

MORE INFO

Books:

Frank, Werner L. *Corporate War: Poison Pills and Golden Parachutes*. Charleston, SC: CreateSpace, 2011.

MacIntosh, Julie. *Dethroning the King: The Hostile Takeover of Anheuser-Busch, an American Icon*. Hoboken, NJ: Wiley, 2010.

Ricardo-Campbell, Rita. *Resisting Hostile Takeovers: The Case of Gillette*. Westport, CT: Praeger, 1997.

See Also:

★ Coping with Equity Market Reactions to M&A Transactions (pp. 721–723)
✔ M&A Regulations: A Global Overview (p. 1130)
✔ Using the Comparable Net Worth Method in Squeeze Outs (p. 1138)
✔ Using the Market-Value Method for Acquisitions (p. 1139)

"The very best takeovers are thoroughly hostile. I've never seen a really good company taken over. I've only seen bad ones." Sir James Goldsmith

  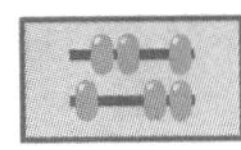   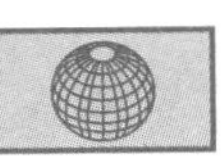   

Using IRR for M&A Financing

DEFINITION

Also known as the economic rate of return, the internal rate of return (IRR) is an indication of the level of growth that can be expected from a project or acquisition. The calculation generates a percentage figure by comparing the value of the proposal's cash outflows with its cash inflows as they vary over the lifetime of the investment.

IRR is frequently used to help assess the outright viability of a project or acquisition by taking into account the cost of capital or the investor's required rate of return. The latter is sometimes referred to as the hurdle rate and is frequently adjusted to take into account the risk levels of different projects.

Acquisitions that are expected to generate returns greater than the cost of capital or the required rate of return are generally accepted, with those falling short typically rejected. IRR is also regularly employed as a means of comparing the expected returns from a number of alternative options, helping to steer investment toward the venture that offers the prospect of the highest returns. In practice, the returns from projects or acquisitions can differ substantially from the levels predicted by the IRR calculation, but the method has retained favor among many potential investors looking for a tool to help decide between alternative investment options.

ADVANTAGES

- IRR generates a relatively simple percentage figure for a project. The method provides a quick and easy way to assess the viability of a project by comparing the projected IRR with the company's risk-adjusted hurdle rate. IRRs can also help investors to select between various options.
- The practical value of the IRR calculation is further underlined by the fact that the calculation takes into account all cash flows, subject to discounting for time.

DISADVANTAGES

- The IRR method does not take into account possible changes in interest rates during the lifespan of the venture. Such changes could significantly alter a company's required hurdle rate given the potential impact on the firm's cost of capital. For short-term projects this limitation can often be overlooked, but the large scope for movements in interest rates over the lifespan of a 10-year project is considerable, compromising the value of the IRR for longer-term projects.
- IRR can sometimes be confused with return on capital employed, as both calculations express results in percentage terms. Care needs to be taken to differentiate between these cash-based and profit-based methods.
- The IRR calculation is based on a presumption that cash generated during the project is subsequently put to work to generate the same return as the average IRR over the lifetime of the project. Although this reinvestment is entirely feasible, in practice reinvested cash often generates lower subsequent returns.

ACTION CHECKLIST

- ✔ To calculate the IRR, we need to establish the various parameters at which the net present value (NPV) of a proposed M&A deal is zero (i.e. the exact level at which the proposed venture is neither a winner nor a loser in dollar terms).
- ✔ Typically, this involves guessing a projected rate of return, *r*, from the investment, and then performing the following calculation:

$$\text{NPV} = \frac{\text{Initial investment} + \text{1st year's income}}{(1+r)^2} + \frac{\text{2nd year's income}}{(1+r)^2} + \frac{\text{3rd year's income}}{(1+r)^3} + \ldots$$

- ✔ Should the resulting NPV figure be positive, the calculation is then repeated using a lower value of *r*. If the NPV is negative, a larger *r* is used. Clearly, the operation is more efficiently performed using a computer spreadsheet than by hand.
- ✔ After repeated calculations, a level of *r* that generates a NPV of zero will be established. This equates to the projected IRR of the deal.

DOS AND DON'TS

DO

- Consider the possibility that any merger or acquisition could involve risks that are difficult or impossible to foresee. To help compensate for such uncertainties, consider how much of a premium a project's IRR should have over the cost of funding.
- Remember that the IRR methodology can accommodate variations in projected annual incomes from proposed deals but does not offer the facility to model changes in funding costs throughout the lifespan of the deal. This can be a major drawback for longer-term project calculations.

DON'T

- Don't interpret IRR as the be all and end all of project financing. Recognize its uses, but at the same time understand its limitations.
- Don't ignore the costs and expenses involved in the acquisition process. Care should be taken to evaluate the costs in terms of management time and resources, as well as in purely financial terms.

MORE INFO

Books:

Reed, Stanley F., Alexandra R. Lajoux, and H. Peter Nesvold. *The Art of M&A: A Merger Acquisition Buyout Guide*. 4th ed. New York: McGraw-Hill, 2007.

Siegel, Joel G., and Jae K. Shim. *Accounting Handbook*. 5th ed. Hauppauge, NY: Barron's Educational Series, 2010.

Articles:

Hartman, Joseph C., and Ingrid C. Schafrick. "The relevant internal rate of return." *Engineering Economist* 49:2 (2004): 139–158. Online at: dx.doi.org/10.1080/00137910490453419

Steele, Anthony. "A note on estimating the internal rate of return from published financial statements." *Journal of Business Finance and Accounting* 13:1 (March 1986): 1–13. Online at: dx.doi.org/10.1111/j.1468-5957.1986.tb01169.x

Websites:

Alliance of Merger & Acquisition Advisers (AMAA): www.amaaonline.org

M&A Source, organization of middle-market intermediaries: www.masource.org

"When it comes to mergers, hope triumphs over experience." Irwin Stelzer

  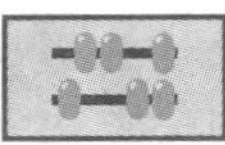   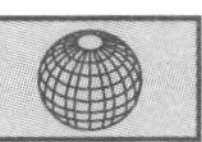   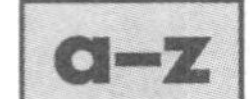

Using the Comparable Net Worth Method in Squeeze Outs

DEFINITION

During the acquisition of a company listed on the stock exchange, a purchaser will frequently manage to acquire a large majority stake as other investors, attracted by the terms of the takeover offer, sell their shares to the acquiring company at the offered terms. However, should a sufficiently small minority of shareholders reject the terms of the acquisition, a squeeze out is a possible route for the purchaser to force a compulsory share buyback from the minority holders, ahead of the company's delisting from one or more stock markets. This only becomes an option if the minority shareholders account for only a small proportion of the company's outstanding capital.

Under such circumstances, relations between the controlling and the minority shareholders can often be strained, due to widely differing views on the true value of the shares or, occasionally, some investors' fundamental reluctance to sell their holding for a variety of reasons. In such cases, should the controlling shareholder decideto try to acquire all remaining shares, the comparable net worth method is often employed to put an appropriate value on the minority shareholders' interests through a comparison of the target company's assets minus liabilities with adjusted equivalent figures for a selection of similar companies. Though this method is only one of several options to help arrive at a valuation, it has found some favor in the United States, becoming one of the officially approved valuation methods in Pennsylvania following a long legal process.

ADVANTAGES

- The primary advantage is that this method uses information that is already public, thus respecting the typical requirements of controlling purchasers that potentially sensitive information such as sales projections are not put into the public domain.
- The method can also be advantageous to the minority shareholders, in that the resulting valuation can sometimes exceed the figure generated by other valuation methods.

DISADVANTAGES

- The method does not produce a definitive valuation, so the result is often subject to dispute. Even the choice of companies forming the comparison group can be contentious.
- The analysis of comparable companies' accounts can be very complex, particularly in terms of the adjustments made according to differing treatments of inventories and receivables across the comparison group.
- From the controlling shareholders' perspective, the valuation resulting from this method (which is often appreciably higher than the figure generated by alternative techniques) can represent a high price to be paid in return for the retention of sensitive information ahead of the squeeze out. However, this higher price can sometimes underline the fundamental value that the acquirer is seeking to unlock with the original takeover move.

ACTION CHECKLIST

- ✔ To make use of the comparable net worth method, first select between five and 10 similar listed companies to form the comparison group. To help address disputes over the choice of companies, an independent third party could be chosen to decide on the composition of the comparison group.
- ✔ Study their accounts in minute detail, making all necessary adjustments in an effort to improve comparability with the target company. In practice, most adjustments are made in areas such
- ✔ as cash and inventories, while other adjustments should be made to take account of cash surpluses or deficits. The adjustment process is best carried out by an independent third party to help address possible disagreements over the methods employed.
- ✔ The result of this adjustment process is a range of comparable net worth numbers that can be weighed against the companies' prevailing stock prices to help in the relative-value calculation.

DOS AND DON'TS

DO

- Remember that the comparable net worth method is one of more than a dozen widely recognized methods of valuing companies, albeit a commonly used valuation tool, when a controlling shareholder wishes to move toward a possible delisting.
- Attempt to find truly comparable companies to form the comparison group. Ideally, the selected companies will be similar to the target company in accounting terms, thereby keeping potentially contentious adjustments to a minimum. In practice, however, closely comparable companies can be very difficult to find.

DON'T

- Don't expect all interested parties to concur with the results of the comparable net worth method. As ever, the valuation is likely to be the subject of ongoing discussions.
- Don't ignore the potential value of discounted cash flow methods. A time-discounted snapshot of future earnings projections, subject to risk adjustments where appropriate, can provide a useful assessment of a company's value. Similarly, the average rate of return and payback methods can be useful starting points for discussion, although the comparable net worth method remains a key valuation tool to squeeze out unwanted minority shareholders.

MORE INFO

Article:

Bates, Thomas W., Michael L. Lemmon, and James S. Linck "Shareholder wealth effects and bid negotiation in freeze-out deals: Are minority shareholders left out in the cold?" *Journal of Financial Economics* 81:3 (September 2006): 681–708. Online at: dx.doi.org/10.1016/j.jfineco.2005.07.009

Websites:

Alliance of Merger & Acquisition Advisers (AMAA): www.amaaonline.org

M&A Source, organization of middle-market intermediaries: www.masource.org

"When you sell 30 percent of a business, it is like taking two limbs off a body—it's not surprising there is a negative effect on the rest of the business." Sir Clive Thompson

        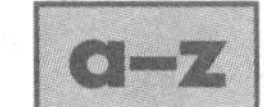

Using the Market-Value Method for Acquisitions

DEFINITION

The capitalization of a publicly traded company is calculated simply by multiplying the market price per share by the number of shares in issue.

For the purposes of valuing a potential acquisition, however, the basic market-value method involves the study of a range of related companies, ideally at a similar stage in the growth cycle and in the same industry or sector, to determine a range of price-to-earnings (P/E) ratios for comparable companies. The resulting lowest and highest of these P/E ratios can subsequently be used to establish a base valuation band for the target company. Alternatively, an average P/E for the group could be used to calculate a central valuation.

This base valuation method assumes that the prevailing market prices across the group of comparable companies fully reflect all available information relating to their businesses and prospects, as the "efficient" market has already priced in all relevant valuation information.

In almost all acquisitions, the valuation will then need to be upwardly adjusted to reflect an appropriate acquisition premium. The level of this premium typically depends on transaction ratings, which are researched based on factors such as the P/Es that are eventually paid for comparable deals, frequently adjusted to reflect present market conditions.

ADVANTAGES

- The market-value method is widely recognized, and was adopted as the industry-standard method of valuing companies ahead of acquisitions. Although other approaches have found favor more recently, the market-value method remains a standard valuation tool for the due-diligence processes undertaken ahead of acquisitions.
- The method provides a fundamentally sound basis for company valuation as long as a number of truly comparable companies can be identified.

DISADVANTAGES

- Because of its reliance on prevailing market prices, the method is applicable only to publicly traded companies. Alternative valuation tools must be employed to establish the values of private companies.
- While P/E ratios are relatively easy to establish for actively traded large-cap stocks, smaller, less liquid stocks may attract infrequent share transactions. For example, microcap stocks traded on junior or fledgling markets may experience sparse trading activity at times, making P/E ratios more difficult to assess.
- Disputes can arise over which companies should be included in the comparables category for calculating P/Es. Because of the lack of hard and fast rules, a prospective buyer could lean towards comparables with lower P/Es, while a more optimistic seller might prefer to include related companies with more demanding P/E multiples.
- The appropriate level for an acquisition premium can be difficult to determine. Proposed acquisition valuations often need to be revised upwards to improve the chances of success of a deal.

ACTION CHECKLIST

- ✔ Before relying on the market-value method, you need to be satisfied that the underlying market is truly efficient. Be aware that some scope exists, particularly among less liquid, sparsely traded smaller companies, for unscrupulous manipulation of market prices ahead of an acquisition.
- ✔ Consider the potential benefits of using a range of P/Es across comparable companies to give a wider valuation band.
- ✔ Research the acquisition premiums paid in comparable acquisitions, making adjustments for changes to the operating environment.

DOS AND DON'TS

DO

- Make every effort to achieve a non-contentious valuation using reasonable comparisons with other companies in the industry.
- Pay close attention to the risk of potential accounting differences between comparable companies, as these could have significant impacts on the resulting average P/E ratios.
- Be prepared to revise the proposed acquisition price depending on stakeholder reaction. In many cases, an improved valuation can have a significantly higher prospect of securing the acquisition.

DON'T

- Don't blindly attempt to use P/E ratios from large-cap companies when seeking to apply the market-value method to smaller companies. Large differences in ratios frequently occur across the capitalization spectrum and can lead to major valuation errors.
- Don't overlook other means of valuing target companies. Although the market-value method was traditionally the industry standard, discounted cash flow techniques have increasingly found favor in recent years, to the extent that they have now largely displaced the market-value approach in all but due-diligence processes.

MORE INFO

Books:

Hitchner, James R. *Financial Valuations: Applications and Models*. 3rd ed. Hoboken, NJ: Wiley, 2011.

Reed, Stanley Foster, Alexandra Lajoux, and H. Peter Nesvold. *The Art of M&A: A Merger Acquisition Buyout Guide*. 4th ed. New York: McGraw-Hill, 2007.

Article:

Weaver, Samuel C., Robert S. Harris, Daniel W. Bielinski, and Kenneth F. MacKenzie. "Merger and acquisition valuation: Panel discussion." *Financial Management* 20:2 (Summer 1991): 85–96. Online at: www.jstor.org/stable/3665732

See Also:

★ Coping with Equity Market Reactions to M&A Transactions (pp. 721–723)
★ Valuing Start-Ups (pp. 769–771)
✔ Acquisition Accounting (p. 1129)
✔ Estimating Enterprise Value with the Weighted Average Cost of Capital (p. 967)

"You might merge with another organization, but two drunks don't make a sensible person." Gary Hamel

     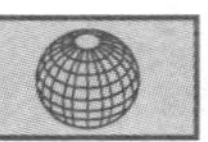   

Applying Cost–Benefit Analysis to Project Appraisal

DEFINITION

Cost–benefit analysis is a widely used, straightforward technique for deciding whether to initiate an action or implement changes. Simply put, it involves adding up the value of the benefits of a course of action and subtracting what it will cost to obtain those benefits. Costs are usually either one-off (for example, start-up costs for materials or equipment) or ongoing (such as staff), whereas benefits tend to unfold over a period of time.

When conducting your analysis, you calculate your payback period, which is the length of time it takes for the benefits to repay the costs of implementing them. It is typical to specify a set payback period of, for example, three years, even if the benefits continue to be reaped long after. The end of the payback period is also known as the breakeven point. This can sometimes be more important than any overall benefits delivered by a project, for example because the organization had to borrow funds to purchase expensive plant. Breakeven is easily calculated by plotting costs and income on a graph—it occurs at the point where the two lines cross. Determining the time span of the payback period is not always easy as many benefits don't have a monetary value or can continue long after the end of payback. The only way to account fully for the effect of time would be to discount all cash flows at the cost of capital.

At its simplest, a cost–benefit analysis assumes that there are only financial costs and financial benefits. For example, a bank needs to train its call centre staff. The analysis would subtract the cost of the training days from the economic benefit that calls will be answered more quickly and efficiently, enabling the bank to handle more calls overall and resolve customer problems more cheaply. Such a simple analysis would not measure the cost of "lost" staff time while they are not on duty, or the benefit of staff having a clearer understanding of standard procedures.

A more sophisticated approach involves trying to work out a monetary value for intangible costs and benefits. This can be highly subjective. For example, when customers praise your call centre staff, how much would it have cost to pay a PR firm to boost the bank's image of handling customer complaints? Calculating intangibles usually raises many questions that need clear answers.

Where very large sums of money are involved, such as in financial market transactions, project evaluation using cost–benefit analysis can be extremely complex, yet of vital importance to ensure that money is spent as wisely as possible.

ADVANTAGES

- The advantage of conducting a cost–benefit analysis is that you can weigh up all the positive and negative impacts of a project using their equivalent financial value to determine whether, on balance, the project is worthwhile.

DISADVANTAGES

- The chief risk in performing a cost–benefit analysis is that the results will only be as accurate as the estimated costs and benefits. Studies have shown that actual costs often turn out to be far higher than estimated, while actual benefits are often lower. This is especially true where intangibles are included in the analysis. It may be safer to perform a straightforward rate-of-return analysis.

ACTION CHECKLIST

✔ Work out how much it will cost to make the change, then calculate the benefit you will gain from it.

✔ Use mapping tools such as Gantt charts or PERT (program evaluation and review technique) to calculate timescales for implementing a project or introducing a change.

✔ A SWOT (strengths, weaknesses, opportunities, threats) analysis can help to keep you focused on what the project should achieve.

✔ Calculate the payback period. This is usually the length of the project, but it may be longer if you are aiming for long-term effects resulting from a limited-term project. Remember that you may need to discount the cash flows at the cost of capital if you want to fully take into account the effect of time.

DOS AND DON'TS

DO

- Remember that benefits are often intangible, i.e. they have no monetary value.
- Make a firm decision on whether to include intangible items within the analysis. As you must estimate a value for these, this inevitably brings an element of subjectivity into the process.

DON'T

- Don't forget to include a risk analysis as part of your overall planning.
- Don't forget to make a cash flow forecast for decisions that will have a purely financial outcome.

MORE INFO

Books:

Brealey, Richard A., Stewart C. Myers, and Franklin Allen. *Principles of Corporate Finance*. 11th ed. New York: McGraw-Hill, 2013.

Chakravarty, Sukhamoy. "Cost–benefit analysis." In Eatwell, John, Murray Milgate, and Peter Newman (eds). *The New Palgrave: A Dictionary of Economics*. Basingstoke, UK: Palgrave Macmillan, 1987; pp. 687–690. (Dictionary online at: www.dictionaryofeconomics.com/dictionary).

Nas, Tevfik F. *Cost-Benefit Analysis: Theory and Application*. Thousand Oaks, CA: Sage Publications, 1996.

See Also:

★ Comparing Net Present Value and Internal Rate of Return (pp. 30–32)
★ Using Decision Analysis to Value R&D Projects (pp. 945–948)
✔ Appraising Investment Opportunities (p. 1143)
✔ Costing a New Project (p. 1155)

"The thought pattern that keeps most people poor: they criticize instead of analyse." Robert Kiyosaki

Applying Stress-Testing to Business Continuity Management

DEFINITION

Business continuity management (BCM) is an important component of the risk management framework for regulated institutions. It increases the resilience to business disruption that may arise from internal or external events and should reduce any adverse impact on business operations, as well as profitability and reputation.

Business operations have become increasingly complex over the years, increasing their vulnerability to disruption by outside events. BCM has thus become an essential part of a company's risk management framework. A whole industry has sprung up devoted to supporting companies on BCM issues.

Although major disruptions to business are rare, few have forgotten the events of 9/11, which resulted in massive disruption to business. External threats from terrorism, computer crime, and viruses are unlikely to go away. Businesses need to put in place continuity plans that are consistent with the scale of their operations.

Stress-testing is crucial to an organization's BCM and its planning for risk management. Stress-testing and scenario analysis both provide management with the information it needs to assess and adjust risks to the organization and to mitigate them effectively. They enable firms to understand how they should deal with certain threats, pick up on any shortfalls, and implement actions to improve their processes for BCM.

Wider use of BCM, stress-testing, and scenario analysis would have a beneficial effect on the robustness of the world's financial systems. There is, however, no simple formula for a company to follow for its own stress-testing and scenario analysis. Depending on its size and global reach, each organization must formulate its own strategies and plans for testing its BCM processes.

ADVANTAGES

Stress-testing of business continuity management should:

- reduce the impact of disruptions to business operations in the event of a problem;
- increase protection to stakeholders and beneficiaries;
- promote confidence in the organization and the whole financial system.

DISADVANTAGES

- The cost of planning and actions.
- The time spent on the whole process.

ACTION CHECKLIST

✔ Put a BCM strategy in place.

✔ Set up methods and routines for stress-testing and scenario analysis.

✔ Carry out regular tests.

✔ Determine follow-up points.

✔ Carry out any necessary actions to improve the BCM plan.

DOS AND DON'TS

DO

- Review your BCM plans and processes regularly.
- Identify actions to update your BCM as appropriate.
- Follow up these actions.

DON'T

- Don't leave your BCM proposals unmonitored once you have put them in place.
- Don't restrict stress-testing to specific threats.

MORE INFO

Books:

Hiles, Andrew (ed). *The Definitive Handbook of Business Continuity Management*. 3rd ed. Chichester, UK: Wiley, 2010.

Osborne, Andy. *Practical Business Continuity Management: Top Tips for Effective, Real-World Business Continuity Management*. Evesham, UK: Word4Word, 2007.

Journal:

Journal of Business Continuity & Emergency Planning. Online at: www.henrystewartpublications.com/jbcep

Websites:

Continuity Central: www.continuitycentral.com

UK Cabinet Office on business continuity: tinyurl.com/77z8rst

See Also:

★ Business Continuity Management: How to Prepare for the Worst (pp. 788–791)
✔ Identifying Your Continuity Needs (p. 1160)
✔ Understanding and Calculating Probable Maximum Loss (PML) (p. 1019)
✔ Understanding Continuity Insurance (p. 1177)
Stress Testing (p. 1255)

"You can't build a reputation on what you are going to do." Henry Ford

Applying Stress-Testing to Operational Risk Exposure

DEFINITION

As global financial markets have become more diversified and complex, many more "new" economies have entered the markets. With the greater number of players and the increased funds available, it has become imperative that all parties with a vested interest in markets and risk exposure—from investment banks to private investors—are properly prepared to assess exposure and able to quantify risk. Stress-testing refers to the various ways that financial and other entities estimate their vulnerability to an exceptional event of plausibility.

The use and practice of stress-testing have increased over the past decade following the occurrence of several notable events in the financial markets: the 1997 Asian crisis, the Enron scandal of 2001, and the collapse of Barings Bank in 1995. As the markets turned bearish in late 2007, it has become standard practice for an institution to acquire the ability to stress-test itself accurately.

Many major institutions stress-test their portfolios on a monthly basis to assess their risk profile and gauge the possible effects of various scenarios on their profit and loss accounts. Stress-testing requires that employees are trained to understand the mathematics and theory behind the process to ensure that the information garnered is both accurate and comprehensive.

Stress-testing can be divided into two distinct categories: simple sensitivity tests (SST), and scenario analysis.

The SST explores changes to a portfolio's value following a change in one risk factor, for example interest rates. It is a very simple yet effective way of flagging major deficiencies and weaknesses in a portfolio. The SST is frequently used by smaller banks and institutions as well as private investors. The drawback of this technique is that it is not plausible that just one variable should change—a massive increase in US interest rates, for example, would have a massive effect on exchange rates and equities.

This is why larger and more complex organizations use scenario analysis, which takes into account a wide range of possible variables such as exchange rates, equity prices, and interest rates, and extrapolates possible outcomes and their probabilities. The process is not dissimilar to forecasting the weather—like the weather, a financial forecast is susceptible to change and must be repeated regularly.

Stress-testing is only as accurate as the information fed into it. Thus, practitioners must have a thorough understanding of economic theory and the effects on the institution's portfolio. It is an exceptionally flexible tool that can be applied to virtually any aspect of an institution's operations that have substantial exposure to risk—country risk, illiquidity exposure, etc. It is not an end-product as stress-testing treats variables separately; companies are currently trying to develop a testing procedure that is more holistic and accumulative in scope.

ADVANTAGES

- A properly conducted stress-test program can help insure against otherwise unnoticed risks and flag problematic investment strategies. If the scenarios and metrics of the system are set clearly, a great deal of benefit can be gained, both for long-term strategy and for day-to-day management. Taking a risk is fine, but it must be accurately gauged, and a properly conducted stress-testing procedure can greatly reduce the potential for error in exposure calculations.

DISADVANTAGES

- If conducted improperly, stress-testing can create a false sense of security. Any stress-test that scored exposure to risk too low would be exceptionally dangerous to an institution. It can be time-consuming and expensive to train employees to use stress-testing, and it must be applied in continually changing environments.

ACTION CHECKLIST

✔ Ensure that the users of the system and the institution's managers understand the limitations, intent, and scope of the process.

✔ Ensure that the results are produced in a comprehensible format.

✔ Ensure that the stress-test is company-wide.

DOS AND DON'TS

DO

- Introduce stress-testing; but
- Make the reports comprehensible and comprehensive.

DON'T

- Don't be deluded into believing that stress-testing is an end in itself. Like all tools, it will only be of benefit if used properly.
- Don't assume that just because a stress-test has been conducted the process is complete.

MORE INFO

Book:

Engelmann, Bernd, and Robert Rauhmeier (eds). *The Basel II Risk Parameters: Estimation, Validation, and Stress Testing*. Berlin: Springer-Verlag, 2006.

Articles:

Sorge, Marco, and Kimmo Virolainen. "A comparative analysis of macro stress-testing methodologies with application to Finland." *Journal of Financial Stability* 2:2 (June 2006): 113–151. Online at: dx.doi.org/10.1016/j.jfs.2005.07.002

Tan, Kok-Hui, and Inn-Leng Chan. "Stress testing using VaR approach—A case for Asian currencies." *Journal of International Financial Markets, Institutions and Money* 13:1 (February 2003): 39–55. Online at: dx.doi.org/10.1016/S1042-4431(02)00025-2

Report:

Sorge, Marco. "Stress-testing financial systems: An overview of current methodologies." Working paper no. 165. Bank for International Settlements, December 2004. Online at: www.bis.org/publ/work165.htm

"Economic distress will teach men, if anything can, that realities are less dangerous than fancies, that fact-finding is more effective than fault-finding." Carl Becker

  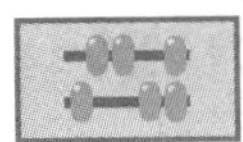   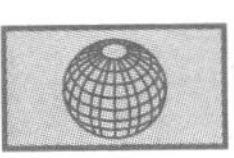   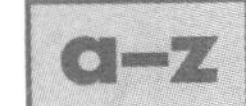

Appraising Investment Opportunities

DEFINITION

As a rule, one of the most critical decisions for any business is long-term investment. This investment can be the purchase of land, buildings, machinery, or other assets in the expectation of earning an income over and above the funds committed. Appraisals are performed to find out whether such investments will yield returns to an organization over a period of time. The appraisals look at the outflows and inflows of funds, the duration of the investment, the scale of risk attached, and the cost of acquiring the funds.

The critical questions in an investment appraisal are:

- What is the extent of the investment, and can the business meet the expense?
- How long will it take to pay back the investment?
- When will the investment start to yield returns?
- What is the return on the investment?
- Would the money be better employed elsewhere?

The methods used when conducting an investment appraisal are:

- Payback: The amount of time needed to repay the initial investment.
- Average rate of return: The profits from an investment as a percentage of the initial capital cost.
- Net present value: Uses opportunity cost (i.e. the cost of an alternative choice when making a decision that must be given up in order to follow a certain action) to put a value on cash inflows from the capital invested.
- Internal rate of return: The annual percentage return on an investment when the sum of the discounted cash inflows over the life of the investment is equal to the sum of the capital invested.

ADVANTAGES

- Investment appraisals allow managers to make long-term plans on the projects that will yield the best returns for the business.
- Payback is easily understood and calculated.
- Average rate of return is easily understood and employs commonly used accounting rules.
- Net present value recognizes that a business incurs costs, such as interest on borrowing.
- Internal rate of return shows how well an investment will perform under different interest rates.

DISADVANTAGES

- The feasibility of the investment appraisal depends on many unknowns, for example the viability of information, financial analysis, and the management skills on which the project is based.
- Payback does not take into account optimal payback time or the effect on profitability.
- Average rate of return does not take into account the duration of the investment or the timing of cash flows.
- Net present value is sensitive to the discount rate applied.
- Management may focus on maximizing the internal rate of return and not net present value.

ACTION CHECKLIST

- ✔ Identify the key investment objectives for the organization and plan around those objectives.
- ✔ Have realistic in-depth budgets been calculated?
- ✔ Will rapid technological change make plant and machinery obsolete sooner and, therefore, will the payback period need to be shortened?
- ✔ Are resources invested in the most profitable objectives, and what alternatives are available?
- ✔ Has a risk analysis been carried out on the project to take into account risks and their impact?

DOS AND DON'TS

DO

- Take into account the duration and timing of cash flows.
- Consider how emerging risks necessitate regular reviews, and how risks such as new technology might affect the long-term viability of the project.
- Involve key stakeholders in an investment appraisal.
- Consider seeking the help of specialist consultants.

DON'T

- Don't make the mistake of being attracted to a project that has not been thoroughly investigated and appraised.
- Don't take risks for granted; although a risk may have been the same in the past, there is no guarantee that it will be the same in the future.

MORE INFO

Books:

Langdon, Ken. *Investment Appraisal*. Oxford: Capstone, 2002.

McLaney, Eddie. *Business Finance: Theory and Practice*. 9th ed. Harlow, UK: Pearson Education, 2011.

Pettinger, Richard. *Investment Appraisal: A Managerial Approach*. Basingstoke, UK: Palgrave Macmillan, 2000.

Websites:

International Federation of Accountants (IFAC): www.ifac.org
Institute of Internal Auditors (IIA): www.theiia.org

See Also:

★ Capital Budgeting: The Dominance of Net Present Value (pp. 20–23)
★ Using Decision Analysis to Value R&D Projects (p. 945)
✔ Understanding Decision-Tree Analysis (p. 1179)
✔ Understanding the Relationship between the Discount Rate and Risk (p. 1001)

"While we stop to think, we often miss an opportunity." Publilius Syrus

     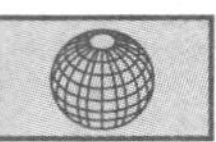   

Assessing Business Performance

DEFINITION

Regular assessments of business performance are vital. It is easy to lose direction and focus only on the day-to-day development of your business. Longer-term and more strategic planning is necessary to get the most out of your business and market opportunities.

Companies need to:

- Review their activities and reevaluate the products that they make or the services they provide. Why are these products or services successful? Are they priced correctly? What could be improved? Is there a market for new or complementary products or services?
- Assess business efficiency. How do you compare with the competition? Are your IT systems adequate? How flexible are your structures? How well do you address customers' needs? Do you have in place an appraisal system for investment opportunities?
- Assess staff. Do you have a high turnover of staff? Are they motivated? Are their skills adequate, or do they need retraining?
- Redefine goals. Where is the business now, where is it going, and how is it going to get there?
- Companies should review their financial statements to help assess their performance:
- The profit and loss statement tells the company whether it is making a profit, as it indicates how revenue is transformed into net income.
- The balance sheet shows assets, liabilities, and shareholders' equity/capital.
- The cash flow forecast or statement identifies the sources and amounts of cash coming into and going out of a business over a given period.

Another way to assess a company's performance is to employ ratio analysis, which uses a combination of financial and/or operating data as a basis for making comparisons with other companies:

- Liquidity ratios give a measure of how readily a company can meet its obligations.
- Profitability ratios give an indication of the earnings and profitability potential of a company.
- Asset management ratios gauge how efficiently a company can change assets into sales.
- Debt management ratios indicate how debt-leveraged a company is, and how it can manage the debt in terms of assets and operating income.
- Dividend/market value ratios measure how well a company uses its assets to generate earnings.
- Profitability ratios indicate earnings and potential profitability.

ADVANTAGES

- Regularly assessing business performance allows for longer-term and more strategic planning, which is necessary to optimize business and market opportunities.
- Ratio analysis permits analysts to read between the lines of financial statements and identify a company's strengths and weaknesses.
- Financial ratios provide lead indications of potential problem areas and allow corrective measures to be taken.

DISADVANTAGES

- Profit and loss statements do not report factors that might be highly relevant but cannot be reliably measured (for example, brand recognition and customer loyalty).
- A balance sheet shows a snapshot of a company's assets, liabilities, and shareholders' equity. It does not show the flows into and out of the accounts during the period.
- Financial ratios are based on past performance; they cannot take into account future events.

ACTION CHECKLIST

✔ What direction should the company take over the next three to five years?

✔ What are the company's markets, and how should it compete?

✔ How can the company gain market advantage and compete better in the future?

✔ What resources will be needed in assets, finance, staff, etc.?

✔ Obtain as much information and compare as many ratios as you can when assessing a business's performance.

DOS AND DON'TS

DO

- Determine whether ratios were calculated before or after adjustments were made to the balance sheet or income statement, such as nonrecurring items and inventory or pro-forma adjustments. In many cases, these adjustments can significantly affect the ratios.

DON'T

- Don't rely solely on ratios when taking decisions. Use market research to confirm the results.
- Don't fall into the trap of thinking that financial ratios are infallible.

MORE INFO

Books:

Porter, Les, and Steven Tanner. *Assessing Business Excellence*. 2nd ed. Oxford: Butterworth-Heinemann, 2004.

Young, Peter C., and Steven C. Tippins. *Managing Business Risk: An Organization-Wide Approach to Risk Management*. New York: AMACOM, 2000.

Websites:

JIT Software: www.jit-software.com

Value Based Management.net: www.valuebasedmanagement.net

See Also:

★ Everything You Need to Know About Benchmarking (pp. 850–853)
★ Using Financial Analysis to Evaluate Strategy (pp. 949–951)
✔ Measuring Financial Health (p. 982)
✔ What Is Benchmarking? (p. 1184)

"Our fixation with financial measures leads us to downplay or ignore less tangible non-financial measures." Tom Peters

Assessing Economies of Scale in Business

DEFINITION

Economies of scale arise when the cost per unit falls as output increases due to efficiencies gained in the production process. Normally, this is because fixed costs are shared across a larger number of goods. Adam Smith believed that the two major steps required to achieve economies of scale were specialization and the division of labor. Diseconomies of scale happen when a firm produces goods or services at an increased cost per unit.

For example, a computer manufacturer producing 1,000 computers at $250 each could expand to produce 2,000 computers at $200 each. The manufacturer's total production costs have risen from $250,000 to $400,000, but the cost of each computer has fallen from $250 to $200. If the manufacturer sells the computers for $350 each, the profit margin per computer rises from $100 to $150.

ADVANTAGES

- The cost per unit falls as output increases, due to efficiencies gained in the production process.
- The sharing of fixed costs over a larger number of goods leads to lower prices.
- Managers in large companies are specialists in particular fields and should be more efficient.
- As their purchasing power increases, businesses are able to obtain lower prices for raw materials.
- Large-scale production normally takes advantage of more technically advanced and more cost-effective machinery.
- Larger firms generally find it easier to raise money at lower interest rates.
- Many marketing and sales costs are fixed, so a larger business can reduce the average marketing cost per unit.

DISADVANTAGES

- A large business is able to pass on lower costs to customers through lower prices and thus increase its market share. This could be a threat to smaller businesses, which might close because of the competition.
- Clogged channels of communication in large businesses can lead to increased costs and duplication of effort.
- Large companies may have a top-heavy workforce, with too many bosses and not enough workers.
- Companies with multiple brands can find that these brands compete with each other.

ACTION CHECKLIST

✔ How efficient is your production process, and how do your unit costs compare with the competition?

✔ Could you use just-in-time (JIT) ordering to make your purchasing process more effective and, at the same time, obtain lower prices for your raw materials?

✔ Conduct an investment appraisal to find out whether the company is using the most cost-effective and technically advanced machinery.

DOS AND DON'TS

DO

- Consider conducting regular reviews of the various aspects of economies of scale to fine tune your production.

DON'T

- Don't forget how diseconomies of scale can upset the best-laid plans.

MORE INFO

Books:

Jeston, John, and Johan Nelis. *Business Process Management: Practical Guidelines to Successful Implementations*. Oxford: Butterworth-Heinemann, 2006.

Longenecker, Justin C., J. William Petty, Leslie E. Palich, and Frank Hoy. *Small Business Management: Launching and Growing Entrepreneurial Ventures*. 16th ed. Mason, OH: South-Western Cengage Learning, 2011.

McClave, James T., P. George Benson, and Terry Sincich. *Statistics for Business and Economics*. 12th ed. Boston, MA: Pearson, 2013.

Article:

Fielding, Roy T. "Economies of scale." *Untangled* (September 22, 2008). Online at: roy.gbiv.com/untangled/2008/economies-of-scale

See Also:

★ Maximizing a New Strategic Alliance (pp. 749–750)
✔ Business Process Reengineering (p. 1150)
✔ Key Components of an Optimal Enterprise Resource Planning System (p. 977)
Jack Welch (p. 1318)

"There are as many foolhardy ways to grow as there are to downsize." Gary Hamel

Assessing the Value of Outsourcing and Offshoring

DEFINITION

The increasingly competitive global business environment and the pace of technological innovation over the last decade have had huge ramifications for the way companies operate. As national borders have shed some of their significance in commercial terms, companies have sought out new ways to focus on their core strengths while seeking to delegate other activities to external parties with specialist expertise in particular fields. Thus, companies with a competitive edge in design could, for example, outsource their manufacturing to a contractor, while other businesses focusing on sectors such as mobile telecoms may choose to outsource their billing and call-centre operations to a specialist third party. However, companies must recognize that, as customers will judge *them*—rather than the outsourcing specialist—by the overall experience they have in buying and using their products, they must ensure that the outsourced services meet the standards expected by customers, or the reputation of the company will suffer.

The increased use of offshoring—the transfer of business processes abroad—over recent years has been further driven by rapid advances in data networking and storage technology. Rather than simply outsource services to specialists in the same country, many companies have seized on opportunities to offshore support services to countries such as India and China, taking advantage of the availability of labor capable of doing the work to the required standard. In most instances, the primary incentive for offshoring is cost, given that the average wage in many developing countries is considerably lower than that demanded by Western employees. However, specialists in the provision of offshoring services claim that using overseas suppliers brings companies other benefits, such as a sharper focus on core activities, better operational efficiency, and improved cultural awareness.

Nevertheless, while offshoring can bring many benefits, the use of overseas external service providers entails some risks. Fraudsters have been quick to investigate opportunities of their own, recognizing that they too can take advantage of cost savings by attempting to bribe employees who have access to secure data, including customer account details. Companies that fall victim to such fraud can run the risk of considerable damage to their reputation and loss of customer confidence.

ADVANTAGES

- Outsourcing and offshoring can bring significant cost benefits.
- Using high-quality specialist external providers can allow companies to capitalize on their strengths and, indirectly, help to improve customers' experiences.
- The use of outsourcing and offshoring can free local employees to focus on strategic planning and other activities.
- External providers can help a company's competitiveness by delivering greater flexibility and responsiveness than would be available in-house.

DISADVANTAGES

- Some in-house employees—even those involved in core activities—could see the use of external specialists as the "thin end of the wedge," taking the view that ultimately their own roles could be outsourced. This could impact on their morale, leading to poor performance.
- Should an external supplier fail to deliver, it is the client company's reputation that stands to suffer most.
- Outsourcing and offshoring can raise control and data security issues.

ACTION CHECKLIST

- ✔ Choose your service suppliers with care, performing adequate checks on their capabilities and conducting due diligence as required.
- ✔ Do not select partners purely on the basis of price; consider a range of factors including their experience, track record, financial stability, and the robustness of the company's technology and equipment.
- ✔ Consider the strength of the local infrastructure—including communications, security, and the availability of resources—when assessing whether to offshore production facilities to a particular overseas location.
- ✔ Be open with your own employees about the logic behind using external specialists for non-core services.
- ✔ Whenever possible, test external providers' capabilities with limited trials before increasing your reliance on them.
- ✔ Ensure that procedures are in place to monitor customer satisfaction levels as external suppliers are introduced, particularly where customers have direct exposure to third-party service providers.

DOS AND DON'TS

DO

- Consider how offshoring production to rapidly developing countries such as China and India could improve your ability to service rising demand in local markets as the spending power of domestic consumers in emerging markets grows.
- Discuss your needs with specialist intermediary consulting companies with direct experience in managing offshore outsourcing. Though this adds to costs, paying for sound advice can prove considerably less expensive than the impact of a poor choice of external provider. Remember that specialist consultants can advise on which activities are most suitable for outsourcing as well as the best choice of external supplier.

DON'T

- Don't see outsourcing and offshoring as exclusively cost-cutting exercises.
- Don't expect the decision to offshore to deliver a constant level of benefits. For example, recognize that higher wage inflation for skilled specialists in developing countries is likely to narrow the gap between salaries in developed and developing economies.

MORE INFO

Books:

Kehal, Harbhajan S., and Varinder P. Singh. *Outsourcing and Offshoring in the 21st Century: A Socio-Economic Perspective*. Hershey, PA: Idea Group, 2006.

Plunkett, Jack W. *Plunkett's Outsourcing & Offshoring Industry Almanac*. Houston, TX: Plunkett Research, 2010.

Article:

Harland, Christine, Louise Knight, Richard Lamming, and Helen Walker. "Outsourcing: Assessing the risks and benefits for organisations, sectors and nations." *International Journal of Operations and Production Management* 25:9 (2005): 831–850. Online at: dx.doi.org/10.1108/01443570510613929

"**There are as many foolhardy ways to grow as there are to downsize.**" Gary Hamel

Basic Steps for Starting a Business

DEFINITION

You think you have a winning idea that's going to make you a fortune. But before you jump in head first, you should carry out some research to see whether your idea really is feasible. That means finding out who your competitors will be and whether there is an opening in the market for your product or service. Do you have the necessary skills to run the business? Gathering and analyzing this information will help you formulate your business plan and goals.

Your initial research should focus on these key questions:

- Is your idea feasible?
- Do you have the financial capacity to carry out the project?
- Is there a market for your product or service?
- How will you protect your idea?
- Who are your competitors, and what differentiates your product from theirs?

Once you have answered these questions satisfactorily, you should draw up a business plan. Most financial institutions provide business plan templates. Alternatively, you could use an off-the-shelf computer program. Your plan should contain:

- a summary describing the elements of your business;
- a description of your business concept;
- an analysis of your business within the market in order to decide how and where your company or products or services fit;
- strategies and goals for the market, and for overcoming the competition you face;
- an outline of how your products or services match your strategies and goals;
- information on how you will market your products;
- an estimate of your sales forecasts;
- what type of financing you will need, who will provide it, and at what cost.

Researching and writing your business plan may seem like a colossal task, but with thorough preparation you will have all the relevant information available and evaluated before you open your doors. As you go through the planning process, you will develop your knowledge and understanding of the proposed business, improve your chances of success, and reduce your risk of failure as a start-up owner. In short, you will be ready to run your business and equipped to compete.

First impressions count, and an accurate, easy-to-read, and well-organized text will convey professionalism and credibility. Have your figures checked by an accountant and the text proofread.

Naming your business accurately is important. Word play might be clever or funny, but it could add to the difficulty customers have in remembering and finding you. It's also tempting to abbreviate your business name to make communications and correspondence easier, but an acronym doesn't say what you do. The general rule is: Keep it simple and try to describe what you do.

ADVANTAGES

- Starting a business allows you to be your own boss and lets you make the decisions that shape your success.
- You get to choose how long and how hard you work.
- The owner receives all the profits, meaning that all earnings go to the sole proprietor.
- If the business is successful, you may be able to reap a tidy sum on retirement by selling the business at a profit.

DISADVANTAGES

- All the responsibility falls on your shoulders. Good or bad, you have to take decisions that may affect the livelihood of your family and employees.
- If you incur debts of any sort, you may have to repay them out of your personal income and assets.
- You may find it difficult to go on vacation or be absent from work for long.

ACTION CHECKLIST

✔ First, do some basic research to see whether your idea really is feasible. Ask yourself whether you have the financial capacity to carry out the project. Is there a market for your product or service, and how will you protect your idea? Who are your competitors, and what distinguishes your product from theirs? If the answers are positive, start to build a detailed business plan.

✔ Second, ask yourself whether you are made of the right stuff to run your own business. Do you have the character, temperament, drive, and staying power?

DOS AND DON'TS

DO

- Take the time to draw up an effective business plan. It might take a month or two, but it will not only help you assess your business idea, it will also tell you whether you are ready and able to carry it out.

DON'T

- Don't use your savings to set up in business without researching and evaluating your ideas. Many chambers of commerce have successful retired business people who will be happy to give you advice on a volunteer basis.

MORE INFO

Books:

Adams, Bob. *Adams Streetwise Small Business Start-Up: Your Comprehensive Guide to Starting and Managing a Business*. Holbrook, MA: Adams Media, 2002.

Kennedy, Joe. *The Small Business Owner's Manual: Everything You Need to Know to Start Up and Run Your Business*. Franklin Lakes, NJ: Career Press, 2005.

The Ultimate Small Business Guide: A Resource for Startups and Growing Businesses. London: Bloomsbury Publishing, 2004.

Websites:

Canada Business: www.canadabusiness.ca/eng/
US Small Business Administration: www.sba.gov

See Also:

★ Assessing Venture Capital Funding for Small and Medium-Sized Enterprises (pp. 451–453)
✔ Assessing Cash Flow and Bank Lending Requirements (p. 964)
✔ Options for Raising Finance (p. 1081)
✔ Steps for Obtaining Bank Financing (p. 1090)

"**The newness of an idea matters less than its ease of use.**" Mari Matsunaga

  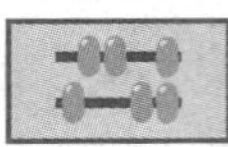      

Building an Efficient Credit and Collection Accounts System

DEFINITION

A credit account relates to credit extended by a business to a customer, which may be another business. A collection account is an account that is in default of the contractual terms (i.e. has passed the due date). It may be assigned to additional collection efforts by the creditor, or passed on to a professional collection agency.

Overdue credit accounts and nonpayment of accounts receivables have an adverse impact on a company's solvency and restrict its dealings. Legal proceedings against defaulting customers cost money and use resources. In addition, they have a detrimental effect on business relationships.

Small businesses must have proper credit and collection policies. Such policies allow a business to collect what they are owed more efficiently from their customers. Good policies help to ensure that a company's customers pay on time or in full. They also help a company to avoid bad accounts, or ditch customers when their accounts turn bad, and keep cash flowing into the business.

As consumer debts increase, competition grows, and interest rates rise, companies are looking at new ways to improve collection rates. Technology is increasingly playing a role in this. Many companies now expect customers to settle debts electronically via BACS (bankers' automated clearing service) transfer, for example, which is cheaper and faster than clearing checks. internet banking now also enables direct debits to be set up quickly. Many companies are also using dedicated software to manage their credit and collection accounts, which reduces dependence on staff or external collection agencies.

The fact is that some debtors fall behind with payments because they can't pay. In such a situation it is better for a company to try to match settlements to the debtor's ability to pay. Slow payment is better than no payment. Information from credit reports and account activity should enable collectors to make better decisions about what payments might best suit a debtor's circumstances.

ADVANTAGES

- Effective collection of debts improves cash flow and helps to grow the bottom line.
- A well-organized credit department can make informed decisions about bad accounts and offer credit only to verified customers.

DISADVANTAGES

- Implementing credit and collection policies can be expensive, at least initially.
- It can also seem like a lot of effort for something that a company hopes to receive without such measures.

ACTION CHECKLIST

- ✔ Analyze your good and bad debtors.
- ✔ Keep a close watch on your cash flow.
- ✔ Ask your debtors if they will be able to pay on time.
- ✔ Indicate penalties for late or nonpayment.
- ✔ Issue a reminder at the end of the payment period.
- ✔ Investigate software options.

DOS AND DON'TS

DO

- Chase up all bad debtors.
- Try to match payment schemes with a debtor's ability to pay.
- Consider the use of technology to improve your collection accounts.

DON'T

- Don't pretend it won't happen. Bad debtors are a fact of business life.
- Don't ignore bad debtors—keep on top of them.
- Don't become a bad debtor yourself as a result of your own bad debts.

MORE INFO

Books:

Bond, Cecil J. *Credit Management Handbook: A Complete Guide to Credit and Accounts Receivable Operations*. New York: McGraw-Hill, 1993.

Schaeffer, Mary S. *Essentials of Credit, Collections, and Accounts Receivable*. Hoboken, NJ: Wiley, 2002.

See Also:

- ✔ Choosing the Right Payment Policy (p. 1151)
- ✔ How to Optimize Stock Control (p. 1159)
- ✔ How to Use Receivables as Collateral (p. 1074)
- ✔ Invoicing and Credit Control for Small and Medium-Sized Enterprises (p. 976)
- ✔ Key Components of an Optimal Enterprise Resource Planning System (p. 977)

"I feel these days like a very large flamingo. No matter what way I turn, there is always a very large bill." Joseph O'Connor

Building an Electronic Invoicing System

DEFINITION

E-invoicing systems can provide a comprehensive solution to the problems associated with large volumes of paper invoices. Traditional paper-based billing processes are inherently vulnerable to errors, particularly when staff are deluged with high volumes of invoices, potentially leading to problems such as missed, duplicate, or unauthorized payments. Paper-based invoicing systems based on multiple staff approvals are also prone to unnecessary payment delays. For example, if one or more of the authorized sign-off managers is absent, paper invoices may be misplaced, ultimately creating payment delays, which can put severe strain on client/supplier relationships. Though increasing the headcount of accounts payable units can improve internal departmental capacity, there may be payment-related problems originating elsewhere within the organization, and also there are significant departmental running costs.

Many companies' first step towards e-invoicing is simply to scan all paper invoices received or to create supplier/client point-to-point invoicing systems. However, centralized, hub-based e-invoicing systems soon come to the fore, supported by legislative changes and the development of e-invoicing standards, typically based on XML (extensible mark-up language) computer code. The design and implementation of an e-invoicing system largely depends on the firm's unique needs, in terms of factors such as invoice volumes, currency conversion needs, approvals process, and the level of integration necessary with other existing management information systems. Another key determinant of successful development is, frequently, the adoption of an e-invoicing system partner with the experience and resources to customize e-invoicing solutions to fit companies' highly specific needs. Among other advantages, e-invoicing system specialists can help clients to overcome compatibility issues between payment system platforms, by supplying a payments hub system with an interface that can be adapted to clients' specific needs.

ADVANTAGES

- A well-implemented e-invoicing system can improve supplier and buyer relationships by making the payments process more reliable.
- E-invoicing can create significant internal cost savings for the business by streamlining the invoice payment process.
- Payment-related information can be supplied directly from the e-invoicing system into management reports as part of a wider management information system.

DISADVANTAGES

- E-invoicing systems can be expensive to introduce, with the necessary investment only recouped if a threshold volume of invoicing makes use of the system.
- There is no universal standard in e-invoicing systems; each company's precise needs are distinct.
- The supplier can sometimes have little short-term incentive to participate in e-invoicing systems, given that the potential cost savings tend to arise on the buyer side. However, in a competitive environment, suppliers can feel under pressure to comply, to retain the business.

ACTION CHECKLIST

✔ A company and its chosen system partners should liaise closely with clients and suppliers when designing and implementing systems—the full benefits of e-invoicing are only achievable if the system is used close to its maximum capacity.

✔ Ask chosen system partners to work with any suppliers holding out for paper-based invoice submission—some e-invoicing hub operators can supply software to help with the transition.

✔ Consult financial advisers over tax considerations ahead of implementing an e-invoicing system. Legal advice in particular jurisdictions is also advised.

✔ Explore how the implementation of e-invoicing systems could improve your company's competitive position, for example, new efficiencies might enable your sales team to win new business ahead of alternate suppliers.

DOS AND DON'TS

DO

- Once your basic e-invoicing system is operational, use the system initially for internal clients to help identify any outstanding post-testing problems, before exposing external clients to any possible gripes.
- When assessing the cost of introducing an e-invoicing system, consider how a well-run system could help to improve the quality of input to wider management information systems.

DON'T

- Don't use e-mail invoices as input to your e-invoicing system as this can expose the network to viruses. Invoice-related communications are best accepted via a secure, closed network.
- Don't choose an e-invoicing system based purely on initial costs. Internally developed systems may appear cheaper initially, but may prove costly in terms of reliability and compatibility issues, while general IT supplier companies may lack relevant specialist e-invoicing and payment systems experience.

MORE INFO

Books:

Groucutt, Jonathan, and Paul Griseri. *Mastering E-Business*. London: Palgrave MacMillan, 2004.

Wille, Patrick, Marc Govers, and I. Desmeytere. *VAT Aspects of Electronic Invoicing and E-Commerce*. Brussels: Intersentia, 2000.

Article:

Corbitt, Terry. "E-invoicing: Are you up to speed?" *Credit Management* (June 2004).

Website:

GXS on invoicing and payments: tinyurl.com/6e4lwag

Business Process Reengineering

DEFINITION

Business process reengineering (BPR) was developed in the early 1990s and refers to a management technique that companies can use to become more efficient. BPR was most famously espoused by management consultants Michael Hammer and James A. Champy in a best-selling book, "Reengineering the Corporation". The authors argued that companies should reinvent the way in which their work was to be accomplished. BPR requires companies to objectively review their business processes and take any necessary measures to maximize customer value and minimize the cost of delivering a product or service, usually through greater use of information technology. The reengineering focused on fundamental business processes as opposed to departments or organizational units.

Hammer and Champy argued that "It is no longer necessary or desirable for companies to organize their work around Adam Smith's division of labor" because task-oriented jobs were becoming obsolete. They recommended that post-industrial companies be "reengineered." The BPR process required a leader with vision, information technologies, close consultation with suppliers to reduce inventories, and empowerment of employees so that decision-making "becomes part of the work."

However, BPR was heavily criticized because it resulted in huge redundancies, and firms that undertook a process of BPR often reported disappointing results. Critics also argued that BPR dehumanized the workplace. Business process management, which seeks to continuously improve processes, has since replaced BPR as the major influence on managerial thinking.

ADVANTAGES

- BPR has proved successful in reinvigorating a wide range of companies, including Ford, Procter & Gamble, American Airlines and General Motors.
- By reviewing the entire business, companies may well be able to spot areas where they can improve efficiency.

DISADVANTAGES

- BPR assumes that a company's existing processes are the main drag on its performance and the main barrier to the company reaching its full growth potential. But this may not be the case.
- BPR has come under fire for its clinical focus on efficiency and technology and for ignoring the human element of an organization that is subjected to a reengineering initiative.
- BPR has been accused of underestimating the resistance to change that is likely to exist in an organization.

ACTION CHECKLIST

✔ Compare the costs and benefits of BPR with those of other methods of improving your business, such as business process management.

✔ Try to determine whether your company needs the radical change demanded by BPR or whether there are other ways in which you could improve performance. This should involve a rigorous analysis of whether your firm is underperforming competitors, and if so, why this is the case.

DOS AND DON'TS

DO

- Consider the potential impact on morale. Implementing BPR can lead to large layoffs that leave remaining staff insecure, overworked, and demotivated. This can adversely affect the efficiency of the business and customer service.
- Talk to other companies that have implemented BPR. Find out whether they regard BPR as a success. What benefits has it delivered and what costs have been incurred?

DON'T

- Don't assume that BPR is a panacea for your company's ills.
- Don't forget that BPR dates back to the early 1990s. It may still have valid points, but new management theories have since been developed.

MORE INFO

Books:

Butler, David. *Business Development: A Guide to Small Business Strategy*. Oxford: Butterworth-Heinemann, 2001.

Hammer, Michael, and James Champy. *Reengineering the Corporation: A Manifesto for Business Revolution*. New York: HarperCollins, 2003.

Joy-Matthews, Jennifer, David Megginson, and Mark Surtees. *Human Resource Development*. 3rd ed. London: Kogan Page, 2004.

Nakayama, Makoto, and Norma Sutcliffe. *Managing IT Skills Portfolios: Planning, Acquisition, and Performance Evaluation*. Hershey, PA: Idea Group Publishing, 2005.

Articles:

Liebowitz, Jay. "Bridging the knowledge and skills gap: Tapping federal retirees." *Public Personnel Management* 33:4 (2004): 421–447.

Lloyd, Jerry. "Skills for business: An evolving network." In "The skill factor," Special supplement, *New Statesman* 132 (March 2003): 8–9. Online at: tinyurl.com/lhpzgm9 [PDF; via archive.org]

Website:

12Manage page on business process reengineering: www.12manage.com/methods_bpr.html

See Also:

★ Reducing Costs and Improving Efficiency by Outsourcing and Selecting Suppliers (pp. 918–920)

★ Reducing Costs through Production and Supply Chain Management (pp. 924–926)

✔ Assessing Business Performance (p. 1144)

✔ Understanding Key Performance Indicators (p. 1180)

ℹ Business Process Reengineering (pp. 1688–1689)

"A memorandum is written not to inform the reader but to protect the writer." Dean Acheson

        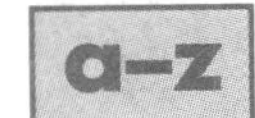

Choosing the Right Payment Policy

DEFINITION

Choosing the right payment policy is critical to the success of any company. To generate revenue, you need to enhance the flow of customers to your business, perhaps by allowing them to pay for a good or service in installments, but at the same time you must generate sufficient cash flow for your business to prosper. You also need to ensure that your customers understand how much they need to pay and when they must settle up. They are more likely to pay you on time if these terms are clearly set out in writing at the start of any business relationship. You can also help your clients, and thus boost income, by being flexible over how you accept payment, for example, by credit card or a loan agreement. Arranging finance for clients can also open up new revenue streams.

On the cost side, negotiating credit terms with your suppliers has obvious advantages. You can, for example, bank revenues and earn interest on them before you need to pay for the goods or services that helped to generate those revenues.

If you adopt a system whereby customers are permitted to pay in installments, you must install a robust credit management system, which is a means of ensuring that your invoices are paid on time. This will minimize the time and effort spent chasing unpaid invoices and will ensure that the resources you expend on credit management are used efficiently. However, it is important to remember that you don't have to adopt the same payment policy for every customer. If you are unsure about the creditworthiness of a particular client, simply insist on cash payment before you supply goods or services.

ADVANTAGES

- Choosing the right payment policy allows you to balance the need to generate sufficient cash flow against the need to encourage sales by offering flexible payment terms.
- If you can offer finance to your clients, you can develop an additional source of income on top of the goods or services you are selling them.
- Negotiating flexible terms with suppliers can also boost your company's finances.

DISADVANTAGES

- Choosing the right payments policy can involve considerable expense and prove time-consuming. Expenses include the cost of purchasing software as well as training staff in the use of this software. You may also have to hire specialist consultants who advise you on which payment policy you should pursue.

ACTION CHECKLIST

- ✔ Simply accepting cash removes the need to install time-consuming and costly credit management systems.
- ✔ Generating immediate cash payments will boost the income you receive from interest.
- ✔ The generation of immediate cash payments may also make your business more attractive to potential purchasers.

DOS AND DON'TS

DO

- Get a lawyer to draw up a payment policy. This will protect your rights as a seller and will give you full ownership of the goods until the customer pays for them in full.
- Install a robust credit management system. Seeking to save money at this stage could prove very costly in the long run.
- Continuously monitor your existing customers' credit histories. Circumstances change, and a business with a good credit rating may not retain that status indefinitely. Increasingly delayed payment could mean that it is in financial trouble.
- Make sure that your payment terms are displayed prominently on any invoice. For example, you could include a box on the front of the document for the customer to sign in acceptance of the terms and conditions of sale.

DON'T

- Don't sell blind. Before you issue credit to new customers, you should first evaluate their ability to pay.
- Don't rule out potential clients just because they have a less than perfect credit history. You can always ask them to pay part or all of the bill immediately, or give them shorter payment terms.

MORE INFO

Books:

Bluman, Allan G. *Business Math Demystified: A Self-teaching Guide*. New York: McGraw-Hill Professional, 2006.

Droms, William G., and Jay O. Wright. *Finance and Accounting for Nonfinancial Managers: All the Basics You Need to Know*. 6th ed. New York: Basic Books, 2010.

Steingold, Fred S. *Legal Guide for Starting & Running a Small Business*. 13th ed. Berkeley, CA: Nolo, 2013.

Articles:

Abad Peiro, J. L., N. Asokan, M. Steiner, and M. Waidner. "Designing a generic payment service." *IBM Systems Journal* 37:1 (1998): 72–88. Online at: dx.doi.org/10.1147/sj.371.0072

Emery, Gary, and Nandkumar Nayar. "Product quality and payment policy." *Review of Quantitative Finance and Accounting* 10:3 (May 1998): 269–284. Online at: dx.doi.org/10.1023/A:1008201701163

Wilson, Nicholas, and Barbara Summers. "Trade credit terms offered by small firms: Survey evidence and empirical analysis." *Journal of Business Finance & Accounting* 29:3–4 (April/May 2002): 317–351. Online at: dx.doi.org/10.1111/1468-5957.00434

See Also:

- ✔ Building an Efficient Credit and Collection Accounts System (p. 1148)
- ✔ Efficient Invoicing Procedures (p. 1158)
- ✔ How to Use Receivables as Collateral (p. 1074)
- ✔ Invoicing and Credit Control for Small and Medium-Sized Enterprises (p. 976)
- ✔ Key Components of an Optimal Enterprise Resource Planning System (p. 977)

"If you don't sell, it's not the product that's wrong, it's you." Estée Lauder

  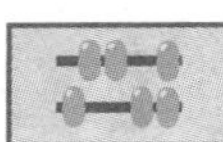      

Commercial Aspects of Licensing

DEFINITION

To license means to give permission to use a certain property in exchange for payment. Such properties can be tangible, such as manufactured products, or intangible, such as intellectual property rights (brand, copyright, trademark, design rights, etc.), or computer software. The parties to a licensing agreement are the owner of the licensed property (the licensor) and the party to whom the license is granted (the licensee).

The licensor and the licensee will usually enter into a licensing agreement which is drafted by the licensor, then negotiated and amended by the licensee.

License agreements can be difficult to understand, and it is advisable for both parties to obtain legal advice to guide them in their negotiations.

Under a licensing agreement, the licensor grants the licensee the right to manufacture certain products or use certain intellectual property rights in a well-defined territory, for a certain period of time, in exchange for a licensing fee. The license can be exclusive or nonexclusive. An exclusive license gives the licensee the sole right to manufacture or use the products in that territory, while a nonexclusive license usually means that there are other licensees using the same rights or manufacturing the same products. Exclusive licenses are, therefore, more expensive and sought after.

Before entering into a licensing agreement, a licensee should thoroughly investigate the market and territory and weigh the advantages and disadvantages of obtaining a license and operating within that market. If the license to be obtained relates to the manufacturing and sale of products, it is advisable to think of the way in which these products will be distributed and sold. A licensor of a top brand will have certain requirements as to how its products are presented and sold. Publicity and marketing will be expensive and should be included in the licensing budget. There will be a difference between the price that the licensee pays to the licensor for a product and the price at which the same product is sold to the consumer. The licensee should weigh these prices carefully in order to assess its profit margin.

For certain products, a royalty fee may be charged to the licensee in addition to the price of the license. This is usually calculated as a percentage of the net takings for the product and will be dealt with in the licensing agreement.

Intellectual property rights usually remain in the ownership of the licensor. The licensee can only use them in accordance with the terms of the license and for the duration of the agreement.

The licensor will include in the agreement certain conditions under which the licensed property can be used. If these conditions are breached, the licensor can revoke the license altogether. It is therefore important that a licensee fully understands such conditions when he enters into the license.

Certain licenses will not allow a licensee to sublicense or assign the license to anyone else without the express written consent of the licensor. This way, a licensor can remain in full control of the distribution of the products in the territory covered by the license.

ADVANTAGES

- Licensing allows a licensor to increase the market for its brand by giving others the right to use it under certain conditions and for a certain price.
- It also allows a licensee to operate a business and to exploit, for the licensee's own benefit and profit, a product that belongs to someone else and that would otherwise be too expensive to acquire.

DISADVANTAGES

- Negotiating a licensing agreement can be complex and time consuming. It involves thorough research of the market and territory in which the products will be sold or used.

ACTION CHECKLIST

✔ Study carefully any license you might acquire. Obtain as much information from as many sources as possible before committing to an expensive licensing agreement.

✔ Know your market and make sure that you have analyzed the consequences for your own business of entering into a licensing agreement.

✔ Be prepared for long and complicated negotiations, which could prove time consuming as well as costly.

✔ Economize by negotiating a reasonable rate with your legal advisers, but remember that it is better to incur costs by obtaining legal advice than to enter into a license under terms that you do not understand.

DOS AND DON'TS

DO

- Involve your solicitors in the evaluation of both the risks and potential benefits of entering into a license.
- Negotiate your rates and make a contingency plan for any cost overrun.
- Plan carefully how the license will operate in the territory.

DON'T

- Don't be attracted by a license that has not been thoroughly investigated.
- Don't overlook the importance of negotiating warranties and indemnities that would protect you in the event that underlying liabilities are discovered.

MORE INFO

Books:

Nimmer, Raymond T., and Jeff C. Dodd. *Modern Licensing Law*. 2008–2009 ed. Eagan, MN: West, 2008.

Sherman, Andrew J. *Franchising and Licensing: Two Powerful Ways to Grow Your Business in Any Economy*. 4th ed. New York: AMACOM, 2011.

Articles:

Loe, Nancy E. "Avoiding the golden fleece: Licensing agreements for archives." *American Archivist* 67:1 (2004): 58–85.

Nimmer, Raymond T. "UCITA and the continuing evolution of digital licensing law." *Computer and Internet Lawyer* 21:2 (2004): 10–16.

"Owning the intellectual property is like owning land: You need to keep investing in it again and again to get a payoff; you can't simply sit back and collect rent." Esther Dyson

  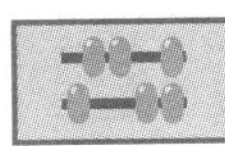   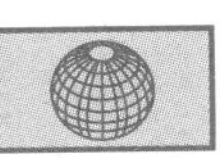   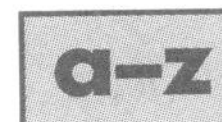

Competition Law: Key Financial Issues

DEFINITION

Competition is one of the main driving forces of economic activity. From the consumer perspective, free and fair competition keeps prices down and helps to ensure the quality of products, while from the producer perspective effective competition boosts productivity, drives efficiency, and promotes innovation. Competition instills discipline in sellers, obliging them to provide quality at an attractive price relative to rivals.

Competition laws, known in the United States as antitrust laws, broadly aim to ensure that competition is free and fair by regulating companies' market power. However, in general terms, most countries' competition legislation aims to set limits for competitors' activities by defining circumstances in which a state or regulator may intervene in the market to ensure that an obstacle to competition is removed, or when the market has effectively ceased to function correctly. Under the major global jurisdictions, competition law permits intervention to tackle many sources of potential market aberrations, such as price manipulation by cartels, the abuse of market power by a monopoly operation, or proposed mergers which could act to the detriment of free and fair competition.

Companies should ensure that they fully understand the intricacies of competition law in all jurisdictions in which they operate, both to meet their own obligations and to help protect their market position and generally defend their rights against rivals. Companies found to be in breach of competition laws risk finding not only that any relevant contracts signed may be unenforceable, but offenders could also face a heavy fine which could, in some cases, threaten the viability of the business. In the United States, the consequences of being found in breach of the Sherman Antitrust Act (1890) can be particularly severe, involving criminal penalties of up to $100 million for a corporation and up to $1 million for an individual, who could also risk spending up to 10 years in prison.

The Organisation for Economic Co-Operation and Development (OECD) recently demonstrated that member states which have implemented reforms to promote competition have actually enjoyed higher levels of economic growth and lower levels of unemployment than those members that are more resistant to change. A 2008 report from the OECD cited the example of Australia, which implemented a series of pro-competitive reforms, both at the national and state levels, in the mid-1990s, measures which helped the country's economy to become one of the OECD's leading performers in the new millennium.

ADVANTAGES

- Competition laws define the boundaries of acceptable trading practices in an effort to create a level playing field for all market participants.
- The laws aim to protect consumers from sharp practices, such as price fixing and other market manipulation.
- Competition laws can promote efficiency and innovation by protecting the rights of companies that bring new or improved products or services to market.
- Trading blocs such as the European Union, NAFTA, Mercosur, and ASEAN have extended the benefits of free trade beyond national borders, promoting and managing trading activities free of import tariffs.

DISADVANTAGES

- Global competition law is something of a misnomer—though international bodies such as the World Trade Organization (WTO) can push initiatives aimed at preventing anticompetitive cross-border trade practices, laws set by individual jurisdictions such as the United States and the European Union apply.
- The boundaries between the passing of laws to protect domestic markets from unfair competition and the introduction of measures purely to protect national producers from overseas competition can often be blurred. Trade disputes between countries or regions can escalate rapidly, with the imposition of crippling import tariffs.
- The pace of technological innovation can create challenges for lawmakers.

ACTION CHECKLIST

✔ Seek professional advice to understand the significance of competition laws in any particular jurisdiction before commencing business activity there.

✔ Competition legislation has grown rapidly over recent years, driven in part by the deregulation of formerly state-controlled industries such as utilities, telecoms, and mail services. It is important to keep abreast of changes that could impact on your business.

✔ Understand that competition laws can represent opportunities for companies driven by innovation, as well as a threat to those who attempt to restrict market choice.

DOS AND DON'TS

DO

- Appreciate the complexity of trying to get to grips with the concept of "global" competition laws; according to the Asian Development Bank there are at least 100 different systems of competition law across the world.
- Consider how competition laws could actually protect your business and help to safeguard investment in areas such as new product development.

DON'T

- Don't make assumptions about competition laws in one country based on experience elsewhere, as significant differences apply between jurisdictions.
- Don't ignore the political element in the way some countries' competition laws are structured, particularly in socially sensitive areas such as utilities.

MORE INFO

Book:

Taylor, Martin D. *International Competition Law: A New Dimension for the WTO?* Cambridge, UK: Cambridge University Press, 2006.

Article:

Kolasky, William. "International comity in antitrust: Advances and challenges." *Legal Backgrounder* 22:16 (May 2007). Online at: tinyurl.com/6xo7gb7 [PDF].

"Thou shalt not covet, but tradition approves all forms of competition." Arthur Hugh Clough

Corporate Insurance Cover: A Primer

DEFINITION

In every country in the world companies are legally required to have a minimum level of insurance cover. It is also prudent to pay for some insurance beyond this basic level. Occasionally, forms of insurance have different names in different countries. This primer uses the British descriptions.

Perhaps the most important form of insurance is employers' liability. This offers cover against bodily injury, illness, or disease suffered in the course of employment.

Public liability ensures that a company is able to pay damages for bodily injury, illness, disease, loss, or damage to property caused by the insured. Product liability covers damages arising from the supply of a defective product. This could include anything from power tools to computer software.

Professional indemnity is mandatory for certain occupations. It protects against legal action by clients claiming damages for what they see as negligent or bad services.

Business interruption insurance is increasingly popular. This provides compensation if, for example, your property is damaged in a way that disrupts your business activities. This may be on the basis of gross profit where a company is making or selling goods. Clubs and other businesses supplying a service may be covered on the basis of gross revenue.

Property and buildings insurance is a complex area with a number of variables. Basic cover will include damage arising, for instance, from fire, lightning, and gas explosions. Additional cover can include threats such malicious damage, flood, or leakage from sprinkler systems. So-called "all-risks" insurance will protect against most eventualities, but not wear and tear or mechanical breakdown.

Contents cover for business assets and equipment is also an area where insurance companies offer a number of different types of policy. Stock is normally covered at cost price, but equipment may be insured for replacement as new or taking into account deterioration. Theft following forcible entry is normally covered, but stealing by employees is generally excluded, although there are special policies for employee dishonesty.

Specific policies insure money lost or stolen from your premises or in transit to the bank. Goods in transit insurance protects against damage to stock carried in your own vehicles, by road hauliers, or by post. A recent addition to policies available protects against damage or consequential loss arising from acts of terrorism.

Many large insurers and brokers offer single policies covering the three main areas of commercial insurance: liabilities; business assets and equipment; and property and buildings. The advantage of this approach is that it should reduce the risk of overlaps or gaps in coverage, although it may be more economical to shop around for specialist policies.

Many organizations will also require other forms of insurance for: commercial vehicles and company cars; business travel; accident and sickness; and employee health. There are also more specialist requirements, such as marine cargo and engineering inspection.

Insurance brokers who specialize in covering commercial clients will be able to offer policies for all these areas.

ADVANTAGES AND DISADVANTAGES

It's not really appropriate to talk of the advantages and disadvantages of taking out corporate insurance, as in many cases having insurance is compulsory.

ACTION CHECKLIST

- ✔ Find a suitable broker who specializes in the type of insurance you need.
- ✔ Check the terms. Not all insurers offer cover for the same thing.
- ✔ Check the laws and regulations for your industry to learn which types of insurance are compulsory for your business.

DOS AND DON'TS

DO

- Shop around to compare premiums and policies.

DON'T

- Don't cut corners. It may be a false economy, and you could end up in court if someone brings a claim you do not have cover for.

MORE INFO

Books:

Blanchard, Ralph H. *Introduction to Risk and Insurance*. Frederick, MD: Beard Books, 2001.

Harrington, Scott E., and Gregory R. Niehaus. *Risk Management and Insurance*. New York: McGraw-Hill/Irwin, 2004.

See Also:

✔ Directors' and Officers' (D&O) Liability Insurance (p. 1116)
✔ Insuring Against Business Interruption (p. 1161)
✔ Insuring Against Financial Loss (p. 975)
✔ Understanding the Components of an Insurance Contract (p. 1021)
Insurance (pp. 1633–1635)

"In the insurance business, there is no statute of limitation on stupidity." Warren Buffett

Costing a New Project

DEFINITION

Before launching any new project, you need to determine its total cost. To ensure that all costs are covered, the first step is to break down all costs into direct and indirect costs. Direct costs include materials and labor that are directly involved in the project. Indirect costs cover operating expenses, such as administrative labor, marketing, office supplies, utilities, and rent.

It is then necessary to estimate each element of direct and indirect costs to obtain the total cost of the project. Some costs, such as labor, or products and services that are bought regularly, are easy to estimate. However, other costs may be more uncertain. You may, for example, have to include a new service or product with unusual specifications. The project budget should then include a design allowance to cover cost overruns. It is also wise to include a contingency sum to cover unexpected events such as unusual weather or problems with suppliers—always a possibility on large projects. So the budget for any new project should contain figures for the estimated cost, plus a contingency fund and design allowance, and any profit. The project manager's role is to keep the actual cost at or below the estimated cost, to use as little of the design allowance and contingency as possible, and to maximize the profit earned from the project.

ADVANTAGES

- Good information is crucial to managing a project well. Understanding the costs of a new project and how they break down is critical in determining whether the project will be profitable or not.
- Producing a detailed project costing enables the project manager to ascertain whether a project is proceeding according to schedule. He can quickly identify areas where costs are running out of control and take steps to rectify these problems.

DISADVANTAGES

- If the project is relatively small, the fees involved in costing the project may be excessive.

ACTION CHECKLIST

- ✔ Draw up a detailed list of all the elements and costs involved in the project. Make sure that you include indirect as well as direct costs.
- ✔ Find out whether project management software could assist in managing project costs.

DOS AND DON'TS

DO

- Talk to all the staff involved in the project to make sure that you have a complete breakdown of costs.
- Talk to suppliers to obtain an idea of the costs of the products and services involved in the project.
- Set aside a contingency fund and a design allowance.

DON'T

- Don't assume that the cost of a particular service or input will remain constant over the lifetime of a project.
- Don't guess the costs of certain elements of a project.

MORE INFO

Books:

Baker, H. Kent, and Gary E. Powell. *Understanding Financial Management: A Practical Guide*. Malden, MA: Blackwell Publishing, 2005.

Bandler, James. *How to Use Financial Statements: A Guide to Understanding the Numbers*. Burr Ridge, IL: Irwin, 1994.

Dickie, Robert B. *Financial Statement Analysis and Business Valuation for the Practical Lawyer*. 2nd ed. Chicago, IL: American Bar Association, 2006.

Articles:

Akintoye, Akintola. "Analysis of factors influencing project cost estimating practice." *Construction Management and Economics* 18:1 (2000): 77–89. Online at: dx.doi.org/10.1080/014461900370979

Munns, A. K., and B. F. Bjeirmi. "The role of project management in achieving project success." *International Journal of Project Management* 14:2 (April 1996): 81–87. Online at: dx.doi.org/10.1016/0263-7863(95)00057-7

Raz, Tzvi, and Dan Elnathan. "Activity based costing for projects." *International Journal of Project Management* 17:1 (February 1999): 61–67. Online at: dx.doi.org/10.1016/S0263-7863(97)00073-2

See Also:

- ✔ Applying Cost–Benefit Analysis to Project Appraisal (p. 1140)
- ✔ Options for Raising Finance (p. 1081)
- ✔ Preparing a Budget (p. 985)
- ✔ Preparing a Cash Flow Forecast (p. 986)

"Perfect numbers, like perfect people, are very rare." René Descartes

  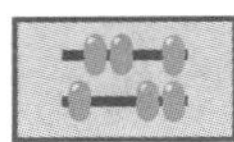      

Creating a Risk Register

DEFINITION

A risk register, also sometimes called a "risk log," is usually used when planning for the future. Future plans may include project plans, organizational plans, or financial plans. Risk registers are used in the area of risk management.

Risk management is a method of managing risks or uncertainty relating to a perceived threat. Risk management will usually involve having strategies in place to deal with risks, whether by avoiding the risk, transferring it elsewhere, reducing its effect, or dealing with the consequences. Financial risk management deals with risks that can be managed using traded financial instruments.

Risk management uses risk registers to identify, analyze, and manage risks in a clear, concise way. A risk register usually takes the form of a table—however long or wide that may end up being.

A risk is an event that, if it occurred, would have an adverse (or positive) impact on a project, investment, or similar. The risk register contains information on each risk that is identified. One of the main skills in risk management is to successfully identify all possible risks. The risk register should contain, in summarized form, the planned response in the event that a risk materializes, as well as a summary of what actions should be taken beforehand to reduce a particular risk. Much financial legislation, such as Basel II, also impels organizations to take steps to reduce risk. Risks are often ranked in order of likelihood, or of their impact. The risk register lists the analysis and evaluation of the risks that have been identified.

ADVANTAGES

- A risk register can identify and make provision for dealing with risks, enabling an organization to save millions if things go wrong.
- Should a risk materialize, there is already a set list of actions to run through immediately to start minimizing the consequences.
- An organization can have the confidence to press on with a project or investment knowing that procedures to deal with any risks arising have been put in place.

DISADVANTAGES

- Much time, effort, and money can be spent on creating risk registers to deal with events that will never occur.

ACTION CHECKLIST

- ✔ Establish a risk management team. The team should meet regularly to discuss the risks associated with each project, investment, etc., to review procedures, and to ensure that the risk register is kept up-to-date. Appoint a team member to keep abreast of any legislative requirements that may affect the risk register.
- ✔ Identify and list all potential risks, and decide on the likelihood of their occurrence. Determine the expected impact if they do occur. Identify any interdependencies with other risks and what knock-on effects there may be.
- ✔ Decide who will bear the risk.
- ✔ Identify countermeasures to mitigate the risk before it occurs.
- ✔ Keep track on the risk register of the current status of any risk that has occurred and what action is being taken.

DOS AND DON'TS

DO

- Create a risk register for each new project or investment.
- List each risk as a separate entry in the register's table.
- Identify an "owner" for each risk, i.e. a person who will be in charge of resolving the risk.
- Follow up on actions and status for each risk identified.
- Revisit the risk register regularly to evaluate any changes to the likelihood of a risk and its potential impact. Changes to projects and investments should also be evaluated for their effect on previously assessed risks or new risks that may arise.

DON'T

- Don't ignore the possibility of risks becoming a reality.
- Don't lose track of the risk register.

MORE INFO

Books:

Ackermann, Fran. *Systemic Risk Assessment: A Case Study*. Management Science Theory Method and Practice Series. Glasgow, UK: Department of Management Science, University of Strathclyde, 2003.

Bateman, Mike. *Tolley's Practical Risk Assessment Handbook*. 5th ed. Boston, MA: Elsevier, 2006.

Brinded, Malcolm. *Perception vs Analysis: How to Handle Risk*. Eighth Annual Royal Academy of Engineering Lloyd's Register Lecture. London: Royal Academy of Engineering, 2000.

Journal:

Risk Management. Published quarterly by Palgrave Macmillan. Online at: www.palgrave-journals.com/rm

Website:

Institute of Risk Management (UK): www.theirm.org

See Also:

★ Quantifying Corporate Financial Risk (pp. 91–93)
✔ Applying Stress-Testing to Operational Risk Exposure (p. 1142)
✔ Establishing a Framework for Assessing Risk (p. 1028)
✔ Understanding and Calculating the Total Cost of Risk (p. 990)

"The art of being wise is the art of knowing what to overlook." William James

Distribution Agreements

DEFINITION

A distributor is an individual or a legal person who has been appointed by another individual or company (the supplier) to distribute its products within a defined territory.

The supplier and distributor enter into a distribution agreement, which is drafted by the supplier, then negotiated and amended by the distributor. Certain distributors can be agents of the supplier, but this is not always the case.

The distributor can be exclusive or nonexclusive. An exclusive distribution agreement gives the distributor the sole right to distribute and sell the products in that territory—the principal will not appoint any other distributors. A nonexclusive arrangement means that there will be other distributors of the same products.

In general, a distributor will purchase the products from the supplier and agrees not to distribute or manufacture during the period that the distribution agreement is valid any goods that compete with the products of the supplier.

A distributor could be an agent of the supplier, but this is unusual as the supplier generally prefers to keep things relatively simple and not give a distributor the power to directly commit it to any contracts that an agency would imply.

Under a distribution agreement, the distributor would have certain obligations, such as: to use all reasonable endeavors to promote the distribution and sale of the products in the territory; to employ a sufficient number of suitably qualified personnel to fulfill its obligation under the agreement; to maintain appropriate levels of stock of the products; and to insure all products against all risks.

A supplier will be also be required to supply the products to the distributor on time and, in the case of exclusive distribution, not to supply the products to anyone else in the territory.

The distribution agreement will contain detailed clauses as to pricing, advertising, and promotion of the products.

In general the distributor will be expected to obtain and comply with all the appropriate import licenses or permits necessary for the entry of the products into the territory.

ADVANTAGES

- A distribution agreement allows a manufacturer or supplier to increase the market for its brand by giving others the right to sell and distribute it under certain conditions and for a certain price.
- It also allows a distributor to operate a business and to exploit, for its benefit, a product that belongs to someone else and would otherwise be too expensive to acquire.

DISADVANTAGES

- Distribution arrangements can be quite expensive for a distributor as thorough research is needed into the obtaining of licenses, permits, and insurance for the products.
- Negotiating a distribution agreement can be complex and time-consuming. It involves thorough research of the market and territory in which the products will be sold or used.
- Exclusive distribution arrangements are expensive.

ACTION CHECKLIST

✔ Study carefully any distribution agreement which you might sign. Obtain as much information from as many sources as you can before committing to an expensive agreement.

✔ Know your market and make sure that you have analyzed the consequences of entering into a distribution agreement for your own business. Plan for contingencies. Take into account any cost of import duties, storage, and insurance.

✔ Be prepared for long and complicated negotiations, which could prove time-consuming as well as costly.

DOS AND DON'TS

DO

- Choose your distributor carefully before you enter into an agreement that could potentially damage your brand.
- Involve your solicitors in the evaluation of both the risks and benefits of entering into a distribution agreement.
- Negotiate your rates and make a contingency plan for any cost overrun.
- Plan carefully how the chain of distribution will operate in the territory.

DON'T

- Don't make the mistake of being attracted by a distributor or supplier that you do not know and has not been thoroughly investigated.
- Don't overlook the importance of negotiating warranties and indemnities that would protect you in the event that the products are damaged while in the care of the distributor.

MORE INFO

Books:

Clasen, T. F. (ed). *International Agency and Distribution Agreements*. Looseleaf ed. London: Lexis Law Publishing, 1991. Also published as *International Agency and Distribution Agreements: Analysis and Forms*. Salem, NH: Butterworth Legal Publishers, 1990.

Singleton, Susan. *Commercial Agency Agreements: Law and Practice*. 3rd ed. Haywards Heath, UK: Bloomsbury Professional, 2010.

See Also:

★ Essentials for Export Success: Understanding How Risks and Relationships Lead to Rewards (pp. 845–847)
★ Reducing Costs through Production and Supply Chain Management (pp. 924–926)
✔ Commercial Aspects of Licensing (p. 1152)
✔ Structuring, Negotiating, and Drafting Agency Agreements (p. 1176)

"Perfect numbers, like perfect people, are very rare." René Descartes

  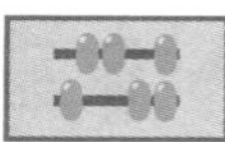      

Efficient Invoicing Procedures

DEFINITION

An invoice is a document issued by a seller to a purchaser that formally requests payment for goods or services supplied. The issuing of an invoice indicates that the buyer must now settle their account with the seller according to the agreed payment terms.

An invoice is usually printed on company stationery and contains certain standard information:

- The word "Invoice."
- A unique reference number.
- Date of the invoice.
- The seller's tax or company registration details, where required.
- The purchaser's name and contact details.
- Description of the goods or services, and date when delivered.
- A purchase order number.
- Unit price, where relevant.
- Total amount payable, including a breakdown of any taxes, if required.
- Payment terms, including method of payment, date due, and details of any applicable late payment charges.

Invoicing legislation varies globally, requiring additional information in some cases. For example, in the United States the Defense Logistics Agency requires an employer identification number; in the European Union a VAT (value added tax) number is needed on invoices if either entity is registered for VAT.

As an important administrative task, it is vital to have good invoicing policies and procedures in place to ensure a smooth cash flow into the business. Conversely, clients generally appreciate knowing your invoicing terms. Set out clear payment terms—30 days is standard in many countries by default, but sometimes it makes sense to shorten or lengthen the payment period.

Figure 1. Example invoice

Invoice No: 032/12

John Smith
Purchasing Manager
Grommet Retail Ltd
15 Brown Street
London W8 9XX

ACME WIDGETS CO. LTD
Acme House
42 Sussex Road
London SE26 2PZ
Tel: 020 8123 4567
Fax: 020 8123 4568

Date: 5 January 2013

INVOICE

Order No. 987654 Delivery No. 321 Delivery date: 4 January 2013

10,000 2mm widgets @ £1.20 per widget (product code: 0042M) £12,000.00

Sub Total	£12,000.00
VAT @ 20%	£ 2,400.00
TOTAL DUE	£14,400.00

Terms of payment 30 days

Please note that late payment is subject to interest charges and associated compensation payment under the UK Late Payment of Commercial Debts (Interest) Act 1998.

Please transfer payment to Acme Widgets Co. Ltd, Clark's Bank, 88 Acacia Avenue, London SE36 1XP, account number 03689043, sort code 20-31-82.

Registered office: Acme House, 42 Sussex Road, London SE26 2PZ
Registered in England number: 98705432 VAT no: 66-777-888

Depending on the size of the company, issuing and/or tracking the status of invoices should be done daily, weekly, or monthly.

ADVANTAGES

- A well thought out invoicing policy not only helps keep cash flowing, it also ensures that its administration is streamlined and easy to maintain.

DISADVANTAGES

- There are no disadvantages to having a clear invoicing process.

ACTION CHECKLIST

✔ Investigate automating your invoicing with suitable software. Various packages exist that can be linked to accounting programs, and some generate invoices as soon as the accounts are updated per client.

✔ Look at the options for e-billing of clients to reduce postal and administrative costs for both parties.

✔ Ensure that clients are aware of the range of payment options. It is possible to pay by BACS (Bankers' Automated Clearing Services) transfer and other electronic payment systems such as PayPal or WorldPay, as well as by standing order, direct debit, and check.

DOS AND DON'TS

DO

- Quote any relevant legislation on late payment on the invoice to encourage clients to pay in good time.
- Consider offering discounts to clients who pay early.
- Prompt clients to pay by emailing a polite reminder a week before the due date. Likewise, a statement of account a week after can galvanize late payers.

DON'T

- Don't get heavy-handed as soon as an invoice is one day overdue. Better to have a clear policy that sets out incremental stages of action for late or nonpayers.

MORE INFO

Book:

Sher, David, and Martin Sher. *How to Collect Debts (And Still Keep Your Customers)*. New York: AMACOM, 1999.

Website:

Better Payment Practice Campaign—A UK-based website with information on late payment legislation and templates for invoices and follow-up action letters: www.payontime.co.uk

"Organizations that are change leaders are designed for change. But people need continuity. . .they do not function well if the environment is not predictable, not understandable, not known." Peter F. Drucker

  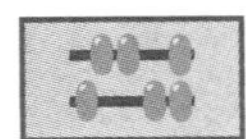      

How to Optimize Stock Control

DEFINITION

Stock control is how an organization ensures that its stocks are at levels that meet predetermined standards of service and allow funds to be released as working capital. Stock control, also known as inventory control, determines how much stock a company has at a given point in time and how it keeps track of it. It applies to every item used to produce a product or service, from raw materials to finished goods, and refers to any kind of stock at every stage of the production process, from purchase and delivery to using and reordering the stock.

Effective practice in stock control requires effort and resources to introduce a system which offers maximum advantage at a reasonable cost and takes into consideration the cost of finance, storage, insurance, handling, obsolescence, and theft. Efficient stock control ensures that a company has the right amount of stock in the right place at the right time, and that minimum capital is tied up. It also helps to protect production should any problems arise with the supply chain.

Holding too much stock can result in a company having too much cash tied up in stock, but holding too little can lose clients. Efficient stock control facilitates "just in time" stock management, with an order schedule that forecasts stock reordering requirements for a period of time ahead, based on factors such as open sales orders, open purchase orders, and the required-by date.

ADVANTAGES

- Good stock control reduces costs and improves efficiency, while ensuring that a company can meet fluctuations in customer demand.

DISADVANTAGES

- Overstocking increases costs, and there is a risk of overestimating the level of demand for products.
- Held stock may become damaged or obsolete, or perish.
- Poor stock control can lead to a potential loss of sales or missed orders, and large stocks may be subject to theft.

ACTION CHECKLIST

- ✔ Choose a suitable stock control system, from simple ledger books and card indexes to highly computerized systems, that will provide knowledge of current stocks on a regular basis and record supplies received and sales, deliveries, outputs, and usage.
- ✔ Use common sense—the cost of the system and its operation should not be greater than the cost of the problem it is intended to solve.
- ✔ Identify current stock levels, record receipts/dispatches, and identify reordering levels and quantities.
- ✔ Establish a regular pattern of auditing and stock checking.
- ✔ Analyze usage of all items in terms of volume and strategic/nonstrategic stock.
- ✔ Identify key products that must be available on demand.
- ✔ Classify products in terms of importance to overall turnover but not in big product families or in other broad product groupings.
- ✔ Focus attention on the items that produce the most revenue.
- ✔ Identify the level of stock that must be held to avoid the risk of missing core opportunities or failing to supply basic needs.

DOS AND DON'TS

DO

- Plan your storage area carefully, locating the most frequently used items in an accessible place, and choose appropriate stacking methods such as pallets, shelving, or bins. Instigate an appropriate labeling system for easy stock identification.
- Implement a stock rotation system and ensure that availability meets requirements.
- Pay attention to environmental conditions, high/low temperatures, and humidity.
- View stock as money.

DON'T

- Don't rule out the possibility of pilferage, excessive waste, or other forms of shrinkage.
- Don't view stocktaking as an annual chore, but do it regularly on a partial basis.
- Don't hold on to stock just to fill the warehouse.
- Don't store every item in the same environment.
- Don't buy speculatively.

MORE INFO

Books:

Baily, Peter, Gerard Tavernier, and Richard Storey. *Stock Control Systems and Records.* 2nd ed. Aldershot, UK: Gower, 1984.

Emmett, Stuart, and David Granville. *Excellence in Inventory Management: How to Minimise Costs and Maximise Service.* Cambridge, UK: Cambridge Academic, 2007.

Wild, Tony. *Improving Inventory Record Accuracy: Getting Your Stock Information Right.* Oxford: Butterworth-Heinemann, 2004.

See Also:

★ Countering Supply Chain Risk (pp. 812–813)
★ Reducing Costs through Production and Supply Chain Management (pp. 924–926)
✔ Business Process Reengineering (p. 1150)
✔ Inventory—How to Control It Effectively (p. 1165)
✔ Managing Working Capital (p. 980)

"All of our long-term suppliers are very profitable." Marcus Sieff

Identifying Your Continuity Needs

DEFINITION

In order for a company to be prepared to recover from the impact of a disaster such as a fire, flood, or explosion, it has to identify its key functions and the risks that are faced. Critical activities and resources can be identified through a business impact analysis (BIA), while a concurrent risk assessment will aid recognition of threats.

The aim of analysis is to create two types of plan, which may overlap. An incident management plan covers the initial impact, including procedures such as evacuation. The longer-term business continuity plan prepares an organization to keep delivering key products and services afterwards.

Plans have to be tested to ensure that they work. Staff also have to be trained in the procedures. The frequency of planning exercises depends on the speed of change within an organization and the outcome of previous drills where weaknesses have been identified.

MORE INFO

Report:

National Fire Protection Association (NFPA). "Standard on disaster/emergency management and business continuity programs." NFPA 1600. 2010. Online at: tinyurl.com/3gpxeze

Websites:

British Standards Institution (BSI) on ISO 22301 Business Continuity Management: www.bsigroup.com/en-gb/iso-22301-business-continuity/

US Federal Emergency Management Agency on business recovery planning: www.fema.gov/protecting-your-businesses

The British Standards Institution (BSI) has developed a standard BS 25999 "Business continuity." In North America the equivalent is the National Fire Protection Association's NFPA 1600 "Standard on disaster/emergency management and business continuity programs." Globally, the International Organization for Standardization (ISO) has published the ISO/-PAS 22399:2007 "Guideline for incident preparedness and operational continuity management."

ADVANTAGES

- Having a continuity plan in place gives peace of mind. You may never need it, but it's there if the worst happens.

DISADVANTAGES

- Failing to prepare for disaster could result in serious financial loss or even bankruptcy if there is a major incident.

ACTION CHECKLIST

1. Undertake a business impact analysis

- ✔ Identify the products and services that will suffer the greatest impact as a result of disruption.
- ✔ Break the results down to analyze the impact on output from disruptions lasting 24 hours, up to two days, up to a week, and up to two weeks.
- ✔ Identify the so-called "maximum period of tolerable disruption" of service and product delivery that the organization can cope with before its viability is threatened.
- ✔ Set a recovery time for each of the key products and services, allowing for unforeseen difficulties.
- ✔ Create a document listing the activities required to deliver the key products and services.
- ✔ Ensure that the necessary resources are allocated to meet the requirements.

2. Carry out a risk assessment

- ✔ Identify the risks to the organization, including loss of staff, key suppliers, utilities, access to premises, IT, and telecommunications systems.
- ✔ Establish the likelihood of each risk.
- ✔ List existing arrangements for dealing with the risks.
- ✔ List arrangements that should be put in place to deal with the risks.
- ✔ Assign a likelihood score to each risk.

3. Decide what action the organization should take for each of the identified risks; for example:

- ✔ Deal with the risk by planning to continue service and product delivery at an acceptable minimum level.
- ✔ Tolerate the risk if the cost of its reduction outweighs the potential benefits.
- ✔ Transfer the risk to a third party or take out insurance.
- ✔ Terminate the activity. In some circumstances, particularly where an item is time-sensitive, it may be appropriate to suspend delivery.

4. Develop, publish, and circulate plans

- ✔ Establish an overall plan then decide how many plans are required within that. This will depend on the size and scope of the organization.
- ✔ State the purpose and scope of each plan.
- ✔ Identify who owns each plan and is responsible for its maintenance.
- ✔ List the individuals and their roles within the plan.
- ✔ Describe the circumstances, methods, and who is responsible for invoking the overall plan and its individual components.
- ✔ List appropriate contact details.
- ✔ For the initial response to an incident, list the tasks, responsibilities, and methods by which they are to be communicated.
- ✔ For business continuity, outline critical activities, the process by which they are to be recovered, and the timescale.

5. Test, maintain, and review plans

- ✔ Parts of the plan can and should be tested, such as back-up power, contact lists, and the process of activation.
- ✔ Staff should be brought together for training to discuss plans and identify weaknesses.
- ✔ Scenario-based desktop exercises can be used to validate plans and train key staff.
- ✔ Live exercises can cover one aspect of a plan, such as evacuation, or to test a full plan.

"What we have found over the years in the marketplace is that derivatives have been an extraordinarily useful vehicle to transfer risk from those who shouldn't be taking it to those who are willing to and are capable of doing so."

Alan Greenspan

  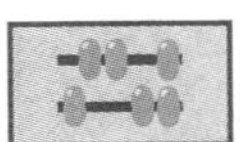   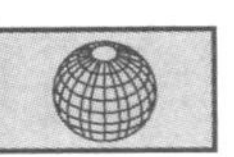   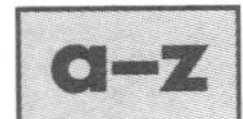

Insuring Against Business Interruption

DEFINITION

Most companies have insurance against specific risks, but they do not always cover the indirect losses arising from an event. A buildings policy will, for instance, commonly include cover for rebuilding after a fire and replacing equipment. If the business is unable to trade and has to move to other premises, it will face considerable loss of income. It will still, however, face continuing costs such as wages, tax, and loan repayments. At the same time there may be additional charges for the rent of emergency accommodation and to pay overtime to staff.

Interruption insurance can fill the gaps in existing policies. It can cover both the continuing and emergency costs faced by the business and the loss of income arising from the enforced shutdown. It is the latter part of the policy that makes this a complex area. Estimating and proving current earnings can be problematic—especially if, for instance, a fire has triggered the payout and destroyed some of the records. In essence an insurer is being asked to pay for sales that the insured believes it would have had. An added complication is that few businesses will restart at the same level they were at before the interruption.

DOS AND DON'TS

DO

- Find a broker who specializes in insurance for business disruption.
- Obtain quotations from several insurers to compare premiums and policies.

DON'T

- Don't be tempted to opt for the cheapest policy as it may be a false economy. If a disaster does occur, you may find you are not covered for everything you need to keep the business running as smoothly as possible while you get back on track.

ACTION CHECKLIST

1. Identify all interruption costs

Ensure that all business interruption costs are covered, including the impact on all areas of the organization if one part is out of action.

2. Identify all sources of income and potential loss

Conduct a thorough review to determine the sources of income that would be lost and other costs or losses that might result from a shutdown.

✔ Forms of income will vary according to the type of business and can be a combination of revenue, fees, or rental.

✔ Penalty payments should be included as a major incident could affect a company's ability to complete a project.

✔ Interruption insurance will probably not cover some forms of income, such as interest on investments or sales of assets.

3. Check the supply chain

Examine the supply chain to make sure there is no over-dependency on one or two suppliers. Consider adding suppliers to the policy if reliance is unavoidable.

4. Coordinate insurance with the continuity plan

Insurance should be coordinated with the company's business continuity plan.

5. Include recovery costs

Ensure that all the costs and time that would be needed to restore the business are covered, including:

✔ Demolition, redesign, and rebuilding.

✔ Replacement of specialist machinery.

✔ Rehiring staff.

6. List all the company's business activities

Some of the items to include here may be less obvious than others.

✔ Include acquisitions, new divisions, and new ventures.

✔ Ensure that long-term projects are covered even if they have not yet produced income.

✔ Consider including key suppliers if damage to their premises could have serious repercussions on your business.

✔ Ensure that power suppliers are included, and check to see when coverage commences. There is a week's "deductible" in many policies.

7. Review the amount insured regularly

In conducting regular reviews of the amount covered, the following points may need consideration:

✔ Many large organizations with multiple profit centers include intergroup sales, which can inflate the premium through double counting.

✔ Make sure the projected figures for lost earnings are accurate for the whole insured period, which may be two or more years.

✔ Consider including a premium adjustment clause to take account of actual rather than projected earnings at the end of the year.

MORE INFO

Books:

Blanchard, Ralph H. *Introduction to Risk and Insurance*. Frederick, MD: Beard Books, 2001.

Harrington, Scott E., and Gregory R. Niehaus. *Risk Management and Insurance*. New York: McGraw-Hill/Irwin, 2004.

See Also:

✔ Corporate Insurance Cover: A Primer (p. 1154)
✔ Insuring Against Financial Loss (p. 975)
✔ Stress Testing to Evaluate Insurance Cover (p. 1016)
✔ Understanding Continuity Insurance (p. 1177)

"You build an expertise around the customer, and that's an investment." Rolf Hueppi

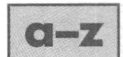

Intellectual Property—Copyright

DEFINITION

Intellectual property is a legal concept that provides for the exclusive ownership of abstract creations. It entitles the owner of such rights to charge for the use of the property or sell it.

Copyright is a concept of intellectual property that gives the author of a creative work the right to be credited for that work and to control its distribution. A copyrighted work may be reproduced only with the copyright owner's permission. There is no standard length of copyright protection, which varies according to the type of work protected and the country where protection is sought.

Copyright is applicable to most creative works, such as literature, drama, music, recordings of sound and film, and broadcasts. It comes into existence purely as a result of the work being produced; the author does not have to apply for copyright. For copyright to be recognized, the work must be original and in a fixed medium. Original ideas cannot be copyrighted unless they take the form of written or broadcasted work. Any items that are already in the public domain cannot be the subject of a copyright claim.

Copyright gives an author a monopoly over certain rights: the right of reproduction, the right to create derivative works, the right to performance, the right to display, the right to distribution, and the right to digitally transmit its performance.

People wanting to publish their work usually enter into a publication and license agreement with a publisher. In the agreement, the author grants exclusive or non-exclusive rights to publish, reproduce, distribute, and use the work in any form for a defined period of time. Nowadays, much work is self-published on websites that support user-generated content, social networks, wikis, and blogs.

Authors are usually asked to give a warranty that what they have written does not defame or invade the privacy of any person, nor infringe anyone's rights.

If copyright infringement occurs, an author may be entitled to an injunction (a court order to stop the infringement), damages, a refund of lawyers' fees relating to the infringement, and an order to confiscate and destroy any copies that infringe the copyright. On the other hand, if a written work infringes the rights of another person, that person will be entitled to damages, which the author will have to pay.

ADVANTAGES

- The author of a creative work is automatically protected by copyright.
- Copyright allows the author of a creative work to profit from it by charging for its use or by selling the copyright.
- Copyright gives the author exclusive rights to the use of the work. This will deter others from copying the work or pretending that they were the authors.
- An author may take legal action against any person who infringes their copyright and is entitled to compensation for that infringement.

DISADVANTAGES

- Copyright is recognized only for work in a fixed form; ideas, however original, are not protected.

ACTION CHECKLIST

✔ Always protect your copyright and take action in relation to any infringement.

✔ Obtain legal advice to protect your copyright if you suspect an infringement.

DOS AND DON'TS

DO

- Balance the cost of taking action against a perceived infringement of a copyright against the consequences of nonaction.
- If necessary, involve your lawyers in the evaluation of both the risks and potential benefits of taking any action.

DON'T

- Don't ignore an infringement of your copyright; take action against it.

MORE INFO

Books:

Poltorak, Alexander I., and Paul J. Lerner. *Essentials of Intellectual Property*. New York: Wiley, 2002.

Stim, Richard W. *Intellectual Property: Patents, Trademarks and Copyrights*. 2nd ed. Florence, KY: Delmar Cengage Learning, 2000.

Articles:

Gordon, Wendy J. "Excuse and justification in the law of fair use: Transaction costs have always been only part of the story." *Journal of the Copyright Society of the USA* 50 (2003): 149.

Novos, Ian E., and Michael Waldman. "The effects of increased copyright protection: An analytical approach." *Journal of Political Economy* 92:2 (April 1984): 236–246. Online at: www.jstor.org/stable/1831385

Websites:

Copyright law of the United States: www.copyright.gov/title17/

Lawdit Solicitors—UK commercial solicitors specializing in intellectual property and litigation: www.lawdit.co.uk

Mandour & Associates, California Intellectual Property law firm: www.mandourlaw.com

Publishing Law Center: www.publaw.com

See Also:

★ Protecting Your Intellectual Property—Nonregistered Rights (pp. 911–912)
★ The Value and Management of Intellectual Property, Intangible Assets, and Goodwill (pp. 118–121)
✔ Intellectual Property—Patents—An International Overview (p. 1163)
✔ Intellectual Property—Registered Designs and Trademarks (p. 1164)
Intellectual Capital: The New Wealth of Organizations (p. 1376)

"What we have found over the years in the marketplace is that derivatives have been an extraordinarily useful vehicle to transfer risk from those who shouldn't be taking it to those who are willing to and are capable of doing so."

Alan Greenspan

Intellectual Property—Patents—An International Overview

DEFINITION

As seen previously, intellectual property is a legal concept that enables the ownership of creations as physical property. It entitles the owner of intellectual property rights to take advantage of his/her ownership and charge for the use of the property or to sell it.

A patent is an intellectual property right that is awarded to an inventor. Each country has its own laws regarding the registration of patents, so to protect a patent in more than one country it has to be registered in each of the relevant countries. A patent gives protection for an average period of 20 years.

A patent prevents others from selling, using, or making the invention in a particular country or importing the invention into that country. Unlike the other intellectual property rights, it grants only the exclusivity nature of that right and not the right itself. An inventor can sell, use, or make his or her invention without a patent.

There are three recognized forms of patent: utility patents, which cover machines and processes; design patents, which cover the design and composition of matter; and plant patents, which are related to plant.

In general, only the inventor can apply for a patent. Any person who falsely claims to be the inventor will be liable to criminal penalties. An inventor can apply for a patent him/herself, but in most cases a specialized patent agent and attorney are appointed to deal with the application. This is because the process itself is complicated and specialist knowledge is required to deal with the application.

Not every invention can be patented. To qualify for a patent, an invention has to be new—which means that it has not been patented before, or described before in any specialized publication—anywhere in the world. The invention also has to have a useful purpose from an operational point of view.

In the United States, applications for patents are made to the US Patent and Trademark Office.

ADVANTAGES

- A patent gives an inventor the right of exclusivity over an invention.
- It allows the inventor to take legal action against any person who uses the invention without permission, and to receive compensation for that use.
- Only the inventor can apply for a patent.
- A patented invention will be more valuable to an investor.

DISADVANTAGES

- Patent registration can be expensive and meticulous in terms of the detail required.
- Not all inventions are patentable.
- In general, patents need to be renewed. The average duration of protection is 20 years.
- Registration is limited to a particular territory. To protect an invention in other countries and territories, new registrations are required.

ACTION CHECKLIST

✔ To avoid future problems, always consider obtaining a patent for your invention.

✔ Obtain advice on whether your invention is patentable.

✔ Investigate the cost of registration and the countries in which your invention may need to be protected.

✔ Balance the cost of obtaining a patent against the possible cost of leaving the invention without a patent and the time spent defending your rights if they are breached.

DOS AND DON'TS

DO

- Consider obtaining a patent for your invention.
- Balance the cost of applying for a patent against the consequences of nonapplication.
- As the application process is complex, budget for instructing a patent agent to apply for you.
- Think carefully about other countries and territories in which your invention may need protection by registering the patent.

DON'T

- Don't think that by inventing something it will automatically qualify for a patent. Not all inventions are patentable.
- Don't ignore a breach or infringement of your patent. Take action.

MORE INFO

Books:

Stim, Richard W. *Intellectual Property: Patents, Trademarks and Copyrights*. 2nd ed. Florence, KY: Delmar Cengage Learning, 2000.

US Department of Commerce. *Patents and How to Get One: A Practical Handbook*. Mineola, NY: Dover Publications, 2003.

Websites:

Intellectual Property Office, UK: www.ipo.gov.uk

Journal of the Patent and Trademark Office Society: www.jptos.org

US Patent and Trademark Office: www.uspto.gov

See Also:

★ Protecting Your Intellectual Property—Registered Rights (pp. 913–914)

★ The Value and Management of Intellectual Property, Intangible Assets, and Goodwill (pp. 118–121)

✔ Intellectual Property—Copyright (p. 1162)

✔ Intellectual Property—Registered Designs and Trademarks (p. 1164)

Intellectual Capital: The New Wealth of Organizations (p. 1376)

     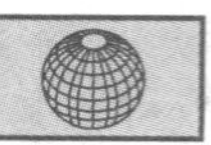   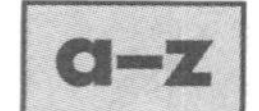

Intellectual Property—Registered Designs and Trademarks

DEFINITION

Intellectual property is a legal concept that provides for the exclusive ownership of abstract creations. It entitles the owner of such rights to charge for the use of the property or sell it.

Design is an intellectual property right that relates to the appearance of a product. Usually, a design right arises automatically when an author creates an original design, but in certain jurisdictions a design has to be registered to guarantee its protection.

A trademark is a registered symbol or sign that is created to distinguish a product from its competitors. A trademark can be a logo, name, shape, color, sound, slogan, or domain name, or any combination of these. To be recognized as a trademark, it must be distinctive—i.e. it must not be similar or identical to other trademarks. It also must not be deceptive or contrary to law. The usual duration of a trademark's registration is 10 years, after which it must be renewed.

A trademark is protected by registering it in a specific territory or country. Each country has its own rules and regulations regarding registration. The registration process can be expensive, but it is important to consider the risks of nonregistration.

Registration of a trademark usually starts with a search to see if there are any conflicting or similar trademarks. An attorney or agent can be instructed to prepare the application. The formal application will be analyzed to determine whether the trademark meets the necessary legal criteria to be registered. Any challenges from third parties must be answered before registration is confirmed.

ADVANTAGES

- Registering a design or trademark allows the owner to control who uses it and how it is used.
- Intellectual property rights allow the author of a creative work to profit from it by charging for its use or by selling or licensing the rights.
- Registration gives the owner exclusive rights to the use of the property. This will deter others from misusing it or pretending that they are the owners.
- Registering a design or trademark allows the owner to take legal action more easily against anyone who uses the design or trademark without permission, and to be compensated for misuse.

DISADVANTAGES

- In certain circumstances registration can be expensive.
- Not all symbols or designs can be registered.
- In general, registration needs to be renewed periodically. Designs are protected for up to 25 years, but trademark registrations need to be renewed every 10 years.
- Registration is limited to a particular territory. To protect designs and trademarks in other territories additional registrations are required.

ACTION CHECKLIST

✔ Always consider protecting your design or trademark to avoid future problems.

✔ Get advice about whether your designs or trademarks can be registered. Check out the cost of registration and the countries in which you would like them to be registered. Try to balance the cost of registration against the possible cost of nonregistration and the time spent dealing with the defense of your rights if they are breached.

DOS AND DON'TS

DO

- Consider registering your designs and trademarks.
- Balance the cost of registering against the risk and complications of being unprotected.
- If necessary, involve your lawyers in the evaluation of both the risks and potential benefits of registering your designs and trademarks.
- Decide carefully in which countries you will protect your intellectual property.

DON'T

- Don't think that having a design or trademark will give you protection without registration.
- Don't assume that all designs or symbols can be registered.
- Don't ignore an infringement of your design or trademark.

MORE INFO

Books:

Poltorak, Alexander I., and Paul J. Lerner. *Essentials of Intellectual Property*. New York: Wiley, 2002.

Stim, Richard W. *Intellectual Property: Patents, Trademarks and Copyrights*. 2nd ed. Florence, KY: Delmar Cengage Learning, 2000.

Articles:

Dinwoodie, Graeme B. "The integration of international and domestic intellectual property lawmaking." *Columbia VLA Journal of Law and the Arts* 23 (2000): 307.

Sosinsky, G. J. "Laudatory terms in trademark law: Square pegs in round holes." *Fordham Intellectual Property, Media and Entertainment Law Journal* 9:2 (Winter 1999): 725–773. Online at: tinyurl.com/5re4a74

Websites:

Lawdit Solicitors—UK commercial solicitors specializing in intellectual property and litigation: www.lawdit.co.uk

Source for trademark clearance searching and monitoring: www.trademark.com

United States Patent and Trademark Office: www.uspto.gov

See Also:

★ Protecting Your Intellectual Property—Registered Rights (pp. 913–914)

★ The Value and Management of Intellectual Property, Intangible Assets, and Goodwill (pp. 118–121)

✔ Intellectual Property—Copyright (p. 1162)

✔ Intellectual Property—Patents—An International Overview (p. 1163)

Intellectual Capital: The New Wealth of Organizations (p. 1376)

"Freedom from activity is never achieved by abstaining from action." Bhagavad Gita

  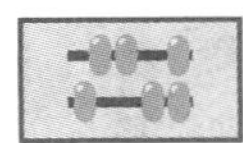      

Inventory—How to Control It Effectively

DEFINITION

Inventory control, or stock control, is concerned with how much stock you have at any one time, and how you keep track of it. Effective inventory control applies to every item you use to produce a product or service, from raw materials to finished goods. It covers stock at every stage of the production process, from purchase and delivery to using and re-ordering the stock.

There are four main types of stock:

- raw materials and components—ready to use in production;
- work in progress—stocks of unfinished goods in production;
- finished goods ready for sale;
- consumables—for example, fuel and stationery.

Effective inventory control is critical to the success of a business. By making sure that capital is not tied up unnecessarily, you can help to lower the cost of running a business and maintain customer loyalty; clients may migrate to other suppliers if you are unable to supply them with the goods they need when they need them. It can protect production if problems arise with the supply chain, and eliminate waste if you are involved in the supply of perishable goods.

Maintaining accurate order records is the first step on the path to controlling inventory. Order sheets should be established by vendor and should include all vital information, such as the name of the customer, their phone number and e-mail address, the date and time the order is placed, the name of the contact person, and other information. You can thus quickly compile a record of all the orders your company receives. From this, it will be possible to determine seasonal and yearly fluctuations in sales and decide which items to discontinue. You will know when to order and will be able to reduce shortages of stock and avoid overordering. Computerizing this system will enable you to manage your inventories in the most efficient manner.

Once you have all this information, you can decide which inventory-control system you wish to adopt. There are three basic systems:

- Minimum stock level—you identify a minimum stock level and re-order when the stock reaches that level. This is known as the “re-order level.”
- Stock review—you regularly review your stock. At every review, you place an order to return stocks to a predetermined level.
- Just in Time (JIT)—this method aims to reduce costs by keeping stock to a minimum. There is a risk that you may run out of stock, so you need to be confident that your suppliers can deliver on demand.

You also need to know the lead time required when ordering some items. This will help you to maintain an optimum level of stock. Ideally, the current stock of an item should be running out just as the new shipment comes in.

ADVANTAGES

- Efficient inventory control allows you to have the right amount of stock in the right place at the right time.
- Keeping an optimum amount of stock, rather than too much, frees up capital that would otherwise be tied up in stock.
- It guards against your customers being disappointed and taking their business elsewhere.
- It prevents stock from deteriorating or simply falling out of fashion.

DISADVANTAGES

- There are no disadvantages involved in efficiently managing your inventories.

ACTION CHECKLIST

✔ Establish accurate order records containing vital information such as the name of the customer, their phone number and e-mail address, the date and time the order was placed, and the name of the contact person.

✔ Decide which inventory-control system suits your business best.

✔ Look to computerize your inventory control. There are software packages that can control your stock for a fraction of the cost of managing it manually.

DOS AND DON’TS

DO

- Make sure that you have good security controls in place to protect your stock. For example, you should mark expensive portable equipment such as computers, and put CCTV in car parking areas and other key locations.
- Make sure that one person is in charge of stock control. Depending on the size of the business, this could either be a dedicated stock controller or an administrator who also undertakes other activities.

DON’T

- Don’t forget that, for security reasons, it is good practice to have different staff responsible for finance and stock.

MORE INFO

Books:

Axsäter, Sven. *Inventory Control*. 2nd ed. New York: Springer, 2006.

Frazelle, Edward. *Supply Chain Strategy: The Logistics of Supply Chain Management*. New York: McGraw-Hill, 2001.

Articles:

Axsäter, Sven. “A framework for decentralized multi-echelon inventory control.” *IIE Transactions* 33:2 (2001): 91–97. Online at: dx.doi.org/10.1080/07408170108936810

Dooley, Frank. “Logistics, inventory control, and supply chain management.” *Choices* 20:4 (4th Quarter 2005): 287–291. Online at: www.choicesmagazine.org/2005-4/supplychain/2005-4-14.htm

See Also:

✔ Business Process Reengineering (pp. 1688–1689)

✔ How to Optimize Stock Control (p. 1159)

✔ Invoicing and Credit Control for Small and Medium-Sized Enterprises (p. 976)

✔ Understanding Yield/Revenue Management (p. 1003)

“**Only recently have people begun to recognise that working with suppliers is just as important as listening to customers.**” Barry J. Nalebuff

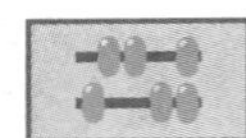

Islamic Commercial Law

DEFINITION

Given that Islam-derived laws encompass all aspects of how Muslims should live their lives and instill a strong sense of the highest moral values, it should be no surprise that Muslims are expected to conduct commercial transactions according to the same principles of equality, justice, and general sense of fair play. Exploitation of any kind is expressly forbidden, including any attempt to capitalize on a counterparty's poor negotiating position due to unforeseen circumstances. Speculative activity of any kind is banned, as are transactions or investments of any kind involving products or services prohibited by Islam, such as alcoholic drink, pork-derived foods, gambling, or pornography. Laws are also structured in such a way to prohibit the charging of interest of any kind, given that Islam expressly forbids any usage of money to make money. Instead, Islamic commercial law supports a partnership-based approach to business with, for example, finance providers treated as stakeholders with an interest in the success of a business rather than external lenders charging interest for the use of their money. Inspired by the Prophet Mohammed's experience as a merchant in Mecca, laws strictly govern agreements such as leasing deals, partnerships, and currency exchanges.

Although aspects of Islam-derived commercial laws bear close comparison with their Western counterparts, other features intended to defend the interest of the counterparties stand in marked contrast to the basic principles of Western commercial laws. For example, while under mainstream Western jurisdictions signed commercial agreements would be binding on both parties unless specific exit clauses are triggered, when applied in modern finance, many basic Islamic contracts can be nonbinding in nature.

Given the trend of increasing commercialism in many Muslim countries as their economies have developed, developments in Islam-inspired commercial law have sought to cater for the needs of Muslims to engage in transactions such as buying their homes, or investing for their future, yet without in any way compromising the principles and moral values enshrined by Islam. Some relatively liberal countries such as Qatar and Bahrain have sought to strike a balance between these potentially conflicting objectives, introducing commercial legal frameworks to enable transactions involving, for example, acceptably low levels of interest or permitting forms of insurance contracts to cover certain types of risk. However, these reforms are not reflected in other countries such as Iran, which retain a strict interpretation of Islamic-led commercial law.

ADVANTAGES

- Islamic commercial law provides a framework for commercial transactions while upholding the high moral values and principles of Islam.
- Laws are structured to support a longer term stakeholder approach, rather than a short-term, "quick return" attitude to business.
- Some countries have chosen to adopt a more business-friendly, progressive attitude to their interpretation of Islamic-inspired law.

DISADVANTAGES

- Some elements of Islam-derived commercial law can be confusing to non-Muslims, notably the nonbinding nature of contracts under certain circumstances.
- While reflecting Islam's rejection of involvement in speculative activities, it could be argued that laws potentially expose businesses to risk, given restrictions on products such as conventional insurance.
- Adherence to traditional ways of overseeing business could mean that Muslim businesses are hampered by legal restrictions.

ACTION CHECKLIST

✔ Recognize how faith and business practices are intertwined in Muslim countries.

✔ Accept that the interpretation of some aspects of *shariah*-inspired laws may be subject to slightly different interpretations in different countries.

✔ Acknowledge the importance of equality, fairness, and compassion in commercial activities in Muslim jurisdictions. Businesses do not simply pay lip service to these concepts; rather, they are fundamental principles on which all transactions are based.

✔ Recognize that individual attitudes to financial products may differ between national jurisdictions. Products such as futures and options may be classed as speculative instruments and, therefore, prohibited in some countries, while others may permit their use as tools to hedge risk.

DOS AND DON'TS

DO

- Acknowledge that law in Muslim countries has a broader role in governing how people live their lives than in the West.
- Take qualified legal advice as to the applicable Islam-inspired law in any particular jurisdiction.

DON'T

- Don't think of Islam-inspired law as a relict of the past. In reality, the influence of *shariah*-inspired law is growing as the prosperity of the followers of Islam across the world grows.

MORE INFO

Books:

Ballantyne, William M., and Howard L. Stovall. *Arab Commercial Law: Principles and Perspectives*. Chicago, IL: American Bar Association Publishing, 2002.

Coulson, Noel J. *Commercial Law in the Gulf States: The Islamic Legal Tradition*. London: Graham & Trotman, 1984.

Hashim Kamali, Mohammad. *Islamic Commercial Law: An Analysis of Futures and Options*. London: Islamic Texts Society, 2000.

Article:

Hegazy, Walid S. "Contemporary Islamic finance: From socioeconomic idealism to pure legalism." *Chicago Journal of International Law* 7:2 (Winter 2007): 581–603.

"If you do things well, do them better. Be daring, be first, be different, be just." Dame Anita Roddick

Islamic Law of Contracts

This checklist offers a brief guide to the nature of contracts in Islam-derived law, and outlines some key differences between these contracts and their Western legal system equivalents.

DEFINITION

The basic prerequisites to establish a valid contract agreement under Islamic law relate to the legal status of the parties seeking to sign the contract, the way the contract is presented or accepted, and finally the subject and consideration of the actual contract.

Parties seeking to engage in a contract may only do so if they are considered legally fit to do so—essentially, adults of sound judgment. Both written and verbal contracts can be considered acceptable, with the proviso that the offer and the acceptance must be performed at the same meeting session, without any interruption or venue change before immediate acceptance. In contrast with Western conventions, Islamic law permits acceptance by conduct; under some circumstances, even not responding to a proposal can imply acceptance. Even once an offer has been accepted during a single session, Islamic law includes the principle that parties retain the right to revoke the contract until the moment either party physically departs the venue. However, interpretation of how this principle can be best applied in practice in the modern era can vary between countries.

In terms of the contract content, Islamic-derived law stresses that the subject of the contract must not relate to prohibited items (such as alcohol, tobacco, or gambling equipment), must be legally owned by one party in the contract and in existence at the time of the contract agreement (i.e. items yet to be built may not be the subject of a standard contract), and must be physically deliverable. As with other legal systems, the exact nature of the goods must be clearly defined in terms of quality and specifications. With the exception of money-exchange deals, the price at which goods will change hands must be agreed at the time of the contract: agreements cannot be based on either future market rates or on the opinion of any external party. While many different types of contract exist, the most common contract for the sale of goods is the *mu'awadat* contract of exchange. These can include a barter-style exchange of goods, a sale of goods in exchange for money, or a money-exchange deal. Another common form of contract is *ijara*, which is commonly used in leasing, either for equipment, real estate, or to provide access to labor.

ADVANTAGES

- Contracts in Islam-derived law fully respect the high moral principles of values expected of all Muslims.
- Islamic contract law is regarded as a product of divine intervention and has been in use for many centuries across North Africa, the Middle East, and Asia.
- Contract law in Muslim countries supports only transactions which would be classified as "ethical" in the West.

DISADVANTAGES

- Islamic contract law can be highly complex, both in terms of its jurisprudence and in its application.
- Technological innovations such as fax and e-mail systems have created some grey areas as to what constitutes a single session of contract discussions.
- Careful consideration needs to be given to the implications of one party failing to honor the contract, given that Islam prohibits any exploitation of another party's genuine misfortunes.

ACTION CHECKLIST

✔ Variations in the details of contract law do occur from country to country. Therefore, acknowledge potential differences in the implementation of Islamic contract law in more liberal Muslim nations such as Qatar, compared to more conservative peers such as Yemen.

✔ When considering potential agreements, *shariah* committees in Islamic financial institutions may pass a judgment on the compatibility of the proposed contract with the ideals of Islam. However, given the subjectivity element, you should appreciate that variations may occur in contracts acceptable to different institutions.

DOS AND DON'TS

DO

- Understand the practicalities of "penalty" clauses that you may wish to insert into a contract. *Shariah* law does not permit the charging of interest (*riba*), and any penalties due may need to be paid to charity under some circumstances.
- Seek expert advice related to Islamic contract law. Given the complexity of many elements of Islamic law of contract, particularly the definition of what constitutes acceptance of a verbal proposal, expert qualified advice should be sought before contract discussions begin, let alone any contract is signed.

DON'T

- Don't assume that the principles of Islamic law bear close comparison with those of Western laws. Contracts agreed under Muslim-derived laws can be less binding in nature than most contracts drawn up under Western legal systems. Take professional advice to determine under what circumstances the agreed contract may not apply in practice.
- Don't assume that the implementation of Islam-derived law takes the same form throughout the Muslim world. Western-leaning countries such as the United Arab Emirates may adopt a more progressive approach to contract law than nations such as Iran or Pakistan.

MORE INFO

Books:

Rayner, Susan. *The Theory of Contracts in Islamic Law*. London: Graham and Trotman, 1991.

Vogel, Frank E., and Samuel L. Hayes. *Islamic Law and Finance: Religion, Risk and Return*. The Hague: Kluwer Law International, 1998.

Articles:

Hussein, Hassan. "Contacts in Islamic law: The principles of commutative justice and liberality." *Journal of Islamic Studies* 13:3 (September 2002): 257–297. Online at: dx.doi.org/10.1093/jis/13.3.257

Islam, M. W. "Dissolution of contract in Islamic law." *Arab Law Quarterly* 13:4 (1998): 336–368. Online at: dx.doi.org/10.1163/026805598125826184

"Only recently have people begun to recognise that working with suppliers is just as important as listening to customers." Barry J. Nalebuff

Managing Bankruptcy and Insolvency

DEFINITION

An insolvent company is one that cannot pay its debts. Cash flow insolvency is the inability to pay debts as they fall due, while balance sheet insolvency occurs when a company has negative net assets and its liabilities exceed the assets. A company can be cash flow insolvent but balance sheet solvent if its assets are illiquid, particularly against short-term debt. Conversely, a company could have negative net assets on the balance sheet but still be cash flow solvent if income can meet debt obligations. Bankruptcy (liquidation in the United Kingdom) occurs when a court rules that a company is unable to pay its creditors. Creditors can force bankruptcy by filing a suit in court against the company in debt, but more usually a company will initiate bankruptcy proceedings itself.

Insolvency law around the world varies, but is generally aimed at protecting creditors' interests and keeping a business afloat. As companies generally want to avoid bankruptcy, the usual practice today is for an insolvent company to file for "bankruptcy protection" (in the United Kingdom, the equivalent is for the company to go into what is called "administration"). An administrator can be appointed by the company directors, or creditors can ask a court to appoint one (without petitioning for bankruptcy). The administrator's job is rescue the business and maintain it as a going concern. To this end, administrators work to restructure the business and its debts in order to pay off creditors and ensure the company emerges in good financial health for the future.

Bankruptcy may follow insolvency, but can also be initiated without going into administration. Bankruptcy laws vary enormously around the world, but all legislation has the aim of winding up the company and paying off creditors. Receivers are appointed by the court to manage this process. The largest creditors will have priority as the debts, or portions of them, are cleared. Some—particularly customers who bought goods but never received them—may never see their money again.

ADVANTAGES

- Appointing administrators is often the smartest option for an insolvent company, as it keeps the company trading and encourages managers to face up to the challenges of learning from their previous errors.
- Bankruptcy may be the best option for a smaller company if its debts are too big to be managed by administration, although there are downsides (see below).

DISADVANTAGES

- Public knowledge of financial problems can cause reputational damage to an insolvent company, possibly hampering the restructuring process and causing customers to decline to do business.
- In many jurisdictions, company directors are banned from running a business for a set period of time if they are involved in a bankruptcy. In some jurisdictions, company directors may be forced to surrender personal assets to clear company debts.
- In some jurisdictions, being made bankrupt can make it very difficult for a company owner to start a new business in the future.

ACTION CHECKLIST

✔ If you need to appoint administrators, choose a firm that has a strong track record in turning ailing businesses around.

✔ It may be worth asking a different firm of accountants to give a second opinion on the company's books to see if there is any other way forward.

DOS AND DON'TS

DO

- Weigh up all the options before embarking on any course of action.
- Take appropriate advice, including consulting your bank and other financial advisers.

DON'T

- Don't rush into making a decision to go bankrupt as other options may be better.
- Don't forget that bankruptcy fraud (concealment of assets, concealment or destruction of documents, making false statements, etc) is a crime.

MORE INFO

Books:

Gilson, Stuart C. *Creating Value through Corporate Restructuring: Case Studies in Bankruptcies, Buyouts and Breakups*. New York: Wiley, 2001.

Hunter, Muir. *Going Bust?: How to Resist and Survive Bankruptcy and Winding Up*. St Albans, UK: XPL Publishing 2007.

Marsh, David, and Roger Sproston. *Bankruptcy Insolvency and the Law: A Straightforward Guide*. 6th ed. Brighton, UK: Straightforward Publishing, 2010.

See Also:

✔ Identifying Your Continuity Needs (p. 1160)
✔ Insolvency/Bankruptcy Regulations in Major Regions (p. 1032)
✔ Islamic Commercial Law (p. 1166)
✔ Practical Techniques for Commercial Mediation (p. 1172)

"Business, more than any other occupation, is a continual dealing with the future; it is a continual calculation, an instinctive exercise in foresight." Henry R. Luce

  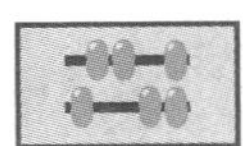      

Nonperformance and Breach of Contract

DEFINITION

A contract is a legally binding agreement between two or more parties. In certain circumstances, a party may not perform its obligations under the contract or may fail to fulfill other terms of the contract. This constitutes a breach of contract, which, if not remedied, can give the other party the right to claim damages.

Contracts can be written or oral and have expressed terms or implied terms. Written contracts are easier to prove than oral contracts.

If a contract has been breached, the party that has been affected by the breach may be entitled, in certain circumstances, to compensation. In general, a party will only be entitled to compensation by way of damages if it can prove that it has suffered a clear financial loss. There is no compensation for distress or hurt feelings.

The person claiming that the contract has been breached (the claimant) has the onus to prove his/her claim. Claims must be well documented and justified.

The courts take the view that a claim is not a means of turning a loss into a profit. The aim is to put the claimant back in the position in which he or she would have been if a certain event had not occurred. The claimant must show that he/she suffered an actual loss caused by the breach, that the loss is not too remote and is recognized as giving rise to entitlement to compensation, and that there is enough evidence that justifies the damages demanded. In certain circumstances and jurisdictions, such as the United States, the courts can force the breaching party to make a payment as a punishment for the breach of contract. These payments are known as punitive damages.

Damages might not be the only remedy sought by the claimant or awarded by the courts. It may be that the court will oblige the party that has breached to specifically perform and execute the contract.

A party that has either breached a contract or suffered a breach should communicate immediately with the other party to explain or discover why the breach has occurred. In many cases, keeping the lines of communication open can prevent the expense and stress of a court action. There are other ways of dealing with a dispute, such as mediation or conciliation, before a court action is considered.

If all such attempts fail, then, as a last resort, a party can sue for breach of contract and damages.

ADVANTAGES

- Contracts are entered into for all sorts of reasons. Respecting the terms of contracts will ensure the smooth running of a business and will help to create a good reputation for a business or individual.

DISADVANTAGES

- Nonperformance and breach of contract can have severe consequences for the reputation of a business or individual. In certain circumstances, a court decision against an individual or business can negatively influence their credit rating.
- The damages awarded for breach of contract, as well as the litigation itself, can be costly.
- Oral contracts are difficult to prove.

ACTION CHECKLIST

- ✔ Study carefully any contract you might enter into. Read the contract's terms and conditions, and ensure that you understand them before you commit.
- ✔ If the terms and conditions offered are not suitable or are too onerous, you may be able to change them through negotiation.
- ✔ Economize by negotiating a reasonable rate with your legal advisers, but remember that it is better to incur costs by obtaining legal advice than to enter into a contract with terms that you do not understand.
- ✔ If you are a consumer, obtain information and advice from relevant consumer protection bodies before entering into a contract.

DOS AND DON'TS

DO

- Read carefully the terms and conditions of any contract.
- If necessary, involve your solicitors in the evaluation of both the risks and potential benefits of entering into a particular contract.
- Negotiate your terms and make a contingency plan for any cost overrun.
- Remember that a claim is not a way of turning a loss into a profit.

DON'T

- Don't make the mistake of being attracted by a contract with terms you do not understand.
- Don't enter into a contract if you do not intend to respect its terms.
- Don't think that you can automatically obtain damages if a contract is breached by the other party.
- Don't overlook the importance of negotiating warranties and indemnities that would protect you in the event that underlying liabilities in the contract are discovered.

MORE INFO

Books:

Blum, Brian A. *Contracts: Examples and Explanations.* 5th ed. New York: Aspen Publishers, 2010.

Farnsworth, E. Allan. *Contracts.* 4th ed. Aspen Student Treatise Series. New York: Aspen Publishers, 2004.

Articles:

Pearce, David, and Roger Halson. "Damages for breach of contract: Compensation, restitution and vindication." *Oxford Journal of Legal Studies* 28:1 (Spring 2008): 73–98. Online at: dx.doi.org/10.1093/ojls/gqm023

Shavell, Steven. "Damage measures for breach of contract." *Bell Journal of Economics* 11:2 (Autumn 1980): 466–490. Online at: tinyurl.com/y9dlqnl

Website:

Attorney/client matching service: www.legalmatch.com

See Also:

★ Human Risk: How Effective Strategic Risk Management Can Identify Rogues (pp. 872–874)
★ International Arbitration: Basic Principles and Characteristics (pp. 887–889)
✔ Practical Techniques for Commercial Mediation (p. 1172)

"**Money you haven't earned is not good for you.**" Robert Maxwell

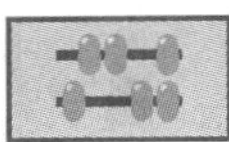

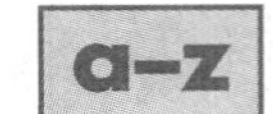

Performing Total Cost of Ownership Analysis

DEFINITION

Originally developed by Gartner Research in 1987, total cost of ownership (TCO) analysis is a tool which aims to systematically calculate the overall costs involved in buying, running, and developing a system or asset over its full life cycle. Frequently employed as a decision support tool in information technology environments, TCO analysis is also widely used to help to assess the likely costs involved in acquiring, installing and operating, then finally developing a wide range of systems or assets, such as production machinery, vehicles, aircraft, or even scientific equipment.

Thorough TCO analysis can help businesses to gain a deeper understanding of the true life cycle costs involved in a potential decision. For example, it can help managers to avoid rushing into a deal that at first glance appears to represent good value on the basis of a low acquisition cost, when analysis of the operational and development costs could paint a very different picture. Detailed TCO studies can help to bring operating costs that are not obvious but nevertheless substantial to light ahead of a critical decision. TCO analysis can be especially valuable in IT-related decisions, when the cost of operating a computer system for several years is usually a large multiple of the initial purchase costs.

To perform TCO analysis, a matrix is usually employed, with one axis listing the full stages of the particular case subject's life cycles. These should include (but not necessarily be limited to) the purchase/procurement phase, the operational/maintenance phase and the development/growth phase. The other axis is typically more complex, detailing all the categories of resources that are set to be required, even to a small degree, from the beginning to the end of the product's useful life cycle. In typical applications such as IT systems, the resources axis could include basic costs related to hardware, software, internal staff expense, external consultancies, and facilities. For more advanced IT systems these broad categories could be expanded considerably. TCO analysis permits the projected costs for each stage in the life cycle to be broken down into individual years, thereby increasing the transparency of the cost patterns.

Table 1. Sample matrix for TCO analysis

	Purchase	Operation	Development and growth
Staff provision			
Hardware			
Software			
External consultancies			
Facilities			

ADVANTAGES

- In its basic form, TCO analysis forms a readily understandable decision-support tool.
- TCO can grow with the complexity of the application, with scope to develop both the resources and life cycle matrices.
- The analysis can help to shed light on costs that could otherwise be simply overlooked.

DISADVANTAGES

- TCO focuses purely on costs, with no consideration given to benefits.
- TCO's analysis on costs risks emphasizing the benefits of the cheaper option rather than a potentially more advantageous but more expensive alternative.
- Even the most thorough cost analysis process cannot guarantee to take account of every conceivable cost that could ever arise.

ACTION CHECKLIST

✔ Identify and understand the full spectrum of your cost base before performing TCO analysis; remember

✔ some costs may be far from obvious.

✔ Consider how technological change could potentially shorten or extend the possible lifespan of the asset.

✔ Use TCO as a means to study how standardized IT costs vary over time; this may help to decide when a product is nearing the end of its commercial life cycle.

DOS AND DON'TS

DO

- Consult as many potential stakeholders as possible when constructing the TCO matrix—some specialists can help to expose otherwise-hidden cost.
- Remember that TCO is most useful when comparing options that deliver similar perceived levels of benefit.
- Use TCO in conjunction with other management aids, such as cost/benefit analysis.

DON'T

- Don't include in the matrix costs that have no relevance to the option under consideration—adding in unnecessary costs only complicates the picture.
- Don't make the mistake of seeing any one single decision-support tool as providing the definitive answer.
- Don't ignore the initial costs associated with TCO analysis, even though TCO has proven its value over the long term in helping companies to choose options involving lower costs across the full life cycle.

MORE INFO

Book:

Devi, Mita. *Total Cost of Ownership: An Introduction*. Hyderabad, India: ICFAI University Press, 2005.

Articles:

Baily, John Taylor, and Stephen R. Heidt. "Why is total cost of ownership important?" *Darwin Magazine* (November 2003).

Ellram, L. M. "Activity based costing and total cost of ownership: A critical linkage." *Journal of Cost Management* 8:4 (1995): 22–30.

"**Money you haven't earned is not good for you.**" Robert Maxwell

  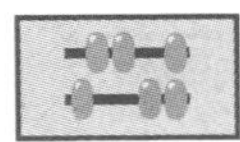     

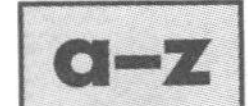

Practical Purchasing Procedures

DEFINITION

A business or organization may buy goods or services either to resell to customers or for its own use. When choosing suppliers and merchandise, you need to consider price, quality, availability, reliability, and technical support. The goal of purchasing is to obtain the highest-quality goods and services at the lowest possible cost to your business. In order to accomplish this successfully, you need to keep abreast of changes affecting both the supply of and demand for products and materials, track market conditions and price trends, and be aware of sales and inventory levels. It is also advisable to have a working technical knowledge of the goods or services to be purchased and to make up a spec sheet for each product to include brand, model, price, service requirements, and payment terms.

ADVANTAGES

- Good purchasing practices will help you to avoid throwing away money by investing in unsuitable and expensive purchases.
- You will save time and money by using spec sheets, as you will be able to select the brand, model, price ceiling or price range, any features, and any other required options.
- By asking for quotes you can often get discounts and perhaps extra information from the supplier, which could help you get a better deal the next time.

DISADVANTAGES

- Many small businesses just don't have the expertise or time to check how much they should be paying for certain goods and services. They could be throwing away money by not getting the best deals.
- In a market such as fashion or technology, where trends can change overnight, it is often almost impossible for businesses to keep up fully with market conditions and price movements.

DOS AND DON'TS

DO

- Consider using a specialist—they can save you time and hassle, as well as using collective bargaining to get better deals.

DON'T

- Don't renew existing contracts out of habit or because it's easier. Check! Your requirements or the market may well have changed.

ACTION CHECKLIST

✔ **Vendors**: Take the time to thoroughly understand the product/service—the more research you do, the better placed you will be to make good judgments. You may want to check out vendors by getting references from other customers, reading product reviews, visiting the vendor's plants, and perhaps sampling the product or service.

✔ **Quotes**: For costly purchases, always ask to see a salesperson, as they can often get you discounts and perhaps recommend more suitable products. You should also try to get at least two or three quotes. Make sure the quotes you are comparing are "like for like". If you need further information, ask your suppliers so that you can make an informed decision. And don't just consider price—quality, service, and added value should also be taken into consideration.

✔ **Spec sheets**: You will need to create a spec sheet for each product you buy. This could specify: brand, model, price ceiling or price range, and any features and options. You should also specify delivery times, warranty or service requirements, and payment terms (for example COD or net 30/60/90 days).

✔ **Purchase orders**: Your purchase order should specify the name of the item or service being purchased and any details specified in your spec sheet, such as brand, quantity, style, type, or color. You will also need to specify packing and receiving requirements, delivery date, delivery address, shipping method, and payment.

✔ **Receiving goods**: Count the number of items delivered and check for any damage. Remember that when you sign for delivery you are generally agreeing that the quantity is correct and that the shipment has suffered no obvious damage. As soon as you can, open the shipment and examine it to check specs, quantity, and quality. If there are any problems, call the supplier immediately.

✔ **Legal aspects**: Check on any legislation affecting your purchasing decisions. Make sure that you are clued up on any legal requirements for the product or service you are buying.

✔ **Contract renewal**: Make a note of contract renewal dates and set yourself a reminder so that you have plenty of time to consider your options.

MORE INFO

Books:

Baily, Peter, David Farmer, Barry Crocker, David Jessop, *et al*. *Procurement Principles and Management*. 10th ed. Harlow, UK: FT Prentice Hall, 2008.

Harding, Michael, Warren Harding, and Mary Lu Harding. *Purchasing*. 2nd ed. Hauppauge, NY: Barron's Educational Series, 2001.

Lysons, Kenneth, and Brian Farrington. *Purchasing and Supply Chain Management*. 8th ed. Harlow, UK: Pearson Education, 2012.

Articles:

Dominick, Charles. "Negotiating successfully in inflationary times." *Next Level Purchasing* (August 2008).

Hardt, Chip W., Nicolas Reinecke, and Peter Spiller. "Inventing the 21st-century purchasing organization." *McKinsey Quarterly* (November 2007).

Websites:

American Purchasing Society (APS): www.american-purchasing.com

Institute for Supply Management (ISM): www.ism.ws

See Also:

✔ Building an Efficient Credit and Collection Accounts System (p. 1148)

"Very often the best way to find out whether something is worth making is to make it, distribute it and then to see, after the product has been around for a few years, whether it was worth the task." Edwin Land

Practical Techniques for Commercial Mediation

DEFINITION

Mediation is a negotiation process between two or more parties to a dispute, assisted by the participation of an independent third party that is assigned the objective of exploring how their differences might be settled without resorting to the law courts. However mediators are chosen, it is important that the parties to a dispute should be satisfied that they are impartial as only then can they explore ways of reaching an agreement that is acceptable to all.

For the mediation process to be most effective, the mediator should not attempt to impose preconditions on the parties before mediation commences. However, it is commonplace for mediators to ask all parties to respect the confidentiality of information presented during the mediation process. This is to remove the risk that the content of a mediation session could be interpreted as an admission of any kind (even, for example, to the extent that it was seen by one party as the basis for subsequent legal action), a risk that could severely undermine the mediation's chances of success.

The mediation process often begins with open discussions involving all parties involved in the dispute, helping the mediator to understand both the issues and the perspectives and concerns of all parties. Individual meetings between each party and the mediator are then normally held to explore the issues in more detail and to allow the mediator to discover exactly which issues are of greatest concern to each party, as well as to identify areas that offer realistic scope for compromise. For this stage of the process to operate effectively, it is important that the mediator has earned the absolute trust of both parties, given the need for each party to take the mediator into their confidence and reveal those points on which they would give ground in exchange for a similar gesture by the other side, whether on the same points or on others. The mediator should be prepared to pose direct questions to each party to help identify both the limits of their flexibility and what they would seek in return for giving ground in particular areas.

Subsequent informal meetings between all parties can frequently generate some kind of resolution of the dispute without either side giving up entirely on the issues that are most important to them. Again, it is worth stressing that *conventional* mediation does not attempt to impose any solution on the parties; agreement is entirely optional. In contrast, *binding* mediation has parallels with court or arbitration hearings, in that compliance with the settlement is binding, with neither party having any assurance that the settlement is one to which they would have agreed in conventional mediation.

ADVANTAGES

- Conventional mediation offers an informal, free exchange of ideas, aiming to come to a resolution of the dispute.
- Costs are generally appreciably lower than those associated with the legal route of dispute resolution.
- Conventional mediation offers a no-obligation route to a possible resolution without the risk of an unacceptable solution being imposed on either party.
- Mediation can often bring about an acceptable resolution in a shorter time frame than a resort to the courts.
- Mediation can bring about a noncontentious resolution, often allowing the parties to maintain a reasonable business relationship. In contrast, litigation is likely to sour relations between parties.

DISADVANTAGES

- Mediation is only possible if all parties to a dispute agree to participate.
- Some parties may be convinced of the strength of their legal position and view mediation as a process that could lead to them needlessly giving ground.
- Mediation offers no guarantee of a resolution. In contrast, litigation will bring about a definite decision.
- Even if unsuccessful, mediation results in costs to be borne by both parties.

ACTION CHECKLIST

- ✔ Select a mediator with a genuine understanding of commercial issues—for example a neutral person with a background in accountancy or law.
- ✔ The parties in dispute must have confidence in the integrity and independence of the mediator.
- ✔ Agree a framework for the discussions and clarify whether the mediation outcome is binding.
- ✔ Ensure that the mediator explores the scope for compromise in a nonjudgmental way.
- ✔ When a solution has been found, the mediator should assist legal representatives in the preparation of a formal resolution agreement.

DOS AND DON'TS

DO

- Ensure that all parties are confident that the mediator is neutral.
- Conduct discussions in a positive, nonconfrontational way.
- Ensure that all parties understand the potential costs of not finding an acceptable compromise through mediation—one of which is a settlement imposed through litigation.

DON'T

- Don't allow needless timescales to be imposed on the mediation process; discussions held in an unpressurized environment are more likely to succeed.
- Don't abandon mediation at the first difficulty—positions may not be as entrenched as they at first appear.
- Don't expect a mediator to play the role of an adviser. Although background commercial awareness is desirable in a mediator, they should not be asked for advice. It is for individual parties to decide for themselves what would be acceptable.

MORE INFO

Books:

Chern, Cyril. *International Commercial Mediation*. London: Informa Law, 2008.

Newmark, Chris, and Anthony Monaghan (eds). *Butterworths Mediators on Mediation: Leading Mediator Perspectives on the Practice of Commercial Mediation*. Haywards Heath, UK: Tottel Publishing, 2005.

Article:

Pribetic, Antonin I. "A strategic functionalist approach to international commercial mediation." *ICFAI Journal of Alternative Dispute Resolution* 7:2 (2008): 37–58.

"Diplomacy is the art of letting someone else have your way." David Frost

  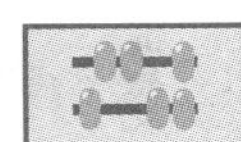      

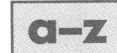

The Principles of Litigation

DEFINITION

Disputes arising between parties can generally be resolved through a process of negotiation. This frequently involves the help of an independent third party, either in the form of a mediator seeking a mutually agreeable compromise, or of an arbitrator who can be granted the authority to impose a settlement on the parties. However, should the negotiation option fail, it may be necessary to seek the decision of a court. The legal process of determining a resolution to a dispute in a law court is known as litigation.

Before the main litigation process can begin, one party to the dispute must make a formal demand on the counterparty setting out their requirements for a resolution. This typically takes the form of an attorney's letter. In many cases this formal step will provoke a response from the counterparty, which previously may have failed to address the issue in dispute. Subsequently, the disputing parties and their lawyers will usually meet to explore possible solutions. However, should no solution be found, the formal process of litigation begins with the lodging of a complaint with the court that specifies what the counterparty did (or did not do) to give rise to the dispute. Once the other party is served with notification of the formal legal process, a response is required within a specified timescale. Should this not be forthcoming, that party is then said to be in default, and loses the action.

If a response is forthcoming but is unsatisfactory to the complainant, there follows a request to the counterparty in an effort to clarify the key issues. This response can lead to further communications to establish the specific issue in dispute. Once the parties have clearly defined the nature of the complaint, the precise issues to be resolved are formally established. Next follows a process of discovery, during which the parties attempt to generate evidence to back up their case, often using documents or the views of witnesses. An important principle of litigation that applies from this stage is that facts must be differentiated from opinions. Next, in a stage known as the motions phase, both parties attempt to define the precise issue or issues in dispute. This is a process that can sometimes result in a decision by a pretrial court or arbitrator, and it may occur when the facts of a case are undisputed, with the judgment depending solely on how the law applies in that case. Should such arbitration fail, the case proceeds to a formal court hearing at which both sides present their case and a judgment is made. Following possible efforts to appeal against the decision, the winning party can then move to claim payment of whatever sum is awarded in the judgment.

ADVANTAGES

- Litigation provides a definitive financial resolution of a dispute.
- The threat of litigation against a secretive corporation can provoke a resolution if it is keen to avoid public disclosure of information in a court.
- The result of litigation can set a legal precedent, and so is an attractive option for parties wishing to bring a test case.

DISADVANTAGES

- Trials can become complicated and expensive procedures compared to other forms of dispute resolution.
- Litigation may result in bad publicity for all parties concerned.
- The process creates ill-feeling between parties, making it difficult to continue business relationships.

ACTION CHECKLIST

✔ Consider whether alternative forms of dispute resolution, such as mediation or arbitration, may be more appropriate.

✔ Take account of the possibility that litigation could require the disclosure of sensitive information in court.

✔ Prolonged litigation can create lingering uncertainty over the outcome for all parties. Consider how much this might disrupt your business before choosing this route.

DOS AND DON'TS

DO

- Assess the possibility of reputational damage before embarking on litigation.
- Pursue all other forms of dispute resolution before embarking on litigation as formal legal action is likely to make an ongoing business relationship with the opposing party impossible.
- Find out whether earlier similar cases have set legal precedents that could be used as leverage in prelitigation negotiations.

DON'T

- Don't underestimate the potential costs of complex litigation proceedings, particularly should the discovery phase of the action involve expert testimony.
- Don't ignore the costs that could be awarded against you if you lose the case.

MORE INFO

Books:

Jeans, James W. *Litigation.* 2nd ed. Charlottesville, VA: Michie Co., 1992.

McElhaney, James W. *McElhaney's Litigation*. Chicago, IL: American Bar Association, 1995.

Articles:

Pannill, William. "Litigator's bookshelf: In the interest of justice." *Litigation Journal* 31:3 (Spring 2005).

Williams, R. Scott, and Mark M. Maloney. "Litigator's perspective: Welcome to bankruptcy court." *American Bankruptcy Institute Journal* 26:10 (December 2007/January 2008): 28.

Website:

American Bar Association (ABA): www.americanbar.org

See Also:

★ International Arbitration: Basic Principles and Characteristics (pp. 887–889)
✔ Nonperformance and Breach of Contract (p. 1169)
✔ Practical Techniques for Commercial Mediation (p. 1172)

Setting Up a Key Risk Indicator (KRI) System

DEFINITION

Key risk indicators (KRI) are measurements that are used by management to show how risky an activity is—a project or an investment, for example. They are called key because they warn of the most obvious areas where problems may arise. KRI help to flag up warnings of a possible adverse impact arising from an activity in the future.

In the United States the Risk Management Association (RMA) manages an initiative that is designed for financial services companies interested in improving their risk management. Going by the name of the KRI Library and Services, its aim is to achieve a degree of consistency and standardization to enable KRI to be compared, analyzed, and reported at the corporate level. The RMA's intention is that the library initiative will lead to distinct improvements in the effective use and benchmarking of KRI with peer groups.

Most companies find the development of effective KRI to be a key challenge. In financial institutions there are plenty of credit risk and market risk indicators, many with frameworks set out within existing financial legislation. However, pulling these data together and developing operational risk indicators is not easy. Conversely, nonfinancial institutions may be in possession of a mass of business and quality information gained from balanced scorecard and quality initiatives. However, their difficulty lies in developing KRI for financial risk or technology risk.

All companies have the awkward task of developing KRI that can provide effective early warning of potential future problems.

It is in the area of forecasting losses that KRI are most likely to gain their stripes, but the majority of companies have yet to master the techniques of setting up effective KRI systems that can do this.

ADVANTAGES

- KRI can provide early warning of future losses or other problems.
- They are useful in supporting management decisions and actions.
- They can be benchmarked both internally and externally.

DISADVANTAGES

- Mastering KRI has proven difficult to date.
- The company has to believe in them, even though past history may not fully support their value.

DOS AND DON'TS

DO

- Make your KRI quantifiable.
- Base KRI on consistent methodologies and standards.
- Track them along a timeline against standards or limits.
- Link KRI to objectives, risk owners, and standard risk categories.
- Run regular overviews to check that your formulae are still relevant and accurate in assessing risk.

DON'T

- Don't complicate risk.
- Don't be too simplistic.
- Don't put 100% faith in your initial KRI.

ACTION CHECKLIST

Some of the following resources can be useful in helping create your own KRI list.

✔ Policies and regulations, particularly those that are aimed at regulating the business activities of the company. Such KRI may include risk exposures relating to compliance with regulatory requirements and standards.

✔ Strategies and objectives. Corporate and business strategies, as established by senior management, are a good source.

✔ Previous losses and incidents. Databases containing historical losses and incidents can provide useful input on what processes or events can cause losses.

MORE INFO

Books:

Alexander, Carol. *Mastering Risk, Volume 2: Applications. Your Single-Source Guide to Becoming a Master of Risk*. Mastering Series. Upper Saddle River, NJ: FT Prentice Hall, 2001.

PricewaterhouseCoopers for Committee of the Sponsoring Organizations of the Treadway Commission (COSO). *Enterprise Risk Management—Integrated Framework.* New York: AICPA, 2004. Hard copies (two volumes) can be ordered from COSO (www.coso.org) or from the Chartered Institute of Internal Auditors (www.iia.org.uk).

Websites:

Institute of Risk Management (IRM; UK): www.theirm.org
KRI Library Services (US): www.kriex.org
Risk Management Association (RMA; US): www.rmahq.org

See Also:

✔ Applying Stress-Testing to Operational Risk Exposure (p. 1142)
✔ Creating a Risk Register (p. 1156)
✔ Establishing a Framework for Assessing Risk (p. 1028)

"In skating over thin ice our safety is in our speed." Ralph Waldo Emerson

  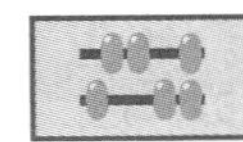   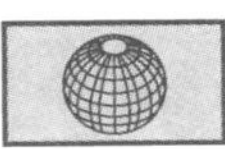   

Structuring and Negotiating Joint Ventures

DEFINITION

Joint ventures are set up for many reasons: to carry out a specific project or simply to assist with the growth and continuation of a business.

The parties to a joint venture can be individuals, partnerships, companies, or other organizations or associations. In certain cases, the joint venture can be created through the incorporation of a company that becomes a party to the joint-venture agreement. In other cases, the parties can sign a collaboration agreement.

The parties must think carefully about what they are trying to achieve through the joint venture. Do the parties want to have a period of exclusive negotiation, will they require a confidentiality undertaking, and will they sign a letter of intent to solidify their intention as a preamble for negotiations?

Things to consider include whether the joint venture will have any limitations in terms of territory in which it will operate. Also, what consents, approvals, licenses, and permits are necessary for the joint venture to operate? If the joint venture will operate at a cross-border level, in which jurisdictions will it be established? Consider also whether there are any laws governing foreign ownership or investment. Are they any exchange controls in force? What relevant taxes and duties are imposed?

The parties to a joint venture can provide their own funding for the joint venture or use external sources for funding. The parties' investment can be cash or payment in kind, such as expertise and resources. The parties must agree the percentage in which they will benefit from the joint venture. They must also agree working-capital requirements, any losses, and think about any expansion costs.

If the joint venture is through a company, the parties must agree the extent to which participation in the joint venture is transferable. Should the joint-venture company be wound-up if one of the parties wants to come out of it?

The joint venture will have to be thoroughly organized. The parties will agree the composition of the board and how the board will operate and vote.

Another very important consideration is whether the parties will be prohibited from competing with the joint venture at all or just in that particular territory.

Deadlock provisions are essential in a joint-venture agreement. This is when the parties cannot agree on certain voting issues and a decision cannot be taken. The joint-venture agreement must deal with this and set up a procedure to be followed in the event of a deadlock. For example, a voting deadlock at board level can be solved by giving a casting vote to the chairman or by involving an independent expert or arbitrator. The agreement must also establish the duration of the joint venture and how it can be terminated. In the event of termination, the agreement must deal with the distribution of assets, the discharge of any outstanding contracts, and the liabilities of the joint venture.

ADVANTAGES

- A joint venture allows two competitors to join forces, increase their market exposure, and compete at a higher level against other, more powerful companies in the same industry.
- It also allows two connected businesses to cooperate on a joint project in a certain market.

DISADVANTAGES

- Negotiating a joint venture can be complex and time consuming. It involves thorough research of the market and territory in which the products will be sold or the project will be organized.
- Joint ventures can be expensive to set up initially.

ACTION CHECKLIST

✔ Study any joint venture you might set up carefully. Obtain as much information from as many sources as you can before committing to an expensive joint-venture agreement. Plan it carefully and set up a realistic business plan with your business partner.

✔ Know your market and make sure that you have analyzed the consequences for your own business of entering into a joint-venture agreement.

✔ Economize by negotiating a reasonable rate with your legal advisers, but remember that it is better to incur costs by obtaining legal advice than to enter into a joint venture under terms that you do not understand.

DOS AND DON'TS

DO

- Choose your partner in the joint venture carefully, as you will be legally bound for a set period of time, under obligations that will prove costly if they are not successfully performed.
- Involve your solicitors in the evaluation of both the risks and potential benefits of entering into a joint venture.
- Negotiate your rates and make a contingency plan for any cost overrun.
- Plan carefully how the joint-venture will operate, how the profits will be distributed and who will take responsibility for what.

DON'T

- Don't make the mistake of being attracted by the idea of a joint venture that has not been thoroughly planned and thought through.
- Don't overlook the importance of setting up a contingency plan in case the joint venture will not work and the relationship breaks down.

MORE INFO

Books:

Glover, Stephen I., and Craig M. Wasserman (eds). *Partnerships, Joint Ventures and Strategic Alliances*. Business Law Corporate Series. New York: Law Journal Press, 2004.

Walmsley, John. *Handbook of International Joint Ventures*. London: Graham & Trotman, 1982.

See Also:

★ Joint Ventures: Synergies and Benefits (pp. 890–892)
★ Maximizing a New Strategic Alliance (pp. 749–750)

"Building trust between partners in a joint venture can be seen as the first necessary step in developing a successful alliance." Jan Selmer

  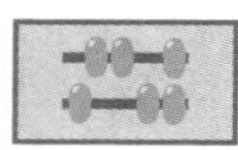      

Structuring, Negotiating, and Drafting Agency Agreements

DEFINITION

An agent is an individual or a legal person who has been appointed by another individual or company (the principal) to act on his, her, or its behalf and to create legal relations between him/her/it and other parties.

The agent and the principal usually enter into an agency agreement, which is drafted by the principal, and then negotiated and amended by the agent. Agency agreements can be oral or written and, in certain cases, can be implied by the conduct of the parties.

An agent can be appointed for many purposes, which can include the distribution, sales, and consignment of goods, or to negotiate, represent, and act on behalf of a principal who is an artist.

From a legal point of view, an agent can exercise all powers given to him or her under the agreement. The agent must carry out with skill and diligence the instructions given by the principal. He or she must promote the principal's interests and must not profit secretly from the agency.

Before entering into an agency agreement, the parties should thoroughly investigate the market and territory and weigh the advantages and disadvantages of establishing an agency and operating within that market. If the agency to be set up relates to the manufacturing and sale of products, it is advisable to think of the way in which these products will be distributed and sold. Under an agency agreement for the sale of goods manufactured by the principal, the principal gives the agent the right to sell its products in a well-defined territory, for a certain period of time, in exchange for a commission fee. The agency can be simple, sole, or exclusive. A *sole agency* means that the principal will not appoint any other agents within that territory but the principal itself is still entitled to sell the goods there. An *exclusive agency* gives the agent the sole right to sell products in that territory: the principal will not appoint any other agents or sell the products itself. A *simple agency* usually means that there are other agents in the territory, as well as the principal, all selling the same products. Exclusive agencies are, therefore, the most expensive and sought after.

The agency agreement should stipulate in detail the commission an agent will be paid. This is usually calculated as a percentage of the gross takings for the product.

An agency agreement must be clear and well structured. It should specify in detail the scope of the agency, the territory where the agency will operate, the obligations of the principal and the agent, the commission, and the payment terms. It should also specify the duration of the agency and any termination clauses. Conflict clauses should be included to deal with nonperformance and breach of contract, with provision for solutions such as mediation.

As an agent will be able to bind a principal to other parties legally, special care should be taken in making sure that the right agent is appointed. Warranties and indemnities should be sought from an agent to cover any potential liabilities a principal may have. On the other hand, an agent should be careful not to take any responsibility for the products of a principal and should seek to be compensated in this respect should it be necessary.

ADVANTAGES

- An agency allows a principal to increase the market for its brand by giving others the right to use it under certain conditions and for a certain price.
- It also allows an agent to operate a business and to exploit, for his or her benefit, a product that belongs to someone else and that would otherwise be too expensive to acquire.

DISADVANTAGES

- Negotiating an agency agreement can be complex and time-consuming. It involves thorough research of the market and territory in which the products will be sold or used.
- Exclusive and sole agencies are more expensive than simple agencies.

ACTION CHECKLIST

✔ Study any agency with which you might sign. Obtain as much information from as many sources as you can before committing to an expensive agency agreement.

✔ Know your market and make sure that you have analyzed the consequences for your own business of entering into an agency agreement.

✔ Be prepared for complicated negotiations, which could prove time-consuming and costly.

✔ Economize by negotiating a reasonable rate with your legal advisers, but remember that it is better to incur costs by obtaining legal advice than to enter into an agency agreement under terms that you do not understand.

DOS AND DON'TS

DO

- Choose your agent carefully.
- Involve your solicitors in the evaluation of both the risks and potential benefits of entering into an agency agreement.
- Negotiate your rates and make a contingency plan for any cost overrun.
- Plan carefully how the agency will operate in the territory.

DON'T

- Don't make the mistake of being attracted by an agency that has not been thoroughly investigated.
- Don't overlook the importance of negotiating warranties and indemnities that will protect you in the event that underlying liabilities are discovered.

MORE INFO

Article:

Lianos, Ioannis. "Commercial agency agreements, vertical restraints, and the limits of Article 81(1) EC: Between hierarchies and networks." *Journal of Competition Law and Economics* 3:4 (December 2007): 625–672. Online at: dx.doi.org/10.1093/joclec/nhm017

"To me the law seems like a sort of maze through which a client must be led to safety; a collection of reefs, rocks and underwater hazards through which he or she must be piloted." John Mortimer

  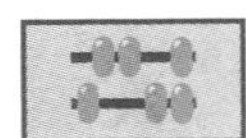      

Understanding Continuity Insurance

DEFINITION

This type of insurance provides a valuable safety net for organizations in the event of a serious disruption and is not a substitute for business continuity planning. It is not sold separately, but either as part of a general package or with buildings insurance.

If an event such as a fire damages a company's premises and prevents it from operating, business continuity insurance covers the profits that would have been earned if the disaster had not happened. The amount of compensation is determined by an examination of the company's business records.

Policies also generally cover operating expenses, such as power bills, which continue even when normal business activities come to a halt. Most policies, however, have a two-day waiting period before claims are covered.

Premiums are determined both by policy limits and the type of business covered. For instance, a restaurant would probably pay more than an office-based business. That is because the risk of a restaurant catching fire is probably greater than an office, and it would be harder to transfer the business to alternative premises.

It is very important that a business continuity or interruption policy is absolutely watertight, even if that takes a great deal of time and effort. If holes are found after a disaster, it could be too late.

ADVANTAGES

- Insurance cover is a useful, even vital, adjunct to a business continuity plan.

DISADVANTAGES

- Insurance can cover lost income following a disaster such as a fire, but it won't restore a company's competitive position in the marketplace if it ceases trading for an extended period.

ACTION CHECKLIST

1. Ensure that insurance is coordinated with the business continuity plan

In particular, indemnity periods should cover the full time it willtake the organization to recover from a disaster, including:

- ✔ Time for demolition, redesign, and rebuilding;
- ✔ How long it will take to replace specialist machinery;
- ✔ Rehiring if staff have been laid off;
- ✔ Also, if there are multiple sites, decide whether the same indemnity period is applicable to all.

2. Identify all sources of income and potential loss

Identify what income would be lost as the result of a shutdown and other costs or losses that might result.

- ✔ Most forms of income can be covered; these vary according to type of business and can be a combination of revenue, fees, or rental.
- ✔ Make sure penalty payments are included if a major incident could affect the company's ability to complete a project.
- ✔ Some income will not be covered, such as interest on investments or sales of assets.

3. List all business activities

In listing business activities you should:

- ✔ Be sure to add acquisitions, new divisions, and new ventures;
- ✔ Ensure that long-term projects are covered even if they have not yet produced income;
- ✔ Consider including key suppliers if damage to their premises could have serious repercussions on your business;
- ✔ Ensure that power suppliers are included, and check to see when coverage commences. There is a week's "deductible" in many policies.

4. Review the amount insured regularly

It may be useful to consider the following points.

- ✔ Many large organizations with multiple profit centers include intergroup sales that can inflate the premium through double counting.
- ✔ Make sure the projected figures for lost earnings are accurate for the whole insured period, which may be two or more years.
- ✔ Consider including a premium adjustment clause to take account of actual rather than projected earnings at the end of the year.

5. Include other potential costs and savings

Include both the increased payroll costs and savings that would follow a disaster:

- ✔ Estimate how many seasonal and other staff could be laid off;
- ✔ Make provision for redundancy payments if necessary;
- ✔ List the key staff who would need to be kept on to enable the company to resume full working.

MORE INFO

Websites:

Continuity Forum provides information and help for business continuity management: www.continuityforum.org

Continuity Insurance & Risk (CIR) Magazine: www.cirmagazine.com

See Also:

★ Business Continuity Management: How to Prepare for the Worst (pp. 788–791)
✔ Applying Stress-Testing to Business Continuity Management (p. 1141)
✔ Identifying Your Continuity Needs (p. 1160)
✔ Stress Testing to Evaluate Insurance Cover (p. 1016)
✔ Understanding the Components of an Insurance Contract (p. 1021)

"Building trust between partners in a joint venture can be seen as the first necessary step in developing a successful alliance." Jan Selmer

  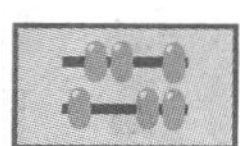      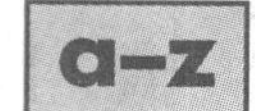

Understanding Crisis Management

DEFINITION

Although any development that poses a serious threat to a business and/or its shareholders can be thought of as a crisis of some kind, events that require rapid and far-reaching action by management to avert significant damage to the organization require some form of crisis management. All businesses should expect to face major challenges from time to time, but the precise form of possible threats to the survival of an organization are very difficult to predict, with the need for the right solutions to be identified and implemented within a tight timescale often adding to the severity of the crisis.

The immediate threat of bankruptcy is an obvious situation that requires crisis management, though struggling companies in need of urgent corporate restructuring or debt refinancing could also employ crisis management techniques. Similarly, companies facing major problems such as a catastrophic computer systems failure, a large-scale industrial accident, a major product recall, or a sudden collapse in sales due to a health scare can also benefit from the implementation of crisis management strategies.

Though the precise nature of potential crises facing businesses varies considerably according to their operating environment, in all cases crisis management presents significant challenges for senior management. When preparing outline crisis management plans in advance, executives should ensure that appropriate personnel structures are in place to help deal with major events that could threaten the business. Management should also impress on their crisis management teams how the company's core values should be reflected in the methodology employed to steer the organization through the crisis. Additionally, emphasis should be placed on how the organization intends to communicate with parties such as employees, clients, and investors during a possible crisis, bearing in mind that loss of support from any of these could in itself pose a grave threat to the business.

In many cases, companies can also improve their state of readiness to deal with potential future crises by testing the mechanisms they have put in place to handle potential threats such as computer failure or product recalls. However, the procedures employed to handle an immediate crisis should integrate effectively with a strategic plan to help the company's overall recovery plan.

ADVANTAGES

- Robust crisis management plans can equip organizations to withstand threats to their survival better.
- Awareness of potential threats can put an organization in a better position to take early action, often helping to avoid more serious problems.
- Effective crisis management plans can help companies to achieve improved levels of regulatory compliance.
- Appropriate planning for potential industry-wide crises can give a company the upper hand over ill-prepared competitors.
- Effective communications during a crisis can help determine how the company's core values and beliefs have helped it to overcome a major challenge, potentially enhancing public perception of the company.

DISADVANTAGES

- Crisis management planning may seem expensive.
- Attempts to plan exhaustively for every conceivable threat can be counterproductive.
- Excessive focus on potential threats can divert management focus on how to capitalize on growth opportunities for the business.

ACTION CHECKLIST

✔ Prepare an overall crisis management plan that encapsulates the company's core values and beliefs.

✔ Establish a crisis management team structure and define roles and responsibilities.

✔ Define and clarify lines of authority reporting.

✔ Ensure that effective structures are in place for communications with key stakeholders.

✔ Link the crisis management plan to a business recovery program.

DOS AND DON'TS

DO

- Recognize the increased operating safety levels associated with effective crisis management planning.
- Appreciate that robust planning to deal with major threats can give a company a competitive advantage.
- Plan for business recovery, not just how to handle the immediate crisis.

DON'T

- Don't ignore the potential long-term benefits of effective crisis management in terms of improved corporate reputation, as doing so can be costly.
- Don't become obsessed with every conceivable challenge that faces the business, as this can be counterproductive.

MORE INFO

Books:

Devlin, Edward S. *Crisis Management Planning and Execution*. Boca Raton, FL: Auerbach Publications, 2007.

Fink, Steven. *Crisis Management: Planning for the Inevitable*. Lincoln, NE: iUniverse, 2002.

Articles:

Chong, John K. S. "Six steps to better crisis management." *Journal of Business Strategy* 25:2 (2004): 43–46. Online at: dx.doi.org/10.1108/02756660410525407

Sturges, David L. "Communicating through crisis: A strategy for organizational survival." *Management Communication Quarterly* 7:3 (February 1994): 297–316. Online at: dx.doi.org/10.1177/0893318994007003004

Website:

Federal Emergency Management Agency (FEMA; US): www.fema.gov

"**The first steps to becoming a really great manager are simply common sense; but common sense is not very common.**"
Gerald M. Blair

     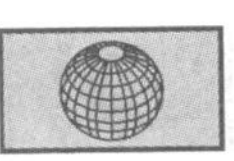   

Understanding Decision-Tree Analysis

DEFINITION

In operational areas, a decision tree—also known as a tree diagram—is a tool for reaching decisions. It uses a diagram or model of decisions and their possible outcomes, including chance events, resource costs, and utility. A decision tree can be used to select the strategy most likely to attain a specific goal. Decision trees are also used as predictive models in data mining (the science of uncovering hidden patterns in data) and machine learning (the development of algorithms and other techniques that enable computers to "learn").

Decision trees have three types of node:

1 Decision nodes: In the diagram these are usually represented by squares;
2 Chance nodes: Represented by circles;
3 End nodes: Represented by triangles.

A tree is usually drawn from left to right, with splitting paths (burst nodes) but no converging paths (sink nodes). Thus, when drawn by hand, the diagram tends to get very big to the right.

Decision trees can be a very effective structure for exploring options and investigating the consequences of choices of action. They can also help to form a picture of the risks and rewards for each possible course of action. In a financial context, decision trees can help to determine the best strategies for investment.

Drawing a decision tree begins with the decision that needs to be made, usually represented by a small square on the left-hand side of a large sheet of paper. For each possible choice a line is drawn out to the right, with a short description written along each line. At the end of each line the result, or outcome, should be stated; this may be an uncertain outcome (circle) or another decision (square), and the result should be written above the symbol. The process is repeated as required from each new decision square, always annotated with descriptions. Once drawn, the tree should be reviewed, as it is unlikely that all possibilities will emerge during the first round.

To work out which option has the greatest value, the decision tree is evaluated by assigning a cash value to each possible outcome. For each circle (an uncertain outcome), the probability of each outcome is estimated as a percentage, with the total of all possible outcomes for each course of action equaling 100%. Obviously, best guesses are often required.

To calculate a tree value, starting on the right-hand side of the tree, each calculation is completed on reaching a node (square or circle) and then recording the result. To calculate the vale of an uncertain outcome (circle), the value of the outcomes is multiplied by the probability as previously estimated.

ADVANTAGES

- Decision trees are simple to understand and interpret.
- They are worth doing even with quite uncertain data. Intuitive insights can be gained based on descriptions of a situation by experts.
- Decision trees lay out a problem clearly so that all options can be explored, and they allow a full analysis of the possible consequences of a decision.
- They provide a method for quantifying the values of outcomes and their probabilities.
- Decision trees assist in making decisions with existing information and best guesses.
- Decision trees can be used to optimize an investment portfolio.

DISADVANTAGES

- Diagrams can become very large when drawn by hand.
- Trees created from numeric datasets can be complex.

ACTION CHECKLIST

✔ Identify the decision you need to make.

✔ Draw a line to the right for each solution with a description.

✔ Consider the outcome at the end of each line.

✔ Repeat the process for each new decision.

✔ When complete, review the tree, evaluate it, and calculate the values.

DOS AND DON'TS

DO

- Review a decision tree often.
- Review the evaluation values regularly.

DON'T

- Don't consider your first effort as final but continually review and revise it.

MORE INFO

Books:

Cai, Jingfeng. *Decision Tree Pruning Using Expert Knowledge: Cost-sensitive Pruning*. Saarbrücken, Germany: VDM Verlag, 2008.

de Ville, Barry. *Decision Trees for Business Intelligence and Data Mining Using SAS Enterprise Miner.* Cary, NC: SAS Institute, 2006.

Rokach, Lior, and Oded Maimon. *Data Mining with Decision Trees: Theory and Applications*. Singapore: World Scientific Publishing, 2008.

Article:

Yuan, Yufei, and Michael J. Shaw. "Induction of fuzzy decision trees." *Fuzzy Sets and Systems* 69:2 (January 27, 1995): 125–139. Online at: dx.doi.org/10.1016/0165-0114(94)00229-Z

Websites:

Time-Management-Guide.com: www.time-management-guide.com/decision-tree.html

The Times 100—Decision tree analysis: tinyurl.com/msoh4o9

Wikipedia—Example of an investment decision tree: tinyurl.com/7t288ce

See Also:

★ Using Decision Analysis to Value R&D Projects (pp. 945–948)

✔ Applying Cost–Benefit Analysis to Project Appraisal (p. 1140)

✔ Costing a New Project (p. 1155)

Amos Tversky (p. 1316)

"To be dilatory about giving orders, but to expect absolute punctuality, that is called being a tormentor." Confucius

Understanding Key Performance Indicators

DEFINITION

A key performance indicator (KPI) is a way for an organization to measure its success or otherwise in reaching its defined goals or objectives. KPIs can be very useful as a means of assessing an organization's current position and deciding on new strategies if necessary. While KPIs are sometimes used to measure progress toward meeting financial goals, such as increasing turnover by 25% within six months, KPIs are more likely to be used to evaluate activities that are normally difficult to measure—for example, levels of customer satisfaction or employee participation. KPIs are probably most effective when used to monitor knowledge-based processes.

Whatever the set goal, KPIs must be measurable. Thus, a general goal of increasing the number of returning customers would be hard to measure using KPIs, but a defined goal of increasing the number of returning customers by 25% within one year would be measurable, as the parameters are clearly set. A KPI metric generally consists of a timeframe, a target, and a benchmark, which together measure the achievability of the goal.

The KPIs used by an organization will vary depending on the nature of its business. A call center operation uses a different set of KPIs from those used by a manufacturing firm.

KPIs are usually measured in real time, but the results are usually stored so that progress can be measured on a daily, weekly, yearly, or otherwise basis—such as hourly. KPIs are often derived from raw data. There are four basic subtypes of KPI:

- *Quantitative indicators* are numerical terms, such as the percentage of customers who buy widgets every year;
- *Practical indicators* interface with existing processes, such as lists of employee capabilities;
- *Directional indicators* demonstrate improvement or progress (or not), such as comparing last month's sales to this month's;
- *Actionable indicators* reflect an organization's ability to effect change, such as KPIs showing that the company would do better by outsourcing some processes.

ADVANTAGES

- KPIs show an organization where it is going wrong, enabling management to make the necessary changes to turn things around.
- KPIs give an organization an edge over its competitors.

DISADVANTAGES

- KPIs can be expensive to use, or even impossible (you cannot quantify staff morale, for example).
- KPIs have limitations to the exactness of results, which often may only be a rough guide rather than a concrete measurement.
- Once designed, KPIs can be difficult to change unless you are prepared to disregard carefully built-up comparison yardsticks, such as year-on-year customer satisfaction levels.
- KPIs may be difficult to compare among peers—competitive analysis may be best left to an external specialist.

ACTION CHECKLIST

✔ Make sure you design each KPI carefully and include all necessary factors to achieve measurable results.

✔ Only use KPIs that focus on whether an organization is achieving its goals or living up to its mission.

DOS AND DON'TS

DO

- Ensure that everyone in the organization is aware that KPIs are in use.
- Focus on meeting the outcomes.
- Use KPI results as a carrot to motivate staff, where you can be reasonably sure they can actually carry out change.

DON'T

- Don't use too many KPIs at the risk of staff spreading their focus too thinly.
- Don't attempt to use a KPI to measure something that cannot be measured at all.

MORE INFO

Books:

Franceschini, Fiorenzo, Maurizio Galetto, and Domenico Maisano. *Management by Measurement: Designing Key Indicators and Performance Measurement Systems*. Berlin: Springer, 2007.

Parmenter, David. *Key Performance Indicators: Developing, Implementing, and Using Winning KPIs*. Hoboken, NJ: Wiley, 2007.

Website:

EPM Review for KPI resources: www.epmreview.com

See Also:

★ Multidimensional Performance Measurement Using the Balanced Scorecard (pp. 897–899)
✔ Assessing Business Performance (p. 1144)
✔ Measuring Financial Health (p. 982)
✔ What Is Benchmarking? (p. 1184)

  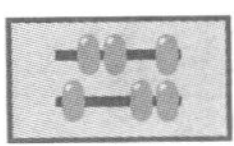      

Understanding Real Options

DEFINITION

Real options, sometimes also referred to as strategic options, are a tool that can be employed in capital budgeting analysis to help companies make better critical strategic decisions. As with financial market traded options, real options can be valued using pricing models. Real options give the holder the right but, importantly, not the obligation, to take a particular course of action. Real options are a mechanism by which a business can attempt to place an actual value on the choice of taking a particular option, and can play a valuable role in helping a company assess the financial implications of various strategic options. Real options are commonly used when dealing with the decision to initiate a new project or to abandon an existing project, depending on how, over time, actual events have differed from the original forecast. Used in conjunction with discounted cash flow techniques, real options provide businesses with a model as to how a certain course of action is likely to impact the business. Without the inclusion of real options, conventional discounted cash flow techniques can provide an incomplete assessment of the viability of a project, as they ignore the option to change course during the life of the project, perhaps taking a charge to abandon, delay, downscale, or even upscale the project.

Potential applications for real options as a decision-support model are many and varied. For example, an energy company may decide to proceed with a production operation if—and only if—the price of crude oil exceeds a level that makes the project commercially worthwhile. While standard discounted cash flow calculations may make the project appear risky and unattractive, the use of real options adds the ability to study the effects of changing course in return for a charge. This course could substantially increase the attractiveness of the venture, by factoring in the cost of the option of an effective escape from a completely negative outcome. Real options effectively make the project less risky by eliminating the "black or white" choice of one or the other. In this energy company example, real options might remove the risk of being stuck with the production costs for the life of the project, even if oil prices slipped to an unfavorable level. By attaching probability and costings on particular strategic options, the inclusion of real options can have significant impacts on expected net present value (NPV) calculations.

In addition to project viability analysis, real options can play an important role in applications such as process input options (for example, to help decide between various options in raw material sourcing), output mix options (for example, switching production from one product to another), production shutdown analysis, and output expansion options, as well project timing decision-making. The study of real options is an exciting, growing field of academic and business research, and the use of real options looks set to become a feature of mainstream business decision-making during the years ahead.

ACTION CHECKLIST

- ✔ Maximize the full potential of the real options methodology by putting all possible strategic options into the mix, not just the obvious ones.
- ✔ Qualify the list to ensure that all strategic options are actually viable.
- ✔ Make use of conventional discounted cash flow techniques.
- ✔ Assign initial inputs for real options.
- ✔ Make use of options modeling software to derive pricing information.

ADVANTAGES

- Real options are a powerful, flexible methodology, bringing together strategic planning with capital budgeting.
- The use of real options can give a business a significant strategic advantage, given their role in helping to identify the optimal timing for a project.
- The use of real options brings a dynamic element to the decision-making process, and can simulate this decision-making process throughout the project life cycle.
- Real options can help companies to avoid the potential pitfalls of pushing ahead with a new venture too early.

DISADVANTAGES

- Given that real options can be more conceptual than discounted cash flow techniques, real options can be more difficult to value with certainty.
- There is a view in some quarters that reliance on the use of real options exposes decision-making to managers' existing personal strategic biases.
- As with any methodology, calculations using real options rely on the quality and reliability of the input data.

DOS AND DON'TS

DO

- Utilize real options analysis alongside conventional techniques to demonstrate the full value of the model.
- As a project progresses, be prepared to refine/amend earlier numerical assumptions.
- Utilize NPV calculations to help verify your strategic analysis.

DON'T

- Don't ignore the value of educating managers and staff about the basic concepts behind real options analysis.
- Don't interpret the results of calculations as "gospel" on which the entire future of a business should be staked.

MORE INFO

Book:

Mun, Johnathan. *Real Options Analysis: Tools and Techniques for Valuing Strategic Investments and Decisions*. 2nd ed. Hoboken, NJ: Wiley, 2006.

Articles:

Boyarchenko, Svetlana, and Sergei Levendorski. "Practical guide to real options in discrete time." *International Economic Review* 48:1 (February 2007): 311–342. Online at: dx.doi.org/10.1111/j.1468-2354.2007.00427.x

Tong, Tony W., and Jeffrey J. Reuer. "Real options in multinational corporations: Organizational challenges and risk implications." *Journal of International Business Studies* 38:2 (March 2007): 215–230. Online at: dx.doi.org/10.1057/palgrave.jibs.8400260

Website:

Real options software provider: www.realoptionsvaluation.com

See Also:

★ Real Options: Opportunity from Risk (pp. 915–917)
★ Using Decision Analysis to Value R&D Projects (pp. 945–948)
✔ Managing the Time Value of Money (p. 979)
✔ Understanding Decision-Tree Analysis (p. 1179)

"The bonus system has proved to be wrong. Substantial cash bonuses do not reward the right kind of behaviour."
Andy Hornby

  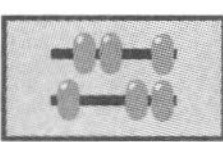      

Understanding Strategy Maps

DEFINITION

A strategy map, devised by Professors Robert S. Kaplan and David P. Norton, is a business management tool aimed at forging a strong link between a company's long-term strategies and its shorter-term operational activities. The concept of strategy mapping was originally developed by Kaplan and Norton in the "balanced scorecard," a means of assessing how successful a company is in terms of delivering on stated goals. While the basic notion of the balanced scorecard is "what you can't measure, you can't manage," further work aimed to help companies reassess their strategic goals. Kaplan and Norton subsequently shifted their focus to the principle of "what you can't measure, you can't describe" as a means to better utilize companies' intangible assets to help them achieve their objectives. The principle of strategic mapping of long-term strategy with shorter-term operational activities, previously merely one element of the balanced scorecard, was elevated to become a central strategy management tool.

Strategy maps aim to illustrate how a company links its macro strategy objectives with its key day-to-day operational elements from the four different perspectives: financial, customer, internal processes, and learning and growth. The financial element focuses primarily on enhancing the cost structure and utilizing assets towards greater productivity, while the customer element encourages companies to understand what sets them apart from their competitors. Though all elements of the strategy framework aim to improve areas such as attitudes to quality, service, partnerships, and company branding, the internal processes element aims to develop better product and service characteristics. Finally, the learning and growth element aims for companies to consider the skills and technologies that are needed to support the company's strategy. In all cases, the strategic mapping process seeks to engrain the appreciation of cause and effect. What can be improved on a "day-to-day level" is significant as, cumulatively, improvements can help improve a company's daily operational activities, helping it to achieve its longer-term strategic objectives. To better demonstrate the connections, the strategy map features a series of arrows linking objectives with individual operational activities.

ADVANTAGES

- Strategy mapping demonstrates to employees how seemingly minute improvements to operational activities can, cumulatively, contribute towards major efficiency and strategic objectives.
- Strategy mapping provides a clear, visual demonstration as to how short-term operational and medium- to long-term strategic objectives are closely aligned, helping to ensure greater "buy-in" from employees at all levels.
- Strategy mapping helps to demonstrate how a company's intangible assets can improve stockholder value.
- Strategy mapping provides a potential solution for managers unable to identify why certain strategies are not delivering tangible performance improvements.

DISADVANTAGES

- Strategy mapping requires "buy in" from individuals across all levels of the organization. If management fails to convince the workforce of the potential benefits of a successful medium- to long-term outcome, employees may feel disenfranchised from the potential benefits of improved corporate performance.
- Though strategic in its macro focus, strategy mapping is unlikely to deliver a single, massive leap forward in any single aspect. Rather, the considerable ultimate benefits of strategic mapping are often comprised of many, seemingly minor, single aspects.

ACTION CHECKLIST

✔ Ensure that everyone within the organization appreciates that strategy mapping is a technique which aims to align individuals' actions with the strategic objective.

✔ As improvements are likely to be incremental, ensure that the benefits are recognized and built on through an emphasis on the feedback/learning input.

DOS AND DON'TS

DO

- Aim to align personal performance improvement goals with those of the company.
- Base remuneration on goals related to improvements in the performance of the overall business. Setting individual performance objectives with related incentive payouts could be counterproductive if individuals shift their focus from delivering collective benefits to the pursuit of personal objectives.

DON'T

- Don't expect giant and immediate leaps forward in terms of operational efficiency, finances or customer experiences. Strategic mapping is more likely to generate numerous, gradual, incremental improvements across the organization.
- Don't set remuneration based on individual targets. Agree only on personal performance goals when you are confident that achieving them will contribute to overall performance improvement across the business.

MORE INFO

Books:

Kaplan, Robert S., and David P. Norton. *Balanced Scorecard: Translating Strategy into Action*. Boston, MA: Harvard Business School Press, 1996.

Kaplan, Robert S., and David P. Norton. *Strategy Maps: Converting Intangible Assets into Tangible Outcomes*. Boston, MA: Harvard Business School Press, 2004.

Articles:

Irwin, D. "Strategy mapping in the public sector." *Long Range Planning* 35:6 (December 2002): 637–647. Online at: dx.doi.org/10.1016/S0024-6301(02)00158-9

Kaplan, Robert S., and David P. Norton "Having trouble with your strategy? Then map it." *Harvard Business Review* (September–October 2000). Online at: tinyurl.com/33zoowa

Scholey, Cam. "Strategy maps: A step-by-step guide to measuring, managing and communicating the plan." *Journal of Business Strategy* 26:3 (2005): 12–19. Online at: dx.doi.org/10.1108/02756660510597065

Website:

Balanced Scorecard Institute: www.balancedscorecard.org

"**If you have someone on a job, use him. If you can't, get rid of him.**" Frederick Herzberg

  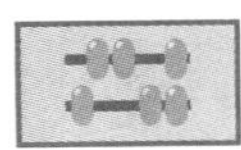   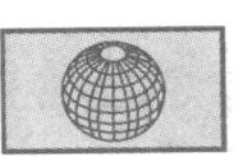   

Understanding the Financial Aspects of Employing People

DEFINITION

The financial aspects of hiring an employee go far beyond the visible cost of paying them a salary. There are many factors and hidden costs that need to be taken into account. National and international legislation also determine a company's financial obligations to an employee to a certain extent. Thus, the true cost of hiring a worker will be more than the agreed wage, and the additional costs need to be budgeted for in the accounts.

Apart from the salary, an employer pays additional up-front costs for items such as the employer's portion of the social security and pension contributions. In many countries employers also have a legal obligation to pay holiday pay and sickness benefit contributions, as well as collecting taxes for the government and paying tax credits to an employee where there is entitlement. Where women of child-bearing age are employed, there is also the cost of maternity leave to consider, the length of which depends on national laws; companies can usually claw most of this back from the government to cover the cost of hiring a temporary replacement. Other legislative issues to consider include matters such as a legal minimum wage and, in some countries, such as the United Kingdom, companies have to meet the cost of running checks to ensure they are not hiring illegal immigrants.

Particularly in the European Union, many countries have employment protection legislation in place, making it difficult for companies to fire staff with little or no notice. Companies therefore need to budget for funds to cover periods when they may need to downsize quickly to reduce costs. Garden leave, where an employee is paid to stay at home instead of working out their notice, is another expense that may need to be covered.

Other staffing costs that need to be budgeted for include items such as training (whether one-off or regular sessions), insurance relating to safety in the workplace, and pay rises. Companies seeking the best staff may wish to offer perks such as private health insurance, travel subsidies to and from the workplace, childcare allowances, and extras such as gym memberships. In very large corporations it is also becoming common practice to use a golden parachute clause in the employment contract. This ensures that an employee will receive certain major benefits if employment is terminated, typically including severance pay, cash bonuses, and share options.

On top of all these costs, there is the additional cost of administration. Whereas small firms often outsource payroll administration, large companies typically have qualified payroll accountants working in-house, as well as a human resources department to handle all the related issues.

ACTION CHECKLIST

- ✔ Have in place accountants experienced in payroll budgeting.
- ✔ Hire or outsource to qualified HR staff who are experienced in the legal and financial aspects of employing staff.
- ✔ Develop a long-term strategy for hiring staff as the business expands or, in some cases, downsizes.
- ✔ Ensure that you have considered and budgeted for all possible scenarios when calculating the salaries you will offer.

DOS AND DON'TS

DO

- Familiarize yourself with the legal requirements in your country.
- Look at tax breaks that are sometimes offered for hiring certain kinds of staff.
- Budget for unexpected costs such as several resignations happening at once, or the costs arising from a legal dispute over the terms of a contract.

DON'T

- Don't try to cut legal corners—the penalties are usually severe.
- Don't forget that even advertising for staff is a cost you need to account for.

MORE INFO

Books:

Ashenfelter, Orley C., and Richard Layard (eds). *Handbook of Labor Economics*. Amsterdam: Elsevier/North-Holland, 1986.

Blundell, Richard, and Thomas MaCurdy. "Labour supply." In Durlauf, Steven N., and Lawrence E. Blume (eds). *The New Palgrave Dictionary of Economics*. 2nd ed. Basingstoke, UK: Palgrave Macmillan, 2008. (Dictionary online at: www.dictionaryofeconomics.com/dictionary).

Stone, Raymond J. *Human Resource Management*. 8th ed. Milton, Australia: Wiley, 2013.

See Also:

★ Managing Retirement Costs (pp. 77–79)

★ Return on Talent (pp. 927–928)

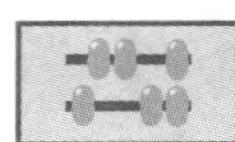

What Is Benchmarking?

DEFINITION

Benchmarking is a tool for analyzing an organization or company's processes and activities to see if they represent best practice. The aim of benchmarking is always to raise an organization's performance to the highest standard.

ACTION CHECKLIST

1. Planning the benchmarking project

- ✔ First understand your own business before making comparisons with others.
- ✔ Look at the business units within your organization and identify their outputs.
- ✔ Decide which are the key processes to benchmark, ensuring that any improvements will be apparent to customers.

2. Select targets

- ✔ Look for processes in your own and other industries that match those of your own organization.
- ✔ Identify the organizations that are best in class for those processes by talking to customers, analysts, trade publications, and suppliers.

3. Decide methodology

- ✔ As there are so many types of process to be measured, information will come from a variety of sources, including structured interviews, surveys, and publicly available data.
- ✔ Make sure your analysis compares "apple with apples" and is as accurate as possible.

4. Collect data and analyze discrepancies

- ✔ Establish what is best practice for each benchmarked process.
- ✔ Compare the gaps between your organization's performance and those benchmarked processes.

5. Make improvements

- ✔ Modify processes to equal or raise your company's performance above that of the highest standard measured.

As the idea is to evaluate the outcome of specific activities, the comparisons do not have to be drawn from competitors. It may be possible to use generic benchmarks based on data from processes that are common across an industry, or functional benchmarks for processes that exist in many unrelated industries. Alternatively, internal benchmarking can compare common activities across the different divisions of an organization.

If it is felt that the most effective data will come from similar businesses, there are two possible approaches: collaborative benchmarking, which is when two or more companies share information on processes; and competitive benchmarking, where the performance of competitors is analyzed. The latter is frequently carried out by a third party.

It is not unusual for competing companies to share benchmarking data. It is not necessary to publish commercially sensitive information in order for a number of companies within an industry to benefit from improvements in efficiency.

The benchmarking information will come from a variety of sources, including interviews, surveys, and published data. Care has to be taken that not only is the information directly comparable, but also that it includes all the relevant areas. It is not uncommon for companies to become fixated on cost-cutting, for example, while ignoring customer care, perhaps because it is less easy to measure.

Once the results of a benchmarking exercise have been presented and agreed, the information can be used as a basis for changes that should improve the organization's processes. These can then provide a baseline for the next round.

ADVANTAGES

- Benchmarking can provide tangible and measurable improvements for an organization.
- It opens up organizations to different ways of operating.
- It provides an objective measure of the success of an organization's processes.
- It encourages focus on key areas for improvement.

DISADVANTAGES

- Benchmarking can be expensive and time-consuming.
- Comparisons may be inappropriate for some processes.
- It can give an organization the answers it wants to hear.
- Comparisons just show that one organization is different from another.
- It can just encourage a process of playing catch-up rather than innovation.

DOS AND DON'TS

DO

- Pick variables that are relatively easy to measure.
- Ensure that the processes being measured are directly comparable.
- Put sufficient human and financial resources into the project.
- Focus on variables that will respond to actions.
- Produce a succinct summary of benefits for senior management.

DON'T

- Don't spread your net too wide by selecting unmanageable areas to research.
- Don't assume your competition's success is solely due to the differences you've measured.
- Don't forget about less easily measured areas such as customer satisfaction.

MORE INFO

Books:

McNair, Carol J., and Kathleen H. J. Leibfried. *Benchmarking: A Tool for Continuous Improvement*. New York: HarperBusiness, 1992.

Watson, Gregory H. *Strategic Benchmarking Reloaded with Six Sigma: Improving Your Company's Performance Using Global Best Practice*. Hoboken, NJ: Wiley, 2007.

Zairi, Mohamed. *Effective Management of Benchmarking Projects: Practical Guidelines & Examples of Best Practice*. Oxford: Butterworth-Heinemann, 1998.

Website:

Global Benchmarking Network: www.globalbenchmarking.org

"The principal weapon companies have to lift efficiency is to apply technology more thoughtfully." Hamish McRae

CALCULATIONS AND RATIOS

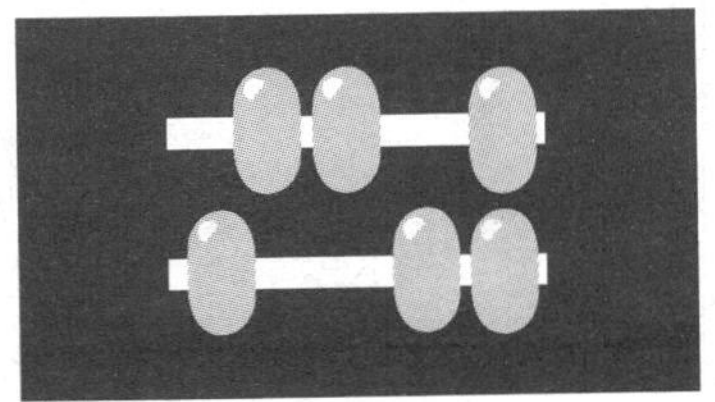

  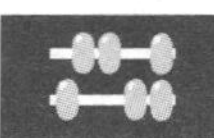      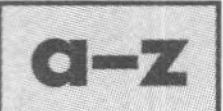

Calculations and Ratios

A Calculations and Ratios concept explains what is being measured, its importance and practical application, and tricks of the trade, which provides the reader with pointers on interpreting the results.

The Calculations and Ratios, written by specialists, provide essential mathematical calculations for target setting and maintaining standards within an enterprise. They not only address key management questions on the day-to-day financial welfare of a business, but also provide indicators that can impact on strategic decision making.

But reader beware, numbers are only a reflection of firm's financial health at any given moment in time, so it is essential to understand the dynamics that sit behind the figures—and which way they are moving.

  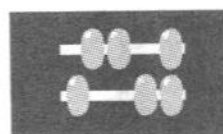   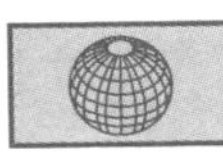  
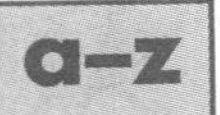

Contents

  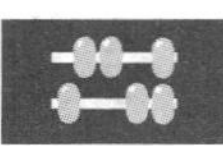      

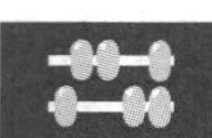

Accounts Payable Turnover Ratio

WHAT IT MEASURES

The rate at which a company pays off its suppliers. The accounts payable turnover ratio is a short-term liquidity measure that quantifies how well a company pays its average payable amount over a single accounting period.

WHY IT IS IMPORTANT

Investors want to know how quickly your company pays its bills, which is why the accounts payable turnover ratio is important. This ratio measures your company's short-term liquidity. Investors consider a falling ratio a sign that the company is taking longer to pay suppliers than before, which might suggest cash flow problems. However, a rising ratio would suggest a relatively short time between purchase of goods and services and payment.

HOW IT WORKS IN PRACTICE

The accounts payable turnover ratio is based on the total purchases made from suppliers, divided by the average accounts payable amount over the same period, as below:

$$\text{APTR} = \frac{\text{Total supplier purchases}}{\text{Average accounts payable}}$$

For example, if a company makes $10 million in purchases from suppliers during a year, and at any given point is owed an average $2 million in accounts payable, then the accounts payable turnover ratio for the period would be 5.

TRICKS OF THE TRADE

- Most companies are required to settle accounts within 30 days to avoid damaging credit relationships, meaning there are 12 risk-free cycles in any year. A ratio of 6 suggests a company is paying its bills less often than is possible, while a ratio above 12 suggests the opposite.
- On its own, the ratio does not tell investors a great deal. The accounts payable turnover ratio must be compared against the industry average to see if the business is competitive. In addition, the ratio should be tracked over successive accounting periods to provide insight into cash flow.
- A falling accounts payable turnover ratio may suggest one of two scenarios. First, the business might be experiencing cash flow problems or disputed invoices with suppliers, which leads to slower payment. However, a successful business may extend payments to make the best possible use of cash and might have negotiated more favorable payment terms with suppliers. Additional analysis is therefore advised when faced with a changing accounts payable turnover ratio.
- An alternative approach that some experts believe is more intuitive than accounts payable turnover ratio is "days payable outstanding." This expresses turnover as the average length of time in days between purchase of goods and services, and payment. To calculate days payable outstanding, simply divide the accounts payable turnover ratio by 365.

MORE INFO

Book:

White, Gerald I., Ashwinpaul C. Sondhi, and Dov Fried. *The Analysis and Use of Financial Statements*. 3rd ed. Chichester, UK: Wiley, 2003.

Article:

Cars, Andreas. "Dynamic current ratio: What it is and how to use it." *Investopedia*. Online at: www.investopedia.com/articles/02/090302.asp

Accounts Receivable Turnover

One of several measures used to assess operating performance, accounts receivable turnover also helps in appraising a company's credit policy and its cash flow.

WHAT IT MEASURES

The number of times in each accounting period, typically a year, that a company converts credit sales into cash.

WHY IT IS IMPORTANT

A high turnover figure is desirable because it indicates that a company collects revenues effectively, and that its customers pay bills promptly. A high figure also suggests that a company's credit and collection policies are sound.

In addition, the measurement is a reasonably good indicator of cash flow, and of overall operating efficiency.

HOW IT WORKS IN PRACTICE

The formula for accounts receivable turnover is straightforward. Simply divide the average amount of receivables into annual credit sales:

$$\text{Receivables turnover} = \frac{\text{Sales}}{\text{Receivables}}$$

If, for example, a company's sales are $4.5 million and its average receivables are $375,000, its receivables turnover is:

$$\frac{4{,}500{,}000}{375{,}000} = 12$$

TRICKS OF THE TRADE

- It is important to use the average amount of receivables over the period considered. Otherwise, receivables could be misleading for a company whose products are seasonal or are sold at irregular intervals.
- The measurement is also helpful to a company that is designing or revising credit terms.
- Accounts receivable turnover is among the measures that comprise asset utilization ratios, also called activity ratios.

MORE INFO

Book:

Salek, John G. *Accounts Receivable Management: Best Practices*. Hoboken, NJ: Wiley, 2005.

See Also:

Asset Utilization (pp. 1195–1196)

  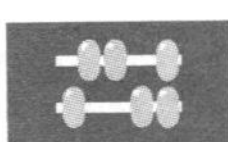      

Accrual Rate

WHAT IT MEASURES

In the pensions world, accrual rate is the rate at which an individual's entitlement to pension benefit builds up related to his or her salary, often in an employer's pension scheme.

WHY IT IS IMPORTANT

It enables an individual to receive a pension benefit that is predictable and fair, while also providing employers with a simple way to predict the potential liabilities of a pension scheme. If your organization's pension is based on an accrual rate, employees earn (or "accrue") a monthly pension amount each year they work. If the employee earns a full pension, they will receive the sum of all those annual accruals as the total pension amount. The higher the accrual, the higher the eventual pension pay-out.

HOW IT WORKS IN PRACTICE

Accrual rates are usually expressed as a fraction of final pay. They vary between different countries and industry sectors, but are generally between 1/50 and 1/80. In the case of an accrual rate of 1/60, this means the employee receives 1/60th of their pensionable earnings for each year of eligible service. To calculate the pension of an employee who retires at the age of 58 after 30 years service on a final salary of $70,000, apply this formula including the accrual rate:

$$\text{Pension liability} = \text{Accrual rate} \times \text{Final salary} \times \text{Years of service}$$

So, in this case the pension liability is:

$$\frac{1}{60} \times \$70,000 \times 30 = \$35,000$$

The lower the denominator in an accrual rate, the higher the accrued benefits for each year of eligible service. So an accrual rate of 1/50 would create a different result:

$$\frac{1}{50} \times \$70,000 \times 30 = \$42,000$$

TRICKS OF THE TRADE

- Accrual rate can be applied to an employee's "final" salary, or may sometimes be applied to what is known as the "best five"—the average of the five highest salaries an employee earns over their entire eligible years of service.
- An accelerated accrual is one that is higher than the typical 1/60 and 1/80 found in occupational pension schemes. They are most frequently used in the public sector.
- An accrual rate can sometimes be expressed as a percentage, such as 1.25% (which is equivalent to 1/80).
- Accrual rates can also be expressed as dollar amounts rather than percentages or fractions. These schemes tend to be less advantageous for employees, since the employer's contribution is not tied to the employee's salary and will not necessarily increase at the same pace.
- Accrual rates can be applied to other employee benefits (commonly holiday and sick pay), but may also be used to refer to the interest added to certain sorts of mortgage loans.

Acid-Test Ratio

A second liquidity ratio that evaluates creditworthiness, the acid-test ratio stands as a more stringent test than the current ratio, hence its name.

WHAT IT MEASURES

How quickly a company's assets can be turned into cash, which is why assessment of a company's liquidity is also known as the quick ratio, or simply the acid ratio.

WHY IT IS IMPORTANT

Regardless of how this ratio is labeled, it is considered a highly reliable indicator of a company's financial strength and its ability to meet its short-term obligations. Because inventory can sometimes be difficult to liquidate, the acid-test ratio deducts inventory from current assets before they are compared with current liabilities—which is what distinguishes it from the current ratio.

Potential creditors like to use the acid-test ratio because it reveals how a company would fare if it had to pay off its bills under the worst possible conditions. Indeed, the assumption behind the acid-test ratio is that creditors are howling at the door demanding immediate payment, and that an enterprise has no time to sell off its inventory, or any of its stock.

HOW IT WORKS IN PRACTICE

The acid-test ratio's formula can be expressed in two ways, but both essentially reach the same conclusion. The more common expression is:

$$\text{Acid-test ratio} = \frac{(\text{Current assets} - \text{Inventory})}{\text{Current liabilities}}$$

If, for example, current assets total $7,700, inventory amounts to $1,200, and current liabilities total $4,500, then:

$$\frac{(7,700 - 1,200)}{4,500} = 1.44$$

A variation of this formula ignores inventory altogether, distinguishes assets as cash, receivables, and short-term investments, and then divides the sum of the three by the total current liabilities:

$$\text{Acid-test ratio} = \frac{(\text{Cash} + \text{Accounts receivable} + \text{Short-term investments})}{\text{Current liabilities}}$$

If, for example, cash totals $2,000, receivables total $3,000, short-term investments total $1,000, and liabilities total $4,800, then:

$$\frac{(2,000 + 3,000 + 1,000)}{4,800} = 1.25$$

There are two other ways to appraise liquidity, although neither is as commonly used: the cash ratio is the sum of cash and marketable securities divided by current liabilities; net quick assets is determined by adding cash, accounts receivable, and marketable securities, then subtracting current liabilities from that sum.

        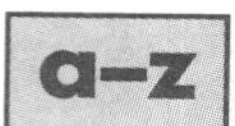

TRICKS OF THE TRADE

- In general, the quick ratio should be 1:1 or better. This means that a company has at least a unit's worth of easily convertible assets for each unit of its current liabilities. A high quick ratio usually reflects a sound, well-managed organization in no danger of imminent collapse, even in the extreme and unlikely event that its sales ceased immediately. On the other hand, companies with ratios of less than 1 could not pay their current liabilities, and should be looked at with extreme care.
- While a ratio of 1:1 is generally acceptable to most creditors, acceptable quick ratios vary by industry, as do almost all financial ratios. No ratio, in fact, is especially meaningful without knowledge of the business from which it originates. For example, a declining quick ratio with a stable current ratio may indicate that a company has built up too much inventory; but it could also suggest that the company has greatly improved its collection system.
- Some experts regard the acid-test ratio as an extreme version of the working capital ratio because it uses only cash and equivalents, and excludes inventory. An acid-test ratio that is notably lower than the working capital ratio often means that inventory makes up a large proportion of current assets. An example would be retail stores.
- Comparing quick ratios over an extended period of time can be used to signal developing trends in a company. While modest declines in the quick ratio do not automatically spell trouble, uncovering the reasons for changes can help to find ways to nip potential problems in the bud.
- Like the current ratio, the quick ratio is a snapshot, and a company can manipulate its figures to make it look robust at a given point in time.
- Investors who suddenly become keenly interested in a company's quick ratio may signal their anticipation of a downturn in the company's business or in the general economy.

MORE INFO

See Also:

✔ Measuring Liquidity (p. 983)
Current Ratio (p. 1213)
Liquidity Ratio Analysis (pp. 1232–1233)

Activity-Based Costing

GETTING STARTED

Activity-based costing (ABC) attempts to create the big picture—crystal-clear, full, and accurate—by painting assorted little pictures.

- ABC identifies the relationship between a business activity and all the resources needed to conduct it by assigning costs to each of those resources, thus presenting the true total expense of the entire activity.
- ABC can account for so-called "soft," or indirect, operating costs, and thus produce a more revealing, and perhaps startlingly different, financial picture than other accounting methodologies such as standard costing might offer.
- Used properly, ABC helps management to distinguish operations that add value from those that do not, permitting more informed decisions about such matters as pricing, product mix, capital investments, and organizational change.
- In turn, ABC's advocates praise it as a more effective tool to identify and control costs, improve productivity, and increase profits.

FAQS

When did ABC start?

ABC came of age in the 1980s amid manufacturers' furious efforts to raise the quality of their products while simultaneously eliminating every unnecessary cost from their operations. The dramatic improvements realized by manufacturers have led to ABC becoming a widely used tool, especially in the manufacturing industry.

What are the basic steps of ABC?

There are five:

1 identify the product or service to be studied;
2 determine all the resources and processes that are required to create the product or deliver the service, and their respective costs;
3 determine the "cost drivers" for each resource: the cost of labor as well as raw materials;
4 collect costs and other data, such as time taken, for each process and resource;
5 use the data to calculate the overall cost of the product or service.

What are ABC's principal advantages?

First, ABC can gauge virtually any activity, be it a manufacturing process, a business process, the performance of a service, or an administrative operation. Second, it considers a much wider variety of resources and materials than more traditional accounting methodologies, and can thus present a more complete picture.

What are ABC's primary weaknesses?

It can be a very time-consuming exercise because of the volume of data it demands. Also, if not managed properly, ABC can transform every manager into an accountant whose energies become fixed on tracking the costs of the activity, rather than on tracking and perfecting the activity itself.

What kind of business sectors use ABC?

The list ranges from accountants to zoologists. It may be especially helpful for knowledge-based businesses that rely primarily on human services and related resources, whose total costs may be difficult to measure with more traditional accounting yardsticks.

What is critical to ABC's success?

Without gaining and maintaining the enduring commitment of all individuals, even a modestly detailed initiative will probably fail. It's also best to start with pilot projects to demonstrate success.

What preliminary steps are needed?

First, an organization must understand its activities and the resources that these require. Second, it must understand thoroughly the amount of information required, and the expense of generating that information. It must also determine what level of accuracy will be acceptable.

MAKING IT HAPPEN

Creating an ABC cost accounting system requires three preliminary steps:

1 converting to an accrual basis of accounting;
2 defining cost centers and cost allocation;
3 determining process and procedure costs.

  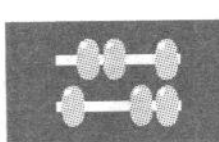 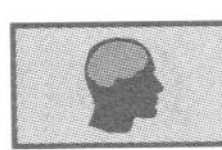  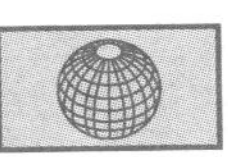   

Businesses have traditionally relied on the cash basis of accounting, which recognizes income when received and expenses when paid. ABC's foundation is the accrual basis. The numbers this statement presents are assigned to the various procedures performed during a given period. Cost centers are a company's identifiable products and services, but also include specific and detailed tasks within these broader activities. Defining cost centers will of course vary by business and method of operation. What is critical to ABC is the inclusion of all activities and all resources. Once these steps have been taken, the results are often more than satisfying.

Banks and financial services firms, for example, have long used ABC-like methods to confirm that investments in automated teller machines would be both cheaper than continuing to rely on tellers and clerks and would be in their customers' best interests.

Railroad companies have used the methodology to determine the cost of processing bills of lading by hand, fax, and the internet. Studying such costs confirmed the wisdom of using e-commerce, generating annual savings of up to $1 million.

Publishers launching "new media" services can more accurately calculate the true costs of creating material for them, then compare such costs to those required to produce traditional publications, and draw more accurate conclusions about what best serves their long- and short-term interests.

Law firms are better positioned to confirm that the hourly fees they charge—no matter how princely they may at first appear—do, in fact, enable them to provide their services profitably.

Finally, healthcare providers use ABC to measure profitability, eliminate unnecessary costs, and plan for change. A medical practice that knows the actual cost of providing a specific service, for example, can make far better decisions about the price of managed health care.

For instance, let's say the Apple-a-Day Medical Clinic includes three physicians, Drs Peel, Core, and Stem. Their clinic has an in-house laboratory and a radiology department. All direct revenues and expenses are allocated to the physician who performs the service and incurs the expense. Indirect variable overhead costs are allocated to each physician based on the proportion of total revenues that each generates in a given period. Fixed overhead costs are divided equally among physicians. Because of their respective incomes and expense allocations, each physician would represent a separate cost center.

Additional cost centers for this medical practice could be laboratory, radiology, and administration. As cost centers are defined, they could further be classified as, say, "patient service centers" or "support centers." In this example, laboratory, radiology, and each individual physician's activity would be patient service centers, while administration would be a support center.

Once cost centers are identified, management teams can begin studying the activities each one engages in and allocating the expenses each one incurs, including the cost of employee services. In this healthcare scenario, activities would range from actual treatment by physicians and nurses, X-rays, medical tests and assessments of their results, plus such administrative support services as personnel, bookkeeping, rent, utilities, property insurance, office supplies, advertising, telecommunications expenses, and equipment costs related to the administrative function. Rent, utilities, and property insurance are usually allocated on the basis of the square footage that the particular activity covers.

Tracking and allocating the detailed costs of individual activities and procedures can be accomplished by different methods, with various degrees of accuracy. The more detailed the cost analysis, of course, the greater the accuracy of the data. Then again, as the detail increases, so does the time and expense.

The most appropriate method is developed from time studies and direct expense allocation. Management teams that choose this method will need to devote several months to data collection in order to generate sufficient information to establish the personnel components of each activity's total cost. The cost of this exercise itself can be significant, but also worthwhile. Proponents say ABC has resulted in cost savings worth as much as 14 times the cost of the exercise. More importantly, the exercise has provided solid documentation for decisions that "seemed correct," as a Chrysler Corporation team once reported, "but could not be supported with hard evidence."

Time studies establish the average amount of time required to complete each task, plus best- and worst-case performances. Only those resources actually used are factored into the cost computation; unused resources are reported separately. These studies can also advise management how best to monitor and allocate expenses which might otherwise be expressed as part of general overhead, or go undetected altogether.

Notably, determining how much of an operation's personnel is underused or unused can significantly help management planning, specifically by exposing activities that are overstaffed or understaffed. This can be especially helpful to any knowledge-based business, since payroll is almost always its highest cost. Moreover, in any business, the more efficiently an enterprise deploys its personnel, the more profitable it will be.

In addition, this type of analysis can also establish useful performance benchmarks within an operation, and might even allow for a comparison of procedure costs with industry averages.

COMMON MISTAKES

Getting Caught Up in the Details

Notwithstanding its successes, ABC remains a tool, not an end in itself. Organizations can lose sight of that fact if they are not careful, and end up allowing it to dominate their working lives.

The enormity and complexity of such a project should never be underestimated. The data requirements alone are daunting. It is all too easy to get caught up in ABC's details and mechanics. In turn, estimating some costs is often recommended, to minimize the level of detail.

At the same time, however, some details are important prerequisites of objectivity and success. For example, if time studies are not used, some other measure must be used to allocate personnel and related costs, as well as indirect costs such as percentage of revenues or income, or the number of customer calls. These methods require far less time for compiling data and are less

MORE INFO

Books:

Burk, Karen B., and Douglas W. Webster. *Activity Based Costing and Performance*. Fairfax, VA: American Management Systems, 1994.

Grossman, Theodore, and John Leslie Livingstone. *The Portable MBA in Finance and Accounting*. 4th ed. Hoboken, NJ: Wiley, 2009.

Article:

Ness, Joseph A., and Thomas G. Cucuzza. "Tapping the full potential of ABC." *Harvard Business Review* (July/August 1995). Online at: tinyurl.com/np4zzv9

Website:

Activity Based Costing Association (ABCA™): abcbenchmarking.com

See Also:

★ Profitability Analysis Using Activity-Based Costing (pp. 908–910)

✔ Understanding Activity-Based Costing (p. 989)

  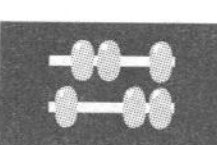      

costly, but drawbacks abound. For one thing, accuracy suffers, and they are almost always subjective, potentially to the point of compromising the entire initiative. Being far less precise, these alternative methods do not differentiate between used and unused personnel resources, and will not provide information on unused capacity or trends in procedure costs.

Without the aid of computer software that has been developed to automate the process, ABC can be hopelessly time-consuming. Indeed, unaided by technology, ABC might well be hoist with its own petard and exposed as an outrageous waste of time.

Like any cost accounting system, activity-based costing is not static. Once established, it needs to be maintained and updated as business conditions and organizations change.

Finally, in delivering its crystal-clear pictures, activity-based costing also has the potential to make individual champions of particular products or services squirm, because it may reveal them to be far more expensive than they might otherwise appear. All the more reason for advocating caution: "Watch out what you wish for!" If a management team is to reduce and eliminate costs, it must first identify them and grasp their impact on specific processes or products. Because activity-based costing can paint a single picture that reveals all the individual direct and indirect costs a business incurs in a given operation, it can be a powerful tool for both assessing current operations and guiding prompt and intelligent reactions as circumstances change. In fact, it's also known as activity-based management (ABM).

Alpha and Beta Values of a Security

Both alpha and beta are investment measures used to quantify risk and reward.

WHAT THEY MEASURE

A security's performance, adjusted for risk, compared to overall market behavior.

WHY THEY ARE IMPORTANT

Just as coaches would expect their most accomplished athletes to perform at a higher level than others, investors expect more from higher-risk investments. Alpha and beta give investors a quick indication of just how risky a stock or fund is.

Alpha is defined as "the return a security or a portfolio would be expected to earn if the market's rate of return were zero."

Beta is a means of measuring the volatility (or risk) of a stock or fund in comparison with the market as a whole. The beta of a stock or fund can be any value, positive or negative, but usually is between +0.25 and +1.75.

Alpha expresses the difference between the return expected from a stock or mutual fund, given its beta rating, and the return actually produced. A stock or fund that returns more than its beta would predict has a positive alpha, while one that returns less than the amount predicted by beta has a negative alpha. A large positive alpha indicates a strong performance, while a large negative alpha indicates a dismal performance.

HOW THEY WORK IN PRACTICE

To begin with, the market itself is assigned a beta of 1.0. If a stock or fund has a beta of 1.2, this means its price is likely to rise or fall by 12% when the overall market rises or falls by 10%; a beta of 0.7 means the stock or fund price is likely to move up or down at 70% of the level of the market change.

In practice, an alpha of 0.4% means the stock or fund in question outperformed the market-based return estimate by 0.4%. An alpha of −0.6% means the return was 0.6% less than would have been predicted from the change in the market alone.

Both alpha and beta should be readily available on request from investment firms, because the figures appear in standard performance reports. It is always best to ask for them, because calculating a stock's alpha rating requires first knowing a stock's beta rating, and calculating beta is a challenge! It is based on linear regression analysis, the week-to-week percentage changes in the given stock's price, and the corresponding week-to-week percentage price change in a market index, over a given period of time, often 24 to 36 months. In short, beta calculations can involve mathematical complexities.

If it's any consolation, calculating alpha is far less taxing, provided the requisite data are available. The formula is:

$$\text{Alpha} = \text{Actual return} - \text{Risk-free return} - \text{Beta} \times (\text{Index return} - \text{Risk-free return})$$

If a mutual fund with a beta rating of 1.1 returned 35%, while its benchmark index returned 30%, and a US Treasury bill returned 4% (T-bill returns are usually used as the "risk-free investment"), then the fund's alpha would equal 2.4%, based on the formula:

$$\begin{aligned} 35\% - 4\% - 1.1 \times (30\% - 4\%) &= 31\% - 1.1 \times 26\% \\ &= 31\% - 28.6\% \\ &= 2.4\% \end{aligned}$$

TRICKS OF THE TRADE

- The underlying rationale for both alpha and beta is that the return of a stock or mutual fund should at least exceed that of a "risk-free" investment such as a US Treasury bill.
- Stocks of many utilities have a beta of less than 1. Conversely, most high-tech, NASDAQ-based stocks have a beta greater than 1; they offer a higher rate of return but are also risky.
- Alpha is often used to assess the performance of a portfolio manager. However, a low alpha score doesn't necessarily reflect poor performance by a fund manager, any more than a high alpha score means that a manager's performance is outstanding. At times, factors beyond a manager's control affect alpha values.

MORE INFO

Reports:

Schwab Performance Technologies. "Troubleshooting an incorrect alpha." September 13, 2012. Online at: tinyurl.com/q4cza7j [PDF].

Schwab Performance Technologies. "Troubleshooting an incorrect beta." July 9, 2012. Online at: tinyurl.com/opb7qel [PDF].

        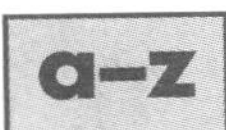

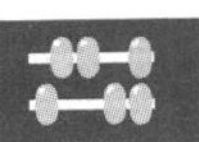

Amortization

Amortization is often regarded as being the same as depreciation, but although the two accounting practices can be difficult to distinguish, there are differences between them. Amortization is also used in connection with loans, although that is not the primary focus here.

WHAT IT MEASURES

Amortization is a method of recovering (deducting or writing off) the capital costs of intangible assets over a fixed period of time. Its calculation is virtually identical to the straight-line method of depreciation.

Amortization also refers to the establishment of a schedule for repaying the principal and interest on a loan in equal amounts over a period of time. Because computers have made this a simple calculation, business references to amortization tend to focus more on the term's first definition.

WHY IT IS IMPORTANT

Amortization enables a company to identify its true costs, and thus its net income, more precisely. In the course of their business, most enterprises acquire intangible assets such as a patent for an invention, or a well-known brand or trademark. Since these assets can contribute to the revenue growth of the business, they can be—and are allowed to be—deducted against those future revenues over a period of years, provided the procedure conforms to accepted accounting practices.

For tax purposes, the distinction is not always made between amortization and depreciation, yet amortization remains a viable financial accounting concept in its own right.

HOW IT WORKS IN PRACTICE

Amortization is computed using the straight-line method of depreciation: divide the initial cost of the intangible asset by the estimated useful life of that asset. For example, if it costs $10,000 to acquire a patent and it has an estimated useful life of 10 years, the amortized amount per year is $1,000.

$$\frac{10{,}000}{10} = \$1{,}000 \text{ per year}$$

The amount of amortization accumulated since the asset was acquired appears on the organization's balance sheet as a deduction under the amortized asset.

While that formula is straightforward, amortization can also incorporate a variety of noncash charges to net earnings and/or asset values, such as depletion, write-offs, prepaid expenses, and deferred charges. Accordingly, there are many rules to regulate how these charges appear on financial statements. The rules are different in each country, and are occasionally changed, so it is necessary to stay abreast of them and rely on expert advice.

For financial reporting purposes, an intangible asset is amortized over a period of years. The amortizable life—"useful life"—of an intangible asset is the period over which it gives economic benefit. Several factors are considered when determining this useful life; for example, demand and competition, effects of obsolescence, legal or contractual limitations, renewal provisions, and service life expectations.

Intangibles that can be amortized include:

- **Copyrights**, based on the amount paid either to purchase them or to develop them internally, plus the costs incurred in producing the work (wages or materials, for example). At present, a copyright is granted for the life of the author plus 70 years. However, the estimated useful life of a copyright is usually far shorter than its legal life, and it is generally amortized over a fairly short period.
- **Cost of a franchise**, including any fees paid to the franchiser, as well as legal costs or expenses incurred in the acquisition. A franchise granted for a limited period should be amortized over its life. If the franchise has an indefinite life, it should be amortized over a reasonable period, not to exceed 40 years.
- **Covenants not to compete**: an agreement by the seller of a business not to engage in a competing business in a certain area for a specific period of time. The cost of the not-to-compete covenant should be amortized over the period covered by the covenant unless its estimated economic life is expected to be shorter.
- **Easement costs** that grant a right of way may be amortized if there is a limited and specified life.
- **Organization costs** incurred when forming a corporation or a partnership, including legal fees, accounting services, incorporation fees, and other related services. Organization costs are usually amortized over 60 months.
- **Patents**, both those developed internally and those purchased. If developed internally, a patent's "amortizable basis" includes legal fees incurred during the application process. Normally, a patent is amortized over its legal life, or over its remaining life if purchased. However, it should be amortized over its legal life or its economic life, whichever is the shorter.
- **Trademarks, brands, and trade names**, which should be written off over a period not to exceed 40 years. However, since the value of these assets depends on the changing tastes of consumers, they are frequently amortized over a shorter period.
- Other types of property that may be amortized include certain intangible drilling costs, circulation costs, mine development costs, pollution control facilities, and reforestation expenditures. They can even include intangibles such as the value of a market share or a market's composition: an example is the portion of an acquired business that is attributable to the existence of a given customer base.

TRICKS OF THE TRADE

- Certain intangibles cannot be amortized, but may be depreciated using a straight-line approach if they have a "determinable" useful life. Because the rules are different in each country and are subject to change, it is essential to rely on specialist advice.
- Computer software may be amortized under certain conditions, depending on its purpose. Software that is amortized is generally given a 60-month life, but it may be amortized over a shorter period if it can clearly be established that it will be obsolete or no longer used within a shorter time.
- Under certain conditions, customer lists that were purchased may be amortized if it can be demonstrated that the list has a finite useful life, in that customers on the list are likely to be lost over a period of time.

MORE INFO

Websites:

Financial Accounting Standards Board (FASB): www.fasb.org
US Copyright Office: www.copyright.gov
US Patent and Trademark Office: www.uspto.gov

 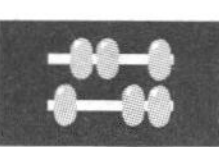   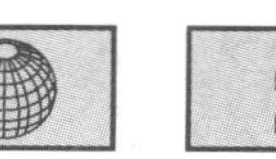   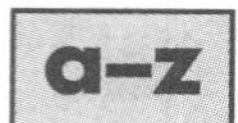

- While leasehold improvements are depreciated for income tax purposes, they are amortized when it comes to financial reporting—either over the remaining term of the lease or their expected useful life, whichever is the shorter.
- Annual payments incurred under a franchise agreement should be expensed when incurred.
- The internet has many amortization loan calculators that can automatically determine monthly payment figures and the total cost of a loan.

Annual Percentage Rate

Different investments typically offer different compounding periods, usually quarterly or monthly. The annual percentage rate, or APR, allows them to be compared over a common period of time, namely one year.

WHAT IT MEASURES

The APR measures either the rate of interest that invested money earns in one year, or the cost of credit expressed as a yearly rate.

WHY IT IS IMPORTANT

It enables an investor or borrower to compare like with like. When evaluating investment alternatives, naturally it's important to know which one will pay the greatest return. By the same token, borrowers want to know which loan alternative offers the best terms. Determining the annual percentage rate provides a direct comparison.

HOW IT WORKS IN PRACTICE

To calculate the APR, apply this formula:

$$\text{APR} = \left(1 + \frac{i}{m}\right)^m - 1$$

where i is the interest rate quoted, expressed as a decimal, and m is the number of compounding periods per year. For example, if a bank offers a 6% interest rate, paid quarterly, the APR would be calculated this way:

$$\begin{aligned}\left(1 + \frac{0.06}{4}\right)^4 - 1 &= (1 + 0.015)^4 - 1 \\ &= 1.015^4 - 1 \\ &= 1.0614 - 1 \\ &= 0.0614 \\ &= 6.14\%\end{aligned}$$

TRICKS OF THE TRADE

- As a rule of thumb, the annual percentage rate is slightly higher than the quoted rate.
- When using the formula, be sure to express the rate as a decimal (that is, 6% becomes 0.06).
- When expressed as the cost of credit, remember to include other costs of obtaining the credit in addition to interest, such as loan closing costs and financial fees.
- APR provides an excellent basis for comparing mortgage or other loan rates; lenders are required to disclose it.
- When used in the context of investment, APR can also be called the "annual percentage yield," or APY.

MORE INFO

See Also:

Fixed-Deposit Compound Interest (pp. 1227–1228)
Nominal and Real Interest Rates (p. 1238)

Asset Turnover

Another of the asset utilization ratios, asset turnover measures the productivity of assets. In some circles it is also referred to as the earning power of assets.

WHAT IT MEASURES

The amount of sales generated for every dollar's worth of assets over a given period.

WHY IT IS IMPORTANT

Asset turnover measures how well a company is leveraging its assets to produce revenue. A well-managed manufacturer, for example, will make its plant and equipment work hard for the business by minimizing idle time for machines.

The higher the number the better—within reason. As a rule of thumb, companies with low profit margins tend to have high asset turnover; those with high profit margins have low asset turnover.

This ratio can also show how capital intensive a business is. Some businesses, such as software developers, can generate tremendous sales per dollar of assets because their assets are modest. At the other end of the scale, electric utilities, heavy industry manufacturers, and even cable TV companies need a huge asset base to generate sales.

Finally, asset turnover serves as a tool to keep managers mindful of the company's balance sheet along with its profit and loss account.

HOW IT WORKS IN PRACTICE

Asset turnover's basic formula is simply sales divided by assets:

$$\frac{\text{Sales revenue}}{\text{Total assets}}$$

Most experts recommend using average total assets in the formula. To determine this figure, add total assets at the beginning of the year to total assets at the end of the year and divide by two.

If, for instance, annual sales totaled $4.5 million, and total assets were $1.84 million at the beginning of the year and $1.78 million at the year end, the average total assets would be $1.81 million, and the asset turnover ratio would be:

$$\frac{4{,}500{,}000}{1{,}810{,}000} = 2.49$$

A variation of the formula is:

$$\frac{\text{Sales revenue}}{\text{Fixed assets}}$$

If average fixed assets were $900,000, then asset turnover would be:

$$\frac{4{,}500{,}000}{900{,}000} = 5$$

TRICKS OF THE TRADE

- This ratio is especially useful for growth companies to gauge whether or not they are growing revenue (for example) turnover, in healthy proportion to assets.
- Asset turnover numbers are useful for comparing competitors within industries. Like most ratios, they vary from industry to industry. As with most numbers, the most meaningful comparisons are made over extended periods of time.
- Too high a ratio may suggest overtrading: too much sales revenue with too little investment. Conversely, too low a ratio may suggest undertrading and an inefficient management of resources.
- A declining ratio may be indicative of a company that overinvested in plant, equipment, or other fixed assets, or is not using existing assets effectively.

MORE INFO

See Also:

Asset Utilization (pp. 1195–1196)
Return on Assets (pp. 1248–1249)

Asset Utilization

Appraising asset utilization is a multi-task exercise conceived and performed in the spirit of "one manages what one measures." There is plenty to measure.

WHAT IT MEASURES

How efficiently an organization uses its resources and, in turn, the effectiveness of the organization's managers.

WHY IT IS IMPORTANT

The success of any enterprise is tied to its ability to manage and leverage its assets. Hefty sales and profits can hide any number of inefficiencies. By examining several relationships between sales and assets, asset utilization delivers a reasonably detailed picture of how well a company is being managed and led—certainly enough to call attention both to sources of trouble and to role-model operations.

Moreover, since all the figures used in this analysis are taken from a company's balance sheet or profit and loss statement, the ratios that result can be used to compare a company's performance with individual competitors and with industries as a whole.

Many companies use this measure not only to evaluate their aggregate success but also to determine compensation for managers.

HOW IT WORKS IN PRACTICE

Asset utilization relies on a family of asset utilization ratios, also called activity ratios. The individual ratios in the family can vary, depending on the practitioner. They include measures that also stand alone, such as accounts receivable turnover and asset turnover. The most commonly used sets of asset utilization ratios include these and the following measures.

Average collection period is also known as days sales outstanding. It links accounts receivable with daily sales and is expressed in number of days; the lower the number, the better the performance. Its formula is:

$$\text{Average collection period} = \frac{\text{Accounts receivable}}{\text{Average daily sales}}$$

For example, if accounts receivable are $280,000 and average daily sales are $7,000, then:

$$\frac{280{,}000}{7{,}000} = 40 \text{ days}$$

Inventory turnover compares the cost of goods sold (COGS) with inventory; for this measure, expressed in "turns," the higher the number the better. Its formula is:

$$\text{Inventory turnover} = \frac{\text{Cost of goods sold}}{\text{Inventory}}$$

For example, if COGS is $2 million and inventory at the end of the period is $500,000, then:

$$\frac{2{,}000{,}000}{500{,}000} = 4$$

Some asset utilization repertoires include ratios like debtor days, while others study the relationships listed below.

Depreciation/Assets measures the percentage of assets being depreciated to gauge how quickly product plants are aging and assets are being consumed.

Depreciation/Sales measures the percentage of sales that is tied up covering the wear and tear of the physical plant.

In either instance, a high percentage could be cause for concern.

Income/Assets measures how well management uses its assets to generate net income. It is the same formula as return on assets.

Income/Plant measures how effectively a company uses its investment in fixed assets to generate net income.

In these two instances, high numbers are desirable.

Plant/Assets expresses the percentage of total assets that is tied up in land, buildings, and equipment.

By themselves, of course, the individual numbers are meaningless. Their value lies in how they compare with the corresponding numbers of competitors and with industry averages. A company with an inventory turnover of 4 in an industry whose average is 7, for example, surely has room for improvement, because the comparison indicates that it is generating fewer sales per unit of inventory and is therefore less efficient than its competitors.

TRICKS OF THE TRADE

- Asset utilization is particularly useful to companies considering expansion or capital investment: if production can be increased

MORE INFO

See Also:

Accounts Receivable Turnover (p. 1188)
Asset Turnover (pp. 1194–1195)
Days Sales Outstanding (pp. 1213–1214)

  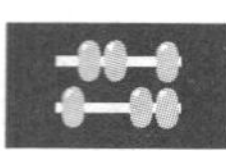      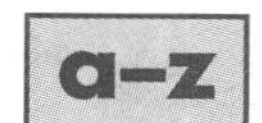

by improving the efficiency of existing resources, there is no need to spend the sums expansion would cost.

- Like all families of ratios, no single number or comparison is necessarily cause for alarm or rejoicing. Asset utilization proves most beneficial over an extended period of time.
- Studying all measures at once can devour a lot of time, although computers have trimmed hours into seconds. Managements in smaller organizations may conduct asset utilization on a continuing basis, tracking particular measures monthly to stay abreast of operating trends.

Basis Point Value

WHAT IT MEASURES

The basis point value (BPV) expresses the change in value of an asset or financial instrument that results from a 0.01 percentage change in yield. BPV is commonly used to measure interest rate risk, and may be referred to as a delta or DV01.

WHY IT IS IMPORTANT

Basis point value is extremely important in assessing the impact of changes to the value or rate of a financial instrument such as an asset or portfolio. Simply stating an absolute percentage can be unclear—a 1% increase to a 10% rate might refer to an increase to 10.1% or 11%, for example.

Basis points can be used to measure changes and differentials in interest rates and margins. For example, a floating interest rate might be set at 25 BPV above Libor. If Libor is 3.5%, this means the floating rate will be 3.75%. Basis points are also useful in describing margins, because percentage changes may be very small or unclear—even while they might have a considerable impact on the bottom line.

BPV is commonly used in financial markets to measure interest rates, and specifically the risk associated with a particular rate. It is popular because it is relatively simple to calculate and can be applied in any scenario where you have a known cash flow.

HOW IT WORKS IN PRACTICE

At its most basic, BPV is 1/100th of 1%. Therefore, there are 30 basis points between a bond with a yield of 10.3% and 10.6%. To calculate simple BPV, therefore, use this formula:

BPV = Yield × 0.0001, or 1% of 1%

It is often useful to take the calculation a step further to define the price value of a basis point (PVBP), which is the change in value of a bond or other financial instrument given a change of one basis point value. Sometimes this is also known as "dollar valuation of 01" or DV01.

To calculate PVBP, apply the following calculation:

PVBP = Initial price − Price if yield changes by 1 BPV

In the financial market, a basis point is used to refer to the yield that a bond or investment pays to the investor. For example, if a bond yield moves from 7.45% to 7.65%, it is said to have risen 20 basis points.

For example, if a bank raises interest rates from 2.5% to 2.75%, you would calculate PVBP as follows:

$0.25 \times 0.0001 \times 100 = 0.025\%$ change

(This is the difference in yield from the account created by a movement of 1 basis point).

TRICKS OF THE TRADE

- Large financial institutions use highly specialized and sophisticated computer systems to calculate the impact of basis point changes (the DV01 figure) in real-time. These figures can be calculated in spreadsheets, but they are difficult to produce accurately, particularly for complex bonds.
- In the bond market, a basis point is used to refer to the yield that a bond pays to the investor. For example, if a bond yield moves from 1.45% to 1.65%, it has risen 20 basis points. Investors will commonly compare bond yields by weighting them according to the BPV.

MORE INFO

Website:

Barbican Consulting guide to BPV:
www.barbicanconsulting.co.uk/bpv

Binomial Distribution

WHAT IT MEASURES

This refers to the number of incidences of a specific outcome in a series of events or trials. For example, how many times you throw the number three when rolling a die 10 times.

WHY IT IS IMPORTANT

The binomial distribution is widely used to test statistical probabilities and significance, and is a good way of visually detecting unexpected values. It is a useful tool in determining permutations, combinations, and probabilities, where the outcomes can be broken down into two probabilities (p and q), where p and q are complementary (i.e., $p + q = 1$).

For example, tossing a coin has only two possible outcomes, heads or tails. Each of these outcomes has a theoretical probability of 0.5. Using the binomial expansion, showing all possible outcomes and combinations, the probability is represented as follows:

$(p+q)^2 = p^2 + 2pq + q^2$, or more simply, $pp + 2pq + qq$

If p is heads and q is tails, the theory shows there is only one way to get two heads (pp), two ways to get a head and a tail ($2pq$), and one way to get two tails (qq).

Common uses of binomial distributions in business include quality control, public opinion surveys, medical research, and insurance problems. It can be applied to complex processes such as sampling items in factory production lines or to estimate percentage failure rates of products and components.

HOW IT WORKS IN PRACTICE

If I toss a coin 100 times and there are 60 instances of heads and 40 of tails:

  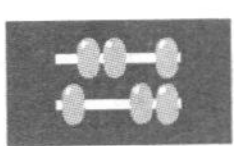   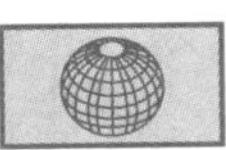   

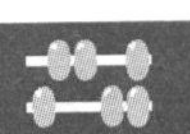

$n = 100$ (the number of opportunities where heads could occur)
$k = 60$ (the number of heads that did occur)
$p = 0.5$ (the statistical probability that heads would occur each time)
$q = 0.5$ (the complementary probability that tails would occur)

At this point, there are three ways to demonstrate probability using a binomial equation. In all three cases, k represents the number of times a specific outcome is observed, p is the probability of heads, and q is the complementary probability of tails.

Method 1
If $n = 100$, exact binomial probabilities can be calculated using repeated applications of the standard binomial formula, as below. This works out the probability of exactly k heads:

$$P(k) = \left[\frac{n!}{k!(n-k!)}\right] p^k q^{n-k}$$

This is considered to be the most accurate calculation of binomial probabilities, since it involves precise calculation. However, it is best used where n is less than 1,000, or where you are using a computer program to perform more complex calculations on larger sample sizes.

Method 2
If both np and nq are greater than 5, then binomial probabilities can be estimated using an approximation to the Normal distribution. This relies on the following formula:

$$Z = \frac{(k - m \pm 0.5)}{\text{sqrt}}$$

where:
$m = np$, or the mean of the binomial sampling distribution
sqrt = the standard deviation of the binomial sampling distribution

Method 3
The final method of estimating binomial distribution is the Poisson probability function, which is used where the number of occurrences (n) is less than 150, and the mean (np) and variance (npq) are within 10% of one another. In this case, you can repeatedly apply the Poisson formula to estimate binomial distribution, as below:

$$P(k \text{ out of } n) = \frac{(e - m)(mk)}{k!}$$

Do keep in mind that the results of the Poisson procedure are only approximations of the true binomial probabilities, valid only in the case that the binomial mean and variance are very close.

TRICKS OF THE TRADE

- To satisfy the requirements of binomial distribution, the event being studied must display certain characteristics:
  - the number of trials or occurrences are fixed
  - there are only two possible outcomes (heads/tails or win/lose, for example)
  - all occurrences are independent of each other (tossing a head does not make it more or less likely you will get the same result next time)
  - all outcomes have the same probability of success
- Binomial distribution is best applied in cases where the population size is at least 10 times the sample size, and not to simple random samples.
- To find probabilities from a binomial distribution, you can perform a manual calculation, but there are online calculators available, or you can use a binomial table or computer spreadsheet.
- The binomial distribution is sometimes called a Bernoulli experiment or trial.
- The binomial *probability* refers to the probability that a binomial experiment results in exactly x successes. In the example above, we see that the binomial probability of getting exactly one head in two coin flips is 0.5.
- A cumulative binomial probability refers to the probability that the binomial random variable falls within a specified range (for example, is greater than or equal to a stated lower limit and less than or equal to a stated upper limit).

MORE INFO

Websites:

Penn State University on binomial distribution (via Internet Archive): tinyurl.com/658qcex
Stat Trek binomial calculator: stattrek.com/online-calculator/binomial.aspx
Texas University binomial calculator: www.stat.tamu.edu/~west/applets/binomialdemo.html

Bond Yield

A bond is a certificate that promises to repay a sum of money borrowed, plus interest, on a specified date, usually years into the future. National, state, and local governments issue bonds, as do corporations and many institutions.

Short-term bonds generally mature in up to 3 years, intermediate-term bonds in 3 to 10 years, and long-term bonds in more than 10 years, with 30 years generally being the upper limit. Longer-term bonds are considered a higher risk because interest rates are certain to change during their lifetime, but they tend to pay higher interest rates to attract investors and reward them for the additional risk.

Bonds are traded on the open market, just like stocks. They are reliable economic indicators, but perform in the reverse direction to interest rates: if bond prices are rising, interest rates and stock markets are likely to be falling, while if interest rates have gone up since a bond was first issued, prices of new bonds will fall.

WHAT IT MEASURES

The annual return on this certificate (the rate of interest) expressed as a percentage of the current market price of the bond.

WHY IT IS IMPORTANT

Bonds can tie up investors' money for periods of up to 30 years, so knowing their yield is a critical investment consideration. Similarly, bond issuers need to know the price they will pay to incur their debt, so that they can compare it with the cost of other means of raising capital.

  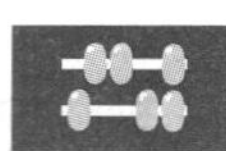 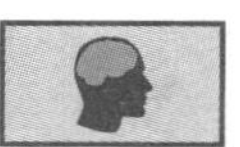     

HOW IT WORKS IN PRACTICE

Bonds are issued in increments of $1,000. To calculate the yield amount, multiply the face value of the bond by the stated rate, expressed as a decimal. For example, buying a new 10-year $1,000 bond that pays 6% interest will produce an annual yield of $60:

$$1,000 \times 0.06 = \$60$$

The $60 will be paid as $30 every six months. At the end of 10 years, the purchaser will have earned $600, and will also be repaid the original $1,000. Because the bond was purchased when it was first issued, the 6% is also called the "yield to maturity."

This basic formula is complicated by other factors. First is the "time-value of money" theory: money paid in the future is worth less than money paid today. A more detailed computation of total bond yield requires the calculation of the present value of the interest earned each year. Second, changing interest rates have a marked impact on bond trading and, ultimately, on yield. Changes in interest rates cannot affect the interest paid by bonds already issued, but they do affect the prices of new bonds.

TRICKS OF THE TRADE

- **Yield to call**. Bond issuers reserve the right to "call," or redeem, the bond before the maturity date, at certain times and at a certain price. Issuers often do this if interest rates fall and they can issue new bonds at a lower rate. Bond buyers should obtain the yield-to-call rate, which may, in fact, be a more realistic indicator of the return expected.
- **Different types of bond**. Some bonds are backed by assets, while others are issued on the strength of the issue's good standing. Investors should know the difference.
- **Zero-coupon bonds**. These pay no interest at all, but are sold at a deep discount and increase in value until maturity. A buyer might pay $3,000 for a 25-year zero bond with a face value of $10,000. This bond will simply accrue value each year, and at maturity will be worth $10,000, thus earning $7,000. These are high-risk investments, however, especially if they must be sold on the open market amid rising interest rates.
- **Interest rates**. Bond values fall when interest rates rise, and rise when interest rates fall, because when interest rates rise existing bonds become less valuable and less attractive.

MORE INFO

See Also:

✔ The Bond Market: Its Structure and Function (p. 1064)
Current Price of a Bond (p. 1212)
Yield (pp. 1263–1264)

Book Value

No-nonsense number-crunchers adore this measure because it presents the value of common stock equity based on historical values and thus helps separate fact from fiction and fancy.

WHAT IT MEASURES

A company's common stock equity as it appears on a balance sheet.

WHY IT IS IMPORTANT

Book value represents a company's net worth to its stockholders, based on the difference between assets and liabilities plus debt. Typically, book value is substantially different from market value, especially in high-tech and knowledge-based industries whose primary assets are intangible and therefore do not appear on the balance sheet.

When compared with its market value, a company's book value helps to reveal how it is regarded by the investment community. A market value that is notably higher than book value indicates that investors have a high regard for the company. A market value that is, for example, a multiple of book value suggests that investors' regard may be unreasonably high—as was shown in the painful plunge of dot-com companies in 2000 and 2001.

The reverse is also true, of course; indeed, it may suggest that a company's stock is a bargain.

A companion measure is book value per stock. It shows the value of the company's assets that each stockholder theoretically would receive if a company were liquidated.

HOW IT WORKS IN PRACTICE

To calculate book value, subtract a company's liabilities and the value of its debt and preferred stock from its total assets. All of these figures appear on a company's balance sheet. For example:

Total assets	$1,300
Current liabilities	–$400
Long-term liabilities, preferred stock	–$250
Book value	**$650**

Book value per stock is calculated by dividing the book value by the number of stocks issued:

$$\text{Book value per stock} = \frac{\text{Book value}}{\text{Number of stocks issued}}$$

If our example is expressed in millions of dollars and the company has 35 million stocks outstanding, the book value per stock would be $650 million divided by 35 million:

$$\frac{650}{35} = \$18.57$$

TRICKS OF THE TRADE

- Related terms include:
  - adjusted book value or modified book value, which is book value after assets and liabilities are adjusted to market value
  - tangible book value, which also subtracts intangible assets, patents, trademarks, and the value of research and development
  - The rationale is that these items cannot be sold outright
- Book value can also mean the value of an individual asset as it appears on a balance sheet, in which case it is equal to the cost of the asset minus any accumulated depreciation.
- Though often considered a realistic appraisal, book value can still contain unrealistic figures. For example, a building might be fully depreciated and have no official asset value but could still be sold for millions, or four-year-old computer equipment that is not fully depreciated might have asset value but no market value, given its age and advances in technology.

MORE INFO

See Also:

Market/Book Ratio (p. 1236)

  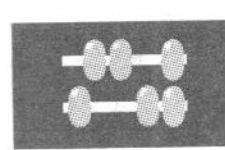   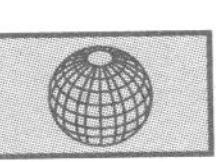   

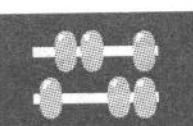

Borrowing Costs and Capitalization

Borrowing costs are the tangible costs of incurring debt, typically expressed in terms of annual interest paid on outstanding debt or as a stated, annual coupon rate. A firm's borrowing costs are a function of its credit quality. Credit quality is determined on the type of debt security issued, capital structure, and capital-intensity of the business. Understanding each of the components of credit quality provides a clear picture of the determinants of a company's cost of debt financing. Borrowing costs also include the expenses incurred to issue debt securities.

GETTING STARTED

The costs of borrowing are primarily made up of interest and issuance expenses. The interest rate assigned to a particular debt instrument is based on the level of default risk assumed by the investor. Several rating agencies assess the default risk of public debt issuances and provide a rating that is indicative of credit quality. The credit quality is greater for secured/collateralized senior debt than for unsecured subordinated debt issued by the same company, and hence the former typically carries a lower rate of interest. Companies that have higher levels of debt must typically pay higher interest rates to investors to compensate them for the increased risk of default. Capital-intensive businesses can usually maintain greater debt-to-capital ratios for the same level of borrowing costs than businesses that are less capital intensive.

FAQS

What are debt issuance costs and are they always incurred when borrowing money?

Debt issuance costs are the underwriting, legal, and administrative fees required to issue the debt. These fees are significant when issuing debt in the public markets, such as bonds. However, other types of debt, such as private placements or bank loans, are cheaper to issue because they require less underwriting, legal, and administrative support. Consequently, the public issuers of debt are typically *Fortune* 500 companies, while middle-market companies tend to issue debt through private placements.

Do borrowing costs increase or decrease for callable bonds or bonds with detachable stock warrants?

When debt securities are issued with a call feature, the debt can be retired at the discretion of the company until some specified future date. The call feature represents value to the issuing company, much like a call option on equity. The issuer must compensate investors for providing this option. Therefore, the interest rate on callable bonds is typically higher than those on noncallable bonds of the same credit quality. That is, the borrowing costs increase on bonds with a call feature.

The opposite is true of bonds with detachable stock warrants. A stock warrant provides the bondholder with the right to purchase shares of common stock in the issuing company at a specified price during a defined period of time. The warrant's strike price is typically at, or higher than, the current market price of the company's stock. Nonetheless, the warrant provides value to the bondholder in the form of a call option on the company's equity. Because these warrants add to the potential total return on the debt, the stated interest rate is usually lower than that on debt issued without warrants of similar credit quality. Borrowing costs are typically lower on bonds with detachable stock warrants.

MAKING IT HAPPEN

When companies borrow money, they enter a formal obligation to make periodic payments of interest and to repay the principal balance outstanding according to an agreed schedule. The interest payments are typically based on a stated, annual percentage of the original amount borrowed. The interest paid on such obligations represents the cost of borrowing, along with the costs to issue the debt.

The Difference between Funded and Unfunded Debt

The debt can be classified as funded or unfunded. Funded debt is long-term debt or debt that has a maturity date in excess of one year. Unfunded debt is short-term debt requiring repayment within a year from issuance. Funded debt is usually issued in the public markets or in the form of a private placement to qualified institutional investors. Most unfunded debt is commercial paper or bank lines of credit.

Senior and Subordinated Debt

Debt can also be classified as senior or subordinated, based on its preference to assets in the event of default by the lender. Subordinated lenders have a junior claim to assets in the event of bankruptcy and are paid only after senior creditors' claims have been satisfied.

Senior credit can be secured or unsecured. Much of the corporate debt outstanding is referred to as a bond. However, a true bond is secured by claims against the company's property, plant, and equipment. For example, many airlines secure their public debt by mortgaging their airplanes. In this example, an airline could be forced to sell its airplanes to pay its public debt if it defaulted on the bonds. Most public debt is secured by the good faith and credit of the issuing company, and is more accurately called a debenture. A company can also pledge certain assets, like accounts receivable, inventory, or property, as collateral for a loan or debt.

Differing Levels of Risk

Even when debt is secured or collateralized, it still does not guarantee repayment by the issuer. A company's underlying asset value and its earnings may be very volatile, increasing the risk of default in a down business cycle. Because this risk can be different from one business to another, there are several national rating agencies that rate public debt based on the creditworthiness of the borrower. Investment-grade debt securities are securities that are rated in the top four categories of creditworthiness by Standard & Poor's or Moody's rating agencies. All debt securities rated below investment-grade are considered to be junk bonds.

Different Types of Interest Rate

Debt can have a fixed or floating rate of interest. Fixed-rate debt pays the same interest rate over its term. Most long-term debt is issued with a fixed rate. Many short-term loans are floating-rate instruments based on the prime lending rate, Libor (London Interbank Offered Rate), or some US Treasury security. When the rates on these securities change, the loan rate changes. For example, a line of credit whose current interest rate is 6%, based on one percentage point above the three-year Libor rate, will change to 6.25% if Libor increases by a quarter of a point. Floating-rate debt is typically used to support a business's working capital requirements.

The Determinants of Credit Quality

The interest rate and, consequently, the borrowing cost is determined by credit quality. Credit quality depends on the type of debt security, the amount of debt relative to total capital, and the capital-intensity of a company's business. All other things being equal, a secured or collateralized debt security is less risky than an unsecured obligation. Therefore, investors require a greater return for the additional risk assumed by investing in unsecured debt. Likewise, an investor will require a greater return for subordinated debt than for senior credit.

Credit quality also deteriorates as the level of debt grows on the balance sheet of a company. Intuitively, the greater the debt-to-capital ratio, the greater the risk of default. By continuing to add financial leverage to its business operations, a company increases the risks that in a bad year it may not be able to cover its debt service. In studies on cost of capital, it was determined that companies experiencing debt-to-capital ratios between 25% and 45% saw their cost of capital increase exponentially, indicating greater risk of financial distress.

Debt-to-Capital Ratios

Finally, companies that are more capital-intensive tend to have greater debt-to-capital ratios. For example, automobile and airline manufacturers typically maintain greater leverage than professional services and software companies. The academic explanation given for this circumstance is the degree of industry maturity, lower earnings volatility, and the ability to secure more debt with tangible assets. Consequently, companies in more capital-intensive industries tend to have lower borrowing costs at a given debt-to-capital ratio than those in less capital-intensive industries.

TRICKS OF THE TRADE

- The costs of borrowing are composed of interest payments and issuance costs. Interest paid on outstanding debt is a function of the creditworthiness of the borrower. The greater the interest rate on a debt security relative to other, similar securities, the lower the credit quality of the issuer. As credit quality falls below investment-grade, the risk of default becomes ominously greater and the costs of borrowing become more exorbitant.
- A company's capital structure is another major determinant of credit quality. There is a direct relationship between debt level and default risk. At a given debt to capital ratio, incremental borrowing costs increase dramatically as the company's risk of financial distress reaches its peak.

MORE INFO

Book:

Brealey, Richard A., Stewart C. Myers, and Franklin Allen. *Principles of Corporate Finance*. 11th ed. New York: McGraw-Hill, 2013.

See Also:

★ Optimizing the Capital Structure: Finding the Right Balance between Debt and Equity (pp. 543–545)
Debt/Capital Ratio (p. 1214)
Debt/Equity Ratio (p. 1215)

Break-Even Analysis

WHAT IT MEASURES

Break-even is the point at which a product or service stops costing money to produce and sell, and starts generating a profit for your business. This means sales have reached sufficient volume to cover the variable and fixed costs of producing and distributing your product.

WHY IT IS IMPORTANT

The ultimate goal of any business is to make money, but break-even analysis can also provide valuable information for profitable businesses in terms of setting price levels, targeting optimal variable/fixed price combinations and determining the financial attractiveness of various strategies for a business.

Break-even analysis allows a business to understand what the minimum level of sales needed is to ensure that it does not make a loss, and how sensitive the break-even point is to changes in fixed or variable expenses. It can help you to understand and examine the profit drivers of your business.

HOW IT WORKS IN PRACTICE

Say you are an entrepreneur looking to sell t-shirts across Europe. You will want to know how many t-shirts you need to sell before your venture generates a profit. This figure can then be compared to your sales forecasts to judge the likely success of your venture. There are two ways of calculating break-even points, as shown below.

The variable cost of producing a single t-shirt is $1. The fixed costs of the business over a year (those costs that won't vary month to month) include items such as telecommunications, rent, and insurance, and total $25,000 in year one. The unit price you are expecting for each t-shirt is $5 and your projected sales in year one are 50,000 units.

To calculate break-even, either draw a chart showing:

- sales revenue at different levels of output;
- fixed costs at different levels of output;
- total costs at different levels of output.

The point where total cost equals total sales revenue is the break-even point.

Or use the data available to calculate the contribution of each unit sold or made. This is the difference between the sales revenue and the variable cost of each unit. Using the example of the t-shirts, each t-shirt brings in $5 of revenue against $1 in variable costs. The contribution of each unit is said to be $4, because the unit makes a $4 contribution towards fixed costs.

The number of units needed to be sold to break even is therefore the total fixed cost divided by the contribution per unit. The t-shirt venture would need to sell enough t-shirts to cover fixed costs ($25,000) divided by the unit contribution ($4)—in other words, 6,250 shirts.

Break-even analysis is particularly useful in comparing alternative scenarios. For example, you might consider what happens if labor costs rise and the variable cost of producing a t-shirt doubles to $2. In this scenario, the contribution per shirt falls to $3 but fixed costs remain $25,000—meaning the business now needs to sell 25,000 ÷ 3 t-shirts to reach break-even (8,334 shirts).

The simple formula for this method is:

$$\text{Break-even sales (\$)} = \frac{\text{Fixed costs}}{\left(\dfrac{\text{Contribution margin}}{\text{Total sales}}\right)}$$

TRICKS OF THE TRADE

- Fundamentally, there are only three ways to reduce break-even: lower direct costs to increase the gross margin; reduce fixed expenses and lower necessary total costs; or raise prices to increase revenues.
- Categorizing costs as fixed or variable is essential for break-even analysis. Fixed costs are those not related

to the volume of production, often referred to as "overheads." These costs will remain static even if you do not produce any goods, and include items such as staff salaries, insurance, property taxes, and interest. Variable costs are those related to production output or sales, and might include raw materials, commission, packaging, and shipping costs. Without a good understanding of your costs, break-even analysis will be meaningless.

- Remember that the break-even point is not a static figure. You should compare projections to real-life results every three to six months, and make adjustments if necessary. In particular, expenses tend to increase over time and you may fall below break-even point because you think it is lower than it has become.
- When conducting break-even analysis, you might want to add in a margin for profit. For example, you might want to target a specific profit margin goal and this can be incorporated into break-even analysis as follows:

$$\text{Break-even (\$)} = \frac{(\text{Fixed costs} + \text{Profit goal})}{\left(\frac{\text{Contribution margin}}{\text{Total sales}}\right)}$$

- Another refinement of the break-even analysis is the "sensitivity analysis." This refers to using the break-even point to evaluate different scenarios. For example, what happens if you increase prices by 25%? What happens if unit sales fall by 20%? Using a spreadsheet, it is very simple to perform such calculations quickly, allowing you to look at different situations.

MORE INFO

Articles:

"Fixed, variable costs and break-even." *The Times 100*. Online at: tinyurl.com/6eeuxkj

"Mind Your Business—Break-even analysis: Debts, revenues and costs." *Biz/ed* (November 18, 2008). Online at: www.bized.co.uk/current/mind/2008_9/181108.htm

Capital Asset Pricing Model

Although at first glance it looks likes a simple formula, the capital asset pricing model (CAPM) represents an historic effort to understand and quantify something that's not at all simple: risk. Conceived by Nobel economist William Sharpe in 1964, CAPM has been praised, appraised, and assailed by economists ever since.

WHAT IT MEASURES

The relationship between the risk and expected return of a security or stock portfolio.

WHY IT IS IMPORTANT

The capital asset pricing model's importance is twofold.

First, it serves as a model for pricing the risk in all securities, and thus helps investors evaluate and measure portfolio risk and the returns they can anticipate for taking such risks.

Second, the theory behind the formula also has fueled—some might say provoked—spirited debate among economists about the nature of investment risk itself. The CAPM attempts to describe how the market values investments with expected returns.

The CAPM theory classifies risk as being either diversifiable, which can be avoided by sound investing, or systematic, that is, not diversified and unavoidable due to the nature of the market itself. The theory contends that investors are rewarded only for assuming systematic risk, because they can mitigate diversifiable risk by building a portfolio of both risky stocks and sound ones.

One analysis has characterized the CAPM as "a theory of equilibrium" that links higher expected returns in strong markets with the greater risk of suffering heavy losses in weak markets; otherwise, no one would invest in high-risk stocks.

HOW IT WORKS IN PRACTICE

CAPM holds that the expected return of a security or a portfolio equals the rate on a risk-free security plus a risk premium. If this expected return does not meet or beat a theoretical required return, the investment should not be undertaken. The formula used to create CAPM is:

$$\text{Expected return} = \text{Risk-free rate} + (\text{Market return} - \text{Risk-free rate}) \times \text{Beta value}$$

The risk-free rate is the quoted rate on an asset that has virtually no risk. In practice, it is the rate quoted for 90-day US Treasury bills. The market return is the percentage return expected of the overall market, typically a published index such as Standard & Poor's. The beta value is a figure that measures the volatility of a security or portfolio of securities compared with the market as a whole. A beta of 1, for example, indicates that a security's price will move with the market. A beta greater than 1 indicates higher volatility, while a beta less than 1 indicates less volatility.

Say, for instance, that the current risk-free rate is 4%, and the S&P 500 index is expected to return 11% next year. An investment club is interested in determining next year's return for XYZ Software Inc., a prospective investment. The club has determined that the company's beta value is 1.8. The overall stock market always has a beta of 1, so XYZ Software's beta of 1.8 signals that it is a riskier investment than the overall market represents. This added risk means that the club should expect a higher rate of return than the 11% for the S&P 500. The CAPM calculation, then, would be:

$$4\% + (11\% - 4\%) \times 1.8 = 16.6\%$$

MORE INFO

Article:

Burton, Jonathan. "Revisiting the capital asset pricing model." *Dow Jones Asset Manager* (May/June 1998): 20–28. Online at: www.stanford.edu/~wfsharpe/art/djam/djam.htm

Website:

Contingency Analysis resource for trading, financial engineering, and financial risk management: www.contingencyanalysis.com

See Also:

✔ Understanding the Relationship between the Discount Rate and Risk (p. 1001)
Expected Rate of Return (p. 1226)
Portfolio Theory and Capital Markets (p. 1409)

What the results tell the club is that given the risk, XYZ Software Inc. has a required rate of return of 16.6%, or the minimum return that an investment in XYZ should generate. If the investment club doesn't think that XYZ will produce that kind of return, it should probably consider investing in a different company.

TRICKS OF THE TRADE

- As experts warn, CAPM is only a simple calculation built on historical data of market and stock prices. It does not express anything about the company whose stock is being analyzed. For example, renowned investor Warren Buffett has pointed out that if a company making Barbie™ dolls has the same beta as one making pet rocks, CAPM holds that one investment is as good as the other. Clearly, this is a risky tenet.
- While high returns might be received from stocks with high beta shares, there is no guarantee that their respective CAPM return will be realized (a reason why beta is defined as a "measure of risk" rather than an "indication of high return").
- The beta parameter itself is historical data and may not reflect future results. The data for beta values are typically gathered over several years, and experts recommend that only long-term investors should rely on the CAPM formula.
- Over longer periods of time, high-beta shares tend to be the worst performers during market declines.

Capital Expenditure

WHAT IT MEASURES

Capital expenditure (capex) refers to the money a business spends purchasing or upgrading fixed assets for future business benefit. Capital expenditure can include money spent for new property that will be resold, or which might be kept for one or more years. Capital expenditure also includes money spent to improve property (or inventory) that you already own. Under international reporting standards, property is considered to be improved only if the money you spend increases or restores an item's value, prolongs its useful life, or enables the item to be used for a new purpose.

WHY IT IS IMPORTANT

Understanding capital expenditure is a vital part of assessing a company's free cash flow. Basically, if a company spends a lot on capital expenditure but doesn't show a corresponding rate of growth, it is considered a less attractive investment. Ideally, healthy companies should generate enough positive cash flow to fund dividends/growth as well as capital expenditure.

HOW IT WORKS IN PRACTICE

To enable cash flow to be properly assessed it is important to calculate accurately the amount of funds necessary to support capital expenditure—and for the business to continue to operate. This is known as capex per share.

First, you should discount any capital expenditure that is discretionary—such as real estate, which might otherwise be leased.

Then use the following formulas to calculate capex per share based on net cash outflow attributable to property, divided by the weighted average number of ordinary shares in issue during the year:

$$\text{Capital expenditure} = \text{Total asset purchases} - \text{Property asset purchases} - \text{Nonproperty asset sales}$$

and

$$\text{Capex per share} = \frac{\text{Capex}}{\text{Weighted average of shares in issue}}$$

TRICKS OF THE TRADE

- Remember that few companies have smooth capex investment over time. Most companies will have a lean capex year, followed by a year or two of heavy investment. Wherever possible, use an average capex calculation—a single figure can be extremely misleading.
- Capital expenditure is only used to refer to one-off purchases of new items or improvements to existing assets which are kept and used by the business. So the cost of buying a truck for your business is a capital expenditure, but the cost of hiring a truck is not.
- It is possible to claim tax relief on a percentage of most capital expenditure, using allowances such as "first year allowance" or "writing down allowance."
- One classic example of capital expenditure is the start-up expenses incurred when you buy or create a new business venture. These expenses are considered capital expenditure because the owner incurs them to acquire property that will be kept. These expenses may be fully deducted in year one, or may be amortized over several years.

MORE INFO

Website:

HMRC (UK) Business Income Manual section on capex: www.hmrc.gov.uk/manuals/bimmanual/BIM35000.htm

Capitalization Ratios

Capitalization ratios, also widely known as financial leverage ratios, provide a glimpse of a company's long-term stability and ability to withstand losses and business downturns.

While not the focus here, capitalization ratio also refers to the percentage of a company's total capitalization contributed by debt, preferred stock, common stock, and other equity.

WHAT THEY MEASURE

By comparing debt to total capitalization, these ratios reflect the extent to which a corporation is trading on its equity, and the degree to which it finances operations with debt.

WHY THEY ARE IMPORTANT

By itself, any financial ratio is a rather useless piece of information. Collectively, and in context, though, financial leverage ratios present analysts and investors with an excellent picture of a company's

  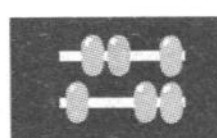   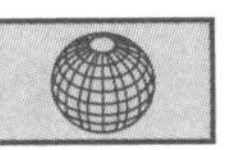   

situation, how much financial risk it has taken on, its dependence on debt, and developing trends. Knowing who controls a company's capital tells one who truly controls the enterprise!

HOW THEY WORK IN PRACTICE

A business finances its assets with either equity or debt. Financing with debt involves risk, since debt legally obligates a company to pay off the debt, plus the interest the debt incurs. Equity financing, on the other hand, does not obligate the company to pay anything. It pays investors dividends—but this is at the discretion of the board of directors. To be sure, business risk accompanies the operation of any enterprise. But how that enterprise opts to finance its operations—how it blends debt with equity—may heighten this risk.

Various experts include numerous formulas among capitalization financial leverage ratios. Three are discussed separately: debt-to-capital ratio, debt-to-equity ratio, and interest coverage ratios. What's known as the capitalization ratio *per se* can be expressed in two ways:

$$\frac{\text{Long-term debt}}{(\text{Long-term debt} + \text{Owners' equity})}$$

and

$$\frac{\text{Total debt}}{(\text{Total debt} + \text{Preferred and common equity})}$$

For example, a company whose long-term debt totals $5,000 and whose owners hold equity worth $3,000 would have a capitalization ratio of:

$$\frac{5{,}000}{(5{,}000 + 3{,}000)} = \frac{5{,}000}{8{,}000} = 0.625$$

Both expressions of the capitalization ratio are also referred to "component percentages," since they compare a company's debt with either its total capital (debt plus equity) or its equity capital. They readily indicate how reliant a company is on debt financing.

TRICKS OF THE TRADE

- Capitalization ratios need to be evaluated over time, and compared with other data and standards. A gross profit margin of 20%, for instance, is meaningless—until one knows that the average profit margin for an industry is 10%; at that point, 20% looks quite attractive. Moreover, if the historical trend of that margin has been climbing for the last three years, it strongly suggests that a company's management has sound and effective policies and strategies in place.
- Also, all capitalization ratios should be interpreted in the context of a company's earnings and cash flow, and those of its competitors.
- Take care in comparing companies in different industries or sectors. The same figures that appear to be low in one industry can be very high in another.
- Some less frequently used capitalization ratios are based on formulas that use the book value of equity (the stock). When compared with other ratios, they can be misleading, because there usually is little relation between a company's book value and its market value—which is apt to be many times higher, since market value reflects what the investment community thinks the company is worth.

MORE INFO

Book:

Walsh, Ciaran. *Key Management Ratios*. 4th ed. London: FT Prentice Hall, 2008.

See Also:

Debt/Capital Ratio (p. 1214)
Debt/Equity Ratio (p. 1215)
Interest Coverage (p. 1231)

Central Limit Theorem

WHAT IT MEASURES

The central limit theorem (CLT) is a statistical theory which holds that, given a sufficiently large sample size from a sufficiently varied population, the mean of all results will be approximately equal to the mean of the population. In addition, samples will roughly follow a normal distribution pattern (i.e., a bell-shaped curve), with variances reflecting the variance of the source population, divided by the sample size. As a rule of thumb, a population sample of 50 is required for CLT to be applied.

WHY IT IS IMPORTANT

CLT is a relatively simple analytical tool that is very important in examining returns from a particular investment. CLT is the foundation for many statistical procedures, including quality control charts, because the distribution of the phenomenon under study does not have to be normal, because the average will be.

HOW IT WORKS IN PRACTICE

CLT states that the average of the sum of a large number of independent, identically distributed random variables with finite means and variances converges to a normal random variable.

For example, if you tossed an ordinary coin 100 times, you would expect sometimes the coin to land on heads, sometimes on tails. If you score one point for each time it lands heads, the result would be the sum of 100 independent, identically distributed random variables.

The central limit theorem states that the distribution of heads will be close to a normal distribution curve. Repeating the experiment more times would create a result that, when plotted on a graph, would closely resemble the normal curve. CLT theory is based on the idea that a large population of independent variables (like the toss of a coin) is subject to independent random effects, which result in a normal distribution.

Expressed as a mathematical formula, CLT is as follows:

Let $X_1, X_2, \ldots, X_n$ be a random sample (independent and identically distributed) from a distribution with well-defined and finite mean (μ_X) and variance ($\sigma^2{}_X$).

As n increases, the sampling distribution of the sample average and the total sum approach Normal distributions with corresponding means and variances.

TRICKS OF THE TRADE

- A very loose form of CLT says that if you add up a large number n of different random variables, and if none of those variables dominate the resultant distribution spread, the sum will eventually look Normal as n gets bigger.

- The CLT almost always holds, but you must be cautious when using it. If the population mean doesn't exist, then CLT is not applicable. Moreover, even if the mean does exist, the CLT convergence to a normal density might be slow, requiring hundreds or even thousands of observations, rather than the few dozen in these examples.

MORE INFO

Websites:

iSixSigma on CLT: tinyurl.com/3mk6we6

Richard Lowry on CLT: vassarstats.net/central.html

Contribution Margin

Finding the contribution margin unearths an important comparison that otherwise would lie hidden in an income statement.

WHAT IT MEASURES

The amounts that individual products or services ultimately contribute to net profit.

WHY IT IS IMPORTANT

Contribution margin helps a business to decide how it should direct or redirect its resources.

When managers know the contribution margin—or margins, as is more often the case—they can make better decisions about adding or subtracting product lines, investing in existing products, pricing products or services (particularly in response to competitors' actions), structuring sales commissions and bonuses, where to direct marketing and advertising expenditures, and where to apply individual talents and expertise.

In short, contribution margin is a valuable decision-support tool.

HOW IT WORKS IN PRACTICE

Its calculation is straightforward:

Contribution margin = Sales price − Variable cost

Or, for providers of services:

Contribution margin = Total revenue − Total variable cost

For example, if the sales price of a good is \$500 and the variable cost is \$350, the contribution margin is \$150, or 30% of the sales price.

This means that 30 cents of every sales dollar remains to contribute to fixed costs and to profit after the costs directly related to the sales are subtracted.

Contribution margin is especially useful to a company comparing different products or services (see the example below).

	Product A	Product B	Product C
Sales price	\$260	\$220	\$140
Variable costs	\$178	\$148	\$65
Contribution margin	\$82	\$72	\$75
Contribution margin	31.5%	32.7%	53.6%

Obviously, Product C has the highest contribution percentage, even though Product A generates more total profit. The analysis suggests that the company might do well to aim to achieve a sales mix with a higher proportion of Product C. It further suggests that prices for Products A and B may be too low, or that their cost structures need attention. Notably, none of this information appears on a standard income statement.

Contribution margin can also be tracked over a long period of time using data from several years of income statements. It can also be invaluable in calculating volume discounts for preferred customers, and break-even sales or volume levels.

TRICKS OF THE TRADE

Contribution margin depends on accurately accounting for all variable costs, including shipping and delivery, or the indirect costs of services. Activity-based cost accounting systems aid this kind of analysis. Variable costs include all direct costs (usually labor and materials). Contribution margin analysis is only one tool to use. It will not show so-called loss leaders, for example. And it doesn't consider marketing factors like existing penetration levels, opportunities, or mature markets being eroded by emerging markets.

MORE INFO

See Also:

Break-Even Analysis (pp. 1200–1201)

Marginal Cost (pp. 1234–1235)

Conversion Price

As often as not, when you need to calculate conversion price, it is not so much the calculation that is at issue, but observation.

WHAT IT MEASURES

The price per share at which the holder of convertible bonds, or debentures, or preferred stock, can convert them into shares of common stock.

Depending on specific terms, the conversion price may be set when the convertible asset is issued.

WHY IT IS IMPORTANT

The conversion price is a key factor in an investment strategy. Knowing it helps investors to determine whether or not it is to their advantage to convert their holdings into shares of stock, sell them on the open market, or retain them until they mature or are called by the issuing company.

At the same time, existing stockholders of the issuing company need to know the point at which the value of their shares could be diluted by the creation of additional shares without the concurrent creation of additional capital.

For companies themselves, a conversion price represents an additional financing option: an opportunity to convert debt into equity, an action that itself has advantages and drawbacks.

HOW IT WORKS IN PRACTICE

If the conversion price is set, it will appear in the indenture, a legal agreement between the issuer of a convertible asset and the holder, which states specific terms. If the conversion price does not appear

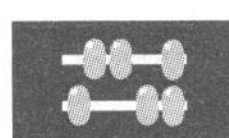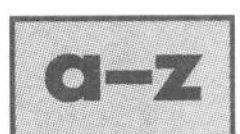

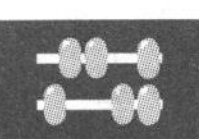

in the agreement, a conversion ratio is used to calculate the conversion price.

A conversion ratio of 25:1, for example, means that 25 shares of stock can be obtained in exchange for each $1,000 of convertible asset held. In turn, the conversion price can be determined simply by dividing $1,000 by 25:

$$\frac{1{,}000}{25} = \$40 \text{ per share}$$

Comparison of a stock's conversion price to its prevailing market price can help to decide the best course of action. If the stock of the company in question is trading at $52 per share, converting makes sense because it increases the value of $1,000 convertible to $1,300 ($52 × 25 shares). But if the stock is trading at $32 per share, then the conversion value is only $800 ($32 × 25), and it is clearly better to defer conversion.

TRICKS OF THE TRADE

- Conversion ratios may change over time according to the terms of the agreement. This is to ensure that a convertible asset holder is not unduly advantaged and that the value of existing stock is not diluted—which, of course, would anger existing stockholders.
- Stockholders, in turn, need to monitor closely a company that decides to issue a large number of convertible assets, since the value of their shares could ultimately be undermined.
- Convertible bonds closely follow the price of the issuing company's underlying stock. Often, in fact, the respective prices of the bond and the shares to be exchanged are almost equal.

MORE INFO

See Also:

Conversion Ratio (p. 1205)
Convertible Preferred Stock (p. 1206)

Conversion Ratio

Conversion ratio and conversion price work in tandem and should be considered together.

WHAT IT MEASURES

The number of shares of common stock an investor will receive on converting a convertible security—a bond, debenture, or preferred stock.

The conversion price may be set when the convertible security is issued, depending on its terms.

WHY IT IS IMPORTANT

Like conversion price, the conversion ratio is an investment strategy tool which is used to determine what the value of a convertible security would be if it were converted immediately. By knowing a convertible's value, an investor can compare it with the prevailing price of the issuing company's common stock and decide whether it is best to convert or to continue holding the convertible.

By the same token, holders of common stock in the company issuing the convertible can use the conversion ratio to help to monitor the value of their stock. For example, a relatively high ratio could mean that the value of their shares would be diluted if large numbers of convertible holders were to exercise their options.

HOW IT WORKS IN PRACTICE

In the same way as conversion price, the conversion ratio may be established when the convertible is issued. If that is the case, the ratio will appear in the indenture, the binding agreement that details the convertible's terms.

If the conversion ratio is not set, it can be calculated quickly: divide the par value of the convertible security (typically $1,000) by its conversion price:

$$\frac{\$1{,}000}{\$40 \text{ per share}} = 25 \text{ shares}$$

In this example, the conversion ratio is 25:1, which means that every bond held with a $1,000 par value can be exchanged for 25 shares of common stock.

Knowing the conversion ratio enables an investor to decide quickly whether his convertibles (or group of them) are more valuable than the shares of common stock they represent. If the stock is currently trading at $30, the conversion value is $750, or $250 less than the par value of the convertible. It would therefore be unwise to convert.

TRICKS OF THE TRADE

- Although it is rare, a convertible's indenture can sometimes contain a provision stating that the conversion ratio will change over the years.
- A conversion ratio that is set when a convertible is issued usually protects against any dilution from stock splits. However, it does not protect against a company issuing secondary offerings of common stock.
- "Forced conversion" means that the company can make holders convert into stock at virtually any time. Convertible holders should also pay close attention to the price at which the bonds are callable.
- Conversion ratio also describes the number of shares of one common stock to be issued for each outstanding share of another common stock when a merger takes place.

MORE INFO

See Also:

Conversion Price (pp. 1204–1205)
Convertible Preferred Stock (p. 1206)

  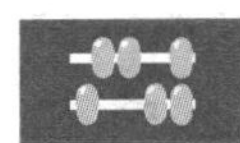      

Convertible Preferred Stock

Convertible preferred stock (known as preference shares in the United Kingdom) gives the holder the right to exchange it at a fixed price for another security, usually common stock. The trick is knowing if, and when, to exercise that right.

GETTING STARTED

- Evaluating convertible preferred stock is principally an analysis of risk rather than of a company.
- Preferred stocks are listed as equity on a balance sheet, but they perform more like bonds than common stock since most of these issues pay a fixed dividend set at the time of issue.
- While holders of preferred stock are entitled to a fixed dividend, they do not usually have voting rights.
- Preferred stocks are usually repayable at par value, and rank above the claims of ordinary stockholders but behind bank and trade creditors.
- An expensive form of capitalization, preferred stock is typically used to finance growth opportunities and capital expenditures, and to repay bank debt and nonbank short-term debt.
- Preferred stocks are often preferred by venture capitalists because they protect their investments better, and offer them greater leverage and growth opportunities.
- US income tax considerations severely limit the appeal of preferred stock among individual investors, but enhance it among corporations.

FAQS

Officially, what is convertible preferred stock?

It is a share of corporation ownership that gives holders a claim on earnings prior to the claim of common stockholders and, generally, on assets in the event of liquidation. It may also be exchanged for a fixed number of shares of common stock. Because no maturity date is stipulated, preferred stock is priced based on a stated dividend yield—in, for example, dollars, pounds, or euros—or as a percentage of par value.

How does preferred stock compare to common stock?

The dividend on common stock is uncertain and variable: high when a company performs well, low or nonexistent when it fares poorly. Holders of preferred stock, however, get a fixed dividend—and one which, if not paid, accrues until it can be. On the other hand, preferred stockholders are not usually able to vote on pertinent resolutions unless dividends fall into arrears, while holders of common stock have voting rights based on the number of shares owned.

Are there different kinds of preferred stock?

Yes. For example, callable preferred stock may be repurchased by the issuing company, typically at par value or slightly higher, while an indirect convertible may be exchanged for another convertible security, such as a bond that can be exchanged for convertible preferred stock. There are also participating preferred stocks, which entitle holders both to receive specified dividends and to participate along with holders of common stock in receiving additional dividends.

Any there other important distinguishing features of preferred stock?

First, there may be an option to receive cash for those who decline to exercise their conversion rights. Most preferred stocks also carry lower interest rates than similar fixed-interest securities, since the investor has the opportunity to convert his holdings to common stock and, in turn, to realize a capital gain if its price rises above its conversion price. Some preferred stocks also permit the investor to require the issuing company to redeem the stock after a predetermined time for an amount that gives the investor a modest profit.

Venture capitalists are known to prefer preferred stock. Why?

It gives them preference in the event of a company's liquidation or sale, which enables venture capitalists to get back their investment before other investors receive any proceeds from such events. A typical convertible preferred stock also enables venture capitalist investors to convert their shares into common stock according to a predetermined formula and to vote on major stockholder issues such as the election of directors and a change of the company's core business activity.

How are repeated conversions of preferred stock prevented from diluting the value of common stock?

The formula used to convert the convertible preferred stock into shares of common stock typically includes an adjustment mechanism—an "anti-dilution provision"—that protects the investor against any dilution in his percentage ownership caused by sale of cheaper stock to later investors. The nature and extent of the protection afforded can be very important also to the holders of the company's common stock: the greater the protection against dilution given to the holder of convertible preferred stock, the more dilution common stockholders are likely to suffer

MAKING IT HAPPEN

Like almost any stock consideration, evaluating convertible preferred stock opportunities and transactions is based on research, market knowledge, and past experience.

It is essential first to understand what a company does and how it generates cash. The next question is determining the likelihood of the company being able to pay its preferred dividends. The tools of choice are, first, a common "coverage ratio" like EBIT or EBITDA, and, second, preferred stock ratings.

EBITDA is the acronym for "earnings before interest, taxes, depreciation, and amortization." It usually measures a company's ability to handle debt service (interest payments), but can easily be adapted to include preferred stock dividends. The ratio is:

$$\frac{\text{EBITDA}}{(\text{Interest expense} + \text{Preferred dividends})}$$

The higher the coverage ratio, the better.

Like corporate bonds, most preferred stocks are rated by such services as Standard & Poor's and Moody's. Each rating service uses a slightly different rating system, but they have a similar basis: "A" is good, "AAA" is better, and so on. A "B" or above is considered investment grade, but anything below that is regarded as very high risk.

Another warning point is that, if a preferred stock is rated only by one of the second-tier rating agencies, the likelihood is that the company's management was unable to get a favorable rating from Standard & Poor's or Moody's. The investor relations offices and websites of most corporations will provide the ratings. If they do not, beware—although the websites of the rating services themselves will probably list them.

  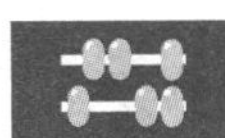      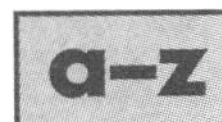

There are also some guidelines to follow. For instance, preferred stocks should have a higher yield than the issuing company's comparable debt (yield is the annual dividend divided by the price). This must be gauged on a case-by-case basis.

There is another long-held contention that higher-quality companies issue standard convertible preferred stock, while lower-quality companies issue convertible exchangeable preferred stock. Similarly, it is maintained that only the "best" companies are consistently able to issue straight debt cost-effectively, while medium-quality companies issue convertible securities, and lower-quality companies or high-risk companies tend to issue additional common stock.

Conversion ratios and prices are other key facts to know about preferred stock. This information is found on the indenture statement that accompanies all issues. Occasionally the indenture will state that the conversion ratio will change over time. For example, the conversion price might be $50 for the first five years, $55 for the next five years, and so forth. Stock splits can affect conversion considerations.

In theory, convertible preferred stocks (and convertible exchangeable preferred stocks) are usually perpetual in time. However, issuers tend to force conversion or induce voluntary conversion for convertible preferred stock within 10 years. Steadily increasing common stock dividends is one inducement tactic used. As a result, the conversion feature for preferred stocks often resembles that of debt securities. Call protection for the investor is usually about three years, and a 30- to 60-day call notice is typical.

About 50% of convertible equity issues also have a "soft call provision." If the common stock price reaches a specified ratio, the issuer is permitted to force conversion before the end of the normal protection period. Converting preferred stock risks diluting common stock, of course, and among mature companies that is a valid concern. Where a company has a good track record and aggressive growth plans, however, it may benefit both investors and the company, especially if the management can maintain (or increase) profit margin.

TRICKS OF THE TRADE

- In any country, tax considerations invariably accompany the exercise of convertible preferred stock transactions. Here are considerations based on US laws:
- Like common stock, preferred stock comes with a prospectus that should answer such basic questions as: Are the dividends cumulative? Are the shares redeemable; if so, when? What is the likelihood of redemption? Has the board of directors ever suspended dividends? (If it has, this is a bad sign indicating cash flow problems).
- At least in the United States, many companies dislike issuing preferred stock because it is an expensive form of capitalization. Preferred stock pays dividends from after-tax profits, while bonds pay interest from pre-tax dollars, thus delivering a tax break that preferred stock cannot match.
- Owning preferred stocks of other companies is another matter, however: corporations are exempt from taxes on up to 80% of preferred dividend income.
- Missing preferred stock dividends is not legally a default, but a company that omits a preferred stock dividend may not pay common stock dividends. Moreover, if subsequent preferred stock dividends are missed, preferred stock shareholders may gain board seats (or more of them), and in some cases also accrue special voting rights.
- Most preferred issues are cumulative, so dividends accrue even if they are not actually paid in a given quarter. Once the dividends are resumed, and before common dividends can be paid, cumulative preferred shareholders must be paid their accrued dividends.
- If a company is liquidated, holders of preferred stock are entitled to receive their investment back before the holders of any common stock receive anything. In other words, "investment" means the amount paid for the preferred stock plus any accrued and unpaid dividends—an important consideration.
- Preferred stocks and other convertible securities offer investors a hedge: fixed-interest income without sacrificing the chance to participate in a company's capital appreciation.
- When a company does well, investors can convert their holdings into common stock that is more valuable. When a company is less successful, they can still receive interest and principal payments, and also recover their investment and preserve their capital if a more favorable investment appears.

MORE INFO

Book:

Jenks, Philip, and Stephen Eckett. *The Global Investor Book of Investing Rules*. London: Harriman House, 2001.

See Also:

Conversion Price (pp. 1204–1205)
Conversion Ratio (p. 1205)

Cost of Goods Sold

WHAT IT MEASURES

For a retailer, cost of goods sold (COGS) is the cost of buying and acquiring the goods that it sells to its customers. For a service company, COGS is the cost of the employee services it supplies. For a manufacturer, COGS is the cost of buying the raw materials and manufacturing its finished products.

WHY IT IS IMPORTANT

Cost of goods sold may help a company to determine the prices to charge for its products and services, and the volume of business that it needs to maintain in order to operate profitably.

For retailers especially, the cost of the merchandise sold is typically the largest expense, and thus is an absolutely critical business factor. However, understanding COGS is an important success factor for any business because it can reveal opportunities to reduce costs and improve operations.

COGS is also a key figure on an income statement, and an important consideration in computing income taxes because of its close relationship to inventory, which tax authorities treat as future income.

HOW IT WORKS IN PRACTICE

Essentially, COGS is equal to a company's opening inventory of goods and services, plus the cost of goods bought and direct costs incurred during a particular period, minus the closing inventory of goods and services.

A critical consideration is the accounting policy that a company adopts to calculate inventory values, especially if raw materials prices change during the year. This may happen often, particularly when inflation is high. Inventory values under a first in first out (FIFO) policy reflect original or older prices of materials, while a last in first out (LIFO) policy reflects current (and often more expensive) prices. Somebody computing COGS first needs to know which policy is being used, because this will affect inventory values.

COGS for a manufacturer will include a variety of items, such as raw materials and energy used in production, labor, benefits for production workers, the cost of raw materials in inventory, shipping fees, the cost of storing finished products, depreciation on production machinery used, and factory overhead expenses.

For a retail company such as Wal-Mart, COGS is generally less complex: the total amount paid to suppliers for the products being sold on its shelves.

COGS is calculated as follows:

Inventory at beginning of period	$20,000
Purchases during period	+ $60,000
Cost of goods available for sale	=$80,000
Less inventory at period end	− $15,000
Cost of goods sold (COGS)	=$65,000

Because the counting of inventory is an exhaustive undertaking for retailers, doing it quarterly or monthly would be open to error. Accordingly, tax authorities allow them to estimate cost of goods sold during the year.

Determining these estimates requires details of the gross profit margin (retailers typically use the preceding year's figure). This figure is then used to calculate the cost ratio.

Begin by assuming that net sales are 100%, then subtract the gross profit margin, say 40%, to produce a cost ratio of 60%: 100% − 40% = 60%. A monthly COGS calculation then looks like this:

Inventory at beginning of month	$10,000
Purchases during month	+ $25,000
Cost of goods available for sale	= $35,000
Less net sales during month	− $28,000
Cost ratio 100% – 40%	= 60%
Estimated cost of goods sold	= $16,800 ($28,000 × 60%)

There is another example to review, because calculating COGS for manufacturers requires additional factors:

Inventory at beginning of year	$20,000
Purchases during year	+ $50,000
Cost of direct labor	+ $15,000
Materials and supplies	+ $12,000
Misc. costs	+ $3,000
Total product expenses	= $100,000
Less inventory at year end	− $15,000
Cost of goods sold (COGS)	= $85,000

TRICKS OF THE TRADE

- Anyone who wants to determine COGS must maintain inventory and know its value!
- Because goods returned affect inventory values and, in turn, cost of goods sold, returns of goods must be reflected in COGS calculations.
- Merchandising companies may use different inventory accounting systems, but the choice has no bearing on the actual costs incurred; it only affects allocation of costs.
- COGS should not include indirect costs like administration and marketing costs, or other activities that cannot be directly attributed to producing or acquiring the product.

Covariance

WHAT IT MEASURES

Covariance measures the relationship between two random variables. For example, we might measure whether a sample population liked drinking wine, and whether they liked eating cheese. Covariance is a form of probability theory that allows us to measure the extent to which those two random variables change together. It's important to remember this does not imply causality—simply because one variable increases along with another does not mean there is necessarily a link between the two variables.

If the two variables tend to change together—showing that people who particularly enjoy drinking wine tend to particularly enjoy eating cheese—there is said to be positive covariance. If the two variables move in opposite directions—people who drink wine tend to be less keen on cheese—the covariance is said to be negative. Random variables that do not relate in either way are said to be uncorrelated.

WHY IT IS IMPORTANT

For investors, covariance is an important way of seeing how one variable is related to another, particularly when analyzing the performance of stocks or investments within a portfolio.

For example, an investor might want to see the impact that multiple changes on a portfolio affect overall returns, or the relationship between a company's debt/equity ratio and working capital cycle. Covariance is often used in measuring the performance of securities.

As a rule of thumb, a high rate of covariance suggests a portfolio that is not diversified, and which presents a high level of risk. For example, if two stock prices tend to rise and fall at the same time, these stocks would not deliver the best diversified earnings.

HOW IT WORKS IN PRACTICE

Covariance provides a way of measuring the strength of correlation between two random variables. The covariance for two random variables x and y, with a sample size of n, is as follows:

$$\text{Covariance } xy = \frac{\sum xx}{n}$$

As an example, imagine we asked four men to rate their liking for both cheese and wine, on a scale of 1 to 10. The results were as follows:

	Cheese (x)	Wine (y)	x	y	zy
A	3	4	−1	−2	2
B	1	4	−3	−2	6
C	3	8	−1	2	−2
D	9	8	5	2	10
Sum	16	24	0	0	16
Mean	4	6	0	0	4

To calculate the covariance, we calculate a mean for both variables. Next, both variables are transformed into deviation scores by subtracting the mean from the relevant score. The products of these deviation scores can then be calculated, summed, and averaged. The result is known as the coefficient of covariance, in this case 4.

Expressed in simpler terms: the sum of the product of variables x and y is 112, and the mean is 28. Subtracting the product of the separate means (28 − 4 × 6 yields the coefficient of covariance equal to 4).

TRICKS OF THE TRADE

- In probability theory, covariance is closely related to the concept of correlation—both of these tools are ways of measuring the similarity of two random variables.
- The coefficient of covariance has no upper or lower limits. Some statisticians point out this indeterminacy is its main disadvantage as compared with the coefficient of correlation.
- In our example, we have calculated covariance by multiplying the correlation of two random variables by the standard deviation. However, you can also calculate covariance by looking at "return surprises" (deviations from an expected return), which can be useful when analyzing securities.

Creating a Balance Sheet

WHAT IT MEASURES

The financial standing, or even the net worth or owners' equity, of a company at a given point in time, typically at the end of a calendar or fiscal year.

WHY IT IS IMPORTANT

The balance sheet shows what is owned (assets), what is owed (liabilities), and what is left (owners' equity). It provides a concise snapshot of a company's financial position.

HOW IT WORKS IN PRACTICE

However they are presented, assets must be in balance with liabilities and stockholders' equity. In other words, assets must equal liabilities plus owners' equity.

Assets include cash in hand and cash anticipated (receivables), inventory of supplies and materials, properties, facilities, equipment, and whatever else the company uses to conduct its business. Assets also need to reflect depreciation in the value of equipment, such as machinery, that has a limited expected useful life.

Liabilities include pending payments to suppliers and creditors, outstanding current and long-term debts, taxes, interest payments, and other unpaid expenses that the company has incurred.

Subtracting the value of aggregate liabilities from the value of aggregate assets reveals the value of owners' equity. Ideally, this should be positive. Owners' equity consists of capital invested by owners over the years and profits (net income) or internally generated capital, which is referred to as "retained earnings;" these are funds to be used in future operations. An example is given opposite.

Assets	*$*
Current	
Cash	8,200
Securities	5,000
Receivables	4,500
Inventory and supplies	6,300
Fixed	
Land	10,000
Structures	90,000
Equipment (less depreciation)	5,000
Intangibles/other	
...	...
Total assets	129,000

Liabilities	*$*
Payables	7,000
Taxes	4,000
Miscellaneous	3,000
Bonds and notes	25,000
Total liabilities	**39,000**
Stockholders' equity (stock, par value × shares outstanding)	80,000
Retained earnings	10,000
Total liabilities and stockholders' equity	**129,000**

TRICKS OF THE TRADE

- The balance sheet does not show a company's market worth, nor important intangibles such as the knowledge and talents of individual people, nor other vital business factors such as customers or market share.
- The balance sheet does not express the true value of some fixed assets. A six-year-old manufacturing plant, for example, is listed at its original cost, even though the price of replacing it could be much higher or substantially lower (because of new technology that might be less expensive or vastly more efficient).
- The balance sheet is not an indicator of past or future performance or trends that affect performance. It needs to be studied along with two other key reports: the income tax return and the cash flow statement. A published balance sheet needs to include prior period comparatives.

MORE INFO

Website:

Conetic Software Systems Inc.: www.conetic.com

See Also:

✔ Preparing Financial Statements: Balance Sheets (p. 1046)
✔ Understanding the Balance Sheet (p. 999)

  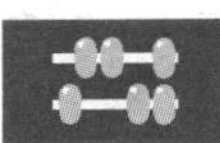      

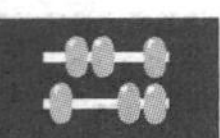

Creating a Cash Flow Statement

WHAT IT MEASURES

Cash inflows and cash outflows over a specific period of time, typically a year.

WHY IT IS IMPORTANT

Cash flow is a key indicator of financial health, and it demonstrates to investors, creditors, and other core constituencies a company's ability to meet obligations, finance opportunities, and generally "come up with the cash" as needs arise. Cash flow that is wildly inconsistent with, say, net income, often indicates operating or managerial problems.

HOW IT WORKS IN PRACTICE

In its basic form, a cash flow statement will probably be familiar to anyone who has been a member of a club that collects and spends money. It reports funds on hand at the beginning of a given period, funds received, funds spent, and funds remaining at the end of the period.

That formula still applies to a business today, even if creating a cash flow document is significantly more complex. Cash flows are divided into three categories: cash from operations; cash investment activities; and cash financing activities. Companies with holdings in foreign currencies use a fourth category: effects of changes in exchange rates on cash.

A standard direct cash flow statement is shown opposite.

TRICKS OF THE TRADE

- A cash flow statement does *not* measure net income, nor does it measure working capital.
- A cash flow statement does not include outstanding accounts receivable, but it does include the preceding year's accounts receivable (assuming these were collected during the year for which the statement is prepared).
- Add to a cash inflow any amounts charged off for depreciation, depletion, and amortization, because cash was actually spent.
- Cash equivalents are short-term, highly liquid investments, although precise definitions may vary slightly by country. These should be included when recalculating the movement of cash in the period.
- There are alternative ways to present cash flow from operations. Some texts, for example, omit earnings and adjustments, and list instead cash and interest received, cash and interest paid, and taxes received.

CRD, Inc. statement of cash flows for year ended December 31, 20__

	$
Cash flows from operations ($)	
Operating profit	82,000
Adjustments to net earnings	
Depreciation	17,000
Accounts receivable	–20,000
Accounts payable	12,000
Inventory	– 8,000
Other adjustments to earnings	4,000
Net cash flow from operations	*87,000*
Cash flows from investment activities ($)	
Purchases of marketable securities	– 58,000
Receipts from sales of marketable securities	45,000
Loans made to borrowers	– 16,000
Collections on loans	11,000
Purchases of plant and real estate assets	– 150,000
Receipts from sales of plant and real estate assets	47,000
Net cash flow from investment activities	*– 121,000*
Cash flows from financing activities ($)	
Proceeds from short-term borrowings	51,000
Payments to settle short-term debts	– 61,000
Proceeds from issuing bonds payable	100,000
Proceeds from issuing capital stock	80,000
Dividends paid	– 64,000
Net cash flow from financing activities	*106,000*
Net change in cash during period	**72,000**
Cash and cash equivalents, beginning of year	27,000
Cash and cash equivalents, end of year	**99,000**

MORE INFO

Website:

International Accounting Standards Consultancy (IASC): www.iasc.co.uk

See Also:

★ Best Practices in Cash Flow Management and Reporting (pp. 16–19)
★ Cash Flow Best Practice for Small and Medium-Sized Enterprises (pp. 28–29)
✔ Preparing a Cash Flow Forecast (p. 986)

Creating a Profit and Loss (P&L) Account

WHAT IT MEASURES

A company's sales revenues and expenses over a period, providing a calculation of profits or losses during that time.

WHY IT IS IMPORTANT

Reading a P&L is the easiest way to tell if a business has made a profit or a loss during a given month or year. The most important figure it contains is net profit: what is left over after revenues are used to pay expenses and taxes.

Companies typically issue P&L reports monthly. It is customary for the reports to include year-to-date figures, as well as corresponding year-earlier figures to allow for comparisons and analysis.

HOW IT WORKS IN PRACTICE

A P&L adheres to a simple rule of thumb: "Revenue minus cost equals profit."

There are two P&L formats, multiple-step and single-step. Both follow a standard set of rules known as "generally accepted accounting principles" (GAAP). These rules generally adhere to requirements established by governments to track receipts, expenses, and profits for tax purposes. They also allow the financial

Multiple-step profit and loss accounts ($)

NET SALES			750,000
Less: cost of goods sold			450,000
Gross profit			300,000
LESS: OPERATING EXPENSES			
Selling expenses			
Salaries & commissions	54,000		
Advertising	37,500		
Delivery/transportation	12,000		
Depreciation/store equipment	7,500		
Other selling expenses	5,000		
Total selling expenses		116,000	
General & administrative expenses			
Administrative/office salaries	74,000		
Utilities	2,500		
Depreciation/structure	2,400		
Misc. other expenses	3,100		
Total general & admin expenses		82,000	
Total operating expenses			198,000
OPERATING INCOME			102,000
LESS (ADD): NONOPERATING ITEMS			
Interest expenses	11,000		
Interest income earned	– 2,800		8,200
Income before taxes			93,800
Income taxes			32,360
Net income			**61,440**

reports of two different companies to be compared. Note that in the United Kingdom and several other nations, sales, revenues, and receipts may all be designated as turnover.

The multiple-step format is much more common, because it includes a larger number of details and is thus more useful. It deducts costs from revenues in a series of steps, allowing for closer analysis. Revenues appear first, then expenses, each in as much detail as management desires. Sales may be broken down by product line or location, while expenses such as salaries may be broken down into base salaries and commissions.

Expenses are then subtracted from revenues to show profit (or loss). A basic multiple-step P&L is shown opposite.

TRICKS OF THE TRADE

- A P&L does not show how a business has earned or spent its money.
- One month's P&L can be misleading, especially if a business generates most of its receipts in particular months. A retail establishment, for example, usually generates a large percentage of its sales in the final three months of the year, while a consulting service might generate the lion's share of its revenues in as few as two months, and no revenues at all in some other months.
- Invariably, figures for both revenues and expenses reflect the judgments of the companies reporting them. Accounting methods can be quite arbitrary when it comes to such factors as depreciation expenses.

MORE INFO

See Also:

✔ Preparing Financial Statements: Profit and Loss Accounts (P&Ls) (p. 1047)

Creditor and Debtor Days

These financial measures are two sides of the same coin, since they respectively measure the flow of money out of and into a business. As such, they are reliable indicators of both efficiency and problems.

WHAT THEY MEASURE

Creditor days is a measure of the number of days on average that a company requires to pay its creditors, while debtor days is a measure of the number of days on average that it takes a company to receive payment for what it sells. It is also called accounts receivable days.

WHY THEY ARE IMPORTANT

Creditor days is an indication of a company's creditworthiness in the eyes of its suppliers and creditors, since it shows how long they are willing to wait for payment. Within reason, the higher the number the better because all companies want to conserve cash. At the same time, a company that is especially slow to pay its bills (100 or more days, for example) may be a company having trouble generating cash, or one trying to finance its operations with its suppliers' funds. Ultimately, companies whose creditor days soar have trouble obtaining supplies.

Debtor days is an indication of a company's efficiency in collecting monies owed. In this case, obviously, the lower the number the better. An especially high number is a telltale sign of inefficiency or worse. It may indicate bad debts, dubious sales figures, or a company being bullied by large customers out to improve their own cash position at another company's expense. Customers whose credit terms are abused also risk higher borrowing costs and related charges.

Changes in both measures are easy to spot, and easy to understand.

HOW THEY WORK IN PRACTICE

To determine creditor days, divide the cumulative amount of unpaid suppliers' bills (also called trade creditors) by sales, then multiply by 365. So the formula is:

$$\text{Creditor days} = \frac{\text{Trade creditors}}{\text{Sales}} \times 365$$

For example, if suppliers' bills total $800,000 and sales are $9,000,000, the calculation is:

$$\frac{800{,}000}{9{,}000{,}000} \times 365 = 32.44 \text{ days}$$

The company takes 32.44 days on average to pay its bills.

To determine debtor days, divide the cumulative amount of accounts receivable by sales, then multiply by 365. For example, if accounts receivable total $600,000 and sales are $9,000,000, the calculation is:

$$\frac{600{,}000}{9{,}000{,}000} \times 365 = 24.33 \text{ days}$$

The company takes 24.33 days on average to collect its debts.

     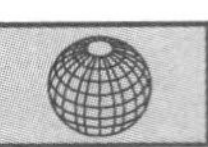   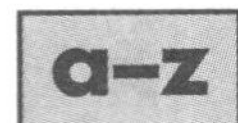

TRICKS OF THE TRADE

- Cash businesses, including most retailers, should have a much lower debtor days figure than noncash businesses, since they receive payment when they sell the goods. A typical target for noncash businesses is 40–50 days.
- An abnormally high creditor days figure may not only suggest a cash crisis, but also the management's difficulty in maintaining revolving credit agreements.
- An increasing number of debtor days also suggests overly generous credit terms (to bolster sales) or problems with product quality.

Current Price of a Bond

WHAT IT MEASURES

The narrow range within which a given bond price falls, based on that bond's current asking price and bid price.

WHY IT IS IMPORTANT

Current prices of comparable bonds are strong indicators of a bond's buying or selling price. Changes in bond prices are also indicators of economic strength and direction.

HOW IT WORKS IN PRACTICE

The price of a bond depends on several factors.

- Interest rates: As rates rise, a bond's price falls, because it pays less interest than current offerings and is thus less attractive. Conversely, a bond becomes more attractive as interest rates fall.
- The risk perceived for the issuing entity, reflected in its credit rating from one of the major rating agencies. The price of a bond of a company in bankruptcy, for instance, will be low because the company may never be able to redeem it. The price of a bond from a strong company may include a premium over its face or "par" value because it is considered a reliable investment: a bond with a face value of $1,000 might sell for $1,050, indicating a $50 premium.
- The issuing of new bonds by corporations or other bodies (and the ratings they receive) affects the prices of existing bonds.

Daily bond tables vary in format, but list the basic information necessary for comparing prices. Only a small fraction of the outstanding bonds trade on any given day, but these representative prices provide sufficient information to estimate what a fair price would be for the bonds being considered.

When considering bonds, several pieces of information are essential:

- the bond's coupon rate—what it will pay in interest;
- how long before the principal amount of the bond matures, or if there is a call date;
- its recent price and current yield.

Essentially, all the tables provide this basic information. The US Treasury table, for example, would be listed as follows:

Rate	Maturity	Bid	Ask	Yield
$7\frac{3}{4}$	Feb 2012	105:12	105:14	5.50
$5\frac{3}{8}$	Feb 2012	99:26	99:27	5.44

In the first row, the security is paying its bondholders $7\frac{3}{4}$% interest and is due to mature in February 2012. Prices in the bid and ask columns are percentages of the bond's face value of $1,000. A bid of 105:12 means that a buyer was willing to pay $1053.75, compared to the seller's lowest asking price, 105:14, or $1054.38, a difference of 63 cents per thousand.

Bond quotes follow certain conventions. Prices are given as percentages of face value, but the digits appearing after the colons are not decimals, being expressed in terms of 1/32. So 12/32, for example, would equal $3.75, which is appended to the 105 before the colon: $1053.75.

The bid and ask prices indicate that an investor who bought the bond at par when it was first issued can make a profit of more than 5% if it were sold now. The last column gives the yield to maturity, an interest rate summarizing the bond's overall investment value.

COMMON MISTAKES

- A bond's yield and its price are not the same. Price is what is paid for a bond; yield expresses the percentage return on the investment. Yield is most useful for comparing fixed-income investments for planning purposes, rather than as an exact measure of the return expected from an investment.
- The number of bond issues outstanding at any given time is far greater than stocks, and most bondholders buy with the intent of holding them until maturity, so the amount of trading is limited.
- There are several bond-rating agencies. A bond's rating indicates its level of risk.
- Listing tables also show the volume traded along with the current yield.
- The internet offers many calculators for quickly determining bond prices and yields.

MORE INFO

Article:

Kamlet, Art, and Chris Lott. "Bonds—Basics." *The Investment FAQ* (July 5, 1998). Online at: www.invest-faq.com/articles/bonds-a-basics.html

Website:

InvestingInBonds.com, from the Securities Industry and Financial Markets Association (SIFMA): www.investinginbonds.com

See Also:

✔ The Bond Market: Its Structure and Function (p. 1064)
⇄ Bond Yield (pp. 1197–1198)

Current Ratio

The current ratio is a key liquidity ratio and a staple for anyone who borrows or lends money.

WHAT IT MEASURES

A company's liquidity and its ability to meet its short-term debt obligations.

WHY IT IS IMPORTANT

By comparing a company's current assets with its current liabilities, the current ratio reflects its ability to pay its upcoming bills in the unlikely event of all creditors demanding payment at once. It has long been the measurement of choice among financial institutions and lenders.

HOW IT WORKS IN PRACTICE

The current ratio formula is simply:

$$\text{Current ratio} = \frac{\text{Current assets}}{\text{Current liabilities}}$$

Current assets are the ones that a company can turn into cash within 12 months during the ordinary course of business. Current liabilities are bills due to be paid within the coming 12 months.

For example, if a company's current assets are $300,000 and its current liabilities are $200,000, its current ratio would be:

$$\frac{300{,}000}{200{,}000} = 1.5$$

As a rule of thumb, the 1.5 figure means that a company should be able to get hold of $1.50 for every $1.00 it owes.

TRICKS OF THE TRADE

- The higher the ratio, the more liquid the company. Prospective lenders expect a positive current ratio, often of at least 1.5. However, too high a ratio is cause for alarm, because it indicates declining receivables and/or inventory—signs that portend declining liquidity.
- A current ratio of less than 1 suggests pressing liquidity problems, specifically an inability to generate sufficient cash to meet upcoming demands.
- Managements use current ratio as well as lenders; a low ratio, for example, may indicate the need to refinance a portion of short-term debt with long-term debt to improve a company's liquidity.
- Ratios vary by industry, however, and should be used accordingly. Some sectors, such as supermarket chains and restaurants, perform nicely with low ratios that would keep others awake at night.
- One shortcoming of the current ratio is that it does not differentiate assets, some of which may not be easily converted to cash. As a result, lenders also refer to the quick ratio.
- Another shortcoming of the current ratio is that it reflects conditions at a single point in time, such as when the balance sheet is prepared. It is possible to make this figure look good just for this occasion: lenders should not, therefore, appraise these conditions by the ratio alone.
- A constant current ratio and falling quick ratio signal trouble ahead, because this suggests that a company is amassing assets at the expense of receivables and cash.

MORE INFO

See Also:

✔ Measuring Liquidity (p. 983)
Acid-Test Ratio (pp. 1189–1190)
Liquidity Ratio Analysis (pp. 1232–1233)

Days Sales Outstanding

Days sales outstanding (DSO) can be considered as a tool for financial troubleshooters.

WHAT IT MEASURES

A company's average collection period, or the average number of days it takes a company to convert its accounts receivable into cash. Commonly referred to as DSO, it is also called the collection ratio.

WHY IT IS IMPORTANT

Knowing how long it takes a company to turn accounts receivable into cash is an important financial indicator. It indicates the efficiency of the company's internal collection, suggests how well a company's customers are accepting its credit terms (net 30 days, for example), and is a figure that is routinely compared with industry averages.

Ideally, DSOs should be decreasing or constant. A low figure means the company collects its outstanding receivables quickly. Typically, DSO is reviewed quarterly or yearly (91 or 365 days).

DSO also helps to expose companies that try to disguise weak sales. Large increases in DSO suggest that a company is trying to force sales either by accepting poor receivable terms or selling products at discount to book more sales for a particular period. An improving DSO suggests that a company is striving to make its operations more efficient.

Any company with a significant change in its DSO merits examination in greater detail.

HOW IT WORKS IN PRACTICE

Regular DSO requires three figures: total accounts receivable, total credit sales for the period analyzed, and the number of days in the period (annual, 365; six months, 182; quarter, 91). The formula is:

$$\text{Days sales outstanding} = \frac{\text{Accounts receivable}}{\text{Total credit sales for the period}} \times \text{Number of days in the period}$$

For example: if total receivables are $4,500,000, total credit sales in a quarter are $9,000,000, and number of days is 91, then:

$$\frac{4{,}500{,}000}{9{,}000{,}000} \times 91 = 45.5 \text{ days}$$

Thus, it takes an average of 45.5 days to collect receivables.

  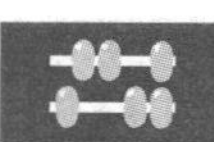      

TRICKS OF THE TRADE

- Companies use DSO information with an accounts receivable aging report. This lists four categories of receivables: 0–30 days, 30–60 days, 60–90 days, and over 90 days. The report also shows the percentage of total accounts receivable that each group represents, allowing for an analysis of delinquencies and potential bad debts—a figure that appears on a profit and loss account.
- A rarely used related calculation, best possible DSO, shows how long it takes a company to collect current receivables. Its formula is:

$$\text{Best possible DSO} = \frac{\text{Current receivables}}{\text{Total credit sales for the period}} \times \text{Number of days in the period}$$

So, current receivables of $3,000,000 and total credit sales of $9,000,000 in a 91-day period would result in a best possible DSO of 30.3 days (3,000,000 ÷ 9,000,000 × 91).

- Only credit sales of merchandise should be used in calculating DSO; cash sales are excluded, as are sales of such items as fixtures, equipment, or real estate.
- Properly evaluating an acceptable DSO requires a standard for comparison. A traditional rule of thumb is that DSO should not exceed one-third to one-half of selling terms. For instance, if terms are 30 days, acceptable DSO would be 40 to 45 days.
- A single DSO is only a snapshot. A fuller picture would require at least quarterly calculations, and some companies review DSO monthly.
- DSO can vary widely by industry as well as company. For example, clothing wholesalers have to have the goods on retailers' shelves for months before they will be sold and the retailer is able to cover invoices. However, a computer wholesaler with a lengthy DSO suggests trouble, since computers become obsolete quickly.

MORE INFO

See Also:

Asset Utilization (pp. 1195–1196)

Debt/Capital Ratio

Whether called debt/capital ratio, debt-to-capital ratio, or simply debt ratio, this is a fundamental tool in analyzing how a company is funded. It is also known as the gearing ratio.

WHAT IT MEASURES

The percentage of total funding represented by debt.

WHY IT IS IMPORTANT

By comparing a company's long-term liabilities to its total capital, the debt/capital ratio provides a review of the extent to which a company relies on external debt financing for its funding and is a measure of the risk to its stockholders.

The debt/capital ratio is also a measure of a company's borrowing capacity, and of its ability to pay scheduled financial payments on term debts and capital leases. Bond-rating agencies and analysts use it routinely to assess creditworthiness. The greater the debt, the higher the risk.

However, it can be misleading to assume that the lowest ratio is automatically the best ratio. A company may assume large amounts of debt in order to expand the business. Utilities, for instance, have high capital requirements, so their debt/capital ratios will be high as a matter of course. So are those of manufacturing companies, especially those developing a new technology or new product.

At the same time, the higher the level of debt, the more important it is for a company to have positive earnings and steady cash flow.

HOW IT WORKS IN PRACTICE

Although there are variations on exactly what goes into this ratio, the most common method is to divide total long-term debt by total assets (total long-term debt plus stockholders' funds), or:

$$\text{Debt/capital ratio} = \frac{\text{Total liabilities}}{\text{Total assets}}$$

For example, if the balance sheet of a corporate annual report lists total liabilities of $9,800,000 and total stockholders' equity of $12,800,000, the debt/capital ratio is (calculating in thousands):

$$\frac{9{,}800}{(9{,}800 + 12{,}800)} = \frac{9{,}800}{22{,}600}$$
$$= 0.434$$
$$= 43.4\%$$

Some formulas distinguish different portions of long-term debt. However, that complicates calculations and many experts regard it as unnecessary. It is also common to express the formula as total debt divided by total funds, which produces the same outcome.

TRICKS OF THE TRADE

- If a company has minority interests in subsidiaries that are consolidated in the balance sheet, they must be added to stockholders' equity.
- Debt calculations should include capital leases.
- One rule of thumb holds that a debt/capital ratio of 60% or less is acceptable, but another holds that 40% is the most desirable.
- A high debt/capital ratio means less security for stockholders, because in bankruptcies debt holders are paid first. It still can be tolerable, however, if a company's return on assets exceeds the rate of interest paid to creditors.
- Do not confuse the debt/capital ratio with debt/capitalization, which compares debt with total market capitalization and fluctuates as the company's stock price changes.

MORE INFO

See Also:

Capitalization Ratios (pp. 1202–1203)
Debt/Equity Ratio (p. 1215)

  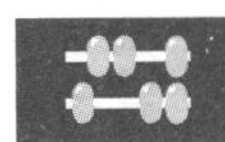      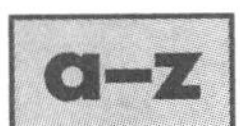

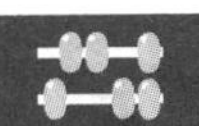

Debt/Equity Ratio

Debt/equity is the most commonly used method of assessing corporate debt, but in fact there is more than one way of expressing essentially the same thing.

WHAT IT MEASURES

How much money a company owes compared with how much money it has invested in it by principal owners and stockholders.

WHY IT IS IMPORTANT

The debt/equity ratio reveals the proportion of debt and equity a company is using to finance its business. It also measures a company's borrowing capacity. The higher the ratio, the greater the proportion of debt—but also the greater the risk.

Some even describe the debt/equity ratio as "a great financial test" of long-term corporate health, because debt establishes a commitment to repay money throughout a period of time, even though there is no assurance that sufficient cash will be generated to meet that commitment.

Creditors and lenders, understandably, rely heavily on the ratio to evaluate borrowers.

HOW IT WORKS IN PRACTICE

The debt/equity ratio is calculated by dividing debt by owners' equity, where equity is, typically, the figure stated for the preceding calendar or fiscal year. Debt, however, can be defined either as long-term debt only, or as total liabilities, which include both long- and short-term debt.

The most common formula for the ratio is:

$$\text{Debt/equity ratio} = \frac{\text{Total liabilities}}{\text{Owners' equity}}$$

In our example, a company's long-term debt is \$8,000,000, its short-term debt is \$4,000,000, and owners' equity totals \$9,000,000. The debt/equity ratio would therefore be (calculating in thousands):

$$\frac{(8{,}000 + 4{,}000)}{9{,}000} = \frac{12{,}000}{9{,}000} = 1.33$$

An alternative debt/equity formula considers only long-term liabilities in the equation. Accordingly:

$$\frac{8{,}000}{9{,}000} = 0.889$$

There is also a third method, which is the reciprocal of the debt-to-capital ratio; its formula is:

$$\text{Debt/equity ratio} = \frac{\text{Owners' equity}}{\text{Total funds}}$$

However, this would be more accurately defined as "equity/debt ratio."

TRICKS OF THE TRADE

- It is important to understand exactly how debt is defined in the ratio presented.
- When calculating the ratio, some prefer to use the market value of debt and equity rather than the book value, since book value often understates current value.
- For this ratio, a low number indicates better financial stability than a high one does; if the ratio is high, a company could be at risk, especially if interest rates are rising.
- A ratio greater than one means assets are mainly financed with debt; less than one means equity provides most of the financing. Since a higher ratio generally means that a company has been aggressive in financing its growth with debt, volatile earnings can result owing to the additional cost of interest.
- Debt/equity ratio is somewhat industry-specific, and often depends on the amount of capital investment required.

MORE INFO

See Also:

Capital Expenditure (p. 1202)
Debt/Capital Ratio (p. 1214)

Defining Assets

WHAT THEY MEASURE

Collectively, the value of all the resources a company uses to conduct business and generate profits. Examples of assets are cash, marketable securities, accounts and notes receivable, inventory of merchandise, real estate, machinery and office equipment, natural resources, and intangibles such as patents, legal claims and agreements, and negotiated rights.

WHY THEY ARE IMPORTANT

No business can continue for very long without knowing what assets it has at its disposal, and using them efficiently. Assets are a reflection of organizational strength, and are invariably evaluated by potential investors, banks, and creditors, and other stakeholders. Moreover, the value of assets is also a key figure that is used to calculate several financial ratios.

HOW THEY WORK IN PRACTICE

Assets are typically broken down into five different categories:

1. **Current assets**. These include cash, cash equivalents, marketable securities, inventory, and prepaid expenses that are expected to be used within one year or a normal operating cycle. All cash items and inventory are reported at historical value. Securities are reported at market value.
2. **Noncurrent assets**, or long-term investments. These are resources that are expected to be held for more than one year. They are reported at the lower of cost and current market value, which means that their values will vary.
3. **Fixed assets**. These include property, plant and facilities, and equipment used to conduct business. These items are reported at their original value, even though current values might well be much higher.

4 **Intangible assets**. These include legal claims, patents, franchise rights, and accounts receivable. These values can be more difficult to determine. Accounts receivable, for example, reflect the amount a business expects to collect, such as $9,000 of the $10,000 owed by customers.
5 **Deferred charges**. These include prepaid costs and other expenditures that will produce future revenue or benefits.

TRICKS OF THE TRADE

- Assets do not necessarily include everything of value, such as the talents of individuals, an organization's collective expertise, or the value of a customer base.
- Classic definitions of assets also often exclude or undervalue trademarks, even though there is universal agreement that these— for example, the three-point star of Mercedes-Benz or Coca-Cola's red logo—can have enormous value.
- Fixed assets are valued at their original cost, because of the prevailing opinion that they are used for business and are not for sale. Moreover, current market value is essentially a matter of opinion.
- Determining the value of patents can be challenging, because a patent has a finite life span, its value declines each year, and its useful life may be even shorter.
- Some experts contend that the principal assets of "knowledge-based" businesses such as consulting firms or real estate development companies are, in fact, its people. In turn, their aggregate value should be calculated by subtracting the net value of assets from market value.

Depreciation

GETTING STARTED

Depreciation is a basic expense of doing business, reducing a company's earnings while increasing its cash flow. It affects three key financial statements: balance sheet; cash flow; and income (or profit and loss). It is based on two key facts: the purchase price of the items or property in question, and their "useful life."

Depreciation values and practices are governed by the tax laws of both national governments, and state or provincial governments, which must be monitored continuously for any changes that are made. Accounting bodies, too, have developed standard practices and procedures for conducting depreciation.

Depreciating a single asset is not difficult: The challenge lies in depreciating the many assets possessed by even small companies, and it is intensified by the impact that depreciation has on income and cash flow statements, and on income statements. It is essential to depreciate with care and to rely on experts, ensuring that they fully understand the current government rules and regulations.

FAQs

What is depreciation?

It is an allocation of the cost of an asset over a period of time for accounting and tax purposes. Depreciation is charged against earnings, on the basis that the use of capital assets is a legitimate cost of doing business. Depreciation is also a noncash expense that is added into net income to determine cash flow in a given accounting period.

What is straight-line depreciation?

One of the two principal depreciation methods, it is based on the assumption that an asset loses an equal amount of its value each year of its useful life. Straight-line depreciation deducts an equal amount from a company's earnings each year throughout the life of the asset.

What is accelerated depreciation?

The other principal method of depreciation is based on the assumption that an asset loses a larger amount of its value in the early years of its useful life. Also known as the "declining-balance" method, it is used by accountants to reduce a company's tax bills as soon as possible, and is calculated on the basis of the same percentage rate each year of an asset's useful life. Accelerated depreciation better reflects the economic value of the asset being depreciated, which tends to become increasingly less efficient and more costly to maintain as it grows older.

What can be depreciated?

To qualify for depreciation, assets must:

- be used in the business;
- be items that wear out, become obsolete, or lose value over time from natural causes or circumstances;
- have a useful life beyond a single tax year.

Examples include vehicles, machines and equipment, computers and office furnishings, and buildings, plus major additions or improvements to such assets. Some intangible assets can also be included under certain conditions.

What cannot be depreciated?

Land, personal assets, inventory, leased or rented property, and a company's employees.

MAKING IT HAPPEN

In order to determine the annual depreciation cost of assets, it is necessary first to know the initial cost of those assets, how many years they will retain some value for the business, and what value, if any, they will have at the end of their useful life.

For example, a company buys a truck to carry materials and finished goods. The vehicle loses value as soon as it is purchased, and then loses more with each year it is in service, until the cost of repairs exceeds its overall value. Measuring the loss in the value of the truck is depreciation.

Straight-line depreciation is the most straightforward method, and is still quite common. It assumes that the net cost of an asset should be written off in equal amounts over its life. The formula used is:

$$\frac{\text{Original cost} - \text{Scrap value}}{\text{Useful life}}$$

For example, if the truck cost $30,000 and can be expected to serve the business for 7 years, its original cost less its scrap value would be divided by its useful life:

$$\frac{(30{,}000 - 2{,}000)}{7} = \$4{,}000 \text{ per year}$$

The $4,000 becomes a depreciation expense that is reported on the company's year-end income statement under "operation expenses."

  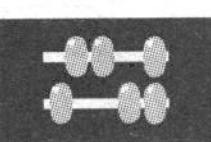      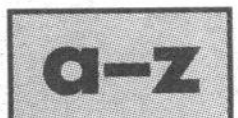

	Straight-line Method		Declining-balance Method	
Year	**Annual Depreciation**	**Year-end Book Value**	**Annual Depreciation**	**Year-end Book Value**
1	\$900 × 20 per cent = \$180	\$1,000 – \$180 = \$820	\$1,000 × 40 per cent = \$400	\$1,000 – \$400 = \$600
2	\$900 × 20 per cent = \$180	\$820 – \$180 = \$640	\$600 × 40 per cent = \$240	\$600 – \$240 = \$360
3	\$900 × 20 per cent = \$180	\$640 – \$180 = \$460	\$360 × 40 per cent = \$144	\$360 – \$144 = \$216
4	\$900 × 20 per cent = \$180	\$460 – \$180 = \$280	\$216 × 40 per cent = \$86.40	\$216 – \$86.40 = \$129.60
5	\$900 × 20 per cent = \$180	\$280 – \$180 = \$100	\$129.60 × 40 per cent = \$51.84	\$129.60 – \$51.84 = \$77.76

In theory, an asset should be depreciated over the actual number of years that it will be used, according to its actual drop in value each year. At the end of each year, all the depreciation claimed to date is subtracted from its cost in order to arrive at its "book value," which would equal its market value. At the end of its useful business life, any undepreciated portion would represent the salvage value for which it could be sold or scrapped.

For tax purposes, some accountants prefer to use accelerated depreciation to record larger amounts of depreciation in the asset's early years in order to reduce tax bills as soon as possible. In contrast to the straight-line method, the accelerated or declining balance method assumes that the asset depreciates more in its earlier years of use. The table compares the depreciation amounts that would be available, under these two methods, for a \$1,000 asset that is expected to be used for five years and then sold for \$100 in scrap.

While the straight-line method results in the same deduction each year, the declining-balance method produces larger deductions in the first years and far smaller deductions in the later years. One result of this system is that, if the equipment is expected to be sold for a higher value at some point in the middle of its life, the declining-balance method can produce a greater taxable gain in that year because the book value of the asset will be relatively lower.

The depreciation method to be used for a particular asset is fixed at the time that the asset is first placed in service. Whatever rules or tables are in effect for that year must be followed as long as the asset is owned.

Depreciation laws and regulations change frequently over the years as a result of government policy changes, so a company owning property over a long period may have to use several different depreciation methods.

TRICKS OF THE TRADE

- With very specific exceptions, it is not possible to deduct in one year the entire cost of an asset if that asset has a useful life substantially beyond the tax year.
- To qualify for depreciation, an asset must be put into service. Simply purchasing it is not enough. There are rules that govern how much depreciation can be claimed on items put into service after a year has begun.
- It is common knowledge that if a company claims more depreciation than it is entitled to, it is liable for stiff penalties in a tax audit, just as failure to allow for depreciation causes an overestimation of income. What is not commonly known is that if a company does not claim all the depreciation deductions it is entitled to, it will be considered as having claimed them when taxable gains or losses are eventually calculated on the sale or disposal of the asset in question.
- While leased property cannot be depreciated, the cost of making permanent improvements to leased property can be (remodeling a leased office, for example). There are many rules governing leased assets; they should be depreciated with care.
- Another common mistake is to continue depreciating property beyond the end of its recovery period. Cars are common examples of this.
- Conservative companies depreciate many assets as quickly as possible, despite the fact that this practice reduces reported net income. Knowledgeable investors watch carefully for such practices.

MORE INFO

Book:

Wolf, Frank K., and W. Chester Finch. *Depreciation Systems*. Ames, IA: Iowa State University Press, 1994.

Websites:

Bankrate.com on Section 179 of the United States Internal Revenue Code: tinyurl.com/y4lc

Business Owner's Toolkit: www.bizfilings.com/toolkit/

See Also:

Residual Value (p. 1248)

Discounted Cash Flow

WHAT IT MEASURES

Discounted cash flow (DCF) is a way of measuring the net present value (NPV) of future cash flow. This allows companies to express the value of an investment today based on predicted future returns. The idea behind discounted cash flow is that \$1 today is worth more than \$1 you might receive in the future. The money you have now can be invested and might generate interest whereas money you haven't yet received can't be used in this way, and there is a risk it might not be received. Therefore, discounted cash flow is a way of adjusting the value of future money over time to reflect its "real" value today.

WHY IT IS IMPORTANT

Discounted cash flow is most useful when future operating conditions and cash flow are variable, or where trading conditions are expected to change significantly over time. It is a good way of assessing the likely value of money the business will receive in future, and therefore DCF is considered one of the best ways of valuing an investment.

HOW IT WORKS IN PRACTICE

To calculate discounted cash flow, you must first determine the forecasted cash flow of a company, and choose a discount rate based on the expected or desired rate of return. The discount rate chosen should reflect the risk that the return will not be achieved—a higher risk should result in a higher discount rate.

Next, use the discount rate for each year to discount cash flow to the "correct" adjusted present value, as shown in the example below. Remember, cash flow will lose value over time because it is discounted for a longer period.

For example:

$$NPV = \frac{CF1}{(1+r)} + \frac{CF2}{(1+r)^2} + \frac{CF3}{(1+r)^3}$$

where NPV is the net present value of cash flows, CF1, CF2, and CF3 are predicted cash flows in years 1, 2, and 3, respectively, and r is the discount rate. It's worth remembering that, unless the series of cash flows has a known finite endpoint, a terminal value will need to be assumed.

TRICKS OF THE TRADE

- Cash flows may represent interest payments or repayments, or in the case of stocks can relate to dividends.
- There are many variations to the calculation illustrated above, and different ways to measure cash flow and discount rates in a DCF calculation. All the different approaches are basically ways of estimating the return from an investment, adjusted for the time value of money.
- Like many calculations, a DCF figure is only as good as the figures used for cash flow and discount rates. Small changes in these figures can result in enormous variation in NPV figures, so it's often wiser to use DCF over a relatively short period of time and to adopt a terminal value approach, rather than discounting to infinity.
- DCF analysis of cash flow should be used when a business case deals with two potential uses of money, and wherever cash flow timing is different.

MORE INFO

Article:

McClure, Ben. "DCF analysis." *Investopedia*. Online at: www.investopedia.com/university/dcf/

Website:

Solution Matrix on DCF: www.solutionmatrix.com/discounted-cash-flow

See Also:

✔ Understanding the Relationship between the Discount Rate and Risk (p. 1001)

Distinguishing between a Capital and an Operating Lease

GETTING STARTED

Determining whether a lease obligation is an operating or capital lease, for financial reporting purposes, requires that it be evaluated on the basis of four criteria established by the FASB (Financial Accounting Standards Board). The criteria are objective rules for making a judgment about who, the lessor or the lessee, bears the risks and benefits of ownership of the leased property.

If a lease is determined to be a capital lease, an asset and corresponding liability are recorded at the present value of the minimum lease payments. The capital asset is depreciated over time, while the liability is amortized as lease payments are made. Rental payments under operating leases are simply expensed as incurred. Due to the complexity of lease agreements, management judgment still plays a large role in distinguishing between operating and capital leases.

FAQS

What are minimum lease payments?

The minimum lease payments are the rental payments to be made during the lease term, plus the amount of the bargain price, guaranteed residual value, or penalty for failure to renew the lease at the end of its original term.

In determining whether a lease should be classified as an operating or capital lease, what interest rate should be used?

The interest rate used to discount the minimum lease payments to their present value is the incremental borrowing rate of the lessee, this being the interest rate that the lessee would have been charged if the assets had been acquired by borrowing the purchase price. If the lessor's implied interest rate for the lease is known and is lower than the lessee's estimated incremental borrowing rate, then the lessee uses the implied rate to discount.

MAKING IT HAPPEN

The Four FASB Criteria

Until the 1970s, many companies used leasing as a means to purchase tangible assets without recognizing their ownership or the lease obligation on the balance sheet. In substance, leases were off-balance-sheet financing. Although all leases were required to be disclosed in the footnotes to the financial statements, even long-term finance leases did not appear as a liability. Because the basic measures of leverage do not consider off-balance-sheet obligations, the accounting profession and the investment community believed that there needed to be more stringent guidelines for classifying leases as operating or financing, and in 1976 the FASB issued Statement no. 13, "Accounting for leases." The statement sets out four criteria to distinguish between an operating and a capital (finance) lease:

- The lease agreement transfers ownership of the assets to the lessee during the term of lease.
- The lessee can purchase the assets leased at a bargain price, such as $1, at the end of the lease term.
- The lease term is at least 75% of the economic life of the leased asset.
- The present value of the minimum lease payments is 90% or greater of the asset's value.

If a lease agreement does not meet any of these criteria, the lessee treats it as an operating lease for accounting purposes. If, however, the agreement meets one of the above criteria, it is treated as a capital lease.

Accounting for a Capital Lease

Capital leases are reported by the lessee as if the assets being leased were acquired and the monthly rental payments as if they were payments of principal and interest on a debt obligation. Specifically, the lessee capitalizes the lease by recognizing an asset and a liability at the lower of the present value of the minimum lease payments or the value of the assets under lease. As the monthly rental payments are made, the corresponding liability decreases. At the same time, the leased asset is depreciated in a manner that is consistent with other owned assets having the same use and economic life.

Accounting for an Operating Lease

If the lease is classified as an operating lease, the monthly lease payments are simply treated as rental expenses and recognized on the income tax return as they are incurred. There is no recognition of a leased asset or liability.

Clearing Up Remaining Confusion

The FASB's attempt to establish objective criteria for distinguishing between operating and capital leases was a good first step. This has enabled companies to make prudent financial decisions in lease versus buy situations, based on the accounting treatment afforded a specific lease structure. Furthermore, financial professionals now have a framework within which to determine what lease terms create a capital lease. However, the use of financial engineering still occurs. Consequently, many leases that are truly financing leases are recorded as operating leases, because their provisions have been altered to avoid qualification as capital leases.

When in doubt, a manager should always ask whether the risks and benefits of ownership have truly been passed from the lessor to the lessee. Facts indicating that the transfer has occurred are when maintenance, insurance, and property tax expenses are borne by the lessee, or when the lessee guarantees a specific residual value on the leased property.

MORE INFO

Websites:

Institute of Chartered Accountants in England and Wales (ICAEW): www.icaew.com

Securities and Exchange Commission (SEC; US): www.sec.gov

See Also:

★ Classification and Treatment of Leases (pp. 309–311)

Dividend Yield

WHAT IT MEASURES

An investment's dividend yield is a measure of the dividend paid on stock, expressed as a percentage over one year. This measure is frequently used in stock quotes and financial reports, and is based upon the company's annual cash dividend per share and the current stock price.

WHY IT IS IMPORTANT

A stock's dividend yield is a crucial measure for potential investors in any company, since it illustrates how much cash flow is generated for each dollar invested in equity, on top of any capital gains made from a rising stock price. A relatively high-paying, stable stock will attract income investors, and the higher the dividend yield, the greater expected return for income investors. Historical data also show that stocks which pay a dividend have generally outperformed non-dividend-paying stocks in the long term.

HOW IT WORKS IN PRACTICE

To calculate a dividend yield, you will need to use the following formula:

$$\text{Dividend yield} = \frac{\text{Annual dividend per share}}{\text{Stock price per share}}$$

For example, Company A has an annual dividend per share of $10, and the average quarterly value of its stock per share is $75. To assess the company's dividend yield, we would divide the dividend by the stock price, as follows:

$$\frac{10}{75} = 0.1333 = 13.33\%$$

On this basis, the stock has a dividend yield of 13.33%.

Company B might also pay an annual dividend per share of $10, but if its stock is trading at $20 per share, then its dividend yield will be 50%—considerably higher than Company A's dividend yield. Assuming other factors are equal, income investors would find Company B a more attractive investment opportunity.

TRICKS OF THE TRADE

- Dividend yield is often simply referred to as a "yield" in financial markets.
- The dividend yield helps to explain a company's value to investors but can vary widely depending on a company's market position, industry, earnings, cash flow, and dividend policy. Therefore, this measure is not always important for long-term investors who are concerned with a company's long-term growth.
- It isn't a guarantee, but many studies show a strong correlation between yield and returns over five years—companies with higher yields tend to offer higher returns, while lower yields lead to lower returns.
- It is common for newspapers to include yield figures in tables showing stock performance and share prices. In general, a yield of around 2–4% is considered average, and most attractive to longer-term growth investors.
- High yields are generally offered by mature, well-established companies while younger companies tend to pay lower yields because they are focused on growth. Many young companies will not pay any dividend at all.
- If a company has a low yield compared to others in the same industry, this could mean the company's stock is over-valued because investors are confident of future growth. Alternatively, it can suggest that the company can't afford to pay the expected dividends.
- If a company has a high yield in comparison to others in the same sector, it could suggest imminent dividend cuts.

MORE INFO

Websites:

Biz/ed on dividend yield: www.bized.co.uk/compfact/ratios/investor8.htm

Investopedia dividend yield calculator: www.investopedia.com/calculator/DivCYield.aspx

See Also:

Earnings per Share (pp. 1220–1221)
Yield (pp. 1263–1264)

  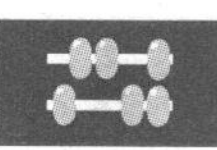   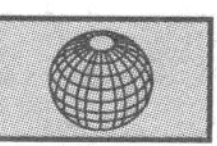   

Earnings at Risk

WHAT IT MEASURES

Earnings at risk (EAR) measures the quantity by which net income might change in the event of an adverse change in interest rates. It is a risk measurement which is closely linked with value at risk (VAR) calculations. The difference is that while VAR looks at the change in the entire value over the forecast horizon, EAR looks at potential changes in cash flows or earnings.

WHY IT IS IMPORTANT

Companies engaged in international business face many risks from changing currency levels to fluctuating interest rates. The challenge for investors and financial professionals is understanding and quantifying how these risks affect the profitability of the business.

Calculating EAR helps you to understand the impact of interest rate changes on your company's financial position, but it can be a challenge to calculate as transaction volumes grow or portfolio complexity increases. For this reason, banks and large corporations will rely on specialist computer applications using the Monte Carlo method to calculate EAR.

HOW IT WORKS IN PRACTICE

There are various models available to calculate EAR, but at heart most will calculate EAR by using a variation of:

$$\text{Principal amount} \times \text{Interest} \times \text{Time period} = \text{Interest income and interest expense}$$

However, EAR is not this simple in reality! Most EAR models will allow you to add in numerous factors that affect interest income and expense, such as time periods for various rates received, outstanding balances, or interest rates received and paid.

In addition, the model will simulate various possible interest rate scenarios over a period of several quarters or years, to determine their potential effect on earnings. There might be dozens of projections covering short-term rates, long-term rates, risk spreads, etc, over the specified time period. For each quarter, the model will calculate income and expense based on assumed interest rates, and can be adapted to reflect hypothetical rate changes, illustrating different strategies and customer behaviors.

If most of the likely scenarios do not seriously reduce earnings, then the organization's interest rate exposure is low. If the scenarios result in unacceptable changes, the organization might consider looking at changes to its strategy.

TRICKS OF THE TRADE

- Because of the number of variables that can be applied to EAR modeling, no two models will look the same, even if applied to the same organization. It is therefore essential to ask for specific details when analyzing any EAR summary.
- A typical EAR model will show analysis for up to a 300 basis point increase or fall in interest rates. These may be shown as a single rise or fall, or gradual change in rates. The EAR will also show a "confidence interval" showing impact according to, for example, a 90% confidence interval.
- Very few organizations devise EAR models from scratch, but will rely on summary results generated by computer. However, managers may well need to analyze EAR reports generated by specialized modeling tools and applications.

MORE INFO

Book:

Lam, James. *Enterprise Risk Management: From Incentives to Controls*. Hoboken, NJ: Wiley, 2003.

Websites:

Approximity on EAR: www.approximity.com/risk/Products/cfar.html

Financial Risk Manager on EAR: tinyurl.com/6b5odvd

Earnings per Share

Earnings per share (EPS) is perhaps the most widely used ratio there is in the investing realm.

WHAT IT MEASURES

The portion of a company's profit allocated to each outstanding share of a company's common stock.

WHY IT IS IMPORTANT

Earnings per share is simply a fundamental measure of profitability that shows how much profit has been generated on a per-share-of-stock basis. Were the term worded as profit per share, the meaning certainly would be much clearer, if not self-evident.

By itself, EPS doesn't reveal a great deal. Its true value lies in comparing EPS figures across several quarters, or years, to judge the growth of a company's earnings on a per-share basis.

HOW IT WORKS IN PRACTICE

Essentially, the figure is calculated after paying taxes and dividends to preferred stockholders and bondholders. Barring extraordinary circumstances, EPS data are reported quarterly, semiannually, and annually.

To calculate EPS, start with net income (earnings) for the period in question, subtract the total value of any preferred stock dividends, then divide the resulting figure by the number of shares outstanding during that period:

$$\text{Earnings per share} = \frac{(\text{Net income} - \text{Dividends on preferred stock})}{\text{Average number of shares outstanding}}$$

By itself, this formula is simple enough. Alas, defining the factors used in the formula invariably introduces complexities and—as some allege on occasion—possible subterfuge.

For instance, while companies usually use a weighted average number of shares outstanding over the reporting period, shares outstanding can still be either "primary" or "fully diluted." Primary EPS is calculated using the number of shares that are currently held by investors in the market and able to be traded. Diluted EPS is the result of a complex calculation that determines how many shares would be outstanding if all exercisable warrants and options were converted into common shares at the end of a quarter. Suppose, for example, that a company has granted a large number of share options to employees. If these options are capable of being exercised

  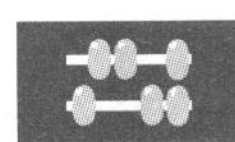   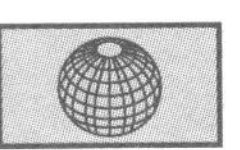   

in the near future, that could alter significantly the number of shares in issue and, thus, the EPS—even though the E part (the earnings) is the same. Often in such cases, the company might quote the EPS both on the existing shares and on the fully diluted version. Which one a person considers depends on their view of the company and how they wish to use the EPS figure. In addition, companies can report extraordinary EPS, a figure which excludes the financial impact of unusual occurrences, such as discontinued operations or the sale of a business unit.

Net income or earnings, meanwhile, can be defined in a number of ways, based on respective nations' generally accepted accounting principles.

For example, "pro-forma earnings" tend to exclude more expenses and income used to calculate "reported earnings." Pro-forma advocates insist that these earnings eliminate all distortions and present "true" earnings that allow pure apples-with-apples comparisons with preceding periods. However, "nonrecurring expenses" seem to occur with such increasing regularity that one may wonder if a company is deliberately trying to manipulate its earnings figures and present them in the best possible light, rather than in the most accurate light.

"Cash" earnings are earnings from operating cash flow—notably, not EBITDA. In turn, cash EPS is usually these earnings divided by diluted shares outstanding. This figure is very reliable because operating cash flow is not subject to as much judgment as net earnings or pro-forma earnings.

TRICKS OF THE TRADE

- Given the varieties of earnings and shares reported today, investors need to determine first what the respective figures represent before making investment decisions. There are cases of a company announcing a pro-forma EPS that differs significantly from what is reported in its financial statements. Such discrepancies, in turn, can affect how the market values a given stock.
- Investors should check to see if a company has issued more shares during a given period, since that action, too, can affect EPS. A similar problem occurs where there have been a number of shares issued during the accounting period being considered. Which number of issued shares do you use, the opening figure, the closing figure, or the mean? In practice the usual method is to use the weighted mean number of shares in issue during the year (weighted, that is, for the amount of time in the year that they were in issue).
- "Trailing" earnings per share is the sum of EPS from the last four quarters and is the figure used to compute most price-to-earnings ratios.
- Diluted and primary shares outstanding can be the same if a company has no warrants or convertible bonds outstanding, but investors should not assume anything, and need to be sure how "shares outstanding" is being defined.

MORE INFO

Article:

Wayman, Rick. "The 5 types of earnings per share." *Investopedia*. Online at: www.investopedia.com/articles/analyst/091901.asp

See Also:

- Dividend Yield (p. 1219)
- Price/Earnings Ratio (p. 1242)
- Return on Stockholders' Equity (pp. 1250–1251)

EBITDA

EBITDA—an acronym that stands for "earnings before interest, taxes, depreciation, and amortization"—is slightly less inclusive than "EBIT"—earnings before interest and taxes. Both focus on profitability, and have gained popularity in the past decade as measures of operating success. But as this popularity has grown, so has the number of the measure's critics.

WHAT IT MEASURES

A company's earnings from ongoing operations, before net income is calculated.

WHY IT IS IMPORTANT

EBITDA's champions contend it gives investors a sense of how much money a young or fast-growing company is generating before it pays interest on debt, taxes, and accounts for noncash changes. If EBITDA grows over time, champions argue, investors gain at least a sense of long-term profitability and, in turn, the wisdom of their investment.

Business appraisers and investors also may study EBITDA to help to gauge a company's fair market value, often as a prelude to its acquisition by another company. It is also frequently applied to companies that have been subject to leveraged buyouts—the strategy being that EBITDA will help to cover loan payments needed to finance the transaction.

EBITDA, and EBIT, too, are claimed to be good indicators of cash flow from business operations, since they report earnings before debt payments, taxes, depreciation, and amortization charges are considered. However, that claim is challenged by many—often rather vigorously.

HOW IT WORKS IN PRACTICE

EBITDA first appeared as leveraged buyouts soared in popularity during the 1980s. It has since become well established as a financial analysis measure of telecommunications, cable, and major media companies.

Its formula is quite simple. Revenues less the cost of goods sold, general and administrative expenses, and the deductions of items expressed by the acronym EBITDA:

$$\text{EBITDA} = \text{Revenue} - \text{Expenses (excluding interest, taxes, depreciation, and amortization)}$$

or

$$\text{EBIT} = \text{Revenue} - \text{Expenses (excluding taxes and interest)}$$

This formula does not measure true cash flow. A communications company, for example, once reported $698 million in EBIT but just $324 million in cash from operations.

TRICKS OF THE TRADE

- As yet no definition of EBITDA is enforced by standards-making bodies, so companies can all but create their own. As a result, EBITDA can easily be manipulated by aggressive accounting policies, which may erode its reliability.
- Ignoring capital expenditures could be unrealistic and horribly misleading, because companies in capital-intensive sectors such as manufacturing and transportation must continually make major capital investments to remain competitive.

  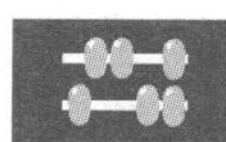      

High-technology is another sector that may be capital-intensive, at least initially.

- Critics warn that using EBITDA as a cash flow indicator is a huge mistake, because EBITDA ignores too many factors that have an impact on true cash flow, such as working capital, debt payments, and other fixed expenses. Interest and taxes can, and do, cost a company cash, they point out, while debt holders have higher claims on a company's liquid assets than investors do.
- Critics further assail EBITDA as the barometer of choice of unprofitable firms because it can present a more optimistic view of a company's future than it has a right to claim. *Forbes* magazine, for instance, once referred to EBIDTA as "the device of choice to pep up earnings announcements."
- Even so, EBITDA may be useful in terms of evaluating firms in the same industry with widely different capital structures, tax rates, and depreciation policies.

Economic Value Added

WHAT IT MEASURES

A company's financial performance—specifically, whether it is earning more or less than the total cost of the capital supporting it.

WHY IT IS IMPORTANT

Economic value added measures true economic profit, or the amount by which the earnings of a project, an operation, or a corporation exceed (or fall short of) the total amount of capital that was originally invested by the company's owners.

If a company is earning more, it is adding value, and that is good. If it is earning less, the company is in fact devouring value, and that is bad, because the company's owners (stockholders, for example) would be better off investing their capital elsewhere.

The concept's champions declare that EVA forces managers to focus on true wealth creation and maximizing stockholder investment. By definition, then, increasing EVA will increase a company's market value.

HOW IT WORKS IN PRACTICE

EVA is conceptually simple and easy to explain: From net operating profit, subtract an appropriate charge for the opportunity cost of all capital invested in an enterprise—the amount that could have been invested elsewhere. It is calculated using this formula:

EVA = Net operating profit less applicable taxes − Cost of capital

A company is considering building a new plant whose total weighted cost over 10 years is $80 million. If the expected annual incremental return on the new operation is $10 million, or $100 million over 10 years, then the plant's EVA would be positive, in this case $20 million:

100,000,000 − 80,000,000 = $20,000,000

An alternative but more complex formula for EVA is:

EVA = [Return on invested capital (%) − Cost of capital (%)] × Original capital invested

TRICKS OF THE TRADE

- EVA is a measure of dollar surplus value, not the percentage difference in returns.
- Purists describe EVA as "profit the way stockholders define it." They further contend that if stockholders expect a 10% return on their investment, they "make money" only when their share of after-tax operating profits exceeds 10% of equity capital.
- An objective of EVA is to determine which business units best utilize their assets to generate returns and maximize stockholder value; it can be used to assess a company, a business unit, a single plant, an office, or even an assembly line. This same technique is equally helpful in evaluating new business opportunities.

MORE INFO

Website:

EVA at Stern Stewart & Co: www.sternstewart.com/?content=proprietary&p=eva

See Also:

★ Creating Value with EVA (pp. 814–816)
★ Why EVA Is the Best Measurement Tool for Creating Shareholder Value (pp. 952–953)
The EVA Challenge: Implementing Value-Added Change in an Organization (p. 1351)

Efficiency and Operating Ratios

For this calculation and related ratios, the lower the numbers the better.

WHAT THEY MEASURE

The portion of operating revenues or fee income spent on overhead expenses.

WHY THEY ARE IMPORTANT

Often identified with banking and financial sectors, the efficiency ratio indicates a management's ability to keep overhead costs low. This measurement is also used by mature industries, such as steel manufacture, chemicals, or auto production, that must focus on tight cost controls to boost profitability because growth prospects are generally modest.

In some industries, the efficiency ratio is called the overhead burden, which is overheads as a percentage of sales.

A different method measures efficiency simply by tracking three other measures: accounts payable to sales, days sales outstanding, and inventory turnover, which indicates how fast a company is able to move its merchandise. A general guide is that if the first two of these measures are low and third is high, efficiency is probably high; the reverse is likewise true.

  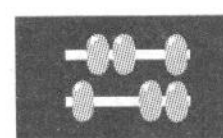   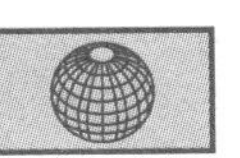   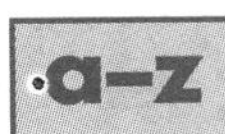

HOW THEY WORK IN PRACTICE

The efficiency ratio is defined as operating overhead expenses divided by fee income plus tax equivalent net interest income. If operating expenses are $100,000, and revenues (as defined) are $230,000, then:

$$\text{Efficiency ratio} = \frac{100{,}000}{230{,}000} = 0.43$$

However, not everyone calculates the ratio in the same way. Some institutions include all noninterest expenses, while others exclude certain charges and intangible asset amortization.

To find the inventory turnover ratio, divide total sales by total inventory. If net sales are $300,000 and inventory is $100,000, then:

$$\text{Inventory turnover ratio} = \frac{300{,}000}{140{,}000} = 2.14$$

To find the accounts payable to sales ratio, divide a company's accounts payable by its annual net sales. A high ratio suggests that a company is using its suppliers' funds as a source of cheap financing because it is not operating efficiently enough to generate its own funds. If accounts payable are $42,000 and total sales are $300,000, then:

$$\text{Accounts payable/sales ratio} = \frac{42{,}000}{300{,}000} = 0.14 = 14\%$$

TRICKS OF THE TRADE

- Identifying "overheads" to calculate the efficiency ratio can itself contribute to overall inefficiency. Some financial experts contend that efficiency can be measured equally well by reviewing earnings per share growth and return on equity.
- Some banks identify amortization of goodwill expense, and pull it out of their noninterest expense in order to calculate what is called the cash efficiency ratio: noninterest expense minus goodwill amortization expense divided into revenue.
- In banking, an acceptable efficiency ratio was once in the low 60s. Now the goal is 50, while better-performing banks boast ratios in the mid 40s. Low ratings usually indicate a higher return on equity and earnings.

Elasticity

Elasticity measures responsiveness, and is very useful when studying the impact of pricing on supply and demand.

WHAT IT MEASURES

The percentage change of one variable caused by a percentage change in another variable.

WHY IT IS IMPORTANT

Elasticity is defined as "the measure of the sensitivity of one variable to another." In practical terms, elasticity indicates the degree to which consumers respond to changes in price. It is obviously important for companies to consider such relationships when contemplating changes in price, demand, and supply.

Demand elasticity measures how much the quantity demanded changes when the price of a product or service is increased or lowered. Will demand remain constant? If not, by how much will demand change?

Supply elasticity measures the impact on supply when a price is changed. It is assumed that lowering prices will reduce supply, because demand will increase—but by how much?

HOW IT WORKS IN PRACTICE

The general formula for elasticity is:

$$\text{Elasticity} = \frac{\text{Change in } x\ (\%)}{\text{Change in } y\ (\%)}$$

In theory, x and y can be any variables. However, the most common application measures price and demand. If the price of a product is increased from $20 to $25, or 25%, and demand in turn falls from 6,000 to 3,000 (−50%), elasticity would be calculated as:

$$\frac{-50}{25} = -2$$

A value greater in magnitude than ±1 means that demand is strongly sensitive to price, while a lesser value means that demand is not price-sensitive.

TRICKS OF THE TRADE

- There are five cases of elasticity:
  - E = 1, or unit elasticity. The proportional change in one variable is equal to the proportional change in another variable: if price rises by 5%, demand falls by 5%.
  - E is greater than 1, or *just elastic*. The proportional change in x is greater than the proportional change in y: for example, if price rises by 5%, demand falls by 3%.
  - E = infinity, or perfectly elastic. This is a special case of elasticity: any change in y will effect no change in x. An example would be prices charged by a hospital's emergency room, where increases in price are unlikely to curb demand.
  - E is less than 1, or *just inelastic*. The proportional change in x is less than the proportional change in y: if prices are increased, say by 3%, demand will fall by 30%.
  - E = 0, or perfectly inelastic. This is another special case of elasticity: any change in y will have an infinite effect on x.
- There are more complex formulae for determining a range of variables, or "arc elasticity."
- Elasticity can be used to affirm two rules of thumb:
  - demand becomes elastic if consumers have an alternative or adequate substitute for the product or service;
  - demand is more elastic if consumers have an incentive to save money.

MORE INFO

See Also:

Price Elasticity (p. 1243)

  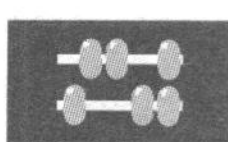      

Enterprise Value

In the financial world, enterprise value has a precise meaning and calculation. It is important to remember this, as many conference planners and consultants routinely rely on "enterprise value" to promote whatever concept they happen to be selling.

WHAT IT MEASURES

It measures what financial markets believe a company's ongoing operations are worth.

Some people also define enterprise value as what it would actually cost to purchase an entire company at a given moment.

WHY IT IS IMPORTANT

Enterprise value is not a theoretical valuation but a firm and finite value, logically determined. It tells an individual investor the underlying value of his stake in an enterprise. For potential acquirers considering a takeover of a company, enterprise value helps them to determine a reasonable price for their desired acquisition.

HOW IT WORKS IN PRACTICE

Although it is a finite figure, enterprise value can be calculated in two ways. One method is quicker, but the other is more thorough and thus more reliable.

The quick way is simply to multiply the number of a company's shares outstanding by the current price per share. Using this approach, the enterprise value of a company with 2 million shares outstanding, and a share price of $25, would be:

$$\text{Enterprise value} = 2{,}000{,}000 \times 25 = \$50{,}000{,}000$$

However, this value is based on the market's perception of the value of its shares of stock; it also ignores some important factors about a company's fiscal health. The second, more complete, method is therefore preferred by many experts. This method calculates enterprise value as the sum of market capitalization, plus debt and preferred stock, minus cash and cash equivalents:

$$\text{Enterprise value} = \text{Market capitalization} + \text{Long-term debt} + \text{Preferred stock} - \text{Cash and equivalents}$$

If market capitalization is $6.5 million, debt totals $1 million, the value of preferred stock is $1.5 million, and cash and equivalents total $2 million, enterprise value would be:

$$6.5 + 1 + 1.5 - 2 = \$7\text{million}$$

This more thorough calculation recognizes the existence of both a company's debt and of the amount of cash and liquid assets on hand. No matter how a stock may fluctuate, these sums are relatively constant, and the amount of debt can be very significant. Debt—and cash too—can be just as important during a company's sale, since new owners assume existing debt and receive any cash on hand. Indeed, more than a few acquisitions are financed in part with funds of the acquired company.

TRICKS OF THE TRADE

- Financial markets often use the market capitalization figure for enterprise value, but they really are not the same thing.
- Experts will occasionally refer to "total enterprise value," but its definition and formula are virtually identical to this second formula for enterprise value. Total enterprise value is only meaningful to those who use the quick method to compute enterprise value.
- A company's value is sometimes expressed as "the total funds being used to finance it." This is increasingly used in place of the price/earnings ratio, and indicates the economic rather than the accounting return that the company is generating on the total value of the capital supporting it. Companies that have borrowed heavily to finance growth, or that have paid large premiums for acquisitions or assets, are more frequently evaluated by this method.

MORE INFO

See Also:

✔ Estimating Enterprise Value with the Weighted Average Cost of Capital (p. 967)

Exchange Rate Risk

Because formulae exist to quantify, at least to a degree, the risks that accompany any investment decision, it is logical to assume that a similar formula exists to quantify what is called both exchange rate risk and currency risk. Such logic is flawed, for no such formula exists.

WHAT IT MEASURES

The risk of a gain or loss in the value of a business activity or investment that results from changes in the exchange rates of world currencies.

WHY IT IS IMPORTANT

Each business day seems to bring more international business transactions, generated by an ever-growing number of enterprises from an ever-increasing number of countries. Enterprises in developing nations, especially, are vying for their share of world commerce.

However, the economies of these developing nations can be especially fragile, while economies of mature nations periodically sputter and suffer recessions. Asia, Latin America, and Eastern Europe have all endured economic turmoil in the past decade, while such regions as the Middle East have been volatile for several decades, principally because of the wide swings in oil prices.

Currency exchange rates can be just as volatile, and this clearly poses risks to any enterprise conducting business in foreign markets and any investor holding either stock in a foreign-based company or an interest in a mutual fund that invests in foreign companies. The effects on a company's earnings, cash flow, and balance sheet can be significant.

The main exchange rate risk to an operation or investment is that any profits realized will be partially reduced—or wiped out altogether—when they are exchanged for the domestic currency, be it US dollars, pounds sterling, the euro, or Japanese yen.

  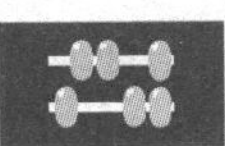   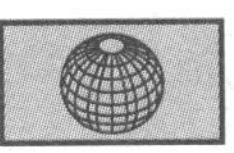   

More often, exchange rate risk will affect a company's price competitiveness in a product or service also offered by a competitor whose costs are incurred in a foreign currency. If the competitor's currency weakens, its relative competitive position improves because its costs decline, enabling the competitor to reduce its price and attract a larger share of a market.

HOW IT WORKS IN PRACTICE

There is a simple way to avoid the risk posed by exchange rates: don't do business abroad! For large companies, as well as an increasing number of small and medium-sized companies, that would be like sticking one's head in the sand.

A second defense against exchange rate risks is almost as unrealistic: conduct all business in your home currency. Requiring foreign customers to pay up only in, say, dollars, puts the burden of currency fluctuations squarely on the customer's shoulders and completely insulates the selling company from any shrinkage of profits from exchange rate differences. The price of such insulation, however, is likely to be a steady loss of customers.

The practical course of action, then, is to gain a basic understanding of exchange rate risks, if only enough to sort out the reams of opinions on the subject, and to select knowledgeable advisers and use their counsel wisely. This is a sophisticated, complex realm that has been examined for over a century. It is certainly no place for amateurs.

At the same time, however, exchange rates, interest rates, and inflation rates have been linked to one another via a classic set of relationships that can serve as leading indicators of changes in risk. These relationships are:

- The **Purchasing Power Parity Theory**. While it can be expressed differently, the most common expression links the changes in exchange rates to those in relative price indices in two countries:

  Rate of change of exchange rate = Difference in inflation rates

- The **International Fisher Effect** (IFE). This holds that an interest rate differential will exist only if the exchange rate is expected to change in such a way that the advantage of the higher interest rate is offset by the loss on the foreign exchange transactions. Practically speaking, the IFE implies that while an investor in a low-interest country can convert funds into the currency of a high-interest country and earn a higher rate, the gain (the interest rate differential) will be offset by the expected loss due to foreign exchange rate changes. The relationship is stated as:

  Expected rate of change of the exchange rate = Interest rate differential

- The **Unbiased Forward Rate Theory**. This holds that the forward exchange rate is the best and unbiased estimate of the expected future spot exchange rate:

  Expected exchange rate = Forward exchange rate

Other than these yardsticks, defending against exchange rate risk is largely a matter of observation. In the floating exchange rate environment that has existed for almost the past 30 years, currency exchange rates respond to a host of factors: political climates, the flow of imports and exports, the flow of capital, inflation rates in various countries, consumer expectations, and confidence levels, to name a few. Frequently, limits are placed on exchange rate fluctuations by government policies—actions that themselves can arouse controversy or debate.

Even so, the exchange rate risks these factors create can be arranged into three primary categories:

- **Economic exposure**. Due to changes in rates, operating costs will rise and make a product uncompetitive in the world market, thus eroding profitability. There's little that can be done about economic risk; it's simply a routine business risk that every enterprise must endure.
- **Translation exposure**. The impact of currency exchange rates will reduce a company's earnings and weaken its balance sheet. In turn, the denominations of assets and liabilities are important, although many experts contend that currency fluctuations have no significant impact on real assets.
- **Transaction exposure**. Caused by an unfavorable move in a specific currency between the time when a contract is agreed and the time it is completed, or between the time when lending or borrowing is initiated and the time the funds are repaid. This is the most common problem that confronts most companies. Requiring payment in advance is rarely practical, and impossible, of course, for borrowing and lending.

To reduce translation exposure, experienced corporate fund managers use a variety of techniques known as currency hedging, which amounts to diversifying currency holdings, monitoring exchange rates, and acting accordingly, depending on specific conditions. Its advocates contend that taking appropriate action can greatly reduce translation risks, if not avoid them altogether. Currency hedging, however, is also technical and sophisticated.

Transaction exposure can be eased by a process known as factoring. Major exporters, in particular, transfer title to their foreign accounts receivable to a third-party factoring house that assumes responsibility for collections, administrative services, and any other services requested. The fee for this service is a percentage of the value of the receivables, anywhere from 5% to 10% or higher, depending on the currencies involved. Companies often include this percentage in selling prices to recoup the cost.

Commercial and country risks can affect exchange rates, too. Commercial risks include the default or bankruptcy of major foreign customers. While this risk mirrors what can also occur at home, foreign-based companies operate under different laws and relationships with their governments. More worrisome are country risks: political or military interventions and currency restrictions that less stable nations might impose. Insurance is available to address such risks, but it can be costly.

TRICKS OF THE TRADE

- Any number of models have been created to explain and forecast exchange rates. None has proved definitive, largely because the world's economies and financial markets are evolving so rapidly.
- A forward transaction is an agreement to buy one currency and sell another on a date some time beyond two business days. It allows an exchange rate on a given day to be locked in for a future payment or receipt, thereby eliminating exchange rate risk.
- Foreign exchange options are contracts which, for a fee, guarantee a worst-case exchange rate for the future purchase of one currency for another. Unlike a forward transaction, the option does not obligate the buyer to deliver a currency on the settlement date unless the buyer chooses to. These options protect against unfavorable currency movements while allowing retention of the ability to participate in favorable movements.

  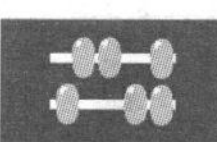      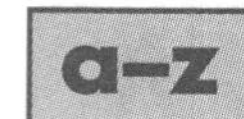

- A producer facing pricing competition caused by fluctuations in exchange rates can also use currency contracts to try to match competitors' cost structures and reduce costs.
- Companies doing larger volumes of business in a foreign country often establish a local office there to pay expenses and collect revenues in local currencies to reduce the impact of sudden and pronounced exchange rate fluctuations.
- Private sector subscription services monitor currencies and publish alerts. One US-based service has established numerical ranges that indicate risk, from 100 (no risk) to 200 (extreme risk or an outright currency crisis).
- Exchange rate risks cannot be insured against *per se*.
- The US Export-Import Bank (Eximbank) may be a source of advice for companies, especially smaller and medium-sized companies, seeking assistance.

MORE INFO

Book:

Giddy, Ian H., and Gunter Dufey. "The management of foreign exchange risk." In Frederick D. S. Choi (ed). *Handbook of International Accounting*. New York: Wiley, 1991. Also online at: www.stern.nyu.edu/~igiddy/fxrisk.htm

Article:

Magos, Alice. "Ask Alice about foreign exchange risk." *Business Owner's Toolkit*. Online at: tinyurl.com/3zdfx4z

See Also:

✔ Hedging Foreign Exchange Risk—Case Studies and Strategies (p. 970)

✔ Identifying and Managing Exposure to Interest and Exchange Rate Risks (p. 974)

Expected Rate of Return

Expected rate of return (ERR) is a measure conceived and crafted in the spirit of "forewarned is forearmed."

WHAT IT MEASURES

The projected percentage return on an investment, based on the weighted probability of all possible rates of return.

WHY IT IS IMPORTANT

No self-respecting businessperson or organization should make an investment without first having some understanding of how successful that investment is likely to be. Expected rate of return provides such an understanding, within certain limits.

HOW IT WORKS IN PRACTICE

The formula for expected rate of return is:

$$\text{Expected rate of return} = \sum_{i=1}^{n} [P(i) \times r_i]$$

where P(*i*) is the probability that the return r_i is achieved, i.e., the sum of the products of all possible returns and their probabilities.

A simple example, as given below, is far easier to grasp, and adequately illustrates the principle which the formula expresses. It will probably be of more practical use to most of those who need to calculate ERR.

The current price of ABC Inc. stock is $10. At the end of the year, ABC shares of stock are projected to be traded:

- 25% higher if economic growth exceeds expectations—a probability of 30%;
- 12% higher if economic growth equals expectations—a probability of 50%;
- 5% lower if economic growth falls short of expectations—a probability of 20%.

To find the expected rate of return, simply multiply the percentages by their respective probabilities and add the results:

$$(30\% \times 25\%) + (50\% \times 12\%) + (20\% \times -5\%) = 7.5 + 6 - 1 = 12.5\%$$

A second example:

- if economic growth remains robust (a 20% probability), investments will return 25%;
- if economic growth ebbs, but still performs adequately (a 40% probability), investments will return 15%;
- if economic growth slows significantly (a 30% probability), investments will return 5%;
- if the economy declines outright (a 10% probability), investments will return 0%.

Therefore the ERR can be calculated:

$$(20\% \times 25\%) + (40\% \times 15\%) + (30\% \times 5\%) + (10\% \times 0\%) = 5 + 6 + 1.5 + 0 = 12.5\%$$

Another method that can be used to project expected return is the capital asset pricing model (CAPM), which is explained separately.

TRICKS OF THE TRADE

- The probability totals must always equal 100% for the calculation to be valid.
- Be sure not to overlook any negative numbers in the calculations, or the results produced will be incorrect.
- An ERR calculation is only as good as the scenarios considered. Wildly unrealistic scenarios will produce an equally unreliable expected rate of return.

MORE INFO

See Also:

Capital Asset Pricing Model (p. 1201)

Rate of Return (p. 1245)

  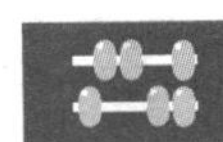      

Fair Value Calculations

WHAT IT MEASURES

Fair value is the value of an asset or liability in a transaction between two parties. It can be used to refer to the complete assets and liabilities of a company that is being acquired by another company, or to calculate the fair value of stock market securities. However, fair value can be applied to almost any assessment of something's value.

WHY IT IS IMPORTANT

In the securities market, fair value explains the relationship between the futures contract on a market and the actual value of the index. In other words, if futures are trading above fair value, investors believe the index will rise. The opposite is true if futures are trading below fair value. If your business invests in futures, this can be crucial in your ability to raise finance. There will always be some variation around fair value because of short-term issues of supply and demand, but futures should generally be close to fair value.

HOW IT WORKS IN PRACTICE

The calculation of fair value is relatively simple as long as you have access to the necessary underlying data. The formula most often used is:

$$\text{Fair value} = \text{Cash} \times \frac{(1 + r \times x)}{360} - \text{Dividends}$$

where Cash is the closing index value, r is the current interest rate, and x is the time remaining until the contract expires, in days.

For example, the fair value calculation for the FTSE 100 where the closing price is 1157 points with a cash index of 1146, the interest rate is 0.57%, with 78 days before expiry of the contract, and a dividend value of 3.47 points, would be calculated as follows:

$$\text{Fair value} = 1146 \times \frac{(1 + 0.0057 \times 78)}{360} - 3.47$$

This calculation gives a fair value of 1156.68 points. If the FTSE is trading at 1157 then the difference between the two figures is 0.32. At this time, the stock is trading below fair value.

TRICKS OF THE TRADE

- Remember that fair value will change on a daily basis depending on the money markets.
- The key purpose of a fair value figure is to give investors a feel for the initial move of the markets "on the open." Futures trading above the fair value number indicate a positive open for the grouping discussed, while numbers below fair value are indicative of negative openings.
- Fair value can also be used to refer more generally to a stock trading at a reasonable level considering price/earning ratios.
- Many financial news websites publish fair value data daily for key global markets, which means that you may not need to do all the calculations manually.

MORE INFO

Website:

Mark Hanes on fair value: tinyurl.com/3lglrxf

Fixed-Deposit Compound Interest

WHAT IT MEASURES

The compound interest paid on fixed deposits, which is usually paid more frequently (monthly or quarterly) than a traditional annual interest rate. As the frequency of compounding increases, so does the effective rate of interest.

WHY IT IS IMPORTANT

The structure of fixed deposits means that a fixed-deposit investment offering a headline interest rate of, perhaps 8%, will in effect pay a rate higher than this. This must be taken into account, along with the frequency of compounding, when calculating the "effective" interest rate paid.

HOW IT WORKS IN PRACTICE

If your company invests \$1 million at a rate of 8% for one year, at the end of the year the investment would be worth \$1,080,000 based on annual compounding.

However, with fixed-deposit compound rates, interest may be paid more frequently, in which case the value of an investment changes. After one year, an investment of \$1 million compounded quarterly would be worth £1,082,432 based on quarterly compounding, for example. This translates into an effective interest rate of 8.24%, rather than 8%.

The formula for calculating fixed deposit compound interest is as follows:

$$\text{FDCI} = p\left(1 + \frac{i}{m}\right)^{mt}$$

where:
p = investment
i = interest rate
m = number of times compounded per year
t = number of years

MORE INFO

Websites:

All Banking Solutions fixed deposit calculator: allbankingsolutions.com/fdcal.htm

MoneyChimp on compound interest: www.moneychimp.com/articles/finworks/fmfutval.htm

Yahoo compound interest calculator: tinyurl.com/6cko88p

See Also:

Annual Percentage Rate (p. 1194)
Nominal and Real Interest Rates (p. 1238)

        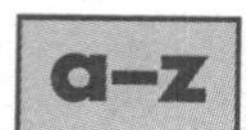

TRICKS OF THE TRADE

- With fixed-deposit investments, investors deposit a sum of money for a fixed period ranging from a few weeks to several years, which attracts a predetermined rate of interest. Fixed deposits are offered by banks and companies, although corporate fixed deposits are considered riskier.
- Fixed deposits offer regular income through interest payments, but won't offer the same returns as a stock portfolio—a typical fixed deposit compound interest rate is between 7% and 10%.

Forward Interest Rates

WHAT THEY MEASURE

Forward interest rates are interest rates which are specified now for a loan or transaction that will occur at a specified future date. As with current interest rates, forward interest rates include a term structure which shows the different forward rates offered on transactions of different maturities. Forward rates are also known as implied forward rates.

WHY THEY ARE IMPORTANT

Forward interest rates are a vital part of forward rate agreements (FRAs), and are important in making any investment decision that is sensitive to interest rates. For corporations, this might include investments or loans, while investors will commonly use forward interest rates to compare forwards and futures for investment potential. Forward rates are also needed when you want to calculate the interest earned between two periods.

Forward rates are extrapolated from a risk-free theoretical spot rate, and should be monitored because they provide an insight into how the market is feeling about future movement of interest rates.

HOW THEY WORK IN PRACTICE

A conventional investment might offer an interest rate of 6.6% per annum, compounded annually. After two years, a $1 investment would return $1.14.

In a forward interest rate agreement, however, an investment and rate is agreed for a future date. For example, you might agree to invest $1 in one year's time, for a period of two years. The interest rate paid is a forward interest rate.

The payments on a forward interest rate agreement can be calculated using the following formula:

$$\text{Payment} = \text{Notional amount} \times \frac{(\text{Reference rate} - \text{Fixed rate} \times \alpha)}{(1 + \text{Reference rate} \times \alpha)}$$

where the reference rate is the base rate, usually taken from Libor, the fixed rate is the interest rate at which the loan is agreed, and α is the time/days involved, using dating conventions.

TRICKS OF THE TRADE

- Future interest rates can be calculated more accurately by incorporating discounted cash flow over the lifetime of the loan/investment. Given a discount function, it is possible to arrange today to borrow $1 at the end of year 1 and pay 1/df(2) at the end of year 2 for a zero net investment, since each sum has a present value of $1.
- Forward rates can cover periods that only last one period, with rates denoted by the starting date. For example, a year one forward rate covers the period from the end of year 1 to the end of year 2, but on terms negotiated today.
- Forward rates are also widely used in foreign currency exchange, where investors predict likely movements in rates over time. They can also be used to price bonds, using forward rates instead of discount rates to value the bond.

MORE INFO

Websites:

Forward rate agreement calculator: www.montegodata.co.uk/consult/FRA/fra.htm

Investopedia on forward rates: tinyurl.com/67pfnah

See Also:

✔ Identifying and Managing Exposure to Interest and Exchange Rate Risks (p. 974)

Future Value

Future value is simply the estimated value of a sum of money at a given point in the future, as in, "What will the $1,000 we have today be worth in two years' time?"

WHAT IT MEASURES

Any amount of any currency.

WHY IT IS IMPORTANT

Future value is a fundamental of investment. Understanding it helps any organization or individual to determine how a sum will be affected by changes in inflation, interest rates, or currency values. Inflation, for instance, will always reduce a sum's value. Interest rates will always increase it. Exchanging the sum for an identical amount in another currency will increase or decrease it, depending on how the respective currencies perform on the world market.

Armed with this knowledge, an organization can make more informed decisions about how to generate the maximum value from its funds in a given period of time: Would it be best to deposit them in simple interest-bearing accounts, exchange them for funds in another currency, use them to expand operations, or use them to acquire another company?

  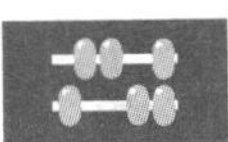      

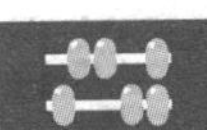

HOW IT WORKS IN PRACTICE

Start with three figures: the sum in question, the percentage by which it will increase or decrease, and the period of time. In this case: $1,000, 11%, and two years.

At an interest rate of 11%, our $1,000 will grow to $1,232 in two years:

$$\$1{,}000 \times 1.11 = \$1{,}110 \text{ (first year)} \times 1.11 = \$1{,}232 \text{ (second year)}$$

Note that the interest earned in the first year generates additional interest in the second year, a practice known as compounding. When large sums are involved, the effect of compounding can be significant.

At an inflation rate of 11%, by contrast, our $1,000 will shrink to $812 in two years:

$$\frac{\$1{,}000}{1.11} = \frac{\$901 \text{ (first year)}}{1.11} = \$812 \text{ (second year)}$$

TRICKS OF THE TRADE

- Express the percentage as 1.11 and multiply and divide by that figure, instead of using 11%. Otherwise, errors will occur.
- Calculate each year, quarter, or month separately, as in our examples.
- It is important always to use the *annual* rates of interest and inflation.
- A more useful tool is "present value," which estimates what value future cash flows would have if they occurred today.

MORE INFO

Website:

Future value calculator: www.calculator.net/future-value-calculator.html

See Also:

✔ Managing the Time Value of Money (p. 979)
Time Value of Money (p. 1258)

Future Value of an Annuity

Calculating the future value of an annuity is another example of the principle that money invested today will be worth more in the future.

WHAT IT MEASURES

The value to which a series of fixed-amount payments made at regular intervals will grow over the specified period of time.

WHY IT IS IMPORTANT

The calculation enables companies to determine the future value of a fund receiving regular payments, such as a pension fund to which contributions are made. Individuals in companies may find the calculation equally useful if they want to establish a fund to pay the cost of future college education: they will know what their annual payments will grow to be in a given number of years.

HOW IT WORKS IN PRACTICE

There are several types of annuity. They vary both in the ways they accumulate funds and in the ways they dispense earnings. The following are some examples:

- A **fixed annuity** guarantees fixed payments to the individual receiving it for the term of the contract, usually until death.
- A **variable annuity** offers no guarantee but has potential for a greater return, usually based on the performance of a stock or mutual fund.
- A **deferred annuity** delays payments until the individual chooses to receive them.
- A **hybrid annuity**, also called a combination annuity, combines features of both the fixed and variable annuity.

Financial calculators and spreadsheet programs will compute annuity calculations automatically. Manual calculations require a future-value-of-annuity table that contains figures based on the interest rate and period in question. The basic formula is:

$$\text{Future value} = \text{Amount invested} \times \text{Table value [interest, period]}$$

If, for example, a pension manager puts $1,000,000 at the end of every year into his company's pension fund, the fund earns 8% interest, and there are no withdrawals, at the end of five years it will be worth:

$$\$1{,}000{,}000 \times 5.867 \text{ [table value]} = \$5{,}867{,}000$$

TRICKS OF THE TRADE

- The formula assumes that payments are made at the end of a given period.
- If a stated interest rate is not an annual rate, it must be adjusted to reflect an annual rate.
- Although their yields are low, annuities are relatively safe investments that provide level streams of cash flow for fixed periods of time.
- In the United States, annuities are tax-deferred, but also often carry an early withdrawal penalty.
- If you are calculating manually, be sure to use the designated future value of an annuity table, and not the future value table; there is a significant difference.
- The mathematical expression for the numbers appearing on a future value of an annuity table is $[(1 + i)^n - 1] \div i$; i is the interest rate, and n is the number of years in question.

MORE INFO

Book:

Walsh, Ciaran. *Key Management Ratios*. 4th ed. London: FT Prentice Hall, 2008.

Website:

Get Objects on future value of annuities: www.getobjects.com/Components/Finance/TVM/fva.html

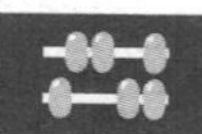

Goodwill and Patents

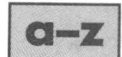

One could define both goodwill and patents as figments of the imagination, the former a financier's and the latter an inventor's. The accounting realm assigns real value to both, based on the theory that both will deliver real benefits in the future.

WHAT IT MEASURES

The value of two intangible assets.

WHY IT IS IMPORTANT

Since both goodwill and patents are intangible assets, their values will be whatever negotiators conclude. Still, their values need to be reflected in financial statements. Goodwill is created in the aftermath of an acquisition, and must appear on a balance sheet. The acquisition of a patent has a cost of its own, be it the price of internal development costs, or the purchase price paid to an inventor.

HOW IT WORKS IN PRACTICE

Ultimately, the assigned values of both assets are matters of opinion, however learned the opinions may be. Each must be considered separately.

Ordinarily, goodwill is completely ignored by accountants. Only when a company has been acquired by another does goodwill become an intangible asset. It then appears on a balance sheet in the amount by which the price paid by the acquiring company exceeds the net tangible assets of the acquired company. In other words:

$$\text{Goodwill} = \text{Purchase price} - \text{Net assets}$$

If, for example, an airline is bought for $12 billion and its net assets are valued at $9 billion, $3 billion of the purchase would be allocated to goodwill on the balance sheet.

The buyer will attribute the difference to any number of reasons that give a competitive advantage, such as a loyal and long-standing customer base, a strong brand, strategic location, or productive employees.

A patent's value, meanwhile, will probably be the sum of its development costs, or its purchase price if acquired from someone else. It is usually to a company's advantage to spread the patent's value over several years. If so, the critical time period to consider is not the full life of the patent (17 years in the United States), but its estimated useful life.

For example, let's say that in January 2000 a company acquired a patent issued in January 1995 at a cost of $100,000. It concludes that the patent's useful commercial life is 10 years, not the 12 remaining before the patent expires. In turn, patent value would be $100,000, and it would be spread (or amortized in accounting terms) over 10 years, or $10,000 each year.

TRICKS OF THE TRADE

- Accounting for goodwill can vary by country, an issue that needs to be considered when evaluating or negotiating acquisitions of foreign-based companies. Moreover, the rules may change from time to time. In the United States, for example, goodwill no longer has to be amortized over 40 years.
- The total value of a patent's development costs may stretch over several years.
- The cost of a patent ultimately may have little bearing on the future revenues and profits it brings.

MORE INFO

Websites:

UK Intellectual Property Office on patents: www.ipo.gov.uk/patent.htm

US Patent and Trademark Office on patents: www.uspto.gov/patents/

See Also:

★ Protecting Your Intellectual Property—Registered Rights (pp. 913–914)

✔ Intellectual Property—Patents—An International Overview (p. 1163)

Gross Profit Margin Ratio

WHAT IT MEASURES

The gross profit margin ratio measures how efficiently a company uses its resources, materials, and labor in the production process by showing the percentage of net sales remaining after subtracting the cost of making and selling a product or service. It is usually expressed as a percentage, and indicates the profitability of a business before overhead costs.

WHY IT IS IMPORTANT

A high gross profit margin ratio indicates that a business can make a reasonable profit on sales, as long as overheads do not increase. Investors pay attention to the gross profit margin ratio because it tells them how efficient your business is compared to competitors. It is sensible to track gross profit margin ratios over a number of years to see if company earnings are consistent, growing, or declining.

For businesses, knowing your gross profit margin ratio is important because it tells you whether your business is pricing goods and services effectively. A low margin compared to your competitors would suggest you are under-pricing, while a high margin might indicate over-pricing. Low profit margin ratios can also suggest the business is unable to control production costs, or that a low amount of earnings is generated from revenues.

HOW IT WORKS IN PRACTICE

To calculate gross profit margin ratio, use the following formula:

$$\text{Gross profit margin ratio} = \frac{\text{Gross profit margin}}{\text{Net sales}}$$

First, determine the gross profit for the business during a specific period of time, such as a financial quarter. This is total revenue minus the cost of sales. The cost of sales includes variable costs associated with manufacturing, packaging, and freight, and should not include fixed overheads such as rent or utilities.

For example, if Company A has net sales of $10 million, while costs for inventory or production total $7 million, then the gross profit margin is $3 million. Next, divide this by net sales. In our example:

$$\frac{3{,}000{,}000}{10{,}000{,}000} = 0.3 = 30\%$$

(Simply multiply the result by 100 to see it expressed as a percentage, here a gross profit margin ratio of 30%.) Tracking several subsequent quarters will allow you to create a more accurate profit margin ratio. A more detailed version of the formula is:

$$\text{Gross profit margin ratio} = \frac{(\text{Total revenue} - \text{Cost of sales})}{\text{Total sales}}$$

TRICKS OF THE TRADE

- Gross profit margins tend to remain stable over time. Significant irregularities or sudden variations might be a potential sign of financial fraud, accounting irregularities, or problems in the business.
- Gross profit margin ratios can be calculated alongside net profit margin ratios (net profit after tax ÷ sales), pre-tax profit margins (net profit before tax ÷ sales), and operating profit margins (net income before interest and taxes ÷ sales) to provide a more comprehensive insight into margins. Net profit margins and gross profit margins can be significantly different because of the impact of interest and tax expenses.
- Profit margin ratios are a popular way to benchmark against competitors. Industries will generally have standard gross profit margin ratios, which are easily discovered.
- If you use an accounting program such as QuickBooks, the software can calculate gross profit margin ratios for you, making it easier to track margin ratios over several years. If you discover fluctuations regularly occur at a particular time of year, you might try to adjust pricing to encourage greater sales at that period.

MORE INFO

Websites:

About.com on gross profit margin: tinyurl.com/e5b3b

BizWiz Consulting on profit margin ratios: tinyurl.com/6aykdyk

Interest Coverage

Interest coverage, or interest cover, describes several ratios used to assess a company's financial strength and capital structure.

WHAT IT MEASURES

The amount of earnings available to make interest payments after all operating and nonoperating income and expenses—except interest and income taxes—have been accounted for.

WHY IT IS IMPORTANT

Interest coverage is regarded as a measure of a company's creditworthiness because it shows how much income there is to cover interest payments on outstanding debt. Banks and financial analysts also rely on this ratio as a rule of thumb to gauge the fundamental strength of a business.

HOW IT WORKS IN PRACTICE

Interest coverage is expressed as a ratio, and reflects a company's ability to pay the interest obligations on its debt. It compares the funds available to pay interest—earnings before interest and taxes, or EBIT—with the interest expense. The basic formula is:

$$\text{Interest coverage ratio} = \frac{\text{EBIT}}{\text{Interest expense}}$$

If interest expense for a year is $9 million, and the company's EBIT is $45 million, the interest coverage would be:

$$\frac{45{,}000{,}000}{9{,}000{,}000} = 5$$

The higher the number, the stronger a company is likely to be. Conversely, a low number suggests that a company's fortunes are looking ominous. Variations of this basic formula also exist. For example, there is:

$$\text{Cash flow interest coverage ratio} = \frac{(\text{Operating cash flow} + \text{Interest} + \text{Taxes})}{\text{Interest}}$$

This ratio indicates the company's ability to use its cash flow to satisfy its fixed financing obligations. Finally, there is the fixed-charge coverage ratio, which compares EBIT with fixed charges:

$$\text{Fixed-charge coverage ratio} = \frac{(\text{EBIT} + \text{Lease expenses})}{(\text{Interest} + \text{Lease expense})}$$

"Fixed charges" can be interpreted in many ways, however. It could mean, for example, the funds that a company is obliged to set aside to retire debt, or dividends on preferred stock.

TRICKS OF THE TRADE

- A ratio of less than 1 indicates that a company is having problems generating enough cash flow to pay its interest expenses, and that either a modest decline in operating profits or a sudden rise in borrowing costs could eliminate profitability entirely.
- Ideally, interest coverage should at least exceed 1.5; in some sectors, 2.0 or higher is desirable.
- Interest coverage is widely considered to be more meaningful than looking at total debt, because what really matters is what an enterprise must pay in a given period, not how much debt it has.
- As is often the case, it may be more meaningful to watch interest coverage over several periods in order to detect long-term trends.
- Cash flow will sometimes be substituted for EBIT in the ratio, because EBIT includes not only cash but also accrued sales and other unrealized income.
- Interest coverage also is called "times interest earned."

  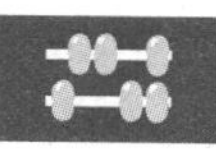   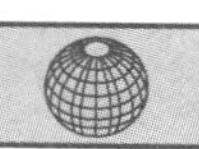   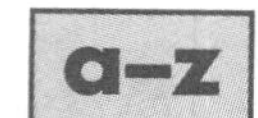

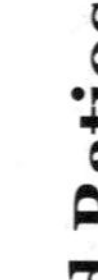

Internal Rate of Return

Internal rate of return (IRR) is another analytical tool based on the time value of money principle. Some regard it as the companion to net present value.

WHAT IT MEASURES

Technically, the interest rate that makes the present value of an investment's projected cash flows equal to the cost of the project; practically speaking, the rate that indicates whether or not an investment is worth pursuing.

WHY IT IS IMPORTANT

The calculation of internal rate of return (IRR) is used to appraise the prospective viability of investments and capital projects. It is also called dollar-weighted rate of return.

Essentially, IRR allows an investor to find the interest rate that is equivalent to the monetary returns expected from the project. Once that rate is determined, it can be compared to the rates that could be earned by investing the money elsewhere, or to the weighted cost of capital. IRR also accounts for the time value of money.

HOW IT WORKS IN PRACTICE

How is IRR applied? Assume, for example, that a project under consideration costs $7,500 and is expected to return $2,000 per year for five years, or $10,000. The IRR calculated for the project would be about 10%. If the cost of borrowing money for the project, or the return on investing the funds elsewhere, is less than 10%, the project is probably worthwhile. If the alternate use of the money will return 10% or more, the project should be rejected, since from a financial perspective it will break even at best.

Typically, management requires an IRR equal to or higher than the cost of capital, depending on relative risk and other factors.

The best way to compute an IRR is by using a spreadsheet (such as Excel) or a financial calculator, which do it automatically, although it is crucial to understand how the calculation should be structured. Calculating IRR by hand is tedious and time-consuming, and requires the process to be repeated to run sensitivities.

If using Excel, for example, select the IRR function. This requires the annual cash flows to be set out in columns, and the first part of the IRR formula requires the cell reference range of these cash flows to be entered. Then a guess of the IRR is required. The default is 10%, written 0.1.

If a project has the following expected cash flows, then guessing IRR at 30% returns an accurate IRR of 27%, indicating that if the next best way of investing the money gives a return of –20%, the project should go ahead.

Now	–2,500
Year 1	1,200
Year 2	1,300
Year 3	1,500

TRICKS OF THE TRADE

- IRR analysis is generally used to evaluate a project's cash flows rather than income because, unlike income, cash flows do not reflect depreciation and therefore are usually more instructive to appraise.
- Most basic spreadsheet functions apply to cash flows only.
- As well as advocates, IRR has critics who dismiss it as misleading, especially as significant costs will occur late in the project. The rule of thumb that "the higher the IRR the better" does not always apply.
- For the most thorough analysis of a project's investment potential, some experts urge using both IRR and net present value calculations, and comparing their results.

MORE INFO

Book:

Walsh, Ciaran. *Key Management Ratios*. 4th ed. London: FT Prentice Hall, 2008.

Article:

Baker, Samuel L. "The internal rate of return." March 28, 2006. Online at: sambaker.com/econ/irr/irr.html

See Also:

★ Comparing Net Present Value and Internal Rate of Return (pp. 30–32)
✔ Using IRR for M&A Financing (p. 1137)

Liquidity Ratio Analysis

WHAT IT MEASURES

Liquidity ratios are a set of ratios or figures that measure a company's ability to pay off its short-term debt obligations. This is done by measuring a company's liquid assets (including those that might easily be converted into cash) against its short-term liabilities.

There are a number of different liquidity ratios, which each measure slightly different types of assets when calculating the ratio. More conservative measures will exclude assets that need to be converted into cash.

WHY IT IS IMPORTANT

In general, the greater the coverage of liquid assets to short-term liabilities, the more likely it is that a business will be able to pay debts as they become due while still funding ongoing operations. On the other hand, a company with a low liquidity ratio might have difficulty meeting obligations while funding vital ongoing business operations.

Liquidity ratios are sometimes requested by banks when they are evaluating a loan application. If you take out a loan, the lender may require you to maintain a certain minimum liquidity ratio, as part of the loan agreement. For that reason, steps to improve your liquidity ratios are sometimes necessary.

HOW IT WORKS IN PRACTICE

There are three fundamental liquidity ratios that can provide insight into short-term liquidity: current, quick, and cash ratios. These work as follows:

  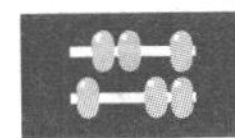      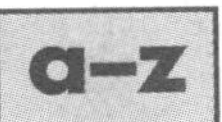

Current Ratio

This is a way of testing liquidity by deriving the proportion of assets available to cover current liabilities, as follows:

$$\text{Current ratio} = \frac{\text{Current assets}}{\text{Current liabilities}}$$

Current ratio is widely discussed in the financial world, and it is easy to understand. However, it can be misleading because the chances of a company ever needing to liquidate all its assets to meet liabilities are very slim indeed. It is often more useful to consider a company as a going concern, in which case you need to understand the time it takes to convert assets into cash, as well as the current ratio.

The current ratio should be at least between 1.5 and 2, although some investors would argue that the figure should be above 2, particularly if a high proportion of assets are stock. A ratio of less than 1 (that is, where the current liabilities exceed the current assets) could mean that you are unable to meet debts as they fall due, in which case you are insolvent. A high current ratio could indicate that too much money is tied up in current assets—for example, giving customers too much credit.

Cash Ratio

This indicates liquidity by measuring the amount of cash, cash equivalents, and invested funds that are available to meet current short-term liabilities. It is calculated by using the following formula:

$$\text{Cash ratio} = \frac{(\text{Cash} + \text{Cash equivalents} + \text{Invested funds})}{\text{Current liabilities}}$$

The cash ratio is a more conservative measure of liquidity than the current ratio, because it only looks at assets that are already liquid, ignoring assets such as receivables or inventory.

Quick Ratio

The third liquidity ratio is a more sophisticated alternative to the current ratio, which measures the most liquid current assets—excluding inventory but including accounts receivable and certain investments.

$$\text{Quick ratio} = \frac{(\text{Cash equivalents} + \text{Short-term investments} + \text{Accounts receivable})}{\text{Current liabilities}}$$

The quick ratio should be around 0.7–1, with very few companies having a cash ratio of over 1. To be absolutely safe, the quick ratio should be at least 1, which indicates that quick assets exceed current liabilities. If the current ratio is rising and the quick ratio is static, this suggests a potential stockholding problem.

TRICKS OF THE TRADE

- All of these ratios have advantages and disadvantages. It is important to remember that any ratio that includes accounts receivable assumes a liquidation of accounts receivable—this may not be possible, practical, or desirable in many situations.
- Liquidity ratios should therefore be considered alongside ratios demonstrating the time it would take to convert assets to cash—a conversion time of several months compared to a few days would seriously affect liquidity.
- Some analysts use a fourth liquidity ratio to measure business performance, known as the "defensive interval." This measures how long a business can survive without cash coming in—and ideally should be between 30 and 90 days.

MORE INFO

Book:

Berman, Karen, and Joe Knight, with John Case. "Liquidity ratios: Can we pay our bills?" In *Financial Intelligence: A Manager's Guide to Knowing What the Numbers Really Mean*. Boston, MA: Harvard Business School Press, 2005. Also available separately.

See Also:

✔ Measuring Liquidity (p. 983)
Acid-Test Ratio (pp. 1189–1190)
Current Ratio (p. 1213)

Management Accounts

WHAT THEY MEASURE

Company accounts fall into two categories: financial and management. While financial accounts are regulated and audited reports of financial transactions and processes, the management accounts are designed to help key business executives understand the overall performance of the business. Most companies produce these reports monthly or quarterly.

WHY THEY ARE IMPORTANT

Rather than focusing on financial metrics, management accounting focuses on operations and the value chain, as opposed to the historical activities of external financial reporting and auditing. They tend to be forward-looking and focused on identifying new revenue, cash flow, profit forecasts, and growth opportunities. Management accounts help executives carry out planning, control, and administration duties effectively. They mean you can see whether profitable parts of the business are subsidizing less successful activities, you can compare performance with forecasts, can identify trends, and manage resources better.

HOW THEY WORK IN PRACTICE

At their most basic, management accounts are reports that provide analysis of business performance and strategy broken down into different business activities or products. Each section of the report should provide an overview of cash flow, profit margins, liabilities, and forecasts for key business metrics.

In practice, management accounts are usually more complex than this. Management accountants may follow any of a number of management accounting methodologies, which will dictate what information is collected, and how it might be presented. Popular approaches to management accounting include:

Lifecycle costing: A form of management accounting that analyses the cost of manufacturing an individual product or service, and looks for how this might be improved.

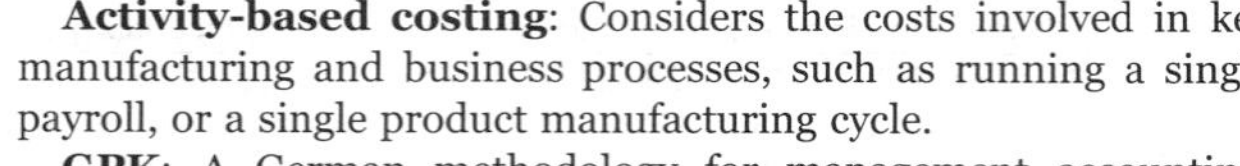

Activity-based costing: Considers the costs involved in key manufacturing and business processes, such as running a single payroll, or a single product manufacturing cycle.

GPK: A German methodology for management accounting, sometimes known as marginal planned cost accounting. This system was created to provide a consistent, accurate view of how managerial costs are calculated and assigned to a company's products and services.

Lean accounting: A management accounting methodology that was designed in the 1990s for use in just-in-time manufacturing environments and service businesses.

Resource consumption accounting: Focuses on identifying areas with potential for business optimization. Governed by the RCA Institute, this approach to accounting promotes consistency and professionalism in management accounts.

Throughput accounting: Recognizes the relationships between the various elements of the modern manufacturing process, and uses calculations to measure the contribution each part makes per unit of resource.

Management accounting can be applied to virtually any business, and each methodology can be tailored to meet the needs of different industries and sizes of company. However, any management accounting program should incorporate most of the following elements:

- variance analysis;
- rate and volume analysis;
- price modeling and profit margin analysis;
- cost analysis;
- cost/benefit analysis;
- lifecycle cost analysis;
- capital budgeting;
- strategic analysis;
- annual budgeting;
- sales and financial forecasting;
- cost allocation.

TRICKS OF THE TRADE

- Management accounting is easier if you build in regular systems to capture key information on a daily or weekly basis. Day to day, business managers should record information into a management accounts spreadsheet or application, including details of transactions made, results of financial changes, and projections of future trade.
- There are many off-the-shelf software packages that can be used for this purpose. The key is to select something easy to use—it's not an effective use of resources to spend weeks learning the intricacies of a financial reporting tool if your job is not financial.
- There is no pre-determined format for management accounts, nor any legal requirement to prepare them—but few businesses can survive without them.

MORE INFO

Website:

Arts Council England management accounts templates: tinyurl.com/ovf7egl

See Also:

Management Accounts: How to Use Them to Control Your Business (p. 1389)

Marginal Cost

Marginal cost is based on the economic theory that the more goods are produced, the lower will be the per-unit cost.

WHAT IT MEASURES

The additional cost of producing one more unit of product, or providing service to one more customer.

WHY IT IS IMPORTANT

Sometimes called incremental cost, marginal cost shows how much costs increase from making or serving one more unit, an essential factor when contemplating a production increase, or seeking to serve more customers.

If the price charged is greater than the marginal cost, then the revenue gain will be greater than the added cost. That, in turn, will increase profit, so the expansion in production or service makes economic sense and should proceed. Of course, the reverse is also true: If the price charged is less than the marginal cost, expansion should not go ahead.

HOW IT WORKS IN PRACTICE

The formula for marginal cost is:

$$\text{Marginal cost} = \frac{\text{Change in cost}}{\text{Change in quantity}}$$

If it costs a company $260,000 to produce 3,000 items, and $325,000 to produce 3,800 items, the change in cost would be:

325,000 − 260,000 = $65,000

The change in quantity would be:

3,800 − 3,000 = 800

When the formula to calculate marginal cost is applied, the result is:

$$\frac{65{,}000}{800} = \$81.25$$

If the price of the item in question were, say, $99.95, expansion should proceed.

TRICKS OF THE TRADE

- A marginal cost that is lower than the price shows that it is not always necessary to cut prices to sell more goods and boost profits.
- Using idle capacity to produce lower-margin items can still be beneficial, because these generate revenues that help cover fixed costs.
- Marginal cost studies can become quite complicated, because the basic formula does not always take into account variables that can affect cost and quantity. Software programs are available, many of which are industry-specific.
- At some point, marginal cost invariably begins to rise; typically, labor becomes less productive as a production run increases, while the time required also increases.
- Marginal cost alone may not justify expansion. It is best to determine also average costs, then chart the respective series of

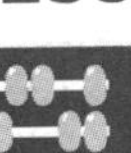
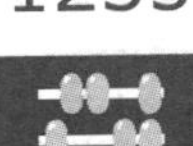

figures to find where marginal cost meets average cost, and thus determine optimum cost.

- Relying on marginal cost is not fail-safe; putting more product on a market can drive down prices and thus cut margins. Moreover, committing idle capacity to long-term production may tie up resources that could be directed to a new and more profitable opportunity.
- An important related principle is contribution: the cash gained (or lost) from selling an additional unit.

Marginal Rate of Substitution

WHAT IT MEASURES

Sometimes referred to as MRS, the marginal rate of substitution measures the rate at which an individual must give up one asset to obtain a single additional unit of a second asset, while keeping overall utility constant. MRS can measure physical goods, but also assets such as labor or time. The result is generally plotted on an "indifference curve," which shows the utility value for each combination of assets. MRS is also often used to show the rate at which a consumer will substitute one product or service with an alternative.

WHY IT IS IMPORTANT

MRS enables businesses to analyze how a rational user/consumer/-organization chooses between two goods. For example, how will a change in the wage rate affect the choice between leisure time and work time? How far will price increases affect a consumer's choice of drinking water?

HOW IT WORKS IN PRACTICE

To calculate MRS, we begin by creating an indifference curve, a line showing all the possible combinations of two goods/assets. The line plots the combinations that result in the same utility or value to the consumer.

In Figure 1, the graph shows a person receives the same utility from 4 hours of work and 6 hours of leisure as from 7 hours of work and 3 hours of leisure.

MRS is the amount of one asset (leisure) that needs to be sacrificed to obtain one unit of the second asset (work) while achieving the same utility (satisfaction).

The simple equation to calculate MRS is as follows:

$$\text{Marginal rate of substitution} = \frac{-dy}{dx}$$

where d = change in good, and x and y represent different goods, products, or services. This calculation assumes utility remains constant.

For example, if the MRS is 2 then the consumer will give up 2 units of y to obtain one additional unit of x.

Using the example above, the marginal rate of substitution between the two selected variables is:

$$\frac{-(6-3)}{(4-7)} = \frac{-3}{-3} = 1$$

TRICKS OF THE TRADE

- Marginal rate of substitution diminishes over time because there is a principle of diminishing marginal utility—so the more units are consumed, the less additional satisfaction each addition creates (in other words, the more we consume something, the more willing we are to substitute it away).
- It is possible to create graphs showing more than one indifference curve—in this case, the resulting graph is called an "indifference curve map."
- A key limitation of MRS is that the relationship between two goods remains constant. In reality, it may be that as a worker increases their salary, they desire more leisure time because they have more disposable income. An increase in tea consumption may decrease the marginal utility of coffee.
- It is common to add a budget line to MRS graphs, to separate affordable and unaffordable consumption possibilities.

Figure 1. An example indifference curve

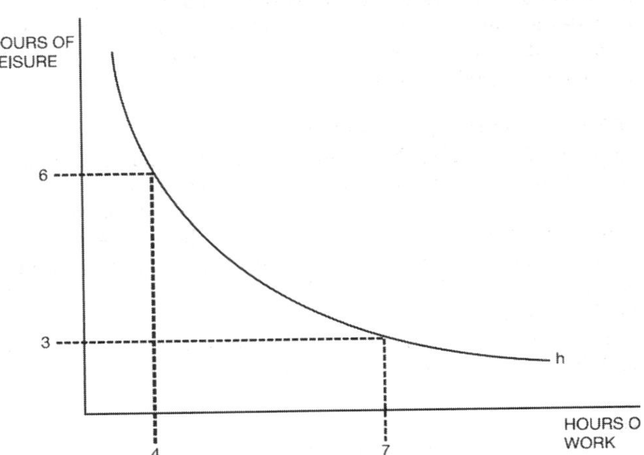

MORE INFO

Book:

Pindyck, Robert S., and Daniel L. Rubinfeld. *Microeconomics*. 7th ed. Upper Saddle River, NJ: Pearson/Prentice Hall, 2008.

Website:

Answers.com on MRS: www.answers.com/topic/marginal-rate-of-substitution

Market/Book Ratio

WHAT IT MEASURES

Market/book ratio, sometimes called price-to-book ratio, is a way of measuring the relative value of a company compared to its stock price or market value.

WHY IT IS IMPORTANT

Market/book ratio is a useful way of measuring your company's performance and making quick comparisons with competitors. It is an essential figure to potential investors and analysts because it provides a simple way of judging whether a company is under or overvalued. If your business has a low market/book ratio, it's considered a good investment opportunity.

HOW IT WORKS IN PRACTICE

At its simplest, market/book ratio measures the market capitalization (expressed as price per stock) of a business divided by its book value (the value of assets minus liabilities). The book value of a company refers to what would be left if the business paid its liabilities and shut its doors, although, of course, a growing business will always be worth more than its book value because it has the ability to generate new sales.

To calculate market/book ratio, take the current price per stock and divide by the book value per stock:

$$\text{Market/book ratio} = \frac{\text{Market price per stock}}{\text{Book value per stock}}$$

For example, Company A might be trading at $2.20 per stock. However, the book value per stock is actually $3.00. This results in a market/book ratio of 0.73, suggesting the company's assets may in fact be undervalued by 27%.

Market-to-book value can alternatively be calculated as follows:

$$\text{Market/book ratio} = \frac{\text{Market price per stock}}{\text{Net asset value per stock}}$$

TRICKS OF THE TRADE

- Like the price-to-earnings ratio, the lower the price-to-book ratio or market/book ratio, the better the value. Investors would use a low price-to-book ratio on stock screens, for instance, to identify potential candidates for new investment. As a rule of thumb, a market/book ratio above one suggests the company is undervalued, while a ratio over one suggests the company might be overvalued.
- A low market/book ratio could suggest a company's assets are undervalued, or that the company's prospects are good and earnings/value should grow.
- Market/book ratios are most useful when valuing knowledge-intensive companies, where physical assets may not accurately or fully reflect the value of the business. Technology companies and other businesses that don't have a lot of physical assets tend to have low book-to-market ratios.

MORE INFO

See Also:

Book Value (p. 1198)

Net Added Value (NAV) and Adjusted NAV

WHAT IT MEASURES

Net added value, or net asset value, is the value of a corporate asset or business based on its assets minus its liabilities. Adjusted NAV refers to the value once it has been adjusted for any known or suspected differences between market value and book value. In share dealing, NAV refers to the value of a portfolio minus its liabilities.

WHY IT IS IMPORTANT

For investors, the NAV gives an idea of appropriate share prices. For example, if a fund's NAV is $10, you should expect that you can buy the fund's shares for $10 each, although there are exceptions to this rule, such as a newly launched fund. NAV is particularly important when valuing shares in companies where much of the value comes from assets rather than the profit stream—such as investment trusts, but also property companies.

HOW IT WORKS IN PRACTICE

To calculate NAV for an investment portfolio, you should use the following formula:

$$\text{Net added value} = \frac{(\text{Market value of all securities} + \text{Cash} + \text{Equivalent holdings} - \text{Liabilities})}{\text{Total shares outstanding}}$$

For example, if a mutual fund holds $10.5 million in securities, $2 million in cash, and has liabilities totaling $0.5 million, with one million shares outstanding, then the NAV calculation would be as follows:

$$\frac{(10.5 + 2 - 0.5)}{1} = \$12$$

TRICKS OF THE TRADE

- When calculating NAV for collective investments such as mutual funds, NAV is the total value of the portfolio less liabilities, calculated on a daily basis. Another alternative measurement for NAV is to add together unit capital and reserves held by a fund.
- In corporate valuations, NAV is the value of assets less liabilities. Assets include anything owned, whether in possession or not, while a liability is anything that is a potential cost to the business. Obviously this means calculating NAV for corporate entities is more difficult, and might be based on book value, carrying value, historical costs, amortized cost, or market value.
- NAV is a good way to keep track of price changes and asset valuations. However, you should keep in mind that the NAV calculation will change from day to day, and does not necessarily reflect the performance of the fund. In the early days of a fund, NAV will rise and fall as the fund's managers take their fees, and each time the fund makes a payout to shareholders. When a fund opens, it often trades at a premium to NAV, later falling to a discount.

  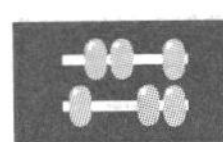      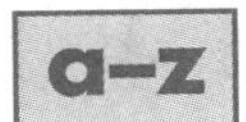

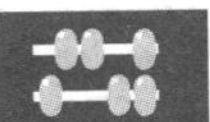

- In general, a low NAV is considered a better investment opportunity than a high NAV. However, because NAV values on investment portfolios are calculated daily, critics argue that they are not a good performance indicator.
- In mutual funds, NAV per share is calculated at the close of trading each day based on closing share prices of securities held in the fund's portfolio. Any buy and sell orders are processed based on the day's NAV.
- The price that investors pay to purchase unit trust units is based on the approximate NAV per unit, plus fees that will be imposed by the unit's managers such as purchase fees.
- While you can calculate NAV for almost any business or fund, it is not of any real use when applied to service companies where there are few assets of value, such as plants, property, or equipment.

MORE INFO

Websites:

Money Terms on NAV: moneyterms.co.uk/nav/

US SEC on NAV: www.sec.gov/answers/nav.htm

Net Present Value

Net present value (NPV) expresses the sum total of an investment's future net cash flows (receipts less payments) minus the investment's initial costs. It is an investment appraisal tool.

WHAT IT MEASURES

The projected profitability of an investment, based on anticipated cash flows and discounted at a stated rate of interest.

WHY IT IS IMPORTANT

Net present value helps management or potential investors weigh the wisdom of an investment—in new equipment, a new facility, or other type of asset—by enabling them to quantify the expected benefits. Those evaluating more than one potential investment can compare the respective projected returns to find the most attractive project.

A positive NPV indicates that the project should be profitable, assuming that the estimated cash flows are reasonably accurate. A negative NPV, of course, indicates that the project will probably be unprofitable and therefore should be adjusted, if not abandoned altogether.

Equally significantly, NPV enables a management to consider the time value of money it will invest. This concept holds that the value of money increases with time because it can always earn interest in a savings account. Therefore, any other investment of that money must be weighed against how the funds would perform if simply deposited and saved.

When the time value of money concept is incorporated in the calculation of NPV, the value of a project's future net cash receipts in "today's money" can be determined. This enables proper comparisons between different projects.

HOW IT WORKS IN PRACTICE

Let's say that Global Manufacturing Inc. is considering the acquisition of a new machine. First, its management would consider all the factors: Initial purchase and installation costs; additional revenues generated by sales of the new machine's products; and the taxes on these new revenues. Having accounted for these factors in its calculations, the cash flows that Global Manufacturing projects will generate from the new machine are:

Year 1	–$100,000 (initial cost of investment)
Year 2	$30,000
Year 3	$40,000
Year 4	$40,000
Year 5	$35,000
Net total	$145,000

At first glance, it appears that cash flows total a whopping 45% more than the $100,000 initial cost, a strikingly sound investment indeed.

Alas, it's not that simple. Time value of money shrinks return on the project considerably, since future dollars are worth less than present dollars in hand. NPV accounts for these differences with the help of present value tables. These user-friendly tables, readily available on the internet and in references, list the ratios that express the present value of expected cash flow dollars, based on the applicable interest rate and the number of years in question.

In our example, Global Manufacturing's cost of capital is 9%. Using this figure to find the corresponding ratios in the present value table, the $100,000 investment cost, and expected annual revenues during the five years in question, the NPV calculation looks like this:

Year	Cash flow	Table factor (at 9%)	Present value
1	– $100,000	× 1.000000	= – $100,000.00
2	$30,000	× 0.917431	= $27,522.93
3	$40,000	× 0.841680	= $33,667.20
4	$40,000	× 0.772183	= $30,887.32
5	$35,000	× 0.708425	= $24,794.88
NPV			$16,873.33

Summing the present values of the cash flows and subtracting the investment cost from the total, the NPV is still positive. So, on this basis at least, the investment should proceed.

TRICKS OF THE TRADE

- Beware of assumptions. Interest rates change, of course, which can affect NPV dramatically. Moreover, fresh revenues (as well as new markets) may not grow as projected. If the cash flows in

MORE INFO

Book:

Walsh, Ciaran. *Key Management Ratios*. 4th ed. London: FT Prentice Hall, 2008.

See Also:

★ Capital Budgeting: The Dominance of Net Present Value (pp. 20–23)

★ Comparing Net Present Value and Internal Rate of Return (pp. 30–32)

 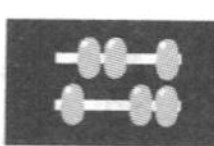      

years 2–5 of our example fall by $5,000 a year, for instance, NPV shrinks to $5,260.89, which is still positive but less attractive.

- NPV calculations are performed only with cash receipts payments and discounting factors. In turn, NPV is a tool, not *the* tool. It ignores other accounting data, intangibles, sheer faith in a new idea, and other factors that may make an investment worth pursuing despite a negative NPV.
- It is important to determine a company's cost of capital accurately.

Nominal and Real Interest Rates

WHAT THEY MEASURE

When calculating interest rates, the nominal rate of interest refers to an interest rate calculated without any adjustment for inflation or for the full effect of compounding. The real interest rate includes compensation for value lost through inflation, whereas the nominal rate excludes this. Finally, the effective interest rate (sometimes known as the annual equivalent rate, or AER) is a rate that takes account of the impact of compounding.

If you purchase a bond for one year that pays 6% interest at the end of the 12 months, a $100 investment would return $106. The 6% interest is a nominal interest rate—it does not account for inflation during that year.

Imagine investing in the same bond and accounting for a 3% inflation rate for the year. If you buy an item for $100 at the start of the year, the same item would cost $103 at the end of the year. If we then invest the $100 into the 6% bond for one year, we lose $3 to inflation—meaning the real interest rate of the bond is actually 3%.

Alternatively, imagine investing the same $100 into the bond over 12 months. At 6%, your money would return $106 after one year. However, if interest is compounded every six months, you will actually earn slightly more. After six months, you would earn $3 interest. At the end of the year, the bond will pay 3% of your new investment total of $103, or $3.09. Your investment would then return $106.09 over a year, making the effective annual rate 6.09%, slightly higher than the nominal interest rate of 6%.

WHY THEY ARE IMPORTANT

When calculating interest rates, most calculations ignore the cost to the lender of not having funds available for a period of time—by the time a loan is repaid, the cost of items may have increased so that the money is now worth less. If you know what inflation is going to be, real interest rates are a powerful tool in analyzing the value of potential investments, because they take account of the erosion of spending power over the lifetime of an investment.

Calculating the effective rate is important because interest on different investments might be paid weekly, monthly, or annually. The effective annual interest rate can compare the returns or costs of different loans more accurately than a nominal interest rate.

HOW THEY WORK IN PRACTICE

The difference between real and nominal interest rates is simply expressed as: Real interest rate = Nominal rate − Inflation. More formally, it can also be described in the equation:

$$(1 + N) = (1 + r) - (1 + i)$$

where:
N is the nominal interest rate;
r is the real interest rate;
i is the rate of inflation.

This calculation is sometimes referred to as the Fisher equation. If you do not know the rate of inflation, it can be predicted using the following formula:

$$i = \frac{(\text{CPI this year} - \text{CPI last year})}{\text{CPI last year}}$$

If you know the nominal interest rate and the number of compounding periods, it is possible to calculate the effective annual rate using the following formula:

$$\text{EAR} = (1 + N/P)^{P-1}$$

where:
N is the nominal rate;
P is the number of compounding periods.

TRICKS OF THE TRADE

- If inflation is positive then the real interest rate will be lower than the nominal interest rate. If the economy is experiencing deflation and the inflation rate is negative, then real interest is higher than nominal interest rates.
- When calculating effective interest rates, remember they will generally not include one-off charges such as set-up fees. In addition, while financial regulators closely control how the APR is expressed, there are fewer controls on the AER.
- The Fisher hypothesis states that, over time, inflation and nominal interest rates move together, so real interest rates are stable in the long term. This theory—sometimes called the Fisher effect, was devised by Irving Fisher.
- Some bonds and savings products link payments to an inflation index, so in effect pay a real interest rate. An example would be government-issued gilt.
- Sometimes it can be beneficial to value investments without taking inflation into account. This can be done by discounting using real interest rates.

MORE INFO

Article:

Moffatt, Mike. "What's the difference between nominal and real? Real variables and nominal variables explained." *About.com*. Online at: tinyurl.com/q25tt

See Also:

Annual Percentage Rate (p. 1194)
Fixed-Deposit Compound Interest (pp. 1227–1228)

  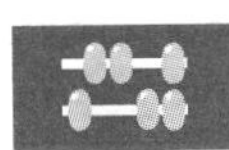      

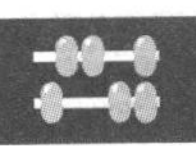

Option Pricing

WHAT IT MEASURES

There are two sorts of options in stock market trading: call and put. Option pricing uses mathematical models to calculate the value of a stock option and how it changes in response to changing conditions.

There are two key components to option pricing: the intrinsic value, which measures the amount by which an option is "in the money;" and the time value, which measures the amount paid for the time the option has before it expires.

WHY IT IS IMPORTANT

Stock traders use option pricing models to predict which options can be used to capture a potential move in a stock, and gain advantage in a trade. Option pricing is also important in risk management, because it can be used to quantify the risk associated with buying, selling, owning, and trading specific options with a high level of accuracy.

HOW IT WORKS IN PRACTICE

To understand option pricing, you must understand the four basic drivers of option prices: current stock price, intrinsic value, time to expiration, and volatility.

Stock price is important because if the price of a stock rises, the cost of a call option will also rise (though not necessarily at the same rate).

Intrinsic value is important because it measures how far an option is "in the money" (ITM), or what proportion of the option's value isn't lost over time. The intrinsic value of the call option is the stock price minus the call strike price.

Time value is the difference between the option's price and its intrinsic value. The more time an option has until it expires, the greater chance it will become "in the money"—and therefore the option becomes more valuable.

Option pricing is related to volatility expected in the market up to the time of expiration. If the market expects little movement in a stock's value, volatility is low, which results in a lower time value.

The most well-known method of modeling option pricing was developed by Fischer Black and Myron Scholes in 1973. The Black–Scholes model works as follows:

$$C = SN(d_1) - Ke^{(-rt)} N(d_2)$$

where:
C = call premium;
S = current stock price;
t = time to expiration;
K = option price;
r = risk-free interest rate;
N = normal distribution;
e = exponential term.

The first part of the calculation, $SN(d_1)$, shows the expected benefit of buying the stock outright. This is calculated by multiplying together the stock price and the change in call premium caused by a change in the underlying stock price.

The second part of the equation shows the present value of paying the exit price on the day the option expires. The fair value of the option price is then calculated by looking at the difference between the option's current value and value at expiration.

The Black–Scholes model of option pricing relies on several assumptions, which should be taken into account. These are:

- the stock pays no dividends during the option's life;
- the stock can only be exercised on the expiration date;
- markets are efficient;
- no commissions are charged;
- interest rates are consistent, predictable, and known;
- returns are normally distributed.

TRICKS OF THE TRADE

- A major potential limitation of the Black–Scholes model is the assumption that no dividends are paid on stock during the lifetime of the option—because most stocks do pay dividends. One way to resolve this is to subtract the discounted value of a future dividend from the stock price.
- In Europe, it is common that options can only be exercised on the expiration date, whereas in the United States they might be exercised at any time. This makes American options more flexible and therefore more valuable.
- The Black–Scholes model has been refined over time by a number of financial scholars, including Merton (who devised a model to take account of dividends) and Ingerson (who devised a model that did not require constant interest rates).

MORE INFO

Article:

Wagner, Hans. "Understanding option pricing." *Investopedia* (April 20, 2009). Online at: tinyurl.com/6l3n837

Website:

Risk Glossary on option pricing theory: tinyurl.com/6gq7u3f

See Also:

✔ Swaps, Options, and Futures: What They Are and Their Function (p. 988)

Option Volatility and Pricing: Advanced Trading Strategies and Techniques (p. 1404)

Payback Period

At first glance, payback is a simple investment appraisal technique, but it can quickly become complex.

WHAT IT MEASURES

How long it will take to earn back the money invested in a project.

WHY IT IS IMPORTANT

The straight payback period method is the simplest way of determining the investment potential of a major project. Expressed in time, it tells a management how many months or years it will take to recover the original cash cost of the project—always a vital consideration, and especially so for managements evaluating several projects at once.

This evaluation becomes even more important if it includes an examination of what the present value of future revenues will be.

HOW IT WORKS IN PRACTICE

The straight payback period formula is:

$$\text{Payback period} = \frac{\text{Cost of project}}{\text{Annual cash revenues}}$$

Thus, if a project costs $100,000 and is expected to generate $28,000 annually, the payback period would be:

$$\frac{100{,}000}{28{,}000} = 3.57 \text{ years}$$

If the revenues generated by the project are expected to vary from year to year, add the revenues expected for each succeeding year until you arrive at the total cost of the project.

For example, say the revenues expected to be generated by the $100,000 project are:

Year	Revenue	Total
1	$19,000	$19,000
2	$25,000	$44,000
3	$30,000	$74,000
4	$30,000	$104,000
5	$30,000	$134,000

Thus, the project would be fully paid for in year 4, since it is in that year that the total revenue reaches the initial cost of $100,000.

The picture becomes complex when the time value of money principle is introduced into the calculations. Some experts insist this is essential to determine the most accurate payback period. Accordingly, present value tables or computers (now the norm) must be used, and the annual revenues have to be discounted by the applicable interest rate, 10% in this example. Doing so produces significantly different results:

Year	Revenue	Present value	Total
1	$19,000	$17,271	$17,271
2	$25,000	$20,650	$37,921
3	$30,000	$22,530	$60,451
4	$30,000	$20,490	$80,941
5	$30,000	$18,630	$99,571

This method shows that payback would not occur even after five years.

TRICKS OF THE TRADE

- Clearly, a main defect of the straight payback period method is that it ignores the time value of money principle, which, in turn, can produce unrealistic expectations.
- A second drawback is that it ignores any benefits generated after the payback period, and thus a project that would return $1 million after, say, six years might be ranked lower than a project with a three-year payback that returns only $100,000 thereafter.
- Another alternative to calculating by payback period is to develop an internal rate of return.
- Under most analyses, projects with shorter payback periods rank higher than those with longer paybacks, even if the latter promise higher returns. Longer paybacks can be affected by such factors as market changes, changes in interest rates, and economic shifts. Shorter cash paybacks also enable companies to recoup an investment sooner and put it to work elsewhere.
- Generally, a payback period of three years or less is desirable; if a project's payback period is less than a year, some contend it should be judged essential.

MORE INFO

See Also:

✔ Appraising Investment Opportunities (p. 1143)
Return on Investment (pp. 1249–1250)

Payout Ratio

Dividend cover, and its US equivalent, payout ratio, is a quick reflection of profitability, which is used to evaluate and select investments.

WHAT IT MEASURES

Dividend cover expresses the number of times a company's dividends to common stockholders could be paid out of its net after-tax profits.

Payout ratio expresses the total dividends paid to stockholders as a percentage of a company's net profit in a given period of time.

WHY IT IS IMPORTANT

Whether defined as dividend cover or payout ratio, it measures the likelihood of dividend payments being sustained, and thus is a useful indication of sustained profitability. However, each ratio must be interpreted independently.

A low dividend cover suggests it might be difficult to pay the same level of dividends in a downturn, and that a company is not reinvesting enough in its future. High cover, therefore, implies just the opposite. Negative dividend cover is unusual, and a clear sign of trouble.

The payout ratio, expressed as a percentage or fraction, is an inverse measure: A high ratio indicates a lack of reinvestment in the business, and that current earnings cannot sustain the current dividend payments. In other words, the lower the ratio, the more secure the dividend—and the company's future.

HOW IT WORKS IN PRACTICE

Dividend cover is so named because it shows how many times over the profits could have paid the dividend. If the figure is 3, for example, a firm's profits are three times the level of the dividend paid to shareholders. To calculate dividend cover, divide earnings per share by the dividend per share:

$$\text{Dividend cover} = \frac{\text{Earnings per share}}{\text{Dividend per share}}$$

If a company has earnings per share of $8, and it pays out a dividend of $2.10, dividend cover is:

$$\frac{\$8}{\$2.10} = 3.80$$

An alternative formula divides a company's net profit by the total amount allocated for dividends. So a company that earns $10 million in net profit and allocates $1 million for dividends has a dividend cover of 10, while a company that earns $25 million and pays out $10 million in dividends has a dividend cover of 2.5:

$$\frac{\$10{,}000{,}000}{\$1{,}000{,}000} = 10$$

$$\frac{\$25{,}000{,}000}{\$10{,}000{,}000} = 2.5$$

The payout ratio is calculated by dividing annual dividends paid on common stock by earnings per share:

$$\text{Payout ratio} = \frac{\text{Annual dividend}}{\text{Earnings per share}}$$

Take the company whose earnings per share is $8 and dividend payout is $2.10. Its payout ratio would be:

$$\frac{2.10}{8} = 0.263 = 26.3\%$$

TRICKS OF THE TRADE

- A dividend cover ratio of 2 or higher is usually adequate, and indicates that the dividend is affordable. By the same token, the payout ratio should not exceed two-thirds of earnings. Like most ratios, however, both vary by industry. US real estate investment trusts, for example, pay out almost all their earnings in dividends because US tax laws exempt them from taxes if they do so. American utilities also offer high payout rates.
- A dividend cover ratio below 1.5 is risky, and a ratio below 1 indicates that a company is paying the current year's dividend with retained earnings from a previous year—a practice that cannot continue indefinitely.
- The higher the dividend cover figure, the less likely the dividend will be reduced or eliminated in the future, should profits fall. Companies that suffer sharp declines or outright losses will often continue paying dividends to indicate that their substandard performance is an anomaly.
- On the other hand, a high dividend cover figure may disappoint an investor looking for income, since the figure suggests directors could have declared a larger dividend.
- A high payout ratio clearly appeals to conservative investors seeking income. However, when coupled with weak or falling earnings it could suggest an imminent dividend cut, or that the company is short-changing reinvestment to maintain its payout.
- A payout ratio above 75% is a warning. It suggests the company is failing to reinvest sufficient profits in its business, that the company's earnings are faltering, or that it is trying to attract investors who otherwise would not be interested.
- Newer and faster-growing companies often pay no dividends at all in order to reinvest earnings in the company's development.
- Historically, dividends have provided more than 40% of a stock investor's total portfolio return. However, the figure has been about half that over the last 20 years.

Portfolio Analysis: Duration, Convexity, and Immunization

WHAT THEY MEASURE

Duration is a measure of how sensitive the price of bonds are to changes in interest rates (otherwise known as interest rate risk). For example, if interest rates rise 1%, a bond with a two-year duration will fall about 2% in value. Convexity is a measure of how prices rise when yields fall, and can also be used to measure interest rate risk.

WHY THEY ARE IMPORTANT

Using a combination of duration and convexity allows traders to hedge investments to minimize or offset the impact of changes in interest rates—a process known as immunization.

HOW THEY WORK IN PRACTICE

Duration is a weighted average of the present value of a bond's payments. It provides an insight into how sensitive a bond or portfolio is to changes in interest rates. The longer the duration, the longer the average maturity and, therefore, the bond's sensitivity to interest rate changes. Securities with the same duration have the same interest rate risk exposure. Duration can be expressed in years (to average maturity) or as a percentage (the percentage change in price for a 1% change in its yield to maturity).

$$\text{Duration} = \frac{(P_- - P_+)}{(2 \times P_0 \times \Delta y)}$$

where:
P_0 = bond price
P_- = bond price when interest rates are incremented
P_+ = bond price when rates are decremented
Δy = change in interest rates (decimal form)

Convexity is a measure of the rate at which duration changes as yields fall, and is expressed in squared time (t + 1). To estimate the convexity of a bond or portfolio, we can use the following formula:

$$\text{Convexity approximation} = \frac{(P_+ + P_- - 2P_0)}{2P_0(\Delta y)^2}$$

Immunization: To immunize a portfolio, you need to know the duration of the bonds and adjust the portfolio so the duration is equal to the investment time horizon. For example, you might select bonds that you know will return $10,000 in five years' time regardless of interest rate changes.

Normally, when interest rates go up, bond prices go down. But if a portfolio is immunized, the investor receives a specific rate of return over time regardless of what happens to interest rates, because the portfolio's duration is equal to the investor's time horizon. This means any changes to interest rates will affect the bond's price and reinvestment at the same rate, keeping the rate of return steady.

        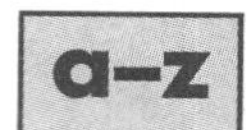

Maintaining an immunized portfolio means rebalancing the portfolio's average duration every time interest rates change, so that the average duration continues to equal the investor's time horizon.

TRICKS OF THE TRADE

- The concept of duration was first developed by Frederick Macaulay in 1938, as a tool for measuring bond price volatility in relation to the length of a bond. However, there are other formulae for calculating duration, including "effective duration" and "modified duration."
- Convexity is usually a positive term, but sometimes the term is negative, such as occurs when a callable bond is nearing its call price. In this case, traders use modified convexity, which is the measured convexity when there is no expected change in future cash flows, or effective convexity, which is the convexity measure for a bond for which future cash flows are expected to change.
- The notion of bond convexity should not be confused with the convexity of the yield curve (see Term Structure of Interest Rates). The latter can assume an arbitrary shape (although a normal yield curve has negative convexity), and complex stochastic models have been proposed for its evolution.

MORE INFO

Article:

Radcliffe, Brent. "Immunization inoculates against interest rate risk." *Investopedia* (February 26, 2009). Online at: tinyurl.com/5vj7ykk

Website:

This Matter on duration and convexity: thismatter.com/money/bonds/duration-convexity.htm

See Also:

✔ The Bond Market: Its Structure and Function (p. 1064)
Current Price of a Bond (p. 1212)

Price/Earnings Ratio

WHAT IT MEASURES

The price/earnings (P/E) ratio is simply the stock price divided by earnings per share (EPS). While EPS is an actual amount of money, usually expressed in cents per share, the P/E ratio has no units—it is just a number. Thus if a quoted company has a stock price of $100 and EPS of $12 for the last published year, then it has a historical P/E of 8.3. If analysts are forecasting for the next year an EPS of, say, $14 then the forecast P/E is 7.1.

WHY IT IS IMPORTANT

Since EPS is the annual earnings per share of a company, it follows that dividing the stock price by EPS tells us how many years of current EPS are represented by the stock price. In the above example, then, the P/E of 8.3 tells us that investors at the current price are prepared to pay 8.3 years of historical EPS for the stock, or 7.1 years of the forecast next year's EPS. Theoretically, the faster a company is expected to grow, the higher the P/E ratio that investors would award it. It is one measure of how cheap or expensive a stock appears to be.

HOW IT WORKS IN PRACTICE

Forecasts can go wrong, of course, resulting in the infamous profit warnings that are issued by some companies. In these they warn that expected profit targets, for various reasons, will not be met. Understandably, a slump in the stock price is the normal reaction, and analysts would then downgrade their existing forecast EPS. If, in the above example, our forecast of $14 for next year was halved to $7 following a profit warning, the forecast P/E on the same price of $100 would immediately double to 14.3—but in practice the price would usually fall substantially, thus cutting back the forecast P/E.

The P/E ratio is mainly useful in comparisons with other stocks rather than in isolation. For example, if the average P/E in the market is 20, there will be many stocks with P/Es well above and well below this, for a variety of reasons. Similarly, in a particular sector, the P/Es will frequently vary quite widely from the sector average, even though the constituent companies may all be engaged in broadly similar businesses. The reason is that even two businesses doing the same thing will not always be doing it as profitably as each other. One may be far more efficient, as demonstrated by a history of rising EPS compared with the flat EPS picture of the other over a series of years, and the market might recognize this by awarding the more profitable stock a higher P/E.

TRICKS OF THE TRADE

- Take care. The market frequently gets it wrong and many high-P/E stocks have in the past been the most awful long-term investments, losing investors huge amounts of money when the promise of future rapid growth proved to be a chimera. In contrast, many low-P/E companies, often in what are perceived as dull industries, have proved over time to be outstanding investments.
- The P/E is an investment tool that is both invaluable and yet requires extreme caution in its application when comparing and selecting investments. It remains, however, by far the most commonly utilized ratio in investment analysis.

MORE INFO

Book:

Walsh, Ciaran. *Key Management Ratios*. 4th ed. London: FT Prentice Hall, 2008.

See Also:

Earnings per Share (pp. 1220–1221)
Price/Sales Ratio (pp. 1243–1244)

  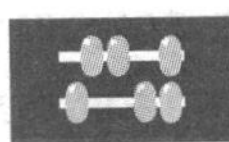      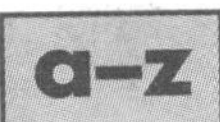

Price Elasticity

WHAT IT MEASURES

Price elasticity (sometimes known as price elasticity of demand, or PED) measures how demand for a product or service changes when the price charged is changed.

WHY IT IS IMPORTANT

Price elasticity enables you to predict how sales will be impacted if the price of a product or service is raised. Elasticity measures the responsiveness of consumers to changes in price, and gives businesses a curve to help analyze demand as it relates to price. Businesses can use elasticity to make effective pricing strategies. For example, if demand is inelastic, it may be possible to increase revenues by increasing the price of a product. If demand is elastic, however, businesses would be more likely to invest in advertising to try and build brand loyalty and create inelastic demand.

HOW IT WORKS IN PRACTICE

The basic formula to calculate price elasticity is as follows:

$$\text{Price elasticity} = \frac{\text{Percentage change in quantity demanded}}{\text{Percentage change in price}}$$

To calculate price elasticity on a product that has changed in price from $10 to $12, we need to know the quantity of goods sold at each price. Imagine that at $10, your company sold 150,000 items but at $12, the company sold 110,000 items.

Next, you need to calculate the percentage change in quantity and the percentage change in price. To calculate the percentage change in quantity demanded, use the following calculation:

$$\frac{(\text{New quantity} - \text{Old quantity})}{\text{Old quantity}}$$

So:

$$\frac{(110{,}000 - 150{,}000)}{150{,}000} = \frac{-40}{150} = -0.2667 = -26.67\%$$

While the percentage change in price is calculated as follows:

$$\frac{(\text{New price} - \text{Old price})}{\text{Old price}}$$

So:

$$\frac{(12 - 10)}{12} = \frac{2}{12} = 0.1667 = 16.67\%$$

Using these two figures we calculate the price elasticity as follows:

$$\frac{-26.67\%}{16.67\%} = -1.6$$

We can therefore conclude, ignoring the minus sign as is conventional, the price elasticity of this product, when the price increases from $10 to $12, is 1.6.

TRICKS OF THE TRADE

- When interpreting elasticity figures, the higher the number, the more sensitive consumers are to price changes. A very high figure suggests that if the price goes up, demand for the product or service will fall steeply. A lower figure suggests demand will not be substantially affected by price increases. This type of product is known as "inelastic."
- As a rule of thumb, an inelastic product will have a price elasticity score of one or less. If the elasticity of demand is exactly one, then a small increase or fall in price would result in value of sales remaining steady—the change in volume will exactly balance.
- Sometimes you will find negative elasticity scores (as in the example above)—when prices increase by 10% and sales fall by 20%, the elasticity score would be −2, for example. However, when using elasticity scores, the negative is ignored and expressed simply as the absolute figure "2."
- Elasticity scores change more dramatically over longer periods. This is because people have time to change buying habits over a period of time. Sales might therefore not be affected much by a price increase in year 1, but be significantly impacted by year 3.
- Goods that are elastic tend to be luxury or expensive purchases (cars, holidays, etc) while inelastic goods are those where there are many alternatives available, and which are bought frequently (bread or milk, for example).
- Elasticity is unlikely to be the same across an entire market. Certain firms will always be able to charge above market rates, while others will tend to under-cut the market price to maintain revenues.

MORE INFO

Websites:

Money Terms on price elasticity: moneyterms.co.uk/price-elasticity/

Quick MBA on price elasticity of demand: www.quickmba.com/econ/micro/elas/ped.shtml

Robert Schenk on price elasticity: ingrimayne.com/econ/elasticity/Elastic1.html

See Also:

Elasticity (p. 1223)

Price/Sales Ratio

WHAT IT MEASURES

The price/sales (P/S) ratio is another measure, like the price/earnings (P/E) ratio, of the relative value of a stock when compared with others.

WHY IT IS IMPORTANT

Like many such price-based ratios, it does not mean too much in isolation but acquires worth when making comparisons. So a figure of 0.33 does not say a lot on its own, until you start to look at how this matches up to the market average or the sector average, for example.

HOW IT WORKS IN PRACTICE

The P/S ratio is obtained by dividing the market capitalization by the latest published annual sales figure. So a company with a capitalization of $1 billion and sales of $3 billion would have a P/S ratio of 0.33.

  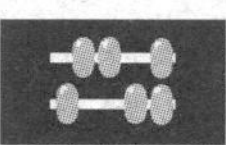      

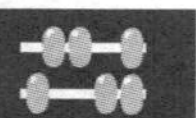

P/S will vary with the type of industry. You would expect, for example, that many retailers and other large-scale distributors of goods would have very high sales in relation to their market capitalizations—in other words, a very low P/S. Equally, manufacturers of high-value items would generally have much lower sales figures and thus higher P/S ratios. Like anything to do with share analysis (this being more of an art than a science), it is not always that clear cut ... but that would be the general trend. If you rank companies by ascending P/S, you will usually find that supermarket chains figure among the lowest.

A company with a lower P/S is cheaper than one with a higher ratio, particularly if they are in the same sector so that a direct comparison is appropriate. The lower P/S means that each share of the company is buying you more of its sales than those of the higher P/S company.

Note, though, that it is cheaper only on P/S grounds; that does not mean it is necessarily the more attractive share. There will often be reasons why it has a lower ratio than another, ostensibly similar, company, most commonly because it is less profitable. As far as corporate efficiency goes, this ratio considers only sales, the top line of the profit and loss account. It is a long way from there to the bottom line, the bit that really counts (that is, how much profit the company has made).

TRICKS OF THE TRADE

- A company with a loss would thus still have a P/S ratio, even though it would have no P/E ratio. In consequence, like all investment analysis tools, P/S has to be used with care—but it can be of use for investors. P/S was cited in an extensive study of the New York Stock Exchange as one leading indicator for selecting very long-term shares that perform well.

MORE INFO

Book:

O'Shaughnessy, James. *What Works on Wall Street: The Classic Guide to the Best-Performing Investment Strategies of All Time*. 4th ed. New York: McGraw-Hill, 2011.

See Also:

Price/Earnings Ratio (p. 1242)

Quantitative Methods

WHAT THEY ARE

Quantitative methods are a number of statistical and mathematical tools that can be used to capture and analyze information on quantitative data—anything that can be measured or counted.

What differentiates quantitative from qualitative methods is that quantitative methods usually rely on a variation of the scientific method to generate measurable results. Quantitative methods are therefore formulae and models used to generate hypotheses, capture and measure data, or evaluate the results.

WHY THEY ARE IMPORTANT

Imagine you wanted to know whether a particular action would increase the yield of a bond portfolio. If you perform the action once and the yield increases, would you be convinced? If it happened three times consecutively, would you be convinced?

Quantitative methods are used to measure and model outcomes, eliminating rogue results and other influences. Formulating a financial problem or hypothesis into a quantitative model allows us to apply statistical analysis to the problem and calculate the probability of certain outcomes—such as how likely a yield is to increase when a specific action is taken.

For investment managers, quantitative methods are most commonly used to value different classes of securities, analyze criteria for guiding investment decisions, measure risk and asset return, and use statistical techniques for forecasting. They can also be used for calculating yields and prices, frequency distributions, risk and probability, correlation, and regression analysis.

HOW THEY WORK IN PRACTICE

As previously discussed, in finance, quantitative methods are used to perform statistical analysis on a range of financial hypotheses and problems. The first stage in any quantitative method is the development of a theory or hypothesis, against which data can be measured or compared, followed by the application of either descriptive or inferential statistical methods.

Descriptive statistical methods describe properties of the data in front of us, while inferential methods allow us to draw conclusions from data in front of us. For example:

"The average income of the portfolio was $2.8 million per annum over the five-year period" is a descriptive statistic, while "The sample of 50 annual yields from the total portfolio indicates the average income of the portfolio was between $2.6 and $2.9 million per annum," is an inferential statistic.

To test your hypothesis, you might use any of a number of statistical tools, the most common including linear regression. The classical linear regression model (CLRM) is used in finance to estimate unknown parameters using statistical methods. Once you have created regression boundaries you can compute confidence intervals and perform hypothesis testing. An alternative approach is the multiple linear regression model (MLRM), which is used for hypothesis testing in scenarios where there is more than one unknown variable.

Other statistical methods used in quantitative analysis include forecasting tools such as correlation analysis, co-efficiency of correlations, and determination and learning curves.

TRICKS OF THE TRADE

- Although quantitative methods have existed since people first recorded numerical data, the modern idea of quantitative methods has its roots in Auguste Comte's positivist framework.
- Quantitative methods also incorporate the basic principles of statistical interference—the process of making inferences from a small sample about the behavior of a larger population. Two main approaches are estimation and hypothesis testing.

MORE INFO

Books:

Brealey, Richard A., Stewart C. Myers, and Franklin Allen. *Principles of Corporate Finance*. 11th ed. New York: McGraw-Hill, 2013.

Gujarati, Damodar N., and Dawn C. Porter. *Essentials of Econometrics*. 5th ed. New York: McGraw-Hill, 2013.

Oakshott, Les. *Essential Quantitative Methods for Business, Management and Finance*. 5th ed. Basingstoke, UK: Palgrave Macmillan, 2012.

  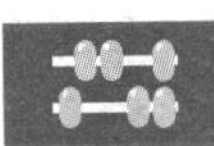      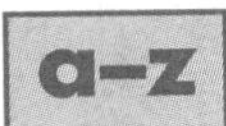

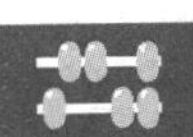

Rate of Return

This may well be as basic and important a computation as there is in finance.

WHAT IT MEASURES

The annual return on an investment, expressed as a percentage of the total amount invested. It also measures the yield of a fixed-income security.

WHY IT IS IMPORTANT

Rate of return is a simple and straightforward way to determine how much investors are being paid for the use of their money, so that they can then compare various investments and select the best—based, of course, on individual goals and acceptable levels of risk.

Rate of return has a second and equally vital purpose: As a common denominator that measures a company's financial performance, for example, in terms of rate of return on assets, equity, or sales.

HOW IT WORKS IN PRACTICE

There is a basic formula that will serve most needs, at least initially:

$$\text{Rate of return} = \frac{(\text{Current value of amount invested} - \text{Original value of amount invested})}{\text{Original value of amount invested}}$$

If $1,000 in capital is invested in stock, and one year later the investment yields $1,100, the rate of return of the investment is calculated like this:

$$\frac{(1100 - 1000)}{1000} = 0.1 = 10\%$$

Now, assume $1,000 is invested again. One year later, the investment grows to $2,000 in value, but after another year the value of the investment falls to $1,200. The rate of return after the first year is:

$$\frac{(2000 - 1000)}{1000} = 1 = 100\%$$

The rate of return after the second year is:

$$\frac{(1200 - 2000)}{2000} = -0.4 = -40\%$$

The average annual return for the two years (also known as average annual arithmetic return) can be calculated using this formula:

$$\text{Average annual return} = \frac{(\text{Rate of return for year 1} + \text{Rate of return for year 2})}{2}$$

Accordingly:

$$\frac{(100\% + -40\%)}{2} = 30\%$$

Be careful, however! The average annual rate of return is a percentage, but one that is accurate over only a short period, so this method should be used accordingly.

The geometric or compound rate of return is a better yardstick for measuring investments over the long run, and takes into account the effects of compounding. As one might expect, this formula is more complex and technical, and beyond the scope of this article.

TRICKS OF THE TRADE

- The real rate of return is the annual return realized on an investment, adjusted for changes in the price due to inflation. If 10% is earned on an investment but inflation is 2%, then the real rate of return is actually 8%.
- Do not confuse rate of return with internal rate of return, which is a more complex calculation.
- Some mutual fund managers have been known to report the average annual rate of return on the investments they manage. In the second example, that figure is 30%, yet the value of the investment is only $200 higher than it was two years ago, or 20%. So, read such reports carefully.

MORE INFO

Book:

Walsh, Ciaran. *Key Management Ratios*. 4th ed. London: FT Prentice Hall, 2008.

See Also:

Expected Rate of Return (p. 1226)
Internal Rate of Return (p. 1232)
Risk-Adjusted Rate of Return (pp. 1251–1252)

Reading an Annual Report

GETTING STARTED

Many companies must publish an annual report to its stockholders as a matter of corporate law. The primary purpose of this report is to inform stockholders of the company's performance. As a legal requirement, the report usually contains a profit and loss account, a balance sheet, a cash flow statement, a directors' report, and an auditors' report. The different elements tell you about different aspects of the company's performance and can be read in a particular order to build up a true picture of how it is doing.

Many companies also provide a lot of other nonstatutory information on their affairs, in the interests of general communication. In some cases, this may be little more than gloss, contrived to illustrate the company's wonderful achievements while remaining strangely silent on negative features.

FAQS

Is there any difference between annual reports from private and public companies?

The main difference is usually length. The reports of privately held companies are far shorter because their mandatory reporting requirements are much reduced. Additionally, they are less concerned with image, and consequently will tend to omit the noncompulsory public relations features that are present in public company reports.

  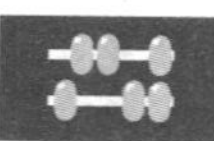   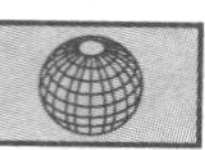   

What guarantee is there that an annual report is a true picture of a company's performance and not just propaganda put out by directors?

All annual reports have to include a report from the auditors, who are independent accountants charged with investigating a company's financial affairs to ensure that the published figures give a true and fair view of performance. Their investigation cannot extend to examining every single transaction (impossible in a company of any size), so they use statistical sampling and other risk-based testing procedures to assess the quality of the company's systems as a basis for producing the annual report. They are not infallible, but they stand between the stockholders and the directors as a way of trying to ensure probity in the running of a company.

MAKING IT HAPPEN

Understanding the Main Contents of an Annual Report

The best way to look at this is to take an example. Standard sections in annual reports can vary from country to country, but the following is the contents list of the annual report of a medium-sized US public company—let's call it X Inc.

- X World;
- Chairman's Statement;
- Chief Executive's Review;
- Financial Review;
- Board of Directors;
- Board Report on Remuneration;
- Directors' Responsibilities;
- Report of the Auditors;
- Financial Statements;
- Five-Year Record;
- Stockholder Information.

Here's what each of these sections is about:

X World: Belongs in the PR area. It tells you about the company, its products and markets.

Chairman's Statement: Comments on the group results for the year and on future developments. It also provides detail on earnings per share and dividends.

Chief Executive's Review: Goes into more detail about individual divisions, breaking down the operating results from areas around the world. It tells us a bit about discontinued businesses and new ones acquired.

Financial Review: Expands on the two previous sections in a more quantitative way, looking at things like cash flow and how it affected group debt; interest charges; the effect of exchange rate fluctuations on profits, assets and liabilities; exceptional items that affect the profits (such as the disposal of a subsidiary company), and so on.

Board of Directors: Lists the directors, with a brief description and photo of each.

Board Report on Remuneration: Describes the work of a committee of nonexecutive directors, who decide the directors' income and that of other senior employees. Their remit includes looking at service contracts, bonus and stock option plans, plus pension plans. It includes an analysis of the pay of each director, with comparable figures for the previous year, plus details of stock options, and so on.

Directors' Responsibilities: A mandatory statement showing exactly what the directors are obliged to discharge with regard to the annual report, maintaining accurate accounting records, and so on.

Report of the Auditors: This is simply what it says. Their findings are published using standard language.

Financial Statements: These are the main purpose of the annual report. In the example of X Inc., they consist of:

- *Consolidated Profit and Loss Account*. The profit and loss account of all the group as one consolidated account.
- *Consolidated and Company Balance Sheets*. The former is the group balance sheet and the latter is for the parent company alone.
- *Consolidated Cash Flow Statement*. A guide to how the money flowing in and out of the company was utilized.
- *Management's Responsibility for Financial Reporting*.
- *Management's Discussion and Analysis*.
- *Notes to the Financial Statements*. These amplify numerous points contained in the figures and are usually critical for anyone wishing to study the financial statements in detail.

Five-Year Record: Shows a very abbreviated set of profit and loss and balance sheet figures for the current and previous four years. Some companies provide a 10-year record.

Stockholder Information: Deals with matters such as the registered office, stockholder registrars, brokers, lawyers, dates for meetings and dividend payments, and other points.

Choosing the Right Order in which to Read the Report

One way is simply to read the report from cover to cover, like a book. However, if you are not experienced with these things, that may lead you to giving equal weight to all the contents and, perhaps, overvaluing the glossy PR bits at the expense of the hard facts shown by the figures.

Start with the Auditors' Report

Remember that this thin gray line of accountants is all that stands between the outside stockholder and the directors. To speed up matters, look at the final paragraph—their opinion. Does that statement give a true and fair view? If so, fine. If not, then it is said to be "qualified." Qualifications vary in depth from the disastrous, meaning that the company has gotten something seriously wrong, to perhaps a difference of opinion between the auditors and the board over some accounting matter. Most auditors' reports are unqualified, but, if there is a qualification present, you will have to judge how much the financial statements can be relied upon as a measure of the company's performance.

Next, Turn to the Five/Ten-Year Review

This is where you build up a mental picture of the company's financial history. Look at earnings per share (EPS)—is it increasing, decreasing, fluctuating wildly? This gives you an idea of how it has been doing over the period. Look at dividends, if any, and consider their pattern. Do they follow EPS or, as is likely, are they showing a smoother picture? Look at company debt, if the information is there, and compare it with stockholders' funds. How is it changing over the years?

Generally, try to build up a view as to whether the company is doing better, worse, or perhaps has no particular pattern over the period. Depending on your reasons for reading the report, a set of prejudices will have begun to develop from this historical picture. If it shows a declining financial situation, this could be a good thing from some points of view—if you wish to acquire the company, for example. If you are an employee though, it would not be very encouraging. So reading reports depends to some extent on which angle you are coming from.

Now Read the Chairman's and Directors' Comments

These will give a deeper feel for the company's business, over and above the raw numerical data. Try to exercise a degree of skepticism in some areas, because it is natural for directors to attempt to play up the good points and play down the less good ones.

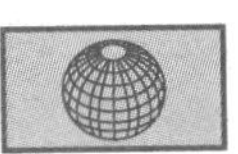

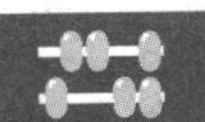

Get to the Heart of the Matter

The kernel of the report is the Financial Statements and the huge number of notes that accompany them. A lot of it is in highly technical accounting terminology, but it gives you the intimate financial detail on the year. Never ignore the notes—they are critical. In fact some investment analysts read the report from the back, because the notes are so important.

Notes have increased dramatically over the years as new legal and accounting standards have been introduced, primarily to enforce standardization so that financial reports are more comparable, but also to avoid "creative accounting," whereby some companies have tried to conceal (legitimately) financially undesirable situations.

Relax with the Glossy Stuff

Having absorbed all that really matters, settle back and read the glossy parts that tell you how wonderful the company is. Just remember to exercise a mild degree of cynicism here—this is the least important, though no doubt the most visually attractive, part of the annual report. The real picture of the company is the numbers, not the photo of the guy in the hard hat standing on an oil rig!

A Common Mistake

Don't pay too much attention to pretty pictures and directors' comments and too little to the accounting data.

This can give a false view of how well, or badly, the company is doing. Understandably, many people have difficulty in comprehending the figures. But if you want to appreciate annual reports properly, then learning to read financial reports is essential.

Some cynics among investment analysts have even expressed the view that there is an inverse relationship between the number of glossy pages in an annual report and the company's actual performance. Maybe that's a little harsh. . .but there might be something in it.

MORE INFO

Websites:

Financial Reporting Council's (FRC; UK) accounting and reporting policy: tinyurl.com/d5qtysr

Securities and Exchange Commission (SEC; US): www.sec.gov

Reserve Ratio

Also called the "reserve requirement," the reserve ratio is a device used both to facilitate financial stability and to influence credit conditions.

WHAT IT MEASURES

In the United Kingdom and in certain European countries there is no compulsory ratio, although banks will have their own internal measures and targets to be able to repay customer deposits as they forecast they will be required. In the United States the policy is more prescriptive, and specified percentages of deposits—specified by the Federal Reserve Board—must be kept by banks in a noninterest-bearing account at one of the 12 Federal Reserve Banks located throughout the country.

WHY IT IS IMPORTANT

To provide stability. In view of the volume and unpredictability of transactions that clear through their accounts every day, banks and financial depositories must maintain a cushion of funds to protect themselves against debits that could leave their accounts overdrawn at the end of the day, and thus subject to penalty.

As a result of the creation of reserve ratios, periods of financial stress are no longer characterized by runs on banks by depositors.

HOW IT WORKS IN PRACTICE

In Europe, the reserve requirement of an institution is calculated by multiplying the reserve ratio for each category of items in the reserve base, set by the European Central Bank, with the amount of those items in the institution's balance sheets. These figures vary according to the institution.

The required reserve ratio in the United States is set by federal law, and depends on the amount of checkable deposits a bank holds. The first $44.3 million of deposits are subject to a 3% reserve requirement. Deposits in excess of $44.3 million are subject to a 10% reserve requirement. These breakpoints are reviewed annually in accordance with money supply growth. No reserves are required against certificates of deposit or savings accounts.

The reserve ratio requirement limits a bank's lending to a certain fraction of its demand deposits. The current rule allows a bank to issue loans to an amount equal to 90% of such deposits, holding 10% in reserve. The reserves can be held in any combination of vault cash and deposit at a Federal Reserve Bank.

A bank facing a reserve deficiency has several options. It can try to borrow reserves for one or more days from another bank, sell marketable assets such as government securities, or bid for funds in the money market, such as large certificates of deposit (CDs) or eurodollars. As a last resort, it can pledge collateral and borrow at the Federal Reserve's discount window.

In order to meet deposit withdrawal contingencies, many banks maintain a margin of excess reserves above the required reserve ratio, since the required reserves are really not available to meet withdrawal liquidity needs. Excess reserves are higher than those needed to meet reserve and clearing requirements, and provide extra protection against overdrafts and deficiencies in required reserves.

TRICKS OF THE TRADE

- Because reserves earn no interest, they have an adverse effect on bank earnings.
- In practice, the required reserve ratio has been adjusted only infrequently by the US Federal Reserve Board.
- US depository institutions hold required reserves in one of two forms: vault cash on hand at the bank or—more significant for monetary policy—required reserve balances in accounts with the Reserve Bank for their respective Federal Reserve District.

Residual Value

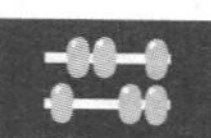

WHAT IT MEASURES

Residual value is the value an asset will have after it has been depreciated, or amortized. Residual value is sometimes referred to as "salvage" value.

WHY IT IS IMPORTANT

According to international financial reporting standards, residual value is the value an asset should have if it is in the expected condition at the end of its useful life, after the cost of selling it.

HOW IT WORKS IN PRACTICE

When calculating the residual value of a business asset, the salvage value is used in conjunction with the purchase price and accounting methods to determine the amount by which the asset depreciates each period. For example, with a straight-line basis, an asset that cost $5,000 and has a salvage value of $1,000 and a useful life of five years would be depreciated at $800 ([5,000 − 1,000] ÷ 5) each year.

This straight-line method uses the following formula to calculate residual value:

$$\text{Depreciation expense} = \frac{\text{(Cost of fixed asset − Scrap value)}}{\text{Lifespan}}$$

An alternative approach is to use the declining-balance method, which assumes that an asset loses value more rapidly in the early part of its useful lifetime. In the case of machinery, this is often a more realistic approach. To calculate residual value using this methodology, each period of depreciation is based on the previous year's net book value, estimated lifespan, and a factor of 2 (known as the double-declining balance). For example:

$$\text{Depreciation expense} = \text{Previous period NBV} \times \frac{\text{Factor}}{\text{N}}$$

For the double-declining balance method, using the vehicle example from above, we compute the depreciation after the first year:

$$17000 \times \frac{2}{5} = \$6800$$

In business accounting there are three common methods of calculating the residual value of a business:

1 Perpetuity business valuation: Using this methodology, the business assumes the company's future cash flow will continue indefinitely, and the residual value of the asset is calculated according to the following formula:

$$\text{Residual value} = \frac{\text{Free cash flow in year } n}{r}$$

where r is the discount rate and n is the last year of the analysis period.

2 Liquidation business valuation: Using this methodology assumes the most conservative way to calculate residual value is to assume the asset will be liquidated at the end of the forecasting period. So, residual value is calculated as being the net liquidation value—the asset's value (including cash, inventory, plant) less liabilities. This value is discounted for the beginning of the period, before adding it to the discounted cash flow, to calculate the company's value.

3 Price earnings valuation: Assumes the best way to determine a venture's residual value is to calculate its market price using the relevant price earning factor as follows:

$$\text{Residual value} = \frac{\text{Net profit in year } n \times \text{Comparative PE}}{r}$$

where r is the discount rate and n is the selected year. Comparative PE refers to the PE of any similar company, or the industry average. The result is then discounted to the beginning of the plan period and added to discounted cash flow.

TRICKS OF THE TRADE

- Residual values should be reviewed annually alongside the useful life of assets, and depreciation adjusted if the residual value of an asset has changed.
- Intangible assets have a zero residual value. Some tangible assets may also have a zero residual value if they cannot be resold, or if there are costs associated with their disposal that outstrip the residual value.
- Residual values used for calculating depreciation should be calculated per asset, but most companies would simplify the calculations by grouping together items into categories.
- Residual value can be built into leases. The residual value of leased assets is the cost of the asset minus less repayments of capital made over the lifetime of the lease.

MORE INFO

Article:

White, Diane. "Depreciation of fixed assets: Straight line, units-of-production, and double declining method." *Suite101.com* (September 15, 2008). Online at: tinyurl.com/5w6625f

Website:

Money Terms on residual value: moneyterms.co.uk/residual-value/

See Also:

Depreciation (pp. 1216–1217)

Return on Assets

Return on assets—or simply ROA—may also be termed return on total assets (ROTA) or return on net assets (RONA). Whatever its designation, it is often referred to as the No. 1 ratio in finance.

WHAT IT MEASURES

A company's profitability, expressed as a percentage of its total assets.

WHY IT IS IMPORTANT

Return on assets measures how effectively a company has used the total assets at its disposal to generate earnings. Because the ROA formula reflects total revenue, total cost, and assets deployed, the ratio itself reflects a management's ability to generate income during the course of a given period, usually a year.

Naturally, the higher the return, the better the profit performance. ROA is a convenient way of comparing a company's performance with that of its competitors, although the items on which the comparison is based may not always be identical.

HOW IT WORKS IN PRACTICE

To calculate ROA, divide a company's net income by its total assets, then multiply by 100 to express the figure as a percentage:

$$\text{Return on assets} = \frac{\text{Net income}}{\text{Total assets}}$$

If net income is $30, and total assets are $420, the ROA is:

$$\frac{30}{420} = 0.0714 = 7.14\%$$

A variation of this formula can be used to calculate return on net assets (RONA):

$$\text{Return on net assets} = \frac{\text{Net income}}{(\text{Fixed assets} + \text{Working capital})}$$

And, on occasion, the formula will separate after-tax interest expense from net income:

$$\text{Return on assets} = \frac{(\text{Net income} + \text{Interest expense})}{\text{Total assets}}$$

It is therefore important to understand what each component of the formula actually represents.

TRICKS OF THE TRADE

- Some experts recommend using the net income value at the end of the given period, and the assets' value from the beginning of the period, or an average value taken over the complete period, rather than an end-of-the-period value; otherwise, the calculation will include assets that have accumulated during the year, which can be misleading.
- While a high ratio indicates a greater return, it must still be balanced against such factors as risk, sustainability, and reinvestment in the business through development costs. Some managements will sacrifice the long-term interests of investors in order to achieve an impressive ROA in the short term.
- A climbing return on assets usually indicates a climbing stock price, because it tells investors that a management is skilled at generating profits from the resources that a business owns.
- Acceptable ROAs vary by sector. In banking, for example, a ROA of 1% or better is a considered to be the standard benchmark of superior performance.
- ROA is an effective way of measuring the efficiency of manufacturers, but can be suspect when measuring service companies, or companies whose primary assets are people.
- Other variations of the ROA formula do exist.

MORE INFO

See Also:

Asset Turnover (pp. 1194–1195)
Asset Utilization (p. 1195)

Return on Investment

Return on investment (ROI) is a ratio that is used frequently—perhaps too frequently. Its definition can vary widely. Indeed, ROI today is not only a family of measurements of the performance of invested capital but also a concept, one used to justify expenditure on almost everything.

WHAT IT MEASURES

In the financial realm, the overall profit or loss on an investment expressed as a percentage of the total amount invested or total funds appearing on a company's balance sheet.

WHY IT IS IMPORTANT

Like return on assets or return on equity, return on investment measures a company's profitability and its management's ability to generate profits from the funds investors have placed at its disposal.

One opinion holds that if a company's operations cannot generate net earnings at a rate that exceeds the cost of borrowing funds from financial markets, the future of that company is grim.

HOW IT WORKS IN PRACTICE

The most basic expression of ROI can be found by dividing a company's net profit (also called net earnings) by the total investment (total debt plus total equity), then multiplying by 100 to arrive at a percentage:

$$\text{Return on investment} = \frac{\text{Net profit}}{\text{Total investment}}$$

If, say, net profit is $30 and total investment is $250, the ROI is:

$$\frac{30}{250} = 0.12 = 12\%$$

A more complex variation of ROI is an equation known as the Du Pont formula:

$$\text{ROI} = \frac{\text{Net profit after taxes}}{\text{Total assets}} = \frac{\text{Net profit after taxes}}{\text{Sales}} \times \frac{\text{Sales}}{\text{Total assets}}$$

If, for example, net profit after taxes is $30, total assets are $250, and sales are $500, then:

$$\frac{30}{250} = \frac{30}{500} \times \frac{500}{250} = 12\% = 6\% \times 2 = 12\%$$

Champions of this formula, which was developed by the Du Pont Company in the 1920s, say that it helps to reveal how a company has both deployed its assets and controlled its costs, and how it can achieve the same percentage return in different ways.

For stockholders, the variation of the basic ROI formula used by investors is:

$$\text{ROI} = \frac{(\text{Net income} + \text{Current value} - \text{Original value})}{\text{Original value}}$$

  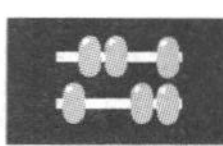      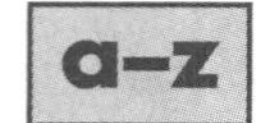

If, for example, somebody invests $5,000 in a company and a year later has earned $100 in dividends, while the value of the stock is $5,200, the return on investment would be:

$$\frac{(100 + 5,200 - 5,000)}{5,000} = \frac{300}{5,000} = 0.06 = 6\%$$

TRICKS OF THE TRADE

- Securities investors can use yet another ROI formula: net income divided by common stock and preferred stock equity plus long-term debt.
- It is vital to understand exactly what a return on investment measures—for example, assets, equity, or sales. Without this understanding, comparisons may be misleading or suspect. A search for "return on investment" on the internet, for example, harvests everything from staff training to e-commerce to advertising and promotions!
- Be sure to establish whether the net profit figure used is before or after provision for taxes. This is important for making ROI comparisons accurate.

MORE INFO

See Also:

✔ Appraising Investment Opportunities (p. 1143)
Payback Period (pp. 1239–1240)

Return on Sales

Although return on sales (ROS) is another tool used to analyze profitability, it is perhaps a better indication of efficiency. In some business environments, it is also called margin on sales percentage, or net margin.

WHAT IT MEASURES

A company's operating profit or loss as a percentage of total sales for a given period, typically a year.

WHY IT IS IMPORTANT

Return on sales (ROS) shows how efficiently management uses the sales dollar, thus reflecting its ability to manage costs and overheads and operate efficiently. It also indicates a company's ability to withstand adverse conditions such as falling prices, rising costs, or declining sales. The higher the figure, the better a company is able to endure price wars and falling prices.

Return on sales can be useful in assessing the annual performances of cyclical companies that may have no earnings during particular months, and of companies whose business requires a huge capital investment and thus incurs substantial amounts of depreciation.

HOW IT WORKS IN PRACTICE

The calculation is very basic:

$$\text{Return on sales} = \frac{\text{Operating profit}}{\text{Total sales}}$$

So, if a company earns $30 on sales of $400, its return on sales is:

$$\frac{30}{400} = 0.075 = 7.5\%$$

TRICKS OF THE TRADE

- While easy to grasp, return on sales has its limits, since it sheds no light on the overall cost of sales or the four factors that contribute to it: Materials, labor, production overheads, and administrative and selling overheads.
- Some calculations use operating profit before subtracting interest and taxes; others use after-tax income. Either figure is acceptable as long as ROS comparisons are consistent. Obviously, using income before interest and taxes will produce a higher ratio.
- The ratio's operating profit figure may also include special allowances and extraordinary nonrecurring items, which, in turn, can inflate the percentage and be misleading.
- The ratio varies widely by industry. The supermarket business, for example, is heavily dependent on volume and usually has a low return on sales.
- Return on sales remains of special importance to retail sales organizations, which can compare their respective ratios with those of competitors and industry norms.

Return on Stockholders' Equity

Return on equity (ROE) is probably the most widely used measure of how well a company is performing for its stockholders.

WHAT IT MEASURES

Profitability, specifically the percentage return that was delivered to a company's owners.

WHY IT IS IMPORTANT

ROE is a fundamental indication of a company's ability to increase its earnings per share and thus the quality of its stock, because it reveals how well a company is using its money to generate additional earnings.

It is a relatively straightforward benchmark, easy to calculate, and is applicable to a majority of industries. ROE allows investors to compare a company's use of their equity with other investments, and to compare the performance of companies in the same industry. ROE can also help to evaluate trends in a business.

Businesses that generate high returns on equity are businesses that pay off their stockholders handsomely and create substantial assets for each dollar invested.

HOW IT WORKS IN PRACTICE

To calculate ROE, divide the net income shown on the income statement (usually of the past year) by stockholders' equity, which appears on the balance sheet:

$$\text{Return on equity} = \frac{\text{Net income}}{\text{Owners' equity}}$$

     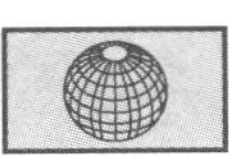   

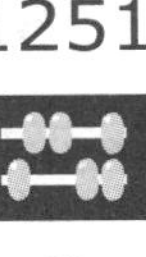

For example, if net income is $450 and equity is $2,500, then:

$$\frac{450}{2{,}500} = 0.18 = 18\%$$

TRICKS OF THE TRADE

- Because new variations of the ROE ratio do appear, it is important to know how the figure is calculated.
- Return on equity for most companies certainly should be in the double digits; investors often look for 15% or higher, while a return of 20% or more is considered excellent.
- Seasoned investors also review five-year average ROE, to gauge consistency.
- A word of caution: Financial statements usually report assets at book value, which is the purchase price minus depreciation; they do not show replacement costs. A business with older assets should show higher rates of ROE than a business with newer assets.
- Examining ROE with return on assets can indicate if a company is debt-heavy. If a company has very little debt, it is reasonable to assume that its management is earning high profits and/or using assets effectively.
- A high ROE also could be due to leverage (a method of corporate funding in which a higher proportion of funds is raised through borrowing than issuing stock). If liabilities are high the balance sheet will reveal it, hence the need to review it.

MORE INFO

Book:

Walsh, Ciaran. *Key Management Ratios*. 4th ed. London: FT Prentice Hall, 2008.

See Also:

Dividend Yield (p. 1219)
Earnings per Share (pp. 1220–1221)

Risk-Adjusted Rate of Return

Knowing an investment's risk-adjusted return goes a long way toward determining just how much "bang for the buck" is really being generated.

WHAT IT MEASURES

How much an investment returned in relation to the risk that was assumed to attain it.

WHY IT IS IMPORTANT

Being able to compare a high-risk, potentially high-return investment with a low-risk, lower-return investment helps to answer a key question that confronts every investor: Is it worth the risk?

By itself, the historical average return of an investment, asset, or portfolio can be quite misleading and a faulty indicator of future performance. Risk-adjusted return is a much better barometer.

The calculation also helps to reveal whether the returns of the portfolio reflect smart investment decisions, or the taking on of excess risk that may or may not have been worth what was gained. This is particularly helpful in appraising the performance of money managers.

HOW IT WORKS IN PRACTICE

There are several ways to calculate risk-adjusted return. Each has its strengths and shortcomings. All require particular data, such as an investment's rate of return, the risk-free return rate for a given period (usually the performance of a 90-day US Treasury bill over 36 months), and a market's performance and its standard deviation.

Which one to use? It often depends on an investor's focus, principally whether the focus is on upside gains or downside losses.

Perhaps the most widely used is the **Sharpe ratio**. This measures the potential impact of return volatility on expected return and the amount of return earned per unit of risk. The higher a fund's Sharpe ratio, the better its historical risk-adjusted performance, and the higher the number the greater the return per unit of risk. The formula is:

$$\text{Sharpe ratio} = \frac{(\text{Portfolio return} - \text{Risk-free return})}{\text{Standard deviation of portfolio return}}$$

Take, for example, two investments, one returning 54%, the other 26%. At first glance, the higher figure clearly looks the better choice, but because of its high volatility it has a Sharpe ratio of 0.279, while the investment with a lower return has a ratio of 0.910. On a risk-adjusted basis the latter would be the wiser choice.

The **Treynor ratio** also measures the excess of return per unit of risk. Its formula is:

$$\text{Treynor ratio} = \frac{(\text{Portfolio return} - \text{Risk-free return})}{\text{Portfolio's beta}}$$

In this formula (and others that follow), beta is a separately calculated figure that describes the tendency of an investment to respond to marketplace swings. The higher the beta, the greater the volatility, and vice versa.

A third formula, **Jensen's measure**, is often used to rate a money manager's performance against a market index, and whether or not an investment's risk was worth its reward. The formula is:

$$\text{Jensen's measure} = \text{Portfolio return} - \text{Risk-free return} - \text{Portfolio beta} \times (\text{Benchmark return} - \text{Risk-free return})$$

TRICKS OF THE TRADE

- A fourth formula, the **Sortino ratio**, also exists. Its focus is more on downside risk than potential opportunity, and its calculation is more complex.

MORE INFO

See Also:

Sharpe Ratio (p. 1253)
Treynor Ratio (p. 1259)

- There are no benchmarks for these values. In order to be useful the numbers should be compared with the ratios of other investments.
- No single measure is perfect, so experts recommend using them broadly. For instance, if a particular investment class is on a roll and does not experience a great deal of volatility, a good return per unit of risk does not necessarily reflect management genius. When the overall momentum of technology stocks drove returns straight up in 1999, Sharpe ratios climbed with them, and did not reflect any of the sector's volatility that was to erupt in late 2000.
- Most of these measures can be used to rank the risk-adjusted performance of individual stocks, various portfolios over the same time, and mutual funds with similar objectives.

Scenario Analysis

WHAT IT MEASURES

Businesses have always planned for "what if" scenarios—and based their decision-making on likely future events. Scenario analysis is simply a formal tool to model the likelihood of various scenarios and their outcomes. Scenario analysis has been widely used in asset management and risk management since the 1970s, to analyze interest rate risks. However, it can be applied to a wide set of corporate and financial activities, including equity prices, exchange rates, commodity prices, and volatility of prices.

WHY IT IS IMPORTANT

Scenario analysis helps companies and investors to measure the expected value of an investment. By combining this information with probability, analysts can make highly accurate predictions about the likelihood of realizing the expected value. Comparing the probability distribution of an event is equivalent to calculating the risk of an investment and important for the same reason—it allows you to make better decisions about business and financial investments.

There are many different approaches to scenario analysis, but one common method is to determine the high/low spread and standard deviation from daily or monthly returns, then compute the value of the portfolio if each security generated returns two or three basis points above and below this average.

This method means the investor or company can have reasonable certainty that the value of a portfolio will remain within expected parameters over a given period of time.

HOW IT WORKS IN PRACTICE

A typical use of scenario analysis would be to consider what happens to the value of a security if interest rates fell, remained static, or increased.

The first step is to consider all the possible outcomes, or paths, that will be taken by relevant risk factors (in this case, interest rates). Each potential outcome is considered over the same time period. In the simple example below, we can see all the relevant outcomes that might be affected by a 100 basis point fall in interest rates, followed by 24 months of static rates:

Time (months)	1-month LIBOR	3-month LIBOR	6-month LIBOR	12-month LIBOR	COFI
0	3.11	3.79	3.84	4.00	3.54
6	2.11	2.79	3.84	4.00	3.54
12	2.11	2.79	3.84	4.00	3.54
18	2.11	2.79	3.84	4.00	3.54
24	2.11	2.79	3.84	4.00	3.54

Once you have identified the scenario, the next step is to project what happens for each of these rates at the given point in time. This extrapolation may be relatively simple, showing the cost of debt in each scenario, or might be more complex—for example, by incorporating other financial data to produce a cash flow forecast, or value at risk metric.

TRICKS OF THE TRADE

- Scenario analysis allows analysts to plan for their "worst-case scenario." Being able to quantify the potential costs of a possible outcome is vital in risk management and forming business strategy. Scenario planning can be highly detailed, and customized to accommodate any number of variables, such as the flattening of the yield curve or narrowing spreads.
- One advantage of scenario analysis is that it is simple to use and very flexible. It can address almost any present or future risk, and can anticipate the impact of future business decisions. However, its major drawback is that it can only consider the impact of risks that are anticipated—outputs are entirely limited to paths suggested by the user, and so if you overlook a risk, it will not be calculated.
- It is also important to remember that if scenario analysis is based on probability, there is still a potential that the low and high extreme values could occur. This is why scenario analysis is often run alongside risk analysis to determine whether these potential risks are within acceptable tolerance levels.
- When dealing with complex scenarios over multiple time periods and involving many possible outcomes (such as the impact on 1,000 clients of 100 different interest rate permutations) scenario analysis can be extremely cumbersome, generating large and complex tables. In such instances, duration analysis can provide more user-friendly analysis.
- Another alternative is to use scenario analysis and the Monte Carlo method, to calculate results based on a large number of random scenarios. This approach is sometimes also referred to as "simulation analysis."

MORE INFO

Website:

Mind Tools on scenario analysis: www.mindtools.com/pages/article/newSTR_98.htm

See Also:

✔ Stress Testing and Scenario Analysis for Keeping Up with Regulation (p. 1054)
✔ Understanding Financial Scenario Analysis for Banking and Insurance Institutions (p. 1020)

  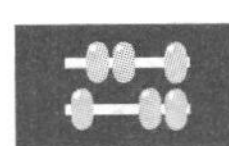      

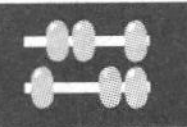

Sharpe Ratio

WHAT IT MEASURES

The Sharpe ratio, devised in 1966 by economist William F. Sharpe, measures the ratio of return from a portfolio to volatility. It is used to compare and select investment options, and identify which portfolio offers the most risk-efficient investment.

WHY IT IS IMPORTANT

The Sharpe ratio provides a simple way compare two assets with the same expected return—showing which will give the greatest return given an equal level of risk. The key advantage of the Sharpe ratio is that it can be easily calculated without needing any additional data regarding the asset's profitability.

HOW IT WORKS IN PRACTICE

The Sharpe ratio is calculated by subtracting the risk-free rate from the return of the portfolio, then dividing by the standard deviation of the portfolio. To use the Sharpe ratio, apply the following formula:

$$\text{Sharpe ratio} = \frac{\text{(Expected rate of return} - \text{Risk-free rate)}}{\text{Standard deviation of the portfolio}}$$

The higher the Sharpe ratio, the better the return for each unit of risk. How does this work in practice?

Imagine that portfolio A generates a return of 15%, while portfolio B generates a return of just 12%. It would seem at first glance that portfolio A has performed better. However, if portfolio A was much riskier then it may be the case that B has a better risk-adjusted rate of return.

If we imagine the risk-free rate in this scenario is 5% and the portfolios have standard deviations of 8% and 5% respectively, then we can see that portfolio A would have a Sharpe ratio of 1.25, while portfolio B would have a Sharpe ratio of 1.4. This suggests that, adjusted for risk, portfolio B presents the better investment.

TRICKS OF THE TRADE

- When using the Sharpe ratio, a score of 1 or better is considered good. A ratio above 2 is considered very good, and 3 would be considered excellent.
- Using the Sharpe ratio doesn't always provide an accurate analysis of return on risk or volatility. This is because portfolio standard deviation can reflect upside or downside returns—and the ratio does not differentiate between these outcomes. Some analysts argue that using standard deviation to measure volatility is not strictly effective, since standard deviation is not a measure of volatility. Instead, standard deviation is really a rough proxy for concepts such as "risk."
- When using the Sharpe ratio, it is wise to adjust the ratio for portfolio analysis. If you are comparing two potential investments for portfolios, then the ratio may not be accurate if one investment is highly correlated with other investments in the portfolio. The solution is therefore to use different Sharpe ratios for different portfolios.
- The Sharpe ratio is unusual in that it can be applied to both ex-ante (expected) returns and ex-poste (historical) returns.

MORE INFO

Article:

Sharpe, William F. "The Sharpe ratio." *Journal of Portfolio Management* (Fall 1994). Online at: www.stanford.edu/~wfsharpe/art/sr/sr.htm

Website:

Hedge Funds Consistency Index on Sharpe ratio: www.hedgefund-index.com/d_sharpe.asp

See Also:

Risk-Adjusted Rate of Return (pp. 1251–1252)
Treynor Ratio (p. 1259)
William F. Sharpe (p. 1309)

Statistical Process Control Methods

WHAT IT MEASURES

Statistical Process Control (SPC) is a tool for monitoring and controlling variation in processes such as manufacturing of goods, testing, or statistical results. It was created in the 1920s by Dr W. Edwards Deming, who claimed the majority of variation was due to operator over-adjustment. SPC requires an organization to:

- determine the process parameters that need to be monitored;
- create a control chart to confirm the process is under control;
- collect data to compare with the control chart to identify process variation.

WHY IT IS IMPORTANT

SPC itself doesn't improve your processes—it can only tell you if variation has increased beyond normal levels. However, this information enables businesses to incorporate or eliminate the changes causing an abnormal variation. This is important because it provides an understanding of business baselines, gives insights into possible process improvements, and shows the value and results of existing processes. SPC can also provide real-time analysis to establish where business processes can be improved, improving decision-making.

HOW IT WORKS IN PRACTICE

The key tool in applying SPC is the control chart that illustrates what a process looks like (statistically) when it is in-control. Control charts typically measure variable data and monitor the process target (mean result) and process range. There are a number of different sorts of control chart but among the most common are the X⁻ chart (pronounced "x bar" but also known as the averages or means chart), and the R chart (also known as the range chart).

This type of control chart has three key elements: a center line, an upper control limit, and a lower control limit. The center line on an X⁻ control chart is the process mean, while the center line on an R chart is the mean range.

The upper and lower control limits (UCL and LCL) are set to represent deviation from the mean that includes 99.7% of all data points (i.e., plus and minus 3 standard deviations from the mean).

Data is then collected from the process and the mean plotted on the X^- and R charts—which can be interpreted to determine if the process is staying in-control or is out-of-control.

In the example below, a company is manufacturing pencils that are 16mm in diameter (mean), and they want to know if the process is in-control, and the level of variation in the pencils created.

The company begins by collecting a series of sample measurements, which are placed in subgroups. Next, the mean of each subgroup is calculated by adding all the measurements together and dividing by the number of measurements in the subgroup.

Next, the company calculates the mean of all of the means—this gives an overall mean for the data. This overall mean is the centre line in the control chart—in our example this is 13.75.

Next, the company must calculate S, the standard deviation of the data points. This can be easily calculated in Excel using the formula =STDEV (data points).

Next, calculate the UCL and LCL as follows:

$$UCL = CL + 3 \times S$$
$$LCL = CL - 3 \times S$$

where CL is the center line or overall mean value. Draw a line on the control chart to represent the UCL and LCL.

On your X^- chart, the x-axis shows the subgroup means from your original calculation. The y-axis represents actual measurements from the process over time. As a rule of thumb, the process is considered out-of-control if any point falls beyond the UCL or LCL lines (i.e., more than 3 standard deviations from the mean).

Control charts may also indicate a process is out-of-control if eight consecutive points fall on the same side of the center line, or if more than two consecutive points are more than one standard deviation point from the mean.

TRICKS OF THE TRADE

- Using a spreadsheet application, it is possible to calculate standard deviation and mean for a set of data. In Excel this is done using the STDEV and AVERAGE functions.
- The benefits of SPC won't be immediately realized in every organization. SPC is best applied where there are clearly defined and consistent processes, and where the organization's leadership is willing to identify and address new problems that might be identified by SPC.

MORE INFO

Books:

Oakland, John. *Statistical Process Control*. 6th ed. Amsterdam: Elsevier Butterworth-Heinemann, 2008.

Stapenhurst, Tim. *Mastering Statistical Process Control: A Handbook for Performance Improvement Using SPC Cases*. Amsterdam: Elsevier Butterworth-Heinemann, 2005.

Website:

MiC Quality SPC course: www.margaret.net/spc/

See Also:

★ Statistical Process Control for Quality Improvement (pp. 939–942)

W. Edwards Deming (p. 1279)

Stochastic Modeling

WHAT IT MEASURES

Stochastic modeling uses thousands of simulations to produce probability distributions for various outcomes. It is widely used to predict how stock markets, bonds, and gilts will perform in the future.

WHY IT IS IMPORTANT

Advocates of stochastic modeling argue that randomness is a fundamental characteristic of financial markets. While some agents may be more successful at predicting future trends than others, modeling the likely outcome of investment activities must take account of probability, and particularly the risk of random events negatively impacting investments.

Many investment tools are "deterministic" in that they are clockwork systems which, given the same starting conditions, will generate exactly the same answer. This approach is not perfect when applied to financial markets, where there is an important element of chance, specifically relating to volatility and distribution.

Stochastic modeling provides a structured way of looking at a portfolio, taking into account random factors such as inflation or risk tolerance. If modeling shows a low probability of reaching investment goals, the fund can be diversified or contribution levels altered.

HOW IT WORKS IN PRACTICE

Stochastic modeling relies upon Monte Carlo simulation to generate random numbers upon which a stochastic formula is applied. This shows what impact specific random events will have on the distribution of probable outcomes.

For example, imagine you wanted to calculate the probability that a million door handles manufactured using four key parts would be too short or long to be used. You would have a million of each of the four different parts, and randomly select the parts to assemble each handle.

To calculate the probability, you would define a range of measurements for each part, and simulate what happens when randomly selected parts are put together. Of course, this is not something that could be calculated manually. Instead, a stochastic model would calculate thousands of probable outcomes based on a large number of random simulations, reflecting the random variation of combinations.

The Monte Carlo method has four key stages:

1 Define a range of possible inputs
2 Generate input randomly from the domain

MORE INFO

Book:

Morgan, Bryon J. T. *Applied Stochastic Modelling*. 2nd ed. Boca Raton, FL: Chapman & Hall/CRC, 2009.

Report:

du Toit, Barry. "Risk, theory, reflection: Limitations of the stochastic model of uncertainty in financial risk analysis." RiskWorX, June 2004. Online at: www.riskworx.com/insights/theory/theory.pdf

3 Perform deterministic computation using these inputs
4 Aggregate the results of the individual computations

TRICKS OF THE TRADE

- Stochastic modeling used to be known as "statistical sampling." Prior to the emergence of computers, it was rarely used because of the number of calculations involved in modeling, but there are now many off-the-shelf computer applications that can handle stochastic modeling quite easily.
- The Monte Carlo model was popularized by von Neumann, Ulam, and Fermi, among others, in the 1930s. The roots of the model actually lie in physics, and the model is still widely used by scientists as well as economists.
- The Monte Carlo simulation model is often used when the model is complex, nonlinear, or involves more than just a couple of uncertain parameters. A simulation can typically involve over 10,000 evaluations of the model, a task which in the past was only practical using super computers.

Stress Testing

WHAT IT MEASURES

Stress testing is a risk management tool that helps to identify how vulnerable a business, portfolio, or venture might be to unusual, negative circumstances. It may involve scenario analysis or simulation, based on hypothetical or historical data.

WHY IT IS IMPORTANT

Stress testing is extremely useful to financial analysts because it provides them with additional information on potential portfolio losses in the event of extreme, but unlikely events. Crucially, stress testing enables risk managers to test how robust a particular investment or instrument will be in the event of a serious change in circumstances.

The current "credit crunch" is a perfect example of the importance of stress testing. Institutions that conducted thorough stress tests based on a simultaneous lack of credit coupled with increased exposure to collateral debt obligations have been less seriously affected, according to financial regulators.

HOW IT WORKS IN PRACTICE

Stress testing is used to test instruments against scenarios such as: What happens if the market collapses by 60%? What happens if interest rates on our loans double? What if our lease costs increase by 75%?

The most common approach to stress testing is to use Monte Carlo simulation. This involves taking a number of randomized scenarios, ranging from modest to extreme outcomes (say a 90% drop in sales, versus a 90% increase in sales), and modeling the results on a probability distribution curve.

Most stress testing exercises involve multiple stressors. There is usually also the ability to test the current ability to cope with a known historical scenario. In recent years, many companies have tested their ability to cope with the kind of recession seen in Europe during the 1990s, for example.

There are three basic kinds of event a stress test can be applied to: Extreme event (current positions combined with historical event); risk factor shock; and external factor shock (shock of any external index factor, such as oil prices or exchange rates).

There are two basic sorts of stress test—sensitivity tests and scenario tests. A sensitivity test assesses the impact of large movement in financial variables on portfolio values without needing a specific reason. For example, you might test what happens if interest rates fall by 20%, or the cost of equity rises by 15%. Sensitivity tests can be run quickly and easily, but lack historical perspective.

Scenario tests are more costly and complex, but provide a better insight into long-term risk. They are constructed either within the context of a specific portfolio or based on a specific set of historical circumstances. Risk managers identify a portfolio's key drivers and test what happens if those drivers are stressed beyond value at risk (VAR) levels. Many risk managers use a hybrid approach of scenario and sensitivity testing.

TRICKS OF THE TRADE

- In many countries, stress testing is a regulatory requirement. In the United Kingdom, for example, the Financial Services Authority (FSA) requires certain financial institutions to conduct stress tests and ensure they have sufficient capital reserves available to handle extreme events.
- Stress testing is mostly used to analyze market risk, and the impact of market changes on portfolios such as interest rates, equity, exchange rates, and commodity instruments. These portfolios are suitable for stress testing because their market prices are regularly updated, giving sufficient data to analyze.
- VAR analysis is a very useful risk management tool, but it is not able to incorporate all possible risk outcomes, particularly sudden, dramatic changes in market circumstances.
- Stress testing is often used as a tool to communicate risk to business leaders. Rather than the hypothetical probabilities of VAR, stress testing provides a response to a very specific set of circumstances.
- Regulators commonly use stress testing to consider the vulnerability of entire financial systems. Stress tests were recently used by the Bank of England as part of a Financial Sector Assessment Program (FSAP), which considered how 10 large domestic banks would deal with a 35% decline in global stock prices, and a 12% decline in domestic property prices.

MORE INFO

Book:

Rösch, Daniel, and Harald Scheule (eds). *Stress-Testing for Financial Institutions: Applications, Regulations and Techniques*. London: Risk Books, 2009.

Article:

Bunn, Philip, Alastair Cunningham, and Mathias Drehmann. "Stress testing as a tool for assessing systemic risks." *Financial Stability Review* (June 2005). Online at: tinyurl.com/6y3e753 [PDF].

See Also:

✔ Applying Stress-Testing to Business Continuity Management (p. 1141)
✔ Applying Stress-Testing to Operational Risk Exposure (p. 1142)
✔ Stress Testing and Scenario Analysis for Keeping Up with Regulation (p. 1054)
✔ Stress Testing to Evaluate Insurance Cover (p. 1016)

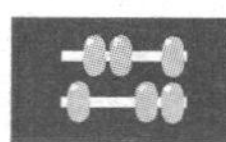

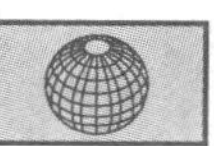

Swap Valuation

WHAT IT MEASURES

In finance, a swap is a derivative in which two parties agree to exchange one stream of cash flow against another. The swap buyer makes a stream of interest payments on a principal sum to the seller, based on the present value of the asset, for a fixed period of time. The seller then receives payments from the seller, which are usually based on a fixed rate, such as Libor. The swap valuation is the price that each party assigns to the components of the swap, and dictates the level of payments made by the buyer of the swap.

WHY IT IS IMPORTANT

Interest rate swaps were originally created to allow large corporations to avoid the cost of exchange controls. Today, they are one of the most popular and flexible financial instruments. They can be used by hedge funds to managed fixed or floating assets and liabilities, while speculators often use swaps to profit from changes in interest rates.

HOW IT WORKS IN PRACTICE

Interest rate swaps do not generate revenue themselves, they merely convert one interest rate basis to another. This type of swap is known as a "plain vanilla" swap, and is by far the most common form of swap.

Because the interest rate swap is simply a series of cash flows occurring at known future dates, it is possible to calculate its value by using a series of estimated discount cash flows.

To calculate a theoretical swap rate (TSR) for the fixed component of a swap contract, use the following formula:

$$\text{TSR} = \frac{\text{Present value of the floating rate payments}}{(\text{Notional principal}_i \times \text{days} \div 360 \times \text{df}_i)}$$

For example, company A and company B agree to a $100 million vanilla swap over three years with company A paying the swap rate, and company B paying six-month Libor floating rate.

Using the formula, it is possible to calculate a swap rate value by using the six-month Libor rate to estimate the present value of the floating rate payments.

First, calculate the present value (PV) of the payment, using Libor forward rates for three years.

As with the floating rate payments, Libor forward rates are used to discount the notional principal for the three-year period. The PV of the notional principal is calculated by multiplying the days in the period and the floating rate forward discount factor.

In our example above, the present value of the notional principal over six bi-annual payments would be calculated at $278,145,000 using the Libor forward rate to discount the cash flow.

To calculate the theoretical swap rate, we would use the following calculation:

$$\text{TSR} = \frac{12{,}816{,}663}{278{,}145{,}000} = 0.046 = 4.6\%$$

In this scenario, the buyer would therefore pay a fixed rate of 4.61% to the seller of the swap, in exchange for receiving six-month Libor interest payments.

TRICKS OF THE TRADE

- Remember, that in an interest rate swap, the principal amount is not exchanged between the counterparties. Rather, interest payments are based on a "notional amount."
- In addition, because the fixed rate component of the swap is based on the rate that values the fixed rate payments at the same present value as the variable rates, there is no advantage to either party at the time of entering a swap and no upfront payment is made. During the life of the swap, the same valuation is used, but since interest rates change, the PV of the variable rate will also change—creating an advantage for one party.
- A swap will typically last for between one and 15 years. The period of the contract is known as the swap's tenor or maturity. The counterparty paying the fixed rate is known as the buyer of the swap, while the floating-rate payer is known as the seller.
- While it is important to understand the theoretical basis of swap valuation, there are a number of computer programs that will perform complex calculations to provide highly accurate valuations.
- You may sometimes see the floating and fixed components of a swap referred to as the "legs" of the swap.

MORE INFO

Books:

Buetow, Gerald W., and Frank J. Fabozzi. *Valuation of Interest Rate Swaps and Swaptions*. New Hope, PA: Frank J. Fabozzi, 2001.

Rogers, Simon. *Swaps in Practice: The Products, Pricing and Applications*. London: Euromoney Books, 2004.

Article:

Duffie, Darrell. "Credit swap valuation." *Financial Analysts Journal* 55:1 (January/February 1999): 73–87. Preprint online at: www.defaultrisk.com/pp_crdrv_57.htm

See Also:

✔ Swaps, Options, and Futures: What They Are and Their Function (p. 988)

Term Structure of Interest Rates

WHAT IT MEASURES

A mathematical description of the relationship between interest rates (or the cost of borrowing) and the time to maturity of a debt in a given currency, often used in relation to fixed securities. The resulting relationship is plotted on a graph that is known as a "yield curve." This curve can then be analyzed to measure the expected yield of securities over time.

WHY IT IS IMPORTANT

The term structure or yield curve graph shows investors how returns compare to government-issued Treasury bonds (which are considered risk-free), and how an investment compares with other fixed-income securities with the same maturity.

By observing the shape of the graph, investors can gain insight into the likely future direction of the economy and identify

trading opportunities. This is important to investors but also to businesses, since most strategic business decisions depend on the availability and cost of capital—which is determined by interest rates.

HOW IT WORKS IN PRACTICE

The yield curve plots the annualized percentage increase in the yield of a specific investment. For example, if a bank account returns an interest rate of 4%, the yield is said to be 4%. However, most investments offer different returns over time. A bank may offer a higher interest rate for deposits that are invested over five years, for example.

The yield is therefore expressed as a function P(*t*), where *t* is the period of time invested over. This means that P(*t*) represents the value today of receiving one unit of currency *t* years in the future. P is usually an increasing function of *t*. The formula for calculating the yield (or interest term structure) for borrowing money of a period of time is as follows:

$$Y_t = \left[\frac{1}{P(t)}\right] - 1$$

The yield curve function P is actually only known with certainty for a few specific maturity dates, the other maturities are calculated by interpolation.

The simplest method of calculating the function P, and therefore the term structure of interest rates, is using the market expectations hypothesis. This states that if investors have an expectation of what one-year interest rates will be, then year-two interest rates will be calculated by compounding the first year's interest rate with the current year's. Over a longer term, rates are calculated as equal to the geometric mean of the yield on short-term rates. This information can be used to construct a simple yield curve.

TRICKS OF THE TRADE

- Critics point out this approach neglects the risk involved in bonds, while other analysts use the liquidity preference model, which includes a premium in the calculation to reflect the benefit of holding long-term bonds (the term premium). This explains the upward curve of most long-term yields.
- There are three basic patterns revealed by term structure graphs:
  a The normal yield curve: The line illustrating normal market conditions, where there are no significant changes expected to the economy and growth is fixed and predictable. In this market, fixed-income securities will likely generate higher yields the further away the maturity date.
  b The flat yield curve illustrates a market that is transitioning and where future movement is unclear, creating a flatter curve than the normal yield curve.
  c The inverted yield curve is rare and seen only during abnormal markets, where investors expect interest rates to decline over time, which will lead to lower yields further into the future.

Tick Value

WHAT IT MEASURES

There are in fact two different uses of the term "tick value."

1. Tick value can refer to the value of the minimum price movement of a traded stock allowed by an exchange. For example, many US stock markets have a tick *size* of 0.01, which translates into a tick *value* of one cent for the NYSE. In contrast, the EUR futures market has a tick value of 0.0001.
2. Tick value can also refer to the number of buyers and sellers of a stock who are bidding above or below the current market value of a stock.

WHY IT IS IMPORTANT

For traded companies, tick value is part of the contractual requirement to be listed on a stock market. Understanding tick value can also help when assessing the risk associated with investment opportunities: Markets with smaller tick values will generate smaller gains and losses with each price movement of a stock.

For investors, tick value also gives a good indication of how many investors are buying a stock on upticks versus downticks, which can be tracked over time to see whether market sentiment is broadly rising or falling.

HOW IT WORKS IN PRACTICE

Stock value relating to market sentiment is calculated according to the number of people placing orders to buy and sell a stock at any given time.

For example, at 9am Company A's stock will have a spread value, based on the difference between highest price buyers will pay, and the lowest bid sellers will accept. For frequently traded stocks, the spread will tend to be relatively small.

A buyer might believe the value of Company A's stock is increasing, and wants to buy stock now. They will therefore place an order for stock, and accept the best offer available from a seller. This sort of transaction is said to have happened on an "up tick" where the market is expected to rise. The opposite, where the seller accepts the best price offered by a buyer, is said to happen on a "down tick."

Stock exchanges calculate tick value by measuring precisely how many trades happen on each of these trajectories every few seconds. For example, on the NYSE, the tick value is taken every six seconds. A tick value of +100 means that 100 more issues traded on down ticks rather than up ticks. Tracking the tick value over time allows you to gain insight into market sentiment.

MORE INFO

Articles:

Porter, David C., and Daniel G. Weaver. "Tick size and market quality." *Financial Management* 26:4 (Winter 1997): 5–26.

Small Investors Software Co. "NYSE tick—Statistical analysis." July 3, 2003. Online at: tinyurl.com/6g8ar8s (via Internet Archive).

Steenbarger, Brett. "A NYSE TICK primer: How to assess intraday sentiment." *TraderFeed* (December 16, 2008). Online at: tinyurl.com/5wcfp6

TRICKS OF THE TRADE

- Among European currency exchanges, the euro futures market has a tick value of $12.50, compared to $6.25 for the British pound futures market. Tick values in stock indexes vary widely, from $5 for the Dow Jones futures market up to $12.50 for the S&P 500.
- Some statisticians have attempted to use tick data to analyze market performance and make predictions based on average ticks over 20 days. Generally speaking, ticks of more than +1000 or less than −800 would suggest excessive market optimism or pessimism.

Time Value of Money

WHAT IT MEASURES

Time Value of Money (TVM) is one of the most important concepts in the financial world. If a business is paid $1 million for something today, that money is worth more than if the same $1 million was paid at some point in the future. The reason money given today is worth more is straightforward: If I have money today, I have the potential to earn interest on the capital.

TVM values how much more a given sum of money is worth now (or at a specific future date) compared to in the future (or, in the case of a future payment, a date that is even further in the future). TVM calculations take into account likely interest gains, discounted cash flow, and potential risk, to create a value figure for a specific amount of money or investment opportunity.

There are several calculations commonly used to express the time value of money, but the most important are present value and future value.

WHY IT IS IMPORTANT

If company A has the opportunity to realize $10,000 from an asset today, or two years in the future, TVM allows the company to calculate exactly how much more that $10,000 is worth if it's received today, as opposed to in the future. It is important to know how to calculate the time value of money because it means you can distinguish between the value of investment opportunities that offer returns at different times.

HOW IT WORKS IN PRACTICE

If a business has the option of receiving a $1 million investment today or a guaranteed payment of the same amount in two years' time, you can use TVM calculations to show the relative value of the two sums of money.

Option A, take the money now: The business might accept the $1,000,000 investment immediately and put the capital into an account paying a 4.5% annual return. In this account, the $1,000,000 would earn $92,025 interest over two years (annually compounded), making the future value of the investment $1,092,025. This can be expressed using the following formula:

$$\text{Future value} = 1{,}000{,}000 \times (1 + 0.045)^2$$

which might be expressed as:

$$\text{Future value} = \text{Original sum} \times (1 + \text{Interest rate per period})^{\text{No of periods}}$$

Obviously, the present value of the $1 million if it is received today would be $1 million. But if the money isn't received for another two years, we can still calculate its present and future values.

The present value of a future $1 million investment is based on how much you would need to receive today to receive $1 million in two years' time. This is done by discounting the $1,000,000 by the interest rate for the period. Assuming an annual interest rate of 4.5%, we can calculate the present value using the following formula:

$$\text{Present value} = \frac{\text{Future value}}{(1 + \text{Interest rate per period})^{\text{No of periods}}}$$

Using this formula, we can see that the present value of a future payment of $1 million in two years' time is:

$$\frac{1{,}000{,}000}{(1 + 0.045)^2} = \$915{,}730$$

In other words, the investment in two years time is the equivalent of receiving $915,730 today, and investing it at 4.5% for two years.

TRICKS OF THE TRADE

- There are five key components in TVM calculations. These are: present value, future value, the number of periods, the interest rate, and a payment principal sum. Providing you know four of these values, you can rearrange the TVM formulae to calculate the fifth.
- When calculating TVM, you may sometimes need to supplement the calculation to discount future payments to take account of risk as well as time value. Discount rates can be adjusted to take account of risks like the other party not paying you back (default risk) or the fact that the item you intended to purchase has become more expensive, reducing the buying power of the money. In this case, the company lending the principal sum might insist on a higher interest rate to compensate for the risk.
- If a future payment is not certain, you can use the capital asset pricing model to calculate the risk involved.

MORE INFO

Websites:

Money-zine TVM calculator: tinyurl.com/6cmtjql

TVMCalcs.com guide: www.tvmcalcs.com/tvm/tvm_intro

See Also:

✔ Managing the Time Value of Money (p. 979)

Future Value (pp. 1228–1229)

Total Return

Total return is one more way to evaluate investment decisions, and because it totals all factors it is perhaps a calculation that investors value most—or should.

WHAT IT MEASURES

The total percentage change in the value of an investment over a specified time period, including capital gains, dividends, and the investment's appreciation or depreciation.

WHY IT IS IMPORTANT

Total return furnishes fundamental information that every investor seeks sooner or later: All things considered, just how much did my investment return?

That in itself makes total return rather important. In addition, there are several sound reasons for paying close attention to each of its components. For those who invest to maximize income, dividends will be very important. For those who invest for long-term growth, capital appreciation will be equally important.

Knowing how much of an investment's total return is attributable to each of the components can help in assessing how volatile the fund is likely to be, how tax-efficient it is, and how much steady income it can be expected to produce.

HOW IT WORKS IN PRACTICE

The total return formula reflects all the ways in which an investment may earn or lose money: dividends as income, capital gains distributions, and capital appreciation—the increase or decrease in the investment's net asset value (NAV):

$$\text{Total return} = \frac{(\text{Dividends} + \text{Capital gains distributions} \pm \text{Change in NAV})}{\text{Initial NAV}}$$

If, for instance, you buy a stock with an initial NAV of $40, and after one year it pays an income dividend of $2 per share and a capital gains distribution of $1, and its NAV has increased to $42, then the stock's total return would be:

$$\frac{(2 + 1 + 2)}{40} = \frac{5}{40} = 0.125 = 12.5\%$$

TRICKS OF THE TRADE

- The total return time-frame is usually one year, and it assumes that dividends have been reinvested.
- If a fund's capital gains exceed its capital losses for the year, most of the net gain must be distributed to stockholders as a capital gains distribution.
- Total return measures past performance only; it cannot predict future results.
- Total return generally does not take into account any sales charges that an investor paid to invest in a fund, or taxes he or she might owe on the income dividends and capital gains distributions received.
- Rules of the US Securities & Exchange Commission require a company to show a comparison of the total return on its common stock for the last five fiscal years with the total returns of a broad market index and a more narrowly focused industry or group index.
- Total return can be a key yardstick in selecting funds once an investor has set objectives and a time horizon, and made decisions about risk and reward.

Treynor Ratio

WHAT IT MEASURES

The Treynor ratio, as devised by Jack Treynor, is a measurement of a portfolio's return earned in excess of what would be earned on a risk-free investment. The higher the Treynor ratio, the better the performance of the portfolio or stock being analyzed.

WHY IT IS IMPORTANT

The Treynor ratio is used to calculate returns over and above what would be generated by a risk-free investment. Whenever the Treynor ratio is high, it denotes that the investor received high yields for each unit of market risk. One of the key advantages of Treynor is that it shows how a fund will perform not in relation to its own volatility but the volatility it brings to an overall portfolio.

HOW IT WORKS IN PRACTICE

The Treynor Ratio divides a portfolio's excess return by its "beta." This is the widely used measure of market-related risk in a stock or collection of stocks. If a stock has a beta of 0.5, it tends to move up or down with the market, but only half as far as the overall market. If a stock has a beta of 1.25 and the market moves up by 10%, that stock would move up by 12.5%.

The formula for the Treynor Ratio is as follows:

$$\text{Treynor ratio} = \frac{(\text{Average portfolio return} - \text{Average risk return of risk-free investment})}{\text{Beta of portfolio}}$$

The formula can be applied to any fund or portfolio where you can find a beta value—the beta is a measurement of market-related risk.

An investor might use the Treynor ratio to calculate the return generated by a fund over the return of short-term Treasury bills. If the fund returns 12% over three years, while the Treasury bill rate is 1.5% and the fund's beta is 0.5, then we can see the Treynor ratio is: $(12 - 1.5) \div 0.5 = 21$.

TRICKS OF THE TRADE

- Like the Sharpe ratio, the Treynor ratio doesn't quantify the value added—it is simply a ranking mechanism. Where the two mechanisms differ is that the Sharpe ratio considers total risk (the standard deviation of the portfolio) while the Treynor ratio considers systematic risk (the beta of a portfolio versus the benchmark).
- In practice, it's possible to simply look up Treynor ratios for many listed equity funds. For example, many newspapers and financial websites will list Treynor figures under "performance" data, usually over three, five, and 10 years.
- It is worth considering how Treynor Ratios change over time and in relation to similar funds—a three-year ratio may be negative while five-year and 10-year figures are positive. This could be because the fund is mismanaged but also could reflect a market downturn or a short-term problem.

MORE INFO

See Also:

Risk-Adjusted Rate of Return (pp. 1251–1252)
Sharpe Ratio (p. 1253)

Value at Risk

WHAT IT MEASURES

Value at risk (VAR) is a useful tool for anyone looking to quantify the risk of a particular project or investment opportunity by measuring the potential loss that might be incurred over a certain period of time. VAR measures what is the most that an investor might lose, based on a specific level of confidence, over a specific period of time. For example, "What's the most I can—with a 95% level of confidence—expect to lose over the next 12 months?"

WHY IT IS IMPORTANT

Most risk measurements focus on volatility whereas VAR focuses specifically on losses. It is commonly used to evaluate risk across a portfolio, but can also be applied to single indexes or anything that trades like a stock. VAR is important because it provides financial executives with a method of quantifying risk that is rigorous but also easily understood by nonfinancial executives.

HOW IT WORKS IN PRACTICE

The most common method of calculating VAR is the variance-covariance approach, sometimes referred to as "parametric VAR." Parametric VAR is a percentile-based risk measure that measures the expected loss of a portfolio over a specific period of time, depending on the confidence. To calculate parametric VAR, use the following formula:

$$\text{Value at risk} = \text{Mean} \times \text{HPR} + [Z - \text{score} \times \text{Std Dev} \times \text{SQRT (HPR)}]$$

where Mean is the average expected (or actual) rate of return, HPR is the holding period, Z-score is the probability, Std Dev is the standard deviation, and SQRT is the square root (of time).

To calculate the VAR of a portfolio worth $1 million with an expected average annual return of 13%, a standard annual deviation of 20% (equal to a daily deviation of 1.26%), and a 95% confidence score, therefore, you would perform the following calculation:

$$13 \times 1 + (95 \times 1.26 \times \text{SQRT}) = 6.037\%$$

This results in a 10-day VAR of $60,370. This means that your biggest potential loss over any 10-day period should not exceed $60,370 more than 5% of the time, or approximately once a year.

TRICKS OF THE TRADE

- VAR is now increasingly accepted as the *de facto* standard for risk measurement. In 1993, when the Bank of International Settlements members met in Basel, they amended the Basel Accord to require banks to hold in reserve enough capital to cover 10 days of losses based on a 95% 10-day VAR.
- A simpler alternative approach to calculating VAR is using the historical method—this simply takes all empirical profit and loss history and puts the returns in order of size. If we had 100 historical returns, the VAR for a 99% confidence score would simply be the second largest loss. Critics argue that very few portfolios have enough historical data to make this approach reliable, however.
- A third approach to calculating VAR is the simulation or Monte Carlo method, which uses computerized simulation to generate thousands of possible returns from a parametric assumption, then ordering them in the same way as with an historical calculation.
- Although VAR is often described as the "maximum possible" loss, this only applies at a single percentage confidence score. It is always possible to lose more by applying a higher confidence level—this is known as the conditional value at risk (CVAR), expected shortfall, or extreme tail loss.

MORE INFO

Books:

Butler, Cormac. *Mastering Value at Risk: A Step-by-Step Guide to Understanding and Applying VAR*. London: FT Prentice Hall, 1999.

Choudhry, Moorad. *An Introduction to Value-at-Risk*. 5th ed. Chichester, UK: Wiley, 2013.

Article:

Harper, David. "An introduction to value at risk (VAR)." *Investopedia* (May 27, 2010). Online at: www.investopedia.com/articles/04/092904.asp

Website:

Risk Glossary on VAR: www.riskglossary.com/link/value_at_risk.htm

See Also:

✔ Calculating Your Total Economic Capital (p. 1005)
Earnings at Risk (p. 1220)
Value at Risk (p. 1430)

Weighted Average Cost of Capital

WHAT IT MEASURES

The weighted average cost of capital (WACC) is the rate of return that the providers of a company's capital require, weighted according to the proportion each element bears to the total pool of capital.

WHY IT IS IMPORTANT

WACC is one of the most important figures in assessing a company's financial health, both for internal use (in capital budgeting) and external use (valuing companies on investment markets). It gives companies an insight into the cost of their financing, can be used as a hurdle rate for investment decisions, and acts as a measure to be minimized to find the best possible capital structure for the company. WACC is a rough guide to the rate of interest per monetary unit of capital. As such, it can be used to provide a discount rate for cash flows with similar risk to that of the overall business.

HOW IT WORKS IN PRACTICE

To calculate the weighted average cost of capital, companies must multiply the cost of each element of capital for a project—which may include loans, bonds, equity, and preferred stock—by its percentage of the total capital, and then add them together.

For example, a business might consider investing $40 million in an expansion program. The financing is raised through a combination of equity (such as $10m of stock with an expected 10% return) and debt (for example, $30m bond issue, with 5% coupon).

In this simple scenario, WACC would be calculated as follows:

Equity ($10m) divided by total capital ($40m)
= 25%, multiplied by cost of equity (10%) = 2.5%

Debt ($30m) divided by total capital ($40m)
= 75%, multiplied by cost of debt (5%) = 3.75%

The two results added together give a weighted cost of capital of 6.25%.

In reality, interest payments are tax deductible, so a more accurate formula for WACC is:

$$WACC = DP \times DC - T + EP \times EC$$

where DP is the proportion of debt financing, DC is the cost of debt financing, T is the company's tax rate, EP is the proportion of equity finance, and EC is the cost of equity finance.

TRICKS OF THE TRADE

- To accurately calculate WACC, you need to know the specific rates of return required for each source of capital. For example, different sources of finance may attract different levels of taxation, or interest, which should be accounted for. A true WACC calculation could therefore be much more complex than the example provided here.
- Critics of WACC argue that financial analysts rely on it too heavily, and that the algorithm should not be used to assess risky projects, where the cost of capital will necessarily be higher to reflect the higher risk.
- Investors use WACC to help decide whether a company represents a good investment opportunity. To some extent, WACC represents the rate at which a company produces value for investors—if a company produces a return of 20% and has a WACC of 11%, then the company creates 9% additional value for investors. If the return is lower than the WACC, the business is unlikely to secure investment.
- Although the WACC formula seems simple, different analysts will often come up with different WACC calculations for the same company depending on how they interpret the company's debt, market value, and interest rates.

MORE INFO

Book:

Pratt, Shannon P., and Roger J. Grabowski. *Cost of Capital: Applications and Examples*. Hoboken, NJ: Wiley, 2008.

Websites:

Money Terms on WACC: moneyterms.co.uk/wacc/

12 Manage on WACC: www.12manage.com/methods_wacc.html

See Also:

✔ Estimating Enterprise Value with the Weighted Average Cost of Capital (p. 967)

✔ Obtaining an Equity Value Using the Weighted Average Cost of Capital (WACC) (p. 1080)

✔ Understanding the Weighted Average Cost of Capital (WACC) (p. 1002)

Working Capital

Working capital is concrete proof of the business axiom "It takes money to make money."

WHAT IT MEASURES

The funds that are readily available to operate a business. Working capital comprises the total net current assets of a business, which are its inventory, debtors, and cash—minus its creditors.

WHY IT IS IMPORTANT

Obviously, it is vital for a company to have sufficient working capital to meet all of its requirements. The faster a business expands, the greater will be its working capital needs.

If current assets do not exceed current liabilities, a company may well run into trouble paying creditors who want their money quickly. Indeed, the leading cause of business failure is not lack of profitability, but rather lack of working capital, which helps to explain why some experts advise: "Use someone else's money every chance you get, and don't let anyone else use yours."

HOW IT WORKS IN PRACTICE

Working capital is also called net current assets or current capital, and is expressed as:

Working capital = Current assets − Current liabilities

Current assets are cash and assets that can be converted to cash within one year or a normal operating cycle; current liabilities are monies owed that are due within one year.

If a company's current assets total $300,000 and its current liabilities total $160,000, its working capital is:

300,000 − 160,000 = $140,000

The working capital cycle describes capital (usually cash) as it moves through a company: It first flows from a company to pay for supplies, materials, finished goods inventory, and wages to workers who produce goods and services. It then flows into a company as goods and services are sold and as new investment equity and loans are received. Each stage of this cycle consumes time. The more time the stages consume, the greater the demands on working capital.

TRICKS OF THE TRADE

- Good management of working capital includes actions like collecting receivables faster and moving inventory more quickly; generating more cash increases working capital.
- While it can be tempting to use cash to pay for fixed assets like computers or vehicles, doing so reduces the amount of cash available for working capital.

MORE INFO

Websites:

PlanWare on working capital: www.planware.org/workingcapital.htm

Study Finance on working capital management: www.studyfinance.com/lessons/workcap/

See Also:

✔ Managing Working Capital (p. 980)

Working Capital Cycle (p. 1262)

Working Capital Productivity (p. 1263)

  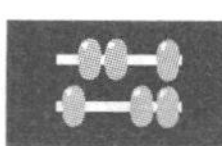      

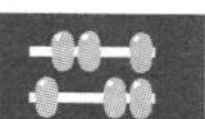

- If working capital is tight, consider other ways of financing capital investment, such as loans, fresh equity, or leasing.
- Early warning signs of insufficient working capital include pressure on existing cash; exceptional cash-generating activities such as offering high discounts for early payment; increasing lines of credit; partial payments to suppliers and creditors; a preoccupation with surviving rather than managing; frequent short-term emergency requests to the bank, for example, to help pay wages, pending receipt of a check.
- Several ratios measure how effectively and efficiently working capital is being used. These ratios are explained separately.

Working Capital Cycle

WHAT IT MEASURES

The working capital cycle measures the amount of time that elapses between the moment when your business begins investing money in a product or service, and the moment the business receives payment for that product or service. This doesn't necessarily begin when you manufacture a product—businesses often invest money in products when they hire people to produce goods, or when they buy raw materials.

WHY IT IS IMPORTANT

A good working capital cycle balances incoming and outgoing payments to maximize working capital. Simply put, you need to know you can afford to research, produce, and sell your product.

A short working capital cycle suggests a business has good cash flow. For example, a company that pays contractors in 7 days but takes 30 days to collect payments has 23 days of working capital to fund—also known as having a working capital cycle of 23 days. Amazon.com, in contrast, collects money before it pays for goods. This means the company has a negative working capital cycle and has more capital available to fund growth. For a business to grow, it needs access to cash—and being able to free up cash from the working capital cycle is cheaper than other sources of finance, such as loans.

Figure 1. A simple working capital cycle diagramWorking capital cycle

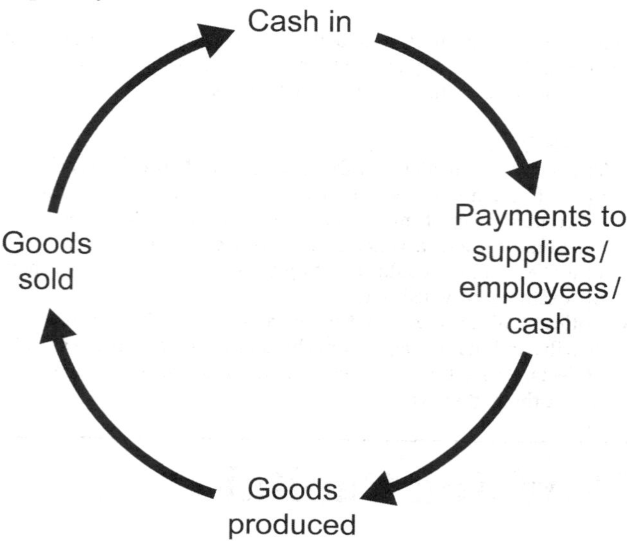

HOW IT WORKS IN PRACTICE

The key to understanding a company's working capital cycle is to know where payments are collected and made, and to identify areas where the cycle is stretched—and can potentially be reduced.

The working capital cycle is a diagram rather than a mathematical calculation. The cycle shows all the cash coming in to the business, what it is used for, and how it leaves the business (i.e., what it is spent on).

A simple working capital cycle diagram is shown in Figure 1. The arrows in the diagram show the movement of assets through the business—including cash, but also other assets such as raw materials and finished goods. Each item represents a reservoir of assets—for example, cash into the business is converted into labor. The working capital cycle will break down if there is not a supply of assets moving continually through the cycle (known as a liquidity crisis).

The working capital diagram should be customized to show the way capital moves around your business. More complex diagrams might include incoming assets such as cash payments, interest payments, loans, and equity. Items that commonly absorb cash would be labor, inventory, and suppliers.

The key thing to model is the time lag between each item on the diagram. For some businesses, there may be a very long delay between making the product and receiving cash from sales. Others may need to purchase raw materials a long time before the product can be manufactured. Once you have this information, it is possible to calculate your total working capital cycle, and potentially identify where time lags within the cycle can be reduced or eliminated.

TRICKS OF THE TRADE

- For investors, the working capital cycle is most relevant when analyzing capital-intensive businesses where cash flow is used to buy inventory. Typically, the working capital cycle of retailers, consumer goods, and consumer goods manufacturers is critical to their success.
- The working capital cycle should be considered alongside the cash conversion cycle—a measure of working capital efficiency that gives clues about the average number of days that working capital is invested in the operating cycle.

MORE INFO

Article:

Harper, David. "Financial statements: Working capital." *Investopedia*. Online at: tinyurl.com/5sgvfau

See Also:

★ Factoring and Invoice Discounting: Working Capital Management Options (pp. 39–41)
Working Capital (pp. 1261–1262)
Working Capital Productivity (p. 1263)

  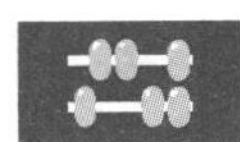      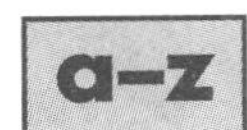

Working Capital Productivity

However expressed or calculated, working capital productivity is a measurement that offers a snapshot of a company's efficiency by comparing working capital with sales or turnover.

WHAT IT MEASURES

How effectively a company's management is using its working capital.

WHY IT IS IMPORTANT

It is obvious that capital not being put to work properly is being wasted, which is certainly not in investors' best interests.

As an expression of how effectively a company spends its available funds compared with sales or turnover, the working capital productivity figure helps to establish a clear relationship between its financial performance and process improvement. The relationship is said to have been first observed by the US management consultant George Stalk while working in Japan.

A seldom-used reciprocal calculation, the working capital turnover or working capital to sales ratio, expresses the same relationship in a different way.

HOW IT WORKS IN PRACTICE

To calculate working capital productivity, first subtract current liabilities from current assets, which is the formula for working capital, then divide this figure into sales for the period.

$$\text{Working capital productivity} = \frac{\text{Sales}}{(\text{Current assets} - \text{Current liabilities})}$$

If sales are $3,250, current assets are $900, and current liabilities are $650, then:

$$\frac{3250}{(900-650)} = \frac{3250}{250} = 13$$

In this case, the higher the number the better. Sales growing faster than the resources required to generate them is a clear sign of efficiency and, by definition, productivity.

The working capital to sales ratio uses the same figures, but in reverse:

$$\text{Working capital/sales ratio} = \frac{\text{Working capital}}{\text{Sales}}$$

Using the same figures in the example above, this ratio would be calculated:

$$\frac{250}{3250} = 0.077 = 7.7\%$$

For this ratio, obviously, the lower the number the better.

TRICKS OF THE TRADE

- By itself, a single ratio means little; a series of them—several quarters' worth, for example—indicates a trend, and means a great deal.
- Some experts recommend doing quarterly calculations and averaging them for a given year to arrive at the most reliable number.
- Either ratio also helps a management compare its performance with that of competitors.
- These ratios should also help to motivate companies to improve processes, such as eliminating steps in the handling of materials and bill collection, and shortening product design times. Such improvements reduce costs and make working capital available for other tasks.

MORE INFO

See Also:

Working Capital (pp. 1261–1262)
Working Capital Cycle (p. 1262)

Yield

WHAT IT MEASURES

Stocks that pay dividends (note that not all do) will produce an annual cash return to the investor. Simply dividing this cash return by the current stock price and expressing that as a percentage is known as the "yield"—that is, the annual percentage income at the current price. As far as newspapers are concerned, the yield figure they publish is usually the historical one.

Analysts will often provide forecasts for dividends in terms of earnings per share (EPS), and thus the forecast yield can then be calculated. Forecasts can, of course, go wrong, and consequently there is some risk in relying on them.

WHY IT IS IMPORTANT

Yield, after the price/earnings ratio, is one of the most common methods of comparing the relative value of stocks, and that is why it is so widely quoted in the press. The majority of investors like to see a cash income from their stocks, although to some extent this is a cultural thing. There are more companies in the United States, for example, that pay no dividends than in the United Kingdom.

HOW IT WORKS IN PRACTICE

You can compare yields against the market average or against a sector average, which in turn gives you some idea of the relative value of the stock against its peers, much like other ratios. Other things being equal, a higher-yield stock is preferable to that of an identical company with a lower yield. The higher-yield stock is cheaper. In practice, of course, there may well be good reasons why the market has decided that the higher yielder should be so—possibly it has worse prospects, is less profitable, and so on. This is not always the case; the market is far from being a perfectly rational place.

An additional feature of the yield (unlike many of the other stock analysis ratios) is that it enables comparison with cash. When you put cash into an interest-bearing source like a bank account or a government stock, you get a yield—the annual interest payable. This

  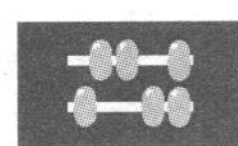   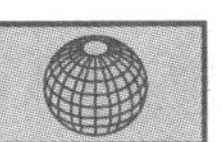   

is usually a pretty safe investment. You can compare the yield from this cash investment with the yield on stocks, which are far riskier. This produces a valuable basis for stock evaluation. If, for example, you can get 4% in a bank without capital risk, you can then look at stocks and ask yourself how this yield compares—given that, as well as the opportunity for long-term growth of both the stock price and the dividends, there is plenty of capital risk.

TRICKS OF THE TRADE

- Care is necessary, however, because unlike banks paying interest, companies are under no obligation to pay dividends at all. Frequently, if they go through a bad patch, even the largest and best-known household name companies will cut dividends or even abandon paying them altogether. So, stock yield is much less reliable than bank interest or government stock interest yield.
- Despite this, yield is an immensely useful feature of stock appraisal. It is the only ratio that tells you about the cash return to the investor, and you cannot argue with cash. EPS, for example, is subject to accountants' opinions, but a dividend once paid is an unarguable fact.

MORE INFO

See Also:

Bond Yield (pp. 1197–1198)
Dividend Yield (p. 1219)

Z-Score

WHAT IT MEASURES

The z-score is a measure of the financial health of a company. Devised in the 1960s by Edward Altman, the score uses statistical techniques to predict the likelihood that a company will fail because of bankruptcy within two years.

The z-score was originally created based on Altman's analysis of 33 bankrupt manufacturing companies with assets averaging $6.4 million and a further 33 nonbankrupt companies with assets between $1 million and $25 million. Altman's analysis showed that 95% of the bankrupt companies had a z-score that suggested financial problems.

WHY IT IS IMPORTANT

Since the 1980s, auditors have used the z-score to help identify companies with serious cash problems. The measure is also used to help score applicants for loans. Stockbrokers commonly use the z-score to determine if a company is a good investment.

HOW IT WORKS IN PRACTICE

The z-score combines five common business ratios and uses a weighting system devised by Altman to produce a score somewhere between -4 and $+8$. Each of the components that make up the final z-score are rated independently, and each component has a different weight in the calculation of the overall z-score. The exact emphasis on each factor can vary slightly from one industry to another, using more specific z-score calculators.

All the information needed to calculate a z-score is available in company financial reports. The original formula to calculate a z-score is as follows:

$$z = 1.2T1 + 1.4T2 + 3.3T3 + 0.6T4 + 0.999T5$$

where:

T1 = working capital ÷ total assets
T2 = retained earnings ÷ total assets
T3 = earnings before interest and tax ÷ total assets
T4 = market value of equity ÷ book value of total liabilities
T5 = sales ÷ total assets

A score can be analyzed as follows:

$>$ 2.99: the company is considered "safe"
1.8–2.99: there is some risk of financial distress
$<$ 1.8: there is serious risk of financial distress

TRICKS OF THE TRADE

- Although the numbers that go into the z-score can be influenced by external events, it is a useful tool to provide a quick analysis of where a company stands compared to competitors, and for tracking the risk of insolvency over time.
- Studies have shown the z-score is an accurate prediction of company failure rates in between seven and eight out of 10 cases.
- The formula was originally devised to be used for public companies, but amendments have since been made to allow z-scores to be calculated for privately held companies. In this case, the calculation that should be used is as follows:

$$0.717T1 + 0.87T2 + 0.420T4 + 0.998T5$$

For private companies, a score of 2.9 is "safe," while a score below 1.23 is considered a serious risk of financial distress.

MORE INFO

Book:

Altman, Edward I. "The z-score bankruptcy model: Past, present, and future." In Edward I. Altman and Arnold W. Sametz (eds). *Financial Crises: Institutions and Markets in a Fragile Environment.* New York: Wiley, 1977.

Website:

EasyCalculation.com z-score business health calculator: easycalculation.com/statistics/altman-z-score.php

See Also:

Measuring Financial Health (p. 982)

FINANCE THINKERS AND LEADERS

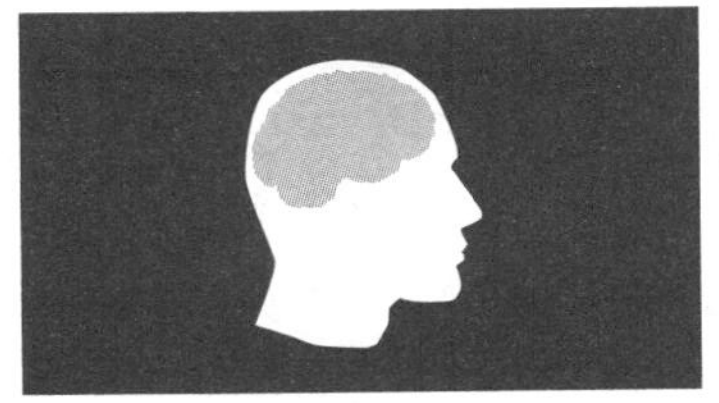

   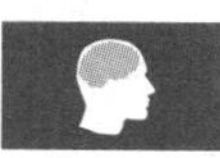  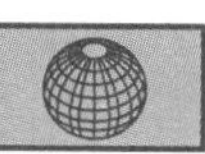   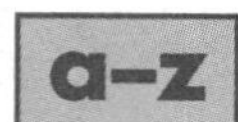

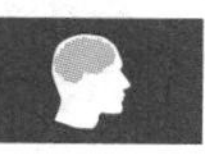

Finance Thinkers and Leaders

Profiling the top finance thinkers and pioneers

This section provides over fifty concise summaries of the some of the most influential finance theorists, practitioners, and thought leaders. The Finance Thinkers and Leaders range from originators of financial theory through to those who created practical applications in real-life situations. One factor links them all—they have all had an impact on current business practice.

The profiles include summaries of the career and thinking of the most important and influential thought leaders and practitioners in the field, as well as an assessment of their contribution to the world of modern finance. We also provide a list of key works and sources if you need to read further.

Our aim has been to identify the key figures who have laid down the foundations of finance and provide the reader with insights behind their practical application.

  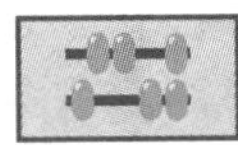      

Contents

Prince Al-Walid bin Talal · Billionaire member of Saudi royal family and international investor

1955 Born in Riyadh, Saudi Arabia.
1979 Received BS in business administration from Menlo College.
1980 Founded Kingdom Holding Company.
1985 Received Master of Social Science degree at the Maxwell School of Citizenship and Public Affairs of Syracuse University.

LIFE AND CAREER

Prince Al-Walid bin Talal bin Abdul Aziz Al Saud, commonly known as Prince Al-Walid, is a member of the Saudi royal family, his grandfather being Abdul Aziz al Saud, the founding king of Saudi Arabia. He is an entrepreneur, businessman, and international investor who began his business career after graduating from Menlo College, funded by a US$30,000 loan from his father and a US$300,000 mortgage on his house. He initially brokered deals with foreign firms wishing to do business in Saudi Arabia, before negotiating land deals in the 1980s, and some major investments in the Saudi banking industry. He continued to amass his fortune through investments in real estate, and the stock market. He is a Lebanese citizen, after his mother, and has been a special envoy for UNICEF. He has received many honorary degrees and academic awards, and is heavily involved in charitable activities across the Middle East, Asia, and Africa. It is estimated that he donates more than US$100 million annually to charity.

KEY THINKING

- Al-Walid is said to be the world's most influential Arab businessman, and one of the richest people in the world, with an estimated net worth of US$30 billion.
- He started his investment career in Saudi Arabia, through joint ventures with foreign companies, reinvesting the profits in real estate in Riyadh that greatly appreciated in value.
- He then focused on the country's banking sector, taking a controlling stake in the unprofitable United Saudi Commercial Bank (USCB) in 1986, returning it to profit within two years.
- In the late 1980s, he extended his investment portfolio out of the Middle East, buying shares in a number of US banks, before focusing all his bank investments in Citicorp.
- After many further strategic investments, the bulk of his fortune is now invested in a variety of high-profile US corporations—he is the largest single foreign investor in the country.
- He donated US$10 million to a relief fund after the attack on the World Trade Center, but became a controversial figure after asking the US to re-examine its policies in the Middle East; Mayor Giuliani returned the donation.
- In the Middle East, however, the confrontation turned him into one of the most respected public figures in the Arab world.
- He has also contributed a considerable amount to educational initiatives focused on uniting the gap between Western and Islamic communities; in 2005, he donated US$20 million each to Harvard and Georgetown universities to fund Islamic studies.
- In 2005, he purchased the Savoy hotel in London for £250 million, and donated US$20 million to the Louvre Museum in Paris, to help fund the construction of a wing for its collection of Islamic art.
- He donated US$500,000 towards a fund to honor former US president, George H. W. Bush in 2002.
- His latest project is the Mile High Tower, to be located in Jeddah; planned to be twice the height of the world's current tallest building, it is expected to cost US$10 billion.

IN PERSPECTIVE

- Al-Walid founded the private investment firm, Kingdom Holding Company, his base for investments in the banking, hotel, and real-estate sectors.
- After his major investments in Citicorp, he made a number of key acquisitions in other faltering blue-chip international businesses, including Eurodisney, New York's Plaza Hotel, London's Canary Wharf, and Apple Computers.
- In 2000, he moved his investments into high-tech companies, such as Compaq, Kodak, eBay, and Amazon.com.
- He is now considered to be the strongest political contender among the third-generation Saudi royals who will one day inherit power.
- He has called for the introduction of elections to Saudi Arabia's 120-member advisory council, to help reduce domestic problems in the country.
- His donations to religious institutions in the Middle East and the building of many new mosques in Saudi Arabia have made him a popular figure in the region.
- He is vocal advocate on women's rights, and hired the first female airline pilot in Saudi Arabia.

MORE INFO

Book:

Khan, Riz. *Alwaleed: Businessman, Billionaire, Prince*. London: HarperCollins, 2005.
The only biography of Al-Walid, it delves into his rise from a modest bank loan into a businessman and investor, with a portfolio containing Citigroup, Disney, Apple, and the Four Seasons Hotels.

See Also:

Saudi Arabia (pp. 1570–1571)

"Banks are the eyes of an economy." Prince Al-Walid bin Talal

   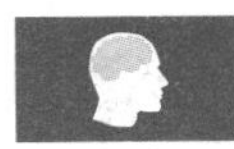  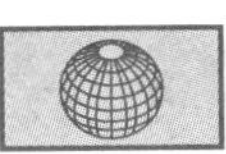   

Louis Bachelier · The father of financial mathematics

1870 Born in Le Havre, France.
1895 Received a Bachelor in Sciences from the Sorbonne.
1897 Received a Certificate in Mathematical Physics.
1900 Publication of his PhD thesis, "The theory of speculation."
1909 Appointed lecturer at the Sorbonne.
1912 Publication of *Calcul des Probabilités*.
1914 Publication of *Le Jeu, la Chance et le Hasard*.
1914 Drafted as a private into the French army.
1919 Appointed assistant professor at University of Besançon.
1922 Appointed assistant professor at University of Dijon.
1925 Appointed associate professor at University of Rennes.
1927 Appointed full professor at University of Besançon.
1937 Appointed professor emeritus at University of Besançon.
1937 Publication of *Les Lois des Grands Nombres du Calcul des Probabilités*.
1937 Retired from academic life.
1938 Publication of *La Spéculation et le Calcul des Probabilités*.
1939 Publication of *Les Nouvelles Méthodes du Calcul des Probabilités*.
1946 Died in Saint-Servan-sur-Mer, France.

LIFE AND CAREER

Louis Bachelier pioneered the study of financial mathematics well before it became central to financial practice. As a young man, he moved to Paris to study at the Sorbonne, where his doctoral thesis, *The Theory of Speculation*, helped originate the mathematics and modeling of finance, and the theory of Brownian motion. He was later offered a permanent professorship at the Sorbonne, with support from the Council of Paris University. However, he was unable to take up the position because World War I intervened and he was drafted into the French army. After the war he returned to academic life, and continued to research and write on financial mathematics, risk and probability. Public acknowledgement of his work, richly deserved for the innovations he brought to financial theory, did not really arrive until after his death, when he was rediscovered by those founding modern financial theory in the 1950s.

KEY THINKING

- Bachelier is credited as the first person to model Brownian motion, as part of his thesis on *The Theory of Speculation*, to show that advanced mathematics could be used in the study of finance to evaluate stock options.
- In mathematics, the Brownian motion is often referred to as the Wiener process, and Bachelier applied its simple stochastic process to modeling random fluctuations in stock prices.
- His work on chance, probability and risk anticipated the random movements of financial market prices and has become an integral part of modern financial theory.
- When he initially applied to join the University of Dijon he was rejected due to a misinterpretation of one of his papers by Paul Lévy, who appeared not to know of Bachelier or his work. Lévy later realized his error, and apologized to Bachelier.

IN PERSPECTIVE

- Bachelier's successful defense of his thesis in 1900 marked the birth of mathematical finance, and it was later published in the influential French journal, *Annales Scientifiques de l'Ecole Normale Supérieure*.
- His analysis of Brownian motion so that it could be applied to the mathematical modeling of price movements, and the evaluation of contingent claims in financial markets, is often thought of as one of the most important mathematical discoveries of the twentieth century.
- His groundbreaking analysis of the stock and option markets included several key ideas for the development of both finance and probability.
- Between 1900 and 1914, he developed the mathematical theory of diffusion processes in a series of papers published in reputed French journals.
- In his book *Le Jeu, la Chance et le Hasard*, Bachelier considered the systematic use of the concept of continuity in probabilistic modeling.
- He introduced many of the concepts of what later became stochastic analysis, in his attempt to find a theory for the valuation of financial options. His findings were similar to the work of Fischer Black, Myron Scholes, and Robert Merton in their seminal paper of 1973.

MORE INFO

Books:

Bachelier, Louis. *Louis Bachelier's Theory of Speculation: The Origins of Modern Finance*. Princeton, NJ: Princeton University Press, 2006. This translation of Bachelier's seminal work also contains a commentary on the development of stochastic analysis and financial economics.

Cootner, Paul H. (ed). *The Random Character of Stock Market Prices*. Cambridge, MA: MIT Press, 1964. A collection of research reprints on the randomness of the market up to 1964. It includes the first full English translation of Bachelier's thesis, "The theory of speculation."

Website:

Bachelier Finance Society, founded in 1996 by researchers in mathematical finance as a forum where academics and practitioners could exchange ideas and discuss their work: www.bachelierfinance.org

"The mathematical expectation of the speculator is zero." Louis Bachelier

  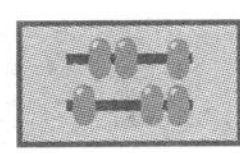 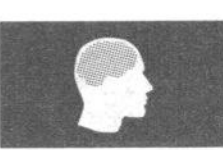  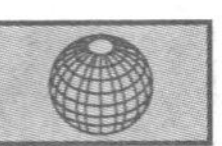   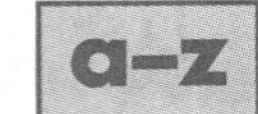

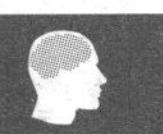

Gary Becker · Nobel Prize-winning economist

1930 Born in Pottsville, Pennsylvania.
1951 Received BA from Princeton University.
1953 Received MA from the University of Chicago.
1954 Appointed assistant professor at the University of Chicago.
1955 Received PhD from the University of Chicago.
1957 Appointed assistant and associate professor of economics at Columbia University.
1957 Appointed member, senior research associate, and research policy adviser, National Bureau of Economic Research.
1957 Publication of *The Economics of Discrimination*.
1960 Appointed professor of economics at Columbia University.
1964 Publication of *Human Capital*.
1967 Received John Bates Clark Medal from the American Economic Association.
1983 Appointed university professor of economics and sociology at the University of Chicago.
1987 Appointed president of the American Economic Association.
1991 Publication of *A Treatise on the Family*.
1992 Received Nobel Memorial Prize in Economic Sciences.
1996 Publication of *Accounting for Tastes*.
2000 Received National Medal of Science.
2007 Received Presidential Medal of Freedom.

LIFE AND CAREER

Gary Becker is an internationally renowned economist, Nobel Prize winner, business writer, and specialist on the sociological aspects of economic theory and analysis. He is regarded as one of the most influential economists of the 20th century, and has inspired much empirical research, due to his innovative work in different areas. He has taught economics at Columbia University for nearly 50 years, written a monthly column for *Business Week* for 20 years, and now coproduces an economics internet blog with Richard Posner. He has previously been on the board of directors at the Manhattan Institute, a member of the Advisory Committee to the Secretary of Defense, a member of the Accenture Energy Advisory Board, and is currently on the board of directors for the New Center for Accelerating Medical Innovations, the Merc Advisory Board on Innovation, and the Hoover Energy Task Force.

KEY THINKING

- Becker focused much of his research on how individuals make choices when investing in human capital based on benefits and cost, and the potential rate of return, in terms of marriage, divorce, fertility, and social welfare.
- He received the Nobel Prize for his work in extending economic theory to new areas of human behavior, including sociology, demography and criminology.
- His economic research also examines the impact of positive and negative habits—such as punctuality and alcoholism—on human capital, the different rates of return, and the resulting macroeconomic implications.
- In his study of discrimination in the workplace, he found it was less prevalent in highly competitive industries that focused on market success, but was greater in regulated industries that were less competitive.
- He also proposed that when minorities are a very small percentage of the population, the cost of discrimination mainly falls on minorities, but when their representation is higher, the cost of discrimination falls on both the minorities and the majority.

IN PERSPECTIVE

- His research considered the overlap between economics and areas of sociology, such as racial discrimination, crime, family organization, and drug addiction.
- He analyzed criminal behavior based on rational decision-making, and how criminals weigh the benefits of their crimes against risks of apprehension, conviction, and punishment.
- This led him to propose the best way to reduce crime was by increasing either the probability or the severity of punishment.
- In *A Treatise on the Family*, he examined social interaction and how time is allocated within the family, using economic theory to explain the reasoning behind decisions to have children and to educate them, and the decisions to marry and to divorce.
- This helped him originate the "rotten kid theorem," which states that children in a family, even if they normally act selfishly, will help one another if sufficiently incentivized.
- He also analyzed the workings of democracy, especially with regard to interest groups exploiting other groups, based on the concept of deadweight loss.

MORE INFO

Books:

Becker, Gary S. *A Treatise on the Family*. Cambridge, MA: Harvard University Press, 1981. His seminal work on the family, in which Becker applies economic theory and assumptions to personal and family decision-making.

Becker, Gary S. *Accounting for Tastes*. Cambridge, MA: Harvard University Press, 1996. A collection of articles that examine issues surrounding the reasoning and impact of preferences and values.

Becker, Gary S. *The Economics of Life: From Baseball to Affirmative Action to Immigration, How Real-World Issues Affect Our Everyday Life*. New York: McGraw-Hill, 1997. Essays from *Business Week* that look at the ways market incentives can influence human behavior.

"Fines are preferable to imprisonment and other types of punishment because they are more efficient." Gary Becker

     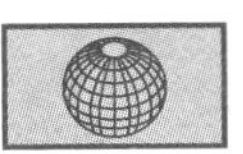   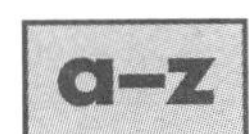

Peter L. Bernstein · The foremost chronicler of risk

1919 Born on January 22.
1941 Graduated from Harvard College with a degree in economics.
1941 Joined the Federal Reserve Board as a researcher.
1951 Appointed chief executive of an investment counsel firm.
1970 Publication of *Economist on Wall Street*.
1973 Founded Peter L. Bernstein Inc.
1974 Became the first editor of the *Journal of Portfolio Management*.
1977 Publication of *Streetwise: The Best of the Journal of Portfolio Management*.
1992 Publication of *Capital Ideas: The Improbable Origins of Modern Wall Street*.
1995 Publication of *Portable MBA in Investment*.
1996 Publication of *Against the Gods: The Remarkable Story of Risk*.
1998 Publication of *Investment Management*.
2004 Publication of *The Power of Gold: The History of an Obsession*.
2005 Publication of *Wedding of the Waters*.
2007 Publication of *Capital Ideas Evolving*.
2009 Died in New York.

LIFE AND CAREER

Peter L. Bernstein is a prolific and award-winning author on finance and risk, and founder and president of Peter L. Bernstein Inc., an international consultancy for institutional investors and corporations. After serving as an intelligence officer in Europe during World War II, he became a member of the research staff at the Federal Reserve Bank of New York. He then taught economics at Williams College and the New School for Social Research in New York, before moving into commercial banking. He was the first editor of the *Journal of Portfolio Management*, and remains consulting editor. He produces a newsletter on the capital markets, and writes regularly for journals and the popular press. He also lectures widely on risk management, asset allocation, portfolio strategy, and market history, and has received major awards for his books.

KEY THINKING

- Bernstein's books are popular and insightful; he has taken difficult concepts in finance, mathematics, philosophy, history, and psychology, and made them accessible for a wide audience.
- In his book, *Capital Ideas*, he traces the origins of Wall Street, and profiles some of the pioneers of modern investment theory over the years, including Louis Bachelier, Harry Markowitz, William Sharpe, Fischer Black, Myron Scholes, Robert Merton, and Franco Modigliani.
- In *Against the Gods*, Bernstein analyzes probability and its applications, using a readable blend of biography, history, and science to examine the role played by famous thinkers in helping the evolution from a superstitious outlook to modern risk management.
- *Against the Gods* also reviews the history of numerical measurement, probability theory, and the history of financial risk instruments.
- The book explains probability, uncertainty, the difference between luck and skill, the interactions between gambling and investing, and rational versus irrational decision-making.

IN PERSPECTIVE

- Bernstein has the ability to combine historical ideas with economics, and the theory and practice of investment management.
- *Capital Ideas* explores the development of new theories in risk, valuation, and investment returns, and focuses on the implementation of these theories in the world of investment management. It shows how these theories explain the link between risk and reward, and the advantages of diversification, and provides a clear framework for valuing financial options.
- Bernstein recently produced a sequel to *Capital Ideas*, called *Capital Ideas Evolving*, which defended the theories of the first book, and extended his examination of the key ideas that drive modern financial practice.
- *Against the Gods* also shows how the concept of risk originated and traces its progression through history, up to our modern understanding of how it affects us all.
- It examined Pascal's Wager in detail, a concept that was ahead of its time in terms of both probability theory and decision theory; it is based on consequences being more important than probabilities.

MORE INFO

Books:

Bernstein, Peter L. *Capital Ideas: The Improbable Origins of Modern Wall Street*. New York: Free Press, 1992.
Bernstein, Peter L. *Against the Gods: The Remarkable Story of Risk*. New York: Wiley, 1996.
Bernstein, Peter L. *Capital Ideas Evolving: The Improbable Origins of Modern Wall Street*. Hoboken, NJ: Wiley, 2007.

See Also:

Against the Gods: The Remarkable Story of Risk (p. 1328)

"The long run ain't what it used to be. Stocks don't have to do well in the future because they did well in the past. In fact, the opposite may be more likely." Peter L. Bernstein

  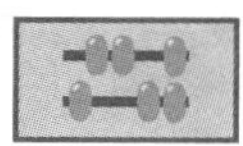 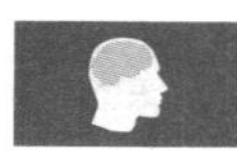     

Fischer Black · The high priest of modern finance

1938 Born in Washington, DC.
1959 Received BA in physics.
1964 Received PhD in applied mathematics from Harvard.
1965 Joined the consulting firm Arthur D. Little.
1969 Founded his own consulting firm, Associates in Finance.
1972 Appointed visiting professor and then full professor at the Graduate School of Business, University of Chicago.
1975 Appointed to MIT Sloan School of Management.
1973 Published seminal paper, "The pricing of options and corporate liabilities," with Myron Scholes.
1984 Joined Goldman Sachs as partner.
1994 Received the Financial Engineer of the Year award from the International Association of Financial Engineers.
1995 Died in New York.
2002 American Finance Association established the Fischer Black Prize.

LIFE AND CAREER

Fischer Black was an economist who applied his analysis of Keynesian and monetarist theories to finance and investment, thereby helping to revolutionize the industry. He was originally an academic at the Graduate School of Business, University of Chicago, where he was Director of the Center for Research in Security Prices, and MIT, before moving to Wall Street and a position at Goldman Sachs. He made the transition at a decisive time, as financial engineering was just emerging, and he played a critical part in applying quantitative strategies to investment practices for the first time. He was the co-author of the famous Black–Scholes equation, which developed an option pricing model that is still used widely today. He would have won the Nobel Prize for Economics but for his untimely death, aged 57, due to cancer.

KEY THINKING

- Black is best known for his work on the problem of how best to price a call option, which had been worked on for many years by researchers taking both a theoretical, and an empirical point of view.
- This research produced the celebrated Black–Scholes formula, based on his 1973 paper with Myron Scholes, "The pricing of options and corporate liabilities."
- The Black–Scholes equation derived the Black–Scholes–Merton differential equation, thereby solving the stock option pricing problem.
- In the announcement of the 1997 Nobel Prize for Economics, awarded to Myron Scholes and Robert Merton, the Nobel committee pointed out Black's key role in their work.

IN PERSPECTIVE

- Black's work on option valuation marked the emergence of continuous time finance, which is now used to value derivative instruments across the industry. Derivatives, now traded in their trillions of dollars each year, are mostly valued using the mathematical methods Black helped develop in the early 1970s.
- In addition to his work with Scholes and Merton, he also made other important contributions, including his work on portfolio insurance, commodity futures pricing, bond swaps and interest rate futures, global asset allocation models, dividend policy, international trade, business cycles, and labor economics.
- He was also the co-developer of the Black–Derman–Toy interest-rate derivatives model, originally created for in-house use by Goldman Sachs in the 1980s.
- He analyzed the capital asset pricing model (CAPM) in terms of monetary policy and Keynesian economics, and discussed the most effective ways it could be used.
- He was a forerunner in the use of computer technology and efficient trading systems.
- He thought that trying to model reality was more important than attempting closed-form analytical solutions.

MORE INFO

Books:

Black, Fischer. *Business Cycles and Equilibrium*. New York: Blackwell, 1987. A collection of essays in which Black examines the role of equilibrium in a developed economy, arguing that mathematical models actually restrain creativity.

Black, Fischer. *Exploring General Equilibrium*. Cambridge, MA: MIT Press, 1995. Here Black assesses general equilibrium theory, and discusses what it reveals about business cycles, growth, and labor economics.

Mehrling, Perry. *Fischer Black and the Revolutionary Idea of Finance*. Hoboken, NJ: Wiley, 2005. A full biography, and an examination of Black's place in the development of modern quantitative finance.

See Also:

Option Pricing (p. 1239)
Robert Merton (p. 1293)
Myron Scholes (p. 1306)

"Most so-called anomalies don't seem anomalous to me at all. They seem like nuggets from a gold mine, found by one of the thousands of miners all over the world." Fischer Black

  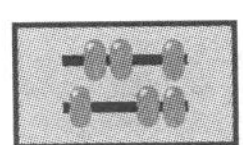 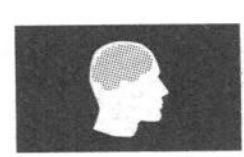  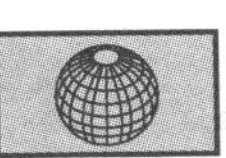   

Warren Buffett · The sage of Omaha

1930 Born in Omaha, Nebraska.
1950 Received BS from the University of Nebraska.
1951 Received MS in economics from Columbia Business School.
1951 Cofounded Buffett-Falk & Co.
1954 Appointed a security analyst at Graham-Newman Corp.
1956 Founded Buffett Partnership Ltd.
1962 Became dollar millionaire.
1965 Acquired Berkshire Hathaway.
1967 Berkshire Hathaway bought National Indemnity Company and National Fire & Marine Insurance Company.
1970 Appointed chairman and chief executive officer of Berkshire Hathaway.
1995 Acquired major stake in McDonald's.
1996 Acquired GEICO.
1998 Bought Executive Jet Corporation.
2001 Became the second-richest man in the US.
2001 Announced new investment strategy.
2003 Acquired Burlington Industries.
2004 Appointed an economic adviser by John Kerry during US presidential elections.
2008 Named by *Forbes* as the richest man in the world, worth US$62.3 billion.
2011 Received Presidential Medal of Freedom.

LIFE AND CAREER

Warren Buffett is a multibillionaire investor, businessman and philanthropist, and one of the most influential people in the financial world. As a child, he quickly started making business deals, before studying at Columbia Business School under investment guru, Benjamin Graham, the first proponent of value investing. He formed the investment firm, Buffett-Falk & Co., and worked as an investment salesman, before Graham offered him a job at the Graham-Newman Corporation. Buffett soon realized he preferred to work independently, so he launched his own family investment partnership at the age of 25, with starting capital of US$100,000. He later decided to turn around one of his acquisitions, the unprofitable Berkshire Hathaway textile company. During the market collapse of 1973, he purchased a series of companies at bargain prices. Berkshire Hathaway is today a massive holdings company for a variety of businesses, with assets and sales totaling many billions of dollars. In 2006, it gave away US$30.7 billion in shares to the Gates Foundation, the largest charitable donation in history.

KEY THINKING

- Buffett was named as the richest man in the world by *Forbes* magazine in early 2008, with a fortune of US$62.3 billion.
- His investing career started with his own personal investment strategy of looking for stocks that offered outstanding value–those that were relatively cheap given their asset value–and then holding those shares for the long term.
- When he took over Berkshire Hathaway, Buffett focused on restructuring the company's financial framework, and using it as a holding company for other investments.
- He grew Berkshire Hathaway into the 12th largest corporation in the US, through the implementation of his investing principles; this strategy proved extremely successful–shareholders who invested US$10,000 in the company in 1965 have made more than US$50 million.
- He avoids stock bubbles that are generated by media coverage, such as the internet boom of the late 1990s; since 2000, he has ignored the technology sector, and focused on bricks, carpets, insulation, and paint.
- He is a Democratic supporter, and acted as an economic adviser to John Kerry, the Democratic candidate for the US presidential elections in 2004.

IN PERSPECTIVE

- Buffett was influenced by investment pioneer Benjamin Graham, in particular his work on value investing. Buffett further developed these theories by researching companies whose shares seemed cheap given their growth prospects.
- This approach was groundbreaking for its time, as it meant also examining a company's intangible assets, such as brand value.
- He invests by sticking rigidly to his own investment principles and avoiding bandwagons–he will not invest in a business he does not understand–but has successfully picked some key stocks at a cheap price, such as Coca-Cola and American Express, when they were at a low point in their business cycle.

MORE INFO

Books:

Hagstrom, Robert G. *The Warren Buffett Way: Investment Strategies of the World's Greatest Investor*. New York: Wiley, 1994. Details Buffett's life and business career and gives a clear overview of his investment techniques and strategies.

Lowenstein, Roger. *Buffett: The Making of an American Capitalist*. New York: Random House, 1996. Looks at his personal life, as well as focusing on his early investments and the long-term growth strategies that made his fortune.

Schroeder, Alice. *The Snowball: Warren Buffett and the Business of Life*. London: Bloomsbury Publishing, 2008. Written with Buffett's full cooperation and collaboration, it combines his business expertise, life story, and philosophy, and is useful for those wanting pointers for investment success.

See Also:

The Snowball: Warren Buffett and the Business of Life (p. 1417)
The Warren Buffett Way (p. 1432)

"Shares are not mere pieces of paper. They represent part-ownership of a business. So, when contemplating an investment, think like a prospective owner." Warren Buffett

  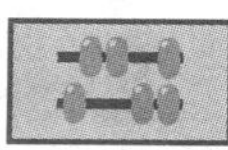   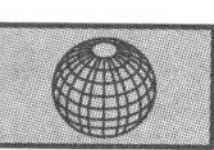   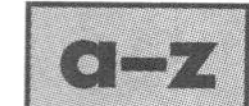

Andrew Carnegie · The original wealthy philanthropist

1835 Born in Dunfermline, Scotland.
1848 Carnegie family left Scotland for America.
1853 Joined the Pennsylvania Railroad.
1856 Took out a loan and made first investment.
1859 Promoted to superintendent at Pennsylvania Railroad.
1861 Invested in an oil company in Pennsylvania.
1865 Founded Keystone Bridge Co.
1875 Opened his first steel plant, the Edgar Thomson Works.
1878 Supplied steel for the Brooklyn Bridge.
1883 Acquired the Homestead Works.
1886 Publication of *Triumphant Democracy*.
1889 Publication of *The Gospel of Wealth*.
1892 Formed Carnegie Steel.
1901 Bought out by J. P. Morgan for US$480 million.
1905 Established Carnegie Teachers' Pension Fund.
1910 Established the Carnegie Endowment for International Peace.
1911 Established the Carnegie Corporation, which gave away 90% of his fortune.
1919 Died in Lenox, Massachusetts.

LIFE AND CAREER

Andrew Carnegie was born into poverty in Scotland and moved to the United States with his family when he was 12. After a succession of jobs he joined the Pennsylvania Railroad, as a telegraph operator and was quickly promoted. He started investing when only 21, and continued to invest wisely, especially in the burgeoning oil industry. By the time he was 30, he was the principal shareholder in several successful companies, a partner in others, and a respected and powerful businessman and industrialist. After building up the steel industry in Pittsburgh, he sold it to J. P. Morgan, and devoted the rest of his life to his philanthropic activities and writing.

KEY THINKING

- Carnegie epitomizes the rags to riches story, a poor immigrant who started his career in a cotton mill when he was 13, working long hours for just US$1.20 a week.
- During the American Civil War, he developed production to aid the provision of munitions to the Union, and later became the first mass producer of railroad lines.
- He established and then dominated the American steel industry.
- He became friends with poets, philosophers, business leaders, and statesmen, and himself became a major player on the political scene.
- Carnegie made US$225,639,000 from selling his business to J. P. Morgan, making him one of the wealthiest men in the world.
- Even before he made his fortune, Carnegie had resolved to give away money if he became rich, as he thought that the rich had a moral obligation to be benevolent.

IN PERSPECTIVE

- He started investing at a young age with the help of his employer at Pennsylvania Railroad Company.
- Bought the Homestead Steel Works in 1888, which helped form part of Carnegie Steel Company, and acquired other specialized companies that eventually became the United States Steel Corporation.
- Carnegie's reputation was affected by accusations of strikebreaking at the Homestead Works in 1892, when the unions fought a pay cut, which resulted in an extended lock-out. Non-unionized workers and detectives were brought in.
- He was bought out by the banker, John Pierpont Morgan, who envisioned a single US-wide, steel-producing organization that could ensure lower prices and better wages.
- Carnegie started writing and contributing to magazines and periodicals, and wrote *Triumphant Democracy*, which examined the progress America had made in society and industry.
- In *The Gospel of Wealth*, he considered the role of the wealthy businessmen in society. He felt that all personal monies above what was needed to live should be used for the benefit of the community.
- During his lifetime, he reportedly gave away more than US$350 million.
- In 1908, he commissioned Napoleon Hill to research a book on how the wealthy had made their fortune, which was successfully published after Carnegie's death as *The Law of Success*, and *Think and Grow Rich*, which are regularly reissued.
- His name lives on in the institutions and awards he founded, such as the Carnegie Corporation of New York, Carnegie Hall in New York, the Carnegie Endowment for International Peace, Carnegie Mellon University, the Carnegie Museum of Art in Pittsburgh (which awards the Carnegie Prize), the Carnegie Museum of Natural History, the Carnegie Medal for literature, and the Carnegie Hero Fund.

MORE INFO

Books:

Carnegie, Andrew, and Gordon Hutner. *The Autobiography of Andrew Carnegie and the Gospel of Wealth*. New York: Signet Classics, 2006.
Krass, Peter. *Carnegie*. New York: Wiley, 2002.
Nasaw, David. *Andrew Carnegie*. New York: Penguin Press, 2006.

"No man can become rich without himself enriching others." Andrew Carnegie

  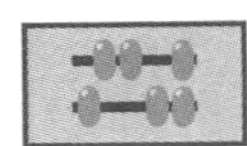 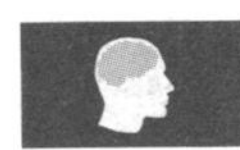  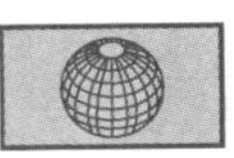   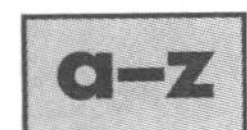

Ronald Harry Coase · Influential economist and social policy innovator

1910 Born in London, England.
1931 Received BSc in economics from the London School of Economics.
1932 Taught at Dundee School of Economics & Commerce.
1937 Published seminal paper on "The nature of the firm."
1938 Appointed lecturer at the London School of Economics.
1947 Appointed reader at the London School of Economics.
1950 Publication of *British Broadcasting: A Study in Monopoly*.
1951 Received PhD in economics from the University of London.
1951 Moved to the United States.
1951 Taught at the University of Buffalo.
1958 Worked at the Center for Advanced Study in the Behavioral Sciences at Stanford University.
1959 Started teaching at the University of Virginia.
1961 Published key paper on "The problem of social cost."
1964 Appointed to the faculty of the Law School at the University of Chicago.
1964 Appointed editor of the *Journal of Law and Economics*.
1977 Appointed senior research fellow at the Hoover Institution, Stanford University.
1991 Appointed visiting distinguished professor at the University of Kansas.
1991 Awarded the Nobel Memorial Prize in Economic Sciences.
1996 Became founding president of the International Society for New Institutional Economics.

LIFE AND CAREER

Ronald Coase is an economist and author, and is the Professor Emeritus of Economics at the University of Chicago Law School. In the early 1940s, he entered government service before becoming an academic in England and then the United States. He has written several crucial papers that have helped the development of economic theory and practice. He won the Nobel Prize in Economics for discovering and explaining the significance of transaction costs and property rights for the institutional structure and functioning of the economy. He is Research Adviser to the Ronald Coase Institute, and his current work focuses on the nature of the firm, producers' expectations, and natural monopolies. He has received many honorary degrees, and is a Fellow of the British Academy, the European Academy, and the American Academy of Arts and Sciences.

KEY THINKING

- Coase is best known for two articles: "The nature of the firm," which introduces the concept of transaction costs to explain the size of firms, and "The problem of social cost," which discusses where to apportion the blame for externalities.
- He takes an approach to economic problems which starts with observation and attempts to understand why things operate as they do, before putting together a working theory.
- His transaction costs approach is influential in modern organizational theory.

IN PERSPECTIVE

- Coase's paper on "The nature of the firm" was to establish the field of transaction cost economics. It explains why the economy is populated by a number of business firms, instead of being only made up of many independent, self-employed people who contract with one another.
- He considers that firms are similar to centrally planned economies, but that firms are formed voluntarily, through people making choices based on "transaction costs."
- The paper on "The problem of social cost" set out what became the *Coase Theorem* and a new field in economic research, law and economics; it is one of the most cited papers in economics.
- He wrote the paper after criticism from a number of senior economists about his theories on the rationale of a property rights system; he met up with them, persuaded them he was right, and they asked him to write up his views for publication.
- He made a crucial contribution to economic debate with the *Coase Conjecture*, which argues that a monopoly in durable goods does not have market power because the monopolist is unable to commit to not lowering its prices in future periods.
- He played a key role in reform of the policy for allocation of the electromagnetic spectrum, due to his paper on "The Federal Communications Commission."

MORE INFO

Books:

Coase, R. H. *The Firm, the Market, and the Law*. Chicago, IL: University of Chicago Press, 1988.

Coase, R. H. *Essays on Economics and Economists*. Chicago, IL: University Of Chicago Press, 1994.

Medema, Steven G. (ed). *The Legacy of Ronald Coase in Economic Analysis*. Aldershot, UK: Edward Elgar, 1995.

Website:

Ronald Coase Institute: www.ronaldcoase.org

"If you torture the data long enough, it will confess." Ronald Harry Coase

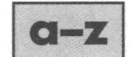

John C. Cox · One of the vanguards of options modeling

1975 Received PhD from the Wharton School at the University of Pennsylvania.
1976 Developed the Cox–Ross–Rubinstein binomial model for options pricing.
1985 Published the Cox–Ingersoll–Ross term-structure model.
1998 Received the IAFE/Infinity Financial Engineer of the Year award.

LIFE AND CAREER

John Cox is an academic and leading theorist on the pricing of derivatives. He was at the forefront of the revolution in options modeling in the 1970s. He is the Nomura Professor of Finance at the Sloan School of Management at MIT, and has been a consultant for a number of securities firms. He has also served as an adviser to government agencies in several countries.

KEY THINKING

- Cox has made a significant contribution to the development of financial engineering technology.
- His work with Stephen Ross explored the foundations of option valuation and established the principle of risk-neutral valuation.
- He is known as one of the developers of the influential Cox–Ross–Rubinstein binomial model for the pricing of options.
- In the mid-1970s, Cox, Stephen Ross of MIT, and Jon Ingersoll of Yale University published a number of papers that led to the Cox–Ingersoll–Ross term-structure model, which provided a consistent approach to the valuation of interest-rate derivatives.
- In a paper co-authored with Fischer Black in 1976, he examined how bond provisions can bring about a firm's bankruptcy or reorganization, one of the first to deal with default premiums and credit spreads.
- In a 1981 article, Cox argued that forward and futures prices will not necessarily be identical.
- In the late 1980s, Cox solved a long-standing problem in portfolio theory with Chi-fu Huang.
- He has studied the use of option technology to analyze corporate securities and intertemporal portfolio policies.

IN PERSPECTIVE

- The Cox–Ross–Rubinstein model became popular due to its relative simplicity and flexibility in that it uses a "discrete-time" model of the varying price over time of the underlying financial instrument, and can be applied to the pricing of American as well as European options.
- The model was built on earlier work on Poisson models by Cox and Ross, and the Cox–Ingersoll–Ross model for the term structure of interest rates.
- The model allowed a better understanding of how derivative securities are priced, as it is based on the fact that investor risk preferences played no part in the pricing of derivatives—the concept of risk-neutral pricing.
- Although there are now computational alternatives to the Cox–Ross–Rubinstein model, the model is still popular due to its value as a teaching tool.
- Cox has also developed a simple numerical scheme for valuing American options that is used by most firms dealing in equity derivatives.
- For dynamic investment strategies, he has examined how best to manage a portfolio over time to meet specific objectives.
- His later research in asset pricing led to a widely used model of the term structure of interest rates.

MORE INFO

Book:

Cox, John C., and Mark Rubinstein. *Options Markets*. Englewood Cliffs, NJ: Prentice Hall, 1985. One of the first popular derivatives textbooks, it examines the options markets in terms of theoretical research and actual trading strategies for puts and calls.

See Also:

Stephen A. Ross (p. 1302)

"Sometimes a little thinking can prevent a lot of misguided math, and sometimes a little math can prevent a lot of misguided thinking." John C. Cox

   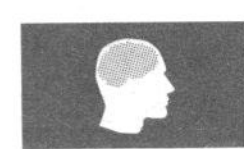  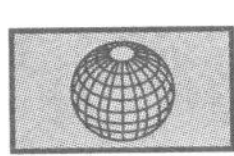   

Herman Daly · The founding father of ecological economics

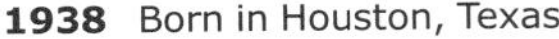

1938 Born in Houston, Texas.
1967 Received doctorate in economics from Vanderbilt University.
1968 Appointed associate professor at Louisiana State University.
1973 Appointed professor at Louisiana State University.
1976 Received the Distinguished Research Master Award from Louisiana State University.
1977 Publication of *Steady-State Economics*.
1983 Appointed alumni professor of economics at Louisiana State University.
1988 Appointed senior economist in the Environment Department of the World Bank.
1989 Publication of *For the Common Good*, which he coauthored.
1994 Appointed senior research scholar, School of Public Affairs, University of Maryland.
1996 Received the Right Livelihood Award.
1996 Received the Heineken Prize for Environmental Science, awarded by the Royal Netherlands Academy of Arts and Sciences.
1996 Publication of *Beyond Growth*.
1999 Publication of *Ecological Economics and the Ecology of Economics*.
2001 Received the Leontief Prize.
2007 Publication of *Ecological Economics and Sustainable Development*.
2008 Named Man of the Year by *Adbusters* magazine.
2010 Received a lifetime achievement award from the National Council for Science and the Environment.

LIFE AND CAREER

Herman Daly has been a greatly influential figure in the development of the interdisciplinary field of ecological economics through his research and study of economic development, sustainability, population, resources, and the environment, and the publication of over 100 articles in scholarly journals and magazines. Although remaining in academia throughout his career, he also worked at the World Bank, where he helped to develop policy guidelines related to sustainable development, and cofounded the International Society for Ecological Economics, and was associate editor of its journal, *Ecological Economics*.

KEY THINKING

- While studying under Nicholas Georgescu-Roegen, he analyzed limitations to economic growth, welfare economics, ecology, and sustainable development to produce a theory of steady-state economics.
- Daly argued that environmental costs must be reflected in the market prices of goods and services, and proposed that a sort of "steady state" can be achieved in which the burden caused by economic production does not exceed the natural capacity of the environment.
- He produced many specific policy proposals for moving to a steady-state economy, including ecological tax reform, limiting inequality in income distribution, freeing up working times to allow for greater flexibility, and re-regulating international commerce.
- He also helped to develop ecological economics, arguing that human economy is embedded in nature and that economic processes are actually biological, physical, and chemical processes and transformations.
- In *For the Common Good* with theologian John Cobb, he examined the consequences of economics moving from an academic discipline to one that is engaged with the real world.
- In *Beyond Growth*, which received worldwide attention, he discussed the impact of unchecked growth on a finite planet and how a sustainable future could be achieved.

IN PERSPECTIVE

- His controversial views on economic growth and environmental protection for sustainable development meant that Daly was seen by many as a maverick.
- He is widely credited with originating the concept of uneconomic growth through his research on environmental problems related to macroeconomic activity.
- He was a key figure in helping ecological economics to become a discipline in its own right, separate from environmental economics.
- He proposed that a sustainable world cannot be achieved through constant growth, but that the focus should be on community rather than the individual, on steady-state economics, the introduction of ecological taxation, and a rejection of free trade.
- At the World Bank, he argued that it is possible to create environmentally sustainable development through a number of means, such as countries taxing labor and income less, maximizing the productivity of natural capital in the short run, and investing in increasing its supply in the long run.
- He sees globalization as a major obstacle to recognizing and addressing the problem of uneconomic growth, and a return to the nation state as a way of avoiding the oligopoly of trading blocs.
- In recent years, Daly has also focused on economic welfare and its measurement, producing the important *Index of Sustainable Economic Welfare*.

MORE INFO

Books:

Daly, Herman E. *Steady-State Economics: The Economics of Biophysical Equilibrium and Moral Growth*. San Francisco, CA: W. H. Freeman, 1977.
Daly, Herman E. *Beyond Growth: The Economics of Sustainable Development*. Boston, MA: Beacon Press, 1996.
Daly, Herman E. *Ecological Economics and Sustainable Development: Selected Essays of Herman Daly*. Cheltenham, UK: Edward Elgar, 2007.

"There is something fundamentally wrong in treating the Earth as if it were a business in liquidation." Herman Daly

  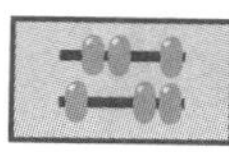 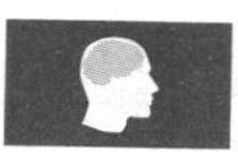  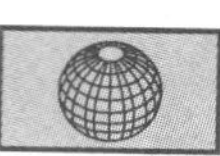  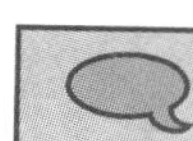 

Joseph de la Vega · Author of *Confusion of Confusions*, the oldest book on the stock exchange business

1650 Born in Espejo, Spain.
1673 Publication of the play *Pardes Shoshannim*.
1683 Publication of *Triumphos del Aguyla y Eclypses de la Luna*.
1683 Publication of *La Rosa, Panegyrico Sacro, Hécho en la Insigne Academia de los Sitibundos*.
1684 Publication of *Rumbos Peligrosos por Donde Navega con Titulo de Novelas la Cosobrante Nave de la Temeridad*.
1685 Publication of *Discursos Academicos, Morales, Retoricos, y Sagrados Que Recitó en la Florida Academia de los Floridos*.
1688 Publication of *Confusion of Confusions*.
1690 Publication of *Retrato de la Prudencia, y Simulacro del Valor, al Augusto Monarca Guilielmo Tercero, Rey do la Gran Bretaña*.
1692 Died in Amsterdam.

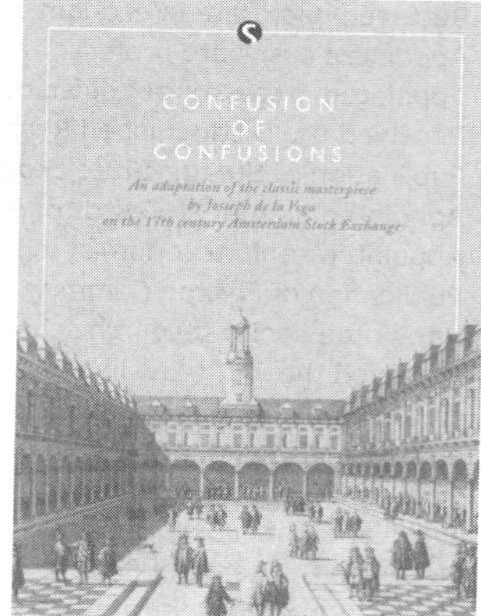

LIFE AND CAREER

Joseph de la Vega (also known as Joseph Penso) was a businessman, writer, and philanthropist who lived in 17th century Amsterdam in a community of Portuguese Jews whose ancestors had fled the Spanish Inquisition. He wrote his first play, *Pardes Shoshannim*, when only 18 and went on to become a respected merchant, and a Spanish poet. He became famous for his masterpiece, *Confusion of Confusions*, the oldest book ever written about stock exchanges. He was elected to several posts in the Jewish, and in the financial communities, including the honorary offices of President of the Academia de los Sitibundos, and Secretary of the Academia de los Floridos. He maintained an extensive correspondence with a number of sovereigns, and other prominent contemporaries.

KEY THINKING

- De la Vega's best-known work, *Confusion of Confusions*, consists of a series of dialogues between a philosopher, a merchant, and a shareholder, describing the workings of the Amsterdam Stock Exchange, the world's first stock exchange.
- It provides a context and understanding of the market participants, the intricacies of speculation and trading, and the financial instruments used at the time, while displaying an affection for the market and its greedy speculators.
- He presents four rules of speculation that are still relevant today: never advise anyone to buy or sell shares; accept both your profits and losses; profits from share dealing never last; you need both money and patience.

IN PERSPECTIVE

- *Confusion of Confusions* was one of the first analytical attempts to describe the different kinds of financial operations taking place at the time. It explores the impact of crowd behavior, and trading trickery on the financial markets.
- Describes the diverse tactics and schemes used by investors playing the Amsterdam market, even though there were only two stocks being traded—the Dutch East India Company and the Dutch West India Company—businesses that depended on risk-laden expeditions around the world.
- He shows that, even then, there were bulls, bears, panics, bubbles, short selling, margin trading, and most of the other features of modern exchanges.
- Discusses trading operations that were complex, involving both options and forward trades; such trading was used both to hedge, and to speculate.
- Shows how many facets of investing are timeless, as he recognizes the value of information and analysis, and how speculators tend to be either optimists or pessimists; de la Vega's advice is to maintain a balance between the two.
- Explains how government regulation banned short selling, but that this was ignored as short sellers were often needed to make markets.

MORE INFO

Book:

Mackay, Charles, and Joseph de la Vega. *Extraordinary Popular Delusions and the Madness of Crowds* and *Confusión de Confusiones*. New York: Wiley, 1996. The two classics combined in one volume, with a translation of De la Vega's first-hand account of the market manipulations of the Amsterdam Stock Exchange.

See Also:

Confusión de Confusiones (p. 1342)

"What really matters is an awareness of how greed and fear can drive rational people to behave in strange ways when they gather in the marketplace." Joseph de la Vega

W. Edwards Deming · The quality and productivity pioneer

1900 Born in Sioux City, Iowa.
1921 Received BSc in electrical engineering from the University of Wyoming.
1925 Received MS in mathematics and physics from the University of Colorado.
1927 Worked as a mathematical physicist at the US Department of Agriculture.
1928 Received PhD in mathematics and physics from Yale University.
1939 Appointed a statistical adviser to the US Census Bureau.
1946 Appointed professor of statistics at New York University.
1947 Worked in Japan on its national census of 1951.
1950 Appointed assistant to the supreme commander of the Allied Powers.
1960 Awarded the Japanese Order of the Sacred Treasure, Second Class.
1982 Publication of *Quality, Productivity, and Competitive Position*.
1986 Publication of *Out of the Crisis*.
1987 Awarded the National Medal of Technology.
1988 Taught at Columbia University's Graduate School of Business.
1988 Received Distinguished Career in Science award from National Academy of Sciences.
1993 Founded the W. Edwards Deming Institute.
1993 Publication of *The New Economics for Industry, Government, Education*.
1993 Died in Washington, DC.

LIFE AND CAREER

W. Edwards Deming was raised on a farm before studying at the University of Wyoming. He went on to do a PhD at Yale while doing an internship at Bell Telephone Laboratories, and then worked at the US Department of Agriculture and the Census Department. He was a census consultant to the Japanese government and taught statistical process control methods to Japanese business leaders, working for many years as a consultant in Japan. He later moved back to the United States, becoming a professor in New York and operating as an independent consultant in Washington, DC. He was also a keen musician and singer, and composed choral compositions and arrangements. He was largely unknown in the United States until a 1980 documentary about industrial competition the country was facing from Japan resulted in greater recognition and demand for his services.

KEY THINKING

- Deming created new methods to help people work together better, allowing individuals and organizations to plan and continually improve themselves, their relationships, processes, products, and services through cooperation and continual improvement.
- His innovations in the workplace included concepts such as pleasing the customer, partnering with suppliers, empowering workers, managing for quality, and eliminating layers of management and hierarchy.
- While in Japan he trained hundreds of engineers, managers, and scholars in statistical process control (SPC) and new concepts of quality as tools for monitoring and controlling variation in processes such as goods manufacture, testing, and statistics.
- In *Out of the Crisis* he presented a theory of management based on his famous 14 points for management, arguing that failing to plan for the future brings significant loss of market and jobs.
- Deming also examined the recurring problems that we experience every day in life, leading him to develop his "red bead experiment" as a learning tool.
- He continued to focus on the impact of nonfinancial measures and the importance of quality, arguing that managers spend too much time analyzing figures and not enough time on the intangibles that really matter.

IN PERSPECTIVE

- Deming was a statistician, academic, writer, and consultant and is widely credited with developing total quality management (TQM) techniques, facilitating the rise of Japan as a manufacturing nation and improving industrial production in the United States during the Cold War.
- He was originally inspired by the work of Walter Shewhart at Bell Telephone Laboratories, especially by his ideas on the causes of variation, helping Deming to develop his management theories.
- Deming extended Shewhart's ideas to manufacturing and management processes, greatly influencing the economics of the industrialized world in the second half of the 20th century.
- He helped the Ford Motor Company to start a quality movement in their operations through questioning the company's culture and management.
- When Japanese manufacturers applied his techniques, the improved quality combined with the lowered cost created an upsurge in demand for Japanese products.
- The Union of Japanese Scientists and Engineers (JUSE) later established the Deming Prize, which continues to greatly influence the development of quality control and management in Japan.

MORE INFO

Books:

Deming, W. Edwards. *Out of the Crisis*. Cambridge, MA: Massachusetts Institute of Technology, 1986.
Deming, W. Edwards. *The New Economics for Industry, Government, Education*. Cambridge, MA: Massachusetts Institute of Technology, 1994.
Voehl, Frank (ed). *Deming: The Way We Knew Him*. Boca Raton, FL: CRC Press, 1995.

Website:
W. Edwards Deming Institute: deming.org

"No one has to change. Survival is optional." W. Edwards Deming

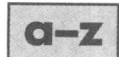

Marc Faber · Contrarian investor and market predictor

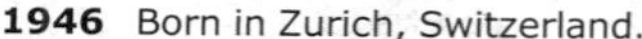

1946 Born in Zurich, Switzerland.
1970 Received PhD in economics from the University of Zurich.
1970 Started work for White Weld & Co. Ltd in New York, Zurich, and Hong Kong.
1973 Moved to Hong Kong.
1978 Appointed managing director at Drexel Burnham Lambert (HK) Ltd.
1990 Founded Marc Faber Ltd.
2002 Publication of *Tomorrow's Gold: Asia's Age of Discovery*.

LIFE AND CAREER

Marc Faber is an economic historian, investment analyst, entrepreneur, and writer. He went to school in Geneva and Zurich, and studied Economics at the University of Zurich. He went on to be a trader and managing director of Drexel Burnham Lambert when the firm was the junk-bond king of Wall Street. He later set up his own business to act as an investment adviser, and fund manager. He is board director of numerous companies, including Ivanhoe Mines. He is also a regular speaker at various investment seminars, and a regular contributor to several leading financial publications around the world. He is now based in Thailand, and publishes a monthly investment newsletter, *The Gloom, Boom & Doom Report*, under the name Dr Doom. He became well known for advising his clients to get out of the stock market one week before the October 1987 crash.

KEY THINKING

- Marc Faber is known for his contrarian investment approach, and he runs his own company based on the same philosophy.
- A regular speaker on the investment circuit, often in the financial press for his non-conformist viewpoint and alternative investment philosophy, he specializes in the Asian markets, and focuses on advising clients on investments that have great potential.
- He is a regular contributor to several leading publications, including the *Herald Tribune*, the *Wall Street Journal*, *Forbes*, and *International Wealth*, as well as several websites.
- His market predictions have been timely: in 1987, he warned his clients to cash out a week before Black Monday on Wall Street; in 1990, he forecast the bursting of the Japanese Bubble; in 1993, he correctly predicted the collapse in US gaming stocks; and in 1997, he foresaw the Asia–Pacific financial crisis.

IN PERSPECTIVE

- He invests and acts as a fund manager to private wealthy clients, and publishes a monthly investment newsletter, *The Gloom, Boom & Doom Report*, which highlights unusual investment opportunities.
- He has given many interviews that reflect his bearish views on a wide variety of investments, including stocks, real estate, and commodities.
- He takes a bearish approach to the long-term outlook for the US dollar, as he believes that the Fed is oversupplying money, which has a negative impact on inflation, and is bad for the value of the currency.
- Since 2000, he has accurately predicted the rise of oil, precious metals, and other commodities, as well as the slide of US dollar from 2002, and various mini-corrections since then.
- He predicted the peak of the US housing bubble earlier than most, and now foresees a new wave of credit collapses across the world.
- In his book, *Tomorrow's Gold: Asia's Age of Discovery*, he predicted the rise of the Chinese market and economy.
- He has been successful in forecasting the performance of US equities over the past few years, and he remains pessimistic about the prospects for the American economy and stock market.
- Believes that there are few value investments still around, except for farmland, and real estate in some emerging markets, such as Argentina and Vietnam.

MORE INFO

Books:

Faber, Marc. *Tomorrow's Gold: Asia's Age of Discovery*. Hong Kong: CLSA, 2003.
A bestselling account of Faber's search for the outperforming asset classes of the future, based on historical analysis, and charting how old investor trends developed. Also assesses how new patterns might emerge.

Vittachi, Nury. *Riding the Millennial Storm: Marc Faber's Path to Profit in the Financial Markets*. Singapore: Wiley, 1998. Discusses Faber's life, investment techniques, and financial predictions.

Website:

Marc Faber Ltd, including the *Gloom, Boom & Doom Report*: www.gloomboomdoom.com

"A mania is a mania, and the experts are caught in it just as the public is." Marc Faber

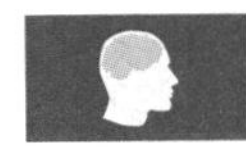

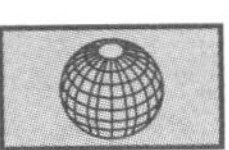

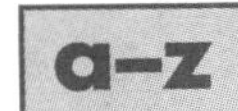

Eugene Fama · Author of the efficient markets hypothesis

1939 Born in Boston, Massachusetts.
1960 Receives a BA from Tufts University.
1963 Received MBA from University of Chicago, Graduate School of Business.
1964 Received PhD from University of Chicago, Graduate School of Business.
1968 Appointed professor of finance, University of Chicago, Graduate School of Business.
1972 Publication of *The Theory of Finance*.
1973 Appointed professor of finance, University of Chicago, Graduate School of Business.
1975 Appointed visiting professor, Catholic University of Leuven and European Institute for Advanced Studies in Management, Belgium.
1982 Appointed visiting professor, Anderson Graduate School of Management, University of California.
1982 Joined board of directors, Dimensional Fund Advisors.
1984 Appointed distinguished service professor of Finance Graduate School of Business, University of Chicago.
2001 Became the first elected fellow of the American Finance Association.
2005 Received the Deutsche Bank Prize in Financial Economics.
2007 Received the Morgan Stanley American Finance Association Award for Excellence in Finance, and the Fred Arditti Innovation Award.
2009 Received the Onassis Prize in Finance.

LIFE AND CAREER

Eugene Fama was a tenured professor at the University of Chicago before he was 30, where he taught portfolio theory before modern finance became established. He has spent his career at the Graduate School of Business, University of Chicago, where he revolutionized thinking on the efficient markets hypothesis, and where he is now Chairman of its Center for Research in Security Prices. He is also Director of Research at Dimensional Fund Advisors, and is an advisory editor of the *Journal of Financial Economics*. He was the first elected Fellow of the American Finance Association, and is also a Fellow of the Econometric Society and the American Academy of Arts and Sciences. He has received numerous honorary degrees, and was the co-winner of the Smith Breeden Prize for the best paper in the *Journal of Finance* in 1992, and received the first Deutsche Bank Prize in Financial Economics in 2005.

KEY THINKING

- Eugene Fama is a prolific author and researcher, having written two books, and published more than 100 articles in academic journals. He is among the most cited of America's financial researchers.
- He is identified with research on markets, particularly with regard to developments in the efficient market hypothesis, and the random walk theory, as well as his work on portfolio theory and asset pricing, both theoretical and empirical.
- Coined the term "efficient markets theory" in a 1970 paper on efficient capital markets, arguing that it is practically impossible for someone to consistently beat the stock market because of the wide availability of information.
- He was the first of many to study how stock prices respond to an event, using price data from a newly available database.
- Focuses much of his study on the relation between risk and return, and the implications for portfolio management.
- Has also made innovations in how we understand the functioning of markets, asset pricing theory, and corporate finance.

IN PERSPECTIVE

- He helped popularize the efficient market hypothesis, and the random walk theory.
- The efficient market hypothesis evolved from his PhD thesis, and suggested that stock markets are efficient because securities will be appropriately priced, and reflect all available information in a market with well-informed investors.
- The random walk theory was discussed in one of his papers, concluding that stock price movements are unpredictable, and follow a random walk.
- His work on efficient markets proposed two key improvements, by classifying three types of efficiency—strong form, semi-strong form, and weak efficiency—and by identifying the notion of market efficiency with the model of market equilibrium.
- His work on the efficiency of markets has helped create many new finance products, and aided the development of new futures contracts for hedging risks.
- He has written a series of papers with Kenneth French that question the validity of the capital asset pricing model (CAPM), as not taking into account market capitalization and book value to market value.
- In portfolio management, Fama and French also developed a successful three-factor model to describe market behavior.

MORE INFO

Books:

Fama, Eugene F. *Foundations of Finance: Portfolio Decisions and Securities Prices*. New York: Basic Books, 1976. A readable introduction to financial theory that examines stocks and portfolios in great detail.

Fama, Eugene F., and Merton H. Miller. *The Theory of Finance*. New York: Holt, Rinehart and Winston, 1972. Provides a systematic grounding in basic financial theory.

See Also:

The Theory of Finance (p. 1423)

"In an efficient market at any point in time the actual price of a security will be a good estimate of its intrinsic value."

Eugene Fama

  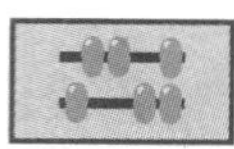 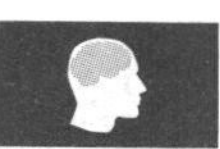     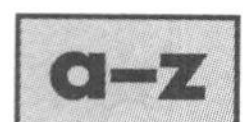

Irving Fisher · Renowned neoclassical economist of the early 20th century

1867 Born in Saugerties, New York.
1888 Received BA from Yale University.
1891 Received PhD in economics from Yale University.
1892 Appointed professor of mathematics at Yale University.
1895 Appointed professor of political economy at Yale University.
1906 Publication of *The Nature of Capital and Income.*
1907 Publication of *The Rate of Interest.*
1910 Publication of *Introduction to Economic Science.*
1912 Became a scientific adviser to the Eugenics Record Office.
1928 Publication of *Money Illusion.*
1929 Appointed professor of economics at Yale University.
1930 Publication of *The Stock Market Crash and After.*
1930 Publication of *The Theory of Interest.*
1895 Appointed professor emeritus at Yale University.
1947 Died in New York.

LIFE AND CAREER

Irving Fisher was a mathematical economist, and a pioneer of neoclassical economics and modern behavioral economics, who contributed to the fields of economics, mathematics, statistics, demography, public health and sanitation, and public affairs. He was the first to earn a PhD in Economics from Yale University, where he taught for his entire academic life. He was also a prolific writer covering a wide array of topics. He was best known for his research on the theory of interest, and capital theory. He lost much of his personal wealth and damaged his reputation in the 1929 Wall Street Crash, after reassuring investors that stock prices were not over-inflated, but were on a new, permanent plateau. He was also a health campaigner, and eugenicist.

KEY THINKING

- He had several concepts named after him, including the Fisher equation, the Fisher hypothesis, and the Fisher separation theorem.
- The Fisher equation estimates the relationship between nominal and real interest rates under inflation, and is used to predict nominal and real interest-rate behavior.
- The Fisher hypothesis proposes that the real interest rate is independent of monetary measures, especially the nominal interest rate.
- The Fisher separation theorem asserts that the firm's investment decisions are independent of the owner's preferences, investment decisions are independent of the financing decision, and that the value of a capital project is independent from methods used to finance the project.
- The International Fisher Effect, which predicts international exchange-rate drift independent of inflation, was also named after him.
- His theories of capital and investment were first presented in *Nature of Capital and Income* and *The Rate of Interest*, and more fully analyzed in his groundbreaking *The Theory of Interest.*
- *The Theory of Interest* examined capital, capital budgeting, credit markets, and the determinants of interest rates, including the rate of inflation, and developed his concept of intertemporal choice.
- His treatment of the *Money Illusion* anticipated later research on the psychology of decision-making by Daniel Kahneman and Amos Tversky; discuss the impact on investors and savers of the tendency to think of currency in nominal, rather than real terms.
- In *The Making of Index Numbers*, he looks at the critical role of index numbers in monetary theory, statistical theory, econometrics, and index number theory.

IN PERSPECTIVE

- Fisher was a central figure of American economics in the first half of the 20th Century, through his analysis of equilibrium price, his theory of capital and investment, his resurrection of the quantity theory of money, the theory of index numbers, the Phillips Curve, and his work on debt deflation.
- He was also one of the first to subject macroeconomic data, including the money stock, interest rates, and price levels, to statistical analysis; in the 1920s, he introduced the technique later called distributed lags.
- He initially made his fortune from inventing an index card system, later known as the Rolodex, but lost it all in the Great Crash.
- Strongly advocated the establishment of a 100% reserve requirement banking system.
- Gained mainstream recognition through his work as a health campaigner and eugenicist, and his bestseller, *How to Live: Rules for Healthful Living Based on Modern Science.*

MORE INFO

Books:

Allen, Robert Loring. *Irving Fisher: A Biography*. Cambridge, MA: Blackwell Publishers, 1993.
Dimand, Roger W., and John Geanakoplos (eds). *Celebrating Irving Fisher: The Legacy of a Great Economist*. Malden, MA: Blackwell, 2005.
Fisher, Irving Norton. *My Father, Irving Fisher.* New York: Comet Press Books, 1956.

"The rate of interest acts as a link between income-value and capital-value." Irving Fisher

  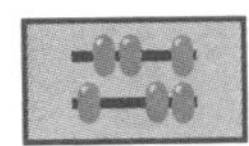 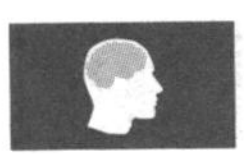     

John Kenneth Galbraith · Leading 20th-century economist and institutionalist

1908 Born in Iona Station, Ontario, Canada.
1931 Received BSc from the Ontario Agricultural College.
1933 Received MSc from the University of California, Berkeley.
1934 Received PhD in agricultural economics from the University of California, Berkeley.
1934 Appointed a tutor at Harvard University.
1939 Taught at Princeton University.
1943 Appointed editor of *Fortune* magazine.
1947 Cofounded Americans for Democratic Action.
1949 Appointed professor of economics at Harvard University.
1952 Publication of *American Capitalism: The Concept of Countervailing Power.*
1954 Publication of *The Great Crash, 1929*.
1958 Publication of *The Affluent Society.*
1961 Appointed US ambassador to India.
1967 Publication of *The New Industrial State*.
1977 Presented *The Age of Uncertainty* for the BBC in the United Kingdom.
1972 Appointed president of the American Economic Association.
1975 Became professor emeritus at Harvard University.
1990 Publication of *A Short History of Financial Euphoria*.
2006 Died in Cambridge, Massachusetts.

LIFE AND CAREER

J. K. Galbraith was one of the most influential and best-known economists and writers of the 20th century. He taught at Harvard and Princeton, before serving as deputy head of the Office of Price Administration during WWII. He was also a leader of the Strategic Bombing Surveys of Europe and Japan, an adviser to post-war administrations in Germany and Japan, and later became US Ambassador to India. During the 1950s and 1960s, his economics books, based on his ideas of liberalism and progressivism, became international best-sellers. As well as teaching at Harvard for many years, he served in the administrations of Franklin D. Roosevelt, Harry Truman, John F. Kennedy, and Lyndon B. Johnson, and was a two-time recipient of the Presidential Medal of Freedom.

KEY THINKING

- Galbraith was a Keynesian economist and liberal, and seen as the rebel of modern economics, due to his advocacy of government spending to combat unemployment, and warnings over the dangers inherent in deregulated markets, corporate greed, and overspending on the military.
- He rejected the technical and mathematical views of neoclassical economics, as being divorced from reality, and argued that most economists were ignoring key areas, such as advertising, corporate ownership, and the influence of government spending.
- In examining the priorities of modern economics, he supported the use of national wealth for public services and not private consumption, the curbing of demand through consumption taxation, and publicly funding education programs aimed at ordinary people.
- He propounded the advantages of countervailing forces in the economy, where groups such as labor unions helped maintain a political and social balance.
- Was also described as the first post-materialist, due to his contention that continually increasing material production was not a sign of economic well-being.

IN PERSPECTIVE

- *The Affluent Society* turned him into a celebrity—it proposed that classical economic theory may have worked for previous eras, but that the rising affluence of the US in the 1950s needed completely new economic theories.
- *American Capitalism* was also a popular success for its critique of the excesses of consumerism, and predictions about the economy becoming dominated by big business, labor, and government.
- In *Economics and the Public Purpose*, he examined the issue of "political capture" by firms, and discussed issues surrounding political processes, public education, and the provision of public goods.
- Followed the views of Thorstein Veblen, that economic activity was not bound by inviolable laws, but was a complicated mix of the cultural and political.
- In *New Industrial State*, he expanded his theory of the firm, arguing that current concepts of the perfectly competitive firm were unsuccessful, but that they were oligopolistic, autonomous institutions vying for market share.
- He was involved in the presidential campaigns of Eugene McCarthy, and George McGovern.
- During the 1980s, he criticized President Reagan and President Bush's policies of trickle-down economics.

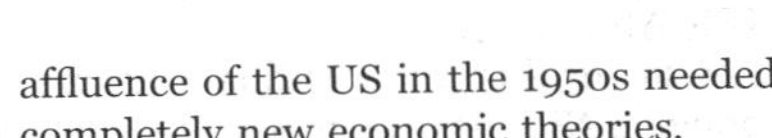

MORE INFO

Books:

Galbraith, John Kenneth. *The Affluent Society*. Boston, MA: Houghton Mifflin, 1958.
Parker, Richard. *John Kenneth Galbraith: His Life, His Politics, His Economics*. New York: Farrar, Straus, and Giroux, 2004.
Stanfield, James Ronald, and Jacqueline Bloom Stanfield (eds). *Interviews with John Kenneth Galbraith*. Jackson, MS: University Press of Mississippi, 2004.

See Also:

The Great Crash, 1929 (p. 1371)

"Trickle-down theory—the less than elegant metaphor that if one feeds the horse enough oats, some will pass through to the road for the sparrows." John Kenneth Galbraith

  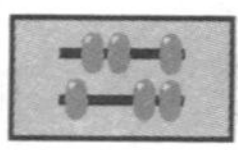 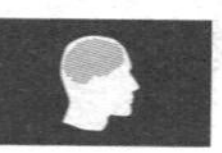     

Nicholas Georgescu-Roegen · The first ecological economist

1906 Born in Constanța, Romania.
1926 Graduated in mathematics from the University of Bucharest.
1930 Received a PhD in statistics and economics from the University of Paris.
1930 Studied at University College London.
1932 Appointed professor of statistics at the University of Bucharest.
1934 Studied at Harvard University.
1948 Fled from Communist-controlled Romania.
1950 Appointed professor at Vanderbilt University, Tennessee.
1966 Publication of *Analytical Economics.*
1971 Publication of *The Entropy Law and the Economic Process.*
1976 Publication of *Energy and Economics Myths: Institutional and Analytical Economic Essays.*
1994 Died in Nashville, Tennessee.

LIFE AND CAREER

After taking his undergraduate degree in Romania, Nicholas Georgescu-Roegen studied in the United Kingdom, France, and the United States before returning to Romania and lecturing at the University of Bucharest. After World War II he held a variety of government posts and was involved in postwar negotiations with the Soviet Union. In 1948 he fled Romania with his wife to avoid arrest by the Communist regime, returning to the United States and becoming a professor at Vanderbilt University, where he stayed until his retirement in 1976. It was there that his work evolved away from neoclassical economics to developing his groundbreaking studies on entropy and ecological economics.

KEY THINKING

- Georgescu-Roegen was the first to formally examine the connection between economic activity and physical laws, demonstrating the thermodynamic foundations of the economic process.
- He is best known for his book *The Entropy Law and the Economic Process*, which proposed that the second law of thermodynamics—the law of entropy—governs economic processes and systems and suggests that an economy faces limits to growth for much the same reasons that useful energy is dissipated.
- In it he also argued that the economic process transforms natural resources into waste—that is, transforms matter/energy from a state of low entropy into a state of high entropy.
- This significant contribution to economics was a building block for his later theories on bioeconomics and ecological economics.
- *Analytical Economics* presents many of the essays that gained him recognition as a pioneer in successfully combining the fields of economics, mathematics, and statistics.
- He helped to formulate a critique of neoclassical production functions and is known for discovering the nonsubstitution theorem and the Hawkins–Simon condition.

IN PERSPECTIVE

- Georgescu-Roegen was a mathematician, statistician, and economist who helped reunite economics with its biophysical foundations.
- His work is usually divided into two categories, his earlier work on consumer and production theory, such as the integrability problem, and his later focus on entropy and bioeconomics.
- As a Rockefeller Fellow at Harvard in the 1930s, he studied under the economist Joseph Schumpeter, who turned him into an economist.
- While at Harvard, he contributed to the theory of choice in "The pure theory of consumer's behavior," a paper that helped to launch his career.
- In 1951 he contributed three important chapters to the renowned monograph by the Cowles Commission on linear programming and general equilibrium.
- He examined problems of the hedonistic valuation framework of neoclassical economics, the conflict between social and hedonistic valuation, and the conflict between individual, social, and environmental values.
- He later became highly critical of neoclassical economics, as he focused on issues of valuation, resource scarcity, and the distribution of economic output.
- He developed a comprehensive theory of economy, society, and biophysical constraints, a new approach to bioeconomics that was based on an understanding of the biophysical and social context of consumption and production.
- In *Analytical Economics* he developed his ideas on a new biological or evolutionary approach to economic theory.

MORE INFO

Books:

Georgescu-Roegen, Nicholas. *The Entropy Law and the Economic Process*. Cambridge, MA: Harvard University Press, 1971. This classic text of ecological and evolutionary economics discusses the key role that the second law of thermodynamics plays in production theory, with implications for the sustainability of economic growth.

Mayumi, Kozo. *The Origins of Ecological Economics: The Bioeconomics of Georgescu-Roegen*. London: Routledge, 2001. This in-depth examination of Georgescu-Roegen's career and theories, written by a protégé, explores his market models and theoretical approaches on the environment and consumer.

Article:

Gowdy, John, and Susan Mesner. "The evolution of Georgescu-Roegen's bioeconomics." *Review of Social Economy* 56:2 (Summer 1998): 136–156. Online at: dx.doi.org/10.1080/00346769800000016. This paper examines the development of Georgescu-Roegen's writings on valuation, and the environmental and social policy recommendations that arise out of his bioeconomic framework.

"Only economists still put the cart before the horse by claiming that the growing turmoil of mankind can be eliminated if prices are right. The truth is that only if our values are right will prices also be so." Nicholas Georgescu-Roegen

  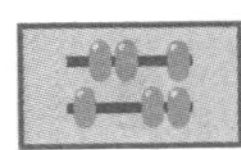 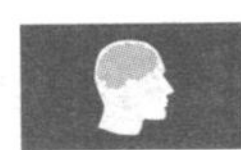  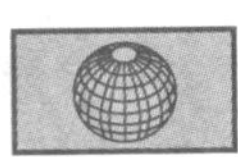   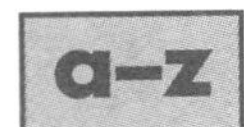

Benjamin Graham · The father of modern security analysis

1894 Born in London.
1895 Moved to New York with his family.
1914 Graduated from Columbia University.
1926 Formed an investment partnership with Jerome Newman.
1926 Started lecturing on finance at Columbia University Business School.
1934 Publication of *Security Analysis.*
1937 Publication of *The Interpretation of Financial Statements.*
1937 Publication of *Storage and Stability: A Modern Ever-normal Granary.*
1944 Publication of *World Commodities and World Currency.*
1949 Publication of *The Intelligent Investor.*
1956 Retired from the faculty of Columbia University Business School.
1976 Died.

LIFE AND CAREER

Benjamin Graham was an economist and investor who defended rigorous security analysis throughout his career. He studied at Columbia University, but declined a teaching position to be a chalker on Wall Street with Newburger, Henderson and Loeb. Bright and ambitious, he was soon undertaking financial research for the firm, and was eventually made a partner. Although the market crash of 1929 almost wiped him out, Graham continued to make useful returns for the firm, while also writing investment books, and lecturing at Columbia. He was a strong advocate of financial analysis training, and helped found the Chartered Financial Analyst (CFA) program. Warren Buffett studied under him at Columbia, and asked him for an investing job, which Graham eventually gave him, starting Buffett on his career.

KEY THINKING

- Graham revolutionized investment thinking by introducing the concepts of security analysis, fundamental analysis, and value investing.
- His books expanded on the definition of a cheap company, based on a principle of "margin of safety." His preference for value investing was based on investors seeking out bargains among undervalued companies, buying into them, and then waiting for their fair value to be realized.
- Two of his books, *Security Analysis* and *The Intelligent Investor*, are considered the bibles for both individual investors, and financial professionals.
- Created an imaginary investor called Mr Market to demonstrate his views about wise investing, and choosing stocks based on their fundamental value rather than because of advice or market direction.

IN PERSPECTIVE

- In *Security Analysis*, he presented his principles of value-oriented investment, using fundamentals in guiding the valuation of securities; he extended this approach in his books, *Interpretation of Financial Statements* and the *Intelligent Investor*.
- Distinguished between the passive and the active investor. The former invests cautiously, looks for value stocks and buys for the long term, while the active investor takes more time getting to know companies to find the best buys in the market.
- Recommended that investors spend time and effort to analyze the financial state of companies.
- Criticized corporations that produced unhelpful financial reports, which hid the real state of their finances from potential investors.
- Advocated dividend payments for shareholders, instead of firms keeping all of their profits as retained earnings. Dividends, he argued, indicated that a company was profitable, and could offer a return even if its stock was performing poorly.
- Popularized the examination of price-to-earnings ratios, debt-to-equity ratios, dividend records, net current assets, book values, and earnings growth.
- In *Storage and Stability*, he examined wider economic issues, such as the effect of deflation on farmers, workers, and producers, and proposed the creation of pools of commodities to act as buffer stocks against general price deflation.
- In *World Commodities and World Currency*, he proposed an international "commodity standard," where macroeconomic policies would focus on a general basket of commodities, a concept supported by Keynes, Hayek, and Friedman.

MORE INFO

Books:

Au, Thomas P. *A Modern Approach to Graham and Dodd Investing*. Hoboken, NJ: Wiley, 2004.

Graham, Benjamin. *The Intelligent Investor: A Book of Practical Counsel*. New York: Harper, 1949.

Graham, Benjamin. *Benjamin Graham, the Memoirs of the Dean of Wall Street*. New York: McGraw-Hill, 1996.

Lowe, Janet. *The Rediscovered Benjamin Graham: Selected Writings of the Wall Street Legend*. New York: Wiley, 1999.

Website:

Advice and information on investing using Graham's techniques: www.grahaminvestor.com

See Also:

The Intelligent Investor (p. 1377)

"Wall Street people learn nothing and forget everything." Benjamin Graham

  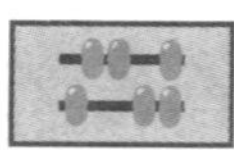      

Alan Greenspan · The longest-serving chairman of the US Federal Reserve

1926 Born in New York.
1948 Received BS in economics from New York University.
1948 Appointed an economic analyst at the Conference Board.
1950 Received MA in economics from New York University.
1955 Appointed chairman and president of Townsend-Greenspan & Co. Inc.
1968 Appointed coordinator of domestic policy for Richard Nixon's nomination campaign.
1974 Appointed chairman of the Council of Economic Advisers.
1977 Received PhD from New York University.
1982 Appointed director of the Council on Foreign Relations.
1987 Appointed chairman of the Board of Governors of the Federal Reserve Board.
2002 Made Knight Commander of the Order of the British Empire (KBE).
2005 Awarded the Presidential Medal of Freedom.
2005 Awarded an honorary doctorate in commercial science by New York University.
2006 Left the Federal Reserve Board.
2007 Appointed a special consultant by PIMCO.
2007 Appointed a special adviser at Deutsche Bank.
2008 Appointed an adviser at Paulson & Co.

LIFE AND CAREER

Alan Greenspan is an economist who dominated the financial world for nearly 20 years as Chairman of the Federal Reserve. He was a respected economic adviser, and long-running President of Townsend-Greenspan & Co, when he took over at the Federal Reserve in 1987, just before the stock market crisis of that year. He was reappointed at successive four-year intervals until retiring in 2006, after an unprecedented tenure as chairman. Following his retirement, Greenspan took up an honorary position at the UK Treasury, and now works as a private adviser and consultant through his company, Greenspan Associates LLC. He has also served as a member of the Group of Thirty, the Washington-based financial advisory body, and as a corporate director for many multinational businesses such as Alcoa, Automatic Data Processing Inc., JP Morgan, and the Mobil Corporation.

KEY THINKING

- Greenspan has been praised as the greatest central banker in memory, running the Federal Reserve during many of the economic events of recent years, and is considered to be the leading authority on American domestic economic and monetary policy.
- His handling of the stock market crash of 1987 just after he took office was the first success of his tenure. His statement that the Fed was ready to provide the necessary liquidity helped minimize the impact of the crash.
- He was also lauded for his handling of the dotcom economic boom of the 1990s, and the transformation of global business that resulted.
- Although he was known for the complexity of his utterances, this was thought to be a useful technique for gaining flexibility in meaning, and avoiding extreme market reaction.

IN PERSPECTIVE

- He became known for the "Greenspan put," the monetary policy that lowered the Fed Funds rate, to improve liquidity and avoid further economic downturn—used to resolved economic problems brought about by the Gulf war, the Mexican crisis, the Asian crisis, the LTCM debacle, Y2K, and the bursting of the dotcom bubble.
- He made a now-famous comment about irrational exuberance and escalating stock prices in 1996—and, as there was an immediate downturn in the international stock markets, the phrase became part of common parlance about economic excess.
- He has come under some criticism for monetary policies that encouraged excessive speculation, and for supporting former US president George W. Bush's demolition of the budget surpluses built up in the Clinton years.
- Considers the current subprime crisis as being a product of the housing bubble, low interest rates, and rising house prices across the world.
- He views the subprime market as being beneficial in allowing people on low incomes to own homes, and believes focus should be on the financial securitization of so-called toxic debt, which has caused the problems.

MORE INFO

Books:

Greenspan, Alan. *The Age of Turbulence: Adventures in a New World*. New York: Penguin Press, 2007.

Martin, Justin. *Greenspan: The Man Behind Money*. Cambridge, MA: Perseus Publishing, 2000.

Woodward, Bob. *Maestro: Greenspan's Fed and the American Boom*. New York: Simon & Schuster, 2000.

See Also:

The Age of Turbulence: Adventures in a New World (p. 1329)
Irrational Exuberance (p. 1385)

"Since becoming a central banker, I have learned to mumble with great incoherence. If I seem unduly clear to you, you must have misunderstood what I said." Alan Greenspan

  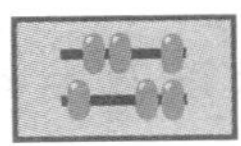 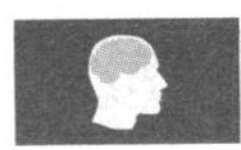  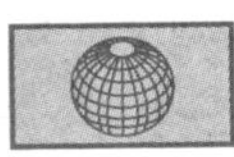   

Friedrich Hayek · Influential social theorist and advocate of free markets

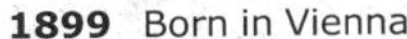

1899 Born in Vienna.
1914 Joined the Austro-Hungarian army in World War I.
1921 Received doctorate in law from the University of Vienna.
1923 Received doctorate in political science from the University of Vienna.
1923 Appointed research assistant at New York University.
1931 Appointed to the faculty of the London School of Economics.
1938 Emigrated to the United Kingdom to avoid the Nazi control of Austria.
1944 Publication of *The Road to Serfdom.*
1950 Appointed professor at the University of Chicago.
1960 Publication of *The Constitution of Liberty.*
1962 Appointed professor at the University of Frieburg.
1974 Received the Nobel Memorial Prize in Economic Sciences, shared with Gunnar Myrdal.
1984 Appointed a member of the Order of the Companions of Honour in the UK.
1988 Publication of *The Fatal Conceit.*
1991 Receives the US Presidential Medal of Freedom.
1992 Died in Freiburg, Germany.

LIFE AND CAREER

Friedrich Hayek was an influential Austrian economist, and political philosopher, known for his defense of classical liberalism and free-market capitalism in the mid-20th century. After being decorated for bravery in World War I, and aiding the Austrian government at the Treaty of Versailles, he founded and served as director of the Austrian Institute for Business Cycle Research, before joining the faculty of the London School of Economics. In 1947, he was an organizer of the Mont Pelerin Society, a group of classical liberals who opposed socialism in various areas. Hayek received the Nobel Prize, along with Gunnar Myrdal, for his work on the theory of money and economic fluctuations, and the interdependence of economic, social, and institutional phenomena. Hayek was a prolific researcher and writer over nearly seven decades, and was seen as a central figure in the move from interventionism and Keynesian policies towards classical liberalism. He was also instrumental in the founding of the Institute of Economic Affairs, the free-market think-tank that inspired Reaganomics and Thatcherism.

KEY THINKING

- Hayek propounded free-market economics, and applied his thinking to issues of political organization, the impact of capital, and the business cycle.
- He opposed government intervention in the marketplace, and was a fierce critic of Keynesian welfare economics.
- His writings also strongly criticized collectivism, as being dependent on a central authority; he argued that the central role of the state should be to maintain the rule of law, and avoid arbitrary intervention as much as possible.
- In *The Road to Serfdom*, his classic work on liberalism, political philosophy, cultural history, and economics, he warned against the dangers of state control, and collectivist principles that can lead to tyranny.
- Using the Soviet Union and Nazi Germany as examples, he explained that in a centrally planned economy, the distribution of resources would always devolve onto a small group, which would not be able to process the necessary information to distribute the resources effectively.
- In *Prices and Production* and *The Pure Theory of Capital*, he explained the origin of the business cycle in terms of central bank credit expansion, and its transmission over time.
- *Prices and Production* introduced the concept of Hayekian triangles, to depict the relationship between the value of capital goods and their place in the temporal sequence of production.
- In *The Pure Theory of Capital*, he described how the economy's structure of production depends on the characteristics of capital goods.

IN PERSPECTIVE

- One of the foremost members of the Austrian school of economics, he advocated individualism, and economic theories based on the basic principles of human action.
- His research on social and political philosophy was based on an understanding of the limits of human knowledge and the concept of *spontaneous order* in social institutions–arguing in favor of organizing society around a market order, where the state is focused on enforcing a free market based around the individual.
- His early works on industrial fluctuations, and prices as signals, were influential, as were his contributions to jurisprudence and cognitive science.

MORE INFO

Books:

Caldwell, Bruce. *Hayek's Challenge: An Intellectual Biography of FA Hayek*. Chicago, IL: University of Chicago Press, 2004. A full biography of Hayek, examining the background to his writings, and discussing his ideas in the context of economic theory.

Ebenstein, Alan. *Friedrich Hayek: A Biography*. New York: Palgrave, 2001. Considers Hayek's life and thinking, and provides a chronological overview of his writings.

Hayek, Friedrich. *The Road to Serfdom*. London: G. Routledge & Sons, 1944. The book which influenced the political ideologies of Thatcher and Reagan, and led to the revival of neoclassical economics in the West, and the lessening of Keynesian influence.

"A claim for equality of material position can be met only by a government with totalitarian powers." Friedrich Hayek

  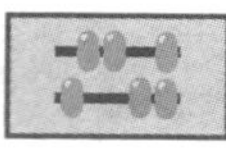 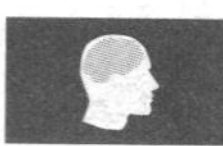  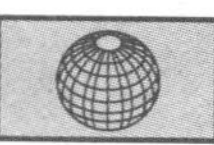   

Daniel Kahneman · Nobel laureate who helped develop prospect theory

1934 Born in Tel Aviv, Israel.
1954 Received BA in psychology and mathematics from Hebrew University, Jerusalem.
1961 Received PhD in psychology from the University of California, Berkeley.
1961 Appointed lecturer in psychology, Hebrew University.
1966 Appointed senior lecturer in psychology, Hebrew University.
1966 Appointed fellow, Center for Cognitive Studies, and lecturer in psychology, Harvard University.
1970 Appointed associate professor, Hebrew University, Jerusalem.
1973 Appointed professor, Hebrew University, Jerusalem.
1977 Appointed fellow, Center for Advanced Studies in the Behavioral Sciences.
1978 Appointed professor of psychology, University of British Columbia.
1982 Received the Distinguished Scientific Contribution Award of the American Psychological Society, with Amos Tversky.
1984 Appointed associate fellow, Canadian Institute for Advanced Research.
1986 Appointed professor of psychology, University of California, Berkeley.
1993 Appointed professor of psychology and public affairs, Woodrow Wilson School, Princeton University.
2000 Appointed fellow, Center for Rationality, Hebrew University, Jerusalem.
2002 Received the Nobel Memorial Prize in Economic Sciences.
2007 Appointed professor of psychology and public affairs emeritus and senior scholar, Woodrow Wilson School, Princeton University.
2007 Received the Distinguished Lifetime Contribution Award, American Psychological Association.
2009 Awarded honorary doctorate by Erasmus University, Rotterdam, The Netherlands.

LIFE AND CAREER

Daniel Kahneman is a psychologist and Nobel laureate, notable for his work on behavioral finance, and hedonic psychology. He spent his childhood years in Paris, before moving to Palestine after World War II. After obtaining his undergraduate degree in Jerusalem, he served in the psychology department of the Israeli Defense Forces. In 1958, he went to the US to study at the University of California, Berkeley. He was also a visiting scientist at the University of Michigan and the Applied Psychological Research Unit in Cambridge. He is now a Senior Scholar at the Woodrow Wilson School of Public and International Affairs, and Professor of Psychology and Public Affairs Emeritus at the Woodrow Wilson School, the Professor of Psychology Emeritus at Princeton University, and a Fellow of the Center for Rationality at Hebrew University, Jerusalem.

KEY THINKING

- Kahneman's early work focused on visual perception and attention, before he went on to research with Amos Tversky and others, establishing a cognitive basis for common human errors using heuristics and biases, and developing prospect theory, which describes decision-making processes in situations that involve risk.
- He and Tversky published a series of important articles on judgment and decision-making, which culminated in the publication of their seminal work on prospect theory in 1979.
- In 2002, he received the Nobel Memorial Prize in Economic Sciences alongside Amos Tversky for their work on decision-making under uncertainty, and for demonstrating how human decisions may systematically depart from those predicted by standard economic theory.

IN PERSPECTIVE

- Kahneman and Amos Tversky started collaborating in 1968, with their first paper together being "Belief in the law of small numbers," published in 1971.
- They published many more articles in peer-reviewed journals over the next few years; apart from "Prospect theory," the most important was "Judgment under uncertainty: Heuristics and biases," published in the journal *Science*.
- Thaler's 1980 paper, "Toward a positive theory of human choice," a key text in the development of behavioral economics, built on Kahneman and Tversky's work on prospect theory.
- During the 1990s, Kahneman began to focus his research more on the field of hedonic psychology, which was becoming more mainstream as part of the positive psychology movement.
- In 1992, he worked with Carol Varey to introduce a method of evaluating moments and episodes, to capture "experiences extended across time."

MORE INFO

Books:

Kahneman, Daniel, Ed Diener, and Norbert Schwarz (eds). *Well-Being: The Foundations of Hedonic Psychology*. New York: Russell Sage Foundation, 1999.
Kahneman, Daniel, Paul Slovic, and Amos Tversky. *Judgment Under Uncertainty: Heuristics and Biases*. New York: Cambridge University Press, 1982.
Kahneman, Daniel, and Amos Tversky (eds). *Choices, Values, and Frames*. New York: Cambridge University Press, 2000.

See Also:

Amos Tversky (p. 1316)

"The brain scientists are the wave of the future in the financial world. If you seek to maximize understanding, whether you're in academia or in the investment community, you'd better pay serious attention to them." Daniel Kahneman

  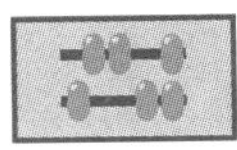 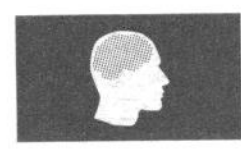  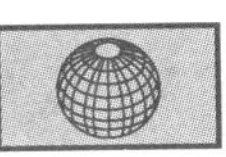   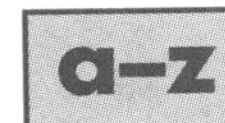

John Maynard Keynes · Key economic thinker of the 20th century

1883 Born in Cambridge, UK.
1897 Received scholarship to Eton.
1902 Attended Cambridge University.
1906 Joined the Civil Service.
1909 Elected fellow of King's College, Cambridge University.
1911 Appointed editor of the *Economic Journal*.
1919 Appointed chief Treasury representative at the Paris Peace Conference.
1919 Publication of *Economic Consequences of the Peace*.
1921 Appointed chairman of the National Mutual Life Insurance Company.
1921 Publication of *Treatise on Probability*.
1923 Publication of *Tract on Monetary Reform*.
1923 Began contributing monthly columns to *The Nation*.
1929 Appointed fellow of the British Academy.
1929 Appointed to the UK government's Macmillan Committee of Enquiry into Finance and Industry.
1930 Publication of *Treatise on Money*.
1936 Publication of *The General Theory of Employment, Interest and Money*.
1940 Appointed a government economic adviser.
1941 Elected to the Court of the Bank of England.
1942 Awarded a peerage.
1944 Represented Britain at the Bretton Woods conference.
1946 Died in Tilton, East Sussex, UK.

LIFE AND CAREER

J. M. Keynes was an internationally renowned economist, who had a major impact on 20th century economic practice and fiscal policy. He was educated at Eton and Cambridge University, before entering the India Office of the Civil Service. He later returned to Cambridge to teach economics, while he developed his economic theories, and wrote some of the major economic texts of his time. He was also involved in the war effort for the Treasury Office, and advised various chancellors between 1940 and 1946. He was central to the creation of the International Monetary Fund and the World Bank, in the aftermath of World War II.

KEY THINKING

- The effect of Keynesian economics and theory still reverberates; his work on economic policy, and social progress was hugely influential in forming modern economic thinking.
- He strongly advocated interventionist policies, and governmental use of fiscal and monetary measures to mitigate the adverse effects of recessions and booms.
- He believed that government borrowing was necessary for undertaking large-scale public works that would stimulate the economy during a recession.
- The promotion of deficit spending to help employment became the basis of government economic policy.
- During World War II, Keynes was actively involved in discussions on the post-war economic landscape, particularly the creation of the International Monetary Fund, the World Bank, and the Bretton Woods system for international currency management.
- At that time, he also met with Roosevelt's economic advisors to counter prevalent laissez-faire policies, and supported the President's New Deal, and the promotion of high employment, production, and purchasing power.
- He was a pivotal figure in the request for American assistance for the UK economy after the war.

IN PERSPECTIVE

- His *Treatise on Probability* explored the foundations of knowledge regarding the meaning and measurement of probability, depicting probability as a logical relation, and therefore objective.
- In *Economic Consequences of the Peace*, he criticized the allies for the harshness of the reparations they imposed on Germany at the end of the World War I. The later rise of Hitler was thought by many to justify this condemnation.
- In *A Tract on Monetary Reform* he called for an end to the Gold Standard, on the basis that devaluation was preferable to deflation, and that sterling was overvalued. The British government later abandoned the Standard, and was forced to devalue sterling by 20%.
- He distinguished between investments and saving, proposing that if investments exceeded saving, it led to inflation, but if saving exceeded investment, there would be recession.
- In *The General Theory of Employment, Interest and Money*, he argued, that unemployment occurs if people don't spend enough money.
- In *How to Pay for the War*, he supported low interest rates, and compulsory saving to prevent the type of inflation that happened after World War I.

MORE INFO

Books:

Davidson, John. *John Maynard Keynes*. Basingstoke, UK: Palgrave Macmillan, 2007.
Keynes, John Maynard. *The General Theory of Employment, Interest and Money*. Basingstoke, UK: Palgrave Macmillan, 2007.
Minsky, Hyman. *John Maynard Keynes*. New York: McGraw-Hill, 2008.

See Also:

Animal Spirits: How Human Psychology Drives the Economy, and Why It Matters for Global Capitalism (p. 1331)

"In the long run, we're all dead." John Maynard Keynes

  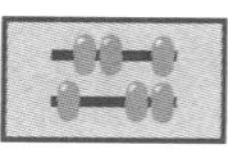   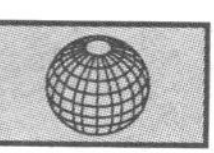   

Edwin Lefèvre · American writer and statesman, best known for his writings on Wall Street

1871 Born in Colon, Colombia.
1901 Publication of *Wall Street Stories.*
1905 Publication of *Golden Flood.*
1907 Publication of *Sampson Rock of Wall Street.*
1909 Appointed an ambassador of the United States.
1916 Publication of *Plunderers.*
1917 Publication of *To the Last Penny.*
1919 Publication of *Simonetta.*
1923 Publication of *Reminiscences of a Stock Operator.*
1943 Died in Dorset, Vermont.

LIFE AND CAREER

Edwin Lefèvre was a journalist, writer, and statesman, and is best known for his writings on Wall Street, which were successful in the 1920s and early 1930s. He was born to American parents, and educated at Michigan Military Academy and Lehigh University. He was an independently wealthy investor, who turned to writing short stories about what he observed on Wall Street. He followed this with several novels about money and finance. During the presidency of William Howard Taft, Lefèvre was appointed an Ambassador of the United States, serving in a number of European countries. After that, he returned to his home in Vermont to continue his writing, publishing short stories in magazines such as *Harper's*, newspapers such as the *Saturday Evening Post*, and writing novels. He retired in the 1930s, at the time of the Great Depression, when interest in the stock market waned.

KEY THINKING

- After operating successfully as a investor, and then writing a number of articles and fictional books about Wall Street, Lefèvre turned to fact for his classic on stock-market trading, *Reminiscences of a Stock Operator*.
- After signing up to work exclusively for the *Saturday Evening Post*, he wrote a series of 12 articles that told the story of a professional stock trader on Wall Street.
- Presented as fiction, the series was generally accepted to be a biography of star trader, Jesse Livermore; the articles subsequently became the book, *Reminiscences of a Stock Operator*.
- The book has been a success ever since it was first published, being continually reprinted, as well as being translated into many languages.
- His writing was insightful and popular, and contained many aphorisms about the financial world.

IN PERSPECTIVE

- Lefèvre offered a perspective of the mindset of a high-stakes speculator in *Reminiscences of a Stock Operator*, explaining the motivation behind their successes as being due to a need to express their own ingenuity.
- Jesse Livermore, dubbed "Larry Livingston" in the book, was an infamous trader who amassed and lost several fortunes, before finally committing suicide with a revolver.
- In *Reminiscences of a Stock Operator*, Lefèvre describes in great detail the bucket shops that operated in the late 19th and early 20th centuries. They were essentially betting parlors where people could wager on stocks.
- They used many tricks to fool their customers, such as falsely reporting stock trades, and arranging "wash sales."
- Lefèvre recognized the role of psychology in investing. He felt that traders should factor in market precedents, the psychology of the public, the limitations of brokers, as well as their own psychological traits and weaknesses.

MORE INFO

Books:

Lefèvre, Edwin. *Wall Street Stories*. New York: McClure, Phillips & Co., 1901. A collection of stories based on well-known investing personalities of the time, this is the book that launched Lefèvre's literary career.

Lefèvre, Edwin. *Reminiscences of a Stock Operator.* New York: George H. Doran Co., 1923. The classic fictionalized biography of the famous speculator, Jesse Livermore. It is a readable and insightful account of making and losing a fortune a few times over.

Lefèvre, Edwin. *Making of a Stockbroker.* New York: George H. Doran Co., 1925. A follow-up to *Reminiscences of a Stock Operator*, but this time the stock trader was a real person, John K. Wing, a senior partner of Bronson and Barnes, a major Boston stock brokerage. Written as a factual biography, Wing's more honest approach to the markets contrasts with that of Livermore.

See Also:

Reminiscences of a Stock Operator (p. 1413)

"After spending many years in Wall Street and after making and losing millions of dollars I want to tell you this: It never was my thinking that made the big money for me. It always was my sitting. Got that? My sitting tight!" Edwin Lefèvre

  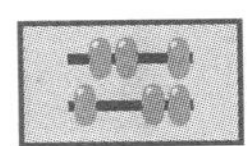 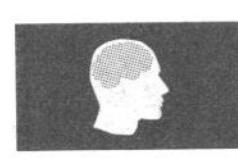  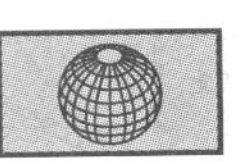   

Burton Malkiel · American economist, and author of classic finance book, *A Random Walk Down Wall Street*

1932 Born in Boston, Massachusetts.
1953 Received BA from Harvard College.
1955 Received MBA from Harvard Graduate School of Business Administration.
1955 Served as a first lieutenant in the Finance Corps of the US Army.
1958 Appointed an associate with Smith Barney & Co.
1964 Received PhD from Princeton University.
1964 Appointed assistant professor at Princeton University.
1966 Appointed associate professor and director of the Financial Research Center, Princeton University.
1966 Publication of *The Term Structure of Interest Rates*.
1968 Appointed professor of economics at Princeton University.
1973 Publication of *A Random Walk Down Wall Street*.
1975 Appointed member of the Council of Economic Advisors.
1978 Appointed president of the American Finance Association.
1980 Publication of *The Inflation Beater's Investment Guide*.
1981 Appointed professor of management studies and dean of Yale School of Management.
1982 Publication of *Winning Investment Strategies*.
2003 Publication of *The Random Walk Guide to Investing*.
2007 Publication of *From Wall Street to the Great Wall*.
2009 Publication of *The Elements of Investing*.

LIFE AND CAREER

Burton Malkiel is an economist and author of the seminal investment book, *A Random Walk Down Wall Street*. He began his career in investment banking for Smith Barney & Co., before teaching at Princeton, where he became Professor of Economics at Princeton University, and Chairman of the Economics Department. He is a past appointee to the President's Council of Economic Advisors, and has served on the boards of several financial corporations, including Prudential Financial, and the Vanguard Group. He has also served on several investment management boards, the advisory panel of the investment management firm, Research Affiliates, and the Investment Committee for the American Philosophical Association.

KEY THINKING

- Malkiel is a leading proponent of the efficient market hypothesis, which contends that prices of publicly traded assets reflect all publicly available information.
- He argues that stocks are priced so efficiently that no professional can exploit differences in pricing with any consistency. For the personal investor, it is even more difficult to beat the market, as they have to pay management fees, trading costs, and taxes.
- Also considers how difficult it is to predict which companies are worth investing in, and contends that chance can predict just as successfully as the experts.
- His solution is to use a widely diversified, low-fee, low-turnover investment strategy such as index funds, or exchange-traded funds.
- Shows how the benefits of broad diversification in a stock portfolio have been proved over the years, and for investors diversifying into other asset categories, such as bonds, real estate, and cash.
- Proposes that it is best to index most of a portfolio, and only undertake some stock speculation around the edges, which reduces the risk involved.
- Describes why investors should place their money in a fund with a level of risk they are comfortable with, and then leave it until retirement.

IN PERSPECTIVE

- In *A Random Walk Down Wall Street*, an investment classic that is now in its ninth edition, Malkiel explains why diversification is critical in a portfolio, and argues that asset allocation should always be done appropriately.
- He has revised the book over the years, re-examining his views on market manias in terms of the internet bubble, and strongly defends efficient markets, and index fund investing.
- His influential article, "The valuation of closed-end investment company shares," in the *Journal of Finance*, discussed why closed-end fund companies trade at market valuations lower than the net value of their assets.
- Compares the different types of mutual funds and hedge funds in terms of investment opportunities.

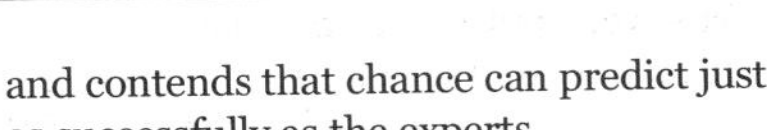

MORE INFO

Books:

Malkiel, Burton G. *A Random Walk Down Wall Street*. New York: WW Norton & Co., 1973. The groundbreaking book that made Malkiel famous, it offers guidance on successful long-term investing, arguing that it is better to buy and hold an index fund than trade in individual stocks, and actively managed funds.

Malkiel, Burton G. *The Random Walk Guide To Investing: Ten Rules for Financial Success*. New York: WW Norton & Co., 2003. The follow-up to his bestseller, this book outlines Malkiel's 10-point plan for investing, and provides practical advice for the beginner.

See Also:

A Random Walk Down Wall Street: The Time-Tested Strategy for Successful Investing (p. 1412)

"A blindfolded monkey throwing darts at a newspaper's financial pages could select a portfolio that would do just as well as one carefully selected by the experts." Burton Malkiel

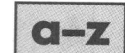

Harry Markowitz · The grandfather of modern portfolio theory

1927 Born in Chicago, Illinois.
1950 Received MA from the University of Chicago.
1952 Appointed a researcher at the RAND Corporation.
1954 Received PhD from the University of Chicago.
1955 Invited to be a student member of the Cowles Foundation for Research in Economics.
1959 Publication of *Portfolio Selection*.
1962 Cofounded CACI International.
1962 Publication of *SIMSCRIPT: A Simulation Programming Language*.
1963 Worked at Consolidated Analysis Centers Inc.
1968 Taught at the University of California, Los Angeles.
1969 Worked at Arbitrage Management Co.
1974 Worked at IBM's TJ Watson Research Center.
1983 Appointed professor of finance at Baruch College, City University of New York.
1990 Received the Nobel Memorial Prize in Economic Sciences.
1994 Appointed professor of economics at the Rady School of Management, University of California, San Diego.

LIFE AND CAREER

Harry Markowitz is an influential economist, best known for his groundbreaking work on modern portfolio theory. He studied at the University of Chicago, and worked at the Cowles Foundation, based at Yale, before joining the RAND Corporation, where he helped develop SIMSCRIPT, the first simulation programming language. He went on to cofound CACI International, and to provide support and training for the program after it was released to the public. He was awarded the Von Neumann Prize in Operations Research Theory in 1989, before receiving the Nobel Memorial Prize in Economic Sciences for his work on portfolio theory, sparse matrix techniques, and SIMSCRIPT, the following year.

KEY THINKING

- Harry Markowitz started specializing in the application of mathematics techniques to the analysis of the stock market while studying at the University of Chicago.
- His work on stock prices and portfolio selection introduced the concept of risk into valuation for the first time, and led to the development of his theory of portfolio allocation under uncertainty, published in 1952 by the *Journal of Finance*.
- His research emphasized the importance of measuring the risk of an entire portfolio, rather than the risk on an individual security level.
- He built his basic concept of portfolio theory on John Burr Williams's *Theory of Investment Value*.

IN PERSPECTIVE

- Harry Markowitz's research focuses on the effects of asset risk, correlation, and diversification on expected investment portfolio returns.
- His work put risk at the center of investing, and attempted to measure the appropriate amount of risk to undertake, as higher returns are dependent on greater risk, and the greater the risk, the greater the possibility of loss.
- Markowitz showed how an investor's portfolio choice can be reduced to balancing just two dimensions: the expected return on the portfolio, and its variance or standard deviation, depending on the circumstances.
- At the RAND Corporation, he researched optimization techniques, developing the critical line algorithm for the identifications of the optimal mean-variance portfolios. This was found to be lying on what was later named the Markowitz Frontier.
- A Markowitz Efficient Portfolio is one where no added diversification can lower the portfolio's risk for a given return expectation, while the Markowitz Efficient Frontier is the set of all portfolios that will give the highest expected return for each given level of risk. These concepts of efficiency were essential to the development of the capital asset pricing model.
- In *Portfolio Selection*, he produced a theory for optimal investment in stocks that differ in their expected return and risk.
- He was the first to place a number on risk relative to investing, defying the traditional view that risk should only be assessed in general terms; he quantified what an investor wants to avoid by using a range of possible return outcomes, based on the past variability of returns.

MORE INFO

Books:

Bernstein, Peter L. *Capital Ideas: The Improbable Origins of Modern Wall Street*. New York: Free Press, 1992.
Markowitz, Harry M. *Portfolio Selection: Efficient Diversification of Investments*. New York: Wiley, 1959.
Williams, John Burr. *Theory of Investment Value*. Cambridge, MA: Harvard University Press, 1938.

See Also:

Merton Miller (p. 1294)
William F. Sharpe (p. 1309)
Portfolio Selection: Efficient Diversification of Investments (p. 1408)

"It's like a crapshoot in Las Vegas, except in Las Vegas the odds are with the house. As for the market, the odds are with you, because on average over the long run, the market has paid off." Harry Markowitz

  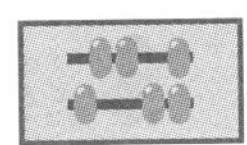 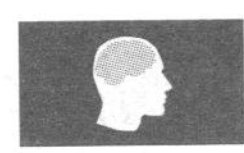  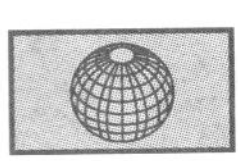   

Robert Merton · Nobel Prize-winning economist and financial innovator

1944 Born in New York.
1966 Received BS in engineering mathematics from Columbia University.
1967 Received MS in applied mathematics from Caltech.
1970 Received PhD in economics from Massachusetts Institute of Technology (MIT).
1974 Appointed professor at Sloan School of Management, MIT.
1979 Appointed research associate, National Bureau of Economic Research.
1986 Appointed president of the American Finance Association.
1987 Appointed visiting professor of finance, Graduate School of Business Administration, Harvard University.
1988 Appointed university professor at Graduate School of Business Administration, Harvard University.
1993 Cofounded Long-Term Capital Management.
1997 Received the Nobel Memorial Prize in Economic Sciences, with Myron Scholes.
1999 Received the Lifetime Achievement in Mathematical Finance award.
2001 Appointed managing director, JP Morgan Chase.
2002 Cofounded Integrated Finance Ltd and appointed chief science officer.
2005 Robert C. Merton professorship in financial economics established at MIT.
2010 Retired from Harvard Business School.

LIFE AND CAREER

Robert Merton is an internationally renowned economist, financial innovator, and recipient of the Noble Memorial Prize in Economic Sciences for his work on stock options. He is best known for his seminal work on the development of the Black–Scholes model, the intertemporal capital asset pricing model, Merton's Portfolio Problem, and the Merton Model, and has been a key figure in the shaping of the global financial system. He was a founder of Long-Term Capital Management, and was recently appointed Chief Science Officer of Trinsum Group, and chairman of the board of directors of Daedalus Software.

KEY THINKING

- Robert Merton was a pioneer in producing models that dealt with risk, and helped revolutionize modern financial theory and practice.
- In particular, he had a great influence on the Black–Scholes formula for pricing stock options which, for the first time, enabled option contracts to be effectively evaluated and priced in an open market.
- He supplied the crucial arbitrage that underpins the logic of the Black–Scholes formula, being the first to publish the differential equation that became known as the Black–Scholes equation, in a paper on continuous-time speculative processes.
- In studying the work done by Black and Scholes on option pricing, he found that the limit of continuous trading was the only circumstance that would provide a risk-free, zero-arbitrage position on the option or stock.
- Merton then produced a more general derivation of the formula, which was acknowledged in a footnote in the celebrated Black and Scholes' paper of 1973.
- He later generalized it further, and it is now applied to many different types of option contracts, and other contingent claim contracts, helping the options markets to become one of the biggest and most active security markets.
- His application of continuous-time financial mathematics to the problem of option pricing earned him the Nobel Prize, shared with Myron Scholes, and which acknowledged the late Fischer Black.

IN PERSPECTIVE

- In 1969, he published Merton's Portfolio Problem, which proposed a formula to help people decide how much of their income they should spend and how much should be used for investing.
- The Merton Model, which he presented in 1970, was a method of valuing a corporate bond based on default probability using a form of the Black–Scholes equation; it was extended by Robert Jarrow and Stuart Turnbull for the Jarrow–Turnbull Model.
- High-profile defaults such as Enron and WorldCom, and the rise of credit derivatives have made the Merton Model more popular among credit analysts.
- In 1973, he introduced the intertemporal capital asset pricing model (ICAPM), which incorporates hedges that investors make to protect themselves from shortfalls in savings.
- In 2002, he was a key figure in the advocacy of expensing the stock options awarded as part of a compensation package.

MORE INFO

Books:

Bodie, Zvi, and Robert C. Merton. *Finance*. Upper Saddle River, NJ: Prentice Hall, 1998.
Merton, Robert C. *Continuous-Time Finance*. Cambridge, MA: Blackwell Publishing, 1990.

Article:

Black, Fisher, and Myron Scholes. "The pricing of options and corporate liabilities." *Journal of Political Economy* 81:3 (May–June 1973): 637–654. Online at: www.jstor.org/stable/1831029

See Also:

Fischer Black (p. 1272)
Myron Scholes (p. 1306)
Finance (p. 1355)

"[Continuous-time finance] is the study of how best to allocate and deploy resources across time in an uncertain environment and of the role of economic organizations in facilitating these allocations." Robert Merton

  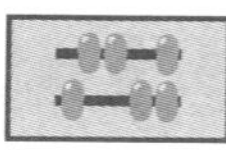 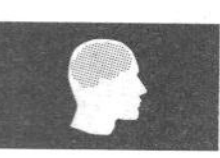  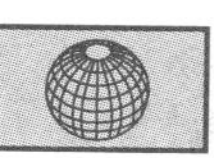   

Merton Miller · Nobel Prize-winning economist, and activist supporter of free-market solutions

1923 Born in Boston, Massachusetts.
1943 Received BA from Harvard University.
1944 Worked at the US Treasury Department.
1952 Received PhD in economics from Johns Hopkins University.
1952 Taught economics at London School of Economics.
1953 Taught economics at Carnegie Mellon University.
1958 Publication of *The Cost of Capital, Corporate Finance and the Theory of Investment.*
1961 Appointed professor of economics at the University of Chicago.
1972 Publication of *The Theory of Finance.*
1975 Appointed fellow of the Econometric Society.
1976 Appointed president of the American Finance Association.
1985 Appointed member of the Chicago Board of Trade.
1990 Appointed member of the Chicago Mercantile Exchange.
1990 Received the Nobel Memorial Prize in Economic Sciences, with Harry Markowitz and William Sharpe.
1991 Publication of *Financial Innovations and Market Volatility.*
1997 Publication of *Merton Miller on Derivatives.*
2000 Died in Chicago, Illinois.

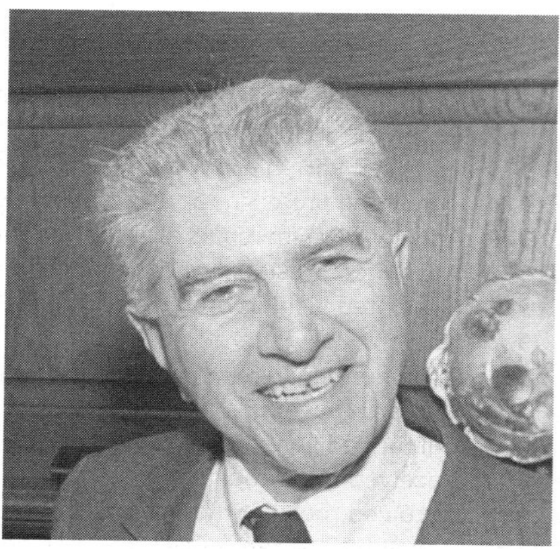

LIFE AND CAREER

Merton Miller was a Professor of Economics, a financial innovator, economist, and renowned financial author. He worked during World War II as an economist in the Division of Tax Research of the US Treasury Department, and subsequently in the Division of Research and Statistics of the Board of Governors of the Federal Reserve System. He then received his doctorate, and was appointed Visiting Assistant Lecturer at the London School of Economics, before being appointed a professor at the University of Chicago. He also served as a public director of the Chicago Mercantile Exchange, and was chairman of its special academic panel considering the 1987 financial market crash.

KEY THINKING

- Merton Miller made pioneering contributions to financial economics through his theory of corporate finance, and the evaluation of firms on markets. He was an influential supporter of a free-market response to economic issues.
- He built on the work of Harry Markowitz on portfolio theory and William Sharpe in the development of the capital asset pricing model, and received the Nobel Prize for his research.
- He built a reputation as one of the most important developers of theoretical and empirical analysis in corporate finance, and collaborated with Franco Modigliani in a seminal article on the cost of capital, and investment theory.
- The Miller–Modigliani Theorem ran against the traditional view that a company should reduce its cost of capital by finding the right debt-to-equity ratio, but argued that there is no right ratio, but that corporate managers are better off reducing their tax liability, and increasing corporate wealth.
- The theorem changed the focus from how investors choose which securities to buy, to how companies decide what securities they should sell.
- He attacked the view that financial innovations have created increasing market volatility, which has a detrimental effect on saving, and business investors.
- He argued that regulators should not use the power of the state to control financial innovation, as this would increase the cost of trading in the domestic markets, while decreasing their international competitiveness.

IN PERSPECTIVE

- Merton Miller helped to interpret the complexities of the futures markets to academia, business, and regulators.
- His analysis of capital structure was critical to resolving the relationship between this and a company's dividend policy, market value, and cost of capital.
- As a public director of the Chicago Board of Trade, his work focused on the economic and regulatory problems of financial services, especially securities and options exchanges.
- When the Chicago markets were blamed for the 1987 stock market crash, he defended them, helping to dissuade regulators from bringing in rules to contain them.
- He argued that the problems between the securities and futures markets centered on Wall Street being unhappy that Chicago was taking business from them.
- He opposed regulation of the exchanges, explaining that futures contracts are similar to other financial products, and have value to those who buy them.

MORE INFO

Books:

Fama, Eugene F., and Merton H. Miller. *The Theory of Finance*. New York: Holt, Rinehart, and Winston, 1972.
Miller, Merton H. *Financial Innovations and Market Volatility*. Cambridge, MA: Blackwell, 1991.
Miller, Merton H. *Merton Miller on Derivatives*. New York: Wiley, 1997.

See Also:

✔ Understanding Capital Structure Theory: Modigliani and Miller (p. 997)
Harry Markowitz (p. 1292)
Franco Modigliani (p. 1296)
William F. Sharpe (p. 1309)
The Theory of Finance (p. 1423)

"What counts is what you do with your money, not where it came from." Merton Miller

  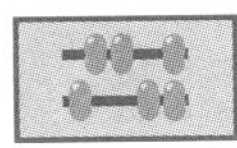 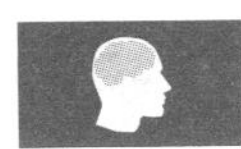  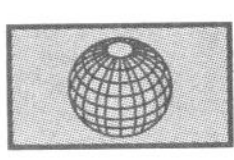   

Hyman Philip Minsky · Maverick economist and financial market theorist

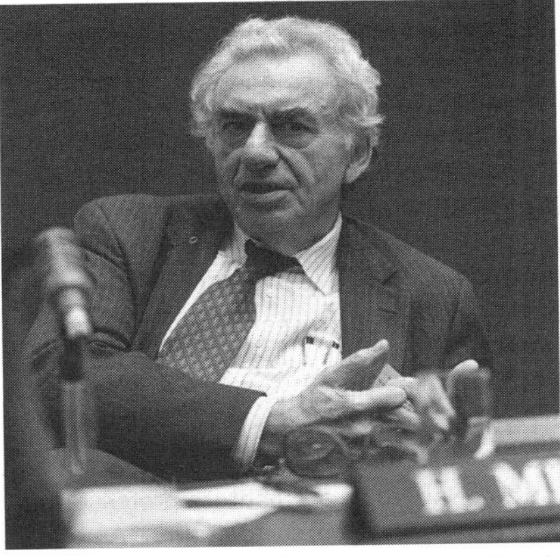

1919 Born in Chicago, Illinois.
1941 Received a BS in mathematics from the University of Chicago.
1943 Joined the US Army.
1947 Received an MPA from Harvard University.
1947 Taught at Carnegie Tech.
1949 Appointed assistant to associate professor at Brown University.
1954 Received a PhD in economics from Harvard University.
1957 Appointed associate professor of economics at the University of California, Berkeley.
1957 Appointed a consultant to the Commission on Money and Credit.
1965 Appointed professor of economics at Washington University in St Louis.
1975 Publication of *John Maynard Keynes*.
1986 Publication of *Stabilizing an Unstable Economy*.
1990 Retired from his professorship.
1990 Appointed Levy Institute distinguished scholar.
1996 Received the Veblen-Commons Award from the Association for Evolutionary Economics.
1996 Died in Rhinebeck, New York.

LIFE AND CAREER

Minsky was born into a family of Menshevik emigrants from Belarus. His mother was involved in the early trade union movement, while his father was active in the Jewish section of the Socialist party of Chicago. At Harvard University, he gained his doctorate, studying under Joseph Schumpeter and Wassily Leontief, while at the University of California, Berkeley, he developed his major theories about lending and economic activity, which he published in his books on *John Maynard Keynes* and *Stabilizing an Unstable Economy*. From 1965 until his retirement in 1990, Minsky was a professor at Washington University in St Louis, and for many years was a director of the Mark Twain Bank, also in St Louis. At the time of his death he was a senior scholar at the Levy Economics Institute of Bard College.

KEY THINKING

- Minsky's work focused on four main themes: his hypothesis of financial fragility, his business cycle theory, his investment theory, and debt inflation.
- He showed how, over a prolonged period of prosperity, corporate cash flow rises beyond what the borrowers can pay off from incoming revenues, creating a speculative euphoria.
- This forces overindebted investors to sell low to make good on their loans, producing a market downturn and a large demand for cash, a financial crisis that has become known as a "Minsky moment."
- As with Keynes, he supported intervention in the financial markets; he considered that the only way to break the pattern of boom and bust was through government and regulation of the financial system, as well as central bank action.
- He argued that financial markets had an innate tendency to excess, which increased the importance of the Federal Reserve as a lender of last resort.
- His work examined the accumulation of debt as the main dynamic that pushes an economy toward crisis, and identified three types of borrowers that contribute to this: hedge borrowers, speculative borrowers, and Ponzi borrowers, the last being the most fragile.
- He studied the cash flow analysis of financial relations, focusing on the flow of incomes from the productive part of the economy that can validate financial obligations.

IN PERSPECTIVE

- Minsky was a post-Keynesian authority on monetary theory and financial institutions; he studied economic fluctuations and recurring instability of the financial system in a capitalist economy, in an attempt to understand and explain the characteristics of financial crises.
- His financial instability hypothesis rejected the mainstream economic concepts of the efficient market hypothesis and the Chicago School of economists.
- He argued that the accumulation of debt must eventually curtail firms' investment, leading to financial retrenchment and recession.
- He interpreted Keynesian economics as an investment theory of the business cycle and a financial theory of investment, which emphasized the tiers approach to the balance of payments.
- Minsky's hypotheses of financial instability and debt accumulation, and the policy implications of his theories, received increased attention in the markets and media during the recent subprime mortgage crisis.
- However, his theories have not really been incorporated into mainstream economic models or central bank policy, and he opposed many of the popular deregulation policies of the 1980s.

MORE INFO

Books:

Bellofiore, Riccardo, and Piero Ferri (eds). *Financial Fragility and Investment in the Capitalist Economy: The Economic Legacy of Hyman Minsky, Vol. II*. Cheltenham, UK: Edward Elgar, 2001.

Minsky, Hyman P. *John Maynard Keynes*. New York: Columbia University Press, 1975.

Minsky, Hyman P. *Can "It" Happen Again? Essays on Instability and Finance*. Armonk, NY: ME Sharpe, 1982.

Minsky, Hyman P. *Stabilizing an Unstable Economy*. New Haven, CT: Yale University Press, 1986.

"A fundamental characteristic of our economy is that the financial system swings between robustness and fragility and these swings are an integral part of the process that generates business cycles." Hyman Philip Minsky

  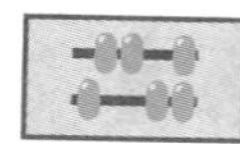 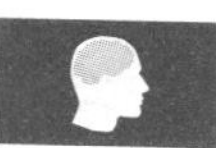  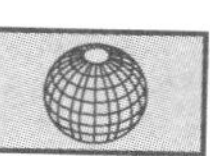   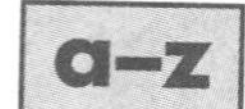

Franco Modigliani · Nobel Prize-winning macroeconomist

1918 Born in Rome.
1939 Received the degree of doctor juris from the University of Rome.
1939 Moved to the United States.
1942 Taught economics and statistics at Columbia University, and Bard College.
1944 Received DSocSci. from the New School for Social Research.
1944 Appointed lecturer and research associate at the Institute of World Affairs.
1948 Joined the faculty at University of Illinois at Urbana-Champaign.
1948 Received the Political Economy Fellowship of the University of Chicago.
1948 Appointed research consultant at the Cowles Commission for Research in Economics.
1952 Appointed professor at the Graduate School of Industrial Administration at Carnegie Mellon University.
1962 Appointed professor of economics at MIT.
1962 Appointed president of the Econometric Society.
1970 Named as an Institute professor at MIT.
1976 Appointed president of the American Economic Association.
1980 Publication of *The Collected Papers of Franco Modigliani.*
1985 Received the Nobel Memorial Prize in Economic Sciences.
1988 Appointed professor emeritus at MIT.
1994 Publication of *Foundations of Financial Markets and Institutions.*
2001 Publication of *Adventures of an Economist.*
2003 Died in Cambridge, Massachusetts.

LIFE AND CAREER

Franco Modigliani was an Italian-American economist, and professor at the MIT Sloan School of Management. He emigrated to the United States a few days before the start of World War II. He was then awarded a fellowship by the Graduate Faculty of Political and Social Science of the New School for Social Research. While there, he studied under Jacob Marschak, who helped him develop solid foundations in economics and econometrics. He went on to develop pioneering macroeconomic and econometric theories that changed the way we look at company behavior, and individual savings. He received the Nobel Prize for Economic Sciences in 1985 for his work on household savings, and the dynamics of financial markets. He also worked as a consultant to the US Treasury, the Federal Reserve System, and a number of European banks.

KEY THINKING

- Modigliani was at the forefront of post-war macroeconomics, and had a great influence on the development of Keynesian economics.
- While at the Cowles Commission, he was involved in two pieces of critical research, on the theory of choice under uncertainty, and statistical inference from non experimental observations.
- His first article in English, "Liquidity preference and the theory of interest and money," was a major contribution to the debate between Keynesian and classical economics.
- In the 1950s and early 1960s, he made two critical contributions to economics: formulating the Modigliani–Miller Theorem, with Merton Miller, and originating the lifecycle hypothesis.
- His research with Miller on financial markets focused on the effects that a company's financial structure, and its future earning potential have on the market value of its stock.
- They concluded that the market value of a company had no real relationship to the size and structure of its debt. Instead, they concluded that stock-market values are determined mainly by what organizations are expected to earn in the future.
- He received the Nobel Memorial Prize in Economics for his research on the lifecycle theory, an analysis of personal savings that had practical applications.

IN PERSPECTIVE

- The Modigliani–Miller Theorem demonstrates that, under certain assumptions, the value of a firm is not affected by whether it is financed by selling shares or borrowing money, and that the market value of a company's stock depends primarily on investors' expectations of what that company will earn in the future.
- His research on the lifecycle hypothesis analyzed individual behavior and aggregate saving, and proposed that consumers would aim for a stable level of income throughout their life, such as by saving during their working years, and spending during their retirement.
- Co-authored a paper on the predictability of social events, when the agent reacts to prediction, which became one of the tenets of the "theory of rational expectations."
- Explored new areas of research, including international finance and the international payment system, inflation, credit rationing, the term structure of interest rates, and the valuation of speculative assets.

MORE INFO

Books:

Fabozzi, Frank J., and Franco Modigliani. *Capital Markets: Institutions and Instruments*. Englewood Cliffs, NJ: Prentice Hall, 1992.

Modigliani, Franco. *Adventures of an Economist*. Rome: Laterza, 1999.

Szenberg, Michael, and Lall Ramrattan. *Franco Modigliani: An Intellectual Biography*. New York: Palgrave Macmillan, 2008.

See Also:

✔ Understanding Capital Structure Theory: Modigliani and Miller (p. 997)
Merton Miller (p. 1294)

"**... challenging the self-evident orthodoxies of the moment, be it that the classics are altogether outdated, or that the rich must save a larger fraction of their income than the poor, or that debt financing is cheaper because the interest rate on high-quality debt is lower than the return on equity.**" Franco Modigliani

  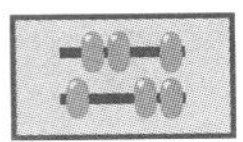 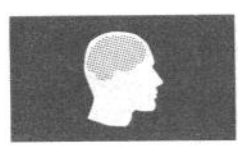  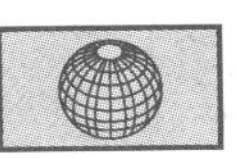   

J. P. Morgan · Legendary American banker

1837 John Pierpont Morgan born in Hartford, Connecticut.
1857 Joined Duncan, Sherman, and Co.
1862 Founded Dabrey, Morgan, and Co.
1871 Teamed up with the firm of Drexel to form Drexel, Morgan, and Co.
1879 Put together stock offering of US$18 million for the New York Central Railroad.
1887 US government passed the Interstate Commerce Act.
1895 Helped avert US financial crisis.
1907 Bailed out US government again.
1912 Appeared before Pujo Committee.
1913 Died in Rome.

LIFE AND CAREER

J. P. Morgan was a renowned banker and businessman. He took an early interest in business, spending time checking receipts, and the expenditure of his allowance rather than playing games. After studying at the University of Göttingen in Germany, he was asked to become an assistant to one of the professors, but he preferred to start out in business, joining Duncan, Sherman, and Co, a firm with which his father had an association. He made money out of the American Civil War, and founded his own company, Dabrey, Morgan, and Co. By 1871, he had teamed up with the firm Drexel, to form Drexel, Morgan, and Co, and quickly established himself as one of the leading financiers in New York. After the war, he continued to build up his banking and business empire. He came to the rescue of the US financial system on a couple of occasions, and also served as president of the Metropolitan Museum of Art.

KEY THINKING

- J. P. Morgan built a portfolio of business interests in the key industries of the day—railways, shipping, and electricity.
- He helped consolidate much of the railroads in the US, create US Steel, and was involved in the creation of General Electric, AT&T, and International Harvester.
- As an industry magnate and a powerful industry figure, he came to be seen as a de facto US central banker, being called upon to assist the financial world in times of trouble, and he helped avert a US financial crisis in 1895.

IN PERSPECTIVE

- Morgan established a reputation as a leading financier, with a considerable salary, and industrialists and governments regularly asked him for advice.
- During the 1870s, he focused on the railway industry, resolving disputes, and organizing private investment from the US and Europe to upgrade the system, and generate operating efficiencies.
- However, he failed in an attempt to unite the railways against the government after the passing of the Interstate Commerce Act in 1887, which banned price-fixing in the industry.
- The financial crisis of 1895 originated from the withdrawal of funds from the US by British investors–as the banks were failing, and the stock market collapsing. So the US government used gold reserves to strengthen the financial system, and asked Morgan for help.
- He suggested an economic and a political answer to the crisis–a syndicate of investors would sell gold coin to the US Treasury, paid for by newly issued bonds; he also guaranteed the scheme to President Cleveland.
- This intervention was successful in halting the slide, and also made him a significant profit.
- He was then involved in a number of high-profile deals, including the financing of US Steel, the largest steel corporation in the world.
- He was also an important figure in the creation of industry trusts, but these were seen as collusive business practices by President Theodore Roosevelt, who started cracking down on this practice, making an example of Morgan in the process.
- By the 1890s, these government attacks had turned him into an unpopular figure in the US, and he spent his later years amassing an art collection, and travelling.

MORE INFO

Books:

Chernow, Ron. *The House of Morgan: An American Banking Dynasty and the Rise of Modern Finance*. New York: Atlantic Monthly Press, 1990. Details the influence and operations of Morgan's banks on economic development since the late 18th century, based on research into the family archives.

Strouse, Jean. *Morgan: American Financier*. New York: Random House, 1999. Examines both Morgan's activities as America's leading banker, and his frenetic social life during the Gilded Age.

Wheeler, George. *Pierpont Morgan and Friends: The Anatomy of a Myth*. Englewood Cliffs, NJ: Prentice Hall, 1973. Examines his career and business partnerships.

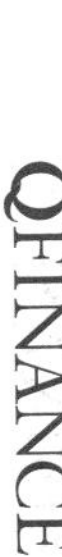

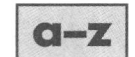

Paul H. O'Neill · Former Secretary to the US Treasury

1935 Born in St Louis, Missouri.
1961 Received degree in economics from Claremont Graduate University.
1961 Appointed a computer systems analyst with the Veterans Administration.
19?? Received master of public administration from Indiana University.
1967 Appointed to the US Office of Management and Budget.
1974 Appointed deputy director of the US Office of Management and Budget.
1977 Appointed vice president of International Paper.
1985 Appointed president of International Paper.
1987 Appointed chairman and chief executive officer of Alcoa.
1995 Appointed chairman of the Rand Corporation.
1997 Cofounded the Pittsburgh Regional Healthcare Initiative.
2001 Appointed US Secretary of the Treasury.
2002 Fired as Secretary of the Treasury by President George W. Bush.
2008 Appointed to the advisory board of the W. Edwards Deming Center for Quality, Productivity, and Competitiveness at Columbia Business School.

LIFE AND CAREER

Paul H. O'Neill is an influential economist, who served under the administrations of Richard Nixon and Gerald Ford, and was the US Secretary of the Treasury under George W. Bush, before resigning, and becoming a harsh critic of the Bush regime. After receiving a bachelor's degree in Economics from California State University, Fresno, he went on to gain further degrees at Claremont Graduate University and Indiana University. He worked at the Veterans' Administration, and the US Office of Management and Budget, was appointed President of International Paper, and then Chairman and Chief Executive Officer of Alcoa. His management of Alcoa was a successful one, with the company increasing its revenues from US$1.5 billion in 1987 to US$23 billion in 2000. He later returned to the public sector under President George W. Bush, where he was noted for taking a different approach, such as touring Africa with singer, Bono, before resigning after disputes with the Bush team over tax issues.

KEY THINKING

- Paul H. O'Neill was US Secretary of the Treasury during part of the first administration of George W. Bush, before resigning in 2002 due to differences in opinion over governmental and tax policies; he has since become a vocal critic of the Bush administration.
- As US Secretary of the Treasury, he was an outspoken member of the administration, often offering opinions that ran counter to the administration's party line.
- He argued against the invasion of Iraq as part of the war on terror, setting himself in opposition to the neo-conservatives in Bush's team.
- He worked hard to push through serious financial and diplomatic engagement in the battle against AIDS in Africa.

IN PERSPECTIVE

- He was asked to be Secretary of Defense by President George H. W. Bush in 1988, but he declined, instead recommending Dick Cheney for the position.
- O'Neill was then appointed to chair an advisory group on education by the president; under his leadership, the advisory group made important recommendations concerning national standards, and unified testing standards.
- While working at the Pittsburgh Regional Healthcare Initiative, he was instrumental in improvements in patient safety and the quality of healthcare; it created a coalition that addressed the existing problems as a region, adopting the scheme of "Perfecting Patient Care."
- A report he commissioned as Treasury Secretary showed that there were potential federal budget deficits of more than US$500 billion, and that massive tax increases or spending cuts would be necessary to meet benefit promises. O'Neill was unhappy that the report's findings were omitted from the 2004 annual budget report.
- As Secretary of the Treasury, his style was often at odds with the financial markets, as well as some of the policy decisions that originated from political advisors who disagreed with the views of leading cabinet officials.
- He questioned President Bush's plans for tax cuts, and his desire to investigate alleged Al-Qaeda funding from some US-allied countries, which led to him being sacked in December 2002.

MORE INFO

Book:

Suskind, Ron. *The Price of Loyalty: George W. Bush, the White House, and the Education of Paul O'Neill*. New York: Simon & Schuster, 2004. An examination of the Bush administration during O'Neill's tenure; it presents Bush's economic policies as irresponsible, claims that he was not greatly involved in meetings, and argues that the war against Iraq was planned in advance.

"Our intention is to give people, however you might stylize it, a tax cut or a pay raise." Paul H. O'Neill

  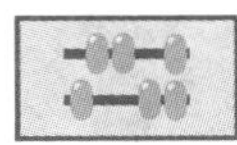 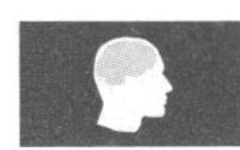  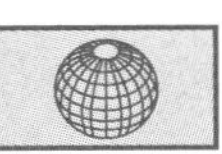   

Michael Eugene Porter · Leading authority on competitive strategy

1947 Born in Ann Arbor, Michigan.
1969 Received BSE in aeronautical engineering from Princeton University.
1971 Received MBA from Harvard Business School.
1973 Received PhD in business economics from Harvard University.
1973 Joined the faculty of Harvard Business School.
1980 Publication of *Competitive Strategy.*
1980 Publication of *Competitive Advantage.*
1983 Publication of *Cases in Competitive Strategy.*
1985 Elected a fellow of the International Academy of Management.
1988 Elected a fellow of the Academy of Management.
1994 Founded and appointed chairman and chief executive officer of the Initiative for a Competitive Inner City.
2006 Publication of *Redefining Health Care.*
2008 Received the Lifetime Achievement Award from the US Department of Commerce.
2008 Publication of *On Competition.*

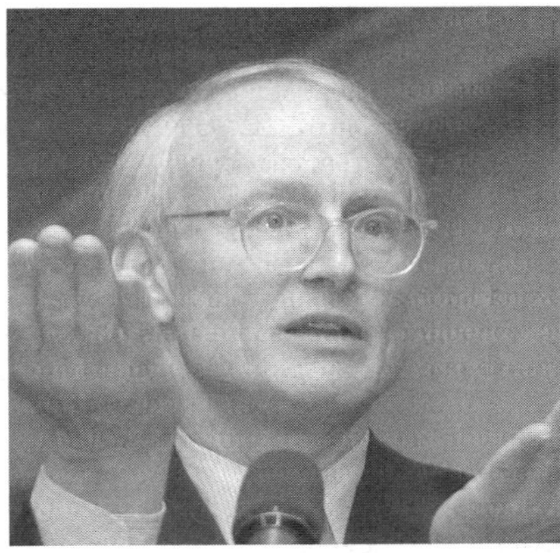

LIFE AND CAREER

Michael Porter is a university professor at Harvard Business School, and an influential thinker on management strategy and economics. His ideas on strategy have become the basis for the required strategy course at the Harvard Business School, and his work is taught in virtually every business school around the world. He also created and chairs Harvard's program for newly appointed CEOs, and he is a leading authority on the competitiveness and economic development of nations, states, and regions. He is the cofounder of the Monitor Group, and has acted as a consultant to businesses, and governments. He is a Fellow Member of the Strategic Management Society. He has played an active role in US economic policy with the Executive Branch, Congress, and international organizations, and is a founding member of the Executive Committee of the Council on Competitiveness. He also chairs the selection committee for the annual Corporate Stewardship Award of the US Secretary of Commerce, and the Global Competitiveness Report.

KEY THINKING

- Michael Porter is at the forefront of advances in research on competitive advantage, by focusing on how a company, region, or country can successfully develop a winning competitive strategy.
- He has shown how this can be achieved through an improvement in organizational innovation, and through factor conditions, demand conditions, related and supporting industries, and company strategy, structure, and rivalry.
- He originated and popularized the concept of the value chain, where products pass through all activities of the chain in order, and increase in value at each activity.
- In *The Competitive Advantage of Nations*, he identifies the fundamental determinants of national competitive advantage in an industry, shows how they work together as a system, and examines "clustering," in which groups of successful firms and industries emerge in one country to gain leading positions in the world market.
- He originated the "Porter hypothesis," which argues that environmental progress and economic competitiveness are more complementary than previously thought.

IN PERSPECTIVE

- Porter's theories on business clusters, and their impact on economic development, have resulted in many cluster initiatives around the world.
- He has explained how, to ensure competitiveness, an organization must choose between three generic strategies: cost leadership, differentiation, and focus.
- These strategies are driven by five competitive forces: the bargaining power of customers, the bargaining power of suppliers, the threat of similar products being brought to market, the threat of new market entrants, and the level of existing competition.
- He focuses on both primary and secondary business activity, with the former being concerned with turning raw materials into products, and the latter relating to activities that support the primary, such as procurement, technology development, human resources, and company infrastructure.
- He produced three critical tests for success: attractiveness, cost-of-entry, and the better-off test, and has introduced seven steps to tackle these questions.
- In a number of articles, he has introduced a new framework for developing strategy in foundations and other philanthropic organizations, and examined how corporations should think strategically about their social responsibility.
- In his latest book, *Redefining Health Care*, he examines competition in the health care system, and looks at ways of improving health care delivery.

MORE INFO

Books:

Porter, Michael. *Competitive Strategy: Techniques for Analyzing Industries and Competitors*. New York: Free Press, 1980.
Porter, Michael. *Cases in Competitive Strategy*. New York: Free Press, 1983.
Porter, Michael. *Competitive Advantage: Creating and Sustaining Superior Performance*. New York: Free Press, 1985.

See Also:

Competitive Strategy: Techniques for Analyzing Industries and Competitors (p. 1341)

"National and economic prosperity is created, not inherited." Michael Eugene Porter

  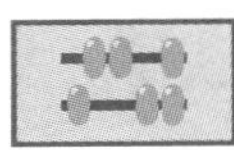 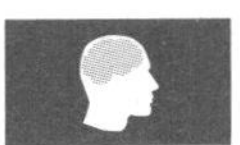     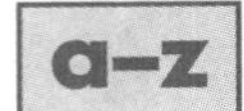

David Ricardo · Founder of the classical school of economics

1772 Born in London.
1786 Started work at the London Stock Exchange.
1810 Publication of *The High Price of Bullion, a Proof of the Depreciation of Bank Notes.*
1814 Retired from business.
1815 Publication of *Essay on Profits.*
1815 Publication of *An Essay on the Influence of a Low Price of Corn on the Profits of Stock.*
1817 Publication of *On the Principles of Political Economy and Taxation.*
1819 Became member of parliament for Portarlington.
1821 Became a founding member of the Political Economy Club.
1823 Died at Gatcombe Park, Gloucestershire, UK.

LIFE AND CAREER

David Ricardo was a political economist and writer, and one of the most important figures in the development of economic theory, introducing the theory of rent, and the concept of comparative advantage to the classical system of political economy. After a brief schooling in Holland, he joined his father at the London Stock Exchange, where he learnt about the financial system, which provided an education on the stock market, and real estate that would prove invaluable to his later work. As a businessman, financier, and speculator, he amassed a considerable fortune, which enabled him to retire from business at the age of 42, to pursue a career in politics, and economic research. He was also a Member of Parliament, and one of the original members of the Geological Society.

KEY THINKING

- Ricardo was one of the most influential economists to develop the classical system of political economy, along with Thomas Malthus, and Adam Smith, and is credited with systematizing economic thought.
- He first gained recognition during the "bullion controversy" of 1809, when he argued that inflation had resulted from the Bank of England's propensity to overissue bank notes.
- In his famous treatise, *Principles of Political Economy and Taxation*, Ricardo laid out the foundations for the principles of a market economy. He also described the guiding concepts behind economic theories such as the law of diminishing returns, and economic rent.
- In *Principles of Political Economy and Taxation*, he integrated his theory of value with his theory of distribution.
- The law of comparative advantage that Ricardo formulated made a significant contribution to political economics. It was developed from Adam Smith's theory of the division of labor, discussed in his seminal work, *An Inquiry into the Nature and Causes of the Wealth of Nations*, and has since become a central tenet of free trade, open markets, and anti-protectionism.
- In *An Essay on the Influence of a Low Price of Corn on the Profits of Stock*, he presented the law of diminishing returns, which states that as more and more resources are combined in production with a fixed resource, the additions to output will diminish.
- In his *Essay on Profits*, he contended that profits depend on high or low wages; wages on the price of necessaries; and the price of necessaries chiefly on the price of food.
- His views have been influential in the work of many more recent economists, including Friedrich Hayek, who discussed the Ricardo Effect based on his theories on the interrelationships between capital, labor, output, and investment.

IN PERSPECTIVE

- Ricardo's law of comparative advantage argues that a nation, which trades in products purchased at a lower cost from another country, is likely to be more prosperous than if it had made the products at home.
- This concept ensures international trade will bring benefits for all countries, but that each country should specialize in making the products in which it possesses a comparative advantage.
- He developed theories of rent, wages, and profits, to explain that as more land was cultivated, farmers would have to start using less-productive land, so that landowners are the ones who gain from productive land.
- He argued that, in the long run, prices reflect the cost of production, calling this long-run price a natural price. The natural price of labor was the cost of its production, the cost of maintaining the laborer.
- His concept of Ricardian equivalence contends that in some circumstances a government's choice of how to pay for its spending might have no effect on the economy.
- Ricardo was admired for his ability to arrive at complex conclusions without the use of mathematics.

MORE INFO

Books:

Henderson, John P., and John B. Davis. *The Life and Economics of David Ricardo*. Boston, MA: Kluwer Academic, 1997. A full examination of Ricardo's life and career, including his later work on money and banking, and international trade.

Ricardo, David. *On the Principles of Political Economy and Taxation*. London: J. Murray, 1817. The groundbreaking book that presents his theory of comparative advantage for the first time, as well as discussing the labor theory of value.

Ricardo, David, and J. R. McCulloch. *The Works of David Ricardo*. London: J. Murray, 1846. An authoritative look at Ricardo's life and work that has been reissued many times.

"There can be no rise in the value of labour without a fall of profits." David Ricardo

  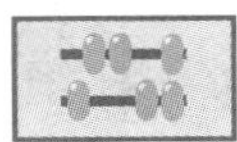 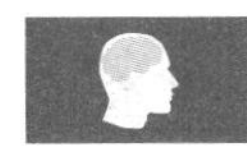  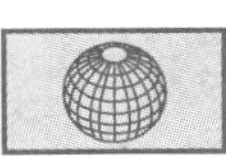   

John D. Rockefeller · American industrialist, and the world's first dollar billionaire

1839 Born in Richford, New York.
1855 Started work at Hewitt & Tuttle.
1859 Founded Rockefeller, Andrews, & Flagler.
1862 Entered oil-refining business.
1869 Rockefeller, Andrews, & Flagler became the Standard Oil Company of Ohio.
1882 The Standard Oil businesses brought under the control of the Standard Oil Company.
1890 Nationwide distribution system reached most towns in the US.
1892 The Trust was dissolved by Ohio government, and reconstituted as Standard Oil Trust.
1900 Standard Oil controlled more than three-quarters of the US petroleum industry.
1904 Standard Oil delivery carts served 80% of US towns.
1911 Resigned as president and Standard Oil Trust was dissolved.
1913 Established Rockefeller Foundation.
1937 Died in Ormond Beach, Florida.

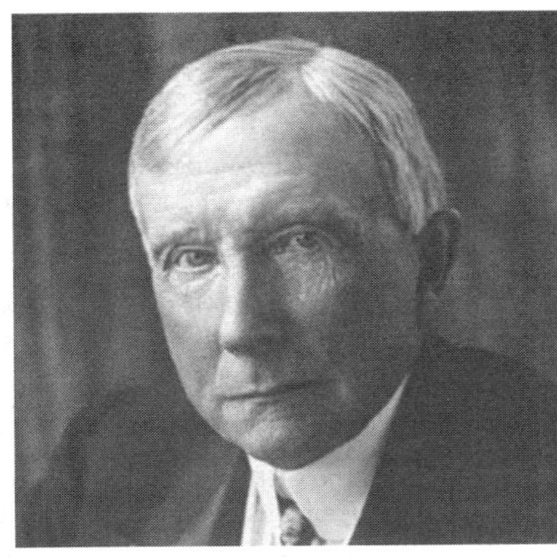

LIFE AND CAREER

John D. Rockefeller was an industrialist, the patriarch of America's best-known family, and the world's richest man of his time. After only a year at high school, and a short time at Folsom Mercantile College, he became an office boy and assistant bookkeeper at the firm of Hewitt & Tuttle. He stayed there for three years, before starting his own business. After this proved successful, he moved into the oil business, buying out most of the local competition, and setting his sights on building a national oil company with a national delivery network. He withdrew from active management of the company in 1897, remaining president until 1911, when the Standard Oil Trust was dissolved by the US government. His final years were devoted to philanthropy, giving away the bulk of his huge fortune through the Rockefeller Foundation.

KEY THINKING

- John D. Rockefeller, the founder of the famously wealthy family dynasty, built up the most powerful oil business in the US, Standard Oil, which refined and marketed nearly 90% of the oil produced in the country.
- His development of Standard Oil to a near-monopolistic position in the US oil industry was part of the larger shift from small business operations to the rise of giant corporations.
- He was extremely successful in creating an empire, and becoming massively wealthy through buying up the competition, and focusing the company on business development and growth.
- His approach received much criticism. There were accusations about the use of unscrupulous tactics, collusion with the railroads, use of predatory pricing, monopolistic practices, and the bribery of political officials.
- The trust that he formed to run Standard Oil was attacked by President Roosevelt, who fought a personal battle against industry trusts in general, and Standard Oil in particular.

IN PERSPECTIVE

- John D. Rockefeller entered the oil industry just as oil was becoming central to the US economy and many refineries were being opened, and he was able to take advantage of the boom.
- Although there was were a large number of companies competing against each other, which forced down prices and made many of them bankrupt, Rockefeller merged his company with the Standard Oil Company of Ohio with US$1 million of capital, and became its president.
- He applied the "combination" strategy to the oil industry that legendary US banker J. P. Morgan had successfully applied to the steel industry—buying up competitors across the country, and spreading the risk inherent in the industry.
- By 1882, his success had enabled him to unite all the businesses of Standard Oil into the single organization of the Standard Oil Trust, which controlled the majority of the oil industry in the US.
- The predominance of the Trust brought criticism, and the Attorney General of Ohio successfully managed to dissolve it. However, it soon reformed as the Standard Oil Company (New Jersey), to take advantage of New Jersey's less-stringent laws.
- In 1911, the US Supreme Court ordered the dissolution of the Standard Oil Company (New Jersey), asserting that it contravened the country's antitrust laws, and all the parts of the business were split into separate entities.
- After his retirement, Rockefeller spent his time on philanthropic work. He donated more than US$35 million to the University of Chicago, founded the Rockefeller Institute for Medical Research, the Rockefeller Foundation, and the Rockefeller Sanitary Commission.
- At its height, Rockefeller's wealth reached US$900 million, but he had given all but US$26,410,837 of it away by the time he died.

MORE INFO

Books:

Chernow, Ron. *Titan: The Life of John D. Rockefeller, Sr.* New York: Random House, 1998.
Morris, Charles R. *The Tycoons: How Andrew Carnegie, John D. Rockefeller, Jay Gould, and J. P. Morgan Invented the American Supereconomy.* New York: H. Holt and Co., 2005.

"The way to make money is to buy when blood is running in the streets." John D. Rockefeller

   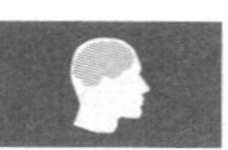     

Stephen A. Ross · Creator of the arbitrage pricing theory

1965 Received BS in physics from CalTech.
1970 Received PhD in economics from Harvard University.
1976 Appointed professor of economics and finance at Yale School of Management.
1979 Developed the Cox–Ross–Rubinstein model.
1985 Developed the Cox–Ingersoll–Ross model.
1988 Publication of *Corporate Finance.*
1988 Appointed president of the American Finance Association.
1991 Publication of *Fundamentals of Corporate Finance.*
1996 Received the Financial Engineer of the Year award from the International Association of Financial Engineers.
1996 Publication of *Essentials of Corporate Finance.*
2005 Publication of *Neoclassical Finance.*
2006 Received the CME-MSRI Prize in Innovative Quantitative Application.
2007 Won the Jean-Jacques Laffont Prize from the Toulouse School of Economics.

LIFE AND CAREER

Stephen Ross is Professor of Financial Economics at the MIT Sloan School of Management, and Chairman of the Investment Advisory Board of IVC International Compensation Valuation Inc. He is also Principal and CIO of Ross Institutional Investors, LLC. After gaining a PhD in Economics from Harvard, he went on teach at the Wharton School and Yale School of Management, before joining MIT. He has founded several investment services firms, acted as a consultant to a number of investment banks and corporations, and served as an adviser to government departments such as the US Treasury, the Commerce Department, and the Internal Revenue Service. He is a former director of Freddie Mac, a Fellow of the Econometric Society, and is a past president of the American Finance Association. He has been the recipient of numerous prizes and awards, including the IAFE Financial Engineer of the Year Award.

KEY THINKING

- Stephen Ross has initiated several important theories, and models in financial economics. He has published more than 100 articles, and one of the classic textbooks on corporate finance.
- He is best known for creating the arbitrage pricing theory, a general theory of asset pricing which argues that the expected return of a financial asset can be modeled as a linear function of various factors, and market indices.
- He was an initiator of the concept of risk-neutral pricing, and the binomial model for pricing derivatives.

IN PERSPECTIVE

- Stephen Ross developed the influential arbitrage pricing theory, an alternative pricing model to the capital asset pricing model (CAPM).
- Unlike CAPM, the arbitrage pricing theory may specify returns as a linear function of more than a single factor.
- He also helped develop the influential Cox–Ross–Rubinstein model, a binomial options pricing model he worked on with John Cox and Mark Rubinstein.
- This model provides a numerical method for the valuation of options, which incorporates a discrete-time model, and a risk-neutrality assumption.
- The financial models he has worked on, including term-structure models and option pricing models, have become standard practice for pricing on the financial markets.
- In 1985, he contributed to the creation of the Cox–Ingersoll–Ross model for interest-rate dynamics, now a central tenet of neoclassical finance.
- This model is a one-factor model that describes the evolution of interest rates, as ascribing movements to market risk alone.
- He gave the inaugural lecture of the Princeton Lectures in Finance in 2001, defending neoclassical finance, including the concepts of efficiency and rationality in the markets.

MORE INFO

Books:

Ross, Stephen A., and Randolph W. Westerfield. *Corporate Finance*. St Louis, MO: Times Mirror/Mosby College Publishing, 1988. A textbook presenting corporate finance that integrates the key features of the subject, and develops the main concepts of modern finance for students.

Ross, Stephen A., Randolph W. Westerfield, and Bradford D. Jordan. *Fundamentals of Corporate Finance*. Homewood, IL: Irwin, 1991. Classic textbook that provides a concise overview of all the basic financial topics in a highly accessible manner.

Ross, Stephen A., Randolph W. Westerfield, and Bradford D. Jordan. *Essentials of Corporate Finance*. Chicago, IL: Irwin, 1996. Distils corporate finance down to its essential features, examining the main concepts and principles for a wide audience.

See Also:

John C. Cox (p. 1276)

"You can't operate a company by fear, because the way to eliminate fear is to avoid criticism. And the way to avoid criticism is to do nothing." Stephen A. Ross

Nouriel Roubini · Leading economic policy adviser

1959 Born in Istanbul, Turkey.
1976 Attended Hebrew University, Jerusalem.
1982 Received BA in economics from Bocconi University, Milan.
1988 Received PhD from Harvard University.
1988 Became a faculty research fellow, National Bureau of Economic Research.
1988 Appointed visiting economist and consultant, International Monetary Fund, Washington, DC.
1991 Became a research fellow at the Centre for Economic Policy Research, London.
1993 Appointed associate professor at the Department of Economics, Yale University.
1995 Appointed associate professor at Stern School of Business, New York University.
1995 Became a consultant for the World Bank, Washington, DC.
1997 Founded RGE Monitor.
1998 Appointed senior economist for international affairs, White House Council of Economic Advisors.
1999 Appointed director of the Office of Policy Development and Review at the US Treasury Department.
2000 Appointed adviser to the US Treasury Department.
2000 Appointed senior adviser to the Under Secretary for International Affairs.
2004 Publication of *Bailouts or Bail-ins? Responding to Financial Crises in Emerging Economies*.
2006 Publication of *New International Financial Architecture*.

LIFE AND CAREER

Nouriel Roubini is Professor of Economics and International Business, Stern School of Business, New York University, and founder and chairman of Roubini Global Economics. After gaining his PhD from Harvard, and joining the faculty of NBER, he worked for the IMF, before returning to academia at Yale, and then Stern School of Business. He has been a Senior Economist for International Affairs on the staff of the President's Council of Economic Advisors, and has served in various roles at the Treasury Department. He is a Member of the Bretton Woods Committee, the Council on Foreign Relations Roundtable on the International Economy, the Academic Advisory Committee, Fiscal Affairs Department, International Monetary Fund, and the Council on Foreign Relation's Roundtable on the International Economy. He also founded the RGE website, a respected economic information resource.

KEY THINKING

- Nouriel Roubini is an internationally known expert in international macroeconomics, and a long-time consultant to the International Monetary Fund, and a number of other public and private institutions, including the US government.
- He has published numerous policy papers and books on key international macroeconomic issues, and is regularly cited as an authority in the media for his views on the future course of the economy.
- He has been a participant and speaker at G-20 meetings of deputy finance ministers, and Central Bank governors' meetings, where he worked on the Asian and global financial crises of 1997–1998, and the subsequent reform of the international financial architecture.
- As Chairman of RGE Monitor, an economic consultancy for financial analysis, he provides strategic financial guidance to businesses.

IN PERSPECTIVE

- Nouriel Roubini's research focuses on international macroeconomics and finance, fiscal policy, political economy, growth theory, and European monetary issues.
- He is known for his bearish views, and was one of the first to forecast a recession in 2006.
- In the book, *Bailouts or Bail-ins?*, he argued that economic policy for troubled emerging markets needed to recognize that each crisis is different and needs to be handled within a framework that provides consistency and predictability to borrowing countries, as well as those who invest in their debt.
- In *Political Cycles and the Macroeconomy*, he explains that the dynamics of political cycles are not short-termist, but more complex, underpinned by an analysis of the relationship between macroeconomic and political policies.

MORE INFO

Books:

Alesina, Alberto, and Nouriel Roubini. *Political Cycles and the Macroeconomy*. Cambridge, MA: MIT Press, 1997. Examines the relationship between political and economic cycles, the timing of elections, government ideology, and how the nature of competition among political parties can influence economic matters.

Roubini, Nouriel, and Brad Setser. *Bailouts or Bail-ins? Responding to Financial Crises in Emerging Economies*. Washington, DC: Institute for International Economics, 2004. Discusses emerging markets, international capital markets, rescue loans, currency devaluations, debt default, and what options are available to resolve the critical issues.

Roubini, Nouriel, and Marc Uzan (eds). *New International Financial Architecture*. Cheltenham, UK: Edward Elgar, 2006. A collection of articles that consider the evolution of international finance during the 1990s.

Website:

Roubini Global Economics: www.roubini.com

"Global imbalances are growing, cross-border financing needs are increasing and a smooth-functioning financial system is now essential for this." Nouriel Roubini

  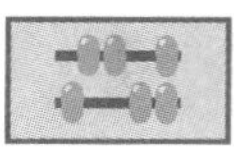 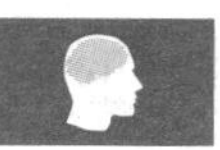  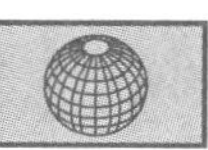   

Paul Samuelson · One of the founders of modern neoclassical economics

1915 Born in Gary, Indiana.
1935 Received BA from the University of Chicago.
1936 Received MA from Harvard University.
1940 Appointed assistant professor of economics at MIT.
1941 Received PhD from Harvard University.
1944 Appointed associate professor of economics at MIT.
1944 Became staff member of the Radiation Laboratory.
1945 Became a part-time professor of international economic relations at Fletcher School of Law and Diplomacy.
1947 Appointed professor of economics at MIT.
1947 Publication of *Foundations of Economic Analysis*.
1947 Awarded the John Bates Clark Medal.
1948 Received Guggenheim Fellowship.
1951 Appointed president of the Econometric Association.
1961 Appointed president of the American Economic Association.
1965 Elected president of the International Economic Association.
1966 Publication of his collected scientific papers begins.
1970 Awarded the Nobel Memorial Prize in Economic Sciences.
2009 Died in Belmont, Massachusetts.

LIFE AND CAREER

Paul Samuelson was an influential economist, academic, and consultant who changed the face of economic theory and practice, through his innovations in many areas of economic research. He worked for the National Resources Planning Board, the War Production Board, and Office of War Mobilization and Reconstruction, the Bureau of the Budget, the Research Advisory Panel to the President's National Goals Commission, the Research Advisory Board Committee for Economic Development, and was a member of the National Task Force on Economic Education. He was an informal consultant for the United States Treasury, and the Council of Economic Advisors. He was also a consultant to the Federal Reserve Bank, and was Economic Adviser to Senator, candidate, and President-elect Kennedy. He was awarded the Nobel Memorial Prize in Economic Sciences for his contribution to neoclassical economic theory.

KEY THINKING

- Paul Samuelson was a leading light of the Harvard generation of 1930s, where he studied under Schumpeter and Leontief, before becoming Professor of Economics at MIT, and creating a powerful economics department.
- He was one of the first economists to generalize and apply mathematical methods developed for the study of thermodynamics to a diverse range of economic issues.
- He helped create the neoclassical synthesis, incorporating Keynesian and neoclassical principles, which now dominates mainstream economics.
- He was one of the progenitors of the Paretian revival in microeconomics, and the neo-Keynesian Synthesis in macroeconomics during the post-war period.

IN PERSPECTIVE

- He took a neoclassical approach to economic theory, focusing on reducing the number of variables, and keeping only a minimum set of simple economic relations and, if possible, rewriting it as a constrained optimization problem.
- His *Foundations of Economic Analysis* was typical of his perspective, as it considers the universal nature of consumer behavior as the key to economic theory, underpinned by mathematical rigor.
- *Foundations of Economic Analysis* helped revive neoclassical economics, and launched the era of mathematization of economics.
- He was one of the first economists to generalize and apply mathematical methods developed from the study of thermodynamics–optimizing behavior of agents, and stability of equilibrium as to economic systems, which was based on classical thermodynamics.
- This innovation established comparative statics in economics, the method for calculating how a change in any parameter affects an economic system.
- Both the multiplier-accelerator macrodynamic model, and his presentation of the Phillips Curve helped make his name.
- In microeconomics, he was responsible for the theory of revealed preference, and also developed the Bergson–Samuelson social welfare functions.
- His work on speculative prices anticipated the efficient markets hypothesis in finance theory, while his research on diversification, and the concept of a "lifetime portfolio" were also respected innovations.
- In international trade theory, he was responsible for the Stolper–Samuelson theorem, and the Factor Price Equalization theorem.

MORE INFO

Books:

Samuelson, Paul A. *Foundations of Economic Analysis*. Cambridge, MA: Harvard University Press, 1947. His magnum opus, a seminal textbook that became a benchmark of neoclassical economics, and helped instigate the mathematization of economics.

Samuelson, Paul A. *Economics*. New York: McGraw-Hill, 1948. Described as the best-selling economics textbook of all time, this classic book gave birth to modern economics.

Szenberg, Michael, Aron A. Gottesman, and Lall Ramrattan. *Paul A. Samuelson: On Being an Economist*. New York: Jorge Pinto Books, 2005. A timely re-examination of Samuelson's career, writings, and research.

"I tell people [investing] should be dull. It shouldn't be exciting. Investing should be more like watching paint dry or watching grass grow. If you want excitement, take $800 and go to Las Vegas." Paul Samuelson

   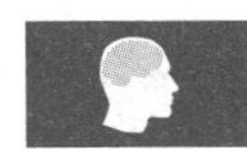  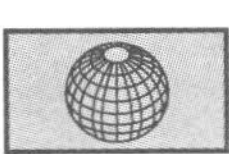   

Jean-Baptiste Say · Early classical political economist

1767 Born in Lyon, France.
1792 Fought as a volunteer in the campaign of Champagne.
1793 Appointed secretary to the Minister of Finance in the French government.
1794 Edited the periodical, *La Decade Philosophique, Litteraire, et Politique.*
1799 Appointed a member of the French Tribunate.
1800 Publication of *Olbie, ou Essai sur les Moyens de Reformer les Moeurs d'une Nation*.
1803 Publication of *A Treatise on Political Economy.*
1819 Appointed to the chair of industrial economy at the Conservatoire des Arts et Métiers.
1820 Publication of *Lettres Malthus.*
1828 Publication of *Cours Complet D'economie Politique Pratique*.
1830 Appointed a member of the Council-General of the Department of the Seine.
1831 Appointed professor of political economy at the Collège de France.
1832 Died in Paris.

LIFE AND CAREER

Jean-Baptiste Say was an economist and businessman, writer, social philosopher, and a successful entrepreneur, and businessman. He initially worked as clerk to a merchant in England before returning to France, where he was employed at a life assurance company. His first published work was a pamphlet on the liberty of the press, published in 1789. He taught at the Conservatoire des Arts and Métiers, and Collège de France and, after being removed from the Tribunate by Napoleon in 1804, he founded a large spinning mill. The restoration of the Bourbon government brought him many honors, and he was subsequently invited to deliver a course of lectures on economics. He is best known as the author of the law of markets, known as Say's Law of Markets (or Say's Law), and as the first to coin the term "entrepreneur."

KEY THINKING

- Say was a central figure in classical economics; he led the revival in the study of political economy, and supported it during a time of opposition to liberal views.
- His most celebrated work was *A Treatise on Political Economy*, which expounded laissez-faire economic principles, and a combination of the utility theory of demand, and Adam Smith's cost theory of supply.
- *A Treatise on Political Economy* was not popular with Napoleon Bonaparte, who demanded he rewrite parts of it to support his move towards protectionism and regulation. When Say refused, Napoleon banned the book and threw him out of the Tribunate.

IN PERSPECTIVE

- Say championed classically liberal principles and argued in favor of competition and free trade, and the lifting of restraints on business.
- He believed that society benefits if the precepts of political economy are widely known, and understood by the people.
- Say's Law of Markets, as outlined in *A Treatise on Political Economy*, states that total demand in an economy cannot exceed or fall below total supply in that economy, so that there can be no demand without supply, and that recession does not occur because of failure in demand, or lack of money.
- Rather, he argued, the more goods that are produced, the more those goods can constitute a demand for other goods, so that prosperity can be increased by stimulating production, not consumption.
- He also proposed that the creation of more money results in inflation. This, he suggested, was because a greater amount of money demanding the same quantity of goods does not represent an increase in real demand.
- Studied the role of entrepreneurs, and their unique importance to the economy as risk-takers and contributors to production, as compared with the manager or the capitalist.

MORE INFO

Books:

Hollander, Samuel. *Jean-Baptiste Say and the Classical Canon in Economics: The British Connection in French Classicism*. London: Routledge, 2005. Examines the similarities and differences between Say's views on economics and the Ricardo School, supported by extensive analysis of Say's writings.

Say, Jean-Baptiste. *A Treatise on Political Economy.* Paris: Déterville, 1803. His most famous book, which helped Say spread his liberal economic ideas, and views on laissez-faire and free trade in many parts of the world.

Whatmore, Richard. *Republicanism and the French Revolution: An Intellectual History of Jean-Baptiste Say's Political Economy.* Oxford: Oxford University Press, 2001. Provides context on the conflict between modern republicanism and other theories of governing societies through Say's writing.

"No set of men are more bigoted to system, than those who boast that they go upon none." Jean-Baptiste Say

  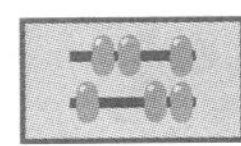 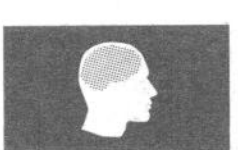     

Myron Scholes · Leading economist, and co-author of the Black–Scholes equation

1941 Born in Timmins, Ontario, Canada.
1961 Received BA in economics from McMaster University, Ontario.
1964 Received MBA.
1968 Appointed associate professor at Sloan School of Management, MIT.
1969 Received PhD from the University of Chicago.
1973 Appointed associate professor at the University of Chicago.
1973 Publication of seminal paper, "The pricing of options and corporate liabilities," with Fischer Black.
1983 Joined Stanford University.
1990 Joined Salomon Brothers as a special consultant.
1992 Publication of *Taxes and Business Strategy: A Planning Approach*.
1994 Cofounded Long-Term Capital Management (LTCM) hedge fund.
1996 Became professor of finance emeritus at Stanford University.
1997 Awarded the Nobel Memorial Prize in Economic Sciences.

LIFE AND CAREER

Myron Scholes is Emeritus Professor of Finance at Stanford, the chairman of Platinum Grove Asset Management, and serves on the boards of various organizations, such as the Chicago Mercantile Exchange, and Dimensional Fund Advisors. In 1973, he published a paper with Fischer Black that presented the Black–Scholes equation, an option-pricing model still widely used in today's markets. In 1990, he joined Salomon Brothers as a managing director, and co-head of its fixed-income derivative sales and trading group, while still conducting research and teaching at Stanford University. He is also a director of the Capital Preservation Fund, a research associate of the National Bureau of Economic Research, and a member of the American Economic Association, and the American Finance Association.

KEY THINKING

- Received the Nobel Prize for developing the Black–Scholes model, a new method for determining the value of derivatives, which provides the framework for options valuation, which has become standard in financial markets.
- The Black–Scholes model is used for a vast number of options trades executed every year, and is the basis for all other binomial option models.
- Wrote several papers on investment banking and incentives with Mark Wolfson, and developed a new theory of tax planning under uncertainty and information asymmetry.
- He has recently focused on the interaction and evolution of markets, and financial institutions.

IN PERSPECTIVE

- Myron Scholes has studied and worked with some of the leading figures in finance and economics, including Fischer Black, Robert Merton, Eugene Fama, Merton Miller, Paul Cootner, and Franco Modigliani.
- While he was at MIT Sloan School of Management, he started working with Black, and Merton, who was also at MIT. They undertook groundbreaking research in asset pricing and derivative pricing models, including the work on their famous option-pricing model.
- They also developed and extended the field of contingent-claims pricing, and examined continuous-time stochastic processes to the problem of devising hedging strategies.
- Scholes worked on testing the capital asset pricing model (CAPM) with Black and Michael Jensen, and developed option-pricing technology with Black.
- At the Graduate School of Business at the University of Chicago, he worked on the effects of taxation on asset prices and incentives, and studied the effects of the taxation of dividends on the prices of securities with Black and Miller.
- Also while at Chicago, he started working with the Center for Research in Security Prices, developing and analyzing high-frequency market data, and helped develop large research data files of daily security prices.
- He examined the efficiency frontier of portfolios—how to construct baskets of assets with optimal trade-offs between risk and return, and focused on the limit of risk-free portfolios.
- In 1994, he joined several colleagues, including John Meriwether and Robert Merton, in founding Long-Term Capital Management (LTCM).
- LTCM was initially extremely successful, with annualized returns of more than 40%; however, in 1998, following crises in the markets in East Asia and Russia, it became the biggest hedge-fund collapse ever seen, losing US$4.6 billion in four months.

MORE INFO

Books:

Lin, Terence, and Andrew W. Lo (eds). *The Derivatives Sourcebook*. Boston, MA: Now Publishers, 2006.

Marlow, Jerry. *Option Pricing: Black–Scholes Made Easy*. New York: Wiley, 2001.

Scholes, Myron. *Taxes and Business Strategy: A Planning Approach*. Englewood Cliffs, NJ: Prentice Hall, 1992.

See Also:

Option Pricing (p. 1239)
Fischer Black (p. 1272)
Robert Merton (p. 1293)
Taxes and Business Strategy: A Planning Approach (p. 1420)

"The world is our laboratory." Myron Scholes

  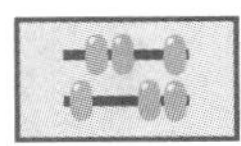 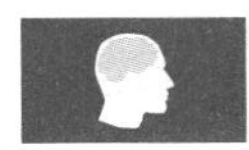  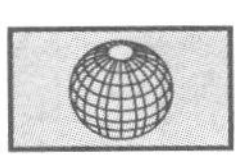   

Ernst Friedrich Schumacher · Internationally renowned economist, and environmentalist

1911 Born in Bonn, Germany.
1930 Rhodes Scholar, New College, Oxford.
1932 Earned diploma in economics, Columbia University, New York.
1933 Appointed assistant lecturer at the School of Banking, Columbia University.
1950 Appointed chief economic adviser to the British Coal Board.
1966 Cofounded the Intermediate Technology Development Group.
1970 Appointed president of the Soil Association.
1973 Publication of *Small Is Beautiful*.
1977 Publication of *A Guide for the Perplexed*.
1977 Died in Romont, Switzerland.
1979 Publication of *Good Work*.

LIFE AND CAREER

Ernst Schumacher was a celebrated economic thinker, with a professional background as a statistician and economist in Britain. He was a Rhodes Scholar at Oxford and continued his studies at Columbia University, before returning to England before the World War II. Although he was interned during the war, his abilities caught the attention of John Maynard Keynes, who organized his release from internment. He was then able to help the British government mobilize both economically and financially during World War II. Keynes also found him a position at Oxford University. After the war, he worked as an economic adviser and then chief statistician for the British Control Commission, rebuilding the German economy. He then worked as chief economic adviser to the British Coal Board for many years, as well as starting his own business producing battery-operated vehicles. He was an author, and one of the chief editorial writers at *The Times* in London, as well as publishing articles in *The Economist* and *Resurgence*.

KEY THINKING

- Ernst Schumacher is best known for his views on the unsustainability of current economic practices, his proposals for human-scale, decentralized, and appropriate technologies, and his economic planning during Britain's post-war economic recovery.
- He proposed the idea of "smallness within bigness," a form of decentralization where large organizations behave like related groups of small organizations to become economically successful.
- His work coincided with the development of mainstream ecology, and he became a renowned figure in the environmental movement.
- His famous essay on Buddhist economics was based on his experiences as advisor to the India Planning Commission, as well as to the governments of Zambia and Burma.
- In *Small Is Beautiful*, he proposed a system of regional economies based on social and ecological principles, and predicted the impending global fuel crisis.
- This book was influential in the development of economics based on humanist principles, reflecting his views on sustainability, and his critique of society as being founded on materialism, greed, and envy.
- While at the National Coal Board, he argued that coal should be preferable to petrol as the main energy source for the world's population. This view was based on his analysis of oil as a finite resource.

IN PERSPECTIVE

- Schumacher's development theories were based around the concepts of intermediate size, and intermediate technology.
- He argued that there should be a shift towards intermediate technologies based on the needs and skills of the people of developing countries, rather than the prevailing ideas of growth, and mass production for its own sake.
- He felt the principles of Buddhist economics focus on the economic rationality of good work as essential to human development, and that production should use local resources, and revolve around local needs.
- He proposed an economic, village-based framework, where human needs and limitations were understood, as was the appropriate use of technology.
- He traveled throughout many developing countries, encouraging local governments to form self-reliant economies, through his development charity, Intermediate Technology Development Group.
- He thought that all major corporations should have a fund for research into, and development of innovative technology.
- He argued against deforestation, and researched the future potential of trees, work that was taken up by the Soil Association after his death.

MORE INFO

Books:

Schumacher, E. F. *Small Is Beautiful: A Study of Economics as if People Mattered*. London: Blond and Bruggs, 1973.
Schumacher, E. F. *A Guide for the Perplexed*. New York: Harper & Row, 1977.
Wood, Barbara. *E. F. Schumacher: His Life and Thought*. London: Jonathan Cape, 1984.

"Man is small, and, therefore, small is beautiful." Ernst Friedrich Schumacher

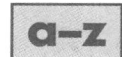

Joseph Schumpeter · Economist, and political scientist

1883 Born in Triesch, Moravia.
1906 Received PhD in law from the University of Vienna.
1909 Appointed professor of economics and government at the University of Czernowitz.
1911 Appointed professor of economics at the University of Graz.
1919 Appointed Austrian Minister of Finance.
1920 Appointed president of the Biederman Bank.
1925 Appointed to a professorship at the University of Bonn.
1932 Lectured at Harvard University.
1934 Publication of *Theory of Economic Development.*
1939 Publication of *Business Cycles.*
1940 Appointed president of the Econometric Society.
1942 Publication of *Capitalism, Socialism and Democracy.*
1948 Appointed president of the American Economic Association.
1950 Died in Taconic, Connecticut.

LIFE AND CAREER

Joseph Schumpeter was an influential economist, classical liberalist, and political scientist, whose research on economic analysis, capitalism, business cycles, and entrepreneurship were central to the development of economic theory in the first half of the 20th century. He was Austrian minister of finance during a period of hyperinflation–which caused his dismissal–before turning to banking. As president of Biederman Bank, he made and lost a fortune, which prompted him to pursue a career in academia. He taught at the University of Bonn, before teaching economics for many years at Harvard, where his pupils included Alan Greenspan and Robert Solow. He was one of the first to study and theorize on the concept of entrepreneurship, and based his research on an attempt to integrate and unite the different social sciences.

KEY THINKING

- Schumpeter was one of the first to analyze the role of entrepreneurs, in *Theory of Economic Development*, arguing that they created innovation and technological change, in the face of competition and falling profits.
- He proposed that the wider economy also benefits from large corporations that have the resources to invest in research and development.
- In *History of Economic Analysis*, he expanded his theory of entrepreneurship and theory of growth into a wider theory of the development of capitalism, also integrating it into theories of the business cycle, and socioeconomic evolution.
- In *Capitalism, Socialism, and Democracy* he defended capitalism as helping to create entrepreneurship, and distinguished inventions from innovations.
- He also discussed how capitalism might evolve, applying the phrase "creative destruction" to describe how traditional ways of doing things are replaced by the new.
- In *Business Cycles*, he develops his arguments against government intervention in industry, first presented in *Theory of Economic Development*.

IN PERSPECTIVE

- Schumpeter believed continual change in the economy meant most businesses fail, becoming victims of innovation by their competitors.
- Argued that entrepreneurs innovate, not just by figuring out how to use inventions, but also by introducing new means of production, new products, and new forms of organization.
- He discounted perfect competition as being the most efficient way to maximize economic wellbeing, viewing some type of monopoly as preferable to holding back competition from innovation.
- He challenged the classical view that democracy is a process by which the electorate choose the politicians who would best carry out the common good, arguing that this was unrealistic, and that politicians set the agenda and manipulate the people.
- He integrated a sociological understanding into his work, as he preferred to use sociology to explain economic principles, rather than the abstract models of his predecessors.
- Helped found the concept of "evolutionary economics," as based on economic change brought about by the interaction between individuals, and the economy as a whole.

MORE INFO

Books:

Backhaus, Jürgen (ed). *Joseph Alois Schumpeter: Entrepreneurship, Style, and Vision*. Boston, MA: Kluwer Academic, 2003. Examines Schumpeter's theories of entrepreneurship and economic development, and contains some of his less well-known, but important works published before he left Europe.

McCraw, Thomas K. *Prophet of Innovation: Joseph Schumpeter and Creative Destruction*. Cambridge, MA: Belknap Press, 2007. Examines the destruction of businesses and careers in the struggle for a better material life.

Schumpeter, Joseph. *Capitalism, Socialism and Democracy*. New York: Harper & Brothers, 1942. Predicts the downfall of capitalism, as it progresses towards a form of hostile corporatism, led by intellectuals amid "creative destruction."

"The ballot is stronger than bullets." Joseph Schumpeter

     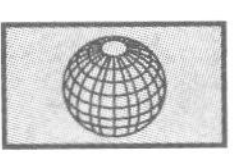   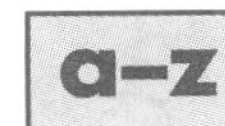

William F. Sharpe · Nobel Prize-winning financial economist

1934 Born in Boston, Massachusetts.
1955 Received BA in economics from the University of California, Los Angeles.
1956 Received MA in economics from the University of California.
1956 Appointed an economist at the Rand Corporation.
1961 Received PhD in economics from the University of California.
1961 Appointed associate professor at the University of Washington.
1968 Appointed professor at the University of California at Irvine.
1970 Appointed professor at Stanford University.
1970 Publication of *Portfolio Theory and Capital Markets*.
1971 Appointed professor of finance at Stanford University.
1978 Publication of *Investments*.
1980 Appointed president of the American Finance Association.
1986 Cofounded and became president of Sharpe-Russell Research.
1987 Publication of *Asset Allocation Tools*.
1989 Became professor emeritus of finance at Stanford University.
1990 Received the Nobel Memorial Prize in Economic Sciences.
1990 Became chairman of William F. Sharpe Associates.
1993 Appointed professor of finance at Stanford University.
1996 Cofounded Financial Engines.
2007 Publication of *Investors and Markets*.

LIFE AND CAREER

William Sharpe is professor of finance emeritus at Stanford University's Graduate School of Business, a Nobel Prize-winning economist, and a key figure in the development of investment theory. He joined the Stanford faculty in 1970, having previously taught at the University of Washington and the University of California at Irvine. He has worked at the National Bureau of Economic Research, studying issues of bank capital adequacy, and has published renowned research articles in a number of professional journals. He has also been a consultant to Merrill Lynch and Wells Fargo, and cofounded Financial Engines in 1996, to provide investment management advice, especially for those in employer-sponsored retirement plans.

KEY THINKING

- Sharpe received the Nobel Prize for his research on the capital asset pricing model (CAPM), where he structured a portfolio's risk into systematic or non-specific risk, and non-systematic or specific risk.
- The research was based on his search for an equilibrium theory of asset pricing and Harry Markowitz's portfolio theory, and is now a foundation for financial economics.
- His research into equilibrium in capital markets focused on its implications for investment portfolio decision-making.
- The model shows how every investment carries two distinct risks—the risk of being in the market, or systematic risk, which cannot be diversified away, and unsystematic risk, which is specific to a company's fortunes.
- One implication of Sharpe's work is that the expected return on a portfolio in excess of a riskless return should be beta times the excess return of the market.

IN PERSPECTIVE

- Sharpe, Harry Markowitz and Merton Miller all shared the Nobel Prize for their contributions to financial economics, which helped establish it as a separate field of study.
- Sharpe showed how CAPM implies a single mix of risky assets fits in every investor's portfolio—those who want a high return should hold a portfolio heavily weighted with the risky asset, while those who want a low return hold a portfolio heavily weighted with a riskless asset.
- He produced a number of innovations in investment analysis, including the Sharpe Ratio for risk-adjusted investment performance analysis—the ratio evaluates the level of risk a fund accepts against the return it delivers.
- He also contributed to the development of the binomial method for the valuation of options, as well as the gradient method for optimizing asset allocation, and returns-based analysis for evaluating the style and performance of investment funds.
- He developed a method for finding approximate solutions to a class of portfolio analysis problems, which has been widely implemented.

MORE INFO

Books:

Sharpe, William F. *Portfolio Theory and Capital Markets*. New York: McGraw-Hill, 1970. His classic book on investment and portfolio theory. It presents his groundbreaking work on the capital asset pricing model, and examines the behavior of the financial markets under different conditions.

Sharpe, William F., Gordon J. Alexander, and Jeffrey V. Bailey. *Investments*. 6th ed. Upper Saddler River, NJ: Prentice-Hall, 1999. His successful textbook, which has been updated and revised over the years, provides the theoretical framework for understanding securities, and the securities markets.

Sharpe, William F. *Investors and Markets: Portfolio Choices, Asset Prices, and Investment Advice*. Princeton, NJ: Princeton University Press, 2007. His most recent book, which is a technical overview of investment theory, and explains his approach to asset pricing in an accessible style. It also summarizes much of Sharpe's seminal work over the years.

See Also:

Sharpe Ratio (p. 1253)
Harry Markowitz (p. 1292)
Merton Miller (p. 1294)
Portfolio Theory and Capital Markets (p. 1409)

"Some investments do have higher expected returns than others. Which ones? Well, by and large they're the ones that will do the worst in bad times." William F. Sharpe

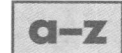

Jeremy Siegel · Renowned finance academic, and writer

1945 Born in Chicago, Illinois.
1967 Received BA in mathematics and economics from Columbia University.
1971 Received PhD in economics from Massachusetts Institute of Technology.
1971 National Science Foundation post-doctoral fellowship at Harvard University.
1972 Appointed assistant professor of business economics, Graduate School of Business, University of Chicago.
1976 Appointed professor of fFinance at the Wharton School of the University of Pennsylvania.
1984 Appointed head of macroeconomics Training for JP Morgan.
1984 Appointed associate editor of the *Journal of Money, Credit and Banking*.
1988 Appointed academic director of the US Securities Institute.
1988 Appointed director in the Trust Department at the Continental Bank.
1990 Taught on the Merrill Lynch economics and finance program.
1991 Appointed advisor to the Asian Securities Industry Association.
1993 Received the Graham and Dodd Award from the Association for Investment Management and Research.
1994 Publication of *Stocks for the Long Run*.
1998 Received the American Library Association Outstanding Academic Book Award for *Stocks for the Long Run*.
2001 Appointed a fellow of the World Economic Forum, Davos, Switzerland.
2005 Publication of *The Future for Investors*.
2005 Received the Nicholas Molodovsky Award from the Chartered Financial Analysts Institute.

LIFE AND CAREER

Jeremy Siegel is professor of finance at the Wharton School of the University of Pennsylvania, and provides analysis of the economy and financial markets in the press, on television networks, and at conferences, and international programs. He writes regular columns for *Kiplinger's Personal Finance* and *Yahoo! Finance*, and is an advisor to Wisdom Tree Investments. He has also contributed articles to the *Wall Street Journal*, *Barron's*, the *Financial Times*, and other national and international news media. He is currently the academic director of the US Securities Industry Institute.

KEY THINKING

- Jeremy Siegel is a staunch proponent of long-term investing, and is a respected teacher, having received the highest teaching rating in a worldwide ranking of business school professors conducted by *Business Week* magazine.
- He has long argued that a diversified basket of inherently risk-laden equities, if retained over a long period, will produce better returns, and be safer than traditional secure investments such as bonds, and bank savings accounts.
- He and Robert Shiller, a professor at Yale School of Management, have frequently debated with each other on TV about the stock market, and its future returns, and have become financial media celebrities.
- In *Revolution on Wall Street*, he analyzes how the market dominance of Wall Street has been overturned by new alternative markets with cheaper transaction systems, government regulation, and bureaucratic problems.
- In *Stocks for the Long Run*, he shows the amateur how to understand market forces, and the best way to put together a successful portfolio, based on an awareness of stock behavior, past trends, and future movements.
- In *The Future for Investors*, he argues that more traditional companies perform better over time than growth stocks, especially those in the technology sector.

IN PERSPECTIVE

- Jeremy Siegel describes stocks as being undervalued for the last 200 years, and that stock markets in the digital age are now more efficient, and safer over the long term.
- He conducted an in-depth study for the New York Stock Exchange in the 1980s, the data for which proved that the compound annual real return on US stocks has been nearly 7% over the past 200 years.
- He has predicted that an unprecedented wave of innovation will create economic growth in the US, which will provide strong returns for those investors who show patience. The prediction is based on his analysis of global trends, such as demographics and shifts in labor, manufacturing capacity, and capital movement.

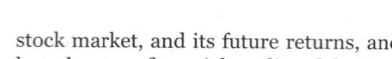

MORE INFO

Books:

Blume, Marshall E., Jeremy J. Siegel, and Dan Rottenberg. *Revolution on Wall Street: The Rise and Decline of the New York Stock Exchange*. New York: WW Norton, 1993.
Siegel, Jeremy J. *Stocks for the Long Run: A Guide for Selecting Markets for Long-Term Growth*. Burr Ridge, IL: Irwin, 1994.
Siegel, Jeremy J. *The Future for Investors: Why the Tried and the True Triumph Over the Bold and the New*. New York: Crown Business, 2005.

Website:

Siegel's own website: www.jeremysiegel.com

See Also:

Stocks for the Long Run: The Definitive Guide to Financial Market Returns and Long-Term Investment Strategies (p. 1418)

"The economy will start screaming uncle eventually." Jeremy Siegel

Adam Smith · The father of modern economics

1723 Born in Kirkcaldy, Great Britain.
1748 Appointed lecturer in literature at Edinburgh University.
1751 Appointed professor of literature at Glasgow University.
1752 Appointed professor of moral philosophy at Glasgow University.
1762 Received the title of doctor of laws from Glasgow University.
1763 Publication of *The Theory of Moral Sentiments*.
1763 Publication of *Lectures on Justice, Police, Revenue, and Arms*.
1763 Appointed tutor to the Duke of Buccleuch.
1764 Publication of *A Treatise on Public Opulence*.
1773 Elected as a fellow of the Royal Society of London.
1775 Elected as a member of the Literary Club.
1776 Publication of *The Wealth of Nations*.
1778 Appointed commissioner of customs in Scotland.
1783 Cofounded the Royal Society of Edinburgh.
1787 Elected lord rector of Glasgow University.
1790 Died in Edinburgh, Great Britain.

LIFE AND CAREER

Adam Smith was a moral philosopher, a pioneer of political economy, and one of the key figures of the Scottish enlightenment in the 18th century. At 14, he won a scholarship to study mathematics and moral philosophy at Glasgow University, before studying at Balliol College, Oxford. He returned to Glasgow University in 1751, to teach literature, before being appointed Professor of Moral Philosophy at the university. He was then appointed tutor to the Duke of Buccleuch, during his grand tour of Europe, when he met Benjamin Franklin, Francois Quesnay, Voltaire, and Rousseau, among others. He spent much of his later life writing on economics, social issues, and philosophy, which brought him great popularity.

KEY THINKING

- Adam Smith was an anti-establishment figure, and a social radical who believed in liberty and equality. His writing focused on the transformation of industry and commerce in Europe.
- His magnum opus and most influential work, *The Wealth of Nations*, was an immediate success, selling out the first edition in only six months, and was the first modern work on economics.
- It helped popularize his laissez-faire arguments for government non-intervention, and provided a rationale for free trade, and capitalism. It hastened the end of the mercantilist era, and ignited a new economic approach based on individualism, and the "natural laws" he espoused.
- The three main concepts he proposed are now the foundation of free market economics: division of labor, the pursuit of self-interest, and the freedom to trade.
- In *The Theory of Moral Sentiments*, he also explores moral judgments within the context of people being motivated by self-interest, while acknowledging that individuals have "social propensities" for sympathy, justice and benevolence.
- This theory of sympathy is based on the argument that, in observing others, we are made aware of our own actions, and the moral context for our behavior.

IN PERSPECTIVE

- In *The Wealth of Nations*, he argued that all human powers are subject to natural, moral, and physical laws, and proposed that government should leave economic matters alone, to work naturally, which he argued would benefit individuals and the state.
- His book expounds the value of individual liberty, and the pursuit of self-interest as being of value for society as a whole. His natural law involves a "law of labor," where the environment provides the products necessary for subsistence, in return for their labor, and that everyone should therefore have the right to do what they need to preserve their existence.
- He found the free market ensured the best balance in goods and services through a so-called "invisible hand"—that society and commerce benefits from people behaving in their own interests.
- He believed that while human motives were often driven by selfishness and greed, the competition in the free market would tend to benefit society as a whole by keeping prices low, while still building in an incentive for the production of a wide variety of goods and services.

MORE INFO

Books:

Buchan, James. *The Authentic Adam Smith: His Life and Ideas*. London: Profile, 2006. This comprehensive study of Smith goes beyond his role as founder of the laissez-faire approach to free markets, to also consider his writings on philosophy, and aesthetics.

Smith, Adam. *The Theory of Moral Sentiments*. London: A. Millar, 1759. Presents a framework for a new system of morals, making it a seminal text in the development of moral and political thought.

Smith, Adam. *An Inquiry into the Nature and Causes of the Wealth of Nations*. London: W. Strahan and T. Cadell, 1776. Ten years in the writing, his most famous work presents a range of ideas that challenged the contemporary mercantilist government, and its protectionist laws.

See Also:

The Money Game (p. 1397)
The Wealth of Nations (p. 1433)

"There is no art which one government sooner learns of another than that of draining money from the pockets of the people." Adam Smith

George Soros · Billionaire philanthropist who "broke" the Bank of England

1930 Born in Budapest, Hungary.
1947 Emigrated to England.
1952 Graduated from the London School of Economics.
1956 Moved to the United States.
1956 Appointed an arbitrage trader at FM Mayer.
1959 Joined Wertheim and Co. as an analyst.
1963 Joined Arnhold and S. Bleichroeder Advisers.
1967 Ran the offshore investment fund, First Eagle, for Arnhold and S. Bleichroeder.
1969 Appointed head of a second fund for Arnhold and S. Bleichroeder, Double Eagle.
1970 Cofounded the Quantum Fund.
1987 Publication of *The Alchemy of Finance*.
2006 Publication of *The Age of Fallibility: Consequences of The War on Terror.*
2008 Pubication of *The New Paradigm for Financial Markets*.

LIFE AND CAREER

George Soros is a financial speculator, stock investor, billionaire, philanthropist, and political activist, and is known for "breaking the Bank of England" on Black Wednesday in 1992. He was 13 when Nazi Germany invaded Hungary. To avoid being apprehended by the Nazis, his father sent him to live with a non-Jewish employee, posing as his godson. His first experience of finance was trading currencies during the Hungarian hyperinflation period of 1945–1946. In 1946, he escaped the Soviet occupation and moved to England to study. After graduating from LSE, he secured a position with London merchant bank, Singer & Friedlander, before becoming a trader and analyst, and then managing increasingly successful investment funds. After making his fortune, he turned to philanthropy, and politics. He is the founder and chairman of Soros Fund Management and the Open Society Institute, and is also a former member of the board of directors of the Council on Foreign Relations, and of the Carlyle Group.

KEY THINKING

- George Soros is probably the most successful speculator of all time; he ascribes his success to being able to recognize when his predictions are wrong.
- The Quantum Fund, which he founded with Jim Rogers, returned 42.6% per year in its first 10 years and helped make Soros' fortune. In 2007, the fund returned almost 32%, netting him US$2.9 billion.
- On Black Wednesday in 1992, he gained celebrity (and money) by selling short more than US$10 billion worth of pounds, earning an estimated US$1.1 billion in the process, when the Bank of England was forced to withdraw the currency from the European exchange rate mechanism (ERM), and to devalue the pound.
- He now spends most of his time writing, focusing on his philanthropic activities, and using his wealth in emerging markets in a bid to encourage them towards democracy.

IN PERSPECTIVE

- He is reported to use the investing technique of buying during the upturns and taking the profit, waiting patiently, and then selling short during the downward cycle.
- Reputed to have given away more than US$6 billion, he has been active as a philanthropist since the 1970s, when he began providing funds to help black students attend the University of Cape Town, South Africa, during apartheid.
- He has increasingly funded projects opposing totalitarian regimes in emerging countries; promoting non-violent democratization in the post-Soviet states, supporting the Solidarity movement in Poland, and the Czechoslovak human rights organization, Charter 77. His funding and organization of Georgia's Rose Revolution was considered critical to its success.
- He has developed a philosophy of "reflexivity," largely influenced by Karl Popper, under whom he studied at the London School of Economics.
- Under reflexivity, events create expectations that influence the financial markets—the markets, in turn, then influence these events, creating a cycle (which can be either "virtuous or vicious").
- He argues that reflexivity, and the biases affecting market transactions, can change the fundamentals of the economy, which are typically marked by disequilibrium rather than equilibrium, and that the efficient market hypothesis does not apply in these situations.
- In 1988, he was accused of insider dealing regarding a takeover attempt of Société Générale, and fined US$2 million by a French court, although he denied any wrongdoing and said news of the takeover was public knowledge.

MORE INFO

Books:

Kaufman. Michael T. *Soros: The Life and Times of a Messianic Billionaire*. New York: Knopf, 2002. The authorized biography of Soros, which looks at how he made his fortune.

Soros, George. *The Alchemy of Finance: Reading the Mind of the Market*. New York: Simon & Schuster, 1987.

Soros, George. *The New Paradigm for Financial Markets: The Credit Crisis of 2008 and What It Means*. New York: PublicAffairs, 2008.

Website:

Soros' website: www.georgesoros.com

See Also:

The Alchemy of Finance: Reading the Mind of the Market (p. 1330)

"My peculiarity is that I don't have a particular style of investing or, more exactly, I try to change my style to fit the conditions." George Soros

Joseph Stiglitz · American economist renowned for his critical view on globalization

1943 Born in Gary, Indiana.
1965 Researcher at University of Chicago.
1966 Appointed assistant professor at Massachusetts Institute of Technology.
1967 Received PhD from Massachusetts Institute of Technology.
1969 Fulbright research fellow at the University of Cambridge.
1979 Received the John Bates Clark Medal.
1995 Appointed chairman of the Council of Economic Advisers.
1997 Appointed chief economist of the World Bank.
2000 Founded the Initiative for Policy Dialogue.
2001 Appointed professor at Columbia University.
2001 Received the Nobel Memorial Prize in Economic Sciences.
2002 Publication of *Globalization and Its Discontents*.
2003 Appointed university professor at Columbia University.
2006 Publication of *Making Globalization Work*.
2008 Publication of *The Three Trillion Dollar War*.
2010 Publication of *Freefall*.

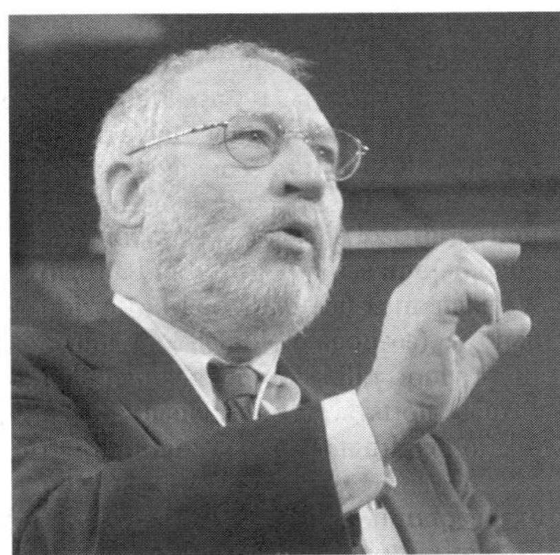

LIFE AND CAREER

Joseph Stiglitz is an economist, a writer on globalization and its effects, and a former senior vice-president and chief economist of the World Bank. He has held professorships at Yale, Duke, Stanford, Oxford, and Princeton universities, and currently teaches at Columbia. He chairs the University of Manchester's Brooks World Poverty Institute, Columbia's Committee on Global Thought, and is President Elect of the International Economic Association. He is the most cited economist in the world, and has served in the Clinton Administration, as chair of the President's Council of Economic Advisors, in which capacity he also served as a member of the cabinet. He has been a member of the Intergovernmental Panel on Climate Change, and was recently appointed to chair a Commission on the Measurement of Economic Performance and Economic Progress.

KEY THINKING

- Stiglitz helped develop a new branch of economics, "the economics of information," which explores information asymmetries; it was based on his research on screening, for which he was awarded the Nobel Prize.
- He has been a critic of the management of globalization, free-market economists, and international institutions such as the International Monetary Fund, and the World Bank.
- His tenure at the World Bank was during protests against globalization, and he was fired as Chief Economist for expressing dissent with its policies.
- In his book, *Stability with Growth*, he focused on macroeconomic policy and capital market liberalization, and developed a new framework for assessing alternative policies, based on real stability and long-term, sustainable, and equitable growth.
- *Making Globalization Work* considers the global economy, and the mechanisms by which developed countries exert an excessive influence over developing nations.
- He argues that through tariffs, subsidies, a complicated patent system, and pollution, economies are being economically and politically destabilized, and that strong, transparent institutions are needed to redress the balance.
- In *Globalization and Its Discontents*, he argues that developing economies are not really developing at all, and blames the IMF for stifling growth and information.
- In *Whither Socialism?*, he analyzes information economics and the theory of markets with imperfect information and imperfect competition, and offers a critique of both free-market and socialist approaches.
- This research counters prevailing neoclassical economics, arguing that markets are only efficient under exceptional circumstances.

IN PERSPECTIVE

- Stiglitz has made major contributions to macroeconomics and monetary theory, to development economics and trade theory, to public and corporate finance, to the theories of industrial organization and rural organization, and to the theories of welfare economics, and of income and wealth distribution.
- He also pioneered such concepts as adverse selection and moral hazard, which have now become standard tools of researchers and policy analysts.
- The Shapiro–Stiglitz model of efficiency wages, which he developed with the economist Carl Shapiro, examines unemployment, and why wages are not bid down to enable full employment.
- The model states that unemployment is driven by the information structure of employment, and dependent on the cost to firms in knowing how much effort their workers are putting in.

MORE INFO

Books:

Chang, Ha-Joon. *The Rebel Within: Joseph Stiglitz and the World Bank*. London: Anthem Press, 2001.
Stiglitz, Joseph. *Globalization and Its Discontents*. New York: WW Norton, 2002.
Stiglitz, Joseph, and Linda J. Bilmes. *The Three Trillion Dollar War: The True Cost of the Iraq Conflict*. New York: WW Norton, 2008.

See Also:

Globalization and Its Discontents (p. 1368)

"Economists often like startling theorems, results which seem to run counter to conventional wisdom." Joseph Stiglitz

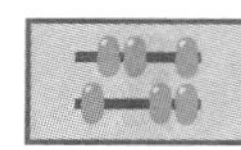
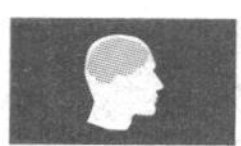

Richard Thaler · Influential thinker on behavioral finance

1945 Born in East Orange, New Jersey.
1967 Received BA from Case Western Reserve University.
1970 Received MS from the University of Rochester.
1974 Received PhD in economics from the University of Rochester.
1978 Appointed assistant professor of economics and public administration, Graduate School of Business and Public Administration, Cornell University.
1980 Appointed associate professor, Johnson Graduate School of Management, Cornell University.
1986 Appointed professor of economics, Johnson Graduate School of Management, Cornell University.
1991 Appointed visiting scholar, Russell Sage Foundation, New York.
1991 Publication of *Quasi-Rational Economics.*
1993 Publication of *The Winner's Curse.*
1993 Publication of *Advances in Behavioral Finance.*
1995 Appointed professor of behavioral science, economics, and finance at the Graduate School of Business, the University of Chicago.
1995 Appointed director of the Center for Decision Research, University of Chicago.
2005 Received the Paul A. Samuelson Award.
2008 Publication of *Nudge.*

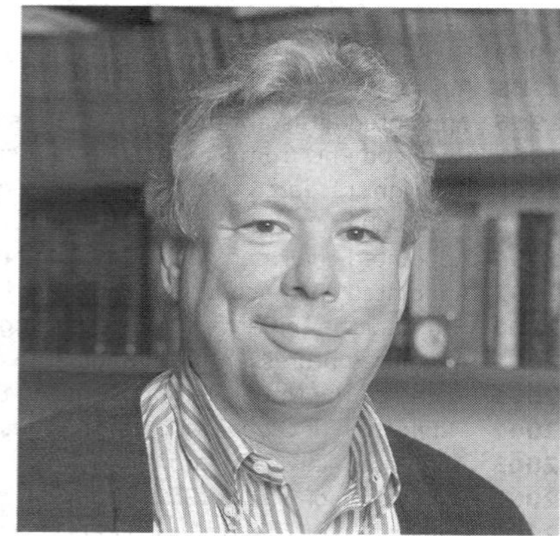

LIFE AND CAREER

Richard Thaler taught at Cornell University and Massachusetts Institute of Technology Sloan School of Management, and is now Professor of Behavioral Science, Economics and Finance at the Graduate School of Business, the University of Chicago, and Director of its Center for Decision Research. He regularly consulted with Barack Obama's economic advisor for the 2008 presidential campaign. Thaler has also organized a series of behavioral finance seminars along with Robert Shiller, another behavioral finance expert, at the Yale School of Management. He is an associate at the National Bureau of Economic Research, co-head of its Behavioral Finance Project, and is the founder of Fuller & Thaler Asset Management Inc.

KEY THINKING

- Richard Thaler is a pioneer in behavioral economics and finance, as well as the psychology of decision-making, helping transform the study of economics by trying to understand how people behave financially.
- He gained attention for a regular column in the *Journal of Economic Perspectives on Anomalies*, where he examined economic behavior that ran counter to traditional microeconomic theory.
- He has written on a wide variety of subjects, from savings and investing, to marketing, decision-making, and financial markets. Recent papers have included an examination of behavior on the television game show, *Deal or No Deal*, and an analysis of the National Football League Draft.
- He has continued to demonstrate the irrationalities inherent in the financial markets, arguing against the neoclassical view that rationality underpins the financial system.
- In *Nudge*, Thaler and co-author Sunstein examine everyday factors that can influence our decisions.
- They argue that institutions, including the government, should use the science of choice and decision-making to impel people to improve their lives, based on the insights of behavioral economics.

IN PERSPECTIVE

- Thaler is considered to have originated the field of behavioral economics, an area of study that integrates psychological research with economic theory.
- He developed the work of Nobel Prize-winning psychologists Daniel Kahneman and Amos Tversky, and their analysis of why people are more concerned with changes in wealth than with their absolute level.
- This research helped explain Thaler's work on anomalies; Kahneman cited his joint work with Thaler as a major factor in his receiving the Nobel Prize in Economics.
- Thaler also focused on "mental accounting," which is based on Kahneman and Tversky's "framing" principle, which examines how the positioning of choices prejudices the outcome.
- He proposed that most people are prone to error, irrationality, and emotion, and that they behave in ways not always consistent with maximizing their own financial wellbeing.
- He received the Paul A. Samuelson Award for his work on the "Save More Tomorrow" project, a plan that allows employees to commit some of their future salary increases toward retirement accounts.

MORE INFO

Books:

Thaler, Richard H. *The Winner's Curse: Paradoxes and Anomalies of Economic Life*. New York: Free Press, 1992.

Thaler, Richard H. (ed). *Advances in Behavioral Finance*. New York: Russell Sage Foundation, 1993.

Thaler, Richard H., and Cass R. Sunstein. *Nudge: Improving Decisions About Health, Wealth, and Happiness*. New Haven, CT: Yale University Press, 2008.

See Also:

Advances in Behavioral Finance (p. 1327)

"We can understand much more about the behavior of markets, even financial markets, if we learn more about the behavior of the people who operate in these markets." Richard Thaler

James Tobin · American economist proponent of Keynesian economics

1918 Born in Champaign, Illinois.
1940 Received BA from Harvard University.
1941 Worked as an economist in the Office of Price Administration and Civilian Supply and the War Production Board in Washington, DC.
1947 Received PhD from Harvard University.
1947 Elected as a junior fellow of Harvard University's Society of Fellows.
1950 Appointed associate professor of economics at Yale University.
1955 Appointed president of the Cowles Foundation.
1957 Appointed Sterling professor at Yale University.
1958 Appointed president of the American Econometric Association.
1955 Received the John Bates Clark medal.
1961 Served as a member of John F. Kennedy's Council of Economic Advisors.
1962 Started work as a consultant.
1971 Appointed president of the American Economic Association.
1971 Publication of *Essays in Economics*.
1972 Publication of *Is Growth Obsolete?*
1977 Appointed president of the Eastern Economics Association.
1981 Received the Nobel Memorial Prize in Economic Sciences.
2002 Died in New Haven, Connecticut.

LIFE AND CAREER

James Tobin was a renowned economist, writer, and Nobel Prize winner, known for his work on portfolio theory, Keynesian economics, Tobin's q, and the Tobit Model. He taught at Yale for many years, and researched and wrote primarily on macroeconomic issues, as well as working as an economics expert, and policy consultant. He was a member of President Kennedy's Council of Economic Advisors, served two terms as president of the Cowles Foundation, and several terms as a member of the board of governors of the Federal Reserve System Academic Consultants. He was also a consultant of the US Treasury Department, and an advisor to 1972 presidential candidate, George McGovern. He received the Nobel Memorial Prize in Economic Sciences in 1981, for his analysis of the financial markets, and their relations to expenditure decisions, employment, production, and prices.

KEY THINKING

- James Tobin was a central figure in the development of economics research and monetary policy in the 20th century.
- He made pioneering contributions to the field of macroeconomics, the study of investment, monetary theory and policy, fiscal policy, and public finance. He was also interested in consumption and saving, unemployment and inflation, portfolio theory, and asset market econometrics.
- His work as a consultant helped design the Keynesian economic policy implemented by the Kennedy administration.
- In 1972, he submitted a proposal for a levy, known as the Tobin Tax, on international currency transactions, as part of an attempt to reduce short-term currency speculation. The tax has recently been at the forefront of discussions about various economic crises.

IN PERSPECTIVE

- His research extended Keynesian economic theory by clarifying issues such as risk, portfolio management, and the role of financial markets in communicating information about underlying economic conditions.
- Tobin's work advanced portfolio theory, and led to the modern theory of portfolio choice asset pricing—that diversification of interests offers the best possibility of security for investors, and that investments should not always be based on highest rates of return.
- He developed Tobin's q, which is a ratio comparing the value of a company given by financial markets with the value of a company's assets, and is calculated by dividing the market value of a company by the replacement value of its assets.
- He introduced the Tobit Model, a frequently used tool for modeling censored variables in econometrics research, and which focuses on the relationship between a non-negative dependent variable and an independent variable.
- Other research included an examination of the inherent pitfalls in financial model building, portfolio balance, and flow-of-funds models, the lifecycle model and social security, and econometric methodology, including the Tobit estimator.
- He also made contributions to mean-variance portfolio demand and asset pricing theory, especially the portfolio separation theorem.

MORE INFO

Books:

Brainard, William C., William D. Nordhaus, and Harold W. Watts (eds). *Money, Macroeconomics, and Economic Policy: Essays in Honor of James Tobin*. Cambridge, MA: MIT Press, 1991.

Tobin, James. *Essays in Economics*. Chicago, IL: Markham Pub. Co., 1971. Presents his macroeconomic writings from the 1940s to 1970.

ul Haq, Mahbub, Inge Kaul, and Isabelle Grunberg (eds). *The Tobin Tax: Coping with Financial Volatility*. New York: Oxford University Press, 1996.

"The miserable failures of capitalist economies in the Great Depression were root causes of worldwide social and political disasters." James Tobin

Amos Tversky · Pioneer of cognitive science

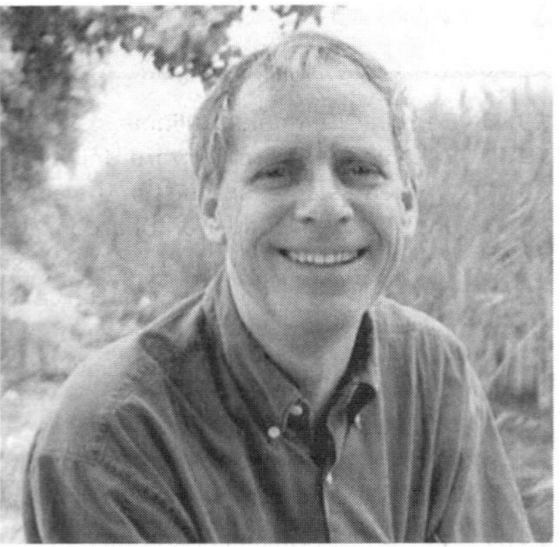

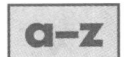

1937 Born in Haifa, Israel.
1961 Received BA from Hebrew University.
1965 Received PhD from the University of Michigan.
1966 Taught at Hebrew University in Jerusalem.
1970 Became a fellow at the Center for Advanced Study in the Behavioral Sciences, Stanford University.
1978 Joined the faculty at Stanford University.
1980 Elected to the American Academy of Arts and Sciences.
1982 Received the American Psychological Association's award for distinguished scientific contribution, with Daniel Kahneman.
1984 Received the MacArthur Fellowship.
1984 Received the Guggenheim Fellowship.
1985 Elected to the National Academy of Sciences.
1991 Became a member of the faculty senate at Stanford University.
1992 Appointed professor of behavioral sciences at Stanford University.
1996 Died in Stanford, California.

LIFE AND CAREER

Amos Tversky became a war hero at the tender age of 19. He was an officer in an elite paratrooper unit, which fought in three wars, when he earned Israel's highest military decoration by saving the life of a fellow soldier. He went on to become one of the world's most respected and influential psychologists, and a pioneer of cognitive science. He was a professor at Stanford, contributing to a number of interdisciplinary programs, and was a cofounder with Kenneth Arrow of the Stanford Center of Conflict and Negotiation. He was also a member of the Academic Council's advisory board to the president and provost. His accomplishments were recognized with many academic honors, and he would also have received the Nobel Memorial Prize in Economic Sciences, but for his untimely death.

KEY THINKING

- Amos Tversky helped create the field of cognitive science with longtime collaborator, Daniel Kahneman, and was a key figure in the discovery of systematic human cognitive bias, and the handling of risk.
- With Kahneman, he originated Prospect Theory to explain irrational human economic choices.
- His work in behavioral economics applied to financial markets, and challenged the efficient market hypothesis.
- His work on the limits of human rationality and decision-making had a major impact on philosophy, social sciences, statistics, political science, law, and medicine.

IN PERSPECTIVE

- His approach was based on counterintuitive results, using practical experiments and formalizations, and drawing on everyday experience to assess the processes and failures of human judgment and decision-making.
- His early work with Kahneman focused on the psychology of prediction, probability judgment, and cognitive illusion, arguing that people repeatedly make errors in judgment, and economic choices that can be predicted and categorized.
- They demonstrated that very small risks are given disproportionate weight, that prospective losses and gains are not treated symmetrically, that the presence or absence of non-selected alternatives can reverse preference orderings, and that the manner in which options are framed can exert an influence on decision-makers.
- They also devised a series of ingenious experiments to expose the illogical ways in which people make decisions that involve probability—including playing roulette, or guessing what someone does for a living.
- Kahneman received the Nobel Prize for the work he did in collaboration with Tversky, and it is assumed that Tversky would have shared the prize but Nobel prizes are not awarded posthumously.
- In his decision-making analysis, he pointed out the misconception in basketball that players tend to get "hot"—that they sometimes score many more consecutive shots than would normally be expected— arguing that this was nothing more than the standard laws of chance, and a problem of human cognition.
- Produced many classic papers focusing on the gap between actual human intellectual performance and the normative standards that should seemingly govern such performance.

MORE INFO

Books:

Kahneman, Daniel, Paul Slovic, and Amos Tversky (eds). *Judgment under Uncertainty: Heuristics and Biases*. Cambridge, UK: Cambridge University Press, 1982. Describes various judgmental heuristics and the biases they produce, not only in laboratory experiments, but also in important social, medical, and political situations.

Kahneman, Daniel, and Amos Tversky (eds). *Choices, Values, and Frames*. New York: Russell Sage Foundation, 2000. Presents an empirical and theoretical challenge to classical utility theory, offering Prospect Theory as a realistic alternative.

Krantz, David H., R. Duncan Luce, Patrick Suppes, and Amos Tversky. *Foundations of Measurement* (3 vols). New York: Academic Press, 1971. A classic series in quantitative measurement.

See Also:

 Daniel Kahneman (p. 1288)

"People use mental approximations to understand an uncertain world. As a result, we make certain types of errors in judgment." Amos Tversky

     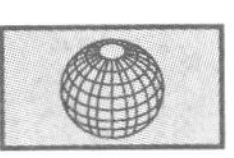   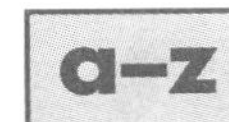

Arnold, Lord Weinstock · One of Britain's most revered industrialists

1924 Born in London.
1944 Graduated from the London School of Economics.
1944 Appointed a junior administrative officer in the Admiralty.
1954 Appointed managing director of Radio & Allied Industries.
1963 Appointed managing director of General Electric Company.
1970 Knighted.
1971 Appointed director of Rolls-Royce.
1980 Made a life peer, as Baron Weinstock of Bowden.
1996 Appointed chairman emeritus of General Electric Company.
2002 Died in Bowden Hill, Wiltshire, UK.

LIFE AND CAREER

Lord Weinstock was an industrialist and business leader during the post-war period. After spending his military service in the Admiralty, working on government procurement in the Production and Priority Branch, he became a civil servant, before going into finance and property development in London. He later joined his father-in-law's electronics company, Radio & Allied Industries Ltd, which he helped merge with General Electric Company, becoming its largest shareholder. He then built GEC into one of the Britain's largest companies, with wide interests in everything from military equipment to trains and telephones. He was an advisor to four British prime ministers, including Margaret Thatcher. He was a trustee of the British Museum, the Royal Philharmonic Orchestra Foundation Fund, and a senior trustee of the Next Century Foundation, a peace process organization he helped establish. He also established the Weinstock Fund, a charitable foundation.

KEY THINKING

- Weinstock led General Electric Company (GEC) for more than three decades, building it into one of the biggest and most successful industrial conglomerates in the UK, during a period of steady decline in manufacturing.
- In the 1960s, he was a pioneer of the hostile takeover and used aggressive tactics to create a monopoly position for GEC in the electrical engineering and defense electronics industries.
- His takeovers were encouraged by Harold Wilson's government, which was keen to make British manufacturing more competitive.
- In the 1970s and 1980s, he continued to grow the business—both organically, and by acquiring rivals.
- During the economic recession of the early 1990s, GEC retained its market leading position by slashing costs, closing inefficient factories, and confronting the unions.
- Weinstock's unbending management style helped the group generate profits of £1 billion a year during the downturn. However, while the company also amassed cash reserves of more than £3 billion, City investors felt that a change was long overdue.
- Weinstock eventually stepped down in 1996 after 33 years as managing director to become honorary "chairman emeritus," and to make way for Lord Simpson of Dunkeld as his chosen successor. Simpson renamed the company Marconi to underline the end of the Weinstock era, and pursued bold new strategies which would ultimately bring it to disaster.

IN PERSPECTIVE

- Weinstock was a central figure in the business world of the 1960s, when he pioneered a wave of mergers, mostly hostile, which changed the face of British industry.
- The largest of these was GEC's takeover of the larger Amalgamated Electrical Industries, backed and financially supported by the government's Industrial Reorganisation Commission.
- His program of rationalization at GEC transformed the UK's electronics industry, as he introduced efficiency measures, stringent cost-cutting, staff reductions, and implemented mergers to inject new growth into the company.
- This returned GEC to profit, and restored the City's confidence in its plans for development.
- Weinstock was known for his uncompromising management style: during his tenure at GEC, he cut the number of employees from 250,000 down to just 57,000.
- His managerial approach in the 1990s set the tone for lean management, and flat organizational structures.
- As GEC's profits and growth started to decrease, it became increasingly unpopular with Prime Minister Margaret Thatcher and the City.
- In an effort to protect GEC from takeover bids, Weinstock formed alliances with Alsthom in France, Siemens in Germany and General Electric in the US. But his actions could not stop the company's decline and, by the time he left GEC, much of the group had been broken up into smaller partnerships.

MORE INFO

Books:

Aris, Stephen. *Arnold Weinstock and the Making of GEC*. London: Aurum Press, 1998. Gives a detailed history of the UK electronics industry, putting in context the meteoric rise of GEC, as well as the effects of technological change, and the evolution of the consumer market.

Brummer, Alex, and Roger Cowe. *Weinstock: The Life and Times of Britain's Premier Industrialist*. London: HarperCollins Business, 1998. An empathetic biography of Weinstock's career, detailing the business and political issues faced during his years in charge of GEC.

"You must live as if you are immortal." Arnold, Lord Weinstock

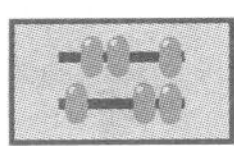
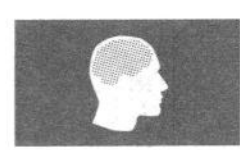

Jack Welch · Innovative and revered business leader

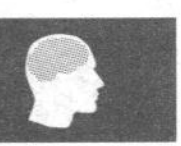

1935 Born in Peabody, Massachusetts.
1957 Received BS in chemical engineering from the University of Massachusetts Amherst.
1960 Received MS and PhD from the University of Illinois at Urbana-Champaign.
1960 Appointed a junior engineer at General Electric.
1963 Put in charge of chemical development at General Electric.
1968 Became General Electric's youngest ever general manager.
1972 Appointed vice president of General Electric.
1977 Appointed senior vice president of General Electric.
1979 Appointed vice chairman of General Electric.
1981 Appointed chief executive officer of General Electric.
1986 Bought RCA.
1995 Introduced Six Sigma at General Electric.
1999 Named as *Fortune*'s Manager of the Century.
2001 Retired as chief executive officer of General Electric.
2001 Publication of *Straight from the Gut*.
2005 Publication of *Winning*.
2006 Began teaching at the MIT Sloan School of Management.

LIFE AND CAREER

Jack Welch was a business leader, and the youngest and most successful Chief Executive Officer of General Electric. After receiving a PhD in Chemical Engineering from the University of Illinois, he joined General Electric in 1960. Over the next few years, he rose through the organization, becoming its head in 1981. With the intention of building it into the world's most valuable company, he transformed its organizational structure during the 1980s, paring down its hierarchy and bureaucracy, and devolving power to individual business units in a move towards decentralization. By 1999, it was the second-most-profitable company in the world, and Welch had become a role model for his generation. Since resigning in 2001, he has been writing as well as teaching at MIT.

KEY THINKING

- Jack Welch built a reputation as one of the world's top executives during his 20-year reign as CEO of General Electric. He helped modernize the company and completely reorganized its structure by introducing Six Sigma—a business management system originally developed by Motorola—in a bid to make it more agile and efficient.
- The result of his leadership and organizational overhaul was a 600% increase in profits and 100 consecutive quarters of increased earnings, turning General Electric into one of the most profitable companies in the world.
- The year before Welch was appointed CEO, General Electric made revenues of around US$26.8 billion. By 2000, this figure had increased to nearly US$130 billion. The company's market value rose from US$14 billion to more than US$410 billion by the end of 2004.
- In the 1980s, he streamlined the company to make it more competitive and, in the 1990s, modernized it by changing its base from manufacturing to financial services, through numerous acquisitions.
- His philosophy was that a company should be one of the top two in a particular industry, or leave it completely.

IN PERSPECTIVE

- Welch's leadership style involved impelling managers to improve performance, rewarding the top 20% with bonuses and stock options, and firing the bottom 10% each year.
- He also strove to eradicate inefficiency by streamlining inventories, trimming obstructive bureaucracy, closing down underperforming business units, and reducing payrolls.
- During the 1980s, he made slashed the workforce, reducing General Electric from 411,000 employees at the end of 1980, to 299,000 by the end of 1985, helping to greatly increase its market capital.
- His attack on stifling bureaucracy was an attempt to develop a company without boundaries; one that was able continually to change and evolve, according to fluctuations in external circumstances. He hoped this would encourage innovation, and the communication of ideas at all levels across the organization.
- He adopted the Six Sigma quality program in the 1990s, in a bid to create products which were close to perfection, based on a rigorous measurement, testing, and implementation process. This led to greatly increased revenues for General Electric.
- Welch resigned from GE in 2001, and was succeeded by Jeffrey Immelt in a highly public succession battle.

MORE INFO

Books:

Slater, Robert. *Jack Welch and the GE Way: Management Insights and Leadership Secrets of the Legendary CEO*. New York: McGraw-Hill, 1999.
Welch, Jack, and John A. Byrne. *Jack: Straight from the Gut*. New York: Warner Books, 2001.
Welch, Jack, and Suzy Welch. *Winning: The Ultimate Business How-to Book*. New York: HarperBusiness, 2005.

See Also:

The Six Sigma Way: How GE, Motorola and Other Top Companies are Honing Their Performance (p. 1415)

"For a large organization to be effective, it must be simple." Jack Welch

   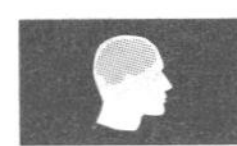  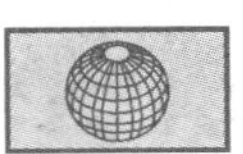   

Muhammad Yunus · Banker to the poor

1940 Born in Chittagong, British India (now Bangladesh).
1960 Received BA in economics from Dhaka University.
1961 Received MA in economics from Dhaka University.
1961 Appointed lecturer in economics at Chittagong College.
1965 Received Fulbright scholarship to study in the US.
1969 Appointed assistant professor of economics at the Middle Tennessee State University.
1971 Received PhD in economics from Vanderbilt University.
1999 Publication of *Banker to the Poor.*
1999 Awarded the Indira Gandhi Prize for Peace, Disarmament and Development.
2006 Received the Nobel Peace Prize, jointly awarded to the Grameen Bank.
2007 Publication of *Creating a World Without Poverty.*
2009 Awarded the Presidential Medal of Freedom.
2010 Publication of *Building Social Business*.
2011 Fired from position at Grameen Bank by Bangladeshi government.

LIFE AND CAREER

Muhammad Yunus is a banker and economist, best known for his work in developing the concept of microcredit, and extending it to the poor in Bangladesh. After receiving his PhD and teaching in the US, he worked at the Bureau of Economics as a research assistant, and ran the Bangladesh Information Center during the Liberation War of Bangladesh. After the war, he returned to Bangladesh, was appointed to the government's Planning Commission, and later became Professor of Economics at Chittagong University, where he first started to apply microcredit, the extension of small loans, to workers and entrepreneurs too poor to qualify for a bank loan. He founded the Grameen Bank and Grameen Foundation to further this concept, and was later awarded the Nobel Peace Prize for his work in alleviating poverty in small Bangladeshi villages. He has also served on the board of directors of the United Nations Foundation, is a founding member of Global Elders, and is a member of the Africa Progress Panel.

KEY THINKING

- Yunus first became involved with poverty reduction after observing the famine of 1974, and established a rural economic program as a research project, a scheme that was adopted by the government.
- In 1976, during visits to the poorest areas near Chittagong University, he realized that very small loans could make a disproportionate difference to alleviating poverty.
- He started making micro-loans to women in a nearby village who were making bamboo furniture, but had to take out expensive loans to buy the bamboo, and then pay the profit back to the moneylenders.
- His first loan was US$27 to 42 women in the village. He soon realized it would be necessary to create an institution which specialized in giving credit to poor people if the project was to develop.
- In 1976, he secured a loan from the government's Janata Bank, specifically for offering loans to the poor. By 1983, the bank had 28,000 customers, and the pilot project grew into a fully-fledged bank, renamed the Grameen Bank.
- The microcredit revolution continued to develop and, by 2007, the Grameen Bank had issued over US$6 billion to 7.4 million borrowers.

IN PERSPECTIVE

- Yunus encountered resistance to his scheme, from politicians, clergy, and some of the men in the villages.
- The conventional banking system had been reluctant to give credit to people with no collateral to guarantee a loan.
- His concept of microcredit was based on the belief that poor people will repay loans if they are given the opportunity to commercialize their ideas, making microcredit a viable business model.
- To ensure repayment, the bank uses a system of small informal groups which apply together for loans, and its members act as co-guarantors of repayment and support one another's efforts.
- Many microcredit projects lend specifically to women—more than 94% of Grameen loans have gone to women, who suffer disproportionately from poverty, and who are more likely than men to give their earnings to their families.
- The concept has also been applied in industrialized nations, including the US, where Yunus has helped introduce microcredit schemes to some of the poorer communities in Arkansas, working with Bill and Hillary Clinton.

MORE INFO

Books:

Bornstein, David. *The Price of a Dream: The Story of the Grameen Bank and the Idea That Is Helping the Poor to Change Their Lives*. New York: Simon & Schuster; 1996. Tells the story behind the bank and the microcredit revolution.

Yunus, Muhammad. *Creating a World Without Poverty: How Social Business Can Transform Our Lives*. New York: Public Affairs, 2007. Shows how social business can be achieved by using the free market to help the poor. It outlines Yunus' vision for this new business model, and tells how some companies are already successfully implementing it.

Yunus, Muhammad, and Alan Jolis. *Banker to the Poor: The Story of the Grameen Bank*. New York: Public Affairs, 1999. The groundbreaking book that first showed how the concept of microcredit can help those trapped in a cycle of poverty, and without access to conventional banking.

Website:

Yunus Centre: www.muhammadyunus.org

See Also:

Banker to the Poor: The Story of the Grameen Bank (p. 1334)
Bangladesh (pp. 1454–1455)

"Poor people are not asking for charity. Charity is not a solution for poverty." Muhammad Yunus

  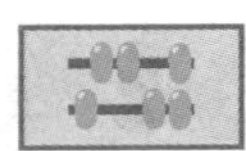 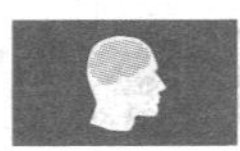     

Robert Zoellick · Former president of the World Bank

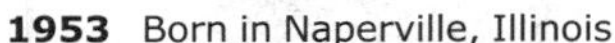

1953 Born in Naperville, Illinois.
1975 Graduated from Swarthmore College.
1981 Received JD from Harvard Law School.
1981 Received master of public policy from Harvard University School of Government.
1982 Served as a law clerk in the United States Court of Appeals for the District of Columbia.
1985 Worked at the US Treasury.
1991 Appointed personal assistant to President Bush for the G7 Summits.
1992 Appointed White House deputy chief of staff.
1992 Received the Knight Commander's Cross of the Order of Merit of the Federal Republic of Germany.
1993 Appointed executive vice president at the Federal National Mortgage Association.
1997 Appointed professor of national security at the US Naval Academy.
1999 Appointed head of the Center for Strategic and International Studies.
2000 Served as a foreign policy adviser to President Bush during the presidential election.
2001 Appointed US trade representative by President Bush.
2005 Appointed Deputy Secretary of State.
2007 Appointed president of the World Bank.

LIFE AND CAREER

Robert Zoellick was president of the World Bank from 2007 to 2012, having previously been US Deputy Secretary of State. After studying at Harvard Law School and Harvard University, he worked at the US Court of Appeals, before moving to the Treasury department. He has also been a managing director at Goldman Sachs, and managing director and chairman of Goldman Sachs' Board of International Advisors. He was appointed President George H. W. Bush's personal representative for the G7 Economic Summits in 1991 and 1992, before being appointed White House Deputy Chief of Staff and Assistant to the President. During the 1990s, he also served on many nonprofit boards, including the Council on Foreign Relations, the European Institute, and the Institute of International Economics. He served in the Executive Office and on the firm's Risk and Business Practices Committees, and was a US Trade Representative between 2001 and 2005.

- In 2000, he aided the new foreign policy directions that would come with a Bush Jr administration; he supported the use of military superiority that would allow the US to manage international order.
- In 2001, he worked on the Doha Development Agenda, and three years later spearheaded the international effort to revitalize the Doha negotiations, by putting together a new framework for the next stage of commitments.
- He also devised the plans to launch a Middle East Free Trade Area, the Enterprise for ASEAN Initiative, and other ventures to increase trade and development.
- At Fannie Mae, he supervised the restructuring of its affordable housing business, as well as the legal, regulatory, government and industry relations, and international services.
- He has been instrumental in making new free-trade agreements with a number of countries, and led the State Department in the NAFTA and Uruguay Round (GATT) negotiations.

IN PERSPECTIVE

- As head of the Office of Oceans, Environment, and Science at the State Department, he guided the US negotiations in achieving the Global Climate Change Framework Agreement of 1992.
- As a counselor at the State Department, and Under Secretary of State for Economics, he was central to the creation of the Asia Pacific Economic Cooperation forum, for which he received the Distinguished Service Award.
- While a US Trade Representative, he was involved in negotiations to bring China and Taiwan into the World Trade Organization.
- He played an important role in the discussions which took place at the end of the Cold War, persuading the US government to support the reunification of West and East Germany, and representing them at the multiparty negotiation over the future of Germany.

KEY THINKING

- Robert Zoellick has been stalwart promoter of US economic interests, and political security issues for many years.
- He has also played leading roles in a number of high-profile administration decisions, including the effort to mediate the crisis in Sudan, where he helped persuade Darfur's rebel leaders to sign a peace accord.

MORE INFO

Books:

Woods, Ngaire. *The Globalizers: The IMF, the World Bank, and Their Borrowers*. Ithaca, NY: Cornell University Press, 2006. Focuses on the political side of how the IMF and World Bank operate, and the relationships between them and their clients.

World Bank. *A Guide to the World Bank*. 3rd ed. Washington, DC: World Bank, 2011. A useful introduction to how the World Bank operates, its governance, structure, organizing principles, and areas of international interest.

"A modern Republican foreign policy recognizes that there is still evil in the world—people who hate America and the ideas for which it stands...The United States must remain vigilant and have the strength to defeat its enemies." Robert Zoellick

FINANCE LIBRARY

  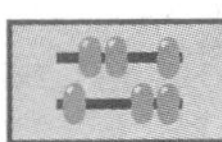   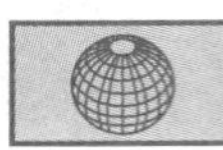   

Finance Library

Summarizing the most influential finance books of all time

There is a vast amount of literature covering the world of finance, and thousands more new publications emerge every year. Finance professionals are time-poor, so we have narrowed the array of titles down to the ground-breaking and most popular works.

The Finance Library extracts the main lessons from the cornerstone titles and the most influential. They include both well-regarded new titles such as Nassim Nicholas Taleb's *The Black Swan*, as well as time-honored classics such as J. K. Galbraith's *The Great Crash* and *Portfolio Theory and Capital Markets* by William F. Sharpe.

Each summary includes a quick analysis of the book's contribution to finance thinking and practice, as well as a list of the key points emerging from the work.

        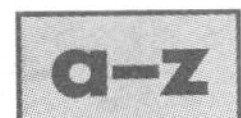

Contents

  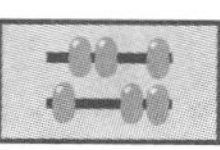      

  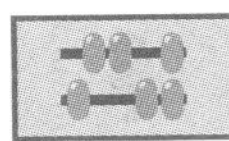   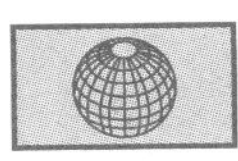 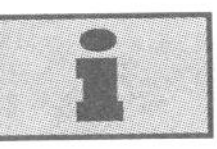  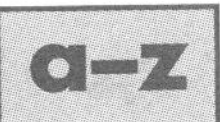

a–z

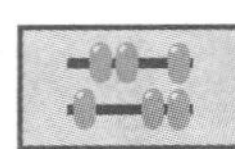

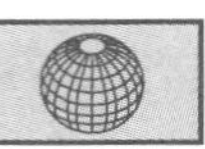

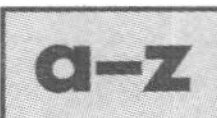

Absolute Returns: The Risk and Opportunities of Hedge Fund Investing

ALEXANDER M. INEICHEN (2003)

WHY READ IT?

- A non-technical, yet sophisticated examination that shows investors how to make educated decisions about hedge fund investment.
- Presents a wide-ranging and detailed examination of hedge funds, which have been much in the headlines, especially due to large failures such as with Long-Term Capital Management.
- Considers the astonishing success of some hedge fund managers, but also points out the common misconceptions, and the risks as well as the rewards.

GETTING STARTED

Absolute Returns is a practical guide to strategies of hedge funds and alternative investments, which examines the complex risks of hedge funds. It reveals how hedge funds really operate, and is written by someone who has worked with them for many years.

AUTHOR

Alexander Ineichen is managing director and senior investment officer in the Alternative Investment Solutions Team at UBS Global Asset Management. He was previously at Swiss Bank Corporation, and is a member of the Chartered Financial Analyst Institute and the Board of Directors of the Chartered Alternative Investment Analyst Association.

CONTEXT

- Details the history, folklore, scandals, personalities, and performance data, of the hedge fund industry.
- Looks at how hedge funds were once limited to an elite group of investors, but are now opening up to less sophisticated, less wealthy speculators.
- Classifies hedge funds according to the strategies they employ, such as relative value, event-driven, and macro, and analyzes the historical performance of the various strategies.
- Looks at how the hedge funds perform better in bear markets, when traditional investment strategies do not.
- Suggests there are two types of investors: pioneers and lemmings (leaders and followers).

IMPACT

- Provides an informed, insider's view of the workings of hedge funds, and the strategies that hedge fund managers use to achieve superior investment performance.
- Argues for hedge funds as a place to invest, and that hedge fund fees aren't excessive on a risk-adjusted return basis. A recurring theme is that hedge funds have outperformed equity indexes, and don't have the same risk.
- Distinguishes between absolute and relative returns, with traditional money managers pursuing returns relative to some benchmark, and hedge fund managers preferring absolute returns.
- Points out the diversification benefits of hedge funds—which are more important to many institutional investors than the purported alpha of hedge funds.

QUOTATIONS

"There are no rules about the game except that it will change. But, most importantly, one should avoid becoming the game."

"The pioneers who were buying into hedge funds during the 1990s were primarily uncomfortable with where equity valuations were heading."

"Managing hedge funds has at least as much to do with risk management as with picking stocks or following a market."

MORE INFO

Books:

Drobny, Steven. *Inside the House of Money: Top Hedge Fund Traders on Profiting in the Global Markets*. Hoboken, NJ: Wiley, 2006. Examines the hidden world of hedge funds and how their star traders operate.

Ineichen, Alexander M. *Asymmetric Returns: The Future of Active Asset Management*. Hoboken, NJ: Wiley, 2007. Ineichen's latest book is a guide for active asset management and achieving an asymmetric return profile.

See Also:

A Demon of Our Own Design (p. 1349)

Hedge Funds, Fund Management, and Alternative Investments (pp. 1729–1732)

"There are no rules about the game except that it will change. But, most importantly, one should avoid becoming the game."

  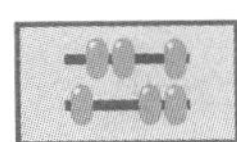   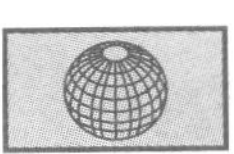   

Advances in Behavioral Finance

RICHARD H. THALER (ED) (1993)

WHY READ IT?

- A team of experts from leading business schools present key papers on this increasingly important topic in finance.
- Considered a major text in the development of theory, containing the latest research on how behavior and psychology affect the financial markets.
- Assesses how individual behavior affects a number of areas, including speculative prices, and when it is best to sell both successful and unsuccessful stocks.

GETTING STARTED

Advances in Behavioral Finance is a collection of seminal research papers from this emerging field of science. It examines discrepancies in the markets, and develops a theoretical basis for explaining each discrepancy based on recent advances in behavioral finance, laying the groundwork for an advanced understanding of the impact of behavior. It also takes an international perspective to examine how behavior affects the international equity markets and exchange risk.

EDITOR

Richard H. Thaler (b. 1945) is professor of behavioral science and economics at Chicago University's Graduate School of Business. He previously taught at Cornell, the University of British Columbia, the Sloan School of Management, and the Center for Advanced Study in Behavioral Sciences, and has received the Paul A. Samuelson Award.

CONTEXT

- Shows how behavioral finance, as one of the most controversial areas of the financial world, argues that not all economic decisions can be described by the equilibrium conditions in the economy and markets.
- Looks at why overreactions occur in the stock market, particularly with regard to the measurement of abnormal performance, and reactions to earnings announcements.
- Discusses aspects of corporate finance, focusing on the behavioral impact of a preference for cash dividends, corporate takeovers, and initial public offerings.

IMPACT

- Examines volatility and movements in stock prices in relation to behavioral characteristics.
- Discusses the effect of noise and information on the markets, such as through trader risk and investor sentiment.
- Considers which types of economic outcome are affected by biased expectations.
- Assesses how economic agents really act in a less that rational way, and the extent and impact of biased expectations.
- Analyzes the failure of competition and high interest rates in the credit card market.

QUOTATIONS

"We can understand much more about the behavior of markets, even financial markets, if we learn more about the behavior of the people who operate in these markets."

"A person with information or insights about individual firms will want to trade, but will realize that only another person with information or insights will take the other side of the trade."

"Noise creates the opportunity to trade profitably, but at the same time makes it difficult to trade profitably."

MORE INFO

Books:

Shefrin, Hersh. *Beyond Greed and Fear: Understanding Behavioral Finance and the Psychology of Investing*. Boston, MA: Harvard Business School Press, 1999. Shows how investors are motivated by fear, hope, overconfidence, and the need for short-term gratification, to help behavioral finance be seen as being just as important as market fundamentals.

Thaler, Richard (ed). *Advances in Behavioral Finance, Vol II*. Princeton, NJ: Princeton University Press, 2005. Gives an overview of the development of behavioral finance from a variety of experts, and examines the importance of behavioral approaches to other areas of economic life.

See Also:

Richard Thaler (p. 1314)
Inefficient Markets: An Introduction to Behavioral Finance (p. 1374)
Behavioral Finance (pp. 1671–1673)

"We can understand much more about the behavior of markets, even financial markets, if we learn more about the behavior of the people who operate in these markets."

  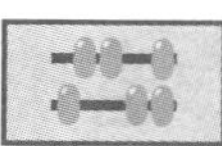      

Against the Gods: The Remarkable Story of Risk

PETER L. BERNSTEIN (1996)

WHY READ IT?

- Provides a fascinating analysis of risk and probability that draws upon history and biography to trace their development and use.
- Without dumbing down, tells the story of a series of scientists and amateurs who discovered the notion of risk, and scientifically linked the present to the future.
- Looks at the basis and context on which people constantly make choices, arrive at decisions, and take risks.

GETTING STARTED

Against the Gods, the international bestseller and winner of the Booz Allen Business Book Award, is a readable analysis of probability and its applications, blending biography with history and science to show how famous thinkers such as Pascal, Bernoulli, Keynes, and Markowitz helped us evolve from superstition to the super computer. The origins, historical progression, and modern understanding of risk are presented in an anecdotal style free of heavy math.

AUTHOR

Peter L. Bernstein (b. 1919) is an author and president of Peter L. Bernstein Inc. He produces a popular semi-monthly analysis of the capital markets and the real economy, and previously taught economics at the Graduate Faculty of the New School for Social Research in New York.

CONTEXT

- Tells the story of risk, from it not existing in the ancient world, through its emergence in Renaissance times, to the evolution of our modern theories of risk management in finance.
- Provides mini biographies of mathematicians, gamblers, and others who made significant contributions to our understanding of probability and risk, making this story one of human endeavor.
- Argues that people had to make an intellectual leap, to believe that outcomes could be influenced by their actions and were not merely in the "hands of the Gods" or a matter of fate. This capacity sets modern civilization apart from all that came before it.
- Reviews the history of numerical measurement, probability theory, and the history of financial risk instruments.

IMPACT

- Looks at how we mistakenly define risk as the "chance of loss," and uncertainty as "not understood," so that we often behave as if the past is the best indication of the future course of events.
- Considers that the understanding of probability that we now have allows us to take informed risks and make the sort of sophisticated decisions critical to progress.
- Brings to life such ideas as probability, uncertainty, the difference between luck and skill, the interactions between gambling and investing, and rational versus irrational decision-making.

QUOTATIONS

"The revolutionary idea that defines the boundary between modern times and the past is the mastery of risk."

"The goal of wresting society from the mercy of the laws of chance continues to elude us."

"Reality is a series of connected events, each dependent on another, radically different from games of chance in which the outcome of any single throw has zero influence on the outcome of the next throw."

MORE INFO

Book:

Bernstein, Peter L. *Capital Ideas: The Improbable Origins of Modern Wall Street*. New York: Free Press, 1992. Shows how a group of academics and economists changed the way that Wall Street ran the world's investments.

See Also:

Peter L. Bernstein (p. 1271)
Fooled by Randomness: The Hidden Role of Chance in Life and in the Markets (p. 1361)
Risk Management (pp. 1785–1789)

"The revolutionary idea that defines the boundary between modern times and the past is the mastery of risk."

  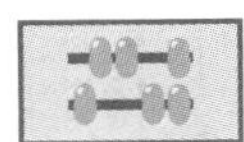   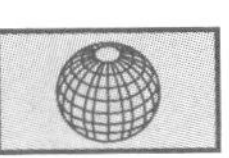   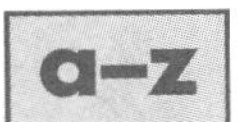

The Age of Turbulence: Adventures in a New World

ALAN GREENSPAN (2007)

WHY READ IT?

- Tells the story of Greenspan's early life, his professional career and his chairmanship of the Federal Reserve Board.
- Details why he thinks the global economy has evolved into a new and turbulent system over the last few years.
- Explains the dynamics behind recent world events through the perspective of his career and experiences.

GETTING STARTED

The Age of Turbulence comprises autobiography and reflections on America's economic history since the 1950s through his experience in business, in government, and as Chairman of the Federal Reserve Board.

It also examines the author's views on global growth, the extent of competition and openness to trade, international institutions, the development of economic policies, and how he expects these to develop over the next few years.

AUTHOR

Alan Greenspan (b. 1926) served as chair of the Council of Economic Advisers between 1974 and 1977, and in 1987 was appointed chairman of the Federal Reserve Board, a position he held until his retirement in 2006.

CONTEXT

- Greenspan chaired the Federal Reserve Board during some of the biggest recent events, including the 1987 stock market crash and 9/11.
- As the dominant force in American economic policy, he became such a key figure that people continually tried to interpret what he said and guess what he would do.
- Comments on a range of key economic issues such as the debt markets, globalization and regulation, equality, pensions, corporate governance, and energy.
- Offers his insider views on a succession of American presidents and British prime ministers.
- Covers the new economy from the standpoint of a neo-classical market economy.

IMPACT

- Examines how he kept the economy steady and growing during economic, financial, and political upheavals.
- Discusses the economic growth of other countries and what they must do to ensure increasing prosperity.
- Talks about President Bush and public spending, the need to raise taxes on energy to encourage conservation, the risk of increased inflation, and whether the Iraq war was about oil.
- Defends his unpopular decision to raise interest rates, and discusses the effect this had on the stock market and real estate.

QUOTATIONS

"Markets have become too huge, complex, and fast-moving to be subject to twentieth-century supervision and regulation."

"Almost all of the developed world is at the edge of a demographic abyss for which there is no precedent."

"Capitalism expands wealth primarily through creative destruction—the process by which the cash flow from obsolescent, low-return capital coupled with new savings is invested in high-return, cutting-edge technologies."

MORE INFO

Book:

Yergin, Daniel, and Joseph Stanislaw. *The Commanding Heights: The New Reality of Economic Power.* New York: Simon & Schuster, 1998. An analysis of the shift of assets from central governments to private enterprise and how deregulation and privatization affect economic power in the world.

See Also:

Alan Greenspan (p. 1286)

"Markets have become too huge, complex, and fast-moving to be subject to twentieth-century supervision and regulation."

  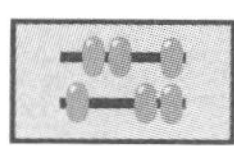      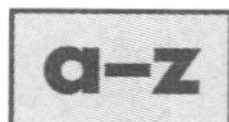

The Alchemy of Finance: Reading the Mind of the Market

GEORGE SOROS (1987)

WHY READ IT?

- Gives insight into Soros's investment strategies, and the decision-making processes of the most successful money manager of our time.
- Depicts how he ran the hugely successful Quantum Fund in the mid-1980s, giving examples of his approach and lessons in how to make money in times of uncertainty.
- He recommends his technique of being adaptive and flexible, as there is no way of knowing how any market situation will turn out.

GETTING STARTED

The Alchemy of Finance analyzes current financial trends, and presents a new paradigm by which to understand the financial market today. It details Soros's innovative investment practices that have made him into a billionaire, along with his views of international finance and the global economy. It is quite philosophical in outlook, and technical in his examination of the connection between thought and reality, and how they apply to the financial markets.

AUTHOR

George Soros (b. 1930) is president of Soros Fund Management, and cofounder and chief investment adviser to the Quantum Fund. A billionaire investor, philanthropist, and author, he is also active in education, culture, and economic aid and development through his Open Society Fund and the Soros Foundation.

CONTEXT

- Provides an in-depth discussion of Soros's "theory of reflexivity," explaining its key analytical principles in the context of boom–bust cycles in financial markets and economies, and its applications in his successful trading system.
- The basic premise of reflexivity is events create expectations that influence the financial markets; the markets, in turn, then influence these events, creating a cycle.
- Offers a unique contrarian insight into our understanding of supposedly obvious economic and financial ideas, such as his denial of the efficient markets hypothesis and financial markets equilibria.
- Argues that the market is a useful early warning system for potential economic catastrophes, as they reflect the fears of investors.
- Proposes a human uncertainty principle that suggests our understanding is often incoherent and always incomplete, inspired by Heisenberg's rule about quantum particles.

IMPACT

- He became famous for making a billion dollars in one day by shorting the British pound against the US dollar and other currencies, and this book provides important business and investing lessons.
- Examines his technique of buying during the upturns and taking the profit, waiting for a while, then sell shorts during the downward cycle.
- Discusses how Soros trades in the currencies and commodities markets, simplifying his model into eight variables.

QUOTATIONS

"I seek to lay the groundwork for a new paradigm that is applicable not only to financial markets but to all social phenomena."

"Financial markets are always wrong in the sense that they operate with a prevailing bias."

"Equilibrium itself has rarely been observed in real life—market prices have a notorious habit of fluctuating."

MORE INFO

Books:

Cunningham, L. A. (ed). *The Essays of Warren Buffett: Lessons for Investors and Managers*. New York: Cardozo Law Review, 1997. A compilation of the writing and thinking of the great investor.

Soros, George. *Soros on Soros: Staying Ahead of the Curve*. New York: Wiley, 1995. Produced in an interview format, revealing his views on investing, global finance, and world affairs.

See Also:

George Soros (p. 1312)
The Intelligent Investor (p. 1377)
Investment (pp. 1736–1741)

"I seek to lay the groundwork for a new paradigm that is applicable not only to financial markets but to all social phenomena."

  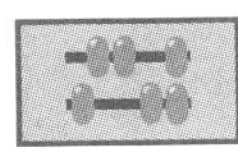   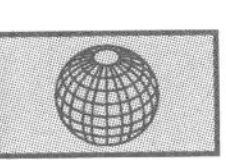   

Animal Spirits: How Human Psychology Drives the Economy, and Why It Matters for Global Capitalism

GEORGE A. AKERLOF and ROBERT J. SHILLER (2009)

WHY READ IT?

- Anyone interested in seeking to understand the causes of the global financial crisis should read this book.
- Akerlof and Shiller seek to explain the functioning of the economy and financial markets by showing the critical influence of human emotions.
- Critically, they show how "animal spirits" led to a blind faith in ever-rising house prices as well as plummeting confidence in capital markets.

GETTING STARTED

John Maynard Keynes, one of the most respected economists of the 20th century and whose insights into the cause of the Great Depression influenced government policy for many decades, argued that much economic activity is governed by animal spirits. He espoused the view that human beings do not behave in a rational manner and that government's role is to contain these spirits rather than allowing markets a free hand. Akerlof and Shiller claim that Keynes's insights must be rediscovered to ensure that the global financial crisis, or another economic catastrophe on the scale of the Great Depression, is not to be repeated.

- They challenge the orthodoxies of the past 30 years, and principally the view—propounded by President Ronald Reagan and Prime Minister Margaret Thatcher—that human behavior, in terms of economics at least, is rational.
- They emphasize Keynes's view that government's role vis-à-vis its citizens is similar to that of a parent toward a child, and that the proper role of the parent is to set limits to prevent the child from overindulging its animal spirits.

IMPACT

- If, as Akerlof and Shiller claim, animal spirits do exert a critical influence on economic behavior, government must play a broad disciplinary role, and should do so on a continuous basis.
- The authors contend that once economic recovery is established governments will come under pressure to allow markets free rein once more, and that they must resist this pressure if another economic or financial disaster is to be prevented.
- They accept that if well directed, animal spirits are a great source of entrepreneurship and innovation.
- They argue that the global financial crisis showed that markets are unable to regulate themselves and that if left to act without restraint the main animal spirits—confidence, fairness, and corruption—can lead to disaster.

AUTHORS

George A. Akerlof is the Koshland professor of economics at the University of California. He was awarded the 2001 Nobel Memorial Prize in Economic Sciences.

Robert J. Shiller is the Arthur M. Okun professor of economics at Yale University. He is author of the best-selling books *Irrational Exuberance* (2005) and *The Subprime Solution* (2008), both published by Princeton University Press.

CONTEXT

- Akerlof and Shiller argue that while Keynes's contention that government must use fiscal levers to control aggregate demand—thus stimulating the economy in times of recession, for example—has long been accepted, his insights into how human emotions drive economic and financial markets have been ignored.
- The authors revisit his work and seek to restore the great economist's view of animal spirits into economic theory, using the greater understanding of human psychology that exists today.

QUOTATIONS

"Such a world of animal spirits gives the government an opportunity to step in. Its role is to set the conditions in which our animal spirits can be harnessed creatively to serve the greater good. Government must set the rules of the game."

"All of those animal spirits tend to drive the economy sometimes one way and sometimes another. Without intervention by the government the economy will suffer massive swings in employment. And financial markets will, from time to time, fall into chaos."

"This book tells us that the solutions to our economic problems can only be reached if we pay due respects in our thinking and in our policies to the animal spirits."

MORE INFO

Books:

Friedman, Milton, and Anna Jacobson Schwartz. *A Monetary History of the United States 1867–1960*. Princeton, NJ: Princeton University Press, 1971. Also published as an e-book, 2008. The counterargument to Keynesianism by the great monetary economist Milton Friedman, whose views influenced both Ronald Reagan and Margaret Thatcher.

Keynes, John Maynard. *The General Theory of Employment, Interest and Money*. London: Macmillan, 1936 (reprinted 2007). The classic economic textbook that sought to explain how the General Depression came about and how government could play a role in stabilizing the economy.

See Also:

John Maynard Keynes (p. 1289)

"Such a world of animal spirits gives the government an opportunity to step in. Its role is to set the conditions in which our animal spirits can be harnessed creatively to serve the greater good. Government must set the rules of the game."

     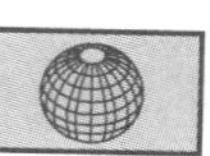   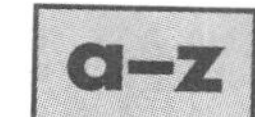

The Ascent of Money: A Financial History of the World

NIALL FERGUSON (2009)

WHY READ IT?

- Provides a comprehensive guide to the history of money, banking, and credit from the ancient world to the modern day.
- Ferguson provides fascinating insights into earlier financial crises such as the South Sea Bubble.
- The author seeks to draw parallels from the past to suggest what might happen following the recent global financial crisis, and asks whether the rise of China might lead to a conflict with the United States.

GETTING STARTED

The Ascent of Money provides an account of credit and banking from the days of the Incas to the global financial crisis that broke in 2008. The author draws parallels between the current global economic and financial crisis and events of the past. Ferguson also seeks to forecast the future and finds three lessons from history, namely: major wars can happen even when globalization is far advanced; the longer the world goes without a major conflict, the harder it becomes to imagine there could be war; and that a crisis which strikes complacent investors does more harm than one that befalls those that have experienced earlier crises.

AUTHOR

Niall Ferguson (b. 1964) is a well-known historian who has written a number of best-selling books, has written and presented a number of TV series, and contributes regularly to newspapers and magazines around the world. He is currently the Laurence A. Tisch professor of history at Harvard University, a senior research fellow of Jesus College, Oxford University, and a senior fellow of the Hoover Institution, Stanford University.

CONTEXT

- Provides an overview of the financial history of the world in a readable and easily digestible format. However, some episodes are inevitably covered only superficially.
- Argues that money is the root of most progress, claiming that "the ascent of money has been essential to the ascent of man."
- Contends that behind each great historical phenomenon there lays a financial secret, "and this book sets out to illuminate the most important of these."
- Argues that poverty is not the result of rapacious financiers exploiting the poor, but rather is due to a lack of financial institutions.
- Says that the financial system reflects and magnifies what we as humans are like. Money, for example, amplifies people's tendency to overreact, and to swing from exuberance when things are going well to depression when they go wrong.
- Contends that few things are harder to predict accurately than the timing and magnitude of financial crises.

IMPACT

- Maintains that economic strength determines political dominance, and that wars are fought to create wealth.
- Presents a convincing case that the development of financial systems has spurred the development of modern societies, by speeding transactions, loans, and investment.
- Explores the economic crisis that began in 2007, and attempts to explain how it happened and who is responsible.
- Looks at the causes of the economic meltdown, examining how, in a globalized world that uses increasingly complex financial instruments, defaults on subprime mortgages in American cities could lead to a global recession.
- Indentifies "Chimerica"—the intertwined economies of America and China—and asks where this relationship will lead in the future.

QUOTATIONS

"The globalization of finance has, among many other things, blurred the old distinction between developed and emerging markets, turning China into America's banker—the Communist creditor to the capitalist debtor, a change of epochal significance."

"The financial crisis that struck the Western world in the summer of 2007 provided a timely reminder of one of the perennial truths of financial history. Sooner or later, every bubble bursts."

"Booms and busts are products, at root, of our emotional volatility."

MORE INFO

Books:

Cooper, George. *The Origin of Financial Crises: Central Banks, Credit Bubbles and the Efficient Market Fallacy*. Petersfield, UK: Harriman House, 2008. Provides a compelling analysis of the forces behind the global economic crisis and an explanation of why financial markets do not obey the efficient market principles described in economic textbooks.

Roberts, J. M., and O. A. Westad. *The History of the World*. 6th ed. New York: Oxford University Press, 2013. A history of the world that covers all ages and all continents.

See Also:

A Farewell to Alms: A Brief Economic History of the World (p. 1352)

This Time Is Different: Eight Centuries of Financial Folly (p. 1425)

"The globalization of finance has, among many other things, blurred the old distinction between developed and emerging markets, turning China into America's banker—the Communist creditor to the capitalist debtor, a change of epochal significance."

  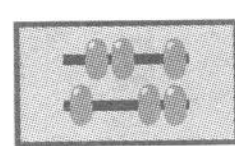   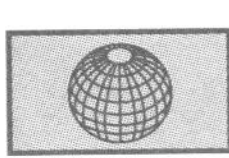   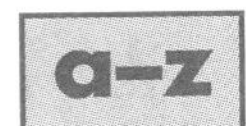

Balanced Scorecard: Translating Strategy into Action

ROBERT S. KAPLAN and DAVID P. NORTON (1996)

WHY READ IT?

- The originators of the Balanced Scorecard present this innovative methodology, and show how managers can use it to maximize the potential of their companies.
- Details how to build a Balanced Scorecard specifically tailored to an organization, and provides the practical tools needed for implementation.
- Describes the impact of using a Balanced Scorecard as a strategic management system, and how it helps clarify both vision and strategy and translate them into action.

GETTING STARTED

Balanced Scorecard focuses on how to successfully execute business strategy using this management model, and provides a guide to building a Balanced Scorecard. It puts in place a new management system for companies to re-focus on the long term for customers, employees, new product development, and systems, rather than concentrating just on short-term profit. It bridges the gap between strategic goals and performance monitoring, and has been implemented by over 300 major organizations.

AUTHORS

Robert S. Kaplan (b. 1940) is professor of leadership development at Harvard Business School, and chairman of the Balanced Scorecard Collaborative. He has previously been on the faculty and dean of the business school at Carnegie Mellon University, and has received numerous awards.

David P. Norton is cofounder and president of Palladium Group. He has also been president of Renaissance Solutions, cofounded and served as president and CEO of the Balanced Scorecard Collaborative, and cofounded and was president of Nolan, Norton & Co.

CONTEXT

- Shows how the Balanced Scorecard works as a measurement and management system for channeling the potential, skills, and knowledge of people towards realizable long-term goals.
- Emphasizes financial results and the human issues that drive them, by integrating a customer perspective, an internal perspective, and a learning and growth perspective.
- Examines the importance of employee learning and growth, internal business processes, and customer knowledge, rather than just short-term financial gain.
- Considers how the scorecard facilitates management processes such as individual and team goal setting, compensation, resource allocation, budgeting and planning, and strategic feedback and learning.
- Analyzes how the scorecard has innovated some of the concepts of previous management models such as Total Quality Management.

IMPACT

- Demonstrates how senior executives are using the Balanced Scorecard to guide current business performance and putting in place targets for future performance.
- Focuses on the vision and strategy of a business, and provides managers with a comprehensive overview of financial performance.
- Shows how to use measures for financial performance, customer knowledge, internal business processes, and learning and growth.
- Considers how the Balanced Scorecard evolves with the organization, unlike many other business models.

QUOTATIONS

"The Balanced Scorecard . . . provides managers with the instrumentation they need to navigate to future competitive success."

"The Balanced Scorecard complements financial measures of past performance with measures of the drivers of future performance."

"The Balanced Scorecard fills the void that exists in most management systems—the lack of a systematic process to implement and obtain feedback about strategy."

MORE INFO

Books:

Kaplan, Robert S., and David P. Norton. *The Strategy-Focused Organization: How Balanced Scorecard Companies Thrive in the New Business Environment*. Boston, MA: Harvard Business School Press, 2001. Explains how companies have used the Balanced Scorecard approach over nearly 10 years, and shows how others can implement it successfully.

Niven, Paul R. *Balanced Scorecard Step-by-Step: Maximizing Performance and Maintaining Results*. New York: Wiley, 2002. Provides practical insight on how best to implement the Balanced Scorecard, based on the author's experience in many organizations.

Olve, Nils-Göran, Jan Roy, and Magnus Wetter. *Performance Drivers: A Practical Guide to Using the Balanced Scorecard*. Chichester, UK: Wiley, 1999. An overview of Balanced Scorecard practice.

See Also:

★ Multidimensional Performance Measurement Using the Balanced Scorecard (pp. 897–899)

"The Balanced Scorecard . . . provides managers with the instrumentation they need to navigate to future competitive success."

Banker to the Poor: The Story of the Grameen Bank

MUHAMMAD YUNUS and ALAN JOLIS (1998)

WHY READ IT?

- Tells the story of how Muhammad Yunus began to assist the poor in Bangladesh with a US$27 loan and ended with the Nobel Peace Prize.
- Shows how the concept of microcredit can help the most needy, those trapped in a cycle of poverty, and without access to traditional banking.
- Explains how the Grameen Bank has grown into a US$2.5 billion enterprise, and microfinancing has spread to over 50 countries, based on the principle of lending to the poorest people in developing countries.

GETTING STARTED

Banker to the Poor recounts the author's early life, and how he first applied the concept of microfinance to alleviating poverty in Bangladesh. He began by helping poor villagers to break the cycle of selling their produce to money lenders for a minimal price, by providing them with a small loan, which they were soon able to repay. Yunus went on to found the Grameen Bank to put microcredit into practice on a larger scale. This has been so successful, it has been copied around the world.

AUTHORS

Muhammad Yunus (b. 1940) was awarded a Fulbright scholarship and then a PhD from Vanderbilt University. After becoming a professor of economics in Bangladesh, he successfully applied microcredit to the poor, became founder of Grameen Bank, and in 2006, he and the bank were jointly awarded the Nobel Peace Prize.

Alan Jolis is a journalist and writer, and has also produced several novels for children.

CONTEXT

- Yunus's work in providing microfinance to the poor was acknowledged by world leaders and the World Bank as a fundamental weapon in the fight against poverty.
- Discusses how microcredit schemes have worked in different countries, and how they have solved many social and economic problems.
- Shows how extending credit to poor people gives them the initiative and self-reliance to help themselves.
- Most of the Grameen Bank's loans are to women, and since its inception, there has been an astonishing loan repayment rate of over 98%.
- Shows how microfinance creates a sense of pride and responsibility, and generates incremental improvements as opposed to charity or donations.

IMPACT

- Details his refusal of assistance from other agencies, the World Bank, and the Bangladeshi government, preferring to stick to independent assets.
- Shows how banks can lend to those unable to raise any collateral and still operate as a profitable business.
- Expounds the belief that poverty is not created by the poor; it is created by the institutions and policies that surround them.
- Details how Grameen has now expanded from loans for income to now include housing and education loans.
- Shows the value of creating self-employment for income-generating activities and housing.
- Encourages women to take loans and work, something of a taboo to Muslim women living in Bangladesh.

QUOTATIONS

"What good were all these elegant [economic] theories when people died of starvation on pavements and on doorsteps?"

"Unless the poor can be liberated from the bondage of the money-lender, no economic programme can arrest the steady process of alienation of the poor."

"I have always believed that the elimination of poverty from the world is a matter of will."

MORE INFO

Books:

Armendairiz, B., and Jonathan Morduch. *The Economics of Microfinance*. Cambridge, MA: MIT Press, 2005. Draws on lessons from academia and international practice to challenge conventional assumptions.

Bornstein, David. *The Price of a Dream: The Story of the Grameen Bank and the Idea That Is Helping the Poor to Change Their Lives*. New York: Simon & Schuster, 1996. Tells the story behind the bank.

Website:

Yunus Centre: www.muhammadyunus.org

See Also:

Muhammad Yunus (p. 1319)
Bangladesh (pp. 1454–1455)
Business Ethics and Codes of Practice (pp. 1683–1686)
Social Responsibility of Management (pp. 1797–1800)

"What good were all these elegant [economic] theories when people died of starvation on pavements and on doorsteps?"

  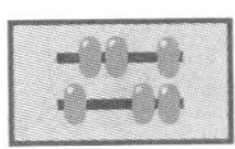   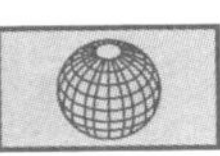   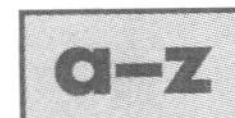

The Black Swan: The Impact of the Highly Improbable

NASSIM NICHOLAS TALEB (2007)

WHY READ IT?

- Discusses how Black Swans—large-scale random occurrences—and chance and luck affect everyday life, and how you cannot predict the future from what happened in the past.
- Explains why we cannot predict large events in life and argues that we should stop trying to forecast them and start taking advantage of the uncertainty.
- Combines an examination of financial theory with Taleb's own philosophy, and provides an account of growing up in war-torn Lebanon.

GETTING STARTED

The book argues that high-impact rare events, Black Swans, are not nearly as rare as people think, and that their impact is so disproportionately large that they affect much of what happens in the world. It argues that we are exposed to randomness all the time, and that Black Swans are unpredictable regardless of the amount of analysis of previous events. It expands on many of the ideas Taleb explored in his previous book, *Fooled by Randomness*, particularly why life doesn't behave as we expect, and how it is important to remember this to avoid mishap.

AUTHOR

Nassim Nicholas Taleb (b. 1960) is professor of marketing at London Business School, adjunct professor of mathematics at the Courant Institute of Mathematical Sciences, New York University, and on the affiliated faculty of Wharton School Financial Institutions Center. He previously held senior positions at major investment banks.

CONTEXT

- Considers the narrative that we impose on our lives to be an illusion that protects us from realizing our life is more random and fragile than we imagine.
- Argues that you cannot eliminate risk, you can only prepare for it, so we should organize our lives to minimize the effect of the negative Black Swans and maximize the impact of the positive ones.
- Taleb calls himself a "skeptical empiricist," as he believes that experience tells us that surprising things will always happen, for which there is supporting evidence all around.
- Disparages a variety of professions that rely on forecasting future trends, such as traders, hedge fund managers, Wall Street bankers, financial risk managers, and economists (even Nobel Prize-winning economists), as unable to predict Black Swans.
- Argues against the use of the Bell Curve of traditional investment theory, which does not tally with his concept of unlikely and extreme events.
- Supports the work of Benoit Mandelbrot, who also thought that Gaussian distributions are not helpful for modeling market behavior.

IMPACT

- Argues that we are permanently exposed to large unexpected events that can wreck all our plans in an instant, and which we can do nothing about.
- Takes a reductivist viewpoint about the uniqueness of experience, and points out that all true learning is based on a few logical truths.
- Finds most specific forecasting to be pointless, as large, rare, and unexpected events will always render forecasts useless.
- Points out the worryingly common flaws in our perceptions with anecdotes and examples, using a range of characters to bring out the essence of his arguments.

QUOTATIONS

"Memory is . . . a self-serving dynamic revision machine: you remember the last time you remembered the event and, without realizing it, change the story at every subsequent remembrance."

"We have far too many possible ways to interpret past events for our own good."

"Black Swan logic makes what you don't know far more relevant than what you do know."

MORE INFO

Book:

Ball, Philip. *Critical Mass: How One Thing Leads to Another.* New York: Farrar, Straus, and Giroux, 2004. Explains social behavior by applying formulas borrowed from physics.

See Also:

Fooled by Randomness: The Hidden Role of Chance in Life and in the Markets (p. 1361)
The (Mis)behavior of Markets (p. 1396)

"Memory is . . . a self-serving dynamic revision machine: you remember the last time you remembered the event and, without realizing it, change the story at every subsequent remembrance."

     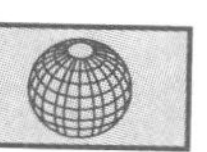   

Blink: The Power of Thinking without Thinking

MALCOLM GLADWELL (2005)

WHY READ IT?

- Analyzes the power of first impressions, how we can know things in an instant, and then make successful decisions based on little or no information.
- Considers how we rapidly and accurately process information in our subconscious and examines the hunches, suspicions, and initial impressions we form without being sure of how or why we make them.
- Argues that we can make better snap judgments if we train our mind and senses to focus only on the most relevant information.

GETTING STARTED

Blink examines how we are continually making quick judgments and how successful these can actually be. Based on research and told in an evocative and anecdotal style, it looks at the many ways that the subconscious makes accurate decisions very quickly, but shows that choices made "in the blink of an eye" will be more accurate if based on experience or preparation. It argues that we should concentrate on the small picture and focus on the meaning of "thin slices" of behavior, rather than over-analyzing matters, as long as we are aware of the potential pitfalls of following our instincts.

AUTHOR

Malcolm Gladwell (b. 1963) was a reporter and then New York bureau chief for the *Washington Post* before becoming a staff writer for the *New Yorker* magazine in 1996. His first book, *The Tipping Point*, is an international bestseller.

CONTEXT

- Discusses how people make instant but successful decisions in a wide range of fields such as psychology and police work.
- Examines the concept of "thin slicing," of how initial judgments are made, and how taking longer to make decisions often reduces their efficacy.
- Considers thin slicing to be about simplifying complexity in our lives and finding patterns in chaos.
- Assesses studies on autism, facial reading, and cardio uptick to argue that training can greatly enhance decision-making.
- Proposes that how we behave is due to a combination of instinct, reaction, and more deliberate analysis, but that we must avoid preconceptions and stereotyping.

IMPACT

- Shows how the "blink factor" occurs when our subconscious makes a decision instantly and in an unemotional way, which it is well suited to.
- Addresses how difficult it is to make decisions in stressful conditions, such as when police and soldiers are expected to make rational choices at times of cognitive overload.
- Examines the problems of snap judgments, which can consistently treat people differently due to their gender, race, age, and clothes, regardless of income, residence, and education.
- Discusses a number of occasions when snap judgments have been failures of judgment, such as the Diallo shooting, the election of Warren G. Harding as US President, and the introduction of New Coke.

QUOTATIONS

"We live in a world that assumes that the quality of a decision is directly related to the time and effort that went into making it."

"... there are moments, particularly in times of stress, ... when our snap judgments and first impressions can offer a much better means of making sense of the world."

"Every moment—every blink—is comprised of a series of distinct moving parts, and every one of these parts offers an opportunity for interventions, for reforms, and for correction."

MORE INFO

Books:

Linden, David J. *The Accidental Mind: How Brain Evolution Has Given Us Love, Memory, Dreams, and God*. Cambridge, MA: Belknap Press, 2007. Argues against the usual assumption that the brain is well designed, maintaining that it has actually evolved to give us our foibles and fallible humanity.

Tavris, Carol, and Elliot Aronson. *Mistakes Were Made (But Not by Me): Why We Justify Foolish Beliefs, Bad Decisions, and Hurtful Acts*. Orlando, FL: Harcourt, 2007. Discusses how our brains are programmed for self-justification, and offers an explanation of how we often deceive ourselves about our decisions.

See Also:

The Tipping Point: How Little Things Can Make a Big Difference (p. 1426)

"We live in a world that assumes that the quality of a decision is directly related to the time and effort that went into making it."

  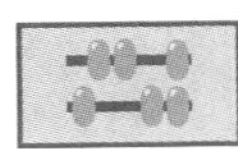   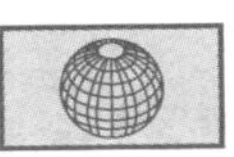   

Blue Ocean Strategy: How to Create Uncontested Market Space and Make the Competition Irrelevant

W. CHAN KIM and RENÉE MAUBORGNE (2005)

WHY READ IT?

- Describes new ways of doing business, by spending less money trying to carve out small profits doing the same thing as ever, and moving into new sectors where there is more opportunity to grow.
- *Blue Ocean Strategy* offers a set of tools and techniques to help you develop a successful business strategy, make the competition irrelevant, and create strong profit growth.
- Covers both strategy formulation and strategy execution, and discusses the BOS principles of value innovation.

GETTING STARTED

Blue Ocean Strategy argues that organizations should pursue new market space where they can develop, rather than being caught up in traditional competition. Based upon a large-scale study that found that differentiation and low cost could make the competition irrelevant and provide new profit areas.

Research in a number of industries brings insight into how success has been achieved through opportunity found in previously neglected markets.

AUTHORS

W. Chan Kim is cofounder and codirector of the INSEAD Blue Ocean Strategy Institute and the Boston Consulting Group, and professor of strategy and international management at INSEAD. He is an advisory member for the European Union, a fellow of the World Economic Forum, and a winner of the Eldridge Haynes Prize.

Renée Mauborgne is cofounder and codirector of the INSEAD Blue Ocean Strategy Institute, and distinguished fellow and a professor of strategy at INSEAD. She is a fellow of the World Economic Forum and a winner of the Eldridge Haynes Prize. She won the 2007 Asia Brand Leadership Award.

CONTEXT

- Puts the emphasis on quality of experience rather than the benefits of a new technology.
- Sets out three key concepts: value innovation, tipping point leadership, and fair process.
- Offers powerful tools to conceptualize the new market space, define it in detail, craft a profit strategy, and actualize its implementation.
- Focuses on creating uncontested market space, creating and capturing new demand, and framing the whole of a company's activities in pursuit of differentiation and low cost.
- Shows how to pursue a strategy that enables a company to free itself from industry boundaries.

IMPACT

- A blue ocean is created where a company's actions favorably affect both its costs and its value for buyers.
- Based primarily on value innovation, when utility, price, and cost are aligned with innovation.
- Identifies key qualities or consumer needs in a market, and then reduces, eliminates, increases, or creates qualities, until new market space is found.

QUOTATIONS

"*Our aim is to make the formulation and execution of blue ocean strategy as systematic and actionable as competing in the red waters of known market space.*"

"*The only way to beat the competition is to stop trying* to beat the competition."

"*Tipping point leadership builds on the rarely exploited corporate reality that in every organization, there are people, acts,* and *activities* that exercise a *disproportionate influence* on performance."

MORE INFO

Books:

Collins, James C., and Jerry I. Porras. *Built to Last: Successful Habits of Visionary Companies*. New York: HarperBusiness, 1994. A visionary book on what makes the difference between a good company and a great one.

Peters, Thomas J., and Robert H. Waterman. *In Search of Excellence: Lessons from America's Best-Run Companies.* New York: Harper & Row, 1982. Ground-breaking analysis of management success.

Porter, Michael E. *Competitive Advantage: Creating and Sustaining Superior Performance*. New York: The Free Press, 1985. Presents a more traditional view of strategic thinking.

Website:

The book's website: www.blueoceanstrategy.com

"Our aim is to make the formulation and execution of blue ocean strategy as systematic and actionable as competing in the red waters of known market space."

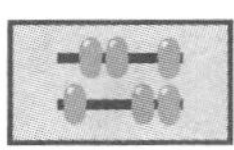

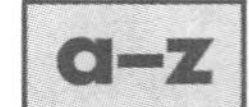

The Bottom Billion: Why the Poorest Countries Are Failing and What Can Be Done About It

PAUL COLLIER (2007)

WHY READ IT?

- A number of the poorest countries have problems that defy traditional approaches to alleviating poverty.
- Describes the failure of current policies to help these countries and proposes new solutions to unlock the poverty trap.
- Looks at how some countries have developed well, and what policies can get the poorest to replicate their success.

GETTING STARTED

The Bottom Billion argues that the economies of the poorest countries in the world have not grown in the last 30 years because they are stuck in one or more of the following traps: the conflict trap, the natural resource trap, the "landlocked with bad neighbours" trap, and the bad governance trap.

It makes three suggestions to help: military intervention; laws, statutes, and charters for improved governance; and trade preferences. Then it explains the strengths and weaknesses of each approach.

AUTHOR

Paul Collier is professor of economics and director of the Centre for the Study of African Economics at Oxford University. Formerly director of development research at the World Bank and adviser to the British government's Commission on Africa, he is one of the world's leading experts on African economies.

CONTEXT

- Recommends focusing only on the very poorest countries, and concentrating not just on aid but a broader range of policy instruments.
- Proposes better delivery of aid, occasional military intervention, international charters, and smarter trade policy as solutions.
- Approach not founded on emotion or guilt, but cost–benefit analysis (for instance, puts a price tag on the cost of a civil war) to help decision makers.
- Aid that is provided must be committed, targeted, and given for over a decade to post-conflict societies.
- Looks at how the WTO could play a more useful role, and how to increase private investment.

IMPACT

- Considers that throwing money at the problem doesn't work after a certain point, but that a combination of different policy instruments can be used to play a key role in helping the poor attain growth.
- Discusses what kinds of aid are most likely to help post-conflict and corrupt countries.
- Criticizes the entrenched elite of certain countries and aid policy that has not worked due to misadministration.
- Argues that anti-globalization is wrong but, with intervention from other nations, reform-minded citizens of problem states can find help to improve their situation.

QUOTATIONS

"The left will find that approaches it has discounted, such as military interventions, trade, and encouraging growth, are critical means to the end it has long embraced. The right will find that, unlike the challenge of global poverty reduction, the problem of the bottom billion will not be fixed automatically by global growth, and that neglect now will become a security nightmare for the world of our children."

"A world with a vast running sore—a billion people stuck in desperate conditions alongside unprecedented prosperity."

"An impoverished ghetto of 1bn people will be increasingly impossible for a comfortable world to tolerate."

MORE INFO

Books:

Calderisi, Robert. *The Trouble with Africa: Why Foreign Aid Isn't Working*. New York: Palgrave Macmillan, 2006. Examines the corruption, greed, and incompetence that undermine the aid effort.

Easterly, William. *The White Man's Burden: Why the West's Efforts to Aid the Rest Have Done So Much Ill and So Little Good*. New York: Penguin Press, 2006. Sees aid as a disaster and emphasizes the need for local solutions to poverty rather than Collier's belief that collective action can benefit the poorest countries.

Sachs, Jeffrey D. *The End of Poverty: Economic Possibilities for Our Time*. New York: Penguin Press, 2005. Argues that poverty can be eradicated with a few simple steps, and approaches global poverty as a problem to be solved through increased Western aid.

See Also:

Banker to the Poor: The Story of the Grameen Bank (p. 1334)

"A world with a vast running sore—a billion people stuck in desperate conditions alongside unprecedented prosperity."

  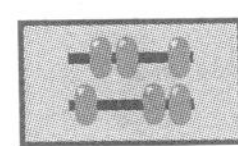   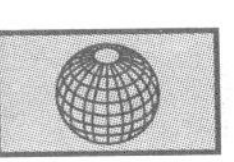   

The Box: How the Shipping Container Made the World Smaller and the World Economy Bigger

MARC LEVINSON (2006)

WHY READ IT?

- A compelling account of how container shipping developed from modest beginnings into a huge industry that made the boom in global trade possible.
- Shows how container shipping transformed global economic geography.
- Explains how the arrival of the shipping container changed the traditional working practices of the large ports, related industries, and cities, along with its impact on longshoremen, labor unions, and governments.

GETTING STARTED

The Box tells the absorbing story of the shipping container: the world worked one way before it came along and in a completely different way in its wake. Levinson shows how a simple idea played a pivotal role in the development of today's global economy. He details the success of the standardized container and its use in international shipping, helping the industry to evolve from old, labor-intensive, manual loading of ships to the mostly automated industry of enormous container ships and specialized ports around the world. Levinson also weaves in tales of the history and politics involved, and shows how the greater efficiency of cargo transferral has dramatically altered global trading.

AUTHOR

Marc Levinson is an economist and author of three previous books. He was formerly finance and economics editor of the *Economist*, a writer at *Newsweek*, and editorial director of the *Journal of Commerce*.

CONTEXT

- Argues that the shipping container was a critical factor in the development of globalization, through cost reduction and increased efficiency.
- Discusses how the dramatic increase in trade brought about by containerization transformed global supply chains, logistics, and outsourcing.
- Provides insight into Malcom McLean, whose drive and entrepreneurism led him to introduce modern containerization methods in 1956 by moving 58 truck trailers on a refitted tanker between Newark and Houston.
- Tells of McLean's struggle to turn containerization into a global industry, the years of high-stakes bargaining needed to win support from two of the titans of organized labor—Harry Bridges and Teddy Gleason—and the sensitivities about standards that would make it possible for a container to travel on any truck, train, or ship.
- Tells how McLean's success in supplying the US forces in Vietnam was pivotal in persuading the world of the container's potential. Details how containerization made possible "just-in-time" manufacturing on a global basis, which meant lower costs and improved productivity.

IMPACT

- Explains why ports such as New York and London were gradually replaced by new deepwater ports designed to facilitate the loading and unloading of containers.
- Discusses the impact of container shipping on the location of manufacturing and industry to make the most of transport infrastructure and cost savings.
- Examines how government regulators tried to obstruct the expansion of containerization to protect commercial interests and limit competition.
- Looks at the shift in economic power that containerization produced, such as the rise of Asia through the provision of inexpensive consumer goods that could be distributed much more cheaply.
- Discusses new uses for shipping containers, such as their potential to be used as designer homes, or even to hide atomic weapons.

QUOTATIONS

"*The container is at the core of a highly automated system for moving goods from anywhere, to anywhere, with a minimum of cost and complication on the way.*"

"*An enormous containership can be loaded with a minute fraction of the labor and time required to handle a small conventional ship half a century ago.*"

"Container shipping . . . has helped some cities and countries become part of the new global supply chains, while leaving others to the side."

MORE INFO

Books:

Cudahy, Brian J. *Box Boats: How Container Ships Changed the World.* New York: Fordham University Press, 2006. An account of the revolution in container ships that covers some of the same ground but focuses more on the transformation of the shipping industry.

Stopford, Martin. *Maritime Economics*. 3rd ed. London: Routledge, 2008. Provides a useful introduction to how global shipping operates, and it examines the economic theory that underpins the industry.

See Also:

Shipping (pp. 1644–1646)

"The container is at the core of a highly automated system for moving goods from anywhere, to anywhere, with a minimum of cost and complication on the way."

Cashflow Reengineering: How to Optimize the Cashflow Timeline and Improve Financial Efficiency

JAMES SAGNER (1997)

WHY READ IT?

- Provides focused advice on how a company can better manage its money and improve organizational decision-making.
- Applies principles of reengineering to the everyday problems of cashflow management.
- Guides you through practical techniques for assessing a cashflow system, including the time-value of money, gross margin analysis, scenario impact analysis, and the payment stream matrix.

GETTING STARTED

Shows how to improve business efficiency through cashflow reengineering, a process that has become increasingly important for companies rethinking and restructuring the way they operate. The reengineering puts them in a much better financial position, increases the available cash, and improves internal processing systems.

Explains how to accurately diagnose a company's cashflow problems and successful treat them through effective management. This means changing the system rather than just patching things up.

AUTHOR

James Sagner is a principal of Sagner/ Marks, a treasury consulting firm, and an expert in treasury management. He was previously a consultant at AT Kearney and chief economist for the Maryland Department of Transportation, and has managed over 250 large-scale company studies.

CONTEXT

- Details 10 management principles and procedures that have helped companies save millions.
- Provides the tools you need to gain the competitive advantages that result from effective cashflow management.
- Shows how people throughout an organization have a significant impact on cash, and offers techniques for working cross-functionally to cut costs without cutting people.
- Complements *Reengineering the Corporation* to help businesses rebuild their internal systems, in this case to manage cash in a more profitable manner.
- Focuses on numerous corporate activities that affect cashflow as well as on the negative side of more traditional methodologies.

IMPACT

- Takes a practical approach to helping you analyze specific situations and create solutions that are useful to your company.
- Implement an efficient cashflow timeline that tracks cash in, through, and out the system.
- Offers specific advice, such as cutting the corporate float, so that money works for you rather than being caught up in the system.
- Helps you determine where outsourcing would be an efficient alternative to in-house systems.
- Provides a useful working model for treasurers.

QUOTATIONS

"Reengineering: the concept of redesigning an organization to save costs and time and to improve service, attempts to determine and implement more efficient business processes."

"The principal areas to benefit from reengineering are those portions of the cashflow timeline that fall outside of traditional financial management."

"At the heart of profitability analysis is the concept of opportunity cost."

MORE INFO

Books:

Graham, Alastair. *Cashflow Control*. New York: AMACOM, 2000. Analyzes cashflow and its management.

Hammer, Michael. *Beyond Reengineering: How the Process-Centered Organization Is Changing Our Work and Our Lives*. New York: HarperBusiness, 1996. Describes the large-scale shift from procedure to process.

See Also:

Financial Management (p. 1357)

"Reengineering: the concept of redesigning an organization to save costs and time and to improve service, attempts to determine and implement more efficient business processes."

  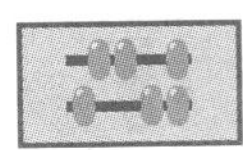   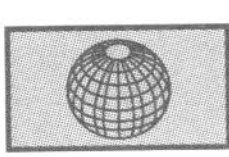   

Competitive Strategy: Techniques for Analyzing Industries and Competitors

MICHAEL E. PORTER (1980)

WHY READ IT?

- A hugely popular book that is taught in most business schools, and read by those interested in business success.
- It put strategic innovation at the forefront of management thinking, and proposes a solution to the eternal strategy dilemma.
- Shows how companies with a clear strategy outperform those whose strategies are unclear, or those that attempt to achieve both differentiation and cost leadership.

GETTING STARTED

Competitive Strategy, a modern classic of business thinking, provides a strong conceptual foundation for developing corporate strategy. It offers a rational and straightforward method for companies to extricate themselves from strategic confusion—and three generic strategies for dealing with competitive forces: differentiation, overall cost leadership, and focus, which for many have become the rules of the game.

AUTHOR

Michael E. Porter (b. 1947) is a professor at Harvard Business School, and has won many fellowships and awards for his work on competitive strategy. He was appointed to the President's Commission on Industrial Competitiveness by President Reagan, and is a four-time recipient of the McKinsey Award.

CONTEXT

- The rules of competition are embodied in competitive forces such as the entry of new competitors, the threat of substitutes, the bargaining power of buyers, and the rivalry among existing competitors.
- Bases its argument around three generic strategies which help avoid losing out to competitors, and five competitive forces, that determine what a company must do to remain competitive.
- Shows how differentiation entails competing on the basis of value added to customers, so that customers will pay a premium to cover higher costs.
- Explains how the strength of the competitive forces determines the ability of companies to earn rates of return on investment in excess of the cost of capital.
- Offers a guide as to whether some particular strategy, once implemented, can produce worthwhile profits.

IMPACT

- Explains how effectively implementing any of these generic strategies usually requires total commitment, which is diluted if there is more than one primary target.
- Argues that if a company fails to focus on any of the three generic strategies it is liable to encounter problems.
- Synthesizes all that economists know about what determines industry and company profitability.
- Presents a rationalist's solution to the long-running strategic dilemma between pragmatism, where companies have to respond to their own specific situations, and responsiveness, which opens up competitive advantage.
- The current consensus contends that the competitive forces are truer to reality than the generic strategies.

QUOTATION

"Strategy is a choice on how to compete."

MORE INFO

Book:

Porter, Michael E. *Competitive Advantage: Creating and Sustaining Superior Performance*. New York: The Free Press, 1985. Presents a traditional view of strategic thinking.

See Also:

Michael Eugene Porter (p. 1299)

"Strategy is a choice on how to compete."

 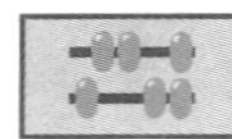   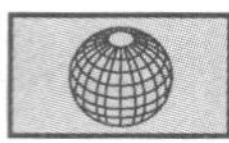   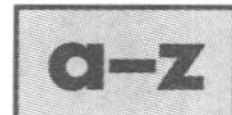

Confusión de Confusiones

JOSEPH DE LA VEGA (1688)

WHY READ IT?

- This is the oldest book ever written about the stock exchange business, and it made de la Vega famous for his insights and stories about speculation in the 17th century.
- Considered a classic, as the type of trading intricacies and market manipulations of the time are still with us today.
- Presents four rules of speculation that are still relevant: never advise anyone to buy or sell shares; accept both profits and losses; profits do not last; you need both money and patience.

GETTING STARTED

Confusión de Confusiones consists of a series of dialogs between a philosopher, a merchant, and a shareholder describing the workings of the Amsterdam Stock Exchange, the first in the world. The dialog gives the perspectives of the various market participants and the particulars of speculation and trading at the time. Although it discusses tactics and schemes used by traders and brokers trying to influence prices and play the market, it also takes an affectionate look at the market and its members.

AUTHOR

Joseph de la Vega (also known as Joseph Penso de la Vega; c. 1650–1692) was a businessman, writer, and philanthropist who lived in Amsterdam in a community of Portuguese Jews whose ancestors had fled the Spanish Inquisition. He was elected to several posts in the Jewish and financial communities, including the honorary office of President of the Academia de los Sitibundos.

CONTEXT

- Only two stocks were traded on the Amsterdam Stock Exchange at the time, the Dutch East India Company and the Dutch West India Company, both businesses dependent on risky operations around the world.
- The trading operations on the exchange were complex, involving options and forward trades to both hedge and speculate.
- There were also a number of other features of modern exchanges, such as bulls, bears, panics, bubbles, short selling, and margin trading.
- Argues that the most successful speculators maintain a balance between optimism and pessimism.
- Describes how the Dutch government banned short selling, but that this was ignored as short sellers were often needed to make markets.

IMPACT

- Gives an overview of who was trading on the Amsterdam Stock Exchange at the time, the types of speculation and trading going on, and the financial instruments used.
- Examines how bull and bear markets can be manipulated and the consequences, teaching how crucial it is to know the rules and think about how they could be used against you.
- Explores the impact of crowd behavior and trading scams on the financial markets.
- Stresses the importance of information and analysis in successful stock trading.

QUOTATIONS

"What really matters is an awareness of how greed and fear can drive rational people to behave in strange ways when they gather in the marketplace."

"[At the stock exchange] concealment of facts, quarrels, provocations, mockery, idle talk, violent desires, collusion, artful deceptions, betrayals, cheatings and even the tragic end are to be found."

"Some gamble for the fun of it, some for vanity, many are spendthrifts, many find satisfaction in their occupation, and quite a few [just] make a living [at the stock exchange."

MORE INFO

Book:

Chancellor, Edward. *Devil Take the Hindmost: A History of Financial Speculation.* New York: Farrar, Straus, Giroux, 1999. Examines the development of stock exchanges and speculative manias through history.

See Also:

Joseph de la Vega (p. 1278)
Reminiscences of a Stock Operator (p. 1413)
Capital Markets and Stock Markets (pp. 1689–1691)

"What really matters is an awareness of how greed and fear can drive rational people to behave in strange ways when they gather in the marketplace."

  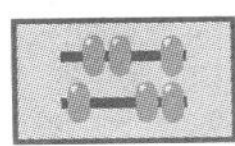   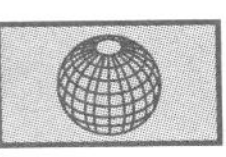   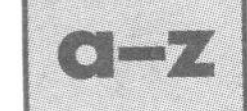

Conquer the Crash: You Can Survive and Prosper in a Deflationary Depression

ROBERT R. PRECHTER, JR (2nd ed 2009, originally 2003)

WHY READ IT?

- Aimed more at the financial amateur than expert, it explains why the boom times are now behind us, and what we can do to face the economic problems that lie ahead.
- Contains practical tips and guidance on how to deal with the stock market, and other financial areas such as real estate, bonds, insurance, banking, annuities, and precious metals.
- Compares the socio-economic mindset of previous boom–bust cycles to that of today to explain why we are repeating history.

GETTING STARTED

Conquer the Crash argues that deflation and depression are now inevitable. Premised on the author's interpretation of the Elliott Wave Principle, and the idea that mass investor psychology drives markets, it explains why the economy is about to enter a depression that few investors are prepared to deal with. Using technical analysis of the nature of the markets, it offers a guide to understanding and avoiding the losses that normally occur in a bear market.

AUTHOR

Robert R. Prechter (b. 1949) is president of Elliott Wave International, executive director of the Socionomic Institute, and has published *The Elliott Wave Theorist*, a monthly forecasting publication for many years. He previously worked at Merrill Lynch, and has served as president of the Market Technicians Association.

CONTEXT

- Introduces the Elliott Wave Principle, which argues that stock market prices rise and fall in discernible patterns and that those patterns can be linked together into waves.
- Some argue that the successful practice of the Elliott Wave Principle relies too heavily on judgement and sentiment, although it appears to be an exact science.
- Explains that there have always been economic cycles, and this will continue due to human activity and nature always adhering to the same fractaled pattern.
- Prechter bases his views on behavioral economics and inefficient market theory that irrational bubbles will form in the markets.
- Relates the current situation to the United States in the early 1930s and Japan over the last 12 years.

IMPACT

- Assembles an array of data to explain how the boom years and market excess of the last decade are now giving way to an extensive bear market.
- Also explores market history, social psychology, and the prevailing money myths to back up this case.
- Advises that we should pay off our bills, pay off our mortgages, buy some precious metals or put our money in a safe bank, not invest in stocks, not rely on the government to protect us, and get ready to profit once we are at the bottom to take advantage of the next uprise.

QUOTATIONS

"It is better to be safe and wrong than exposed and wrong."

"In essence, bull and bear markets are social mood trends."

"The underlying trend of human progress is upward."

MORE INFO

Books:

Brussee, Warren. *The Second Great Depression.* Bangor, ME: Booklocker.com, 2005. Highlights the growing problems from huge consumer debt that are starting to beset the global marketplace.

Frost, A. J., and Robert R. Prechter. *The Elliott Wave Principle: Key to Market Behavior.* Chappaqua, NY: New Classics Library, 1978. A classic text that examines the Elliott Wave Principle for forecasting stock market behavior.

Schiff, Peter D. *Crash-proof: How to Profit from the Coming Economic Collapse.* Hoboken, NJ: Wiley, 2007. Similar in approach, as it offers useful tips on how to depression-proof your finances, and assesses the financial problems we face.

"It is better to be safe and wrong than exposed and wrong."

        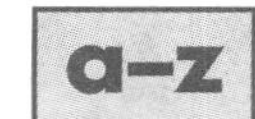

Corporate Financial Management

GLEN ARNOLD (5th ed 2012, originally 1998)

WHY READ IT?

- A comprehensive introductory text on corporate finance that helps the beginner move up to an intermediate level of knowledge.
- Sets out the basic principles of finance in a clear style, while working through the main elements of business management.
- Examines financial decision-making, and how the financial markets operate, while integrating it into a practical analysis of how companies operate.

GETTING STARTED

Corporate Financial Management is a comprehensive introduction to corporate finance that covers all the relevant topics, as well as emerging issues such as risk management using derivatives and shareholder value analysis. It is a practical and focused textbook that is used on many undergraduate and business courses.

AUTHOR

Glen Arnold is professor of finance at Salford Business School, Manchester, and the director of the Finance, Accounting and Banking Research Interest Group, as well as being a bestselling finance textbook author.

CONTEXT

- Aimed primarily at second/third-year undergraduates of accounting and finance, economics, business studies/management.
- Provides an overview of the financial world, from an extensive treatment of the investment decision, risk and return, and sources of finance, to a comprehensive analysis of corporate value, including mergers, risk management using derivatives, and managing exchange rate risk.
- Explores the theory behind corporate finance, and looks at where it impacts on real-world practice. The emphasis is on connecting finance theory to practical management, and examining current theoretical re-evaluations.
- Uses extensive case studies and examples to explain financial theory, and worked examples and questions in each chapter to aid learning.

IMPACT

- The core principles of corporate financial management are explained with the beginner in mind.
- Uses a learning format, and includes *Financial Times* articles, and key concepts summarized at the end of each chapter.
- Has been internationally developed to the quality of a typical US finance textbook.
- Non-technical treatment, as equations and math are kept to a minimum.
- Contains useful references to other materials for further learning.

QUOTATIONS

"Without a vibrant and adaptable finance sector all parts of the economy would be starved of investment and society would be poorer."

"It is vital for the health of the firm and the economic welfare of the finance providers that management employ the best techniques available when analysing which of all the possible investment opportunities will give the best return."

"Defining and measuring future receipts and outlays accurately is central to successful project appraisal."

MORE INFO

Books:

Arnold, Glen. *Essentials of Corporate Financial Management*. Harlow, UK: Pearson, 2013. Textbook aimed at courses on the core topics of finance.

Emery, Douglas R., and John D. Finnerty. *Corporate Financial Management*. London: Prentice Hall International, 1997. Connects theory and practice, with many useful examples from the corporate world.

Weaver, Samuel C., and Fred Weston. *Strategic Financial Management: Application of Corporate Finance*. Mason, OH: Thomson/South-Western, 2008. Works through the tools, techniques, and concepts for understanding financial management.

See Also:

Principles of Corporate Finance (p. 1410)

"Without a vibrant and adaptable finance sector all parts of the economy would be starved of investment and society would be poorer."

  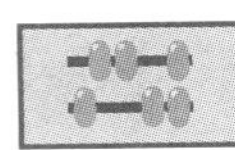   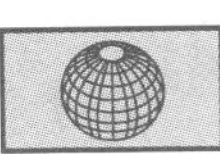 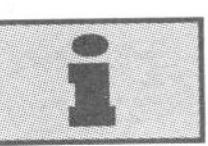  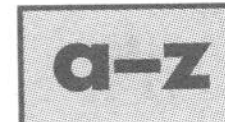

Corporate-Level Strategy: Creating Value in the Multibusiness Company

MICHAEL GOOLD, ANDREW CAMPBELL, and MARCUS ALEXANDER (1994)

WHY READ IT?

- Argues that because most large companies are now multibusiness organizations, there is a great need to change how they are structured to help them add value.
- Recommends that multibusiness organizations should aim for a tighter fit between individual company strategies and the overall corporate strategy.
- Suggests that although large conglomerates claim to add value through synergy and economies of scale, this is not really the case.

GETTING STARTED

Corporate-Level Strategy puts the case for a tight fit between the main parent company's strategy and its businesses' strategies, arguing that this will promote success. This needs to be thought through properly, to ensure that the most is made from company structure and interactions.

AUTHORS

Michael Goold is founding director of the Ashridge Strategic Management Centre. Before joining Ashridge, he was a senior fellow at the London Business School. He was also a vice president and director of the Boston Consulting Group.

Andrew Campbell is a director of Ashridge Strategic Management Centre. Before joining Ashridge, he was a fellow of the Centre for Business Strategy at London Business School. He has also worked at McKinsey & Co.

Marcus Alexander is a director of the Ashridge Strategic Management Centre, and a professor at the London Business School. He has previously worked in investment banking, at the Boston Consulting Group, and in business.

CONTEXT

- Notes that while individual businesses within the organization often have strategies, the corporation as a whole may not.
- Introduces the concept of heartland businesses and shows how it can help corporations improve their overall performance, as this type of business is more broad-ranging and can cover different industry sectors, markets, and technologies.
- Discusses successful corporate strategies for multibusiness organizations, exploring the role of the parent, its distinctive characteristics, and how each parent will only be effective with certain sorts of businesses.
- Argues that corporate strategy should be driven by parenting advantage to create more value in the portfolio of businesses than would be achieved by any rival. To do so requires a fundamental change in perspective on the role of the parent and the approach of the organization.

IMPACT

- Discusses how there must be a clear vision regarding the role of the parent organization, that the parent must concentrate on "heartland businesses" that it understands.
- Separates the concept of heartland businesses from core businesses, with the former being a better fit with the parent organization.
- Calculates that in most multibusiness companies the whole is worth less than the sum of its parts.
- The research runs counter to the findings of authors such as Alfred Chandler in *Strategy and Structure* and Peter Drucker in *The Practice of Management*, in that it is possible for the corporate level to add value.

QUOTATIONS

"The parent has an innate feel for its heartland that enables it to make difficult judgments and decisions with a high degree of success."

"Heartland businesses are well understood by the parent; they do not suffer from inappropriate influence and meddling that can damage less familiar businesses."

MORE INFO

Books:

Goold, Michael, and Andrew Campbell. *Designing Effective Organizations: How to Create Structured Networks.* San Francisco, CA.: Jossey-Bass, 2002. Winner of the Igor Ansoff Strategic Management Award, it takes on corporate-level organizational design.

Porter, Michael E. *Competitive Advantage: Creating and Sustaining Superior Performance*. New York: The Free Press, 1985. Presents a traditional view of strategic thinking.

See Also:

Blue Ocean Strategy: How to Create Uncontested Market Space and Make the Competition Irrelevant (p. 1337)

Corporate Strategy: An Analytic Approach to Business Policy for Growth and Expansion (p. 1346)

Corporate Strategy (pp. 1701–1704)

"The parent has an innate feel for its heartland that enables it to make difficult judgments and decisions with a high degree of success."

     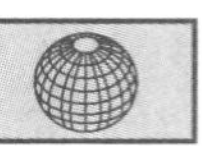   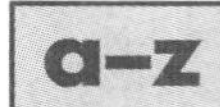

Corporate Strategy: An Analytic Approach to Business Policy for Growth and Expansion

H. IGOR ANSOFF (1965)

WHY READ IT?

- Was the first book to concentrate entirely on strategy, and remains one of the classics of management literature.
- Provides a powerful, rational model by which strategic and planning decisions can be made.
- Ansoff was the originator of the strategic management concept, and responsible for establishing strategic planning as a management activity in its own right.

GETTING STARTED

Corporate Strategy develops a series of concepts and procedures that managers can use to promote strategic decision-making within an organization. The book is based on the author's experiences as a strategist at Lockheed, and argues that, in developing strategy, it is essential to systematically anticipate future environmental challenges to an organization, and draw up appropriate strategic plans for responding to them.

AUTHOR

H. Igor Ansoff (1918–2002) was vice president at Lockheed Aircraft Corporations, and professor of industrial administration at the Carnegie Institute of Technology. He also taught at a number of other universities, and was named as distinguished professor emeritus at the United States International University on his retirement.

CONTEXT

- Saw strategic planning as a complex sequence, or cascade, of decisions and defined two main concepts essential to understanding its nature, and, therefore, to implementing it successfully.
- Examines how decision planning is central to the concept of gap analysis: see where you are, identify where you wish to be, and identify the tasks that will take you there.
- Introduces the word "synergy" to the management vocabulary. Although the term has become overused, Ansoff 's explanation (2 + 2 = 5) remains memorably simple.
- Presents the strategy tool known as the Ansoff matrix, which depicts the product and market choices available to an organization.
- Provides a rational model for decision-making that concentrates on corporate expansion and diversification, rather than on strategic planning as a whole.

IMPACT

- Discusses several new theoretical concepts such as partial ignorance, business strategy, capability and competence profiles, and synergy.
- Sees strategic management as a powerful applied theory, offering a degree of coherence and universality lacking in the more traditional, functionally dominated management theories.
- While it was a remarkable book for its time, its flaws have been widely acknowledged, most honestly by Ansoff himself. It is highly prescriptive and advocates heavy reliance on analysis.
- Attempts to prove that strategic management can be a dynamic tool able to cope with the unexpected twists of turbulent markets.
- Helped to create the language and processes that allowed modern industrial companies to address the deep questions of corporate strategy for the first time.
- Examined corporate advantage long before its more modern analysis in the 1980s.

QUOTATION

"Paralysis by analysis."

MORE INFO

Book:

Porter, Michael E. *Competitive Advantage: Creating and Sustaining Superior Performance*. New York: The Free Press, 1985. Presents a traditional view of strategic thinking.

See Also:

Corporate-Level Strategy: Creating Value in the Multibusiness Company (p. 1345)
Corporate Strategy (pp. 1701–1704)

"Paralysis by analysis."

  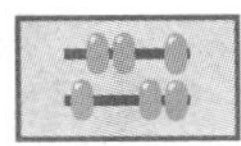   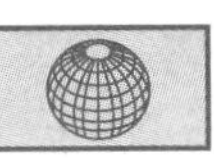   

Cost and Effect: Using Integrated Cost Systems to Drive Profitability and Performance

ROBERT S. KAPLAN and ROBIN COOPER (1997)

WHY READ IT?

- Two highly respected academics present a resource for understanding and implementing activity-based cost management, and show how to improve company profits and performance.
- Provides a detailed blueprint to enable managers to make better decisions and to promote organizational learning.
- Explains why activity-based costing has great benefits, not only for accounting but also management and business strategy.
- Explains how cost and performance measurement systems can enhance organizational profitability and performance.

GETTING STARTED

Cost and Effect demonstrates how the principles of activity-based costing and other advanced cost management techniques, such as target and kaizen costing, can drive business performance. It can be seen as a guidebook for managers to gain benefits from these techniques. Thought of as a classic in managerial accounting literature, the book helps the business and finance communities rethink how a company should handle cost.

AUTHORS

Robert S. Kaplan (b. 1940) is professor of leadership development at Harvard Business School, and chairman of the Balanced Scorecard Collaborative. He has previously been on the faculty and dean of the business school at Carnegie Mellon University, and has received numerous awards.

Robin Cooper is a professor at Goizueta Business School, Emory University, and was formerly professor of management at Claremont University. He was previously on the faculty of the Harvard Business School, and is a fellow of the Institute of Chartered Accountants in England and Wales.

CONTEXT

- Focuses on the need for accurate financial reporting and cost management, by integrating financial reporting processes built around activity-based costing.
- Assists in determining where improvements in quality, efficiency, and productivity will have the highest payoffs.
- Offers practical guidance on negotiating more effectively on price, product features, quality, delivery, and service.
- Uses examples from leading companies to show how to create integrated, knowledge-based systems that provide meaningful information on performance.
- Examines how to design products and services that meet customers' expectations, and that can be produced and delivered at a profit.

IMPACT

- Reveals that most managers don't know how to measure accurately, influence, or understand the fundamental cost drivers in their businesses.
- Analyzes the different systems in managerial cost accounting, and presents quality and productivity improvement systems such as TQM and Six Sigma that could contribute to company performance.
- Shows how to integrate activity-based cost systems into reporting and budgeting processes.
- Links the advantages of activity-based costing to economic value added and enterprise systems.

QUOTATIONS

"We use two powerful concepts . . . that enable the finance function to shift from being the passive reporter of the past to a proactive influencer of the future."

"In today's highly competitive environments, it is not enough to be the most efficient player; it is also necessary to be part of the most efficient supply chain."

"[We provide a] guided tour for how companies can migrate from inadequate, traditional cost systems to a destination where cost and performance measurement systems are explicitly designed to produce the right information at the right time for essential managerial learning, decisions, and control."

MORE INFO

Books:

Cokins, Gary. *Activity-Based Cost Management Making it Work: A Manager's Guide to Implementing and Sustaining an Effective ABC System.* Chicago, IL: Irwin Professional Publishing, 1996. Explains how and why you should implement an effective ABC management system.

Kaplan, Robert S., and Steven R. Anderson. *Time-Driven Activity-Based Costing: A Simpler and More Powerful Path to Higher Profits.* Boston, MA: Harvard Business School Press, 2007. Provides a model for managers wanting to estimate the resource demands imposed by each transaction, product, or customer.

See Also:

★ Profitability Analysis Using Activity-Based Costing (pp. 908–910)
✔ Understanding Activity-Based Costing (p. 989)
Activity-Based Costing (pp. 1190–1192)

"We use two powerful concepts . . . that enable the finance function to shift from being the passive reporter of the past to a proactive influencer of the future."

  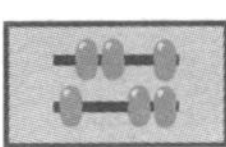      

Damodaran on Valuation: Security Analysis for Investment and Corporate Finance

ASWATH DAMODARAN (2nd ed 2006, originally 1994)

WHY READ IT?

- Combining analysis of both the theory and practice of business valuation, this is a highly regarded text on how to best measure the value of a particular asset.
- Damodaran has a great reputation as a teacher and authority, and he here critically evaluates the leading valuation models to help pick the right model for any scenario.
- Provides practical frameworks for addressing the key issues of company valuation.

GETTING STARTED

Damodaran on Valuation provides focused guidance on asset valuation for practitioners involved in securities analysis, portfolio management, M&A, and corporate finance. It offers a systematic examination of the three basic approaches to valuation—discounted cash flow valuation, relative valuation, and contingent claim valuation—and explains the concepts and techniques of valuation in an understandable manner.

AUTHOR

Aswath Damodaran is professor of finance at the Stern School of Business, and has also taught at the University of California, Berkeley. He was the youngest winner of the University-wide Distinguished Teaching Award, and profiled in *Business Week* as one of the top 12 business school professors.

CONTEXT

- Examines a variety of real-life firms where the direct application of valuation models has failed, identifies the problems, and offers solutions.
- Explains the value and limitations of models in order to illustrate key techniques.
- Assists the development of the skills needed to select the right model for any valuation scenario.
- Presents how to implement the right model, and the kinds of firms to which it is best applied.
- Discusses many of the common myths of valuation, regarding objectivity, supposed timelessness, precision, quantitativeness, and process.
- Focuses throughout on application, including how to develop an understanding of stock fundamentals.

IMPACT

- Emphasizes the usefulness and benefits of the variety of valuation models available to businesses.
- Presents tools designed for a variety of demands, such as estimating the cost of equity, estimating growth rates, measuring free cash flow to equity, valuing firms, estimating the value of assets by looking at the pricing of comparable assets, and measuring the value of assets that share option characteristics.
- Provides spreadsheets that have been prepared to allow readers to apply what they are learning immediately.

QUOTATIONS

"Reasonable estimates of value can be made for most assets and that the same fundamental principles determine the value of all types of assets, real as well as financial."

"Valuation is not an objective exercise, and any preconceptions and biases that an analyst brings to the process will find its way into the value."

"Matching the valuation model to the asset or firm being valued is as important a part of valuation as understanding the models and having the right inputs."

MORE INFO

Books:

Damodaran, Aswath. *Study Guide for Damodaran on Valuation: Security Analysis for Investment and Corporate Finance*. New York: Wiley, 1994. A supporting learning resource for the main book.

Damodaran, Aswath. *The Dark Side of Valuation: Valuing Old Tech, New Tech, and New Economy Companies*. Upper Saddle River, NJ: FT Prentice Hall, 2001. Details various ways to adapt conventional valuation methods for companies.

See Also:

Investment Banking: Valuation, Leveraged Buyouts, and Mergers and Acquisitions (p. 1382)
Valuation: Measuring and Managing the Value of Companies (p. 1429)
Corporate Valuation (pp. 1704–1707)

"Reasonable estimates of value can be made for most assets and that the same fundamental principles determine the value of all types of assets, real as well as financial."

A Demon of Our Own Design

RICHARD BOOKSTABER (2007)

WHY READ IT?

- A timely book on the risks underpinning the hedge fund industry, and the markets in general.
- Bookstaber was involved in the design of some of the complex options and derivatives described in the book, which are contributing to the market downturn.
- Discusses why, although there is greater market sophistication, improved technology, and improved oversight and regulation, the markets are becoming more risky all the time.

GETTING STARTED

A Demon of Our Own Design provides an entertaining guide to how the markets work, the dynamics of the hedge fund industry, and the risks inherent in financial innovation. It examines some of the financial disasters of the last 25 years in a readable style, and worries us with the premise that the financial products developed over the past few decades have become too complicated for our own good.

AUTHOR

Richard Bookstaber (b. 1950) is a finance writer and runs an equity hedge fund, having also been at Ziff Brothers Investments and Moore Capital Management. He was previously a managing director at Salomon Brothers and on their Risk Management Committee.

CONTEXT

- Shows how the very things done to make markets safer have actually created a world that is far more dangerous, and examines the dynamics behind such financial calamities as the 1987 crash and the demise of Long-Term Capital Management.
- Takes an insider's perspective on the management decisions made by some of the world's most powerful financial operators, including Warren Buffett, Sandy Weill, and John Meriwether.
- Recounts the author's own contribution to market calamities, and the market complexity due to derivatives and structured products.

IMPACT

- Argues that the increasing specialization of financial instruments means that there will be greater uncertainty, and we will be more vulnerable to larger problems.
- Discusses the crises occurring from tight coupling, where the close interlinking of factors is causing problems in different industries.
- Considers much that is currently relevant in risk management, the capital markets, and the liquidity crisis.
- Calls for a slower rate of market innovation and trading, which originates from his economist background and distaste for risk.
- Explains the many complex relationships between securities in an understandable style.
- Thinks of financial markets as inherently unstable, and says this should limit how far we should go in pursuit of profit.

QUOTATIONS

"The financial markets that we have constructed are now so complex, and the speed of transactions so fast, that apparently isolated actions and even minor events can have catastrophic consequences."

"Virtually all mishaps over the past decades had their roots in the complex structure of the financial markets themselves."

"The danger to the system is the system."

MORE INFO

Book:

Knee, Jonathan A. *The Accidental Investment Banker: Inside the Decade That Transformed Wall Street.* Oxford: Oxford University Press, 2006. A look at the role of the investment banker and the deal culture, from one who has been there.

See Also:

- Liar's Poker: Rising Through the Wreckage on Wall Street (p. 1386)
- Traders, Guns, and Money: Knowns and Unknowns in the Dazzling World of Derivatives (p. 1427)
- Hedge Funds, Fund Management, and Alternative Investments (pp. 1729–1732)

"The financial markets that we have constructed are now so complex, and the speed of transactions so fast, that apparently isolated actions and even minor events can have catastrophic consequences."

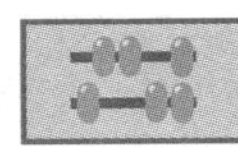

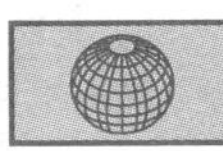

The Essence of Financial Management

DAVID R. MYDDELTON (1995)

WHY READ IT?

- Useful as a reference for managers wanting to improve their knowledge and skills in financial management.
- Examines the current issues and topics of financial management and corporate finance.
- Takes a practical approach to the subject, showing how to implement the concepts and techniques discussed.

GETTING STARTED

The Essence of Financial Management provides a comprehensive overview of the theory and main techniques of financial management. It assists managers new to financial matters, and gives them a full understanding of the financial objectives of a business, the environment in which the business operates, and fundamental accounting concepts such as the balance sheet, P&L statement, and return on investment.

AUTHOR

David R. Myddelton taught at the School of Management, Cranfield University, for 40 years until retirement in 2005, having been professor of finance and accounting since 1972. He is now emeritus professor of finance and accounting at the School.

CONTEXT

- Aimed at those new to finance who are looking for a sound and useful primer on the topic.
- Defines the basic concepts and themes involved in financial management.
- Explores the problems financial managers face on a daily basis: time, uncertainty, liquidity, inflation, tax planning, and other critical issues.
- Includes a useful glossary.

IMPACT

- Presents all the financial management techniques a non-financial manager needs to know.
- Presents the four basic accounting concepts: going concern, accruals, consistency, and prudence.
- Advises on how to treat the components of interest rates, from term structure to short-termism.
- Details the uses of cash, working capital, and capital project appraisal.
- Examines borrowing and the cost of debt, and the main impact areas.
- Gives an overview on shares, the markets, and modern portfolio theory.
- Discusses corporate finance, including cost of capital, gearing, and mergers.

QUOTATIONS

"Both cash and profit matter, but people sometimes wonder whether one matters more than the other."

"Equity investors cannot avoid market risk, which stems from the uncertainties of the whole economy."

"Any change in the future prospects of a business—especially its future earnings or the risks involved—may affect a share's present market value."

MORE INFO

Book:

Brigham, Eugene F., and Joel F. Houston. *Fundamentals of Financial Management.* Hinsdale, IL: Dryden Press, 1978. Focused guidance for teaching undergraduate corporate finance, with an online student assessment and tutorial resource.

"Both cash and profit matter, but people sometimes wonder whether one matters more than the other."

The EVA Challenge: Implementing Value-Added Change in an Organization

JOEL M. STERN and JOHN S. SHIELY (2001)

WHY READ IT?

- The cofounder of the EVA concept explains how it can be used for measuring a company's true profitability and providing a strategy for enhancing corporate and shareholder wealth.
- Shows how to customize EVA initiatives for different types of organization, to improve corporate economic value by focusing on corporate, financial, and market performance.
- Compares EVA with other performance measures and financial management systems, and presents the benefits of knowing how value can be best created and maintained.

GETTING STARTED

The EVA Challenge is an introductory overview on the benefits of using Economic Value Added to measure corporate performance, and increase shareholder value. It is a means to alter organizational priorities and behavior, and acts as a basis for incentive compensation, and unity between management actions and shareholder needs. It was created as an alternative to the Generally Accepted Accounting Procedures (GAAP), and has been utilized by many large companies to improve shareholder value.

AUTHORS

Joel M. Stern is managing partner of Stern Stewart & Co., and currently serves on the faculties of five graduate business schools. He is a writer, and a columnist for the *Sunday Times* of London.

John S. Shiely is president of Briggs & Stratton. He began his career as a tax accountant at Arthur Andersen & Co., before working as a lawyer with Hughes Hubbard & Reed and Allen-Bradley/Rockwell Automation.

CONTEXT

- Presents a completely new way for companies to value and measure their performance, drawing on strategy, management, accounting, finance, and economics, to attain a tailored model of EVA implementation.
- Analyzes how GAAP-based corporate reporting rules were designed to protect lenders by depicting a company's liquidation value, making it a conservative and inaccurate picture of financial strength.
- Argues that EVA is ideal for knowledge-based companies making heavy infrastructure investments today for any anticipated return later.
- Proposes that an EVA program must have the full backing of the management board.

IMPACT

- Covers all stages of EVA, including strategy development, organizational design, training, and incentive compensation.
- Shows that to get the most out of EVA, companies should install all of its systems—measurement, management, and incentive.
- Explains why the opportunity cost of capital has been miscalculated, due to the split between ownership and control, and traditional accounting measurements being mis-applied.
- Discusses how EVA can improve the accuracy of corporate reporting by more accurately reflecting the value of intangible assets.

QUOTATIONS

"EVA is the profit that remains after deducting the cost of the capital invested to generate that profit."

"EVA is simple and easy enough for non-financial types to grasp and to apply."

"EVA is the prime mover of shareholder value."

MORE INFO

Books:

Ehrbar, Al. *EVA: The Real Key to Creating Wealth.* New York: Wiley, 1998. A senior VP of Stern Stewart outlines the applications and benefits that can be gained by employing EVA.

Grant, James L. *Foundations of Economic Value Added.* New Hope, PA: Frank J. Fabozzi Associates, 1997. Examines the role of economic profit analysis in the process of wealth creation.

Young, S. David. *EVA and Value-Based Management: A Practical Guide to Implementation.* New York: McGraw-Hill, 2001. Looks at how to implement both EVA and VBM successfully.

See Also:

★ Creating Value with EVA (pp. 814–816)
★ Why EVA Is the Best Measurement Tool for Creating Shareholder Value (pp. 952–953)
Economic Value Added (p. 1222)

"EVA is the profit that remains after deducting the cost of the capital invested to generate that profit."

  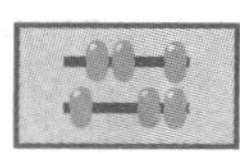 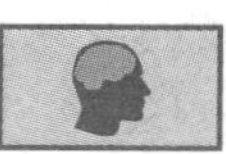     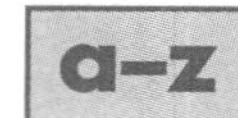

A Farewell to Alms: A Brief Economic History of the World

GREGORY CLARK (2007)

WHY READ IT?

- Attempts to answer why some countries have become developed and comparatively rich while others have not and remain poor.
- Finds that income inequality between societies has increased in recent years.
- Proposes the theory that social evolution explains economic growth, and that stability and security were essential to the development of a thriving economy.

GETTING STARTED

A Farewell to Alms aims to uncover the laws underlying human history through quantitative research, and explain the unbalanced nature of economic development.

It looks at why some parts of the world are rich and others poor, and why the industrial revolution occurred in 18th century England. Clark suggests that culture and a gradual improvement in economic rigor explains the differences.

AUTHOR

Gregory Clark (b. 1957) is professor of economics and chair of the economics department at the University of California, Davis. His main research is on long-run economic growth and the wealth of nations; he teaches undergraduate and graduate world economic history, and helps organize the economic history seminar.

CONTEXT

- Argues that, throughout history, population was at equilibrium—whenever technological improvements increased productivity, the result was not better living conditions, but higher population.
- Explains that the rich had twice as many offspring as the poor, which meant that the skills and behaviors of the rich seeped down to eventually trigger the industrial revolution.
- In the past, he notes that markets were much less regulated; property rights were more secure, and there was more balance on the return on human capital.
- Finds that cultural differences were shaped by selective pressures that people experience differently from each other.

IMPACT

- Argues against current thinking that industrialization happened because of improved institutional stability.
- Finds that the average person in 1800 was no better off in terms of life expectancy and stature than the average person in 100,000 BC.
- Challenges the belief in the superiority of free markets and the faith in the equality of mankind.
- Considers that the poor can be helped by outside assistance only through a radical change in the way that things are structured.

QUOTATIONS

"Though the book is about economics, we shall see that in the long run economic institutions, psychology, culture, politics, and sociology are deeply interwoven."

"The gap in incomes between countries is of the order of 50:1. There walk the Earth now both the richest people who ever lived and the poorest."

"Money will buy happiness, but that happiness is transferred from someone else, not added to the common pool."

MORE INFO

Books:

Landes, David S. *The Wealth and Poverty of Nations: Why Some Are So Rich and Some So Poor.* New York: WW Norton, 1998. Considers the growing gulf between rich and poor.

Pomeranz, Kenneth. *The Great Divergence: China, Europe, and the Making of the Modern World Economy.* Princeton, NJ: Princeton University Press, 2000. A similar treatment examining the divergence in economies.

See Also:

The Ascent of Money: A Financial History of the World (p. 1332)

The Wealth of Nations (p. 1433)

"Though the book is about economics, we shall see that in the long run economic institutions, psychology, culture, politics, and sociology are deeply interwoven."

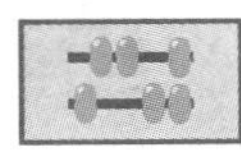

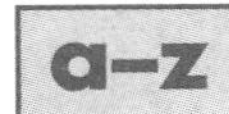

Fault Lines: How Hidden Fractures Still Threaten the World Economy

RAGHURAM G. RAJAN (2010)

WHY READ IT?

- A powerful investigation into the initial causes of the global economic crisis, explaining them as being caused by rising inequality and stagnant wages.
- Analyzes the inherent problems of a global market system that is dependent on US consumerism for growth and reliability.
- Argues that the fault lines in the international economic system are more hidden and widespread than previously thought.
- Winner of the *Financial Times* and Goldman Sachs Business Book of the Year award 2010, being cited as a profound and compelling book that "should be required reading for policymakers and those in the financial services industry."

GETTING STARTED

Fault Lines is a comprehensive exploration of the origins of the recent economic and financial crisis, presenting some difficult choices in for public policy and a range of reforms necessary to ensure a full recovery. As chief economist of the IMF, Rajan had warned central bankers that the financial sector was facing disaster; in this book, he takes a wider perspective on the growing gap between rich and poor as a major reason behind the crisis. He also proposes a raft of general policy recommendations to help avoid a similar financial calamity in the future.

AUTHOR

Raghuram G. Rajan (b. 1963) is professor of finance at the University of Chicago Booth School of Business and a former chief economist at the International Monetary Fund. He received an MBA from the Indian Institute of Management and a PhD from MIT, has worked as a consultant for the Indian Finance Ministry, the World Bank, and the Federal Reserve Board, and coauthored *Saving Capitalism from the Capitalists.*

CONTEXT

- Examines how failings in the US economy, such as the increasing wage gap, unequal access to education, and lack of affordable healthcare created financial instability and put pressure on governments to fix things in the short term.
- Assesses the economic fall-out from government intervention, and how the fault lines in the global economy forced both the bankers and the government into the financial crisis.
- Shows that the decisions collectively made by bankers, government officials, and ordinary homeowners created the economic downturn.
- Warns that the financial markets will only repeat their mistakes unless effective reforms are made.

IMPACT

- Focuses on the political and economic aspects of the recent crisis, not just the failures of the banking sector.
- Changes the focus from the usual suspects of bankers, regulators, and borrowers, instead arguing that their actions were part of a bigger picture impacted by politics.
- Discusses how the finance sector provided home equity loans, subprime mortgages, and auto loans in response to a need for credit due to the gap between purchasing power and the cost of living.
- Proposes changes that counteract social inequality and dependency on export-led growth to help us avoid the next financial disaster.
- Suggested reforms include revamping bankers' pay systems and developing capital buffers in the global credit system, so that there is less need to bail out companies seen as too important or big to fail.

QUOTATIONS

"There are no silver bullets. Reforms will require careful analysis and sometimes tedious attention to detail."

"Governments have to do more to help their citizens build capabilities that will allow them to be productive. But they also have to step back in other areas to allow the market to function effectively."

"There is substantial evidence that government intervention and regulatory failure had as much a role to play in this crisis as private-sector failure."

MORE INFO

Books:

French, Kenneth R., *et al*. *The Squam Lake Report: Fixing the Financial System*. Princeton, NJ: Princeton University Press, 2010. Discusses how to improve the financial markets and make effective regulatory reforms to avoid future financial crises, written by a group of 15 leading US economists, including Raghuram G. Rajan.

Rajan, Raghuram G., and Luigi Zingales. *Saving Capitalism from the Capitalists: How Open Financial Markets Challenge the Establishment and Spread Prosperity to Rich and Poor Alike*. New York: Crown Business, 2003. Considers how vested interests have tried to protect their wealth and power by ensuring the markets work in their favor, but argues that free financial markets actually allow countries to be competitive and prosperous.

Roubini, Nouriel, and Stephen Mihm. *Crisis Economics: A Crash Course in the Future of Finance*. New York: Penguin Press, 2010. The renowned macroeconomist provides an overview of how the recent financial crisis came about, and how we can avoid the boom and bust cycle from continuing to damage the economy.

See Also:

Freefall: Free Markets and the Sinking of the Global Economy (p. 1365)

IOU: Why Everyone Owes Everyone and No One Can Pay (also published as Whoops) (p. 1384)

"There are no silver bullets. Reforms will require careful analysis and sometimes tedious attention to detail."

FIASCO: The Inside Story of a Wall Street Trader

FRANK PARTNOY (1997)

WHY READ IT?

- This is an insider's account of working as a derivatives salesman at Morgan Stanley in the 1990s.
- It was the first book to examine the derivatives trading industry in detail, and it warned of the dangers of buying and selling products so complex that many of the traders did not understand them.
- Tells the story behind many of the best-known derivatives fiascos, including Orange County, Barings, and Procter & Gamble, where collectively billions of dollars were lost.

GETTING STARTED

FIASCO tells the story of the author's time in the financial jungle of Wall Street and of his experience at Morgan Stanley as a young derivatives salesman. He was taught how to buy and sell billions of dollars worth of derivative securities, many of which were so complex that even the traders didn't understand them properly. The book acts as an introduction to derivatives on a practical level, examines some of the most infamous fiascos and the largely unregulated market in derivatives products, and criticizes the whole field of financial investments.

AUTHOR

Frank Partnoy is professor of law at the University of San Diego. Prior to that, he worked as an investment banker at Credit Suisse First Boston and Morgan Stanley in New York, and as an attorney at Covington & Burling in Washington, DC.

CONTEXT

- Takes the reader through the author's time on Wall Street, most of which was spent in Morgan Stanley's high-profile derivatives group.
- Discusses the little-known world of structuring, marketing, and selling derivatives, and the macho attitudes and fierce competition within the investment banks.
- Exposes the contempt that the salesmen had for their clients, and the lack of ethics in an industry that was awash with money.
- Provides insights into the types of exotic products being structured by the investment banks, and the reasons for doing so, making them understandable for a nonspecialist reader.

IMPACT

- Provides an insider's record of the financial world in New York and Tokyo during the 1990s, and analyzes the losses suffered as a result of misguided betting in the derivatives market.
- Tells the story through the characters he worked with, accompanied by vivid descriptions of the derivatives transactions his firm once thrived on.
- Discusses the trader mentality, working terminology, and aggressive approach to selling that was integral to how the salesmen operated and how the investment banks drive their performance.
- Provides real-life examples of biased and self-aggrandizing behavior in the major investment banks.
- Examines the thriving practice of "off-balance-sheet" derivative speculation.

QUOTATIONS

"What lessons did I draw from my experience selling derivatives? I believe derivatives are the most recent example in the history of finance: Wall Street bilks Main St."

"Wall Street has made, and continues to make, a huge amount of money on derivatives by trickery or deceit."

"Derivatives remain unseen, yet ubiquitous. Time bombs are ticking away, concealed in the underbelly of our investment portfolios."

MORE INFO

Books:

Partnoy, Frank. *Infectious Greed: How Deceit and Risk Corrupted the Financial Markets*. New York: Times Books, 2003. The sequel to *FIASCO*, it demonstrates how companies have hidden their exposure to risk from shareholders and manipulated the markets.

Stewart, James B. *Den of Thieves*. New York: Simon & Schuster, 1991. Tells the story behind the biggest insider-trading ring in Wall Street history during the 1980s.

See Also:

Liar's Poker: Rising Through the Wreckage on Wall Street (p. 1386)

"What lessons did I draw from my experience selling derivatives? I believe derivatives are the most recent example in the history of finance: Wall Street bilks Main St."

 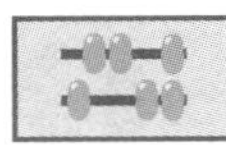   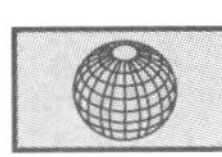   

Finance

ZVI BODIE and ROBERT C. MERTON (2000)

WHY READ IT?

- Works through all the main topics of corporate finance, as well as ranging into other topics, giving the book a broader scope than usual for such textbooks.
- Focuses on practical financial decision-making and applied finance.
- Aimed at MBA and undergraduate students and business professionals, using an integrated approach to teach the basics of finance.

GETTING STARTED

Two leading finance academics provide an overarching and focused approach to the teaching of finance that will be of use to students on different levels, and teachers needing a practical guide that covers all the specifics of the subject.

Finance encompasses all the main subfields of finance—corporate finance, investments, financial institutions and markets—within a single unifying conceptual framework, to provide a book that works as a self-study guide or a textbook that instructs on all the main concepts of finance.

AUTHORS

Zvi Bodie (b. 1943) is professor of finance and economics at Boston University School of Management. He has served on the finance faculties at Harvard Business School and Sloan School of Management, and is a member of the Pension Research Council at the Wharton School.

Robert C. Merton (b. 1944) is a professor at the Harvard Business School. He previously served on the finance faculty of Sloan School of Management, and is a senior fellow of the International Association of Financial Engineers. He is a past president of the American Finance Association, and a member of the National Academy of Sciences. Dr Merton received the Nobel Memorial Prize in Economic Sciences in 1997.

CONTEXT

- Published after rigorous development, input, and review from hundreds of colleagues teaching introductory finance courses.
- As a teaching resource, the text organizes the key principles of finance into three analytical silos: optimization over time, asset valuation, and risk management.
- Using a full array of learning features, including examples, concept questions, special-interest boxes, end of chapter problems, an instructor's manual, a set of spreadsheet templates, and an accompanying CD that includes a spreadsheet modeling handbook.
- Provides a useful overview of resource allocation over time under conditions of uncertainty.

IMPACT

- Encompasses all the subfields of finance within a single unifying framework and incorporates international material.
- Tries to change the way finance is taught in business schools, to incorporate other key topics not normally covered.
- Sets out the basic principles of the discipline, from defining what finance is to complex portfolio theory, then applies them to a wide variety of situations.
- Integrates all the main concepts throughout.
- Useful for non-finance specialists, as well as those interested in business and personal finance.

QUOTATIONS

"Finance as a scientific discipline is the study of how to allocate scarce resources over time under conditions of uncertainty."

"A basic tenet of finance is that the ultimate function of the system is to satisfy people's consumption preferences."

"Asset prices and interest rates provide critical signals to managers of firms in their selection of investment projects and financing arrangements."

MORE INFO

Book:

Ross, Stephen A., Randolph W. Westerfield, and Jeffrey Jaffe. *Corporate Finance*. St. Louis: Times/Mirror/Mosby College Publishing, 1988. Examines the fundamentals of the subject in an integrated manner.

See Also:

Robert Merton (p. 1293)
Corporate Financial Management (p. 1344)
Principles of Corporate Finance (p. 1410)

"Finance as a scientific discipline is the study of how to allocate scarce resources over time under conditions of uncertainty."

Financial Accounting and Reporting

BARRY ELLIOTT and JAMIE ELLIOTT (16th ed 2013, originally 1993)

WHY READ IT?

- Offers clear and well-structured analysis of the main issues in financial accounting and reporting.
- Includes extensive coverage of International Accounting Standards (IASs) and International Financial Reporting Standards (IFRSs), and uses the latest International Accounting Standards as a framework.
- Examines the underlying tension between theory and practice, and analyzes the use of company accounts.

GETTING STARTED

Financial Accounting and Reporting provides you with the necessary knowledge and skills to understand and apply current financial reporting methods, as well as the relevant financial accounting standards. It is a comprehensive text for university students studying the subject, as well as the industry professional, and includes numerous exercises, varying in level of difficulty.

AUTHORS

Barry Elliott is a training consultant; he has extensive teaching experience and as an external examiner at all levels of professional education.

Jamie Elliott is a director with Deloitte & Touche. Prior to this he was a university lecturer, and then an assistant professor on MBA and executive programs at the London Business School.

CONTEXT

- Discusses, in detail, income and asset value measurement systems, the regulatory framework, balance sheets, consolidated accounts, how to interpret financial accounts, and the issue of accountability.
- Gives you the tools to critically appraise the underlying accounting concepts and financial reporting methods.
- Focuses on financial accounting, reporting, and analysis modules for second and final-year undergraduate courses in accounting, business studies, MBAs, specialist MSc courses, and professional courses that prepare for professional accountancy examinations.
- Outlines recent developments in corporate governance by regulators prompted by accounting scandals and stakeholder activism.

IMPACT

- Provides an overview of UK accounting standards, as well as covering International Financial Reporting Standards, and International Accounting Standards.
- Uses practical applications and illustrations taken from real-world international company reports and accounts.
- Discusses the dynamics between those who prepare financial reports, stakeholders, auditors, academic accountants, and standard setters.

QUOTATIONS

"The accountant needs to be skilled in identifying the information that is needed and conveying its implication and meaning to the user."

"To be useful, the financial information . . . needs to be comparable over time and between companies and understandable."

"Corporate governance guidelines are developed so that it can be seen whether the directors are maximising returns to shareholders, the business risk is set at a reasonable level, that a director or a board of directors do not become dominant to the detriment of the shareholders, and that the remuneration of the directors is reasonable."

MORE INFO

Books:

Alexander, David, and Anne Britton. *Financial Reporting: The Theoretical and Regulatory Framework.* London: Chapman and Hall, 1993. Combines financial accounting theory with a detailed examination of the legal and regulatory framework of accounting.

Moscove, Stephen A., Mark G. Simkin, and Nancy A. Bagranoff. *Core Concepts of Accounting Information Systems.* New York: Wiley, 1997. Offers concise and user-friendly coverage of the key topics.

Stolowy, Hervé, and Michel J. Lebas. *Corporate Financial Reporting: A Global Perspective.* London: Thomson Learning, 2002. Introduces financial accounting for business students.

See Also:

★ Understanding the Requirements for Preparing IFRS Financial Statements (pp. 423–424)
✔ International Financial Reporting Standards (IFRS): The Basics (p. 1039)

"The accountant needs to be skilled in identifying the information that is needed and conveying its implication and meaning to the user."

Financial Management

JAE K. SHIM and JOEL G. SIEGEL (3rd ed 2009, originally 1986)

WHY READ IT?

- Is a comprehensive primer that provides a good depth of discussion without being too theoretical.
- Emphasizes the practical application of principles, concepts, and tools of financial management.
- Offers a complete overview of the subject using easy learning features, and can be used to reinforce course material for students.

GETTING STARTED

Financial Management, part of the popular Schaum's Outlines series of textbooks, is a basic run through of all the main aspects of current financial practice. It is used for quick learning or exam preparation, and has been fully updated to reflect changes in the rules and regulations governing corporate finance, including the Sarbanes–Oxley Act, passed in 2002.

AUTHORS

Jae K. Shim is professor of business administration at California State University at Long Beach. He has written extensively, and is a recipient of the 1982 Credit Research Foundation Award for an article on financial management.

Joel G. Siegel was professor of finance and accounting at Queens College of the City University of New York. He received the Outstanding Educator of America Award in 1972.

CONTEXT

- Examines the essentials of financial analysis, financial forecasting, planning, budgeting, and the management of working capital.
- Also gives a useful perspective on such critical aspects of financial management as short-term financing, risk, return, valuation, capital budgeting, cost of capital, leverage and capital structure, options, futures, mergers and acquisitions, and multinational finance.
- Discusses the Sarbanes–Oxley Act and its implications in detail, and features new sections on risk management, corporate governance, real options, and behavioral finance.

IMPACT

- Offers step-by-step solutions, additional practice problems, with answers supplied, clear explanations of financial management concepts and practices, and a comprehensive exam to test your mastery of the material.
- Helps you refresh knowledge, prepare for tests, and study quickly and effectively, without having to take the time to read lengthy textbooks.
- Presents the material in a straightforward and easy-to-understand manner, and is suited to real-world application.
- Designed for both undergraduate and graduate students, and offers a short cut to a faster understanding of key topics.
- Can be used as preparation for Certified Management Accountant and Chartered Financial Analyst exams, or for independent study.

QUOTATIONS

"The focus on wealth maximization continues in the new millennium."

"Financial statement analysis involves the calculation of various ratios."

"Financial forecasting, an essential element of planning, is the basis for budgeting activities and estimating future financing needs."

MORE INFO

Books:

Brigham, Eugene F., and Michael C. Ehrhardt. *Financial Management: Theory and Practice*. 14th ed. Eagan, MN: Cengage Learning, 2013. Covers all the main financial management topics in a practical way.

Damodaran, Aswath. *Corporate Finance: Theory and Practice*. New York: Wiley, 1997. Takes a more applied approach to corporate finance than is usual, using real companies and real data throughout.

See Also:

Corporate Financial Management (p. 1344)

"The focus on wealth maximization continues in the new millennium."

  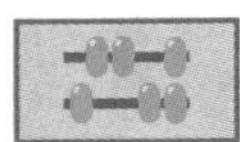      

Financial Management for the Small Business

COLIN BARROW (6th ed 2006, originally 1984)

WHY READ IT?

- Designed to assist with the basics of business finance for the managers of small businesses.
- Focuses on key areas, informing on financial statements, financial analysis, business plans, and budgets.
- Gives advice on successful financial planning and control, and how to operate a small business from a solid financial platform.

GETTING STARTED

Financial Management for the Small Business provides an introduction to financial management, aimed primarily at those who have little experience with business accounts. As the most common cause of business failure is poor financial control due to an ignorance of business finance, it is essential to have a sound knowledge of the basics of financial management; this book gives that grounding in a practical and focused way.

AUTHOR

Colin Barrow was head of the Enterprise Group at Cranfield School of Management for many years. He is the author of many business books, and was previously in industry before teaching at Stirling University, and being a visiting professor at Suffolk University, Boston.

CONTEXT

- Provides advice on proper financial planning and control, making it an important resource for both existing small businesses and entrepreneurs considering launching one.
- Helps the beginner become financially literate, and have the tools to undertake all the standard financial operations of a business.
- Covers the essentials of financial management such as balance sheets, P&L accounts, cash flow, control of working capital and fixed assets, costs, pricing and profit decisions, budgeting and bookkeeping, improving performance, and writing and presenting business plans.

IMPACT

- Focuses on business planning and budgeting, a vital area of finance for businesses looking to launch or those wanting to expand.
- Helps to clarify difficult terms and concepts for those who find business finance confusing.
- Reinforces essential points through the use of questions within each section, and includes a glossary of key accounting terms.

QUOTATIONS

"The first steps towards an understanding of finance are the most difficult."

"All methods of financing have important implications for your tax and financial position."

"While bad luck plays a part in some failures, a lack of reliable financial information plays a part in most."

MORE INFO

Books:

Barrow, Colin. *The Business Plan Workbook.* London: Kogan Page, 2005. A guide to the processes and procedures required to put together a successful business plan.

Wilson, Peter. *The Barclays Guide to Financial Management for the Small Business.* Oxford: Blackwell, 1990. Advice for small businesses wanting to improve their understanding of financial and management accounts.

See Also:

i Small and Growing Businesses (pp. 1792–1797)

"The first steps towards an understanding of finance are the most difficult."

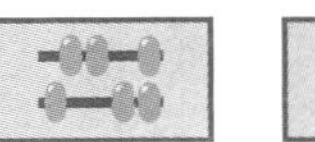

The Financial Times Handbook of Financial Management

STEVE ROBINSON (1995)

WHY READ IT?

- For the business professional who is lacking a basic knowledge of financial concepts and tools.
- Provides essential guidance for the manager's toolkit, to help them achieve financial objectives in their work.
- Summarizes the role of finance in key international business issues, enabling the manager to make the right business decisions.

GETTING STARTED

The Financial Times Handbook of Financial Management helps you understand financial ideas and terms used by financial professionals and bankers. It brings a greater understanding of the dynamics of business and how companies measure and report, and gives insight into enhancing shareholder value through sound financial principles.

AUTHOR

Steve Robinson (b. 1943) is head of open executive programmes, School of Growth, Innovation and Enterprise, Henley Management College. He joined Henley in 2002 after 14 years at Ashridge Management College, the last seven as MBA director. He is also a business consultant.

CONTEXT

- Examines the key financial elements of the business world, from starting a company, to undertaking a business valuation or financial appraisal of a forthcoming project.
- Uses clear language to explain complex terms, and illustrate the main issues through recent case examples of how companies have handled key areas of financial management.
- Looks at other critical elements of business financing, funding, and borrowing, offering practical guidance.
- Gives a framework for decision-making based on sound financial principles, such as completing financial analyses, and carrying out project appraisals and valuations.
- Shows how to measure business performance and examines the use of key financial data.
- Provides insight into accounting and market measures, as well as how to best manage assets and liabilities.

IMPACT

- Presents a synopsis of finance as a refresher or thorough grounding for non-specialists
- Shows how to manage operational financial decisions, such as pricing, outsourcing, and profitability analysis.
- Details how to manage money internationally, and covers currency risk.
- Contains useful case studies that highlight the impact of financial decisions on a company's operations.
- Examines the multi-disciplinary role of finance within a corporate framework.
- Helps with an appreciation of the relationship between financial markets and other markets.

QUOTATIONS

"Comprehensive analysis of business performance must include both absolute and relationship numbers to enable comparison with competition and industry standards."

"Strategy defines the broad direction of the business, operational tactics determine the precise route and pace."

"Much of the financial information available to investors concentrates on the past, yet returns will only come in the future."

MORE INFO

Books:

Brigham, Eugene F., and Joel F. Houston. *Fundamentals of Financial Management.* Hinsdale, IL: Dryden Press, 1978. An introductory guide to corporate finance and financial management.

Emery, Douglas R., and John D. Finnerty. *Corporate Financial Management.* London: Prentice Hall International, 1997. Connects theory and practice, with many useful examples from the corporate world.

See Also:

Corporate Financial Management (p. 1344)

"Comprehensive analysis of business performance must include both absolute and relationship numbers to enable comparison with competition and industry standards."

  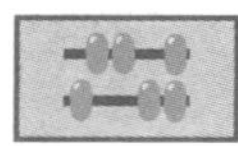      

Financial Strategy

JANETTE RUTTERFORD, MARTIN UPTON, and DEVENDRA KODWANI (EDS) (2006)

WHY READ IT?

- An edited collection of writing from key figures in the business strategy and financial planning community.
- Outlines the major ways in which financial strategy can add value to a business, especially in the areas of investment, performance, value, risk management, and governance.
- Can be used as course material for MBA and advanced undergraduate students of financial strategy and financial management, but also of benefit for finance professionals.

GETTING STARTED

Financial Strategy is a collection of writing from some of the leading thinkers in financial strategy; with an emphasis on added value for organizations, each chapter looks at different ways to ensure this, particularly through investment, financing, and risk management. It also covers the debate on corporate governance and performance measurement, and focuses on the place of financial strategy in the modern business.

EDITORS

Janette Rutterford is a professor of financial management at the Open University Business School, having previously worked in corporate finance and investment at Credit Lyonnais and Rothschild.

Martin Upton is a senior lecturer in finance and head of the Centre for Accounting and Finance at the Open University Business School. Previously he worked for 17 years in the financial services industry, including 12 years as treasurer of the Nationwide Building Society.

Devendra Kodwani is a senior lecturer in finance and director of the MBA course at the Open University Business School.

CONTEXT

- Reflects the recent developments in financial strategy, which have added value to organizations, and gives a useful overview of best practice.
- Discusses innovations such as financial restructuring, the role of real options, financial engineering, and economic value added, and their impact on business strategy.
- Examines how derivatives can be used to alter the risk-return profile for risks such as currency, interest rate, or credit, to suit organizational preferences.

IMPACT

- Focuses on decision-making as a pivotal factor in business success—investment, financing, and risk management decisions.
- Shows how performance measurement is critical to successful strategic planning—cash flows, regulatory standardization to ensure compatibility of financial reporting, and financial performance measures.
- Examines the changed relationship between accounting and finance within the organizational structure.
- Discusses the application of financial strategy to organizations in the public and private sectors internationally.
- Looks at how choosing the right capital structure can add value, regardless of production or marketing decisions.
- Addresses issues relevant to UK and US-listed companies, as well as an international audience.

QUOTATIONS

"It has become clear that financial strategy on its own can have a major impact on organisations."

"Future changes to [risk management] practices seem inevitable if only because it is naïve to believe that current systems have eradicated the potential for any future financial calamities."

"The more emphasis that the financial markets place on earnings ... the more pressure there is on managers to deliver the expected performance."

MORE INFO

Books:

Pike, Richard, and Bill Neale. *Corporate Finance and Investment: Decisions and Strategies*. London: Prentice Hall, 1993. Takes a practical approach to key concepts and techniques on a broad range of contemporary issues in corporate finance.

Stern, Joel N., and Donald H. Chew, Jr (eds). *The Revolution in Corporate Finance*. Oxford: Blackwell, 1986. Although this textbook of collected writings has a similar structure, it is focused less on shareholder value than the practical implications of recent theoretical advances.

See Also:

Corporate Financial Management (p. 1344)

"It has become clear that financial strategy on its own can have a major impact on organisations."

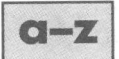

Fooled by Randomness: The Hidden Role of Chance in Life and in the Markets

NASSIM NICHOLAS TALEB (2nd ed 2005, originally 2001)

WHY READ IT?

- The author is a professional trader and mathematics professor who wants to change how we think about risk, probability, and random events.
- A readable account of the tendency to explain random events as due to cause and effect rather than chance.
- Considers the real nature of success and failure among traders, and compares this to other professions, where skill and practice bring improvement and success.

GETTING STARTED

Fooled by Randomness examines what randomness means in practical terms and why human beings are so prone to mistake luck for skill. It argues that we shouldn't attribute success to skill alone, and that it is also wrong to assume intelligence is a necessary condition for wealth. We get an excellent insight into the role of probability in the markets as well as in daily life, and the role that randomness plays in practically everything we do.

AUTHOR

Nassim Nicholas Taleb (b. 1960) is professor of marketing at London Business School, adjunct professor of mathematics at the Courant Institute of Mathematical Sciences, New York University, and on the affiliated faculty of Wharton School Financial Institutions Center. He previously held senior positions at major investment banks.

CONTEXT

- Distils all Taleb's empirical thoughts on the nature of chance, through statistics, probability, philosophy, trading, economics, pop culture, classical literature, and psychology.
- Considers that traders are successful due to statistics and good fortune, rather than skill, and compares this unfavorably with other professions. Examines why attributing causes to explain events is a basic human instinct, driven by the need for control and not being at the mercy of chance. Argues against the prevalent feeling that if something has happened before, then it will necessarily happen again.
- Claims that we should ignore much of the information we are normally exposed to, and that investment advice from any source has no value.
- Gives advice on successful investing, based on not chasing fads, or looking at your investments too often, and being open to both sides of any argument.

IMPACT

- Considers how we have lost the distinction between noise and signal: noise (market volatility) is mistaken for signal (predictable responses), so that luck is mistaken for skill.
- Shows disdain and frustration at the abuse of statistics and logic by experts.
- Proposes that the human mind is just not made to understand randomness. Provides insights into the world of quantitative finance that also hold true for the wider world.
- Presents a framework for what to expect when speculating, and avoiding self-delusion and common mistakes.
- Examines the concept of alternate outcomes and alternate histories, especially for extreme events.

QUOTATIONS

"We underestimate the share of randomness in just about everything."

"Mild success can be explainable by skills and labor. Wild success is attributable to variance."

"Mixing forecast and prophecy is symptomatic of randomness-foolishness."

MORE INFO

Website:

Nassim Nicholas Taleb's website: www.fooledbyrandomness.com

See Also:

- Against the Gods: The Remarkable Story of Risk (p. 1328)
- The Black Swan: The Impact of the Highly Improbable (p. 1335)
- The (Mis)behavior of Markets (p. 1396)

"We underestimate the share of randomness in just about everything."

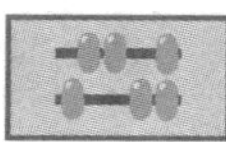

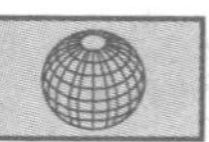

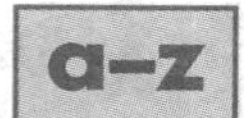

Foundations of Multinational Financial Management

ALAN C. SHAPIRO and ATULYA SARIN (6th ed 2008, originally 1991)

WHY READ IT?

- A focused and practically oriented textbook that examines real-life financial management decision-making in an international context.
- Provide a clear strategy for understanding the impact of financial management processes on business operations.
- Demystifies and simplifies the subject in a clear conceptual framework that helps learning.

GETTING STARTED

Foundations of Multinational Financial Management explores all the main traditional areas of corporate finance, including working capital management, capital budgeting, cost of capital, and financial structure, from the perspective of a multinational corporation. It lays out the key concepts and processes in an understandable style, which has made it a core text for dedicated courses on financial management in business schools.

AUTHORS

Alan C. Shapiro is professor of banking and finance at Marshall School of Business, University of Southern California. He was previously an assistant professor at Wharton, and has been a visiting professor at Yale and a number of business schools.

Atulya Sarin is professor of finance in the Leavey School of Business at Santa Clara University. He publishs in leading finance, economics, and management journals and served on the editorial board of the *Journal of Financial Research*.

CONTEXT

- Examines international financial management as a logical extension of the principles and valuation framework provided by domestic corporate financial management.
- Treats international financial management as part of a natural development of the principles learned on foundational courses in financial management.
- Focuses on the macroeconomic issues of how a multinational firm operates.
- This is a concise version of the authors' bestselling textbook, *Multinational Financial Management*.

IMPACT

- Provides insight on how being a multinational firm creates business difference, and how to take advantage of this in practical terms.
- Offers a variety of real-life examples, both numerical and institutional, that demonstrate the use of financial analysis and reasoning in solving international financial problems.
- Provides a clear conceptual framework for analyzing key financial decisions and the particular characteristics of multinational firms.
- Emphasizes broad concepts and practices rather than providing extensive theoretical or quantitative material.
- Discusses how the United States is gaining competitive advantage from the new era of price and service competition, deregulation, increased technology, wider corporate control, mergers and leveraged buy-outs, and global standardization.

QUOTATIONS

"Companies today operate within a global marketplace and can ignore this fact only at their peril."

"The true multinational corporation is characterized more by its state of mind than by the size and worldwide dispersion of its assets."

"In a world in which change is the rule and not the exception, the key to international competitiveness is the ability of management to adjust to change and volatility at an ever faster rate."

MORE INFO

Books:

Desai, Mihir A. *International Finance: A Casebook*. Hoboken, NJ: Wiley, 2007. Offers a unique perspective on making financial decisions in a globalizing world, based on how firm financing and investment decisions must adapt to circumstances in the international marketplace.

Shapiro, Alan C. *Multinational Financial Management*. 9th ed. Hoboken, NJ: Wiley, 2009. Shapiro's full textbook, which gives an overview of how to make sound financial decisions in the multinational firm.

See Also:

The Essence of Financial Management (p. 1350)
Multinational Business Finance (p. 1400)

"Companies today operate within a global marketplace and can ignore this fact only at their peril."

  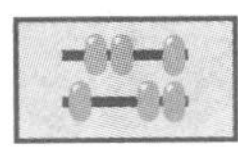   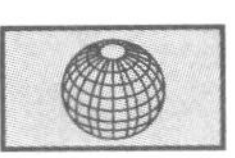   

Frank Wood's Business Accounting, Volumes 1 and 2

FRANK WOOD and ALAN SANGSTER (12th ed 2011, originally 1967)

WHY READ IT?

- Provides a clear and straightforward introduction to the core techniques and skills required to fully understand the foundations of financial and business accounting.
- Each key topic is reinforced through worked examples and self-assessment material to help monitor progress and learning.
- Useful for anyone new to accountancy and bookkeeping, or those who wish to update their bookkeeping skills.

GETTING STARTED

Frank Wood's Business Accounting is one of the most popular textbooks on accounting and bookkeeping in business, and is used on a wide variety of courses, both at secondary and tertiary level, and for those studying for professional qualifications. Now in its 11th edition, it is a good primer to all the key principles and processes of the discipline.

AUTHORS

Frank Wood (1926–2000) was a bestselling author of books on accountancy and bookkeeping. As well as being a highly successful author, publisher, and teacher, he used his influence to raise money for charity.

Alan Sangster is professor of accounting at the Open University Business School, and was previously at Queen's University of Belfast, the University of Aberdeen, and the University of Strathclyde.

CONTEXT

- Comprehensive analysis of how to prepare accounts for sole traders, partnerships, companies, and groups, with a detailed examination of the key differences.
- Provides a primer to accounting—clear and well laid out, with plenty of useful examples.
- Takes a universal approach that is useful to students from a broad range of educational backgrounds.
- Bases its teaching around the information needed to accord with the criteria and requirements established by various prominent examination boards.
- Contains real exam questions at the end of every chapter, with exam guidance to help students prepare better and improve their results.

IMPACT

- Intensive coverage of the underlying techniques and skills of accounting.
- Provides a full understanding of double-entry bookkeeping and the preparation of accounting information.
- Features hundreds of review questions, activities and multiple-choice questions, so that students can judge how well they understand, and can apply what they are learning.
- Follows a logical progression and focused activities designed to reinforce an understanding of key concepts.

QUOTATIONS

"Accounting involves deciding what amounts of money are, were, or will be involved in transactions (often buying and selling transactions) and then organising the information obtained and presenting it in a way that is useful for decision making."

"The primary objective of accounting is to provide information for decision making."

"Management accounting produces the financial forecasts that guide planning."

MORE INFO

Books:

Drury, Colin. *Management Accounting for Business Decisions*. London: International Thomson Business Press, 1997. Comprehensive and detailed text that uses real-world examples to good effect.

Kimmel, Paul D., Jerry J. Weygandt, and Donald E. Kieso. *Financial Accounting: Tools for Business Decision Making.* New York: Wiley, 1998. Teaches fundamental accounting procedures with an emphasis on the relationship between the procedure and fundamental accounting.

Website:

There is a regularly updated companion website at www.pearsoned.co.uk/wood, which includes further self-test questions and accounting standards updates.

See Also:

Financial Accounting and Reporting (p. 1356)
Accounting (pp. 1658–1661)

"Accounting involves deciding what amounts of money are, were, or will be involved in transactions (often buying and selling transactions) and then organising the information obtained and presenting it in a way that is useful for decision making."

  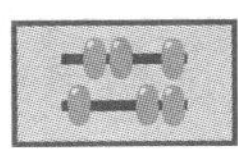      

Freakonomics: A Rogue Economist Explores the Hidden Side of Everything

STEVEN D. LEVITT and STEPHEN J. DUBNER (2005)

WHY READ IT?

- Urges the reader to look deeper into the underlying causes of everyday events.
- Examines the use of incentives and how they drive human behavior.
- Provides insight into a range of issues such as why crack dealers live with their parents, and trends in baby names.
- Examines other off-beat questions such as why the Ku Klux Klan are like a group of real estate agents, what makes a perfect parent, where have all the criminals gone, and what is the link between schoolteachers and sumo wrestlers.

GETTING STARTED

Freakonomics examines a number of everyday events, and challenges the received wisdom and myths of each through detailed analysis of underlying data. It brings economics (and statistics) into the mainstream through an accessible look at a wide range of behaviors and social issues. Combining economics lite and unorthodoxy to uncover new truths, and show that nothing is what it seems and that assumptions can be dangerous.

AUTHORS

Steven D. Levitt teaches economics at the University of Chicago. His economic research areas include themes such as guns and game shows and have triggered debate in media and academic circles. He recently received the American Economic Association's John Bates Clark Medal.

Stephen J. Dubner writes for the *New York Times* and the *New Yorker*, and is the author of *Turbulent Souls* and *Confessions of a Hero-Worshipper*.

CONTEXT

- Avoids being academic in style, but is based on stringent research and data analysis.
- Proposes that we should challenge orthodoxy through questioning the underlying causes of typical aspects of social events.
- It goes beyond correlations to seek causation, for instance attributing the dramatic fall of US crime rates in the 1990s to greater access to abortion 20 years earlier, rather than traditional explanations like improved policing methods.

IMPACT

- Brings economic analysis and what economists actually do to a wider audience.
- Explains that the main interest of economists is the study of incentives, causes, and behavior, illustrating this with many reader-friendly examples.

QUOTATIONS

"If morality represents an ideal world, then economics represents the actual world."

"It wasn't gun control or a strong economy or new police strategies that finally blunted the American crime wave. It was, among other factors, the reality that the pool of potential criminals had dramatically shrunk."

"The gulf between the information that we publicly proclaim and the information that we know to be true is often vast. (Or, put a more familiar way: we say one thing and do another)."

MORE INFO

Book:

Landsburg, Steven E. *The Armchair Economist: Economics and Everyday Life.* New York: Free Press, 1993. Key issues in economics explained in a humorous way.

Website:

Book website, including reviews, articles, and a blog: www.freakonomicsbook.com

See Also:

The Tipping Point: How Little Things Can Make a Big Difference (p. 1426)
The Undercover Economist (p. 1428)

"If morality represents an ideal world, then economics represents the actual world."

     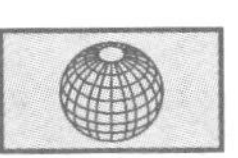   

Freefall: Free Markets and the Sinking of the Global Economy

JOSEPH STIGLITZ (2010)

WHY READ IT?

- Describes the course of the global financial crisis, which began in 2007, and the underlying causes.
- Argues that much more radical reforms are needed than those currently being implemented, if the world is to avoid similar systemic crises in the future.
- Shows why the bailout has been only marginally effective and explains how it could have had a much more positive impact.

GETTING STARTED

Freefall describes how the United States' addiction to consumption rather than saving caused the global financial crisis. Stiglitz argues that the crisis originated in an overheated housing market, which was stimulated by politicians' desire to encourage lending and keep the economy growing, despite the obvious risks involved. The author is highly critical of the US government's policy responses, which he describes as a series of disasters. Consequently, Stiglitz believes that the United States' failure to address the problems of excess borrowing, high consumption, and low wages means that the country will experience a Japanese-style recovery.

AUTHOR

Joseph Stiglitz (b. 1943) was chief economist at the World Bank until 2000. He is currently university professor of the Columbia Business School and chair of the Management Board and director of Graduate Summer Programs, Brooks World Poverty Institute, University of Manchester. He won the Nobel Memorial Prize in Economic Sciences in 2001 and is the author of various best-selling books including *Globalization and Its Discontents*, *The Roaring Nineties*, *Making Globalization Work*, and *The Three Trillion Dollar War*.

CONTEXT

- Following the Asian financial crisis of 1997, Stiglitz warned that free-market ideologues at the US Treasury and the International Monetary Fund had botched the policy response to the crisis.
- He forecast that unless these institutions entered into a dialog with their critics, further crises would follow.
- Explains in a lucid, easily digestible style how the crisis was inevitable, given that the United States' deregulated financial markets were awash in liquidity as a result of low interest rates.
- Argues that these factors, when combined with a global real-estate bubble and skyrocketing subprime lending, created a toxic bubble.
- Attacks the Federal Reserve Chairman Alan Greenspan and his successor Ben Bernanke for failing to indentify and prevent the housing bubble from developing.
- Argues that the problems that the United States and the world face entail more than a small adjustment to the financial system.
- Calls for the authorities to seize the opportunity created by the crisis to establish a new financial and economic system that will generate meaningful jobs and narrow inequalities in society.

IMPACT

- Stiglitz's long-standing record as a critic of unfettered free-market capitalism, and his constant warnings of the dangers posed by deregulated financial markets, give added credibility to the book.
- However, there is also a sense that Stiglitz is settling scores with his critics, and the book is undermined by the fact that a sustainable global economic recovery now appears to be underway.
- Provides a stinging indictment of the failed government policies that led to the crisis and a coherent attack on those who believe that the free market is self-regulating and self-correcting.
- Argues that the cost of the recovery should be borne by the financial sector for compelling economic reasons, as well as for reasons of natural justice.
- A must-read for policy makers as well as anyone who is interested in how the global financial crisis came about and how future crises can be prevented.

QUOTATIONS

"*The only surprise about the economic crisis of 2008 was that it came as a surprise to so many.*"

"*America's economic hegemony will no longer be taken for granted in the way that it was.*"

"*If the United States is going to succeed in reforming its economy, it may have to begin by reforming economics.*"

MORE INFO

Book:

Krugman, Paul. *The Return of Depression Economics and the Crisis of 2008*. London: Penguin, 2008. The Nobel Prize-winning economist, who specializes in recessions, takes us through the history of why they happen.

See Also:

- Joseph Stiglitz (p. 1313)
- Fault Lines: How Hidden Fractures Still Threaten the World Economy (p. 1353)
- Globalization and Its Discontents (p. 1368)
- IOU: Why Everyone Owes Everyone and No One Can Pay (p. 1384)

"The only surprise about the economic crisis of 2008 was that it came as a surprise to so many."

  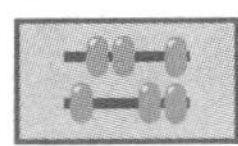      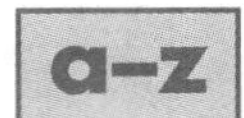

Futures, Options, and Swaps

ROBERT W. KOLB and JAMES A. OVERDAHL (5th ed 2007, originally 1994)

WHY READ IT?

- A comprehensive educational tool for those wanting a detailed grounding in these complex derivatives.
- Explains difficult concepts that the student needs to understand in this very technical subject area.
- Useful for non-quantitative capital market professionals who are looking for a broad introduction to derivative instruments.

GETTING STARTED

Futures, Options, and Swaps is a widely used textbook that provides a practical introduction to derivatives and their use in the capital markets. It analyzes basic theory to aid understanding of the role that financial engineering plays in pricing and hedging these instruments, and also examines the basic principles of finance engineering.

AUTHORS

Robert W. Kolb (b. 1949) is professor of finance and chair of applied ethics at the business school, Loyola University. He has held appointments at the University of Florida, Emory University, University of Miami, and was professor of finance and assistant dean for business and society at the University of Colorado at Boulder.

James A. Overdahl is chief economist at the Commodity Futures Trading Commission in Washington, DC, and has held senior positions in the Risk Analysis Division of the Office of the Comptroller of the Currency and at the Securities and Exchange Commission. He was also an adjunct professor of finance at Georgetown University, the University of Maryland, George Washington University, and Johns Hopkins University.

CONTEXT

- Provides a practical orientation, covering futures, options, and swaps from the perspective of implementation.
- A clear and readable account of all the key topics, providing learning material in a concise style that doesn't miss any of the main steps.
- Balances introductory analysis with more advanced treatment, and offers coverage of several major types of financial derivatives and their use.
- Makes no assumption about the knowledge level of the reader.

IMPACT

- Offers commentary throughout as to why one might use a certain financial instrument for a given reason or problem, making it a thorough, practical resource.
- Is the only non-AIMR text that is required reading for all three CFA exams.
- Preferred by many over Options, Futures, and Other Derivatives, for those whose background is not mathematics, engineering, or hard sciences. Although technical, it avoids complex terminology.
- Includes advanced formulas in the latter part of the book if you want to get deeper.

QUOTATIONS

"While financial derivatives are undeniably risky in some applications, they also provide a powerful tool for limiting risks that individuals and firms face in the ordinary conduct of their business."

"Large pension funds and investment banking firms trade options in conjunction with stock and bond portfolios to control risk and capture additional profits."

"In the short time since they started trading . . . , options have helped to revolutionize finance."

MORE INFO

Books:

Chisholm, Andrew. *Derivatives Demystified: A Step-by-Step Guide to Forwards, Futures, Swaps and Options.* Chichester, UK: Wiley, 2004. Explains derivative products in a straightforward way, focusing on applications and intuitive explanations.

Wilmott, Paul. *Paul Wilmott on Quantitative Finance.* Chichester, UK: Wiley, 2000. Introduces fundamental mathematical tools and financial concepts to help understand quantitative finance, portfolio management, and derivatives.

See Also:

Options, Futures, and Other Derivatives (p. 1405)
Derivatives and Quantitative Finance (pp. 1711–1713)

"While financial derivatives are undeniably risky in some applications, they also provide a powerful tool for limiting risks that individuals and firms face in the ordinary conduct of their business."

     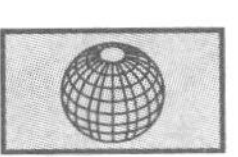   

The Global Financial System: A Functional Perspective

DWIGHT B. CRANE, KENNETH A. FROOT, SCOTT P. MASON, ANDRÉ F. PEROLD, ROBERT C. MERTON, ZVI BODIE, ERIK R. SIRRI, and PETER TUFANO (1995)

WHY READ IT?

- A collection of eight essays written by top finance academics and thinkers at Harvard Business School.
- Places a focus on how the performance of the financial system is evolving, and the implications this has for the future.
- Examines how each of the main functions of the financial system meets a basic organizational need.

GETTING STARTED

In *The Global Financial System* leading financial scholars present essays examining the performance of the global financial systems, and how a focus on functional and strategic perspectives can inform on the changes underway in the financial system. Covering such critical functions as the financial environment, payment systems, pooling, resource transfer, and the allocation of risk, it takes a critical but analytical overview of how to impose best practice on the financial system.

AUTHORS

Dwight B. Crane was a member of the Finance Faculty at Harvard Business School, and was also previously senior associate dean, and the chair of the School's European Research Initiative. Prior to joining the faculty, he was an economist and a director at Mellon Bank.

Kenneth A. Froot is professor of business administration at Harvard University's Graduate School of Business Administration. He is a founding partner of FDO Partners and State Street Associates, and was a consultant to the IMF, the World Bank, and the Federal Reserve.

Scott P. Mason (1948–1998) was professor of finance and banking at Harvard Business School, and was the chair of the finance department. He was previously with Goldman Sachs, and went on to become president and chief executive officer of Investment Technology Group.

André F. Perold is professor of finance and banking at the Harvard Business School, and served as senior associate dean. He is also a founder and chair of the Investment Committee of HighVista Strategies.

Robert C. Merton (b. 1944) is a professor at Harvard Business School, a senior fellow of the International Association of Financial Engineers, a past president of the American Finance Association, and a member of the National Academy of Sciences; he was awarded the Nobel Memorial Prize in Economic Sciences in 1997.

Zvi Bodie is professor of management at Boston University, and has served on the finance faculty at the Harvard Business School and MIT Sloan School of Management. He has published widely on pensions and investment strategy.

Erik R. Sirri is the director of market regulation at the Securities and Exchange Commission. He is currently on leave as professor of finance at Babson College, and was previously at Harvard Business School, worked at NASA, and was a governor of the Boston Stock Exchange.

Peter Tufano is professor of financial management at Harvard Business School, and has served as a senior associate dean at the school. He was previously director of faculty development and head of the Finance Unit at HBS.

CONTEXT

- Provides a collection of cutting-edge essays that examine the performance of the basic financial functions underlying global financial systems.
- Discusses the impact of key elements such as payments, lending and investing, pooling funds, allocating risk, providing information, and dealing with incentive issues, to evaluate the new financial environment.
- Looks at the challenges facing managers of financial institutions and public policy officials.
- Examines the needs of government as user, producer, and overseer of the financial system.
- Looks at why corporations hedge by themselves, and also how asymmetric information affects financial instruments.

IMPACT

- Identifies the fundamental changes occurring in the basic functions of financial systems, and presents insights about the future development of the financial institutions and markets.
- Considers the dynamics of financial change and the design of financial products and services.
- Discusses how the rapidly changing geopolitical, regulatory, and technological boundaries have rendered strategic and public policy decision-making increasingly difficult and complex.
- Includes recommendations on issues of public policy and regulation.

QUOTATIONS

"Institutional form follows function."

"Even when the outward identities are the same, the functions financial institutions perform often differ dramatically."

"The basics functions performed by the financial system are stable across time and place, but the institutional ways that they are performed are not."

MORE INFO

Books:

Abdelal, Rawi. *Capital Rules: The Construction of Global Finance.* Cambridge, MA: Harvard University Press, 2007. Focuses on the lowering of national borders to movement of capital, and its impact on the international economy.

Allen, Larry. *The Global Financial System: 1750–2000*. London: Reaktion Books, 2001. Traces the history and development of global finance.

Valdez, Stephen. *An Introduction to Global Financial Markets.* Basingstoke, UK: Macmillan Business, 1997. Provides a broad introduction to the financial markets.

"Institutional form follows function."

  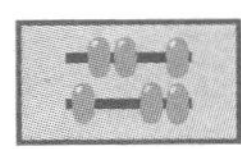   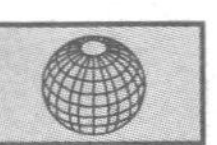   

Globalization and Its Discontents

JOSEPH STIGLITZ (2002)

WHY READ IT?

- One of the main authorities on the global economy and international finance examines the impact of economic policies and development in an easy-to-understand manner.
- Focuses on the real impact that economic theory has on people's lives.
- Offers solutions as well as criticisms, rather than just being an attack on the effects of globalization.

GETTING STARTED

Globalization and Its Discontents considers the functions and powers of the main institutions that govern globalization—the IMF, the World Bank, and the World Trade Organization—along with the ramifications of their policies. Examines the effect of global economics on the lives of people in developing countries, concluding that pursuit of free trade in these countries has been disastrous, and explaining why.

AUTHOR

Joseph Stiglitz (b. 1943) is a professor at Columbia University, and has taught at Yale, Princeton, Stanford, MIT, and Oxford. He has been chairman of the Council of Economic Advisers, and chief economist and senior vice president of the World Bank. He was awarded the Nobel Memorial Prize in Economics in 1971.

CONTEXT

- Informs on Stiglitz's tenure as an economic adviser to the White House and the Chief Economist at the World Bank.
- Analyzes the original roles of the IMF, the World Bank, and the WTO, and how they do not live up to their mandates.
- Examines how the critical transition of a country to a market economy is being carried out, and demands more focus on improving the infrastructure before it happens.

IMPACT

- Believes that globalization can be a positive force against poverty, but only if the IMF, World Bank, and WTO become more transparent and improve how they operate.
- Argues that standard IMF policy has tended to approach countries in financial crises with the same rather crude economics as that used on Wall Street.
- Regards the IMF as being unhelpful to poorer countries, making them rein in during recessions, and assisting international lenders to get their money when there is the chance a developing country might go bankrupt.
- Explains that the removal of barriers to free trade and the closer integration of national economics has the potential to enrich everyone in the world, if only it is managed better.
- Examines the interactions between exchange rates, exchange rate support, inflation, liquidity, government deficits, and monetary and structural reform.

QUOTATIONS

"[At the World Bank] decisions were made on the basis of what seemed a curious blend of ideology and bad economics, dogma that sometimes seemed to be thinly veiling special interests."

"Those who vilify globalization too often overlook its benefits."

"[The IMF has changed] from serving global economic interests to serving the interests of global finance."

MORE INFO

Books:

Kuttner, Robert. *Economic Illusion: False Choices between Prosperity and Social Justice.* Boston, MA: Houghton Mifflin, 1984. An examination of the fit between capitalism and political democracy.

McMillan, John. *Reinventing the Bazaar: A Natural History of Markets.* New York: Norton, 2002. An accessible description of markets, as well as an explanation of their underlying mechanisms.

Monbiot, George. *Manifesto for a New World Order.* New York: New Press, 2004. Examines the flaws on the left and right, and offers instead a radical vision of a new global democratic order that transcends the traditional nation-state.

See Also:

Joseph Stiglitz (p. 1313)
International Finance (pp. 1734–1736)

"[At the World Bank] decisions were made on the basis of what seemed a curious blend of ideology and bad economics, dogma that sometimes seemed to be thinly veiling special interests."

  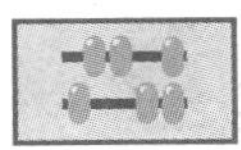   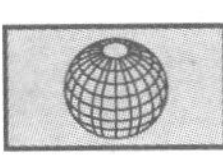   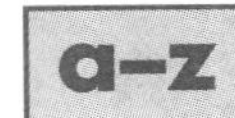

Good Value: Reflections on Money, Morality, and an Uncertain World

STEPHEN GREEN (2009)

WHY READ IT?

- Stephen Green is an unusual bank chief. A priest, he can offer a rare moral, ethical, and religious insight into the world of finance.
- The author has credibility as a commentator on the current state of the banking world. HSBC, the bank he leads, did not require any government bailouts during the credit crisis.
- Rather than preaching, Green asks some important questions which the banking industry must address if it is to regain the public's confidence.

GETTING STARTED

In *Good Value* the author examines how the human impulse to explore and to trade has shaped our globalized, urban world, and he concludes that capitalism, while clearly flawed, remains the best system for increasing material wealth. He asks how the financial sector should respond to the global financial crisis that broke in 2008.

- He contends that although economic progress and globalization gathered pace in the 1990s, the distribution of the world's wealth became more unequal.
- He shows how "casino capitalism" led to the global financial crisis and says that at the very least the crisis has demonstrated that the idea that the market is inherently self-stabilizing is wrong.

AUTHOR

Stephen Green (b. 1948) is currently chairman of HSBC, having joined the bank in 1982 and served as chief executive from 2003 to 2006. He was ordained as a priest in the Church of England in 1988. Green is chairman of the British Bankers' Association and is the chair of the Prime Minister's Business Council for Britain. He is also a trustee of the British Museum.

CONTEXT

- As a priest and one of the most powerful bankers in the world, Stephen Green is uniquely placed to ponder how we align capitalism and the need for economic progress to alleviate human suffering with our spiritual and psychological needs.
- He explores how the process of globalization, which gathered pace in the 19th century, was halted by the outbreak of the First World War.
- He argues that the lights of progress, global integration, and economic expansion remained out until at least the 1950s and that, as some say, the First World War did not end until 1989.

IMPACT

- Green defends globalization, arguing that it is righting huge wrongs by empowering all sections of society. He argues that globalization has shown that women, for example, can "flourish and lead commercially, professionally, politically . . . "
- He argues that capitalism, although sometimes brutal, unpredictable, and imperfect, remains the world's best hope for eradicating poverty.
- He claims that global warming could be the prolog to a tragedy of unimaginable scale and that government must give the market direction in addressing this issue.
- He contends that we can all help to improve the world by behaving in an ethical manner at all times rather than compartmentalizing our lives.

QUOTATIONS

"*Maybe we are so satisfied and at ease with the immediate pleasures on offer that we have made the decision to still our conscience for a nice car and a detached house and exotic but risk-less holidays. Maybe we have made some kind of Faustian bargain.*"

"*We need to be able to look ourselves in the mirror and ask two questions about our role in the global bazaar: how is what I am doing contributing to human welfare? And why am I specifically doing it?*"

"*Globalized market capitalism is in the dock as it has not been for a generation.*"

MORE INFO

Books:

Ferguson, Niall. *The Ascent of Money: A Financial History of the World*. New York: Penguin, 2008. An account of the history of financial transactions and their role in shaping history.

Strange, Susan. *Casino Capitalism*. Manchester, UK: Manchester University Press, 1997. A prophetic book describing how a new world of global finance, independent of states and industrial production, began to emerge in the 1970s.

See Also:

The Box: How the Shipping Container Made the World Smaller and the World Economy Bigger (p. 1339)

Globalization and Its Discontents (p. 1368)

"Maybe we are so satisfied and at ease with the immediate pleasures on offer that we have made the decision to still our conscience for a nice car and a detached house and exotic but risk-less holidays. Maybe we have made some kind of Faustian bargain."

  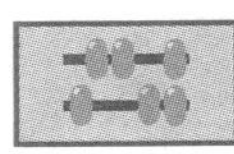      

Governance and Risk: An Analytical Handbook for Investors, Managers, Directors, and Stakeholders

GEORGE DALLAS (ED) (2004)

WHY READ IT?

- A team of expert authors offer a global overview on corporate governance trends, and how integral risk has become for any organization.
- Shows how to assess the complex issues of governance and risk management that have been highlighted by scandals and corporate collapses, and the increasing need for a rigorous governance system.
- Examines the key aspects of corporate governance and risk practices, and links them to practical performance steps that companies should follow.

GETTING STARTED

Governance and Risk has been written by a group of experts, mostly affiliated with Standard & Poor's, including senior members from their Governance Services group, to offer a comprehensive state-of-play report. Aimed at analysts and business professionals, it provides a clear analytical framework for examining and benchmarking governance standards in all companies, using a balanced and rational approach.

EDITOR

George Dallas is managing director and global practice leader for corporate governance at Standard & Poor's, where he has also served as head of global emerging markets and regional head for S&P's ratings services in Europe. He previously worked at Wells Fargo Bank.

CONTEXT

- Presents the analytical framework used by Standard & Poor's in its governance scoring and evaluation process for individual companies.
- Details corporate governance practices around the world, and examines the diversity of governance practices that global investors need to understand through a common analytical framework.
- Analyzes the impact of governance and risk issues from a variety of perspectives, including the economic, legal, and social.

IMPACT

- Covers all the main topics of governance and an increasingly critical set of wider themes, such as social and environmental reporting, directors' liability, and managed fund governance.
- Discusses how realistic it is to expect market participants to practice self-governance in the current financial climate, and the inherently conflicting interests within the modern corporation.
- Explores ownership structures and external influences, shareholder rights and stakeholder relations, transparency, disclosure and audit, and board structure and effectiveness.
- Argues for thinking of corporate governance as a risk factor, and provides a practical scoring methodology that helps rate a company.
- Takes a cross-disciplinary approach, setting out a framework for examining the different facets of corporate governance.

QUOTATIONS

"The development and institutionalization of corporate governance analysis is a long-term journey."

"Good governance should be rewarded, and bad governance should be punished."

"The market needs strong analytical tools and reliable benchmarks to assess governance risk."

MORE INFO

Books:

Coyle, Brian. *Risk Awareness and Corporate Governance*. Canterbury, UK: Financial World, 2002. A guide to the principles of risk awareness and management, and the requirements of corporate law and directors' responsibilities.

Monks, Robert A. G., and Nell Minow. *Corporate Governance*. 5th ed. Chichester, UK: Wiley, 2011. Explains the key concepts of corporate governance in a textbook format.

Shaw, John C. *Corporate Governance and Risk: A Systems Approach*. Hoboken, NJ: Wiley, 2003. Provides a framework for redesigning decision-making, risk, and governance processes.

"The development and institutionalization of corporate governance analysis is a long-term journey."

  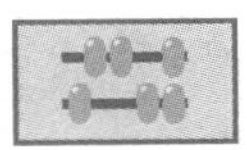      

The Great Crash, 1929

JOHN KENNETH GALBRAITH (1955)

WHY READ IT?

- Entertaining account of the market mania and resulting historic crash of 1929.
- Tells a relevant and timely story of over-investment and market frenzy, and why financial bubbles since then have always been compared to the Great Crash.
- Traces the market fluctuations of the time, showing how the crash evolved and helped ignite a full economic depression.

GETTING STARTED

The Great Crash, 1929 depicts a time of rampant speculation, record trading volumes, and assets bought not because of their value but because of a gold-rush mentality. An enjoyable read, it offers an explanation of the market dynamics during the late 1920s, and how people got caught up in the stock market frenzy that led to the 1929 crash, and how the aftermath affected the economy.

AUTHOR

John Kenneth Galbraith (1908–2006) was an influential economist and author. He was an economics professor at Harvard, and later became an adviser to President Kennedy, president of Americans for Democratic Action, president of the American Economic Association, and was awarded the Presidential Medal of Freedom on two occasions.

CONTEXT

- Shows the sustained mania for investment of the time in terms of crowd psychology—the investors wanted to believe that speculation would lead to great wealth.
- Shows in detail the impact of speculative enthusiasm and how it caused the market to become extremely overvalued, and that despite the losses, people kept buying for the rise.
- Details how government inaction enabled financial firms to operate in too risky and unethical a fashion.
- Explodes a few myths about the crash, such as that it was caused by a lack of available securities, and that it hugely increased the suicide rate.

IMPACT

- Explains the increase in embezzlement of the time, euphemistically called "informal financial arrangements," and how the crash impacted on some of the big names of the time.
- Details the cause of the crash as also being due to a mixture of bad income distribution, bad corporate structure, bad banking structures, and lack of economic intelligence.
- The similarities to more recent market downturns are unmistakable, from the trends toward corporate mergers and industry consolidations to the bubbles around certain sectors—investment trusts in the late 1920s and tech stocks in the late 1990s, and the current subprime and housing market problems.
- Uses the story to show why economies are not self-sustaining after all, but susceptible to supply and demand shifts.

QUOTATIONS

"As a protection against financial illusion or insanity, memory is far better than law."

"A roaring boom was in progress in the stock market and, like all booms, it had to end."

"But now, as throughout history, financial capacity and political perspicacity are inversely correlated."

MORE INFO

Books:

Gow, Mary. *The Stock Market Crash of 1929: Dawn of the Great Depression.* Berkeley Heights, NJ: Enslow, 2003. Captures this key part of American history through firsthand accounts and quotes, and examines subsequent economic crises.

Sobel, Robert. *The Great Bull Market: Wall Street in the 1920s.* New York: Norton, 1968. An informative and enjoyable account of the times.

Williams, Andrea D. (ed). *The Essential Galbraith.* Boston, MA: Houghton Mifflin, 2001. A selection of Galbraith's writings that show how relevant he still is.

See Also:

John Kenneth Galbraith (p. 1283)
Lords of Finance: The Bankers Who Broke the World (p. 1387)

"As a protection against financial illusion or insanity, memory is far better than law."

  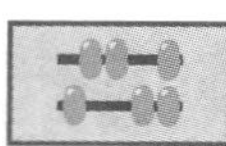      

The Gridlock Economy: How Too Much Ownership Wrecks Markets, Stops Innovation, and Costs Lives

MICHAEL HELLER (2008)

WHY READ IT?

- Analyzes how too much ownership, especially of property, is blocking economic development and innovation.
- Shows why property, whether physical or intellectual, is now broken down into such small units that it lacks full value or usefulness.
- Examines the obstructions to an efficiently working economy, and offers means to identify and resolve the difficulties brought about by gridlock.

GETTING STARTED

The Gridlock Economy considers many important social and economic problems, and shows how they are created and exacerbated by the structure of ownership and property rights. Gridlock occurs when ownership, competition, and usage are not working properly, and affects many different areas of our lives. It examines the impact of excessive property rights that create underused resources, and looks at issues such as patent rights, copyright laws, airport delays, robber barons, and rap music, and how real estate laws lead to a loss of family estates. Heller argues that all the examples he provides are part of the same problem of gridlock stifling efficiency, productivity, and innovation.

AUTHOR

Michael Heller (b. 1962) is professor of real estate law at Columbia Law School. He was previously a fellow at the Center for Advanced Study in the Behavioral Sciences, taught at the University of Michigan Law School, UCLA, and NYU. He also worked at the World Bank.

CONTEXT

- Examines private ownership and the effect it has on the economy; it generates wealth, but it can also create gridlock if there is too much ownership in the wrong place.
- Considers the social impact of having too many competing owners, and the risks and costs of gridlock.
- Argues that when too many people own a part of a resource, cooperation can be replaced by discord, which can contribute to a loss of wealth, and problems over usage.
- Explains why gridlock doesn't have to happen, that it is a result of choices we make about our resources.
- Offers insights into how to identify gridlock, and how it can be overcome to improve the economy, identifying entrepreneurship as critical to resolving some of the problems.

IMPACT

- Describes what Heller calls the "tragedy of the anti-commons," the lack of individual property rights, that means traditional methods of ownership are blocking wealth creation in the modern economy.
- Considers the complexity of property ownership in modern economies is increasing the amount of gatekeepers, those who have to give permission for things to be done.
- Shows how this complexity is escalating the likelihood of gridlock, describing ownership conflict as similar to traffic congestion, blocking innovation.
- Provides examples of gridlock in different industries, such as why new runways aren't built to ease air travel delays, the problems of patent owners blocking pharmaceutical companies from developing a cancer cure, and why most of the cell phone broadcast spectrum isn't being used.
- Analyzes the current mortgage crisis, and how it is affected by the gridlock of loans being repackaged and sold to investors many times over, distorting ownership and making it very difficult to restructure the loans.

QUOTATIONS

"We can unlock the grid once we know where to start."

"Gridlock is a paradox. Private ownership usually increases wealth, but too much ownership has the opposite effect: it wrecks markets, stops innovation, and costs lives."

"Underuse results from mistakes and gaps in economic, legal, and social organization. It is an artifact of ownership gone awry."

MORE INFO

Book:

Fox, Merritt B., and Michael A. Heller (eds). *Corporate Governance Lessons from Transition Economy Reforms*. Princeton, NJ: Princeton University Press, 2006. A collection of essays that highlight how corporate governance has developed in post-socialist economies.

Website:

Book's official website: www.gridlockeconomy.com

See Also:

Freakonomics: A Rogue Economist Explores the Hidden Side of Everything (p. 1364)
The Tipping Point: How Little Things Can Make a Big Difference (p. 1426)

"We can unlock the grid once we know where to start."

  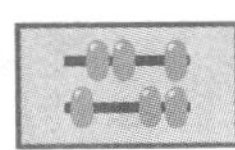   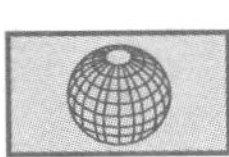   

How the Stock Market Works: A Beginner's Guide to Investment

MICHAEL BECKET (4th ed 2012, originally 2002)

WHY READ IT?

- Introduces the stock market, from defining shares, to all the major financial products, trading, investing, share picking, understanding company accounts, and the markets.
- Provides all the information and advice necessary to start investing in the markets, explained in simple language.
- With the current problems in the stock exchanges, it is even more important to have the correct information for trading.

GETTING STARTED

A comprehensive guide to the main aspects of the stock market, aimed at beginners. A starting point for anyone thinking about investing in shares and needing a strong overview about what is involved.

Helps the reader understand the variety of different exchanges and how to invest in them. With the ever-increasing amount of markets and products, it has become easier and cheaper to trade, but less easy to trade successfully.

AUTHOR

Michael Becket is a financial journalist who was the *Daily Telegraph*'s small business editor for 10 years. He is currently freelancing for a number of journals and is the author of several successful books, including *An A to Z of Finance.*

CONTEXT

- This book is not just for investors, but for anyone who wishes to understand our financial system—how it works, and how we all fit into it.
- Sets out the fundamental rules and the ways that systems operate—what is being traded, how it is traded, and who does the trading.
- Explains the wide variety of different products on offer, such as shares, gilts, futures, and options.
- Cuts through the mystique with useful information for the amateur.

IMPACT

- There is still money to be made in the market, but you need essential guidance of the type provided by this book, as well as caution, common sense, and luck.
- Gives you the knowledge to ask the right questions, make better choices, and not to be fooled by the wrong guidance.
- Answers key questions on share ownership, costs, where and when to buy and sell, and how to understand financial information.

QUOTATIONS

"The money that can be released for shares depends on personal risk/reward calculations."

"The odds are way ahead of other forms of gambling, and the return is better than other forms of investment, and careful research, monitoring and evaluation can certainly reduce risks on the stock market."

"Competition among stockbrokers is... increasing with the number of sites on the internet rising daily, so the cost could start coming down, and with it the minimum economic investment."

MORE INFO

Books:

Gough, Leo. *How the Stock Market Really Works: The Guerrilla Investor's Secret Handbook.* London: FT Prentice Hall, 2001. A guide to intelligent private investing.

Wyss, B. O'Neill. *Fundamentals of the Stock Market.* New York: McGraw-Hill, 2001. A practical guide to understanding the stock markets.

See Also:

i Capital Markets and Stock Markets (pp. 1689–1691)

"The money that can be released for shares depends on personal risk/reward calculations."

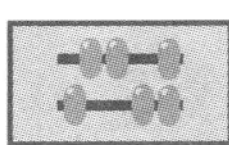

Inefficient Markets: An Introduction to Behavioral Finance

ANDREI SHLEIFER (2000)

WHY READ IT?

- Provides a broad introduction to the current opportunities and challenges in behavioral finance, the study of how people make decisions under financial uncertainty.
- Useful for those responsible for managing money or involved in trading in the financial markets.
- Presents a model of investor sentiment regarding individual decision-making under conditions of uncertainty.

GETTING STARTED

Inefficient Markets provides the theoretical framework of modern finance theory and the efficient markets hypothesis, a key tenet in the financial markets for the last few years. Taking a new approach, it builds on the economic analysis of real-world markets, focusing on investor sentiment and limits to arbitrage.

AUTHOR

Andrei Shleifer (b. 1961) is professor of economics at Harvard University. After obtaining his AB and PhD, he has held a post in the Department of Economics at Harvard since 1991. In 1999, he received the John Bates Clark Medal; he is ranked among the 10 top economists in the world by IDEAS/RePEc.

CONTEXT

- Examines the three main forms of efficient markets hypothesis: technical analysis, fundamental analysis, and insider trading.
- Discusses investor sentiment, the limits of arbitrage, the closed-end fund puzzle, positive feedback investment, and both market overreaction and underreaction to news.
- Presents and evaluates models of inefficient markets that both explain the available financial data better than does the efficient markets hypothesis and generates new empirical predictions.
- Shows how investor sentiment can form a positive trading environment in which arbitrage can actually destabilize the market.
- Stresses that risky arbitrage means that it is difficult to take advantage of pervasive irrationality.

IMPACT

- Explains that arbitrage is of limited usefulness in relatively competitive markets, much less in more complicated environments.
- Observes that the assumptions of investor rationality and perfect arbitrage are contradicted by psychological and institutional evidence.
- Demonstrates the limits of arbitrage in maintaining efficient markets through a model for predicting the returns of arbitrageurs and noise traders.
- Develops a model of investor sentiment based on investors' patterns of psychological reaction.
- Admits that it is hard to prove with certainty that financial markets are or are not efficient.

QUOTATIONS

"Remarkably, the EMH does not live or die by investor rationality."

"The field of behavioral finance . . . has presented financial economics with a new body of theory, a new set of explanations of empirical regularities, as well as a new set of predictions."

"Behavioral finance has provided both theory and evidence which suggest what the deviations of security prices from fundamental values are likely to be, and why they persist over time without being eliminated by arbitrage."

MORE INFO

Books:

Shefrin, Hersh. *Beyond Greed and Fear: Understanding Behavioral Finance and the Psychology of Investing*. Boston, MA: Harvard Business School Press, 2000. A general treatment of the subject that helps us understand the behavior behind stock selection, financial services, and corporate financial strategy.

Thaler, Richard H. *The Winner's Curse: Paradoxes and Anomalies of Economic Life.* New York: Free Press, 1992. A good introduction to behavioral finance, which challenges received wisdoms in many financial transactions.

See Also:

Advances in Behavioral Finance (p. 1327)
Behavioral Finance (pp. 1671–1673)

"Remarkably, the EMH does not live or die by investor rationality."

  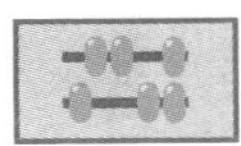      

Innovation Corrupted: The Origins and Legacy of Enron's Collapse

MALCOLM S. SALTER (2008)

WHY READ IT?

- Analyzes the collapse of Enron, and the management behavior and practices that took the company from the most lauded of its generation to bankruptcy.
- Examines how Enron's risk analysis and control system failed to counteract its management style, and why success built without ethical foundation can lead to disaster.
- Recommends actions that can be taken to prevent similar corporate breakdowns in the future, including changes to regulatory oversight, executive compensation, and performance measurement.

GETTING STARTED

Innovation Corrupted is a well-researched and analytically rigorous examination of the causes of the collapse of Enron in 2001, the largest bankruptcy in American economic history. Salter examined the technical analysis and sworn testimonies in court documents, obtained internal Enron documents, and interviewed former Enron executives and staff. He shows how Enron executives maximized opportunities for enormous personal gain, distracting them from the responsibilities of institutional integrity, sound corporate governance, and ethical working practices.

AUTHOR

Malcolm S. Salter is professor of business administration emeritus at the Harvard Business School, where he has been a member of the faculty since 1967. He has previously taught at the Harvard Law School and the Kennedy School of Government. He was president of Mars & Co. from 1986 to 2006.

CONTEXT

- Presents a historical overview of Enron's rise, strategic successes and failures, its business model, and how its top executives managed the business.
- Discusses how warning flags were ignored both within the business and by others, who instead focused on the capital markets and profit-making.
- Analyzes why external watchdogs, such as security analysts, credit rating agencies, and regulatory authorities, failed to publicize Enron's problems.
- Looks at how Enron sold overvalued and underperforming assets off-balance-sheet, and how these complex entities managed reported earnings and minimized reported debt to support the company's credit rating and stock price.
- Recommends a private-equity model of corporate governance to help solve possible governance breakdowns in public companies, proposing that directors should adopt such a model to ensure proper oversight.

IMPACT

- Shows the impact of declining corporate ethical standards, failings at board level, and the collusion of external intermediaries in the collapse of Enron.
- Proposes practical recommendations for preventing future Enron-type disasters, including board members having a sound knowledge of the business, improved executive incentivization, and ethical discipline being instilled throughout the organization.
- Considers the collapse in terms of managerial arrogance, which led to ill-advised diversification and badly implemented administrative processes.
- Discusses why Enron's board failed to detect and prevent violations of accounting principles and rules.
- Examines the collusion of investment banks in misrepresenting the financial conditions at Enron.

QUOTATIONS

"Enron's collapse involved the corruption of a remarkable strategy of innovation."

"Before fraud at Enron there was fatal thoughtlessness and incompetence among its executives."

"Overwhelmed regulatory systems were vulnerable to manipulation and evasion—particularly at Enron's creative hands."

MORE INFO

Book:

Swartz, Mimi, and Sherron Watkins. *Power Failure: The Inside Story of the Collapse of Enron.* New York: Doubleday, 2003. The story of the Enron accountant who first tried to alert management to the accounting fraud.

See Also:

The Smartest Guys in the Room: The Amazing Rise and Scandalous Fall of Enron (p. 1416)
What Went Wrong at Enron: Everyone's Guide to the Largest Bankruptcy in US History (p. 1434)

"Enron's collapse involved the corruption of a remarkable strategy of innovation."

  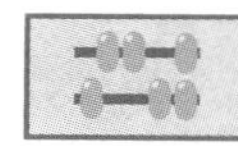      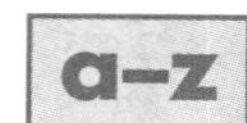

Intellectual Capital: The New Wealth of Organizations

THOMAS A. STEWART (1997)

WHY READ IT?

- The definitive guide to understanding and managing intangible assets, from the pioneer of knowledge management.
- Shows how theories on knowledge management are valuable to any organization that wants to improve the return on its intellectual capital.
- Argues that knowledge working will change the pattern of careers in the 21st century.

GETTING STARTED

Intellectual Capital is a guide to the strategic and practical issues of identifying, capturing, and using knowledge to improve a company's competitive advantage. It explains not only why intellectual capital will be the foundation of corporate success in the future, but also offers practical guidance to companies about how to make best use of their intangible assets.

AUTHOR

Thomas A. Stewart (b. 1948) is the chief marketing and knowledge officer of Booz & Company and was the editor and managing director of the *Harvard Business Review* from 2002 to 2008. Prior to this, he was the editorial director of *Business 2.0*, and a member of the Board of Editors of *Fortune*. He is also a fellow of the World Economic Forum.

CONTEXT

- Details how the emphasis has shifted from traditional capital, with financial or physical characteristics, to intangible assets and intellectual capital.
- Breaks intellectual capital down into three areas—human capital, customer capital, and structural capital—and examines the impact of each type on how a business operates.
- Argues that real value comes from capturing and deploying intellectual capital to best advantage, but that you cannot define and manage intellectual assets unless you know what you want to do with them.
- Discusses 10 key principles for managing intellectual capital: who owns it, how to manage it, how to create usable human capital, its scarcity, the place of information and knowledge, and how human, structural, and customer capital can work together.
- Shows why knowledge has become the pre-eminent economic resource and why managing it properly is an essential economic task.

IMPACT

- Discusses knowledge working and individual career paths, and how careers have become a series of gigs rather than steps.
- Looks at why project management is now important for career building, and observes that expertise is more relevant than power.
- Argues that either insiders or outsiders can perform most roles, which has an impact on how businesses are structured.
- Proposes that the fundamental career choice is not between one company and another, but between specializing and generalizing.

QUOTATIONS

"Intellectual capital is intellectual material—knowledge, information, intellectual property, experience—that can be put to use to create wealth. It is collective brainpower. It's hard to identify and harder still to deploy effectively. But once you find it and exploit it, you win."

"You cannot define and manage intellectual assets unless you know what you want to do with them."

MORE INFO

Books:

Davenport, Thomas H., and Laurence Prusak. *Working Knowledge. How Organizations Manage What They Know.* Boston, MA: Harvard Business School Press, 1998. Asserts that learning how to identify, manage, and foster knowledge is vital for companies who hope to compete in the global economy.

Stewart, Thomas A. *The Wealth of Knowledge: Intellectual Capital and the Twenty-First Century Organization.* New York: Currency, 2001. Emphasizes the importance of intellectual, as well as bricks and mortar and other forms of capital, in accounting for the worth of corporations.

See Also:

Knowledge Management (pp. 1745–1749)

"Intellectual capital is intellectual material—knowledge, information, intellectual property, experience—that can be put to use to create wealth. It is collective brainpower. It's hard to identify and harder still to deploy effectively. But once you find it and exploit it, you win."

  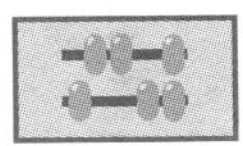      

The Intelligent Investor

BENJAMIN GRAHAM (1949)

WHY READ IT?

- Presents many of the principles of investing that the author created and taught, and which investors still use today.
- Graham was a mentor to Warren Buffett, who developed many of the methods covered in this book to make his fortune.
- Shows how to excel at making money in the stock market without taking big risks, centered round his concept of margin of safety.

GETTING STARTED

The Intelligent Investor, often described as the bible of value investing, gives a strong grounding in how to approach the stock market. Value investing helps shield investors from substantial error and teaches them to develop long-term strategies. It considers everything you need to know about investing, not only in stocks, but in business generally.

- Invest for the long-term in large, steady, straightforward businesses that adhere to certain financial criteria, but only when the market price is a bargain.
- Discusses different approaches to investing and compares defensive investing, investing using analysis, and speculating.

IMPACT

- Proposes that an investor should look at the market as if it were a business partner who is offering to buy you out, or sell you his interest daily.
- Introduces the idea of examining a company's stock as though you might buy the whole company.
- Advocates the use of market psychology, that by using the fear and greed of the market, you can find advantage.
- Argues strongly about looking at the returns one can expect from the market compared with a company one actively manages.
- Considers that shareholders should act more like owners and not simply submit to management practices.

AUTHOR

Benjamin Graham (1894–1976) was widely recognized as the father of value investing, and his "margin of safety" concept changing the landscape of investing. He taught for nearly 30 years at Columbia University's business school, and his advocacy for financial analysis training was a catalyst for the chartered financial analyst (CFA) program.

CONTEXT

- Examines the philosophy of value investing.
- Discusses the concept of margin of safety, where investments should be based on the fundamentals and be below the intrinsic value.
- Covers useful metrics for valuing a company, and states that avoiding losses is more important than making gains.

QUOTATIONS

"The stock market often goes far wrong, and sometimes an alert and courageous investor can take advantage of its patent errors."

"... to have a true investment there must be present a true margin of safety [which] can be demonstrated by figures, by persuasive reasoning, and by reference to a body of actual experience."

"... the chief losses to investors come from the purchase of low-quality securities at times of favorable business conditions."

MORE INFO

Books:

Arnold, Glen. *The Financial Times Guide to Investing.* London: FT Prentice Hall, 2004. An introduction to investing, and how to invest successfully.

Buffett, Warren. *The Essays of Warren Buffett: Lessons for Corporate Investors.* New York: L. Cunningham, 2001. Financial acumen from the successful protégé.

See Also:

Warren Buffett (p. 1273)
Benjamin Graham (p. 1285)

"The stock market often goes far wrong, and sometimes an alert and courageous investor can take advantage of its patent errors."

  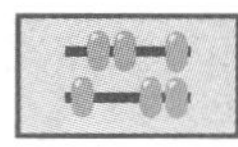      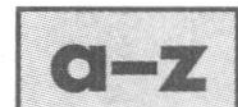

International Financial Management

CHEOL S. EUN and BRUCE G. RESNICK (6th ed 2011, originally 1998)

WHY READ IT?

- Combines an analysis of the essential financial concepts with a practical approach to implementation.
- Offers a conceptually solid treatment of international financial topics, teaching what is necessary to become an effective global financial manager.
- Used as course material by many of the top business schools, including Wharton, Stanford, Northwestern, and INSEAD.

GETTING STARTED

International Financial Management examines the fundamentals of the macroeconomic environment. Now in its fourth edition, this textbook provides a comprehensive overview of the tools and techniques of international financial management.

AUTHORS

Cheol S. Eun is a professor of finance and chair in international finance at Georgia Institute of Technology. Before that he taught at a number of universities, received the Krowe Teaching Excellence Award at the University of Maryland, and worked as a consultant.

Bruce G. Resnick is a professor of management at the Babcock Graduate School of Management, Wake Forest University. He has also taught at a number of other universities, and worked as a consultant.

CONTEXT

- Provides a comprehensive overview of the financial environment in which the multinational firm and its managers functions.
- Analyzes foreign exchange management and financial management in a multinational firm.
- Looks at how to deal with exchange risk and market imperfections, using the various instruments and tools available.
- Emphasizes financial theory, rather than the usual textbook focus on business processes.

IMPACT

- Teaches how to be an effective global financial manager.
- Helps the reader have a practical understanding of the techniques necessary to work in the foreign exchange markets.
- Provides you with the requisite knowledge, and illustrative examples, rather than showing how to implement key concepts.
- Useful as a textbook that can be used as a companion to course notes, it often presents material in the form of a tutorial.
- Can be used as preparation for the CFA charter examinations, or for senior-level finance undergraduates and MBA students, as well as finance professionals needing a reference on investments.

QUOTATIONS

"We are now living in a world where all the major economic functions—consumption, production, and investment—are highly globalized. It is thus essential for financial managers to fully understand vital international dimensions of financial management."

"There is a growing consensus around the world that it is vitally important to strengthen corporate governance to protect shareholder rights, curb managerial excesses, and restore confidence in capital markets."

"The market for foreign exchange is the largest financial market in the world by virtually any standard."

MORE INFO

Books:

Hill, Charles W. L. *International Business: Competing in the Global Marketplace*. Burr Ridge, IL: Irwin, 1994. Discusses the internationalization process, why businesses choose to go global, and the managerial implications of doing so.

Madura, Jeff. *International Finance Management*. 11th ed. Mason, OH: South-Western, Cengage Learning, 2011. Provides a background to international finance, and focuses on the managerial aspects from a corporate perspective.

Shapiro, Alan C. *Multinational Financial Management*. 9th ed. Hoboken, NJ: Wiley, 2009. Focuses on decision-making in an international context.

See Also:

Foundations of Multinational Financial Management (p. 1362)

"We are now living in a world where all the major economic functions—consumption, production, and investment—are highly globalized. It is thus essential for financial managers to fully understand vital international dimensions of financial management."

        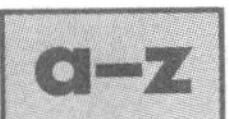

Introduction to Accounting

PRU MARRIOTT, J. R. EDWARDS, and H. J. MELLETT (3rd ed 2002, originally 1989)

WHY READ IT?

- Provides an accessible introduction to accounting for students.
- Analyzes the basic accounting techniques and concepts and shows how to apply them in a practical way.
- Flexible learning resource that can be easily used for working on your own or in a classroom.

GETTING STARTED

Introduction to Accounting is a practical textbook for those studying accounting who need a rigorous overview and practical focus on the main aspects and standards in the accounting profession. It covers the key concepts, processes, and features for those wanting extensive analysis and a reference resource, and the guidance necessary for successful specialization on this topic.

AUTHORS

Pru Marriott is head of the Department of Accounting, Economics and Finance at Winchester Business School. She has over 20 years experience of teaching and managing undergraduate and postgraduate accounting programmes, and is a member of the editorial board of the *Journal of Accounting Education*.

John Richard Edwards is professor and head of the accounting and finance Section at the University of Cardiff, a fellow of the Institute of Chartered Accountants in England and Wales, and an associate of the Chartered Institute of Taxation.

Howard Mellett is professor of accounting at the University of Cardiff, head of section, and joint coordinator of the Financial Reporting and Business Communication Research Unit at the University.

CONTEXT

- Examines key topics such as accounting frameworks, balance sheets, calculating profit, the double entry system, asset valuation, partnerships, company accounts and how to understand them, decision making, and costing and budgetary control.
- Uses detailed questions, many of which have been taken from major accounting examination bodies.
- Includes recent developments in reporting financial performance and the treatment of goodwill and intangible fixed assets, and discusses issues of research and development, and regulatory updates.
- Provides fully illustrated and worked examples to help learning.

IMPACT

- Aimed at the non-specialist and those intending to specialize in accounting at undergraduate or postgraduate level.
- One of the best primers on accounting, which has been used extensively on courses as a key educational tool.
- Examines the various stages in the accounting and decision-making processes to show the reader how to successfully integrate accounting techniques into corporate performance and strategic development.

QUOTATIONS

"The financial aspects of human enterprise cannot be ignored; the activities of almost any undertaking have financial consequences that should be measured and controlled."

"Accounting statements should contain only those financial facts that are material, or relevant, to the decision being taken by the recipient of the report."

"standards and budgets . . . help ensure the most efficient use of available resources."

MORE INFO

Books:

Ainsworth, Penne, and Dan Deines. *Introduction to Accounting: An Integrated Approach.* Chicago, IL: Irwin, 1997. Takes an unusual approach by integrating financial and managerial accounting, and focusing on the business process.

Black, Geoff. *Introduction to Accounting and Finance.* Harlow, UK: FT Prentice Hall, 2005. A student textbook that is applied, and includes interactivity for learning.

Horngren, Charles T. *Introduction to Financial Accounting.* Englewood Cliffs, NJ: Prentice Hall, 1981. Combines financial statement analysis with coverage of cash flows for MBA introductory courses or higher-level undergraduate courses.

Website:

Solutions website: www.sagepub.co.uk/resources/marriott

See Also:

Accounting (pp. 1658–1661)

"The financial aspects of human enterprise cannot be ignored; the activities of almost any undertaking have financial consequences that should be measured and controlled."

  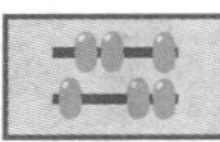   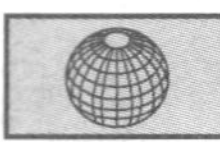   

An Introduction to Islamic Finance Theory and Practice

ZAMIR IQBAL and ABBAS MIRAKHOR (2007)

WHY READ IT?

- Two of the best-known authorities in Islamic economics, finance, and banking provide an insightful and comprehensive introduction to Islamic financial principles and practice.
- Offers a concise background on the development of Islamic finance, and a practical overview of the main products and processes.
- Reflects on the progress that Islamic financial markets have made over the last few years, which has helped create an appetite for the Western finance and banking industry to expand into this emerging market.

GETTING STARTED

An Introduction to Islamic Finance Theory and Practice explains the fundamental principles of an economic and financial system governed by Sharia law (Islamic law), and introduces all of the key elements and concepts of Islamic finance. It shows how the surge of interest in Islamic finance practices is based on a demand for more ethical investing, and a greater appreciation of the principles of, and potential under, Islamic law.

AUTHORS

Zamir Iqbal is a principal financial officer in the Risk and Analytics Department in the Treasury of the World Bank. He has previously been a member of the adjunct faculty of international finance at the George Washington University.

Abbas Mirakhor is an executive director of the IMF, and has taught at various universities in the United States and Iran. He has received several awards, including the Order of Companion of Volta for service to Ghana, and the Quaid-e Azam star for service to Pakistan.

CONTEXT

- Places Islamic finance and banking within the context of Islamic teachings and principles, as well as modern Western finance and banking practices.
- Explains the fundamental principles and functions of an economic, banking, and financial system operating under Sharia law.
- Offers an overview of the principal concepts, focusing on financial contracting, instruments and intermediation, capital markets, regulation and governance, and how risk relates to Islamic finance.
- Examines the numerous tenets of Islam and how they impact on finance and banking, such as social justice, equality, preservation of property rights, sanctity of contracts, and the prohibition of *riba*.

IMPACT

- Useful as a resource for those seeking to invest in the Islamic finance markets, and also Islamic banks and financial institutions who are redesigning their risk management and diversifying their portfolios.
- Assesses the historical systems and financial instruments used by Muslim societies, and discusses the key tenets of Islam in relation to the economic behavior of individuals, society, and state.
- Examines the challenges of globalization, and how Islamic finance is developing to meet them.
- Provides insights into the fast-growing Islamic financial services industry, and incorporates examples and practical discussions which help give an understanding of this evolving market.

QUOTATIONS

"Islam propounds the guiding principles, and prescribes a set of rules, for all aspects of human life, including the economic aspect."

"... the foremost priority of Islam and its teachings on economics is about 'Justice and Equity'."

"Islam's unconditional prohibition of Riba *(interest)... changes the landscape of the Islamic financial system."*

MORE INFO

Books:

Ayub, Muhammad. *Understanding Islamic Finance.* Hoboken, NJ: Wiley, 2007. Introduces this growing market, with a detailed overview and descriptions of all the major products and processes.

Iqbal, Munawar. *A Guide to Islamic Finance.* London: Risk Books, 2007. A focused report that explains the precepts of Islamic finance and how to develop products that would comply with Islamic principles.

Saiful, AzharRosly. *Critical Issues on Islamic Banking and Financial Markets: Islamic Economics, Banking and Finance, Investments, Takaful and Financial Planning.* Bloomington, IN: AuthorHouse, 2005. A primer on modern Islamic financial transactions and the principles of Sharia financial instruments.

See Also:

i Islamic Finance (pp. 1741–1745)

"Islam propounds the guiding principles, and prescribes a set of rules, for all aspects of human life, including the economic aspect."

  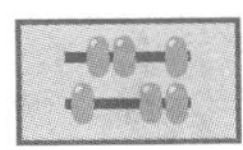   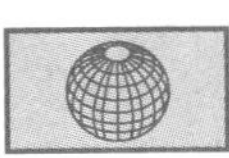   

Inventing Money: The Story of Long-Term Capital Management and the Legends Behind It

NICHOLAS DUNBAR (2000)

WHY READ IT?

- Tells the story of the unfolding drama and high-profile collapse of one of the biggest hedge funds in the world.
- Gives insight into the arcane workings of the hedge fund industry and its biggest players, including Nobel Prize winners.
- Looks at the opportunities and risks of derivatives, and their use by LTCM.

GETTING STARTED

Inventing Money leads the reader through the beginnings of the financial revolution partly initiated by Robert Merton and Myron Scholes, on through John Meriwether's infamous bond arbitrage group, to their formation of LTCM, probably the most famous hedge fund in history.

The book explains the background to how the collapse happened: the involvement of losses around Russian government debt, credit spreads in the world markets, stampeding investors, and borrowings that took LTCM's total exposure over US$100 billion.

- One of the founders of LTCM was John Meriwether, who was also featured in Michael Lewis' *Liar's Poker*.
- Also covers the same ground as *When Genius Failed*, but looks more at derivatives use and the arbitrage theories upon which the fund was based.
- Explains clearly what went wrong and how such intelligent people could fail in such a big way.
- Although it was the failure of lauded financial theories that brought down the fund, central to it all was also the fact that key risk management systems proved unsuccessful.

IMPACT

- Exposes the truths behind the LTCM collapse by focusing on the individuals and institutions involved.
- Provides a telling account of the world of derivatives and markets not easily accessible for those not in them.
- The reader can understand the financial positions taken by LTCM, and understand how artificially engineered financial instruments can generate such an enormous impact on the markets and international economics.
- It succeeds in explaining how these supposedly "risk-free" trades manage to make profit and be perfectly hedged.

AUTHOR

Nicholas Dunbar (b. 1965) studied physics at Manchester, Cambridge, and Harvard. After working in feature films and television, he turned to finance and science writing, focusing on the derivatives industry, joining *Risk* magazine in 1998 as technical editor, and is now also editor of *Life & Pensions* magazine.

CONTEXT

- Provides an overview of modern portfolio theory for a non-technical reader.
- LTCM was founded by some of those who revolutionized the finance markets in recent years.

QUOTATIONS

"Just as the engineering of digital bits would eventually lead to the internet, the mathematically driven engineering of stocks, bonds and other securities would create the modern trillion-dollar financial system."

"At $4 billion, LTCM experienced the greatest derivatives loss in the history of finance."

"...economic analysts paid by investment banks to produce daily reports for clients were lost for words, as the market appeared to go insane."

MORE INFO

See Also:

Liar's Poker: Rising Through the Wreckage on Wall Street (p. 1386)
When Genius Failed: The Rise and Fall of Long-Term Capital Management (p. 1435)

"Just as the engineering of digital bits would eventually lead to the internet, the mathematically driven engineering of stocks, bonds and other securities would create the modern trillion-dollar financial system."

Investment Banking: Valuation, Leveraged Buyouts, and Mergers and Acquisitions

JOSHUA ROSENBAUM and JOSHUA PEARL (2009)

WHY READ IT?

- This authoritative guide to buyout and M&A valuation is accessible for all levels, from nonprofessional interested in finding out more, to the experienced investment professional needing to update their knowledge.
- Gives a comprehensive overview of the main skill set needed to be a successful investment banking professional.
- Offers practical advice on all the main methodologies and valuation procedures for mergers and acquisitions (M&A) and leveraged buyout (LBO) transactions.

GETTING STARTED

Investment Banking is a practical and topical guide to the analysis of valuation that lies at the heart of investment banking, corporate finance, and private equity. It helps the reader to develop practical judgment skills and a wider perspective of the processes involved. With the approaches and products of investment banking changing all the time, this timely book provides the necessary fundamental technical know-how, with a focus on valuation analysis.

AUTHORS

Joshua Rosenbaum (b. 1971) is an executive director at UBS Investment Bank in the Global Industrial Group, specializing in structures, M&A, corporate finance, and capital markets transactions. He has previously worked at the International Finance Corporation, the direct investment division of the World Bank. Joshua received an AB from Harvard and an MBA with honors from Harvard Business School.

Joshua Pearl (b. 1971) structures and executes leveraged loan and high-yield bond financings, as well as LBOs and restructurings, for the Leveraged Finance Group at Deutsche Bank. He has previously worked at AG Edwards, and has designed and taught corporate finance training courses. He received a BS in business from the Kelley School of Business.

CONTEXT

- Gives the banking professional the knowledge and skills to work successfully in transaction-related finance.
- Combines a practical overview of the fundamentals of LBOs with analysis of an organized M&A sale process.
- Appraises the basics of valuation and critical due diligence underpinned by a step-by-step approach and the use of diagrams and numerical examples.
- Explores many of the institutional concepts of investment banking that are not usually covered, and provides definitions of key terms, financial concepts, and processes.
- Comprehensively codifies the valuation process.

IMPACT

- Focuses on the main valuation methodologies used in the financial markets, such as discounted cash flow, leveraged buy-out analysis, comparable companies, and precedent transactions.
- Explains how these methodologies can be used effectively to determine a valuation for public and private companies within the context of M&A transactions, LBOs, IPOs, restructurings, and investment decisions.
- Proposes an innovative structure for issues involving how much you should pay for a business and how to finalize the deal.
- The structure takes a grounded approach to risk and the range of value drivers available.

QUOTATIONS

"In the constantly evolving world of finance, a solid technical foundation is an essential tool for success."

"Companies with stable and predictable cash flow, as well as substantial assets, generally represent attractive LBO candidates due to their ability to support larger quantities of debt."

"Once the decision to sell has been made, the sell-side advisor seeks to achieve the optimal mix of value maximization, speed of execution, and certainty of completion among other deal-specific considerations for the selling party."

MORE INFO

Books:

Damodaran, Aswath. *Investment Valuation: Tools and Techniques for Determining the Value of Any Asset*. 3rd ed. Hoboken, NJ: Wiley, 2012. Revised and updated to reflect market conditions, this authoritative guide to investment valuation offers guidance on how to value virtually any type of asset by the renowned finance expert.

Fleuriet, Michel. *Investment Banking Explained: An Insider's Guide to the Industry*. New York: McGraw-Hill, 2008. This overview of investment banking provides a comprehensive analysis of investment banking approaches and techniques, with each area of specialty being explored in detail.

Liaw, K. Thomas. *The Business of Investment Banking: A Comprehensive Overview*. 3rd ed. Hoboken, NJ: Wiley, 2011. This topical examination of investment banking and valuation offers an accessible guide to the industry and its key operations and methodologies, including new developments that have been adopted by practitioners and the challenges posed by globalization.

See Also:

- Damodaran on Valuation: Security Analysis for Investment and Corporate Finance (p. 1348)
- Valuation: Measuring and Managing the Value of Companies (p. 1429)
- Corporate Valuation (pp. 1704–1707)

"In the constantly evolving world of finance, a solid technical foundation is an essential tool for success."

  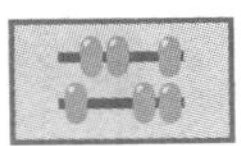      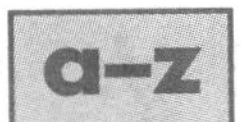

Investments

ZVI BODIE, ALEX KANE, and ALAN J. MARCUS (9th ed 2010, originally 1989)

WHY READ IT?

- Introduces financial concepts, markets, and instruments; shows how to develop a basic finance toolbox, and how to apply it in a portfolio setting.
- Analyzes all the core concepts in investment, and explains market structure and environment.
- Blends practical and theoretical coverage, and is useful for those wanting to develop a greater knowledge of portfolio theory.

IMPACT

- Introduces the most basic financial concepts that are used in portfolio construction and management.
- Emphasizes asset allocation, and provides a broader assessment of futures, options, and other derivative security markets than most investment texts.
- Not for those wanting a deep understanding of the background research that developed the theories.
- Provides a variety of real-life examples to supplement their explanations, which provides context for some of the abstract concepts.
- Contains helpful guidance for the Professional Risk Manager Certification, and is used in the certification programs of the Financial Planning Association and the Society of Actuaries.

GETTING STARTED

Investments, now in its ninth edition, is an introductory textbook that focuses on the practical aspects of investing and investment strategy. It is the leading textbook for the graduate/MBA investments market, as it gives a good overview of investment techniques and opportunities, and offers a comprehensive analysis of investment theory and the concepts involved.

- Examines why the security markets are nearly efficient, and how this ensures that securities are priced appropriately, given their risk and return attributes.
- Balances theory and application of both the basics and advanced topics, and explains the pros and cons of various financial models.
- Although not overly technical, does assume some basic mathematical knowledge.

AUTHORS

Zvi Bodie is professor of management at Boston University, and has served on the finance faculty at the Harvard Business School and MIT Sloan School of Management. He has published widely on pension finance and investment strategy.

Alex Kane is professor of finance and economics at the School of International Relations and Pacific Studies, University of California, San Diego. He is a member of the American Economic Association and the American Finance Association, and has held academic appointments at UCLA and Harvard.

Alan J. Marcus is professor of finance at the School of Management, Boston College. He also currently serves on the Research Foundation Advisory Board of the CFA Institute.

CONTEXT

- Communicates complex investment concepts to those with little or no background in finance.
- Helps you understand, analyze, and utilize all the major investment tools.
- Discusses concepts such as derivatives, which can alter the characteristics of portfolios.

QUOTATIONS

"When complex derivatives are misunderstood, firms that believe they are hedging might in fact be increasing their exposure to various sources of risk."

"Securities in the capital market are much more diverse than those found within the money market."

"For some firms, macroeconomic and industry circumstances might have a greater influence on profits than the firm's relative performance within its industry."

MORE INFO

Books:

Bodie, Zvi, Alex Kane, and Alan J. Marcus. *Student Solutions Manual to Accompany Investments*. New York: Irwin/McGraw-Hill, 2006.

Brown, Keith, and Frank K. Reilly. *Investment Analysis and Portfolio Management*. Hinsdale, IL: Dryden Press, 1979. Takes a more quantitative approach to the valuation of various assets and is more comprehensive.

Sharpe, William, Gordon J. Alexander, and Jeffrey W. Bailey. *Investments*. Englewood Cliffs, NJ: Prentice Hall, 1978. More of a technical and detailed coverage of the same topics.

Website:

Book website including spreadsheets directly related to the content: www.mhhe.com/bkm

See Also:

i Investment (pp. 1736–1741)

"When complex derivatives are misunderstood, firms that believe they are hedging might in fact be increasing their exposure to various sources of risk."

  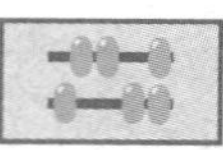      

IOU: Why Everyone Owes Everyone and No One Can Pay (also published as Whoops)

JOHN LANCHESTER (2010)

WHY READ IT?

- Explains the developments that precipitated the global financial crisis in terms that anyone can understand.
- Provides new insights into how the financial crisis developed in a lucid and witty manner.
- Points out that the critical factor that caused the crisis was that banks could sell loans on to investors, removing the relationship between lenders and borrowers—it no longer mattered whether the lender thought the borrower could repay the loan.

GETTING STARTED

IOU explains the events that led up to and precipitated the global financial crisis in a humorous and easily understandable manner. However, the prose, while simple, is never simplistic. The book describes the main characters involved, ranging from the mathematicians that invented the new derivatives based on subprime loans, and the bankers who sold these products on to gullible investors, to the politicians and central bankers who failed to understand or supervise what was going on.

AUTHOR

John Lanchester (b. 1962) is a novelist, journalist, and winner of the Whitbread First Novel award and the EM Forster award, among other prizes. He says that he began studying the global economic crisis as the background to a novel and then realized that he had "stumbled across the most interesting story I've ever found." He adds that as an outsider to economics and finance, he sought to understand the issues that led to the crisis and explain these to the layman.

CONTEXT

- John Lanchester's painstaking research has enabled him to discover how the derivatives that caused the financial crisis—credit defaults swaps (CDS)—were developed.
- Provides detailed explanations of these financial instruments and how they work.
- Reveals that the trade in derivatives exceeds the total annual economic output of the world by an enormous factor, "perhaps tenfold," and details how this gigantic, unstable bubble was allowed to grow to dangerous proportions.
- Analyses failures of risk management in banks, and provides insights into the American housing market, looking at how the subprime market developed partly as a result of political pressure from Washington.
- Explains how policy failures in general, and the loose money policy adopted by the Federal Reserve in particular, created the credit bubble that preceded the financial crisis.
- Shows how the ratings agencies defied common sense by assigning triple-A credit ratings to instruments that were composed of subprime debt.

IMPACT

- This is one of the most readable accounts of the financial instruments and the main characters involved in the events that led to the global financial crisis.
- Describes how sophisticated theories of risk, based on the analysis of past data, asserted that a sustained collapse in American house prices was a hugely improbable event, even though such events had happened in the past.
- Shows how these theories of risk led to "predatory lending" to some of the poorest people in the United States, including "ninja" loans, to applicants with "no income, no job, no assets."
- Explains how the original sellers of these loans were able to escape exposure by bundling up the loans and selling them on to investors who then took out insurance with companies such as AIG.
- Warns that although everybody is hoping for an economic recovery, that is when the public will receive the bill for the measures taken to avoid another global Great Depression.

QUOTATIONS

Lanchester explains the 20-year evolution of the credit derivatives and their ultimate impact by saying, "*It's as if people used the invention of seat belts as an opportunity to take up drunk driving.*"

"*I am going to arraign a number of culprits for the crash: derivatives are prominent in the line-up, but among derivatives it was CDS which were the chief baddy, the gang leader, the mafia don, the most destructive of the WMDs.*"

"*Many bright, literate people have no idea about all sorts of economic basics, of a type that financial insiders take as elementary facts about how the world works.*"

MORE INFO

Books:

Krugman, Paul. *The Return of Depression Economics and the Crisis of 2008*. London: Penguin, 2008. The Nobel Prize-winning economist, who specializes in recessions, takes us through the history of why they happen.

Shiller, Robert J. *The Subprime Solution: How Today's Global Financial Crisis Happened, and What to Do About It*. Princeton, NJ: Princeton University Press, 2008. The American economist, academic, and best-selling author provides a snappy but far-reaching account of the global financial crisis.

Smith, David. *The Age of Instability: The Global Financial Crisis and What Comes Next*. London: Profile Books, 2010. The economics editor of the *Sunday Times* asks how an apparently clear blue economic sky masked the approaching ferocious storm.

See Also:

Fault Lines: How Hidden Fractures Still Threaten the World Economy (p. 1353)
Freefall: Free Markets and the Sinking of the Global Economy (p. 1365)

Lanchester explains the 20-year evolution of the credit derivatives and their ultimate impact by saying, "It's as if people used the invention of seat belts as an opportunity to take up drunk driving."

  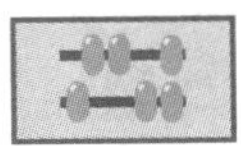      

Irrational Exuberance

ROBERT J. SHILLER (2nd ed 2005, originally 2000)

WHY READ IT?

- Uses a combination of economics, econometrics, sociology, and psychology to analyze stock market movements, and explain how speculative bubbles come about.
- Cautions that the market in 2000 was overvalued by historical standards, which made it inherently unstable, and therefore liable to crash.
- Analyzes why the current housing market crisis is part of a speculative bubble, which may trigger declining home prices for many years.

GETTING STARTED

Irrational Exuberance looks at how unstable the financial markets can be under a free-market economy. It explains how Alan Greenspan's phrase "irrational exuberance," which he used to describe the behavior of investors who had driven the value of shares on the New York Stock Exchange to record levels, is a valid one to describe the mood of bull markets and psychology of investing. Originally published just before the market downturn, it made Shiller famous as a guru of speculative bubbles, and has been recently republished to cover other volatile markets in the same context.

AUTHOR

Robert J. Shiller is professor of economics at Yale University, and professor of finance and fellow at the International Center for Finance, Yale School of Management. He received the Paul A. Samuelson Award, and has served as vice president of the American Economic Association, and president of the Eastern Economic Association.

CONTEXT

- Discusses factors that were driving stocks up when the book was published, including increased internet usage, greater coverage of financial news, optimistic punditry, low inflation, and the rise of the mutual fund industry.
- Assesses different stock market booms over the years, which betrayed all the signs of a speculative bubble; during each, there was much talk of it being a "new era."
- Looks at how people make decisions in uncertain situations by preferring familiar patterns, especially when determining their stock picking and timing.
- Demonstrates that financial markets occasionally get out of sync with economic fundamentals, and that trends or herd influences pull markets around in an exaggerated way.

IMPACT

- Warns that there is too great a reliance on stocks as the only investment vehicle worth using, and recommends that investors consider looking beyond stocks as a way to diversify and hedge against the inevitable downturn.
- Lays out an intuitive case for how to avoid investing in major market excesses when they occasionally occur.
- Attempts to disprove that stocks or real estate are necessarily the best thing to invest in on a long-term basis.
- Argues that private pension plans that depend on the stock market should be modified, and offers a solution that includes improved public institutions and a broader array of investment options.

QUOTATIONS

"Emotions and heightened attention to the market create a desire to get into the game. Such is irrational exuberance today in the United States."

"The emotional state of investors when they decide on their investments is no doubt one of the most important factors causing the bull market."

"Stock market expansions have often been associated with popular perceptions that the future is brighter or less uncertain than it was in the past."

MORE INFO

Books:

Kindleberger, Charles P., and Robert Z. Aliber. *Manias, Panics, and Crashes: A History of Financial Crises*. 6th ed. Basingstoke, UK: Palgrave Macmillan, 2011. An account of how the mismanagement of money and credit has led to financial disasters over the years.

Shiller, Robert J. *The New Financial Order: Risk in the 21st Century*. Princeton, NJ: Princeton University Press, 2003. Describes a number of fundamental ideas that use information technology and financial theory to manage some of the risks that are generally ignored by risk management institutions.

See Also:

Fooled by Randomness: The Hidden Role of Chance in Life and in the Markets (p. 1361)

"Emotions and heightened attention to the market create a desire to get into the game. Such is irrational exuberance today in the United States."

  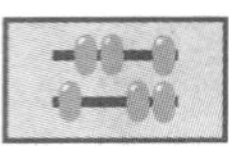      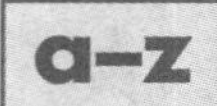

Liar's Poker: Rising Through the Wreckage on Wall Street

MICHAEL LEWIS (1989)

WHY READ IT?

- Shows the reality behind bond trading in the 1980s—the deals, the salaries, the greed, and the ambition.
- A funny and absorbing insight into human nature, it explores the drivers of success and failure in a complex, dynamic financial environment.
- Examines how a culture of excessive competition contributed to Salomon's financial collapse.

GETTING STARTED

Liar's Poker explores the characters and forces behind Salomon Brothers' bond-trading empire in the 1980s. It gives an entertaining autobiographical account of the author's time there, and analyzes the benefits and costs of competition between individuals and between firms. It also provides a behind-the-scenes exposé of a successful dealing house during its heyday, and how Salomon failed to use information to understand its competitors—just as in poker, this is essential to success.

AUTHOR

Michael Lewis (b. 1960) is a bestselling author, and a journalist with the *New York Times* and Bloomberg. Prior to this, he was a bond salesman at Salomon Brothers both on Wall Street and in London. He is also a visiting fellow at the University of California, Berkeley.

CONTEXT

- The title of the book is based on the game that is occasionally played on Wall Street, involving gambling on the serial number of a dollar bill.
- Depicts how an organization's culture is critical to its success by examining how Salomon's culture of bond trading became increasingly competitive and ambitious.
- Shows how actively competing with others is often key to success in a business environment, but competition at the expense of teamwork can be disastrous.
- Attributes Salomon's difficulties after 1987 to its management's lack of focus and their behaving more like traders than managers—seeking to "manage by numbers."
- Highlights the character traits of a successful trader as fast, ambitious, and addicted to gambling.

IMPACT

- Provides a lesson in market failure, where Salomon operated a near monopoly in such areas as mortgage bonds and made enormous, but unsustainable, profits.
- Examines how remuneration of traders became an issue, and notes that the unwillingness to pay substantial bonuses to successful young traders caused discontent.
- Details how the collapse of Salomon's mortgage department was the result of poor communication between business units, a lack of market awareness, and dwindling employee loyalty.
- Looks at how Salomon failed to maintain customer loyalty, as their traders focused exclusively on commission-based bonuses, and appeared neither to value customers nor to show loyalty to their firm.

QUOTATION

"In any market, as in any poker game, there is a fool."

MORE INFO

See Also:

- Inventing Money: The Story of Long-Term Capital Management and the Legends Behind It (p. 1381)
- When Genius Failed: The Rise and Fall of Long-Term Capital Management (p. 1435)

"In any market, as in any poker game, there is a fool."

  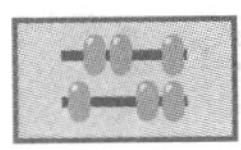   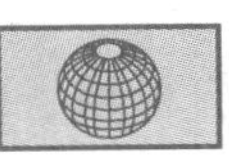   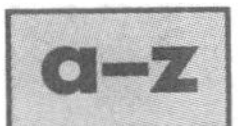

Lords of Finance: The Bankers Who Broke the World

LIAQUAT AHAMED (2009)

WHY READ IT?

- *Lords of Finance* provides a fascinating insight into the policy failures that led to the Wall Street Crash and the Great Depression.
- It explores the parallels and the differences between the dramatic events that took place in the late 1920s and early 1930s and the global financial crisis that developed in 2008.
- The author gives new insights into how financial crises develop and the enormous impact that central bankers can have on the lives of ordinary people.

GETTING STARTED

The book tells the story of the events that led up to the Wall Street Crash and the subsequent Great Depression through the lives of four central bankers dubbed by the press of the time as belonging to the "most exclusive club in the world." It describes how the economic disaster unfolded, beginning after the First World War when the Allies, and France in particular, insisted that a bankrupt Germany pay massive reparations. But if the central bankers cannot entirely be blamed for the issue of reparations, they more than anyone else, according to Ahamed, were responsible for the second fundamental error of economic policy in the 1920s: the decision to take the world back on to the gold standard.

AUTHOR

Liaquat Ahamed has been a professional investment manager for 25 years. He has worked at the World Bank in Washington, DC, and was the chief executive of the New York-based partnership of Fischer Francis Trees & Watts. He is currently an adviser to several hedge fund groups, including the Rock Creek Group and Rohatyn Group, and is a director of Aspen Insurance. He is also on the board of trustees of the Brookings Institution.

CONTEXT

- Ahamed's painstaking research uncovers the characters of the four Lords of Finance: Benjamin Strong of the Federal Reserve Bank of New York; Montagu Norman of the Bank of England; Émile Moreau of the Banque de France; and Hjalmar Schacht, in charge of Germany's Reichsbank. Together these four sought to manage the international financial system in the 1920s.
- He describes in gripping prose how, instead of averting a catastrophe and saving the world, the four piloted the global economy into the abyss.
- He analyzes how too loose a monetary policy in the United States created the stock market bubble that preceded the Wall Street Crash.
- He explains why the economic orthodoxies of the time—the nostrum that currencies should be backed by the gold standard and the belief that governments should cut spending during an economic downturn—helped to create the greatest economic disaster the modern world has seen.
- He shows how the central bankers' belief that struggling banks should be allowed to fail undermined confidence in the financial system and contributed to the economic collapse.
- He demonstrates how the Great Depression led to the rise of Hitler and the Second World War.

IMPACT

- Many books about the Great Depression are tinder dry. Ahamed's book is inspired and its timing could not have been better. It is highly readable and provides a gripping account of the terrible downward spiral known as the Great Depression.
- The book describes how it took a noneconomist, but a man with an incisive mind and clear intuition, President Franklin Delano Roosevelt, to realize that what the world needed was inflation, not further measures that would only compound deflation.
- It shows how financial crises are invariably preceded by investor overconfidence and a belief that economic systems have entered a new era that allows stocks to move higher and higher.
- It warns that even before the First World War there was a widespread view that globalization and the increasing interdependence of economies meant that war was no longer a rational option.
- Let us hope that a well-thumbed copy of *Lords of Finance* lies on the desk of every official of the major central banks today so that they do not make the same blunders as their well-intentioned predecessors.

QUOTATIONS

"[By 1932] industrial production in the United States had fallen in half, prices had tumbled by 30%, and national income had contracted from over US$100 billion to US$55 billion."

"Asked by a reporter in August 1932 if there had ever been anything like this before, Keynes responded: 'Yes, It was called the Dark Ages, and it lasted four hundred years'."

"Don't forget what desperate straits the allies drove us to ... Just try to imagine what a cultured people like the Germans had to go though to fall for a demagogue like Hitler ... All we wanted was some possibility of export, for trade, to live somehow."

MORE INFO

Book:

Krugman, Paul. *The Return of Depression Economics and the Crisis of 2008*. New York: WW Norton & Co., 2009. The Nobel Prize-winning economist who specializes in recessions takes us through the history of why they happen.

See Also:

The Great Crash, 1929 (p. 1371)

"[By 1932] industrial production in the United States had fallen in half, prices had tumbled by 30%, and national income had contracted from over US$100 billion to US$55 billion."

  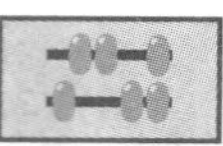      

Macroeconomics

N. GREGORY MANKIW (8th ed 2012, originally 1992)

WHY READ IT?

- It explains concepts clearly and uses relevant examples to convey meaning.
- Covers all the main macroeconomic topics, including science, data, money, inflation, unemployment, short-run and long-run factors, and the business cycle.
- Incorporates real-world issues and data throughout, rather than being overly academic.

IMPACT

- Examines the long run when prices are flexible before moving on to the short run when prices are sticky.
- Emphasizes the empirical and experiential throughout, to ensure relevancy.
- Is clear about the limits regarding what economists really know about the economy.
- Analyzes how changes in policies and variables affect aggregate functions.
- Discusses key concepts such as the IS-LM model, Solow steady state, and the Keynesian consumption function.
- Presents the economic ideas of one of the key figures in the Bush White House.

GETTING STARTED

Macroeconomics is a widely adopted intermediate-level textbook that communicates the principles of macroeconomics in a comprehensible style.

It integrates many learning tools such as case studies, information boxes, graphs, mathematical notes, chapter summaries, key concepts, questions for review, problems, and applications, to ensure it can be used by students and teachers, as well as those needing a refresher on the topic.

- Examines the economic behavior of human beings as well as nations and the economic interactions between nations, including aspects of the economy such as money, savings, growth, stocks and flows, inflation, unemployment, taxation, and national budgets.
- Ensures that the math is understandable and applicable.

AUTHOR

N. Gregory Mankiw (b. 1958) is professor of economics at Harvard University. He has been a research associate of the National Bureau of Economic Research, and an adviser to the Federal Reserve Bank of Boston and the Congressional Budget Office. From 2003 to 2005 he served as chairman of the President's Council of Economic Advisers.

CONTEXT

- A focused and practical textbook that balances its coverage between short- and the long-run macroeconomic issues.
- Integrates Keynesian and classical ideas to give a pedagogical overview of the issues.
- Uses a variety of simple models to put its points across.

QUOTATIONS

"I incorporate many of the contributions of the classical economists before Keynes and the new classical economists of the past three decades."

"Instead of pretending that there is one model that is complete enough to explain all facets of the economy, I encourage students to learn how to use and compare a set of prominent models."

"The basic principles of macroeconomics do not change from decade to decade, but the macroeconomist must apply these principles with flexibility and creativity to meet changing circumstances."

MORE INFO

Books:

Blanchard, Olivier. *Macroeconomics*. Upper Saddle River, NJ: Prentice Hall, 1997. Presents a unified view of macroeconomics, connecting the short run, medium run, and long run.

Chamberlin, Graeme, and Linda Yueh. *Macroeconomics*. London: Thomson Learning, 2006. A general textbook that takes an international perspective.

Website:

Author blog: gregmankiw.blogspot.com

"I incorporate many of the contributions of the classical economists before Keynes and the new classical economists of the past three decades."

Management Accounts: How to Use Them to Control Your Business

TONY SKONE (1995)

WHY READ IT?

- Explains management accounts in an easily understandable style, especially for managers needing to make strategic decisions regarding their business.
- The emphasis throughout the book is on applying the information.
- Explains the jargon, identifies both what is important and what is irrelevant, and advises on what accounts information you should be receiving.

GETTING STARTED

To run a business successfully it is essential that you be able to analyze the well-being of your business, and make informed decisions about future operations. *Management Accounts* gives you the tools to do this, and shows how individual decisions affect the profitability, cashflow and risk profile of a business. It helps you improve your contribution to the planning and financial control of an organization.

AUTHOR

Tony Skone (b. 1939) is a financial, tax, and cost consultant, principal of Management and Training Consultants, and has lectured at business schools as well as holding a post as senior lecturer at the University of Westminster. He is author and coauthor of several business finance books.

CONTEXT

- Use your management accounts to get the full picture of how your business has been performing in many different areas. The accuracy and relevancy of the financial information should underpin future decision making.
- Provides a guide to management accounts written from the perspective of the user.
- Use your management accounts to examine sales revenue and expected cashflow.
- Includes guidance on how to analyze data on sales, purchasing, and fixed assets.
- Helps an understanding of the differences between expected and actual achievements.
- Illustrates the control mechanisms available, including the control of budgets and working capital.

IMPACT

- Suggests a variety of spreadsheet applications using numbers and graphs, and provides two formulas for calculating break-even and profit.
- Demonstrates how to develop your ratio analysis, and the use of spreadsheets and the financial scorecard.
- Helps you spot worrying trends, such as stock levels increasing against flat sales.

QUOTATIONS

"What accountants have to do is to become better communicators while managers have to become financially literate, that is, they have to learn to speak the language of business—money."

"It is people who make things happen, not money."

"The selection of appropriate ratios and the keeping of some form of financial scorecard will provide the basis for more effective control of the business."

MORE INFO

Books:

Mott, Graham. *Accounting for Managers.* London: Kogan Page, 1994. Part of a fast-track MBA series.

Terry, Leslie Alfred. *Business Accounts.* London: Pitman & Sons, 1935. An introduction to business accounting.

See Also:

Management Accounts (pp. 1233–1234)

"What accountants have to do is to become better communicators while managers have to become financially literate, that is, they have to learn to speak the language of business—money."

  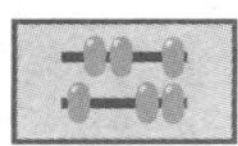      

Managing Financial Resources

MICK BROADBENT and JOHN CULLEN (3rd ed 2003, originally 1993)

WHY READ IT?

- Addresses the complexities of financial planning and control, and explains key concepts.
- Focuses on finance for the non-financial manager, helping them understand the principles involved in managing financial resources.
- Makes it easier for educators to prepare materials, and structure courses for students at different levels.
- Includes 20 self-contained tutorial sessions, each containing activities, session plans and outcomes.

GETTING STARTED

Managing Financial Resources examines relevant issues such as performance measures and cost analysis, methods of improving profitability, and techniques of financial monitoring and control, concentrating on how to apply accountancy to managerial issues. It also provides a full range of tutorials on managing resources, and assists in teaching management courses at certificate and diploma level.

AUTHORS

Mick Broadbent is head of department, Accounting, Finance and Economics, and professor of accounting, acting head of the Business School, University of Hertfordshire. He is a Quality Assurance Agency Collaborative Provision Auditor and a member of the Chartered Institute of Management Accountants Expert Assessment Panel.

John Cullen is professor of management accounting at the Management School, Sheffield University. He is vice chairman of the committee of heads of accounting, is also a member of the Freight Logistics Research Group at the Department for Transport, and undertakes supply chain consultancy projects.

CONTEXT

- Analyzes relevant topics such as public sector management issues, audit commission, and capital investment decisions.
- Discusses essential finance resource topics such as stakeholder analysis for published reports and accounts, intellectual property, performance measurement, outsourcing, and new developments in the public sector.
- Helps the reader to develop essential and relevant management skills.
- Real examples and case studies are used throughout to illustrate the main points in a practical way.

IMPACT

- Suitable for managers on the Diploma in Management or part one of the Postgraduate Diploma, especially those accredited by the Chartered Management Institute and Edexcel.
- Can also be used as a practical resource by managers and MBA students.
- Easy to use and able to be customized for different courses.
- Examines key issues, including break-even analysis and how to assess financial performance.
- Based on the Management Charter Initiative's Occupational Standards for Management NVQs and SVQs at level 4.

QUOTATIONS

"The recording of financial information within an enterprise is a natural part of good business practice."

"The key to understanding management accounting is to recognize that costs are classified in many different ways depending upon the purpose for which the information is to be used."

"An understanding of cost behaviour is crucial for both short and long-term decision making."

MORE INFO

Book:

Ryan, Bob. *Finance and Accounting for Business.* London: Thomson Learning, 2004. An introductory overview of financial accounting, management accounting, and financial management for non-specialist students.

"The recording of financial information within an enterprise is a natural part of good business practice."

     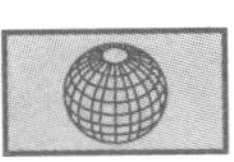   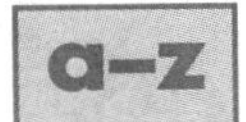

Market Wizards: Interviews with Top Traders

JACK D. SCHWAGER (1989)

WHY READ IT?

- Shows how successful traders have beaten the markets and made millions, through detailed interviews that discuss their strategies and trading techniques.
- Provides a number of themes that offer useful advice for all levels of investors wanting to improve their trading approach and methodologies.
- Discusses traders from a variety of areas, such as the futures and currency markets, equity trading, and floor trading, and examines the psychology of trading.

GETTING STARTED

Market Wizards was the first in a trilogy of interview-based, bestselling books that Schwager published, which provide insight into the backgrounds, personalities, experiences, and techniques of top traders. It offers advice on how to be a successful market speculator, how to implement a sound trading philosophy, and how to use effective techniques and disciplines to beat the market. Each interview has an introduction to the trader, an edited transcript of the interview, and a brief summary of their trading strategies.

AUTHOR

Jack D. Schwager (b. 1948) is a managing director and principal of the Fortune Group, and a finance author. He worked for many years on Wall Street as a director of futures research and the coprincipal of a commodity trading advisory firm. He is also a regular seminar speaker.

CONTEXT

- Gives a useful overview of trading and investing techniques in different types of markets over the last 30 years, as most interviewees started trading in the 1970s and are still operating successfully now.
- Examines the human side of trading, as the interviews discuss the investors' experiences, how they honed their skills and developed personal philosophies and styles, and examine aspects of their daily trading operations.
- Common characteristics of the traders include a strong desire for success, confidence about their abilities over the long run, a winning strategy that they stuck with, risk awareness, being patient until the right trade came along, acting independently, and understanding that losing is part of the game.
- Provides the opportunity to understand and apply well-established trading rules to your own investing.
- Learn the importance of creating your own individual trading system that plays to personal strengths.

IMPACT

- Reveals the money and risk management tips and philosophies of professional traders.
- Outlines a number of key trading principles, such as "cut your losses, let your winners run," "have patience to wait for the right trade to come along," and "getting your ego out of trading decisions."
- Demonstrates the success of a wide variety of trading and investing styles.
- Examines the mistakes that most traders make during their careers, and compares the characteristics of losing traders with those of successful ones.
- Discusses key trading concepts such as discipline, capital preservation, risk management, individual responsibility, flexibility, intellectual honesty, and consistency.
- Emphasizes the importance of planning your trades, and the best time to buy and sell.
- Explains program trading, portfolio insurance, and options, in appendixes.

QUOTATIONS

"Diversification is a hedge for ignorance. I think you are much better off owning a few stocks and knowing a great deal about them."

"One of the jobs of a good trader is to imagine alternative scenarios. I try to form many different mental pictures of what the world should be like and wait for one of them to be confirmed."

"You don't need any education at all to [trade]. The smarter you are, the dumber you are. The more you know, the worse it is for you."

MORE INFO

Books:

Schwager, Jack. *A Complete Guide to the Futures Markets: Fundamental Analysis, Technical Analysis, Trading, Spreads, and Options.* New York: Wiley, 1984. The seminal reference book on the futures markets, which examines price forecasting in the commodity futures market.

Schwager, Jack. *Stock Market Wizards: Interviews with America's Top Stock Traders.* New York: Harper Business, 2001. The third volume in this series, providing more insights into the trading styles of top traders.

See Also:

Reminiscences of a Stock Operator (p. 1413)

"Diversification is a hedge for ignorance. I think you are much better off owning a few stocks and knowing a great deal about them."

Mastering Financial Management: Demystify Finance and Transform Your Financial Skills of Management

STEPHEN BROOKSON (1998)

WHY READ IT?

- Enables business managers and executives to master the essentials of financial management, and to learn techniques of immediate use.
- Explains commercially vital concepts, processes, practices, and terminology, and shows how they should best be adopted and implemented.
- Covers finance and accounting in a way that brings competitive advantage to those previously with little knowledge of the subject.

GETTING STARTED

Mastering Financial Management provides practical coaching in financial accounting, management accounting and financial management. With guidance on financial statements and financial information, it helps you understand and use financial techniques and improve individual and organizational performance.

AUTHOR

Stephen Brookson is a chartered accountant, and was a consultant with Ernst & Young, before leaving to set up his own training consultancy business. He presents seminars and training events in both the public and private sectors.

CONTEXT

- Provides a practical guide to financial accounting, budgetary control, and management accounting.
- Offers a framework for understanding the relationship between the company and its providers of capital.
- Examines the principles and structure of financial management and details the main techniques for strategic, tactical, and operational decision-making based on sound budgeting and financial planning.
- Helps you respond to current business challenges through relevant knowledge of management finance.
- Covers the finance basics on accounts, balance sheets, assets and liabilities, and ratios.
- Advises on corporate financial health and how to analyze business performance.
- Discusses the rules governing accounting, and looks at the fundamentals of taxation and its commercial implications.

IMPACT

- Gives you the essentials of managing company finances, either for a department or the whole business, and the confidence to develop the full range of key attributes.
- Aimed just as much at personal development as job skills, it helps those needing a financial grounding as a critical business expertise.
- In line with others in the Masters in Management series, it is aimed at decision-makers, general managers, team leaders and implementers, and senior-level executives.
- Enables effective decision-making and investment appraisal.
- Offers a variety of practical learning features throughout, such as key questions, action checklists, activities, guides to best practice, key learning points, and key management concepts.

QUOTATIONS

"Finance is the critical business skill to possess before you can set course for a successful business career."

"It is a common fault that most people preen their profit and loss accounts incessantly, whilst paying only lip service to their balance sheets and cash flow."

"Those managers who may have an inkling that all is not well with the costs are excluded by jargon and witchcraft, and so the errors continue."

MORE INFO

Books:

Brigham, Eugene F., and Joel F. Houston. *Fundamentals of Financial Management.* Hinsdale, IL: Dryden Press, 1978. An introductory guide to corporate finance and financial management.

Whiteley, John. *Mastering Financial Management.* Basingstoke, UK: Palgrave Macmillan, 2004. Introduces financial management in a practical way, and usefully examines company accounts, with guidance on how to make your financial reports interesting and influential.

See Also:

The Financial Times Handbook of Financial Management (p. 1359)

"Finance is the critical business skill to possess before you can set course for a successful business career."

  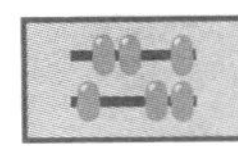   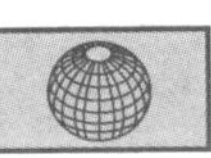   

Mastering Risk, Volume 1: Concepts

JAMES PICKFORD (ED) (2000)

WHY READ IT?

- An impressive cast of contributors bring the latest ideas on the management of financial risk and offer a guide to best practice.
- Provides a comprehensive overview of the key concepts of risk management.
- The practical relevance of these concepts is highlighted throughout with recent examples and short case studies.

GETTING STARTED

Mastering Risk is a collection of all 10 issues of the respected Mastering Risk supplement to the *Financial Times*. It contains 50 articles from contributors working in top business schools and the business community, to take the reader through a broad range of risk issues, from the traditional insurance type risks to more high-level financial risk management, and covers both core areas and emerging fields of importance.

EDITOR

James Pickford is the business life editor of the *Financial Times*.

CONTEXT

- Brings you the current thinking from some of the leading authorities on risk, to examine the concept of risk control in all aspects of business and finance management.
- The variety of backgrounds of the risk experts featured ensures this a balanced perspective on risk.
- Traces the development of attitudes, and introduces the latest ideas and approaches from the US and Europe.
- Contains definitive explanations of the types of risk, and helps an understanding of the nature of these risks.
- Approaches risk measurement, risk categorization, and risk perception in a variety of ways to give a perceptive overview of how they can be tackled.

IMPACT

- Covers the essentials of risk measurement, risk strategy, financial risk, operational risk, regulation and political risk, insurance and systemic risk, and extreme events.
- Analyzes the techniques used to identify and measure risk, the methods of managing financial and non-financial risk, and investigates emerging areas of risk such as e-commerce and reputation management.
- Explains the methods of assessing and controlling risks, and the role that different parts of the organization should play in risk management.
- Avoids the mathematics of risk, to focus on accessible definitions and explanations of the subject.
- In examining risk, it also delves into other disciplines, such as psychology, investment, law, statistics, and marketing.

QUOTATIONS

"Companies that implement a well-designed risk management strategy increase their shareholders' wealth."

"The perception of risk is a complex and subjective process."

"The enormous growth and development in both financial and electronic technologies have created a richer palette of risk management techniques."

MORE INFO

Books:

Alexander, Carol (ed). *Mastering Risk, Volume 2: Application.* Harlow, UK: FT Prentice Hall, 2001. The second part, consisting of specially commissioned chapters that cover the application side of risk management.

Borge, Dan. *The Book of Risk.* New York: Wiley, 2001. Examines the process of decision-making in an uncertain world, and the role of risk management.

See Also:

Against the Gods: The Remarkable Story of Risk (p. 1328)

Risk Management (pp. 1785–1789)

"Companies that implement a well-designed risk management strategy increase their shareholders' wealth."

  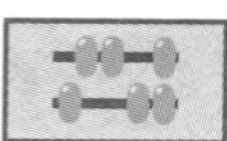      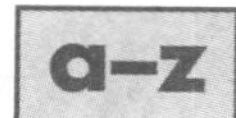

Mastering the VC Game: A Venture Capital Insider Reveals How to Get from Start Up to IPO on Your Terms

JEFFREY BUSSGANG (2010)

WHY READ IT?

- An insider's account for entrepreneurs and business heads looking for capital and a successful working partnership with a venture capitalist (VC).
- Shows how to choose the best investor for a venture, and work with them over the course of a funding.
- Discusses how VCs work with companies, and the types of businesses they prefer to fund.

GETTING STARTED

The author brings his own background and experience as a former entrepreneur and now venture capitalist to inform on how VCs operate and how they combine with entrepreneurs to fund and grow companies. Based around a series of interviews with leading venture capitalists and entrepreneurs, *Mastering the VC Game* explores how to pick the most suitable VC, pitch to them, and negotiate the right deal, in ways suitable for a particular business.

AUTHOR

Jeffrey Bussgang is a general partner at venture capital firm Flybridge Capital Partners, and previously worked as an entrepreneur in a number of start-ups and as a management consultant with the Boston Consulting Group. He received an MBA from Harvard Business School and a BA in computer science from Harvard College.

CONTEXT

- Follows the process of how entrepreneurs can effectively achieve investment capital by persuading venture capitalists to risk their money on an idea for a new business enterprise.
- Presents guidance on ways of cashing out on a business, such as selling the company and undertaking an initial public offering (IPO).
- Provides practical advice backed up by interesting anecdotes and personal insights from the author's experience on both sides of the divide.
- Analyses the typical types of business start-ups and how they usually originate.
- Gives an overview of how the VC industry operates a variety of countries around the world.

IMPACT

- Presents interviews with the founders of successful start-ups, including Jack Dorsey from Twitter and Reid Hoffman from LinkedIn, as well as a number of leading venture capitalists.
- Offers a practical guide for entrepreneurs into the inner world of the VC, and an overview of the current venture capital industry.
- Shows how to achieve the support to finance, develop, and launch new ventures.
- Recounts how the author moved from entrepreneurial start-ups to becoming a VC.
- Explores how to find a VC, undertake a successful pitch, and then work with a VC as a partner and adviser.
- Investigates the operations and processes of the entrepreneur, and how they focus on passion and wanting to change their industries, and not just make money.

QUOTATIONS

"Entrepreneurs have to persuade investors to risk capital in a concept that is often little more than a glimmer of an idea."

"A critical thing for entrepreneurs when fund-raising is to find a firm that's going to be a good fit with their capital profile."

"Many entrepreneurs make the mistake of playing down the risk of their venture in the pitch for capital."

MORE INFO

Books:

Berkery, Dermot. *Raising Venture Capital for the Serious Entrepreneur.* New York: McGraw-Hill, 2008. This sourcebook for entrepreneurs looking for venture capital explains the main strategies for raising new business capital and all the processes involved in achieving effective valuation.

Gladstone, David, and Laura Gladstone. *Venture Capital Handbook: An Entrepreneur's Guide*. Revised and updated ed. Upper Saddle River, NJ: Prentice Hall, 2002. This classic guide takes you through the entire VC funding process in a practical way, showing exactly how to get funded quickly and effectively.

Livingston, Jessica. *Founders at Work: Stories of Startups' Early Days*. Berkeley, CA: Apress, 2007. A series of interviews in which founders of well-known technology companies such as Apple, Flickr, Hotmail, and PayPal talk about their original ideas, and what their businesses do to create value and achieve competitive advantage.

See Also:

★ Assessing Venture Capital Funding for Small and Medium-Sized Enterprises (pp. 451–453)
★ Sources of Venture Capital (pp. 601–603)
✔ Dealing with Venture Capital Companies (p. 1067)

"Entrepreneurs have to persuade investors to risk capital in a concept that is often little more than a glimmer of an idea."

  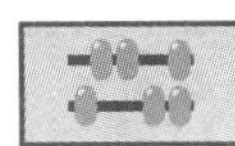 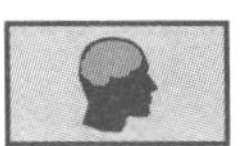  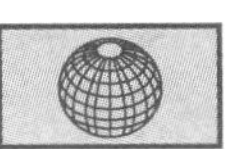   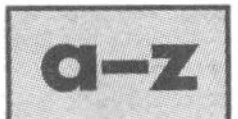

The Mesh: Why the Future of Business Is Sharing

LISA GANSKY (2010)

WHY READ IT?

- Explains how Mesh businesses have reengineered the way companies operate through the sharing of products and services rather than outright purchase.
- Explains how the collaborative approach provides organizations with a better idea of what consumers are actually looking for and when.
- Discusses how the Mesh approach allows the consumer to receive flexible, reliable, and more sustainable products and services.

GETTING STARTED

The Mesh explores how businesses based on shared networks and nontraditional approaches to ownership are already proving successful and could be the business model of the future. It examines the structure of Mesh enterprises, how they use web and mobile data networks to organize focused information, and discusses how full connectivity and networks allow consumers to receive online services, products, or related products that are more in line with their needs.

AUTHOR

Lisa Gansky (b. 1958) is an entrepreneur and environmentalist, and CEO, cofounder, and chairman of consumer services company Ofoto. She was previously at Kodak, has been a vice president of internet services at AOL, and was cofounder and CEO of GNN, the first commercial website. She is an adviser, investor, and board member of a number of new internet ventures.

CONTEXT

- Explores how Mesh companies use new technology, data, networks, and social media to offer goods and services when people actually need them.
- Looks at a variety of business types that can be developed through the Mesh approach and offers a practical overview of Mesh design and implementation.
- Explains how to develop an effective strategy for using the Mesh on the basis that online collaboration is both an inexpensive and an accessible way to conduct business operations.
- Examines the role of consumer data, market trends, and usage patterns in developing efficient Mesh businesses.
- Explores how Mesh companies can offer the same product many times, helping to expand all the related opportunities.

IMPACT

- Explores how in the future businesses will share and collaborate using the internet, and how companies will be able to offer more effective services and products using this approach.
- Analyzes how information can be used to ensure that products and services are personalized and offered on a timely basis.
- Shows how products and services can be tailored for different people in an easy and cheap way.
- Discusses the benefits of personal recommendations and social networking for Mesh operations.
- Explains how the Mesh business model is environmentally friendly, as it cuts down on the need to own things that are rarely used.
- Presents a series of interesting and focused case studies of firms that are already using the Mesh system, such as Netflix, Zipcar, and Ofoto.

QUOTATIONS

"*. . . some things are better shared.*"

"*The new share-based businesses are bolstered and built on social media. Using web-enabled mobile networks, they can define and deliver highly targeted, very personal goods and services at the right time and location.*"

"*The Mesh is made possible by the way in which we are all increasingly connected to everything else—to other people, businesses, organizations, and things.*"

MORE INFO

Books:

Botsman, Rachel, and Roo Rogers. *What's Mine Is Yours: The Rise of Collaborative Consumption*. New York: HarperBusiness, 2010. This argues that consumption as we know it is no longer sustainable, and that technological innovation is helping a drive toward collaborative consumption and concepts such as Freecycle and eBay.

Fried, Jason, and David Heinemeier Hansson. *Rework*. New York: Crown Business, 2010. This book of practical business knowledge presents a series of rules and advice for entrepreneurial success, focusing on strategy, customers, and how to become more productive.

Godin, Seth. *Purple Cow: Transform Your Business by Being Remarkable*. New York: Portfolio, 2003. This bestseller from the marketing guru explores how traditional approaches are failing and why companies now have to differentiate themselves in order to be noticed. It looks at companies that have successfully achieved this path to growth.

See Also:

Wikinomics: How Mass Collaboration Changes Everything (p. 1437)

"**. . . some things are better shared.**"

The (Mis)behavior of Markets

BENOIT MANDELBROT and RICHARD L. HUDSON (2004)

WHY READ IT?

- The founder of fractal geometry re-evaluates the standard tools and models of modern financial theory.
- Examines how the traditional finance models originated, arguing that, since financial markets are unpredictable and far riskier than first thought, it is necessary to find alternatives.
- Presents a different method of predicting stock price movements, founded on his fractal theories.

GETTING STARTED

The (Mis)behavior of Markets explains what a fractal view of the world of finance would look like, based on applying Mandelbrot's theory of fractal geometry to equity prices and their movements. Also integrating economics and chaos theory, it considers the failings of modern financial theory, and shows how his mathematical model based on fractals can improve on the existing financial models, such as the Black–Scholes formula for option pricing and the capital asset pricing model.

AUTHORS

Benoit Mandelbrot (b. 1924) is professor of mathematical sciences at Yale University and a fellow emeritus at IBM's Thomas J. Watson Laboratory. As the originator of fractal geometry, he received the Wolf Prize in Physics, the Japan Prize in science and technology, and an award from the US National Academy of Sciences.

Richard L. Hudson was a reporter and editor for the *Wall Street Journal* for 25 years, before being appointed the managing editor of its European edition. He graduated from Harvard University and was a Knight Fellow of MIT in 1991.

CONTEXT

- Argues that current models of financial theory are flawed, as they do not properly explain real market prices and their fluctuations, and are inadequate to control actual levels of investment risk.
- Considers that these models, such as modern portfolio theory, the capital asset pricing model, and Black–Scholes, depend on the mistaken belief that investments conform to the simple distribution of the bell curve.
- Demonstrates that the Gaussian Normal distribution is an oversimplification of financial prices due to "fat tails," concentration, and extreme events.
- Presents empirical evidence showing that the commodity, futures, money, stock, and other market price movements are not generally Normally distributed.
- Proposes instead the use of predictive ideas based on fractal geometry, which better reflect the inherent turbulence and volatility of the market.
- Describes 10 heresies of finance, including market turbulence and riskiness, timing, market similarities and uncertainties, and the inevitability of bubbles.

IMPACT

- Criticizes how economic and modern financial theory has developed, in terms of theories of price movements.
- Analyzes how the markets really behave, suggesting that a "multifractal" approach is preferable to the random walk and efficient market theories, which assume that prices changes conform to the bell curve.
- Argues that returns follow a multifractal—a fractal both in value and in time; this model can create pictures of financial returns that are similar to real financial returns.
- Admits that multifractals should be researched further and are not presently able to build a successful model for a particular market.
- Discusses the observation that prices are not random but have inherent patterns, which substantiates a new way of looking at markets: "econophysics."

QUOTATIONS

"Patterns are the fool's gold of financial markets."

"Continuity is a fundamental assumption of conventional finance."

"What passes for orthodoxy in economics and finance, proves on closer examination to be shaky business."

MORE INFO

Books:

Mandelbrot, Benoit. *Fractals and Scaling in Finance: Discontinuity, Concentration, Risk.* New York: Springer, 1997. Combines new material with reprints of Mandelbrot's classic papers, which helped an analysis of evaluating the risks involved in trading strategies.

Peters, Edgar E. *Fractal Market Analysis: Applying Chaos Theory to Investment and Economics.* New York: Wiley, 1994. An accessible study of how to use fractals to explain behavior and understand price movements.

See Also:

Fooled by Randomness: The Hidden Role of Chance in Life and in the Markets (p. 1361)

"Patterns are the fool's gold of financial markets."

  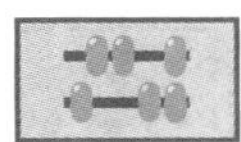      

The Money Game

ADAM SMITH (1976)

WHY READ IT?

- An influential and thought-provoking book about money and how to make it, based on the experiences of a Wall Street insider.
- A classic book, oft-quoted by investors, that foreshadows almost every major investment paradox or problem that is faced today.
- Can be thought of as one of the first books about behavior finance, in its descriptions of trading, crowd psychology, and the stock markets.

GETTING STARTED

The Money Game describes the psychological factors influencing the stock market of the 1960s. Based on a set of essays submitted by the fictitious Mr Smith to a variety of financial publications between the mid-1960s and the early 1970s, it is a well-written, humorous, and intelligent examination of the money machine. It describes the style of the boardrooms and trade pits of Wall Street in the 1960s, and a new generation of Wall Street money managers, referred to as "the gunslingers," who approach the management of other people's money with a distinct lack of care.

AUTHOR

Adam Smith is a pseudonym for George J. W. Goodman (b. 1930), a business journalist who also wrote novels, investment books, and a television show. He also presented lectures on the media at Princeton for several years, and was editor of the *Institutional Investor*.

CONTEXT

- Depicts a trading culture where money is how you keep score—if you make lots of money, you are winning the game. The game is there to be played—win, lose, or draw—and the money managers cannot help but play.
- Offers timeless insights into how and why players, amateur and professional, really play the money game, all within the context of the excesses of the 1960s.
- Discusses such diverse subjects as crowd psychology, inkblots, and random walks, and their application to the markets from an original point of view.
- Looks at the fundamental principles of fear and greed in the context of investment strategy.
- Examines the success of technical analysis, fundamental analysis, efficient market theory, the random walk, and Dow theory, and finds them all lacking.

IMPACT

- Discusses the fallibility of numbers, trends, and data analysis as systems dependent on the reading of the past to determine the future.
- Shows how professional money managers operate, and notes that even though they have more money and information than the amateur, they still are unable to accurately predict the markets.
- Advises that people thinking about getting involved in investing would do well to look inward to find their own trading style before making any outward financial moves.

QUOTATIONS

"If I really had a system for making money in the market and it worked all the time, first of all, I wouldn't tell anybody and second of all, I would soon have just about all the money there is."

"The real object of the Game is not money, it is the playing of the Game itself."

"If you are going to operate with intuition—or judgment—then it follows that the first thing you have to know is yourself."

MORE INFO

Book:

Smith, Adam. *Supermoney*. New York: Random House, 1972. The follow-up to *The Money Game*, which has recently been re-issued with a new foreword and preface.

See Also:

Adam Smith (p. 1311)
One Up on Wall Street: How to Use What You Already Know to Make Money in the Market (p. 1403)
Reminiscences of a Stock Operator (p. 1413)

"If I really had a system for making money in the market and it worked all the time, first of all, I wouldn't tell anybody and second of all, I would soon have just about all the money there is."

  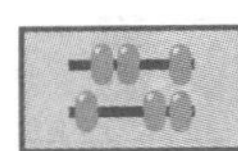      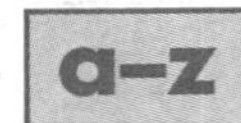

Monkey Business: Swinging Through the Wall Street Jungle

JOHN ROLFE and PETER TROOB (2000)

WHY READ IT?

- Gives a searing expose of the life of investment bankers in a mergers and acquisitions department at a leading Wall Street bank.
- Through personal stories and anecdotes, we learn about the processes and practices of young investment bankers, as well as the boredom and drudgery of their daily lives—which is far from the glamour that led them to apply in the first place.
- Reveals the macho mentality of their workplace, the invective, belittling of others, lack of sleep, and visits to less than glamorous nightspots.

GETTING STARTED

Monkey Business tells of two young business school graduates who were lured to Wall Street with high hopes of making their fortunes and leading life in the fast lane. Rolfe and Troob give an insider's account of how the business is run, through an entertaining, sarcastic, and somewhat pessimistic view of the life of an investment banker. The combination of a lack of values, the vulgar and patriarchal approach of their colleagues, and the extreme hours and endless work, which are related in amusing detail, finally convinces the young men that investment banking is not for them.

AUTHORS

John Rolfe taught at Virginia Tech and the University of Florida, before doing broadcast research in New York. In 1993 he was at the Wharton School of Business. He then joined Donaldson, Lufkin & Jenrette, before becoming a principal with a private investment organization. He is now a freelancer.

Peter Troob worked for Kidder Peabody in New York, and in 1993 entered the graduate program at the Harvard Business School. He later joined Donaldson, Lufkin & Jenrette, and is currently a partner with a private investment organization.

CONTEXT

- The story of a journey from MBA to Wall Street that shows how many young people enter investment banking dreaming of big bonuses and a glamorous lifestyle, but without an awareness of what life is really like as a trainee in this world.
- Through a range of personal stories, the authors give an insight into what to expect as a junior investment banker at a major firm.
- Shows the business processes and how money is made in the M&A departments of investment banks, covering deal origination, preparing a pitch book, how a company's valuation is reached, and how to read a prospectus that has been through countless drafts.
- Provides a useful understanding of the valuation process and the methods involved in valuing a company for an acquisition or a stock offering.
- Gives an account of due diligence, with stories about traveling to many different countries in a short period of time, making the authors too exhausted to remain awake during presentations.

IMPACT

- Details the authors' appointment as junior associates at the elite Wall Street investment bank Donaldson, Lufkin & Jenrette, tempted by visions of money and glamour.
- Explains that what they actually found was relentless hard work, boredom, bureaucracy, and incompetence, which they depict as representative of the whole banking sector.
- The continuous tensions between work and leisure, money and time, provide an understanding of how banks operate and use junior staff to build business.
- Discusses the working lifestyle of young investment bankers, what happens behind the scenes of the deal making, and what they will do to generate fees.
- Provides a guide on what to avoid, and how not burn out in the investment banking jungle.

QUOTATIONS

"We realized that the compensation levels and the perks weren't in place because being an associate in investment banking was a great job. They were in place because the job sucked."

"The investment banking community has long been an oligopoly, with only a handful of real players with the size and scale to drive through the big deals."

"Investment banking is a profession characterized by extremes. Whether it's money, booze, food, sex, or work hours, the typical banker believes that more is better."

MORE INFO

See Also:

- Liar's Poker: Rising Through the Wreckage on Wall Street (p. 1386)
- Traders, Guns, and Money: Knowns and Unknowns in the Dazzling World of Derivatives (p. 1427)

"We realized that the compensation levels and the perks weren't in place because being an associate in investment banking was a great job. They were in place because the job sucked."

More Money than God: Hedge Funds and the Making of the New Elite

SEBASTIAN MALLABY (2010)

WHY READ IT?

- Provides a detailed look at the hedge fund industry, the type of people that work in it, and of their successes and failures.
- Shows how hedge funds have revolutionized the world of finance and the global economy.
- Shortlisted for the 2010 *Financial Times* and Goldman Sachs Business Book of the Year award and a *New York Times* bestseller.

GETTING STARTED

More Money than God delves into the innermost workings of the hedge fund industry to tell the story of how it originated in the 1960s and 1970s, its confrontations with central banks during the 1980s and 1990s, up to their part in the recent financial crisis. It focuses on some of the key players, and the different style they brought to investing, based on the author's knowledge of and access to hedge funds.

AUTHOR

Sebastian Mallaby (b. 1964) is a journalist and public speaker, senior fellow in international economics at the Council on Foreign Relations and director of the Center for Geoeconomic Studies (CGS). He is a columnist for the *Washington Post*, having previously worked on *The Economist*, and is also a two-time Pulitzer Prize finalist. He has a degree in modern history from the University of Oxford.

CONTEXT

- Provides an insight into how related concepts from economics, mathematics, and psychology have facilitated the growth of the industry.
- Explains how hedge funds work to achieve their higher investment returns in terms of the balance between long and short positions and the use of derivatives.
- Examines how hedge funds have helped the development of new exotic instruments that have changed the way finance operates.
- Discusses how hedge funds operate without regulation, without much leverage, and by offering huge performance incentives.
- Argues that hedge funds help economic growth because they correct anomalies in the market and do not do as much damage as the banking sector.
- Offers insights into the effect of hedge funds when the credit crisis started to impact the industry.

IMPACT

- Investigates the secretive world of the hedge fund industry, and explores its current state.
- Offers a guide to some of the key personalities that have populated the industry through the years, such as Paul Tudor Jones, Jim Simons, Michael Steinhardt, and Ken Griffin.
- Considers historic events in fund history, including George Soros's shorting of sterling and John Paulson's more recent shorting of subprime mortgages.
- Praises the giants of the hedge fund industry and their contrarian investment approach and ability to predict the market.
- Argues that hedge funds came out of the crisis better than the rest of the investment world, due to the way they are structured.
- Sees the importance of hedge funds as continuing, and sees them as a force for growth and innovation in the industry.

QUOTATIONS

"The hedge-fund titans were the new Rockefellers, the new Carnegies, the new Vanderbilts. They were the new American elite—the latest act in the carnival of creativity and greed that powers the nation forward."

"Hedge funds are the vehicles for loners and contrarians, for individualists whose ambitions are too big to fit into established financial institutions."

"Capitalism works only when institutions are forced to absorb the consequences of the risks that they take on. When banks can pocket the upside while spreading the cost of their failures, failure is almost certain."

MORE INFO

Books:

Biggs, Barton. *A Hedge Fund Tale of Reach and Grasp ... Or What's a Heaven For?* Hoboken, NJ: Wiley, 2010. Biggs offers a fictional but detailed narrative of the industry through the life of a poor boy who becomes wealthy from working in a hedge fund.

Mallaby, Sebastian. *After Apartheid: The Future of South Africa.* New York: Times Books, 1992. Mallaby's portrait of South Africa in the post-apartheid era examines the legacy and its social and political consequences, covering a wide range of issues, such as the rise of AIDS, township violence, and tribalism.

Mallaby, Sebastian. *The World's Banker: A Story of Failed States, Financial Crises, and the Wealth and Poverty of Nations*. New York: Penguin Press, 2004. An engaging insight into the World Bank and its president between 1995 and 2005, James Wolfensohn. It examines the organization's processes, public policy, and economic development during those years.

See Also:

- Absolute Returns: The Risk and Opportunities of Hedge Fund Investing (p. 1326)
- A Demon of Our Own Design (p. 1349)
- Inventing Money: The Story of Long-Term Capital Management and the Legends Behind It (p. 1381)
- When Genius Failed: The Rise and Fall of Long-Term Capital Management (p. 1435)
- Hedge Funds, Fund Management, and Alternative Investments (pp. 1729–1732)

"The hedge-fund titans were the new Rockefellers, the new Carnegies, the new Vanderbilts. They were the new American elite—the latest act in the carnival of creativity and greed that powers the nation forward."

Multinational Business Finance

DAVID K. EITEMAN, ARTHUR I. STONEHILL, and MICHAEL H. MOFFETT
(13th ed 2012, originally 1973)

WHY READ IT?

- Helps managers of multinational enterprises recognize and capitalize on the unique characteristics of the global markets.
- Communicates the background and complexities of international finance, maintaining a managerial focus.
- Examines the environment that the multinational business operates in, and offers guidance on the specific financial and business measures that need to be taken into account for varying circumstances.

GETTING STARTED

Multinational Business Finance is a textbook that provides practical insights into current financial management practices, and is a learning resource for students of international finance, as well as being useful as focused training for professionals. Now in its 11th edition, it can also be seen as a reference resource on the tools and techniques of business finance, as it works through the complexities of international finance in an authoritative manner.

AUTHORS

David K. Eiteman is professor emeritus at Anderson School of Management, UCLA, and has held appointments at a number of academic institutions. He is a former president of the International Trade and Finance Association, the Society for Economic and Management in China, and the Western Finance Association.

Arthur I. Stonehill is a professor of finance and international business emeritus at Oregon State University, and has held appointments at a number of academic institutions. He is a former president of the Academy of International Business, and a Western director of the Financial Management Association.

Michael H. Moffett is associate professor of finance at Thunderbird, the American Graduate School of International Management. He was formerly associate professor of finance at Oregon State University, and has held a number of other teaching appointments.

CONTEXT

- Provides a number of real-world case studies that apply key concepts to the types of situations an international manager would face, in order to help them make financial decisions that increase firms' values.
- Does not go extensively into all the mathematical theory, but covers the requisite practical information of international business finance.
- Analyzes accounting exposures, and the impact of foreign affiliates on financial statements, and what this means for the operations of multinational business.
- Considers the essential and developing financing issues underpinning the global firm, such as cost of capital, financial structures, sourcing equity, and sourcing debt on a global basis.
- Covers issues of foreign investment decisions, particularly as they affect corporate strategy, capital budgeting, international acquisitions and valuation, and the necessary risk adjustments.

IMPACT

- Updated to provide insights into current financial management practices, and features a streamlined presentation, expanded attention to emerging markets, several new chapters, and four new decision cases with an emerging markets focus.
- Examines the changing attitudes towards the impact multinational corporations have on local businesses.
- Offers a number of tests, guidelines, and key issues, with teaching cases and internet coverage, to aid learning.

QUOTATIONS

"[Multinational enterprises] face unique risks that do not hamper domestic firms as much. These risks are related to foreign exchange risks and political risks."

"An important task of the financial manager is to measure foreign exchange exposure and to manage it so as to maximize the profitability, net cash flow, and market value of the firm."

"The ability of a firm to achieve a globally competitive cost and availability of capital depends on its success at attracting international portfolio investors."

MORE INFO

Books:

Butler, Kirt C. *Multinational Finance*. Cincinnati: South-Western, 1997. Provides a concise treatment of the investment and financial decisions facing the multinational corporation.

Moffett, Michael H. *Cases in International Finance*. Boston, MA: Addison-Wesley, 2001. Further decision cases that complement the textbook.

Shapiro, Alan C. *Multinational Financial Management*. 9th ed. Hoboken, NJ: Wiley, 2009. Treats international financial management as a natural extension of financial management principles.

Website:

Companion website for the 13th edition: wps.prenhall.com/bp_eiteman_mbf_13/

See Also:

International Finance (pp. 1734–1736)

"[Multinational enterprises] face unique risks that do not hamper domestic firms as much. These risks are related to foreign exchange risks and political risks."

  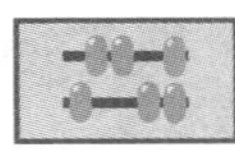      

My Life as a Quant

EMANUEL DERMAN (2004)

WHY READ IT?

- An honest and engaging account of the author's life, career, and experiences as a physicist and in quantitative finance.
- Shows how and why Derman made the transition from academia to Wall Street, and details the differences between the two worlds.
- Analyzes how the quantitative finance industry evolved, and its place in the investment community.

GETTING STARTED

Derman was one of the first physicists to move into finance and use his skills in quantitative modeling and trading during the emergence of financial engineering and exotic derivatives in the 1980s and 1990s. In *My Life as a Quant*, he describes coming to terms with such a complete mindshift, and how he was able to apply his scientific skills to a burgeoning new area of research.

AUTHOR

Emanuel Derman is a professor and director of the financial engineering program at Columbia University. He was previously a managing director at Goldman Sachs, and has been named the SunGard/IAFE Financial Engineer of the Year, and appointed to the Risk Hall of Fame.

CONTEXT

- Describes Derman's interactions with famous scientists and big players on Wall Street, including Fischer Black, with whom he collaborated on the widely used Black–Derman–Toy model.
- Analyzes the development of quantitative finance as a practical discipline and its place in the hierarchy of finance, where traits like salesmanship, practical trading skills, and internal politicking are more of a dominant culture.
- Explains how the best financial quants combine mathematics, intuition, financial insight, business knowledge, and technology.

IMPACT

- Follows Derman's transformation from young scientist to Managing Director and head of the renowned quantitative strategies group at Goldman Sachs.
- Analyzes the varying styles and approaches of quants and traders and their incompatibility.
- Provides insights into how investment banks work, and the role that quants play in developing new products and trading strategies.
- Examines the nature of discovery in physics and how this compares with computational and theoretical finance.
- Derman comes across as humble, self-critical, philosophical, and intelligent as he reflects on his life and career; he feels that he wasn't able to be a success in his physics career, and that there was a wide disparity between youthful ideals and mature compromises.

QUOTATIONS

"When you do physics you're playing against God; in finance, you're playing against God's creatures."

"Traders and quants are genuinely different species."

"Personality plays a larger part in economic writing because truth's part is smaller."

MORE INFO

Books:

Bernstein, Peter L. *Capital Ideas: The Improbable Origins of Modern Wall Street.* New York: Free Press, 1992. Shows how a group of academics and economists changed the way that Wall Street ran the world's investments.

Mehrling, Perry. *Fischer Black and the Revolutionary Idea of Finance.* Hoboken, NJ: Wiley, 2005. Describes Black's life, and examines the history, players, and ideas of the evolving risk management industry.

See Also:

Fooled by Randomness: The Hidden Role of Chance in Life and in the Markets (p. 1361)

"When you do physics you're playing against God; in finance, you're playing against God's creatures."

  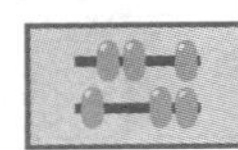      

A Non-Random Walk Down Wall Street

ANDREW W. LO and A. CRAIG MACKINLAY (1999)

WHY READ IT?

- Two distinguished researchers and authors offer an in-depth and technical exposition of the movements of markets.
- Examines and challenges in detail the random walk hypothesis, which is considered one of the foundations of financial theory and modeling.
- Finds that markets are not completely random, and that predictable components do exist in recent stock and bond returns, confronting a precept of financial economics and many investment strategies.

GETTING STARTED

A Non-Random Walk Down Wall Street puts the random walk hypothesis to the test. As a compilation of key research and writing from two reputed academics, it analyzes the markets and their non-randomness in detail, using a mathematically rigorous approach to reinforce their arguments.

AUTHORS

Andrew W. Lo is professor of finance at the MIT Sloan School of Management and the director of MIT's Laboratory for Financial Engineering. He is also a governor of the Boston Stock Exchange, and founder and chief scientific officer of AlphaSimplex Group.

A. Craig MacKinlay is professor of finance at Wharton. He has received the Paul A. Samuelson Award, and is a research associate of the National Bureau of Economic Research.

CONTEXT

- Focuses on financial economics, and the techniques used in advanced econometric analysis, to clarify common myths about efficient market theory and the random walk hypothesis.
- Examines the techniques for detecting predictabilities, and evaluates their statistical and economic significance.
- Concludes that the random walk model is not consistent with the behavior of weekly returns.
- Argues that day traders tend to overreact to news, making it possible to profit by taking the opposite side of their trades.

IMPACT

- Argues that the random walk hypothesis is false, that the financial markets are not inherently random, and that day-to-day movements in stock prices are not what many models predict.
- Tracks the course of the authors' research on the predictability of stock prices, from early work on rejecting random walks in short-horizon returns to their analysis of long-term memory in stock market prices.
- Attempts to show that the financial markets do contain a certain degree of predictability, and illustrate this by analyzing empirical data and through mathematical proof.
- Presents an enquiry into the pitfalls of "data-snooping biases" that have arisen from the use of the same historical databases for discovering anomalies and developing seemingly profitable investment strategies.

QUOTATIONS

"The Random Walk Hypothesis and ... the Efficient Market Hypothesis have become icons of modern financial economics that continue to fire the imagination of academics and investment professionals alike."

"Unforecastable prices need not imply a well functioning financial market with rational investors, and forecastable prices need not imply the opposite."

"The apparent inconsistency between the broad support for the Random Walk Hypothesis and our empirical findings is largely due to the common misconception that the Random Walk Hypothesis is equivalent to the Efficient Market Hypothesis."

MORE INFO

Book:

Campbell, John Y., Andrew W. Lo, and A. Craig MacKinlay. *The Econometrics of Financial Markets.* Princeton, NJ: Princeton University Press, 1997. Covering a broad sweep of empirical finance, it combines theory and practice to examine statistical techniques and their application to finance.

See Also:

The Intelligent Investor (p. 1377)
A Random Walk Down Wall Street: The Time-Tested Strategy for Successful Investing (p. 1412)

"The Random Walk Hypothesis and ... the Efficient Market Hypothesis have become icons of modern financial economics that continue to fire the imagination of academics and investment professionals alike."

One Up on Wall Street: How to Use What You Already Know to Make Money in the Market

PETER LYNCH (1989)

WHY READ IT?

- An introduction to the stock market, and what to look for when investing your money, without relying on what the experts tell you.
- Presents the author's proven strategies and principles on stock investing in a readable manner.
- Argues that small investors can research stocks better than most professionals, and that they should focus on quality, undervalued companies they can understand, and use common sense to identify those that will grow.

GETTING STARTED

One Up on Wall Street considers stock market investing from the standpoint of the amateur, arguing that the most successful type of investor does their homework, studies the fundamentals of a company, and then invests for the long term only in what they can understand. A bestseller, it provides an easy to understand and entertaining approach, and a set of fundamental rules that are easy to put into practice.

AUTHOR

Peter Lynch (b. 1944) is a successful fund manager and stockpicker. He previously managed the Fidelity Magellan Fund, the top-ranked general equity mutual fund in America, and has written several bestselling stock investing books. He was previously an analyst, and also writes a column for *Worth* magazine.

CONTEXT

- Lynch is a proponent of stock analysis and value investing, and focuses on analyzing company fundamentals such as sales, earnings, and growth rates.
- Categorizes different types of companies—stalwarts, fast growers, slow growers, cyclicals, asset plays, and turnarounds—in terms of their investment opportunity.
- Asserts that amateurs can be as good or even better than investment professionals as long as they are alert for opportunity, and invest in what they know, using local knowledge as much as possible.
- Shows how difficult it is to time the market, so you should ignore the experts and think for yourself, focusing on quality stocks at reasonable prices.
- Discusses the qualitative aspects of investing, including portfolio balance, picking winners, and when best to buy and sell.

IMPACT

- Advises that it is better to understand what kind of company to invest in and set specific investment objectives before purchase of a stock.
- Shows how to categorize the companies, and what strategy to use when investing in each of them.
- Informs on how to identify companies, how to analyze their prospects for growth, and how to continue monitoring potential growth.
- Argues that to beat the market you should choose a small portfolio of stocks that grow at a higher rate than the market average.

QUOTATIONS

"I continue to think like an amateur as frequently as possible."

"Stocks are most likely to be accepted as prudent at the moment they're not."

"Only invest what you could afford to lose."

MORE INFO

Book:

Lynch, Peter. *Beating the Street.* New York: Simon & Schuster. 1993. A book aimed at all levels of investors, shows how to spot companies that will outperform.

See Also:

The Intelligent Investor (p. 1377)

Stocks for the Long Run: The Definitive Guide to Financial Market Returns and Long-Term Investment Strategies (p. 1418)

"I continue to think like an amateur as frequently as possible."

  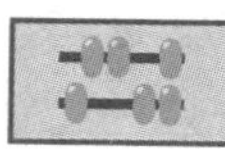      

Option Volatility and Pricing: Advanced Trading Strategies and Techniques

SHELDON NATENBERG (1994)

WHY READ IT?

- One of the most widely read books among active option traders around the world.
- Although geared primarily towards professionals and traders, it will also be useful for amateurs interested in how to trade options.
- Points out the key concepts essential to successful trading, including option pricing, and strategies for training up to a desired level.

GETTING STARTED

Option Volatility and Pricing presents the fundamentals of option theory, and shows how it can be used to identify and exploit trading opportunities. It works through many of the classic trading strategies, so that the trader can select the best strategy for themself in terms of market conditions and personal risk tolerance. It considers the technicalities of how traded options work without being too mathematical.

AUTHOR

Sheldon Natenberg, a recipient of the Traders' Hall of Fame Lifetime Achievement, began his trading career in 1982 at the Chicago Board Options Exchange. Since 1985 he has been trading commodity options at the Chicago Board of Trade, and conducting seminars at many of the world's exchanges.

CONTEXT

- Discusses the most current developments and trends in option products and trading strategies, such as pricing models, volatility considerations, basic and advanced trading strategies, and risk management techniques.
- Explains the underlying fundamentals in an understandable way.
- Looks at option strategies and definitions of different popular pricing models, as well as what goes into developing a theoretical option-pricing model.
- Describes how to determine if an option is over or undervalued.

IMPACT

- Examining both the theory and reality of option trading, it shows that option pricing and modeling cannot be an exact science due to volatility.
- Explains the essentials of volatility in great detail, and how to apply it to different option positions.
- Reveals the mechanics of how to price an option.
- Discusses the Normal distribution and how it relates to volatility and investing in options.

QUOTATIONS

"The direction in which the underlying market moves can have a significant effect on the profitability of an option strategy."

"Every trader who enters the marketplace must balance two opposing considerations, reward and risk."

"Only a trader who fully understands what a model can and cannot do will be able to make the model his servant rather than his master."

MORE INFO

Book:

Cohen, Guy. *The Bible of Options Strategies: The Definitive Guide for Practical Trading Strategies*. London: FT Prentice Hall, 2005. A reference of the world's 60 best options trading strategies.

See Also:

Futures, Options, and Swaps (p. 1366)
Options, Futures, and Other Derivatives (p. 1405)
Derivatives and Quantitative Finance (pp. 1711–1713)

"The direction in which the underlying market moves can have a significant effect on the profitability of an option strategy."

  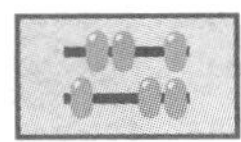      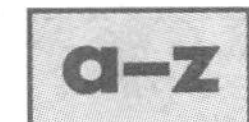

Options, Futures, and Other Derivatives

JOHN C. HULL (8th ed 2011, originally 1989)

WHY READ IT?

- Introduces the world of derivatives, pricing, and risk management in clear and understandable terms.
- Provides a practitioner-focused overview of market dynamics and a feel of real market conditions.
- Offers a comprehensive overview of all the most relevant materials on the range of derivatives, together with derivations of all the formulas.

GETTING STARTED

Options, Futures, and Other Derivatives has long been the standard text for learning about financial engineering and derivatives; now in its seventh edition, it is a comprehensive treatment of all the main topics in mathematical finance. Widely used by academics and practitioners, especially traders, it is one of the most cited books on derivatives, teaching you how to analyze and trade these products.

AUTHOR

John C. Hull (b. 1946) is professor of derivatives and risk management at the Rotman School of Management, University of Toronto. He has acted as consultant to several financial institutions, won many teaching awards, and was voted Financial Engineer of the Year by the International Association of Financial Engineers in 1999.

CONTEXT

- Bridges the gap between the theory and practice of derivatives, and helps develop a working knowledge of how derivatives can be analyzed.
- Examines in detail the valuation of derivatives, presenting a unifying framework for derivative valuation.
- Provides a good grounding in pricing derivatives and explains clearly all the techniques you need for numerical valuation.
- Describes the basic principles of derivatives theory, and presents them in an intuitive way.

IMPACT

- The mathematics is stripped down to essentials, allowing you to quickly grasp the key assumptions underlying various models.
- Suitable for practitioners who want to acquire a working knowledge of how to analyze derivatives, and by MBAs who need a solid grounding in derivatives but want to avoid too much math.
- Updated to include new material on using futures for hedging, numerical procedures, swaps, credit risk, real options, insurance, and derivative crises.
- Includes MS Excel-based software that allows users to calculate options prices, imply volatilities, and calculate Greeks for European options, American options, exotic options, and interest rate derivatives.

QUOTATIONS

"We have now reached the stage where anyone who works in finance needs to understand how derivatives work, how they are used, and how they are priced."

"To avoid the sort of problems Barings encountered, it is very important for both financial and nonfinancial corporations to set up controls to ensure that derivatives are being used for their intended purpose."

"It is essential that all companies define in a clear and unambiguous way limits to the financial risks that can be taken."

MORE INFO

Books:

Baxter, Martin, and Andrew Rennie. *Financial Calculus: An Introduction to Derivative Pricing*. Cambridge, UK: Cambridge University Press, 1996. Follows a pure math approach, focusing theory around mathematical theorems.

Wilmott, Paul. *Derivatives: The Theory and Practice of Financial Engineering.* Chichester, UK: Wiley, 1998. Takes a more applied math approach.

Website:

Support material from the author: www-2.rotman.utoronto.ca/~hull/ofod/

See Also:

Futures, Options, and Swaps (p. 1366)

Derivatives and Quantitative Finance (pp. 1711–1713)

"We have now reached the stage where anyone who works in finance needs to understand how derivatives work, how they are used, and how they are priced."

  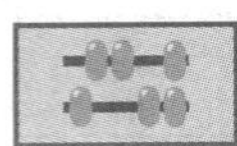   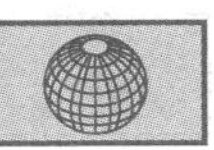   

Poor Economics: A Radical Rethinking of the Way to Fight Global Poverty

ABHIJIT V. BANERJEE and ESTHER DUFLO (2011)

WHY READ IT?

- Examines individual rationality and daily existence for the poor, highlighting issues including the potential detrimental effects of healthcare for the poor, and why they are less likely to take up financial services such as health insurance.
- Based on the authors' fieldwork in 18 countries, it explains why traditional anti-poverty policies are failing due to a lack of real insight, and avoids standard generalizations of either the pro-aid, top-down strategies or the bottom-up, anti-aid approach.
- In an accessible way, it points to how a lack of effective government in some developing countries leads the poor to take on too much responsibility for issues including health, education, and welfare.

GETTING STARTED

Poor Economics, the winner of the 2011 *Financial Times* and Goldman Sachs Business Book of the Year award, seeks solutions for improving the lot of millions of poor people around the world, so that they can contribute to economic and social progress. It explores a range of possible approaches, such as more-effective subsidies, insurance, better jobs, and less education, and argues from the standpoint of behavioral economics that there is no magic bullet, but that economic change should be based on a microeconomic approach to field data.

AUTHORS

Abhijit V. Banerjee (b. 1961) is a professor of economics at MIT and co-founder of the Abdul Latif Jameel Poverty Action Lab. He has also been president of the Bureau for Research and Economic Analysis of Development (BREAD), a research associate of National Bureau of Economic Research (NBER), and is a fellow of both the American Academy of Arts and Sciences and the Econometric Society.

Esther Duflo (b. 1972) is a professor of poverty alleviation and development economics at MIT. She co-founded the Abdul Latif Jameel Poverty Action Lab, and is an NBER research fellow, a BREAD board member, and director of the development economics program at the Center for Economic and Policy Research (CEPR).

CONTEXT

- Contends that rigorous field experimentation, rather than ideological change, is the best way to identify the underlying reasons for poverty and to pinpoint the best ways to overcome it.
- Proposes that a new approach to policymaking is needed from the standpoint of identifying causes.
- Discusses everyday issues for the poor and how they can be resolved, such as obtaining usable water, the value of mosquito nets, and the effectiveness of anti-HIV education campaigns.

IMPACT

- The book is based around the concept of randomized controlled trials, comparing the performance of groups being exposed to different methods.
- Examines many of the paradoxes inherent in a life of poverty, including the impact of borrowing to save, the failures of incentive-driven aid, and the lack of growth of small businesses.
- Offers a strong case that micro-businesses and self-employment are only popular in developing countries due to a lack of full-time jobs.
- Blames the markets for financial services such as health insurance for failing to support development.
- Finds that despite acting rationally, the poor's lack of information on issues such as immunization constrains them from improving their lot.

QUOTATIONS

"Our focus is on the world's poorest. The average poverty line in the fifty countries where most of the poor live is 16 Indian rupees per person per day."

"Recognizing that schools have to serve the students they do have, rather than the ones they perhaps would like to have, may be the first step to having a school system that gives a chance to every child."

"Ideology, ignorance, and inertia—the three Is—on the part of the expert, the aid worker, or the local policy maker, often explain why policies fail and why aid does not have the effect it should."

MORE INFO

Books:

Sachs, Jeffrey D. *The End of Poverty: Economic Possibilities for Our Time*. New York: Penguin Press, 2005. A sustained analysis of how to end poverty and achieve economic success based on an explanation of why wealth and poverty have diverged, and how it is possible to solve the problem through effective change.

Sen, Amartya. *Development As Freedom*. New York: Knopf, 1999. Details the underlying reasons why so many people are without basic freedoms and are constrained by poverty, social deprivation, political tyranny, or cultural authoritarianism, arguing that freedom and sustainability are key to so many potential improvements around the world.

See Also:

Banker to the Poor: The Story of the Grameen Bank (p. 1334)
The Bottom Billion: Why the Poorest Countries Are Failing and What Can Be Done About It (p. 1338)

"Our focus is on the world's poorest. The average poverty line in the fifty countries where most of the poor live is 16 Indian rupees per person per day."

  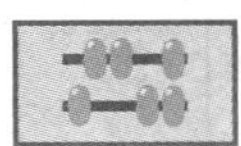   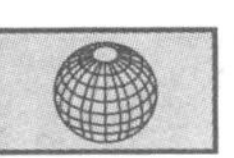   

The Portable MBA in Finance and Accounting

THEODORE GROSSMAN and JOHN LESLIE LIVINGSTONE (EDS)
(4th ed 2009, originally 1992)

WHY READ IT?

- Provides a simplified learning resource for understanding finance and accounting as an organizational tool, especially for those who do not have time to do an MBA.
- Helps explain how the numbers work, how they can be used for competitive advantage, and how to use them for managing a business more effectively.
- Written by a team of professors from top business schools, it offers an overview of all the key concepts, topics, and terms.

GETTING STARTED

The Portable MBA in Finance and Accounting, now in its fourth edition, is a practical handbook on all the main aspects of the subject. It covers the basics for the financial management of companies of any size, including start-ups, and nonprofit organizations. It offers a thorough grounding in applying finance and accounting to business needs, and the skills in budgeting and financial planning that are critical to running a business.

- Explains the main elements of pricing products and making profitable bids, business valuations, and managing financial risks with options, hedges, and derivatives.
- Also focuses on a range of practical topics, such as the responsibilities of governors and directors, bankruptcy, M&A, income tax, managing foreign exchange risk, activity-based costing, and creating a successful business plan.

EDITORS

Theodore Grossman is a senior member of the faculty of Babson College, and was founder of TRG Systems Inc. He consults nationally for retailers and suppliers of retail technology.

John Leslie Livingstone directs his own consulting company. He was previously a professor at Ohio State University, chair at Georgia Institute of Technology, chairman of the Department of Accounting at Babson College, and a senior partner at Coopers & Lybrand.

CONTEXT

- A useful reference for business managers needing an update on finance and accounting tools, techniques, and processes.
- Shows how to quickly grasp financial statements, analyze profitability, develop and use sophisticated cost-analysis tools, and perform financial forecasting and strategic budgeting.

IMPACT

- Provides practical and accessible definitions of key finance and accounting topics.
- Discusses strategies used in leading companies and business units on a daily basis.
- Illustrates how a manager can use spreadsheets to monitor how prices and costs affect business performance, and how financials can be used to build an effective strategy.
- Details how day-to-day business activities translate into the standard accounting reports.
- Assumes no prior financial and accounting knowledge or experience, and avoids excessive mathematics.
- Each chapter has useful internet links and further reading.

QUOTATIONS

"All successful businesspeople should have a good basic understanding of financial statements and of the main financial ratios."

"An estimation of the sustainable portion of earnings should be the centerpiece of analyzing business earnings."

"Businesses cannot operate effectively without estimating the financial implications of their strategic plans and monitoring their progress throughout the year."

MORE INFO

Books:

Bruner, Robert F., Mark R. Eaker, R. Edward Freeman, Robert E. Spekman, Elizabeth Olmsted Teisberg, and S. Venkataraman. *The Portable MBA*. 4th ed. Hoboken, NJ: Wiley, 2003. Based on the first year of an MBA program, this is a comprehensive overview on marketing, economics, ethics, technology, and strategy.

Siciliano, Gene. *Finance for Non-Financial Managers.* New York: McGraw-Hill, 2003. Guide to understanding financial reports, and how to use them to make informed decisions.

Silbiger, Steven. *The Ten-Day MBA: A Step-by-Step Guide to Mastering the Skills Taught in America's Top Business Schools.* New York: W. Morrow, 1993. A reference for MBAs and those in business, providing a basic framework for business courses.

"All successful businesspeople should have a good basic understanding of financial statements and of the main financial ratios."

  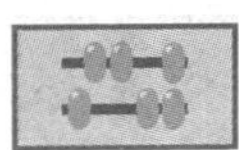      

Portfolio Selection: Efficient Diversification of Investments

HARRY M. MARKOWITZ (2nd ed 1991, originally 1959)

WHY READ IT?

- An acknowledged classic in the evolution of modern finance by a Nobel Prize-winning academic.
- A practical starting point for anyone interested in the efficient management and diversification of financial portfolios.
- Introduces the concepts around portfolio management and explains them in an easily understandable way.

GETTING STARTED

Portfolio Selection is based on the theory that investors should focus on selecting optimal portfolios as opposed to optimal assets, the first major breakthrough in the field of modern financial theory. This seminal work provides an insight into the early thinking and development of portfolio theory, and is a strong reference for individuals and financial institutions selecting optimal portfolios.

AUTHOR

Harry Markowitz (b. 1927) is adjunct professor of finance at Rady School of Management. He developed his seminal theory of portfolio allocation under uncertainty in 1952, and went on to receive a PhD from the University of Chicago. He won the Nobel Memorial Prize in Economic Sciences in 1990, while a professor of finance at Baruch College.

CONTEXT

- Explains the theory upon which modern portfolio theory is based in an accessible manner without recourse to unnecessary mathematical terminology, and combines finance, economics, research, and computers to do so.
- Was the first book to consider risk along with return in portfolio management.
- The concepts are still used today by some of the world's biggest financial institutions to help them optimize returns.
- It created the mathematics of portfolio selection in a model that has turned out to be the indispensable building block from which the theory of the demand for risky securities is constructed.
- Shows the investor how to protect their portfolio and maximize returns.

IMPACT

- Argues that risk is what drives return, rather than being a by-product of the search for higher returns.
- Describes how the portfolio should dominate its constituent assets.
- Shows that the way to minimize risk for a given level of expected return is to minimize the covariance of returns of the assets within that portfolio.
- Provided the foundation for financial economics and computational economics, and the basis for concepts such as the Capital Asset Pricing Model, Efficient Markets Hypothesis, and behavioral finance.

QUOTATIONS

"To reduce risk, it is necessary to avoid a portfolio whose securities are all highly correlated with each other."

"To understand the general properties of large portfolios we must consider the averaging together of large numbers of highly correlated outcomes."

"The results of a portfolio analysis are no more than the logical consequences of its information concerning securities."

MORE INFO

Books:

Elton, Edwin J., and Martin J. Gruber. *Modern Portfolio Theory and Investment Analysis.* New York: Wiley, 1981. Examines the characteristics and analysis of individual securities, as well as the theory and practice of optimally combining securities into portfolios.

Sharpe, William. *Investors and Markets: Portfolio Choices, Asset Prices, and Investment Advice.* Princeton, NJ: Princeton University Press, 2007. Another Nobel Prize winner, this time focusing more on helping investment professionals make better portfolio choices by improving on their asset pricing.

See Also:

Harry Markowitz (p. 1292)
Portfolio Theory and Capital Markets (p. 1409)
Value Investing: Tools and Techniques for Intelligent Investment (p. 1431)
Investment (pp. 1736–1741)

"To reduce risk, it is necessary to avoid a portfolio whose securities are all highly correlated with each other."

  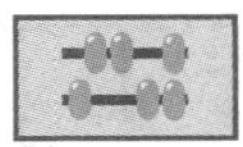      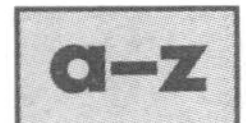

Portfolio Theory and Capital Markets

WILLIAM SHARPE (1970)

WHY READ IT?

- A classic text on investment and portfolio theory, it presents Sharpe's groundbreaking work on the Capital Asset Pricing Model (CAPM).
- It examines how the financial markets operate and how investors can best deal with the uncertainties of pricing and risk.
- Still relevant today for investors and portfolio managers choosing investment portfolios.

GETTING STARTED

Portfolio Theory and Capital Markets introduces the Capital Asset Pricing Model, which has had a profound impact on modern finance and investment. The CAPM details why every investment contains two distinct risks, the systematic risk due to being in the market, and the unsystematic risk of a company's operations, and how they should be assessed in terms of individual securities and portfolios.

AUTHOR

William Sharpe (b. 1934) is professor of finance emeritus at Stanford University's Graduate School of Business. He has served as president of the American Finance Association, been a consultant to Merrill Lynch, and cofounded William F. Sharpe Associates. He was the winner of the 1990 Nobel Memorial Prize in Economic Sciences.

CONTEXT

- The book that introduced CAPM to the investment community, and helped make Sharpe a recognized leader in financial research.
- Discusses the impact of the CAPM on investment theory and practice, and describes its use as a model for measuring portfolio risk along with the return an investor can expect for taking that risk.
- Explains how pricing and risk inform all investments, and the uncertainties and relationship between them impact on market knowledge.
- Discusses the implications of capital market theory, and the measures that can be used to understand the data, including the now widely used Sharpe ratio.

IMPACT

- Provides the theoretical underpinning of and groundwork for such investment standards as modern portfolio theory, derivatives pricing and investment, and equity index funds.
- Synthesizes many related areas of portfolio theory and the capital markets into a practical treatment that takes into account market volatility and uncertainty.
- Integrates historical research and analysis to improve portfolio construction and evaluation.
- Gives a useful overview of applying the economic model to a variety of securities, and how to calculate the payoff of the portfolio.
- Explains how to turn the theories into successful investment practice, and examines the impact this has.

QUOTATIONS

"Almost all empirical research deals with ex post manifestations of investor's expectations and their predictions of risk and correlations, and that such measures are subject to considerable error."

"The theoretical superiority of the market portfolio led directly to the concept of the index fund."

"[Portfolio theory] extends the classical economic model of investment under conditions of complete certainty."

MORE INFO

Books:

Elton, Edwin J., Martin J. Gruber, Stephen J. Brown, and William N. Goetzmann. *Modern Portfolio Theory and Investment Analysis.* New York: Wiley, 1981. Examines the characteristics and analysis of individual securities, as well as the theory and practice of optimally combining securities into portfolios.

Sharpe, William. *Investors and Markets: Portfolio Choices, Asset Prices, and Investment Advice.* Princeton, NJ: Princeton University Press, 2007. Sharpe's most recent work, showing why investment professionals fail to make good portfolio choices unless they properly understand the determinants of asset prices.

See Also:

William F. Sharpe (p. 1309)
Portfolio Selection: Efficient Diversification of Investments (p. 1408)
Value Investing: Tools and Techniques for Intelligent Investment (p. 1431)
Capital Markets and Stock Markets (pp. 1689–1691)

"Almost all empirical research deals with ex post manifestations of investor's expectations and their predictions of risk and correlations, and that such measures are subject to considerable error."

        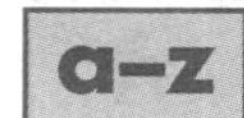

Principles of Corporate Finance

RICHARD A. BREALEY, STEWART C. MYERS, and FRANKLIN ALLEN
(11th ed 2013, originally 1983)

WHY READ IT?

- Provides a comprehensive and practical introduction to the basic concepts and techniques of corporate finance.
- Can be beneficial throughout your career, from learning the basics as a student, to job training, to further learning such as an MBA, or as a reference for practicing financial managers.
- No previous knowledge is needed as the book takes you through all the basic information for implementing financial techniques.

GETTING STARTED

Principles of Corporate Finance is considered the bible of corporate finance, and is a teaching resource in many of the top business schools; now in its ninth edition, it teaches managers how to use financial theory to solve practical problems and to respond to change by implementing financial solutions.

AUTHORS

Richard A. Brealey is visiting professor of finance at the London Business School, and a special adviser to the governor of the Bank of England. He was previously a faculty member at LBS, the former president of the European Finance Association, and director of the American Finance Association.

Stewart C. Myers is professor of financial economics at MIT Sloan School of Management, and a past president of the American Finance Association. He is also a research associate at NBER, and a director of the Cambridge Endowment for Research in Finance.

Franklin Allen is codirector of the Wharton Financial Institutions Center and the Nippon Life professor of finance and economics at the Wharton School, University of Pennsylvania. His is director of the Glenmede Fund and the Glenmede Portfolios, and is scientific adviser to the Central Bank of Sweden.

CONTEXT

- Enables a beginner to gain an in-depth and clear understanding of finance, investment, and the capital markets, demystifying many of the more complex topics.
- Acts as both a practical resource and learning tool on all the main tenets of financial performance and management, from the basic ideas on discounting to option pricing and innovative finance concepts.
- Explores both the theory and practice of corporate finance, as well as the essentials of economic value, the function and structure of the firm, the opportunity cost of capital, the capital asset pricing model, measures of return, risk return payoffs, financing decisions, and modern portfolio theory.

IMPACT

- Useful not only for theoretical study but also for practical work in financial positions, and preparing for examinations.
- Can be used for reviewing first principles, as well as integrating current research.
- Discusses in detail net present value and the best way to value a business.
- Incorporates lesson objectives at the start of each chapter, key points, and summary sections, to facilitate learning.
- Provides straightforward explanations, diagrams, formulas, and examples, and explains the math used in the examples.

QUOTATIONS

"Most investors are not adrenaline junkies; they don't enjoy taking risks. Therefore they require a higher expected return from risky investments."

"Long before the development of modern theories linking risk and expected return, smart financial managers adjusted for risk in capital budgeting."

"Smart managers know that it is often worth paying today for the option to buy or sell an asset tomorrow."

MORE INFO

Books:

Damodaran, Aswath. *Corporate Finance: Theory and Practice.* New York: Wiley, 2000. Extremely applied and practical.

Ross, Stephen A., and Randolph Westerfield. *Fundamentals of Corporate Finance.* Chicago, IL: Irwin, 1995. Presents a unified valuation approach, with a management focus.

Watson, Denzil, and Antony Head. *Corporate Finance: Principles and Practice.* London: Pitman, 1998. Accessible and concise introduction to the key topic areas, incorporating a range of real-world examples.

See Also:

Corporate Financial Management (p. 1344)

"Most investors are not adrenaline junkies; they don't enjoy taking risks. Therefore they require a higher expected return from risky investments."

  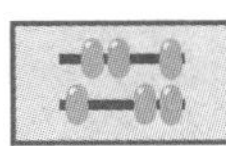   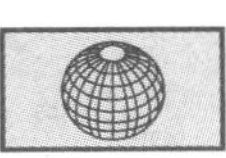   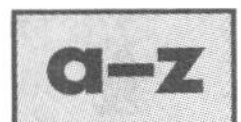

Private Empire: ExxonMobil and American Power

STEVE COLL (2012)

WHY READ IT?

- Examines the history, growth, and cult-like corporate culture of the ExxonMobil Corporation since its formation in 1999.
- Looks inside its corporate headquarters and lobbying offices, particularly at its CEO Lee Raymond and his replacement Rex Tillerson, and at a culture based on discipline and secrecy.
- Includes analysis of the lead-up and consequences of the *Exxon Valdez* accident in 1989, when hundreds of thousands of barrels of crude oil were spilled in Alaskan waters after the tanker ran aground.

GETTING STARTED

Private Empire, the winner of the 2012 *Financial Times* and Goldman Sachs Business Book of the Year award, examines ExxonMobil in the context of the oil industry as a whole, and its ability to affect American foreign policy. It discusses the background to the merger between Exxon and Mobil and ExxonMobil's consequent exponential growth, and highlights how the company has faced many of the challenges of the oil industry—including kidnapping, threats of blackmail, and civil wars—and the problem of maintaining reserves.

AUTHOR

Steve Coll (b. 1958) is an American journalist and writer who has twice won the Pulitzer Prize, and is president of the New America Foundation public policy institute. He previously worked at the *New Yorker* and as a managing editor of the *Washington Post*. His books include *The Bin Ladens* and *Ghost Wars*.

CONTEXT

- Based on over 450 interviews and offering balanced analysis without prejudging such a secretive corporation, it highlights many of the inner operations and uncovers many of the secrets of the company.
- Shows how Exxon moved on from the *Exxon Valdez* incident to become a leading global oil company.
- Details many of the corporation's activities around the world, including problems of collaborating with countries led by dictators, such as Azerbaijan and Kazakhstan, and how its global power is used to help increase its profits and scope.
- Presents some of the huge revenue figures that the company has achieved over the years.

IMPACT

- Discusses how its political lobbying on oil and gas taxes, as well as regulatory change, has had an effect on issues such as global warming.
- Highlights how the scale of the company means that it practically operates its own foreign policy, and shows how this has impinged on or accorded with US policy.
- Demonstrates how ExxonMobil operates within the confines of increasing public interest in the ethical standpoint of large multinational corporations, such as concerns about damage to the environment from overuse of fossil fuels.

QUOTATIONS

"Exxon's size and the nature of its business model meant that it functioned as a corporate state within the American state."

"Compromise was not the Exxon way."

"The early-twenty-first-century politics of global oil and gas production turned on security, nationalism, climate change, and taxation."

MORE INFO

Books:

Ammann, Daniel. *The King of Oil: The Secret Lives of Marc Rich*. New York, St Martin's Press, 2009. A detailed biography of controversial billionaire oil trader Marc Rich, which explores his invention of the spot oil market and dealings with Iran, Angola, South Africa, and Israel, as well as his private life.

Bergin, Tom. *Spills and Spin: The Inside Story of BP*. London: Random House Business Books, 2011. Presents a history of the oil giant, detailing its growth and key figures, and examining the explosion and catastrophic oil spill in the Gulf of Mexico in 2010.

Yergin, Daniel. *The Prize: The Epic Quest for Oil, Money, and Power*. 2nd ed. New York: Free Press, 2008. Provides a summary of the history of the oil industry, highlighting some of the main players in its development and the importance of oil for the world economy and politics, as well as corporate interests.

See Also:

United States of America (pp. 1599–1605)
Oil and Gas (pp. 1638–1639)

"Exxon's size and the nature of its business model meant that it functioned as a corporate state within the American state."

A Random Walk Down Wall Street: The Time-Tested Strategy for Successful Investing

BURTON G. MALKIEL (10th ed 2012, originally 1973)

WHY READ IT?

- An investing classic that is also an entertaining read, this is a concise guide for the novice that challenges all preconceptions about investing.
- Shows how to manage money effectively regardless of personal income, savings, and age, and that diversification is critical to investment success.
- Also of interest to professionals, as it discusses aspects of investment such as the random walk hypothesis, the efficient market hypothesis, and portfolio theory with great insight.

GETTING STARTED

A Random Walk Down Wall Street has been a recognized classic of personal investment since it was published. Now updated and expanded for its ninth edition, it contains new analysis of behavioral finance and strategies for rearranging a retirement portfolio. It provides a history of investing, insights into how professionals invest, and the development of modern portfolio theory, and discusses how this can all be applied to managing an investment portfolio effectively. While warning against get-rich-quick schemes, it advocates asset allocation that is appropriate to both the age and the risk tolerance of the investor.

AUTHOR

Burton G. Malkiel (b. 1932) is professor of economics at Princeton University. He was previously professor of management studies, and dean, at Yale School of Management. He is a past appointee to the President's Council of Economic Advisors, and is a past president of the American Finance Association.

CONTEXT

- Describes a variety of investment types and styles, and recommends which investors should use, depending on personal circumstance.
- Examines market speculations that have spiraled out of control, from the tulip craze and the South Sea bubble, right up to the recent growth and the tech stocks bubbles.
- Believes in a diluted version of the efficient market hypothesis that has occasional inefficiencies, which even good money managers find it difficult to take advantage of, never mind amateur investors.
- Argues against trying to make a profit from either technical or fundamental analysis, but offers some simple rules for stock picking for those determined to invest.
- Considers some of the more complex investment topics such as modern portfolio theory and the capital asset pricing model.

IMPACT

- Provides a guide to investing that is of use to investors of any age, looks at the pitfalls and opportunities of investing, how investors often repeat their mistakes, and how they can be avoided.
- Evaluates the full range of investment opportunities, from stocks, bonds and money markets, to insurance, home ownership, gold, and collectibles.
- Explains the impact of financial risk and the riskiness of practically anything that can be invested in.
- Discusses the difference between having an attitude toward risk and a capacity to deal with it.
- Recommends ignoring the advice of all financial publications and newsletters.

QUOTATIONS

"Greed run amok has been an essential feature of every spectacular boom in history."

"The psychology of speculation is a veritable theatre of the absurd."

"The extent to which the stock market is usefully predictable has been vastly overstated."

MORE INFO

Books:

Bernstein, William J. *Four Pillars of Investing: Lessons for Building a Winning Portfolio*. New York: McGraw-Hill, 2002. With a blend of market history, investing theory, and behavioral finance, this book enables investors to be self-sufficient, and provides the necessary tools to construct successful portfolios.

Malkiel, Burton G. *The Random Walk Guide to Investing: Ten Rules for Financial Success*. New York: WW Norton, 2003. A cut-down version of his classic, which condenses his thoughts into three basic points and 10 rules.

See Also:

Burton Malkiel (p. 1291)

"Greed run amok has been an essential feature of every spectacular boom in history."

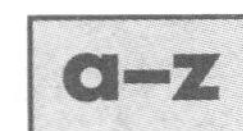

Reminiscences of a Stock Operator

EDWIN LEFÈVRE (1923)

WHY READ IT?

- Remains the most widely read, highly recommended investment book ever written.
- Provides a highly entertaining account of a famous and successful speculator's career in the markets of the early 1900s.
- Offers insights into the workings of "bucket shops" from the turn of the century until the 1920s.
- Contains analysis by financial historian Charles Geisst that gives the readers an understanding of both the financial and cultural contexts.
- Observes the investing, speculating, and market of the time in acute detail.

GETTING STARTED

Reminiscences of a Stock Operator is widely agreed to be a fictionalized biography of Jesse Livermore, a hugely successful American speculator of the early 1900s, who won and lost millions of dollars playing the stock and commodities markets. First published as a series of articles and illustrations in *The Saturday Evening Post*, the entire collection has been revised and published each year since its first publication, with the most recent edition including the original illustrations as they appeared in *The Saturday Evening Post*.

- Shows how Livermore was eventually banned from the bucket shops because of how successful he was.
- Tells the story of how Livermore went on to speculate on Wall Street, where he made and lost his fortune several times over.
- Provides an accessible insight into the stock markets of the time, and how other big traders played the markets.

AUTHOR

Edwin Lefèvre (1871–1943) originally trained as a mining engineer, before becoming a reporter for the *New York Sun*. He was then appointed as US ambassador to various countries, but returned to writing both books, and short stories for such magazines as the *Saturday Evening Post*.

CONTEXT

- Written in the 1920s as a series of articles for the *Saturday Evening Post*, and considered to be the fictionalized biography of Jesse Livermore, a famous trader who operated during the early 20th Century.

IMPACT

- Offers a rare view of an emerging industry before the introduction of modern day technology and legislation.
- Assesses crowd psychology and market timing in a way that is still relevant today.
- Provides a study of a successful, lucrative career begun on a small budget.
- Examines both good and bad practice of the time in an historical context, based on actual events and real people.

QUOTATIONS

"Without faith in his own judgment no man can go very far in this game."

"And still the public loses money as easily as ever, because, though methods change and laws multiply and predatory wealth is curbed, the sucker is still the sucker."

"I always made money when I was sure I was right before I began. What beat me was not having brains enough to stick to my own game."

MORE INFO

Book:

Livermore, Jesse. *How to Trade In Stocks: The Livermore Formula for Combining Time, Element and Price.* New York: Duel, Sloan & Pearce, 1940. The most successful stock trader who ever lived offers traders their first account of his trading system.

See Also:

Edwin Lefèvre (p. 1290)
The Money Game (p. 1397)

  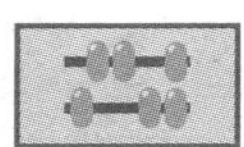      

The Rise and Fall of Strategic Planning

HENRY MINTZBERG (1994)

WHY READ IT?

- Analyzes the history of corporate strategy and its rise to prominence in business thinking, and the current dissatisfaction with strategic planning as being far from effective.
- Thinks that strategic planning is a contradictory concept, as planning encourages stability, while strategy is a more flexible idea, the direction of which can change more easily.
- Shows how over-emphasizing analysis and hard facts limits strategic planning; rather, planning should be visionary and creative.

GETTING STARTED

The Rise and Fall of Strategic Planning argues that strategy cannot be planned as business planning is concerned with analysis, while strategy making is primarily concerned with synthesis. Due to this dichotomy, strategic planning is not working, and can neither provide creativity, nor deal with it when it emerges.

AUTHOR

Henry Mintzberg is professor of management studies at McGill University, Canada, and a visiting scholar at INSEAD, France. He has also been elected as an Officer of the Order of Canada, and as a Distinguished Scholar by the Academy of Management.

CONTEXT

- Describes strategic planners as tending to be detached from the reality of the organization, making false assumptions that discontinuities can be predicted, that the future will resemble the past, and that strategy making can be formalized.
- Examines why planners have typically gathered hard data on their industry, markets, and competitors. Soft data—such as networks of contacts, talking with customers, suppliers, and employees—have been ignored.
- Argues that to gain useful understanding of an organization's competitive situation, soft data need to be dynamically integrated into the planning process as the key to strategy making.
- Sees strategy formulation as having been dominated by logic and analysis, which narrow options, and promotes intuition and creativity as important to the process.
- Describes planners as having value, but only as strategy finders, analysts, and catalysts for change. They need to do more.

IMPACT

- Considers the three main pitfalls of planning practice as the assumptions that discontinuities can be predicted, that planners are in touch with the reality of the organization, and that strategy making can be formalized.
- Points out that if the system does the thinking, then strategy must be separated from business operations—and the thinkers from the doers—something the author thinks lies at the root of the problem with strategic planning.
- Challenges strategists such as Michael Porter about the alternatives for business change.

QUOTATION

"Strategy cannot be planned."

MORE INFO

Books:

Mintzberg, Henry, Bruce Ahlstrand, and Joseph B. Lampel. *Strategy Safari: A Guided Tour Through the Wilds of Strategic Management*. New York: Free Press, 1998. Defines what strategy really means for management decision-making, and draws together the various strands of strategic thought.

Mintzberg, Henry, Bruce Ahlstrand, and Joseph B. Lampel. *Strategy Bites Back*. Harlow, UK: FT Prentice Hall, 2005. Shows how the most interesting and most successful companies have creative, inspiring, and even playful, strategies.

Porter, Michael E. *Competitive Strategy: Techniques for Analyzing Industries and Competitors*. New York: Free Press, 1980. Shows how companies with a clear strategy outperform those whose strategy is unclear.

"Strategy cannot be planned."

 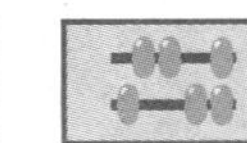   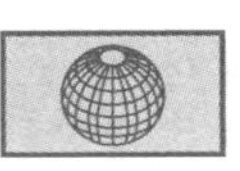   

The Six Sigma Way: How GE, Motorola and Other Top Companies are Honing Their Performance

PETER S. PANDE, ROBERT NEUMAN, and ROLAND R. CAVANAGH (2000)

WHY READ IT?

- The authors are Six Sigma experts who have taught major firms how to effectively implement this business management strategy.
- Explains how Six Sigma operates as a useful and straightforward tool that integrates a quest for perfection into organizational planning.
- Shows you how to launch a Six Sigma initiative, with examples from companies that have introduced the program.

GETTING STARTED

Shows how the Six Sigma strategy can be used to identify problems in manufacturing and business processes, and how these can then be resolved. It explains how the principles of Six Sigma can be applied to reduce costs, improve productivity, increase market share, and have a generally beneficial effect on any type of organization. This is a comprehensive guide for adapting and implementing this established quality management system, originally popularized by Jack Welch when he ran General Electric.

AUTHORS

Peter S. Pande is founder and president of Pivotal Resources, an international consulting firm that has helped companies such as Citicorp and Chevron implement Six Sigma systems.

Robert Neuman is a senior consultant with Pivotal Resources, and speaker on business improvement methods and Six Sigma.

Roland R. Cavanagh is a professional engineer and consultant with Pivotal Resources, who has worked with companies such as America West Airlines, Commonwealth Edison, and Tencor Instruments.

CONTEXT

- Examines how Six Sigma operates as a data-driven management system, with performance objectives that are based on perfect attainment.
- Shows how Six Sigma generates sustained success, introduces performance goals, improves value to customers, promotes learning, and executes strategic change.
- Focuses on the practical implementation and fundamentals, key stages, and quality improvement tools in the Six Sigma system.
- Debunks certain myths around the system, such as the view that it's only of benefit to manufacturing companies, and that it uses a plethora of high-level statistics.
- Examines the differences between Six Sigma and other business strategies such as Total Quality Management.
- Incorporates examples from business leaders and managers that have used Six Sigma in their companies.

IMPACT

- Identifies key elements that can be applied to different business activities and challenges, to help maximize performance.
- Looks at how the benefits of Six Sigma can be achieved by a whole enterprise, or even just a single department within it.
- Presents a roadmap for introducing a Six Sigma program, focusing on basic measurement and analysis techniques, and showing how to achieve support from management and staff.

QUOTATIONS

"Six Sigma can inspire and motivate better ideas and performance from people—and create synergy between individual talents and technical prowess."

"Any level of Six Sigma effort takes an investment in time, energy, and money."

"Results come much faster when an organizations is willing to admit to its shortcomings, learn from them, and start setting priorities to correct them."

MORE INFO

Books:

Breyfogle, Forrest W. *Implementing Six Sigma: Smarter Solutions Using Statistical Methods.* New York: Wiley, 1999. A useful reference on the key tools and how a Six Sigma program is typically implemented.

Pande, Peter S., Robert Neuman, and Roland R. Cavanagh. *The Six Sigma Way Team Fieldbook: An Implementation Guide for Process Improvement Teams.* New York: McGraw-Hill, 2002. A companion guide that focuses on the work of the project management teams.

Pyzdek, Thomas. *The Six Sigma Handbook: The Complete Guide for Greenbelts, Blackbelts, and Managers at All Levels.* New York: McGraw-Hill, 2001. Analyzes the systems and statistical tools that underpin this approach to management.

See Also:

i Business Appraisal and Performance Measurement (pp. 1680–1683)

"Six Sigma can inspire and motivate better ideas and performance from people—and create synergy between individual talents and technical prowess."

  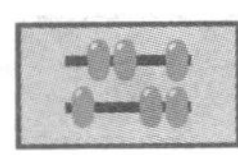      

The Smartest Guys in the Room: The Amazing Rise and Scandalous Fall of Enron

BETHANY MCLEAN and PETER ELKIND (2003)

WHY READ IT?

- Tells of Enron's rise and dramatic fall from a US$70 billion company to bankruptcy.
- Hailed as one of the biggest success stories in corporate America for a generation, the success was shown to be illusory and based on deception. This book details the full story of its downfall and the greed that led to it.
- Examines the corporate culture, where the behavior of senior executives allowed things to escalate.

GETTING STARTED

The Smartest Guys in the Room covers the history of the celebrated and then notorious energy company Enron from its inception to spectacular collapse, the first of a series of major corporate scandals. It details the combination of intelligence and arrogance that helped create an environment that was hailed as visionary but where financial maneuvering for profit overstepped into the illegal.

AUTHORS

Bethany McLean (b. 1970) is editor-at-large for *Fortune*. In 2001 she was one of the first reporters to raise questions about Enron. She was previously an analyst at Goldman Sachs, and has a BA in English and mathematics from Williams College.

Peter Elkind is editor-at-large for *Fortune*. He has twice won the World Leadership Forum's Journalist of the Year award, and has been a guest on numerous radio and television programs. He graduated with honors from Princeton University.

CONTEXT

- Bethany McLean was the first journalist to question the accounting validity of the profits that Enron was making—within a year of her original article, Enron was facing the largest bankruptcy in US history.
- Tells of the top executives: CEO Kenneth Lay, Jeff Skilling, and CFO Andrew Fastow, the huge salaries and bonuses, and the complicity of the lawyers and accountants.
- Details the stories of employees who lost their jobs, disappointed shareholders, executives receiving prison sentences, and even suicide.
- Describes the culture of landing big deals, particularly in new industries and markets, and the subsequent failure to follow through and financially contribute to the company.

IMPACT

- Exposes the complicity of the investment banks, the accountants, and the lawyers that directly benefited without looking into the details behind their profit-making.
- Questions key aspects of corporate governance, such as business performance being pegged to the stock price, so that executives ensured strong financial statements to obscure the fact that the profits were not real.
- Examines Enron's use of "mark to market" accounting, which was largely responsible for obscuring the losses that had been made.
- Depicts the creative accounting methods such as hiding massive debt in off-balance-sheet schemes so that Enron could present itself as fantastically profitable.

QUOTATIONS

"The Enron scandal grew out of a steady accumulation of habits and values and actions that began years before and finally spiraled out of control."

"The tale of Enron is a story of human weakness, of hubris and greed and rampant self-delusion; of ambition run amok; of a grand experiment in the deregulated world; of a business model that didn't work; and of smart people who believed their next gamble would cover their last disaster—and who couldn't admit they were wrong."

"The government [indictment] portrayed Enron as a company that was operated to create the illusion of prosperity, not the reality. In other words: a fraud."

MORE INFO

Books:

Eichenwald, Kurt. *Conspiracy of Fools: A True Story*. New York: Broadway Books, 2005. Also on the Enron story, but portrayed in more of a novelistic style.

Swartz, Mimi, and Sherron Watkins. *Power Failure: The Inside Story of the Collapse of Enron*. New York: Doubleday, 2003. The personal story from Watkins, who was the Enron accountant who tried to alert Kenneth Lay about the accounting improprieties.

Movie:

Gibney, Alex (dir). *Enron: The Smartest Guys in the Room*. Magnolia Pictures, 2005. DVD documentary based on the book.

See Also:

Innovation Corrupted: The Origins and Legacy of Enron's Collapse (p. 1375)

What Went Wrong at Enron: Everyone's Guide to the Largest Bankruptcy in US History (p. 1434)

"The Enron scandal grew out of a steady accumulation of habits and values and actions that began years before and finally spiraled out of control."

  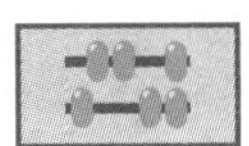   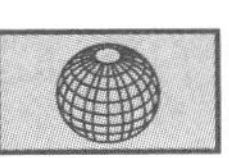   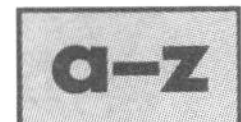

The Snowball: Warren Buffett and the Business of Life

ALICE SCHROEDER (2008)

WHY READ IT?

- The first full biography of Warren Buffett, the most famous investor of all time, written with his full cooperation and collaboration.
- Gives a lucid account of his life and career, from his first financial forays to becoming a revered investment guru.
- Analyses his business deals and strategies, as well as mistakes, by looking at the development of his investing style, his many investment partnerships, and how he built up his fortune.

GETTING STARTED

The Snowball is a comprehensive and revealing biography, based on interviews with Buffett, his wife, children, friends, and business associates—with the help of unprecedented access to his files. It covers the narrative of his upbringing in a middle-American family, his early pursuit of profitable business ideas, how he became a millionaire by the time he was 30, and the deals that helped grow Berkshire Hathaway into a multibillion dollar company. Through this fascinating financial success story, we learn about his personality, intellect, and humanity, as well as about the investment philosophy and worldview that has helped him to great wealth.

AUTHOR

Alice Schroeder is an insurance analyst and a managing director at Morgan Stanley. She received an MBA from the University of Texas at Austin, before becoming a certified public accountant, working for Ernst & Young.

CONTEXT

- *Snowball* is a thorough and inclusive biography of the world's greatest investor, examining his family history, his youthful adventures, and how he developed his investment acumen.
- It shows how Buffett came from a line of small business owners, and how his parents toiled through the Great Depression, and how his somewhat unbalanced mother shaped his outlook on life.
- Reveals that his investment career took off with the purchase of textile firm Berkshire Hathaway, and explains how he grew it into the 12th largest corporation in the United States.
- It combines biographical detail with an examination of his business deals, focusing on the development of his expertise, strategy, and investment philosophy.
- Lays bare the real Buffett—his moral viewpoint, honesty, and integrity, as well as his many contradictions, such as his frugality, eccentric eating habits, and choice of clothing.
- Details how he built up his business expertise, and the success of his many investment partnerships.

IMPACT

- Gives a detailed account of his investments over the years, how he selected companies in which to invest, his definition of risk, and how he decided how much to actually invest in each company.
- Shows his successful preference for long-term investing in sound businesses that he can understand, as well as belief in stewardship and integrity towards these companies.
- Examines how he has evolved into the figurehead of value investing after his guru Benjamin Graham, rather than as someone who follows market bubbles, such as the tech boom of the late 1990s.
- Looks at his dependence on friends and a network of business associates, and how his collaboration with other investment managers proved essential to his success.
- Provides insight into Buffett's focus on customer loyalty, the quality of management, choosing allies carefully, and avoiding unnecessary diversity.
- Shows how he was one of the first to point out the inherent danger in derivative products, and how they could affect the financial system.
- Argues that he prefers being involved in new ventures to personal leadership of his investments.

QUOTATIONS

"Warren may have said he wanted to become a millionaire, but he never said that he would stop there."

"Berkshire's best opportunities always came at times of uncertainty, when others lacked the insight, resources, and fortitude to make the right judgments and commit."

"Cash combined with courage in a crisis is priceless."

MORE INFO

Books:

Buffett, Warren. *The Essays of Warren Buffett: Lessons for Corporate America.* New York: Cardozo Law Review, 1997. A valuable overview of his thinking and strategy, with much financial wisdom from the annual reports he writes for Berkshire Hathaway.

Lowenstein, Roger. *Buffett: The Making of an American Capitalist.* New York: Random House, 1995. An entertaining biography of the man, which delves into his personality as well as investing career. Provides useful detail on the Buffett strategy of betting on the long-term growth of only a few companies.

See Also:

Warren Buffett (p. 1273)

The Warren Buffett Way (p. 1432)

"Warren may have said he wanted to become a millionaire, but he never said that he would stop there."

Stocks for the Long Run: The Definitive Guide to Financial Market Returns and Long-Term Investment Strategies

JEREMY J. SIEGEL (5th ed 2013, originally 1994)

WHY READ IT?

- Siegel is one of the most respected investment strategists, and he here updates his most famous book to cover today's financial world and markets.
- Is of benefit to professional investors, as well as those new to investing and wanting to know how the market works.
- Takes a long-term approach to value investing, arguing that you have to be in it for the long haul to be successful.

GETTING STARTED

Stocks for the Long Run, now in its fourth edition, examines today's turbulent stock market with the strategies, tools, and techniques investors need to achieve meaningful stock returns over time. It provides an understanding of how to implement a reliable investment strategy, and draws upon historical market data to make a compelling case for stocks as the most dependable investment strategy.

AUTHOR

Jeremy J. Siegel (b. 1945) is professor of finance at Wharton, and has also taught at the Graduate School of Business of the University of Chicago. He has worked at JP Morgan, is currently the academic director of the US Securities Industry Institute, and appears frequently in the media.

CONTEXT

- Provides a powerful summary of the historical data available on investing and market returns, to support Siegel's preference for empiricism and a scientific method to choosing stocks.
- Examines the various investment theories and styles that can be used, as well as the economic influences that impact on investing, and the newer products available, such as exchange-traded funds.
- Discusses the value of patience and understanding your timescales before fixing on a particular investment mix.
- Considers how behavior influences investment decisions and potential success.

IMPACT

- Argues for a long-term and patient approach to stock investing and maintaining a long-term portfolio, especially given the regular fluctuations of the stock market.
- Analyzes the merits of short and long-term stock investing, and shows why the latter yields superior performance and lower risk.
- Covers the entire spectrum of opportunities that exist for investors, from international markets to the debate over growth versus value stocks.
- Shows what the long-term investor must address in organizing their portfolio, from diversification to tax advantages.
- Explains how to calculate stock returns and more technical aspects of analyzing stocks.

QUOTATIONS

"Investing in international equities [is] not only important but critical to developing a comprehensive investment strategy."

"The worst course an investor can take is to follow the prevailing sentiment about economic activity."

"Which stocks you own is secondary to whether you own stocks, especially if you maintain a balanced portfolio."

MORE INFO

Book:

Ellis, Charles D. *Winning the Loser's Game: Timeless Strategies for Successful Investing*. 6th ed. New York: McGraw-Hill, 2013. Offers strategies for controlling your investments, by working with the markets instead of against them.

Website:

Jeremy Siegel's website: www.jeremysiegel.com

See Also:

Jeremy Siegel (p. 1310)
The Intelligent Investor (p. 1377)
A Random Walk Down Wall Street: The Time-Tested Strategy for Successful Investing (p. 1412)

"Investing in international equities [is] not only important but critical to developing a comprehensive investment strategy."

     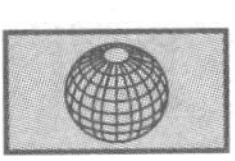   

Take On the Street: What Wall Street and Corporate America Don't Want You to Know

ARTHUR LEVITT (2002)

WHY READ IT?

- Describes how the US securities markets work, their differences, the relationships within them, and why they act as they do.
- Explains the relationship between brokers, analysts, corporations, and politicians.
- A guide to what is happening with an investor's money and how it is possible to maintain control of it.

GETTING STARTED

Take On The Street examines the US stock markets, the dangers faced by individual investors when they invest money in them, and how these dangers can be avoided. It takes the reader through many real examples of malpractice, and uses them to examine how the industry works. The main message is that investors need to research all aspects of the market before investing.

AUTHOR

Arthur Levitt (b. 1931) was the longest-serving chairman of the US Securities and Exchange Commission, which he ran between 1993 and 2001. After working on Wall Street as a broker, and later chairing the American Stock Exchange, he became chairman of the NYC Economic Development Corporation. He has been a senior adviser to the Carlyle Group since leaving the SEC.

CONTEXT

- Provides a personal account of the author's time as the Chairman of the SEC.
- Shows the influence of political parties and individuals on the US stock markets.
- Explains how the brokerage system works, what commissions, bonuses, and fees to expect, and how and when these are paid.
- Offers advice on how to make the most of investments, and how to influence the workings of the markets.
- Examines the Enron collapse to show how the policy changes he championed could help remove corruption within the industry.
- Shows the bigger picture when it comes to trading on the US markets.

IMPACT

- Controversially analyzes the workings of an industry commonly regarded as complex and difficult for outsiders to understand.
- Examines the nature of political influence on those that work within the US markets and how this helped to shape an industry the author believes to be fundamentally corrupt.
- Includes correspondence between the author and key players such as senators and the chief executive of Enron.
- Intended as a warning to market investors, but also as a guide to how to be successful and use the system to advantage.

QUOTATIONS

"By learning about conflicts, motivations, and political favoritism, investors can become more discerning in how they use the power of their money and the power of their shareholder vote."

"America's markets operate by a set of rules that are half written and half custom. That makes the individual's responsibility to discern hidden motivations and conflicts of interest as important as any law or regulation."

"If you understand the basic mechanics of how stocks trade, you'll be better equipped to watch out for your own interests."

MORE INFO

Books:

Casparino, Charles. *Blood on the Street: The Sensational Inside Story of How Wall Street Analysts Duped a Generation of Investors.* New York: Free Press, 2005. A detailed account of the US stock markets in the late 1990s, the Internet bubble, and how doctored research on Internet companies was created by large investment banks at the expense of smaller investors.

Schwager, Jack D. *New Market Wizards: Conversations with America's Top Traders.* New York: HarperBusiness, 1992. A series of interviews with traders focused on the trading psychology, and information and advice on how to be a successful trader.

See Also:

How the Stock Market Works: A Beginner's Guide to Investment (p. 1373)

One Up on Wall Street: How to Use What You Already Know to Make Money in the Market (p. 1403)

"By learning about conflicts, motivations, and political favoritism, investors can become more discerning in how they use the power of their money and the power of their shareholder vote."

Taxes and Business Strategy: A Planning Approach

MYRON S. SCHOLES, MARK A. WOLFSON, MERLE M. ERICKSON, EDWARD L. MAYDEW, and TERRENCE J. SHEVLIN (4th ed 2008, originally 1992)

WHY READ IT?

- Focuses on the importance of effective tax planning in the business and investment decision-making process.
- Presents the implications of certain taxation issues in a straightforward and understandable fashion.
- Analyzes the main tax issues faced by investment bankers, making it an essential resource for planning tax and business strategy.
- Uses an abundance of examples that can be applied directly to situations that arise in the real world.

GETTING STARTED

Taxes and Business Strategy, now in its fourth edition, addresses contemporary tax issues and provides a clear framework for understanding how taxation influences asset prices, equilibrium returns, and the form and content of contractual agreements. It analyzes the critical issues in tax accounting, economics, and corporate strategy in a readable and practical way.

AUTHORS

Myron S. Scholes (b. 1941) is professor of finance emeritus at the Stanford University Graduate School of Business, and chairman of Platinum Grove Asset Management. He has previously been president of the American Finance Association, and was awarded the Nobel Memorial Prize in Economic Sciences in 1997.

Mark A. Wolfson is consulting professor at the Stanford Graduate School of Business. He is a managing partner of Oak Hill Capital Management.

Merle M. Erickson is professor of accounting at the University of Chicago Booth School of Business, and is a coeditor of the *Journal of Accounting Research*. He has received several awards from the American Taxation Association

Edward L. Maydew is the David E. Hoffman distinguished professor of accounting at the Kenan-Flagler Business School, University of North Carolina. He also serves as director of research for the UNC Tax Center.

Terrence J. Shevlin is professor of accounting, the Paul Pigott-PACCAR professor of business administration, and chair, Department of Accounting, at the Foster School of Business, University of Washington.

CONTEXT

- Provides extensive analysis of technical tax rules applied to corporate mergers and acquisitions, an explanation of accounting for income taxes, a discussion on college savings plans, and a practical evaluation of the new tax rates on dividends and capital gains.
- Examines the pervasive impact of tax rules on the investment and financial decisions of businesses.
- Highlights important economic issues found in a multitude of tax-related transactions.
- Focuses more clearly on the economic consequences of alternative contractual arrangements than on the precise tax laws governing the arrangements.

IMPACT

- Relevant for those in investment banking, law, private equity, and other fields where tax plays a large role in determining the outcome and structure of deals and compensation.
- Provides a multi-perspective framework for thinking about tax issues and how taxes can impact the value of a transaction.
- Serves as a guide for any investment banker or experienced professional wanting to develop more efficient structuring alternatives for clients.
- Integrates an understanding of the tax laws with fundamentals of corporate finance and microeconomics.
- Shows how accountants and economists can unify the way they think about taxation.
- Useful as course material for studying tax strategy, investment banking, corporate finance, strategy consulting, money management, and venture capital.

QUOTATIONS

"Traditional approaches to tax planning fail to recognize that effective tax planning and tax minimization are very different things."

"We view efficient tax planning as part of the larger problem of the efficient design of organizations."

"From a social policy standpoint, tax rules are most controversial when they are designed to discriminate among different economic activities."

MORE INFO

Books:

Block, Cheryl D. *Corporate Taxation: Examples And Explanations.* New York: Aspen Law & Business, 1998. Builds your understanding through application of hypothetical examples.

Karayan, John E., Charles W. Stenson, and Joseph W. Neff. *Strategic Corporate Tax Planning.* Hoboken, NJ: Wiley, 2002. A corporate guide to understanding the basic tax implications of everyday business.

See Also:

Myron Scholes (p. 1306)

"Traditional approaches to tax planning fail to recognize that effective tax planning and tax minimization are very different things."

  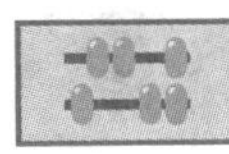   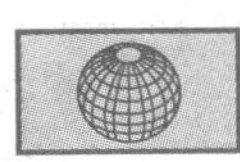   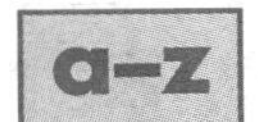

Technical Analysis of the Financial Markets: A Comprehensive Guide to Trading Methods and Applications

JOHN J. MURPHY (1999)

WHY READ IT?

- Offers a clear and concise explanation of the underlying concepts and practical uses of technical analysis in a way that anyone approaching the markets can understand.
- Provides a guide to understanding and interpreting stock and commodity charts, and stock market movements.
- Covers all the essentials for learning how to use technical analysis, before tackling the more advanced principles and the linkages between them.

GETTING STARTED

Technical Analysis of the Financial Markets is known as the "bible" on TA; it is useful both for beginners and experienced traders, as it describes all the main tools, techniques, and applications for market trading and investment based on charting and historic data. Murphy interprets the role of the technical forecasters in today's financial climate, and explains how they apply their techniques to the financial markets.

AUTHOR

John J. Murphy (b. 1952) is founder and president of MurphyMorris Inc. He was previously a director of technical analysis for Merrill Lynch, and was the technical analyst for CNBC TV for many years.

CONTEXT

- Shows how TA uses historic trading data, especially prices, volume, and open interest, in order to predict future prices of securities, currencies, and commodities.
- Examines all the key techniques, such as chart construction, fundamental vs technical analysis, trends, major technical pattern recognition, moving averages, oscillators, times cycles, and computer trading systems.
- Covers different methods of charting, including bar, point, figure, and candlestick, and how patterns and indicators are used.
- Considers all that is needed to understand the underlying structure and psychology of the financial markets.
- Reviews quantitative techniques, such as moving averages, oscillators, and Boillinger Bands.

IMPACT

- Examines the basic structure of all major TA techniques, to help choose the best method for specific trading and investment decisions.
- Details how to apply basic and sophisticated TA methods, emphasizing charting techniques, numerical indicators, and the importance of trend in the financial markets.
- Many believe that technical analysis of stock charts helps you make better trades and more consistent profits; some prefer fundamental analysis, or a combination of the two.
- Provides examples and analysis of market moves and quotes from the author's newsletter.
- Recognized by the main industry associations, and is required reading for both the Chartered Market Technicians designation and the Diploma of International Technical Analysis.

QUOTATIONS

"The statement 'market action discounts everything' forms what is probably the cornerstone of technical analysis."

"The fundamentalist studies the cause of market movement, while the technician studies the effect."

"By following all the markets [the technician] gets an excellent feel for what markets are doing in general, and avoids the 'tunnel vision' that can result from following only one group of markets."

MORE INFO

Books:

Edwards, Robert D., John Magee, and W. H. Charles Bassetti. *Technical Analysis of Stock Trends*. 10th ed. Boca Raton, FL: CRC Press, 2012. Was the first to produce a methodology for interpreting the predictable behavior of investors and markets.

Murphy, John J. *Study Guide for Technical Analysis of the Financial Markets: A Comprehensive Guide to Trading Methods and Applications*. New York: New York Institute of Finance, 1999. Study guide that enables the reader to monitor and review their progress.

Pring, Martin J. *Technical Analysis Explained: The Successful Investor's Guide to Spotting Investment Trends and Turning Points*. New York: McGraw-Hill, 1985. Provides a practical introduction, explaining how to understand, interpret, and predict major market moves.

"The statement 'market action discounts everything' forms what is probably the cornerstone of technical analysis."

Test Your Financial Awareness

JOHN HODGSON (2000)

WHY READ IT?

- Gives an introduction to the basics of finance and what you need to know to successfully operate as a financial manager.
- Uses a question and answer format to help you hone financial skills and knowledge.
- Helps provide an understanding of the "black art" that is finance.

GETTING STARTED

Test Your Financial Awareness introduces basic financial awareness, tests understanding, and enables you to calculate key financial measures as well as make better business decisions. It is useful for those responsible for utilizing assets, and analyzing sales revenues, costs, and expenses; there are financial awareness quizzes throughout to explain all the concepts.

AUTHOR

John Hodgson is a founder of RH International & Associates and CEO of RH America. He also operates as an external tutor on behalf of the Institute of Management and the Institute of Directors, and is on the board of several multinational manufacturing organizations.

CONTEXT

- Provides a basic financial awareness, and assesses financial knowledge and capability with a before-and-after test.
- Explains how to calculate relevant financial measures, and how to improve business decisions based on financial data and analysis.
- Describes a framework for financial management and commercial business processes as part of the core competencies for managers.
- Presents all the key terms in an accessible manner, using diagrams and examples to increase insight and aid retention.
- Helps to clarify confusing financial concepts by highlighting different descriptions used in business, the professional services, and in other countries.

IMPACT

- Addresses the more difficult areas of finance, such as the relationship between the P&L account and the balance sheet.
- Helps you understand how to measure the productivity of a company, and how to improve it.
- Explains the significance of financial accounts in analyzing and improving business performance.
- Assesses the organizational reality behind financial data to provide an understanding of the real health of the company.

QUOTATIONS

"More and more people . . . are expected to make decisions based on financial input."

"To improve return on investment a company aims to maximise the return and minimise the investment parts of the equation."

"The productivity equation can be used by everybody in every organisation to improve company results."

MORE INFO

Books:

Fitzgerald, Ray. *Business Finance for Managers: An Essential Guide to Planning, Control and Decision Making.* 3rd ed. London: Kogan Page, 2002. Practical advice for managers with little financial experience.

Ryan, Bob. *Finance and Accounting for Business.* London: Thomson Learning, 2004. Introduces financial accounting, management accounting and financial management for non-specialists.

"More and more people . . . are expected to make decisions based on financial input."

  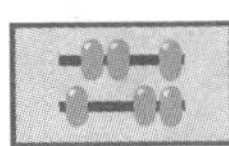   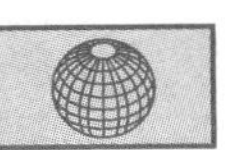   

The Theory of Finance

EUGENE F. FAMA and MERTON H. MILLER (1972)

WHY READ IT?

- Helped shape the field of finance as a separate discipline, and became a landmark book across business schools worldwide.
- Examines the essential theoretical frameworks of finance, and also provides a resource to understanding how the building blocks of finance are organized.
- Uses a framework for learning that combines a variety of approaches to give a full perspective on key concepts.

GETTING STARTED

The Theory of Finance provides a systematic and rigorous grounding in the basic theory of finance by two of the most reputable names in the history of finance. Acting as a textbook rather than an exposition of a single view, it is a groundbreaking treatment of all the developing concepts of finance as we now know them.

AUTHORS

Eugene F. Fama (b. 1939) is professor of finance at the University of Chicago Graduate School of Business. He was the first elected fellow of the American Finance Association, and has received numerous honors. He is a fellow of the Econometric Society and the American Academy of Arts and Sciences.

Merton H. Miller (1923–2000) was a professor at the University of Chicago Graduate School of Business, and a fellow of the Econometric Society, the American Academy of Arts and Sciences, and the American Economic Association. He was awarded the Nobel Memorial Prize in Economic Sciences in 1990.

CONTEXT

- Analyzes certainty models in terms of models of the accumulation and allocation of wealth, durable commodities and investment, market value, dividends, and criteria for optimal investment decisions.
- For uncertainty models, focuses on financing and investment decisions, cost of capital, the expected utility approach to the problem of choice under uncertainty, two-period consumption-investment models, risk, return and market equilibrium, and multi-period models.
- Ensures that all the main points are covered in a variety of ways: mathematically, verbally, graphically, and, in a few cases, by numerical examples.

IMPACT

- Assumes that all securities are traded in perfect markets, but avoids the danger of focusing only on models based on perfect market assumptions by discussing the pitfalls of applying these models to real-world problems without thinking.
- Relies much more on the standard apparatus of economic theory than is typically the case in finance books.
- Its emphasis on essential theory means there's little analysis on practical management or business.
- Does not provide examples about how to apply the theory in quantitative terms, or empirically, to real-world decision problems.
- Presents the material in order of difficulty and logical priority, and keeps mathematical requirements to a minimum.

QUOTATIONS

"The theory of finance is concerned with how individuals and firms allocate resources through time."

"The financing decisions of firms are a matter of indifference to their security holders—it follows that operating and financing decisions are separable."

"There is much evidence in support of the position that perfect market models ... have substantial value in describing real-world economic phenomena."

MORE INFO

Books:

Copeland, Thomas E., and J. Fred Weston. *Financial Theory and Corporate Policy.* Reading, MA: Addison-Wesley, 1983. A useful textbook that presents a unified treatment of finance, combining theory, empirical evidence and applications.

Tirole, Jean. *The Theory of Corporate Finance.* Princeton, NJ: Princeton University Press, 2006. An empirical study structured around the basic finance models.

See Also:

Eugene Fama (p. 1281)
Merton Miller (p. 1294)

"The theory of finance is concerned with how individuals and firms allocate resources through time."

  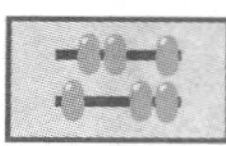      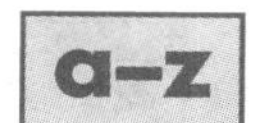

The Theory of Social and Economic Organization

MAX WEBER (1924)

WHY READ IT?

- Weber was a key theorist in the history of social and economic development.
- This is a crucial study for understanding how modern organizations work.
- Argues that bureaucracy is the most efficient way of implementing the rule of law if undertaken properly.

GETTING STARTED

The Theory of Social and Economic Organization grew out of Weber's philosophical inquiries into the nature of authority and how it is transmitted. He identified three types of authority: the charismatic, based on the individual qualities of a leader and reverence for them among his or her followers; the traditional, based on custom and usage; and the rational-legal, based on the rule of objective law.

AUTHOR

Max Weber (1864–1920) was a sociologist and economist, and professor of political economy at the universities of Freiburg and Heidelberg in Germany. He is best known today as one of the founding fathers of modern sociology, and for his scholarly writings.

CONTEXT

- Describes bureaucracy as the most efficient and rational means of organization, and without a realistic substitute.
- Shows how the purely bureaucratic type of administrative organization is, from a purely technical point of view, capable of attaining the highest degree of efficiency. It is, in this sense, the most rational known means of carrying out imperative control over human beings.
- Considers that aspects of the bureaucratic model remain alive and well in a great many organizations where hierarchies, demarcations, and exhaustive rules dominate.
- Found that the most important feature of bureaucracy—its main strength as well as its main weakness—is its impersonality. Discusses how this impersonality is a strength, in that it minimizes the potential abuse of power by leaders, but is a weakness as delays in information movement make bureaucracies slow to react.
- Analyzes the main principles identified as rational-legal bureaucracy, concerning how organizations are structured, specific areas of competence, the structuring of functions, the separation of administration from the means of production, and the recording of the rules and decisions.

IMPACT

- Bureaucratic organization as expounded by Max Weber became the model for the 20th-century organization, and was encapsulated in Alfred Sloan's General Motors and Harold Geneen's ITT.
- Strictly implemented, and in combination with regimented mass-production as practiced by Henry Ford, who echoed some of Weber's thoughts on strict demarcations and a mechanistic approach, it could produce a nightmare scenario for the world of work in the future.
- Today's organizations are imagined as more elusive and ever changing, rather than efficient and static. The regularity of the machine age has given way to the complexity of the information age.

QUOTATION

"Large organizations require that the people involved put the cause of the organization before their own aspirations."

MORE INFO

Books:

Allen, Kieran. *Max Weber: A Critical Introduction*. London: Pluto Press, 2004. Summarizes Weber's ideas and writing.

Giddens, Anthony. *Capitalism and Modern Social Theory: An Analysis of the Writings of Marx, Durkheim and Max Weber*. London: Cambridge University Press, 1971. Provides a basic framework and context for these major writers.

Weber, Max. *The Protestant Ethic and the Spirit of Capitalism*. London: George Allen and Unwin, 1930. Weber's best-known and most controversial work, it contends that the Protestant ethic made possible and encouraged the development of capitalism in the West.

"Large organizations require that the people involved put the cause of the organization before their own aspirations."

This Time Is Different: Eight Centuries of Financial Folly

CARMEN M. REINHART and KENNETH S. ROGOFF (2009)

WHY READ IT?

- Provides a comprehensive guide to a wide range of financial crises across the world over the past eight centuries and argues that these events are universal rites of passage for emerging and advanced economies.
- The authors draw upon the lessons of history to show how much (and how little) we have learned.
- Using clear and sharp analysis the authors explain that crises occur in clusters, and strike with surprisingly consistent frequency, duration, and ferocity.

GETTING STARTED

This Time Is Different provides a detailed quantitative history of financial crises stretching back to the 12th century. The book does not seek to offer a historical narrative, but rather aims to present all the known facts about these crises, and includes a large database illustrated by tables and charts. The book thus provides a source of reference on the causes and consequences of financial crises. It also gives interesting insights into the recent global financial crisis and argues that, if history is a guide, the consequences of the events that began in 2007 are likely to be felt for many years.

AUTHORS

Carmen M. Reinhart (b. 1955) is professor of economics at the University of Maryland and is a regular lecturer at the International Monetary Fund and the World Bank.

Kenneth S. Rogoff (b. 1953) is the Thomas D. Cabot professor of public policy and professor of economics at Harvard University. He is a frequent contributor to the *Wall Street Journal* and the *Financial Times.*

CONTEXT

- Provides a quantitative history of financial crises and a simple message: "We have been here before."
- Argues that no matter how different the latest financial frenzy or crisis always appears, there are usually remarkable similarities with past experience from other countries and from history.
- Claims that recognizing these analogies and precedents is an essential step toward improving our global financial system, both to reduce the risk of future crises and to better handle catastrophes when they do happen.
- Identifies a common theme to the vast range of crises covered by the book, namely that excessive debt accumulation, whether it be by government, banks, corporations, or consumers, often poses greater systemic risks than is apparent during the boom.
- Aims to look at long spans of history to catch sight of rare events that are all too often forgotten, although they turn out to be far more common and similar than people seem to think.
- Contends that government debt is more often the cause of financial disasters than private debt.
- Concludes that international policy-making organizations, such as the International Monetary Fund, have a major responsibility to provide government debt accounts that are more transparent than those available today.

IMPACT

- Provides a wealth of data that interested observers can use to try to compare the causes of the recent global financial crisis with similar episodes in the past, aiding those who wish to analyze the causes and the likely outcomes of the current economic situation.
- Reveals that the widespread belief that modern sovereign default is a phenomenon confined to Latin America and a few poorer European countries is wrong, and that the spell between 2003 and 2008, in which governments generally honored their debt obligations, is far from usual.
- Presents a convincing argument that financial crises follow a rhythm of boom and bust through the ages. Quite simply, it says that while countries, institutions, and financial instruments may change across time, human nature does not.
- Provides food for thought for those who believe that the global financial crisis is over. The authors argue that profound financial crises, such as that which broke in 2008, cause government debt to explode not primarily because of the cost of bailouts, but due to collapsing tax revenues, and that the impact on unemployment, house prices, and output can be long-lasting.

QUOTATIONS

"The essence of the this-time-is-different syndrome is simple. It is rooted in the firmly held belief that financial crises are things that happen to other people in other countries at other times."

"We would argue that there is tremendous scope to strengthen macroprudential supervision by improving the reporting of current data and investing in the development of long-term data so as to gain more perspective on patterns and statistical regularities."

"Policymakers must recognize that banking crises tend to be protracted affairs."

MORE INFO

Book:

Krugman, Paul. *The Return of Depression Economics and the Crisis of 2008*. London: Penguin, 2008. The Nobel Prize-winning economist, who specializes in recessions, takes us through the history of why they happen.

See Also:

The Ascent of Money: A Financial History of the World (p. 1332)
A Farewell to Alms: A Brief Economic History of the World (p. 1352)
The Great Crash, 1929 (p. 1371)

"The essence of the this-time-is-different syndrome is simple. It is rooted in the firmly held belief that financial crises are things that happen to other people in other countries at other times."

  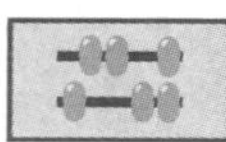   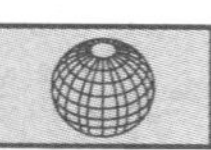   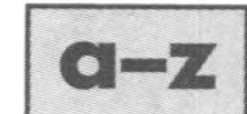

The Tipping Point: How Little Things Can Make a Big Difference

MALCOLM GLADWELL (2000)

WHY READ IT?

- The "tipping point": who does not now know this phrase, first coined in Gladwell's entertaining and instructive bestseller to describe how the culmination of a buildup of small changes can effect a big change?
- Gladwell suggests that ideas, products, messages, and behaviors spread like viruses so that we infect one another with preferences and recommendations, until we reach a tipping point, after which a social epidemic becomes contagious and crosses a threshold to reach saturation point.
- Events such as crime waves and fashion trends are used to explore how ideas spread rapidly, and how once the tipping point is reached, things accelerate and take on a life of their own.
- *The Tipping Point* is itself an example of viral marketing, representing the actual theories discussed in the book.

GETTING STARTED

The Tipping Point examines how social epidemics and trends in different areas, such as fashion, education, business, and crime, reach a "tipping point," where interest moves from being small-scale and contained to having a widespread impact. Using an intriguing metaphor, it suggests this is similar to a viral epidemic, as contagious behavior is caused by only a few people but can spread rapidly once it reaches a certain level. *The Tipping Point* also discusses the types of people that originate major new trends, and the various contexts within which they occur.

AUTHOR

Malcolm Gladwell (b. 1963) was a reporter and then New York bureau chief for the *Washington Post* before becoming a staff writer for *New Yorker* magazine in 1996. His second book, *Blink*, is an international bestseller. His latest book, *Outliers: The Story of Success*, was published in November 2008.

CONTEXT

- Examines what factors must converge to bring about dramatic transformations in society.
- Analyzes trends and looks at recent behavioral research to explain why we are so affected by them.
- Discusses how important context is to creating moments of critical mass and changes to group and societal behavior.
- Looks at how the "broken windows" theory—which argues that leaving things unrepaired leads to further disrepair—was used to reduce crime in New York.
- Presents other examples such as the resurgence in popularity of Hush Puppies, how suicides escalated in Micronesia, and the techniques used to develop *Sesame Street* into a groundbreaking and popular program.

IMPACT

- Looks at why epidemics of viruses, ideas, and behavior do not always originate or spread as you would expect.
- Considers tipping points to be due to three main factors: the power of the messenger, the strength of the message, and the context in which the message is communicated.
- Discusses how the messenger must be highly connected, an expert in a specific area, or a salesman who is persuasive and can spread information.
- Shows how the message is affected by its "stickiness," so that it has an impact and is memorable, and looks at how best to create a sticky message.
- Explains why the power of context and environment is critical to reaching a tipping point and to a trend becoming widespread.

QUOTATIONS

"In a given process or system some people matter more than others."

"...that one dramatic moment in an epidemic when everything can change all at once is the Tipping Point."

"...the world of the Tipping Point is a place where the unexpected becomes expected, where radical change is more than a possibility. It is—contrary to all our expectations—a certainty."

MORE INFO

Books:

Cialdini, Robert. *Influence: How and Why People Agree to Things.* New York: Morrow, 1984. A classic book on persuasion that was an influence on *The Tipping Point*, it attempts to explain why people agree to things, and shows how to become a skilled persuader.

Goleman, Daniel. *Emotional Intelligence.* New York: Bantam Books, 1995. Argues that the traditional IQ is too narrow a measure, and makes the case for "emotional intelligence" being the strongest indicator of human success.

See Also:

Blink: The Power of Thinking without Thinking (p. 1336)

"In a given process or system some people matter more than others."

  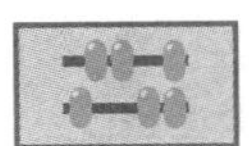      

Traders, Guns, and Money: Knowns and Unknowns in the Dazzling World of Derivatives

SATYAJIT DAS (2006)

WHY READ IT?

- An entertaining introduction to derivatives trading and its impact on the financial markets by a veteran of the industry.
- Tells the inside story of how derivatives began, how they are used, their benefits, and their dangers.
- Describes the mechanics of the financial markets and difficult concepts in a clear, amusing, and somewhat cynical style.

GETTING STARTED

Traders, Guns, and Money is written like a series of vignettes, telling of the author's professional life in finance, and how he got involved with financial derivatives. It describes the complex workings of the industry in an engaging and informative style to provide a behind-the-scenes, warts-and-all examination of the markets.

AUTHOR

Satyajit Das is an expert on derivatives, having worked for the Commonwealth Bank of Australia, Citicorp Investment Bank, and Merrill Lynch, as well as being treasurer of the TNT Group. He now acts as a consultant, advising banks and corporations, and presenting seminars on derivatives.

CONTEXT

- Details the market personalities, their motivations, weaknesses, and ability to resort to questionable tactics to make money.
- Analyzes several well-known examples of the use of derivatives as speculative bets or hedges, and explains their complex nature and significant risks.
- Gives an insightful account of how trading transactions are structured and can easily go wrong.
- Describes how the banks mistakenly believe they understand and properly hedge their own exposure.
- Helps to make sense of some of the more complex derivatives such as CDOs, CCOs, currency swaps, interest rate swaps, and inverse floaters.

IMPACT

- Shows how many of the transactions in the markets are based on misrepresentation and deception, due to the trading culture that drives the business.
- Explains the frustrations involved in working at every level of a bank, as well as the tensions and dynamics between the different functions.
- Outlines why the trading floors of the major financial centers resemble casinos.
- Shows how products are created that have integrated profit for the banks, but although they are marketed as a panacea for investors, this ignores their inherent risk and that they are little understood.
- Provides a useful critique of the run-up to the recent credit crisis.

QUOTATIONS

"The entire investment process is flawed—projected returns are too high and actual returns are measured with tools that the fund managers and asset consultants choose. It is like getting a student to mark their own exams."

"Banks make a lot of money trading, but no money is really ever made in financial markets. They merely transfer wealth: the trick is to tap into the money that flows through the markets."

"Mathematical finance lends credibility and false precision to the dismal reality of risk management."

MORE INFO

See Also:

- A Demon of Our Own Design (p. 1349)
- FIASCO: The Inside Story of a Wall Street Trader (p. 1354)
- Liar's Poker: Rising Through the Wreckage on Wall Street (p. 1386)
- Derivatives and Quantitative Finance (pp. 1711–1713)

"The entire investment process is flawed—projected returns are too high and actual returns are measured with tools that the fund managers and asset consultants choose. It is like getting a student to mark their own exams."

        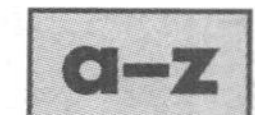

The Undercover Economist

TIM HARFORD (2006)

WHY READ IT?

- Makes economics easier to understand by showing why it is central to how we live.
- Unlocks many of the economic mysteries of daily life in an interesting way.
- Considers how economic policy can influence how we make decisions and allocate resources more efficiently without us realizing it.

GETTING STARTED

The Undercover Economist explores the economic world in an accessible way. While providing an introduction to a variety of economic situations and anomalies, it looks at familiar situations in unfamiliar ways, and gives fresh explanations for the way fundamental principles of the modern economy work.

From why there is a Starbucks on every corner to why good and cheap healthcare is so difficult to achieve, Harford brings to life the underlying reasons why things are as they are.

AUTHOR

Tim Harford (b. 1973) writes editorials and two columns for the *Financial Times*, one inspired by this book, and has presented a TV series, *Trust Me, I'm an Economist*. He has worked at the World Bank, Shell, and as an economics tutor at Oxford University.

CONTEXT

- Offers a new take on economics, explaining unusual aspects of the economy, mainly through the author walking around and observing what he sees, and explaining the underlying economic ideas.
- Examines some key principles of economics such as demand–supply interaction, market failure, perfect markets, globalization, international trade, and comparative advantage, in an interesting way and in non-technical terms.
- Illuminates his concepts with examples from around the world to reveal the intricate pressures that drive not only the economy at large but the everyday choices we make.

IMPACT

- Concentrates on the economics of a situation rather than pushing particular political viewpoints.
- Explores how choices and pricing are used to create the appearance of competitiveness while encouraging those who are price-insensitive to pay as much as possible.
- Discusses the irrationality of everyday economic decisions.
- Defends free markets and sweatshops as a necessary step for progress, contending that the market will dictate standards.
- Leaves the reader to make their own decision about whether a particular practice or action is good or bad.

QUOTATIONS

"Economics is partly about modelling, about articulating basic principles and patterns that operate behind seemingly complex subjects like the rent on farms or coffee bars."

"When economists see the world, they see hidden social patterns, patterns that become evident only when one focuses on the essential underlying processes."

"In the end, economics is about people—something that economists have done a very bad job at explaining."

MORE INFO

Books:

Kay, John. *Everlasting Lightbulbs: How Economics Illuminates the World*. London: Erasmus Press, 2004. Tries to make economics fun and relevant.

Landsburg, Steven E. *The Armchair Economist: Economics and Everyday Life.* New York: Free Press, 1993. Offers an economist's view of human behavior, examining everyday situations.

See Also:

Freakonomics: A Rogue Economist Explores the Hidden Side of Everything (p. 1364)

"Economics is partly about modelling, about articulating basic principles and patterns that operate behind seemingly complex subjects like the rent on farms or coffee bars."

  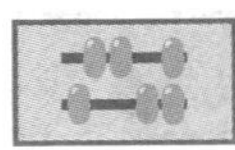   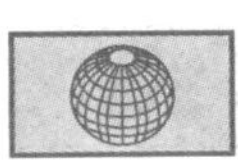   

Valuation: Measuring and Managing the Value of Companies

TIM KOLLER, MARC GOEDHART, and DAVID WESSELS (5th ed 2010, originally 1990)

WHY READ IT?

- Describes how to value companies, and the impact of various business decisions on corporate value.
- Advocates a systematic approach to company valuation, especially when estimating the value of alternative corporate and business strategies.
- Shows how to assess the financial impact of key business transactions such as mergers and acquisitions.

GETTING STARTED

Valuation shows how companies can create shareholder value through effective planning and implementing sound management techniques, based on the measuring and managing the value of a company. The book incorporates the practical experience and valuation knowledge of the consultants McKinsey, where the authors worked.

AUTHORS

Tim Koller is a partner in McKinsey & Co.'s New York office. He leads the firm's Corporate Performance Center and is a member of the leadership group of the firm's global corporate finance practice, as well as leading the firm's research activities in valuation and capital markets. He was formerly with Stern Stewart & Co., and Mobil Corporation.

Marc Goedhart is an associate principal in McKinsey's Amsterdam office and a member of the leadership group of the firm's corporate finance practice in Europe. He taught finance as an assistant professor at Erasmus University in Rotterdam.

David Wessels is an adjunct professor of finance at the Wharton School of the University of Pennsylvania and has been named by *Business Week* as one of America's top business school instructors. He is also a director in Wharton's executive education group, serving on the executive development faculties of several Fortune 500 companies. He was formerly a consultant with McKinsey & Co.

CONTEXT

- Encourages business leaders, corporate finance professionals, and bankers to be more disciplined on corporate valuation, describing a framework for best practice, particularly if undertaking or funding a corporate acquisition.
- Examines existing corporate valuation techniques in relation to company strategies.
- Provides detailed analysis of the discounted cash flow valuation process—how it should be developed, where particular data goes.
- Offers different perspectives, such as value-based management, on how to manage companies in order to create wealth.

IMPACT

- Provides practical guidance for investors who want to use valuation techniques to make passive investments in public companies, and managers who buy or sell business assets for their firms.
- Relies on practice, rather than academic theory, and is useful for those who have no idea how to start the valuation process.
- Real-life examples and detailed explanations of models help an understanding of the key concepts and terms.
- Ensures that all models and formulas suggested in the book can be applied using MS Excel.

QUOTATIONS

"The business environment has become extremely unstable...[which] demands that companies rethink their overall corporate and business-unit strategies almost continuously."

"Businesses are facing a stream of unprecedented challenges—challenges that will have a major impact on shareholder value."

"The essence of corporate strategy is to figure out how the corporation, as intermediary, can add value to the businesses it oversees."

MORE INFO

Books:

Damodaran, Aswath. *Investment Valuation: Tools and Techniques for Determining the Value of Any Asset.* New York: Wiley, 1996. Shows how to value most types of asset, and examines the theory and application of valuation models, highlighting their strengths and weaknesses.

Rappaport, Alfred. *Creating Shareholder Value: The New Standard for Business Performance.* New York: Free Press, 1986. Describes the value-based management concept that Rappaport helped create.

Stewart, G. Bennett. *The Quest for Value.* New York: HarperBusiness, 1991. Looks at the processes that influence and control share prices, and provides a framework for corporate decision-making.

See Also:

Damodaran on Valuation: Security Analysis for Investment and Corporate Finance (p. 1348)
Investment Banking: Valuation, Leveraged Buyouts, and Mergers and Acquisitions (p. 1382)
Corporate Valuation (pp. 1704–1707)

"The business environment has become extremely unstable... [which] demands that companies rethink their overall corporate and business-unit strategies almost continuously."

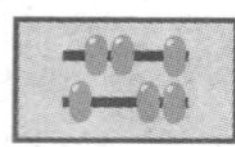

Value at Risk

PHILIPPE JORION (3rd ed 2006, originally 1997)

WHY READ IT?

- Jorion is an acknowledged VAR expert, as well as a respected author and speaker.
- Offers a good introduction and overview of financial risk management and the Value at Risk approach.
- A key text on risk management that has been regularly updated, it examines critical developments for managing a variety of financial risk types.

GETTING STARTED

Value at Risk covers a technical subject in an accessible way, providing insight into risk management, as well as the potential downside of complex derivatives. It details how VAR has evolved over the past two decades, and examines how different risks have been assumed, new risk management techniques have been developed, new regulation has come into being, and how the approach has expanded beyond finance.

AUTHOR

Philippe Jorion (b. 1955) is a professor of finance at the Paul Merage School of Business, University of California at Irvine, where he is also chancellor's professor. He has previously taught at the universities of Columbia, Northwestern, Chicago, and British Columbia.

CONTEXT

- Explains how important it is to use sophisticated risk assessment tools, as proven by the high-profile failures at Barings Bank and Orange County.
- Offers an understandable overview of VAR, explaining that it is a single number that shows how much an investment portfolio may lose, although the actual calculation is a complex operation.
- Provides the most current information available on how to understand and implement VAR, as well as manage more recent dimensions of financial risk.
- Used by the Global Association of Risk Professionals as their main text for the Financial Risk Manager examination.

IMPACT

- Covers the different risk aspects, and discusses how risk management is achieved in banking, investment management, pension funds, and in the corporate world.
- Discusses new developments in risk management, such as extreme value theory, principal components, and copulas.
- Examines how VAR is used for measuring and controlling risk, and creating backtesting models to forecast risk and correlations.
- Details how VAR is also widely used in investment management, as it offers a conceptual framework for risk budgeting and monitoring.
- Analyzes the Basel II capital adequacy rules for commercial banks.
- Includes short questions and exercises at the end of each chapter to help monitor progress.

QUOTATIONS

"Initially confined to measuring market risk, VAR is now being used to control and manage risk actively, well beyond derivatives."

"Corporations are in the business of managing risks."

"The common denominator for any risk management activity is efficient use of capital."

MORE INFO

Books:

Allen, Linda, Jacob Bodoukh, and Anthony Saunders. *Understanding Market, Credit, and Operational Risk: The Value at Risk Approach.* Malden, MA: Blackwell, 2004. A practical guide to using VAR models, and applying the VAR approach to the measurement of market risk, credit risk and operational risk.

Holton, Glyn A. *Value-at-Risk: Theory and Practice.* Boston, MA: Academic Press, 2003. Authoritative guide to implementing real-world VAR measures.

Website:

Solutions to questions and exercises in the book: www.pjorion.com/var

See Also:

Value at Risk (p. 1260)

"Initially confined to measuring market risk, VAR is now being used to control and manage risk actively, well beyond derivatives."

  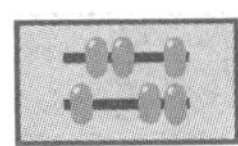   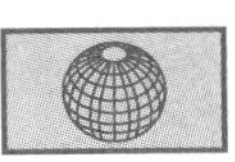   

Value Investing: Tools and Techniques for Intelligent Investment

JAMES MONTIER (2009)

WHY READ IT?

- Provides a compendium of pieces and speeches from the author, written while chief strategist at Société Générale.
- Rejects the precepts of modern portfolio theory (MPT) and almost all of its tools and techniques, including the capital asset pricing model (CAPM).
- Sets out the core principles involved in following a value approach, via Montier's "ten tenets" of investing.

GETTING STARTED

Value Investing argues that MPT hinders rather than helps investors, and explains the most dangerous (and one of the most common) errors that investors make—that is, overpaying for the hope of growth. He provides empirical evidence to support his beliefs. Uniquely, Montier describes how short selling can be a valuable tool for an investor. He also supplies real-time analysis of the market's behavior over the recent financial crisis, one of the most turbulent periods in investment history.

AUTHOR

James Montier is a member of GMO's asset allocation team. Prior to that, he was global strategist for Société Générale and Dresdner Kleinwort. He has been the top-rated analyst in the annual Extel survey for most of the last decade. He is visiting fellow at the University of Durham and a fellow of the Royal Society of Arts.

CONTEXT

- Explains why the value investment approach has allowed the small minority of investors who have adopted this strategy (which has been recognized for at least 75 years) to outperform the market.
- Compares the efficient market hypothesis (EMH) to Monty Python's Dead Parrot—believers just won't accept that it doesn't work.
- Argues that there is an overwhelming body of evidence that shows that CAPM simply does not work, and explains why this is the case.
- Contends that in the world of finance a love of numbers has replaced a desire for critical thinking, and that investment professionals are guilty of using pseudoscience to promote an illusion of safety.
- Argues that diversification "lies close to the heart of many financial disasters" and that holding too many stocks in a portfolio is a key source of underperformance.
- Sets out his 10 core principles of investing, including a focus on value, and adopting a contrarian, unconstrained, and skeptical approach.
- Concludes that valuation is the primary determinant of long-term returns.

IMPACT

- Provides an excellent guide to value investing, written by an expert in this area but in a way that any layman can understand.
- Presents a compelling argument in favor of value investing by using real examples and data to support this approach.
- Convincingly argues that many of the investment tools, techniques, and theories used by investment professionals simply do not work.
- Explains how an investor can use the 10 tenets of Montier's investment creed to adopt the value approach.
- A must-read for investment professionals and individual investors who wish to outperform the market over the long term.

QUOTATIONS

"The efficient market hypothesis (EMH) is the financial equivalent of Monty Python's Dead Parrot. No matter how much you point out that it is dead, the believers just respond that it is simply resting."

"The promise of growth has a seductive allure, much like the siren's song. However, it rarely pays for investors to do what is comfortable."

"Perhaps the most persistent 'mistake' I encounter among investors is overpaying for the hope of growth. Nowhere is this behavior currently more evident than in the context of emerging markets."

MORE INFO

Books:

Graham, Benjamin, and David Dodd. *Security Analysis*. 6th ed. New York: McGraw Hill, 2008. Graham is often described as the first proponent of value investing, and this book first brought the concept to the public's attention. Now updated with commentary.

Greenwald, Bruce C. N., Judd Kahn, Paul D. Sonkin, and Michael van Biema. *Value Investing: From Graham to Buffett and Beyond*. New York: Wiley, 2001. A book that seeks to update and expand Benjamin Graham's ideas.

See Also:

★ Viewpoint: Only White Swans on the Road to Revulsion (pp. 222–223)

Portfolio Selection: Efficient Diversification of Investments (p. 1408)

Portfolio Theory and Capital Markets (p. 1409)

"The efficient market hypothesis (EMH) is the financial equivalent of Monty Python's Dead Parrot. No matter how much you point out that it is dead, the believers just respond that it is simply resting."

  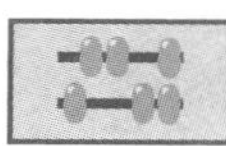      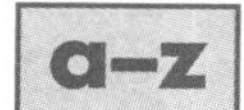

The Warren Buffett Way

ROBERT G. HAGSTROM (2nd ed 2004, originally 1994)

WHY READ IT?

- Shows how Buffett made his name as the most successful investor of our time, and how his investment strategies made his fortune.
- Examines his numerous investments and deals, and the investment strategies and techniques he has used to beat the market over the years, regardless of market fluctuation.
- The author has himself successfully implemented many of Buffett's investment methods, and shows how the individual investor can apply them to their stock market investments.

GETTING STARTED

The Warren Buffett Way is an international bestseller that details Warren Buffett's life, experiences in business and investing in the early days—what companies he invested in and why, and how he made his huge wealth. It explains Buffett's investing strategies in an understandable way, showing how he took up a value investing approach, and underpinned all his work with rigorous research and pragmatism.

AUTHOR

Robert G. Hagstrom (b. 1956) is a business writer, senior vice president and director of Legg Mason Focus Capital, and portfolio manager of the Legg Mason Focus Trust.

CONTEXT

- Provides an insightful summary and overview of the key principles and practices that led to Buffett becoming one of the world's richest men.
- Under the headings of business, management, financial, and value, it discusses the tenets that have guided Buffett's investing.
- Shows how Buffett's philosophy is straightforward, as it depends on buying into companies with business potential, which have a responsible management team, and show continuous growth.
- Argues that the most effective investment methods are based on taking a long-term view, usually picking businesses that are traditional and understandable.
- Other core principles include not worrying about the economy, focusing on the business rather than the stock, and managing a portfolio of businesses.
- Reviews the main influences on Buffett and his career, including Benjamin Graham, Philip Fisher, and Charlie Munger, and illustrates how he integrated their investment philosophies.

IMPACT

- Examines which companies Buffett has invested in over the years, explaining why he decided to buy into them based on his investing principles.
- Discusses the value investing approach, decision-making based on real business value, and the impact of price and value on stock picking.
- Advocates focusing on the return on equity rather than earnings per share, calculating owner earnings to get a true reflection of value, and looking for companies with high profit margins.
- Examines in detail the shareholder reports from Berkshire Hathaway, which can usually only be seen if you are a shareholder.
- Shows how Buffett spends a great deal of time reading annual reports to learn about a company, and offers some of his tips for spotting accounting problems and irregularities in financial documents.

QUOTATIONS

"Warren Buffett is idiosyncratic—it is a source of his success—but his methodology, once understood, is applicable to individuals and institutions alike."

"Warren Buffett's approach to investing is uniquely his own, yet it rests on the bedrock of philosophies absorbed from four powerful figures: Benjamin Graham, Philip Fisher, John Burr Williams, and Charles Munger."

"Buffett believes that a business should achieve good returns on equity while employing little or no debt."

MORE INFO

Book:

Lowenstein, Roger. *Buffett: The Making of an American Capitalist.* New York: Random House, 1995. An entertaining biography of the great man—his life and investments.

See Also:

Warren Buffett (p. 1273)
The Snowball: Warren Buffett and the Business of Life (p. 1417)

"Warren Buffett is idiosyncratic—it is a source of his success—but his methodology, once understood, is applicable to individuals and institutions alike."

  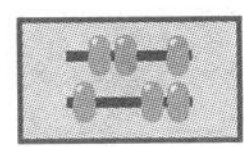      

The Wealth of Nations

ADAM SMITH (1776)

WHY READ IT?

- A classic and seminal work, it is a broad-ranging exploration of commercial and economic first principles that has influenced Western economics ever since it was written.
- Was the first comprehensive exploration of the foundations, workings, and machinations of a free market economy, concepts that are still relevant today.
- Proposes that the invisible hand of free-market competition ensures both the vitality of commercial activity and the ultimate good of all a nation's citizens.

GETTING STARTED

The Wealth of Nations, published in the same year as the signing of the American Declaration of Independence, is a keystone in the philosophical foundations of modern capitalism and the modern market economy. There are few economists over the last 200 years—and fewer politicians of a free-market persuasion—who have not been influenced by it. Smith helped shape the economic policies of British prime ministers and chancellors of the exchequer from the time of Lord North (1770–1782) to the current day.

AUTHOR

Adam Smith (1723–1790) was a political economist and philosopher, professor of logic, and later the chair of moral philosophy, at Glasgow University. He also became a tutor to the Duke of Buccleuch, and was appointed commissioner of customs in Scotland.

CONTEXT

- The central thesis is that capital can best be used for the creation of both individual and national wealth in conditions of minimal interference by government.
- Propounds the concept of the invisible hand; as attempts to better the lot of a nation and its population are generally doomed to failure, and the unintended cumulative effects of self-interested striving are far more effective.
- Argues that the value of a particular good or service is determined by the costs of production. If something is expensive to produce, then its value is similarly high.

IMPACT

- Written without knowledge of the power and scope of modern corporations, let alone the power of brand names and customer loyalty, yet has a powerful relevance for the place of these in the way that Western economies are now run.
- Continues to be thought of as a right-wing manifesto, a logical exposition of the power of market forces.
- The appeal is not only to the right wing in politics, as the system of demarcation and functional separation that Smith expounded also provided the basis for the management theorists of the early 20th century, such as Frederick Winslow Taylor, and practitioners such as Henry Ford.
- The book's legacy to scientific management was the concept of the division of labor.

QUOTATIONS

"The real and effectual discipline which is exercised over a workman is not that of his corporation, but that of his customers."

"[Every individual] intends only his own gain, and he is in this, as in many other cases, led by an invisible hand to promote an end which was no part of his intention."

MORE INFO

Books:

Buchan, James. *The Authentic Adam Smith: His Life and Ideas*. London: WW Norton, 2006. A portrait of the man and his work.

O'Rourke, P. J. *On the Wealth of Nations*. New York: Atlantic Monthly Press, 2007. Entertaining and accessible introduction to the great work.

Smith, Adam. *The Theory of Moral Sentiments*. London: A. Millar, 1759. More of a philosophical work, focusing on the nature of morality.

See Also:

Adam Smith (p. 1311)

"The real and effectual discipline which is exercised over a workman is not that of his corporation, but that of his customers."

  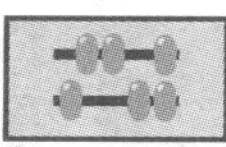   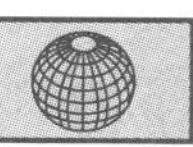   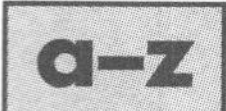

What Went Wrong at Enron: Everyone's Guide to the Largest Bankruptcy in US History

PETER C. FUSARO and ROSS M. MILLER (2002)

WHY READ IT?

- Explains how the biggest collapse in US corporate history occurred, in an interesting and understandable style.
- Discusses how a hugely successful energy company moved away from its core competency to become a major player in many new markets.
- Shows how chasing profits at all costs, and not admitting mistakes, created a corporate culture that was deeply flawed.

GETTING STARTED

In a non-technical manner, *What Went Wrong at Enron* depicts the increasing breakdown in trust and the range of factors that contributed to such a spectacular corporate implosion. It examines the management personalities, company culture, use of special purpose entities, and the executive deception that led to Enron's collapse. Enron is shown to be a corporate product of both a willingness to bend the rules and also the opportunity to do so.

- Provides insight into the problems of mark-to-market accounting principles, the lack of full disclosure, how being the counterparty to every arbitrage trade, and the deals financed by its high stock price, brought about Enron's troubles.
- Looks at what lessons can be learned from Enron's downfall, including the need for improvements in corporate ethics and truthfulness, honesty, and transparency and disclosure in accounting and corporate structures.

IMPACT

- Exposes the lack of strategic knowledge brought about by the separation of senior management and those on an operational level.
- Discusses the problems associated with competing goals within Enron.
- Shows the damage caused by the constant positive spin that was put on performance and style, and how this led to even more exaggeration and fraudulent reporting.
- Looks at how other factors such as debt, competition, inadequate planning, and the loss of investor confidence contributed to the bankruptcy.
- Examines the failings due to self-interest and an intimidatory corporate culture.

AUTHORS

Peter C. Fusaro is chairman of Global Change Associates, cofounded the Energy Hedge Fund Center, and is an energy industry expert.

Ross M. Miller has served as a consultant to several financial institutions, authored many articles, and appeared on TV as an industry expert.

CONTEXT

- Explains how Enron first flourished in the deregulated energy and utility markets, and became a huge corporate success story.
- Shows how Enron became innovative as a key market maker in expanding areas such as water supply, pollution credits, and weather-related risks.
- Discusses the controversial use of special-purpose vehicles.

QUOTATIONS

"The idea that drove Ken Lay and fueled Enron was that of the power of the free market system."

"A series of missteps (both accidental and calculated) and just plain bad luck brought Enron's more nefarious dealings to light, precipitating its ultimate collapse."

"For Enron, everything was beginning to go wrong at once."

MORE INFO

Books:

Cruver, Brian. *Anatomy of Greed: The Unshredded Truth from an Enron Insider.* New York: Carroll & Graf, 2002. An account of Enron's fall, told by a young MBA who joined the company shortly before the scandal broke.

Swartz, Mimi, and Sherron Watkins. *Power Failure: The Inside Story of the Collapse of Enron.* New York: Doubleday, 2003. As told by the Enron accountant who first tried to alert management to the accounting fraud.

See Also:

The Smartest Guys in the Room: The Amazing Rise and Scandalous Fall of Enron (p. 1416)

"The idea that drove Ken Lay and fueled Enron was that of the power of the free market system."

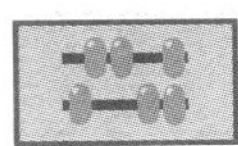

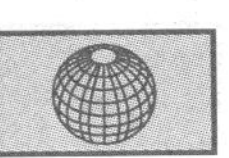

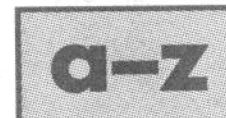

When Genius Failed: The Rise and Fall of Long-Term Capital Management

ROGER LOWENSTEIN (2001)

WHY READ IT?

- Tells the story behind the biggest hedge fund collapse ever seen, that sent shock waves through the whole banking system.
- Provides perceptive detail into all the main characters involved, including two Nobel Prize winners.
- Gives an absorbing account of the Federal Reserve Board's unprecedented move to bail out the fund after thousands of its derivatives contracts started failing.

GETTING STARTED

When Genius Failed uncovers and examines the personalities, academic expertise, professional relationships, and finances behind LTCM's collapse. It details John Meriwether's move from Salomon Brothers, where he formed its renowned arbitrage group by hiring academia's top financial economists, through his founding of LTCM and hiring of former colleagues and future Nobel Prize laureates Robert Merton and Myron Scholes, to create the most successful hedge fund in the world. It was a fund that was based on betting big, so when things turned bad, they had a lot to lose.

AUTHOR

Roger Lowenstein reported for the *Wall Street Journal* for over a decade. His first book was *Buffett: The Making of an American Capitalist*. His work has also appeared in the *New York Times* and *New Republic*, and he writes a column for *SmartMoney Magazine*.

CONTEXT

- Explains how the huge wealth and success of LTCM was based on investing through finding small mispricings of one security versus another, "as if it were vacuuming nickels that others couldn't see," as Myron Scholes put it.
- Shows how the trade modelers failed to give enough importance to freak events in their trading strategy, leading to its downfall.
- When the problems arose, billions disappeared quickly in these arbitrage trades. LTCM assumed that things would swing back and moved too slowly to unwind the trades.

IMPACT

- Explains how the company managed to leverage up so many times on its trades, allowing it to have an exposure to the market over a 100 times its capitalization.
- Shows how the lack of supervision and due diligence contributed to the collapse.
- Details how LTCM was built around consensus in the financial markets, so that the reputation of such famous names overcame concerns about the trades.
- Lines of credit from every major financial institution in these markets entangled the banking system in the problems.
- Exposes major weaknesses in the financial system.

QUOTATIONS

"This one obscure arbitrage fund had amassed an amazing $100 billion in assets, virtually all of it borrowed."

"Every bet was losing simultaneously. The dice were not being thrown at random, or at least they seemed as if tossed by the same malevolent hand."

"Unlike at banks, where independent risk managers watch over traders, Long-Term's partners monitored themselves. Though this enabled them to sidestep the rigidities of a big organization, there was no one to call the partners to account... The traders were their own watchdogs."

MORE INFO

See Also:

Inventing Money: The Story of Long-Term Capital Management and the Legends Behind It (p. 1381)

Liar's Poker: Rising Through the Wreckage on Wall Street (p. 1386)

"This one obscure arbitrage fund had amassed an amazing $100 billion in assets, virtually all of it borrowed."

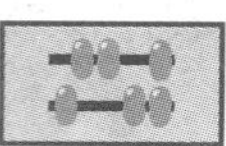

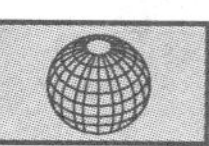

When Markets Collide: Investment Strategies for the Age of Global Economic Change

MOHAMED A. EL-ERIAN (2008)

WHY READ IT?

- Analyzes the origins of the current financial crisis, and how to identify investment opportunities that take advantage of the financial turmoil.
- Examines the recent transformation of the global economy and the capital markets, and presents practical strategies for both investors and policy makers.
- Provides a means for investors to differentiate between the random noise generated by the financial system and key investment signals that should be understood and exploited.

GETTING STARTED

When Markets Collide argues that the current financial market upheaval is a collision between the markets of the past and those in the future. It offers an overview of the rapidly changing international financial system, and describes strategies that capitalize on the opportunities available in the new investment landscape. It also describes how to identify and manage the new types of risks that have emerged, while providing guidance on how best to allocate assets on a long-term basis.

AUTHOR

Mohamed El-Erian (b. 1958) is chief executive officer of PIMCO, one of the largest investment management companies in the world. He was formerly president and chief executive officer of Harvard Management Company, and spent 15 years at the International Money Fund, working on policy, capital market, and multilateral economic issues.

CONTEXT

- Examines the impact of the evolving markets on investment approaches, business strategy, and policy making.
- Provides a range of tools and techniques that aid improved investment, focusing on the mortgage markets, the emerging markets, sovereign wealth funds, and monetary policy.
- Offers insights on the credit crisis from the perspectives of academic economists, policy officials, investment bankers, and fund managers.

IMPACT

- Proposes an action plan for long-term investment success, based on the opportunities offered by this global market shift.
- Discusses the concept of "noise" in the financial system, arguing that it signals important structural changes and realignments affecting the whole investment world.
- Examines the increasing influence of sovereign wealth funds as permanent sources of investment capital with long-term investment objectives.
- Details the reasons why the emerging markets will have a much greater influence on the world economy and capital flows in the future, as developing countries increasingly hold significant and sustainable sources of global growth.
- Shows why China in particular will become a major player in the global markets, driven by an increased focus on consumer demand, and a greater resistance to Western economic downturns.

QUOTATIONS

"The forces behind the recent financial crises have not gone away. Instead, underlying global transformations will play a major role in defining and influencing the investment and policy landscape for years to come."

"Market participants need to adjust if they wish to remain successful in this new age."

"The outcome will be nothing less than a regime change in which the next stage in globalization and integration."

MORE INFO

Books:

Ferguson, Niall. *The Ascent of Money: A Financial History of the World.* New York: Penguin, 2008. An accessible and entertaining examination the history of finance and the money markets, that argues that only by looking back can we work out what to do next to avoid recurrent bubbles and crashes.

Schiff, Peter, with John Downes. *Crash Proof: How to Profit from the Coming Economic Collapse.* Hoboken, NJ: Wiley, 2007. Discusses the economic forces and structural weaknesses underlying the current financial downturn, and the measures that can be taken to protect investments and savings while it lasts.

Soros, George. *The New Paradigm for Financial Markets: The Credit Crisis of 2008 and What It Means.* New York: PublicAffairs, 2008. The investment guru examines the credit crunch, why financial experts and economists need to understand financial bubbles better, and explores why free markets behave as they do.

See Also:

Investment (pp. 1736–1741)

"The forces behind the recent financial crises have not gone away. Instead, underlying global transformations will play a major role in defining and influencing the investment and policy landscape for years to come."

  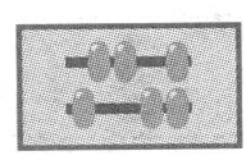   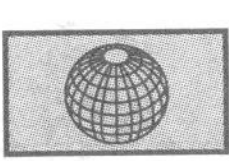   

Wikinomics: How Mass Collaboration Changes Everything

DON TAPSCOTT and ANTHONY D. WILLIAMS (2006)

WHY READ IT?

- Examines the emergence of online mass collaboration, ideas sharing, and peer production, and discusses the future potential.
- Collaboration is changing the way traditional business operates and transforming the economy in unpredictable ways.
- Looks at how companies can access more expert knowledge through idea markets, and develop new capabilities.

GETTING STARTED

Wikinomics argues for a new way of working that is collaborative and ideas driven. A wiki is software that allows anyone with access to a computer to create, edit, and link web-pages, and is part of the development in which users of the web generate content.

The book discusses current collaborations to produce collective results and examines the possibilities of mass collaboration, open-source software, and new innovative working practices.

AUTHORS

Don Tapscott (b. 1947) is chief executive and founder of New Paradigm, a think-tank and strategy consulting company. He teaches at the Rotman School of Management at the University of Toronto, and is the author of a number of books on business strategy and the digital economy.

Anthony D. Williams has been writing about trends in technology and society for over a decade. He advises Fortune 500 firms and international institutions, including the World Bank. He holds a masters in research from the London School of Economics and is vice president and executive editor at New Paradigm.

CONTEXT

- Discusses the new web approach, where sites such as MySpace, YouTube, and Flickr allow mass collaboration from participants in the online community.
- Examines the success of Wikipedia, the user-edited online encyclopedia that is the main example of online collaborative efforts.
- Provides ideas on how to apply wiki frameworks in your daily business.
- Shows how you can expand your business capabilities and deliver value using collective intelligence.
- Analyzes why it isn't possible to apply traditional business techniques to the internet, but that new strategies are needed to accommodate change to the way organizations are run.

IMPACT

- Proposes that sharing your company's dealings with the online community is good for its health and future progress.
- Provides detail on how communities are being formed, and how individuals share ideas and intelligence, accelerate new product development, and efficiently create new revenue streams.
- Discusses business benefits such as the reduced transaction costs possible with mass collaboration, and the new business models benefiting from openness, peering, sharing, and acting globally.

QUOTATIONS

"As a growing number of firms come see the benefits of mass collaboration, this new way of organizing will eventually displace the traditional corporate structures as the economy's primary engine of wealth creation."

"The web is now the foundation for new dynamic forms of community and creative expression."

"[Mass collaboration is] a new way for people to socialize, entertain, innovate, and transact in self-organizing peer-to-peer communities of their choosing."

MORE INFO

Books:

Locke, Christopher, Rick Levine, and Doc Searls. *The Cluetrain Manifesto: The End of Business as Usual*. Cambridge, MA: Perseus Books, 2000. How businesses should embrace new collaborative methods of communication.

Sunstein, Cass R. *Infotopia: How Many Minds Produce Knowledge*. Oxford: Oxford University Press, 2006. How to share information and improve our lives.

Tapscott, Don. *Digital Economy: Promise and Peril in the Age of Networked Intelligence*. New York: McGraw-Hill, 1996. A review of the state of technology innovation at the time.

See Also:

The Mesh: Why the Future of Business Is Sharing (p. 1395)

"As a growing number of firms come see the benefits of mass collaboration, this new way of organizing will eventually displace the traditional corporate structures as the economy's primary engine of wealth creation."

  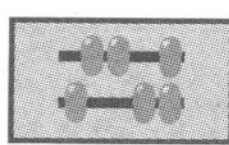   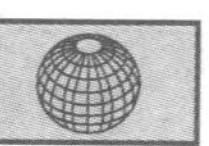   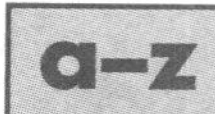

Winning in Emerging Markets: A Road Map for Strategy and Execution

TARUN KHANNA and KRISHNA G. PALEPU (2010)

WHY READ IT?

- Examines the business potential of emerging markets, and offers strategies for success in those markets.
- Offers a new approach to dealing with the opportunities and risks in emerging markets effectively.
- Focuses on institutional voids that occur in developing countries, and the opportunities they bring for both multinationals and local businesses.

GETTING STARTED

Winning in Emerging Markets is aimed at executives and management, as well as policymakers in developing countries who are looking for effective guidance on successfully operating in those markets. It proposes a new strategic approach for organizations operating there, based on defining their structure and finding innovative ways to exploit the opportunities provided by the institutional voids in that structure.

AUTHORS

Tarun Khanna is a professor at Harvard Business School, where he teaches in the executive education programs, and is faculty chair for HBS activities in India. He serves on the boards of a few companies and NGOs, and has been published in a number of economics and management journals. He received an engineering degree from Princeton University and a PhD from Harvard University.

Krishna G. Palepu is professor of business administration and senior associate dean for international development at Harvard Business School. He chairs the HBS executive education programs, and has served on the board of a number of public companies and NGOs. He has a doctorate in management from MIT, and an honorary doctorate from the Helsinki School of Economics and Business Administration.

CONTEXT

- Shows businesses how to develop entry strategies for new markets.
- Proposes a framework for executives wanting to operate globally and make the most of opportunities in the emerging markets, based on identifying institutional voids.
- Explores these voids as being due to a lack of financial organizations that help to ensure effective business operations.
- Shows how to recognize these institutional voids, such as in labor, product, and capital markets, and features of social and political systems.
- Discusses how to create or improve such market institutions for competitive advantage, and recommends a structure for making the most of these opportunities, such as studying the market and developing new capabilities.
- Works as a practical guide backed by real-life useful examples.

IMPACT

- Offers guidance to help companies compete in emerging markets, as a key requisite of the current global economy.
- Explores the various operating conditions in emerging markets.
- Based on many years of hands-on research into the way international companies function in emerging markets.
- Provides toolkits for entrepreneurs in emerging markets to help them evolve these countries into the developed ones, and to collaborate for the good of their societies.
- Discusses how entrepreneurs and governments can assist emerging countries to raise themselves out of poverty.
- Helps to define and execute sustainable business strategies in developing economies.

QUOTATIONS

"For executives of multinationals, emerging markets are growth drivers amid stagnation and financial crisis in developed countries—and the home turfs of powerful new corporate competitors."

"By developing a granular understanding of the underlying market structure of emerging economies ... companies can tailor their strategies and execution in emerging markets to avoid mistakes and outcompete rivals."

"Unshackled by economic liberalization, entrepreneurs and domestic companies in emerging markets are aggressively pursuing growth opportunities at home and overseas."

MORE INFO

Books:

Khanna, Tarun. *Billions of Entrepreneurs: How China and India Are Reshaping Their Futures and Yours*. Boston, MA: Harvard Business School Press, 2007. Khanna's examination of how young Chinese and Indian entrepreneurs are developing new business models and helping to improve social problems and historic tensions in these two growth countries.

Pacek, Nenad, and Daniel Thorniley. *Emerging Markets: Lessons for Business Success and the Outlook for Different Markets*. 2nd ed. London: Profile Books, 2007. This guide to a range of business opportunities in the emerging markets, including China, Russia, East Asia, and Eastern Europe, shows how to avoid mistakes others have made and be aware of problems with current emerging market strategies.

Palepu, Krishna G., and Paul M. Healy. *Business Analysis and Valuation Using Financial Statements: Text and Cases*. 4th ed. Mason, OH: Thomson/South-Western, 2007. Palepu coauthored this student guide into using financial statements to assess company value, financial performance, and creditworthiness. It combines analysis of both accounting and financial techniques, backed by real-life case studies.

See Also:

★ How to Manage Emerging Market Risks with Third Party Insurance (pp. 866–868)
ℹ Emerging Market Finance (pp. 1716–1718)

"For executives of multinationals, emerging markets are growth drivers amid stagnation and financial crisis in developed countries—and the home turfs of powerful new corporate competitors."

COUNTRY AND SECTOR PROFILES

Country and Sector Profiles

This section provides users with an up-to-date world finance almanack in two parts. The first focuses on countries and the second on industries. The information on the countries and industries will be updated online at qfinance.com, so that potential investors, or those interested in conducting business with these countries or within the industries, can quickly ascertain the current state of a particular economy or the latest developments in an industry.

Just over 100 countries are analyzed by our experienced *QFINANCE* writers, who provide up-to-date analysis of the recent and near-term financial outlook for each country using official government sources as well as respected organizations such as the World Bank, the OECD, and the IMF.

Added to this is a wealth of in-depth reference content from the "Countries of the World" section of *Whitaker's Almanack 2013*, published yearly since 1868, comprising:

- Geographical information
- Climate and terrain
- History and politics
- Defence
- Economy and trade
- Education and health
- Culture
- Communications
- External territories

The countries profiled include EU, OECD, and OPEC members, plus composites of MSCI, emerging markets, and MENA indices. We have also included offshore banking centers and the major global financial centers.

The second part of this section provides profiles of 26 of the world's leading industries. These are analyzed on a global basis. Each profile contains the following components:

- Major industry developments—we provide an overview of the main commercial developments affecting the industry in the previous 12 months.
- Market analysis—our writers analyze the key developments in each industry, covering areas such as changes in the regulatory environment, in market share, and in the corporate arena.

Contents

  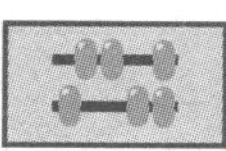      

Algeria

Al-Jumhuriyah al-Jaza'iriyah ad Dimuqratiyah ash Sha'biyah—People's Democratic Republic of Algeria
Area—2,381,741 sq. km
Capital—Algiers (El Djazair, Al Jaza'ir); population, 2,740,000 (2009 est)
Major cities—Djelfa, Batna, Constantine (Qacentina), Oran (Wahran)
Currency—Algerian dinar (DA) of 100 centimes
Population—34,994,937 rising at 1.17% a year (2011 est); Arab-Berber (99%) (est)
Religion—Muslim (Sunni 99%); Christian and Jewish (1%) (est)
Language—Arabic (official), French, Berber dialects
Population density—15 per sq. km (2010)
Urban population—66.5% (2010 est)
Median age (years)—27.6 (2011 est)
National anthem—'Kassaman' ['We Pledge']
National day—1 November (Revolution Day)
Death penalty—Retained (not used since 1993)
CPI score—2.9 (2011)

FINANCIAL OUTLOOK

The IMF's latest country report on Algeria expects the country's economy to grow at around 3.4% through 2013, building on what the IMF anticipates will be growth of 2.5% in 2012. Key to this is the country's buoyant non-hydrocarbon sector and strong domestic consumer demand. The current account surplus was expected to reach 8.1% of GDP in 2012, as higher hydrocarbon prices offset lower export volumes, and to stabilize at 7.0% of GDP in 2013. In 2012 and 2013, the country's foreign-exchange reserves will remain comfortable, the IMF says, at about three years of imports, and external debt levels will remain low. Algeria's oil stabilization fund, net of public debt will stay at around 26% of GDP through 2013, although the government may well come under pressure to release funds prematurely, the IMF says. Inflation remains a concern, as it reached 8.4% in 2012, a 15-year high, and well up from the 4.5% seen in 2011. In May 2012, the Banque d'Algérie raised the required reserve rate from 9% to 11% to reduce liquidity in the economy to combat inflation, but the effect was limited.

CLIMATE AND TERRAIN

Algeria, the second-largest country in Africa after Sudan, is dominated by the Sahara desert, which covers over 80% of its territory. Elevation extremes range from 3,003m (Mt Tahat) to −40m (Chott Melrhir, a salt lake). The mountains are subject to earthquakes, and to flooding during the rainy season (November–March). The temperate northern coastal areas receive the greatest and most frequent rainfall, whereas the interior plateaux are drier and experience cold winters and hot summers.

HISTORY AND POLITICS

Algeria's 1976 constitution was amended in 1989 to reintroduce political pluralism, and was revised in 2008, most notably to remove the limit on presidential terms. The president is directly elected for a five-year term, which may be renewed. The bicameral *Barlaman* comprises the National People's Assembly, the lower house, and the National Council. The assembly has 389 members, directly elected for a five-year term. The National Council has 144 members; 48 are appointed by the president, and 96 are indirectly elected for a six-year term by electoral colleges formed by local councils; half of these elected members are re-elected every three years. Although Algeria is no longer a one-party state, parties based on religion or on race, language, gender or region, are banned under the constitution.

In the 2012 legislative election, the ruling National Liberation Front-led coalition won the most seats and retained control in both houses. In 2009, President Bouteflika was re-elected for a third term, although the coalition suffered a blow in early 2012 after the Movement of Society for Peace party pulled out of the presidential alliance citing political differences.

HEAD OF STATE

President, Defence, Abdelaziz Bouteflika, *elected* 15 April 1999, *re-elected* 2004, 2009

SELECTED GOVERMENT MEMBERS *as at June 2012*

Prime Minister, Ahmed Ouyahia
Deputy Prime Minister, Noureddine Yazid Zerhouni
Finance, Karim Djoudi
Foreign Affairs, Mourad Medelci

ALGERIAN EMBASSY

54 Holland Park, London W11 3RS
T 020-7221 7800
E info@algerianembassy.org.uk
W www.algerianembassy.org.uk
Ambassador Extraordinary and Plenipotentiary, HE Amar Abba, *apptd* 2010

BRITISH EMBASSY

3 Chemin Capitaine Hocine Slimane, Ex Chemin des Glycines, Algiers
T (+213) (770) 085 000
E britishembassy.algiers@fco.gov.uk
W ukinalgeria.fco.gov.uk
Ambassador Extraordinary and Plenipotentiary, HE Martyn Roper, *apptd* 2010

DEFENCE

All aged 16–49, 2010 est	*Males*	*Females*
Available for military service	10,273,129	10,114,552
Fit for military service	8,622,897	8,626,222

Military expenditure—US$8,170m (2011)
Conscription—19–30 years of age; 18 months

ECONOMY AND TRADE

Recent economic reforms and the initiation of a privatisation programme in 1997, combined with high oil prices, resulted in trade surpluses, record foreign exchange reserves and the reduction of foreign debt for Algeria, but diversification away from the energy sector and development of the financial system is slow because of difficulty in attracting foreign investment. A wave of economic protests at the start of 2011 prompted the government to offer more than US$23bn (£14.5bn) in public grants and retroactive benefit increases.

Algeria has substantial oil and gas reserves and the hydrocarbon industry accounts for 30% of GDP, nearly 60% of government revenue and over 95% of export earnings. Services provide 30.2% of GDP, industry 61.5% and agriculture 8.3%. Industries other than oil and gas production and processing include mining, electrical goods, food processing and light industries.

Algeria's main trading partners are the USA, France, Italy, other EU countries and China. The chief imports are capital goods, foodstuffs and consumer goods.

GNI—US$155,537; US$4,450 per capita (2010)
Annual average growth of GDP—2.9% (2011 est)
Inflation rate—4% (2011 est)
Population below poverty line—23% (2006 est)
Unemployment—10% (2010 est)
Total external debt—US$4,421 (2011 est)
Imports—US$40,228m (2010)
Exports—US$57,718m (2010)

BALANCE OF PAYMENTS
Trade—US$17,490m surplus (2010)
Current Account—US$411m surplus (2009)

Trade with UK	*2010*	*2011*
Imports from UK	£345,666,316	£574,130,392
Exports to UK	£592,122,932	£1,498,994,225

EDUCATION AND HEALTH
Literacy rate—76.2% (2008 est)
Gross enrolment ratio (percentage of relevant age group)—primary 110%; tertiary 31% (2010 est)
Health expenditure (per capita)—US$268 (2009)
Hospital beds (per 1,000 people)—1.7 (2004–9)
Life expectancy (years)—74.26 (2010 est)
Mortality rate—4.69 (2011 est)
Birth rate—16.69 (2011 est)
Infant mortality rate—25.81 (2011 est)

COMMUNICATIONS
International airports—11, including Algiers and Constantine
Telecommunications—2.923 million fixed lines (2009); there were 4.7 million internet users in 2009
Internet code—dz; 213 (from UK), 44 (to UK)
Major broadcaster—Enterprise Nationale de Télévision
WPFI score—47,33 (133)

Angola

Republica de Angola—Republic of Angola
Area—1,246,700 sq. km; includes the exclave of Cabinda
Capital—Luanda; population, 4,511,000 (2009 est)
Major cities—Cabinda, Huambo, Lubango
Currency—Kwanza (Kzrl) of 100 centimos
Population—13,338,541 rising at 2.03% a year (2011 est); Ovimbundu (37%), Kimbundu (25%), Bakongo (13%), other African, including Lunda-Chokwe and Ngangela (22%), mestico (2%) (est)
Religion—Christian (predominantly Roman Catholic; indigenous African Christian denominations 25%, Protestant 10%) (est). Some of the rural population practises animism or indigenous religions
Language—Portuguese (official), Bantu
Population density—15 per sq. km (2010)
Urban population—58.5% (2010 est)
Median age (years)—18.1 (2011 est)
National anthem—'Angola Avante' ['Forward Angola']
National day—11 November (Independence Day)
Life expectancy (years)—38.76 (2010 est)
Mortality rate—23.4 (2011 est)
Birth rate—42.91 (2011 est)
Infant mortality rate—175.9 (2011 est)
HIV/AIDS adult prevalence—2% (2009 est)
Death penalty—Abolished for all crimes (since 1992)
CPI score—2.0 (2011)
Literacy rate—70% (2009 est)
Gross enrolment ratio (percentage of relevant age group)—primary 124% (2010 est)
Health expenditure (per capita)—US$204 (2009)
Hospital beds (per 1,000 people)—0.8 (2004–9)

FINANCIAL OUTLOOK
The Angolan economy is expected to have achieved growth of 8.2% in 2012, once all the numbers are in, and the expected growth for 2013 is only slightly lower at 7.1%. The country is in the middle of an IMF program that aims to tighten fiscal and monetary policy along with introducing reforms to the exchange-rate system and the creation of greater financial transparency to stamp out corruption. Widespread poverty means that the government will face large demands on its budget to provide a social safety net for large numbers of people. The social spending side of the budget is expected to continue to amount to some 33.3% of the overall budget for 2012, double what the country spends on defense and public order. In 2013, revenues are expected to start flowing from the Angolan liquefied natural gas (LNG) project. Inflation for 2012 was down slightly on 2011 at around 10% and is expected to fall slightly in 2013.

CLIMATE AND TERRAIN
The land rises from a narrow coastal plain to a vast interior plateau, with desert to the south. The highest point of elevation is 2,620m (Morro do Moco) and the lowest is 0m (Atlantic Ocean). The climate is tropical in the north—with a cool, dry season from April to September and a hot, rainy season from October to March—and sub-tropical in the south and along the coast to Luanda.

HISTORY AND POLITICS
Under the 2010 constitution, the president is chosen by the party with the largest number of seats in the legislature. The unicameral National Assembly has 223 members, elected by proportional representation for a five-year term.

Political pluralism was introduced under the 1991 peace agreement and multiparty elections were held in 1992, though National Union for Total Independence of Angola (UNITA) refused to accept the results. The first legislative elections since 1992 were held in 2008; the People's Movement for the Liberation of Angola won, with 191 seats to UNITA's 16 seats, and formed a new government. A presidential election has not been held since 1992; the new constitution introduced in 2010 ended direct election of the president, created the office of vice-president and abolished the post of prime minister.

  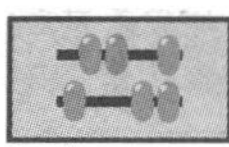      

HEAD OF STATE
President, Jose Eduardo dos Santos, *re-elected* 30 September 1992
Vice-President, Fernando da Piedade dos Santos

SELECTED GOVERNMENT MEMBERS *as at June 2012*
Defence, Candido Pereira dos Santos Van-Dunem
Finance, Carlos Alberto Lopes
Foreign Affairs, George Rebelo Pinto Chicoty
Interior, Sebastiao Jose Antonio Martins

EMBASSY OF THE REPUBLIC OF ANGOLA
22 Dorset Street, London W1U 6QY
T 020-7299 9850
E embassy@angola.org.uk
W www.angola.org.uk
Ambassador Extraordinary and Plenipotentiary, vacant

BRITISH EMBASSY
Rua 17 de Setembro (Caixa Postal 1244), Luanda
T (+244) (22) 233 4583
W ukinangola.fco.gov.uk
Ambassador Extraordinary and Plenipotentiary, HE Richard Wildash, *apptd* 2010

Secession

In the oil-rich northern exclave of Cabinda, separatists have conducted a low-level guerrilla war since the mid-1970s. The government has been unable to end the fighting either through negotiation or by military means. A ceasefire and peace agreement reached in 2006 has not been observed by all parties.

DEFENCE

Aged 16–49, 2010 est	Males	Females
Available for military service	3,062,438	2,964,262
Fir for military service	1,546,781	1,492,308

Military expenditure—US$3,281m (2011)

ECONOMY AND TRADE

The economy is still recovering from decades of mismanagement, corruption and war, but liberalisation and stabilisation are being achieved. Post-war increases in oil, diamond and agricultural production have driven strong economic growth, although the economy contracted in 2009 as the global downturn reduced demand for exports. The extractive industries and infrastructure projects have attracted foreign investment despite the corruption and stifling bureaucracy that have deterred investors in other sectors.

Angola, especially Cabinda, is rich in natural resources. The main industries involve extracting and processing oil (oil production and related activities account for around 85% of GDP), diamonds, metals and other minerals, forestry, fishing, food processing and the manufacture of cement, metal products, tobacco products and textiles, and ship repair. Angola has large areas of good farmland, but the prevalence of unexploded landmines has reduced the area under cultivation and forced many areas back to subsistence agriculture, although coffee, sisal and cotton are produced for export. Despite rising production, the country still imports half of its food.

The main trading partners are China, the USA and Portugal. The principal exports are crude oil, diamonds, refined petroleum products, coffee, sisal, fish, timber and cotton. The main imports are machinery and electrical equipment, vehicles and spare parts, medicines, food, textiles and military goods.

GNI—US$75,515m; US$3,940 per capita (2010)
Annual average growth of GDP—3.7% (2011 est)
Inflation rate—14.3% (2011 est)
Population below poverty line—40.5% (2006 est)
Total external debt—US$19,740m (2011 est)
Exports—US$40,100m (2009)

BALANCE OF PAYMENTS
Trade—US$29,864m surplus (2010)
Current Account—US$7,572 deficit (2009)

Trade with UK	2010	2011
Imports from UK	£534,742,729	£375,797,026
Exports to UK	£43,142,776	£316,477,088

COMMUNICATIONS

Airports—193, including 31 with paved runways
Waterways—Main ports include Luanda, Lobito and Namibe
Roadways—51,429km
Railways—2,764km
Telecommunications—303,200 fixed lines and 8.909 million mobile subscriptions (2010)
Internet code and IDD—ao; 244 (from UK), 44 (to UK)
WPFI score—28,50 (104)

Antigua and Barbuda

Area—442.6 sq. km; Antigua 280 sq. km; Barbuda 161 sq. km; Redonda 1.6 sq. km
Capital—St John's; population, 26,580 (2009 est)
Currency—East Caribbean dollar (EC$) of 100 cents
Population—87,884; rising at 1.28% a year (2011 est)
Religion—Christian 74% (Anglican 26%, Catholic, Methodist and Moravian each less than 10%, Evangelical 25%, Jehovah's Witness 1%), Rastafarian 1% (2001)
Language—English (official)
Population density—202 per sq. km (2010)
Urban population—30% (2010 est)
Median age (years)—30.3 (2011 est)
National anthem—'Fair Antigua, We Salute Thee'
National day—1 November (Independence Day)
Life expectancy (years)—75.48 (2011 est)
Mortality rate—5.73 (2011 est)
Birth rate—16.31 (2011 est)
Infant mortality rate—14.63 (2011 est)
Death penalty—Retained
Literacy rate—99.0% (2009 est)

FINANCIAL OUTLOOK

In the budget for 2013, Antigua's finance and economy minister, Harold Lovell, said that the government expected to see between

1.0% and 1.2% growth in the Antiguan economy in 2013. This would greatly increase government revenues and would be boosted by tax administration system reforms, he said. Antigua should see growth of between 3% and 4% in the medium term, given the implementation of policies that are attractive to investment, he said. Revenue from sales tax is expected to increase by 9% over the sums received in 2012, again, largely on the back of economic growth. The government expects to see recurrent revenue of US$757.8 million, some 7% higher than in 2012, while spending cutbacks mean that expenditure will be around US$5.9 million less than in 2012. Lovell promised that the government would create a business- and investor-friendly environment to secure economic growth.

CLIMATE AND TERRAIN

Unlike most other Leeward Islands, Antigua has few high hills and little forest cover. Its elevation extremes range from 402m (Boggy Peak) to 0m (Caribbean Sea). Barbuda, 48km north of Antigua, is a flat coral island with a large lagoon. Both islands are tropical, but drier than most of the West Indies. They lie within the hurricane belt and are subject to tropical storms and hurricanes between August and October.

HISTORY AND POLITICS

Prehistoric settlers were succeeded by the Arawaks, then the Caribs. Although the islands were discovered by Columbus in 1493, the European (English) settlement of Antigua began only in 1632. Barbuda was colonised from Antigua in 1661. Administered as part of the Leeward Islands Federation from 1871 to 1956, it became internally self-governing in 1967 and fully independent on 1 November 1981.

The head of state is Queen Elizabeth II, represented by the governor-general. The bicameral parliament comprises a senate of 17 members, appointed by the governor-general on the advice of the prime minister and opposition leader, and a House of Representatives of 17 directly elected members; both chambers serve a five-year term.

The United Progressive Party defeated the Antigua Labour Party, which had been in office since 1976, in the 2004 election and was re-elected in 2009.

Governor-General, HE Dame Louise Lake-Tack, GCMG, *apptd* 2007

SELECTED GOVERNMENT MEMBERS *as at June 2012*

Prime Minister, Foreign Affairs, Baldwin Spencer

Minister of Finance and Economy, Harold Lovell

National Security, Leon Errol Cort

HIGH COMMISSION FOR ANTIGUA AND BARBUDA

2nd Floor, 45 Crawford Place, London W1H 4LP

T 020-7258 0070

E enquiries@antigua-barbuda.com

W www.antigua-barbuda.com

High Commissioner, HE Dr Carl Roberts, CMG, *apptd* 2004

BRITISH HIGH COMMISSION

High Commissioner, HE Paul Brummell, *apptd* 2009, resident at Bridgetown, Barbados

DEFENCE

Aged 16–49, 2010 est	*Males*	*Females*
Available for military service	21,141	24,056
Fit for military service	17,676	19,960

Military budget—US$33m (2010)

ECONOMY AND TRADE

The economy is largely based on tourism and related services (contributing over half of GDP), with light manufacturing (bedding, handicrafts, electronic components) for export, and agriculture (livestock, sea island cotton, market gardening, fishing) for local consumption. Economic growth and fiscal reform between 2004–7 enabled the government to reduce public debt. However, from 2008, a decline in tourism caused by the global economic downturn and the collapse of Alan Stanford's Antigua-based financial group (which included Antigua's major financial institution) hit the economy badly and public debt is rising again.

GNI—US$1,179m; US$13,170 per capita (2010)

Annual average growth of GDP—2% (2011 est)

Inflation rate—2.5% (2011 est)

Total external debt—US$359.8m (2006)

BALANCE OF PAYMENTS

Trade—US$472m deficit (2010)

Current Account—US$156 deficit (2010)

Trade with UK	*2010*	*2011*
Imports from UK	£10,727,437	£13,775,238
Exports to UK	£2,261,243	£1,355,432

COMMUNICATIONS

Major broadcasters—The Antigua Labour Party and the Bird family owns or controls many of the country's television and radio stations. Antigua's first independent radio station, Observer Radio, began broadcasting in 2001

Internet code and IDD—ag; 1 268 (from UK), 011 44 (to UK)

Argentina

República Argentina—Argentine Republic

Area—2,780,400 sq. km

Capital—Buenos Aires; population, 12,987,800 (2009 est)

Major cities—Córdoba, La Plata, Mar del Plata, Mendoza, Rosario, Salta, San Miguel de Tucumán, Santa Fé

Currency—Peso of 100 centavos

Population—42,192,494 rising at 0.997% a year (2012 est)

Religion—Christian (Roman Catholic 76%, Pentecostal 8%), Muslim 1% (of which Sunni 60%, Shia 40%) (est)

Language—Spanish (official), Italian, English, German, French

Population density—15 per sq. km (2010)

Urban population—92.4% (2010 est)

Median age (years)—30.5 (2011 est)

National anthem—'Marcha de la Patria' ['March of the Fatherland']

National day—25 May (Revolution Day)

Death penalty—Abolished for all crimes (since 2008)

CPI score—3.0 (2011)

  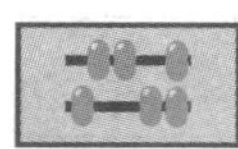      

FINANCIAL OUTLOOK

Booming commodity prices supported a long boom in Argentina until 2012, when growth slowed to just 1.9%, the slowest pace since 2009. Growth averaged 7.8% from 2003 to 2011, reaching 8.9% in 2011. Sluggish global demand, high inflation, a weak 2011–12 grains harvest, and the impact of government import and currency controls on investment lay behind the slowdown. However, the current account balance of payments ran a surplus of US$479 million in 2012, compared with a revised deficit of US$1.57 billion in 2011. The government of President Cristina Fernández de Kirchner continues to pursue controversial economic policies. In 2012, for example, it nationalized the subsidiary of Spain's Repsol, infuriating Spain, one of Argentina's largest foreign investors. In February 2013, the IMF censured Argentina for failing to supply accurate economic data, the first time the global crisis lender has taken such an action against a member.

CLIMATE AND TERRAIN

The Andes mountain range runs the full length of the country, along its western border with Chile, and the area is prone to earthquakes. East of the Andes, the north is mostly subtropical rainforest, the centre contains the vast grasslands of the pampas, and the southern Patagonian plateau is arid and desolate, with glaciers in the far south. The highest point of elevation is 6,960m (Cerro Aconcagua) and the lowest is – 105m (Laguna del Carbon). Temperatures range from subtropical in the north to subantarctic in the south. In Buenos Aires average temperatures are between 17°C and 29°C in January and 5°C and 14°C in June.

HISTORY AND POLITICS

Following constitutional amendments agreed in 1994, the executive president is directly elected for a four-year term, renewable once. The bicameral National Congress consists of a 72-member senate (three members for each province and three for Buenos Aires) and a 257-member Chamber of Deputies. Deputies are directly elected for a four-year term, with half of the seats renewable every two years. Senators are directly elected for a six-year term, with one-third of seats renewable every two years.

The Argentine Republic is a federation of 23 provinces, each with an elected governor and legislature, plus the federal district of Buenos Aires, which has an elected mayor and autonomous government.

The 2011 presidential election was won in the first round by Cristina Fernández de Kirchner, who gained re-election with 54% of the overall vote. The Front for Victory, the pro-presidential wing of the internally divided Judicialist Party, a Peronist grouping, regained control of both houses of the legislature, previously lost in the 2009 mid-term legislative elections.

HEAD OF STATE

President, Cristina Fernández de Kirchner, *sworn in* 10 December 2007, *re-elected* 10 December 2011
Vice-President, Amado Boudou

SELECTED GOVERNMENT MEMBERS *as at June 2012*

Cabinet Chief, Juan Manuel Abal Medina
Defence, Arturo Puricelli
Economy, Hernan Lorenzino
Foreign Relations, Héctor Timerman
Interior, Anibal Randazzo

EMBASSY OF THE ARGENTINE REPUBLIC

65 Brook Street, London W1K 4AH
T 020-7318 1300
E info@argentine-embassy-uk.org
W www.argentine-embassy-uk.org
Ambassador Extraordinary and Plenipotentiary, HE Osvaldo Marsico, *apptd* 2009

BRITISH EMBASSY

Dr Luis Agote 2412, 1425 Buenos Aires
T (+54) (11) 4808 2200
W ukinargentina.fco.gov.uk
Ambassador Extraordinary and Plenipotentiary, HE Shan Morgan, CMG, *apptd* 2008

DEFENCE

Aged 16–49 years, 2010	Males	Females
Available for military service	10,038,967	9,959,134
Fit for military services	8,458,362	8,414,460

Military expenditure—US$3,167m (2011)

ECONOMY AND TRADE

The economy recovered rapidly from the economic collapse of 2001–2, experiencing strong growth from 2003. Argentina restructured its defaulted debt in 2005 and repaid its IMF loan in 2006. Inflation rose sharply in 2007–8 and remains high, pushing up prices, despite a recession in 2008–9 caused by the global downturn. A shortfall in energy supplies remains a problem.

The country is rich in natural resources, particularly lead, zinc, tin, copper, iron ore, manganese, uranium, oil and coal. The fertile pampas supports a strong and export-orientated agricultural sector; the main crops are cereals, oil-bearing seeds, fruit, tea, tobacco and livestock products, especially beef, mutton and wool.

The main industrial activities are food processing (meat-packing, flour-milling, sugar-refining, wine production) and the production of motor vehicles, consumer durables, textiles, chemicals, petrochemicals, printing, metallurgy and steel.

The main trading partners are Brazil, China and the USA. The principal exports include soya beans and derivatives, petroleum and gas, motor vehicles and cereals. The major imports are machinery, motor vehicles, petroleum and natural gas, chemicals and plastics.

GNI—US$358,618m; US$8,620 per capita (2010)
Annual average growth of GDP—8% (2011 est)
Inflation rate—22% (2010 est)
Population below poverty line—30% (2010)
Unemployment—7.8% (2010 est)
Total external debt—US$1,360m (2011)
Imports—US$48,048m (2010)
Exports—US$64,722m (2010)

BALANCE OF PAYMENTS

Trade—US$16,674m surplus (2010)
Current Account—US$6,468m surplus (2009)

Trade with UK	*2010*	*2011*
Imports from UK	£329,605,990	£382,950,498
Exports to UK	£601,594,040	£589,282,548

        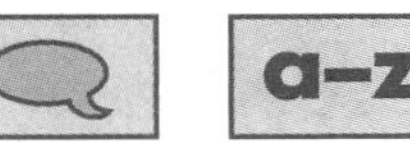

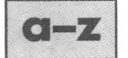

COMMUNICATIONS

Airports—Four major airports, including Buenos Aires, Córdoba, Salta and Rio Gallegos; 156 with paved runways
Waterways—11,000km of inland waterways
Railways—36,966km (state owned)
Roadways—231,374km (69,412km surfaced and 734km motorway)
Telecommunications—10 million fixed lines and 57.3 million mobile phone subscriptions (2010); there were 13.694 million subscribers in 2009
Internet code and IDD—ar; 54 (from UK), 44 (to UK)
Major broadcasters—Telefe, America, Canal 9, Canal 13 (all privately owned)
Press—Over 150 daily newspapers (mainly in Spanish, with some in English and German), including seven major dailies published in Buenos Aires
WPFI score—16,35 (55)

EDUCATION AND HEALTH

Education is compulsory until the age of 14.
Literacy rate—97.7% (2009 est)
Gross enrolment ratio (percentage of relevant age group)—primary 117%; secondary 86%; tertiary 69% (2008 est)
Health expenditure (per capita)—US$730 (2009)
Hospital beds (per 1,000 people)—4.0 (2004–9)
Life expectancy (years)—76.95 (2011 est)
Mortality rate—7.38 (2011 est)
Birth rate—17.54 (2011 est)
Infant mortality rate—10.81 (2011 est)

ARGENTINE ANTARCTIC TERRITORY

The Argentine Antarctic Territory consists of the Antarctic Peninsula and a triangular section extending to the South Pole, defined as the area between 25°W and 74° W and 60°S. This overlaps with both Britain's and Chile's claimed areas. Administratively, the territory is a department of the province of Tierra del Fuego, Antarctica and South Atlantic Islands. The population varies seasonally between approximately 150 and 300 people, all of whom are scientific researchers and their dependents.

Australia

Commonwealth of Australia
Area—7,692,024 sq. km (excluding overseas territories)
Capital—Canberra, in the Australian Capital Territory; population, 384,091 (2009 est)
Major cities—Adelaide, Brisbane, Melbourne, Perth, Sydney
Currency—Australian dollar ($A) of 100 cents
Population—22,0158,576 rising at 1.126% a year (2012 est)
Religion—Christian (Roman Catholic 26%, Anglican 19%, other 19%), Buddhist 2%, Muslim 2%, Hindu 1% (est)
Language—English, Chinese, Italian, Aboriginal languages
Population density—3 per sq. km (2010)
Urban population—89% (2010 est)
Median age (years)—37.7 (2011 est)
National anthem—'Advance Australia Fair'
National day—26 January (Australia Day)
Death penalty—Abolished for all crimes (since 1985)
CPI score—8.8 (2011)

FINANCIAL OUTLOOK

According to official figures released in January 2013, the Australian economy grew by 3.1%, the unemployment rate was at 5.2%, and inflation at 2.0% in 2012, while underlying inflation stood at 2.5%. During the course of the year, the Royal Bank of Australia repeatedly expressed concern over the economy. A resources boom that propelled growth in recent years has lost momentum, largely as a result of the slowdown in China. In addition, the strong Australian dollar has squeezed the profits of manufacturers that rely on overseas markets. Falling inflation towards the end of 2012 gave the central bank scope to cut interest rates. Consumer prices rose 2.2% in Q4 2012, compared with Q4 2011, and 0.2% up on Q3 2012, according to the Australian Bureau of Statistics. Economists had been expecting a 2.4% rise from FY2011. The central bank cut its benchmark cash rate incrementally over the course of 2012 to 3%, matching the low reached in the depths of the global financial crisis, and is targeting an inflation rate of 2–3%.

CLIMATE AND TERRAIN

The majority of Australia is a plateau, with hills, low mountain ranges and sparsely populated deserts in the interior, and tropical wetlands and rainforest in the north-east. Mountain ranges running down the east coast are the source of the Murray and Darling river systems, which flow across the densely populated fertile plain in the south-east. Off the north-east coast is the Great Barrier Reef, the world's largest coral reef. Elevation ranges from 2,229m (Mt Kosciuszko) to −15m (Lake Eyre). The climate is arid or semi-arid in the interior, tropical in the north and temperate in the south and east.

HISTORY AND POLITICS

Under the 1901 constitution, the Commonwealth of Australia is a federation of six states. The constitution defines the powers of the federal government, and residuary legislative power remains with the states.

The head of state is Queen Elizabeth II, represented by the governor-general, who is appointed on the advice of the Australian prime minister. The bicameral parliament consists of the senate and the House of Representatives. The constitution provides that the number of members of the House of Representatives shall be proportionate to the population of each state, with a minimum of five members for each state, and that the number of senators shall be, as nearly as is practicable, half the number of representatives. There are currently 150 members, including two members for the Northern Territory and two for the Australian Capital Territory; they are directly elected for a three-year term. There are 76 senators; each state returns 12 senators, who are directly elected for a six-year term, with half retiring every third year. The Australian Capital Territory and the Northern Territory each return two senators, who are directly elected for a three-year term.

Each of the six states has its own constitution, executive, legislature and judicature. Executive authority is vested in a governor (appointed by the Crown), assisted by a council of ministers or executive council headed by a state premier. There are ten territories, and three—the Australian Capital Territory, Northern Territory and Norfolk Island—have limited self-government, with an executive authority headed by an administrator (appointed by the governor-general), and legislative assembly led by a chief minister. The other territories are directly administered by the federal government.

The Australian Labor Party's (ALP) resounding victory in the 2007 general election ended 11 years of government by a Liberal Party–National Party coalition. Under Kevin Rudd, the ALP reversed many of the previous government's policies, signing the Kyoto protocol on climate change, apologising for past abuses of Aborigines and promising an end to the detention of asylum seekers on small Pacific island states. In June 2010 Mr Rudd was replaced as ALP party leader by deputy prime minister Julia Gillard, who became Australia's first female prime minister. In a general election in August 2010 the ALP won 72 seats, and Ms Gillard formed a minority government with the support of independents.

Governor-General, Quentin Bryce, *apptd* 2008

SELECTED GOVERNMENT MEMBERS *as at May 2012*
Prime Minister, Julia Gillard
Deputy Prime Minister, Treasurer, Wayne Swan
Defence, Stephen Smith

AUSTRALIAN HIGH COMMISSION
Australia House, Strand, London WC2B 4LA
T 020-7379 4334
W www.uk.embassy.gov.au
High Commissioner, HE John Dauth, LVO, *apptd* 2008

BRITISH HIGH COMMISSION
Commonwealth Avenue, Yarralumla, Canberra, ACT 2600
T (+61) (2) 6270 6666
E ukinaustralia@fco.gov.uk
W ukinaustralia.fco.gov.uk
High Commissioner, HE Paul Madden, *apptd* 2011

STATES AND TERRITORIES

	Area (sq. km)	Population (2011 est)	Capital	Premier (2011)
Australian Capital Territory (ACT)	2,358	365,400	Canberra	Katy Gallagher†
New South Wales (NSW)	800,642	7,303,700	Sydney	Barry O'Farrell
Northern Territory (NT)	1,349,129	230,200	Darwin*	Paul Henderson†
Queensland (Qld)	1,730,648	4,580,700	Brisbane	Anna Bligh
South Australia (SA)	983,482	1,657,000	Adelaide	Jay Weatherill
Tasmania (Tas.)	68,401	510,600	Hobart	Lara Giddings
Victoria (Vic.)	227,416	5,624,100	Melbourne	Ted Baillieu
Western Australia (WA)	2,529,875	2,346,400	Perth	Colin Barnett

* Seat of administration † Chief Minister

DEFENCE

Aged 16–24, 2010 est	Males	Females
Available for military service	5,316,464	5,116,722
Fit for military service	4,411,958	4,239,985

Military expenditure—US$22,955m (2011)

ECONOMY AND TRADE

Australia has a highly diversified and internationally competitive market economy that saw sustained strong growth from the early 1990s until 2008. It weathered the global downturn better than most developed countries, avoiding recession through a government fiscal stimulus package and low interest rates. Recent problems have been climate related, with agricultural output, a key export sector, down by about 20% in 2006 owing to the worst drought in a century, and agriculture, mining and infrastructure hit badly by extensive flooding in Queensland, the eastern seaboard and Victoria in 2010–11. The service sector contributes 71.2% of GDP and employs 75% of the workforce; industry accounts for 24.8% of GDP and 21.1% of labour; and agriculture contributes 4% of GDP and employs 3.6% of the workforce.

The diversity of Australia's climate and soil conditions means that a wide range of crops can be grown, although most are confined to specific regions. Scant or erratic rainfall, limited scope for irrigation and unsuitable soils or topography have restricted intensive agriculture, although wheat is a major export and sugar cane and fruit are important crops. Cattle and sheep ranching is widespread, providing meat, meat derivatives, wool and dairy products.

Significant natural resources include bauxite, coal, copper, diamonds, gold, iron ore, lead, mineral salts, nickel, silver, tin, tungsten, uranium, zinc, oil and natural gas. The main industrial activities are mining, the production of industrial and transport equipment, chemicals and steel, and food processing. Production and processing of hydrocarbons are expected to increase once the oil and gas fields in the Timor Sea begin production.

Over the past 20 years, the focus of Australia's trade, like its foreign policy, has shifted from Europe to Asia and the Pacific region. It is a leading member of the Asia-Pacific Economic Cooperation forum, and a free-trade agreement (FTA) between Australia and the ASEAN countries entered into force in 2010; it is also negotiating for FTAs with China, Japan, South Korea and Malaysia. Major trading partners include China, Japan, South Korea, India, Thailand, Singapore and Germany. The chief exports are coal, iron ore, gold, meat, wool, alumina, wheat, machinery and transport equipment. The main imports are machinery and transport equipment, computers, office and telecommunications equipment, crude oil and petroleum products.

GNI—US$900,676m; US$43,770 per capita (2009)
Annual average growth of GDP—1.8% (2011 est)
Inflation rate—3.4% (2011 est)
Unemployment—5.2% (2010 est)
Total external debt—US$1,377,000m (2011)
Imports—US$201,641m (2010)
Exports—US$212,358m (2010)

BALANCE OF PAYMENTS
Trade—US$10,718m surplus (2010)
Current Account—US$33,089m deficit (2010)

Trade with UK	2010	2011
Imports from UK	£3,328,979,042	£4,179,093,807
Exports to UK	£4,305,486,888	£2,408,042,382

COMMUNICATIONS

Airports—326 (with paved runways); there are international airports in each of the eight territories
Waterways—2,000km; major ports in all of the state capitals except Hobart
Railways—38,445km
Roadways—818,356km
Telecommunications—8.66 million fixed lines and 22.5 million mobile phone subscriptions (2010); there were 15.81 million internet subscribers in 2009
Internet country code and IDD—au; 61 (from UK), 11 41 (to UK)

  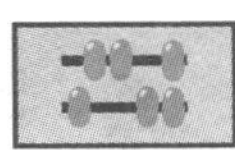      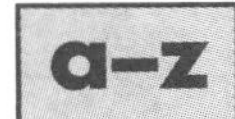

Major broadcasters—The Australian Broadcasting Corporation (ABC) and Special Broadcasting Service (SBS); other major television networks include Australia Network and Foxtel (owned by News Corporation)
Press—Four major media groups—including Rupert Murdoch's News Corporation—own 80% of newspaper titles; major publications include *The Sydney Morning Herald*, *The Australian* and *The Daily Telegraph*
WPFI score—5,38 (18)

EDUCATION AND HEALTH

Education is administered by each state and territory, and is compulsory between the ages of five and 16 (15 in New South Wales and the Northern Territory, 17 in Western Australia).
Gross enrolment ratio (percentage of relevant age group)—primary 104%; secondary 129%; tertiary 76% (2009 est)
Health expenditure (per capita)—US$3,867 (2009)
Hospital beds (per 1,000 people)—3.8 (2004–9)
Life expectancy (years)—81.81 (2011 est)
Mortality rate—6.88 (2011 est)
Birth rate—12.33 (2011 est)
Infant mortality rate—4.61 (2011 est)

CULTURE

Australia's diverse indigenous communities continue to practise traditional music and art forms, which for thousands of years have been used as the media for relating a community's history and folklore. Painting, carvings and sculpture are sources of income for many communities. Influential artists include Johnny Warangkula Tjupurrula (*c.* 1925–2001), pioneer of the commercially successful Aboriginal dot painting technique, and Rover Thomas (1926–98).

Since the colonial era, Australia has been dominated by European, and latterly US, culture. Prominent literary figures include T.S. Eliot Prize-winning poet Les Murray (*b.* 1938), Nobel Prize winner Patrick White (1912–90), and double Booker Prize-winner Peter Carey (*b.* 1943). Germaine Greer (*b.* 1939) and Clive James (*b.* 1939) are internationally respected cultural commentators.

The country's cinema industry enjoyed a renaissance in the 1980s with success for both art-house films and mass-market franchises such as *Mad Max* and *Crocodile Dundee*. Director Baz Luhrmann (*b.* 1962) and actors Russell Crowe (*b.* 1964) and Nicole Kidman (*b.* 1967) are established figures in Hollywood.

Sport is an integral part of the culture. Cricket and Australian rules football are the most popular sports; cricketer Don Bradman (1908–2001) is widely considered the country's sporting hero.

EXTERNAL TERRITORIES

Most of the territories are administered by the federal government through the Department of Regional Australia, Regional Development and Local Government; the Australian Antarctic Territory and the Territory of Heard Island and McDonald Islands are administered through the Australian Antarctic Division of the Department of Sustainability, Environment, Water, Population and Communities.

Ashmore and Cartier Islands

The Ashmore Islands (comprising Middle, East and West Islands) and Cartier Island are situated in the Indian Ocean 320km off Australia's north-west coast. The islands became an Australian territory in 1933. A nature reserve was established on Ashmore Reef in 1983 and a marine reserve around Cartier Island in 2000.

The Australian Antarctic Territory

The Australian Antarctic Territory was established in 1933 and is 5,896,500 sq. km. It comprises all the islands and territories, other than Adélie Land, that are situated south of latitude 60° S. and lying between 160° E. longitude and 45° E. longitude.

Christmas Island

Area—135 sq. km
Population—1,496 (2012 est)
Christmas Island is situated in the Indian Ocean about 1,565km north-west of Northwest Cape in Western Australia. The island was annexed by Britain in 1888. Sovereignty was transferred to Australia in 1958. The Shire of Christmas Island (SOCI) is responsible for local government services on the island; its council has nine members directly elected for a four-year term. The main activities are phosphate mining, tourism and the government sector.
Administrator, Brian Lacy

Cocos (Keeling) Islands

Area—14 sq. km
Population—596 (2012 est)
The Cocos (Keeling) Islands are two separate atolls (North Keeling Island and, 24km to the south, the main atoll) comprising 27 small coral islands, situated in the Indian Ocean, about 2,950km north-west of Perth. The two inhabited islands of the southern atoll are West Island and Home Island, where around 80% of the population lives, including most of the Cocos Malay community.

The islands were declared a British possession in 1857. In 1886 Queen Victoria granted all land in the islands to George Clunies-Ross and his heirs, who established coconut plantations worked by imported Malay labour. Sovereignty was transferred to Australia in 1955, and the government purchased the Clunies-Ross land and property in 1978, 1984 and 1993. The land is held in trust for the residents, with the local government body, the Shire of the Cocos (Keeling) Islands, as trustee. In 1984 the Cocos community, in a UN-supervised Act of Self-Determination, voted to integrate with Australia. The seven-member Shire Council of Cocos (Keeling) Islands is responsible for local government services. The public sector is the main employer and there is a little tourism; coconuts are the only cash crop.
Administrator, Brian Lacy

Coral Sea Islands Territory

The Coral Sea Islands Territory lies east of Queensland between the Great Barrier Reef and longitude 156° 06′ E., and between latitudes 12° and 24° S. It comprises scattered islands, spread over a sea area of 780,000 sq. km. There is a manned meteorological station on Willis Island but otherwise the islands are uninhabited. Established in 1969, the territory is now a nature reserve, administered jointly by the Department of Sustainability, Environment, Water, Population and Communities and the Department of Agriculture, Fisheries and Forestry.

Heard Island and McDonald Islands

The Territory of Heard Island and the McDonald Islands, about 4,100km south-west of Perth, comprises all the islands and rocks lying between 52° 30′ and 53° 30′ S. latitude and 72° and 74° 30′ E. longitude. The subantarctic islands, which have active volcanoes, were discovered in the 1850s and sovereignty was transferred from Britain to Australia in 1947. The islands are now part of a marine reserve established in 2002.

 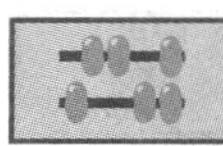      

Jervis Bay Territory
Area—73 sq. km
Population—611 (2001 census)
The territory consists of 65 sq. km of land on the southern shore of Jervis Bay, 8 sq. km of marine waters and Bowen Island (0.5 sq. km), and lies about 200km south of Sydney. Originally part of New South Wales, the territory was acquired by the federal government in 1915 to provide Canberra with access to the sea. Much of the land and water now comprises Booderee National Park, leased from the Wreck Bay Aboriginal Community who since the 1980s have been granted 90% of the land. The main economic activity is tourism.

Norfolk Island
Area—36 sq. km
Population—2,182 rising at 0.006% a year (2012 est)
Seat of government—Kingston
National day—8 June (Bounty Day)
Discovered by Captain Cook in 1774, Norfolk Island is situated in the South Pacific Ocean, about 1,600km north-east of Sydney. In 1856, 194 descendants of the *Bounty* mutineers accepted an invitation to leave Pitcairn and settle on Norfolk Island, which had served as a penal colony.

The island became a territory in 1914 and has been internally self-governing since 1979. The nine-member legislative assembly is directly elected for a three-year term, and elects the five-member executive council. This advises the Administrator, who represents the federal government. The economy is dependent on tourism; other economic activities include the sale of postage stamps and pine and palm seeds, livestock-rearing and agriculture.
Administrator, Owen Walsh

Austria

Republik Österreich—Republic of Austria
Area—83,871 sq. km
Capital—Vienna (Wien); population, 1,693,430 (2009 est)
Major cities—Graz, Innsbruck, Klagenfurt, Linz, Salzburg
Currency—Euro (€) of 100 cents
Population—8,219,743 rising at 0.026% a year (2012 est); Austrian (91.1%), former Yugoslav (4%), Turkish (1.6%) (2001)
Religion—Christian (Roman Catholic 66%, Protestant 4%, Eastern Orthodox 2%), Muslim 4% (est)
Language—German (official), Croatian and Hungarian (official in Burgenland), Slovene (official in Carinthia), Turkish, Serbian
Population density—102 per sq. km (2010)
Urban population—67.6% (2010 est)
Median age (years)—43 (2011 est)
National anthem—'Land der Berge, Land am Strome' ['Land of Mountains, Land on the River']
National day—26 October (date law of neutrality passed, 1955)
Death penalty—Abolished for all crimes (since 1968)
CPI score—7.8 (2011)

FINANCIAL OUTLOOK

Austria has weathered the eurozone crisis better than many other EU member states. The economy grew by 0.7% in 2012, while many other countries languished in recession. GDP in Q4 2012 fell 0.2% from Q3 2012, when it rose 0.1%, according to the government-backed Wifo Institute. However, the European Commission's winter forecast, published in February 2013, forecast that Austria would post GDP growth of 0.7%, compared with an expected 0.3% contraction across the whole eurozone. Furthermore, in January 2013, Standard & Poor's raised its outlook on the country to stable, from negative, and said it expects the economy to sidestep most of the negative impact from Europe's sovereign debt crisis. Austria also has one of the lowest jobless rates in the EU. Unemployment stood at 4.9% in January 2013 compared to an EU average of 10.8%.

CLIMATE AND TERRAIN

The north and east of the country feature rolling hills in the river Danube basin, while the west and south contain the eastern Alps, which cover nearly two-thirds of the country. The highest point of elevation is 3,798m (Grossglockner) and the lowest is 115m (Lake Neusiedl). The climate is continental in the lowlands, and alpine in the mountains, with average temperatures in Vienna ranging from lows of −4°C in January to highs of 25°C in July.

HISTORY AND POLITICS

Under the 1955 constitution, the federal president is directly elected for a six-year term, renewable once. There is a bicameral legislature, the *Parlament*, consisting of the National Council *(Nationalrat)*, which has 183 members directly elected for a four-year term, and the Federal Council *(Bundesrat)*, which has 62 members elected for terms of five to six years by the provincial assemblies. Some powers may only be exercised by both houses acting together as the Federal Assembly *(Bundesversammlung)*. The executive is headed by the federal chancellor, who is appointed by the president.

The 2004 presidential election was won by Heinz Fischer of the Social Democrats (SPÖ), who was re-elected in 2010. A snap legislative election was held in 2008 after the SPÖ-led coalition collapsed. The SPÖ and the Austrian People's Party (ÖVP) remained the largest parties after this election, but both lost ground to far-right parties. No party had an outright majority, and a new SPÖ–ÖVP coalition was formed under the new SPÖ leader, Werner Faymann.

HEAD OF STATE

Federal President, Heinz Fischer, *took office* 8 July 2004, *re-elected* 2010

SELECTED GOVERNMENT MEMBERS *as at May 2012*

Chancellor, Werner Faymann
Vice-Chancellor, Foreign Affairs, Michael Spindelegger
Defence, Norbert Darabos
Finance, Maria Fekter

EMBASSY OF AUSTRIA

18 Belgrave Mews West, London SW1X 8HU
T 020-7344 3250
E london-ob@bmeia.gv.at
W www.bmeia.gv.at//london
Ambassador Extraordinary and Plenipotentiary, HE Emil Brix, *apptd* 2010

BRITISH EMBASSY

Jaurèsgasse 12, 1030 Vienna
T (+43) (1) 716 130
E viennaconsularenquiries@fco.gov.uk
W ukinaustria.fco.gov.uk

Ambassador Extraordinary and Plenipotentiary, HE Susan le Jeune d'Allegeershecque, *apptd* 2011

Federal Structure

There are nine provinces *(Länder)*: Burgenland, Carinthia, Lower Austria, Salzburg, Styria, Tyrol, Upper Austria, Vienna and Vorarlberg. Each has its own assembly and government.

DEFENCE

Aged 16-49, est 2010	*Males*	*Females*
Available for military service	1,941,110	1,910,434
Fit for military service	1,579,862	1,554,130

Military expenditure—US$3,305m (2011)
Conscription duration—6 months (9–10 months for officers, NCOs and specialists)

ECONOMY AND TRADE

Austria has a well-developed market economy which is closely linked to other EU states. Its strong commercial links with central, eastern and south-eastern Europe, an attraction for foreign investors in the past, increased its vulnerability in the global economic downturn, and its financial sector required state support. The economy went into recession in 2008 but started to recover from late 2009.

The services sector contributes most to GDP (69% in 2011), followed by industry (29.5%) and the small but highly developed agricultural sector (1.5%). The main industries include tourism (about 16% of GDP), construction, manufacturing of machinery, vehicles and parts, food processing, timber and wood processing, production of metals and metal goods, chemicals, paper and cardboard, and communications equipment.

Austria's main trading partners are Germany, Italy and Switzerland. Principal exports include the goods produced by the main industries, iron and steel, and textiles. The main imports are machinery and equipment, vehicles, chemical products, metal goods, oil and oil products, and foodstuffs.

GNI—US$377,062m; US$47,060 per capita (2010)
Annual average growth of GDP—3.3% (2011 est)
Inflation rate—3.3% (2011 est)
Population below poverty line—6% (2008)
Unemployment—6.9% (2010 est)
Total external debt—US$883,500m (2011)
Imports—US$149,792m (2010)
Exports—US$144,476m (2010)

BALANCE OF PAYMENTS

Trade—US$5,316m deficit (2010)
Current Account—US$10,294m surplus (2010)

Trade with UK	*2010*	*2011*
Imports from UK	£1,428,060,153	£1,641,708,344
Exports to UK	£2,585,566,519	£2,931,540,216

COMMUNICATIONS

Airports—Principal airports include Vienna, Salzburg and Innsbruck; 55 in total, 25 with paved runways
Waterways—358km of navigable waterways; considerable trade through Danube ports (Vienna, Krems, Enns, Linz)
Railways—6,399km
Roadways—110,778km
Telecommunications—3.245 million fixed line and 12.241 million mobile phone subcriptions (2010); there were 6.143 million internet subscribers in 2009
Internet code and IDD—at; 43 (from UK), 44 (to UK)
Major broadcasters—Österreichischer Rundfunk (ÖRF) and ATV
Press—There are five main daily titles, *Die Presse, Kronen Zeitung, Wiener Zeitung, Der Standard* and *Der Kurier*
WPFI score—0,50 (7)

EDUCATION AND HEALTH

Education is free and compulsory from six to 15.
Gross enrolment ratio (percentage of relevant age group)—primary 100%; secondary 100%; tertiary 60% (2009 est)
Health expenditure (per capita)—US$5,037 (2009)
Hospital beds (per 1,000 people)—7.7 (2004–9)
Life expectancy (years)—79.78 (2011 est)
Mortality rate—10.14 (2011 est)
Birth rate—8.67 (2011 est)
Infant mortality rate—4.32 (2011 est)

CULTURE

From the 18th to the 20th centuries Vienna was one of Europe's greatest cultural centres. Musicians included Haydn (1732–1809), Mozart (1756–91), Beethoven (1770–1827), the Strauss family, Mahler (1860–1911) and Schoenberg (1874–1951). The late 19th century produced the writers Rainer Maria Rilke (1875–1926) and Robert Musil (1880–1942), the pioneering psychoanalyst Sigmund Freud (1856–1939), and the notable scientists Gregor Mendel (1822–84), whose research laid the foundations of modern genetics, and Erwin Schrödinger (1887–1961), who contributed to the development of quantum mechanics.

In art, the symbolist paintings of Gustav Klimt (1862–1918) are among the most recognisable of the Art Nouveau period. Film director Fritz Lang (1890–1976) produced two of cinema's earliest classics: *Metropolis* (1927) and *M* (1931).

The Bahamas

Commonwealth of the Bahamas
Area—13,880 sq. km
Capital—Nassau, on New Providence; population, 247,659 (2009 est)
Major city—Freeport, on Grand Bahama
Currency—Bahamian dollar (B$) of 100 cents
Population—316,182 rising at 0.9% a year (2012 est)
Religion—Christian (Baptist 35%, Anglican 15%, Roman Catholic 14%, Pentecostal 8%, Church of God 5%, Seventh-day Adventist 5%, Methodist 4%) (est)
Language—English (official), Creole
Population density—34 per sq. km (2010)
Urban population—84.1% (2010 est)
Median age (years)—30.2 (2011 est)
National anthem—'March on, Bahamaland'
National day—10 July (Independence Day)
Life expectancy (years)—71.18 (2011 est)
Mortality rate—6.91 (2012 est)
Birth rate—15.951 (2012 est)

Infant mortality rate—13.49 (2011 est)
HIV/AIDS adult prevalence—3.1% (2009 est)
Death penalty—Retained

FINANCIAL OUTLOOK

In October 2012, the ratings agency Standard & Poor's warned that the Bahamas faced "at least a one in three chance" of having its sovereign credit rating downgraded by 2014. What was concerning S&P was the fact that the Bahamas' fiscal deficits were set to remain higher than anticipated in the short term. The 2013–14 budget is due to be presented to Parliament in May 2013 and S&P wants to see a significant reduction in the Bahamas' US$504 million deficit run up in 2011–12. For its part, the Bahamas government has promised to introduce far-reaching tax reforms to improve its tax revenue receipts, but there is concern that introducing such changes to the tax system is a project that will take years to implement and so cannot be relied on to deliver any meaningful fiscal deficit reduction in the short term. The IMF expects the country's economy to grow at 2.5% in 2013, following a similar performance in 2012.

CLIMATE AND TERRAIN

The Bahamas consist of more than 700 islands and 2,400 cays, all low-lying. The highest point is 63m (Mt Alvernia, on Cat Island) and the lowest 0m (Atlantic Ocean). The principal islands include: Abaco Islands, Acklins, Andros, Berry Islands, Bimini, Cat Island, Crooked Island, Eleuthera, Exuma, Grand Bahama, Harbour Island, Great Inagua, Long Island, Mayaguana, New Providence, Ragged Island, Rum Cay, San Salvador and Spanish Wells. The 14 major islands are inhabited, as are a few of the smaller islands. The climate is semitropical. The hurricane season is June to November.

HISTORY AND POLITICS

The islands were discovered by Columbus in 1492, settled by the British from the 17th century and became a crown colony in 1717. The Bahamas became internally self-governing in 1964 and gained independence on 10 July 1973.

The Progressive Liberal Party (PLP) held power for 25 years until the Free National Movement (FNM) won an absolute majority in the 1992 general election. Power has subsequently alternated between the two parties. The PLP regained its majority in the 2012 legislative election, winning 29 of the 38 seats.

The head of state is Queen Elizabeth II, who is represented by a governor-general. The bicameral parliament has a senate of 16 appointed members and a House of Assembly of 41 members; both chambers serve a five-year term.

Governor-General, HE Sir Arthur Foulkes, *apptd* 2010

SELECTED GOVERNMENT MEMBERS *as at July 2012*

Prime Minister, Perry Christie
Deputy Prime Minister, Philip Davies
National Security, Keith Bell

HIGH COMMISSION OF THE COMMONWEALTH OF THE BAHAMAS

10 Chesterfield Street, London W1J 5JL
T 020-7408 4488
E information@bahamashclondon.net
W www.bahamashclondon.net
High Commissioner, HE Paul Farquharson, *apptd* 2008

BRITISH HIGH COMMISSION

High Commissioner, Howard Drake, *apptd* 2010, resident in Kingston, Jamaica

DEFENCE

Aged 16–49, 2010 est	Males	Females
Available for military service	85,568	–
Fit for military service	63,429	64,645

Military budget—US$46m (2010)

ECONOMY AND TRADE

The economy is dominated by tourism and offshore financial services, which together contribute about 90% of GDP. A tightening of financial regulations in 2000 caused a number of international businesses to relocate elsewhere, and visitor numbers from the USA (over 80% of all visitors) have declined since 2006. The effects of the global downturn have caused the economy to contract further, although the decline was diminished as tourism and investment returned in 2011.

Manufacturing and agriculture account for 10% of GDP and employment. Agriculture produces mainly fresh vegetables, fruit, meat and eggs. Mineral reserves produce aragonite and salt for export. Other activities include cement, rum, pharmaceuticals and steel pipe production, and the provision of oil trans-shipment services.

The main trading partners are the USA, Singapore, South Korea, Japan and Poland. The chief exports are mineral products and salt, animal products, rum, chemicals, fruit and vegetables. Imports are chiefly machinery and transport equipment, manufactured articles, chemicals, fuel, foodstuffs and livestock.

GNI—US$6,940m; US$20,610 per capita (2009)
Annual average growth of GDP—2% (2011 est)
Inflation rate—3.4% (2011 est)
Population below poverty line—9.3% (2004)
Unemployment—7.6% (2006 est)
Total external debt—US$342.6m (2004 est)
Imports—US$2,863m (2010)
Exports—US$620m (2010)

BALANCE OF PAYMENTS

Trade—US$2,243m deficit (2010)
Current Account—US$900m deficit (2010)

Trade with UK	*2010*	*2011*
Imports from UK	£32,881,433	£17,253,054
Exports to UK	£2,476,742	£5,251,917

COMMUNICATIONS

Airports—International airports are operated from Andros, Chubb Cay, Eleuthera, Exuma, Grand Bahama and New Providence
Waterways—The main ports are Nassau (New Providence), Freeport and South Riding Point (Grand Bahama). The Bahamas is a major ship registry, and 1,080 of the 1,170 ships registered in 2010 were foreign-owned
Roadways—2,717km, 1,560km of which are paved
Railways—none
Telecommunications—129,300 fixed lines (2009) and 428,400 mobile phone subscriptions (2010); there were 115,800 internet users in 2009
Internet code and IDD—bs; 1 242 (from UK), 011 44 (to UK)
Press—The government-owned ZNS-TV is the country's principal television broadcaster; daily newspapers include *The Nassau Guardian*, *The Tribune* and *The Freeport News*

Bahrain

Mamlakat al-Bahrayn—Kingdom of Bahrain
Area—760 sq. km
Capital—Manama; population, 163,311 (2009 est)
Major towns—Al Muharraq, Ar Rifa
Currency—Bahraini dinar (BD) of 1,000 fils
Population—1,248,348 (including 235,108 non-nationals) rising at 2.652% a year (2012 est); Bahraini (62.4%) (2001). The non-Bahraini population includes large numbers of Europeans and South Asians
Religion—Muslim 99% (of which Shia 60%, Sunni 40%) (est); Islam is the state religion
Language—Arabic (official), English, Farsi, Urdu
Population density—1,660 per sq. km (2010)
Urban population—88.6% (2010 est)
Median age (years)—30.9 (2011 est)
National anthem—'Bahrainona' ['Our Bahrain']
National day—16 December (date of independence from British protection, 1971)
Life expectancy (years)—78.15 (2011 est)
Mortality rate—2.63 (2012 est)
Birth rate—14.41 (2012 est)
Infant mortality rate—10.43 (2011 est)
Death penalty—Retained
CPI score—5.1 (2011)
Literacy rate—91.4% (2009 est)

FINANCIAL OUTLOOK

The economy expanded by 3.9% in 2012, according to the Economic Development Board, which forecast that GDP would expand by 6.2% in 2013 before easing to 3.4% in 2014. The economy grew by just 1.9% in 2011, recovering gradually since it was hit hard in the first quarter of 2011 by pro-democracy protests, led mainly by majority Shi'ite Muslims. Sporadic unrest has continued since then, weighing on foreign investment and the tourism industry. Technical problems disrupted production at the Abu Safa oil field, which Bahrain shares with Saudi Arabia, for most of 2012, hurting growth, according to the board. Bahrain relies on the field for around 70% of its budget revenue. However, the technical problems were fixed in November and this is expected to boost economic growth in 2013, along with higher output from an onshore Bahraini oil field, the board said.

CLIMATE AND TERRAIN

Bahrain consists of an archipelago of 36 low-lying islands situated approximately halfway down the Persian Gulf, some 32km off the east coast of Saudi Arabia. The largest of these, Bahrain Island, is about 48km long and 16km wide at its broadest. Elevation extremes range from 122m (Jabal ad Dukhan) to 0m at sea level. The climate is arid, hot and humid, with average maximum temperatures ranging from 20°C to 38°C.

HISTORY AND POLITICS

Bahrain was ruled by Persia (Iran) from 1602 until it was ousted in 1783 by the al-Khalifa family, who remain in power. The emirate was a British protectorate from 1820 until 1971, when it became independent. In 1975 the legislature was suspended and the emir assumed virtually absolute power after clashes between Sunni and Shia factions. Moves to return to democratic rule were made in response to civil agitation in the 1990s, until Sheikh Hamad succeeded to the throne and initiated the transition to a constitutional monarchy. The 2002 constitution established Bahrain as a kingdom and a constitutional monarchy, and legalised elections. There has been ongoing agitation for further democratisation, particularly by the Shia majority against the predominantly Sunni authorities. In February 2011 this flared up into mass demonstrations that were repressed brutally by the government from March, when martial law was declared and the Pearl monument, the focal point of the demonstrations in Manama, was demolished. A report into the unrest, commissioned by Sheikh Hamad, was released in November 2011 and confirmed the practice of torture and infringements of human rights; in response, the ruler vowed to 'learn lessons' from the unrest and promised to reform the country's laws to make them compatible with international standards.

In the 2010 legislative election, the radical Shia group al-Wefaq remained the largest bloc, with 18 seats. A number of ministers resigned in spring 2011 after protesting at the treatment of demonstrators. A by-election was held in September 2011 after al-Wefaq withdrew from the National Assembly; the seats were taken by independent candidates following low voter turnout.

Under the 2002 constitution, the country is a hereditary constitutional monarchy with the king as head of state. The king appoints the cabinet. The bicameral National Assembly consists of a lower house, the Council of Representatives, and an upper house, the Consultative Council. The lower house has 40 members directly elected for a four-year term, and the upper house has 40 members appointed by the king for a four-year term. The 2002 constitution granted women the right to vote and to stand for election.

HEAD OF STATE

HH The King of Bahrain, Sheikh Hamad bin Isa al-Khalifa, KCMG *succeeded as emir* 6 March 1999, *proclaimed king* 14 February 2002
Crown Prince, Chair of the National Economic Development Council, Sheikh Salman bin Hamad al-Khalifa

SELECTED GOVERNMENT MEMBERS *as at May 2012*

Prime Minister, HH Sheikh Khalifa bin Salman al-Khalifa
Deputy Prime Ministers, Sheikh Mohammed bin Mubarak al-Khalifa; Sheikh Ali bin Khalifa al-Khalifa; Jawad bin Salem al Oraied; Sheikh Khalid bin Abdullah al-Khalifa
Foreign Affairs, Sheikh Khalid bin Ahmed bin Mohammed al-Khalifa
Defence, Sheikh Mohammad bin Abdullah al-Khalifa
Finance, Sheikh Ahmed bin Mohammed al-Khalifa

EMBASSY OF THE KINGDOM OF BAHRAIN

30 Belgrave Square, London SW1X 8QB
T 020-7201 9170
E information@bahrainembassy.co.uk
W www.bahrainembassy.co.uk
Ambassador Extraordinary and Plenipotentiary, HE Alice Thomas Samaan, *apptd* 2011

BRITISH EMBASSY

PO Box 114, 21 Government Avenue, Manama 306
T (+973) 1757 4100
W ukinbahrain.fco.gov.uk
Ambassador Extraordinary and Plenipotentiary, HE Iain Lindsay, OBE, *apptd* 2011

  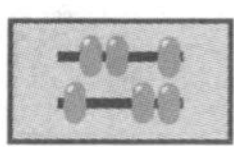      

DEFENCE

Aged 16–49, 2010 est	Males	Females
Available for military service	508,863	290,801
Fit for military service	423,757	245,302

Military expenditure—US$883m (2011)

ECONOMY AND TRADE

Bahrain was one of the first Gulf states to discover oil, in the 1930s, but reserves and production are lower than in neighbouring countries. It has diversified its economy, developing particularly as a regional financial and business centre, and as a tourist destination. Petroleum production and refining still accounts for an estimated 11% of GDP, 70% of government revenue and 60% of total exports. Other industries include petrochemicals, aluminium smelting, and shipbuilding and repair. Bahrain's main trading partners are Saudi Arabia, the EU, Far Eastern countries and the USA.

GNI—US$20,979m; US$25,420 per capita (2008)
Annual average growth of GDP—1.5% (2011 est)
Inflation rate—0.3% (2011 est)
Unemployment—15% (2005 est)
Total external debt—US$15,200m (2011 est)
Imports—US$9,800m (2010)
Exports—US$15,400m (2010)

BALANCE OF PAYMENTS

Trade—US$5,600m surplus (2010)
Current Account—US$564m surplus (2009)

Trade with UK	2010	2011
Imports from UK	£228,848,890	£236,284,142
Exports to UK	£61,080,729	£163,488,475

COMMUNICATIONS

Airports—Bahrain International Airport is one of the main air traffic centres of the Gulf and acts as a stopover point for other airlines on routes between Europe and Australia and the Far East
Waterways—There are two major ports, including Khalifa bin Salman Port, based in Manama, and a smaller terminal in Sitra
Roadways—3,121km of paved roads; the four main islands are connected by causeways, and a 25km causeway links Bahrain Island to Saudi Arabia
Telecommunications—228,000 main lines and 1.567 million mobile phone subscriptions (2010); there were 419,500 internet users in 2009
Internet code and IDD—bh; 973 (from UK), 44 (to UK)
Major broadcasters—State-run Bahrain Radio and Television Corporation operates five terrestrial TV networks
Press—Major daily newspapers include *Akhbar al-Khaleej*, *Al-Ayam* and *Al-Wasat*
WPFI score—51,38 (144)

Bangladesh

Gana Prajatantri Bangladesh—People's Republic of Bangladesh
Area—143,998 sq. km
Capital—Dhaka; population, 14,251,300 (2009 est)
Major cities—Chittagong, Khulna, Narayanganj
Currency—Taka (Tk) of 100 paisa
Population—161,083,804 rising at 1.579% a year (2012 est); Bengali (98%) (1998 est)
Religion—Muslim (Sunni 90%), Hindu 9% (est); Islam is the state religion
Language—Bengali (official), English
Population density—1,142 per sq. km (2010)
Urban population—28.1% (2010 est)
Median age (years)—23.3 (2011 est)
National anthem—'Amar Shonar Bangla' ['My Golden Bengal']
National day—26 March (Independence Day)
Death penalty—Retained
CPI score—2.7 (2011)

FINANCIAL OUTLOOK

The economy grew by 4.4% in 2012, down from 5.8% in 2011, according to the UN World Economic Situation and Prospects (WESP) 2013 report published in March 2013. Despite the slowdown, Bangladesh outpaced many of its neighbors. Robust expansion in private investment and consumption and a steady increase in worker remittances sent from abroad were the main drivers of the economy. The UN forecast that Bangladesh would continue to enjoy steady growth at 6.3% and 6.4% in 2013 and 2014, respectively. The country's external balances are also in a healthy position. Strong exports and inward remittances lay behind the surplus of nearly US$1 billion recorded in the current account in the first half of the 2012–13 fiscal year ending in June 2013, the central bank reported in March. Inflation remains a problem, however, running at an annual pace of 7.87% in February 2013.

CLIMATE AND TERRAIN

Although hilly in the south-east and north-east, over 75% of the country is less than 3m above sea-level, situated on the alluvial plain and delta of the Ganges (Padma)–Brahmaputra (Jamuna)–Meghna river system, which empties into the Bay of Bengal, the largest estuarine delta in the world. The highest elevation is 1,230m (Keokradong) and the lowest 0m at the Indian Ocean. The climate is tropical, with a monsoon season (June–September) during which heavy rainfall causes flooding in around one-third of the country each year; annual rainfall in most of the country is up to 2,000mm.

HISTORY AND POLITICS

Bangladesh consists of what was the eastern part of Bengal province and the Sylhet district of Assam province in British India. On independence in 1947, these territories acceded to Pakistan, forming the province of East Bengal (renamed East Pakistan in 1955). Tensions between East and West Pakistan (separated by over 1,600km) caused the East to secede in 1971. After months of civil war, and following the intervention of India, Bangladesh achieved independence from Pakistan on 16 December 1971.

Since independence, Bangladesh has experienced periods of political instability, with a number of coups and attempted coups, the assassinations of President Mujibar Rahman (1975) and President Zia (1981), and periods of government under martial law (1975–8, 1982–6) or a state of emergency (1987–8, 2007–8).

Parliamentary government has remained in place since 1991, despite occasional boycotts of parliament. Governments have

been formed, or coalition governments led, by one of the two main parties: the Bangladesh Nationalist Party (BNP), led by Khaleda Zia (widow of President Zia), in 1991–6 and 2001–6; and the Awami League, led by Sheikh Hasina Wajed (daughter of President Mujibar Rahman), in 1996–2001 and since January 2009.

The BNP-led coalition government headed by Khaleda Zia stepped down in 2006 when its term of office expired. Following violent protests over the choice of an interim government and the impartiality of election preparations, the president declared a state of emergency and appointed a caretaker administration until a new parliament was convened after the December 2008 legislative election. The election was won by the Awami League, with 230 of the 345 seats. Zillur Rahman was elected president in February 2009.

The head of state is the president, elected by the legislature for a five-year term. The unicameral parliament, *Jatiya Sangsad*, has 345 members directly elected for a five-year term; under a 2004 constitutional amendment, 45 seats are reserved for women. The president appoints the prime minister, and the cabinet on the advice of the prime minister.

HEAD OF STATE
President, Zillur Rahman, *elected* 11 February 2009

SELECTED GOVERNMENT MEMBERS *as at May 2012*
Prime Minister, Defence, Sheikh Hasina Wajed
Finance, Abu Maal Abdul Muhith
Foreign Affairs, Dipu Moni
Law, Justice and Parliamentary Affairs, Shafiq Ahmed

HIGH COMMISSION FOR THE PEOPLE'S REPUBLIC OF BANGLADESH
28 Queen's Gate, London SW7 5JA
T 020-7584 0081
E info@bhclondon.org.uk
W www.bhclondon.org.uk
High Commissioner, HE Dr Mohammad Sayeedur Rahman Khan, *apptd* 2009

BRITISH HIGH COMMISSION
PO Box 6079, United Nations Road, Baridhara, Dhaka 1212
T (+880) (2) 882 2705
E consular.bangladesh@fconet.fco.gov.uk
W ukinbangladesh.fco.gov.uk
High Commissioner, HE Robert Winnington, CMG, OBE, *apptd* 2011

DEFENCE

Aged 16–49, 2010 est	*Males*	*Females*
Available for military service	36,520,491	–
Fit for military service	30,486,086	35,616,093

Military expenditure—US$1,367m (2011)

ECONOMY AND TRADE

Bangladesh is a poor country, highly dependent on foreign aid. Although poverty has been reduced by 1–2% a year since 1990, over a third of the population lives below the poverty line. Many migrate to the Gulf states and south-east Asia to find work, and their remittances and garment manufacturing are the mainstay of the economy. These have fuelled the steady growth of 5–6% a year since the mid-1990s, which has continued throughout the global downturn. However, inefficient state-owned enterprises, slow implementation of economic reforms, corruption and unreliable power supplies are obstacles to greater growth.

The service and industrial sectors account for 53% and 28.6% of GDP respectively. Although the smallest contributor to GDP (18.4%), agriculture is the primary occupation of 45% of the workforce. The chief industries are based on processing agricultural and fisheries products such as cotton, jute, tea, sugar, fish and seafood, the manufacture of textiles, garments, newsprint, cement and fertiliser, and light engineering. Most exports are to the USA and EU countries; imports come mainly from China, India and other Asian countries.

GNI—US$109,694m; US$700 per capita (2010)
Annual average growth of GDP—6.3% (2011 est)
Inflation rate—10.7% (2011 est)
Population below poverty line—40% (2010 est)
Unemployment—5.1% (2010 est)
Total external debt—US$24,930m (2011 est)
Imports—US$26,071m (2010)
Exports—US$14,195m (2010)

BALANCE OF PAYMENTS
Trade—US$11,877m deficit (2010)
Current Account—US$3,137m surplus (2009)

Trade with UK	*2010*	*2011*
Imports from UK	£114,292,581	£135,753,803
Exports to UK	£1,182,581,509	£1,488,538,761

COMMUNICATIONS

Airports—Three international airports (at Dhaka, Cittagong and Sylhet) and 14 other airports and airfields
Waterways—Principal seaports are Chittagong and Mongla, and there are smaller ports in Chalna and Khulna; the 8,370km of waterways are a key element of the transport infrastructure, although reduced to 5,200km in dry season
Roadways—239,226km (22,726km surfaced)
Railways—2,622km
Telecommunications—900,000 fixed lines (2010), 68.65 million mobile phone subscriptions (2009); there were 617,300 internet users in 2009
Internet country code and IDD—bd; 880 (from UK), 44 (to UK)
Major broadcasters—The government-run Bangladesh Television and Radio Bangladesh are the principal broadcasters; other television broadcasters include ATN Banglia, Channel i and NTV
Press—Major newspapers include English-language dailies *The Daily Star, The New Nation* and *The Independent*
WPFI score—42,50 (126)

EDUCATION AND HEALTH

Education is compulsory and free for children aged 6 to 10, but drop-out rates are high.
Literacy rate—55.9% (2009 est)
Gross enrolment ratio (percentage of relevant age group)—primary 103%; secondary 49% (2009 est)
Health expenditure (per capita)—US$18 (2009)
Hospital beds (per 1,000 people)—0.4 (2004–9)
Life expectancy (years)—69.75 (2011 est)
Mortality rate—5.71 (2012 est)
Birth rate—22.53 (2012 est)
Infant mortality rate—50.73 (2011 est)

  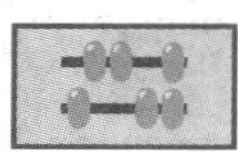      

Barbados

Area—430 sq. km
Capital—Bridgetown, in the parish of St Michael; population, 112,154 (2009)
Currency—Barbados dollar (BD$) of 100 cents
Population—287,733 rising at 0.35% a year (2012 est)
Religion—Christian 75% (Protestant 63%, of which the largest denomination is Anglican), Muslim 1% (2008 est)
Language—English (official)
Population density—636 per sq. km (2010)
Urban population—40.8% (2010)
Median age (years)—36.5 (2011 est)
National anthem—'In Plenty and in Time of Need'
National day—30 November (Independence Day)
Death penalty—Retained
CPI score—7.8 (2011)

FINANCIAL OUTLOOK

The Barbados government committed itself to a total expenditure of just over US$3.6 billion in its budget for the 2012–13 tax year, up 8.9% on the budget for 2011–12. Almost a third of this, US$1.1 billion, represents the repayment of principal and debt interest on the government's debt. Projected revenues for the period fall some way short of the US$3.6 billion figure for expenditure, at US$2.62 billion, showing that were it not for its debt burdens, the Barbados government would be running a fiscally neutral budget. In presenting the budget in June 2012, Peter Sinckler, the minister for finance and economic affairs, said that unemployment had risen above 11% but also pointed out that there had been a 20% increase in growth in new business registrations in Barbados's offshore and financial services sector. The government would not go down the road of extreme austerity to correct its financial problems but would seek a "balanced response," he said.

CLIMATE AND TERRAIN

Barbados is the most easterly of the Caribbean islands. The land rises gently to central highlands, and elevation extremes range from 336m (Mt Hillaby) to 0m (Atlantic Ocean). The climate is tropical with a wet season from July to November, when the island is subject to occasional hurricanes.

HISTORY AND POLITICS

Early settlers were succeeded by the Arawaks and then the Caribs. The island was uninhabited when settled by the English in 1627 and was a crown colony from 1652, achieving self-government in 1961. It became an independent state on 30 November 1966.

Since independence, power has alternated between the two main political parties, the Barbados Labour Party (BLP) and the Democratic Labour Party (DLP). In the 2008 general election the BLP was defeated by the DLP, which won 20 of the 30 seats and took office under David Thompson. He died in October 2010 and was succeeded as prime minister by his deputy, Freundel Stuart.

The head of state is Queen Elizabeth II, represented by the governor-general. The bicameral parliament consists of a senate of 21 appointed members and a House of Assembly of 30 directly elected members; both chambers serve a five-year term.

There are 11 administrative areas (parishes): St Michael, Christ Church, St Andrew, St George, St James, St John, St Joseph, St Lucy, St Peter, St Philip and St Thomas.

Governor-General, HE Sir Elliott Belgrave, GCMG, *apptd* June 2012

SELECTED GOVERNMENT MEMBERS *as at June 2012*
Prime Minister, Freundel Stuart
Attorney-General, Home Affairs, Adriel Brathwaite
Finance, Christopher Sinckler
Foreign Affairs, Maxine McClean

BARBADOS HIGH COMMISSION
1 Great Russell Street, London WC1B 3ND
T 020-7631 4975
E london@foreign.gov.bb
High Commissioner, HE Hugh Arthur, *apptd* 2008

BRITISH HIGH COMMISSION
PO Box 676, Lower Collymore Rock, Bridgetown
T (+1) (246) 430 7800
E ukinbarbados@fco.gov.uk
W ukinbarbados.fco.gov.uk
High Commissioner, HE Paul Brummell, *apptd* 2009

DEFENCE

Aged 16–49, 2010 est	*Males*	*Females*
Available for military service	73,820	73,835
Fit for military service	58,125	58,016

Military budget—US$34m (2010)

ECONOMY AND TRADE

Historically, Barbados's chief products were sugar, rum and molasses. Since independence, tourism, offshore finance and information services, and light industry have become more significant. The global economic downturn affected tourism in particular, causing the economy to contract in 2009.

The main trading partners are Trinidad and Tobago, the USA and Jamaica. Chief exports are manufactured goods, sugar and molasses, rum, other food and beverages, chemicals and electronic components.

GNI—US$3,517m (2009); US$12,660 per capita (2009)
Annual average growth of GDP—1.8% (2011 est)
Inflation rate—7.4% (2011 est)
Unemployment—10.7% (2003 est)
Total external debt—US$668m (2003)
Imports—US$1,562m (2010)
Exports—US$429m (2010)

BALANCE OF PAYMENTS
Trade—US$1,133m deficit (2010)
Current Account—US$247m deficit (2009)

Trade with UK	*2010*	*2011*
Imports from UK	£40,467,489	£42,324,513
Exports to UK	£19,506,750	£29,620,977

COMMUNICATIONS

Airports—The Grantley Adams International near Bridgetown is the only international airport on the island
Waterways—Bridgetown, the only port of entry, has a deep-water harbour

Roadways—There are 1,600km of roads, all of which are surfaced
Telecommunications—137,500 fixed lines and 350,100 mobile phone subscriptions (2010); there were 188,000 internet users in 2008
Internet country code and IDD—bb; 1 246 (from UK), 011 44 (to UK)
Major broadcasters—Caribbean Broadcasting Corporation, which also operates MCTV, a multi-channel and pay TV service
Press—Major newspapers include *The Barbados Advocate* and *The Nation*

EDUCATION AND HEALTH

Education is free in government schools at primary (ages four to 11), secondary (ages 11 to 18) and tertiary levels, and is compulsory until the age of 15.
Literacy rate—99.7% (2004 est)
Life expectancy (years)—74.52 (2012 est)
Mortality rate—8.39 (2012 est)
Birth rate—12.23 (2012 est)
Infant mortality rate—11.86 (2011 est)
HIV/AIDS adult prevalence—1.4% (2009 est)

Belgium

Koninkrijk Belgie/Royaume de Belgique/Königreich Belgien—Kingdom of Belgium
Area—30,528 sq. km
Capital—Brussels; population, 1,892,000 (2009 est)
Major cities—Antwerp, Bruges, Charleroi, Ghent, Liège
Currency—Euro (€) of 100 cents
Population—10,438,353 rising at 0.06% a year (2012 est); Fleming (58%), Walloon (31%) (est)
Religion—Christian (Roman Catholic 45%, Protestant 1%), Muslim 4% (est).
Language—Dutch (Flemish), French, German (all official)
Population density—359 per sq. km (2010)
Urban population—97.4% (2010 est)
Median age (years)—42.3 (2011 est)
National anthem—'La Brabançonne' ['The Song of Brabant']
National day—21 July (Accession of King Leopold I, 1831)
Death penalty—Abolished for all crimes (since 1996)
CPI score—7.5 (2011)

FINANCIAL OUTLOOK

The Belgian economy contracted by 0.2% in 2012, according to the European Central Bank, compared to the 1.8% expansion seen in 2012. Private consumption fell by 0.6% during the year, while exports grew by just 0.4%. Consumer price inflation averaged 2.6%, compared to 3.4% in 2011. The state forecasting agency cut its growth outlook in February 2013 to 0.2% for 2013, suggesting that the government will have to make bigger than expected cuts to its budget if it is to meet its budget target. The budget is currently based on a growth estimate of 0.7% for the year. In March 2013, a committee advising the government estimated that an additional €2.8 billion (US$3.66 billion) in savings had to be found if Belgium was to end 2013 with a deficit of 2.15% of GDP. The Belgian government estimates its deficit in 2012 at 2.96% of GDP.

CLIMATE AND TERRAIN

There are two distinct regions: the west is generally low-lying and fertile, while in the east the forested hills of the Ardennes are more rugged with poorer soil. Elevation extremes range from 0m on the North Sea coast to 694m (Signal de Botrange). The polders near the coast, which are protected against floods by dykes, cover an area of around 500 sq. km. Average temperatures range from 2°C in January to 18°C in July.

HISTORY AND POLITICS

Belgium is a constitutional monarchy with a hereditary monarch as head of state. Amendments to the constitution since 1968 have devolved power to the regions. The national government retains competence only in foreign and defence policies, the national budget and monetary policy, social security, and the judicial, legal and penal systems. The bicameral legislature, the Federal Chambers, consists of a senate and a Chamber of Representatives. The latter has 150 members, directly elected by proportional representation for a four-year term. The senate has 71 members, who serve a four-year term; 40 are directly elected, the Flemish and French communities receive ten members each and the German community one, with the remaining ten co-opted by the elected members.

There are three language communities: Flemish, Francophone and Germanophone. Each community has its own assembly, which elects the community government. At this level, Flanders is covered by the Flemish community assembly; most of Wallonia is covered by the Francophone community assembly, and areas of Wallonia lying in the German-speaking communities of Eupen and Malmédy are covered by the Germanophone community assembly; Brussels is covered by a joint community commission of the Flemish and Francophone community assemblies.

At regional level, Belgium is divided into the three regions of Wallonia, Brussels and Flanders. Each region has its own directly elected assembly and government.

The ten provinces of Belgium are: Antwerp, East Flanders, Flemish Brabant, Hainaut, Liège, Limburg, Luxembourg, Namur, Walloon Brabant and West Flanders. In addition, 589 communes form the lowest level of local government.

Early elections were held in June 2010 and the New Flemish Alliance, a Flemish separatist party, emerged as the largest party in what was a heavily contested Chamber of Representatives. Negotiations over budget and immigration issues, and voting rights between the French-speaking and Flemish communities, continued for a record 541 days before Socialist Party leader Elio Di Rupo formed a coalition government comprising of the country's principal parties; Di Rupo was sworn into office in December 2011.

Minister-President of the Brussels Capital Government, Charles Picqué
Minister-President of the Flemish Community and Flemish Region, Kris Peeters
Minister-President of the French Community and Walloon Region, Rudy Demotte
Minister-President of the German-speaking Community, Karl-Heinz Lambertz

HEAD OF STATE

HM The King of the Belgians, King Albert II, *born* 6 June 1934; *acceded* 9 August 1993
Heir, HRH Prince Philippe Léopold Louis Marie, *born* 15 April 1960

  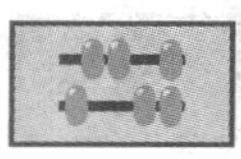      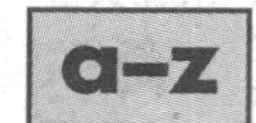

SELECTED GOVERNMENT MEMBERS *as at May 2012*
Prime Minister, Elio Di Rupo
Deputy Prime Ministers, Joëlle Milquet *(Interior)*; Laurette Onkelinx *(Social Affairs and Public Health)*; Didier Reynders *(Foreign Affairs)*; Steven Vanackere *(Finance and Sustainable Development)*
Defence, Pieter De Crem

EMBASSY OF BELGIUM
17 Grosvenor Crescent, London SW1X 7EE
T 020-7470 3700
E london@diplobel.fed.be
W www.diplomatie.be/london
Ambassador Extraordinary and Plenipotentiary, HE Johan Verbeke, *apptd* 2010

BRITISH EMBASSY
Avenue d'Auderghem 10, Oudergemlaan, 1040 Brussels
T (+32) (2) 287 6211
E info@britain.be
W ukinbelgium.fco.gov.uk
Ambassador Extraordinary and Plenipotentiary, HE Jonathan Brenton, *apptd* 2010

DEFENCE

The headquarters of NATO, and of its Supreme Headquarters Allied Powers Europe, are in Belgium.

Aged 16–49, 2010 est	*Males*	*Females*
Available for military service	2,359,232	2,291,689
Fit for military service	1,934,957	1,877,268

Military expenditure—US$5,136m (2011)

ECONOMY AND TRADE

Belgium has a free-market economy with highly diversified industrial and commercial sectors. With few natural resources, industry is based largely on processing imported raw materials for export. This makes the economy dependent on the state of world markets; public debt remained close to 100% of GDP in 2011, although the Belgian GDP grew by around 2% the same year. The banking sector was severely affected by the international banking crisis and government bailouts caused the budget deficit to worsen, although the deficit has since been reduced to around 4% of GDP.

Principal industries are engineering and metal products, vehicle assembly, transport equipment, scientific instruments, food processing and beverages, chemicals, base metals, textiles, glass, petroleum and diamonds. Industry accounts for 21.6% of GDP and 25% of employment. There is a large service sector, partly owing to the location in Brussels of EU institutions, NATO headquarters and a number of other international organisations. The service sector accounts for 77.7% of GDP. There is a small agricultural sector (0.7% of GDP).

Around three-quarters of trade is with other EU states, especially Germany, France and the Netherlands. External trade statistics relate to Luxembourg as well as Belgium, as the two countries formed an economic union in 1921.

GNI—US$477,643m; US$45,910 per capita (2010)
Annual average growth of GDP—2% (2011 est)
Inflation rate—3.1% (2011 est)
Population below poverty line—15.2% (2007 est)
Unemployment—8.3% (2010 est)
Total external debt—US$1,399,000m (2011)
Imports—US$390,176m (2010)
Exports—US$411,272m (2010)

BALANCE OF PAYMENTS
Trade—US$21,097m surplus (2010)
Current Account—US$4,891m surplus (2010)

Trade with UK	*2010*	*2011*
Imports from UK	£12,940,306,643	£15,383,714,421
Exports to UK	£16,981,334,281	£18,726,103,530

COMMUNICATIONS

Airports—The main airports are at Antwerp, Brussels, Liège and Ostend
Waterways—There are 2,043km of inland waterways, of which 1,528km are in regular commercial use; ship canals link Ostend and Zeebrugge with Bruges and Ghent, Ghent with Terneuzen in the Netherlands, Brussels with Charleroi and Willebroek Rupel, and Liège with Antwerp. The Meuse (Maas), Sambre and Schelde rivers form an integral part of the network. The major inland ports are located in Brussels, Ghent and Antwerp
Roadways—There are 153,595km of roadways, including 1,763km of motorways
Railways—The rail system is run by Belgian National Railways and, at 3,233km, the network is one of the densest in the world
Telecommunications—4.64 million main lines and 12.154 million mobile phones subscriptions (2010); there were 8.113 million internet users in 2009
Internet code and IDD—be; 32 (from UK), 44 (to UK)
Major broadcasters—Major television broadcaster include French-language RTBF and Dutch-language VRT
Press—Major newspapers include Dutch-language daily *Het Nieuwsblad* and French-language daily *Le Soir*
WPFI score—4,00 (14)

EDUCATION AND HEALTH

Nursery schools provide free education for children from two-and-a-half to six years of age. The official school-leaving age is 18.
Gross enrolment ratio (percentage of relevant age group)—primary 105%; secondary 111%; tertiary 67% (2009 est)
Health expenditure (per capita)—US$5,104 (2009)
Hospital beds (per 1,000 people)—6.6 (2004–9)
Life expectancy (years)—79.51 (2011 est)
Mortality rate—10.57 (2011 est)
Birth rate—10.06 (2011 est)
Infant mortality rate—4.33 (2011 est)

Bermuda

Area—54 sq. km
Capital—Hamilton, on Main Island; population, 11,535 (2009 est)
Currency—Bermuda dollar of 100 cents
Population—68,679 rising at 0.594% a year (2011 est)

Religion—Christian (Protestant 52%, Roman Catholic 15%) (est)
Language—English (official), Portuguese
Population density—1,292 per sq. km (2010 est)
Flag—British red ensign with the coat of the arms in the fly
National day—24 May (Bermuda Day)
Life expectancy (years)—80.71 (2011 est)
Mortality rate—7.57 (2011 est)
Birth rate—11.42 (2011 est)
Infant mortality rate—2.47 (2011 est)

FINANCIAL OUTLOOK

In 2012, Bermuda's GDP was expected to have been flat like in 2011, at US$5.5 billion, with the low-to-no growth environment potentially continuing deep into 2013. The US$5.5 billion GDP figure means Bermuda is back to pre-2008 global financial crash levels. Much of Bermuda's business is tied to the long economic relationship it has enjoyed with the United States. By the end of 2011, two-way trade in services between the United States and Bermuda was worth in excess of US$75 billion. By 2011 and continuing through 2012 and into 2013, Bermuda was the leading supplier of reinsurance services into the United States and the leading export market for the US primary insurance sector. The country is also the 10th-largest market for US exports as far as banking and investment funds are concerned. Bermuda is the 10th-largest portfolio capital investor in the United States and the fourth-largest investor in US government bonds. The country benefits from the fact that US and Asian investors, particularly those domiciled in Hong Kong, China, Taiwan, and Singapore, have found a Bermuda-domiciled holding company to be a very valuable and useful way of organizing investment flows between Asia and the United States.

CLIMATE AND TERRAIN

Bermuda is a group of over 130 small islands, of which about 20 are inhabited, in the North Atlantic Ocean. All the islands are volcanic in origin, with hilly interiors, surrounded by coral reefs. Elevation extremes range from 76m (Town Hill) to 0m (Atlantic Ocean). The climate is subtropical, regulated by the Gulf Stream, with an average temperature of 22°C.

HISTORY AND POLITICS

Bermuda was discovered by the Spanish in 1503 but colonised by the British from the early 17th century, becoming a colony in 1684. Independence from the UK was rejected in a 1995 referendum.

Internal self-government was introduced in 1968. The governor is responsible for external affairs, defence, internal security and the police, although administrative matters for the police service have been delegated to the minister of labour, home affairs and public safety. The cabinet comprises the premier and six elected assembly members. The legislature consists of the senate of 11 appointed members and the House of Assembly with 36 members elected for a five-year term. At the 2007 election, the ruling Progressive Labour Party (PLP) retained its 22 seats and continued in office. Ewart Brown stepped down as PLP leader in 2010 and was replaced by Paula Cox. An election is due to be held by the end of 2012.

Governor, HE Sir Richard Gozney, KCMG,*apptd*2007
Premier, Hon. Paula Cox

ECONOMY

The economy is based on offshore financial services for international business (especially re-insurance), and tourism. Other activities include light manufacturing (re-exports of pharmaceuticals are the main export) and construction.

Trade—US$1,292m deficit (2010)

Trade with UK	*2009*	*2011*
Imports from UK	£20,922,122	£17,453,125
Exports to UK	£863,642	£7,756,574

COMMUNICATIONS

The main islands are connected by a series of bridges and causeways. There are 447km of roads, all of which are paved, and one airport, near Ferry Reach on St David's Island. The main ports are at Hamilton, Freeport and St George. The telephone system is extensive, and mobile telephone distribution is widespread.

Bolivia

Estado Plurinacional de Bolivia—Plurinational State of Bolivia
Area—1,098,581 sq. km
Capital—La Paz, the seat of government; population, 1,641,950 (2009 est); Sucre, the legal capital and seat of the judiciary; population, 280,925 (2009 est)
Major cities—Cochabamba, El Alto, Oruro, Potosí, Santa Cruz
Currency—Boliviano ($b) of 100 centavos
Population—10,290,003 rising at 1.664% a year (2012 est); Quechua (30%), mestizo (30%), Aymara (25%) (est)
Religion—Christian (Roman Catholic 78%, Protestant 16%, other 3%) (est)
Language—Spanish, 36 indigenous languages (all official); Quechua and Aymara are the main indigenous languages
Population density—9 per sq. km (2010)
Urban population—66.5% (2010 est)
Median age (years)—22.5 (2011 est)
National anthem—'Himno Nacional de la República de Bolivia' ['National Anthem of the Republic of Bolivia']
National day—6 August (Independence Day)
Death penalty—Retained for certain crimes (last used 1974)
CPI score—2.8 (2011)

FINANCIAL OUTLOOK

In a report on Bolivia's economy in May 2012, the IMF estimated that real GDP growth for 2012 as a whole would amount to 5%, helped by strong gas export volumes and what the IMF called "mildly expansionary policies," which are helping to drive consumer spending in the country. Bolivia is also in the fortunate position of being able to enjoy a small surplus in its external current account and in its fiscal position. The biggest risk is rising prices caused by an overheating economy and demand outstripping supply, as the country's output gap shrinks to nothing. This is a situation that could easily hand pricing power to producers. One of the great successes of the country's policymaking in 2012 is the fact that access to financial services by all the population has been greatly expanded and this will continue through 2013. The Bolivian central bank will have to watch the expansion of credit in the country closely in 2013 and there will be a need for strengthened supervision, the IMF says. The IMF expects Bolivia to see inflation of around 4% in 2013, down 0.5% from 2012.

CLIMATE AND TERRAIN

Landlocked Bolivia's main topographical feature is its great central plateau, the Altiplano. Over 800km in length and at an average

altitude of 3,750m above sea level, this plateau lies between two great chains of the Andes that traverse the country from north to south. Lake Titicaca, shared with Peru, lies on the Antiplano. Elevation extremes range from 6,542m (Nevado Sajama) to 90m (Rio Paraguay). The low-lying north and eastern plains are drained by the principal rivers, the Itenez, Beni, Mamoré and Madre de Dios. The climate varies dramatically between regions: on the lowlands of the Amazon basin, temperatures average around 25°C; above 500m on the Altiplano, conditions are subpolar. The south is prone to droughts. The wet season is November to April.

HISTORY AND POLITICS

The 1967 constitution was revised in 1994 and 2009. It provides for an executive president who is directly elected for a five-year term, which may be renewed once. The bicameral Plurinational Legislative Assembly, or National Congress, consists of a 36-member Chamber of Senators and a 130-member Chamber of Deputies; members of both chambers are directly elected for a five-year term.

President Morales, leader of the Movement Towards Socialism (MAS), took office in 2006 after winning the 2005 presidential elections, and was re-elected in 2009. After the 2005 legislative elections, the MAS had an outright majority in the lower chamber of the legislature but the Social and Democratic Power party was the largest party in the upper chamber. The MAS won a majority in both chambers in the 2009 legislative elections.

HEAD OF STATE

President, Evo Morales Ayma, *elected* 18 December 2005, *sworn in* 22 January 2006, *re-elected* 2009
President of the Senate, Vice-President, Alvaro Garcia Linera

SELECTED GOVERNMENT MEMBERS *as at June 2012*

Defence, Ruben Saavedra Soto
Economy and Public Finance, Luis Alberto Arce Catacora
Foreign Affairs, David Choquehuanca Cespedes
Interior, Wilfredo Chavez

BOLIVIAN EMBASSY

106 Eaton Square, London SW1W 9AD
T 020-7235 4248/4255
E embol@bolivianembassy.co.uk
Ambassador Extraordinary and Plenipotentiary, Vacant

BRITISH EMBASSY

PO Box 694, Avenida Arce 2732, La Paz
T (+591) (2) 243 3424
E ukinbolivia@gmail.com
W ukinbolivia.fco.gov.uk/en/
Ambassador Extraordinary and Plenipotentiary, HE Ross Denny, *apptd* 2011

DEFENCE

Aged 16–49, 2010 est	Males	Females
Available for military service	2,472,490	2,535,768
Fit for military service	1,762,260	2,013,281

Military expenditure—US$316m (2011)

ECONOMY AND TRADE

The country is one of the poorest and least developed in South America, although steady growth since the 1990s has lowered the proportion of the population living below the poverty line from over half to under one-third. Economic growth slowed in the 2000s owing to lower commodity prices and political instability, and the economy contracted in 2009 because of the global downturn, recovering strongly in 2010 as commodity prices rose. The renationalised energy industry is the mainstay of the economy but development is hampered by lack of investment. There are plans, some already implemented, to nationalise other key industries and utilities.

Mining (principally for zinc, tin and gold) and smelting, natural gas and oil production, agriculture and textiles are the principal industries. Industry contributes 38% of GDP, agriculture 12% and services 50%.

The main trading partners are Brazil, the USA, Argentina and Peru. Principal exports are natural gas, soya beans and soya products, crude oil, zinc ore and tin. The main imports are petroleum products, plastics, paper, aircraft and aircraft parts, processed food, vehicles and insecticides.

GNI—US$18,789m; US$1,810 per capita (2010)
Annual average growth of GDP—5% (2011 est)
Inflation rate—10.1% (2011 est)
Population below poverty line—30.3% (2009 est; defined as living on less than US$2 a day)
Unemployment—7.8% (2010)
Total external debt—US$6,856m (2011 est)
Imports—US$5,182m (2010)
Exports—US$6,179m (2010)

BALANCE OF PAYMENTS

Trade—US$998m surplus (2010)
Current Account—US$813m surplus (2009)

Trade with UK	2010	2011
Imports from UK	£15,514,489	£17,814,773
Exports to UK	£27,580,655	£20,308,559

COMMUNICATIONS

Airports—Bolivia has 881 airports and airfields, including four international airports serving the major cities
Waterways—Bolivia has 10,000km of commercially navigable waterways, with an inland port on the river Paraguay at the border with Brazil. It has free port privileges at seaports in Argentina, Brazil, Chile and Paraguay, and a lease on a free-trade zone at the Peruvian port of Ilo
Roadways—Of the 13,602km of roads, fewer than 4,990km are surfaced
Railways—The 3,652km of railways form an eastern network and an Andean network
Telecommunications—848,200 main lines in use (2010), 7.179 million mobile telephones in use (2010); there were 1.103 million internet users in 2009
Internet code and IDD—bo; 591 (from UK), 10/11/12/13 44 (to UK; depends on area and/or carrier)
Major broadcasters—Television broadcasters include the government-run Television Boliviana and the commercially-run Bolivision and Unitel broadcasters; Radio Panamericana and the state-run Radio Illimani are some of the country's major radio broadcasters
Press—There are six national daily newspapers, including *La Razon*, *El Deber* and *El Mundo*
WPFI score—28,13 (103)

EDUCATION AND HEALTH

Elementary education is compulsory and free from the ages of five to 17.
Literacy rate—90.7% (2008 est)

Gross enrolment ratio (percentage of relevant age group)—primary 108%; secondary 81%(2008 est)
Health expenditure (per capita)—US$85 (2009)
Hospital beds (per 1,000 people)—1.1 (2004–9)
Life expectancy (years)—67.57 (2011 est)
Mortality rate—6.85 (2011 est)
Birth rate—24.71 (2011 est)
Infant mortality rate—42.16 (2011 est)

Botswana

Republic of Botswana
Area—581,730 sq. km
Capital—Gaborone; population, 195,894 (2009 est)
Major cities—Francistown, Molepolole, Selebi-Phikwe
Currency—Pula (P) of 100 thebe
Population—2,098,018 rising at 1.477% a year (2012 est); Tswana (79%), Kalanga (11%), Basarwa (3%) (est)
Religion—Christian 70% (predominantly Protestant) (est)
Language—English (official), Setswana, Kalanga, Sekgalagadi
Population density—4 per sq. km (2010)
Urban population—61.1% (2010 est)
Median age (years)—22.3 (2011 est)
National anthem—'Fatshe Leno La Rona' ['Blessed Be This Noble Land']
National day—30 September (Botswana Day)
Death penalty—Retained
CPI score—6.1 (2011)

FINANCIAL OUTLOOK

According to Business Monitor International, Botswana should see GDP growth of about 5.3% through 2013, on top of growth of the order of 5% for 2012. Inflation in Botswana is coming down. Historically, from 2001 to 2012, the rate of inflation averaged 8.48%. According to the Botswana Central Statistics Office, the rate in 2012 fell to 7.4% by December, as against the record high of 15.1% in August 2008. The country is on course to run a balanced budget through 2013, having achieved this in 2012 through a program of fiscal consolidation. BMI points out that this has created some discontent internally, but that the president has a tight grip on power and is expected to achieve a 10th election victory for the ruling party in 2014, so there is little chance of popular unrest posing a threat to fiscal consolidation. Botswana is expected to run a small current account surplus of 1.3% in 2013.

CLIMATE AND TERRAIN

Botswana lies on an undulating plateau and is covered by the Kalahari desert in the south and west. To the east, streams run into the Marico, Notwani and Limpopo rivers. In the north lies a flat region comprising the Makgadikgadi salt pans and the swampland of the Okavango delta. Elevation extremes range from 1,489m (Tsodilo Hills) to 513m (junction of the Limpopo and Shashe rivers). The climate is subtropical in the north, arid in the south and west, and more temperate in the east, which has regular rain. Average temperatures range from 13°C in July to 26°C in January.

HISTORY AND POLITICS

The Tswana people were predominant in the area from the 17th century. In 1885, at the request of indigenous chiefs fearing invasion by the Boers, Britain formally took control of Bechuanaland, and the northern part of the territory was declared the Bechuanaland Protectorate, while land to the south of the Molopo river became British Bechuanaland, which was later incorporated into the Cape Colony and eventually South Africa. In 1964, the Bechuanaland Protectorate became self-governing, and on 30 September 1966 it became an independent republic under the name Botswana. Since independence, Botswana has been stable and relatively prosperous owing to the diamond mining industry. There is a high level of HIV/AIDS among the population, and although an advanced treatment programme in place since 2001 is reducing the level of infection, the country faces serious demographic and social problems.

President Festus Mogae stood down in 2008, having completed two terms of office, and was succeeded by the vice-president, Lt.-Gen. Ian Khama, son of the country's first president. The 2009 legislative election was won by the Botswana Democratic Party (BDP), with 45 seats. President Khama, of the BDP, was elected president two days later.

Under the 1966 constitution, the executive president is elected by the legislature for a five-year term, renewable once. He appoints the vice-president and the cabinet. The unicameral National Assembly has 57 members directly elected for a five-year term, plus a variable number of members (currently four) nominated by the president and elected by the assembly. A 15-member House of Chiefs advises on tribal matters and constitutional changes.

HEAD OF STATE

President, Lt.-Gen. (retd) Ian Khama, *sworn in* 1 April 2008, *elected* 18 October 2009
Vice-President, Mompati Merafhe

SELECTED GOVERNMENT MEMBERS *as at June 2012*

Finance and Development Planning, Kenneth Matambo
Foreign Affairs, Phandu Skelemani
Defence, Dikgakgamatso Seretse

BOTSWANA HIGH COMMISSION

6 Stratford Place, London W1C 1AY
T 020-7499 0031
E bohico@govbw.com
High Commissioner, HE Roy Blackbeard, *apptd* 1998

BRITISH HIGH COMMISSION

Private Bag 0023, Plot 1079-1084 Main Mall, off Queens Road, Gaborone
T (+267) 395 2841
W ukinbotswana.fco.gov.uk
High Commissioner, HE Jennifer Anderson, *apptd* 2010

DEFENCE

Aged 16–49, 2010 est	*Males*	*Females*
Available for military service	557,647	531,095
Fit for military service	340,949	302,332

Military expenditure—US$344m (2011)

ECONOMY AND TRADE

Botswana has been relatively prosperous since independence because of its mining industry, political stability and sound economic management. Despite this, about 30% of the population lives below the poverty line. Longer-term problems are the impact of the high levels of HIV/AIDS among the workforce and the levelling off of diamond production, which usually accounts for 70 to 80% of export earnings; diamond exports declined owing to the global downturn, causing the economy to contract sharply in 2009. The government has sought to reduce the economy's dependence on the diamond industry by diversifying; safari tourism and financial services in particular have grown in recent years, and the services sector now contributes 52.9% of GDP. The industrial sector contributes 45% of GDP, mainly from mining diamonds, copper, nickel, salt, soda ash, potash, coal, iron ore and silver. Agriculture is predominantly pastoral and accounts for 2.1% of GDP.

The main trading partners are EU and southern African countries. Principal exports are diamonds, copper, nickel, soda ash, meat and textiles. The main imports are foodstuffs, machinery, electrical goods, transport equipment, textiles, fuel and petroleum products.

GNI—US$14,771m; US$6,790 per capita (2010)
Annual average growth of GDP—6.2% (2011 est)
Inflation rate—7.8% (2011 est)
Population below poverty line—30.3% (2003)
Unemployment—7.5% (2007)
Total external debt—US$2,684m (2011 est)
Imports—US$5,700m (2010)
Exports—US$4,700m (2010)

BALANCE OF PAYMENTS
Trade—US$1,000m deficit (2010)
Current Account—US$668m deficit (2009)

Trade with UK	2010	2011
Imports from UK	£11,023,942	£16,643,191
Exports to UK	£561,035,901	£2,416,299,677

COMMUNICATIONS
Airports—There are 78 airports and airfields, including the international airport in Gaborone
Roadways—There are 25,798km of roads, of which 8,410km are paved
Railways—The only railway is the 888km line from Zimbabwe to South Africa, which passes through eastern Botswana
Telecommunications—137,400 fixed lines and 2.363 million mobile subscriptions (2010); there were 120,000 internet users in 2009
Internet code and IDD—bw; 267 (from UK), 44 (to UK)
Major broadcasters—State-run television broadcaster Botswana TV was established in 2000; state-run Radio Botswana operates a commercial FM station from Gaborone
Press—Major daily newspapers include the *Daily News* and the privately-owned *Mmegi*
WPFI score—17,50 (62)

EDUCATION AND HEALTH
Botswana does not have a compulsory education policy, although many children receive 12 years of education (seven years of primary education, three years of junior secondary and two years of senior secondary). In 2006 fees were reintroduced for state secondary schools, which had been free of charge for over 20 years.
Literacy rate—84.1% (2009 est)
Gross enrolment ratio (percentage of relevant age group)—primary 109%; secondary 82% (2007 est)
Health expenditure (per capita)—US$612 (2009)
Hospital beds (per 1,000 people)—1.8 (2004–9)
Life expectancy (years)—58.05 (2011 est)
Mortality rate—10.57 (2011 est)
Birth rate—22.31 (2011 est)
Infant mortality rate—11.14 (2011 est)
HIV/AIDS adult prevalence—24.8% (2009)

Brazil

Republica Federativa do Brasil—Federative Republic of Brazil
Area—8,514,877 sq. km
Capital—Brasilia; population, 3,788,820 (2009 est)
Major cities—Belo Horizonte, Fortaleza, Porto Alegre, Recife, Rio de Janeiro (the former capital), Salvador, Sao Paulo
Currency—Real of 100 centavos
Population—205,716,890 rising at 1.102% a year (2012 est)
Religion—Christian (Roman Catholic 74%, Protestant 15%) (est)
Language—Portuguese (official), Spanish, German, Italian, Japanese, English, Amerindian languages
Population density—23 per sq. km (2010)
Urban population—86.5% (2010 est)
Median age (years)—29.3 (2011 est)
National anthem—'Hino Nacional Brasileiro' ['Brazilian National Anthem']
National day—7 September (Independence Day)
Death penalty—Retained for certain crimes (last used 1855)
CPI score—3.8 (2011)

FINANCIAL OUTLOOK
According to a Reuters report, the Brazilian economy probably grew by no more than 1.03% in 2012. This is less than the IMF is forecasting for the economies of Japan and the United States, and about the same as that of Germany. The prediction comes from a survey by the Brazilian Central Bank of 100 financial institutions. The survey predicts somewhat stronger growth for the economy in 2013, amounting to 3.5%. This is a downwards revision from an identical survey carried out a year earlier, when growth in 2013 was expected to be 3.7%. In 2012, Brazil's manufacturers faced the triple whammy of an overvalued currency, high labor costs, and a general softening in the global economy. The country also needs a great deal more investment. Targeted tax reductions by President Dilma Rousseff's government are helping to drive some growth. The central bank has cut interest rates 10 times in a row, to a record low of 7.25%. More stimulus is expected through 2013.

CLIMATE AND TERRAIN
Brazil has six distinct topographical areas: the Amazon basin (north and west of the country), the Parana-Paraguay river basin (south; the Parana drains the Pantanal, the world's largest freshwater wetland), the Guiana Highlands (north of the Amazon), the Mato Grosso plateau (centre), the Brazilian Highlands (south of the Amazon) and the coastal strip. Elevation

extremes range from 2,994m (Pico da Neblina) to 0m (Atlantic Ocean). Brazil has the world's largest rainforest, as well as large expanses of savannah *(cerrado)*. The climate is mostly tropical, with the equator passing through the north and the Tropic of Capricorn through the south-east. The Amazon basin sees annual rainfall of up to 2,000mm a year and there is no dry season (average temperature 30°C). The north-east is the driest area of the country and can experience long periods of drought (maximum average temperature 38°C). The southern states have a seasonal temperate climate (average temperatures between 17°C and 19°C).

HISTORY AND POLITICS

The Federative Republic of Brazil is composed of the Federal District of Brasilia in which the capital lies, and 26 states: Acre, Alagoas, Amapa, Amazonas, Bahia, Ceara, Espirito Santo, Goias, Maranhao, Mato Grosso, Mato Grosso do Sul, Minas Gerais, Para, Paraiba, Parana, Pernambuco, Piaui, Rio de Janeiro, Rio Grande do Norte, Rio Grande do Sul, Rondonia, Roraima, Santa Catarina, Sao Paulo, Sergipe and Tocantins. Each state has its own governor and legislative assembly.

Under the 1988 constitution (amended in 1997), the executive president is directly elected for a four-year term, which is renewable once. The National Congress consists of an 81-member federal senate (three senators per state, directly elected for an eight-year term) and a 513-member Chamber of Deputies which is directly elected every four years; the number of deputies per state depends upon the state's population.

Dilma Rousseff of the Workers' Party (PT) was elected in 2010, becoming Brazil's first female president. In the 2010 legislative election, the PBSM alliance led by the PT and the Brazilian Democratic Movement Party (PMDB) won a majority in both houses of Congress. President Rousseff appointed a coalition government dominated by the PT and including the PMDB, five other parties and independents; her government was dogged by corruption allegations throughout 2011 and early 2012.

HEAD OF STATE

President, Dilma Rousseff, *sworn in* 1 January 2011
Vice-President, Michel Temer

SELECTED GOVERNMENT MEMBERS *as at July 2012*

Defence, Celso Amorim
Foreign Affairs, Antonio Patriota
Finance, Guido Mantega
Attorney-General, Luis Inacio Lucena Adams

EMBASSY OF BRAZIL

32 Green Street, London W1K 7AT
T 020-7499 0877
E infolondres@brazil.org.uk
W www.brazil.org.uk
Ambassador Extraordinary and Plenipotentiary, HE Roberto Jaguaribe, *apptd* 2010

BRITISH EMBASSY

Setor de Embaixadas Sul, Quadra 801, Lote 8, CEP 70408-900, Brasilia DF
T (+55) (61) 3329 2300
W ukinbrazil.fco.gov.uk
Ambassador Extraordinary and Plenipotentiary, HE Alan Charlton, CMG, *apptd* 2008

DEFENCE

All aged 16–49, 2010 est	*Males*	*Females*
Available for military service	53,530,703	53,433,918
Fit for military service	38,993,989	44,841,661

Military budget—US$31,576m (2011)
Conscription duration—12 months (can be extended to 18)

ECONOMY AND TRADE

Historically subject to boom and bust cycles, the economy was stabilised by reforms in the 1990s. Tight fiscal management, IMF programmes, a growth in output and an expanding export base have produced steady growth since 2003, although poverty is still widespread. Brazil's economy, based on well-developed agriculture, mining, manufacturing and service sectors, is now the eighth largest in the world, giving the country growing global influence. Although the economy contracted in the global downturn, it weathered the crisis better than many other countries and is recovering steadily, despite a faltering industrial sector and rising currency.

The country is rich in mineral deposits, including iron ore (haematite), bauxite, gold, manganese, nickel, platinum and uranium. It produces oil, gas and hydroelectricity, and is close to self-sufficiency in oil. Brazil is the world's largest producer of coffee; the other main agricultural products are soya beans, wheat, rice, maize, sugar cane, cocoa, citrus fruit and beef. The expansion of agriculture and forestry threaten the rainforest, although recent governments' attempts to prevent further depredations by loggers and farmers have slowed the rate of deforestation considerably. Tourism is a growing industry. In 2011, services generated 67.3% of GDP, industry 26.9% and agriculture 5.8%.

Brazil's main trading partners are the USA, China, Argentina and Germany. Principal exports are transport equipment, iron ore, soya beans, footwear, coffee and vehicles. The main imports are machinery, electrical and transport equipment, chemical products, oil, vehicle parts and electronics.

GNI—US$2,049,163m; US$9,390 per capita (2010)
Annual average growth of GDP—2.8% (2011)
Inflation rate—6.9% (2011 est)
Population below poverty line—26% (2008)
Unemployment—6.7% (2010 est)
Total external debt—US$410,000m (2011)
Imports—US$191,464m (2010)
Exports—US$201,915m (2010)

BALANCE OF PAYMENTS

Trade—US$10,451m surplus (2010)
Current Account—US$47,365m deficit (2010)

Trade with UK	*2010*	*2011*
Imports from UK	£2,128,960,731	£2,321,919,662
Exports to UK	£3,694,788,983	£2,800,504,758

COMMUNICATIONS

Airports—There are 4,072 airports and airfields; international flights operate to the major cities
Waterways—In remote regions, transport is primarily by air or water, utilising the 50,000km of navigable waterways, although a severe drought in 2010 left water levels so low that ferries and other craft were unable to operate
Roadways—1,751,868km; the Trans-Amazonian Highway connects the Amazon region with the rest of the country, although it is mostly unpaved and often becomes impassable in the rainy season

  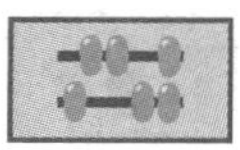      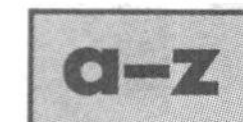

Railways—28,538km
Telecommunications—42.141 million fixed lines and 202.994 million mobile subscriptions (2010); there were 23.79 million internet users in 2011
Internet—br; 55 (from UK), 14/15/21/23/31 44 (to UK, varies depending on area and/or carrier)
Major broadcasters—Domestic conglomerates, most notably Globo, dominate the market and run television and radio networks, newspapers and subscription television stations
Press—There are six major daily newspapers, including *O Dia*, *O Correio Brazilinese* and *Jornal do Brasil*
WPFI score—16,60 (58)

EDUCATION AND HEALTH

Public education is free at all levels, and is compulsory between the ages of seven and 14.
Literacy rate—90.0% (2008 est)
Gross enrolment ratio (percentage of relevant age group)—primary 120%; secondary 90%; tertiary 38% (2009 est)
Health expenditure (per capita)—US$734 (2009)
Hospital beds (per 1,000 people)—2.4 (2004–9)
Life expectancy (years)—72.53 (2011 est)
Mortality rate—6.36 (2011 est)
Birth rate—17.79 (2011 est)
Infant mortality rate—21.17 (2011 est)

British Virgin Islands

Area—151 sq. km
Capital—Road Town, on Tortola; population, 9,384 (2009 est)
Currency—US dollar (US$) of 100 cents
Population—25,383 rising at 1.741% a year (2011 est)
Religion—Christian (Protestant 86%, Roman Catholic 10%) (est)
Language—English (official)
Population density—146 per sq. km (2005)
Flag—British blue ensign with the coat of arms in the fly
National day—1 July (Territory Day)
Life expectancy (years)—77.63 (2011 est)
Mortality rate—4.49 (2011 est)
Birth rate—14.5 (2011 est)
Infant mortality rate—13.63 (2011 est)

FINANCIAL OUTLOOK

The 2013 budget speech emphasized that the British Virgin Islands (BVI) had seen a "gradual but slow recovery" through 2010 and 2011, with growth of 2.01% and 2.4%, respectively, with the number of new incorporations in the country's financial services sector going up by 8% (26% in 2009). However, the country's tourism industry continues to struggle. By the end of 2011, the numbers of arrivals had still not recovered to pre-2008 crisis levels, with the 2011 figure still 24% down on 2007, driven mainly by reductions in cruise passenger visits. The recovery in the BVI economy since 2007 has been largely driven, therefore, by the recovery in the financial services sector. Inflation has been low and stable for the last decade, staying in the low single digits. The BVI is anticipating GDP growth to be 4% for 2012, well up on the 2.4% recorded in the prior year. However, cruise passenger numbers fell by 22.5% in the first half of 2012, resulting in a 13.3% drop in tourists to the BVI in that period. Larger cruise ship sizes mean that the BVI has to invest in upgrading its port infrastructure if it wants to see a return to boom times in the cruise market, and that won't happen in time to improve results for 2013. The recovery in the financial services sector looks set to continue through 2013, however, helping to keep GDP growth in the low single digits.

CLIMATE AND TERRAIN

The easternmost part of the Virgin Islands archipelago in the Caribbean Sea, the British Virgin Islands comprise Tortola, Anegada, Virgin Gorda, Jost Van Dyke and about 40 islets and cays; 16 of the islands are inhabited. Apart from Anegada, which is flat, the British Virgin Islands are hilly with coral reefs offshore. The highest point of elevation is 521m (Mt Sage, on Tortola). The climate is sub-tropical, with little variation in temperature, which typically ranges between 25°C in January and 27°C in July. The hurricane season is from June to November.

HISTORY AND POLITICS

Initially settled by Arawak Indians, the islands were named by Christopher Columbus in 1493 and colonised by the Dutch in the early 17th century. Annexed by the British in 1672, the islands were part of the Leeward Islands colony from 1872 to 1960. After a period of direct rule, a measure of self-government was introduced by the 1977 constitution and extended in 2000.

Under the 2007 constitution, the governor, appointed by the crown, retains responsibility for defence, security, external affairs and the civil service. The executive council comprises the premier, four other elected Assembly members and the attorney-general. The House of Assembly consists of a speaker, one *ex-officio* member (the attorney-general) and 13 members elected for a four-year term.

The 2011 election was won by the opposition National Democratic Party with nine seats.
Governor, HE Boyd McCleary, CMG, CVO, *apptd* 2010
Premier, Hon. Orlando Smith, OBE

ECONOMY

The main industries are tourism, which generates about 45% of GDP, and offshore financial services. Other industries include construction and light manufacturing. The major exports are rum, fresh fish, fruit, livestock, gravel and sand. Chief imports are building materials, cars, foodstuffs and machinery.

Trade with UK	*2009*	*2011*
Imports from UK	£31,380	£31,003,194
Exports to UK	£10,630,295	£15,658,019

COMMUNICATIONS

The principal airport is on Beef Island, linked by bridge to Tortola, and there are also airfields on Anegada and Virgin Gorda. Road Harbour, at Road Town, is the main port, and ferry services connect the main islands. Many of the 200km of roads are steep and narrow.

  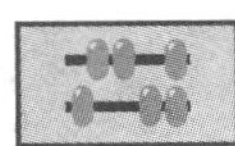      

Brunei

Negara Brunei Darussalam—Brunei Darussalam
Area—5,765 sq. km
Capital—Bandar Seri Begawan; population, 22,228 (2009 est)
Major towns—Kuala Belait, Seria, Kampong Ayer
Currency—Brunei dollar (B$) of 100 sen (fully interchangeable with Singapore currency)
Population—408,786 rising at 1.691% a year (2012 est); Malay (66.3%), Chinese (11.2%) (2004 est)
Religion—Muslim 82% (predominantly Shafi'i, a school of Sunni Islam), Buddhist 7%, Christian 3% (est); Islam is the state religion
Language—Malay (official), English, Chinese
Population density—76 per sq. km (2010)
Urban population—75.7% (2010 est)
Median age (years)—28.4 (2011 est)
National anthem—'Allah Peliharakan Sultan' ['God Bless the Sultan']
National day—23 February (date of independence from British protection, 1984)
Death penalty—Retained (no known use since 1992)
CPI score—5.2 (2011)

FINANCIAL OUTLOOK

Brunei's economy is dominated by the petroleum sector. Energy production, which accounts for two-thirds of nominal GDP and 92% of government revenues, has allowed the government to fund high levels of social benefits and public-sector employment, according to the IMF. In December 2012, officials predicted that GDP would expand by 1.6% in 2012, down from 2.2% in 2011. In its latest report on the economy, published in April 2012, the Asian Development Bank said that substantial fiscal and current account surpluses provide a cushion against shocks. Diversifying sources of growth is the main challenge for the economy. Government price controls and subsidies keep inflation low; it averaged 0.5% in 2013, according to the Department of Economic Planning and Development. The Brunei dollar is pegged to the Singapore dollar through a currency board arrangement, and appreciated against the US dollar for much of 2012 but lost ground in the first quarter of 2013.

CLIMATE AND TERRAIN

The country lies on the north-west coast of the island of Borneo. It is surrounded and divided in two by the Malaysian state of Sarawak. The terrain is around 70% rainforest (although current estimates vary), with extensive mangrove swamps along the coastal plain. There are mountains on the border with Sarawak. Elevation extremes range from 1,850m (Bukit Pagon) to 0m (South China Sea). The climate is tropical, with high humidity, and an annual average daily temperature of 27°C.

HISTORY AND POLITICS

Formerly a powerful Muslim sultanate that controlled Borneo and parts of the Philippines, Brunei was reduced to its present size by the mid-19th century and came under British protection in 1889. It chose to remain a British dependency in 1963 rather than joining the Federation of Malaysia. Internally self-governing from 1959, Brunei gained full independence on 1 January 1984.

In 1962 the legislative election was annulled after it was won by a party that sought to remove the sultan; a state of emergency was declared and the sultan has ruled by decree ever since. A ministerial system of government was introduced in 1984. Some political liberalisation and modernisation has taken place since 2004, when the legislature was reconvened after 20 years.

Parts of the 1959 constitution have been suspended since the state of emergency began in 1962. Supreme executive authority is vested in the sultan, a hereditary monarch who presides over and is advised by a privy council, a religious council and the council of cabinet ministers. The legislative council was reconvened in 2004 with 21 members appointed by the sultan; it has passed constitutional amendments to increase its size to 45 members, 15 of whom will be directly elected. No date has been set for an election.

HEAD OF STATE

HM The Sultan of Brunei, Prime Minister, Defence, Finance, HM Hassanal Bolkiah, GCB, *acceded* 5 *October* 1967, *crowned* 1 August 1968
HM Crown Prince, Senior Minister in the Prime Minister's Office, Prince Al-Muhtadee Billah

SELECTED GOVERNMENT MEMBERS *as at May 2012*

Foreign Affairs, Prince Mohamed Bolkiah
Home Affairs, Pehin Dato Ustaz Badaruddin bin Pengarah Othman

BRUNEI DARUSSALAM HIGH COMMISSION

19–20 Belgrave Square, London SW1X 8PG
T 020-7581 0521
E info@bdhcl.co.uk
High Commissioner, HE Mohd Aziyan Del Abdullah, *apptd* 2010

BRITISH HIGH COMMISSION

2.01, 2nd Floor, Block D, Kompleks Yayasan Sultan Haji Hassanal Bolkiah, Bandar Seri Begawan, BS 8711
T (+673) (2) 222 231
E brithc@brunet.bn
W ukinbrunei.fco.gov.uk
High Commissioner, Robert Fenn, *apptd* 2009

DEFENCE

All aged 16–49, 2010 est	Males	Females
Available for military service	112,688	117,536
Fit for military service	95,141	99,386

Military expenditure—US$373m (2011)

ECONOMY AND TRADE

The economy is based on the production of oil and natural gas and the income from overseas investments. Royalties and taxes from these operations form the bulk of government revenue and have enabled the construction of free health, education and welfare services. However, oil and gas reserves are declining and Brunei is now trying to diversify its economy, developing financial services and tourism. A new monetary authority was established in January 2011 with a view to develop and monitor the country's growing financial institutions.

Agriculture accounts for 0.9% of GDP, industry 72.3% and services 26.8%. The main trading partners are Japan, Singapore, Indonesia, Malaysia and South Korea. Principal exports are crude oil, natural gas and clothing. The main imports are machinery and transport equipment, manufactured goods, food (over 80% of domestic requirements is imported) and chemicals.

GNI—US$10,784m; US$31,800 per capita (2009)
Annual average growth of GDP—2.8% (2011 est)

Inflation rate—2% (2011)
Unemployment—3.7% (2008)

BALANCE OF PAYMENTS
Trade—US$5,601m surplus (2010)
Current Account—US$4,318m surplus (2009)

Trade with UK	2010	2011
Imports from UK	£151,419,603	£57,016,887
Exports to UK	£14,151,157	£33,722,842

COMMUNICATIONS
Airports—There are two airports, one in Seria and one in Bandar Seri Begawan
Waterways—There are ports at Kuala Belait, Muara and Tanjong Salirong; the 209km of internal waterways are navigable only by shallow craft.
Roadways—2,971km
Railways—None
Telecommunications—79,900 fixed lines in use and 435,100 mobile subscriptions; there were 314,900 internet users in 2009
Internet code and IDD—bn; 673 (from UK), 44 (to UK)
Major broadcasters—The only broadcast media organisation, Radio Television Brunei (RTB), is state-owned; it broadcasts in Malay and English
WPFI score—51,00 (142)

EDUCATION AND HEALTH
All levels of education are free.
Literacy rate—95.3% (2009 est)
Gross enrolment ratio (percentage of relevant age group)—primary 111%; secondary 107%; tertiary 19% (2009 est)
Life expectancy (years)—76.17 (2011 est)
Mortality rate—3.35 (2011 est)
Birth rate—17.87 (2011 est)
Infant mortality rate—11.51 (2011 est)

Bulgaria

Republika Balgariya—Republic of Bulgaria
Area—110,879 sq. km
Capital—Sofia; population, 1,191,890 (2009 est)
Major cities—Burgas, Plovdiv, Varna
Currency—Lev of 100 stotinki
Population—7,037,935 falling at 0.79% a year (2012 est); Bulgarian (83.9%), Turkish (9.4%), Roma (4.7%) (2001)
Religion—Christian 85% (Bulgarian Orthodox 84%), Muslim 13% (predominantly Sunni) (est)
Language—Bulgarian (official), Turkish, Romani
Population density—69 per sq. km (2010)
Urban population—71.7% (2010 est)
Median age (years)—41.9 (2011 est)
National anthem—'Mila Rodino' ['Dear Motherland']
National day—3 March (Liberation Day)
Death penalty—Abolished for all crimes (since 1998)
CPI score—3.3 (2011)

FINANCIAL OUTLOOK
According to a Bloomberg report, Bulgaria's 2013 budget brought in a 10% tax on interest from deposits, and targets growth of between 1.2% and 1.9% for 2013. "The budget sets a sustainable macroeconomic environment and encourages quicker economic recovery," said Finance Minister Simeon Djankov, when presenting the budget. Bulgaria managed to avoid borrowing from lenders abroad during the economic crisis, despite being the poorest, per capita, in the European Union. The budget assumes a deficit of 1.3% of GDP, the same as in 2012. Revenues for the government in 2013 are expected to amount to US$20.13 billion, or 37.5% of GDP, while spending is projected at 38.8% of GDP. Inflation is expected to be around 3.4% through 2013, rising from 2.6% in 2012. Public debt is capped at 17.6% of GDP for 2013. Personal and corporate tax rates remain very favorable at a flat rate of 10%, in an attempt to attract inward investment and boost growth.

CLIMATE AND TERRAIN
The Balkan Mountains cross the country from west to east, averaging 2,000m in height and the Rhodope Mountains in the south-west climb to almost 3,000m. Elevation extremes range from 2,925m (Musala) to 0m (Black Sea). The lowland plains of the north and south-east are in the basins of the main rivers: the Danube in the north, which forms much of the border with Romania, and the Maritsa, which divides the Balkan and Rhodope ranges. The climate is temperate, with cold, damp winters and hot, dry summers. Average temperatures in Sofia range from −1°C in January to 20°C in July.

HISTORY AND POLITICS
Under the 1991 constitution, the president is directly elected for a five-year term, renewable once. The head of government is the prime minister, who is appointed by the president, and is usually the leader of the largest party in the legislature. There is a unicameral National Assembly of 240 members who are directly elected for a four-year term.

In the 2009 legislative election, the new centre-right party Citizens for European Development of Bulgaria (GERB) won the most seats, but without an overall majority, and formed a minority government with support from small right-wing parties. Rosen Plevneliev of the GERB won the 2011 presidential election, picking up 40% of the vote; he was inaugurated on 21 January 2012.

HEAD OF STATE
President, Rosen Plevneliev, *elected* 30 October 2011
Vice-President, Margarita Popova

SELECTED GOVERNMENT MEMBERS *as at May 2012*
Prime Minister, Boiko Borisov
Deputy Prime Ministers, Simeon Djankov *(Finance)*, Tsvetan Tsvetanov *(Interior)*
Defence, Anyu Angelov
Foreign Affairs, Nikolay Mladenov

EMBASSY OF THE REPUBLIC OF BULGARIA
186–188 Queen's Gate, London SW7 5HL
T 020-7584 9400
E info@bulgarianembassy.org.uk
W www.bulgarianembassy-london.org
Ambassador Extraordinary and Plenipotentiary, HE Lyubomir Kyuchukov, *apptd* 2009

        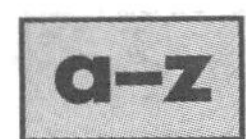

BRITISH EMBASSY
9 Moskovska Street, Sofia 1000
T (+359) (2) 933 9222
E britembsof@mbox.cit.bg
W ukinbulgaria.fco.gov.uk
Ambassador Extraordinary and Plenipotentiary, HE Jonathan Allen, *apptd* 2011

DEFENCE

Aged 16–49, 2010 est	*Males*	*Females*
Available for military service	1,637,470	1,621,532
Fit for military service	1,320,955	1,337,616

Military expenditure—US$722m (2011)

ECONOMY AND TRADE

The government adopted radical economic reforms in 1996 and the economy achieved stability and attracted significant foreign investment, although administrative corruption and organised crime remain potential deterrents. Despite steady economic growth in 2004–8 and responsible fiscal management, the economy contracted in the global economic downturn as industrial production and exports declined. Recovery has been slow.

Natural resources include copper, lead, zinc, other minerals, coal and timber. Fertile arable land produces vegetables, fruit, tobacco, wine, wheat, barley, sunflowers and livestock. Agriculture employs 7.1% of the workforce and accounts for 5.2% of GDP. Industries include energy generation, food processing, beverages, tobacco, machinery and equipment, base metals, chemicals, mining and oil refining. Tourism is growing.

The main trading partners are EU countries, Russia and Turkey. Principal exports are clothing and footwear, iron and steel, machinery and equipment, and fuels. The main imports are predominantly machinery and raw materials for the industrial sector.

GNI—US$46,025m; US$6,270 per capita (2010)
Annual average growth of GDP—2.2% (2011 est)
Inflation rate—4% (2011 est)
Population below poverty line—21.8% (2008 est)
Unemployment—9.5% (2010 est)
Total external debt—US$39,280m (2011)
Imports—US$25,361m (2010)
Exports—US$20,608m (2010)

BALANCE OF PAYMENTS
Trade—US$4,753m deficit (2010)
Current Account—US$473m deficit (2010)

Trade with UK	*2010*	*2011*
Imports from UK	£238,895,611	£320,718,423
Exports to UK	£227,822,635	£282,100,216

COMMUNICATIONS
Airports—The main airports are at Sofia, Plovdiv, Burgas and Varna
Waterways—There are 470km of waterways, and inland ports include Vidin, Lom and Ruse on the river Danube; The main ports are Burgas and Varna on the Black Sea
Roadways—There are 40,231km of roads, including 418km of motorways
Railways—4,151km
Telecommunications—2.2 million fixed lines and 10.585 million mobile telephone subscriptions (2010); there were 3.395 million internet users in 2009
Internet code and IDD—bg; 359 (from UK), 44 (to UK)
Major broadcasters—Public service broadcasters Bulgarian National Radio and Bulgarian National Television share the market with a vigorous commercial sector that provides national and regional broadcasting
Press—There are seven major daily newspapers, including *Dnevnik*, *Trud*, and the business-orientated *Pari*
WPFI score—19,00 (70)

EDUCATION AND HEALTH
Education is free and compulsory from seven to 14 years.
Literacy rate—98.3% (2009 est)
Gross enrolment ratio (percentage of relevant age group)—primary 103%; secondary 88%; tertiary 53% (2009 est)
Health expenditure (per capita)—US$475 (2009)
Hospital beds (per 1,000 people)—6.5 (2004–9)
Life expectancy (years)—73.59 (2011 est)
Mortality rate—14.32 (2011 est)
Birth rate—9.32 (2011 est)
Infant mortality rate—16.68 (2011 est)

Canada

Area—9,984,670 sq. km
Capital—Ottawa; population, 1,170,310 (2009 est; includes Gatineau)
Major cities—Calgary, Edmonton, Hamilton, Montréal, Québec, Toronto, Vancouver, Winnipeg
Currency—Canadian dollar (C$) of 100 cents
Population—34,300,083 rising at 0.784% a year (2012 est)
Religion—Christian (Roman Catholic 44%, Protestant 29%, other 4%), Muslim 2%, Jewish 1%, Buddhist 1%, Hindu 1%, Sikh 1% (2001)
Language—English, French (both official)
Population density—4 per sq. km (2010)
Urban population—80.6% (2010 est)
Median age (years)—41 (2011 est)
National anthem—'O Canada'
National day—1 July (Canada Day)
Death penalty—Abolished for all crimes (since 1998)
CPI score—8.7 (2011)

FINANCIAL OUTLOOK
The Canadian economy grew by 1.8% in 2012, according to Statistics Canada, down from 2.6% in 2011. In March 2013, the Bank of Canada forecast growth of 2.0% in 2013. The central bank signaled that it was in no rush to raise interest rates after a prolonged pause, but added that the next move would be a hike rather than a cut. Despite the economic slowdown, the unemployment rate fell to a four-year low of 7.1% in December 2012. Canada's housing market has become a matter of concern, with prices having nearly doubled since 2000. The market has boomed in recent years and some economists have warned that it is a bubble that could burst. The announcement in November 2012 that Bank of Canada governor Mark Carney, credited

  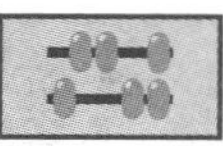      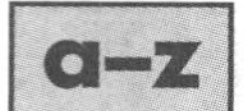

with helping to steer Canada though the global financial crisis, was leaving to take charge of the Bank of England, was one of the major developments in Canada's financial environment in 2012.

CLIMATE AND TERRAIN

The six main geographic divisions of Canada are: the Appalachian-Acadian region; the Canadian Shield, which comprises more than half the country; the St Lawrence-Great Lakes lowland; the interior plains; the Cordilleran region; and the Arctic archipelago, which lies under continuous permafrost. The most southerly point is Middle Island in Lake Erie. Elevation extremes range from 5,959m (Mt Logan) to 0m (Atlantic Ocean) at the lowest. The climate varies from temperate in the south to subarctic and arctic in the north. The east and centre experience greater extremes than in corresponding latitudes in Europe, but the climate is milder in the south-western part of the prairie region and the southern parts of the Pacific slope. The tornado season is April to September, peaking in June and early July in southern Ontario, Alberta and Québec, Saskatchewan and Manitoba through to Thunder Bay. The interior of British Columbia and western New Brunswick are also tornado zones.

HISTORY AND POLITICS

Under the 1982 constitution, the head of state is Queen Elizabeth II, represented by a governor-general appointed on the advice of the Canadian prime minister.

The bicameral parliament consists of a senate and a House of Commons. The senate comprises 105 members, who serve until the age of 75, appointed by the governor-general on the recommendation of the prime minister; seats are assigned on a regional basis. A reform bill introduced in 2011 proposed nine-year non-renewable terms for senators. The House of Commons has 308 members, directly elected for a four-year term. Representation is proportional to the population of each province. Each province is largely self-governing, with its own lieutenant-governor and unicameral legislative assembly. The territories are administered by the federal government.

A parliamentary vote of no confidence ended 12 years of Liberal government in 2005. In snap general elections in 2006 and 2008, the Conservative Party won the most seats, but not a majority, and formed minority governments under Stephen Harper. His government won a snap general election in May 2011, increasing its seats to achieve an overall majority.

GOVERNOR-GENERAL

Governor-General, HE David Johnston, *apptd* 2010

SELECTED GOVERNMENT MEMBERS *as at June 2012*

Prime Minister, Stephen Harper
Finance, James Flaherty
Foreign Affairs, John Baird
Defence, Peter MacKay

CANADIAN HIGH COMMISSION

Macdonald House, 1 Grosvenor Square, London W1K 4AB
T 020-7258 6600
E 1dn@international.gc.ca
W www.unitedkingdom.gc.ca
High Commissioner, HE Gordon Campbell, *apptd* 2011

BRITISH HIGH COMMISSION

80 Elgin Street, Ottawa, Ontario K1P 5K7
T (+1) (613) 237 1530
W ukincanada.fco.gov.uk
High Commissioner, HE Andrew Pocock, CMG, *apptd* 2011

Federal Structure

Provinces or Territories (with official contractions)	*Population (2011)*	*Area (sq. km)*	*Capital*	*Premier*
Alberta (AB)	3,645,257	640,081	Edmonton	Alison Redford
British Columbia (BC)	4,400,057	922,509	Victoria	Christy Clark
Manitoba (MB)	1,208,268	552,329	Winnipeg	Greg Selinger
New Brunswick (NB)	751,171	71,377	Fredericton	David Alward
Newfoundland and Labrador (NL)	514,536	370,510	St John's	Kathy Dunderdale
Northwest Territories (NT)	41,462	1,143,793	Yellowknife	Bob McLeod
Nova Scotia (NS)	921,727	52,939	Halifax	Darrell Dexter
Nunavut (NU)	31,906	1,877,787	Iqaluit	Eva Aariak
Ontario (ON)	12,851,821	908,607	Toronto	Dalton McGuinty
Prince Edward Island (PE)	140,240	5,685	Charlottetown	Robert Ghiz
Québec (QC)	7,903,001	1,356,547	Québec City	Jean Charest
Saskatchewan (SK)	1,033,381	588,239	Regina	Brad Wall
Yukon Territory (YT)	33,897	474,712	Whitehorse	Darrell Pasloski

DEFENCE

The Canadian armed forces are unified and organised into three functional commands: land force command, maritime command and air command.

All aged 16–49, 2010 est	*Males*	*Females*
Available for military service	8,031,266	7,755,550
Fit for military service	6,633,472	6,389,669

Military expenditure—US$23,082m (2011)

ECONOMY AND TRADE

Canada has a highly developed, industrialised and diversified market economy, which was transformed from a predominantly rural to an industrial economy in the second half of the 20th century by the growth of mining, manufacturing and services. Tight management of government finances resulted in balanced budgets from the late 1990s until 2007, and free-trade agreements with the USA in 1989 and 1994 (NAFTA) stimulated trade. The economy went into recession in 2008 owing to the global downturn, although the financial sector proved more stable than that of many other major economies; recovery began in 2010 and achieved marginal growth in 2011.

Canada's wealth of natural resources make it the world's largest exporter of timber, pulp and newsprint (over half the land is tree-covered), and it is one of the world's largest exporters of minerals, particularly uranium (of which it is the world's second largest single producer) and diamonds (of which it is the world's third largest producer). About 5% of the land area is farmed, of which 4.6% is under cultivation, mostly in the prairie region of western Canada. The country is one of the world's leading food producers, particularly of wheat, barley, oilseed, tobacco, fruit, vegetables and dairy products. The fishing industry is also significant but has declined in recent years because of restrictions introduced to protect stocks after decades of overfishing. Oil, natural gas and hydroelectricity production is high enough for Canada to be a net exporter of energy; oil production, in particular, has become a significant economic driver, and Canada's oil reserves are ranked

third in the world behind Saudi Arabia and Venezuela. The government has plans to develop the oil and gas-rich Arctic area but the assertion of its sovereignty has attracted criticism from other Arctic countries and is complicated by the lack of international agreement on countries' territorial claims.

In 2011, the services sector contributed 71% of GDP, industry 27.1% and agriculture 1.9%.

The USA is Canada's main trading partner, taking 74.9% of exports and providing 50.4% of imports. The main exports are motor vehicles and parts, industrial machinery, aircraft, telecommunications equipment, chemicals, plastics, fertilisers, forestry products, energy products (including crude oil, natural gas and electricity) and aluminium.

GNI—US$1,549,652m; US$43,270 per capita (2010)
Annual average growth of GDP—2.2% (2011 est)
Inflation rate—2.8% (2011 est)
Unemployment—8% (2010 est)
Total external debt—US$1,181,000m (2011)
Imports—US$390,526m (2010)
Exports—US$386,011m (2010)

BALANCE OF PAYMENTS
Trade—US$4,515m deficit (2010)
Current Account—US$49,375m deficit (2010)

Trade with UK	2010	2011
Imports from UK	£4,868,802,524	£4,847,556,053
Exports to UK	£12,151,704,468	£6,252,336,196

COMMUNICATIONS
Airports—There are over 1,400 airports and airstrips, of which 26 serve major cities
Waterways—There are over 300 ports, the most significant of which are Vancouver and Prince Rupert on the Pacific coast and Montréal, Halifax, Port Cartier, Sept-Iles/Pointe Noire, Saint John and Québec in the east. Most deep-water ports are open all year, and Churchill, on Hudson's Bay, is ice-free for longer periods as a result of climate change. In addition, the Great Lakes/St Lawrence Seaway system, the world's longest inland waterway for ocean-going shipping, provides access to the North American interior
Railways—The 46,552km railway network transports over 270 million tonnes of freight a year
Roadways—1,042,300 km, including 17,000km of motorways
Telecommunications—17 million fixed lines in use, 24 million mobile telephones subscriptions (2011); there were 26.96 million internet users in 2009
Internet code and IDD—ca; 1 (from UK), 011 44 (to UK)
Major broadcasters—The public broadcaster, the Canadian Broadcasting Corporation (CBC), transmits programmes in English and French, and provides services for indigenous peoples in the north of the country. Société Radio-Canada is the French-language public broadcasting service.
Press—Major newspapers include *The Toronto Sun*, *National Post* and *Le Journal de Montreal*
WPFI score—7,00 (21)

EDUCATION AND HEALTH
Education is compulsory from ages six to 16 (18 in Ontario and New Brunswick).
Gross enrolment ratio (percentage of relevant age group)—primary 99%; secondary 101% (2008 est)
Health expenditure (per capita)—US$4,380 (2009)
Hospital beds (per 1,000 people)—3.4 (2004–9)
Life expectancy (years)—81.38 (2011 est)
Mortality rate—7.98 (2011 est)
Birth rate—10.28 (2011 est)
Infant mortality rate—4.92 (2011 est)

CULTURE
Canada has produced a number of successful actors, directors, musicians and comedians, including Jim Carrey (*b.* 1962), David Cronenberg (*b.* 1943), Joni Mitchell (*b.* 1943), Neil Young (*b.* 1945), and Donald (*b.* 1935) and Kiefer (*b.* 1966) Sutherland. Writers include the Nobel laureate Saul Bellow (1915–2005), International Booker prize winner Alice Munro (*b.* 1931), Carol Shields (1935–2003), who won the Pulitzer prize, and the Booker prize winner Margaret Atwood (*b.* 1939).

Cayman Islands

Area—264 sq. km
Capital—George Town, on Grand Cayman; population, 31,723 (2009 est)
Currency—Cayman Islands dollar (CI$) of 100 cents
Population—51,384 rising at 2.287% a year (2011 est)
Religion—Christian (Protestant 68%, Roman Catholic 13%) (est)
Language—English (official), Spanish
Population density—234 per sq. km (2010 est)
Flag—British blue ensign with the coat of arms in the fly
National day—first Monday in July (Constitution Day)
Life expectancy (years)—80.68 (2011 est)
Mortality rate—5.1 (2011 est)
Birth rate—12.24 (2011 est)
Infant mortality rate—6.63 (2011 est)
GNI—US$43,703 per capita (2002)
Annual average growth of GDP—1.1% (2008)

FINANCIAL OUTLOOK
The Cayman Islands had a long struggle with the UK Treasury over its 2012–13 budget and was asked to rewrite it to lower the debt the government felt it needed to incur through 2013. Premier McKeeva Bush's agreed budget forecasts operating revenues of US$651.4 million and operating expenses of US$582.8 million, creating a net surplus of US$68.6 million. The revenue figure includes some 24 new revenue-raising measures, including increases to existing fees and some new fees, bringing in some US$90 million in new revenue for the government. Fees to be charged to directors for various regulated and unregulated entities are expected to bring in some US$21.3 million. The government will not be increasing its long-term borrowings in 2013 and, in fact, expects to pay down long-term debt by some US$26.4 million through the year. This is the first budget within a four-year frame agreed with the United Kingdom to put the Cayman Islands government's finances on a stable and sustainable footing.

CLIMATE AND TERRAIN
The Cayman Islands comprise Grand Cayman, Cayman Brac and Little Cayman. Situated about 240km south of Cuba, the low-lying islands are divided from Jamaica, 268km to the south-east, by the Cayman Trench, the deepest part of the Caribbean Sea. The average temperature is 27°C. Hurricane season is from July to November.

HISTORY AND POLITICS

The territory derives its name from the Carib word *caymanas* (crocodile). The islands were ceded to Britain by Spain in 1670, and permanent settlement began in the 1730s. A dependency of Jamaica from 1863, the islands came under direct rule after 1962, and a measure of self-government was granted in 1972.

The 1972 constitution (revised 1994 and 2009) provides for a governor, a legislative assembly and a cabinet. The governor is responsible for the police, civil service, defence and external affairs, and chairs the cabinet. The cabinet comprises two appointed official members (the deputy governor and attorney-general) and five of the assembly's elected members. The legislative assembly has 15 members elected for a four-year term and the two appointed official members of the cabinet, as well as a speaker.

The election in May 2009 was won by the opposition United Democratic Party.

Governor, HE Duncan Taylor, CBE, *apptd* 2010
Leader of Government Business, Hon. W. McKeeva Bush, OBE

CAYMAN ISLANDS GOVERNMENT OFFICE
6 Arlington Street, London SW1A 1RE
T 020-7491 7772
W www.gov.ky

ECONOMY

The mainstays of the economy are offshore financial services (largely owing to the absence of direct taxation) and tourism. Government revenue is derived from fees and duties.

Trade with UK	2009	2011
Imports from UK	£10,163,692	£9,721,656
Exports to UK	£2,003,173	£42,254,176

COMMUNICATIONS

The islands are served by airports at George Town and on Cayman Brac and by an airfield on Little Cayman. George Town is the main port. There are 785km of surfaced roads.

Chile

República de Chile—Republic of Chile
Area—756,102 sq. km
Capital—Santiago; population, 5,883,040 (2009 est)
Major cities—Antofagasta, Concepción, Iquique, Puente Alto, Punta Arenas, Temuco, Valparaíso
Currency—Chilean peso of 100 centavos
Population—17,067,369 rising at 0.884% a year (2012 est)
Religion—Christian (Roman Catholic 70%, Protestant 15%) (est)
Language—Spanish (official), Mapudungun, German, English
Population density—23 per sq. km (2010)
Urban population—89% (2010 est)
Median age (years)—32.1 (2011 est)
National anthem—'Himno Nacional de Chile' ['National Anthem of Chile']
National day—18 September (Independence Day)
Death penalty—Retained for certain crimes (last used 1985)
CPI score—7.2 (2011)

FINANCIAL OUTLOOK

The Chilean economy expanded by 5.6% in 2012, according to the central bank, on the back of strong export demand for copper—Chile is the world's top producer. The central bank expects Chile, which also exports wine, salmon, fruits, and wood products, to expand by between 4.25% and 5.25% in 2013. The bank held the benchmark interest rate at 5%, following a surprise cut in January 2012. The strong peso, which gained 8.48% in 2012, one of the strongest performances by an emerging-market currency, has helped to suppress inflation. Inflation in the 12 months to February 2013 amounted to 1.3%, below the bottom end of the central bank's 2–4% tolerance range. It is the lowest 12-month figure since at least January 2011, according to the INE, Chile's national statistics institute.

CLIMATE AND TERRAIN

Chile extends over 4,600km from the arid north around Arica to Cape Horn, with an average breadth of 180km. The Atacama desert lies in the north. In the central zone there is a fertile valley between the Andes and the low coastal range of mountains, with a Mediterranean climate; two-thirds of the population live here. Chilean Patagonia, in the south, extends into subantarctic terrain, with glaciers and icefields; the climate is cool with high precipitation. Elevation extremes range from 6,880m (Nevado Ojos del Salado) to 0m (Pacific Ocean). Its Pacific island possessions include the Juan Fernández group and Easter Island, and the Chilean Antarctic Territory covers the Antarctic peninsula and an area of the landmass that extends from 53°W to 90°W along a latitude of 60°S.

HISTORY AND POLITICS

Chile was conquered in the 16th century by the Spanish, who subjugated the indigenous population. It remained under Spanish rule until 1810, when the first autonomous government was established. Independence was achieved in 1818 after a revolutionary war.

A military coup in 1973 overthrew the Marxist president Salvador Allende. General Augusto Pinochet, the coup leader, assumed the presidency and retained the office until elections were held in 1989, beginning the transition to full democracy. Between 1998 and his death in 2006, a number of unsuccessful attempts were made to bring Gen. Pinochet to trial for human rights atrocities committed during his time in office. A massive earthquake, registering 8.8 in magnitude, hit central Chile in 2010, killing about 500 people and causing widespread devastation.

In the 2009 legislative elections, the right-wing Coalition for Change (APC) won one more seat than the incumbent Coalition of Parties for Democracy (CPD) in the lower chamber, and each grouping won half the seats in the senate. Sebastián Piñera, the candidate of the National Renewal party (part of the APC), won the 2010 presidential election and formed a government consisting of members of the APC and independents.

The 1981 constitution was amended in 1989 and 2005. The executive president is directly elected for a four-year term that is not renewable. The bicameral National Congress comprises a senate of 38 members elected for an eight-year term (half renewed every four years) and a Chamber of Deputies of 118 members directly elected for a four-year term.

HEAD OF STATE

President, Sebastián Piñera, *elected* 17 January 2010, *sworn in* 11 March 2010

  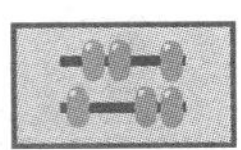      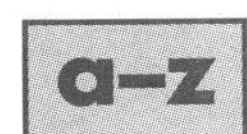

SELECTED GOVERNMENT MEMBERS *as at June 2012*
Defence, Andrés Allamand
Economy, Pablo Longueira
Finance, Felipe Larrain Bascunan
Interior, Rodrigo Hinzpeter Kirberg

EMBASSY OF CHILE
37–41 Old Queen Street, London SW1H 9JA
T 020-7222 2361
E embachile@embachile.co.uk
W www.chileabroad.gov.cl/reino-unido
Ambassador Extraordinary and Plenipotentiary, HE Tomás E. Müller Sproat, *apptd* 2010

BRITISH EMBASSY
Avda. El Bosque Norte 0125, Las Condes, Santiago
T (+56) (2) 370 4100
E embsan@britemb.cl
W ukinchile.fco.gov.uk/en
Ambassador Extraordinary and Plenipotentiary, HE Jon Benjamin, *apptd* 2009

DEFENCE

All aged 16–49, 2010 est	*Males*	*Females*
Available for military service	4,324,732	4,251,954
Fit for military service	3,621,732	3,561,099

Military expenditure—US$7,392m (2011)

ECONOMY AND TRADE
Economic reforms in the late 1970s and the 1980s and sound financial management have made Chile one of the most successful economies in Latin America; in 2010 it became the first South American country to join the OECD. Growth is based on high copper prices, a strong export base and growing domestic demand. Although the economy contracted slightly in 2009 owing to the global downturn, it began to recover later that year and GDP grew over five% in both 2010 and 2011.

Chile is the world's largest producer of copper, and the world's only commercial producer of nitrate of soda (Chile saltpetre) from natural resources. The chief industries are mining, forestry, fishing, food and fish processing, and winemaking.

The main trading partners are the USA, China, Brazil, Argentina and Japan. Principal exports are copper, fruit, fish products, paper and pulp, chemicals and wine. The main imports are petrol and petroleum products, chemicals, electrical and telecommunications equipment, industrial machinery, vehicles and natural gas.

GNI—US$197,330m; US$10,120 per capita (2010)
Annual average growth of GDP—6.5% (2011 est)
Inflation rate—3.3% (2011 est)
Population living below poverty line—11.5% (2009)
Unemployment—7.1% (2010 est)
Total external debt—US$98.68m (2011 est)
Imports—US$58,956m (2010)
Exports—US$71,028m (2010)

BALANCE OF PAYMENTS
Trade—US$12,073m surplus (2010)
Current Account—US$3,802m surplus (2010)

Trade with UK	*2010*	*2011*
Imports from UK	£584,394,080	£739,647,988
Exports to UK	£509,366,459	£591,199,175

COMMUNICATIONS
Airports—There are 366 airports and airfields; the principal airport is at Santiago
Waterways—The main ports are Arica, Antofagasta, Coquimbo, Valparaíso, San Antonio and Talcahuano
Railways—7,082km (2010)
Roadways—80,505km, of which 16,745km is surfaced
Telecommunications—3.458 million fixed lines in use and 19.582 million mobile subscriptions (2010); there were around 7 million internet users in 2009
Internet code and IDD—cl; 56 (from UK), 44 (to UK)
Major broadcasters—The National Television of Chile is state-owned but under direct government control; Radio Cooperativa is a news-based private network which broadcasts alongside numerous other private radio stations
Press—Major newspaper publications include *El Mercurio*, a conservative daily, and *La Nación*, a government-owned daily
WPFI score—10,50 (33)

EDUCATION AND HEALTH
Education is free and compulsory for 12 years, although the education system has suffered from underinvestment and mismanagement resulting in ongoing student protests.
Literacy rate—98.6% (2009 est)
Gross enrolment ratio (percentage of relevant age group)—primary 106%; secondary 88%; tertiary 59% (2009 est)
Health expenditure (per capita)—US$787 (2009)
Hospital beds (per 1,000 people)—2.1 (2004–9)
Life expectancy (years)—77.7 (2011 est)
Mortality rate—5.9 (2011 est)
Birth rate—14.33 (2011 est)
Infant mortality rate—7.34 (2011 est)

China

Zhonghua Renmin Gongheguo—People's Republic of China
Area—9,596,961 sq. km
Capital—Beijing; population, 12,213,900 (2009 est)
Major cities—Changchun, Chengdu, Chongqing, Guangzhou, Harbin, Nanjing, Shanghai, Shenyang, Tianjin, Taiyuan, Wuhan, Xi'an
Currency—Renminbi (RMB) or yuan (Y) of 10 jiao or 100 fen
Population—1,343,239,923 rising at 0.481% a year (2012 est); Han Chinese (91.5%), around 55 ethnic minorities 8.5% (2000)
Religion—officially atheist, but permits four state-registered religions: Buddhism, Taoism, Islam, and Catholic and Protestant Christianity. It is difficult to estimate numbers, as many congregations worship in private; Mahayana Buddhism and Taoism are the predominant faiths but Christianity is growing rapidly
Language—Mandarin (official), Cantonese, Shanghainese, Fuzhou, Xiang, Gan, Taiwanese
Population density—143 per sq. km (2010)

Urban population—44.9% (2010 est)
Median age (years)—35.5 (2011 est)
National anthem—'Yiyongjun Jinxingqu' ['The March of the Volunteers']
National day—1 October (Founding of People's Republic)
Death penalty—Retained
CPI score—3.6 (2011)

FINANCIAL OUTLOOK

China's economic growth eased to a 13-year low of 7.8% in 2012, down from 9.2% in 2011, and 10.3% in 2010. In 2012, the government cut the forecast rate for the first time in eight years, from a longstanding annual goal of 8%. It is predicting growth of 7.5% in 2013. However, growth expanded 7.9% in the final three months of 2012 from a year earlier, the first pickup in eight quarters. Weak external demand and measures to cool inflation have taken a toll on the economy in recent years. The government is continuing to bear down on inflation, reducing its consumer price index target to around 3.5% in 2013, from 4% in 2012. Inflation cooled to 2.6% in 2012. However, the authorities are also trying to stimulate growth. The central bank cut interest rates twice in 2012, and reduced the amount banks must keep in reserve in an attempt to encourage lending.

Hong Kong

The fortunes of the territory's economy are closely connected to those of China, and the slowdown in the mainland affected Hong Kong in 2012. According to the Census and Statistics Department, GDP grew by 1.4% in 2012, following 4.9% growth in 2011. The government estimates GDP growth of 1.5% to 3.5% in 2013, lower than the average of 4.5% of the past decade. The government is forecasting an average headline inflation rate of 4.5% in 2013, compared to 4.15% in 2012. The government announced a fiscal surplus of HK$64.9 billion (US$8.4 billion) in 2012, buoyed by rising land sales and taxes on corporate profits. Authorities had previously forecast a deficit of HK$3.4 billion. In February 2013, the government sought to curb the booming property market, which has been fuelled by low interest rates, tight supply, and abundant liquidity, by raising stamp duty and attempting to restrict home sales.

Macau

In mid-December 2012, Macau's legislative assembly approved the budget proposal for 2013, which includes expenditure of 82.57 billion patacas (US$10.321 billion) and a surplus of 52.23 billion patacas (US$6.528 billion). The proposal presented by the government projects growth of 17% in overall revenues to 134.8 billion patacas (US$16.850 billion), and 6.74% in expenditure to 82.57 billion patacas (US$10.321 billion). Despite an expected rise in expenditure, the government also expects significant growth in revenues, based on increased taxes on gaming and gambling. This rise takes account of, and is on top of a package of tax incentives and other benefits due to be introduced next year to boost Macau's major industry of gambling. Current account revenues are expected to rise by 10.48% to 113.75 billion patacas, but most of the revenues come from direct taxes for which the government projects a rise of 9.3% to 99.48 billion patacas. In direct gaming and gambling taxes alone, charged at a rate of 35% on gross casino revenues and included in direct taxes, the government expects revenues of 92.4 billion patacas, or 7.4 billion patacas more than projected for the whole of 2012.

CLIMATE AND TERRAIN

China is twice the size of western Europe and contains a vast range of landscapes and climates. The highest mountains are on the Tibetan plateau, in the west of the country, where the highest elevation is 8,850m (Mt Everest). To the north of the Tibetan plateau, the land drops to the arid, semi-desert steppes bisected by the Tian Shan mountains; the country's lowest elevation is −154m at Turpan Pendi. The southern plains and east coast have the most fertile land, irrigated by the Huang He (Yellow), Chang Jiang (Yangtze) and Xi Jiang (West) rivers, and are the most heavily populated areas.

There are seven climate zones. The north-east has cold winters, fierce winds, warm and humid summers and erratic rainfall. The mountainous south-west has mild winters and warm summers. Inner Mongolia has cold winters and hot summers. Central China has warm and humid summers with occasional tropical cyclones. South China is partly tropical with heavy rainfall. The high Tibet plateau is subject to harsh winters. Xinjiang and the west have a desert climate, with cold winters and little rain.

HISTORY AND POLITICS

The Communist Party of China is the dominant political party, and all elements of the political system are subordinate to it. A party congress is held every five years and elects the Politburo and its standing committee. This standing committee is the policy- and decision-making body and the *de facto* government.

Under the 1982 constitution, the National People's Congress is the highest organ of state power. It has 2,987 members, indirectly elected for a five-year term, and holds only one full session a year; between sessions, its work is delegated to its standing committee. The congress elects the premier and, on his nomination, the State Council. The head of state is the president, also elected by the congress, who serves a five-year term, renewable once.

Deputies to people's congresses at the primary level are directly elected by the voters from a list of approved candidates. These congresses elect the deputies to the congress at the next highest level. Deputies to the National People's Congress are elected by the provincial and municipal people's congresses, and by the armed forces.

Local government is conducted through people's governments at provincial/municipal, prefecture/city, county/district, township and village levels. There are 22 provinces (Taiwan is claimed as a 23rd province), four municipalities directly under the central government, five autonomous regions, and two special administrative areas; provinces may contain autonomous counties or towns for ethnic minorities.

In 2003 Hu Jintao was elected by the National People's Congress as the new state president and Wen Jaibao was elected as premier; both were re-elected to their posts at the 2008 party congress. Hu is pursuing policies in health, education, the environment and other areas which are intended to address the social inequalities created by the economic growth of recent years.

HEAD OF STATE

President, Hu Jintao, *elected* 15 March 2003, *re-elected* March 2008
Vice-President, Xi Jinping

STATE COUNCIL *as at May 2012*

Premier, Wen Jiabao
Vice-Premiers, Zhang Dejiang; Li Keqiang; Hui Liangyu; Wang Qishan

  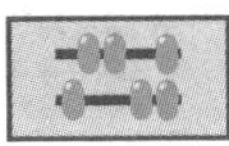      

State Councillors, Dai Bingguo; Liang Guanglie *(National Defence)*; Meng Jianzhu *(Public Security)*; Ma Kai *(Secretary-General of the State Council)*; Liu Yandong

SELECTED GOVERNMENT MEMBERS *as at May 2012*
Civil Affairs, Li Liguo
Finance, Xie Xuren
Foreign Affairs, Yang Jiechi

EMBASSY OF THE PEOPLE'S REPUBLIC OF CHINA
49–51 Portland Place, London W1B 1JL
T 020-7299 4049
W www.chinese-embassy.org.uk
Ambassador Extraordinary and Plenipotentiary, HE Liu Xiaoming, *apptd* 2010

BRITISH EMBASSY
11 Guang Hua Lu, Jian Guo Men Wai, Beijing 100600
T (+86) (10) 5192 4000
E consular.beijing@fco.gov.uk
W ukinchina.fco.gov.uk
Ambassador, HE Sebastian Wood, *apptd* 2010

Human Rights

Liberalisation has allowed ordinary people greater personal choice: they can now travel freely, for example, or change professions. However, freedom of expression, religion and association are still tightly controlled, and the regime firmly suppresses dissent by ethnic minorities or other groups that it perceives as a threat to its authority. This has led to moves against separatists from the Uygur Muslim minority group in Xinjiang Autonomous Region since the 1990s, the banning of the Falun Gong spiritual movement in 1999 and the violent suppression of demonstrations in Tibet in 2008. Religious gatherings that have not been approved by the state-sanctioned religious bodies are broken up by the authorities and their leaders harassed; despite this, all religions are experiencing a revival throughout China, and underground Protestant churches in particular are growing rapidly.

DEFENCE

All three military arms are parts of the People's Liberation Army (PLA).

All aged 16–49, 2010 est	*Males*	*Females*
Available for military service	385,821,101	363,789,674
Fit for military service	318,265,016	300,323,611

Military expenditure—US$129,272m (2011)
Conscription duration—24 months (selective)

ECONOMY AND TRADE

Liberalisation since the 1980s has transformed the economy, developing a more autonomous state sector, a rapidly growing private sector and a leading presence in global trade and investment. A massive industrial base and transport infrastructure have been constructed, especially in the coastal regions, and the economy has become a free market in all but name, with several stock markets and Shanghai's emergence as a financial centre. China attracts considerable foreign investment and has become a major investor overseas. GDP has grown more than ten-fold since 1978, and by some measures China's economy is now the second-largest in the world.

Although some 250 million people who migrated to urban areas have been lifted out of poverty in the past two decades, the effects of the rapid transformation have been unevenly distributed. In 2012 it was reported China's city dwellers outnumber China's rural population for the first time; there are wide income differences between urban and rural areas, poor healthcare provision, lack of access to public services for migrant workers, rampant official corruption and environmental degradation of land, water and air. The government is also keen to increase domestic consumption (a priority of the 2011–16 five-year plan), and so reduce the economy's reliance on exports for growth, especially as foreign demand slowed in 2008 and plummeted in 2009 owing to the global economic downturn.

China's expansion boosted its need for oil and coal, met initially by imports but increasingly by domestic production. However, to achieve its aim of reducing environmental degradation, China is looking more to nuclear power (although nuclear approval has been suspended indefinitely owing to safety concerns following the Fukushima Daiichi plant disaster in Japan) and alternative energy generation, such as hydroelectric power from the Three Gorges Dam.

Although rural areas have seen few benefits from the economic transformation and are suffering the effects of rural depopulation and pollution, agriculture remains important; it contributes 10.1% of GDP but employs 36.7% of the workforce. The main crops are rice, cereals, vegetables, peanuts, tea, fruit, cotton and oilseed crops. Livestock is raised in large numbers. Silk farming is one of the oldest industries. Cotton, woollen and silk textiles are manufactured in large quantities.

The highly diversified industrial sector, encompassing heavy industry, manufacturing and construction, contributes 46.8% of GDP and employs 28.7% of the workforce. The services sector accounts for 43.1% of GDP and 34.6% of employment. Tourism is now a major industry.

Exports include machinery, electrical equipment, data processing equipment, garments, textiles, iron and steel, and optical and medical equipment. The principal imports are electrical and other machinery, oil and mineral fuels, optical and medical equipment, metal ores, plastics and organic chemicals. The main trading partners are the USA, Hong Kong, Japan, South Korea, and Germany, although trade with Latin America and Africa is growing.

GNI—US$5,957,012m; US$4,270 per capita (2010)
Annual average growth of GDP—9.5% (2011 est)
Inflation rate—5.4% (2011 est)
Population below poverty line—2.8% (2007 est; based on a poverty line of US$125 per year)
Unemployment—9% (2009 est)
Total external debt—US$635,500m (2011 est)
Imports—US$1,394,690m (2010)
Exports—US$1,578,270m (2010)

BALANCE OF PAYMENTS
Trade—US$183,580m surplus (2010)
Current Account—US$305,300m surplus (2010)

Trade with UK	*2010*	*2011*
Imports from UK	£7,305,572,838	£8,772,626,567
Exports to UK	£33,886,950,033	£30,155,983,037

COMMUNICATIONS

Airports—There are over 500 airports and airfields and several national air carriers
Waterways—The main seaports are Shanghai and Dalian in the north, and Guangzhou in the south; there are 110,000km of

  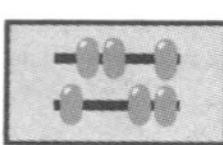      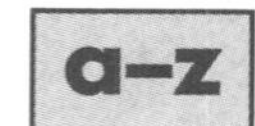

navigable waterways, Nanjing is the largest river port, and the Huang He (Yellow), Chang Jiang (Yangtze) and Xi Jiang (West) are the most significant river routes
Railways—The rail system has 86,000km of track, although only 36,000km is electrified; extension of the Qinghai–Tibet railway is opening up the remote western province
Roadways—The 3.8 million km road network allows access to all towns and villages, and the major cities are linked by 65,000km of modern highways
Telecommunications—294.3 million fixed lines in use and 859 mobile subscriptions (2010); there were 389 million internet users in 2009
Internet code and IDD—cn; 86 (from UK) 44 (to UK)
Major broadcasters—The Communist Party maintains a firm grip on the media and the internet. Television is the most popular medium in a huge media industry; state-run stations offer around 2,100 channels, and in 2010 over 175m households had cable subscription services
Press—Every city has its own newspaper, as well as a local Communist Party publication; approximately 2,000 newspapers are published every week
WPFI score—84,67 (171)

EDUCATION AND HEALTH

Primary education lasts six years and secondary education six years (three years in junior middle school and three optional years in senior middle school).
Literacy rate—94.0% (2009 est)
Gross enrolment ratio (percentage of relevant age group)—primary 111%; secondary 80%; tertiary 24% (2009 est)
Health expenditure (per capita)—US$177 (2009)
Hospital beds (per 1,000 people)—4.1 (2004–9)
Life expectancy (years)—74.68 (2011 est)
Mortality rate—7.03 (2011 est)
Birth rate—12.29 (2011 est)
Infant mortality rate—16.06 (2011 est)

CULTURE

The Chinese language has many dialects, notably Cantonese, Hakka, Amoy, Foochow, Changsha, Nanchang, Wu (Shanghai) and the northern dialect. The common speech, or *putonghua* (often referred to as Mandarin), is based on the northern dialect. The Communists have promoted it as the national language and it is taught throughout the country. Because *putonghua* encourages the use of the spoken language in writing, the old literary style and ideographic form of writing has fallen into disuse. Since 1956, simplified characters have been introduced to make reading and writing easier. In 1958 the National People's Congress adopted a system of romanisation known as *pinyin*.

TIBET

Area—1,199,164 sq. km
Population—2,610,000 (2001 est)
Capital—Lhasa

Tibet is a plateau, seldom lower than 3,000m, in south-west China. It forms the frontier with India (boundary imperfectly demarcated), from which it is separated by the Himalayas from Kashmir to Myanmar; Nepal and Bhutan also border it to the south. The Indus, Brahmaputra, Mekong and Yangtze rivers all rise on the Tibet plateau.

Tibet was under Mongol rule almost continuously from the 13th to the 17th centuries. Chinese control grew from the 18th century and direct rule began in 1910, but with the collapse of the Chinese Empire in 1911, Tibet declared its independence and the Dalai Lama ruled undisturbed until Communist rule was established in China. In 1950 Chinese Communist forces invaded Tibet, and in 1951 the Tibetan authorities signed a treaty agreeing joint Chinese-Tibetan rule. A series of revolts against Chinese rule culminated in a 1959 uprising in the capital, which was crushed following several days of fighting after which military rule was imposed. The Dalai Lama fled to India where he and his followers were granted political asylum and established a government in exile. Tibet became an Autonomous Region of China in 1965. Martial law was declared in Tibet in 1989.

The Panchen Lama, the second-highest Lama, remained in Lhasa after 1959; when he died in 1989, China rejected the Dalai Lama's choice of successor and enthroned its own candidate. Subsequent appointments have been handled in a similar manner. Despite occasional talks between the Chinese government and representatives of the Dalai Lama, relations remain poor. In March 2011, the Dalai Lama announced his intention to withdraw from political life, transferring leadership to Lobsang Sangay, prime minister of the Tibetan parliament.

Another source of tension is the large number of Chinese migrants who have settled in Tibet since the 1970s, a development that the Tibetan government-in-exile regards as an attempt to eradicate the culture of the Tibetan people. Chinese now considerably outnumber Tibetans and have benefited disproportionately from the economic development of recent years.

Peaceful anti-Chinese demonstrations in Tibet increased in early 2008 as the imminence of the Beijing Olympics put China's human rights record under greater international scrutiny. The violence of the Chinese crackdown was condemned worldwide, and pro-Tibet activists abroad disrupted the Olympic torch relay in several countries. Resistance and unrest continue: in 2009, in a show of passive resistance, farmers in Tibet and neighbouring provinces refused to till the fields or plant crops; in 2011, demonstrations sparked by the self-immolation of a Tibetan monk in the Sechuan province led to hundreds of arrests.

SPECIAL ADMINISTRATIVE REGIONS

Hong Kong

Xianggang Tebie Xingzhengqu—Hong Kong Special Administrative Region
Area—1,104 sq. km
Currency—Hong Kong dollar (HK$) of 100 cents
Population—7,153,519 rising at 0.421% a year (2012 est)
Population density—6,783 per sq. km (2010)
Flag—Red, with a white bauhinia flower of five petals each containing a red star
National day—1 July (Establishment Day)
Death penalty—Abolished for all crimes (since 2003)
CPI score—8.4 (2011)

Climate and Terrain

Hong Kong consists of Hong Kong Island, Kowloon and the New Territories (on a peninsula of the mainland in Guangdong province) and over 260 islands, including Lantau Island. Hong Kong Island is about 18km long and 3–8km wide. It is separated from the mainland by a narrow strait. The highest point is Tai Mo Shan (958m). The climate is subtropical, with hot, wet summers and cool, dry winters. Mean monthly temperatures range from 16°C to 29°C. Tropical cyclones occur between May and November, and over 75% of the average annual rainfall of 2,398mm falls between May and September.

History and Politics

Hong Kong developed as a major regional trading port because of its location on the main Far Eastern trade routes. Hong Kong Island was first occupied by Britain in 1841 and formally ceded to Britain in

1842. Kowloon was acquired in 1860, and the New Territories by a 99-year lease signed in 1898.

In 1984, the UK and China agreed that China would resume sovereignty over Hong Kong in 1997, and on 1 July 1997, Hong Kong became a Special Administrative Region (SAR) of the People's Republic of China. The 1984 joint declaration and the Basic Law (1990) guarantee that the SAR's social and economic systems will remain unchanged for 50 years and grant it a high degree of autonomy.

Although the Basic Law provides for the development of democratic processes, political reform has been slow, prompting frequent demonstrations to demand full democracy or to oppose measures perceived to be repressive. In 2007 the Chinese government said that the chief executive could be directly elected from 2017 and the legislature members from 2020.

Leung Chun-ying was elected chief executive in March 2012, beating closest rival Henry Tang; Chun-ying replaced Donald Tsang, who served two terms between 2005 and 2012. In the 2008 legislative elections, pro-China parties won 35 seats and pro-democracy parties won 23, sufficient for the pro-democracy parties to veto constitutional changes.

The Basic Law, approved in 1990, has served as Hong Kong's constitution since 1997. Its government is headed by the chief executive, who is elected by a 1200-member electoral committee and serves a five-year term. The chief executive is aided by an executive council consisting of 15 principal officials, who are the heads of administrative departments, and 14 non-official members. The legislative council consists of 70 members, 35 directly elected by geographic constituencies, and 30 elected by functional, occupation-based constituencies; they serve a four-year term.

Chief Executive, Leung Chun-ying, *elected* 25 March 2012, *sworn in* 1 July 2012

SELECTED GOVERNMENT MEMBERS *as at July 2012*
Chief Secretary for Administration, Carrie Lam Cheng Yuet-ngor
Financial Secretary, John Tsang Chun-wah
Secretary for Justice, Rimsky Yuen Kowk-Keung

BRITISH CONSULATE-GENERAL
PO Box 528, 1 Supreme Court Road, Central Hong Kong
T (+852) 2901 3000
E consular@bcg.org.hk
W ukinhongkong.fco.gov.uk
Consul-General, Andrew Seaton, *apptd* 2008

Economy and Trade

The economy has moved away from manufacturing (which has mostly relocated to mainland China) and is now service-based, with a high reliance on international trade and re-exports. It has developed into a regional corporate and banking centre, and has benefited in recent years from closer integration with China through increased trade, tourism and financial links. Although badly affected by the global economic downturn in 2008–9, the strength of the Chinese economy helped it to recover quickly.

The economy is dominated by the service sector, which accounts for 92.6% of GDP. The main contributors to this are tourism, financial services and shipping. Industry contributes 7% of GDP. Principal products are textiles, clothing, electronics, plastics, toys, clocks and watches.

The principal export markets are China (52.4%), the USA and Japan. China is Hong Kong's principal supplier of imported goods (44.9%).

GNI—US$229,164m; US$32,780 per capita (2010)
Annual average growth of GDP—5% (2011 est)
Inflation rate—5.3% (2011 est)
Unemployment—3.4% (2011 est)
Imports—US$433,193m (2010)
Exports—US$390,174m (2010)

BALANCE OF PAYMENTS
Trade—US$43,019m deficit (2010)
Current Account—US$13,933m surplus (2010)

Trade with UK	2010	2011
Imports from UK	£4,463,649,783	£5,062,150,395
Exports to UK	£5,377,455,132	£7,325,899,831

Education and Health

Education is free and compulsory for children up to age 15.
Gross enrolment ratio (percentage of age group)—primary 102%; secondary 83%; tertiary 60% (2010 est)
Life expectancy (years)—82.12 (2012 est)
Birth rate—7.54 (2012 est)
Mortality rate—7.23 (2012 est)
Infant mortality rate—2.9 (2012 est)

Communications

Airports—There are two airports, one accommodating international flights
Waterways—Hong Kong has one of the world's finest natural harbours, and is the fifth-busiest container port in the world. Dockyard facilities include eight floating drydocks; the largest is capable of docking vessels of up to 150,000 tonnes deadweight
Roadways—There are 2,067km of roads (2010)
Telecommunications—4.345 million fixed lines and 13.146 million mobile subscriptions (2010); there were 4.873 million internet users in 2009
Internet code and IDD—hk; 852 (from UK) 1 44 (to UK)
WPFI score—10,75 (35)

Macau (Aomen)

Aomen Tebie Xingzhengqu—Macau Special Administrative Region
Area—28.2 sq. km
Currency—Pataca of 100 avos
Population—578,025 rising at 0.866% a year (2012 est)
Population density—19,416 per sq. km (2010)
Flag—Green, with a white lotus flower above a white stylised bridge and water, under a large gold five-point star and four gold stars in crescent
National day—20 December (Establishment Day)
CPI score—5.1 (2011)
Internet code and IDD—mo; 853 (from UK), 44 (to UK)

Climate and Terrain

Macau consists of the Macau peninsula and the islands of Coloane and Taipa. It is situated at the western side of the mouth of the Pearl river, bordering Guangdong province in south-east China. It is 64km from Hong Kong. Its area has nearly doubled since the 19th century due to land reclamation. The highest point is Coloane Alto (172m). The climate is subtropical.

History and Politics

The first Portuguese ship arrived at Macau in 1513 and trade with China commenced in 1553. Macau became a Portuguese colony in 1557; China recognised Portugal's sovereignty over Macau by treaty

       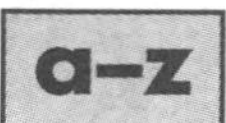

in 1887. An agreement to transfer the administration of Macau to China was signed in 1987, and Macau became the Macau Special Administrative Region (MSAR) of China on 20 December 1999. Fernando Chui was elected unopposed as chief executive in 2009, and the most recent legislative election was held in September 2009.

The Basic Law (1993) has served as Macao's constitution since 1999. The chief executive is elected by a 300-member election committee and serves a five-year term of office, which may be renewed once. The chief executive is assisted by the ten-member executive council. The legislative assembly has 29 members, who serve for four years; 12 are directly elected in geographic constituencies, ten are indirectly elected in functional constituencies and seven are appointed by the chief executive.

Chief Executive, Fernando Chui Sai On, *elected* July 2009, *sworn in* 20 December 2009

SELECTED GOVERNMENT MEMBERS *as at May 2012*
Economy and Finance, Francis Tam Pak Yuen
Secretary for Administration and Justice, Florinda Rosa Silva Chan

CONSUL-GENERAL
Andrew Seaton, *apptd* 2008, resident at Hong Kong

Economy and Trade
The economy is based on tourism and gambling, which have grown rapidly since 2001, and garment and textile manufacturing, which is in decline. Visitors totalled nearly 25 million in 2010, the majority coming from mainland China, where gambling is illegal. The service sector contributes about 97.1% of GDP and industry 2.8%. The principal products and exports are clothing, textiles, footwear, toys, electronics, machinery and parts. The main trading partners are Hong Kong, China and the USA.

GNI—US$20,738m; US$39,550 per capita (2009)
Annual average growth of GDP—1% (2009 est)
Inflation rate—3.9% (2011)
Imports—US$5,527m (2010)
Exports—US$870m (2010)
BALANCE OF PAYMENTS
Trade—US$4,657m deficit (2010)
Current Account—US$6,238m surplus (2009)

Trade with UK	*2010*	*2011*
Imports from UK	£31,516,776	£36,855,901
Exports to UK	£12,898,778	£24,008,315

Colombia

República de Colombia—Republic of Colombia
Area—1,138,910 sq. km
Capital—Bogotá; population, 8,261,650 (2009 est)
Major cities—Barranquilla, Cali, Cartagena, Medellín
Currency—Colombian peso of 100 centavos
Population—45,239,079 rising at 1.128% a year (2012 est)
Religion—Christian (Roman Catholic 80%, other denominations 14%) (est)
Language—Spanish (official)
Population density—42 per sq. km (2010)
Urban population—75.1% (2010 est)
Median age (years)—28 (2011 est)
National anthem—'Himno Nacional de la República de Colombia' ['National Anthem of the Republic of Colombia']
National day—20 July (Independence Day)
Death penalty—Abolished for all crimes (since 1910)
CPI score—3.4 (2011)

FINANCIAL OUTLOOK
The government of Colombia raised its 2013 budget by 12.2% over 2012, to US$103.5 billion. Spending on defense and police will rise by 7.8% to 26.3 trillion pesos in 2013. Some 46.5 trillion pesos of the budget is set aside for debt repayments in order to give the government some insulation from any future shocks to the economy, according to Colombia's finance minister, Juan Carlos Echeverry. Colombia's central bank forecasts GDP growth of between 2% and 5% for 2013, with a marked degree of uncertainty over the final figure as Europe's sovereign debt problems creates a volatile market for Colombia's oil, coffee, and precious metals exports. This is more or less the same as the GDP growth expected for 2012. In July 2012, the central bank cut interest rates for the first time since 2010 to counteract a marked slowdown in the economy. There are also fears that inflation could rise in 2013, particularly if the El Niño weather phenomenon creates a spike in food prices. Inflation in 2012 was 3%.

CLIMATE AND TERRAIN
The western, central and eastern ranges of the Andes run from south-west to north-east of Colombia, separating the arid north-eastern peninsula and the tropical coastal regions in the north and west from the densely forested south-eastern lowlands and the vast tablelands in the east. This last region, having a temperate climate, is the most densely populated part of the country. Elevation extremes range from 5,775m (Pico Cristobal Colon) to 0m (Pacific Ocean). The principal rivers are the Magdalena, which flows into the Caribbean; the Guaviare and Meta, tributaries of the Orinocco; and the Caquetá and Putumayo, which drain into the Amazon basin. The predominantly tropical climate is moderated by altitude in the interior.

HISTORY AND POLITICS
Spanish settlement of the region began in 1525, and Colombia was ruled as part of a vice-royalty until 1810, when independence was declared. In 1819, Simón Bolivar established the Republic of Gran Colombia, consisting of the territories now known as Colombia, Panama, Venezuela and Ecuador, after finally defeating the Spanish. In 1829–30 Venezuela and Ecuador withdrew, and in 1831 the remaining territories formed a separate state, which adopted the name of Colombia in 1866; Panama seceded in 1903.

Power alternated between the Conservative and Liberal parties from the mid-19th century. In 1949, a civil war broke out which lasted until 1957, when the Conservative and Liberal parties formed a coalition government known as the National Front. This arrangement continued until 1974 and was revived in 1978 in an attempt to maintain the rule of law in the face of violence by drugs cartels, a left-wing insurgency and counter-attacks by right-wing paramilitaries. Despite foreign assistance and increased military spending, drug trafficking continues to be widespread, although less of a threat to civil order than hitherto, but the government has been unable to suppress or reach a negotiated settlement with insurgents' leaders despite sporadic peace talks.

  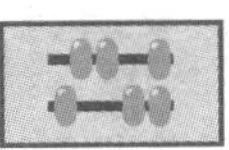 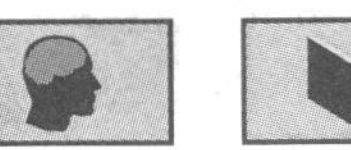     

In the 2010 legislative elections, parties that supported President Uribe won the majority of seats in both chambers. The 2010 presidential election was won in the second round by former defence minister Juan Manuel Santos Calderón.

Under the 1991 constitution, amended in 2005, the executive president is directly elected for a four-year term, which is renewable once. The bicameral congress comprises the 166-member House of Representatives, and the 102-member senate. All members are directly elected for a four-year term. Two senate seats are reserved for representatives of indigenous people.

HEAD OF STATE

President, Juan Manuel Santos Calderón, *elected* 20 June 2010, *sworn in* 7 August 2010

Vice-President, Angelino Garzón

SELECTED GOVERNMENT MEMBERS *as at June 2012*

Defence, Juan Carlos Pinzon

Finance, Juan Carlos Echeverry

Foreign Affairs, Maria Angela Holguin

Interior, Justice, German Vargas Lleras

EMBASSY OF COLOMBIA

3 Hans Crescent, London SW1X 0LN

T 020-7589 9177

E elondres@cancilleria.gov.co

W www.colombianembassy.co.uk

Ambassador Extraordinary and Plenipotentiary, HE Mauricio Rodriguez Munera, *apptd* 2009

BRITISH EMBASSY

Carrera 9, No 76–49, Piso 8, Edificio ING Barings, Bogotá D.C.

T (+57) (1) 326 8300

E inquiries.bogota@fco.gov.uk

W ukincolombia.fco.gov.uk

Ambassador Extraordinary and Plenipotentiary, HE John Dew, *apptd* 2008

Insurgencies

Colombia has been dogged by violence since the 1960s, initially from insurgency by left-wing guerrilla groups, mainly the Revolutionary Armed Forces of Colombia (FARC) and the National Liberation Army (ELN), countered by right-wing paramilitaries affiliated with the United Self-Defence Forces of Colombia (AUC), which was suspected of having links with the security forces. In the 1980s, lawlessness increased with the rise of drug-producing and -trafficking cartels. The guerrillas and paramilitaries became involved in these and other crimes, including kidnapping, and often act to protect these sources of funding as much as to further their political aims.

Action against the insurgents and drug cartels since 2002 has extended state control so that the government now has a presence in every municipality. Talks between the government and the FARC and ELN have made little headway, but talks with the AUC from 2004 led to demobilisation of most units in 2006.

Neighbouring countries are affected by the overspill from the violence in Colombia, and cross-border incursions by Colombian forces in pursuit of the FARC, ELN or AUC have affected relations with both Ecuador and Venezuela in recent years. Venezuela also strongly opposes the USA's military presence in Colombia to counter drug-trafficking.

DEFENCE

All aged 16–49, 2010 est	Males	Females
Available for military service	11,692,647	11,727,625
Fit for military service	9,150,400	9,861,760

Military expenditure—US$10,290m (2011)

ECONOMY AND TRADE

An improving security situation, economic liberalisation and international investment aided economic growth from 2002 to 2008. Although the economy contracted in 2009 owing to the global downturn, it recovered strongly and GDP grew by 5.7% in 2011. The government has encouraged diversification to reduce dependence on a limited range of commodities and markets, and this has led to the growth of new export-orientated industries (particularly textiles, clothing and footwear), and a broader range of export markets.

Services account for around 53.1% of GDP, industry 38% and agriculture 8.9%. Coal, oil, natural gas and hydroelectricity resources are exploited, and hydrocarbons account for about half of mining output; iron ore, nickel, gold, emeralds, copper and other minerals account for the remainder. Major cash crops are coffee, bananas and cut flowers. Cattle are raised in large numbers, and forestry is also important.

The principal trading partners are the USA, China and the EU. Main exports are oil, coffee, coal, nickel, emeralds, garments, bananas and cut flowers. Imports include industrial and transport equipment, consumer goods, chemicals, paper products and fuels.

GNI—US$276,072m; US$5,510 per capita (2010)

Annual average growth of GDP—4.9% (2011 est)

Inflation rate—3.4% (2011 est)

Population below poverty line—45.5% (2009)

Unemployment—11.8% (2010 est)

Total external debt—US$69,890m (2011 est)

Imports—US$40,683m (2010)

Exports—US$39,710m (2010)

BALANCE OF PAYMENTS

Trade—US$973m deficit (2010)

Current Account—US$5,141m deficit (2009)

Trade with UK	2010	2011
Imports from UK	£217,847,335	£293,389,897
Exports to UK	£618,806,284	£880,115,314

COMMUNICATIONS

Airports—There are 990 airports and airstrips, although only 116 have surfaced runways; the principal airports are at Bogotá, Barranquilla and Cali

Waterways—18,000km of inland waterways; the main seaports are Barranquilla and Cartagena on the Caribbean Sea and Buenaventura on the Pacific coast

Roadways and railways—141,374km of roadways; 874km of railways

Telecommunications—6.809 million fixed lines in use and 43.405 million mobile subscriptions (2010); there were 22.538 million internet users in 2009

Internet code and IDD—co; 57 (from UK), 5/7/9 44 (to UK)

Major broadcasters—The state-run Senal Columbia is one of the largest television broadcasters in the country; Caracol runs several radio networks across the country alongside the state-run Radio Nacional de Columbia

  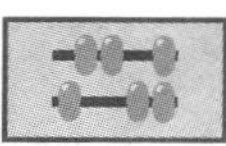      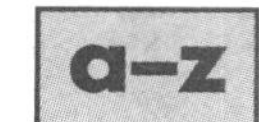

Press—Colombia is one of the most dangerous countries in the world for journalists, who are often targeted by guerrillas and paramilitary groups. There are seven major daily newspapers, including *El Tempo* and *El Nuevo Siglo*
WPFI score—51,50 (145)

EDUCATION AND HEALTH
Elementary education is free and compulsory for ten years. Health care is provided through a mixture of contributory and subsidised health schemes by both the private and the public sector.

Literacy rate—93.2% (2009 est)
Gross enrolment ratio (percentage of relevant age group)—primary 115%; secondary 96%; tertiary 39% (2010 est)
Health expenditure (per capita)—US$323 (2009)
Hospital beds (per 1,000 people)—1.0 (2004–9)
Life expectancy (years)—74.55 (2011 est)
Mortality rate—5.26 (2011 est)
Birth rate—17.49 (2011 est)
Infant mortality rate—16.39 (2011 est)

Croatia

Republika Hrvatska—Republic of Croatia
Area—56,594 sq. km
Capital—Zagreb; population, 685,128 (2009 est)
Major cities—Zadar, Osijek, Rijeka (Fiume), Split
Currency—Kuna of 100 lipa
Population—4,480,043 falling at 0.09% a year (2012 est); Croat (89.6%), Serb (4.5%) (2001)
Religion—Christian (Roman Catholic 85%, Serbian Orthodox 6%), Muslim and Jewish minorities (est)
Language—Croatian (official), Serbian
Population density—79 per sq. km (2010)
Urban population—57.8% (2010 est)
Median age (years)—41.4 (2011 est)
National anthem—'Lijepa Nasa Domovino' ['Our Beautiful Homeland']
National day—8 October (Independence Day)
Death penalty—Abolished for all crimes (since 1990)
CPI score—4.0 (2011)

FINANCIAL OUTLOOK
In its January 2013 report on Croatia, the IMF saw a further contraction in the Croatian economy for 2012 of – 1.5%, following a stagnant year in 2011, and two years of contraction in 2010 and 2009. The best the IMF could see for the Croatian economy in 2014 was a modest return to positive growth of less than 1% (0.75%). However, the IMF pointed out that the risks to this level of growth were large, given Croatia's restricted ability to absorb any further shocks from further negative developments in the European Union's sovereign debt crisis, or contractions in the Balkan economies. Croatia is pressing on with financial consolidation and is achieving the target reduction in its budget deficit for 2012. It will have to make further efforts during 2013 and beyond to return to fiscal sustainability, the IMF warned. Inflation continues to hover at around 3% and the external current account deficit is likely to widen to 4.25% of GDP by 2017. Croatia still has a lot of work to do to address barriers to investment and employment growth, the IMF said.

CLIMATE AND TERRAIN
There are three major geographic areas: the plains of the Pannonian region in the north, the central mountain belt, and the Adriatic coast region of Istria and Dalmatia, which has 1,185 islands and islets and 1,777km of coastline. Elevation extremes range from 1,831m (Dinara) to 0m (Adriatic Sea) at the lowest. The climate varies significantly between the Dalmatian coast, where the winters are mild and the summers hot, and inland areas, which have colder temperatures and rain in the summer. Average temperatures in Zagreb range from 2°C in December to 20°C in July.

HISTORY AND POLITICS
The 1990 constitution was amended in 2000 to increase the powers of the legislature, making the presidency a largely ceremonial role, and in 2001 to abolish the upper house of the legislature. The head of state is a president, who is directly elected for a five-year term. The legislature, the Croatian Assembly, has one chamber, the House of Representatives, which has 151 members directly elected for a four-year term. The prime minister is appointed by the legislature and appoints the cabinet.

The 2010 presidential election was won by Ivo Josipovic, who picked up 20% more votes than the nearest competitor (Milan Bandic) in the second round of voting. In the 2011 legislative election, a coalition consisting of the Social Democratic Party of Croatia (SDP), the Croatian People's Party and two smaller parties (the Kukuriku coalition) overtook the Croation Democratic Union to secure an overall majority in the parliament. SDP leader Zoran Milanovic was named prime minister in December 2011 and set about forming a government based on the Kururiku coalition.

HEAD OF STATE
President, Ivo Josipovic, *elected* 10 January 2010, *sworn in* 18 February 2010

SELECTED GOVERNMENT MEMBERS *as at May 2012*
Prime Minister, Zoran Milanovic
Deputy Prime Ministers, Radimir Cacic *(Economy)*, Neven Mimica, Milanka Opacic, Branko Grcic
Defence, Ante Kotromanovic
Foreign Affairs, Vesna Pusic
Interior, Ranko Ostojic

EMBASSY OF THE REPUBLIC OF CROATIA
21 Conway Street, London W1T 6BN
T 020-7387 2022
E croemb.london@mvp.hr
W uk.mvp.hr
Ambassador Extraordinary and Plenipotentiary, HE Dr Ivica Tomic, *apptd* 2009

BRITISH EMBASSY
Ivana Lucica 4, 10000 Zagreb
T (+385) 600 9100
E british.embassyzagreb@fco.gov.uk
W ukincroatia.fco.gov.uk
Charge d'Affaires, Nicole Davison

DEFENCE

All aged 16–49, 2010 est	Males	Females
Available for military service	1,016,234	1,017,355
Fit for military service	770,710	839,732

Military expenditure—US$1,037m (2011)

ECONOMY AND TRADE

As part of Yugoslavia, Croatia was a prosperous and industrialised area, but the conflict in 1991–5 damaged its infrastructure, large areas of farmland, industrial productivity and the tourist industry. From 2000 to 2007 there was steady economic growth, led by a recovery in tourism, banking and public investment. However, a growing trade deficit, high unemployment, the size of the public sector, and the economy's over-reliance on tourism are longer-term problems that left the economy vulnerable in the global economic downturn and slow to recover. The World Bank predicted Croatia would enter recession in 2012 and urged the new government to address the country's fiscal overspending.

The service sector accounts for 70.1% of GDP, industry for 24.2%, and agriculture for 5.5%. Tourism is a major contributor to GDP. Industry produces chemicals and plastics, machine tools, metals and metal products, electronics, wood products, construction materials and textiles, and includes food processing, shipbuilding and oil refining. Agricultural production includes cereals, pulses, fruit and vegetables, livestock and dairy products. Most trade is with EU and neighbouring countries.

GNI—US$58,805m; US$13,870 per capita (2010)
Annual average growth of GDP—0.8% (2011 est)
Inflation rate—3.2% (2011 est)
Population below poverty line—17% (2008)
Unemployment—17.6% (2010 est)
Total external debt—US$66,300m (2011 est)
Imports—US$20,051m (2010)
Exports—US$11,806m (2010)

BALANCE OF PAYMENTS
Trade—US$8,244m deficit (2010)
Current Account—US$666mm deficit (2010)

Trade with UK	2010	2011
Imports from UK	£165,949,905	£146,613,393
Exports to UK	£95,200,061	£104,486,399

COMMUNICATIONS
Airports—There are 23 airports, with international terminals in Zagreb and Split
Waterways—There are 785km of inland waterways and frequent ferry services to the many Adriatic islands
Roadways and railways—There are 2,722km of railways and 29,343km of roads, including 1,047km of motorway
Telecommunications—1.866 million fixed lines and 6.362 million mobile subscriptions (2010); there were 2.234 million internet users in 2009
Internet code and IDD—hr; 385 (from UK), 44 (to UK)
Major broadcasters—Croatian Radio-Television (HRT) is the national state-owned public service broadcaster
Press—There are three main news publications: *Vecernji List* (daily), *Jutarnji List* (daily) and *Nacional* (weekly)
WPFI score—17,50 (62)

EDUCATION AND HEALTH
Literacy rate—98.8% (2009 est)
Gross enrolment ratio (percentage of relevant age group)—primary 93%; secondary 95%; tertiary 49% (2009 est)
Health expenditure (per capita)—US$1,120 (2009)
Hospital beds (per 1,000 people)—5.5 (2004–9)
Life expectancy (years)—75.79 (2011 est)
Mortality rate—11.91 (2011 est)
Birth rate—9.6 (2011 est)
Infant mortality rate—6.16 (2011 est)

Cyprus

Kypriaki Dimokratia/Kibris Cumhuriyeti—Republic of Cyprus
Area—9,251 sq. km, of which 3,355 sq. km are in the Turkish Cypriot-administered area
Capital—Nicosia; population 239,859 (2009 est)
Major cities—Larnaca, Limassol, Paphos (south of the partition); Famagusta, Kyrenia (north)
Currency—Euro (€) of 100 cents (south), Turkish lira (north)
Population—1,138,071 rising at 1.57% a year (2012 est); Greek (77%), Turkish (18%) (2001 est)
Religion—Christian (Greek Orthodox 95%) south of the partition; Sunni Muslim (98%) in the north
Language—Greek, Turkish (both official), English
Population density—119 per sq. km (2010)
Urban population—70% (2010 est)
Median age (years)—34.8 (2011 est)
National anthem—'Imnos eis tin Eleftherian' ['Hymn to Freedom']
National day—1 October (Independence Day)
Life expectancy (years)—77.82 (2011 est)
Mortality rate—6.45 (2011 est)
Birth rate—11.41 (2011 est)
Infant mortality rate—9.38 (2011 est)
Death penalty—Abolished for all crimes (since 2002)
CPI score—6.3 (2011)
Literacy rate—97.9% (2009 est)

FINANCIAL OUTLOOK

Cyprus has been one of the economies worst affected by the eurozone sovereign debt crisis. In March 2013, Cyprus agreed a €10 billion bailout with the EU and the IMF in an attempt to stave off the collapse of its banking sector and the wider economy. Cyprus has agreed to a significant restructuring of its banking sector, along with other measures such as tax rises and privatizations. The measures are designed to raise billions towards the bailout, but protect bank customers with deposits of €100,000 or less. Cyprus's second-largest bank, Laiki Bank, will be closed down and deposits above €100,000 moved into a "bad bank." However, in April it was reported that the cost of the bailout for Cyprus had increased to €23 billion, according to a draft document prepared by the country's creditors. The new total means Cyprus will have to find €13 billion to secure €10 billion from the EU and the IMF, and there are doubts that it can raise such a sum.

CLIMATE AND TERRAIN

Cyprus is the third-largest island in the Mediterranean. It has two mountain ranges, the Pentadaktylos along the north coast, and the Troodos in the centre and west. Plains lie between the two ranges and on parts of the south coast. Elevation extremes range from 1,951m (Mt Olympus, Troodos range) to 0m (Mediterranean Sea). The climate is Mediterranean, with very warm summers.

HISTORY AND POLITICS

The 1960 constitution provides for power-sharing between the Greek and Turkish Cypriots but some of these provisions have been in abeyance since 1963, when the Turkish Cypriots withdrew from the power-sharing arrangements. The executive president is directly elected for a five-year term. The unicameral legislature, the House of Representatives, has 80 members, directly elected for a five-year term; elections to the 24 seats reserved for Turkish Cypriots have not taken place since 1963.

Demetris Christofias, the candidate of the Progressive Party of the Working People (AKEL), was elected president in 2008. The legislative elections held in May 2011 resulted in gains for both AKEL and the opposition Democratic Rally (DISY) party; AKEL maintained its majority in the House of Representatives through a coalition with the Democratic Party (DIKO), although a munitions blast in the south of the country July 2011 forced a major cabinet reshuffle and the resignation of key coalition members.

HEAD OF STATE

President, Demetris Christofias, *elected* 24 February 2008, *sworn in* 28 February 2008

SELECTED GOVERNMENT MEMBERS *as at May 2012*

Defence, Demetris Eliades
Finance, Vassos Shiarlys
Foreign Affairs, Erato Marcoullis
Interior, Eleni Mavrou

HIGH COMMISSION FOR THE REPUBLIC OF CYPRUS

13 St James's Square, London SW1Y 4LB
T 020-7321 4100
E cyphclondon@btconnect.com
High Commissioner, HE Alexandros Zenon, *apptd* 2008

BRITISH HIGH COMMISSION

PO Box 21978, Alexander Pallis Street, 1587 Nicosia
T (+357) 2286 1100
W ukincyprus.fco.gov.uk
High Commissioner, HE Matthew Kidd, apptd 2010

British Sovereign Base Areas

The Sovereign Base Areas (SBAs) of Akrotiri and Dhekelia are those parts of Cyprus that remained under British sovereignty and jurisdiction after independence, and have the status of a UK overseas territory. They are around 254 sq. km in size. There are approximately 15,700 residents: 7,700 Cypriots, and 8,000 military and UK-based civilian personnel and their dependants.

Administrator of the British Sovereign Base Areas, Air Vice-Marshal Graham Stacey, *apptd* 2010

DEFENCE

A military airfield in Paphos provides a base for Greek military aircraft, as Cyprus does not possess its own air force.

All aged 16–49, 2010 est	*Males*	*Females*
Available for military service	327,875	287,891
Fit for military service (All Greek Cypriot National Guard)	275,842	239,862

Military expenditure—US$494m (2011)
Conscription duration—24 months

ECONOMY AND TRADE

The Greek Cypriot economy is dominated by the service sector, which accounted for 81.3% of GDP in 2011; this was derived mainly from tourism and financial services. Tourism represents a major part of the total GDP, making the economy vulnerable to fluctuations; reduced visitor numbers due to the global economic downturn contributed to the economy entering recession in 2009 and registering no growth in 2011. Shipping services are also important; about 20% of the world's shipping is Cypriot-registered. Industry contributes 16.4% of GDP and agriculture 2.3%. The main products for export are citrus fruits, potatoes, pharmaceuticals, cement and garments. Imports are primarily consumer goods, fuel and lubricants, machinery and transport equipment. Over half of trade is with other EU countries.

The Turkish Cypriot economy suffers from a small domestic market, international isolation and a bloated public sector. It is heavily dependent on financial support from the Turkish government. Services accounted for about 69.1% of GDP in 2006, industry for 22.5% and agriculture for 8.6%. The main products for export are citrus fruits, dairy products, potatoes and textiles. The main imports are vehicles, fuel, cigarettes, food, minerals, chemicals and machinery. The tourist industry is small because the only international transport links are via Turkey, but a drop in tourist numbers and the global downturn had a serious impact on the economy in 2009.

GNI—US$22,539m; US$29,430 per capita (2010)
Annual average growth of GDP—0% (2011 est)
Inflation rate—3.3% (2011 est)
Unemployment—4.6% (2010 est)
Total external debt—US$32,610m (2008 est)
Imports—US$8,568m (2010)
Exports—US$1,514m (2010)

BALANCE OF PAYMENTS

Trade—US$7,054m deficit (2010)
Current Account—US$1,794 deficit (2010)

Trade with UK	*2010*	*2011*
Imports from UK	£540,913,187	£669,052,154
Exports to UK	£105,631,055	£126,576,116

COMMUNICATIONS

Airports—Larnaca and Paphos (Greek area); flight connections to Turkish areas are via Turkey
Waterways—Principal ports are Limassol, Larnaca and Paphos (Greek area), and Famagusta and Kyrenia (Turkish area)
Railways and roadways—There are no railways; the road network (12,321km in the Greek part of the island and 2,350km in the Turkish part) serves the main population centres
Telecommunications—414,700 (Greek area) and 86,228 (Turkish area) fixed lines in use and 1.03 million (Greek area) and 147,522 (Turkish area) mobile subscriptions (2010); there were 433,900 internet users in 2009
Internet code and IDD—cy; 357 (from UK) 44 (to UK)

Major broadcasters—The state-run Cyprus Broadcasting Corporation competes with a number of privately owned television and radio stations. The Turkish north operates its own services and broadcasts
Press—Major newspapers include *Cyprus Daily* (English language), *Politis* (Greek language daily) and *Kibris Gazete* (Turkish language)
WPFI score—13,40 (45)

TURKISH REPUBLIC OF NORTHERN CYPRUS

In 1974, a Greece-backed coup against the Cypriot government led Turkey, fearing the coup was a precursor to the union of Cyprus with Greece, to invade northern Cyprus and occupy over a third of the island. The following year, a Turkish Federated State of Cyprus was declared, and in 1983 a declaration of statehood was issued which purported to establish the Turkish Republic of Northern Cyprus. The declaration was condemned by the UN security council and only Turkey has recognised the republic. A constitution was adopted in 1985, and election have been held at regular intervals since.

Reunification talks were unsuccessful in the 1980s and 1990s, and although Turkish Cypriots approved a UN-sponsored reunification plan put to simultaneous referendums in 2004, it was rejected by Greek Cypriots. Since 2004, the EU has given aid to the area to promote and ease reunification, and UN-facilitated talks began in 2008.

The 2009 legislative election was won by the National Unity Party, which favours unification with Turkey. Dervis Eroglu won the 2010 presidential election, replacing Mehmet Ali Talat.

DE FACTO HEAD OF STATE
President, Dervis Eroglu, *elected* 18 April 2010, *sworn in* 23 April 2010
Prime Minister, Irsen Kucuk

Czech Republic

Ceska Republika—Czech Republic
Area—78,867 sq. km
Capital—Prague (Praha); population, 1,161,770 (2009 est)
Major cities—Brno (Brünn), Ostrava, Plzen (Pilsen)
Currency—Koruna (Kcs) of 100 haleru
Population—10,177,300 falling at 0.13% a year (2012 est); Czech (90.4%), Moravian (3.7%), Slovak (1.9%) (2001)
Religion—Christian (Roman Catholic 27%, Protestant 3%, Czech Hussite 1%)
Language—Czech (official), Slovak
Population density—136 per sq. km (2010)
Urban population—73.5% (2010 est)
Median age (years)—40.8 (2011 est)
National anthem—'Kde Domov Muj?' ['Where is My Homeland?']
National day—28 October (Founding Day)
Death penalty—Abolished for all crimes (since 1990)
CPI score—4.4 (2011)

FINANCIAL OUTLOOK

The Czech economic recession stretched into the longest on record in the fourth quarter of 2012, as the government extended its austerity program and the eurozone crisis curbed demand for exports. GDP shrank by 0.2% in Q4 2012, the fourth consecutive quarter of decline. On a year-on-year basis, output fell by 1.7%, the steepest drop in three years. Exports account for about 75% of Czech GDP, but grew by just 1.9% (Q-on-Q) in Q4 2012, the weakest performance since the final quarter of 2009. Weak domestic demand compounded the impact of soft export orders. The central bank attempted to offset the impact of public spending cuts by reducing borrowing costs three times in 2012, to effectively zero. Retail sales fell by 5.1% in December 2012, highlighting the weakness of domestic demand, while the jobless rate rose to 8% in January, the highest reading on record, according to Labor Ministry data. Moreover, industrial output fell by 12.5% in December 2012, year-on-year, the biggest decline in more than three years.

CLIMATE AND TERRAIN

The landlocked republic is composed of Bohemia (the west and centre) and Moravia (the east). Bohemia contains the fertile plains of the river Elbe and the surrounding low mountains, while the hilly region of Moravia extends towards the basin of the river Danube. Roughly a third of the country is covered by forest. Elevation extremes range from 1,602m (Snezka) to 115m (river Elbe). The climate is continental, with warm, humid summers and cold, dry winters. The average temperature in Prague ranges from −1°C in January to 17°C in July and August.

HISTORY AND POLITICS

The 1992 constitution provided for the separation of the Czech Republic and Slovakia; federal laws remain in place unless superseded by Czech ones. The president is elected by a joint session of both chambers of the legislature for a five-year term, renewable once. The bicameral *Parlament* comprises a 200-member Chamber of Deputies, directly elected for a four-year term, and an 81-member senate directly elected for a six-year term, one-third being elected every two years. The council of ministers is appointed by the president on the recommendation of the prime minister.

Vaclav Klaus of the Civic Democrat Party (ODS) was elected president at the third attempt in 2003; he was narrowly re-elected in 2008. Legislative elections in May 2010 gave a combined majority to three centre-right parties—the ODS, Top09 and the Public Affairs party—which formed a coalition government under ODS leader Petr Necas. The partial senate elections in autumn 2010 resulted in a slight majority for the opposition, enabling it to disrupt the government's austerity programme.

HEAD OF STATE
President, Vaclav Klaus, *elected* 28 February 2003, *sworn in* 7 March 2003, *re-elected* 2008

SELECTED GOVERNMENT MEMBERS *as at June 2012*
Prime Minister, Petr Necas
Foreign Affairs, Karel Schwarzenburg
Defence, Alexandr Vondra
Interior, Jan Kubice
Finance, Miroslav Kalousek

EMBASSY OF THE CZECH REPUBLIC
26 Kensington Palace Gardens, London W8 4QY
T 020-7243 1115
E london@embassy.mzv.cz
W www.czechembassy.org.uk
Ambassador Extraordinary and Plenipotentiary, HE Michael Zantovsky, *apptd* 2009

  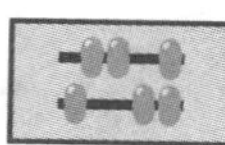      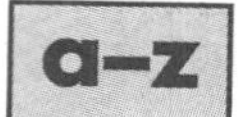

BRITISH EMBASSY
Thunovska 14, 11800 Prague 1
T (+420) (2) 5740 2111
W ukinczechrepublic.fco.gov.uk
Ambassador Extraordinary and Plenipotentiary, HE Sian MacLeod, *apptd* 2009

DEFENCE

All aged 16–49, 2010 est	Males	Females
Available for military service	2,506,826	2,407,634
Fit for military service	2,072,267	1,988,839

Military expenditure—US$2,254m (2011)

ECONOMY AND TRADE

Economic reforms and accession to the EU have produced a stable and prosperous market economy, as well as contributing to steady growth by expanding export markets and encouraging foreign investment. The global economic downturn caused the economy to contract in 2009, largely because of a reduced demand for the country's major exports. A slow recovery began in late 2009.

Services account for 59% of GDP, industry for 38.7% and agriculture for 2.2%. The principal agricultural products are cereal crops, sugar beet and potatoes; the timber industry is also important. The country has been industrialised since the 19th century, and motor vehicles, metals, machinery, glass and armaments are major products. Electricity is also exported. The principal trading partners are EU countries—especially Germany—and China and Russia.

GNI—US$179,432m; US$17,890 per capita (2010)
Annual average growth of GDP—1.8% (2011 est)
Inflation rate—1.9% (2011 est)
Unemployment—9% (2010 est)
Total external debt—US$96,940m (2011 est)
Imports—US$125,697m (2010)
Exports—US$132,142m (2010)

BALANCE OF PAYMENTS
Trade—US$6,445m surplus (2010)
Current Account—US$7,188m deficit (2010)

Trade with UK	2010	2011
Imports from UK	£1,751,657,135	£1,856,721,358
Exports to UK	£3,948,048,160	£4,222,098,843

COMMUNICATIONS
Airports—There are 122 airports across the country; the principal airport is at Prague
Waterways—Navigable inland waterways include 664km on the Elbe, Vltava, and Oder and other rivers, lakes and canals
Roadways and railways—Extensive road (127,797km) and rail (9,449km) networks link the main population centres
Telecommunications—2.19 million fixed lines and14.33 million mobile subscriptions (2010); there were 6.68 million internet users in 2009
Internet code and IDD—cz; 420 (from UK) 44 (to UK)
Major broadcasters—The public broadcaster Ceska Televize (CT) runs two networks and a 24-hour news channel alongside two major private television stations. Czech public radio, Cesky Rozhlas (CRo), operates three national networks and local services
Press—There are four major daily newspapers:*Lidove Noviny, Mlada Fronta Dnes, Pravo* and *Blesk*
WPFI score—7,50 (23)

EDUCATION AND HEALTH
Education is free and compulsory for all children from the age of six to 15.
Gross enrolment ratio (percentage of relevant age group)—primary 106%; secondary 90%; tertiary 61% (2009 est)
Health expenditure (per capita)—US$1,384 (2009)
Hospital beds (per 1,000 people)—7.2 (2004–9)
Life expectancy (years)—77.19 (2011 est)
Mortality rate—10.86 (2011 est)
Birth rate—8.7 (2011 est)
Infant mortality rate—3.73 (2011 est)

Denmark

Kongeriget Danmark—Kingdom of Denmark
Area—43,094 sq. km (excluding the Faeroe Islands and Greenland)
Capital—Copenhagen; population, 1,173,680 (2009 est)
Major cities—Aalborg, Aarhus, Esbjerg, Odense
Currency—Danish krone (DKr) of 100 ore
Population—5,543,453 rising at 0.23% a year (2012 est)
Religion—Christian (Lutheran 81%, Roman Catholic 1%), Muslim 4% (est). The Evangelical Lutheran Church is the state church
Language—Danish (official), Faroese, Greenlandic, German. English is widely spoken as a second language
Population density—131 per sq. km (2010)
Urban population—87.2% (2010 est)
Median age (years)—40.9 (2011 est)
National anthem—'Det er et Yndigt Land' ['There is a Lovely Land']
National day—5 June (Constitution Day)
Death penalty—Abolished for all crimes (since 1978)
CPI score—9.4 (2011)

FINANCIAL OUTLOOK
After a further contraction in its economy of −0.4% for 2012, Denmark's near-term economic outlook is expected to return to modest growth in 2013, lifted mostly by private consumption and moderate business investment growth, according to a January 2013 report from the IMF. Denmark's public expenditure is the highest in the OECD when considered as a share of GDP, largely due to a bloated state sector that employs around a third of the country's labor force, and has done for the last 30 years. The country has a "cradle-to-grave" welfare system, which entails significant spending on disability and family benefits as well as on labor market policies. Nevertheless, Denmark's public debt to GDP ratio is well inside the EU's 60% ceiling, though the IMF questions the stability of this high level of social welfare spending in the medium term, given the pressures of an ageing population and declining productivity, along with a tailing-off of North Sea oil and gas revenues. Denmark's currency was seen as a safe haven up to 2011, which meant that while Italy was paying close to 7% on its bonds, Denmark only had to offer 0.3%, which in real terms after inflation was a negative rate of interest, meaning that investors were paying Denmark to safeguard their cash. Annual inflation was at 2.8% at the end of 2012, although average salary increases were only 2%.

CLIMATE AND TERRAIN

Denmark consists of most of the Jutland peninsula and 406 islands, mainly in the Baltic Sea or among the northern Frisian Islands in the North Sea. The largest islands are Sjaelland (Zealand), Fyn, Lolland, Faister and Bornholm. It is a low-lying country, indented by fjords on its east coast and with lagoons and sand dunes along the west coast; Lim Fjord nearly bisects the north of Jutland. Elevation extremes range from 171m (Mollehoj) to −7m (Lammefjord). The climate is temperate, with cold winters and warm summers. Average temperatures range from 0°C in January to 17°C in July.

HISTORY AND POLITICS

The Danes were at the forefront of Viking expansionism from the eighth century. Denmark was unified in the tenth century and was the centre of a short-lived empire, also including Norway and England, created by Cnut (Canute) in the 11th century. The Union of Kalmar (1397) brought Norway and Sweden (including Finland) under Danish rule. Danish power waned during the 16th century, enabling Sweden to re-establish its independence in 1523, and Norway was ceded to Sweden under the Treaty of Kiel in 1814. Denmark was neutral during the First World War, but in the Second World War it was invaded and occupied by Germany until May 1945.

Denmark joined the European Community in 1973. In a 2000 referendum, it rejected adopting the euro.

In the 2011 legislative election, the Liberal Party remained the largest party in parliament, but a surge of support for the Red Bloc (a political alliance consisting of centre-left parties including the Social Democrats) gave them an overall majority with 97 seats. Helle Thorning-Schmidt, leader of the Social Democrats, formed a coalition with other member parties of the Red Bloc, and took office in October 2011.

The country is a constitutional monarchy, with a hereditary monarch as head of state. The head of government is the prime minister, who appoints the cabinet. The unicameral legislature, the *Folketing*, has 179 members, including two for the Faeroes and two for Greenland; members are elected for a four-year term by proportional representation.

HEAD OF STATE

HM The Queen of Denmark, Queen Margrethe II, KG, *born* 16 April 1940, *acceeded* 14 January 1972

Heir, HRH Crown Prince Frederik, *born* 26 May 1968

SELECTED GOVERNMENT MEMBERS *as at May 2012*

Prime Minister, Helle Thorning-Schmidt

Deputy Prime Minister, Magrethe Hansen *(Economic Affairs and Interior)*

Defence, Nick Haekkerup

Finance, Bjarne Corydon

ROYAL DANISH EMBASSY

55 Sloane Street, London SW1X 9SR

T 020-7333 0200

E lonamb@um.dk

W www.denmark.org.uk

Ambassador Extraordinary and Plenipotentiary, HE Anne Hedensted Steffensen, *apptd* 2011

BRITISH EMBASSY

Kastelsvej 36–40, 2100 Copenhagen O

T (+45) 3544 5200

W ukindenmark.fco.gov.uk

Ambassador Extraordinary and Plenipotentiary, Nick Archer, MVO, *apptd* 2008

DEFENCE

All aged 16–49, 2010 est	Males	Females
Available for military service	1,236,337	1,224,182
Fit for military service	1,014,560	1,003,921

Military expenditure—US$4,515m (2011)

Conscription duration—4–12 months

ECONOMY AND TRADE

Denmark has a diversified and industrialised market economy with a high dependence on exports. It is a net exporter of food and energy (oil and natural gas). Slowing growth from 2007 and then the global downturn pushed the economy into recession in 2009; a modest recovery began in 2010 but the economy re-entered a technical recession at the beginning of 2011. The service sector contributes 76.4% of GDP, industry 19.1% and the highly efficient agricultural sector 4.5%. Metals, pharmaceuticals, shipping and renewable energy are key industries.

The main trading partners are other EU countries, especially Germany and Sweden. Principal exports are machinery and instruments, meat and meat products, dairy products, fish, pharmaceuticals, furniture and windmills. The main imports are machinery and equipment, industrial raw materials and semi-manufactures, chemicals, grain and foodstuffs, and consumer goods.

GNI—US$315,664m; US$59,050 per capita (2010)

Annual average growth of GDP—1.5% (2011 est)

Inflation rate—2.8% (2011 est)

Population below poverty line—12.1% (2007)

Unemployment—6% (2010 est)

Total external debt—US$626,900m (2011)

Imports—US$84,469m (2010)

Exports—US$96,813m (2010)

BALANCE OF PAYMENTS

Trade—US$12,344m surplus (2010)

Current Account—US$15,715m surplus (2010)

Trade with UK	*2010*	*2011*
Imports from UK	£2,667,281,654	£2,950,108,199
Exports to UK	£4,023,222,364	£6,056,271,951

COMMUNICATIONS

Airports—The principal airports are at Copenhagen, Aarhus, Aalborg and near Vejle

Waterways—The main ports are Aarhus, Odense, Copenhagen, Aalborg and Esbjerg

Railways—2,667km of railway, of which 640km is electrified

Roadways—73,197km, including 1,111km of motorways

Telecommunications—2.623 million fixed lines and 6.905 million mobile subscriptions (2010); there were 4.75 million internet users in 2009

Internet code and IDD—dk; 45 (from UK), 44 (to UK)

Major broadcasters—The public broadcaster is Danmarks Radio, which operates two television networks and national and regional radio stations

Press—There are six major daily newspapers, including *Morgenavisen Jyllands-Posten*, *Berlingske Tidende* and *Ekstra Bladet*

WPFI score—2,50 (11)

EDUCATION AND HEALTH

Education is free and compulsory for nine years.

Gross enrolment ratio (percentage of relevant age group)—primary 99%; secondary 117%; tertiary 74% (2009 est)
Health expenditure (per capita)—US$6,273 (2009)
Hospital beds (per 1,000 people)—3.6 (2004–9)
Life expectancy (years)—78.63 (2011 est)
Mortality rate—10.19 (2011 est)
Birth rate—10.29 (2011 est)
Infant mortality rate—4.24 (2011 est)

THE FAEROE ISLANDS

Area—1,393 sq. km
Capital—Torshavn; population, 20,082 (2009 est)
Population—49,483 rising at 0.447% per year (2012 est)
National day—29 July (Olaifest)
Internet code and IDD—fo; 298 (from UK), 44 (to UK)

The Faeroe (Sheep) Islands are a group of 18 rugged islands (17 inhabited) and a few islets in the North Atlantic Ocean, between the Shetland Islands and Iceland. First settled in the ninth century, the islands were a Norwegian province and, with Norway, came under Danish rule in the 14th century. Since 1948 the Faeroes have been self-governing and are not part of the EU.

The sovereign is represented in the islands by a high commissioner, and the islands elect two representatives to the Danish legislature. The Faroese government *(Landsstyri)* is responsible for internal affairs. The parliament *(Loegting)* has 33 members, elected for a four-year term. In the 2011 election, the Union Party overtook the Republican Party to become the largest party in parliament; the incumbent prime minister Kaj Leo Johannesen continued to head a coalition government comprising the Union Party, the Social Democrats and the People's Party.

Prime Minister, Kaj Leo Johannesen

Economy and Trade

The economy has grown steadily in recent years, although it slowed during the global downturn. It remains highly dependent on fishing and fish processing; fish and fish products account for 95% of exports. Offshore oil discoveries raise the possibility of future diversification and less dependence on Danish government subsidies.

BALANCE OF PAYMENTS

Trade—US$90m deficit (2003)
Current Account—US$7m deficit (2003)

Trade with UK	2010	2011
Imports from UK	£20,127,655	£12,540,975
Exports to UK	£119,085,555	£151,095,381

BRITISH CONSULATE

P/F Damfar, PO Box 1154, Niels Finsengota 5, FR-110 Torshavn
T (+298) 35 00 77
Honorary Consul, Tummas H. Dam

GREENLAND (KALAALLIT NUNAAT)

Area—2,166,086 sq. km
Capital—Nuuk (Godthab); population 15,182 (2009 est)
Population—57,695 rising at 0.038% per year (2012 est)
National day—21 June (longest day)
Internet code and IDD—gl; 299 (from UK), 44 (to UK)

Greenland, the world's largest island, lies between the Atlantic and Arctic oceans, to the east of Canada and to the west of Iceland. Most of Greenland is within the Arctic Circle, with permafrost covering about 80% of the island, although this ice cap is beginning to melt. Elevation extremes range from 3,700m (Gunnbjorn) to 0m (Atlantic Ocean).

Greenland was first discovered by small groups of hunters and nomadic groups who migrated from Canada *c.* 500 BC. In the late tenth century Icelanders established settlements along the south-eastern coast, but these colonies had died out by the 16th century. Danish colonisation began in the 18th century. Greenland was integrated into Denmark in 1953 and was granted internal autonomy in 1979; greater autonomy was granted in 2009. Greenland negotiated its withdrawal from the EU, without discontinuing relations with Denmark, and left in 1985. The USA maintains air bases on the island.

The sovereign is represented by a high commissioner, and Greenland elects two representatives to the Danish legislature. The Greenlandic government *(Landsstyre)* is elected by the parliament *(Landsting)*, which has 31 members, elected for a four-year term. In the 2009 election to the *Landsting*, the Siumut (Forward) party, in power since the 1970s, was defeated by the Inuit Ataqatigiit (Brotherhood of the People) party, which won 14 seats.

Prime Minister, Kuupik Kleist

Economy and Trade

The economy is dependent on Danish subsidies (56% of government revenue) and fishing; fish and fish products comprise 89% of exports. Natural resources include zinc, iron ore, lead, coal, molybdenum, gold, platinum and uranium, some of which are mined. Mineral exploration and mining operations are being extended as the ice cap shrinks. This is also benefiting offshore oil exploration, and global warming is extending the growing season. Tourism is being encouraged.

Trade with UK	2010	2011
Imports from UK	£39,430,761	£71,654,409
Exports to UK	£7,347,501	£21,263,693

Dominica

Commonwealth of Dominica
Area—751 sq. km
Capital—Roseau; population, 14,266 (2009 est)
Currency—East Caribbean dollar (EC$) of 100 cents
Population—73,126 rising at 0.216% a year (2012 est)
Religion—Christian (Roman Catholic 61%, Pentecostal 6%, Seventh-day Adventist 6%, Baptist 4%, Methodist 4%) (est)
Language—English (official), Creole
Population density—90 per sq. km (2010)
Urban population—74.6% (2010 est)
Median age (years)—30.8 (2011 est)
National anthem—'Isle of Beauty, Isle of Splendour'
National day—3 November (Independence Day)
Life expectancy—75.98 (2011 est)
Mortality rate—8.06 (2011 est)
Birth rate—15.62 (2011 est)

  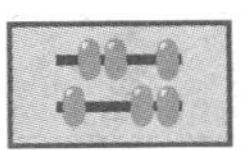      

Infant mortality rate—12.78 (2011 est)
Death penalty—Retained
CPI score—5.2 (2011)
Literacy rate—88.0% (2008 est)

FINANCIAL OUTLOOK
Economic growth has faltered in recent years. GDP growth declined from 7.8% in 2010 to 4.5% in 2011, and to a projected 4% in 2012, according to an IMF report published in March 2013. A large increase in government spending in 2012 was partly offset by declining private-sector demand. More positively, headline inflation declined below 3% in 2012, well below the central bank's target range of 4.5–6.5%. However, the IMF added that the large fiscal expansion, an easing of monetary policy, and limited exchange-rate flexibility increased public-sector debt, kept the external current account deficit high, and fueled losses in international reserves. The fiscal deficit in 2012 rose to an estimated 8.5% of GDP, while the stock of public debt reached nearly 45% of GDP, compared with 35% of GDP in 2007–08. The central bank lowered its overnight deposit rate during May–August 2012 by a total of 175 basis points to 5%.

CLIMATE AND TERRAIN
Dominica, the most northerly of the Windward Islands, is 46km long and 25km wide, with a mountainous and forested centre. Its peaks include volcanic craters, one of which contains Boiling Lake, the world's second-largest thermally active lake. Elevation extremes range from 1,447m (Morne Diablotins) to 0m (Caribbean Sea). The climate is tropical, with an average temperature of 25°C. The island is located within the hurricane zone.

HISTORY AND POLITICS
Dominica was discovered by Columbus in 1493, when it was a stronghold of the Caribs, the sole inhabitants of the island until the French founded settlements in the 18th century. It was ceded to the British in 1763 but passed back and forth between France and Britain until 1805, after which British possession was unchallenged. From 1871 until the 1960s Dominica was administered by Britain as part of various federations of West Indian islands. Internal self-government from 1967 was followed on 3 November 1978 by independence as a republic.

President Nicholas Liverpool was the sole candidate nominated in the 2008 presidential election and was returned for a second term. The Dominica Labour Party (DLP), in power since 2000, won the legislative election in 2009 and continued in government.

Under the 1978 constitution, the president is elected by the legislature for a five-year term, renewable once. The unicameral House of Assembly has 30 members, 21 directly elected, and nine appointed senators; all members serve a five-year term.

HEAD OF STATE
President, Nicholas Liverpool, *elected* 2003, *re-elected* 26 July 2008

SELECTED GOVERNMENT MEMBERS *as at June 2012*
Prime Minister, Finance, Foreign Affairs, Roosevelt Skerrit
National Security, Charles Savarin
Attorney-General, Levi Peter

OFFICE OF THE HIGH COMMISSIONER FOR THE COMMONWEALTH OF DOMINICA
1 Collingham Gardens, London SW5 0HW
T 020-7370 5194
E info@dominicahighcommission.co.uk
W www.dominicahighcommission.co.uk
High Commissioner (acting), Janet Charles

BRITISH HIGH COMMISSIONER
High Commissioner, HE Paul Brummell, *apptd* 2009, resident at Bridgetown, Barbados

ECONOMY AND TRADE
The economy, traditionally dependent on banana exports, struggled in the early 2000s as EU preferential access for the fruit was phased out; the industry also suffered serious hurricane damage in 2007. Economic restructuring from 2003 led to steady growth, with an emphasis on eco-agriculture and eco-tourism, until the global downturn caused the economy to contract in 2009, picking up only slightly in 2011. Diversification into offshore financial services and light industry is also being encouraged, and exploitation of geothermal energy, fishing and forestry resources is planned.

Agriculture is the principal occupation, employing 40% of the workforce but producing only 21.4% of GDP. Services contribute 56.3% of GDP and industry 32.8%. The main trading partners are Japan, the UK, the USA, other Caribbean countries and China. Principal exports are bananas, soap, bay oil, vegetables and citrus fruits. The main imports are manufactured goods, machinery and equipment, food and chemicals.

GNI—US$454m; US$6,760 per capita (2010)
Annual average growth of GDP—0.9% (2011 est)
Inflation rate—3.5% (2011 est)
Total external debt—US$213m (2004)
Imports—US$200m (2010)

BALANCE OF PAYMENTS
Trade—US$205m deficit (2010)
Current Account—US$103m deficit (2010)

Trade with UK	*2010*	*2011*
Imports from UK	£5,789,611	£5,676,295
Exports to UK	£3,993,404	£2,462,322

COMMUNICATIONS
Airports and waterways—The principal airports are Melville Hall on the north-east tip of the island and Canefield, just outside Roseau; the main seaports are located at Portsmouth and Roseau
Roadways—780km
Telecommunications—15,500 fixed lines and 98,100 mobilesubscriptions (2010); there were 28,000 internet users in 2009
Internet code and IDD—dm; 1 767 (from UK), 011 44 (to UK)
Major broadcasters—There is no national television on the island, but cable television provider Marpim Telecom and Broadcasting covers parts of the island

Ecuador

República del Ecuador—Republic of Ecuador
Area—283,561 sq. km
Capital—Quito; population, 1,800,850 (2009 est)
Major cities—Cuenca, Guayaquil, Machala, Manta, Santo Domingo de los Colorados
Currency—US dollar (US$) of 100 cents

  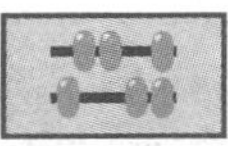      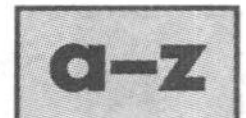

Population—15,223,680 rising at 1.419% a year (2012 est)
Religion—Christian (Roman Catholic 85%) (est)
Language—Spanish (official), Quechua, other Amerindian languages
Population density—58 per sq. km (2010)
Urban population—66.9% (2010 est)
Median age (years)—25.7 (2011 est)
National anthem—'Salve, Oh Patria' ['We Salute You, Our Homeland']
National day—10 August (Independence Day)
Death penalty—Abolished for all crimes (since 1906)
CPI score—2.7 (2011)

FINANCIAL OUTLOOK

Ecuador's economy should see GDP growth of above 4% for 2013, largely supported by a boom in the country's construction industry, according to the Ecuadoran finance minister, Patricio Rivera. The minister said that Ecuador was expecting to grow above the 4% average for Latin America in 2013. However, the Central Bank of Ecuador has cut its generous 2013 growth forecast of 5.4% back to 4.8%. Reuters says that high oil revenues and increased tax collection have allowed the government to ramp up spending on roads, hospitals, and schools over the last few years, stimulating growth. One of the major downside risks to the forecast level of growth is a possible drop in the price of oil. In 2011, the country saw growth of 7.8%, more than doubling the prior year's growth rate of 3.6%. According to the central bank, oil exports saw a slight decrease in value in the first quarter of 2012. The leftist government of President Rafael Correa is expected to continue to spend heavily in the run-up to presidential elections to be held in February 2013.

CLIMATE AND TERRAIN

The Andes run north to south through the centre of Ecuador, dividing the coastal plain in the west from the low-lying rainforest in the east, and between two local Andean chains lie the central highlands. Elevation extremes range from 0m (Pacific Ocean) to 6,267m (Chimborazo). Other Andean peaks include Cotopaxi (5,896m) and Cayambe (5,790m) in the Eastern Cordillera. Ecuador is located in an earthquake zone and five of its volcanoes have erupted since 2000—most recently Tungurahua in April 2011. The country has four different climatic zones, and is one of the most bio-diverse countries on earth; its territory includes the Galápagos Islands in the Pacific Ocean. The average temperature in Quito is 15°C.

HISTORY AND POLITICS

The kingdom of the Caras, around Quito, was conquered by the Incas of Peru in the 15th century. After the Spanish defeated the Incas in Peru, Ecuador was conquered in 1534 and added to the Spanish viceroyalty of Peru. Independence from Spain was achieved in a revolutionary war that culminated in the battle of Mt Pichincha (1822). Ecuador then formed part of Gran Colombia with Colombia, Panama and Venezuela, but left this union to become a fully independent state in 1830. After independence, the country experienced periods of political instability interspersed with dictatorships and military rule. Democratic rule under civilian government was restored in 1979.

The exploitation of oil reserves funded economic and social transformation from the 1970s onwards but also caused rapid inflation and increased foreign debt. In recent years, these problems have worsened because of economic recession, leading to strikes and demonstrations. The most notable of these were by indigenous people, who have benefited least from the oil boom but been hardest hit by the economic downturn. Civil unrest forced three presidents from office between 1997 and 2003.

Presidential and legislative elections were held in 2009 after a new constitution was approved by a national referendum in 2008. President Correa was re-elected in the first round of voting and his party, the left-wing PAIS Alliance, won the most seats in the new legislature.

The 2008 constitution provides for an executive president who is directly elected for a four-year term, renewable once. The unicameral National Assembly has 124 members elected on a party-list proportional representation basis for a four-year term. The republic is divided into 24 provinces.

HEAD OF STATE

President, Rafael Correa, *took office* 15 January 2007, *re-elected* April 2009
Vice-President, Lenin Moreno

SELECTED GOVERNMENT MEMBERS *as at June 2012*

Finance, Patricio Rivera Yanez
Foreign Affairs, Ricardo Patino
National Defence, Javier Ponce Cevallos

EMBASSY OF ECUADOR

Flat 3B, 3 Hans Crescent, London SW1X 0LS
T 020-7584 1367
E eecugranbretania@mmrree.gov.ec
W www.consuladoecuador.org.uk
Ambassador Extraordinary and Plenipotentiary, HE Ana Alban Mora, *apptd* 2010

BRITISH EMBASSY

PO Box 17-17-830, Citiplaza Building, Av. Naciones Unidas y Republica de El Salvador, Piso 14, Quito
T (+593) (2) 2970 800
E britembq@interactive.net.ec
W ukinecuador.fco.gov.uk
Ambassador Extraordinary and Plenipotentiary, HE Patrick Mullee, *apptd* 2012

DEFENCE

All aged 16–49, 2010 est	*Males*	*Females*
Available for military service	3,728,906	3,844,918
Fit for military service	2,834,213	3,269,535

Military expenditure—US$2,209m (2011)
Conscription duration—12 months (selective)

ECONOMY AND TRADE

Structural reforms in 2000, including the adoption of the US dollar, in response to the severe economic crisis of 1999 paved the way for strong growth from 2002 to 2006. Growth has slowed since owing to the uncertainty created by windfall taxes imposed on foreign oil companies, a fall in oil production since 2007, the government defaulting on 80% of private external debt in 2008, and the cancellation of a number of bilateral investment treaties in 2009. The global downturn further reduced oil revenue, remittances from expatriate workers (who number nearly one million) and export earnings, although the economy started to recover and recorded 6.5% growth in 2011.

Oil is Ecuador's principal export, accounting for over half of export earnings and a third of government revenue in recent years. After oil, agriculture, fishing and forestry are the most important activities, providing products both for export and for the food- and wood-processing industries. The main exports are oil, bananas, cut flowers, fish, cacao, coffee, hemp and timber. The main imports are industrial materials, fuels and lubricants, and consumer goods. Principal trading partners are the USA and other South American countries; China, moreover, has become Ecuador's largest foreign bilateral lender, allowing the government to address social spending.

GNI—US$56,924m; US$3,850 per capita (2010)
Annual average growth of GDP—5.8% (2011 est)
Inflation rate—4.7% (2011 est)
Population below poverty line—33.1% (2010)
Unemployment—7.6% (2010 est)
Total external debt—US$19,620m (2011)
Imports—US$20,591m (2010)
Exports—US$17,415m (2010)

BALANCE OF PAYMENTS
Trade—US$3,176m deficit (2010)
Current Account—US$1,917m deficit (2010)

Trade with UK	2010	2011
Imports from UK	£54,453,817	£71,819,838
Exports to UK	£69,170,088	£112,332,470

COMMUNICATIONS
Airports—There are 428 airports and airfields, of which 105 have surfaced runways, and international flights operate to Quito and Guayaquil
Waterways—The main ports are Guayaquil and Esmeraldas
Railways—965km
Roadways—43,670km of roads, 6,472km of which are surfaced
Telecommunications—2.086 million fixed lines and 14.78 million mobile subscriptions (2010); there were 3.35 million internet users in 2009
Internet code and IDD—ec; 593 (from UK), 44 (to UK)
Major broadcasters—Six private television broadcasters dominate broadcasting, including TC Television and Ecuavia
Press—Six newspapers are published daily, including *El Comercio*, *El Teimpo* and the Guayaquil-based daily *El Universo*
WPFI—27,50 (101)

EDUCATION AND HEALTH
Elementary education is free and compulsory until age 14.
Literacy rate—84.2% (2009 est)
Gross enrolment ratio (percentage of relevant age group)—primary 114%; secondary 80% (2009 est)
Health expenditure (per capita)—US$255 (2009)
Hospital beds (per 1,000 people)—1.5 (2004–9)
Life expectancy (years)—75.73 (2011 est)
Mortality rate—5 (2011 est)
Birth rate—19.96 (2011 est)
Infant mortality rate—19.65 (2011 est)

GALÁPAGOS ISLANDS
The Galápagos (Giant Tortoise) Islands, about 960km from the mainland, were annexed by Ecuador in 1832. The 12 large and several hundred smaller islands lie on the equator, and most form part of a national park where unique marine birds, iguanas and the giant tortoises are conserved. This wildlife provided naturalist Charles Darwin (1809–82) with inspiration and research material for his theory of evolution by natural selection, expounded in *On the Origin of Species* (1859). The islands were declared a UNESCO World Heritage Site in 1978.

Egypt

Jumhuriyat Misr al-Arabiyah—Arab Republic of Egypt
Area—1,001,450 sq. km
Capital—Cairo; population, 10,902,500 (2009 est); stands on the Nile about 22km from the head of the delta
Major cities—Alexandria (founded 332 BC by Alexander the Great; the capital for over 1,000 years), Giza, Port Said, Suez, Shubra al-Khema
Currency—Egyptian pound (£E) of 100 piastres or 1,000 millièmes
Population—83,688,164 rising at 1.92% a year (2012 est); Egyptian (including Berber and Bedouin) 99.6% (2006). The Bedouin of the Western and Eastern deserts are traditionally semi-sedentary tent-dwellers. The Nubians of the Nile Valley are of mixed Arab and African descent
Religion—Muslim 90% (almost all Sunni), Christian 10% (Coptic 9%) (est)
Language—Arabic (official), English, French
Population density—81 per sq. km (2010)
Urban population—42.8% (2010 est)
Median age (years)—24.3 (2011 est)
National anthem—'Biladi, Biladi, Biladi' ['My Homeland, My Homeland, My Homeland']
National day—23 July (Revolution Day)
Death penalty—Retained
CPI score—2.9 (2011)

FINANCIAL OUTLOOK
The political unrest that began in 2011 and led to the overthrow of President Mubarak weighed heavily on the Egyptian economy in 2012. The economy grew by around 2%, according to official figures, around the same level as population growth. However, in December 2012, Standard & Poor's downgraded Egypt's long-term credit rating, citing "deepening political turbulence undermining efforts to prop up the economy and public finances." In March 2013, the central bank increased interest rates for the first time since 2011 in a bid to curb inflation. In March 2013, the government pushed ahead with a US$4.8 billion loan request that had been stalled in late 2012 as officials revised an economic plan sought by the IMF. Meanwhile, the country's foreign currency reserves had fallen to US$3.6 billion at the end of January, from US$36 billion at the start of the uprising.

CLIMATE AND TERRAIN
There are four broad regions: the Western Desert, which covers nearly two-thirds of the country to the west of the Nile valley; the Eastern Desert, which lies between the Nile and the mountains along the Red Sea coast; the fertile Nile valley and delta, where most of the population lives; and the Sinai peninsula, where a coastal plain on the Mediterranean rises to mountains in the south. The deserts are arid plateaux, with depressions in the Western Desert whose springs irrigate oases, while the Eastern Desert is dissected by wadis (dry watercourses). Elevation extremes range from 2,629m (Mt Catherine, Sinai) to −133m (Qattara depression). The country has a desert climate, with hot, dry summers and mild winters. Temperatures increase further south, and rainfall increases nearer the coast. Average daily temperatures in Cairo range from 13°C to 28°C.

HISTORY AND POLITICS

The 1971 constitution was suspended after President Mubarak's resignation, and substantial changes to it were approved by referendum in March 2011. It now provides for an executive president who is directly elected for a four-year term, which is renewable once. It also included the appointment of a 100-member constituent assembly to draft a new constitution in preparation for a referendum; the assembly was suspended in April 2012, however, following accusations of under-representation and religious bias.

The unicameral People's Assembly has 508 members, who serve a five-year term; 498 members are directly elected and ten are appointed by the president. The Consultative Council has an advisory role; its 264 members include 176 who are directly elected and 88 presidential appointees, all serving a six-year term.

In November 2011, the first legislative election since President Mubarak's departure from office saw the Freedom and Justice Party (FJP, founded by the Muslim Brotherhood) win the most seats in the People's Assembly but fail to win a majority; the FJP also won the most seats in the Consultative Council.

In the first presidential election in the country's history, FJP candidate Mohammed Mursi narrowly defeated former National Democratic Party candidate Ahmed Shafiq and was inaugurated on 30 June 2012.

HEAD OF STATE

President, Mohammed Mursi, *elected* 24 June 2012, *sworn-in*, 30 June 2012

Leader of the Supreme Council of the Armed Forces, Minister of Defence, Field Marshal Mohammed Tantawi

SELECTED GOVERNMENT MEMBERS *as at July 2012*

Prime Minister, Hisham Quandril
Finance, Momtaz El-Nour
Foreign Affairs, Mohamed Kamel Ali Amr
Interior, Mohamed Ibrahim Yasef Ahmed

EMBASSY OF THE ARAB REPUBLIC OF EGYPT

26 South Street, London W1K 1DW
T 020-7499 3304
E eg.emb_london@mfa.gov.eg
W www.egyptembassyuk.org
Ambassador Extraordinary and Plenipotentiary, HE Hatem Seif el-Nasr, *apptd* 2008

BRITISH EMBASSY

7 Ahmed Ragheb Street, Garden City, Cairo
T (+20) (2) 2791 6000
E info@britishembassy.org.eg
W ukinegypt.fco.gov.uk
Ambassador Extraordinary and Plenipotentiary, HE James Watt, *apptd* 2011

Insurgencies

Militant Islamic fundamentalists emerged in the 1980s. Their campaign against the government became increasingly violent from the early 1990s, and was eventually directed against foreign tourists as well as domestic targets. Although the largest fundamentalist organisation, Gamaat-i-Islamiya, renounced violence in 1999, attacks continue, often targeting foreigners.

DEFENCE

All aged 16–49, 2010 est	*Males*	*Females*
Available for military service	21,012,199	20,145,021
Fit for military service	18,060,543	17,244,838

Military expenditure—US$4,107m (2011)
Conscription duration—12–36 months

ECONOMY AND TRADE

Economic liberalisation in recent years has attracted foreign investment and promoted exports, producing strong growth in GDP, but political uncertainty significantly reduced government revenues in 2012, and Eygpt may be forced to look for fiscal support from IMF in 2012-13. The unrest in January 2011 triggered increased social spending by the government, yet living standards for most of the population remain low, with a fifth living below the poverty line. There is a growing budget deficit, partly owing to price subsidies for basic necessities, and high public debt. Although the dams on the Nile have expanded the area of land under cultivation, other factors, such as population growth, put resources under pressure.

The services sector contributes 45.8% to GDP and employs 51% of the workforce. Tourism is the largest component of this sector (visitor numbers have increased by over 50% since the late 1990s), along with Suez Canal revenues and expatriate remittances. Industry accounts for 39.5% of GDP and 17% of employment, but despite increasing industrialisation, agriculture still employs 32% of the workforce, contributing 14.4% of GDP. Egypt is a net importer of foodstuffs, especially grain, and a food security programme has been set up with the aim of achieving self-sufficiency.

The main cash crop is cotton, of which Egypt is one of the world's main producers. Other important crops are rice, maize, wheat, vegetables, fruit and livestock. Industry is centred on oil and gas extraction, processing hydrocarbons, cotton and other agricultural products, producing textiles, chemicals and pharmaceuticals. Oil is the backbone of the economy and helps, alongside considerable reserves of natural gas and the hydroelectric power produced by the Aswan and High dams, to make Egypt self-sufficient in energy.

The main trading partners are the USA, Italy, China and Germany. Principal exports are crude oil and petroleum products, cotton, textiles, metal products, chemicals and processed food. The main imports are machinery and equipment, foodstuffs, chemicals, wood products and fuels.

GNI—US$214,529m; US$2,420 per capita (2010)
Annual average growth of GDP—1.2% (2011 est)
Inflation rate—13.3% (2011 est)
Population below poverty line—20% (2005 est)
Unemployment—9% (2010 est)
Total external debt—US$37,280m (2011)
Imports—US$52,923m (2010)
Exports—US$26,438m (2010)

BALANCE OF PAYMENTS

Trade—US$26,485m deficit (2010)
Current Account—US$4,318m deficit (2010)

Trade with UK	*2010*	*2011*
Imports from UK	£1,134,696,883	£1,038,811,140
Exports to UK	£600,616,526	£792,906,718

COMMUNICATIONS

Airports—There are 86 airports and airfields; the principal airports are at Cairo, Sharm el-Sheikh, Luxor, Alexandria and Hurghada

Waterways—Egypt has 3,500km of waterways, including the River Nile and Lake Nasser, the Alexandria–Cairo waterway, numerous small canals in the Nile delta and the Suez Canal (opened 1869; closed 1967–75). The main seaports are Alexandria, Damietta and Port Said on the Mediterranean Sea and Suez on the Red Sea
Railways and roadways—A road network of 65,050km and a rail network of 5,083km link the Nile valley and delta with the main development areas east and west of the river, but there are few routes in the interior
Telecommunications—9.62 million fixed lines and 70.66 million mobile subscriptions (2010); there were 20.14 million internet users in 2009
Internet code and IDD—eg; 20 (from UK), 44 (to UK)
Major broadcasters—Two state-run national television channels and six regional channels compete with the country's thriving satellite television industry, which is watched throughout the Arab-speaking world
Press—Four major newspapers are published daily, including *Al-Ahram*, the oldest newspaper in the Arab world
WPFI score—43,33 (127)

EDUCATION AND HEALTH

Education is free between the ages of six and 15.
Literacy rate—66.4% (2008 est)
Gross enrolment ratio (percentage of relevant age group)—primary 100%; tertiary 29% (2007 est)
Health expenditure (per capita)—US$113 (2009)
Hospital beds (per 1,000 people)—1.7 (2004–9)
Life expectancy (years)—72.66 (2011 est)
Mortality rate—4.82 (2011 est)
Birth rate—24.63 (2011 est)
Infant mortality rate—25.2 (2011 est)

CULTURE

Egyptian culture dates back 5,000 years to one of the earliest-known civilisations on Earth; ancient Egyptian hieroglyphic scripts provide some of the world's oldest records of written communication. The country has experienced periods of Hellene, Christian, Arab and Islamic culture, and remains most famous for the pyramids of Giza, the library of Alexandria and the art and architecture of its ancient periods (beginning in the fourth millennium BC and waning around 31 BC). Modern Egypt has the highest number of Nobel laureates in Africa, including author Naguib Mahfouz (1911–2006) and diplomat Mohamed ElBaradei (*b.* 1942); actor Omar Sharif (*b.* 1932) is an Academy Award winner, while Cairo is home to Al-Ahly, the most widely supported football club in Africa.

Estonia

Eesti Vabariik—Republic of Estonia
Area—45,228 sq. km
Capital—Tallinn; population, 399,027 (2009 est)
Major towns—Kohtla-Jarve, Narva, Parnu, Tartu
Currency—Euro (€) of 100 cents
Population—1,274,709 falling at 0.65% a year (2012 est); Estonian (68.7%), Russian (25.6%), Ukrainian (2.1%), Belarusian (1.2%), Finn (0.8%) (2008)
Religion—Christian (Lutheran 14%, Orthodox 13%) (est)
Language—Estonian (official), Russian
Population density—32 per sq. km (2010)
Urban population—69.5% (2010 est)
Median age (years)—40.5 (2011 est)
National anthem—'Mu Isamaa, Mu Onn Ja Room' ['My Native Land, My Joy and Delight']
National day—24 February (Independence Day)
Death penalty—Abolished for all crimes (since 1998)
CPI score—6.4 (2011)

FINANCIAL OUTLOOK

The Estonian central bank has raised its growth forecast for 2012 to 2.9%, and to 3% for 2013, although it warns of downside risks to that projection for the year ahead. These risks come mainly from the ongoing sovereign debt crisis in Europe and from weakness in the economies of its major trading partners in the region. Inflation is higher than the EU average, at 4.3% for 2012. This is expected to subside somewhat in 2013, to around 3.6%. Commenting on the Estonian economy in 2012, the vice-president of Estonia's central bank said that the year had been "surprisingly good" despite a slowdown in the fourth quarter of the year. The bank is forecasting growth of between 4% and 5% for 2014. If achieved, this would make Estonia one of the fastest-growing economies in the region. However, the bank emphasizes that, as a small, open economy, Estonia could expect to be greatly influenced by the fortunes of its major trading partners. Inflation was rising faster than expected, the bank warned, and there was a continued risk from rising global oil prices.

CLIMATE AND TERRAIN

The country is mostly a plain of lakes, marshes and forests, with a range of low hills in the south-east. Elevation extremes range from 318m (Suur Munamagi) to 0m (Baltic Sea). Part of the border with Russia runs through the large Lake Peipsi. The climate is maritime, with average temperatures ranging from −5°C in February to 16°C in July.

HISTORY AND POLITICS

The area came under Swedish control between 1561 and 1629, and was ceded to the Russian Empire in 1721. An Estonian nationalist movement developed in the late 19th century and fought against occupying German forces during the First World War. Estonia declared its independence in February 1918 and defended it against Soviet forces until 1920, when independence was recognised by the USSR. However, the USSR annexed Estonia in 1940, and the country was subsequently occupied by German forces when they invaded the USSR in 1941. In 1944 the USSR expelled the Germans and reannexed the country, beginning a process of 'Sovietisation'.

There was a resurgence of nationalist sentiment in the 1980s, and in 1989 the Estonian Supreme Soviet declared the republic to be sovereign and its 1940 annexation by the USSR to be illegal. In 1990, the Communist Party's monopoly of power was abolished and, following multiparty elections in which pro-independence candidates won the majority of seats, a period of transition to independence was inaugurated, culminating in its declaration on 20 August 1991. The last Russian troops withdrew in 1994. Since independence, Estonia has pursued pro-Western policies. It joined NATO and the EU in 2004.

In 2011 Toomas Hendrik Ilves was re-elected president by an electoral assembly. In the 2011 legislative election, the Reform Party

(ER), the main partner in the coalition government since 2005, remained the largest party and formed a coalition with the Union of Pro Patria and Res Publica (IRL).

Under the 1992 constitution, the president is elected for a five-year term by the legislature by a two-thirds majority or, if no candidate receives this majority after three rounds of voting, by an electoral assembly composed of the legislature members and 266 local government representatives. The unicameral legislature, the *Riigikogu*, has 101 members, directly elected for a four-year term. The prime minister is appointed by the president and nominates the government. Members of the government need not be members of the *Riigikogu*.

HEAD OF STATE
President, Toomas Hendrik Ilves, *elected by electoral assembly* 23 September 2006, *sworn in* 9 October 2006, *re-elected* 2011

SELECTED GOVERNMENT MEMBERS *as at June 2012*
Prime Minister, Andrus Ansip
Defence, Mart Laar
Finance, Jurgen Ligi
Foreign Affairs, Urmas Paet
Internal Affairs, Ken-Marti Vaher

EMBASSY OF THE REPUBLIC OF ESTONIA
16 Hyde Park Gate, London SW7 5DG
T 020-7589 3428
E london@mfa.ee
W www.estonia.gov.uk
Ambassador Extraordinary and Plenipotentiary, HE Aino Lepik von Wiren, *apptd* 2010

BRITISH EMBASSY
Wismari 6, Tallinn 10136
T (+372) 667 4700
W ukinestonia.fco.gov.uk
Ambassador Extraordinary and Plenipotentiary, HE Christopher Holtby, *apptd* 2012

DEFENCE

All ages 16–49, 2010 est	*Males*	*Females*
Available for military service	291,801	302,696
Fit for military service	210,854	251,185

Military expenditure—US$336m (2011)
Conscription duration—8–11 months

ECONOMY AND TRADE

Economic reforms and restructuring since 1992 have resulted in a market economy, the growth of which was boosted by the country's accession to the EU. Estonia entered recession in 2008 after an investment and consumption slump and a drop in demand for exports. Prudent financial management has enabled the economy to recover slowly, and it met the accession criteria for the eurozone, which Estonia joined in January 2011; it has since garnered one of the highest GDP growth rates in Europe.

Agriculture engages 4.2% of the workforce and accounts for 2.6% of GDP, the main products being cereals, vegetables, livestock, dairy products and fish. Industry accounts for 20.2% of employment and 29.2% of GDP, concentrating on engineering, electronics, wood and wood products, textiles, information technology and telecommunications; electronics and telecommunications are particularly strong. The services sector accounts for 75.6% of employment and 68.2% of GDP.

The main trading partners are other EU countries, particularly Finland, Sweden and Russia. Principal exports are machinery and electrical equipment, wood and wood products, metals, furniture, vehicles and parts, food products and textiles. The main imports are machinery and electrical equipment, fuels, foodstuffs, plastics and textiles. Estonia remains dependent on Russian natural gas supplies.

GNI—US$18,419m; US$14,460 per capita (2010)
Annual average growth of GDP—6.5% (2011 est)
Inflation rate—5% (2011 est)
Population below poverty line—19.7% (2008)
Unemployment—16.9% (2010 est)
Total external debt—US$25,400m (2011 est)
Imports—US$12,282m (2010)
Exports—US$11,607m (2010)

BALANCE OF PAYMENTS
Trade—US$675m deficit (2010)
Current Account—US$875m surplus (2009)

Trade with UK	*2010*	*2011*
Imports from UK	£185,109,178	£271,681,225
Exports to UK	£162,221,871	£189,734,167

EDUCATION AND HEALTH

Primary and secondary level education is compulsory between the ages of seven and 15.
Gross enrolment ratio (percentage of relevant age group)—primary 99%; secondary 104%; tertiary 63% (2009 est)
Health expenditure (per capita)—US$1,004 (2009)
Hospital beds (per 1,000 people)—5.7 (2004–9)
Life expectancy (years)—73.33 (2011 est)
Mortality rate—13.55 (2011 est)
Birth rate—10.45 (2011 est)
Infant mortality rate—7.06 (2011 est)
HIV/AIDS adult prevalence—1.2% (2009 est)

COMMUNICATIONS

Airports—The are 19 airports and airfields; the principal international airport is based in Tallinn
Waterways—There are 320km of year-round navigable waterways; the main seaports are at Tallinn, Parnu and Haapsalu Jahtklubi
Roadways—There are 58,034km of roadways
Railways—There are 1,200km of railways
Telecommunications—482,200 fixed lines and 1.65 million mobile subscriptions (2010); there were 971,700 internet users in 2009
Internet code and IDD—ee; 372 (from UK), 44 (to UK)
Major broadcasters—Public broadcasters Eesti Televisioon and Eesti Radio compete with private-sector, usually Swedish or Norwegian-owned broadcasters
Press—Major newspapers include *Postimees*, and *Eesti Paevaleht*
WPFI score—2,00 (9)

Finland

Suomen tasavalta/Republiken Finland—Republic of Finland
Area—338,145 sq. km
Capital—Helsinki (Helsingfors); population, 1,106,910 (2009 est)
Major cities—Espoo (Esbo), Oulu (Uleaborg), Tampere (Tammerfors), Turku (Aabo), Vantaa (Vanda)
Currency—Euro (€) of 100 cents
Population—5,262,930 rising at 0.07% a year (2012 est); Finnish (93.4%), Swedish (5.6%), Sami (0.1%) (2006 est)
Religion—Christian (Lutheran 81%, Orthodox 1%), Muslim 1% (predominantly Sunni) (est)
Language—Finnish, Swedish (both official)
Population density—18 per sq. km (2010)
Urban population—63.9% (2010 est)
Median age (years)—42.5 (2011 est)
National anthem—'Maamme'/'Vart Land' ['Our Land']
National day—6 December (Independence Day)
CPI score—9.4 (2011)

FINANCIAL OUTLOOK

The Finnish economy continues to be affected by the slowdown in the EU generally, with GDP growth in 2012 expected to come in at around 1%, buoyed up by domestic demand. Private investment is contracting in comparison with 2011, and the Finnish government expects to see a drop in both exports and imports, based on weak demand from the country's eurozone trading partners. Growth is expect to remain constant at 1% during 2013, although this is predicated on an anticipated increase in exports of 2.5%, with domestic consumption remaining at 2012 levels. This rate of growth will not be sufficient to prevent unemployment rising in 2013, which is projected to reach 8.1%. Inflation is expected to decrease slightly in 2013, from the forecast level for 2012 of 2.6%. Under Finland's framework agreement between labor unions and employers, the nominal index of wage and salary earnings will rise by 3.5% in 2012, falling back somewhat in 2013. Commenting on the economy in its budget review, the Finnish Ministry of Finance warned that while the Finnish economy remains one of the strongest in the EU, as a small, open economy it is very vulnerable to economic shocks.

CLIMATE AND TERRAIN

Much of the centre of the country is a glaciated plateau of forests and lakes, with low hills along the eastern border with Russia and in the far north. Forests cover around 70% of the country, including those of the coastal peatlands in the south west. There are over 60,000 lakes, with an average depth of 7m. Elevation extremes range from 1,328m (Haltiatunturi, or Halti) to 0m (Baltic Sea). A quarter of the country lies north of the Arctic Circle; temperatures there can range from −50°C in January to 17°C in July. Average temperatures in Helsinki range from −6°C in February to 16°C in July.

Owing to isostatic uplift (the rise of land mass no longer depressed by the weight of glaciers), the surface area of Finland is growing by around 7 sq. km a year.

HISTORY AND POLITICS

Finland was part of the Swedish Empire from the 12th century until it was ceded to Russia in 1809, when it became an autonomous grand duchy of the Russian Empire. After the Russian Revolution in 1917, Finland declared its independence. An attempted coup by Finnish Bolsheviks led to a short civil war that ended in their defeat in 1918, and in 1919 a republic was established. It resisted the 1939 invasion by the USSR but was defeated in 1940 and forced to cede territory; in the hope of recovering this territory it joined Germany's attack on the USSR in 1941. After agreeing an armistice with the USSR in 1944, Finland concluded a peace treaty in 1947 that conceded further territory to the USSR and obliged it to pay reparations. A Soviet-Finnish cooperation treaty in 1948 forced Finland to demilitarise its Soviet border and to adopt a stance of neutrality; these terms lasted until the demise of the USSR in 1991.

Since the mid-1960s the majority of Finnish governments have been coalitions of centre and moderate left-wing parties, usually led by the Social Democratic Party (SDP) or the Centre Party (KESK). Finland joined the EU in 1995 and the European Monetary Union in 1998.

The results of the legislative election in April 2011 were inconclusive, with the four leading parties winning similar numbers of seats. After two months of negotiations, a six-party coalition government, comprising the National Coalition Party (KOK), the Social Democratic Party (SDP) and four smaller parties, took office under the SDP leader Jyrki Katainen. KOK candidate Sauli Niinisto won the 2012 preseidential election, picking up 37% of the overall vote.

Under the 2000 constitution, the president is directly elected for a six-year term. There is a unicameral legislature, the *Eduskunta*, with 200 members directly elected for a four-year term. The prime minister is elected by the *Eduskunta* and appointed by the president.

HEAD OF STATE

President, Sauli Niinisto, *elected* 5 February 2012, *inaugurated* 1 March 2012

SELECTED GOVERNMENT MEMBERS *as at June 2012*

Prime Minister, Jyrki Katainen
Deputy Prime Minister; Finance, Jutta Urpilainen
Defence, Stefan Wallin
Foreign Affairs, Erkki Tuomioja
Interior, Paivi Rasanen

EMBASSY OF FINLAND

38 Chesham Place, London SW1X 8HW
T 020-7838 6200
E sanomat.lon@formin.fi
W www.finemb.org.uk
Ambassador Extraordinary and Plenipotentiary, HE Pekka Huhtaniemi, *apptd* 2010

BRITISH EMBASSY

Itainen Puistotie 17, 00140 Helsinki
T (+358) (9) 2286 5100
W ukinfinland.fco.gov.uk
Ambassador Extraordinary and Plenipotentiary, HE Matthew Lodge, *apptd* 2010

DEFENCE

All aged 16–49, 2010 est	*Males*	*Females*
Available for military service	1,115,368	1,106,193
Fit for military service	955,151	912,983

Military expenditure—US$3,656m (2011)
Conscription duration—6–12 months

ECONOMY AND TRADE

The country has a highly industrialised market economy which has thrived as a result of its telecommunications and electronics industries, particularly the manufacture of mobile phones, as well as

  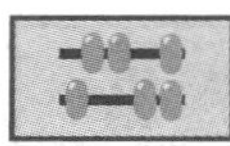      

its traditional timber and metals industries. The drop in exports and domestic demand due to the global economic downturn pushed the economy into recession in 2009, but recovery began in 2010. The economy is particularly vulnerable to fluctuations in trade with Russia, both its own trade (Russia is its leading supplier of imports and a major export market) and foreign trade, for which Finland is a major transit point.

The main trade partners are Russia, Germany and Sweden. Principal exports are electrical and optical equipment, machinery, transport equipment, paper and pulp, chemicals, base metals and timber. The main imports are foodstuffs (especially grain), petroleum and petroleum products, chemicals, transport equipment, iron and steel, machinery, textile yarn and fabrics, and components for manufactured goods. Finland is a net importer of energy.

GNI—US$242,899m; US$47,720 per capita (2010)
Annual average growth of GDP—2.7% (2011 est)
Inflation rate—3.3% (2011 est)
Unemployment—7.8% (2011 est)
Total external debt—US$518m (2011)
Imports—US$68,474m (2010)
Exports—US$69,594m (2010)

BALANCE OF PAYMENTS
Trade—US$1,120m surplus (2010)
Current Account—US$7,396m surplus (2010)

Trade with UK	2010	2011
Imports from UK	£1,447,999,568	£1,614,054,567
Exports to UK	£2,162,791,050	£2,441,044,052

COMMUNICATIONS
Airports—The principal airports are at Helsinki, Turku and Tampere
Waterways—The main seaports are Helsinki, Kotka, Rauma and Turku, and there are passenger services to Sweden, Estonia and Germany as well as countries outside the Baltic
Roadways and railways—The 78,141km road network and 5,919km rail network are concentrated in the southern half of the country, where most of the population and industry are located
Telecommunications—1.25 million fixed lines and 8.39 million mobile telephone subscriptions (2010); there were 4.393 million internet users in 2009
Internet code and IDD—fi; 358 (from UK), 44 (to UK)
Major broadcasters—There are both commercial and state-owned broadcasters; the state broadcaster, Yleisradio Oy (YLE), is funded by licence fees and provides radio and television services in Swedish and Finnish, with radio in Sami (Lappish)
Press—Newspapers appear in both Finnish and Swedish; major publications include *Helsingin Sanomat*, *Hufvudstadsbladet* and the English-language *Helsinki Times*
WPFI score—0,00 (1)

EDUCATION AND HEALTH
Basic education is free and compulsory for children from seven to 16 years.
Gross enrolment ratio (percentage of relevant age group)—primary 99%; secondary 108%; tertiary 92% (2009 est)
Health expenditure (per capita)—US$4,310 (2009)
Hospital beds (per 1,000 people)—6.5 (2004–9)
Life expectancy (years)—79.41 (2012 est)
Mortality rate—10.33 (2012 est)
Birth rate—10.36 (2012 est)
Infant mortality rate—3.4 (2012 est)
Death penalty—Abolished for all crimes (since 1972)

France

République française—French Republic
Area—551,500 sq. km (excluding overseas territories)
Capital—Paris; population, 10,410,000 (2009 est)
Major cities—Bordeaux, Lille, Lyon, Marseille, Montpellier, Nantes, Nice, Reims, Rennes, Strasbourg, Toulouse. The chief towns of Corsica are Ajaccio and Bastia
Currency—Euro (€) of 100 cents
Population—65,630,692 (excluding overseas territories), rising at 0.5% a year (2012 est)
Religion—Christian (Roman Catholic 64%, Protestant 2%), Muslim 8%, Jewish 1%, Buddhist 1% (est)
Language—French (official)
Population density—118 per sq. km (2010) (excluding overseas territories)
Urban population—77.8% (2010 est)
Median age (years)—39.9 (2011 est)
National anthem—'La Marseillaise' ['Song of Marseille']
National day—14 July (Fête de la Fédération/Fête Nationale)
Death penalty—Abolished for all crimes (since 1981)
CPI score—7.0 (2011)

FINANCIAL OUTLOOK
The French economy registered 0% growth in 2012, down from 1.7% in the previous year. In February 2013, the European Commission cut its forecast for France to 0.1% for 2013, from 0.4%. The economy's low growth rate is pushing up unemployment, which reached a 13-year high of 10.6% in the final quarter of 2012, putting further strain on the government's finances. In November 2012, the credit ratings agency Moody's downgraded France's sovereign rating from AAA to AA1. Moody's said the primary reason for the downgrade had been France's "persistent structural economic challenges," and the threats they pose to economic growth and the government's coffers. French finance minister Pierre Moscovici said that France was still committed to cutting its public deficit to 3% of output in 2013. However, in February 2013 the European Commission said that it expects the deficit to reach 3.7% of GDP this year, and 3.9% in 2014 if the government makes no changes to its policies.

CLIMATE AND TERRAIN
The north and west consist of flat plains, particularly in the basins of the Somme, Seine, Loire and Garonne rivers, with some low hills. The centre of the south is occupied by the Massif Central plateau, which is divided by the valley of the Rhone and Soane rivers from the mountains—the French Alps, the Jura and the Vosges—on the eastern border. The Pyrenees range lies along the southern border with Spain. Elevation extremes range from 4,807m (Mt Blanc, Alps) to −2m (Rhône delta). The climate is generally temperate, though the south has a Mediterranean climate and the east a continental climate.

HISTORY AND POLITICS

Under the 1958 constitution, the head of state is a president directly elected for a five-year term, which is renewable once. The legislature, the *Parlement*, consists of the National Assembly and the senate. The National Assembly has 577 deputies, 555 for metropolitan France and 22 for the overseas departments and territories; members are directly elected for a five-year term. The senate has been enlarged gradually over the past decade; from the September 2011 elections there will be 348 senators (328 for metropolitan France and the overseas departments, eight for overseas collectivities and territories, and 12 for French nationals abroad) elected by an electoral college to serve a six-year term, with half elected every three years.

The prime minister is nominated by the National Assembly and appointed by the president, as is the council of ministers. They are responsible to the legislature, but as the executive is constitutionally separate from the legislature, ministers may not sit in the legislature and must hand over their seats to a substitute.

The constitution was amended in 2003 to pave the way for the devolution to the 22 metropolitan regions and 96 metropolitan departments of powers over economic development, transport, tourism, culture and further education.

The 2012 presidential election was won in the second round by Socialist Party candidate François Hollande. In the 2012 legislative elections, the Socialist Party won an overall majority, defeating Nicolas Sakozy's Union for a Popular Movement party by 86 seats.

HEAD OF STATE

President of the French Republic, François Hollande, *elected* 6 May 2012

SELECTED GOVERNMENT MEMBERS *as at June 2012*

Prime Minister, Jean-Marc Ayrault
Defence, Jean-Yves Le Drian
Economy, Pierre Moscovici
Foreign Affairs, Laurent Fabius

EMBASSY OF FRANCE

58 Knightsbridge, London SW1X 7JT
T 020-7073 1000
E presse.londres-amba@diplomatie.gouv.fr
W www.ambafrance-uk.org
Ambassador Extraordinary and Plenipotentiary, HE Bernard Emié, *apptd* 2011

BRITISH EMBASSY

35 rue du Faubourg St Honoré, 75363 Paris Cédex 08
T (+33) (1) 4451 3100
W ukinfrance.fco.gov.uk
Ambassador Extraordinary and Plenipotentiary, HE Sir Peter Ricketts, GCMG, *apptd* 2012

Insurgencies

Corsican separatists have pursued a campaign of bombings and shootings since the 1970s apart from a ceasefire in 2003–5 observed by the main separatist faction. The French government's proposals to combine the island's two departments and to give the Corsican regional parliament greater autonomy were narrowly rejected in a 2003 referendum.

DEFENCE

All aged 16–49, 2010 est	*Males*	*Females*
Available for military service	14,563,662	14,238,434
Fit for military service	12,025,341	11,721,827

Military expenditure—US$58,244m (2011)

ECONOMY AND TRADE

The economy is in transition from extensive government ownership and intervention to a more liberal and market-oriented form; reform was initiated in response to poor economic growth and high unemployment. Implementation has been slow because of the constraints of eurozone membership, and strong resistance to the government's plans for privatisation and reform of labour, pensions and welfare. The new government, under president François Hollande, advocates pro-growth economic policies and the implementation of new banking reforms, as well as the introduction of a new top bracket income tax.

Over one-third of the land area of metropolitan France is utilised for agricultural production and a further quarter is covered by forests. Viniculture is extensive, although France has lost market share to other countries in recent years. Cognac, liqueurs and cider are also produced. Other important agricultural products include cereals, sugar beet, potatoes, beef, dairy products and fish. Agriculture employs 3.8% of the workforce and contributes 1.7% of GDP.

Oil is produced from fields in the Landes area, but France is a net importer of crude oil, for processing by its oil-refining industry. Natural gas is produced in the foothills of the Pyrenees.

Industry contributes 18.5% of GDP, employing 24.3% of the workforce. The sector is highly diversified and includes the production of machinery, iron, steel, aluminium, chemicals, vehicles, aircraft, electronic goods, textiles and processed food. The service sector contributes 79.8% of GDP and employs 71.8% of the workforce. Tourism is an important contributor to GDP.

The main trading partners are other EU countries, especially Germany. Principal exports are machinery, vehicles, aircraft, plastics, chemicals, pharmaceutical products, iron and steel, and beverages. The main imports are raw materials for industry (eg crude oil, chemicals, plastics), machinery and equipment, vehicles and aircraft.

GNI—US$2,606,779m; US$42,390 per capita (2010)
Annual average growth of GDP—1.7% (2011 est)
Inflation rate—2% (2011 est)
Population below poverty line—6.2% (2004)
Unemployment—9.1% (2011 est)
Total external debt—US$5,633,000m (2011)
Imports—US$599,176m (2010)
Exports—US$519,737m (2010)

BALANCE OF PAYMENTS

Trade—US$79,439m deficit (2010)
Current Account—US$44,657m deficit (2010)

Trade with UK	*2010*	*2011*
Imports from UK	£20,183,783,626	£23,194,002,926
Exports to UK	£23,352,365,811	£23,170,898,113

COMMUNICATIONS

Airports—There are two international airports serving Paris, and many regional airports capable of accepting international flights
Waterways—The principal seaports are Marseille on the Mediterranean Sea, Bordeaux and Nantes on the Atlantic coast, and Le Havre, Calais and Dunkirk on the Channel coast. There are 8,501km of navigable inland waterways, 1,621km navigable by large vessels, and Paris, Rouen and Strasbourg are significant river ports. The French mercantile marine consisted in 2011 of 162 ships of 1,000 gross tonnage or over, 151 of which are registered overseas

  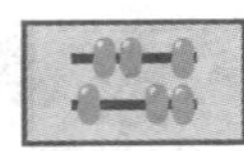      

Roadways—951,200km, including 11,100km of motorways
Railways—29,640km
Telecommunications—36.154 million fixed lines in use, 64 mobile subscriptions (2010); there were 45.262 million internet users in 2009
Internet code and IDD—fr; 33 (from UK), 44 (to UK)
Major broadcasters—TV5 is an international French-language television channel co-financed by Belgium, Canada, France and Switzerland. The main domestic channel, TF1, was privatised in 1987. A global news channel, France 24, was launched in 2006 and broadcasts in French, English and Arabic
Press—France has over 100 daily newspapers, including *Le Monde*, *Le Figaro* and *Libération*.
WPFI score—13,38 (44)

EDUCATION AND HEALTH

Education is compulsory and free between the ages of six and 16. There are three types of *lycée—général, technique* and *professionel*—and each leads to its own *baccalauéat* qualification. Specialist schools are numerous.

Gross enrolment ratio (percentage of relevant age group)—primary 111%; secondary 113%; tertiary 55% (2009 est)
Health expenditure (per capita)—US$4,797 (2009)
Hospital beds (per 1,000 people)—7.1 (2004–9)
Life expectancy (years)—81.46 (2012 est)
Mortality rate—8.85 (2012 est)
Birth rate—12.72 (2012 est)
Infant mortality rate—3.37 (2012 est)

CULTURE

Two of the earliest masterpieces of French literature are the medieval *Song of Roland* and *The Romance of the Rose*. Literature flowered particularly in the 19th century with the novels of Victor Hugo (1802–85), Alexandre Dumas (1802–70), Gustave Flaubert (1821–80), Jules Verne (1828–1905) and Émile Zola (1840–1902). French contributions to philosophy and critical theory in the 20th century included the works of Henri Bergson (1859–1941), Jean-Paul Sartre (1905–80), Simone de Beauvoir (1908–86), Albert Camus (1913–60), Michel Foucault (1926–84) and Jacques Derrida (1930–2004).

France's artistic movements range from the classicism of Nicholas Poussin (1594–1665) and the Romanticism typified by Eugène Delacroix (1798–1863) to Impressionism, one of France's most productive artistic movements, whose prominent figures include Édouard Manet (1832–83), Edgar Degas (1834–1917), Claude Monet (1840–1924), Pierre-Auguste Renoir (1841–1919) and Mary Cassatt (1844–1926). The work of Post-Impressionists Paul Cézanne (1839–1906) and Paul Gauguin (1848–1903) informed later movements such as Fauvism, which includes the early work of Henri Matisse (1869–1954), and Cubism, developed by Georges Braque (1882–1963) in collaboration with Picasso. Eminent French sculptors include Auguste Rodin (1840–1917) and Marcel Duchamp (1887–1968).

French cinema is characterised by experimental auteurs such as Jean-Luc Godard (*b.* 1930) and François Truffaut (1932–1984), while actors such as Brigitte Bardot (*b.* 1934), Catherine Deneuve (*b.* 1943) and Juliette Binoche (*b.* 1964) succeeded in Hollywood as well as France. In music, Edith Piaf (1915–63) and Serge Gainsbourg (1928–91) are the best-known proponents of the French musical form *chanson*. In classical music, Hector Berlioz (1803–69), Georges Bizet (1838–75) and Claude Debussy (1862–1918) are among the country's best-known composers.

OVERSEAS DEPARTMENTS/REGIONS

French Guiana, Guadeloupe, Martinique and Réunion have had departmental status since 1946. They were given regional status with greater powers of self-government and elected assemblies in 1982, and were redesignated as Overseas Regions in 2003. Their regional and departmental status is identical to that of regions and departments of metropolitan France, and they can choose to replace these with a single structure by merging their regional and departmental assemblies. The French government is represented by a *prefect* in each. In referendums in 2010, French Guiana and Martinique rejected proposals for granting greater autonomy to their local governments.

French Guiana

Area—83,534 sq. km
Capital—Cayenne; population, 62,437 (2009 est)
Population—237,200 (2011 est)

Situated on the north-eastern coast of South America, French Guiana is flanked by Suriname to the west and by Brazil to the south and east. Under the administration of French Guiana are the Îles du Salut group of islands (St Joseph, Île Royal and Île du Diable). The European Space Agency rocket launch site is situated at Kourou, and accounts for 25% of GDP. Fishing, forestry and mining are the main activities, and the economy is dependent on government subsidies. The main exports are timber, shrimp and gold. Tourism is restricted by the lack of infrastructure, as much of the interior is only accessible by river.

Prefect, Denis Labbé, *apptd* 2011

Guadeloupe

Area—1,628 sq. km
Capital—Basse-Terre; population 12,000 (2007 est), on Guadeloupe
Population—403,257 (2009 est)

The Guadeloupe archipelago consists of a number of islands in the Leeward Islands group in the West Indies, including Guadeloupe (or Basse-Terre), Grande-Terre, Marie-Galante, La Désirade and the Îles des Saintes. The main towns are Les Abymes, Pointe-à-Pitre (Grande-Terre) and Grand Bourg (Marie-Galante). The main industries are tourism, agriculture, sugar refining and rum distilling. Bananas, sugar, rum and vanilla are the main exports.

Prefect, Jean-Luc Fabre, *apptd* 2009

Martinique

Area—1,100 sq. km
Capital—Fort-de-France; population, 87,787 (2009 est)
Population—398,733 (2009 est)

An island in the Windward Islands group in the West Indies, Martinique lies between Dominica in the north and St Lucia in the south. It is dominated by Mt Pelée (1,397m), an active volcano that last erupted in 1902. Tourism is a major industry. The main exports are bananas, rum and petroleum products.

Prefect, Laurent Prevost, *apptd* 2011

Mayotte

Area—374 sq. km
Capital—Mamoudzou; population, 53,022 (2007 est)
Population—223,765 (2009 est)

Part of the Comoros archipelago, Mayotte remained a French dependency when the other three islands became independent as the Comoros Republic in 1975. It became a *collectivité territoriale* in 1976, and an overseas department/region in 2011. The main products are vanilla, ylang-ylang (perfume essence), coffee, copra, lobster and shrimp. The economy is dependent on French subsidies.

Prefect, Hubert Derache, *apptd* 2009

Réunion

Area—2,513 sq. km
Capital—St-Denis; population 140,906 (2009 est)

Population—821,168 (2009 est)
A French possession since 1638, Réunion lies in the Indian Ocean, about 650km east of Madagascar and 180km south-west of Mauritius. The main industries are tourism and sugar and rum production.
Prefect, Michel Lalande, *apptd* 2010

TERRITORIAL COLLECTIVITIES

Overseas *collectivités* are administrative divisions with a degree of autonomy but without the status of a similar administrative division in metropolitan France; each has its own laws and an elected assembly and president. The French government is represented by a *prefect* or high commissioner in each. Constitutional changes in 2003 redesignated most of the former overseas territories as *collectivités*; New Caledonia is treated in this category because this is its *de facto* status at present, but its official designation depends upon the outcome of independence referendums to be held between 2014 and 2018.

French Polynesia

Area—4,167 sq. km
Capital—Papeete, on Tahiti; population, 132,980 (2009 est)
Population—274,512; rising at 1.02% a year (2012 est)
French Polynesia consists of over 118 volcanic or coral islands and atolls in the South Pacific. There are five archipelagos: the Society Islands (Windward Islands group includes Tahiti, Moorea, Makatea, Mehetia, Tetiaroa, Tubuai Manu; Leeward Islands group includes Huahine, Raiatea, Tahaa, Bora-Bora, Maupiti), the Tuamotu Islands (Rangiroa, Hao, Turéia etc), the Gambier Islands (Mangareva etc), the Tubuai Islands (Rimatara, Rurutu, Tubuai, Raivavae, Rapa etc) and the Marquesas Islands (Nuku-Hiva, Hiva-Oa, Fatu-Hiva, Tahuata, Ua Huka etc). Some of the atolls were used by France for testing nuclear weapons between 1966 and 1996. The main industries are tourism, pearl-farming, deep-sea fishing, coconut products and vanilla production.
High Commissioner, Richard Didier, *apptd* 2010

New Caledonia

Area—18,575 sq. km
Capital—Nouméa; population, 143,577 (2009 est)
Population—260,166 rising at 1.49% a year (2012 est)
New Caledonia is a large island in the western Pacific, 1,120km off the eastern coast of Australia. Its dependencies are the Isle of Pines, the Loyalty Islands (Mahé, Lifou, Urea, etc), the Bélep Archipelago, the Chesterfield Islands, the Huon Islands and Walpole. New Caledonia was discovered in 1774 and annexed by France in 1853. Agitation for independence from the 1980s ended with the Nouméa accord in 1998, under which an increasing degree of autonomy will be transferred to the territory up to 2018, with a referendum on independence to be held between 2014 and 2018. The territory is divided into three provinces, each with a provincial assembly; these combine to form the territorial assembly.

A quarter of the world's nickel deposits are found in the territory, and nickel mining and smelting are the main industries, along with tourism and fishing. Ferronickel, nickel ore and fish are the main exports. About 20% of food has to be imported.
High Commissioner, Albert Dupuy, *apptd* 2010

St Barthélemy

Area—21 sq. km
Capital—Gustavia
Population—7,332 (2011 est)
The island lies in the Caribbean Sea about 240km north-west of Guadeloupe. It was settled by the French from 1648. France sold the island to Sweden in 1784 but bought it back again in 1878 and it was under the administration of Guadeloupe until 2007, when it became a *collectivité territoriale*. The economy is based on luxury tourism and duty-free commerce in luxury goods. Freshwater sources are limited, so all food and energy and most manufactured goods are imported.
Prefect, Philippe Chopin, *apptd* 2011

St Martin

Area—54.4 sq. km
Capital—Marigot
Population—30,959 (2012 est)
The territory occupies the northern part of the island of St Martin, 250km to the north-west of Guadeloupe; the southern part (Sint Maarten) is a territory of the Netherlands. The island was claimed for Spain by Columbus in 1493 but the Spanish relinquished it in 1648 to the Dutch and French, who divided the island between them. The French part was administered from Guadeloupe until it was made a *collectivité territoriale* in 2007. The economy is dependent on tourism, which employs 84% of the workforce. Nearly all food, energy and manufactured goods are imported.
Prefect, Philippe Chopin, *apptd* 2011

St Pierre and Miquelon

Area—242 sq. km
Capital—St-Pierre; population, 5,888 (2011 est)
Population—5,831 falling at 0.98% a year (2012 est)
These two small groups of eight islands off the south coast of Newfoundland became a *collectivité territoriale* in 1985. The main industry of fishing and servicing fishing fleets has declined in step with the decline in cod stocks, and fish farming, crab fishing and agriculture are being developed. Tourism is of growing importance, but the economy is dependent on government subsidies.
Prefect, Patrice Latron, *apptd* 2011

Wallis and Futuna Islands

Area—142 sq. km
Capital—Mata-Utu, on Uvea, the main island of the Wallis group; population, 1,112 (2009 est)
Population—15,453 rising at 0.36% a year (2012 est)
The two groups of islands (the Wallis Archipelago and the Îles de Horne) lie in the South Pacific, north-east of Fiji. They became a French protectorate from the 1840s and were administered from New Caledonia until 1961. The main products are copra, vegetables, bananas, livestock products, fish and timber.
Administrator, Michel Jeanjean, *apptd* 2010

OVERSEAS TERRITORIES

Territory of the French Southern and Antarctic Lands

Created in 1955 from former Réunion dependencies, the territory comprises the islands of Amsterdam (55 sq. km) and St Paul (7 sq. km), the Kerguelen Islands (7,215 sq. km) and Crozet Islands (352 sq. km) archipelagos, Adélie Land (302,500 sq. km) in the Antarctic continent and, since 2007, the islands of Bassas da India (80 sq. km), Europa (28 sq. km), les Glorieuses (5 sq. km), Juan de Nova (4.4 sq. km) and Tromelin (1 sq. km). The population consists only of staff of the meteorological and scientific research stations.
Administrator, Pascal Bolot, *apptd* 2012

The French Community of States

The 1958 constitution envisaged the establishment of a French Community of States. A number of former French colonies in Africa have seceded from the community but for all practical purposes continue to enjoy the same close links with France as do those that remain formal members. Most former French African colonies are closely linked to France by financial, technical and economic agreements.

  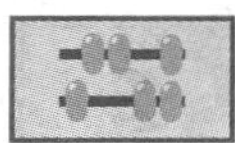      

Germany

Bundesrepublik Deutschland—Federal Republic of Germany
Area—357,022 sq. km
Capital—Berlin; population, 3,437,780 (2009 est)
Major cities—Bremen, Cologne, Dortmund, Dresden, Düsseldorf, Essen, Frankfurt, Hamburg, Hannover, Leipzig, Munich, Nuremberg, Stuttgart
Currency—Euro (€) of 100 cents
Population—81,305,856 falling at 0.2% a year (2012 est); German (91.5%), Turkish (2.4%) (est)
Religion—Christian 63% (Protestant 32%, Roman Catholic 31%), Muslim 5% (predominantly Sunni) (est)
Language—German (official)
Population density—234 per sq. km (2010)
Urban population—73.8% (2010 est)
Median age (years)—44.9 (2011 est)
National anthem—'Das Deutschlandlied' ['The Song of Germany']
National day—3 October (Unity Day)
Death penalty—Abolished for all crimes (since 1949 in FRG and 1987 in GDR)
CPI score—8.0 (2011)

FINANCIAL OUTLOOK

The German economy expanded by just 0.7% in 2012, compared with 3% in 2012, as the crisis in the eurozone, the country's main export market, weighed on growth. In February 2013, the Bundesbank said that the economy should grow by 0.4% in 2013 as industrial production picks up. Unemployment fell to just 5.3% in December 2012. However, productivity in the manufacturing sector fell in Germany between 2007 and 2011, the last period for which OECD data is available, while rising in stricken eurozone countries such as Spain, which saw a rise of 2.4%. This may affect future growth prospects. Figures released by the Bundesbank in February 2013, for example, showed foreign direct investment flows into Germany fell in 2012 for the first time in eight years, dipping by €2.4 billion after rising by €29.1 billion in 2011 and €35.4 billion in 2010.

CLIMATE AND TERRAIN

The north of the country is low-lying, rising in the centre to uplands and Alpine foothills, then to the Bavarian Alps in the south. Elevation extremes range from 2,963m (Zugspitze, Bavaria) to −3.54m (Neuendorf bei Wilster). The Rhine, Weser and Elbe rivers flow from the south to the North Sea, the Oder and Neisse rivers flow north to the Baltic Sea, and the Danube flows east from its source in the south of the country to the Austrian border. Nearly a third of the land is covered by forest or woodland. The climate is temperate, with average temperatures in Berlin ranging from −1°C in January to 19°C in July.

HISTORY AND POLITICS

The Basic Law was adopted in 1949 as the constitution of West Germany; at unification in 1990, Berlin and the five reformed *Länder* (states) of East Germany acceded to the Federal Republic. The president is elected for a five-year term by the *Bundesversammlung*, an electoral college comprising the members of the *Bundestag* (*see* below) and an equal number of representatives elected by the state legislatures. The bicameral legislature comprises a lower house, the Federal Assembly *(Bundestag)*, with 622 members elected by a mixed constituency and proportional representation system for a four-year term. The Federal Council *(Bundesrat)* has 69 members appointed by the governments of the *Länder* in proportion to their populations; their term of office is determined by their *Land*'s constitution. The head of government is the chancellor, who is proposed by the president and elected by the *Bundestag*.

Angela Merkel, leader of the Christian Democratic Union of Germany and the Christian Social Union of Bavaria (CDU/CSU), became Germany's first female chancellor in 2005 at the head of a CDU/CSU and Social Democratic Party (SPD) coalition following inconclusive legislative elections. At the 2009 elections, the CDU increased its number of seats, while the SPD lost ground, and Angela Merkel was re-elected Chancellor at the head of a CDU/CSU coalition with the Free Democrats (FDP). Independent candidate Joachim Gauck won the 2012 presidential election, picking up 991 votes; he replaced Christian Wulf following the the president's resignation amid allegations of corruption.

HEAD OF STATE

Federal President, Joachim Gauck, *elected and sworn in* 23 March 2012

SELECTED GOVERNMENT MEMBERS *as at June 2012*

Federal Chancellor, Angela Merkel
Foreign Affairs, Guido Westerwelle
Defence, Thomas de Maizière
Finance, Wolfgang Schäuble

EMBASSY OF THE FEDERAL REPUBLIC OF GERMANY

23 Belgrave Square, London SW1X 8PZ
T 020-7824 1300
W www.london.diplo.de
Ambassador Extraordinary and Plenipotentiary, HE Georg Boomgaarden, *apptd* 2008

BRITISH EMBASSY

Wilhelmstrasse 70, 10117 Berlin
T (+49) (30) 204 570
W ukingermany.fco.gov.uk
Ambassador Extraordinary and Plenipotentiary, HE Simon McDonald, CMG, *apptd* 2010

Federal Structure

Germany is a federal republic composed of 16 states *(Länder)* (ten from the former FRG, five from the former GDR, and Berlin). Each *Land* has its own directly elected legislature and government led by a minister-president (prime minister) or equivalent. The 1949 Basic Law vests executive power in the *Länder* governments except in those areas reserved for the federal government.

State	*Capital*	*Population (millions) (2005 est)*
Baden-Württemberg	Stuttgart	10.7
Bavaria	Munich	12.5
Berlin	—	3.4
Brandenburg	Potsdam	2.6
Bremen	—	0.7
Hamburg	—	1.7
Hesse	Wiesbaden	6.1
Lower Saxony	Hannover	8.0
Mecklenburg-West Pomerania	Schwerin	1.7
North Rhine-Westphalia	Düsseldorf	18.1

Rhineland-Palatinate	Mainz	4.1
Saarland	Saarbrücken	1.1
Saxony	Dresden	4.3
Saxony-Anhalt	Magdeburg	2.5
Schleswig-Holstein	Kiel	2.8
Thuringia	Erfurt	2.3

DEFENCE

All aged 16–49, 2010 est	*Males*	*Females*
Available for military service	18,529,299	17,888,543
Fit for military service	15,027,866	14,510,527

Military expenditure—US$43,478m (2011)
Conscription duration—9 months. Conscription was phased out in July 2011

ECONOMY AND TRADE

Germany has one of the world's largest economies but decades of strong economic performance gave way in the 1990s to a severe recession, largely an aftermath of reunification and of macro-economic stagnation. Although the economy as a whole began to grow again in 2006, in the east it remains weak despite costly modernisation and integration measures. However, the revival was largely export-led and a decline in demand due to the global economic downturn caused a recession in 2008–9. The government's economic stimulus measures pushed the budget deficit slightly beyond the eurozone's 3% threshold in 2010, although it remained at 1.7% in 2011.

The country has a modern, diverse, highly industrialised and technologically advanced market economy. The services sector contributes 71% of GDP, industry 28.1% and agriculture 0.8%. The industrial sector is among the world's largest producers of iron, steel, coal, cement, chemicals, machinery, vehicles, machine tools, electronics, food and beverages, ships and textiles. Germany depends on imports to meet its oil and natural gas needs, but it remains a net exporter of electricity; in the wake of Japan's Fukushima crisis in March 2011, the German government revoked a decision to extend the life of the country's 17 nuclear power stations (which supply about 25% of its electricity). All stations are expected to close by 2022.

The main trading partners are other EU countries, the USA and China. Machinery, vehicles, chemicals, metals and manufactures, foodstuffs and textiles are the principal imports and exports.

GNI—US$3,341,390m; US$43,110 per capita (2010)
Annual average growth of GDP—2.7% (2011 est)
Inflation rate—2.2% (2011 est)
Unemployment—5.7% (2011 est)
Total external debt—US$5,624,000m (2011)
Imports—US$1,068,054m (2010)
Exports—US$1,271,352m (2010)

BALANCE OF PAYMENTS

Trade—US$203,299m surplus (2010)
Current Account—US$187,232m surplus (2010)

Trade with UK	*2010*	*2011*
Imports from UK	£28,520,245,056	£33,161,548,587
Exports to UK	£45,733,533,350	£49,202,693,173

COMMUNICATIONS

Airports—The busiest airport is at Frankfurt; other major airports include Berlin, Munich and Bonn

Waterways—Around 20% of domestic freight is carried on 7,467km of inland waterways. The Rhine and the Danube are linked by the Rhine-Maine-Danube canal, creating a through route from the North Sea to the Black Sea. The Kiel canal links the North Sea and the Baltic Sea. The main river ports are Duisburg, Frankfurt, Karlsruhe and Mainz; the main seaports are Hamburg, Bremen, Bremerhaven, Lübeck, Rostock and Wilhemshaven
Roadways—There is an extensive 644,480km road network, including 12,800km of motorways
Railways—41,981km
Telecommunications—45.6 million fixed lines in use and 105 million mobile subscriptions (2010); there were 65.1 million internet users in 2009
Internet code and IDD—de; 49 (from UK), 44 (to UK)
Major broadcasters—National and regional public television competes with a large private sector, with about 90% of households having access to cable or satellite stations; broadcasters include ARD (which operates Das Erste, the main national public TV channel) and ZDF
Press—Major newspapers include *Frankfurter Allgemeine Zeitung* and *Süddeustche Zeitung*
WPFI score—4,25 (17)

EDUCATION AND HEALTH

Education is free and compulsory between the ages of six and 18.

The largest universities are in Munich, Berlin, Hamburg, Bonn, Frankfurt and Cologne. Germany's oldest university is Heidelberg, founded in 1386.

Gross enrolment ratio (percentage of relevant age group)—primary 102%; secondary 103% (2009 est)
Health expenditure (per capita)—US$4,629 (2009)
Hospital beds (per 1,000 people)—8.2 (2004–9)
Life expectancy (years)—80.19 (2012 est)
Mortality rate—11.04 (2012 est)
Birth rate—8.33 (2012 est)
Infant mortality rate—3.51 (2012 est)

CULTURE

Germany has produced a wealth of composers, including Johann Sebastian Bach (1685–1750), Beethoven (1770–1827), Schubert (1797–1828), Wagner (1813–83) and Brahms (1833–97). Philosophers include Immanuel Kant (1724–1804), Karl Marx (1818–83), Friedrich Engels (1820–95) and Friedrich Nietzsche (1844–1900). The works of playwrights Goethe (1749–1832) and Schiller (1759–1805) had a Europe-wide influence. Novelists Thomas Mann (1875–1955), Hermann Hesse (1877–1962) and Günter Grass (*b.* 1927) have all received the Nobel prize for literature.

Key figures in the visual arts are Albrecht Dürer (1471–1528), Hans Holbein the Younger (1497–1543), surrealist Max Ernst (1891–1976) and Joseph Beuys (1921–86). Film directors Friedrich Murnau (1888–1931), Leni Riefenstahl (1902–2003), Werner Herzog (*b.* 1942) and Wim Wenders (*b.* 1945), and actor Klaus Kinski (1926–91), all gained Hollywood recognition.

Physicist Albert Einstein (1879–1955) is perhaps the world's best-known modern scientist, having introduced his theory of special relativity to the wider world in 1905. Other notable German scientists include Wilhelm Röntgen (1845–1923), Max Planck (1858–1947), Hans Geiger (1882–1945) and Werner Heisenberg (1901–1976).

  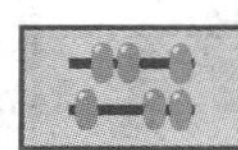      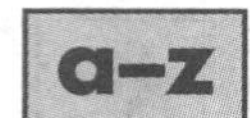

Ghana

Republic of Ghana
Area—238,533 sq. km
Capital—Accra; population, 2,268,500 (2009 est)
Major cities—Kumasi, Sekondi-Takoradi, Tamale
Currency—Cedi of 100 pesewas
Population—25,241,998 rising at 1.79% a year (2012 est); Akan (45.3%), Mole-Dagbon (15.2%), Ewe (11.7%), Ga-Dangme (7.3%), Guan (4%), Gurma (3.6%), Grusi (2.6%) (2000)
Religion—Christian 69% (including Pentecostal/Charismatic 24%, Protestant 19%), Muslim 16% (predominantly Sunni), indigenous and other religions 9% (est)
Language—English (official), Asante, Ewe, Fante, Boron, Dagomba, Dangme, Dagarte, Akyem, Ga, Akuapem
Population density—107 per sq. km (2010)
Urban population—51.5% (2010 est)
Median age (years)—21.4 (2011 est)
National anthem—'God Bless Our Homeland Ghana'
National day—6 March (Independence Day)
Death penalty—Retained (not used since 1993)
CPI score—3.9 (2011)

FINANCIAL OUTLOOK

According to the Centre for Policy Analysis (CEPA), overall GDP growth for Ghana was expected to slow from 14.1% in 2011 to 8.5% in 2012, before picking up again to 10.5% for 2013. The non-oil sector is projected to grow at a trend growth rate of 8.6% through to 2014. The country's overall growth rate tends to be volatile, and dependent on both the price of oil and changes in expected production levels at the massive Jubilee oilfield. This has suffered persistent setbacks, although corrective strategies were implemented in time to see a pick-up in production levels, from 70,000 barrels of oil per day to 90,000 by the end of 2012. Oil production schedules in 2013 are expected to see further improvements, levelling out at 120,000 bpd. Inflation at the end of December 2011 stood at 8.6%, well within the Central Bank of Ghana's acceptable range of 6.5–10.0%. However, foreign direct investment flows into Ghana, driven by rising oil production, have hammered the country's currency, and the cedi depreciated by around 15% in the first five months of 2012. The Ghana Statistical Service records inflation falling from 9.3% in November 2012 to 8.8% by the end of 2012. According to CEPA, Ghana is slipping into the Dutch disease syndrome (whereby a wealthy resource center destroys production in the non-oil economy) and the government will need to take strong corrective measures to boost the non-oil sector through 2013 and 2014.

CLIMATE AND TERRAIN

Ghana consists mostly of plains dissected by the Volta river basin and the great central Lake Volta, rising to the Ashanti plateau in the west. There is dense rainforest in the south and west and forested hills in the north, with savannah in the east and far north. Elevation extremes range from 885m (Mt Afadjato) to 0m (Atlantic Ocean). The climate is tropical but with cooler temperatures on the south-east coast, and less rainfall in the south-east and north. Temperatures in Accra average between 23°C and 31°C.

HISTORY AND POLITICS

First reached by Europeans in the 15th century, after which it became a centre for gold and slave trading, the constituent parts of Ghana came under British administration at various times. The original Gold Coast colony was constituted in 1874 and Ashanti and the Northern Territories Protectorate in 1901. Trans-Volta-Togoland, part of the former German colony of Togo, was mandated to Britain by the League of Nations after the First World War and was integrated with the Gold Coast colony in 1956 following a plebiscite. The colony became independent as Ghana on 6 March 1957. It was proclaimed a republic in 1960.

Ghana became a one-party state in 1964 and from 1966 experienced long periods of military rule (1966–9, 1972–9, 1981–91) interspersed with short-lived civilian governments (1969–72, 1979–81). Flt. Lt. Jerry Rawlings, who had ousted the military regime in 1979 and deposed the civilian government in 1981, was elected president in 1992 when the country returned to multiparty politics after a referendum approved a new constitution.

Since the mid-1990s there have been intermittent clashes over land ownership between ethnic groups in the north; a state of emergency was in place there for two years after the last major outbreak of ethnic violence in 2002.

In the 2008 elections, John Atta Mills, the candidate of the National Democratic Congress (NDC), was elected president, and the NDC became the largest party in the legislature, winning half of the seats. Vice-president John Dramani Mahama took over the presidency following the death of John Atta Mills in July 2012. Presidential and legislative elections are due to take place in December 2012.

Under the 1993 constitution, the executive president is directly elected for a four-year term, renewable once. The president appoints members of the council of ministers subject to approval by the legislature. The unicameral parliament has 230 members who are directly elected for a four-year term.

HEAD OF STATE

President, National Security (acting), John Dramani Mahama, *apptd* 24 July 2012

SELECTED GOVERNMENT MEMBERS *as at June 2012*

Defence, Joseph Smith
Finance, Kabwena Duffuor
Foreign Affairs, Mohammed Mumuni
Interior, William Aboah

OFFICE OF THE HIGH COMMISSION FOR GHANA

13 Belgrave Square, London SW1X 8PN
T 020-7201 5921
E ghmfa31@yahoo.com
W www.ghanahighcommissionuk.com
High Commissioner, Prof. Kwaku Danso-Boafo, *apptd* 2009

BRITISH HIGH COMMISSION

PO Box 296, Osu Link, off Gamel Abdul Nasser Avenue, Accra
T (+233) (302) 213 250
E high.commission.accra@fco.gov.uk
W ukinghana.fco.gov.uk
High Commissioner, HE Peter Jones, *apptd* 2011

DEFENCE

All aged 16–49, 2010 est	*Males*	*Females*
Available for military service	6,268,191	6,194,339
Fit for military service	4,136,406	4,220,761

Military expenditure—US$96m (2011)

ECONOMY AND TRADE

Ghana has abundant natural resources, but high foreign debt and budget and trade deficits make it dependent on international financial and technical aid to fund its economic and social development programmes. It has benefited from tighter government management of the economy since 2001, and from debt relief in 2002 and 2006.

The sale of gold and coca helped sustain GDP growth between 2008 and 2011. Agriculture, mostly at subsistence level, forms the basis of the economy, along with forestry and fishing. The sector employs 56% of the workforce and generates 28.3% of GDP. The main cash crops are cocoa, timber and tuna. Industry employs 15% of the workforce and contributes 21% of GDP, mainly from mining (gold, manganese, bauxite, diamonds), forestry, light manufacturing, aluminium smelting, food processing and shipbuilding. Services employ 29% and account for 50.7% of GDP. Hydroelectric power is generated at dams on Lake Volta and is transmitted to most of Ghana, and to Togo and Benin. Oil was discovered offshore in 2007 and production began in 2010.

The main export markets are EU countries, Ukraine and Malaysia. Principal exports are gold, cocoa, timber, tuna, metals, minerals and diamonds. Imports are provided mainly by China, Nigeria, the USA, Côte d'Ivoire, India and the EU. The main imports are capital equipment, fuel and foodstuffs.

GNI—US$30,775m; US$1,230 per capita (2010)
Annual average growth of GDP—13.5% (2011 est)
Inflation rate—8.8% (2011 est)
Population below poverty line—28.5% (2007 est)
Total external debt—US$7,779m (2011 est)
Imports—US$11,000m (2010)
Exports—US$8,100m (2010)

BALANCE OF PAYMENTS

Trade—US$2,900m deficit (2010)
Current Account—US$2,252m deficit (2010)

Trade with UK	*2010*	*2011*
Imports from UK	£353,686,641	£426,136,132
Exports to UK	£219,473,671	£341,166,884

EDUCATION AND HEALTH

The government provides ten years of compulsory basic education for all children free of charge. Ghana has one of Africa's oldest universities, at Legon in Accra (established in 1948).

Literacy rate—66.6% (2009 est)
Gross enrolment ratio (percentage of relevant age group)—primary 106%; secondary 58%; tertiary 9% (2009 est)
Health expenditure (per capita)—US$45 (2009)
Hospital beds (per 1,000 people)—0.9 (2004–9)
Life expectancy (years)—61.45 (2012 est)
Mortality rate—8.57 (2012 est)
Birth rate—26.99 (2012 est)
Infant mortality rate—47.26 (2012 est)
HIV/AIDS adult prevalence—1.8% (2009 est)

COMMUNICATIONS

Airports and waterways—There are four major airports, including an international terminal in Accra; there 1,293km of navigable waterways
Roadways and railways—There are 62,221km of railways and 947km of railways
Telecommunications—277,900 fixed lines in use and 17.43 million mobile subscriptions; there were 1.29 million internet users in 2009
Internet code and IDD—gh; 233 (from UK), 44 (to UK)
WPFI score—8,00 (26)

Gibraltar

Area—6.5 sq. km
Capital—Gibraltar
Currency—Gibraltar pound of 100 pence
Population—28,956 rising at 0.27% a year (2011 est)
Religion—Christian (Roman Catholic 78%, other 10%), Muslim 4%, Jewish 2%, Hindu 2% (est)
Language—English (official), Spanish, Italian, Portuguese
Population density—3,105 per sq. km (2009 est)
Flag—White with a red stripe along the lower edge; over all a red castle with a key hanging from its gateway
National day—10 September
Life expectancy (years)—78.68 (2011 est)
Mortality rate—8.18 (2011 est)
Birth rate—14.23 (2011 est)
Infant mortality rate—6.69 (2011 est)

FINANCIAL OUTLOOK

In its budget for 2013, the Gibraltar government introduced a number of new tax measures aimed at stimulating growth and attracting entrepreneurial activity. These included a transitory tax bracket designed to effect a slow reduction over three years of income below the top tax rate to 25%, plus some incentives to industry. Tax on income up to €60,000 will be reduced to 29% from 32% in 2014, and to 25% in 2015. The rate of tax above this threshold stays at 35%. Gibraltar is also reintroducing tax exemption for EU cross-border mergers. This measure was repealed several years ago, and its reintroduction will make it much easier for companies to grow by acquisition, or for larger groups with European interests to restructure divisions. Existing companies providing seed funding to new enterprises will be able to claim a tax deduction of up to €30,000. The economy grew at an estimated 5.1% during 2012, with blue-chip gaming companies providing much of the increase in GDP, which currently stands at around £1.137 billion. This is expected to grow to £1.64 billion by 2014/15. The island currently enjoys full employment, with around 22,247 jobs registered in October 2011. Inflation to July 2012 stood at 2.2%, while average earnings rose 9.6% to £25,830.

CLIMATE AND TERRAIN

Gibraltar is a rocky promontory, 426m at its highest point, that juts southwards from the south-east coast of Spain, with which it is connected by a low isthmus. It is about 32km from the coast of Africa, across the Strait of Gibraltar.

HISTORY AND POLITICS

Gibraltar was captured in 1704, during the War of the Spanish Succession, by a combined Dutch and English force, and was ceded to Britain by the Treaty of Utrecht (1713).

Spanish claims to the territory were a source of tension for many years, but after the overwhelming rejection of a joint sovereignty arrangement in a referendum in 2002, Spain moderated its attitude and the previously bilateral Anglo-Spanish talks about the territory became tripartite with the inclusion of Gibraltar from 2006.

Gibraltar is part of the EU (with the UK government responsible for enforcing EU directives affecting Gibraltar), but is not a full member and is exempt from the common policies on customs, commerce, agriculture, fisheries and VAT. Gibraltarians have voted in EU elections since 2004.

The 1969 constitution made provision for self-government in respect of certain domestic matters, but full internal autonomy came into effect with the 2006 constitution. This limited the governor's responsibilities to external affairs, defence, internal security and public service. The House of Assembly was restyled the Gibraltar Parliament, and may determine its own size; at present, it consists of an appointed speaker and 17 members elected for a four-year term. The government is formed by the chief minister (who is the leader of the majority party) and ministers from among the elected members of parliament.

The 2011 elections were won by the incumbent Gibraltar Social Democrats with ten seats.

Governor, HE Vice-Admiral Sir Adrian Johns KBE, CBE, *apptd* 2009

Chief Minister, Hon. Fabian Picardo

GOVERNMENT OF GIBRALTAR
150 Strand, London WC2R 1JA
T 020-7836 0777
W www.gibraltar.gov.uk

ECONOMY

The economy is dominated by tourism (especially retail for day visitors), offshore financial services and shipping, and these three sectors account for about 85% of GDP. Diversification efforts have encouraged telecommunications in particular and Gibraltar has become a centre for internet businesses, especially internet gaming. A shift from a predominantly public-sector to a private-sector economy has occurred in recent years, although government spending still has a significant impact on the local economy. The chief sources of government revenue are port dues, the rent of the crown estate in the town, and duties on consumer items (although value added tax is not applied in the territory).

GNI—US$5,000 per capita (2001)

Trade with UK	*2009*	*2011*
Imports from UK	£359,370,965	£529,025,701
Exports to UK	£13,532,504	£40,814,697

COMMUNICATIONS

Gibraltar has one international airport. The 29km road network is all surfaced; road links to Spain reopened in the 1980s. The port services the large shipping industry, cruise liners and a regular ferry service to Tangiers (Morocco).

Greece

Elliniki Dhimokratia—Hellenic Republic
Area—131,957 sq. km
Capital—Athens; population, 3,252,250 (2009 est)
Major cities—Iraklion (Heraklion) on Crete, Larisa, Patrai (Patras), Piraeus, Thessaloniki (Salonika)
Currency—Euro (€) of 100 cents
Population—10,767,827 rising at 0.06% a year (2012 est)
Religion—Christian (Greek Orthodox 95%) (est)
Language—Greek (official)
Population density—88 per sq. km (2010)
Urban population—61.4% (2010 est)
Median age (years)—42.5 (2011 est)
National anthem—'Imnos eis tin Eleftherian' ['Hymn to Freedom']
Death penalty—Abolished for all crimes (since 2004)
CPI score—3.4 (2011)

FINANCIAL OUTLOOK

Greece's economy shrank by about 6.5% in 2012, according to figures released in March 2013, having endured a 7.1% contraction in 2011. Greek GDP has contracted by about 20% since the recession began in 2008. The economy is expected to experience its fifth year of recession in 2013, with the central bank forecasting a decline of around 4.5% before recovery begins in 2014. By the end of 2012, the unemployment rate climbed to 24%. However, average unit labor costs have declined 14% since the 2009 peak. The effect of this, together with weak domestic demand, has been a steady improvement in the current account deficit, which fell to 5% in September 2012, from 16% in 2009. Public debt is expected to amount to around 180% of GDP in 2013. In January, the IMF said the country would need further assistance to reach the target of 124% of GDP by 2020. Athens is aiming for a primary budget surplus in 2013 for the first time since 2002.

CLIMATE AND TERRAIN

The main areas of Greece are: Macedonia, Thrace, Epirus, Thessaly, Continental Greece, the Peloponnese and Attica on the mainland and the island of Crete. The main island groups are the Sporades, the Dodecanese or Southern Sporades and the Cyclades in the Aegean Sea, and the Ionian islands, including Corfu, to the west of the mainland. Low-lying coastal areas rise to a hilly or mountainous interior on the mainland and the islands. The Pindos mountains form a spine down the centre of the mainland, continuing down the Peloponnese, which is divided from the mainland by the Gulf of Corinth, the largest of the gulfs and bays indenting the coast. Elevation extremes range from 2,917m (Mt Olympus) to 0m (Mediterranean Sea). The climate is temperate; the coastline and islands have a Mediterranean climate but the weather is cooler at higher altitudes. The average temperature in Athens ranges from 9°C in January to 28°C in July and August.

HISTORY AND POLITICS

Under the 1975 constitution, the head of state is the president, elected by the legislature for a five-year term, renewable once. The unicameral legislature, the *Vouli*, has 300 members directly elected for a four-year term.

Karolos Papoulias was elected president in 2005, and was re-elected in 2010. A legislative election was held in October 2009, nearly two years early, and Panhellenic Socialist Movemnet (PASOK) returned to government after winning an outright majority of seats. In 2010 the PASOK government pushed through unpopular austerity measures to address the severe financial crisis, and agreed a three-year programme of economic reforms with the IMF and other EU countries in return for financial help to avoid defaulting on its debt. Prime minister George Papandreou tendered his resignation in November 2011 in order to enable a government of national unity to pass controversial austerity measures in parliament; he was replaced by economist Lucas Papademos, who subsequently resigned in preparation for the country's legislative elections in 2012. The New Democracy party (ND) won the most seats in the 2012 legislative elections but was unable to form a coalition government; the party increased its number of seats in the subsequent election and ND leader Antonis Samaras was sworn into office on 20 June 2012.

HEAD OF STATE

President of the Hellenic Republic, Karolos Papoulias, *elected* 8 February 2005, *sworn in* 12 March 2005, *re-elected* 2010

SELECTED GOVERNMENT MEMBERS *as at June 2012*

Prime Minister, Antonis Samaras
Interior, Evripidis Styliandis
Foreign Affairs, Dimitris Avramopolous
Finance, Yannis Stournas

EMBASSY OF GREECE

1A Holland Park, London W11 3TP
T 020-7727 3071
W www.greekembassy.org.uk
Ambassador Extraordinary and Plenipotentiary, Aristidis Sandis, *apptd* 2010

BRITISH EMBASSY

1 Ploutarchou Street, 106 75 Athens
T (+30) (210) 727 2600
E information.athens@fco.gov.uk
W ukingreece.fco.gov.uk
Ambassador Extraordinary and Plenipotentiary, HE Dr David Landsman, OBE, *apptd* 2009

DEFENCE

All aged 16–49, 2010 est	*Males*	*Females*
Available for military service	2,485,389	2,469,854
Fit for military service	2,032,378	2,016,552

Military expenditure—US$7,502m (2011)
Conscription duration—Up to 9 months

ECONOMY AND TRADE

Greece has a capitalist economy, with a large public sector which currently accounts for 40% of GDP, although several state enterprises are being privatised as part of the government's economic reforms. It experienced rapid economic growth in the final quarter of the 20th century, owing largely to increased tourism and its accession to the EC. But in the 2000s, high government spending, low fiscal revenue and recession contributed to a growing budget deficit, which soared to over 15% of GDP in 2009 and left the country particularly vulnerable in the global economic downturn. The New Democracy government's persistent failure to address the public finances crisis contributed to Greece's international debt rating being downgraded in late 2009, amid fears of an imminent default on its debt. The PASOK government's austerity measures, and financial assistance from the IMF and other EU countries, saw the budget deficit reduced to 9% of GDP in 2011 but unemployment rose by over 5% causing many economists to doubt the effectiveness of the government's fiscal policies.

Despite substantial industrialisation in the 20th century, agriculture still employs 12% of the workforce, contributing 3.3% of GDP. The most important agricultural products are cereals, vegetables, fruit, tobacco, beef and dairy products. Industrial activities, which contribute 17.9% of GDP, include food and tobacco processing, textiles, chemicals, metal products, mining and petroleum production. The service sector employs 65% of the workforce and generates 78.9% of GDP; much of this is derived from tourism, which accounts for about 15% of GDP, and shipping. Greece is a net importer of energy, including oil for refining and re-export.

The main trading partners are other EU countries (especially Germany and Italy) and China. Principal exports are food and drink, manufactured goods, petroleum products, chemicals and textiles. The main imports are machinery, transport equipment, fuels and chemicals.

GNI—US$292,874m; US$26,940 per capita (2010)
Annual average growth of GDP—−6% (2011 est)
Inflation rate—2.9% (2011 est)
Population below poverty line—20% (2009 est)
Unemployment—17% (2011 est)
Total external debt—US$583,300m (2011)
Imports—US$63,777m (2010)
Exports—US$21,586m (2010)

BALANCE OF PAYMENTS

Trade—US$42,191m deficit (2010)
Current Account—US$31,926m deficit (2010)

Trade with UK	*2010*	*2011*
Imports from UK	£1,337,325,672	£1,127,254,578
Exports to UK	£671,070,949	£654,356,475

COMMUNICATIONS

Airports—There are 81 airports and airfields, of which 67 have surfaced runways; the main airports are at Athens, Thessaloniki, Iraklion (Crete) and Corfu town (Corfu)
Waterways—The main seaports are Piraeus, Thessaloniki and Patrai on the mainland and Iraklion on Crete. An extensive ferry system connects the islands to one another and to the mainland. The 6km Corinth canal across the Corinth isthmus shortens the sea journey by 325km
Roadways—There are 116,771km of roads, including 948km of motorways
Railways—The 2,548km of railways are state-owned (with the exception of the Athens–Piraeus Electric Railway) but the loss-making state-controlled rail network operator TrainOSE is being privatised
Telecommunications—5.2 million fixed lines in use and 12.3 million mobile subcriptions (2010); there were 4.97 million internet users in 2009
Internet code and IDD—gr; 30 (from UK), 44 (to UK)
Major broadcasters—ERT operates a number of regional and cultural channels; private broadcasters include Mega TV and ANT 1
Press—There are three major daily news publications: *Eleftherotypia*, *Ta Nea*, and *Kathimerini*
WPFI score—19,00 (70)

  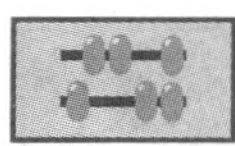      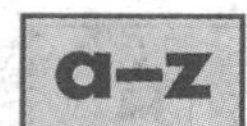

EDUCATION AND HEALTH
Education is free and compulsory between the ages of six and 14, and is maintained by state grants.
Literacy rate—97.2% (2009 est)
Health expenditure (per capita)—US$3,041 (2009)
Hospital beds (per 1,000 people)—4.8 (2004–9)
National day—25 March (Independence Day)
Life expectancy (years)—80.05 (2012 est)
Mortality rate—10.8 (2012 est)
Birth rate—9.08 (2012 est)
Infant mortality rate—4.92 (2012 est)

CULTURE
Greek civilisation emerged *c.*1300 BC and underpins the philosophy, politics, literature, art and mathematics of the Western world. The epic poems of Homer, the *Iliad* and the *Odyssey*, are thought to date from *c.*800 BC, making them the earliest recorded works in Western literature. Dramatists whose work has survived include Aeschylus (*c.*525–*c.* 456 BC), who is credited with inventing modern drama, Euripedes (480–406 BC) and Aristophanes (446–388 BC), author of the earliest known comedies. Socrates (470–399 BC), Plato (*c.* 428–*c.* 348 BC) and Aristotle (384–322 BC), whose *Poetics* is the earliest work of literary criticism, are considered the founders of western philosophy. Hippocrates (*c.* 460–370 BC) was the first to separate medicine from philosophy and religion.

Hungary

Magyar Koztarsasag—Republic of Hungary
Area—93,028 sq. km
Capital—Budapest; population, 1,704,710 (2009 est)
Major cities—Debrecen, Gyor, Miskolc, Pecs, Szeged
Currency—Forint of 100 filler
Population—9,958,453 falling at 0.18% a year (2012 est); Hungarian (92.3%), Roma (1.9%) (2001). There are also smaller groups of ethnic Germans, Serbs, Romanians and Slovaks
Religion—Christian (Roman Catholic 55%, Protestant 18%), Jewish (1%) (est)
Language—Hungarian (official)
Population density—112 per sq. km (2010)
Urban population—68.3% (2010 est)
Median age (years)—40.2 (2011 est)
National anthem—'Himnusz' ['Hymn']
National day—20 August (St Stephen's Day)
Death penalty—Abolished for all crimes (since 1990)
CPI score—4.6 (2011)

FINANCIAL OUTLOOK
According to the IMF, funding pressures on Hungary's government eased slightly in 2012 with some improvement in the global economy, but the outlook remains difficult. The economy is in the midst of its second recession in four years, with consumption and investment falling and unemployment remaining stubbornly high. While the fiscal deficit was reduced significantly in 2012, partly to offset an earlier loosening, policies to achieve this worsened the investment climate, the IMF says. GDP for 2012 is expected to show a contraction of 1.5%, with both investment and private consumption dwindling. While the export manufacturing sector is doing reasonably well, the rest of the economy is struggling. On the basis of current policies, economic activity is expected to stagnate in 2013, with a modest positive contribution from net exports likely to be offset by continued weak domestic demand. The government believes that higher eurozone growth, strategic agreements with selected companies in the manufacturing sector, and faster absorption of EU funds are the keys required to spur growth in the coming years. On the positive side, the government is experiencing surging private flows into government debt, especially by non-residents, which is helping Hungary to cover its large fiscal financing needs. The IMF is concerned that Hungary's fiscal deficit is likely to increase by around 3% per year in the period from 2013–15.

CLIMATE AND TERRAIN
Hungary lies mostly on the vast plain created by the Danube and Tisza rivers, with hills and mountains along the northern border. Elevation extremes range from 1,014m (Mt Kekes) to 78m (river Tisza). Lake Balaton lies in the west. Average temperatures range from −1°C in January to 21°C in July.

HISTORY AND POLITICS
The 1949 constitution will be superseded in 2012 by a new constitution approved by the legislature in April 2011. The president is elected by the legislature for a five-year term, renewable once; under the new constitution, he or she nominates the prime minister who is then elected by parliament. The unicameral National Assembly has 386 members directly elected for a four-year term.

The 2010 legislative election was won by the opposition Fidesz and Christian Democratic People's Party bloc with an overwhelming majority and it formed a government under Viktor Orban (prime minister 1998-2002). The 2010 presidential election was won outright at the first vote by Pal Schmitt of the Fidesz party, who subsequently resigned from office in April 2012 after admitting he had plagiarised much of his doctoral thesis; the Fidesz party elected Janos Ader as Schmitt's replacement in a vote that was boycotted by the opposition Socialist party.

HEAD OF STATE
President, Janos Ader, *elected* 2 May 2012, *sworn in* 10 May 2012

SELECTED GOVERNMENT MEMBERS *as at June 2012*
Prime Minister, Viktor Orban
Deputy Prime Ministers, Tibor Navracsics; Zsolt Semjen
Economy, Gyorgy Matolcsy
Foreign Affairs, Janos Martonyi
Defence, Csaba Hende

EMBASSY OF THE REPUBLIC OF HUNGARY
35 Eaton Place, London SW1X 8BY
T 020-7201 3440
E office.lon@kum.hu
W www.mfa.gov.hu/emb/london
Ambassador Extraordinary and Plenipotentiary, Janos Csak, *apptd* 2011

BRITISH EMBASSY
Harmincad Utca 6, 1051 Budapest

  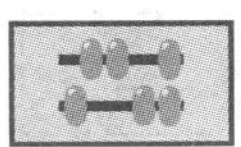      

T (+36) (1) 266 2888
E info@britemb.hu
W ukinhungary.fco.gov.uk
Ambassador Extraordinary and Plenipotentiary, HE Jonathan Knott, *apptd* 2012

DEFENCE

All aged 16–49, 2010 est	Males	Females
Available for military service	2,349,948	2,290,568
Fit for military service	1,902,639	1,897,378

Military expenditure—US$1,287m (2011)

ECONOMY AND TRADE

Hungary made a successful transition to a market economy after 1989, attracting high levels of foreign direct investment, and over 80% of GDP is now generated by the private sector. This strong economic growth started to slow in 2006–7, partly as a result of a government austerity programme intended to reduce the budget deficit and public debt. The global economic downturn left Hungary struggling to service both state and private debt in the face of rising interest rates and falling export demand, and the government had to obtain international assistance in 2008. The economy achieved growth in 2011 but the government had to seek further international financial assistance at the end of the year.

Nearly half the land is under cultivation, but agriculture accounts for only 3.7% of GDP; the main crops are cereals, sunflower seeds, vegetables, livestock and dairy products. Industry contributes 31.3% of GDP; the main activities include mining, metallurgy, food processing, and the production of construction materials, textiles, chemicals (especially pharmaceuticals) and motor vehicles. The main trading partners are Germany, other EU countries, Russia and China. Machinery and manufactured goods account for 90% of exports and 50% of imports. The country is a net importer of fuels and electricity.

GNI—US$122,372m; US$12,850 per capita (2010)
Annual average growth of GDP—1.8% (2011 est)
Inflation rate—3.7% (2011 est)
Unemployment—10.9% (2011 est)
Population below poverty line—13.9% (2010 est)
Total external debt—US$185,000m (2011 est)
Imports—US$87,612m (2010)
Exports—US$94,759m (2010)

BALANCE OF PAYMENTS
Trade—US$7,147m surplus (2010)
Current Account—US$2,696m deficit (2010)

Trade with UK	2010	2011
Imports from UK	£1,047,387,553	£1,147,863,219
Exports to UK	£3,242,161,824	£3,071,432,773

COMMUNICATIONS
Airports—There are 43 airports and airfields, 22 of which have surfaced runways; the principal airport is at Budapest
Waterways—There are 1,622km of permanently navigable waterways, mainly on the river Danube, which has several major river ports and harbours including Budapest
Roadways and railways—Hungary has 197,519km of roads, 74,993km of which are surfaced, and 8,057km of railways (including a cross-border line to Austria jointly managed by the two countries)
Telecommunications—2.98 million fixed lines in use and 12.01 million mobile subscriptions (2010); there were 6.18 million internet users in 2009
Internet code and IDD—hu; 36 (from UK), 44 (to UK)
Major broadcasters—Magyar Televizio operates two public channels alongside private channels TV2 and RTL Klub; Duna TV operates satellite channels for Hungarian minorities living in neighbouring states
Press—There are four daily newspapers, including *Nepszabadsag* and *Magyar Hirlap*
WPFI score—7,50 (23)

EDUCATION AND HEALTH
Hungarians have ten years of compulsory education until age 16; a further two years at secondary level is optional.
Literacy rate—99.4% (2009 est)
Gross enrolment ratio (percentage of relevant age group)—primary 102%; secondary 98%; tertiary 62% (2009 est)
Health expenditure (per capita)—US$938 (2009)
Hospital beds (per 1,000 people)—7.0 (2004–9)
Life expectancy (years)—75.02 (2012 est)
Mortality rate—12.7 (2012 est)
Birth rate—9.49 (2012 est)
Infant mortality rate—5.24 (2012 est)

Iceland

Lydveldid Island—Republic of Iceland
Area—103,000 sq. km
Capital—Reykjavik; population, 198,093 (2009 est)
Major towns—Hafnarfjordur, Kopavogur
Currency—Icelandic krona (Kr) of 100 aurar
Population—313,183 rising at 0.67% a year (2012 est)
Religion—Christian (Lutheran 84%, Roman Catholic 3%) (est)
Language—Icelandic (official), English, German
Population density—3 per sq. km (2010)
Urban population—92.3% (2010 est)
Median age (years)—35.6 (2011 est)
National anthem—'Lofsongur' ['Hymn']
National day—17 June (Independence Day)
Life expectancy (years)—81 (2012 est)
Mortality rate—7.02 (2012 est)
Birth rate—13.23 (2012 est)
Infant mortality rate—3.18 (2012 est)
Death penalty—Abolished for all crimes (since 1928)
CPI score—8.3 (2011)
Military expenditure—US$10.6m (2009)
Gross enrolment ratio (percentage of relevant age group)—primary 99%; secondary 107%; tertiary 74% (2009 est)

FINANCIAL OUTLOOK
Iceland is gradually moving to a sounder economic footing after the disastrous collapse of its financial sector. The economy expanded by 2.6% in 2011, according to the IMF, and achieved an equivalent

growth (2.4%) in 2012, with GDP expected to achieve further growth of 2.3% in 2013. Unemployment is down to 6%, from its peak of 9.2% in September 2010, and is expected to fall to 5.7% in 2013. According to the IMF, Iceland is on track to reduce its massive public debt, and its current budget envisages an annual fiscal deficit of 2.7% in 2012, and a further deficit of 1.2% in 2013. According to a report from Dansk Bank, investment activity in Iceland is good and should see increases of around 8–9%, year-on-year, for 2012 and 2013. The expectation for inflation is that it will be 3.7% for 2012, falling slightly to 3.1% in 2013. The bank expects unemployment in Iceland to fall to 5.8% for 2012, and to 5.2% by the end of 2013.

CLIMATE AND TERRAIN

Iceland is a volcanic island in the North Atlantic Ocean, to the east of Greenland and to the west of Norway, and its northernmost point reaches the Arctic Circle. Some parts of the coastline have narrow strips of low-lying land, others are sheer cliffs. An inland plateau of glaciers, lakes and lava fields covers most of the interior, with mountainous areas in the north and at the four glaciers in the centre and south. Elevation extremes range from 2,110m (Hvannadalshnukur, on the Oraefajokull volcano) to 0m (North Atlantic Ocean). There are geysers and hot springs owing to the numerous active volcanoes, which can create new islands, such as Surtsey in 1963; the volcano under the Eyjafjallajokull glacier has been active since March 2010. It is estimated that over the past 500 years, Iceland has emitted a third of the earth's total lava flow. The climate is influenced by the Gulf Stream; average temperatures range from −3°C in January to 11°C in July.

HISTORY AND POLITICS

The first major settlement occurred from around AD 870 onwards, as turmoil in Scandinavia drove migrants to seek new homelands. Iceland hosted a flourishing Viking culture in the ninth and tenth centuries, becoming a fully Christian country in 1000. Iceland recognised Norwegian sovereignty in 1263 and, with Norway, came under Danish rule in 1397. When Norway was ceded to Sweden in 1814, Iceland remained Danish territory, achieving autonomy in domestic affairs in 1874. Although it became an independent state with the same sovereign as Denmark in 1918, Copenhagen continued to control its foreign policy and defence. The treaty of union with Denmark expired in 1943, while Denmark was under German occupation, and in a referendum Icelanders voted to become a fully independent republic, proclaimed on 17 June 1944.

The country's dependence on the fishing industry has led occasionally to fraught foreign relations. The introduction and extensions of an exclusive fishing limit around Iceland in 1958, 1972 and 1975 caused the so-called 'Cod War' disputes with the UK.

Post-independence politics was dominated by the conservative Independence Party (SSF) until January 2009, when the country's economic crisis forced the government first to call an early election, then to resign with immediate effect. The Social Democratic Alliance, the junior party in the outgoing coalition, formed a new coalition with the Left-Green Movement (VGF) which then won the legislative election in April. Incumbent president Olafur Ragnar Grimsson was re-elected for a fourth term in June 2012.

Under the 1944 constitution, the head of state is the president, who is directly elected for a four-year term, which is renewable. The unicameral legislature, the *Althing*, has 63 members, who are directly elected for a four-year term. Founded in AD 930, the *Althing* is the world's oldest functioning parliament.

HEAD OF STATE

President, Olafur Ragnar Grimsson, *elected* 29 June 1996, *re-elected* 2000, 2004, 2008, 2012

SELECTED GOVERNMENT MEMBERS *as at June 2012*

Prime Minister, Johanna Sigurdardottir
Economic Affairs, Steingrimur Sigfusson
Finance, Oddny Hardardottir
Foreign Affairs, Ossur Skarphedinsson

EMBASSY OF ICELAND

2A Hans Street, London SW1X 0JE
T 020-7259 3999
E icemb.london@utn.stjr.is
W www.iceland.is//uk
Ambassador Extraordinary and Plenipotentiary, HE Benedikt Jonsson, *apptd* 2009

BRITISH EMBASSY

Laufasvegur 31, PO Box 460, 121 Reykjavík
T (+354) 550 5100
E info@britishembassy.is
W ukiniceland.fco.gov.uk
Ambassador Extraordinary and Plenipotentiary and Consul-General, HE Ian Whitting, *apptd* 2008

ECONOMY AND TRADE

Iceland has a market economy with an extensive welfare system. While it remains heavily dependent on the fishing industry, which accounts for more than 12% of GDP and 40% of export earnings, there has been recent diversification into aluminium smelting, ferrosilicon production, software production, biotechnology and tourism, encouraged by the plentiful supply of geothermal power. A major area of diversification was into banking, but aggressive expansion in the 2000s led to over-exposure in foreign markets. In the 2008 global financial crisis, the three largest banks collapsed and the government required over US$10bn in loans to stabilise its currency and financial system. The economy contracted sharply, causing widespread unemployment and rapid inflation, and has been in recession since 2009; GDP, however, rose by 2.4% in 2011 and the country has begun compensation payments to international claimants of failed Icelandic banks.

The main trading partners are EU countries, Norway and the USA. Principal exports are fish and fish products, aluminium, animal products, ferrosilicon and diatomite. The main imports are machinery, petroleum products, foodstuffs and textiles.

GNI—US$9,974m; US$32,710 per capita (2010)
Annual average growth of GDP—2.4% (2011 est)
Inflation rate—4.5% (2011 est)
Unemployment—6% (2011 est)
Total external debt—US$124,500m (2011 est)
Imports—US$3,932m (2010)
Exports—US$4,601m (2010)

BALANCE OF PAYMENTS

Trade—US$669m surplus (2010)
Current Account—US$1,287m deficit (2010)

Trade with UK	2010	2011
Imports from UK	£127,241,888	£233,664,218
Exports to UK	£353,323,319	£482,896,783

COMMUNICATIONS

Airports and waterways—Iceland has 99 airports and airfields, the principal ones being at Keflavik, near Reykjavik, in the south, and Akureyri in the north; there are no waterways

Roadways and railways—Although the country has 12,869km of roads, about two-thirds are unsurfaced; there are no railways
Telecommunications—204,000 fixed lines and 348,100 mobile subcriptions (2010); there were 301,600 internet users in 2009
Internet code and IDD—is; 354 (from UK), 44 (to UK)
Major broadcasters—Icelandic National Broadcasting Service operates radio and television services across the country
Press—There are three major daily newspapers:*Frettabladid*, *Morgunbladid* and *DV*
WPFI score—0,00 (1)

India

Bharatiya Ganarajya—Republic of India
Area—3,287,263 sq. km
Capital—New Delhi; population, 294,783 (2001 est). Delhi urban agglomeration; population, 21,719,700 (2009 est)
Major cities—Ahmadabad, Bengaluru (Bangalore), Chennai (Madras), Hyderabad, Jaipur, Kanpur, Kolkata (Calcutta), Mumbai (Bombay), Pune, Surat
Currency—Indian rupee (Rs) of 100 paise
Population—1,205,073,612 rising at 1.31% a year (2012 est); Indo-Aryan (72%), Dravidian (25%) (2000 est)
Religion—Hindu 81%, Muslim 13% (of which Sunni 85%, Shia 15%), Christian 2%, Sikh 2% (est)
Language—Hindi (official national language), English, Assamese, Bengali, Bodo, Dogri, Gujarati, Kannada, Kashmiri, Konkani, Maithili, Malayalam, Manipuri, Marathi, Nepali, Oriya, Punjabi, Sanskrit, Santhali, Sindhi, Tamil, Telugu, Urdu (all official)
Population density—394 per sq. km (2010)
Urban population—30.1% (2010 est)
Median age (years)—26.2 (2011 est)
National anthem—'Jana Gana Mana' ['Thou Art the Ruler of the Minds of all People']
National day—26 January (Republic Day)
Death penalty—Retained
CPI score—3.1 (2011)

FINANCIAL OUTLOOK

India saw growth threatening to fall below 6% in 2012, having had growth of 8.4% during 2010 and 2011, according to the IMF. The country continues to run a current account deficit of around 2.5% of GDP, financed largely from inflows from direct and institutional investors, and from inflows into deposit accounts by non-resident Indians. India still operates capital account restrictions, which it is easing partially by lifting foreign institutional investor quotas on local currency bond investments. The IMF would like to see the Indian government allowing banks more flexibility in borrowing abroad and increasing the ceiling for bond investments. The level of external borrowings by large Indian corporates is broadly stable at about 5% of GDP. The Reserve Bank of India requires banks to verify that their corporate clients' borrowings do not exceed one-third of assets. India's financial sector is diversified and expanding rapidly, comprising commercial banks, other credit institutions, insurance companies, pension funds, and mutual funds. The sector's overall assets amount to 140% of GDP. The expectation is that India's GDP will continue to show positive growth at around 6% or higher for 2013 and beyond. According to the Global Manufacturing Competitiveness Index, Indian manufacturing is expected to become the world's second most competitive over the next five years.

CLIMATE AND TERRAIN

India has three well-defined regions: the mountain range of the Himalayas, the Indo-Gangetic plain and the southern peninsula. The Himalayas along the northern border reach 8,598m (Kanchenjunga), then drop to the northern plains formed by the basins of the Indus, Ganges and Brahmaputra rivers before rising to low hills running east to west that mark the division with the southern Deccan peninsula. The peninsula has narrow coastal plains rising to a central plateau, with the Western Ghats and Eastern Ghats ranges of hills lying along the west and east coasts respectively. The Thar Desert lies in the north-west. The climate varies from tropical in the south to temperate in the north. It is influenced by the south-west monsoon; the main rainy season is June to October. During the drier season from December to May, the weather is cooler until February and then becomes increasingly hot until the monsoon breaks. The average temperature in New Delhi ranges from 14°C in January to 34°C in June.

HISTORY AND POLITICS

Under the 1950 constitution, the president is elected for a five-year term by an electoral college consisting of members of both chambers of the legislature. The president appoints the prime minister, who is responsible to the legislature. The vice-president, who is elected by both chambers for a five-year term, is *ex-officio* chair of the upper chamber. The legislature, the *Sansad*, consists of two chambers. The upper chamber, the Council of States *(Rajya Sabha)*, has up to 250 members, who serve a six-year term; up to 238 members are elected by the state legislative assemblies as individual terms expire, and the rest are nominated by the president. The House of the People *(Lok Sabha)* has 545 members; 543 are directly elected for a five-year term, and two representatives of the Anglo-Indian community are nominated by the president.

There are 28 states and seven union territories (including the national capital territory). Each state has its own executive, comprising a governor, who is appointed by the president for a five-year term, and a council of ministers. All states have a legislative assembly, and some also have a legislative council, elected directly for a maximum period of five years. The states have considerable autonomy, although the union government controls such matters as foreign policy, defence and external trade. The union territories are administered, except where otherwise provided by parliament, by a lieutenant-governor or an administrator appointed by the president

The 2012 presidential election was won by Pranab Mukherjee. In the 2009 legislative elections, the India National Congress (INC) and its coalition partners won the most seats in the *Lok Sabha* (*see* below), and were only ten seats short of an outright majority. A new INC-led coalition government was formed under Manmohan Singh, prime minister since 2004.

HEAD OF STATE

President, Pranab Mukherjee, *elected* 19 July 2012, *took office* 25 July 2012
Vice-President, Hamid Ansari

SELECTED GOVERNMENT MEMBERS *as at June 2012*

Prime Minister, Manmohan Singh
Defence, A. K. Antony

  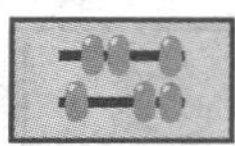      

Finance, Pranab Mukherjee
Home Affairs, Palaniappan Chidambaram

OFFICE OF THE HIGH COMMISSIONER FOR INDIA
India House, Aldwych, London WC2B 4NA
T 020-7836 8484
E administration@hcilondon.in
W www.hcilondon.net
High Commissioner, vacant

BRITISH HIGH COMMISSION
Chanakyapuri, New Delhi 110021
T (+91) (11) 2419 2100
E web.newdelhi@fco.gov.uk
W www.ukinindia.fco.gov.uk
High Commissioner, Sir James Bevan, KCMG, *apptd* 2011

Internal Unrest

Tensions between India's Hindu majority and large Muslim minority have never been fully resolved. Violence between the two at the time of partition in 1947 is thought to have cost up to one million lives. The rise of Hindu nationalism in the 1990s accompanied a rise in communal clashes. In 1992, a mosque in the town of Ayodhya was destroyed by Hindus who claimed it was built on the birthplace of the Hindu god Rama. Anti-Muslim mobs rampaged through many parts of India and the army was called upon to restore order. Intercommunal violence flared up again in 2002 when the massacre of pilgrims returning from Ayodhya prompted revenge killings.

There have been separatist campaigns or insurgencies in Manipur, Meghalaya, Mizoram, Nagaland and Tripura since 1947; in Assam since 1979; by Islamists in Kashmir since 1989; and by ethnic Gurkhas in Darjeeling in 1986–8 and since 2008. Sikh separatist agitation for an independent state in the Punjab became increasingly violent in the 1980s. The suppression of Sikh militants, and in particular the Indian army assault on the militant-occupied Golden Temple at Amritsar in 1984, led to the assassination of Indira Gandhi by her Sikh bodyguards later that year.

A peasant uprising in Naxalbari, West Bengal, in 1967 has developed into a Maoist uprising with the declared aim of overthrowing the government by 2050. By 2010 the insurgency affected 223 districts in 20 states, and the Maoists controlled a 'red corridor' between the east coast and the Nepalese border. Nationwide federal operations to tackle the insurgents in 2009 and 2010 have been met by a series of attacks by the Maoists.

Foreign Relations

Since partition, sovereignty over the predominantly Muslim state of Jammu and Kashmir has been disputed by India and Pakistan. A short war in 1947–8 resulted in the state being partitioned between the two countries; its status remains unresolved, despite further outbreaks of war in 1965 and 1971, low-level conflict for control of the Siachen glacier since 1985 and occasional increases in military exchanges, most recently in 1999–2002 and 2003. Tension was exacerbated by Pakistan's support of the Muslim insurgency in the Indian part of the state, which began in the late 1980s and has included terrorist attacks in Indian cities, and by both countries' acquisition of nuclear weapons. Moves towards a peaceful settlement began in 2003, when diplomatic missions were reopened and the resumption of transport links was initiated. Formal diplomatic talks began in 2004 and have achieved several accords intended to reduce tension between the two countries, although the status of Kashmir has yet to be addressed. Talks were temporarily suspended by the Indian government after the 2008 terrorist attacks on Mumbai but resumed in 2010.

In the Sino-Indian war in 1962, India lost territory to China. In addition, China claims Arunachal Pradesh and does not recognise Indian sovereignty over Sikkim. Talks between India and China in 2003 resulted in India's formal recognition of the Tibetan Autonomous Region as a part of China and a cross-border trade agreement on Sikkim.

DEFENCE

All aged 16–49, 2010 est	Males	Females
Available for military service	319,129,420	296,071,637
Fit for military service	249,531,562	240,039,958

Military expenditure—US$44,282m (2011)

ECONOMY AND TRADE

The economy was closed for several decades after independence, with high import tariffs and limits on foreign investment to stimulate domestic growth. Since 1991, economic liberalisation and increased foreign investment have generated rapid expansion, with GDP growing by an average 7% a year since 1997, apart from a brief contraction in 2008–9 during the global economic downturn.

India's large skilled workforce has enabled it to develop knowledge-based industries, and become a global centre for manufacturing and services. Other areas of growth are pharmaceuticals, tourism and the provision of services to the burgeoning urban middle class. The service sector now accounts for 55.6% of GDP and industry for 26.3%, employing 34% and 14% of the workforce respectively.

Although about 1% of the population has been lifted out of poverty each year since 1997, rural areas have benefited disproportionately little from the economic growth. Since 2004 the government has initiated schemes intended to reduce rural poverty, which has been exacerbated by prolonged drought in some areas and the effects of the Indian Ocean tsunami of 2004. Agriculture, forestry and fishing support 52% of the population and contribute 18.1% of GDP. The main food crops are rice, cereals (principally wheat) and pulses. The major cash crops include cotton, jute, tea and sugar cane. Agriculture and forestry are threatened by deforestation, soil erosion, over-grazing and desertification.

Despite recent advances, the economy faces a number of problems, chief among which is population growth. Economic constraints on continued growth include underinvestment in infrastructure, shortfalls in energy generation, excessive regulation and corruption.

The main trading partners are the USA, the UAE, and China. Principal exports include petroleum products, precious stones, machinery, iron and steel, chemicals, vehicles and garments. Its main imports are crude oil, precious stones, machinery, fertiliser, iron and steel, and chemicals.

GNI—US$1,712,645m; US$1,330 per capita (2010)
Annual average growth of GDP—7.8% (2011 est)
Inflation rate—6.8% (2011 est)
Population below poverty line—25% (2007 est)
Unemployment—9.8% (2011 est)
Total external debt—US$267,100m (2011 est)
Imports—US$323,622m (2010)
Exports—US$216,867m (2010)

BALANCE OF PAYMENTS
Trade—US$106,755m deficit (2010)
Current Account—US$42,807m deficit (2010)

Trade with UK	*2010*	*2011*
Imports from UK	£4,017,261,290	£5,410,581,663
Exports to UK	£5,380,470,481	£5,868,749,453

COMMUNICATIONS

Airports—There are 352 airports and airfields, principally at Delhi, Mumbai, Chennai and Kolkata

Waterways—The chief seaports are Mumbai, Kolkata, Haldia, Chennai, Cochin, Visakhapatnam, Mangalore and Tuticorin. There are 340 ships of over 1,000 tonnes in the merchant fleet. There are 485km of canals and the great rivers provide around 5,200km of navigable waterways

Railways and roadways—There are 3.3 million km of roads and 63,974km of railways

Telecommunications—35.1 million fixed lines and 752 million mobile subscriptions (2010); there were 61.34 million internet users in 2009

Internet code and IDD—in; 91 (from UK), 44 (to UK)

Major broadcasters—The public-owned Doordarshan network operates several national, regional and local services, and All India Radio is the country's largest radio broadcaster

Press—Eight major daily newspapers make up a lively press sector; these include *The Times of India*, *The Hindu* and *India Today*

WPFI score—38,75 (122)

EDUCATION AND HEALTH

Education is free and became compulsory for children aged six to 14 years in April 2010.

Literacy rate—66.8% (2008 est)

Gross enrolment ratio (percentage of relevant age group)—primary 118%; secondary 60% (2008 est); tertiary 16% (2009 est)

Health expenditure (per capita)—US$45 (2009)

Hospital beds (per 1,000 people)—0.9 (2004–9)

Life expectancy (years)—67.14 (2012 est)

Mortality rate—7.43 (2012 est)

Birth rate—20.6 (2012 est)

Infant mortality rate—46.07 (2012 est)

Indonesia

Republik Indonesia—Republic of Indonesia

Area—1,904,569 sq. km

Capital—Jakarta; population, 9,120,730 (2009 est)

Major cities—Bandung, Bekasi, Depok, Makasar, Medan, Palembang, Semarang, Surabaya, Tangerang

Currency—Rupiah (Rp) of 100 sen

Population—248,216,193 rising at 1.04% a year (2012 est); Javanese (40.6%), Sundanese (15%), Madurese (3.3%), Minangkabau (2.7%), Betawi (2.4%), Bugis (2.4%), Banten (2%), Banjar (1.7%) (2000)

Religion—Muslim 88% (predominantly Sunni), Christian 9%, Hindu 2% (est)

Language—Bahasa Indonesia (official), English, Dutch, Javanese, over 580 languages and dialects

Population density—132 per sq. km (2010)

Urban population—53.7% (2010 est)

Median age (years)—28.2 (2011 est)

National anthem—'Indonesia Raya' ['Great Indonesia']

National day—17 August (Independence Day)

Life expectancy (years)—71.62 (2012 est)

Mortality rate—6.28 (2012 est)

Birth rate—17.76 (2012 est)

Infant mortality rate—26.99 (2012 est)

Death penalty—Retained

CPI score—3.0 (2011)

Literacy rate—92.2% (2008 est)

Gross enrolment ratio (percentage of relevant age group)—primary 117%; secondary 75%; tertiary 22% (2009 est)

Health expenditure (per capita)—US$55 (2009)

FINANCIAL OUTLOOK

The Indonesian economy, southeast Asia's largest, grew by 6.2% in 2012, down from 6.5% in 2011. Weak exports offset strong domestic demand. Exports fell by 6.6% in 2012, contributing to a trade deficit of US$1.63 billion during the year. The government is targeting an expansion of 6.5–6.8% in 2013. The central bank has maintained its key interest rate at 5.75% since cutting it by 25 basis points in February 2012, and has avoided cutting rates further because of the weakness of the currency, which was among the worst performers in Asia in 2012. The headline inflation rate rose to 5.31% in February 2013, with core inflation at 4.29%. The central bank targets inflation of 4.5%, plus or minus 1 percentage point. In April 2012, Standard and Poor's warned that policy threatened the economy, and that consequently it would not upgrade the country's credit rating to investment grade. Indonesia was awarded investment grade status by Fitch in December 2011, and by Moody's in January 2012.

CLIMATE AND TERRAIN

Indonesia is an archipelago of over 17,500 islands, of which about 6,000 are inhabited. They include the islands of Sumatra, Java, Madura, Bali, Lombok, Sumbawa, Sumba, Flores, the Riouw-Lingga archipelago, Bangka and Billiton, part of the island of Borneo (Kalimantan), Sulawesi (formerly Celebes), the Maluku (formerly Moluccas) archipelago and others comprising the provinces of East and West Nusa Tenggara, and the western halves of the islands of New Guinea (Papua; formerly Irian Jaya) and Timor. Many of the islands have narrow coastal plains with hilly or mountainous interiors, and around half of the country is covered by tropical rainforest. Elevation extremes range from 5,030m (Puncak Jaya, in Papua) to 0m (Indian Ocean). The climate is tropical; the average temperature is 28°C, but rainfall peaks in January and February and is lowest in August.

The country is located near to an intersection of tectonic plates, making it susceptible to seismic activity such as earthquakes and volcanic eruptions. Its weather patterns are being affected by climate change.

HISTORY AND POLITICS

Hindu and Buddhist kingdoms existed in some parts of the Indonesian islands until the 14th century. Islam was introduced in the 13th century and spread over the next three centuries. Trading by the Portuguese began in the 16th century, but the Portuguese were displaced by the Dutch who, lured by the rich spice trade, came to dominate Indonesia by the early 20th century. Opposition to Dutch rule grew in the 1920s and the Japanese occupation of Indonesia during the Second World War strengthened nationalism, leading to a declaration of independence after liberation in 1945. This was not recognised by the Dutch, who attempted to reassert control, but after four years of guerrilla warfare they granted independence to the Netherlands Indies in 1949. Irian Jaya (now Papua) was annexed in 1963. Timor–Leste was invaded and annexed in 1975 but gained its independence in 2002.

Achmed Soekarno, the foremost proponent of self-rule since the 1920s, became president in 1949 but was deposed in 1966 in a military coup suppressed by General Suharto, who subsequently became president. Suharto remained in power until 1998 when, amid economic and social upheaval, he was succeeded by his deputy B. J. Habibie. Habibie's cautious introduction of social and economic reforms led to him being defeated in 1999 by Abdurrahman Wahid, in the first democratic elections for 44 years. President Wahid was impeached for alleged financial corruption and in 2001 the legislature appointed Megawati Soekarnoputri (daughter of Achmed Soekarno) to replace him.

Susilo Bambang Yudhoyono, of the Democratic Party, was elected president in 2004, and he was re-elected in 2009. In the 2009 legislative elections, the Democratic Party won the greatest number of seats but without an overall majority, and a coalition government was appointed by the president.

The 1959 constitution was amended in 2001 to provide for the establishment of the upper chamber of the legislature, and in 2002 to provide for the direct election of the president and the abolition of parliamentary seats reserved for the armed forces.

The executive president is directly elected for a five-year term, renewable once, and appoints the cabinet. The bicameral People's Consultative Assembly comprises the House of Representatives, which has 560 members directly elected for a five-year term, and the House of Representatives of the Regions, which has 132 members, four for each province, directly elected on a non-partisan basis for a five-year term.

HEAD OF STATE
President, Susilo Bambang Yudhoyono , *sworn in* 20 October 2004, *re-elected* 2009
Vice-President, Boediono

SELECTED GOVERNMENT MEMBERS *as at June 2012*
Defence, Purnomo Yusgiantoro
Finance, Agus Martowardojo
Foreign Affairs, Marty Muliana Natalegawa

EMBASSY OF THE REPUBLIC OF INDONESIA
38 Grosvenor Square, London W1K 2HW
T 020-7499 7661
E kbri@btconnect.com
W www.indonesianembassy.org.uk
Ambassador Extraordinary and Plenipotentiary, HE Teuku Mohammad Hamzah Thayeb, *apptd* 2012

BRITISH EMBASSY
Jalan M. H. Thamrin 75, Jakarta 10310
T (+62) (21) 2356 5200
W ukinindonesia.fco.gov.uk
Ambassador Extraordinary and Plenipotentiary, HE Mark Canning, *apptd* 2011

Insurgencies

Separatist movements developed in several parts of Indonesia after independence, including Maluku, which fought an unsuccessful separatist war in the 1950s; Irian Jaya (now Papua), which was granted greater autonomy in 2002, although separatist agitation continues; Timor–Leste, from its annexation in 1975 until independence in 2002; and Aceh province in Sumatra, which was granted a degree of autonomy in 2005.

Since the fall of Suharto in 1998, tensions between different ethnic and religious groups have surfaced, and there has been inter-communal violence in Kalimantan (1996–7, 1999, 2001), Sulawesi (1998–2000, 2001, 2005) and Maluku (1999–2002, 2004).

At least two Muslim extremist groups are based in Indonesia and claim links with al-Qaida. They have been held responsible for bombings in Bali in 2002 and 2005 and Jakarta in 2003, 2004 and 2009.

Political System

The 1959 constitution was amended in 2001 to provide for the establishment of the upper chamber of the legislature, and in 2002 to provide for the direct election of the president and the abolition of parliamentary seats reserved for the armed forces.

The executive president is directly elected for a five-year term, renewable once, and appoints the cabinet. The bicameral People's Consultative Assembly comprises the House of Representatives, which has 560 members directly elected for a five-year term, and the House of Representatives of the Regions, which has 132 members, four for each province, directly elected on a non-partisan basis for a five-year term.

HEAD OF STATE
President, Susilo Bambang Yudhoyono , *sworn in* 20 October 2004, *re-elected* 2009
Vice-President, Boediono

SELECTED GOVERNMENT MEMBERS *as at June 2012*
Defence, Purnomo Yusgiantoro
Finance, Agus Martowardojo
Foreign Affairs, Marty Muliana Natalegawa

EMBASSY OF THE REPUBLIC OF INDONESIA
38 Grosvenor Square, London W1K 2HW
T 020-7499 7661
E kbri@btconnect.com
W www.indonesianembassy.org.uk
Ambassador Extraordinary and Plenipotentiary, HE Teuku Mohammad Hamzah Thayeb, *apptd* 2012

BRITISH EMBASSY
Jalan M. H. Thamrin 75, Jakarta 10310
T (+62) (21) 2356 5200
W ukinindonesia.fco.gov.uk
Ambassador Extraordinary and Plenipotentiary, HE Mark Canning, *apptd* 2011

DEFENCE

All aged 16–49, 2010 est	*Males*	*Females*
Available for military service	65,847,171	63,228,017
Fit for military service	54,264,299	53,274,361

Military expenditure—US$5,220m (2011)
Conscription duration—24 months (selective)

ECONOMY AND TRADE

The economy struggled from the late 1990s until recent years, hit in succession by the Asian financial crisis, the political turmoil following the fall of Suharto, a downturn in tourism following the

Bali bombings and a number of natural disasters since 2004. President Yudhoyono's government introduced significant economic reforms which reduced debt, unemployment and inflation and boosted growth in 2004–8. Although growth slowed in 2008, government stimulus measures countered the effect of the global downturn in 2009 and by 2011 Indonesia's credit rating was raised to investment grade due mainly to its low rates of inflation and small current account surplus. Poverty, poor infrastructure, corruption, a complex regulatory regime and inequitable resource distribution among Indonesia's regions continue to present problems.

Natural resources include oil, tin, natural gas, nickel, timber, bauxite, copper, coal, gold and silver. However, a lack of investment in prospecting for new sources has led to a decline in oil production and Indonesia has been a net importer since 2004. The exploitation and processing of mineral assets, production of textiles, clothing, cement, fertilisers, plywood and rubber, and tourism are the main industrial activities; industry accounts for 46% of GDP and services 39.1%, employing 12.8% and 48.9% of the workforce respectively. Agriculture contributes only 14.9% of GDP but employs 38.3% of the workforce. The main crops are rice, cassava, peanuts, rubber, cocoa, coffee, palm oil, copra and livestock products.

The main trading partners are Singapore, Japan, China, the USA, South Korea and other Pacific Rim nations. Principal exports are oil and natural gas, electrical appliances, plywood, textiles and rubber. The main imports are machinery and equipment, chemicals, fuel and foodstuffs.

GNI—US$686,633m; US$2,500 per capita (2010)
Annual average growth of GDP—6.4% (2011 est)
Inflation rate—5.7% (2011 est)
Population below poverty line—13.3% (2010)
Unemployment—6.7% (2011 est)
Total external debt—US$158,800m (2011 est)
Imports—US$132,099m (2010)
Exports—US$157,823m (2010)

BALANCE OF PAYMENTS
Trade—US$25,724m surplus (2010)
Current Account—US$5,643m surplus (2010)

Trade with UK	*2010*	*2011*
Imports from UK	£438,877,161	£630,948,764
Exports to UK	£1,373,289,047	£1,300,130,610

COMMUNICATIONS
Airports—There are 684 airports and airfields, of which 171 have surfaced runways; each of the main islands has a major airport, with most capable of accepting international flights
Waterways—There are nine major ports, usually the chief towns of the major islands, and the merchant fleet contains 1,340 ships of over 1,000 tonnes
Roadways and railways—There are 437,759km of roadways and 5,042km of railways
Telecommunications—37.96 million fixed lines in use, 220 million mobile subscriptions (2010); there were 20 million internet users in 2009
Internet code and IDD—id; 62 (from UK) 1 44/ 8 44 (to UK)
Major broadcasters—Radio and Televisi Republik Indonesia, the country's principal broadcaster, operates six television and two radio networks
Press—*The Jakarta Post* and *The Jakarta Globe* dominate a competitive market which includes eight other dailies
WPFI score—35,83 (117)

Iran

Jomhuri-ye Eslami-ye Iran—Islamic Republic of Iran
Area—1,648,195 sq. km
Capital—Tehran; population 7,190,400 (2009 est)
Major cities—Ahvaz, Esfahan, Karaj, Mashhad, Qom, Shiraz, Tabriz
Currency—Iranian rial of 100 dinar
Population—78,868,711 rising at 1.24% a year (2012 est); Persian (51%), Azeri (24%), Gilaki and Mazandarani (8%), Kurdish (7%), Arab (3%), Lur (2%), Baloch (2%), Turkmen (2%) (est)
Religion—Muslim (Shia 89%, Sunni 9%) (est); small Zoroastrian, Jewish, Christian and Baha'i minorities; Sufism is growing, but Shia orders of Sufism are being persecuted by the state
Language—Persian (official), Turkic, Kurdish, Luri, Balochi, Arabic, Turkish
Population density—45 per sq. km (2010)
Urban population—69.5% (2010 est)
Median age (years)—26.8 (2011 est)
National anthem—'Sorud-e Melli-e Jomhuri-ye Eslami-ye Iran' ['Anthem of the Islamic Republic of Iran']
National day—1 April (Republic Day)
Death penalty—Retained
CPI score—2.7 (2011)

FINANCIAL OUTLOOK
The Iranian economy grew by 0.36% in 2012, according to the Mehr News Agency, citing the parliament's research center. IMF figures released in October 2012 forecast an economic contraction in Iran of 0.9% in 2012, and growth of 0.8% in 2013. The economy grew by 4.67% in the year ended March 19, 2012, according to the Statistical Centre of Iran. Iran's oil and gas exports, which had accounted for three-quarters of total exports, plunged in 2012 because of international sanctions, according to the International Energy Agency. It estimated that Iran's oil exports may have dropped below 1 million barrels per day in January 2013, from 2.2 million bpd in late 2011, costing the country more than US$40 billion in lost revenues over the course of the year. Meanwhile, year-on-year inflation hit 27.4% at the end of 2012, according to official data. The slide in the rial, which lost around two-thirds of its value against the dollar in 2012, is fueling inflation.

CLIMATE AND TERRAIN
Apart from narrow coastal plains on the Gulf coasts and the shores of the Caspian Sea, the interior is a plateau consisting of barren desert in the centre and east. This is enclosed by high mountains in the west and north, with smaller ranges on the eastern border and the southern coast. Elevation extremes range from 5,671m (Kuh-e Damavand) to −28m (Caspian Sea). Earthquakes are frequent. The climate is arid or semi-arid in the interior, and subtropical on the Caspian shores. Average temperatures in Tehran are 1°C in January and 31°C in July.

HISTORY AND POLITICS
Under the 1979 constitution, overall authority rests with the spiritual leader of the republic, who is appointed for life by the

Assembly of Experts; this consists of 83 clerics who are directly elected and decide religious and spiritual matters. The executive president is directly elected for a four-year term, renewable once. Ministers are nominated by the president but must be approved by the legislature. The unicameral Consultative Council *(Majlis al-Shoura)* has 290 members who are directly elected for a four-year term on a non-party basis; five seats are reserved for religious minorities. Laws passed by the legislature must be approved by the Council of Guardians of the Constitution, six theologians appointed by the spiritual leader and six jurists nominated by the judiciary and approved by the legislature; it also has a supervisory role in elections. In 1997, the Constitutional Surveillance Council, a five-member body, was established to supervise the proper application of constitutional laws.

The incumbent president Mahmoud Ahmadinejad was declared the outright winner after the first round of voting in the 2009 presidential election, but the result was challenged by the other candidates, who alleged electoral fraud. Following massive protest rallies, the Council of Guardians confirmed Ahmadinejad's victory and ruled out an annulment; further popular protests were suppressed. Since the protests in summer 2009, the regime has ruthlessly suppressed opposition (the Green Movement) and purged liberals from official positions. Conservative candidates retained the majority of seats in the *Majlis* in the 2012 legislative election.

Spiritual Leader of the Islamic Republic and C.-in-C. of Armed Forces, Ayatollah Seyed Ali Khamenei, *appointed* June 1989
President, Mahmoud Ahmadinejad, *elected* 24 June 2005, *re-elected* 2009
First Vice-President, Mohammad Reza Rahimi

SELECTED GOVERNMENT MEMBERS *as at June 2012*
Defence, Ahmad Vahidi
Economic Affairs and Finance, Shamseddin Hosseini
Foreign Affairs, Ali Akbar Salehi

EMBASSY OF THE ISLAMIC REPUBLIC OF IRAN
16 Prince's Gate, London SW7 1PT
T 020-7225 4208
E consulate@iran-embassy.org.uk
W www.iran-embassy.org.uk
Ambassador Extraordinary and Plenipotentiary, vacant

BRITISH EMBASSY
198 Ferdowsi Avenue, 113116–91144 Tehran
T (+98) (21) 6405 2000
W ukiniran.fco.gov.uk
Ambassador Extraordinary and Plenipotentiary, vacant

Foreign Relations

Between 1980 and 1988, Iran was engaged in a bitter war with Iraq over the Shatt-al-Arab waterway. Iran remained neutral in the Gulf War (1991) and the Iraq War (2003), but it has been accused since of subverting reconstruction in Iraq by arming Shia insurgents.

Since the 1978 revolution, Iran's relations with the West, and especially the USA, have been strained. It has not cooperated with international efforts to achieve peace in the Middle East, and has long been suspected of sponsoring terrorism by Islamic fundamentalists, especially in Lebanon and Palestine, and now is believed to be supplying arms to the Taliban.

Since 2002 international relations have deteriorated further because of concerns over Iran's nuclear and ballistic missile programmes, especially its acquisition of the ability to enrich uranium. Iran insists that this is for power generation and is not a precursor to developing nuclear weapons, but refuses to halt the programme or cooperate with the IAEA. The UN has passed six resolutions since 2006 calling on Iran to suspend uranium enrichment and reprocessing and to comply with its IAEA obligations and responsibilities; four of the resolutions imposed or extended sanctions on trade and travel. In an escalation of the nuclear row, the European Union imposed an oil embargo on Iran in January 2012, after the country reportedly began to enrich uranium at its underground plant in Fordo. Economic sanctions were strengthened following an attack on the British embassy in November 2011, followed by the expulsion of the British ambassador to Tehran.

DEFENCE

All aged 16–49, 2010 est	*Males*	*Females*
Available for military service	23,619,215	22,628,341
Fit for military service	20,149,222	19,417,275

Military expenditure—US$7,463m (2008)*
* Figure does not include paramilitary spending

ECONOMY AND TRADE
Iran was one of the best-performing economies in the Middle East owing to its vast reserves of oil and natural gas, but its performance has been deteriorating; the predominantly state-controlled economy is inefficient and inflexible, with little diversification and only a limited, small-scale private sector. Unemployment and underemployment are serious problems, and there is a flourishing unofficial economy. Falling oil prices in 2008–10 and UN sanctions since 2008 have exacerbated Iran's economic problems.

Oil and gas extraction and processing dominate the economy, but other industries include petrochemicals, textiles, construction materials, food processing, metal fabrication and armaments. Agricultural production includes wheat, rice, other grains, sugar beet and sugar cane, fruit, nuts, cotton, dairy products, wool and caviar.

The main trading partners are China, the UAE, South Korea, Japan and India. Principal exports are petroleum (80%), chemical and petrochemical products, fruit and nuts, and carpets. The main imports are industrial raw materials and intermediate goods, capital goods, foodstuffs, consumer goods and technical services.

GNI—US$328,593m; US$4,520 per capita (2009)
Annual average growth of GDP—2.5% (2011 est)
Inflation rate—22.5% (2011 est)
Population below poverty line—18% (2007 est)
Unemployment—15.3% (2011 government est)
Total external debt—US$17,900m (2011 est)
Imports—US$62,700m (2010)
Exports—US$100,900m (2010)

BALANCE OF PAYMENTS
Trade—US$38,200m surplus (2010)
Current Account—US$24,406m surplus (2010)

Trade with UK	*2010*	*2011*
Imports from UK	£285,807,268	£179,844,606
Exports to UK	£194,666,672	£359,333,086

  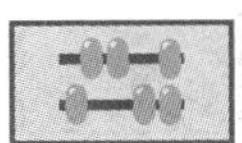      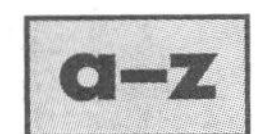

COMMUNICATIONS

Airports—There are 319 airports and airfields; the principal airports are at Tehran and Shiraz

Waterways—Iran's seaports include Asaluyeh, Bushehr and Abadan on the Persian Gulf and Bandar Abbas on the Strait of Hormuz. The 850km of navigable waterways are mainly on the river Karun and Lake Urmia

Roadways and railways—There are 172,927km of roadways, including 1,429km of motorways; there are 8,442km of railways

Telecommunications—26.85 million fixed lines in use and 67,5 million mobile subscriptions (2010); there were 8.2 million internet users in 2009

Internet code and IDD—ir; 98 (from UK), 44 (to UK)

Major broadcasters—The state-run IRIB network operates national and international networks in an industry dominated by satellite channels

Press—Major newspapers include the English-laguage daily *Tehran Times* and the conservative daily *Kayhan*

WPFI score—94,56 (175)

EDUCATION AND HEALTH

Primary education, between age six and 14, is compulsory and free.

Literacy rate—85% (2008 est)

Gross enrolment ratio (percentage of relevant age group)—primary 108%; secondary 84% (2009 est); tertiary 43% (2010 est)

Health expenditure (per capita)—US$269 (2009)

Hospital beds (per 1,000 people)—1.4 (2004–9)

Life expectancy (years)—70.35 (2012 est)

Mortality rate—5.94 (2012 est)

Birth rate—18.52 (2012 est)

Infant mortality rate—41.11 (2012 est)

Iraq

Jumhuriyat al-Iraq—Republic of Iraq

Area—438,317 sq. km

Capital—Baghdad; population, 5,751,210 (2009 est)

Major cities—Arbil, Basra, Kirkuk, Mosul, Najaf, Sulaymaniyah

Currency—New Iraqi dinar (NID) of 1,000 fils

Population—31,129,225 rising at 2.35% a year (2012 est); Arab (75–80%), Kurdish (15–20%) (est)

Religion—Muslim 97% (of which Shia 65%, Sunni 35%), Christian 3% (predominantly Chaldean Catholic) (est)

Language—Arabic (official), Kurdish (official in Kurdish Autonomous Region), Turkoman, Assyrian, Armenian

Population density—73 per sq. km (2010 est)

Urban population—66.4% (2010 est)

Median age (years)—20.9 (2011 est)

National anthem—'Mawtini' ['My Homeland']

National day—14 July (Republic Day)

Death penalty—Retained

CPI score—1.8 (2011)

FINANCIAL OUTLOOK

The economy grew by 10% in 2012, up from around 5% in 2011, and is expected to expand by a further 9% in 2013, helped by a surge in oil production, according to the central bank. It also estimates that foreign reserves reached US$110 billion by the end of 2012, while oil production surpassed 3 million barrels per day for the first time in 30 years, reaching 3.4 million bpd, an increase of 40% in just three years. Meanwhile, inflation in 2012 was relatively moderate at 5%. The International Energy Agency estimates that Iraq will account for 45% of the globe's marginal oil production over the next two decades, and will replace Russia as the world's second-biggest oil exporter. Iraqi policymakers are planning to increase oil production expansion to 3.7 million bpd in 2013. Iraq's production increases have matched the relative production decreases in Iran.

CLIMATE AND TERRAIN

The north-west and south of Iraq consist of an almost barren desert plain. The area between the Euphrates and Tigris rivers, which run across the country from north-west to south-east, is fertile, irrigated and heavily cultivated. The rivers run through marshland to their outflow in the Persian Gulf, on which Iraq has a 58km coastline. In the north-east the land rises to the Kurdistan mountains. Elevation extremes range from 3,611m to 0m (Persian Gulf). The climate is mostly desert, though colder and wetter in the mountains. Average temperatures in Baghdad range from 8°C in January to 34°C in July.

HISTORY AND POLITICS

Under the 2005 constitution, the president is elected by the legislature for a four-year term, renewable once. The president nominates the prime minister, subject to the approval of the legislature. The unicameral Council of Representatives *(Majlis al-Nuwab)* has 325 members, of whom 82 must be women and 15 from minorities; members are directly elected for a four-year term.

Following the invasion and occupation between March and May 2003, a coalition provisional authority became the occupying authority in Iraq before handing over sovereignty in June 2004 to the Iraqi interim governing council.

In the March 2010 legislative elections, the Iraqi National Movement (al-Iraqiya) bloc led by former prime minister Iyad Allawi won the most seats, but only by a narrow margin over the State of Law (SL) bloc led by incumbent prime minister Nouri al-Maliki. After several months of negotiations, the al-Iraqiya, SL and Kurdistan Alliance (KA) blocs agreed in November 2010 to form a coalition government under Nouri al-Maliki, and this was sworn in on 21 December. Jalal Talabani, the Kurdish president of the interim government in 2005 and re-elected to the office in 2006, was re-elected for a second term in November 2010.

HEAD OF STATE

President, Jalal Talabani, *elected* 6 April 2005, *re-elected* 22 April 2006, November 2010

Vice-Presidents, Tariq al-Hashimi; Khodeir al-Khaozai

SELECTED GOVERNMENT MEMBERS *as at June 2012*

Prime Minister, National Security (interim), Interior (interim), Nouri Jawad al-Maliki

Deputy Prime Ministers, Saleh Mutlaq; Hussain al-Shahristani; Roj Nouri Shawis

Foreign Affairs, Hoshyar al-Zebari

EMBASSY OF THE REPUBLIC OF IRAQ

4 Elvaston Place, London SW7 5QH

  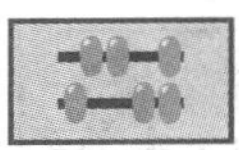      

T 020-7594 0180
W www.iraqembassy.org.uk
Chargé d'affaires, Muhieddin Hussien Abdullah Al-Taaie

BRITISH EMBASSY
International Zone, Baghdad
T (+964) 790 192 6280
E britembbaghdad@fco.gov.uk
W ukiniraq.fco.gov.uk
Ambassador Extraordinary and Plenipotentiary, HE Michael Aron, CMG, LVO, *apptd* 2011

Internal Unrest

There are about four million Kurds in north-east Iraq, in areas adjoining the predominantly Kurdish areas in Iran and Turkey. Iraq's Kurdish nationalists have demanded an autonomous homeland, Kurdistan, since the 1960s, and turned to militant tactics in the 1970s. Their demands were opposed by Saddam Hussein's regime with great brutality. An uprising after the Gulf War (1991) was suppressed by Iraqi troops, prompting the creation of UN safe havens which enabled the Kurds to set up a semi-autonomous region in the north. An air exclusion zone was also established, but there was further conflict with Iraqi forces and between the two main Kurdish parties in the 1990s. During the war in 2003, Kurdish fighters fought alongside US troops in the north, taking control of the northern cities and establishing an administration in the area, which is now autonomous. The boundary of the autonomous area has yet to be defined, and its precise location will decide control of Kirkuk and of oilfields in the region; this issue is the cause of tension between the central and regional governments, and of some intercommunal violence between Arabs and Kurds in the area.

The Shias in southern Iraq also rebelled after the Gulf War and were brutally suppressed. The UN established an air exclusion zone over southern Iraq in 1992 to protect the population, but persecution continued until 2003.

After May 2003, there was insurgent activity throughout the country, particularly in the Baghdad area, the predominantly Sunni-populated towns in the centre and west of the country, and in and around Mosul. Initially the targets were foreign troops, Iraqi military and police, and foreign aid and reconstruction workers, but from early 2005 the attacks became increasingly sectarian in nature. The level of violence has dropped since 2007 because of the US military 'surge', a ceasefire by one of the main militias, the Mahdi Army, from August 2007, and a key Sunni militia, the Awakening movement, turning against al-Qaida. There was an upsurge of violence in 2008 as the government mounted offensives against militias in Basra, Mosul and parts of Baghdad, and another upsurge in 2009–10 in the run-up to the legislative election and in the months following its inconclusive result. The approximate number of deaths as at December 2010 was: Iraqi civilians 99,000–108,000; US troops 4,400; and other coalition troops 318.

DEFENCE

All aged 16–49, 2010 est	*Males*	*Females*
Available for military service	7,767,329	7,461,766
Fit for military service	6,591,185	6,421,717

Military expenditure—US$5,568m (2011)

ECONOMY AND TRADE

The economy suffered three decades of state intervention, mismanagement, corruption, militarisation, war and international sanctions as well as the looting, insurgency and sabotage that followed the 2003 Allied invasion. With the improvement in the security situation, economic activity has increased, the institutions required to implement economic policy are being put in place and a debt reduction programme has been arranged. However, regulatory restrictions, inadequate infrastructure and corruption hamper economic development, and unemployment remains high (15%).

Oil is the main resource and export, and production has returned to pre-2003 levels. Other industries include chemicals, textiles, construction materials, food processing and metal fabrication.

The main trading partners are the USA (24.3% of exports), Turkey (24.2% of imports), Syria and India. Principal exports are crude oil (84%), other crude materials, food and livestock. The main imports are food, medicine and manufactured goods.

GNI—US$77,842m; US$2,340 per capita (2010)
Annual average growth of GDP—9.6% (2011 est)
Inflation rate—6% (2011 est)
Population below poverty line—25% (2008 est)
Total external debt—US$45,290m (2011 est)

BALANCE OF PAYMENTS
Trade—US$19,077m surplus (2010)
Current Account—US$2,619m deficit (2010)

Trade with UK	*2010*	*2011*
Imports from UK	£194,430,226	£203,672,614
Exports to UK	£2,190,965	£2,447,687

COMMUNICATIONS

Airports—There are 104 airports; the main international airport is at Baghdad
Waterways—The 5,279km of waterways are primarily on the Tigris and Euphrates rivers
Roadways and railways—There are 44,900km of roads and 2,272km of railways
Telecommunications—1.6 million fixed lines nd 24 million mobile subscriptions (2010); there were 325,900 internet users in 2009
Internet code and IDD—iq; 964 (from UK), 44 (to UK)
Major boradcasters—The television and radio stations set up by the coalition provisional authority now form part of the publicly funded Iraqi Public Broadcasting Service
Press—There are more than 100 newspapers and periodicals, many with an ethnic or religious affiliation; publications include the state-run *Al-Sabah* and *Al-Mada*
WPFI score—45.58 (130)

EDUCATION AND HEALTH

Since 2003 the country's education system has been reviewed, and over 2,500 schools have been refurbished. Primary education is compulsory.
Literacy rate—78.1% (2009 est)
Health expenditure (per capita)—US$98 (2009)
Hospital beds (per 1,000 people)—1.3 (2004–9)
Life expectancy (years)—70.85 (2012 est)
Mortality rate—4.73 (2012 est)
Birth rate—28.19 (2012 est)
Infant mortality rate—40.25 (2012 est)

  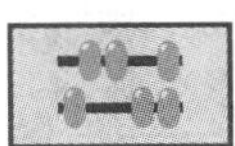      

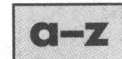

Ireland

Eire—Ireland
Area—70,273 sq. km
Capital—Dublin *(Baile Átha Cliath)*; population, 1,084,160 (2009 est)
Major cities—Cork (Corcaigh), Galway (Gaillimh), Limerick (Liumneach), Swords (Sord Cholm Cille), Waterford (Port Láirge)
Currency—Euro (€) of 100 cents
Population—4,722,028 rising at 1.11% a year (2012 est)
Religion—Christian (Roman Catholic 87%, Anglican 3%, Presbyterian 1%), Muslim 1% (est)
Language—English, Irish (Gaelic) (both official)
Population density—65 per sq. km (2010)
Urban population—61.9% (2010 est)
Median age (years)—34.8 (2011 est)
National anthem—'Amhran na bhFiann' ['The Soldier's Song']
National day—17 March (St Patrick's Day)
Death penalty—Abolished for all crimes (since 1990)
CPI score—7.5 (2011)

FINANCIAL OUTLOOK

In February 2013, the European Commission forecast that the Irish economy would expand by 1.1% in 2013, and 2.2% in 2014, outpacing the rest of the eurozone. GDP grew by 0.7% in 2012. In February 2013, the government said that it was confident of emerging from an EU/IMF bailout in 2013 following a promissory note deal. The exchange of promissory notes for long-date government bonds should reduce the government's debt-servicing costs and lower the refinancing risk to the country. Ireland became the second eurozone country to be bailed out in November 2010. However, the government deficit remained high at 8% of GDP in 2012, but is expected to fall to 7.5% in 2013. In February 2012, Standard & Poor's upgraded its outlook on the Irish economy from "negative" to "stable." However, it warned Ireland still has a large deficit, and the domestic economy faces uncertain growth prospects.

CLIMATE AND TERRAIN

The greatest length of the island of Ireland is 486km, from Torr Head in the north-east to Mizen Head in the south-west, and the greatest breadth is 280km, from Dundrum Bay in the east to Annagh Head in the west. Northern Ireland, in the north-east, is part of the UK. The republic has a central plain broken by hills and numerous lakes and bogs. It is surrounded by low mountains, including the Wicklow, Knockmealdown, Galty and Boggeragh mountains, and drained by the principal river, the Shannon (386km), which flows into the Atlantic Ocean. On the north coast of Achill Island (Co. Mayo) are the highest cliffs in the British Isles, 609m above sea level. Elevation extremes range from 1,041m (Carrauntoohil, Co. Kerry) to 0m (Irish Sea).

HISTORY AND POLITICS

Under the 1937 constitution, the president *(Uachtaran na Eireann)* is directly elected for a seven-year term, renewable once. The bicameral National Parliament *(Oireachtas)* consists of the House of Representatives *(Dail Eireann)* and the senate *(Seanad Eireann)*. The *Dail* has 166 members, elected for a five-year term by proportional representation. The *Seanad* has 60 members, who serve a five-year term; of these, 11 are nominated by the prime minister *(Taoiseach)* and 49 are elected, six by the universities and 43 from panels of candidates representing various sectoral interests.

The *Taoiseach* is appointed by the president on the nomination of the *Dail*, while other members of the government are appointed by the president on the nomination of the *Taoiseach* with the previous approval of the *Dail*. The *Taoiseach* appoints a member of the government to be the deputy prime minister *(Tanaiste)*.

The 1997 presidential election was won by Mary McAleese, and she was confirmed in office unopposed in 2004. The coalition government of the Fianna Fail, Progressive Democrats and Green Party lost the early election called in February 2011 because of the country's economic crisis. The opposition Fine Gail (FG) won the most seats but without a majority, and formed a coalition government with the Labour Party; the FG leader Enda Kenny was elected prime minister. Labour Party candidate Michael D. Higgins won the 2011 presidential election, picking up over half of the total vote.

HEAD OF STATE

President, Michael D. Higgins, *elected* 27 October 2011, *confirmed in office* 11 November 2011

SELECTED GOVERNMENT MEMBERS *as at June 2012*

Taoiseach (Prime Minister), Enda Kenny
Tanaiste (Deputy PM), Foreign Affairs, Eamon Gilmore
Defence, Alan Shatter
Finance, Michael Noonan

EMBASSY OF IRELAND

17 Grosvenor Place, London SW1X 7HR
T 020-7235 2171
W www.embassyofireland.co.uk
Ambassador Extraordinary and Plenipotentiary, HE Bobby McDonagh, *apptd* 2009

BRITISH EMBASSY

29 Merrion Road, Ballsbridge, Dublin 4
T (+353) (1) 205 3700
W britishembassyinireland.fco.gov.uk
Ambassador Extraordinary and Plenipotentiary, HE Dominick Chilcott, CMG, *apptd* 2012

DEFENCE

All aged 16–49, 2010 est	Males	Females
Available for military service	1,179,125	1,163,728
Fit for military service	977,631	965,900

Military expenditure—US$1,207m (2011)

ECONOMY AND TRADE

Since the 1980s Ireland's economy has been transformed from a mainly agricultural to a modern, export-led economy that experienced strong growth from the mid-1990s. But an over-inflated property sector and high levels of personal debt left the economy exposed in the 2008 global financial crisis, causing it to contract rapidly and go into a deep recession which put severe pressure on the financial system and government finances. Stabilisation of the financial system pushed the budget deficit to nearly 32% of GDP in 2010, despite austerity budgets in 2009 and

  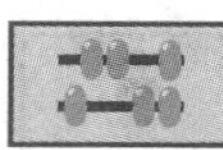      

2010, and in November 2010 the government agreed loan packages with the IMF and EU to avoid defaulting on its sovereign debt.

Agriculture now accounts for 2% of GDP and 5% of employment; services contribute 69% and industry 29% of GDP, and the sectors account for 76% and 19% of employment respectively. Major industries include mining, pharmaceuticals, chemicals, computer hardware and software, food and drink production, and tourism. Although the Kinsale gas field off the south coast meets some of Ireland's gas needs, and hydroelectric power is generated from the Shannon barrage and other schemes, the country is a net importer of energy.

The main trading partners are other EU countries and the USA. Principal exports are machinery, computers, chemicals, pharmaceuticals, livestock and livestock products. The main imports are data processing equipment, other machinery, chemicals, petroleum and petroleum products, textiles and clothing.

GNI—US$171,259m; US$41,000 per capita (2010)
Annual average growth of GDP—1.1% (2011 est)
Inflation rate—2.4% (2011 est)
Population below poverty line—5.5% (2009 est)
Unemployment—14.3% (2011 est)
Total external debt—US$2,357,000m (2011)
Imports—US$60,438m (2010)
Exports—US$118,583m (2010)

BALANCE OF PAYMENTS
Trade—US$58,145m surplus (2010)
Current Account—US$1,010m surplus (2010)

Trade with UK	2010	2011
Imports from UK	£16,316,524,067	£17,302,436,715
Exports to UK	£12,814,052,101	£12,985,760,277

COMMUNICATIONS
Airports—The principal airport is at Dublin, with others at Shannon, Waterford, Cork, Killarney, Galway and Knock
Waterways—There are over 950km of waterways, although these are used only by leisure craft. The main ports are Cork, Dun Laoghaire, Galway, Limerick and Waterford
Roadways and railways—Ireland has 96,036km of roads and 3,237km of railways
Telecommunications—2.08 million fixed lines and 4.7 million mobile subscriptions (2010); there were 3.04 million internet users in 2009
Internet code and IDD—ie; 353 (from UK), 44 or 048 for Northern Ireland (to UK)
Major broadcasters—The main radio and television broadcaster is the state-run Raidio Telefis Eireann (RTE), whose competitors include a handful of Irish commercial stations and British terrestrial and satellite services
Press—There are three national newspapers: the *Irish Times*, *Irish Independent* and *Irish Examiner*
WPFI score—2,00 (9)

EDUCATION AND HEALTH
Primary education is directed by the state and education is compulsory until age 16.
Gross enrolment ratio (percentage of relevant age group)—primary 106%; secondary 117%; tertiary 63% (2009 est)
Health expenditure (per capita)—US$4,952 (2009)
Hospital beds (per 1,000 people)—5.2 (2004–9)
Life expectancy (years)—80.32 (2012 est)
Mortality rate—6.38 (2012 est)
Birth rate—15.81 (2012 est)
Infant mortality rate—3.81 (2012 est)

Israel and Palestinian Territories

Medinat Yisra'el/Dawlat Isra'il—State of Israel
Area—20,072 sq. km (includes Jerusalem and the Golan Heights)
Capital—The legislature and most government departments are in Jerusalem; population 767,634 (2009 est). A resolution proclaiming Jerusalem as the capital of Israel was adopted by the *Knesset* in 1950. It is not, however, recognised as the capital by the UN because East Jerusalem is part of the Occupied Territories captured in 1967; the UN and international law consider the Tel Aviv (population, 392,500) to be the capital
Major cities—Haifa; Rishon Le'Zion
Currency—New Israeli Shekel (NIS) of 100 agora
Population—7,590,758 rising at 1.54% a year (2012 est); includes about 508,600 settlers in the occupied areas. Since independence, Israel has had a policy of granting an immigration visa to every Jew who expresses a desire to settle in the country; between 1948 and 2009, over 3 million immigrants entered Israel from over 100 different countries
Religion—Jewish 76% (of which secular 44%, 'traditional religious' or 'traditional non-religious' 39%, Orthodox 10%, *Haredi* 7%), Muslim 16.5% (predominantly Sunni; Druze 2%), Christian 2% (predominantly Eastern Orthodox) (est)
Language—Hebrew, Arabic (both official), English
Population density—352 per sq. km (2010)
Urban population—91.7% (2010 est)
Median age (years)—29.4 (2011 est)
National anthem—'Hatikvah' ['The Hope']
National day—fifth day of Jewish month of Iyar (anniversary of Independence Day, 1948); falls on 25 April in 2012
Death penalty—Retained for certain crimes (last used 1962)
CPI score—5.8 (2011)

FINANCIAL OUTLOOK
Economic growth slowed to 3.3% in 2012, compared with 4.6% in 2011 and 5% in 2010, according to the Israeli Central Bureau of Statistics. Slowing global growth has had a moderating effect on the expansion of the export-dependent economy. Tax revenues have also been affected, and the government had a budget deficit of 4.2% of GDP in 2012. Prime Minister Binyamin Netanyahu, who raised taxes in mid-2012 to help boost revenue, called early elections for January 2013 after failing to reach an agreement with coalition parties regarding the 2013 budget. The government's debt-to-GDP ratio is expected to total 73.5% in 2012, compared to 74.1% in 2011. Meanwhile, annual inflation continued to fall in 2012, reaching its lowest level in the past six years at 1.6%, according to the Central Bureau of Statistics, compared to 2.2% in 2011, and 2.7% in 2010.

CLIMATE AND TERRAIN
Israel comprises the partly forested hill country of Galilee and parts of Judea and Samaria, the coastal plain from the Gaza Strip to north

  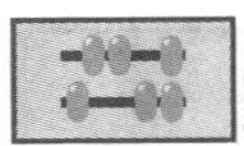      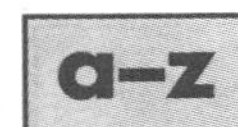

of Acre (including the plain of Esdraelon running from Haifa Bay to the south-east); the Negev, a triangular rocky desert in the south; and parts of the Jordan valley, including the Hula region, Lake Tiberias and the south-western part of the Dead Sea. Elevation extremes range from 1,208m (Har Meron) to −408m (Dead Sea), which is the Earth's deepest depression. The climate is temperate, with hotter, drier conditions in the south and east. Average temperatures in Tel Aviv range from 12°C in January to 26°C in August.

HISTORY AND POLITICS

There is no written constitution; most constitutional provision is set out in the basic law on government. The head of state is the president, elected by the legislature for a seven-year term, which is not renewable. The unicameral *Knesset* has 120 members elected by proportional representation for a four-year term. The prime minister is responsible to the *Knesset*, and appoints the cabinet, subject to the approval of the *Knesset*.

The 2007 presidential election was won by Shimon Peres. In September 2008, Tzipi Livni was elected head of the governing Kadima party but her attempts to form a new coalition were unsuccessful and an election was held in February 2009. Although Kadima won 28 seats to Likud's 27 seats, Likud succeeded in forming a coalition government with the Labour party and three smaller parties under Benjamin Netanyahu; the government took office in March 2009. In May 2012, Kadima agreed to join Netanyahu's coalition with a majority of 94, one of the biggest in the country's history.

HEAD OF STATE

President, Shimon Peres, *elected* 13 June 2007, *sworn in* 15 July 2007

SELECTED GOVERNMENT MEMBERS *as at June 2012*

Prime Minister, Benjamin Netanyahu
Vice Prime Ministers, Silvan Shalom; Moshe Ya'alon
Deputy Prime Ministers, Ehud Barak *(Defence)*; Avigdor Liberman *(Foreign Affairs)*; Dan Meridor; Eliyahu Yishai *(Interior)*
Finance, Yuval Steinitz

EMBASSY OF ISRAEL

2 Palace Green, London W8 4QB
T 020-7957 9500
E info@london.mfa.gov.il
W london.mfa.gov.il
Ambassador Extraordinary and Plenipotentiary, HE Daniel Taub, *apptd* 2011

BRITISH EMBASSY

1 Ben Yehuda Street, Migdalor Building, 15th Floor, Tel Aviv 63801
T (+972) (3) 725 1222
E webmaster.telaviv@fco.gov.uk
W ukinisrael.fco.gov.uk
Ambassador Extraordinary and Plenipotentiary, HE Matthew Gould, MBE, *apptd* 2010

DEFENCE

All aged 16–49, 2010 est	*Males*	*Females*
Available for military service	1,797,960	1,713,230
Fit for military service	1,517,510	1,446,132

Military expenditure—US$15,209m (2011)
Conscription duration—24–48 months (Jews and Druze only; Christians, Circassians and Muslims may volunteer)

ECONOMY AND TRADE

Israel has a technically advanced market economy, having developed its agriculture and industry intensively since the 1970s despite limited natural resources. After a short recession in the early 2000s, structural reforms and tighter fiscal control were implemented, resulting in steady growth from 2003 to 2007, increased foreign investment and a rising demand for exports. Despite the high level of external debt, the economy proved resilient in the global downturn, although it contracted slightly in 2008–9. Its debt and deficits are covered by foreign aid and loans; the USA is the main source of economic and military aid and is Israel's main creditor, owed about half of its external debt.

Israel has developed a strong technology sector, central to which are the aviation, electronics, biotechnology, communications and software industries. Other important industries include timber and paper, mineral and metal products, cement, chemicals, plastics, textiles, diamond cutting and tourism, which is reviving. The country is also an important producer of citrus fruits, vegetables, cotton, beef, poultry and dairy products. Service industries account for 64.7% of GDP, industry for 1.2% and agriculture for 2.5%.

The main trading partners are the USA (32.1% of exports), Belgium, other EU states and China. Principal exports are high-technology machinery and equipment, software, cut diamonds, agricultural products, chemicals, textiles and clothing. The main imports are raw materials, military equipment, investment goods, rough diamonds, fuels, grain and consumer goods.

GNI—US$210,352m; US$27,170 per capita (2010)
Annual average growth of GDP—4.8% (2011 est)
Inflation rate—3.2% (2011 est)
Population below poverty line—23.6% (2007; defined as less than US$7.30 per day)
Unemployment—5.6% (2011 est)
Total external debt—US$112,000m (2011)
Imports—US$61,209m (2010)
Exports—US$58,392m (2010)

BALANCE OF PAYMENTS

Trade—US$2,817m deficit (2010)
Current Account—US$6,385m surplus (2010)

Trade with UK	*2010*	*2011*
Imports from UK	£1,333,199,223	£1,566,873,435
Exports to UK	£1,465,322,511	£2,185,869,315

COMMUNICATIONS

Airports—There are 48 airports and airfields; the chief international airport is Ben Gurion, between Tel Aviv and Jerusalem
Waterways—The chief seaports are Haifa and Ashdod on the Mediterranean, and Eilat on the Red Sea; Acre has an anchorage for small vessels
Roadways and railways—There are 18,290km of roads, including 146km of motorway; Israel State Railways operates a network of 975km
Telecommunications—3.27 million fixed lines and 9.87 million mobile subscriptions (2010); there were 4.53 million internet users in 2009
Internet code and IDD—il; 972 (from UK), 44/012/013/014 (to UK)

  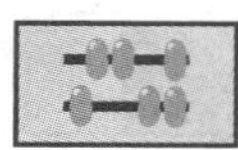      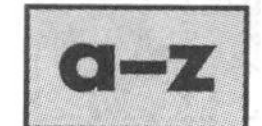

Major broadcasters—The Israel Broadcasting Authority operates public television and radio services across the country

Press—There are five main daily newspapers, including *Yediot Aharonot, Ha'aretz* and *Jerusalem Post*

WPFI score—23,25 (86)

EDUCATION AND HEALTH

Education is compulsory between the ages of five and 16 and is free.

Literacy rate—97.1% (2008 est)

Gross enrolment ratio (percentage of relevant age group)—primary 113%; secondary 91%; tertiary 62% (2009 est)

Health expenditure (per capita)—US$1,966 (2009)

Hospital beds (per 1,000 people)—5.8 (2004–9)

Life expectancy (years)—81.07 (2012 est)

Mortality rate—5.5 (2012 est)

Birth rate—18.97 (2012 est)

Infant mortality rate—4.07 (2012 est)

PALESTINIAN AUTONOMOUS AREAS

Area—The total area is 6,231 sq. km. The area which is fully autonomous is 412 sq. km, of which the Gaza Strip is 352 sq. km and the Jericho enclave 60 sq. km

Capital—Although Palestinians claim East Jerusalem as their capital, the administrative capital was established in 1994 in Gaza City; population 479,400 (2005 est); since 2007 the president and transitional government have been located in Ramallah, on the West Bank; population, 69,479 (2009 est)

Major towns—Jabalia, Khan Yunis, Rafah in the Gaza Strip; Hebron, Jericho, Nablus and Ramallah on the West Bank

Population—4,119,083 (2003 est)

Religion—Muslim 98% (predominantly Sunni); small Jewish and Christian minorities (est)

Flag—Three horizontal stripes of black, white, green with a red triangle based on the hoist (the PLO flag)

National anthem—'Fidai, Fidai' ['Freedom Fighter, Freedom Fighter']

Death penalty—Retained

Literacy rate—93.8% (2007 est)

History and Politics

The Interim Agreement of 1995 invested the Palestinian Authority with executive, legislative and judicial authority, but not sovereignty, in the autonomous areas.

The executive president is directly elected for a five-year term. The unicameral Palestinian Legislative Council *(Majlis al-Tashri'i)* has one seat reserved for the president and 132 seats for members elected from party lists for a five-year term. The president appoints the prime minister, who appoints the council of ministers, which must be approved by the legislature.

SELECTED GOVERNMENT MEMBERS *as at June 2012*

President, Mahmoud Abbas, *elected* 9 January 2005

Prime Minister, Finance, Salam Khaled Abdallah Fayyad

Interior, Sa'id Abu Ali

Foreign Affairs, Riyad Najib Abd-al-Rahman al-Maliki

PALESTINIAN GENERAL DELEGATION

5 Galena Road, London W6 0LT

T 020-8563 0008 www.palestinianmission.com

General Delegate, Prof. Manuel Hassassian

BRITISH CONSULATE-GENERAL

PO Box 19690, 19 Nashashibi Street, Sheikh Jarrah Quarter, East Jerusalem 97200

T (+972) (2) 541 4100

W ukinjerusalem.fco.gov.uk

Consul-General, Sir Vincent Fean, KCVO, *apptd* 2010

Economy and Trade

The *intifada*, and Israeli security restrictions in response to it, have damaged infrastructure and severely constrained economic activity in the Palestinian areas and external trade since 2000. Incomes had dropped and poverty risen sharply even before 2006, when the policies of the new Hamas government led to an embargo by international funding providers, and Israel stopped remitting customs dues collected on behalf of the Palestinian Authority. Emergency aid, provided through channels that bypass the Hamas government, was resumed in late 2006. The effects were and remain most severe in Gaza, where the population is dependent on food aid. On the West Bank, some Israeli restrictions have been eased since 2007, and the president's economic and structural reforms since 2008, underpinned by foreign aid donors, have stimulated economic development.

Most economic activity consists of small family businesses engaged in farming, quarrying and small-scale manufacturing of construction materials and textiles, metal goods, handicrafts and agricultural processing. The main exports are stone, fruit, olives, vegetables and flowers, and the main trading partners are Israel, Jordan and Egypt.

Inflation rate—9.9% (2009 est)

Population below poverty line—West Bank 46% (2007 est); Gaza Strip 70% (2009 est)

Trade with UK	*2010*	*2011*
Imports from UK	£1,622,039	£3,447,197
Exports to UK	£884,571	£804,336

Italy

Repubblica Italiana—Italian Republic

Area—301,340 sq. km

Capital—Rome; population, 3,357,470 (2009 est). The 'Eternal City' was founded, according to legend, by Romulus in 753 BC. It was the centre of the Latin civilisation and capital of the Roman republic and empire

Major cities—Bari, Bologna, Florence, Genoa, Milan, Naples, Turin, Venice, Verona. The chief town of Sicily is Palermo, and of Sardinia is Cagliari

Currency—Euro (€) of 100 cents

Population—61,261,254 rising at 0.38% a year (2012 est)

Religion—Christian (Roman Catholic 87%) (est)

Language—Italian (official), German, French, Slovene

Population density—206 per sq. km (2010)

Urban population—68.4% (2010 est)

Median age (years)—43.5 (2011 est)

National anthem—'L'Inno di Mameli' ['Mameli's Hymn']

National day—2 June (Republic Day)

  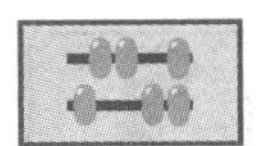      

Death penalty—Abolished for all crimes (since 1994)
CPI score—3.9 (2011)

FINANCIAL OUTLOOK

Italy's economy is expected to have shrunk by 2.3% in 2012, with a further contraction of −0.5% expected by the end of 2013, according to the Italian statistics office, Istat. This was a more pessimistic assessment than that given by the Italian government in September 2012, when it forecast a contraction of just −0.2% for 2013. The large contraction in 2012 was due to a slump in domestic demand and falling investment. The recession in 2013 would be deeper and longer than that forecast if any of a number of possible factors came to pass. These include a revival of the EU sovereign debt crisis, with widening sovereign credit risk spreads on Italian bonds, and also include the risk of a possible slowdown in the global economy, which would have an amplifying effect on recessionary conditions in Italy. According to the IMF, the difficult business environment, allied to Italy's fragmented labor market and limited competition in services, have created the conditions for weak growth and to a loss in competitiveness. Reforms are needed to address these weaknesses or the country can expect potential growth to remain low over the medium term. The IMF can only see Italy's GDP improving by a 10th of a percentage point each year from 2014 to 2017, with plenty of downside risks to this assessment.

CLIMATE AND TERRAIN

Italy consists of a peninsula, the islands of Sicily, Sardinia, Elba and about 70 smaller islands. The smaller islands include Pantelleria, the Pelagian islands, the Aeolian islands, Capri, the Flegrean islands, the Pontine archipelago, the Tremiti islands and the Tuscan archipelago. Most of the islands are mountainous.

The peninsula is also largely mountainous, but between the spine of the Apennines and the eastern coastline are two large fertile plains: Emilia-Romagna in the north and Apulia in the south. Italy is divided from France and Switzerland by the Alps, and from Austria and Slovenia by both the Alps and the Dolomites. Three volcanoes, Vesuvius, Etna and Stromboli, are still active. Elevation extremes range from 4,748m (Mt Bianco di Courmayeur) to 0m (Mediterranean Sea). At the foot of the Alps lie the great lakes of Como, Maggiore and Garda. The chief rivers are the Po (651km) and the Adige, flowing through the northern plain to the Adriatic Sea, and the Arno (Florentine plain) and the Tiber (flowing through Rome to Ostia), which flow to the west coast. The climate is Mediterranean, with warm dry summers and mild winters.

HISTORY AND POLITICS

The 1948 constitution has been amended several times, notably in 2001 to provide for greater autonomy for the 20 regions in tax, education and environment matters. The president, who must be over 50 years of age, is elected for a seven-year term by an electoral college consisting of both chambers of the legislature and 58 regional representatives. The bicameral *Parlamento* comprises a 630-member Chamber of Deputies and a senate with 315 members directly elected on a regional basis and a variable number of life senators, who are past presidents and senators appointed by incumbent presidents. Elected members of both chambers serve a five-year term.

The 2006 presidential election was won, after four rounds of voting, by Giorgio Napolitano. In the 2008 legislative election, the People of Freedom party (PdL), with the support of the Northern League and the Movement for Autonomy, achieved a majority in both chambers. PdL leader Silvio Berlusconi resigned from government in November 2011 following the loss of the PdL's legislative majority and intensifying economic problems; he was replaced by economist Mario Monti who formed an interim non-party government and began to push through new austerity measures.

HEAD OF STATE

President, Giorgio Napolitano, *elected* 11 May 2006, *took office* 15 May 2006

SELECTED GOVERNMENT MEMBERS *as at June 2012*

Prime Minister, Mario Monti
Foreign Affairs, Giulio Terzi di Sant'agata
Defence, Adm. Giampaolo Di Paola
Interior, Anna Maria Cancellieri

ITALIAN EMBASSY

14 Three Kings Yard, Davies Street, London W1K 4EH
T 020-7312 2200
E ambasciata.londra@esteri.it
W www.amblondra.esteri.it
Ambassador Extraordinary and Plenipotentiary, HE Alain Economides, *apptd* 2010

BRITISH EMBASSY

Via XX Settembre 80a, I-00187 Rome
T (+39) (6) 4220 2431
W ukinitaly.fco.gov.uk
Ambassador Extraordinary and Plenipotentiary, HE Christopher Prentice, CMG, *apptd* 2011

DEFENCE

All aged 16–49, 2010 est	*Males*	*Females*
Available for military service	13,865,688	14,003,755
Fit for military service	11,247,446	11,348,695

Military expenditure—US$31,946m (2011)

ECONOMY AND TRADE

Economically, Italy is divided between a prosperous and industrially developed north and a largely agricultural and welfare-dependent south that has high unemployment levels. There is a large unofficial economy that is estimated to be worth 17% of GDP, but measures to tackle this and wider structural reforms have made slow progress because of political opposition and sluggish economic performance. The growth rate has been low in recent years, and the global economic downturn caused a recession in 2008–9. A budget deficit that is above the 3% eurozone limit and public debt of over 120% of GDP has forced the government to pass a series of austerity packages to reduce its debt burden and balance its budget by 2013.

Tourism is the largest industry. Other major industries include precision machinery, iron and steel, chemicals, food processing, textiles, motor vehicles, fashion clothing, footwear, ceramics and electrical goods. The services sector contributes 67.8% of GDP, industry 28.3% and agriculture 3.9%. The main trading partners are other EU states, especially Germany and France. Principal exports are the products of the main industries, plus food, beverages, minerals and non-ferrous metals. The main imports are engineering and energy products, industrial raw materials and transport equipment.

GNI—US$2,023,915m; US$35,150 per capita (2010)
Annual average growth of GDP—0.6% (2011 est)

  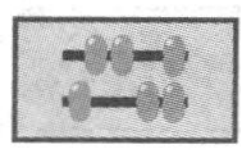      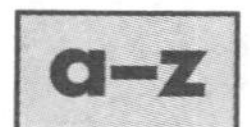

Inflation rate—2.3% (2011 est)
Unemployment—8.4% (2011 est)
Total external debt—US$2,684,000m (2011 est)
Imports—US$486,598m (2010)
Exports—US$447,463m (2010)

BALANCE OF PAYMENTS
Trade—US$39,135m deficit (2010)
Current Account—US$67,646m deficit (2010)

Trade with UK	2010	2011
Imports from UK	£8,761,376,789	£9,912,865,302
Exports to UK	£14,188,652,849	£14,212,011,950

COMMUNICATIONS
Airports—There are 132 airports and airfields, the major ones being at Rome, Milan, Naples and Venice, Palermo and Catania (Sicily) and Cagliari (Sardinia)
Waterways—The main seaports are Naples, Genoa, Livorno, Trieste, Venice, Palermo and Catania
Roadways—A 6,700km network of motorways *(autostrade)* covers the country but there are 487,700km of roads in total
Railways—There are 20,255km of railways; the main railway system is run by the state-owned *Ferrovia dello Stato*. In 2001, Italy and France agreed plans to build a 52km rail tunnel through the Alps as part of a high-speed rail link between Turin and Lyon; commissioning of the project is scheduled for 2012
Telecommunications—21.6 million fixed lines and 82 million mobile subscriptions (2010); there were 29,23 million internet users in 2009
Internet code and IDD—it; 39 (from UK), 44 (to UK)
Major broadcasters—Rai is Italy's public radio and television broadcaster and competes with a number of private television broadcasters, the leading one being Mediaset, part of the media empire of former prime minister Silvio Berlusconi
Press—The press is highly regionalised, although there are five national dailies, including *La Stampa* and *La Repubblica*
WPFI score—15,00 (49)

EDUCATION AND HEALTH
Education is free and compulsory between the ages of six and 16.
Literacy rate—98.9% (2009 est)
Gross enrolment ratio (percentage of relevant age group)—primary 103%; secondary 99%; tertiary 66% (2009 est)
Health expenditure (per capita)—US$3,328 (2009)
Hospital beds (per 1,000 people)—3.7 (2004–9)
Life expectancy (years)—81.86 (2012 est)
Mortality rate—9.93 (2012 est)
Birth rate—9.06 (2012 est)
Infant mortality rate—3.36 (2012 est)

CULTURE
Florence, the capital of Tuscany, was the 'cradle' of the Renaissance in the 14th to 16th centuries; many of the greatest names in Italian art flourished there, including Donatello (1386–1466), Botticelli (1445–1510), Leonardo da Vinci (1452–1519) and Michelangelo (1475–1564), often under the patronage of the Medici family. Other significant artists include Titian (*c.* 1490–1576), Caravaggio (1571–1610) and Modigliani (1884–1920).

Italy's wealth of composers includes Monteverdi (1567–1643), whose *Orfeo* (1607) is the oldest opera still regularly performed, Vivaldi (1678–1741), Verdi (1813–1901) and Puccini (1858–1924).

Dante Alighieri (1265–1321) and Boccaccio (1313–75) were two of the earliest Europeans to write in the vernacular. The works of the poet Petrarch (1304–74), politician Niccoló Machiavelli (1469–1527) and diplomat Baldassare Castiglione (1478–1529) strongly influenced other European writers. Notable modern writers include Primo Levi (1919–1987), Italo Calvino (1923–1985), Dario Fo (*b.* 1926), winner of the Nobel prize for literature in 1997, and Umberto Eco (*b.* 1932).

Italian cinema has produced world-renowned auteurs such as Luchino Visconti (1906–76), Federico Fellini (1920–93) and Michelangelo Antonioni (1912–2007). Director Sergio Leone (1929–89) and composer Ennio Morricone (*b.* 1928) are famed for their work on spaghetti westerns.

Japan

Nihon-koku/Nippon-koku—Japan
Area—377,915 sq. km
Capital—Tokyo; population, 36,506,600 (2009 est)
Major cities—Fukuoka, Hiroshima, Kawasaki, Kobe, Kyoto (the ancient capital), Nagoya, Osaka, Saitama, Sapporo, Yokohama
Currency—Yen of 100 sen
Population—127,368,088 falling at 0.07% a year (2012 est)
Religion—Shinto 82%, Buddhist 70%, Christian 2% (est); much of the population adheres to more than one religion, most commonly combining Shinto and Buddhist beliefs
Language—Japanese (official)
Population density—350 per sq. km (2010)
Urban population—66.8% (2010 est)
Median age (years)—44.8 (2011 est)
National anthem—'Kimi ga Yo' ['May Your Reign Last Forever']
National day—23 December (Birthday of Emperor Akihito)
Death penalty—Retained
CPI score—8.0 (2011)

FINANCIAL OUTLOOK
Japan's economy contracted for the third consecutive quarter in the three months to the end of December 2012. The economy shrank by 0.1% compared with the previous three months. Weak export demand in key markets, as well as subdued domestic consumption, has hurt the economy. The new government, elected in December 2012, said that reviving the economy is its top priority. In January 2013, it approved a fresh ¥10.3 trillion (US$116 billion) stimulus package, which included infrastructure spending, as well as incentives for businesses to boost investment. Japan's central bank also expanded its asset purchase program in January, and is expected to pump billions of yen into the economy. In February 2013, the government nominated Haruhiko Kuroda as the next governor of the country's central bank. Kuroda is seen as a supporter of aggressive monetary easing to help revive the economy.

CLIMATE AND TERRAIN
Japan consists of four large islands: Honshu (or Mainland), Shikoku, Kyushu and Hokkaido, and many smaller islands.

        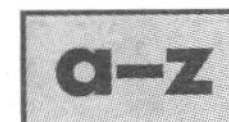

Typically, the islands have coastal plains and wooded, mountainous interiors; 67% of Japan's land area is forested. The mountains running across the mainland from the Sea of Japan to the Pacific Ocean include a number of volcanoes, mainly extinct or dormant. Elevation extremes range from 3,776m (Mt Fuji) to −4m (Hachirogata). The climate varies from temperate in the north to tropical in the south. Average temperatures in Tokyo range from 5°C in January to 27°C in August.

The islands are located at the intersection of three tectonic plates and are prone to seismic activity; 20% of the world's major earthquakes occur in this area. A magnitude-9 earthquake and the ensuing tsunami devastated the north-east of Honshu in March 2011.

HISTORY AND POLITICS

The 1947 constitution established Japan as a constitutional monarchy with a hereditary emperor as head of state. The bicameral Diet comprises the House of Representatives (the lower house) and the House of Councillors. The House of Representatives has 480 members directly elected for a four-year term, including 180 by proportional representation. The House of Councillors has 242 members, including 96 elected by proportional representation, who serve six-year terms, with half elected every three years; unlike the lower house, it cannot be dissolved by the prime minister. The prime minister is formally elected by the House of Representatives and appoints the cabinet.

The Liberal Democrat Party (LDP) has dominated post-war politics, holding power continuously from 1955 to 1993, and then—usually as the main party in coalition governments—from 1994 to 2009. In 2010, it regained control of the upper house of the legislature from the Democratic Party of Japan (DPJ); prime minister and leader of the DPJ-led coalition, Naoto Kan, subsequently resigned from office in August 2011, and was replaced by former finance minister Yoshihiko Noda.

HEAD OF STATE

HIM The Emperor of Japan, Akihito, *born* 23 December 1933, *succeeded* 8 January 1989, *enthroned* 12 November 1990

Heir, HRH Crown Prince Naruhito Hironomiya, *born* 23 February 1960

SELECTED GOVERNMENT MEMBERS *as at June 2012*

Prime Minister, Yoshihiko Noda
Finance, Jun Azumi
Foreign Affairs, Koichiro Gemba
Defence, Naoki Tanaka

EMBASSY OF JAPAN

101–104 Piccadilly, London W1J 7JT
T 020-7465 6500
E info@ld.mofa.go.jp
W www.uk.emb-japan.go.jp
Ambassador Extraordinary and Plenipotentiary, HE Keiichi Hayashi, *apptd* 2011

BRITISH EMBASSY

No. 1 Ichiban-cho, Chiyoda-ku, Tokyo 102–8381
T (+81) (3) 5211 1100
W ukinjapan.fco.gov.uk
Ambassador Extraordinary and Plenipotentiary, HE Sir David Warren, KCMG, *apptd* 2008

DEFENCE

The constitution prohibits the maintenance of armed forces, although internal security forces were created in the 1950s and their mission was extended in 1954 to include the defence of Japan against aggression. In the 1990s, legislation was passed permitting limited participation by the armed forces in UN peacekeeping missions and allowing them to enter foreign conflicts in order to rescue Japanese nationals. A revision to the USA–Japan defence cooperation guidelines agreed in 1997 permits Japan to play a supporting role in US military operations in areas surrounding Japan; Japanese troops were also deployed in Iraq to assist with post-war reconstruction between 2003 and 2006.

All aged 16–49, 2010 est	*Males*	*Females*
Available for military service	27,301,443	26,307,003
Fit for military service	22,390,431	21,540,322

Military expenditure—US$54,529m (2011)

ECONOMY AND TRADE

Japan has the third-largest economy in the world after the USA and China. Its rapid post-war economic growth, based largely on car and consumer electronics manufacturing, experienced a marked contraction from 1990. Exacerbated by the 1997 Asian economic crisis, the recession lasted 14 years, causing unprecedented levels of bankruptcy, unemployment and homelessness and a huge public debt (estimated at 192% of GDP in 2009). Reforms introduced from 2001, particularly to the corporate and public sectors, improved economic growth from 2002 to 2007, but the economy went into recession again in 2008 owing to the global downturn. Government stimulus packages and an increase in global demand spurred the start of a recovery from late 2009, but the drop in production and cost of reconstruction following the 2011 earthquake and tsunami are expected to reverse this.

High-technology industries remain the mainstay of the economy, producing vehicles, electronic equipment, machine tools, steel and other metals, ships, chemicals, textiles and processed food. Financial services is also a major sector, supplying a global market. Agriculture is constrained by the mountainous terrain but intensive cultivation produces high yields, and there is a large fishing industry. The service sector contributes 74.6% of GDP, industry 24% and agriculture 1.4%.

The main trading partners are China, the USA, other Pacific Rim countries and the Gulf states. Principal exports include transport equipment, motor vehicles, semiconductors, electrical machinery and chemicals. The main imports are machinery and equipment, fuels, foodstuffs, chemicals, textiles and raw materials.

GNI—US$5,601,557m; US$41,850 per capita (2010)
Annual average growth of GDP—−0.5% (2011 est)
Inflation rate—0.4% (2011 est)
Unemployment—4.8% (2011 est)
Total external debt—US$2,719,000m (2011)
Imports—US$692,566m (2010)
Exports—US$770,003m (2010)

BALANCE OF PAYMENTS

Trade—US$77,438m surplus (2010)
Current Account—US$195,856m surplus (2010)

Trade with UK	*2010*	*2011*
Imports from UK	£3,328,979,042	£4,394,992,532
Exports to UK	£8,624,970,671	£8,509,383,029

COMMUNICATIONS

Airports—There are 144 airports and airfields; the principal airports include Haneda (Tokyo), Narita, Kansai and Chubu

Waterways—Japan has a large merchant fleet, with 684 ships of over 1,000 tonnes in 2011. The main seaports are Tokyo, Osaka, Nagoya, Yokohama, Kobe and Kawasaki

Roadways—1,210,251km, including 7,083 of motorways

Railways—27,182km

Telecommunications—40.41 million fixed lines and 121 million mobile subscriptions (2010); there were 99.18 million internet users in 2009

Internet code and IDD—jp; 81 (from UK); 1 44/010 44/41 44/61 44 (to UK)

Major broadcasters—A public broadcaster, NHK, provides radio and television services; satellite and cable television is widespread and digital broadcasting is expanding

Press—Around 80% of the population reads a daily newspaper, creating huge markets for publications such as *Asahi Shimbun* and English-language title *The Japan Times*

WPFI score—2,50 (11)

EDUCATION AND HEALTH

Elementary education is free and compulsory at elementary level (six-year course) and lower secondary (three-year course).

Gross enrolment ratio (percentage of relevant age group)—primary 103%; secondary 102%; tertiary 59% (2009 est)

Health expenditure (per capita)—US$3,321 (2009)

Hospital beds (per 1,000 people)—13.8 (2004–9)

Life expectancy (years)—83.91 (2012 est)

Mortality rate—9.15 (2012 est)

Birth rate—8.39 (2012 est)

Infant mortality rate—2.21 (2012 est)

Jordan

Al-Mamlakah al-Urduniyah al-Hashimiyah—Hashemite Kingdom of Jordan

Area—89,342 sq. km

Capital—Amman; population, 1,087,910 (2009 est)

Major cities—Al Aqaba, Az Zarqa, Irbid

Currency—Jordanian dinar (JD) of 10 dirhams

Population—6,508,887 falling at 0.96% a year (2012 est); Arab (98%), Circassian (1%), Armenian (1%) (est)

Religion—Muslim (Sunni 95%), Christian 2% (est)

Language—Arabic (official), English

Population density—69 per sq. km (2010)

Urban population—78.5% (2010 est)

Median age (years)—22.1 (2011 est)

National anthem—'As-Salam al-Malaki al-Urdoni' ['Long Live the King']

National day—25 May (Independence Day)

Death penalty—Retained

CPI score—4.5 (2011)

FINANCIAL OUTLOOK

Jordan's economy increased slightly to 2.8% in 2012, according to an IMF report published in March 2013. It said that following the liberalization of fuel prices in late 2012, inflation increased to 7.2% at the year-end, but eased to 6.7% at the end of January 2013. Reflecting lower grants and higher energy imports, the external current account deficit widened to about 18% of GDP in 2012, but a stronger capital account helped bring the overall balance of payments in line with expectations, the IMF added. It expects growth to accelerate to above 3% in 2013, as a result of increased government capital spending, higher domestic consumption, and a recovery in exports. Inflation is expected to decline to 3.2% by the end of 2013. Factors weighing on the economy in 2012 included the conflict in Syria, and related large refugee inflows, as well as high energy and food prices.

CLIMATE AND TERRAIN

Most of the country is a desert plateau, with the valley of the River Jordan and the Dead Sea in the west marking the border with Israel. The Jordan Valley and its extension from the Dead Sea to the Gulf of Aqaba are part of the Great Rift Valley in Africa. The only hills lie in the south, along the edge of the Great Rift Valley, although there is a hilly outcrop in the centre of the desert. Elevation extremes range from 1,854m (Jabal Umm ad Dami) to −408m (Dead Sea). The climate is arid, but with a rainy season in the west from November to April. Summers are very hot, and temperatures in the Jordan Valley have been known to reach 49°C. Winters can be cold, with frost and snow on the plateau.

HISTORY AND POLITICS

The 1952 constitution provides for a monarchy with a hereditary king as head of state. The bicameral National Assembly comprises a House of Deputies and a senate or House of Notables. The House of Deputies has 120 members, directly elected for a four-year term; 12 seats are now reserved for women. The senate has 55 members, who are appointed by the king for a four-year term. The king appoints the prime minister, who chooses the council of ministers.

The legislature was dissolved halfway through its term in November 2009. After the legislative election in November 2010, over 85% of seats were won by pro-government candidates; the announcement of this result led to rioting. Since January 2011, Jordan has experienced demonstrations similar to those elsewhere in the Arab world, with protestors demanding political reform, lower food prices and measures to tackle unemployment. This led to the king dismissing the government in February 2011 and to the appointment of four prime ministers in 14 months, with Fayez Tarawneh replacing outgoing head of government Awn-al-Khasawneh in April 2012.

HEAD OF STATE

HM The King of Jordan, Abdullah II, *born* 30 January 1962, *succeeded* 7 February 1999

Crown Prince, Hamzeh ibn al-Hussein, *born* 29 March 1982

SELECTED GOVERNMENT MEMBERS *as at July 2012*

Prime Minister, Defence, Fayez Tarawneh

Minister of the Interior, Ghabib Al Zu'bi

Finance, Suleiman Al Hafez

Foreign Affairs, Nasser Judah

EMBASSY OF THE HASHEMITE KINGDOM OF JORDAN

6 Upper Phillimore Gardens, London W8 7HA

T 020-7937 3685
E london@fm.gov.jo
W www.jordanembassy.org.uk
Ambassador Extraordinary and Plenipotentiary, HE Mazen Kemel Homoud, *apptd* 2011

BRITISH EMBASSY
PO Box 87, Abdoun, Amman 11118
T (+962) (6) 590 9200
E amman.enquiries@fco.gov.uk
W ukinjordan.fco.gov.uk
Ambassador Extraordinary and Plenipotentiary, HE Peter Millett, *apptd* 2011

DEFENCE

All aged 16–49, 2010 est	*Males*	*Females*
Available for military service	1,674,260	1,611,315
Fit for military service	1,439,192	1,384,500

Military expenditure—US$1,310m (2011)

ECONOMY AND TRADE

Jordan's economic development has been hindered by its lack of natural resources, influxes of refugees from the West Bank in 1967 and Iraq since 2003, and the impact of conflict on its trade with Israel and Iraq. High levels of poverty, unemployment and government debt are long-term problems. Since 1999, King Abdullah has implemented economic reforms, and these measures have increased productivity and exports, begun to attract foreign direct investment, and won agreement to debt rescheduling from international donors. Even so, the economy is still dependent on foreign aid, of which the USA is the largest provider, and in 2011 the government agreed two economic relief packages to improve the living conditions for the middle and poor classes.

Jordan has no oil reserves of its own and few water resources. Since 2003, several Gulf states have temporarily extended aid to Jordan in order to compensate for the loss of its usual oil supplies from Iraq. The country also imports natural gas, but aims to become a net exporter of electricity via its national grid's links with those of Syria and Egypt. It is currently considering nuclear power generation to ensure an adequate future supply. Jordan has also begun joint ventures with Israel and Syria to guarantee water supplies.

The service sector, including tourism, accounts for 65.2% of GDP. Industry generates 30.3%, from activities that include garment manufacturing, fertilisers, potash and phosphate mining, pharmaceuticals, oil refining, cement, inorganic chemicals and light manufacturing. Agriculture, which accounts for 4.4% of GDP, produces citrus and stone fruits, tomatoes, cucumbers, olives, sheep, poultry and dairy products.

The main trade partners are the USA, Iraq, India, China and Saudi Arabia. Principal exports are clothing, fertilisers, potash, phosphates, vegetables and pharmaceuticals. The main imports are crude oil, machinery, transport equipment, iron and cereals.

GNI—US$27,820m; US$4,340 per capita (2010)
Annual average growth of GDP—2.5% (2011 est)
Inflation rate—6.4% (2011 est)
Unemployment—12.3% (2011 est)
Total external debt—US$7,296m (2011 est)
Imports—US$15,085m (2010)
Exports—US$7,023m (2010)

BALANCE OF PAYMENTS
Trade—US$8,062m deficit (2010)
Current Account—US$1,296m deficit (2010)

Trade with UK	*2010*	*2011*
Imports from UK	£222,755,820	£254,606,813
Exports to UK	£19,976,041	£32,259,166

COMMUNICATIONS
Airports—There are 18 airports and airfields; the principal airports are at Amman and Aqaba
Waterways—Amman is linked to Jordan's seaport at Aqaba, the Saudi Arabian port of Jeddah and the Syrian and Iraqi capitals by roads which are of considerable importance in the overland trade of the Middle East
Roadways and railways—There are 7,891km of roads and 507km of railways
Telecommunications—485,000 fixed lines and 6.62 million mobile subscriptions (2010); there were 1.64 million internet users in 2009
Internet code and IDD—jo; 962 (from UK), 44 (to UK)
Major broadcasters—Jordan Radio and Television, the state-run broadcaster, operates three terrestrial television channels and a satellite channel as well as radio services in Arabic, English and French
Press—Major daily newspapers include *Ad Dustour*, *Al Ra'y* and *Al Ghadd*
WPFI score—37,00 (120)

EDUCATION AND HEALTH
Literacy rate—91.1% (2008 est)
Gross enrolment ratio (percentage of relevant age group)—primary 97%; secondary 91% (2008 est); tertiary 42% (2009 est)
Health expenditure (per capita)—US$336 (2009; includes contributions from the UN Relief and Works Agency for Palestinian refugees)
Hospital beds (per 1,000 people)—1.8 (2004–9)
Life expectancy (years)—80.18 (2012 est)
Mortality rate—2.74 (2012 est)
Birth rate—26.52 (2012 est)
Infant mortality rate—15.83 (2012 est)

Korea

Taehan-min'guk—Republic of Korea
Area—99,720 sq. km
Capital—Seoul; population, 9,777,720 (2009 est)
Major cities—Busan, Daegu, Daejon, Gwangju, Incheon, Changwon, Urusan, Suwon,
Currency—Won of 100 jeon
Population—48,860,500 rising at 0.20% a year (2012 est)
Religion—Christian (Protestant 18%, Roman Catholic 11%), Buddhist 23% (predominantly the Jogye order of the Seon (Zen) school) (est)
Language—Korean (official), English
Population density—504 per sq. km (2010)

Urban population—81.9% (2010 est)
Median age (years)—38.4 (2011 est)
National anthem—'Aegukka' ['The Patriotic Song']
National day—15 August (Liberation Day)
Death penalty—Retained (not used since 1997)
CPI score—5.4 (2011)

FINANCIAL OUTLOOK

The weakness of the Japanese yen is forecast to take a toll on the economy in 2013. Japan is one of South Korea's main export competitors. The central bank cut interest rates in July and October 2013 to 2.75%, remaining unchanged in April 2013. The export-driven economy grew 2.0% in 2012—the slowest pace in three years—compared with 3.6% growth in 2011. The deceleration was largely blamed on sagging global demand caused by the eurozone debt crisis and a slowdown in China. The central bank has forecast economic growth of 2.8% in 2013. However, the government aims to boost the country's growth rate to more than 3% in the second half of 2013 and create in excess of 300,000 jobs. The authorities plan to front-load more than 60% of the annual budget into the first half, and to expand financial support for small and mid-sized exporters that are struggling to compete with Japanese rivals.

CLIMATE AND TERRAIN

The country occupies the southern part of the mountainous Korean peninsula, with highlands and mountains accounting for around 70% of the land area. Elevation extremes range from 1,950m (Halla-san) to 0m (Sea of Japan). The climate is temperate, although winters are very cold for the latitude. Average temperatures in Seoul range from −5°C in January to 26°C in August. The rainy season lasts from June to September.

HISTORY AND POLITICS

From 1948, South Korea experienced over 40 years of mostly authoritarian, often military, rule and great industrial development. Syngman Rhee, president from 1948, resigned in 1960 in the face of popular protests at corruption and electoral fraud. A military coup in 1961 brought General Park Chung-hee to power and he instigated a programme of industrial development; by the time of his assassination in 1979 Korea was a leading shipbuilding nation and producer of electronic goods.

Following riots against the interim government, General Chun Do-hwan assumed power in 1980 after martial law was declared. Pro-democracy agitation in the mid-1980s led to constitutional changes in 1987 and the first multiparty legislative elections in 1988, but despite the anti-corruption campaign of the new democratically elected president Roh Tae-woo, politics continued to be plagued by allegations of corruption and fraud, and was subject to military influence. The first civilian president and the first wholly civilian government since 1961 were appointed in 1993. Kim Dae-jung's inauguration as president in 1998 saw the adoption of the 'sunshine policy' of engagement with North Korea.

The 2007 presidential election was won by Lee Myung-bak, the Grand National Party (GNP) candidate. Lee Myung-bak's government reversed the 'sunshine policy' in 2008, and imposed sanctions on North Korea in 2010, blaming North Korea for the sinking of one of its warships in March 2010. In the 2012 legislative election, the GNP won a small overall majority in the National Assembly.

A new constitution was adopted when the Sixth Republic was inaugurated in 1988. Under this, the president is directly elected for a five-year term, which is not renewable. He appoints the prime minister with the approval of the legislature, and members of the state council (cabinet) on the recommendation of the prime minister. The president is also empowered to take wide-ranging measures in an emergency, including the declaration of martial law, but must obtain the agreement of the legislature. The unicameral National Assembly has 300 members who are directly elected for a four-year term.

HEAD OF STATE

President, Lee Myung-bak, *elected* 19 December 2007, *sworn in* 25 February 2008

SELECTED GOVERNMENT MEMBERS *as at June 2012*

Prime Minister, Kim Hwang-sik
Finance, Bahk Jae-wan
Defence, Gen. Kim Kwan-jin
Foreign Affairs, Kim Sung-hwan

EMBASSY OF THE REPUBLIC OF KOREA

60 Buckingham Gate, London SW1E 6AJ
T 020-7227 5500
E koreanembinuk@mofat.go.kr
W gbr.mofat.go.kr
Ambassador Extraordinary and Plenipotentiary, HE Choo Kyu-ho, *apptd* 2010

BRITISH EMBASSY

Sejong-daero 19-gil 24, Jung-gu, Seoul 100-120
T (+82) (2) 3210 5500
E enquiry.seoul@fco.gov.uk
W ukinrok.fco.gov.uk
Ambassador Extraordinary and Plenipotentiary, HE Scott Wightman, CMG, *apptd* 2011

DEFENCE

All aged 16–49, 2010 est	*Males*	*Females*
Available for military service	13,185,794	12,423,496
Fit for military service	10,864,566	10,168,709

Military expenditure—US$28,280m (2011)
Conscription duration—26 months

ECONOMY AND TRADE

Industrialisation from the 1960s transformed South Korea from a predominantly agrarian country into one of the Asian 'miracle' economies by the 1980s. Initially based on shipbuilding and electrical goods, production shifted towards electronics and IT goods in the 1980s. By 1997 South Korea was the world's eleventh-largest economy, with an annual GDP growth rate of 8%. However, the dominating conglomerates *(chaebols)* were experiencing difficulties which, exacerbated by the Asian financial crisis in 1997, caused a number to collapse in the late 1990s and the economy to contract sharply. Corporate and financial reforms were introduced and GDP growth resumed, from the early 2000s. The global downturn in 2008 caused another brief contraction in 2009 but the economy recovered strongly in 2010-11.

Services contribute 58.6% to GDP, industry 39.2% and agriculture 2.6%. Major manufacturing industries include electronics, telecommunications, motor vehicles, chemicals, shipbuilding and steel. Tourism is of growing importance.

The main trading partners are China, Japan and the USA (the US-South Korea Trade Agreement was first signed in 2007 and ratified in 2011). Principal exports are semiconductors, telecommunications equipment, motor vehicles, computers, steel, ships and petrochemicals. The main imports are machinery, electronics and electronic equipment, oil, steel, transport equipment, organic chemicals and plastics.

GNI—US$1,014,759m; US$19,890 per capita (2010)
Annual average growth of GDP—3.9% (2011 est)
Inflation rate—4.2% (2011 est)
Population below poverty line—15% (2006 est)
Unemployment—3.4% (2011 est)
Total external debt—US$397,300m (2011 est)
Imports—US$425,212m (2010)
Exports—US$466,384m (2010)

BALANCE OF PAYMENTS
Trade—US$41,172m surplus (2010)
Current Account—US$28,214m surplus (2010)

Trade with UK	2010	2011
Imports from UK	£2,204,852,690	£2,515,653,610
Exports to UK	£2,436,034,094	£2,536,493,519

COMMUNICATIONS
Airports—There are 116 airports and airfields, including international airports at Seoul (Kimpo), Kimhae (near Busan), Daegu, Cheju city and Incheon
Waterways—Busan, Incheon and Pohang are the major ports, although development and operations at Incheon are hampered by tidal variations of 9–10m.
Roadways—There are 103,029km of roads, of which 3,367km are motorways
Railways—There are 3,381km of railway in commercial operation, of which 1,843km are electrified. A high-speed railway line is being constructed between Seoul and Busan, and between Cheongwong county and Gwangju; there are plans to extend the service across the country by 2020
Telecommunications—28.543 million fixed lines and 50.76 million mobile telephone subscriptions (2010); there were 39.4 million internet users in 2009
Internet code and IDD—kr; 82 (from UK), 1 44/2 44 (to UK)
Major broadcasters—Korea has a number of public radio and television broadcasters, including Korea Broadcasting System (KBS) and Munhwa Broadcasting Corporation (MBC), as well as a diversified commercial sector
Press—Major newspapers include *Korea Daily* and English-language daily *Korea Herald*
WPFI score—13,33 (42)

EDUCATION AND HEALTH
Primary education is free and compulsory for nine years from the age of six.
Gross enrolment ratio (percentage of relevant age group)—primary 104%; secondary 97%; tertiary 104% (2009 est)
Health expenditure (per capita)—US$1,108 (2009)
Hospital beds (per 1,000 people)—12.3 (2004–9)
Life expectancy (years)—79.3 (2012 est)
Mortality rate—6.38 (2012 est)
Birth rate—8.42 (2012 est)
Infant mortality rate—4.08 (2012 est)

Kuwait

Dawlat al-Kuwayt—State of Kuwait
Area—17,818 sq. km
Capital—Kuwait City (Al Kuwayt); population, 2,229,990 (2009 est)
Currency—Kuwaiti dinar (KD) of 1,000 fils
Population—2,646,314 rising at 1.88% a year (2012 est); Kuwaiti (45%), other Arab (35%), South Asian (9%), Iranian (4%) (est)
Religion—Of citizens, Muslim (Sunni 70%, the remainder predominantly Shia) (est); Christian, Hindu and Parsi minorities, mostly expatriates
Language—Arabic (official), English
Population density—154 per sq. km (2010)
Urban population—98.4% (2010 est)
Median age (years)—28.5 (2011 est)
National anthem—'Al-Nasheed al-Watani' ['National Anthem']
National day—25 February
Death penalty—Retained
CPI score—4.6 (2011)

FINANCIAL OUTLOOK
The Kuwaiti economy is forecast to slow to 1.9% growth in 2013, from 6.3% in 2012, the central bank said in March 2013. A contraction in the contribution of the oil sector, as the crude exporter trims output, lies behind the downturn. The central bank forecasts non-oil GDP growth of 5.3% in 2013, up slightly from 5.1% in 2012. The government posted a record budget surplus of 13.2 billion dinars (US$47 billion) in the 2012–13 fiscal year, as oil production and prices rose. The government is seeking to spend heavily on large infrastructure projects, which should ease the economy's dependence on growth in the consumer sector. However, political wrangling has delayed implementation of the National Plan adopted in 2010. The country saw some of the largest protests in its history in 2012, with demonstrators demanding democratic reforms. In October 2012, the central bank cut its interest rate to 2% to boost growth.

CLIMATE AND TERRAIN
Kuwait is an almost entirely flat desert plain, with elevation extremes ranging from 306m to 0m (Persian Gulf). Its territory includes the island of Bubiyan and others at the head of the Persian Gulf. The climate is arid, with little rainfall but high levels of humidity. Average temperatures range from 13°C in January to 37°C in July.

HISTORY AND POLITICS
The area was under the nominal control of the Ottoman Empire from the late 16th century, but in 1756 an autonomous sheikhdom was founded that has been ruled by the al-Sabah family ever since. Kuwait entered into a treaty of friendship with Britain in 1899, in order to protect itself from Ottoman and Saudi domination, and it became a British protectorate in 1914. The borders with Saudi Arabia and Iraq were agreed between 1922 and 1933. Full independence was achieved in 1961, although Britain retained a military presence in the country until 1971.

An attempted Iraqi invasion shortly after independence in 1961 was discouraged by British troops in the Gulf. However, in August

1990 Iraq invaded and occupied Kuwait, proclaiming it a province of Iraq. In 1991, a short military campaign by a US-led alliance expelled the Iraqi forces, although there were further Iraqi incursions in 1993 before Iraq renounced its claim and recognised the new UN-demarcated border in 1994. Extensive damage was caused to the country's infrastructure and environment during the Iraqi occupation and the liberation campaign, and reconstruction was a priority throughout the 1990s. In 2003, Kuwait was a base for forces involved in the Iraq War, and it remains an important transit route for military and civilian traffic into and out of Iraq.

In recent years, there have been clashes between security forces and militant Islamists, some of whom are alleged to have links to al-Qaida.

Although Kuwait was the first Arab country in the Gulf to have an elected legislature, this was suspended from 1977–81, 1986–92 and in 1999. Since 1999 it has sat regularly, and its assertiveness has caused clashes with the government; two elections were held in 12 months in 2008–9 owing to its efforts to subject the government to parliamentary scrutiny. Pro-reform demonstrations took place in spring 2011 forcing Sheikh Nasser al-Muhammad al-Ahmed al-Sabeh's government to resign from office; the cabinet was replaced by a new government headed by Sheikh Jaber Mubarak al-Hamad al-Sabeh who retained power until the next election. The 2012 legislative election saw Islamists retain the largest bloc in the National Assembly, after which Sheikh Jaber was re-appointed prime minster.

The 1962 constitution was amended in 2005 to extend the franchise to women. The head of state is the emir, chosen from among the ruling family. He exercises executive power through the council of ministers; in 2003, the post of prime minister was separated from the role of heir to the throne for the first time. The unicameral National Assembly has 50 members directly elected for a four-year term. There are no political parties.

The country is divided into six governorates: Capital, Hawalli, Al-Ahmadi, Al-Jahrah, Al-Farwaniya and Mubarak Al-Kabeer.

HEAD OF STATE

HH The Emir of Kuwait, Sheikh Sabah al-Ahmad al-Jaber al-Sabah, *born* 1929, *acceded* 29 January 2006

Crown Prince, HH Sheikh Nawaf al-Ahmad al-Jaber al-Sabah

SELECTED GOVERNMENT MEMBERS *as at June 2012*

Prime Minister, Sheikh Jaber Mubarak al-Hamad al-Sabah

First Deputy Prime Minister, Interior, Sheikh Ahmad Hamoud al-Jaber al-Sabah

Deputy Prime Minister, Defence, Sheikh Ahmad Khalid al-Hamad al-Sabah

Deputy Prime Minister, Foreign Affairs, Sheikh Sabah Khaled al-Hamad al-Sabah

EMBASSY OF THE STATE OF KUWAIT

2 Albert Gate, London SW1X 7JU

T 020-7590 3400

E kuwait@dircon.co.uk

Ambassador Extraordinary and Plenipotentiary, HE Khaled al-Duwaisan, GCVO, *apptd* 1993

BRITISH EMBASSY

PO Box 2, Arabian Gulf Street, Safat 13001

T (+965) 2259 4320

W ukinkuwait.fco.gov.uk

Ambassador Extraordinary and Plenipotentiary, HE Frank Baker, OBE, *apptd* 2010

DEFENCE

All aged 16–49, 2010 est	*Males*	*Females*
Available for military service	1,002,480	616,958
Fit for military service	840,912	523,206

Military expenditure—US$5,178m (2011)

ECONOMY AND TRADE

Oil was discovered in 1938 and the development of the oil industry after 1945 transformed the country from one of the poorest in the world to one of the richest. Petroleum accounts for 95% of export revenues and 95% of government income. Income from foreign reserves and investment is also high, cushioning the economy from the effects of dependency on oil. Economic reform is slow owing to the tensions between the government and legislature, but a development plan passed in 2011 aims to diversify the economy, attract more investment and stimulate the private sector.

The climate and terrain limit agriculture and, with the exception of fish, all food is imported; the primary sector contributes only 0.3% of GDP. Services account for 51.8% of GDP and industry for 48%. Apart from the oil and petrochemical industries, activities include the production of cement and construction materials, shipbuilding and repair, water desalination and food processing.

The main export markets are Japan, South Korea, India, the USA and China, and the main sources of imports are the USA, China, Saudi Arabia and Japan. Principal exports are oil and refined products, and fertilisers. The main imports are food, construction materials, vehicles and vehicle parts, and clothing.

GNI—US$117,187m (2009); US$47,790 per capita (2007)
Annual average growth of GDP—5.7% (2011 est)
Inflation rate—5.6% (2011 est)
Unemployment—2.2% (2004 est)
Total external debt—US$44,450m (2011 est)
Imports—US$22,000m (2010)
Exports—US$66,000m (2010)

BALANCE OF PAYMENTS

Trade—US$44,000m surplus (2010)
Current Account—US$36,884m surplus (2010)

Trade with UK	*2010*	*2011*
Imports from UK	£530,434,798	£506,464,078
Exports to UK	£958,351,509	£1,469,137,436

COMMUNICATIONS

Airports—There are seven airports and airstrips; the international airport is at Kuwait City
Waterways—The main seaports are Ash Shu'aybah and Ash Shuwaykh
Roadways and railways—Kuwait has 5,749km of roads, most of which are surfaced, but no railway
Telecommunications—566,300 fixed lines and 2.2 million mobile subscriptions; there were 1.1 million internet users in 2009
Internet code and IDD—kw; 965 (from UK), 44 (to UK)
Major broadcasters—State-run radio and television broadcasters compete with commercial stations; satellite television is also widely watched
WPFI score—23,75 (87)

EDUCATION AND HEALTH

Education is free and compulsory from six to 14 years.

Literacy rate—93.9% (2008 est)
Gross enrolment ratio (percentage of relevant age group)—primary 106%; secondary 101% (2008 est)
Health expenditure (per capita)—US$1,416 (2009)
Hospital beds (per 1,000 people)—1.8 (2004–9)
Life expectancy (years)—77.28 (2012 est)
Mortality rate—2.13 (2012 est)
Birth rate—20.96 (2012 est)
Infant mortality rate—7.87 (2012 est)

Latvia

Latvijas Republika—Republic of Latvia
Area—64,589 sq. km
Capital—Riga; population, 710,637 (2009 est)
Major cities—Daugavpils, Jelgava, Liepaja
Currency—Lats of 100 santims
Population—2,191,580 falling at 0.59% a year (2012 est); Latvian (59.3%), Russian (27.8%), Belarusian (3.6%), Ukrainian (2.5%), Polish (2.4%), Lithuanian (1.3%) (2009 est)
Religion—Christian (Roman Catholic 23%, Lutheran 20%, Orthodox 17%) (est)
Language—Latvian (official), Russian, Lithuanian
Population density—36 per sq. km (2010)
Urban population—68.2% (2010 est)
Median age (years)—40.6 (2011 est)
National anthem—'Dievs, Sveti Latviju' ['God Bless Latvia']
National day—18 November (Independence Day)
Death penalty—Abolished for all crimes (since 2012)
CPI score—4.2 (2011)

FINANCIAL OUTLOOK

At the start of 2012, the Latvian government took a very cautious view of the country's growth prospects, forecasting GDP growth of between 1% and 2%. In reality, growth for 2012 turned out to be very much better at 5%, making Latvia the fastest-growing economy in the European Union. Industrial output and export volumes are already ahead of pre-crisis levels, and the "brain drain" of skilled workers leaving the country in search of better salaries elsewhere, seems to have ended. Unemployment, however, still stands at 13.5%, which is higher than in Latvia's two neighbors, Estonia and Lithuania. Income in Latvia is currently 60% of the EU average, but the expectation is that this will gradually move to mirror the EU norm. (It is worth remembering that in 1995 the average income in Latvia was only 30% of the EU norm.) Latvia is expected to meet all the Maastricht criteria and to receive an invitation to join the EU, and is en route to becoming an OECD member nation. Latvia has long had an employment problem. In the period from 1996 to 2011, the country typically saw unemployment of 13%. However, the IMF expects Latvia's output gap, now up to 5% of GDP, to be closed by 2015. The natural unemployment rate should shrink to 10% by 2017, it said.

CLIMATE AND TERRAIN

Latvia is a flat, low-lying country on the eastern shore of the Baltic Sea, with low hills and many lakes in the south-east. Elevation extremes range from 312m (Gaizinkalns) to 0m (Baltic Sea). The climate is temperate, and average temperatures in Riga range from −3°C in January and February to 17°C in July.

HISTORY AND POLITICS

Conquered and Christianised in the 13th century by the Teutonic Knights, Latvia was successively under Polish, Lithuanian and Swedish rule in the 16th and 17th centuries until it was incorporated into the Russian Empire in 1721. Under partial German occupation during the First World War, it declared its independence in 1918 and successfully defended this against the Bolsheviks in 1918–20. A dictatorship was established in 1934 following a period of political instability and economic depression. The USSR invaded and annexed Latvia in 1940, and regained control in 1944 after ousting the German forces that had invaded in 1941. Latvia suffered huge civilian losses during the Second World War, including the destruction of its large Jewish community. Many more Latvians died after the war in purges and deportations ordered by Stalin.

Agitation by nationalist groups grew from the mid-1980s. In May 1990 the legislature declared independence. The last Russian troops left in 1994 but a large Russian minority remains and there are intercommunal tensions. Latvia joined NATO and the EU in 2004.

In the 2011 legislative election, the pro-Russian Harmony Centre party won a small majority of seats, and Valdis Dombrovskis, prime minister since 2009, formed a new coalition government. Andris Berzins was elected president in June 2011 after his nomination by five members of the Green and Farmers' Union (ZZS).

The 1922 constitution was restored in 1993. The head of state is a president, who is elected by the legislature for a four-year term which may be renewed once. The president appoints the prime minister, who appoints the cabinet subject to approval by the legislature. The unicameral *Saeima* has 100 deputies who are directly elected for a four-year term.

HEAD OF STATE

President, Andris Berzins, *elected* 2 June 2011, *sworn in* 8 July 2011

SELECTED GOVERNMENT MEMBERS *as at June 2012*

Prime Minister, Valdis Dombrovskis
Deputy Prime Minister, Defence, Artis Pabriks
Finance, Andris Vilks
Foreign Affairs, Edgars Rinkevics

EMBASSY OF THE REPUBLIC OF LATVIA

45 Nottingham Place, London W1U 5LY
T 020-7312 0040
E embassy.uk@mfa.gov.lv
W www.london.mfa.gov.lv
Ambassador Extraordinary and Plenipotentiary, HE Eduards Stiprais, *apptd* 2009

BRITISH EMBASSY

5 J. Alunana Street, Riga 1010
T (+371) 6777 4700
E british.embassy@apollo.lv
W ukinlatvia.fco.gov.uk
Ambassador Extraordinary and Plenipotentiary, HE Andrew Soper, *apptd* 2010

DEFENCE

All aged 16–49, 2010 est	*Males*	*Females*
Available for military service	546,090	540,810
Fit for military service	401,691	447,638

  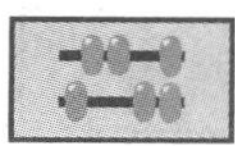      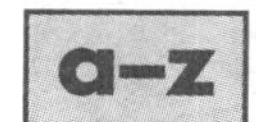

Military expenditure—US$267m (2011)

ECONOMY AND TRADE
The country made the transition from a planned to a market economy in the decade after independence, although a few large enterprises remain in state ownership. The economy grew rapidly from 2004 to 2007, but was severely affected by the global economic downturn because of its large current account deficit and private-sector debt. The economy contracted by 20% in 2008–9 and was slow to return to growth. The IMF, the World Bank and the EU provided aid in 2008–9 to avoid devaluation of the lat in return for a 40% cut in public spending. The IMF programme was successfully concluded in December 2011 and the country posted a reduction in its fiscal deficit of 4% of GDP at the end of the year.

The economy has shifted towards service industries since independence. Services, especially transit services and banking, is the largest sector, contributing 74.9% of GDP. Industry contributes 21% of GDP and includes food processing and the manufacture of processed wood products, textiles, processed metals, pharmaceuticals, rail transport vehicles, synthetic fibres and electronics. The agricultural sector accounts for 4.1% of GDP, employs 8.8% of the workforce and specialises in rearing livestock, dairy farming and crops including grain, rapeseed, potatoes and other vegetables.

The main trading partners are other EU states and Russia. Principal exports are food products, timber and wood products, metals, machinery and equipment, and textiles. The main imports are machinery and equipment, consumer goods, chemicals, fuel and vehicles.

GNI—US$24,072m; US$11,620 per capita (2010)
Annual average growth of GDP—4% (2011 est)
Inflation rate—4.3% (2011 est)
Unemployment—13% (2011 est)
Total external debt—US$41,080m (2011 est)
Imports—US$11,064m (2010)
Exports—US$8,817m (2010)

BALANCE OF PAYMENTS
Trade—US$2,247m deficit (2010)
Current Account—US$861m surplus (2010)

Trade with UK	2010	2011
Imports from UK	£162,221,871	£230,971,377
Exports to UK	£386,085,481	£380,356,706

COMMUNICATIONS
Airports and waterways—The main airports are at Riga, Ventspils and Liepaja; there are two major ports at Riga and Ventspils
Roadways and railways—73,074km of roadways and 2,239km of railways
Telecommunications—532,100 fixed lines and 2.3 million mobile subscriptions (2010); there were 1.5 million internet users in 2009
Internet code and IDD—lv; 371 (from UK), 44 (to UK)
Media—There are around 140 newspapers in circulation, including many in Russian. Television and radio output is provided by public service broadcaster Latvian Television and a number of commercial stations
WPFI score—8,50 (30)

EDUCATION AND HEALTH
Education is compulsory from the age of seven until 16 years, after which there is the option for a further three years of either secondary or vocational study.
Literacy rate—99.8% (2009 est)
Gross enrolment ratio (percentage of relevant age group)—primary 100%; secondary 94%; tertiary 66% (2009 est)
Health expenditure (per capita)—US$750 (2009)
Hospital beds (per 1,000 people)—6.4 (2004–9)
Life expectancy (years)—72.93 (2012 est)
Mortality rate—13.6 (2012 est)
Birth rate—9.97 (2012 est)
Infant mortality rate—8.24 (2012 est)

Lebanon

Al-Jumhuriyah al-Lubnaniyah—Lebanese Republic
Area—10,400 sq. km
Capital—Beirut (Bayrut); population, 1,909,410 (2009 est)
Major city—Sidon, Tripoli (Tarabulus)
Currency—Lebanese pound (L£) of 100 piastres
Population—4,140,289 falling at 0.38% a year (2012 est); Arab (95%), Armenian (4%) (est)
Religion—Muslim 59% (Sunni 27%, Shia 27%, Druze 5%), Christian 41% (Maronite 21%, Greek Orthodox 8%, Greek Catholic 5, other 7%) (est)
Language—Arabic (official), French, English, Armenian
Population density—413 per sq. km (2010)
Urban population—87.2% (2010 est)
Median age (years)—29.8 (2011 est)
National anthem—'Lebanese National Anthem'
National day—22 November (Independence Day)
Death penalty—Retained
CPI score—2.5 (2011)

FINANCIAL OUTLOOK
The conflict in neighboring Syria has not taken as large a toll as might have been expected on the Lebanese economy, which expanded by just 0.8% in 2012, down from 1.8% in 2011, according to the Institute of International Finance. The IIF said the decline had rather been mainly caused by internal tensions adversely affecting investment, tourism, exports, and foreign direct investment. In a separate report published in March 2013, Deutsche Bank forecast that the economy would grow by 2.8% in 2013, compared with an average of 5% per year from 2000 to 2010. The central bank's foreign currency reserves, estimated at about US$35 billion, provide a cushion to external imbalances, and the country's banking sector, which holds the majority of the state's public debt, remains well capitalized, according to the bank. The high public debt of about US$56 billion, accounting for 135% of GDP, weighs on growth.

CLIMATE AND TERRAIN
A narrow plain along the Mediterranean Sea coast is backed by the Lebanon Mountains, along which the Anti-Lebanon range runs parallel, forming the border with Syria. Between the two ranges lies the fertile Bekaa valley, the northern extremity of Africa's Great Rift Valley. Elevations range from 3,088m (Qurnat as Sawda') to om (Mediterranean Sea). The climate is Mediterranean, although the mountains usually receive snow in winter. Average temperatures in Beirut are 12°C in January and 26°C in July and August.

HISTORY AND POLITICS

The constitution dates from 1926 but has been heavily amended, most significantly in 1943, when the National Covenant set out the division of power between the religious communities, and in 1990 to incorporate the provisions of the Ta'if accord. By convention, the presidency is held by a Maronite Christian, the prime minister is a Sunni Muslim and the speaker is a Shia Muslim.

The president is elected by the legislature for a six-year term, which is not renewable. The unicameral National Assembly has 128 members, directly elected for a four-year term; seats are divided equally between Christians and Muslims, whose quotas are subdivided by confession according to the distribution formalised in the 2008 election law. The prime minister is appointed by the president following consultation with the legislature.

The failure to agree on a successor to President Emile Lahoud after his term of office ended in November 2007 created a political vacuum that led to a rise in factional violence. After rival political leaders concluded the Doha agreement in May 2008, a neutral candidate, General Michel Suleiman, the head of the armed forces, was elected president. In the 2009 legislative election, the governing anti-Syria '14 March' coalition won 68 seats, the opposition '8 March' bloc won 57 and independents aligned with the '14 March' coalition won three seats. After months of negotiation the '14 March' leader Saad Hariri formed a national unity government which took office in November 2009. This government collapsed in January 2011 with the withdrawal of pro-Syria parties, and although Najib Mikati was elected prime minister-designate later that month, it took him until June to form a new coalition government; this comprised 18 ministers nominated by Hezbollah and its allies, and 11 nominated by either the president, the prime minister or the Druze leader.

HEAD OF STATE

President, Gen. Michel Suleiman, *elected* 25 May 2008, *sworn in* 26 May 2008

SELECTED GOVERNMENT MEMBERS *as at July 2012*

Prime Minister, Mohammad Najib Mikati
Deputy Prime Minister, Samir Mokbel
Finance, Mohammad Safadi
Foreign Affairs, Adnan Mansour

EMBASSY OF LEBANON

21 Palace Gardens Mews, London W8 4RA
T 020-7727 6696
E info@lebaneseembassy.org.uk
W www.lebaneseembassy.org.uk
Ambassador Extraordinary and Plenipotentiary, HE Inaam Osseiran, *apptd* 2007

BRITISH EMBASSY

PO Box 11-471, Armies Street, Zkak al-Blat, Serail Hill, Beirut Centre-Ville, Beirut
T (+961) (1) 960 800
W ukinlebanon.fco.gov.uk
Ambassador Extraordinary and Plenipotentiary, HE Tom Fletcher, CMG, *apptd* 2011

DEFENCE

All aged 16–49, 2010 est	*Males*	*Females*
Available for military service	1,081,016	1,115,349
Fit for military service	920,825	941,806

Military expenditure—US$1,657m (2011)

ECONOMY AND TRADE

The civil war seriously damaged Lebanon's economy and infrastructure, as well as its role as an entrepôt and financial services centre for the region. Reconstruction was almost complete when the Israeli attacks in 2006 caused an estimated US$3.6bn (£2.1bn) of infrastructure damage. Recovery was hindered by internal instability, which also postponed the introduction of the economic reforms that were a condition of international funding for reconstruction. Economic growth began anew in 2008, though it was slowed by the collapse of the government in early 2011.

The service sector contributes 79.7% of GDP, largely through banking and tourism, which are the two main economic activities. Industry accounts for 15.9%, through food processing, wine production and the manufacture of jewellery, cement, textiles, mineral and chemical products, timber and furniture, oil refining and metal fabrication. Agriculture contributes 4.5% of GDP, producing fruit, vegetables, tobacco and livestock.

The main export markets are Switzerland, the UAE, Saudi Arabia and Syria, while imports come mainly from the USA, the EU, China and Turkey. Principal exports include jewellery, base metals, chemicals, consumer goods, fruit, vegetables, tobacco and construction materials. The main imports are petroleum products, cars, medicines, clothing, meat, livestock and consumer goods.

GNI—US$39,051m; US$8,880 per capita (2010)
Annual average growth of GDP—1.5% (2011 est)
Inflation rate—5.2% (2011 est)
Unemployment—9.2% (2007 est)
Total external debt—US$35,060m (2011 est)
Imports—US$18,500m (2010)
Exports—US$5,000m (2010)

BALANCE OF PAYMENTS

Trade—US$13,500m deficit (2010)
Current Account—US$4,284m deficit (2010)

Trade with UK	*2010*	*2011*
Imports from UK	£398,796,927	£409,300,768
Exports to UK	£33,388,595	£41,929,205

COMMUNICATIONS

Airports and waterways—There are seven airports and airfields, including the international airport at Beirut. The principal seaports are Beirut and Tripoli
Roadways and railways—There are 6,970km of roads and 401km of railways
Telecommunications—887,800 fixed lines and 2.87 million mobile subscriptions (2010); there were 1 million internet users in 2009
Internet code and IDD—lb; 961 (from UK), 44 (to UK)
Major broadcasters—Tele-Liban is the state-run broadcaster and competes with several commercial stations, including pro-Hezbollah al-Manar TV and the market-leading Lebanese Broadcasting Corporation and Future TV
Press—There are a number of daily newspapers, including French- and English-language publications
WPFI score—20,50 (78)

EDUCATION AND HEALTH

There are nine years of compulsory education.
Literacy rate—89.6% (2008 est)
Gross enrolment ratio (percentage of relevant age group)—primary 105%; secondary 81%; tertiary 54% (2010 est)

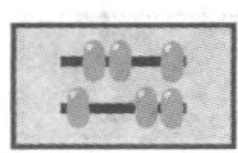

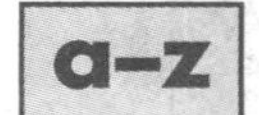

Health expenditure (per capita)—US$663 (2009)
Hospital beds (per 1,000 people)—3.5 (2004–9)
Life expectancy (years)—75.23 (2012 est)
Mortality rate—6.63 (2012 est)
Birth rate—14.92 (2012 est)
Infant mortality rate—15.32 (2012 est)

Libya

Al-Jumahiriyah al-Arabiyah al-Libiyah ash Shabiyah al-Ishtirakiyah al-Uzma—Great Socialist People's Libyan Arab Jamahiriya
Area—1,759,540 sq. km
Capital—Tripoli (Tarabulus); population, 1,095,110 (2009 est)
Major cities—al-Hums, az-Zawiyah, Benghazi, Misratah, Tarhunah, Zuwarah
Currency—Libyan dinar (LD) of 1,000 dirhams
Population—6,733,620 rising at 2% a year (2012 est); Arab–Berber (97%), with some Tuareg in the south-west
Religion—Sunni Muslim 97%, Christian (Coptic 1%) (est)
Language—Arabic (official), Italian, English
Population density—4 per sq. km (2010)
Urban population—77.9% (2010 est)
Median age (years)—24.5 (2011 est)
National day—1 September (Revolution Day)
Death penalty—Retained
CPI score—2.0 (2011)

FINANCIAL OUTLOOK

The Libyan economy doubled in size in 2012, according to an IMF report published in March 2013, as the economy continued its recovery from the 2011 revolution, which ousted the dictatorial regime of Muammar Gaddafi. The financial situation began to normalize after most of the UN sanctions that had frozen Libya's foreign assets were lifted on December 16, 2011, allowing the central bank to provide foreign-exchange liquidity to banks, and help normalize commercial banking operations. Libya's economy is forecast to grow about 16.7% in 2013, after surging 121.9% in 2012, the IMF reported. In 2011, Libya's had economy contracted by about 60%. The IMF added that the hydrocarbon sector should see a full recovery in production in 2013, while the recovery in the non-hydrocarbon sector would be completed in 2014. However, according to a report on ABC News published in March 2013, unemployment, officially at 15%, is estimated by some analysts to be as high as 50%.

CLIMATE AND TERRAIN

Apart from hills on the north-west and north-east coasts and in the far south, the country is made up of plains and plateaux, with some depressions; 90% is desert or semi-desert. Elevation extremes range from 2,267m (Bikku Bitti) to −47m (Sabkhat Ghuzayyil). The climate is Mediterranean on the coast, and arid desert in the interior. Average temperatures in Tripoli range from 12°C in January to 27°C in July and August.

HISTORY AND POLITICS

Following the overthrow of the 'Leader of the Revolution', Col. Muammar al-Gaddafi, the National Transitional Council (NTC) announced its own draft constitution in August 2011. The Constitutional Declaration sets out plans for a 'political democratic regime to be based upon the political multitude and multi-party system'. The new draft constitution guarantees the rights of minority groups and sets out steps towards the appointment of an electoral commission and a Public National Conference (PNC) of 200 elected members. The PNC is charged with appointing the prime minister, who nominates an interim government.

HEAD OF STATE
Chair of the National Transitional Council, Mustafa Abdel Jalil

SELECTED GOVERNMENT MEMBERS *as at July 2012*
Prime Minister, Abdurrahim al-Keib
First Deputy Prime Minister, Mustafa abu Shagour
Second Deputy Prime Minister, Omar Abdallah Abdelkarim
Third Deputy Prime Minister, Haramain Mohammad al-Haramain
Economy, Ahmed Salim al-Koshli

EMBASSY OF LIBYA
61–62 Ennismore Gardens, London SW7 1NH
T 020-7589 6120
W www.libyan-embassy.co.uk
Ambassador Extraordinary and Plenipotentiary, Vacant

BRITISH EMBASSY
24th Floor, Tripoli Towers, Tripoli
T (+218) (21) 335 1084
E tripoli.press@fco.gov.uk
W ukinlibya.fco.gov.uk
Ambassador Extraordinary and Plenipotentiary, HE Hon. Dominic Asquith, CMG, *apptd* 2011

DEFENCE

All aged 16–49, 2010 est	Males	Females
Available for military service	1,775,078	1,714,194
Fit for military service	1,511,144	1,458,934

Military expenditure—US$1,116m (2008 est)*
Conscription duration—12 to 24 months (selective)
* Does not include spending on paramilitary forces

ECONOMY AND TRADE

Normalisation of international relations stimulated economic liberalisation and the start of a slow transition towards a more market-orientated economy, as well as attracting more foreign direct investment.

The state-controlled oil industry dominates the economy, accounting for 95% of export earnings and about 65% of GDP and 80% of government revenue; as the population is small, this gives the country a relatively high per capita GDP, although the benefits are not felt by much of the population. The considerable oil and natural gas reserves are relatively undeveloped, and further exploration has been licensed in recent years in auctions open to foreign companies. Attempts to diversify the economy have led to expansion of the manufacturing and construction sectors, which together account for more than 50% of GDP, to include the production of petrochemicals, iron, steel and aluminium in addition to food processing. Owing to the terrain and climate, agriculture is a small sector, contributing only 3.6% of GDP.

The main trading partners are Italy, Germany, other EU countries and China. Principal exports are crude oil, refined petroleum products, natural gas and chemicals. The main imports are machinery, semi-finished goods, food, transport equipment and consumer products.

GNI—US$61,985m; US$12,320 per capita (2009)
Annual average growth of GDP—4.2% (2010 est)
Inflation rate—6.1% (2011 est)
Population below poverty line—7.4% (2005 est)
Unemployment—30% (2004 est)
Total external debt—US$5,285m (2011 est)
Imports—US$10,500m (2010)
Exports—US$46,100m (2010)

BALANCE OF PAYMENTS
Trade—US$35,600m surplus (2010)
Current Account—US$10,266m surplus (2010)

Trade with UK	2010	2011
Imports from UK	£377,241,478	£86,398,079
Exports to UK	£1,253,812,362	£418,620,786

COMMUNICATIONS
Airports—There are 137 airports and airfields; the principal airports are at Tripoli, Benghazi and Sebha
Waterways—The main seaports are Benghazi, Tripoli and Tubruq
Roadways and railways—There are 100,024km of roads; the coastal road running from the Tunisian frontier through Tripoli, Benghazi and Tubruq to the Egyptian border serves the main population centres; there are no railways
Telecommunications—1.23 million fixed lines and 10.9 million mobile subscriptions (2010); there were 353,900 internet users in 2009
Internet code and IDD—ly; 218 (from UK), 44 (to UK)
Major broadcasters—Libyan Radio and TV is the successor to the Gaddafi-era state broadcaster; it was launched in April 2011 following the uprising
Press—The press has undergone a radical shift since the removal of Gaddafi; Benghazi has emerged as a publishing hub, distributing dailies such as *February* and *New Quryna*
WPFI score—63,50 (160)

EDUCATION AND HEALTH
There are six years of primary education and six of secondary, nine of which are compulsory.
Literacy rate—88.9% (2009 est)
Health expenditure (per capita)—US$417 (2009)
Hospital beds (per 1,000 people)—3.7 (2004–9)
Life expectancy (years)—77.83 (2012 est)
Mortality rate—3.41 (2012 est)
Birth rate—23.47 (2012 est)
Infant mortality rate—19.34 (2012 est)

Liechtenstein

Fürstentum Liechtenstein—Principality of Liechtenstein
Area—160 sq. km
Capital—Vaduz; population, 5,151 (2009 est)
Major town—Schaan
Currency—Swiss franc of 100 rappen (or centimes)
Population—36,713 rising at 0.79% a year (2012 est)
Religion—Christian (Roman Catholic 78%, Protestant 8%, Orthodox 1%), Muslim 5% (2000)
Language—German (official), Alemannic (dialect)
Population density—225 per sq. km (2010)
Median age (years)—41.8 (2011 est)
National anthem—'Oben am Jungen Rhein' ['High Above the Young Rhine']
National day—15 August (Feast of the Assumption)
Life expectancy (years)—81.5 (2012 est)
Mortality rate—6.78 (2012 est)
Birth rate—10.76 (2012 est)
Infant mortality rate—4.39 (2012 est)
Death penalty—Abolished for all crimes (since 1987)
Gross enrolment ratio (percentage of relevant age group)—primary 106%; secondary 70%; tertiary 34% (2009 est)

FINANCIAL OUTLOOK
The Liechtenstein government introduced changes to the principality's tax law in November 2012, following a shortfall announced in its planned budget for 2013. The government had already introduced two other fiscal measures aimed at narrowing the fiscal deficit but they had proved insufficient, so tax rises were the only way forward, it said. After discussions with industry, the government went ahead and adopted a proposal for increased tax on high earners. The tiny principality's economy expanded by 8.7% in 2010, and has averaged 3.91% for the last 40 years. Although the country is famous as a financial center and as an onshore tax haven—a status that is being regularized through a series of bilateral information-sharing agreements with advanced economies interested in pursuing tax avoiders—the country's main contributor to GDP is its manufacturing sector. This accounts for some 36% of GDP, with financial services in second position with 33%, followed by general services, which contributes a further 25%.

CLIMATE AND TERRAIN
Liechtenstein is a small, mountainous landlocked principality in the Alps. The land falls in the west, in the valley of the river Rhine, which forms the western border. Elevation extremes range from 2,599m (Grauspitz) to 430m (Ruggeller Riet). The climate is continental, with heavy snowfall in winter; average temperatures in the lowlands range from 4°C in January to 20°C in July.

HISTORY AND POLITICS
Although there was a sovereign state within the present boundaries from the 14th century, the present state of Liechtenstein was formed from the lordships of Schellenberg and Vaduz in 1719. Part of the Holy Roman Empire, the principality became a member of the Confederation of the Rhine that succeeded the Empire in 1806, and then of the German Confederation from 1815 until 1866. It was the only German principality to remain outside the German Empire

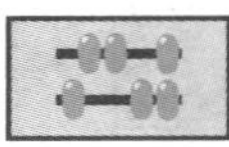

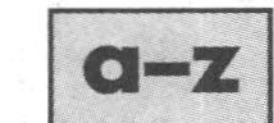

formed in 1871. The country abolished its armed forces and declared permanent neutrality in 1868. This was maintained in world wars.

Economic decline in the years following the First World War led Liechtenstein to adopt the Swiss currency in 1921 and to enter into a Swiss customs union in 1923. The country became extremely prosperous as an international finance centre after the Second World War. Since 2000 it has tightened its laws to prevent money laundering, and since 2008 it has started to meet international financial transparency standards.

Governments in the 20th and 21st centuries have been formed by the two main parties, the northern-based Progressive Citizens' Party (FBP) and the southern-based Fatherland Union (VU). Usually they have formed a coalition government, although the FBP formed a single-party government from 2001 to 2005. However, the government's power is limited by that of the monarchy, whose powers over the government and judiciary were increased by a 2003 referendum. Prince Hans Adam II remains head of state but in 2004 he handed over day-to-day responsibility for government to his son, Prince Alois.

The VU won an overall majority in the 2009 election. The coalition government formed with the FBP in 2005 continued, although the premiership passed from the FBP to the VU's Klaus Tschütscher.

Under the 1921 constitution, Liechtenstein is a constitutional monarchy, with the hereditary prince as head of state. The unicameral legislature, the *Landtag*, has 25 members directly elected for a four-year term. The cabinet is appointed by the prince on the advice of the *Landtag* and consists of the head of government and four ministers.

HEAD OF STATE

HSH The Prince of Liechtenstein, Hans Adam II, *born* 14 February 1945, *succeeded* 13 November 1989

Heir, HSH Prince Alois, *born* 11 June 1968

SELECTED GOVERNMENT MEMBERS *as at June 2012*

Head of Government, Finance, Klaus Tschütscher

Deputy Head of Government, Economy, Martin Meyer

Foreign Affairs, Aurelia Frick

Home Affairs, Hugo Quaderer

BRITISH AMBASSADOR

HE Sarah Gillett, CMG, MVO, resident at Bern, Switzerland

ECONOMY AND TRADE

Liechtenstein has a prosperous, highly industrialised and diversified economy. Its mainstay is the financial services sector, which, with other service industries such as tourism, employs over half of the workforce. A light industrial base produces electronics, metal manufactures, dental products, ceramics, pharmaceuticals, food products, precision instruments and optical instruments, and employs 41.3% of the workforce. Over half the workforce commutes daily from Austria, Switzerland and Germany.

Liechtenstein became a member of the European Free Trade Association in 1991, and of the European Economic Area in 1995. Most of its trade is with EU countries and Switzerland. The principal exports are its industrial products. The main imports are agricultural products, industrial raw materials, energy, machinery, metal goods, textiles, foodstuffs and vehicles.

GNI—US$4,816m; US$137,070 per capita (2009)

Annual average growth of GDP—1.8% (2008 est)

Inflation rate—0.7% (2010)

Unemployment—2.8% (2009)

Trade with UK	*2010*	*2011*
Imports from UK	£24,297,711	£13,783,856
Exports to UK	£13,139,570	£8,005,362

COMMUNICATIONS

Transport—Liechtenstein has no airports and only 380km of roads, 28km of waterways, and 9km of rail track which is part of the Austrian system connecting Austria and Switzerland

Telecommunications—19,600 fixed lines and 35,500 mobile subscriptions (2010); there were 23,000 internet users in 2009

Internet code and IDD—li; 423 (from UK), 44 (to UK)

Media—The country has a very small media sector; its citizens rely on foreign broadcasters for most television and radio services. News publications include *Liechtensteiner Vaterland* and *Liechtensteiner Volksblatt*

Lithuania

Lietuvos Respublika—Republic of Lithuania

Area—65,300 sq. km

Capital—Vilnius; population, 545,970 (2009 est)

Major cities—Kaunas, Klaipeda

Currency—Litas of 100 centas, pegged to the euro

Population—3,525,761 falling at 0.28% a year (2012 est); Lithuanian (84%), Polish (6.1%), Russian (4.9%), Belarusian (1.1%) (2009 est)

Religion—Christian (Roman Catholic 80%, Orthodox 5%, Lutheran 1%) (est)

Language—Lithuanian (official), Russian, Polish

Population density—53 per sq. km (2010)

Urban population—67.2% (2010 est)

Median age (years)—40.1 (2011 est)

National anthem—'Tautiska Giesme' ['National Song']

National day—16 February (Independence Day)

Death penalty—Abolished for all crimes (since 1998)

CPI score—4.8 (2011)

FINANCIAL OUTLOOK

In its latest country report on Lithuania, the IMF says that the country has come a long way in reducing the imbalances that were at the root of the 2008 crisis, thanks to determined policy implementation. As a result, the broad-based economic recovery of the Lithuanian economy that began in 2011 continued through 2012, albeit at a much slower pace. However, the IMF warned that external risks pose challenges to the recovery. Unemployment is high, and remaining vulnerabilities still need to be fully addressed. Key policy priorities for the Lithuanian government are the need to complete fiscal consolidation, while continuing to strengthen the resilience of the banking system. Structural reforms need to be put in place to boost potential growth and promote sustainable job creation. Inflation in 2012 edged up to 4%, mostly on the back of rising food and energy prices. In 2011, Lithuania achieved GDP growth of nearly 6%. This fell back to 2.75% in 2012, but headline inflation also dropped to around 3%. The IMF expected the Lithuanian fiscal deficit to be an acceptable 3% for 2012, and said

that this should be brought down to 2% for 2013, with the aim of running a balanced budget in 2015.

CLIMATE AND TERRAIN

Lithuania is a low-lying country with low hills in the west and south-east. It contains around 6,000 lakes and lagoons—over 2,800 of them sizeable—mostly lying in the east, although the Courland lagoon on the west coast is a major feature. Elevation extremes range from 294m (Aukstojas Hill) to 0m (Baltic Sea). The climate is mainly continental, and average temperatures range from −11°C in January to 23°C in July.

HISTORY AND POLITICS

Lithuania became a nation in the 13th century. It remained pagan for far longer than the rest of Europe, only becoming fully Christian in the 15th century when the Samogitians and the Aukstaitiai, the two main ethnic groups in the region, were converted. In the 14th century, a grand duchy was formed that stretched from the Baltic to the Black Sea and eastwards almost as far as Moscow. It confederated with Poland in the 16th century, before coming under Russian rule in 1795. The country joined Poland in rebelling against Russian domination twice in the 19th century.

Occupied by Germany during the First World War, Lithuania declared its independence in 1918 and successfully defended its autonomy against the Bolsheviks in 1918–19. However, the province and city of Vilnius were occupied by the newly independent Poland from 1920 until 1939. The USSR invaded and annexed Lithuania in 1940, but the country revolted in 1941 and briefly established its own government before being invaded and occupied by the Germans in their 1941 offensive against the USSR. Around 210,000 Lithuanians, mainly Jews, were killed during the German occupation. Soviet troops ousted the Germans in 1944 and re-established Soviet control, against which Lithuanians carried on a guerrilla war until 1952.

Growing nationalist sentiment led to the formation of the pro-democracy *Sajudis* ('The Movement') in 1988 to campaign for greater autonomy. A unilateral declaration of independence in 1990 was blocked by the USSR but following the failed coup in Moscow in 1991, Lithuania declared its independence a second time, and this was internationally recognised. The last Russian troops left the country in 1993. Lithuania joined NATO and the EU in 2004.

In the 2008 legislative elections, the Homeland Union–Lithuanian Christian Democrats became the largest party but without a majority. Its leader, Andrius Kubilius, became prime minister at the head of a four-party coalition government. The 2009 presidential election was won by Dalia Grybauskaite, who became the country's first female president. The next legislative election is due in October 2012.

Under the 1992 constitution, the head of state is a president, who is directly elected for a five-year term, renewable once. The unicameral *Seimas* has 141 members who are directly elected for a four-year term; 71 members are elected in first-past-the-post constituencies and 70 by proportional representation. The prime minister is appointed by the president with the approval of the *Seimas*, and ministers are appointed upon the recommendation of the prime minister.

HEAD OF STATE

President, Dalia Grybauskaite, *elected* 17 May 2009, *sworn in* 12 July 2009

SELECTED GOVERNMENT MEMBERS *as at July 2012*

Prime Minister, Andrius Kubilius
Defence, Rasa Jukneviciene
Foreign Affairs, Audronius Azubalis
Interior, Arturas Melianas

EMBASSY OF THE REPUBLIC OF LITHUANIA

Lithuania House, 2 Bessborough Gardens SW1V 2JE
T 020-7592 2840
E amb.uk@urm.lt
W www.lithuanianembassy.co.uk
Ambassador Extraordinary and Plenipotentiary, HE Oskaras Jusys, *apptd* 2009

BRITISH EMBASSY

2 Antakalnio, Vilnius 10308
T (+370) (5) 246 2900
W ukinlithuania.fco.gov.uk
Ambassador Extraordinary and Plenipotentiary, HE David Hunt, *apptd* 2011

DEFENCE

All aged 16–49, 2010 est	*Males*	*Females*
Available for military service	890,074	875,780
Fit for military service	669,111	724,803

Military expenditure—US$405m (2011)
Conscription duration—12 months

ECONOMY AND TRADE

Lithuania's transition to a market economy is nearly complete, with the private sector now accounting for about 80% GDP. The transition initially caused a recession, but the economy recovered and grew steadily from 2004 to 2008 before being plunged into a deep recession by the global economic downturn. Drastic government cuts in public spending and the halving of imports in 2009 restored the current account deficit, which had soared to 15% of GDP in 2007–8, to a surplus. GDP grew 1.3% in 2010 before jumping to 5.8% in 2011, making the country one of the fastest growing economies in the EU. Despite high unemployment, the government is working vigorously to develop foreign investment and export markets, and has recently began to reform its energy networks to reduce its dependence on Russian output.

The economy is diverse, and industries include metal-cutting machine tools, electric motors, domestic appliances, oil refining, shipbuilding, furniture making, textiles and amber extraction and jewellery making. Industry contributes 28% to GDP, services 68.8% and agriculture3.2%.

The main trading partners are Russia and other EU countries. Principal exports are mineral products, machinery and equipment, chemicals, textiles, foodstuffs and plastics. The main imports are mineral products, machinery, transport equipment, chemicals, textiles, clothing and metals.

GNI—US$35,686m; US$11,390 per capita (2010)
Annual average growth of GDP—6% (2011 est)
Inflation rate—4% (2011 est)
Population below poverty line—4% (2008)
Unemployment—15.6% (2011 est)
Total external debt—US$27,670m (2011 est)
Imports—US$23,378m (2010)
Exports—US$20,814m (2010)

BALANCE OF PAYMENTS

Trade—US$2,564m deficit (2010)
Current Account—US$667m surplus (2010)

  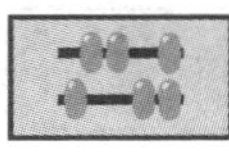      

Trade with UK	2010	2011
Imports from UK	£221,071,227	£264,005,698
Exports to UK	£548,490,845	£557,891,109

COMMUNICATIONS

Airports and waterways—The 81 airports and airfields include major airports at Vilnius, Kaunas and Palanga; the main seaport is at Klaipeda

Roadways and railways—There are 81,030km of roads, and a railway system of 1,767km linking the major towns with Vilnius and Klaipeda

Telecommunications—733,700 fixed lines and 4.89 million mobile subscriptions (2010); there were 1.96 million internet users in 2009

Internet code and IDD—lt; 370 (from UK), 44 (to UK)

Media—Lithuanian National Radio and Television operates several networks, in competition with a number of thriving commercial stations. There are ten major national newspapers available, in Lithuanian, Russian, Polish and English

WPFI score—2,50 (11)

EDUCATION AND HEALTH

Education is free and compulsory from seven to 16 years, with the system comprising primary school (four years), lower secondary school (six years) and upper secondary education (two years).

Literacy rate—99.7% (2009 est)

Gross enrolment ratio (percentage of relevant age group)—primary 97%; secondary 98%; tertiary 77% (2009 est)

Health expenditure (per capita)—US$730 (2009)

Hospital beds (per 1,000 people)—6.8 (2004–9)

Life expectancy (years)—75.55 (2012 est)

Mortality rate—11.4 (2012 est)

Birth rate—9.34 (2012 est)

Infant mortality rate—6.18 (2012 est)

Luxembourg

Groussherzogtom Lëtzebuerg/Grand-Duché de Luxembourg/ Großherzogtum Luxembourg—Grand Duchy of Luxembourg

Area—2,586 sq. km

Capital—Luxembourg; population, 89,814 (2009 est)

Major towns—Esch-sur-Alzette, Dudelange

Currency—Euro (€) of 100 cents

Population—509,074 rising at 1.13% a year (2012 est); Luxembourger (63.1%), Portuguese (13.3%), French (4.5%), Italian (4.3%), German (2.3%), other EU 7.3% (2000)

Religion—Christian (Roman Catholic 90%, Orthodox 1%), Muslim 2% (est)

Language—Luxembourgish, French, German (all official)

Population density—195 per sq. km (2010)

Urban population—82.2% (2010 est)

Median age (years)—39.4 (2011 est)

National anthem—'Ons Heemecht' ['Our Homeland']

National day—23 June (official birthday of Grand Duchess Charlotte)

Life expectancy (years)—79.75 (2012 est)

Mortality rate—8.5 (2012 est)

Birth rate—11.7 (2012 est)

Infant mortality rate—4.39 (2012 est)

Death penalty—Abolished for all crimes (since 1979)

CPI score—8.5 (2011)

Military expenditure—US$294m (2007)

Health expenditure (per capita)—US$8,183 (2009)

Gross enrolment ratio (percentage of relevant age group)—primary 100%; secondary 98%; tertiary 11% (2008 est)

FINANCIAL OUTLOOK

Luxembourg has recovered relatively well from the 2008 crash, and its financial sector has remained stable despite the demise of Dexia, which had a major subsidiary in Luxembourg. The general double-dip recession experienced in the European Union in mid-2012 turned growth flat as far as Luxembourg's economy was concerned. Weakened external demand from EU trading partners, itself a consequence of eurozone fiscal consolidation, held back exports in the second half of 2012, and what the IMF calls "lingering uncertainties" weighed on domestic demand. Luxembourg has a massive investment fund industry, and while funds saw large outflows in the aftermath of the 2008 crash, the sector now has assets under management that are larger than in pre-crisis times. However, the IMF warns that an upsurge in eurozone turbulence could see massive outflows from Luxembourg's investment fund sector. Preserving Luxembourg's hallmark stability and its business-friendly climate will require continued efforts from the government to limit financial sector vulnerabilities, ensure fiscal sustainability, and promote growth. Growth in jobs will require labor market reforms to address disincentives to work, as well as product market reforms to improve productivity. GDP growth in 2012 was virtually flat at 0.2%, and is only expected to reach 0.7% in 2013. Inflation averaged 2.5% in 2012, and is set to fall slightly to 2.3% through 2013.

CLIMATE AND TERRAIN

Luxembourg has the forested plateau of the Ardennes in the north, forming part of the Natural Germano-Luxembourg Park which extends east into Germany. The south of the country is mainly fertile farmland, and in the east is the wine-growing region of the Moselle valley. Elevation extremes range from 559m (Buurgplaatz) to 133m (Moselle river). The climate is modified continental, and average temperatures in Luxembourg city range from 1°C in January to 18°C in July.

HISTORY AND POLITICS

The area was part of the Roman Empire and then became part of the Frankish Empire in the fifth century AD. It became autonomous within the Holy Roman Empire under Siegfried, Count of Ardennes, and was given the status of a duchy in 1354. Controlled by a succession of European powers after 1437 (when the House of Luxembourg died out), it was made a grand duchy under Dutch rule after the Napoleonic wars. Much of Luxembourg joined the Belgians in their revolt against the Netherlands in 1830; in 1838 the western, French-speaking region was assigned to Belgium, and the remainder became an independent grand duchy in 1839. The Treaty of London in 1867 confirmed its independence and neutrality. Occupation by Germany in both world wars prompted Luxembourg to give up its neutrality and it was a founding member of NATO in 1949.

  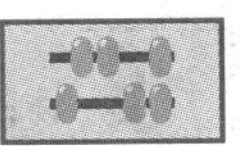      

Luxembourg entered into economic union with Belgium in 1921 and joined the Benelux economic union in 1948. It was a founder member of the EEC in 1958 and joined the eurozone in 1999.

The Christian Social Party (CSV) has held power almost continuously since the First World War, usually as the main partner in coalition governments. It remained the largest party in the legislature after the 2009 election, but without an overall majority. A new coalition government was formed under the leadership of Jean-Claude Juncker of the CSV, who has been prime minister since 1995.

Under the 1868 constitution, the head of state is a hereditary grand duke, whose role is now largely ceremonial. The unicameral legislature, the Chamber of Deputies, has 60 members directly elected for a five-year term. There is also a Council of State, which has 21 members nominated by the grand duke; this acts as the supreme administrative tribunal and has some legislative functions. The prime minister is appointed by the grand duke on the basis of the election results and appoints the cabinet.

HEAD OF STATE
HRH The Grand Duke of Luxembourg, Grand Duke Henri, *born* 16 April 1955;*succeeded* 7 October 2000
Heir, HRH Prince Guillaume, *born* 11 November 1981

SELECTED GOVERNMENT MEMBERS *as at July 2012*
Prime Minister, Jean-Claude Juncker
Deputy Prime Minister, Foreign Affairs, Jean Asselborn
Interior, Jean-Marie Halsdorf
Finance, Luc Frieden

EMBASSY OF LUXEMBOURG
27 Wilton Crescent, London SW1X 8SD
T 020-7235 6961
E londres.amb@mae.etat.lu
W londres.mae.lu
Ambassador Extraordinary and Plenipotentiary, HE Alphonse Berns, *apptd* 2011

BRITISH EMBASSY
5 Boulevard Joseph II, L-1840, Luxembourg
T (+352) 229 864
W ukinluxembourg.fco.gov.uk
Ambassador Extraordinary and Plenipotentiary, HE Hon. Alice Walpole, *apptd* 2011

ECONOMY AND TRADE
The economy is stable, with steady growth, low unemployment and low inflation providing an exceptionally high standard of living. The government offset the contraction in the economy in 2008–9 with economic stimulus measures, which led to a budget deficit in 2009 but growth resumed in 2010. Banking and financial services are the dominant sector, contributing 28% of GDP. Steel production used to dominate the industrial sector, but this has diversified to include IT, telecommunications, freight transport, food processing, chemicals, metal products and engineering. Tourism is also important. The small agricultural sector consists mainly of family-owned farms. Services account for 80.6% of GDP, industry for 17,2% and agriculture for 2.2%. Around 60% of the workforce commutes daily from France, Belgium and Germany.

The main trading partners are other EU countries and China. Principal exports are the products of industrial activities. The main imports are minerals, metals, foodstuffs and quality consumer goods.

GNI—US$37,925m; US$77,160 per capita (2010)
Annual average growth of GDP—3.6% (2011 est)
Inflation rate—3.4% (2011 est)
Unemployment—6% (2011 est)
Total external debt—US$2,146,000m (2011 est)
Imports—US$20,536m (2010)
Exports—US$13,927m (2010)

BALANCE OF PAYMENTS
Trade—US$6,608m deficit (2010)
Current Account—US$4,319m surplus (2010)

Trade with UK	2010	2011
Imports from UK	£235,072,289	£271,013,105
Exports to UK	£567,886,054	£897,278,117

COMMUNICATIONS
Transportation—Luxembourg has one airport. There are 5,227km of roads (including 147km of motorways), and 275km of railways. The Moselle river provides 37km of navigable waterway
Telecommunications—272,400 fixed lines and 727,000 mobile subscriptions (2010); there were 424,500 internet users in 2009
Internet code and IDD—lu; 352 (from UK) 44 (to UK)
Media—Luxembourg is the headquarters of the Société Européenne des Satellites (SES), which operates Europe's largest satellite operation; RTL Tele Letzebuerg is the country's principal domestic network and popular national dailies include *Luxemburger Wort* and *Tageblatt*
WPFI score—4,00 (14)

Malaysia

Area—329,847 sq. km
Capital—Kuala Lumpur; population, 1,493,500 (2009 est); Putrajaya is the administrative capital
Major cities—Ampang Jaya, Ipoh, Johor Bahru, Klang, Kota Kinabalu, Kuching, Petaling Jaya, Shah Alam, Kuantan
Currency—Malaysian ringgit (RM) of 100 sen; also known as Malaysian dollar
Population—29,179,952 rising at 1.54% a year (2012 est); Malay (50.4%), Chinese (23.7%), indigenous (11%), Indian (7.1%) (2004 est)
Religion—Muslim 60% (predominantly Shafi'i, a school of Sunni Islam), Buddhist 19%, Christian 9%, Hindu 6%, Chinese traditional religions 3% (est)
Language—Bahasa Malaysia (Malay) (official), English, Cantonese, Mandarin, Tamil, Telugu, Malayalam, Punjabi, Thai, Iban, Kadazan
Population density—86 per sq. km (2010)
Urban population—72.2% (2010 est)
Median age (years)—26.8 (2011 est)
National anthem—'Negaraku' ['My Country']

 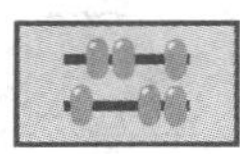      

National day—31 August (Independence Day)
Death penalty—Retained
CPI score—4.3 (2011)

FINANCIAL OUTLOOK

The Malaysian economy grew by 5.6% in 2012 with growth accelerating in the final months of the year, up from 5.1% in 2011. GDP expanded by 6.4% in the final quarter of 2012, the country's fastest quarterly pace since Q2 2010. Domestic demand was the main driver in Q4 2012, expanding by 7.5% and with gross fixed capital formation growing by 15%. The central bank expects domestic demand to continue to drive activity in 2013. Higher wages and bonuses for civil servants, along with cash handouts to thousands of low-income earners ahead of the national elections due in 2013, have helped spur consumption. Heavy spending to develop the country's infrastructure, under the government's Economic Transformation Program, has also supported public investment. Malaysia's unemployment rate rose to 3.3% in December 2012, from 2.9% in the November 2012, according to the Department of Statistics.

CLIMATE AND TERRAIN

Malaysia comprises the 11 states of peninsular Malaya plus the states of Sabah and Sarawak on the island of Borneo. The Malay peninsula, which extends from the isthmus of Kra to the Singapore Strait, is a plain with two highland areas in the north. The Malaysian part of Borneo is mostly high plateau, rising to mountains in western Sabah and eastern Sarawak, while Sarawak also has lower-lying land along the coast and in the Rajang valley; both states are densely forested. Elevation extremes range from 4,100m (Gunung Kinabalu, Sabah)to 0m (Indian Ocean). The climate is tropical, experiencing the south-west monsoon from May to September and the north-east monsoon from November to March. Temperatures in Kuala Lumpur range between 22°C and 33°C all year round.

HISTORY AND POLITICS

The federal *Parlimen* has two houses, the House of Representatives and the senate. The former is the lower house and has 222 members, directly elected for a five-year term. The senate has 70 members who serve a three-year term; the legislative assembly of each state elects two members, and 44 are nominated by the head of state.

Each of the 13 states has its own constitution, which must not be inconsistent with the federal constitution. The Malay rulers are either chosen or succeed to their position in accordance with the custom of their particular state; in other states of Malaysia, choice of the head of state is at the discretion of the *Yang di-Pertuan Agong* after consultation with the chief minister of the state. The ruler or governor acts on the advice of an executive council appointed on the advice of the chief minister and a single-chamber legislative assembly. The legislative assemblies are elected on the same basis as the lower chamber of the federal legislature.

The *Barisan Nasional* coalition won the 2008 legislative election, but with a majority reduced from 198 to 140 seats after a significant swing to the opposition parties. Abdullah Ahmed Badawi, prime minister since 2003, stood down in 2009 and was replaced as leader of UMNO and prime minister by his deputy, Najib Tun Abdul Razak.

The 1957 constitution provides for a federal government and a degree of autonomy for the state governments. The supreme head of state *(Abdul Halim al-Marhum Badlishah)* is elected by the nine hereditary rulers of the peninsular states from among their number and serves a five-year term.

HEAD OF STATE

Supreme Head of State, HM Tuanku Abdul Halim al-Marhum Badlishah, *sworn in* 13 December 2011
Deputy Head of State, HM Sultan Muhammad V

SELECTED GOVERNMENT MEMBERS *as at July 2012*

Prime Minister, Finance, Najib Tun Abdul Razak
Deputy Prime Minister, Muhyiddin bin Mohamed Yasin
Foreign Affairs, Anifah Aman
Defence, Ahmad Zahid Hamidi

MALAYSIAN HIGH COMMISSION

45 Belgrave Square, London SW1X 8QT
T 020-7235 8033
E mwlon@btconnect.com
W www.jimlondon.net
High Commissioner, HE Datuk Zakaria Sulong, *apptd* 2010

BRITISH HIGH COMMISSION

PO Box 11030, 185 Jalan Ampang, 50450 Kuala Lumpur
T (+60) (3) 2170 2200
W ukinmalaysia.fco.gov.uk
High Commissioner, HE Simon Featherstone, *apptd* 2010

DEFENCE

All aged 16–49, 2010 est	Males	Females
Available for military service	7,501,518	7,315,999
Fit for military service	6,247,306	6,175,274

Military expenditure—US$4,223m (2011)

ECONOMY AND TRADE

The economy has grown vigorously since the 1970s, transforming the country into a diversified emerging economy. The government's goal is to achieve developed nation status by 2020. To this end, it has encouraged investment in high technology industries, medical technology and pharmaceuticals, and growth as a regional financial hub, especially for Islamic finance. Growth has largely been driven by export-orientated manufacturing, dependence on which the government aims to reduce.

The agricultural sector produces the raw materials for its highly developed industries. Industrial production includes rubber manufacturing, palm oil processing, pharmaceuticals, medical technology, electronics, tin mining and smelting, and logging and timber processing; in addition, oil is produced in Sabah and Sarawak, and refined in Sarawak. Tourism is a major industry. The services sector contributes 48% of GDP, industry 40% and agriculture 12%.

The main trading partners are China, Singapore, the USA, Japan and other south-east Asian countries. Principal exports are electronic equipment, petroleum and liquefied natural gas, timber and wood products, palm oil, rubber, textiles and chemicals. The main imports are electronics, machinery, petroleum products, plastics, vehicles, iron and steel products, and chemicals.

GNI—US$229,565m; US$7,760 per capita (2010)
Annual average growth of GDP—5.2% (2011 est)
Inflation rate—3.3% (2011 est)
Unemployment—3.1% (2011 est)
Total external debt—US$78,180m (2011 est)
Imports—US$164,734m (2010)
Exports—US$198,800m (2010)

BALANCE OF PAYMENTS

Trade—US$34,067m surplus (2010)
Current Account—US$27,363m surplus (2010)

Trade with UK	2010	2011
Imports from UK	£1,229,730,172	£1,458,816,735
Exports to UK	£1,875,724,207	£1,800,697,821

COMMUNICATIONS

Airports—The main international airports are at Kuala Lumpur, Kota Kinabalu, Kuching and Penang
Waterways—There are six main seaports in peninsular Malaysia, plus Kota Kinabalu (Sabah) and Kuching (Sarawak), and a merchant fleet of 315 ships of more than 1,000 tonnes; there are 7,200km of navigable waterways
Roadways and railways—There are 98,721km of roads and 1,849km of railways
Telecommunications—4.573 million fixed lines and 34.46 million mobile subscriptions (2010); there were 15.36 million internet users in 2009
Internet country code and IDD—my; 60 (from UK), 44 (to UK)
Major broadcasters—The state-run Radio Television Malaysia provides services in competition with commercial operators, which broadcast in Malay, Tamil, Chinese and English
Press—The four main national daily newspapers are in English: *The Star*, *Business Times*, *New Straits Times* and *The Malay Mail*
WPFI score—50,75 (141)

EDUCATION AND HEALTH

There are six years of compulsory education.
Literacy rate—92.5% (2009 est)
Gross enrolment ratio (percentage of relevant age group)—secondary 69%; tertiary 37% (2008 est)
Health expenditure (per capita)—US$336 (2009)
Hospital beds (per 1,000 people)—1.8 (2004–9)
Life expectancy (years)—74.04 (2012 est)
Mortality rate—4.95 (2012 est)
Birth rate—20.74 (2012 est)
Infant mortality rate—14.57 (2012 est)

Malta

Repubblika ta' Malta—Republic of Malta
Area—316 sq. km
Capital—Valletta; population, 199,283 (2009 est)
Major towns—Birkirkara, Mosta, Qormi, Saint Paul's Bay (San Pawl il-Bahar)
Currency—Euro (€) of 100 cents
Population—409,836 rising at 0.36% a year (2012 est)
Religion—Christian (Roman Catholic 95%), Muslim 2% (est)
Language—Maltese, English (both official)
Population density—1,291 per sq. km (2010)
Urban population—94.7% (2010 est)
Median age (years)—40 (2011 est)
National anthem—'L-Innu Malti' ['Hymn of Malta']
National day—21 September (Independence Day)
Life expectancy (years)—79.85 (2012 est)
Mortality rate—8.72 (2012 est)
Birth rate—10.31 (2012 est)
Infant mortality rate—3.65 (2012 est)
Death penalty—Abolished for all crimes (since 2000)
CPI score—5.6 (2011)

FINANCIAL OUTLOOK

The Maltese economy is dominated by foreign-owned, non-financial corporations, and relies heavily on FDI flows and EU funds to drive investment. This makes the economy very vulnerable to external economic shocks. There is a very large financial sector with assets of eight times Malta's GDP. Malta's economy performed well in 2011 despite turbulence in its near neighbor, north Africa, and the European Union's sporadic sovereign debt crises, and achieved 2% GDP growth. The tiny country's real GDP is actually 1.5% higher now than it was pre-crisis, making it unique among EU member states. Real GDP fell back to 1.2% for 2012, and is expected to return to 2% growth through 2013. Inflation is currently running at 3.5%, and is expected to flatten down to 2% through 2013. Malta's government debt is largely held domestically, so the downgrade of the country by ratings agencies, as part of a general downgrade of a number of EU member states, had little impact. Malta's domestic banks also hold very little EU peripheral sovereign debt, which gives the sector considerable resilience against sovereign risk events in Europe. Compared to eurozone peers, the IMF says, Maltese banks continue to outperform in terms of profits and capital adequacy.

CLIMATE AND TERRAIN

Malta is an archipelago of six islands in the Mediterranean Sea; Malta, Gozo and Comino are the largest. The island of Malta has a coastal plain in the north-east, rising to low hills in the south-west. Elevation extremes range from 253m (Ta'Dmejrek) to 0m (Mediterranean Sea). Average temperatures in Valetta range from 12°C in January to 27°C in August.

HISTORY AND POLITICS

The islands were ruled successively by the Phoenicians, Greeks, Carthaginians, Romans, Arabs, Spanish and the Sovereign Military Order of Malta (known as the Knights of St John), which held them from 1530 until a French invasion in 1798. Liberated from French rule with British naval support in 1800, the island of Malta became a British colony in 1814, and was developed into a substantial naval base and dockyard. Malta was strategically important in both world wars, but particularly the second, when it was blockaded and subjected to aerial bombardment for five months. Its resistance led to the people of Malta being awarded the George Cross, the UK's highest award for civilian bravery, in 1942.

Malta gained its independence in 1964 and became a republic in 1974. In the 1970s it developed close links with communist and Arab states, but more pro-European and pro-US policies were adopted after the election of the Nationalist Party in 1987. Malta became a member of the EU in 2004, and adopted the euro in 2008. Since joining the EU, Malta has experienced a marked increase in illegal immigration from northern Africa.

The Nationalist Party was returned to power in the 2008 legislative election with a modest overall majority. George Abela, the only nominee, was elected president in 2009.

Under the 1974 constitution, the president is elected by the legislature for a five-year term, renewable once. The unicameral legislature, the House of Representatives, has 69 members directly elected for a five-year term; if a party wins the majority of votes in a general election without winning a majority of seats, new seats are created until that party holds a majority of one seat. The prime minister is appointed by the president and nominates the other ministers.

  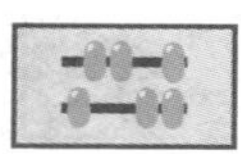      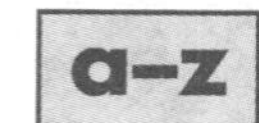

HEAD OF STATE
President, George Abela, *elected* 12 January 2009, *took office* 4 April 2009

SELECTED GOVERNMENT MEMBERS *as at July 2012*
Prime Minister, Defence, Lawrence Gonzi
Deputy Prime Minister, Foreign Affairs, Tonio Borg
Home Affairs, Carmelo Mifsud Bonnici
Finance and Economy, Tonio Fenech

MALTA HIGH COMMISSION
Malta House, 36–38 Piccadilly, London W1J 0LE
T 020-7292 4800
E maltahighcommission.london@gov.mt
W www.foreign.gov.mt
High Commissioner, HE Joseph Zammit Tabona, *apptd* 2009

BRITISH HIGH COMMISSION
Whitehall Mansions, Ta' Xbiex Seafront, Ta' Xbiex XBX 1026
T (+356) 2323 0000
W ukinmalta.fco.gov.uk
High Commissioner, HE Louise Stanton, *apptd* 2009

DEFENCE

All aged 16–49, 2010 est	Males	Females
Available for military service	95,499	90,919
Fit for military service	79,645	75,684

Military expenditure—US$58.7m (2011)

ECONOMY AND TRADE
The mainstay of the economy for over a century was the dockyard, and shipbuilding and ship repairs remain significant industries, but since the 1980s Malta has developed into a tourist destination, financial services centre and freight trans-shipment point. Tourism is now the main source of income, followed by foreign trade and manufacturing, especially of electronics and pharmaceuticals. All were adversely affected by the global downturn in 2009, and new fiscal measures contributed further to a deterioration in public finances in 2011, leading to a warning from the EU that Malta would risk sanctions if it failed to bring debt levels under control. The service sector accounts for 80.9% of GDP, industry for 17.2% and agriculture for 1.9%.

The main trading partners are other EU states, Singapore, Hong Kong and China. Principal exports are electrical machinery, mechanical appliances, fish and shellfish, pharmaceuticals and printed material. The main imports are mineral fuels and oil, machinery, aircraft and other transport equipment, semi-manufactured goods, food, beverages and tobacco.

GNI—US$7,697m; US$19,270 per capita (2010)
Annual average growth of GDP—2.5% (2011 est)
Inflation rate—2.7% (2011 est)
Unemployment—6.2% (2010)
Total external debt—US$48,790m (2011 est)
Imports—US$4,423m (2010)
Exports—US$2,747m (2010)

BALANCE OF PAYMENTS
Trade—US$1,676m deficit (2010)
Current Account—US$397m deficit (2010)

Trade with UK	2010	2011
Imports from UK	£384,141,058	£437,694,011
Exports to UK	£158,447,044	£161,621,134

COMMUNICATIONS
Airports and waterways—There is an international airport based in Luqa, south-west of Valletta; the main ports are Marsaxlokk (Malta's freeport) and Valletta; there is a large merchant fleet of 1,650 ships of over 1,000 tonnes
Roadways and railways—There are 3,096km of roads, but no railways
Telecommunications—247,300 fixed lines and 455,400 mobile subscriptions (2010); there were 240,600 internet users in 2009
Internet code and IDD—mt; 356 (from UK), 44 (to UK)
Media—There are public-service radio and television broadcasters, as well as a thriving private sector
WPFI score—4,00 (14)

EDUCATION
Education is free at all levels and compulsory between the ages of five and 16.
Literacy rate—92.4% (2008 est)
Gross enrolment ratio (percentage of relevant age group)—primary 95%; secondary 105%; tertiary 33% (2009 est)

Mauritius

Republic of Mauritius
Area—2,040 sq. km (includes Rodrigues and other islands)
Capital—Port Louis; population, 149,286 (2009 est)
Major towns—Beau Bassin-Rose Hill, Curepipe, Quatre Bornes, Vacoas-Phoenix
Currency—Mauritius rupee of 100 cents
Population—1,313,095 rising at 0.71% a year (2012 est); Indo-Mauritian (68%), Creole (27%), Sino-Mauritian (3%), Franco-Mauritian (2%) (est)
Religion—Hindu 48%, Christian 33% (of which Roman Catholic 73%), Muslim 17% (of which Sunni 90%) (est)
Language—English (official), Creole, French, Bhojpuri
Population density—631 per sq. km (2010)
Urban population—42.6% (2010 est)
Median age (years)—32.7 (2011 est)
National anthem—'Motherland'
National day—12 March (Independence Day)
Death penalty—Abolished for all crimes (since 1995)
CPI score—5.1 (2011)

FINANCIAL OUTLOOK
The latest IMF report on Mauritius was issued in January 2013, when the IMF delegation found that the government of Mauritius had continued to implement prudent macroeconomic policies during 2012, with good inflation and fiscal outcomes. The challenge in 2013 will be to find ways of accelerating growth in a difficult external environment. The government must look to lay the

  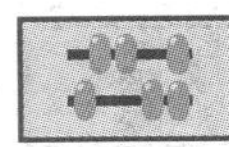      

foundations for future growth through increased public and private investment, and through productivity enhancements. The IMF expects GDP growth for 2013 to increase to 3.7%, fueled by strong growth in fishery, information and communications technology, and financial services. Investment is likely to increase, driven by public investment projects, while private investment is expected to remain subdued. At around 4%, inflation is currently regarded as reasonable, but inflationary pressures could emerge in 2013 from wage pressures in the private sector linked to the decision to increase public-sector wages, and from possible adjustments in some administered prices. The IMF projects headline consumer price index inflation to accelerate to 5.7% on average in 2013, and decline thereafter.

CLIMATE AND TERRAIN

The republic is an island group in the Indian Ocean, approximately 885km east of Madagascar. The volcanic island of Mauritius rises from narrow coastal plains to a central plateau ringed by mountains. Elevation extremes range from 828m (Mt Piton) to 0m (Indian Ocean). The island of Rodrigues, formerly a dependency but now part of Mauritius, is about 563km east of Mauritius, with an area of 108km; the population is 37,837 (2010). The islands of Agalega and St Brandon are dependencies of Mauritius; their total population is 289 (2010).

There is a tropical climate, modified by south-east trade winds, and little variation in temperature throughout the year. The cyclone season (December–April) brings rain but cyclones usually miss the islands.

HISTORY AND POLITICS

The islands were first visited in the tenth century, but were settled only after 1638 by the Dutch, who introduced sugar cane cultivation; the colonists withdrew in 1710. A decade later they were replaced by the French, who established plantations that were worked by African slaves. In 1814 Mauritius was ceded to the British, who had occupied it in 1810. The British abolished slavery in 1834 and imported indentured Indian and Chinese labourers to work on the plantations. Independence was achieved on 12 March 1968 and the state became a republic in 1992.

The Militant Socialist Movement (MSM) under Sir Anerood Jugnauth held power from 1983 until 1995, and then returned to power in 2000 in coalition with the Mauritian Militant Movement (MMM). Jugnauth stood down as party leader and prime minister in 2003; he was elected president later that year and again in 2008. The MSM-MMM coalition lost the 2005 election to the opposition Socialist Alliance, which included the Mauritius Labour Party (MPT) led by Navinchandra Ramgoolam, who became prime minister. The MPT-led Alliance of the Future, now also including the MSM, won the 2010 legislative election. President Jugnauth resigned from office in March 2012 following disagreements with prime minister Ramgoolam; vice-president Monique Ohsan-Bellepeau took over as acting president.

The 1968 constitution was amended in 1992 to introduce a republican form of government, and in 2001 to give the island of Rodrigues a degree of autonomy.

The president is elected by the legislature for a five-year term, renewable once. The unicameral National Assembly has 62 elected members (including two representing Rodrigues) and eight appointed members, all of whom serve a five-year term; the electoral commission allocates the appointed seats on a 'best loser' basis to give more equitable representation to ethnic minorities. The prime minister is the leader of the majority party in the legislature.

Rodrigues has had an 18-member regional assembly, a chief commissioner and a chief executive since 2002.

HEAD OF STATE
President (Acting), Monique Ohsan-Bellepeau, *took office* 30 March 2012

SELECTED GOVERNMENT MEMBERS *as at July 2012*
Prime Minister, Defence, Interior, Navinchandra Ramgoolam
Deputy Prime Minister, Ahmed Rashid Beebeejaun
Foreign Affairs, Arvin Boolell

MAURITIUS HIGH COMMISSION
32–33 Elvaston Place, London SW7 5NW
T 020-7581 0294
E londonmhc@btinternet.com
High Commissioner, HE Abhimanu Kundasamy, *apptd* 2005

BRITISH HIGH COMMISSION
PO Box 1063, Les Cascades Building, Edith Cavell Street, Port Louis
T (+230) 202 9400
E bhc@bow.intnet.mu
W ukinmauritius.fco.gov.uk
High Commissioner, HE Nick Leake, *apptd* 2010

DEFENCE

All aged 16–49, 2010 est	Males	Females
Available for military service	343,828	–
Fit for military service	280,596	283,317

Military expenditure—US$8.8m (2011)

ECONOMY AND TRADE

Since independence Mauritius has developed from an economy dependent on agriculture to one with prospering tourist, manufacturing (primarily of textiles and garments) and financial sectors. Although sugar remains an important commodity (sugar cane is grown on 90% of cultivated land and produces 15% of export earnings), both the sugar and textile industries are beginning to decline. Diversification into fish processing, information and communications technology, hospitality and property development is being encouraged. The services sector accounts for 71.8% of GDP, industry for 23.8% and agriculture for 4.4%.

The main trading partners are France, the UK and India. Principal exports are clothing, textiles, sugar, cut flowers, molasses and fish. The main imports are manufactured goods, capital equipment, food, fuels and chemicals.

GNI—US$9,798m; US$7,750 per capita (2010)
Annual average growth of GDP—4.2% (2011 est)
Inflation rate—6.7% (2011 est)
Population below poverty line—8% (2006 est)
Unemployment—7.8% (2011 est)
Total external debt—US$6,002m (2011 est)
Imports—US$4,403m (2010)
Exports—US$2,239m (2010)

BALANCE OF PAYMENTS
Trade—US$2,164m deficit (2010)
Current Account—US$797m deficit (2010)

Trade with UK	2010	2011
Imports from UK	£58,809,581	£71,483,537
Exports to UK	£241,969,049	£252,369,014

COMMUNICATIONS

Airports and waterways—The international airport is located near Plaisance; the main port is at Port Louis

Roadways—There are 2,066km of roads

Telecommunications—387,700 fixed lines and 1.19 million mobile subscriptions (2010); there were 290,000 internet users in 2009

Internet code and IDD—mu; 230 (from UK), 44 (to UK)

Media—The state-owned Mauritius Broadcasting Corporation runs television and radio services funded through advertising and a licence fee

WPFI score—18,00 (65)

EDUCATION AND HEALTH

Twelve years of education are free and compulsory.

Literacy rate—87.9% (2009 est)

Gross enrolment ratio (percentage of relevant age group)—primary 99%; secondary 89% (2010 est); tertiary 25% (2008 est)

Health expenditure (per capita)—US$383 (2009)

Hospital beds (per 1,000 people)—3.3 (2004–9)

Life expectancy (years)—74.71 (2012 est)

Mortality rate—6.73 (2012 est)

Birth rate—13.78 (2012 est)

Infant mortality rate—11.2 (2012 est)

HIV/AIDS adult prevalence—1% (2009 est)

Mexico

Estados Unidos Mexicanos—United Mexican States

Area—1,964,375 sq. km

Capital—Mexico City; population, 19,318,500 (2009 est)

Major cities—Ecatepec, Ciudad Juárez, Guadalajara, León, Monterrey, Puebla, Tijuana

Currency—Peso of 100 centavos

Population—114,975,406 rising at 1.09% a year (2012 est)

Religion—Christian (Roman Catholic 88%) (est)

Language—Spanish (official), 66 Mayan, Nahuatl and other regional languages

Population density—58 per sq. km (2010)

Urban population—77.8% (2010 est)

Median age (years)—27.1 (2011 est)

National anthem—'Himno Nacional Mexicano' ['Mexican National Anthem']

National day—16 September (Independence Day)

Death penalty—Abolished for all crimes (since 2005)

CPI score—3.0 (2011)

FINANCIAL OUTLOOK

The strength and resilience of the recovery of Mexico's economy after the global crisis has since been put on a sound footing by the Mexican government's strong policy frameworks, and skillful macroeconomic management, according to the IMF. The recognition of Mexico as a predictable and prudently managed economy, with market-friendly and transparent regulations for foreign investment, and open and liquid financial markets, has bolstered large foreign investment inflows in recent years. GDP growth is expected to be around 3.5% for 2013, and the same again for 2014. However, Mexico is highly integrated with international capital markets, which makes it vulnerable to any surge in the sovereign debt crisis plaguing the European Union. Another risk is that the inflows of capital, which mean that the equity and debt portfolio holdings of foreign investors amount to around 30% of Mexico's GDP, could reverse suddenly if a bout of risk aversion sweeps through the global economy. A significant slowdown in the US economy would also hurt the Mexican economy. However, these are downside risks, not present realities. Mexico is currently running a GDP current account deficit of no more than 1%. Public debt has stabilized at around 43% of GDP.

CLIMATE AND TERRAIN

The Rio Grande river forms the eastern part of the border with the USA. South of this, coastal plains rise to a central plateau which lies between two spines of high mountains, the Western and the Eastern Sierra Madre, running from the north-west to south-east. The mountains include volcanoes such as Popocatepetl, and in the south are covered with dense jungle. The Yucatán peninsula in the south-east is low-lying, and marshy on the coast. The narrow Baja California peninsula, separated from the rest of the country by the Gulf of California, has a range of hills running along it. Elevation extremes range from 5,700m (Volcan Pico de Orizaba) to −10m (Laguna Salada). The north has a desert climate, while the south is tropical. The temperature in Mexico City can be as low as 5°C in January and up to 27°C in April.

HISTORY AND POLITICS

Under the 1917 constitution, the federal republic consists of 31 states and the federal capital. The head of state is an executive president, directly elected for a single six-year term. The bicameral legislature is the Congress of the Union: the lower house, the Chamber of Deputies, has 500 members, directly elected for a three-year term, and the senate has 128 members, directly elected for a six-year term. The president appoints the cabinet.

Each of the states has its own constitution and is administered by a governor, elected for a six-year term, and a state chamber of deputies, elected for a three-year term.

The Institutional Revolutionary Party's (PRI) political dominance ended at the 1997 election, when it lost its absolute majority in the lower house of the legislature, although it continued in government until 2000 and was again in power from 2003 until 2006. The 2006 presidential election was won by Felipe Calderón of the Partido Accion Nacional (PAN); Lopez Obrador, Calderón's closest rival, refused to accept the result, alleging voting irregularities. Lopez Obrador also stood in the 2012 presidential elction, eventually losing to PRI's Enrique Pena Nieto in another election marred by accusations of voting irregularities. PRI became the largest party in the Chamber of Deputies in the 2012 legislative election, picking up 93 more seats than nearst rival PAN.

HEAD OF STATE

President, Felipe Calderón, *elected* 2 July 2006, *sworn in* 1 December 2006

President-elect, Enrique Pena Nieto, *elected* 1 July 2012

SELECTED GOVERNMENT MEMBERS *as at July 2012*

Defence, Gen. Guillermo Galván Galván

Economy, Bruno Ferrari García de Alba

Foreign Affairs, Patricia Espinosa Cantellano

Interior, Alejandro Poiré

EMBASSY OF MEXICO
16 St George Street, London W1S 1FD
T 020-7499 8586
W embamex.sre.gob.mx/reinounido/
Ambassador Extraordinary and Plenipotentiary, HE Eduardo Medina-Mora, *apptd* 2010

BRITISH EMBASSY
Río Lerma 71, Col. Cuauhtémoc, 06500 Mexico City
T (+52) (55) 1670 3200
E ukinmexico@fco.gov.uk
W ukinmexico.fco.gov.uk
Ambassador Extraordinary and Plenipotentiary, HE Judith Macgregor, CMG, LVO, *apptd* 2009

DEFENCE

All aged 16–49, 2010 est	*Males*	*Females*
Available for military service	28,815,506	30,363,558
Fit for military service	23,239,866	25,642,549

Military expenditure—US$5,723m (2011)

ECONOMY AND TRADE

Mexico had a relatively closed economy until the mid-1980s, but increased trade and domestic liberalisation in the 1990s stimulated economic growth and development, particularly in the industrial sector. However, although it has free trade agreements with over 50 countries, covering 90% of its trade, its economy is still closely tied to that of the USA and experienced a deep recession in 2009 as the global downturn affected its main export market. Despite posting positive growth in 2010 and 2011, Mexico remains a poor country and President Calderón has prioritised job creation and poverty reduction measures.

Agriculture is diverse and productive; major crops include maize, wheat, soya beans, rice, beans, cotton, coffee, fruit, tomatoes, beef, poultry and dairy products. Agriculture accounts for 3.9% of GDP and 13.7% of employment. The main industries include production of food, beverages, tobacco, chemicals, iron and steel, textiles, clothing, motor vehicles, consumer durables, oil production, mining and tourism. Tourism is now the fourth-largest revenue earner. The services sector accounts for 63.4% of GDP and industry for 32.8%.

The main trading partner is the USA (73.5% of exports; 60.6% of imports). Canada is the other main export market, and China and South Korea the other main source of imports. Principal exports include manufactured goods, oil and oil products, silver, fruit, vegetables, coffee and cotton. The main imports include metal-working machines, steel mill products, agricultural machinery, electrical equipment, car parts for assembly, vehicle repair parts, aircraft and aircraft parts.

GNI—US$1,020,287m; US$8,890 per capita (2010)
Annual average growth of GDP—3.8% (2011 est)
Inflation rate—3.5% (2011 est)
Population below poverty line—18.2% (2008)
Unemployment—5.1% (2011 est)
Total external debt—US$204,000m (2011 est)
Imports—US$301,482m (2010)
Exports—US$298,138m (2010)

BALANCE OF PAYMENTS
Trade—US$3,344m deficit (2010)
Current Account—US$5,626m deficit (2010)

Trade with UK	*2010*	*2011*
Imports from UK	£919,218,074	£951,838,614
Exports to UK	£1,477,738,521	£1,055,540,715

COMMUNICATIONS

Airports—The main international airport is at Mexico City, with nearly 250 others around the country
Waterways—Veracruz, Tampico and Coatzacoalcos are the chief seaports on the east coast, and Guaymas, Mazatlán, Lázaro Cárdenas and Salina Cruz on the Pacific; there are 2,900km of navigable rivers and coastal canals
Roadways and railways—There are 366,095km of roads, of which 132,289km are surfaced and 17,166km of railways. The Baluarte bridge, the highest cable-stayed bridge in the world, is due to be completed in late 2012 and will stretch 1,124m across the Durango-Mazatlán motorway in the north
Telecommunications—19.89 million fixed lines and 91.36 million mobile subscriptions (2010); there were 31.02 million internet users in 2009
Internet code and IDD—mx; 52 (from UK), 44 (to UK)
Major broadcasters—The Televisa group used to dominate broadcasting but now competes with other television channels and a huge number of independent radio stations
Press—There are six national daily newspapers, representing a variety of political opinions
WPFI score—47,50 (136)

EDUCATION AND HEALTH

Education is compulsory in Mexico for ten years from age six, although attainment varies among states.
Literacy rate—93.4% (2009 est)
Gross enrolment ratio (percentage of relevant age group)—primary 115%; secondary 87%; tertiary 27% (2009 est)
Health expenditure (per capita)—US$515 (2009)
Hospital beds (per 1,000 people)—1.6 (2004–9)
Life expectancy (years)—76.66 (2012 est)
Mortality rate—4.9 (2012 est)
Birth rate—18.87 (2012 est)
Infant mortality rate—16.77 (2012 est)

Monaco

Principauté de Monaco—Principality of Monaco
Area—2 sq. km
Capital—Monaco
Major town—Monte Carlo
Currency—Euro (€) of 100 cents
Population—30,510 falling at 0.07% a year (2012 est); French (47%), Monegasque (16%), Italian (16%) (est)
Religion—Christian (predominantly Roman Catholic)
Language—French (official), English, Italian, Monegasque
Population density—17,704 per sq. km (2010)
Urban population—100% (2010 est)
Median age (years)—49.4 (2011 est)
National anthem—'Hymne Monégasque' ['Hymn of Monaco']
National day—19 November (St Rainier's Day)
Life expectancy (years)—89.68 (2012 est)
Mortality rate—8.52 (2012 est)

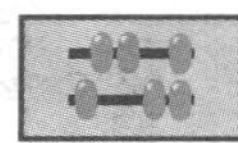

Birth rate—6.85 (2012 est)
Infant mortality rate—1.8 (2012 est)
Death penalty—Abolished for all crimes (since 1962)

FINANCIAL OUTLOOK
Monaco's prosperity has been built on tourism and its status as a tax haven. Monaco has also developed a banking sector, and has encouraged the formation of small, high-value-added, non-polluting industries. The government appears intent on maintaining the policies that have created its economic success, namely levying no income tax and only low business taxes. The government also retains monopolies in a number of sectors, including tobacco, the telephone network, and the postal service, which it shows no sign of relinquishing. Prince Albert is a committed champion of environmental issues. In a speech to the Governing Council of the United Nations Environment Programme (UNEP) in February 2008, he announced that one of his key ambitions for Monaco "is for it to become a preferred destination for entrepreneurs and investment professionals involved in the research, development, and marketing of new technologies with regards to the environment." The principality has an Energy Climate Plan and is committed to reducing its greenhouse gas emissions by 20% over 1990 levels by 2020. The principality has more than 110 industries, representing some 11% (US$3 billion) of the national economy. There are some 150 shipping companies based in Monaco, generating 4% of the national economic turnover. The country is home to one of the most famous oceanographic institutes in the world, and is a leader in marine environmental research.

CLIMATE AND TERRAIN
Monaco lies on 4km of steep, rugged coastline. It has been expanded by 0.3 sq. km with land reclaimed from the sea by infilling. Elevation extremes range from 140m (Mt Agel) to 0m (Mediterranean Sea). The climate is Mediterranean, with average temperatures ranging from 10°C in January to 24°C in August.

HISTORY AND POLITICS
Monaco has been ruled by the Grimaldi family since the 13th century. Monarchical France recognised Monaco's independence in the 15th century, but Revolutionary France annexed it in 1793. Although the prince was restored to power in 1814, Monaco did not regain its independence until 1861. It was occupied by the Italians and subsequently by the Germans in the Second World War. The principality's foreign relations and security have been aligned to those of France since 1861 by various treaties; the terms were changed in 2005 to allow Monaco greater control over its foreign relations and internal administration.

The 1962 constitution was amended in 2002 to allow the throne to pass in the female line in the absence of male heirs. Legislative power is held jointly by the prince and a 24-member National Council, which is directly elected for a five-year term. Executive power is exercised by the prince and a six-member Council of Government, headed by a minister of state who is nominated by the prince and approved by the French government. The judicial code is based on that of France.

In the 2008 legislative election, the Union for Monaco (UPM) retained its 21 seats, an overwhelming majority, in the legislature. Michel Roger replaced Jean-Paul Proust as head of the government in March 2010.

HEAD OF STATE
HSH The Prince of Monaco, Prince Albert II (Alexandre Louis Pierre), *born* 14 March 1958, *succeeded* 6 April 2005
Heir, HSH Princess Caroline von Hannover, *born* 23 January 1957

SELECTED GOVERNMENT MEMBERS *as at July 2012*
Minister of State, Michel Roger
Finance and Economy, Marco Piccinini
Interior, Paul Masseron
Foreign Affairs, José Badia

EMBASSY OF THE PRINCIPALITY OF MONACO
7 Upper Grosvenor Street, London W1K 2LX
T 020-7318 1083
E embassy.uk@gouv.mc
W www.monaco-embassy-uk.gouv.mc
Ambassador Extraordinary and Plenipotentiary, Evelyne Genta, *apptd* 2010

BRITISH HONORARY CONSULATE
PO Box 265, 33 Boulevard Princesse Charlotte, 98005 Monaco
T (+377) 9350 9966

ECONOMY AND TRADE
The economy has diversified away from its historic dependence on tourism and gambling, and over half its revenue now comes from financial services, retail, real estate, construction and light industry (chemicals, pharmaceuticals, cosmetics, medical devices, plastics, electronics). A large floating jetty, installed in 2002, has extended the harbour facilities, doubling the port's capacity to handle cruise ships. As the state collects no taxes from individuals and little from businesses, it has become a tax haven for wealthy expatriates and foreign companies. The state retains monopolies in a number of sectors, including tobacco, the telephone network and the postal service. Since 1963 Monaco has been in a customs union with France, and through this it participates in the EU market. Over half its trade is with EU countries, particularly Italy.

GNI—US$6,108m; US$183,150 per capita (2009)
Unemployment—0% (2005 est)

COMMUNICATIONS
Transport—The nearest international airport is the Cote d'Azur airport in Nice, France; the port of Monaco is the main source of transportation. There are 77km of roads and a single railway station, Monaco-Monte Carlo
Telecommunications—34,100 fixed lines and 26,300 mobile subscriptions (2010); there were 23,000 internet users in 2009
Internet code and IDD—mc; 377 (from UK), 44 (to UK)
Media—Monaco has one television station and the principality's news is covered by the French press

Montserrat

Area—102 sq. km
Capital—Plymouth (abandoned 1997); the seat of government is now at Brades, in the north, population, 823 (2009 est); a new capital is under construction at nearby Little Bay
Currency—East Caribbean dollar (EC$) of 100 cents
Population—5,140 rising at 0.447% a year (2011 est)
Language—English (official)
Population density—55 per sq. km (2005 est)

  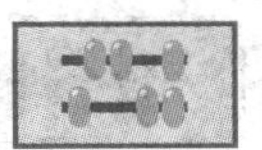      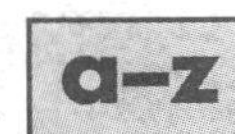

Flag—British blue ensign with the coat of arms in the fly
National day—Second Saturday in June (birthday of Queen Elizabeth II)
Life expectancy (years)—73.16 (2011 est)
Mortality rate—7.2 (2011 est)
Birth rate—11.67 (2011 est)
Infant mortality rate—15.23 (2011 est)

FINANCIAL OUTLOOK
Montserrat has made enormous progress in its recovery from the 1995 eruption of a long-dormant volcano, with substantial support from the United Kingdom and the European Union. However, the volcano, which remains intermittently active, has had a large and lasting demographic, economic, and social impact, and in some respects the recovery is still under way. Donor support also buffered the impact of the global crisis in 2009–10. The failure of two regional insurance companies (CLICO and BAICO) weakened several financial institutions, and the authorities are working on a strategy to address vulnerabilities arising from this. According to the IMF, there are several opportunities for Montserrat to enhance its long-term growth prospects and viability. The construction of a new capital and port is the keystone of its public investment program, and this needs to be pushed forward in 2013, the IMF says. Montserrat's budget is currently sustained by grants from the United Kingdom, which account for some 50% of expenditure. Public-sector debt remains low at about 5% of GDP, and consists mostly of loans from the Caribbean Development Bank for the construction of Montserrat's former port, which was destroyed by the volcano. The IMF expects growth to peak at about 3%, largely driven by the government's capital projects.

CLIMATE AND TERRAIN
Montserrat is a mountainous volcanic island in the Leeward group in the Caribbean Sea. Its lowest point of elevation is 0m (Caribbean Sea); its highest point was 914m (Chances Peak), although a lava dome in a crater in the Soufrière Hills volcano is estimated to be over 930m. Volcanic activity since 1995 has left over half of the island devastated by lava flows and ash. The climate is tropical and the average temperature is 27°C.

HISTORY AND POLITICS
Discovered by Columbus in 1493, Montserrat became a British colony in 1632. It was fought over by the French and British throughout the 17th and 18th centuries, before being finally restored to Britain in 1783.

Volcanic activity by the Soufrière Hills volcano between 1995 and 2008 has left over half of the island uninhabitable, and prompted the migration of two-thirds of the population in the late 1990s. A 'special vulnerable area', to which access is restricted, covers two-thirds of the island and two maritime exclusion zones extend between 2km and 4km offshore.

The 1990 constitution was amended in 1999 after more than half of the constituencies were made uninhabitable by volcanic activity. Following modernisation talks, a new constitution came into force in September 2011, which established a new National Advisory Council to enhance democracy and governance. Under the new constitution, the cabinet is chaired by the governor and comprises the premier and three other elected members and two *ex-officio* members (the attorney-general and the financial secretary). The legislative assembly consists of nine members elected for a five-year term and two *ex-officio* members. In the 2009 general election the Movement for Change and Prosperity won the most seats.
Governor, HE Adrian Davis, *apptd* 2011
Chief Minister, Hon. Reuben Meade

GOVERNMENT OF MONTSERRAT
180–186 Kings Cross Road, London WC1X 9DE
T 020-7520 2622

ECONOMY
Continuing volcanic activity has restricted economic activity to the northern third of the island. Activity includes mining and quarrying, construction (mostly public sector), financial and professional services, and tourism. Communications improved with the opening of Gerald's airport in the north in 2005, allowing regular commercial air services to resume. There are port facilities at Little Bay, and a ferry service to and from Antigua was reintroduced in December 2009.

Trade with UK	*2009*	*2011*
Imports from UK	£637,817	£570,320
Exports to UK	£268,965	£153,006

Morocco

Al-Mamlakah al-Maghribiyah—Kingdom of Morocco
Area—446,550 sq. km
Capital—Rabat; population, 1,769,590 (2009 est)
Major cities—Agadir, Casablanca, Fez, Marrakesh, Meknes, Tangier
Currency—Dirham (DH) of 100 centimes
Population—32,309,239 rising at 1.05% a year (2012 est); Arab–Berber (99%) (est)
Religion—Muslim 99% (predominantly Sunni), Christian 1% (est)
Language—Arabic (official), French, Berber dialects
Population density—72 per sq. km (2010)
Urban population—56.7% (2010 est)
Median age (years)—26.9 (2011 est)
National anthem—'Hymne Chérifien' ['Hymn of the Sharif']
National day—30 July (Throne Day)
Death penalty—Retained (not used since 1993)
CPI score—3.4 (2011)

FINANCIAL OUTLOOK
Economic growth is estimated to have slowed in 2012 to 3.2%, from 5% in 2011, according to an IMF report published in February 2013. The IMF said a lower-than-average cereal crop lay behind the slowdown, while non-agricultural GDP growth is believed to have remained robust at around 4.5%. The IMF expected the fiscal deficit to have declined to about 6% of GDP in 2012, from 6.8% in 2011, thanks to a combination of measures, notably the increase in some energy-administered prices in June, and the control of nonessential spending. Meanwhile, the current account deficit is expected to have increased to 8.8% of GDP in 2012 as import growth, pushed by energy-related imports, outpaced slow export growth. Tourism receipts and remittances are projected to have fallen slightly relative to 2011, reflecting the deterioration in the European economy.

CLIMATE AND TERRAIN

Fertile coastal plains in the west rise to a mountainous centre, with ranges, including the Atlas range, running north-east to south-west. The Rif mountains lie along the northern, Mediterranean coast. Elevation extremes range from 4,165m (Jebel Toubkal) to −55m (Sebkha Tah). The climate is Mediterranean, becoming more extreme in the interior. Average temperatures in Rabat range from 13°C in January to 22°C in July and August, although summer temperatures in the desert can reach over 40°C.

HISTORY AND POLITICS

From the tenth century BC, the northern coast was settled by the Phoenicians. Morocco was part of the Roman Empire from the first century AD until it was invaded by first the Vandals and then the Visigoths in the fifth and sixth centuries. Arab conquest of the area began in the seventh century but Morocco was independent from about the ninth century, successfully resisting inclusion in the Ottoman Empire in the 16th century. The current Alawite dynasty was founded in the mid-17th century. Morocco remained isolated until the mid-19th century, when the country opened up to European trade. The subsequent growth in Spanish and French influence resulted in its partition into two protectorates from 1912. In the Second World War, Morocco was a base for the Allied offensives that drove German forces out of North Africa.

Nationalist campaigning for independence began in the 1940s. French and Spanish forces withdrew in 1956, leaving Morocco independent under Sultan Mohammed V, who adopted the title of king in 1957; the coastal towns of Ceuta and Melilla remain under Spanish control. King Hassan II, who ruled from 1961 to 1999, annexed the mineral-rich Western Sahara region in 1975.

Since the accession of King Mohammed VI in 1999, Morocco has been moving away from absolute monarchy, increasing civil liberties and addressing human rights issues. Pro-reform demonstrations in spring 2011 led to a referendum in July in which an overwhelming majority voted in favour of constitutional changes that would make the prime minister, rather than the king, the head of government.

In the 2011 legislative election the Justice and Development Party (PJD) became the largest party in the House of Representatives. Its leader, Abdelilah Benkirane, was appointed prime minister and formed a coalition government that includes three other parties.

The 1992 constitution was amended in 1996 to introduce a bicameral legislature. The head of state is a hereditary constitutional monarch. The king appoints the prime minister, who appoints the members of the council of ministers. There is a bicameral legislature; the lower house, the House of Representatives *(Majlis al-Nuwab)* has 325 members who are directly elected for a five-year term. The House of Councillors *(Majlis al-Mustasharin)* has 270 members, elected by local councils, professional organisations and the 'salaried classes'; one-third of its members is elected every three years, to serve a nine-year term.

HEAD OF STATE

HM The King of Morocco, King Mohammed VI (Sidi Mohammed Ben Hassan), *born* 21 August 1963, *acceded* 23 July 1999, *crowned* 30 July 1999

Heir, HRH Crown Prince Moulay Hassan, *born* 2003

SELECTED GOVERNMENT MEMBERS *as at July 2012*

Prime Minister, Abdelilah Benkirane
Economy and Finance, Nizar Baraka
Foreign Affairs, Saad-Eddine El Othmani
Interior, Mohand Laenser

EMBASSY OF THE KINGDOM OF MOROCCO

49 Queen's Gate Gardens, London SW7 5NE
T 020-7581 5001
E ambalondres@maec.gov.ma
W www.moroccanembassylondon.org.uk
Ambassador Extraordinary and Plenipotentiary, HH Princess Lalla Joumala Aaoui, *apptd* 2009

BRITISH EMBASSY

28 Avenue SAR Sidi Mohammed, Souissi 10105 (BP45), Rabat
T (+212) (0) 537 633 333
W ukinmorocco.fco.gov.uk
Ambassador Extraordinary and Plenipotentiary, HE Timothy Morris, *apptd* 2008

DEFENCE

All aged 16–49, 2010 est	*Males*	*Females*
Available for military service	8,252,682	8,691,419
Fit for military service	7,026,016	7,377,045

Military expenditure—US$3,186m (2011)
Conscription duration—18 months

ECONOMY AND TRADE

Economic liberalisation since 1999 has attracted foreign direct investment, and the industrial and service sectors are being developed. Despite steady growth, Morocco remains a poor country, with unemployment at around 9%, though it is often nearer 20% in urban areas, and in 2005 the king launched a poverty-alleviation programme. The remittances of expatriate workers are crucial to the domestic economy but these, along with tourism and export demand, declined in 2008–9 owing to the global downturn; recovery is slow because of dependence on the sluggish European market and, more recently, the increasing prices in the fuel and food markets.

The large agrarian sector generates 16.6% of GDP and engages 44.6% of the workforce, producing cereals, citrus fruits, vegetables, wine, olives and livestock. It faces environmental problems such as desertification and soil erosion. Another major sector is the exploitation of mineral reserves, especially phosphate. Other industries include food processing, textiles, leather goods, construction and tourism. Industry accounts for 32.3% of GDP and services for 51%.

The main trading partners are EU countries, especially France and Spain. Principal exports are clothing, textiles, electrical components, inorganic chemicals, transistors, crude minerals, fertilisers, petroleum products, fruit and vegetables. The main imports are crude petroleum, fabrics, telecommunications equipment, wheat, gas and electricity.

GNI—US$88,577m; US$2,850 per capita (2010; includes Western Sahara)
Annual average growth of GDP—4.6% (2011 est)
Inflation rate—1.9% (2011 est)
Population below poverty line—15% (2007 est)
Unemployment—9.2% (2011 est)
Total external debt—US$28,080m (2011 est)
Imports—US$35,522m (2010)
Exports—US$17,559m (2010)

BALANCE OF PAYMENTS

Trade—US$17,963m deficit (2010)
Current Account—US$3,943m deficit (2010)

  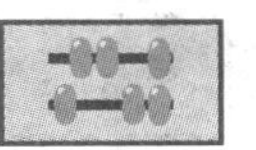 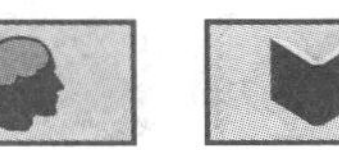    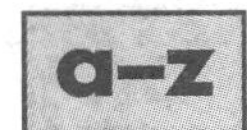

Trade with UK	2010	2011
Imports from UK	£527,085,424	£546,194,510
Exports to UK	£318,839,858	£422,152,950

COMMUNICATIONS

Airports and waterways—The principal airports are at Rabat, Agadir, Casablanca and Marrakesh; the main ports are Tangier, Casablanca and Agadir, on the Atlantic coast
Roadways and railways—There are 2,067km of railways linking the major towns and 58,256km of roads; a 39,480km network of surfaced roads connects the main towns
Telecommunications—3.75 million fixed lines and 31.92 million mobile subscriptions (2010); there were 13.21 million internet users in 2009
Internet code and IDD—ma; 212 (from UK), 44 (to UK)
Major broadcasters—The government owns Radio-Television Marocaine and has a stake in 2M, the other main television network
Press—There are a number of daily newspapers, including the semi-offical *Le Matin*
WPFI score—47,40 (135)

EDUCATION AND HEALTH

Education is compulsory between the ages of six and 15.
Literacy rate—56.1% (2009 est)
Gross enrolment ratio (percentage of relevant age group)—primary 111% (2010 est); tertiary 13% (2009 est)
Health expenditure (per capita)—US$156 (2009)
Hospital beds (per 1,000 people)—1.1 (2004–9)
Life expectancy (years)—76.11 (2012 est)
Mortality rate—4.76 (2012 est)
Birth rate—18.97 (2012 est)
Infant mortality rate—26.49 (2012 est)

WESTERN SAHARA

Al-Jumhuriyya al-'Arabiyya as-Sahrawiyya ad-Dimuqratiyya—Sahrawi Arab Democratic Republic
Area—266,000 sq. km. Neighbours: Morocco (north), Algeria (north-east), Mauritania (east and south)
Population—522,928 rising at 3.03% a year (2012 est)
Administrative centre—El-Aaiun (Laayoune); population, 213,000 (2009 est)
Religion—Muslim (99%) (est)
Language—Arabic, Hassaniyya Arabic, Spanish
Flag—Three horizontal stripes of black, white and green with a red crescent and a five-pointed star in the centre and a red triangle based on the hoist

Western Sahara came under Spanish rule in 1884, and became a province in 1934. Following Spain's withdrawal in 1976, Morocco and Mauritania annexed the territory and divided it between them. The Polisario Front declared the Western Sahara's independence as the Sahrawi Arab Democratic Republic in 1976, and began a guerrilla war to win the territory, setting up a government in exile. In 1979, Mauritania withdrew from its part of the territory, which was annexed by Morocco.

A ceasefire was established in 1991 following both sides' agreement in 1988 to UN proposals for a peace settlement, which included holding a referendum on the future status of Western Sahara. But the precise terms of the referendum have proved a sticking point and an impasse was reached that has still not been overcome despite further negotiations in 2001–4; Polisario agreed to a referendum offering the options of independence, semi-autonomy or integration for Western Sahara, but Morocco is only prepared to accept semi-autonomy or integration. Talks have taken place intermittently since 2007 but have made no progress.

Nauru

Republic of Nauru
Area—21 sq. km
Capital—Yaren District (unofficial)
Currency—Australian dollar ($A) of 100 cents
Population—9,378 rising at 0.61% a year (2012 est); Nauruan (58%), other Pacific Islander (26%), Chinese (8%), European (8%) (est)
Religion—Christian (Protestant 46%, Roman Catholic 33%) (2002)
Language—Nauruan (official), English
Urban population—100% (2010 est)
Median age (years)—24.2 (2011 est)
National anthem—'Nauru Bwiema' ('Song of Nauru')
National day—31 January (Independence Day)
Life expectancy (years)—65.7 (2012 est)
Mortality rate—5.97 (2012 est)
Birth rate—27.08 (2012 est)
Infant mortality rate—8.51 (2012 est)
Death penalty—Retained (not used since 1968)

FINANCIAL OUTLOOK

The former British colony of Nauru is the world's smallest republic. The tiny Pacific island once generated a huge per capita income. However, the source of this wealth—phosphates—is nearing exhaustion, leaving the islanders facing an uncertain future. Financial crises have caused a slide into bankruptcy and a dependence on aid. The country had to sell off its assets in Australia to pay off a multi-million-dollar debt to a US corporation. It has attempted but failed to develop alternative industries, including tourism and offshore banking. According to the Asian Development Bank (ADB), the country's population amounted to just over 10,000 in 2011, with a GDP of A$69.5 million, increasing by 2.2% during the year, having fallen by 0.9% in 2010. The ADB says that Nauru's phosphate exports grew strongly to 519,000 tonnes in FY2012 (ended June 30, 2012), supporting GDP growth estimated at 4.8%. This was the highest production recorded since phosphate production resumed in 2006.

CLIMATE AND TERRAIN

Nauru is a low-lying island in the southern Pacific Ocean, 42km south of the equator and 4,000km north-east of Sydney, Australia. There is a fertile coastal plain but about 60% of the land area consists of the central plateau, formed of phosphate, which has been extensively mined. The plateau rim is the highest point, at 61m; the lowest is 0m at sea level. The climate is tropical, with a rainy season from November to February.

HISTORY AND POLITICS

Nauru was first settled by Polynesian and Melanesian groups. The first Europeans to visit the island were British whalers in 1798 and by 1888 Nauru was annexed by Germany. At the outbreak of the First World War, Nauru was occupied by Australia, which continued to administer the island under a League of Nations mandate from 1920. The island was occupied by the Japanese in 1942–3, but in

  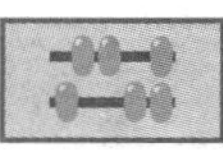      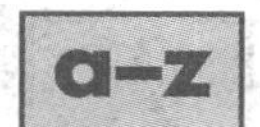

1947 UN trusteeship status superseded the mandate and Nauru continued to be administered by Australia until it became independent on 31 January 1968.

A financial crisis since 2003 has caused some political instability, with five changes of president between January and August 2003 and two different presidents in 2004. A more stable period during Ludwig Scotty's second presidency (2004–7) saw the introduction of austerity measures and public sector reform, but Scotty lost a vote of confidence in December 2007 and was replaced by Marcus Stephen. The 2008 legislative election succeeded in breaking a parliamentary deadlock over the budget, but by early 2010 a realignment of political allegiances had produced another stalemate. President Stephen resigned in 2011 amid allegations of corruption and was replaced temporarily by Frederick Pitcher; the latter was removed from office after a vote of no confidence some five days later and was replaced by former transport minister Sprent Dabwido.

Under the 1968 constitution, the executive president is elected by the legislature from among its members for a three-year term. The unicameral parliament has 18 members, who are directly elected for a three-year term. The president appoints the cabinet. Although there are active political parties, most parliamentary candidates stand as independents.

HEAD OF STATE

President, Foreign Affairs, Sprent Dabwido, *elected* 15 November 2011

SELECTED GOVERNMENT MEMBERS *as at June 2012*

Finance, Justice, Roland Kun

Commerce, Industry and Environment, Marcus Stephen

HONORARY CONSULATE

Romshed Courtyard, Underriver, Sevenoaks, Kent TN15 0SD

T 01732-746061

E nauru@weald.co.uk

Honorary Consul, Martin Weston

BRITISH HIGH COMMISSIONER

High Commissioner, HE Martin Fidler (acting), *apptd* 2011, resident at Suva, Fiji

ECONOMY AND TRADE

Phosphate is the only resource and its extraction is the sole industry, but reserves will be exhausted before the mid-21st century. Profits derived from the mining industry were invested in trust funds to provide for the post-mining future, but heavy spending from the funds has left the country virtually bankrupt, causing it to default on loans and have assets seized in 2004. Nauru accommodated asylum seekers for Australia between 2001 and 2008, but the loss of this revenue has left the economy dependent on international aid (principally from Australia) and revenue from the sale of fishing licences. Diversification efforts include offshore banking and small-scale tourism.

The main trading partners are Australia and New Zealand. The only export is phosphate. All food, fuel, manufactured goods, machinery and construction materials are imported.

Unemployment—90% (2004 est)

Total external debt—US$33.3m (2004 est)

Trade with UK	*2010*	*2011*
Imports from UK	£220,576	£19,562
Exports to UK	£2,928	£25,407

EDUCATION AND COMMUNICATIONS

Education—Free of charge and compulsory between the ages of six and 17

Transport—The island has one international airport and 24km of roadways

Telecommunications—1,900 fixed lines (2010); there were 8,161 internet users in 2009

Internet code and IDD—nr; 674 (from UK), 44 (to UK)

Media—The government-owned Nauru Television is the island's principal broadcaster; there are no daily newspapers

The Netherlands

Koninkrijk der Nederlanden—Kingdom of the Netherlands

Area—41,543 sq. km

Capital—Amsterdam; population, 1,043,700 (2009 est)

Seat of government—The Hague (Den Haag or, in full, 's-Gravenhage), population 629,185 (2009 est)

Major cities—Almere, Eindhoven, Rotterdam, Tilburg, Utrecht

Currency—Euro (€) of 100 cents

Population—16,730,632 rising at 0.45% a year (2012 est); Dutch (80.7%), Indonesian (2.4%), Turkish (2.2%), Surinamese (2%), Moroccan (2%) (2008 est)

Religion—Christian 50% (Roman Catholic 30%, Protestant 20%), Muslim 6% (2006)

Language—Dutch, Frisian (both official); English is widely spoken

Population density—492 per sq. km (2010)

Urban population—82.9% (2010 est)

Median age (years)—41.1 (2011 est)

National anthem—'Het Wilhelmus' ['The William']

National day—30 April (Queen's Day)

Death penalty—Abolished for all crimes (since 1982)

CPI score—8.9 (2011)

FINANCIAL OUTLOOK

In February 2013, the European Commission cut its forecast for the Dutch economy, and projected a second year of contraction because of depressed domestic demand. It forecast GDP would shrink by 0.6% in 2013, followed by 1.1% growth in 2014, while the budget deficit is forecast to narrow to 3.6% of GDP in 2013, down from 4.1% in 2012. The economy contracted by 0.2% in 2012. In a March 2013 report, the IMF said that balance-sheet deleveraging would continue to be a drag on the recovery. In early 2013, Fitch cut the outlook on the Netherlands' credit rating to negative, citing the level of public debt, problems at some Dutch banks, and a property-market slump (house prices fell by 20% between 2008 and the end of 2012, according to the IMF). However, Fitch added that the country's AAA sovereign rating was still underpinned by its flexible, diversified, high value-added, and competitive economy, as well as current account surpluses and positive net international investment position.

CLIMATE AND TERRAIN

The Netherlands is a low-lying country; about a quarter is below sea level, making it susceptible to flooding despite the coastal defences and a network of dykes and canals. Its land area has been extended

over the centuries by land reclamation (polders), found especially in the west around the huge freshwater lake of Yssel, created in the 1930s by damming the Zuider Zee. The country is crossed by three major European rivers, the Rhine, Maas (Meuse) and Scheldt, whose estuaries are in the south-west. Mount Scenery (862m), on the Caribbean island of Saba, is considered the highest point of the Kingdom of the Netherlands. Elevation extremes in the Netherlands itself range from 322m (Vaalserberg) to −7m (Zuidplaspolder). The climate is temperate, with average temperatures in De Bilt ranging from −1°C in January to 22°C in July.

HISTORY AND POLITICS

Under the 1983 constitution, the head of state is a hereditary constitutional monarch. The States-General *(Staten-Generaal)* consists of the First Chamber *(Eerste Kamer)* of 75 members, elected for a four-year term by the Provincial States; and the Second Chamber *(Tweede Kamer)* of 150 members, directly elected for a four-year term. The head of government is the prime minister, who is responsible to the legislature.

Although it is a stable democracy, one party has rarely commanded a sufficient parliamentary majority to govern alone in the post-war period; governments have usually been coalitions of two or more parties. The collapse of a coalition of the Christian Democratic Alliance (CDA), the Labour Party (PvdA) and the Christian Union (CU) in February 2010 led to an election in June in which the People's Party for Freedom and Democracy (VVD) won 31 seats to the PvdA's 30 and CDA's 21. The VVD formed a minority government with the CDA and is dependent on the support of the Freedom Party (24 seats) to pass legislation.

HEAD OF STATE

HM The Queen of the Netherlands, Queen Beatrix Wilhelmina Armgard, KG, GCVO, *born* 31 January 1938; *succeeded* 30 April 1980

Heir, HRH Prince Willem Alexander, *born* 27 April 1967

SELECTED GOVERNMENT MEMBERS *as at July 2012*

Prime Minister, Mark Rutte
Deputy Prime Minister, Maxime Verhagen
Defence, Hans Hillen
Foreign Affairs, Uri Rosenthal

ROYAL NETHERLANDS EMBASSY

38 Hyde Park Gate, London SW7 5DP
T 020-7590 3200
E lon@minbuza.nl
W www.dutchembassyuk.org

Ambassador Extraordinary and Plenipotentiary, HE Pieter Waldeck, *apptd* 2007

BRITISH EMBASSY

Lange Voorhout 10, The Hague, 2514 ED
T (+31) (70) 427 0427
E ukinnl@fco.gov.uk
W ukinnl.fco.gov.uk

Ambassador Extraordinary and Plenipotentiary, HE Paul Arkwright, *apptd* 2009

DEFENCE

All aged 16–49, 2010 est	Males	Females
Available for military service	3,911,098	3,817,031
Fit for military service	3,201,328	3,122,889

Military expenditure—US$10,945m (2011)

ECONOMY AND TRADE

The Netherlands has a highly industrialised and diversified market economy, and is a major European transportation hub. The economy depends heavily on foreign trade and financial services, and contracted sharply in 2009 as exports fell by almost 25% in the global economic downturn. The government nationalised two banks to stabilise the financial sector and introduced stimulus measures, creating a budget deficit; the implementation of new fiscal measures in early 2011, however, reduced the budget deficit, which remained at 3.8% of GDP by the end of the year.

The highly mechanised agricultural sector employs only 2% of the workforce but output supplies the food processing industries and the export as well as the domestic market. Flower bulbs and cut flowers are a major contributor to this sector, as is the fishing industry. The industrial sector contributes 24.2% of GDP; major industries include food processing, and the manufacture of metal and engineering products, electrical machinery and equipment, chemicals, oil refining, construction and micro-electronics. The service industries represent 73% of the economy. Other EU countries, China and the USA account for most overseas trade. Principal exports are machinery and equipment, chemicals, fuels and foodstuffs. The main imports are machinery and transport equipment, chemicals, fuels, foodstuffs and clothing.

GNI—US$772,747m; US$49,050 per capita (2010)
Annual average growth of GDP—1.6% (2011 est)
Inflation rate—2.3% (2011 est)
Population below poverty line—10.5% (2005)
Unemployment—5.2% (2011 est)
Total external debt—US$2,655,000m (2011 est)
Imports—US$440,619m (2010)
Exports—US$492,267m (2010)

BALANCE OF PAYMENTS

Trade—US$51,647m surplus (2010)
Current Account—US$55,724m surplus (2010)

Trade with UK	2010	2011
Imports from UK	£20,565,717,098	£22,788,829,694
Exports to UK	£26,097,522,275	£28,232,441,059

COMMUNICATIONS

Airports—The principal airports are at Amsterdam, Rotterdam, Eindhoven and Maastricht, with a further 23 smaller airports and airfields around the country

Waterways—The main seaport is Rotterdam, although there are a number of other ports on river estuaries or linked to the coast by the canals; 6,214km of inland waterways are navigable by ships of up to 50 tonnes. The large merchant fleet includes 744 ships of over 1,000 tonnes

Roadways and railways—There are 136,827,km of roads and 2,896km of railways, of which 2,195km are electrified

Telecommunications—7.17 million fixed lines and 19.31 million mobile subscriptions (2010); there were 14.87 million internet users in 2009

Internet code and IDD—nl; 31 (from UK), 44 (to UK)

Major broadcasters—A competitive broadcasting sector includes Nederlandse Omroep Stichting (NOS), which oversees the country's broadcasting

Press—There are seven national daily newspapers, including *Algemeen Dagblad*, *NRC Handelsblad* and *De Telegraaf*

  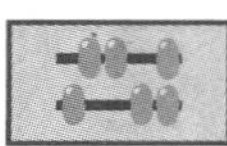      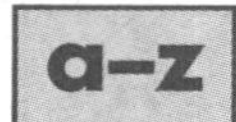

WPFI score—0,00 (1)

EDUCATION AND HEALTH

Thirteen years of compulsory primary and secondary education are provided by denominational and state schools. The principal universities are at Leiden, Utrecht, Groningen, Amsterdam, Nijmegen, Maastricht and Rotterdam.

Gross enrolment ratio (percentage of relevant age group)—primary 108%; secondary 120%; tertiary 63% (2009 est)
Health expenditure (per capita)—US$5,164 (2009)
Hospital beds (per 1,000 people)—4.3 (2004–9)
Life expectancy (years)—80.91 (2012 est)
Mortality rate—8.39 (2012 est)
Birth rate—10.89 (2012 est)
Infant mortality rate—3.73 (2012 est)

OVERSEAS TERRITORIES

The Kingdom of the Netherlands consists of four autonomous elements: the Netherlands (European and Caribbean Netherlands), Aruba, Curacao and St Maarten; the latter two were part of the Netherlands Antilles until its dissolution on 10 October 2010. The other three islands of the Netherlands Antilles, the 'Caribbean Netherlands', comprising Bonaire, St Eustatius and Saba, are now autonomous special municipalities of the Netherlands.

Aruba

Area—193 sq. km
Capital—Oranjestad; population, 33,112 (2009 est)
Major town—Sint Nicolaas
Currency—Aruban guilder/florin of 100 cents
Population—107,635 rising at 1.41% a year (2012 est)
Language—Dutch (official), Papiamento, Spanish, English
National Day—18 March (Flag Day)

The Caribbean island was colonised by the Dutch in the 17th century. It was part of the Netherlands Antilles until 1986, when it became a separate, autonomous territory. The Dutch government is responsible for external affairs and represented by a resident governor. Internal government is in the hands of the prime minister and council of ministers, who are responsible to the 21-member unicameral legislature (*Staten*), directly elected for a four-year term.

The principal economic activities are tourism and offshore financial services.

Governor, Fredis Refunjol, *apptd* 2004
Prime Minister, Mike Eman, *elected* 2009

Curacao

Area—444 sq. km
Capital—Willemstad; population, 123,355 (2009 est)
Currency—Netherlands Antilles guilder of 100 cents; to be replaced by the Caribbean guilder in 2013
Population—142,180 (2010 est)
Language—Dutch (official), Papiamento, English, Spanish

The island was colonised by the Dutch in the 17th century and was part of the Netherlands Antilles from 1954 until 10 October 2010, when it became a separate, autonomous territory. The Dutch government is responsible for external affairs and represented by a resident governor. Internal affairs are in the hands of a prime minister and council of ministers, who are responsible to the 21-member unicameral legislature (*Staten*), which serves a four-year term.

The principal economic activities are tourism, oil refining and offshore financial services.

Governor, Gen. Frits Goedgedrag, *apptd* 2002
Prime Minister, Gerrit Schotte, *elected* 2010

St Maarten

Area—34 sq. km
Capital—Philipsburg
Currency—Netherlands Antilles guilder of 100 cents; to be replaced by the Caribbean guilder in 2013
Population—37,429 (2010)
Language—Dutch, English (official), Spanish, Creole

The territory forms the southern part of the island of St Martin in the Caribbean; the north is French territory. Possession of the island was disputed between the Dutch and the Spanish until 1648, when the Spanish relinquished it to the Dutch and French, who divided it between them. The Dutch territory was part of the Netherlands Antilles from 1954 until 10 October 2010, when it became a separate, autonomous territory. The Dutch government is responsible for external affairs and represented by a governor. Internal affairs are in the hands of a prime minister and council of ministers, who are responsible to the 15-member unicameral legislature (*Staten*), which serves a four-year term.

The principal economic activities are tourism and sugar production.

Governor, Eugene Holiday, *apptd* 2010
Prime Minister, Sarah Westcott-Williams, *apptd* 2010

New Zealand

Aotearoa—New Zealand
Area—267,710 sq. km (includes outlying islands)
Capital—Wellington; population, 391,201 (2009 est)
Major cities—Auckland, Christchurch, Dunedin, Hamilton, Manakau, North Shore, Tauranga, Waitakere
Currency—New Zealand dollar (NZ$) of 100 cents
Population—4,327,944 rising at 0.86% a year (2012 est); European (56.8%), mixed (9.7%), Asian (8%), Maori (7.4%), Pacific Islander (4.6%) (2006)
Religion—Christian (Anglican 14%, other Protestant 16%, Roman Catholic 13%, other 10%), Hindu 2%, Buddhist 1%, other 2% (2006)
Language—English, Maori, New Zealand Sign Language (all official)
Population density—17 per sq. km (2010)
Urban population—86.8% (2010 est)
Median age (years)—37 (2011 est)
National anthem—'God Defend New Zealand'/'God Save the Queen'
National day—6 February (Waitangi Day)
Death penalty—Abolished for all crimes (since 1989)
CPI score—9.5 (2011)

FINANCIAL OUTLOOK

The economy grew by 2.5% in 2012, the highest annual growth in GDP since March 2008, when the economic recession began. GDP rose by 1.5% in the December 2012 quarter, the strongest quarterly growth since December 2009, according to Statistics New Zealand. However, the current account deficit for the year ended December 2012 was US$10.5 billion, or 5% of GDP. The increase in the deficit

from US$9.9 billion, or 4.7% of GDP, for the year ended September 2012, was mainly the result of a fall in exports of goods and services of US$1.3 billion. Exports of dairy and crude oil were both lower in the last quarter of 2012 than for the year ended September 2012, while expenditure by overseas visitors to New Zealand also fell. In March 2013, the IMF highlighted a strengthening housing market as one of the risks facing the New Zealand economy over the next 12 months.

Cook Islands

The Cook Islands economy was expected to grow by 5.4% in 2012 and by 3% in 2013. However, the Asian Development Bank says that for fiscal year 2012 (ending 30 June 2012), the Islands' economy actually grew by just 3.4%, well short of the forecast 5.4%. The ADB also reduced its GDP growth forecast for 2013 down to 2%. Much of the growth in 2012 was expected to come from increased visitor arrivals on the islands. In fact, visitor numbers were lower than anticipated, and capital spending by government was also somewhat reduced. However, the growth actually achieved was still higher than the 2.4% recorded for 2011. The government has embarked on a program of large infrastructure works on roads, water and energy, which is expected to underpin the growth expected in 2013. Increased phosphate exports from Nauru are expected to boost that island's economy by 4.8% in 2012, and 4.2% in 2013. Inflation during fiscal year 2012 averaged 3.0% (estimated) and is projected to rise to 4.2% in 2013, largely driven by increases in fuel prices. Merchandise exports from the Cook Islands fell by 40.9% in the first half of fiscal year 2012, largely caused by a marked drop in shipments of fresh fish.

CLIMATE AND TERRAIN

New Zealand consists of North Island, South Island and neighbouring coastal islands such as Stewart Island, and outlying islands that include the Chatham, Kermadec, Three Kings, Bounty, Antipodes, Snares, Auckland and Campbell groups in the South Pacific Ocean. The two larger islands, North Island and South Island, are separated by the relatively narrow Cook Strait. The island groups are much smaller and more widely dispersed.

Much of the North and South Islands is mountainous. The North Island mountains include several volcanoes, three of which are active. The principal range is the Southern Alps, extending the entire length of the South Island to the west of the Canterbury Plains. There are geysers and hot springs in the Rotorua district and glaciers in the Southern Alps. Elevation extremes range from 3,754m (Aoraki/Mt Cook) to 0m (Pacific Ocean). The climate is temperate, though with marked regional variations; average temperatures in Christchurch (South Island) range from 5°C in July to 20°C in January. The country is subject to seismic activity; a major earthquake devastated Christchurch in February 2011.

HISTORY AND POLITICS

Settled by Polynesian tribes, the ancestors of the Maori, from about the tenth century, New Zealand was sighted by the Dutch navigator Abel Tasman in 1642 but he did not land. The British explorer James Cook surveyed the coastline in 1769, the year in which the islands were claimed by the British. The Maori accepted British sovereignty in 1840, under the Treaty of Waitangi, in return for land rights and the rights of British subjects. Large-scale European immigration and the 1860s gold rush led to encroachment by settlers and 'land wars' with the Maori in 1860 and 1872; Maori resistance was defeated but concessions such as parliamentary representation were won. A tribunal was set up in 1975 to consider grievances caused by breaches of the Waitangi Treaty, and in the 1990s the Maori were compensated for land lost to European settlers.

New Zealand was administered as part of Britain's New South Wales colony until 1841, when it became a separate colony. In 1907 it was granted dominion status; in 1931 the Statute of Westminster tacitly acknowledged its independence, which was formally confirmed in 1947.

New Zealand forces took part in the Boer War, both world wars, the Korean War and the Vietnam War. Since the UK's entry into the EEC in 1973, the focus of New Zealand's foreign and trade policies has shifted to Asia and the Pacific region.

Post-war politics has been dominated by the National Party and the Labour Party, either forming governments on their own or in coalition with smaller parties; coalitions have been the norm since a proportional representation voting system was introduced in 1993. In the 2011 legislative election, the National Party won the most seats but failed to gain an overall majority by one seat; the party, led by John Key, formed a coalition government with the support of three smaller parties.

There is no written constitution. The head of state is Queen Elizabeth II, represented by the governor-general, who is appointed on the advice of the New Zealand government. The unicameral House of Representatives currently has 122 members (usually 120), elected for a three-year term; there are 70 members from single-member constituencies, which include seven Maori constituencies, and 52 (usually 50) allocated from party lists; if a party wins a significantly larger proportion of constituency seats relative to their party list vote, this can result in an 'overhang' of extra seats. The prime minister and cabinet are appointed by the governor-general on the advice of the legislature.

GOVERNOR-GENERAL

Governor-General, HE Lt.-Gen. Sir Jerry Mateparae, *sworn in* August 2011

SELECTED GOVERNMENT MEMBERS *as at June 2012*

Prime Minister, John Key
Deputy Prime Minister, Finance, Bill English
Defence, Jonathan Coleman
Internal Affairs, Chris Tremain

NEW ZEALAND HIGH COMMISSION

New Zealand House, 80 Haymarket, London SW1Y 4TQ
T 020-7930 8422
E aboutnz@newzealandhc.org.uk
W www.nzembassy.com/uk
High Commissioner, HE Derek Leask, *apptd* 2008

BRITISH HIGH COMMISSION

PO Box 1812, 44 Hill Street, Wellington 6011
T (+64) (4) 924 2888
E consularmail.wellington@fco.gov.uk
W ukinnewzealand.fco.gov.uk
High Commissioner, HE Victoria Treadell, MVO *apptd* 2010

DEFENCE

With Australia and the USA, New Zealand formed the ANZUS Pacific Security Treaty in 1951, but its non-nuclear military policy led to disagreements with the USA and France in 1985, and in 1986 the USA suspended its ANZUS obligations towards New Zealand.

All aged 16–49, 2010 est	*Males*	*Females*
Available for military service	1,019,798	1,003,429
Fit for military service	843,526	828,779

Military expenditure—US$1,566m (2011)

ECONOMY AND TRADE

Since the 1980s industrial and service sectors have developed to complement the large, efficient agricultural sector. Growth has been driven by trade, particularly in agricultural products, but various factors had pushed the economy into recession in 2008 before the global downturn. Government stimulus measures were introduced to cushion the effects of the recession in 2009, after which a fragile recovery began.

The agricultural sector contributes 4.7% of GDP and employs 7% of the workforce. The main products are dairy products, meat, cereals, pulses, fruit, vegetables, wool and fish. The major industries are food processing, wood and paper products, textiles, machinery, transport equipment, financial services, mining, and tourism, which is overtaking agriculture as the main source of foreign exchange revenue. Non-metallic minerals such as coal, limestone and dolomite are heavily exploited, and gold and iron production is economically important. Natural gas deposits in offshore and onshore fields are used for electricity generation, though a significant amount of the country's energy is derived from sustainable sources such as hydroelectric power. Industry contributes 24% of GDP and services 71.3%.

The main trading partners are Australia, China, the USA and Japan. Principal exports are dairy products, meat, wood, wood products, fish and machinery. The main imports are machinery and equipment, vehicles and aircraft, petroleum, electronics, textiles and plastics.

GNI—US$121,435m; US$28,770 per capita (2009)
Annual average growth of GDP—2% (2011 est)
Inflation rate—4.5% (2011 est)
Unemployment—6.5% (2011 est)
Total external debt—US$84,540m (2011 est)
Imports—US$29,487m (2010)
Exports—US$30,123m (2010)

BALANCE OF PAYMENTS
Trade—US$636m surplus (2010)
Current Account—US$5,743m deficit (2010)

Trade with UK	2010*	2011**
Imports from UK	£390,760,955	£507,448,504
Exports to UK	£766,875,068	£860,797,751

* Includes Tokelau, Cook Islands and Niue
** Includes Cook Islands and Niue

COMMUNICATIONS

Airports—The principal airports are at Auckland, Wellington (North Island), Christchurch and Dunedin (South Island) and there are nearly 120 smaller airports around the country
Waterways—Tauranga, Christchurch, New Plymouth, Auckland and Napier are the main seaports
Roadways and railways—There are 93,911km of roads, of which about 65% are surfaced; there are 4,128km of railways
Telecommunications—1.87 million fixed lines and 5.02 million mobile subscriptions (2010); there were 3.4 million internet users in 2009
Internet code and IDD—nz; 64 (from UK), 44 (to UK)
Major broadcasters—The state-owned Television New Zealand competes with two other private networks; Niu FM is the national government-funded station for the Pacific island communities
Press—The Auckland-based *New Zealand Herald* has the largest circulation, alongside Wellington-based *Dominion Post* and Christchurch-based *The Press*

WPFI score—1,50 (8)

EDUCATION AND HEALTH

Education is free of charge and compulsory between the ages of 5 and 16.
Gross enrolment ratio (percentage of relevant age group)—primary 101%; secondary 125%; tertiary 83% (2009 est)
Health expenditure (per capita)—US$2,634 (2009)
Hospital beds (per 1,000 people)—6.2 (2002–7)
Life expectancy (years)—80.71 (2012 est)
Mortality rate—7.2 (2012 est)
Birth rate—13.57 (2012 est)
Infant mortality rate—4.72 (2012 est)

TERRITORIES

Tokelau

Area—12 sq. km
Population—1,368 (2012 est)
Tokelau consists of three atolls, Fakaofo, Nukunonu and Atafu, in the southern Pacific Ocean. Formerly part of Britain's Gilbert and Ellice Islands colony, Tokelau was transferred to New Zealand administration in 1926 and proclaimed part of New Zealand in 1949.

The territory is self-administering, but has rejected greater autonomy in two referendums (2006 and 2007). The Council for the Ongoing Government (cabinet) comprises three *Faipule* (village leaders) and three *Pulenuku* (village mayors), one from each atoll; the position of *Ulu-o-Tokelau* (leader) is rotated among the three *Faipule* members annually. The *General Fono*, which has 20 members elected for a three-year term, has legislative powers. Each atoll has a *Taupulega* (council of elders).

The economy is dependent on New Zealand budgetary aid, with some revenue derived from remittances and the sale of fishing rights, stamps, coins and the use of its internet suffix. The main activities are subsistence farming, copra production and handicrafts.
Administrator, Jonathan Kings, *apptd* 2011

The Ross Dependency

New Zealand has administrative responsibility for the Ross Dependency. This is defined as all the Antarctic islands and territories between 160° E. and 150° W. longitude which are situated south of the 60° S. parallel, including Edward VII Land and portions of Victoria Land.

ASSOCIATED STATES

Cook Islands

Area—236 sq. km
Population—10,777 (2012 est)
Capital—Avarua, on Rarotonga
The Cook Islands consist of 15 volcanic islands and coral atolls in the southern Pacific Ocean. A former British protectorate, since 1965 the islands have been self-governing in free association with New Zealand.

Queen Elizabeth II has a representative on the islands, and the New Zealand government is represented by a high commissioner. There is a 24-member legislative assembly, and the House of Ariki, made up of 15 traditional leaders who advise on traditional matters. Executive power is exercised by a prime minister and a cabinet responsible to the legislature.

The main economic activities are tourism, agriculture (especially tropical fruits), fruit processing, fishing, garment manufacturing, handicrafts and pearl-farming; black pearls are the main export.

HM Representative, Sir Frederick Goodwin, KBE, *apptd* 2001
Prime Minister, Henry Puna *apptd* 2010

Niue

Area—260 sq. km
Population—1,269 (2012 est)
Capital—Alofi; population, 547 (2009 est)

Although part of the Cook Islands group, Niue was administered separately after 1903. Since 1974 the island has been self-governing in free association with New Zealand.

A New Zealand high commissioner represents both the Queen and the New Zealand government. There is a 20-member legislative assembly; executive power is exercised by a prime minister and a three-member cabinet drawn from the assembly's members.

The principal economic activities are agriculture, fishing, tourism, handicrafts, food processing and the sale of postage stamps and the use of its internet suffix.

New Zealand High Commissioner, Mark Blumsky, *apptd* 2011
Premier, Toke Talagi

Nigeria

Federal Republic of Nigeria
Area—923,768 sq. km
Capital—Abuja (since 1991); population, 1,857,230 (2009 est)
Major cities—Aba, Benin City, Ibadan, Ilorin, Kaduna, Kano, Lagos (the former capital), Port Harcourt, Warri
Currency—Naira (N) of 100 kobo
Population—170,123,740 rising at 2.55% a year (2012 est); Hausa and Fulani (29%), Yoruba (21%), Igbo (18%), Ijaw (10%), Kanuri (4%), Ibibio (3.5%), Tiv (2.5%) (est)
Religion—Muslim 50% (predominantly Sunni), Christian 40%, indigenous beliefs 10% (est); many Christians and Muslims also follow indigenous beliefs
Language—English (official), Hausa, Yoruba, Igbo, Fula, over 500 other languages
Population density—174 per sq. km (2010)
Urban population—49.8% (2010 est)
Median age (years)—19.2 (2011 est)
National anthem—'Arise O Compatriots, Nigeria's Call Obey'
National day—1 October (Independence Day)
Death penalty—Retained
CPI score—2.4 (2011)

FINANCIAL OUTLOOK

In December 2012, the Nigerian National Assembly passed a US$31.6 billion budget for 2013, which basically aims to cut back on "heritage" saving of oil money, and use more oil revenue for social spending. The formula previously used by the Nigerian government was that anything above US$75 a barrel went into the "Excess Crude Account." Parliament raised that to US$79 a barrel, even though the global price of crude held more or less constant through the year. A sovereign wealth fund aimed at ring-fencing Nigeria's oil savings, instead of having it channeled by lawmakers into constituency spending, is due to be launched in 2013. The budget assumes that economic growth in 2013 will be 6.5%, with inflation of 9.5%, and an exchange rate of 160 Nigerian niara to the US dollar. Nigeria also intends to launch a proposed infrastructure Euro Bond of around US$1 billion (N160 billion) to complete gas pipeline and other infrastructure developments.

CLIMATE AND TERRAIN

The north is arid savannah and semi-desert plains, which rise to central hills and plateaux. There are mountains along the south-eastern border, but the south is generally low-lying and covered in tropical rainforest, with mangrove swamps along the coast and hills in the south-east. Elevation extremes range from 2,419m (Chappal Waddi) to 0m (Atlantic Ocean). The river Niger flows across the country from the north-west to the south coast, where it forms a broad delta on the Gulf of Guinea. The climate is equatorial in the south, tropical in the centre and arid in the north. The north has one rainy season (June to September), while the south has two (March–July, September–October); average temperatures in Lagos range between 21°C and 33°C all year round.

HISTORY AND POLITICS

The country is a federal democratic republic. Under the 1999 constitution, the executive president is directly elected for a four-year term, renewable once. The president appoints the federal executive council, which must be approved by the senate. The bicameral National Assembly comprises the 360-member House of Representatives and the 109-member senate, both elected for a four-year term.

The People's Democratic Party (PDP) has dominated politics since 1999, and retained its majority in both legislative chambers in the 2007 and 2011 elections. President Goodluck Jonathan, elected as vice-president in 2007, succeeded to the presidency after the death of President Yar'Adua in May 2010, and was elected president in the first round of voting in April 2011.

HEAD OF STATE

President, Goodluck Jonathan, *sworn in* 6 May 2010, *elected* 16 April 2011
Vice-President, Namadi Sambo

SELECTED GOVERNMENT MEMBERS *as at August 2012*

Finance, Ngozi Okonjo-Iweala
Foreign Affairs, Olugbenga Ashiru
Internal Affairs, Abba Moro

HIGH COMMISSION FOR THE FEDERAL REPUBLIC OF NIGERIA

Nigeria House, 9 Northumberland Avenue, London WC2N 5BX
T 020-7839 1244
E chancery@nigeriahc.org
W www.nigeriahc.org.uk
High Commissioner, HE Dr Dalhatu S. Tafida, *apptd* 2008

BRITISH HIGH COMMISSION

19 Torrens Close, Maitama, PMB 4808, Abujaa
T (+234) (9) 462 2200
E information.abuja@fco.gov.uk
W ukinnigeria.fco.gov.uk
High Commissioner, HE Andrew Lloyd, *apptd* 2011

Federal Structure

The federal republic is divided into 36 states and the Federal Capital Territory: Abia, Adamawa, Akwa Ibom, Anambra, Bauchi, Bayelsa, Benue, Borno, Cross River, Delta, Ebonyi, Edo, Ekiti, Enugu, Gombe, Imo, Jigawa, Kaduna, Kano, Katsina, Kebbi, Kogi, Kwara, Lagos, Nassarawa, Niger, Ogun, Ondo, Osun, Oyo, Plateau, Rivers,

Sokoto, Taraba, Yobe and Zamfara. Each state has an elected governor and legislature.

DEFENCE

All aged 16–49, 2010 est	Males	Females
Available for military service	37,087,711	35,232,127
Fit for military service	20,839,976	19,867,683

Military expenditure—US$2,215m (2011)

ECONOMY AND TRADE

Nigeria is the leading sub-Saharan oil producer, enjoying an oil boom in the 1970s and recently benefiting again from high oil prices. However, mismanagement and corruption, which dissipated the profits of the 1970s boom, mean that the majority of the population has yet to derive much benefit, and nearly three-quarters live below the poverty line. Past governments also failed to diversify the economy away from its dependence on oil, which accounts for 80% of government revenue and 95% of foreign exchange earnings. However, since 2008 economic reforms have been introduced to improve fiscal and monetary management, curb inflation and address regional agitation for wider distribution of oil revenues. Factors such as security and inadequate infrastructure remain obstacles to growth, but infrastructure improvements are a priority, especially in electricity supply and roads. Recent high oil revenues and debt relief or cancellation have freed Nigeria from much of its large foreign debt.

The mainstay of the economy is agriculture, mostly at subsistence level, which generates 35.4% of GDP and engages 70% of the labour force. The main crops include cocoa, peanuts, cotton, palm oil, maize, rice, sorghum, millet and rubber. However, agricultural output has failed to keep pace with rapid population growth, changing Nigeria from a net food exporter to a food importer. Industrial activities include oil and natural gas production, mining (coal, tin, columbite), processing agricultural products, textiles, cement and other construction materials and footwear. Industry contributes 33.6% of GDP and services 31%.

The main trading partners are the USA (37.4% of exports), China, India, Brazil and the EU. Principal exports are oil and oil products, cocoa and rubber. The main imports are machinery, chemicals, transport equipment, manufactured goods, food and live animals.

GNI—US$176,768m; US$1,180 per capita (2010)
Annual average growth of GDP—6.9% (2011 est)
Inflation rate—10.8% (2011 est)
Population below poverty line—70% (2007 est)
Unemployment—21% (2011 est)
Total external debt—US$12,060m (2011 est)
Imports—US$39,000m (2009)
Exports—US$52,500m (2009)

BALANCE OF PAYMENTS

Trade—US$13,500m surplus (2009)
Current Account—US$21,899m surplus (2009)

Trade with UK	2010	2011
Imports from UK	£1,367,745,985	£1,523,368,179
Exports to UK	£796,614,837	£2,236,055,927

COMMUNICATIONS

Airports—There are 54 airports and airfields, including the principal airports at Lagos, Abuja, Kano and Port Harcourt
Waterways—There are 8,600km of waterways, mostly on the Niger and Benue rivers; the main seaports are Lagos, Port Harcourt, Warri and Calabar.
Roadways and railways—There are 193,200km of roads; the Nigerian railway network, which is controlled by the Nigerian Railway Corporation, has 3,505km of track
Telecommunications—1.05 million fixed lines and 87.29 million mobile subscriptions (2010); there were 43.99 million internet users in 2009
Internet code and IDD—ng; 234 (from UK), 9 44 (to UK)
Major broadcasters—The state-run Nigerian Television Authority reaches nearly half of the population
Press—*The Guardian* is one of the most influential news publications in the country; the government-backed *New Nigerian* prints separate editions in Lagos and Kaduna
WPFI score—51,50 (145)

EDUCATION AND HEALTH

Literacy rate—60.8% (2009 est)
Gross enrolment ratio (percentage of relevant age group)—primary 83%; secondary 44% (2010 est)
Health expenditure (per capita)—US$69 (2009)
Hospital beds (per 1,000 people)—0.5 (2004–9)
Life expectancy (years)—52.05 (2012 est)
Mortality rate—13.48 (2012 est)
Birth rate—39.23 (2012 est)
Infant mortality rate—74.36 (2012 est)
HIV/AIDS adult prevalence—3.6% (2009 est)

Norway

Kongeriket Norge—Kingdom of Norway
Area—386,224 sq. km, of which Svalbard and Jan Mayen have a combined area of 62,422 sq. km
Capital—Oslo; population, 874,695 (2009 est)
Major cities—Bergen, Stavanger, Trondheim
Currency—Krone of 100 ore
Population—4,707,270 rising at 0.33% per year (2012 est)
Religion—Christian (Lutheran 79%, other Protestant 4%, Roman Catholic 1%), Muslim 2% (est)
Language—Bokmal and Nynorsk Norwegian (both official), Finnish, Sami (official in six municipalities)
Population density—16 per sq. km (2010)
Urban population—77.6% (2010 est)
Median age (years)—40 (2011 est)
National anthem—'Ja, Vi Elsker Dette Landet' ['Yes, We Love This Country']
National day—17 May (Constitution Day)
Death penalty—Abolished for all crimes (since 1979)
CPI score—9.0 (2011)

FINANCIAL OUTLOOK

In its 2013 budget, Norway pointed out that employment has increased for the last eight quarters, to the point where there are now more jobs than there were before the 2008 global financial crisis. As a consequence, unemployment is now well below the

  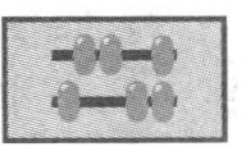      

average for the last 25 years, and considerably lower than in most other industrialized countries. GDP growth in 2013 is expected to be around 3%, while unemployment is around 2.5%, which means that Norway's mainland economy is starting to run into capacity constraints. Wage costs are running well above the EU average, which is damaging Norway's competitiveness, making exporters vulnerable to changes in retail prices, or to further appreciation of the Norwegian krone. Low interest rates and high wages are fueling strong consumer demand, boosting the construction and retail sectors. Private consumption growth is estimated at 3.75% in 2012, and 4% in 2013. House prices have risen 35% since the 2008 crash. Investment in the petroleum sector increased by 13% year-on-year and was an important driver behind the pick-up in the Norwegian economy.

CLIMATE AND TERRAIN

The terrain is mostly mountainous, with elevated, barren plateaux separated by deep, narrow valleys; the north is arctic tundra. The coastline is deeply indented with numerous fjords and fringed with thousands of rocky islands and islets; Geirangerfjord and Naeroyfjord are UNESCO World Heritage Sites. Elevation extremes range from 2,469m (Galdhopiggen) to 0m (Norwegian Sea).

Nearly half of the country lies north of the Arctic Circle, and at North Cape the sun does not appear to set between about 14 May and 29 July, causing the phenomenon known as the midnight sun; conversely, there is no apparent sunrise from about 18 November to 24 January. The climate is temperate on the coast but colder and wetter inland; average temperatures in Oslo range from −7°C in January to 22°C in July, but winter temperatures in parts of the north can drop to −40°C.

HISTORY AND POLITICS

Norway became a unified country under the rule of King Harald Fairhair in c.900 but dissolved after his death and was reunified by Olav II in c. 1016–28. Canute brought Norway under Danish rule in 1028 but the throne reverted on his death to Magnus I. When the royal house died out in the 14th century, the Danish monarch was the nearest heir and in 1397 Norway, Denmark and Sweden were united under a single monarch in the Kalmar Union. Sweden seceded from the union in 1523, but Norway continued to be ruled by the Danish crown until 1814, when it was ceded to Sweden.

Although internal self-government was established in 1814, growing tension over constraints on the Norwegian government led to the union being dissolved, and Norway became independent in 1905. The first king of the newly independent country was a Danish prince, who took the throne as King Haakon VII.

The country was neutral in the First World War, but in the Second World War Norway was invaded and occupied by Germany from 1940 until 1945. Norway joined NATO in 1949 and was a founder member of the European Free Trade Association in 1960. Membership of the EU was rejected in referendums in 1972 and 1994.

After 1945, governments pursued policies of economic planning and an extensive welfare state. The Labour Party dominated politics from the 1930s to the early 1980s, governing either on its own or in coalition with smaller parties. It was returned to power in 2005 after winning a majority of seats in the legislative election, forming a coalition government with the Socialist Left and Centre parties. In the 2009 legislative election the governing coalition was returned with a one-seat majority.

Norway is a constitutional monarchy with a hereditary monarch as head of state. Under the 1814 constitution, the unicameral *Storting* has 169 members who are directly elected for a four-year term; a 2007 constitutional amendment abolished a bicameral division within the *Storting*, which took effect from the 2009 election. The prime minister, who is responsible to parliament, appoints the cabinet.

HEAD OF STATE

HM The King of Norway, King Harald V, KG, GCVO, *born* 21 February 1937; *succeeded* 17 January 1991
Heir, HRH Crown Prince Haakon Magnus, *born* 20 July 1973

SELECTED GOVERNMENT MEMBERS *as at July 2012*

Prime Minister, Jens Stoltenberg
Defence, Espen Barth Eide
Finance, Sigbjorn Johnsen
Foreign Affairs, Jonas Gahr Store

ROYAL NORWEGIAN EMBASSY

25 Belgrave Square, London SW1X 8QD
T 020-7591 5500
E emb.london@mfa.no
W www.norway.org.uk
Ambassador Extraordinary and Plenipotentiary, HE Kim Traavik, *apptd* 2010

BRITISH EMBASSY

Thomas Heftyesgate 8, 0264 Oslo
T (+47) 2313 2700
E britemb@online.no
W ukinnorway.fco.gov.uk
Ambassador Extraordinary and Plenipotentiary, HE Jane Owen, *apptd* 2010

DEFENCE

All aged 16–49, 2010 est	*Males*	*Females*
Available for military service	1,079,043	1,051,210
Fit for military service	888,761	865,697

Military expenditure—US$7,083m (2011)
Conscription duration—12 months plus refresher training

ECONOMY AND TRADE

Norway's prosperity depends primarily upon oil and gas extraction, which accounts for nearly half of exports, and its fisheries. Oil production is declining, but exploration for oil and gas in the Barents Sea, and other areas that are becoming more accessible as the Arctic ice cap retreats, is ongoing. Norway has planned for the time when reserves are exhausted by investing revenue from this sector in a government fund. The state retains a majority share in key enterprises, including the oil industry.

The nature of the terrain restricts agriculture, which generates 2.7% of GDP. The main industries apart from oil and gas are fishing, forestry, food processing, shipbuilding, pulp and paper products, metals, chemicals, mining and textiles. Shipping freight services are also significant, with Norwegian companies controlling over 5% of the world's shipping fleet by tonnage. Industry contributes 38.3% of GDP and services 59%.

The main trading partners are EU countries, the USA and China. Principal exports are oil and petroleum products, machinery and equipment, metals, chemicals, ships and fish. The main imports are machinery and equipment, chemicals, metals and foodstuffs.

GNI—US$413,979m; US$84,290 per capita (2010)
Annual average growth of GDP—1.7% (2011 est)
Inflation rate—1.4% (2011 est)
Unemployment—3.4% (2011 est)
Total external debt—US$644,500m (2011)

 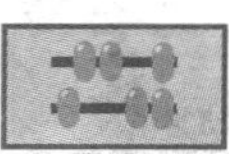      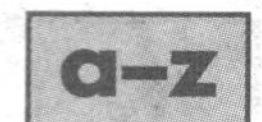

Imports—US$77,252m (2010)
Exports—US$131,395m (2010)

BALANCE OF PAYMENTS
Trade—US$54,144m surplus (2010)
Current Account—US$51,284m surplus (2010)

Trade with UK	2010	2011
Imports from UK	£2,982,853,211	£3,294,965,087
Exports to UK	£19,223,317,249	£24,244,871,138

COMMUNICATIONS
Airports—There are 98 airports and airfields, including the principal airports at Oslo, Bergen, Stavanger and Trondheim
Waterways—The main ports are Oslo, Bergen, Kristiansand, Tonsberg, Stavanger and Narvik, and there is a large merchant fleet, with 585 ships of over 1,000 tonnes registered in Norway and 974 registered abroad
Roadways and railways—There are 93,509km of roads and 4,169km of railways
Telecommunications—1.70 million fixed lines and 5.52 million mobile subscriptions (2010); there were 4.43 million internet users in 2009
Major broadcasters—The public broadcaster NRK operates radio and television channels, in competition with a number of commercial rivals
Press—*VG* has the largest circulation amongst the country's daily news publications; other newspapers include *The Norway Post* and *Dagbladet*
WPFI score—0,00 (1)

EDUCATION AND HEALTH
Education from six to 16 is free and compulsory in the basic schools, and free from 16 to 19 years.
Gross enrolment ratio (percentage of relevant age group)—primary 99%; secondary 110%; tertiary 74% (2009 est)
Health expenditure (per capita)—US$7,662 (2009)
Hospital beds (per 1,000 people)—3.5 (2004–9)
Life expectancy (years)—80.32 (2012 est)
Mortality rate—9.22 (2012 est)
Birth rate—10.8 (2012 est)
Infant mortality rate—3.5 (2012 est)

TERRITORIES
Svalbard
Area—62,045 sq. km
Population—1,970 (2012 est); Norwegian 55%, Russian and Ukrainian 44%

The Svalbard archipelago consists of Spitsbergen, North East Land, the Wiche Islands, Barents Island, Edge Island, Prince Charles Foreland, Hope Island and Bear Island. It lies north of the Arctic Circle, and glaciers and snow cover around 60% of the area, although the west coast is ice-free for about half the year. Some 65% of the Svalbard archipelago is protected to ensure biodiversity; there are seven national parks, six large nature reserves, 15 bird sanctuaries and one geotopic protected area. A global seed repository has been established on Spitsbergen. Norway's sovereignty was recognised by treaty in 1920 but the other signatories were granted equal rights to exploit mineral deposits, although this right is now only exercised by Russia. The territory is administered by a governor, who is responsible to the Ministry of Justice and Police. The main economic activities are coal mining, tourism, and research and education.

Jan Mayen Island
Area—377 sq. km
Population—the only residents are the staff of the radio and meteorological stations

The island is barren, volcanic and partially covered by glaciers, with no exploitable natural resources. It lies in the North Atlantic Ocean about 950 km west of Norway and is home to the Beerenberg volcano, the northernmost active volcano on earth. It was annexed by Norway in 1922 and integrated into the kingdom in 1930; since 1995 it has been administered by the governor of Nordland county.

Norwegian Antarctic Territory
The Norwegian Antarctic Territory consists of Queen Maud Land, Bouvet Island and Peter the First Island. Claimed in 1938, Queen Maud Land is a sector of the Antarctic continent which extends from 45° E. to 20° E. Peter the First Island was formally claimed in 1931 and is the only claimed area covered under the Antarctic Treaty that is not part of the main land mass. Bouvet Island was claimed in 1930.

Pakistan

Jamhuryat Islami Pakistan—Islamic Republic of Pakistan
Area—796,095 sq. km
Capital—Islamabad; population, 832,002 (2009 est)
Major cities—Faisalabad, Gujranwala, Hyderabad, Karachi, Lahore, Multan, Peshawar, Quetta, Rawalpindi
Currency—Pakistan rupee of 100 paisa
Population—190,291,129 rising at 1.55% a year (2012 est); Punjabi (44.7%), Pashtun (15.4%), Sindhi (14.1%), Sariaki (8.4%), Muhajirs (7.6%), Balochi (3.6%) (est)
Religion—Muslim 95% (predominantly Sunni) (est); small Christian and Hindu minorities; Islam is the state religion
Language—Urdu, English (both official), Punjabi, Sindhi, Siraiki, Pashto, Balochi, Hindko, Brahui, Burushaski
Population density—225 per sq. km (2010)
Urban population—37% (2010 est)
Median age (years)—21.6 (2011 est)
National anthem—'Qaumi Tarana' ['National Anthem']
National day—23 March (Republic Day)
Death penalty—Retained
CPI score—2.5 (2011)

FINANCIAL OUTLOOK
The Pakistan 2013 budget began with a look back to the disastrous position the country found itself in at the start of its transition to democracy in 2008. The rupee depreciated from the 60s to the 80s against the US dollar, the Karachi KSE-100 index dropped by one-third, which meant the market had to be closed, and gross reserves dropped from US$16 billion to US$6 billion. Pakistan immediately went to the IMF and entered a program that helped to stabilize the economy. The economy has now improved, despite shocks such as

  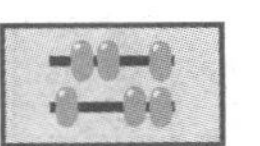      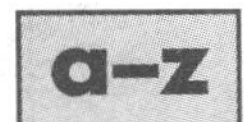

the great floods of 2010, to the point where growth in 2011 and 2012 averaged around 3.4%, by comparison with 2% in 2009 and 2010. The rate of growth for 2013 is expected to be 3.7%. The country has repaid US$1.2 billion of loans to the IMF. The central government has transformed funding to the provinces and has made them directly responsible for health and education in their areas, which is expected to have long-term benefits to the economy. A social safety net has been introduced for the poorest families and covers some 7 million vulnerable households. Electricity is provided at one-sixth of the cost of production to some 8 million families. The days of 25% inflation, seen in 2008, are over; inflation was down to 11% in 2012, with single-digit inflation targeted for 2013.

CLIMATE AND TERRAIN

The arid Thar desert in the east gives way to the fertile Indus valley in the centre of the country. The terrain then rises to the Makran, Kirthar and Sulaiman mountain ranges in the west and the Karakoram and Himalayan ranges in the north. Elevation extremes range from 8,611m (K2) to 0m (Indian Ocean). The climate varies greatly across the country. For most areas, the rainy season runs from July to September and is accompanied by very high humidity. Average temperatures in Lahore range from 12°C in January to 33°C in June. Pakistan is prone to earthquakes, the most recent in 2005 and 2008, and flooding; following heavy monsoon rains in 2010 the entire length of the Indus valley was flooded, displacing millions of people.

HISTORY AND POLITICS

Pakistan is a federal republic. The 1973 constitution has been suspended and restored several times, amended in 1985, 2002 and 2003, and in 2010 was reinstated in its original form, returning some of the president's powers to the prime minister.

The president is elected by the legislature for a five-year term. The parliament *(Majlis as-Shura)* comprises a lower house, the National Assembly and the senate. The National Assembly has 342 members, of whom 60 are women and ten are elected by non-Muslim minorities; members serve a five-year term. The senate has 104 members, 92 elected by provincial assemblies, eight chosen by tribal agencies and four elected by the National Assembly; they serve a six-year term, with half elected every three years. The prime minister is nominated by and is responsible to the legislature.

There are four provinces: Balochistan, Khyber Pukhtoonkhwa (formerly North-West Frontier Province), Punjab and Sindh. Each has a provincial assembly and government. In addition, there are the Federally Administered Tribal Areas and the Islamabad Capital Territory.

The legislative elections originally scheduled for January 2008 were postponed to February after the assassination of Benazir Bhutto in December 2007. The two main opposition parties, Bhutto's Pakistan People's Party (PPP) and the Pakistan Muslim League–Nawaz Sharif (PML-N), won the most seats and formed a coalition government with two smaller parties; the PML-N withdrew from the coalition government in August 2008. The presidential election in September 2008 was won by Asif Ali Zadari, the widower of Benazir Bhutto. Two smaller parties withdrew from the coalition government in December 2010, and a new PPP-led coalition was formed in February 2011. The Pakistan Muslim League–Quaid-e-Azam party joined the coalition in April 2011.

HEAD OF STATE
President, Asif Ali Zardari, *elected* 6 September 2008, *sworn in* 9 September 2008

SELECTED GOVERNMENT MEMBERS *as at August 2012*
Prime Minister, Raja Ashruf
Defence, Naveed Qamar
Foreign Affairs, Hina Khar
Finance, Abdul Hafiz Sheikh

HIGH COMMISSION FOR THE ISLAMIC REPUBLIC OF PAKISTAN
34–36 Lowndes Square, London SW1X 9JN
T 020-7664 9200
W www.phclondon.org
High Commissioner, HE Wajid Shamsul Hasan, *apptd* 2008

BRITISH HIGH COMMISSION
PO Box 1122, Diplomatic Enclave, Ramna 5, Islamabad
T (+92) (51) 282 2000
E consularenquiries.karachi@fco.gov.uk
W ukinpakistan.fco.gov.uk
High Commissioner, HE Adam Thomson, CMG, *apptd* 2010

Insurgencies

Balochistan, Punjab and Sindh provinces have all been affected since the 1980s by conflict between Shia and Sunni fundamentalists. Balochistan and, since the early 1990s, Sindh (especially Karachi) have experienced violence by armed militants seeking greater autonomy for each province.

Civil order has always been harder to maintain in the North-West Frontier Province and the federally administered tribal areas than in the rest of the country. These areas became havens for the Taliban and al-Qaida fleeing Afghanistan after 2001 and for like-minded Pakistani militants, who became entrenched along the Afghan border, radicalising and destabilising increasingly wide areas. Government military and security forces are struggling to maintain control in over half of these areas. The government conceded the imposition of Shariah law in the Swat valley as part of a cease-fire agreement with the Taliban in early 2009, but when the Taliban attempted to extend their influence further into the country, the army began a counter-insurgency offensive to retake the area in April 2009, subsequently moving against the Taliban in other strongholds such as South Waziristan. These offensives led to an increase in militants' attacks in the major cities, while by 2010 the Taliban began to reassert its influence in some of the areas cleared by the army offensives in 2009.

Foreign Relations

Since partition, sovereignty over the predominantly Muslim state of Jammu and Kashmir has been disputed between Pakistan and India. A short war in 1947–8 resulted in the state being partitioned between the two countries; its status remains unresolved, despite further outbreaks of war in 1965 and 1971, low-level conflict for control of the Siachen glacier since 1985 and occasional increases in military exchanges, most recently in 1999–2002 and 2003. Tension was exacerbated by Pakistan's support of the Muslim insurgency in the Indian part of the state, which began in the 1980s, and by both countries' acquisition of nuclear weapons. Moves towards a peaceful settlement began in 2003, when diplomatic missions were reopened and the resumption of transport links was initiated. Formal diplomatic talks began in 2004 and have achieved several accords intended to reduce tension between the two countries, although the status of Kashmir has yet to be addressed. Talks were temporarily suspended by the Indian government after the Mumbai terrorist attacks in 2008, but resumed in 2010.

International concern was raised in 2004 by disclosures that Pakistan has sold its nuclear technology to other countries.

DEFENCE

All aged 16–49, 2010 est	Males	Females
Available for military service	48,453,305	44,898,096
Fit for military service	37,945,440	37,381,549

Military expenditure—US$5,685m (2011)*
* Figure does not include paramilitary spending

ECONOMY AND TRADE
Decades of political instability, inefficiency, corruption and high military expenditure have left Pakistan a poor and underdeveloped country. In the 2000s economic reforms, international aid and greater foreign investment produced steady growth of 5–8% a year until 2008, notably in the industrial and service sectors, and reduced poverty levels by 10% between 2001 and 2007. However, slower growth in 2008 caused budget and fiscal deficits that forced Pakistan to seek IMF assistance; inflation, already a persistent problem, rose to 20.3% in 2008 and remains high. These problems were exacerbated by the 2010 floods, which left millions homeless, destroyed crops and damaged infrastructure. A large proportion of the country's labour force works abroad, especially in the Middle East, providing valuable remittances but also causing use of child labour within Pakistan.

Agriculture employs 45% of the workforce, producing cotton, wheat, rice, sugar cane, vegetables, milk, meat and eggs, and contributing 20.9% of GDP. Significant manufacturing industries include textiles and clothing, food processing, pharmaceuticals, construction materials, paper products, fertiliser and seafood. Industry accounts for 25.8% of GDP and services for 53.3%.

The main trading partners are the UAE, the USA, China, Saudi Arabia and Afghanistan. Principal exports are textiles (clothing, bed linen, cotton cloth and yarn), rice, leather goods, sports goods, chemicals, carpets and rugs. The main imports are petroleum, machinery, plastics, transport equipment, edible oils, paper, iron, steel and tea.

GNI—US$183,619m; US$1,050 per capita (2010)
Annual average growth of GDP—2.4% (2011 est)
Inflation rate—13.9% (2011 est)
Population below poverty line—24% (2005–6 est)
Unemployment—5.6% (2011 est)
Total external debt—US$59,390m (2011 est)
Imports—US$37,783m (2010)
Exports—US$21,409m (2010)

BALANCE OF PAYMENTS
Trade—US$16,373m deficit (2010)
Current Account—US$3,946m deficit (2010)

Trade with UK	2010	2011
Imports from UK	£442,345,621	£508,872,030
Exports to UK	£745,966,440	£852,978,445

COMMUNICATIONS
Airports—The principal airports are at Karachi, Islamabad, Lahore, Peshawar and Sialkot
Waterways—The main seaports are Karachi and Port Muhammad bin Qasim, and there is a deepwater port at Gwadar
Roadways and railways—There are 260,760km of roads and 7,791 of railways
Telecommunications—3.42 million fixed lines and 111 million mobile subscriptions (2010); there were 20.4 million internet users in 2009
Internet code and IDD—pk; 92 (from UK), 44 (to UK)
Media—There are eight national daily newspapers, and the state-owned broadcaster, Pakistan Television Corporation Ltd, competes with around 50 private channels
WPFI score—56,17 (151)

EDUCATION AND HEALTH
Education is free to upper secondary level.
Literacy rate—55.5% (2008 est)
Gross enrolment ratio (percentage of relevant age group)—primary 95%; secondary 34% (2010 est); tertiary 5% (2008 est)
Health expenditure (per capita)—US$23 (2009)
Hospital beds (per 1,000 people)—0.6 (2004–9)
Life expectancy (years)—66.35 (2012 est)
Mortality rate—6.8 (2012 est)
Birth rate—24.3 (2012 est)
Infant mortality rate—61.27 (2012 est)

Panama

República de Panamá—Republic of Panama
Area—75,420 sq. km
Capital—Panama City; population, 1,346,260 (2009 est)
Major cities—Colón, Davíd
Currency—Balboa of 100 centésimos; at parity with the US dollar, which is used as paper currency. Both Panamanian and US coins are used
Population—3,510,045 rising at 1.41% a year (2012 est)
Religion—Christian (Roman Catholic 75%, Protestant 15%) (est)
Language—Spanish (official), English
Population density—47 per sq. km (2010)
Urban population—74.8% (2010 est)
Median age (years)—27.5 (2011 est)
National anthem—'Himno Istmeño' ['Hymn of the Isthmus']
National day—3 November (Independence Day)
Death penalty—Abolished for all crimes (since 1922)
CPI score—3.3 (2011)

FINANCIAL OUTLOOK
Panama increased its 2013 budget by 12.57% over the expenditure allocated for its 2012 budget, setting a record expenditure figure of US$16.268 billion. This figure includes US$7 billion for investment in the continued construction of the new Metro subway system in Panama City. The minister of economy and finance, Frank De Lima, said that the budget takes account only of "real income," and he does not plan to use cash raised from the sale of state assets in joint ventures. Panama's GDP growth for 2013 is expected to be around 8%, with a similar performance forecast for 2014. The expansion in the economy is bringing in more tax revenues, while at the same time the government of Ricardo Martinelli is enforcing a much stricter clampdown on tax-dodging through improved enforcement

and collection procedures. These two factors combined justify the 12.57% hike in expenditure. Much of the major work on expanding the Panama Canal will take place in 2013. The Minera Panama copper mine, a US$6 billion venture, will also see massive investment in 2013.

CLIMATE AND TERRAIN

Panama lies on the isthmus connecting North and South America. A mountain range runs along the centre, falling to coastal plains on both coasts. There is dense tropical rainforest in the east. Elevation extremes range from 3,475m (Volcan Baru) to 0m (Pacific Ocean). The climate is tropical, with a prolonged wet season from May to January. Average temperatures are relatively constant throughout the year, and range between 22°C and 32°C.

HISTORY AND POLITICS

Panama was visited by Spanish explorers from 1502, and in 1519 became part of the Viceroyalty of New Andalucia, later New Grenada. It became a strategically important centre of trade. When it gained its independence from Spain in 1821, Panama joined the confederacy of Gran Colombia (comprising Colombia, Venezuela, Ecuador, Peru and Bolivia). The confederacy split up in 1830 and Panama became part of Colombia until 1903, when it achieved its independence.

In the 1880s, the French attempted to construct a canal across Panama to link the Atlantic and Pacific oceans. In 1903 the USA bought the rights to build the canal, which was completed in 1914 and opened in 1919. The USA was also given control of the canal and land to either side of it, known as the Canal Zone, in perpetuity but, under a 1977 agreement, sovereignty over the Canal Zone was transferred to Panama in 2000.

Panama was under the military rule of General Omar Torrijos from 1968 until his death in 1981. In 1983, General Manuel Noriega seized power and instigated a period of military rule, supported by the USA until 1987. An internal coup to unseat Noriega was unsuccessful in 1988, but in 1989 US forces invaded and deposed him. Noriega surrendered in 1990 and was tried and sentenced in the USA on drug-trafficking and money-laundering charges in 1992.

The 2009 presidential election was won by Ricardo Martinelli of the Democratic Change party. In the simultaneous legislative election, the governing *Partido Revolucionario Democrática* (PRD) was again the individual party with the most seats, but the combined seats of the four-party Alliance for Change coalition led by Martinelli constituted a majority.

Under the 1972 constitution, as amended in 1983, the executive president is directly elected for a five-year term, which is not renewable. The unicameral National Assembly has 71 members, who are directly elected for a five-year term. The president, who is responsible to the legislature, appoints the cabinet.

HEAD OF STATE

President, Ricardo Martinelli, *elected* 3 May 2009, *sworn in* 1 July 2009
First Vice-President, Foreign Affairs, Juan Carlos Varela

SELECTED GOVERNMENT MEMBERS *as at July 2012*

Interior, Jorge Ricardo Fabrega
Economy and Finance, Frank de Lima

EMBASSY OF PANAMA

40 Hertford Street, London W1J 7SH
T 020-7493 4646
E panama1@btconnect.com
Ambassador Extraordinary and Plenipotentiary, HE Ana Delgado, *apptd* 2011

BRITISH EMBASSY

PO Box 0816–07946, Torre MMG, Calle 53, Marbella, Panama City 1
T (+507) 269 0866
E britemb@cwpanama.net.pa
W ukinpanama.fco.gov.uk
Ambassador Extraordinary and Plenipotentiary, HE Michael Holloway, OBE, *apptd* 2011

DEFENCE

All ages 16–49, 2010 est	*Males*	*Females*
Available for military service	890,006	–
Fit for military service	731,254	728,329

Military expenditure—US$0m (2011)

ECONOMY AND TRADE

The economy is based on a large service sector and has experienced steady growth in recent years, although this slowed in 2009 because of the global economic downturn. However, the distribution of wealth is uneven: about one-quarter of the population lives below the poverty line, although unemployment has reduced significantly from 12% to less than 3% of the labour force in 2011.

The service sector accounts for 79.1% of GDP, derived from the operation of the Panama Canal and the Colón free trade zone, financial services, container ports, ship registry and tourism. Enlargement of the canal to take more and larger vessels is scheduled for completion in 2014. Industry, which contributes 18.6% of GDP, includes construction, brewing, sugar refining and the manufacture of cement and other construction materials. Agriculture, which accounts for 4.3% of GDP, is centred on bananas, rice, maize, coffee, sugar cane, vegetables, livestock and shrimp.

The main trading partners are Japan, the USA, Singapore, South Korea, EU countries and China. Principal exports are bananas, shrimp, sugar, coffee and clothing. The main imports are capital goods, foodstuffs, consumer goods and chemicals.

GNI—US$25,036m; US$6,970 per capita (2010)
Annual average growth of GDP—7.4% (2011 est)
Inflation rate—5.9% (2011 est)
Population below poverty line—29% (2011 est)
Unemployment—4.5% (2011 est)
Total external debt—US$14,240m (2011 est)
Imports—US$9,145m (2010)
Exports—US$832m (2010)

BALANCE OF PAYMENTS

Trade—US$8,313m deficit (2010)
Current Account—US$2,992m deficit (2010)

Trade with UK	*2010*	*2011*
Imports from UK	£169,746,784	£168,781,246
Exports to UK	£18,209,303	£26,012,043

COMMUNICATIONS

Airports—There are 118 airports and airfields; the principal airport is at Panama City
Waterways—The Panama Canal connects the Pacific and Atlantic oceans. Each year the canal handles about 5% of world trade and over 40% of trade between Asia and the east coast of the USA. The chief ports are Colón, Cristóbal and Balboa, at either end of the

canal. Because of its role as a ship registry, there were 6,413 Panamanian- and 5,162 foreign-owned ships of over 1,000 tonnes registered under its flag in 2011
Roadways and railways—There are 11,978km of roads and 76km of railways
Telecommunications—553,100 fixed lines and 6.49 million mobile subscriptions; there were 959,800 internet users in 2009
Internet code and IDD—pa; 507 (from UK), 44 (to UK)
Media—Broadcasting is dominated by the private sector, and there are several television networks and about 100 radio stations. *La Prensa*, *Panama News* and *El Siglo* are among the leading newspapers
WPFI score—21,83 (81)

EDUCATION AND HEALTH
There are nine years of compulsory education.
Literacy rate—93.6% (2009 est)
Gross enrolment ratio (percentage of relevant age group)—primary 108%; secondary 74% (2010 est); tertiary 45% (2009 est)
Health expenditure (per capita)—US$591 (2009)
Hospital beds (per 1,000 people)—2.2 (2004–9)
Life expectancy (years)—77.96 (2012 est)
Mortality rate—4.69 (2012 est)
Birth rate—19.17 (2012 est)
Infant mortality rate—11.32 (2012 est)

Peru

República del Perú—Republic of Peru
Area—1,285,216 sq. km
Capital—Lima; population (including Callao), 8,769,350 (2009 est)
Major cities—Arequipa, Chiclayo, Iquitos, Piura, Trujillo
Currency—New sol of 100 centimos
Population—29,549,517 rising at 1.01% a year (2012 est)
Religion—Christian (Roman Catholic 81%, Protestant 13%) (2007 est)
Language—Spanish, Quechua (both official), Aymara, other Amerindian languages
Population density—23 per sq. km (2010)
Urban population—71.6% (2010 est)
Median age (years)—26.2 (2011 est)
National anthem—'Himno Nacional del Perú' ['National Anthem of Peru']
National day—28 July (Independence Day)
Death penalty—Retained for certain crimes (last used 1979)
CPI score—3.4 (2011)

FINANCIAL OUTLOOK

Peru's economy grew faster than expected in 2012, although it slowed somewhat in the fourth quarter, to finish around 6.3%. Surplus capacity in the economy (the output gap) has all but vanished. This has been achieved despite a weaker export performance than in 2011, with domestic demand and private investment being the major drivers, according to the IMF. Inflation declined to 2.7% in November, well within the 1–3% target range set by the Central Reserve Bank of Peru. This was largely down to the "normalization" of food prices, which had been unduly elevated. Peru's current account deficit ran to almost 4% of GDP in 2012, mostly as a result of deteriorating terms of trade (weaker export prices), and strong import growth. However, this was turned into a positive flow by strong foreign direct investment movements. The Peruvian government has focused its macroeconomic strategy on managing the surge in foreign direct investment into the country, and on trying to take some of the steam out of strong credit growth. Monetary conditions were tightened, with the central bank increasing reserve requirements by a cumulative 375 basis points during 2012. The currency, the nuevo sol, appreciated by around 4.75% in real terms in 2012. The IMF warns that downside risks from the global economy, such as a prolonged slowdown in China, could have profound negative consequences on the Peruvian economy.

CLIMATE AND TERRAIN

Peru has three main regions: the Costa, the coastal desert plain west of the Andes; the Sierra (mountain range) of the Andes, which runs parallel to the Pacific coast; and the Montaña (or Selva), a vast area of jungle stretching from the eastern foothills of the Andes to the country's eastern and north-eastern borders. Elevation extremes range from 6,768m (Nevado Huascaran) to 0m (Pacific Ocean). The climate is arid in the west, temperate in the mountains and tropical in the east. Occasionally, due to the El Niño weather system, the northern districts experience a period of higher temperatures accompanied by torrential rain. Average temperatures in Lima range from 18°C from June to October to 23°C in February.

HISTORY AND POLITICS

The Inca Empire centred on Cuzco superseded earlier civilisations in Peru and flourished from the 13th to the 15th century, when the empire reached its zenith before falling to Spanish conquistadores led by Francisco Pizarro in 1532–3. The territory formed the Viceroyalty of Peru and its gold and silver mines made Peru the principal source of wealth in Spain's American empire. After 1810, Peru became the centre of Spanish colonial government as its other colonies rebelled. Although Peru declared its independence in 1821, this was achieved only with the final defeat of Spanish forces in 1824.

Peru entered into several border disputes with its neighbours in the 19th and 20th centuries, including the Pacific War (1879–83) in which it lost three southern coastal provinces to Chile. A border dispute with Ecuador was renewed in 1981, leading to a short, inconclusive war in 1995, but was resolved in 1998 following adjudication. A border dispute with Chile ended in 1999 with the implementation of accords first agreed in 1929.

Following independence, Peru alternated between periods of military dictatorship and democratic rule. Two left-wing insurgencies, by the Maoist *Sendero Luminoso* (Shining Path) and the *Movimento Revolucionario Tupac Amaru* (MRTA), began in the 1980s. The activities of the *Sendero Luminoso* in particular destabilised the government and the economy; the conflict caused about 69,000 deaths and saw human rights abuses by both the security forces and the guerrillas. By the late 1990s both insurgencies had been overcome, although a few Maoists remain active. The conflict has left a legacy of criminal violence, much of it related to drug production and trafficking.

Alberto Fujimori, elected president in 1990 on a platform of economic reform, subverted democratic institutions in Peru during his decade in power, suspending the legislature for three years, sacking judges and imposing order through an 'emergency national reconstruction government'. He fled to Japan in 2000 to escape corruption charges, but was extradited and convicted in 2007 of abuse of power and in 2009 of human rights abuses.

In the 2011 legislative election, the Peru Wins alliance gained the most seats but without a majority. The presidential election was won in the second round in June 2011 by the Peruvian Nationalist Party candidate Ollanta Humala.

Political System

Under the 1993 constitution, the executive president is directly elected for a five-year term, renewable once. The unicameral legislature, the Congress of the Republic, has 130 members, directly elected for a five-year term. The president, who is responsible to the legislature, appoints the council of ministers.

HEAD OF STATE
President, Ollanta Humala, *elected* 5 June 2011, *sworn in* 28 July 2011
First Vice-President, Marisol Espinoza

SELECTED GOVERNMENT MEMBERS *as at July 2012*
President of Council of Ministers, Juan Jimenez
Defence, Pedro Cateriano
Economy and Finance, Luis Castilla Rubio
Foreign Affairs, Rafael Roncagliolo

EMBASSY OF PERU
52 Sloane Street, London SW1X 9SP
T 020-7235 1917
E postmaster@peruembassy-uk.com
W www.peruembassy-uk.com
Ambassador Extraordinary and Plenipotentiary, Vacant

BRITISH EMBASSY
PO Box 854, Torre Parque Mar (Piso 22), Avenida José Larco 1301, Lima
T (+51) (1) 617 3000
E belima@fco.gov.uk
W ukinperu.fco.gov.uk
Ambassador Extraordinary and Plenipotentiary, HE James Dauris, *apptd* 2010

DEFENCE

All aged 16–49, 2010 est	Males	Females
Available for military service	7,385,588	7,727,623
Fit for military service	5,788,629	6,565,097

Military expenditure—US$1,978m (2011)

ECONOMY AND TRADE

The economy has grown steadily since 2002, driven by increased agricultural, fisheries and mining exports, major infrastructure developments and tourism. Poverty remains widespread, but the benefits of economic growth are starting to be felt in the poorer regions and the poverty rate has declined by 19% since 2002. Economic growth slowed in the global downturn, owing to reduced demand for exports and lower commodity prices, but recovered strongly in 2010 and continued to grow in 2011 due partly to private investment.

Mineral resources, including copper, gold, silver, zinc, oil and natural gas, are abundant, and extracting and refining these is the mainstay of the economy, although this makes it vulnerable to global price fluctuations. Other industries include steel and metal fabrication, fishing and fish processing, textiles and clothes manufacture and food processing. Agriculture is centred on asparagus, coffee, cocoa, cotton, sugar cane, rice, cereals, vegetables, fruit, coca, medicinal plants, meat and dairy products. Services contribute 54% to GDP, industry 38% and agriculture 8%.

The main trading partners are the USA, China, Switzerland, Japan, other South American countries and Canada. Principal exports are copper, gold, zinc, tin, crude oil and petroleum products, natural gas, coffee, vegetables and fruit. The main imports are oil and petroleum products, chemicals, plastics, machinery, vehicles, telecommunications equipment, iron and steel, and food.

GNI—US$146,999m; US$4,700 per capita (2010)
Annual average growth of GDP—6.2% (2011 est)
Inflation rate—3% (2011 est)
Population below poverty line—31.3% (2010 est)
Unemployment—7.7% (2011 est)
Total external debt—US$37,690m (2011 est)
Imports—US$28,818m (2010)
Exports—US$35,565m (2010)

BALANCE OF PAYMENTS
Trade—US$6,747m surplus (2010)
Current Account—US$2,315m deficit (2010)

Trade with UK	2010	2011
Imports from UK	£119,231,578	£146,561,870
Exports to UK	£221,149,418	£242,061,748

COMMUNICATIONS

Airports and waterways—There are over 210 airports and airstrips, including the international airport at Lima; there are 8,808km of inland waterways and the main seaports are Callao and Matarani
Roadways and railways—There are 137,327km of roads, including sections of the east-west Andean Highway, linking the Pacific and Atlantic coasts, and the north–south Pan-American Highway running along the Pacific coast. The state-run railways have 1,906km of track
Telecommunications—3.16 million fixed lines and 29.11 million mobile subscriptions (2010); there were 9.16 million internet users in 2009
Internet code and IDD—pe; 51 (from UK), 44 (to UK)
Media—The state-owned Television Nacional de Peru broadcasts alongside a number of commercial television channels; daily newspapers include *El Bocon* and *La Republica*
WPFI score—30,00 (109)

EDUCATION AND HEALTH

Education is free and compulsory for 11 years.
Literacy rate—89.6% (2007 est)
Gross enrolment ratio (percentage of relevant age group)—primary 109%; secondary 92% (2009 est)
Health expenditure (per capita)—US$201 (2009)
Hospital beds (per 1,000 people)—1.5 (2004–9)
Life expectancy (years)—72.73 (2012 est)
Mortality rate—5.95 (2012 est)
Birth rate—19.13 (2012 est)
Infant mortality rate—21.5 (2012 est)

  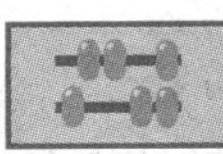      

The Philippines

Republika ng Pilipinas—Republic of the Philippines
Area—300,000 sq. km
Capital—Manila; population (Metro Manila, including Quezon City), 11,449,200 (2009 est)
Major cities—Bacolod, Cagayan de Oro, Cebu, Davao, General Santos (Dadiangas), Iloilo, Zamboanga
Currency—Philippine peso (P) of 100 centavos
Population—103,775,002 rising at 1.87% a year (2012 est); Tagalog (28.1%), Cebuano (13.1%), Ilocano (9%), Bisaya (7.6%), Hiligaynon Ilonggo (7.5%), Bikol (6%), Waray (3.4%) (2000)
Religion—Christian (Roman Catholic 81%, other 12%), Muslim 5% (predominantly Sunni) (est)
Language—Filipino (based on Tagalog), English (both official), Tagalog, Cebuano, Ilocano, Hiligaynon, Bicol, Waray, Pampango, Pangasinan
Population density—313 per sq. km (2010)
Urban population—66.4% (2010 est)
Median age (years)—22.9 (2011 est)
National anthem—'Lupang Hinirang' ['Chosen Land']
National day—12 June (Independence Day)
Death penalty—Abolished for all crimes (since 2006)
CPI score—2.6 (2011)

FINANCIAL OUTLOOK

The improving outlook for the global economy in 2013 is very positive for the Philippines, the ratings agency Standard & Poor's said in March 2013. However, the agency said that it expected GDP growth in 2013 to slow to 5.9%, down from 6.6% in 2012. It allocated a "positive" outlook to the country, which means the current rating may be raised to investment grade if favorable trends continue. These include the improving fiscal condition of the government, the robust pace of economic growth, benign inflation, a stable banking sector, and rising foreign-exchange reserves. The IMF said in January 2013 that the Philippines economy would grow faster than initially forecast in 2013, citing the resilience of domestic consumption, government spending, and low interest rates. These economic drivers, if sustained, would likely push the country into a higher growth trajectory in the future, IMF officials said.

CLIMATE AND TERRAIN

The Philippines comprises over 7,100 islands in the western Pacific Ocean. The principal islands are Luzon, Mindanao, Mindoro, Samar, Negros, Palawan, Panay and Leyte; other groups include the Sulu islands, Babuyanes and Batanes, Calamian and Kalayaan islands. The islands mostly have mountainous interiors and narrow coastal plains. The mountain ranges are volcanic, and some volcanoes are still active. Elevation extremes range from 2,954m (Mt Apo) to 0m (Philippine Sea). The climate is tropical, with relatively constant temperatures throughout the year which in Manila vary between averages of 22°C in January and February and 34°C in May and June, when the humidity is particularly oppressive. The country is affected by the monsoons, which cause the rainy season between July and October. During this period the country is also susceptible to typhoons, which frequently cause widespread damage and loss of life.

HISTORY AND POLITICS

The Philippine islands were settled first by Malays, then by Chinese, Indonesian and Arab traders. Islam was introduced in the 14th century and became the dominant religion in the south. The islands were discovered by Spain and then settled from 1565 by the Spanish, who introduced Roman Catholicism. Colonial rule lasted until 1898, when Spain ceded the colony to the USA following the Spanish-American War. The country became internally self-governing in 1935, was occupied by Japan from 1942 to 1944, and achieved independence from the USA in 1946.

Ferdinand Marcos was elected president in 1965, imposing martial law in 1972. His regime became increasingly repressive, corrupt and violent, and when he falsified election results in 1986 to prevent Corazon Aquino from taking office as president, a popular uprising forced him to flee the country. Aquino survived political unrest and ten attempted military coups to introduce a new constitution and entrench democratic politics.

Fidel Ramos, Aquino's successor in 1992, built on her work, raised the country's international profile and instigated peace talks with insurgents (*see* below). Joseph Estrada, elected president in 1998, was overthrown in 2001 in a popular uprising; his term was completed by Vice-President Gloria Arroyo. President Arroyo retained the presidency in the 2004 presidential election, but her popularity plummeted and her anti-corruption measures and economic reforms were undermined by corruption scandals and impeachment attempts.

The 2010 presidential election was won by Benigno ('Noynoy') Aquino III, son of former president Corazon Aquino.

A communist insurgency by the New People's Army (NPA) began in the late 1960s. The NPA is based in Mindanao but has groups in rural areas throughout the country. Peace talks between the government and the NPA's political front, the National Democratic Front, stalled in 2004 but were resumed in early 2011.

There has been a Muslim (Moro) insurgency in the southern islands, particularly Mindanao, since the 1970s. The Moro National Liberation Front (MNLF) concluded a peace agreement with the government in 1996 that ended its insurgency and established the Autonomous Region of Muslim Mindanao (ARMM). The Moro Islamic Liberation Front (MILF) agreed a ceasefire with the government in 2003, but negotiations over a Muslim 'homeland' broke down in 2008; a resumption of violence in 2009 displaced over 300,000 people until another ceasefire was agreed and peace talks resumed in late 2009. Talks broke-down in October 2011, however, after air strikes on MILF areas in Zamboanga left 35 people dead.

The radical Muslim separatist group Abu Sayyaf, based on Jolo and Basilan, is viewed as a terrorist organisation and the government refuses to negotiate with it. It has links with Jamaah Islamiyah, the group responsible for the Bali bombings, and possibly with al-Qaida. Since 2001 it has carried out a series of violent kidnappings and bombings, but military operations since 2006 have depleted its numbers and its leadership.

Under the 1987 constitution, the executive president is directly elected for a six-year term, which is not renewable. There is a bicameral Congress. The lower house, the House of Representatives, has 286–8 members, of whom 231 are directly elected and the rest appointed from party and minority group lists; all serve a three-year term. The senate has 24 members directly elected for a six-year term, with half re-elected every three years.

The Autonomous Region of Muslim Mindanao comprises the provinces of Lanao del Sur and Maguindanao on Mindanao and the island provinces of Sulu, Tawi-Tawi and Basilan. It has a 24-member regional assembly and a governor.

HEAD OF STATE

President, Benigno ('Noynoy') Aquino III, *elected* 10 May 2010, *sworn in* 30 June 2010

Vice-President, Jejomar Binay

SELECTED GOVERNMENT MEMBERS *as at June 2012*
Finance, Cesar Purisima
Trade and Industry, Gregory Domingo
Foreign Affairs, Albert del Rosario
Defence, Voltaire Gazmin

EMBASSY OF THE REPUBLIC OF THE PHILIPPINES
6–8 Suffolk Street, London SW1Y 4HG
T 020-7451 1780
E embassy@philemb.co.uk
W philembassy-uk.org
Ambassador Extraordinary and Plenipotentiary, HE Enrique Manalo, *apptd* 2011

BRITISH EMBASSY
120 Upper McKinley Road, McKinley Hill, Taguig City 1634, Manila
T (+63) (2) 858 2200
E ukinthephilippines@fco.gov.uk
W ukinthephilippines.fco.gov.uk
Ambassador Extraordinary and Plenipotentiary, HE Stephen Lillie, *apptd* 2009

DEFENCE

All aged 16–49, 2010 est	*Males*	*Females*
Available for military service	25,614,135	25,035,061
Fit for military service	20,142,940	21,427,792

Military expenditure—US$2,225m (2011)

ECONOMY AND TRADE

The economy has been one of the best-performing in the region since 2002, owing to growth in exports, agricultural output and the service industries. Despite this, poverty has increased as economic expansion struggles to offset the high rate of population growth, and nearly a third of the population lives below the poverty line. Remittances from the millions of Filipinos working abroad are vital and helped to cushion the economy in 2009 from the effects of the global downturn, although the government was forced to announce a stimulus effort after growth slowed significantly in 2011.

Major industries include electronics assembly, manufacture of clothing, footwear, pharmaceuticals, chemicals and wood products, food processing, oil refining and fishing. The large agricultural sector employs 33% of the workforce, producing sugar cane, coconuts, rice, maize, tropical fruits and livestock products. Agriculture accounts for 12.3% of GDP, industry for 33.3% and services for 54.4%.

The main trading partners are the USA, Japan, China, Singapore, other Asian states and the EU. Principal exports are semiconductors and electronic products, transport equipment, clothing, copper products, petroleum products, coconut oil and fruit. The main imports are electronic products, fuels, machinery and transport equipment, iron and steel, fabrics, grains, chemicals and plastics.

GNI—US$199,897m; US$2,060 per capita (2010)
Annual average growth of GDP—4.7% (2011 est)
Inflation rate—5.3% (2011 est)
Population below poverty line—32.9% (2006 est)
Unemployment—7.2% (2011 est)
Total external debt—US$62,410m (2011 est)
Imports—US$58,229m (2010)
Exports—US$51,432m (2010)

BALANCE OF PAYMENTS
Trade—US$6,797m deficit (2010)
Current Account—US$8,465m surplus (2010)

Trade with UK	*2010*	*2011*
Imports from UK	£285,673,790	£285,362,823
Exports to UK	£674,036,683	£453,530,270

COMMUNICATIONS

Airports and waterways—There are 254 airports and airfields, including international airports at Manila, Cebu and Davao City. The main ports are Manila (Luzon), Cebu, Davao, Subic Bay, Batangas and Iloilo, and there are over 420 smaller ports
Roadways and railways—There are 213,151km of roads, and Philippine National Railway operates 995km of railways
Telecommunications—6.78 million fixed lines and 79.89 million mobile subscriptions (2010); there were 8.28 million internet users in 2009
Internet code and IDD—ph; 63 (from UK), 44 (to UK)
Major broadcasters—The government-owned IBC television network competes with two commercial broadcasters and over 700 radio stations
Press—There are four main national newspapers, including the *Daily Tribune* and *Malaya*
WPFI score—60,00 (156)

EDUCATION AND HEALTH

There are seven years of free and compulsory primary education, followed by three years of free but non-compulsory secondary education.
Literacy rate—95.4% (2008 est)
Gross enrolment ratio (percentage of relevant age group)—primary 106%; secondary 85% (2009 est); tertiary 29% (2008 est)
Health expenditure (per capita)—US$67 (2009)
Hospital beds (per 1,000 people)—0.5 (2004–9)
Life expectancy (years)—71.94 (2012 est)
Mortality rate—4.98 (2012 est)
Birth rate—24.98 (2012 est)
Infant mortality rate—18.75 (2012 est)

Poland

Rzeczpospolita Polska—Republic of Poland
Area—312,685 sq. km
Capital—Warsaw; population, 1,709,560 (2009 est)
Major cities—Bydgoszcz, Gdansk, Katowice, Krakow, Lodz, Lublin, Poznan, Szczecin, Wroclaw
Currency—Zloty of 100 groszy
Population—38,415,284 falling at 0.08% a year (2012 est)
Religion—Christian (Roman Catholic 94%, other 5%) (est)
Language—Polish (official)
Population density—126 per sq. km (2010)

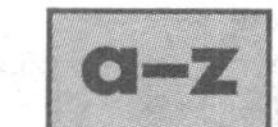

Urban population—61.2% (2010 est)
Median age (years)—38.5 (2011 est)
National anthem—'Mazurek Dabrowskiego' ['Dabrowski's Mazurka']
National day—3 May (Constitution Day)
Death penalty—Abolished for all crimes (since 1997)
CPI score—5.5 (2011)

FINANCIAL OUTLOOK

The Polish economy is feeling the effects of headwinds from Europe, according to a report by the IMF in January 2013. Growth is moderating rapidly amid weaker export demand and greater levels of uncertainty, which are causing private investment and domestic consumption to slow. All this is being compounded by lower public investment. Economic activity is projected to slow further in 2013. Risks are on the downside, as a deeper or more protracted slowdown in Europe or a re-intensification of the crisis would affect Poland through substantial trade and financial channels, including through possible disorderly deleveraging by European parent banks. As a result, Poland has asked the IMF for a new, two-year precautionary funding line worth 22 billion in special drawing rights. The IMF has said it sees no objection to the loan. IMF officials congratulated the Polish government at the end of its 2012 Article IV Consultation, for its implementation of sound macro-economic management in a challenging environment. Poland's external financing needs continue to be high, running at 22% of GDP in 2013. Polish government bonds have seen strong inflows from investors outside Poland, increasing external investors' share of Poland's sovereign debt to 36%, a record high. Poland managed to reduce its fiscal deficit from 7.9% of GDP in 2010 to 5% in 2011, and to reduce it further in 2012. Public debt is limited to 60% of GDP. The economy is expected to grow by 2% in 2013, having grown by 2.4% in 2012.

CLIMATE AND TERRAIN

Poland lies mostly in a great plain crossed by the Oder, Neisse and Vistula rivers. The land rises to the Carpathian, Tatra and Sudeten mountains along the southern border. Elevation extremes range from 2,499m (Rysy) to −2m (Raczki Elblaskie). The climate is continental, and average temperatures in Warsaw range from −6°C in January to 24°C in July.

HISTORY AND POLITICS

Under the 1997 constitution, the head of state is the president, who is directly elected for a five-year term, renewable once. The president nominates the prime minister and has the right to be consulted over the appointment of the foreign, defence and interior ministers. The National Assembly is bicameral; the lower house, the Diet *(Sejm)*, has 460 members elected by proportional representation for a four-year term. The senate has 100 members elected on a provincial basis for a four-year term.

President Lech Kaczynski, elected in 2005, was killed in a plane crash in Russia in April 2010; his successor, acting president Bronislaw Komorowski of the PO, was elected in July. The Civil Platform (PO), led by Donald Tusk, remained the largest party in both houses of the National Assembly in the 2011 legislative election, picking up 207 of the 460 seats in the lower chamber.

HEAD OF STATE

President, Bronislaw Komorowski, *elected* 4 July 2010, *sworn in* 6 August 2010

SELECTED GOVERNMENT MEMBERS *as at July 2012*

Prime Minister, Donald Tusk
Deputy Prime Minister, Economy, Waldemar Pawlak
Defence, Tomasz Siemoniak
Finance, Jan Vincent-Rostowski

EMBASSY OF THE REPUBLIC OF POLAND
47 Portland Place, London W1B 1JH
T 020-7291 3520
E london@msz.gov.pl
W london.polemb.net
Ambassador Extraordinary and Plenipotentiary, HE Barbara Tuge-Erecinska, *apptd* 2006

BRITISH EMBASSY
ul. Kawalerii 12, 00-468 Warsaw
T (+48) (22) 311 0000
E info@britishembassy.pl
W ukinpoland.fco.gov.uk
Ambassador Extraordinary and Plenipotentiary, HE Robin Barnett, *apptd* 2011

DEFENCE

All aged 16–49, 2010 est	Males	Females
Available for military service	9,531,855	9,298,593
Fit for military service	7,817,556	7,766,361

Military expenditure—US$9,149m (2011)

ECONOMY AND TRADE

Poland's successful transition to a market economy in the 1990s came at the cost of high levels of public debt, unemployment and inflation, which were reduced by subsequent governments. The economy has grown steadily since 1992 and particularly since accession to the EU in 2004, avoiding recession in 2008–9. Further economic development is hindered by inefficiency, rigidity and low-level corruption, although the Tusk government is committed to further privatisation and restructuring public finances.

Poland has vast mineral resources, especially coal, and nearly half its area is fertile arable land. The large agricultural sector has been modernised but remains inefficient; it employs 17% of the workforce but contributes only 3.4% of GDP. The main crops are vegetables, fruit, wheat, meat, eggs and dairy products. The main industries are machine-building, iron and steel production, coal-mining, chemicals, shipbuilding, food processing, glass, beverages and textiles. Industry accounts for 33.6% of GDP.

The main trading partners are other EU countries (especially Germany) and Russia. Principal exports include machinery and vehicles, manufactured and semi-manufactured goods, food and livestock. The main imports are machinery and vehicles, semi-manufactured goods, chemicals, minerals, fuels and lubricants.

GNI—US$452,275m; US$12,440 per capita (2010)
Annual average growth of GDP—3.8% (2011 est)
Inflation rate—4% (2011 est)
Population below poverty line—17% (2003 est)
Unemployment—12% (2011 est)
Total external debt—US$306,900m (2011 est)
Imports—US$173,752m (2010)
Exports—US$155,796m (2010)

BALANCE OF PAYMENTS

Trade—US$17,956m deficit (2010)

  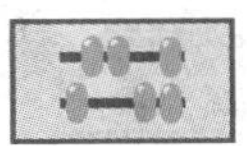      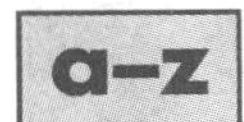

Current Account—US$20,982m deficit (2010)

Trade with UK	2010	2011
Imports from UK	£3,665,850,931	£4,197,322,144
Exports to UK	£5,929,319,644	£7,108,149,476

COMMUNICATIONS

Airports and waterways—Nearly 130 airports and airfields are in use; the principal airports are at Warsaw, Krakow, Katowice and Wroclaw; the principal seaports are Gdansk, Gdynia, Swinoujscie and Szczecin and there are 3,997km of navigable rivers and canals
Roadways and railways—There are 423,997km of roads and 19,428km of railways
Telecommunications—9.45 million fixed lines and 46 million mobile subscriptions (2010); there were 22.45 million internet users in 2009
Internet code and IDD—pl; 48 (from UK), 44 (to UK)
Major broadcasters—State-owned television (TVP) still has the largest national audience share for its output, although there are competitive commercial and subscription services
Press—*Gazeta Wyborcza* and *Fakt* are the principal mass-circulation dailies
WPFI score—8,88 (32)

EDUCATION AND HEALTH

Elementary education (ages seven to 15) is free and compulsory. Secondary education is also free, but optional.
Literacy rate—99.5% (2009 est)
Gross enrolment ratio (percentage of relevant age group)—primary 97%; secondary 97%; tertiary 71% (2009 est)
Health expenditure (per capita)—US$804 (2009)
Hospital beds (per 1,000 people)—6.6 (2004–9)
Life expectancy (years)—76.25 (2012 est)
Mortality rate—10.24 (2012 est)
Birth rate—9.96 (2012 est)
Infant mortality rate—6.42 (2012 est)

Portugal

República Portuguesa—Portuguese Republic
Area—92,090 sq. km
Capital—Lisbon; population, 2,808,190 (2009 est)
Major cities—Oporto
Currency—Euro (€) of 100 cents
Population—10,781,459 rising at 0.18% a year (2012 est)
Religion—Christian (Roman Catholic 84%, other 2%) (est)
Language—Portuguese, Mirandese (both official)
Population density—116 per sq. km (2010)
Urban population—60.7% (2010 est)
Median age (years)—40 (2011 est)
National anthem—'A Portuguesa' ['The Portuguese Song']
National day—10 June (Portugal Day)
Death penalty—Abolished for all crimes (since 1976)
CPI score—6.1 (2011)

FINANCIAL OUTLOOK

Portugal has been one of the hardest hit of the peripheral eurozone countries. GDP fell by 3.2% in 2012, according to the statistics institute, its sharpest downturn since 1975. The Bank of Portugal predicted in January 2013 that the economy would contract by 1.9% in 2013, more than previously forecast, as export growth slows. Economic growth has averaged less than 1% per annum for the past decade, placing Portugal among Europe's weakest performers. The government's austerity measures are compounding export weakness. Huge tax hikes and plans to cut €4 billion in spending are expected to take place in 2013. The government forecasts public debt to peak at 122.3% of GDP in 2014, after reaching 122.2% in 2013. In 2012, unemployment stood at 17.6%, the third-highest rate in the eurozone after Greece and Spain.

CLIMATE AND TERRAIN

The terrain is mountainous north of the river Tagus, with rolling hills and plains in the south. Elevation extremes range from 2,351m (Ponta do Pico, Azores) to 0m (Atlantic Ocean). Forests of pine, cork oak and eucalyptus cover about 38% of the country. The climate is temperate, with average temperatures in Lisbon ranging from 8°C in January to 28°C in August.

HISTORY AND POLITICS

Part of the Roman Empire from the second century BC, the country was overrun by Vandals and Visigoths in the fifth century AD. The Visigoths were ousted by Muslims from north Africa in the eighth century, but Christian reconquest began in the tenth century and an independent Christian kingdom was established in the 12th century.

Portuguese navigators led the 15th-century European age of exploration and the country soon became a major commercial and colonial power, its empire expanding to include Brazil, parts of China and large areas of Africa. In 1807 Portugal was invaded by Napoleonic France and then became the base from which Allied forces liberated Portugal and Spain in the Peninsular War. The 19th century was politically turbulent, with power struggles between conservative and liberal politicians and between different factions of the royal family. In 1910 an armed uprising in Lisbon drove King Manuel II into exile and a republic was declared.

A period of political instability ensued until the military intervened in 1926. The constitution of 1933 gave formal expression to the authoritarian *Estado Novo* (New State) introduced by Dr Antonio Salazar, prime minister from 1932 until 1968. Marcello Caetano succeeded Salazar in 1968 but the regime's failure to liberalise at home or to conclude wars in the African colonies resulted in the government's overthrow in a military coup in 1974. Great political turmoil followed in 1974–5, a period in which most of the country's colonies gained their independence. Elections in 1976 stabilised the situation and full civilian government was restored in 1982. Portugal joined the EEC in 1986 and adopted the euro in 2002.

The 2006 presidential election was won by the Social Democrat candidate Anibal Cavaco Silva (prime minister 1985–95), and he was re-elected in January 2011. The Socialist Party government, in power since 2005 but as a minority government since the 2009 election, resigned after its austerity programme was defeated in March 2011. In the legislative election in June, the Social Democratic Party (PSD) won the most seats but not an overall majority, and formed a coalition with the Democratic and Social Centre-People's Party and independents under the PSD leader Pedro Passos Coelho.

Under the 1976 constitution, amended in 1982 and 1989, the head of state is a president who is directly elected for a five-year term, renewable once. The unicameral Assembly of the Republic has

  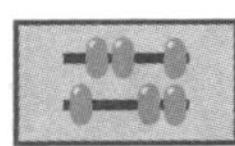      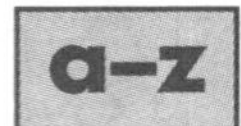

230 members, directly elected by proportional representation for a four-year term. The prime minister, appointed by the president, is usually the leader of the largest party in the assembly.

HEAD OF STATE
President of the Republic, Anibal Cavaco Silva, *elected* 22 January 2006, *sworn in* 9 March 2006, *re-elected* 2011

SELECTED GOVERNMENT MEMBERS *as at July 2012*
Prime Minister, Pedro Passos Coelho
Foreign Affairs, Paulo Portas
Interior, Miguel Macedo
Finance, Vitor Gaspar

EMBASSY OF PORTUGAL
11 Belgrave Square, London SW1X 8PP
T 020-7235 5331
E london@portembassy.co.uk
Ambassador Extraordinary and Plenipotentiary, HE Joao de Vallera, *apptd* 2011

BRITISH EMBASSY
Rua de Sao Bernardo 33, 1249-082 Lisbon
T (+351) (21) 392 4000
E ppa.lisbon@fco.gov.uk
W ukinportugal.fco.gov.uk
Ambassador Extraordinary and Plenipotentiary, HE Jill Gallard, *apptd* 2011

DEFENCE

All aged 16–49, 2010 est	*Males*	*Females*
Available for military service	2,566,264	2,458,297
Fit for military service	2,103,080	2,018,004

Military expenditure—US$4,285m (2011)
Military personnel—43,340: army 26,700, navy 10,540, air force 7,100; paramilitary 47,700

ECONOMY AND TRADE

Portugal's economy was transformed after it joined the EU in 1986 into a diversified and increasingly service-based economy. The rapid growth of the 1990s slowed in 2001–8, and the global downturn pushed the economy into recession in 2009. Despite government austerity measures, a budget deficit treble the eurozone limit led to the country's credit rating being downgraded in 2010 amid concerns about the country's ability to service its sovereign debt; in April 2011 the government obtained EU financial support.

Nearly 12% of the workforce is engaged in agriculture, contributing 2.5% of GDP. The chief products are grain, fruit and vegetables, livestock, fish, dairy products and timber and cork from the forests. The main industries are tourism, manufacturing (textiles, footwear, cork, pulp and paper, chemicals, motor vehicle components), metalworking, winemaking, oil refining, and shipbuilding and repair. Natural resources are being exploited to generate electricity from hydroelectric and solar sources to reduce dependence on imported fuel and energy. Industry accounts for 22.8% of GDP and services for 74.5%.

The main trading partners are other EU countries, particularly Spain and Angola. Principal exports are agricultural products, food, wine, oil products, wood products, other industrial products, machinery and tools. The main imports include agricultural products, chemicals, vehicles, optical and precision instruments, computer and IT components.

GNI—US$221,242m; US$21,880 per capita (2010)
Annual average growth of GDP—-2.2% (2011 est)
Inflation rate—3.2% (2011 est)
Population below poverty line—18% (2006 est)
Unemployment—12.4% (2011 est)
Total external debt—US$548,300m (2011)
Imports—US$75,590m (2010)
Exports—US$48,742m (2010)

BALANCE OF PAYMENTS
Trade—US$26,848m deficit (2010)
Current Account—US$22,669m deficit (2010)

Trade with UK	*2010*	*2011*
Imports from UK	£1,770,801,944	£1,700,566,298
Exports to UK	£1,720,545,975	£1,787,611,144

COMMUNICATIONS

Airports and waterways—There are 65 airports and airfields, including international airports at Lisbon, Oporto, Faro, Santa Maria (Azores) and Funchal (Madeira). The main ports are Aveiro, Figueira da Foz, Leixoes, Lisbon, Setubal and Sines
Roadways and railways—There are 82,900km of roadways and 3,319km of railways
Telecommunications—4.49 million fixed lines and 15.19 million mobile subscriptions (2010); there were 5.17 million internet users in 2009
Internet code and IDD—pt; 351 (from UK), 44 (to UK)
Major broadcasters—The monopoly of the public broadcaster RTP ended in 1992, and commercial stations now dominate the market
Press—Principal national newspapers include the daily titles *Diario de Noticias*, *Correio da Manha* and *Jornal de Noticias*
WPFI score—12,36 (40)

EDUCATION AND HEALTH

Education is free and compulsory for nine years from the age of six. The university at Coimbra was founded in 1290.
Literacy rate—94.9% (2009 est)
Gross enrolment ratio (percentage of relevant age group)—primary 114%; secondary 107%; tertiary 62% (2009 est)
Health expenditure (per capita)—US$2,410 (2009)
Hospital beds (per 1,000 people)—3.4 (2004–9)
Life expectancy (years)—78.7 (2012 est)
Mortality rate—10.86 (2012 est)
Birth rate—9.76 (2012 est)
Infant mortality rate—4.6 (2012 est)

AUTONOMOUS REGIONS

Madeira and the Azores are both autonomous regions, each with its own locally elected assembly and government.
MADEIRA is a group of islands in the Atlantic Ocean about 990km south-west of Lisbon, and consists of Madeira, Porto Santo and three uninhabited islands. Total area is 801 sq. km; population, 267,938 (2011 est). Funchal on Madeira, the largest island, is the capital.
THE AZORES is an archipelago of nine islands in the Atlantic Ocean 1,400–1,800km west of Lisbon, and consists of Flores, Corvo, Terceira, Sao Jorge, Pico, Faial, Graciosa, Sao Miguel and Santa Maria. Total area is 2,322 sq. km; population, 246,102 (2011 est). Ponta Delgada, on Sao Miguel, is the capital.

Qatar

Dawlat Qatar—State of Qatar
Area—11,586 sq. km
Capital—Doha; population, 426,617 (2009 est)
Major cities—Ar Rayyan, Al Wakrah
Currency—Qatar riyal of 100 dirhams
Population—1,951,591 rising at 4.93% a year (2012 est); Arab (40%), Indian (18%), Pakistani (18%), Iranian (10%) (est)
Religion—Muslim 77% (predominantly Sunni), Christian 8%, other 14% (2004)
Language—Arabic (official), English
Population density—152 per sq. km (2010)
Urban population—95.8% (2010 est)
Median age (years)—30.8 (2011 est)
National anthem—'As-Salam al-Amiri' ['Peace to the Amir']
National day—18 December
Life expectancy (years)—78.09 (2012 est)
Mortality rate—1.55 (2012 est)
Birth rate—10.23 (2012 est)
Infant mortality rate—6.81 (2012 est)
Death penalty—Retained
CPI score—7.2 (2011)
Literacy rate—94. 7% (2009 est)

FINANCIAL OUTLOOK

The Qatari economy grew by 11% in 2012, according to preliminary estimates released by the central bank in March 2013. The bank forecast growth of 5.5% in 2013. However, this is significantly down on the 19% estimated by the IMF in 2011. The slowdown reflects lower hydrocarbon sector growth, as a self-imposed moratorium on increasing liquefied natural gas (LNG) capacity commences. With Qatar hosting the 2022 soccer World Cup, the economy is likely to gain a significant boost from infrastructure spending in the coming years. Over the next 10 years, Qatar is intending to embark on US$150 billion of infrastructure spending. The most dramatic growth is expected to occur between 2013 and 2014, when many of the World Cup construction projects are expected to start. However, in January 2013, the IMF warned Qatar to contain its inflation rate in the medium term on the back of pressures emerging from the state's investment program.

CLIMATE AND TERRAIN

Qatar occupies a peninsula in the Persian Gulf and is mostly a low-lying desert plain, with sand dunes in the south. Elevation extremes range from 103m (Qurayn Abu al-Bawl) to 0m (Persian Gulf). The country has a desert climate, with low rainfall and average temperatures ranging from 13°C in January to 42°C in July. Humidity along the coast often reaches 90% in summer.

HISTORY AND POLITICS

Towns on the Qatari coast developed into important trading centres from the 18th century. Persian rule of the area ended in the mid-18th century and after a period of conflict, the peninsula became a dependency of Bahrain in the 1850s. A revolt against Bahraini rule in the 1860s was suppressed, but Britain intervened in 1867, recognising the dependency as a separate entity. Nominally under the rule of the Ottoman Empire from 1871 until the outbreak of the First World War, Qatar became a British protectorate in 1916, when the al-Thani family was recognised as the ruling house. It became independent in 1971.

In 1972 Sheikh Ahmad was overthrown by the crown prince and prime minister, Sheikh Khalifa. Sheikh Khalifa was overthrown in 1995 by his son and heir, Sheikh Hamad, who has since introduced liberal reforms. Municipal elections, the first democratic polls since independence, were held in 1999. A referendum in 2003 approved a new constitution, which came into force in 2005. Elections to the partially elected consultative council established by the constitution have yet to take place.

A new constitution came into force in 2005. The head of state is a hereditary absolute monarch, the amir. There is no legislature at present, although the 2005 constitution provides for a legislative council with 45 members, 30 directly elected and 15 appointed by the amir, and this will have legislative powers. At present there is an advisory council with 35 members appointed by the amir. There are no political parties. Women have been permitted to vote and stand for election since 1999.

HEAD OF STATE

HH Amir of Qatar, Defence, Sheikh Hamad bin Khalifa al-Thani, KCMG, *assumed power* 27 June 1995
Crown Prince, HH Sheikh Tamim bin Hamad al-Thani

SELECTED GOVERNMENT MEMBERS *as at June 2012*

Prime Minister, Foreign Affairs, HH Sheikh Hamad bin Jassem bin Jabr al-Thani
Deputy Prime Minister, Abdullah bin Hamad al-Attiyah
Internal Affairs, Sheikh Abdulla bin Khalid al-Thani
Economy and Finance, Yousef Hussain Kamal

EMBASSY OF THE STATE OF QATAR

1 South Audley Street, London W1K 1NB
T 020-7493 2200
E london@mofa.gov.qa
W www.qatarembassy.info
Ambassador Extraordinary and Plenipotentiary, HE Khalid Rashid al-Hamoudi al-Mansouri, *apptd* 2005

BRITISH EMBASSY

PO Box 3, Doha
T (+974) 496 2000
E embassy.qatar@fco.gov.uk
W ukinqatar.fco.gov.uk
Ambassador Extraordinary and Plenipotentiary, Michael O'Neill, *apptd* 2012

DEFENCE

All aged 16–49, 2010 est	Males	Females
Available for military service	389,487	165,572
Fit for military service	321,974	140,176

Military expenditure—US$2,355m (2008)

ECONOMY AND TRADE

The economy is based largely on the production of oil and gas, which account for more than 50% of GDP, about 85% of export earnings and 70% of government revenues. The state-owned Qatar General Petroleum Corporation controls the industry, and is responsible for oil production onshore and offshore. There has been

substantial foreign investment in exploitation of Qatar's large gasfields, and the country is now the world's leading exporter of liquefied natural gas.

Other industries include oil refining, production of ammonia, fertilisers, petrochemicals, steel and cement, and ship repairing. Industry contributes 79% of GDP and services 20.9%.

The main export markets are Japan, South Korea and Singapore; the chief sources of imports are the USA, EU states, South Korea and Japan. Principal exports are liquefied natural gas, petroleum products, fertilisers and steel. The main imports are machinery and transport equipment, food and chemicals.

Annual average growth of GDP—18.7% (2011 est)
Inflation rate—2.8% (2011 est)
Unemployment—0.4% (2011 est)
Total external debt—US$82,050m (2011 est)
Imports—US$22,000m (2010)
Exports—US$61,500m (2010)

BALANCE OF PAYMENTS
Trade—US$39,500m surplus (2010)
Current Account—US$32,183m surplus (2010)

Trade with UK	2010	2011
Imports from UK	£990,362,856	£1,126,050,593
Exports to UK	£2,165,745,117	£4,768,793,275

COMMUNICATIONS
Airports and waterways—Doha is the principal airport, and also the main seaport
Roadways—Qatar has 7,790km of roads
Telecommunications—298,100 fixed lines and 2.33 million mobile subscriptions (2010); there were 563,800 internet users in 2009
Internet code and IDD—qa; 974 (from UK), 44 (to UK)
Media—Domestic television and radio are exclusively state-run; Al-Jazeera is the principal broadcaster and one of the largest broadcasters in the Middle East
WPFI score—38,00 (121)

Romania

Area—238,391 sq. km
Capital—Bucharest; population, 1,933,200 (2009 est)
Major cities—Brasov, Cluj-Napoca, Constanta, Craiova, Galati, Iasi, Timisoara
Currency—New leu (plural lei) of 100 bani
Population—21,848,504 falling at 0.26% a year (2012 est); Romanian (89.5%), Hungarian (6.6%), Roma (2.5%) (2002); small minority of Sasi (Transylvanian Saxons)
Religion—Christian (Orthodox 87%, Protestant 7%, Roman Catholic 5%, Greek Catholic 1%) (2002); small Muslim and Jewish minorities
Language—Romanian (official), Hungarian, Romani, German
Population density—93 per sq. km (2010)
Urban population—54.6% (2010 est)
Median age (years)—38.7 (2011 est)
National anthem—'Desteapta-te, Romane' ['Awake Thee, Romanian']
National day—1 December (Unification Day)
Death penalty—Abolished for all crimes (since 1989)
CPI score—3.6 (2011)

FINANCIAL OUTLOOK
The IMF completed its most recent review of Romania's economy in late January 2013. Real GDP growth in 2012 was almost flat, but is projected to pick up to around 1.6% in 2013, mainly driven by domestic demand. Inflation increased to 5% at end-2012, partly due to higher food prices following the bad harvest, and is expected to come down in the second half of 2013 to slightly above 3.5% by year-end. The current account deficit is expected to remain at around 4% of GDP in 2013. It looks as if Romania's 2012 budget deficit in accrual terms will be below 3% of GDP, as planned. The 2013 budget targets a deficit of 2.4% of GDP in accrual terms, and 2.1% in cash terms. The budget allows for the increase of public-sector wages so as to restore them to pre-crisis levels, and a 4% increase in pensions. The authorities expressed their commitment to resume public enterprise reform and a privatization program of state assets is underway. The secondary public offering of 15% of the capital of Transgaz will be finalized in the coming months, and a majority share in CFR Marfa will be sold to a strategic investor. Efforts to appoint professional boards and managers in public enterprises will be stepped up. The roadmaps for electricity and natural gas price deregulation will be strictly followed, while measures will be taken to protect the most vulnerable households.

CLIMATE AND TERRAIN
The Carpathian mountain range runs south from the Ukrainian border into the centre of the country and then turns west (the Transylvanian Alps) and north. The mountains enclose the central Transylvanian plateau and divide it from the southern Wallachian plain, part of the basin of the river Danube, which runs along most of the southern border, and the eastern Moldavian plateau, through which the river Siret flows, and the Black Sea coast. The mountains are thickly forested. Elevation extremes range from 2,544m (Moldoveanu) to 0m (Black Sea). The climate is continental, with average temperatures in Bucharest ranging from −6°C in January to 30°C in July and August.

HISTORY AND POLITICS
The 1991 constitution was amended in 2003 to bring it into line with EU requirements. The president is directly elected for a five-year term, renewable once. The bicameral parliament comprises the Chamber of Deputies with 334 seats, of which 18 are reserved for ethnic minorities, and the senate with 137 seats. Both houses are directly elected for a four-year term by proportional representation. The prime minister is appointed by the president.

In the 2008 legislative election, an alliance of the Social Democratic Party (PSD) and the Conservative Party (PC) remained the largest bloc, although the Democratic Liberal Party (PD-L) was the largest party. The PD-L formed a coalition government with the PSD under Emil Boc. The PSD withdrew from the coalition in October 2009, leaving a minority government which resigned after losing a vote of confidence. After failed attempts to form a government by other candidates, Emil Boc was reappointed prime minister in December 2009 at the head of a coalition of the PD-L, the Democratic Union of Hungarians in Romania and several independents. Boc was forced to resign in February 2012 following widespread protests over the government's austerity measures; his replacement, Mihai-Razvan

Ungureanu, lost a vote of no-confidence in April and was subsequently replaced by Victor Ponta, who formed a new coalition government.

HEAD OF STATE
President of the Republic, Traian Basescu, *elected* 12 December 2004, *re-elected* 2009

SELECTED GOVERNMENT MEMBERS *as at July 2012*
Prime Minister, Victor Ponta
Deputy Prime Minister, Florin Georgescu
Interior, Mircea Dusa
Defence, Corneliu Dobritoiu
Economy, Daniel Chitoiu

EMBASSY OF ROMANIA
Arundel House, 4 Palace Green, London W8 4QD
T 020-7937 9666
E roemb@roemb.co.uk
W www.londra.mae.ro
Ambassador Extraordinary and Plenipotentiary, HE Dr Ion Jinga, *apptd 2008*

BRITISH EMBASSY
24 Strada Jules Michelet, 010463 Bucharest
T (+40) (21) 201 7200
E Press.Bucharest@fco.gov.uk
W ukinromania.fco.gov.uk
Ambassador Extraordinary and Plenipotentiary, HE Martin Harris, *apptd* 2010

DEFENCE

Under an agreement signed in 2005, the USA is allowed to use military bases in Romania.

All aged 16–49, 2010 est	Males	Females
Available for military service	5,601,234	5,428,939
Fit for military service	4,550,409	4,507,880

Military expenditure—US$1,945m (2011)

ECONOMY AND TRADE

Transition to a market economy made sluggish progress until 2000, accelerating after 2004 in order to meet the requirements for EU accession. Although the economy grew steadily from 2000 to 2008, it was from a low base and the effects only recently started to have an impact on the country's widespread poverty. The economy contracted sharply in 2009 owing to the global downturn, and the government sought IMF and EU funding in spring 2009, but political volatility in late 2009 delayed the implementation of measures to address the economic problems. Following austerity measures, which delayed recovery from the recession, the economy returned to positive growth in 2011.

Agriculture remains inefficient, employing about 30% of the workforce but contributing only 7.9% of GDP. The principal crops are grains, sugar beet, sunflower seeds, vegetables and livestock products. Vines and fruit are grown, and extensive forests support an important timber industry. There are reserves of natural gas and oil, but Romania is a net importer of fossil fuels, although it exports electricity. Mineral deposits, including coal, iron ore, bauxite, chromium and uranium support a mining industry. Other industries include manufacturing, electrical and light machinery and car assembly, metallurgy, food processing and oil refining.

The main trading partners are EU states (especially Italy and Germany), Turkey and China. Principal exports include machinery and equipment, textiles, footwear, metals and metal products, minerals and fuels, chemicals and agricultural products. The main imports are machines and equipment, fuels, minerals, chemicals, textiles, base metals and agricultural products.

GNI—US$159,027m; US$7,840 per capita (2010)
Annual average growth of GDP—1.5% (2011 est)
Inflation rate—6.1% (2011 est)
Population below poverty line—21.1% (2010 est)
Unemployment—7% (2011 est)
Total external debt—US$136,900m (2011 est)
Imports—US$61,885m (2010)
Exports—US$49,357m (2010)

BALANCE OF PAYMENTS
Trade—US$12,528m deficit (2010)
Current Account—US$6,958m deficit (2010)

Trade with UK	2010	2011
Imports from UK	£756,794,798	£928,900,532
Exports to UK	£1,195,170,284	£1,281,195,431

COMMUNICATIONS

Airports and waterways—The main airports are at Bucharest and Timisoara; navigable waterways include 1,599km on the river Danube and its tributaries and 132km of canals. The main ports are Braila, Constanta, Galati and Tulcea
Roadways and railways—There are 71,154km of surfaced roads, of which 321km are motorway; there are 10,785km of railways, over one-third of which are electrified
Telecommunications—4.5 million fixed lines and 24.64 million mobile subscriptions (2010); there were 7.79 million internet users in 2009
Internet code and IDD—ro; 40 (from UK), 44 (to UK)
Major broadcasters—The state-owned Televiziunea (TVR) is the country's principal broadcaster
Press—There are several daily newspapers, including *Adevarul*, and *Libertatea*
WPFI score—16,00 (52)

EDUCATION AND HEALTH

Primary and secondary education is free and compulsory for ten years.
Literacy rate—97.7% (2009 est)
Gross enrolment ratio (percentage of relevant age group)—primary 96%; secondary 95%; tertiary 64% (2009 est)
Health expenditure (per capita)—US$408 (2009)
Hospital beds (per 1,000 people)—6.5 (2004–9)
Life expectancy (years)—74.22 (2012 est)
Mortality rate—11.84 (2012 est)
Birth rate—9.49 (2012 est)
Infant mortality rate—10.73 (2012 est)

  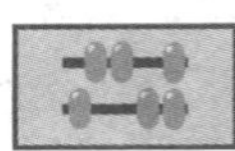      

Russia

Rossiyskaya Federatsiya—Russian Federation

Area—17,098,242 sq. km. Includes the Kalingrad exclave, between Lithuania and Poland. Neighbours: Norway, Finland, Estonia, Latvia, Belarus, Ukraine (west), Georgia, Azerbaijan, Kazakhstan, China, Mongolia, North Korea (south)

Capital—Moscow; population, 10,522,900 (2009 est). Founded in around 1147, it became the centre of the rising Moscow principality and in the 15th century the capital of the whole of Russia (Muscovy). In 1703 Peter the Great transferred the capital to St Petersburg, but Moscow became the capital again in 1918

Major cities—Chelyabinsk, Kazan, Nizhniy Novgorod (Gorky 1932–90), Novosibirsk (Novonikolayevsk until 1926), Omsk, Perm, Rostov, St Petersburg (Petrograd 1914–24; Leningrad 1924–91), Samara (Kuibyshev 1935–90), Ufa, Volgograd (Stalingrad 1925–61), Yekaterinburg (Sverdlovsk 1924–91)

Currency—Rouble of 100 kopeks

Population—138,082,178 falling at 0.48% a year (2012 est); Russian (79.8%), Tatar (3.8%), Ukrainian (2%), Bashkir (1.2%), Chuvash (1.1%), and a further 150 nationalities (2002)

Religion—Christian (Russian Orthodox 70%, other 2%), Muslim 10%, Buddhist 1% (est); small Jewish minority

Language—Russian (official); many minority languages

Population density—9 per sq. km (2010)

Urban population—72.8% (2010 est)

Median age (years)—38.7 (2011 est)

National anthem—'Gosudarstvenny Gimn Rossiyskoy Federatsii' ['State Anthem of the Russian Federation']

National day—12 June (Russia Day)

Death penalty—Retained (not used since 1999)

CPI score—2.4 (2011)

FINANCIAL OUTLOOK

The IMF completed its most recent review of Russia's economy in late January 2013. Growth is moderate, but historically low unemployment and high capacity utilization suggest that economic activity is close to its potential. In 2012, consumption-driven growth momentum slowed from the beginning of Q2 2012, with economic activity dampened by a dip in oil prices, and slowing investment and export growth. Annual growth is estimated at 3.6% for both 2012 and 2013. The 2013 growth figure is based on a fairly pessimistic scenario, where oil prices stay flat and external demand remains weak. Despite decelerating economic activity, headline inflation at around 7% remains above the medium-term target, but is expected to ease somewhat to 6% in 2013. Bringing inflation down further will require monetary policy initiatives, which could damp down growth. Rapid credit growth constitutes a danger for 2013, and is weakening the reserve position and liquidity of Russian banks, but the IMF says that the Russian authorities have strengthened their policy capacity to manage volatility and crises. This has been achieved, mainly through a more flexible exchange-rate policy and through increased reserve buffers, with the Reserve Fund now standing at some 4.5% of GDP. However, the target for the fund is 7% of GDP, and this remains some way off. An ageing population and negative demographics make Russia's current pension system unsustainable, and the IMF wants to see changes.

CLIMATE AND TERRAIN

Russia includes the easternmost areas of Europe and the whole of northern Asia. It lies mostly on plains which extend eastwards to the Ural mountains and then from the Urals to the Yenesei river. To the east of the Yenesei are plateaux, with lowlands in northern Siberia. Mountainous areas lie along the southern borders, in eastern Siberia and the Kamchatka peninsula. The terrain varies from the tundra of the Arctic region, through the taiga (the largest zone) of the north and centre, to the grassy plains (steppe) between the forests and the mountains. Elevation extremes range from 5,633m (Mt El'brus, Caucasus) to −28m (Caspian Sea). Russia has the longest Arctic coastline in the world (over 27,000km); it also has Baltic, Black Sea and Pacific coastlines.

The most important rivers are the Volga, the Northern Dvina, the Neva, the Don and the Kuban in the European part, and in the Asiatic part the Ob, the Irtysh, the Yenisei, the Lena, the Amur and, further north, the Khatanga, Olenek, Yana, Indigirka and Kolyma. Lake Baikal in eastern Siberia is the deepest lake in the world. Part of the Caspian Sea lies within Russia.

The climate is mostly continental, but varies with latitude and terrain from arctic conditions in the north to subtropical in the far east and on the Black Sea coast. Average temperatures in Moscow range from −14°C in January and February to 24°C in July. Rainfall is low to moderate in most of the country.

HISTORY AND POLITICS

The 1993 constitution introduced multiparty democracy and enshrines various human rights and civil liberties; amendments in 2008 extended the terms of office for the presidency and the State Duma from the 2012 elections. The head of state is a president, who is directly elected for a six-year term, renewable once consecutively. The bicameral Federal Assembly comprises the State Duma (lower house) of 450 members, all elected by proportional representation for a five-year term, and the Council of the Federation, which has 166 members (two from each member of the federation), appointed for terms of varying lengths. The president appoints the chairman of the council of ministers (prime minister), subject to the approval of the legislature, but is also entitled to chair sessions of the council.

In the 2011 legislative elections, the pro-Vladimir Putin United Russia party retained its overall majority in the *Duma* but with a reduced majority. Putin (elected president between 2000-8) also retained the presidency in March 2012, picking up 63.6% of the overall vote in a highly controversial presidential election. He was inaugurated as president in May 2012 and duly appointed former president Dmitry Medvedev to be chair of the Council of Ministers.

HEAD OF STATE

President, Vladimir Putin, *elected* 4 March 2012, *took office* 7 May 2012

SELECTED GOVERNMENT MEMBERS *as at July 2012*

Prime Minister, Dmitry Medvedev

First Deputy Chair, Igor Shuvalov

Deputy Chairs, Vladislav Surkov; Dmitry Rogozin; Dmitry Kozak; Arkady Dvorkovich; Olga Golodets

EMBASSY OF THE RUSSIAN FEDERATION

6–7 Kensington Palace Gardens, London W8 4QP

T 020-7229 6412

E info@rusemb.org.uk

W www.rusemb.org.uk

Ambassador Extraordinary and Plenipotentiary, HE Alexander Yakovenko, *apptd* 2011

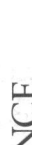

BRITISH EMBASSY
Smolenskaya Naberezhnaya 10, 121099 Moscow
T (+7) (495) 956 7200
E moscow@britishembassy.ru
W ukinrussia.fco.gov.uk
Ambassador Extraordinary and Plenipotentiary, HE Tim Barrow, DCMG, LVO, MBE, *apptd* 2011

Insurgencies

Chechnya occupies an area that is strategically important to Russia because routes from central Russia to the Black Sea and Caspian Sea, and oil and gas pipelines from neighbouring countries, pass through it. The republic declared itself independent in 1991 but its attempts to assert its independence led to two wars with the federal government. The first of these, in 1994–6, resulted in the signing of the Khasavyurt accords. After the peace broke down and Russia invaded Chechnya again in 1999, President Putin refused negotiations and imposed direct rule from Moscow in 2000. Rebels continued with terrorist attacks, although these have decreased since 2007. Russia announced the end of counter-terrorism operations in Chechnya in 2009, but has had to reinstate these in some areas where rebels remain active.

The conflict in Chechnya has destabilised the whole of the northern Caucasus, especially Ingushetia and Dagestan, where violence has increased in recent years. The violence has also affected other parts of Russia, where extremists linked to Chechen separatists have carried out suicide bombings and attacks such as the Moscow theatre siege in 2002, the Beslan school siege in 2004, and the bombing of Moscow's metro system in 2010.

Federal Structure

Following the break-up of the USSR in 1991, a new federal treaty was signed in 1992 between the central government and the autonomous republics of the Russian Federation. Tatarstan and Bashkortostan signed the treaty in 1994 after securing considerable legislative and economic autonomy.

The Russian Federation comprises 46 *oblasti* (regions), 9 *krai* (autonomous territories), 21 *respubliki* (autonomous republics), 4 *okrugi* (autonomous areas), two cities with federal status (Moscow and St Petersburg) and one autonomous Jewish *oblast*, Yevrey. The *oblasti* are Amur, Arkhangelsk, Astrakhan, Belgorod, Bryansk, Chelyabinsk, Irkutsk, Ivanovo, Kaliningrad, Kaluga, Kemerovo, Kirov, Kostroma, Kurgan, Kursk, Leningrad, Lipetsk, Magadan, Moscow, Murmansk, Nizhny Novgorod, Novgorod, Novosibirsk, Omsk, Orenburg, Orel, Penza, Pskov, Rostov, Ryazan, Sakhalin, Samara, Saratov, Smolensk, Sverdlovsk, Tambov, Tomsk, Tula, Tver, Tyumen, Ulyanovsk, Vladimir, Volgograd, Vologda, Voronezh and Yaroslavl. The *krai* are Altai, Kamchatka, Khabarovsk, Krasnodar, Krasnoyarsk, Perm, Primorski, Stavropol and Zabaykalsk. The *respubliki* are Adygeia, Altai, Bashkortostan, Buryatia, Chechnya, Chuvashia, Dagestan, Ingushetia, Kabardino-Balkaria, Kalmykiya, Karachayevo-Cherkessia, Karelia, Khakassia, Komi, Mari-El, Mordovia, North Ossetia, Sakha, Tatarstan, Tuva and Udmurtia. The *okrugi* are Chukotka, Khanty-Mansi, Nenets and Yamalo-Nenets.

DEFENCE

Since the demise of the USSR, Russia's armed forces have been considerably reduced and major army reform is ongoing.

The CIS Collective Security Treaty enables Russia to station troops in Armenia, Belarus, Kazakhstan, Kyrgyzstan and Tajikistan. The Black Sea fleet was divided between Russian and Ukraine under an agreement signed in 1997. In April 2010, the Strategic Arms Reduction Treaty (START) was renewed by president Medvedev and US president Obama; the bilateral treaty, originally drafted in 1991, is an agreement between the two states to continue to significantly reduce the number of operational strategic nuclear weapons.

All aged 16–49, 2010 est	Males	Females
Available for military service	34,132,156	34,985,115
Fit for military service	20,431,035	26,381,518

Military expenditure—US$64,123m (2011)
Conscription duration—12 months

ECONOMY AND TRADE

Under the Soviet regime, an essentially agrarian economy in 1917 was transformed by the early 1960s into the second-greatest industrial power in the world. However, by the early 1970s the concentration of resources on the military-industrial complex had caused stagnation in the civilian economy. Economic reforms were introduced by President Gorbachev, including the legalisation of small private businesses, the reduction of state control over the economy, and denationalisation and privatisation. Mass privatisation of state industries began in 1992, and 80% of the economy had been privatised by 1996. The largest and most economically significant industries, oil and gas, were partially renationalised from 2004.

The transition to a market economy caused severe economic crises in 1993 and 1998, but from 1999 to 2008 the economy sustained growth averaging 7% a year, and unemployment and poverty declined. Banking and fiscal reforms stimulated foreign investment, although political and economic uncertainties, corruption, excessive red tape and a lack of trust in institutions continue to inhibit growth. Other problems include the economy's vulnerability to fluctuations in global prices of key commodities and a dilapidated infrastructure. Some of these factors exacerbated the impact on Russia of the global financial crisis in autumn 2008, when a sharp fall in oil prices coincided with turmoil in the banking system and a 70% drop in the stock market. Despite US$200bn in government aid to the financial sector, credit problems, a severe drop in production and rising unemployment caused a sharp contraction in the economy until late 2009, before high oil prices buoyed economic growth towards the end of 2011.

Russia has some of the world's richest natural resources, especially mineral deposits and timber. The recent growth in the economy is founded on the exploitation and export of its oil and natural gas reserves. Russia is now the world's leading oil producer (surpassing Saudi Arabia in 2011) and exporter of hydrocarbons, and the leading supplier to European countries and China, a position that has led the country into disputes with some of its neighbours; Ukraine, Georgia and Belarus have all had gas supplies cut for short periods during price negotiations. Oil and natural gas account for 70% of exports, 45% of federal budget revenue and over 25% of GDP. Economic diversification, especially into high technology sectors, is a government priority.

Mining (coal, iron ore, aluminium and other non-ferrous metals) and oil and natural gas extraction are concentrated in the region south of Moscow, the Volga valley, the northern Caucasus, the Urals, Siberia and the far east and north. Russia is also keen to exploit the shrinking of the Arctic ice-cap to prospect for previously inaccessible deposits under the Arctic Sea. The main industries are extracting and processing oil, gas and minerals, forestry, all forms of machine building (including transport, communications, agricultural, construction, and power generating and transmitting equipment), defence industries, shipbuilding, medical and scientific instruments, consumer durables, textiles, food processing and handicrafts.

The vast area and the great variety in climatic conditions are reflected in the structure of agriculture. In the far north, only

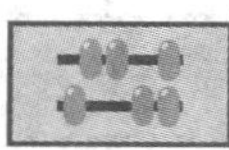

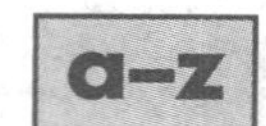

reindeer breeding, hunting and fishing are possible; further south, forestry is combined with grain growing. In the southern half of the forest zone and in the adjacent forest-steppe zone, the acreage under grain crops is larger and agriculture more complex. The southern part of the Western Siberian plain is an important grain-growing and stock-breeding area. In the extreme south, cotton is cultivated. Vine, tobacco and other southern crops are grown on the Black Sea shore of the Caucasus.

The service sector is the largest, accounting for 58.9% of GDP and employing 62.7% of the workforce; industry contributes 37% of GDP and employs 27.5%; and agriculture accounts for 4.2% of GDP and 9.8% of employment.

Russia's main trading partners are EU countries (especially Germany), China, Ukraine, the USA and Turkey. Principal exports are oil and petroleum products, natural gas, metals, timber and wood products, chemicals, manufactured goods, military vehicles and defence equipment. The main imports are machinery, vehicles, pharmaceutical products, plastics, semi-finished metal products, meat, fruits and nuts, optical and medical equipment, iron and steel.

GNI—US$1,431,120m; US$9,900 per capita (2010)
Annual average growth of GDP—4.3% (2011 est)
Inflation rate—8.9% (2011 est)
Population below poverty line—13.1% (2010)
Unemployment—6.8% (2011 est)
Total external debt—US$519,400m (2011 est)
Imports—US$229,655m (2010)
Exports—US$397,668m (2010)

BALANCE OF PAYMENTS
Trade—US$168,013m surplus (2010)
Current Account—US$71,129m surplus (2010)

Trade with UK	2010	2011
Imports from UK	£3,450,871,453	£4,781,128,266
Exports to UK	£5,286,091,964	£7,264,459,857

COMMUNICATIONS
Airports—There are 1,213 airports and airfields, although only 593 have surfaced runways. The principal international airports are at Moscow, St Petersburg and Novosibirsk
Waterways—Major ports include Kaliningrad on the Baltic Sea and Novorossiysk on the Black Sea. Two of the three northern ports, St Petersburg and Arkhangelsk, are icebound during winter; only Murmansk is accessible. There is a large merchant fleet of 1,143 ships of 1,000 tonnes and over, with a further 439 ships registered in other countries. There are 102,000km of waterways, supplemented by a 72,000km system of canals which provides a through route between the White Sea and Baltic Sea in the north and the Black Sea, Caspian Sea and the Sea of Azov in the south
Roadways—There are 982,000km of roads, 776,000km of which are surfaced
Railways—The railways are state-run, with 87,157km of the network used for passenger transport plus 30,000km by industry
Telecommunications—44.96 million fixed lines and 238 million mobile subscriptions (2010); there were 40.85 million internet users in 2009
Internet code and IDD—ru; 7 (from UK), 810 44 (to UK)
Major broadcasters—Broadcasting is dominated by the Russian State Television and Radio Broadcasting Company (VGTRK) and stations part-owned by the government or whose owners have close ties to it
Press—There are over 400 major newspapers printed every week, including mass-circulation dailies *Komsomolskaya Pravda* and *Moskovsky Komsomolets*
WPFI score—49,90 (140)

EDUCATION AND HEALTH
There are 11 years of compulsory education: nine at basic school level and a further two at senior secondary level.
Literacy rate—99.6% (2009 est)
Gross enrolment ratio (percentage of relevant age group)—primary 99%; secondary 89%; tertiary 76% (2009 est)
Health expenditure (per capita)—US$475 (2009)
Hospital beds (per 1,000 people)—9.7 (2004–9)
Life expectancy (years)—66.46 (2012 est)
Mortality rate—16.03 (2012 est)
Birth rate—10.94 (2012 est)
Infant mortality rate—9.88 (2012 est)
HIV/AIDS adult prevalence—1% (2009 est)

St Kitts and Nevis

Federation of St Christopher and Nevis (Federation of St Kitts and Nevis)
Area—261 sq. km
Capital—Basseterre; population, 12,847 (2009 est)
Major town—Charlestown, the chief town of Nevis
Currency—East Caribbean dollar (EC$) of 100 cents
Population—50,726 rising at 0.81% a year (2012 est)
Religion—Christian (Anglican 50%, Roman Catholic 25%) (est)
Language—English (official)
Population density—202 per sq. km (2010)
Urban population—32.4% (2010 est)
Median age (years)—32 (2011 est)
National anthem—'Oh Land of Beauty!'
National day—19 September (Independence Day)
Life expectancy (years)—74.84 (2012 est)
Mortality rate—7.08 (2012 est)
Birth rate—13.9 (2012 est)
Infant mortality rate—9.43 (2012 est)
Death penalty—Retained (last used 2008)

FINANCIAL OUTLOOK
According to the latest IMF report on St Kitts and Nevis, in November 2012, the authorities have done well in implementing its IMF-supported program, which aims to reduce the two islands' massive deficit of some 170% of GDP. The near-term outlook for the economy is for a modest recovery, the IMF says. Significant progress has been made in restructuring public debt. In order to limit the impact on the islands' financial sector, and to further buttress the fiscal position through lower interest payments, the authorities need to push on with this, including finalizing negotiations with remaining domestic and external creditors. The authorities are in the process of elaborating a budget for 2013. In line with their IMF-supported program's aim of securing gains from

the reduction in public debt, due emphasis will need to be given to bolstering the tax base, containing current outlays, and increasing capital spending, as well as the capacity to buffer shocks. Over the near to medium term, it will be important to accelerate the pace of structural reforms to further boost revenue, and promote growth-enhancing public expenditure. The financial system has remained resilient, with adequate capitalization and continued deposit growth. Inflation declined from 2.9% at the end of 2011, to 1.9% in 2012. The authorities met all the IMF's program targets to end-March 2012 and end-June 2012, and were on target to reduce the external debt to 100% of GDP by the end of 2012.

CLIMATE AND TERRAIN

The volcanic islands of St Kitts (St Christopher) (168 sq. km) and Nevis (93 sq. km) are part of the Leeward group in the eastern Caribbean Sea. The centre of St Kitts is forest-clad and mountainous, with the Great Salt Pond occupying the tip of its southern peninsula; elevation extremes range from 1,156m (Mt Liamuiga) to 0m (Caribbean Sea). Nevis, separated from the southern tip of St Kitts by a strait 3km wide, is dominated by Nevis Peak (985m). The climate is tropical, moderated by north-east trade winds, and a wet season occurs from May to September. The islands are in the hurricane belt.

HISTORY AND POLITICS

The islands were inhabited by Carib, or Kalinago, people when discovered in 1493 by Christopher Columbus, who gave St Christopher its name. Colonisation by the British began in 1623–4, when St Kitts became the first British colony in the West Indies, and French settlement began shortly after. The island was held jointly from 1628 to 1713, although there were skirmishes between the British and French settlers in the 17th century; France dropped its claims after 1783. Nevis was settled by the British from 1628. The two islands were part of the Leeward Islands colony from 1871 to 1956, and then of the West Indies Federation from 1958 to 1962. They achieved internal self-government in 1967 and became independent in September 1983.

A separatist movement was formed on Nevis in 1970. A referendum on the issue in 1998 resulted in a 61.8% vote in favour of secession, which fell short of the two-thirds majority required.

The Labour Party, which has been in power since 1995, retained its overall majority in the 2010 legislative election, and began its fourth term of office under Denzil Douglas.

Under the 1983 constitution, the head of state is Queen Elizabeth II, represented by a governor-general appointed on the advice of the prime minister. The unicameral National Assembly has 15 members: 11 directly elected for a five-year term, a speaker, and three appointed by the governor-general on the advice of the prime minister and the leader of the opposition. The prime minister, who is responsible to the legislature, and the cabinet are appointed by the governor-general.

Nevis is responsible for its own internal affairs. It has an eight-member Nevis Island assembly and is governed by the Nevis Island administration, headed by the premier.

Governor-General, HE Sir Cuthbert Sebastian, GCMG, OBE, *apptd* 1996

SELECTED GOVERNMENT MEMBERS *as at July 2012*
Prime Minister, Finance, Denzil Douglas
Deputy Prime Minister, Foreign Affairs, National Security, Sam Condor

HIGH COMMISSION FOR ST KITTS AND NEVIS
10 Kensington Court, London W8 5DL
T 020-7937 9718
E info@sknhc.co.uk
High Commissioner, HE Kevin Isaac, *apptd* 2011

BRITISH HIGH COMMISSIONER
High Commissioner, HE Paul Brummell, *apptd* 2009, resident at Bridgetown, Barbados

ECONOMY AND TRADE

The sugar industry was the mainstay of the economy for over 300 years but was closed down in 2005 after decades of operating at a loss. Tourism (the chief source of foreign exchange revenue), offshore financial services and manufacturing, especially distilling, food processing, clothing and electronics, are being developed. Services now account for 74.7% of GDP, industry for 22.8% and agriculture for 2.4%. The economy of Nevis relies on farming, but a sea-island cotton industry is being developed for export. The economy is restricted by one of the world's highest public debt burdens (estimated at 200% of GDP in 2011) and the country remains vulnerable to costly damage from natural disasters and shifts in tourism demand.

The main trading partners are the USA and Trinidad and Tobago. Principal exports are machinery, food, electronic equipment, beverages and tobacco. The main imports are machinery, manufactured goods, food and fuels.

GNI—US$620m; US$11,740 per capita (2010)
Annual average growth of GDP—1.5% (2011 est)
Inflation rate—4.6% (2011 est)
Total external debt—US$211.3m (2011 est)

BALANCE OF PAYMENTS
Trade—US$183m deficit (2010)
Current Account—US$179m deficit (2009)

Trade with UK	2010	2011
Imports from UK	£5,249,278	£5,885,456
Exports to UK	£340,719	£195,494

COMMUNICATIONS

Airports and waterways—There are two airports; that on St Kitts can take most large jet aircraft. Basseterre is a port of registry and has deep-water harbour facilities; there are regular ferries between Basseterre and Charlestown
Roadways and railways—The islands have a total of 383km of roads, of which 163km are surfaced, and 50km of narrow-gauge railways on St Kitts
Telecommunications—20,600 fixed lines and 84,600 mobile subscriptions (2009); there were 17,000 internet users in 2009
Internet code and IDD—kn; 1 869 (from UK), 011 44 (to UK)
Media—The government-owned broadcaster ZIZ operates national television and radio networks; *The Sun* is the sole daily newspaper

Saudi Arabia

Al-Mamlakah al-Arabiyah as Suudiyah—Kingdom of Saudi Arabia
Area—2,149,690 sq. km
Capital—Riyadh (Ar-Riyadh); population, 4,725,270 (2009 est)
Major cities—Dammam, Jeddah, Mecca, Medina, Tabuk, At Taif
Currency—Saudi riyal (SR) of 100 halalas
Population—26,534,504 rising at 1.52% a year (2012 est); includes some 5,576,076 non-nationals (2012 est)
Religion—Muslim (Sunni 85%, predominantly Wahhabi; Shia 10%) (est). Public practice of other religions is forbidden
Language—Arabic (official)
Population density—14 per sq. km (2010)
Urban population—83.6% (2010 est)
Median age (years)—25.3 (2011 est)
National anthem—'As-Salaam al Malaki' ['The Royal Salute']
National day—23 September (Unification Day)
Death penalty—Retained
CPI score—4.4 (2011)

FINANCIAL OUTLOOK

Saudi Arabia's economy grew by 6.8% in 2012, driven by the oil sector and non-oil sector, according to the Saudi Economic Developments and Outlook report by the National Commercial Bank. However, the NCB forecast that GDP growth would level off to 3% in 2013. Oil output rose by 7.2% in 2012, averaging 9.92 million bpd, which boosted the oil sector's GDP by 5.5%, the fastest pace of growth since 2005. The world's top oil exporter has recovered since the 2009 downturn, fueled by heavy public spending on welfare and housing construction, driven in part by the government's reaction to unrest elsewhere in the Arab world. The government is planning to increase public spending by 15% in 2013, to US$266.6 billion. Much of this investment will be directed towards construction of residential, educational, and health facilities, and the transport infrastructure.

CLIMATE AND TERRAIN

Saudi Arabia comprises about 80% of the Arabian peninsula. The Hejaz region (north-west) runs along the northern Red Sea coast to the Asir and contains the holy cities of Mecca and Medina. The mountainous Asir (south-west) and the coastal plain of the Tihama lie along the southern Red Sea coast from the Hejaz to the border with Yemen. The Nejd plateau extends over the centre, including the Nafud and Dahna deserts. The Hasa (east) is low-lying and largely desert. The Empty Quarter (south) is the world's largest sand desert. Elevation extremes range from 3,133m (Jabal Sawda) to 0m (Persian Gulf). There is a desert climate, with extremes of temperature in the interior; coastal areas are more temperate but extremely humid. Average temperatures in Riyadh range from 3°C in January to 45°C in July.

HISTORY AND POLITICS

The Arabian peninsula was the birthplace of the Muslim faith in the seventh century and the base from which the religion and a Muslim empire expanded, eventually stretching from India to Spain. When this empire declined in the 12th century, Arabia became isolated and internally divided. The rise of the al-Saud family began in the 18th century, when it united the Nejd in support of the Wahhabi religious movement. The modern state was the culmination of a 30-year campaign by Abd-al Aziz al-Saud (often known as Ibn Saud) to unite the four tribal regions of the Hejaz, Asir, Najd and Hasa; the Kingdom of Saudi Arabia was proclaimed on 23 September 1932.

The ruling family preserved stability for many years by suppressing dissent and resisting calls for greater democracy, with some of its actions raising international concerns over human rights abuses. Internal tension grew in the 1990s because of the continuing presence of foreign, particularly US, troops in the country after the 1991 Gulf War; troops, and foreign nationals became terrorist targets. Despite the troops' redeployment to Qatar in early 2003, the frequency of attacks increased following the start of the Iraq War in 2003 and included Saudi as well as foreign victims. Some dissident groups are believed to have links with al-Qaida. Since 2003 demand for political reform has grown and become more militant. In 2005, the country's first nationwide elections were held for half the seats on municipal councils, with voting by universal male suffrage.

King Abdullah acceded to the throne after the death of his half-brother King Fahd in 2005.

There is no written constitution; constitutional practice is provided for by articles of government based on the Qur'an and the teachings and sayings of the Prophet Muhammad *(Sunnah)* and issued by royal decree.

Saudi Arabia is a hereditary monarchy. The king is head of government and appoints the council of ministers (established in 1953), whose term of office was fixed in 1993 at four years.

There is no legislature; the Consultative Council *(Majlis-al-Shura)* debates policy, proposes legislation in certain areas and makes recommendations to the king. The council's 150 members are appointed by the king and serve a four-year term. Its decisions are taken by majority vote. There are no political parties.

Each of the 13 provinces has a governor appointed by the king and a council of prominent local citizens to advise the governor on local government, budgetary and planning issues.

HEAD OF STATE
The King of Saudi Arabia, Custodian of the Two Holy Mosques, Prime Minister, King Abdullah bin Abdul Aziz al-Saud, *born* 1923, *succeeded* 2 August 2005
HRH Crown Prince, Deputy Prime Minister, Defence, Prince Salman bin Abdul Aziz al-Saud

SELECTED GOVERNMENT MEMBERS *as at July 2012*
Finance, Ibrahim bin Abdel Aziz al-Assaf
Foreign Affairs, HRH Prince Saud al-Faisal bin Abdul Aziz al-Saud
Economy, Khaled bin Mohammad al-Qussaibi

ROYAL EMBASSY OF SAUDI ARABIA
30 Charles Street, London W1J 5DZ
T 020-7917 3000
E ukemb@mofa.gov.sa
W www.saudiembassy.org.uk
Ambassador Extraordinary and Plenipotentiary, HE HRH Prince Mohamed bin Nawaf bin Abdul Aziz al-Saud, *apptd* 2005

BRITISH EMBASSY
PO Box 94351, Diplomatic Quarter, Riyadh 11693
T (+966) (1) 488 0077
E PressOffice.Riyadh@fco.gov.uk
W ukinsaudiarabia.fco.gov.uk
Ambassador Extraordinary and Plenipotentiary, HE Sir Tom Phillips, KCMG, *apptd* 2010

DEFENCE

All aged 16–49, 2010 est	Males	Females
Available for military service	8,644,522	6,601,985
Fit for military service	7,365,624	5,677,819

Military budget—US$46,219m (2011)

ECONOMY AND TRADE

The economy is based on oil extraction and processing, but since 1970 the government has used five-year development plans to encourage diversification, and the non-oil sector now accounts for over half of GDP. The 2010–14 development plan aims to increase natural gas production and to promote the growth of small- and medium-sized businesses, partly through further privatisation; it also partially opened the Saudi stock market to foreign investors, and between 2010 and 2014 intends to spend over $373bn on social development and infrastructure projects on six 'economic cities' across the country.

Oil extraction since the 1940s has brought great wealth. Saudi Arabia has the largest proven reserves of oil in the world (about 20% of the world total) and the fifth-largest reserves of recoverable gas. The oil and gas industry contributes around 45% of GDP and about 80% of government revenue.

The main industries apart from oil extraction and refining include production of petrochemicals, ammonia, industrial gases, caustic soda, cement, fertiliser, plastics and metals, commercial ship and aircraft repair and construction. Industry accounts for 69.1% of GDP and the service sector for 28.9%. Agriculture contributes 2% but is limited by the terrain, although productivity has been increased by extensive irrigation, desalination and the use of aquifers. The main products are grains, fruit, meat and dairy.

The main trading partners are the USA, China, Japan and South Korea. Oil and petroleum products constitute 90% of exports. The principal imports are machinery and equipment, foodstuffs, chemicals, motor vehicles and textiles.

GNI—US$381,276m; US$16,190 per capita (2009)
Annual average growth of GDP—6.5% (2011 est)
Inflation rate—5% (2011 est)
Unemployment rate—10.9% (males only) (2011 est)
Total external debt—US$101,000m (2011 est)
Imports—US$97,077m (2010)
Exports—US$251,100m (2010)

BALANCE OF PAYMENTS

Trade—US$154,023m surplus (2010)
Current Account—US$20,983m surplus (2009)

Trade with UK	2010	2011
Imports from UK	£3,076,566,521	£3,074,720,984
Exports to UK	£424,447,489	£1,234,646,163

COMMUNICATIONS

Airports and waterways—There are 217 airports and airfields; the three international airports are at Riyadh, Jeddah (serving Mecca) and Dammam; the main cargo ports are Jeddah on the Red Sea coast and Dammam on the Gulf coast. The main oil port (the world's largest) is Ras Tanura
Roadways and railways—The road network totals 221,372km, including a 3,891km motorway system; there are 1,378km of railways, operated by the state-run Saudi Railway Organisation
Telecommunications—4.16 million fixed lines and 51.56 million mobile subscriptions (2009); there were 9.77 million internet users in 2009
Internet code and IDD—sa; 966 (from UK), 44 (to UK)
Major broadcasters—Television and radio networks are operated by the state-run Broadcasting Service of Saudi Arabia
Press—There are around seven daily newspapers, including *Al Watan* and the English-language *Arab News*
WPFI score—61,50 (157)

EDUCATION AND HEALTH

With the exception of a few schools for expatriate children, all schools are segregated and supervised by the government.
Literacy rate—86.1% (2009 est)
Gross enrolment ratio (percentage of relevant age group)—primary 106%; secondary 104%; tertiary 37% (2010 est)
Health expenditure (per capita)—US$714 (2009)
Hospital beds (per 1,000 people)—2.2 (2004–9)
Life expectancy (years)—74.35 (2012 est)
Mortality rate—3.32 (2012 est)
Birth rate—19.19 (2012 est)
Infant mortality rate—15.61 (2012 est)

Seychelles

République des Seychelles/Repiblik Sesel—Republic of Seychelles
Area—455 sq. km
Capital—Victoria, on Mahé; population, 26,001 (2009 est)
Currency—Seychelles rupee of 100 cents
Population—90,024 rising at 0.92% a year (2012 est)
Religion—Christian 93% (Roman Catholic 82%, Anglican 6%), Hindu 2%, Muslim 1% (2002)
Language—English, French, Creole (all official)
Population density—188 per sq. km (2010)
Urban population—55.3% (2010 est)
Median age (years)—32.5 (2011 est)
National anthem—'Koste Seselwa' ['Seychellois Unite']
National day—18 June (Constitution Day)
Life expectancy (years)—73.77 (2012 est)
Mortality rate—6.9 (2012 est)
Birth rate—15.1 (2012 est)
Infant mortality rate—11.35 (2012 est)
Death penalty—Abolished for all crimes (since 1993)
CPI score—4.8 (2011)
Literacy rate—91.8% (2009 est)

FINANCIAL OUTLOOK

Following the re-election of President James Michel, the Seychelles government maintained a fiscal policy aimed at reducing public debt, as per the terms of an IMF-backed reform plan. It posted a budget surplus in 2012, and is projected to do the same in 2013. The planned introduction of value-added tax (VAT) in 2012 has helped finances. According to African Economic Outlook, the government is making progress in improving the investment climate regulatory framework. Amendments to the Financial Institutions Act have established the legal basis for new financial products, boosted competition, and reduced the state's role in the

  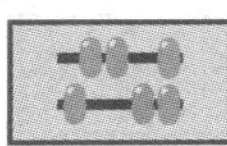      

financial sector. Seychelles recently prepared the new Seychelles Sustainable Development Strategy (SSDS) 2011–20. The IMF warns that there is little scope to relax medium-term fiscal policy, given the authorities' objective to bring down public debt below 50% of GDP by 2018. Policies in 2013 aim to attenuate balance of payments pressures stemming from declining foreign direct investment, and strong import demand through fiscal adjustment, providing room for a gradual decline in interest rates from double-digit levels. GDP growth hit 6.7% in 2010, but declined in both 2011 and 2012 to 5% and 4%, respectively. Tourism will continue to be the main driver of economic growth in 2012–13.

CLIMATE AND TERRAIN

Seychelles consists of 115 islands spread over 643,737 sq. km of the south-west Indian Ocean, north of Madagascar. There is a relatively compact granitic group of 32 islands, with high hills and mountains, of which Mahé is the largest and most populated (about 90% of the population lives on Mahé), and an outlying coralline group, for the most part only slightly above sea-level. Elevation extremes range from 905m (Morne Seychellois) to 0m (Indian Ocean). The climate is tropical, with average temperatures between 24°C and 31°C throughout the year, and a wet season from November to March.

HISTORY AND POLITICS

The uninhabited islands were proclaimed French territory in 1756, but settlement of the Mahé group began only in 1770. The group was a dependency of Mauritius, and was ceded to Britain with Mauritius in 1814. In 1903 these islands, together with the coralline group, were formed into a colony separate from Mauritius. On 29 June 1976, the islands became an independent republic.

Following a coup d'état in 1977, when France-Albert René became president, Seychelles became a one-party state ruled by the Seychelles People's Progressive Front (SPPF) in 1979. Opposition parties were permitted from 1991 and in 1993 President René reintroduced a multiparty constitution. Power has remained with the SPPF under the pluralist system, although opposition parties are beginning to achieve a greater share of the vote.

President René stepped down in mid-term in 2004 and the rest of his term was served by the vice-president, James Michel, who was elected president in 2006 and re-elected in May 2011. In the 2011 legislative election, the SPPF retained its overall majority.

Under the 1993 constitution, the executive president is directly elected for a five-year term, with a maximum of three consecutive terms. The unicameral National Assembly has up to 34 members: 23 directly elected by constituencies and up to 11 allocated by proportional representation; members serve a five-year term. The council of ministers is appointed by the president.

HEAD OF STATE

President, Defence, James Michel, *assumed office* 14 April 2004, *elected* July 2006, *re-elected* 2011
Vice-President, Danny Faure

SELECTED GOVERNMENT MEMBERS *as at July 2012*

Foreign Affairs, Jean-Paul Adam
Home Affairs, Joel Morgan

SEYCHELLES HIGH COMMISSION

4th Floor, 111 Baker Street, London W1U 6RR
T 020-7935 7770
E consulate@seychelles-gov.net
W www.seychelles-gov.net
High Commissioner, HE Patrick Pillay, *apptd* 2010

BRITISH HIGH COMMISSION

PO Box 161, Oliaji Trade Centre, Victoria, Mahé
T (+248) 283 666
E bhcvictoria@fco.gov.uk
W ukinseychelles.fco.gov.uk
High Commissioner, HE Matthew Forbes, OBE, *apptd* 2009

DEFENCE

All aged 16–49, 2010 est	*Males*	*Females*
Available for military service	26,257	23,996
Fit for military service	20,231	19,891

Military expenditure—US$9.4m (2011)

ECONOMY AND TRADE

Seychelles prospered after independence owing to the development of tuna fishing and tourism, which employs about 30% of the workforce. The economy struggled in 2008–9 owing to external debt, high deficits, food and oil price rises and a reduction in foreign exchange earnings after tourism declined in the global economic downturn, but recovered in 2010–11.

Agriculture, small-scale manufacturing and offshore financial services are being developed to diversify the economy. Apart from fishing and tourism, the main industries involve processing fish, coconuts and vanilla, producing coir rope, furniture and beverages, boat-building and printing.

The main trading partners are EU countries, Saudi Arabia and South Africa. The principal exports are canned tuna, frozen fish, cinnamon bark, copra and re-exports of petroleum products. The principal imports are machinery and equipment, foodstuffs, petroleum products and chemicals.

GNI—US$854m; US$9,760 per capita (2010)
Annual average growth of GDP—5% (2011 est)
Inflation rate—2.7% (2011 est)
Unemployment rate—2% (2006 est)
Total external debt—US$1,682m (2011 est)
Imports—US$989m (2010)
Exports—US$400m (2010)

BALANCE OF PAYMENTS

Trade—US$588m deficit (2010)
Current Account—US$316m deficit (2009)

Trade with UK	*2010*	*2011*
Imports from UK	£21,240,368	£22,703,725
Exports to UK	£45,835,878	£53,574,532

COMMUNICATIONS

Airports and waterways—The principal airport is at Mahé; the main port is Victoria, and ferries run regularly between Mahé, Praslin and La Digue
Roadways—There are 508km of roads
Telecommunications—22,000 fixed lines and 117,600 mobile subscriptions (2009); there were 32,000 internet users in 2008
Media—The state-run Seychelles Broadcasting Corporation operates various channels across the country;*Seychelles Nation* is the main government-owned daily newspaper
WPFI score—18,00 (65)

  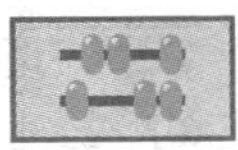      

Singapore

Xinjiapo Gongheguo/Republik Singapura/Cinkappur Kutiyaracu—Republic of Singapore
Area—697 sq. km
Capital—Singapore
Currency—Singapore dollar (S$) of 100 cents
Population—5,353,494 rising at 1.99% a year (2012 est); Chinese (76.8%), Malay (13.9%), Indian (7.9%) (2000)
Religion—Buddhist 42%, Muslim 15% (predominantly Sunni), Christian 15%, Taoist 8%, Hindu 4% (est)
Language—Mandarin, English, Malay, Tamil (all official), Hokkien, Cantonese, Teochew
Population density—7,252 per sq. km (2010)
Urban population—100% (2010 est)
Median age (years)—40.1 (2011 est)
National anthem—'Majulah Singapura' ['Onward, Singapore']
National day—9 August (Independence, 1965)
Life expectancy (years)—83.75 (2012 est)
Mortality rate—3.41 (2012 est)
Birth rate—7.72 (2012 est)
Infant mortality rate—2.65 (2012 est)
Death penalty—Retained
CPI score—9.2 (2011)
Literacy rate—94.7% (2009 est)
Health expenditure (per capita)—US$1,501 (2009)
Hospital beds (per 1,000 people)—3.1 (2004–9)

FINANCIAL OUTLOOK

Singapore's economy expanded by approximately 1.3% in 2012, with growth accelerating towards the end of the year as global economic conditions improved. Singapore's trade-dependent economy is a bellwether for the global economic cycle. The economy grew by 3.3% in the three months to the end of December 2012, on a quarter-on-quarter basis. A slump in manufacturing as a result of the global slowdown has hurt Singapore's growth in recent years. Officials said the rebound was helped by growth in the biomedical manufacturing and transport engineering sectors, which helped offset a decline in the output of the electronics sector. The government is forecasting growth for 2013 of 1–3%. However, it cautioned that if the economic situation in the US or eurozone deteriorated, Singapore's economic growth "could come in lower than expected." Meanwhile, inflation remains subdued, with the consumer price index in January 2013 rising by 3.6% on January 2012, after increasing by 4.3% in December.

CLIMATE AND TERRAIN

Singapore consists of the island of Singapore and 63 islets situated off the southern extremity of the Malay peninsula, from which it is separated by the Straits of Johor. The land rises from the shore to a low, undulating central plateau. Elevation extremes range from 166m (Bukit Timah) to 0m (Singapore Strait). The state is just north of the Equator and the climate is tropical, subject to monsoons in June to September and December to March. The average temperature is 27°C, and there is frequent rain and high humidity.

HISTORY AND POLITICS

Singapore, a trading site since the 13th century, was established as a British trading post by Sir Stamford Raffles in 1819 and was ceded to Britain in perpetuity in 1824. In 1826 it was incorporated with Penang and Malacca to form the Straits Settlements and they became a crown colony in 1867. Singapore became the commercial and financial hub of south-east Asia in the 19th century, and the principal British military base in the Far East in the 1920s. In 1942, during the Second World War, it fell to Japanese forces. Liberated in 1945, it became a separate colony in 1946, and internal self-government was introduced in 1959. It became part of the Federation of Malaysia in 1963, before withdrawing to become an independent sovereign state in 1965.

Although Singapore is a multiparty state, the People's Action Party (PAP) has dominated politics since 1959; opposition candidates were elected to parliament for the first time in 1981.

Independent candidate Tony Tan was elected president in August 2011, replacing PAP's Sellapan rama Nathan. In the 2011 general election, the PAP retained its large majority with 81 seats, but opposition parties won an unprecedented six seats. Lee Hsien Loong, the son of Lee Kuan Yew, continued in office as prime minister, a post he has held since 2004.

The 1959 constitution was amended in 1965 to end the affiliation with Malaysia and make Singapore a republic, and in 1991 to make the presidency directly elected. The president is directly elected for a six-year term, which is renewable. The president appoints the prime minister and, on his advice, the members of the cabinet. There is a unicameral parliament with 87 directly elected members and up to nine extra members from opposition parties (NCMPs) (currently three), depending on their share of the vote; all members serve a five-year term. Up to nine members can also be nominated by the government for a two-year term (NMPs) to bring the opposition numbers up to 18.

HEAD OF STATE

President, Tony Tan, *took office* 1 September 2011

SELECTED GOVERNMENT MEMBERS *as at July 2012*

Prime Minister, Lee Hsien Loong
Deputy Prime Minister, Rear-Adm. Teo Chee Hean *(Home Affairs)*
Foreign Affairs, K. Shanmugam
Finance, Tharman Shanmugaratnam

HIGH COMMISSION FOR THE REPUBLIC OF SINGAPORE

9 Wilton Crescent, London SW1X 8SP
T 020-7235 8315
E singhc_lon@sgmfa.gov.sg
W www.mfa.gov.sg/london
High Commissioner, HE Thambynathan Jasudasen, *apptd* 2011

BRITISH HIGH COMMISSION

100 Tanglin Road, Singapore 247919
T (+65) 6424 4200
E commercial.singapore@fco.gov.uk
W ukinsingapore.fco.gov.uk
High Commissioner, HE Antony Phillipson, *apptd* 2011

DEFENCE

All aged 16–49, 2010 est	*Males*	*Females*
Available for military service	1,255,902	–
Fit for military service	1,018,839	1,087,134

 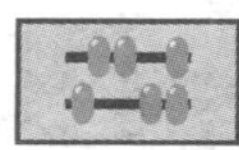      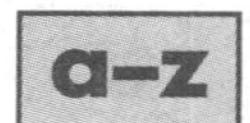

Military expenditure—US$8,302m (2011)
Conscription duration—24 months

ECONOMY AND TRADE

Historically based on trade in raw materials from surrounding countries and on entrepot trade in finished products, the economy industrialised rapidly after independence and diversified, becoming a regional financial and technology centre and a tourist destination. Economic growth has rarely flagged since 1965; although the global economic downturn pushed the economy into recession in 2008, it recovered strongly in 2010 and grew 4.9% in 2011 due to a renewed export market.

Agriculture is limited and contributes little to GDP. Industries include manufacturing (especially consumer electronics, information technology products, biomedical sciences, pharmaceuticals and chemicals), engineering, oil refining, rubber processing, food processing and ship repair; industry contributes 26.6% of GDP. The service sector (financial and business services, entrepot trade, tourism) accounts for 73.4% of GDP and employs 80.3% of the workforce.

The main trading partners are the USA, Malaysia, China, Indonesia, Japan and Hong Kong. Principal exports are machinery and equipment (especially electronic), consumer goods, pharmaceuticals and other chemicals and mineral fuels. The main imports are machinery and equipment, mineral fuels, chemicals, food and consumer goods.

GNI—US$201,050m; US$40,070 per capita (2010)
Annual average growth of GDP—5.3% (2011 est)
Inflation rate—4.6% (2011 est)
Unemployment—2% (2011 est)
Total external debt—US$23,590m (2011 est)

Imports—US$310,791m (2010)
Exports—US$351,867m (2010)

BALANCE OF PAYMENTS

Trade—US$41,076m surplus (2010)
Current Account—US$49,454m surplus (2010)

Trade with UK	2010	2011
Imports from UK	£3,313,867,465	£3,641,161,676
Exports to UK	£2,876,405,069	£3,825,152,793

COMMUNICATIONS

Airports and waterways—Singapore is one of the busiest seaports in the world, although there is a high risk of piracy in the South China Sea. It has a large merchant fleet of 1,599 ships of over 1,000 tonnes, with 344 registered in other countries, while 966 foreign-owned ships are registered in Singapore. There is one international airport, at Changi
Roadways and railways—There are 3,356km of roads and an extensive light rail system on the island
Telecommunications—1.98 million fixed lines and 7.3 million mobile subscriptions (2009); there were 3.23 million internet users in 2009
Internet code and IDD—sg; 65 (from UK), 1/2/8 44 (to UK)
Major broadcasters—Broadcasting is dominated by MediaCorp, owned by a state investment agency
Press—Singapore Press Holdings, which has close links to the ruling party, has a virtual monopoly on the newspaper industry, and publishes 17 newspapers
WPFI score—47,50 (136)

Slovakia

Slovenska Republika—Slovak Republic
Area—49,035 sq. km
Capital—Bratislava; population, 428,003 (2009 est)
Major city—Kosice
Currency—Euro (€) of 100 cents
Population—5,483,088 rising at 0.1% a year (2012 est); Slovak (85.8%), Hungarian (9.7%), Roma (1.7%), Ruthenian/Ukrainian (1%) (2001)
Religion—Christian (Roman Catholic 69%, Lutheran 7%, other 8%) (2001)
Language—Slovak (official), Hungarian, Romani, Ukrainian
Population density—113 per sq. km (2010)
Urban population—56.8% (2010 est)
Median age (years)—37.6 (2011 est)
National anthem—'Nad Tatrou sa blýska' ['Lightning Over the Tatras']
National day—1 September (Constitution Day)
Life expectancy (years)—76.03 (2012 est)
Mortality rate—9.64 (2012 est)
Birth rate—10.38 (2012 est)
Infant mortality rate—6.47 (2012 est)
Death penalty—Abolished for all crimes (since 1990)
CPI score—4.0 (2011)
Gross enrolment ratio (percentage of relevant age group)—primary 102%; secondary 89%; tertiary 54% (2009 est)
Health expenditure (per capita)—US$1,373 (2009)
Hospital beds (per 1,000 people)—6.6 (2004–9)

FINANCIAL OUTLOOK

The economy has remained relatively resilient to the troubles affecting the country's main trading partners in the eurozone. GDP grew by around 2% in 2012, according to government estimates, down from 3.2% in 2011. Officials said that economic growth was driven exclusively by foreign demand. Slovakia probably benefited from stronger demand for its products, such as new auto models, according to economists. Domestic demand stagnated as consumers concerned about high unemployment cut their spending, while public spending is also under pressure. The government cut the fiscal deficit to 4.6% in 2011, from 8%, and is aiming to cut the public-finance gap to less than the EU's limit of 3% of GDP by 2013. In March 2013, the central bank forecast that the economy would grow much more slowly than previously predicted—by 0.7%, as opposed to the earlier forecast of 1.3%. The bank blamed sluggish domestic and foreign demand.

CLIMATE AND TERRAIN

Slovakia is landlocked and mountainous, lying in the western Carpathian range which includes the Tatra and Beskid mountains to the north. The mountains fall to plains in the south-east and south-west; the latter is the plain of the river Danube and its tributary the Vah, which rises in the Tatras. Elevation extremes range from 2,655m (Gerlachovsky stit) to 94m (Bodrog river). The climate is temperate, with warm humid summers and cold dry winters.

Average temperatures in Kosice range from −7°C in January to 26°C in July.

HISTORY AND POLITICS

The 1993 constitution has been amended several times, most recently in 1999 to allow direct elections to the presidency. The president is directly elected for a five-year term, renewable once. The unicameral National Council has 150 members, who are directly elected for a four-year term by proportional representation. The prime minister, who is appointed by the president, nominates the cabinet.

The 2004 presidential election was won by Ivan Gasparovic; he was re-elected in 2009. Direction-Social Democracy (Smer-SD) remained the largest party after the 2010 legislative election, but four centre-right parties held a majority of seats and formed a coalition government. Smer-SD won the 2012 legislative election, gaining an overall majority and forming a government under Robert Fico.

HEAD OF STATE

President, Ivan Gasparovic, *elected* 17 April 2004, *sworn in* 15 June 2004, *re-elected* 2009

SELECTED GOVERNMENT MEMBERS *as at July 2012*

Prime Minister, Robert Fico
Defence, Martin Glvac
Foreign Affairs, Miroslav Lajcak
Interior, Robert Kalinak

EMBASSY OF THE SLOVAK REPUBLIC
25 Kensington Palace Gardens, London W8 4QY
T 020-7313 6470
E cons.london@mzv.sk
W www.slovakembassy.co.uk
Ambassador Extraordinary and Plenipotentiary, Miroslav Wlachovsky, *apptd* 2011

BRITISH EMBASSY
Panska 16, Bratislava 811 01
T (+421) (2) 5998 2000
E bebra@internet.sk
W ukinslovakia.fco.gov.uk
Ambassador Extraordinary and Plenipotentiary, HE Susannah Montgomery, *apptd* 2011

DEFENCE

All aged 16–49, 2010 est	*Males*	*Females*
Available for military service	1,405,310	1,369,897
Fit for military service	1,156,113	1,139,380

Military expenditure—US$968m (2011)
Conscription duration—6 months

ECONOMY AND TRADE

Slovakia has nearly completed the transition from a centrally planned to a free-market economy, following structural reforms and privatisation begun after 1998. As a result, foreign investment has risen, especially in the vehicle and electronics industries, and GDP grew steadily in 2000–8. The economy contracted in 2009 because of the global economic downturn, recovering in 2010.

Natural resources include brown coal and lignite, natural gas, oil, iron ore, copper and manganese. Major industries include production of metal and metal products, food and beverages, fuel and energy (electricity, gas, coke, oil and nuclear), chemicals and synthetic fibres, machinery, paper and printing, ceramics, transport vehicles, textiles and electrical and optical equipment. Industry accounts for 35.5% of GDP, services 60.7% and agriculture 3.8%.

The main trading partners are other EU countries (especially Germany and the Czech Republic) and Russia. Principal exports are machinery and electrical equipment, vehicles, base metals, chemicals, minerals and plastics. The main imports are machinery and transport equipment, mineral products, vehicles, base metals, chemicals and plastics.

GNI—US$86,077m; US$16,830 per capita (2010)
Annual average growth of GDP—3.3% (2011 est)
Inflation rate—4% (2011 est)
Unemployment—13.5% (2011 est)
Total external debt—US$75,900m (2011 est)
Imports—US$67,700m (2010)
Exports—US$64,505m (2010)

BALANCE OF PAYMENTS

Trade—US$3,195m deficit (2010)
Current Account—US$3,022m deficit (2010)

Trade with UK	*2010*	*2011*
Imports from UK	£451,164,856	£532,557,255
Exports to UK	£1,610,662,647	£1,507,527,491

COMMUNICATIONS

Airports and waterways—The principal airport is at Bratislava and the main Danube ports are Bratislava and Komarno
Roadways and railways—There are 43,761km of roads, including 384km of motorways and 3,622km of railways
Telecommunications—1.09 million fixed lines and 5.9 million mobile subscriptions (2009); there were 4.06 million internet users in 2009
Internet code and IDD—sk; 421 (from UK), 44 (to UK)
Major broadcasters—The public broadcasters, Slovak TV and Slovak Radio, operate national networks in competition with private companies
Press—The major daily newspapers, including *Pravda* and *Sme* are all privately owned
WPFI score—11,50 (35)

Slovenia

Republika Slovenija—Republic of Slovenia
Area—20,273 sq. km
Capital—Ljubljana; population, 260,092 (2009 est)
Major city—Maribor
Currency—Euro (€) of 100 cents
Population—1,996,617 falling at 0.18% a year (2012 est); Slovene (83.1%), Serb (2%), Croat (1.8%), Bosniak (1.1%) (2002)
Religion—Christian (Roman Catholic 58%, Orthodox 2%), Muslim 2% (2002)
Language—Slovene (official), Serbo-Croat; Hungarian and Italian are also official in designated municipalities
Population density—102 per sq. km (2010)
Urban population—48% (2010 est)
Median age (years)—42.4 (2011 est)

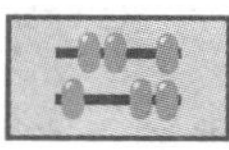

National anthem—'Zdravljica' ['A Toast']
National day—25 June (Statehood Day)
Death penalty—Abolished for all crimes (since 1989)
CPI score—5.9 (2011)

FINANCIAL OUTLOOK

The crisis affecting key neighboring eurozone markets has weighed heavily on the Slovenian economy. In February 2013, Standard & Poor's cut its rating by one notch from A to A−, citing the country's rising debt burden and uncertain growth prospects. The ratings agency said Slovenia had a higher-than-anticipated debt burden, as a resulting of supporting its state-owned banks' pressures. S&P said these factors are constraining Slovenia's ability to further implement policy responses to help boost its banking system, public finances, and growth prospects. Slovenia's fiscal deficits averaged 5.5% of GDP from 2009 to 2012, and the country's general government debt ratio increased to about 48% of GDP last year, compared with 16% in 2008. In August 2012, both Fitch and Moody's also cut their ratings on Slovenia. In February 2013, the European Commission forecast that the economy would shrink by 2% in 2013, following a 2.3% decline in 2012.

CLIMATE AND TERRAIN

The Alps cover 42% of the country, towards the north, and the south lies on the high Karst plateau. The only low-lying areas are the Pannonian plain in the east and north-east, and the short (47km) narrow coastal belt on the Adriatic Sea. Elevation extremes range from 2,864m (Triglav) to 0m (Adriatic Sea). The climate is continental in most of the country but Mediterranean on the coast. Average temperatures in Ljubljana range from −7°C in January to 27°C in July.

HISTORY AND POLITICS

Under the 1991 constitution, the president is directly elected for a five-year term. The unicameral National Assembly has 90 members directly elected for a four-year term. The National Council, which has 40 members indirectly elected for a five-year term, has an advisory role. The prime minister, who is nominated by the president and elected by the legislature, appoints the cabinet.

The 2007 presidential election was won by an independent candidate, Danilo Turk; the next presidential election is due in October 2012. The 2011 legislative election was won by the centre-right Positive Slovenia party, led by Ljubljana mayor Zoran Jankovic; the Social Democrats, which held the largest number of seats in the 2008 election, lost nearly two-thirds of its seats.

HEAD OF STATE

President, Danilo Turk, *elected* 11 November 2007; *sworn in* 22 December 2007

SELECTED GOVERNMENT MEMBERS *as at July 2012*

Prime Minister, Janez Jansa
Defence, Ales Hojs
Foreign Affairs, Karl Erjavec

EMBASSY OF THE REPUBLIC OF SLOVENIA

10 Little College Street, London SW1P 3SH
T 020-7222 5700
E vlo@gov.si
W london.embassy.si
Ambassador Extraordinary and Plenipotentiary, HE Iztok Jarc, *apptd* 2009

BRITISH EMBASSY

4th Floor, Trg Republike 3, 1000 Ljubljana
T (+386) (1) 200 3910
E info@british-embassy.si
W ukinslovenia.fco.gov.uk
Ambassador Extraordinary and Plenipotentiary, HE Andrew Page, *apptd* 2009

DEFENCE

All aged 16–49, 2010 est	Males	Females
Available for military service	477,592	464,301
Fit for military service	392,075	380,077

Military expenditure—US$668m (2011)

ECONOMY AND TRADE

Always the most prosperous republic of the former Yugoslavia, Slovenia's transition to a market economy was smoothed by good infrastructure and a well-educated workforce, and it has successfully re-orientated its exports towards Western markets. Much of the economy remains in state ownership and taxes are high, deterring foreign investment and inhibiting its international competitiveness. The economy contracted sharply in 2009 owing to the global downturn; it started to recover in 2010, although unemployment rose to nearly 11% in 2011.

Agriculture contributes 2.5% of GDP, industry 6.9% and the service sector 90.5%. The main agricultural products are potatoes, hops, wheat, sugar beet, maize, grapes and livestock. Industries include mining and mineral processing (iron ore, aluminium, lead, zinc), electronics (including for military purposes), vehicles, electric power equipment, wood products, textiles, chemicals and machine tools.

The main trading partners are other EU countries (particularly Germany and Italy) and Croatia. Principal exports are manufactured goods, machinery and transport equipment, chemicals and food. These items, along with fuels and lubricants, are also the main imports.

GNI—US$46,216m; US$23,860 per capita (2010)
Annual average growth of GDP—1.1% (2011 est)
Inflation rate—1.9% (2011 est)
Population below the poverty line—12.3% (2008 est)
Unemployment—10.8% (2011 est)
Total external debt—US$61,230m (2011 est)
Imports—US$26,050m (2010)
Exports—US$24,182m (2010)

BALANCE OF PAYMENTS

Trade—US$1,868m deficit (2010)
Current Account—US$394m deficit (2010)

Trade with UK	2010	2011
Imports from UK	£211,990,082	£235,973,309
Exports to UK	£354,381,123	£357,090,835

COMMUNICATIONS

Airports and waterways—The international airports are at Ljubljana, Maribor and Portoroz; Koper is the main port
Roadways and railways—There are 38,925km of roads and 1,228km of railways
Telecommunications—913,600 fixed lines and 2.12 million mobile subscriptions (2009); there were 1.29 million internet users in 2009
Internet code and IDD—si; 386 (from UK), 44 (to UK)

Media—The television market is mainly shared between the public service, RTV Slovenia, and private stations; daily newspapers include *Dnevnik* and *Slovenske Novice*
WPFI score—13,44 (46)

EDUCATION AND HEALTH
Education is free and compulsory between the ages of six and 15.
Literacy rate—99.7% (2009 est)
Gross enrolment ratio (percentage of relevant age group)—primary 98%; secondary 97%; tertiary 87% (2009 est)
Health expenditure (per capita)—US$2,175 (2009)
Hospital beds (per 1,000 people)—4.7 (2004–9)
Life expectancy (years)—77.48 (2012 est)
Mortality rate—11 (2012 est)
Birth rate—8.76 (2012 est)
Infant mortality rate—4.12 (2012 est)

South Africa

Republic of South Africa
Area—1,219,090 sq. km
Capital—The seat of government is Pretoria (Tshwane): population, 1,403,880 (2009 est); the seat of the legislature is Cape Town: population, 3,352,890 (2009 est); and the seat of the judiciary is Bloemfontein: population, 436,356 (2009 est)
Major cities—Durban, Johannesburg, Port Elizabeth
Currency—Rand (R) of 100 cents
Population—48,810,427 falling at 0.41% a year (2012 est)
Religion—Christian 80% (African Independent Churches 26%, other 54%); small minorities of Muslims, Hindus, Jews and Buddhists (est). Many combine Christian and indigenous beliefs
Language—Afrikaans, English, isiNdebele, isiXhosa, isiZulu, Sepedi, Sesotho, Setswana, siSwati, Tshivenda, Xitsonga (all official); the most widely spoken are isiZulu, isiXhosa and Afrikaans, but English is the lingua franca
Population density—41 per sq. km (2010)
Urban population—61.7% (2010 est)
Median age (years)—25 (2011 est)
National anthems—'Nkosi Sikelel' iAfrika' ['God Bless Africa'], incorporating 'Die Stem van Suid Afrika' ['The Call of South Africa']
National day—27 April (Freedom Day)
Death penalty—Abolished for all crimes (since 1997)
CPI score—4.1 (2011)

FINANCIAL OUTLOOK
In its assessment of the South African economy in September 2012, the IMF concluded that the two main challenges facing the country's economy were the difficulties of conducting policy in the face of a highly uncertain global environment, allied to the need to continue to make firm progress on reforms, to ensure that growth filters down to benefit all levels of the population, to maintain social cohesion. South Africa needed to make more of an effort to expand employment opportunities, secure better education and health outcomes, and build more efficient infrastructure. The IMF acknowledged that this will be made more difficult by the fact that the slowdown in Europe, South Africa's main trading partner, will lead to growth below 3% in 2012. Unemployment remains stubbornly high, and inflation is at the upper limit of the South African Reserve Bank's target band, driven by higher food and fuel prices. Growth should return to around 3% in 2013, with a continuing output gap holding inflation in check. Gross government debt is expected to peak at around 45% of GDP in 2014–15, and to start coming down thereafter.

CLIMATE AND TERRAIN
South Africa occupies the southernmost part of the African continent, with the exception of Lesotho and Swaziland. Its territory includes Prince Edward and Marion Islands, 1,920km to the south-east of Cape Town. The narrow coastal plain is separated by a mountainous escarpment, including the Drakensberg range, from a high inland plateau (the Great Karoo and the Highveld), an area of semi-arid scrubland in the west merging into grasslands or savannah in the centre and east. Elevation extremes range from 3,408m (Njesuthi) to 0m (Atlantic Ocean). The main rivers are the Orange and the Limpopo and their tributaries. The country lies at the convergence of the Atlantic and Indian oceans, and the climate is influenced by the cold Benguela current along the west coast and the warm Agulhas current along the east, as well as by the altitude of the interior. These influences cause cooler, drier conditions in the west and almost subtropical warmth and rainfall in the east. Average temperatures in Pretoria (Tshwane) range from 3°C in July to 28°C in December.

HISTORY AND POLITICS
Under the 1997 constitution, the executive president is elected by the National Assembly for a five-year term, renewable once. The president, who is responsible to the legislature, appoints the cabinet. The bicameral parliament consists of the National Assembly, the lower house, and the National Council of Provinces. The National Assembly has 400 members directly elected by proportional representation for a five-year term. The National Council of Provinces has 90 members, ten for each province, selected by the provincial legislatures for a five-year term.

South Africa is divided into nine provinces: Eastern Cape, Free State, Gauteng, KwaZulu-Natal, Limpopo, Mpumalanga, Northern Cape, North-West, and Western Cape. Each province has its own premier, legislature and constitution.

The ANC has won all the legislative elections since 1994, but is increasingly racked by internal tensions and tainted by corruption allegations. In April 2009 its majority in the National Assembly was reduced by 13 seats and it lost one of the provincial assemblies as two of the opposition parties began to challenge its dominance. In May 2009, Jacob Zuma of the ANC was elected president.

HEAD OF STATE
President, Jacob Zuma, *elected* 6 May 2009, *sworn in* 9 May 2009
Deputy President, Kgalema Motlanthe

SELECTED GOVERNMENT MEMBERS *as at July 2012*
Defence, Lindiwe Nonceba Sisulu
Finance, Pravin Gordhan
Home Affairs, Nkosazana Dlamini-Zuma

SOUTH AFRICAN HIGH COMMISSION
South Africa House, Trafalgar Square, London WC2N 5DP

  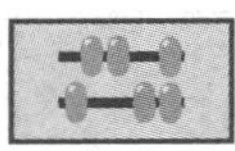      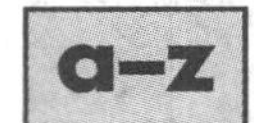

T 020-7451 7299
W www.southafricahouseuk.com
High Commissioner, HE Dr Zola Skweyiya, *apptd* 2009

BRITISH HIGH COMMISSION
255 Hill Street, Arcadia 0002, Pretoria (Tshwane)
T (+27) (12) 421 7500
E media.pretoria@fco.gov.uk
W ukinsouthafrica.fco.gov.uk
High Commissioner, HE Dr Dame Nicola Brewer, DCMG, *apptd* 2009

DEFENCE

The South African National Defence Force (SANDF) was created in 1994 from the merger of the South African Defence Forces (SADF), the Umkhonto we Sizwe (MK) armed wing of the ANC, the Azanian People's Liberation Army (APLA) of the Pan Africanist Congress of Azania, and the defence forces of the four former 'independent' homelands.

All aged 16–49, 2010 est	*Males*	*Females*
Available for military service	13,439,781	12,473,641
Fit for military service	7,617,063	6,476,264

Military expenditure—US$4,827m (2011)

ECONOMY AND TRADE

The economy varies between the sophisticated and well-developed, based on manufacturing, mining and financial services; the living eked out by the very poor, mostly through subsistence agriculture; and a large informal sector. Growth was strong until 2008, when the global economic downturn caused a contraction in the economy from which recovery is slowly being made. State-owned enterprises are being used to create jobs and raise incomes. However, unemployment remains high and poverty widespread (about half the population lives below the poverty line), and productivity and trade are constrained by outdated infrastructure in some sectors; power cuts have been frequent since 2007 because of the unreliability of the electricity supply.

Agriculture, forestry and fishing account for 2.5% of GDP and employ 9% of the workforce. Principal crops are maize, wheat, sugar cane, fruit and vegetables. Livestock farming, cotton and viticulture are also widespread.

The largest industry is mining; South Africa is the world's largest producer of gold, platinum and chromium, as well as producing diamonds, manganese, coal, copper, iron ore, tin, uranium and titanium. Other industries include car assembly, metalworking, food processing, ship repair and production of machinery, textiles, iron and steel, chemicals and fertiliser; manufacturing is concentrated most heavily around Johannesburg, Pretoria (Tshwane) and the major ports. Tourism is a significant industry, with over nine million visitors in 2007, and South Africa is a major transit point for its landlocked neighbours. Industry contributes 31.6% of GDP and services 65.9%.

Fossil-fuel based electricity generation is being supplemented by nuclear power; one nuclear power station is in operation and others are planned. Water resources are inadequate to meet demand, so water is imported from the highlands of Lesotho.

The main trading partners are China, Germany, the USA and Japan. Principal exports are gold, diamonds, platinum, other metals and minerals, and machinery and equipment. Principal imports are machinery and equipment, chemicals, petroleum products, scientific instruments and foodstuffs.

GNI—US$356,475m; US$6,090 per capita (2010)
Annual average growth of GDP—3.4% (2011 est)
Inflation rate—5% (2011 est)
Unemployment—23.9% (2011 est)
Total external debt—US$47,660m (2011 est)
Imports—US$80,131m (2010)
Exports—US$81,822m (2010)

BALANCE OF PAYMENTS
Trade—US$1,691m surplus (2010)
Current Account—US$10,114m deficit (2010)

Trade with UK	*2010*	*2011*
Imports from UK	£3,015,164,053	£3,335,748,545
Exports to UK	£6,025,605,168	£2,910,714,272

COMMUNICATIONS

Airports—There are 578 airports and airfields, with international airports at Johannesburg, Durban and Cape Town
Waterways—Durban is the largest seaport. Other major ports are Cape Town, Port Elizabeth, East London, Saldanha, Mossel Bay and Richards Bay
Roadways and railways—There are 362,099km of roads and 20,192km of railways, including the high-speed Gautrain which links Johannesburg's main international airport and will eventually connect with Pretoria
Telecommunications—4.22 million fixed lines and 50.37 million mobilesubscriptions (2009); there were 4.4 million internet users in 2009
Internet code and IDD—za; 27 (from UK), 44 (to UK)
Major broadcasters—The South African Broadcasting Corporation (SABC) is the country's major, state-owned television and radio broadcaster
Press—*The Star* is Johannesburg's oldest daily newspaper, while the *Sunday Times* is the longest running weekly title; *Beeld* is a popular Afrikaans daily title
WPFI score—12,00 (38)

EDUCATION AND HEALTH

Education is compulsory between the ages of seven and 15.
Literacy rate—88.7% (2007 est)
Gross enrolment ratio (percentage of relevant age group)—primary 102%; secondary 94% (2009 est)
Health expenditure (per capita)—US$485 (2009)
Hospital beds (per 1,000 people)—2.8 (2004–9)
Life expectancy (years)—49.41 (2012 est)
Mortality rate—17.23 (2012 est)
Birth rate—19.32 (2012 est)
Infant mortality rate—42.67 (2012 est)
HIV/AIDS adult prevalence—17.8% (2009 est)

  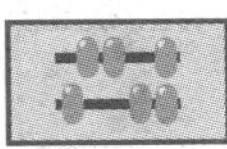      

Spain

Reino de España—Kingdom of Spain
Area—505,370 sq. km
Capital—Madrid; population, 5,762,050 (2009 est)
Major cities—Barcelona, Bilbao, Las Palmas (Gran Canaria), Málaga, Murcia, Palma (Majorca), Seville, Valencia, Zaragoza
Currency—Euro (€) of 100 cents
Population—47,042,984 rising at 0.65% a year (2012 est)
Religion—Christian (Roman Catholic 73%) (est)
Language—Castilian (Spanish) (official), Catalan, Galician, Basque (all are official in certain regions)
Population density—92 per sq. km (2010)
Urban population—77.4% (2010 est)
Median age (years)—40.5 (2011 est)
National anthem—'La Marcha Real' ['The Royal March']
National day—12 October
Death penalty—Abolished for all crimes (since 1995)
CPI score—6.2 (2011)

FINANCIAL OUTLOOK

The downward spiral in the Spanish economy continued unabated in 2012, even worsening in the final months of the year. The economy shrank by 1.4% in 2012, while GDP falling by 0.8% in Q4 from Q3 2012, the worst performance in Spain since the 2009 global recession. In February 2013, Prime Minister Mariano Rajoy indicated that the economy would continue to contract throughout the first half of 2013, but that the public-sector deficit had narrowed to 6.7% of GDP in 2012, from 8.9% in 2011. Spain is committed to reducing its deficit to below the 3% of GDP limit for EU member states by the end of 2014. Additionally in February 2013, the nationalized lender Bankia posted record losses of €19.2 billion in 2012, the biggest ever recorded by a Spanish company. The troubled banking sector, excessive household and company debts, harsh government austerity, and a lack of competitiveness inside the eurozone are weighing on the economy.

CLIMATE AND TERRAIN

Spain occupies over 80% of the Iberian peninsula, and includes two archipelagos and territories on or just off the Moroccan coast. The interior consists of an elevated plateau surrounded and traversed by mountain ranges: the Pyrenees on the border with France, the Cantabrian Mountains (north-west), the Sierra de Guadarrama, Sierra Morena, Montes de Toledo (centre) and the Sierra Nevada (south). Elevation extremes range from 3,718m (Pico de Teide, Tenerife, Canary Islands) to 0m (Mediterranean Sea). The principal rivers are the Duero, the Tajo (Tagus), the Guadiana, the Guadalquivir, the Ebro and the Miño. The climate is Mediterranean in the southern and eastern coastal areas, and temperate further inland and at altitude. Average temperatures in Madrid range from 0°C in January to 33°C in July.

HISTORY AND POLITICS

The 1978 constitution has been amended at various times to devolve powers to the 19 autonomous regions. The head of state is a hereditary constitutional monarch. There is a bicameral legislature, the *Cortes Generales*, comprising a 350-member Congress of Deputies directly elected for a four-year term, and a senate with 264 members, 208 directly elected and 56 appointed by the assemblies of the autonomous regions, for a four-year term.

There are 19 autonomous regions: Andalucía, Aragón, Asturias, Balearic Islands, the Basque Country, Canary Islands, Cantabria, Castilla-La Mancha, Castilla y León, Catalonia, Ceuta, Extremadura, Galicia, La Rioja, Madrid, Melilla, Murcia, Navarra and Valencia. Each has its own elected legislature and government. In 2006 a referendum endorsed the *Cortes'* approval of greater autonomy for Catalonia.

In the 2011 early legislative elections the Popular Party won an overall majority in both houses. Mariano Rajoy, leader of the PP, was appointed prime minister in December 2011, replacing José Luis Rodríguez Zapatero.

HEAD OF STATE

HM The King of Spain, King Juan Carlos I de Borbón, KG, GCVO, *born* 5 January 1938, *acceded to the throne* 22 November 1975
Heir, HRH The Prince of the Asturias (Prince Felipe Juan Pablo Alfonso y Todos los Santos), *born* 30 January 1968

SELECTED GOVERNMENT MEMBERS *as at July 2012*

Prime Minister, Mariano Rajoy
Vice President, Soraya Saenz de Santamaria
Foreign Affairs, Jose Manuel Garcia Margallo
Interior, Jorge Fernandez Diaz
Defence, Pedro Morenes Eulate

EMBASSY OF SPAIN

39 Chesham Place, London SW1X 8SB
T 020-7235 5555
E emb.londres@maec.es
W www.mae.es/embajadas/londres/es/home
Ambassador Extraordinary and Plenipotentiary, HE Carles Casajuana Palet, *apptd* 2008

BRITISH EMBASSY

Torre Espacio, Paseo de la Castellana 259D, 28046 Madrid
T (+34) (91) 714 6300
W ukinspain.fco.gov.uk
Ambassador Extraordinary and Plenipotentiary, HE Giles Paxman, LVO, *apptd* 2009

Insurgencies

The Basque separatist organisation ETA (*Euzkadi ta Azkatasuna—*Basque Nation and Liberty), formed in 1959, began a terrorist campaign of bombings, shootings and kidnappings in 1961 in an attempt to gain independence for the Basque country. ETA rejected regional autonomy for the Basque country in 1979 as insufficient and continued its campaign, but was greatly weakened in the early 1990s by increased cooperation between Spanish security forces and their European counterparts. ETA announced a permanent ceasefire in January 2011.

DEFENCE

All aged 16–49, 2010 est	*Males*	*Females*
Available for military service	11,759,557	11,204,688
Fit for military service	9,603,939	9,116,928

Military budget—US$10,200m (2010)

ECONOMY AND TRADE

Conservatism and isolation held back economic development until the mid-20th century, but the economy improved from the 1950s with industrialisation and the development of tourism. The mixed capitalist economy showed above-average growth, stimulated by liberalisation, privatisation and deregulation, from the mid-1990s until 2007. In 2008 it entered a severe recession because of the global economic downturn. This pushed unemployment to 21% in 2011 (from 8% in 2007). The downturn in construction and the property market left many banks struggling in 2010, and rising public-sector debt led to Spain's international credit rating being downgraded; the government introduced austerity measures in response but concern continues over the impact on the eurozone of Spain's sovereign debt.

The generally fertile country produces grains, vegetables, olives, sugar beets, citrus and other fruits, meat and dairy products. Viticulture is widespread. Spain also has one of Europe's largest fishing industries. The agricultural sector contributes 3.2% of GDP and employs 4.2% of the workforce. Abundant mineral resources include coal, iron ore, copper, zinc, lead, uranium and tungsten. Metal extraction and the manufacture of metal products, including steel, are major industries. A diverse industrial sector includes manufacturing (principally textiles, clothing, footwear, beverages, chemicals, cars, machine tools, clay products, pharmaceuticals and medical equipment), food processing, shipbuilding and tourism. Industry accounts for 25.8% of GDP and the service sector for 71%.

The main trading partners are other EU countries, especially France and Germany. Principal exports include machinery, vehicles, foodstuffs, pharmaceuticals, medicines and other consumer goods. The main imports are machinery and equipment, fuels, chemicals, semi-finished goods, foodstuffs, consumer goods, and measuring and medical control instruments.

GNI—US$1,388,744m; US$31,750 per capita (2010)
Annual average growth of GDP—0.8% (2011 est)
Inflation rate—3.1% (2011 est)
Population below the poverty line—19.8% (2005)
Unemployment—20.8% (2011 est)
Total external debt—US$2,570,000m (2011 est)
Imports—US$315,548m (2010)
Exports—US$246,274m (2010)

BALANCE OF PAYMENTS

Trade—US$69,274m deficit (2010)
Current Account—US$64,227m deficit (2010)

Trade with UK	2010	2011
Imports from UK	£9,630,415,364	£9,479,918,601
Exports to UK	£9,973,111,067	£10,828,754,226

COMMUNICATIONS

Airports and waterways—Of the 145 airports, the principal terminals are at Madrid, Barcelona, Alicante, Málaga, Valencia and Bilbao; the main ports are Algeciras, Alicante, Barcelona, Bilbao, Cádiz, Santander and Valencia, and Las Palmas in the Canary Islands. There are also 1,000km of navigable inland waterways
Roadways and railways—There are 681,298km of roads and 15,293km of railways
Telecommunications—19.9 million fixed lines and 51.5 million mobile subscriptions (2009); there 28.12 million internet users in 2009
Internet code and IDD—es; 34 (from UK), 44 (to UK)
Major broadcasters—Public radio and television services are run by Radio Television Espanola (RTVE), which is funded by advertising and state subsidies
Press—Popular newspaper titles include *El Mundo*, *ABC*, *El País* and *El Periodico de Catalunya*.
WPFI score—12,25 (39)

EDUCATION AND HEALTH

Education is free from age six to 18, and compulsory to the age of 16.
Literacy rate—97.7% (2009 est)
Gross enrolment ratio (percentage of relevant age group)—primary 107%; secondary 119%; tertiary 73% (2009 est)
Health expenditure (per capita)—US$3,075 (2009)
Hospital beds (per 1,000 people)—3.2 (2004–9)
Life expectancy (years)—81.27 (2012 est)
Mortality rate—8.88 (2012 est)
Birth rate—10.4 (2012 est)
Infant mortality rate—3.37 (2012 est)

ISLANDS AND ENCLAVES

THE BALEARIC ISLES form an archipelago off the east coast of Spain. There are four large islands (Majorca/Mallorca, Minorca, Ibiza and Formentera) and seven smaller ones (Aire, Aucanada, Botafoch, Cabrera, Dragonera, Pinto and El Rey). Area 4,992 sq. km; population 1,106,049 (2010 est). The archipelago forms a province of Spain. The capital is Palma, on Majorca.

THE CANARY ISLANDS are an archipelago in the Atlantic off the African coast, consisting of seven islands and six islets. Area 7,447 sq. km; population 2,118,519 (2010 est). The Canary Islands form two provinces of Spain: Las Palmas, comprising Gran Canaria, Lanzarote, Fuerteventura and six islets, with the seat of administration at Las Palmas, in Gran Canaria; and Santa Cruz de Tenerife, comprising Tenerife, La Palma, La Gomera and El Hierro, with the seat of administration at Santa Cruz, in Tenerife.

ISLA DE FAISANES an uninhabited Franco-Spanish condominium, at the mouth of the Bidassoa in La Higuera bay.

CEUTA is a fortified post on the Moroccan coast, opposite Gibraltar. Area 19 sq. km; population 80,579 (2010 est). Ceuta is an autonomous city of Spain.

MELILLA is a town on a rocky promontory of the Moroccan coast, connected with the mainland by a narrow isthmus. Area 13 sq. km; population 76,034 (2010 est). Melilla is an autonomous city of Spain.

OVERSEAS TERRITORIES

The following territories, which are Spanish settlements on the Moroccan seaboard, come under direct Spanish administration. They are uninhabited other than by military personnel.

PENON DE ALHUCEMAS is a bay including six islands.

PENON DE LA GOMERA (or Peñón de Velez) is a fortified rocky islet.

THE CHAFFARINAS (or Zaffarines) is a group of three islands near the Algerian frontier.

  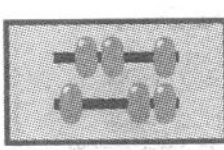      

Sri Lanka

Shri Lamka Prajatantrika Samajaya di Janarajaya/Ilankai Jananayaka Choshalichak Kutiyarachu—Democratic Socialist Republic of Sri Lanka

Area—65,610 sq. km

Capital—Colombo; population, 681,484 (2009 est), Sri Jayewardenepura Kotte; population, 123,090 (2009 est) is the administrative capital

Major cities—Dehiwala-Mount Lavinia, Jaffna, Kalmunai, Kandy, Moratuwa, Negombo, Trincomalee, Vavuniya

Currency—Sri Lankan rupee of 100 cents

Population—21,481,334 rising at 0.91% a year (2011 est); Sinhalese (73.8%), Sri Lankan Moor (7.2%), Indian Tamil (4.6%), Sri Lankan Tamil (3.9%) (2001 est; excludes predominantly Tamil areas then held by rebels)

Religion—Buddhist 70% (predominantly Theravada), Hindu 15%, Christian 8% (predominantly Roman Catholic), Muslim 7% (predominantly Sunni) (est)

Language—Sinhala (official), Tamil, English

Population density—333 per sq. km (2010)

Urban population—15.1% (2010 est)

Median age (years)—30.8 (2011 est)

National anthem—'Sri Lanka Matha' ['Mother Sri Lanka']

National day—4 February (Independence Day)

Life expectancy (years)—75.94 (2012 est)

Mortality rate—5.96 (2012 est)

Birth rate—17.04 (2012 est)

Infant mortality rate—9.47 (2012 est)

Death penalty—Retained (not used since 1976)

CPI score—3.3 (2011)

Literacy rate—90.6% (2008 est)

Gross enrolment ratio (percentage of relevant age group)—primary 95% (2009 est)

Health expenditure (per capita)—US$84 (2009)

Hospital beds (per 1,000 people)—3.1 (2004–9)

FINANCIAL OUTLOOK

Growth in the first quarter of 2012 remained robust, with real GDP expanding by 8%, supported by a rebound in agriculture and strong activity in the construction sector. However, growth then became more moderate in response to policy tightening by the government, aimed at reducing Sri Lanka's external current account deficit. Real GDP growth for 2012 is now expected to be around 6.75%, with headline inflation in May 2012 standing at 7%, and was expected to peak at around 10% by the end of 2012. Core inflation is more like 5%, according to the IMF. The government is expected to succeed in narrowing its current account deficit to around 5.5% of GDP in 2012. The Central Bank of Sri Lanka increased interest rates sharply during 2012, in an attempt to mop up liquidity, and damp down rising inflation, and an overheating of credit expansion to the private sector. The CBSL is now also virtually allowing the Sri Lankan rupee to find its own level in the foreign exchange markets.

CLIMATE AND TERRAIN

Sri Lanka (formerly Ceylon) is an island in the Indian Ocean, separated from India by the narrow Palk Strait. The land is low-lying in the north and along the coasts, rising to a central massif with hills and mountains in the south and centre. Forests, jungle and scrub cover the greater part of the island. In areas over 600m above sea level, grasslands *(patanas* or *talawas)* are found. Elevation extremes range from 2,524m (Pidurutalagala) to 0m (Indian Ocean). The climate is tropical with little seasonal variation in conditions and humidity, which often reaches around 90%. The island experiences the south-west monsoon from May to September and the north-east monsoon from October to January.

HISTORY AND POLITICS

The 1978 constitution was amended in 1983 to ban parties advocating separatism, in 1987 to create provincial councils, and in 2010 to remove the limit on presidential terms. The executive president is directly elected for a six-year term, which may be renewed. The unicameral parliament has 225 members directly elected by proportional representation for a six-year term. The president appoints the prime minister and cabinet.

Elected councils were set up in the nine provinces in 1987 in an attempt to defuse ethnic tensions. The Northern and Eastern provinces were merged into one from 1988 to 2006.

The 2005 presidential election was won by the Sri Lanka Freedom Party (SLFP) leader Mahinda Rajapaksa, and he was re-elected in an early election in January 2010. The legislative election in April 2010 was won by the SLFP-led United People's Freedom Alliance, with an increased majority.

HEAD OF STATE

President; Defence; Finance, Mahinda Rajapaksa, *elected* 17 November 2005, *re-elected* 2010

SELECTED GOVERNMENT MEMBERS *as at July 2012*

Prime Minister, Dissanayake Jayaratne
Home Affairs, John Seneviratne
Foreign Affairs, G. L. Peiris

HIGH COMMISSION OF THE DEMOCRATIC SOCIALIST REPUBLIC OF SRI LANKA

13 Hyde Park Gardens, London W2 2LU
T 020-7262 1841
E mail@slhc-london.co.uk
W www.srilankahighcommission.co.uk
High Commissioner, HE Chrisantha Nonis, *apptd* 2011

BRITISH HIGH COMMISSION

389 Bauddhaloka Mawatha, Colombo 7
T (+94) (11) 539 0639
E bhctrade@slt.lk
W ukinsrilanka.fco.gov.uk
High Commissioner, HE John Rankin, *apptd* 2011

DEFENCE

All aged 16–49, 2010 est	*Males*	*Females*
Available for military service	5,342,147	5,466,409
Fit for military service	4,177,432	4,574,833

Military expenditure—US$1,403m (2011)

ECONOMY AND TRADE

Despite the 26-year civil war and the 2004 Indian Ocean tsunami, which destroyed tourist resorts and the fishing industry, the economy saw sustained growth throughout the 2000s. The 2008–9 global downturn affected productivity only slightly, but high

  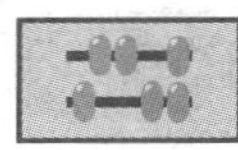      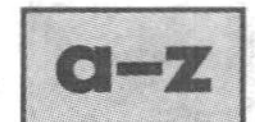

government debt and budget deficits obliged the government to seek an IMF loan, which in turn resulted in two years of strong growth. The once predominantly agricultural economy has become increasingly industrialised and diversified, with service industries such as tourism now making the greatest contribution to GDP. Remittances from expatriate workers are also economically significant.

Agriculture still accounts for 13% of GDP and over 32.7% of employment. The main crops are rice, sugar cane, grains, pulses, oilseed, spices, vegetables, fruit, tea, rubber, coconuts, livestock products and fish. Manufacturing is based on processing the main cash crops of rubber, tea, coconuts, tobacco and other commodities, and production of textiles, clothing, beverages and cement; other industries include oil refining and mining gemstones. Service industries such as telecommunications, banking and insurance, information technology services and tourism are also important. The service sector accounts for 57.4% of GDP and industry for 29.6%.

The main trading partners are India, the USA, China, the UK and Singapore. Principal exports are textiles and clothing, tea, rubber manufactures, spices, diamonds, emeralds, rubies, coconut products and fish. The main imports are oil, textile fabrics, machinery, transport equipment, building materials, mineral products and foodstuffs.

GNI—US$48,916m; US$2,240 per capita (2010)
Annual average growth of GDP—7% (2011 est)
Inflation rate—7.7% (2011 est)
Unemployment—4.2% (2011 est)
Population below poverty line—8.9% (2009 est)
Total external debt—US$21,740m (2011 est)
Imports—US$13,512m (2010)
Exports—US$8,307m (2010)

BALANCE OF PAYMENTS
Trade—US$5,205m deficit (2010)
Current Account—US$1,418m deficit (2010)

Trade with UK	*2010*	*2011*
Imports from UK	£129,526,294	£155,079,838
Exports to UK	£681,028,624	£804,399,620

COMMUNICATIONS
Airports and waterways—The principal airport is Bandaranaike International, to the north of the capital; Colombo is the main port although the first phase of a deep-water container port opened in 2010 at Hambantota
Roadways and railways—There are 91,907km of roads and 1,449km of railway
Telecommunications—3.58 million fixed lines and 17.36 million subscriptions (2010); there were 1.78 million internet users in 2009
Internet code and IDD—lk; 94 (from UK), 44 (to UK)
Media—The state-owned Sri Lanka Rupavahini Corporation operates two major channels; there are eight daily newspapers, published in Sinhala, Tamil and English
WPFI score—62,50 (158)

Sweden

Konungariket Sverige—Kingdom of Sweden
Area—450,295 sq. km
Capital—Stockholm; population, 1,278,820 (2009 est)
Major cities—Gothenburg, Malmo, Uppsala
Currency—Swedish krona of 100 ore
Population—9,103,788 rising at 0.17% a year (2012 est)
Religion—Christian (Lutheran 71%, other Protestant 4%), Muslim 5% (est)
Language—Swedish (official), Finnish, Sami dialects, Meankieli, Romani, Yiddish (all official national minority languages)
Population density—23 per sq. km (2010)
Urban population—84.7% (2010 est)
Median age (years)—42 (2011 est)
National anthem—'Du Gamla, Du Fria' ['Thou Ancient, Thou Freeborn']
National day—6 June (Flag Day)
Death penalty—Abolished for all crimes (since 1972)
CPI score—9.3 (2011)

FINANCIAL OUTLOOK
Sweden's export-driven economy grew by 0.8% in 2012, down from 3.7% in the previous year, mainly as a result of the impact of the slowdown in the eurozone. Sweden is among those EU member states that do not belong to the euro. However, exports account for about half of output and are primarily sold in Europe. Encouragingly, activity picked up in the final quarter of 2012, with the economy expanding by a faster-than-expected 1.4% compared to Q4 2011. Household consumption grew by 1.5% in 2012, while exports gained 0.7%. The government expects the economy to grow by 1.1% in 2013, while the central bank projects an expansion of 0.9%. The Riksbank cut rates four times in 2012, to 1%, and said in February 2013, it would maintain its main lending rate at this level for about a year to speed up growth subdued by weak demand for the country's sales abroad.

CLIMATE AND TERRAIN
The terrain is mostly flat or rolling lowlands in the south and along the east coast, with mountains in the west. Elevation extremes range from 2,111m (Kebnekaise) to − 2.4m (reclaimed bay of Lake Hammarsjon). There are many lakes, including Vanern, Vattern, Malaren and Hjalmaren in the south, and over 20,000 islands off the coast near Stockholm. The climate is temperate in the south and subarctic in the north; average temperatures in Stockholm range from − 5°C in January to 22°C in July.

HISTORY AND POLITICS
Sweden is a hereditary constitutional monarchy. The 1975 constitution was amended in 1979 to vest the succession in the monarch's eldest child irrespective of sex. The unicameral legislature, the *Riksdag*, has 349 members directly elected by proportional representation for a four-year term. The prime minister appoints the council of ministers.

After the 2010 general election, the Social Democrats remained the largest single party in the legislature but with fewer seats than the four-party Alliance for Sweden coalition government (comprising the Moderate Party, Centre Party, Liberal People's Party and Christian Democrats) that had been in government since the 2006 election. The Alliance for Sweden coalition continued in office as a minority government.

  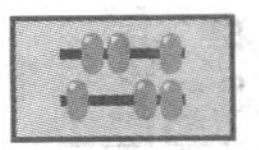      

Sweden is divided into 21 counties *(lan)* and 290 municipalities *(kommun)*.

HEAD OF STATE

HM The King of Sweden, King Carl XVI Gustaf, KG, *born* 30 April 1946, *succeeded* 15 September 1973

Heir, HRH Crown Princess Victoria Ingrid Alice Desiree, Duchess of Vastergotland, *born* 14 July 1977

SELECTED GOVERNMENT MEMBERS *as at July 2012*

Prime Minister, Fredrik Reinfeldt
Deputy Prime Minister, Jan Bjorklund
Defence, Karin Enstrom
Finance, Anders Borg

EMBASSY OF SWEDEN

11 Montagu Place, London W1H 2AL
T 020-7917 6400
E ambassaden.london@foreign.ministry.se
W www.swedenabroad.com/london
Ambassador Extraordinary and Plenipotentiary, HE Nicola Clase, *apptd* 2010

BRITISH EMBASSY

PO Box 27819, Skarpogatan 6–8, 115 93 Stockholm
T (+46) (8) 671 3000
E info@britishembassy.se
W ukinsweden.fco.gov.uk
Ambassador Extraordinary and Plenipotentiary, HE Paul Johnston, *apptd* 2011

DEFENCE

Sweden has a policy of non-alignment in peace and neutrality in war, and has declined to become a member of NATO.

All aged 16–49, 2010 est	Males	Females
Available for military service	2,065,691	1,996,764
Fit for military service	1,709,055	1,650,432

Military expenditure—US$5,960m (2011)
Conscription—abolished from July 2010

ECONOMY AND TRADE

Sweden developed from an agricultural to an industrial economy in the early 20th century. The prosperity that had funded the generous welfare state after 1946 ended in the early 1990s, when Sweden experienced a deep recession. It recovered to experience strong growth before briefly entering recession again in 2008–9 as a result of the global downturn; 2010 and 2011 saw a strong rebound, however, and the government is implementing measures in 2012 to weather the effects of the international economic crisis.

The main, export-orientated industries are engineering and high-tech manufacturing, mining and forestry. Mineral resources include iron ore, lead, zinc, sulphur, granite, marble, precious and heavy metals (the latter not exploited) and extensive deposits of low-grade uranium ore. The engineering sector provides 50% of output and exports, particularly specialised machinery and systems such as electrical and electronic equipment and armaments, and motor vehicles and aircraft; other industries produce pharmaceuticals, plastics and chemicals.

Agriculture contributes 1.1% of GDP, industry 28.2% and services 70.7%.

The main trading partners are other EU states, Norway and China. Principal exports include machinery, vehicles, paper products, pulp and wood, iron and steel products, and chemicals. The main imports are machinery, oil and petroleum products, chemicals, vehicles, iron and steel, foodstuffs and clothing.

GNI—US$467,253m; US$50,110 per capita (2010)
Annual average growth of GDP—4.4% (2011 est)
Inflation rate—2.5% (2011 est)
Unemployment—7.6% (2011 est)
Total external debt—US$1,016,000m (2011)
Imports—US$148,429m (2010)
Exports—US$158,085m (2010)

BALANCE OF PAYMENTS

Trade—US$9,656m surplus (2010)
Current Account—US$29,007m surplus (2010)

Trade with UK	2010	2011
Imports from UK	£5,372,739,533	£6,157,828,199
Exports to UK	£6,532,167,636	£7,520,948,846

COMMUNICATIONS

Airports and waterways—The principal airports are at Stockholm, Gothenburg, Lulea, Malmo and Umea; the main ports are Gothenburg, Helsingborg, Malmo and Stockholm
Roadways and railways—There are 572,900km of roads and 11,633km of railways
Telecommunications—5.01 million fixed lines and 10.65 million mobile subscriptions (2009); there were 8.39 million internet users in 2009
Internet code and IDD—se; 46 (from UK), 44 (to UK)
Major broadcasters—Public television is run by Sveriges Television (SVT)
Press—There are four Stockholm-based daily newspapers, one based in Gothenburg and one in Malmo
WPFI score—0,00 (1)

EDUCATION AND HEALTH

The state education system provides nine years of free and compulsory schooling from the age of seven to 16 in the comprehensive elementary schools.

Gross enrolment ratio (percentage of relevant age group)—primary 100%; secondary 100%; tertiary 71% (2009 est)
Health expenditure (per capita)—US$4,252 (2009)
Life expectancy (years)—81.18 (2012 est)
Mortality rate—10.21 (2012 est)
Birth rate—10.24 (2012 est)
Infant mortality rate—2.74 (2012 est)

  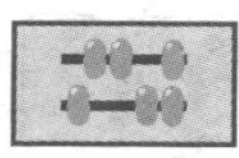      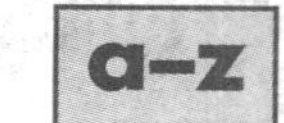

Switzerland

Schweizerische Eidgenossenschaft/Confédération suisse/Confederazione Svizzera/Confederaziun svizra—Swiss Confederation
Area—41,277 sq. km
Capital—Bern; population, 345,720 (2009 est)
Major cities—Basel, Geneva, Lausanne, Zurich
Currency—Swiss franc of 100 rappen (or centimes)
Population—7,655,628 rising at 0.2% a year (2012 est); German (65%), French (18%), Italian (10%), Romansch (1%) (est)
Religion—Christian (Roman Catholic 42%, Protestant 35%, Orthodox 2%), Muslim 4% (majority Sunni) (2000)
Language—German, French, Italian, Romansch (all official), Serbo-Croatian, Albanian, Portuguese, Spanish, English
Population density—196 per sq. km (2010)
Urban population—73.6% (2010 est)
Median age (years)—41.7 (2011 est)
National anthem—'Schweizerpsalm'/'Cantique suisse'/'Salmo svizzero'/'Psalm svizzer' ['Swiss Psalm']
National day—1 August (Confederation Day)
Death penalty—Abolished for all crimes (since 1992)
CPI score—8.8 (2011)

FINANCIAL OUTLOOK

The strong Swiss franc and the crisis in key neighboring eurozone economies weighed on Switzerland in 2012, with the economy expanding by just 1% compared to 1.9% growth in 2011. In December 2012, the Swiss government predicted 1.3% growth in 2013. Investors unnerved by the eurozone and uncertain US economic prospects have fled to the perceived safety of the Swiss franc. The central bank has sought to prevent the Swiss franc from gaining too much in value against the euro. It has repeatedly vowed to maintain a euro exchange-rate ceiling of CHF1.20, imposed in September 2011 to avoid hurting Swiss exports. The currency has risen by around 20% since the global financial crisis struck in 2008. The central bank has held its benchmark interest rate at zero since August 2011. Swiss exports rose by just 1.7% in 2012.

CLIMATE AND TERRAIN

Switzerland is the most mountainous country in Europe. The central plateau of hills, plains and over 1,500 lakes is enclosed by mountains. The Jura mountains lie in the north-west and the Alps, which cover two-thirds of the country, occupy the south and east. Elevation extremes range from 4,634m (Dufourspitze, Alps) to 195m (Lake Maggiore). Lakes Neuchâtel, Lucerne and Zurich lie wholly within the country, but Lake Maggiore is shared with Italy, Lake Geneva with France and Lake Constance with Germany and Austria. The Rhine, Rhône and Inn rivers all rise in the Alps. The climate is temperate, with conditions that vary with altitude. Average temperatures in Zurich range from −4°C in January to 23°C in July.

HISTORY AND POLITICS

The area was conquered by the Romans in 58 BC and then overrun by Germanic tribes in the fourth century AD. It was a province of the medieval Holy Roman Empire from 1033. The Swiss confederation began in 1291 as a defensive alliance of three cantons to protect their autonomy, and expanded during the following centuries, becoming independent of the Habsburgs in the 14th century. Its independence was recognised by the Treaty of Westphalia in 1648. French revolutionary forces captured Switzerland in 1789 and named it the Helvetic Republic. Independence was restored in 1814, and the congress of Vienna (1815) joined Geneva, Neuchatel and Valais to the confederation and recognised the country's perpetual neutrality in international affairs. A new constitution was adopted in 1848 which replaced the loose confederation of cantons with a federal state and enhanced the powers of the central government.

Many policy decisions are submitted to national referendums. Although the federal government has pursued a policy of gradual integration with the EU and applied for membership in 1992, referendums have rejected membership of the European Economic Area (1992), approved bilateral trade agreements with the EU (2000), and rejected EU membership (2001).

Proportional representation, introduced in 1919, resulted in coalition governments throughout the 20th and into the 21st century. Apart from a 12-month period in 2007–8, since 1959 the federal government has been a coalition of four parties: the Swiss People's Party (SVP), the Social Democratic Party, the Christian Democratic People's Party and the Radical Democratic Party. The SVP, in coalition with the Democratic Centre Union, remained the largest party in the National Council in the 2011 legislative election, while the Conservative Democratic Party candidate Eveline Widmer-Schlumpf was elected president.

Under the 1998 constitution, the head of state is a president elected annually (along with the vice-president) for a one-year term by the federal legislature from the members of the Federal Council; consecutive terms may not be served. The bicameral legislature, the Federal Assembly, has two chambers: the National Council has 200 members, directly elected for a four-year term; the Council of States has 46 members (two from each canton and one from each half-canton) directly elected within each canton for a four-year term.

Executive power is in the hands of a Federal Council of seven members, elected for a four-year term by the Federal Assembly after every legislative election. The Federal Council is chaired by the president. Not more than one person from the same canton may be elected a member of the Council; however, there is a tradition that Italian- and French-speaking areas should between them be represented on the council by at least two members.

Any citizen able to obtain 100,000 voters' signatures in support of holding a referendum on a given issue can initiate a national referendum.

SELECTED GOVERNMENT MEMBERS *as at July 2012*

President of the Swiss Confederation, Eveline Widmer-Schlumpf
Vice-President, Ueli Maurer
Public Economy, Johann Schneider-Ammann
Interior, Alain Berset

EMBASSY OF SWITZERLAND

16–18 Montagu Place, London W1H 2BQ
T 020-7616 6000
E lon.vertretung@eda.admin.ch
W www.eda.admin.ch/london
Ambassador Extraordinary and Plenipotentiary, HE Anton Thalmann, *apptd* 2010

BRITISH EMBASSY

Thunstrasse 50, 3005 Bern
T (+41) (31) 359 7700
E info@britishembassy.ch
W ukinswitzerland.fco.gov.uk

  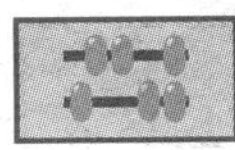      

Ambassador Extraordinary and Plenipotentiary, HE Sarah Gillett, CMG, MVO, *apptd* 2009

Confederal Structure

There are 23 cantons, three of which are subdivided, making 20 cantons and six half-cantons, or 26 in all. Each canton and half-canton has its own government and a substantial degree of autonomy. The main language in 19 of the cantons is German; in six others it is French and one Italian.

DEFENCE

All aged 16–49, 2010 est	*Males*	*Females*
Available for military service	1,828,043	1,786,552
Fit for military service	1,493,509	1,459,450

Military expenditure—US$4,618m (2011)*
Conscription duration—18 weeks, then 3-week refresher courses
* Figure des not include paramilitary spending

ECONOMY AND TRADE

Switzerland has a prosperous and stable market economy with low unemployment and a highly skilled labour force. Its prosperity is based on banking, financial services and export-orientated industrial manufacturing. The economy went into recession in 2009 owing to slower export demand and the impact on the banking sector during the 2008 global financial crisis; the largest bank required government support. Although not an EU member, Switzerland has brought many practices in line with the EU's to maintain its competitiveness, and it is currently adopting OECD standards on tax administration and transparency.

Agriculture is practised in the mountain valleys and the central plateau, where grains, fruits and vegetables are grown. Dairy farming and stock-raising are also important. The industrial sector is noted for precision, electrical and mechanical engineering, pharmaceuticals, chemicals, telecommunications, food processing and packaging, and graphics. Banking, insurance and tourism are the major service industries. Agriculture contributes 1.3% of GDP, industry 27.5% and services 71.3%.

The main trading partners are EU countries (especially Germany) and the USA. Principal exports are machinery, chemicals, metals, watches and agricultural products. The main imports are machinery, chemicals, vehicles, metals, agricultural products and textiles.

GNI—US$568,639m; US$71,530 per capita (2010)
Annual average growth of GDP—2.1% (2011 est)
Inflation rate—0.4% (2011 est)
Unemployment—3.1% (2011 est)
Population below poverty line—6.9% (2010 est)
Total external debt—US$1,346,000m (2011 est)
Imports—US$166,910m (2010)
Exports—US$185,774m (2010)

BALANCE OF PAYMENTS
Trade—US$18,865m surplus (2010)
Current Account—US$83,539m surplus (2010)

Trade with UK	*2010*	*2011*
Imports from UK	£11,110,540,359	£5,374,724,104
Exports to UK	£7,498,280,114	£7,688,286,706

COMMUNICATIONS

Airports and waterways—The principal airports are at Zurich, Basel, Bern and Geneva; the Rhine carries commercial shipping on the 65km stretch from Basel-Rheinfelden and Schaffhausen-Bodensee, and there are 12 navigable lakes
Roadways and railways—There are 71,454km of roads, including 1,790km of motorways and 4,876km of railways
Telecommunications—4.38 million fixed lines and 9.53 million mobile subscriptions (2009); there were 6.15 million internet users in 2009
Internet code and IDD—ch; 41 (from UK), 44 (to UK)
Major broadcasters—The public-service Swiss Broadcasting Corporation (SRG/SSR), which is funded mainly through licence fees, dominates broadcasting
Press—Newspapers tend to be regional, reflecting linguistic divisions: there are two German-language dailies based in Zurich, two French-language dailies in Geneva and an Italian-language daily in Lugano
WPFI score—0,00 (1)

EDUCATION AND HEALTH

Education is controlled by cantonal and communal authorities and is free and compulsory from ages seven to 16.
Gross enrolment ratio (percentage of relevant age group)—primary 102%; secondary 95%; tertiary 51% (2009 est)
Health expenditure (per capita)—US$7,141 (2009)
Hospital beds (per 1,000 people)—5.3 (2004–9)
Life expectancy (years)—81.17 (2012 est)
Mortality rate—8.8 (2012 est)
Birth rate—9.51 (2012 est)
Infant mortality rate—4.03 (2012 est)

Syria

Al-Jumhuriyah al-Arabiyah asSuriyah—Syrian Arab Republic
Area—185,180 sq. km
Capital—Damascus; population, 2,527,260 (2009 est)
Major cities—Aleppo (Halab), Hama (Hamah), Homs (Hims), Latakia (Al Ladhiqiyah)
Currency—Syrian pound (S£) of 100 piastres
Population—22,530,746 falling at 0.8% a year (2012 est)
Religion—Muslim (Sunni 74%, Druze 3%; other 13%, including Alawite sect), Christian 10% (est) (of which Greek Orthodox is the largest denomination)
Language—Arabic (official), Kurdish, Armenian, Aramaic, Circassian, French
Population density—111 per sq. km (2010)
Urban population—54.9% (2010 est)
Median age (years)—21.9 (2011 est)
National anthem—'Homat el Diyar' ['Guardians of the Homeland']
National day—17 April (Independence Day)
Death penalty—Retained
CPI score—2.6 (2011)

        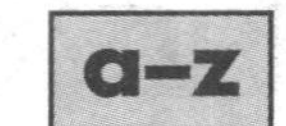

FINANCIAL OUTLOOK

The civil war that erupted in Syria in 2011 has taken a devastating toll on the economy. The economy shrank by a fifth in 2012, and all of Syria's foreign reserves could be spent by the end of 2013, according to the Washington-based Institute for International Finance (IIF). In December 2012, the IIF estimated that since a revolt that descended into civil war started in March 2011, inflation had risen to 40% and the Syrian pound's official exchange rate against the US dollar had fallen by 51%. Sanctions have compounded the economic downturn. In January 2012, the Syrian Center for Policy Research estimated that overall the Syrian economy, to the end of 2012, amounted to around US$48.4 billion, equal to 81.7% of GDP in 2010. About 1.5 million Syrians have lost their jobs because of the war, the report said, adding that the unemployment rate had reached a record high of 34.9% by the end of 2012.

CLIMATE AND TERRAIN

There is a narrow coastal plain and ranges of mountains in the west, and the fertile basin of the river Euphrates in the north-east. The centre and south of the interior consist of semi-arid and desert plateaux. Elevation extremes range from 2,814m (Mt Hermon) to −200m (unnamed location near Lake Tiberias). There is a desert climate in much of the country, moderated by altitude in the mountains, and a Mediterranean climate on the coast. Average temperatures in Damascus range from 2°C in January to 37°C in August.

HISTORY AND POLITICS

The 1973 constitution declares that the Arab Socialist Renaissance (Ba'ath) Party is the leading party in the state and society. The executive president is elected for a seven-year term by the legislature and confirmed in office by a national referendum. The president appoints the council of ministers. The unicameral People's Council *(Majlis al-Sha'ab)* has 250 members directly elected for a four-year term. The only candidates permitted to stand in elections are those from the Ba'ath Party, parties allied with it or independents.

The Arab Socialist Renaissance (Ba'ath) Party has been the ruling party since 1963. Hafez al-Assad seized power in a coup in 1970 and was elected president in 1971. He remained president until his death in 2000, when he was succeeded by his son, Bashar al-Assad, who was re-elected unopposed in 2007. Pro-democracy protests have spread to all the major cities since early 2011 and peaked during the country's 2012 legislative elections, in which the Ba'ath Party retained its overall majority. The 2012 election was the first election contested by opposition parties.

HEAD OF STATE

President, Lt-Gen. Bashar al-Assad, *elected* 27 June 2000, *confirmed by referendum* 10 July 2000, *re-elected* 2007
Vice-Presidents, Farouk al-Shara; Najah al-Attar

SELECTED GOVERNMENT MEMBERS *as at July 2012*

Prime Minister, Riyad Fareed Hijab
Defence, Dawoud Rajha
Finance, Mohammad al-Jleilati
Foreign Affairs, Walid al-Muallem

EMBASSY OF THE SYRIAN ARAB REPUBLIC

8 Belgrave Square, London SW1X 8PH
T 020-7245 9012
W www.syremb.com
Ambassador Extraordinary and Plenipotentiary, HE Sami Khiyami, *apptd* 2004

BRITISH EMBASSY

PO Box 37, Kotob Building, Mohammad Kurd Ali Street, Malki, Damascus
T (+963) (11) 339 1513
E british.embassy.damascus@fco.gov.uk
W ukinsyria.fco.gov.uk
Ambassador Extraordinary and Plenipotentiary, HE Simon Collis *apptd* 2007

DEFENCE

Aged 16–49, 2010 est	*Males*	*Females*
Available for military service	5,889,837	5,660,751
Fit for military service	5,055,510	4,884,151

Military expenditure—US$2,490m (2011)
Conscription duration—30 months

ECONOMY AND TRADE

The economy is state-controlled and predominantly state-owned, although recent political unrest and international sanctions have slowed economic growth.

Oil and agriculture account for nearly half of GDP, but other activities, such as financial services, telecommunications, tourism and non-oil industry and trade, are becoming increasingly important. Gas is produced for domestic use, and phosphate is mined and processed; other non-oil industry includes the manufacture of textiles, processed food, beverages, tobacco and cement, and car assembly. Agriculture contributes 16.9% of GDP, industry 27.4% and services 55.7%.

The main export markets are Iraq, Lebanon, Germany and Italy; imports come chiefly from Saudi Arabia, China, Turkey and Egypt. Principal exports are crude oil, minerals, petroleum products, fruit and vegetables, cotton fibre, textiles, clothing, meat, livestock and wheat. The main imports are machinery and transport equipment, electric power machinery, food and livestock, metals and metal products, chemicals, plastics, yarn and paper.

GNI—US$57,265m; US$2,750 per capita (2010)
Annual average growth of GDP— −2% (2011 est)
Inflation rate—7% (2011 est)
Population below poverty line—11.9% (2006 est)
Unemployment—8.1% (2011 est)
Total external debt—US$8,006m (2011 est)
Imports—US$17,000m (2010)
Exports—US$14,000m (2010)

BALANCE OF PAYMENTS

Trade—US$3,000m deficit (2010)
Current Account—US$1,946m deficit (2009)

Trade with UK	*2010*	*2011*
Imports from UK	£132,954,421	£85,310,110
Exports to UK	£17,009,001	£20,915,700

COMMUNICATIONS

Airports and waterways—The principal airports are at Aleppo and Damascus; the main port is Latakia
Roadways and railways—The country has 68,157km of roads and 2,052km of railways
Telecommunications—4.07 million fixed lines and 11.69 million mobile subscriptions (2009); there were 4.47 million internet users in 2009
Internet code and IDD—sy; 963 (from UK), 44 (to UK)

Major broadcasters—The state-run Syrian TV operates domestic and satellite networks
Press—The government-owned *Al-Baath* and *Al-Thawra* newspapers are published on a daily basis
WPFI score—91,50 (173)

EDUCATION AND HEALTH
Education is under state control. Elementary education is free at state schools and is compulsory from the age of seven.
Literacy rate—84.2% (2009 est)
Gross enrolment ratio (percentage of relevant age group)—primary 118%; secondary 72% (2010 est)
Health expenditure (per capita)—US$72 (2009)
Hospital beds (per 1,000 people)—1.5 (2004–9)
Life expectancy (years)—74.92 (2012 est)
Mortality rate—3.67 (2012 est)
Birth rate—23.52 (2012 est)
Infant mortality rate—15.12 (2012 est)

Taiwan

T'ai-wan—Taiwan (Republic of China)
Area—35,980 sq. km
Capital—Taipei; population, 2,646,474 (2001 est)
Major cities—Kaohsiung, Taichung, Tainan
Currency—New Taiwan dollar (NT$) of 100 cents
Population—23,113,901 rising at 0.17% a year (2012 est); Han Chinese 98% (Holo 70%, Hakka 14%), indigenous (2%) (est)
Religion—Buddhist 35%, Taoist 33%, Christian 2% (est). Many combine Buddhism and Taoism, and may also practise Chinese folk beliefs. About 3% belong to the Falun Gong spiritual movement
Language—Mandarin (official), Taiwanese (Min-Nan), Hakka dialects
Population density—618 per sq. km (2001)
Median age—37.6 (2011 est)
National anthem—'San Min Chu I' ['Three Principles of the People']
National day—10 October (Republic Day)
Life expectancy (years)—78.48 (2012 est)
Mortality rate—7.12 (2012 est)
Birth rate—8.81 (2012 est)
Infant mortality rate—5.1 (2012 est)
Death penalty—Retained (last used 2011)
CPI score—6.1 (2011)

FINANCIAL OUTLOOK
Taiwan's economy struggled in 2012, growing just 1.25%, its slowest pace for three years, with shrinking exports being largely to blame. You have to go back to 2009, just after the 2008 global financial meltdown, to find an equivalent performance, with the economy growing at just 1.81% that year. Nevertheless, this was a modest improvement on the dire 1.13% that had been forecast by the end of November, with the figure being lifted by a sudden pick-up in foreign trade and domestic spending. Growth for the fourth quarter of 2012 was demonstrated this pick-up, coming in at 3.42%. The economy is projected to grow at 3.53% for 2013, as overseas demand for the island's highly desired electronics and telecoms products picks up. According to Taiwan Asia Strategy Consulting, the economy is likely to show positive growth in 2013 thanks to a continued pick-up in Taiwan's key export markets. Tourist arrivals in 2012 were up 46% on a year earlier, including some 2.8 million tourists from China (around 30% of all tourists visiting the island in 2012).

CLIMATE AND TERRAIN
The island of Taiwan (formerly Formosa) lies 145km east of the Chinese mainland. Mountains run the length of the island, covering over half the terrain, with lowlands in the west. Elevation extremes range from 3,952m (Yu Shan) to 0m (South China Sea). Taiwan shares the tropical monsoon climate of southern China, with large seasonal variations in temperature, dry winters and wet summers. The typhoon season lasts from May to November, with particularly high humidity between July and September. Average temperatures in Taipei range from 12°C in January and February and 33°C in July.

Territories include the Penghu (Pescadores) islands (80.47 sq. km), some 56km west of Taiwan, as well as Kinmen (Quemoy) (109 sq. km) and Matsu (7 sq. km), which are only a few kilometres from mainland China.

HISTORY AND POLITICS
Settled by Chinese from about the 12th century, the island was annexed by China in the 17th century, and ceded to Japan in 1895 at the end of the Sino-Japanese War. It was returned to China after Japan's defeat in the Second World War. The Kuomintang (KMT) government, led by Gen. Chiang Kai-shek, withdrew to Taiwan in 1949 after being defeated by the communists in mainland China. The territory remained under Chiang Kai-shek's presidency until his death in 1975. He was succeeded as president by his son, Gen. Chiang Ching-kuo, who ruled until his death in 1988. Martial law was lifted in 1987 after 38 years. In 1991 the Taiwanese government declared an end to the state of war with China, officially recognising the People's Republic of China for the first time, and ended emergency measures that had frozen political life in Taiwan since 1949.

Democratisation of the authoritarian one-party state began in the 1980s and led to the first multiparty elections in 1992. The 'Senior Parliamentarians' who had retained their seats since being elected on the mainland in 1948 were forcibly retired in 1991–2. From this point, power shifted away from the mainlanders to the native Taiwanese, and 50 years of KMT rule ended when the Democratic Progressive Party (DPP), which favours self-determination, won the presidency in 2000 and the 2001 legislative election.

The DPP retained the presidency and continued in government after the 2004 elections. However, in the 2008 elections the KMT returned to power, and the KMT candidate, Ma Ying-jeou, was elected president. The KMT retained its majority in the 2012 legislative election and Ma Ying-jeou gained re-election, picking up over 51% of the vote.

Most nations acknowledge the position of the Chinese government that Taiwan is a province of the People's Republic of China, and as a result Taiwan has formal diplomatic relations with only 23 countries and no seat at the UN. China has sanctioned the use of force to prevent Taiwan declaring itself independent.

Contacts between Taiwan and China began in the 1980s and have led to a gradual relaxation of restrictions on direct economic, trade and transport links, and on travel and tourism. Since the KMT returned to power in 2008, Taiwan has sought greater economic cooperation and integration with China.

The 1947 constitution (which originally applied to the whole of China) has been amended a number of times since 1991. In 2004 an amendment provided for future proposed constitutional changes to be put to a referendum instead of the National Assembly (formerly the upper house of the legislature), which was disbanded under 2005 provisions that also reduced the number of legislative seats with effect from the 2008 election.

The president is directly elected for a four-year term, renewable once. The unicameral Legislative Yuan has 113 members: 73 directly elected, 34 elected proportionately by party and six elected by indigenous peoples in two constituencies; all serve a four-year term. The president appoints the premier and, on the premier's advice, the cabinet.

HEAD OF STATE
President, Ma Ying-jeou, *elected* 22 March 2008, *re-elected* 14 January 2012
Vice-President, Wu Den-yih

SELECTED GOVERNMENT MEMBERS *as at July 2012*
Premier, Sean Chen-Chun
Defence, Kao Hua-chu
Economy, Shih Yen-shiang
Foreign Affairs, Timothy Yang Chin-tien

DEFENCE

All aged 16–49, 2010 est	Males	Females
Available for military service	6,183,567	6,006,676
Fit for military service	5,074,173	4,951,088

Military expenditure—US$8,888m (2011)
Conscription duration—12 months

ECONOMY AND TRADE

Since the 1950s Taiwan has transformed itself from a mainly agricultural country into a highly developed industrial economy. This transition was driven by exports. There has been a gradual shift away from state domination of the economy, with a reduction in government influence on investment and foreign trade, and privatisation in the financial and industrial sectors. Taiwan's export markets suffered severely in the global economic downturn and the economy contracted sharply in 2008–9, but it recovered strongly in 2010.

Only a quarter of the land area is suitable for agriculture but the soil is very fertile, producing rice, corn, vegetables, fruit, tea, flowers, meat and dairy products. The industrial base includes electronics, communications and information technology products, oil refining, armaments, chemicals, textiles, iron and steel, machinery, cement, food processing, vehicles, consumer goods, pharmaceuticals and fishing. Agriculture contributes 1.3% of GDP, industry 32% and services 66.9%.

The main trading partners are China (28.1% of exports), Japan (20.7% of imports), the USA and Hong Kong. Principal exports are electronic and computer equipment, flat panels, machinery, metals, textiles, plastics, chemicals and precision instruments. The main imports are electronic and electrical equipment, machinery, crude oil and precision instruments.

Average annual growth of GDP—5.2% (2011 est)
Inflation rate—1.6% (2011 est)
Population below poverty line—1.16% (2010 est)
Unemployment—4.3% (2011 est)
Total external debt—US$116,000m (2011 est)
Imports—US$251,500m (2010)
Exports—US$274,600m (2010)

BALANCE OF PAYMENTS
Trade—US$23,100m surplus (2010)
Current Account—US$39,900m surplus (2010)

Trade with UK	2010	2011
Imports from UK	£1,049,063,249	£1,298,519,598
Exports to UK	£3,027,826,270	£3,336,213,203

COMMUNICATIONS

Airports and waterways—There are international airports at Taoyuan (near Taipei), Kaohsiung and Taichung; the main ports are Keelung, Kaohsiung and Taichung
Roadways and railways—There are 41,475km of roadways and 1,580km of railways
Telecommunications—16.43 million fixed lines and 27.84 million mobile subscriptions (2009); there were 16.14 million internet users in 2009
Internet code and IDD—tw; 886 (from UK), 2 44 (to UK)
Media—The government runs a non-profit public broadcaster, Public Television Service, alongside various commercial companies; there are six daily newspapers, including the *United Daily News* and the *China Times*

Thailand

Ratcha Anachak Thai—Kingdom of Thailand
Area—513,120 sq. km
Capital—Bangkok (Krung Thep); population, 6,901,690 (2009 est)
Major cities—Chon Buri, Nonthaburi, Samut Prakan, Udon Thani
Currency—Baht of 100 satang
Population—67,091,089 rising at 0.54% a year (2012 est); Thai, including Lao (75%), Chinese (14%) (est)
Religion—Buddhist 94% (predominantly Theravada), Muslim 5% (predominantly Sunni) (est); many Buddhists also incorporate Brahmin-Hindu and animist practices
Language—Thai (official), English
Population density—135 per sq. km (2010)
Urban population—34% (2010 est)
Median age (years)—34.2 (2011 est)
National anthem—'Phleng Chat' ['National Song']
National day—5 December (Birthday of the King)
Death penalty—Retained (last used 2009)
CPI score—3.4 (2011)

FINANCIAL OUTLOOK

In 2012, the Thai economy continued to deal with the aftermath of the devastating floods that had struck the country during 2011. By the final quarter of 2012, the recovery appeared complete, with GDP surging by 18.9% in the October–December period, compared to Q4 2011. Most analysts had forecast a figure close to 15%. Compared with Q3 2012, the economy grew by 3.6%. The floods hit some of Thailand's biggest industrial area, resulting in many factories shutting and damaging exports, one of the biggest drivers of Thai economic growth. The government implemented various steps to boost domestic demand in an attempt to offset the decline in exports. Minimum wages, for example, rose by 40% in April 2012, and the government announced US$65 billion of infrastructure spending. The central bank also loosened monetary policy. In February 2013, the Bank of Thailand raised its GDP growth forecast for 2013 to 4.9%, up from the 4.6% projected in October 2012.

CLIMATE AND TERRAIN

Thailand is divided geographically into four regions: the north is mountainous and forested; to the north-east is the semi-arid Korat plateau; the centre is a fertile plain lying in the Chao Phraya basin; and the south is the narrow, mountainous isthmus of Kra. Extremes of elevation range from 2,576m (Doi Inthanon) to 0m (Gulf of Thailand). The principal rivers are the Chao Phraya and its tributaries in the central plains and the Mekong on the north and eastern borders. The climate is tropical, with a monsoon season from June to October and high humidity.

HISTORY AND POLITICS

Thailand is a constitutional monarchy with a hereditary monarch as head of state. The 2007 constitution provides for a bicameral National Assembly comprising a 500-member House of Representatives, elected for a four-year term, and a senate with 150 members: 76 elected members (one from each province) and 74 members appointed by a selection committee; senators serve a six-year term. The prime minister is appointed by the king and approved by and responsible to the House of Representatives.

In the legislative election in July 2011, the For Thai party (PTP), a successor party to the People Power Party (PPP), won an overall majority and its leader, Yingluck Shinawatra (sister of former prime minister Thaksin Shinawatra), formed a coalition government with four smaller parties.

HEAD OF STATE

HM The King of Thailand, King Bhumibol Adulyadej (Rama IX), *born* 5 December 1927, *succeeded* 9 June 1946
Heir, HRH Crown Prince Maha Vajiralongkorn, *born* 28 July 1952

SELECTED GOVERNMENT MEMBERS *as at July 2012*

Prime Minister, Yingluck Shinawatra
Deputy Prime Ministers, Yongyuth Wichaidit; Chalerm Yubamrung; Yuthasak Sasiprapha; Kittirat na Ranong *(Finance)*
Defence, Sukampol Suwannatat
Foreign Affairs, Surapong Towichukchaikul

ROYAL THAI EMBASSY

29–30 Queen's Gate, London SW7 5JB
T 020-7589 2944
E thaiduto@btinternet.com
W www.thaiembassyuk.org.uk
Ambassador Extraordinary and Plenipotentiary, HE Kitti Wasinondh, *apptd* 2007

BRITISH EMBASSY

14 Wireless Road, Bangkok 10330
T (+662) 305 8333
E info.bangkok@fco.gov.uk
W ukinthailand.fco.gov.uk
Ambassador Extraordinary and Plenipotentiary, HE Asif Ahmad, *apptd* 2010

Insurgency

The Muslim minority is concentrated in the isthmus of Kra. A separatist campaign in the region began in the 1970s but died down in the 1980s. Violence resumed in 2004 and has since claimed over 3,000 lives.

Foreign Relations

Sovereignty over border territory around the Hindu temple complex at Preah Vihear has been disputed with Cambodia for over a century. Although the temple complex was awarded to Cambodia in 1962, the status of adjacent territory remains unsettled. Tensions increased in 2008, when Cambodia had the temple listed as a UNESCO World Heritage Site, and there has been frequent sporadic fighting in the area between the countries' troops.

DEFENCE

All aged 16–49, 2010 est	*Males*	*Females*
Available for military service	17,689,921	17,754,795
Fit for military service	13,308,372	14,182,567

Military expenditure—US$5,114m (2011)
Conscription duration—24 months

ECONOMY AND TRADE

Thailand was transformed from an agricultural to an export-orientated industrial economy in the last quarter of the 20th century, sustaining steady growth after its quick recovery from the 1997 economic crisis. The 2008 global economic downturn caused the export-dependent economy to contract sharply, and flooding in October and November 2011 reduced growth to only 0.1% in 2011; the government anticipates growth in 2012, however, as the industrial sector recovers and the private sector improves.

The agricultural sector generates 13.3% of GDP and employs 40.7% of the workforce. The main crops are rice, cassava, rubber, maize, sugar cane, coconuts and soya beans. In recent years fishing and livestock production have grown in importance. There are reserves of natural gas, lignite, tin, tungsten and lead.

The main industry is tourism, which has been the chief foreign exchange earner since the 1980s. Other industries include textiles and clothing, agricultural processing, beverages, tobacco, cement, mining and light manufacturing (jewellery, electrical appliances, computers and parts), furniture, plastics and cars and vehicle parts. Industry contributes 34% of GDP and services 52.7%.

The main trading partners are Japan, China, the USA and Malaysia. Principal exports are textiles and footwear, fish products, rice, rubber, jewellery, cars, computers and electrical appliances. The main imports are capital goods, intermediate goods and raw materials, consumer goods and fuels.

GNI—US$304,811m; US$4,150 per capita (2010)
Annual average growth of GDP—1.5% (2011 est)
Inflation rate—4.1% (2011 est)
Population below poverty line—8.1% (2009 est)
Unemployment—0.7% (2011 est)
Total external debt—US$84,160m (2011 est)
Imports—US$184,591m (2010)
Exports—US$195,375m (2010)

BALANCE OF PAYMENTS

Trade—US$10,784m surplus (2010)
Current Account—US$14,784m surplus (2010)

Trade with UK	*2010*	*2011*
Imports from UK	£1,508,795,014	£1,368,229,536
Exports to UK	£2,393,659,088	£2,487,613,977

  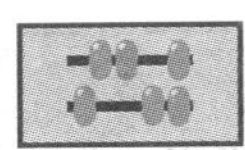      

COMMUNICATIONS

Airports and waterways—Bangkok is the main international airport and the main seaports are located in Bangkok and Sattahip; there are also 3,701km of inland waterways

Roadways and railways—There are 180,053km of roadways and 4,071km of railways

Telecommunications—7 million fixed lines and 69.68 million mobile subscriptions (2009); there were 17.48 million internet users in 2009

Internet and IDD—th; 66 (from UK), 1 44 (to UK)

Media—Newspapers are largely privately run, with popular titles including *Bangkok Post* and *Thairath*; chief broadcasters include the government-owned Thai TV3 and the military-owned TV5

WPFI score—56,83 (153)

EDUCATION AND HEALTH

Primary and lower secondary education is compulsory and free, and upper secondary education is free in government schools.

Literacy rate—93.5% (2005 est)

Gross enrolment ratio (percentage of relevant age group)—primary 91% (2009 est); secondary 77%; tertiary 46% (2010 est)

Health expenditure (per capita)—US$168 (2009)

Life expectancy (years)—73.83 (2012 est)

Mortality rate—7.38 (2012 est)

Birth rate—12.81 (2012 est)

Infant mortality rate—15.9 (2012 est)

HIV/AIDS adult prevalence—1.3% (2009 est)

Tunisia

Al-Jumhuriyah at-Tunisiyah—Tunisian Republic

Area—163,610 sq. km

Capital—Tunis; population, 758,729 (2009 est)

Major cities—Ariana (Aryanah), Sfax

Currency—Tunisian dinar of 1,000 millimes

Population—10,732,900 rising at 0.96% a year (2012 est)

Religion—Muslim 99% (predominantly Sunni; Shia less than 1%) (est); small minorities of Christians and Jews. Sunni Islam is the official religion

Language—Arabic (official), French

Population density—68 per sq. km (2010)

Urban population—67.3% (2010 est)

Median age (years)—30 (2011 est)

National anthem—'Humat al-Hima' ['Defenders of the Homeland']

National day—20 March (Independence Day)

Death penalty—Retained (not used since 1991)

CPI score—3.8 (2011)

FINANCIAL OUTLOOK

In a report on Tunisia's economy in September 2012, the IMF praised the way the country had moved steadily forward with its political transition, including through peaceful national elections, the formation of a coalition government, and the authorization of more than 100 new political parties. However, the Tunisian revolution has brought about economic and financial uncertainty, and downside risks loomed large amid a legacy of social and economic challenges and increased vulnerabilities, the IMF said. Nevertheless, stepped-up government spending and a rebound in tourism have helped improve prospects for Tunisia's economy for 2013 and 2014. This is in sharp contrast to 2011, when domestic unrest and conflict in neighboring Libya took a heavy toll on the economy. Tunisia's economic activity contracted by 1.8% in 2011, as tourism and activity in other sectors affected by strikes declined sharply. The overall fiscal deficit widened to 3.7% of GDP in 2011 from 1.1% in 2010, as the government increased spending on an expanded wage bill, almost doubled food and energy subsidies to offset higher international prices, and implemented new social measures, including revamped youth unemployment programs. Unemployment stood at 18.9%, with youth unemployment at 40%. GDP growth in 2012 is expected to reach 2.7%.

CLIMATE AND TERRAIN

A central plain rises to mountains in the north, and in the semi-arid south merges into the Sahara desert. There are salt lakes in the west. Elevation extremes range from 1,544m (Jebel ech Chambi) to −17m (Shatt al Gharsah). The northern and coastal regions have a Mediterranean climate, while there is a desert climate in the south. Average temperatures in Tunis range from 7°C in January to 32°C in August.

HISTORY AND POLITICS

The area was ruled successively by the Phoenicians, Carthaginians, Romans, Byzantines and Arabs before becoming a largely autonomous part of the Ottoman Empire in the 16th century. In the 19th century French influence grew and it was formally declared a French protectorate in 1883. It was briefly occupied by Germany during the Second World War (1942–3), and became independent as a monarchy under the bey in 1956. In 1957 the bey was deposed and the country became a republic under one-party rule with Habib Bourguiba as president.

There was a growing demand throughout the 1970s for the legalisation of other political parties and the government's resistance to these led to serious unrest. Multiparty legislative elections were held in 1981, but the ruling party, the Constitutional Democratic Rally (RCD), retained its grip on power until 2011. Although proclaimed president for life in 1975, President Bourguiba was deposed in 1987 on the grounds of senility by the prime minister Zine el-Abidine Ben Ali. Ben Ali was subsequently elected president in unopposed elections in 1989 and 1994, and in multiparty elections in 1999, 2004 and 2009.

Ben Ali's authoritarian regime maintained tight constraints on the political opposition, with electoral laws and media access weighted in favour of the RCD. However, nationwide protests over unemployment and political restrictions from December 2010 forced Ben Ali to leave office and flee the country in January 2011, and the RCD was dissolved by the courts in March 2011. Moncef Marzouki was elected interim president by the new Constituent Assembly in December 2011; his nomination followed legislative elections in which the former opposition party En-Nahda won the most seats but not an overall majority.

Under the 2002 constitution, the executive president is directly elected for a five-year term. The parliament *(Barlaman)* comprises the Chamber of Deputies *(Majlis al-Nuwaab)*, with 214 members directly elected for a five-year term, and the Chamber of Councillors *(Majlis al-Mustasharin)*, which has 126 members (85 elected by municipal councils, professional organisations and trade unions, and 41 appointed by the president), who serve a six-year term, with half elected every three years. In October 2011 a

Constituent Assembly *(Majlis al-Watani at-Tasisi)* was implemented with 217 seats.

HEAD OF STATE
Interim President, Moncef Marzouki, *took office* 12 December 2011

SELECTED GOVERNMENT MEMBERS *as at July 2012*
Prime Minister, Hamadi Jebali
Defence, Abdelkarim Zbidi
Finance, Houcine Dimassi
Foreign Affairs, Rafik Ben Abdessalem
EMBASSY OF TUNISIA
29 Prince's Gate, London SW7 1QG
T 020-7584 8117
E london@tunisianembassy.co.uk
Ambassador Extraordinary and Plenipotentiary, HE Hatem Atallah, *apptd* 2010

BRITISH EMBASSY
Rue du Lac Windemere, Les Berges du Lac, 1053 Tunis
T (+216) (71) 108 700
E british.embassy@planet.tn
W ukintunisia.fco.gov.uk
Ambassador Extraordinary and Plenipotentiary, HE Chris O'Connor, *apptd* 2008

DEFENCE

All aged 16–49, 2010 est	*Males*	*Females*
Available for military service	2,846,572	2,952,180
Fit for military service	2,397,716	2,484,097

Military expenditure—US$583m (2011)
Conscription duration—12 months (selective)

ECONOMY AND TRADE

The economy is diverse and an increasing proportion is in private ownership, with further liberalisation planned. Growth was steady from the late 1990s until 2008, although the economy contracted in 2009 as export demand dropped. The downfall of the Ben Ali regime sent the country's economy into freefall in 2011 and the new government faces challenges in stabilising spending and increasing output.

Agriculture and fisheries account for 10.6% of GDP; the main products are olives, grain, tomatoes, citrus fruits, sugar beets, dates, almonds, meat and dairy products. The main industries are oil production, mining (principally phosphates and iron ore), tourism, processing agricultural products and manufacture of textiles, footwear and beverages. Tourism is the chief foreign exchange earner.

The main trading partners are EU countries, especially France and Italy. Principal exports are clothing, semi-finished goods and textiles, agricultural products, mechanical goods, phosphates and chemicals, hydrocarbons and electrical equipment. The main imports are textiles, machinery and equipment, hydrocarbons, chemicals and foodstuffs.

GNI—US$42,020m; US$4,160 per capita (2010)
Annual average growth of GDP—0% (2011 est)
Inflation rate—3.7% (2011 est)
Population below poverty line—3.8% (2005 est)
Unemployment—16% (2011 est)
Total external debt—US$25,270m (2011 est)
Imports—US$22,218m (2010)
Exports—US$16,427m (2010)

BALANCE OF PAYMENTS
Trade—US$5,791m deficit (2010)
Current Account—US$2,124m deficit (2010)

Trade with UK	*2010*	*2011*
Imports from UK	£202,102,779	£145,692,700
Exports to UK	£624,665,751	£228,395,069

COMMUNICATIONS

Airports and waterways—The principal airports are at Tunis, Monastir and Djerba and the main ports include Bizerte, Sfax and Rades
Roadways and railways—There are 19,232km of roadways and 2,165km of railways
Telecommunications—1.29 million fixed lines and 11.11 million mobile subscriptions (2009); there were 3.5 million internet users in 2009
Internet code and IDD—tn; 216 (from UK), 44 (to UK)
Major broadcasters—National Tunisian TV operates two national TV channels
Press—There are five daily newspapers, including *La Presse* and *Esshafa*
WPFI score—72,50 (164)

EDUCATION AND HEALTH

There are 11 years of free and compulsory education.
Literacy rate—77.6% (2008 est)
Gross enrolment ratio (percentage of relevant age group)—primary 109%; secondary 90%; tertiary 34% (2009 est)
Health expenditure (per capita)—US$240 (2009)
Hospital beds (per 1,000 people)—2.1 (2004–9)
Life expectancy (years)—75.24 (2012 est)
Mortality rate—5.87 (2012 est)
Birth rate—17.28 (2012 est)
Infant mortality rate—24.98 (2012 est)

Turkey

Turkiye Cumhuriyeti—Republic of Turkey
Area—783,562 sq. km
Capital—Ankara (Angora), in Asia; population, 3,845,610 (2009 est)
Major cities—Adana, Antalya, Bursa, Gaziantep, Istanbul, Izmir, Konya
Currency—New Turkish lira (TL) of 100 kurus
Population—79,749,461 rising at 1.2% a year (2012 est); Turkish (70–75%), Kurdish (18%) (2008 est)
Religion—Muslim 99% (predominantly Hanafi, a school of Sunni Islam; a large minority are Alevi, a Shia sect); small Christian and Jewish minorities (est)
Language—Turkish (official), Kurdish, Dimli, Azeri, Kabardian
Population density—95 per sq. km (2010)
Urban population—69.6% (2010 est)
Median age (years)—28.5 (2011 est)
National anthem—'Istiklal Marsi' ['The Independence March']

National day—29 October (Republic Day)
Death penalty—Abolished for all crimes (since 2004)
CPI score—4.2 (2011)

FINANCIAL OUTLOOK

Turkey is recovering from an overheated credit market, which had fueled a domestic demand boom that pushed inflation to double digits in 2010, and created a current account deficit of 10% of GDP in 2011 (the second largest in the world in dollar terms). According to the IMF, this opened up the Turkish economy to the risk of capital fleeing the country, creating a hard landing for the economy. However, Turkey tightened its macroeconomic policy towards the end of 2011 and exports held up well, despite a softening in the global economy. Robust trade with the Middle East and Africa has offset weakened demand from Turkey's eurozone trading partners. Turkey continues to suffer from its need for external financing equal to 25% of GDP, and from the fact that Turkey's banks are overly dependent on short-term foreign borrowings. GDP growth shrank from 9.1% in the second quarter of 2011 to 2.9% by the second quarter of 2012. Unemployment, however, is at a 10-year low at below 9%. Core inflation is now around 7%. In June 2012, the fiscal tightening and general improvements to the economy through government policies led the ratings agency Moody's to upgrade the country's debt by one notch, to just below investment grade.

CLIMATE AND TERRAIN

Turkey in Europe consists of the relatively low-lying area of Eastern Thrace, including the cities of Istanbul and Edirne, and is separated from Asia by the Bosporus at Istanbul and by the Sea of Marmara and the Dardanelles (a strait about 64km in length, with a width varying from 1.6km to 6.4km).

Turkey in Asia comprises the whole of Asia Minor or Anatolia. Western Anatolia consists of a high central plateau with narrow coastal plains fringed by mountains in the north and south. Eastern Anatolia is mountainous, the land falling to a plateau between the mountains and the Syrian border. Elevation extremes range from 5,166m (Mt Ararat) to 0m (Mediterranean Sea). The Euphrates and Tigris rivers rise in the eastern mountains, which also contain many lakes, including Lake Van. Anatolia is prone to earthquakes.

The climate is temperate, but more extreme in the interior. Average temperatures in Ankara range from −4°C in January to 30°C in August.

HISTORY AND POLITICS

The 1982 constitution has been amended several times, mostly recently in 2010; the 2010 amendments increase parliamentary control over the judiciary and the military. The current president was elected by the legislature for a single seven-year term; from 2014, the president will be directly elected for a four-year term, renewable once. The unicameral Turkish Grand National Assembly has 550 members who were directly elected for a four-year term. The prime minister is appointed by the president and appoints the cabinet.

Tension between secularists and Islamists has grown in recent years, particularly since the Islamic-based Justice and Development Party (AKP), led by Recep Tayyip Erdogan, came to power in 2002. Seculists' concerns about the AKP's agenda caused a four-month political crisis in 2007, preventing the election of a new president and leading outgoing President Sezer to refuse approval of constitutional amendments. The impasse was ended by early legislative elections in July 2007, in which the AKP won a greatly increased majority. In August the AKP candidate, Abdullah Gul, was elected president in the third round of voting. The AKP retained its overall majority in the legislative election in June 2011.

HEAD OF STATE

President, Abdullah Gul, *elected* 27 August 2007

SELECTED GOVERNMENT MEMBERS *as at July 2012*

Prime Minister, Recep Tayyip Erdogan
Deputy Prime Ministers, Besir Atalay; Ali Babacan; Bulent Arinc; Bekir Bozdag
Finance, Mehmet Simsek
Foreign Affairs, Ahmet Davutoglu

EMBASSY OF THE REPUBLIC OF TURKEY

43 Belgrave Square, London SW1X 8PA
T 020-7393 0202
E turkemb.london@mfa.gov.tr
W www.londra.be.mfa.gov.tr
Ambassador Extraordinary and Plenipotentiary, HE Unal Cevikoz, *apptd* 2010

BRITISH EMBASSY

Sehit Ersan Caddesi 46/A, Cankaya, Ankara
T (+90) (312) 455 3344
E britembinf@turk.net
W ukinturkey.fco.gov.uk
Ambassador Extraordinary and Plenipotentiary, HE David Reddaway, CMG, MBE, *apptd* 2009

Insurgencies

Turkey's 12 million Kurds are the majority population in the south-east of the country, and have sought greater political and cultural rights for many years. The Kurdistan Workers' Party (PKK) has fought a guerrilla war for an ethnic homeland in the south-east since 1984 and has been blamed for bombings in other parts of Turkey. Conflict on the Turkey–Iraq border has caused tension in relations with Iraq, especially in 2008 after Turkish military incursions into the autonomous Kurdish area in northern Iraq, where PKK fighters have taken refuge. The government started to seek a political solution to the violence in 2009, introducing measures to increase Kurdish language rights and reduce the military presence in the south-east. Iran and Turkey agreed in October 2011 to work together to defeat Kurdish militants.

A number of bombings attributed to Muslim extremists occurred in Istanbul in 2003 and 2004.

DEFENCE

All aged 16–49, 2010 est	*Males*	*Females*
Available for military service	21,079,077	20,558,696
Fit for military service	17,664,510	17,340,816

Military expenditure—US$18,687m (2011)
Conscription duration—15 months

ECONOMY AND TRADE

The economy combines modern industry and commerce with a traditional agriculture sector. The private sector is growing steadily following large-scale privatisations of basic industry, banking, transport and communications. Financial and fiscal reforms from 2002 achieved growth averaging over 5% a year from 2005 to 2007, although large current account and trade deficits remain.

The agricultural sector accounts for 9.3% of GDP and employs 25.5% of the workforce. The principal crops are tobacco, cotton, grain, olives, sugar beets, pulses, nuts, citrus and other fruits, and livestock products. A diverse industrial sector is dominated by textiles and clothing (which employ one-third of the industrial workforce), food processing, vehicle assembly, electronics, mining, iron and steel, oil, construction, timber and paper. Turkey is also a destination and a transit route for oil and gas from central Asian countries. Tourism is a major industry and source of foreign revenue. Industry contributes 28.1% of GDP and services 62.6%.

The main trading partners are EU countries (especially Germany), Russia, China and the USA. Principal exports are clothing, foodstuffs, textiles, metal manufactures and transport equipment. The main imports are machinery, chemicals, semi-finished manufactures, fuels and transport equipment.

GNI—US$727,056m; US$9,890 per capita (2010)
Annual average growth of GDP—6.6% (2011 est)
Inflation rate—7.8% (2011 est)
Population below poverty line—16.9% (2010 est)
Unemployment—10.3% (2011 est)
Total external debt—US$313,600m (2011)
Imports—US$185,541m (2010)
Exports—US$113,979m (2010)

BALANCE OF PAYMENTS
Trade—US$71,562m deficit (2010)
Current Account—US$48,424m deficit (2010)

Trade with UK	*2010*	*2011*
Imports from UK	£3,665,850,931	£3,698,072,909
Exports to UK	£4,832,536,063	£5,397,836,674

COMMUNICATIONS
Airports and waterways—The principal airports are at Istanbul and Ankara and the main ports are at Istanbul (Europe) and Izmir (Asia)
Roadways and railways—There are 352,046km of roadways and 8,699km of railways
Telecommunications—16.2 million fixed lines and 61.77 million mobile subscriptions (2009); there were 27.23 million internet users in 2009
Internet code and IDD—tr; 90 (from UK), 44 (to UK)
Major broadcasters—Turkey has one state television and radio broadcaster, TRT, over 300 private television channels and more than 1,000 private radio stations
Press—There are around 40 national daily newspapers, including *Hurriyet*, *Milliyet* and *Cumhuriyet*
WPFI score—49,25 (138)

EDUCATION AND HEALTH
Education is free, secular and compulsory from the ages of six to 14.
Literacy rate—90.8% (2009 est)
Gross enrolment ratio (percentage of relevant age group)—primary 102%; secondary 78%; tertiary 46% (2009 est)
Health expenditure (per capita)—US$571 (2009)
Hospital beds (per 1,000 people)—2.4 (2004–9)
Life expectancy (years)—72.77 (2012 est)
Mortality rate—6.1 (2012 est)
Birth rate—17.58 (2012 est)
Infant mortality rate—23.07 (2012 est)

Turks and Caicos Islands

Area—430 sq. km
Capital—Cockburn Town, on Grand Turk; population, 6,195 (2009 est)
Currency—US dollar (US$) of 100 cents
Population—48,819 rising at 3.485% a year (2011 est)
Religion—Christian (Protestant 86%) (est)
Language—English (official)
Population density—40 per sq. km (2010 est)
Flag—British blue ensign with the coat of arms in the fly
National day—30 August (Constitution Day)
Life expectancy (years)—79.11 (2011 est)
Mortality rate—2.99 (2011 est)
Birth rate—17.76 (2011 est)
Infant mortality rate—11.97 (2011 est)

FINANCIAL OUTLOOK
The main drivers of the economy are tourism and offshore financial services. There is also a sizeable fishing industry, which is a valuable export earner. The only other notable industry is construction, which is largely geared towards improving tourism infrastructure. Most capital goods and food for domestic consumption are imported. The economy was sluggish in the early part of this decade, but has expanded strongly since 2003, growing by 13.9% in 2005. However, some aid from the United Kingdom is still needed to balance the budget, and fund capital projects. Under pressure from London, the European Union, and global organizations such as the OECD, the government has committed to improving transparency, establishing better exchange of information in tax matters, and has introduced a tighter regulatory structure to prevent fraud and money-laundering. The islands are currently in the midst of advanced preplanning processes for the preparation of a long-term, 10-year, sustainable development plan. The aim is to create a knowledge-driven and internationally competitive economy, with particular regard to those sectors that generate foreign exchange for the country. Specific economic goals include maintaining rates of balanced growth in the high-single digits; diversifying the economy, including with the assistance of foreign investment; greater local participation, and; exploiting the islands' resources to create a sustainable economy. For the first six months of the 2012–13 financial year, the government saw an overall revenue surplus of £5.2 million, £0.9 million over budget. The government now publishes quarterly financial statements as part of a transparency drive brought about by the UK-led interim administration.

CLIMATE AND TERRAIN
Around 40 islands and cays make up the the Turks and Caicos Islands, of which eight are permanently inhabited. The climate is marine tropical, moderated by trade winds; the average annual temperature is 26°C. Flamingo Hill on East Caicos is the highest elevation, at 48m.

  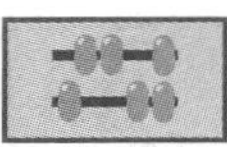      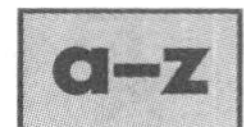

HISTORY AND POLITICS

The islands changed hands several times between the French, Spanish and British between their discovery in 1512 and the arrival of the first settlers, a group of Bermudans, in the 1670s. They achieved separate colonial status under the administration of the Bahamas in 1848, and since 1973 the territory has had its own governor and internal self-government.

The 2006 constitution provided for ministerial government and a partially elected legislature, with the governor retaining responsibility for defence, external affairs, internal security and the regulation of financial services. Following an inquiry into alleged political corruption in 2008–9, on 14 August 2009 the UK government suspended parts of the constitution, dismissed the House of Assembly and imposed direct rule by the governor for a period of at least two years, during which time legislative, administrative and financial reforms were to be implemented. New elections are due by 2013 while the UK foreign office commited to paying off old government debts and cover revenue shortfalls.

Governor, HE Damian Roderic Todd, *apptd* 2011

GOVERNMENT OF TURKS AND CAICOS ISLANDS

42 Westminster Palace Gardens, 1–7 Artillery Row, London SW1P 1RR
T 020-7222 9024

ECONOMY

The main industries are tourism, offshore financial services and fishing. The USA is the main source of tourists.

Trade with UK	*2009*	*2011*
Imports from UK	£3,257,817	£1,898,037
Exports to UK	£2,915	£395,231

COMMUNICATIONS

The principal airports are on the islands of Grand Turk and Providenciales and provide international air links; the main seaports are on Grand Turk and Providenciales. The islands also have a total of 121km of roads, 24km of which are surfaced.

Ukraine

Ukrayina—Ukraine
Area—603,550 sq. km
Capital—Kiev (Kyiv); population, 2,778,850 (2009 est)
Major cities—Dnipropetrovsk, Donetsk, Kharkiv, L'viv, Odesa, Zaporizhzhya
Currency—Hryvnia of 100 kopiykas
Population—44,854,065 falling at 0.63% a year (2012 est); Ukrainian (77.8%), Russian (17.3%); small Belarusian, Moldovan, Crimean Tatar, Bulgarian, Romanian, Polish, Hungarian and Greek minorities (2001)
Religion—Christian (Ukrainian Orthodox 84%, Greek Catholic 8%, Roman Catholic 2%, Protestant 2%), Muslim 1% (predominantly Sunni) (est)
Language—Ukrainian (official), Russian
Population density—79 per sq. km (2010)
Urban population—68.1% (2010 est)
Median age (years)—39.9 (2011 est)
National anthem—'Shche ne vmerla, Ukrainy' ['Ukraine's Glory Has Not Perished']
National day—24 August (Independence Day)
Death penalty—Abolished for all crimes (since 1999)
CPI score—2.3 (2011)

FINANCIAL OUTLOOK

The Ukrainian government was recently slammed by the ratings agency Moody's for allowing "a deterioration in the country's institutional strength against a background of poor policy predictability," which is an elaborate way of saying that the government has lost its way—not a good indicator for economic success. The best hope for the Ukrainian economy in 2013 is that global demand for its exports, particularly steel, firms up. Many firms in the Ukraine are working well below capacity and have not yet fully recovered from the 2008 crash. Weak investment activity is also eroding the manufacturing sector's ability to compete. According to the IMF, the Ukraine's business environment suffers from uneven administrative decisions and weak governance, which is dampening enthusiasm for investing, and chilling growth prospects. At US$3,600, the Ukraine's per capita income is only 10% of the average of the European Union's 27 member states. The economy saw 5.2% growth in 2011, but growth fell away in 2012 to under 2%. Headline inflation has come down from 12% in mid-2011 to a deflationary −0.5% in May 2012, although core inflation remains at 4%, and wage increases have outpaced productivity growth. The international bond markets are also no longer open to the Ukraine, which is now seen as too high a risk. Progress has been made on banking sector reforms but bank balance sheets remain weak. GDP growth in 2013 is expected to be around 3.5%, largely on the back of anticipated growth in its trading partners.

CLIMATE AND TERRAIN

Much of the country lies in a plain (steppe), with the Carpathian mountains in the west and mountains in the south of the Crimean peninsula. Elevation extremes range from 2,061m (Hora Hoverla) to 0m (Black Sea). The main rivers are the Dnieper, which runs through the centre of the country, the Dniester in the west, the Southern Buh and the Northern Donets (a tributary of the Don). The climate is continental, and Mediterranean in the southern Crimea. Average temperatures in Kiev range from −9°C in January to 26°C in July.

HISTORY AND POLITICS

The 1996 constitution was amended in 2006 to transfer some powers from the president to the legislature; the constitutional court returned these powers to the president in late 2010. The president is directly elected for a five-year term. The unicameral Supreme Council has 450 members, who are directly elected for a five-year term. The prime minister is appointed by the president, subject to the legislature's approval.

The country is divided into 24 provinces, the autonomous republic of Crimea and two municipalities (Kiev and Sevastapol) with provincial status.

Tensions between pro-Russian and pro-western political blocs, and divisions within the pro-western parties, have caused political instability since 2004, with two legislative elections and several changes of government. The 2007 legislative election was called after a power struggle between President Yushchenko and the prime minister, Viktor Yanukovych, produced a political impasse. Yanukovych's Party of Regions (PR) remained the largest party in the legislature but without an outright majority, and

President Yushchenko's Our Ukraine–People's Self Defence Bloc (OUPSD) and the Yulia Tymoshenko Bloc (YTB) formed a coalition government headed by Yulia Tymoshenko (prime minister February–September 2005). This government collapsed in September 2008 after disagreements over its response to Russia's use of force in Georgia; an early legislative election was called for December, but was cancelled when the OUPSD and YTB joined with the Lytvyn Bloc to reconstitute the coalition government. The government resigned after losing a vote of confidence in March 2010 and was replaced by a four-party coalition led by the PR. Viktor Yanukovych was elected president in January 2010 and former prime minister Yulia Tymoshenko was controversially jailed in October 2011 for abuse of power during her time in office.

HEAD OF STATE

President, Viktor Yanukovych, *elected* 7 February 2010, *sworn in* 25 February 2010

SELECTED GOVERNMENT MEMBERS *as at August 2012*

Prime Minister, Mykola Azarov

First Deputy Prime Minister, Valerii Khoroshkovskyi

Deputy Prime Ministers, Borys Kolesnikov; Serhiy Tyhypko

Finance, Yurii Kolobov

EMBASSY OF UKRAINE

60 Holland Park, London W11 3SJ

T 020-7727 6312

E emb_gb@mfa.gov.ua

W www.ukremb.org.uk

Ambassador Extraordinary and Plenipotentiary, HE Volodymyr Khandogiy, *apptd* 2010

BRITISH EMBASSY

Desyatinna 9, Kiev 01025

T (+380) (44) 490 3660

E ukembinf@gmail.com

W ukinukraine.fco.gov.uk

Ambassador Extraordinary and Plenipotentiary, HE Simon Smith, *apptd* 2012

Foreign Relations

In the aftermath of the USSR's disintegration in 1991, relations between Ukraine and Russia were strained by disputes over the Black Sea fleet and the status of Crimea. An agreement was reached in 1997 over the division of the fleet and Russia's lease of a naval base in Sevastopol. Disputes over Crimea have flared up intermittently, most recently in 2003 over a border in the region. The main causes of tension are the pro-Western policies pursued by some recent governments, particularly the possibility of Ukraine joining NATO, and the economic interdependence of the two countries; Ukraine is heavily dependent on Russia for gas supplies, and pipelines carrying much of Russia's gas exports to Europe pass through Ukraine. Price disputes have led to Russia suspending gas supplies on four occasions, but relations have improved since the election of President Yanukovych.

Ukraine signed a partnership and cooperation agreement with the EU in 1994 and an association agreement is under negotiation; President Yanukovych is less committed to EU membership than his predecessor. Ukraine was involved in NATO's Partnership for Peace programme in the 1990s. It applied for NATO membership during Viktor Yushchenko's presidency, but President Yanukovych's preference is for a strengthened relationship short of membership.

DEFENCE

All aged 16–49, 2010 est	Males	Females
Available for military service	10,984,394	11,260,000
Fit for military service	6,893,551	8,792,504

Military budget—US$3,747m (2011)

Conscription duration—18–24 months

ECONOMY AND TRADE

The first decade of independence was characterised by economic mismanagement and opposition to economic restructuring. Reform began in the late 1990s and brought economic growth, with rises in output and exports and a reduction in inflation. However, the slow progress of reform has been a drag on the economy, leaving it vulnerable to external factors such as the global economic downturn; the economy contracted severely in 2009 after key commodity prices and export demand fell. The government sought IMF support in autumn 2008, but some funding has been delayed owing to political volatility.

The agricultural sector is large and productive, with over half the land under cultivation. The main crops are grain, sugar beet, sunflower seeds and vegetables; stock-raising and dairy-farming are also important. Agriculture accounts for 9.4% of GDP and 16% of employment. There are large deposits of coal, iron ore and other minerals. The main industrial activities are mining and metal processing, manufacture of machinery and transport equipment and chemicals, electricity generation and food processing, especially sugar. Ukraine imports three-quarters of its oil and gas, principally from Russia; supplies have been suspended on occasions by price disputes with Russia, but in 2009 the two countries signed 10-year gas supply and transit agreements.

The main trading partners are Russia (24.1% of exports; 33.9% of imports), China, Germany and Turkey. Principal exports are ferrous and non-ferrous metals (especially steel), fuel and petroleum products, chemicals, machinery and transport equipment, and foodstuffs. The main imports are energy (primarily gas), machinery and equipment, and chemicals.

GNI—US$135,920m; US$3,000 per capita (2010)

Annual average growth of GDP—4.7% (2011 est)

Inflation rate—9% (2011 est)

Population below poverty line—35% (2009)

Unemployment—7.9% (2011 est)

Total external debt—US$111,700m (2011 est)

Imports—US$60,740m (2010)

Exports—US$51,431m (2010)

BALANCE OF PAYMENTS

Trade—US$9,309m deficit (2010)

Current Account—US$2,884m deficit (2010)

Trade with UK	*2010*	*2011*
Imports from UK	£442,600,929	£542,955,371
Exports to UK	£213,297,887	£361,727,671

COMMUNICATIONS

Airports and waterways—The principal airports are at Kiev and Odesa and the main seaports are Mariupol on the Sea of Azov, and Kherson, Mykolayiv, Odesa and Sevastopol on the Black Sea

  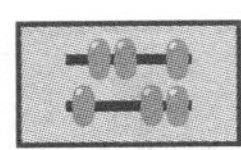      

Roadways and railways—There are 169,496km of roadways and 21,684km of railways
Telecommunications—12.94 million fixed lines and 53.93 million mobile subscriptions (2009); there were 7.77 million internet users in 2009
Internet code and IDD—ua; 380 (from UK), 44 (to UK)
Major broadcasters—The National TV Company of Ukraine operates the popular UT1, UT2, and UT3 channels
Press—Major titles include *Fakty i Kommentarii*, *Silski Visti* and *Segodnya*
WPFI score—46,83 (131)

EDUCATION AND HEALTH
Literacy rate—99.7% (2009 est)
Gross enrolment ratio (percentage of relevant age group)—primary 99%; secondary 96%; tertiary 79% (2010 est)
Health expenditure (per capita)—US$180 (2009)
Hospital beds (per 1,000 people)—8.7 (2004–9)
Life expectancy (years)—68.74 (2012 est)
Mortality rate—15.76 (2012 est)
Birth rate—9.59 (2012 est)
Infant mortality rate—8.38 (2012 est)
HIV/AIDS adult prevalence—1.1% (2009 est)

United Arab Emirates

Al-Imarat al-Arabiyah al-Muttahidah—United Arab Emirates
Area—83,600 sq. km
Capital—Abu Dhabi; population, 666,360 (2009 est)
Major cities—Ajman, Al-Ain, Ash Shariqah, Dubai
Currency—UAE dirham (Dh) of 100 fils
Population—5,314,317 rising at 3.06% a year (2012 est); Emirati nationals 20.1%, non-nationals 79.9% (2005 est); of the non-nationals, about half are from South Asia and a quarter are Arab or Iranian
Religion—Muslim 76%, Christian 9% (est), large Hindu and Buddhist minorities; Islam is the state religion, and 90% of nationals are Muslim (Sunni 85%, Shia 15%)
Language—Arabic (official), Persian, English, Hindi, Urdu
Population density—90 per sq. km (2010)
Urban population—78% (2010 est)
Median age (years)—30.2 (2011 est)
National anthem—'Ishy Bilady' ['Long Live My Homeland']
National day—2 December (Independence Day, 1971)
Death penalty—Retained
CPI score—6.8 (2011)

FINANCIAL OUTLOOK
The UAE economy is expected to sustain an annual growth rate above 4% in 2013, the minister for the economy said in February 2013. GDP is estimated to have expanded by 4.9% in 2012. Growth was driven largely by high global prices for crude oil, which is the mainstay of the country's exports. A partial rebound in the property market, a resurgence in consumer confidence, and an improved performance in the banking sector also helped Dubai recover from the impact of the 2008 financial crisis. The UAE's central bank has taken steps to ensure economic growth is better balanced. In December 2012, it announced plans to cap mortgage lending. However, Moody's said in March 2013 that Dubai faces "a pivotal year" in 2014, as government debt repayments of US$20 billion loom. The rating agency believes there is a high chance that oil-rich Abu Dhabi will continue to support its indebted smaller neighbor of Dubai, the Gulf's commercial center.

CLIMATE AND TERRAIN
The United Arab Emirates (UAE) is situated in the south-east of the Arabian peninsula. Six of the emirates lie on the shore of the Gulf, between the Musandam peninsula in the east and the Qatar peninsula in the west, while the seventh, Fujairah, lies on the Gulf of Oman. A flat coastal plain merges into the desert of the interior, and there are mountains in the east. Elevation extremes range from 1,527m (Jabal Yibir) to 0m (Persian Gulf). There is a desert climate, although it is cooler in the mountains, with high humidity on the coast. Average temperatures in Sharjah range from 12°C in January to 39°C in August.

HISTORY AND POLITICS
The United Arab Emirates (formerly the Trucial States) is composed of seven emirates. Six of these came together as an independent state on 2 December 1971 when they ended their individual special treaty relationships with the British government, and they were joined by Ras al-Khaimah on 10 February 1972. On independence, the union government assumed full responsibility for all internal and external affairs apart from those internal matters that remain the prerogative of the individual emirates.

Sheikh Zayed of Abu Dhabi was president from independence until his death in 2004. He was succeeded as Sultan of Abu Dhabi by his son, Sheikh Khalifa, who was also elected president of the UAE. The first national elections were held in 2006, when half the members of the Federal National Council (FNC) were elected by a small electoral college of 6,600 voters. The size of the electoral college increased significantly, to 129,274 voters (women comprised just under half of this total), in the most recent legislative election held in September 2011.

The 1971 provisional constitution, approved in 1996, was amended in 2008 to convert the Federal National Council from a consultative ino a legislative body and to extend its original two-year term to 2011. Overall authority lies with the Supreme Council, comprising the hereditary rulers of the seven emirates, each of whom also governs in his own territory. The president and vice-president are elected every five years by the Supreme Council from among its members. The president appoints the prime minister and the council of ministers. The unicameral Federal National Council has 40 members, eight members each from Abu Dhabi and Dubai, six each from Sharjah and Ras al-Khaimah and four each for Fujairah, Umm al-Qaiwain and Ajman; half are elected by an electoral college and half are appointed by the rulers of each emirate.

HEAD OF STATE
President, HH Sheikh Khalifa bin Zayed al-Nahyan *(Abu Dhabi)*, *elected* 3 November 2004, *re-elected* 2009
Vice-President, Prime Minister, Defence, HH Sheikh Mohammed bin Rashid al-Maktoum *(Dubai)*

SELECTED GOVERNMENT MEMBERS *as at July 2012*
Deputy Prime Ministers, Lt.-Gen. Sheikh Saif bin Zayed al-Nahyan *(Interior)*; Sheikh Mansour bin Zayed al-Nahyan

        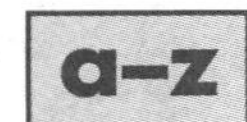

Finance, HH Sheikh Hamdan bin Rashid al-Maktoum
Foreign Affairs, Sheikh Abdullah bin Zayed al-Nahyan

EMBASSY OF THE UNITED ARAB EMIRATES
30 Prince's Gate, London SW7 1PT
T 020-7581 1281
E informationuk@mofa.gov.ae
W www.uae-embassy.ae/uk
Ambassador Extraordinary and Plenipotentiary, HE Abdul Rahman Ghanim al-Mutaiwee, *apptd* 2009

BRITISH EMBASSY
PO Box 248, Khalid bin al-Waleed Street (Street 22), Abu Dhabi
T (+971) (2) 610 1100
E chancery.abudhabi@fco.gov.uk
W ukinuae.fco.gov.uk
Ambassador Extraordinary and Plenipotentiary, HE Dominic Jermey, OBE, *apptd* 2010

Federal Structure

The emirates are: Abu Dhabi, Ajman, Dubai, Fujairah, Ras al-Khaimah, Sharjah and Umm al-Qaiwain. Each emirate has its own government, judicial system and penal code. Abu Dhabi has an executive council chaired by the crown prince.

DEFENCE

All aged 16–49, 2010 est	*Males*	*Females*
Available for military service	2,676,928	981,649
Fit for military service	2,229,366	842,759

Military expenditure—US$16,062m (2010)

ECONOMY AND TRADE

Exploitation of the territories' oil reserves began in the 1960s and transformed the UAE from poor rural principalities into modern states with a high standard of living. Oil and gas production dominate the economy, although diversification means that output now accounts for less than 25% of GDP. The economy is also dependent on foreign workers, but the government aims to increase opportunities for its citizens through improved education and expansion of the private sector. The economy was badly hit by the global downturn, particularly in Dubai, which was heavily exposed when property prices crashed; its debt crisis has been alleviated by loans from federal and Abu Dhabi institutions.

Agriculture is limited by the terrain but the area under cultivation has been extended by irrigation and water desalination projects. The main products are dates, vegetables, watermelons, poultry, eggs and dairy products. Non-hydrocarbon industries include fishing, aluminium, cement, petrochemicals, fertilisers, commercial ship repair, construction materials, handicrafts, textiles, boat-building, financial services and tourism. Several free-trade zones are attracting foreign investment.

The main export markets are Japan, South Korea and India; imports come chiefly from China, India, the USA, Germany and Japan. Principal exports are crude oil (45%), natural gas, re-exports, dried fish and dates. The main imports are machinery and transport equipment, chemicals and food.

GNI—US$273,547m; US$41,930 per capita (2009)
Annual average growth of GDP—3.3% (2011 est)
Inflation rate—2.5% (2011 est)
Population below poverty line—19.5% (2003)
Total external debt—US$167,200m (2011 est)
Imports—US$170,000m (2010)
Exports—US$235,000m (2010)

BALANCE OF PAYMENTS
Trade—US$65,000m surplus (2010)
Current Account—US$21,240m surplus (2010)

Trade with UK	*2010*	*2011*
Imports from UK	£4,177,961,866	£4,714,617,878
Exports to UK	£937,768,948	£1,888,032,585

COMMUNICATIONS

Airports and waterways—There is an international airport in every emirate except Ajman and significant ports in Jebel Ali, Khor Fakkan, Mina Zayed, Mina Rashid, Mina Saqr and Mina Khalid
Roadways—There are 4,080km of roadways and no railways
Telecommunications—1.48 million fixed lines and 10.92 million mobile subscriptions (2009); there were 3.44 million internet users in 2009
Internet code and IDD—ae; 971 (from UK), 44 (to UK)
Media—MBC operates two major channels across the Emirates; major newspapers include *Al Bayan* and *Gulf News*
WPFI score—23,75 (87)

EDUCATION AND HEALTH

Education is free in state schools and compulsory from ages six to 14.
Literacy rate—90.0% (2005 est)
Health expenditure (per capita)—US$1,520 (2009)
Hospital beds (per 1,000 people)—1.9 (2004–9)
Life expectancy (years)—76.71 (2012 est)
Mortality rate—2.04 (2012 est)
Birth rate—15.76 (2012 est)
Infant mortality rate—11.59 (2012 est)

United Kingdom

United Kingdom of Great Britain and Northern Ireland
Area—243,122 sq. km
Capital—London; population, 8,173,900 (2011)
Major cities—Belfast, Birmingham, Cardiff, Edinburgh, Glasgow, Leeds, Liverpool, Manchester
Currency—Pound sterling (£) of 100 pence
Population—63,047,162 rising at 0.55% a year (2011 est)
Religion—Christian 72% (Anglican 29%, Roman Catholic 10%, other Protestant 14%), Muslim 3%, Hindu 1% (est); small Jewish, Sikh and Buddhist minorities
Language—English, Welsh, Lowland Scots, Scottish Gaelic, Irish
Population density—257 per sq. km (2010)
Urban population—90.1% (2010 est)
Median age (years)—40 (2011 est)

  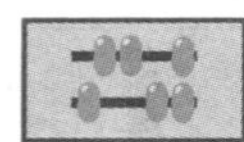      

National anthem—'God Save the Queen'
Death penalty—Abolished for all crimes (since 1998)
CPI score—7.8 (2011)

FINANCIAL OUTLOOK

The UK economy grew by 0.2% in 2012, according to revised official figures released in February 2013. Earlier that month, the UK was downgraded from its prized sovereign debt AAA-rating for the first time since 1978, on expectations that growth will "remain sluggish over the next few years," according to Moody's. The ratings agency added that the government's debt reduction program faced significant "challenges" ahead and that the UK's huge debts were unlikely to reverse until 2016. The UK's net sovereign debt was the equivalent of 68% of the country's annual economic output, or GDP, at the end of 2012. Despite the sluggish economy, unemployment fell in 2012, the trend continuing into 2013. UK unemployment fell in the three months to December by 14,000 to 2.5 million, while the number of people in work jumped to a new record of 29.7 million. More than 580,000 more people were employed over the course of the year. The jobless total fell by 14,000 between October and December 2012 to 2.5 million, according to official figures.

Guernsey

Guernsey's budget for 2013 introduced a 10% intermediary tax for some insurance companies that had previously paid zero tax, bringing Guernsey's business tax regime more into line with Jersey's. The measure is expected to raise £12 million per year, and will see the finance industry making a larger contribution to the island's tax receipts. The budget also introduced a 3% increase in personal income tax allowances and a 6% increase in the rate of duty on tobacco, with a 3% increase on alcohol and fuel.

Isle of Man

In its 2012-13 budget, the Isle of Man decided not to tackle its deficit head on, but instead to introduce a four-year plan with the goal of having a balanced budget by year four. That said, the government achieved savings of £12 million in 2011-12, adding to the £51 million of savings achieved in 2010-11. It has also reduced spending by £35 million below the total envisaged for 2012-13 in its previous budget. Staff posts have been reduced by 170. Personal taxation remains at 10% for the lower rate and 20% for the higher rate. The aim of the rebalanced four-year budget plan is to eliminate any requirement to use reserves to finance fiscal spending commitments by the end of 2015-16. A revision in the public-sector pension scheme is on course to remove the current £6 million annual deficit on expenditure in five years. The Isle of Man increased VAT to 20% in 2011, in part to counterbalance a reduction in revenues from the renegotiation of revenue-sharing arrangements with the UK.

Jersey

Jersey's 2013 budget was approved in early December 2012. There were no tax increases, an increase in personal tax exemptions, and first-time buyers got increased tax relief through an extension of the stamp duty limit to dwellings priced at £450,000 and above. The budget also increased income tax exemptions by 3%, in line with inflation and retained income tax allowances unchanged from 2012. Jersey's gross value added fell by 1% through 2011 and the non-financial sector declined by 2%. The budget retained the goods and services tax at 5%.

CLIMATE AND TERRAIN

The terrain of Great Britain is higher in the north and west, with low mountains and rugged hills in Scotland, northern England and Wales; the land declines towards the south and east, with its lowest points in the south-east. Northern Ireland is more low-lying, with low mountains in the north and east. The heavily indented coastline varies in height between high cliffs and sea level. Elevation extremes range from 1,343m (Ben Nevis, Scotland) to – 4m (the Fens, eastern England). Although Scotland contains numerous large lochs and northern England includes an area known as the Lake District, the largest freshwater lake is Lough Neagh in Northern Ireland. The main rivers are the Thames, the Severn and the Trent in England and Wales, and the Tay in Scotland. The climate is temperate and extremes are rare, but the convergence of Atlantic, Arctic and European weather systems produces unusually changeable weather conditions. Average temperatures in London range from 2°C in January to 22°C in July.

HISTORY AND POLITICS

There is no written constitution. The head of state is a hereditary constitutional monarch. The bicameral parliament consists of the House of Commons, the lower house, and the House of Lords. The House of Commons has 650 members, directly elected for a five-year term. The House of Lords is appointed and numbers vary; in July 2012 it had 816 members, comprising 26 archbishops and bishops of the Church of England, 698 life peers and 92 hereditary peers. The prime minister is the leader of the majority party or coalition in the House of Commons.

Powers over certain internal matters were devolved in 1999 to Scotland, Wales and Northern Ireland, each of which has its own legislature and government; devolution was suspended in Northern Ireland several times between 2000 and 2007 owing to the breakdown of power-sharing arrangements.

The Labour government elected in 1945 pursued socialist economic and welfare policies, nationalising key industries, setting up the National Health Service and expanding the social security system. Economic decline continued until the 1980s, when it was reversed by the Conservative government led by Margaret Thatcher, the country's first woman prime minister. Her administration privatised nationalised industries, opened up welfare services to market forces and reduced the role of local government, polarising politics and public opinion. She also established a close relationship with the USA that was supportive of its foreign policy. This has been continued by her successors, most recently in the support for the US 'war on terror' and the deployment of British forces in Afghanistan since 2001, Iraq from 2003 to 2009, and in Libyan air space in 2011.

At the 2010 legislative election, the Conservative party won the most seats but without an outright majority. After negotiations with the Liberal Democrat party, a coalition government was formed under the Conservative leader, David Cameron, with the Liberal Democrat leader, Nick Clegg, as deputy prime minister.

HEAD OF STATE

HM The Queen of the United Kingdom of Great Britain and Northern Ireland, Queen Elizabeth II, *born* 21 April 1926; *succeeded* 6 February 1952; *crowned* 2 June 1953
Heir, HRH The Prince of Wales (Prince Charles Philip Arthur George), *born* 14 November 1948

SELECTED GOVERNMENT MEMBERS *as at September 2012*

Prime Minister, First Lord of the Treasury, Civil Service, David Cameron
Deputy Prime Minister, Nick Clegg
Chancellor of the Exchequer, George Osborne
Foreign and Commonwealth Affairs, William Hague
Justice, Lord Chancellor, Chris Grayling

Home Affairs, Theresa May
Defence, Philip Hammond

DEFENCE

All aged 16–49, 2010 est	Males	Females
Available for military service	14,856,917	14,307,316
Fit for military service	12,255,452	11,779,679

Military expenditure—US$57,875m (2011)

ECONOMY AND TRADE

The UK has a highly developed and technologically advanced economy that is now dominated by services and trade. It was the first industrialised nation, developing an economy in the 19th century based on heavy industry, mass manufacturing and global trade. It became less predominant as industrialisation spread to other countries, and the demands of the Second World War caused a postwar industrial decline that left the economy less efficient than many of its competitors and increasingly undercut by cheaper production in the developing world. In the 1980s, privatisation of state industries and constraints on public spending improved government finances, and primary industrial activities were increasingly replaced by service industries. After emerging from recession in the early 1990s, the economy experienced its longest-recorded period of expansion, outperforming the rest of the EU states, until 2008. The global economic downturn, tight credit and the end of the property boom caused the economy to go into recession from early 2008 until late 2009 and again at the start of 2012. The banking sector in particular was badly affected by the global financial crisis in 2008 and government intervention was necessary to stabilise the financial system, including nationalising or part-nationalising major banks. These measures left the government with a massive public-sector debt to service, and the new coalition government announced tight constraints on public spending from 2010.

The service sector, especially banking, insurance and business services, electronics, telecommunications and tourism, now contributes 77.8% of GDP and employs 80.4% of the workforce. Agriculture is intensive, highly mechanised and efficient, employing 1.4% of the workforce, although contributing only 0.7% of GDP. The UK has large but declining reserves of oil, gas and coal, and the country became a net importer of energy in 2005. Other industrial output is mostly of manufactured goods, including machine tools, electrical power equipment, automation and transport equipment, aircraft, ships, motor vehicles and parts, electronics and communications equipment, metals, chemicals, paper and paper products, food processing, textiles, clothing and other consumer goods.

The main trading partners are other EU countries, the USA and China. The principal exports are manufactured goods, fuels, chemicals, food, beverages and tobacco. The main imports are manufactured goods, machinery, fuels and foodstuffs.

GNI—US$2,280,718m; US$38,370 per capita (2010)
Annual average growth of GDP—1.1% (2011 est)
Inflation rate—4.5% (2011)
Population below poverty line—14% (2006 est)
Unemployment—7.9% (2011 est)
Total external debt—US$9,836,000m (2011)
Imports—US$561,514m (2010)
Exports—US$410,169m (2010)

BALANCE OF PAYMENTS
Trade—US$151,344m deficit (2010)
Current Account—US$37,319m deficit (2009)

COMMUNICATIONS

Airports—There are around 140 licensed civil airports, of which Heathrow (the world's busiest international airport), Gatwick, Stansted and Manchester handle the highest volume of passengers
Waterways—Traditionally a seafaring nation, the UK has a large merchant navy, with 504 ships of over 1,000 tonnes registered in the UK and 308 ships registered overseas. The main ports are at Grimsby and Immingham, London, Milford Haven, Southampton, Tees and Hartlepool, Forth, Liverpool, Felixstowe, Dover and Belfast
Roadways—There are 394,295km of roadways, including 3,571km of motorways
Railways—The 16,454km of rail network is operated by 23 rail companies
Telecommunications—33.32 million fixed lines and 80.79 million mobile subscriptions (2009); there were 51.44 million internet users in 2009
Major broadcasters—The British Broadcasting Corporation is a public service broadcaster and provides radio and television programmes, in competition with several commercial radio and television stations, including cable and satellite services
Press—The lively and occasionally controversial newspaper press publishes around ten newspapers daily, including *The Times*, *The Guardian* and *The Sun*
WPFI score—6,00 (19)

EDUCATION AND HEALTH

Full-time education is compulsory between the ages of five and 16 in Great Britain and four and 16 in Northern Ireland. Education between the ages of 16 and 18 is voluntary, but under recent government legislation, will become compulsory from 2013.
Gross enrolment ratio (percentage of relevant age group)—primary 106%; secondary 102%; tertiary 59% (2009 est)
Health expenditure (per capita)—US$3,285 (2009)
Hospital beds (per 1,000 people)—3.4 (2004–9)
Life expectancy (years)—80.17 (2012 est)
Mortality rate—9.33 (2012 est)
Birth rate—12.27 (2012 est)
Infant mortality rate—4.56 (2012 est)

OVERSEAS TERRITORIES

See Bermuda, the British Virgin Islands, the Cayman Islands, Gibraltar, Montserrat, and the Turks and Caicos Islands.

United States of America

Area—9,826,675 sq. km
Capital—Washington, District of Columbia; population, 4,420,650 (2009 est)
Major cities—Chicago, Dallas, Houston, Los Angeles, New York, Philadelphia, Phoenix, San Antonio, San Diego, San José
Currency—US dollar (US$) of 100 cents

Population—313,847,465 rising at 0.9% a year (2011 est); white 80%, black 12.9%, Asian 4.4%, Amerindian and Alaskan native 1%, native Hawaiian and other Pacific islander 0.2%; Hispanic 15.1% (persons of Hispanic origin may be of any race or ethnic group) (2007 est)
Religion—Christian (Protestant 51%, Roman Catholic 24%, Mormon 2%, other 2%), Jewish 2%, Buddhist 1%, Muslim 1% (est)
Language—English, Spanish, Hawaiian (official in Hawaii)
Population density—34 per sq. km (2010)
Urban population—82.3% (2010 est)
Median age (years)—36.9 (2011 est)
National anthem—'The Star-Spangled Banner'
National day—4 July (Independence Day)
Death penalty—Abolished in 16 states, District of Columbia and US insular territories
CPI score—7.1 (2011)

FINANCIAL OUTLOOK

The US's economic recovery gathered pace in 2012 despite political turbulence over budget cuts. GDP grew by 2.2% during 2012, helped by an improving housing market and reviving consumer spending. Sales of new homes, a lead component of past recoveries, surged 16% in January to a 437,000 annual pace, the highest rate since July 2008. At the end of 2012, Congress and the White House agreed a deal to avoid what was dubbed the "fiscal cliff," which included expiring tax breaks and the sequester (deep budget cuts that began to take effect in March 2013). The latter was drawn up in mid-2011, as Congress and the White House clashed over raising the debt ceiling and how to slash the huge deficit. However, in March 2013, President Obama signed into effect the sequester, after he and Republican congressional leaders failed to agree on measures to avoid them. Obama warned that the cuts—if fully realized—would slow US economic growth by 0.5%, and cost 750,000 jobs.

CLIMATE AND TERRAIN

The coastline has a length of about 3,329km on the Atlantic Ocean, 12,268km on the Pacific, 1,705km on the Arctic, and 2,624km on the Gulf of Mexico. The principal river is the Mississippi-Missouri-Red (5,970km long), traversing the whole country from Montana to its mouth in the Gulf of Mexico. The Rocky Mountains range runs the length of the western portion of the country. West of this, bordering the Pacific coast, the Cascade Mountains and Sierra Nevada form the outer edge of a high tableland, consisting partly of stony and sandy desert and partly of grazing land and forested mountains, and including the Great Salt Lake, which extends to the Rocky Mountains. A vast central plain lies between the Rockies and the hills and low mountains of the eastern states, where large forests still exist, remnants of the forests which formerly extended over the entire Atlantic slope. Elevation extremes range from 6,194m (Mt McKinley, Alaska) to −86m (Death Valley, California). The climate varies with latitude but is mostly temperate, with semi-arid conditions on the great plains and arid in the south-west. Average temperatures in Washington DC range from −1°C from December–February to 31°C in July.

Two states are detached: Alaska and Hawaii. Alaska occupies the north-western extremity of North America, separated from the rest of the USA by the Canadian province of British Columbia. The terrain is arctic tundra with mountain ranges, and the climate is arctic. The state of Hawaii is a chain of about 20 mountainous volcanic islands in the north Pacific Ocean, of which the chief islands are Hawaii, Maui, Oahu, Kauai and Molokai. The climate is tropical.

The Pacific coast and Hawaii are prone to seismic activity. The Atlantic and Gulf of Mexico coasts frequently experience hurricanes.

HISTORY AND POLITICS

By the constitution of 17 September 1787 (which has been amended 15 times, most recently in 1992), the government of the USA is entrusted to three separate authorities: the federal executive (the president and cabinet), the legislature (Congress, which consists of a senate and a House of Representatives) and the judicature. The president is indirectly elected by an electoral college to serve a four-year term, and may serve a maximum of two consecutive terms. If a president dies in office, the vice-president serves the remainder of his term. The president appoints the cabinet officers and all the chief officials, subject to confirmation by the senate. He makes recommendations of a general nature to Congress, and when laws are passed, he may return them to Congress with a veto. But, if a measure so vetoed is again passed by both houses by a two-thirds majority in each house, it becomes law, notwithstanding the objection of the president.

Each of the 50 states has its own executive, legislature and judiciary. In theory, they are sovereign, but in practice their autonomy is increasingly circumscribed.

PRESIDENTIAL ELECTIONS

Candidates for the presidency must be at least 35 years of age and a native citizen of the USA. The electoral college for each state is directly elected by universal adult suffrage in the November preceding the January in which the presidential term expires. The number of members of the electoral college is equal to the whole number of senators and representatives to which the state is entitled in the national congress. The electoral college for each state meets in its state in December and each member votes for a presidential candidate by ballot. The ballots are sent to Washington, and opened on 6 January by the president of the senate in the presence of Congress. The candidate who has received a majority of the whole number of electoral votes cast is declared president for the ensuing term. If no one has a majority, then from the highest on the list (not exceeding three) the House of Representatives elects a president, the votes being taken by states, the representation from each state having one vote. A presidential term begins at noon on 20 January.

The 2008 presidential election was won by the Democrat candidate Barack Obama, the first African-American to hold the office. In the 2008 legislative elections, the Democrat Party retained its majorities in both houses of congress. The Democrat majority in the senate was lost in early 2010 but a narrow majority was regained at the November 2010 elections. In the 2010 elections to the House of Representatives, the Democrats lost heavily to the Republicans.

HEAD OF STATE

President, Barack Obama, *elected* 2008, *sworn in* 20 January 2009
Vice-President, Joseph Biden

SELECTED GOVERNMENT MEMBERS *as at July 2012*
Secretary of State, Hillary Clinton
Defence, Leon Panetta
Interior, Ken Salazar
Treasury, Timothy Geithner
Secretary for Homeland Security, Janet Napolitano

THE CONGRESS

Legislative power is vested in the bicameral Congress, comprising the senate and the House of Representatives. The senate has 100

members, two from each state, elected for a six-year term, with one-third elected every two years. The House of Representatives has 435 members directly elected in each state for a two-year term; a resident commissioner from Puerto Rico and a delegate each from American Samoa, the District of Columbia, Guam, the Northern Mariana Islands and the Virgin Islands serve as non-voting members of the house.

Members of the 112th congress were elected on 2 November 2010 and sworn into office on 5 January 2011. As at July 2012, the 112th congress is constituted as follows:
Senate: Democrats 51; Republicans 47; Independent 2
House of Representatives: Democrats 191; Republicans 240
President of the Senate, The Vice-President
Senate majority leader, Harry Reid *(D), Nevada*
Speaker of the House of Representatives, John Boehner *(R), Ohio*
House majority leader, Eric Cantor *(R), Virginia*

THE JUDICATURE
The federal judiciary consists of three sets of federal courts: the Supreme Court at Washington, DC, consisting of a Chief Justice and eight Associate Justices; the US court of appeals, consisting of 179 circuit judges within 12 regional circuits and one federal circuit; and the 94 US district courts served by 678 district court judges.

THE SUPREME COURT
US Supreme Court Building, Washington DC 20543
Chief Justice, John Roberts, *apptd* 2005

UNITED STATES EMBASSY
24 Grosvenor Square, London W1A 1AE
T 020-7499 9000
W www.usembassy.org.uk
Ambassador Extraordinary and Plenipotentiary, HE Louis B. Susman, *apptd* 2009

BRITISH EMBASSY
3100 Massachusetts Avenue NW, Washington DC 20008
T (+1) (202) 588 6500
E washi@fco.gov.uk
W ukinusa.fco.gov.uk
Ambassador Extraordinary and Plenipotentiary, Sir Peter Westmacott, KCMG, LVO, *apptd* 2012

THE STATES OF THE UNION

The USA is a federal republic consisting of 50 states and the federal District of Columbia, and also of organised territories. Of the present 50 states, 13 are original states, seven were admitted without previous organisation as territories, and 30 were admitted after such organisation.
§ The 13 original states
(D) Democratic Party; (I) Independent; (R) Republican Party

State (date and order of admission)	*Area sq. km*	*Population**	*Capital*	*Governor (end of term in office)*
Alabama (AL) (1819, 22)	133,915	4,779,736	Montgomery	Robert Bentley (R), Jan. 2015
Alaska (AK) (1959, 49)	1,530,694	710,231	Juneau	Sean Parnell (R), Dec. 2014
Arizona (AZ) (1912, 48)	295,259	6,392,017	Phoenix	Jan Brewer (R), Jan. 2015
Arkansas (AR) (1836, 25)	137,754	2,915,918	Little Rock	Mike Beebe (D), Jan. 2015
California (CA) (1850, 31)	411,047	37,253,956	Sacramento	Jerry Brown (D), Jan. 2015
Colorado (CO) (1876, 38)	269,595	5,029,196	Denver	John Hickenlooper (D), Jan. 2015
Connecticut (CT) § (1788, 5)	12,997	3,574,097	Hartford	Dan Malloy (D), Jan. 2015
Delaware (DE) § (1787, 1)	5,297	897,934	Dover	Jack Markell (D), Jan. 2013
Florida (FL) (1845, 27)	151,939	18,801,310	Tallahassee	Rick Scott (R), Jan. 2015
Georgia (GA) § (1788, 4)	152,576	9,687,653	Atlanta	Nathan Deal (R), Jan. 2015
Hawaii (HI) (1959, 50)	16,760	1,360,301	Honolulu	Neil Abercrombie (D), Dec. 2014
Idaho (ID) (1890, 43)	216,430	1,567,582	Boise	C. L. (Butch) Otter (R), Jan. 2015
Illinois (IL) (1818, 21)	145,933	12,830,632	Springfield	Patrick Quinn III (D), Jan. 2015
Indiana (IN) (1816, 19)	93,719	6,483,802	Indianapolis	Mitchell E. Daniels (R), Jan. 2013
Iowa (IA) (1846, 29)	145,752	3,046,355	Des Moines	Terry Branstad (R), Jan. 2015
Kansas (KS) (1861, 34)	213,097	2,853,118	Topeka	Sam Brownback (R), Jan. 2015
Kentucky (KY) (1792, 15)	104,661	4,339,367	Frankfort	Steve Beshear (D), Dec. 2015
Louisiana (LA) (1812, 18)	123,677	4,533,372	Baton Rouge	Bobby Jindal (R), Jan. 2016
Maine (ME) (1820, 23)	86,156	1,328,361	Augusta	Paul LePage (R), Jan. 2015
Maryland (MD) § (1788, 7)	27,091	5,773,552	Annapolis	Martin O'Malley (D), Jan. 2015
Massachusetts (MA) § (1788, 6)	21,455	6,547,629	Boston	Deval Patrick (D), Jan. 2015
Michigan (MI) (1837, 26)	151,584	9,883,640	Lansing	Rick Snyder (R), Jan. 2015
Minnesota (MN) (1858, 32)	218,600	5,303,925	St Paul	Mark Dayton (D), Jan. 2015
Mississippi (MS) (1817, 20)	123,514	2,967,297	Jackson	Phil Bryant (R), Jan. 2016
Missouri (MO) (1821, 24)	180,514	5,988,927	Jefferson City	Jeremiah (Jay) Nixon (D), Jan. 2013

 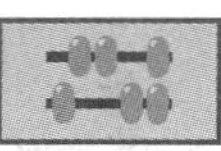       

Montana (MT) (1889, 41)	380,848	989,415	Helena	Brian Schweitzer (D), Jan. 2013
Nebraska (NE) (1867, 37)	200,349	1,826,341	Lincoln	Dave Heineman (R), Jan. 2015
Nevada (NV) (1864, 36)	286,352	2,700,551	Carson City	Brian Sandoval (R), Jan. 2015
New Hampshire (NH) § (1788, 9)	24,033	1,316,470	Concord	John Lynch (D), Jan. 2013
New Jersey (NJ) § (1787, 3)	20,168	8,791,894	Trenton	Chris Christie (R), Jan. 2014
New Mexico (NM) (1912, 47)	314,925	2,059,179	Santa Fé	Susana Martinez (R), Jan. 2015
New York (NY) § (1788, 11)	127,189	19,378,102	Albany	Andrew Cuomo (D), Jan. 2015
North Carolina (NC) § (1789, 12)	136,412	9,535,483	Raleigh	Beverly Perdue (D), Jan. 2013
North Dakota (ND) (1889, 39)	183,117	672,591	Bismarck	Jack Dalrymple (R), Dec. 2014
Ohio (OH) (1803, 17)	107,044	11,536,504	Columbus	John Kasich (R), Jan. 2015
Oklahoma (OK) (1907, 46)	181,185	3,751,351	Oklahoma City	Mary Fallin (R), Jan. 2015
Oregon (OR) (1859, 33)	251,418	3,831,074	Salem	John Kitzhaber (D), Jan. 2015
Pennsylvania (PA) § (1787, 2)	117,347	12,702,379	Harrisburg	Tom Corbett (R), Jan. 2015
Rhode Island (RI) § (1790, 13)	3,139	1,052,567	Providence	Lincoln Chafee (I), Jan. 2015
South Carolina (SC) § (1788, 8)	80,582	4,625,364	Columbia	Nikki R. Haley (R), Jan. 2015
South Dakota (SD) (1889, 40)	199,730	814,180	Pierre	Dennis Daugaard (R), Jan. 2015
Tennessee (TN) (1796, 16)	109,153	6,346,105	Nashville	Bill Haslem (R), Jan. 2015
Texas (TX) (1845, 28)	691,027	25,145,561	Austin	Rick Perry (R), Jan. 2015
Utah (UT) (1896, 45)	219,888	2,763,885	Salt Lake City	Gary Herbert (R), Jan 2013
Vermont (VT) (1791, 14)	24,900	625,741	Montpelier	Peter Shumlin (D), Jan. 2013
Virginia (VA) § (1788, 10)	105,586	8,001,024	Richmond	Bob McDonnell (R), Jan. 2014
Washington (WA) (1889, 42)	176,479	6,724,540	Olympia	Christine Gregoire (D), Jan. 2013
West Virginia (WV) (1863, 35)	62,761	1,852,994	Charleston	Earl Ray Tomblin (D), Jan. 2013
Wisconsin (WI) (1848, 30)	145,436	5,686,986	Madison	Scott Walker (R), Jan. 2015
Wyoming (WY) (1890, 44)	253,324	563,626	Cheyenne	Matthew Mead (R), Jan. 2015
Dist. of Columbia (DC) (1791)	179	601,723	–	Vincent Gray (D), Jan. 2015 *(Mayor)*

Outlying Territories and Possessions

	Area sq. km	*Population**	*Capital*	*Governor (end of term in office)*
American Samoa	199	68,061	Pago Pago	Togiola Tulafono (D), Jan. 2013
Guam	541	185,674	Hagatna	Eddie Calvo (R), Jan. 2015
Northern Mariana Islands	477	44,582	Saipan	Benigno Fitial (C), Jan. 2015
Puerto Rico	13,790	3,998,905	San Juan	Luis G. Fortuño (R), Jan. 2013
US Virgin Islands	363	109,574	Charlotte Amalie	John de Jongh Jr (D), Jan. 2015

* States 2010 estimate; outlying territories 2011 estimate

DEFENCE

Each military department is separately organised and functions under the direction, authority and control of the Secretary of Defence (except the Coast Guard, which is part of the Department of Homeland Security created in 2002). The air force has primary responsibility for the Department of Defence space development programmes and projects.

Military expenditure—US$689,591m (2011)

All aged 16–49, 2010 est	*Males*	*Females*
Available for military service	73,270,043	71,941,969
Fit for military service	60,620,143	59,401,941

ECONOMY AND TRADE

The USA is one of the world's leading industrial nations, with a sophisticated market economy that saw huge growth during the 20th century. Economic development was due in part to the mechanisation of the agrarian economy, the expansion of the transport infrastructure and large amounts of relatively cheap migrant labour; more recently it has been driven by rapid advances in technology. In the late 20th century, the economy shifted emphasis from industry to services, and government involvement in the economy was steadily reduced. Until 2008, the economy experienced steady growth, with low unemployment and inflation, although there were large budget and trade deficits, high levels of personal debt and an increasingly uneven distribution of wealth.

The US sub-prime mortgage crisis in 2007 triggered a global economic downturn, and falling property prices and tight credit pushed the domestic economy into recession by mid 2008. Following the failure of several investment banks, Congress passed a US$700bn relief programme to stabilise the financial markets in October 2008, and in spring 2009 a US$787bn fiscal stimulus package and a record US$3.6 trillion budget for 2010 were approved. Despite these measures, the economy still experienced the collapse of key industries (such as vehicle manufacturing), and rising unemployment and inflation before growth restarted in late 2009 after the USA's longest and deepest recession since the 1930s; the budget and trade deficits remain very high. The USA's triple 'A' credit rating was reduced in August 2011 following a deficit reduction plan passed by Congress.

Agriculture is a major industry in the USA; principal crops are wheat, maize, other grains, fruit, vegetables, cotton, meat and dairy products. Agriculture, fishing and forestry contribute 1.2% of GDP and employ 0.7% of the workforce.

Mining and extraction are important to the economy. Large quantities of coal, iron ore, phosphate rock, copper, zinc and lead are mined. About one-third of the country's oil requirements are supplied by domestic production, principally from fields in the Gulf of Mexico. Natural gas is also produced. Despite its domestic oil and natural gas resources and its electricity generating capacity, the USA is a net importer of energy.

The industrial sector is highly diversified and technologically advanced. The main manufacturing industries produce steel, vehicles, aircraft and aerospace equipment, telecommunications equipment, chemicals, electronic equipment and consumer goods, and process food. Industry contributes 19.2% of GDP and services account for 79.6% of GDP.

The main trading partners are Canada, China, Mexico, Japan, Germany and the UK. Principal exports are capital goods (chiefly transistors, aircraft, vehicle parts, computers, telecommunications equipment), industrial supplies (e.g. organic chemicals), consumer goods (cars, medicines) and agricultural produce (soya beans, fruit, maize). The main imports are industrial goods (especially crude oil), consumer goods (cars, clothing, medicines, furniture, toys), capital goods (computers, telecommunications equipment, vehicle parts, office machines, electric power machinery) and agricultural products.

GNI—US$14,635,600m; US$47,390 per capita (2010)
Annual average growth of GDP—1.5% (2011 est)
Inflation rate—3% (2011 est)
Population below poverty line—15.1% (2010 est)
Unemployment—9.1% (2011 est)
Total external debt—US$14,710,000m (2011)
Imports—US$1,968,070m (2010)
Exports—US$1,277,580m (2010)

BALANCE OF PAYMENTS
Trade—US$690,490m deficit (2010)
Current Account—US$470,898m deficit (2010)

Trade with UK	2010	2011
Imports from UK	£37,436,308,922	£38,979,793,542
Exports to UK	£34,889,461,456	£30,295,972,028

COMMUNICATIONS

Airports—There are over 15,000 airports; nearly 200 are capable of handling international flights, the rest cater for the high domestic demand
Waterways—The main seaports are at Baton Rouge, Corpus Christi, Hampton Roads, Houston, Long Beach, Los Angeles, Miami, New Orleans, New York, Oaklands, Plaquemines, Port Canaveral, Port Everglades, Savannah, Seattle, Tampa and Texas City
Roadways—There are 6,506,204km of roads, including 75,238km of motorways
Railways—There are 224,792km of railways
Telecommunications—151 million fixed lines and 279 million mobile subscriptions (2009); there were 245 million internet users in 2009
Internet code and IDD—us; 1 (from UK), 011 44 (to UK)
Major broadcasters—The major television networks are ABC, CBS, NBC, CNN, Fox, MTV, HBO and the Public Broadcasting System, which serves around 350 local member stations and is partially funded by the government and by private grants
Press—There are more than 1,500 daily newspapers, including *The Wall Street Journal, USA Today, The Washington Post* and *The New York Times*
WPFI score—6,75 (20)

EDUCATION AND HEALTH

All the states have compulsory school attendance laws. In general, children are obliged to attend school from seven to 16 years of age.
Gross enrolment ratio (percentage of relevant age group)—primary 104%; secondary 96%; tertiary 89% (2009 est)
Health expenditure (per capita)—US$7,410 (2009)
Hospital beds (per 1,000 people)—3.1 (2004–9)
Life expectancy (years)—78.49 (2012 est)
Mortality rate—8.39 (2012 est)
Birth rate—13.68 (2012 est)
Infant mortality rate—5.98 (2012 est)

CULTURE

The culture of the USA is indebted to the diverse origins of its immigrants; European, African and Latin American influences are particularly strong.

The best-known writers include Mark Twain (1835–1910), Henry James (1843–1916), and poets Walt Whitman (1819–92) and Emily Dickinson (1830–86) in the 19th century; William Faulkner (1897–1962), Ernest Hemingway (1899–1961), John Steinbeck (1902–68), poet Robert Frost (1874–1963) and dramatist Eugene O'Neill (1888–1953) in the early 20th century; and Saul Bellow (1915–2005), John Updike (1932–2009), Philip Roth (*b.* 1933) and playwrights Arthur Miller (1915–2005) and Tennessee Williams (1911–83) among the post-war generation. African-American literature has been assimilated into the literary canon through the works of James Baldwin (1924-87), Maya Angelou (*b.* 1928), Toni Morrison (*b.* 1931) and Alice Walker (*b.* 1944).

The Hollywood film industry is the most wide-reaching in the world; celebrated film-makers include Walt Disney (1901–66), Orson Welles (1915–85), Stanley Kubrick (1928–99), Martin Scorsese (*b.* 1942) and Steven Spielberg (b. 1946).

Renowned artists include Edward Hopper (1882–1967), Jackson Pollock (1912–56), Roy Lichtenstein (1923–97) and Andy Warhol (1928–87).

Musical icons include Elvis Presley (1935–77) and Bob Dylan (*b.* 1941) in rock, Hank Williams (1923–53) and Johnny Cash (1932–2003) in country music, Leadbelly (1888–1949) and Muddy Waters (1915–83) in blues, and Louis Armstrong (1901–71), Miles Davis (1926–91) and John Coltrane (1926–67) in jazz.

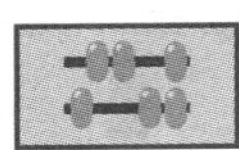

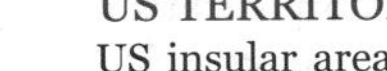

US TERRITORIES ETC

US insular areas are territories that are not part of one of the 50 US states or a federal district. The US Department of the Interior's Office of Insular Affairs has jurisdiction over American Samoa, Guam, the Northern Mariana Islands, the US Virgin Islands, part of Palmyra Atoll (4 sq. km) and Wake Atoll (6.4 sq. km), the latter shared with the US army's Space and Strategic Defence Command. The US Fish and Wildlife Service has jurisdiction over Baker Island (1.5 sq. km), Howland Island (2.5 sq. km), Jarvis Island (4.2 sq. km), Johnston Atoll (2.5 sq. km, shared with the Defence Threat Reduction Agency), Midway Atoll (5.2 sq. km), Navassa Island (7.8 sq. km), Kingman Reef and part of Palmyra Atoll. The Aleutian Islands (17,666 sq. km) form part of the Alaskan archipelago.

American Samoa

Territory of American Samoa
Area—199 sq. km
Capital—Pago Pago
Population—68,061 rising at 1.21% per year (2011 est)
National day—17 April (Flag Day)
American Samoa consists of the islands of Tutuila, Aunu'u, Ofu, Olosega, Ta'u, Rose Island and Swains Island. The islands were discovered by Europeans in the 18th century and the USA took possession in 1900. Those born in American Samoa are US non-citizen nationals, although some have acquired citizenship through service in the US armed forces or other naturalisation procedures. American Samoa is represented in Congress by a non-voting delegate, who is directly elected for a two-year term. Under the 1966 constitution, American Samoa has a measure of self-government, with certain powers reserved to the US Secretary of the Interior. The governor and deputy governor are directly elected for a four-year term. The bicameral legislative assembly comprises a 21-member House of Representatives (one appointed member and 20 members directly elected for a two-year term) and an 18-seat senate with members elected from among the traditional chiefs for a four-year term. Tuna fishing and canning are the principal economic activities. The economy and infrastructure were severely damaged by a tsunami in 2009.
Governor, Togiola Tulafono (D)

Guam

Guahan—Territory of Guam
Area—541.3 sq. km
Capital—Hagatna (also known as Agana); population, 149,000 (2007 est)
Population—185,674 rising at 1.28% per year (2011 est); Chamorro (37%), Filipino (26%), other Pacific islander (11%). The official languages are Chamorro (a language of the Malayo-Polynesian family with admixtures of Spanish) and English; most Chamorro residents are bilingual
National day—first Monday in March (Discovery Day)
Guam is the largest of the Mariana Islands, in the north Pacific Ocean. A Spanish colony for centuries, it was ceded to the USA in 1898 after the Spanish–American War. Guam was occupied by the Japanese in 1941 but was recaptured by US forces in 1944. Any person born in Guam is a US citizen. Guam is represented in Congress by a non-voting delegate, who is directly elected for a two-year term. Under the Organic Act of Guam 1950, Guam has statutory powers of self-government. The governor and lieutenant-governor are directly elected for a four-year term. The 15-member unicameral legislature is directly elected every two years. The main sources of revenue are tourism (particularly from Japan) and US military spending; the military installation is one of the most strategically important US bases in the Pacific.
Governor, Eddie Calvo (R)

Trade with UK	2010	2011
Imports from UK	£1,077,570	£3,162,433
Exports to UK	£13,646	£6,342

Northern Mariana Islands

Commonwealth of the Northern Mariana Islands
Area—464 sq. km
Seat of government—Saipan
Population—44,582 falling at 2.45% per year (2011 est)
National day—8 January (Commonwealth Day)
The USA administered the Northern Mariana Islands, a group of 14 islands in the north-west Pacific Ocean, as part of a UN trusteeship until the trusteeship agreement was terminated in 1986, when the islands became a commonwealth under US sovereignty. Those resident in 1976 or subsequently born in the islands are US citizens. The islands are represented in Congress by a non-voting representative, who is directly elected for a two-year term. Under the 1978 constitution, the islands are self-governing. The governor and lieutenant-governor are directly elected for a four-year term. The bicameral legislature comprises a 20-member House of Representatives and a nine-member senate; members are directly elected, representatives for two years and senators for four years. Tourism and manufacturing, especially of clothing, are the main industries.
Governor, Benigno Fitial (R)

Puerto Rico

Commonwealth of Puerto Rico
Area—13,790 sq. km
Capital—San Juan; population, 2,729,980 (2009 est). Other major towns are: Bayamón, Carolina, Poncel
Population—3,998,905 rising at 0.24% per year (2011 est); most people are of Spanish descent. The official languages are Spanish and English
National day—25 July (Constitution Day)
Puerto Rico (Rich Port) is an island of the Greater Antilles group in the Caribbean Sea and was discovered in 1493 by Columbus. It was a Spanish possession until 1898, when it was ceded to the USA after the Spanish–American War. Residents have been US citizens since 1917, and Puerto Rico is represented in Congress by a non-voting resident commissioner, who is directly elected for a four-year term. Under its 1952 constitution, Puerto Rico is a self-governing commonwealth. The governor is directly elected for a four-year term. The bicameral legislative assembly consists of a 27-member senate and a 51-member House of Representatives, whose members serve four-year terms. Tourism, pharmaceuticals, electronics, clothing and food processing are the main economic activities.
Governor, Luis G. Fortuño (R)

The United States Virgin Islands

Area—1,910 sq. km
Capital—Charlotte Amalie, on St Thomas; population, 53,526 (2009 est)
Population—109,574 falling at 0.09% per year (2011 est)
National day—31 March (Transfer Day)
There are three main islands, St Thomas, St Croix and St John, and about 50 small islets or cays. These constituted the Danish part of

the Virgin Islands from the 17th century until purchased by the USA in 1917. Those born in the US Virgin Islands are US nationals. The Virgin Islands are represented in Congress by a non-voting representative, who is directly elected for a two-year term. Under the provisions of the Revised Organic Act of 1954, the islands have powers of self-government. The governor and lieutenant-governor are directly elected for a four-year term. The unicameral senate has 15 members directly elected for a two-year term. Tourism, oil refining and manufacturing are the main industries.

Governor, John de Jongh Jr (D)

Venezuela

República Bolivariana de Venezuela—Bolivarian Republic of Venezuela

Area—912,050 sq. km

Capital—Caracas; population, 3,050,770 (2009 est)

Major cities—Barquisimeto, Ciudad Guayana, Maracaibo, Valencia

Currency—Bolívar fuerte (Bs. F) of 100 céntimos

Population—28,047,938 rising at 1.47% a year (2012 est)

Religion—Christian (Roman Catholic 96%, Protestant 2%); other 2% (est)

Language—Spanish (official), several indigenous languages

Population density—33 per sq. km (2010)

Urban population—94% (2010 est)

Median age (years)—26.1 (2011 est)

National anthem—'Gloria al Bravo Pueblo' ['Glory to the Brave People']

National day—5 July (Independence Day)

Death penalty—Abolished for all crimes (since 1863)

CPI score—1.9 (2011)

FINANCIAL OUTLOOK

With President Hugo Chavez battling cancer, key economic decisions in Venezuela, such as when and by how much to devalue the currency in the face of 25–30% inflationary prospects, were harming the country's troubled economy at the start of 2013. Matters were not helped by Chavez's death in March 2013. His successors seem likely to continue his brand of "petro-socialism" while running down the non-oil economy through incompetence. The*Venezuelan Daily Brief*, which provides bi-weekly summaries of key news items affecting bulk commodities in Venezuela, reports that 67% of businessmen in the country believe they will have "some problems in supplying goods and services in the next six months." Since taking office in 1999, Chavez seized more than 1000 companies, but international money markets have stayed open to Venezuela since Chavez used the country's oil revenues to repay interest on bonds. Agriculture-related exports have dropped 90% over the past decade, while other MERCOSUR nations have seen a 304% increase in agricultural exports over that time. Inflation has run at 26.5% for the last five years. Although the country runs an average deficit of no more than 5.6% per year, the nation's debt has jumped from 23% of GDP in 2008 to 51% of GDP by 2012. Much of the cause for this is thought to be the flight of cash into US dollars despite Venezuela's stringent currency control regime. A report from Barclays Capital shows that some US$150 billion has fled the country by backdoor routes since Chavez introduced currency controls in 2003—almost triple the amount that was leaving the country before the imposition of capital controls.

CLIMATE AND TERRAIN

The Andean mountains, of which the main range is the Sierra Nevada de Mérida, run across the north-west of the country, separating the northern coast from the central plains *(llanos)*. The Guiana Highlands occupy the south-east of the country. Elevation extremes range from 5,007m (Pico Bolivar) to 0m (Caribbean Sea). The Orinoco flows across the centre of the country to its delta on the Atlantic coast. Its upper waters are united with those of the Rio Negro (a Brazilian tributary of the Amazon) by a natural river or canal, known as the Brazo Casiquiare. The coastal lowlands contain many lagoons and lakes, including Lake Maracaibo (area 13,351 sq. km), the largest lake in South America. The climate varies from tropical to alpine, depending on altitude, and most areas experience a wet season from May to November. Average temperatures in Caracas range from 14°C in January to 27°C in April and May.

HISTORY AND POLITICS

Columbus landed on the coast in 1498, and the first Spanish settlement was established at Cumaná in 1520. Venezuela became part of the Viceroyalty of New Granada in the early 18th century. There were several revolts against Spanish colonial rule, and a declaration of independence in 1811 was followed by several years of struggle until troops led by Simón Bolivar defeated the Spanish at the battle of Carabobo in 1821. Venezuela became part of Gran Colombia (with Colombia, Ecuador and Panama), and then an independent republic in 1830 under the first of a series of *caudillos* (military leaders). The first truly democratic elections were held in 1947 but the government was overthrown by the military within months. An enduring civilian democracy was established in 1958 and introduced a period of relative political stability.

Oil revenues supported a buoyant economy in the 1970s but a price collapse in the mid-1980s led to economic difficulties and widespread poverty, causing social unrest and a number of attempted coups. Since he came to power in 1998, President Hugo Chávez's economic and social reforms and his authoritarian style have polarised domestic opinion, provoking strikes and demonstrations, an attempted military coup in 2002 and a recall referendum in 2004, which he won.

President Chávez was re-elected again in 2006. In the 2010 legislative election, the president's United Socialist Party of Venezuela and its allies won an overall majority, but lost its two-thirds majority (needed to change the constitution) as opposition parties won 67 seats.

Under the 1999 constitution, the executive president is directly elected for a six-year term; the limit on the number of successive terms was abolished in 2009. The unicameral National Assembly has 165 members, 162 directly elected and three representing indigenous people, who serve a five-year term. The president appoints the vice-president and the council of ministers.

The country is divided into 23 states, one capital district and one federal dependency composed of 11 island groups (72 individual islands). The states have considerable autonomy and each has its own legislature and elected governor.

HEAD OF STATE

President, Col. (retd) Hugo Chávez Frías, *elected* 6 December 1998, *sworn in* 2 February 1999, *re-elected* 2000, 2006

Vice-President, Elías Jaua Milano

  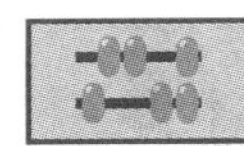      

SELECTED GOVERNMENT MEMBERS *as at July 2012*
Interior and Justice, Tarek El Aissami
Defence, Henry Silva
Trade, Richard Canan

EMBASSY OF THE BOLIVARIAN REPUBLIC OF VENEZUELA
1 Cromwell Road, London SW7 2HW
T 020-7584 4206
E info@venezlon.co.uk
W www.embavenez-uk.org
Ambassador Extraordinary and Plenipotentiary, HE Samuel Moncada, *apptd* 2007

BRITISH EMBASSY
Edificio Torre la Castellana, Piso 11, Avenida la Principal de la Castellana, Caracas 1601
T (+58) (212) 263 8411
E britishembassy@internet.ve
W ukinvenezuela.fco.gov.uk
Ambassador Extraordinary and Plenipotentiary, HE Catherine Nettleton, *apptd* 2010

DEFENCE

All aged 16–49, 2010 est	*Males*	*Females*
Available for military service	7,013,854	7,165,661
Fit for military service	5,614,743	6,074,834

Military expenditure—US$3,115m (2011)
Conscription duration—30 months (selective)

ECONOMY AND TRADE

Much of industry is state-owned, and since President Chávez came to power an increasing proportion of the private sector, some foreign-owned, has been nationalised, including oil, electricity, financial, steel, construction and agribusiness companies. Laws passed in December 2010 will increase government control of the economy, which is struggling because of imbalances, high inflation and electricity shortages after a severe drought in 2009–10 left hydroelectric plants inoperable.

Oil and gas are the mainstays of the economy, providing over 95% of exports and over 40% of government revenue, but heavy dependence on them makes the economy vulnerable to global price fluctuations. The economy went into recession in 2009 owing to lower prices and the global downturn.

Other major industries are mining (coal, iron ore, bauxite, gold), production of construction materials, textiles, steel and aluminium, food processing and vehicle assembly. Industry contributes 35.8% of GDP and services 60.4%.

Agriculture comprises large-scale commercial farms and subsistence farming. Land distribution is uneven, but redistribution of land to the rural poor, breaking up larger estates, has begun. Agricultural products include maize, sorghum, sugar cane, rice, bananas, vegetables and coffee. There is an extensive beef and dairy farming industry. Agriculture provides 3.8% of GDP and engages 7.3% of the workforce.

The main trading partners are the USA (38.7% of exports; 26.6% of imports), Colombia, China and Brazil. Principal exports are oil, bauxite and aluminium, minerals, chemicals, agricultural products and basic manufactures. The main imports are agricultural products, raw materials, machinery, transport equipment and construction materials.

GNI—US$389,037m; US$11,590 per capita (2010)
Annual average growth of GDP—2.8% (2011 est)
Inflation rate—28.9% (2011 est)
Population below poverty line—27.4% (2011 est)
Unemployment—7.3% (2011 est)
Total external debt—US$89,600m (2011 est)
Imports—US$33,815m (2010)
Exports—US$65,800m (2010)

BALANCE OF PAYMENTS
Trade—US$31,985m surplus (2010)
Current Account—US$14,378m surplus (2010)

Trade with UK	*2010*	*2011*
Imports from UK	£217,847,335	£300,936,705
Exports to UK	£379,821,201	£392,297,029

COMMUNICATIONS

Airports and waterways—There are over 400 airports, the principal airports being at Caracas and Maracaibo; the main ports are Maracaibo, Puerto Cabello and Caracas-La Guaira
Roadways and railways—There are 96,155km of roads and 806km of railways
Telecommunications—7.08 million fixed lines in use and 27.88 million mobile subscriptions (2009); there were 8.9 million internet users in 2009
Internet code and IDD—ve; 58 (from UK), 44 (to UK)
Major broadcasters—Radio Caracas Television had its terrestrial licence terminated in 2007; other networks include the government-run Venezolana de Television
Press—There are six daily newspapers, including *El Mundo* and *El Nacional*
WPFI score—47,33 (133)

EDUCATION AND HEALTH

There are nine years of compulsory education.
Literacy rate—95.2% (2007 est)
Gross enrolment ratio (percentage of relevant age group)—primary 103%; secondary 83% (2010 est); tertiary 78% (2009 est)
Health expenditure (per capita)—US$686 (2009)
Hospital beds (per 1,000 people)—1.3 (2004–9)
Life expectancy (years)—74.08 (2012 est)
Mortality rate—5.2 (2012 est)
Birth rate—19.88 (2012 est)
Infant mortality rate—20.18 (2012 est)

Vietnam

Cong Hoa Xa Hoi Chu Nghia Viet Nam—Socialist Republic of Vietnam
Area—331,210 sq. km
Capital—Hanoi; population, 2,667,800 (2009 est)
Major cities—Bien Hoa, Da Nang, Haiphong, Ho Chi Minh City (Saigon)
Currency—Dong of 10 ho or 100 xu

  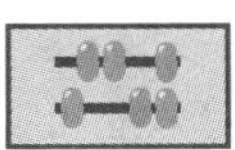      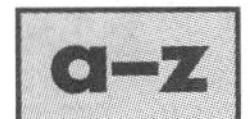

Population—91,519,289 rising at 1.05% a year (2012 est); Kinh (85.7%), Tay (1.9%), Thai (1.8%), Muong (1.5%), Khmer (1.5%), Hmong (1.2%), Nung (1.1%) (2009)
Religion—Buddhist 50% (predominantly Mahayana), Christian (Roman Catholic 7%, Protestant 1%), Cao Dai 3%, Hoa Hao 2% (est). Cao Dai is a syncretistic religion that combines elements of several faiths. Hoa Hao is a branch of Buddhism
Language—Vietnamese (official), English, French, Chinese, Khmer; Mon-Khmer and Malayo-Polynesian are spoken in mountain areas
Population density—280 per sq. km (2010)
Urban population—28.8% (2010 est)
Median age (years)—27.8 (2011 est)
National anthem—'Tien Quan Ca' ['Army March']
National day—2 September (Independence Day)
Death penalty—Retained
CPI score—2.9 (2011)

FINANCIAL OUTLOOK

The economy grew by 5.08% in 2012, down from 5.9% in 2011, the lowest level in 13 years, according to official figures. High-profile corruption scandals, falling investor confidence, and record levels of bad debt, partly caused by a burst property bubble, weighed on the economy. A credit squeeze prompted a record number of business failures in 2011 and 2012. In 2012, the central bank increased its estimate of the total ratio of banks' bad debt to 8.8%, the highest in South-East Asia. However, Standard Chartered believes the true figure is much higher at 15–20%. In December 2012, the World Bank forecast that Vietnam's economy would expand by 5.5% in 2013. The central bank cut its refinancing for the sixth time in December 2012. However, in January 2013, the World Bank warned that the country faces the risk of double-digit inflation in 2013.

CLIMATE AND TERRAIN

The country is mostly mountainous, apart from the densely populated fertile plains around the deltas of the Hong (Red River) in the north and the Mekong in the south. Elevation extremes range from 3,144m (Fan Si Pan) to 0m (South China Sea). The climate is tropical and affected by the monsoon cycle. The wet season lasts from May to September, although the coast, being affected by typhoons and tropical storms, receives most rain between September and January.

HISTORY AND POLITICS

The 1992 constitution was amended in 2001 to allow small-scale capitalism greater freedom. The president is elected by the legislature to serve a five-year term. The unicameral National Assembly *(Quoc-Hoi)* has 500 members, who are directly elected for a five-year term. The head of government is the prime minister, who is responsible to the National Assembly, which appoints the council of ministers. However, effective power lies with the Communist Party of Vietnam. Its highest executive body is the Central Committee, elected by the national party congress held every five years. The politburo and the secretariat of the central committee, which exercise the real power, are elected at the party congress.

After the 2006 Communist Party Congress, the president and prime minister resigned to allow a younger leadership to be appointed; Nguyen Minh Triet was elected president to complete his predecessor's term of office, and he appointed Nguyen Tan Dung as prime minister. Both were re-elected to their posts in 2007, but the former lost the 2011 presidential race to Truong Tan Sang. In the May 2011 legislative election, the Communist Party and its allies held all the seats apart from four won by independent candidates.

HEAD OF STATE

President, Truong Tan Sang, *elected* 25 July 2011
Vice-President, Nguyen Thi Doan

SELECTED GOVERNMENT MEMBERS *as at July 2012*

Prime Minister, Nguyen Tan Dung
Deputy Prime Ministers, Vu Van Ninh; Nguyen Thien Nhan; Hoang Trung Hai; Nguyen Xuan Phuc
Finance, Vuong Dinh Hue
Internal Affairs, Nguyen Thai Binh

EMBASSY OF THE SOCIALIST REPUBLIC OF VIETNAM

12–14 Victoria Road, London W8 5RD
T 020-7937 1912
E consular@vietnamembassy.org.uk
W www.vietnamembassy.org.uk
Ambassador Extraordinary and Plenipotentiary, HE Vu Quang Minh, *apptd* 2011

BRITISH EMBASSY

Central Building, 31 Hai Ba Trung, Hanoi
T (+84) (4) 936 0500
E behanoi02@vnn.vn
W ukinvietnam.fco.gov.uk
Ambassador Extraordinary and Plenipotentiary, HE Dr Antony Stokes, LVO, *apptd* 2010

DEFENCE

All aged 16–49, 2010 est	Males	Females
Available for military service	25,649,738	24,995,692
Fit for military service	20,405,847	21,098,102

Military expenditure—US$2,487m (2011)
Conscription duration—24–36 months

ECONOMY AND TRADE

The economy struggled for a decade after 1975 owing to the devastation of war and the imposition of a centrally planned economy. Since economic liberalisation and international integration were adopted in 1986, the economy has grown substantially, albeit from a low base, and export-driven industries are being developed. Poverty was reduced by over 40% between 1993 and 2007, although more remote rural areas have yet to benefit. The global downturn reduced economic growth in 2008–9, and in early 2012 the government introduced a three-fold economic reform programme, proposing a restructuring of the banking sector, public spending and state-owned enterprises.

Agriculture's contribution is gradually shrinking, but still accounts for 22% of GDP and employs 48% of the workforce. The main industries are food processing, clothing and footwear, machine building, coal mining, steel, cement, chemical fertiliser, glass, tyres and paper, and oil and gas production from large offshore reserves. Industry now contributes 40.3% of GDP and services 37.7%.

The main trading partners are China, Japan, the USA and South Korea. Principal exports are clothing, footwear, fish and seafood, crude oil, electronics, wood products, rice and machinery. The main imports are machinery and equipment, petroleum products, steel products, raw materials, electronics, plastics and vehicles.

GNI—US$102,007m; US$1,160 per capita (2010)
Annual average growth of GDP—5.8% (2011 est)

Inflation rate—18.9% (2011 est)
Population below poverty line—14.5% (2010 est)
Unemployment—2.3% (2011 est)
Total external debt—US$37,340m (2011 est)
Imports—US$83,800m (2010)
Exports—US$71,700m (2010)

BALANCE OF PAYMENTS
Trade—US$12,100m deficit (2010)
Current Account—US$3,928m deficit (2010)

Trade with UK	2010	2011
Imports from UK	£276,293,147	£325,334,242
Exports to UK	£1,236,732,020	£1,666,605,141

COMMUNICATIONS
Airports and waterways—The principal airports and ports are at Ho Chi Minh City, Hanoi and Da Nang
Roadways and railways—There are 180,549km of roads and 2,632km of railways
Telecommunications—16.4 million fixed lines and 154 million mobile subscriptions (2009); there were 23.38 million internet users in 2009
Internet code and IDD—vn; 84 (from UK), 44 (to UK)
Major broadcasters—VTV is the state-run broadcaster
Press—There are over a hundred different newspapers and magazines, including *Nhan Dan*, the Communist Party daily and the English-language *Vietnam Economic Times*
WPFI score—75,75 (165)

EDUCATION AND HEALTH
Literacy rate—92.8% (2009 est)
Gross enrolment ratio (percentage of relevant age group)—primary 106% (2010 est); secondary 77% (2008 est); tertiary 22% (2010 est)
Health expenditure (per capita)—US$80 (2009)
Hospital beds (per 1,000 people)—2.9 (2004–9)
Life expectancy (years)—72.41 (2012 est)
Mortality rate—5.95 (2012 est)
Birth rate—16.83 (2012 est)
Infant mortality rate—20.24 (2012 est)

  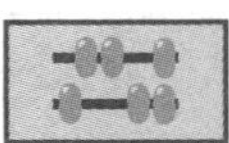      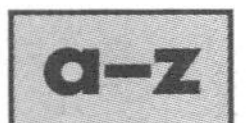

Automobiles

MAJOR INDUSTRY TRENDS

Far-reaching innovations in technology, plus rising demand and increased manufacturing capacity in emerging markets are set to change the automotive sector dramatically. A report by Deloitte (2009) argues that the current situation, with 15 major players located in just four countries, is inevitably going to see a contraction in manufacturer numbers, even as it sees India and China joining the ranks of top automotive producing countries.

According to the Deloitte report, we will see the number of original equipment manufacturers (OEMs) capable of producing high volumes of vehicles shrinking to 10, spread across six major markets instead of the current four. Major players will look to establish headquarters and/or operations in the new manufacturing hubs in China and India, and both these countries will become centers of design and manufacturing for OEMs, breaking the current dominance enjoyed by Western Europe, Japan, Korea, and the United States.

The key technology trends that will drive the industry through this period, the report says, are advances in powertrain technology and the move to electric motors, the shift from mechanics to electronics, and what the report calls "low-tech mobility." This latter term simply points to the huge potential market for low-cost, attractive, but extremely basic vehicles such as the Tata Nano in India, which comes without power steering and with few of the features of a modern even sub-£10,000 car. This is the vehicle type that will sell best to a rising lower-middle class consumer base with little disposable income.

The shift in power to emerging markets from advanced markets is underscored by an APCO Worldwide (2010) report on China's automotive industry. Sales of 17 million vehicles in China in 2010 matched the highest total ever recorded in the United States. In 2012, according to the China Association of Automobile Manufacturers (CAAM), automobile production in China reached 15,720,100 units by October, with two months' production still to come. Since October's production alone was just over 1.5 million cars, that suggests that total production for 2012 could be in excess of 18 million units.

By comparison, according to a report by Rosen and DuBord (2012) on the US auto industry, US producers and importers were expected to sell some 13.8 million cars in 2012, including a large number of foreign brands. With a large proportion of these sales being small, fuel-efficient Japanese and European cars, US domestic car production will be dwarfed by China's levels.

The Impact of Climate Change on Auto Demand and Design

Customer demand and regulatory pressure driven by climate change concerns are already interacting to transform the way manufacturers think about vehicle and engine design. Fuel efficiency is fundamental to reducing CO_2emissions, so there is already a considerable effort underway to improve powertrain technology. In its report on the auto industry to 2020, Deloitte argues that improved fuel efficiencies from advanced combustion engines will enable petrol and diesel engines to extend their reign over alternative engines such as electrical and gas-driven engines. However, Deloitte sees scope for considerable advances in electric vehicles, with the bulk of the demand coming from advanced markets, while emerging markets favor flex-fuels such as ethanol and natural gas.

Government policies will have a very important role in determining engine preferences at a national level. In setting these policies, governments will be driven by at least two major factors. One will, of course, be a desire to tighten carbon emission standards. The second consideration for a number of countries will be the desire to lessen the state's dependence on foreign energy resources. By 2020, Deloitte says, electric cars and other "green" vehicles will represent up to a third of total global sales in developed markets, and up to 20% in urban areas of emerging markets.

The recent joint report from the International Energy Agency, the Rocky Mountain Institute, and Clean Energy Ministerial (IEA et al., 2012) points out that a number of cities around the world either already have or are busy formulating transport policies within their environs that will mandate the use of electric vehicles, as these cities work to become fossil fuel-free. The IEA is working with a group of cities that are collaborating to launch the World EV (electric vehicle) Cities and Ecosystems web portal, the aim of which is to share best practice in EV deployment. "By working together and sharing knowledge, cities from diverse regions and countries will realize the benefits of electric mobility and achieve a sustainable energy future," the foreword to the report says. All of this will have a real impact on the auto sector over the next few years. With transportation accounting for approximately one-fifth of global primary energy use, and a quarter of all energy-related CO_2-emissions, governments have a considerable incentive to prioritize "green" vehicles, despite any strides the auto industry might make in developing fuel-efficient combustion engines.

According to the report, thanks to the cumulative national targets for EV and plug-in hybrid EV (PHEV) vehicles announced by Electric Vehicle Initiative (EVI) member governments, there is likely to be some 20 million EVs on the road by 2020, amounting to 6% of total vehicle sales each year. The IEA recognizes that there are real challenges to the widespread deployment of EVs, but it points out that some 40,000 EV cars were sold worldwide through 2011, the highest total to date.

The Deloitte report is somewhat more subdued on the subject of EVs, pointing out that of the 49.6 million cars on the road in Germany, for example, only around 1,500 of them are EVs, with a further 22,300 being hybrid models. Deloitte highlights four major challenges to the widespread adoption of EVs: the elevated cost, their limited range, the lack of infrastructure, and the lack of government incentives or subsidies to hasten their adoption.

The Growth of Cities and the Demand for Cars

The continuing movement of global populations into cities and away from the countryside is going to have an inevitable impact on the kinds of vehicles that consumers are going to want. In addition to the likelihood that city planners and authorities will want to prioritize fossil fuel-free vehicles within the environs of their cities, crowded city roads and limited parking spaces will drive consumer choice towards smaller, more compact vehicles. According to the Deloitte report, about three-quarters of the population in developed countries currently lives in urban centers, while the figure for developing country populations is around 45%, and is set to rise strongly in a number of countries. By 2020, the world will have at least 24 megacities with populations in excess of 10 million. Current research suggests that by far the biggest demand in these cities will be for compact EV cars with great infotainment systems.

MARKET ANALYSIS

Economic Crisis and Structural Transformation

Deloitte points out that the economic crisis which began in 2008 and is likely to continue until at least 2015, has accelerated deep structural change in the automotive industry. "High-cost exporting countries will see domestic capacity closed as vehicle production continues to migrate to the 'new Detroits,' namely lower-cost centers dotted across India and China, and other locations in the regional trade zones of the North American Free Trade Agreement (NAFTA) and the European Union," the report says.

Manufacturers are already reconfiguring their production capacity around high-volume global platform architectures. To support this, we will see the emergence of new business models characterized by alliances with key players in other industry sectors that have the new skills required by advances in technology and electronics. There will also be a "recalibration" of the automotive industry supply chain, which was forced on the sector by the decline in sales during the period from 2009 to 2012. This, together with the emergence of new manufacturing capacity in India and China, has created global overcapacity, which is particularly evident in plants in Europe and North America. "Profitability for OEMs has been hurt and margins for suppliers have sunk below the break-even level," the report warns. A rash of bankruptcies and the high-profile government bailout of key auto industry players in the United States and elsewhere underscore this point. The future, however, looks brighter for a reconfigured automotive sector, with current predictions cited by the report pointing to around 70 million units being sold worldwide by 2015.

The Major Players

Volkswagen once again came out as the world's top auto manufacturer in Forbes's survey of the world's top 2000 companies (Campbell, 2012). It ranked 17th in the survey, up seven places from 2011, and has had a stellar 2012. Volkswagen Group recorded a 10.2% increase, to 7.5 million vehicles, in the nine months from January to October 2012, with output rising to 14.6% in October, at 788,700 vehicles. There were strong performances in North America, China, and Russia. Volkswagen grew its sales to customers in North America by 25.4%, and in Russia by 46.7%, albeit from a much smaller base. In the Asia-Pacific region, sales grew by 19%, with some 2.15 million vehicles being sold. However, difficult market conditions in Europe saw Volkswagen's sales there sliding by 5.8% (Volkswagen, 2012).

Toyota came in as the second in the industry, ranked 25th overall. Up to October 2012, the company had produced 8.469 million vehicles worldwide in the calendar year, with October seeing the first increase in Toyota production for two months, thanks to increased production in Australia, Asia, Latin America, and North America (Toyota, 2012b). Of the company's two other brands, Daihatsu enjoyed its second consecutive month of increased production, and Hinos its 16th. Announcing its financial results for the first half of fiscal 2013, Toyota (2012a) reported net revenues were up by 36.1%, compared with the same period last year, a significant rebound which saw a loss of ¥32.6 billion turned around into a profit of ¥693.7 billion. Toyota put the turnaround down to good marketing and cost reductions of some ¥230 billion.

Daimler, which owns Mercedes-Benz, is the next-highest-placed auto manufacturer in 37th, up six places on 2011. The company reported net profits of €1,205 million for the third quarter of 2012, slightly down on the same quarter in 2011, but Group revenues were up by 8%, to €28.6 billion (€26.4 billion in Q3 2011). Daimler's chairman, Dieter Zetsche, who also heads up Mercedes-Benz, called the results good, in light of difficult market conditions.

Ford came up 10 places to 44th, followed by Japan's **Honda Motors** at 59, with Germany's **BMW** coming in at 61. Next was **General Motors** at 63, down two places from 2011.

MORE INFO

Articles:

Campbell, Matt. "Rankings: World's biggest car companies." *Drive.com.au* (April 20, 2012). Online at: tinyurl.com/lnqatb8

Toyota. "TMC announces first half fiscal year 2013 financial results." November 5, 2012a. Online at: tinyurl.com/m7vj6bx [PDF].

Toyota. "TMC announces results for October 2012." November 29, 2012b. Online at: www2.toyota.co.jp/en/news/12/11/1129.html

Volkswagen. "News." November 16, 2012. Online at: tinyurl.com/m6f4vb7

Reports:

APCO Worldwide. "Market analysis report: China's automotive industry." November 2010. Online at: tinyurl.com/k33fkbo [PDF].

Rosen, Jeffrey S., and Kimberly N. DuBord. "State of the U.S. motor vehicle industry: 2012." *Briefing.com* (February 9, 2012). Online at: tinyurl.com/n3rshn7 [PDF].

Deloitte. "A new era. Accelerating towards 2020—An automotive industry transformed." 2009. Online at: tinyurl.com/mqpjq55

International Energy Agency (IEA), Rocky Mountain Institute (RMI), and Clean Energy Ministerial (CEM). "EV city casebook 2012: A look at the global electric vehicle movement." 2012. Online at: www.iea.org/evi/evcitycasebook.pdf

See Also:

Transport and Logistics (pp. 1651–1652)

Aviation

MAJOR INDUSTRY TRENDS

This report covers the entire aviation industry, including the airline and aerospace sectors. It focuses upon the civil sector of the aerospace business. The military sector is included in the separate sector profile on Defense.

The Economic Cycle and Aviation

The civil aviation industry is highly cyclical, being extremely sensitive to the economic cycle. In times of economic hardship, people simply fly less often than they do in the good times. In addition to being hostage to the economic cycle, the airline industry is struggling with two major factors, namely fuel costs, which seem to be on a perpetual path upwards, and the need to "green up." As the Economist (2012) has pointed out, the world's airlines operate on the tightest of margins, and the least ill wind can push even the most established players into administration or bankruptcy.

However, necessity, as the old saying has it, is often the mother of invention, and the big engine manufacturers that target the sector, such as Pratt & Whitney, Rolls-Royce, and GE, along with several innovative competitors, have all been looking to design more-efficient, leaner engines that use less fuel per mile and that are generally quieter, putting them comfortably inside the industry's latest noise abatement measures.

Connectivity

Connectivity is undoubtedly one of the biggest trends in the sector, with airlines racing to re-equip their cabins to provide passengers with internet capability and telephone connectivity while in flight.

Another development that has already made great advances in the business aviation sector, where price is often not an overriding consideration, is opening up the cabin management system (CMS) to the new "bring your own device" world. Major equipment providers such as Honeywell are already giving customers the option of using their tablet PCs, iPads, and iPods to watch movies and to interact with the entertainment resources on board. With commercial airlines, this trend will affect first-class cabins first, and will probably be slower to filter down to premium and economy-class cabins.

Supersonic Flight

Interestingly, while supersonic flight came to an end in commercial airline operations with the demise of Concorde in 2003, the business aviation world has a couple of players that are going flat out to try to bring both supersonic and hypersonic jets to market. Aerion is partnering with NASA to overcome the design issues involved in producing a supersonic business jet that will be capable of cutting hours off a long-range journey such as New York to Tokyo. Another company, HyperMach, now headquartered in the United Kingdom, is working on what would be the first hypersonic business jet. HyperMach CEO, Richard Lugg, reckons that his revolutionary hybrid electric and jet-fuel turbine engine will take his SonicStar aircraft with 24 passengers from London to New York in 55 minutes. These are exciting developments and show that the dream of supersonic and hypersonic flight has not died.

MARKET ANALYSIS

The current state of the global commercial airline business continues to be difficult at best. One of the deep structural issues that the industry faces is that it is very difficult to take overcapacity out of the sector while so many national airlines are propped up in various ways by government subsidies. What happens in other industries faced with overcapacity, namely a spate of mergers and takeovers, along with some high-profile failures, has all sorts of systemic barriers to overcome in the airline sector. This arguably prevents the market from functioning the way competitive markets should function.

By way of example, two of the biggest mergers in recent years, the merger between Air France and KLM, and the merger between British Airways and Iberia, were both accomplished through holding companies, with the result that both parties to the merger stayed largely independent of each other and could continue to be national in character. Part of the problem is that for an international airline to fly between two countries, the airline requires the bilateral agreement of both governments. This either involves the country concerned requiring a stake in the incoming airline or requiring reciprocity from that airline's government for its flag carrier. So far, no solution to this problem has been found and the only way in which the airline industry can seem to be truly global to its millions of passengers, is via alliances between airlines. These alliances allow baggage forwarding, through ticketing, and a multi-country network, which gives them an international flavor even as all the participants retain their domestic links.

The global airline industry has made a multi-billion-dollar loss in seven of the last 12 years. There is scarcely a major airline that is immune from potential bankruptcy, apart from the Gulf airlines, which are all cash-rich and expanding their businesses. Any sector with a profit margin of 3% or under is living on the edge. In fact, on December 13, 2012, the International Air Transport Association (IATA) announced that the net post-tax margin for the industry as a whole will barely amount to 1.0% for 2012 and 1.3% for 2013. That is such a wafer-thin margin that even a modest spike in fuel costs could tip the industry into yet another annual loss in 2013. In any event, IATA estimates that the industry needs a profit of between 7% and 8% to recover the cost of capital deployed. That does not look on the cards any time soon. IATA director-general Tony Tyler said in December 2012 that it seems likely that the world's airlines will return a profit of US$6.7 billion in 2012, which represents a downward revision of IATA's October 2012 prediction of US$7.5 billion. This amounts to just US$2.25 for every one of the 2.97 billion passengers carried in 2012, not much of a profit margin for a multi-billion-dollar sector.

Despite the thin-to-non-existent profits, passenger numbers continue to grow. In fact IATA points out that, despite high fuel prices and a slowing world economy, airline profits and cash flows held up at levels similar to 2006, when oil prices were US$45 per barrel lower and the world economy was growing at 4.0%.

Commenting on the numbers, Tyler said: "With global GDP growth close to the 'stall speed' of 2.0%, and with oil at US$109.55 a barrel, we expected much weaker performance. But airlines have adjusted to this difficult environment through improving efficiency and restructuring. That is protecting cash flows against weak economic growth and high fuel prices."

General aviation—The Scale of the Business and VIP Jet Market

As the international industry body, the General Aviation Manufacturers Association (GAMA), points out in its compilation of statistics on the sector (GAMA, 2012), the corporate and private jet sector is responsible for getting on for two million jobs worldwide and generates billions of dollars in revenue. This "general aviation" (GA) sector is defined as encompassing all aviation other than military and commercial aircraft, and includes everything from two-seater trainers to intercontinental business jets such as Bombardier's Lear 850 or the Gulfstream 650. There are more than 320,000 GA aircraft worldwide, and more than two-thirds of these are based in the United States, the world's largest GA market by far.

GA contributes more than US$150 billion to the US economy annually and employs some 1.265 million people. GA aircraft fly some 35 million hours annually in the US and carry around 166 million people. There are nearly 4,000 paved GA airports in the United States open to business jets. By contrast, there are just 500 commercial airports. At a stroke, this highlights one of the major reasons for the continued use of business jets by corporates and high-net-worth individuals. Even in the United States, there are a large number of town and city pairs that are not on commercial airline routes and that would require road trips of more than an hour or two for travelers to get from their desired destination to a commercial airport. In the emerging economies of India and China, business aviation has an even stronger case to make.

General aviation has always had to struggle against the public (and political) stereotypical view of private jets as toys for the super-rich. As the National Business Aviation Association (NBAA) points out in its "No Plane No Gain" campaign for 2012 and 2013, legislation follows perception, so the sector has to wage a constant struggle to avoid penal taxes being imposed, which would damage growth and jobs in the sector. One of the perennial ideas pushed by US politicians from time to time is a GA usage fee tax of US$100 per flight. When you consider that a corporate with an eight-seater jet will do at least 300 hours flying time each year, or around 30 trips with six to eight managers and executives flying to meetings with clients and suppliers, that amounts to 30 times 6 times 100, or a tax on the company of US$18,000. To a multinational such as Walmart, which works its corporate jets hard ferrying generally mid and low-level managers, buyers, and supplier relationship representatives out to the regions, the tax on the business would not be trivial.

The NBAA commissioned the research house NEXA to report on business jet usage by S&P 500 companies. It found that, between 2003 and 2009, users of business aircraft outnumbered non-users by three to one, and that users typically used business aircraft to drive increased revenues, profitability, and efficiencies. Business aircraft users outperformed non-users on several important financial measures for the period 2003 to 2007. On a market-cap-weighted basis, annual growth in revenues was 116% higher for users, earnings growth was 434% higher, and average annual EBIT growth was 83% higher. According to GAMA, more than two-thirds of all the hours flown by general aviation are for business purposes, and this includes all the leisure hours flown by small propeller and turbo-prop two-seater and four-seater aircraft.

Airbus and Boeing Growth Predictions for Sales of Commercial Aircraft

Despite the very thin profit margins experienced by commercial airlines worldwide, passenger numbers are continuing to climb. In its latest industry forecast for the period 2013–20, Boeing notes that passenger numbers for 2011 rose 6% above the figure for 2010. Boeing expects world passenger traffic to grow at 5% annually for the next 20 years. Air cargo traffic actually shrank slightly in 2011, down 2.4% on the figure for 2010. However, Boeing argues that emerging-market economies, with their hunger for goods and their thriving export engines, will foster a continuing need for air cargo, which Boeing expects to grow at an average annual rate of 5.2% up to 2031.

Taking these two facts into account, Boeing is forecasting a long-term demand for some 34,000 new airplanes to 2030, with a total value of US$4.5 trillion. "These new airplanes will replace older, less-efficient airplanes, benefiting airlines and passengers, and stimulating growth in emerging markets and innovation in airline business models," it says. The bulk of new orders, some 23,240 airplanes, will be single-aisle regional jets, reflecting growth in emerging markets such as China and India. The larger, twin-aisle segment of the market, which currently has an approximately19% share of today's fleet, will increase to 23% by 2031, Boeing says. These planes tend to be the intercontinental jets, so their arrival will foster the continuing globalization of trade and travel.

Airbus sees new-build demand for 2031 rising to 28,200 passenger and freight aircraft, somewhat down on Boeing's figures. Traffic growth between advanced and emerging air transport markets will run at an average annual rate of 5.1%, it says. This is ahead of the average global growth figure of 4.7%, and not far off the 6.6% growth anticipated for flights between emerging markets. Airbus also thinks that around 42% of all the aircraft larger than 100 seats in size will be delivered to carriers in the EU and North America.

Technological Developments

Aircraft makers are focused on reducing fuel consumption, and operating costs in general, in the battle to win orders from airlines. Fuel costs, which can account for 50% of an airline's operating costs, can make or break an airline. Boeing says that its 787 Dreamliner cuts fuel use by 20%, thanks to new engines, and the use of lightweight, composite materials. Meanwhile, Airbus says that the A380 is the first long-haul aircraft to consume less than three liters of fuel per passenger per 100 km, a rate comparable to an economical family car. It claims that the A380's efficiency and advanced technology result in 15–20% lower seat-mile costs than those of competitor aircraft. Fuel-efficient engines and the use of advanced composite materials have played a vital role in reducing the A380's operating costs. The airframe is made up of some 25% composite material by weight, while the Airbus A350XWB, which entered production in 2010, utilizes around 50% composite material.

Boeing and Airbus are also engaged in developing alternative fuels. Engine-makers Pratt & Whitney, Rolls-Royce, and General Electric are all involved, and momentum is being maintained, even though oil prices have fallen considerably from their mid-2008 peaks. IATA has a goal of 10% alternative fuels by 2017 while, in the United States, the Federal Aviation Administration is encouraging the use of new fuels. Several flights have already taken place using biofuels. In April 2010, for example, the Boeing F/A-18 Super Hornet, nicknamed the "Green Hornet," carried out a biofuel-powered flight and became the first US Navy fighter to be powered by a biofuel blend. The Navy noted that the F414 engine performed as expected during the 45-minute flight, and indicated "the aircraft did not know the difference between the bioblend and its traditional fuel source."

MORE INFO

Article:

Economist. "Struggling to take off." Economist Gulliver blog (October 1, 2012). Online at: tinyurl.com/lajemwa

Report:

General Aviation Manufacturers Association (GAMA). "2012 general aviation statistical databook and industry outlook." 2012. Online at: tinyurl.com/m4uulto

Websites:

Aerion: www.aerion.com

Aerospace Technology, analysis and news on aerospace-industry projects: www.aerospace-technology.com

Airbus, Global Market Forecast, 2012–31: www.airbus.com/company/market/forecast/

Boeing, Current Market Outlook, 2012–31: www.boeing.com/commercial/cmo

General Aviation Manufacturers Association (GAMA): www.gama.aero

HyperMach: www.hypermach.com

International Air Transport Association (IATA), provides statistics and information on the international aviation industry: www.iata.org

National Business Aviation Association (NBAA; US): www.nbaa.org

See Also:

Defense (pp. 1618–1620)

Transport and Logistics (pp. 1651–1652)

Banking and Financial Services

MAJOR INDUSTRY TRENDS

While regulation continues to be the biggest challenge facing the banking and financial services sector during 2013, banks are facing challenges on a number of other fronts. In its 2012 report on the banking sector, consultancy Accenture points out that some of the key strategies that the largest banks favored to boost earnings before the financial crash have now been discarded. The requirement to hold more capital for what are deemed to be riskier loans will reinforce the tendency to be risk-averse.

Proprietary dealing desks are already under threat, although banks have had some success in arguing with the regulator to the effect that it is impossible to distinguish between some kinds of proprietary trading and the bank simply providing traditional hedging services for its commercial clients.

One instance of the more restricted world that banks will be operating in lies in securitization deals, or rather their absence in the current climate. Banks will have plenty of disincentives predisposing them against going in for securitization plays. These had been seen as highly profitable in the run-up to the crash, but mortgage-backed securitization packages turned out to be one of the most toxic items on bank books during the crash of 2008, and the appetite for large-scale securitizations has yet to return.

As mainstream banks increasingly withdraw from lending to corporates with C-grade investment ratings, other players from outside the banking world are emerging to "cherry-pick" clients that the banks no longer want. "New risk-takers—outside the classic banking system—will emerge to raise and deploy capital," says the Accenture report. Already there are a number of new lenders interested in providing three to five-year loans to mid-range corporates at rates that are only slightly more expensive than traditional bank rates.

Another major trend that banks are grappling with is the emergence of innovative, mobile payments systems. This trend is bringing banks into direct competition with a range of new service providers. In a report on banking trends, Deutsche Bank (2012) points out that leading IT and software firms like Google and Apple, along with traditional payment services providers such as PayPal, are all active in bringing mobile payment systems to market. Card firms, too, are repositioning themselves to take advantage of payment via mobile phones, and telecoms providers are also potential suppliers, as they have systems designed to bill at periodic intervals for small amounts (individual phone calls).

This same theme emerged in a recent roundtable seminar hosted by IBM and FST Media. Brett King, a technology expert and futurologist, argued at the seminar that banks are going to find that customers are increasingly finding banks and traditional banking services irrelevant. The digitization of money and its disbursement electronically through the ubiquitous mobile phone represents a major threat to the bank's traditional relationship with its retail customers, and can leave bank branch networks looking woefully underutilized. Banks are going to have to respond rapidly, both by building relationships with new players like Google, and by "going mobile" themselves.

MARKET ANALYSIS

By the start of 2013, the debate between those who want to see big banks broken up to get rid of the "too big to fail" trap once and for all, and those who simply want better regulation of the banking sector still had to be resolved. Many senior bankers argue that as companies operate in an increasingly global world, they need the spread of services and geographies that only the biggest banks can provide, and that unitary banks, which combine investment and deposit-taking activities, are best placed to provide that full range of services. Bank services directly affect the economy for good or ill, so the power of the banking lobby to restrict political efforts to regulate the sector should not be underestimated.

The other factor is fear of regulatory arbitrage. If most countries regulate banks heavily but a few do not, those few could see a number of banks relocating to their territory, with beneficial consequences for them and negative consequences for the rest. So far, while there is some movement towards an international consensus, actually achieving it remains elusive.

There is an obvious relationship between bank regulation and its potential impact on the economy, particularly when the regulatory authorities are concerned—as they rightly should be—with ensuring that banks hold sufficient capital to be able to weather reasonable levels of stress in the market. The debate here is all about how much capital banks should be made to hold in reserve, and how quickly they should be asked to improve their capital adequacy. There are real fears that making banks hold more capital in reserve, and calculating the amount of capital required with reference to the risks inherent in the bank's lending book, will naturally lead to banks curtailing their lending to weaker companies. Clearly, cutting off riskier lending is one option, and in many instances it is seen as a more attractive option than raising more capital.

Basel III sets out minimum standards for enhancing bank capital requirements, and reducing the amount of leverage that banks should be allowed to consider prudent. It has been fiercely attacked by bankers as being far too pro-cyclical, i.e. likely to amplify positive and negative trends. The banking lobby also argues that Basel III is likely to pull money out of the economy (by making banks hold more capital) just when the economy most needs additional lending.

In addition to Basel III, there is a continuing effort by national regulators in general, and in the United Kingdom by the Financial Services Authority (FSA) and, as of April 1, 2013, its two replacement bodies, the Prudential Regulatory Board (PRB) and the Financial Conduct Authority (FCA), to work out what will be required to bring about an orderly resolution of any large, failed bank. Still another arm to this regulatory debate is the European Central Bank's proposal, put forward in June 2012 and apparently strongly underwritten at the EU summit on October 17, 2012, for a unitary banking regulator and a single resolution fund that would be capable of bailing out any failed European bank without need for recourse to that bank's sovereign government.

At a stroke, this is seen as the solution to breaking the pernicious negative feedback loop between failing banks and failing states, taking considerable pressure off the likes of Spain. It is important to note that the three regulatory initiatives aimed at banks, namely Basel III, the so-called "living wills" debate over how to manage the orderly failure of large banks, and a single European banking regulator, are all interrelated but somewhat independent regulatory projects. The single banking supervisory authority proposal was first mooted seriously by the European Union in June 2012, but in a fairly watery sort of way, with a lot of "wriggle room." The October 2012 meeting of heads of state sharpened this up remarkably, calling for legislators to draft legislation to bring a unitary banking regulator into existence by January 2013.

However, the path to banking union in the European Union is not going to be a smooth one. Speaking at a conference in Frankfurt on November 19, 2012, Jens Weidman, the head of the Bundesbank, warned that a banking union would not of itself cure the current crisis. There were only two paths that would lead to a solution, he told his audience. Either member states would have to take greater ownership and responsibility individually for their own problems, or they would have to move to a full fiscal union, ceding national sovereignty to a European central state.

The Rise of Asian Banks

The last five years have seen Chinese banks moving to the top of the banking league tables. China now has three of the top 10 global banks in ICBC, China Construction Bank, and Bank of China, and it has seven of the top 10 fastest-growing banks, according to The Banker. Japan's banks are also doing well, and have been involved in some major acquisitions. In December 2011, Mitsubishi UFJ Financial Group paid US$457.5 million for a 15% stake in AMP Capital Holdings, for example, and that deal was dwarfed by Sumimoto Mitsui Financial Group's US$7.3 billion acquisition of the UK-based Royal Bank of Scotland's aircraft leasing business.

The rise of strong regional banks focused on regional trade, rather than on trying to develop a global footprint, is a potentially serious competitive threat to the big global banks, already under threat from regulators.

The US Banking Sector—Not Out of the Woods Yet

In its report in September 2012, "Banking system outlook," the ratings agency Moody's said that the outlook for the US banking sector remained negative. Moody's had the giant US banks, including Bank of America, Citigroup, Goldman Sachs Group, JPMorgan Chase & Co, and others, squarely in the frame, arguing that the macroeconomic environment could well undo much that the big US banks had achieved by way of steadying the ship in the years since the 2008 global financial crash. "US banks remain in recovery mode, which is prone to reversal if the economy takes a turn for the worse. Nonperforming asset levels are still high, and legacy issues from the financial crisis will take years to resolve," Moody's said. In sum, the next few years are going to be difficult for banks in the United States and Europe, while Asian banks are likely to see their growth spurt continue.

MORE INFO

Report:

Deutsche Bank. "The future of (mobile) payments: New (online) players competing with banks." December 20, 2012. Online at: tinyurl.com/lj5oakt [PDF].

Website:

European Commission on financial services: ec.europa.eu/internal_market/finances/index_en.htm

See Also:

★ Banking Transparency and the Robustness of the Banking System (pp. 135–137)
★ Outsourcing and the Banks (pp. 226–228)
✔ Banks "Planning for Failure"—Living Wills as Resolution and Recovery Plans (p. 1004)
✔ The Interbank Market: Its Structure and Function (p. 1008)
✔ Merchant Banks: Their Structure and Function (p. 1012)
✔ Retail Banks: Their Structure and Function (p. 1014)

Chemicals

MAJOR INDUSTRY TRENDS

With the number of "useful" chemical compound molecules approaching 10,000, and with chemicals playing a huge role in so much of what modern societies use, eat, clean, manufacture, and do each day, it might be thought that the global chemicals industry should be set for perpetual boom times. In fact, as the European Chemical Industry Council (Cefic), the body representing the European chemicals industry, observes in its report (Cefic, 2004), things are not looking particularly encouraging for the sector, at least in Europe.

The Cefic report sketches out the probable future of the sector to 2015, and one of its themes is that the European chemicals industry, which historically included the largest group of chemicals producers on the planet, is in danger of falling behind rival producers in Asia and the Americas, and is already trailing behind its "sister" industry, the pharmaceuticals sector.

While it is not always easy to separate the two sectors, Cefic argues that over the past decade or so, trends in pharmaceuticals and chemicals have "decoupled." "There is a strong asymmetry between the two sectors, with regard to the growth of output, trade surplus, and employment. [Our] analysis shows that growth in chemicals output is lower than in pharmaceuticals," it says.

Even outside the European Union, although the global chemicals trade surplus is still increasing, it shows considerably less dynamism than the growth in pharmaceuticals outputs around the world. Moreover, the number of people directly employed by chemicals is falling dramatically, while employment in pharmaceuticals continues to show what Cefic calls "an encouraging increase."

Whereas the chemicals sector output grew at an average of 2.8% from 1996 to 2001, manufacturing output generally grew at 2.9%, and pharmaceuticals output grew at an average annual rate of 5.5%, Cefic says. It makes the point, too, that if one strips out pharmaceuticals-related growth from general chemicals growth, the picture looks even bleaker, as the share of EU pharmaceuticals trade surplus in the total chemicals surplus (which includes pharmaceuticals) has grown considerably, from 23% in 1990 to 40% in 2002.

The most recent figures from the European Commission date to 2007, and show that the manufacture of pharmaceutical preparations and basic pharmaceutical products was the principal activity of around 4,500 businesses in the 27 member states, while the sector employed 611,000 people and generated around €73.7 billion.

According to Cefic, the decoupling of pharmaceuticals and chemicals is the result of a number of factors. These include the introduction of different technologies, changes in downstream markets, approaches to innovation, and changing shareholder expectations.

The chemicals sector itself breaks down into bulk chemicals and fine chemicals, and into a further category of petrochemicals and plastics. In 2002, total world chemicals production (excluding pharmaceuticals) was worth around €1.3 trillion, with the European Union's share of that being €360 billion, followed by the United States (25.6%), and Asia (33%). According to the latest figures from the United Nations Environment Programme (UNEP, 2013), the global industry has grown dramatically since 2002. The value of total output from the sector is now some US$4.1 billion, by comparison with just US$171 million in 1970. As the UNEP report emphasizes, there is hardly an industry where chemicals are not used, and millions of people throughout the world see direct benefits from the sector. However, UNEP points out that while chemicals are major contributors to national and world economies, their sound management throughout their life cycle is essential in order to avoid significant and increasingly complex risks to human health and ecosystems, resulting in substantial costs to national economies as well as to considerable individual suffering. The exact number of chemicals on the global market is not known, but under the pre-registration of the European Union's chemicals regulation, REACH, approaching 144,000 chemical substances have been pre-registered, which UNEP says provides a reasonable guide to the number of chemicals traded globally.

According to the OECD (2012), annual global chemical sales have doubled over the period from 2000 to 2009, with one clear trend being the way developing economies are increasing their share of global output while the share of OECD member states decreases. The latest figures from the OECD, which date to 2009, show member states' share decreasing from 77% of global output in 2000, to 63% by 2009, and that contraction would have increased significantly by 2013.

Within this, the European Union's share of global output has benefited somewhat from the enlargement process, as many of the east European accession countries have their own chemicals industries. However, Cefic points out that closer inspection of the data shows that even with enlargement, the EU's position is still eroding. A decade ago, the European Union's share was 32%, or 4% higher than its current 28% share of global output.

The main reasons for the decline are slow demand growth in Europe versus high demand growth in Asia, particularly in China, compounded by increasing imports into the European Union from Asia and the Middle East, creating pressure on prices and margins. The internationalization of trade, with customer industries moving manufacturing out of Europe to low-wage economies, is also a contributing factor, as is regulatory arbitrage, with Europe constituting a highly regulated zone, versus Asia as a less-regulated zone, and therefore a more favorable location for manufacturers. The problem for the European industry, as Cefic notes, is that as it declines, a smaller budget is allocated to R&D, and, as the sector thrives on innovation, spending less on R&D would accelerate the decline, and erode the industry's skills base in Europe.

Another issue for the European sector is that the Asian region's rate of industrial production growth is outpacing that of much of the rest of the world, creating a very strong demand for a wide range of chemicals. Moreover, Asia's greater focus on agriculture, manufacturing, and durable goods creates a more chemicals-intensive demand than developed economies, where the service sector plays a much larger role. Add to this the importance of the electronics, electrical, and textiles sectors, plus construction, leather, and plastics processing, and the result, again, is very strong and sustained demand for chemical products.

The question posed by Cefic, given all of the above, is whether Europe could still be regarded as a growth area for chemicals to 2015. Its answer, following an extensive modeling exercise, was that only in the most optimistic scenarios could the growth rates of the whole chemical industry be expected to outstrip GDP growth in Europe. The more likely scenario is that growth in demand will lag behind GDP growth, and could even become negative. If this happens, it would mean a major structural change.

"This would entail major consequences for the European chemical industry, but also, because of the leverage effects from raw materials supply and innovation, for European industry as a whole, and therefore on the whole European economy," the report warns.

MARKET ANALYSIS

The overall health of the global chemicals sector is highly susceptible to the global economic cycle, reflecting the fact that it mainly processes raw materials, and manufactures and supplies intermediates (semi-processed raw materials) to other manufacturing industries worldwide. Consequently, the global economic downturn that began in 2008 and continued into 2009 had a severe impact on the industry. However, things began to pick up in 2010, and by June 2011 Cefic was revising upwards its forecast for the EU chemicals industry for 2011. The picture reversed in 2012, however. In a press release dated November 15, 2012, Cefic said that EU chemical production fell by 2.2% in the first eight months of 2012, by comparison with the same period in 2011. "Data for the first eight months of 2012 point to EU chemicals production being 5.8% below the 2007 peak levels," it said. However, prices increased by 2.7% over the year, helping the industry to achieve a net trade surplus for the first seven months of €29.1 billion.

Accounting firm PricewaterhouseCoopers (PwC) points out that M&A activity in the global chemicals industry held relatively constant through 2011 and 2012, with the sector seeing a number of mega deals (more than US$1 billion in value) and large deals (between US$250 million and US$1 billion). "Many chemical producers have seen gains in liquidity over the past two years, indicating that potential acquirers are becoming better capitalized, despite issues relating to decelerating growth as the chemical industry faces headwinds and higher costs," PwC says. Some 121 deals over US$50 million were recorded in the global chemicals sector in 2011, worth a total of US$79.3 billion. By the end of the third quarter of 2012, some 92 deals had been done, with a total value of US$48.6 billion.

Regulatory Trends

The global chemicals industry has long been aware that the production and use of chemicals can have an adverse impact on both human health and the environment, and there has been a host of initiatives over the years aimed at developing coherent, industry-wide support for best-practice standards on the use, production, transportation, and safe disposal of chemicals.

The industry's Responsible Care program has been in existence for close to two decades. As the International Council of Chemical Associations (ICCA) observes, some 15 years ago, just a handful of countries had launched Responsible Care programs in their chemicals sector. By 2002, the program had been adopted by 47 countries worldwide.

The UN has been pushing for the global adoption of its strategic approach to international chemicals management (SAICM) since 2002. The SAICM concept and framework was endorsed by the World Summit on Sustainable Development in 2002, and by many global conferences since.

There is little argument against, and almost universal support for, the UN goal that, by 2020, chemicals across the world should be produced and used in ways that minimize significant adverse effects on human health and the environment (known as the Johannesburg Plan of Implementation).

SAICM objectives are grouped around five headings: risk reduction; knowledge and information; governance; capacity building and technical assistance; and, lastly, illegal international traffic—the last being a continuing problem in the sector.

The UN's argument has a number of strands to it. The increased use of chemicals frequently accompanies economic development, and chemicals can play an important role in the improvement of living standards, including in relation to disease eradication, safe drinking water, and the alleviation of hunger. At the same time, the sound management of chemicals is essential for environmental sustainability, which, in turn, is a prerequisite for sustainable development as a whole.

UNEP says that there is increasing recognition, at the level of national governments, and by national chemical producers, of the importance of the sound management of chemicals in meeting the internationally agreed goals of the Millennium Declaration, and of the potential for exposure to toxic substances to undermine development, health, and poverty-alleviation investments.

"Many people living in poverty have weakened immune systems, leaving them more vulnerable to diseases caused or exacerbated by toxic substances, and many lack knowledge of toxic substances in their community. Inadequate living conditions often leave them exposed to hazards of toxic substances, and many work in occupations such as agriculture and mining, which constantly expose them to harmful substances. Chemical exposures can also interfere with primary education by impairing children's physical growth and emotional development, and, in the case of metals such as lead and mercury, can have serious and irreversible adverse effects on children's mental development," UNEP warns.

The ICCA set up the Responsible Care Global Charter in 2006, for companies and national associations to sign, as part of meeting the sustainable development challenge. Cefic itself is an enthusiastic supporter of the charter.

In addition, the European Union has a chemicals policy called REACH (Registration, Evaluation, and Authorization of Chemicals), which became applicable in law on June 1, 2007. REACH makes businesses responsible for the chemicals they use, and the onus is on them to show that these chemicals are safe in the way that they are being used. It also streamlines and improves the previous legislative framework on chemicals for the European Union.

The thrust of REACH is to encourage the replacement of hazardous chemicals with safer ones, and to act as a stimulus to businesses and the chemicals sector to research and develop safer products.

The United Nations has a globally harmonized system, called GHS, for identifying hazardous chemicals, and to convey information to the public and to users about these hazards, through standard symbols and phrases on packaging and labels, and through safety data sheets. GHS originated with the World Summit on Sustainable Development, held in Johannesburg in September 2002. This encouraged countries to implement GHS as a harmonized basis for providing consistent physical, environmental, and safety information on hazardous chemical substances and mixtures.

On December 16, 2008, the European Parliament and the Council adopted a new regulation on the classification, labeling, and packaging (CLP) of substances and mixtures, which aligns existing EU legislation with the UN's GHS regime. CLP was published in the Official Journal on December 31, 2008 and came into force on January 20, 2009. The deadline for substances to be classified according to CLP is December 1, 2010, and for mixtures, June 1, 2015. The CLP Regulations will ultimately replace two earlier directives: the directive on the classification, labeling, and packaging of substances, and the directive on "preparations." However, chemical companies are being given a period of time to make the transition. The deadline for substance reclassification is November 30, 2010, and for mixtures, May 31, 2015.

Companies

The ICIS Top 100 Chemical Companies (see More Info) includes all chemical firms around the world with sales greater than US$2.5 billion.

MORE INFO

Reports:

Cefic. "Horizon 2015: Perspectives for the European chemical industry." March 2004. Online at: tinyurl.com/nxuq665 [PDF].

OECD. "OECD environmental outlook to 2050: The consequences of inaction." June 2012. Online at: tinyurl.com/kxhmx5x

UNEP. "Global chemicals outlook: Towards sound management of chemicals." February 15, 2013. Online at: tinyurl.com/c4sbwu2

Websites:

European Chemical Industry Council (Cefic): www.cefic.be

ICIS Top 100 Chemical Companies: www.icis.com/pages/top-100-2012/

International Council of Chemical Associations (ICCA): www.icca-chem.org

Registration, Evaluation, Authorisation and Restriction of Chemicals (REACH): tinyurl.com/ygwr75

Strategic Approach to International Chemicals Management (SAICM): www.saicm.org

See Also:

Healthcare and Pharmaceuticals (pp. 1630–1632)

Construction and Building Materials

MAJOR INDUSTRY TRENDS

The construction sector is in an interesting phase of its evolution, not quite yet global in nature, but with some players active in more than one national market and the largest players becoming involved in multiple projects in Europe, North America, and Asia, particularly China. The sector includes companies from the smallest to the largest. At the bottom of the scale are small house-builders, followed at the mid-range by regional and national companies capable of handling multiple projects within one country, to larger players with specialist interests, for example, in shopping mall construction or office blocks, operating in multiple countries. The industry has a clear overlap with civil engineering on infrastructure projects, particularly where groundworks and ground preparation for site construction are concerned.

The sector, of necessity, works in partnership with a range of other professions, such as architects, quantity surveyors, and structural engineering consultants, who may be external to the construction company, or part of the company. Legal and financial advice on contracts, joint ventures, and project financing, as well as on litigation—the construction sector is associated with more than its fair share of litigation—are also essential services for the sector.

After a number of boom years, the global downturn started to have a real impact around August 2008, and had a severe effect on the sector across the developed world, in all areas except public works and infrastructure. Much of the European and US construction sector was still in difficulties at the start of 2013. In most developed markets, construction still lags behind other sectors. Severe repossession and vacancy rates in the US housing market, and in a number of European countries, continue to prevent the construction sector from moving forward.

The housing sector crash that followed the bursting of the housing and speculative commercial building bubble sent numbers of smaller house-builders into administrative insolvency, while larger construction firms have implemented layoffs, which, in many instances, will damage their ability to go forward rapidly when the upturn finally arrives.

The stimulus packages that were implemented by governments globally all had as a common theme: the idea of bringing forward or initiating major infrastructure projects to pump public money into the economy. However, infrastructure is not a market in which smaller players can get involved so government programs have brought only limited relief to the vast bulk of the construction sector.

The industry also has a clear and very close relationship with related industries specializing in building materials, including cement, plastics, wood, steel, and glass, as well as innovative new product types, with particular strength, thermal, or low-maintenance properties.

The industry has always had a tendency to be national and local in its focus, rather than massively cross-border, although in Europe there is an increasing trend towards cross-border joint ventures in projects such as shopping mall construction.

There are huge difficulties in the way of construction companies moving outside their own national "turf." Every country has its own planning laws, building materials laws, and building regulations for residential, office, leisure, retail, and industrial building. Moreover, construction is very materials- and skills-intensive, and bringing materials to the site and organizing the necessary skills, labor, and project management is a challenge for one location, never mind for multiple locations in multiple jurisdictions.

Cross-border construction projects provide a way of ensuring that local knowledge is applied, and provides the incoming company with a way of acquiring a sufficient base of experience in the new jurisdiction's regulations and requirements. These projects can be expected, over time, to result in a more international sector as various players build up the necessary network of relationships to make building outside the home country feasible, and tendering for projects in foreign states a practical proposition.

For this reason, many international infrastructure projects tend to be project-managed by large civil engineering companies, who may use their own construction arms, or a range of large and smaller local construction companies, or some combination of all of these to get the job done.

While both the residential house-building and commercial office markets in the United Kingdom and Europe are in deep recession at present, 2009 was a vintage year for the launching of grand infrastructure projects in Europe and the United States. Italy, for example, revived one of Prime Minister Silvio Berlusconi's top projects, the Messina Bridge, which will have a central span of 3.3 kilometers. Once completed, at a projected cost of €6.1 billion, the Messina Bridge will be the longest in the world, and will link the island of Sicily to the Italian mainland's Calabria region. It is to be part of a €17.8 billion public works program announced by the Italian government in March 2009, designed to counteract the effects of the global slowdown on Italian jobs and the Italian economy.

The new spending is a supplement to the €16.6 billion on new infrastructure spending announced by the Italian government in November 2008, to include new schools, prisons, and a flood barrier for the ancient city of Venice. Before the original Messina Bridge project was canceled by the short-lived Socialist government, it involved a truly international consortium of construction and civil engineering companies, including Italy's Impregilo, Condotte, Aci Consorzio Stabile, Cooperativa Muratori & Cementisti (CMC), and Impresa Grassetto, alongside Spain's Sacyr Vallehermoso, and Ishikawajima-Harima Heavy Industries (IHI) from Japan.

One of the biggest construction projects in Latin America at present is the US$5.25 billion expansion of the Panama Canal, to accommodate modern vessels that are longer and wider than was the case when the canal was originally built. The expansion program includes the construction of new locks on the Atlantic side, on the east side of the Gatun Locks, and on the Pacific side, to the southwest of the existing Miraflores Locks. It also involves the excavation of new access channels and the widening of existing channels, plus a modest raising of the level of Lake Gatun to accommodate the additional flows of water into the new locks at each locking. Already, three consortia of international companies have put in bids to construct the lock basins, which will take around half of the projected budget.

However, much of the globe's infrastructure spending is now being undertaken by emerging economies, and Western companies are fighting to gain contracts in countries such as China and India. In 2010, the Indian prime minister, Manmohan Singh, said that India needed to double infrastructure spending from US$500 billion (£325 billion) to US$1 trillion in the next five-year plan if the country's plans to lift millions out of poverty are to be successful, beginning in 2013. Roads and highways are a particular focus of attention, and the government's highways minister, Kamal Nath, set himself a target of 20 kilometers of roads a day from June 2010, meaning 7,000 kilometers a year, and 20,000 kilometers of work in progress. It could easily be the biggest and the most ambitious infrastructure rollout in the world.

China pledged to spend US$585 billion on infrastructure in 2010 and 2011. Projects include building a bridge almost 50 kilometers across the Pearl River delta from Hong Kong to the city of Zhuhai, adjoining the former Portuguese colony of Macau. The bridge, costing about US$7 billion, and which for much of its length will soar 200 meters above the waterway leading to some of China's busiest ports, is expected to be completed in 2016.

MARKET ANALYSIS

Building Materials—Industry Trends

The building materials sector is extremely diverse and constitutes a sizeable chunk of the industrial base of developed countries. It includes a highly diverse range of suppliers, from cement manufacturers (an area that is under tremendous pressure to both innovate and to "green up"), to specialty glass and steel manufacturers, as well as providing a large market to white goods manufacturers, furniture manufacturers, paint and wiring manufacturers, and a host of other related industries.

One of the biggest boosts for the building materials sector is the seemingly endless raising of the bar by various national planning departments on "green" building. The green building materials market was worth some US$60 billion in 2009 in the United States alone, with the residential market being a major driver. One of the biggest segments of this market is the green floor-coverings sector, with renewable products such as woven floor coverings, bamboo, or cork being in huge demand.

According to one of the leading green building and sustainability consultants, Jerry Yudelson, who publishes an annual "Top 10 Megatrends" for the global green building industry, 2013 is going to be a very good year for the sector globally. Yudelson points out that more and more countries are creating their own green building incentive schemes, and developing their own Green Building Councils and rating schemes. There are now nearly 90 countries with startup or established green building organizations, and these will drive growth in the sector. In many countries around the world, Leadership in Energy and Environmental Design (LEED) certification, developed and managed by the US Green Building Council, is now the recognized standard for measuring building sustainability. It includes a third-party commissioning process that provides confidence that the developer has achieved the set goals on zero or near-zero emissions. Although LEED was developed as a US standard, by the end of 2012 around 40% of all LEED-registered projects were located outside the United States, and LEED projects are now being carried forward in some 130 countries. According to Yudelson, zero-net energy buildings will become increasingly commonplace in both residential and commercial sectors around the world.

Another growth area is concrete production from recycled materials, such as ash from power furnaces. Wood from proven, sustainable forests is another area that is set to boom, as are water-efficient plumbing fixtures and energy-efficient lighting fixtures, both of which were expected to see double-digit growth every year to 2013, according to a green building materials report by market analysts the Freedonia Group.

In the residential homes sector, construction companies are often pulled and pushed in two opposing directions simultaneously by regulations, when it comes to innovations in building materials. On the one hand, anything that helps to "green" a home, by improving its thermal efficiency, or lowering its energy consumption, is regarded as good. On the other hand, local planning offices tend to be very prescriptive on the kinds of materials that are regarded as suitable, and it can be an uphill struggle for new materials to gain acceptance.

There are ways around this. Australia, for example, has a Building Products Innovation Council, whose job it is to promote the most efficient and innovative use of building products across the sector, while still seeing that construction companies adhere to a consistent regulatory framework for building. The council includes senior representation from across the spectrum of the building materials and products side of the building industry, which ensures that the council stays abreast of new product innovations.

The construction sector is, in many ways, both an ideal test bed for scientific innovation, and a powerful economic driver of innovation; successful products can be taken up in enormous quantities on a worldwide scale. The range of innovation opportunities is as broad as the designer's imagination. One company that specializes in building product innovation, DuPont, has products on offer that range from new materials to construct "storm rooms" to keep families safe in high-risk tornado and hurricane areas, to kitchen counter tops, such as its Zodiaq range, which incorporates quartz crystal to create an exceptionally durable and scratch-resistant surface. Many innovations address thermal loss from homes to make them more energy-efficient. Phase-change materials, for example, release or absorb large quantities of heat when changing state from one phase to the other. Companies such as BASF and Ciba, which specialize in surface coatings, have come up with micro-encapsulation waxes that enable glass manufacturers to incorporate phase-change materials into window construction (for example, esBITS from PCM Innovations).

Innovation need not be limited to new building materials; it can also be innovation in the way standard materials are used. The German Passivhaus standard is a low-energy house, built around a set of principles applied to building design. There are some 15,000 Passivhaus builds in the world, and the design principle is promoted by the Passivhaus Institute in Germany. The core is a super-insulated, airtight envelope boosted by the use of glass to promote solar gain, and the result cuts heating requirements by up to 85%.

Home and buildings designers and planners have to think about both materials and the building regulations that are likely to appear in a world dominated by calls for action to cut carbon emissions. Current building requirements are likely to be amended further, almost year on year, to minimize the impact of the built environment on the planet, which means cutting emissions and energy usage. We are at the dawn of "smart" buildings, which react both to energy usage and to the needs of occupants, but many leading architects and designers are already thinking about zero-emissions buildings, or massively taller buildings, or buildings that are themselves virtual "cities"—all concepts that will provide a fertile ground for innovation in building materials.

MORE INFO

Websites:

American Forest & Paper Association report on China's construction boom: www.cintrafor.org

Dupont, buildings materials innovation: www.dupont.com

esBITS from PCM Innovations: www.esbits.com

Passive House Institute: passiv.de/en/

Portland Cement Association: www.cement.org

What's New in Building, UK construction industry site: www.whatsnewinbuilding.com

Yudelson Associates: www.greenbuildconsult.com

See Also:

Engineering (pp. 1626–1628)
Mining (pp. 1637–1638)
Real Estate (pp. 1641–1642)
Steel (pp. 1646–1647)

Defense

MAJOR INDUSTRY TRENDS

Defense Spending and the Global Economic Downturn

Defense spending is clearly the key determinant of the health of the defense industry. It is sensitive to the economic cycle, with democratically elected governments preferring to focus their resources on politically sensitive areas, such as healthcare and welfare spending, or on measures to boost employment, when their revenues come under pressure during an economic slowdown. Plainly, however, when a country is at war it has little option but to maintain defense spending, regardless of the economic circumstances, and no country is willing to sacrifice its long-term security for the sake of short-term savings.

Military budgets have proven buoyant over the past few years, driven by the wars in Iraq and Afghanistan, and higher spending by developing countries. According to a report in April 2012 from the Stockholm International Peace Research Institute (SIPRI), world military expenditure in 2011 totaled US$1.74 trillion, almost unchanged from 2010 in real terms. The small rise of just 0.3%, SIPRI says, marks the end of a continuous series of increases in military spending running from 1998 to 2010, with the average annual increase over the last decade being around 4.5%.

The cutback during 2011 was largely the result of six of the world's top military spenders, Brazil, France, Germany, India, the United Kingdom, and the United States, cutting military budgets in 2011, mostly as an attempt to find savings as part of the "austerity" debt reduction programs in those countries. "The after-effects of the global economic crisis, especially deficit-reduction measures in the USA and Europe, have finally brought the decade-long rise in military spending to a halt, at least for now," commented Dr. Sam Perlo-Freeman, head of SIPRI's Military Expenditure Project.

Military expenditure in the United States fell by 1.2% in real terms, and this was expected to continue during 2012 and 2013. The withdrawal from Iraq and the drawdown of US forces from Afghanistan will lead to additional falls in spending, to go along with further budget cuts in 2013, now being argued over between Republicans and Democrats in the US Congress and Senate.

According to SIPRI, the deepest cuts in Europe in military spending have been made by France, with its defense budget falling by 4% since 2008. By comparison, cuts in the United Kingdom and Germany have been more modest, being just 1.4% for the latter and only 0.6% for the United Kingdom. One of the biggest increases has come from Russia, where military spending was increased by 9.3% in 2011, reaching a total of US$71.9 billion, making the country the world's third-largest military spender, ahead of both the United Kingdom and France. Russia has embarked on a decade-long program to replace the majority of its Soviet-era weaponry and military equipment with modern equivalents by 2020.

Military spending in Asia and Oceania rose by 2.4%, mostly as a result of a 6.7% increase by China (US$8.2 billion). India's military budget, by way of contrast, fell by 3.9%, or US$1.9 billion in real terms, with high inflation in the country canceling out a nominal budget increase. In Africa, most of the region's increase of 8.6% came from a massive increase of 44% in the Algerian military budget to counter concerns over the conflict in Libya. SIPRI has little data on military spending in Iran and the United Arab Emirates, but says that there is a clear pattern across the Middle East of an increasing spend on military budgets. Latin America, on the other hand, saw a decline in military spending of 3.3% during 2011. This was almost entirely due to the fact that the region's biggest spender on military budgets, Brazil, cut its 2011 military budget by 8.2% as part of efforts to cool its overheating economy and to reduce inflationary pressures.

In general, countries have difficulty cutting their defense spending by significant amounts in the short term. Defense programs can last for decades, and, if a project is already underway, it is often difficult for a government to cancel its order. Defense spending can also be politically sensitive. Cutting back on equipment orders may simply add to unemployment during a recession.

The United States is by far the largest market for defense equipment, and is likely to remain so for the foreseeable future. Even with a built-in assumption that the wars in Iraq and Afghanistan will be concluded before 2015, US defense spending in that year is still projected to be at a higher level, adjusted for inflation, than in any year in the entire post-World War II period prior to 2005. The United States spends almost as much on defense as every other country in the world combined. In 2015, spending on defense and other "security" activities will take up close to 20% of the federal budget. However, the United States has been taking the axe to many programs as the Obama administration curbs defense spending, which doubled during the Bush years. Among them are the costly F-22 fighter plane, a new communications satellite, shipbuilding programs, and missile development.

The need to cut its massive deficit has prompted swingeing cuts in the United Kingdom's defense budget. However, analysts are warning that the United Kingdom is going to have to choose between continuing a high-profile military and diplomatic role, and winding back its military expenditure. In December 2012, the Treasury confirmed that the Ministry of Defence (MoD) will be looking at some £735 million of cuts to its core budget for the period 2013–15. The MoD will also be expected to absorb around one-fifth of all new spending department reductions. Spending on military operations in Afghanistan is also falling by a further £650 million as British troops prepare to return home. However, the Treasury also announced that in future it would be giving the MoD the power to carry over unspent budget from prior years.

MARKET ANALYSIS

Arms Race Developing in the Asia-Pacific Region

Many analysts believe that growing friction between the United States and China will define the coming decades. Certainly, China is in the midst of an ambitious bid to modernize its military by the middle of this century. A key part of this effort is to downsize its army—the world's largest—while beefing up its air force and navy. This will enable China to project military force farther beyond its borders. China's total spending is second only to that of the United States, but it is low as measured by per capita spending. However, China has expanded its military spending at a double-digit pace in the past decade, and it became the world's second-largest military power, surpassing France, in 2009. In March 2011, the Chinese government announced that it would be raising its official military budget by 12.7%, to US$91.5 billion. This marks a surge forward in military spending and reverses the government's 2010 position, when it reined in military spending to a mere 7.5% increase. The 2010 military budget was the first to fall below 10% since 1989. Military experts in the United States and elsewhere have said Beijing's real military spending is at least double the announced figure. A 2009 Pentagon report estimated China's total military spending to be between US$105 billion and US$150 billion. While growing rapidly, China's military spending is still dwarfed by that of the United States.

China clearly now intends to develop a military capability to match its new-found economic status, and is spending more on its navy and air force, and cutting back on its land forces. The idea is to put the country in a better position to project force outside its own borders. China's insatiable appetite for raw materials and energy has also widened the military's mission to protect China's strategic economic interests overseas. The country's naval and air forces certainly appear determined to impose their dominance in the South China Sea—through which vital oil supplies pass, and where several islands are in dispute—and in the East China Sea, where China and Japan are in dispute over mineral rights, and a number of contested islands. The government says that most of the increased military expenditure is focused on improving the historically poor living conditions of soldiers in the People's Liberation Army.

In addition, the authorities intend to increase spending on "informatization," in an attempt to close the gap on the United States's use of "smart" technology. Defense companies in the West could benefit from China's attempts to upgrade its military technology, although it is extremely doubtful whether Washington would allow American companies to supply technology to China.

Some analysts contend that if China's economic growth remains robust, and the country is thus able to continue to expand its defense spending significantly each year, it will pose a threat to the United States' military dominance of the globe by the mid-21st century, or earlier. In early 2009, Beijing confirmed plans to build aircraft carriers, with the apparent intent of projecting "blue water" naval power eastwards into the Pacific, bringing it into potential conflict with the United States. For its part, Beijing fears that the United States is trying to "encircle" China, by using India, and allies such as Japan and Australia, as proxies to contain China's increasing military strength. China's concerns have some validity—military ties between Washington and New Delhi, for example, are growing in a number of areas.

India is also growing into a major purchaser of US military equipment, an about-turn for a country that relied on Soviet weapons during the Cold War. In a groundbreaking deal, India agreed to buy six Lockheed C130J transport planes for around US$1 billion in January 2008—New Delhi had previously procured transport aircraft from the USSR or Russia.

India is expected to spend US$100 billion in the next decade on its military. India's defense minister, Arackaparambil Kurien Antony, has made it clear that he expects military spending, currently 2.5% of GDP, to increase substantially as the nation's robust economy continues to grow.

Other Major Trends: The Environment

It might appear surprising, but the US military is arguably doing more to save the planet than any other organization on earth. The US Defense Department is investing huge sums in the search to develop renewable sources of energy, as well as improving energy efficiency. The key drivers behind this trend include: national security—the United States does not want to be dependent upon energy imported from politically unstable regions; cost reasons—even a 5% cut in the fuel bill would save the Department of Defense US$635 million (based on the 2007 figure); and, finally, because it makes sound military sense—many lives are lost transporting fuel to the frontline in vulnerable convoys.

The US military is already one of the largest consumers of renewable energy in the world, and it has set a goal that 25% of its

  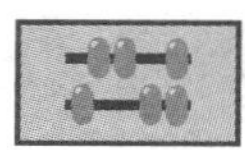      

energy should come from renewable sources by 2025. The US Air Force's goal is that 50% of all the fuels used in domestic training flights will come from synthetic, or non-petroleum, sources by 2016. The US military is also investing heavily in solar and wind power.

Technological Advances
The military is one of the key drivers of technological advances. There are certainly some remarkable developments taking place. The F-35 Joint Strike Fighter, being developed by Lockheed Martin, Northrop Grumman, and BAE Systems, for example, features some extraordinary features. These include technology that allows the pilot to look through the structure of the aircraft. The aircraft also features voice commands that significantly reduce the pilot's workload.

The military is also investing heavily in information technology on land. Military units constantly transmit huge amounts of data back and forth to report their position, generate situational awareness, and share information on enemy tactics. Soldiers with access to laptops, for example, can provide vital information to military commanders. Real-time management of information enables rapid decision-making, meaning that military operations can proceed quickly, possibly providing a decisive advantage during a battle.

Cyberspace: The New Battlefield
Unsurprisingly, given the new emphasis on information technology, governments around the world are investing heavily in measures to protect their computer networks from attacks, and to launch their own cyber attacks. In 2010, the *Guardian* reported (January 13, 2010) that the Chinese military has been developing capabilities to spy on, infiltrate, and compromise adversaries' computer networks for years. "Informatized war" is an integral component of its "three warfares" (*san zhong zhanfa*) strategic concept, and the achievement of information superiority is viewed as a requirement for battlefield supremacy. Many large defense companies have already branched out into cyber-security and information-technology services.

MORE INFO
Websites:
DefenseLINK, official website of the US Department of Defense: www.defenselink.mil
Jane's Defence Weekly, long-established and respected source of information on developments in global defense matters: www.janes-defence-weekly.com
Stockholm International Peace Research Institute (SIPRI), which details trends in military spending: www.sipri.org

E-Commerce

MAJOR INDUSTRY TRENDS

Electronic commerce, or e-commerce, involves the sale of goods and services via electronic means—principally over the internet, although sales via television (terrestrial, cable, and satellite) are also included. E-commerce can be further divided into the following sectors: business-to-business (B2B), business-to-government (B2G), consumer-to-consumer (C2C), government-to-business (G2B), government-to-citizen (G2C), and business-to-consumer (B2C). Retailers that rely primarily on e-commerce to sell goods or services are often referred to as e-tailers.

Retailing over the internet generally takes one of two forms:

- Cybermalls—the most famous cybermall is eBay, which offers access to products from a variety of independent retailers.
- Individual websites—most major retailers now have their own websites, which complement their traditional bricks-and-mortar outlets. Some retailers operate solely over the internet.

An interesting additional development has been the gradual emergence of "connected TVs," i.e. television sets that have internet connectivity so that TV program-makers can draw on the power of the internet to enhance and transform both TV advertising and the kind of television selling that has long been a staple part of the medium, Over the last few decades, television selling via programs on dedicated shopping channels generally featured a presenter demonstrating products on air. Viewers buy these products by telephoning an order line with their credit card details, or, in the case of interactive television services, by using their remote control. Recent years have seen the development of a variety of selling techniques, including on-air auctions.

In June 2011, Time ran an article by a technology industry analyst which spoke of the imminent arrival of what the analyst called "t-commerce." By this, he meant that the advent of internet connected TVs will drive new commerce opportunities via the ubiquitous home TV set. By 2014, the expectation is that there will be around 123 million connected TV sales globally. "Smarter" TVs will be able to target advertising more directly to the individual, using similar technologies to that applied by Amazon and other e-tailers with their "if you bought this, you'll probably also like these..." approach. Combining this with social media and "big data" mining by e-tailers opens up the possibility of putting a "social widget" on the screen, showing a consumer which of their online friends also recently bought that same product—all via the TV set.

If this sounds futuristic, consider the history of e-commerce and the internet and the series of leaps forward we have seen in e-commerce since the mass adoption of the internet. E-commerce initially became possible with the opening up of the internet to commercial users in the early 1990s. However, it took a while for the initial expectations to start to be fulfilled, and it wasn't until the latter half of the decade that companies really began to harness the internet's commercial potential. A number of the start-up companies from that era, such as Amazon and eBay, have emerged as retailing behemoths in their own right. However, e-commerce has largely been developed by established large retailers, which regard it as simply another sales channel. The gigantic grocery retailers that have expanded away from food and into a wide variety of other areas, such as clothing and electronic goods, have been particularly quick to appreciate its potential.

The medium has also created opportunities for very small businesses. It is now possible to buy over the internet a wide range of specialized products that are not available in shopping malls. Thus, the internet has provided a lifeline for many small producers, and has allowed entrepreneurs to enter the retailing sector without the need to invest heavily in physical retail outlets.

E-commerce has proven so successful because it offers significant advantages to both consumers and retailers. Consumers can compare products and prices from an array of retailers with a few touches on the screen or a few clicks of a mouse, giving the consumer a power that never existed previously. In itself, this changes the game for retailers as it raises huge issues of customer retention.

Online retailers often sell products and services at a significant discount to those offered by traditional outlets. Buying online is

convenient: consumers can make their purchases from the comfort of their own homes, and have them delivered to their doors. Furthermore, online shopping appeals to the environmentally conscious. In March 2009, researchers at Heriot-Watt University in the United Kingdom revealed that online shopping is 24 times "greener" than taking the car to the shops, and seven times greener than taking the bus. The researchers compared the carbon footprint of a typical delivery from a local depot with average carbon footprints for shopping trips by car and bus, and found that home deliveries involved much lower levels of carbon emissions. In June 2009, a study by the Carnegie Mellon Green Design Institute in the United States found that shopping online can reduce "our environmental impact by as much as 66%."

For businesses, the advantages of e-commerce lie mainly in the low cost of setting up and maintaining a business. Firms do not need to invest heavily in a physical presence, or in sales staff. However, they do have to organize payment systems, distribution, and returns.

Industry Suitability

Undoubtedly, some industries are more suited to e-commerce than others at the present stage of technology. This type of retailing is most applicable to goods that are fairly simple, commoditized, and do not require on-the-spot input from knowledgeable sales staff. Thus, grocery retailing is ideally suited to e-commerce, whereas consumers generally need to try on clothing before they make a purchase. Technology will change this. Progress in 3D avatars and more computing power will allow viewers to try on clothes virtually on an avatar of themselves, rotating the image from every angle to form their buy-don't buy decision, and social networking will allow them to get instant feedback from their friends. Similarly, advances in computing power and technology will make even the most complex items purchasable online, with full advice being provided by an avatar of a shop assistant. These features will probably be standard by 2016 or so as broadband connectivity moves towards an average of around 20 megabytes per second, and the computing power in the various devices, tablets and PCs increases in accordance with Moore's law.

As e-commerce is still a relatively recent development, its penetration is often high in some sectors of a given market, but low in others. In financial services, for example, purchasing of insurance or a loan, both highly commoditized products, is ideally suited to the internet. However, many people prefer to buy a sophisticated financial product, such as a pension, on a face-to-face basis, as they will almost certainly require advice before making their choice. Generally, it is difficult to make online sales of sophisticated goods and services that require a large amount of advice or input from the retailer.

Technological Advances

The growth of broadband internet connections around the globe has undoubtedly boosted online shopping by dramatically speeding up the process of accessing websites and buying goods. Broadband is at least ten times as fast as dial-up. Having access to broadband means that consumers are more likely to use the internet to purchase everyday items such as groceries. However, faster connection speeds also allow users to download larger files, such as music, video clips, and movies, or to compete in online gaming, further boosting the potential revenues generated by e-commerce.

Traditionally, individuals and businesses have ordered goods or services online via computers, but the increase in data connection speeds on mobile phones with the introduction of 3G and 4G (3rd and 4th generation) technology has opened up another avenue for e-tailers, who are now very much aware of the potential of the mobile phone. In fact, the scale of the opportunity looming from the combination of fast mobile access to the Internet and very intuitive "smart" tablets and phones, is enormous. For example, in April 2012, a report by Capital Economics suggested that 4G mobile networks in the United Kingdom will be worth 0.5% of GDP by 2020, in other words, around £75 billion in today's figures. The research was commissioned by Everything Everywhere, the owners of the Orange and T-mobile networks. According to Capital Economics 4G will attract some £5.5 billion of private investment in the United Kingdom alone and will create or safeguard some 125,000 jobs. The United States, South Korea, and Germany are the global leaders so far in 4G, with relatively mature networks, but by the start of 2013 the United Kingdom already had the highest levels of smartphone usage and mobile commerce, even given the embryonic nature of 4G networks at that stage.

Surprisingly, given that the United States is generally regarded as the most advanced economy in the world, its broadband penetration rates are relatively low, according to the Organization for Economic Cooperation and Development (OECD), which publishes data on the subject (see More Info). The OECD's latest figures, announced in December 2011, showed Switzerland topping the fixed broadband rankings for the first time, with an average of 39.9 subscribers per 100 inhabitants, with the Netherlands (39.1) and Denmark (37.9) in second and third place. The United States was in 15th position, with around 27 connected citizens for every 100 of the population. The figures are produced by the OECD's Directorate for Science, Technology and Industry. The importance of internet-based commerce to the OECD was confirmed in the Seoul Declaration of 2008, where ministers agreed that access to a high-speed internet was critical to economic growth, but also to the protection of individual liberties and as a critical component of a democratic, culturally diverse community. "We share a vision that the internet economy . . . will strengthen our ability to improve the quality of life for all our citizens . . ." the Seoul Declaration proclaims. In March 2012, the OECD produced a paper, Laying the foundations for the Internet Economy, which emphasized the importance of governments promoting the development of high-speed broadband infrastructures in their respective countries.

MARKET ANALYSIS

Calculating the overall size of the global e-commerce market is complicated by the relatively high levels of cross-border sales that take place. Furthermore, few research companies measure all of the various sectors of the market (B2B, B2C, etc). However, estimates from various analysts suggest the global market was worth around US$500 billion in 2009. According to IMRWorld, the UK industry association for global e-retailing, by 2013 the estimated value of the UK online retail market stood at £87 billion, while in 2012 mobile commerce grew by some 300%. By 2013, China had the highest number of internet users, with one in every four users being based in China. South Korea had the highest percentage of mobile broadband subscriptions, with 91%.

Statistics from the government-linked China Internet Network Information Center (CINIC) showed that around 51 million new Chinese users accessed the internet in 2012, bringing the number of online users in the country up to 564 million, an increase of 10% on the 2011 numbers. Some 41.1% of the country is now online, CINIC claims. The Chinese Ministry of Industry and Information Technology estimates that the country's internet population will reach roughly 800 million users by 2015.

Varying Business Models

Companies have adopted differing business models for their e-commerce operations. Amazon operates from vast warehouses, as

  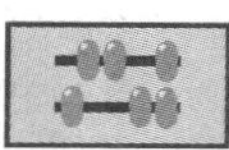      

does Ocado, a grocery retailer based in the United Kingdom. In the Ocado model, pickers inside the warehouse service thousands of internet orders, which are stacked, packed into pods that are attached to big trucks, and then transported all over the United Kingdom to car parks, where the pods are slotted onto individual vans for street-level deliveries. Other retailers pursue different models. The United Kingdom's Tesco, the third-largest retailer in the world, bases its online shopping business at individual stores. Tesco's website sends orders to the store nearest to the shopper, and pickers visit the store's shelves to fill the orders. Tesco vans then take the orders out locally.

Amazon is regarded as one of the pioneers of e-commerce, and continues to go from strength to strength. Founded in 1995 by Jeff Bezos to sell books, Amazon now sells a wide range of consumer products, and is one of the best-known internet retailers. By the end of the 1990s, Amazon's revenue was around US$1.5 billion a year, but it was still making a loss—it had to borrow around US$1 billion each year just to keep afloat. However, it managed to survive the financial storm, and, by the middle of the current decade, was making a healthy profit. Indeed, in 2005, on Amazon's 10th birthday, Bezos said that his aim was to turn Amazon into the Wal-Mart of electronic retailing, with a company mantra of "get big fast." In the year ending December 31, 2009, Amazon's net sales increased 28% year-on-year to US$24.51 billion. By Q3 2012, Amazon's net sales had reached US$13.81 billion, which would create annual sales for the full year 2012 of around double the 2009 figure.

MORE INFO

Articles:

Bajarin, Ben. "TV meets e-commerce: Are you ready for 't-Commerce'? "*Time* (June 17, 2011). Online at: tinyurl.com/p3pnq73

Swann, Allan. "4G mobile will boost UK economy by £75bn. "*Computer Business Review* (April 30, 2012). Online at: tinyurl.com/peuxjf9

Websites:

IMRG, UK industry association for online retail: www.imrg.org

OECD Key ICT Indicators: www.oecd.org/internet/broadbandandtelecom/oecdkeyictindicators.htm

See Also:

Information Technology (pp. 1632–1633)
Retail (pp. 1642–1644)

Electronics

MAJOR INDUSTRY TRENDS

If there is one sector that is changing the nature of the world we live in faster than any other, it is electronics. From mobile phones to the internet, from telecommunications to satellite TV, electronics are ubiquitous, and advancing by leaps and bounds, with more power being crammed into less space year on year. It is fashionable at this point to quote Moore's law. Geoffrey Moore was the co-founder of the PC chip company, Intel, and the man famous for predicting that the number of transistors on the same-sized piece of silicon would double every two years—without bothering even to imply an end date for this process.

A few years ago, it was thought that Moore's law was running out of steam, as circuits were (a) becoming small enough for quantum effects to introduce instability in current flow, and (b) becoming crowded enough for the heat generated from operating the chip to start to be a real problem. However, advances in silicon substrate technology (the introduction of metal oxide gates, for example) opened up the door again, and Moore's law still holds good. Instead of Intel merely producing one central processing unit (CPU, the calculating "heart" of a microcomputer) on a chip, it produced first two CPUs per chip, then four, then eight, and we are very close to 16-CPU chips, with higher multiples possible and planned beyond this.

Simultaneously, the software industry is on a steep learning curve as it rewrites its applications to take full advantage of the vast amounts of processing power becoming available, whether at the server, on people's desks, or on a plethora of handheld devices, from palmtop computers to mobile phones and tablet PCs. These were first popularized by Apple's iPad, but by 2011 virtually every hardware manufacturer seemed to be producing a tablet PC.

As the amount of cheap computer power available to engineers has increased, the power of electronics to transform the world has moved forward in leaps and bounds. No part of industry is now untouched. The ability to simulate real physics inside "the box" has allowed car makers to stress-test both virtual parts and the whole design, long before metal goes anywhere near being machined. In advanced medicine, biosciences companies model molecules and processes to predict drug interactions on target proteins or cell constituents, before any real-world work is done. In the oil and gas sector, vast data sets from seismic and advanced scanning of reservoirs are turned into visual, three-dimensional models that geologists can "walk through," to examine reservoirs "from the inside" before any well is drilled.

The ability to create and explore real physics through virtual models increases dramatically with each new breakthrough in processing power. Advances in electronics truly have the power to change the rules for whole industries.

The electronics manufacturing sector is generally separated from the electrical manufacturing sector by a technical distinction. Under this, the term "electronics" refers to the flow of charge through non-metal conductors, such as silicon in semiconductor implementations, and "electrical" refers to the flow of charge through metal conductors. Electrical is all about wires, and electronics is all about semiconductors, broadly speaking. The latter leads to printed circuit boards (PCBs) and memory chips, while the former leads to white goods and power stations (with the proviso that almost all electrical goods these days have some PCB-controlled circuitry somewhere).

MARKET ANALYSIS

From an industry perspective, electronics has spawned a vast range of specialist industries, from the IT industry (dominated by the likes of IBM, and its competitors, at the mainframe end, and Intel and AMD at the PC end), to the mobile phone market. It includes TV set manufacturers, videogame consoles, and, across an array of industry sectors, a vast army of specialist control-systems manufacturers, not to mention the aviation and auto sectors, both of which could not exist in their present forms without massive input from the electronics sector. Then there is the medical devices market, and so on.

Asia, today, is regarded as the powerhouse of PCB and memory-chip production, yet it all began through a combination of some breakthrough research in Japan, and US companies outsourcing first PCB assembly, then PCB fabrication, to Asia to take advantage of cheap labor rates. Today, Asia's dominance in motherboard and memory-chip manufacturing has reached the point where a US air force colonel, Charles Howe, was prompted to write a strategic study looking at the potential impact on US national security of having so much of the electronics industry outside the United States.

The point is not without irony, as the semiconductor industry began in the United States with innovations such as Texas Instruments' invention of the integrated circuit in 1958, and Intel's production of the first 8-bit microprocessor, the 8008, in 1972. Howe's study gives a very clear account of the integrated circuit (IC) design process. The basic design process requires electronic design automation (EDA) software in the hands of experts. Fabrication involves "etching" or imprinting the designs onto silicon wafers.

Each new generation of chip tends to require either a totally retooled fabrication plant ("fab"), or a new plant built from scratch. Each plant costs around US$3 billion, which means that each new generation of chip represents a huge bet by the manufacturer that it can sell vast numbers of its chips to the various global markets.

Very few companies in the world can bet on that scale and get it wrong twice, so semiconductor chip manufacturing is a game with very high entry costs, and is played for very high stakes. Asian chip companies generally play a safer game, and focus on producing not CPUs, but peripheral components, such as motherboards and memory chips.

The entire semiconductor industry is tremendously vulnerable to downturns in the economy, as in all markets, from PCs to mobile phones, the sale of new products is predicated on global growth. There is no doubt that the semiconductor industry suffered heavily from the global downturn of 2008 as both businesses and consumers cut their discretionary spending. For businesses, this meant cutting back on IT projects, and for consumers it frequently meant economies, such as not replacing last year's mobile phone with this year's latest model. The impact on sales was marked, with the sector recording its first year-on-year drop in sales, at the end of 2008, since the dot.com crash of 2001.

Since then, things have improved markedly but the vulnerability of the sector to headwinds in the global economy remains a problem. In its November 2012 forecast for the global semiconductor sector, the World Semiconductor Trade Statistics organization (WSTS) predicted that the semiconductor market would recover somewhat in 2013 after a slight contraction in 2012. The WSTS forecast that when all the figures are in, the world semiconductor market in 2012 will be seen to have fallen short by some 3.2% on its performance in 2011, a drop in revenues for the sector of some US$290 billion. However, the WSTS sees a recovery of some 4.5% of growth for 2013, with revenues topping US$303 billion. This is some way short of the 7.2% growth in 2013 that the WSTS was predicting back in Spring 2012, and the WSTS blames the shortfall on "growing uncertainty in the world economy, including China's slowdown."

No one escaped the pull back in 2012, with all regions showing negative growth for all product categories, apart from logic and optoelectronics. The WSTS expects Europe to be the hardest hit, with production set to decline by 10.7% by comparison with 2011, to US$33 billion.

If the decline reverses in 2013 as the WSTS anticipates, then the world market should grow by 5.2%, to US$319 billion in 2014, with most regions seeing solid mid-single-digit growth in most product categories.

The Consumer Electronics Association (CEA), in association with the market research firm GfK, comes in slightly under the WSTS figure, as it is concerned with electronics sales generally. The worldwide electronics industry's sales should be worth some $1.105 billion in 2013, reversing the 1% drop in 2012. The 2012 drop was not, however, evenly spread. Sales in advanced economies contracted by some 4% while emerging markets grew sales by some 3%, resulting in the headline 1% drop.

Devices such as smartphones and tablets are expected to be a major driver of growth in 2013, but the growth in tablet sales is partially at the expense of PC sales, which are in fairly dramatic decline. In the United States, some 44% of homes now have tablets, by comparison with just 1% of homes in July 2010, with 55% of homes having one or more smartphones.

The Asian Semiconductor Industry

The Asian semiconductor industry began in the 1960s, with small pockets of foreign investment. Japan established a semiconductor industry in the 1970s, and in 1979 Fujitsu became the first company to mass-produce 64KB memory chips, with Japan cornering the world market in memory chips by the mid-1980s, passing the United States in semiconductor production volumes. By the late 1980s, South Korea had developed a thriving memory-chip industry, with companies such as Samsung enjoying rapid growth. Taiwanese investment generated the world's first "on-demand, fab-for-hire" plant, and Singapore, Malaysia, and China have all developed significant chip industries.

According to Colonel Howe's study, the first US outsourcing investment in the sector was by Fairchild Semiconductor in Hong Kong in 1961. Outsourcing began with chip assembly (bringing the various components together to complete a printed circuit board), then moved to fabrication, and, later, in the 1980s, to chip design.

Asia now accounts for around 60% of global sales, and is home to many of the world's leading chipmakers. According to the Semiconductor Equipment and Materials International (SEMI), the global industry association serving the manufacturing supply chain for the micro and nanoelectronics industries, investment in fab equipment continued during 2012, despite the disappointing second half to the year. SEMI was originally expecting installed capacity in fab plants around the world to increase by 5.3% in 2012. By May 2012, it had revised that figure down to just 3.6%. Logic chips will be a good part of this growth, with a 6% capacity increase, followed by foundries, with 5% growth and memory chips are expected to see growth of 3%. By the end of 2012, some 10 companies would control around 50% of total global capacity, SEMI says. In 2013, a number of new fabs are expected to be built, with equipment spending at record levels. The growth in capacity should reach 7% during 2013, SEMI says. Top of the regional list for fab spending in 2013 will be the Americas, with US$2.8 billion of spending, followed by Taiwan (US$1.3 billion) and Korea (US$1.1 billion).

The semiconductor industry has already enabled software designers to go some way down the road to "virtualizing" our world, creating immensely powerful tools for solving real-world problems far faster than ever before, and enabling new products,

  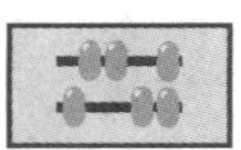      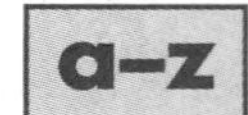

new drugs, and new forms of entertainment (of which the videogames console and the mobile phone are two stunning examples) to be brought to market extremely rapidly.

It is a safe bet that this sector is going to change life as we know it almost beyond recognition over the coming decades. As such, it is certainly a sector worth watching.

MORE INFO

Report:

Spillman, Mark S. "The Asian semiconductor industry and it's potential impacts to US national security." 2007. Washington, DC: Industrial College of the Armed Forces. Online at: tinyurl.com/9gndx66 [PDF; via archive.org].

Websites:

Electronic Industry Alliance (EIA): www.eia.org

Semiconductor Industry Association (SIA): www.sia-online.org

SEMI, the global industry organization for the micro and nanoelectronics industries: www.semi.org

See Also:

Information Technology (pp. 1632–1633)

Energy

MAJOR INDUSTRY TRENDS

Energy is the lifeblood of any economy, and global demand for energy has risen inexorably in the last 150 years, in step with industrial development and population growth. Most global energy needs are supplied by coal, oil and gas—the fossil fuels that formed long ago from the carbon-rich remains of dead plants and animals.

Concern has grown in recent decades about environmental impact. Climate scientists have warned that greenhouse gas emissions, caused by burning fossil fuels and other human activities, must be substantially reduced to avoid climate change. Pressure to replace fossil fuels has focused more attention on renewable sources, e.g. solar and wind.

New technology called fracking is enabling the industry to drill for vast new deposits of oil and gas, which hold the potential to transform the global energy industry, the global economy, and the geopolitical forces that have shaped the world for decades. Fracking involves pumping a mixture of water, sand, and some chemicals into a well under high pressure, allowing oil and gas molecules to be extracted from dense shale rock formations. The technology is being used to the greatest extent in the gas industry in the United States. Indeed, the International Energy Agency (IEA) estimated in 2013 that the United States will replace Russia as the world's largest producer of natural gas in only two years. The Americans could also become the world's top petroleum producers by 2017.

According to a report by PricewaterhouseCoopers, published in February 2013, shale oil production could also boost the world economy by up to US$2.7 trillion by 2035. The extra supply could reach up to 12% of global oil production, or 14 million barrels a day, and push global oil prices down by up to 40%. PwC added that the level of global growth could increase by around as much as 3.7% by the extra supply of shale oil, which is the equivalent of adding an economy roughly the size of the United Kingdom to the total world economy by 2035. But the benefits of oil-price reductions as a result of shale oil production are likely to vary significantly by country. Current major oil exporters, such as Russia and the Middle East, could be "significant net losers in the long term unless they can develop their own shale oil resources on a large scale", it said.

Low natural gas prices—the price of natural gas in the United States is only a quarter of what it was in 2008—have led many analysts to predict a resurgence of American industry. The US government estimates that the shale boom could generate 600,000 new jobs, while other experts even believe that up to three million new jobs could be created in the coming years.

Other countries with large shale reserves are believed to include China, Argentina, Poland, France, and Germany. The United States, however, is likely to be the key beneficiary.

A study by Germany's foreign intelligence agency, the BND, concludes that Washington's discretionary power in foreign and security policy will increase substantially as a result of the country's new energy riches. According to the BND study, the political threat potential of oil producers such as Iran will decline. It is possible, some argue, that, in about 15 years the United States will no longer station aircraft carriers in the Persian Gulf.

Releasing its World Energy Outlook report in November 2012, the IEA confirmed the changes taking place in the global energy marketplace. "North America is at the forefront of a sweeping transformation in oil and gas production that will affect all regions of the world, yet the potential also exists for a similarly transformative shift in global energy efficiency."

Under its central scenario, the IEA forecast that the United States would become a net exporter of natural gas by 2020, and would be almost self-sufficient in energy, in net terms, by 2035. It added that North America's emergence as a net oil exporter would accelerate the switch in direction of international oil trade, with almost 90% of Middle Eastern oil exports being drawn to Asia by 2035.

Links between regional gas markets would also strengthen as liquefied natural gas trading becomes more flexible, and contract terms evolve. It forecast that global energy demand would continue to grow, increasing by more than one-third to 2035. China, India, and the Middle East would account for 60% of the growth, while demand would remain largely unchanged in the OECD, although there would be a pronounced shift towards gas and renewables.

Fossil fuels would remain dominant, supported by subsidies that, in 2011, jumped by almost 30% to US$523 billion, mainly as a result of subsidy increases in the Middle East and North Africa. Global oil demand would grow by seven million bpd to 2020 and would exceed 99 million bpd in 2035, by which time oil prices would reach US$125/barrel in real terms (above US$215/barrel in nominal terms).

The IEA believes that renewables will become the world's second-largest source of power generation by 2015. However, this rapid increase hinges critically on continued subsidies. In 2011, these subsidies (including for biofuels) amounted to US$88 billion, but over the period to 2035 need to amount to US$4.8 trillion.

MARKET ANALYSIS

According to BP, global energy consumption grew by 2.5% in 2011, broadly in line with the historical average but well below the 5.1% seen in 2010. Once again, emerging economies accounted for all of the net growth in energy consumption, with demand in the OECD falling for a third time in the last four years, China alone accounting for 71% of global energy consumption growth. Consumption in OECD countries fell by 0.8%, the third decline in the past four years. The fall in OECD consumption was led by a sharp decline in Japan—in volumetric terms, the world's largest decline. Non-OECD consumption grew by 5.3%, in line with the 10-year average. Global consumption growth decelerated in 2011 for all fuels, as did total energy consumption for all regions. The data suggests that growth in global CO2 emissions from energy use continued in 2011, but at a slower rate than in 2010.

Fossil fuels still dominate energy consumption, with a market share of 87%. Renewable energy continues to gain, but today accounts for only 2% of energy consumption globally. Meanwhile, the fossil fuel mix is changing as well. Oil,á still the leading fuel, has lost market share for 12 consecutive years. In 2011, coal was once again the fastest-growing fossil fuel, with predictable consequences for carbon emissions.

Nuclear Energy

The global future of nuclear as a power source was called into question after the disaster that occurred in March 2011, when a Japanese earthquake and tsunami rocked the reactors at Fukushima, leaving radioactivity leaking from the plant. However, many governments are continuing to pursue nuclear energy as a key part of their energy strategies. In the UK, for example, all but one of the country's 16 reactors—supplying almost a fifth of the UK's power—are set to close by 2023, but replacements planned.

In March 2013, the British minister Vince Cable said: "Nuclear power has the potential to play an increasing role in meeting the UK's future energy needs. It is a source of low-carbon energy and can contribute to the UK's energy mix and security of supply longer-term. This strategy—like those for offshore wind and oil and gas—will achieve a more effective alignment and integration of energy and industrial policy to enable the UK to deliver competitive energy technologies in future, with significant input from UK-based industry." The British government said that £930 billion will be invested globally in building reactors over the next 20 years, with £250 billion being spent on decommissioning disused stations.

However, Germany has adopted a more radical solution, vowing to phase out the country's nuclear power plants by 2022, while expanding the use of renewables. The decision, announced in May 2011, makes Germany the biggest industrial power to announce plans to give up nuclear energy. Chancellor Angela Merkel set up a panel to review nuclear power following the crisis at Fukushima in Japan. Nearly a quarter of German's electricity currently comes from nuclear power.

Biofuels

Controversy also continues to surrounds biofuels, with many reports that it is contributing to an increase in food prices, which is hurting the world's poorest people. In August 2012, however, Harald von Witzke, Professor of Agricultural Economics at Humboldt University in Berlin, told the BBC that only 3% of the world's farmland was being used for biofuel. This, he estimated, was responsible for perhaps one-tenth of the doubling in food prices since 2000, suggesting that reports of the impact of biofuels on food prices has been exaggerated. However, in October 2012, the EU said it was changing its policy on biofuels to encourage energy production from waste rather than from crops.

The European Commission said that clearing land in order to plant biofuel crops can often cancel out the environmental benefits of biofuel. In some cases, forests are chopped down. The EU is putting a cap of 5% on the food-based biofuel allowed in the renewable energy used for transport. New biofuel installations will have to meet a minimum 60% threshold in terms of their efficiency in reducing greenhouse gas emissions. Meanwhile, the UN has appointed a special rapporteur on the right to food, Olivier De Schutter, who has sharply criticized the direct and indirect effects of biofuels on the poor.

According to BP's 2012 Statistical Review, world biofuels production grew by 0.7% in 2011, the smallest increase since 2000. Increased output in North America was offset by declines in South and Central America, and Europe. Biodiesel accounts for just 27.5% of global biofuels output, but accounted for all of its growth in 2011. Global ethanol output declined by 1.4%.

Renewables

According to BP's 2012 Statistical Review, the rapid growth of renewable power generation continued in 2011. Global growth was 17.7%, only marginally slower than in 2010, and the ninth successive year of double-digit growth. It was the largest-ever volume growth, at 129 TWh, contributing 20% of the growth in global power generation, and representing 10% of world energy growth.

OECD countries remain the main source of renewable power generation (76% of the world total in 2011), according to BP, but non-OECD growth has accelerated sharply, and has exceeded OECD growth in percentage terms in each of the six years to 2011. The share of renewable power in global power generation reached 3.9% in 2011, up from 1.5% in 2000. Renewables accounted for 6% of OECD power generation in 2011, compared to 1.8% in the non-OECD. While the aggregate shares remain low, for some individual countries renewables now contribute a significant share of power. Fourteen countries now have a renewables share of more than 10%, up from just eight countries in 2010.

However, according to a PricewaterhouseCoopers report published in February 2013, the worldwide expansion of relatively cheap shale oil could put investment in renewable energy and global emissions targets under threat, as well as posing other environmental risks. The report also noted that cheaper oil could displace production from higher cost and more environmentally sensitive areas, such as the Arctic and Canadian tar sands, while tax windfalls could provide finance for carbon capture and storage, and other low-carbon technologies.

Energy Outlook

In its report, "The Outlook for Energy: A view to 2040," published in early 2013, Exxon Mobil made the following predictions as to how the global energy market will develop over the next 30 or so years:

- Efficiency will continue to play a key role in solving global energy challenges. Energy-saving practices and technologies, such as hybrid vehicles and high-efficiency natural gas power plants, will help OECD countries—including those in North America and Europe—to keep energy use essentially flat, even as OECD economic output grows by around 80%.
- Energy demand in developing nations (non-OECD) will rise by 65% by 2040 compared to 2010, reflecting growing prosperity and expanding economies. Overall, global energy demand will growá by 35%, even with significant efficiency gains, as the

world's population expands from about seven billion people today, to nearly nine billion people by 2040, led by growth in Africa and India.

- This growth will generate greater demand for electricity. Electricity generation represents the largest driver of demand for energy. By 2040, it will account for more than half of the increase in global energy demand.
- Growth in transport demand will be fueled expanding commercial activity. However, energy consumed by personal vehicles will gradually peak, and then begin to fall as vehicles become much more fuel-efficient.
- Technology is enabling the safe development of once hard-to-produce energy resources, significantly expanding available supplies to meet the world's changing energy needs. Oil will remain the number one global fuel, while natural gas will overtake coal for the number two spot. Use of nuclear power and renewable energy will grow, while demand for coal peaks, and then begins a gradual decline.
- Evolving demand and supply patterns will open the door for increased global trade opportunities. By around 2030, North America will likely become a net exporter of oil and oil-based products.

MORE INFO

Article:

Der Spiegel. "Full throttle ahead: US tips global power scales with fracking." February 1, 2013. Online at: tinyurl.com/ang2hfo

Reports:

BP. "Statistical review of world energy." June 2012. Online at: tinyurl.com/q7h9qn4

ExxonMobil. "The outlook for energy: A view to 2040." 2013. Online at: www.exxonmobil.co.uk/Corporate/files/news_pub_eo.pdf

PricewaterhouseCoopers. "Shale gas: A renaissance in US manufacturing?" February 2012. Online at: tinyurl.com/8ze7pr6

See Also:

★ Viewpoint: Challenges in Global Energy and Their Potential Impact on the Cost of Energy (pp. 144–146)

★ Viewpoint: Energy Self-Sufficiency through Shale Gas Changes the Game for the United States (pp. 170–172)

Mining (pp. 1637–1638)

Oil and Gas (pp. 1638–1639)

Engineering

MAJOR INDUSTRY TRENDS

The engineering sector encompasses a bewildering array of possible roles, and touches virtually all other industry segments. The discipline of engineering is generally subdivided into mechanical, electrical, and chemical engineering on the macro scale. However, with its connotations of pragmatic manipulation, as in using a body of skill and techniques to achieve a designated impact in the real world, engineering as a term is now readily applied to fields as diverse as software, genetics, and finance.

On this last point, the College of Engineering at the University of Michigan, for example, offers a financial engineering degree, teaching students how to use applied mathematics to analyze financial derivatives. In fact, the original financial engineers, whom many blame for devising some of the complex derivatives that played such a big role in the current global banking crisis, were drawn from the fields of process and operations engineering, as well as from applied mathematics backgrounds.

Understanding the behavior of complex systems, such as near-turbulent water flows, is, after all, an engineering specialty, and is an essential part of propeller design. There are also numerous other classic engineering problems involving near-chaotic systems. Moving from this to spotting short-lasting, predictable trends in complex data flows, such as trades on millions of stocks, is not that big a jump.

For those concerned with educating the next generation of engineers, the way in which new fields, such as nanotechnology or genetics, are opening up rich, new seams for engineering, is not surprising. The US National Academy of Engineering (NAE) holds a symposium every year under the banner, "Frontiers of Engineering—Reports on leading-edge engineering" (see www.nae.edu). The 2011 symposium took place from September 19th to 21st at Google Headquarters and looked at four cutting-edge areas: additive manufacturing; engineering sustainable buildings; semantic processing; and neuroprosthetics. It is safe to say that none of these topics would have been on an engineering agenda a few decades back, demonstrating yet again that this is a field that is constantly changing.

With drug delivery systems, advances in new materials have opened up new ways of administering drugs to patients using, for example, engineered particles providing sustained release of therapies over an extended time frame. With nanoelectronic devices, the search is on to find circuit concepts and sensor functionalities, such as new switches, that can develop new technologies for information processing to create wholly new kinds of computers.

In a book, The Engineering of 2020: Visions of Engineering in the New Century, published in 2004 by the NAE, the academy points out that, in the past, "changes in the engineering profession and engineering education have followed changes in technology and society. Disciplines were added and curricula were created to meet the critical challenges in society, and to provide the workforce required to integrate new developments into the economy."

However, today, technological change is occurring at a faster and faster pace. Engineering needs to apply some of its skills to anticipating future necessary advances, and adapting the education of future generations of engineers to be "ahead of the curve," insofar as that is possible, the NAE argues.

In fact, this is likely to be where the real locus of competition between nations and, indeed, between multinational and multidisciplinary engineering companies will lie in a few years' time. Firms and nations that are best placed with innovative answers to emerging global challenges, be these to do with food crises, or aberrant weather patterns, or power or water shortages, will become the leaders in the field.

Simultaneously with all this, of course, established international engineering companies specializing in a huge array of disciplines, are essential generators of GDP growth in virtually all the developed, and many developing economies. This leads directly to the topic of outsourcing, which is one of the major themes in manufacturing, engineering, and design today.

Writing in the January 2012 edition of Oracle's Profit magazine, Scott Bartlett argues that the three dominant trends in engineering in 2012 were: (a) construction projects will continue to increase in complexity; (b) increased globalization with increased competition for the same projects; and c) increased reporting as owners of major projects seek to cut costs through analyzing processes. On point (a) in particular, Bartlett points out that major projects are now the rule rather than the exception, and cites the 2,700 feet tall Burj Khalifa in Dubai as an example, along with China's massive South-North water diversion project. Today, most of the really complex large infrastructure projects are outside North America, with only three of the current crop of 20 mega infrastructure projects being based in the United States.

MARKET ANALYSIS

A few years ago, it was fashionable for governments in Europe and the United States, and particularly in the United Kingdom, to urge manufacturers to "go up the value chain," to avoid competition from low-wage economies. The point followed logically enough from the fact that volume manufacturing, of the "pile 'em high, sell 'em cheap" variety, is essentially about price, and the lower the wages paid, the cheaper the price of the end-product.

It followed that manufacturers based in China or India, where wages were a lot lower than in advanced economies, would drive their counterparts based in high-wage economies out of business.

To counter this, the argument went, Western manufacturers should use their engineering and design know-how to focus on high-value, complex products. The problem with this argument, many people noticed, is that it presupposes that low-wage economies are trapped forever doing low-wage, "grunt" jobs, and will not be able to do high-quality engineering and design work to innovate and compete on complex, high-value-added projects.

This argument began to fall away when people took account of just how many engineers and scientists low-wage economy countries such as India and China were producing. It vanished entirely when Western companies started outsourcing design and innovation to offshore centers, as Indian and Chinese engineers are also "lower wage" than their colleagues in developed economies, at least for the present.

A team at the Pratt School of Engineering, Duke University, United States, has specialized in studying the quality and quantity of engineering graduates being produced by Indian and Chinese institutions, and the impact of globalization on the engineering profession. Their aim was to explore the factors driving the US trend to engineering outsourcing, and to look at what could be done to enable the United States to retain any edge it still has in this field.

The comparative annual numbers most frequently cited for engineering graduates in the United States, India, and China, they point out, are 70,000 undergraduate engineers in the United States, 350,000 for India, and 700,000 for China. However, when the Duke University team checked the numbers, they found huge difficulties around semantics.

Chinese does not distinguish particularly, as far as terms go, between a motor mechanic and a nuclear engineer, both are "engineers." The team checked 200 universities in China and 100 in India. Their analysis showed that while a realistic figure for China for 2004 was probably more like 360,000 conventionally trained engineering graduates, versus 139,000 in India, and almost 138,000 for the United States, there was, nevertheless, a very real and obvious ramping-up in the number of engineers China is now producing.

This increase stems from initiatives taken by the Chinese government in 1999, and those initiatives are now bearing fruit. What has really worked for the Chinese, the Duke team found, as far as numbers at least are concerned, is to transform science and engineering education from "elite education" to "mass education," by increasing enrolment in engineering programs. The downside of this is that an improvement of 140% in numbers of students has taken place at the expense of dramatic increases in class sizes, creating some serious quality problems for qualification standards.

In other words, the quality of engineering dropped off dramatically outside some 10 to 15 top Chinese engineering institutions, even as the numbers went up. The Duke team, therefore, argue that China is likely to find it at least as difficult as the United States does to generate a large number of extremely well-skilled engineers over time.

India, by way of contrast, has benefited from engineering education places being offered by a number of private colleges and training institutions. Most of these face quality issues, the Duke team says, but a few are recognized as producing high-quality graduates. Indian companies told the team that they felt comfortable hiring the top graduates from a wide range of Indian institutions (a reverse of the situation in China).

A key fact that emerged from a survey of US companies carried out by the Duke University team was that the vast majority of these companies said they would move at least part of their R&D to emerging markets, in order to respond to the big opportunities in these growing markets. They also said that their units there would increasingly be catering for worldwide needs.

On the positive side, by staying open to the brightest and the best, the United States—and, by implication, Europe—continues to benefit from the ability to attract very-high-caliber students from both China and India, many of whom stay in Europe after completing their studies, often making very substantial contributions in their own right to innovation and progress, and ultimately to the GDP of the host country.

The question of who will "out-innovate" whom may quite possibly prove to be irrelevant in the longer term, itself becoming a victim of the increasingly global and multinational nature of engineering operations.

Regulatory Issues

Engineering is a prime example of a discipline bounded on all sides by political and social "rules." The European Union's Waste Electrical and Electronic Equipment Directive, known as WEEE, on the disposal of end-of-life electronic and electrical equipment is one obvious example. One of the goals of WEEE is to force manufacturers to think much more carefully about the way they engineer products.

By getting manufacturers to think of the waste that results at the end of a product's lifecycle, and by making them pay for the ultimate disposal of those products at expensive, special-purpose, hazardous waste sites, the idea is that manufacturers will improve the recyclable content of their products (less going to landfill or hazardous waste disposal sites equals less cost per product).

In other words, the goal being set for engineers is no longer, "does this product do the job well?" The dimension, "can this product be cost-effectively disposed of at the end of its life?" has been added. From an engineer's standpoint, that is just another design challenge, and one that gives their company yet another opportunity to craft something better than their competitors have yet managed.

Equally relevant are the various moral limits on what may and may not be "engineered." The debates over genetic manipulation of crops are now familiar ground. Engineers and scientists face similar emotive debates over the topic of cloning, a subject that emerges very readily out of breakthrough research into DNA, the "blueprint" of life.

Today, and for the foreseeable future, plant cloning is "in," human cloning is "out," and the "in" and the "out" here have nothing to do with natural limits on engineering, and everything to do with the moral limits that society places on engineers.

The NAE points out that the biotechnology "revolution," for example, holds great potential but it is a field in which political and societal implications intervene to set limits on what is acceptable. In other words, there are very clear issues that have an impact on technological change that are beyond the scope of engineering.

Finally, there is much to be hoped for from the fact that engineering has a tremendous role to play in facilitating international cooperation. As the NAE notes, engineering itself "speaks through an international language of mathematics, science, and technology," and, as such, bodies of professionals across the globe very quickly find themselves on common ground when dealing with engineering concepts. It looks at least possible that the real future of engineering lies on a global, rather than on any particular merely national stage—particularly as the challenges facing engineering are themselves increasingly global in nature.

MORE INFO

Article:

Bartlett, Scott. "Top three trends in 2012 for the engineering and construction industry. "*Profit* (January 2012). Online at: tinyurl.com/p9qspn8

Websites:

Grand Challenges for Engineering, National Academy of Engineering (US): www.engineeringchallenges.org

National Academy of Engineering (US): www.nae.edu

Prism, journal of the American Society for Engineering Education (ASEE): www.prism-magazine.org

See Also:

Chemicals (pp. 1614–1616)
Construction and Building Materials (pp. 1616–1618)
Electronics (pp. 1622–1624)

Food and Agribusiness

MAJOR INDUSTRY TRENDS

Despite the accelerating industrialization of the globe over the past 100 years, and the rapid growth of manufacturing industry across the developing world over the past 20 years, around four in 10 of the total global population remain involved in agriculture, according to the United Nations Food and Agriculture Organization (FAO). The FAO says that, in 2009, more than one billion people were engaged in agriculture, or around one in three workers. There are huge variations across the globe. In sub-Saharan Africa around 60% of the workforce is engaged in farming. In the United States, by contrast, less than one per cent of the population claims farming as an occupation.

Food Prices

Food price inflation at the retail level has fallen significantly from its peak in 2008, and its contribution to overall inflation has become more moderate. Nevertheless, food price inflation remains high in many developing countries and is still outpacing overall inflation in a majority of countries. A surge in food prices during the summer of 2012, fuelled by the worst drought in more than half a century in the United States, and dry weather in other major exporting countries, raised fears of a new food crisis such as the one seen in 2008. However, food prices fell for the third month running in December 2012. Nonetheless, food prices will stay at high levels in 2013, and low stocks pose the risk of sharp price increases if crops fail, the FAO warned in January 2013. The FAO's Food Price Index, which measures monthly price changes for a basket of cereals, oilseeds, dairy, meat, and sugar, averaged 212 in 2012, down 7% compared to 2011, but still at historically high levels. The FAO's index is below a peak of 238 points hit in February 2011, when high food prices helped drive the Arab Spring uprisings in the Middle East and North Africa.

Western Diets (and Health Problems) Sweep the Globe

Rising living standards and changing patterns of food consumption in emerging countries are other key factors driving global demand for food, and putting upward pressure on commodity prices. Consumption of dairy products in countries such as India and China used to be very low, but is now surging to such an extent that it is driving up prices for dairy products around the world. Similar trends are occurring in meat, vegetable oils, and many other areas.

In 2011, the UN's World Health Organization (WHO) warned that the number of overweight African children under five had tripled to 13.5 million in 20 years. Poor diet, low rates of breastfeeding, and a sedentary lifestyle were largely to blame for the sharp rise in overweight children in developing nations, the WHO said. In Africa, the jump was from four million in 1990 to 13.5 million in 2010, an increase from 4% of the total under-five population to 8.5%, it said. In Asia, the corresponding gain over the same period was from 3.2% to 4.9%.

The Growing Power of Supermarkets and the Impact on Agribusiness

The growing power of supermarkets around the world is also having an enormous impact on agribusiness and the food chain. The phenomenon has already been well documented in Western countries. Up until the early 1960s, small neighborhood grocery shops, independent butchers, and local fruit and vegetable shops dominated food retailing in many Western countries, such as the United Kingdom. Today, supermarkets account for more than 90% of UK food sales. Furthermore, four major chains—Tesco, Asda (part of US giant, Wal-Mart), Sainsbury's, and Morrisons—account for around 75% of sales, with Tesco alone taking more than £3 of every £10 spent on food in the country. Similar trends can be seen in other developed countries, and, increasingly, in emerging economies around the world. Supermarkets entered Latin America in the early 1990s, and South-East Asia in the latter part of the decade. They are now sweeping across India, China, Eastern Europe, and parts of Africa. In many countries, supermarkets now account for around 50% of food sales.

While suppliers and wholesalers could once dictate prices, and even tell retailers which products they could sell, the balance of power has now shifted decisively to the retailers, which are in a position to demand ever-lower prices and improved terms. The major supermarket chains increasingly source their produce from around the world, placing further pressure on local suppliers, which either meet the demands of the major chains, or go under. Inevitably, this trend affects the person at the bottom of the supply chain: the farmer. The supermarkets are also using the increasing acceptance and popularity of their own brands to exert pressure on suppliers.

MARKET ANALYSIS

The Size of the Global Food Market

According to Frost & Sullivan's Food & Agricultural Research Practice, the cumulative value of all revenue derived from the global food and beverage value chain—from farm to fork—was well over US$20 trillion dollars in 2012, representing nearly 30% of the world's entire economy.

Global Trends by Commodity: Cereals

The FAO's forecast for world cereal production in 2012 (published in February 2013) estimated output of 2,302 million tonnes (including rice in milled terms), 2% down from the previous year's record. However, the FAO says that early prospects for 2013 point to increased global wheat output. Contributing largely to this outlook is an estimated 4-5% increase in the winter wheat area in the EU where, additionally, winter weather conditions have been generally favorable. Elsewhere in Europe, prospects are satisfactory in the Russian Federation and Ukraine, where winter plantings remained similar to 2011's levels, and moisture conditions are somewhat improved except in those southern parts of Russia worst affected by drought in 2012, according to the FAO. The organization adds that in Asia, winter wheat prospects are reported as being favorable in China, where higher minimum purchase prices have encouraged farmers to maintain last year's crop production. In India, plantings are around the respectable level seen in 2012, and another bumper crop is in prospect. In the United States, the outlook is less favorable. Despite an estimated 1% increase in winter wheat plantings, and prospects for spring wheat areas to expand, severe drought conditions continue to plague the southern Great Plains, where the condition of crops is reported to be very poor.

In terms of coarse grains, the first 2013 prospects for maize crops in South America's main producing countries are favorable. In Southern Africa, prospects for the 2013 maize harvest, due to start from April/May, are generally favorable, despite the late onset of seasonal rains in parts.

Rice

Rice is the staple food for around 2.5 billion people, or more than one-third of the global population. The global price of rice has been increasing for much of the past decade. According to the International Rice Research Institute (IRRI), a non-profit research and education center, this is because the world is consuming more rice than it is producing, and global stocks are becoming rapidly depleted (current stocks are at their lowest levels since 1988). A number of factors are causing this imbalance between supply and demand. They include:

- A slowdown in the growth of rice yield. In South Asia, for example, average yield growth decreased from 2.14% per year between 1970 and 1990 to 1.40% per year between 1990 and 2005, according to IRRI.
- In Asia, pressure on land is limiting the scope for increasing the area devoted to the cultivation of rice.
- Governments are devoting decreasing resources to agricultural research and development. IRRI says that declining rice prices in the 1990s led to complacency about the need for R&D among governments.
- Rice has become an increasingly popular food in Africa, leading to further pressure on global supplies.
- Population growth is outstripping growth in rice production, a problem that is projected to worsen.
- Rapid economic growth is increasing the pressure on agricultural land. IRRI says that highly productive rice land has been lost to housing and industrial development, or to the cultivation of vegetables and other cash crops.

In its November 2012 Food Outlook, the FAO said that world rice production in 2012 may surpass 2011's record, supported by favorable growing conditions. Steadfast import demand, together with very ample export availabilities, were sustaining an expansion of trade in 2012, with a further, albeit small, increase foreseen in 2013.

In terms of rice production in 2013, the FAO says the outlook is positive in Indonesia. In Sri Lanka, plantings of the main 2013 crop late last year were again constrained by lingering drought and, subsequently, floods. In Australia, the area under rice expanded by more than 12%, its highest level since 2002, but extreme heat is raising concern about possible negative impacts on yields. In Southern Africa, prospects for 2013 crops remain uncertain, as much of the sub-region has witnessed a late arrival and erratic progress of the seasonal rains.

Meat and Meat Products

Global demand for meat has risen more than five-fold in the past 50 years, according to the FAO. However, the FAO says that in late 2012/early 2013, global meat markets are challenged by high feed prices, stagnating consumption, and falling profitability, with growth in total output slowing down to 2%. Virtually all of the sector growth in 2012 is forecast to stem from the feed-dependent poultry and pig meat sectors, as gains in both bovine and sheep meat outputs are anticipated to be modest.

Concerns about the profitability of the meat sector have been compounded by a weakening of the growth of export markets, with trade expansion anticipated to slow down to 2% from 8% in 2011, according to the FAO. Global meat exports are expected to edge up by about 600,000 tonnes to 29.4 million tonnes in 2012, mainly sustained by increased poultry and pig meat flows, and with much of the market expansion likely to be captured by developing countries, in particular Brazil and India.

Escalating feed prices and slowing meat production growth pushed up international meat prices in late 2012, to levels approaching the highs attained in 2011. Accordingly, the FAO meat price index, averaged 174 points between January and October, which compares with 176 for the same period in 2011. Most of the recent increase in the meat price index reflect price gains for poultry and pig meat.

Fish and Fish Products

Fish is the main source of protein for around a billion people. As with meat, demand for fish is also increasing rapidly, driven by population growth and rising incomes. Indeed, global per capita consumption of fish increased from 9 kg in 1961 to an estimated 16.5 kg in 2003, and around 17.1 kg in 2008, according to the FAO. In 2011, trade volumes and prices both saw a positive uplift, sustained by dynamic demand globally, but particularly from emerging economies. Supply fell short of demand for many farmed species, including Atlantic salmon, trout, sea bass, and sea bream. In addition, growing domestic consumption of local fish products, especially in Asia and South America, is constraining export availability.

Dairy Products, Eggs, Oils, and Fats

International prices of dairy products began to strengthen in mid-2012, reversing the steady decline that had characterized the previous 12 months. The change in trend resulted from a tightening of supplies to the world market. The FAO believed that global supply

 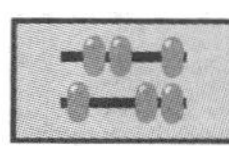      

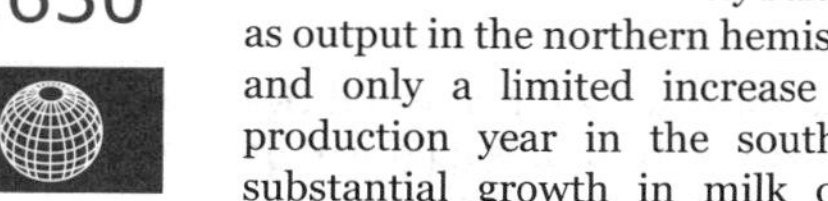

and demand would be finely balanced until at least the end of the year, as output in the northern hemisphere moved seasonally downwards and only a limited increase was anticipated during the new production year in the southern hemisphere. The absence of substantial growth in milk output in the principal exporting countries is likely to mean a further upward movement in prices.

World milk production in 2012 is forecast to have grown by 3% to 760 million tonnes—a higher rate than the average for recent years, according to the FAO. Asia is expected to account for most of the increase, with output also growing in Oceania and South America. The FAO believes that the world trade in dairy products continued expanding in 2012. Demand remained firm, with imports anticipated to have reached 52.9 million tonnes of milk equivalent, up 4.6% from 2011. Most of the growth in demand is coming from Asia, followed by Africa.

MORE INFO

Reports:

United Nations Food and Agriculture Organization (FAO). "Food outlook, June 2013." 2013. Published biannually. Online at: www.fao.org/giews/english/fo

United Nations Food and Agriculture Organization (FAO). "The state of food and agriculture 2013: Food systems for better nutrition." 2013. Published annually. Online at: www.fao.org/publications/sofa

Websites:

International Food Policy Research Institute (IFPRI): www.ifpri.org
International Rice Research Institute (IRRI): www.irri.org
US Department of Agriculture (USDA): www.usda.gov

Healthcare and Pharmaceuticals

MAJOR INDUSTRY TRENDS

Healthcare and pharmaceuticals are two distinct industries, but they are interdependent and are subject to similar trends, which is why they are covered together in this profile. Both are benefiting from ageing populations in many advanced economies, and various developing countries, such as China. In addition, important medical discoveries, including the decoding of the human genome, are fueling scientific advances, and facilitating the release of new drugs and treatments.

The Impact of Austerity on Healthcare Budgets

Governments in many developed countries are being forced to hike taxes and contain and even cut public spending to curb large deficits and growing debt mountains. This is particularly true in many peripheral eurozone countries. In Greece, for example, total health spending accounted for 10.2 % of GDP 2010, down from 10.6% in 2009, according to the OECD. The financial and economic crisis initially led to a rapid increase in the health spending to GDP ratio, as the Greek economy slumped but health spending was maintained. However, a subsequent cut in public spending has seen the health share of GDP fall, says the OECD.

The same is true in other countries, according to *The Economist*. In an article published in June 2012, it points out that eight OECD countries cut spending in 2010, while only three increased it by more than 3% in real terms. Greece's healthcare spending declined by 6.5% in 2010, while Ireland cut healthcare spending by 7.6% in 2010. However, *The Economist* points out that the cuts follow nearly a decade of generous increases. In 2010, OECD governments spent an average of 9.5% of their GDP on healthcare, up from 6.9% in 1990. Indeed, spending increased by a real annual average of 4.8% between 2000 and 2009. However, in 2010 healthcare spending across the 34 countries of the OECD was largely flat.

The OECD says that most of the reductions in public spending in Greece have been achieved through cuts in wages and actual reductions in the number of health workers, as well as price decreases for pharmaceuticals. As in many other countries hard-hit by the recession, investment plans have also been put on hold.

The public sector is the main source of health funding in all OECD countries, except Chile, Mexico, and the United States, according to the OECD. Health spending accounted for 17.6% of GDP in the United States in 2010, down slightly from 2009 (17.7%) and by far the highest share in the OECD, and a full eight percentage points higher than the OECD average of 9.5%. Following the United States were the Netherlands (at 12.0% of GDP), and France and Germany (both at 11.6% of GDP).

Spending by Country

The United States spent US$8,233 on health per capita in 2010, two and a half times more than the OECD average of US$3,268 (adjusted for purchasing power parity), according to the OECD Health Data report issued in June 2012. Norway and Switzerland, which spent more than US$5,250 per capita were the next largest spenders. Americans spent more than twice as much as relatively rich European countries such as France, Sweden, and the United Kingdom.

Despite the relatively high level of health expenditure in the United States, there are fewer physicians per capita in the country than in most other OECD countries. In 2010, America had 2.4 practicing physicians per 1,000 population, below the OECD average of 3.1. By contrast, there were 11 nurses per 1,000 population in the US in 2010, a higher number than the average of 8.7 across OECD countries.

The number of curative care hospital beds in the United States was 2.6 per 1,000 population in 2009 (latest year available), lower than the OECD average of 3.4 beds. The OECD says that, in common with other members, the number of hospital beds per capita has fallen over the past 25 years in the United States. This decline has coincided with a reduction in average length of stays in hospitals and an increase in day surgeries. In the United States, the number of computed tomography (CT) scanners and magnetic resonance imaging (MRI) units is much greater than in most other OECD countries. There were 40.7 CT scanners per million population in 2011, a number that is almost double the OECD average of 22.6, and 31.6 MRIs per million population, two and a half times the OECD average of 12.5.

Health Status and Risk Factors

Most OECD countries have enjoyed large gains in life expectancy over the past decades. In the United States, life expectancy at birth increased by almost nine years between 1960 and 2010, but this is less than the increase of more than 15 years in Japan and above 11 years on average in OECD countries. As a result, while life expectancy in the United States used to be 1.5 years above the OECD average in 1960, it is now, at 78.7 years in 2010, more than one year below the average of 79.8 years. Japan, Switzerland, Italy, and Spain are the OECD countries with the highest life expectancy, exceeding 82 years.

The proportion of smokers among the adult population has shown a marked decline over recent decades across most OECD countries. In the United States, the proportion of adults who smoke daily has fallen by more than half over the past 30 years, from 33.5% in 1980 to 15.1% in 2010. This is the lowest rate among OECD countries after Sweden and Iceland. At the same time, obesity rates have increased in recent decades in all OECD countries, although there are notable differences. In the United States, the obesity rate among adults—based on actual measures of height and weight—was 35.9% in 2010, up from 15% in 1978. This is the highest rate among OECD countries. The average for the 15 OECD countries with measured data was 22.2% in 2010. The OECD warns that the growing prevalence of obesity foreshadows increases in the occurrence of health problems (such as diabetes and cardiovascular diseases), and higher healthcare costs in the future.

Ageing Populations

Ageing populations are driving demand for healthcare services and pharmaceutical products around the globe. Older people tend to require more healthcare and are subject to higher levels of chronic illness than younger people.

The older population—persons aged 65 years or older—numbered 40.4 million in 2010 in the United States (the most recent year for which data are available), according to the US Department of Health & Human Services. This represents 13.1% of the US population, or more than one in every eight Americans. The number of older Americans has increased by 5.4 million or 15.3% since 2000, compared to an increase of 8.7% for the under-65 population. However, the number of Americans aged 45-64 who will reach 65 over the next two decades increased by 31% during this period.

Since 1900, the percentage of Americans aged 65-plus has more than tripled (from 4.1% in 1900 to 13.1% in 2010), and the number has increased almost 13 times (from 3.1 million to 40.4 million). The older population itself is increasingly older. In 2010, the 65-74 age group (20.8 million) was 10 times larger than in 1900. In contrast, the 75-84 group (13.1 million) was 17 times larger and the 85-plus group (5.5 million) was 45 times larger.

In 2009, persons reaching age 65 had an average life expectancy of an additional 18.8 years (20.0 years for females and 17.3 years for males). A child born in 2009 could expect to live 78.2 years, about 30 years longer than a child born in 1900. Much of this increase occurred because of reduced death rates for children and young adults. However, the period of 1990-2007 also has seen reduced death rates for the population aged 65-84, especially for men: by 41.6% for men aged 65-74, and by 29.5% for men aged 75-84. Life expectancy at age 65 increased by only 2.5 years between 1900 and 1960, but increased by 4.2 years from 1960 to 2007. Nonetheless, some research has raised concerns about future increases in life expectancy in the US compared to other high-income countries, primarily due to past smoking and current obesity levels, especially for women aged 50 and over (National Research Council (2011)).

As the proportion of older people in the population grows, so does their political importance, and this is partly why democratically elected governments are loathe to cut healthcare spending. In the UK, for example, the coalition government elected in 2010 is committed to reducing the public sector deficit, yet has ring-fenced healthcare spending.

Scientific and Technological Advances

Enormous progress has been made over the past decade in developing drugs that treat previously incurable illnesses. The BBC reported in January 2013, for example, on what the "Brave New World of personalized medicine", opened up by our new understanding of the human genome, may look like. It reported on the results of research, published in January 2013, carried out the Brighton and Sussex Medical School and colleagues at the University of Dundee, which had focused on the substantial minority of severely asthmatic children who respond poorly to the leading conventional drug treatment, Salmeterol.

The drug, which is found in Seretide and Servant inhalers, acts on beta-2 receptors in the lining of the airways, but previous research had shown that as many as one in seven children carry a gene variant—arginine-16—that undermines its effectiveness. The study showed that by substituting salmeterol for an alternative anti-inflammatory medicine, montelukast, outcomes for severely asthmatic children with the arginine-16 gene variant were substantially improved. The children experienced increased quality of life, and attendance at school and in sports activities improved, while the number of visits to out-of-hours GPs' surgeries declined.

For the price of a simple spit test—costing about £15 a head—existing treatments for a chronic and debilitating condition can be revised and tailored to fit a specific genetic sub-group within a population. It provides an example of stratified or personalized medicine working its way into practice. The BBC concluded that the better targeting of existing medicines within groups of patients "may show us how the hype over personalized medicine could begin to be realized."

Developed Economy Dominance of the Pharmaceutical Industry Under Pressure from Emerging Economies

After a long period of strong US market dominance, the United Kingdom, and Europe as a whole, are facing increasing competition from emerging economies, such as China, Brazil, and India, according to the Association of the British Pharmaceutical Industry (ABPI).

From 2003 to 2007, the UK was ranked as the fifth or sixth nation in the worldwide pharmaceutical market, but has since fallen to 10th position. China has remained one of the strongest growing countries in the world throughout the recession. The United States remains the largest market in the world, with spending of around US$22 billion in 2011. It is followed by Japan with spending of around US$111 billion, and China with around US$65 billion, says the ABPI, quoting figures from *IMS World Review 2012 Analyst*.

MARKET ANALYSIS

Healthcare Spending

The total global expenditure for health amounted to around US$6.5 trillion in 2010, according to the World Health Organization, and health expenditure as a percentage of GDP has been increasing among all major economies.

Spending on healthcare varies widely from country to country, as do outcomes. Nor is there necessarily a correlation between the amount of money spent and the effectiveness of the healthcare system. The United States spends more on healthcare than any other country, in both relative and absolute terms, yet its healthcare system scores poorly in terms of its overall performance, according to the Commonwealth Fund Commission, a US private foundation that supports independent research on healthcare issues. The Fund produced a report on the performance of the US health system in 2008 ("National scorecard on US health system performance"). The scorecard aimed to measure and monitor healthcare outcomes, quality, access, efficiency, and equity in the United States. It ranked the United States last out of 19 countries on a measure of mortality amenable to medical care. In June 2010, the Commonwealth Fund Commission published an update which found that the US healthcare system ranks last or next to last on five dimensions of a high performance health system: quality, access, efficiency, equity, and healthy lives.

MORE INFO

Article:

The Economist. "Health-care spending." June 30, 2012. Online at: www.economist.com/node/21557793

Reports:

Davis, Karen, Cathy Schoen, and Kristof Stremikis. "Mirror, mirror on the wall: How the performance of the U.S. health care system compares internationally." Commonwealth Fund, June 2010. Online at: tinyurl.com/3t2sc72

Organisation for Economic Co-operation and Development. "OECD health data 2012: How does Greece compare." November 2012. Online at: www.oecd.org/greece/BriefingNoteGREECE2012.pdf

World Health Organization. "World health statistics 2012." Online at: www.who.int/gho/publications/world_health_statistics/EN_WHS2012_Full.pdf

Websites:

Association of the British Pharmaceutical Industry (ABPI): www.abpi.org.uk

OECD Health Data 2012: www.oecd.org/health/healthdata

See Also:

Chemicals (pp. 1614–1616)

Information Technology

MAJOR INDUSTRY TRENDS

The term information technology (IT), sometimes called information and communications technology or ICT, encompasses a vast range of activities. These include:

- computer programming;
- computer consultancy;
- computer gaming;
- computer networking activities;
- computing facilities management;
- data processing;
- data hosting activities;
- internet service provision;
- telecommunications;
- web portals.

The sector is highly innovative and subject to constant technological development. It is also the source of dramatic changes in business practices in all other industrial sectors. Consumers and businesses now expect to be able to communicate with each other instantly and IT has driven huge increases in productivity in recent decades. A process of convergence has also been underway for some time between IT and telephony, driven by transforming voice traffic from an analogue signal to a digital packet, indistinguishable from other data packets travelling through a computer network.

Cloud computing services are now providing yet another catalyst for ICT convergence, and a revolution in the way businesses operate. Telecommunications carriers are gradually moving IT systems and internet data centers into the cloud, while uniform standards are being developed to speed rapid cloud development. One of the main advantages of cloud computing for businesses is that they no longer need to buy or maintain expensive and energy-draining servers. IT administration, including licensing issues, software updates, and IT security management, is looked after by the cloud computing provider. Cloud computing also allows a dispersed workforce to work effectively, and collaborate easily, even if they are stretched around the globe.

In November 2012, Gartner released a report that said that public cloud services are simultaneously cannibalizing and stimulating demand for external IT services spending. Infrastructure as a service (IaaS) adoption—the most basic and fundamental form of cloud computing service—has expanded beyond development and test use cases, the company said. The Gartner survey found that 19% of organizations are using cloud computing for most of their production computing, and 20% percent are using storage as a service for all, or most, storage requirements. Gartner surveyed 556 organizations, between June and July 2012, across nine countries and multiple industries where cloud planning is a critical issue.

One other key trend is the integration of smart devices, which is changing the way consumers use their home devices (television sets, smartphones, and personal computers or PCs), and blurring the boundaries between these formerly separate industries. As a result of advances in smartphones and tablets, consumers are increasingly using these devices to access the internet. The difference between mobile phones and tablets is also blurring, with phones becoming mobile computers rather than simply a device for making calls or sending text messages.

In January 2013, Gartner said tablets had dramatically changed the device landscape for PCs, not so much by cannibalizing PC sales, but because PC users are shifting consumption to tablets rather than replacing older PCs. Whereas once a world in which individual users would have both a PC and a tablet as personal devices was imagined, Gartner increasingly suspect that most individuals will shift consumption activity to a personal tablet, and perform creative and administrative tasks on a shared PC. There will be some individuals who retain both, but it is believed they will be exception and not the norm.

Software subdivides into numerous specialist areas, from relational database technologies to enterprise applications, to "horizontal" office applications characterized by Microsoft Office, for example.

Somewhat off the main track of IT at present, but very much related to both increases in processor power, and to work in simulation and artificial intelligence, is the field of robotics. This lies outside the scope of this profile, but the linkages between robotics and IT are already transforming both manufacturing and defense.

In addition, the IT arena is characterized by a number of key trends and emerging technologies which, again, have the potential to transform the way businesses currently use IT and carry out their operations, for example, outsourcing IT services, such as desktop PC support, or whole IT-supported functions, such as accounts processing. In technology, the trend to virtualization refers to the ability of large servers to be subdivided into a number of virtual machines, which can be either virtual PCs or virtual servers.

Virtualization carries with it a number of benefits, including stopping what, at one stage, looked like an endless proliferation of servers inside companies. Splitting one large server into a number of virtual servers enables the organization to reduce the number of servers it has to manage. Server virtualization should not be confused with another powerful trend: the creation of virtual environments inside the machine. The fact that desktop processors are now powerful enough to mimic real-world physics in computer space is transforming both design and entertainment.

MARKET ANALYSIS

According to the latest forecast by IT market analysis firm Gartner, worldwide IT spending is projected to total US$3.7 trillion in 2013, a 4.2% increase from 2012 spending of $3.6 trillion. The 2013 outlook for IT spending growth in US dollars has been revised upward from 3.8% in the Q3 2012 forecast. Gartner said much of this spending increase is the result of projected gains in the value of foreign currencies versus the dollar. When measured in constant dollars, 2013 spending growth is forecast to be 3.9%.

In June 2011, Gartner revised its estimate of total spend on IT in 2011 upwards for the second time in the year. It now estimates that global IT spending will grow by 7.1% over 2010's figure, to US$3.67 trillion.

Worldwide devices spending, which includes PCs, tablets, mobile phones, and printers, is forecast to reach US$666 billion in 2013, up 6.3% from 2012. However, this is a significant reduction in the outlook for 2013 compared with Gartner's previous forecast of US$706 billion in worldwide devices and 7.9% growth. The long-term forecast for worldwide spending on devices has been reduced as well, with growth from 2012 to 2016 now expected to average 4.5% annually in current US dollars (down from 6.4%), and 5.1% annually in constant dollars (down from 7.4%). These reductions reflect a sharp fall in the forecast growth in spending on PCs and tablets, which is only partially offset by marginal increases in forecast growth in spending on mobile phones and printers.

Gartner says that the tablet market has seen greater price competition from Android devices as well as smaller, low-priced devices in emerging markets, and this shift towards relatively lower-priced tablets has led the company to lower its average selling prices forecast for 2012 until 2016. These lower prices are also responsible for slowing device spending growth in general, and PC and tablet spending growth in particular.

Gartner forecasts that worldwide enterprise software spending will total US$296 billion in 2013, a 6.4% increase from 2012. This segment will be driven by key markets such as security, storage management, and customer relationship management. However, beginning in 2014, markets aligned to big data and other information management initiatives, such as enterprise content management, data integration tools, and data quality tools, will begin to see increased levels of investment.

The global telecom services market continues to be the largest IT spending market. Gartner analysts predict that growth will be predominately flat over the next few years, as revenue from mobile data services compensates for the decline in total spending for both the fixed and mobile voice services markets. By 2016, Gartner forecasts that mobile data will represent 33% of the total telecom services market, up from 22% in 2012.

Worldwide mobile phone sales to end-users totaled 1.75 billion units in 2012, a 1.7% decline from 2011 sales, according to Gartner. By the end of Q1 2013, smartphones will account for more than half of all mobile phones shipped worldwide according to Gartner. Data from Q4 2012 revealed that smartphone shipments hit a record high of 44% of the overall mobile phone market of 472 million. With smartphone numbers growing by almost 40% year on year every quarter, while shipments of so-called feature phones drop by around 20% in the same period, that would put smartphones substantially ahead of feature phone shipments—at 286 million against 211 million—during the first quarter of 2013. Samsung dominated both the mobile phone and smartphone markets, shipping a total of 107 million units globally in the final quarter of 2012, of which about 64 million were smartphones. Nokia was the second-largest player, accounting for 85 million shipments, while Apple was third with 43.4 million shipments. Apple and Samsung together accounted for 52% of the smartphone market, up from 46.4% in the third quarter, according to Gartner.

Gartner added that Samsung's resources and ability to build a broad market reach are advantages that no other competitor can easily match. However, the competition will intensify in 2013 as players such as Sony and Nokia improve. With Samsung commanding more than 42.5% of the Android market globally, and the next vendor at just a 6% share, the Android operating system is being overshadowed by Samsung's brand, with the Galaxy name nearly a synonym for Android phones in consumers' minds.

MORE INFO

Websites:

Gartner: www.gartner.com
IDC: www.idc.com

See Also:

✔ Auditing Information Technology and Information Systems (p. 1023)
E-Commerce (pp. 1620–1622)
Electronics (pp. 1622–1624)
Telecoms (pp. 1647–1649)

Insurance

MAJOR INDUSTRY TRENDS

The insurance sector is highly cyclical. Enormous sums can be lost when a series of weather-related catastrophes go against the sector. These losses then tend to be made up during the course of the next few years as insurance companies regroup by raising their premium charges. That increased premium in turn attracts large amounts of new money into the sector, which initiates a new round of price competition and insurance company profits fade. The cycle is repeated over and over, which some have argued ultimately means that the sector is not really bearing risk, as losses are foisted onto clients, and the market in general, via higher premiums, with a one or two-year time lag. These switches are labeled a hard cycle, when insurance companies can get a "fair price", and a soft cycle, when price competition in the sector drives down premiums.

By general agreement 2011 was a bad year for the sector, with a series of natural catastrophes around the world. On the plus side, global catastrophes were at a lower level during 2012 than in either 2011 or 2010. A recent report by Aon Benfield, a division of Aon plc, found that insurers generally had very strong capital positions in 2012, and that this was reflected in substantially lower demand by insurers for reinsurance services. (Reinsurance is the process whereby insurers lower the risk to themselves on specific contracts or portfolios of contracts, by farming out some of their portfolio to specialist third-party "reinsurers.")

According to Aon, a great deal of new money flowed into the reinsurance sector during 2012, with the result that the supply of available reinsurance money exceeded demand in most, if not all, global regions. At the same time, with large amounts of cash on their balance sheets, insurance companies were able to absorb larger amounts of business themselves, without turning to the reinsurance market. While there were weather catastrophes in 2012, the scale of the loss to shareholders of the major reinsurance players was bearable. As far as Hurricane Sandy, the storm that hit the east coast of the United States is concerned, reinsurers on average reported that losses directly attributable to policies relating to Hurricane Sandy amount to only 5.2% of shareholders' funds. This compares very favorably for them to the 17.5% that they lost on average in 2011 because of extreme weather events.

Apart from the weather and its impacts, the insurance sector faces some major trends and challenges. These were summed up in a recent report by accountant PwC as: (a) demographic shifts; (b) the rise of emerging markets; and (c) changing customer behaviors, largely driven through social networking and technology changes. These trends affect all three major business areas (i.e. personal, commercial and life, and annuity and retirement) for the insurance sector. The whole sector is going to have to face the fact that growth in major advanced economies is likely to be slow, particularly in comparison with emerging markets. What insurers operating in emerging markets need to do is to find ways of reshaping some mainstream, advanced market insurance products for their own particular markets. At the same time, social trends are changing and are shaking up traditional business patterns in the insurance industry, very much to the benefit of the customer, PwC says. Instead of working through brokers, for example, customers are showing an increasing preference for working directly with insurance providers, if the right internet-based or telephone channels are available. This is driving a switch to insurance products being "bought" by customers, rather than being sold by brokers and agents. The shift to mobile and online shared social networking sites is another factor to be coped with. "Leading insurers will get better at targeting customers, and customizing product and service attributes to meet the specific needs of a particular group of customers," PwC says.

As consumers become ever more comfortable with the likes of Facebook, social networks are likely to foster some dramatic changes. For a start, customers are increasingly likely to use their social network as a way of testing a particular insurer's credibility, so insurance companies have to find ways of marketing to social networking sites in order to promote their own reputation, and avoid or neutralize harm.

At the same time, improvements in technology will enable the leading insurers to become better at targeting customers and customizing their product for each and every one of their client base. Eventually, the online social networks could turn into pooling mechanisms for self-insurance, PwC says. This will change the role of insurers at a primary level, from product manufacturers to administration services providers.

A cluster of technological developments have helped the insurance sector to achieve much greater efficiencies in the last few years. PwC identifies the key developments as a) the growth in smart phones and tablets, which provide constant access to the internet; b) the massive increases in computing power and storage available to companies, which makes it possible to analyze masses of data to spot trends; and c) the growth in active sensors and devices connected to the internet. On this last point, PwC says that on top of the fact that commercial insurers are already looking to connected devices and sensors to develop risk- and loss-management systems, it expects life and health insurers to start using "smart" devices as well. The medical service and treatment model is evolving towards the customization of health care. Personalized medicine and highly customized healthcare offer the sector a way of containing costs as longevity continues to improve.

PwC and the Centre for the Study of Financial Innovation produced a study in 2011 that analyzed the risks run by the insurance sector across the life, non-life reinsurance, and London market sectors. Interestingly, in a year of major catastrophes, the risk that insurers themselves most prioritize is the risk posed to their business models by regulatory changes. Without doubt, this reflects the global industry's dissatisfaction with Solvency II, the major regulatory form being faced by the sector as regulators seek to prevent another meltdown such as the US$188 billion loss suffered by American International Group (AIG). AIG had to be bailed out by US taxpayers, and was one of the first casualties of the 2008 financial crash.

In general, though, the insurance sector was not nearly as badly damaged by the crisis as the global banking sector. In a considered paper on the impact on the sector of the crisis, Zurich Re author Marian Bell argued that, although insurers and banks were both suppliers of financial services, and together constituted the bulk of the financial services industry, they remained very distinct businesses, with different regulatory regimes, and a different approach to risk. Thus, it is not surprising that the financial crisis affected the two related businesses of banking and insurance differently.

The insurance sector was exposed to the global financial crisis in several ways. It invests in equities, and, substantially, in banking stocks (which gave it exposure to bank losses through share-price losses in its investment portfolio), and in corporate investment-grade bonds, about 60% of which come from the finance sector. Insurance companies have also, in recent years, become much more involved in the capital markets, with some insurance lines being securitized and sold to the capital markets. However, this did not pose as great a risk as the banks investing in asset-backed securities, many of which turned toxic as the US subprime mortgage crisis developed.

MARKET ANALYSIS

In its first report on the global insurance industry, the International Association of Insurance Supervisors gave a reasonably optimistic account of how the industry had weathered the series of catastrophes in Asia in 2011, stating that by 2012 it was clear that most non-life insurers and reinsurers had recovered most of their losses during 2012, and were doing reasonably well. This recovery gains more significance when one remembers that 2010 was also a very bad year for the sector. In 2010, total insured losses for the global reinsurance industry from natural catastrophes and man-made disasters amounted to US$108 billion, more than double the total losses for 2009, and coming close to the all-time record of 2005, when hurricanes Katrina, Wilma, and Rita generated claims well in excess of US$100 billion in the US alone. The record books were rewritten in 2011 when one looks at total economic losses rather than total insured losses, with the former amounting to a staggering US$350 billion. The earthquake and tsunami in Japan in March 2011 accounted for the vast bulk of this. One of the big worries for insurers in 2011 and during virtually the whole of 2012 was the extent to which investments by the sector remain exposed to the risk of sovereign debt defaults in Europe. Insurers are also heavily exposed to debt instruments issued by European banks. The fact that the start of 2013 saw an upturn in optimism in Europe, labeled a "positive contagion" by European Central Bank President, Mario Monti, will be a great relief to the sector.

Commenting on the prospects for the insurance industry in 2013, David Law, global insurance leader at accountant PwC, said that the turbulent conditions in the global equities markets at the start of 2013, allied to the upheavals the sector is going through as it attempts to grapple with regulatory initiatives such as Solvency II, are having a chilling effect on the sector. "The immediate pressures of market volatility and regulatory upheaval have left little space in boardroom agendas for insurers to think about how to remain competitive in the years ahead," he said in the course of a recent interview (Friel, 2012).

Lloyd's of London chairman, John Nelson, said in a speech in September 2012, that whereas 2011 had been an "annus horribilis" in terms of natural catastrophes, things had picked up in 2012 apart from continuing shocks from the eurozone sovereign debt crisis. The real challenge ahead, he said, was finding ways to grow in a no- to low-growth environment. "For us, the City, the biggest challenge is how large, established, financial services—and other—businesses can grow in a period when Europe may be recording negative or negligible growth rates, and when the US may struggle to make it over the 3% GDP growth mark," he said. The storm is not going to blow over, or at least not for a very long while, so the sector needs to change if it wants to grow. Bankers and insurers are servers of the wider economy and they need to put the customer first, focusing on improving services by paying claims quicker and modernizing back-office processes. Winning more business from fast-growing economies will be the key for Lloyd's and, indeed, for all advanced market insurers who want to grow faster than their domestic economies, he suggested.

In a report on the outlook for the insurance sector for 2013–14, Swiss Re pointed out that there were some positive factors, suggesting that 2013 could be a better economic environment for the insurance sector. An improving housing market in the United States, fiscal and monetary stimulus in China, and an improvement in the euro could all boost growth in 2013, while accommodative monetary policy by banks in the United States, Japan, Europe, and the United Kingdom should continue well into 2015, it said. The industry saw growth in non-life premiums improving during 2012, and should continue into 2013, with some improvement in premium pricing. The impact of Hurricane Sandy in the United States is expected to depress reinsurance sector profits in 2013, as reinsurers tend to be more exposed than insurers to losses from natural catastrophes. Global primary life premium growth was next to zero in 2012, but is expected to be better in 2013. One of the positive factors here will be regulatory and legislative changes already passed in China and India, as the rising middle classes there develop an increased appetite for protection products. Premiums are expected to rise in 2013 in life products in advanced markets, making up for any shortfalls in 2012, Swiss Re concludes.

MORE INFO

Article:

Friel, Martin. "PwC: Companies must adapt to changing market dynamics. "*Insurance Age* (February 17, 2012). Online at: tinyurl.com/phe3xto

Reports:

Nelson, John. "City dinner speech 2012." Lloyd's, September 6, 2012. Online at: tinyurl.com/pqdxjn6

Swiss Re. "Global insurance review 2012 and outlook 2013/14." December 2012. Online at: tinyurl.com/o39w3y8 [PDF].

Website:

International Association of Insurance Supervisors (IAIS): www.iaisweb.org

See Also:

★ Climate Change and Insurance (pp. 149–150)
★ Insurance—Bruised, Not Crushed (pp. 190–191)
★ Islamic Insurance Markets and the Structure of *Takaful* (pp. 202–203)
★ Solvency II—A New Regulatory Framework for the Insurance Sector (pp. 247–248)
★ Viewpoint: The Global Risk Map and the Current Credit Crunch (pp. 182–183)
★ Viewpoint: The Role of Insurance in Bringing Resilience to Societies Challenged by Global Warming (pp. 235–236)

Media

MAJOR INDUSTRY TRENDS

The term "media" refers both to various forms of communication, and to the organizations behind this communication, including the press and news-reporting agencies. It can also refer to different types of data storage. This sector profile looks at the media in all its communication activities.

A century, the media was simply composed of the printed press. Today, there is a vast range of communication channels, including TV, radio, cinema, and the internet, as well as print. However, common industry trends can still be identified, despite the increasingly diverse nature of the market.

Convergence

Convergence has been one of the buzzwords in the industry for many years. It relates to the emergence of digital technology, which has allowed media organizations to deliver text, audio, and video material over the same wired, wireless, or fiber-optic connections. The development of the internet has played a critical role in media convergence, as it now allows people to read newspapers, listen to the radio, watch TV, and download music and movies (and play both) on their computers, or, increasingly, on handheld devices. Consumers are now watching movies on their mobile phones and tablets, and making phone calls from their personal computers.

 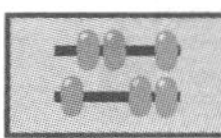      

Technological advances also mean that consumers can watch TV programs on demand, that is, when and where they want, rather than when the TV schedulers decide to broadcast them.

The convergence of smartphones and tablets suggests that more and more media will be consumed on these products rather than TVs, or even PCs or laptops. In January 2013, for example, the South Korean firm Pantech unveiled the biggest smartphone to date, with a screen capable of showing 1080p high-definition (HD) video at full resolution. The Vega No 6 has a 5.9-in (15 cm) display, which packs in 373 pixels per inch (ppi). Earlier, China's Huawei unveiled a 6.1-in handset, but it had only a 720p display.

They add to the so-called "phablet" category, as manufacturers test how big customers are willing to go for phone size. When Samsung helped pioneer the format with its 5.3 in Galaxy Note in 2011, many analysts suggested its size was too large to find favor. Dell had previously released a 5-in phone—the Streak 5—but had ended up discontinuing the line to focus on a larger 7-in tablet.

However, the Note proved a success for the South Korean firm, leading Samsung to announce a larger successor in August 2012. In late 2012 and early 2013, other firms, including Sony, LG, HTC and ZTE, unveiled smartphones with 5-inch and larger screens. More super-sized handsets are expected in 2013.

Broadcasters Under Threat

Advertising continues to migrate away from traditional broadcasters. In early 2013, Google's chief business officer, Nikesh Arora, said that offline advertisers will become increasingly more comfortable with online advertising, resulting in hundreds of billions of dollars of ad money shifting online. Five years from now, Arora believes there is a "reasonable probability" that more than 50% of total advertising spending will go online. Currently, around US$100 billion of the global ad spend of US$800 billion is spent online.

Google believes that internet-connected, or smart, TVs will be the key driver of this trend, as these devices go will from "nice to have" to "must have" in the minds of consumers, forcing marketers to allocate more ad dollars online. Internet TV is attractive to advertisers because it invites the possibility of a two-way interactive user experience, and allows advertisers to target niche interests on a truly global scale at a substantially lower cost than the traditional broadcast model.

In February 2013, Intel said it had been negotiating with major content companies and would introduce a set-top box and internet television platform before the end of 2013. Intel Media said that it planned to offer a full service of "catch-up" television, on the model of BBC's iPlayer, giving subscribers digital access to every program for seven days after transmission, without having to program a DVR. The service would also include an expanded video-on-demand library similar to what most cable, satellite, and telecom companies are offering to compete with Hulu and Netflix's libraries. Finally, it would offer "TV everywhere"-style delivery of the service to every screen, including mobile phones.

Technological Developments

Apart from convergence, other technological developments are likely to have a dramatic impact on the media industry over the next 5–10 years. 3D TV was launched in 2010, but has failed to attract consumers in significant numbers. TV makers are now seeking new strategies to revive their flagging operations, which are suffering as more and people watch TV on smartphones and tablets. Thus, TV makers are looking at expanding screen sizes, boosting image quality, and making TVs "smarter" and more user-friendly.

So-called 4K UHD, or ultra-high-definition, models are one key trend expected to develop in 2013. A 4K panel has four times as many pixels compared with the full HD panels installed in many of current TV models. When screens get bigger, even HD screens become less clear. Thus, 4K was introduced to continue to provide rich, sharp images. With the growth of smartphones and tablets, people can view videos and movies anytime and anywhere, but the screens of these devices are small, so televisions able to display rich, realistic images on big screens that provide exciting viewing experiences for consumers is becoming ever more critical, according to TV makers.

However, 4K sets remain very expensive. In early 2013, Sony's 84-inch Bravia KD-84X9005 had a price tag of US$25,000. However, some broadcasters such as the BBC are already filming programs in 4K, while some TV makers are investigating the possibility of 8K TVs. Sharp already has an 8K, 85 in (216 cm) TV, which offers more detail than a 33-megapixel photo.

MARKET ANALYSIS

Pay TV Shines in the Global Media Sector

Pay TV has been one of the growth areas of broadcasting, and has continued to expand in most areas of the globe in recent years. However, the number of pay-TV subscribers in Western Europe dropped by 384,000 in 2012, the first decline since the launch of the industry in the 1980s, according to research firm Informa. The decline reflects the severity of the downturn in the eurozone. While subscriber numbers grew in the UK in 2012, big drops elsewhere, particularly in Spain and Italy, weighed on the overall numbers. The region had about 92.6 million pay-TV subscribers at the end of 2012, down from 93 million at year-end 2011, Informa Telecoms & Media said. However, the firm also forecast that pay-TV subscribers in western Europe would rise to 94 million this year.

However, the global pay-TV market added nearly 47 million subscribers in 2012, reaching a total of 864 million subscribers. The growth in satellite, cable, and IPTV (internet-protocol television) markets was strong, although digital terrestrial TV growth was flat in 2012, according to ABI Research. The company expects that the pay-TV market will continue to grow in 2013, to reach 907 million subscribers.

The worldwide IPTV subscriber base has been increasing rapidly in the past few years. In 2013, the worldwide IPTV subscriber base is expected to add more than nine million subscribers, to reach 79.3 million. More than half of the net addition will be from Asia-Pacific; China alone is expected to add more than three million subscribers. The cable TV market will also remain strong, especially as a result of growth in Asia-Pacific markets such as China and India, according to ABI. Cable TV is expected to maintain the largest market share of the overall pay-TV market in 2013. However, rapidly growing IPTV is forecastto cause cable's market share to decline to 65.4% in 2013 from 66.2% in 2012.

At present, 33% of worldwide pay-TV subscribers are using HDTV services. HDTV penetration is the highest in North America, followed by Western Europe, accounting for 84% and 76% of total pay-TV subscriptions, respectively. As many of the countries in different regions are trying to switch over to digital transmission, the number of HD channels and packages offered by the operators is increasing.

In the US, the pay-TV business lost 127,000 subscribers in Q3 2012. Over the first nine months of the year, pay-TV subscriber numbers were flat. Given the economic improvement seen in the US over this period, it appears likely that pay TV in the US is coming under pressure as consumers switch to the internet.

Growth of the Internet Hits Newspapers

The newspaper industry is in long-term decline as readers migrate to the internet. In 2001, the newspaper industry in the US employed 414,000 people, but by 2011 that number had fallen to 246,020

  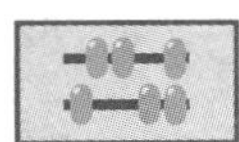      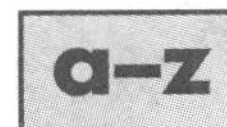

people. The industry is declining at an average annual rate of 6.4%, according to IBISWorld, and it s expected to continue to decline by an average annual rate of 4.2% until at least 2017. The loss of advertising revenue has been the greatest challenge for newspaper publishers. According to the Newspaper Association of America (NAA), total advertising revenues have declined by more than 50% percent in just five years, from US$49.3 billion in 2006 to US$23.9 billion in 2011.

However, some newspaper executives remain optimistic that the industry can adapt to a digital world. In August 2012, the Newspaper Association Managers released a study showing that 25% of newspaper executives believe the industry will be more relevant five years from now than it is today, while only about 16% say it will be less relevant. The industry is banking on developing new digital products and new revenue streams to successfully make the transition from its dependence on print advertising.

MORE INFO

Websites:

ABI Research: www.abiresearch.com

IBISWorld: www.ibisworld.com

Informa: www.informa.com

Newspaper Association of America (NAA): www.naa.org

See Also:

★ Viewpoint: Every Company Is a Media Company (pp. 848–849)

Mining

MAJOR INDUSTRY TRENDS

The mining sector covers everything that companies extract by way of geological materials from the earth: from base and precious metals to coal, uranium, diamonds, rock salt, and potash. (Oil and gas extraction is covered in a separate sector profile and will not be considered here.) This profile will focus on the commodities aspect of mining rather than on extraction techniques, while the fortunes of particular companies in the sector will be touched on collectively, through an examination of merger and acquisition deals conducted during 2012–13.

The sector, along with agricultural products such as grain and coffee beans, constitutes the commodities sector, which is notorious for price volatility and boom-and-bust cycles. This has certainly been true in recent years. The price of many metals soared from around mid-2005 until the advent of the global financial crisis in 2008. Prices then plunged, but have been reviving gradually since the end of 2009. The price of commodities is clearly correlated to the global economic cycle, but the growth of emerging economies, particularly China, has also become a key driver in recent years. However, according to an IMF Working Paper published in May 2012, China's impact on world commodity markets is rising but, perhaps surprisingly, remains smaller than that of the United States.

The paper says that China is a large consumer of a broad range of primary commodities. As a percentage of global production, China's consumption during 2010 accounted for about 20% of non-renewable energy resources, 23% of major agricultural crops, and 40% of base metals. The paper adds that China's commodity intensity of demand has been growing particularly fast, and is now unusually high. In terms of broad commodity groups, China has come to play a dominant role in base metals markets, and, to a somewhat lesser extent, agricultural raw material markets. In contrast, China has not yet assumed a large role in global food and energy markets, although its share of world imports is rising gradually.

The price of iron ore has also experienced a rollercoaster ride in recent years, with demand from China being a key driver. By the end of February 2013, the price of iron ore had jumped almost 80% since hitting a low of US$87 per tonne in September 2012, and analysts have been upgrading their profits forecast for the big iron ore miners. In February 2013, for example, UBS calculated earnings at BHP and Rio Tinto in 2013 would jump by 22% and 23%, respectively, while Fortescue's earnings could jump by 54%, if spot iron ore prices were sustained. The upturn largely reflects hopes that Chinese economic output is picking up, and that the country's demand for iron ore will also recover strongly. Other factors driving prices up include panic buying due to an expected cyclone in the Pilbara region of Western Australia, which led steel mills to replenish their stock, and political factors that led to many mines shutting down in India.

Rio de Janeiro-based Vale is the world's largest iron ore producer and exporter. It posted net earnings of US$5.51 billion in 2012, down 75.9% from a record US$22.89 billion the previous year, partly reflecting the slump in iron ore prices in 2012. Vale reported a net loss of US$2.65 billion in Q4 2012, compared to net earnings of US$4.67 billion in Q4 2011. The company saw record sales of iron ore and pellets in 2012 of 303Mt, up 1.4% from the previous record of 299Mt in 2011.

One of the consequences of the adverse macroeconomic scenario seen in 2012 was a general decline in minerals and metals prices. "In this context, our financial performance was adversely affected," said Vale CEO, Murilo Ferreira. "In 2013, we expect a less volatile market and an increased demand for raw materials, as 2012 was one of the most challenging years for the company."

Copper prices also came under downward pressure in 2012, a development that also affected earnings at the big copper miners. In February 2013, for example, Kazakhstan's largest copper producer, Kazakhmys plc, reported lower earnings as a result of a drop in copper prices, and output earnings before interest, taxation, depreciation, and amortization (EBITDA), excluding special items, dropped 30% to US$1.36 billion for the 12 months to December 31, 2012, compared with US$1.96 billion in 2011, missing analysts' expectations. Revenue dropped 5.9% to US$3.35 billion, from US$3.56 billion in 2011,as the average copper price dropped 10% during the year, missing analysts' expectations of US$3.41 billion.

Copper prices have continued on their downward trend in 2013. According to the Copper Development Association, 40% of copper demand is derived from the construction industry, as copper electrical wires and pipes are essential to both residential and commercial construction. However, housing demand remains weak in the United States and China. Concerns regarding China's housing demand also increased after the Chinese government ordered cities to promptly curb housing purchases. China currently accounts for approximately 40% of the world's copper demand.

Gold has seldom been far from the headlines in recent years. Demand for the precious metal has steadily risen since 2000, with much of it down to developing nations using their new-found wealth to fill their reserves with bullion. The increased popularity of gold jewelry, particularly in India, has also helped. But the asset is

  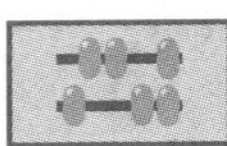      

regarded as a safe haven that holds its value in times of trouble; demand surged following the global financial crisis, with many investors worried that the extremely loose monetary policies pursued by central banks around the world would reignite inflation. The gold price surged, eventually hitting a high of US$1,895 in 2011. Gold's last bull market was at the tail-end of the inflation surge of the 1970s. However, by February 2013 the gold price had plunged to US$1,600 per troy ounce.

MARKET ANALYSIS

According to PricewaterhouseCoopers (PwC), the volume of global mining mergers and acquisitions (M&A) deals fell more than 30%, to 940 transactions in the first half of 2012, compared to 1,371 for the same period in 2011. The total value of deals for the first six months of 2012 was US$79 billion, slightly higher than US$71 billion for the same period a year earlier, but this includes Glencore International plc's US$53.6 billion offer for Xstrata plc. Excluding that deal, the total value of transactions announced drops to US$25 billion, one-third of 2011's first half-year total, reflecting global market uncertainty. In 2011, more than 2,600 M&A deals worth US$149 billion were announced in the global mining sector. Volumes were close to historic highs, and values were 33% higher than 2010. Buyers were plentiful, bidding wars ensued, and valuations were high. Not at all the kind of behaviors expected in a cyclical downturn, according to PwC.

PwC said that the top 40 mining companies invested US$98 billion in capital projects in 2011, and were planning for a further US$140 billion for 2012 in an effort to increase supply. The market, however, doesn't seem to be buying the industry's long-term growth story, which has sent share prices lower; 2011 marks the start of the growing disconnect.

PwC reported that:

- 2011 was a year of great contrast for the mining industry—record profits for the top 40 companies of US$133 billionn, but market capitalization fell 25%.
- The market does not appear to buy the long-term growth story of the emerging world, as the European debt crisis lingers.
- While net profits increased, net profit margins remained steady reflecting a changed cost base.
- Supply will be a focus for future years as the industry has undergone a structural change in the cost base, as cost increased 25% on 2010.
- The industry invested a record US$98 billion in capital projects in 2011 and planed for a further US $140 billion in 2012, but shareholders and investors are demanding greater returns of cash.

MORE INFO

Report:

Roache, Shaun K. "China's impact on world commodity markets." Working paper no. WP/12/115. IMF, May 2012. Online at: www.imf.org/external/pubs/ft/wp/2012/wp12115.pdf

Website:

PwC on mining: www.pwc.com/gx/en/mining

See Also:

★ The Role of Commodities in an Institutional Portfolio (pp. 585–588)
✔ Trading in Commodities: Why and How (p. 1093)
Construction and Building Materials (pp. 1616–1618)
Energy (pp. 1624–1626)
Oil and Gas (pp. 1638–1639)
Steel (pp. 1646–1647)

Oil and Gas

MAJOR INDUSTRY TRENDS

Oil

Brent oil averaged around US$111.26 per barrel in 2011, an increase of 40% from the 2010 level. The loss of Libyan supplies early in the year, combined with smaller disruptions in a number of other countries, pushed prices sharply higher despite a large increase in production among other OPEC members following the Libyan outages, and a release of strategic stocks from International Energy Agency (IEA) member countries.

Crude oil prices rose during the first quarter of 2012 as concerns about possible international supply disruptions pushed up petroleum prices. Prices then fell during the second quarter, before turning sharply upward at the start of the third quarter. They remained at these relatively elevated levels during the final quarter of the year.

The development of shale oil resources in the United States holds the potential to transform the global oil and gas industry. The US Energy Information Administration (EIA) said in early 2013 that US oil production would jump by a quarter by 2014, to its highest level in 26 years. This is mainly because of the discovery of vast reserves of shale oil. New technology, colloquially known as fracking, has allowed the United States to access oil and gas in shale rock. Fracking is the process of blasting water at high pressure into shale rock to release oil or gas held within it. It has become widespread in the United States and domestic gas prices have plummeted as a result.

The technology is also now having an impact on the US oil industry. The EIA, for example, forecast average global oil prices would fall from US$112 per barrel in 2012, to US$99 in 2014. It added that US oil imports would fall by a quarter between 2012 and 2014, because of rising domestic production and the discovery of shale gas. US oil imports have been falling since 2005, when they stood at 12.5 million barrels per day (bpd). By 2014, imports are expected to have halved to six million barrels, the EIA said.

Domestic oil production, which stood at 6.4 million barrels in 2012, is forecast to rise to 7.9 million barrels in 2013, the highest level since 1988. Meanwhile, the IEA has said it expects the United States to overtake Russia as the world's biggest gas producer by 2015, and to become "all but self-sufficient" in its energy needs by about 2035.

The United States will also overtake Saudi Arabia as the world's biggest oil producer "by around 2020", the IEA predicted at the end of 2012 in World Energy Outlook. It expects that the US will be producing 11.1 million bpd by 2020, compared with 10.6 million from Saudi Arabia. Currently, the US imports about 20% of its total energy needs.

Gas

The IEA also expects the United States to overtake Russia as the world's biggest gas producer by 2015, again thanks to fracking. In December 2012, Royal Dutch Shell's chief executive, Peter Voser, said the US economy is set for a revolution as the country becomes self-sufficient in energy. He and other experts have argued that the an abundance of low-cost energy will drive the re-industrialization of the economy. Nonetheless, the shale revolution is not without its critics. Environmentalists fear it could increase seismic risks and pollute drinking water. However, US officials question these concerns, and say that thanks to the higher proportion of gas use, the United States has had its lowest CO2 emissions in 20 years.

Interest in exploiting shale gas reserves is spreading across the globe. In early 2013, Shell signed a US$10 billion shale gas deal with Ukraine—the biggest contract yet in Europe—which could help Ukraine ease its reliance on Russian gas imports. Ukraine is said to have Europe's third-largest shale gas reserves at 42 trillion ft3 (1.2 trillion m3), according to the EIA. Its reserves are dwarfed by those of France, however, which are estimated to be Europe's largest at 180 trillion ft3. However, France has banned fracking. By contrast, the German government of Chancellor Angela Merkel wants to jump-start the extraction of shale gas deposits in the country, essentially ending a hold on the practice because of public concern and safety worries. Legal guidelines for fracking are to be introduced before the German general election in Fall 2013.

MARKET ANALYSIS

Oil

Global oil reserves rose by 31 billion barrels to 1,653 billion barrels in 2011, according to BP. Iraq added 28 billion bbl and Russia, Brazil, and Saudi Arabia all increased reserves by 1 billion bbl. Proved reserves remain concentrated in OPEC, which controls 72% of the world's oil reserves, the highest proportion since 1998. Overall, the long-term trend is that globally reserves are increasing in proportion to the amount being used. Global proved oil reserves at the end of 2011 reached 1652.6 billion bbl, sufficient to meet 54.2 years of global production.

Annual global oil production in 2011 increased by 1.1 million bpd, or 1.3%. Nearly all the net growth was in OPEC, with large increases in Saudi Arabia, the UAE, Kuwait, and Iraq more than offsetting the loss of the Libyan supply. Output reached record levels in Saudi Arabia, the UAE, and Qatar. Non-OPEC output was broadly flat, with increases in the United States, Canada, Russia, and Colombia offsetting continued declines in mature provinces such as the United Kingdom and Norway, as well as unexpected outages in a number of other countries.

Gas

Global natural gas reserves increased by 12.3 trillion m3 to 208.4 trillion m3 in 2011, according to BP. Meanwhile, global natural gas production grew by 3.1%. The United States recorded the largest volumetric increase despite lower gas prices, and remained the world's largest producer. Consumption growth was below average in all regions except North America, where low prices drove robust growth. Outside North America, the largest volumetric gains in consumption were in China, Saudi Arabia, and Japan These increases were partly offset by the largest decline on record in EU gas consumption.

Analysts expect global gas demand to grow rapidly over the coming decades. The key drivers of this growth are likely to be:

- Aggressive gas usage plans in China and India;
- The emergence of domestic shale gas as a preferred fuel source in the United States;
- The discovery and utilization of gas resources in Latin America;
- The move away from nuclear power in Japan and some European countries in response to the Fukushima Dai-ichi nuclear accident;
- Europe's continued reduction of greenhouse gas emissions;
- Russian plans to search for gas in its Far Eastern region;
- The search for shale and other unconventional gas resources in currently gas-poor countries.

Shell, for example, expects global natural gas demand to increase by 60% from 2010 to 2030, reaching 25% of the global primary energy mix, and, within that, strong growth in liquefied natural gas (LNG). According to Shell, LNG demand doubled to 200 million tonnes per annum (mtpa) in the first decade of this century. Shell expects LNG demand to double again to 400 mtpa by 2020, and potentially reach 500 mtpa by 2025. Meeting this demand growth will require substantial industry investment—potentially more than US$700 billion—and continued innovation and interdependency between supplier and customer countries.

The IEA's view is more conservative, saying that demand for natural gas could rise more than 50% by 2035, from 2010. However, this growth would depend upon whether a significant portion of the vast global resources of shale gas, tight gas and coal-bed methane could be developed profitably, and in an environmentally acceptable way. The IEA said the surge in North American production of unconventional gas, thanks to technology advances, held out the prospect of further output increases in the United States and Canada, and "the emergence of a large-scale unconventional gas industry in other parts of the world, where sizeable resources are known to exist." This would help bring about greater energy diversity, boost energy security, and also result in global benefits in the form of reduced energy costs, it said. Gas could have a 25% share of the global energy mix by 2035, overtaking coal to become the second-largest primary energy source after oil, in the IEA's most positive scenario for unconventional gas.

MORE INFO

Article:

Der Spiegel. "Full throttle ahead: US tips global power scales with fracking." February 1, 2013. Online at: tinyurl.com/ang2hfo

Reports:

BP. "Statistical review of world energy." June 2012. Online at: tinyurl.com/q7h9qn4

Organization of Petroleum Exporting Countries. "Monthly oil market report." December 2012. Online at: tinyurl.com/nknoa39 [PDF].

PricewaterhouseCoopers. "Shale gas: A renaissance in US manufacturing?" February 2012. Online at: tinyurl.com/8ze7pr6

See Also:

★ The Role of Commodities in an Institutional Portfolio (pp. 585–588)
★ Viewpoint: Challenges in Global Energy and Their Potential Impact on the Cost of Energy (pp. 144–146)
★ Viewpoint: Energy Self-Sufficiency through Shale Gas Changes the Game for the United States (pp. 170–172)
✔ Trading in Commodities: Why and How (p. 1093)
Energy (pp. 1624–1626)
Mining (pp. 1637–1638)

Professional Services

INTRODUCTION

This report covers the market for professional services around the world. It encompasses areas such as accountancy, audit, legal services, information technology, property management, architecture, advertising, and management consultancy. While large companies often have in-house lawyers and accountants, many

small and medium-sized companies rely on the services supplied by firms that specialize in these areas, or else outsource the work to contractors. Big global companies outsource many functions to external suppliers. Management consultancy and services in areas such as architecture, for example, tend to be supplied by external firms or contractors that focus on these areas.

Given the diversity of the sector, it is difficult to find meaningful data on its size or growth rate. Definitions of what is included in the sector also vary from one country to another, but there is little doubt that it accounts for a large proportion of GDP, particularly in developed economies. Professional, scientific, and technical services accounted for 7.5% of GDP in the United States, for example, in 2010, while the real estate sector accounted for a further 12.7%.

MAJOR INDUSTRY TRENDS

Emergence of Global Standards in Accountancy

The drive towards global standards in areas such as accountancy appears to be gathering pace, and has been given added impetus by the global financial crisis. Indeed, by 2013, more than 120 countries around the world—including EU member states and China—now use international financial reporting standards (IFRS). Around 85 of those countries require IFRS reporting for all domestically listed companies. It had been thought that United States would favor the adoption of IFRS in place of US Generally Accepted Accounting Principles (GAAP). Many US companies already use IFRS. However, in 2012, US regulators questioned whether US companies would benefit, and expressed skepticism that international accounting standards are applied consistently in the countries where they are already used. Officials from the Securities and Exchange Commission (SEC) are reportedly adopting a wait-and-see attitude toward incorporating IFRS into the US financial system.

Governments Seek to Liberalize the Legal Profession

Countries around the world are seeking to liberalize the legal sector, but with varying degrees of success. In 2012, for example, both Malaysia and Singapore took steps to open up their legal professions to foreign lawyers. In the United Kingdom, the government has passed legislation that encourages new entrants to the market, in the hope of increasing competition, and the consumer experience, in terms of price, access, and service. The legislation allow firms to be owned, invested in, and run by non-lawyers. The legislation also enables law firms to merge with other companies, such as supermarkets. Indeed, according to some analysts the Legal Services Act of October 2011 made the UK legal market one of the most liberalized in the world. However, in January 2013, the Office of Fair Trading said that the process for creating "alternative business structures" (ABSs) was too slow, and could inhibit new service providers in a £23 billion market.

MARKET ANALYSIS

Advertising

The global advertising market reached US$495bn in 2012, up 3.8% on 2011, and is expected to grow 3.1% in 2013, according to the "Magna Global advertising forecast 2013," published by M&M Global.

The United States remains the largest market, attracting US$152.3 billion in ad revenues, followed by Japan (US$51.2 billion), China (US$38 billion), Germany (US$25.1 billion), and Brazil (US$20.5 billion). Magna Global's 2012 estimate is slightly lower (−1.0%) than its earlier prediction in June 2012, owing largely to a slowdown in western Europe.

Western Europe saw a 2.8% decline in ad revenues in 2012, as challenging economic conditions continued to take their toll on ad spend. However, the region's two biggest markets—Germany and the United Kingdom—managed to grow, with 0.5% and 2.2% growth, respectively. They are expected to show modest growth in 2013, and the region as a whole is predicted to see a decrease of 0.1%.

All of southern Europe saw declines this year. The rate of decline ranges from a modest drop in France (−2.5%) to double-digit declines in Italy, Spain and, as expected, in Greece (−28%). Overall, the region is expected to see a 4.3% decline in growth in 2013.

The central and eastern European markets of Hungary, Croatia, Romania, Bulgaria, Poland, and the Czech Republic saw declines, but this was offset by 10.4% growth in Russia and 8.4% growth in Turkey. Overall, ad revenues in the region grew 5.5% and are expected to grow 7% next year.

Political advertising and the London 2012 Olympics contributed to 4% growth in the US ad market. The US election cycle brought almost US$3 billion of incremental ad revenues, the bulk of which went to local TV stations, marking its biggest year ever.

Ad revenues in Asia-Pacific grew by an average 5.5% in 2012. Both China and India slowed to single-figure ad growth at 9.2% and 2.6%, respectively, yet this is expected to return to double figures in 2013-14. Japan saw stronger-than-expected growth of 4.1%, following four consecutive years of declines. In 2013, Asia-Pacific is expected to grow by 4.8%.

In 2012, Latin America posted growth of 13%, despite slowing economic growth and high inflation prices in some markets. Brazil (up 13%) and Argentina (up 22%) had a strong showing, while growth in Mexico was more moderate at 6.4%. Next year, the region is predicted to see growth of 11.9%.

Among the traditional media categories, TV was most resilient, with 5% growth in 2012. However, newspapers and magazines saw declines of 4.5% and 5.7% respectively. Radio posted 1.6% growth and out-of-home benefited from the rise in digital formats, with 6.1% growth.

M&M Global's 2013 forecast predicts ad revenues to grow by 3.1% in 2014, down slightly from its June 2012 forecast of 4.5% growth. Of the 69 markets covered by the forecast, 57 are expected to see growth while 12 will decline.

Digital ad revenues are forecast to increase by 13.5% next year, as marketers shift their budgets towards online video and mobile formats.

"Tablets have been the fastest device ever to reach 50 million users in less than three years," according to Magna. "As they become more affordable, we are seeing an explosion in the volume and the nature of mobile media usage.

"Marketers are gradually embracing the new marketing and branding opportunities: mobile advertising already represents US$6 billion globally, i.e. 6% of digital advertising and 1% of total advertising," adds Magna, which is predicting the format to grow to US$24 billion by 2017, reaching 14% of global digital advertising and 4% of overall advertising revenues.

IT spending

Worldwide IT spending is projected to total US$3.7 trillion in 2013, a 4.2% increase from 2012 spending of US$3.6 trillion, according to a forecast published by Gartner, Inc in 2013.

Gartner analysts said much of this spending increase is the result from projected gains in the value of foreign currencies versus the dollar. When measured in constant dollars, 2013 spending growth is forecast to be 3.9%.

Worldwide devices spending, which includes PCs, tablets, mobile phones, and printers, is forecast to reach US$666 billion in 2013, up 6.3% from 2012. However, this is a significant reduction in the outlook for 2013 compared with Gartner's previous forecast of US$706 billion in worldwide devices and 7.9% growth. The long-term forecast for worldwide spending on devices has been reduced

as well, with growth from 2012 to 2016 now expected to average 4.5% annually in current US dollars (down from 6.4%), and 5.1% annually in constant dollars (down from 7.4%). These reductions reflect a sharp reduction in the forecast growth in spending on PCs and tablets, which is only partially offset by marginal increases in forecast growth in spending on mobile phones and printers.

MORE INFO

Articles:

Baker, Jenny. "Global ad spend reaches $495bn in 2012." *M&M Global* (December 3, 2012). Online at: tinyurl.com/qj4rosg

Gartner. "Gartner says worldwide IT spending forecast to reach $3.7 trillion in 2013." January 3, 2013. Online at: www.gartner.com/newsroom/id/2292815

Website:

The Lawyer: www.thelawyer.com

See Also:

✔ Financial Intermediaries: Their Role and Relation to Financial Markets (p. 1069)
✔ Structuring, Negotiating, and Drafting Agency Agreements (p. 1176)
Banking and Financial Services (pp. 1612–1614)
Insurance (pp. 1633–1635)

Real Estate

INTRODUCTION

This report coversreal estatearound the world, looking at the residential sector as well as the market forcommercial property.

MAJOR INDUSTRY TRENDS

Outlook for Commercial Sector Improves

According to Jones Lang LaSalle, the global real estate market began 2013 with a more confident stride, following an exceptional rally in the final quarter of 2012 that served "to demonstrate the strength of investors' appetite for commercial property." The search for yield in a low-interest-rate environment, combined with a perceived reduction in macroeconomic risks and a selective improvement in debt markets, has supported increasing investor activity, according to Jones Lang LaSalle. The real estate services firm said it expects investment volumes to grow in 2013 by a further 10-15% on 2012 levels, "with upside potential in the best secondary markets, which are now beginning to attract investor interest with their more attractive yields."

However, the company says leasing markets have been less resilient as corporates focus on productivity gains and cost savings, rather than on expansion, but that even in this area it detects an improvement in optimism that should translate into renewed growth in leasing activity during 2013, with momentum gathering pace during the second half of the year. It says that prime rents are projected to increase modestly, by an average of 2–3% in 2013, but given shortages of high-quality space and low levels of new construction pipeline, even a modest uptick in absorption above Jones Lang LaSalle's baseline projections could trigger rental spikes in some markets.

Jones Lang LaSalle sees investment volumes of between US$450 and US$500 billion in 2013, their highest level since 2007. While leasing markets are less resilient, improving business confidence could translate into higher volumes in the second half of the year, the company adds. Supply is largely under control and, with shortages of high-quality space, rental spikes could appear in some markets later in the year, and into 2014. The greatest upside potential is offered by US markets, while austerity measures will constrain recovery across parts of Europe, according to the company. Meanwhile, investment volumes in Asia-Pacific are forecast to increase by around 15%, with Asian sovereign wealth funds and pension funds deploying more capital in their home region.

The global office vacancy rate, which stood at 13.2% at the end of 2012, is expected to edge down further in 2013 to 12.9% by the end of the year, with the largest falls likely in the United States. The decline in vacancy will be supported by continued low levels of new supply; while global office completions are forecast to rise by nearly a third in 2013 (on 2012 levels), they will remain well below the long-term trend during 2013 and 2014, according to Jones Lang LaSalle.

Residential Market Stabilizes

According to a number of analysts, the residential sector also saw signs of recovery in 2012 and early 2013. ScotiaBank of Canada, for example, said the downward pressure on pricing in a number of national housing markets appeared to have eased over the summer and early fall of 2012. In the majority of advanced and emerging nation property markets, average inflation-adjusted house prices were negative on a year-on-year (YoY) basis in the third quarter of 2012. However, many are showing some tentative signs of stabilization, including the United States, the United Kingdom, Australia, and China, supported in part by highly accommodative monetary policy.

According to the bank, housing markets remain weakest in Europe, not unexpectedly given ongoing recessionary conditions, fragile consumer confidence, and high joblessness. The eurozone-wide unemployment rate rose to a record 11.7% in October 2012, while for young workers under 25 it soared to almost 24%. Wage compression and emigration are further reducing the pool of potential homebuyers. These markets are expected to remain under pressure during 2013, according to the bank.

ScotiaBank found that conditions were relatively stable in most other advanced nations in the third quarter of 2012. Cyclical and fundamental factors favor the United States over the overvalued housing markets in Canada, Australia, and Sweden, where years of rising prices have eroded affordability. Even so, the still-sluggish pace of US job growth is expected to have a moderating effect on the recovery. Among emerging nations, Latin American housing

  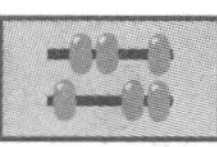 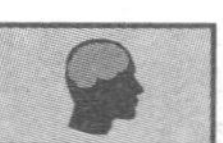     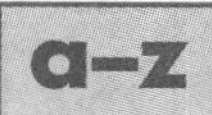

markets are generally outperforming those in Asia, supported by solid domestic activity and labor markets.

US Residential Market Recovering

It is well known that the epicenter of the global financial crisis lay in the US housing market. Having led the global economy into recession, the US housing market now appears to be leading the recovery. Home prices, pending sales, and construction activity all increased towards the end of 2012, while the number of existing houses for sale continued to drop. At the same time, home values remain depressed, while what is expected to be slow economic growth in 2013 could hinder the housing sector's recovery.

Encouragingly, the supply of new homes has fallen to its lowest level in years, which is helping to drive up prices as buyers compete against one another. The nation's inventory of existing homes for sale, which is not seasonally adjusted, fell 4.9% from December 2012 to January 2013 to 1.74 million, the lowest level since December 1999. Existing home sales rose by 0.4% in January 2013 to a seasonally adjusted annual rate of 4.92 million units, the second-highest rate of sales since November 2009, when a federal tax credit for home buyers was due to expire. Steady job creation helped the housing sector in 2012, when it added to economic growth for the first time since 2005. Many Americans are holding back from putting their homes on the market because they owe more on their mortgages than their homes are worth. A sharp drop in inventories over the last year has given developers more incentive to build homes.

The availability of credit is likely to be the most factor in 2013. Major banks continue to restrict loans because of the ultra-low interest rates mortgages carry, preferring to husband their capital or to focus on more lucrative business lines, such as trading. Lenders also can typically make more money refinancing an existing mortgage than issuing a new one.

As a result, the nation's biggest banks continue to set high requirements for borrowing, especially as many of these lenders are still dealing with the legal and financial fallout of the bad loans they issued during the housing boom. However, this is creating opportunities for smaller, local banks, which typically have a better understanding of individual real estate markets, to step up their lending.

MARKET ANALYSIS

While central banks in many developed countries continue to adopt measures designed to boost liquidity and support asset prices, many developing countries are likely to adopt further measures to cool overheated real estate markets. There have been concerns for some time, for example, that a real estate bubble is developing in China. In the last few decades, China has loosened property purchase laws, enabling its citizens to invest in the sector. However, with the escalating pace of home prices, the government has introduced stricter regulations in the last three years to avoid a housing crisis. The regulations include tougher mortgage qualification requirements, higher down-payments and, more recently, caps on property purchases.

However, the mortgage market remains small, with the ratio of home mortgage loans to GDP standing at just 10%, despite the rapid growth of outstanding loans. Moreover, the government has raised the minimum cash component of purchases to 30%, and many people put down much larger sums. Many properties are simply bought outright with cash.

Meanwhile, the Hong Kong government adopted a number of measures aimed at curbing the property market in February 2013. It doubled the sales tax on properties costing more HK$2 million, and targeted commercial real estate for the first time as the risk of a bubble spreads from apartments to parking spaces, shops, and hotels. The stamp duty will increase to 8.5% of the purchase price for all properties, financial secretary John Tsang said. The Hong Kong Monetary Authority also tightened mortgage terms for commercial properties and parking spaces, which have attracted a lot of speculative money. Home prices had doubled in Hong Kong in the previous four years on near-record low mortgage rates, an influx of mainland Chinese buyers, and a lack of new supply.

In January 2013, Singapore introduced new measures that included an increase in stamp duty for homebuyers by between five and seven percentage points, and stamp duty for sellers of industrial buildings, starting at 15% if the property is sold within a year.

MORE INFO

Websites:

Foresight Analytics, provides real-estate market analysis and projections for investors, lenders, and developers: www.foresightanalytics.com

Jones Lang LaSalle's "Global market perspective" report, published quarterly: tinyurl.com/3wormle

Retail

MAJOR INDUSTRY TRENDS

Retailing involves the sale of commodities to the public. Outlets can vary from family-run stores to global behemoths such as Wal-Mart, the world's largest retailer, with two million employees (or "associates," as Wal-Mart prefers to call them), and sales of US$444 billion during the fiscal year ending January 31, 2012. The industry also covers a wide range of sectors, from general products, such as food and clothing, to specialist goods, such as sports equipment and automobile accessories. Despite the diverse nature of the industry, a number of common trends can be identified.

Industry Concentration

Around the world, small independent outlets, known as "mom and pop" stores in the United States, are coming under pressure from national and, increasingly, global giants, such as Wal-Mart and Tesco, which can exploit their vast buying power to extract the best possible price from suppliers. It is often impossible for the independents, or even relatively large retail chains, to compete on price with the largest retailers.

Whereas once a consumer might have visited the butcher, the baker, and the candlestick-maker on Main Street, they are now most likely to drive to an out-of-town retailer such as Wal-Mart in the United States, Tesco in the United Kingdom, or Carrefour in France, and buy meat and bread, towels, duvets, and TVs all under one roof—a phenomenon known as one-stop shopping.

While the power of the giant retailers is already entrenched in advanced economies—the biggest four retailers account for 75% of grocery sales in the United Kingdom—these retailers are also making rapid inroads into emerging economies. This is largely because their domestic markets are close to saturation point, and because the biggest retailers account for such a large share of their own market that taking over a domestic rival could trigger opposition from the relevant competition authorities.

The pattern seen in the grocery market is being repeated in other retailing sectors, such as clothing and electronics, with sales increasingly concentrated through a relatively small number of retailers. Many of these companies are also expanding internationally. For example, the Spanish clothing retailer Inditex, which opened its first store in 1975, had 6,009 stores around the world by the end of 2012, and an international presence that stretches from the Americas to Asia. Sales reached €15.9 billion during the year ending January31, 2013.

Brands under Pressure

The growth of the giant retailers means that they can now dictate terms to suppliers of even iconic brands. Whereas once suppliers sold their goods through a wide range of small shops, and could tell these retailers how much to charge for their goods and where they should be positioned in the store, the balance of power is now firmly in the hands of the retailer. Companies such as Tesco, which commands nearly a third of the UK grocery market, can have an enormous impact on a brand simply by refusing to stock it.

The growing popularity of own brands, also known as own labels or private labels, has given even more power to the giant retailers. Own-label goods are products sold under the retailer's brand. Some companies focus solely on supplying own-brand goods. Dailycer, which supplies own-brand breakfast cereals to European retailers, is one example. However, own brands are also supplied by companies that produce branded goods. Indeed, the own brand may be identical to its branded counterpart.

In the 1960s and 1970s, retailer own brands were focused on the "value" end of the market. In other words, retailers focused on supplying goods that offered a cheap alternative to brands, but did not try to compete on quality. That changed in the 1980s and 1990s, as retailers increased the range of own brands that they offered. During that period, many supermarkets offered goods in the value, standard, and premium segments of the market. In the late 1990s and in the current decade, supermarket own brands have become increasingly sophisticated. Now, supermarkets target consumers by lifestyle, as well as by income. Thus, in the food sector, retailers now offer "healthy" own brands, which are low in fat or sugar, as well as ethical, fairtrade products, and brands that appeal to a particular sector, such as organic foods. All this activity has inevitably strengthened the share that own brands take in the average supermarket. In the United Kingdom, which is generally thought to have the most sophisticated own-brand market, they account for around 42% of all sales, according to the market-research publisher Key Note Ltd.

The global economic downturn appears to have given retailers even greater power over suppliers. Hard-pressed consumers are increasingly turning to own-brand value goods to stretch their spending power. In the UK, *The Guardian* reported in January 2013 that nearly a quarter (22%) of shoppers plan to buy more own-brand food and drink in 2013 according to market researchers (him! Research and Consultancy). The newspaper added that more own-label products were launched in 2011 than branded equivalents, and that own labels have moved from the margins to become the rising star of the supermarket shelves. "Once aimed at those on a low income, the leveling effect of a grim economy means today own brand is popular with everyone—so much so that upmarket grocer Waitrose got in on the act, launching its 'essential' range as a response to the recession," the newspaper reported.

The Guardian quoted retail analysts Datamonitor as saying: "The cost of ingredients is going up for food brands while there's been a decline in spend from the consumers. Something's got to give—and so more consumers are buying own label." Own label's rise has been nothing short of spectacular, according to the newspaper, which quoted Datamonitor as saying that in most of the food and drink categories they analyze, own label outperforms well-known household brands.

Technological Advances and E-Commerce

The giant retailers have been quick to exploit the benefits of advances in IT, as well as the growth of the internet. The latter medium has created new retailing giants such as Amazon, but it has largely been exploited by established retailers, which view it as simply another distribution channel, and a means to drive sales. Sales via the internet are certainly growing rapidly. Tesco, of the United Kingdom, the third-largest global retailer, said in February 2012 that it expected to double its online grocery revenue to £5.5 billion in the next five years, as the popularity of internet food shopping grows.

Director of internet retailing Ken Towle was quoted as saying that the growth is achievable if the market continues to develop at a rapid rate, and that Tesco is already on the cusp of a 50% market share in food online. In February 2012 it stood at 48%. Towle said online accounts for a small proportion of total food spend across the industry at present—about 3%—but that more people buy over the internet than this figure suggests. He said: "The proportion of people who shop online is much higher—around 20% of people have tried to buy grocery online at some point. We can see online shopping at Tesco doubling over the next five years in grocery."

At present, the internet accounts for a relatively small proportion of sales in many sectors; analysts estimate, for example, that online sales of clothing represent just 5–10% of the total clothing market. However, those same analysts expect this figure to grow rapidly.

Advances in IT and communications have been exploited by retailers in a number of other ways. Inditex, for example, is credited with creating the concept of fast fashion, which gives shoppers the latest styles just a few weeks after they first appear on the catwalk, at prices that mean they can wear an outfit once or twice, and then replace it. IT enables Inditex to sell clothes in its stores two weeks after they have been designed. At Inditex, information is also continually transmitted from the company's stores to a design team of more than 200 professionals, informing them of customers' needs and concerns, allowing the company to respond very rapidly to changing tastes.

Meanwhile, companies have used IT to harness information about their customers and refine their marketing programs. Tesco, for example, uses data collected from its Clubcard loyalty scheme to identify shopping trends, and refine existing brands and marketing campaigns as a result. In its 2011 annual report, Tesco also pointed out that its advanced weather forecasting system now has a very substantial input into store stocking programs, adjusting both goods carried and quantities based on detailed weather pattern analysis.

Global Sourcing

The major retailers are increasingly sourcing goods from around the world, rather than just their own domestic markets. This not only allows retailers to find the cheapest suppliers in the world, but also has other advantages. Grocery retailers, for example, can now supply what were once seasonal foods all year round. In the middle of winter, a shopper in London can buy strawberries flown in from Chile.

Tesco has a global sourcing office in Hong Kong, which supplies more than 60% of all clothing and 40% of other non-food products sold in Tesco's UK stores, as well as most of the non-food items sold in the 12 other countries in which Tesco operates. The Hong Kong office is responsible for design, sourcing, overseeing production, quality control, and arranging the customs documentation for approximately 50,000 Tesco product lines. Many of the goods are sourced from mainland China. Recently, however, a stumbling block to the continued expansion of global sourcing had emerged in the shape of concerns over the contribution of global sourcing policies to global warming. The concept of food miles, the distance food has to travel to arrive on supermarket shelves, has started to gain ground as environmental groups focus on the carbon footprint associated with supermarket sourcing habits. This issue still has some way to play out in the next few years, but already many supermarkets are emphasizing a "buy local, shop local" dimension to their activities as they attempt to "green up."

Supermarkets Expand Out of Food

The major supermarket operators around the world have expanded into a whole range of areas beyond their traditional role as suppliers of food and household goods. They now sell clothing, household equipment, music, electronics, health and beauty products, and pharmaceutical goods, as well as financial services, and even cars. This trend is being driven by various factors. For example, in many countries, there are now so many supermarkets that the market has reached saturation point. In addition, items such as electronics offer higher margins than traditional groceries.

MARKET ANALYSIS

The five largest retailers in the world are Wal-Mart (United States), Carrefour (France), Tesco (United Kingdom), Ahold (the Netherlands), and Delhaize (Belgium). All have long since expanded outside their domestic markets, and now operate on a global basis.

Thus, Wal-Mart operated more than 10,000 retail units in 27 countries around the world in 2012. Its two million employees serve more than 200 million customers every week. Carrefour is Europe's biggest supermarket operator and is the second-biggest retailer in the world, beaten only by Wal-Mart. In March 2013, it said the year ahead would be difficult due to the impact of the eurozone crisis on demand. Carrefour's giant stores have been hurt by competition from specialist stores and online shopping. The company is trying to cut costs and compete harder on prices. It had expanded in emerging markets, including China and Brazil, but pulled out of non-core areas, such as Singapore and Colombia in 2012. As of December 31, 2012, Carrefour group operated more than 9,994 stores in 33 countries.

Tesco operated just over 6,000 stores around the world in 2012, of which 2,979 were in the United Kingdom, and employed almost 520,000 people in 14 countries, including China, the Czech Republic, France, Hungary, Japan, Malaysia, Poland, the Republic of Ireland, Slovakia, South Korea, Thailand, Turkey, the United Kingdom, and the United States. Tesco says it "has a well-established and consistent strategy for growth, which has allowed us to strengthen our core UK business and drive expansion into new markets." However, in October 2012, it announced its first fall in profits since 1994, which was due to spending on the retailer's £1 billion investment program to improve its UK stores. In December 2012, Tesco announced a review of its American operations, which may lead to the closure of the business.

Ahold, based in Amsterdam, operates grocery stores in the United States, the Netherlands, the Czech Republic, Slovakia, Sweden, Norway, and the Baltic States. In the United States, Ahold owns the Stop & Shop and Giant-Landover supermarkets, and in the Netherlands it owns the Albert Heijn grocery network. At the end of 2011, it had 3,008 stores, 218,000 employees, and total sales of €30.3 billion.

Delhaize is a Belgian international food retailer with activities in six countries on three continents. At the end of 2011, Delhaize Group's sales network consisted of 3,458 stores. In 2011, Delhaize Group posted €21.1 billion in revenues and an operating profit of €812 million. Delhaize Group employs approximately 160,000 "associates."

MORE INFO

Websites:

Key Note Ltd, provides research on a wide range of markets, including retailing: www.keynote.co.uk

Market-research website giving information on a wide range of reports, including those on retailing: tinyurl.com/3zqc7ve

Wal-Mart: www.walmartstores.com

See Also:

E-Commerce (pp. 1620–1622)

Shipping

MAJOR INDUSTRY TRENDS

The shipping industry has basically been at stall speed since the global economic slowdown, apart from a brief but illusory flurry of positive activity in 2010. Shipping relies heavily on global trade flows and growth in emerging markets to generate demand for tankers, bulk ore carriers, and container ships to ply from East to West and back again. As soon as trade slackens or the infrastructure build-out in the developing economies of China and India slows, the shipping industry is in trouble.

The industry has its own, highly accurate barometer of demand in the shape of the Baltic Dry Index. This is an index of freight shipping maintained by the Baltic Exchange, based in London. It provides a measure of the daily average cost of shipping bulk dry commodities such as iron ore, coal, and grain. Shipping contracts are struck months in advance of the goods actually being shipped, so the Baltic Dry Index offers a very good window into whether the world's trade is contracting or expanding. The higher the demand for bulk freight around the world, the higher the index. If the Baltic Dry starts to fall away, that is a sign that trade will contract sharply some months hence. By April 2010, the Baltic Dry Index, had risen by 58.5% over the previous 12 months, and there was considerable optimism that the world had moved into a recovery phase, with strong emerging market growth pulling advanced markets out of their slump. However, by mid-2011 virtually all that optimism had faded in the face of the European sovereign debt crisis, and persistent weakness in the US economy. Inevitably, the shipping industry suffered as a result, and its woes continued during 2012, which by consensus was a very bad year, and into 2013.

A CNBC report on the sector in June 2012 pointed out that the Baltic Dry had dropped by around 40% by mid-2012. Charter rates for ships were down to around US$8,000 a day, by comparison with their pre-crisis peak of US$22,000 a day, and many ships were swinging empty at anchor, tying up their owners' money, and generating zero income.

In an interview on December 12, 2012 with the BBC, Thomas Riber Knudsen, the Asia head of Maersk Line, said that the shipping industry suffers enormously from the fact that over the last few years it has only been able to generate a 1% or 2% return on its investment. "For an industry like ours, this is simply not sustainable," he told the BBC. In common with a number of major players in the industry, Maersk Shipping's parent company, the Maersk Group, has made some very substantial investments over the last few years in E-class container ships, the largest of the current container ships. However, the group has no intention of making any further investments in its shipping arm for the foreseeable future, Knudsen says, citing the low return on investment, and the fact that there are other businesses in the group that are able to generate a better return. There could hardly be a clearer indication of the predicament the sector is in.

What makes matters worse is that many companies in the sector invested heavily in new shipping at the height of the boom in 2006 and 2007. By the time these ships were delivered demand for shipping had crashed, so the industry was left with a surplus of very modern, very large vessels, and a greatly reduced order book. Because of the long lead time in building ships, new ships were being launched into that glut for some time after it became apparent that there was insufficient demand to justify expansion. Unfortunately, at the height of the 2007 boom, just prior to the global downturn, the global shipping sector committed itself to some of the biggest bets in the sector's history. These bets took the form of billions of dollars spent on a new generation of extra-large container vessels, which take anything from 18 months to three years to build.

The bulk dry carrier sector, too, saw fleet additions picking up strongly in the period from 2004 to 2007. During 2004–08, the average annual growth rate for the dry bulk fleet hovered around 7%, significantly above the levels of previous decades. More recently, there has been a major step change in fleet additions. In 2009, the total dry bulk fleet expanded by 10% year on year, or 42 million deadweight tonnage (dwt), the strongest growth in the fleet's history, ending the year with 460 million dwt of capacity. On top of that, the fleet grew another 12% in 2010, adding a further 55 million dwt, after accounting for cancellations, delays, and fleet scrappage.

By way of contrast to all the gloom and doom, the specialist liquefied natural gas (LNG) carrier section looks as if it is about to see real boom times. The sector had a false start at the height of the boom in early 2007, when investing in LNG tankers looked like an excellent idea. The world was hungry for gas as a cleaner alternative to oil, and a major global power production program based on newly built gas-generation power plants fueled demand for security of supply. However, by March 2010, there were reports that freight rates for transporting spot cargoes of LNG had dropped by at least 20% since December 2009. In a briefing note to clients, the Japanese broker Nomura warned that, "the sustainability of very large crude carrier (VLCC) and chemical tanker rates looks less than clear, with vessel overhang risks remaining."

Since then, however, the rising excitement over the extraction of natural gas from vast shale deposits in the United States and China has created a real buzz in the sector. Chinese shipyards have begun building LNG tankers in competition with established shipyards in Japan and South Korea. The first LNG carrier built by a Chinese shipyard was launched in 2008, out of Hudong-Zhonghua Shipbuilding, a subsidiary of the state-owned China State Shipbuilding. In January 2011, Hudong-Zhonghau Shipbuilding won a US$1 billion contract to build four LNG carriers for ExxonMobil and Japan's Mitsui OSK lines, and, in September 2012, it won an order from a consortium that includes Australia's Origin Energy, the United States' ConocoPhillips, and China's China Petroleum and Chemical Corporation (Sinopec), for four to six LNG carriers. In 2002, there were just 126 LNG carriers in the world. By 2015, the number is expected to rise to 485.

The main drama, however, is being played out in the container market. Containers were the invention of the North Carolina entrepreneur Malcom McLean back in 1956. They have completely revolutionized the transport of goods and cargoes worldwide, as containers make it very easy for many manufacturers to ship their specific products as part of a large, general shipment. When McLean invented the container, it cost almost US$6 a ton to hand-load a ton of cargo onto or off a ship. Using containers, that price comes down to US$0.16 (source: Wikipedia). The container was a huge step beyond the previous best "invention," namely palleted goods in break bulk cargoes.

The novel element in McLean's approach was the idea of a sealed, steel box that was never opened in transit, and that could be speedily loaded, unloaded, and transshipped, or switched from rail to ship to road freight. The transformation of the whole process of shipping goods around the world was immense. Instead of having to unload ships by hand (or, in more modern times, by cranes swinging pallets of goods onshore to be checked, then warehoused until they could be freighted out), containerized goods take very little time to shift from ship to shore, or vice versa, and there is no checking of goods because the containers are sealed.

From there, the shipping industry slowly but surely moved in the direction of economies of scale. The fixed overhead costs associated with shipping a container come down when the number of containers being shipped goes up. When the world is booming, and the demand for container shipments is huge, this approach provides a fast route to superior profits. The largest of today's container ships are some 400 meters in length and 55 meters wide. They can carry 13,000 containers, or 50% more containers than the biggest ships in 2003–04.

MARKET ANALYSIS

In a penetrating analysis of the current state of the shipping market, Danish Ship Finance (DSF) points out that ship owners have stopped investing for the time being. Shipyard orders are contracting, and shipyards around the world are currently running at only 30% of capacity. Some 13 million compensated gross tonnage (CGT) has contracted. DSF predicted that around 4% of the world's shipyards would close or go inactive in 2012. By 2013 and 2014, many yards will be running out of orders. By the end of 2014, DSF believes that global capacity will have retreated back to 2008 levels.

However, DSF points out that despite overcapacity in the container shipping market, in general shipping lines have been very disciplined about keeping rates up, and simply resting overcapacity instead of getting into price wars. Slow steaming has been a feature as well, which cuts fuel burn, and keeps utilization rates higher than would otherwise be the case. DSF expects supply growth to continue to outstrip demand during 2013, which does not bode well for the sector, the main reason for this being the arrival of new ships already in the build pipeline.

There is also a large and growing oversupply of tonnage in the crude tanker market. "The outlook for 2013 is dominated by the challenge of absorbing both the previous overhang of tonnage and another large inflow of vessels," DSF says. Freight rates and asset values are expected to continue to remain low in 2013.

MORE INFO

Article:

Volkov, Matthew, Alexander Gladstone, and Ivy Zhang. "A rising tide lifts all ships." *Financial Times* (October 22, 2012). Online at: tinyurl.com/ndldmmu

Report:

Danmarks Skibskredit. "Shipping market review." October 2012. Online at: tinyurl.com/or7zv23 [PDF].

Websites:

Baltic Exchange: www.thebaltic.com

BBC News video, "Shipping industry faces tough times amid global slowdown": www.bbc.co.uk/news/business-20778405

Lloyd's List: www.lloydslist.com

Transpacific Stabilization Agreement (TSA): www.tsacarriers.org

See Also:

The Box: How the Shipping Container Made the World Smaller and the World Economy Bigger (p. 1339)

Transport and Logistics (pp. 1651–1652)

Steel

MAJOR INDUSTRY TRENDS

The world steel industry is struggling with overcapacity, but its output is essential to virtually every other industry. According to the World Steel Association, the industry directly employs in excess of two million people worldwide, with a further two million contractors and another four million employed in supporting industries. However, when you take steel's position as the key product supplier to a range of industries, including automotive, construction, transport, power, and machine goods, it is reasonable to use a multiplier of 25:1. This means that the steel industry is at the heart of the employment of more than 50 million people worldwide.

Not surprisingly, the world's use of steel continues to grow, even in the flat to low growth environment that advanced economies are currently experiencing. World crude steel production has increased from 851 megatonnes (Mt) in 2001 to 1,527 in 2011 (1 Mt = 1 million tonnes), and the average steel use per capita has increased from 150 kg in 2001 to 215 kg in 2011. The World Steel Association (WSA) points out that steel is at the heart of the green economy, as it is the main material used in delivering renewable energy from solar, marine, and wind power generation sources. Moreover, all steel created in the last 150 years can be recycled and reused today in new products and applications.

By sector, global steel recovery rates for recycling are estimated at 85% for construction, 85% for automotive, 90% for machinery, and 50% for electrical and domestic appliances. This leads to a global weighted average of over 70%. It is a measure of the increased efficiency of the steel sector over the last three decades that it now takes 50% less energy to produce a tonne of steel than it did 30 years ago. The industry also strives to return water used in the production of steel back to rivers and other sources in a condition that is at least as good or better than when it was extracted.

China is far and away the world's leading steel producer, and has increased production almost fivefold from 2002, when it produced some 182.249 million tones, to 2011, when it produced 683.883 Mt. In fact, the whole shape of steel production has changed dramatically over the last six or seven decades. From 1910 until 1960, the United States was far and away the world's largest steel producer, with almost half the global steel production coming from there. Then Japan and China came to the fore. Japan produced 107.6 Mt in 2011, while US production for the whole of 2012 was 97.22 million, according to the American Iron and Steel Institute (ANSI). Brazil and Turkey have also moved up the ranks of steel-producing nations. At seventh place, Germany is the only EU member in the top 10, with Ukraine in eighth place.

The entire global steel industry—and arguably the development of much of modern society, which depends on steel for everything from construction to automobiles—owes a huge debt to Henry Bessemer, the inventor of the Bessemer process, which he patented in 1855. This was the world's first inexpensive industrial process for the mass production of steel from molten pig iron, and was a huge contributing factor to the growth of the United States from 1865 until the early 1900s.

The top 10 steel-producing companies in the world at the end of 2011 were:

1. ArcelorMittal (Luxemborg), 98 Mt;
2. Baosteel (China), 37 Mt;
3. Posco (South Korea), 35.4 Mt;
4. Nippon Steel (Japan), 35 Mt;
5. JFE Holdings (Japan), 31.1 Mt;
6. Jiangsu Shagang Group (China), 23.2 Mt;
7. Tata Steel (India), 23.2 Mt;
8. US Steel (USA), 22.3 Mt;
9. Anshan Iron & Steel Group (China), 22.1 Mt;
10. Gerdau (Brazil), 18.7 Mt.

The world's largest steel producer, Arcelor Mittal, is the result of the 2006 merger between Arcelor and the Indian steel-maker, Mittal, owned by Lakshmi Mittal. The new company produces about 10% of the world's steel, and is headquartered in Luxembourg. However, overcapacity in the sector has hurt the company, which in 2012 idled some nine of 25 blast furnaces, and in October 2012 it closed two permanently.

  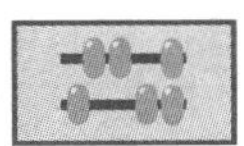      

MARKET ANALYSIS

In its October 2012 Short Range Outlook, the WSA predicted that global apparent steel use will have increased by 2.1% in 2012, once all the figures are in. This is a considerable reduction from the 6.2% growth achieved in 2011. The WSA expects things to pick up in 2013, when demand should grow by 3.2%, it says, to a new record high of 1.4 trillion tonnes.

Commenting on the results, Hans Jürgen Kerkhoff said that while the WSA had anticipated the second half of 2012 to continue to show the improvement seen during the first half of the year, following the marked slowdown at the end of 2011, this had not happened. "The economic situation deteriorated due to continued uncertainty arising from the debt crisis in the eurozone and a sharper than expected slowdown in China," he said. These factors hammered business and manufacturing confidence around the world, and curtailed the demand for steel.

However, provided the United States manages to balance the need for growth with the need for some fiscal tightening to reduce its huge deficit, and provided the eurozone crisis is contained and China manages to achieve 8% growth, then 2013 may turn out to be reasonable. That prediction, however, contains a good many imponderables and could well be disproved as the year progresses. "Since the 2008 crisis, uncertainty and volatility has become the norm for the steel industry, but it is worth noting that world steel demand has maintained positive growth despite all the headwinds and lingering difficulties," he concluded.

Steel demand in China is expected to increase by 3.1% during 2013, to 659 Mt, partially as a result of stimulus measures taken by the government to improve the economic situation. Demand in India, however, is likely to contract somewhat from previous highs, and will be no more than 5% in 2013.

Iron Ore Prospects for 2013

The price of iron ore is one of the key influences on the steel industry. On December 12, Australia, comfortably the world's largest exporter of iron ore, raised its price estimate for 2013 because it expects infrastructure spending, and stimulus spending by the Chinese government to create a steady boost to demand. According to the Australian Bureau of Resources and Energy Economics (BREE), prices will average US$106 a tonne in 2013, up US$5 from a September forecast of US$101 a tonne. This would still be a considerable falling away from prices achieved in 2012, when the average was US$128 as of end December 2012. However, BREE says that the price drop is not because of falling demand, but because Australia's competitors have ramped up supply to meet what the industry as a whole sees as a healthy level of demand during 2013.

Australia expects to have shipped slightly in excess of 480 Mt in 2012, rising to 543 million in 2013, the latter being an increase in the 528 Mt figure BREE predicted in September 2012. The impact of Chinese demand on the world iron ore prices is huge. In December 2012, the price climbed to its highest in more than four months, as the market grew confident that the Chinese economy was finally emerging from a seven-quarters-long slowdown. Market sentiment was buoyed by the fact that November 2012 was the second highest monthly import of iron ore by China ever, at 65.8 Mt. The monthly record is currently held by January 2011, when China imported 68.97 Mt. According to BREE, China's imports of iron ore for 2013 are expected to total around 770 Mt, up around 5.3% from the 2012 figure of 704 Mt. China's crude steel production rose 14% in 2012, with output reaching 57.4 Mt in November 2012. However, while this is good news for iron ore exporters such as Australia and Brazil, the ratings agency Standard & Poor's points out that there is overcapacity in China in steel production, and that the outlook for steel prices in Asia generally during 2013 is weak as a result of overcapacity in the sector. "We maintain our negative outlook on the steel sector in Asia. However, we are seeing some signs of price stability and improved demand, which, if sustained, could change our negative outlook to stable within the next quarter," S&P said (cited in *Inquirer Business*).

MORE INFO

Article:

Dumlao, Doris C. "Gold, copper sales to improve in 2013, prospects not as bright for other metals." *Inquirer Business* (December 6, 2012). Online at: tinyurl.com/psdvp3j

Report:

PricewaterhouseCoopers. "Forging ahead: Global metals deals 2013 outlook and 2012 review." January 2013. Online at: tinyurl.com/nko7g6g

Websites:

South East Asia Iron and Steel Institute (SEAISI): www.seaisi.org

World Steel Association: www.worldsteel.org

ThomasNet News produces industry trend analyses for the sector: news.thomasnet.com

See Also:

Construction and Building Materials (pp. 1616–1618)
Mining (pp. 1637–1638)

Telecoms

MAJOR INDUSTRY TRENDS

Growing Popularity of Mobile Threatens Fixed-Line Sector

The telecoms industry can be divided into two principal sectors: fixed-line services and mobile services. The mobile sector has been the main engine of growth over the past decade, and has proved a boon to many consumers in emerging economies who have little or no access to fixed-line services. The growth of mobile services is also threatening the position of traditional fixed-line operators in developed economies, particularly with the advent of smartphones, which combine the abilities of a powerful computer with the phone, and allow users to access the internet as well as simply making calls and sending texts. Meanwhile, mobiles are converging with tablets. Tablets are now available in 7-inch screen form factors, with some smart phones pushing up to 5-inch screen size, while "voice" and "content consumption" patterns as computing appliance functions are also converging across mobiles and tablets.

New Mobile Technologies

In October 2012, Gartner outlined the top technologies and trends that will drive mobile phones and other segments of the rapidly converging IT sector in 2013. These included the following.

  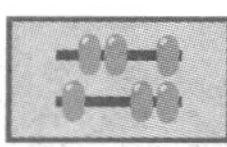      

Mobile Device Battles

Gartner predicts that by 2013 mobile phones will overtake PCs as the most common web access device worldwide, and that by 2015 more than 80% of the handsets sold in mature markets will be smartphones. However, only 20% of those handsets are likely to be Windows phones. By 2015, media tablet shipments are forecast to reach around 50% of laptop shipments, while the Windows 8 operating system is expected to be in third place behind Google's Android and Apple's iOS. Windows 8 is Microsoft's big bet; its platform styles should be evaluated to get a better idea of how they might perform in real-world environments, as well as how users will respond. Consumerization will mean enterprises will not be able to force users to give up their iPads or prevent the use of Windows 8 to the extent consumers adopt consumer targeted Windows 8 devices. Enterprises will need to support a greater variety of form factors, reducing the ability to standardize PC and tablet hardware. The implications for IT is that the era of PC dominance, with Windows as the single platform, will be replaced with a post-PC era where Windows is just one of a variety of environments IT will need to support.

Mobile Applications and HTML5

The market for tools to create consumer and enterprise facing apps is complex, with well over 100 potential tools vendors. Currently, Gartner separates mobile development tools into several categories. For the next few years, no single tool will be optimal for all types of mobile application, so enterprises should expect to employ several. Six mobile architectures—native, special, hybrid, HTML5, message, and noo client—will remain popular. However, Gartner predicts a long-term shift away from native apps to web apps as HTML5 becomes more capable. Nevertheless, native apps are unlikely to disappear, and will always offer the best user experiences and most sophisticated features. Developers will also need to develop new design skills to deliver touch-optimized mobile applications that operate across a range of devices in a coordinated fashion.

Personal Cloud

The personal cloud is forecast to gradually replace the PC as the location where individuals keep their personal content, access their services and personal preferences, and center their digital lives. It will be the glue that connects the web of devices they choose to use during different aspects of their daily lives. The personal cloud entails the unique collection of services, web destinations, and connectivity becoming the home of their computing and communication activities. Users will see it as a portable, always-available place where they go for all their digital needs. In this world, no one platform, form factor, technology, or vendor will dominate, and managed diversity and mobile device management will be an imperative. The personal cloud shifts the focus from the client device to cloud-based services delivered across devices.

Enterprise App Stores

Enterprises face a complex app store future as some vendors will limit their stores to specific devices and types of apps, forcing the enterprise to deal with multiple stores, multiple payment processes, and multiple sets of licensing terms. By 2014, Gartner believes many organizations will deliver mobile applications to workers through private application stores. With enterprise app stores, the role of IT shifts from that of a centralized planner to that of a market manager providing governance and brokerage services to users, and potentially an ecosystem to support app entrepreneurs.

The Internet of Things

The internet of things (IoT) is a concept that describes how the internet will expand as physical items such as consumer devices and physical assets are connected to it. Key elements of the IoT that are being embedded in a variety of mobile devices include embedded sensors, image recognition technologies, and NFC (near field communication, or contactless) payment. As a result, mobile no longer refers only to use of cellular handsets or tablets. Cellular technology is being embedded in many new types of devices, including pharmaceutical containers and automobiles. Smartphones and other intelligent devices don't just use the cellular network, they communicate via NFC, bluetooth, and wifi to a wide range of devices and peripherals, such as wristwatch displays, healthcare sensors, smart posters, and home entertainment systems. The IoT will enable a wide range of new applications and services, while raising many new challenges.

Hybrid IT and Cloud Computing

As employees have been asked to do more with less, IT departments must play multiple roles in coordinating IT-related activities, and cloud computing is now pushing that change to another level. A recently conducted Gartner IT services survey revealed that the internal cloud services brokerage (CSB) role is emerging, as IT organizations realize they have a responsibility to help improve the provisioning and consumption of inherently distributed, heterogeneous, and often complex cloud services, for both their internal users and external business partners. The internal CSB role represents a means for the IT organization to retain and build influence inside its organization, and to become a value center in the face of challenging new requirements in relation to the increasing adoption of cloud as an approach to IT consumption.

Strategic Big Data

So-called big data is moving from a focus on individual projects to an influence on enterprises' strategic information architecture. Dealing with data volume, variety, velocity, and complexity is forcing changes to many traditional approaches. This realization is leading organizations to abandon the concept of a single enterprise data warehouse containing all information needed for decisions. Instead they are moving towards multiple systems, including content management, data warehouses, data marts, and specialized file systems, tied together with data services and metadata, which will become the "logical" enterprise data warehouse.

Actionable Analytics

Analytics are increasingly delivered to users at the point of action, and in context. With the improvement of performance and costs, IT leaders can afford to perform analytics and simulation for every action taken in the business. The mobile client linked to cloud-based analytic engines and big data repositories potentially enables use of optimization and simulation everywhere and every time. This new step provides simulation, prediction, optimization, and other analytics, to empower even more decision flexibility at the time and place of every business process action.

In-Memory Computing

In-memory computing (IMC) can also provide transformational opportunities. The execution of certain types of hours-long batch processes can be squeezed into minutes or even seconds, allowing these processes to be provided in the form of real-time, or near real-time services, that can be delivered to internal or external users in the form of cloud services. Millions of events can be scanned in a matter of a few tens of milliseconds to detect correlations and patterns pointing at emerging opportunities and threats, "as things happen." The possibility of concurrently running transactional and analytical applications against the same dataset opens unexplored possibilities for business innovation. Numerous vendors are

predicted to deliver in-memory-based solutions over the next two years, driving this approach into mainstream use.

Integrated Ecosystems

The market is undergoing a shift to more integrated systems and ecosystems, and away from loosely coupled heterogeneous approaches. Driving this trend for users is the desire for lower cost, simplicity, and more assured security. Driving the trend for vendors is the ability to have more control of the solution stack and obtain greater margin on a sale, as well as offer a complete solution stack in a controlled environment, but without the need to provide any actual hardware. The trend is manifested in three levels. Appliances combine hardware and software, and software and services are packaged to address an infrastructure or application workload. Cloud-based marketplaces and brokerages facilitate purchase, consumption, and/or use of capabilities from multiple vendors, and may provide a foundation for independent software vendors' (ISV) development and application runtime. In the mobile world, vendors including Apple, Google and Microsoft drive varying degrees of control across and end-to-end ecosystem extending the client through the apps.

MARKET ANALYSIS

Smartphones Selling Well

Worldwide mobile phone sales to end-users fell in 2012, down on 2011 figures, mainly as a result of the sluggish global economy, according to Gartner Inc. A total of 1.75 billion mobile phones were sold worldwide in 2012, 1.7% fewer than in 2011, and the first year-on-year handset sales decline since 2009. Tough economic conditions, shifting consumer preferences, and intense market competition weakened the worldwide mobile phone market in 2012.

However, record sales of 207.7 million smartphones in the fourth quarter of 2012 —a 38.3% hike year on year—helped to support overall sales. Demand for feature phones remained weak. Sales of feature phones totaled 264.4 million units in the fourth quarter, down 19.3% year on year. The research firm expects worldwide sales of smartphones to dominate the overall market in 2013—reaching close to 1 billion units—whereas total mobile phone sales are predicted to touch 1.9 billion units this year. Feature phone sales are expected to keep falling.

iPhone-maker Apple Inc and South Korea's Samsung Electronics Co. dominated the smartphone segment with a combined market share of 52% in the fourth quarter, up from 46.4% in Q3 2012, according to Gartner. The company added that the success of Apple and Samsung is based on the strength of their brands as much as their actual products. Their direct competitors, including those with comparable products, struggle to achieve the same brand appreciation among consumers, who, in a tough economic environment, go for cheaper products over brand.

Former market leader, Finland's Nokia's handset sales in the fourth quarter were boosted by a good response to its Asha mobile phones, and the launch of the latest Lumia Windows Phone 8 models. However, Nokia lost further market share, which fell to its lowest-ever level, Gartner said. In 2012, Nokia achieved 39.3 million smartphone sales worldwide, down 53.6% from 2011.

Gartner added that: "Nokia needs to build on momentum around Asha in 2013 by adding devices and apps to further enhance its overall value proposition and, in doing so, moving up the price point slightly to achieve better margins breaching the gap left by Symbian."

Fixed-Line Sector

The number of fixed-line subscribers around the world as a proportion of the population has been in decline since 2005, according to the International Telecommunication Union (ITU). The number of mobile broadband subscribers overtook the number of fixed-line subscribers globally in 2010. The figure of fixed-line subscribers amounted to 17.3 per 100 inhabitants in 2011, down from 17.8 in 2009, according to the ITU's World Telecommunication/ICT Indicators database.

By contrast, there were 87.3 mobile phone subscriptions per 100 inhabitants in 2011, compared to 67 in 2009. Households with internet access amounted to 34.1%, while 32.5% of individuals used the internet. New information and communication technologies (ICTs) continue to penetrate countries in all regions of the world, as more and more people get connected. There was persistent growth in 2011 in ICT uptake worldwide, with an increase in all key indicators except the number of fixed telephone lines, according to the ITU.

Based on the ubiquity of mobile telephones, the introduction of mobile broadband services in the majority of countries in the world, coupled with the availability of smartphones and tablet computers, has sparked a steep increase in mobile broadband subscriptions, which have experienced average annual growth of 41% since 2007 (see Chart 1.2). The trend away from traditional mobile services, such as voice and SMS, towards mobile web services and uptake is gradually shifting mobile traffic volumes from voice to data, with all this implies in terms of speed, price, available spectrum, revenue, and investment. At the same time, fixed-broadband internet is still growing continuously—albeit at lower rates in developing than in developed countries, where mobile broadband services are fulfilling the demand for internet access.

MORE INFO

Report:

International Telecommunication Union. "Measuring the information society." Published annually. Online at: www.itu.int/ITU-D/ict/publications/idi/

Websites:

CCS Insight, provides market information, analysis and intelligence for companies focusing on the mobile and wireless sector: www.ccsinsight.com

Gartner, supplies information-technology research: www.gartner.com

Informa Telecoms and Media, supplies business intelligence and strategic services for the global telecoms and media markets: www.informatandm.com

iSuppli, provides information on the electronics-industry value chain: www.isuppli.com

See Also:

Information Technology (pp. 1632–1633)

Tourism and Hotels

MAJOR INDUSTRY TRENDS

Spending on tourism and hotels is closely related to the economic cycle. Certainly, spending on leisure activities such as holidays tends to be one of the first things that consumers cut back in times of economic hardship. The travel and hotel industry is further affected by reduced demand from the business sector, as travel is one of the first areas that the corporates axe when the economy slows.

The United Nations World Tourism Organization (UNWTO) says that international tourist arrivals for business, leisure, and other purposes grew by 4% in 2012 to reach 1.035 billion, according to the latest UNWTO World Tourism Barometer. Emerging economies (4.1%) grew faster than advanced economies (3.6%), with Asia-Pacific showing the strongest results, reflecting their superior economic growth over the period. UNWTO says that growth is expected to continue in 2013 at only slightly below the 2012 level (3-4%) and in line with its long-term forecast.

International tourist arrivals to Europe, the most visited region in the world, were up by 3%; a very positive result in view of the economic situation, and following a strong 2011 (6%). Total arrivals reached 535 million, 17 million more than in 2011. By sub-region, Central and Eastern Europe destinations (8%) experienced the best results, followed by Western Europe (3%). Destinations in southern Mediterranean Europe (2%) consolidated their excellent performance of 2011, and returned in 2012 to their normal growth rates.

Asia-Pacific (7%) was up by 15 million arrivals in 2012, reaching a total 233 million international tourists. South-East Asia (9%) was the best performing sub-region, largely as a result of the implementation of policies that foster intraregional cooperation and coordination in tourism. Growth was also strong in North-East Asia (6%), as Japanese inbound and outbound tourism recovered, while it was comparatively weaker in South Asia (4%) and in Oceania (4%).

The Americas (4%) saw an increase of 6 million arrivals, reaching 162 million in total. Leading the growth were destinations in Central America (6%), while South America, up by 4%, showed some slowdown compared to the double-digit growth of 2010 and 2011. The Caribbean (4%), on the other hand, performed above the previous two years, while North America (3%) consolidated its 2011 growth.

Africa (6%) recovered well from its setback in 2011, when arrivals declined by 1% largely because of the negative results of North Africa. Arrivals reached a new record (52 million) as a result of the rebound in North Africa (9%, compared to a 9% decline in 2011), and the continued growth of Sub-Saharan destinations (5%). Results in thea Middle East (−5%) improved after a 7% decline in 2011, yet the region recorded an estimated 3 million fewer international tourist arrivals in 2012, despite the clear recovery in Egypt.

Top Tourism Destinations

Among the top 10 tourist destinations, receipts were up significantly in the first nine months of 2012, with Hong Kong (China) gaining 16%, the United States (10%), the United Kingdom (6%), and Germany (5%), according to UNWTO. A significant number of destinations around the world saw receipts from international tourism increase by 15% or more—Japan (37%), India and South Africa (both 22%), Sweden and the Republic of Korea (both 19%), Thailand (18%), and Poland (16%).

Although the highest growth rates in expenditure abroad among the 10 top markets came from emerging economies—China (42%) and Russia (31%)—important traditional source markets showed particularly good results, according to UNWTO. In Europe, and despite economic pressures, expenditure on international tourism by Germany held well at 3%, while the United Kingdom (5%) returned to growth after two flat years. In the Americas, both the United States and Canada grew 7%. On the other hand, France (−7%) and Italy (−2%) registered declines in travel expenditure.

Smaller markets with significant growth, according to UNWTO, were Venezuela (31%), Poland (19%), the Philippines (17%), Malaysia (15%), Saudi Arabia (14%), Belgium (13%), Norway and Argentina (both 12%), Switzerland and Indonesia (both 10%).

The Role of Tourism in the Global Economy

Travel and tourism are significant contributors to the world economy. The OECD points out that international tourism has been growing at a slightly faster pace than the world economy in recent years, and has played a critical role in sustaining economic growth and employment, and in generating foreign currency receipts for countries. In OECD countries, the employment growth rate in the hotel and restaurant industry was above 2% every year from 2000 to the start of the global downturn, and by 2011 had recovered to similar levels. This is more than a percentage point above total employment growth, and demonstrates the importance of the sector in job creation. During the last 20 years, the growth rate of non-resident tourist arrivals in OECD countries, while 1.6% below the worldwide rate has averaged 2.8% a year, well ahead of the average OECD country growth rate of 2.4%.

The EU has also released data highlighting the importance of tourism in many EU member states. In September 2012, the EU said that the economic importance of international tourism can be measured by looking at the ratio of international travel receipts in relation to GDP; the data are from balance of payments statistics and include both business travel and travel for pleasure. In 2011, the ratio of travel receipts to GDP was highest in Malta (14.0 %) and Cyprus (10.2 %), confirming the importance of tourism to these island nations; an even higher ratio was observed in Croatia (14.7 %). In absolute terms, the highest international travel receipts in 2011 were recorded in Spain (€43.026 million) and France (€38.682 million), followed by Italy, Germany, and the United Kingdom.

Geopolitical Turbulence Can Have a Dramatic Impact

The revolts that began in Tunisia at the end of 2010 and spread across the Middle East and North Africa had a devastating impact on tourism, but not everyone lost out. Tourism in Egypt and Tunisia plunged more than 30% in 2011 amid the popular upheavals sweeping the Arab world, according to UNWTO. Tourism fell by about 80% in Tunisia after the unrest began in the first months of 2011. Egypt counts on foreign visitors for 16% of its GDP and 14% of jobs, while in Tunisia, tourism accounts for 17% of GDP and more than 15% of jobs, according to the World Travel & Tourism Council (WTTC). However, a marketing campaign targeting European holidaymakers, in particular, resulted in a 30% rise in the number of visitors in 2012, compared to the previous year, with almost 6 million arriving in 2012. Tourist numbers also grew in Dubai, rising by 10% in 2012. Dubai has remained free of unrest, and has used its Emirates airline and strategic location midway between Europe, Africa, and Asia to persuade transit passengers to spend at least a couple of days there. It has become a short-break destination in itself. The Arab Spring uprisings have also been credited with boosting visitor numbers in Spain.

Growth of Budget Airlines

Since first emerging in the mid-1990s, budget airlines have had a dramatic impact on the tourism industry. Apart from boosting overall numbers, budget airlines have also opened up lesser-known destinations, and encouraged greater independent travel. However, their impact has not been entirely positive, with some countries claiming that the advent of budget airlines has hurt the domestic tourism industry. Australian travel agents have warned that this is the case in their country, for example. Thus, in December 2011, Alan Dodson, the managing director of travel company Holiday Planet, said he was finding it harder and harder to market Australia as a destination, with low-cost carriers such as AirAsia and Jetstar offering such cheap packages to Asia. Spanish tourism officials have also criticized the budget airlines operating across Europe that fly to the country and its islands, saying the low fares led to tourists who wouldn't spend the savings they had made on their flights while on their holiday, but would instead spend the duration of their time trying to get equally cheap accommodation, food, and drink.

Environmental Concerns Pose Long-Term Threat to Industry

One of the biggest international problems grabbing the attention of the media and the political classes is that of climate change. Air travel, in particular, has attracted the ire of environmentalists, and proved a useful scapegoat for politicians keen to polish their green credentials. Certainly, governments around the world have been quick to impose taxes on air travel. To the cynics, this has simply been an exercise in raising revenue, while environmentalists have called for even higher taxes, and the introduction of draconian measures to curb air travel. Given the slump in air travel that has occurred as a result of the global economic slowdown, the immediate urgency to adopt measures to discourage air travel has evaporated. In the long term, the issue may come back to haunt the industry. However, the aerospace industry is investing heavily in technology to boost fuel efficiency, as well as in research to develop alternative fuels. Indeed, it is doubtful whether anything—even concern about the environment—can stop the long-term growth of the industry, given its potential in countries such as India and China as living standards rise.

MARKET ANALYSIS

The Global Market

Tourism is now one of the largest industries in the world. According to UNWTO, the export income generated by international tourism ranks fourth after fuels, chemicals, and automotive products. Furthermore, UNWTO points out that, for many developing countries, tourism is one of the main income sources of foreign exchange, and creates much-needed employment and opportunities for economic development. The industry has also enjoyed staggering growth over the past six decades. The WTO says that from 1950 to 2012, international tourist arrivals grew from 25 million to 1.035 billion.

The industry is expected to continue to grow rapidly in the long term. The WTTC, a "forum for business leaders in the travel and tourism industry," says that, globally in 2011, travel and tourism employed approximately 260 million people, or 7.6% of total employment, and generated US$6 trillion, or 9.0% of world GDP. The WTTC anticipates that, by 2021, travel and tourism will generate nearly 300 million jobs, and account for 10% of global GDP.

MORE INFO

Websites:

International Air Transport Association (IATA): www.iata.org
United Nations World Tourism Organization (UNWTO): www.unwto.org
World Travel and Tourism Council (WTTC): www.wttc.org

Transport and Logistics

MAJOR INDUSTRY TRENDS

Air Traffic Looks for Upturn in 2013

The fortunes of the transport and logistics industry are closely connected to the economic cycle. When economic activity is buoyant, demand for transport and logistics services is equally strong. Consumer and business demand for goods and services inevitably translates into higher demand for transport and logistics services. Thus, the slump in global economic growth that occurred in the second half of 2008 and during the course of 2009 caused global trade volumes to plummet, and had a severe impact on the transport and logistics industry. However, the International Air Transport Association (IATA) expects some rebound in 2013, fueled by better prospects for the global economy.

Both air travel and air cargo saw a pick-up in volume at the end of 2012. Air travel was 4.6% up in November 2012 by comparison with the same month in 2011, building on the October improvement, year on year, of 2.6%. Air freight volumes, which saw a further year-on-year drop in October 2012 of 2.6%, saw growth of 1.6% in November. While positive, these are still rather thin indicators of growth, and IATA's director general, Tony Tyler, pointed out that the level of demand for air travel was only 2% higher at the end of 2012 than it was at the start, a much weaker level of growth than the historic average for the sector. Tyler said that it was "premature" to consider that air cargo had turned the corner, and was now set to resume normal trend growth. However, coupled with positive developments in the US economy and a general improvement in business confidence, things were looking positive for 2013. IATA's growth forecast for the year, however, is extremely modest, at 1.4% for air cargo. Passenger volume growth is expected to be somewhat better at 4.5% worldwide.

Nevertheless, this is a real improvement on the position the sector was in after the 2008 global crash. By December 2008, cargo volumes had fallen by 22.6%, and by 23.2% year on year by January 2009, at which point the then-CEO of IATA, Giovanni Bisignani, said that the cargo industry was in crisis, with demand having "fallen off a cliff." Bisignani called 2009 the worst year in aviation history in terms of demand, predicting that airlines would lose US$5.6 billion on a net basis in 2010, after losing US$11 billion in 2009.

According to IATA, air cargo represents about 10% of the airline industry's revenues. As 35% of the value of goods traded internationally are transported by air, air cargo is a barometer of global economic health.

The shipping industry is, if anything, in a worse position than air transport, with its recovery from the 2008 crash, which looked promising in 2010, now seemingly stalled, and the sector still suffering from overcapacity. The Baltic Dry Index, which provides the daily average cost to ship bulk dry commodities (such as grain products or coal) around the world, is highly sensitive to global economic activity. Because the freight costs it measures move in response to demand for shipping services, the index is another excellent barometer of world trade. By April 2010, the Baltic Dry Index had risen by 58.5% over the previous 12 months, and there was considerable optimism that the world had moved into a recovery phase, with strong emerging market growth pulling advanced markets out of their slump. However, by mid-2011 virtually all that optimism had faded in the face of the European sovereign debt crisis, and persistent weakness in the US economy. Inevitably, the shipping industry suffered as a result and its woes continued through 2012, which by consensus was a very bad year, and the problems look set to continue in 2013.

Drewry, the specialist research and advisory organization for the maritime sector, said in its January 2013 report on container shipping that, despite attempts by shippers to withdraw capacity to keep freight rates up, weaker cargo volumes had negated much of their efforts. Freight rates actually declined from around US$2,700 per feu (forty-foot equivalent units) in early March 2012 to US$2,400 by early January 2013. "While this is not a disaster for the carriers, it proves that there is a fundamental weakness in the market, compounded by low volumes on the back of a non-existent peak season in 2012," Drewry said. Competition among carriers, particularly in the Asia-Mediterranean trade, continued to depress load factors (as carriers were introducing too much capacity in an attempt to win market share), with average load factors being in the 75-85% range for most of the second half of 2012. With another 40 ships of at least 10,000 teu (twenty-foot equivalent units) due for delivery in 2013, carriers were facing a near-impossible task in finding ways of deploying this capacity without doing further damage to the supply demand balance, Drewry said.

Logistics Industry Rebuilds after the Crash of 2008

Road and rail traffic freight hauliers and general logistics businesses have had much the same experience as their peers in the air cargo and shipping industries. In August 2012, Deutsche Post DHL, the world's largest postal and logistics group, called the economic environment "difficult," but expected to grow revenues by roughly 5% year on year. Its third-quarter results were up 5.7% on the same period for 2011. "Looking beyond the current year, the company remains optimistic and expects the positive earnings trend to continue," it said.

In its commentary on the outlook for the UK logistics industry, Barclays said that while the sector had seen a rebound in 2010 and early 2011, this had been followed by slowing activity in the first half of 2012. "Fuel costs have weighed heavily on the sector in recent years, and continue to represent a major cost pressure. A brief decline in oil prices earlier in 2012 provided some limited respite for transport operators, but this has subsequently reversed," it said.

Environmental Laws Could Hit Transport Firms

Air freight companies may be affected by stricter environmental regulations over the next few years, according to Cargonews Asia. The website said that the likely advent of more stringent global environmental regulations, "would impact not only the economics of using air transport, but would also possibly result in punitive sanctions against goods produced with environmentally questionable practices." It added that the latter element would significantly erode the comparative advantage enjoyed by manufacturers in Asia, which have fueled the growth in demand for air cargo in recent years. These concerns appear to be shared by IATA. Cargonews Asia quoted the organization's chief economist, Brian Pearce, as saying that "the cost of protectionism and deglobalization, higher taxes, and climate-change policies will all have an impact on the industry."

MARKET ANALYSIS

Aviation Industry Cuts Jobs and Capacity, While Mergers Increase

The slump in global trade hit the airlines and shipping companies hard. Airlines cut capacity, routes, and jobs in 2008 and 2009. The downturn has also hurried the consolidation of the industry. In November 2009, British Airways and Spanish airline Iberia said that they had reached a preliminary agreement for a merger, which completed in late 2010. In May 2010, Continental Airlines and UAL Corporation's United Airlines merged to create the world's largest airline. The new airline is a US$3 billion company capable of carrying 144 million passengers per year. Sector analysts generally approve of mergers as they allow carriers to pool costs, and to raise fares on routes where they used to compete. However, this latter reason is also why regulators scrutinize potential merger deals very closely before giving their approval.

Overcapacity Plagues Shipping Industry

The shipping sector is suffering from a combination of plummeting demand and an oversupply of ships, as vessels ordered during the growth years are delivered. The shipping industry enjoyed five boom years until 2007, but the global recession has sapped demand for the transportation of Asian-made goods. In 2010, many shipping companies reported that, although demand had picked up, overcapacity affected both rates and their profits. In April 2009, for example, China Cosco Holdings Co., the world's largest operator of dry bulk ships, announced an annual loss after rates for hauling commodities, while container prices tumbled on overcapacity.

Global Economic Slump Hits Logistics Specialists

Many of the major logistics firms were affected by the global economic slump, but made a reasonable recovery through to the first half of 2011. In its 2009 annual results, the CEO of the logistics giant TNT, Peter Bakker, said: "While 2008 was a year of two halves, with the second half clearly marked by the impact of the global economic crisis, 2009 has seen the impact of the economic crisis for its full duration." The company said that its express business, with its cyclical nature, was most severely affected. "Many customers in Europe have chosen slower and cheaper forms of transport, leading to a move away from air towards road express. The result was an unprecedented drop in volumes of air express of 25% in the beginning of the year, with road volume declines also building up during the year to double digit levels." Looking forward, TNT said that the fourth quarter of 2009 showed the return of positive growth in express volumes, compared to the dramatic lows in the final quarter of 2008. Bakker said in the Group's 2010 Annual Report (for the year ending December 31, 2010) that 2010 had been a year of large operating challenges for logistics companies, complicated by both the volcanic ash cloud that had grounded large numbers of European flights, and by the extreme winter conditions experienced in 2010. However, the year also saw growth returning to both advanced markets and, more robustly, to emerging markets. The company's express delivery volumes rose to pre-economic crisis levels, and the volume growth in the company's parcels business continued.

MORE INFO

Article:

Drewry. "Container forecaster 4Q12." January 9, 2012. Online at: www.drewry.co.uk/news.php?id=164

Report:

Barclays. "UK transport and logistics: Sector outlook. Third quarter 2012." Online at: tinyurl.com/q64rdkg

Websites:

Cargonews Asia, providing news on transport and logistics in Asia: www.cargonewsasia.com

Drewry, independent maritime research, consultancy, and publishing company: www.drewry.co.uk

International Air Transport Association (IATA): www.iata.org

Port Strategy, providing information on the global shipping industry: www.portstrategy.com

See Also:

Automobiles (pp. 1609–1610)
Aviation (pp. 1610–1612)
Shipping (pp. 1644–1646)

Water

MAJOR INDUSTRY TRENDS

Water and the Global Economic Downturn

Water is an essential requirement of life, as well as of economic development. However, water scarcity is an increasing problem as global demand rises while supplies are limited. Around 97% of the water on the planet is seawater, and the remaining 3% fresh, of which two percentage points is locked in ice. Over the past 40 years, the world's population has doubled, yet water usage has quadrupled, while the amount of water has remained unchanged.

Moreover, water management is made more complicated by climatic and geographical variations. Freshwater supplies are erratically distributed in time and space, and there can be considerable variations in the amount of rainfall within a region from season to season, and from one year to the next. Moreover, according to the United Nations, the state of water resources is influenced by withdrawals to meet socioeconomic demands. This, in turn, is affected by drivers such as population growth, economic development and dietary changes, as well as the need for control of water resources to protect settlements in flood plains and drought-prone regions.

Given its essential nature, the provision of water is generally highly regulated in most countries. Some countries, the United Kingdom, for example, create social tariffs to reduce the charges of customers who would otherwise struggle to meet their bills. High levels of regulation remain a characteristic of the industry, even though in some countries the water industry has been privatized. The industry in the United Kingdom, for example, was privatized as long ago as 1989. However, the supply of water remains publicly owned in many countries. In Germany, for example, local municipalities are generally responsible for supplying water.

In the United States, local governments traditionally have owned and operated public water systems, but in recent years an increasing number of municipalities have elected to sell or outsource their water operations to private companies. Government-owned systems make up the vast majority of the US water and wastewater utility segment, accounting for approximately 84% of all community water systems, and approximately 98% of all community wastewater systems.

The utility segment of the water industry is highly fragmented, with approximately 53,000 community water systems, and approximately 16,000 community wastewater facilities, according to the United States Environmental Protection Agency (EPA). There are a few large water utilities, and of these, American Water is the largest investor-owned water and wastewater utility company in the United States.

Demand for water also tends to be fairly constant almost irrespective of the economy. In stock market terms, it is therefore regarded as a "defensive" sector, i.e. the shares can be a safe haven during times of economic hardship as earnings remain steady. However, demand for water could grow at a faster pace than was previously the case, according to some analysts. In February 2013, for example, the International Energy Agency (IEA) forecast that global water consumption by the energy industry would double from the current 66 billion m3 of water to about 135 billion m3 by 2035. This is water used for cooling, irrigating, and fracking, etc. The IEA predicted that half of this consumption will be required for coal-fired energy plants, and 30% for use in biofuel production.

Indeed, there has been concern for a number of years that growing demand for water could lead to geopolitical conflict. At current rates of growth, demand for water may exceed supplies by 40%, according to the World Bank-sponsored 2030 Water Resources Group. In March 2012, the US Director of National Intelligence warned that the risk of conflict would grow, as water demand is set to outstrip sustainable current supplies by 40% by 2030. Already, around 780 million people lack access to safe drinking water, according to the UN. By 2030, around 47% of the world's population will be living in areas of high water stress, according to the OECD's Environmental Outlook to 2030.

Rapid population growth and increased industrial demand has led to a three-fold increase in demand for water over the past 30 years, according to the UN. It says that 30 countries will be classified as water-scarce (defined as areas with less than 1,000 m3 of water per adult per annum) by 2025, up from 20 countries in 1980. The growth of agriculture is also blamed for the rapid growth of water demand. Agriculture accounts for 70% of all water withdrawn by the agricultural, municipal, and industrial (including energy) sectors, according to the UN.

Indeed, in September 2012, the Stockholm International Water Institute warned that the world's population may have to become vegetarian over the next 40 years because of growing water scarcity. Foods rich in animal protein require five to 10 times as much water to produce as vegetarian diets, according to the organization. The global population is expected to reach nine billion by the middle of the 21st century, up from the current seven billion; feeding this additional two billion people will place enormous pressure on already strained land and water resources, according to the Swedish institute.

Desalination is one solution to the shortage of water, and governments and companies across the globe are investing heavily in these plants. By the end of 2011, desalination plants were producing around 6.7 billion m3, around double the level seen 10 years earlier. By the beginning of 2013, around 16,000 plants were operating globally, and the industry is growing by around 15% a year. China is investing particularly heavily in desalination, and is on track to become the world's biggest producer of desalinated water. It plans to produce around 2.2 million m3 a day by 2015, according to the Chinese National Development and Reform Commission. The water would supply around 15% of the needs of factories on the country's eastern seaboard, according to the commission. However, desalinated water costs around 15 times more than regular water to produce. It also burns polluting fossil-fuel energy, as solar-powered desalination is in its infancy.

MARKET ANALYSIS

The Global Market

In February 2013, the investment advisory firm, WaterTech Capital, in Plano, Texas, was reported as saying that the global water industry receives revenues amounting to US$620 billion per year, and, that over the next 25 years, up to US$25 trillion could be spent on global water and wastewater infrastructure expenses. It added that there are around 400 water-related companies globally, most of which are in the United States. The United States alone will need to spend at least US$500 billion over the next 20 years to replace ageing infrastructure such as pipelines, according to government agencies. Municipalities and for-profit utilities will bear the brunt of these costs. At the same time, some emerging countries are laying new systems to deliver clean water.

Huge Investment Needed in Water Industry

The privatization of the water industry in many parts of the globe spurred huge investor interest in the water industry, which they had previously regarded as a safe and rather boring area. However, according to the UN's Fourth World Water Development Report, published every three years and last issued in 2012, raising commercial finance for water has become more difficult as a result of the global financial situation since 2007. It has discouraged new private interest in water infrastructure projects, and has also unsettled partners in existing private/public partnership (PPP) ventures. In early 2009, the International Finance Corporation (IFC), part of the World Bank, reported that US$200 billion of PPP projects had been postponed, or had become 'at risk', 15–20% of which were in water supply and sanitation. The UN says many local water utilities are funded by revenues from users or public budgets that are insufficient to exceed their day-to-day operating costs. As a result, they lack adequate cash flow to borrow money. Such utilities cannot fund long-term investments if they do not receive grant subsidies. However, many that might have adequate cash flows remain unable to finance investments through borrowings, either because lenders perceive them as an unacceptable risk, or because their potential rating results in loans with short terms and high interest rates.

Climate Change and Water Supplies

Many agencies, including the UN, have warned that climate change is exacerbating the problem of water scarcity. One argument is that climate warming causes polar ice to melt into the sea, which turns fresh water into sea water, although this has little direct effect on the water supply. Climate warming also increases the amount of water that the atmosphere can hold, which in turn can lead to greater and heavier rainfall when the air cools, which means it is harder to save and store this rainfall. Warmer air also increases evaporation rates and causes inland glaciers to melt, while in the sub-tropics climate change is likely to lead to reduced rainfall in already dry regions. The overall effect is that both flooding and droughts become more commonplace.

According to the Intergovernmental Panel on Climate Change (IPCC), despite global increases in rainfall, many dry regions including the Mediterranean and southern Africa will suffer badly from reduced rainfall and increased evaporation. Consequently, the IPCC estimates that around one billion people in dry regions may face increasing water scarcity.

MORE INFO

Websites:

WaterTech: www.watertechservices.com

Intergovernmental Panel on Climate Change: www.ipcc.ch

UN World Water Development Report 2012: unesdoc.unesco.org/images/0021/002156/215644e.pdf

FINANCE INFORMATION SOURCES

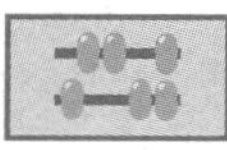

Finance Information Sources

Providing the quickest and easiest route to the best finance information available

Sometimes it's easy to grasp the basics about a topic, such as accounting, risk management, or investment. More often than not, it's difficult to know where to start—or where to go next. There is plenty of free world-class finance advice out there—but where is it?

Finance Information Sources is a highly selective and well-researched collection of sources: it's designed to give you the quickest and easiest route to the information you need, in a variety of media.

We cite thousands of sources of the best finance information from around the world, divided up into over 50 subject areas. These include the best websites, the most informative books, magazines, and journals, and the most authoritative organizations.

  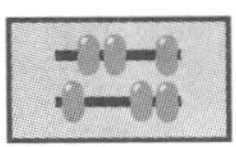   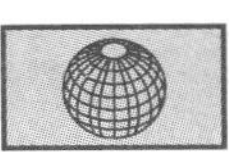   

Contents

Accounting

BOOKS

Accounting in a Nutshell: Finance for the Non-Specialist, 3rd ed

Janet Walker

Oxford: Chartered Institute of Management Accountants, 2008
368pp, ISBN: 978-0-7506-8738-6

This introductory text is designed for nonspecialist managers and students who need an understanding of the basic principles of financial and management accounting. The topics covered include accounting statements, profit and loss accounts, cost analysis, and budget planning and control.

The Best Small Business Accounts Book (Blue Version)

Peter Hingston, Stuart Ramsden

Hereford, UK: Hingston Publishing, 2004
64pp, ISBN: 978-0-906555-23-1

There are three versions of this book, all designed for the UK tax system. The blue version, which has a monthly layout, is ideal for non-VAT-registered credit-based businesses. Updated since its initial publication in 1991, this book allows the small business owner to keep the accounts in one compact book. It provides full instructions and worked examples to help the user to achieve correct and effective bookkeeping, including 16 columns to analyze checks and an easy-to-do monthly bank statement check.

Book-Keeping and Accounting for the Small Business: How to Keep the Books and Maintain Financial Control over Your Business, 7th ed

Peter Taylor

Oxford: How To Books, 2003
256pp, ISBN: 978-1-85703-878-1

Aimed at both students and anyone running, or responsible for, the accounts of a small business, this guide offers structured advice on the essentials of bookkeeping.

CIMA Dictionary of Finance and Accounting

London: A&C Black Publishers, 2003
352pp, ISBN: 978-0-7475-6689-2

With the stamp of approval of the Chartered Institute of Management Accountants, this is an authoritative and reliable finance and accounting dictionary. It is a useful reference for both practitioners and students of all areas of business.

Corporate Financial Reporting: Text and Cases, 4th ed

E. Richard Brownlee, Kenneth R. Ferris, Mark E. Haskins

Maidenhead, UK: McGraw-Hill, 2000
944pp, ISBN: 978-0-07-118107-5

The book is written for those who require a substantial appreciation and understanding of the issues, problems, and practices of financial accounting. The topics covered are: the institutional setting and fundamental concepts of accounting; the measurement and reporting of income, financial position, and cash-flows; the measurement and reporting of assets, liabilities, and stockholders' equity; selected reporting and disclosure issues; and assessing the quality of reported earnings and financial position.

Essentials of Credit, Collections and Accounts Receivable

Mary S. Schaeffer

Chichester, UK: Wiley, 2002
272pp, ISBN: 978-0-471-22074-9

This paperback will help the reader stay up to date with the latest strategies, developments, and technologies in credit, collections, and accounts receivable. With tips, techniques, and real-world examples, the book offers practical solutions for the credit and collection professional.

FASB Current Text 2008

Financial Accounting Standards Board

Hoboken, New Jersey: Wiley, 2008
ISBN: 978-0-470-39691-9

This two-volume set is a collection of generally accepted accounting principles (GAAP) organized by topic. Material in the book is drawn from the Financial Accounting Standards Board's Statements on Financial Accounting Standards and Interpretations, the AICPA's Accounting Research Bulletins, and APB Opinions. Volume 1 is a collection of GAAP that has general applicability to all businesses. Volume 2 contains standards that apply to specific industries and nonprofit organizations. The book is updated annually to reflect new standards promulgated during the year.

Finance and Accounting for Nonfinancial Managers: All the Basics You Need to Know, 6th ed

William G. Droms

Cambridge, Massachusetts: Perseus Books Group, 2010
304pp, ISBN: 978-0-7382-0818-3

This helpful book demystifies the complex world of finance and accounting and makes it accessible to managers of all levels.

The Financial Times Guide to Using and Interpreting Company Accounts, 3rd ed

Wendy McKenzie

Harlow, UK: FT Prentice Hall, 2003
416pp, ISBN: 978-0-273-66312-6

This book is essential for any nonfinancial manager who needs to understand more about a company's accounts and wants to make more informed financial decisions. It explains what information can be found in the accounts, how to analyze accounts, and how to use the analysis.

The Green Bottom Line: Environmental Accounting for Management Current Practice and Future Trends

Martin Bennett, Peter James (editors)

Sheffield, UK: Greenleaf Publishing, 1998
432pp, ISBN: 978-1-874719-24-3

The editors have brought together a collection of papers on research and best practice in the area of environmental management accounting, with a strong focus on the analysis of financial costs and the benefits of environmentally friendly behavior in business. The papers are grouped in four sections: general concepts; empirical research; case studies of individual companies; and practical suggestions on how environment-related management accounting can be implemented.

How to Read a Financial Report, 7th ed

John A. Tracey

Chichester, UK: Wiley, 2009
216pp, ISBN: 978-0-470-40530-7

Tracey provides guidance on interpreting company accounts (with relation to US practice), paying particular attention to the three essential parts of every financial report—the balance sheet, the income statement, and the cash-flow statement. His explanations are illustrated with many examples.

Intermediate Accounting, 13th ed

Donald E. Keiso, Jerry J. Weygandt, Terry D. Warfield

Chichester, UK: Wiley, 2010
1440pp, ISBN: 978-0-470-41891-8

The book covers the conceptual framework underlying financial accounting, financial reporting standards and statements, and more complex topics and transactions that are encountered in today's business environment. Specific guidance is provided for numerous topics, including accounting for cash and receivables, inventory, intangible assets, current and long-term liabilities, income taxes, leases, shareholders' equity, and revenue recognition.

International Financial Reporting Standards (IFRSs) 2010

International Accounting Standards Board (IASB)

London: IASB, 2010
2944pp, ISBN: 978-1-907026-59-1

The official printed edition of the IASB's authoritative pronouncements. It is comprised of the latest version of International Financial Reporting Standards (IFRSs), International Accounting Standards (IASs), IFRIC, and SIC interpretations, and supporting documents. These standards are endorsed by many countries in the European Union. Many leading companies, both inside and outside the European Union, prepare their financial statements accordingly.

Managerial Accounting, 3rd ed

James Jiambalvo

Chichester, UK: Wiley, 2007
624pp, ISBN: 978-0-470-03815-4

The author presents the fundamental concepts of managerial accounting including job-order and process costing, cost-volume-profit analysis, cost allocation and activity-based costing, capital budgeting decisions, and standard cost and variance analysis. Unlike many cost and managerial accounting texts that focus on accounting skills, the book approaches the subject matter from a manager's perspective.

The Meaning of Company Accounts, 8th ed

Walter Reid, D. R. Myddleton

Aldershot, UK: Gower Publishing, 2005
310pp, ISBN: 978-0-566-08660-1

The authors aim to help people to gain a firm grasp of what company accounts mean and to understand how they relate to business activities. Managers without formal accounting or financial training should find the book useful. It will also provide a basic introduction to company accounts for those taking formal accounting or business studies courses.

Teach Yourself Book Keeping

Andrew G. Piper, Andrew Lymer

Teach Yourself Series
London: Hodder Arnold, 2003
356pp, ISBN: 978-0-340-85942-1

This book aims to demystify the areas of bookkeeping that are essential for small business owners and managers. Offering plenty of examples to help explain key terms and concepts, it covers the double-entry system and the processes of recording purchases and different types of transactions. Profit and loss accounts and balance sheets are also explained, and the book includes helpful completed exam pages with worked examples.

Tolley's Tax Guide 2008–09

Arnold Homer, Rita Burrows

London: LexisNexis, 2008
ISBN: 978-0-7545-3285-9

Useful for both tax professionals and those who assess themselves, this book presents all the latest tax legislation accessibly. It covers the entire range of UK taxes and also features roughly 150 worked examples as well as useful checklists and planning tools. Tables of tax rates and allowances and summaries of recent changes are also included.

MAGAZINES

Accountancy

Institute of Chartered Accountants in England and Wales
Chartered Accountants' Hall, PO Box 433, Moorgate Place, London, EC2P 2BJ, UK
T: +44 (0) 20 7920 8100
F: +44 (0) 20 7920 0547
www.accountancymagazine.com
ISSN: 0001-4664

Published by Croner, but the official publication of the ICAEW, the magazine contains a wide range of news and articles relating to the practice of accountancy and fields such as auditing, taxation, finance, business, and management, as well as news about the ICAEW itself as a professional body.

Accountancy Age

Incisive Media
Haymarket House, 28–29 Haymarket, London, SW1Y 4RX, UK
T: +44 (0) 20 7316 9000
F: +44 (0) 20 7316 9250
www.accountancyage.com
ISSN: 0001-4672

Accountancy Age contains news on all aspects of accountancy practice, including financial reporting, taxation, law, business recovery, software programs, and auditing.

Accounting and Business

Association of Chartered Certified Accountants
2 Central Park Quay, 89 Hydepark Street, Glasgow, G3 8BW, UK
T: +44 (0) 141 582 2000
F: +44 (0) 141 582 2222
www.accaglobal.com/members/publications/accounting_business/
ISSN: 1460-406X

This magazine publishes articles on all aspects of, and developments in, professional accounting, and is aimed at executive agencies and professional partnerships, as well as at accounting and financial professionals.

Accounting Horizons

American Accounting Association
5717 Bessie Drive, Sarasota, FL 34233–2399, USA
T: +1 941 921 7747
F: +1 941 923 4093
aaahq.org/pubs/horizons.htm
ISSN: 0888-7993

Published quarterly, this reviewed magazine thoroughly covers all aspects of banking and finance, business, and accounting. The theory and application of business finance is paramount in this journal.

The Accounting Review

American Accounting Association
5717 Bessie Drive, Sarasota, FL 34233–2399, USA
T: +1 941 921 7747
F: +1 941 923 4093
aaahq.org/pubs/acctrev.htm
ISSN: 0001-4826

The *Review* contains news and articles on all aspects of teaching and research in the field of accounting.

Accounting Today

Accountants Media Group/Thomson
PO Box 966, Fort Worth, TX 76101, USA
T: +1 800 260 2793
F: +1 817 252 4400
www.webcpa.com/current_issue.cfm?pub=ato
ISSN: 1044-5714

Published bimonthly, this magazine is an essential resource for accounting professionals. Covering the latest trends in finance, it is a useful source of current information.

Financial Management

Chartered Institute of Management Accountants
26 Chapter Street, London, SW1P 4NP, UK
T: +44 (0) 20 8849 2251
www.cimaglobal.com/cps/rde/xchg/live/root.xsl/1673.htm
ISSN: 1471-9185

The magazine of the Chartered Institute of Management Accountants, *Financial Management* features news from the field of management accounting and articles on subjects including business performance and appraisal.

Journal of Accountancy

AICPA
1211 Avenue of the Americas, New York, NY 10036, USA
T: +1 212 596 6200
F: +1 212 596 6213
www.aicpa.org/pubs/jofa
ISSN: 1945-0729

Published monthly, this journal provides articles, interviews, and legislative updates on all aspects of accounting. The magazine is the publication of the American Institute of Certified Public Accountants.

JOURNALS

Accounting, Organizations and Society

Elsevier
The Boulevard, Langford Lane, Kidlington, Oxford, OX5 1GB, UK
T: +1 877 839 7126
F: +1 407 363 1354
www.elsevier.com/locate/inca/486
ISSN: 0361-3682

Accounting, Organizations & Society is a major international journal concerned with all aspects of the relationship between accounting and human behavior, organizational structures and processes, and the changing social and political environment of the enterprise.

Advances in Accounting, Incorporating Advances in International Accounting

Elsevier
The Boulevard, Langford Lane, Kidlington, Oxford, OX5 1GB, UK
T: +1 877 839 7126
F: +1 407 363 1354
www.elsevier.com/wps/product/cws_home/714520
ISSN: 0882-6110

This series focuses on the academic and theoretical side of the profession in the areas of financial accounting, accounting education and auditing. Articles range from empirical and analytical, to the development of new technologies.

International Journal of Accounting

Elsevier
The Boulevard, Langford Lane, Kidlington, Oxford, OX5 1GB, UK
T: +1 877 839 7126
F: +1 407 363 1354
www.elsevier.com/locate/inca/620179
ISSN: 0020-7063

The aims of the *International Journal of Accounting* are to advance the academic and professional understanding of accounting theory and practice from an international perspective and viewpoint.

International Journal of Accounting Information Systems

Elsevier
The Boulevard, Langford Lane, Kidlington, Oxford, OX5 1GB, UK
T: +1 877 839 7126
F: +1 407 363 1354
www.elsevier.com/locate/issn/1467–0895
ISSN: 1467-0895

  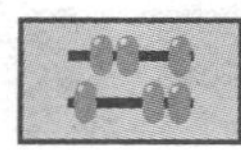      

Publishes articles that examine the rapidly evolving relationship between accounting and information technology.

Journal of Accounting Education

Elsevier
The Boulevard, Langford Lane, Kidlington, Oxford, OX5 1GB, UK
T: +1 877 839 7126
F: +1 407 363 1354
www.elsevier.com/locate/jaccedu
ISSN: 0748-5751

This is a refereed journal dedicated to promoting and publishing research on accounting education issues and to improving the quality of accounting education worldwide.

Journal of Business Finance & Accounting

Blackwell Publishing
9600 Garsington Road, Oxford, OX4 2DQ, UK
T: +44 (0) 1865 791 100
F: +44 (0) 1865 791 347
www.wiley.com/bw/journal.asp?ref=0306-686X
ISSN: 0306-686X

This journal publishes research papers in accounting and finance, relating to financial reporting, asset pricing, financial markets and institutions, market microstructure, corporate finance, corporate governance, and the economics of internal organization and management control.

Journal of International Financial Management & Accounting

Blackwell Publishing
9600 Garsington Road, Oxford, OX4 2DQ, UK
T: +44 (0) 1865 791 100
F: +44 (0) 1865 791 347
www.wiley.com/bw/journal.asp?ref=0954-1314
ISSN: 0954-1314

The *Journal of International Financial Management & Accounting* publishes original research dealing with international aspects of financial management and reporting, banking and financial services, auditing and taxation.

INTERNET

Accountants World

www.accountantsworld.com

This is an extensive portal based in the United States with links to a wide range of websites of interest to accountants. It relates mainly to US accounting practice.

Accounting Web

www.accountingweb.co.uk

This site is an extensive online resource based in the United Kingdom. It contains material intended for accountancy and finance professionals from a number of providers. It has received an award as the New Media Business Website of the Year.

Financial Accounting Standards Board

www.fasb.org

This is the website for the Financial Accounting Standards Board, the independent private-sector entity that establishes generally accepted accounting principles (GAAP). The Board issues formal accounting guidance on the treatment and reporting of financial transactions and performance.

Internal Revenue Service

www.irs.gov

One of the best-known American institutions, the Internal Revenue Service (IRS) is the main body in charge of US taxes. It oversees tax laws and their enforcement, and tax collection. It also has numerous resources available online, from helpful agencies to forms for download.

Tax and Accounting Sites Directory

www.taxsites.com

Created by Dennis Schmidt, Professor of Accounting at the University of Northern Iowa, this site has numerous links to additional accounting and tax information across a broad spectrum. Easy to navigate and simple to make sense of, the directory helps businesses and individuals to find what they need quickly.

ORGANIZATIONS

Europe

Association of Accounting Technicians (AAT)

140 Aldersgate Street, London, EC1A 4HY, UK
T: +44 (0) 20 7397 3000
F: +44 (0) 20 7837 6970
E: aat@aat.org.uk
www.aat.co.uk

The AAT awards certificates in accounting at NVQ levels 2, 3, and 4. An accounting technician is qualified to a slightly lower level than a fully qualified accountant.

Association of Chartered Certified Accountants (ACCA)

2 Central Park Quay, 89 Hydepark Street, Glasgow, G3 8BW, UK
T: +44 (0) 141 582 2000
F: +44 (0) 141 582 2222
E: info@accaglobal.com
www.acca.co.uk

The Association is a professional and examining body in accountancy, recognized under the Companies Act 1989.

Chartered Institute of Management Accountants (CIMA)

26 Chapter Street, London, SW1P 4NP, UK
T: +44 (0) 20 8849 2251
www.cimaglobal.com

CIMA is the leading UK professional organization for management accountants, but it also has a global reach: it represents more than 85,000 students and 65,000 members in more than 150 countries.

Chartered Institute of Public Finance and Accountancy (CIPFA)

3 Robert Street, London, WC2N 6RL, UK
T: +44 (0) 20 7543 5600
F: +44 (0) 20 7543 5700
E: corporate@cipfa.org
www.cipfa.org

CIPFA is a UK professional accountancy body whose main aim is to train managers to understand public finance and manage public money. Its members are drawn from both the public and private sectors. In addition to providing membership services, running courses, and awarding certification, it organizes conferences and produces publications.

Institute of Chartered Accountants in England and Wales (ICAEW)

Chartered Accountants' Hall, PO Box 433, London, EC2P 2BJ, UK
T: +44 (0) 20 7920 8100
F: +44 (0) 20 7920 0547
E: dsbds@icaew.co.uk
www.icaew.co.uk

This, the largest professional accountancy organization in Europe with over 120,000 members, is responsible for educating and training Chartered Accountants and maintaining standards of professional conduct among its members.

Institute of Chartered Accountants of Scotland (ICAS)

CA House, 21 Haymarket Yards, Edinburgh, EH12 5BH, UK
T: +44 (0) 131 347 0100
F: +44 (0) 131 347 0105
E: enquiries@icas.org.uk
www.icas.org.uk

The ICAS is the leading professional accounting body in Scotland, and the oldest professional body of accountants in the world.

USA

American Accounting Association (AAA)

5717 Bessie Drive, Sarasota, FL 34233–2399, USA
T: +1 941 921 7747
F: +1 941 923 4093
E: office@aaahq.org
aaahq.org

The American Accounting Association promotes worldwide excellence in accounting education, research and practice. Founded in 1916 as the American Association of University Instructors in Accounting, its present name was adopted in 1936. The Association is a voluntary organization of persons interested in accounting education and research.

American Institute of Certified Public Accountants (AICPA)

1211 Avenue of the Americas, New York, NY 10036–8775, USA
T: +1 212 596 6200
F: +1 212 596 6213
www.aicpa.org

This organization provides information, continuing education, accreditation, advocacy, and leadership to certified public accountants in the United States. The AICPA's Audit and Attest Standards team directs and develops standards for audit, attestation, and review services performed by CPAs.

Financial Accounting Standards Board (FASB)

401 Merritt 7, PO Box 5116, Norwalk, CT 06856–5116, USA
T: +1 203 847 0700

F: +1 203 849 9714
E: fasbpubs@fasb.org
www.fasb.org

Since 1973, the Financial Accounting Standards Board (FASB) has been the designated organization in the private sector for establishing standards of financial accounting and reporting in the US.

National Society of Accountants

1010 North Fairfax Street, Alexandria, VA 22314, USA
T: +1 703 549 6400
F: +1 703 549 2984
E: members@nsacct.org
www.nsacct.org

The National Society of Accountants is a nonprofit organization of some 30,000 professionals which provides accounting, tax preparation, financial and estate planning, and management advisory services to an estimated 19 million individuals and business clients. Most of the society's members are independent practitioners or partners in small- to mid-size accounting and tax firms.

BRIC

Chinese Institute of Certified Public Accountants (CICPA)

6th Floor, Guangyuan Building, 5 Guangyuanzha, Haidian District, Beijing 100081, China
T: +11 8610 6872 1166
F: +11 8610 6848 3041
www.cicpa.org.cn/english

The CICPA provides services to its members, monitors the service quality and professional ethics of members, regulates the CPA profession according to relevant laws, and coordinates the relationship within and beyond the CPA profession in China.

Institute of Chartered Accountants of India (ICAI)

Bhawan, Indraprastha Marg, Post Box No. 7100, New Delhi – 110 002, India
T: +91 11 3989 3989
E: icaiho@icai.org
www.icai.org

ICAI is a statutory body for the regulation of the profession of Chartered Accountants in India. During nearly six decades of existence, ICAI has achieved recognition as a premier accounting body not only in the country but also globally, for its contribution in the fields of education, professional development, maintenance of high accounting, auditing, and ethical standards. ICAI now is the second largest accounting body in the world.

Institute of Cost and Works Accountants of India (ICWAI)

12 Sudder Street, Kolkata, 700 016, India
T: +91 33 2252 1031
F: +91 33 2252 7993
E: ceo@icwai.org
www.myicwai.com

A professional institution actively associated with the industrial and economic development of India. Cost and Works Accountants are called Management Accountants outside of India.

The Institute of Professional Accountants of Russia (IPAR)

Tverskaya Street, 22B/3, Moscow, 125009, Russia
T: +7 499 788 72 00
F: +7 495 699 46 45
E: info@ipbr.ru
www.ipbr.ru/?page=english

IPAR is professional, non-profit, self-regulatory organization of certified accountants that assists in developing standards of professional ethics as well as accounting and auditing standards. It develop the accounting profession as a key element of the governance system, arranges and conducts the training, retraining, and certification of accountants and financial managers, and aims to improve the image of accounting profession.

Acquisitions, Takeovers, and Mergers

BOOKS

Acquisition: Strategy and Implementation, 2nd ed

Nancy Hubbard

Basingstoke, UK: Palgrave, 2001
320pp, ISBN: 978-0-333-94548-3

The process of acquisition is explored through an in-depth look at its key stages: preacquisition planning, communication during the deal, and implementation. The book also gives an overview of the history of acquisitions, global trends, and the reasons for success and failure. Case studies demonstrate different approaches and degrees of success. The new edition includes a chapter on new technology and e-commerce acquisitions.

After the Merger: The Authoritative Guide to Integration Success, 2nd ed

Price Pritchett, Donald Robinson, Russell Clarkson

New York: McGraw-Hill, 1997
158pp, ISBN: 978-0-7863-1239-9

This book features the six main errors that managers regularly make regarding mergers, and shows how to avoid them. It also presents best practices for handling the four major categories of a merger, ways to handle cultural problems that can destroy mergers, and offers separate checklists for executives on both sides of the deal.

The Art of M&A Integration: A Guide to Merging Resources, Processes and Responsibilities, 2nd ed

Alexandra Reed Lajoux

New York: McGraw-Hill, 2005
450pp, ISBN: 978-0-07-144810-9

The Art of M&A Integration provides readers with updated facts on integration of compensation plans, new FASB and GAAP accounting rules, strategies for merging IT systems and processes, and more. This book is a comprehensive guide of post–merger integration, covering the following areas: planning and communications; integration of resources; processes and management systems; technology and innovation; and commitments to customer suppliers, shareholders and employees.

Barbarians at the Gate: The Fall of RJR Nabisco, Revised ed

Bryan Burrough, John Helyar

HarperBusiness
New York: HarperBusiness, 2009
624pp, ISBN: 978-0-06-165555-5

Now hailed as a classic, this is an expose of the largest-ever leveraged buyout, of RJR Nabisco by private equity group Kohlberg Kravis Roberts. Also made into a film, its portrayal of oversized egos and greed seemed to sum up an era, and contributed greatly to the negative image of private equity in the 1980s.

Capitalize on Merger Chaos: Six Ways to Profit from Your Competitors' Consolidation and Your Own

Thomas M. Grubb, Robert B. Lamb

New York: Free Press, 2001
224pp, ISBN: 978-0-684-86777-9

The authors suggest that, although merger mania is at an all-time high, up to 80% of mergers fail because of culture clashes, mismanagement, and the chaos that ensues. They examine the growth and profit opportunities that can arise from competitors' merger chaos, and identify strategies which managers can adopt to exploit them. They further illustrate their argument by considering the winning strategies devised by companies such as AOL, General Electric, Dell, and Vodafone, and the failures at Coca-Cola, Boeing, and Compaq.

Complete Guide to Mergers & Acquisitions: Process Tools to Support M&A Integration at Every Level, 2nd ed

Timothy J. Galpin, Mark Herndon

Jossey-Bass Business and Management Series
San Francisco, California: Jossey-Bass, 2007
336pp, ISBN: 978-0-7879-9460-0

The authors present an updated and expanded guide to the process of planning and managing the M&A process. The revised edition not only updates case studies and presents recent integration research, but it also adds new tools. The authors draw from their experience with numerous Fortune 500 companies; this resource will help organizations attain deal synergies more quickly and effectively. The book addresses dos and don'ts, people dynamics, common mistakes, communications strategies, and specific actions taken to create positive results throughout the integration process.

Due Diligence: Definitive Steps to Successful Business Combinations

Denzil Rankine, Graham Stedman, Mark Bomer

Harlow, UK: FT Prentice Hall, 2003
256pp, ISBN: 978-0-273-66101-6

Due diligence is a key part of the (often fraught) acquisitions process in business. Done properly, it means that potential risks are reduced and chances of success increased. This book is a useful guide to the process and offers advice, cases studies, and analysis.

Harvard Business Review on Mergers & Acquisitions
Harvard Business School Press
Boston, Massachusetts: Harvard Business School Press, 2001
224pp, ISBN: 978-1-57851-555-4

This examines current various mergers, buyouts, and joint ventures, and provides guidance on what companies should take part. From valuation to integration, it helps managers understand the importance of each strategic move for their organization.

HR Know-How in Mergers and Acquisitions
Sue Cartwright, Cary L. Cooper
Developing Practice Series
London: Chartered Institute of Personnel and Development, 2000
128pp, ISBN: 978-0-85292-634-5

The authors offer guidance on the human factors involved in mergers and acquisitions. The topics they cover include: influencing the decision to merge; establishing effective communication; handling job insecurity; pay and benefits; downsizing, early retirement, and relocation; support systems and counseling; creating a new corporate culture; and establishing new roles and training. Case studies are included.

Intelligent M&A: Navigating the Mergers and Acquisitions Minefield
Scott Moeller, Chris Brady
Chichester, UK: Wiley, 2007
328pp, ISBN: 978-0-470-05812-1

Mergers and acquisitions are essential for growing companies but most fail to reach their target. This examines the full cycle of a merger or an acquisition, identifying areas where business intelligence can result in the attainment of a specific target. It discusses techniques developed by governmental intelligence services, and includes a wide range of case studies, quotations, and anecdotes.

International Business Acquisitions: Major Legal Issues and Due Diligence, 3rd ed
Michael Whalley, Franz-Jorg Semler (editors)
Alphen aan den Rijn, The Netherlands: Kluwer Law International, 2007
568pp, ISBN: 978-90-411-2483-8

This examines aspects of international acquisitions, including accessing foreign markets, providing foreign production or marketing capacity, obtaining regulatory approvals, acquiring complementary product or service lines, and spreading product, service, and market risk. It also provides useful information on the key legal issues and the process of gaining informed due diligence in each jurisdiction.

International Mergers and Acquisitions
Tony Edwards, Ali Budjanovcanin, Stuart Woollard
London: Chartered Institute of Personnel and Development, 2008
60pp, ISBN: 978-1-84398-213-5

To understand the how organizations learn from their international merger experience and how the knowledge is transferred, the involvement of HR in merger and acquisition activity is crucial. This book examines the challenges for the HR function, knowledge transfer in international mergers and acquisitions, and international policy-making and networking.

Mergers and Acquisitions: Business Strategies for Accountants, 3rd ed
William J. Gole, Joseph Morris
Hoboken, New Jersey: Wiley, 2007
416pp, ISBN: 978-0-470-04242-7

This provides a step-by-step guide to reviewing an acquisition candidate, setting up and implementing computer system transactions for the business combination, tax compilation, and regulatory considerations. It also features practical procedurals and useful examples of application.

Mergers and Acquisitions in a Nutshell, 2nd ed
Dale A. Oesterle
St Paul, Minnesota: Thomson West, 2006
313pp, ISBN: 978-0-314-15956-4

This accessible reference provides a brief description of the law on mergers and acquisitions for students and lawyers needing a reliable guide.

The Morning After: Making Corporate Mergers Work After the Deal Is Sealed
Stephen J. Wall, Shannon Rye Wall
Cambridge, Massachusetts: Perseus Books Group, 2000
288pp, ISBN: 978-0-7382-0523-6

This book deals with merger management. It offers insights for recognizing when a merger is in danger, and advice on issues such as communicating effectively with stakeholders. It includes several case studies.

Reducing the M&A Risks: The Role of IT in Mergers and Acquisitions
Frank Vielba, Carol Vielba
Basingstoke, UK: Palgrave Macmillan, 2006
216pp, ISBN: 978-1-4039-4678-2

The lack of adequate and timely IT involvement in the merger and acquisition process costs companies millions of dollars every year. Current research shows that IT accounts for a growing percentage of the post-acquisition benefits in a merger or acquisition. This provides analysis of some of the key approaches by IT managers to reducing risk within the M&A process.

MAGAZINES

Acquisitions Monthly
Thomson Financial
Aldgate House, 33 Aldgate High Street, London, EC3N 1DL, UK
T: +44 (0) 20 7369 7000
F: +44 (0) 20 7369 7373
www.aqm-e.com
ISSN: 0592-3618

This monthly journal for financial executives, directors, bankers, and accountants provides information on international mergers, acquisitions, and management buyouts.

Mergers and Acquisitions: The Dealmaker's Journal
Source Media
1 State Street Plaza, 27th Floor, NY 10004, USA
T: + 1 212 803 8200
www.acg.org/global/library/mergersandacquisitionsjournal.aspx
ISSN: 0026-1101

This monthly journal offers complete listings of all M&A deals, including pricing, deal structure, and the sales and profit levels of merger partners. In-depth feature articles cover trends in the industry and provide practical advice.

JOURNALS

Journal of Financial Economics
Elsevier
11830 Westline Industrial Drive, St Louis, MO 63146, USA
T: +1 314 453 7076
F: +1 314 523 5153
www.elsevier.com/locate/jfec
ISSN: 0304-405X

This quarterly journal offers a section on M&A papers and case studies, which provides an outlet for events and practice. It is also a source of data that illustrates or challenges accepted theory and can lead to new insights.

INTERNET

Acquisitions Monthly
www.aqm-e.com

The site provides M&A news and data worldwide, and information on trends, industries, and sectors. Some services are subscription-based.

Antitrust Division, Department of Justice (US)
www.usdoj.gov/atr

This US government site provides information on antitrust enforcement, case filings, and links to competition authorities worldwide.

BizBuySell
www.bizbuysell.com

As well as databases of businesses for sale and e-mail notification of listings, this US-based site includes articles on how to go about buying or selling a business. Users may search for their target company by category or location.

@brint.com
www.brint.com

  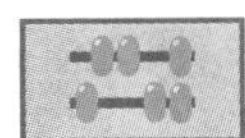      

This extensive portal and community network for e-business, information, technology, and knowledge management contains news, articles, book reviews, and links to relevant websites in the featured areas.

Competition Matters—BERR (UK)

www.berr.gov.uk/whatwedo/businesslaw/competition

This site provides information and guidance on UK and EU legislation and procedures from the UK Department for Business Enterprise and Regulatory Reform.

Daily Deal

www.thedeal.com

This website provides up-to-date analysis on the M&A activities of various companies around the world.

European Commission—Competition

ec.europa.eu/competition

This Brussels-based site provides information on European competition policy and legislation. All material is available in a variety of languages.

FactSet Mergerstat

www.mergerstat.com

This site covers all the key concepts of M&A, as well as providing links to its publications for further coverage.

MergerNetwork

www.mergernetwork.com

This site acts as a marketplace for buyers and sellers of companies, predominantly in North America but increasingly also in Europe, Asia, and South America. Users may search the databases of buyer profiles and businesses for sale free of charge, but must pay for contact information.

The Takeover Panel

www.thetakeoverpanel.org.uk

The Panel on Takeovers and Mergers is an independent body whose main functions are to issue and administer the City Code on Takeovers and Mergers, and to supervise and regulate takeovers and other matters to which the Code applies. Its central objective is to ensure fair treatment for all shareholders in takeover bids.

ORGANIZATIONS

Europe

Competition Commission (UK)

Victoria House, Southampton Row, London, WC1B 4AD, UK
T: +44 (0) 20 7271 0100
E: info@cc.gsi.gov.uk
www.competition-commission.org.uk

The Competition Commission (CC) is one of the independent public bodies that woks to ensure healthy competition between companies in the UK, for the benefit of companies, customers, and the economy. It concentrates on areas of concern in mergers, preventing competition in a particular market, and regulated sectors.

USA

Alliance of Merger and Acquisition Advisors (AMAA)

200 East Randolph Street, 24th Floor, Chicago, IL 60601, USA
T: +1 877 844 2535
F: +1 312 729 9800
www.amaaonline.org

This association was formed to bring together all professionals who work with mergers and acquisitions. AMAA provides national certification for members, as well as various opportunities for networking with other organization members.

Federal Trade Commission (US)

600 Pennsylvania Avenue NW, Washington, DC 20580, USA
T: +1 202 326 2222
E: antitrust@ftc.gov
www.ftc.gov

The US Fair Trade Commission practices efficient law enforcement, advances consumers' interests by sharing its expertise with federal and state legislatures and US and international government agencies. It develops policy and research tools through hearings, workshops, and conferences. It also works to ensure that consumers have choices in price, selection, and service.

BRIC

Competition Commission of India

B Wing, HUDCO Vishala, 14 Bhikaji Cama Place, New Delhi 110 066, India
T: +91 11 2670 1619
F: +91 11 2610 3861
E: cci-bunker@nic.in
www.cci.gov.in

Established under India's Competition Act 2002, the Competition Commission of India has regulatory and quasi-judicial powers. Its duties are eliminating practices having an adverse effect on competition, promoting and sustaining competition, and protecting the interests of consumers, within the jurisdictions of anticompetitive agreements, abuse of dominant positions, M&A, and training/public awareness.

Fair Trade Commission, Taiwan

12–14 F, No. 2–2 Jinan Rd., Sec. 1, Jhongjheng (Zhongzheng) District, Taipei City 100, Taiwan
T: +886 2 2351 7588
E: ftcpub@ftc.gov.twl
www.ftc.gov.tw/internet/english

The Fair Trade Commission is the main authority in charge of competition policy and fair trade law in Taiwan. Its duties include drafting fair trade policy, laws, regulations, and investigating and handling various activities impeding competition, such as monopolies, mergers, concerted actions, and other restraints on competition or unfair trade practices on the part of enterprises.

Federal Antimonopoly Service of the Russian Federation

Sadovaya Kudrinskaya, 11, Moscow, D-242, GSP-5, 123995, Russia
T: +7 495 252 70 48
E: international@fas.gov.ru
fas.gov.ru/english

The Federal Antimonopoly Service of the Russian Federation was formed in 2004, replacing the Ministry of the Russian Federation for Antimonopoly Policy and Support to Entrepreneurship in terms of its function as the federal antimonopoly body, control over the activity of natural monopolies, and observance of the legislation on advertising.

International

International Network of M&A Partners (IMAP)

6000 Cattleridge Drive, Suite 300, Sarasota, FL 34232, USA
T: +1 941 378 5500
F: +1 941 378 5505
E: info@imap.com
www.imap.com

Founded in 1971 and formerly called the International Association of Merger and Acquisition Consultants, the IMAP is a global networking organization with over 50 members. It is dedicated to helping middle-market companies obtain confidential business information on available merger and acquisition prospects. It also assists individuals in a variety of financial transactions, such as the sale of private or public companies, the purchase of product lines, leveraged buyouts, financing and investment banking services, and mezzanine financing.

M&A Source

401 North Michigan Avenue, Suite 2200, Chicago, IL 60611–4267, USA
T: +1 888 686 4222
F: +1 312 673 6599
E: admin@masource.org
www.masource.org

Founded in 1991, M&A Source proclaims itself to be the world's largest organization of middle-market intermediaries. With a focus on the enhancement of the skills and abilities of its members and their professional development, this organization provides them with the guidance needed to assist clients. M&A Source also keeps them up to date with the latest issues and trends in mergers and acquisitions.

  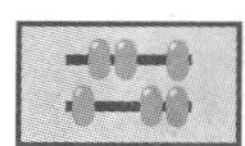      

Analytical Techniques and Statistics

BOOKS

Accelerated Testing: Statistical Models, Test Plans, and Data Analysis, 2nd ed
Wayne B. Nelson
Wiley Series in Probability and Statistics
Hoboken, New Jersey: Wiley, 2004
624pp, ISBN: 978-0-471-69736-7

This practical resource presents modern, statistical methods for accelerated testing including test models, analyses of data, and plans for testing. Each topic is self-contained for easy reference, and the coverage is broad and detailed enough to serve as a text or reference. It also features real test examples along with data analyses, computer programs, and references to the literature.

Basic Business Statistics: Concepts and Applications, 11th ed
Mark L. Berenson, David M. Levine
Upper Saddle River, New Jersey: Prentice Hall, 2009
936pp, ISBN: 978-0-13-500936-9

This book deals with the techniques of analyzing and presenting business data. It explains probability, normal distribution, estimation, hypothesis testing, analysis of variance, and linear and multiple regression models. It will be helpful for students to know how statistics is used in each functional area of business.

Doing Research in Business and Management: An Introduction to Process and Method
Dan Remenyi et al.
London: Sage Publications, 1998
336pp, ISBN: 978-0-7619-5950-2

After first highlighting the different contexts and purposes, strategies and tactics, and programs and processes of management research, the authors then move on to a more detailed review of the relevant research approaches and methods. They discuss the interrelationship of theoretical and empirical research and examine how these different approaches are used in practice. The implications of using quantitative and qualitative methods are reviewed, and the book also contains practical advice on available analysis techniques and software packages.

Effective Use of Statistics: A Practical Guide for Managers, 2nd ed
Tim Hannagan
Business Skills Series
London: Kogan Page, 1999
160pp, ISBN: 978-0-7494-2969-0

Hannagan provides a statistical foundation for managers, focusing on integrating statistical information into everyday work and presenting it effectively. An appendix offers basic math for managers, and the book comes with an accompanying computer disk with a data file in Microsoft Word for Windows.

Essential Quantitative Methods for Business Management and Finance, 4th ed
Les Oakshott
Basingstoke, UK: Palgrave, 2009
528pp, ISBN: 978-0-230-21818-5

This is a student guide to the major topics likely to be taught on a quantitative methods course. Excel and SPSS software is included, along with extra support for lecturers.

Implementing Global Performance Measurement Systems: A Cookbook Approach to Evaluation
Ferdinand Tesoro, Jack Tootson
San Francisco, California: Jossey-Bass, 2000
176pp, ISBN: 978-0-7879-4744-6

This practical guide presents a step-by-step approach to evaluating and measuring ongoing business performance. Following an overview of performance measurement, it examines how to establish the business case, identify the right performance metrics, implement the performance measurement system, and leverage results to improve performance. Guidance is offered on constructing a line graph, a cause–effect diagram, and a scatter diagram.

Practical Business Statistics, 5th ed
Andrew Siegel
Maidenhead, UK: McGraw-Hill, 2002
730pp, ISBN: 978-0-07-282125-3

Though this is a college textbook, it is not simply filled with formulas and equations. It offers a less theoretical approach to statistics, focusing on examples using real data, on applications, and on the underlying reasons for using statistical analysis in business.
It is especially useful because the text acknowledges that much of what is done in business statistics and analysis is now done by computer programs, rather than by unhappy, squinting workers in visors with scientific calculators.

Quantitative Approaches in Business Studies, 7th ed
Claire Morris
Harlow, UK: FT Prentice Hall, 2008
528pp, ISBN: 978-0-273-70889-6

This textbook uses a driven approach for student of business courses and management on undergraduate, Masters and professional courses. It aims to demonstrate effectiveness of quantitative methods. The four parts cover: handling numbers; numbers as a basis for deduction; and numbers as a tool of planning.

Quantitative Methods for Business, 4th ed
Donald Waters
Harlow, UK: FT Prentice Hall, 2007
648pp, ISBN: 978-0-273-69458-8

Quantitative Methods for Business has been thoroughly revised and updated for this 4th edition, and continues to provide a simple and practical introduction to an area that students can find difficult. The book takes a nonthreatening approach to the subject, avoiding excessive mathematics and abstract theory. It shows how to apply quantitative ideas to the real problems faced by managers.

Statistical Methods for Survival Data Analysis, 3rd ed
Elisa T. Lee, John Wenyu Wang
Wiley Series in Probability and Statistics
New York: Wiley, 2003
534pp, ISBN: 978-0-471-36997-4

This examines the statistical methods for analyzing survival data from laboratory studies of animals, clinical and epidemiological studies of humans, and other appropriate applications.
It provides a thorough discussion of the most common parametric and nonparametric methods in survival analysis, as well as guidelines for the planning and design of clinical trials. The methods are suitable for applications in industrial reliability, the social sciences, and business.

Statistics, Data Analysis, and Decision Modeling, 4th ed
James R. Evans
Upper Saddle River, New Jersey: Prentice Hall, 2010
592pp, ISBN: 978-0-13-606600-2

This book covers the basic concepts of business statistics, data analysis, and management science in a contemporary spreadsheet environment. It particularly emphasizes the practical applications of its approaches to business decision-making. A software package on CD is included.

Trend Forecasting with Intermarket Analysis: Predicting Global Markets with Technical Analysis, 2nd ed
Louis B. Mendelsohn
Columbia, Maryland: Marketplace Books, 2008
224pp, ISBN: 978-1-59280-332-3

This examines the limitations of traditional technical trading/intermarket analysis, and methods for identifying reoccuring patterns within individual financial markets and between related global markets. It shows how combining technical, fundamental, and intermarket analysis into one framework can provide an advantage in forecasting trends. It also describes trading strategies and limitations of traditional technical analysis methods, and how they can be overcome.

JOURNALS

Brazilian Journal of Probability and Statistics
Brazilian Statistical Association
Rua do Matão, 1010 sala 250A Cep,

05508–090 São Paul, Brazil
T: +55 11 3091 6261
F: +55 11 3812 5067
www.imstat.org/bjps
ISSN: 0103-0752

The *Brazilian Journal of Probability and Statistics* is an official publication of the Brazilian Statistical Association and is supported by the Institute of Mathematical Statistics (IMS). It is published twice a year, in June and December, and publishes papers in applied probability, applied statistics, computational statistics, mathematical statistics, probability theory, and stochastic processes.

Journal of Statistical Research

Institute of Statistical Research and Training
University of Dhaka, Dhaka 1000, Bangladesh
www.isrt.ac.bd/jsr
ISSN: 0256-422X

The *Journal of Statistical Research* is an official publication of the Institute of Statistical Research and Training. It is a method of transfer and communication of statistical knowledge for the developing nations across the globe, and publishes original research articles both in theoretical and applied statistics areas. The Journal is published twice a year, one in June and the other in December.

Journal of the American Statistical Association (JASA)

American Statistical Association
732 North Washington Street, Alexandria,
VI 22314–1943, USA
T: +1 703 684 1221
F: +1 703 684 2037
pubs.amstat.org/loi/jasa
ISSN: 0162-1459

JASA was established in 1888 and is published in March, June, September, and December. Subjects covered include statistical applications and statistical education.

INTERNET

Milner Library, Illinois State University

www.mlb.ilstu.edu/learn/stat

This is an online tutorial called "Finding Statistics." Via a series of internet pages, it covers (a) finding statistics, (b) understanding them, and (c) evaluating their usefulness. A self-assessment tool, or quiz, is included in each section. On this site, the reader can find answers to a number of basic questions, such as what the general definitions and terminology are in statistical research, how to locate statistics easily, how to determine whether statistics are reliably relevant, and what statistical databases are available. This is an excellent primer on the subject.

ORGANIZATIONS

Europe

Royal Statistical Society (RSS)

12 Errol Street, London, EC1Y 8LX, UK
T: +44 (0) 20 7638 8998
F: +44 (0) 20 7614 3905
E: rss@rss.org.uk
www.rss.org.uk

Founded in 1834, the RSS has 6,500 members in the United Kingdom and internationally. It holds a number of meetings annually, including an annual international conference, and offers several professional qualifications to members. The society also publishes the *Journal of the Royal Statistical Society* (in four series), and a monthly news magazine, *RSS News*.

Staple Inn Hall

High Holborn, London, WC1V 7QJ, UK
T: +44 (0) 20 7632 2100
F: +44 (0) 20 7632 2111
E: institute@actuaries.org.uk
www.actuaries.org.uk

The Faculty's objective is to unite those practicing as actuaries in the UK, as well as those promoting actuarial education.

USA

American Statistical Association (ASA)

732 North Washington Street, Alexandria,
VI 22314–1943, USA
T: +1 703 684 1221
F: +1 703 684 2037
E: asainfo@amstat.org
www.amstat.org

Founded in 1839, this is an educational society for professional statisticians that boasts Florence Nightingale, Alexander Graham Bell, and Andrew Carnegie among its former members. It now has some 16,000 members in the United States, Canada, and throughout the world. The ASA publishes or copublishes a number of journals, including the Journal of the American Statistical Association. The Association's website has a searchable database of relevant events.

BRIC

Indian Statistical Association

Department of Statistics, University of Poona, Poona, 411 007, India
T: + 91 212 336062

The Indian Statistical Association was formed to promote research in statistics. The General Assembly of the Association meets each year towards the end of December or early in January to elect the Governing Council.

International Chinese Association

University of Connecticut,
215 Glenbrook Road, Storrs,
CT 06269–4120, USA
T: +1 860 486 6984
F: +1 860 486 4113
E: mhchen@stat.uconn.edu

The International Chinese Statistical Association (ICSA) is a non-profit organization dedicated to educational, charitable, and scientific purposes. Its membership is open to all individuals and organizations in all statistics-related areas.

Asset and Liability Management

BOOKS

Asset and Liability Management: The Banker's Guide to Value Creation and Risk Control, 2nd ed

Jean Dermine, Youssef F. Bissada
Financial Times Series
Harlow, UK: FT Prentice Hall, 2007
187pp, ISBN: 978-0-273-71001-1

The increasing emphasis on measuring bank performance against value creation means effective ALM, and the control of value and risk, are now even more relevant. This book provides an understanding of these measures, by presenting the essential concepts, showing how to evaluate performances on a risk-adjusted basis, and price loans to ensure they create value, and covers more recent topics such Basel II and credit derivatives.

Asset and Liability Management Tools: A Handbook for Best Practice

Bernd Scherer (editor)
London: Risk Books, 2003
333pp, ISBN: 978-1-904339-06-9

This is a multi-author volume that provides a non-technical and practical overview of current ALM issues and techniques. A strong team of writers examine how to develop an enhanced understanding and competency of ALM, as well as pension finance, foundations, actuarial mathematics, fair valuation of pension liabilities, scenario simulation, and portfolio optimization.

Asset Liability Management: Individual and Institutional Approaches

Hainaut Donatien
Saarbrücken, Germany: VDM Verlag, 2008
220pp, ISBN: 978-3-8364-9178-5

This approaches ALM in terms of maximizing expected lifetime utility, focusing on both individual and institutional investors as economic agents. It analyzes asset allocation problems, such as wealth maximization under a Value at Risk constraint, and also examines the individual asset allocation decision at retirement.

Asset/Liability Management for Financial Institutions: Maximising Shareholder Value through Risk-Conscious Investing

Leo M. Tilman (editor)
London: Euromoney Books, 2003
386pp, ISBN: 978-1-84374-124-4

This is a guide to the management, techniques, and practices of ALM across financial institutions, which shows how to develop a consistent

  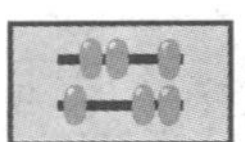   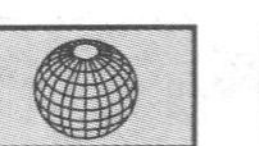   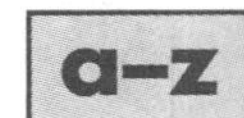

framework for risk management. A leading group of contributors examine the challenges facing the industry, and offer advice and analysis to financial and corporate executives, treasurers, portfolio managers, investment bankers, traders, actuaries, modelers, academics, and regulators.

Bank Asset and Liability Management: Strategy, Trading, Analysis

Moorad Choudhry
Wiley Finance Series
Singapore: Wiley, 2007
1,415pp, ISBN: 978-0-470-82135-0

This is a comprehensive examination of the techniques, products, and art of ALM. Aimed at anyone involved in banking and the debt capital markets, it covers bank capital, money market trading, risk management, hedging, regulatory capital, securitization and balance sheet management, yield curve analysis, structured finance products, and their role in ALM treasury operations and group transfer pricing.

Financial Risk Management in Banking: The Theory and Application of Asset and Liability Management

Dennis G. Uyemura, Donald R. van Deventer
Chicago, Illinois: McGraw-Hill, 1992
361pp, ISBN: 978-1-55738-353-2

This is a useful overview of ALM, and the risks and volatility inherent in bank financial management. It presents basic financial concepts and practices, and shows how ALM can strengthen the capital position of a financial institution. It covers the impact of accounting concepts on ALM, currency and international funds risk, and the relationship between cash flow, market value, and risk.

Goal Programming Techniques for Bank Asset Liability Management

Kyriaki Kosmidou, Constantin Zopounidis
Applied Optimization Series
Boston, Massachusetts: Kluwer, 2004
166pp, ISBN: 978-1-4020-8104-0

A comprehensive textbook that combines an analysis of the more general concepts of bank ALM with an examination of the contribution that goal programming techniques can make to more effective asset and liability management. Aimed at academics and practitioners in operations research, management scientists, financial managers, bank managers, economists, and risk analysts.

Handbook of Asset and Liability Management, Volume 1: Theory and Methodology

S. A. Zenios, W. T. Ziemba
Amsterdam: Elsevier, 2006
508pp, ISBN: 978-0-444-50875-1

The first volume focuses on the theories and methods that align operations and business strategy with its uncertain environment. It examines the relationship between optimization tools and financial decision-making, term and volatility structures, interest rates, risk-return analysis, dynamic asset allocation strategies in discrete and continuous time, the use of stochastic programming models, and bond portfolio management.

Handbook of Asset and Liability Management, Volume 2: Applications and Case Studies

S. A. Zenios, W. T. Ziemba
Amsterdam: Elsevier, 2007
684pp, ISBN: 978-0-444-52802-5

This second volume analyzes applications, models, and case studies in a practical way, showing how the operations research and mathematical finance tools described in the first volume can be exploited profitably by pension funds, insurance companies, banks, and major and individual investors. It also presents a framework for controlling interest rate and liquidity risks.

Handbook of Asset and Liability Management: From Models to Optimal Return Strategies

Alexandre Adam
Wiley Finance Series
Chichester, UK: Wiley, 2008
550pp, ISBN: 978-0-470-03496-5

This is a comprehensive and practical guide to asset and liability management tools, techniques, and issues, which also examines balance sheet items, product modeling, and optimal returns strategies. It presents a framework based on accounting obligations (for IFRS and IAS), organization, and regulation (for both Basel II and Solvency II), and discusses the more relevant sources of risk.

The Handbook of Asset/Liability Management: State-of-the-Art Investment Strategies, Risk Controls and Regulatory Requirements, 2nd ed

Frank J. Fabozzi, Atuso Konishi (editors)
Chicago, Illinois: Irwin Professional, 1996
506pp, ISBN: 978-1-55738-800-1

This is a revised and updated reference source for practitioners needing guidance on keeping a portfolio and market risk under control, and an understanding of the benefits of effective risk management. It also examines asset securitization, how to best measure interest rate and yield curve risk, hedge with derivatives, and implement controls for managing derivative positions.

Liabilities, Liquidity, and Cash Management: Balancing Financial Risks

Dimitris N. Chorafas
New York: Wiley, 2002
316pp, ISBN: 978-0-471-10630-2

Offers guidance on how to deal with liabilities and overexposure, and implement better internal controls on liability and overexposure. It provides tools, strategies, and advice tailored to the needs of companies facing overexposure and debt risk in a volatile economy, and discusses loss of capitalization, derivatives, globalization, sensitivity analysis, gap analysis, stress testing, and real-time financial reporting.

Liquidity Risk: Managing Asset and Funding Risks

Erik Banks
Finance and Capital Markets Series
Basingstoke, UK: Palgrave Macmillan, 2005
230pp, ISBN: 978-1-4039-3399-7

This examination of liquidity risk focuses on the nature of the risk, issues that can arise in asset and funding liquidity, and mechanisms that can be developed to monitor, measure, and control such risks. It examines how to manage assets and risk, in order to avoid the problems of losses in asset/liability portfolios and off balance sheet activities, and even financial distress and insolvency.

Liquidity Risk Measurement and Management: A Practitioner's Guide to Global Best Practices

Leonard Matz, Peter Neu (editors)
Wiley Finance Series
Singapore: Wiley, 2007
395pp, ISBN: 978-0-470-82182-4

With financial crises over the last few years increasing the need for banks to operate effective systems and processes for identifying, measuring, monitoring, and controlling liquidity risks, practical guidance is important. This book offers best practice in tools and techniques for bank liquidity risk measurement and management, from day-to-day funding management to worst-case contingency planning.

Managing Financial Institutions: An Asset/Liability Approach, 4th ed

Mona J. Gardner, Dixie L. Mills, Elizabeth S. Cooperman
Dryden Press Series in Finance
Fort Worth, Texas: Dryden Press, 1999
960pp, ISBN: 978-0-03-022054-8

This provides coverage of asset and liability management tools and techniques for financial institutions such as depository institutions, finance companies, insurance companies, pension funds, mutual funds, securities firms, and diversified financial services firms, which are operating in an increasingly competitive environment. It is also suitable for courses on financial institutions and commercial bank management.

Worldwide Asset and Liability Modeling

William T. Ziemba, John M. Mulvey (editors)
Publications of the Newton Institute Series
Cambridge, UK: Cambridge University Press, 1998
665pp, ISBN: 978-0-521-57187-6

This is an introductory overview to ALM modeling, which examines the strategic and the technical issues currently facing the industry. It takes a broad approach, combining theoretical papers with practical discussions of models, and shows how to invest assets over time to achieve satisfactory returns subject to uncertainties, various constraints, and liability commitments, and presents some new techniques.

MAGAZINES

Bank Asset/Liability Management

Sheshunoff Information Services
807 Las Cimas Parkway, Suite 300, Austin, Texas

        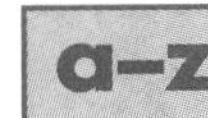  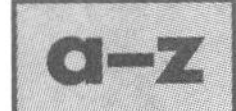

78746, USA
T: +1 512 472 2244
F: +1 512 305 6575
www.aspratt.com/store/805.php

This monthly newsletter provides practical guidance on how to reduce exposure to interest rate risks, from either the asset or liability side of the balance sheet. It covers the latest information on the full range of bank ALM topics, such as using gap analysis, duration analysis, income simulation analysis, economic value sensitivity analysis, back-testing, and management goals, policies, procedures, and systems.

JOURNALS

Journal of Asset Management

Palgrave Macmillan
Brunel Road, Houndmills, Basingstoke, Hampshire, RG21 6XS, UK
T: +44 (0) 1256 357893
F: +44 (0) 1256 328339
www.palgrave-journals.com/jam
ISSN: 1470-8272

This bimonthly journal publishes applied academic research, commercial best practice, and regulatory and legal interests, offering the latest thinking, techniques, and developments for the fund management industry. It covers new investment strategies, methodologies and techniques, new products and trading developments, and emerging trends in asset management. Core areas include asset allocation, hedge fund strategies, risk definition and management, index tracking, and performance measurement.

INTERNET

ALM Professional

www.almprofessional.com

This is a website dedicated to the ALM community, with a large global membership of industry professionals, which offers information and guidance on managing an institution's asset liability management process. Its features include articles, recommended reading, market watch, policies and procedures, calendar, news-letters, jobs listings, and a discussion board.

ORGANIZATIONS

Europe

European Fund and Asset Management Association

Chair: Mathias Bauer
18/2 Square de Meeûs, 1050 Brussels, Belgium
T: +32 2513 3969
F: +32 2513 2643
www.efama.org

EFAMA is the representative association for the European investment and asset management industry, representing its member associations and corporate members. It aims include supporting investor protection through the promotion of high ethical standards, integrity, and professionalism in the industry, promoting the completion of an effective single market for investment management, strengthening the competitiveness of the industry, and promoting relevant scientific research.

USA

The North American Asset/Liability Management Association

USA
www.nalma.net

NALMA is an industry association for senior practitioners in the field of asset and liability management and related areas of risk management. Its aim is to facilitate the exchange of ideas, to advance industry best practice, risk management problems, and to influence the development of regulatory measures.

Auditing and Management Audit

BOOKS

Auditing: A Business Risk Approach, 6th ed

Larry E. Rittenberg, Bradley J. Schwieger, Karla Johnstone
Cincinnati, Ohio: South-Western College Publishing, 2007
864pp, ISBN: 978-0-324-37558-9

This provides a thorough understanding of current auditing processes with the hands-on practice that's critical to business success. It introduces the audit process within the context of business risk–explaining why it is important to first understand the organization's business environment, and how to apply the risk model.

Auditing: An Integrated Approach, 8th ed

Alvin A. Arens
Upper Saddle River, New Jersey: Prentice Hall, 2000
798pp, ISBN: 978-0-13-082735-7

This book is intended as an introduction to auditing for students who have had no significant experience of the subject.

Auditing and Assurance Services, 12th ed

Alvin Arens, Randal Elder, Mark Beasley
Harlow, UK: Prentice Hall, 2008
888pp, ISBN: 978-0-13-245225-0

The integrated concepts approach shows students the auditing process from start to finish. It uses an illustrative example of key audit decisions for a public company audit throughout, with an emphasis on audit planning, including risk assessment processes and evaluating internal controls, and collecting and evaluating evidence in response to risks, to prepare students for real-world audit decision-making.

The Essential Handbook of Internal Auditing

K. H. Spencer Pickett
Chichester, UK: Wiley, 2005
298pp, ISBN: 978-0-470-01316-8

This shows the reader how to understand the audit context and how this context fits into the wider corporate agenda. The new context is set firmly within the corporate governance, risk management, and internal control arena.

The Internal Auditing Handbook, 3rd ed

K. H. Spencer Pickett
Hoboken, New Jersey: Wiley, 2010
1088pp, ISBN: 978-0-470-51871-7

The book is a comprehensive guide to audit standards, internal controls, planning and risk analysis, statistical sampling, client interviews and flowcharting. It provides many examples of the application of audit theory by means of case studies and assignments with suggested solutions. *The Internal Auditing Handbook* also deals with special engagements and topics including computer audits, fraud investigations, establishing an audit function, and training audit staff. It is organized in four major parts that cover theory, techniques, internal audit management, and specialist auditing.

Montgomery's Auditing, 12th ed

Vincent M. O'Reilly et al.
New York: Wiley, 1999
336pp, ISBN: 978-0-471-34605-0

The book outlines all the information needed to understand and apply generally accepted auditing standards. It assists auditors in developing an enterprise plan, testing specific accounting cycles and accounts, and producing the final audit report. The book is organized in five parts that cover the audit environment, theory and concepts, auditing specific accounts, completing the audit and reporting results, and auditing specialized industries.

Quantitative Analysis for Management, 10th ed

Barry Render, Ralph M. Stair, Michael E. Hanna
Upper Saddle River, New Jersey: Prentice Hall, 2008
768pp, ISBN: 978-0-13-603625-8

This textbook for students combines coverage of traditional management science techniques with modern technology solutions. It includes a CD-ROM.

Sawyer's Internal Auditing: The Practice of Modern Internal Auditing, 5th ed

Lawrence B. Sawyer, Mortimer A. Dittenhofer, James H. Scheiner, Anne Graham, Paul Makosz
Altamonte Springs, Florida: Institute of Internal Auditors, 2003
1446pp, ISBN: 978-0-89413-509-5

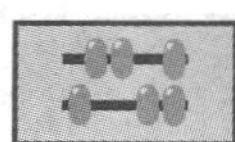

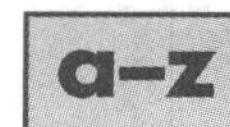

This provides a new global perspective reflecting the recent transformation in the way organizations do business. It analyzes how new ideas about internal auditing are reshaping the profession, what the new competency framework means, the importance of alignment with management, the implications of outsourcing the internal audit function, and value-added approaches that are redefining the role of the internal auditor.

The Smartest Guys in the Room: The Amazing Rise and Scandalous Fall of Enron

Bethany McLean, Peter Elkind

New York: Portfolio, 2004

464pp, ISBN: 978-1-59184-053-4

Written by two *Fortune* journalists, this book attempts to lay bare the extraordinary story behind Enron's collapse in 2001. A tale of jaw-dropping corporate arrogance, it shows the impact of incompetence and greed on the notion of corporate governance.

MAGAZINES

ABI Journal

American Bankruptcy Institute
44 Canal Center Plaza, Suite 400, Alexandria, VA 22314, USA
T: +1 703 739 0800
F: +1 703 739 1060
www.abiworld.org/journal

The *ABI Journal* is published ten times a year. It is written by experts from the insolvency community and addresses issues such as consumer bankruptcy, the intersection of state laws and the Bankruptcy Code, valuation, turnaround management concerns, and recent legislative developments.

Internal Auditing

International Council for Small Business
GWU School of Business, 2201 G Street NW, Funger Hall, Suite 315, Washington, DC 20052, USA
T: +1 314 977 3628
F: +1 314 977 3627
www.iia.org.uk/en/Publications/IA_and_BR_Magazine

This magazine, the journal of the IIA-UK, covers all aspects of internal auditing and of risk assessment and risk management.

Internal Auditor

Institute of Internal Auditors
247 Maitland Avenue, Altamonte Springs, FL 32701-4201, USA
T: +1 407 937 1100
F: +1 407 937 1101
www.theiia.org/intauditor
ISSN: 0020-5745

This magazine, the journal of the IIA in the United States, covers auditing techniques and applications, internal control systems, and corporate governance, besides containing practical case studies.

JOURNALS

Accounting, Auditing and Accountability Journal

Emerald
60/62 Toller Lane, Bradford, West Yorkshire, BD8 9BY, UK
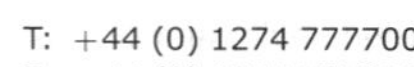
T: +44 (0) 1274 777700
F: +44 (0) 1274 785200
www.emeraldinsight.com/0951-3574.htm
ISSN: 0951-3574

The *Accounting, Auditing & Accountability Journal* is dedicated to the advancement of accounting knowledge and provides a forum for the publication of high-quality papers concerning the interaction between accounting/auditing and their socio-economic and political environments.

Auditing: A Journal of Practice & Theory

American Accounting Association
5717 Bessie Drive, Sarasota, FL 34233-2399, USA
T: +1 941 921 7747
F: +1 941 923 4093
aaahq.org/audit/ajpt.htm
ISSN: 0278-0380

This is a scholarly journal that publishes original papers on research that contributes to improvements in auditing theory or auditing methodology. It provides news and analysis of accounting and is very influential in the auditing world.

International Journal of Accounting, Auditing and Performance Evaluation

Inderscience Enterprises
World Trade Center Building, 29 route de Pre-Bois, Case Postale 896, CH-1215, Geneva, 15, Switzerland
T: +44 (0) 1234 240515
F: +41 22 791 08 85
www.inderscience.com/ijaape
ISSN: 1740-8008

IJAAPE encourages contributions especially from emerging markets and economies in transition and studies whose results are applicable across nation states or capable of being adapted to the different accounting and business environments.

International Journal of Auditing

Blackwell Publishing
9600 Garsington Road, Oxford, OX4 2DQ, UK
T: +44 (0) 1865 791 100
F: +44 (0) 1865 791 347
www.wiley.com/bw/journal.asp?ref=1090-6738
ISSN: 1090-6738

IJA is a high-quality, specialist journal that publishes articles from the broad spectrum of auditing. Its primary aim is to communicate clearly, to an international readership, the results of original auditing research conducted in research institutions and/or in practice.

Managerial Auditing Journal

Emerald
60/62 Toller Lane, Bradford, West Yorkshire, BD8 9BY, UK
T: +44 (0) 1274 777 700
F: +44 (0) 1274 785 200
www.emeraldinsight.com/0268-6902.htm
ISSN: 0268-6902

The *Managerial Auditing Journal* addresses the changing function of the auditor and examines both the professional and the managerial aspects of the role. Its articles are mainly concerned with the latest developments in auditing theory and practice, research, and case studies.

INTERNET

The American Institute of Certified Public Accountants (AICPA)

www.aicpa.org

This is the website of a large membership organization that provides information, continuing education, accreditation, advocacy, and leadership to certified public accountants in the United States. The AICPA's Audit and Attest Standards team directs and develops standards for audit, attestation, and review services performed by CPAs.

Information Systems Audit and Control Association (ISACA)

www.isaca.org

This is the website of the Information Systems Audit and Control Association, a recognized leader in information technology assurance, control, and governance. With 50,000 members in more than 140 countries, the organization provides CISA (Certified Information Systems Auditor) certification and develops worldwide standards for information systems auditing and control.

The Institute of Internal Auditors (IIA)

www.theiia.org

This is the website of a nonprofit organization with more than 117,000 members from all over the world. Its purpose is to serve as the profession's international watchdog and primary resource for certification, continuing education, research, and technological issues related to internal audits.

ORGANIZATIONS

Europe

Auditing Practices Board (APB)

5th Floor, Aldwych House, 71-91 Aldwych, London, WC2B 4HN, UK
T: +44 (0) 20 7492 2300
F: +44 (0) 20 7492 2301
E: j.grant@frc-apb.org.uk
www.frc.org.uk/apb

Part of the Financial Reporting Council. The APB is committed to leading the development of auditing practice in the United Kingdom and the Republic of Ireland, to establish high standards of auditing, meet the developing needs of users of financial information, and ensure public confidence in the auditing process.

USA

Association to Advance Collegiate Schools of Business (AACSB International)

777 South Harbour Island Boulevard, Suite 750, Tampa, FL 33602-5730, USA
T: +1 813 769 6560
F: +1 813 769 6559
www.aacsb.edu

Founded in 1916, AACSB International acts as an accrediting agency for bachelor's, master's, and doctoral degree programs in business administration and accounting.

BRIC

National Audit Office of the People's Republic of China (CNAO)

1 Beiluyuan, Zhanlan Road, Beijing, 100830, China
F: +11 86 10 6833 0958
E: cnao@audit.gov.cn
www.cnao.gov.cn

As the supreme audit institution of China, the CNAO, directly under the leadership of the Premier, organizes and administers audit work of the whole country, in accordance with the law and subject to no interference by any administrative organ or public organization or individual, and reports its work to the State Council. Chinese auditing standards are unique because they originated in a socialist period in which the state was the sole owner of industry.

International

The International Federation of Accountants (IFAC)

545 Fifth Avenue, 14th Floor, New York, NY 10017, USA
T: +1 212 286 9344
F: +1 212 286 9570
E: elizabethconde@ifac.org
web.ifac.org

IFAC is the global organization for the accountancy profession. It works with its 158 members and associates in 122 countries and jurisdictions to protect the public interest by encouraging high quality practices by the world's accountants. IFAC members and associates, which are primarily national professional accountancy bodies, represent 2.5 million accountants employed in public practice, industry and commerce, government, and academia.

Bankruptcy and Business Failure

BOOKS

Bankruptcy Explained: The Bankruptcy Association's Practical Guide to UK Insolvency Laws, 2nd ed
John McQueen
Lancaster, UK: Bankruptcy Association, 2005
88pp, ISBN: 978-1-905069-01-9

The Enterprise Act 2002 has introduced several amendments to the now longstanding Insolvency Act 1986. *Bankruptcy Explained* deals with the resultant changes in the various aspects of bankruptcy law. This book is the Bankruptcy Association's most popular practical guide book to the United Kingdom's insolvency legislation. It covers the law throughout the United Kingdom, and includes coverage of deals with limited companies.

The Consistency Gap: Overcoming Failure in Consistently Executing the Business Plan
Mark S. Turner
Bloomington, Indiana: iUniverse, 2005
108pp, ISBN: 978-0-595-33807-8

The Consistency Gap provides a range of practical methods and solutions to the issues of information and tolerance. The author uses imagery and outline for setting goals and explaining how to achieve those goals.

Corporate Bankruptcy: Tools, Strategies and Alternatives
Grant A. Newton
Hoboken, New Jersey: Wiley, 2003
256pp, ISBN: 978-0-471-33268-8

In its examination of the complexities of restructuring and bankruptcy, this book provides a working knowledge of the bankruptcy process and of its benefits and challenges for both companies and their creditors. Supported by actual case studies, it assesses the legal and practical problems facing both debtors and creditors. It is a useful reference tool for every bankruptcy practitioner.

Corporate Failure by Design: Why Organizations Are Built to Fail
Jonathan I. Klein
Westport, Connecticut: Quorum Books, 2000
328pp, ISBN: 978-1-56720-297-7

Despite all that has been written on the subject of making organizations succeed, the reality is that an overwhelming majority of businesses fail within five years and almost all fail within 10 years. The author suggests that this tendency is inherent in the organization and explains his theory of organizational self-destruction. Besides analyzing the causes and processes of failure, however, he also points out the lessons that can be learned from it.

Corporate Financial Distress and Bankruptcy: Predict and Avoid Bankruptcy, Analyze and Invest in Distressed Debt, 3rd ed
Edward I. Altman and Edith Hotchkiss
Wiley Finance Series
Hoboken, New Jersey: Wiley, 2006
368pp, ISBN: 978-0-471-69189-1

This 3rd edition of the most authoritative finance book on the topic updates and expands its discussion of corporate distress and bankruptcy, as well as the related markets dealing with high-yield and distressed debt, and offers state-of-the-art analysis and research on the costs of bankruptcy, credit default prediction, the post-emergence period performance of bankrupt firms, and more.

Corporate Turnaround: How Managers Turn Losers into Winners
Donald B. Bibeault
Frederick, Maryland: Beard Group, 1998
482pp, ISBN: 978-1-893122-02-4

This is a reprint of a classic book that remains a source of effective advice on financial crisis management. It distills the experiences of close to 100 managers who successfully restored companies to profitability and constitutes a practical guide to management strategies to prevent bankruptcy.

Creating Value through Corporate Restructuring: Case Studies in Bankruptcies, Buyouts, and Breakups
Stuart C. Gilson
New York: Wiley, 2010
814pp, ISBN: 978-0-470-50352-2

Management buyouts are a common form of business restructuring. This collection of recent case studies from the United States and several other countries illustrates the real-world techniques and strategies that are common to all types of restructuring. It demystifies the complex financial issues surrounding business valuation and gives the reader a better understanding of the possibilities when dealing with corporate restructuring.

Elements of Bankruptcy, 5th ed
Douglas G. Baird
New York: Foundation Press, 2010
270pp, ISBN: 978-1-59941-725-7

Baird's book gives an overview of current law and practice in the United States. Recent changes in the law and topical issues are discussed and placed in context.

The Executive Guide to Corporate Bankruptcy
Thomas J. Salerno, Jordan A. Kroop, Craig D. Hansen
Frederick, Maryland: Beard Group, 2001
736pp, ISBN: 978-1-58798-026-8

This book was written to provide a comprehensive resource for managers of financially troubled companies facing Chapter 11 bankruptcy proceedings. The authors outline the history of American bankruptcy law and explain bankruptcy terminology for the lay person, then provide a step-by-step guide to the bankruptcy and reorganization process, including sample documents.

Financial Shenanigans: How to Detect Accounting Gimmicks and Fraud in Financial Reports, 3rd ed
Howard M. Schilit
New York: McGraw-Hill, 2010
304pp, ISBN: 978-0-07-170307-9

This examines the current climate of accounting fraud. It provides practical tips and suggestions for potentially affected people from misleading business valuations, including investors and lenders. It is also useful for managers and auditors wanting to research and read financial reports, and to identify early warning signs of a company's problems.

  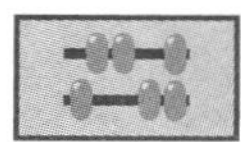      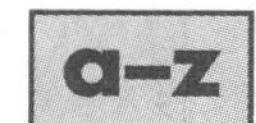

International Insolvency Law: Themes and Perspectives

Paul J. Omar

Markets and the Law Series
Aldershot, UK: Ashgate Publishing, 2008
452pp, ISBN: 978-0-7546-2427-1

This is a new study that examines the phenomenon of cross-border incorporations and the conduct of business in more than one jurisdiction. It is a compilation of essays by academics and practitioners in the field who trace the development of the subject, and provide an account of economics, legal history and private international law. It demonstrates its relationship with finance and security issues as well as the importance of business rescue, and how new international instruments function, as well as how this area is being challenged by other areas of law.

Surviving a Downturn: Building a Successful Business . . . Without Breaking the Bank

Jeremy Kourdi

Business on a Shoestring Series
London: A&C Black Publishers, 2007
208pp, ISBN: 978-0-7136-7547-4

All businesses go through difficult times but how they react can make the difference between survival and going to the wall. Realistic but inspiring and packed with ideas that really work, this book helps small business owners face and tackle the challenges of a downturn.

JOURNALS

British Accounting Review

Elsevier
11830 Westline Industrial Drive, St Louis, MO 63146, USA
T: +1 314 453 7076
F: +1 314 523 5153
www.elsevier.com/locate/issn/0890-8389
ISSN: 0890-8389

The *British Accounting Review* is the official journal of the British Accounting Association. The journal is diverse and contributions are included from a wide range of research methodologies, including analytical, archival, experimental, survey, and qualitative case methods, and topics, such as financial accounting, management accounting, finance and financial management, auditing, public sector accounting, social and environmental accounting, accounting education, and accounting history.

Corporate Governance: The International Journal of Effective Board Performance

Emerald
60/62 Toller Lane, Bradford, West Yorkshire, BD8 9BY, UK
T: +44 (0) 1274 777 700
F: +44 (0) 1274 785 200
www.emeraldinsight.com/1472-0701.htm
ISSN: 1472-0701

This journal publishes a range of theoretical, methodological and substantive debates, as well as practical developments in the field of corporate governance worldwide. It focuses on areas such as the impact of changes of business/corporate governance forms and practices on people, the sustainability of different governance models, how improvements in performance can be achieved through effective governance, and the legacy from contradicting governance philosophies.

Financial Analysts Journal

CFA Institute
560 Ray C. Hunt Drive, Charlottesville, VA 22903-2981, USA
T: +1 434 951 5499
F: +1 434 951 5262
ejournals.ebsco.com/direct.asp?JournalID=108977
ISSN: 0015-198X

This quarterly journal, published by the Chartered Financial Analyst Institute, is dedicated to the advancement of knowledge and understanding of the practice of investment management through the publication of high-quality, practitioner-relevant research. It serves as a bridge between academic research and practice by seeking academically rigorous papers that have direct relevance to practitioners.

Insolvency Intelligence

Sweet & Maxwell
100 Avenue Road, Swiss Cottage, London, NW3 3PF, UK
T: +44 (0) 20 7393 7000
F: +44 (0) 20 7393 7010
www.sweetandmaxwell.co.uk/Catalogue/ProductDetails.aspx?recordid=426&productid=6958
ISSN: 0950-2645

This magazine, published 10 times each year, provides immediate, concise and authoritative coverage of insolvency law, practice and procedure.

Insolvency Law and Practice

LexisNexis
Tolley House, 2 Addiscombe Road, Croydon, CR9 5AF, UK
T: +44 (0) 20 8662 2000
F: +44 (0) 20 8662 2012
www.lexisnexis.co.uk
ISSN: 0267-0771

Aimed at legal practitioners, students, and accountants, this magazine covers all aspects of insolvency law and accountancy. It appears six times each year.

International Insolvency Review

Wiley
The Atrium, Southern Gate, Chichester, West Sussex, PO19 8SQ, UK
T: +44 (0) 1243 779 777
F: +44 (0) 1243 775 878
www.interscience.wiley.com/jpages/1180-0518
ISSN: 1180-0518

The *IIR* is published three times each year, in association with INSOL (the International Federation of Insolvency Professionals), and provides an international perspective on developments in insolvency law and practice, in addition to covering issues relating to cross-border insolvency.

International Small Business Journal

Sage Publications
1 Oliver's Yard, 55 City Road, London, EC1Y 1SP, UK
T: +44 (0) 20 7324 8500
F: +44 (0) 20 7324 8600
isb.sagepub.com
ISSN: 0266-2426

The *International Small Business Journal* (*ISBJ*) is a quarterly journal that aims to provide a forum for the discussion and dissemination of views and research on the small business sector. Papers published in the *ISBJ* cover theoretical, methodological, and empirical studies of small firms from a broad range of disciplines and perspectives. The papers are aimed at academics, policy makers, and analysts, in government and business, trade and business institutions, small business representative bodies, and those in support agencies.

INTERNET

ABIWorld

www.abiworld.org

ABIWorld is sponsored by the American Bankruptcy Institute and is a major source of US bankruptcy information. The site includes news and statistics, information and opinions on bankruptcy cases, information on international bankruptcy legislation, an interactive newsletter, and information on how to find a bankruptcy professional. Some sections are restricted to ABI members.

American Bankruptcy Institute

www.abiworld.org

The American Bankruptcy Institute is a nonprofit, nonpartisan organization promoting education, research, and the analysis of bankruptcy issues. Its website provides access to current news and legislation pertaining to bankruptcy and business failures, an interactive newsletter, and research and analysis.

Bankruptcy for Business

www.bankruptcyforbusiness.net

This site focuses on bankruptcy for business, providing guidance and articles on how to file and how to avoid bankruptcy, based on the premise that business turnaround is usually the cheaper alternative.

Business Bankruptcy Info

www.creditworthy.com/topics/bankruptcy.html

Hosted by Creditworthy, this website provides links to business bankruptcy information covering the United States, Canada, and the United Kingdom. It includes information on, and links to, a US bankruptcy dictionary, an overview of the US Bankruptcy Code, and statistics and research on bankruptcy filings.

Filing for Bankruptcy Online

www.filingforbankruptcyonline.com/businessbankruptcy.html

This US site provides practical information on bankruptcy for businesses, and a range of related areas involving legal issues, documentation, software, tax issues, mortgage, and credit.

Insolvency Services

www.insolvency.gov.uk

This government-sponsored site provides practical information and advice on personal and

  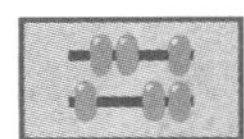      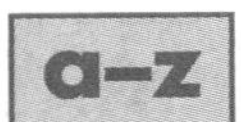

corporate insolvency in the United Kingdom, including statistics and a database of insolvency practitioners.

InsolvencyAsia

www.insolvencyasia.com

This site, based in Hong Kong, provides insolvency-related news together with information on bankruptcy legislation and listings of consultants, associations, and regulatory authorities in Asian countries.

InterNet Bankruptcy Library

www.bankrupt.com

Sponsored by the Bankruptcy Creditors' Service and the Beard Group, this site is aimed particularly at creditors. It includes a news archive, a database of bankruptcy professionals, information on legal rules in American states, and details of publications, as well as providing access to discussion groups.

United States Bankruptcy Courts

www.uscourts.gov/bankruptcycourts.html

Since there are specialized courts that settle bankruptcy claims in America, this site offers information about the courts themselves, offers downloadable forms, has an FAQ section, and has links to the individual courts for particular areas.

ORGANIZATIONS

Europe

Bankruptcy Association

Freepost LA1118, 4 Johnson Close, Lancaster, LA1 5BR, UK
T: +44 (0) 1539 469 474
E: johnmcqueennospam@theba.org.uk
www.theba.org.uk

The association was founded by John McQueen in 1983 to provide information and advice to debtors and bankrupts in the United Kingdom and to campaign for reform of insolvency legislation.

Insolvency Practitioners Association (IPA)

Valiant House, 4–10 Heneage Lane, London, EC3A 5DQ, UK
T: +44 (0) 20 7623 5108
F: +44 (0) 20 7623 5127
E: secretariat@insolvency-practitioners.org.uk
www.insolvency-practitioners.org.uk

The IPA, founded in 1961, is a professional organization for insolvency practitioners. Its main objectives are to promote training and education in insolvency administration and to maintain the standards of performance and conduct of those working in the field.

R3, The Association of Business Recovery Professionals

8th Floor, 120 Aldersgate Street, London, EC1A 4JQ, UK
T: +44 (0) 20 7566 4200
F: +44 (0) 20 7566 4224
E: association@r3.org.uk
www.r3.org.uk

R3 (Rescue, Recovery, Renewal), founded in 1990 and formerly known as the Society of Practitioners of Insolvency, is a professional organization for insolvency practitioners and turnaround managers which places a growing emphasis on reconstruction, turnaround management, and corporate recovery. Its activities include courses, conferences, and producing publications–including the quarterly journal *Recovery*.

USA

American Bankruptcy Institute

44 Canal Center Plaza, Suite 400, Alexandria, VA 22314, USA
T: +1 703 739 0800
F: +1 703 739 1060
E: support@abiworld.org
www.abiworld.org

American Bankruptcy Institute is the largest multi-national organization dedicated to research and education on matters related to insolvency. The ABI membership includes more than 11,500 attorneys, auctioneers, bankers, judges, lenders, professors, turnaround specialists, accountants, and other bankruptcy professionals. It provides a forum for the exchange of ideas and information, and is involved in a number of publications both for the insolvency practitioner and the public.

The National Association of Bankruptcy Trustees

1 Windsor Cove, Suite 305, Columbia, SC 29223, USA
T: +1 803 252 5646
F: +1 803 765 0860
E: info@nabt.com
www.nabt.com

The association is committed to improving the administration of bankruptcy by promoting professionalism, education, and the open exchange of ideas among its members and other members of the bankruptcy community.

BRIC

Managers under the Chamber of Commerce and Industry of the Russian Federation (SOAM)

6 St Ilyinka, Moscow, 109012, Russia
T: +7 495 620 0009
F: +7 495 620 0360
E: tpprf@tpprf.ru
www.soautpprf.ru/site.xp/049049056049.html

The Chamber of Commerce and Industry of the Russian Federation is a non-governmental, non-profit organization which aims to meet the tasks and goal objectives set out in the Russian Federation Law on Chambers of Commerce and Industry. It represents the interests of small, medium-size, and big business, and encompasses all business sectors.

International

INSOL International

2–3 Philpot Lane, London, EC3M 8AQ, UK
T: +44 (0) 20 7929 6679
F: +44 (0) 20 7929 6678
E: heather@insol.ision.co.uk
www.insol.org

INSOL is a grouping of member associations that aims to facilitate the exchange of information and ideas and to encourage international cooperation within the insolvency profession. It participates in governmental advisory groups, supports research, and promotes the development of international guidelines and codes of practice. Its activities include the organization of seminars and conferences and the publication of newsletters, reports, and a journal.

International Association of Restructuring, Insolvency & Bankruptcy Professionals

2–3 Philpot Lane, London, EC3M 8AQ, UK
T: +44 (0) 20 7929 6679
F: +44 (0) 20 7929 6678
E: heather@insol.ision.co.uk
www.insol.org

INSOL International is a global alliance of national associations for accountants and lawyers who focus on turnaround and insolvency. It consists of 40 member associations from around the world, with over 10,000 professionals participating as members of INSOL International.

Behavioral Finance

BOOKS

Advances in Behavioral Finance, Volume I

Richard H. Thaler (editor)
New York: Russell Sage Foundation, 1993
597pp, ISBN: 978-0-87154-844-3

A groundbreaking and insightful overview of behavioral finance, the 21 papers discuss different behavioral issues and anomalies that occur in the financial markets. In the first book published on this emerging topic, the authors develop theories to help explain the effects of financial agents behaving in ways that are not fully rational.

Advances in Behavioral Finance, Volume II

Richard H. Thaler (editor)
Roundtable Series in Behavioral Economics
Princeton, New Jersey: Princeton University Press, 2005
728pp, ISBN: 978-0-691-12175-8

The second volume, published 12 years later, focuses on the large changes that have occurred in behavioral finance since the first volume was published. It shows how financial markets often fail to behave as they would if trading was

  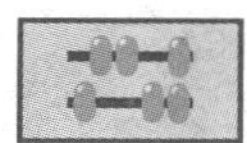      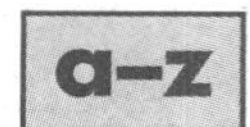

undertaken by fully rational investors, and discusses the impact of behavioral finance approach on areas such as asset pricing and investor behavior.

A Behavioral Approach to Asset Pricing, 2nd ed
Hersh Shefrin
Academic Press Advanced Finance Series
Oxford: Academic Press, 2008
618pp, ISBN: 978-0-12-374356-5

Shefrin here presents a practical approach to the application of behavioral economics and finance to a range of pricing issues, such as portfolio management, trading, and the pricing of equities, bonds and options.

Behavioral Corporate Finance: Decisions that Create Value
Hersh Shefrin
McGraw-Hill/Irwin Series in Finance, Insurance, and Real Estate
Boston, Massachusetts: McGraw-Hill/Irwin, 2007
203pp, ISBN: 978-0-07-284865-6

Focuses on behavior and decision making in the corporate sector, identifying psychological obstacles to success. It considers how behavioural finance can be used to advantage and for enhancing corporate value if the impact of these obstacles is minimized.

Behavioral Finance
Joachim Goldberg, Rudiger von Nitzsch
Wiley Finance Series
New York: Wiley, 2001
238pp, ISBN: 978-0-471-49784-4

Examines how a behavioral approach to finance can explain and rationalize the fundamental principles of technical analysis. It offers practical analysis and advice on key behavioural issues, such as forecasting, strategies for crisis management, the consequences of psychological needs, and successful trading.

Behavioral Finance
Hersh Shefrin (editor)
International Library of Critical Writings in Financial Economics Series
Northampton, Massachusetts: Edward Elgar Publishing, 2001
2,088pp, ISBN: 978-1-84064-274-2

A three-volume collection of essays that examines the overlap between psychology, decision-making, and finance. It combines many of the classic approaches to both psychology and finance, and discusses the debate between the behavioural school and the efficient market school of finance.

Behavioral Finance and Wealth Management: How to Build Optimal Portfolios that Account for Investor Biases
Michael M. Pompian
Wiley Finance Series
Hoboken, New Jersey: Wiley, 2006
336pp, ISBN: 978-0-471-74517-4

This is a wide-ranging introduction to irrational investor behavior and the practical application of behavioral finance, and how to adjust portfolios for individual investors to account for behavioral biases. It also provides a history of behavioral finance, a detailed review of some of the most commonly found biases, and examines how to incorporate investor behavior into the asset allocation process.

Behavioural Finance: Insights into Irrational Minds and Markets
James Montier
Chichester, UK: Wiley, 2002
193pp, ISBN: 978-0-470-84487-8

Provides a practical overview of behavioral finance, with insights into the irrational nature of investment decisions. Montier links the underlying theory to real-life applications in financial products through an examination of measurable variables, and presents useful advice on how institutional investors can improve their decision-making through an awareness of behavioral research and finance.

Behavioural Investing: A Practitioners Guide to Applying Behavioural Finance
James Montier
Wiley Finance Series
Chichester, UK: Wiley, 2007
728pp, ISBN: 978-0-470-51670-6

This book for professional investors focuses on methods for improving investment behavior by considering behavioral decision-making biases. It reviews the applications of behavioral finance, and examines the possible errors and mental pitfalls, and discusses how to avoid them having a negative impact on returns.

Beyond Greed and Fear: Understanding Behavioral Finance and the Psychology of Investing
Hersh Shefrin
Financial Management Association Survey and Synthesis Series
Boston, Massachusetts: Harvard Business School Press, 2007
368pp, ISBN: 978-0-19-530421-3

Discusses how biases, perception, and other psychology patterns can affect investment behavior. It considers investors as being motivated by fear, hope, overconfidence, and the need for quick returns, which can push them to unnecessary errors. It also provides examples of investment mistakes, and analyzes them from a behavioral-finance perspective.

Inefficient Markets: An Introduction to Behavioral Finance
Andrei Shleifer
Clarendon Lectures in Economics Series
New York: Oxford University Press, 2000
224pp, ISBN: 978-0-19-829227-2

A classic of behavioral finance, this was one of the first books published on the subject. It examines some of the most important early ideas in behavioral finance, and is aimed at financial economists who are looking for a source of empirical facts, as well as wanting to explore new ideas in this emerging area of finance.

Nudge: Improving Decisions about Health, Wealth, and Happiness
Richard H. Thaler, Cass R. Sunstein
New Haven, Connecticut: Yale University Press, 2008
293pp, ISBN: 978-0-300-12223-7

This new book on decision-making discusses how organizations can help people make better choices in their lives. Using a range of everyday activities as examples, it shows how we are susceptible to various biases, and shows how to design environments to nudge people into making better decisions.

Rumors in Financial Markets: Insights into Behavioral Finance
Mark Schindler
Wiley Finance Series
Hoboken, New Jersey: Wiley, 2007
210pp, ISBN: 978-0-470-03196-4

A new look at behavioral finance, providing insights into how finance, psychology and sociology act as the foundations for rumors in the marketplace. It integrates behavioral finance with experimental finance, to examine how rumors evolve, spread and are used, and discusses the effect this has on volatility, price movements, and herding behavior.

The Story of Behavioral Finance
Brandon Adams, Brian Finn
Bloomington, Indiana: iUniverse, 2006
82pp, ISBN: 978-0-595-39690-0

A useful primer on behavioral finance and its application to the real world. It concisely summarizes a number of related core concepts, such as the efficient market hypo-thesis and the Capital Asset Pricing Model, and discusses a number of key questions about the impact of behavioral finance on different market phenomena, such as investor psychology and limits to arbitrage.

The Winner's Curse: Paradoxes and Anomalies of Economic Life
Richard H. Thaler
Princeton, New Jersey: Princeton University Press, 1994
240pp, ISBN: 978-0-691-01934-5

The author, a leading figure in behavioral economics, here analyzes a number of examples of recognizable anomalies, arguing that winners are often the real losers. He relates this to the debate over market efficiency, countering the received wisdom that economic choice rests on a foundation of rationality.

JOURNALS

Behavioral & Experimental Finance
SSRN, USA
www.ssrn.com/update/fen/fen_behav-exper-fin.html

This electronic journal publishes working and accepted paper abstracts covering all aspects of behavioral and experimental finance. It strives for greater explanation and insight into finance and investments based on research from the social sciences, and to foster a better understanding of those elements of human psychology, both

  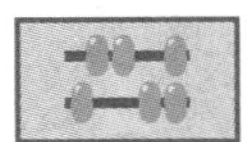      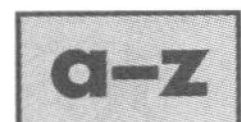

cognitive and affective, that influence the decision-making process.

The Icfai University Journal of Behavioral Finance

The Icfai University Press
6-3-354/1, Stellar Sphinx, Road No. 1, Banjara Hills, Panjagutta, Hyderabad - 500 034, Andhra Pradesh, India
T: +91 40 2343 0448
F: +91 40 2343 0447
www.iupindia.org/behavioralfinance.asp
ISSN: 0972-9089

This is a quarterly journal that focuses on behavioral economics, behavior of markets, behavioral aspects influencing investment decisions of managers and behavioral aspects in corporate finance decision. It provides a platform for cutting-edge research in understanding the human behavior in relation to finance and economics.

The Journal of Behavioral Finance

The Institute of Behavioral Finance and Lawrence Erlbaum Associates
1900 Preston Road #267, Suite 310, Plano, TX 75093, USA
www.journalofbehavioralfinance.org
ISSN: 1542-7560

This journal publishes papers analyzing developments in behavioral finance, and addresses the implications of current work on individual and group emotion, cognition, and behavior in markets, aiming to foster debate among groups who have keen insights into the behavioral patterns of markets.

The Journal of Economic Behavior and Organization

Elsevier
1598 South Main Street, Room 16, JMU, MSC 5505, Harrisonburg, VA 22807, USA
F: +1 540 801 8650
www.elsevier.com/wps/find/journaldescription.cws_home/505559/description#description
ISSN: 0167-2681

This journal publishes theoretical and empirical research concerning economic decision, organization and behavior and to economic change in all its aspects. Its aim is to explore the interrelations of economics with other disciplines, such as biology, psychology, law, anthropology, sociology and mathematics.

Journal of Risk and Uncertainty

Springer Verlag
Tiergartenstr. 17, 69121 Heidelberg, Germany
T: +49 622 1487 8575
www.springer.com/economics/economic+theory/journal/11166
ISSN: 0895-5646

This journal publishes theoretical and empirical papers that analyze risk-bearing behavior and decision-making under uncertainty, and is an outlet for research in decision analysis, economics and psychology dealing with choice under uncertainty.

INTERNET

Behavioral Finance Net

www.behaviouralfinance.net

This is an online resource on for researchers in behavioral finance. It contains key information on a large number of associated topics, and includes definitions and quotes, bibliography, people, history, links, glossary, and links topics with papers.

ORGANIZATIONS

USA

The Behavioral Finance Forum

Chair: Shlomo Benartzi, Warren Cormier
USA
www.rand.org/labor/centers/befi

The Behavioral Finance Forum (BeFi) is a collective of academic, financial and government leaders promoting behavioral research for practical application. It aims to help consumers worldwide make better financial decisions, and the financial industry to use this information to produce innovative product and service ideas with a unique marketing advantage. Founded in 2006, it hosts an annual conference, and conducts a number of web seminars each year; the non-profit RAND Corporation recently took on the management of its activities.

The Institute of Behavioral Finance

Harborside Financial Center, Plaza 10, Suite 800, Jersey City, NJ 07311, USA
T: +1 201 793 2015
E: vilieva@journalofbehavioralfinance.org
www.journalofbehavioralfinance.com

The Institute of Behavioral Finance was established to study the impact of psychology on investor decision-making and, through its publication, The Journal of Behavioral Finance, and sponsored conferences, it promotes new research in all areas of the subject. It also addresses important new issues by involving interested practitioners and academics in related fields to better explain both investor decision-making and market anomalies.

International

The Institute of Behavioral Finance

Chair: Theo Vorster
Fountain Grove Office Park, Cnr William Nicol & 2nd Road, Hyde Park, Johannesburg, South Africa
T: +27 011 888 5088
F: +27 011 888 5088
E: gerdavdl@lantic.net
www.ibfsa.co.za

The Institute of Behavioral Finance is an independent research and training institution aimed at the study and promotion of the behavioral finance discipline. It incorporates the work of researchers and academics to discuss investor decision-making and market anomalies, and add value to the professional status of the investment sector in South Africa.

Benchmarking

BOOKS

Benchmarking: The Search for Industry Best Practices That Lead to Superior Performance

Robert C. Camp
New York: Productivity Press, 2006
320pp, ISBN: 978-1-56327-352-0

This provides a guide through the historic 10-step benchmarking process that the author developed while at Xerox, a process that is credited with reviving that company when it was floundering in 1979. It presents other examples of the process, including its dramatic application to L. L. Bean. He uses these examples to show managers how to relate benchmarking to their own circumstances, and presents strategy and tips for efficiently undertaking best performance.

The Benchmarking Book

Tim Stapenhurst
Oxford: Butterworth-Heinemann, 2009
450pp, ISBN: 978-0-7506-8905-2

This essential guide to process improvement through benchmarking provides all the information you need to carry out effective benchmarking studies and improve performance. Focused on best practice across different industries, it offers crucial guidance on how to analyze data, avoid pitfalls and structure reports to achieve the best results.

Benchmarking Strategies: A Tool for Profit Improvement

Rob Reider, Harry Reider
Chichester, UK: Wiley, 2000
276pp, ISBN: 978-0-471-34464-3

This is a practical manual covering benchmarking principles, techniques, and implementation. It examines how corporations perform various tasks in identifying and implementing internal and external best practices in a program of continuous improvement.

Best Practices: Building Up Your Business with Customer-focused Solutions

R. Hiebeler, T. B. Kelly, C. Ketteman
Carmichael, California: Touchstone Books, 2000
240pp, ISBN: 978-0-684-84804-4

From case studies of over 40 best practice companies, this book draws lessons on how to focus on customers, create growth, reduce costs, and increase profits. It discusses new insights beyond benchmarking, best practices auditing, understanding markets and customers, involving customers in the design of products and services, selling products and services, how best to serve customers, managing customer information, and putting best practices to work.

  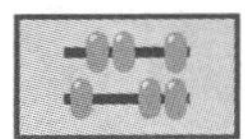      

Best Practices in Planning and Management Reporting: From Data to Decisions, 2nd ed

David A. J. Axson

Chichester, UK: Wiley, 2007
288pp, ISBN: 978-0-470-00857-7

This examines the process of improving business performance through the adoption of best practices. It introduces the technique of best practice benchmarking, and explains how best practices may be used to drive change. The issues of strategic planning, operational and financial planning, management reporting, forecasting, and the use of technology are discussed, as well as the use of benchmarking as a starting point.

Driving Your Company's Value: Strategic Benchmarking for Value

Michael J. Mard, Robert R. Dunne, Edi Osborne, James S. Rigby, Jr

Chichester, UK: Wiley, 2005
193pp, ISBN: 978-0-471-64855-0

Driving Your Company's Value is a step-by-step book presenting a valuation-oriented methodology that helps companies maximize shareholder value. It offers clear, concise, and concrete methods for management to create and preserve value, complete with case study applications.

Effective Management of Benchmarking Projects: Practical Guidelines and Examples of Best Practice

Mohamed Zairi

Oxford: Butterworth-Heinemann, 1998
348pp, ISBN: 978-0-7506-3987-3

This book begins with a profile of Rank Xerox—where the benchmarking story started. It examines the strategic application of benchmarking for best practice, as well as topics such as partner selection, the ethics of benchmarking, and the value of industrial visits and benchmarking awards. It also describes the process of benchmarking in practice.

Strategic Benchmarking Reloaded with Six Sigma: Improving Your Company's Performance Using Global Best Practice

Gregory H. Watson

Chichester, UK: Wiley, 2007
360pp, ISBN: 978-0-470-06908-0

Strategic Benchmarking Reloaded with Six Sigma updates benchmarking, by adding statistical concepts from Six Sigma. These two methodologies combine to form a powerful platform for improving any company's overall performance. This new revision reviews the first 25 years of development in benchmarking, and features new appendices, case studies, and topics.

Winning Business: How to Use Financial Analysis and Benchmarks to Outscore Your Competition

Rich Gildersleeve

Houston, Texas: Gulf Professional Publishing Company, 1999
334pp, ISBN: 978-0-88415-898-1

Financial analysis, with all its detailed measurements and calculations, is often overlooked as a benchmarking tool. This provides clear explanations of the fundamental terms used to analyze and understand financial statements, and demonstrates their value in benchmarking companies. The benchmarking indicators presented can be used to track key measurements or as a metric by which to measure your company against others.

JOURNALS

Benchmarking: An International Journal

Emerald
60/62 Toller Lane, Bradford, West Yorkshire, BD8 9BY, UK
T: +44 (0) 1274 777 700
F: +44 (0) 1274 785 200
www.emeraldinsight.com/1463-5771.htm
ISSN: 1463-5771

The journal focuses on the theory and practice of benchmarking, with articles on recent academic research as well as real-life case studies of benchmarking activities by companies. Contributors are from a wide range of countries.

Business Process Management Journal

Emerald
60/62 Toller Lane, Bradford, West Yorkshire, BD8 9BY, UK
T: +44 (0) 1274 777 700
F: +44 (0) 1274 785 200
www.emeraldinsight.com/1463-7154.htm
ISSN: 1463-7154

This journal is published in association with the European Centre for Total Quality Management. Contributions from both academics and practitioners are included, and the focus is on the management of business processes for efficiency and competitive success.

Measuring Business Excellence

Emerald
60/62 Toller Lane, Bradford, West Yorkshire, BD8 9BY, UK
T: +44 (0) 1274 777 700
F: +44 (0) 1274 785 200
www.emeraldinsight.com/1368-3047.htm
ISSN: 1368-3047

Measuring Business Excellence provides international insights into non-financial methods of measuring business improvements. It shows how to apply best practice, implement innovative thinking, and learn how to use different improvement tools within an organization.

INTERNET

APQC's Benchmarking and Best Practice

www.apqc.org/best

This site summarizes the benefits of benchmarking, outlines a methodology, and lists the keys to success in the area. The "free resources" section includes articles, case studies, and white papers to guide you through the benchmarking process.

Avoid These Ten Benchmarking Mistakes

www.benchmarkingplus.com.au/mistakes.htm

Many sites tell you how to benchmark. This site lists the 10 most common mistakes in benchmarking so that you can avoid making them yourself.

Benchmarking Exchange

www.benchnet.com

This is an extremely comprehensive site with a lot of information on benchmarking practices for both members and nonmembers. Members can conduct benchmark surveys online and have the information collected and returned through the Exchange as replies are received.

Benchmarking Network

www.benchmarkingnetwork.com

This is another comprehensive site. Members share information about best practice in a wide range of operations across all industry sectors.

Best-Practice.com

www.Best-Practice.com

Providing a range of information on benchmarking, this site has links to more detailed research and tools that can be purchased direct from the various partners in the network. Membership is free.

The Business Performance Improvement Resource

www.bpir.com

The Business Performance Improvement Resource is an internet-based benchmarking and business information service. It provides access to benchmarks, best practices, performance measures, business excellence tools, self-assessments, and over 250,000 articles from around the world. It is run by the Centre for Organisational Excellence Research (COER).

Global Benchmarking Council

www3.best-in-class.com/gbc

Members have access to a benchmarking database, regular meetings, and research reports, plus a range of other services and detailed information.

ORGANIZATIONS

Europe

Best Practice Club

The Atrium, Curtis Road, Dorking, Surrey, RH4 1XA, UK
T: +44 (0) 1306 646 555
F: +44 (0) 1306 646 556
E: enquiries@bpclub.com
www.bpclub.com

With an international membership, this organization promotes organizational excellence through members networking and comparing their practice. Member companies come from both the manufacturing and the service sectors and pool their experience.

 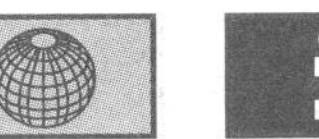 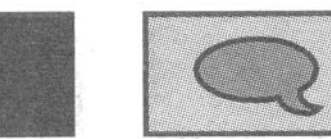  

Centre for Interfirm Comparison (CIFC)

32 Thomas Street, Winchester, Hampshire, SO23 9HJ, UK
T: +44 (0) 1962 844 144
F: +44 (0) 1962 843 180
E: enquiries@cifc.co.uk
www.cifc.co.uk

The centre helps businesses of all types and in all sectors to assess their performance through confidential, detailed comparison of their financial ratios and other data with those of similar businesses, and to target improvements in specific areas of their operations. It provides a wide range of benchmarking and related consulting services.

USA

American Productivity and Quality Center (APQC)

123 North Post Oak Lane, 3rd Floor, Houston, TX 77024, USA
T: +1 713 681 4020
F: +1 713 681 1182
E: apqcinfo@apqc.org
www.apqc.org

Founded in 1977, APQC works with organizations of all sizes to improve productivity and quality. Its aim is to research and understand both emerging improvement methods and methods whose effectiveness is already proven, and it distributes its findings through education, advice, and information services. In 1992 it set up the International Benchmarking Clearinghouse to promote and facilitate the process of learning from best practice.

International

Centre for Organisational Excellence Research (COER)

Massey University, Private Bag 11 222, Palmerston North, New Zealand
T: +64 (0) 6 350 5445
E: r.s.mann@massey.ac.nz
www.coer.org.nz

The Centre for Organisational Excellence Research (COER), led by Dr Robin Mann, undertakes benchmarking and business excellence research and consultancy. They also operate the www.bpir.com site, which focuses on best practice sharing.

The Global Benchmarking Network (GBN)

c/o Informationszentrum Benchmarking (IZB), Fraunhofer IPK, Pascalstrasse 8–9, 10587 Berlin, Germany
T: +49 (0) 30 39 006
F: +49 (0) 30 393 25 03
E: gbn@ipk.fhg.de
www.globalbenchmarking.org/

The GBN is a membership-based organization for those organizations that promote and support benchmarking within their country. Currently it represents over 25 countries. The purpose of the GBN is to promote and support benchmarking worldwide and the international exchange of best practices. Its members consist of the world's leading experts in benchmarking, and its president is Dr Robert Camp, the founder of benchmarking.

Bonds/Fixed Income

BOOKS

The Bond Bible

Marilyn Cohen
New York: New York Institute of Finance, 2000
238pp, ISBN: 978-0-7352-0138-5

This is a comprehensive guide to bonds and fixed-income investments, discussing their characteristics, stability, equilibrium, and the benefits they bring to portfolio diversification. It demystifies bond investing, and discusses the increase in bond usage and markets, how to identify a bargain, where to buy from, and how to avoid the pitfalls of the bond market.

The Bond Book: Everything Investors Need to Know About Treasuries, Municipals, GNMAs, Corporates, Zeros, Bond Funds, Money Market Funds, and More, 2nd ed

Annette Thau
New York: McGraw-Hill, 2001
394pp, ISBN: 978-0-07-135862-0

This comprehensive introduction to bonds explains how they work, the historic returns for each type of fund, how to buy and sell them, and acts as a practical guide to safer investing and using cash flow assets. It provides useful information and tools for integrating bonds, and more recent innovations such as inflation-indexed bonds, savings bonds, CMOs, and emerging market bonds, into a portfolio.

Bond Markets, Analysis and Strategies, 7th ed

Frank J. Fabozzi
Boston, Massachusetts: Addison-Wesley, 2008
792pp, ISBN: 978-0-13-607897-5

This new textbook on fixed-income securities and bond markets shows how to understand the bond market and the necessary tools for managing bond portfolios. Taking a practical approach, it presents a detailed account of each type of bond, their investment characteristics, technology for valuing them, portfolio strategies for using them, and shows how to quantify exposure to changes in interest rates.

Bonds: The Unbeaten Path to Secure Investment Growth

Hildy Richelson, Stan Richelson
New York: Bloomberg Press, 2007
387pp, ISBN: 978-1-57660-243-0

This focuses on the use of bonds and fixed income as successful investment vehicles, explaining how to use the asset class for achieving specific financial goals. It argues that an all-bond portfolio is preferable to one with an equity mix, as it will produce higher returns, and describes the array of bond-investment options, and how to purchase bonds at the best price.

Charlie D.: The Story of the Legendary Bond Trader

William D. Falloon
New York: Wiley, 1997
230pp, ISBN: 978-0-471-15672-7

This biography of the famous trader, thought by many to be the greatest ever, details his life, accomplishments, and trading strategies from the Treasury bond pit at the Chicago Board of Trade, the world's largest futures trading arena. It describes his entrepreneurial style, trading integrity, and philanthropy, and looks at the risk-taking style that helped him achieve such enormous daily trading positions.

European Fixed Income Markets: Money, Bond, and Interest Rate Derivatives

Jonathan A. Batten, Thomas A. Fetherston, Peter G. Szilagyi (editors)
Wiley Finance Series
Chichester, UK: Wiley, 2004
484pp, ISBN: 978-0-470-85053-4

This analysis of fixed-income instruments and associated derivatives provides a useful overview of the euro and non-euro markets. A team of leading international academics and market practitioners examine the main features of these markets, and the increase in scope of individual national debt markets, and offer detailed country analyses, as well as discussing the post-euro landscape in these markets.

First Steps in Bonds: Successful Strategies without Rocket Science

Peter Temple
Boston, Massachusetts: FT Prentice Hall, 2002
197pp, ISBN: 978-0-273-65657-9

This is a practical bond primer that offers a comprehensive and accessible overview to the techniques and tools used by professional investors to integrate bonds into a balanced portfolio. It examines how to analyze and value bonds, key market issues, trading strategies, and discusses each of the main parts of the market, including government bonds, corporate bonds, and Eurobonds.

Fixed-Income Securities: Valuation, Risk Management and Portfolio Strategies

Lionel Martellini, Philippe Priaulet, Stéphane Priaulet

  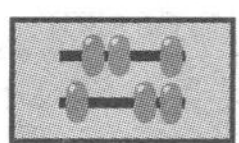      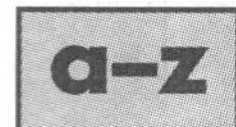

Wiley Finance Series
Chichester, UK: Wiley, 2003
631pp, ISBN: 978-0-470-85277-4

This comprehensive textbook covers all areas of bonds, including techniques for valuing them, portfolio management, and risk management in bond markets. It examines how various types of derivative securities can be used to manage the risks inherent in fixed-income securities, and presents worked examples on valuation, risk management, and portfolio strategies, as well as discussing yield curves, credit spreads, and hedging interest rate risk.

Fixed Income Analysis, 2nd ed

Frank J. Fabozzi (editor)

CFA Institute Investment Series
Hoboken, New Jersey: Wiley, 2007
768pp, ISBN: 978-0-470-05221-1

This practical guide provides complete coverage of fixed-income tools and techniques, and how they can be applied to the investment process and portfolio construction. It focuses on the fixed-income marketplace, the risks associated with investing in fixed-income securities, the fundamentals of valuation and interest rate risk, features of structured products, principles of credit analysis, and the valuation of fixed-income securities with embedded options.

Fixed Income Securities: Tools for Today's Markets, 2nd ed

Bruce Tuckman

Hoboken, New Jersey: Wiley, 2002
512pp, ISBN: 978-0-471-06322-3

This describes the latest fixed-income concepts, securities, analytical techniques, and models, using a topical approach to application and risk control. As new securities are introduced that are an increasingly risky, this presents a useful framework for pricing and hedging fixed-income securities in an accessible way, backed up by a range of examples, applications, and case studies.

Fixed Income Securities and Derivatives Handbook: Analysis and Valuation

Moorad Choudhry (editor)

Princeton, New Jersey: Bloomberg Press, 2005
355pp, ISBN: 978-1-57660-164-8

This comprehensive guide presents a combination of academic theory and market practice to describe the full range of methodologies, techniques, and applications used in the analysis and valuation of principal debt market instruments and their associated derivatives. It shows how bonds are structured, valued, and traded, and presents a framework for understanding fixed-income analytics in a practical way, based around individual requirements.

Fixed Income Strategy: A Practitioner's Guide to Riding the Curve

Tamara Mast Henderson

Wiley Finance Series
Chichester, UK: Wiley, 2003
204pp, ISBN: 978-0-470-85063-3

This presents a practical approach to developing a successful fixed-income investing and trading strategy, combining an understanding of both theoretical models and practical market experience. It shows how to use models to your advantage, how to structure trades that are based on different strategic perspectives, and introduces the most relevant aspects of risk management necessary for practitioners.

The Handbook of Fixed Income Securities, 7th ed

Frank J. Fabozzi (editor)

New York: McGraw-Hill, 2005
1,495pp, ISBN: 978-0-07-144099-8

This authoritative guide to fixed-income securities, now in its seventh edition, is a popular reference, written by a team of leading academics and practitioners. It provides all the necessary details and formulas to keep pace with recent changes, focusing on applications, electronic trading, and global portfolio management, as well as containing new analysis of Eurobonds, emerging market debt, credit risk modeling, synthetics, credit derivatives, and transition management.

An Introduction to Bond Markets, 3rd ed

Moorad Choudhry

Securities Institute Series
Chichester, UK: Wiley, 2006
405pp, ISBN: 978-0-470-01758-6

This bond market primer describes the different types of bonds traded in the capital markets, and the analytical techniques used by traders and fund managers. It presents the latest developments and market practice in bonds, focusing on bond yield measurement, interest rate risk, the UK gilt market and corporate debt markets, risk management, off-balance sheet instruments, including swaps and options, and the emerging markets.

Investing in Fixed Income Securities: Understanding the Bond Market

Gary Strumeyer

Wiley Finance Series
Hoboken, New Jersey: Wiley, 2005
514pp, ISBN: 978-0-471-46512-6

This is a practical overview of fixed-income securities and markets for both investors and market professionals. It presents the basic bond market concepts and terminology, compares different debt instruments, and describes strategies for managing a diversified portfolio. It also offers advice on maximizing investment value, applying appropriate valuation methods to a variety of fixed-income securities, and explains macro-economic concepts and their impact on the bond market.

Naked Guide to Bonds: What You Need to Know—Stripped Down to the Bare Essentials

Michael V. Brandes

Hoboken, New Jersey: Wiley, 2003
242pp, ISBN: 978-0-471-46221-7

Using plenty of examples from the bond market, this primer for investors describes the best way to achieve a balanced, diversified portfolio. It presents insights into the full range of instruments, characteristics, structures, and strategies for the fixed-income asset class in an easy learning style, focusing on the most important factors in the investment decision process.

The Only Guide to a Winning Bond Strategy You'll Ever Need: The Way Smart Money Preserves Wealth Today

Larry E. Swedroe, Joseph H. Hempen

New York: St. Martin's Press, 2006
260pp, ISBN: 978-0-312-35363-6

This accessible guide explains the standard techniques for investing in bonds and other fixed-income securities, describing their use, how the bond market works, and how and why each security may or may not be suitable for a portfolio. It also presents useful investment tips, such as buying bonds with the highest ratings, avoiding buying hybrid securities, and not trying to time the market.

Strategic Asset Allocation in Fixed Income Markets: A Matlab Based User's Guide

Ken Nyholm

Wiley Finance Series
Hoboken, New Jersey: Wiley, 2008
186pp, ISBN: 978-0-470-75362-0

With Matlab now used by most investment banks, this guide shows how to implement financial and econometric models using applying Matlab-based computational techniques, with an emphasis on fixed-income finance. It introduces all concepts and techniques from a basic level, from fundamental aspects such as price-yield conversions to more complex topics such as term structure modeling and strategic asset allocation, with detailed descriptions of the programming steps involved.

Valuing Fixed Income Futures

David Boberski

McGraw-Hill Library Investment and Finance Series
New York: McGraw-Hill, 2007
239pp, ISBN: 978-0-07-147541-9

This is a practical assessment of the role of futures in the fixed-income marketplace, which analyzes how to measure the performance of Treasury and Eurodollar futures, and build empirical models to measure risk. It discusses major changes in trading, and explains the technology for understanding price behavior, and the development of frameworks for solving embedded option valuation in Treasury and Eurodollar futures.

JOURNALS

Journal of Fixed Income

Institutional Investor
Journals Group, 225 Park Avenue South, New York, NY 10003, USA
T: +1 212 224 3570
F: +1 212 224 3197
www.iijournals.com/JFI
ISSN: 1059-8596

This quarterly journal provides research and case studies on both bond theory and practice. Its papers are focused on the analysis of fixed-income structuring, performance tracking, and risk management, and cover bonds, municipals, ABSs,

MBSs, CDOs, and credit derivatives. It also discusses relative risk and return features between different securities and markets, security performance under varying economic conditions, valuation techniques, and distressed securities.

INTERNET

Bond Market Prices

www.bondmarketprices.com

This website is for private investors, and offers access to the TRAX database of bond prices and other information produced by international bond dealers. It includes data on both sterling-denominated and foreign currency bonds trading in the international capital markets.

Bondscape

www.bondscape.net

This website is a free service that provides easy access to the bond market in the UK, and offers price and yield analysis, and research. It provides brokers and other professional investment advisers with the ability to trade bonds in smaller sizes, offering equity-style online dealing capabilities with multiple market makers.

Fixed Income Investor

www.fixedincomeinvestor.co.uk

This online resource provides visibility, education, and research on bonds and other sterling-denominated, fixed-income securities. It is aimed at private investors and their advisers wanting an understanding of these markets, to be able to compare and evaluate the available securities, and identify investment opportunities. It provides analysis and comment, as well as coverage of bond prices and yields, monthly bankers, and model portfolios.

InvestinginBonds.com

www.investinginbonds.com

This is a resource on bonds created by the Securities Industry and Financial Markets Association to help educate investors. It is for all level of investor wanting bond price information, and includes a wide variety of market data, news, commentary, and information about the bond markets.

Reuters Fixed Income Services Financial Glossary

www.ejv.com/bp/html/glossary3.html

This is an online glossary that provides definitions on all the main terminology relating to fixed-income products and markets.

ORGANIZATIONS

Europe

Committee of European Securities Regulators

Chair: Eddy Wymeersch
11–13 avenue de Friedland, 75008 Paris, France
T: +33 1 58 36 43 21
F: +33 1 58 36 43 30
E: secretariat@cesr.eu
www.cesr-eu.org

CESR is an independent committee that works to improve co-ordination among securities regulators, to develop effective operational network mechanisms to enhance day-to-day consistent supervision and enforcement of the single market for financial services, and act as an advisory group to assist the EU Commission.

USA

Fixed Income Analysts Society

Chair: Alex Golbin
244 Fifth Avenue, Suite L230, New York, NY 10001, USA
T: +1 212 726 8100
E: fiasi@fiasi.org
www.fiasi.org

FIASI is a non-profit, professional society of fixed-income professionals from all disciplines and all sectors, which is dedicated to the education of its membership and the fixed-income community at large. It provides a member forum on issues affecting the industry, and sponsors educational programs and workshops covering topics of current interest.

BRIC

The Fixed Income Money Market and Derivatives Association of India

Chair: V. Srikanth
52, 5th Floor, Mittal Chambers, Nariman Point, Mumbai 400021, India
T: +011 91 2202 5725
F: +011 91 2202 5739
E: fimmda@fimmda.org
www.fimmda.org

FIMMDA is a voluntary association for the bond, money, and derivatives markets, comprising of commercial banks, financial institutions, and primary dealers in India. It represents members, promotes the development of these markets, works with regulators, adopts and develops international standard practices and a code of conduct, and undertakes development, training, and the standardization of best market practices.

International

Commercial Mortgage Securities Association

Chair: J. Christopher Hoeffel
30 Broad Street, 28th Floor, New York, NY 10004-2304, USA
T: +1 212 509 1844
F: +1 212 509 1895
E: info@cmsaglobal.org
www.cmsaglobal.org

This is an international, member-driven, trade association for the commercial real estate capital markets. It acts to promote the liquidity, and viability of commercial real estate capital market finance worldwide, and in setting industry standards, and educating professionals. It represents the full range of the industry's market participants, including senior bank executives, rating agencies, insurance companies, investors, lenders, and service providers.

International Capital Market Association

Chair: Hans-Joerg Rudloff
Talacker 29, PO Box, 8022 Zurich, Switzerland
T: +41 44 363 4222
F: +41 44 363 7772
www.icmagroup.org

ICMA is a self-regulatory organization that represents a broad range of capital market interests, including global investment banks, regional banks, asset managers, exchanges, central banks, law firms, and other professional advisers. Its market conventions and standards provide a framework of rules governing market practice, it promotes the capital markets by bringing together market participants, and also undertakes educational and research programs.

The International Organization of Securities Commissions

Chair: Jean-Pierre Jouyet
C/Oquendo 12, 28006 Madrid, Spain
T: +34 91 417 55 49
F: +34 91 555 93 68
E: mail@iosco.org
www.iosco.org

This international body promotes co-operation among securities commissions to assist high standards of regulation and just, efficient and sound markets, the exchange of information to promote the development of domestic markets, efforts to establish standards and effective surveillance of international securities transactions, and mutual assistance to promote the integrity of the markets by a rigorous application of the standards and by effective enforcement.

Securities Industry and Financial Markets Association

Chair: Timothy Ryan
120 Broadway, 35th Floor, New York, NY 10271-0080, USA
T: +1 212 313 1200
F: +1 212 313 1301
E: inquiry@sifma.org
www.sifma.org

SIFMA, created through a merger of the Bond Market Association and the Securities Industry Association, is a global, member-driven organization for professionals in the financial services industry. With offices in the US, Europe and Asia, it represents investment banks, broker-dealers, and asset managers, and other institutions, such as exchanges, government-sponsored enterprises, rating agencies, service providers, industry utilities, and law firms.

     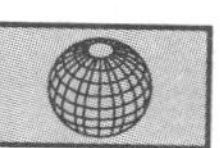   

Budgeting

BOOKS

Beyond Budgeting: How Managers Can Break Free from the Annual Performance Trap

Jeremy Hope, Robin Fraser

Boston, Massachusetts: Harvard Business School Press, 2003

256pp, ISBN: 978-1-57851-866-1

An enlightening read for all managers, not just finance specialists, this book posits that traditional budgeting processes are unproductive. Recognizing the fact that many executives are forced to spend their time "making the numbers work" rather than making the most of their company's potential, the book offers an alternative way forward. Case studies and findings from the *Beyond Budgeting* Roundtable are also included.

Budgeting: Technology, Trends, Software Selection and Implementation

Nils H. Rasmussen, Christopher J. Eichorn

New York: Wiley, 2000

304pp, ISBN: 978-0-471-39207-1

Describing itself as a guide to "essential budget planning for the 21st century corporation," this practically oriented book introduces and explains new trends in budgeting and budgeting software. By means of various report and contract samples, questionnaires, and interviews with leading managers, it guides the reader through the range of considerations that are crucial to streamlining the budget-planning process.

Budgeting Basics and Beyond, 3rd ed

Jae K. Shim, Joel G. Siegel

Chichester, UK: Wiley, 2008

448pp, ISBN: 978-0-470-38968-3

Budgeting Basics and Beyond takes the reader through every step to handle budgeting process. Some of the extra features include Balanced Scorecard, budgeting for nonprofit organizations, business simulations for executive and management training.

Capital Budgeting: Theory and Practice

Pamela P. Peterson, Frank J. Fabozzi

New York: Wiley, 2002

243pp, ISBN: 978-0-471-21833-3

The book covers the underlying principles of capital budgeting, including discounted net cash-flows, risk assessment, and leases. It explains the importance of making wise decisions when investing in long-lived assets, and provides quantitative decision-making tools that assist managers in choosing between options.

Capital Budgeting Decision: Economic Analysis of Investment Projects

Harold Bierman, Jr, Seymour Smidt

Abingdon, UK: Routledge, 2006

402pp, ISBN: 978-0-415-40004-6

This provides the corporate decision-maker with practical information on choices related to the elements of risk and time. It focuses on the theme of Net Present Value (NPV), and how it can be used as a single measure of value. It also covers areas such as distribution policy and capital budgeting, form investing in a second firm, and investing in current assets. The book is easy to understand and will enable readers to make smart capital budgeting decisions for any corporation.

Cash Flow Strategies: Innovation in Nonprofit Financial Management

Richard S. Linzer, Anna O. Linzer

San Francisco, California: Jossey-Bass, 2007

272pp, ISBN: 978-0-7879-8147-1

Cash Flow Strategies provides nonprofit organizations with new methods for handling financial management. It emphasizes the use of cash flow concepts that help an organization gain the working capital it needs. This book includes illustrative examples, tools, and templates which can be applied to any institution.

Cash Management: Making your Business Cash-Rich... Without Breaking the Bank

Tony Dalton

Business on a Shoestring Series

London: A&C Black Publishers, 2007

208pp, ISBN: 978-0-7136-7706-5

If you run your own business, keeping an eye on your cash is one of your most important tasks. Packed with ideas that really work, real-life examples, step-by-step advice and sources of further information.

Credit Risk Management: A Guide to Sound Business Decisions

H. A. Schaeffer, Jr

Chichester, UK: Wiley, 2000

288pp, ISBN: 978-0-471-35020-0

This book examines the steps leading to a sound business credit decision. It is divided into four main sections: analysis for creative credit management; building up essential business credit information; considering all factors that affect the business credit decision; and making a decision or recommendation. Detailed case studies are provided, illustrating common problems along with their solutions.

Foundations of Multinational Financial Management, 6th ed

Alan C. Shapiro, Atulya Sarin

Steps to Success Series

Hoboken, New Jersey: Wiley, 2008

542pp, ISBN: 978-0-470-12895-4

This focuses on expansive practices, and provides a clear conceptual framework for analyzing key financial decisions in multinational firms. It treats international financial management as a natural and logical extension of the principles learned in the foundations course in financial management. It also builds on and extends the valuation framework provided by domestic corporate finance, to account for aspects that are unique to international finance.

Get to Grips with Budgets: How to Take the Stress Out of Working with Numbers

London: A&C Black Publishers, 2005

96pp, ISBN: 978-0-7475-7734-8

Aimed at anyone who has to work with numbers but who feels uncomfortable with them, this is a practical and down-to-earth guide to budgeting. Featuring a special jargon-busting section, it covers a wide range of key issues including drawing up and managing budgets, keeping on top of costs, solving cash-flow problems, and interpreting balance sheets and profit and loss accounts.

Good Finance Guide for Small Businesses: How to Raise, Manage and Grow Your Company's Cash

London: A&C Black Publishers, 2007

288pp, ISBN: 978-0-7136-8209-0

Cash—or the lack of it—keeps small business owners awake at night more than anything else. This one-stop guide to small business finance is invaluable for anyone who needs to raise money to launch or grow a business, or manage the finances of one they run already. It covers five key areas: getting off the ground; managing your money; getting paid on time; company admin, tax and payroll, and coping in a crisis.

Implementing Beyond Budgeting: Unlocking the Performance Potential

Bjarte Bogsnes

Hoboken, New Jersey: Wiley, 2008

240pp, ISBN: 978-0-470-40516-1

Implementing Beyond Budgeting presents practices from real-life cases. It explains how an organization can fully utilize a performance climate with teams attaining the same target, rewards, and value creation, and examines how every organization can motivate the ambition and energy of its people under pressure from the budgeting process.

Management Accounting in Health Care Organizations, 2nd ed

David W. Young

San Francisco, California: Jossey-Bass, 2008

688pp, ISBN: 978-0-470-30021-3

This provides a clear understanding of accounting principles, concepts, and techniques that lead to managerial decision-making in health care. It also covers full-cost accounting, differential cost accounting, and responsibility accounting. Case-based problems are presented which highlight the lessons, and each chapter includes learning objectives, standard introductions, and key terms.

Managing by the Numbers

Chuck Kremer, Ron Rizzuto, John Case

Cambridge, Massachusetts: Perseus Books Group, 2000

198pp, ISBN: 978-0-7382-0256-3

In this text, Chuck Kremer and Ron Rizzuto present a practical approach to reading financial statements and to managing the three core issues of business financial performance: net profit, operating cash-flow, and return on assets. The book features numerous exercises and examples (with associated templates available on the web), a powerful new management tool known as The Financial Scoreboard, and an extensive glossary.

Mastering Spreadsheet Budgets and Forecasts: How to Save Time and Gain Control of Your Business

Malcolm Secrett

Smarter Solutions Series
Harlow, UK: FT Prentice Hall, 1999
272pp, ISBN: 978-0-273-64491-0

This step-by-step, jargon-free guide demonstrates the advantages and potential of using spreadsheets to prepare and present budgets and forecasts. It includes examples of budgets and forecasts, followed through completely from beginning to end.

Total Business Budgeting: A Step-by-Step Guide with Forms, 2nd ed

Robert Rachlin

Chichester, UK: Wiley, 1999
321pp, ISBN: 978-0-471-35103-0

Rachlin provides an introduction to a wide range of budgetary techniques and applications and shows how to analyze outside influences, develop performance targets and budgeting segments, and administer the right budgeting processes. He includes detailed instructions, forms, examples, schedules, and formats.

MAGAZINES

Business Performance Management

Penton Technology Media
221 East 29th Street, Loveland, CO 80538, USA
T: +1 847 763 9504
F: +1 913 514 3621
bpmmag.net
ISSN: 1556-813X

BPM magazine educates business, finance, and IT employees about the opportunities for changing their organization's effectiveness through the application of BPM processes. It includes analysis and advice on BPM best practices, industry trends, and research results, as well as features such as case studies where corporate users of BPM explain how they fully utilize these processes and technologies. It is published quarterly.

CMA Management

Certified Management Accountants of Canada
1 Robert Speck Parkway, Suite 1400, Mississauga, ON, L4Z 3M3, Canada
T: +1 905 949 4200
F: +1 905 949 0888
www.managementmag.com
ISSN: 1490-4225

CMA is a monthly magazine that covers all aspects of management. It includes trends, views, media, business strategies, government issues and global views.

Strategic Finance

Institute of Management Accountants
10 Paragon Drive, Suite 1, Montvale, NJ 07645, USA
T: +1 201 573 9000
F: +1 201 474 1600
www.imanet.org/publications_sfm.asp
ISSN: 1524-833X

Strategic Finance magazine provides information about practices and trends in finance, accounting, and information management that will impact members (mostly controllers, CFOs, and their staff) and their jobs. It offers advice to help financial professionals perform their jobs more effectively, advance their careers, grow personally and professionally, and make their organizations more profitable.

INTERNET

Accountants World

www.accountantsworld.com

This is an extensive portal based in the United States with links to a wide range of websites of interest to accountants. It relates mainly to US accounting practice.

Accounting Web

www.accountingweb.co.uk

This site is an extensive online resource based in the United Kingdom. It contains material intended for accountancy and finance professionals from a number of providers. It has received an award as the New Media Business Website of the Year.

CFO.com—Tools and Resources for Financial Executives

www.cfo.com

CFO.com is a great resource for anyone in a business financial setting. With multiple articles to read, CFO.com also has a newsletter, webcasts, and a magazine, which was named Magazine of the Year by the American Society of Business Publication Editors (ASBPE).

The Dyer Partnership

www.dyerpartnership.us

The site provides a wide range of information on UK tax and accounting matters and other business issues of interest to owners and managers of UK businesses.

Institute of Management Accountants

www.imanet.org

This is the website of the Institute of Management Accountants (IMA), a professional organization that promotes management accounting and financial management. The IMA is responsible for the education and certification of professionals involved in management accounting, including operational and capital budgeting responsibilities. Members of the IMA receive information and educational materials on financial budgeting and control, capital budgeting, and management accounting topics.

ORGANIZATIONS

Europe

Institute of Credit Management (ICM)

The Water Mill, Station Road, South Luffenham, Oakham, Leicestershire, LE15 8NB, UK
T: +44 (0) 1780 722 900
F: +44 (0) 1780 721 333
E: info@icm.org.uk
www.icm.org.uk

The Institute of Credit Management (ICM) is the largest organization of credit professionals in Europe, and the focal point in the United Kingdom for all matters relating to credit management and its ancillary functions. The ICM sets professional standards and tests and assesses those who wish to gain its professional qualification. It also provides advice to government and other national bodies.

Institute of Financial Accountants (IFA)

Burford House, 44 London Road, Sevenoaks, Kent, TN13 1AS, UK
T: +44 (0) 1732 458 080
F: +44 (0) 1732 455 848
E: mail@ifa.org.uk
www.ifa.org.uk

The Institute of Financial Accountants, established in 1916, is the largest professional body of its type in the world. It represents members and students in more than 80 countries around the world and provides a qualification and continuing professional development for those who want to become financial accountants. It also sets both technical and ethical standards within the profession.

BRIC

The Association of Certified Treasury Managers

52, Nagarjuna Hills, Panjagutta, Hyderabad, 500 082, India
T: +91 040 335 3411/1071/3748
E: k_seethapathi@actmindia.org

ACTM is a non-profit society that helps to develop new treasury professionals through a certification program in treasury and forex management and standards for professional practice and ethics. It develops and regulates the growth of the profession of treasury management on sound ethical lines, organizes seminars, workshops and training programs in treasury management, foreign exchange management, risk management and allied areas, undertakes research, and offers industry publications.

The National Association of Financial Market Institutions

Av. República do Chile, 230/13o andar, Centro, Rio de Janeiro 20031-170, Brazil
T: +55 21 3814 3800
F: +55 21 3814 3960
E: brazildebt@fazenda.gov.br

ANDIMA is a non-profit civil entity that brings together several financial institutions in Brazil. It is a service-provider, offering technical and operating support to these institutions, provides daily monitoring of market behavior with the dissemination of statistical data, monitoring legislation, preparing analyses, studies and reports on key economic issues, and produces a program of professional training.

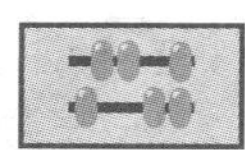

Business Appraisal and Performance Measurement

BOOKS

Assessing Business Excellence: A Guide to Self Assessment, 2nd ed

Les Porter, Steve Tanner

Oxford: Butterworth-Heinemann, 2004
468pp, ISBN: 978-0-7506-5517-0

A strategic framework to help companies achieve business excellence and total quality management is presented in this well-informed guide. The main quality frameworks are introduced and compared, before the self-assessment process is examined.

The Balanced Scorecard

Robert S. Kaplan, David P. Norton

Boston, Massachusetts: Harvard Business School Press, 1996
322pp, ISBN: 978-0-87584-651-4

This book demonstrates to managers how to utilize their people to fulfill the company's mission. It shows how to channel the energies, abilities, and specific knowledge belonging to each individual into the achievement of long-term strategic goals for the company. The balanced scorecard is a measurement tool, but it is also a management tool for investing in the long term in customers, employees, new product development, and systems.

The Balanced Scorecard Step-by-Step: Maximizing Performance and Maintaining Results, 2nd ed

Paul R. Niven

Chichester, UK: Wiley, 2006
336pp, ISBN: 978-0-471-78049-6

This book gives valuable advice on developing a performance management system. Areas covered in this text include: the development of performance objectives and measures; the finalizing of cause and effect links; methods of embedding the balanced scorecard in the organization and sustaining its implementation; and procedures for implementing the balanced scorecard in nonprofit and public sector organizations.

Beyond Registration: Getting the Best from ISO9001 and Business Improvement, 3rd ed

Steve Tanner, Mike Bailey, Charles Pertwee

London: British Standards Institution, 2007
120pp, ISBN: 978-0-580-50363-4

The first part of this book covers ISO9001 and the Malcolm Baldrige EFQM excellence models, while the second looks at a wide range of business improvement approaches, including the balanced scorecard, benchmarking, business process reengineering, Charter Mark, failure mode effect analysis, Investors in People, kaizen/continuous improvement, Six Sigma, statistical process control, theory of constraints, total productive maintenance, and total quality management (TQM).

Business Performance Measurement: Unifying Theory and Integrating Practice, 2nd ed

Andy Neely (editor)

Cambridge, UK: Cambridge University Press, 2008
528pp, ISBN: 978-0-521-85511-2

Drawing together contributions from leading thinkers around the world, this reviews recent developments in the theory and practice of performance measurement and management. Significantly updated and modified from the first edition, it includes 10 new chapters which review performance measurement from the perspectives of accounting, marketing, operations, public services, and supply-chain management.

Corporate Valuation: Tools for Effective Appraisal and Decision Making

Bradford Cornell

Business One Series
Maidenhead, UK: McGraw-Hill, 1993
303pp, ISBN: 978-1-55623-730-0

This book illustrates the best practices for measuring and predicting value by combining the science of business appraisal with the art of perceived value. It provides a tool for comparing various valuation techniques, and shows how to rethink the investment process into the future.

Cost Benefit Analysis: Concepts and Practice

Anthony E. Boardman, David H. Greenberg, Aidan R. Vining, David Leo Weimer

Harlow, UK: Prentice Hall, 2006
560pp, ISBN: 978-0-13-143583-4

This book includes a number of up-to-date illustrations and examples to show how theories and techniques are applied to real-world situations. It provides readers with a practical orientation and introduction to cost-benefit analysis through problem solving. There are problems and exercises at the end of all chapters.

Determining Value: Valuation Models and Financial Statements

Richard Barker

Harlow, UK: FT Prentice Hall, 2001
232pp, ISBN: 978-0-273-63979-4

This is designed for members of the professional and private investment community, including stockbrokers, fund managers, corporate financiers and bankers, and advanced students of finance and accounting. It provides a comprehensive overview of valuation methods such as price-earnings ratio, dividend yield and EVA (economic value added), and analyzes the quality and availability of the financial data used in these models. It also covers stock market valuation, dividends and stock prices, price-earnings ratio, measuring earnings, measuring return on capital, and cash-flow models from stockholder value analysis to cash-flow return on investment (CFROI).

Essentials of Balanced Scorecard

Mohan Nair

Essentials Series
Chichester, UK: Wiley, 2004
248pp, ISBN: 978-0-471-56973-2

Taking simplicity as a guiding principle, this sets out to help managers understand the fundamentals of the balanced scorecard. The concept is introduced and the four perspectives that make up the methodology are outlined. The relationship of the balanced scorecard to strategy and performance management is also examined. It also identifies and describes six factors that make for success in implementing the balanced scorecard and discusses the 11 deadly sins that can lead to failure.

Essentials of Corporate Performance Measurement

George T. Friedlob, Lydia L. F. Schleifer, Franklin J. Plewa

Essentials Series
New York: Wiley, 2002
216pp, ISBN: 978-0-471-20375-9

The most common way to evaluate the success of investment is by measuring the return on investment (ROI). This practical guide explains the importance of ROI and examines its use to analyze performance. Different forms of ROI are described and its use in analyzing sales revenues, costs, and profits is considered. The techniques of return on technology investment (ROTI and ROIT) are also covered, as are residual performance measures (RI and EVA).

The EVA Challenge: Implementing Value-Added Change in an Organization

Joel M. Stern, John S. Shiely

New York: Wiley, 2004
250pp, ISBN: 978-0-471-47889-8

This is an accessible and practical account of EVA, which measures the financial performance of a company, and presents a strategy for creating corporate and shareholder wealth. It details what exactly EVA is, how to calculate it, what information it can provide shareholders, and how to customize and implement EVA at any level of a company.

Evaluation in Organizations: A Systematic Approach to Enhancing Learning, Performance, and Change, 2nd ed

Darlene Russ-Eft, Hallie Preskill

Harvard Business Review Paperbacks Series
Cambridge, Massachusetts: Perseus Books Group, 2009
416pp, ISBN: 978-0-465-01866-6

This book is a guide to the context of evaluation and to its implementation in a three-phase system. It includes an audit mechanism and comprehensive resources.

  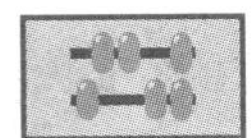      

Harvard Business Review on Measuring Corporate Performance

Boston, Massachusetts: Harvard Business School Press, 1998
224pp, ISBN: 978-0-87584-882-2

A collection of articles from leading management thinkers, this book shows how to evaluate performance measures and discusses the importance of aligning corporate strategy with them. It includes discussion of the balanced scorecard, customer relationships, internal business processes, and employee learning.

How to Use The Model: Implementing the EFQM Excellence Model

British Quality Foundation

London: British Quality Foundation, 2002
48pp, ISBN: 978-1-899358-50-2

This booklet provides an introduction to the EFQM business excellence model, describes in detail the criteria used in it, and sets out the procedures that an organization needs to consider, plan, and complete. It should help anyone who is trying to raise awareness of the Excellence Model within their organization, encourage self-assessment, and improve the organization's efficiency and effectiveness.

Implementing Global Performance Measurement Systems: A Cookbook Approach to Evaluation

Ferdinand Tesoro, Jack Tootson

San Francisco, California: Jossey-Bass, 2000
176pp, ISBN: 978-0-7879-4744-6

This practical guide presents a step-by-step approach to evaluating and measuring ongoing business performance. Following an overview of performance measurement, it examines how to establish the business case, identify the right performance metrics, implement the performance measurement system, and leverage results to improve performance. Guidance is offered on constructing a line graph, a cause–effect diagram, and a scatter diagram.

Making Scorecards Actionable: Balancing Strategy and Control

Nils-Goran Olve et al.

Chichester, UK: Wiley, 2003
304pp, ISBN: 978-0-470-84871-5

Focusing on the experiences of a broad range of companies and looks at the challenges and key design issues that emerge as scorecards are put into operation. Practical guidance on operational issues is provided, which covers assigning roles and responsibilities, balancing the incentive system, and using IT. Case studies of a number of well-known companies such as Skandia, British Airways, Ericsson, Xerox, Volvo, and Hewlett Packard are included.

Natural Capitalism: Creating the Next Industrial Revolution

Paul Hawken, Amory Lovins, L. Hunter Lovins

Boston, Massachusetts: Back Bay Books, 2000
396pp, ISBN: 978-0-316-35300-7

This discusses how top companies are carrying out a modern form of industrialism which runs more smoothly, increases profits, lessens damage to the environment, and creates more jobs. They call this system "natural capitalism" and give several examples of organizations which have benefited the environment.

Oliver Wight ABCD Checklist for Operational Excellence, 5th ed

Oliver Wight International

New York: Wiley, 2000
176pp, ISBN: 978-0-471-38819-7

The Oliver Wight ABCD Checklists are a widely recognized tool used by organizations as part of an appraisal of their performance. The aim of this checklist is to become an industry standard for operational performance measurement. Beginning with an explanation of the use of the performance measures, the assessment tool then focuses on strategic planning, people and teams, total quality and continuous improvement, new product development, and planning and control.

The Organizational Measurement Manual

David Wealleans

Aldershot, UK: Gower Publishing, 2001
178pp, ISBN: 978-0-566-08349-5

Divided into three parts—the concept of measurement, establishing a process measurement program, and looking beyond the basics—this book gives a guide to performance measurements at the working level. It identifies procedures for using measurements and shows how to relate them to organizational objectives and initiatives. Wealleans demonstrates a best-practice approach, and illustrates his text with figures and tables throughout.

Performance Scorecards

Richard Y. Chang, Mark W. Morgan

San Francisco, California: Jossey-Bass, 2000
224pp, ISBN: 978-0-7879-5272-3

The authors contend that many corporations have too many performance measurements, which causes them to lose sight of the ones that are really important. They advocate customizing performance scorecards to suit an organization's strategy. The book uses a fictional storyline to illustrate the six steps that go into performance scorecards: collect, create, cultivate, cascade, connect, and confirm.

Strategy-Focused Organization: How Balanced Scorecard Companies Thrive in the New Business Environment

Robert S. Kaplan, David P. Norton

Boston, Massachusetts: Harvard Business School Press, 2000
416pp, ISBN: 978-1-57851-250-8

This book presents case studies of over twenty companies that have adopted the balanced scorecard approach. Five principles for strategy-focused organizations, drawn from their experiences, are outlined in this text. These are: translating the strategy into operational terms; aligning the organization to strategy; making strategy everyone's everyday job; making strategy a continual process; and mobilizing change through effective leadership.

Strategy Maps: Converting Intangible Assets into Tangible Outcomes

Robert S. Kaplan, David P. Norton

Boston, Massachusetts: Harvard Business School Press, 2003
324pp, ISBN: 978-1-59139-134-0

This book explores what a strategy map is—a tool that can provide the missing link between strategy formulation and implementation. Derived from the balanced scorecard technique devised by the authors, *Strategy Maps* provides a blueprint for describing, measuring, and aligning tangible assets for superior performance. Through numerous examples of private, public, and nonprofit organizations, the process of creating customized strategy maps is explained.

Total Performance Scorecard: Redefining Management to Achieve Performance with Integrity

Hubert K. Rampersad

Oxford: Butterworth-Heinemann, 2003
336pp, ISBN: 978-0-7506-7714-1

Rampersad introduces a new concept of improvement and change management called the Total Performance Scorecard (TPS). This model integrates aspects of the balanced scorecard, total quality management and competence management. It is based around a cyclical process of continuous improvement, development, and learning and also takes account of the connections between personal and organizational development. Model appraisal forms and scorecard questions are included in appendices.

Valuation: Measuring and Managing the Value of Companies, 4th ed

Tim Koller, Marc Goedhart, David Wessels

Chichester, UK: Wiley, 2005
768pp, ISBN: 978-0-471-70218-4

At the crossroads of corporate strategy and finance lies valuation. And in today's economy, whether you're a seasoned manager or a budding business professional, it's essential to excel at measuring, managing, and maximizing shareholder and company value. This book explains how to do just that.

Valuation Workbook: Step-by-Step Exercises and Tests to Help You Master Valuation, 4th ed

Tim Koller, Marc Goedhart, David Wessels, Jeffrey P. Lessard

Chichester, UK: Wiley, 2006
200pp, ISBN: 978-0-471-70216-0

The ideal companion to *Valuation*. This comprehensive study guide provides you with an invaluable opportunity to explore your understanding of the strategies and techniques covered in the main text, before putting it to work in real-world situations.

The Value Mindset: Returning to the First Principles of Capitalist Enterprise

Erik Stern, Mike Hutchinson

Chichester, UK: Wiley, 2004
456pp, ISBN: 978-0-471-65029-4

In *The Value Mindset* the authors present their ideas as to how companies can transform themselves to deliver value and returns to shareholders. Building on their experience of EVA (Economic Value Added) programs at Stern Stewart, they explain the development of the WAI (Wealth Added Index) performance metric and illustrate the concept of the value mindset through real-world success stories, such as those of Isadore Sharp at the Four Seasons hotel chain and Roberto Goizueta at Coca-Cola. The theory and practice of strategic reconfiguration is described, and a number of related issues including financial architecture and the motivation of managers and employees are explored.

Valuing a Business: The Analysis and Appraisal of Closely-Held Companies, 5th ed

Shannon P. Pratt, Robert F. Reilly, Robert P. Schweihs

Maidenhead, UK: McGraw-Hill, 2007

1000pp, ISBN: 978-0-07-144180-3

This latest edition, originally published in 1981, includes significant revisions and ten new chapters. Its coverage now extends to topics such as credentials and standards, analyzing financial statements, control and acquisition premiums, valuing debt securities and litigation support. The book is a standard reference for defining the methodology of business valuation—for businesses of all sizes—and then arriving at an accurate and supportable estimation of value.

MAGAZINES

Balanced Scorecard Report

Harvard Business School Press
PO Box 257, Shrub Oak, NY 10588-0257, USA
T: +1 800 668 6705
F: +1 914 962 1338
hbp.harvardbusiness.org/ep
ISSN: 1526-145X

This monthly newsletter, developed in conjunction with David S. Kaplan and David P. Norton, creators of the balanced scorecard, provides the latest research and implementation news from companies using the balanced scorecard management system.

The Value Examiner

The National Association of Certified Valuation Analysts
1111 Brickyard Road, Suite 200, Salt Lake City, UT 84106-5401, USA
T: +1 801 486 0600
F: +1 801 486 7500
www.nacva.com/examiner/examiner.asp

This bimonthly magazine focuses on the latest developments regarding industry issues. It covers a variety of industry related topics, such as trends, forecasts and the latest technology resources, and provides the resources needed for business appraisal professionals.

JOURNALS

Business Valuation Review

American Society of Appraisers
555 Herndon Parkway, Suite 125, Herndon, VI 20170, USA
T: +1 703 478 2228
F: +1 703 742 8471
www.bvappraisers.org/issuestore
ISSN: 0882-2875

This quarterly journal features articles on the practice and theory of appraisal. The articles present various opinions on the latest trends in business. The journal will be beneficial for any business valuation professional.

Performance Evaluation: An International Journal

Elsevier
Radarweg 29, Amsterdam 1043 NX, The Netherlands
T: +31 20 485 3911
F: +31 20 485 2457
www.elsevier.com/locate/peva
ISSN: 0166-5316

This journal provides information relative to performance aspects, promotes interdisciplinary flow of technical information among researchers and professionals, and serves as a publication medium for various special interest groups in the performance community at large.

INTERNET

Balanced Scorecard Collaborative

www.thepalladiumgroup.com

The website of Robert Kaplan and David Norton, creators of the balanced scorecard. Their professional services company provides training, networking events, and BSC software certification. The bimonthly *Balanced Scorecard Report* magazine is also available to members through the website.

College of Performance Management

www.pmi-cpm.org

Sponsored by a nonprofit professional organization, the site offers news, information about events and conferences, and links.

Execution Premium

hbp.harvardbusiness.org/ep/

The website of performance Gurus Robert S. Kaplan and David P. Norton, which contains their blog, publication information, and other resources.

Interthink Consulting, Inc.

www.interthink.ca

Sponsored by a Canadian consulting firm, the site includes research on topics including assessment, processes, training, and implementation, and a newsletter of industry events.

ORGANIZATIONS

Europe

British Chambers of Commerce

65 Petty France, London, SW1H 9EU, UK
T: +44 (0) 20 7654 5800
F: +44 (0) 20 7654 5819
E: info@britishchambers.org.uk
www.britishchambers.org.uk

This is an umbrella body for a national network of chambers of commerce serving local businesses and providing advice on exporting and export services to member companies.

British Quality Foundation (BQF)

32-34 Great Peter Street, London, SW1P 2QX, UK
T: +44 (0) 20 7654 5000
F: +44 (0) 20 7654 5001
www.quality-foundation.co.uk

The BQF is a nonprofit membership organization that promotes business excellence to other public and private sector organizations in the United Kingdom. It undertakes numerous activities in pursuit of this aim, most of which have the Business Excellence Model at their core. It also sponsors the UK Business Excellence Award.

European Foundation for Quality Management (EFQM)

Avenue des Pléiades 15, 1200 Brussels, Belgium
T: +33 2 775 35 11
F: +33 2 775 35 35
E: info@efqm.org
www.efqm.org

The EFQM introduced the European Excellence Model in the early 1990s to help businesses assess and improve their performance.

USA

American Society of Appraisers (ASA)

555 Herndon Parkway, Suite 125, Herndon, VI 20170, USA
T: +1 703 478 2228
F: +1 703 742 8471
E: asainfo@appraisers.org
www.appraisers.org

Founded in 1952, this organization has more than 6,000 members. ASA is a professional appraisal educator and represents all the disciplines of appraisal specialists. The society requires a mandatory certification program for all of its members, including the ASA Ethics Exam and the Uniform Standards of Professional Appraisal Practice Examination.

Institute of Business Appraisers (IBA)

PO Box 17410, Plantation, FL 33318, USA
T: +1 954 584 1144
F: +1 954 584 1184
E: ibahq@go-iba.org
www.go-iba.org

Established in 1978, the Institute of Business Appraisers is the oldest professional society devoted to the appraisal of closely held businesses. It is a nationally recognized organization with a membership of over 3,000, and seeks to educate the public in all aspects of business valuation and appraisal, and is involved in monitoring and supporting national legislation that affects the business valuation community.

MeasureNet

2115 West Lawn Avenue, Madison, WI 53711, USA
T: +1 608 256 9993
F: +1 435 304 8452
E: greg@measure.net
www.measure.net

This organization is concerned with extending and improving corporate performance measurement strategies. It provides information for measuring performance within a company, and for managing a business. To this end, it is involved in research, education and consulting services, and also conducts various seminars and courses.

  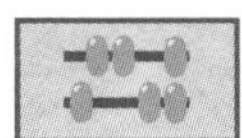      

The National Association of Certified Valuation Analysts (NACVA)

1111 Brickyard Road, Suite 200, Salt Lake City, UT 84106–5401, USA
T: +1 801 486 0600
F: +1 801 486 7500
E: nacva1@nacva.com
www.nacva.com

Supports the users of business and intangible asset valuation services and financial forensic services, including damages determinations of all kinds and fraud detection and prevention, by training and certifying financial professionals in these disciplines. NACVA training includes Continuing Professional Education (CPE) credit and is available to both members and non-members.

International

Foundation for Performance Measurement (FPM)

c/o Metapraxis Ltd, Hanover House, Coombe Road, Kingston-Upon-Thames, Surrey, KT2 7AH, UK
T: +44 (0) 20 8541 1696
F: +44 (0) 20 8546 2105
E: info@fpm.com
www.fpm.com

With both UK and US Chapters, this foundation serves as a source of information, a forum for research and debate, and as a link to tools and resources for organizations interested in developing practical new ways of measuring enterprise performance. It links businesses that have successfully implemented new performance measures with those that are endeavoring to do.

Business Ethics and Codes of Practice

BOOKS

Absolute Honesty: Building a Corporate Culture That Values Straight Talk and Rewards Integrity
Larry Johnson, Bob Phillips
New York: AMACOM, 2003
304pp, ISBN: 978-0-8144-0781-3

This book starts out from the belief that honesty can produce economic as well as moral rewards, in terms of improved productivity, competitive advantage, morale, and public trust. It asserts the need to reestablish a culture of openness and truth in communication methods, grounded in absolute honesty. To this end it sets out a framework of six laws of absolute honesty and gives advice on implementing them within an ethical infrastructure.

Business Ethics and Ethical Business
Robert Audi
New York: Oxford University Press, 2008
176pp, ISBN: 978-0-19-536910-6

Business Ethics and Ethical Business gives a concise introduction and is organized into three parts that cover the role of business in society, the ethics of internal management, and the challenges of international business. It introduces the standards essential in business ethics, explores a wide range of issues using concrete examples, and provides analytical tools for guiding ethical decisions in the real world. Its features include short case scenarios, explanation of different ethics, and a glossary of many key terms in business ethics.

Business Ethics and Values: Individual, Corporate and International Perspectives, 3rd ed
Colin Fisher, Alan Lovell
Harlow, UK: FT Prentice Hall, 2008
640pp, ISBN: 978-0-273-71616-7

Fisher and Lovell offer the reader a comprehensive introduction to the ideas and complexities of ethics in the contemporary business world. It ensures a relevancy for today's business students through the inclusion of frequent interesting examples and activities, helping consideration of ethical questions.

Business Ethics: Ethical Decision Making and Cases, 7th ed
O. C. Ferrell, John Fraedrich, Linda Ferrell
Boston, Massachusetts: Houghton Mifflin, 2007
496pp, ISBN: 978-0-618-74934-8

Business Ethics: Ethical Decision Making and Cases consists of text and cases that offer a critically-based clear approach to workplace ethics. Its purpose is to help the reader make an informed ethical decision without depending on any particular philosophy or process. It also covers dilemmas, ethical decision-making frameworks, behavioral simulations, interactive games, e-ethics sites, and self tests.

Business Ethics: Managing Corporate Citizenship and Sustainability in the Age of Globalization, 3rd ed
Andrew Cane, Dirk Matten
Oxford: Oxford University Press, 2010
648pp, ISBN: 978-0-19-928499-3

This book covers the foundations of business ethics and applying these theories, concepts, and tools to each of the corporation's major stakeholders. It is written from a European perspective, and considers the implications of three major challenges facing the corporation: corporate citizenship, globalization and sustainability. This second edition has been thoroughly revised and updated, and includes new content on personal values and Asian perspectives.

Business Ethics: The Ethical Revolution of Minority Shareholders
Jacques Cory
Dordrecht, The Netherlands: Springer, 2001
269pp, ISBN: 978-0-387-23040-5

This book deals with the relationships between companies and minority stockholders, from the perspective of business ethics. It highlights the inefficiency of traditional safeguards of the rights of small stockholders and discusses the new "vehicles" that can bring about an ethical revolution for minority shareholders and tilt the balance in their favor. It provides cases of companies to show how minority stockholders can lose their investments. The purpose is to analyze why and how companies do not act ethically towards their minority shareholders, not how many, which, to what degree or where.

Developing a Code of Business Ethics: A Guide to Best Practice including the IBE Illustrative Code of Business Ethics
Simon Webley
London: Institute of Business Ethics, 2003
64pp, ISBN: 978-0-9539517-4-1

This pamphlet provides a practical step-by-step guide to developing a code of business ethics. Webley argues the case for introducing a code, and discusses the issues involved in developing one, including ethical dilemmas and cross-cultural problems. The IBE Illustrative Code of Business Ethics, which includes checklists and sample wordings, is presented as a guide.
A number of sample codes are included in an appendix.

Does Business Ethics Pay? Ethics and Financial Performance
Simon Webley, Elise More
London: Institute of Business Ethics, 2003
64pp, ISBN: 978-0-9539517-3-4

This pamphlet reports on research undertaken to measure the commitment to ethics and corporate responsibility of certain businesses and to compare the results against financial performance measures. It concludes that there is strong evidence to indicate that larger UK companies with codes of ethics outperform those without codes on the basis of both financial and other indicators. A summary of related research is also included, together with a glossary and sources of further information.

The Earthscan Reader in Business and Sustainable Development
Richard Starkey, Richard Welford (editors)
London: Earthscan, 2001
364pp, ISBN: 978-1-85383-659-6

This collection of work by leading authors in the field of business and sustainable development contains 17 chapters in sections covering business opportunities, environmental accounting, critical perspectives, and trade and sustainable development.

Just Business: Business Ethics in Action, 2nd ed

Elaine Sternberg

Oxford: Oxford University Press, 2000
320pp, ISBN: 978-0-19-829663-8

The author presents an ethical decision model that can be used as a conceptual framework for resolving questions of business ethics and corporate governance in all their variety and complexity. The book is intended for active businessmen and presupposes no knowledge of philosophy, it provides a reasoned philosophical approach to determining what constitutes ethical conduct in business.

Leading with Soul, 2nd ed

Lee G. Bolman, Terrence E. Deal

Chichester, UK: Wiley, 2001
272pp, ISBN: 978-0-7879-5547-2

This is a contemporary parable about an executive's quest for passion and purpose in work and in life. The authors draw upon many spiritual traditions, poetry, philosophy, and social science teachings on leadership and organizations. They demonstrate how to lead with soul and how to ignite the soul of an organization. This second edition has a new introduction, new material, and includes letters written by readers of the first edition.

Managing Business Ethics: Straight Talk About How to Do It Right, 4th ed

Linda K. Trevino, Katherine A. Nelson

Hoboken, New Jersey: Wiley, 2007
407pp, ISBN: 978-0-471-75525-8

Managing Business Ethics offers a practical examination of ethics in the workplace, and presents a guide to identifying and solving ethical dilemmas. It also explains why people behave in a certain way and how to design a culture that promotes ethical behavior.

Managing Values and Beliefs in Organisations

Tom McEwan

Harlow, UK: FT Prentice Hall, 2001
408pp, ISBN: 978-0-273-64340-1

This is a book, written as a student text, that summarizes the origins of corporate responsibility, business ethics, and corporate governance, and reviews the similarities and differences between them. The specific issues covered include: moral meaning and applied ethics; values, beliefs, and ideologies; individual morality in organizations; unethical behavior by individuals; international business and the developing world; ethical investment; organization culture and stakeholder theory; and corporate social performance, ethical leadership, and reputation management.

Perspectives on Corporate Social Responsibility

David Crowther, Lez Rayman-Bacchus (editors)

Aldershot, UK: Ashgate Publishing, 2004
264pp, ISBN: 978-0-7546-3886-5

This book aims to explore different perspectives on what is meant by corporate social responsibility (CSR), based on the experiences of people in different parts of the world. Contributors investigate the theoretical aspects of socially responsible behavior, its application in practice, and its ethical dimension. Specific topics covered include: assessing trust in, and the legitimacy of, the Corporate; limited liability or limited responsibility; the power of networks—organizing versus organization; and social performance in government.

Private Business, Public Battleground: The Case for 21st Century Stakeholder Companies

John Egan, Des Wilson

Basingstoke, UK: Palgrave, 2002
210pp, ISBN: 978-0-333-92939-1

The authors put forward the view that companies can no longer operate in isolation from the world around them, or ignore the concerns of their stakeholders. The relationship between business and the community is explored, covering the impact of global capitalism, environmental sustainability, the rise of the stakeholder company, and corporate citizenship. A case history of BAA (formerly the British Airports Authority) is also included.

Trust or Consequences: Build Trust Today or Lose Your Market Tomorrow

Al Golin

New York: AMACOM, 2006
248pp, ISBN: 978-0-8144-7388-7

In a climate of public skepticism toward business there is a need for organization to create a trust bank of goodwill to communicate that they are trustworthy, it is claimed. This book deals with the creation of trust strategies using the author's tried-and-tested methods in various international organizations. The book's three sections cover, respectively, an assessment of external and internal trends that have contributed to the debate; the steps organizations can take; and a framework of strategies and scenarios for action. Case studies are also included.

Value Shift: Why Companies Must Merge Social and Financial Imperatives to Achieve Superior Performance

Lynn Sharp Paine

New York: McGraw-Hill, 2003
304pp, ISBN: 978-0-07-142733-3

This book argues the case for a new style of management that will align company performance with today's ethical standards. It argues that there is now a dichotomy between traditional management and the expectations of business in contemporary society. Acknowledging it is no longer enough simply to produce goods and services and create wealth, the author discusses today's corporate leaders' need to make a shift in management values to incorporate high ethical standards along with strong financial results.

What Matters Most? Business Social Responsibility and the End of the Era of Greed

Jeffrey Hollender, Stephen Fenichell

London: Random House, 2004
240pp, ISBN: 978-1-84413-397-0

Jeffrey Hollender, CEO of Seventh Generation, a world leader in manufacturing environmentally friendly household products, is a frequent commentator on corporate responsibility. This book, coauthored with Stephen Fenichell, puts forward an approach to corporate strategy that is said to help integrate concerns related to social responsibility into an organization's culture, systems, and activities.

Working Ethics: Strategies for Decision Making and Organizational Responsibility

Marvin T. Brown

San Francisco, California: Jossey-Bass, 2000
219pp, ISBN: 978-1-889059-55-6

This book explores the role of ethics as a tool in decision-making, showing how ethical behavior can improve organizational effectiveness by fostering open communications, resolving disputes, and enhancing employee–management relations. It highlights the fact that arguments centering on an open expression of disagreements can lead to better relations, and provides examples and practical exercises for building an organization that makes morally and socially responsible decisions.

JOURNALS

Business and Professional Ethics Journal

Public Interest Enterprises
PO Box 15017, Gainesville, FL 32604, USA
T: +1 325 392 2084
F: +1 325 392 0057
www.ethics.ufl.edu/BPEJ/index.html
ISSN: 0277-2027

Published four times each year, this journal contains articles that focus on the ethical issues encountered by business professionals working in large organizations.

Business and Society Review

Wiley Periodicals
350 Main Street, Malden, MA 02148, USA
T: +1 781 388 8598
www.wiley.com/bw/journal.asp?ref=0045-3609
ISSN: 0045-3609

This quarterly publication covers the debate on the role of business in society and covers a wide range of ethical issues relating to business, society, and the public good. Contributors include business professionals, researchers, government administrators, and legal experts.

Business Ethics: A European Review

Blackwell Publishing
9600 Garsington Road, Oxford, OX4 2DQ, UK
T: +44 (0) 1865 791 100
F: +44 (0) 1865 791 347
www.wiley.com/bw/journal.asp?ref=0962-8770
ISSN: 0962-8770

    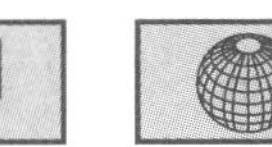   

Offering rigorous analysis of ethical issues faced by business worldwide, this quarterly is primarily an academic research journal. However, it is readable and user-friendly, and its focus is not exclusively European.

Business Ethics Quarterly: The Journal of the Society for Business Ethics

Philosophy Documentation Center
Society for Business Ethics, Philosophy Documentation Center, PO Box 7147, Charlottesville, VI 22906–7147, USA
T: +1 434 220 3300 or 800 444 2419
F: +1 434 220 3301
www.societyforbusinessethics.org/index.php?option=com_content&task=view&id=57&Itemid=103
ISSN: 1052-150X

This learned peer-reviewed journal explores the application of ethics to international business. It focuses on theoretical and methodological questions that can advance ethical inquiry and enhance the ethical performance of business organizations.

Journal of Business Ethics

Springer
PO Box 358, Dordrecht, 3300 AA, The Netherlands
T: +31 78 657 6392
F: +31 78 657 6474
www.springer.com/philosophy/ethics/journal/10551
ISSN: 0167-4544

From 2004 this monthly journal has incorporated *The International Journal of Value-Based Management* and *Teaching Business Ethics*. It covers a wide range of ethical issues related to business and includes empirical research reports. The use of specialist jargon is avoided as the publication is intended for a wide constituency including the business community, universities, government, and consumer groups.

Journal of Business Ethics and Education

Neilson Journals Publishing
151 Whitehouse Loan, Edinburgh, EH9 2EY, UK
T: +44 (0) 131 447 3300
F: +44 (0) 131 464 0300
www.neilsonjournals.com/JBEE
ISSN: 1649-5195

JBEE publishes educational materials suitable for use in ethics courses or in other business courses where ethical issues are discussed. These include case studies, lecture articles for student use, articles and ethical analyses for instructors, role-playing material, and syllabi and curricula. It covers areas such as the proper role of ethics in business education, integrating ethics into other business courses, and the relative merits of integration versus stand-alone courses.

Journal of Human Values

Sage Publications
1 Oliver's Yard, 55 City Road, London, EC1Y 1SP, UK
T: +44 (0) 20 7324 8500
F: +44 (0) 20 7324 8600
jhv.sagepub.com
ISSN: 0971-6858

The *Journal of Human Values* focuses the effect of human values on all dimensions. Some of the dimensions are the relevance in today's world and human values at the organizational level. Its purpose is to provide an understanding of how individuals, organizations, and societies can function effectively. The journal provides an international platform for the exchange of ideas, principles and processes.

INTERNET

Business Impact

www.bitc.org.uk/index.html

This site contains information from Business in the Community's Business Impact task force, including a news directory and general information on corporate social responsibility.

Center for the Study of Ethics in the Professions

ethics.iit.edu/codes

This site makes available 850 codes of ethics from professional societies, corporations, government, and academic institutions, as well as a literature review and a user guide.

Ethics Connection

www.scu.edu/SCU/Centers/Ethics

This site, run by the Markkula Center for Applied Ethics at Santa Clara University, offers case briefings, articles, and dialogue in all fields of applied ethics, including business and technology.

Ethics Resource Center

www.ethics.org

A range of resources from this Washington-based ethics education organization can be accessed here. These include articles from *Ethics Today* magazine, useful links, book reviews, and details of training resources and events.

Global Business Society Resource Center

www.bsr.org

Business for Social Responsibility offers an introduction to issues of social responsibility and business ethics on this site. The site also includes a news archive, information about company practices and policies, award and recognition programs, and publications. A special feature is the facility it provides for creating reports on selected topics.

GlobeEthics.net

www.globethics.net

Globethics.net is a global network of people and institutions interested in different fields of applied ethics. It offers resources on ethics and collaborative web-based researches.

ORGANIZATIONS

Europe

Business in the Community

137 Shepherdess Walk, London, N1 7RQ, UK
T: +44 (0) 870 600 2482
E: information@bitc.org.uk
www.bitc.org.uk

Business in the Community was set up as a partnership between business, government, local authorities, and labor unions to promote corporate community involvement. It has a support network aimed particularly at helping new and developing businesses to become involved in the community.

Institute of Business Ethics (IBE)

24 Greencoat Place, London, SW1P 1BE, UK
T: +44 (0) 20 7798 6040
F: +44 (0) 20 7798 6044
E: info@ibe.org.uk
www.ibe.org.uk

Launched in 1986 by the then Lord Mayor of London, Alderman Sir Allan Davis, the Institute aims to emphasize the essentially ethical nature of wealth creation, to encourage the highest standards of behavior by companies, and to publicize the best ethical practices. Its activities include research, conferences, seminars, and the development of codes of practice and resource material.

The Office of Fair Trading

Fleetbank House, 2–6 Salisbury Square, London, EC4Y 8JX, UK
T: +44 (0) 20 7211 8000
E: enquiries@oft.gsi.gov.uk.
www.oft.gov.uk

The OFT is the UK's consumer and competition authority. Their mission is to make markets work well for consumers. They encourage businesses to comply with competition and consumer law and to improve their trading practices. The OFT is a non-ministerial government department established by statute in 1973.

USA

Business for Social Responsibility (BSR)

111 Sutter Street, 11th Floor, San Francisco, CA 94104, USA
T: +1 415 984 3200
F: +1 415 984 3201
www.bsr.org

Founded in 1992, this organization provides resources–including information, news, publications, training, and consulting–designed to help member companies succeed in business while respecting ethical values. Based in the United States, BSR has developed regional networks and alliances with similar organizations worldwide.

Ethics & Compliance Officer Association

411 Waverley Oaks Road, Suite 324, Waltham, MA 02452, USA
T: +1 781 647 9333
E: msonin@theecoa.org
www.theecoa.org/AM/Template.cfm?Section=About

The Ethics & Compliance Officer Association (ECOA) is a nonconsulting, member-driven association exclusively for individuals responsible for their organization's ethics, compliance, and business conduct programs. It is the largest group of business ethics and compliance practitioners in the world.

        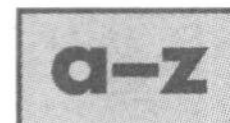

Institute for Business and Professional Ethics
1 East Jackson, Chicago, IL 60604, USA
T: +1 312 362 8000
commerce.depaul.edu/ethics

The mission of this institute is to maintain and encourage ethical deliberation by stirring the moral conscience and by developing models for ethical decision-making in business and the professions.

Society for Business Ethics (SBE)
School of Business Administration, Loyola University Chicago, 25 East Pearson Avenue, Chicago, IL 60611-2196, USA
T: +1 312 915 6112
F: +1 312 915 7207
sba.luc.edu

The SBE is an international association of scholars and professionals that aims to promote the study of business ethics, to improve the way they are taught, and to provide a forum for the exchange of ideas in the field.

International

Institute for Global Ethics
PO Box 563, Camden, ME 04843, USA
T: +1 207 236 6658
F: +1 207 236 4014
www.globalethics.org

A nonsectarian membership organization funded by private foundations, sponsors, and members, the institute fosters public discussion of and practical action on ethical issues and promotes the teaching of "ethical fitness." It has an international board of directors, an international advisory council, and branch offices in the United Kingdom and Canada. Its activities are centered on three areas: corporate services, educational programs, and public policy. Visitors to IBE's online site may register free for the weekly *Ethics Newsline* e-newsletter.

Business Plans and Planning

BOOKS

The Business Plan Workbook, 6th ed
Colin Barrow, Paul Barrow, Robert Brown
London: Kogan Page, 2008
384pp, ISBN: 978-0-7494-5231-5

The processes and procedures required to write a business plan are brought together in this workbook, and are illustrated with examples from actual business plans. The seven-phase approach focuses on: the business history and position to date; market research; competitive business strategies; operations; forecasting results; business controls; and writing up and presenting your business plan. Appendices give market research information sources and sources of finance for new and small businesses.

Business Plans in a Week
Iain Maitland
In a Week Series
London: Profile Books, 2002
96pp, ISBN: 978-0-340-84963-7

This succinct guide to the process of compiling and writing a business plan explains how to identify goals, make preparatory notes, compile the financial and commercial sections, and present the finished plan effectively.

The Complete Book of Business Plans: Simple Steps to Writing a Powerful Business Plan
Joseph A. Covello, Brian J. Hazelgren
Naperville, Illinois: Sourcebooks, 1994
320pp, ISBN: 978-0-942061-41-3

This classic presents the key questions to bear in mind when writing a plan for a new business, and encourages the reader to look for answers to the kinds of questions that investors ask, to develop marketing strategies and financial presentations, and to find ways to stay ahead of the competition.

The Definitive Business Plan: The Fast Track to Intelligent Business Planning for Executives and Entrepreneurs, 2nd ed
Richard Stutley
Harlow, UK: FT Prentice Hall, 2006
320pp, ISBN: 978-0-273-71096-7

Written for both the newcomer and the experienced planner, this text provides a concise guide to the business planning process, and focuses attention on strategic planning and strategic and operational controls. The practical aspects of constructing various types of business plan are explained in some detail.

How to Prepare a Business Plan, 5th ed
Edward Blackwell
Sunday Times Business Enterprise Guide Series
London: Kogan Page, 2008
192pp, ISBN: 978-0-7494-4981-0

This highly recommended title takes the owner/manager through the process of developing a business plan for start-up or expansion. This book covers financial forecasting and planning and gives useful case studies of businesses preparing and following business plans.

How to Really Create a Successful Business Plan, 4th ed
David E. Gumpert
Boston, Massachusetts: Inc Publishing, 2003
236pp, ISBN: 978-0-9701181-7-2

This book provides a step-by-step method for completing a high-quality business plan. It also provides models of business plans from a number of highly successful US companies.

How to Write a Great Business Plan
William A. Sahlman
Harvard Business Review Classics Series
Boston, Massachusetts: Harvard Business School Press, 2008
64pp, ISBN: 978-1-4221-2142-9

Sahlman shows how to avoid creating an over-elaborate and off-the-point business plan by ensuring that your plan assesses the factors critical to every new venture: the people, the opportunity, the context, what can go wrong and right, and how the entrepreneurial team will respond.

The Mission Primer: Four Steps to an Effective Mission Statement
Richard O'Halloran, David O'Halloran
Richmond, Virginia: Mission Incorporated, 2000
130pp, ISBN: 978-0-9676635-0-0

Including an easy-to-use guide, examples of model mission statements, and a glossary of useful terms, this book will enable you to analyze your situation and create your own mission statement.

The Successful Business Plan: Secrets and Strategies, 4th ed
Rhonda M. Abrams, Paul Barrow
Palo Alto, California: Running R Media, 2008
478pp, ISBN: 978-1-84112-807-8

This book is designed to help readers create a business plan that will attract the funding they need to get started. It presents insights from some 200 business owners, venture capitalists, and CEOs, but, in addition, contains worksheets and sample business plans, provides tools to help in number-crunching, and offers guidance on the length of an ideal plan and the way it should be worded and formatted.

Your First Business Plan: A Simple Question and Answer Format Designed to Help You Write Your Own Plan, 5th ed
Brian Hazelgren
Naperville, Illinois: Sourcebooks, 2005
256pp, ISBN: 978-1-4022-0412-8

With little or no company history, the first business plan can be the most difficult. By outlining each part of the business plan and making suggestions for what to focus on and what to avoid, this book will help your writing. Also included are a glossary and a sample business plan.

JOURNALS

Long Range Planning: International Journal of Strategic Management
Elsevier
Radarweg 29, Amsterdam 1043 NX, The Netherlands
T: +31 20 485 3911

F: +31 20 485 2457
www.elsevier.com/locate/lrp
ISSN: 0024-6301

LRP, published in association with the Strategic Planning Society and the European Strategic Planning Federation, is a leading international journal in the field of strategic management. Aimed at senior managers, administrators, and academics, it includes articles from academics and practitioners.

INTERNET

Allindialive Business Planning Portal

www.allindialive.org

An Indian Blogger offering help on business planning. The site provides many links and publications on the topic.

Business Link

www.businesslink.gov.uk

The UK Small Business Service runs this site to provide advice for small business owners and anyone thinking of setting up a small business in England. The site is packed with helpful information and easily navigable. Business Link offers a telephone support line on 0845 600 9006 and also has a network of 45 operators across the country which puts you in touch with an adviser.

Business Plan Guide

www.business-plans.co.uk

Sponsored by Miller Consultancy, this site provides information on business planning resources. It includes books, links to websites, and articles.

Business Plans

www.bplans.com

This site, created by Palo Alto Software, offers planning advice for small businesses and a substantial range of sample plans, which subscribers to bplans' software can download and edit. It also includes a resource center with links to other websites, as well as an "ask the experts" section.

Businessballs.com

www.businessballs.com/freebusinessplansandmarketingtemplates.htm

This section of the extensive businessballs.com site offers a useful list of key business planning terms as well as advice on the best information to include and what to leave out. Links to sources of further help are also provided.

More Business

www.morebusiness.com

This site has a lengthy business and marketing plans section and provides some useful sample business plans.

Planware.org

www.planware.org

This site offers free business planning software, freeware, templates, samples, and online tools, and offers advice and guides.

United States Small Business Administration

www.sba.gov

This website, run by the US government organization dedicated to helping small business owners, provides sources for technical, managerial, and financial advice and assistance. It also includes a small business planner with a model business plan.

Venture Associates

www.venturea.com/business.htm

Produced by an investment banking and management consulting firm, the site provides freely available information on various aspects of business planning. It also includes a useful business plan outline.

Venture Capital Resource Library

www.vfinance.com

This site provides a business plan template, general articles, and texts of SEC and UCC rules and regulations, as well as leads to sources of venture capital.

ORGANIZATIONS

Europe

Chartered Management Institute (CMI)

Management House, Cottingham Road, Corby, Northamptonshire, NN17 1TT, UK
T: +44 (0) 1536 204 222
F: +44 (0) 1536 201 651
E: enquiries@managers.org.uk
www.managers.org.uk

Formed in 1992, the CMI is the largest organization for professional management in the United Kingdom, representing almost 89,000 individual members and embracing 560 corporate partners. It exists to promote the art and science of management through research, publications, the provision of information services, networking opportunities, education and training, and the objective presentation of managers' views and opinions.

USA

American Management Association (AMA)

1601 Broadway, New York, NY 10019, USA
T: +1 212 586 8100
F: +1 212 903 8168
E: customerservice@amanet.org
www.amanet.org

Founded in 1923, this association has over 80,000 members. With a focus on practical training, the AMA provides business forums and seminars worldwide. Members can enhance their business skills and develop successful planning strategies by studying the best practices of various world-class organizations. Seminars are geared to every professional level, from CEO to administrative assistant. The AMA also publishes valuable print resources that cover a wide range of topics including business plans, career building, and technology.

Chief Executive Officers' Club

47 West Street, New York, NY 10013, USA
T: +1 212 925 7911
F: +1 212 925 7463
E: mail@ceoclubs.org
ceoclubs.org/main/default.htm

Established in 1978, this association serves as a management resource for entrepreneurs and their professional advisers. Membership is by invitation only. Membership is restricted to CEOs of businesses that have over $2m in annual sales. The organization selects publications on developing business plans and conducts seminars on the entrepreneurial process.

United States Small Business Administration

409 Third Street, SW, Washington, DC 20416, USA
T: 1 800 827 7722
www.sba.gov

Providing multiple resources for the small business covering a wide range of topics, such as starting your business, financing your business, managing your business, and business opportunities, this link, provided by the United States government, is a handy stop for anyone interested in business planning.

BRIC

Indian Institutes of Management (IIMs)

Diamond Harbour Road, Joka, Kolkata 700104, West Bengal, India
T: +91 33 2467 9178
F: +91 33 2467 9178
E: pgpadmissions@iimcal.ac.in
www.iimcal.ac.in/

The IIMs are top business schools created by the government of India, to create a pool of highly educated managers to lead India's economy. The institutes also carry out research in emerging areas.

Business Process Reengineering

BOOKS

The Aftermath of Reengineering: Downsizing and Corporate Performance

Tony Carter

Binghamton, New York: The Haworth Press, 1999
165pp, ISBN: 978-0-7890-0720-9

Carter takes a much needed, thorough look at the effectiveness of reengineering and both its positive and negative human, strategic, and societal consequences. Every chapter concludes with a case study that illustrates the topic, and the final chapter of the book provides an evaluation of reengineering best practices from a variety of companies and industries.

Beyond Reengineering: How the Process-centered Organization Is Changing

Michael Hammer

New York: HarperCollins, 1997
304pp, ISBN: 978-0-88730-880-2

This book explores the strategy and structure of the process-centered organization, and the consequences of reengineering.

Cases on Information Technology and Business Process Reengineering

Mehdi Khosrow-Pour

Cases on Information Technology Series
Hershey, Pennsylvania: IGI Publishing, 2006
357pp, ISBN: 978-1-59904-396-8

The technological innovation of information technology is driving businesses and organizations to reassess their structures and processes to achieve a higher level of efficiency and effectiveness using IT. In this ongoing process, the wisdom and experiences of other organizations can be a roadmap to successful IT implementation.

Making Sense of Change Management: A Complete Guide to the Models, Tools and Techniques of Organizational Change, 2nd ed

Esther Cameron and Mike Green

London: Kogan Page, 2009
304pp, ISBN: 978-0-7494-5310-7

This book is for students and professionals. It explains how change happens, and what needs to be done to make change a welcome rather than a dreaded concept. It offers considered insights in frameworks, models, and ways of approaching change, and helps the reader to apply the right approach to each unique situation.

The Reengineering Alternative: A Plan for Making Your Current Culture Work

William E. Schneider

Maidenhead, UK: McGraw-Hill, 1999
173pp, ISBN: 978-0-07-135981-8

Reengineering has virtually become business dogma, yet there are viable, and perhaps even preferable, alternatives. Mechanistic approaches to reengineering often fail to take into account one of a company's most vital and enduring resources—its culture. This book describes an approach to change management that focuses on a company's unique existing strengths and corporate objectives, and shows how to work effectively to foster improvement according to four basic corporate culture types.

Reengineering Business for Success in the Internet Age: Business-to-Business E-Commerce Strategies, 3rd ed

Debra Cameron

Charleston, South Carolina: Computer Technology Research Corporation, 2000
197pp, ISBN: 978-1-56607-084-3

The publisher is now out of business—another casualty of the e-commerce nosedive—but this report may still be purchased through online booksellers. It applies reengineering strategies to the dynamic e-business environment.
Topics range from integrating legacy systems to implementing B2B security strategies, with special emphasis on the unique role of XML in reengineering for e-business.

JOURNALS

Industrial Management & Data Systems

Emerald
60/62 Toller Lane, Bradford, West Yorkshire, BD8 9BY, UK
T: +44 (0) 1274 777 700
F: +44 (0) 1274 785 200
www.emeraldinsight.com/0263-5577.htm
ISSN: 0263-5577

This journal addresses the requirements of re-engineering information needed by organizations whose existence is dependent on coping with rapidly changing requirements. Reengineering examines and alters the system to reconstitute in a new form and the subsequent implementation of the new form.

Knowledge and Process Management

Wiley
The Atrium, Southern Gate, Chichester, West Sussex, PO19 8SQ, UK
T: +44 (0) 1243 779 777
F: +44 (0) 1243 775 878
www.interscience.wiley.com/jpages/1092-4604
ISSN: 1092-4604

Formerly called *Business Change and Reengineering: Journal of Corporate Transformation*, this quarterly journal aims to meet the needs of executives responsible for organizational performance improvement. Articles focus on the areas of knowledge management, organizational learning, core competences, and process management. Emphasis is placed on the practical lessons learned from the experience of organizations.

TQM Journal

Emerald
60/62 Toller Lane, Bradford, West Yorkshire, BD8 9BY, UK
T: +44 (0) 1274 777 700
F: +44 (0) 1274 785 200
www.emeraldinsight.com/1754-2731.htm
ISSN: 1754-2731

Known as the *TQM Magazine* until the end of 2007, this journal examines the management concept of business process reengineering (BPR), arguing that while little is really new, the need for organizations to embrace process improvement is high. It discusses some key success factors for organizations using BPR.

INTERNET

Brint.com Business Process Reengineering

www.brint.com/BPR.htm

A comprehensive collection of links to BPR resources.

Business Process Reengineering (BPR) Online Learning Center

www.prosci.com

This online learning center features seven series of multiple online tutorials on various aspects of business process reengineering, together with best practice benchmarking studies, a change management resource library, and a project trouble shooter.

Business Process Reengineering (BPR)—An Introductory Guide

www.teamtechnology.co.uk/business-process-reengineering.html

This website provides a detailed introduction to the field of business process re-engineering.

National Center for Public Productivity

www.ncpp.us

Affiliated with Rutgers University, the website for this center is a gateway to federal, state, and international resources on productivity in the public sector, and for "citizen-driven government performance."

ORGANIZATIONS

BRIC

Business Process Industry Association of India

c/o Confederation of Indian Industry, 249-F, Phase-IV, Udyog Vihar, Sector 18, Gurgaon, 122 015 (Haryana), India
T: +91 124 410 104
F: +91 124 401 4080
E: info@bpiai.org
www.bpiai.org

The Business Process Industry Association of India (BPIAI) provides a network for members to jointly address challenges facing the call centre industry. It aims to create opportunities for networking

  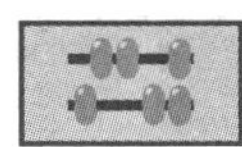      

within the industry through events and conferences, and take up policies and infrastructure-related issues with the government.

International

Business Modeling & Integration (BMI) Domain Task Force (DTF)

140 Kendrick Street, Building A, Suite 300,
Needham, MA 02494, USA
T: +1 781 444 0404
F: +1 781 444 0320
E: info@omg.org
www.bpmi.org

OMG is international, open membership, non-profit computer industry consortium, which ensures that every organization, large and small, has a effective voice in their running. The membership includes hundreds of organizations, with half being software end-users in over two dozen vertical markets, and the other half representing virtually every large organization in the computer industry, as well as many smaller ones.

Business Process Management Group (BPMG)

The Manor, Haseley Business Centre, Warwick,
Warwickshire, CV35 7LS, UK
T: + 44 1926 864 477
F: + 44 (0) 20 7691 7132
E: editor@bpmg.org
www.bpmg.org

The BPMG is a business interest group, established in the United Kingdom in 1992, which now has over 15,000 members worldwide. Its aims are to advance the understanding and application of business process management, to raise business awareness of BPM, and to provide a forum for the exchange of information relevant to BPM.

Workflow and Reengineering International Association (WARIA)

2436 North Federal Highway 374, Lighthouse Point,
FL 33064, USA
T: +1 954 782 3376
F: +1 954 782 6365
E: waria04@waria.com
www.waria.com

WARIA is a nonprofit organization concerned with issues that arise at the intersection between BPR, knowledge management, electronic commerce, and workflow management. It encourages the sharing of information on issues common to these fields by providing networking opportunities.

Capital Markets and Stock Markets

BOOKS

Capital Market Liberalization and Development

Joseph E. Stiglitz, Jose Antonio Ocampo (editors)
New York: Oxford University Press, 2008
375pp, ISBN: 978-0-19-923844-6

This is a new examination of the impact of liberalization on the capital markets, a development that has been central to the debate on the effects of globalization. It brings together some of the leading researchers and practitioners in the field, to provide an analysis of both the risks associated with capital market liberalization and the alternative policy options available to enhance macroeconomic management.

Capital Market Revolution: The Future of Markets in an Online World

Patrick Young, Thomas Theys
Harlow, UK: FT Prentice Hall, 1999
212pp, ISBN: 978-0-273-64232-9

The book that spread an awareness of what the coming electronic age would mean for the financial markets. At a time when much trading was still done on a face-to-face basis, it predicted the move to fully automated markets and electronic trading. It presciently warned that traders and exchanges would have to change or they would be doomed.

Capital Markets

K. Thomas Liaw
Mason, Ohio: Thomson/South-Western, 2004
603pp, ISBN: 978-0-324-02420-3

A strong overview of the financial markets and institutions, with a focus on global financial centers, including the Euromarkets, European Monetary Union, and the capital markets in Japan, Asia, Russia, and Latin America. It considers the impact of globalization, deregulation, consolidation, and technology, and examines the securities markets, and current market practice.

Capital Markets: A Global Perspective

Thomas H. McInish
Boston, Massachusetts: Blackwell Publishing, 2000
429pp, ISBN: 978-0-631-21159-4

This book provides an international overview of the main financial products, principles, and operating structure of the global marketplace. It examines integration across equities, debt securities, derivatives, and foreign exchange, and focuses on market microstructure in terms of prices, risks, and transaction costs of the four product types.

Capital Markets: Institutions and Instruments, 4th ed

Frank J. Fabozzi, Franco Modigliani
Upper Saddle River, New Jersey: Prentice Hall, 2009
696pp, ISBN: 978-0-13-602602-0

This is a comprehensive and wide-ranging examination of the capital markets, by two of the most respected writers and researchers in the business. It evaluates and explains the instruments, institutions, players, and principles of valuation in a detailed and accessible way. It combines theory and practice to provide a detailed reference for professionals working in the markets.

The Complete Guide to Capital Markets for Quantitative Professionals

Alex Kuznetsov
McGraw-Hill Library of Investment and Finance Series
New York: McGraw-Hill, 2007
554pp, ISBN: 978-0-07-146829-9

Aimed at those with a technical background who are planning to enter the financial sector, and need a solid grounding in the fundamentals of how the financial sector operates. It offers advice about the type of jobs they should be contemplating, and focuses on the mechanics of trading in the markets, and the use of financial models and systems.

Financial Institutions, Markets, and Money, 10th ed

David S. Kidwell, David W. Blackwell, David A. Whidbee, Richard L. Peterson
Hoboken, New Jersey: Wiley, 2008
671pp, ISBN: 978-0-470-17161-5

This is an introduction to how the US financial system, focusing on its institutions, markets, and financial instruments, and the impact of technology and globalization. It examines the Federal Reserve System and how it conducts monetary policy, and explores the risks faced by financial institutions on interest rates, credit, liquidity, and foreign exchange, and how they can be managed effectively.

Fundamentals of the Stock Market

B. O'Neill Wyss
New York: McGraw-Hill, 2001
245pp, ISBN: 978-0-07-136096-8

A practical examination of market basics, such as how to trade, the major exchanges, different types of stock, and where to look for financial news, up to more advanced concepts, such as technical analysis, short selling, modern portfolio theory overview of stocks and mutual funds, and how trends and policies affect markets.

The Great Crash of 1929

John Kenneth Galbraith
Boston, Massachusetts: Houghton Mifflin, 1997
206pp, ISBN: 978-0-395-85999-5

An examination of the stock market crash of 1929, which heralded the Great Depression in US. Galbraith provides insights into the unbridled speculation, the high trading volumes, the market hysteria, and the inaction of the government to resolve the crisis, and records in detail the run up to the crash, and the effect it had on the US economy and society.

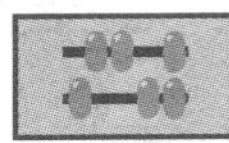

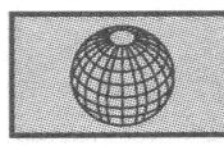

Handbook of World Stock, Derivatives and Commodity Exchanges

Herbie Skeete (editor)

London: GMB Publishing, 2008
1,200pp, ISBN: 978-1-84673-115-0

This is a useful directory and reference source on around 250 exchanges in over 100 countries. It contains trading, settlement and organizational information, as well as equities, futures and options traded, and contact details and a host of key facts about each exchange.

A History of the Global Stock Market: From Ancient Rome to Silicon Valley

B. Mark Smith

Chicago, Illinois: University of Chicago Press, 2004
344pp, ISBN: 978-0-226-76404-7

A thorough market history through the ages, it examines how stock markets became a focus for investment, and so integral to the global economy. Smith recounts the development of a financial market system through a series of entertaining stories, while arguing that speculative bubbles are not inevitable, and that globalization of the market is nothing new.

How the Stock Market Works, 3rd ed

John M. Dalton

New York Institute of Finance Series
New York: Prentice Hall, 2001
422pp, ISBN: 978-0-7352-0183-5

Provides a comprehensive examination of the workings of the markets, and basic concepts such as market operations, understanding the financial press, initial public offerings, brokering, the mutual fund market, the globalization of the markets, and finance theory. It includes a detailed glossary as a reference tool.

An Introduction to Capital Markets: Products, Strategies, Participants

Andrew Chisholm

Wiley Finance Series
New York: Wiley, 2002
448pp, ISBN: 978-0-471-49866-7

This is a useful primer to the capital markets, which explains in easy terms the basics with the aid of real-world case studies and examples. It provides a useful overview for those entering investment banking or asset management, as it details the markets, participants, equity and debt instruments, the main derivative products, as well as risk management tools and strategies.

Money and Capital Markets, 10th ed

Peter S. Rose, Milton H. Marquis

New York: McGraw-Hill/Irwin, 2008
767pp, ISBN: 978-0-07-128432-5

Provides a thorough view of the financial sector and how it operates. All the major types of financial institutions and financial instruments are considered, as well as how the current global system of money and financial markets is evolving. Money and Capital Markets also usefully describes how interest rates and security values are determined.

Portfolio Theory and Capital Markets

William F. Sharpe

New York: McGraw-Hill, 2000
316pp, ISBN: 978-0-07-135320-5

The bible of modern portfolio theory by the Nobel Prize-winning researcher and author William Sharpe. It introduced the Capital Asset Pricing Model—which became pivotal to modern investment theory—to a wider audience and established Sharpe as a giant of financial thought, crucial as it was to the formulation of modern portfolio theory, derivatives pricing and investment.

Trading Strategies for Capital Markets

Joseph Benning

New York: McGraw-Hill, 2008
356pp, ISBN: 978-0-07-146496-3

Explains how the capital markets work in practice, what the main drivers are and how to recognize them, and the best way to develop and implement effective trading strategies for securities and derivatives. It presents real examples of successful trading strategies, guidance on how they operate, and discusses trading psychology and risk management.

Why Stock Markets Crash: Critical Events in Complex Financial Systems

Didier Sornette

Princeton, New Jersey: Princeton University Press, 2003
421pp, ISBN: 978-0-691-11850-5

A book focused on crises in the financial system; rather than the usual explanation of crashes as based on market failings in the run up to a crash, Sornette explores underlying causes months and years before the event, that can contribute to a dangerous market bubble. Also covers a range of related concepts, such as game theory, fractals, catastrophe theory, and critical phenomena.

MAGAZINES

Bloomberg Markets

Bloomberg
Bloomberg Tower, 731 Lexington Avenue, New York 10022, USA
T: +1 212 318 2000
F: +1 917 369 5000
www.bloomberg.com/news/marketsmag
ISSN: 1531-5061

This is a monthly magazine for professional investors, which provides news, articles, special reports, and commentary on the markets, companies, and hedge funds, as well as covering more general issues. It also goes out to all Bloomberg professional service subscribers.

Capital Market Magazine

Capital Market Publishers
101 Swastik Chambers, Umarshi Bappa Chowk, Sion-Trombay Road, Chembur, Mumbai 400 071, India
T: +91 022 2522 9720
F: +91 022 2522 0954
www.capitalmarket.com

This fortnightly magazine has been published since 1985, and was a pioneer in rating IPOs on a 100-point scale. It features information and commentary on the markets, analyst meetings and AGMs, market beat, market cap, bulletins, broker research, corporate results, sector trends, and company profiles.

The Stock Market Journal

Unitron Media
2605 72nd Avenue E, M/S 344, Ellenton, Florida 34222, USA
T: +1 941 932 8234
F: +1 941 870 7831
www.thestockmarketjournal.com

This financial and investment newspaper journal is aimed at traders of stocks, futures, options and forex, covering small emerging public companies and service providers in the micro-cap and small cap markets. It offers strategies, techniques, and resources related to personal investing and commentary on personal finance issues.

INTERNET

Bloomberg

www.bloomberg.com

A large-scale resource that provides a range of financial and capital market information, commentary, and analysis, as well as covering news, market data, and investment tools, and more general topics such as arts and culture, sports, and science.

Financial Times

www.ft.com

This is an international site for the *Financial Times* newspaper, that presents a wide coverage of financial news, market information, issues, and analysis, and also encompasses world events, politics, and the arts.

ORGANIZATIONS

Europe

Federation of European Securities Exchanges

Chair: Spyros Capralos

Avenue de Cortenbergh 52, 1000 Brussels, Belgium
T: +32 2 551 01 80
F: +32 2 512 49 05
E: info@fese.eu
www.fese.be

FESE represents 42 securities exchanges in 23 different countries, and is one of the founding members of the European Capital Markets Institute. It links up with the international regulatory industry, and aims to promote the global competitiveness and recognition of European exchanges, provide a forum for debate on capital markets, advocate improved regulation and competition in securities markets, and improve the efficiency of clearing and settlement of securities.

Financial Services Authority

Chair: Lord Turner of Ecchinswell

25 North Colonnade, Canary Wharf, London, E14 5HS, UK
T: +44 (0) 20 7066 1000
F: +44 (0) 20 7066 1099
www.fsa.gov.uk

  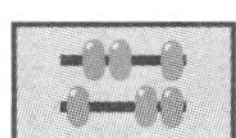      

The Financial Services Authority (FSA) is an independent non-governmental body, which regulates the financial services industry in the UK. It acts as the authority for listing of shares on a stock exchange, and has four statutory objectives: market confidence, public awareness, consumer protection, and reduction of financial crime. It also has the strategic aims of promoting efficient, orderly and fair markets, helping retail consumers achieve a fair deal, and improving our business capability and effectiveness.

USA

Financial Industry Regulatory Authority

Chair: Mary L. Schapiro
1735 K Street, Washington, DC 20006, USA
T: +1 301 590 6500
www.finra.org

FINRA is the largest independent regulator for all securities firms doing business in the US, and has the role of protecting investors by maintaining the fairness of the US capital markets. It is involved in virtually every aspect of the securities business, including registering and educating industry participants, examinations of securities firms, writing rules that govern the conduct of the industry, and enforcing those rules and the federal securities laws.

Institute for Financial Markets

Chair: Peter F. Borish
2001 Pennsylvania Avenue NW, Suite 600, Washington, DC 20006, USA
T: +1 202 223 1528
F: +1 202 296 3184
E: info@theIFM.org
www.theifm.org

The IFM is a non-profit organization, and an autonomous affiliate of the Futures Industry Association. It has no members and does not engage in any lobbying or political activities, but provides unbiased information, education, ethics and data, to industry professionals, market-users, investors, and decision makers in the financial services industry.

US Securities and Exchange Commission

Chair: Christopher Cox
100 F Street NE, Washington, DC 20549, USA
T: +1 202 942 8088
E: help@sec.gov
www.sec.gov

The mission of the SEC is to protect investors, maintain fair, orderly, and efficient markets, and facilitate capital formation. It oversees the key participants in the securities world, requires public companies to disclose meaningful financial and other information to the public, and works to uncover cases of insider trading, accounting fraud, and the provision of false or misleading information about securities and the companies that issue them.

International

ACI

Chair: Manfred Wiebogen
8 Rue du Mail, 75002, Paris, France
T: +33 1 42 97 51 15
F: +33 1 42 97 51 16
E: deputymanager@aciforex.com
www.aciforex.com

The ACI is a global association for financial market professionals engaged within the financial trading or sales environment in the global financial markets, representing foreign exchange, interest rate products and other securities, banknotes and bullions, precious metals and commodities and their various kinds of derivatives.

International Association of Options Exchanges and Clearing Houses

Chair: Hugh Freedberg
www.world-exchanges.org/ioma

IOMA includes most of the major exchanges trading options on equities, equity indexes, debt instruments, currencies, futures, and commodities, and is affiliated to the World Federation of Exchanges. It conducts the annual survey of options markets, and maintains a directory of IOMA members.

World Federation of Exchanges

Chair: William J. Brodsky
France
T: +33 (0) 1 58 62 54 00
F: +33 (0) 1 58 62 50 48
E: secretariat@world-exchanges.org
www.world-exchanges.org

The WFE, formerly the International Federation of Stock Exchanges, is an international trade organization for securities and derivative markets such as stock exchanges, and its exchanges are home to over 46,000 listed companies. Membership is considered by some governments and national associations of asset managers as a criteria for preferential investment policy and taxation for these markets.

Central Banking

BOOKS

Asian States, Asian Bankers: Central Banking in Southeast Asia

Natasha Hamilton-Hart
Cornell Studies in Political Economy Series
Ithaca, New York: Cornell University Press, 2002
215pp, ISBN: 978-0-8014-3987-2

An investigation of central banks, governments, and private bankers in Southeast Asia, that shows how the development and attributes of central banks and state financial institutions shape their interactions with private bankers and affect how they manage the financial sector.

Central Bank Directory 2008

Robert Pringle (editor)
London: Central Banking Publications, 2008
290pp, ISBN: 978-1-902182-51-3

A key information resource on central banks, containing details on over 4,000 key contacts in 162 Central Banks, a short history of each bank, current legislative arrangements, terms of appointment, and past governors. Now in its 17th year, this annual directory is extensively revised every year.

Central Bank Modernisation

Peter Nicholl (editor)
London: Central Banking Publications, 2005
230pp, ISBN: 978-1-902182-38-4

A compilation of papers by leading industry experts that examine how central banks are developing their governance, strategic planning, and process reforms during a time of great upheaval in the financial sector. Uses case studies to illustrate how many leading central bankers have reformed their institutions, and are now focusing on greater efficiency and competitiveness.

Central Banking as Global Governance: Constructing Financial Credibility

Rodney Bruce Hall
Cambridge Studies in International Relations Series
Cambridge, UK: Cambridge University Press, 2009
280pp, ISBN: 978-0-521-72721-1

A new academic study that analyses central banking in terms of governance, explaining how central banking and monetary economics should be approached in the wider context of international finance. It offers an original assessment of the mechanisms of governance, arguing that they are based more on social than material processes.

Central Banking in Theory and Practice

A. S. Blinder
Lionel Robbins Lectures Series
Cambridge, Massachusetts: MIT Press, 1998
92pp, ISBN: 978-0-262-52260-1

Argues for the greater use of academic theory in the monetary policies of central banks, and offers advice for concentrating research on providing practical solutions to central banking problems. Also discusses the goals of monetary policy, the choice of monetary instrument, central bank credibility, central bank independence, and the relationship between the central bank and financial markets.

Central Banks as Economic Institutions

Jean-Philippe Touffut (editor)
Cournot Centre for Economic Studies Series
Cheltenham, UK: Edward Elgar Publishing, 2008
256pp, ISBN: 978-1-84844-108-8

A collection of papers by distinguished economists and central bankers that evaluate how central banks function, develop their policies, choose their economic instruments, and examines the implications of their increased focus on independence and inflation targeting. It also considers issues around accountability, transparency, monetary policy, and policy problems relating to globalization and financial imbalances.

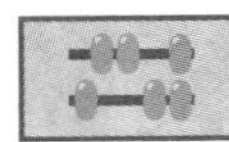

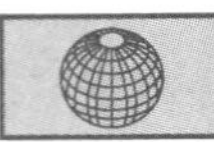

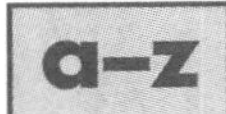

Central Banks in the Age of the Euro: Europeanization, Convergence, and Power

Kenneth Dyson, Martin Marcussen (editors)

Oxford, UK: Oxford University Press, 2009
384pp, ISBN: 978-0-19-921823-3

A new study on the impact of Europeanization on central banks since the introduction of the euro, which analyses how the euro has altered the power and convergence of central banks. It also uses case studies to consider how EU central banks have evolved in terms of monetary policy, financial market supervision, accountability and transparency, and research.

Challenges for Central Banking

Anthony M. Santomero, Staffan Viotti, Anders Vredin (editors)

Boston, Massachusetts: Kluwer Academic, 2001
274pp, ISBN: 978-0-7923-7346-9

Provides a comprehensive analysis of the role and operations of central banks, and looks at the key problems that they are going to face in the future. Also discusses the challenges of financial innovations for the supervision and stability of financial institutions.

The Changing Face of Central Banking: Evolutionary Trends Since World War II

Pierre L. Siklos

Studies in Macroeconomic History Series
New York: Cambridge University Press, 2008
372pp, ISBN: 978-0-521-03449-4

This is a comprehensive and wide-ranging overview of how central banks have transformed themselves into major players in national and international policy making over the last 60 years. It is based on a study of 20 industrial countries, and examines the economic, political and institutional influences that have affected central banks and their relationship with government.

The European Central Bank: The New European Leviathan?, 2nd ed

David J. Howarth, Peter H. Loedel

Basingstoke, UK: Palgrave Macmillan, 2005
296pp, ISBN: 978-1-4039-4159-6

Takes a comprehensive overview of the antecedents of European monetary authority, how the European Central Bank originated, its difficult first years, how it operates in the current economic climate, and explores different national perspectives on central bank independence.

Evolution and Procedures in Central Banking

David E. Altig, Bruce D. Smith (editors)

Cambridge, UK: Cambridge University Press, 2003
334pp, ISBN: 978-0-521-81427-0

A revealing overview of the institutional nature of central banking, which analyzes their overall development, operating framework, and the challenges they face in the future. Through a series of rigorous articles, this book presents a combination of historical observation and economic theory and experimentation to provide a comprehensive overview of central banking.

Financial Stability and Central Banks: A Global Perspective

Richard Brearley, Juliette Healey, Peter J. N. Sinclair, Charles Goodhart, David T. Llewellyn, Chang Shu (editors)

Central Bank Governors' Symposium Series
London: Routledge, 2001
272pp, ISBN: 978-0-415-25776-3

Written by practicing policy makers, Financial Stability and Central Banks provides an important overview of current policy issues and the legal, regulatory, managerial and economic issues that are affecting central banks. It is also a topical examination of the role of central banks in protecting the banking and payments system from risks and crises.

Handbook of Central Banking and Financial Authorities in Europe: New Architectures in the Supervision of Financial Markets

Donato Masciandaro

Elgar Original Reference Series
Cheltenham, UK: Edward Elgar Publishing, 2005
566pp, ISBN: 978-1-84376-789-3

This is a comprehensive overview of the changes in regulation and supervision of the banking and financial industry in Europe. Written by a team of industry experts, it focuses on the role of national central banks, the financial supervisory authorities, and the European Central Bank, and highlights the emerging role of new integrated financial authorities.

A History of Central Banking in Great Britain and the United States

John H. Wood

Cambridge, UK: Cambridge University Press, 2008
456pp, ISBN: 978-0-521-74131-6

Examines the early emergence of central banks and monetary policy in Great Britain and the United States in terms of the knowledge and behavior of central bankers and their interactions with economists and politicians. It focuses on how the continuity in central banking contributed to the stability of the financial markets.

International Economic Indicators and Central Banks

Anne Dolganos Picker

Wiley Finance Series
Hoboken, New Jersey: Wiley, 2007
295pp, ISBN: 978-0-471-75113-7

Discusses the importance of using the movement of international economic indicators to understand global economic events as they occur, which helps awareness of how the decisions of foreign central banks can affect market behavior. This approach can effectively improve investment decisions in international markets.

New Horizons in Central Bank Risk Management

Robert Pringle, Nick Carver

London: Central Banking Publications, 2004
269pp, ISBN: 978-1-902182-25-4

Discusses how central banks are identifying and managing the new risks they are facing, presents some of the new frameworks being introduced, and the best approach to effective risk mitigation throughout an organization. Also covers key issues such as business failure, litigation, deflation, and systemic failures, and contains a survey on the diversity and emerging trends in central bank risk management around the world.

The Origin of Financial Crises: Central Banks, Credit Bubbles and the Efficient Market Fallacy

George Cooper

Petersfield, UK: Harriman House, 2008
208pp, ISBN: 978-1-905641-85-7

A timely examination of the underlying forces behind the global economic and financial crisis; Cooper takes a contentious look at the consensus of economic theory and practice, arguing that financial markets do not actually follow the efficient market principles depicted in textbooks, but rather are inherently unstable and prone to regular upheaval and crisis.

The Past and Future of Central Bank Cooperation

Claudio Borio, Gianni Toniolo, Piet Clement (editors)

Studies in Macroeconomic History Series
Cambridge, UK: Cambridge University Press, 2008
256pp, ISBN: 978-0-521-87779-4

A timely and thoroughly researched analysis and history of central bank cooperation, demonstrating how such cooperation helps prevent or limit financial crises, as well as the potentially disastrous consequences of non-cooperation. It explores how the cooperation between central banks is crucial to maintaining monetary and financial stability, and the smooth functioning of the international financial system.

The Quiet Revolution: Central Banking Goes Modern

A. S. Blinder

Arthur M. Okum Memorial Lectures Series
New Haven, Connecticut: Yale University Press, 2004
144pp, ISBN: 978-0-300-10087-7

Looks at the evolution of central banking in the last few years, focusing on the move toward transparency, the evolution from individual to committee decision-making, and the more attentive approach to the financial markets. It is based on the author's experiences as a former vice chairman of the Federal Reserve System and member of President Clinton's Council of Economic Advisers.

MAGAZINES

The Banker

Financial Times
1 Southwark Bridge, London, SE1 9HL, UK
T: +44 (0) 20 7873 3000
www.thebanker.com
ISSN: 0005-5395

This monthly magazine, established in 1926, provides investigative comment and expert analysis on the key developments in the global banking arena. It produces articles, special reports, awards, industry rankings, database, archive, as well as free monthly electronic newsletters on cash and securities services, capital markets, FX and derivatives, news and comment, retail banking, and technology.

JOURNALS

Central Banking

Central Banking Publications, Incisive Media, Haymarket House, 28–29 Haymarket, London, SW1Y 4RX, UK
T: +44 (0) 20 7484 9700
F: +44 (0) 20 7930 2238
www.centralbanking.co.uk/publications/journals/cbj.htm
ISSN: 0960-6319

This quarterly journal is focused on reporting, analyzing, and commenting on the activities of the central banks around the world. It is aimed at senior staff and key decision-makers from central banks, and provides analysis of key developments affecting them. It also features interviews with leading central bankers, special issues on key central banks, and articles from internationally renowned academics and commentators.

International Journal of Central Banking

DG Research, European Central Bank, Postfach 16 03 19, D-60066 Frankfurt, Germany
T: +49 69 1344 7623
F: +49 69 1344 8553
www.ijcb.org
ISSN: 1815-4654

This quarterly international journal is an initiative of the Bank for International Settlements (BIS), the European Central Bank, the Group of Ten (G-10) central banks, and other central banks and sponsoring organizations. It features articles on central bank theory and practice, with a special emphasis on research relating to monetary and financial stability.

INTERNET

Bank for International Settlements

www.bis.org/cbanks.htm

The Bank for International Settlements (BIS) is an international organization that fosters international monetary and financial cooperation, and serves as a bank for central banks. Its website contains links to central banks of each country, listed alphabetically.

CentralBankNews.com

www.centralbanknews.com

This online resource, established in 2000, provides daily updates and an independent commentary on news and research in the fields of monetary policy and interest rates, financial regulation, reserve management, payment systems and public debt management. It also monitors the activities of the major international financial institutions such as the IMF.

ORGANIZATIONS

Europe

European Central Bank

Chair: Jean-Claude Trichet
Postfach 16 03 19, 60066 Frankfurt am Main, Germany
T: +49 69 13 44 0
F: +49 69 13 44 60 00
E: info@ecb.europa.eu
www.ecb.int

The European Central Bank is one of the most important central banks, having responsibility for monetary policy for the Eurozone. Its main task is to maintain the euro's purchasing power and price stability in the euro area, the 15 European Union countries that have introduced the euro since 1999. It works closely with the national central banks of all euro area countries, and focuses on decision-making, independence, transparency, accountability, corporate governance, and capital subscription.

USA

Federal Reserve System

Chair: Ben Bernanke
Eccles Building, Constitution Avenue, Washington, DC 20551, USA
T: +1 202 452 3000
www.federalreserve.gov

The Federal Reserve System is the central banking system of the US. It comprises the Board of Governors, the Federal Open Market Committee, 12 regional Federal Reserve Banks, many private US member banks, and a number of advisory councils. In its role as the central bank of the US, the Fed serves as both a banker's bank and the government's bank, helping to assure the safety and efficiency of the payments system, and processing a variety of financial transactions.

International

World Bank

Chair: Robert Zoellick
1818 H Street NW, Washington, DC 20433, USA
T: +1 202 473 1000
F: +1 202 477 6391
www.worldbank.org

The World Bank is a source of financial and technical assistance to developing countries for development programs with the stated goal of reducing poverty. It is made up of the International Bank for Reconstruction and Development (IBRD), and the International Development Association (IDA), which itself incorporates the International Finance Corporation, the Multilateral Investment Guarantee Agency, and the International Centre for Settlement of Investment Disputes.

Contingency, Crisis, Disaster Management

BOOKS

Business Continuity Planning: A Step-by-Step Guide with Planning Forms on CD-ROM, 3rd ed

Kenneth L. Fulmer
Brookfield, Connecticut: Rothstein Associates, 2005
190pp, ISBN: 978-1-931332-21-7

This detailed workbook will help you build a corporate disaster plan. It covers factors such as choosing an alternate location and selecting vendors to enable your organization to resume business as soon as possible. It reviews how to choose a planning coordinator and recovery team, how to write a planning document, and stresses the need for testing the plan to be sure it works.

Business Continuity Planning: Protecting Your Organization's Life

Ken Doughty (editor)
Best Practices Series
Boca Raton, Florida: Auerbach, 2000
408pp, ISBN: 978-0-8493-0907-6

Contributions from a range of experts provide a comprehensive overview of business continuity planning. They indicate the importance of analyzing the risks to which an organization is exposed and of developing a plan for the resumption of business after a crisis. They also give detailed guidance on building, testing, maintaining, and updating a business continuity plan.

Business Continuity Strategies: Protecting Against Unplanned Disasters, 3rd ed

Kenneth N. Myers
Chichester, UK: Wiley, 2006
224pp, ISBN: 978-0-470-04038-6

Employing a thorough and practical approach, this edition provides a proven methodology for implementing a realistic and cost-efficient business contingency program. It shows corporate leaders how to prepare a logical "what if" plan that would enable an organization to retain market share, service customers, and maintain cash flow if a disaster occurs.

The Definitive Handbook of Business Continuity Management, 2nd ed

Andrew Hiles, Peter Barnes (editors)
Chichester, UK: Wiley, 2007
666pp, ISBN: 978-0-470-51638-6

This revised and updated edition tackles business continuity from two perspectives: the first part discusses the key concepts and provides an overview of the type of events which can interrupt business; the second takes the form of a practical how-to guide. Further resources, including case studies and standards for business continuity practitioners, are listed in appendices.

Disaster Management: A Guide to Management and Crisis Communication

Chris Skinner, Gary Mersham

Oxford: Oxford University Press, 2002
192pp, ISBN: 978-0-19-578313-1

This practical guidebook is about achieving a state of preparedness for all types of disaster, natural or human, that can affect a company. It provides the insights and tools required to manage the situation and any associated publicity this might incur. Relevant for students and professionals in the fields of human resource management, personnel management, public relations, and communications, it includes case studies, and offers operational guidelines and checklists for implementing a crisis management plan, and for handling media relations.

Disaster Recovery Planning: Preparing for the Unthinkable, 3rd ed

Jon William Toigo

Harlow, UK: Prentice Hall, 2003
512pp, ISBN: 978-0-13-046282-4

This volume provides the information needed to develop a plan to protect your company's data in case of an emergency. Filled with interviews with vendors and practitioners, it walks the reader through the steps that those responsible for an organization's information technology must take to ensure that organizational data will be available in the aftermath of a disaster.

Managing Communications in a Crisis

Peter Ruff, Khalid Aziz

Aldershot, UK: Gower Publishing, 2003
176pp, ISBN: 978-0-566-08294-8

This book details how crisis situations can be identified and dealt with to ensure that risks to an organization's financial well-being and reputation are minimized. Part I considers the definitions of a crisis and the theory behind dealing with crisis communications, both externally and internally. Practicalities of crisis management communications dealt with in Part II include the identification of audiences and how and by whom each should be dealt with. Checklists and supporting information on the key aspects of the communication process are also supplied, together with brief case studies.

Managing Crises Before They Happen, 2nd ed

Ian I. Mitroff, Gus Anagnos

New York: AMACOM, 2005
192pp, ISBN: 978-0-8144-7328-3

Having explained the specific features of corporate culture that enable crises to happen, the authors present a framework for preventing such crises happening and for controlling the damage they cause.

Risk Issues and Crisis Management: A Casebook of Best Practice, 4th ed

Michael Regester, Judy Larkin

PR in Practice Series
London: Kogan Page, 2008
256pp, ISBN: 978-0-7494-5107-3

This book deals with the successful handling of crisis situations so that damage and disruption are minimized. Case studies and models are included and illustrate how complex crises have been handled in practice, both successfully and unsuccessfully.

Secure Online Business Handbook: E-Commerce, IT Functionality, and Business Continuity, 4th ed

Jonathan Reuvid

London: Kogan Page, 2006
256pp, ISBN: 978-0-7494-4642-0

This practical handbook, divided into five sections, contains a collection of contributions from a range of experts in the field of information technology and e-commerce and addresses the need for effective management of business risk. Information at risk and the business case for security are considered first. Points of exposure and the range of threats to privacy and integrity are explored, and methods of software protection such as firewalls, encryption, digital signatures and biometrics are covered. In the operational management section, the need for a culture of workplace security is also discussed, and data recovery, disaster management, and forensics are covered under the heading of contingency planning.

MAGAZINES

Continuity

Business Continuity Institute
10 Southview Park, Marsack Street, Caversham, Berkshire, RG4 5AF, UK
T: +44 (0) 870 603 8783
F: +44 (0) 870 603 8761
www.thebci.org/continuity.htm
ISSN: 1460-1451

Continuity is the official journal of the Business Continuity Institute. It appears quarterly and includes articles, news, and reports of research projects.

Disaster Recovery Journal

Richard L. Arnold
PO Box 510110, St Louis, MO 63151, USA
T: +1 314 894 0276
F: +1 314 894 7474
www.drj.com
ISSN: 1079-736X

The *DRJ* was founded in 1987 and is published quarterly. It covers the field of business continuity and disaster recovery.

JOURNALS

Disaster Prevention and Management

Emerald
60/62 Toller Lane, Bradford, West Yorkshire, BD8 9BY, UK
T: +44 (0) 1274 777 700
F: +44 (0) 1274 785 200
www.emeraldinsight.com/0965-3562.htm
ISSN: 0965-3562

This journal appears five times a year and focuses on the latest research into the prevention and mitigation of natural and man-made disasters. Each issue includes articles by international experts in the field, news, product reviews, case studies, and details of events, conferences, and resources.

Journal of Contingencies and Crisis Management

Blackwell Publishing
9600 Garsington Road, Oxford, OX4 2DQ, UK
T: +44 (0) 1865 791 100
F: +44 (0) 1865 791 347
www.wiley.com/bw/journal.asp?ref=0966-0879
ISSN: 0966-0879

This is a quarterly journal for managers with responsibilities in the area of risk and crisis management.

Journal of Small Business and Enterprise Development

Emerald
60/62 Toller Lane, Bradford, West Yorkshire, BD8 9BY, UK
T: +44 (0) 1274 777 700
F: +44 (0) 1274 785 200
www.emeraldinsight.com/1462-6004.htm
ISSN: 1462-6004

The *JSBED* is a peerreviewed journal that disseminates research findings and best practice and aims to bridge the gap between theory and practice in the field of small business and enterprise development. The journal contains articles, case studies, and book reviews, and is aimed at those responsible for the management of SMEs, those who provide support and assistance to entrepreneurs and owner-managers, and those involved in the development of enterprise policy.

INTERNET

Crisis Management and Disaster Recovery

www.crisismanagement-disasterrecovery.com

This site provides information and links for both crisis management and disaster recovery. It links you with companies that can help with crisis management plans or disaster recovery plans, and gives information about crisis management and disaster management.

Crisis Management and Disaster Recovery Group

www.crisis-management-and-disaster-recovery.com

This site provides information on how to create and maintain a disaster recovery or crisis management plan and provides access to leading support resources.

Disaster Recovery Journal

www.drj.com

This journal's website provides access to a great deal of free material and resources including articles, a vendor directory, and chat groups.

Federal Emergency Management Agency

www.fema.gov

This US federal government site features GEMS (Global Emergency Management System), a searchable database of reviewed websites in fields related to emergency management, and a virtual library including practical guides and checklists.

globalcontinuity.com
www.globalcontinuity.com

This is a portal site for business recovery and continuity planning information, featuring a database of suppliers and including news, articles, surveys, and related links.

London Prepared
www.londonprepared.gov.uk

The UK government has launched this site to give advice and information on how to protect you business against all sorts of threats. The site is part of London Resilience, a broad project that helps people in London to prepare themselves for emergencies.

ORGANIZATIONS

Europe

Emergency Planning Society
The Media Centre, Culverhouse Cross, Cardiff, CF6 6XJ, UK
T: +44 (0) 845 600 9587
F: +44 (0) 29 2059 0396
www.the-eps.org

The society was formed in 1993 through the merger of the Emergency Planning Association and the County Emergency Planning Officers Society. Its aims are to foster effective emergency planning and management in the United Kingdom and to promote the professional interests of its members, who include representatives of the emergency services, local and central government, the health services, industry, consultants, and voluntary organizations. It is active in the areas of training, professional development, networking, representation, and publications.

USA

Contingency Planning Exchange, Inc. (CPE)
11 Hanover Square, Suite 501, New York, NY 10176-3099, USA
T: +1 212 344 4003
F: +1 212 344 2016
E: headquarters@cpeworld.org
www.cpeworld.ciom

The CPE is a professional organization for disaster recovery specialists which provides a forum for members to exchange information, and represents the views of members to government agencies and the wider business community.

Federal Emergency Management Agency (FEMA)
500 C Street S.W., Washington, DC 20472, USA
T: +1 800 621 3362
www.fema.gov

An independent agency of the federal government of the United States, FEMA was founded in 1979, but can trace its origins back to the Congressional Act of 1803. The mission of the agency is to reduce loss of life and property and to protect the national infrastructure from all types of hazard through an emergency management program that includes preparation, mitigation, response, and recovery.

BRIC

BCM Institute
315 Outram Road #15-04, Tan Boon Liat Building, Singapore, 169074, Singapore
T: +65 6323 1500
F: +65 6323 0933
E: info@bcm-institute.org
www.bcm-institute.org

Covering most of Asia, including India and China, and represented in Africa, the BCM was erected to create a common base knowledge of business continuity (BC) management and disaster recovery (DR) planning, to certify qualified individuals, and to create credibility and professionalism in certified BC and DR professionals.

International

Association of Contingency Planners (ACP)
Technical Enterprises, 7044 South 13th Street, Oak Creek, WI 53154, USA
T: +1 414 768 8000
E: acp_membership@techenterprises.net
www.acp-international.com

The ACP is a nonprofit trade association for contingency planners, business continuity professionals, and emergency managers. The organization, which began informally in 1983 and was incorporated in 1985, provides an international forum for networking and information exchange. Activities include a branch network, a quarterly newsletter, and an annual international symposium.

Business Continuity Institute (BCI)
10 Southview Park, Marsack Street, Caversham, RG4 5AF, UK
T: +44 (0) 870 603 8783
F: +44 (0) 870 603 8761
E: bci@thebci.org
www.thebci.org

The BCI is a professional organization founded in 1994 to promote high standards of professional competence and ethics in the provision of business continuity planning and services. It has developed standards of competence, a code of ethics, and an accreditation scheme for continuity practitioners. Additional activities include seminars, conferences, and the Business Continuity Awards. The organization has over 1,100 members in 32 countries.

Disaster Preparedness and Emergency Response Association (DERA)
PO Box 280795, Denver, CO 80228, USA
E: dera@disasters.org
www.disasters.com

DERA is a nonprofit professional association, established in 1962, whose members include emergency management specialists, government officials, consultants, business managers, volunteers, researchers, and educators. It sponsors research projects in the field and publishes a newsletter, *DisasterCom*.

DRI International
1400 Eye Street, NW, Suite 1050, Washington, DC 20005, USA
T: +1 202 962 3979
F: +1 202 962 3939
www.drii.org

Formerly the Disaster Recovery Institute, DRI International was formed in 1988 by a group of professionals in St. Louis, Missouri, who saw a need for education in business continuity. The organization is a nonprofit one; it sets standards of competence for business continuity and has developed a certification program.

Emergency Preparedness for Industry and Commerce Council (EPICC)
9800, 140 Street, Surrey, British Columbia, V3T 4M5, Canada
T: +1 604 580 7373
F: +1 604 586 4334
E: epicc@telus.net
www.epicc.org

The aim of this organization is to help businesses and communities prepare to survive disasters through education and representation. It organizes workshops and forums, and publishes a newsletter.

International Association of Emergency Managers (IAEM)
201 Park Washington Court, Falls Church, VI 22046-4527, USA
T: +1 703 538 1795
F: +1 703 241 5603
E: info@iaem.com
www.iaem.com

The IAEM is a nonprofit educational organization; it created the Certified Emergency Manager program to maintain professional standards in emergency management. Members receive a monthly newsletter and can participate in internet discussion groups.

  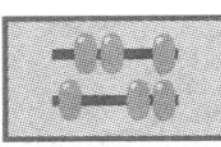   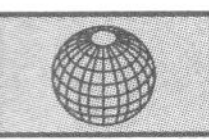   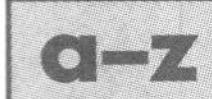

Corporate Insurance

BOOKS

Alternative Risk Strategies: A New Approach to Handling Risk

Morton Lane (editor)

London: Risk Books, 2002
684pp, ISBN: 978-1-899332-63-2

This comprehensive and wide-ranging analysis of the overlap between insurance and finance examines new areas of risk financing and their effect on traditional methods of insurance. It provides an overview of the reinsurance industry and recent developments, research, and current practice, and a detailed approach to contingent financing, terrorism risk, captives, finite risk, loss portfolio transfers, the financial impact of catastrophic natural events, and modeling techniques.

Alternative Risk Transfer: Integrated Risk Management through Insurance, Reinsurance, and the Capital Markets

Erik Banks

Wiley Finance Series
Chichester, UK: Wiley, 2004
226pp, ISBN: 978-0-470-85745-8

This is a practical exploration of alternative risk transfer (ART) and how it has evolved into an integral part of the financial system. It focuses on risk and the ART market, insurance and reinsurance, the capital markets, and enterprise risk management, and examines its potential as a source of risk solutions and risk capacity, as well as for integrating corporate risk management programs.

Captive Insurance Companies: An Introduction to Captives, Closely-Held Insurance Companies, and Risk Retention Groups

Jay D. Adkisson

Bloomington, Indiana: iUniverse, 2006
370pp, ISBN: 978-0-595-42237-1

This introduction to the captive insurance sector discusses its main features, such as wealth transfer, and accumulation and preservation advantages of captives, as well providing an overview of the types of captives, their taxation, and domiciles. It examines how they are formed, and their potential to develop into a full insurance companies seeking to profit from underwriting the risks of others.

Captive Insurance Companies in Risk Management

Florian Klingenschmid

Saarbrücken, Germany: VDM Verlag, 2008
68pp, ISBN: 978-3-639-01170-8

This explores captive insurance as an innovative form of alternative risk transfer, and how companies use it to manage their risks effectively. It explains the basics of captive insurance, the different types of captives, why they are created, and the international features of the industry, as well as focusing on the influence that captives have on the risk management and credit rating of their parent company.

Dictionary of Insurance Terms, 5th ed

Harvey W. Rubin

Barron's Business Guides Series
Hauppauge, New York: Barron's Educational Series, 2008
576pp, ISBN: 978-0-7641-3884-3

This popular insurance dictionary, now in its fifth edition, provides clear definitions, descriptions, and examples of the terminology used in the industry. It is a reference for agents, brokers, actuaries, underwriters, and consumers, presenting around 4,500 key terms relevant to life, health, property, and casualty insurance, as well as to home owners' insurance, professional liability insurance, pension plans, and individual retirement accounts.

Fundamentals of Risk and Insurance, 10th ed

Emmet J. Vaughan, Therese M. Vaughan

Hoboken, New Jersey: Wiley, 2008
704pp, ISBN: 978-0-470-08753-4

This textbook addresses the principles of risk management as they relate to the insurance industry, and reviews the impact of risk on both the individual and society. It describes how insurance can effectively resolve risk management issues and problems, and discusses the key concepts of insurance theory, focusing on insurance products and the use of insurance within the risk management framework.

The Guide to Understanding Business Insurance Products: How to Safeguard Businesses from Financial Risk

A. M. Best Company

Charleston, South Carolina: BookSurge Publishing, 2007
24pp, ISBN: 978-1-4196-6635-3

This handbook on corporate insurance products provides a valuable resource, explaining what each coverage protects against, who needs it, how it works, and itys key details. Produced for insurance clients, prospects, staff, brokers, agents and carriers, it describes most areas of commercial insurance coverage, including business owners' policy, commercial general liability, commercial property insurance, employment practices liability, intellectual property, and product liability.

Hide! Here Comes the Insurance Guy: A Practical Guide to Understanding Business Insurance and Risk Management

Rick Vassar

Bloomington, Indiana: iUniverse, 2006
196pp, ISBN: 978-0-595-38608-6

This is an accessible resource for reducing business and commercial insurance costs, taken from a risk management perspective. It provides understandable explanations and practical solutions, and a series of steps for reducing expenses in current insurance programs, based on understanding the language, knowing the players, developing a strategy for maximizing coverage for minimal cost, and investing the time to gain real financial benefit.

Inside the Minds: The Insurance Business

Martin D. Feinstein, Constantine Iordanou, Mark E. Watson, James J. Maguire, John W. Hayden

Inside the Minds Series
Boston, Massachusetts: Aspatore Books, 2004
128pp, ISBN: 978-1-58762-423-0

This provides insights from senior executives representing many leading insurance companies, as they explore how to be successful in this fast-changing industry. It gives an overview of current and future trends in the industry, presents strategies for revenue growth, examines the inner workings of the business, and identifies the biggest risks companies face, and how to hedge them.

Insurance: From Underwriting to Derivatives: Asset Liability Management in Insurance Companies

Eric Briys, François de Varenne

Wiley Finance Series
Chichester, UK: Wiley, 2001
165pp, ISBN: 978-0-471-49227-6

This offers a detailed examination of the convergence between the insurance industry and the capital markets, as traditional insurance is overtaken by its new role as an asset class. It discusses the main issues and trends affecting the industry, how it is responding to increasing market pressure, and how insurance risks are now being priced and exchanged on the markets.

Introduction to Risk Management and Insurance, 9th ed

Mark S. Dorfman

Upper Saddle River, New Jersey: Prentice Hall, 2008
567pp, ISBN: 978-0-13-224227-1

This primer on risk and insurance focuses on problem solving for the insurance practitioner, examining the business characteristics of risk management and insurance, as well as consumer applications. It covers professional financial planning, and insurance regulation and contracts, as well as topics such as homeowners insurance, annuities, standard life insurance contract provisions and options, commercial property insurance, general and special liability insurance, and employee benefits.

Modelling Extremal Events: For Insurance and Finance

Paul Embrechts, Claudia Klüppelberg, Thomas Mikosch

Stochastic Modelling and Applied Probability Series
Berlin: Springer, 1997
655pp, ISBN: 978-3-540-60931-5

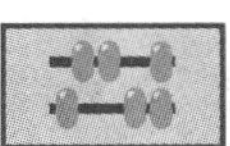
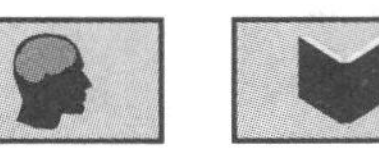

This comprehensive practitioner reference to extremal events modelling presents a wide range of theory and applications of extremal processes in an accessible way. It combines key concepts in extreme value theory with extreme event modelling, and analyzes a number of issues relevant to both insurance and financial applications, such as large insurance claims, large fluctuations in financial data, stock market shocks, and risk management.

Reinsurance: Fundamentals and New Challenges, 4th ed
Ruth Gastel (editor)
New York: Insurance Information Institute, 2004
218pp, ISBN: 978-0-932387-50-9

This is a collection of essays by a number of industry experts that provides a basic introduction to reinsurance, and how it functions as a way for insurance to spread risk. It covers all the main technical aspects of the subject, and the challenges currently facing the industry, and will appeal to those needing a practical overview, such as regulators and the wider financial community.

Risk Management and Insurance: Perspectives in a Global Economy
W. Jean Kwon, Harold D. Skipper
Malden, Massachusetts: Wiley, 2007
751pp, ISBN: 978-1-4051-2541-3

This examines the main aspects of risk management and insurance for both students and practitioners. It explores key aspects of international risk management and insurance, how they operate, and the economic, social, political, and regulatory landscape of the global risk and insurance markets. Using real-world case studies, discussion questions, and exercise modules, it describes the different types of risk businesses face, including financial, political, environmental, social, and health.

Risk Management for Insurers: Risk Control, Economic Capital and Solvency II
René Doff
London: Risk Books, 2007
204pp, ISBN: 978-1-904339-79-3

With the insurance industry focused on risk exposure, and the supervisory rules for regulatory capital for insurance companies being transformed, this shows how to implement risk management best practice. It presents key risk management techniques, tools, and terms, analyzes the impact of Solvency II on the regulatory framework of the industry, and explores how risk management and value creation can be integrated into the management control framework of insurance companies.

Structured Finance and Insurance: The ART of Managing Capital and Risk, 2nd ed
Christopher L. Culp
Wiley Finance Series
Hoboken, New Jersey: Wiley, 2006
892pp, ISBN: 978-0-471-70631-1

This introduction to alternative risk transfer (ART) provides an overview of the key financing and risk management innovations in both insurance and capital markets. It examines the development and benefits of this new generation of products for managing market, credit, operational, legal, and other risks, and explains the theory and practice of risk transfer through either balance sheet mechanisms or insurance.

MAGAZINES

Best's Review
A. M. Best Company
Ambest Road, Oldwick, NJ 08858, USA
T: +1 908 439 2200
www.bestreview.com
ISSN: 1527-5914

This monthly insurance magazine offers news coverage of the global insurance industry. It focuses on topical areas such as trends in the reinsurance/capital markets, new technology, health/employee benefit issues, the property/casualty sector, life insurance, agent/brokers, changes in regulation and law, and provides exclusive lists and rankings.

Business Insurance
Crain Communications
711 Third Avenue, New York, NY 10017-4036, USA
T: +1 212 210 0100
F: +1 212 210 0223
www.businessinsurance.com
ISSN: 0007-6864

This weekly newspaper on business insurance features news, comment, and analysis on the industry, as well as a number of industry directories, a knowledge center, an industry focus, details of jobs, and email news alerts.

Business Insurance Europe
Crain Communications
9–17 Perrymount Road, Haywards Heath, RH16 3DH, UK
T: +44 (0) 1444 475 650
F: +44 (0) 8456 777 804
www.bieurope.com
ISSN: 1759-1295

This fortnightly publication is a source of news, views, and analysis on the European risk and commercial insurance business. It provides coverage on the latest developments, comment on topical issues, special feature articles, case studies, regulatory updates, and the latest trends and views from leading industry professionals.

Claims
The National Underwriter Company
5081 Olympic Boulevard, Erlanger, KY 41018, USA
T: +1 859 692 2128
F: +1 859 692 2246
www.claimsmag.com

This monthly magazine focuses on the business of loss for property/casualty insurance claims professionals and corporate risk managers. It provides reports on disasters, insurance crime, emerging trends in insurance claims, regulatory, judicial and legislative changes, and expert advice and educational articles that cover techniques for handling insured losses.

Continuity Insurance & Risk
Perspective Publishing
6th Floor, 3 London Wall Buildings, London, EC2M 5PD, UK
T: +44 (0) 20 7562 2401
F: +44 (0) 20 7374 2701
www.cirmagazine.com
ISSN: 1479-862X

This professional magazine, published bimonthly, provides authoritative news and analysis for business continuity, risk management, and insurance practitioners.

Global Reinsurance
Newsquest
30 Cannon Street, London, EC4M 6YJ, UK
T: +44 (0) 20 7618 3456
F: +44 (0) 20 7618 3420
www.globalreinsurance.com
ISSN: 1358-7420

This monthly magazine provides breaking news, analysis, and industry comment on reinsurance. It offers features such as insurance agenda, catastrophe risk, research, people news, jobs, supplements, and a range of special reports covering reinsurance buying strategies, insurance-linked securities, enterprise-wide risk management, and Europe and UK market run-off.

Insurance & Technology
United Business Media
TechWeb, 11 West 19th Street, New York, NY, 10011, USA
T: +1 212 600 3000
F: +1 212 600 3060
www.insurancetech.com
ISSN: 1054-0733

This monthly magazine offers breaking news, analysis, insurance agenda, catastrophe risk, supplements, research, reinsurance jobs, and a range of special reports covering reinsurance buying strategies, insurance-linked securities, enterprise-wide risk management, and analysis of specific industry sectors.

Insurance Age
Incisive Media
32–34 Broadwick Street, London, W1A 2HG, UK
T: +44 (0) 20 8606 7516
F: +44 (0) 20 7316 9313
www.insuranceage.com
ISSN: 0143-8085

This monthly magazine is published for insurance brokers/intermediaries and companies serving the broker community, including insurance companies, loss adjusters, claims management and IT providers. It offers news and analysis, product reviews, market sector comment, and job postings.

Insurance Day
Informa
Informa House, 30–32 Mortimer Street, London, W1W 7RE, UK
T: +44 (0) 20 7017 5000
www.insuranceday.com

This is the only daily newspaper dedicated to the international insurance, reinsurance, and risk industry. It comments on a wide range of market sectors, and provides expert comment and opinion, company profiles and results, current

  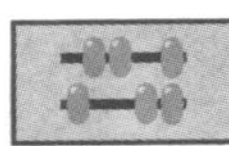      

rates, regulation and forecasts, and technology developments, and coverage and guidelines of both the life and non-life insurance markets.

Insurance Journal

Wells Publishing
3570 Camino del Rio North, Suite 200, San Diego, CA 92108, USA
T: +1 619 584 1100
F: +1 619 584 1200
www.insurancejournal.com
ISSN: 0020-4714

This fortnightly magazine is an authoritative source of news and information on property and casualty insurance for independent insurance agents and brokers. It provides news, comment, and analysis on key industry topics, and offers features such as regional stories, classifieds, e-newsletter, forums, events, and a technology center.

Insurance Networking News

SourceMedia
550 West Van Buren Street, Suite 1100, Chicago, IL 60607, USA
T: +1 312 913 1334
F: +1 312 913 1366
www.insurancenetworking.com
ISSN: 1542-4901

This monthly magazine produces information on how technology is being implemented to support insurers' strategic business objectives, and analysis on the use of technology for automating key processes. Its coverage includes claims management, automated underwriting, fraud detection, agency automation, disaster planning, web services, business intelligence, data management, regulatory compliance, new products, and competitive strategies.

Insurance Times

Newsquest
30 Cannon Street, London, EC4M 6YJ, UK
T: +44 (0) 20 7618 3456
F: +44 (0) 20 7618 3420
www.insurancetimes.co.uk
ISSN: 1466-8149

This weekly insurance newspaper publishes breaking news, analysis, and features, including insurance agenda, comment/blogs, profiles, events, research, jobs, and a focus on regional brokers. It also offers regular supplements, including BIBA Times, Top 50 Brokers, and Top 50 Insurers.

InsuranceNewsNet Magazine

InsuranceNewsNet.com
355 North 21st Street, Suite 211, Camp Hill, PA 17011, USA
T: +1 866 707 6786
www.insurancenewsnetmagazine.com

This new, free magazine for life, health, and annuity producers in the US offers analysis of annuity sales secrets, life insurance trends, and health marketing. It publishes articles by leading industry experts, and coverage of life insurance sales strategies, and health insurance marketing and business growth.

Post

Incisive Media
Haymarket House, 28–29 Haymarket, London, SW1Y 4RX, UK
T: +44 (0) 20 7484 9700
F: +44 (0) 20 7484 9797
www.postonline.co.uk
ISSN: 1365-4284

This weekly magazine provides comprehensive and authoritative coverage of all issues of interest to the UK insurance industry, through news and analysis, comment, topical features, and technical articles, and supplements. It also features information on recruitment, and hosts conferences and annual awards.

Professional Broking

Incisive Media
32–34 Broadwick Street, London, W1A 2HG, UK
T: +44 (0) 20 7484 9700
www.professionalbroking.co.uk
ISSN: 1355-0519

This monthly magazine is produced for insurance broker managers, and delivers business intelligence on topics such as the tax implications of green strategies, and the latest employee benefits, as well as on wider economic and business issues. It also offers supplements, competitions, management events, insurance directories, ratings search, interviews, and surveys.

Property and Casualty Magazine

The National Underwriter Company
33–41 Newark Street, 2nd Floor, Hoboken NJ 07030, USA
T: +1 201 526 1230
F: +1 201 526 1260
www.propertyandcasualtyinsurancenews.com

This weekly magazine focuses on the commercial insurance business, and the wider insurance industry, covering key developments affecting buyers, sellers, and manufacturers of insurance products and related services. It discusses industry topics such as legislation, mergers and acquisitions, technology trends, compliance issues, and new product news, and publishes special reports and directories on specialty markets and technology breakthroughs.

Reinsurance

Incisive Media
Haymarket House, 28–29 Haymarket, London, SW1Y 4RX, UK
T: +44 (0) 20 7316 9000
F: +44 (0) 20 7316 9313
www.reinsurancemagazine.com
ISSN: 0048-7171

This monthly magazine presents news and analysis from the global markets and Lloyd's, as well as country reports, technical reports, statistics and surveys, views and opinions from leading industry figures, and commentary on developments in regulation, legislation and litigation.

The Review

Informa
Informa House, 30–32 Mortimer Street, London, W1W 7RE, UK
T: +44 (0) 20 7017 5000
www.thereview.biz

This monthly publication delivers reinsurance news and analysis for the global risk management industry, especially those with a responsibility for buying, distributing, or underwriting reinsurance and related risk management products.

Risk & Insurance

LRP Publications
Suite 500, 747 Dresher Road, PO Box 980, Horsham, PA 19044-0980, USA
T: +1 215 784 0910
F: +1 215 784 0275
www.riskandinsurance.com
ISSN: 1050-9232

This magazine, published 15 times each year, covers business risks and mitigation strategies, such as insurance, employee benefits, alternative risk transfer, and emerging risks. It provides features, articles, industry risk reports, in-depth series, and special reports, as well as resources and tools such as a power broker directory, risk innovators, case studies, industry events, workers' compensation forum, and vendor directories.

The Risk Retention Reporter

Insurance Communications
PO Box 50147, Pasadena, CA 91115, USA
T: +1 626 796 4972
F: +1 626 796 2363
www.rrr.com

This monthly magazine provides risk retention industry news and the latest legislative and judicial developments, and monitors hundreds of risk retention and purchasing groups. It also offers a monthly roundup, articles by industry experts, profiles, special reports, and market surveys.

JOURNALS

The Geneva Papers on Risk and Insurance

International Association of Insurance Supervisors
IAIS Secretariat, c/o Bank for International Settlements, CH-4002 Basel, Switzerland
T: +41 61 225 73 00
F: +41 61 280 91 51
www.palgrave-journals.com/gpp
ISSN: 1018-5895

This quarterly journal, sponsored by the Geneva Association, publishes papers that advance an understanding of individual and firm behavior under uncertainty. The papers tend to be theoretical, but it also publishes empirical and/or experimental research if it tests competing theories and expands knowledge of insurance economics.

Insurance: Mathematics and Economics

Elsevier
Radarweg 29, 1043 NX Amsterdam, The Netherlands
F: +31 20 485 2180
www.elsevier.com/wps/find/journaldescription.cws_home/505554/description
ISSN: 0167-6687

This bimonthly international journal is aimed at individuals and groups who produce and apply research results in insurance and finance. It publishes papers of international interest, concerned with either the theory of insurance mathematics and economics, or the inventive

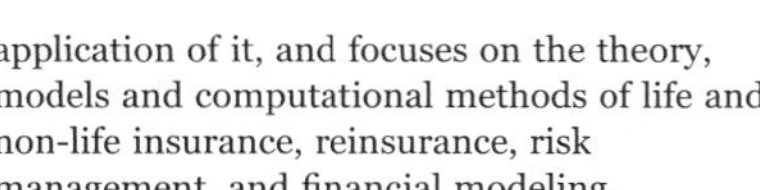

application of it, and focuses on the theory, models and computational methods of life and non-life insurance, reinsurance, risk management, and financial modeling.

Journal of Risk and Insurance

American Risk and Insurance Association
716 Providence Road, Malvern,
PA 19355-3402, USA
T: +1 610 640 1997
F: +1 610 725 1007
www.journalofriskandinsurance.org
ISSN: 0022-4367

This quarterly academic journal publishes original theoretical and empirical research in insurance and risk management. It covers such areas as the industrial organization of insurance markets, the management of risks, insurance finance, economics of employee benefits, utility theory, asymmetric information, insurance regulation, econometric, actuarial, and statistical methodology, economics of insurance institutions, and insurance cycles and economic cycles of insurance markets.

Risk Management and Insurance Review

American Risk and Insurance Association
716 Providence Road, Malvern,
PA 19355-3402, USA
T: +1 610 640 1997
F: +1 610 725 1007
www.wiley.com/bw/journal.asp?ref=1098-1616
ISSN: 1098-1616

This biannual journal publishes applied research, opinion, and discussion on risk and insurance. Its publishes original research on applications and applied techniques, perspectives on research literature, business practice, and public policy, and educational papers that provide a repository of model lectures in risk and insurance, as well as discussing and evaluating instructional techniques.

INTERNET

Insurance Day

www.insuranceday.com

This is a subscription-only service that provides the latest insurance industry news, as well as information on insurance law and insurance regulation changes.

Insurance Directories

www.insurance-directories.com

This is a useful online search facility for professional insurance services, products, and companies.

Insurance News Net

www.insurancenewsnet.com

This is an online provider of focused insurance industry information, news, analysis and commentary, aimed at producers, distributors, and carriers in the insurance and financial services industry. It organizes, analyzes, and filters insurance news from sources around the world, and produces weekly industry e-newsletters.

ORGANIZATIONS

Europe

Association of British Insurers

Chair: Stephen Haddrill
51 Gresham Street, London, EC2V 7HQ, UK
T: +44 (0) 20 7600 3333
F: +44 (0) 20 7696 8999
E: info@abi.org.uk
www.abi.org.uk

The ABI is the representative body for the UK insurance industry. It speaks out on issues of common interest, participates in debates on public policy, and advocates high standards of customer service in the insurance industry. Its policy work focuses on general insurance, life and pensions, financial regulation and taxation, and investment affairs, and it also organizes conferences, and publishes research reports and policy documents.

Association of Insurance and Risk Managers

Chair: Julia Graham
6 Lloyd's Avenue, London, EC3N 3AX, UK
T: +44 (0) 20 7480 7610
F: +44 (0) 20 7702 3752
www.airmic.com

AIRMIC is the UK membership body for risk and insurance managers. Its activities include lobbying, campaigning, risk management, insurance best practice, networking, and training, as well as research into new technology and business continuity.

British Insurance Brokers' Association

Chair: Derek Thornton
8th Floor, John Stow House, 18 Bevis Marks, London, EC3A 7JB, UK
F: +44 (0) 20 7626 9676
E: enquiries@biba.org.uk
www.biba.org.uk

BIBA is a general insurance organization that represents the interests of insurance brokers, intermediaries, and their customers in the UK. It acts as the voice of the industry, advising members, regulators, government, consumer bodies, and other stakeholders on key insurance issues, and provides facilities, technical advice, guidance on regulation, business support, and works to raise and maintain industry standards.

CEA

Chair: Tommy Persson
Square de Meeûs 29, 1000 Brussels, Belgium
T: +32 2 547 58 11
F: +32 2 547 58 19
www.cea.eu

The CEA is a European insurance and reinsurance federation that represents all types of insurance and reinsurance undertakings. It promotes the strategic interests of its members, raises awareness of insurers' and reinsurers' roles in providing insurance protection and security, advocates a competitive and open market, and acts as the voice of the European insurance industry at European and international level.

Chartered Insurance Institute

Chair: Alexander Scott
42–48 High Road, South Woodford, London, E18 2JP, UK
T: +44 (0) 20 8989 8464
F: +44 (0) 20 8530 3052
E: customer.serv@cii.co.uk
www.cii.co.uk

The CII is a professional and educational organization for the insurance and financial services industry in the UK. It provides accreditation and professional qualifications, and promotes competence through the provision of relevant knowledge for employees at all levels and across all sectors of the industry. It also supports fair dealing and integrity through a code of ethics and conduct to which all members subscribe.

European Federation of Insurance Intermediaries

Avenue Albert-Elisabeth 40, 1200
Brussels, Belgium
T: +32 2 735 60 48
F: +32 2 732 14 18
E: bipar@skynet.be
www.bipar.eu

BIPAR is a Europe-wide organization that promotes the interests of insurance agents and brokers in European public affairs. Its membership consists of representative national associations of professional insurance agents and brokers from within Europe, and it also represents self-employed and corporate professional insurance intermediaries.

Federation of European Risk Management Associations

Chair: Marie-Gemma Dequae
Avenue Louis Gribaumont 1, 1150 Brussels, Belgium
T: +32 2 761 94 32
F: +32 2 771 87 20
E: info@ferma.eu
www.ferma.eu

FERMA is comprised of member associations across Europe, and is dedicated to widening and raising the culture of risk management throughout Europe to its members and the risk management and insurance community.
It promotes an awareness of risk management through the media, by information sharing, educational, and research projects.

Institute of Insurance Brokers

Higham Business Centre, Midland Road, Higham Ferrers, Northamptonshire, NN10 8DW, UK
T: +44 (0) 1933 410 003
F: +44 (0) 1933 410 020
E: inst.ins.brokers@iib-uk.com
www.iib-uk.com

The IIB is a non-profit, professional association dedicated to representing the interests of insurance brokers and their clients throughout the UK. It promotes their interests to government, regulatory authorities, and other relevant bodies throughout the world, and encourages debate on topical issues, through bulletins, meetings, and a professional forum.

Institute of Risk Management

Chair: Simone Wray
6 Lloyd's Avenue, London, EC3N 3AX, UK
T: +44 (0) 20 7709 9808
F: +44 (0) 20 7709 0716
E: enquiries@theirm.org
www.theirm.org

        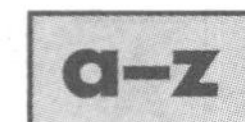

IRM is a non-profit organization that provides education, training, and qualifications at a range of levels for the risk management community. It approaches risk management as a multi-disciplinary field, and works closely with other specialist institutes and associations and represents a broad set of stakeholders, with its membership being drawn from industry, commerce, consultancy, and the public sector.

USA

American Association of Insurance Services

Chair: Paul Baiocchi
1745 South Naperville Road, Wheaton, IL 60189–8132, USA
T: +1 630 681 8347
F: +1 630 681 8356
E: info@AAISonline.com
www.aais.org

AAIS is a product development resource for insurance providers, with expertise in product research and design, actuarial analysis, and regulatory filings. It introduces new programs, product innovations, and services that respond to changes in the insurance marketplace, and offers programs of forms, rules, and rating information for personal and commercial insurance, statistical reporting plans, support services for custom product development, automation, and training.

American Insurance Association

Chair: Leigh Ann Pusey
2101 L Street, NW, Suite 400, Washington, DC 20037, USA
T: +1 202 828 7100
F: +1 202 293 1219
E: info@aiadc.org
www.aiadc.org

AIA is a property-casualty insurance trade organization, its member companies offering all types of property and liability coverage. It aims to provide constructive solutions to industry issues, and operate on promote the views of its member companies, consumers, regulators, and business leaders.

American Risk and Insurance Association

Chair: Tony Biacchi
716 Providence Road, Malvern, PA 19355-3402, USA
T: +1 610 640 1997
F: +1 610 725 1007
E: aria@cpcuiia.org
www.aria.org

ARIA is an academic organization devoted to the study and promotion of knowledge about risk management and insurance. It comprises insurance scholars, risk management and insurance professionals, and institutional sponsors, and provides resources, information, and support for professional growth and education, and offers a forum for scholarly discussion of risk management and insurance issues.

Risk & Insurance Management Society

Chair: Mary Roth
1065 Avenue of the Americas, 13th Floor, New York, NY 10018, USA
T: +1 212 286 9292
www.rims.org

RIMS is a non-profit organization dedicated to advancing the practice of risk management, and which connects risk management professionals throughout North America and the world. It represents industrial, service, non-profit, charitable, and governmental entities, and provides information, education, networking and advocacy, promotes the well-being of the industry, and supports the integration of risk management throughout an organization.

Society of Insurance Research

Chair: Ed Budd
631 Eastpointe Drive, Shelbyville, IN 46176, USA
T: +1 317 398 3684
F: +1 317 642 0535
E: sir.mail@comcast.net
www.sirnet.org

SIR is an international, interdisciplinary organization of insurance research practitioners focused on identifying, understanding, and communicating industry trends, emerging issues, and innovations. It provides a forum for technical education, networking, and professional growth for members, who are insurance professionals with responsibilities in research, product development, competitive intelligence, actuarial science, strategic planning, marketing, and other disciplines.

BRIC

All-Russian Insurance Association

Russia
T: +7 495 956 65 87
F: +7 495 956 65 87
E: mail@ins-union.ru
www.ins-union.ru

ARIA is a national association that promotes its members interests, and the development and improvement of the Russian insurance industry. It works to improve key areas such as insurance legislation, insurance market infrastructure, conditions for insurance, and standards of professional ethics, and produces education and training programs, conferences and seminars, and industry publications.

General Insurance Council of India

Chair: K. K. Srinivasan
5th Floor, Royal Insurance Building, 14, Jamshedji TATA Road, Churchgate, Mumbai 400020, India
T: +91 22 2281 7511
F: +91 22 2281 7515
E: gicouncil@gicouncil.in
www.gicouncil.in

The GI Council represents the collective interests of the non-life insurance companies in India, provides leadership and guidance to the industry, and participates in forming public policy. It also promotes issues of common interest, works to improve the legal and regulatory framework, and act as an advocate for high standards of customer service in the industry.

International

Asia-Pacific Risk and Insurance Association

Chair: Y. U. Ziyou
The APRIA Secretariat, c/o Singapore College of Insurance, 9, Temasek Boulevard, #14-01/02/03 Suntec Tower 2, Singapore 038989, Singapore
T: +65 221 2336
F: +65 220 6684
E: apria@scidomain.org.sg
www.apria.org

APRIA is an international association for academics, executives, researchers, and government leaders interested in risk management, insurance, actuarial science, and related areas. It provides a forum for sharing ideas and engaging in collaborative research, discusses market developments, and publishes a biannual newsletter.

International Association for the Study of Insurance Economics

Chair: Jacques Aigrain
53 Route de Malagnou, 1208 Geneva, Switzerland
T: +41 22 707 66 00
F: +41 22 736 75 36
E: secretariat@genevaassociation.org
www.genevaassociation.org

Better known as The Geneva Association, this global research institution examines the growing importance of worldwide insurance activities in all sectors of the economy. It identifies trends and strategic issues in the insurance sector, and develops and encourages initiatives concerning the evolution of risk management and the notion of uncertainty. It also provides a forum for senior insurance executives to exchange ideas and discuss these issues.

International Association of Insurance Supervisors

Chair: Yoshihiro Kawai
IAIS Secretariat, c/o Bank for International Settlements 4002 Basel, Switzerland
T: +41 61 225 73 00
F: +41 61 280 91 51
E: iais@bis.org
www.iaisweb.org

IAIS is an international organization for national insurance regulators and supervisors. It issues global insurance principles, standards and guidance papers, provides training and support on issues related to insurance supervision, and organizes meetings and seminars for insurance supervisors, as well as working with other financial sector standard setting bodies and international organizations to promote financial stability.

International Insurance Society

Chair: Brian Duperreault
101 Murray Street New York, NY 10007, USA
T: +1 212 815 9291
F: +1 212 815 9297
E: jeastmond@iisonline.org
www.iisonline.org

This is a non-profit organization that provides a resource for insurance executives, academicians, and others interested in insurance to share interests and ideas on relevant global issues. It connects the international insurance community, providing information, education, and networking opportunities for companies and individuals seeking contacts, cross-border

  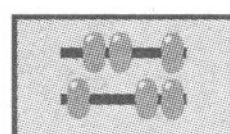   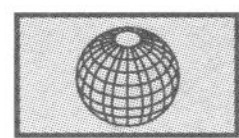   

exchanges, and knowledge on a global scale. It also produces annual seminars, insurance studies, reports, awards, and research.

World Federation of Insurance Intermediaries

Avenue Albert Elisabeth, 40, B-1200 Brussels, Belgium
F: +32 2 732 60 42
E: wfii@skynet.be
www.wfii.org

WFII is a non-profit federation that represents insurance agents and brokers from around the world. It works to increase the awareness of the role played by professional intermediaries with international institutions, and provides a voice for the interests of its members, innovative solutions at international level, and enable the exchange of information on global issues and goals that all national associations of intermediaries have in common.

Corporate Strategy

BOOKS

The Boston Consulting Group on Strategy: Classic Concepts and New Perspectives, 2nd ed
Carl W. Stern, Michael S. Deimler (editors)
Chichester, UK: Wiley, 2006
432pp, ISBN: 978-0-471-75722-1

This anthology of articles on strategy and management is a companion for executives rethinking their businesses. Whether the task is to defeat new or entrenched competitors, it is often necessary to go back to the basics and to consider radical departures. It shows readers how to do both through concepts about reducing costs and gaining market share, as well as new thinking on the power of networks, pricing and segmentation, and the impact of ever cheaper communications and distribution.

Business Strategy: A Guide to Effective Decision Making
Jeremy Kourdi
London: Economist Books, 2003
256pp, ISBN: 978-1-86197-459-4

This practical guide provides help for those involved in making strategic decisions. The text also examines the decision making process in detail. The forces shaping major decisions, including social, cultural, and commercial, are explained, and various rational and intuitive frameworks are introduced. Practical insights and techniques for handling decisions are also outlined.

Competing for the Future: How Digital Innovations Are Changing the World
Henry Kressel
Cambridge, UK: Cambridge University Press, 2007
422pp, ISBN: 978-0-521-86290-5

This offers expert personalized answers to questions such as the significance of going digital, the miniaturization of circuit boards, the role of venture capital in financing the revolution, and the importance of research and development. It explains how the technology works, why it matters, how it is financed, and what the key lessons are for public policy.

Competitive Strategy: Techniques for Analyzing Industries and Competitors
Michael E. Porter
New York: Free Press, 2004
432pp, ISBN: 978-0-684-84148-9

This work, researched by Porter during the 1970s, is regarded as a management classic and has shaped and influenced mainstream thinking on competition and strategy. The author argues that in order to retain competitive capability companies need to choose from three generic strategies (cost leadership, differentiation, and focus), which are driven by five competitive forces (customers, suppliers, the threat of similar products, existing competition, and the threat of new market entrants).

Contemporary Strategy Analysis: Concepts, Techniques, Applications, 6th ed
Robert M. Grant
Oxford: Blackwell Publishing, 2007
496pp, ISBN: 978-1-4051-6309-5

This text reflects current academic thinking and management practice and presents the tools required to formulate and implement strategies. In this edition, extra coverage is given to value creation in electronic commerce, the new economy, complexity and self-organization, and strategic innovation.

Essentials of Strategic Management, 4th ed
J. David Hunger, Thomas L. Wheelen
Harlow, UK: Pearson Education, 2006
208pp, ISBN: 978-0-13-148523-5

This text provides the essentials of the most important concepts and techniques in strategic management. The topics covered by the authors are: basics of strategic management; corporate governance and social responsibility; environmental scanning and industry analysis; internal scanning; strategy formulation; strategy implementation; evaluation and control; and suggestions for analysis.

Every Business Is a Growth Business
Noel M. Tichy, R. Charan
Chichester, UK: Wiley, 1999
352pp, ISBN: 978-0-471-98763-5

In this title, the authors outline how to turn an ordinary company into one that grows. The book gives two main pointers for successful growth; first, to redefine your market and increase demand by seeing things from your customers' point of view, and, second, to reinvigorate the corporate culture to enable growth. The authors give many real-life examples to support these central points.

The New Market Leaders: Who's Winning and How in the Battle for Customers
Fred Wiersema
New York: Free Press, 2002
272pp, ISBN: 978-0-7432-0466-8

This offers insights into successful customer service strategies, based on a six-year study of 5,000 global companies; it examines 100 of these companies in detail, including General Electric, Wal-Mart, Microsoft, Intel and AOL Time Warner, arguing that executives and managers can no longer blame the internet or the New Economy for their customer service failings. It argues that the most successful companies focus on being at the forefront of new technology and, most importantly, try to learn from other winning companies.

Exploring Corporate Strategy, 8th ed
Gerry Johnson, Kevan Scholes
Exploring Corporate Strategy Series
Harlow, UK: Prentice Hall, 2008
664pp, ISBN: 978-0-273-71191-9

This classic textbook provides an overview of the principles and practice of corporate strategy in a variety of contexts. The areas of strategic analysis, resource allocation, strategic choice, strategy implementation, and managing strategic change are covered. Recent developments in the field of strategy, including core competence knowledge and learning, have been incorporated into the seventh edition, which also includes a list of recommended key reading and work assignments for students.

Financial Times Guide to Strategy, 3rd ed
Richard Koch
Harlow, UK: FT Prentice Hall, 2008
334pp, ISBN: 978-0-273-70877-3

This title offers executives the help needed to build a strategic structure for a business, to organize a marketplace, and to create a business model. The book also reveals how strategy can help to raise profits and analyses the views on strategic thinking that have emerged over the last 40 years.

5 Kick-Ass Strategies Every Business Needs: To Explode Sales, Stun the Competition, Wow Customers and Achieve Exponential Growth
Robert Grede
Naperville, Illinois: Sourcebooks, 2006
336pp, ISBN: 978-1-4022-0640-5

This business-growth guide presents actual case studies, visual elements, and strategic steps, to help in reaching, and exceeding, growth goals. In this handbook, Robert Grede provides the essential strategies for improving each area of your business. It also examines how to create a strategic growth plan, the benefits of buying

  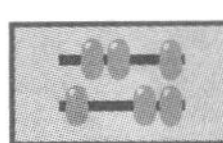      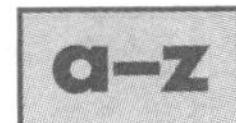

market share, ways to hunt for business, how to sell more to your current customers, and how to introduce new products.

Good to Great: Why Some Companies Make the Leap . . . and Others Don't

Jim Collins

London: Random House Business Books, 2001
320pp, ISBN: 978-0-7126-7609-0

Written by one of the world's bestselling business writers and based on extensive research of over 1,000 businesses, this book focuses on eleven of the world's leading corporations and analyzes their successes. Concluding that an excellent corporate culture is the way forward, this book offers advice and useful tactics for all aspiring business builders.

Gurus on Business Strategy

Tony Grundy

London: Thorogood, 2004
224pp, ISBN: 978-1-85418-262-3

The author presents a guide to well-known writers and thinkers on business strategy and the practical lessons which can be learnt from their ideas. The work opens with an introduction to strategy as a management concept, focusing on management of the external environment, development of competitive advantage, and strategic decision-making. Subsequent sections provide introductions to the wisdom of around 40 business thinkers.

The Interactive Strategy Workout: Analyze and Develop the Fitness of Your Business Strategy, 3rd ed

Cyril Levicki

Harlow, UK: FT Prentice Hall, 2003
368pp, ISBN: 978-0-273-65912-9

This title is a step-by-step guide to creating a successful strategy, both for business purposes and for everyday life. It is accompanied by a CD-ROM.

On the Fly: Executive Strategy in a Changing World

Stephen J. Wall

Chichester, UK: Wiley, 2004
240pp, ISBN: 978-0-471-46484-6

Businesses operate in a volatile external environment where rapid change is the norm, and it is always difficult for them to formulate a clear sense of sustained strategic direction for the future. While emphasizing the case for strong corporate identity grounded in strategic focus, this book offers a model for combining a flexible response to external factors with the analytical tools of strategic planning.

One Stop Strategy

Jeremy Kourdi

One Stop Series
Hemel Hempstead, UK: ICSA Publishing, 2000
268pp, ISBN: 978-1-86072-086-4

This is a practical guide for managers looking to do more than just plan organizational activities. Key topics in a range of areas such as allocating resources, structuring the organization, controlling systems and processes, and managing people are arranged in alphabetical order. Short case studies, checklists, and summaries are included.

The Portable MBA in Strategy, 2nd ed

Liam Fahey, Robert M. Randall

Chichester, UK: Wiley, 2000
414pp, ISBN: 978-0-471-19708-9

This comprehensive guide features contributions from internationally recognized leaders in strategic thought and practice. Topics covered include: strategic management practices; analysis of customers, markets, and competitors; identification and assessment of strategic alternatives; and threats and opportunities facing business.

The Rise and Fall of Strategic Planning

Henry Mintzberg

New York: Free Press, 1994
464pp, ISBN: 978-0-02-921605-7

Mintzberg traces the history of strategic planning since the 1960s and gives his own perspective on past failures. The various planning models are reviewed and analyzed, the pitfalls identified, and a new approach is put forward.

Strategic Management and Organisational Dynamics: The Challenge of Complexity to Ways of Thinking about Organisations, 5th ed

Ralph D. Stacey

Harlow, UK: FT Prentice Hall, 2007
496pp, ISBN: 978-0-273-70811-7

The author of this work takes a radically different approach to strategic management. He is concerned with unpredictability and the limitations of control, factors that militate against the rational models of planning and control presented by other authors. The book explores strategy and organizational dynamics, and includes European case studies.

Strategy-Focused Organization: How Balanced Scorecard Companies Thrive in the New Business Environment

Robert S. Kaplan, David P. Norton

Boston, Massachusetts: Harvard Business School Press, 2000
416pp, ISBN: 978-1-57851-250-8

This book presents case studies of over twenty companies that have adopted the balanced scorecard approach. Five principles for strategy-focused organizations, drawn from their experiences, are outlined in this text. These are: translating the strategy into operational terms; aligning the organization to strategy; making strategy everyone's everyday job; making strategy a continual process, and mobilizing change through effective leadership.

Strategy and Planning: A Manager's Guide, 5th ed

David Hussey

Chichester, UK: Wiley, 2000
289pp, ISBN: 978-0-471-50006-3

This work explores strategic thinking in the context of the major functional areas—marketing, manufacturing, finance, and human resources—as well as examining the major issues and steps in the development of a corporate strategy.

Strategy Process: Concepts, Contexts and Cases, 4th ed

Henry Mintzberg, James Brian Quinn

Harlow, UK: Pearson Education, 2003
1040pp, ISBN: 978-0-13-047913-6

This book is designed to support the teaching and practice of strategy formulation. A collection of readings covers the concepts and contexts of strategy and is supplemented by US and international case studies. Discussion questions for students are included.

Strategy Safari: A Guided Tour through the Wilds of Strategic Management

Henry Mintzberg, Bruce Ahlstrand, Joseph Lampel

London: Simon & Schuster, 1998
304pp, ISBN: 978-0-684-84743-6

This book provides a thorough critique of the contributions and limitations of ten different approaches to strategic planning. These include such schools of thought as entrepreneurial, cognitive, cultural, and environmental. The book then goes on to show how these alternative schools can be merged and shaped to produce one coherent approach to strategy formation.

MAGAZINES

Harvard Business Review

Harvard Business School Press
60 Harvard Way, Boston, MA 02163, USA
T: +1 800 988 0886
F: +1 617 783 7555
hbr.harvardbusiness.org
ISSN: 0017-8012

HBR is a leading magazine for business leaders and senior executives, which emphasizes current best practice and the application of leading-edge research to business problems. Coverage is wide-ranging with a strong focus on strategy. Each issue includes feature articles written by experts and an interview with a business leader.

Journal of Business Strategy

Emerald
60/62 Toller Lane, Bradford, West Yorkshire, BD8 9BY, UK
T: +44 (0) 1274 777 700
F: +44 (0) 1274 785 200
www.emeraldinsight.com/products/journals/journals.htm?id=jbs
ISSN: 0275-6668

This is a bimonthly magazine featuring practical articles on current business topics written by senior executives and strategists.

JOURNALS

Business Strategy Review

Blackwell Publishing
9600 Garsington Road, Oxford, OX4 2DQ, UK

  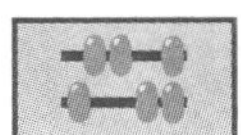   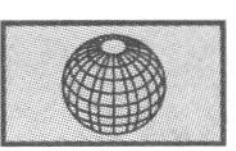   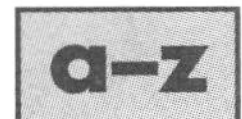

T: +44 (0) 1865 791 100
F: +44 (0) 1865 791 347
www.wiley.com/bw/journal.asp?ref=0955-6419
ISSN: 0955-6419

Business Strategy Review is a quarterly journal published on behalf of the London Business School. It includes articles on strategic issues relevant to modern business, taking a multi-disciplinary approach, and aiming for accessibility to a wide audience, including students and academics.

Business Strategy Series

Emerald
60/62 Toller Lane, Bradford, West Yorkshire, BD8 9BY, UK
T: +44 (0) 1274 777 700
F: +44 (0) 1274 785 200
www.emeraldinsight.com/1751-5637.htm
ISSN: 1751-5637

Business Strategy Series brings 50 exclusive briefing papers to your desktop, covering all aspects of strategy development and implementation. It brings together the strategic thought leaders behind many of the world's leading corporations, including senior executives, top-flight consultants, and business school gurus.

Journal of Economics & Management Strategy

Wiley Periodicals
350 Main Street, Malden, MA 02148, USA
T: +1 781 388 8598
www.wiley.com/bw/journal.asp?ref=1058-6407
ISSN: 1058-6407

The *Journal of Economics & Management Strategy* provides a leading forum for interaction and research on the competitive strategies of managers and the organizational structure of firms. The journal covers theoretical and empirical industrial organization, applied game theory, and management strategy.

Journal of Strategy and Management

Emerald
60/62 Toller Lane, Bradford, West Yorkshire, BD8 9BY, UK
T: +44 (0) 1274 777700
F: +44 (0) 1274 785200
www.emeraldinsight.com/1755-425X.htm
ISSN: 1755-425X

The *Journal of Strategy and Management* is an international journal dedicated to improving the existing knowledge and understanding of strategy development and implementation globally in private and public organizations, and encouraging new thinking and innovative approaches to the study of strategy.

Long Range Planning: International Journal of Strategic Management

Elsevier
PO Box 211, 1000 AE Amsterdam, The Netherlands
T: +31 20 485 3911
F: +31 20 485 2457
www.elsevier.com/locate/lrp
ISSN: 0024-6301

LRP, published in association with the Strategic Planning Society and the European Strategic Planning Federation, is a leading international journal in the field of strategic management. Aimed at senior managers, administrators, and academics, it includes articles from academics and practitioners.

MIT Sloan Management Review

MIT Sloan School of Management
77 Massachusetts Avenue, Cambridge, MA 02139-4307, USA
T: +1 617 253 7170
F: +1 617 258 9739
sloanreview.mit.edu
ISSN: 1532-9194

Founded in 1959, this quarterly journal aims to provide senior managers with the best of current management theory and practice. It has a strong focus on corporate strategy and leadership.

Strategic Change

Wiley
The Atrium, Southern Gate, Chichester, West Sussex, PO19 8SQ, UK
T: +44 (0) 1243 779 777
F: +44 (0) 1243 775 878
www.interscience.wiley.com/jpages/1086-1718
ISSN: 1086-1718

Eight issues of *Strategic Change* are published annually. The journal aims to provide authoritative and topical research papers addressing the strategic management of change and its implementation in an increasingly globalized business environment.

Strategic Management Journal

Wiley
The Atrium, Southern Gate, Chichester, West Sussex, PO19 8SQ, UK
T: +44 (0) 1243 779 777
F: +44 (0) 1243 775 878
www.interscience.wiley.com/jpages/0143-2095
ISSN: 0143-2095

SMJ is a monthly journal devoted to the theory and practice of strategic management. It is aimed at academics and practicing managers and has a strong emphasis on research.

Strategy and Leadership

Emerald
60/62 Toller Lane, Bradford, West Yorkshire, BD8 9BY, UK
T: +44 (0) 1274 777 700
F: +44 (0) 1274 785 200
www.emeraldinsight.com/1087-8572.htm
ISSN: 1087-8572

This bimonthly journal for business leaders publishes articles describing effective practice in strategy and leadership and new theories that have the potential to advance the art of strategy development and its implementation.

INTERNET

Asian Pacific Management Forum

www.apmforum.com

This association provides a business news portal for Asia, a research center, an archive of relevant industry articles, and publishes an electronic magazine.

Business.com Strategic Planning

www.business.com

The strategic planning section (in the business directory) under "Management" includes a comprehensive collection of links to websites, associations, and publications.

Centre of Management Research (ICMR)

www.icmrindia.org

On their case studies and management resources website, which is popular in Asia, they feature many very helpful strategy case studies. The case studies focus on cases in Asia, but also cover a variety of Western countries.

Knowledge@Wharton

knowledge.wharton.upenn.edu

The section on strategic management on this site, sponsored by the Wharton School at the University of Pennsylvania, includes articles and useful links.

Strategic Management Club Online

www.strategyclub.com

This website, developed by Dr. Fred David for graduate and undergraduate students, provides links, templates, a discussion forum, and a chat facility.

Strategy + Business

www.strategy-business.com

This online version of Strategy + Business magazine offers a selection of articles on corporate strategy as well as a useful search and browse facility. Subscribers to the magazine can also sign up for a free regular e-mail newsletter on this topic.

Thinking Managers

www.thinkingmanagers.com

This is a free advice resource run by management thinkers Edward de Bono and Robert Heller. The strategy section, under business management, provides useful links and self-written blogs.

ORGANIZATIONS

Europe

Strategic Planning Society (SPS)

Buxton House, 7 Highbury Hill, London, N5 1SU, UK
T: +44 (0) 845 056 3663
F: +44 (0) 870 751 8216
E: membership@sps.org.uk
www.sps.org.uk

The SPS is a professional organization, founded in 1967, which aims to promote knowledge and understanding of strategic management through publications, training events, conferences, and special interest groups.

USA

Association for Strategic Planning

12021 Wilshire Boulevard, Suite 286, Los Angeles, CA 90025-1200, USA
T: +1 877 816 2080
F: +1 323 954 0507

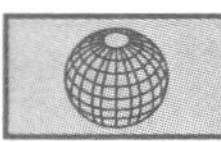

E: executivedirector@strategyplus.org
www.strategyplus.org

This professional association aims to promote effective strategic thinking, planning, and action in public and private organizations.

Strategy Institute

230 Park Avenue, 10th Floor, New York, NY 10169, USA
T: +1 866 298 9343
F: +1 866 298 9344
E: info@strategyinstitute.com
www.strategyinstitute.com

A knowledge source for corporate North America, the Strategy Institute is an independent, research-based organization which monitors and communicates changes and trends in business and business strategy.

International

Global Business Network (GBN)

5900-X Hollis Street, Emeryville, CA 94608, USA
T: +1 510 547 6822
F: +1 510 547 8510
E: info@gbn.com
www.gbn.com

The GBN was founded in 1987 by Peter Schwartz, Jay Ogilvy, Napier Collyns, and Stewart Brand, with the collaboration of European colleagues Kees van der Heijden, Arie de Geus, and Bo Ekman. The founders' aim was to develop a worldwide community of individual members and subscribing organizations interested in increasing their understanding of change in the business environment and in developing ideas and tools for planning and innovation. The organization has a strong focus on the use of scenarios.

Strategic Management Society (SMS)

Purdue University, Krannert Center, 425 West State Street, West Lafayette, IN 47907–2056, USA
T: +1 765 494 6984
F: +1 765 494 1533
E: sms@exchange.purdue.edu
www.smsweb.org

The Strategic Management Society is an international organization founded in 1981 with members in more than 50 countries. It focuses on the development and dissemination of insights into strategic management, combining the contributions of practitioners and academics. It holds an international conference and smaller special interest conferences annually, and supports publications such as the *Strategic Management Journal* and a book series.

Strategos Institute

820 West Jackson Boulevard, Suite 450, Chicago, IL 60607, USA
T: +1 312 655 0826
F: +1 312 655 8334
E: contact@strategos.com
www.strategos.com

The Strategos Institute is a consortium of world-class companies working on the development of tools, processes, and metrics for strategy innovation. Business practitioners, consultants, and business school professors are involved, and the writer and thinker Gary Hamel is the chairman.

Corporate Valuation

BOOKS

Brealey & Myers on Corporate Finance: Capital Investment and Valuation

Richard A. Braeley, Stewart C. Myers

New York: McGraw-Hill, 2002
500pp, ISBN: 978-0-07-138377-6

Offers a comprehensive analysis of corporate investment and asset valuation, the best strategies for increasing value, and how they can be implemented. It explores the theory and mechanics of valuation and investing, the risks involved, the cost/benefit analyses of mergers, buyouts, issues in capital budgeting, financing and project value, the use of options, and strategies for creating shareholder value through integrated investment and operating programs.

Business Valuation: An Integrated Theory, 2nd ed

Z. Christopher Mercer, Travis W. Harms

Wiley Finance Series
Hoboken, New Jersey: Wiley, 2008
288pp, ISBN: 978-0-470-14816-7

This new, concise treatment of business valuation presents both a theoretical analysis and a guide to implementation and current modeling issues. It explains how to apply fundamental valuation concepts, how to define various levels of value, and better understand business appraisal reports, and discusses the impact of valuation on growth, risk, and reward, alternative investments, present value, and valuation premiums and discounts.

Corporate Finance: A Valuation Approach

Simon Benninga, Oded Sarig

New York: McGraw-Hill/Irwin, 1997
445pp, ISBN: 978-0-07-005099-0

This early classic on company valuation was designed for courses in corporate finance, and provides a detailed description of the valuation process, and an integrated method for valuing assets, firms, and securities across a wide variety of industries. It examines financial and accounting techniques, and assists in the development of pro-forma financial statements and their translation into values.

Corporate Finance and Valuation

Bob Ryan

London: Cengage Learning, 2007
623pp, ISBN: 978-1-84480-271-5

This textbook examines the unique challenges to business growth and valuation in an accessible way. It clearly presents the relevant theory, mathematics, key concepts and principles through practical examples, and explores the themes of value, return, and risk, offering a managerial perspective on identifying and solving financial problems in the real world.

Corporate Valuation: A Guide for Managers and Investors

Phillip R. Daves, Michael C. Ehrhardt, Ron E. Shrieves

Mason, Ohio: Thomson/South-Western, 2004
301pp, ISBN: 978-0-324-27428-8

This is an accessible handbook to company valuation, which provides guidance on how to obtain real world data, how to structure spreadsheet valuation models, and the use of spreadsheets in simplifying and standardizing accounting processes in financial statements. It offers a range of examples of valuing different types of company, and explains the fundamental economic forces that underlie a company's value.

Corporate Valuation: An Easy Guide to Measuring Value

David Frykman, Jakob Tolleryd

London: FT Prentice Hall, 2003
208pp, ISBN: 978-0-273-66161-0

This practical guide discusses the key issues of valuation, and the importance of measuring a company's health to maximize shareholder value, in the context of past results, the current situation, and prospects for the future. It covers commonly used valuation methods, and examines scenarios, ratio-based and DCF methods, techniques for reflecting industry structure and intellectual capital, and value-based management.

Creating Shareholder Value: A Guide for Managers and Investors, 2nd ed

Alfred Rappaport

New York: Free Press, 1998
205pp, ISBN: 978-0-684-84410-7

Rappaport, described as the father of shareholder value, here offers investors and corporate managers a practical guide to the practical tools needed to generate superior returns. He focuses on a shareholder value approach that uses sales/growth rates, operating profit margins, and cost of capital to measure value, rather than traditional performance metrics such as price-to-earnings ratios, return on investment, and equity measures.

Damodaran on Valuation: Security Analysis for Investment and Corporate Finance, 2nd ed

Aswath Damodaran

Wiley Finance Series
Hoboken, New Jersey: Wiley, 2006
685pp, ISBN: 978-0-471-75121-2

Written by a renowned teacher, author, and valuation expert, this is a guide to all aspects of

  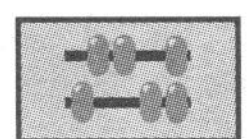      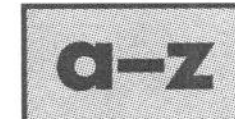

valuation, from the valuation process, and key valuation models, to the different valuation scenarios that can be faced. It also presents techniques for assessing the effect on value of employee stock options, methodologies for using valuation models to value intangible assets, and the effect of illiquidity on value.

EVA and Value-Based Management: A Practical Guide to Implementation

S. David Young, Stephen F. O'Byrne
New York: McGraw-Hill, 2001
493pp, ISBN: 978-0-07-136439-3

This objective analysis of two key management tools discusses the advantages and disadvantages of their implementation, focusing on performance measurement, value drivers, and management compensation to increase shareholder value. It explains the main steps in their successful application for an organization, as well as providing definitions, and a practical rationale for their introduction.

The EVA Challenge: Implementing Value-Added Change in an Organization

Joel M. Stern, John S. Shiely
New York: Wiley, 2004
250pp, ISBN: 978-0-471-47889-8

This is an accessible and practical account of economic value added (EVA), which measures the financial performance of a company, and presents a strategy for creating corporate and shareholder wealth. It details what exactly EVA is, how to calculate it, what information it can provide shareholders, and how to customize and implement EVA at any level of a company.

Financial Valuation: Applications and Models, 2nd ed

James R. Hitchner (editor)
Wiley Finance Series
Hoboken, New Jersey: Wiley, 2006
1,336pp, ISBN: 978-0-471-76117-4

This major practitioner resource on business valuation covers the most effective valuation procedures, and the latest in valuations for financial reporting. Written by a number of respected industry figures, it also examines the models and methods that can be used to navigate a valuation project, how to value pass-through entities, and value consulting and company analysis using the concept of strategic benchmarking for value.

Intangible Assets: Valuation and Economic Benefit

Jeffrey A. Cohen
Wiley Finance Series
Hoboken, New Jersey: Wiley, 2005
161pp, ISBN: 978-0-471-67131-2

This presents a practical framework for addressing the valuation and economics of intangibles, their treatment under current accounting rules, and how basic valuation methodologies apply to intangible assets.
It examines how to identify and value intangible assets such as intellectual property, brands, patents, copyrights, trademarks, and trade secrets, and how value is created and sustained.

Principles of Private Firm Valuation

Stanley J. Feldman
Wiley Finance Series
Hoboken, New Jersey: Wiley, 2005
179pp, ISBN: 978-0-471-48721-0

This offers insights into the factors that determine private firm value for finance professionals, exploring the valuation issues, and the best tools and techniques that can be used. It also discusses the influence of taxes, the cost of capital, the size of the marketability discount, the value of control, and the importance of transparency and liquidity in establishing the value of a private firm.

The Quest for Value

G. Bennett Stewart
New York: HarperBusiness, 1991
781pp, ISBN: 978-0-88730-418-7

This bible of financial management provides a practical framework that managers can use in goal setting, resource allocation, strategy development, valuation of acquisitions, financial policy setting, incentive compensation planning, and building shareholder value. It presents corporate strategy for enhancing shareholder value, and examines issues surrounding dividends, earnings per share, and what really drives share price.

Valuation: Avoiding the Winner's Curse

Kenneth R. Ferris, Barbara S. Pecherot Petitt
Upper Saddle River, New Jersey: Prentice Hall, 2002
225pp, ISBN: 978-0-13-034804-3

This introduces and illustrates the most important valuation techniques and models, such as discounted cash flow analysis, earnings multiples analysis, adjusted present value analysis, economic value analysis, and real option analysis. It offers advice for acquiring and valuing target companies, describes key financial reporting, accounting, and tax considerations, and presents examples and case studies from many industry sectors.

Valuation: Measuring and Managing the Value of Companies, 4th ed

Tim Koller, Marc Goedhart, David Wessels
Hoboken, New Jersey: Wiley, 2005
739pp, ISBN: 978-0-471-70218-4

This classic guide to valuation has been updated to reflect the volatile global economy, and provides practical advice on how to create, manage, and measure company value, and case studies that illustrate valuation techniques in real-world situations. It also presents a framework for managers, and shows how to analyze historical performance, forecast performance, estimate the cost of capital, and interpret the results of a valuation.

Valuation: Mergers, Buyouts and Restructuring, 2nd ed

Enrique R. Arzac
Wiley Finance Series
Hoboken, New Jersey: Wiley, 2008
448pp, ISBN: 978-0-470-12889-3

This focused guide to valuation presents both a theoretical and practical overview of the valuation tools, techniques, and applications that create the foundation for mergers, buyouts and restructuring. It discusses core valuation, LBOs, options pricing, and deal structuring, as well as contract design to resolve disagreements about value, and the valuation of special offer structures.

Valuation: The Art and Science of Corporate Investment Decisions

Sheridan Titman, John Martin
Addison-Wesley Series in Finance
Boston, Massachusetts: Addison Wesley, 2008
556pp, ISBN: 978-0-321-33610-1

This textbook offers an overview of valuation and an integrated approach to both project and enterprise valuation. It moves beyond usual discounted cash flow analysis to include valuation methods such as comparables, simulations, and real options. It also discusses project analysis using DCF, cost of capital, and enterprise valuation techniques.

Valuation Workbook: Step-by-Step Exercises and Tests to Help You Master Valuation, 3rd ed

Tom Copeland, Tim Koller, Jack Murrin, William Foote
Hoboken, New Jersey: Wiley, 2006
185pp, ISBN: 978-0-471-70216-0

This successful companion workbook and practical study guide to the book, Corporate Valuation, can be used to test understanding of the subject and the necessary calculation skills to help apply the principles to realize shareholder value. It covers such essentials as value creation, M&As, valuation frameworks, analyzing historical information, estimating the cost of capital, forecasting performance, and calculating results.

Value Based Management: The Corporate Response to the Shareholder Revolution

John D. Martin, J. William Petty
Boston, Massachusetts: Harvard Business School Press, 2000
249pp, ISBN: 978-0-87584-800-6

Examines how a value-based management program can be used by financial managers to plan, monitor, and control a firm's operations, and to enhance shareholder value. It looks at the link between operational and financial choices and shareholder value, and discusses why maximizing shareholder value should be differentiated from maximizing earnings per share, and is based on a study of firms that have successfully implemented VBM systems

Valuing a Business: The Analysis and Appraisal of Closely Held Companies, 5th ed

Shannon P. Pratt, Robert F. Reilly, Robert P. Schweihs
Maidenhead, UK: McGraw-Hill, 2007
1000pp, ISBN: 978-0-07-144180-3

This latest edition, originally published in 1981, includes significant revisions and ten new chapters. Its coverage now extends to topics such as credentials and standards, analyzing financial statements, control and acquisition premiums, valuing debt securities and litigation support. The book is a standard reference for defining the methodology of business valuation—for businesses of all sizes—and then arriving at an accurate and supportable estimation of value.

Valuing Small Businesses and Professional Practices, 3rd ed

Shannon P. Pratt, Robert F. Reilly, Robert P. Schweihs

McGraw-Hill Library of Investment and Finance Series
New York: McGraw-Hill, 1998
1,056pp, ISBN: 978-0-7863-1186-6

The classic reference source and practical tool on small business valuation focuses on valuation theory, value estimation and analyses, and professional practices, and explains the valuation process, as well as valuation for estate plans, useful data sources for small businesses, the legal context, value drivers and their impact on valuation methods, employee stock ownership plans, and corporate partnership dissolutions/buyouts.

MAGAZINES

Business Valuation Update

Business Valuation Resources
1000 SW Broadway, Suite 1200, Portland, OR 97205, USA
T: +1 503 291 7963
F: +1 503 291 7955
www.bvlibrary.com/ProductServices/psBVU.aspx

This monthly newsletter presents a wide range of news, analyses, and expert debate on valuation issues and trends. It publishes articles by industry experts, news updates, special reports, legal and court case abstracts, data and publications notices, cost of capital updates, and a calendar of business valuation events.

CPA Expert

American Institute of Certified Public Accountants
220 Leigh Farm Road, Durham, NC 27707, USA
T: +1 888 777 7077
www.cpa2biz.com/AST/Main/CPA2BIZ_Primary/BusinessValuationandLitigationServices/LitigationServices/PRDOVR~PC-CPX-XX/PC-CPX-XX.jsp

This quarterly newsletter, published by the American Institute of Certified Public Accountants, provides news and analysis on trends, practices, concepts, and methodologies of business valuation, as well as the latest legislation and court rulings, emerging practice trends, and service and technical innovations.

Valuation Strategies

Thomson Reuters
ria.thomsonreuters.com/EStore/detail.aspx?ID=VLRP
ISSN: 1557-2919

This bimonthly journal provides information and analysis on all types of valuation issue, the tools required to ensure transactional accuracy, and valuation in a wide variety of tax planning and compliance matters. It also provides analysis of the latest appraisal techniques used for businesses, real estate, and personal property, and discusses emerging trends affecting valuation of both tangible and intangible assets.

The Value Examiner

National Association of Certified Valuation Analysts
1111 Brickyard Road, Suite 200, Salt Lake City, UT 84106-5401, USA
T: +1 801 486 0600
F: +1 801 486 7500
www.nacva.com/ecommerce/product.asp?pc=03VE

This bimonthly magazine on value offers news and articles for professionals involved in business valuation, forensic accounting, and litigation support services. It publishes substantive, peer-reviewed articles from consulting disciplines such as fraud deterrence and detection, mergers and acquisitions, exit planning strategies, intellectual property, and practice development.

JOURNALS

Business Valuation Review

American Society of Appraisers
555 Herndon Parkway, Suite 125, Herndon, VA 20170, USA
T: +1 703 478 2228
F: +1 703 742 8471
www.bvappraisers.org/IssueStore
ISSN: 0897-1781

This quarterly journal aimed at practitioners focuses on business appraisal and valuation topics. It presents academically rigorous and technical articles that analyze new concepts relevant to valuation learning, and which reiterate the teachings presented in American Society of Appraisers Business Valuation educational courses.

INTERNET

CPA2Biz

www.cpa2biz.com

CPA2Biz is a leading e-commerce site for the accounting profession, and a subsidiary of the American Institute of CPAs, the main association for certified public accountants in the US. It markets a selection of professional products and services to financial professionals across the country, and offers articles, online literature, continuing professional education, and career resources.

ValuationResources.Com

www.valuationresources.com

This free online resource for business appraisers provides a guide to business valuation, industry and company information, economic data, and offers relevant information on books and publications, financial ratios, salary surveys, economic data, cost of equity capital, public market data, M&A transaction data, valuation multiples, and legal and tax issues.

ORGANIZATIONS

USA

American Business Appraisers

USA
www.businessval.com

The ABA provides a national network business for valuation expertise and services, especially in taxation, litigation, transactions, and compliance. Their qualified members can act as either an independent and objective business appraiser or consultants for deal negotiation, supporting an unambiguous value for a business interest or asset, testifying in court, defending an audit, or participating in regulatory hearings to support conclusions.

American Institute of Certified Public Accountants

Chair: Barry C. Melancon
220 Leigh Farm Road, Durham, NC 27707, USA
T: +1 888 777 7077
E: service@aicpa.org
www.aicpa.org

AICPA is the main professional association for certified public accountants in the US. Its mission is to provide members with resources, information, and leadership, focusing on advocacy, certification and licensing, communications, recruitment and education, and standards and performance.

American Society of Appraisers

Chair: Terry J. Allen
555 Herndon Parkway, Suite 125, Herndon, VA 20170, USA
T: +1 703 478 2228
F: +1 703 742 8471
E: asainfo@appraisers.org
www.bvappraisers.org

This is an international organization for professional valuers and appraisers, representing all of the disciplines of appraisal specialists, including business valuation.

Appraisal Foundation

Chair: Shawn McGowan
1155 15th Street NW, Suite 1111, Washington, DC 20005, USA
T: +1 202 347 7722
F: +1 202 347 7727
E: info@appraisalfoundation.org
www.appraisalfoundation.org

The Appraisal Foundation, a not-for-profit organization dedicated to the advancement of professional valuation, is main source of appraisal standards, appraiser qualifications and standards of ethical conduct in all valuation disciplines, and which aims to foster public trust in the valuation profession.

Business Valuation Association

Chair: John Worthen
500 North Plum Grove Road, Palatine, IL 60067, USA
T: +1 847 776 1976
F: +1 847 776 1980
E: info@businessvaluationassociation.org
www.businessvaluationassociation.org

BVA is a non-profit organization comprising more than 200 members in and around the Chicago area, which focuses on promoting professionalism among business valuation practitioners through continuing education. It offers a number of presentations, seminars, and special forums on the latest valuation standards and techniques by industry experts each year.

Institute of Business Appraisers

PO Box 17410 Plantation, FL 33318, USA
T: +1 954 584 1144
F: +1 954 584 1184
E: hqiba@go-iba.org
www.go-iba.org

This institute is devoted to the appraisal of closely held businesses, and the promotion of business appraisal education and professional accreditation. It focuses on increasing awareness of business valuation as a specialized profession, ensuring that the services of qualified, ethical appraisers are available, expanding the knowledge of valuation, developing and providing information, programs and services for members, and improving national policy and law affecting the valuation community.

National Association of Certified Valuation Analysts

1111 Brickyard Road, Suite 200, Salt Lake City, UT 84106-5401, USA
T: +1 801 486 0600
F: +1 801 486 7500
E: nacva1@nacva.org
www.nacva.com

NACVA supports professional education, the development of valuation software and databases, tools for providing valuation services, research support, and standards setting for the valuation industry. Its membership comprises CPAs and other valuation and consulting professionals involved in business valuation, litigation forensics consulting, fraud deterrence, and related services serving the legal and business communities.

International

International Association of Consultants, Valuators and Analysts

Chair: James P. Catty
707 Eglinton Avenue West, Suite 501, Toronto, Ontario M5N 1C8, Canada
T: +1 416 865 9665
F: +1 416 865 1249
E: info@iacva.org
www.iacva.org

IACVA provides worldwide support to professionals who either perform valuations or are engaged in fraud deterrence, with the objective of supporting best practice in both. For valuation, it promotes the uniform application of valuation theory, approaches, methods and models, and for fraud deterrence and forensic accounting it encourages the development and dissemination of consistent and demonstrable systems and techniques for the detection and prevention of fraud.

International Valuation Standards Council

12 Great George Street, London, SW1P 3AD, UK
T: +44 (0) 1442 879306
E: ivsc@ivsc.org
www.ivsc.org

The IVSC is an independent, not-for-profit, private sector organization that produces standards for many types of assets, intangible assets and businesses, and for different applications such as financial reporting and bank lending. Its objectives are to be the international voice of the valuation profession, and to create and maintain independent and transparent international valuation standards.

Credit and Debt Management

BOOKS

The Bank Credit Analysis Handbook: A Guide for Analysts, Bankers and Investors, 2nd ed

Jonathan Golin
Wiley Finance Series
Singapore: Wiley, 2008
800pp, ISBN: 978-0-470-82157-2

This explains the role and methodologies of bank credit analysts, and how rating agencies assign credit ratings to banks. Aimed at both investors and practitioners, it provides suggestions and insights for understanding and complying with the Basel Accords, examines the basic elements of the CAMEL model for assessing a bank's performance and financial condition, and discusses the processes of peer and trend analysis.

Credit Analysis of Financial Institutions, 2nd ed

Waymond A. Grier
London: Euromoney Books, 2000
350pp, ISBN: 978-1-84374-274-6

This discusses the most effective approach to credit analysis for banks, insurance companies, investment banks, finance companies, leasing companies, investment management companies, and pension funds. It examines key issues such as IFRS, Basel II, hedge fund growth, the explosion in credit derivatives, and market sensitivity analysis, and provides a framework to enable a banker or analyst to gain a meaningful view of any institution.

Credit Derivatives: A Primer on Credit Risk, Modeling, and Instruments

George Chacko, Anders Sjöman, Hideto Motohashi, Vincent Dessain
Upper Saddle River, New Jersey: Wharton School Publishing, 2006
272pp, ISBN: 978-0-13-146744-6

This provides an overview of the credit risk market in a clear way, from the underlying principles surrounding credit risk, to current methods and instruments for managing it. It introduces total return swaps, credit spread options, credit-linked notes, and other instruments, demonstrating how each of them can be used to isolate risk and sell it on.

Credit Derivatives: Risk Management, Trading and Investing

Geoff Chaplin
Wiley Finance Series
Chichester, UK: Wiley, 2005
336pp, ISBN: 978-0-470-02416-4

This is a useful analysis of the key credit derivatives products, applications, risks, and alternative means of trading, which also provides insight into typical trades, such as basis trading, hedging, and credit structuring. It examines the industry standard 'default and recovery' and Copula models, and emphasizes the management of a portfolio or book of credit risks, and methods of correlation risk.

Credit Risk Modeling Using Excel and VBA

Gunter Loeffler, Peter N. Posch
Chichester, UK: Wiley, 2007
280pp, ISBN: 978-0-470-03157-5

This is a practical introduction to credit risk modeling, which shows how to implement analytical methods, and mathematical modeling tools and techniques, using Excel and VBA. It shows how to use option theoretic and statistical models to estimate default risk, and how portfolio models can be validated or used to access structured credit products such as CDOs.

Credit Risk Scorecards

Naeem Siddiqi
Hoboken, New Jersey: Wiley, 2005
208pp, ISBN: 978-0-471-75451-0

This is a practical guide to developing, implementing, and monitoring successful predictive credit scorecards. It presents the key steps in a straightforward way, and provides a strong grounding in the technical issues involved in building, validating, and implementing credit scoring models, making it a useful resource for scorecard specialists, credit risk managers, and other consumer credit professionals.

Debt for Sale: A Social History of the Credit Trap

Brett Williams
Philadelphia, Pennsylvania: University of Pennsylvania Press, 2005
160pp, ISBN: 978-0-8122-1886-2

An examination of the credit and debt industry, and the social and economic impact it has had on people's lives. From the introduction of charge cards, to the advent of computers and the deregulation of banking that helped expand credit

  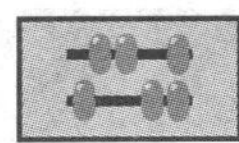   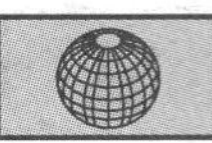   

card use and consumer debt, Debt for Sale examines why it is in the best interest of banks, corporations, and their shareholders, to keep consumer debt at high levels.

Euromoney Encyclopedia of Debt Finance
Tony Rhodes (editor)
London: Euromoney Books, 2007
276pp, ISBN: 978-1-84374-269-2

With contributions from leading authors and international financial institutions, this is a useful reference for both new entrants and specialists into the debt markets. It summarizes the range of debt products and markets, and provides examples of the use of these markets in practice.

Guide to Measuring and Managing Credit Risk
Arnaud de Servigny, Olivier Renault
New York: McGraw-Hill, 2004
388pp, ISBN: 978-0-07-141755-6

This is an authoritative exploration of credit risk measurement and management tools and techniques, which includes a detailed review of the most popular portfolio models. It provides practical analysis of issues such as the determinants of credit risk and loss given default, how credit risk is reflected in the prices and yields of individual securities, and how derivatives and securitization instruments can be used to transfer and repackage credit risk.

Managing Bank Risk: An Introduction to Broad-Base Credit Engineering
Morton Gantz
Amsterdam: Academic Press, 2002
600pp, ISBN: 978-0-12-285785-0

With a focus on new approaches to fundamental analysis and credit administration, this offers useful models, programs, and documents for creating a sound credit risk environment, credit granting processes, and appropriate administrative and monitoring controls.
It presents analytic methods and traditional credit management processes to help bankers judge asset quality and value.

Managing Credit Risk: The Next Great Financial Challenge, 2nd ed
John B. Caouette, Edward I. Altman, Paul Narayanan, Robert Nimmo
Hoboken, New Jersey: Wiley, 2008
628pp, ISBN: 978-0-470-11872-6

This is an extensive examination of the global credit markets, exploring all the relevant topics that can influence them. It introduces some of the most effective credit risk management tools, techniques, and vehicles currently available, and offers credit risk solutions for different types of organization, including credit derivatives, and approaches that can be used to analyze counterparty credit risk.

The New Paradigm for Financial Markets: The Credit Crisis of 2008 and What It Means
George Soros
New York: PublicAffairs, 2008
208pp, ISBN: 978-1-58648-683-9

Soros examines the financial crisis in terms of how individuals and institutions manage the boom and bust cycles that dominate global economic activity, and discusses the extent of the problem in the markets around the world. He also analyzes the origins of the crisis and its implications for the future.

Standard & Poor's Fundamentals of Corporate Credit Analysis
Blaise Ganguin, John Bilardello
New York: McGraw-Hill, 2004
428pp, ISBN: 978-0-07-144163-6

This guide to the processes and tools of fundamental credit analysis focuses on credit risk, cash flow modeling, debt structure analysis, and other key risks to a company. It also explains the impact of debt instruments and debt structures on a firm's recovery prospects should it become insolvent, presenting a scoring system for assessing the ability to repay debt and evaluate recovery prospects in the event of financial distress.

The Structured Credit Handbook
Arvind Rajan, Glen McDermott, Ratul Roy
Wiley Finance Series
Hoboken, New Jersey: Wiley, 2007
496pp, ISBN: 978-0-471-74749-9

This is a comprehensive introduction to all types of credit-linked financial instruments, such as collateralized debt obligations, collateralized loan obligations, credit derivatives such as credit default swaps and swaptions, and iBoxx indexes. It provides a solid grounding in the investment rationale, risks, and rewards associated with structured credit investments, with little financial jargon or mathematical complexity.

The Subprime Solution: How Today's Global Financial Crisis Happened, and What to Do About It
Robert J. Shiller
Princeton, New Jersey: Princeton University Press, 2008
208pp, ISBN: 978-0-691-13929-6

This is a forward thinking and sometimes controversial account of the subprime and credit crisis. It argues that bailouts of distressed borrowers are important for restoring confidence, that more financial engineering would prevent similar occurrences, and proposes a major restructuring of the institutional foundations of the financial system.

Surviving Your Business Debt: A Financial Survival Guidebook for Business Owners, Financial Managers, and CFOs
Kenneth Easton
Exeter, New Hampshire: PublishingWorks, 2007
363pp, ISBN: 978-1-933002-50-7

This is an examination of the tactics and strategies business owners need to know to attain funding, and ensure they receive credit approval. It provides guidance about personal guarantees, lender fees, interest rates, managing the problems inherent in business debt, how to re-evaluate a business' credit situation, and put in place an effective debt strategy.

MAGAZINES

Business Credit
National Association of Credit Management
8840 Columbia 100 Parkway, Columbia, Maryland 21045-2158, USA
T: +1 410 740 5560
F: +1 410 740 5574
www.nacm.org

Published 10 times a year, this magazine of the National Association of Credit Management is aimed at those responsible for extending business and trade credit and risk management for their companies. It features analysis of new trends, and important legislative, bankruptcy, business ethics, trade finance, asset protection, benchmarking, risk management, technology, and scoring issues.

Credit
Incisive Media
Haymarket House, 28–29 Haymarket, London, SW1Y 4RX, UK
T: +44 (0) 20 7484 9700
F: +44 (0) 20 7484 9797
www.creditmag.com

This monthly magazine covers the entire credit market, and includes regular features on credit derivatives, structured credit, loans and convertibles. It aims to provide a forum for bondholders, borrowers, banks, and investors to discuss the key issues of the credit market, and features industry profiles, product news, people moves, regulatory issues, events, awards, technology updates, and surveys.

Credit Today
Athene Publishing
Axe & Bottle Court, 70 Newcomen Street, London, SE1 1YT, UK
T: +44 (0) 844 477 4740
F: +44 (0) 20 7940 4843
www.credittoday.co.uk

This monthly magazine for the commercial and consumer credit industry is focused on breaking news, information, and industry debate. It also organizes a number of educational and networking events, and its website acts as a popular online credit news hub, and also features jobs and event information, and has a directory of suppliers and an industry forum.

JOURNALS

The Journal of Credit Risk
Risk Journals
Haymarket House, 28–29 Haymarket, London, SW1Y 4RX, UK
T: +44 (0) 20 7484 9700
F: +44 (0) 20 7484 9797
www.journalofcreditrisk.com
ISSN: 1744-6619

This is an international quarterly journal that publishes refereed papers on the measurement and management of credit risk, the valuation and hedging of credit products, and the promotion of

  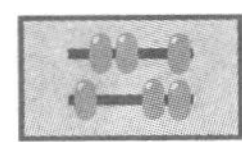      

greater understanding in the area of credit risk theory and practice. It features technical credit risk research from both industry and academia.

Journal of Money, Credit and Banking

Ohio State University Press
1070 Carmack Road, Columbus, Ohio 43210, USA
T: +1 614 292 7834
F: +1 614 247 7814
web.econ.ohio-state.edu/jmcb
ISSN: 0022-2879

This professional journal is published seven times a year, and is aimed at academics, researchers, and policymakers, in the areas of money and banking, credit markets, regulation of financial institutions, international payments, portfolio management, and monetary and fiscal policy.

ORGANIZATIONS

USA

National Association of Credit Management

Chair: Jim Fried
8840 Columbia 100 Parkway, Columbia, Maryland 21045-2158, USA
T: +1 410 740 5560
F: +1 410 740 5574
www.nacm.org

NACM and its network of affiliated associations are key resource for credit and financial management, and provide a full range of services, such as pre-collection services, final demand notices, industry groups, and commercial credit reports. It aims to assist members by offering accessible, products, services and programs.

Currency and Foreign Exchange

BOOKS

Adventures of a Currency Trader: A Fable about Trading, Courage, and Doing the Right Thing

Rob Booker
Wiley Trading Series
Hoboken, New Jersey: Wiley, 2007
221pp, ISBN: 978-0-470-04948-8

An entertaining and educational guide to successful currency trading, told through the story of a fictional trader, Harry Banes. It tells of his start in the foreign currency market, learning how to trade, finding the best trading approach, avoiding the most common trading mistakes, and demonstrating in a readable way the strategies and pitfalls of currency trading.

The Complete Guide to Currency Trading & Investing: How to Earn High Rates of Return Safely and Take Control of Your Investments

Jamaine Burrell
Ocala, Florida: Atlantic Publishing, 2007
288pp, ISBN: 978-1-60138-119-4

With currency trading gaining in popularity and accessibility all the time, this guide provides practical instruction in the basics of successfully trading in the largest market in the world. Comprehensive and well-researched, it covers everything you need to know to get started, including effective investment strategies, advice on all aspects of the FX markets, and how best to avoid the main risks involved.

Currencies and Crises

Paul Krugman
Cambridge, Massachusetts: MIT Press, 1992
240pp, ISBN: 978-0-262-61109-1

This is a collection of writing on currencies by Nobel Prize winner Paul Krugman. The papers focus on his view of international monetary economics from the late 1970s onwards, and explain the role of exchange rates in balance-of-payments adjustment policy, how speculation affects the functioning of exchange-rate regimes, emerging market debt, and the development of an international monetary system.

Currency Strategy: The Practitioner's Guide to Currency Investing, Hedging and Forecasting, 2nd ed

Callum Henderson
Wiley Trading Series
Chichester, UK: Wiley, 2006
264pp, ISBN: 978-0-470-02759-2

For the more advanced reader, this takes a broad view of the currency markets, explaining the main tools for predicting, managing, and optimizing currency changes, and shows how to develop new techniques and use mathematical models to take advantage of them. This new edition also examines recent changes impacting the Chinese currency markets.

Currency Wars: How Forged Money is the New Weapon of Mass Destruction

John Cooley
New York: Skyhorse Publishing, 2008
320pp, ISBN: 978-1-60239-270-0

An investigation into the use of counterfeit money, thought to cause greater economic damage than terrorism. Cooley tells many entertaining stories of forged money through history, focusing on how counterfeiting has been used by states for political and economic reasons, to destabilize enemy governments as a sort of aggressive economic warfare.

Day Trading the Currency Market: Technical and Fundamental Strategies to Profit from Market Swings

Kathy Lien
Wiley Trading Series
Hoboken, New Jersey: Wiley, 2006
256pp, ISBN: 978-0-471-71753-9

Intended for all levels of day trader, it presents all the necessary market basics and currency characteristics, and shows how to build an effective trading approach. It also discusses the emergence of the foreign exchange market, the major players, and emphasizes how to take advantage of movements in the currency market from both a technical and fundamental perspective.

A Foreign Exchange Primer, 2nd ed

Shani Shamah
Wiley Trading Series
Chichester, UK: Wiley, 2008
250pp, ISBN: 978-0-470-75437-5

This is a new edition of the accessible beginner's guide to working in the foreign exchange market, that takes you through all the practical skills necessary to trade, and examines the main products and techniques, the key institutions and players, and the terminology used.

Forex Conquered: High Probability Systems and Strategies for Active Traders

John L. Person
Wiley Trading Series
Hoboken, New Jersey: Wiley, 2007
304pp, ISBN: 978-0-470-09779-3

Provides the essentials of the foreign exchange market, the strategies and systems, and how to manage the risks involved. Written more for the experienced trader, it also explains technical topics such as candlestick charting, Elliott wave theory and Fibonacci price corrections.

Forex Patterns & Probabilities: Trading Strategies for Trending & Range-Bound Markets

Ed Ponsi
Wiley Trading Series
Hoboken, New Jersey: Wiley, 2007
272pp, ISBN: 978-0-470-09729-8

Offers practical strategies and trading methodologies based on the author's experience as a professional trader and educator. A clear presentation of how to trade like a professional, it introduces a variety of elements essential to currency trading success, from as the best ways to enter, exit, and manage trades, to real-life examples of effective trading.

The Forex Trading Course: A Self-Study Guide to Becoming a Successful Currency Trader

Abe Cofnas
Wiley Trading Series
Hoboken, New Jersey: Wiley, 2007
240pp, ISBN: 978-0-470-13764-2

This is a practical and user-friendly handbook on currency trading, which teaches the trading basics, through to an understanding of the complexities of applying fundamental and technical analysis to identify patterns and trends. It also shows how to develop an effective trading plan, with appropriate strategies for different size accounts, and how to use emotional intelligence to improve trading performance.

Mastering Foreign Exchange & Currency Options: A Practical Guide to the New Marketplace, 2nd ed

Francesca Taylor
Market Editions Series
Harlow, UK: FT Prentice Hall, 2003
432pp, ISBN: 978-0-273-66295-2

Now in its second edition, this is a handbook for those involved in the market at any level, whether looking for practical guidance on forex trading, tips on how to improve your currency dealing, or how to keep appraised of new developments in this fast-changing market. It also has a useful focus on how new technology has changed the market.

Mathematical Methods for Foreign Exchange: A Financial Engineer's Approach

Alexander Lipton
Singapore: World Scientific, 2001
700pp, ISBN: 978-981-02-4823-9

A classic, albeit technical, examination of the mathematics that underpins a successful financial engineering approach to foreign exchange. It takes a systematic approach to financial modeling of the currency markets, and explains the mathematical, economic and trading background of this approach, and its uses in derivative pricing.

The Money Changers: A Guided Tour through Global Currency Markets

Robert G. Williams
Black Point, Nova Scotia: Fernwood Publishing, 2006
256pp, ISBN: 978-1-84277-695-7

A readable exploration of the workings of the foreign exchange markets, which provides an international perspective on the movement of currencies and exchange rates around the world. This is an important overview of the markets, systems, strategies, and people that make it work.

Technical Analysis of the Currency Market: Classic Techniques for Profiting from Market Swings and Trader Sentiment

Boris Schlossberg
Wiley Trading Series
Hoboken, New Jersey: Wiley, 2006
224pp, ISBN: 978-0-471-74593-8

A trading primer for the currency markets that focuses on using technical analysis to trade successfully in a wide range of market situations. It provides a practical approach to the use of currency trading tools and strategies, and is aimed at giving you the skill and confidence to trade in the global currency market.

MAGAZINES

Currency Trader

161 North Clark, Suite 4915, Chicago, IL 60601, USA
T: +1 312 775 5422
www.currencytradermag.com

This is a monthly magazine that covers trading strategies, systems, analysis, news, and issues of risk control and money management, for FX and currency futures traders. It includes special strategy articles that explore behavioral characteristics and tendencies in different currencies, and the relationships between currencies and economic data.

e-Forex

ASP Media
Suite 10, 3 Edgar Buildings, George Street, Bath, BA1 2FJ, UK
T: +44 (0) 1249 814466
F: +44 (0) 1249 814477
www.e-forex.net

This is an international quarterly magazine focused on electronic and online trading of FX and OTC financial instruments. Targeted at both sell-side and buy-side, it provides the latest industry news and technical developments, and evaluates the benefits of e-FX trading, and assesses the functionality and capabilities of retail or institutional online trading platforms.

Euromoney Weekly FiX

Euromoney
Nestor House, Playhouse Yard, London, EC4V 5EX, UK
T: +44 (0) 20 7779 8888
F: +44 (0) 20 7779 8602
www.euromoneyfix.com

The Weekly FiX is an online magazine that builds on Euromoney's coverage of foreign exchange, to provide news, analysis of FX market trends and regulation, commentary, Q&As with industry experts, people moves, market data and market analysis, and analysis of the institutions, people and products in the global FX business.

The Forex Journal

One Raffles Place, OUB Centre #18-01, Singapore 048616, Singapore
T: +65 9 788 8141
F: +65 6 312 8091
www.forexjournal.com
ISSN: 1793-2149

This is a monthly magazine designed for both advanced and novice traders in the foreign exchange markets. It covers the major Forex market basics, as well as examining issues such as factors that impact price movements in the currency market, the best times to trade for individual currency pairs, trade parameters for different market conditions, and technical and fundamental trading strategies.

FX&MM

Russell Publishing
Court Lodge, Hogtrough Hill, Brasted, Kent, TN16 1NU, UK
T: +44 (0) 1959 563311
F: +44 (0) 1959 563317
www.fx-mm.com

This is a monthly magazine that examines the issues bankers, corporate treasurers, fund managers, traders, and brokers face in the international finance markets. Through in-depth global news, features, interviews and case studies on leading products and personalities in the foreign exchange and money market industry, and provides guidance on managing currency and interest rate fluctuations.

FX Week

Incisive Media
Incisive Media, Haymarket House, 28–29 Haymarket, London, SW1Y 4RX, UK
T: +44 (0) 20 7484 9700
F: +44 (0) 20 7930 2238
www.fxweek.com
ISSN: 1050-0782

This is a monthly industry newsletter for foreign exchange and money market professionals working within banks, brokerages, institutions and corporate treasuries. It produces news stories, special reports, the latest currency forecasts index, analysis and commentary, technology news, and people moves within the industry. It also produces quarterly supplements covering CLS, emerging markets, e-FX, currency derivatives, white labeling and retail FX.

INTERNET

Forex Directory

www.forexdirectory.org

The Forex Directory is an online resource for the foreign exchange and currency market, that provides listings and links to brokers, quotes, associations, training, risk management, alerts and signals, competitions, online trading and accounts, charts, magazines, accountants, legal advisers, hedge funds, and software.

Forexsites

www.forexsites.com

Provides a balanced flow of independent information for foreign exchange and currency traders around the world. It delivers real-time quotes, live news feeds, charting, technicals, fundamentals, tutorials, forums, and information specific to the major currencies.

OANDA

www.oanda.com

OANDA is one of the main internet-based forex trading and currency information services, and a market maker and a source for currency data for those involved in the market. It has access to one of the world's largest historical, high frequency, filtered currency databases; it is estimated that about a fifth of the global online spot forex transactions take place on its servers.

Derivatives and Quantitative Finance

BOOKS

All About Derivatives

Michael Durbin

New York: McGraw-Hill, 2006
253pp, ISBN: 978-0-07-145147-5

This introduces you to derivatives, how they work, and how they can enhance profits and control market risk. It presents the main features and methods for all the main products, and explains their contracts, techniques for pricing and trading, terminology, the mechanics of storage, settlement, valuation, and payoff, hedging strategies, and leverage.

The Bible of Options Strategies: The Definitive Guide for Practical Trading Strategies

Guy Cohen

Upper Saddle River, New Jersey: FT Press, 2005
356pp, ISBN: 978-0-13-171066-5

This is an accessible guide to options trading that analyzes the most popular strategies, and explains how and when each one should be used, and the hazards to look out for. It covers all of the best income, volatility, leveraged, synthetic, and sideways market strategies, helping the trader to identify and implement the most effective strategy for every opportunity, trading environment, and desired outcome.

The Complete Guide to Capital Markets for Quantitative Professionals

Alex Kuznetsov

McGraw-Hill Library of Investment and Finance Series
New York: McGraw-Hill, 2007
554pp, ISBN: 978-0-07-146829-9

Offering practical advice for those with a science and technology background who need a greater understanding of how the capital markets work, this book assumes no previous knowledge of financial analytics. It explains the business models of different types of institution, and discusses the different type of job role that those with technical backgrounds can apply for.

The Complete Guide to Option Pricing Formulas, 2nd ed

Espen Gaarder Haug

New York: McGraw-Hill, 2007
536pp, ISBN: 978-0-07-138997-6

This is a comprehensive resource that contains a complete listing of nearly every options pricing formula. This practitioner-focused listing is presented in a dictionary format, and now contains more than 60 new option models and formulas, with author commentary and accompanying programming code. The new edition covers option sensitivities, discrete dividend, commodity options, and numerical methods covering trees, finite difference and Monte Carlo Simulation.

Derivatives: Markets, Valuation, and Risk Management

Robert E. Whaley

Wiley Finance Series
Hoboken, New Jersey: Wiley, 2006
930pp, ISBN: 978-0-471-78632-0

This provides an overview of derivatives products and markets, and offers guidance on using derivatives to manage the different types of risks faced by individuals, corporations, and governments. It gives a solid understanding of derivative contract valuation and risk management, as well as the structure of the markets within which they trade.

Derivatives Demystified: A Step-by-Step Guide to Forwards, Futures, Swaps and Options

Andrew M. Chishom

Wiley Finance Series
Chichester, UK: Wiley, 2004
233pp, ISBN: 978-0-470-09382-5

This describes derivative products in straightforward terms, focusing on applications and intuitive explanations of how they are used. It examines the basic building blocks of derivatives, and how they are applied to different markets and various risk management and trading problems. It also offers guidance on the underlying theory, and case studies and examples of how the products are used to solve real-world problems.

Derivatives Markets, 2nd ed

Robert L. McDonald

Boston, Massachusetts: Addison-Wesley, 2006
964pp, ISBN: 978-0-321-54308-0

A comprehensive examination of derivatives markets, which provides an in-depth treatment of the theory, institutions, and applications of derivatives, in an accessible manner. It also offers insights into derivatives pricing models, a tiered approach to the underlying mathematics, an emphasis on the application of the tools and models, and a computation-friendly approach, with pricing functions also available in accompanying spreadsheets.

Financial Derivatives: Pricing, Applications, and Mathematics

Jamil Baz, George Chacko

Cambridge, UK: Cambridge University Press, 2008
352pp, ISBN: 978-0-521-06679-2

This demonstrates the principles and mathematics of financial derivatives pricing and portfolio allocation decisions, including mean-reverting processes and jump processes, and the related tools of stochastic calculus. It also develops generic pricing techniques for assets and derivatives, and discusses key concepts such volatility and time, random walks, geometric Brownian motion, and Ito's lemma.

How I Became a Quant: Insights from 25 of Wall Street's Elite

Barry Schachter, Richard Lindsey

Hoboken, New Jersey: Wiley, 2007
386pp, ISBN: 978-0-470-05062-0

In a series of personal insights and recollections from some of the most successful names on Wall Street, they detail their backgrounds, varying career paths, and contributions to finance, as well as explaining what exactly they do and how they do it. It explains how they introduced techniques for managing risks through trading financial instruments, and the transformation of the financial markets they instigated.

An Introduction to Derivatives and Risk Management, 7th ed

Don Chance, Robert Brooks

Mason, Ohio: Thomson/South-Western, 2006
653pp, ISBN: 978-0-324-32139-5

This is a comprehensive primer to the pricing, trading, and strategy relating to the use of derivatives in trading and risk management. It combines institutional material, theory, and practical applications, and a flexible mathematical approach, to discuss options, futures, forwards, swaps, and risk management, as well as mortgage-backed securities, structured notes, derivatives accounting, and best practices benchmarks for risk management.

Mastering Derivatives Markets: A Step-by-Step Guide to the Products, Applications and Risks, 3rd ed

Francesca Taylor

Market Editions Series
Harlow, UK: FT Prentice Hall, 2007
426pp, ISBN: 978-0-273-70978-7

This comprehensive overview of derivative processes and instruments for the professional investor offers practical advice on the markets in an understandable way. It discusses changes in derivative trading, explains key products across the main asset classes, and covers topics such as credit derivatives, what happens after the deal is done, benchmarking, the STP market, how technology is evolving, the new accounting regulations, and the impact of MiFID.

My Life as a Quant: Reflections on Physics and Finance

Emanuel Derman

Hoboken, New Jersey: Wiley, 2004
292pp, ISBN: 978-0-470-19273-3

This is a wide-ranging and personal autobiography by one of the pioneering quants that transformed the financial markets. Derman, co-author of some of the most influential financial models, provides an entertaining account of his move to Wall Street, how the academics brought their new financial science to the business world, the incompatibility between traders and quants, and the dissimilar nature of knowledge in physics and finance.

  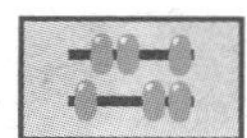      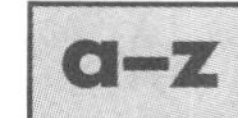

Options, Futures, and Other Derivatives, 7th ed
John C. Hull
Prentice Hall Series in Finance
Upper Saddle River, New Jersey: Prentice Hall, 2008
821pp, ISBN: 978-1-4082-1743-6

Regarded as the classic text on derivatives, this updated and revised bestselling introduction to futures and options markets is aimed at professionals with limited math background working in the markets, financial engineering, and risk management. It provides a unifying approach to the valuation of derivatives, bridging the gap between the theory and practice, supported by clear explanations and examples.

Paul Wilmott Introduces Quantitative Finance, 2nd ed
Paul Wilmott
Chichester, UK: Wiley, 2007
695pp, ISBN: 978-0-470-31958-1

This is a concise and accessible primer on the classical side of quantitative finance, adapted from Wilmott's renowned books on derivatives and quantitative finance. It presents a thorough overview of futures, options and numerical methods, and includes software to help visualize the most important ideas, and to show how techniques are implemented in practice.

Traders, Guns & Money: Knowns and Unknowns in the Dazzling World of Derivatives
Satyajit Das
Harlow, UK: FT Prentice Hall, 2006
334pp, ISBN: 978-0-273-70474-4

This is an insider's view of the business of trading and marketing derivatives, providing a sensational and controversial first-person account in the spirit of Liar's Poker. It details the nature of the industry, the players, the culture, games, how other people's money is made and lost, and the deceptions that underpin the entire process.

MAGAZINES

FOW
Euromoney Institutional Investor, UK
T: +44 (0) 20 7779 8219
www.fow.com
ISSN: 0953-6620

This is a monthly magazine for the global derivatives and risk management industry. it offers news and analysis on all financial asset classes and commodity derivatives, including fixed income, equity, foreign exchange, technology, new products, personal and corporate profiles, people moves, market reports and key data.

Futures
Summit Business Media
5081 Olympic Boulevard, Erlanger, KY 41018-3164, USA
T: +1 859 692 2100
www.futuresmag.com
ISSN: 0746-2468

This monthly magazine for the derivatives industry covers the futures markets, as well as the options, forex and stock markets. It publishes articles and features on fundamental and technical trading strategies, market news, managed money and fund reviews, new products, technology updates, and trader profiles.

Risk
Incisive Media
Haymarket House, 28–29 Haymarket, London, SW1Y 4RX, UK
T: +44 (0) 20 7484 9700
F: +44 (0) 20 7484 9932
www.risk.net
ISSN: 0952-8776

This is a monthly magazine that focuses on financial risk management and the global derivatives industry. It covers new developments in the derivatives markets, provides updates on the movements and activities of key players and personalities in the industry, and showcases technical papers and the latest research into derivatives tools and techniques.

Wilmott
Wiley
The Atrium, Southern Gate, Chichester, West Sussex, PO19 8SQ, UK
T: +44 (0) 1243 779777
F: +44 (0) 1243 775878
www.wilmott.com
ISSN: 1540-6962

Published every two months, *Wilmott* offers new research, innovative models, products, software, analysis, solutions, and tests the latest quantitative finance theories with practical examples. It publishes technical articles from all the functional areas of quantitative finance, derivatives, risk management, finance, and behavioral finance, usually written by quantitative analysts in banks and academia, mathematicians, econophysicists and economists.

JOURNALS

Derivatives & Financial Instruments
International Bureau of Fiscal Documentation (IBFD)
PO Box 20237, 1000HE Amsterdam, The Netherlands
T: +31 20 554 0100
F: +31 20 620 8626
www.ibfd.org/portal/Product_dfijournal.html
ISSN: 1389-1863

This bimonthly journal provides information and analysis for tax professionals and financial market experts around the world. It publishes articles on the taxation of swaps, futures, options, forward contracts, credit derivatives, synthetic equities, securitization, index-linked and unit-linked contracts and forward rate agreements, as well as on legislation, government documents, case reports, and assessments of recent events in the taxation of financial instruments.

International Journal of Theoretical and Applied Finance
World Scientific
5 Toh Tuck Link, Singapore 596224, Singapore
T: +65 6466 5775
F: +65 6467 7667
www.worldscinet.com/ijtaf
ISSN: 0219-0249

This technical journal is published eight times a year, and offers research papers, review papers, and book reviews on the quantitative tools used in finance. It focuses on the mathematical modeling of financial instruments, the application of these models to global financial markets, and the development and application of modern stochastic methods in finance.

Journal of Derivatives & Hedge Funds
Palgrave Macmillan
The Macmillan Building, 4 Crinan Street, London, N1 9XW, UK
T: +44 (0) 20 7843 4684
www.palgrave-journals.com/jdhf
ISSN: 1753-9641

This is a quarterly journal that examines the derivatives market and hedge funds. Formerly known as *Derivatives Use, Trading & Regulation*, it has evolved its coverage to take into account the enormous growth in hedge funds. It focuses on trading, legal and other derivative issues, and the many challenges facing the hedge fund industry, such as transparency, liquidity risk, and risk management control.

Journal of Derivatives
Institutional Investor Journals
225 Park Avenue South, 8th Floor, New York, NY 10003, USA
T: +1 212 224 3570
F: +1 212 224 3197
www.iijournals.com/JOD
ISSN: 1074-1240

This quarterly journal, the official publication of the International Association of Financial Engineers, offers practitioner-oriented research in the area of derivatives. The articles published are academically rigorous, and focused on applicable research.

Journal of Financial and Quantitative Analysis
115 Lewis, Box 353200, Seattle, WA 98195-3200, USA
T: +1 206 543 4598
F: +1 206 616 1894
www.jfqa.org
ISSN: 0022-1090

This quarterly journal publishes theoretical and empirical research in financial economics, focusing on corporate finance, investments, capital and security markets, and quantitative methods of particular relevance to financial researchers.

The Journal of Futures Markets
Wiley
989 Market Street, San Francisco, CA 94103-1741, USA
T: +1 415 433 1767
F: +1 415 951 8553
www3.interscience.wiley.com/journal/34434/home
ISSN: 0270-7314

This monthly journal presents the latest developments in financial futures and derivatives, written by leading finance

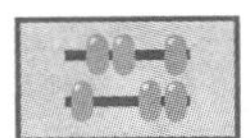

academics and professionals. It covers both practical and theoretical topics, such as risk management and control, financial engineering, new financial instruments, hedging strategies, analysis of trading systems, legal, accounting, and regulatory issues, and portfolio optimization.

Quantitative Finance

Routledge
Informa House, 30–32 Mortimer Street, London, W1W 7RE, UK
T: +44 (0) 20 7017 5532
F: +44 (0) 20 7017 4781
www.tandf.co.uk/journals/rquf
ISSN: 1469-7688

This journal publishes eight issues each year, and provides an interdisciplinary forum for both theoretical and empirical approaches to quantitative methods in finance. It has a broad remit, offering technical papers from researchers and practitioners across a range of specialisms and within a variety of organizations.

Review of Derivatives Research

Springer, USA
www.springer.com/business/finance/journal/11147
ISSN: 1380-6645

Publishes three times a year, this journal is aimed at financial institutions, institutional investors, and corporations who use sophisticated quantitative techniques and financial instruments. It offers articles on the pricing and hedging of derivative assets on any underlying asset, and provides an international forum for researchers involved in the general areas of derivative assets.

Review of Quantitative Finance and Accounting

Springer, USA
www.springer.com/business/finance/journal/11156
ISSN: 0924-865X

This research-based quarterly journal focuses on presenting theoretical and methodological results with the support of empirical applications. It presents papers on the interaction of finance with accounting, economics and quantitative methods, as well as relevant topics that use finance theory and methodology, such as managerial accounting and auditing, macroeconomics, and managerial economics.

INTERNET

Derivatives Strategy

www.derivativesstrategy.com

This website, once the online presence of the monthly Derivatives Strategy magazine, now provides a forum for news and information on the global derivatives market from a US perspective. It is for users of derivatives products, rather than quants, and tries to explain complex derivatives issues in an understandable way.

DW Online

www.iiderivatives.com

An online resource for news on all derivatives types across all regions, as well as producing analysis and information on credit, equity, currencies, people and firms, regulation and documentation, conferences, and market data.

Futures and Options Intelligence

www.fointelligence.com

This website provides market data, research, news, insight, analysis, alerts, and details on volumes, exchanges, and contracts for the global exchange-traded derivatives market.

Global Derivatives

www.global-derivatives.com

This is an online resource for the quantitative finance and financial engineering industry, that offers news, forums, options databases, education, pricing models, a financial mathematics glossary, quant finance 101s, book reviews, working papers, and job postings.

Quantnotes.com

www.quantnotes.com

This is a quantitative finance website that provides articles and downloadable publications on derivatives and other financial instruments, as well as links to relevant software and calculators, book reviews, discussion forums, and listings of events and jobs.

ORGANIZATIONS

Europe

The Futures and Options Association

Chair: Steve Sparke
2nd Floor, 36–38 Botolph Lane, London, EC3R 8DE, UK
T: +44 (0) 20 7929 0081
F: +44 (0) 20 7621 0223
www.foa.co.uk

The FOA is a European industry trade association for firms and institutions carrying on business in futures, options and other derivatives, or which use such products in their business. Its principal role is to represent the interests of its members in the public and regulatory domain, and deliver a wide range of support services to its members.

USA

Commodity Futures Trading Commission

Chair: Walter Lukken
Three Lafayette Centre, 1155 21st Street NW, Washington, DC 20581, USA
T: +1 202 418 5000
F: +1 202 418 5521
E: questions@cftc.gov
www.cftc.gov

The mission of the CFTC is to protect market users and the public from fraud, manipulation, and abusive practices related to the sale of commodity and financial futures and options, and to foster open, competitive, and financially sound futures and option markets, and the integrity of the clearing process. It enables the futures markets to provide a means for price discovery and offsetting price risk.

Futures Industry Association

Chair: Kenneth M. Ford
2001 Pennsylvania Avenue NW, Suite 600, Washington, DC 20006, USA
T: +1 202 466 5460
F: +1 202 296 3184
www.futuresindustry.org

The FIA provides a means for the exchange of ideas, and works with commodity exchanges to promote and preserve free marketing and a high standard of ethics, a high quality of service to the public. It also examines ways of reducing the costs and increasing the volume of trading in the business, eliminating credit abuse, improving education, and protecting firms from fraudulent warehouse receipts.

International Association of Financial Engineers

Chair: David Jaffe
630 9th Avenue, Suite 802, New York, NY 10036, USA
T: +1 646 736 0705
F: +1 646 417 6378
E: main@iafe.org
www.iafe.org

This not-for-profit, professional society is dedicated to promoting quantitative finance by providing platforms to discuss key industry issues. It is composed of individual academics and practitioners from banks, broker dealers, hedge funds, pension funds, asset managers, technology firms, regulators, accounting, consulting and law firms, and universities around the world.

International Swaps and Derivatives Association

360 Madison Avenue, 16th Floor, New York, NY 10017, USA
T: +1 212 901 6000
F: +1 212 901 6001
E: isda@isda.org
www.isda.org

ISDA encourages the development of the privately negotiated derivatives industry by promoting the efficient conduct of the business, promoting the development of sound risk management practices, fostering high standards of commercial conduct, advancing international public understanding, and educating members and others on legislative regulatory, legal, accounting, tax, and other issues affecting them.

National Futures Association

Chair: W. Robert Felker
300 South Riverside Plaza, #1800, Chicago, IL 60606-6615, USA
T: +1 312 781 1300
F: +1 312 781 1467
E: information@nfa.futures.org
www.nfa.futures.org

This is an independent, self-regulatory organization for the US futures industry. It develops rules, programs and services to safeguard market integrity, protect investors and help their members meet regulatory responsibilities.

  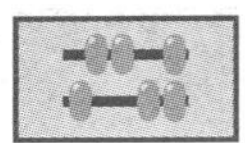      

Econometrics

BOOKS

Applied Econometrics: A Modern Approach Using Eviews and Microfit, revised ed

Dimitrios Asteriou, Stephen Hall

New York: Palgrave Macmillan, 2007
256pp, ISBN: 978-0-230-50640-4

A solid overview of current econometric thinking, it provides a practical guide to econometric data, econometrics tests and methods of estimation for those studying econometrics or quantitative economics. It also presents a step-by-step approach to using the popular software packages, and includes a section on panel data, that contains the latest developments in panel unit roots and panel cointegration.

A Concise Introduction to Econometrics: An Intuitive Guide

Philip Hans Franses

New York: Cambridge University Press, 2002
117pp, ISBN: 978-0-521-52090-4

A short and practical introduction to the subject, this guide reviews the basic econometric concepts, focusing on a select number of key methods. It emphasizes the importance of specification, evaluation, and implementation of models appropriate to the data, and also provides a series of questions in various economic disciplines, to be answered using econometric methods and models.

Econometric Analysis, 6th ed

William H. Greene

Upper Saddle River, New Jersey: Prentice Hall, 2007
1,216pp, ISBN: 978-0-13-513245-6

Provides an introduction to econometrics and its tools, as well as a resource on the professional literature on the subject that links specialized areas. Combining an applied approach with a theoretical underpinning, it covers a wide range of topics such as Classical, Bayesian, GMM, and maximum likelihood, and emphasizes new areas such a time series and panels.

Econometric Models and Economic Forecasts, 4th ed

Robert Pindyck, Daniel Rubinfeld

Boston, Massachusetts: McGraw-Hill/Irwin, 1998
634pp, ISBN: 978-0-07-913292-5

A strong textbook that focuses on modeling and model building, explaining what type of model to build, how to test it statistically, and then apply the model to practical problems in forecasting and analysis. It also analyses time series and forecasting, single-equation and the multiple regression models, and has an expanded treatment of nonlinear and maximum-likelihood estimation.

Econometric Theory and Methods

Russell Davidson, James G. MacKinnon

New York: Oxford University Press, 2004
750pp, ISBN: 978-0-19-512372-2

A textbook that unifies modern econometric theory and practical econometric methods, and examines a wide range of tools and techniques, including the geometrical approach to least squares, the method of moments, and bootstrap and Monte Carlo tests. Each chapter contains useful exercises, many involving simulation, to aid learning.

Econometrics

Fumio Havashi

Princeton, New Jersey: Princeton University Press, 2000
690pp, ISBN: 978-0-691-01018-2

Acting as an introduction to the subject, it presents all the standard material necessary for understanding the various estimation techniques, through a mix of theory and applications. Generalized methods of moments (GMM) are helpfully used as an organizing principle throughout, and there is also a detailed analysis of stationary and non-stationary time series.

The Econometrics of Financial Markets

John Y. Campbell, Andrew W. Lo, A. Craig MacKinlay

Princeton, New Jersey: Princeton University Press, 1997
611pp, ISBN: 978-0-691-04301-2

This is a technical but accessible examination of financial econometrics by three leading researchers, presenting cutting-edge statistical techniques and the techniques of financial modeling. It examines much of empirical finance in detail, including the Random Walk Hypothesis, event analysis, the Capital Asset Pricing Model, Arbitrage Pricing Theory, statistical fractals, and chaos theory.

Essentials of Econometrics, 3rd ed

Damodar Gujarati

Boston, Massachusetts: McGraw-Hill/Irwin, 2006
553pp, ISBN: 978-0-07-313594-6

Now in its 3rd edition, this focused examination of the principles of econometrics provides an introduction to the subject for the beginner. It is accessible for those wanting a quick understanding of econometric techniques, especially linear regression analysis. It presents all the main econometric theory and techniques through extensive examples and explanations, and has an accompanying CD.

Financial Econometrics: From Basics to Advanced Modeling Techniques

Svetlozar T. Rachev, Stefan Mittnik, Frank J. Fabozzi, Sergio M. Focardi, Teo Jasic

Frank J. Fabozzi Series
Hoboken, New Jersey: Wiley, 2007
553pp, ISBN: 978-0-471-78450-0

This is a comprehensive guide to financial econometrics that uses numerous examples to help an understanding of the main issues. It provides a thorough overview of all the key topics, concepts, and theories, including background material on probability theory and statistics, and uses real-world data and the results of published research where possible.

A Guide to Econometrics, 6th ed

Peter Kennedy

Malden, Massachusetts: Blackwell Publishing, 2008
585pp, ISBN: 978-1-4051-8257-7

This is a supplement and guide to the main econometrics textbooks, which provides analysis and practical advice for all levels of econometrics classes. This new edition contains new chapters on instrumental variables and on computation considerations, and an introduction to wavelets.

A Guide to Modern Econometrics, 3rd ed

Marno Verbeek

Chichester, UK: Wiley, 2008
472pp, ISBN: 978-0-470-51769-7

The new edition of this textbook takes a practical approach to analysing some of the alternative econometric techniques available. It also introduces new material on panel data and pseudo panels, and takes a closer look at some of the more complex topics, such as multicollinearity, instrumental variables, and robust inference.

Introduction to Econometrics, 2nd ed

James H. Stock, Mark W. Watson

Addison-Wesley Series in Economics
Boston, Massachusetts: Pearson/Addison Wesley, 2007
796pp, ISBN: 978-0-321-27887-6

A primer in applied econometrics that combines modern theory and practice. It integrates real-world questions and data with current thinking, and covers a wide range of key topics, such as program evaluation, panel data methods, instrumental variables regression, and regression with time series data.

Introductory Econometrics: A Modern Approach, 4th ed

Jeffrey M. Wooldridge

Mason, Ohio: South Western, Cengage Learning, 2009
865pp, ISBN: 978-0-324-58162-1

A new edition of this guide to the fundamentals of econometrics, that focuses on current approaches and techniques, and incorporates relevant applications in many places. It includes analysis of a wide range of topics that are common in research, such as panel data, and a balance of mainstream models, equations, examples, and intuitive descriptions.

Introductory Econometrics for Finance, 2nd ed

Chris Brooks

Information Technology & Law Series
Cambridge, UK: Cambridge University Press, 2008
648pp, ISBN: 978-0-521-69468-1

This successful textbook is a strong primer for finance students needing the basics of econometrics tailored for their learning needs.

It has been updated to include new analysis of panel data and limited dependent variable models, as well as the standard topics. It assumes no prior knowledge of econometrics, and focuses more on intuitive understanding than formulae.

Practical Financial Econometrics

Carol Alexander

Market Risk Analysis Series
Chichester, UK: Wiley, 2008
426pp, ISBN: 978-0-470-99801-4

Part of the Market Risk Analysis series, *Practical Financial Econometrics* introduces the most common econometric techniques in finance, with a unique focus on applications to asset pricing, fund management and problem solving in market risk analysis. It also covers equity factor models, volatility and correlation, GARCH, cointegration, copulas, Markov switching, forecasting and model evaluation.

Principles of Econometrics, 3rd ed

R. Carter Hill, Wiliam E. Griffiths, Guay C. Lim

Hoboken, New Jersey: Wiley, 2008
579pp, ISBN: 978-0-471-72360-8

A rigorous overview of econometrics and how to use the basic tools for estimation, inference, and forecasting, put in the context of real-life economic problems. It offers clear descriptions of simple economic models, as well as how to estimate key economic parameters, test economic hypotheses, and predict economic outcomes, in terms of motivation, understanding, and implementation.

JOURNALS

Applied Econometrics and International Development

Euro-American Association of Economic Development Studies
Faculty of Economics, Room 119-B, Econometrics, University of Santiago de Compostela 15782, Spain
T: +34 981 563 100
www.usc.es/~econome t/aeid.htm
ISSN: 1578-4487

Currently publishing twice yearly, this journal places an emphasis on economic development with an international and quantitative approach, and its main aim is to foster international cooperation to development.

Econometric Reviews

Taylor & Francis
325 Chestnut Street, Suite 800, Philadelphia, PA 19106, USA
T: +1 215 625 8900
F: +1 215 625 2940
www.tandf.co.uk/journals/titles/07474938.asp
ISSN: 0747-4938

This is a bimonthly review journal that examines the limits of econometric knowledge, featuring regular refereed articles and book reviews, as well as retrospective surveys of current or developing topics. Special issues of the journal are developed on a variety of specific themes in econometrics.

Econometric Theory

Cambridge University Press
40 West 20th Street, New York, NY 10022-4211, USA
T: +1 212 924 3900
F: +1 212 691 3239
korora.econ.yale.edu/et
ISSN: 0266-4666

This is an international bimonthly journal dedicated to advancing theoretical research in econometrics. It provides an outlet for original theoretical contributions in all of the major areas of econometrics, and seeks to foster the multidisciplinary features of econometrics that extend beyond the subject of economics.

Econometrica

The Econometrics Society
Department of Economics, Princeton University, Fisher Hall, Princeton, NJ 08544-1021, USA
T: +1 609 258 4768
F: +1 609 258 8844
www.econometricsociety.org
ISSN: 0012-9682

This is a bimonthly respected journal that publishes original articles in all branches of economics—theoretical and empirical, abstract and applied. The articles explore a range of topics, from the frontier of theoretical developments in many new and important areas, to research on current and applied economic problems, to methodologically innovative, theoretical and applied studies in econometrics.

The Econometrics Journal

Royal Economic Society
Lauriergracht 123, 1016 RK Amsterdam, The Netherlands
T: +31 20 598 9898
F: +31 20 598 9899
www.ectj.org
ISSN: 1368-4221

This is a journal, published three times a year, for econometric research, open to all areas of econometrics, whether applied, computational, methodological or theoretical. It seeks to promote the general advancement and application of econometric methods and techniques to problems of relevance to modern economics.

International Journal of Applied Econometrics and Quantitative Studies

Euro-American Association of Economic Development Studies
Faculty of Economics, Room 119-B, Econometrics, University of Santiago de Compostela 15782, Spain
T: +34 981 563 100
www.usc.es/~econome t/ijaeqs.htm
ISSN: 1698-4153

This refereed twice-yearly journal is mainly focused on policy-oriented quantitative studies of socio-economic interest. It focuses on special topics, including key questions linking economics research and policies, studies by country, including interesting quantitative studies with special priority for articles related with education, social well-being, international trade, investment and cooperation to development in one or more countries, and reports and other studies.

Journal of Applied Econometrics

Wiley
Faculty of Economics, University of Cambridge, Sidgwick Avenue, Cambridge, CB3 9DD, UK
T: +44 (0) 1223 335291
F: +44 (0) 1223 335471
jae.wiley.com
ISSN: 0883-7252

This is a bimonthly international journal that publishes articles on the application of existing as well as new econometric techniques to a wide variety of problems in economics and related subjects, covering topics in measurement, estimation, testing, forecasting, and policy analysis.

Journal of Business and Economic Statistics

American Statistical Association
732 North Washington Street, Alexandria, VA 22314-1943, USA
T: +1 703 684 1221
F: +1 703 684 2037
www.amstat.org/publications/jbes
ISSN: 0735-0015

This is a quarterly journal that publishes a range of articles, primarily applied statistical analyses of microeconomic, macroeconomic, forecasting, business, and finance related topics. It also publishes relevant papers in statistics, econometrics, computation, simulation, and graphics.

Journal of Econometrics

Elsevier
Radarweg 29, 1043 NX Amsterdam, The Netherlands
T: +31 20 485 3757
F: +31 20 485 3432
www.elsevier.com/wps/find/journaldescription.cws_home/505575/description#description
ISSN: 0304-4076

This is a monthly journal serving as an outlet for new research in both theoretical and applied econometrics. Its scope includes papers dealing with estimation and other methodological aspects of the application of statistical inference to economic data, as well as papers dealing with the application of econometric techniques to substantive areas of economics. Econometric research in the traditional divisions of the discipline, or in the newly developing areas of social experimentation, are also covered.

Journal of Financial Econometrics

Oxford University Press
Great Clarendon Street, Oxford, OX2 6DP, UK
T: + 44 (0) 1865 353907
F: +44 (0) 1865 353485
jfec.oxfordjournals.org
ISSN: 1479-8409

This is a quarterly journal dedicated to this fast-growing area of research. It addresses substantive statistical issues in econometrics, and aims to reflect and advance the relationship between econometrics and finance, both at the methodological and at the empirical levels.

  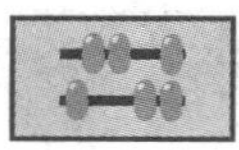      

Review of Economics and Statistics
MIT Press
Harvard University, 79 JFK Street, Box 134, Cambridge, MA 02138, USA
T: +1 617 495 2111
F: +1 617 495 5147
www.mitpressjournals.org/loi/rest
ISSN: 0034-6535

This is a quarterly journal of applied and quantitative economics that has published some of the most important articles in empirical economics. It also publishes collections of papers or symposia devoted to a single topic of methodological or empirical interest.

INTERNET

Econometric Links
www.econometriclinks.com

This is an online journal and resource, extensively annotated, and updated monthly. It focuses on general collections and preprint sites, departments and societies, software links, books, conferences, journals and mailing lists.

Econometric-Research
www.jiscmail.ac.uk/lists/econometric-research.html

This is an online forum for applied and theoretical research in econometrics and associated statistical theory, and functions as a dissemination list for research resources such as conferences, seminars, academic jobs, and free software.

Econometric Resources on the Internet
www.oswego.edu/~kane/econometrics

Although this is a site designed to accompany an econometrics textbook, it does contain useful annotated links to econometrics resources for both students and researchers, including links to data sources, economic associations, economic journals, datasets, government sites, newsgroups and software.

Econometrics Laboratory Software Archive
elsa.berkeley.edu

This site contains links to introductory tutorials on LaTeX, Perl, SAS, TCP/IP, Maple, MATLAB, as well as links to documentation and help for other software. It also includes a large selection of links to sources of econometric data, and a software archive for GAUSS and MATLAB.

ORGANIZATIONS

Europe

The Applied Econometrics Association
Chair: Orhan Güvenen
53, rue Saint Denis, 75 001 Paris, France
T: +33 1 4221 1172
F: +33 958 888 232
E: aea08@fed-eco.org
www.aea-eu.com

The purpose of The Applied Econometrics Association is to encourage and develop econometric applications in a spirit of open-minded scientific research, and it aims to bring its proposals before public and governmental bodies, firms, teaching and professional training institutions. Its areas of speciality are employment, finance, health, sector-based analysis, macro- and microeconomics, and management.

USA

Cowles Foundation
Yale University, PO Box 208281, New Haven, CT 06520-8281, USA
T: +1 203 432 3702
F: +1 203 432 6167
E: marleen.vega-perez@yale.edu
cowles.econ.yale.edu

The Cowles Foundation, continuing the work of the Cowles Commission for Research in Economics, founded in 1932 by Alfred Cowles, conducts and encourages research in economics and related fields. It seeks to foster the development and application of rigorous logical, mathematical, and statistical methods of analysis, and provides financial support for research, visiting faculty, postdoctoral fellowships, workshops, and graduate students.

The Econometric Society
Chair: Torsten Persson
Claire Sashi, General Manager, Department of Economics, New York University, 19 West Fourth Street, 6th Floor, New York, NY 10012, USA
T: +1 212 998 3820
F: +1 212 995 4487
E: sashi@econometricsociety.org
www.econometricsociety.org

This is an international society for the advancement of economic theory in its relation to statistics and mathematics, and which promotes studies that aim at a unification of the theoretical-quantitative and empirical-quantitative approach to economic problems. The main activities of the Society are the publication of the journal, Econometrica, the publication of a monograph series, the organization of scientific meetings around the world, and the conduct of elections for Fellow of the Econometric Society.

Emerging Market Finance

BOOKS

Bailouts or Bail-Ins: Responding to Financial Crises in Emerging Economies
Nouriel Roubini, Brad Setser
Washington, DC: Institute for International Economics, 2004
348pp, ISBN: 978-0-88132-371-9

Examines the recurring economic problems and short-term financial crises in developing markets, such as a lack of foreign reserves that prevent access to international capital markets. It looks at the role of the International Monetary Fund and the G-7 countries, rescue loans, currency devaluation and default, arguing that a flexible response and a consistent framework is crucial, as every crisis is different.

Bank Risk Analysis in Emerging Markets
Howard Palmer
London: Euromoney Books, 1998
212pp, ISBN: 978-1-85564-478-6

This is designed to help build a strategic bank risk portfolio, and understand the techniques and concepts of bank risk analysis, including loan provisions, liquidity ratios, cost/income ratios, the role of correspondent banking, and the future of bank risk indicators. It shows how to appraise the risks involved in dealing with banks in emerging economies, with greater transaction risks, and less reliance on supervision and potential rescue of banks in difficulty.

Emerging Capital Markets and Globalization: The Latin American Experience
Augusto De La Torre, Sergio Schmukler
Latin American Development Forum Series
Palo Alto, California/Washington, DC: Stanford University Press/World Bank, 2007
209pp, ISBN: 978-0-8213-6543-4

This examines why the development of local capital markets in most of Latin America has not been as successful as in other emerging economies, and puts this into the context of global trends in the capital markets. It analyzes the factors for this, discusses the implications for capital market reform in Latin America, and the need for revisions to the current policy agenda.

Emerging Capital Markets in Turmoil: Bad Luck or Bad Policy?
Guillermo A. Calvo
Cambridge, Massachusetts: MIT Press, 2005
563pp, ISBN: 978-0-262-03334-3

This collection of essays analyzes the struggle of emerging markets with capital flow volatility, and the limitations and vulnerabilities these economies face. It focuses on exchange rate issues, explores the reasons why emerging market economies have been affected by such dramatic highs and lows, and the increasing role of stocks and the financial sector in containing financial crises.

Emerging Markets: A Practical Guide for Corporations, Lenders, and Investors
Jeffrey C. Hooke
New York: Wiley, 2001
283pp, ISBN: 978-0-471-36099-5

This provides both Western investors and development professionals with a guide to the opportunities and problems associated with dealing with emerging markets. It defines what emerging markets are and discusses why

  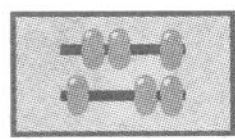   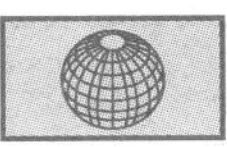   

multinational firms should invest in them, reviews some of the obstacles to investment, and discusses patterns of business behavior and market conditions in the context of developing countries.

Emerging Markets: Lessons for Business Success and the Outlook for Different Markets, 2nd ed

Nenad Pacek, Daniel Thorniley

London: Economist, 2007
245pp, ISBN: 978-1-86197-843-1

This practical discussion on business in emerging markets examines why some firms fail and some succeed, and provides an extensive review of the outlook for different emerging markets. Based on real experiences of companies, it is aimed at both managers who are involved in emerging markets for the first time and managers already operating in them.

Emerging Markets and Financial Globalization: Sovereign Bond Spreads in 1870-1913 and Today

Paolo Mauro, Nathan Sussman, Yishay Yafeh

Oxford, UK: Oxford University Press, 2008
208pp, ISBN: 978-0-19-922613-9

This is an exploration of the development of financial globalization based on an examination and comparison of the data on sovereign bonds issued by borrowing developing countries in this earlier period and in the present day. It shows the characteristics of successful borrowers in the two periods, and informs both on how the world used to operate and on the current international financial environment.

Financial Decisions in Emerging Markets

Jaime Sabal

New York: Oxford University Press, 2002
280pp, ISBN: 978-0-19-514459-8

This examines the context and characteristics of emerging market finance and the problems they present, such as the relative lack of market efficiency. It focuses on investment and financing decisions as they relate to investors in emerging markets, and proposes relevant approaches for investment analysis in these countries. It also reviews relevant financial theory, and is aimed at practitioners, development experts, and students of finance.

Financial Markets Volatility and Performance in Emerging Markets

Sebastian Edwards, Marcio G. P. Garcia (editors)

National Bureau of Economic Research Conference Report Series
Chicago, Illinois: University of Chicago Press, 2008
287pp, ISBN: 978-0-226-18495-1

This is a collection of articles that examine the increasing globalization of the financial markets in the context of capital flows and crises, domestic credit, international financial integration, and economic policy. It discusses the balance between capital mobility and capital controls for developing countries as they operate in the complex world of private investors, hedge funds, large corporations, and international institutions.

Getting Started in Emerging Markets

Christoher Poillon

New York: Wiley, 2000
206pp, ISBN: 978-0-471-39545-4

This introduction to emerging markets describes what they are, the opportunities for high returns and portfolio diversification, the risks in each, and presents a systematic process for successful investing in the markets. It lists each country, with information about their government, markets, GDP, inflation, unemployment, and index funds, and includes a review of online investing, stock data, and investment software.

Harvard Business Review on Emerging Markets

Harvard Business Review Paperback Series
Boston, Massachusetts: Harvard Business School Press, 2008
224pp, ISBN: 978-1-4221-2649-3

This is a review of the unique challenges of doing business in developing regions, which explores the different types of risk that can be faced, strategies for capturing fast-growing consumer markets in emerging economies, and ways to develop new local businesses in collaboration with social activists. It supports its guidance with real-world examples, to provide insight into potential issues and dangers.

Institutional Banking for Emerging Markets: Principles and Practice

Wei-Xin Huang

Wiley Finance Series
Hoboken, New Jersey: Wiley, 2007
274pp, ISBN: 978-0-470-03076-9

This explores how banks can prosper in the emerging countries, and discusses some of the unique functions of institutional banking in these markets, such as problem solving, the importance of communication, and the problems caused by the irregularity of the market and non-transparency of the financial and legal systems. It contains examples and case studies that show how institutional banking works in the real world.

Investing in Emerging Fixed Income Markets, 2nd ed

Frank J. Fabozzi, Efstathia Pilarinu (editors)

Frank J. Fabozzi Series
New York: Wiley, 2002
374pp, ISBN: 978-0-471-21836-4

This is an investor's guide to understanding and benefiting from opportunities in the fixed income markets of emerging economies. A team of leading experts analyze these markets as a potentially lucrative area of investment, addressing issues affecting the corporate bond market, valuation techniques, credit analysis, and risk management, and show how to develop an investment approach to enhance long-term returns.

Macroeconomics in Emerging Markets

Peter J. Montiel

Cambridge, UK: Cambridge University Press, 2003
445pp, ISBN: 978-0-521-78060-5

This textbook examines why emerging markets face a different set of challenges to developed economies, and provides an overview of the main issues, such as debt, high inflation, and lack of credibility, and the debate on policy reform. It combines a clear analytical framework with a comprehensive discussion of monetary, fiscal, and exchange rate policy concerns in emerging markets.

Risk Management in Emerging Markets: How to Survive and Prosper

Carl Olsson

London: FT Prentice Hall, 2002
311pp, ISBN: 978-0-273-65618-0

With understanding risk in emerging markets being a critical factor for successful businesses, this book defines risk management and related technical concepts, and offers guidance on the basics of identification, measurement and management of risk in the context of the emerging markets. It also argues that risk management is about controlled decision-making rather than risk avoidance, and that balancing risk and reward is increasingly important.

Six Sizzling Markets: How to Profit from Investing in Brazil, Russia, India, China, South Korea, and Mexico

Pran Tiku

Hoboken, New Jersey: Wiley, 2008
374pp, ISBN: 978-0-470-17888-1

This lays out the case for investing in the emerging economies of BRIC, South Korea, and Mexico, and analyzes each nation's investment opportunities and successful industries. The overview is based around the tenets of demographics, economic performance, technology, open trade, infrastructure development, transparency and rule of law, education and training, and sound financial systems and policies.

Understanding Emerging Markets: China and India

Peter Enderwick

London: Routledge, 2007
249pp, ISBN: 978-0-415-37085-1

Understanding Emerging Markets offers guidelines on the opportunities and the risks involved in doing business in large emerging markets, especially China and India, and how these countries are responding to the challenge of globalization. It discusses the challenges faced by Western businesses, the market volatility, the social and informational risk, and the implications for management and global restructuring caused by the enormous expansion of those countries.

Valuation of Companies in Emerging Markets

Luis E. Pereiro

New York: Wiley, 2002
507pp, ISBN: 978-0-471-22078-7

This is a comprehensive exploration of evaluating potential acquisitions in the emerging markets, presenting corporate and private investors with tools, data, and practical examples for valuing both new ventures and

  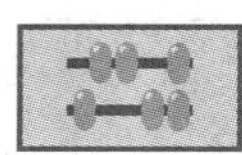      

established companies. It shows how to investigate emerging economies for opportunities to expand, define the relevant features of such a market, why traditional valuation techniques prove inadequate, and assesses the importance of unsystematic risk.

MAGAZINES

Emerging Markets

Euromoney Institutional Investor
Nestor House, Playhouse Yard, London, EC4V 5EX, UK
T: +44 (0) 20 7440 6023
F: +44 (0) 20 7440 6085
www.emergingmarkets.org

This newspaper, providing analysis of finance in developing economies, is published over the course of the annual meetings of the main multilateral development banks, and is also delivered free to delegates of these meetings. It runs breaking news stories and commentary by journalists, bankers, academics and others, offering a broad range of features and analysis.

JOURNALS

Emerging Markets Finance and Trade

M. E. Sharpe
PO Box 1943, Birmingham, Alabama 35201, USA
T: +1 205 981 4007
www.mesharpe.com/mall/results1.asp?ACR=REE
ISSN: 1540-496X

Published bimonthly, this journal focuses on the financial and economic aspects of emerging economies. It provides an outlet for research that is policy oriented and interdisciplinary, employing sound econometric methods, using macro, micro, financial, institutional, and political economy data. One or two issues each year are special issues, presenting selected papers from major research conferences worldwide.

Emerging Markets Review

Elsevier
Finance and Decision Sciences Journals,
Radarweg 29, 1043 NX Amsterdam, The Netherlands
F: +31 20 485 2370
www.elsevier.com/wps/find/journaldescription.cws_home/620356/description#description
ISSN: 1566-0141

This quarterly journal publishes high impact empirical and theoretical studies in emerging markets finance. Its coverage emphasizes comparative studies with a global and regional perspective, single country studies that address critical policy issues and have significant global and regional implications, and includes papers that examine the interactions of national and international financial architecture.

Global Financial Stability Report

The International Monetary Fund
700 19th Street NW, Washington, DC 20431, USA
T: + 1 202 623 7000
F: + 1 202 623 4661
www.imf.org/external/pubs/ft/gfsr

These twice-yearly reports by the IMF provide comprehensive coverage of both mature and emerging financial markets as part of their tracking of financial markets. They focus on market developments and issues, assessing the global financial system and markets, structural or systemic issues relevant to international financial stability, and emerging market financing in a global context.

International Journal of Emerging Markets

Emerald Group Publishing
Howard House, Wagon Lane, Bingley, BD16 1WA, UK
T: +44 (0) 1274 777 700
F: +44 (0) 1274 785 201
info.emeraldinsight.com/products/journals/journals.htm?id=IJOEM
ISSN: 1746-8809

IJoEM publishes the latest theoretical and empirical management research from the field of management and business studies in the emerging markets. It provides this research for both the academic and business world, and also covers marketing, strategy, finance and accounting, operations and decision sciences, organizational behavior and cross-cultural management, international trade, and business economics.

Journal of Emerging Market Finance

Sage Publications
B17 Greater Kailash Enclave 2, 2nd Floor,
New Delhi 110 048, India
emf.sagepub.com
ISSN: 0972-6527

This journal, with three issues each year, publishes papers on finance and economics in emerging market economies. It is aimed at the experienced practitioner, but also offers an outlet for application-oriented research, and covers models of portfolio risk management, exchange rate risks, global banking, derivative pricing, equity market structures, policy impacts on financial markets, and financial indicators.

The Journal of Emerging Markets

The Peter J. Tobin College of Business
St. John's University, 8000 Utopia Parkway, Queens, NY 11439, USA
T: +1 718 990 7305
F: +1 718 990 1868
new.stjohns.edu/academics/graduate/tobin/research/jem
ISSN: 1083-9798

This quarterly journal publishes the results of basic or applied research on the operation and structure of emerging markets, economic-financial developments in developing countries and transitional economies, and the relation between emerging and international capital markets. Articles focus on government policies, institutional frameworks and other environmental factors, and also present empirical analysis on individual countries, market sectors, or financial instruments.

INTERNET

The Emerging Markets Companion

www.emgmkts.com

This is an online financial information source on the emerging markets for the global investor. Articles from market participants and news organizations are updated throughout the day, and it provides a forum on investing in the developing economies. It offers news on asset prices, closing levels of major emerging markets, political, economic, and financial events, global research, commentary and analysis.

ORGANIZATIONS

USA

Emerging Markets Private Equity Association

Chair: Roger S. Leeds
1055 Thomas Jefferson Street NW, Suite 650,
Washington, DC 20007, USA
T: +1 202 333 8171
F: +1 202 333 3162
E: info@empea.net
www.empea.net

EMPEA is a broad-based organization that focuses on the emerging private equity markets of Africa, Asia, Central and Eastern Europe, Russia, Latin America and the Middle East. It is comprised primarily of private equity fund managers, but also includes institutional investors, service providers, and others with an interest in the asset class, and promotes greater understanding of private equity investing in emerging markets.

EMTA

360 Madison Avenue, 18th Floor, New York,
NY 10017, USA
T: +1 212 313 1100
F: +1 212 313 1016
www.emta.org

Formerly the Emerging Markets Traders Association, this trade association for the emerging markets is a not-for-profit corporation that promotes the development of fair, efficient and transparent trading markets for emerging markets instruments, and the integration of the emerging markets into the global financial marketplace. It provides a forum for market participants to identify issues of importance to the trading and investment community.

  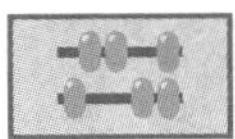      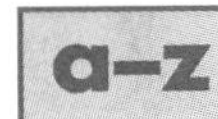

Energy and Commodity Finance

BOOKS

Carbon Finance: The Financial Implications of Climate Change

Sonia Labatt, Rodney R. White

Wiley Finance Series
Hoboken, New Jersey: Wiley, 2007
268pp, ISBN: 978-0-471-79467-7

This examination of the developing carbon finance market assesses the financial opportunities and challenges available in banking, insurance, and investment. It describes how the carbon markets operate, the expanding range of financial products, the difficulties facing companies managing their emissions, new markets in carbon currencies, risk transfer measures, and the Kyoto Protocol.

Commodities and Commodity Derivatives: Modelling and Pricing for Agriculturals, Metals and Energy

Hélyette Geman

Wiley Finance Series
Chichester, UK: Wiley, 2005
396pp, ISBN: 978-0-470-01218-5

This is a technical examination of hard and soft commodities and related derivatives for academics and market professionals looking for a solid grounding in the subject. It provides an overview of the commodity markets, and a detailed analysis of commodity price and volume risk, stochastic modeling of commodity spot prices and forward curves, real options valuation, and hedging of physical assets in the energy industry.

Commodity Fundamentals: How to Trade the Precious Metals, Energy, Grain, and Tropical Commodity Markets

Ronald C. Spurga

Wiley Trading Series
Hoboken, New Jersey: Wiley, 2006
196pp, ISBN: 978-0-471-78851-5

This is an accessible primer on commodity trading, which examines the profit potential in trading precious metals, energy, grains, and tropical commodities. It offers guidance on techniques such as spread trades, and cash and carry trades, as well as trends in the global commodities market, and aspects of diversification, risks, and rewards, as well as how to integrate commodities into an overall trading strategy.

Commodity Investing: Maximizing Returns through Fundamental Analysis

Adam Dunsby, John Eckstein, Jess Gaspar, Sarah Mulholland

Wiley Finance Series
Hoboken, New Jersey: Wiley, 2008
290pp, ISBN: 978-0-470-22310-9

This is a detailed exploration of the investment opportunities available in the expanding commodity markets. It describes the basics of a range of commodities, and the necessary tools for integrating them effectively into a portfolio, and covers the key elements of a commodity-based trading strategy, trend following, anchor variables, the shape of the futures curve, and risk control methodologies.

Commodity Modeling and Pricing: Methods for Analyzing Resource Market Behavior

Peter Schaeffer (editor)

Wiley Finance Series
Hoboken, New Jersey: Wiley, 2008
298pp, ISBN: 978-0-470-31723-5

This is a comprehensive examination of the key issues relating to commodity price behavior and pricing. Leading industry experts and academics discuss how to apply the latest methods for analyzing, modeling, and forecasting the commodity markets, and the role that resource commodity markets play in economic development, international trade, and global economic stability.

Commodity Trader's Almanac 2008

Jeffrey A. Hirsch, Scott W. Barrie

Almanac Investor Series
Hoboken, New Jersey: Wiley, 2007
192pp, ISBN: 978-0-470-10986-1

This reference work presents information and analysis on futures and commodities, and describes the markets for those trading or hedging. It is organized in a calendar format, and features monthly almanac pages based around the three major groupings of metals, petroleum, and agriculture. It also provides market-based data and information on different market tendencies, and monthly and daily reminders of market opportunities.

Emissions Trading: Principles and Practice, 2nd ed

T. H. Tietenberg

Washington, DC: RFF Press, 2006
233pp, ISBN: 978-1-933115-31-3

This classic guide to emissions trading provides a comprehensive overview of pollution reform and the first large-scale attempt to use economic incentives in environmental policy in the US. It analyzes how the use of transferable permits to control pollution became central to the US program on acid rain and the European approach to greenhouse gases, surveys environmental policy, and identifies best practices for the design of effective programs.

Energy and Power Risk Management: New Developments in Modeling, Pricing and Hedging

Alexander Eydeland, Krzysztof Wolyniec

Wiley Finance Series
Hoboken, New Jersey: Wiley, 2003
490pp, ISBN: 978-0-471-10400-1

This is an authoritative guide to managing energy price risk in the natural gas and power markets. It examines the key issues in the development of the energy industry, the challenges for energy traders and energy risk management professionals, and presents the latest developments in modeling, pricing, hedging the risks of the relevant derivative structures, as well as how to understand the data used in energy models.

Energy Budgets at Risk (EBaR): A Risk Management Approach to Energy Purchase and Efficiency Choices

Jerry Jackson

Wiley Finance Series
Hoboken, New Jersey: Wiley, 2008
300pp, ISBN: 978-0-470-19767-7

This new, non-technical examination of risk management and energy budgeting focuses on energy costs, price, and efficiency, and the key elements in developing a balanced approach to facility energy risk management. It introduces a new energy management framework that reduces energy costs and energy-efficiency investment risk, and increase cash flows, by applying risk management tools developed in the financial industry.

Energy Commodity Hedge Funds: A Practitioner's Guide

John P. Thompson, Erik Serrano Berntsen

Wiley Finance Series
Hoboken, New Jersey: Wiley, 2009
448pp, ISBN: 978-0-470-51940-0

This is a practical guide to energy commodity hedge funds, which examines the key factors in setting up and operating funds trading in these markets. It outlines the necessary due diligence process for evaluating and investing in the funds, and discusses the opportunities and risks of all energy commodity markets as hedge fund investments.

Energy Price Risk: Trading and Price Risk Management

Tom James

Basingstoke, UK: Palgrave Macmillan, 2003
538pp, ISBN: 978-1-4039-0340-2

This is a practical examination of methods for optimizing company performance through effective price risk strategies and tools in the energy markets. It discusses critical aspects of risk management and its impact on energy pricing, and presents the mitigation tools and strategies available in the market. It covers the full range of energy products, and offers useful worked examples and solutions.

Energy Risk: Valuing and Managing Energy Derivatives, 2nd ed

Dragana Pilipovic

New York: McGraw-Hill, 2007
400pp, ISBN: 978-0-07-148594-4

This quantitative approach to energy risk analyzes the guidelines and tools for using energy derivatives, and strategies for trading in the energy markets. It explores the main factors that influence energy risk, such as spot price behavior,

volatility, and the forward price curve, market behavior, seasonal effects, how to use energy-specific models, and methods for valuing energy derivatives.

The Handbook of Commodity Investing
Frank J. Fabozzi, Roland Fuss, Dieter G. Kaiser
Frank J. Fabozzi Series
Hoboken, New Jersey: Wiley, 2008
986pp, ISBN: 978-0-470-11764-4

This guide to commodity investment examines the basic techniques, products, markets, and sectors, as well as more technical aspects such as performance measurement, risk management, and asset allocation. It explains the mechanics of the commodity market, how to understand and incorporate commodities into a portfolio, and outlines key principles for effective risk management of commodity futures portfolios.

Handbook of Financing Energy Projects
Albert Thumann, Eric Woodruff
Lilburn, Georgia: Fairmont Press, 2005
432pp, ISBN: 978-0-8493-3667-6

This practical guide to project finance in the energy sector assesses the full range of current financing, such as energy service performance contracting, rate of return analysis, and energy savings measurement and verification. It examines the importance of funding, outlines key techniques for effectively structuring a financed energy project, how to present a proposal with positive cash flow, and innovative financing methods.

Hot Commodities: How Anyone Can Invest Profitably in the World's Best Market
Jim Rogers
New York: Random House, 2004
250pp, ISBN: 978-0-8129-7371-6

This is an accessible primer on commodity investing, which explains the fundamental concepts, the relationship between the stock and commodities markets, the relative risks involved, and describes a range of techniques and strategies that can be used to trade effectively. It also offers practical advice on information sources, opening an account, index funds, industry terminology, and the place of commodities in a balanced portfolio.

Intelligent Commodity Investing: New Strategies and Practical Insights for Informed Decision Making
Hilary Till, Joseph Eagleeye (editors)
London: Risk Books, 2007
350pp, ISBN: 978-1-904339-63-2

This collection of new writing by range of investors, consultants, hedge funds, index providers, risk managers, and academics describes the range of innovative investment techniques currently being utilized in the commodity markets. It explores the characteristics, benefits, and challenges of these capital assets, and discusses asset allocation, investment strategies, and risk control, to provide a practical framework and reference on active and passive natural resources investing.

Profiting from Clean Energy: A Complete Guide to Trading Green in Solar, Wind, Ethanol, Fuel Cell, Carbon Credit Industries, and More
Richard W. Asplund
Wiley Trading Series
Hoboken, New Jersey: Wiley, 2008
370pp, ISBN: 978-0-470-11799-6

This guide to the basics of clean energy investment explains the technology and industry structure behind various sectors of this field, and discusses the opportunities available in each. It presents the full range of investment techniques that are applicable, such as individual stocks, green exchange-traded funds or mutual funds, or trading the biofuel and carbon credit markets.

Risk Management in Commodity Markets: From Shipping to Agriculturals and Energy
Hélyette Geman (editor)
Wiley Finance Series
Chichester, UK: Wiley, 2009
320pp, ISBN: 978-0-470-69425-1

This edited collection provides a guide to the main risk management issues associated with commodities such as energy, weather, agriculturals, metals and shipping. It discusses the modeling of spot and forward prices, the use of options and other derivative contract forms for hedging purposes, and the freight derivatives markets and products used to manage shipping and freight risk in the commodity markets.

Timing Strategies for Commodity Futures Markets: Effective Strategy and Tactics for Short-Term and Long-Term Traders
Colin Alexander
New York: McGraw-Hill, 2007
352pp, ISBN: 978-0-07-149601-8

This is a detailed analysis of commodity futures, which focuses on timing issues, and provides advice on setting up monthly, weekly, daily, and intraday charts with indicators for effective trading. It presents a proven approach to evaluating markets, and explores how to define a trend, avoid high-risk and marginal trades, build and read charts, and implement current market indicators.

Trading Commodities and Financial Futures: A Step-by-Step Guide to Mastering the Markets, 3rd ed
George Kleinman
Boston, Massachusetts: FT Press, 2005
258pp, ISBN: 978-0-13-147654-7

This bestselling primer shows you how to trade effectively in the commodities markets. It examines the fundamentals of each market, the best technical tools available, and how to recognize key market movements and trends. It also discusses the impact of trading psychology, electronic trading, and the latest contracts, and introduces a useful methodology, with details on its implementation.

Voluntary Carbon Markets: An International Business Guide to What They Are and How They Work
Ricardo Bayon, Amanda Hawn, Katherine Hamilton
Environmental Markets Insight Series
London: Earthscan Publications, 2007
164pp, ISBN: 978-1-84407-417-4

This guide to the international voluntary carbon markets provides a source of knowledge, information, ideas, and trends about the business potential in this new sector. It explores how business and individuals can enter the market, describes what voluntary carbon markets are, where they are, how they work, and how to capitalize on the opportunities they present for economic and environmental benefit.

MAGAZINES

Energy Risk
Incisive Media
Haymarket House, 28–29 Haymarket, London, SW1Y 4RX, UK
T: +44 (0) 20 7484 9700
F: +44 (0) 20 7484 9797
www.energyrisk.com
ISSN: 1362-5403

This monthly magazine is dedicated to the financial, political, and legal risks in the global energy markets. It provides news, analysis, and education on the latest industry developments, and features updates on regulation issues, case studies, risk management workshops, market statistics and data, technology reviews, a regional focus, and special reports on issues facing market professionals.

Power Finance & Risk
Institutional Investor
225 Park Avenue South, New York, NY 10003, USA
T: +1 212 224 3300
www.iipower.com

PFR is a weekly magazine that provides coverage of corporate finance and restructuring, deals, mergers and acquisitions, and risk management trends and activity, and worldwide regulatory news in the power industry. It offers features such as a generation auction and sale calendar, a directory of ongoing generation asset sales, electric power indices, financing record, and a weekly recap of publicly reported power news stories.

World Energy
Loomis Publishing Services
3300 South Gessner, Suite 200, Houston, Texas 77063, USA
T: +1 713 626 5369
F: +1 713 627 1638
www.worldenergysource.com/wes/stores/1/World-Energy-Magazine-C27.aspx

Published eight times each year, this magazine provides a forum for the exchange of ideas and debate on the global energy markets. It presents a range of articles by leading industry executives, decision-makers, and energy officials, who discuss key issues such as manpower shortages, global warming, and the pricing of crude and natural gas.

JOURNALS

Energy Economics

Elsevier
Radarweg 29, 1043 NX Amsterdam, The Netherlands
F: +31 20 485 2370
www.elsevier.com/wps/ find/journaldescription. cws_home /30413/description#description
ISSN: 0140-9883

This bimonthly journal provides a forum for research papers relating to the economic and econometric modeling and analysis of energy systems and issues. It takes a broad approach to the subject, covering issues related to forecasting, financing, pricing, investment, taxation, development, policy, conservation, regulation, risk management, insurance, portfolio theory, fiscal regimes, accounting, and the environment.

Journal of Energy Markets

Risk Journals
Incisive Media, Haymarket House, 28–29 Haymarket, London, SW1Y 4RX, UK
T: +44 (0) 20 7004 7531
F: +44 (0) 20 7484 9758
www.journalofenergymarkets.com
ISSN: 1756-3615

This quarterly journal publishes new empirical work on the price, risk, and investment behavior of energy commodities. It focuses on the evolution and performance of electricity, gas, oil and other energy markets, both wholesale and retail, as well as new methodologies on modeling energy markets for academics and energy professionals.

Resource and Energy Economics

Elsevier
Radarweg 29, 1043 NX Amsterdam, The Netherlands
F: +31 20 485 2370
www.elsevier.com/wps/find/journaldescription. cws_home/505569/description#description
ISSN: 0928-7655

This quarterly journal offers a forum for high-level economic analysis of the utilization and development of natural resources. This encompasses questions of optimal production and consumption affecting energy, minerals, land, air and water, and includes analysis of firm and industry behavior, environmental issues, and public policies.

INTERNET

Sustainable Alternatives Network

www.sustainablealternatives.net

SANet, a United Nations initiative, offers a tailor-made advisory service with access to local experts, one-on-one consulting, and a host of online information resources, including case studies of businesses that have successfully switched to cleaner technologies. It also provides a resource library, as well as in-person, local services in selected countries.

Sustainable Energy Finance Directory

www.sef-directory.net

This is a free online database of lenders and investors who actively provide finance to the sustainable energy sector worldwide. It is designed to help project developers and entrepreneurs identify sources of potential capital in the renewable energy and energy efficiency industry, and provides searchability on finance type, technology type, and geographic focus, as well as by criteria.

ORGANIZATIONS

International

International Association for Energy Economics

Chair: Georg Erdmann
28790 Chagrin Blvd., Ste. 350, Cleveland, Ohio 44122, USA
T: +1 216 464 5365
E: iaee@iaee.org
www.iaee.org

IAEE is an independent, global, non-profit organization that provides an interdisciplinary forum for the exchange of ideas, research, development, experiences, and issues among professionals interested in the field of energy economics. It publishes two periodicals, organizes international and regional conferences, and builds networks of energy-concerned practitioners.

The International Energy Credit Association

Chair: Denis Vermette
8325 Lantern View Lane, St. John, IN 46373, USA
www.ieca.net

IECA is an international, non-profit organization of credit and financial management professionals in the energy industry. It encourages communications between credit professionals, practitioners, and industry service providers worldwide, and provides continuing education, publications, conferences, and industry-specific seminars, with the aim of increasing recognition of the global energy credit community.

Financial Economics

BOOKS

Economic and Financial Decisions Under Risk

Louis Eeckhoudt, Christian Gollier, Harris Schlesinger
Princeton, New Jersey: Princeton University Press, 2005
234pp, ISBN: 978-0-691-12215-1

Presents an accessible introduction that bridges the gap between economic and finance theory and practice, and explains the fundamentals of risk measurement and risk aversion, and how to model risk effectively. It presents a summary of basic multi-period decision-making under risk, and how to apply these concepts to insurance decisions and portfolio choice in a one-period model.

Economics for Financial Markets

Brian Kettell
Quantitative Finance Series
Oxford, UK: Butterworth-Heinemann, 2002
359pp, ISBN: 978-0-7506-5384-8

This wide-ranging treatment covers the basics of financial economics, financial market valuation, and market behavior. It provides traders, investment managers, risk managers, and finance professionals with a sound grounding in the necessary economics, especially what type of information to concentrate on. It also examines how the new economy has changed financial market behavior, the impact of the euro on currency markets, and the actions of central banks.

The Economics of Financial Markets

Roy E. Bailey
Cambridge, UK: Cambridge University Press, 2005
528pp, ISBN: 978-0-521-61280-7

This is a comprehensive textbook on the key theoretical concepts and topics in financial economics and the capital markets. It explores the underlying economic principles and theories, and describes how they relate to different financial markets. It also examines market microstructure, and the randomness of stock market prices, and discusses how the economics of uncertainty can be applied to financial decision-making.

The Economics of Financial Markets

Hendrik S. Houthakker, Peter J. Williamson
New York: Oxford University Press, 1996
361pp, ISBN: 978-0-19-504407-2

This popular financial economics textbook informs on the critical issues of increasingly complex financial markets faced by investors, traders, speculators and brokers. It shows how the concepts and tools of economics can help an understanding of the way financial markets move, and draws on data from the financial behavior of households, corporations, and governments, as well as the prices of individual securities.

The Economics of Money, Banking and Financial Markets, 8th ed

Frederic S. Mishkin
MyEconLab Series
Boston, Massachusetts: Addison Wesley, 2006
661pp, ISBN: 978-0-321-42780-9

This student textbook provides an overview and analysis of the key concepts, models, and issues in money and banking. It offers an insight into the monetary policy process, the regulation and supervision of the financial system, and the internationalization of financial markets, with an emphasis on application. It comes with an online suite of student and instructor tools built around the textbook.

The Economics of Risk and Time, 2nd ed

Christian Gollier

Cambridge, Massachusetts: MIT Press, 2004
465pp, ISBN: 978-0-262-57224-8

This treatise on the impact of risk and time on finance theory and practice presents a unified analysis of the expected utility model as applied to risk analysis, financial decision-making, macroeconomics, and environmental economics. It explores many of the key concepts of choice under uncertainty involving two different assets, and the equilibrium price of risk and time in an Arrow–Debreu portfolio.

Financial Accounting in an Economic Context, 7th ed

Jamie Pratt

Hoboken, New Jersey: Wiley, 2009
792pp, ISBN: 978-0-470-23398-6

This analyzes which accounting tools generate the best return on equity and create long-term shareholder value, including economic factors, measurement issues, and the principles of decision-making. It also describes how performance metrics, shareholder value creation, and market value are interwoven, and discusses methods used to account for operating, investing, and financing transactions, and new regulatory developments.

Financial Economics, 2nd ed

Zvi Bodie, Robert Merton, David Cleeton

Prentice Hall Series in Finance
Upper Saddle River, New Jersey: Prentice Hall, 2009
500pp, ISBN: 978-0-13-185615-8

This guide examines a broad range of themes, principles, and topics in financial economics, beyond the usual focus on corporate finance. It takes a balanced approach to the three key areas of optimization over time, asset valuation, and risk management, presents an overview of resource allocation over time under conditions of uncertainty, and also covers some personal finance topics, including saving and investing, and asset valuation.

Financial Economics

Chris Jones

New York: Routledge, 2008
320pp, ISBN: 978-0-415-37584-9

This is an introduction to classical finance models and financial economics, integrating both the institutional aspects of financial markets and general equilibrium analysis. It analyzes economic activity in the financial markets, focusing on how capital assets are priced and how these prices change over time, and how individuals use financial securities to choose their current and future consumption flows.

Foundations for Financial Economics

Chi-fu Huang

Englewood Cliffs, New Jersey: Prentice Hall, 1998
364pp, ISBN: 978-0-13-500653-5

This is an examination of individual consumption and portfolio decisions under uncertainty based on formal derivations of financial theory, and their implication for the valuation of securities, helping an understanding of modern financial economics. It features most of the relevant concepts, including risk aversion and stochastic dominance, capital asset pricing models and arbitrage pricing models, option pricing, and signaling models.

Global Financial Meltdown: How We Can Avoid the Next Economic Crisis

Colin Read

New York: Palgrave Macmillan, 2009
256pp, ISBN: 978-0-230-22218-2

This is new and accessible account of the problems inherent in the modern financial markets and the regulatory structure describes the reasons behind the subprime mortgage crisis and economic downturn. It explains many of the key topics in economics, connecting them to real world financial problems, and makes recommendations for how the financial system can operate more effectively, without regular upheavals.

Handbook of the Economics of Finance: Corporate Finance, Volume 1A

George M. Constantinides, Milton Harris, René M. Stulz (editors)

Amsterdam: Elsevier, 2003
576pp, ISBN: 978-0-444-51362-5

This handbook focuses on corporate finance (Volume 1B examines the economics of financial markets), and discusses many key features relating to how economics impacts on the theory and practice of corporate finance. With contributions by many leading industry experts, it explores the financing decisions behind how businesses obtain and allocate capital, and the way in which managers can maximize the wealth of shareholders.

Intermediate Financial Theory, 2nd ed

Jean-Pierre Danthine, John B. Donaldson

Amsterdam: Elsevier, 2005
377pp, ISBN: 978-0-12-369380-8

An introductory textbook to financial asset pricing theory, this also discusses the many variations of asset pricing models, and the basic concepts of financial economics without recourse to complex mathematics. It also emphasizes the distinction between the equilibrium and the arbitrage perspectives on valuation and pricing, with this new edition including new coverage of asset management for the long-term investor.

International Financial Economics: Corporate Decisions in Global Markets, 2nd ed

Thomas J. O'Brien

New York: Oxford University Press, 2006
302pp, ISBN: 978-0-19-517504-2

This updated and revised treatment of international financial management applies the core concepts of financial economics to explaining how international corporate finance decisions are made in the real world. It takes a financial perspective rather than an economic one, offering a comprehensive discussion of economic foreign exchange exposure, hedging, and the cost of capital and accounting for overseas investments.

International Monetary and Financial Economics, 2nd ed

Joseph P. Daniels, David D. VanHoose

Mason, Ohio: Thomson/South-Western, 2002
580pp, ISBN: 978-0-324-06362-2

This is a comprehensive overview of all the main elements of international money and finance, open-economy macroeconomics, and international banking. It integrates theory with real-world policy and business applications, and discusses the relevance of international monetary and financial economics to international affairs and business.

Introduction to the Economics of Financial Markets

James Bradfield

Oxford, UK: Oxford University Press, 2007
489pp, ISBN: 978-0-19-531063-4

This non-technical introduction to financial theory and concepts examines all the main areas of financial economics, and shows how economists analyze the way in which financial markets allocate scarce resources. It focuses on the economics of securities markets and their operation, and explains risk-return trade-offs, the market efficiency concept, futures and options, and the economic implications of debt and equity contracts.

Microeconomics of Banking, 2nd ed

Xavier Freixas, Jean-Charles Rochet

Cambridge, Massachusetts: MIT Press, 2008
363pp, ISBN: 978-0-262-06270-1

This examines the main issues relating to the microeconomic theory of banking that has emerged over recent years, and looks at the use of the asymmetric information model for explaining the role of banks in the economy and for pinpoint structural weaknesses in the banking sector. It also covers financial intermediaries, macroeconomic consequences of financial imperfections, risk management inside the banking firm, and bank regulation.

Microfoundations of Financial Economics: An Introduction to General Equilibrium Asset Pricing

Yvan Lengwiler

Princeton, New Jersey: Princeton University Press, 2006
287pp, ISBN: 978-0-691-12631-9

This textbook explores the basics of modern asset pricing theory and microeconomic principles for masters or PhD students specializing in financial economics. It analyzes issues of general economic theory and financial economics, the consequences of heterogeneity, how welfare theorem is used in asset pricing theory, term structure models, the deficiencies in the standard asset pricing models.

  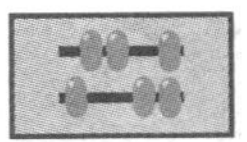   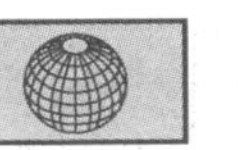   

Principles of Financial Economics

Stephen F. LeRoy, Jan Werner

Cambridge, UK: Cambridge University Press, 2001
280pp, ISBN: 978-0-521-58605-4

This introductory guide to financial economics focuses on the link between financial economics and equilibrium theory, describing the connection at each stage of its analysis. It avoids some of the more specific finance areas, such as the valuation of derivatives, to act as a primer for students of economics needing a better grasp of financial economics.

Quantitative Financial Economics: Stocks, Bonds and Foreign Exchange, 2nd ed

Keith Cuthbertson, Dirk Nitzsche

Chichester, UK: Wiley, 2004
720pp, ISBN: 978-0-470-09171-5

This successful introduction to the modeling of economic behavior in financial markets, now updated to take account of recent advances, focuses on theoretical innovation, model testing, and discrete time series analysis. It shows how to develop and implement an investment process, and contains new coverage of Monte Carlo simulation, and mean-variance and intertemporal asset allocation.

JOURNALS

Applied Financial Economics

Taylor & Francis
4 Park Square, Milton Park, Abingdon, Oxfordshire, OX14 4RN, UK
T: +44 (0) 20 7017 6000
F: +44 (0) 20 7017 6336
www.tandf.co.uk/journals/journal.asp?issn=0960-3107&subcategory=EB050000
ISSN: 0960-3107

This journal, increasing its issue rate to 24 per year in 2009, provides an international forum for applied research on financial markets, including the bond and equity markets, derivative securities markets, the foreign exchange market, corporate finance, and market microstructure.

Applied Financial Economics Letters

Taylor & Francis
4 Park Square, Milton Park, Abingdon, Oxfordshire, OX14 4RN, UK
T: +44 (0) 20 7017 6000
F: +44 (0) 20 7017 6336
www.tandf.co.uk/journals/titles/17446546.asp
ISSN: 1744-6546

This bimonthly companion journal to Applied Financial Economics publishes short accounts of new and original research in financial economics. It encourages discussion of previously published letters or papers, and offers occasional special features such as software reviews, book reviews, conference reports, and industry announcements.

International Journal of Finance & Economics

Wiley
1 Oldlands Way, Bognor Regis, West Sussex, PO22 9SA, UK
T: +44 (0) 1243 843 335
F: +44 (0) 1243 843 232
onlinelibrary.wiley.com/journal/10.1002/(ISSN)1099-1158
ISSN: 1076-9307

This quarterly journal publishes articles on issues in international finance that impact on national and global economies. It offers technical, empirical and theoretical papers, each prefaced by a non-technical summary, on a range of relevant issues such as exchange rates, balance of payments, financial institutions, risk analysis, international banking and portfolio management, and financial market regulation.

International Research Journal of Finance and Economics

EuroJournals
www.eurojournals.com/finance.htm
ISSN: 1450-2887

IRJFE is a bimonthly, international research journal that publishes articles and short research notes on issues in international finance and economics which impact on national and global economies. It also focuses on international banking and portfolio management, financial economics, international political economy, financial analysis, financial market regulation, financial risk analysis, and related areas.

International Review of Economics & Finance

Elsevier
Radarweg 29, 1043 NX Amsterdam, The Netherlands
F: +31 20 485 2370
www.elsevier.com/wps/find/journaldescription.cws_home/620165/description#description
ISSN: 1059-0560

IREF is a quarterly journal that publishes theoretical and empirical articles in all areas of international economics, macroeconomics and financial economics. It focuses on open economy macroeconomics, exchange rates and financial issues, and contains a book review section.

Journal of Economics and Finance

Springer
233 Spring Street, New York, NY 10013, USA
T: +1 212 460 1500
F: +1 212 460 1575
www.springer.com/economics/journal/12197
ISSN: 1055-0925

This journal, published three times each year, is the official journal of the Academy of Economics and Finance. It publishes theoretical and empirical research papers in economics and finance and related fields, such as decision sciences, marketing and accounting, with a primary focus on empirical studies with an emphasis on the policy relevance of the findings.

Journal of Economics and Finance Education

Academy of Economics and Finance
Department of Economics, Armstrong Atlantic State University, 11935 Abercorn Street, Savannah, Georgia 31419-1997, USA
T: +1 912 921 3781
F: +1 912 921 3782
www.jeandfe.org
ISSN: 1543-0464

This electronic journal, published twice yearly by the Academy of Economics and Finance, has a primary purpose of providing an outlet for scholarship in the areas of economics and finance education. It is a general interest publication, which encourages empirical and methodological contributions, as well as the occasional theoretical article.

Journal of Financial Economics

Simon School of Business
University of Rochester, Rochester, NY 14627, USA
T: +1 407 345 4020
F: +1 407 363 1354
www.jfe.rochester.edu
ISSN: 0304-405X

This monthly journal provides a forum for research on financial economics and the theory of the firm. It focuses on publishing analytical, empirical, and clinical papers on the capital markets, financial institutions, corporate finance, corporate governance, and the economics of organizations.

Journal of Financial Stability

Elsevier
Radarweg 29, 1043 NX Amsterdam, The Netherlands
F: +31 20 485 2370
www.elsevier.com/wps/find/journaldescription.cws_home/702019/description#description
ISSN: 1572-3089

This quarterly journal provides an international forum for applied research on theoretical and empirical macro and micro economic and financial analysis of the causes, management, resolution and preventions of financial crises. It also aims to publish papers that identify potential risks to financial stability, and develop means for preventing, mitigating or managing these risks both within and across countries.

Journal of Monetary Economics

Elsevier
Radarweg 29, 1043 NX Amsterdam, The Netherlands
F: +31 20 485 2370
www.elsevier.com/wps/find/journaldescription.cws_home/505566/description#description
ISSN: 0304-3932

JME, published eight times each year, offers research papers on issues in monetary economics and analysis, the operations and structure of financial institutions, the role of various institutional arrangements, the consequences of specific changes in banking structure, the workings of the credit markets, and aspects of the behavior of rates of return on assets.

The North American Journal of Economics and Finance

Elsevier
Radarweg 29, 1043 NX Amsterdam, The Netherlands
F: +31 20 485 2370
www.elsevier.com/wps/find/journaldescription.cws_home/620163/description
ISSN: 1062-9408

This journal, published three times each year by the International Banking, Economics and Finance Association, focuses on the economics of integration of goods, services, financial markets, at both regional and global levels, and economic policy. It also offers theoretical and empirical

 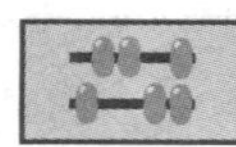      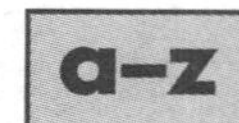

papers related to globalization, and the policy implications of governments, and domestic and international institutions.

The Quarterly Review of Economics and Finance
Elsevier
Radarweg 29, 1043 NX Amsterdam, The Netherlands
F: +31 20 485 2370
www.elsevier.com/wps/find/journaldescription.cws_home/620167/description#description
ISSN: 1062-9769

QREF is a quarterly journal that covers topics in the areas of economics, financial economics, and finance. It offers theoretical, empirical, or policy related papers, and usually one special issue is published each year, devoted to a single theme with contributions by well-known authors.

Review of Financial Economics
Elsevier
Radarweg 29, 1043 NX Amsterdam, The Netherlands
F: +31 20 485 2370
www.elsevier.com/wps/find/journaldescription.cws_home/620170/description#description
ISSN: 1058-3300

This quarterly journal takes a broad approach to finance, covering corporate finance, investments, financial institutions and international finance, and economics, covering monetary theory, fiscal policy, and international economics amongst other topics. It also publishes original research on the application of economic principles to financial decision-making, as well as the behavior of security prices, and monetary and fiscal policy.

INTERNET

Financial Economics Network
www.ssrn.com/fen/index.html

This major online research resource is part of the influential Social Science Research Network (SSRN). It features announcements and details on conferences, professional meetings, calls for papers, and professional job listings, and provides a research paper series, a conference management service, and a professional directory, which encourages direct communication within the SSRN community.

ORGANIZATIONS

Europe

European Economics and Finance Society
Chair: George M. Agiomirgianakis
Riga Ferreou 169 & Tsamadou, Patra 26222, Greece
T: +30 2610 367 440
F: +30 2610 367442
E: gmagios@eap.gr
www.eefs.eu

EEFS is an international association of professional economists working mainly in the area of international economics, specializing in trade theory and international macroeconomics, and international finance. It promotes scientific research and scholarly work, encourages communication among economists working in related fields, facilitates a wide dissemination of research output through its conferences and scientific meetings, and fosters the development of young economists.

International Economics and Finance Society, UK Chapter
Chair: Keith Pilbeam
Department of Economics, City University, Northampton Square, London, EC1V 0HB, UK
E: k.s.pilbeam@city.ac.uk
www.iefs.org.uk

This is an association of economists working in international economics, international macroeconomics, and international finance. It focuses on promoting research, encouraging communication in the industry, producing conferences and the publications, and providing relevant information for its members. It also encourages economists working as practitioners in government, business or other organizations to participate in events and discussions.

USA

Academy of Economics and Finance
Chair: William Sackley
USA
www.economics-finance.org

This is a scholarly association focused on economics and finance, with its membership being mostly financial economists and finance specialists. It is affiliated with both the Journal of Economics and Finance (JEF) and the Journal of Economics and Finance Education (JEFE).

Financial Economists Roundtable
Chair: George G. Kaufman
Loyola University, 820 North Michigan Avenue, Chicago, Illinois 60611, USA
T: +1 312 915 7075
F: +1 312 915 8508
E: gkaufma@luc.edu
www.luc.edu/orgs/finroundtable

FER is made up of a group of senior financial economists who have made significant contributions to financial research. It focuses on microeconomic issues in investments, corporate finance, and financial institutions and markets, and provides a forum for analysis of current policy issues in order to raise the level of public and private policy debate, and improve the quality of policy decisions.

BRIC

Association of Indian Economic & Financial Studies
Chair: Suhas L. Ketkar
Department of Economics, Vanderbilt University, VU Station B # 351819, 2301 Vanderbilt Place, Nashville, TN 37235-1819, USA
T: +1 615 343 2473
E: kwketkar@hotmail.com
www.vanderbilt.edu/econ/aiefs

AIEFS is an academic organization that promotes interest in the study of Indian economics and finance, and encourages inquiry into, and analysis of, the problems facing the Indian economy. It also facilitates communication and discussion among scholars, to reflect the growing importance of financial markets in India's economic development.

International

International Banking, Economic and Finance Association
Chair: James A. Brox
USA
T: +1 214 922 5050
F: +1 214 922 5364
E: niki.l.maas@dal.frb.org
www.ibefa.org

IBEFA is a non-profit, international organization dedicated to the study of banking, economic, and financial issues in countries and across the global economy and financial markets. It provides a framework for the exchange of research and ideas, promotes individual and collective research, and fosters friendly relationships and collaborations with other economic and finance professional associations throughout the world.

Financial Modeling

BOOKS

Building Financial Models: The Complete Guide to Designing, Building, and Applying Projection Models, 2nd ed
John S. Tjia
New York: McGraw-Hill, 2009
464pp, ISBN: 978-0-07-160889-3

This explains how to design, build, and implement core valuation/projection models for interpreting financial statements, determining company value, and projecting future performance. It provides a guide to using Excel and other spreadsheet programs for creating a dynamic financial model, and then customizing it for specific situations, and explains the underlying and accounting principles of each model.

Building Financial Models with Microsoft Excel: A Guide for Business Professionals
K. Scott Proctor

Wiley Finance Series
Hoboken, New Jersey: Wiley, 2004
347pp, ISBN: 978-0-471-66103-0

This provides a clear overview of understanding and constructing fully functioning financial models using Excel. It presents step-by-step instructions for their use in financial accounting reports, including the balance sheet, the income statement, and the statement of cash flows, and covers key topics such as budgeting, valuation, sensitivity analysis, contribution margin and financial ratios, and the basics of building and using a capitalization table.

Business Models: A Strategic Management Approach

Allan Afuah

New York: McGraw-Hill/Irwin, 2003
415pp, ISBN: 978-0-07-288364-0

This introduction to business models used in corporate finance examines research in strategic management to explore how to effectively implement the most relevant models. It presents an integrated framework regarding the relationship between a company's activities, revenue model, cost structure, resources, capabilities, and competition, focusing on strategic models that benefit from the link between resources, product-market positions, and profits.

Business Models

David Watson

Petersfield, UK: Harriman House, 2005
316pp, ISBN: 978-1-897597-58-3

This is an accessible guide to investment in a company or sector, detailing a large number of models that can help an investor analyze competitive advantage. It provides scoring charts and sets of criteria for both company and sector business models, as well as other key tools such as growth at a reasonable price, technical analysis, scuttlebutting, accounting for growth, and investment axioms.

Dynamic Term Structure Modeling: The Fixed Income Valuation Course

Sanjay K. Nawalkha, Gloria M. Soto, Natalia A. Beliaeva

Wiley Finance Series
Hoboken, New Jersey: Wiley, 2007
683pp, ISBN: 978-0-471-73714-8

This is a thorough reference on modern dynamic term structure modeling and valuing fixed income derivatives, focusing on the practical implementation of the relevant models, supported by solution techniques using trees, PDE methods, Fourier methods, and approximations. It provides a description of the continuous time interest rate models, and presents equilibrium and no-arbitrage models in a new framework, and an analysis of the yield curve dynamics.

The Econometric Modelling of Financial Time Series

Terence C. Mills, Raphael N. Markellos

Cambridge, UK: Cambridge University Press, 2008
456pp, ISBN: 978-0-521-71009-1

This textbook on the econometrics of financial modeling presents the latest research in economic time series, and explains how it can be applied to an analysis of the financial markets. It focuses on volatility, nonlinearity, non-linear models used to analyze financial data at high frequencies, the long memory characteristics found in financial time series, and the modeling of trends and structural breaks.

An Engine, Not a Camera: How Financial Models Shape Markets

Donald MacKenzie

Inside Technology Series
Cambridge, Massachusetts: MIT Press, 2008
377pp, ISBN: 978-0-262-63367-3

This book argues that the emergence of modern economic theories had a profound impact on how the modern financial system evolved. It discusses how new structures in financial markets and the growth of derivative products was dependent on these economic theories explaining how they worked and giving them legitimacy. It also explores finance theory in terms of recent financial crises.

A Fast Track to Structured Finance Modeling, Monitoring and Valuation: Jump Start VBA

William Preinitz

Wiley Finance Series
Hoboken, New Jersey: Wiley, 2009
744pp, ISBN: 978-0-470-39812-8

This is a practical guide to structured modeling using VBA, and which works through modeling problems of differing complexity. It focuses on using monitoring and valuation models to track deal performance, shows how to implement simple tasks into VBA code using a critical subset of the features of the language, and covers general modeling concepts, and organizing and creating VBA modules to hold model code.

Financial Modeling, 3rd ed

Simon Benninga

Cambridge, Massachusetts: MIT Press, 2008
1,132pp, ISBN: 978-0-262-02628-4

This respected guide to financial modeling and analysis provides insight and instruction for using spreadsheets to solve real-world problems in corporate finance, investments, and derivatives. It presents a step-by-step approach to finding financial data, building programs to analyze it, and improving financial decision-making. It explains each model and how it can be solved using Microsoft Excel, with examples taken from actual company data.

Financial Modeling Using Excel and VBA

Chandan Sengupta

Wiley Finance Series
Hoboken, New Jersey: Wiley, 2004
857pp, ISBN: 978-0-471-26768-3

This comprehensive textbook provides a clear approach to developing financial models in all major areas of finance. It shows how to model a wide range of finance problems using the most common programs, Excel and VBA, and presents a toolkit for any level of application. It also explains all the relevant financial theory and concepts to aid effective implementation of real-world financial models.

Financial Modelling in Practice: A Concise Guide for Intermediate and Advanced Level

Michael Rees

Wiley Finance Series
Hoboken, New Jersey: Wiley, 2008
270pp, ISBN: 978-0-470-99744-4

This is a detailed and practical examination of financial modeling, from basic Excel functions, to designing, structuring, and building effective and appropriate models. It also explores application issues, such as modeling financial statements, cash flow valuation, risk analysis, options, and real options, the use of VBA, and discusses sensitivity analysis techniques, and the application of statistical functions.

Interest Rate Models—Theory and Practice: With Smile, Inflation and Credit, 2nd ed

Damiano Brigo, Fabio Mercurio

Springer Finance Series
Berlin: Springer, 2006
981pp, ISBN: 978-3-540-22149-4

This technical guide to interest rate modeling and derivatives combines theory and practice to provide the necessary mathematical expertise for quantitative analysts, advanced traders, and students. It analyzes the effectiveness of different models, and presents updates on hybrid products, credit derivatives, the smile issue in the LIBOR market model, calibrations to real market data, and stochastic volatility models.

Interest Rate Risk Modeling: The Fixed Income Valuation Course

Sanjay K. Nawalkha, Gloria M. Soto, Natalia A. Beliaeva

Wiley Finance Series
Hoboken, New Jersey: Wiley, 2005
396pp, ISBN: 978-0-471-42724-7

This is comprehensive introduction to interest rate risk, which details the most common models used for pricing and risk analysis of various fixed income securities and their derivatives. It explains how to measure and manage interest rate risk, how the various modeling techniques are used by fixed-income professionals, and illustrates the application of these models to a range of products.

Linear Factor Models in Finance

John Knight, Stephen Satchell (editors)

Quantitative Finance Series
Oxford, UK: Butterworth-Heinemann, 2005
282pp, ISBN: 978-0-7506-6006-8

This is a detailed exploration of one of the most widely used techniques for asset pricing, a central tenet in modern investment theory. It examines its impact on the pricing of stocks, bonds, options, futures, and derivatives, and appraises asset valuation, portfolio theory and applications, dynamic asset allocation strategies, portfolio performance measurement, risk management, international perspectives, and the use of derivatives.

  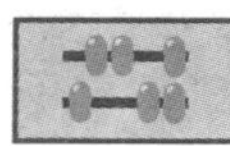      

Martingale Methods in Financial Modelling, 2nd ed

Marek Musiela, Marek Rutkowski

Stochastic Modelling and Applied Probability Series

Berlin: Springer, 2007

680pp, ISBN: 978-3-540-20966-9

This detailed analysis of martingales in pricing and hedging derivative securities takes a practical approach to financial modeling, focusing on the most common techniques available. It presents the latest term structure research, and provides a through overview of advanced modern financial mathematics, particularly fixed income models and stochastic volatility.

Mastering Financial Modelling in Microsoft Excel: A Practitioner's Guide to Applied Corporate Finance, 2nd ed

Alastair Day

Market Editions Series

Harlow, UK: FT Prentice Hall, 2007

497pp, ISBN: 978-0-273-70806-3

This is a guide for the professional use of Excel in corporate finance, an increasingly important tool for business managers, which explores the different ways that financial models can improve business decision-making. It explores how to use spreadsheets more effectively by quickly building and applying Excel models, how to add advanced features, and how to model more in-depth corporate finance techniques.

The Mathematics of Financial Modeling and Investment Management

Sergio M. Focardi, Frank J. Fabozzi

Frank J. Fabozzi Series

Hoboken, New Jersey: Wiley, 2004

778pp, ISBN: 978-0-471-46599-7

This analyzes the overlap between mathematics and finance, focusing on financial decision-making and its economic foundations, and how key mathematical techniques can be applied in the world of modern finance. It examines mathematical tools that provide an understanding of financial econometrics and financial economics, and discuss financial applications such as arbitrage pricing, interest rate modeling, derivative pricing, credit risk modeling, and risk management.

Microsoft Office Excel 2007: Data Analysis and Business Modeling, 2nd ed

Wayne L. Winston

Redmond, Washington: Microsoft Press, 2007

624pp, ISBN: 978-0-7356-2396-5

This describes the main techniques for using Excel for data analysis, modeling, and decision-making. It provides real-world examples and exercises to explain how to create scenarios for sales, estimate a product's demand curve, forecast using trend and seasonality, and determine which product mix will yield the greatest profit. It also covers topics such as asset allocation modeling, and how to optimize bidding strategies and portfolios.

Modeling for Insight: A Master Class for Business Analysts

Stephen G. Powell, Robert J. Batt

Hoboken, New Jersey: Wiley, 2008

466pp, ISBN: 978-0-470-17555-2

This is an introduction to building spreadsheet models and using them for effective business decision-making. It explains the problem-solving process—frame the problem, diagram the problem, build a model, and generate insights—and presents specific modeling tools, such as influence diagrams, spreadsheet engineering, parameterization, sensitivity analysis, strategy analysis, and iterative modeling, to achieve this, and describes the software packages used.

Modeling Risk: Applying Monte Carlo Simulation, Real Options Analysis, Forecasting, and Optimization Techniques

Johnathan Mun

Wiley Finance Series

Hoboken, New Jersey: Wiley, 2006

605pp, ISBN: 978-0-471-78900-0

This is a technical exploration of the main techniques for identifying, predicting, quantifying, valuing, hedging, diversifying, and managing risk. It describes modeling and analyzing risk within a business environment, applications for risk analysis, corporate strategy, and asset allocation, and covers model building, Monte Carlo simulation, real options analysis, forecasting, and optimization.

The Oxford Guide to Financial Modeling: Applications for Capital Markets, Corporate Finance, Risk Management and Financial Institutions

Thomas S. Y. Ho

Oxford, UK: Oxford University Press, 2004

735pp, ISBN: 978-0-19-516962-1

This comprehensive and applied guide to financial modeling shows how to incorporate models into corporate decision-making, problem solving, and enterprise risk management. It analyzes all the main models, including the present value model, the capital asset pricing model, interest rate models, and option models, and relates them to financial statements, risk management, and asset/liability management with illiquid instruments.

Practical Financial Modelling: A Guide to Current Practice

Jonathan Swan

London: CIMA Publishing, 2008

282pp, ISBN: 978-0-7506-8647-1

This handbook on financial modeling is aimed at finance and management professionals developing or using spreadsheets and financial models, particularly in areas such as financial budgeting and financial planning. It presents a simple approach to building and using financial models that reduces complexity, and which has been used for creating simple cash flow forecasts as well as modeling intensive transactions.

Structured Finance Modeling with Object-Oriented VBA

Evan Tick

Wiley Finance Series

Hoboken, New Jersey: Wiley, 2007

332pp, ISBN: 978-0-470-09859-2

This guide to modeling complex financial structures examines how to use object-oriented VBA in an Excel environment to produce flexible and effective models. It explains object-oriented programming for modeling structured products, and also covers stochastic models, optimization techniques, and object-oriented architecture. It presents models and their implementation, with examples of them in practice, as well as empirical studies of their sensitivities.

JOURNALS

Applied Stochastic Models in Business and Industry

Wiley

1 Oldlands Way, Bognor Regis, West Sussex, PO22 9SA, UK

T: +44 (0) 1243 843 335

F: +44 (0) 1243 843 232

www3.interscience.wiley.com/journal/117943444/grouphome/home.html

ISSN: 1524-1904

This bimonthly journal offers both technical and practical papers on subjects within stochastic modeling and data analysis, and their applications in business, finance, insurance, management, and production. It presents new results that solve real-life problems, and new methods for solving such problems, such as optimization, database management, knowledge acquisition, expert systems, computer-aided decision supports, and neural computing.

Economic Modelling

Elsevier

Radarweg 29, 1043 NX Amsterdam, The Netherlands

F: +31 20 485 2370

www.elsevier.com/wps/find/journaldescription.cws_home/30411/description#description

ISSN: 0264-9993

This quarterly journal publishes theoretical and applied papers on economic modeling, and complete versions of many large-scale models that have been developed for policy analysis. It also covers national macroeconomic models, growth models, optimization models, planning models, international trade models, general equilibrium modeling of national economies, modeling structural adjustments, and the sensitivity of econometric models to alternative macroeconomics policies.

Journal of Empirical Finance

Elsevier

Radarweg 29, 1043 NX Amsterdam, The Netherlands

F: +31 20 485 2180

www.elsevier.com/wps/find/journaldescription.cws_home/523106/description#description

ISSN: 0927-5398

This international journal, issued five times each year, is dedicated to empirical research in the intersection of econometrics and finance. It publishes papers on the testing of theories using financial data, the measurement of variables relevant in financial decision-making, the econometric analysis of financial market data, and the development of new econometric methodology with finance applications.

The Journal of Risk Model Validation

Incisive Media
Haymarket House, 28–29 Haymarket, London, SW1Y 4RX, UK
T: +44 (0) 20 7004 7531
F: +44 (0) 20 7484 9758
www.journalofriskmodelvalidation.com
ISSN: 1753-9579

This quarterly journal publishes technical research papers on the implementation and validation of risk models. It promotes a greater understanding of key issues, such as the empirical evaluation of existing models, pitfalls in model validation, stress testing, the development of new methods, and regulatory factors.

INTERNET

Financial Modeling Guide

www.financialmodelingguide.com

This is an online resource that provides free financial modeling tutorials, advice, tips and tricks for all levels of user. It offers simple guidelines for structuring and laying out spreadsheets for a financial model, and for managing their development and auditing results.

Financial Modelling.net

www.financialmodelling.net

This useful online resource, run by a financial modeler, has the aim of improving standards in business decision-making and financial modeling, and includes guidance on best practice, resources, links, and industry discussion.

Modelling Excel

www.westnet.net.au/balson/ModellingExcel

This is a resource on Excel modeling that provides a range of advice and practical tools and tips on its application. It includes guidance on how to modify default settings to improve the look of worksheets, tables and charts, and reduce complexity using structural templates and automation techniques.

VB Users

vbusers.com

This site provides free source code in C#, Visual Basic and VBA, as well as numerous applications and ActiveX objects. It also provides a number of resources for submitting source code and problem resolution, and features downloads, source code, report bugs, discussion groups, services, commercial software, and industry links.

Forecasting and Scenario Planning

BOOKS

Building Financial Models: A Guide to Creating and Interpreting Financial Statements

John S. Tjia

Maidenhead, UK: McGraw-Hill, 2004
340pp, ISBN: 978-0-07-140210-1

This book provides step-by-step instructions for the design and development of financial projection models according to Generally Accepted Accounting Principles (GAAP) using Microsoft Excel software. In-depth explanations of the principles of accounting, including income statements, balance sheets, and cash-flow statements, and the concepts of model building are given. The book also describes the use of spreadsheet functions and tools and offers guidelines for making useful business forecasts.

Business Forecasting, 9th ed

John E. Hanke, Dean Wichern

Upper Saddle River, New Jersey: Pearson Education, 2008
576pp, ISBN: 978-0-13-230120-6

This book is written in a simple, straightforward style, presenting basic statistical techniques using practical business examples to teach how to predict long-term forecasts. It can also be used to teach undergraduate and postgraduate students.

The Change Game: How Today's Global Trends are Shaping Tomorrow's Companies

Peter Lawrence

London: Kogan Page, 2004
288pp, ISBN: 978-0-7494-4269-9

Based on interviews with managers from around the world, this book is an account of change in business in the West. The text provides insights into the major global trends and issues that are influencing organizations today, and what they mean for the future. The new management consensus is examined, including the gains it has made and some of the blind spots to which it has given rise. The text also addresses the ideas of competitive advantage and the unique business proposition.

Creating Futures: Scenario Planning as a Strategic Management Tool, 2nd ed

Michel Godet

London: Economica, 2006
349pp, ISBN: 978-2-7178-5244-8

This offers a collection of effective methodologies for strategic planning. It shows that with the right tools and attitude, people can learn how to create a new future. It presents these planning methods with examples and illustrative and informative case studies.

How to Forecast: A Guide for Business

James Morrell

Aldershot, UK: Gower Publishing, 2002
224pp, ISBN: 978-0-566-08492-8

Drawing on his experience as a forecaster, the author considers the key areas that affect businesses. These are divided into those that lie beyond the control of an organization and those that are under its control. The former include the national economy, government policy, the global market, population and social trends, and technological change. The latter include long-term strategy and investment, costs and prices, and profits and share prices. Each section of this book provides a set of practical conclusions and a listing of key sources of information. The book closes with a set of simple rules and guidelines for successful forecasting.

HR Forecasting and Planning

Paul Turner

Developing Practice Series
London: Chartered Institute of Personnel and Development, 2002
288pp, ISBN: 978-0-85292-933-9

The role of the human resource department in strategy formulation is widely recognized. This book offers practical step-by-step guidelines to help HR executives add value to the strategy-setting process. The author uses a three-part model: part one looks at issues surrounding forecasting, strategy, and planning, and the role of HR in these; part two presents the strategic human resources forecast; and part three outlines the human resource plan.

Learning from the Future: Competitive Foresight Scenarios

Liam Fahey, Robert Randall

New York: Wiley, 1997
288pp, ISBN: 978-0-471-30352-7

Aimed at managers, consultants, and leaders, this book comprises a selection of articles that explain how to construct and model the outcomes of a variety of strategic decisions. Four key areas are addressed: the basics of scenario learning; approaches to constructing scenarios; scenario application in diverse contexts; and managing scenario learning in the organizational context.

The Living Company: Habits for Survival in a Turbulent Business Environment

Arie de Geus

Boston, Massachusetts: Harvard Business School Press, 2002
240pp, ISBN: 978-1-57851-820-3

This book, by one of the gurus of scenario planning, focuses on his belief that businesses are like living organisms and must be managed as such if they are to survive over time and become what he calls "living companies."

The Oxford Handbook of Organizational Decision Making

Gerard P. Hodgkinson, William H. Starbuck (editors)

Oxford: Oxford University Press, 2008
720pp, ISBN: 978-0-19-929046-8

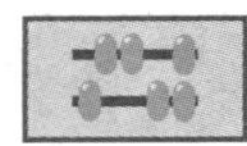

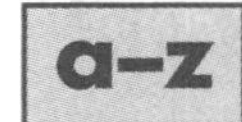

The Oxford Handbook of Decision-Making surveys theory and research on organizational decision-making. It emphasizes psychological perspectives, while encompassing the insights of economics, political science, and sociology. It provides coverage at the individual, group, organizational, and inter-organizational levels of analysis, while case studies illustrate the practical implications of the work surveyed.

Quantitative Analysis for Management, 10th ed

Barry Render, Ralph M. Stair, Michael E. Hanna

Upper Saddle River, New Jersey: Prentice Hall, 2008
768pp, ISBN: 978-0-13-603625-8

This textbook for students combines coverage of traditional management science techniques with modern technology solutions. It includes a CD-ROM.

Scenario Planning, 2nd ed

Gill Ringland

Chichester, UK: Wiley, 2006
490pp, ISBN: 978-0-470-01881-1

Updated for this new edition, this book focuses on how scenarios can be used effectively to manage the future. It is aimed at practicing managers. The book includes extensive case studies, checklists, and practical advice.

Scenarios: The Art of Strategic Conversation, 2nd ed

Kees van der Heijden

Chichester, UK: Wiley, 2004
380pp, ISBN: 978-0-470-02368-6

Aimed at strategic managers, this book explores the relationship between the strategy process and scenario planning in order to facilitate effective decisions. Drawing on his own experiences while working for Shell, and on the experiences of the company as a whole, the author explores the principles, practices, implementation, and applications of scenario planning.

The Sixth Sense: Accelerating Organizational Learning with Scenarios

Kees van der Heijden et al.

Chichester, UK: Wiley, 2002
320pp, ISBN: 978-0-470-84491-5

The key issue of this book revolves around addressing the flaws at individual, organizational, and community levels that inhibit organizational change. The text highlights a link between organizational learning and scenario planning in order to overcome these flaws. It suggests that by motivating learners to develop a deeper perspective on the long-term business environment, and scenario planners to see their work in the context of organizational survival and development, creative limitations can be overcome and a favorable environment for multiple futures developed. This book explains why scenario thinking is important, why it is valuable as a catalyst for innovative and creative thinking, how it enhances strategic dialog, how it helps organizational learning and development, and how it can be assimilated within the strategic organizational learning framework.

Trajectory Management: Leading a Business Over Time

Paul Strebel

Chichester, UK: Wiley, 2003
222pp, ISBN: 978-0-470-86290-2

Paul Strebel believes that the search for universal best practice has given rise to the impression that there is "one true way" to business success. To work effectively, however, best practice must be adapted to the particular conditions facing the organization at the time. The author aims to help business leaders succeed over time by identifying and adapting internal business drivers to exploit changing conditions. This is the art of trajectory management, which will enable organizations to succeed in differing conditions. He considers drivers such as: governance roles, leadership styles, organization modes, and business models. He also explains the process of shaping, sustaining, and switching trajectory drivers.

20–20 Foresight: Crafting Strategy in an Uncertain World

Hugh Courtney

Boston, Massachusetts: Harvard Business School Press, 2001
207pp, ISBN: 978-1-57851-266-9

This book sets out to help managers understand the concept of "residual uncertainty" in today's business environment—that is, the difference between what can be known and what can't be known—so that they can develop 20/20 foresight and create competitive advantage. A five-piece management toolkit of scenario planning, game theory, decision analysis, system dynamics models, and management flight simulators can be used to plot strategy against uncertainty.

MAGAZINES

Business Credit

National Association of Credit Management
8840 Columbia 100 Parkway, Columbia, MA 21045–2158, USA
T: +1 410 740 5560
www.nacm.org/business-credit-magazine.html
ISSN: 0897-0181

Business Credit Magazine is published ten times a year and targets readers who are responsible for extending business and trade credit and risk management for their companies. The magazine has up-to-date trends and important legislative, bankruptcy, business ethics, trade finance, asset protection, benchmarking, and scoring issues.

Journal of Business Forecasting

Institute of Risk Management
Lloyd's Avenue House, 6 Lloyd's Avenue, London, EC3N 3AX, UK
T: +44 (0) 20 7709 9808
F: +44 (0) 20 7709 0716
www.ibf.org/index.cfm?fuseaction=showObjects&objectTypeID=20
ISSN: 0278-6087

This is a quarterly journal aimed at business executives and managers which provides practical forecasting ideas plus guidance on recognizing and using effective forecasting models for key business decisions. The *Journal* also includes forecasts on the international economic outlook and corporate earnings.

JOURNALS

European Journal of Operational Research

Elsevier
11830 Westline Industrial Drive, St Louis, MO 63146, USA
T: +1 314 453 7076
F: +1 314 523 5153
www.elsevier.com/locate/ejor
ISSN: 0377-2217

The *European Journal of Operational Research* (*EJOR*) publishes papers that discuss the methodology of operational research and decision making. EJOR presents the following types of papers: invited reviews, innovative applications, theory and methodology papers, and short communications.

International Journal of Applied Forecasting

International Institute of Forecasters
140 Birchwood Drive, Colchester, VT 05446, USA
T: +1 781 234 4077
F: +1 509 357 5530
forecasters.org/ijf
ISSN: 0169-2070

This organization is dedicated to the research and development of forecasting techniques, with the aim of bridging the gap between forecasting theory and practice and contributing to the professional development of forecasters. The site includes information on events and conferences, its journal, time series data, and links to other forecasting sites.

International Journal of Forecasting

Elsevier
Regional Sales Office, Customer Support Department, PO Box 211, 1000 AE Amsterdam, The Netherlands
T: +31 20 485 3757
F: +31 20 485 3432
www.elsevier.com/locate/ijforecast
ISSN: 0169-2070

This is the official journal of the International Institute of Forecasters, whose aims and scope it shares: to unify the field of forecasting; to bridge the gap between theory and practice; and to make forecasting useful and relevant for decision and policy makers. It publishes high-quality refereed papers on all aspects of forecasting.

Journal of Forecasting

Wiley
The Atrium, Southern Gate, Chichester, West Sussex, PO19 8SQ, UK
T: +44 (0) 1243 779777
F: +44 (0) 1243 775878
www.interscience.wiley.com/jpages/0277-6693
ISSN: 0277-6693

This international journal, published eight times each year, presents papers on theoretical, practical, and computational approaches to forecasting across a range of

sectors including business, technology, and government. Individual issues include research reports, review articles, and book and software reviews.

INTERNET

Applied Forecasting

www.appliedforecasting.com

Applied Forecasting is an independent website that contributes to the forecasting community. The focus is to serve researchers, practitioners and students worldwide with updated information and facilitating online interaction.

Forecasting: Methods and Applications

www.robhyndman.info/forecasting

This site is based on the book of the same name and offers hundreds of forecasting data sets plus links to forecasting resources and software on the internet.

Global Business Network

www.gbn.org

This is the premier site for those interested in scenario planning, including amongst its founders and members some of those who were involved in Royal Dutch/Shell's groundbreaking work in this area.

International Institute of Forecasters

www.forecasters.org

The organization is dedicated to the research and development of forecasting techniques, with the aim of bridging the gap between forecasting theory and practice and contributing to the professional development of forecasters. Its site includes information on events and conferences, information on its journal, *Foresight*, time series data, and links to other forecasting sites.

Principles of Forecasting

www.forecastingprinciples.com

This site summarizes useful knowledge about forecasting for researchers, practitioners, and educators. It features guidelines, prescriptions, rules, conditions, action statements, and advice about what to do in given situations.

Scenario Planning Resources

www.well.com/~mb/scenario_planning

This website contains references and articles about scenario planning. Some are good for orientation, while others are more technical, show how to develop method, and explore new areas of application.

World Future Society

www.wfs.org

This nonprofit educational and scientific organization provides information about the technological and social forces that shape the future and are fundamental to scenario planning and forecasting.

ORGANIZATIONS

Europe

Lancaster University Centre for Forecasting

c/o The Management School, Lancaster University, Lancaster, Lancashire, LA1 4YX, UK
T: +44 (0) 1524 593 879
F: +44 (0) 1524 844 885
E: r.fildes@lancaster.ac.uk
www.lums.lancs.ac.uk/research/forecast.htm

This center is part of the Management School at Lancaster University. It aims to promote the development of new approaches to forecasting and business models, supports the integration of forecasting theory and practice, and offers research and consultancy services to industry, commerce, and government. Its services corporate research, courses for practitioners, and consultancy services. The site also offers advice for special interest groups.

University of Bath Research Center

c/o School of Management, University of Bath, BA2 7AY, UK
T: +44 (0) 1225 383 594
F: +44 (0) 1225 826 473
E: p.goodwin@bath.ac.uk
www.bath.ac.uk/management/research/office/centres.html

This center is part of the Science School at Bath University. It aims to research the integration of judgment and models in forecasting and decision-making. Its aim is to design forecasting software that will provide support to managers in their use of judgment, so that these problems are reduced and greater forecast accuracy can be achieved.

USA

Institute of Business Forecasting

PO Box 670159, Flushing, New York, NY 11367–0159, USA
T: +1 516 504 7576
E: info@ibf.org
www.ibf.org

The aims of this member-based organization are to disseminate knowledge about business forecasting and planning, and to provide products and services to help business executives in their planning and forecasting efforts.

International

International Institute of Forecasters

140 Birchwood Drive, Colchester, VT 05446, USA
T: +1 781 234 4077
F: +1 509 357 5530
E: forecasters@forecasters.org
www.forecasters.org

The organization is dedicated to the research and development of forecasting techniques, with the aim of bridging the gap between forecasting theory and practice, and contributing to the professional development of forecasters. Its site includes information on events and conferences, information on its journal, time series data, and links to other forecasting sites.

Hedge Funds, Fund Management, and Alternative Investments

BOOKS

Absolute Returns: The Risk and Opportunities of Hedge Fund Investing

Alexander Ineichen
Wiley Finance Series
New York: Wiley, 2002
514pp, ISBN: 978-0-471-25120-0

A practical analysis of hedge fund investing, that takes a practical look at the strategies and techniques that hedge fund managers use to achieve superior investment performance, especially absolute return strategies. It also discusses methods for integrating hedge fund investment into traditional portfolios to increase returns and balance risk exposure.

Fundamentals of Fund Administration: A Guide

David Loader
Elsevier Finance Series
Boston, Massachusetts: Elsevier, 2007
224pp, ISBN: 978-0-7506-6798-2

This is a guide to the role of the fund administrator, the underlying market infrastructures, operations functions related to funds, and related issues. It provides comprehensive analysis of each stage from trade to settlement, helping those responsible for managing and supervising fund administration services understand the decisions, actions and problems involved for completion and regulatory compliance.

The Fundamentals of Hedge Fund Management: How to Successfully Launch and Operate a Hedge Fund

Daniel A. Strachman
Wiley Finance Series
Hoboken, New Jersey: Wiley, 2007
177pp, ISBN: 978-0-471-74852-6

Teaches how to build and maintain a successful hedge fund business, presented

  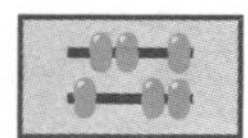      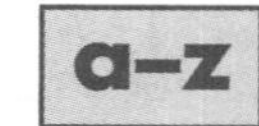

in an accessible way. It covers all the essentials, from choosing a lawyer, and the documentation needed, to an awareness of what markets attract investors. Based on real-life cases of leading funds, it provides a practical insight into what makes a hedge fund work.

Handbook of Hedge Funds

Francois-Serge l'Habitant
Wiley Finance Series
Chichester, UK: Wiley, 2006
637pp, ISBN: 978-0-470-02663-2

A comprehensive reference on hedge funds for all those involved in the industry. It offers practical guidance on their operational, legal, and regulatory characteristics, as well as historical information, analysis of investment strategies, hedge fund indices and databases, advice on portfolio construction, and coverage of structured products and funds of hedge funds.

The Hedge Fund Handbook: A Definitive Guide for Analyzing and Evaluating Alternative Investments

Stefano Lavinio
New York: McGraw-Hill, 2000
192pp, ISBN: 978-0-07-135030-3

A guide to hedge funds, which examines the techniques and strategies used by a successful fund managers, and gives insights into how best to identify and select which funds to invest in. It gives a clear overview of the dynamics of hedge fund behavior, and the financial innovations available in alternative investments, while also discussing the risk management side of their operation.

Hedge Fund of Funds Investing: An Investor's Guide

Joseph G. Nicholas
Princeton, New Jersey: Bloomberg Press, 2004
259pp, ISBN: 978-1-57660-124-2

A concise guide, which details how to create, combine, and manage investments with multiple hedge funds as a fund of funds. It shows how to evaluate risks, estimate potential returns, and choose statistical measurement methods, as they can help to balance risks and can be incorporated into a portfolio to attain investment objectives and build diversification.

Hedge Funds: An Analytic Perspective

Andrew W. Lo
Advances in Financial Engineering Series
Princeton, New Jersey: Princeton University Press, 2008
337pp, ISBN: 978-0-691-13294-5

A new examination of the hedge fund industry by a leading financial economist, Hedge Funds discusses the need for a systematic framework for managing hedge fund investments. It outlines the basic properties of hedge fund returns, trading strategies, risk characteristics, and potential for illiquidity, and presents new tools for analyzing their dynamics.

Hedge Funds and Prime Brokers

Mark Berman (editor)
London: Risk Books, 2006
206pp, ISBN: 978-1-904339-90-8

A collection of articles that examine the changing relationship between the funds and prime brokers. It discusses some of the key areas between them, such as the level of regulation, trading, legal, regulatory and jurisdictional issues, the role of hedge fund service providers, and how prime brokers affect the development of hedge funds and their trading strategies.

Hedge Hunters: Hedge Fund Masters on the Rewards, the Risk, and the Reckoning

Katherine Burton
New York: Bloomberg Press, 2007
206pp, ISBN: 978-1-57660-245-4

Based on interviews with a number of rising stars in the hedge fund industry, these profiles focus on the personal and business qualities needed to build a successful asset management business, and provide revealing details into the challenges they face, and how they trade successfully.

Hedgehogging

Barton Biggs
Hoboken, New Jersey: Wiley, 2006
308pp, ISBN: 978-0-470-06773-4

Written by a legendary figure in the hedge fund industry, it provides an illuminating view of hedge fund investing, of some of the personalities involved, and what goes on behind the scenes in these funds. Biggs presents an insiders view of hedge funds, and explains how he has earned successful returns out of such a complex and risky approach.

Inside the House of Money: Top Hedge Fund Traders on Profiting in the Global Markets

Steven Drobny
Hoboken, New Jersey: Wiley, 2006
370pp, ISBN: 978-0-471-79447-9

Providing insight into the often hidden world of hedge funds, this book presents a collection of detailed interviews with a number of leading money managers. They tell of their personal trading strategies, their experiences during recent financial crises, and also examines the trend towards increased competition and specialization, and the impact this is having on their approach to investment.

An Introduction to Fund Management, 3rd ed

Ray Russell
Securities Institute Series
Chichester, UK: Wiley, 2006
178pp, ISBN: 978-0-470-01770-8

This is a primer on fund management that provides a comprehensive overview, and details the different types of fund, how they are established, their processes, performance measurement, fund administration, and their investment strategies. This updated edition provides a practical description of investment funds and fund management from a number of perspectives, and contains new material on regulatory changes and industry developments.

Investment Strategies of Hedge Funds

Filippo Stefanini
Wiley Finance Series
Hoboken, New Jersey: Wiley, 2006
315pp, ISBN: 978-0-470-02627-4

Opens up the hidden world of hedge funds to offer guidance on the opportunities for investment they provide. It details how hedge funds operate, and the tools that investors need to access these types of funds, and discusses each hedge fund strategy, with trading examples by successful hedge fund managers, to show how to create high investment returns.

MAGAZINES

Absolute Return

HedgeFund Intelligence
Nestor House, Playhouse Yard, London, EC4V 5EX, UK
T: +44 (0) 20 7779 7330
F: +44 (0) 20 7779 7331
www.hedgefundintelligence.com/ar
ISSN: 1740-4282

This is a monthly magazine that covers current events in the hedge fund industry, with an emphasis on US hedge funds. It features new fund launches, analysis of regulatory developments, interviews, industry surveys, performance data, league tables of the best performing funds, and weekly email news updates. It is available to qualified investors and industry professionals only.

Alpha

Institutional Investor
225 Park Ave South, New York, NY 10003, USA
T: +1 212 224 3300
www.iimagazine.com/alpha
ISSN: 1930-8434

Alpha is a monthly magazine that provides a link between the hedge fund industry, its users, and those who provide advisory, financial and technological services to the sector. It covers all areas of hedge fund business, including investment fund strategies, hedge fund operations, rankings, reports on tax and regulatory measures, and new fund launches.

Hedge Fund Alert

Harrison Scott Publications
5 Marine View Plaza, #400, Hoboken, NJ 07030-5795, USA
T: +1 201 659 1700
F: +1 201 659 4141
www.hfalert.com
ISSN: 1530-7832

This is a weekly newsletter that provides news and analysis for the alternative investment community. Its coverage includes fund marketing strategies, competition among prime brokers and other service providers, fund launches, new products, regulatory and legal issues, personnel moves, shifts in investor allocations, as well as developments that can affect the hedge fund industry.

The Hedge Fund Journal

31 Davies Street, London, W1K 4LP, UK
T: +44 (0) 20 7409 0888
F: +44 (0) 20 7409 0905

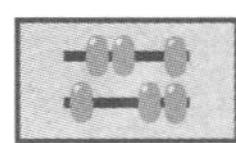

www.thehedgefundjournal.com
ISSN: 1756-3453

This journal is published 10 times a year, and is a major source of information on the hedge fund industry. It combines detailed profiles and interviews with news summaries, commentary, research, expert opinion and analysis, special reports, and appointments.

Hedge Funds Review

Incisive Media
Haymarket House, 28–29 Haymarket, London, SW1Y 4RX, UK
T: +44 (0) 20 7484 9700
F: +44 (0) 20 7484 9932
www.hedgefundsreview.com
ISSN: 1471-8855

This is a monthly magazine for the hedge fund industry, which aims to provide hedge fund managers, investors, and service providers with news and analysis on the trends and developments affecting their business and investment decisions. It offers news and comment, strategy analysis, interviews, trading tips, hedge fund investment mandates, fund closure lists, performance data, and special reports.

The Nordic Hedge Fund Journal

Nordic Hedge Fund Index
Kigkurren 8G, 4. tv - DK-2300 Copenhagen S, Denmark
T: +45 8 830 0000
F: +45 3 313 3730
www.hedgenordic.com/?pageid=63

This is a monthly newsletter that acts as a concise source of information on the Nordic hedge fund industry, and providing updates on the developments, performance, and challenges within the industry. It features industry interviews with asset managers, pension funds and other institutional investors.

Total Alternatives

Institutional Investor
225 Park Ave South, New York, NY 10003, USA
T: +1 212 224 3300
www.totalalternatives.com
ISSN: 1544-7596

This is an online news source for hedge funds, private equity, and other alternative investments. It contains stories on new strategies, fund launches, and reorganizations at major firms. It features the latest market news, daily email summaries, a resource of hedge fund news items in other media, and a data zone on hedge funds that includes information on strategy, rate of returns, annualized volume, and assets.

JOURNALS

Journal of Alternative Investments

Institutional Investor
225 Park Avenue South, New York, NY 10003, USA
T: +1 212 224 3570
www.iijournals.com/JAI
ISSN: 1520-3255

This quarterly journal provides research and expert analysis on managing investments in hedge funds, private equity, distressed debt, commodities, futures, energy, funds of funds, and other non-traditional instruments. It examines the growth of hedge funds and alternatives, how to measure and track portfolio performance, and includes coverage of asset allocation, risk management, indexing, regulation and taxation.

Journal of Derivatives & Hedge Funds

Palgrave Macmillan
The Macmillan Building, 4 Crinan Street, London, N1 9XW, UK
T: +44 (0) 20 7843 4684
www.palgrave-journals.com/jdhf
ISSN: 1753-9641

This is a quarterly journal that examines the derivatives market and hedge funds. Formerly known as Derivatives Use, Trading & Regulation, it has evolved its coverage to take into account the enormous growth in hedge funds. It focuses on trading, legal and other derivative issues, and the many challenges facing the hedge fund industry, such as transparency, liquidity risk, and risk management control.

INTERNET

Albourne Village

www.village.albourne.com

This is an online knowledge economy for the Alternative Investment community, designed as an environment for evolving hedge-fund news, intellectual property, content and debates on current issues. It revolves around the elements of village life—village pub, library, hedge fund mall, job centre, and data farm. There is also a conference center and Village school, and a range of shops run by financial institutions, software companies, and publishers.

The Hedge Fund Service Provider Guide

www.iihedgefundguide.com

The Hedge Fund Service Provider Guide is an internet directory of companies serving the hedge fund industry, including accounting firms, administrators, compliance vendors, consultants and advisers, CRM, executive search, information providers, legal services, prime brokerage, risk management vendors, technology providers, and trading services. It is composed of over 550 entries, helping firms and individuals looking for service providers within their market sectors.

Hedge Funds and Compliance for Hedge Funds

www.hedge-fund-manager.net

This is a portal for information on hedge funds, which contains details on funds, managers and management, strategies, software, books, forums, compliance, certification, jobs.

HedgeWeek

www.hedgeweek.com

An online resource that provides information and reports on hedge fund news, and features jobs, events, comments and opinions, interviews, forum, and an industry directory.

HedgeWorld

www.hedgeworld.com

This is an information source for news, research, analysis, investigative reports, interviews, and profiles, aimed at individual and institutional investors and their professional advisers, fund managers and service providers in the global hedge fund industry.

HFN

www.hedgefund.net

This is resource for hedge fund news and performance data industry news, monitor existing hedge fund investments, and review fund information in anticipation of making allocations to the asset class. It is available only to accredited investors, who can access a database of information on more than 8,000 hedge funds, funds-of-funds and commodity products.

ORGANIZATIONS

USA

The Hedge Fund & Private Equity Resource Center

1225 Franklin Avenue, Suite 325, Garden City, NY 11530, USA
T: +1 516 992 3417
E: info@hfpe.net
www.hfpe.net

This is a private, non-partisan institution dedicated to independent research and education on issues of government, politics, regulatory oversight and supervision involving private investment firms. It assists in the formulation of innovative policy solutions, and its research activities involve representative members of the private investment industry, professionals, and academics.

International Association of Hedge Funds Professionals

Chair: George Lekatis
George Lekatis, Compliance LLC, 1200 G Street NW, Suite 800, Washington, DC 20005, USA
T: +1 302 342 8828
E: lekatis@hedge-funds-association.com
www.hedge-funds-association.com

This is an industry association for hedge funds manager, administrators, analysts, and others working with hedge funds. It aims to explain to the outside world what hedge funds professionals do and how their consultants operate, discuss the regulation and control of hedge funds, and also provide information on services for education and training.

100 Women in Hedge Funds

331 W 57th Suite 239, New York, NY 10019, USA
www.100womeninhedgefunds.org

This is an international association of more than 10,000 professional women

in the hedge fund industry. It provides educational programming, professional leverage initiatives, and philanthropy. There is also a version of the association based in London, with its own Board of Directors and Executive Committee.

International

Alternative Investment Management Association

Chair: Florence Lombard
2nd Floor, 167 Fleet Street, London, EC4A 2EA, UK
T: +44 (0) 20 7822 8380
www.aima.org

This international, not-for-profit, trade association represents nearly 1,300 corporate members worldwide, including hedge fund managers, fund of hedge funds managers, prime brokers, legal and accounting services, and fund administrators. The association influences policy development, industry initiatives, and is involved in regulation. It also focuses on developing industry skills and education standards, and is a co-founder of the Chartered Alternative Investment Analyst designation (CAIA).

The Chartered Alternative Investment Analyst Association

Chair: Peter Douglas
29 South Pleasant Street, Amherst, MA 01002, USA
T: +1 413 253 7373
F: +1 413 253 4494
E: info@caia.org
www.caia.org

The CAIA is an independent, not-for-profit, global organization that is committed to education and professionalism in the field of alternative investments. It provides information on alternative investments, promotes professional development through education, advocates high standards of professional conduct, and is the sponsoring body for the CAIA designation, the educational standard for the alternative investment industry.

The Hedge Fund Association

Chair: David Friedland
2875 NE 191st Street, Suite 900, Aventura, Florida 33180, USA
T: +1 202 478 2000
F: +1 202 478 1999
E: info@thehfa.org
www.thehfa.org

This is a not-for-profit international association for hedge fund professionals, which provides a forum for industry leaders, innovators, practitioners, and investors. It represents the industry through the education of investors, the media, regulators and legislators, lobbies at government level, and sets industry standards for fund administrators and other service providers who collect, collate, and analyze information related to hedge funds.

Intellectual Property

BOOKS

The Change Function: Why Some Technologies Take Off and Others Crash and Burn

Pip Coburn
London: A&C Black Publishers, 2007
240pp, ISBN: 978-0-7136-8207-6

This draws on the author's experiences to explain why some technologies are successful while others fail. It argues that consumers are only ready to change when the "pain" of their current position outweighs the potential pain of trying something new. It will be of interest to investors in new technology, and those involved in new product development.

Copyright: Interpreting the Law for Libraries, Archives and Information Services, 5th ed

Graham Cornish
London: Library Association Publishing, 2009
224pp, ISBN: 978-1-85604-664-0

Cornish's book explains the provisions of the Copyright, Designs, and Patent Act 1988 and supporting legislation, in an accessible Q&A format. New sections cover licensing schemes and developments in electronic copyright issues, including the legal deposit of electronic materials.

Copyright in a Week, 2nd ed

Graham Cornish
London: Profile Books, 2002
96pp, ISBN: 978-0-340-84944-6

This introductory text will help you understand what copyright is, why it is important to respect it, and how to make use of copyright law in business, management, and everyday life.

Essentials of Licensing Intellectual Property

Alexander I. Poltorak, Paul J. Lerner
Chichester, UK: Wiley, 2004
240pp, ISBN: 978-0-471-43233-3

Poltorak and Lerner have compiled a concise and useful primer for professionals who need answers fast and novices who would like to learn more about this subject. The book goes from the basics of the intellectual property field to copyright laws, as well as exploring current strategies and technologies.

From Ideas to Assets: Investing Wisely in Intellectual Property

Bruce M. Berman (editor)
Chichester, UK: Wiley, 2001
672pp, ISBN: 978-0-471-40068-4

Based on the experience of expert contributors, this argues that corporations need to understand what their intellectual property assets are and how to protect their rights to them. It covers such topics as maximizing returns on intellectual property assets, valuing those assets, and discerning performance variables.

Patent It Yourself, 14th ed

David Pressman
Berkeley, California: Nolo Press, 2009
596pp, ISBN: 978-1-4133-1058-0

As an experienced patent attorney and former patent examiner of the US Patent and Trademark Office, David Pressman has developed a very useful guide containing all the instructions and forms necessary to patent an invention in the United States. The book offers comprehensive and up-to-date advice for obtaining a high-quality patent and presents the information in a user-friendly, jargon-free, and well-illustrated way.

Patents, Copyrights and Trademarks for Dummies

Henri J. A. Charmasson
Chichester, UK: Wiley, 2008
384pp, ISBN: 978-0-470-33945-9

Patents, Copyrights and Trademarks For Dummies explains, in layman's terms, the basic nature, function, and application of intellectual property (IP) rights, including how you can acquire those rights, wield them effectively against your competitors, or exploit them lucratively through licensing agreements and other rewarding adventures.

Protecting Your #1 Asset: Creating Fortunes from Your Ideas: An Intellectual Property Handbook

Michael A. Lechter
Rich Dad's Advisors Series
Boston, Massachusetts: Back Bay Books, 2003
320pp, ISBN: 978-0-446-67831-5

Placing its emphasis on protecting intellectual property (IP), this book makes the case for understanding developments in this sector. It covers topics such as identifying and benefiting from IP assets, using IP assets to build barriers to competition, licensing IP assets, and using IP assets to raise capital.

The Strategic Management of Intellectual Capital and Organizational Knowledge: A Collection of Readings

Nick Bontis, Chun Wei Choo (editors)
Oxford: Oxford University Press, 2002
748pp, ISBN: 978-0-19-513866-5

This collection of articles addresses central themes in the strategic management of intellectual capital. It is designed to assist organizations in understanding the strategic and operational roles of intellectual property, and in developing organizational infrastructures and cultures that foster the creation, development, sharing, and mentoring of intellectual capital.

Valuation of Intellectual Property and Intangible Assets, 3rd ed

Gordon V. Smith, Russell L. Parr
Intellectual Property Series

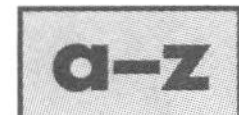

Chichester, UK: Wiley, 2000
638pp, ISBN: 978-0-471-36281-4

This book argues that intellectual property and intangible assets represent the core of most corporations' value, and offers advice on how to identify, define, and exploit these assets. It also includes a discussion of setting royalty rates based on rates of return, and recent developments in the field.

Value Driven Intellectual Capital: How to Convert Intangible Corporate Assets into Market Value

Patrick H. Sullivan

Intellectual Property Series
Chichester, UK: Wiley, 2000
240pp, ISBN: 978-0-471-35104-7

This book explores the expanding world of intellectual assets, where translating an innovative idea into bottom-line profits involves a tightly focused strategy. It offers suggestions for turning corporate knowledge, know-how, and intellectual property into a sustainable competitive weapon that will build reputation and market share.

MAGAZINES

Copyright World

Informa Law
30–32 Mortimer Street, London, W1W 7RE, UK
T: +44 (0) 20 7017 4046
F: +44 (0) 20 7453 2221
www.ipworld.com/ipwo/public/publications/article-list.htm?publication_id=copyrightworld
ISSN: 0950-2505

This publication contains international news and updates on copyright and intellectual property matters, covering both legal and practical issues.

Managing Intellectual Property

Euromoney Legal Media Group
Nestor House, Playhouse Yard, London, EC4V 5EX, UK
T: +44 (0) 20 7779 8610
F: +44 (0) 20 7779 8602
www.managingip.com
ISSN: 0960-5002

Published 10 times each year, this international magazine for intellectual property owners, especially senior in-house counsel in multinational companies. It provides news, comment, data, and analysis of the industry, and offers regular surveys and supplements on patents, trademarks, and copyright.

JOURNALS

Journal of Intellectual Property Law & Practice

Oxford Journals
Great Clarendon Street, Oxford, OX2 6DP, UK
T: +44 (0) 1865 353 907
F: +44 (0) 1865 353 485
jiplp.oxfordjournals.org
ISSN: 1747-1532

JIPLP is a peer-reviewed journal dedicated to intellectual property law and practice. Published monthly, coverage includes the full range of substantive IP topics, practice-related matters such as litigation, enforcement, drafting and transactions, plus relevant aspects of related subjects such as competition and world trade law.

Journal of World Intellectual Property

Blackwell Publishing
9600 Garsington Road, Oxford, OX4 2DQ, UK
T: +44 (0) 1865 791 100
F: +44 (0) 1865 791 347
www.wiley.com/bw/journal.asp?ref=1422-2213
ISSN: 1747-1796

This bimonthly journal is dedicated to intellectual property in relation to trade and investment, with particular focus on the WTO and TRIPS (the Agreement on Trade-Related Aspects of Intellectual Property Rights).

INTERNET

Copyright and Fair Use: Stanford University Libraries

fairuse.stanford.edu

The site provides a quick search facility and overview of copyright law, with links to internet resources, current legislation, cases, judicial opinions, regulations, treaties, and conventions.

Copyright Clearance Center

www.copyright.com

Copyright Clearance Center, Inc., the largest licenser of text reproduction rights in the world, was formed to facilitate compliance with US copyright law. It provides licensing systems for the reproduction and distribution of copyrighted materials in print and electronic formats throughout the world.

The Copyright Licensing Agency

www.cla.co.uk

The agency is the UK's reproduction rights organization—the UK equivalent of the US Copyright Clearance Center.

Franklin Pierce Law Center

www.fplc.edu

Sponsored by a law school, the site offers an extensive list of articles relating to intellectual property.

International Intellectual Property Alliance

www.iipa.com

Sponsored by a private-sector coalition formed to protect US copyrighted material around the world, this site offers articles on a variety of intellectual property topics and country-specific copyright information.

Intellectual Property Office

www.ipo.gov.uk

The website of the UK government department responsible for intellectual property—copyright, patents, designs, and trademarks—has a section of links to government, academic, and general intellectual property sites.

United States Copyright Office

www.copyright.gov

The US Copyright Office is located in the Library of Congress. The site has a section for FAQs and another for requests relating to the Freedom of Information Act, as well as material on copyright legislation, and an international section with links to the World Intellectual Property Organization.

United States Patent and Trademark Office

www.uspto.gov

The PTO promotes industrial and technological progress in the US, and strengthens the national economy by administering the laws relating to patents and trademarks, and advising the US government on patent, trademark, and copyright protection, and on trade related aspects of intellectual property.

World Intellectual Property Organization (WIPO)

www.wipo.org

WIPO is a specialized agency of the United Nations whose mandate is to promote the protection of intellectual property worldwide. With 182 countries among its member states, WIPO administers 23 treaties in the field of intellectual property. The first general group of treaties defines internationally agreed basic standards of intellectual property in each of the member states.

ORGANIZATIONS

Europe

European Patent Office

Av. de Cortenbergh 60, Brussels 1000, Belgium
T: + 49 89 2399 4636
www.epo.org

The European Patent Office (EPO) provides a uniform application procedure for individual inventors and companies seeking patent protection in up to 38 European countries. It is the executive arm of the European Patent Organisation and is supervised by the Administrative Council.

Intellectual Property Institute UK

36 Great Russell Street, London, WC1B 3QB, UK
T: +44 (0) 20 7436 3040
F: +44 (0) 20 7323 5312
E: pleonard@ip-institute.org.uk
www.ip-institute.org.uk

The purpose of the institute, a non-profit membership organization, is to increase the contribution of intellectual property to economic well-being, by timely, relevant, and authoritative research, and by informing policy makers and public debate.

Intellectual Property Office (IPO)

Concept House, Cardiff Road, Newport, South Wales, NP10 8QQ, UK
T: +44 (0) 1633 814 000
F: +44 (0) 1633 817 777
E: enquiries@ipo.gov.uk
www.ipo.gov.uk/

This is the official government body responsible for granting intellectual property (IP) rights in the United Kingdom. These rights

include patents, designs, trademarks, and copyright.

USA

American Intellectual Property Law Association (AIPLA)

241 18th Street South, Suite 700, Arlington, VI 22202, USA
T: +1 703 415 0780
F: +1 703 415 0786
E: aipla@aipla.org
www.aipla.org

Founded in 1897 and having more than 16,000 members, AIPLA comprises national bar association lawyers practising in the fields of patents, trademarks, and copyrights. It also promotes the improvement of US intellectual property systems.

Intellectual Property Owners Association (IPO)

1501 M Street NW, Suite 1150, Suite 200, Washington, DC 20005, USA
T: +1 202 507 4500
F: +1 202 507 4501
E: info@ipo.org
www.ipo.org

This group comprises over 400 major corporations and lawyers that deal with intellectual property issues and concerns. The IPO works to support and strengthen the patent, trademark, copyright, and trade secret laws of the United States, and also monitors legislative activities.

United States Patent and Trademark Office (USPTO)

PO Box 1450, Alexandria, VI 22313–1450, USA
E: usptoinfo@uspto.gov
www.uspto.gov

The PTO promotes industrial and technological progress in the United States, and works to strengthen the national economy by administering the laws relating to patents and trademarks, and advising the US government on patent, trademark, and copyright protection, and on trade-related aspects of intellectual property.

BRIC

Federal Reserve for Intellectual Property, Patents and Trademarks (ROSPATENT)

30–1 Berezhkovskaya nab., Moscow G-59, GSP-5 123995, Russia
F: +7 499 240 6179
E: rospatent@rupto.ru
www.fips.ru/ruptoen

Federal Reserve for Intellectual Property, Patents and Trademarks (ROSPATENT) in Russia is a federal executive authority performing functions of control and supervision in the area of the legal protection and exploitation of intellectual property rights, including patents and trademarks.

Institute Nacional da Propriedade Industrial (INPI)

Rua Mayrink Veiga, nº 9, Centro, Rio de Janeiro, Brazil
T: +55 21 2139 3000
www.inpi.gov.br

The Brazilian National Patent Office is responsible for the registration of brands, patents, trademarks, software programs, geographical indications, industrial design, and for transferring technology.

Intellectual Property Office India

The Patent Office, Boudhik Sampada Bhawan, Near Antop Hill Post Office, S.M.Road, Antop Hill, Mumbai 400 037, India
T: +91 22 2413 7701
F: +91 22 2413 0387
E: mumbai-patent@nic.in
www.patentoffice.nic.in

The Intellectual Property Office India registers patents, trademarks, designs and geographical indications across the country.

State Intellectual Property Office of China (SIPO)

6 Xitucheng Road, Haidian District, Bejing, 100088, China
www.sipo.gov.cn/sipo_English

SIPO organizes and coordinates intellectual property rights protection work across China, works to improve the protection system and standardize patent administration, laws, and regulations, draws up the policies of foreign-related IP work, organizes development programs for the patent work nationwide, and lays down the criteria of affirming the exclusive rights of patents, and publicizes patent laws, regulations and policies.

International

The International Intellectual Property Institute (IIPI)

4401-A Connecticut Ave NW, Box 235, Washington, DC 20008, USA
T: +1 202 544 6610
F: +1 202 478 1955
www.iipi.org

The International Intellectual Property Institute (IIPI) is a non-profit 501(c)(3) corporation located in Washington, DC. As an international development organization and think tank, IIPI is dedicated to increasing awareness and understanding of the use of intellectual property as a tool for economic growth, particularly in developing countries.

World Intellectual Property Organization (WIPO)

34, chemin des Colombettes, Geneva, Switzerland
T: +41 22 338 91 11
F: +41 22 733 54 28
www.wipo.org

WIPO is a specialized agency of the United Nations whose mandate is to promote the protection of intellectual property worldwide. Counting 182 countries among its member states, WIPO administers 23 treaties in the field of intellectual property. The first general group of treaties defines internationally agreed basic standards of intellectual property in each of the member states.

International Finance

BOOKS

Country Risk Assessment: A Guide to Global Investment Strategy

Michel Henry Bouchet, Ephraim Clarke, Bertrand Groslambert
Wiley Finance Series
Hoboken, New Jersey: Wiley, 2003
271pp, ISBN: 978-0-470-84500-4

This is a comprehensive analysis of the various economic, financial, geopolitical, sociological, and historical factors that contribute to country risk. It examines the various sources of country risk, and details information sources and country risk service providers, strategies for international risk assessment and management, and the opportunities that have arisen from the integration of international finance markets.

Finance of International Trade

Eric Bishop
Essential Capital Markets Series
Amsterdam: Elsevier, 2004
207pp, ISBN: 978-0-7506-5908-6

This introduction to international trade finance provides a guide to each phase of a typical transaction, and examines the relationships between the various parties involved, and the facilities employed. It also explores the type of banking instruments and techniques available, when to apply a particular form of finance, the risks involved, and how they can be managed.

Fixing Global Finance

Martin Wolf
Forum on Constructive Capitalism Series
Baltimore, Maryland: Johns Hopkins University Press, 2008
230pp, ISBN: 978-0-8018-9048-2

This is a timely analysis of the structural problems impacting the global financial system. It explains the imbalances of the world economy and how they cause regular financial crises, how the current recession began, and how further disruptions to international finance can be avoided. It also explores international economics and exchange rates, and reviews various theories about market downturns.

Global Banking, 2nd ed

Roy C. Smith, Ingo Walter

Oxford, UK: Oxford University Press, 2003
438pp, ISBN: 978-0-19-513436-0

This is a practical overview of recent developments in international banking and how the financial markets operate, as well as outlining competitive strategies for the future. It focuses on international commercial banking, including issues of cross-border risk evaluation and exposure management, and regulatory oversight within the context of global competition. It also tackles international investment banking and its overlap with commercial side of the industry.

Global Corporate Finance: Text and Cases, 6th ed

Suk Kim, Seung Kim

Malden, Massachusetts: Blackwell Publishing, 2006
569pp, ISBN: 978-1-4051-1990-0

This comprehensive textbook on international finance provides a guide to global financial problems and techniques. It analyzes corporate finance and governance, international markets, global financial dynamics and strategies, and risk management techniques, with each chapter starting with a real-world case study illuminating the theories and research presented.

Global Governance of Financial Systems: The International Regulation of Systemic Risk

Kern Alexander, Rahul Dhumale, John Eatwell

Oxford, UK: Oxford University Press, 2006
320pp, ISBN: 978-0-19-516698-9

This is an examination of regulation and the system of committees, organizations, rules, and guidelines that now oversee the international financial system. It argues that the current framework fails to take account of the macroeconomic consequences that follow from the failure of financial institutions, and analyzes the role of the International Monetary Fund, the Basel committees on banking, and the Asian financial crises in financial governance.

The Global Securities Market: A History

Ranald Michie

Oxford, UK: Oxford University Press, 2006
399pp, ISBN: 978-0-19-928062-9

This is an authoritative account of the global securities market from its earliest developments to the present day. It presents a full history of the securities markets, of stocks and bonds, established and emerging markets, stock exchanges, over-the-counter trading, and its bubbles and crashes, from its beginnings in Medieval Venice, to Amsterdam and London, up to the current global market system.

Globalization and Finance

Tony Porter

Cambridge, UK: Polity, 2005
230pp, ISBN: 978-0-7456-3119-6

This comprehensive overview of the interrelationship between economic globalization and the international financial system guides the reader through the debate on the impact of a global marketplace on how we live. It discusses the structure of public-sector and non-governmental institutions and practices that influence financial globalization and offers some solutions for its regulation. It also focuses on the role of banking, securities markets, and foreign direct investment.

The Handbook of International Trade and Finance: The Complete Guide to Risk Management, International Payments and Currency Management, Bonds and Guarantees, Credit Insurance and Trade Finance

Anders Grath

London: Kogan Page, 2008
198pp, ISBN: 978-0-7494-5320-6

This practical guide to international trade and finance provides a useful discussion of the main factors involved, such as risk management, international payments, currency management, bonds and guarantees, and trade finance. It explains how to reduce risks and improve cashflow, identify the most competitive finance alternatives, structure the best payment terms, and minimize finance and transaction costs.

International Business Finance

Michael Connolly

New York: Routledge, 2007
212pp, ISBN: 978-0-415-70153-2

This textbook for foundation courses provides a useful introduction to the main building blocks of international business finance, focusing on the foreign exchange market, reviewing spot, forwards, futures and options. It also discusses the corporate aspects of international trade, presents a study of the instruments used by currency traders and hedgers, and explores the role of managers in international corporations.

International Finance: Transactions, Policy and Regulation, 15th ed

Hal S. Scott

University Casebook Series
New York: Foundation Press, 2008
1,115pp, ISBN: 978-1-59941-547-5

This introductory casebook to international finance, policy, and regulation focuses on the international aspects of major domestic markets, the infrastructure for financial markets, instruments and offshore markets, emerging markets, and the impact of terrorism. It discusses basic financial concepts and transactions, the expansion of US capital market regulation, and the implementation of international accounting standards.

International Finance, 3rd ed

Keith Pilbeam

Basingstoke, UK: Palgrave Macmillan, 2006
497pp, ISBN: 978-1-4039-4837-3

This popular textbook provides an introduction to international finance, particularly the theories and differing policies on the balance of payments, exchange rates and the international monetary system. Various strands of research are explained in an understandable way, and related to current financial practice, aided by extensive figures, tables and graphs to illustrate the analysis.

International Financial Management

Geert Bekaert, Robert J. Hodrick

Prentice Hall Series in Finance
Upper Saddle River, New Jersey: Prentice Hall, 2009
810pp, ISBN: 978-0-13-116360-7

This new textbook covering the main aspects and trends of international financial management presents the necessary analytical tools for financial decision-making in the current competitive global environment. It examines the markets, their institutional aspects, and sources of risks that have an impact on them, and how they can be managed.

International Financial Management, 9th ed

Jeff Madura

Mason, Ohio: Thomson/South-Western, 2008
673pp, ISBN: 978-0-324-59347-1

This abridged edition of the popular textbook balances theory with practical applications to examine the latest trends in international finance. It shows how to develop the management skills needed to succeed in the competitive financial marketplace, focusing on management decisions that maximize a firm's value, backed up by practical examples from a variety of multinational corporate projects.

International Investments, 5th ed

Bruno Solnik, Dennis McLeavey

Boston, Massachusetts: Addison Wesley, 2003
760pp, ISBN: 978-0-321-22389-0

This accessible exploration of the international capital markets provides a comprehensive analysis of all the main international investment concepts and theories. It is aimed at advanced undergraduates and MBA students, but also has relevance for professionals working in the investment sector, and has been selected by the AIMR as recommended reading for the Chartered Financial Analysts exam.

International Money and Finance, 3rd ed

C. Paul Hallwood, Ronald MacDonald

Malden, Massachusetts: Blackwell Publishing, 2000
568pp, ISBN: 978-0-631-20462-6

This comprehensive and analytic textbook covers a broad range of topics relating to the international financial system. It investigates theory, evidence, policy, and institutions from a monetary, neoclassical, and neo-Keynesian perspective, to provide a resource for those studying international economy and finance. This updated edition also explores European monetary union, transition economies, and developing countries.

International Trade Finance, 8th ed

Paul Cowdell, Derek Hyde (editors)

London: Global Professional Publishing, 2003
390pp, ISBN: 978-0-85297-721-7

Now in its eighth edition, this standard text on international trade finance provides a guide for all students and practitioners wanting an introduction to the main concepts and trends, including foreign exchange, and support services, such as documentary credits, for exporters, importers and merchants.

Multinational Business Finance, 11th ed

David K. Eiteman, Arthur I. Stonehill, Michael H. Moffett

Addison-Wesley Series in Finance
Boston, Massachusetts: Addison Wesley, 2007
746pp, ISBN: 978-0-321-35796-0

This regularly updated treatment of how multinational businesses function provides a comprehensive examination of international finance, explaining how to recognize and capitalize on the unique characteristics of global markets. It offers case studies throughout to apply concepts to the real-life problems that managers of multinational firms face, and presents new analysis of multinational business finance in the emerging markets.

Multinational Financial Management, 8th ed

Alan C. Shapiro

New York: Wiley, 2006
745pp, ISBN: 978-0-471-73769-8

This respected textbook provides a conceptual framework for analyzing key financial decisions in multinational firms, and the opportunities available to them in the global marketplace. It shows how they can avoid the threats and risks of international trade, as well as examining the increase of diversification, the ability to arbitrage between imperfect capital markets, and the impact of Chinese economic expansion on the global economy.

MAGAZINES

Global Finance

Global Finance
411 Fifth Avenue, New York, NY 10016, USA
T: +1 212 447 7900
F: +1 212 447 7750
www.gfmag.com
ISSN: 0896-4181

This monthly magazine offers market intelligence, news, and analysis on the latest trends and developments in international finance. It covers corporate finance, M&A, country profiles, capital markets, e-business initiatives, investor relations, currencies, banking, risk management, custody, direct investment, and money management, and reports on how companies fund their operations, and financial groups use money and finance.

Global Money Management

Institutional Investor
FL 7, 225 Park Ave S, New York, NY 10003, USA
T: +1 212 224 3300
www.globalmoneymanagement.com
ISSN: 1529-6679

This monthly newsletter provides information, news, and analysis of new products and offerings, M&A activity, and major regulatory developments in the international institutional investment sector. It also features investment manager and consultant search-and-hire activity, plan sponsor interviews, country reports, league tables, and consultant profiles, and reports on investment strategies, performance measurement, and the developing markets.

JOURNALS

Global Finance Journal

Elsevier
Radarweg 29, 1043 NX Amsterdam, The Netherlands
F: +31 20 485 2370
www.elsevier.com/wps/find/journaldescription.cws_home/620162/description#description
ISSN: 1044-0283

This journal, issued three times each year, provides a forum for the exchange of ideas, applied research, and industry techniques among academicians and practitioners in global financial management. It publishes scholarly papers that integrate theory and practice in areas such as financial management, investment, banking and financial services, accounting, and taxation.

International Finance

Wiley
PO Box 808, 1–7 Oldlands Way, Bognor Regis, PO21 9FF, UK
T: +44 (0) 1865 778315
www.wiley.com/bw/journal.asp?ref=1367-0271&site=1
ISSN: 1367-0271

This journal, published three times each year, presents scholarly, theoretical and policy research on problems in macroeconomics and finance. It offers broad coverage of key policy areas, such as exchange rates, political economy, monetary policy, financial markets, corporate finance, transition economics, and the analysis of complex market issues.

Journal of International Banking Law & Regulation

Sweet & Maxwell
100 Avenue Road, London, NW3 3PF, UK
T: +44 (0) 20 7393 7000
www.sweetandmaxwell.co.uk/Catalogue/ProductDetails.aspx?recordid=508&productid=7242
ISSN: 0267-937X

This monthly international journal on banking law and securities provides detailed, practical analysis of international legal and regulatory issues from around the world. It presents papers on topical issues and future trends, and analytical pieces that combine practical information with academic opinion, as well as expert reviews of the latest publications.

Journal of International Financial Management & Accounting

Wiley
350 Main Street, Malden, MA 02148, USA
T: +44 (0) 1865 778315
www.wiley.com/bw/journal.asp?ref=0954-1314
ISSN: 0954-1314

JIFMA, published three times each year, presents original research on international aspects of financial management and reporting, banking and financial services, auditing and taxation. It provides a forum for academics and professionals on new developments and emerging trends in the industry, including the impact of institutional, regulatory, and accounting differences across countries.

Journal of International Financial Markets Institutions and Money

Elsevier
Radarweg 29, 1043 NX Amsterdam, The Netherlands
F: +31 20 485 2370
www.elsevier.com/wps/find/journaldescription.cws_home/600113/description#description
ISSN: 1042-4431

This journal, issued five times each year, produces informed analysis of international trade, financing and investments, and the related cash and credit transactions. It also covers relevant areas such as the international financial markets, international securities markets, foreign exchange markets, international commercial and investment banking, central bank intervention, and balance of payments.

Journal of International Money and Finance

Elsevier
Radarweg 29, 1043 NX Amsterdam, The Netherlands
F: +31 20 485 2370
www.elsevier.com/wps/find/journaldescription.cws_home/30443/description#description
ISSN: 0261-5606

This journal, published eight times each year, offers theoretical and empirical research in international economics and finance for researchers and financial market professionals. It focuses on international monetary economics, international finance, and the overlap between the two, as well as research on exchange rate behavior, foreign exchange options, international capital markets, international monetary and fiscal policy, and international transmission.

Investment

BOOKS

The Accidental Investment Banker: Inside the Decade that Transformed Wall Street

Jonathan A. Knee

New York: Random House, 2007
260pp, ISBN: 978-0-8129-7804-9

This insider's account of investment banking takes a humorous look at the extraordinary growth of high finance during the 1990s. It describes the importance of doing deals, generating revenue, and getting noticed, and provides pen portraits of some of the characters involved. It also depicts how far professional standards have fallen, and the fundamental changes that occurred in the industry during that boom-and-bust decade.

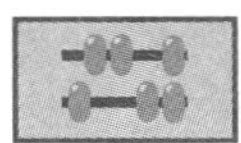

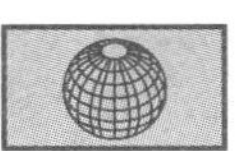

The Business of Investment Banking: A Comprehensive Overview, 2nd ed

K. Thomas Liaw

Hoboken, New Jersey: Wiley, 2006
440pp, ISBN: 978-0-471-73964-7

This guide to investment banking describes how investment banks are dealing with the challenges of new competition, changes in regulation, the impact of globalization, and innovations in information technology. It compares financial holding companies, full-service investment banks, and boutique investment banks, and examines strategies for risk management, career opportunities, key operations, trading fundamentals, and ethics and professionalism.

Common Stocks and Uncommon Profits and Other Writings

Philip A. Fisher

Wiley Investment Classics Series
New York: Wiley, 2003
320pp, ISBN: 978-0-471-44550-0

This classic on investment techniques by a pioneer of modern investment theory introduced Fisher's investment philosophies and theories, and discussed a stock's worth in terms of potential growth for the first time. It laid the foundation for current investment practices, describing the benefits of long-term growth stocks and their emerging value, as opposed to short-term trades for quick profit.

The Financial Times Guide to Investing

Glen Arnold

London: FT Prentice Hall, 2004
410pp, ISBN: 978-0-273-66309-6

This authoritative examination of investing shows how to build a successful personal financial portfolio, and invest in the capital markets in an effective way. It explains the key information, data, facts, and comments available to the investor, describes how financial assets and markets operate, and how to invest effectively in shares, bonds, funds and derivatives, using the same tools and techniques as the professional investor.

The Four Pillars of Investing: Lessons for Building a Winning Portfolio

William J. Bernstein

New York: McGraw-Hill, 2002
316pp, ISBN: 978-0-07-138529-9

This investment guide presents the necessary concepts, tools, and processes for constructing a successful portfolio, combining market history, investing theory, and behavioral finance for achieving long-term investing success. It describes historical and market data, risk and reward in the capital markets, how to mix different asset classes in a portfolio, and the dangers of picking individual stocks.

Fundology: The Secrets of Successful Fund Investing

John Chatfeild-Roberts

Petersfield, UK: Harriman House, 2006
166pp, ISBN: 978-1-897597-77-4

This explains the essentials of fund investing, while avoiding the common mistakes that can lead to poor results. Focusing on unit trusts and open-ended investment companies, it explains how to buy and sell investment funds in a clear style, why funds are a good investment, how unit trusts and OEICs work, how to pick the best managers, and how to become an expert fund investor.

Global Perspectives on Investment Management: Learning from the Leaders

Rodney N. Sullivan (editor)

Charlottesville, Virginia: CFA Institute, 2007
352pp, ISBN: 978-1-932495-64-5

This presents a range of practical new ideas and fundamental areas of concern in investment management from some of the leading experts in the industry. It re-evaluates some key assumptions about investments, markets, and decision-making, and covers such topics as risk management and uncertainty, seeking value in equities, the corporate debt market, and the role of commodities in portfolios.

How to Create and Manage a Mutual Fund or Exchange-Traded Fund: A Professional's Guide

Melinda Gerber

Wiley Finance Series
Hoboken, New Jersey: Wiley, 2008
351pp, ISBN: 978-0-470-12055-2

This guide to mutual funds and exchange-traded funds presents a complete business plan for their launch and management, describing each stage, from initial idea to selling shares. It discusses the importance of profiling customers and identifying the competition, picking the team, producing a diverse marketing plan, and assesses new products, regulations, scandals, the inclusion of timelines, and common mistakes to avoid.

The Intelligent Investor: The Classic Text on Value Investing

Benjamin Graham

New York: HarperBusiness, 2005
269pp, ISBN: 978-0-06-075261-3

This bestselling book, first published in 1949, is written by the revered investment expert and father of value investing. It explains his methodology for shielding investors from error, buying stocks at less than their intrinsic value, and developing long-term investment strategies. This paperback edition contains a commentary that relates Graham's ideas to current market practices, as well as reinforcing some of his teachings and principles.

Investment Banking and Investment Opportunities in China: A Comprehensive Guide for Finance Professionals

K. Thomas Liaw

Hoboken, New Jersey: Wiley, 2007
560pp, ISBN: 978-0-470-04468-1

This comprehensive resource examines the Chinese investment banking industry, and the investment opportunities available in the financial services sector. It focuses on what information investors and bankers need to operate in business and the financial markets in China, and examines features of investment banking such as privatization and market reforms, growth and value investing, and financial instruments for foreign investors.

Investment Planning for Finance Professionals

Geoffrey A. Hirt, Stanley B. Block, Somnath Basu

New York: McGraw-Hill, 2006
369pp, ISBN: 978-0-07-143721-9

This comprehensive reference for financial planners and investment professionals presents a range of tools, and techniques for maximizing returns on their clients' investments and reduce levels of risk tolerance. It describes ways of diversifying and balancing a portfolio of investments, the types and uses of investment vehicles, types and measures of investment risk, measures of investment returns, portfolio management and measurement concepts, and tax issues.

Investments, 8th ed

Zvi Bodie, Alex Kane, Alan J. Marcus

Boston, Massachusetts: McGraw-Hill/Irwin, 2009
1,056pp, ISBN: 978-0-07-338237-1

This is a leading textbook for graduate/MBA students of investment markets. It combines theoretical and practical coverage of the topic, and presents a unifying theme of security markets as nearly efficient, that most securities are usually priced appropriately given their risk and return attributes. It focuses on asset allocation, offering a broader treatment of futures, options, and other derivative security markets.

An Investor's Guide to Analysing Companies and Valuing Shares: How to Make the Right Investment Decision

Michael Cahill

London: FT Prentice Hall, 2003
278pp, ISBN: 978-0-273-66363-8

This analytical guide to share buying examines the decision making process, based on a common sense investing approach, and the belief that a company's share price is determined by its fundamental value. It describes what to look for in assessing the real value of a business and its share price, emphasizing the importance of research, and how to understand the stock market's assessment of the company.

The Little Book of Common Sense Investing: The Only Way to Guarantee Your Fair Share of Stock Market Returns

John C. Bogle

Hoboken, New Jersey: Wiley, 2007
216pp, ISBN: 978-0-470-10210-7

This investment guide provides practical advice and strategies for investing in the long term, arguing that putting money into low-cost index funds is the best way to ensure greater stock market returns, and avoid investment costs, taxes, and inflation. Bogle eschews investing trends,

  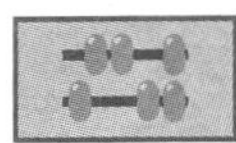   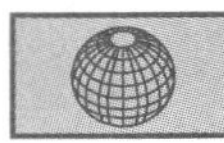   

describing how with index funds you actually own the entire market, creating a useful diversification of stocks.

Monkey Business: Swinging Through the Wall Street Jungle

John Rolfe, Peter Troob

New York: Warner Books, 2000

273pp, ISBN: 978-0-446-67695-3

Based on the authors' experiences as junior associates at a major investment bank, this exposé of life on Wall Street provides an entertaining snapshot of their daily routine, pitch book development, fee generation, and company valuation. It describes their extravagant lifestyles, as well as the mundane reality of their work, and why they could not last in that environment.

Mutual Fund Industry Handbook: A Comprehensive Guide for Investment Professionals

Lee Gremillion

Hoboken, New Jersey: Wiley, 2005

381pp, ISBN: 978-0-471-73624-0

This reference to mutual funds provides an overview of their history and structure, investment management, portfolio operations, accounting, auditing, compliance, distribution, globalization, e-commerce, and the trends affecting the industry. It also examines their benefits in offering professional management, easy diversification, liquidity, convenience, and regulatory protection, and includes real-life examples of how specific functions are performed at various firms.

One Up on Wall Street: How to Use What You Already Know to Make Money in the Market, 2nd ed

Peter Lynch

New York: Simon & Schuster, 2000

304pp, ISBN: 978-0-7432-0040-0

This classic guide to investing offers advice and effective rules for trading as a professional, explaining how investment opportunities can be discovered by observing ordinary, understandable businesses that are successful, and by reviewing a company's financial statements. It also describes how to beat the expert by identifying 'tenbaggers', stocks that appreciate tenfold or more, and provides guidelines for investing in cyclical, turnaround, and fast-growing companies.

Pioneering Portfolio Management: An Unconventional Approach to Institutional Investment, 2nd ed

David F. Swensen

New York: Free Press, 2009

432pp, ISBN: 978-1-4165-4469-2

This describes the investment process that underpins the author's own institutional investment success, and describes his often counterintuitive strategies for structuring a well-diversified equity-oriented portfolio. It analyzes asset-allocation structures, active fund management, as explores how to handle risk, select advisers, and survive market downturns, based on the key elements of trust, expertise, fortitude, and a long-term perspective.

A Random Walk Down Wall Street: The Time-Tested Srategy for Successful Investing, 9th ed

Burton G. Malkiel

New York: W. W. Norton, 2007

414pp, ISBN: 978-0-393-33033-5

This oft-updated, bestselling investment guide evaluates the full range of investment opportunities, from stocks, bonds, and money markets, to real estate investment trusts and insurance, home ownership, and tangible assets such as gold and collectibles. It presents the author's guide to investing throughout the life-cycle, with this edition including new analysis of behavioral finance, and insights into investment strategies for retirement.

Real Estate Finance & Investments, 13th ed

William B. Brueggeman, Jeffrey D. Fisher

Boston: McGraw-Hill, 2008

688pp, ISBN: 978-0-07-352471-9

This regularly revised and updated textbook on real estate finance and investments is a rigorous and practical overview of the tools needed to understand and analyze real estate markets and the investment alternatives available to both debt and equity investors. New content has been added on current trends in mortgage finance and investment techniques.

Smarter Investing: Simpler Decisions for Better Results

Tim Hale

Harlow, UK: FT Prentice Hall, 2006

371pp, ISBN: 978-0-273-70800-1

This accessible investment guide examines how to invest rationally and simply, to achieve better returns. It provides a simple and powerful approach to investing, helping you to build a balanced investment portfolio suited to your needs, emphasizing the importance of establishing what you want from your money, and how much you need to achieve your goals.

Stocks for the Long Run: The Definitive Guide to Financial Market Returns and Long Term Investment Strategies, 4th ed

Jeremy J. Siegel

New York: McGraw-Hill, 2008

380pp, ISBN: 978-0-07-149470-0

This popular guide to investing presents research, data, and analysis to support the case for an investment strategy based on understanding market forces, and building a successful long-term portfolio that provides enhanced returns and reduced risk. It compares exchange-traded funds, mutual funds, and index options and futures, with this edition featuring new analysis of global investing, behavioral finance, and the latest index instruments.

Vault Career Guide to Investment Banking, 6th ed

Tom Lott

New York: Vault, 2008

176pp, ISBN: 978-1-58131-532-5

This handbook on working in the investment banking industry examines the fundamentals of the financial markets, such as walk-throughs of equity and fixed income offerings, and M&A private placements and reorganizations, and discusses career paths and job responsibilities in corporate finance, sales and trading, research, and syndicate.

The Warren Buffett Way, 2nd ed

Robert G. Hagstrom

Hoboken, New Jersey: Wiley, 2005

245pp, ISBN: 978-0-471-74367-5

This describes Buffett's life, business career, and investment principles, strategies, and practices, detailing the companies he has invested in and why, his value investing approach, and how he built up his fortune over the years. It also examines his perspective on long-term investing, speculation on traditional and understandable businesses, portfolio management, and the influence of investment experts such as Benjamin Graham on his investment philosophy.

When Markets Collide: Investment Strategies for the Age of Global Economic Change

Mohamed El-Erian

New York: McGraw-Hill, 2008

344pp, ISBN: 978-0-07-159281-9

This examination of the current financial turbulence argues that the upheaval is due to a collision between historical markets and future ones, and describes where the evolving economic landscape can provide investment opportunities. It shows how to differentiate between random noise and key investment signals, the increasing role of China in the global economy, and how to allocate assets on a long-term basis.

MAGAZINES

Barron's

Dow Jones & Company

200 Liberty Street, 9th Floor, New York, NY 10281, USA

T: +1 212 416 2000

online.barrons.com

ISSN: 1077-8039

This respected weekly consumer magazine provides news, commentary, market analyses, insights, and statistics on companies, industries, sectors, the economy, and financial markets for individual investors, institutional investors, financial professionals, and senior corporate decision-makers. It also features stock picks and pans, markets, technology, funds, portfolio, data and tools, and a daily stock alert.

CFA Magazine

CFA Institute

PO Box 3668, Charlottesville, VA 22903, USA

T: +1 434 951 5499

F: +1 434 951 5262

www.cfapubs.org/loi/cfm

This is a bimonthly, practice-based, professional member magazine, which updates members on CFA Institute initiatives, and presents local financial reporting and regulatory developments, industry coverage, debate, and technical articles on practical applications.

  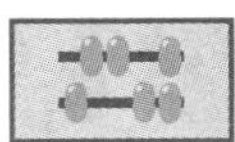      

Global Investor

Euromoney Institutional Investor
Nestor House, Playhouse Yard, London, EC4V 5EX, UK
T: +44 (0) 20 7779 8610
F: +44 (0) 20 7779 8602
www.globalinvestormagazine.com
ISSN: 0951-3604

This respected monthly specialist magazine is aimed at global investment management professionals, and examines the latest developments in the financial markets from an investor's perspective. It focuses on the full range of topics related to international investment, and features a range of supplements, people moves, a summary of mandate wins and corporate activity, opinion pieces, technical challenges, interviews, and profiles.

Institutional Investor

Institutional Investor
225 Park Ave South, New York, NY 10003, USA
T: +1 212 224 3300
www.iimagazine.com
ISSN: 0020-3580

This weekly global magazine for leading financiers, corporate executives and government officials offers market analysis and intelligence, breaking stories, a newsletter, and a range of proprietary research and rankings. It focuses on the capital markets, investing and trading, research, asset management, trading technology, pensions, international markets, and opinion.

International Investment

Incisive Media
Haymarket House, 28–29 Haymarket, London, SW1Y 4RX, UK
T: +44 (0) 20 7034 2600
www.intinv.com

This monthly magazine for international financial advisers covers fund launches, banking news, cross-border life-based investment services, and the latest regulatory and tax changes facing high-net worth individuals. It also news, features, and expert opinion on stock and bond markets, portfolio construction, performance analysis, and tax and legal issues.

Investment Dealers' Digest

SourceMedia
1 State Street Plaza, 26th Floor, New York, NY 10004, USA
T: +1 212 803 8333
www.iddmagazine.com
ISSN: 0021-0080

This weekly magazine provides news and analysis for investment bankers, to help them identify market opportunities and new deal structures. It offers late-breaking news, features, and key data on the financial markets, listings of newly registered securities and new issues, and league tables.

Investment Week

Incisive Media
Haymarket House, 28–29 Haymarket, London, SW1Y 4RX, UK
T: +44 (0) 20 7484 9700
F: +44 (0) 20 7484 9994
www.investmentweek.co.uk
ISSN: 1469-1876

This weekly magazine provides news, commentary, features, fund analysis, investment strategies and product analysis on all aspects of the investment industry for investment advisers, discretionary portfolio managers, fund of funds managers, heads of investment selection, and investment researchers. It also incorporates conferences, seminars, forums, an email bulletin, and awards.

Investors Chronicle

Financial Times
1 Southwark Bridge, London, SE1 9HL, UK
T: +44 (0) 20 7775 6582
F: +44 (0) 20 7775 6501
www.investorschronicle.co.uk
ISSN: 0261-3115

This respected weekly magazine provides private investors with weekly stock market analysis, offering feature articles on many aspects of successful investing, supplements on investment products, and a range of statistical and reference information.

JOURNALS

Financial Analysts Journal

CFA Institute
560 Ray C. Hunt Drive, Charlottesville, VA 22903-2981, USA
T: +1 434 951 5499
www.cfapubs.org/loi/faj

FAJ is a bimonthly publication of the CFA Institute that presents articles dedicated to the practice of investment management. It acts as a bridge between academic research and practice by offering academically rigorous papers of relevance to practitioners.

Journal of Alternative Investments

Institutional Investor
225 Park Avenue South, New York, NY 10003, USA
T: +1 212 224 3570
www.iijournals.com/JAI
ISSN: 1520-3255

This quarterly journal provides research and expert analysis on managing investments in hedge funds, private equity, distressed debt, commodities, futures, energy, funds of funds, and other non-traditional instruments. It examines the growth of hedge funds and alternatives, how to measure and track portfolio performance, and includes coverage of asset allocation, risk management, indexing, regulation and taxation.

Journal of Investing

Institutional Investor
225 Park Avenue South, New York, NY 10003, USA
T: +1 212 224 3570
F: +1 212 224 3197
www.iijournals.com/JOI
ISSN: 1068-0896

This quarterly journal for investment professionals offers research and analysis on maximizing assets and effective portfolio management, mutual funds, exchange-traded funds, asset allocation, and performance measurement. It also publishes papers on such areas as assessing the risk/return characteristics of traditional and alternative asset classes, effective strategies for structuring a global portfolio, identifying new market opportunities, and optimizing allocation in traditional and alternative investments.

Journal of Investment Compliance

Emerald Group Publishing
Howard House, Wagon Lane, Bingley, BD16 1WA, UK
T: +44 (0) 1274 777 700
F: +44 (0) 1274 785 201
www.emeraldinsight.com/Insight/viewContainer.do?containerType=JOURNAL&containerId=22667
ISSN: 1528-5812

JOIC is a quarterly professional journal that publishes articles on regulatory and compliance issues relevant to broker–dealers, investment advisers, mutual funds, hedge funds, and other types of investment companies. It offers practical advice on future directions for the industry and the compliance implications, and covers issues such as research analyst independence, employment law, registration with regulators, and preparing for regulatory examinations and investigations.

Journal of Money, Investment and Banking

EuroJournals
www.eurojournals.com/JMIB.htm
ISSN: 1450-288X

This bimonthly, international research journal publish both theoretical and empirical papers on issues relating to money, investment, international banking, and finance. It offers research papers, research notes, discussion articles, book reviews, software reviews, editorials, and letters on its core areas, as well as on financial economics, e-finance, financial analysis, risk management, financial derivatives, mathematical finance, financial accounting, financial engineering, and credit rating.

Journal of Portfolio Management

Institutional Investor
225 Park Avenue South, New York, NY 10003, USA
T: +1 212 224 3570
F: +1 212 224 3197
www.iijournals.com/JPM
ISSN: 0095-4918

This quarterly journal provides analysis and research on practical techniques in institutional investing, asset allocation, performance measurement, market trends, risk management, and portfolio optimization. It describes new and classic portfolio management techniques, with articles covering different products, equities, market behavior, international investing, and new asset classes.

Journal of Property Investment & Finance

Emerald Group Publishing
Howard House, Wagon Lane, Bingley, BD16 1WA, UK
T: +44 (0) 1274 777 700
F: +44 (0) 1274 785 201

www.emeraldinsight.com/Insight/viewContainer.do?containerType=Journal&containerId=12267
ISSN: 1463-578X

Published bimonthly, this journal provides information and ideas relating to property valuation and investment, property management, and decision-making in the commercial property market. It publishes papers by both academics and practitioners, covering the latest research, real estate law and new legislation, internet sites and recent publications, market data, and changes in the property market.

INTERNET

Global Investor

www.global-investor.com

This is one of main online resources in the financial industry. It provides a range of investment sites, such as The Global Investor Bookshop and other branded bookshops for client websites, a popular financial glossary, information about financial events, conferences, and training, and offers courses on the investment techniques, and strategies.

Investegate

www.investegate.co.uk

This is a comprehensive online source of announcements from UK quoted companies, which presents regulatory and other published information, and offers company announcements feeds, as well as analysis of companies and sectors in the news, and a live features column.

Investing in Bonds

www.investinginbonds.com

This is a source of bond price information and other market data, news, commentary and information about bonds. It was founded by The Securities Industry and Financial Markets Association to help educate investors.

Investor Links

www.investorlinks.com

This is a financial resource website that offers a comprehensive financial directory, and links and descriptions to thousands of financial websites. It also provides a portfolio tracker, e-mailed news alerts, message boards, stock quotes, and indices.

ORGANIZATIONS

Europe

Alternative Investment Management Association

Chair: Florence Lombard
2nd Floor, 167 Fleet Street, London, EC4A 2EA, UK
T: +44 (0) 20 7822 8380
www.aima.org

This is international, not-for-profit, trade association represents nearly 1,300 corporate members worldwide, including hedge fund managers, fund of hedge funds managers, prime brokers, legal and accounting services, and fund administrators. The association influences policy development, industry initiatives, and is involved in regulation. It also focuses on developing industry skills and education standards, and is a co-founder of the Chartered Alternative Investment Analyst designation (CAIA).

The Association of Investment Companies

9th Floor, 24 Chiswell Street, London, EC1Y 4YY, UK
T: +44 (0) 20 7282 5555
F: +44 (0) 20 7282 5556
E: enquiries@theaic.co.uk
www.theaic.co.uk

AIC is the trade organization for the closed-ended investment company industry. It represents a broad range of closed-ended investment companies, incorporating investment trusts, offshore investment companies, and venture capital trusts which are traded on the London Stock Exchange, AIM, and Euronext. It supports the development of the investment company market, helps directors discharge their obligations to shareholders, and works with management groups and the wider industry.

The Association of Private Client Investment Managers and Stockbrokers

Chair: David Bennett
22 City Road, Finsbury Square, London, EC1Y 2AJ, UK
T: +44 (0) 20 7448 7100
F: +44 (0) 20 7638 4636
E: info@apcims.co.uk
www.apcims.co.uk

APCIMS is the trade association of wealth management and broking firms who provide services to private investors. It promotes the interests of its members with governments, regulators, financial institutions, and all participants in financial services, and provides information and assistance to members across a wide range of regulatory, market, and business issues.

Association of Solicitors and Investment Managers

Riverside House, River Lawn Road, Tonbridge, Kent, TN9 1EP, UK
T: +44 (0) 1732 783 548
F: +44 (0) 1732 362 626
www.asim.org.uk

ASIM is a non-profit organization that supports the provision of high-quality investment management services by firms of solicitors and investment firms. It runs training programs on regulatory and investment issues, and provides a forum through which members can exchange information and experience on commonly encountered portfolio investment service issues.

The CFA Society of the UK

Chair: Joe Biernat
2nd Floor, 135 Cannon Street, London, EC4N 5BP, UK
T: +44 (0) 20 7280 9620
F: +44 (0) 20 7280 9636
E: info@cfauk.org
www.cfauk.org

CFA UK, part of the Chartered Financial Analyst Institute, leads the development of the investment profession in the UK through the promotion of the high standards of ethical behavior, and the provision of education, professional development, information, career support, and advocacy on behalf of its members.

European Fund and Asset Management Association

Chair: Mathias Bauer
Square de Meeus 18, 1050 Brussels, Belgium
T: +32 2 513 3969
F: +32 2 513 2643
www.efama.org

EFAMA is the representative association for the European investment and asset management industry, representing its member associations and corporate members. It aims include supporting investor protection through the promotion of high ethical standards, integrity and professionalism in the industry, promoting the completion of an effective single market for investment management, strengthening the competitiveness of the industry, and promoting relevant scientific research.

Investment Management Association

65 Kingsway, London, WC2B 6TD, UK
T: +44 (0) 20 7831 0898
F: +44 (0) 20 7831 9975
E: ima@investmentuk.org
www.investmentuk.org

IMA's aims are to improve the legal, regulatory and fiscal environment in which its members operate, maintain and enhance the reputation and standing of the industry, and provide a center of excellence for the development of knowledge and understanding of the industry. Its principles are based on customer focus, accountability, responsible stewardship, professionalism, efficiency, and transparency.

London Investment Banking Association

Chair: Jonathan Taylor
6 Frederick's Place, London, EC2R 8BT, UK
T: +44 (0) 20 7796 3606
F: +44 (0) 20 7796 4345
E: liba@liba.org.uk
www.liba.org.uk

LIBA is the trade association in the United Kingdom for firms active in the investment banking and wholesale securities industry. It acts to promote its members' views to legislators, regulators, and opinion-formers, works with other trade associations, provides a forum for the exchange of views, promotes London as a location for the conduct of investment banking business, and represents the London offices of investment banks from around the world.

Securities & Investment Institute

Chair: Scott Dobbie
8 Eastcheap, London, EC3M 1AE, UK
T: +44 (0) 20 7645 0600
F: +44 (0) 20 7645 0601
www.sii.org.uk

The SII is a professional body for those in the securities and investment industry in the UK and around the world. It promotes the advancement and dissemination of knowledge in securities and investments, develops high ethical standards for practitioners in securities and investments, and acts as an authoritative body for the purpose of consultation and research in matters of education or public interest concerning investment in securities.

        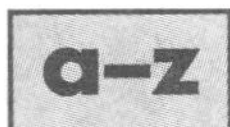

USA

CFA Institute

Chair: John D. Rogers
560 Ray C. Hunt Drive, Charlottesville,
VA 22903-2981, USA
T: +1 434 951 5499
E: info@cfainstitute.org
www.cfainstitute.org

This is a major, global, non-profit association for the global investment community. It provides a range of educational opportunities online and around the world, strives to make the financial markets equitable, free, and efficient, works on behalf of the ultimate investor, and fosters high ethical principles and self-regulatory standards.

The Chartered Alternative Investment Analyst Association

Chair: Peter Douglas
29 South Pleasant Street, Amherst, MA 01002, USA
T: +1 413 253 7373
F: +1 413 253 4494
E: info@caia.org
www.caia.org

The CAIA is an independent, not-for-profit, global organization that is committed to education and professionalism in the field of alternative investments. It provides information on alternative investments, promotes professional development through education, advocates high standards of professional conduct, and is the sponsoring body for the CAIA designation, the educational standard for the alternative investment industry.

Investment Recovery Association

638 West 39th Street, Kansas City, MO 64111, USA
T: +1 816 561 5323
F: +1 816 561 1991
E: info@invrecovery.org
www.invrecovery.org

This is the professional association for managers of surplus and idle assets, and acts as a resource for companies and individuals engaged in profit-driven asset management. It aims to assist members and their companies make the most of their past investments through strategic use of recycling, redeployment, reselling, and other techniques.

New York Society of Security Analysts

Chair: Jan Jackrel
1177 Avenue of the Americas, 2nd Floor, New York, NY 10036-2714, USA
T: +1 212 541 4530
F: +1 212 541 4677
E: staff@nyssa.org
www.nyssa.org

NYSSA is a non-profit educational organization that provides a forum for the investment community. It aims to establish and maintain a high standard of professional ethics in the security analysis field, improve analytical techniques, foster the interchange of ideas and information among security analysts, and promote proper understanding of the function of financial and security analysis and the operation of the security markets.

Professional Association for Investment Communications Resources

Chair: Lisa Bosley
191 Clarksville Road, Princeton Junction, NJ 08550, USA
T: +1 609 799 4382
F: +1 609 799 7032
www.paicr.com

PAICR is a non-profit organization that aims to empower investment marketing and communications professionals through opportunities for professional development, continuing education and networking at association events throughout North America.

International

Investment and Financial Services Association

Chair: David Deverall
Level 24, 44 Market Street, Sydney NSW 2000, Australia
T: +61 2 9299 3022
F: +61 2 299 3198
E: ifsa@ifsa.com.au
www.ifsa.com.au

IFSA is a non-profit organization that represents the retail and wholesale funds management, superannuation, and life insurance industries. It aims to assist in the development of the social, economic and regulatory framework in which their members operate, thereby assisting members to serve their customers better.

Islamic Finance

BOOKS

Critical Issues on Islamic Banking and Financial Markets: Islamic Economics, Banking and Finance, Investments, Takaful and Financial Planning

Saiful Azhar Rosly
Bloomington, Indiana: AuthorHouse, 2005
618pp, ISBN: 978-1-4184-6930-6

This is an accessible guide to modern Islamic finance, which provides a practical discussion of the underlying principles of Shariah financial instruments, and Islamic banking, insurance, and fund management. It examines the growth of Islamic funds and transactions, and their integration into the international financial system, and explains key concepts and terms, such as Shariah, sukuk, riba, al-bay', and maisir.

Financial Risk Management for Islamic Banking and Finance

Ioannis Akkizidis, Sunil Kumar Khandelwal
New York: Palgrave Macmillan, 2008
300pp, ISBN: 978-0-230-55381-1

This guide to risk management in Islamic finance presents a methodology for assessing and managing risk in Shariah-compliant financial products and services. It details how to practically implement a risk management framework for Islamic financial institutions, to manage the increase in financial products and services, and number of Islamic financial institutions managing funds.

A Guide to Islamic Finance

Munawar Iqbal
London: Risk Books, 2007
118pp, ISBN: 978-1-904339-85-4

This focused and practical report explains the basic theory, practice, and limitations of Islamic banking and finance. It shows how to develop products that comply with Islamic principles, that perform financial intermediation functions without the involvement of interest, and explains the objectives and sources of Islamic law and the guidelines for business contracts, and offers an extensive glossary of relevant Arabic terms.

Handbook of Islamic Banking

M. Kabir Hassan, Mervyn K. Lewis (editors)
Cheltenham, UK: Edward Elgar Publishing, 2007
443pp, ISBN: 978-1-84542-083-3

This authoritative handbook examines how Islamic banking and finance operates, and assesses its role within the international banking and capital markets, as an alternative to conventional interest-based financing methods. It details the variety of financial instruments and investment vehicles, and other key topics such as governance and risk management, securities and investment, structured financing, accounting and regulation, economic development, and globalization.

The International Handbook of Islamic Banking and Finance

Elisabeth Jackson-Moore
London: Global Professional Publishing, 2009
300pp, ISBN: 978-1-906403-31-7

This comprehensive guide provides an overview of current practices in Islamic banking and finance, and the essential elements of Shariah compliance. It examines the issues faced by bankers, scholars, regulators and others interested in understanding the objectives and challenges of Islamic finance and its growing role in the global financial markets.

Introduction to Islamic Banking and Finance

Brian Kettell
London: Islamic Banking Training, 2008
251pp, ISBN: 978-0-9558351-0-0

This comprehensive primer to Islamic banking and finance details the fundamental points of convergence and divergence between Shari'ah-compliant finance and conventional interest-based finance. It analyzes the key principles, components, and techniques of the industry, the introduction

  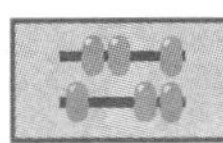      

of services free from interest, and the use of profit and loss sharing as a method of resource allocation and financial intermediation.

An Introduction to Islamic Finance: Theory and Practice
Zamir Iqbal, Abbas Mirakhor
Wiley Finance Series
Singapore: Wiley, 2007
332pp, ISBN: 978-0-470-82188-6

This is a concise resource on the fundamental principles of Islamic finance, an economic and financial system governed by Shariah Islamic law. It provides guidance and insight on all of main essential topics, products, and processes, discusses the context of Islamic finance within modern finance and banking practices, and examines Islamic tenets that influence economic behavior in the fast growing Islamic financial services industry.

Islamic Economics and Finance: A Glossary, 2nd ed
Muhammad A. Khan
London: Routledge, 2003
195pp, ISBN: 978-0-415-45925-9

An updated and enlarged edition of this useful glossary, it explains terms used in Islamic banking, taxation, insurance, accounting, and auditing by Muslim scholars, historians and legal experts, from Arabic, Urdu, Turkish, Malaysian, and English sources. It provides a reference for all interested in Islamic economics and finance, including economists, bankers, accountants, students and researchers.

Islamic Finance: A Guide for International Business and Investment
Roderick Millar, Habiba Anwar (editors)
London: GMB Publishing, 2008
216pp, ISBN: 978-1-84673-078-8

This guide to Islamic financial practice aimed at banking professionals and corporate investors examines the tenets of Islamic investment that exclude areas such as gambling, alcohol, weapons, and products that are high-risk and high-return. It analyzes the differences between Islamic and conventional banking, and the reasons for investors and asset managers becoming increasingly attracted to financial products and the institutions that comply with Shariah principles.

Islamic Finance: A Practical Guide
Rahail Ali (editor)
London: Globe Law and Business, 2008
175pp, ISBN: 978-1-905783-13-7

This practitioner approach to Islamic finance analyzes market trends, key developments and structures for sukuk, syndications, types of Shariah-compliant fund, takaful, project financing, and Islamic liquidity management, as well as the relevant legal issues. It provides a practical guide for sovereigns, financial institutions, multinationals, and corporates on the essentials of Islamic finance, including Islamic bonds, and corporate, retail, and acquisition.

Islamic Finance: Law, Economics, and Practice
Mahmoud A. El-Gamal
Cambridge, UK: Cambridge University Press, 2006
221pp, ISBN: 978-0-521-74126-2

This is an overview of Islamic finance practices, which analyzes the constraints that Islam imposes on financial relations in attempting to replicate financial instruments, markets, and institutions, arguing that this is failing to serve the objectives of Islamic law. Instead, it proposes a fundamental reform in Islamic finance, to focus more on issues of community banking, micro-finance, and socially responsible investment.

Islamic Finance: The Regulatory Challenge
Rifaat Ahmed Abdel Karim, Simon Archer (editors)
Wiley Finance Series
Singapore: Wiley, 2007
418pp, ISBN: 978-0-470-82189-3

This examines the regulatory aspects of Islamic finance, and the development of structured regulatory, supervisory, and legal frameworks appropriate for the Islamic financial services industry worldwide. It discusses principles of Islamic commercial jurisprudence, the role of the Islamic Financial Services Board, the potential for growth in Islamic financial services, corporate governance and supervision issues, and the nature of risk in Islamic banking.

Islamic Finance in the Global Economy, 2nd ed
Ibrahim Warde
Edinburgh, UK: Edinburgh University Press, 2008
272pp, ISBN: 978-0-7486-2777-6

This is a comprehensive reference to the political economy of Islamic finance, for those interested in Islamic and Middle Eastern economics, business and finance. It provides an overview of modern Islamic finance, analyzes the connection between Islamic finance and politics, explores the underlying economic, cultural, and political principles, and discusses Islamic finance in the context of the global political and economic system.

Islamic Retail Banking and Finance: Global Challenges and Opportunities
Jaffer Sohail (editor)
London: Euromoney Books, 2005
222pp, ISBN: 978-1-84374-198-5

This is an international treatment of Islamic finance and banking, which details the development of the sector over the last few years, and issues such as the increasing focus by Western banks on Islamic financial services, and Islamic retail banking in Europe. It provides an overview of the creation of Islamic mortgages, savings, insurance, and retail investment products in terms of increasing competition with conventional financial products, and their basis in Islamic law.

A Mini Guide to Islamic Banking & Finance
Centre for Research and Training
Kuala Lumpur, Malaysia: CERT Publications, 2006
123pp, ISBN: 978-983-42785-4-0

This concise introduction to Islamic banking, finance, and accountancy examines the basic requirements, obligatory prohibitions, and Shariah-compliant transactions, as well as permissible investment and insurance alternatives. It also offers a useful set of Q&As, bibliography, and glossary.

New Issues in Islamic Finance and Economics: Progress and Challenges
Hossein Askari, Zamir Iqbal, Abbas Mirakhor
Wiley Finance Series
Hoboken, New Jersey: Wiley, 2008
320pp, ISBN: 978-0-470-82293-7

This review of the main issues and challenges facing Islamic finance focuses on governance, institutions, public finance, and economic development within an Islamic financial system. It looks at the development of Islamic finance, and argues that its future success will depend on factors such as economic and financial reform in Islamic countries, institutional reform, governance and regulatory oversight, and research into suitable financial products.

The Politics of Islamic Finance
Clement Henry, Rodney Wilson (editors)
Edinburgh, UK: Edinburgh University Press, 2004
307pp, ISBN: 978-0-7486-1837-8

This exploration of the political aspects of Islamic finance examines the experiences of Islamic banking in a range of countries, and the political implications of the increase in Islamic capital. It also explores the connections between Islamic finance and Islamic political movements, the perceived connection between Islamic finance and money laundering and terrorism, and common misconceptions about Islamic banking and finance.

Risk Analysis for Islamic Banks
Hennie van Greuning, Zamir Iqbal
Washington, DC: World Bank Publications, 2007
330pp, ISBN: 978-0-8213-7141-1

This is a focused exploration of the assessment, analysis, and management of various types of risks in the field of Islamic banking. It introduces a high-level framework that takes into account the current realities of changing economies and Islamic financial markets, and discusses the accountability of key players in the corporate governance process in terms of the management of different dimensions of Islamic financial risk.

Structuring Islamic Finance Transactions
Thomas Abdulkader, Stella Cox, Bryan Kraty (editors)
London: Euromoney Books, 2005
234pp, ISBN: 978-1-84374-213-5

This explains the fundamental principles of Islamic finance instruments and compliance with Islamic law in the context of recent financial developments and the growth of Islamic financial institutions. It discusses the complex structures and applications of Islamic transactions, such as sukuk and debt-like products, risk management and derivative-like products, and the emerging regulatory environment for Islamic finance products and transactions.

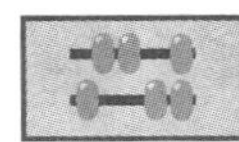

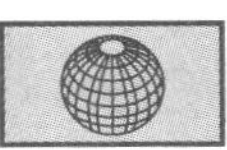

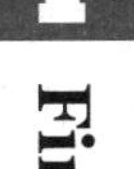

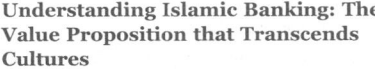

Understanding Islamic Banking: The Value Proposition that Transcends Cultures

Joseph A. DiVanna

Cambridge, UK: Leonardo and Francis Press, 2006
174pp, ISBN: 978-1-905687-00-8

This is a guide to the principles and practice of Islamic banking, which provides a framework for contemporary retail banks to be accessible for investors of any faith. It also explores the essentials of a bank's value proposition, such as brand, innovation, investment strategy, and shareholder and consumer value, as attributes of Islamic banking identifiable by Muslims and non-Muslims.

Understanding Islamic Finance

Muhammad Ayub

Wiley Finance Series
Hoboken, New Jersey: Wiley, 2007
516pp, ISBN: 978-0-470-03069-1

This introduction to Islamic finance explains all the key concepts, principles, products, and processes of this growing market. It presents a clear background and history, exploring how the concepts are rooted in Islamic law, the Islamic economic system, and Shariah compliance. It discusses Islamic economics as a rule-base system better understood as a set of contracts, and examines how to design financial instruments compatible with Islamic jurisprudence.

MAGAZINES

Arab Banker

The Arab Bankers Association
43 Upper Grosvenor Street, London, W1K 2NJ, UK
T: +44 (0) 20 7659 4889
F: +44 (0) 20 7659 4658
www.arab-banker.com
ISSN: 0261-2925

This journal, published twice yearly by the Arab Bankers' Association, covers current affairs, commentary, people in the news, company news, and bank results.

Islamic Banking & Finance

New Millennium Publishing
Suite 3, 20 Old Steine, Brighton, East Sussex, BN1 1EL, UK
T: +44 (0) 560 116 9695
F: +44 (0) 700 603 4010
www.islamicbankingandfinance.com
ISSN: 1814-8042

This magazine, published six times each year, reports on all aspects of Islamic banking and finance, and core topics such as takaful, law, software, and property. It features news, analysis, micro-finance, viewpoints, business scope, latest products and services, data from the latest Dow Jones Islamic Market Indices, and regular special country reports.

Islamic Finance Asia

REDmoney
21/F, Menara KUB, 12, Jalan Yap Kwan Seng, 50450 Kuala Lumpur, Malaysia
T: +603 2162 7800
F: +603 2162 7810
www.islamicfinanceasia.com

This bimonthly global magazine is distributed free to all qualified corporate individuals within the Islamic finance market. It provides research and commentary on takaful and retakaful, retails, ratings, and funds, and features information a review of Asian and global activity, as well as reviews, moves, and events.

Islamic Finance News

REDmoney
21/F, Menara KUB, 12, Jalan Yap Kwan Seng, 50450 Kuala Lumpur, Malaysia
T: +603 2162 7800
F: +603 2162 7810
www.islamicfinancenews.com

This weekly e-newsletter focuses on the global Islamic financing market and related instruments. It produces news briefs, detailed country and industry sector reports, a research review, retail news, legal updates, and information on moves and promotions, events and training courses, and league tables. Its website carries all content from the newsletter, in addition to useful supplements, books, directories, and a database.

Quantum

Qatar Financial Centre Authority, Qatar
T: +44 (0) 20 8670 1922
www.quantummagazine.com

This quarterly magazine presents a global perspective in its analysis of significant international and regional trends in the financial services industry. It encourages debate, and provides a forum for leading decision makers to present arguments and challenge conventional wisdoms. Its contributors include senior market practitioners, analysts, academics, and journalists.

True Banking

Al Huda Center of Islamic Banking and Islamic Economics
Suite 9, 2nd Floor, Gohar Center, Wahdat Road, Lahore, India
T: +92 42 591 2771
F: +92 42 585 8990
www.truebanking.com.pk

This is a monthly magazine dedicated to the banking and financial services sector, focusing on industry news and analysis, new financial products, research and development, market analysis, training, and education in Islamic banking, takaful, and investment.

JOURNALS

International Journal of Islamic and Middle Eastern Finance and Management

Emerald Group Publishing
Howard House, Wagon Lane, Bingley, BD16 1WA, UK
T: +44 (0) 1274 777700
F: +44 (0) 1274 785201
www.emeraldinsight.com/products/journals/journals.htm?id=imefm
ISSN: 1753-8394

This quarterly journal provides original research and analysis into the growth of Islamic banking, finance and financial services, and personal finance, including hedge funds, Islamic bonds, retail and corporate lines of Islamic credit and derivatives, mortgages, auto financing, and consumer finance. It offers dedicated sections on news, new products, market/sector reports, and extended book reviews.

Islamic Economic Bulletin

4\1914, Faridi House, S. S. Nagar, Aligarh, 202002, India
T: +91 571 240 1028

This academic newsletter, published six times each year by the Indian Association for Islamic Economics, aims to create awareness of the latest development in theory and practice of Islamic economics.

Islamic Economic Studies

Islamic Research and Training Institute
PO Box 9201, Jeddah 21413, Saudi Arabia
T: +966 2636 1400
F: +966 2637 8927
www.irti.org/irj/portal/anonymous/IRTIJournal

This journal, published biannually in Muharram and Rajab, according to the Islamic calendar, offers papers that make a contribution to Islamic economics, either theoretical or applied, or discuss an economic issue from an Islamic perspective.

Journal of Islamic Banking & Finance

International Association of Islamic Banks

This quarterly journal publishes research and analysis of Islamic principles relating to banking, finance and economics, and produces reports about financial institutions and banks in Middle East and other Islamic countries.

The Review of Islamic Economics

International Association of Islamic Economics and the Islamic Foundation
Markfield Conference Centre, Ratby Lane, Markfield, Leicestershire, LE67 9SY, UK
T: +44 (0) 1530 244 944
F: +44 (0) 1530 244 946
www.islamic-foundation.org.uk
ISSN: 0962-2055

This biannual journal, published by the International Association of Islamic Economics and the Islamic Foundation, presents research articles in the field of Islamic economics, banking and finance. It focuses on theoretical issues in economics dealt with from an Islamic perspective, empirical studies about the economies of Muslim countries, applied Islamic economics, and survey articles in various fields of Islamic economics.

INTERNET

American Journal of Islamic Finance

ajif.org

American Journal of Islamic Finance is an online resource on Islamic Finance, which provides a range of useful information on the operations of Islamic banking, securities, and finance. It offers research papers on subjects such as money management, capital markets, economics, regulation, and treasury.

Islam Online

www.islamonline.com/news/category.php?catid=10

This respected information resource includes a section covering the Islamic finance and banking industry, offering news from a variety of sources.

Islamic-Finance.com

www.islamic-finance.com

This is an independent online resource that features news and commentary, as well articles, research, institutional information, market updates, a glossary, and details of events, books, jobs, resources.

The Islamic Banker

www.theislamicbanker.com

This is a respected, professional online magazine covering the Islamic financial services industry. It focuses on promoting the Islamic banking industry, enhancing employee and organizational performance through the provision of Islamic financial news, information, and details about events and conferences.

Islamic Banking, Investment & Takaful

islamic-finance.startpagina.nl

This useful references contains more than 300 links in the field of Islamic finance, detailing news, studies, forum, shared risk/ethical banking, economics, finance index, jobs, risk management, networks, and advisers.

Islamic Banking & Finance News

www.alhudacibe.com/magdetail.php

This monthly online magazine has the objective of promoting a better awareness of the Islamic banking and finance industry worldwide. It provides national and international news, analysis, research, interviews, round table discussions, product reviews, and partners with different international Islamic financial institutions to offer Islamic banking and finance information services to financial institutions.

The Islamic Banking Portal

www.islamicbanking.com

This portal provides a comprehensive and useful list of Islamic banks and financial institutions, and gathers news from a variety of international sources.

Islamic Banks and Financial Institutions Information

www.ibisonline.net

This online portal is targeted at researchers and finance professionals working in the area of Islamic economics and finance. It provides data, information, research, and literature on the activities of Islamic finance institutions, and offers an Islamic banks database, and tools for online analysis and download.

Islamic Business & Finance Network

www.iiibf.org

IBF Net is a global network of students, researchers, bankers, and finance professionals interested in Islamic business and finance. It offers an online discussion forum, and sponsors the International Institute of Islamic Business and Finance in their educational, training, and publication programs in India and overseas.

Islamic Finance Information Source

www.securities.com/ifis

This information resource provides key Islamic research, and features newswatch, company information, Islamic bonds, Islamic banking, Islamic deals and transactions, Islamic capital markets and Islamic investments, Islamic funds, Islamic insurance, and Islamic finance league tables.

Islamicity

www.islamicity.com/finance

This website aims to encourage international understanding of Islam and Muslims, and offers a wide range of information and services, including financial news, products, banking, loans, investment, insurance.

ORGANIZATIONS

Europe

Academy for International Modern Studies

244 Robin Hood Lane, Blue Bell Hill, Chatham, Kent, ME5 9JY, UK
www.learnislamicfinance.com

AIMS is an international organization that promotes industry professionalism and best practice in Islamic banking and finance. Their academic partnership program, developed in response to the growth in the Islamic finance industry, is led by a committee of Islamic Shariah scholars, and they offer customized training programs, seminars, workshops, and several certifications on areas of Islamic banking, finance and insurance.

The Arab Bankers Association

Chair: George Kardouche
43 Upper Grosvenor Street, London, W1K 2NJ, UK
T: +44 (0) 20 7659 4889
F: +44 (0) 20 7659 4658
E: arab-bankers@btconnect.com
www.arab-bankers.co.uk

This association seeks to develop ties between Arab professionals working in the financial services sector, and encourages the exchange of views, information, and expertise between the banking and financial sectors in the Arab world, and their counterparts in the United Kingdom and other countries. It also provides services to the Arab banking and financial community, and fosters an awareness of recent financial developments in the region.

Institute of Islamic Banking and Insurance

12–14 Barkat House, 116–118 Finchley Road, London, NW3 5HT, UK
T: +44 (0) 20 7245 0404
F: +44 (0) 20 7245 9769
E: iibi@islamic-banking.com
www.islamic-banking.com

This UK-based organization provides professional education, training, research, and related activities with the purpose of increasing knowledge and understanding of Islamic principles in international finance. It contributes to the education and training of people in Islamic banking and insurance through a post-graduate diploma course, publications, lectures, seminars, workshops, research, Shariah advisory services, and a website.

International

Accounting and Auditing Organization for Islamic Financial Institutions

Block 304, Al Muthana Road, Yateem Center, Building 71, 4th Floor, Office 403, Manama, Bahrain
T: +973 244 496
F: +973 250 194
E: aaoifi@batelco.com.bh
www.aaoifi.com

AAOIFI is an Islamic independent, international, non-profit organization that prepares accounting, auditing, governance, ethics, and Shariah standards for Islamic financial institutions and the industry, and which also offers professional qualification programs.

Al Huda Center of Islamic Banking and Islamic Economics

Chair: M. Zubair Mughal
Suite 9, 2nd Floor, Gohar Center, Wahdat Road, Lahore, India
T: +92 42 591 2771
F: +92 42 585 8990
E: info@alhudacibe.com
www.alhudacibe.com

This organization provides education, training, workshops, awareness, and practice.

Association of Islamic Banking Institutions Malaysia

Chair: Dato' Zukri Samat
23rd Floor, Menara Tradewinds (Menara Tun Razak), Jalan Raja Laut, 50350 Kuala Lumpur, Malaysia
T: +60 3 2694 8002
F: +60 3 2694 8012
E: admin@aibim.com
www.aibim.com

On Islamic banking, finance, takaful, and sukuk, mostly in Pakistan. It aims to train and develop bankers and finance professionals in the spiritual and intellectual heritage of Islam, and promote professional growth in this sector.

The General Council for Islamic Banks and Financial Institutions

Chair: Saleh Kamel
www.islamicfi.com

This is an international, non-profit organization formed jointly by the Islamic Development Bank and other Islamic financial institutions to improve the public awareness of Islamic Shariah concepts, rules, and provisions related to the development of the Islamic financial industry. It works to enhance co-operation among its members, and provides information related to Islamic financial institutions.

  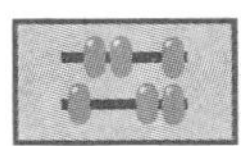      

International Association of Islamic Banks

Saudi Arabia

This association promotes links amongst Islamic financial institutions, and promotes cooperation in the industry. It also fosters the concept of Islamic banking, coordinates with Islamic banks to resolve common problems, provides assistance in manpower development, maintains a databank of all Islamic financial institutions, offers technical assistance in Islamic banking, and represents the interests of Islamic banks at all levels.

International Institute of Islamic Business & Finance

G-51/3-B Fourth Floor, Abul Fazal Enclave II, Shaheen Bagh, Okhla, New Delhi 110025, India
T: +91 989 102 9390
E: shafeeq@iiibf.org
www.iiibf.org

IIIBF, sponsored by IBF Net, offers education, training, workshops, seminars, and publication programs in India and overseas.

International Islamic Financial Market

Chair: Khalid Hamad
PO Box 11454, Bahrain Tower, Office 171, 17th Floor, Building 20, Al Khalifa Avenue Block 305, Road 385, Manama, Bahrain
T: +973 17 500 161
F: +973 17 500 171
E: iifm@batelco.com.bh
www.iifm.net

IIFM is an organization founded by the central banks and monetary agencies of several countries, which advocates the establishment, development, self-regulation, and promotion of Islamic capital and money markets. It focuses on the advancement and standardisation of Islamic financial instrument structures, contracts, product development, and infrastructure, as well as the issuance of guidelines and recommendations for the enhancement of Islamic capital and money markets globally.

Islamic Banking and Finance Institute Malaysia

Chair: Tan Sri Dato' Sri Dr. Zeti Akhtar Aziz
Malaysia

IBFIM is an industry-owned institute dedicated to improving the training and competence of those working in the Islamic finance and banking industry, with the aim of assisting the growth and professionalism of the sector.

Islamic Financial Services Board

Chair: Hamad Al- Sayari
3rd Floor, Block A, Bank Negara Malaysia Building, Jalan Dato' Onn, 50480 Kuala Lumpur, Malaysia
T: +603 2698 4248
F: +603 2698 4280
E: ifsb_sec@ifsb.org
www.ifsb.org

This organization serves as an international standard-setting body of regulatory and supervisory agencies focused on ensuring the soundness and stability of the Islamic financial services industry. It promotes the sector through international standards consistent with Shariah principles, and ensures its work complements regulatory development by other international institutions.

Islamic International Rating Agency

Chair: Khaled M. Al-Aboodi
Al-Zamil Tower, 7th Floor, Government Avenue, Manama 305, PO Box 20582, Bahrain
T: +973 1721 1606
F: +973 1721 1605
E: iira@iirating.com
www.iirating.com

IIRA is a credit rating agency that assists the Islamic financial services industry is gaining recognition, both locally and internationally, as strong and capable financial institutions,
and promotes greater standards of disclosure and transparency. It also supports the development and functioning of the regional capital market, and acts as a resource for credit ratings in accordance with Shariah principles.

Islamic Research and Training Institute

Chair: Ahmad Mohamed Ali Al-Madani
PO Box 9201, Jeddah 21413, Saudi Arabia
T: +966 2636 1400
F: +966 2637 8927
E: irti@isdb.org
www.irti.org

IRTI undertakes research on economic, financial, and banking activities in Muslim countries, to conform to Shariah, and offers training facilities for professionals engaged in Islamic economics and banking in IDB member countries. It also organizes and co-ordinates research on models and their application in economics, finance and banking.

Knowledge Management

BOOKS

Advanced Methods for Inconsistent Knowledge Management

Ngoc Thanh Nguyen
Advanced Information and Knowledge Processing Series
London: Springer, 2008
356pp, ISBN: 978-1-84628-888-3

Advanced Methods for Inconsistent Knowledge Management, aimed at researchers and students in the field of knowledge management, conflict solution, and intelligent systems, describes many random problems of inconsistent knowledge management. It provides a general overview of intelligent technologies for inconsistency resolution, as well as formal models of inconsistency and algorithms for its resolution.

Beyond Knowledge Management: Dialogue, Creativity, and the Corporate Curriculum

Bob Garvey, Bill Williamson
Harlow, UK: FT Prentice Hall, 2002
224pp, ISBN: 978-0-273-65517-6

In this book the authors explore the ways in which learning and knowledge processes link to the success of an organization. They encourage managers to think critically and offer useful frameworks for identifying and releasing tacit knowledge. They draw on a unique triad framework of strategic capability, knowledge productivity, and corporate curriculum, and stress the use of critical dialogue, learning histories, narratives, and metaphors. The implications of the knowledge economy on corporations today are explored and debated.

Building a Knowledge-Driven Organization

Robert H. Buckman
Maidenhead, UK: McGraw-Hill, 2004
272pp, ISBN: 978-0-07-138471-1

The author, chairman and CEO emeritus of Buckman Laboratories, describes how the company pioneered the development of a knowledge sharing culture as opposed to a knowledge hoarding one. The lessons learned in the process are presented with the aim of assisting others to change organizational culture and develop a knowledge-based strategy. There is a strong focus on the people aspects of implementing a knowledge system, breaking down organizational hierarchies and motivating employees to share their expertise. Aspects of knowledge management also covered include: the choice between customized and off-the-shelf information systems: the creation of communities and virtual teams; the importance of customer centricity; the development of new knowledge-based products and services; and the measurement of outcomes.

Capitalizing On Knowledge: From E-Business to K-Business

David J. Skyrme
Oxford: Butterworth-Heinemann, 2001
336pp, ISBN: 978-0-7506-5011-3

Knowledge management and e-business are rapidly converging into the emerging field of k-business. A k-business is one that turns an organization's knowledge assets into knowledge products and services, and uses the internet to market and deliver them. The book provides models and frameworks with checklists and case examples to help unravel the next phase of the knowledge and dot-com economy. Sections cover the nature of knowledge and e-business, new markets and models for conducting k-business, knowledge markets, and the 10 Ps of using the internet for marketing. Assessment tools and checklists

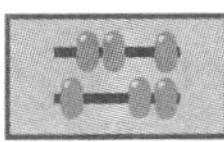

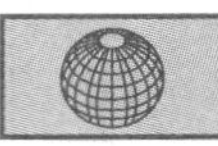

are provided that cover readiness for k-business, online market evaluation, website evaluation, and website project planning.

Common Knowledge: How Companies Thrive by Sharing What They Know

Nancy M. Dixon

Boston, Massachusetts: Harvard Business School Press, 2000
188pp, ISBN: 978-0-87584-904-1

Creating successful knowledge transfer systems requires matching the type of knowledge to be shared to the method best suited for transferring it effectively. Based on an in-depth study of several organizations that are leading the field in successful knowledge transfer (including Ernst & Young, Bechtel, Ford, Chevron, British Petroleum, Texas Instruments, and the US Army), *Common Knowledge* reveals groundbreaking insights into how organizational knowledge is created, how it can be effectively shared, and why transfer systems work when they do.

Cross-Cultural Management: A Knowledge Management Perspective

Nigel Holden

Harlow, UK: FT Prentice Hall, 2001
352pp, ISBN: 978-0-273-64680-8

The author treats culture as an object of knowledge management, and as an organizational knowledge resource. Previous writing on cross-cultural management is discussed, and the idea of knowledge management is described. The two are linked through four case studies, of Novo Nordisk, Matsushita Electric, LEGO, and Sulzer Infra. The final part of the book is concerned with the redesign of cross-cultural management as a knowledge domain.

Cultivating Communities of Practice: A Guide to Managing Knowledge

Etienne Wenger, Richard McDermott, William M. Snyder

Boston, Massachusetts: Harvard Business School Press, 2002
288pp, ISBN: 978-1-57851-330-7

It is argued that while knowledge drives today's marketplace, leveraging knowledge remains a challenge. Leading companies are adopting communities of practice as a keystone of an effective knowledge strategy. Such communities may form naturally, but organizations need to become proactive to develop and integrate them into their strategy. Practical methods and models for nurturing communities of practice to their full potential are described.

Effective Knowledge Management: A Best Practice Blueprint

Sultan Kermally

Chichester, UK: Wiley, 2002
208pp, ISBN: 978-0-470-84449-6

Kermally discusses best practice transfer and benchmarking and the creation of organizational knowledge of external changes. He also deals with the importance of managing knowledge, the creation and transfer of knowledge within the organization, the role of new technology, and leadership, together with intangible assets and their management. The book includes many case studies.

Enabling Knowledge Creation: How to Unlock the Mystery of Tacit Knowledge and Release the Power of Innovation

Georg von Krogh, Kazuo Ichijo, Ikujiro Nonaka

Oxford: Oxford University Press, 2000
192pp, ISBN: 978-0-19-512616-7

Written as a sequel to the authors' work *The Knowledge-Creating Company*, this book examines how organizations can encourage and enable the creation of knowledge and the generation of ideas. Knowledge management, it suggests, has overemphasized information technology and measurement tools and focused on controlling rather than supporting knowledge. The authors then introduce five activities that they term "knowledge enablers": instilling a knowledge vision; managing conversations; mobilizing knowledge activists; creating the right context; and globalizing local knowledge. A case study of Gemini Consulting is included in the text.

From Know-how to Knowledge: The Essential Guide to Understanding and Implementing Knowledge Management

Bryan Gladstone

London: Thorogood, 2000
224pp, ISBN: 978-1-85835-880-2

The concept of knowledge management is defined and explored under the headings: knowledge management; better information management is not enough; knowledge creation cycle; why knowledge management is important now; process of knowledge management; being a knowledge manager; and the future of knowledge management.

Intellectual Capital: Core Asset for the Third Millennium

Annie Brooking

London: Caspian Publishing, 1996
224pp, ISBN: 978-1-86152-408-9

Brooking identifies and analyzes four primary categories of intellectual capital: market assets, intellectual property assets, human-centered assets, and infrastructure assets. This book is particularly suitable for corporations evaluating these assets prior to reengineering or downsizing, or for corporations looking to acquire a knowledge-intensive organization.

Key Issues in the New Knowledge Management

Joseph M. Firestone, Mark W. McElroy

Oxford: Butterworth-Heinemann, 2003
352pp, ISBN: 978-0-7506-7655-7

The authors present their concept of The New Knowledge Management (TNKM) as a broadening of the scope of knowledge management from a concern with the sharing, dissemination and retrieval of knowledge to a concern with its creation or production. They discuss definitions of information, data, and knowledge, introduce the knowledge life cycle, and describe its applications. They also explore the relationships between knowledge management concepts and the practical management issues of organizational learning, culture, and strategy.

The Knowing–Doing Gap: How Smart Companies Turn Knowledge into Action

Jeffrey Pfeffer, Robert I. Sutton

Boston, Massachusetts: Harvard Business School Press, 1999
336pp, ISBN: 978-1-57851-124-2

This book is all about turning knowledge to practical account. The subject headings of its main sections give a good idea of its content and approach: knowing what to do is not enough; when talk substitutes for action; when memory is a substitute for thinking; when fear prevents acting on knowledge; when measurement obstructs good judgment; when internal competition turns friends into enemies; firms that surmount the knowing–doing gap; turning knowledge into action.

The Knowledge Activist's Handbook: Adventures from the Knowledge Trenches

Victor Newman

Oxford, UK: Capstone, 2003
182pp, ISBN: 978-1-84112-320-2

The author's own consulting experiences are used to demonstrate how emotion and reflection can effectively combine to create knowledge. Rejecting an academic approach, the style is discursive and entertaining, indeed openly critical of the "tedium" of knowledge management literature. Generally structured around a collection of easy-to-read, thematically connected anecdotes of between 700 to 1500 words, each section ends with a series of punchlines or implications for the reader to consider.

Knowledge Entrepreneur: How Your Business Can Create, Manage, and Profit from Intellectual Capital

Colin Coulson-Thomas

London: Kogan Page, 2003
240pp, ISBN: 978-0-7494-3946-0

Knowledge Entrepreneur examines theories in knowledge management, and shows how to boost revenues and profit by significantly improving the performance of existing activities and creating new offerings that generate additional income. It deals with problems and makes suggestions for practical, knowledge-based, job-support tools, and provides features such as lists of possible commercial ventures, detailed checklists that can be used for identifying and analyzing opportunities for knowledge entrepreneurship, and exercises for assessing entrepreneurial potential and possible products and services.

Knowledge Management and Organizational Competence

Ron Sanchez (editor)

Oxford: Oxford University Press, 2003
264pp, ISBN: 978-0-19-925928-1

     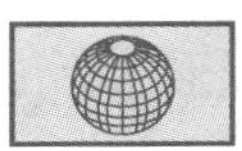   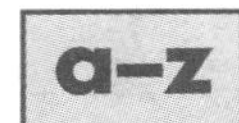

A collection of papers from notable management scholars offers a framework for understanding organizational knowledge and its role in building and leveraging competences. New insights into various kinds of knowledge that are of value to organizations are discussed.

Knowledge Management Casebook: Siemens Best Practices, 2nd ed

Thomas H. Davenport, Gilbert J. B. Probst

Munich, Germany: Publicis, 2002
336pp, ISBN: 978-3-89578-181-0

Siemens has been recognized as one of the top ten knowledge management companies worldwide. This case study describes the best of the corporation's practical applications and experiences. The six sections cover: knowledge strategy, knowledge transfer, communities of practice, added value of knowledge management, learning and knowledge management, and visualizing more of the value creation.

Knowledge Networking: Creating the Collaborative Enterprise

David J. Skyrme

Oxford: Butterworth-Heinemann, 1999
311pp, ISBN: 978-0-7506-3976-7

This book offers a comprehensive overview of the strategic application of knowledge management within global corporations. With an emphasis on good leadership practice, it shows how companies have successfully leveraged the knowledge dispersed and fragmented throughout their companies to deliver organizational benefits and create new opportunities. It gives guidance on how to innovate quickly and exploit human networks, wherever they are based, and provides examples of how global companies can harness employees' accumulated knowledge and apply it to specific problems. It also contains toolkits and checklists for individual, team, organizational, and collaborative enterprises.

Leading Organizational Learning: Harnessing the Power of Knowledge

Marshall Goldsmith, Howard Morgan, Alexander J. Ogg (editors)

New York: Jossey-Bass, 2004
368pp, ISBN: 978-0-7879-7218-9

This book brings together contributions from experts in the field of organizational learning and knowledge management including Fons Trompenaars, Jon Katzenbach, Margaret J. Wheatley, and many others. These are grouped in five sections covering: the challenges and dilemmas of knowledge management; processes for managing knowledge and learning; the role of leaders in the knowledge organization; changes for the future, including the development of new ideas and case studies and examples.

Learning to Fly: Practical Lessons from One of the World's Leading Knowledge Companies, 2nd ed

Chris Collinson, Geoff Parcell

Chichester, UK: Capstone, 2004
332pp, ISBN: 978-1-84112-124-6

Based on the authors' experiences at BP, as a detailed case study, the book sets out to provide a practical, jargon-free overview of what knowledge is, how it can be harnessed, stored, and—most importantly—shared throughout any organization. This updated edition includes a CD-ROM.

Managing Knowledge: An Essential Reader

Stephen Little, Paul Quintas, Tim Ray (editors)

Basingstoke, UK: Palgrave, 2002
400pp, ISBN: 978-0-7619-7213-6

This book provides general background on the major themes in the field. A critical overview of the theories is offered, and the four parts cover: creating knowledge; resources and capabilities; communicating and sharing knowledge; and knowledge, innovation and human resources. Some reprints of significant articles and papers are collected together to give key theoretical work, and critical case studies are included as well as newly written chapters.

Managing Knowledge: Building Blocks for Success

Gilbert Probst, Steffen Raub, Kai Romhardt

Chichester, UK: Wiley, 1999
368pp, ISBN: 978-0-471-99768-9

Based on many years of research and experience, the ideas put forward in *Managing Knowledge* result from intensive collaboration with many major organizations. The book provides a road map of the most important stages of the knowledge management process; it presents a wide range of knowledge techniques, assesses their possible effects, and addresses key questions faced by managers. It is illustrated throughout with examples from managerial practice and is designed to prompt critical thinking and assist practitioners to chart their own path through the knowledge jungle.

Managing Knowledge Security: Strategies for Protecting Your Company's Intellectual Assets

Kevin C. Desouza

London: Kogan Page, 2007
200pp, ISBN: 978-0-7494-4961-2

Managing Knowledge Security gives a clear and inclusive perspective on how to secure the physical and intangible assets owned by a business. It explains how vital it is to take measures to retain key assets and to avoid data and knowledge falling into the hands of competitors, and offers practical strategies and real-life examples from companies such as Hewlett Packard, Microsoft, Google, Boeing and Amazon.

Managing Knowledge Work, 2nd ed

Sue Newell et al.

Basingstoke, UK: Palgrave, 2009
288pp, ISBN: 978-0-230-52201-5

This textbook looks at the nature and management of knowledge work in a wide range of organizational contexts. The introduction examines the nature of knowledge and the shifts in society that have made knowledge work central to wealth creation. The book covers the knowledge intensive organization, the importance of teamworking in knowledge creation, the impact of HRM policies in knowledge work, the relationship between knowledge and information and communication technologies (ICT), the value and management of communities of practice and the link between knowledge management and innovation. A final section draws conclusions about the key challenges in the management of knowledge work. Case studies are included.

Organizing Knowledge: An Introduction to Managing Access to Information, 4th ed

Jennifer Rowley, John Farrow

Aldershot, UK: Gower Publishing, 2008
392pp, ISBN: 978-0-7546-4431-6

This is a standard text on knowledge organization and retrieval. The different sections focus on: the nature of information and knowledge and their incorporation into documents; the use of electronic databases; the range of tools for accessing information resources, including indexing, classification, and catalogs; and the electronic contexts in which knowledge can be stored.

Profiting from Intellectual Capital: Extracting Value from Innovation

Patrick H. Sullivan

Chichester, UK: Wiley, 2001
384pp, ISBN: 978-0-471-41747-7

This volume provides examples from companies' best practices in knowledge management, with a focus on getting value from intellectual capital. The book offers an overview of essential knowledge-management concepts and detailed coverage of strategies for measuring, monitoring, and assigning value to existing knowledge assets. It provides practical advice for those familiar with the basics of knowledge generation and information sharing.

Sharing Expertise: Beyond Knowledge Management

Mark S. Akerman, Volkmar Pipek, Volker Wulf (editors)

Cambridge, Massachusetts: MIT Press, 2003
432pp, ISBN: 978-0-262-01195-2

A new approach to knowledge management (KM), "expertise sharing," focuses on what can be gained from the cognitive, social and organizational, or human expertise aspect in knowledge work. A literature review, overview, and background are provided, and expertise sharing in organizational settings is explored empirically. The tools, technology, and architectures designed for expertise management are also discussed.

Smart Things to Know about Knowledge Management

Thomas M. Koulopoulos, Carl Frappaolo

Smart Series
Oxford: Capstone, 1999
240pp, ISBN: 978-1-84112-041-6

In the new economy, say the authors, knowledge management is vital. It allows companies to

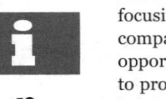

leverage their most precious assets, collective know-how, talent, and experience, and only by focusing on these valuable resources can companies handle new market challenges and opportunities. The aim of this book, therefore, is to provide a framework for practical action, helping people to understand knowledge management and how it can benefit their organization, to position it at the heart of their business, to measure success in a knowledge-based economy, and to become the knowledge management champions in their organizations.

The Wealth of Knowledge: Intellectual Capital and the Twenty-First Century Organization

Thomas A. Stewart

New York: Currency/Doubleday, 2001
400pp, ISBN: 978-0-385-50072-2

This book builds on Stewart's 1997 book *Intellectual Capital*, which outlined organizational assets in a knowledge economy. It analyzes corporate practices in managing intellectual capital, providing the basics of knowledge organization theory and real-world examples. A four-step process is used to describe the day-to-day management of knowledge and how it can improve productivity and profitability.

Working Knowledge: How Organizations Manage What They Know

Thomas H. Davenport, Laurence Prusak

Boston, Massachusetts: Harvard Business School Press, 2000
240pp, ISBN: 978-1-57851-301-7

The authors break down knowledge management into four activities—accessing, generating, embedding, and transferring—and identify the key processes involved in each. They discuss skills and techniques, knowledge-management technologies, and best practices from their work with leading companies. They also emphasize the importance of corporate culture in fostering knowledge creation and sharing.

MAGAZINES

Knowledge Management Review

Melcrum
First Floor, Chelsea Reach, 79–89 Lots Road, London, SW10 0RN, UK
T: +44 (0) 20 7795 2205
F: +44 (0) 20 7795 2156
www.melcrum.com/products/journals/kmr.shtml
ISSN: 1369-7633

This journal provides the latest trends, techniques, and ideas in knowledge management through corporate case studies, practitioners' insights, and practical articles.

JOURNALS

European Journal of Innovation Management

Emerald
60/62 Toller Lane, Bradford, West Yorkshire, BD8 9BY, UK
T: +44 (0) 1274 777 700
F: +44 (0) 1274 785 200
www.emeraldinsight.com/1460–1060.htm
ISSN: 1460-1060

The journal aims to be a European forum for information and knowledge in the field of innovation. It publishes high-quality papers by both academics and industrialists, which capture leading developments, both in practice and theory.

International Journal of Entrepreneurship and Innovation Management

Inderscience Enterprises
World Trade Center Building, 29 route de Pre-Bois, Case Postale 896, 1215, Geneva, 15, Switzerland
T: +44 (0) 1234 240515
F: +41 22 791 08 85
www.inderscience.com/ijeim
ISSN: 1368-275X

IJEIM provides a source of information and an international platform for the field of entrepreneurship and innovation management, business corporate strategy, and government economic policy. The journal publishes theory-based empirical papers, review papers, case studies, conference reports, relevant reports and news, book reviews, and briefs.

International Journal of Innovation Management

World Scientific
www.worldscinet.com/ijim/ijim.shtml
ISSN: 1363-9196

The *International Journal of Innovation Management* (*IJIM*) is a quarterly publication dedicated to promoting academic research and management practice in the field of innovation management. It offers papers which integrate the management of technological, market, and organizational innovation. Contributions are based on original empirical research, as well as the observations of experienced managers, providing a platform for academics, practicing managers, and consultants.

Journal of Knowledge Management

Emerald
60/62 Toller Lane, Bradford, West Yorkshire, BD8 9BY, UK
T: +44 (0) 1274 777 700
F: +44 (0) 1274 785 200
www.palgrave-journals.com/kmrp/index.html
ISSN: 1367-3270

This quarterly, peer-reviewed publication includes original research and case studies on strategies, tools, and techniques and technologies for knowledge management. It focuses on the identification of innovative knowledge management strategies and the application of theoretical concepts to real-world situations.

Knowledge Management: Research and Practice

Palgrave Macmillan
Houndmills, Basingstoke, Hampshire, RG21 6XS, UK
www.palgrave-journals.com/kmrp/index.html
ISSN: 1477-8238

KMRP is a forum for articles on all aspects of managing knowledge, organizational learning, intellectual capital, and knowledge economics, from both a theoretical and practical perspective. It places a particular emphasis on cross-disciplinary approaches, and a mix of technological, cultural, and motivational issues. Contributions from both academics and practitioners are welcomed.

INTERNET

International Knowledge Management Network

www.cibit.com

This site offers news, conference and seminar details, a discussion forum, an archive of literature resources, and weblinks. Visitors need to register to use parts of the site.

The KNOW Network

www.knowledgebusiness.com

This site contains a knowledge management library consisting of news, summaries of trends, market research, a diary, links, and a KM resources guide to publications, reviews, and websites. It also acts as the gateway to the KNOW Network—a group of leading knowledge organizations dedicated to the identification and exchange of best practice. Some of the site can only be accessed by joining the KNOW Network.

Knowledge Management Online Open Source

www.knowledge-management-online.com

This is a unique knowledge management online site offering open source KM education and open source KM consulting methods, tools and techniques.

Sveiby Knowledge Management Library

www.sveiby.com

This website provides access to Karl-Erik Sveiby's collected works on knowledge management, along with some of his favorite articles. The texts may be downloaded for research purposes and for personal viewing.

WWW Virtual Library on Knowledge Management

www.brint.com/km

This site provided by @brint.com offers full-text articles, book reviews, weblinks, and a discussion forum on various issues relating to knowledge management.

ORGANIZATIONS

Europe

International Knowledge Management Network

Secretariat, Kenniscentrum CIBIT, Arthur van Schendelstraat 570, PO Box 19210, Utrecht, 3501 AD, The Netherlands
T: +31 30 230 8900
F: +31 30 230 8999
E: info@cibit.nl
www.cibit.com

Set up in 1994, the network evolved from the experiences of the Dutch Knowledge Management Network and is now a worldwide organization for exchanging ideas and experiences in the knowledge management field.

The KNOW Network
4 St George's Road, Bedford, Bedfordshire, MK40 2LS, UK
T: +44 (0) 1234 314 197
F: +44 (0) 1234 308 824
E: info@knowledgebusiness.com
www.knowledgebusiness.com

A web-based network of some of the world's foremost knowledge-based organizations, the network is dedicated to the identification and exchange of best practice for competitive advantage.

USA

Knowledge Management Benchmark Association
USA
T: +1 281 440 5044
F: +1 281 440 6677
www.kmba.org

The Knowledge Management Benchmarking Association assembles knowledge management professionals from a variety of companies. KMBA conducts benchmarking studies to identify practices that improve the effectiveness of Knowledge Management activities. Its objective is use the competence of the association to gain process performance data and related best practices regarding knowledge management.

Knowledge Management Consortium International
c/o Joseph M. Firestone, 309 Yoakum Parkway, #603, Alexandria, VA 22304, USA
T: +1 703 461 8823
E: help@kmci.org

KMCI was founded in 1997 as an international professional association of knowledge management practitioners. Its purpose is to enhance an organization's capacity to detect problems, solve, or dispose of them, or share or present the solutions to others. It does this by enhancing organizational learning and innovation processes.

Knowledge Management Professional Society
PO Box 16444, Alexandria, VA 22302, USA
T: +1 757 460 6500
F: +1 757 460 6672
E: support@kmpro.org
www.kmpro.org

This is a non-profit association committed to promoting knowledge management worldwide. It is created by and for KM professionals actively engaged in implementation, change management, information management, innovation, human/intellectual capital strategy, and intangible asset valuation. One of its goals is to form alliances with people who share their vision, ethics, values, and beliefs.

BRIC

Asian Knowledge Management Association
Suite 2B, Max Share Centre, 367–373 King's Road, North Point, Hong Kong
T: +852 2512 0113
F: +852 2570 4207
www.akma.com.hk/index.php

AKMA is a forum for professional learning, networking, research, and cooperation among governments, academics, business practitioners, and knowledge workers in Asia-Pacific region. The association assists companies in Asia wanting to transform and gain competitive advantage in knowledge management.

Knowledge Management India
249 – F, Sector 18, Udyog Vihar, Gurgaon 122 015, India
T: +91 12 44 0140 6067
F: +91 12 44 014 080

KM India aims to create an environment that can generate economic value through knowledge and intellectual capital, within knowledge-based organizations and industries. Its intention is to create a better understanding of research and practical applications in KM.

Leadership

BOOKS

The Accidental Leader: What to Do When You're Suddenly in Charge
Harvey Robbins, Michael Finley
New York: Jossey-Bass, 2003
208pp, ISBN: 978-0-7879-6855-7

Written in an easy to read anecdotal style, this practical toolkit can act as a resource book and inspiration for those who have been thrust suddenly into a position of responsibility. Part one addresses self-management and areas such as coping with responsibility and meeting the team. Part two deals with technical issues such as planning and creating a learning environment; and part three explores people management.

Alpha Leadership: Tools for Business Leaders Who Want More from Life
Anne Deering, Robert Dilts, Julian Russell
Chichester, UK: Wiley, 2002
240pp, ISBN: 978-0-470-84483-0

This "how to" book is based on the authors' research that shows that the successful leader has three related strengths: anticipation, alignment, and action. Each of these areas is covered, and tools and frameworks are provided.

Arc of Ambition: Defining the Leadership Journey
James Champy, Nitin Nohria
Chichester, UK: Wiley, 2001
282pp, ISBN: 978-0-471-53020-6

Champy and Nohria explore the fascinating dimensions of ambition through the stories of dozens of achievers, past and present, who exemplify both its positive and negative qualities. From the quest of Giuseppe Garibaldi for a unified Italy to the vision of Alfred Sloan for General Motors, which changed management practice forever, and the boyhood dream of Michael Dell to have a building with a flag out front, ambition comes in many guises. Champy and Nohria outline how it can be channeled toward creative and enriching endeavors at the personal, organizational, and even national levels.

Are Leaders Born or Are They Made? The Case of Alexander the Great
Manfred F. R. Kets de Vries, Elisabet Engellau
London: Karnac Books, 2004
128pp, ISBN: 978-1-85575-315-0

In this text, the life story of Alexander the Great and how he created and administered an empire that spanned most of the ancient world is examined. The authors go on to analyze his personality and behavior from a clinical perspective, examining the psychological forces that shaped his character, the leadership qualities that brought him success, and his strengths and weaknesses as a leader. Finally, the key leadership lessons that contemporary leaders in business and politics can learn from his life are identified.

The Art and Science of Leadership, 5th ed
Afsaneh Nahavandi
Harlow, UK: Prentice Hall, 2009
272pp, ISBN: 978-0-13-208995-1

The author presents a broad overview of the field of leadership, focusing on the history of leadership theory, popular current trends, and prospects for the future. This edition includes expanded coverage of personality traits, abilities, values, and skills. Contingency models of leadership are also examined, and separate chapters cover participative management and team leadership, change-oriented leadership, and strategic leadership. The book is intended for students of leadership and each chapter includes details of relevant research, examples of innovative practices, ethical dilemmas faced by leaders, and case studies of real-life leaders.

The Center for Creative Leadership Handbook of Leadership Development, 3rd ed
Ellen Van Velsor, Cynthia D. McCauley, Marian N. Ruderman (editors)
New York: Jossey-Bass, 2010
528pp, ISBN: 978-0-470-38739-9

This handbook explores the essence of leadership development, reveals how individuals can effectively enhance their leadership skills, and demonstrates what organizations can do to help build leaders and leadership capacity. Part one focuses on individual leader development. Part two explores leader development across gender and race, cross-cultural issues, global roles, and lifelong adult development. Part three looks at organizational capacity for leadership and development.

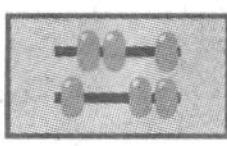

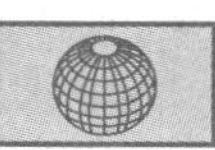

Complete Leadership: A Practical Guide for Developing Your Leadership Talents

Susan Bloch, Philip Whiteley

Harlow, UK: Pearson Education, 2003
192pp, ISBN: 978-1-84304-025-5

This book is a personal coaching manual with questionnaires, guides and case studies for readers to evaluate and improve their leadership style. The book covers the following: how your style affects your staff, how it affects the organization, looking at your leadership type, how your team views you, self-awareness, personal development and progress.

Connective Leadership: Managing in a Changing World

Jean Lipman-Blumen

Oxford: Oxford University Press, 2000
432pp, ISBN: 978-0-19-513469-8

A new form of leadership is needed in an era of increasing interdependence and diversity, the author suggests. She reviews the psychological and historical foundations of leadership and develops a new model of connective leadership based around nine behavioral facets. The book draws on the results of qualitative interview research and quantitative survey research on achieving styles, conducted among over 5,000 leaders. A final section examines how the connective leadership model relates to new organizational structures and the wider social context.

Develop Your Leadership Skills

John Adair

Creating Success Series
London: Kogan Page, 2007
89pp, ISBN: 978-0-7494-4919-3

Develop your Leadership Skills is John Adair's most accessible title on leadership. Providing a useful range of exercises and checklists, it helps to boost confidence levels, and act as a guide to leadership excellence.

Effective Strategic Leadership

John Adair

Indianapolis, Indiana: PanMacmillan, 2002
352pp, ISBN: 978-0-330-48787-0

This readable and practical analysis of the nature of strategic leadership starts from a historical (ancient world) and military perspective, defining the different types of leadership with specific reference to the strategic variety. The second part of the book looks at the practical aspects of becoming a strategic leader, with many suggestions, exercises and a large number of short case studies of leaders through the ages from all walks of life.

First, Break All the Rules

Marcus Buckingham, Curt Coffman

London: Simon & Schuster, 1999
256pp, ISBN: 978-1-4165-0266-1

This book is based directly on a huge research project into the behavior of managers and how they conduct business matters to achieve success. Acknowledging that good managers are pivotal to realizing a company's potential, the authors cite instances of successful employee selection and development techniques that reflect the quality of excellent management.

The Five Most Important Questions You Will Ever Ask about Your Organization, 3rd ed

Peter F. Drucker

New York: Jossey-Bass, 2008
144pp, ISBN: 978-0-470-22756-5

This assesses Peter Drucker's five questions: What is our mission? Who is our customer? What does the customer value? What are our results? What is our plan? It provides a response to these key areas by five prominent thought leaders, and offers a close analysis of what drives their organizations.

Focus on Leadership: Servant-Leadership for the 21st Century

Larry C. Spears, Michele Lawrence (editors)

Chichester, UK: Wiley, 2001
400pp, ISBN: 978-0-471-41162-8

Focus on Leadership expands on Robert K. Greenleaf's idea of a servant-leader, an individual who seeks to improve and enhance the workplace and the community rather than focusing on company profit. This book offers writings from some of the leading thinkers on management and leadership, including Margaret Wheatley, Danah Zohar, Warren Bennis, and Stephen Covey.

The Future of Leadership: Today's Top Leadership Thinkers Speak to Tomorrow's Leaders

Warren Bennis, Gretchen M. Spreitzer, Thomas G. Cummings (editors)

New York: Jossey-Bass, 2001
320pp, ISBN: 978-0-7879-5567-0

Nineteen essays written by some of the leading thinkers in management today. The essays are arranged in the sections: including the leader of the future; how leaders stay on top of their game; insights from young leaders; and some closing thoughts. Contributors include Warren Bennis, Edward E. Lawler III, Charles Handy, Thomas H. Davenport, Tom Peters, Jeffrey Sonnenfeld, Philip Slater, and James O'Toole.

Geeks and Geezers: How Era Values and Defining Moments Shape Leaders

Warren G. Bennis, Robert J. Thomas

Boston, Massachusetts: Harvard Business School Press, 2002
224pp, ISBN: 978-1-57851-582-0

A study of two groups of leaders is presented: geeks—young leaders under 35 —and geezers—older leaders over 70. The authors interviewed both groups on their experiences of leadership and success to gain an insight into how they were shaped by the times in which they grew up and to identify the qualities that enabled them to become successful leaders. Brief biographies of geezers and geeks are included.

Improving Leadership in Nonprofit Organizations

Ronald E. Riggio, Sarah Smith Orr (editors)

New York: Jossey-Bass, 2008
320pp, ISBN: 978-0-470-40179-8

Leadership issues and challenges for nonprofit organizations are discussed by various authors, including Jay Conger. Areas covered include future challenges, ethical challenges, board leadership, pay in nonprofit organizations, succession, and assessment.

In Search of Leaders

Hilarie Owen

Chichester, UK: Wiley, 2000
192pp, ISBN: 978-0-471-49197-2

Leadership is discussed as a potential that all individuals have and can develop, rather than as a phenomenon based on hierarchical authority or a heroic chairman. The author offers a three-stage model for a journey of self-discovery. She outlines the "seven essences" of leadership and explores transformational ideas about leadership to help individuals develop their own inner leadership potential.

Inner Leadership: Realize Your Self-Leading Potential

Simon Smith

People Skills for Professionals Series
London: Nicholas Brealey Publishing, 2000
256pp, ISBN: 978-1-85788-271-1

The concept of the "leader in each of us" is explored here through case studies, business examples, and exercises. The author presents a four-stage model (REAL) as a method of reaching individual potential. The four stages are: recognizing the depth and diversity of resources and qualities; exploring the parts of yourself which influence decisions and actions; actualizing qualities and values to achieve leadership goals; and leading yourself.

Inspiring Leadership: Learning from Great Leaders

John Adair

London: Nicholas Brealey Publishing, 2002
368pp, ISBN: 978-1-85418-207-4

This book discusses some of the great leaders in history, aiming to identify the main lessons of leadership that can be learnt from them. Each section takes a particular theme, illustrated by one or more individuals. Amongst the many individuals described are Socrates, Lao Tzu, Jesus Christ, Alexander the Great, Churchill, Machiavelli, Nelson, Shackleton, Margaret Thatcher, and Nelson Mandela.

John Adair's 100 Greatest Ideas for Effective Leadership and Management

John Adair

Chichester, UK: Capstone, 2002
192pp, ISBN: 978-1-84112-140-6

Adair offers accessible advice relating leadership to areas including time management, leadership functions, skills and team management, creativity and innovation, and communication. These are organized under the headings: getting your act together; understanding leadership; performing as a leader; thinking as a leader; power through the people; and getting the message across.

Lead to Succeed: Creating Entrepreneurial Organisations

Colin Turner

London: Texere Publishing, 2002
240pp, ISBN: 978-1-58799-124-0

  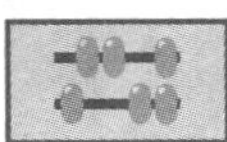      

In this book the author puts forward his ideas on creating an entrepreneurial culture in established organizations. Part one examines the essential attributes of entrepreneurial leaders and how the OILS (opportunity, innovation, leadership, and service) of entrepreneurship can be applied. In part two the principles and practices of entrepreneurial leadership are outlined. Finally it looks at creating entrepreneurial people, culture, customer ethos and opportunities.

Leadership: Theory, Application, Skill Development, 4th ed

Robert N. Lussier, Christopher F. Achua

Cincinnati, Ohio: South-Western College Publishing, 2009
544pp, ISBN: 978-0-324-59655-7

By providing new, engaging ways to learn, including role-playing and using the internet for readings and exercises, this textbook seeks to expand the user's knowledge about leadership. It is divided into three sections that focus on individual, team, and organizational leadership.

Leadership: Theory and Practice, 5th ed

Peter G. Northouse

London: Sage Publications, 2010
416pp, ISBN: 978-1-4129-4161-7

This book is a major source of insights and perspectives for all those studying on leadership courses in both the business and education sectors. It is also an excellent source for school leaders and educators who want to increase their understanding of all the key aspects of leadership.

Leadership and the New Science, 3rd ed

Margaret J. Wheatley

San Francisco, California: Berrett-Koehler, 2006
218pp, ISBN: 978-1-57675-344-6

This updated version of the original 1992 title discusses the effect of quantum physics on the way we organize our lives, how biology and chemistry influence the way we live, and how leadership is affected by science and chaos theory.

The Leadership Challenge, 4th ed

James M. Kouzes, Barry Z. Posner

San Francisco, California: Jossey-Bass, 2008
416pp, ISBN: 978-0-7879-8492-2

This key title aims to help people to further their abilities to lead others to get "extraordinary" things done, presenting principles and practices that are based in solid research. It describes the five practices of exemplary leadership, discussing the characteristics that people most admire in leaders, the motives of leaders, how leaders foster collaboration and create a climate for high performance, and how leadership practices can be learnt by anyone.

The Leadership Crash Course: How to Create Personal Leadership Value, 2nd ed

Paul Taffinder

London: Kogan Page, 2006
192pp, ISBN: 978-0-7494-4638-3

The Leadership Crash Course is designed to help readers develop their skills and effectiveness. Split into seven sections, this book aims to build personal capability.

Leadership in Organizations: Current Issues and Key Trends, 2nd ed

John Storey (editor)

London: Routledge, 2010
352pp, ISBN: 978-0-415-31033-8

This study not only strongly criticizes many currently available leadership training and development approaches, but also suggests alternatives. Areas covered include post-transformational leadership, leadership competencies, leader integrity, leadership learning, corporate university solutions, public sector leadership development, leadership and business strategy, and leadership career development.

Leadership on the Line: Staying Alive through the Dangers of Leading

Ronald A. Heifetz, Marty Linsky

Boston, Massachusetts: Harvard Business School Press, 2002
256pp, ISBN: 978-1-57851-437-3

The book describes the difficulties, risks and rewards of leadership, and discusses some strategies for surviving the dangers. It also shows how a leader may manage his or her own personal needs and vulnerabilities, and how the spirit may be sustained during difficult times. Examples are drawn from politics, business, and family life.

The Leadership Pipeline: How to Build the Leadership-Powered Company

Ram Charan, Stephen Drotter, James Noel

New York: Jossey-Bass, 2001
256pp, ISBN: 978-0-7879-5852-7

The authors show how to identify future leaders, assess their competence, plan their development, and measure the results. They also show how this process may be integrated with succession planning, so that the supply of leaders at all levels may be constantly renewed. Six critical stages in the leadership development pipeline are identified and separately addressed.

Leadership—The Inner Side of Greatness: A Philosophy for Leaders

Peter Koestenbaum

New York: Jossey-Bass, 2002
384pp, ISBN: 978-0-7879-5956-2

The author explores how to be an exceptional and passionate leader in today's complex world. He presents his Leadership Diamond Model that challenges managers to transform their thinking and approach everything with fresh effectiveness. Insights into the characteristics great leaders have in common—vision, reality, ethics, and courage—are presented and strategies that all managers can use are described.

Leading at the Edge: Leadership Lessons from the Extraordinary Saga of Shackleton's Antarctic Expedition

Dennis N. T. Perkins et al.

New York: AMACOM, 2000
268pp, ISBN: 978-0-8144-0543-7

This book records the adventures of Sir Ernest Shackleton on his Antarctic expedition and examines through the lens of business the extraordinary leadership skills he displayed. Ten lessons on what it takes to be a great leader are drawn from the account. Contemporary business case studies further illustrate leadership at the edge, and the behaviors, attitudes, and ways of thinking about life that help individuals to realize their full potential as leaders are discussed.

Leading Beyond the Walls

Frances Hesselbein, Marshall Goldsmith, Iain Somerville (editors)

San Francisco, California: Jossey-Bass, 2001
320pp, ISBN: 978-0-7879-5555-7

Twenty-nine of the world's leading management thinkers explore the need for a new paradigm in leadership. In today's fast-paced global society, leaders must be adept at establishing diverse partnerships, alliances, and networks by building and maintaining relationships both within and outside their own organization. *Leading Beyond the Walls* brings together Peter Drucker, Stephen Covey, Peter Senge, Jim Collins, Noel Tichy, Regina Herzlinger, C. K. Prahalad, Sally Helgesen, and other thought leaders to describe new ways of building relationships, new approaches to strategy and marketing, new models of employee relations, and other innovative ways of thinking and acting.

Leading the Professionals: How to Inspire and Motivate Professional Service Teams

Geoff Smith

London: Kogan Page, 2004
256pp, ISBN: 978-0-7494-3996-5

This book supplies practical advice for those who lead professionals. It suggests an encouraging and supportive approach to meet the challenges of managing highly qualified or creative individuals and of developing high performing teams. Smith reviews keys to success such as objectives and values, and communication and coaching, and suggests ways to resolve performance problems and conflicts.

Leading the Way: Three Truths from the Top Companies for Leaders

Robert Gandossy, Marc Effron

Chichester, UK: Wiley, 2004
224pp, ISBN: 978-0-471-48301-4

Three leadership truths are identified and these are said to be the fundamental building blocks used by top companies to build a sustainable pipeline of great leaders. Advice is given on identifying the leadership capabilities necessary for your organization and the process for building them, as well as considering the challenges, opportunities, and solutions that lie ahead.

A Manager's Guide to Leadership

Mike Pedler, John Burgoyne, Tom Boydell

Maidenhead, UK: McGraw-Hill, 2004
284pp, ISBN: 978-0-07-710423-8

This is a practical self-development guide that is designed to help managers meet key leadership

tasks and challenges. Part one helps you establish your leadership strengths and weaknesses and consider personal goals. Part two examines the leadership practices of power, risk taking, critical questioning, facilitation, and networking. Part three helps you develop your leadership skills by addressing the challenges to be found in the workplace.

Managing the Dream: Reflections on Leadership and Change

Warren G. Bennis

Cambridge, Massachusetts: Perseus Books Group, 2000
317pp, ISBN: 978-0-7382-0332-4

This book contains over ten of the author's most significant essays on leadership. The majority of the essays concentrate on how to make leadership possible and how to cope with change, while others discuss the character and ethics of a good leader.

The New Leaders: Transforming the Art of Leadership

Daniel Goleman, Richard E. Boyatzis, Annie McKee

Amsterdam: Time Warner, 2003
336pp, ISBN: 978-0-7515-3381-1

Psychologist Daniel Goleman is best known for his bestseller Emotional Intelligence, after which EI became a buzzword for many in the world of management. Goleman argues that our self-awareness, personal motivation, and ability to relate to others are more important than the narrow 'raw' intelligence which is measured by intelligence tests. He here unites with two academics to explore the consequences of emotional intelligence for leaders and organizations.

The Inspirational Leader: How to Motivate, Encourage, and Achieve Success

John Adair

London: Kogan Page, 2009
208pp, ISBN: 978-0-7494-5478-4

This book explores the nature and practice of leadership and reinforces the author's argument that leaders are not born but made. It takes the form of conversations between a young chief executive and the author. Each aspect of leadership is studied and discussed so that the key skills are revealed for anyone to adopt and use.

On Becoming a Leader, 2nd ed

Warren Bennis

Cambridge, Massachusetts: Perseus Books Group, 2003
256pp, ISBN: 978-0-7382-0817-6

In this key title, updated for the new millennium, the author outlines the characteristics that determine whether a person will become a leader and, using key figures from a range of business areas as examples, the various ways companies treat such people.

Practicing Servant-Leadership: Succeeding Through Trust, Bravery, and Forgiveness

Larry C. Spears, Michele Lawrence (editors)

New York: Jossey-Bass, 2004
336pp, ISBN: 978-0-7879-7455-8

Practicing Servant-Leadership brings together a group of exceptional thinkers, who offer a compendium of new ideas on bringing servant-leadership into the daily lives of business leaders. Each contributor focuses on their area of expertise, and explore how servant-leadership works in the real world, using examples from a variety of organizations such as businesses, nonprofit organizations, churches, schools, foundations, and leadership organizations.

Primal Leadership: Realizing the Power of Emotional Intelligence

Daniel Goleman, Richard Boyatzis, Annie McKee

Boston, Massachusetts: Harvard Business School Press, 2002
352pp, ISBN: 978-1-57851-486-1

The authors describe six styles that account for all critical management behavior: visionary, coaching, affiliative, democratic, pace-setting, and commanding. Good leaders use different styles according to the situation. They explain that the importance of these styles is that the right style used with the right team will generate "good feelings" and that style is a critical factor, not only in managing and leading but also in generating organizational profits. The book is based on studies of nearly 4,000 executives.

Ruthless Leader: Three Classics of Strategy and Power

Alistair McAlpine (editor)

Chichester, UK: Wiley, 2000
272pp, ISBN: 978-0-471-37247-9

The texts of three classic works on leadership make up this compilation: *The Prince* by Nicolò Machiavelli, *The Servant* by Alistair McAlpine, and *The Art of War* by Sun Tzu. The introduction places these texts in their contemporary contexts, and compares and contrasts them, drawing out their major themes and demonstrating their application to modern business organizations.

The Smartest Guys in the Room: The Amazing Rise and Scandalous Fall of Enron

Bethany McLean, Peter Elkind

New York: Portfolio, 2004
464pp, ISBN: 978-1-59184-053-4

Written by two *Fortune* journalists, this book attempts to lay bare the extraordinary story behind Enron's collapse in 2001. A tale of jaw-dropping corporate arrogance, it shows the impact of incompetence and greed on the notion of corporate governance.

The Snowball: Warren Buffett and the Business of Life, updated ed

Alice Schroeder

New York: Bantam Books, 2009
832pp, ISBN: 978-0-553-38461-1

This examines in detail the life, career, and financial success story of the revered investment guru.

Test Your Leadership Skills

Brian O'Neill

Test Yourself Series
London: Profile Books, 2000
95pp, ISBN: 978-0-340-78208-8

This book is intended to enable you to: discover your potential as a visionary, integration, or fulfillment type of leader; assess your leadership style—as expert, friend, guide, hero, or driver; fit your leadership to what your followers and organization require; develop outstanding teams; and anticipate future demands and opportunities.

The Transparency Edge: How Credibility Can Make or Break You in Business

Barbara Pagano, Elizabeth Pagano

Maidenhead, UK: McGraw-Hill, 2005
224pp, ISBN: 978-0-07-145884-9

This text argues that, in line with a growing culture of transparency in business, the demand for clear and transparent leadership is becoming a priority. The authors demonstrate the benefits of clear and open business policy and transparent leadership practices. This book helps leaders to develop the "transparent edge" through nine key behavioral patterns that build and enhance credibility for leaders and consequently for business.

The Trusted Leader: Bringing Out the Best in Your People and Your Company

Robert Galford, Anne Seibold Drapeau

New York: Free Press, 2003
272pp, ISBN: 978-0-7432-3539-6

The importance of trust within organizations is outlined, and the difference between being trustworthy and building trust is explained. The characteristics and competencies of the trusted leader are established, and the identification and application of the tools of trusted leaders are examined through a series of interactive exercises and diagnostic tools.

21 Leaders for the 21st Century: How Innovative Leaders Manage in the Digital Age

Fons Trompenaars, Charles Hampden-Turner

Chichester, UK: Wiley, 2005
250pp, ISBN: 978-1-84112-463-6

Leaders of global corporations, it is argued, are beset by a series of dilemmas, pairs of conflicting propositions that clamor for their attention. Successful leadership depends on the capacity to integrate these demands and create powerful strategies that unite them. 21 corporate giants reveal their personal experiences of business dilemmas and these are used to show how managers understand and use the seven dilemmas of leadership.

Up Your Business: 7 Steps to Fix, Build, or Stretch Your Organization, 2nd ed

Dave Anderson

Chichester, UK: Wiley, 2007
320pp, ISBN: 978-0-470-06856-4

  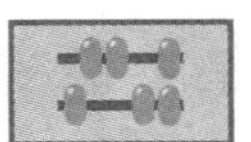   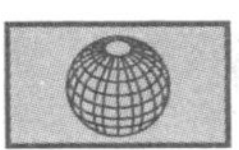   

Achieving the highest organizational performance is about quality leadership; and without the right team, vision, strategy, and values are worthless. This book encourages reflection on leadership style and strategy and discusses areas such as recruitment, culture, employee development, goal setting, and growth. Written from a nonacademic, anti-intellectual stance, it is based on real-world experience.

Why Most Things Fail: Evolution, Extinction and Economics

Paul Ormerod
Hoboken, New Jersey: Wiley, 2007
272pp, ISBN: 978-0-470-08919-4

In what could be a wake-up call for many senior leaders, this book tackles one of the great unspoken truths of the business world: most things do not work. Drawing on the author's experience as a professor of economics and reflecting on the raft of scandals witnessed since the fall of Enron, this book sets out to equip readers with the knowledge they need to avoid a similar fate.

JOURNALS

Harvard Business Review (HBR)

Harvard Business School Press
60 Harvard Way, Boston, MA 02163, USA
T: +1 617 783 7500
F: +1 (617) 783-7555
hbr.harvardbusiness.org
ISSN: 0017-8012

The *HBR* is a leading magazine for business leaders and senior executives that emphasizes current best practice and the application of leading edge research to business problems. Coverage is wide-ranging with a strong focus on leadership and strategy. Each issue includes feature articles written by experts and an interview with a business leader.

Leadership and Organization Development Journal

Emerald
60/62 Toller Lane, Bradford, West Yorkshire, BD8 9BY, UK
T: +44 (0) 1274 777 700
F: +44 (0) 1274 785 200
www.emeraldinsight.com/0143-7739.htm
ISSN: 0143-7739

This bimonthly journal for business leaders publishes articles that describe effective practice in strategy and leadership, as well as new theories that have the potential to advance the art of strategy development and its implementation.

Leadership Quarterly

Elsevier
PO Box 211, 1000 AE Amsterdam, The Netherlands
T: +31 20 485 3757
F: +31 20 485 3432
www.elsevier.com/locate/leaqua
ISSN: 1048-9843

Published four times each year, this journal analyzes the many factors that contribute to outstanding leadership. Executive managers and upper-level administrators will find the information presented in this journal will enhance and improve their leadership skills. It provides current information on the latest in leadership research. There is also an annual review of leadership topics.

INTERNET

12 Manage

www.12manage.com/i_l.html

Under the Leadership link, this site offers information, forums and multiple links on leadership, methods, models, and theory.

Forbes.com

www.forbes.com/leadership

Under the Leadership link, this site offers articles, special reports, links, networks, a question and answer platform, and newsletters on leadership and related topics.

Leader to Leader

www.leadertoleader.org

This site offers access to a contents listing from the *Drucker Foundation Journal* and selected articles written by today's leading thinkers from the private, public, and social sectors.

Leaders Direct

www.leadersdirect.com

Offering extensive tips for managers and leaders, this site focuses on the nature and development of leadership.

weLEAD, Incorporated

www.leadingtoday.org

weLEAD is a nonprofit organization that believes that everyone is capable of being a great leader. The site includes an online magazine, tips, and book reviews. Extra services, including access to an article archive and related useful links, are available for members.

ORGANIZATIONS

Europe

The Leadership Trust Foundation

Weston-under-Penyard, Ross-on-Wye, Herefordshire, HR9 7YH, UK
T: +44 (0) 1989 767 667
F: +44 (0) 1989 768 133
www.leadership.org.uk

The foundation provides courses, postgraduate education, grants, and bursaries for those in pursuit of excellence in leadership.

USA

Center for Creative Leadership

1 Leadership Place, PO Box 26300, Greensboro, NC 27438-6300, USA
T: +1 336 545 2810
F: +1 336 282 3284
E: info@leaders.ccl.org
www.ccl.org

The Center for Creative Leadership is a nonprofit educational institution that is an internationally recognized resource for understanding and expanding the leadership capabilities of individuals and organizations.

The Global Leadership Network

The Center for Corporate Citizenship at Boston College, 55 Lee Road, Chesnut Hill, MA 02467, USA
E: info@globalleadershipnetwork.org
www.globalleadershipnetwork.org

This is an initiative of The Center for Corporate Citizenship at Boston College USA, AccountAbility in London, UK, and Rever Consulting in Brazil.

The Greenleaf Centre for Servant Leadership

770 Pawtucket Drive, Westfield, IN 46074, USA
T: +1 317 669 8050
F: +1 317 669 8055
E: lyoder@greenleaf.org
www.greenleaf.org

This international, non-profit organization promotes the understanding and practice of servant leadership worldwide. The USA-based center also has a European counterpart (www.servantleadershipcenter.net) in The Netherlands.

BRIC

Brazilian Association for Leadership Development (ABDL)

Av. Prof. Almeida Prado, n° 532 prédio 31 térreo, Cidade Universitária Butantã, 05508-901 São Paulo, Brazil
T: +55 11 3719 1532
F: +55 11 3714 4222
E: abdl@abdl.org.br
www.abdl.org.br/article/view/2907

ABDL is an autonomous Brazilian organization and a member of the LEAD International network (Leadership for Environment and Development), with support from several domestic and international partners who believe in the future and in the methodology of building capacity for action. ABDL is a non-profit organization with the mission of articulating leadership for a sustainable world.

Businessworld (BW)

ABP Pvt. Ltd., 3rd Floor, Express Building, 9-10, Bahadur Shah Zafar Marg, New Delhi 110 002, India
T: +11 23 7021 7079
F: +11 23 702 077
E: bwonline@bworldmail.com
www.businessworld.in/index.php/BW-Leadership

Businessworld has a separate heading for BW-Leadership, through which it offers links, a forum, listings, coaching, and news on leadership in India.

China Executive Leadership Academy Pudong (CELAP)

99 Qiancheng Road, Pudong New Area, Shanghai 201204, China
T: +86 21 2828 8888
F: +86 21 5059 5935
www.celap.org.cn

CELAP is a Shanghai-based, national institution funded by the central government. It focuses on social improvement and economic development, and provides training for leaders from government and top executives from the business community.

  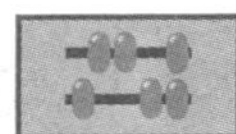      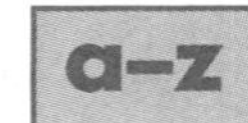

The Institute of Strategy, Leadership and Innovations

3, Volkhovskiy pereulok, Saint Petersburg, 199004, Russia
T: +7 812 323 8464
F: +7 812 329 3234
E: niim@gsom.pu.ru
www.gsom.pu.ru/en/niim/welcome

The institute is part of the Graduate School of Management at the St Petersburg State University, and focuses on research.

International

Association for Corporate Growth (ACG)

International Headquarters,
Suite 1, 1926 Waukegan Road,
Glenview,
IL 60025–1770, USA
T: +1 847 657 6730
F: +1 847 657 6819
E: acghq@tcag.com
www.acg.org

The ACG was founded in 1954 for professional managers involved in corporate growth and development in middle-market companies. The organization now has 5,000 members in the United States, Mexico, Canada, and the United Kingdom, and undertakes a range of activities including conferences. It also publishes a newsletter and offers networking opportunities.

Management Buyouts

BOOKS

The Art of M&A: A Merger Acquisition Buyout Guide, 4th ed

Stanley Foster Reed, Alexandra Reed Lajoux, H. Peter Nesvold

New York: McGraw-Hill, 2007
1100pp, ISBN: 978-0-07-140302-3

This book provides clear, in-depth answers and explanations on everything from the SEC rules and new tax guidelines to documents and key players . The authors give up-to-the-minute information on avoiding mishaps and completing the deal. It gives real-world insights through synopsis of dozens of landmark cases and includes sample forms and checklists.

Barbarians at the Gate: The Fall of RJR Nabisco, revised ed

Bryan Burrough, John Helyar

HarperBusiness
New York: HarperBusiness, 2009
624pp, ISBN: 978-0-06-165555-5

Now hailed as a classic, this is an expose of the largest-ever leveraged buyout, of RJR Nabisco by private equity group Kohlberg Kravis Roberts. Also made into a film, its portrayal of oversized egos and greed seemed to sum up an era, and contributed greatly to the negative image of private equity in the 1980s.

The Buyout Book: The Insider's Guide to Buying Your Own Company

Rick Rickersten et al.

New York: AMACOM, 2001
304pp, ISBN: 978-0-8144-0626-7

This book gives you the tools and strategies you need to lead a successful management buyout. It includes everything from how to select the company you want to buy, through due diligence issues and finding equity partners, to running the company when you succeed in your buyout.

Creating Value through Corporate Restructuring: Case Studies in Bankruptcies, Buyouts, and Breakups

Stuart C. Gilson

New York: Wiley, 2010
814pp, ISBN: 978-0-470-50352-2

Management buyouts are a common form of business restructuring. This collection of recent case studies from the United States and several other countries illustrates the real-world techniques and strategies that are common to all types of restructuring. It demystifies the complex financial issues surrounding business valuation and gives the reader a better understanding of the possibilities when dealing with corporate restructuring.

How to Do a Leveraged Buyout

Christopher Jansen

Morrisville, North Carolina: Lulu.com, 2008
492pp, ISBN: 978-1-4357-1832-6

This book provides a step-by-step guide to successfully completing the leveraged buyout of any business. It offers specific advice on the key processes, techniques, and concepts involved in acquiring a business and financing its purchase.

Management Buyout: A Guide for the Prospective Entrepreneur, 2nd ed

Ian Webb

Aldershot, UK: Gower Publishing, 1990
176pp, ISBN: 978-0-566-02810-6

This book provides an introduction to the process of achieving a successful buyout and considers the financial and legal issues involved. It reviews the development of the buyout market in the United Kingdom and considers the relevance of an entrepreneurial mindset to buyout situations. Five case studies are included.

The MBO Deal: Inside the Management Buyout

Richard Westcott

Harlow, UK: FT Prentice Hall, 2002
131pp, ISBN: 978-0-273-65920-4

Management teams undertaking an MBO need to understand the complexities and risks involved. This briefing provides a detailed insight into the workings of an MBO, the processes involved, the risks, the financing, the documentation, and the negotiation of the deal itself.

Private Equity and Management Buy-Outs

Mike Wright and Hans Bruining

Cheltenham, UK: Edward Elgar Publishing, 2008
528pp, ISBN: 978-1-84720-725-8

Private Equity and Management Buy-Outs provides a balanced view of the often polarized private equity debate. This careful and objective analysis of private equity in buy-out firms reviews the effects of this ownership transfer in terms of firm performance and survival, placing private equity in the broader context of its implications for value creation.

MAGAZINES

Buyouts Newsletter

Thomson Financial
195 Broadway, 10th Floor, New York, NY 10007, USA
T: +1 646 822 2000
F: +1 646 822 3230
www.buyoutsnews.com
ISSN: 1040-0990

Buyouts is a biweekly newsletter offering news, data, and analysis relating to the buyout industry. Listings of deals and funds in the United States are published quarterly. Readers can sign up for the newsletter on the website.

European Management Buyout Review

Chartered Institute of Public Finance and Accountancy
3 Robert Street, London, WC2N 6RL, UK
T: +44 (0) 20 7543 5600
F: +44 (0) 20 7543 5700
www.nottingham.ac.uk/business/cmbor/EBR.html

The *Review* focuses on trends in the European buyout market and covers 14 Western European countries.

Management Buyouts: A Quarterly Review

Chartered Institute of Public Finance and Accountancy
3 Robert Street, London, WC2N 6RL, UK
T: +44 (0) 20 7543 5600
F: +44 (0) 20 7543 5700
www.nottingham.ac.uk/business/cmbor/QR.html

This review includes feature articles on current topics as well as analyses of trends and reports on activity on the UK buyout scene.

JOURNALS

Journal of Management Studies

Blackwell Publishing
9600 Garsington Road, Oxford, OX4 2DQ, UK
T: +44 (0) 1865 791 100
F: +44 (0) 1865 791 347

  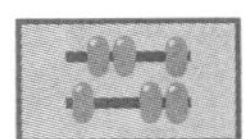      

www.wiley.com/bw/journal.asp?ref=0022-2380
ISSN: 0022-2380

JMS, published eight times each year, offers empirical studies, theoretical developments, and practical applications on innovation and excellence in management research organization theory and behavior, strategic and human resource management, cross-cultural comparisons of organizational effectiveness, and reviews of the latest publications in management studies.

Journal of Small Business and Enterprise Development

Emerald
60/62 Toller Lane, Bradford, West Yorkshire, BD8 9BY, UK
T: +44 (0) 1274 777 700
F: +44 (0) 1274 785 200
www.emeraldinsight.com/1462-6004.htm
ISSN: 1462-6004

The *JSBED* is a peer-reviewed journal that disseminates research findings and best practice and aims to bridge the gap between theory and practice in the field of small business and enterprise development. The journal contains articles, case studies, and book reviews, and is aimed at those responsible for the management of SMEs, those who provide support and assistance to entrepreneurs and owner-managers, and those involved in the development of enterprise policy.

Management Decisions

Emerald
60/62 Toller Lane, Bradford, West Yorkshire, BD8 9BY, UK
T: +44 (0) 1274 777 700
F: +44 (0) 1274 785 200
www.emeraldinsight.com/0025-1747.htm
ISSN: 0025-1747

Management Decisions consists of articles that analyze the link between management buyouts and the entrepreneurial process. It examines evidence to support the MBO-entrepreneur link, and that MBOs encourage entrepreneurial activity.

INTERNET

Are You Management Buyout Material?

www.cfo.com/Article?article=2117

Management buyouts are not for everyone. It takes the right team with appropriate backing. This checklist can help you determine whether you have what it takes to be successful.

Is a Management Buyout in Your Future?

www.imakenews.com/rcwmirus/e_article000017429.cfm

This article from the Mirus Online Newsletter describes management buyouts and identifies the characteristics of typical candidate companies. It outlines what each side is looking for and presents financing options that can be used.

Orchestrating a Management Buyout

www.southflorida.bizjournals.com/milwaukee/stories/1996/12/09/focus1.html

Describing the management buyout experience as a roller coaster ride, this article points out that perseverance is often a key element in completing the buyout successfully. It provides real-world examples of how obstacles can be overcome.

ORGANIZATIONS

Europe

The British Private Equity and Venture Capital Association

3 Clements Inn, London, WC2A 2AZ, UK
T: +44 (0) 20 7025 2950
F: +44 (0) 20 7025 2951
E: bvca@bvca.co.uk
www.bvca.co.uk/index.html

The BVCA is the industry body for the UK private equity and venture capital industry. It consists of 400 members and promotes the industry to entrepreneurs and investors, as well as provides services and best practice standards to its members.

Centre for Management Buyout Research (CMBOR)

Nottingham University Business School, Jubilee Campus, Wollaton Road, Nottingham, Nottinghamshire, NG8 1BB, UK
T: +44 (0) 115 951 5493
F: +44 (0) 115 951 5204
E: margaret.burdett@nottingham.ac.uk
www.nottingham.ac.uk/business/cmbor

CMBOR was founded by Barclays Private Equity Limited and Deloitte & Touche at the Nottingham University Business School in March 1986 to monitor and analyze management buyouts in a comprehensive and objective way. A database of MBOs in the United Kingdom and Europe has been developed, and quarterly reviews and research papers are published.

BRIC

India Venture Capital Association

301–302, Delhi Blue Apartments, Main Ring Road, New Delhi 110 029, India
T: +91 11 4162 8566
F: +91 11 4162 8863
E: info@indiavca.org
www.indiavca.org/abt_mission.aspx

Indian Venture Capital and Private Equity Association (IVCA) is a member-based, national organization that represents venture capital and private equity firms, promotes the industry within India and the rest of the world, and encourages investment in high-growth companies.

Mathematical Finance

BOOKS

Arbitrage Theory in Continuous Time, 2nd ed

Tomas Björk
Oxford Finance Series
Oxford, UK: Oxford University Press, 2004
466pp, ISBN: 978-0-19-927126-9

This is an introduction to the classical underpinnings of mathematical finance, which combines sound mathematical principles with economic applications. It focuses on the probabilistic theory of continuous arbitrage pricing of financial derivatives, including stochastic optimal control theory and Merton's fund separation theory. It includes a solved example for every new technique presented, and contains numerous exercises.

Aspects of Mathematical Finance

Marc Yor (editor)
Berlin: Springer, 2008
80pp, ISBN: 978-3-540-75258-5

This short but insightful treatment is based on a series of public lectures given in Paris by internationally renowned experts in mathematical finance, which promoted an understanding of the fundamental ideas, techniques and new tools of the financial industries. It develops topics such as risk measures, the notion of arbitrage, and dynamic models involving fundamental stochastic processes.

The Concepts and Practice of Mathematical Finance, 2nd ed

Mark S. Joshi
Mathematics, Finance and Risk Series
Cambridge, UK: Cambridge University Press, 2008
539pp, ISBN: 978-0-521-51408-8

Written by one of the most respected figures in mathematical finance, this book is an introduction to the discipline of mathematical and quantitative finance. It provides a clear understanding of the intuition behind derivatives pricing, how models are implemented and used, and how they are used and adapted in practice.

An Elementary Introduction to Mathematical Finance: Options and Other Topics, 2nd ed

Sheldon M. Ross
Cambridge, UK: Cambridge University Press, 2003
253pp, ISBN: 978-0-521-81429-4

This primer to mathematical finance covers the basics of option pricing in an accessible way for both professional traders and undergraduates studying the fundamentals of finance. It offers explanations of arbitrage, the Black–Scholes option pricing formula, and other topics such as utility functions, optimal portfolio selections, the Capital Asset Pricing Model, and Value at Risk.

Financial Calculus: An Introduction to Derivative Pricing

Martin Baxter, Andrew Rennie
Cambridge, UK: Cambridge University Press, 1996
233pp, ISBN: 978-0-521-55289-9

One of the most respected treatments in the field, this practical introduction to the pricing of

derivatives is an accessible account of the mathematics behind the pricing, construction and hedging of derivative securities. It provides real examples from stock, currency, and interest rate markets, and describes key concepts such as martingales, change of measure, and the Heath–Jarrow–Morton model.

Introduction to the Mathematics of Finance: From Risk Management to Options Pricing

Steven Roman

Undergraduate Texts in Mathematics Series
New York: Springer, 2004
354pp, ISBN: 978-0-387-21364-4

This textbook on the mathematics of financial derivatives examines discrete derivative pricing models, offering a complete derivation of the Black–Scholes option pricing formula as a limiting case of the Cox–Ross–Rubinstein discrete model. It assumes no previous experience in finance, as it explores the basics of options, and also analyzes American options, and the Capital Asset Pricing Model.

Introduction to the Mathematics of Finance

R. J. Williams

Graduate Studies in Mathematics Series
Providence, Rhode Island: American Mathematical Society, 2006
150pp, ISBN: 978-0-8218-3903-4

This is an introduction to the theory and practice of mathematical finance, which assesses the development of hedging and pricing of European and American derivatives in the discrete setting of binomial tree models. It presents tools from probability such as conditional expectation, filtration, and martingales, and describes the Black–Scholes model, for which pricing and hedging of European and American derivatives are developed.

Introduction to the Mathematics of Financial Derivatives, 2nd ed

Salih Neftci

Academic Press Advanced Finance Series
San Diego, California: Academic Press, 2000
527pp, ISBN: 978-0-12-515392-8

This is an accessible, self-contained primer on the fundamentals of mathematical finance, especially the mathematics utilized in the pricing models of derivative instruments. It is aimed at derivatives traders, risk managers, and other users and developers of derivatives models, and helps reduce the cost of entry into the mathematical world of valuation, hedging, and risk measurement for derivatives positions.

Mastering Financial Mathematics with Excel: A Practical Guide for Business Calculations

Alastair L. Day

Market Editions Series
Harlow, UK: FT Prentice Hall, 2005
350pp, ISBN: 978-0-273-68866-2

This is an examination of the use of spreadsheets tools to enable business managers to carry out financial calculations. It acts as a practical guide to the basic calculations and key financial formulas, and provides a set of tools and methods for applying Excel to solving mathematical problems. It includes a CD for working through the chapters and examples, and provides a menu of basic templates.

Mathematical Finance: Theory, Modeling, Implementation

Christian Fries

Hoboken, New Jersey: Wiley, 2007
520pp, ISBN: 978-0-470-04722-4

This is an introduction to the theoretical foundations and real-world applications of mathematical finance, aimed at students in mathematical finance, computational finance, and derivative pricing courses. It discusses the mathematical concepts and common characteristics that are the foundation of commonly used derivative pricing models, as well as providing key techniques and tips for the construction of these models.

Mathematical Techniques in Finance: Tools for Incomplete Markets

Ales Cerny

Princeton, New Jersey: Princeton University Press, 2004
378pp, ISBN: 978-0-691-08807-5

This is a comprehensive exploration of pricing and risk measurement in incomplete markets, a key area of current research. It offers a blend of numerical applications and theoretical grounding in economics, finance, and mathematics, and focuses on asset pricing throughout the book. It also contains useful exercises, figures, worked examples, computer programs, and spreadsheets.

Mathematics for Finance: An Introduction to Financial Engineering

Marek Capinski, Tomasz Zastawniak

Springer Undergraduate Mathematics Series
London: Springer, 2003
310pp, ISBN: 978-1-85233-330-0

This is an introduction to the mathematics of derivatives, interest rates, and portfolio management. It builds on mathematical models of bonds, focusing on Black–Scholes' arbitrage pricing of options, Markowitz portfolio optimization theory and the Capital Asset Pricing Model, and interest rates and their term structure. It is designed as a textbook, containing useful worked examples and exercises.

Methods of Mathematical Finance, 3rd ed

Ioannis Karatzas, Steven E. Shreve

New York: Springer, 2001
422pp, ISBN: 978-0-387-94839-3

This technical exploration of mathematical finance methods presents techniques of practical importance, as well as advanced methods for research. It focuses on applications of stochastic analysis and optimal control theory to various problems, and provides analysis of portfolio optimization and valuation problems under constraints, as well as contingent claim pricing and optimal consumption/investment in both complete and incomplete markets.

Monte Carlo Methods in Financial Engineering

Paul Glasserman

Stochastic Modelling and Applied Probability Series
New York: Springer, 2004
596pp, ISBN: 978-0-387-00451-8

With Monte Carlo simulation now seen as a key tool in the pricing of derivative securities and in risk management, this practical guide develops the use of Monte Carlo methods in finance and uses simulation as a vehicle for presenting models and ideas from financial engineering. It also examines the foundations of derivatives pricing, and describes techniques for improving simulation accuracy and efficiency.

New Directions in Mathematical Finance

Paul Wilmott, Henrik Rasmussen (editors)

Wiley Finance Series
Chichester, UK: Wiley, 2002
192pp, ISBN: 978-0-471-49817-9

This compilation brings together the leading names in quantitative finance to discuss modeling techniques in a variety of areas of financial engineering. It presents many ideas on quantitative finance, including a discussion of mean-variance strategies, passport options and Value at Risk, and new techniques for risk management, equity modeling, and interest rate modeling.

Numerical Methods for Finance

John Miller, David Edelman, John Appleby

Chapman & Hall/CRC Financial Mathematics Series
Boca Raton, Florida: CRC Press, 2008
293pp, ISBN: 978-1-58488-925-0

This examination of numerical methods provides practical insights on credit risks, exotic/hybrid options, retirement plans/pensions, life insurance, portfolio selection, incentive schemes, and interest rate modeling. It presents a variety of mathematical methods involving finite-difference, Monte Carlo, and fast Fourier transform techniques, alternatives to the Value at Risk approach, and identifies the potential pitfalls of standard methodologies.

Stochastic Calculus for Finance II: Continuous-Time Models, 2nd ed

Steven E. Shreve

Springer Finance Series
New York: Springer, 2008
550pp, ISBN: 978-0-387-40101-0

The second volume in this respected and comprehensive two-volume work examines continuous-time models, and the key ideas in the mathematical theory of securities pricing based upon the ideas of classical finance. It includes a self-contained treatment of the probability theory needed for stochastic calculus, including Brownian motion and its properties, as well as technical topics including foreign exchange models, forward measures, and jump-diffusion processes.

  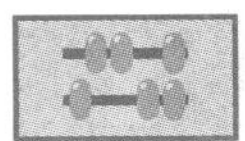      

JOURNALS

Applied Mathematical Finance

Routledge
4 Park Square, Milton Park, Abingdon, Oxfordshire, OX14 4RN, UK
T: +44 (0) 20 7017 6000
F: +44 (0) 20 7017 6336
www.tandf.co.uk/journals/routledge/1350486X.html
ISSN: 1350-486X

Published bimonthly, this journal presents theoretical and empirical research on applied mathematics and mathematical modeling in finance. It publishes papers on the modeling of financial and economic primitives, such as interest rates and asset prices, the modeling of market behaviour and market imperfections, the pricing of financial derivative securities, hedging strategies, numerical methods, and financial engineering.

Finance and Stochastics

Springer
ETH Zürich, Department of Mathematics, ETH-Zentrum, CH-8092 Zürich, Switzerland
T: +41 44 63 23580
F: +41 44 63 21474
www.math.ethz.ch/~finasto
ISSN: 0949-2984

A quarterly journal that provides a forum for research in all areas of finance based on stochastic methods. It publishes papers on a range of relevant topics, such as probability theory, statistics, stochastic analysis, theory and analysis of financial markets, continuous time finance, derivatives research, portfolio selection, and term structure models, and also presents special issues and surveys in developing research areas.

The Journal of Computational Finance

Incisive Media
Haymarket House, 28–29 Haymarket, London, SW1Y 4RX, UK
T: +44 (0) 20 7004 7531
F: +44 (0) 20 7484 9758
www.journalofcomputationalfinance.com
ISSN: 1460-1559

This quarterly journal focuses on advances in numerical and computational techniques in pricing, hedging and risk management of financial instruments. It publishes technical papers on quantitative risk research, methods that provide numerical solutions of pricing equations, optimization techniques in hedging and risk management, fundamental analysis relevant to finance, and developments in free-boundary problems in finance.

The Journal of Risk Model Validation

Incisive Media
Haymarket House, 28–29 Haymarket, London, SW1Y 4RX, UK
T: +44 (0) 20 7004 7531
F: +44 (0) 20 7484 9758
www.journalofriskmodelvalidation.com
ISSN: 1753-9579

This quarterly journal publishes technical research papers on the implementation and validation of risk models. It promotes a greater understanding of key issues, such as the empirical evaluation of existing models, pitfalls in model validation, stress testing, the development of new methods, and regulatory factors.

Mathematical Finance

Wiley
350 Main Street, Malden, MA 02148, USA
T: +1 781 388 8598
www.wiley.com/bw/journal.asp?ref=0960-1627&site=1
ISSN: 0960-1627

This quarterly journal is devoted to the mathematical aspects of finance theory from such fields as finance, economics, mathematics, and statistics. It publishes articles on the latest theoretical developments in financial theory, financial engineering, and related mathematical and statistical techniques, and new work that assesses mathematical tools in both research and practice.

INTERNET

CQF

www.cqf.info

This is a forum dedicated to mathematical finance, quantitative finance, and related fields, including all aspects of quantitative analysis. It provides information, articles, and discussions on areas such as probability, statistics, econometrics, and optimization. It features forums, problems, literature, technical questions, mathematical finance events, computers and programming, jobs, interviews, and interview questions.

FinMath

www.finmath.com

This is an online resource for information on books relating to mathematical finance, categorized by publisher and subject area. It presents all their covers, and links to conferences, seminars, workshops, events, jobs, and relevant websites.

Mathfinance

www.mathfinance.de

This site features investment banking and academic research in mathematical finance, and information on derivative consulting, model development, implementation in C++, pricing tools in Excel, Mathematica, derivation of formulae, products, and valuation for structured products in foreign exchange or equity. It also contains details on quant jobs, courses and conferences, an industry networking forum, and a long-running fortnightly email newsletter.

ORGANIZATIONS

Europe

The Bachelier Finance Society

Chair: Ernst Eberlein
Department of Mathematical Stochastics, University of Freiburg, Eckerstraße 1, D-79104 Freiburg, Germany
T: +49 761 203 5660
F: +49 761 203 5661
E: eberlein@stochastik.uni-freiburg.de
www.bachelierfinance.com

The society encourages the advancement of finance under the application of the theory of stochastic processes, statistical and mathematical theory. It actively promotes interrelationships between industry and academia in these areas, and organizes conferences and workshops, and a prestigious world congress every two years.

Money Laundering

BOOKS

Anti-Money Laundering: International Law and Practice

Wouter H. Muller, Christian H. Kalin, John G. Goldsworth (editors)
Chichester, UK: Wiley, 2007
813pp, ISBN: 978-0-470-03319-7

This provides a review of international anti-money laundering rules around the world, and summarizes the approach of organizations such as the United Nations and the European Council. It examines new techniques for fighting money laundering and terrorist financing, and compares current money laundering legislation and rules in each country, and the interconnected system of regulations that international financial professionals need to understand.

Bank Secrecy Act/Anti-Money Laundering

Lilian B. Klein
New York: Nova Science Publishers, 2008
118pp, ISBN: 978-1-60456-624-6

This provides an assessment and overview of current legislation that the US government is using to prevent drug trafficking, money laundering, and related crimes. It describes in detail the Bank Secrecy Act, and its use for preventing banks from being intermediaries for criminal activity, and other laws that made money laundering a criminal activity, and help to identify money-laundering schemes in financial institutions.

Black Finance: The Economics of Money Laundering

Donato Masciandaro, Elöd Takáts, Brigitte Unger
Cheltenham, UK: Edward Elgar, 2007
257pp, ISBN: 978-1-84720-215-4

This offers a systematic analysis of the economics of money laundering and its connection with

  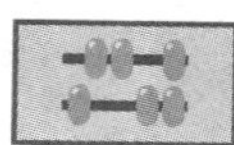   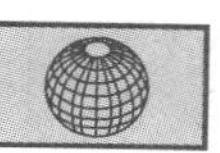   

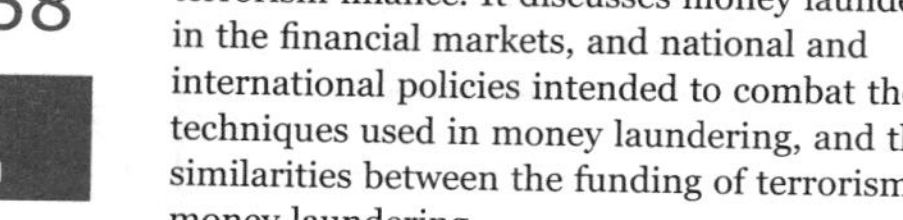

terrorism finance. It discusses money laundering in the financial markets, and national and international policies intended to combat them, techniques used in money laundering, and the similarities between the funding of terrorism and money laundering.

Capital, Payments and Money Laundering in the European Union

John Handoll

Oxford, UK: Oxford University Press, 2006
386pp, ISBN: 978-1-904501-51-0

This provides a comprehensive analysis of EU frameworks governing free movement of capital and payments, covering the definition of capital payments, the prohibition of restrictions on free movement, and permitted exceptions, derogations, and safeguard measures. In this context, it also examines the EU framework for combating money laundering, focusing on provisions, the international environment, and the impact on financial services.

Combating Money Laundering and Terrorist Financing: A Model of Best Practice for the Financial Sector, the Professions and Other Designated Businesses, 2nd ed

London: Commonwealth Secretariat, 2006
190pp, ISBN: 978-0-85092-842-6

This discusses international measures to combat money laundering and terrorist financing, focusing on global issues, national issues and strategy formulation, and financial and professional sector procedures. It examines the international standards developed by the Financial Action Task Force on Money Laundering, and systems created to help compliance with global standards.

Countering Terrorist Finance: A Training Handbook for Financial Services

Tm Parkman, Gill Peeling

Aldershot, UK: Gower Publishing, 2007
220pp, ISBN: 978-0-566-08725-7

This is a specialist resource for compliance officers in financial institutions that have responsibility for developing awareness amongst relevant employees. It provides guidance on how to train staff in the necessary processes and skills for countering terrorist financing activities, and assesses international legal responses and obligations, and the financing techniques used in recent international terrorist attacks.

Global Financial Crime: Terrorism, Money Laundering, and Off Shore Centres

Donato Masciandaro (editor)

Global Finance Series
Aldershot, UK: Ashgate Publishing, 2004
256pp, ISBN: 978-0-7546-3707-3

This is a multidisciplinary examination of money laundering, terrorism financing, and tax crime, which provides a systematic assessment of international policies on offshore countries. It focuses on ways to combat the increase in financial crime due to the globalization of the financial markets, and analyzes the economic, institutional, and political impact of offshore and onshore financial centers.

Handbook of Anti-Money Laundering

Dennis Cox

Hoboken, New Jersey: Wiley, 2009
608pp, ISBN: 978-0-470-06574-7

This practical guide takes an international approach to money laundering and money laundering deterrence, international standards and rules, and specific country rules and regulations. It examines current regulatory oversight, and its implications for banks and other financial organizations, and provides advice on how to implement the regulations, and protect and prevent against money laundering.

Money Laundering: A Concise Guide for All Business

Doug Hopton

Aldershot, UK: Gower Publishing, 2006
182pp, ISBN: 978-0-566-08639-7

This is a practical guide to anti-money laundering regulations, international law, and standards that have been introduced by governments to combat global terrorism and criminality. It also examines the basis of money laundering and how it works, corporate responsibilities and liabilities, and what procedures businesses should establish, and how and when to report suspicious activity.

Money Laundering: A Guide for Criminal Investigators, 2nd ed

John Madinger

Boca Raton, Florida: CRC Press, 2006
530pp, ISBN: 978-0-8493-3395-8

This authoritative resource provides an overview of money-laundering practices, and explains the investigative and legislative processes that are being used for detection and prevention. It examines current legislation and how it affects money-laundering investigation, strategies needed to combat new money laundering techniques, and the increasing importance of uncovering terrorist financing.

Money Laundering: Business Compliance

Stuart Bazley, Caroline Foster

London: Tolley, 2004
383pp, ISBN: 978-0-7545-2623-0

This is an assessment of the effect money laundering and terrorist financing is having on business operations, and the regulatory controls that have been imposed. It discusses UK law that requires regulated companies be aware of their obligations, and examines the implications for failing to comply with anti-money laundering provisions, including financial penalties and potential criminal sanctions.

Money Laundering, 2nd ed

Toby Graham, Evan Bell, Nicholas Elliott

Butterworth's Compliance Series
Oxford, UK: Butterworth-Heinemann, 2003
200pp, ISBN: 978-0-406-93248-8

This is a practical guide that presents a unified examination of criminal, civil, and regulatory elements in money laundering law and practice. It examines the inherent connections between each, and discusses new laws and agencies that have been created to help deterrence, investigation, and prosecution.

Money Laundering and the Proceeds of Crime: Economic Crime and Civil Remedies

M. Michelle Gallant

Cheltenham, UK: Edward Elgar, 2005
153pp, ISBN: 978-1-84376-951-4

This examines national and international strategies to combat money laundering by investigating the financial proceeds of criminal activity, a key element of current crime control. It looks at new methods related to terrorism funding, focusing on developments in the civil strategy of the US and UK, and analyzes the proceeds of crime laws, and anti-money laundering regimes.

Money Laundering Compliance, 2nd ed

Tim Bennett

Haywards Heath, UK: Tottel Publishing, 2007
559pp, ISBN: 978-1-84766-052-7

This examines the changes in UK regulatory supervision, and the role, liabilities, and obligations of trustees, practitioners and their professional advisers with regard to money laundering. It examines the range of offences and the application of principles in a number of jurisdictions, and practical issues such as know your client, reporting procedures, and the conflict between tipping-off and disclosure.

Reference Guide to Anti-Money Laundering and Combating the Financing of Terrorism, 2nd ed

Paul Allan Schott

Washington, DC: World Bank Publications, 2006
288pp, ISBN: 978-0-8213-6513-7

This is a comprehensive reference, providing practical information and guidance on combating money laundering and terrorist financing. It analyzes the effects of these crimes, how countries can work to mitigate them, and the role international organizations and international standards can play in the process, presenting tools for developing a program to effectively prevent, detect, and prosecute money laundering and terrorist financing.

The Scale and Impacts of Money Laundering

Brigitte Unger

Cheltenham, UK: Edward Elgar, 2007
228pp, ISBN: 978-1-84720-223-9

This is an overview of current money-laundering techniques and strategies, which assesses the link between money laundering and fraud, and the increasing international scope and economic impact of financial crimes. It also describes economic models that have been designed to measure money-laundering activities, and research into techniques and the potential effects of money laundering.

  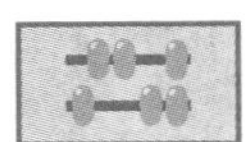      

Suppressing Terrorist Financing and Money Laundering: The Evolution and Implementation of International Standards
Jae-myong Koh
New York: Springer, 2006
243pp, ISBN: 978-3-540-32518-5

This describes the development of international standards for countering terrorist financing from the perspective of international criminal law, as well as the theoretical and operational focus of anti-money laundering strategy since 9/11.
It also assesses the functioning of organizations such as the UN Security Council, Financial Action Task Force, IMF, World Bank, and the Asia/Pacific Group on Money Laundering.

MAGAZINES

AML Compliance Alert

Eli Financial
PO Box 90324, Washingtion DC 20090, USA
www.elifinancial.com/aml_compliance.html

This new monthly newsletter provides information and news on the fight against money laundering and terrorism financing. It aims to assist bank professionals and their advisers increase the effectiveness of their asset liability programs, and focuses on terrorism, organized crime, and money laundering.

Anti-Money Laundering

Australian Financial Markets Association
Level 3 Plaza Building, 95 Pitt Street, Sydney 2000, NSW 2001, Australia
T: +61 2 9776 7955
F: +61 2 9776 4488
www.afma.com.au/scripts/nc.dll?AFMAV6.1573196:STANDARD:1648505960:pc=L1C2S2

This magazine, published by the Australian Financial Markets Association, is a source of information and education for the financial services sector on anti-money laundering and counter-terrorist financing. It provides a forum for debate and analysis on the key implementation challenges facing financial institutions across the region, and focuses on regulation, customer identification, monitoring, legal, and technology.

Money Laundering Bulletin

Informa
Telephone House, 69–77 Paul Street, London, EC2A 4LQ, UK
T: +44 (0) 20 7017 5532
www.informaprofessional.com/publications/newsletter/money_laundering_bulletin
ISSN: 1462-141X

This is a monthly newsletter that provides information and news on money-laundering schemes, methods, trends, and policing. It offers the latest legal, regulatory, and practical developments in preventing and detecting money laundering and terrorist financing for businesses.

JOURNALS

Journal of Financial Crime

Emerald Group
Howard House, Wagon Lane, Bingley, BD16 1WA, UK
T: +44 (0) 1274 777 700
F: +44 (0) 1274 785 201
info.emeraldinsight.com/products/journals/journals.htm?id=jfc
ISSN: 1359-0790

This quarterly journal is an authoritative resource for information on methods used in economic crime and the steps that can be taken to avoid and combat it. It offers a series of analyses, briefings, and updates for practitioners concerned with the prevention, detection, and prosecution of financial crime and the protection of assets.

Journal of International Money and Finance

Elsevier
Radarweg 29, 1043 NX Amsterdam, The Netherlands
F: +31 20 485 2370
www.elsevier.com/wps/find/journaldescription.cws_home/30443/description#description
ISSN: 0261-5606

Published eight times each year, this scholarly journal is devoted to theoretical and empirical research in the fields of international monetary economics, international finance, and the rapidly developing overlap area between them. It focuses on research on exchange rate behavior, foreign exchange options, international capital markets, international monetary and fiscal policy, and international transmission.

Journal of Money Laundering Control

Emerald Group
Howard House, Wagon Lane, Bingley, BD16 1WA, UK
T: +44 (0) 1274 777 700
F: +44 (0) 1274 785 201
info.emeraldinsight.com/products/journals/journals.htm?id=jmlc
ISSN: 1368-5201

This quarterly journal publishes analysis, briefings, and updates on the latest laws, regulation, techniques, and best practice in the prevention, identification and prosecution of money laundering. It publishes on areas such as legislation in jurisdictions around the world, terrorist financing, suspicious transaction reporting requirements, monitoring patterns of suspicious payments, and new and emerging techniques in money laundering.

INTERNET

IBA Anti-Money Laundering Forum

www.anti-moneylaundering.org

This online network, run by the International Bar Association, provides a guide for lawyers in dealing with their responsibilities regarding new anti-money laundering legislation and compliance requirements. It offers detailed information, categorized by jurisdiction and region, and works to increase awareness of the difficulties in preventing and detecting money laundering among legal professionals and their clients throughout the world.

International Money Laundering Information Network

www.imolin.org

IMoLIN is an internet-based network that works to assist governments, organizations, and individuals in the fight against money laundering and the financing of terrorism. It was developed through the cooperation of leading anti-money laundering organizations, and offers a database on legislation and regulations throughout the world, an electronic library, and a calendar of events.

MoneyLaundering.com

www.moneylaundering.com

This is a site providing money-laundering news from around the world. It covers the basics of anti-money laundering, compliance guidelines, enforcement actions, government reports, international resources, laundering cases, laws and regulations, money laundering alert, research tools, and US regulatory information, as well as conferences and seminars, products. and services.

ORGANIZATIONS

Europe

Institute of Money Laundering Prevention Officers

Chair: Steve Lock
6 Millside Place, Old Isleworth, Middlesex, TW7 6BU, UK
T: +44 (0) 20 8847 4074
E: info@imlpo.com
www.imlpo.com

IMLPO is a cross-representative forum of anti-money laundering professionals, which provides a forum for the sharing of views, experiences, and concerns on the business of combating money laundering. It also facilitates the further education and professional development of its members, and provides a broad representation for issues concerning money-laundering prevention.

USA

Association of Certified Anti-Money Laundering Specialists

Chair: John J. Byrne
Brickell Bayview Center, 80 Southwest 8th Street, Suite 2350, Miami, FL 33130, USA
T: +1 305 373 0020
F: +1 305 373 7788
E: info@acams.org
www.acams.org

ACAMS provides information, education, career development, and professional networking opportunities in the anti-money laundering sector. It promotes the development and implementation of sound anti-money laundering policies and procedures, and offers resources for financial institutions and related businesses that help train, identify, and locate practitioners in money-laundering control policies, procedures and regulations.

FIBA Anti Money Laundering Institute

80 SW 8th Street, Suite 2505, Miami, FL 33130, USA
T: +1 305 579 0086
F: +1 305 579 0969
E: fibatraining@fiba.net
fibatraining.net

This institute, run by the Florida International Bankers Association, focuses on providing in-depth and practical professional training and courses to ensure the highest level of competency in the industry. It also organizes two certification courses

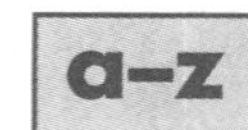

for anti-money laundering compliance officers, as well as targeted professional continuing education courses in the areas of correspondent banking, private banking, outside directors, and management.

International

Asia/Pacific Group on Money Laundering
Chair: Mick Keelty, Ong Hian Sun

E: mail@apgml.org
www.apgml.org

The APG is an autonomous and collaborative international organization committed to the effective implementation and enforcement of internationally accepted standards against money laundering and the financing of terrorism. It assesses compliance, co-ordinates technical assistance and training, participates in the international anti-money laundering network, and conducts research and analysis into money laundering and terrorist financing trends and methods.

Offshore Group of Banking Supervisors
www.ogbs.net

The aims of the OGBS are to identify and discuss issues of mutual interest to its members, participate with relevant international organizations in setting and promoting the implementation of international standards for cross-border banking supervision, combating money-laundering/terrorist financing, encouraging high standards of supervision, and promoting best practice for trust and company service providers.

The Society of Anti Money Laundering Professionals
Hong Kong
www.socamlpro.org

This global organization draws on best practice, expertise, and mentoring from senior members of the profession from around the world. It provides a forum for industry professionals, and the interchange of ideas, education and training for those engaged in combating financial crime, money laundering, and terrorist financing.

Mortgage Finance

BOOKS

Commercial Mortgage-Backed Securitisation: Developments in the European Market
Andrew V. Petersen (editor)
London: Sweet & Maxwell, 2006
596pp, ISBN: 978-0-421-96090-9

This provides comprehensive legal and regulatory guidance on the rapidly expanding area of commercial mortgage-backed securitization in Europe. It looks at current practice, how to set up new transactions, the administration of existing arrangements, and examines related economic and technological issues. It also discusses tools such as key lending agreements, and compares European practice with that of the United States.

Commercial Real Estate Analysis and Investments, 2nd ed
David M. Geltner, Norman G. Miller, Jim Clayton, Piet Eichholtz
Mason, Ohio: Thomson/South-Western, 2007
880pp, ISBN: 978-0-324-38212-9

This presents the essential concepts, principles and tools for the analysis of commercial real estate from an investment perspective. It attempts to bridge the gap between mainstream finance and current professional real estate practice, and examines urban and financial economics, international real estate investments, real options application to real estate development, and the streamlining of data returns.

Economics of the Mortgage Market: Perspectives on Household Decision Making
David Leece
Real Estate Issues Series
Oxford, UK: Blackwell Publishing, 2004
258pp, ISBN: 978-1-4051-1461-5

This provides an organised research resource for financial analysts in real estate, as well as researchers in real estate finance, real estate economics, housing economics and urban economics. It examines the link between household behavior and issues in mortgage market economics and mortgage valuation, and emphasizes the increasing importance of the secondary mortgage market.

Financial Shock: A 360° Look at the Subprime Mortgage Implosion, and How to Avoid the Next Financial Crisis
Mark Zandi
Upper Saddle River, New Jersey: FT Press, 2009
270pp, ISBN: 978-0-13-714290-3

This new book presents an account of the economic, political, and regulatory forces behind the crisis in the subprime mortgage market. It discusses how internet technology and access to global capital transformed the mortgage industry, the impact of housing market problems on the global financial system, and offers advice on recognizing emerging bubbles, improving oversight, and surviving downturns.

The Handbook of Mortgage-Backed Securities, 6th ed
Frank J. Fabozzi (editor)
New York: McGraw-Hill, 2006
1,238pp, ISBN: 978-0-07-146074-3

This practical guide to MBS fundamentals and trading strategies provides a resource for both private investors and professional portfolio managers. It covers the full range of MBS products and derivatives, and explores the many advantages and potential pitfalls in herent in the market. It includes new analysis of collateralized mortgage obligations, prepayment derivatives, loan level determinants of repayments, and innovative approaches to MBS valuation.

Mortgage and Real Estate Finance: Latest Innovations and Opportunities
Stefania Perrucci (editor)
London: Risk Books, 2008
350pp, ISBN: 978-1-906348-12-0

This examination of the complex structured market of mortgage and real estate finance focuses on ways of taking advantage of the current market distress, and avoiding its pitfalls. Providing a history of the market and overview of both the primary and secondary mortgage markets, it also analyses the latest innovations in the market, risk management of mortgage securities, and other relevant areas of mortgage finance.

Mortgage Markets Worldwide
Danny Ben-Shahar, Charles Ka Yui Leung, Seow Eng Ong
Real Estate Issues Series
Chichester, UK: Blackwell Publishing, 2008
312pp, ISBN: 978-1-4051-3210-7

This theoretical and empirical study of selected mortgage markets explores problems of housing finance in each country, steps taken to solve these problems, and the expected future developments of the market. It examines issues relating to housing finance efficiency and contract heterogeneity, the integration of mortgage markets with capital markets, and how particular institutional frameworks interact with mortgage markets.

Real Estate Finance: Theory and Practice, 5th ed
Terrence M. Clauretie, G. Stacy Sirmans
Mason, Ohio: Thomson/South-Western, 2005
557pp, ISBN: 978-0-324-30550-0

This is a textbook that examines the techniques and strategies of real estate finance, based on sound economic and finance principles. It applies the theoretical aspects of financial economics to explain how real estate financial institutions and markets have developed over time, and examines how real estate financial markets operate in today's environment. It also discusses the impact of federal legislation on real estate finance.

Real Estate Finance & Investments, 13th ed
William B. Brueggeman, Jeffrey D. Fisher
Boston: McGraw-Hill, 2008
688pp, ISBN: 978-0-07-352471-9

     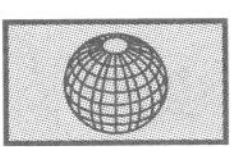    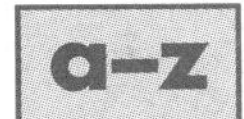

This regularly revised and updated textbook on real estate finance and investments is a rigorous and practical overview of the tools needed to understand and analyze real estate markets and the investment alternatives available to both debt and equity investors. New content has been added on current trends in mortgage finance and investment techniques.

Real Estate Finance and Investment Manual, 9th ed

Jack Cummings

Hoboken, New Jersey: Wiley, 2008
669pp, ISBN: 978-0-470-26040-1

This guide to financing for real estate investors covers all the financing options, new real estate investment strategies, and insider techniques available. It shows how to set realistic investment goals, practice effective negotiation, use leverage to maximize investment returns, choose between conventional and creative financing methods, understand wraparound and blanket mortgages, and uncover real estate tax loopholes.

Real Estate Finance in a Nutshell, 6th ed

Jon W. Bruce

Mason, Ohio: Thomson/South-Western, 2008
317pp, ISBN: 978-0-314-18354-5

This primer presents a thorough overview of the law of real estate finance. It discusses the mortgage market, real estate financing devices, the underlying obligation, mortgaged property, and transfer of both the mortgagor's interest and the mortgagee's interest. It also covers rights and obligations after default and before foreclosure, and considers the legal principles underpinning real estate finance.

Real Estate Investment: A Capital Market Approach

Gerald R. Brown, George A. Matysiak

Harlow, UK: FT Prentice Hall, 2000
708pp, ISBN: 978-0-13-020063-1

Examines the effect on real estate markets of the recent economic upheaval, which has increased the degree of risk of investment assets. It focuses on three major areas of financial and economic importance within the real estate profession: the time value of money and the valuation of cash flows, risk and return in real estate, and portfolio management.

Salomon Smith Barney Guide to Mortgage-Backed and Asset-Backed Securities

Lakhbir Hayre

New York: Wiley, 2001
876pp, ISBN: 978-0-471-38587-5

This provides a comprehensive guide to these fixed-income securities, now the largest sector of the bond market. It presents a framework for modeling of prepayment rates on residential mortgage loans, and discusses how the internet has affected the mortgage origination process, option-adjusted spreads, and other types of MBS and ABS. It is useful for investment professionals, institutional investors, pension funds, and hedge funds.

Subprime Mortgage Credit Derivatives

Laurie S. Goodman, Shumin Li, Douglas J. Lucas, Thomas A. Zimmerman, Frank J. Fabozzi

Frank J. Fabozzi Series
Hoboken, New Jersey: Wiley, 2008
334pp, ISBN: 978-0-470-24366-4

This new book discusses the topical area of subprime mortgage credit derivatives, addressing areas such as mortgage credit, mortgage securitizations, and credit default swaps on mortgage securities. It outlines the origins of the subprime crisis, and examines current instruments and strategies for managing a portfolio of mortgage credits in the current volatile climate.

Your Successful Career as a Mortgage Broker

David Reed

New York: Amacom, 2007
246pp, ISBN: 978-0-8144-7370-2

This detailed and informative guide to successful mortgage broking offers practical advice on how to quote interest rates, get approved by wholesale lenders, negotiate the steps of the loan process, market and prospect effectively, licensing and educational requirements, as well as information on the different career options available as a mortgage broker, mortgage banker, and correspondent mortgage banker.

MAGAZINES

Commercial Mortgage Alert

Harrison Scott Publications
5 Marine View Plaza, #400, Hoboken,
NJ 07030-5795, USA
T: +1 201 659 1700
F: +1 201 659 4141
www.CMAlert.com
ISSN: 1520-3697

This weekly newsletter provides news, analysis, and statistics on the commercial mortgage market and traditional real estate finance. It discusses financing opportunities, and key moves by big lenders and borrowers, and covers financing needs of REITs and private developers, CMBS offerings, new trends, career openings for real estate finance and securitization professionals, and the latest rankings of key players in the real estate capital markets.

Inside Mortgage Finance

Inside Mortgage Finance Publications
7910 Woodmont Avenue, Suite 1000, Bethesda,
MD 20814-7019, USA
T: +1 301 951 1240
F: +1 301 656 1709
www.imfpubs.com/issues/imfpubs_imf
ISSN: 8756-0003

This weekly magazine offers statistics and analysis of legislative developments, regulatory changes, and market trends in the mortgage markets. It also produces surveys on these markets, extensive data, rankings, and charts, analysis and competitive intelligence, as well as information on the private mortgage insurance industry, the latest moves from Fannie Mae and Freddie Mac, and guidance on non-traditional loans.

Mortgage Banking

Mortgage Bankers Association
1331 L Street NW, Washington, DC 20005, USA
T: +1 202 557 2700
www.mortgagebankingmagazine.com
ISSN: 0730-0212

This monthly magazine focused on real estate finance provides coverage and analysis of the critical issues and trends affecting the industry. It features news, strategic information, research, and executive profiles for real estate finance industry leaders, senior financial services executives, mortgage bankers, and brokers.

Mortgage Finance Gazette

Metropolis Business Publishing
6th Floor, Davis House, 2 Robert Street, Croydon,
CR0 1QQ, UK
T: +44 (0) 20 8253 8618
www.mfgonline.co.uk
ISSN: 0964-7988

This is a monthly magazine that provides all the latest industry news on people, jobs, products and organisations, as well as a number of special reports covering issues in the mortgage finance industry.

Mortgage Originator

Summit Business Media
1801 Park 270 Drive, Suite 550, St. Louis,
MO 63146, USA
T: +1 314 824 5500
F: +1 314 824 5640
www.mortgageoriginator.com
ISSN: 1070-5708

This is a monthly magazine for mortgage originators, which acts as a resource for mortgage brokers, retail loan officers, lenders, and other mortgage professionals. It presents industry news and company highlights, and features a marketing resource center, podcasts, a resource directory, and an e-bookstore.

Mortgage Solutions

Incisive Media
Haymarket House, 28-29 Haymarket, London,
SW1Y 4RX, UK
T: +44 (0) 20 7484 9700
F: +44 (0) 20 7930 2238
www.mortgagesolutions-online.com
ISSN: 1475-8008

This is a weekly magazine for mortgage intermediaries, which delivers news, editorial comment, analysis, and features on all aspects of the mortgage market. It offers articles on training, interviews with the industry figures, a regular regional housing market focus, and a market debate, and produces specialist supplements on key topics such as subprime, buy to let, and regulation.

National Mortgage News

SourceMedia
1 State Street Plaza, 27th Floor, New York,
NY 10004, USA
T: +1 212 803 8333
F: +1 212 292 5216
www.nationalmortgagenews.com
ISSN: 1050-3331

A weekly newspaper that offers news and analysis, and discusses the trends and events that are

affecting the mortgage industry. It is aimed at mortgage bankers, commercial bankers, savings institutions, brokerage firms, insurance companies, and government enterprises, and covers commercial lending, mortgage servicing, technology and e-commerce, default management, B&C lending, the latest M&A developments, and industry rankings.

JOURNALS

Briefings in Real Estate Finance

Wiley
111 River Street, Hoboken, NJ 07030, USA
T: +1 201 748 6645
www3.interscience.wiley.com/journal/110484210
ISSN: 1473-1894

A quarterly publication providing a practical understanding of the processes and challenges associated with the funding of real estate. It discusses current techniques, approaches, and best practice in all aspects of the subject, and addresses such issues as risk management, structuring finance, finance for trading, development and investment, sources of funding and terms available, and changes in taxation.

Journal of European Real Estate Research

European Real Estate Society
Howard House, Wagon Lane, Bingley, BD16 1WA, UK
T: +44 (0) 1274 777 700
F: +44 (0) 1274 785 201
info.emeraldinsight.com/products/journals/journals.htm?id=jerer
ISSN: 1753-9269

This quarterly journal publishes theoretical and practical papers relating to commercial and residential property in Europe, aimed at improving property appraisal, finance and investment skills, and an understanding of the differences between the various real estate markets across the continent. Coverage includes REITs and financial derivatives, housing and residential markets, indirect property investment, cross-border portfolio diversification, and comparative market analysis.

Journal of Property Investment & Finance

Emerald Group Publishing
Howard House, Wagon Lane, Bingley, BD16 1WA, UK
T: +44 (0) 1274 777 700
F: +44 (0) 1274 785 201
www.emeraldinsight.com/Insight/viewContainer.do?containerType=Journal&containerId=12267
ISSN: 1463-578X

Published bimonthly, this journal provides information and ideas relating to property valuation and investment, property management, and decision-making in the commercial property market. It publishes papers by both academics and practitioners, covering the latest research, real estate law and new legislation, internet sites and recent publications, market data, and changes in the property market.

The Journal of Real Estate Finance and Economics

Kluwer Academic Publishers
298B Brooks Hall, Terry College of Business, The University of Georgia, Athens, Georgia 30602-6255, USA
T: +1 706 542 3805
F: +1 706 542 4295
www.jrefe.org
ISSN: 0895-5638

This is a quarterly journal that publishes empirical and theoretical papers on real estate, finance, and economics. It covers topics such as the working and structure of markets, the role of various institutional arrangements, mortgages and asset securitization, risk management and valuation, and public policy and regulation.

The Journal of Real Estate Research

American Real Estate Society
California State University, Fullerton, College of Business & Economics, Department of Finance, Fullerton, CA 92834-6848, USA
T: +1 714 278 4363
F: +1 714 278 2161
www.business.fullerton.edu/Finance/Journal
ISSN: 0896-5803

This quarterly journal, produced by the American Real Estate Society, is devoted to promoting business decision-making applications through scholarly real estate research. It presents analytical and empirical papers on real estate development, economics, finance, investment, law, management, marketing, secondary markets, and valuation.

Real Estate Economics

American Real Estate and Urban Economics Association
PO Box 9958, Richmond, VA 23228, USA
T: +1 866 273 8321
F: +1 877 273 8323
www.areuea.org/publications/ree
ISSN: 1080-8620

This quarterly journal provides research information and ideas by academic researchers and industry professionals in the field of real estate economics. It focuses on improving the analysis of real estate decisions, and covers such areas as tax rules and the sale or leaseback of corporate real estate, and methods for measuring efficiency in the savings and loan industry.

Real Estate Finance

Aspen Publishers, USA
T: +1 301 698 7100
www.aspenpublishers.com
ISSN: 0748-318X

Published bimonthly, this journal provides tools for decision-making in real estate finance, written by investment managers and advisers, bankers and insurers, developers, property managers, tax planners, lawyers, accountants, government officials, and academics. Coverage includes volatility risk, pricing REITS and mortgage-backed securities, valuing overseas investment opportunities, and the default characteristics of real estate loans.

INTERNET

Broker Universe

www.brokeruniverse.com

This website for mortgage brokers and originators provides practical information on techniques and technologies for optimizing performance in the mortgage markets, and a daily email newsletter.

MortgageMag

www.mortgagemag.com

This online resource for mortgage industry professionals features company listings, forums, people's choice, opinions, products and services, resumé and job postings, and instant messages/email updates.

ORGANIZATIONS

Europe

The Council of Mortgage Lenders

Bush House, North West Wing, Aldwych, London, WC2B 4PJ, UK
T: +44 (0) 845 373 6771
F: +44 (0) 845 373 6778
www.cml.org.uk

This is the trade association for the mortgage lending industry, which aims to improve the operating environment in the UK housing and mortgage markets. It represents the residential mortgage lending industry, and provides economic, statistical, and legal research and other market information. Its membership comprises of banks, building societies and other mortgage lenders.

European Mortgage Federation

Chair: Pasquale Giamboi
Avenue de la Joyeuse Entrée 14/2, 1040 Brussels, Belgium
T: +32 2 285 40 30
F: +32 2 285 40 31
E: emfinfo@hypo.org
www.hypo.org

The EMF promotes the interests of mortgage lenders at European level, uniting institutions with a special interest in the mortgage industry and the housing sector, such as mortgage banks, commercial banks, savings banks, co-operative banks, building societies, umbrella companies, and insurance companies. It encourages mortgage lending, advises EU institutions, and provides industry statistics.

European Real Estate Society

Chair: Ramon Sotelo
Hanna Kaleva, c/o KTI Kiinteistötieto Oy, KTI Finland, Eerikinkatu 28, 00180 Helsinki, Finland
T: +358 (0) 20 7430 124
F: +358 (0) 20 7430 131
www.eres.org

ERES is a non-profit organization that promotes the advancement of real estate research throughout Europe, and incorporates national property research societies, academic researchers, and real estate practitioners. It encourages professionalism in the industry, and improved communication in real estate in academia, and organizes events on real estate, including an annual conference, industry seminars, and education seminars.

USA

American Real Estate and Urban Economics Association

Chair: Frank E. Nothaft
PO Box 9958, Richmond, VA 23228, USA
T: +1 866 273 8321
F: +1 877 273 8323
E: areuea@areaue.org
www.areuea.org

The aim of AREUEA is to encourage greater information and analysis in the fields of real estate development, planning and economics. It promotes the exchange of information and opinions among academic, professional and governmental people, publishes a journal, and holds three conferences each year which promote research in the fields of real estate and urban economics.

American Real Estate Society

Chair: Mauricio Rodriguez
Clemson University, Department of Finance,
314 Sirrine Hall, Clemson, SC 29634-1343, USA
T: +1 864 656 1373
F: +1 864 656 3748
www.aresnet.org

ARES is dedicated to producing and disseminating knowledge and research related to real estate decision-making and the functioning of real estate markets. Its membership is comprised of academics in a wide variety of fields such as economics, finance, marketing, geography, and professional researchers, analysts, and appraisers. It publishes a number of industry journals, and provides listings of academic and senior research positions worldwide.

The Federal Home Loan Mortgage Corporation

Chair: David M. Moffett
8200 Jones Branch Drive, McLean,
VA 22102-3110, USA
T: +1 703 903 2000
www.freddiemac.com

Commonly known as Freddie Mac, this is a stockholder-owned corporation chartered by Congress to keep money flowing to mortgage lenders in support of homeownership and rental housing. Its mission is to provide liquidity, stability and affordability to the housing market.

The Federal National Mortgage Association

Chair: Herbert M. Allison
3900 Wisconsin Avenue NW, Washington,
DC 20016-2892, USA
T: +1 202 752 7000
E: headquarters@fanniemae.com
www.fanniemae.com

Commonly known as Fannie Mae, this is a stockholder-owned corporation chartered by Congress as a government-sponsored enterprise. Its purpose is to purchase and securitize mortgages in order to ensure that funds are consistently available to the institutions that lend money to home buyers, and provides services, products, and solutions to lender partners and a broad range of housing partners.

International Mortgage Lenders Association

2398 East Camelback Road, Suite 935, Phoenix,
AZ 85016, USA
T: +1 602 667 3500
E: tkelley@imigrouponline.com
www.internationalmla.org

The IMLA serves the international mortgage lending community in the areas of lending, brokering, real estate, title/escrow, appraising, legal, and services. It promotes research and the exchange of ideas, the review of public policy matters, best practices, and standards to increase efficiency, and supports the educational needs of the international real estate finance industry.

The Mortgage Bankers Association

Chair: David G. Kittle
1331 L Street NW, Washington, DC 20005, USA
T: +1 202 557 2700
www.mbaa.org

This national association represents the real estate finance industry, its members comprising mortgage companies, mortgage brokers, commercial banks, thrifts, life insurance companies, and others in the mortgage-lending field. It provides news and information on strategic tools, industry trends and resources, and promotes fair lending practices and professional excellence through a wide range of educational programs and a variety of publications.

The Mortgage Insurance Companies of America

USA
E: info@micadc.org
www.privatemi.com

MICA is the trade association representing the private mortgage insurance industry. Its members help loan originators and investors make funds available to home buyers for low down payment mortgages, by protecting these institutions from a major portion of the financial risk of default. It provides information on legislative and regulatory issues, and represents the industry to government.

National Association of Mortgage Brokers

Chair: Marc S. Savitt
7900 Westpark Drive, Suite T309, McLean,
VA 22102, USA
T: +1 703 342 5900
F: +1 703 342 5905
E: jotto@namb.org
www.namb.org

This is a national trade association that represents the mortgage broker industry, and promotes the industry through programs and services such as education, professional certification, and government affairs representation.

Operations Management

BOOKS

Cases in Operations Management: Building Customer Value through World-Class Operations

Robert D. Klassen,
Larry J. Menor (editors)
The Ivey Casebook Series
Thousand Oaks, California: Sage Publications, 2006
425pp, ISBN: 978-1-4129-1371-3

This approaches operations management from a real-world decision-making perspective, presenting a range of focused case studies from an international context. It describes the basic concepts while exploring economic, political, and cultural issues relating to the key areas of process design, quality, supply chain management, and customer value, and offers resources such as case notes, preparation questions, and discussion questions.

Introduction to Operations and Supply Chain Management, 2nd ed

Cecil Bozarth, Robert B. Handfield
Upper Saddle River, New Jersey: Prentice Hall, 2008
576pp, ISBN: 978-0-13-179103-9

This new textbook examines the key topics that are taught in courses on operations management, covering relevant service theory and applications, as well as manufacturing applications and theory. It assesses operations management from a cross-functional perspective, linked to other areas of an organization, and explores the impact of technology on business operations, and the integration of the value chain.

Operations and Process Management: Principles and Practice for Strategic Impact, 2nd ed

Nigel Slack, Stuart Chambers, Robert Johnston, Alan Betts
Harlow, UK: FT Prentice Hall, 2009
568pp, ISBN: 978-0-273-71851-2

This practical textbook examines operations management takes an integrative approach to services and manufacturing operations. It explains the core principles and processes fundamental to managing business operations, and provides a toolkit for assessing and improving the operations and processes in a company. Interactive cases are presented for working through the decision-making process to solve operations problems.

Operations Management: An Integrated Approach, 3rd ed

R. Dan Reid, Nada R. Sanders
Hoboken, New Jersey: Wiley, 2007
671pp, ISBN: 978-0-471-79448-6

This integrative approach explores the critical impact that operations management now

has in the business world. It provides detailed coverage of key topics, connecting these throughout, and focuses on problem solving to provide effective decision-making expertise and an understanding of the main techniques involved, and how operations management relates to every department within an organization.

Operations Management: Creating Value Along the Supply Chain, 6th ed

Roberta S. Russell, Bernard W. Taylor

Hoboken, New Jersey: Wiley, 2007

776pp, ISBN: 978-0-470-09515-7

This comprehensive textbook offers an introduction to operations management, and assesses value by analyzing the quantitative and qualitative aspects of operations and supply chain management. It presents both managerial issues and quantitative techniques, relating everything to real business methods and problems, and discusses how companies manage key processes such as inventory and forecasting.

Operations Management: Goods, Service, and Value Chains, 2nd ed

David Alan Collier, James R. Evans

Mason, Ohio: Thomson/South-Western, 2007

830pp, ISBN: 978-0-324-17939-2

This textbook for business students provides coverage of the main concepts, techniques, and applications of current operations management, covering topics such as supply chain design, capacity management, quality control, and project management. It includes an assessment of contemporary and relevant service and manufacturing theory and applications, and approaches operations as linked to all other functional areas of an organization.

Operations Management: Integrating Manufacturing and Services, 5th ed

Mark Davis, Janelle Heineke

Boston, Massachusetts: McGraw-Hill/Irwin, 2005

679pp, ISBN: 978-0-07-299435-3

This textbook presents a wide-ranging and non-quantitative analysis of operations management, for students in general business studies. It describes the main fundamental principles and concepts in both manufacturing and services, and integrates learning with real-life case studies to aid understanding.

Operations Management: Processes and Value Chains, 8th ed

Lee J. Krajewski, Larry P. Ritzman, Manoj K. Malhotra

Upper Saddle River, New Jersey: Prentice Hall, 2007

728pp, ISBN: 978-0-13-169739-3

This examines current operational management issues, and presents a range of analytic techniques for use in operational decision-making. It offers a broad picture of the strategic operations, as well as process orientation in both service and manufacturing, and presents strategic and managerial issues, and the operations tools and techniques for problem solving, for aligning operation management activities with corporate strategy across the business.

Operations Management, 9th ed

Jay Heizer, Barry Render

Upper Saddle River, New Jersey: Prentice Hall, 2007

784pp, ISBN: 978-0-13-812878-4

This successful textbook emphasizes the practical elements of operations management, providing students with a sound knowledge of how companies work, and how to apply their learning to real company challenges and best practices. It does this through an extensive array of integrated problems, and examining service applications and firms and their operations activity in the real world.

Operations Management, 2nd ed

Terry Hill

Basingstoke, UK: Palgrave Macmillan, 2005

764pp, ISBN: 978-1-4039-3466-6

This analyzes the fundamental concepts of operations management, and how operations can deliver competitive advantage for organizations. It explores the responsibilities and strategic role of the operations manager, how operational decision-making is driven by market demand, enterprise resource planning, and supply chain issues, and includes case studies that assess management issues in both service and production operations.

Operations Management, 5th ed

Nigel Slack, Stuart Chambers, Robert Johnston

New York: FT Prentice Hall, 2007

728pp, ISBN: 978-1-4058-4700-1

This is a comprehensive, practical, and strategic examination of the role of operations management within business. It focuses on how organizations create and deliver products at lower cost and with higher revenue, meet the challenges posed by changes in customer preferences, internet-based technologies and global supply networks, supply-chain planning, outsourcing, and the 'greening' of operations, and provides numerous examples of operations in practice.

Operations Management, 10th ed

William J. Stevenson

McGraw-Hill/Irwin Series on Operations and Decision Sciences

Boston, Massachusetts: McGraw-Hill/Irwin, 2008

906pp, ISBN: 978-0-07-728409-1

This new edition presents the latest concepts and applications in operations management, as well as detailed explanations of key process to aid an understanding of how to apply the main operations management tools and methods in real-life situations.

Operations Management for Competitive Advantage, 11th ed

Richard Chase, F. Robert Jacobs, Nicholas Aquilano

Boston, Massachusetts: McGraw-Hill/Irwin, 2006

806pp, ISBN: 978-0-07-312166-6

This regularly updated textbook on using effective operations management to ensure competitive advantage provides a thorough introduction to the concepts, processes, and methods of managing and controlling operations in manufacturing or service settings. It covers all the key areas, from high-tech manufacturing to high-touch services, and integrates topical issues such as globalization, supply chain strategy, e-business, and enterprise resource planning.

Operations Management for MBAs, 3rd ed

Jack R. Meredith, Scott M. Shafer

Hoboken, New Jersey: Wiley, 2007

445pp, ISBN: 978-0-471-35142-9

This practical student textbook examines key strategic operational issues that can have a critical impact on the success of an organization, focusing on international problems and cases. It discusses the growing importance of new technologies, and the rise of service organizations, as well as Six Sigma improvement projects, project management, enterprise resource planning, lean management, outsourcing and offshoring, supply chain management, and process design and planning.

Principles of Operations Management, 7th ed

Jay Heizer, Barry Render

Upper Saddle River, New Jersey: Prentice Hall, 2007

671pp, ISBN: 978-0-13-234328-2

This introductory textbook on operations management provides a comprehensive overview of the fundamental principles of operations and how they relate to effectively producing goods and services, and related decision-making processes. Keeping math to a minimum, it examines economic and international issues, and activities such as operations strategy for competitive advantage, forecasting, managing quality, operations technology, enterprise resource management, and supply chain management.

Quantitative Survival Guide for Operations Management, 2nd ed

Thomas Kratzer

New York: Wiley, 2005

71pp, ISBN: 978-0-471-67877-9

This is a concise reference that describes the quantitative skills and methods necessary in operations management. It analyzes the relevant mathematical concepts, and presents a series of examples of the types of problems that a student will encounter in a typical operations management textbook, as well as guidance on working through them.

Service Operations Management, 3rd ed

Robert Johnston, Graham Clark

Harlow, UK: FT Prentice Hall, 2008

533pp, ISBN: 978-1-4058-4732-2

This textbook describes the key terms, principles, tools, frameworks, and techniques

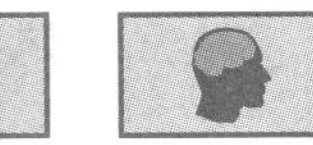   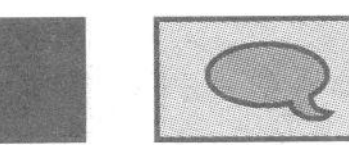 

for operational analysis and improvement, is aimed at students on services-orientated operations management courses. It assesses operations management within the wider business context, describes the impact of other management functions and issues, and explores the operations decisions that managers face in controlling their resources and delivering services to customers.

JOURNALS

Annals of Operations Research

Springer
233 Spring Street, New York, NY 10013, USA
T: +1 212 460 1500
F: +1 212 460 1575
www.springer.com/business/operations+research/journal/10479
ISSN: 0254-5330

Published eight times each year, this is a series of volumes dedicated to key aspects of operations research, including theory, practice, computation, and emerging trends. Each volume has a guest editor, and features research articles, short notes, expositions and surveys, reports on computational studies, and case studies that present new and innovative practical applications.

International Abstracts in Operations Research

International Federation of Operational Research Societies
Palgrave Macmillan, Brunel Road, Houndmills, Basingstoke, Hampshire, RG21 6XS, UK
T: +44 (0) 1256 357 893
F: +44 (0) 1256 328 339
www.palgrave-journals.com/iaor/index.html
ISSN: 0020-580X

IAOR, published eight times each year, offers abstracts from journals worldwide, to provide a comprehensive synopsis of current operations research literature. Further abstracts are selected from supplemental and specialized journals, if relevant to the philosophy, methodology, or practice of operations research. The topics are divided into the categories of process, application, technique, and professional.

International Journal of Operations & Production Management

Emerald Group
Howard House, Wagon Lane, Bingley, BD16 1WA, UK
T: +44 (0) 1274 777 700
F: +44 (0) 1274 785 201
www.emeraldinsight.com/products/journals/journals.htm?id=ijopm
ISSN: 0144-3577

IJOPM is a monthly journal that publishes insights into the latest theoretical and practical developments and research on operations management. It provides a means of communication for all those working in the operations management field, including academics, practitioners, and consultants, and focuses on management topics, rather than technical content.

International Transactions in Operational Research

International Federation of Operational Research Societies
Wiley, 350 Main Street, Malden, MA 02148, USA
T: +1 781 388 8598
www.wiley.com/bw/journal.asp?ref=0969-6016&site=1
ISSN: 0969-6016

ITOR is a bimonthly journal that that aims to advance the understanding and practice of operational research and management science internationally. Its scope includes international problems, international work done by industry leaders, studies of worldwide interest from nations with emerging operational research communities, national or regional work which has the potential for application in other nations, and technical developments of international interest.

Journal of Operations Management

Elsevier
Radarweg 29, 1043 NX Amsterdam, The Netherlands
F: +31 20 485 2370
www.elsevier.com/wps/find/journaldescription.cws_home/523929/description
ISSN: 0272-6963

This bimonthly journal publishes high-quality research papers in the field of operations management, with the aim of furthering the understanding of the subject among researchers and practitioners, and clarifying and advancing the role of operations management within organizations.

Operations Management

The Institute of Operations Management
Earlstrees Court, Earlstrees Road, Corby, Northants, NN17 4AX, UK
T: +44 (0) 1536 740 105
F: +44 (0) 1536 740 101
www.iomnet.org.uk/control-and-news/default.aspx
ISSN: 1529-5648

This journal, published bimonthly by the Institute of Operations Management, offers technical articles, reports, and case studies by practitioners, consultants, and academics, as well as industry news, book reviews, and information on activities and forthcoming events.

Production and Operations Management

Production and Operations Management Society, USA
www.poms.org/journal
ISSN: 1059-1478

This bimonthly journal is dedicated to research in operations management in manufacturing and services. It offers scientific research into the problems, interest, and concerns of managers, and covers all topics in product and process design, operations, and supply chain management.

INTERNET

Operations Research: The Science of Better

www.scienceofbetter.org

This online resource, run by the Institute for Operations Research and the Management Sciences, offers guidance and explanations on operations research, what it can do, and how to start using it, and features information on awards, leadership, and case studies.

ORGANIZATIONS

Europe

European Operations Management Association

Chair: Ann Vereecke
EurOMA Secretariat, c/o EIASM, Place De Brouckère Plein 31, 1000 Brussels, Belgium
T: +32 (0) 2 226 66 60
F: +32 (0) 2 512 19 29
E: euroma@eiasm.be
www.euroma-online.org

EurOMA is a leading European professional association for those involved in operations management. It comprises of an international network of academics and practitioners who are interested in the continuing development of operations management as an area of research and best practice, and offers international links for the share of knowledge, experiences, and ideas.

The Institute of Operations Management

Earlstrees Court, Earlstrees Road, Corby, Northants, NN17 4AX, UK
T: +44 (0) 1536 740 105
F: +44 (0) 1536 740 101
E: info@iomnet.org.uk
www.iomnet.org.uk

The institute provides a professional community of practitioners, consultants, academics, and thought leaders that promote the theory of, techniques for, and best practice in operations management. It is committed to excellence, continuous improvement and professionalism in operations management, and offers education and training in all its forms for the manufacturing and service industries.

USA

The Association for Operations Management

Chair: Thomas J. Krupka
8430 West Bryn Mawr Avenue, Suite 1000, Chicago, IL 60631, USA
T: +1 773 867 1777
F: +1 773 409 5576
E: service@apics.org
www.apics.org

APICS is the global association dedicated to operations management, including production, inventory, supply chain, materials management, purchasing, and logistics. It provides industry training, internationally recognized certifications, comprehensive resources, and a worldwide network of accomplished industry professionals.

Association of Business Process Management Professionals

Chair: Brett Champlin
47 West Polk Street, Suite 100–279, Chicago, IL 60605-2085, USA
www.abpmp.org

ABPMP is a non-profit, vendor-independent, professional organization dedicated to the advancement of business process management concepts and its practices. It has local chapters in several US areas, with more being formed in the US and internationally.

Institute for Operations Research and the Management Sciences

Chair: Don N. Kleinmuntz
7240 Parkway Drive, Suite 300, Hanover, Maryland 21706-1300, USA
T: +1 443 757 3500
F: +1 443 757 3515
E: onlineservices@informs.org
www.informs.org

INFORMS is a global association for professionals in the field of operations research. It serves the scientific and professional needs of operations research educators, investigators, scientists, students, managers, and consultants, as well as the organizations they serve, by publishing scholarly journals and a magazine, and organizing national and international conferences.

Production and Operations Management Society

Chair: Cheryl Gaimon
USA
E: poms@fiu.edu
www.poms.org

POMS is an international professional organization that represents the interests of industry professionals around the world. Its objectives include extending and integrating knowledge pertaining to production and operations management, disseminating information, and promoting the improvement and teaching on the subject to manufacturing and service organizations throughout the world.

International

International Federation of Operational Research Societies

Chair: Elise del Rosario
E: secretary@ifors.org
www.ifors.org

IFORS is an international umbrella organization dedicated to operational research, representing national societies around the world. It sponsors international meetings and other means for exchanging information on operational research, encourages nations to establish operational research societies, supports standards of competence in operational research, promotes operational research education, and promotes the growth of both existing and new fields of operational research.

Outsourcing

BOOKS

The Black Book of Outsourcing: How to Manage the Changes, Challenges, and Opportunities

Douglas Brown, Scott Wilson
Hoboken, New Jersey: Wiley, 2005
386pp, ISBN: 978-0-471-71889-5

This useful and comprehensive introduction to outsourcing is an essential guide to this growing (and often controversial) area. This book is as useful for those trying to carve out a career in this industry as it is for those who need to know the nuts and bolts, such as how to manage an outsourcing program.

Business Process Outsourcing: Process, Strategies, and Contracts, 2nd ed

John K. Halvey, Barbara Murphy Melby
Hoboken, New Jersey: Wiley, 2007
600pp, ISBN: 978-0-470-04483-4

In this guide for businesses looking to outsource some of their business functions, the topics dealt with address the process involved in contracting out key services, including the request for proposal (RFP) and selecting and contracting with an outsourcing vendor.

Outsourcing for Dummies

Ed Ashley
Hoboken, New Jersey: Wiley, 2008
368pp, ISBN: 978-0-470-22687-2

This practical, plain-English guide helps you plan an effective sourcing strategy. There are tips on negotiating with vendors, drafting a binding contract, and verifying and maintaining compliance. It also explains the importance of communicating with vendors, finding ways to measure performance, productivity, and cost-effectiveness, troubleshooting and solving outsourcing problems, and advice on ending the deal.

The Outsourcing Handbook: How to Implement a Successful Outsourcing Process

Mark J. Power, Kevin Desouza, Carlo Bonifazi
London: Kogan Page, 2006
222pp, ISBN: 978-0-7494-4430-3

The book provides detailed insight into the processes, issues, pitfalls, and successes for any type of outsourcing activity. It provides a valuable set of customer outsourcing methodology activities, and does not assume any prior knowledge of the subject.

Outsourcing IT: The Legal Aspects, 2nd ed

Rachel Burnett
Aldershot, UK: Gower Publishing, 2009
276pp, ISBN: 978-0-566-08597-0

This comprehensive guide to outsourcing the information technology function focuses on the need to obtain a properly negotiated formal contract. It discusses the structure of such a contract, and then goes on to cover the provisions that relate to staffing, location, software, costs, management liaison, allowing for change, security, duration, termination, and other matters. It also gives advice on public procurement and choosing a supplier.

The Outsourcing Process: Strategies for Evaluation and Management

Ronan McIvor
Cambridge, UK: Cambridge University Press, 2005
326pp, ISBN: 978-0-521-84411-6

This book provides a framework for an up-to-date understanding of the outsourcing process and the key issues associated with it. It integrates a number of contemporary topics, including benchmarking, buyer-supplier relationships, organizational behavior, competitor analysis, and technology influences.

What's This India Business? Offshoring, Outsourcing and the Global Services Revolution

Paul Davies
London: Nicholas Brealey Publishing, 2008
252pp, ISBN: 978-1-904838-21-0

Many businesses have outsourced some of their operations to India, and this book is a practical guide for anyone planning or simply investigating such a route. Packed with advice on how to gain competitive advantage from outsourcing to India, the books also has helpful hints on etiquette and Indian business culture.

JOURNALS

Strategic Outsourcing: An International Journal

Emerald
60/62 Toller Lane, Bradford, West Yorkshire, BD8 9BY, UK
T: +44 (0) 1274 777 700
F: +44 (0) 1274 785 200
www.emeraldinsight.com/1750-614X.htm
ISSN: 1750-614X

This journal aims to foster and lead the international debate on global sourcing and outsourcing. It provides a central, authoritative, and independent forum for the critical evaluation and dissemination of research and development, applications, processes and current practices relating to the design, implementation, and undertaking of strategic outsourcing.

INTERNET

BPO Watch India

www.bpowatchindia.com

This is a leading source for news and research on the business process outsourcing (BPO) industry.

National Outsourcing Association

www.noa.co.uk

  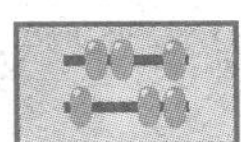      

This site provides access to recent articles by members and details of association events. It also has a members-only section.

Outsource World

www.outsource-world.com

Outsource World offers conferences, exhibitions, links, and networks through this site.

Outsourcing Center

www.outsourcing-center.com

This website provides comprehensive information and links regarding outsourcing. Its content includes industry-specific outsourcing information, research, outsourcing processes, and an online journal. It also provides material on suppliers and legal issues.

The Outsourcing Institute

www.outsourcing.com

The Outsourcing Institute is a professional association providing information and networking resources related to outsourcing. Its website offers information on the outsourcing process, including needs assessment and the selection of service providers. It also has information targeted at buyers and sellers of outsourcing services. Registration is required for some information; online membership is free.

The Outsourcing Management Zone

www.theoutsourcerzone.com

This site is aimed at both outsourcing professionals and those new to the concept. It provides numerous articles, a directory, and information on outsourcing, and also explains how and why outsourcing can affect your business.

Outsourcing Research Center

www.cio.com/topic/1513/Outsourcing

The site provides online access to recent articles on outsourcing, as well as providing details of forthcoming events.

silicon.com

www.silicon.com/tags/outsourcing.htm

This business technology site offers a range of news, articles, and links on outsourcing.

TechWeb Business Technology Network

www.techweb.com

This site focuses on recent news and articles on IT outsourcing, plus links to events in its "Tech Calendar."

Virtual Corporations and Outsourcing

www.brint.com

A selection of articles on outsourcing can be sourced from this site.

ORGANIZATIONS

Europe

National Outsourcing Association (NOA)

44 Wardour Street, London, W1D 6QZ, UK
T: +44 (0) 20 7292 8686
F: +44 (0) 20 7287 2905
E: admin@noa.co.uk
www.noa.co.uk

The NOA is the only outsourcing trade association in the UK. Formally established as a non-profit company, it operates as an independent organization, with a principle objective of boosting the effectiveness and success of outsourcing, through the promotion of best practice and innovation in the application and development of outsourcing.

Network Outsourcing Association

Keswick House, 44 Wardour Street, London, W1D 6QZ, UK
T: +44 (0) 20 7292 8686
F: +44 (0) 20 8778 8402
E: admin@noa.co.uk
www.noa.co.uk

The Association is an independent body, formed in the early 1990s, that acts as a forum for the business technology outsourcing community. Its membership is made up of UK and other companies with experience in outsourcing, and suppliers and consultants who support the industry.

USA

The Outsourcing Institute

Jericho Atrium, 500 North Broadway, Suite 141, Jericho, New York, NY 11753, USA
T: +1 516 681 0066
F: +1 516 938 1839
E: customerservice@outsourcing.com
www.outsourcing.com

This professional body, founded in 1993, provides outsourcing professionals worldwide with access to a business-to-business marketplace and an independent advisory network, as well as with information and education on outsourcing best practice. Membership is free.

BRIC

China Sourcing

F12 Baiyan Building, 238, Beisihuan Zhong Road, Haidian District, Beijing 100191, China
T: +86 10 823 31717
F: +86 10 8233 2323
E: ruby.guan@chinasourcingguide.com
www.chinasourcingguide.com

The objective of China Sourcing is to raise awareness of China as a provider of highly skilled technology services and gain recognition for China's vibrant technology outsourcing industry. Its participants are the Beijing Municipal Science & Technology Commission, the Beijing Municipal Bureau of Commerce, and the Beijing Software Industry Productivity Center.

Export Promotion Bureau of Bangladesh (EPB)

Export Promotion Bureau, TCB Bhaban, 1–2, Kawran Bazar C/A Dhaka 1215, Bangladesh
T: +880 2 9144 821 4
F: +880 2 9119 531
E: info@epb.gov.bd
www.epb.gov.bd

This government organization, run by the Ministry of Commerce, promotes export and international trade. It is pivotal when entering into a trade agreement with a Bangladeshi company.

Outsourcing Malaysia (OM)

1106, Block B, Phileo Damansara II, 15, Jln 16/11, 46350 Petaling Jaya, Selangor Darul Ehsan, Malaysia
T: +60 3 7955 2922
F: +60 3 7955 2933
www.outsourcingmalaysia.org.my

Outsourcing Malaysia (OM) is an initiative of the outsourcing industry and a chapter of PIKOM. With the support from its institutional partners, such as the Multimedia Development Corporation and the Malaysia Debt Ventures, and senior leaders from the global services industry, it promotes the capabilities and competencies of the Malaysian outsourcing industry.

Pension Fund Finance

BOOKS

Dealing with the New Giants: Rethinking the Role of Pension Funds

Tito Boeri, Lans Bovenberg, Benoit Coeure, Andrew Roberts
Geneva Reports on the World Economy Series
London: Centre for Economic Policy Research, 2006
140pp, ISBN: 978-1-898128-94-6

This examines the role of pension funds as major institutional investors in global financial markets, their impact of risk sharing, and imperfect markets in which they operate. It argues for a reform of public pension systems, mandatory participation in standalone, collective pension plans, a new governance structure for pension funds, the harmonization of accounting standards, and the development of innovative hybrid collective pension schemes.

Fiduciary Management: Blueprint for Pension Fund Excellence

Anton van Nunen
Wiley Finance Series
Hoboken, New Jersey: Wiley, 2008
274pp, ISBN: 978-0-470-17103-5

This practical guide examines fiduciary management as an increasingly popular strategy for organizing the management of institutional investment portfolios. It describes its rise to prominence, the benefits of fiduciary management, and the key functions of the fiduciary manager. It also analyzes it in terms of asset-liability modeling, constructing portfolios,

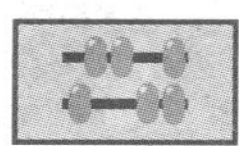

selecting and overseeing investment managers, benchmarking and performance measurement, and reporting.

Foundation and Endowment Investing: Philosophies and Strategies of Top Investors and Institutions

Lawrence E. Kochard, Cathleen M. Rittereiser
Wiley Finance Series
Hoboken, New Jersey: Wiley, 2008
320pp, ISBN: 978-0-470-12233-4

This offers a number of profiles of top Chief Investment Officers in the foundation and endowment industry, where they discuss their investment philosophies, their strategies for improving the financial health of their organizations, and how they applied them in real-world market conditions. It also provides a practical perspective on institutional investing, and issues such as asset allocation and the emergence of alternative asset classes.

Frontiers in Pension Finance

Dirk Broeders, Sylvester Eijffinger, Aerdt Houben (editors)
Cheltenham, UK: Edward Elgar Publishing, 2008
337pp, ISBN: 978-1-84720-660-2

This is a guide to the latest insights into pension finance, pension system design, pension governance, and risk-based supervision, which attempts to meet the challenges currently faced by this fast-changing industry. A team of international experts examine the pressure of an ageing population, the shift from pay-as-you-go pension systems to pre-funded plans, the delivery of adequate pension benefits at reasonable costs, and attempts to increase the efficiency of pension systems.

How to Select Investment Managers & Evaluate Performance: A Guide for Pension Funds, Endowments, Foundations, and Trusts

G. Timothy Haight, Stephen O. Morrell, Glenn E. Ross
Frank J. Fabozzi Series
Hoboken, New Jersey: Wiley, 2007
260pp, ISBN: 978-0-470-04255-7

This is a comprehensive and accessible guide to selecting and evaluating external investment professionals, improving their effectiveness, and gauging their ability to meet clients' investment goals, objectives, and needs. It is useful for trustees of pension plans, endowments, and trusts responsible for governing and overseeing the investment of their funds, and covers such aspects as return measures, fixed income and duration, manager searches, and committee meetings.

Innovations in Pension Fund Management

Arun Muralidhar
Stanford, California: Stanford Economics and Finance, 2001
327pp, ISBN: 978-0-8047-4521-5

This is a theoretical and practical guide to current thinking on pension fund investment strategy, asset allocation, human financial resource management, risk management, and performance evaluation and implementation. It covers asset liability management, current practices of plan sponsors and investment managers, how to best measure and manage risk, and provides a framework for the use of derivatives in funds, and the benefits of leverage.

Investing in Pension Funds and Endowments: Tools and Guidelines for the New Independent Fiduciary

Russell L. Olson
New York: McGraw-Hill, 2003
409pp, ISBN: 978-0-07-141336-7

This is an accessible, practical reference to all aspects of investing for pension funds, endowments, trusts, and foundations. It analyzes the opportunities and pitfalls for fund managers, and describes how to produce superior pension management returns without sacrificing fiduciary responsibilities. It also provides practical guidance on risk, asset allocation, types of potential investments, master trustees and custodians, governance, and liabilities.

The Money Flood: How Pension Funds Revolutionized Investing

Michael J. Clowes
New York: Wiley, 2000
308pp, ISBN: 978-0-471-38483-0

This is a history of the growth of corporate pension funds over the last fifty years, which details their impact on investing, the financial markets, the labor force, corporate management, and the general economy. It also provides a warning regarding the potential consequences of these changes, the power of fund managers in the global financial markets, and the shift from defined benefit pension plans to defined contribution plans.

No Small Change: Pension Funds and Corporate Engagement

Tessa Hebb
Ithaca, New York: Cornell University Press, 2008
152pp, ISBN: 978-0-8014-4696-2

This is an exploration of how pension funds are meeting the challenge of the long-term value of the stocks they hold, the risks faced, and the pressure of now being major owners of corporations. It examines the ability of pension funds to change corporate practices by adding share value, ensuring the retirement benefits of their members, and also using their influence to raise the environmental, social, and governance standards of companies.

Pension Finance

David Blake
Chichester, UK: Wiley, 2006
465pp, ISBN: 978-0-470-05843-5

This provides a comprehensive overview of theory and practice in pension finance from a multi-disciplinary perspective. It explains the different types of investment assets, different asset classes, corporate pension finance, the financial aspects of defined contribution and defined benefit pension plans, the role of pension funds and pension fund management, pension fund performance measurement and attribution, and risk management in pension funds.

Pension Fund Excellence: Creating Value for Stakeholders

Keith P. Ambachtsheer, D. Don Ezra
New York: Wiley, 1998
238pp, ISBN: 978-0-471-24655-8

This comprehensive handbook to effective pension fund management focuses on the integration of pension fund governance, management, and operations, decision structures, fiduciary responsibilities, pension economics, and the markets for financial capital and investment management services. It examines the rise of defined contribution plans, how to fix problematic national social security schemes, and discusses the growing economic power of pension funds.

Pension Fund Governance: A Global Perspective on Financial Regulation

John Evans, Michael Orszag, John Piggott (editors)
Cheltenham, UK: Edward Elgar Publishing, 2008
269pp, ISBN: 978-1-84720-485-1

This technical treatment of pension fund governance combines original contributions from industry experts around the world, based on both theoretical analysis and empirical study. It provides frameworks for pension fund governance, and examines private and public pensions, global governance practice and experience on pension funds in the United States and Australia, and discusses the role of government guarantees.

Pension Fund Investment Management, 2nd ed

Frank J. Fabozzi
Hoboken, New Jersey: Wiley, 1997
301pp, ISBN: 978-1-883249-26-7

The new edition of this wide-ranging handbook examines the essentials of pension fund investment management, before discussing current developments and issues in pension fund governance, operations, and value creation. It is written by a team of leading industry experts, and is aimed at all investment professionals concerned with the management of pension funds.

Pension Fund Trustee Handbook, 9th ed

Roger Self
Haywards Heath, UK: Tottel Publishing, 2005
365pp, ISBN: 978-1-84592-175-0

This is a comprehensive guide to the role and duties of occupational pension fund trustees, providing a useful reference regardless of level of legal expertise. This updated edition examines both statutory and trust law, the role of the sponsoring employer, the rights of the scheme members, requirements for advisers, and looks at breaches of trust, protection for trustees, and trustee powers and discretions.

  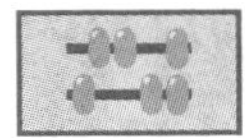      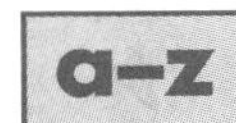

Pension Revolution: A Solution to the Pensions Crisis

Keith P. Ambachtsheer

Wiley Finance Series
Hoboken, New Jersey: Wiley, 2007
336pp, ISBN: 978-0-470-08723-7

This examination of the current failings of retirement plans offers strategic analysis of pension governance, benefit design, investment policy, funding, organizational structure, the distribution of risk, performance measurement, and results disclosure. It details the design features that have helped create the pension crisis, and explains how to bring about fundamental changes to ensure that the provision of retirement income is sustainable.

Risk-Based Supervision of Pension Funds: Emerging Practices and Challenges

Greg Brunner, Roberto Rocha, Richard Hinz (editors)

Directions in Development Series
Washington, DC: World Bank, 2008
250pp, ISBN: 978-0-8213-7493-1

This is a review of risk-based pension fund supervision and the increasing focus on risk management in both banking and insurance based on capital requirements, supervisory review, and market discipline. It examines the modifications needed to apply the method to pension funds, particularly for defined contribution funds, and presents a range of cases on the diversity of pension systems and approaches to risk-based supervision.

Risk Management for Pensions, Endowments, and Foundations

Susan M. Mangiero

Wiley Finance Series
Hoboken, New Jersey: Wiley, 2005
268pp, ISBN: 978-0-471-23485-2

This approach to the risk management process for endowments, foundations, and pension funds examines the important links among the accounting, corporate governance, and economic aspects of hedging. It analyzes the corporate governance rationale for risk management education, the basics of risk, futures, options, and swaps, the risk management concepts and processes, and issues such as valuation and reporting.

State and Local Pension Fund Management

Jun Peng

Public Administration and Public Policy Series
Boca Raton, Florida: Taylor & Francis, 2008
263pp, ISBN: 978-0-8493-0548-1

This is a systematic guide to the major issues facing those responsible for state and local public retirement programs. It provides a history of the public pension system, and looks at pension benefit design, actuarial valuation and funding methods, financial reporting, and pension asset investment management, before focusing on policy issues such as the management of public pension programs, and pension benefit reforms.

MAGAZINES

European Pensions & Investment News

Financial Times Group
1 Southwark Bridge, London, SE1 9HL, UK
T: +44 (0) 20 7873 3000
www.epn-magazine.com

This fortnightly magazine provides news, information, and analysis on all aspects of the investment of employer-supported retirement institutions, including traditional defined benefit and defined contribution company pension funds. It focuses on investment trends, the operation of the institutional fund management industry, analysis of regulatory changes both on a national and EU level, and analysis of the investment intentions of retirement institutions.

Global Pensions

Incisive Media
28–29 Haymarket, London, SW1Y 4RX, UK
T: +44 (0) 20 7484 9700
F: +44 (0) 20 7234 0702
www.globalpensions.com
ISSN: 1743-3312

This monthly magazine, with daily and weekly online updates, is a news-driven, campaigning publication that provides opinion and analysis of current information on institutional pension schemes worldwide. It focuses on regional pensions news, new investment products, current trends in the industry, and also offers round table discussions.

Investment & Pensions Europe

IPE International Publishers
320 Great Guildford House, 30 Great Guildford Street, London, SE1 0HS, UK
T: +44 (0) 20 7261 0666
www.ipe.com
ISSN: 1369-3727

This monthly magazine is aimed at those responsible for running pension funds in Europe. It provides coverage of the major challenges that are facing the industry in meeting the retirement needs of ageing populations, and the opportunity this provides for the asset management industry, and offers a database of pension funds country-by-country, and monthly supplements on a wide range of topics.

Pensions & Investments

Crain Communications
711 Third Avenue, New York, NY 10017, USA
T: +1 212 210 0100
F: +1 212 210 0117
www.pionline.com
ISSN: 1050-4974

This fortnightly international newspaper on money management provides news, research, and analysis to pension, portfolio, and investment managers in the institutional investment market. It provides coverage of events affecting the money management business, including business and financial news, legislative reports, global investments, product development, technology, investment performance, executive changes, and corporate governance.

Pensions Age

Perspective Publishing
6th Floor, 3 London Wall Buildings, London, EC2M 5PD, UK
T: +44 (0) 20 7562 2401
F: +44 (0) 20 7374 2701
www.pensionsage.com

This monthly magazine for pensions professionals covers a wide range of topics, including personal and occupational schemes, employee benefits, investment management, legislative changes and technology. It offers news, market surveys, product developments, and features on the main issues in both the private and public sectors.

Pensions Management

Financial Times Group
1 Southwark Bridge, London, SE1 9HL, UK
T: +44 (0) 20 7873 3000
www.pensions-management.co.uk

This monthly magazine is source of information and debate on the UK pension and investment markets. It reports on the latest developments in the pensions sector, interviews industry experts, presents key fund statistics, and provides surveys, features, roundtables, awards, investment, people, politics/policy, and product news.

Professional Pensions

Incisive Media
28–29 Haymarket, London, SW1Y 4RX, UK
T: +44 (0) 20 7484 9700
F: +44 (0) 20 7034 2750
www.professionalpensions.com

This weekly publication for the occupational pensions industry in the UK offers news and commentary on the key issues facing schemes and their sponsors. It offers regular roundtable and panel debates on a range of investment, administrative and legal topics, industry sector reports on property investment, specialist managers, local authority schemes, group risk and consultants, as well as fund performance statistics, job opportunities, and interviews.

JOURNALS

Journal of Pension Economics and Finance

Cambridge University Press
The Edinburgh Building, Shaftesbury Road, Cambridge, CB2 8RU, UK
T: +44 (0) 1223 326 070
F: +44 (0) 1223 325 150
journals.cambridge.org/action/displayJournal?jid=PEF
ISSN: 1474-7472

JPEF is a quarterly journal that focuses on the economics and finance of pensions and retirement income. It offers research on a variety of topics, including pension fund management, the regulation of pensions, and pensions and labor markets, and current public policies, and provides a forum for international debate on the impact of demographic factors on the pensions industry.

Journal of Pension Planning and Compliance

Aspen Publishers
76 Ninth Avenue, New York, NY 10011, USA

  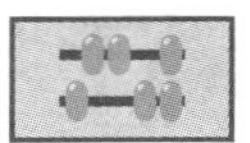      

T: +1 301 698 7100
www.aspenpublishers.com/product.asp?catalog_name=Aspen&product_id=SS01482181
ISSN: 0148-2181

This quarterly journal publishes technical articles on major issues confronting the pension community. It covers pension compliance and design issues, plan qualification problems, new developments in employee benefits, and current legislative trends, as well as aspects of non-discrimination regulations, plan administration, tax law, and fiduciary liability.

Pensions: An International Journal

Palgrave Macmillan
Houndmills, Basingstoke, RG21 6XS, UK
www.palgrave-journals.com/pm
ISSN: 1478-5315

Pensions is quarterly journal for pensions professionals that is dedicated to the practice of pensions administration, law, compliance, and investment. It provides briefings, analyses, and updates on areas such as investment policy, benefits practices, actuarial prediction, trustee responsibility, regulation, advisory services, pensions management, government policy, accounting and reporting practices, dispute resolution, and legislation and case law.

INTERNET

IPE.com

www.ipe.com

This is a major European website that provides daily news, articles, web conferencing, white papers, and links for the pensions community. It also offers useful resources, such as a guide to managing pension funds, seminars, a real estate investment managers guide, an asset manager database, a pension funds database, and industry job information.

PensionsNet

www.pensionsnet.com

This is an online resource that presents news, features, a free weekly email service, seminars, and surveys on recent pensions and investments news.

ORGANIZATIONS

Europe

European Federation for Retirement Provision

Chair: Angel Martinez-Aldama
Koningsstraat 97 rue Royale, 1000 Brussels, Belgium
T: +32 (0) 2 289 14 14
F: +32 (0) 2 289 14 15
E: efrp@efrp.org
www.efrp.org

EFRP represents occupational/supplementary pension plans throughout the European Union, and acts as a centre of expertise within Europe. It promotes national diversity in financial vehicles to fund occupational pension schemes, the view that pension provision can be combined to form one single retirement income, the balance between the protection of pension fund ben eficiaries and the efficiency of financing the liabilities, and the rights of pension funds as wholesale consumers.

National Association of Pension Funds

Chair: Joanne Segars
NIOC House, 4 Victoria Street, London, SW1H 0NX, UK
T: +44 (0) 20 7808 1300
F: +44 (0) 20 7222 7585
E: napf@napf.co.uk
www.napf.co.uk

The NAPF is an industry association dedicated to workplace pensions in the UK, representing those involved in designing, operating, advising, and investing in all aspects of pensions and other retirement provision. It offers information, conferences, seminars, and events for its members, who are pension schemes, businesses that provide services to the pensions sector, local authorities, and other organizations that provide pensions for their employees.

Pensions Institute

Chair: David Blake
Cass Business School, 106 Bunhill Row, London, EC1Y 8TZ, UK
T: +44 (0) 20 7040 8951
E: d.blake@city.ac.uk
www.pensions-institute.org

The institute undertakes high quality research in all fields related to pensions, including microeconomics, fund management and performance, contingency analysis and valuation, law and regulation, accounting, taxation and administration, and the marketing of private sector pension schemes. It also disseminates the results to academics and professionals, establishes international networks of pension researchers, and provides expert advice to the pensions industry and government.

Pensions Management Institute

Chair: Steve Delo
PMI House, 4–10 Artillery Lane, London, E1 7LS, UK
T: +44 (0) 20 7247 1452
F: +44 (0) 20 7375 0603
E: enquiries@pensions-pmi.org.uk
www.pensions-pmi.org.uk

PMI is a non-lobbying professional body that promotes professionalism amongst those working in the field of pensions. It offers four levels of membership and nine different examinations, as well as providing a range of support services for ongoing personal development, a series of national and regional events, a number of publications, and a network of nine regional groups.

Pensions Policy Institute

Chair: Baroness Greengross
King's College, Room 311, 3rd Floor, 26 Drury Lane, London, WC2B 5RL, UK
T: +44 (0) 20 7848 3744
F: +44 (0) 20 7848 1786
E: info@pensionspolicyinstitute.org.uk
www.pensionspolicyinstitute.org.uk

The PPI is an educational organization that provides non-political, independent comment and analysis on pension policy in the UK. It provides relevant and accessible information on the extent and nature of retirement provision, analysis and commentary on the policy-making process, encourages pension research and debate, acts as a sounding board for providers, policy makers and opinion formers, and informs the public debate on pensions issues.

Pensions Research Accountants Group

Chair: Jeff Highfield
c/o Deloitte & Touche, 4 Brindley Place, Birmingham, B1 2HZ, UK
E: feedback@prag.org.uk
www.prag.org.uk

PRAG is an independent research and discussion group for the development and exchange of ideas in the pensions field. It focuses on the main areas of reporting and accounting by pension schemes, and produces reports on related matters.

Society of Pension Consultants

Chair: Duncan Howorth
St Bartholomew House, 92 Fleet Street, London, EC4Y 1DG, UK
T: +44 (0) 20 7353 1688
F: +44 (0) 20 7353 9296
E: info@spc.uk.com
www.spc.uk.com

SPC is a representative body for providers of advice and services to work-based pension schemes, and their sponsors across the private pensions sector. It aims to influence policy and strategy, provide members with access to technical information on key policy debates, and helps to raise the profile of its members and address practical industry issues on their behalf.

USA

American Society of Pension Professionals & Actuaries

Chair: Brian H. Graff
4245 North Fairfax Drive, Suite 750, Arlington, VA 22203, USA
T: +1 703 516 9300
F: +1 703 516 9308
E: asppa@asppa.org
www.asppa.org

ASPPA is a national, non-profit, professional organization for career retirement plan professionals, its members being comprised of disciplines supporting retirement income management and benefits policy. Its aims are to educate retirement plan and benefits professionals, and preserve and enhance the private pension system. It offers educational programs for its members, and tracks legislative and regulatory activities affecting retirement benefits and pension policy.

National Institute of Pension Administrators

Chair: Theresa Conti
401 North Michigan Avenue, #2200, Chicago, Illinois 60611-4267, USA
F: +1 312 245 1085
E: nipa@nipa.org
www.nipa.org

NIPA is a national organization that educates and trains pension plan administrators. It encourages active participation in order to maintain our profession at the highest

possible standards, and provides educational forums such as courses, workshops, and seminars on various aspects of plan administration.

The Pension Research Council

Chair: Olivia S. Mitchell
The Wharton School, 3620 Locust Walk, 3000 Steinberg Hall–Dietrich Hall, Philadelphia, PA 19104-6302, USA
T: +1 215 898 7620
F: +1 215 573 3418
E: prc@wharton.upenn.edu
www.pensionresearchcouncil.org

The Pension Research Council is a non-profit organization based at the Wharton School of the University of Pennsylvania, and is committed to generating debate on key policy issues affecting pensions and other employee benefits. It sponsors interdisciplinary research on private pension and social security programs, as well as related benefit plans worldwide. It holds conferences and symposia, research projects, and publishes books, preprints, and working papers.

International

International Federation of Pension Fund Administrators

Avda. 11 de septiembre 2155, Tower C, Office 901, Floor 9, Providencia, Santiago, Chile
T: +56 2 381 1723
F: +56 2 381 2655
E: fiap@fiap.cl
www.fiap.cl

FIAP is a non-profit organization that disseminates, promotes, defends, and publicizes the development of social security systems based on saving and individual capitalization, through pension fund administrators. Its aims include the uniting of associations, chambers, and similar institutions in countries which have legally constituted systems of pension fund administrators, the promotion of private pension fund systems, and representing the concerns of its members in an international context.

The International Organisation of Pension Supervisors

Chair: Ross Jones
OECD Bureau Ingres 278, 2 Rue Andre Pascal, 75116 Paris, France
E: andre.laboul@oecd.org
www.iopsweb.org

IOPS is an independent international body that represents those involved in the supervision of private pension arrangements. It covers all levels of economic development and brings together all types of pension and supervisory systems. It acts as worldwide forum for policy dialogue and the exchange of information, as well as a standard setting body for promoting good practices in pension supervision.

Pricing

BOOKS

Asset Pricing

John Howland Cochrane
Princeton, New Jersey: Princeton University Press, 2001
530pp, ISBN: 978-0-691-07498-6

Asset Pricing covers the pricing of all assets, focusing on the concept of price equals expected discounted payoff. It examines empirical work using the Generalized Method of Moments, which studies sample average prices and discounted payoffs to determine whether price does equal expected discounted payoff. It also includes review of recent empirical work on return predictability and value.

International Transfer Pricing: A Study of Cross-Border Transactions

J. Elliott, C. R. Emmanuel
London: CIMA Publishing, 2000
96pp, ISBN: 978-1-85971-346-4

Directed at managers and theorists, this report is based on a research project investigating international transfer pricing (ITP) in 12 organizations. It presents the findings from interviews aimed at acquiring an in-depth understanding of single ITP transactions undertaken by participants in each of the multinational organizations involved. Key issues and trends are summarized in the last section.

Market-oriented Pricing: Strategies for Management

Michael H. Morris, Gene Morris
Lincolnwood, Illinois: Quorum Books, 2001
224pp, ISBN: 978-0-8442-3460-1

Using company case studies and examples, this manual for marketers and managers leads its readers through the steps involved in developing and implementing market-based pricing strategies. The areas covered include the psychology of pricing, market and competitor analysis, negotiating prices, using price elasticity, and computer aids in pricing.

The Price Advantage, 2nd ed

Michael V. Marn, Eric V. Roegner, Craig C. Zawada
Hoboken, New Jersey: Wiley, 2010
384pp, ISBN: 978-0-470-48177-6

Price advantage suggests that many companies neglect the opportunities offered by pricing strategy for increasing profitability and outperforming the competition. Drawing on their experience of advising businesses, the authors offer a practical pricing guide for managers. A three-level framework for identifying and exploiting pricing opportunities, covering industry strategy, product and market strategy and transaction level, is set out. Pricing issues in specific contexts such as the introduction of new products, packaged offerings, price wars, post-merger pricing and practical issues such as the use of technology and the regulatory framework are also addressed. These are then placed within overall organizational strategy. The text is illustrated throughout with case studies.

Price Advantage, 2nd ed

Michael V. Marn, Eric V. Roegner, Craig C. Zawada
Hoboken, New Jersey: Wiley, 2010
384pp, ISBN: 978-0-470-48177-6

Price advantage suggests that many companies neglect the opportunities offered by pricing strategy for increasing profitability and outperforming the competition. Drawing on their experience of advising businesses, the authors offer a practical pricing guide for managers. A three-level framework for identifying and exploiting pricing opportunities, covering industry strategy, product and market strategy, and transaction level, is set out. Pricing issues in specific contexts such as the introduction of new products, packaged offerings, price wars, post-merger pricing and practical issues such as the use of technology and the regulatory framework are also addressed. These are then placed within overall organizational strategy. The text is illustrated throughout with case studies.

Pricing for Profitability: Activity-Based Pricing for Competitive Advantage

John L. Daly
Chichester, UK: Wiley, 2001
288pp, ISBN: 978-0-471-41535-0

The authors suggest that activity-based pricing helps companies set appropriate prices which both generate sales and result in a profit. Activity-based pricing analyzes the interdependence between price, cost and sales volume, resulting in a disciplined approach to the process of price development. Other topics included in the book are estimating customer demand, pricing law in the United States, the ethics of pricing, planning profit, and tips for successful price negotiations.

Pricing on Purpose: Creating and Capturing Value

Ronald J. Baker
Hoboken, New Jersey: Wiley, 2006
416pp, ISBN: 978-0-471-72980-8

This book explains the theory of value, and details how any business can use the various pricing strategies to create, communicate, and capture the value of their products and services. It takes a new approach by focusing on the external value as perceived by the customer, and advocates matching price to value. It can be useful for new executives, professional pricers, and marketers.

Professional's Guide to Value Pricing, 6th ed

Ronald J. Baker
Chicago, Illinois: CCH, 2005
640pp, ISBN: 978-0-7355-4806-0

This book lets readers see how pricing by the hour, instead of pricing by the value, can have a negative effect on your business. Through examples and clear and powerful writing, Baker leads the businessperson to achieve a better system of charging by the services rendered to the client.

Profitable Buying Strategies: How to Cut Procurement Costs and Buy Your Way to Higher Profits
Mike Buchanan
London: Kogan Page, 2008
256pp, ISBN: 978-0-7494-5238-4

This book gives clear and self-explanatory advice of cost reduction techniques which can be applied in any business. It examines how to improve your staff's skills in negotiation, e-procurement, market testing, and outsourcing. It also covers relevant contract laws for ensuring effective buying operations.

The Strategy and Tactics of Pricing: A Guide to Growing More Profitably, 4th ed
Thomas T. Nagle, Reed K. Holden
Harlow, UK: Prentice Hall, 2006
368pp, ISBN: 978-0-13-204358-8

The Strategy and Tactics of Pricing provides a comprehensive, practical, step-by-step guide to pricing analysis and strategy development. Ideal for MBA students, this book is a practical guide to pricing strategy. Concepts are fully illustrated with examples, and this new edition features many drawn from the world of e-commerce.

Transfer Pricing Methods: An Applications Guide
Robert Feinscreiber
Chichester, UK: Wiley, 2004
320pp, ISBN: 978-0-471-57360-9

This practical guide is designed to assist managers in mid-sized businesses with the techniques of transfer pricing. The subject is introduced and the application of specific transfer pricing techniques is explained. Also explored are various international transfer pricing issues.

Winning the Profit Game: Smarter Pricing and Smarter Branding
Robert G. Docters et al.
Maidenhead, UK: McGraw-Hill, 2003
320pp, ISBN: 978-0-07-143472-0

In order to improve profitability, it is argued that organizations now need to focus on the top line, and that the two fundamental tools for doing this are price and brand. The need to take a fresh look at price and brand is explained, and the process of developing an integrated price brand strategy is examined. This focuses on setting price and creating revenue, managing ongoing revenues, and building revenue capabilities.

JOURNALS

Journal of Product and Brand Management
Emerald
60/62 Toller Lane, Bradford, West Yorkshire, BD8 9BY, UK
T: +44 (0) 1274 777 700
F: +44 (0) 1274 785 200
www.emeraldinsight.com/1061-0421.htm
ISSN: 1061-0421

This academic journal, published seven times each year, explores the practice of product and brand management, as well as the understanding of product and pricing issues. It presents practical problems and solutions through case histories and examines the deployment of advertising, sales, promotion, packaging, research, consumer psychology, and other elements in branding.

Journal of Revenue and Pricing Management
Palgrave Macmillan
Houndmills, Basingstoke, Hampshire, RG21 6XS, UK
www.palgrave-journals.com/rpm/index.html
ISSN: 1476-6930

This journal, published five times each year, offers commentary and analysis on this growing sector. It focuses on revenue management, also known as yield management, and related areas, such as operations research/management science, statistics, economics, human resource management, software development, marketing, economics, e-commerce, consumer behavior, and consulting in their use for managing demand for a firm's products or services.

INTERNET

Professional Pricing Society
www.pricingsociety.com

Sponsored by a professional society dedicated to pricing management, the site offers forums, mailing list archives, products for purchase, webinars, and a bookstore for related books. Membership services are also available, as is a free newsletter.

Strategic Pricing Group
www.strategicpricinggroup.com

Sponsored by a consulting firm that specializes in strategic pricing, this site provides articles, recommended reading, a calendar of events, and information on educational services and consulting.

ORGANIZATIONS

Europe

Chartered Institute of Marketing (CIM)
Moor Hall, Cookham, Maidenhead, Berkshire, SL6 9QH, UK
T: +44 (0) 1628 427 500
F: +44 (0) 1628 427 499
E: marketing@cim.co.uk
www.cim.co.uk

The CIM is the main organization for professional marketers in the United Kingdom. It runs courses, holds examinations, produces publications, and offers information services covering all aspects of marketing.

USA

Fordham University Pricing Center
113 West, 60th Street, New York, NY 10023, USA
www.fordham.edu/cba/pricecenter

The Fordham University Pricing Center is a research institution dedicated to developing a better understanding of prices and pricing, from both academic and managerial perspectives. It conducts academic research, and sponsors research and practitioner seminars, and also acts as an advocate for pricing education in business school curricula.

Professional Pricing Society
3535 Roswell Road, Suite 59, Marietta, GA 30062, USA
T: +1 770 509 9933
F: +1 770 509 1963
E: contactus@pricingsociety.com
www.pricingsociety.com

PPS is an association for price decision makers and price management personnel; its members are primarily pricing and marketing executives. It offers its members conferences and workshops, monthly and quarterly publications, consulting services, and pricing workbooks.

BRIC

Association of Mutual Funds in India
709 Raheja Centre, Free Press Journal Marg, Nariman Point, Mumbai 400 021, India
T: +91 22 6610 1886
F: +91 22 6610 1889
www.amfiindia.com/index.asp

The Association of Mutual Funds in India focuses on developing the Indian mutual fund industry on professional and ethical lines, and enhancing and maintaining standards in all areas, to help protect and promote the interests of mutual funds and their unit holders.

National Investment Information Network
Brazil
T: +55 61 2109 7055
F: +55 61 2109 7047
E: renai@desenvolvimento.gov.br
investimentos.desenvolvimento.gov.br/renai_en/index.asp

The National Investment Information Network (RENAI) is an information network for investment activity in Brazil, supported by the Ministry of Development, Industry and Foreign Trade, with the assistance of other partners. The network aims to make such information available for wide use by investors, development incentive entities, research organisms, public bodies, and international agencies.

Private Equity

BOOKS

Adding Value in Private Equity: Lessons from Mature and Emerging Markets

Eric D. Cruikshank

London: Euromoney Books, 2006
271pp, ISBN: 978-1-84374-218-0

This is a practical guide to the events and strategies that can add or undermine value in private companies throughout the investment period and exit. It explains the different stages of funding, how to determine value, the effects of globalization on private equity values, deal structuring, pre- and post-investment adding value, and adding value in the exit strategy.

Barbarians at the Gate: The Fall of RJR Nabisco, revised ed

Bryan Burrough, John Helyar

HarperBusiness
New York: HarperBusiness, 2009
624pp, ISBN: 978-0-06-165555-5

Now hailed as a classic, this is an expose of the largest-ever leveraged buyout, of RJR Nabisco by private equity group Kohlberg Kravis Roberts. Also made into a film, its portrayal of oversized egos and greed seemed to sum up an era, and contributed greatly to the negative image of private equity in the 1980s.

Beyond the J Curve: Managing a Portfolio of Venture Capital and Private Equity Funds

Thomas Meyer, Pierre-Yves Mathonet

Wiley Finance Series
Chichester, UK: Wiley, 2005
366pp, ISBN: 978-0-470-01198-0

This is a comprehensive guide to how private equity funds operate in today's business environment, and achieve high returns. It presents a toolset for designing and managing portfolios, what it takes to select an effective fund manager, how to determine the funds' economic value, and the importance of monitoring.

Exposed to the J-Curve: Understanding and Managing Private Equity Fund Investments

Ulrich Grabenwarter, Tom Weidig

London: Euromoney Books, 2005
181pp, ISBN: 978-1-84374-149-7

This is an insightful review of the private equity fund industry, how to manage fund investments, and how institutional and private investors can safely invest into private equity funds. It discusses private equity as an asset class, how it fits into an alternative investment programme, and examines the different types of risks faced by private equity investors.

Getting a Job in Private Equity: Behind the Scenes Insight into How Private Equity Funds Hire

Brian Korb, Aaron Finkel

Glocap Guide Series
Hoboken, New Jersey: Wiley, 2008
198pp, ISBN: 978-0-470-29262-4

An insight into how the private equity hiring process works, the skills and qualifications required by hiring firms, with example interview questions, and useful case studies of successful job candidates. It shows how to improve your chances of successful employment, and how to build a long-term career in this competitive industry.

J-Curve Exposure: Managing a Portfolio of Venture Capital and Private Equity Funds

Pierre-Yves Mathonet, Thomas Meyer

Wiley Finance Series
Chichester, UK: Wiley, 2007
449pp, ISBN: 978-0-470-03327-2

A follow-up to the authors' earlier book, this presents new analysis and advanced guidance on the practical questions faced by institutions when setting up and managing a successful private equity investment program. It also examines the factors that can prevent institutions using venture capital, as well as regulatory issues, the prioritization of fund distributions, and techniques for track record analysis.

Lessons from Private Equity Any Company Can Use

Orit Gadiesh, Hugh MacArthur

Memo to the CEO Series
Boston, Massachusetts: Harvard Business School Press, 2008
126pp, ISBN: 978-1-4221-2495-6

This is a concise treatment of private equity, laid out in the format of a memo. It describes the rise of private equity in the marketplace, and its ability to maximize investor value more successfully than traditional companies, and presents a number of reasons for this, including measurement strategies, use of capital structure, and timeframe.

Private Equity, Corporate Governance and the Dynamics of Capital Market Regulation

Justin O'Brien (editor)

London: Imperial College Press, 2007
411pp, ISBN: 978-1-86094-847-3

Examines the implications of private equity for the governance of corporations and the capital markets. It appraises the type and amount of risk posed by private equity by placing it in the wider context of the financial system, and addresses a number of key concepts, such as conflicts of interest, fiduciary duties, enforcement, systems of regulation, compliance, and accountability.

Private Equity: History, Governance, and Operations

Harry Cendrowski, James P. Martin, Louis W. Petro, Adam A. Wadecki

Wiley Finance Series
Hoboken, New Jersey: Wiley, 2008
457pp, ISBN: 978-0-470-17846-1

Provides a comprehensive overview of private equity, its history and development as an asset class, the private equity process, terms of investment, and key players. It describes its ability to generate wealth for investors and the companies, and the mechanisms by which private equity achieves success, and presenting a framework for the analysis of private equity investments.

Private Equity and Venture Capital: A Practical Guide for Investors and Practitioners

Rick Lake, Ronald A. Lake (editors)

London: Euromoney Books, 2000
297pp, ISBN: 978-1-85564-691-9

This is an edited collection of articles from experts in private equity finance appraises this expanding asset class in the main US and UK markets, as well as in the developing markets. It focuses on the risks and returns involved in private equity investment, and discusses a number of essential features of this sector, such as investment management techniques, leveraged buyouts, and corporate governance.

Private Equity as an Asset Class

Guy Fraser-Sampson

Wiley Finance Series
Hoboken, New Jersey: Wiley, 2007
284pp, ISBN: 978-0-470-06645-4

This is a practical guide to understanding how private equity operates as an asset class. It presents basic concepts and definitions, the structure of private equity vehicles and returns, and the emerging area of total return investing. It also examines the differences between private equity and other asset classes, and the techniques used to measure and analyse performance.

The Private Equity Edge: How Private Equity Players and the World's Top Companies Build Value and Wealth

Arthur B. Laffer, William J. Hass, Shepherd G. Pryor IV

New York: McGraw-Hill, 2009
432pp, ISBN: 978-0-07-159078-5

A new treatment of private equity, and the potential innovation and returns it brings to business. It examines value, how people can have an impact on success, the risk element, and the macroeconomic perspective, and explores the techniques that successful private equity players use to increase shareholder value and wealth for their partners.

Private Equity Exits: Divestment Process Management for Leveraged Buyouts

Stefan Povaly

Berlin: Springer, 2007
411pp, ISBN: 978-3-540-70953-4

Provides a comprehensive analysis of private equity divestment processes, or "exits," for European buyouts. It examines features of the divestment process, and the efficiency of exits, and an improved understanding of exit behavior, and also makes recommendations for integrated and exit-oriented private equity portfolio management.

  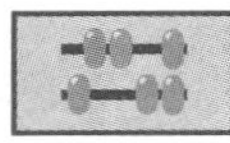      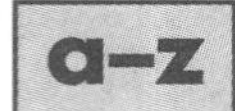

Structuring Venture Capital, Private Equity and Entrepreneurial Transactions

Jack Levin

New York: Aspen Publishers, 2008
1,326pp, ISBN: 978-0-7355-7468-7

Examines how to structure deals on a transaction-by-transaction basis, and how to ensure the tax, legal, and economic structuring consequences of deal-making works is conducted favorably. It presents practical detail on maximizing returns on transactions, controlling future rights to exit a profitable investment, and guidance on turning each transaction into a effective venture.

Venture Capital and Private Equity: A Casebook, 4th ed

Josh Lerner, Felda Hardymon, Ann Leamon

Hoboken, New Jersey: Wiley, 2009
545pp, ISBN: 978-0-470-22462-5

Now in its 4th edition, this casebook provides an overview of the industry at a time of great change in the industry, including rapid globalization. It focuses on how private equity funds are raised and structured, the interactions between private equity investors and the entrepreneurs, the process through which private equity investors exit their investments, and possible future developments.

Who's Who in Private Equity 2009, 19th ed

London: Incisive Media, 2008

An annual reference guide that contains details on over 2,300 industry professionals, from over 600 companies in 15 European countries. It provides key contact, investment and company profile information, and includes legal advisers as well as investors and corporate and leveraged finance companies.

MAGAZINES

The Elevator

HEPT
Grand Rue 114, 1820 Montreux, Switzerland
T: +41 21 944 11 80
F: +41 21 944 11 83
www.the-elevator.net
ISSN: 1754-4912

This is a quarterly up-market magazine for the private equity industry. It features a number of private equity projects and deals in each issue, discusses industry related topics with experts, and provides reviews of bespoke travel destinations and luxury products.

Emerging Private Equity

Greenland Publishing
34A Greenland Road, London, NW1 0AY, UK
T: +44 (0) 20 7870 7185
www.emergingpe.com
ISSN: 1755-3326

Aimed at private equity professionals in Africa, Asia, Central and Eastern Europe, Latin America, and the Middle East, this magazine focused on the emerging private equity markets also produces special reports, people news, and data analysis.

European Venture Capital & Private Equity Journal

Thomson Reuters
33 Aldgate High Street, London, EC3N 1DL, UK
T: +44 (0) 20 7369 7516
www.evcj.com
ISSN: 0954-1675

This magazine for the European venture capital and private equity industry is published 10 times a year, providing data and analysis on key developments in these markets. It covers every relevant activity, offers a comprehensive list of companies seeking buyers in Europe and announced deals every month, and produces supplements on issues such as mezzanine finance, MBOs, and new legal and regulatory developments.

Private Equity Europe

Incisive Media
Haymarket House, 28–29 Haymarket, London, SW1Y 4RX, UK
T: +44 (0) 20 7484 9700
F: +44 (0) 20 7004 7548
www.privateequityeurope.com
ISSN: 1465-9719

This is monthly magazine that provides fully validated pan-European coverage, statistics and analysis on the latest fundraising, buyout and exit news. It offers commentary on current issues surrounding institutional investment into the private equity asset class, as well as a deal forecast and mezzanine monitor.

Private Equity Insider

Harrison Scott Publications
5 Marine View Plaza, #400, Hoboken, NJ 07030-5795, USA
T: +1 201 659 1700
F: +1 201 659 4141
www.peinsider.com
ISSN: 1551-093X

This weekly newsletter provides the latest news and early intelligence on market developments in the private equity industry, involving operators of buyout funds, venture capital firms, funds of funds, secondaries, and other types of private equity vehicles. It covers marketing, capital raising innovations, successes and failures, infighting, fund launches, investor relations, market trends, career opportunities, valuation standards, and competition among service providers.

Private Equity International

PEI
2nd Floor, Sycamore House, Sycamore Street, London, EC1Y 0SG, UK
T: +44 (0) 20 7566 5444
www.peimedia.com/pei

This international magazine provides relevant information and insight to institutional investors and market practitioners who have an active interest in private equity. Published 10 times each year, it offers market insight and intelligence covering this global asset class, and substantive articles on the technical issues and challenges facing the market.

Private Equity News

Financial News
2nd Floor, Stapleton House, 29–33 Scrutton Street, London, EC2A 4HU, UK
T: +44 (0) 20 7426 3333
F: +44 (0) 20 7739 9954
www.penews.com
ISSN: 1741-9085

This weekly magazine provides daily news and analysis for Europe's private equity industry. It focuses on fundraising, deals, debt, advisory services, and comment, with its website also providing in-depth features, roundtables, reports and surveys on key topics and regional activity.

Real Deals Europe

Caspian Publishing
198 Kings Road, London, SW3 5XP, UK
T: +44 (0) 20 7368 7138
F: +44 (0) 20 7368 7178
www.realdeals.eu.com

This is a fortnightly magazine on the European private equity industry, which provides comment, news analysis, features, sector reports and supplements, as well as a daily news and deals email service, analysis of every European private equity deal, industry awards, and events.

Total Alternatives

Institutional Investor
225 Park Ave South, New York, NY 10003, USA
T: +1 212 224 3300
www.totalalternatives.com
ISSN: 1544-7596

This is an online news source for hedge funds, private equity, and other alternative investments. It contains stories on new strategies, fund launches, and reorganizations at major firms. It features the latest market news, daily email summaries, a resource of hedge fund news items in other media, and a data zone on hedge funds that includes information on strategy, rate of returns, annualized volume, and assets.

Unquote

Incisive Media
Haymarket House, 28–29 Haymarket, London, SW1Y 4RX, UK
T: +44 (0) 20 7484 9700
F: +44 (0) 20 7004 7548
www.unquote.com
ISSN: 1467-0062

This fortnightly newsletter presents news from the private equity and venture capital markets in the UK and Ireland, and is aimed at general partners, institutional investors, and intermediaries. It provides coverage from early-stage and expansion deals to buyouts and portfolio management, breakdowns of fundraising programs, exits, P2Ps, IPOs, and people moves, as well as in-depth analysis on key industry topics.

JOURNALS

The Journal of Private Equity

Institutional Investor
225 Park Avenue South, New York, NY 10003, USA
T: +1 212 224 3570
www.iijournals.com/JPE
ISSN: 1096-5572

This quarterly journal presents strategies and techniques for venture investing, and practical research and analysis for the venture capital and private equity markets. It delves into each

  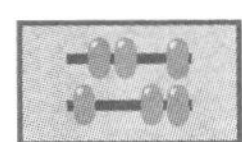      

successful deal, with detailed explanations, analysis, and real-life case studies, and covers early-stage, mezzanine and later-stage private companies and financings, with articles also on financial applications of structuring and exit strategies, cross-border issues, industry analyses, and management methods.

INTERNET

Albourne Village

www.village.albourne.com/private_equity

This is an online knowledge economy for the private equity community, designed as an environment for evolving news, intellectual property, content and debates on current issues. It revolves around the elements of village life—village pub, library, hedge fund mall, job centre, and data farm. There is also a conference center and village school, and a range of shops run by financial institutions, software companies, and publishers.

The International Private Equity and Venture Capital Valuation Guidelines

www.privateequityvaluation.com

This resource was developed by European private equity and venture capital associations, to reflect the need for greater comparability across the industry and for consistency with IFRS and US GAAP accounting principles. The valuation guidelines are used by the private equity and venture capital industry for valuing private equity investments, and provide a framework for fund managers and investors to monitor the value of existing investments.

NVST

www.nvst.com

This portal for the global private equity and finance community provides a broad range of private equity investment resources. It offers access to venture capital and M&A investment opportunities, online business tools, industry publications, research databases and educational resources for professional training.

Private Equity Central

www.privateequitycentral.net

This site is available to accredited individual and institutional investors, providing a source for news, data, and commentary on the fast-changing private equity market. It offers daily news about the funds, deals and people, interviews with managers, weekly market commentary, a directory of more than 1,000 private equity firms, a list of funds in the market, and searchable archives.

Private Equity Info

www.privateequityinfo.com

This is an informational resource of financial buyers, hedge funds, mezzanine investors, small business investment companies, valuation firms, M&A advisory firms, and real estate investors, and features a database of thousands of firms. It is aimed at middle market investment banks and M&A transaction-related professionals.

Private Equity Insight

www.privateequityinsight.com

This is an online database focused on the private equity industry, providing searchable data going back to 1990. This data is designed to help trend analysis, and an understanding of industry/geographic activity and competitor behavior in deal origination, portfolio management, benchmarking and strategic development, fundraising and investor relations, and performance.

Private Equity Wire

www.privateequitywire.co.uk

This site provides information on industry jobs, events, comments and opinions, interviews, and a free daily news bulletin.

ORGANIZATIONS

Europe

The British Private Equity and Venture Capital Association

Chair: Simon Walker
3 Clements Inn, London, WC2A 2AZ, UK
T: +44 (0) 20 7025 2950
F: +44 (0) 20 7025 2951
E: bvca@bvca.co.uk
www.bvca.co.uk/index.html

This is the industry body representing the UK private equity and venture capital industry. It promotes private equity for the benefit of entrepreneurs, investors, practitioners, and provides services, best practice standards to members, publications, research reports, and training courses. Its members are private equity companies active in making equity investments, and associate members who are professional firms including accountants, lawyers, and consultants.

European Private Equity and Venture Capital Association

Chair: Javier Echarri
Bastion Tower, Place du Champ de Mars 5, 1050 Brussels, Belgium
T: +32 2 715 0020
F: +32 2 725 0704
E: info@evca.eu
www.evca.eu

This is a member-based, non-profit trade association based in Brussels. It represents, promotes, and protects the interests of the European private equity and venture capital industry, and has over 1,300 members in Europe. Its activities cover the whole range of private equity, and provides network opportunities, training, co-ordination of public affairs, research initiatives, related publications, and an annual conference and seminars.

USA

The Hedge Fund & Private Equity Resource Center

1225 Franklin Avenue, Suite 325, Garden City, NY 11530, USA
T: +1 516 992 3417
E: info@hfpe.net
www.hfpe.net

This is a private, non-partisan institution dedicated to independent research and education on issues of government, politics, regulatory oversight and supervision involving private investment firms. It assists in the formulation of innovative policy solutions, and its research activities involve representative members of the private investment industry, professionals, and academics.

National Venture Capital Association

Chair: Dixon Doll
1655 North Fort Myer Drive, Suite 850, Arlington, Virginia 22209, USA
T: +1 703 524 2549
F: +1 703 524 3940
www.nvca.org

This is the main trade association representing the US venture capital industry. It is a member-based organization consisting of venture capital firms that manage pools of risk equity capital. Its mission is to foster greater understanding of the importance of venture capital to the US economy, support entrepreneurial activity and innovation, represent the public policy interests of the venture capital community, maintain professional standards, provide industry data, and sponsor professional development.

The Private Equity CFO Association

Chair: Chuck Woodard
c/o Citizens Bank, 53 State Street, 8th Floor, Boston, MA 02109, USA
E: charles.c.woodard@citizensbank.com
www.privateequitycfo.org

This association consists of over 650 private equity, venture capital and fund of funds CFOs in the New England, New York, Midwest, Mid-Atlantic and West Coast regions of the US, and provides communication, education, and networking opportunities for members. Membership is open to those responsible for the financial management in private equity, venture capital and fund of funds firms, and is not intended for asset management firms, investment bankers, industry consultants, vendors or service professionals.

BRIC

Indian Venture Capital and Private Equity Association

Chair: Saurabh Srivastava
301–302, Delhi Blue Apartments, Main Ring Road, New Delhi 110 029, India
T: +91 11 4162 8566
F: +91 11 4162 8863
E: info@indiavca.org
www.indiavca.org

This is a national organization that represents venture capital and private equity firms, promotes the industry within India and throughout the world, and encourages investment in high-growth companies. Its members comprise venture capital firms, institutional investors, banks, incubators, angel groups, corporate advisers, accountants, lawyers, government bodies, academic institutions and other service providers to the venture capital and private equity industry.

  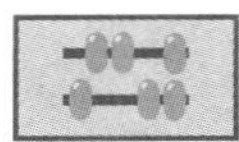      

Process Control and Statistical Process Control

BOOKS

The Desk Reference of Statistical Quality Methods, 2nd ed

Mark L. Crossley

Milwaukee, Wisconsin: ASQ Quality Press, 2008
560pp, ISBN: 978-0-87389-725-9

Arranged in alphabetical order for quick reference, this book provides the quality practitioner with a single resource that illustrates, in a practical manner, how to execute specific statistical methods frequently used in the quality sciences.

Managing Six Sigma: A Practical Guide to Understanding, Assessing, and Implementing the Strategy That Yields Bottom-Line Success

Forrest W. Breyfogle, III, James M. Cupello, Becki Meadows

London: Bantam Doubleday Dell Books, Random House, 2000
288pp, ISBN: 978-0-471-39673-4

This book provides detailed coverage of the Six Sigma techniques. Case studies describe some of the successes and pitfalls encountered in their successful implementation at Motorola and General Electric. Plans, checklists, and other materials are presented to help managers achieve a smooth and successful implementation.

The Quality Improvement Handbook, 2nd ed

John E. Bauer, Grace L. Duffy, Russell T. Westcott (editors)

Milwaukee, Wisconsin: ASQ Quality Press, 2006
242pp, ISBN: 978-0-87389-690-0

This book is for anyone who wants to improve themselves and/or their organization. It is particularly salient for those at the beginning stages of learning about the history, concepts, and tools of continual quality improvement.

Six Sigma: The Breakthrough Management Strategy Revolutionizing the World's Top Corporations

Mikel Harry, Richard Schroeder

London: Bantam Doubleday Dell Books, Random House, 2006
320pp, ISBN: 978-0-385-49437-3

This is an explanation of Six Sigma, in which the authors cite examples of companies (such as Polaroid) where the concept is currently in practice. Essentially, Six Sigma is a process that "guides companies into making fewer mistakes in everything they do—from filling out a purchase order to manufacturing airplane engines." A guide to achieving cost-effective quality within large corporations, this book is especially pertinent to managers and investors.

The Six Sigma Handbook, 3rd ed

Thomas Pyzdek

Maidenhead, UK: McGraw-Hill, 2009
560pp, ISBN: 978-0-07-162338-4

If improving the quality of your manufacturing processes is your goal, and the extraordinarily successful Six Sigma program at GE is one you want to emulate, this book will help you implement that approach. The author examines the philosophy underlying the program and explores the management and organization of Six Sigma, then explains the statistical tools and problem-solving techniques needed to implement it.

Six Sigma Revolution: How General Electric and Others Turned Process into Profits

George Eckes

Chichester, UK: Wiley, 2000
272pp, ISBN: 978-0-471-38822-7

Presenting Six Sigma as a quantitative approach to quality that has boosted productivity and increased profits for a number of large businesses, the author explains how and why it is superior to other quality improvement methods and describes how to create and sustain a Six Sigma initiative in an organization.

Statistical Methods for Quality Improvement, 2nd ed

Thomas P. Ryan

Wiley Series in Probability and Mathematical Statistics
Chichester, UK: Wiley, 2000
592pp, ISBN: 978-0-471-19775-1

Ryan provides a detailed introduction to the mathematics and statistics that form the basis of a range of fundamental quality control and statistical methods.

Statistical Process Control, 6th ed

John S. Oakland

Oxford: Butterworth-Heinemann, 2007
472pp, ISBN: 978-0-7506-6962-7

This new edition of a leading text reflects recent thinking in the field and provides a reliable reference source for statistical process control. The broad issues covered include understanding processes, process variability, process control, process capability, and process improvement.

Statistical Process Control for Quality Improvement: The Deming Paradigm and Beyond, 2nd ed

James R. Thompson, Jacek Koronacki

Boca Raton, Florida: Chapman & Hall/CRC Press, 2001
464pp, ISBN: 978-1-58488-242-8

The authors draw upon their experience of presenting short seminars to workers, foremen, and managers to create this introduction to SPC. They provide an overview of the subject for those with little knowledge of statistics, but the remaining, more detailed explanations of the analytical techniques of SPC are written for statisticians and production engineers with a higher level of mathematical understanding.

MAGAZINES

Quality Progress

World Alliance for Quality
600 North Plankinton Avenue, Milwaukee, WI 53203, USA
T: +1 414 272 8575
F: +1 414 272 1734
www.qualityprogress.com

ASQ's flagship publication, which features in-depth articles that describe the application of innovative methods. Topics include knowledge management, process improvement, and organizational behavior.

Six Sigma Forum Magazine

World Alliance for Quality
600 North Plankinton Avenue, Milwaukee, WI 53203, USA
T: +1 414 272 8575
F: +1 414 272 1734
www.asq.org/pub/sixsigma

This quarterly magazine offers feature articles focusing on companies such as Motorola and GE that have benefited from the practice of Six Sigma, and is aimed at Six Sigma professionals at all levels of experience.

JOURNALS

Total Quality Management and Business Excellence

Routledge
4 Park Square, Milton Park, Abingdon, Oxfordshire, OX14 4RN, UK
T: +44 (0) 20 7017 6000
F: +44 (0) 20 7017 6336
www.tandf.co.uk/journals/titles/14783363.asp
ISSN: 1478-3363

This international journal acts as a forum for new thinking and research in all aspects of total quality management, and provides a forum for the discussion and dissemination of research results. The journal is designed to appeal to both the academic and professional community working in this area.

INTERNET

American Society for Quality

www.asq.org

This ASQ site includes a profile of Walter A. Shewhart, the first honorary member of the Society and acclaimed father of modern quality control.

iSixSigma

www.isixsigma.com

This is an online content resource for the Six Sigma community. It offers resources to businesses at every stage of their Six Sigma maturity for professionals at all levels. It presents guidance for learning new skills, career advancement, and contributing to the success of an organization through a wide range of articles, tools, conferences, and practitioner forums.

Six Sigma Forum

www.sixsigmaforum.com

The site of this recently formed Forum provides some introductory information on Six Sigma and its application. There are links to related informative case studies and news, but you have to become a member to access these items.

ORGANIZATIONS

Europe

European Society for Quality

36–38 rue Joseph II, Brussels 1000, Belgium
T: +32 2 219 59 09
E: eoq@eoq-org.eu
www.eoq.org

The European Organization for Quality (EOQ) is an autonomous, nonprofit association that acts as a forum for members of the quality industry across Europe.

USA

American Society for Quality (ASQ)

600 North Plankinton Avenue, Milwaukee, WI 53203, USA
T: +1 414 272 8575
F: +1 414 272 1734
E: cs@asq.org
www.asq.org

Founded in 1946, the ASQ is a society of individual and organizational members dedicated to the development and promotion of the concepts, principles, and techniques of quality. It has recently launched the Six Sigma Forum.

BRIC

Indian Society for Quality (ISQ)

52 Community Centre, II Floor, East of Kailash, New Delhi 110065, India
T: +91 11 4652 6000
F: +91 11 4657 2982
E: info@isqnet.org
www.isqnet.org

This is a membership-based forum on quality management. It promotes an awareness of quality management, conducts research, publishes on the subject, and awards prizes to companies that excel in the field of quality management.

Programa Gaucho da Qualidade e Produtividade (PGQP)

Rua Washington Luiz 820, cj. 302 90010–460, Porto Alegre RS, Brazil
T: +55 51 3221 2663
www.mbc.org.br/mbc/pgqp/

PGQP is a nonprofit organization based around voluntary work, which promotes and deploys the use of total quality management concepts and tools as a way of teaching organizational objectives and recognizing individual achievements.

Russian National Benchmarking Centre (RNBC) / The Benchmarking Club

2nd Mashinostroyeniya St., 17, 115088, Moscow, Russia
T: +7 495 771 6652
F: +7 495 771 6653
E: benchmarkingclub@mirq.ru
www.benchmarkingclub.ru

This non-profit organization is run by the Russian Organisation for Quality's (ROQ) Business Excellence Department. It aims to systematize and disseminate advanced principles of excellence and techniques for their implementation, and organize and offer practical assistance in exchange of experience between members in Russia and abroad.

Six Sigma Quality Management Research Center of RUC

School of Statistics of Renmin University, Beijing, 100872, China
T: +86 10 5198 6383
F: +86 10 6251 5246
E: hxq00@263.net
stat.ruc.edu.cn/en/research/centers/21698.html

This research center is run by the School of Statistics, Renmin University of China, and works to expand an awareness of applied statistics, and to promote the application of statistical methods and techniques in practice.

International

World Alliance for Quality (WAQ)

600 North Plankinton Avenue, Milwaukee, WI 53203, USA
T: +1 414 272 8575
F: +1 414 272 1734
waq.asq.org

The WAQ is an international organization, hosted by the American Society for Quality (ASQ), that strives to be the leader in fostering international cooperation for issues related to quality. It promotes the use of quality philosophies, principles, techniques, and tools to benefit society at large by supporting its application for activities such as resolution of global conflict and efficient use of all global resources.

Project Finance

BOOKS

Advanced Modelling for Project Finance

Charles T. Haskell
London: Euromoney Books, 2005
97pp, ISBN: 978-1-84374-214-2

This is a technical workbook that provides guidance on pricing and negotiating a project finance deal through the use of key industry models. It offers new perspectives on financial modeling, and features worked examples of how to build and analyze each step of a project finance model, to give a comprehensive understanding of the processes involved.

Advanced Project Financing

Richard Tinsley
London: Euromoney Books, 2000
294pp, ISBN: 978-1-85564-834-0

This technical overview of project finance provides timely analysis of the major risks in the sector, backed up by a range of real-world case studies where each choice of risk structure, such as currency risk and credit risk, is explained and assessed. It also describes and analyzes the impact of counterparties, joint venture documentation, and the emerging markets.

Financing Large Projects: Using Project Finance Techniques and Practices

M. Fouzul Kabir Khan, Robert J. Parra
Singapore: Prentice Hall, 2003
639pp, ISBN: 978-0-13-101634-7

This is a comprehensive examination of the techniques employed to finance large start-up projects, which addresses the financial, technical, legal, and environmental aspects of complex projects. It follows the project development cycle, from how projects are initiated, through to financial closure, and also explores the complexities of international law as it relates to project finance.

Identifying and Managing Project Risk: Essential Tools for Failure-Proofing Your Project, 2nd ed

Tom Kendrick
New York: Amacom, 2009
304pp, ISBN: 978-0-8144-1340-1

This new practical guide to project risk aims to help project managers that are time constrained, facing technical challenges, and working with inadequate resources. It describes how to minimize the possibility of project failure, by examining where possible risks can occur at each step of a project, and analyzes aspects such as project scope, scheduling, and how to use high-level risk assessment tools.

International Project Analysis and Finance

Gerald Pollio
Ann Arbor, Michigan: University of Michigan Press, 1999
235pp, ISBN: 978-0-472-11095-7

This book combines an analysis of project assessment with the necessary funding aspects needed to achieve the potential of both private and public sector investment projects. It examines concepts such as capital budgeting, limited recourse debt, and risk management, particularly in relation to natural resource projects, offering a theoretical and practical reference for economic analysts, finance specialists, lending institutions, students, and researchers.

  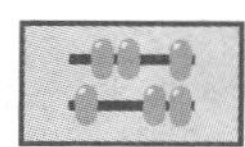      

International Project Financing, 4th ed

Ronald F. Sullivan

Huntington, New York: Juris Publishing, 2004
350pp, ISBN: 978-1-57823-193-5

This treatment of PF is aimed at lawyers practicing in the area of international project financing, and the problems counsels face when negotiating and drafting agreements relating to project finance. It integrates a discussion of particular contract provisions relevant to the topic of each chapter, as well as references to different examples of these provisions contained in the forms of agreement published at the end of the book.

Introduction to Project Finance

Andrew Fight

Essential Capital Markets Series
Boston, Massachusetts: Elsevier, 2005
208pp, ISBN: 978-0-7506-5905-5

This provides a practical grounding in the basics of project finance. It describes the key risks involved and how to mitigate them, methods of project evaluation, recourse and non-recourse funding, feasibility, the various parties involved, techniques for cash flow preparation, building cash flow statements, and the key variables impacting financial performance.

Megaprojects and Risk: An Anatomy of Ambition

Bent Flyvbjerg, Nils Bruzelius, Werner Rothengatter

Cambridge, UK: Cambridge University Press, 2003
207pp, ISBN: 978-0-521-00946-1

This is a comprehensive examination of the global megaprojects phenomenon, combining theoretical analysis with empirical research to explore the main issues—the impact of costs, revenues, the environment, and economic development—behind numerous projects around the world. It also examines how the promoters of these expensive megaprojects had them approved and built, their dealings with parliaments, the public, and the media.

Modern Project Finance: A Casebook

Benjamin C. Esty

New York: Wiley, 2004
562pp, ISBN: 978-0-471-43425-2

This financial casebook focuses on the structuring and valuing of projects, how to manage project risk, and finance projects, and is based on real cases from a range of geographic locations and industrial sectors. It explores why companies use project finance, the role of banks, how project loans should be priced, why some projects fail, and the reduction of agency costs.

Principles of Project and Infrastructure Finance

Willie Tan

London: Taylor & Francis, 2007
280pp, ISBN: 978-0-415-41577-4

This holistic approach to project finance issues provides both an introductory and analytical guide to the key areas within project finance from a project manager's perspective. It offers a range of relevant case studies that illustrate integration in selected sectors, and is aimed at students, researchers, and project finance practitioners, such as company directors, project managers, lawyers, architects, contractors, engineers, regulators, insurers, and investors.

Principles of Project Finance

Edward Yescombe

Amsterdam: Academic Press, 2002
344pp, ISBN: 978-0-12-770851-5

This introduction for project finance practitioners offers a comprehensive examination of the key concepts and techniques, integrating legal, contractual, scheduling, and other relevant aspects. It describes sources of project finance, typical commercial contracts and their impact on the project finance structure, project finance risk assessment, the structuring of project finance debt, and issues in negotiating a project finance debt facility.

Project Finance, Securitisations and Subordinated Debt, 2nd ed

Philip R. Wood

London: Sweet & Maxwell, 2007
262pp, ISBN: 978-1-84703-211-9

This is a practical guide to international project finance, which explains how the key concepts are applied in commercial situations. It examines project finance structures, securitisation contracts and financial agreements, as well as securitization issues. It describes the different international jurisdictions and relevant laws, discusses the different classes of subordination agreement, and presents a global survey of the law of subordinated debt.

Project Finance, 3rd ed

Graham D. Vinter, Gareth Price

London: Sweet & Maxwell, 2006
473pp, ISBN: 978-0-421-90950-2

This overview of project finance focuses on the issues involved in the tendering, negotiation, financial structuring, and management of infrastructure and energy projects. It provides guidance on legal factors of typical project financing, commercial and financial planning, current market practice, as well as coverage of documentation, bid structuring, public-private partnerships, risk allocation, cover ratios, and export credit agencies.

Project Finance in Theory and Practice: Designing, Structuring, and Financing Private and Public Projects

Stefano Gatti

Academic Press Advanced Finance Series
Burlington, Massachusetts: Academic Press, 2008
414pp, ISBN: 978-0-12-373699-4

This comprehensive overview combines a discussion of project finance theory with a presentation of best practice. It examines project finance techniques, processes, and practices, creating a resource for both practitioners and researchers, explains the roles and objectives of the different parties, the legal issues, the role of advisers, and provides useful new analysis of PPPs, and credit risk measurement problems under Basel II.

Project Financing: Asset-Based Financial Engineering, 2nd ed

John D. Finnerty

Wiley Finance Series
Hoboken, New Jersey: Wiley, 2007
476pp, ISBN: 978-0-470-08624-7

This practical guide aims to provide insight into the complexities, challenges, and processes involved in project financing, and is aimed at project sponsors, regulators, host governments, and corporate financiers, as well as advisers, senior strategists, bankers, and large private investors. It examines the rationale behind project financing, the risks, security arrangements, legal structure, how to prepare the financial plan, and unsuccessful project financing cases.

Project Financing, 7th ed

Peter K. Nevitt, Frank Fabozzi

London: Euromoney Books, 2000
498pp, ISBN: 978-1-85564-791-6

This comprehensive guide to all aspects of project finance examines the key criteria for success, including the choice of financial advisers and banks, types and sources of equity and debt finance, effective project structuring, and types of risk and risk appraisal. It describes the concepts and structures that can be applied at any stage in project financing, illustrated by numerous examples and case studies.

Project Financing and the International Financial Markets

Esteban C. Buljevich, Yoon S. Park

Boston, Massachusetts: Kluwer Academic, 1999
302pp, ISBN: 978-0-7923-8524-0

This professional reference guide examines the increasing use of the global capital markets and international financing techniques for privately funding project finance initiatives. It describes the use of derivative instruments for asset and liability management, the different risk management techniques available, the impact of cross-border project financing, and reviews the various marketable debt securities actively used in the international financial markets.

Public-Private Partnerships: A Practical Analysis

Nicholas Avery

London: Globe Law and Business, 2006
199pp, ISBN: 978-1-905783-00-7

This practical textbook focuses on public-private partnership (PPP) financing, analyzing topical developments and the latest techniques in the main sectors in which it operates. It features coverage of issues such as the role of financing institutions, EU procurement, and developments in the debt and equity financial markets relevant to PPP, for lawyers, facility managers, technical advisers, and those in government departments and agencies.

  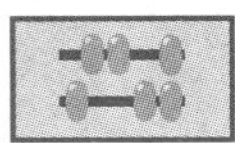      

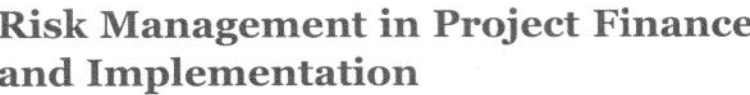

Risk Management in Project Finance and Implementation

Henri L. Beenhakker

Westport, Connecticut: Quorum Books, 1997
274pp, ISBN: 978-1-56720-106-2

This offers a comprehensive examination of all the main risk management concepts involved in project finance, including financial structures and techniques, the development of efficient portfolios, and investment risks and taxes. It takes a multifaceted approach to the subject, and combines an analysis of both theory and practice, for professionals with investment responsibilities in both the public and private sectors.

MAGAZINES

Infrastructure Journal

Emap
Greater London House, Hampstead Road, London, NW1 7EJ, UK
T: +44 (0) 20 7728 5407
F: +44 (0) 20 7728 5299
www.ijonline.com
ISSN: 1460-468X

This subscription-only online news and research journal is for professionals involved in the global project finance of infrastructure transactions. It offers news and data for the international infrastructure investment market, as well as research and analysis, a projects database, league tables, awards, a global directory, forums, opinion, case studies, and a weekly review.

PPP Bulletin

Rockcliffe
20a Hillgate Place, 18–20 Balham Hill, London, SW12 9ER, UK
T: +44 (0) 20 8772 6648
F: +44 (0) 20 8675 0950
www.pppbulletin.com
ISSN: 1752-7007

This monthly subscription-based magazine provides in-depth updates on international public-private partnerships legislation, regulation, working procedure and market potential. It provides international news, interviews with the top industry figures, in-depth market reports, country reports, industry jobs, and a business leads section about new projects.

Project Finance

Euromoney Institutional Investor
Nestor House, Playhouse Yard, London, EC4V 5EX, UK
T: +44 (0) 20 7779 8610
F: +44 (0) 20 7779 8602
www.projectfinancemagazine.com
ISSN: 1462-0014

This bimonthly magazine features in-depth articles that evaluate a range of project finance issues, from new financing instruments to deal round-ups. The industry sectors covered include telecoms, power, oil, gas, rail, roads, bridges, tunnels, water, ports, airports, property and tourism development, petrochemicals, mining, and private and public partnerships.

Project Finance International

Reuters Professional Publishing
Aldgate House, 33 Aldgate High Street, London, EC3N 1DL, UK
T: +44 (0) 20 7369 7000
www.pfie.com
ISSN: 0967-5914

Published every two weeks, PFI offers global project finance news and information by industry sector, as well as regional news, features, people and markets, supplements, roundtables, project pipeline, completed deals, and league tables. It reports on the entire lifecycle of deals, from the initial concept through to post-completion analysis.

Public Works Financing

Public Works Financing
147 Elmer Street, Westfield, New Jersey 07090, USA
T: +1 908 654 6572
F: +1 908 654 6573
www.pwfinance.net

This monthly magazine provides project case studies, news updates, project leads, political trends, analyses of successful financings, profiles of key industry players, and a directory of the most experienced advisers. Features also examine the role played by the main parties, as well as the alignment of risks and rewards on publicly sanctioned projects.

JOURNALS

Journal of Public Works & Infrastructure

Henry Stewart Publications
Russell House, 28/30 Little Russell Street, London, WC1A 2HN, UK
T: +44 (0) 20 7404 3040
F: +44 (0) 20 7404 2081
www.henrystewart.com/jpwi
ISSN: 1755-0955

This quarterly journal publishes contributions from public works and infrastructure professionals on best practice and new thinking in the strategic management and operational delivery of public works projects and services. It offers papers on best practice, industry briefings, case studies, and empirical research that show how projects and services have been specified, designed, financed and delivered in practice.

Journal of Structured and Product Finance

Institutional Investor Journals
225 Park Avenue South, 8th Floor, New York, NY 10003, USA
T: +1 212 224 3570
F: +1 212 224 3197
www.iijournals.com/JPF
ISSN: 1082-3220

This quarterly journal offers research and commentary on all aspects of structured and project finance, including detailed analysis of the regulatory, financial and legal aspects of project finance deals. It also focuses on a range of real-life securitization deals and their investment implications, as well as environmental and political issues, to provide a strategic understanding of the products, applications, and market.

INTERNET

Project Finance Portal

www.people.hbs.edu/besty/projfinportal

This online resource, run by Harvard Business School, provides a reference guide for practitioners, researchers, and students seeking information about project finance and public-private partnerships. It presents bibliographical references for books, articles, and case studies, and hundreds of links to related sites, as well as information about particular projects and companies/organizations involved with project finance.

ORGANIZATIONS

Europe

International Project Finance Association

Chair: Geoff Haley
Linton House, 164–180 Union Street, London, SE1 0LH, UK
T: +44 (0) 20 7620 1883
F: +44 (0) 20 7620 1886
E: info@ipfa.org
www.ipfa.org

IPFA is a non-profit association that promotes and represents the interests of private sector companies involved in project finance and public-private partnerships around the world. It offers a range of information resources on current issues and developments throughout the industry, and aims to raise awareness and understanding globally about project finance and PPPs, and the role they play in infrastructure and economic development.

The Major Projects Association

Chair: Sir Robert Walmsley
Egrove Park, Kennington, Oxford, OX1 5NY, UK
T: +44 (0) 1865 422581
F: +44 (0) 1865 326068
E: mpa@majorprojects.org
www.majorprojects.org

This international, multi-industry association provides a forum for organizations concerned with large complex projects,
with the aim of sharing knowledge, experience, and good practice. It covers all industrial, government and commercial sectors, and brings together the major players in every aspect of major projects, such as funders, promoters, designers, contractors, suppliers, operators, regulators, professional contributors, and government.

USA

INFRADEV & Infrastructure Experts Group

Chair: Barbara C. Samuels II
79 Fifth Avenue, Suite 1129B, New York, NY 10003, USA
T: +1 212 229 5901
F: +1 212 229 5903
E: infradev@globalclearinghouse.org
www.infradev.org

INFRADEV operates as an information exchange, offering a resource and financing for development tool to mobilize private capital for developing country infrastructure. It aims to enhance the capacity of developing country governments and development agencies to mobilize private sector investment and resources for infrastructure projects.

Purchasing and Supply Chain Management

BOOKS

B2B: How to Build a Profitable E-Commerce Strategy

Michael Cunningham

Cambridge, Massachusetts: Perseus Books Group, 2002
224pp, ISBN: 978-0-7382-0522-9

This book presents a definitive blueprint for creating a profitable business-to-business e-commerce strategy. Showcasing successful initiatives designed by industry leaders such as Cisco Systems and Dell Computers, as well as lesser-known trailblazers such as VerticalNet and eCredit.com, the author clearly identifies the key issues in assessing opportunities, building technological and organizational capabilities, and designing a successful business-to-business strategy using the full power of the internet.

Designing and Managing the Supply Chain, 3rd ed

David Simchi-Levi, Philip Kaminsky, Edith Simchi-Levi

New York: McGraw-Hill, 2007
544pp, ISBN: 978-0-07-334152-1

The book provides state-of-the-art models, concepts, and methods that are critical for the design, control, operation, and management of supply chain systems. In particular, the authors attempt to convey the intuition behind many key supply chain concepts, and to provide simple techniques that can be used to analyze various aspects of the supply chain.

Harvard Business Review on Supply Chain Management

Harvard Business School Press

Harvard Business Review Paperback Series
Boston, Massachusetts: Harvard Business School Press, 2006
211pp, ISBN: 978-1-4221-0279-4

Many of today's companies struggle with the task of delivering products to customers when and where they want them. Using tactics from articles in this volume, any company can learn how to beat the competition, and reduce waste in each step of their value-delivery process.

Logistics and Supply Chain Management: Creating Value-Adding Networks, 3rd ed

Martin Christopher

Harlow, UK: FT Prentice Hall, 2004
320pp, ISBN: 978-0-273-68176-2

The goal of supply chain management is to link the marketplace, the distribution network, the manufacturing process, and the procurement activity in such a way that customers are serviced at higher levels and yet at lower total cost. The author explores the role of logistics in achieving these goals. He examines the relationship between logistics and competitive strategy, the customer service dimension, measuring logistics costs and performance, and benchmarking and managing the supply chain.

Managing the Global Supply Chain, 3rd ed

Philip B Schary, Tage Skjott-Larsen

Copenhagen, Denmark: Copenhagen Business School Press, 2007
459pp, ISBN: 978-87-630-0171-7

The book shows how structure, process, and organization may build a supply network comprising distribution, production, and procurement within one integrated system. The importance of the supply chain in corporate strategy is also emphasized. This new edition stresses customer relationships and reflects recent changes in technology and practice.

Managing the Supply Chain: The Definitive Guide for the Business Professional

David Simchi-Levi, Philip Kaminsky, Edith Simchi-Levi

Maidenhead, UK: McGraw-Hill, 2003
320pp, ISBN: 978-0-07-141031-1

Interest in supply chain management has grown rapidly over past years and continues to increase. To meet this interest the authors introduce a range of state-of-the-art concepts and techniques that are important for the design, control, operation and management of supply chain systems. They focus on supply chain integration network planning, supply chain alliances, outsourcing and supply contracts, product design, customer value, and global issues in supply chain management. Numerous examples illustrate the key issues.

New Directions in Supply Chain Management: Technology Strategy and Implementation

Tonya Boone, Ram Ganeshan

New York: AMACOM, 2002
384pp, ISBN: 978-0-8144-0637-3

This collection of 18 original essays examines the efficiencies new technology has brought to supply chain management and how new strategies and solutions based on these changes can be implemented. They are grouped into three sections covering the integration of new technologies into supply chain operations, technology-based product and service development, and knowledge management and supply-chain integration issues.

Partners.com

Michael Cunningham

Cambridge, Massachusetts: Perseus Books Group, 2002
256pp, ISBN: 978-0-7382-0687-5

Partners.com shows businesses how to forge leading-edge internet partnerships fast with competitors, customers, employees, and other businesses. The book reveals the specifics of these new and better ways of doing business. It presents a clear picture of companies such as eBay, Altra, GoFish, Egghead, VerticalNet, and Yahoo, that are utilizing technology-driven partnerships.

Purchasing and Supply Chain Management, 7th ed

Kenneth Lysons, Brian Farrington

Harlow, UK: FT Prentice Hall, 2005
736pp, ISBN: 978-0-273-69438-0

A much revised and enlarged version of a successful textbook, this edition meets the requirements for an integrated approach to supply chain management, drawing on the many disciplines, from ethics and human resources to suppliers, sourcing, and strategy, that contribute to a full knowledge of purchasing practice and techniques.

The Sourcing Solution: A Step-by-Step Guide to Creating a Successful Purchasing Program

Larry Paquette

New York: AMACOM, 2007
224pp, ISBN: 978-0-8144-0038-8

Larry Paquette believes that, as purchasing options and technologies become more plentiful, they also become more complex. In this text, he sets out to help managers sort through alternatives, identify the strategies that make sense, and implement them in ways that complement the overall business strategy. He explains how to make the most of vendor relationships and partnerships, opportunities for cost reduction, electronic and paperless inventory management, product knowledge and company information, different production models, global sourcing opportunities, scheduling, and contracts and negotiations.

Supply Chain Excellence: A Handbook for Dramatic Improvement Using the SCOR Model, 2nd ed

Peter Bolstorff, Robert Rosenbaum

New York: AMACOM, 2007
403pp, ISBN: 978-0-8144-0926-8

The SCOR (Supply Chain Operations Reference) model, developed by the Supply-Chain Council in the United States, is introduced in this handbook, which also examines in detail the process of applying the model and describes the achieving of supply chain excellence over a 17-week period.

Supply Chain Management

John T. Mentzer (editor)

London: Sage Publications, 2001
512pp, ISBN: 978-0-7619-2111-0

A group of collaborating authors present a comprehensive definition and model of supply chain management (SCM) on the basis of their interviews with top supply chain managers from 20 companies. The book distinguishes types of chain, and discusses SCM as a management philosophy and in terms of its prerequisites and its potential effects on business and channel performance.

Supply Chain Management Best Practices

David Blanchard

Hoboken, New Jersey: Wiley, 2007
320pp, ISBN: 978-0-471-78141-7

This book offers a comprehensive look at the development of supply chain management. It presents success stories from practitioners and experts at competitive companies of all sizes and in various industries, who share their secrets, experiences, and accomplishments to provide guidance on best practice.

The Supply Management Handbook, 7th ed

Joseph L. Cavinato, Ralph G. Kauffman, Anna E. Flynn

New York: McGraw-Hill, 2006
1000pp, ISBN: 978-0-07-144513-9

This successful handbook is for purchasing and supply professionals in every field and industry, and provides comprehensive updates that examine the shift from simple purchasing to a new, more technology-based imperative–identifying and managing supply chain sources and strategies.

MAGAZINES

Purchasing

Reed Business Information
8878 Barrons Boulevard, Highlands Ranch, CO 80129–2345, USA
T: +1 800 446 6551
F: +1 303 470 4280
www.purchasing.com
ISSN: 0033-4448

This is a bimonthly magazine which focuses on total supply management. It has served 93,500 professionals working in manufacturing, process, and service companies throughout the full spectrum of business for 85 years. The magazine makes available the information required by purchasing professionals to do their jobs. It provides news, identifies trends, interprets events, makes forecasts, and presents exclusive information and data sources.

Supply Management

Redactive Publishing
1 Benjamin Street, London, EC1M 5EA, UK
T: +44 (0) 20 7880 6200
F: +44 (0) 20 7814 0981
www.supplymanagement.co.uk
ISSN: 1362-2021

The journal of the Chartered Institute of Purchasing and Supply, it combines international and UK news, features, regular columns on the law and academic research, book and video reviews, news from CIPS, and a special section on key prices and economic indicators. *Supply Management* provides the essential information purchasing professionals need to carry out their jobs, together with analysis of the main strategic issues facing the profession today.

JOURNALS

Journal of Supply Chain Management: A Global Review of Purchasing and Supply

Institute for Supply Management
PO Box 22160, Tempe, AZ 85285–2160, USA
T: +1 480 752 6276
F: +1 480 752 7890
www.ism.ws/pubs/journalscm/index.cfm?navItemNumber=5474
ISSN: 1055-6001

A quarterly publication produced specifically for purchasing professionals, this journal provides coverage and analysis of key management issues, leading research, one-to-one interviews, and supplier relationship applications. Abstracts of the articles and the one-to-one interviews can be accessed on the web.

Journal of Supply Chain Management

Blackwell Publishing
9600 Garsington Road, Oxford, OX4 2DQ, UK
T: +44 (0) 1865 791 100
F: +44 (0) 1865 791 347
www.wiley.com/bw/journal.asp?ref=1523–2409
ISSN: 1523-2409

This quarterly journal is aimed at supply chain management scholars, through the publication of high-quality, high-impact behavioral methodologies focusing on theory-building and empirical research.

Supply Chain Forum: An International Journal

The Institute for Supply Chain Excellence of BEM
BEM – ISLI, 680, Cours de la Libération, 33405 Talence, France
T: +33 (0) 5 56 84 55 70
F: +33 (0) 5 56 84 55 80
www.supplychain-forum.com
ISSN: 1625-8312

Supply Chain Forum explores all the aspects of logistics, supply chain and operations management. It is concerned with the management and optimization of flows in the supply chain from primary supplier to final customer, and provides research articles and company case studies that enrich both the knowledge of the discipline and the practices of supply chain management.

Supply Chain Management: An International Journal

Emerald
60/62 Toller Lane, Bradford, West Yorkshire, BD8 9BY, UK
T: +44 (0) 1274 777 700
F: +44 (0) 1274 785 200
www.emeraldinsight.com/1359–8546.htm
ISSN: 1359-8546

This bimonthly journal is broad based, but with a strategic focus, covering aspects of marketing, logistics and information technology, economics, management, and organizational behavior in relation to the operation of supply chains in all sectors. It encourages the development and implementation of supply chain systems which achieve higher levels of service and substantial savings in costs.

INTERNET

CAPS Research

www.capsresearch.org

This site is offered by the Center for Advanced Purchasing Studies, a nonprofit independent research organization co-sponsored by Arizona State University and the National Association of Purchasing and Supply. It provides full access to a range of recent research and benchmarking reports and their journal *Practix*. Access is free, but you must register to view articles. There are also links to related sites.

Chartered Institute of Purchasing and Supply

www.cips.org

While this site is designed to promote the training and research services and activities of CIPS, it does allow nonmembers access to its comprehensive bookstore with details of over 350 specialist publications.

Institute for Supply Management

www.ism.ws

This is the home site of the Institute for Supply Management. The amount of information available to nonmembers is limited, but there is access to selected articles or abstracts of recent articles in the institute's journals.

International Purchasing and Supply Education and Research Association

www.ipsera.com

IPSERA is an active network of academics and practitioners dedicated to the development of understanding on matters concerning the future of purchasing and supply management. The site provides general information about the association, details about membership, and advice on applying for funding.

Responsible Supply Chain Management Portal

www.csr-supplychain.org

This website offers information and advice for buyers and suppliers on corporate social responsibility in the supply chain, from a number of top companies. The site covers international standards and principles, practical guidelines, supplier training, codes of conducts for vendors, audit self-assessments, and details on how to implement supply chain programs. Topics covered include health and safety, ethics, and child labor.

Supply Chain Online

www.supplychainonline.com.br

Brazil's portal to supply chain management offers information, articles, expert opinions, news, events, software, and technological applications on supply chain management.

supplymanagement.com

www.supplymanagement.com

Managed by the Chartered Institute of Purchasing and Supply, this site offers selected content from

 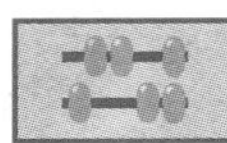      

the print magazine, breaking news stories, plus a range of online-only features, including streaming business and political news, archive of past articles, searchable events diary, e-mail news alerts, and a commodity price database.

ORGANIZATIONS

Europe

Chartered Institute of Purchasing and Supply

1 Easton House, Easton-on-the-Hill, Stamford, Lincolnshire, PE9 3NZ, UK
T: +44 (0) 1780 756 777
F: +44 (0) 1780 751 610
www.cips.org

Based in the United Kingdom, CIPS is an international education and qualification organization serving the international purchasing and supply profession. It is dedicated to promoting best practice through the provision of a wide range of services for the benefit of members and the wider business community. These include a program of continuous improvement in professional standards, and raising awareness of the contribution that purchasing and supply makes to corporate, national, and international prosperity. CIPS gained a Royal Charter in 1992.

European Supply Chain Institute (ESCI)

www.escinst.org

The European Supply Chain Institute is an international association with a mandate to research the technologies that drive the supply chain, and examine its applications. The largest research program over recent years has been regarding the application of RFID and how the technology can transform an organization's manufacturing and supply chain operations.

BRIC

China Supply Chain Council (CSCC)

Unit A, 10F, Bldg. 2, 543 Xin Hua Road, Shanghai, 200052, China
T: +86 21 5102 1617
F: +86 21 5258 3864
www.supplychain.cn

CSCC is the largest professional organization dedicated to furthering the knowledge, understanding, and career development of executives, managers, and professionals in the field of supply chain, logistics, and procurement management in China.

Indian Institute of Materials Management

Plot Nos. 102 & 104, Sector 15, Institutional Area, CBD Belapur, Navi Mumbai 400614, India
T: +91 22 2756 5741
F: +91 22 2756 5592
E: iimmedu@mtnl.net.in
www.iimm.org

This is a membership-based institute that advocates efficient supply management, provides information and research, and promotes the professional status of people working in supply management.

International

Canadian Association of Supply Chain and Logistics Management

7270 Woodbine Avenue, Suite 204, Markham, Ontario, L3R 4B9, Canada
T: +1 905 513 7300
F: +1 905 513 1248
E: members@infochain.org
www.sclcanada.org

Established in 1967, SCL is a nonprofit membership organization which aims to advance the logistics and supply chain profession in Canada. Through a range of activities, research, and informal discussion, members are encouraged to further their understanding of logistics and the art and science of its management.

Global Institute of Logistics

245 Park Avenue, 24th and 39th Floors, New York, NY 10167, US
T: +1 212 672 1846
F: +1 212 792 4001
E: ceo@globeinst.org
www.globeinst.org

The institute acts as a bridge between the academic world and business, educating the global supply chain community on the latest academic thinking on the subject.

Purchasing Management Association of Canada

777 Bay Street, Suite 2701, PO Box 112, Toronto, Ontario, ON M5G 2C8, Canada
T: +1 416 977 7111
F: +1 416 977 8886
E: info@pmac.ca
www.pmac.ca

PMAC is a national, nonprofit association and is a leading source of education, training, and development in the purchasing and supply management field in Canada. The association operates with ten provincial institutes, which can be contacted through the website.

The Supply-Chain Council (SCC)

1331 H Street NW, Suite 500, Washington, DC 20005, US
T: + 1 202 962 0440
F: + 1 202 962 3939
E: info@supply-chain.org
www.supply-chain.org

The Supply-Chain Council (SCC) is a global, non-profit trade association open to all types of organizations. It sponsors and supports educational programs, including conferences, retreats, benchmarking studies, and development of the Supply-Chain Operations Reference-Model (SCOR), as well as the Design-Chain Reference-Model (DCOR), the process reference models designed to improve users' efficiency and productivity. The council is also dedicated to improving the supply chain efficiency of its practitioner members.

Retail Banking

BOOKS

Analyzing and Managing Banking Risk: Framework for Assessing Corporate Governance and Financial Risk, 2nd ed

Hennie Van Greuning, Sonja Brajovic Bratanovic

Washington, DC: World Bank, 2003
384pp, ISBN: 978-0-8213-5418-6

This provides a comprehensive discussion of the assessment, analysis, and management of financial risks in banking. It considers the principles of risk management, and presents a framework for identifying the key players in the risk management and corporate governance processes. Coverage includes the treasury function, investment management, proprietary trading, asset liability management, components, and transparency in financial statements.

The Art of Better Retail Banking: Supportable Predictions on the Future of Retail Banking

Hugh Croxford, Frank Abramson, Alex Jablonowski

Chichester, UK: Wiley, 2005
276pp, ISBN: 978-0-470-01320-5

This is a wide-ranging examination of the issues facing the retail banking industry, and how it may develop over the next few years. It considers retail banking within an integrated framework, looking at how banks operate, management strategies, how they make and lose money, and how they fit into the various banking models. It emphasizes the importance of leadership, creativity, and teamwork for future success.

Bank Management, 6th ed

Timothy W. Koch, S. Scott MacDonald

Mason, Ohio: Thomson Higher Education, 2006
562pp, ISBN: 978-0-324-28927-5

Bank Management explains how managers can implement strategies to maximize stockholders wealth by balancing the trade-off between banking risks and returns. It also demonstrates how risk management decisions in different areas affect each other and the overall profitability and risk of the institution, and provides an Excel template for practising cash flow analysis and bank performance analysis.

  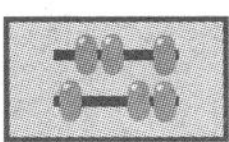   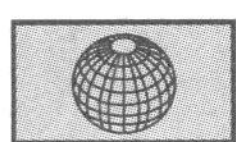   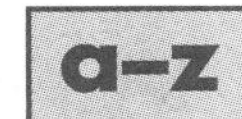

Bank Management: Text and Cases, 5th ed

George H. Hempel, Donald G. Simonson

Hoboken, New Jersey: Wiley, 2008
700pp, ISBN: 978-0-471-16960-4

This is a comprehensive introduction to bank management that examines basic asset, liability and capital management decisions. It covers the lending function of commercial banks, such as credit analysis, loan pricing and structuring a loan, and emphasizes integrative management techniques, including a description of the use of new financial products and methods of pricing in bank management.

Commercial Banking: The Management of Risk, 3rd ed

Benton E. Gup, James W. Kolari

Hoboken, New Jersey: Wiley, 2005
548pp, ISBN: 978-0-471-46949-0

This is a practical introduction to bank management and current banking practices used to control different kinds of risk. It examines the factors that affect the value of a bank, and techniques for managing that value, and explores the principal lending activities to businesses and individuals. A comprehensive coverage of banking operations includes brokerage services, insurance, trust activities, and regulatory and legal changes.

The Economics of Banking, 2nd ed

Kent Matthews, John Thompson

Chichester, UK: Wiley, 2008
295pp, ISBN: 978-0-470-51964-6

This textbook is mathematically accessible and provides a microeconomic context, enabling students to understand contemporary trends and operations in banking. It provides a sound theoretical basis for understanding bank behavior, and focuses on bank performance, the competitive nature of the banking market, bank and financial regulation, international banking, and risk management, especially in terms of trading risk and bank book risk management.

Essentials of Banking

Deborah K. Dilley

Essentials Series
Hoboken, New Jersey: Wiley, 2008
273pp, ISBN: 978-0-470-17088-5

This guide to the banking industry explores the basic elements of banking, and is a practical resource for traditional bankers, online bankers, and finance professionals. It examines how banking has evolved from being product-centered to having a more customer-driven focus, and the increasing use of multiple channels. It covers deposit insurance, regulatory compliance, ethics, customer service, and cross-industry affiliations.

The Future of Retail Banking

Joseph DiVanna

New York: Palgrave Macmillan, 2003
224pp, ISBN: 978-1-4039-1126-1

This exploration of the banking and financial services industry details how the sector can develop strategic initiatives to improve operations and increase competitiveness. It also addresses current trends influencing competition, such as globalization, market structure, technology and demographics, and how these will impact upon companies and their organization, business opportunities, revenue streams, branding and customer behavior.

The Future of Retail Banking in Europe: A View from the Top

Oonah McDonald, Kevin Keasey

New York: Wiley, 2002
193pp, ISBN: 978-0-471-89277-9

This is an exploration of the current banking sector in Europe, and is aimed at middle managers in the banking and financial services sectors, suppliers, investors, and MBA students. It analyzes the banking structures in all the major European markets, the challenges currently being faced, and predicts future trends for retail banking in Europe through a series of insights from the CEOs of major European banks.

Introduction to Banking

Barbara Casu, Claudia Girardone, Philip Molyneux

Harlow, UK: FT Prentice Hall, 2006
560pp, ISBN: 978-0-273-69302-4

This is a comprehensive introduction to theoretical and applied issues relating to the global banking industry. It introduces banking basics, before discussing central banking and bank regulation, bank management concerns such as risk management techniques, comparative banking markets, and global trends in different banking markets.

Managing Bank Risk: An Introduction to Broad-Base Credit Engineering

Morton Glantz

Amsterdam: Academic Press, 2003
667pp, ISBN: 978-0-12-285785-0

This is an examination of the concepts of credit risk management as they relate to techniques in banking and portfolio management. It focuses on new approaches to fundamental analysis and credit administration, discusses tools for understanding and measuring credit risk, credit analysis, and new credit engineering tools for the banking sector, and shows how to assimilate these tools.

Microeconomics of Banking, 2nd ed

Xavier Freixas, Jean-Charles Rochet

Cambridge, Massachusetts: MIT Press, 2008
363pp, ISBN: 978-0-262-06270-1

This examines the main issues relating to the microeconomic theory of banking that has emerged over recent years, and looks at the use of the asymmetric information model for explaining the role of banks in the economy and for pinpoint structural weaknesses in the banking sector. It also covers financial intermediaries, macroeconomic consequences of financial imperfections, risk management inside the banking firm, and bank regulation.

Modern Banking

Shelagh Heffernan

Chichester, UK: Wiley, 2005
716pp, ISBN: 978-0-470-09500-3

This is a textbook focused on the theory and practice of banking, and its prospects for the future. It considers a number of fundamental issues, such as core banking functions, different types of banks and diversification of bank activities, issues and techniques in risk management, global regulation, banking in emerging markets, bank failure and financial crises, and competitive factors.

Retail Banking

Keith Pond

London: Financial World Publishing, 2007
192pp, ISBN: 978-0-85297-777-4

This examines the current priorities in retail banking, as well as the legal and practical environment in which they operate. It explains banking fundamentals, the main economic concepts that underpin much banking activity, and bank risk. It also reviews key banking transactions, their regulation by national and international bodies, and bank profitability from the perspective of annual accounts.

Risk Management in Banking, 2nd ed

Joël Bessis

New York: Wiley, 2002
792pp, ISBN: 978-0-471-89336-3

This classic text examines the changing nature of financial risk management in the banking sector. It emphasizes conceptual and implementation issues of risk management, and presents the latest techniques and practical issues, such as Value at Risk, asset liability management, credit risk, interest rate risk, funds transfer pricing, credit derivatives, market portfolio risk, capital management, and loan portfolio models.

MAGAZINES

ABA Banking Journal

American Banking Journal
345 Hudson Street, 12th Floor, New York, NY 10014, USA
T: +1 212 620 7200
F: +1 212 633 1165
www.ababj.com
ISSN: 0194-5947

This monthly magazine, published by the American Bankers Association, is aimed at managers and executives at commercial and savings banking institutions operating in the competitive financial services market. It provides news and commentary, and identifies and explores business and societal trends, as well as legislative and regulatory issues.

American Banker

SourceMedia
1 State Street Plaza, 27th Floor, New York, NY 10004, USA
T: +1 212 803 8200
F: +1 212 843 9600
www.americanbanker.com
ISSN: 0002-7561

American Banker is a daily paper and information resource that serves the banking and financial services community. It offers news and analysis of the issues, strategies, and people that influence events in the banking sector in the United States, as well as feature articles, data applications, and special reports.

The Asian Banker

TAB International
10 Hoe Chiang Road, #14-06 Keppel Tower, Singapore 089315, Singapore
T: +65 6236 6500
F: +65 6236 6530
www.theasianbanker.com

This magazine, published 10 times a year, covers news and developments in commercial banking and financial services in Asia. It examines critical issues, trends, and best practices, and produces a comprehensive ranking of the top 300 commercial banks in Asia Pacific by asset size and strength, as well as special reports and regular tele-consultation sessions with industry experts.

Bank Accounting & Finance

CCH, USA
T: +1 978 369 6285
www.bankaccountingandfinance.com
ISSN: 0894-3958

This bi monthly magazine for bank accounting and financial officers provides practitioners' perspectives on industry best practices and trends for financial reporting, risk management, and performance analysis. It also covers issues such as financial and management accounting, profitability measurement, asset/liability management, liquidity issues, new financial instruments and capital markets products, mergers and acquisitions, and regulation.

Bank Director

Board Member
5110 Maryland Way, Suite 250, Brentwood, TN 37027, USA
T: +1 615 309 3200
F: +1 615 371 0899
www.bankdirector.com

Bank Director is a quarterly publication that examines pertinent issues in the banking sector, such as mergers and acquisitions, technology, board accountability, and marketing and business development. It is aimed at directors and top officers in financial institutions, including chairmen, presidents, chief executives, and other directors of institutions large and small, national and international.

The Banker

Financial Times
1 Southwark Bridge, London, SE1 9HL, UK
T: +44 (0) 20 7873 3000
www.thebanker.com
ISSN: 0005-5395

This monthly magazine investigates the critical developments and trends in the global banking sector. It provides in-depth financial intelligence, and covers comments and analysis, capital markets and investment banking, securities services and payments, environments and resources, retail banking, technology, special reports, regions, and features awards, database, archive, and events.

Banking Strategies

BAI
115 South LaSalle Street, Suite 3300, Chicago, IL 60603-3801, USA
T: +1 312 683 2464
F: +1 312 683 2373
www.bai.org/bankingstrategies
ISSN: 1091-6385

This magazine is published bimonthly, and presents the latest in best practices and thought leadership, and covers and interprets strategic and managerial trends in the financial services industry.

Retail Banker International

VRL KnowledgeBank
34 Porchester Road, London, W2 6ES, UK
T: +44 (0) 20 7563 5600
F: +44 (0) 20 7563 5602
www.vrlpublishing.com/retailbankerinternational.php?id=4
ISSN: 0261-1740

This newsletter is published 20 times each year, and tracks and analyzes issues related to the global retail financial services industry. It focuses on retail banking and consumer financial services on an international basis, in particular products and product innovation, marketing, distribution, technology, interim and annual results analysis, regulation and legislation, and mergers and acquisitions.

US Banker

SourceMedia
1 State Street Plaza, 27th Floor, New York, NY 10004, USA
T: +1 212 803 8200
F: +1 212 843 9600
www.americanbanker.com/usb.html
ISSN: 0148-8848

This is a monthly business management magazine that provides analysis and commentary on the industry players, financial and economic market trends, regulations, business strategies, and innovations taking place in the banking and financial services sector. It also offers guidance on improving shareholder value, business revenue and profitability, operations, and business growth, and produces rankings and series of events.

JOURNALS

Academy of Banking Studies Journal

Allied Academies
PO Box 2689, 145 Travis Road, Cullowhee, North Carolina 28723, USA
T: +1 828 293 9151
F: +1 828 293 9407
www.alliedacademies.org/Public/Journals/JournalDetails.aspx?jid=3
ISSN: 1939-2230

This journal, focused on research in the banking sector, is currently published twice yearly.

Journal of Banking & Finance

Elsevier
Radarweg 29, 1043 NX Amsterdam, The Netherlands
F: +31 20 485 2370
www.ees.elsevier.com/jbf
ISSN: 0378-4266

This is a monthly publication aimed at providing an outlet for academic research concerning financial institutions and the money and capital markets within which they function. Its emphasis is on theoretical developments and their implementation, empirical, applied, and policy-oriented research in banking and other domestic and international financial institutions and markets.

Journal of Commercial Banking and Finance

Allied Academies
PO Box 2689, 145 Travis Road, Cullowhee, North Carolina 28723, USA
T: +1 828 293 9151
F: +1 828 293 9407
www.alliedacademies.org/Public/Journals/JournalDetails.aspx?jid=3
ISSN: 1544-0028

This practitioner-oriented journal, issued once each year, publishes theoretical and empirical papers on banking and financial management, with the aim of furthering an understanding of the discipline of banking and institutional finance.

INTERNET

Bankers Almanac

www.bankersalmanac.com

This is a major online source of reference data solutions to the banking industry for payments, due diligence, compliance, risk assessment and financial research in the banking industry.

The Islamic Banker

www.theislamicbanker.com

This is a leading professional online magazine for the Islamic financial services industry. It provides financial news and information, coverage of Islamic financial institutions, events, and conferences, and promotes Islamic banking, employee and organizational performance.

ORGANIZATIONS

Europe

British Bankers Association

Chair: Angela Knight
Pinners Hall, 105–108 Old Broad Street, London, EC2N 1EX, UK
T: +44 (0) 20 7216 8800
F: +44 (0) 20 7216 8811
E: info@bba.org.uk
www.bba.org.uk

This is the leading trade association for the UK banking and financial services sector. It speaks for 223 banking members from 60 countries on the full range of UK or international banking issues, and engages with 37 associated professional firms. Its activities include market-pricing benchmarks, such as the BBA LIBOR rates.

European Banking Federation

Chair: Michel Pebereau
10 rue Montoyer, 1000 Brussels, Belgium
T: +32 (0) 2 508 37 11
F: +32 (0) 2 511 23 28
E: ebf@ebf-fbe.eu
www.ebf-fbe.eu

The EBF represents the interests of the whole European banking sector. It provides a forum for best practice, proposes and debates legislative proposals and initiatives, helps to position the European banking industry within European and global regulatory frameworks, and promotes the interests of its members and member associations, and the development of the industry.

The Worshipful Company of International Bankers

Chair: Henry Angest
3rd Floor, 12 Austin Friars, London, EC2N 2HE, UK
T: +44 (0) 20 7374 0214
F: +44 (0) 20 7374 0207
E: tim.woods@internationalbankers.co.uk
www.internationalbankers.co.uk

This guild represents the banking and financial services sector in the City of London, and combines tradition with a modern outlook on the financial services sector. Its main aim is to promote the original purposes of the Livery Companies and Guilds, that of fellowship, charity, education, and the promotion of trades and professions.

USA

American Bankers Association

Chair: Arthur R. Connelly
1120 Connecticut Avenue NW, Washington, DC 20036, USA
T: +1 202 663 5087
www.aba.com

The ABA works to enhance the competitiveness of the nation's banking industry, strengthen the US economy and communities, and serve its members by enhancing the role of financial services institutions as providers of financial services. It does this through federal legislative and regulatory activities, legal action, communication, consumer education, research, and products and services.

BRIC

Association of Russian Banks

Chair: Garegin Ashotovich Tosunyan
Building 1, Skatertnyi per., 20, 121069, Moscow, Russia
T: +7 495 691 8098
F: +7 495 691 6666
E: arb@arb.ru
www.arb.ru

ARB is a non-governmental, non-commercial organization that unites commercial banks and other credit organizations, as well as organizations involved in the functioning of the finance-and-credit system in Russia. It represents the interests of all types and size of bank, develops the Russian banking system, and suggests and promotes amendments to legislative acts and by-laws, and improvements to tax legislation.

China Banking Association

12F China Reinsurance Mansion, 11 Jinrong Street, Beijing 100034, China
T: +86 10 6655 3358
F: +86 10 6655 3356
www.china-cba.net

CBA represents 81 full members and 37 associate members in a variety of banking institutions in China. Its aim is to best represent the interests of the industry, and actively encourage its members to self-regulate and communicate, regulate operation and management, as well as protecting the legal rights of its members, and promoting the development of the banking sector.

Indian Banks Association

Chair: T. S. Narayanasami
World Trade Centre, 6th Floor, Centre 1 Building, World Trade Centre Complex, Cuff Parade, Mumbai 400 005, India
E: webmaster@iba.org.in
www.iba.org.in

This is a trade association that represents public sector banks, private sector banks, foreign banks having offices in India, and urban co-operative banks. It promotes sound and progressive banking principles, practices, and conventions, provides services to members and the banking industry, and develops and implements new ideas and innovations in banking services, operations and procedures.

Latin Bankers Association

E: emerson.pieri@latinbankers.com
www.latinbankers.com

This is an internet-based association focused on bringing value to professional banking networks in Latin America. It brings together Latin and international financial services professionals to connect financial people in the region and beyond, to assist in the development of their business, expertise, and knowledge.

International

The Bankers' Association for Finance and Trade

Chair: Charles H. Silverman
1120 Connecticut Avenue NW, 5th Floor, Washington, DC 20036, USA
T: +1 202 663 7575
F: +1 202 663 5538
E: baft@aba.com
www.baft.org

This is a financial trade association representing a broad range of internationally active financial institutions and companies that provide important services to the global financial community. It provides a forum for analysis, discussion and action among international financial professionals on a wide range of topics affecting international trade and finance, including legislative/regulatory issues.

The International Bankers Association

Chair: Paul Kuo
14th Floor, Ark Mori Building, 1-12-32 Akasaka, Minato-ku, Tokyo 107-6014, Japan
T: +81 03 5545 7511
F: +81 03 5545 0502
E: g-info@ibajapan.org
www.ibajapan.org

The IBA represents of the interests of the international financial community in Japan, and promotes cooperation among financial groups, banks, securities firms, and representative offices in the country. It also encourages the development of banking and capital markets, as well as the interests of its members, and works closely with government authorities, regulators, and non-governmental bodies.

The International Banking Federation

Chair: Sally Scutt
Pinners Hall, 105–108 Old Broad Street, London, EC2N 1EX, UK
E: sally.scutt@bba.org.uk
www.ibfed.org

This is the representative body for a group of key national banking associations and federations—the US, Australia, Canada, Japan, China, and India, and the European Banking Federation. Its main objective is to increase the effectiveness of the industry's response to multilateral and national government issues affecting their common interests, and functions as the main international forum for addressing legislative, regulatory and other issues of interest to the global banking industry.

Risk Management

BOOKS

The Book of Risk

Dan Borge
Chichester, UK: Wiley, 2001
240pp, ISBN: 978-0-471-32378-5

Dan Borge breaks down the concept and application of risk management into basic ideas to facilitate a more thorough understanding. He describes the techniques professional risk managers use for determining probabilities and personal preferences, and explores their use for more effective actions. The book explains how we are all already risk managers, and the aim is to help managers become better risk managers.

Business Continuity: Helping Directors Build a Strategy for a Secure Future

Institute of Directors
Directors Guide Series
London: Kogan Page, 2000
80pp, ISBN: 978-0-7494-3563-9

In this book managing risk has been singled out explicitly as a key board responsibility. The guide introduces the crucial value of business continuity and illustrates the steps directors can take to manage the threat and reality of business interruptions. The overriding message is positive: a planned approach to risk management and business continuity will not only avoid unnecessary crisis, it will also provide a clear competitive edge.

Managing Business Risk: An Organization-Wide Approach to Risk Management

Peter C. Young, Steven C. Tippins

New York: AMACOM, 2001
448pp, ISBN: 978-0-8144-0461-4

This is a practical textbook that explains to managers the essentials of risk management. A model, called "organizational risk management," is presented to facilitate a cost saving, company-wide approach to risk management. The techniques covered include risk assessment, risk control, asset and liability exposures to risk, risk financing principles, and insurance.

Managing Corporate Reputation and Risk: Developing a Strategic Approach to Corporate Integrity Using Knowledge Management

Dale Neef

Amsterdam: Elsevier/Butterworth-Heinemann, 2003
156pp, ISBN: 978-0-7506-7715-8

Looking at best practice techniques in risk management, this title explores the management of corporate integrity through the establishment of ethical policies, risk management through knowledge management techniques, and bottom line reporting.

Managing Environmental Risks and Liabilities

Paul Pritchard

Business and Environmental Practitioner Series
London: Earthscan, 2000
240pp, ISBN: 978-1-85383-598-8

Recent developments in environmental risk management are discussed in this book, which focuses on the nature of environmental risks and their relation to property, financial risk transfer, decision making, risk-management integration, and risk-management frameworks.

Managing Project Risk and Uncertainty

Chris Chapman, Stephen Ward

Chichester, UK: Wiley, 2002
512pp, ISBN: 978-0-470-84790-9

This focuses on the scope of recent approaches to the management of risk and uncertainty in projects and related operational strategic management. It consists of a number of real cases that explore project-related problems, including cost estimation, pricing competitive bids, risk allocation and incentive contract design, evaluation of threats and opportunities, buffer management in a supply chain, investment appraisal, portfolio management, and strategy formulation.

Managing Risk in Nonprofit Organizations: A Comprehensive Guide

Melanie L. Herman et al.

Chichester, UK: Wiley, 2003
336pp, ISBN: 978-0-471-23674-0

This practical guide shows managers in nonprofit organizations how to implement sound risk management procedures. It is divided into three sections: the nature and purposes of risk management; recognizing the context for risk management; and risk financing for nonprofits. Potential risks covered include human resource issues, fundraising, internet use, mergers, and volunteer management.

Operational Risk: Measurement and Modelling

Jack L. King

Chichester, UK: Wiley, 2001
272pp, ISBN: 978-0-471-85209-4

Operational risk, it is reported, is concerned with the risk to the performance of a firm, due to how the firm is operated as opposed to how it is financed. The authors present a new approach to measuring operational risk. This enables firms to better control the variability or risk of earnings in their operations.

Practical Risk Management: An Executive Guide to Avoiding Surprises and Losses

Erik Banks, Richard Dunn

Chichester, UK: Wiley, 2003
176pp, ISBN: 978-0-470-84967-5

This book looks at the world of financial risk management and offers practical approaches to managing financial risk based on the authors' experiences. It explores the challenges of risk management and how these can be overcome by focusing on governance and accountability. The book aims to provide an understanding of the different financial risks, the various measurement tools available, and how to construct a practical risk process that is consistent with corporate strategy.

Project Risk Assessment in a Week, 2nd ed

Donald Teale

Business in a Week Series
London: Profile Economist Books, 2003
96pp, ISBN: 978-0-340-84972-9

This book guides you step by step through the process of identifying and analyzing the key risks to a project. Guidelines are provided for identifying the risks, assessing the impact of each risk, analyzing the combined impact of the risks on the project objectives, assigning adequate contingency to the project budget and schedule, and producing a risk management plan to assist in risk mitigation.

Project Risk Management: An Essential Tool for Managing and Controlling Projects

D. van Well-Stam, F. Lindenaar, S. van Kinderen, B. P. can den Bunt

London: Kogan Page, 2004
180pp, ISBN: 978-0-7494-4275-0

This is a detailed and practical exploration of managing risk in projects. It shows how to deal effectively with unforeseen problems or requirements that can delay a project.

Project Risk Management: Processes, Techniques and Insights, 2nd ed

Chris Chapman, Stephen Ward

Hoboken, New Jersey: Wiley, 2003
408pp, ISBN: 978-0-470-85355-9

Project Risk Management examines the key issues and concepts involved in effective risk and uncertainty management in a clear and accessible way, providing a comprehensive discussion of risk management processes set firmly in the context of the project management task as a whole. It focuses on improving performance, and methodologies and techniques that are applicable to all kinds and all sizes of project.

Risk Analysis: A Quantitative Guide, 3rd ed

David Vose

Chichester, UK: Wiley, 2008
752pp, ISBN: 978-0-470-51284-5

Quantitative risk analysis (QRA), combined with Monte Carlo simulation, offers a useful method for dealing with uncertainty and variability in a problem. This focused text guides the reader through the necessary steps to produce an accurate risk analysis model, and offers general and specific techniques to cope with most modeling problems.

Risk from the CEO and Board Perspective

Mary Pat McCarthy, Timothy P. Flynn

Maidenhead, UK: McGraw-Hill, 2003
304pp, ISBN: 978-0-07-143471-3

Corporate decision-making is about navigating the business environment with one eye on the present and the other on the risks associated with each action. This text sets out to explain how corporate leaders are confronting and controlling risk in their organizations. Drawing upon their wealth of experience, the authors explore how to uncover and address sources of risk within an organization, manage risk without undermining ongoing initiatives, and link governance and risk management initiatives.

Risk Management

Michel Crouhy, Dan Galai, Robert Mark

Maidenhead, UK: McGraw-Hill, 2000
512pp, ISBN: 978-0-07-135731-9

This book suggests ways to implement a risk management system to effectively manage financial and economic risk as well as regulatory capital. It analyzes developments in risk management techniques used in the financial world and provides an up-to-date look at modern risk management tools.

Risk Management: Helping Directors to Identify and Control Business Risks Effectively, revised ed

Institute of Directors and AXA Insurance

IOD Director's Guide Series
London: Kogan Page, 2006
80pp, ISBN: 978-1-904520-44-3

This guide will assist senior decision-makers to develop a practical risk management strategy, to identify possible threats, and to introduce appropriate measures. The main areas of risk in any business are reviewed, and a wide range of advice and information provided. Case studies are included.

Risk Management: Ten Principles

Jacqueline Jeynes

Oxford: Butterworth-Heinemann, 2001

144pp, ISBN: 978-0-7506-5036-6

The ten main risk areas of a business are identified at the outset as premises, product, purchasing, people, procedures, protection, processes, performance, planning, and policy. The following sections identify and evaluate the risks and hazards relevant to each of these ten areas, and discuss ways in which the risks can be controlled. Case studies from service-based and production-based industries are included. Overall risk management strategies and policies are then described.

The Risk Management Universe: A Guided Tour, 2nd ed

David Hillson

London: British Standards Institution, 2007

424pp, ISBN: 978-0-580-50346-7

The Risk Management Universe combines the views of leading experts in the risk management field, who share their insights on various risks. It discusses the impact of new developments to maximize the effectiveness of risk management in all its diverse areas of application.

Risky Business: Corruption, Fraud, Terrorism, and Other Threats to Global Business, 2nd ed

Stuart Poole-Robb, Alan Bailey

London: Kogan Page, 2003

304pp, ISBN: 978-0-7494-4031-2

Organizations in today's world are subject to a range of risks over and above the standard expectations of terrorism and fraud, including organized crime, corruption and civil unrest. The authors' company has significant experience of these risks and the forces behind them and the book includes many case studies in areas such as Indonesia, Russia, and Asia and the Far East. Part one deals with the implications of risk for investment; part two looks at renowned trouble spots; and part three considers threats and defenses.

The Road to Audacity: Being Adventurous in Life and Work

Stephen Carter, Jeremy Kourdi

Basingstoke, UK: Palgrave Macmillan, 2003

160pp, ISBN: 978-1-4039-0617-5

The authors argue that risk-taking is an inevitable part of life and work, and that responding to uncertainty and risk is not just a matter of calculation and an attempt at objective prediction. The audacity factor is what makes the difference between caution and action. Drawing upon various examples, the book explores the way audacity can be developed and explains its importance to any individual or organization that wants to change, explore, or be different.

Secure Online Business Handbook: E-Commerce, IT Functionality, and Business Continuity, 4th ed

Jonathan Reuvid

London: Kogan Page, 2006

256pp, ISBN: 978-0-7494-4642-0

This practical handbook, divided into five sections, contains a collection of contributions from a range of experts in the field of information technology and e-commerce and addresses the need for effective management of business risk. Information at risk and the business case for security are considered first. Points of exposure and the range of threats to privacy and integrity are explored, and methods of software protection such as firewalls, encryption, digital signatures and biometrics are covered. In the operational management section, the need for a culture of workplace security is also discussed, and data recovery, disaster management, and forensics are covered under the heading of contingency planning.

Value at Risk: The Benchmark for Controlling Market Risk, 3rd ed

Philippe Jorion

Maidenhead, UK: McGraw-Hill, 2006

544pp, ISBN: 978-0-07-146495-6

This book is aimed at helping professional risk managers understand and operate within today's dynamic new risk environment. This edition updates the original book, which focused on "Value at Risk" as a financial technique to measure risks run by trading and investment operations. New developments include a chapter on liquidity risk, and information on the latest risk instruments and the expanded derivatives market.

MAGAZINES

Public Risk Magazine

Public Risk Management Association

500 Montgomery Street, Suite 750, Alexandria, VA 22314, USA

T: +1 703 528 7701

F: +1 703 739 0200

www.primacentral.org/content.cfm?sectionid=33

ISSN: 0891-7183

Public Risk Magazine, published 10 times each year, provides risk managers in the public sector with timely, focused information in an easy-to-read format. It features articles from risk management practitioners as well as industry experts.

Risk

Incisive Media

Haymarket House, 28–29 Haymarket, London, SW1Y 4RX, UK

T: +44 (0) 20 7316 9000

F: +44 (0) 20 7316 9250

www.risk.net

ISSN: 0952-8776

This monthly magazine covers news, analysis, and developments in financial risk management. It is aimed at financial managers, academics, bankers, and investment bankers.

Risk and Continuity

CHI Publishing

17a Everard Road, Birkdale, Southport, Merseyside, PR8 6NN, UK

T: +44 (0) 1704 512 512

F: +44 (0) 1704 512 212

www.chi-publishing.com

ISSN: 1463-1628

This journal provides best practice information on risk and continuity management strategies. It also covers IT security, disaster management, related human factors, and legal issues, together with company and product news.

Risk Management: An International Journal

Palgrave Macmillan

Houndmills, Basingstoke, Hampshire, RG21 6XS, UK

www.palgrave-journals.com/rm

ISSN: 1460-3799

The purpose of this quarterly journal is to generate ideas and promote good practice for all those involved in managing risk. It takes a multidisciplinary approach and aims to facilitate the exchange of information and expertise across the world.

RMA Journal

Risk Management Association

1 Liberty Place, 1650 Market Street, Suite 2300, Philadelphia, PA 19103–7301, USA

T: +1 215 446 4096

F: +1 215 446 4101

www.rmahq.org/RMA/RMAUniverse/ProductsandServices/RMABookstore/RMAJournal

ISSN: 1531-0558

Published ten times a year, this, the official journal of the Risk Management Association of the United States, covers the latest trends, techniques, and challenges that lending, credit, and risk management professionals have to deal with.

JOURNALS

Journal of Credit Risk

Risk Journals, Incisive Media

Haymarket House, 28–29 Haymarket, London, SW1Y 4RX, UK

T: +44 (0) 20 7316 9000

F: +44 (0) 20 7316 9250

www.journalofcreditrisk.com

ISSN: 1744-6619

JCR is a quarterly journal dedicated to the measurement and management of credit risk, focusing on various aspects of portfolio credit risk and the pricing of credit products.

Journal of Operational Risk

Risk Journals, Incisive Media

Haymarket House, 28–29 Haymarket, London, SW1Y 4RX, UK

T: +44 (0) 20 7316 9000

F: +44 (0) 20 7316 9250

www.journalofoperationalrisk.com

ISSN: 1744-6740

JOP is a quarterly journal dedicated to the measurement and management of operational risk. Each issue features technical research papers and a forum to promote active discussions of current issues in operational risk, and the impact of the Basel II Accord.

Journal of Risk

Risk Journals, Incisive Media

Haymarket House, 28–29 Haymarket, London,

  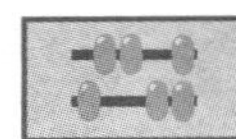   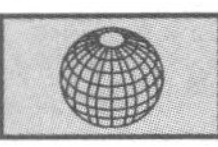   

SW1Y 4RX, UK
T: +44 (0) 20 7316 9000
F: +44 (0) 20 7316 9250
www.thejournalofrisk.com
ISSN: 1465-1211

This quarterly journal is a leading forum for research into financial risk management, which covers the latest innovations on theoretical and empirical studies in financial risk management, including the management of market and credit risk, capital allocation, and volatility estimation.

Journal of Risk Model Validation

Risk Journals, Incisive Media
Haymarket House, 28–29 Haymarket, London, SW1Y 4RX, UK
T: +44 (0) 20 7316 9000
F: +44 (0) 20 7316 9250
www.journalofriskmodelvalidation.com
ISSN: 1753-9579

JRMV is a quarterly journal that focuses on the implementation and validation of risk models, and the promotion of the greater understanding in the area of new developments in the theory and practice of risk model validation.

Risk Analysis: An International Journal

Blackwell Publishing
9600 Garsington Road, Oxford, OX4 2DQ, UK
T: +44 (0) 1865 791 100
F: +44 (0) 1865 791 347
www.wiley.com/bw/journal.asp?ref=0272-4332
ISSN: 0272-4332

The journal is an official publication of the Society for Risk Analysis. It covers new developments in risk analysis and other topics which should be of interest to scientists and managers from a wide range of disciplines.

INTERNET

RMISWEB, the Internet Resource for Risk Management Information Systems

www.rmisweb.com

This site provides access to journal and review articles and press releases on risk management. It also contains recent news items, a directory of software providers, a list of consultants, and links to other risk and insurance sites.

ORGANIZATIONS

Europe

Alarm – The Public Risk Management Association

Ladysmith House, High Street, Sidmouth, EX10 8LN, UK
T: +44 (0) 1395 519 083
F: +44 (0) 1395 517 990
E: admin@alarm-uk.org
www.alarm-uk.org

This Association creates effective risk management programs, and focuses on reducing total losses as well as explaining the effects of those which do occur and require corporate and individual commitment. They aim to provide guidance in best practice for both new and experienced risk managers.

Association of Insurance and Risk Managers

Lloyd's Avenue House, 6 Lloyd's Avenue, London, EC3N 3AX, UK
T: +44 (0) 20 7480 7610
F: +44 (0) 20 7702 3752
E: enquiries@airmic.co.uk
www.airmic.com

This membership organization, founded in 1963, brings together over 900 UK and overseas risk managers within industry, commerce, and the public sector. It offers a valuable source of contacts and practical operational support to its members, as well as assisting their self-development, technical awareness, and internal working relationships.

Business Continuity Institute

10 Southview Park, Marsack Street, Caversham, Berkshire, RG4 5AF, UK
T: +44 (0) 870 603 8783
F: +44 (0) 870 603 8761
E: bci@thebci.org
www.thebci.org

The BCI is a professional organization founded in 1994 to promote high standards of professional competence and ethics in the provision of business continuity planning and services. It has developed standards of competence, a code of ethics, and an accreditation scheme for continuity practitioners. Additional activities include seminars, conferences, and the Business Continuity Awards. The organization has over 1,100 members in 32 countries.

Federation of European Risk Management Associations

Avenue Louis Gribaumont, 1, 1150, Brussels, Belgium
T: +32 2 761 94 32
F: +32 2 771 87 20
E: info@ferma.eu
www.ferma.eu/Home/tabid/70/Default.aspx

FERMA's objective is to promote and raise risk management throughout Europe. It achieves its aims by promotion and raising awareness of risk management through the media, by information sharing, and educational and research projects.

Institute of Risk Management

Lloyd's Avenue House, 6 Lloyd's Avenue, London, EC3N 3AX, UK
T: +44 (0) 20 7709 9808
F: +44 (0) 20 7709 0716
E: enquiries@irmgt.co.uk
www.theirm.org

Besides providing advice and consultation, this membership organization, founded in 1986, also runs educational courses and examinations in risk management, and undertakes research.

USA

Global Association of Risk Professionals

111 Town Square Place, Suite 1215, Jersey City, New Jersey 07310, USA
T: +1 201 719 7210
F: +1 201 222 5022
E: frm@garp.com
www.garp.com

Global Association of Risk Professionals is an independent association dedicated to financial risk management. Members work in regional and global banks, asset management firms, insurance companies, central banks, securities regulators, hedge funds, universities, large industrial corporations, and multinationals. It offers comprehensive programs and resources from leading financial risk professionals.

Global Association of Risk Professionals

28 East 18th Street, 2nd Floor, New York, NY 10003, USA
T: +1 212 995 0930
F: +1 212 995 0835
E: membership@garp.com
www.garp.com

Originally an independent organization of risk management practitioners and researchers, founded by a group of risk managers from the finance industry, GARP is now a diverse association of over 15,000 professionals sharing a common interest in risk management. Its activities include facilitating the exchange of information, developing educational programs, and promoting standards in the area of financial risk management.

Public Risk Management Association

500 Montgomery Street, Suite 750, Alexandria, VA 22314, USA
T: +1 703 528 7701
F: +1 703 739 0200
E: info@primacentral.org
www.primacentral.org

The Public Risk Management Association is an industry body that provides educational programs, risk resources, and networking opportunities for public sector risk managers. It promotes effective risk management in the public interest as an essential component of public administration.

Risk and Insurance Management Society, Inc.

655 Third Avenue, 2nd Floor, New York, NY 10017, USA
T: +1 212 286 9292
www.rims.org

This is a nonprofit organization dedicated to advancing the practice of risk management. It serves its members by providing quality products, services, and information designed to manage all forms of business risk. It also offers educational opportunities and aims to develop a responsive and productive network.

Risk Management Association

1 Liberty Place, 1650 Market Street, Suite 2300, Philadelphia, PA 19103-7301, USA
T: +1 215 446 4096
F: +1 215 446 4101
E: customers@rmahq.org
www.rmahq.org

RMA is a membership organization for lending, credit, and risk management professionals in the financial services industry. Members have access to a number of benefits including professional development and networking opportunities, benchmarking tools, RMA products, and a journal. It was formerly known as Robert Morris Associates.

  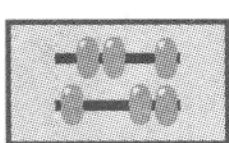   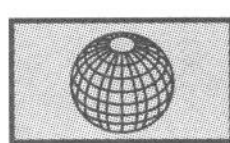   

Society for Risk Analysis

1313 Dolley Madison Boulevard, Suite 402, McLean, VI 22101, USA
T: +1 703 790 1745
E: sra@burkinc.com
www.sra.org

Providing an open forum for those interested in risk analysis in its broadest sense, this organization devotes itself to risks of concern to individuals, the public and private sectors, and society in general. Membership is multidisciplinary and international.

BRIC

Brazalian Risk Management Association

Rua Alberto Leal, 71, São Paulo – SP, Brazil
T: +55 11 5581 3569
E: abgr@abgr.com.br
www.abgr.com.br

Risk Management Association of India

25, Baranashi Ghosh Street, Calcutta, 700 007, India
T: +91 33 239 4184
F: +91 33 233 6612
E: insurance@prgindia.com
www.prgindia.com/rsk_mgmt.php

The Risk Management Association of India promotes risk management through a forum for the exchange of views among those engaged in the risk management profession and insurance, an understanding of risk management and safety techniques, guidance and information on the latest developments in the industry, courses and lectures, and assists members in the matters of dispute.

International

International Risk Management Benchmarking Association

USA
T: +1 281 440 5044
www.irmba.com

Selling and Salesmanship

BOOKS

Boosting Sales: Increasing Profits . . . Without Breaking the Bank

Bob Gorton

Business on a Shoestring Series
London: A&C Black Publishers, 2007
208pp, ISBN: 978-0-7136-7541-2

Boosting your company's sales is essential if you're going to make a success of your business. Packed with ideas that really work, real-life examples, step-by-step advice and sources of further information, this book helps you to make the most of every sales opportunity.

Can I Change Your Mind?

Lindsay Camp

London: A&C Black Publishers, 2007
224pp, ISBN: 978-0-7136-7849-9

Everyone needs to be able to argue a case effectively in writing. Drawing on his long experience as a leading copywriter, Lindsay Camp shows how it's done, whether the "end product" is a magazine ad, a new business proposal, a page for the company website, or an email to your boss. Engaging, entertaining and—as you'd expect—highly persuasive, this book will change the way you think about the words you use for ever.

Clients Forever: How Your Clients Can Build Your Business for You

Doug Carter, Jenni Green

Maidenhead, UK: McGraw-Hill, 2003
256pp, ISBN: 978-0-07-140256-9

This book shows you how to build your business through solid, long-term relationships with your favorite kind of clients. It provides the know-how and confidence to focus your efforts on the people you most enjoy working with, generate better results with less effort, build relationships with clients, and develop an approach that accentuates your personal strengths.

Dalrymple's Sales Management: Concepts and Cases, 10th ed

William L. Cron, Thomas E. DeCarlo

Hoboken, New Jersey: Wiley, 2008
528pp, ISBN: 978-0-470-16965-0

This practical guide introduces the key issues, strategies, and relationships for managing an effective sales force. It places emphasis on developing a sales force program and managing strategic account relationships, and explores team development, diversity in the work force, problem-solving skills, and financial issues, to provide a useful guide for a career in sales management.

Delighting Your Customers: Delivering Excellent Customer Service . . . Without Breaking the Bank

Avril Owton

Business on a Shoestring Series
London: A&C Black Publishers, 2007
176pp, ISBN: 978-0-7136-7542-9

Your relationship with your customers is probably one of the most important you'll ever have. No business can survive without them, but reaching customers in the first place is a big challenge for small companies. This book will help you do just that by offering invaluable advice on a range of key issues including: understanding your customers; hiring the right people; coping with complaints; adding a personal touch; and learning from your competitors.

Global Account Management: A Complete Action Kit of Tools and Techniques for Managing Key Global Customers

Peter Cheverton

London: Kogan Page, 2008
242pp, ISBN: 978-0-7494-5227-8

This book explains the challenges of establishing a global account strategy and guides the reader through the process of decisions and actions required to manage global accounts successfully, and provides a template for all businesses with global clients. It also highlights the difference between an international company operating in different markets and one that can be considered truly global, explaining that company directors need to understand whether a client has consistent needs across different countries, possesses a global operational structure, and has the ability to implement global decisions.

Global Account Management: Creating Value

H. David Hennessey, Jean-Pierre Jeannet

Chichester, UK: Wiley, 2003
272pp, ISBN: 978-0-470-84892-0

The globalization of many industries, it is suggested, has created a unique opportunity to interact with a client on a coordinated global basis. The handling of large global customers requires special expertise, systems, and organizational alignment. This book examines the key aspects of the practice of global account management and of developing and managing global customers, and illustrates these with case studies.

How to Become a Rainmaker: The Rules for Getting and Keeping Customers and Clients

Jeffrey J. Fox

London: Vermilion, 2001
176pp, ISBN: 978-0-09-187654-8

This book is written to assist in identifying, attracting and keeping customers. It identifies "rainmakers" (people who bring revenue into organizations), who may be CEOs, owners, partners, sales representatives, or fundraisers. Jeffrey J. Fox explains how the reader can become a rainmaker, enabling him or her to attract more customers and rise above the competition in any company.

Improving Customer Satisfaction, Loyalty, and Profit: An Integrated Measurement and Management System

Michael D. Johnson, Anders Gustafsson

San Francisco, California: Jossey-Bass, 2000
240pp, ISBN: 978-0-7879-5310-2

By outlining in detail five key areas, this book offers ways to improve customer loyalty. By outlining key measures of customer satisfaction and giving suggestions for marketing strategy and product development, the book enables a more cohesive measurement and management system.

  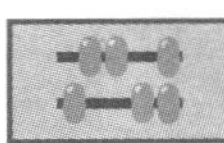      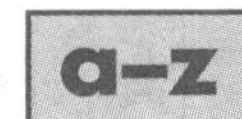

Key Account Management: A Complete Action Kit of Tools and Techniques for Achieving Profitable Key Supplier Status, 4th ed

Peter Cheverton

London: Kogan Page, 2008
368pp, ISBN: 978-0-7494-5277-3

This comprehensive textbook takes a broad perspective on key account management (KAM), starting from the premise that it is not just to do with selling but with developing profitable relationships between customers and suppliers. Peter Cheverton starts by defining KAM and explains how to understand the customer's perspective, put in place the organizational systems and processes required, identify key accounts, develop management strategies, and meet customer needs. Advice on developing key account plans and keeping track of progress and examples of good and bad practice are provided throughout.

Key Account Management: Learning from Supplier and Customer Perspectives, 2nd ed

Malcolm McDonald, Beth Rogers

Oxford: Butterworth-Heinemann, 2006
416pp, ISBN: 978-0-7506-6246-8

Key account management, it is suggested, is rapidly becoming more important as purchasing power is increasingly concentrated in the hands of fewer, larger buyers. This text, based on research by Cranfield School of Management, presents a new framework for understanding the development of key account relationships. It explains the processes of identifying and targeting key accounts, key account planning, the role and skills of key account managers, and the positioning of key account activity. The book also considers the future of key account management.

Key Account Management and Planning: The Comprehensive Handbook for Managing Your Company's Most Important Strategic Asset

Noel Capon

London: Simon & Schuster, 2001
480pp, ISBN: 978-0-7432-1188-8

With a greater level of competition and increased costs of selling, the nature of the selling process has changed. Using research, real-life stories of successes and failures, and clarifying figures, the author presents his four-part "congruence model" of key account management. He explains: how to select the key account portfolio; how to manage key accounts; how to recruit, select, train, reward and retain key account managers, and how to formulate and execute key account strategies.

Knock Your Socks Off Selling

Jeffrey Gitomer, Ron Zemke

New York: AMACOM, 1999
208pp, ISBN: 978-0-8144-7030-5

Offering an overview of sales techniques, from basic selling to developing relationships, the book is appropriate for salespeople at every level. It places emphasis on making a partnership out of the buyer-seller relationship and discusses networking, generating leads, making presentations, and following through.

Marketing and Selling Professional Services: Practical Approaches to Practice Development, 3rd ed

Patrick Forsyth

London: Kogan Page, 2003
320pp, ISBN: 978-0-7494-4090-9

With the aim of helping professionals of all kinds to develop successful strategies for marketing what are essentially intangible services, the author starts by explaining the importance and role of marketing in professional service businesses, and goes on to explore a range of practical issues, including marketing planning, promotional mix, advertising, and postal promotion. A second section deals with professional personal selling, and covers persuasive writing and communication, and systematic client development.

The New Strategic Selling: The Unique Sales System Proven Successful by the World's Best Companies, 3rd ed

Stephen E. Heiman et al.

London: Kogan Page, 2003
304pp, ISBN: 978-0-7494-4130-2

Following the strategic selling process outlined in this book, the authors lay out an effective plan that leverages the key benefits of the sellers/buyers solution, and minimizes price as the principal buying criterion. The book provides a process for what successful sales people do consistently—plan.

The Sales Bible: The Ultimate Sales Resource

Jeffrey H. Gitomer

New York: HarperCollins, 2008
304pp, ISBN: 978-0-06-137940-6

Designed as a book to be read by those within the sales industry, this book targets aspiring salesmen/women and gives them practical advice on how to reconsider and reevaluate the whole selling process. Fundamentally challenging prevailing perceptions, this text offers a comprehensive range of new ideas and strategies.

Sales Genius: A Master Class in Successful Selling

Tony Buzan, Richard Israel

Aldershot, UK: Gower Publishing, 2000
272pp, ISBN: 978-0-566-08209-2

The authors present 12 traits that can be found in professional salespeople and 12 strategies that they deploy. They then create a program of activities based on these traits.

Selling from the Heart: The Total Success System for Mastering Business Relationships

Steven Lloyd

Arlington, Texas: Sterling & Pope, 2000
240pp, ISBN: 978-0-9678-6160-9

The main focus of the book is "emotional selling" but it also provides practical, hands-on advice on salesmanship. It covers topics including prospecting, sales presentations, customer relationships, follow-up, and building a career in sales.

Selling to Big Companies

Jill Konrath

New York: Kaplan Business, 2005
256pp, ISBN: 978-1-4195-1562-0

This presents a range of sales strategies for effectively accessing big accounts, reducing the sales cycle, and closing more business. It also provides an Account Entry Toolkit, which explains how to apply this process to your own business.

The Seven Keys to Managing Strategic Accounts

Sallie Sherman, Joseph Sperry, Samuel Reese

Maidenhead, UK: McGraw-Hill, 2003
256pp, ISBN: 978-0-07-141752-5

Offering market-proven strategies for generating competitive advantage by identifying and looking after your best customers, this book provides decision-makers with a strategy for profitably managing their largest and most critical accounts.

The SPIN Selling Fieldbook: Practical Tools, Methods, Exercises and Resources

Neil Rackham

Maidenhead, UK: McGraw-Hill, 2007
208pp, ISBN: 978-0-07-052235-0

Full of case studies and practical information, this book shows the reader how to put into practice the help and advice given in *SPIN Selling*.

The 25 Sales Habits of Highly Successful Salespeople, 3rd ed

Stephan Schiffman

Avon, Massachusetts: Adams Media Corporation, 2008
128pp, ISBN: 978-1-59869-757-5

This insightful guide shows how to convert leads to sales, motivate yourself and motivate others, give killer presentations, while retaining a sense of humor. It includes new examples that use the latest advances in sales presentation technology, cases of these successful habits in action, and tips on how to overcome mistakes, set sales timetables, and reexamine processes to shore up weaknesses.

The Ultimate Sales Letter: Attract New Customers, Get Face Time, Boost Your Sales, 3rd ed

Dan S. Kennedy, Daniel Kennedy

Avon, Massachusetts: Adams Media Corporation, 2006
224pp, ISBN: 978-1-59337-499-0

This text provides clear examples to assist in writing focused sales letters that target specific customer bases. Tips and features include creating powerful headlines, improving readability, when to use bullet points, which font to use, and which demographics to target. All this is performed within 28 structured steps, and should interest sales reps, business owners, and advertising people.

Why People Don't Buy Things: Five Proven Steps to Connect with Your Customers and Dramatically Increase Your Sales

Harry Washburn, Kim Wallace

Cambridge, Massachusetts: Perseus Books Group, 1999
208pp, ISBN: 978-0-7382-0157-3

The authors provide a methodical approach to understanding customers' motivations and show how to customize an entire sales strategy to customers' shopping patterns. In identifying different sales profiles, they reveal strategies to break out of unproductive patterns, create fresh relationships, and gain a loyal customer base.

Why We Buy: The Science of Shopping

Paco Underhill

London: Texere Publishing, 2008
320pp, ISBN: 978-1-4165-9524-3

This book is filled with retail insights, revealing, for example, how men are starting to shop like women and how women have changed the way supermarkets are designed. Looking to the future, Underhill predicts huge retail opportunities concomitant with an ageing baby-boom population, and shows how online retailing will change shopping malls.

MAGAZINES

Sales and Marketing Management

Nielsen Business Media
770 Broadway, New York, NY 10003–9595, USA
www.salesandmarketing.com
ISSN: 0163-7517

This monthly magazine features articles, profiles, and interviews written for top executives who have direct responsibility for all aspects of sales, marketing, and management. Featured topics include case studies and marketing strategies from the world's most successful companies.

Sales Leader

Dartnell Corporation
360 Hiatt Drive, Palm Beach Gardens, FL 33418, USA
T: +1 800 621 5463
F: +1 561 622 2423
www.dartnellcorp.com/sales_leader.htm

This newsletter is published 12 times each year. Written for novice and experienced sales personnel, it offers tips and advice on how to capture sales. The articles are written by expert salesmen with years of experience in closing the deal on buying decisions. Sales tactics in a variety of major industries are covered.

Sales Promotion

Market Link Publishing
The Mill, Bearwalden Business Park, Wendens Ambo, Saffron Walden, Essex, CB11 4GB, UK
T: +44 (0) 1799 544 215
F: +44 (0) 1799 544 202
www.salespromo.co.uk
ISSN: 0957-6193

Published monthly, this magazine covers promotional marketing and incentive strategy. Its target readership consists of marketing directors, brand managers, and sales promotion agencies.

Winning Edge

International Network of M&A Partners
6000 Cattleridge Drive, Suite 300, Sarasota, FL 34232, USA
T: +1 941 378 5500
F: +1 941 378 5505
www.ismm.co.uk/magazine.php
ISSN: 0264-3200

The official journal of the Institute of Sales and Marketing Management, it is published ten times a year and covers topics such as market intelligence, sales techniques, and strategies for marketing.

JOURNALS

Journal of Personal Selling and Sales Management

M. E. Sharpe
80 Business Park Drive, Armonk, NY 10504, USA
T: +1 800 541 6563
F: +1 914 273 2106
www.jpssm.org
ISSN: 0885-3134

JPSSM is a quarterly journal that seeks to advance the theory and practice of personal selling and sales management, and bridge the gap between the academic and business communities. It provides a forum for 'cross-talk' among sales educators, researchers, and practitioners.

Journal of Selling & Major Account Management

Northern Illinois University, College of Business
College of Business, Northern Illinois University, DeKalb, IL 60115–2897, USA
T: +1 815 753 5000
www.cob.niu.edu/jsmam
ISSN: 1463-1431

The main objective of this journal is to provide a focus for collaboration between practitioners and academics for the advancement of education, research, and best practice in the areas of selling and major account management. It is aimed at both practitioners in industry and academics researching in sales.

INTERNET

BestOfSales.com

www.bestofsales.com

A list of links to sales resources on the internet is given on this site.

Just Sell

www.justsell.com

This site offers a selection of useful sales checklists and evaluation tools for sales professionals. Users must register to access the information, but registration is free.

Sales Rep Central

www.salesrepcentral.com

A portal for sales professionals, the site contains news, articles, a community message board, jobs, sales leads, and travel services.

Saleslinks.com

www.saleslinks.com/links

Run by Mentor Associates, this site is aimed at anyone who is engaged in selling for a living. It includes links to sales resources on the internet, arranged in categories.

Salesmanship

www.dmoz.org/Business/Marketing_and_Advertising

Maintained as part of the Open Directory Project, this site contains a large list of other websites, each with a brief description, relating to all aspects of salesmanship.

SalesVault

www.salesvault.com

This site is aimed at professional salespeople. It also includes articles, news, and advice, and also advertises courses that users may wish to take up for a fee.

Selling Power

www.sellingpower.com

The online counterpart to *Selling Power* magazine, the site offers archived issues of the magazine, electronic newsletters on several sales-related topics, and advice on motivation and management. Much of the information on the site can be viewed by nonmembers, but to access other areas you will need to register. Registration is free.

ORGANIZATIONS

Europe

Direct Selling Association UK

29 Floral Street, London, WC2E 9DP, UK
T: +44 (0) 20 7497 1234
F: +44 (0) 20 7497 3144
E: info@dsa.org.uk
www.dsa.org.uk

The DSA aims to promote the understanding of direct selling as a distribution channel. Its benefits are potentially huge, as the site cites figures which claim that direct selling is worth more than ú1.6 billion each year. The DSA's website has four major categories: protecting the consumer, direct selling today, information on the association, and "A Business of Your Own," which gives information on how direct selling can be helpful to start-up businesses.

Institute of Sales and Marketing Management

Harrier Court, Lower Woodside, Bedfordshire, LU1 4DQ, UK
T: +44 (0) 1582 840 001
F: +44 (0) 1582 849 142
www.ismm.co.uk

Established in 1966, the ISMM is a professional body for salespeople in the United Kingdom. It promotes standards of excellence in the industry and provides qualifications and training. Its members are individuals at all levels from students to sales directors. The organization holds a conference in Birmingham every October.

Institute of Sales Promotion

Arena House, 66–68 Pentonville Road, London, N1 9HS, UK
T: +44 (0) 20 7837 5340
F: +44 (0) 20 7837 5326
E: enquiries@isp.org.uk
www.isp.org.uk

The Institute of Sales Promotion was set up in 1979. It offers education, training, legal advice, and networking opportunities for members.

Society of Sales and Marketing

40 Archdale Road, East Dulwich, London, SE22 9HJ, UK
T: +44 (0) 20 8693 0555
F: +44 (0) 709 234 2170
E: info@ssam.co.uk
www.ssam.co.uk

This professional body was established in 1980. It exists to encourage the study of selling and sales management, marketing principles and practice, retail management, and international trade. It provides professional status for salespeople and accredits educational programs.

USA

Direct Selling Association

1667 K Street, NW, Suite 1100, Washington, DC 20006–1660, USA
T: +1 202 347 8866
F: +1 202 452 9010
E: info@dsa.org
www.dsa.org

DSA is a trade association for firms that manufacture and distribute goods and services sold directly to consumers. It offers its members research services, a monthly newsletter, a resource guide, conferences, networking councils, legislative lobbying, and salesforce support.

National Association of Sales Professionals

37557 Newburgh Park Circle, Livonia, MI 48152, USA
T: +1 480 951 4311
F: +1 480 483 2860
E: info@nasp.cpm
www.nasp.com

Founded in 1991, NASP states that its mission is to cater for the needs of salespersons, to help in their professional development in a changing field, and to upgrade the career status of those working in sales. It runs the Certified Professional SalesPerson program, and administers the International Registry of Accredited Salespersons.

BRIC

Direct Selling Association of Hong Kong (HKDSA)

c/o Amway Hong Kong, Amway Asia Pacific, Hong Kong Branch, 38/F, The Lee Gardens, 33 Hysan Avenue, Hong Kong
T: +86 852 296 96333
F: +86 852 280 73920
E: angela_keung@amway.com
www.hkdsa.org.hk

HKDSA is a trade association of person-to-person marketing companies in Hong Kong. A wide range of products and services are marketed and distributed directly to consumers through these companies' salespeople. The HKDSA is a full member of the World Federation of Direct Selling Associations.

Direct Selling Association of Russia

Ulanky Per. 4, Building 1, Moscow, Russia
T: +7 495 705 9311
F: +7 495 792 3641
E: info@rdsa.ru
www.rdsa.ru/eng.html

DSA is the national trade association of the leading firms that manufacture and distribute goods and services sold directly to consumers in Russia. Its mission is to protect, serve and promote the effectiveness of member companies and the independent business people they represent, and ensure that the marketing by member companies of products and/or the direct sales opportunity is conducted with the highest level of business ethics and service to consumers.

Indian Direct Selling Association (IDSA)

c/o Sangeet Shyamala Cultural Institute, A-12, Vasant Vihar, New Delhi 110 070, India
T: +91 11 2615 2045
F: +91 11 2615 2045
E: idsasg@idsa.co.in
www.indiandsa.co.in

The Indian Direct Selling Association is an association of companies engaged in the business of direct selling in India. Its members are of high national and international repute, having set standards in delivering quality goods and in following ethical business practices.

International

Sales and Marketing Executives International, Inc.

PO Box 1390, Sumas, Washington, DC 98295–1390, USA
T: +1 312 893 0751
F: +1 604 855 0165
E: smeihq@smei.org
www.smei.org

SME International is a worldwide association of sales and marketing managers whose members are top executives. Founded in 1935, it provides education in both sales and management, along with workshops, newsletters, meetings, and discussions.

World Federation of Direct Selling Associations (WFDSA)

1667 K Street, NW, Suite 1100, Washington, DC 20006, USA
T: +1 202 452 8866
F: +1 202 452 9010
E: info@wfdsa.org
www.wfdsa.org

The WFDSA is a global, nongovernmental, voluntary organization that represents the direct selling industry as a federation of national direct selling associations.

Small and Growing Businesses

BOOKS

Business Services in European Economic Growth

Luis Rubalcaba, Henk Kox (editors)

Basingstoke, UK: Palgrave, 2007
320pp, ISBN: 978-0-230-00202-9

This provides a comprehensive approach from an applied economics perspective, focusing on the contribution of business services to European economic growth, and exploring all the major mechanisms through which this contribution operates.

The E-Myth Revisited: Why Most Small Businesses Still Don't Work and What You Can Do About Yours, 2nd ed

Michael E. Gerber

London: HarperCollins, 2004
288pp, ISBN: 978-0-88730-728-7

First published in 1986, this best-selling book provides information and guidance on starting and maintaining a small business or franchise. "E-myth" stands for "entrepreneurial myth" and refers to Gerber's belief that entrepreneurs do not necessarily make good business people. The book shows the reader how to simplify the systems involved in running a business, and instead create an incredibly organized and regimented plan, so that the systems can more or less run themselves, freeing the entrepreneur's mind to focus on long-term strategy.

Enterprise Planning and Development: Small Business and Enterprise Start-Up and Growth, 2nd ed

David Butler

Oxford: Butterworth-Heinemann, 2006
432pp, ISBN: 978-0-7506-8064-6

This book aims to help owner-managers of small businesses draw up a plan for the long-term future. The subjects covered include: reviewing performance, resource implications, sales and marketing strategy, market expansion, staffing, and financial performance. The standards for business development established by the Small Firms Enterprise Development Institute (SFEDI) are appended.

Financial Management for the Small Business: A Practical Guide, 6th ed

Colin Barrow

Business Enterprise Series
London: Kogan Page, 2006
256pp, ISBN: 978-0-7494-4563-8

The author provides practical advice on proper financial planning and control for the small business. The three main sections cover key financial statements, financial analysis tools, and business plans and budgeting. A list of further reading and sources of information is included.

Finding Your Perfect Work: The New Career Guide for Making a Living, Creating a Life

Paul Edwards, Sarah Edwards

New York: Penguin Putnam, 2003
480pp, ISBN: 978-1-58542-216-6

This book is aimed at those in the crucial first phase of setting up a business: assessing yourself. Considering what you really want to do and get from your own business is explored in depth here, and the book contains worksheets to help readers pinpoint their own strengths, weaknesses, and goals.

Go It Alone: The Streetwise Secrets of Self-Employment

Geoff Burch

Chichester, UK: Capstone, 2003
336pp, ISBN: 978-1-84112-470-4

This easy-to-read, practical guide for those thinking of starting their own business is packed with anecdotal advice drawn from the author's wealth of experience in entrepreneurship and sales and is conveyed in a style that is both original and humorous.

Good Finance Guide for Small Businesses: How to Raise, Manage and Grow Your Company's Cash

London: A&C Black Publishers, 2007
288pp, ISBN: 978-0-7136-8209-0

Cash—or the lack of it—keeps small business owners awake at night more than anything else. This one-stop guide to small business finance is invaluable for anyone who needs to raise money to launch or grow a business, or manage the finances of one they run already. It covers five key areas: getting off the ground; managing your money; getting paid on time; company admin, tax and payroll; and coping in a crisis.

Growing a Private Company: Commercial Strategies for Building a Business Worth Millions

Ian Smith

London: Kogan Page, 2000
256pp, ISBN: 978-0-7494-3280-5

This book is aimed at owners of private companies and provides guidance on strategy, operational efficiency, growth techniques, venture capital, acquisitions, and exit options.

Growing Business Handbook: Inspiration and Advice from Successful Entrepreneurs and Fast Growing UK Companies, 12th ed

Adam Jolly (editor)

London: Kogan Page, 2009
480pp, ISBN: 978-0-7494-5548-4

Designed to help businesses with an established market position, this handbook presents a range of practical strategies for managing growth. The contributors, who come from a variety of backgrounds, provide advice in areas including funding options, competition, managing the risks, making the most of IT, external relations, and competitive purchasing.

Growing Your Own Business: Growth Strategies for Meeting New Challenges and Maximizing Success

Gregory F. Kishel, Patricia Gunter Kishel

Lincoln, Nebraska: iUniverse, 2000
256pp, ISBN: 978-0-595-14792-2

Focusing on the key decisions needed for creating and maintaining your business from start-up to maturity, this book offers information and guidance in areas such as planning, financing, team building, marketing, expansion, taxation, and transition.

Kick Start Your Dream Business: Getting It Started and Keeping You Going

Romanus Wolter

Berkeley, California: Ten Speed Press, 2001
304pp, ISBN: 978-1-58008-251-8

This book contains practical advice for anyone thinking about starting a small business as well as supportive real-life examples of successful entrepreneurship.

The Loyalty Effect: The Hidden Force Behind Growth, Profits, and Lasting Value

Frederick F. Reichheld

Boston, Massachusetts: Harvard Business School Press, 2001
352pp, ISBN: 978-1-57851-687-2

Loyalty is not dead, and this book explains why, demonstrating the power of loyalty-based management as a profitable alternative to a constant flux of employees, investors, and customers.

Managing by the Numbers

Chuck Kremer, Ron Rizzuto, John Case

Cambridge, Massachusetts: Perseus Books Group, 2000
198pp, ISBN: 978-0-7382-0256-3

In this text, Chuck Kremer and Ron Rizzuto present a practical approach to reading financial statements and to managing the three core issues of business financial performance: net profit, operating cash-flow, and return on assets. The book features numerous exercises and examples (with associated templates available on the web), a powerful new management tool known as "The Financial Scoreboard," and an extensive glossary.

Managing Difficult People: A Survival Guide for Handling Any Employee

Marilyn Pincus

Avon, Massachusetts: Adams Media Corporation, 2005
224pp, ISBN: 978-1-59337-186-9

While you may have a marvelous business idea, you may not be the world's most confident manager, and as your business grows, that's something you'll need to work on. If you work with someone with a challenging personality, this book will help you find practical ways of dealing with them so that you can both get on with your job. Offering practical help on how to get a tricky situation back on track, this book profiles several different types of awkward colleagues, including the Bully, the Complainer, the Procrastinator, the Know-it-All, and the Silent Type.

Marketing Your Service Business

Ian Ruskin-Brown

London: Thorogood, 2005
296pp, ISBN: 978-1-85418-316-3

This examines the key differences between the marketing of products based on goods and those which are based on services, or which use services to gain a competitive advantage. It presents current real life examples and exercises to illustrate the ideas discussed, and a sample workbook for use in training staff in customer service.

The Next Level: Essential Strategies for Achieving Breakthrough Growth

James B. Wood

Cambridge, Massachusetts: Perseus Books Group, 1999
224pp, ISBN: 978-0-7382-0159-7

An accessible guide to planning and managing the stages of company growth, *The Next Level* centers around the use of a powerful, field-tested diagnostic tool, the Inc Growth Strategy Analysis. James Wood carefully shows entrepreneurs and established business leaders alike how to analyze their organization's growth potential, identify the key constraints to future growth, and put into practice the strategies that will enable them to arrive at new levels of expansion and profit generation.

The On-Purpose Business: Doing More of What You Do Best More Profitably

Kevin W. McCarthy

Colorado Springs, Colorado: Navpress Publishing Group, 2002
192pp, ISBN: 978-1-57683-321-6

Written in a story format and with a spiritual backdrop, this book examines the principles of management and introduces the "On-Purpose" model, which focuses on all areas where each individual joins, belongs, and contributes to an organization.

101 Best Businesses to Start, 3rd ed

Philip Lief Group, Russell D. Roberts, Sharon Kahn

New York: Random House, 2000
720pp, ISBN: 978-0-7679-0659-3

This popular book offers helpful, practical advice on where to start if you are looking for a new business opportunity. Each of the businesses listed is described fully and entries include profit projections, information on costs, strategies for success, and assistance on planning staff requirements.

Outsmarting Goliath: How to Achieve Equal Footing with Companies That Are Bigger, Richer, Older and Better Known

Debra Koontz Traverso

London: Kogan Page, 2000
288pp, ISBN: 978-1-57660-031-3

The author presents practical advice on how to help small businesses present a professional image, produce high-quality marketing materials, and win contracts that may seem out of reach for a small company. The book also outlines innovative ways to enhance company profile.

Patent It Yourself, 14th ed

David Pressman

Berkeley, California: Nolo Press, 2009
596pp, ISBN: 978-1-4133-1058-0

As an experienced patent attorney and former patent examiner of the US Patent and Trademark Office, David Pressman has developed a very useful guide containing all the instructions and forms necessary to patent an invention in the United States. The book offers comprehensive and up-to-date advice for obtaining a high-quality patent and presents the information in a user-friendly, jargon-free, and well-illustrated way.

Setting Up a Limited Company, 2nd ed

Mark Fairweather, Rosy Border

Pocket Lawyer Series
London: The Stationery Office, 2004
160pp, ISBN: 978-1-85941-857-4

This is a practical guide to the procedures for setting up a limited company in the United Kingdom. The text covers considering the options, roles, and responsibilities, and completing the required forms. Sample letters, minutes, resolutions, and articles of association are included in the text and on disk. Listings of frequently asked questions and useful contacts are also provided.

Setting Up and Running a Limited Company: A Comprehensive Guide to Forming and Operating a Company as a Director and Shareholder, 4th ed

Robert Browning

Oxford: How To Books, 2003
192pp, ISBN: 978-1-85703-866-8

This guide is aimed at anyone thinking of establishing a limited company and addresses statutory requirements as well as advising on best practice. The book includes information on: the responsibilities of shareholders and directors; setting up your business; preparing financial records; sourcing venture capital; and retreating gracefully if things don't go to plan.

Small Business Management, 6th ed

David Stokes, Nicholas Wilson

London: Thomson Financial, 2010
480pp, ISBN: 978-1-4080-1799-9

This is a practical textbook, written by some of the most respected writers on small business in the United Kingdom.

Small Business Marketing Management

Ian Chaston, Terry Mangles

Basingstoke, UK: Palgrave, 2002
272pp, ISBN: 978-0-333-98075-0

This book is designed to give undergraduate and postgraduate students an understanding of the small business marketing process, including positioning, competitive advantage, product management, pricing, and distribution. The impact of e-commerce and the internet, the marketing of services, and international marketing are also covered. The text is supported by real-life case studies and published research findings.

Small Time Operator: How to Start Your Own Business, Keep Your Books, Pay Your Taxes, and Stay Out of Trouble, 11th ed

Bernard B. Kamoroff

Willits, California: Bell Springs Publishing, 2010
232pp, ISBN: 978-0-917510-30-4

Kamoroff presents the reader with the essentials of building a business, from obtaining initial permits and licenses, to seeking financing, locating the right business area, establishing an accounts and bookkeeping system, and taking on new staff. The text is continually updated in order to reflect the very latest thinking in tax and business management.

So You Want to Start a Business: 8 Steps to Take Before Making the Leap

Edward D. Hess, Charles F. Goetz

Upper Saddle River, New Jersey: FT Press, 2008
224pp, ISBN: 978-0-13-712667-5

This identifies the main "killer mistakes" in business services, provides advice on the knowledge and tools to avoid them, and ensure your business thrives.

Spare Room Tycoon: Succeeding Independently—The 70 Lessons of Sane Self-Employment, 2nd ed

James Chan

London: Nicholas Brealey Publishing, 2006
224pp, ISBN: 978-1-85788-252-0

Written by a entrepreneur with over 20 years' experience of working from home, this book is aimed at anyone thinking of setting up a home-based business. It offers support and tips on how to avoid isolation and to spread the word about your business. The book focuses on "soft" skills, such as work–life balance, building confidence, and coping with the emotional demands of being your own boss, and offers reassuring anecdotal advice.

Start and Run a Creative Services Business, 2nd ed

Susan Kirkland

Start & Run Series
Bellingham, Washington: Self-Counsel Press, 2009
192pp, ISBN: 978-1-55180-607-5

This book for creative designers shows how to make money designing anything from print ads to book jackets, logos to letter-heads, and much more. Industry-specific information is presented in a logical order, appealing to the novice as well as the seasoned designer who needs advice on a particular situation.

Starting Your Own Business: The Bestselling Guide to Planning and Building a Successful Enterprise, 6th ed

Jim Green

Oxford: How To Books, 2010
320pp, ISBN: 978-1-84528-420-6

This practical guide examines the steps that need to be taken before starting a business. These include preparing a business plan, raising finance, and developing marketing strategies. The role of the internet is also considered. The book includes a directory of sources of advice and information.

Ultimate Start-Up Directory, 2nd ed

James Stephenson

Irvine, California: Entrepreneur Press, 2007
320pp, ISBN: 978-1-932531-98-5

This book offers an extensive listing of business ideas, covering more than 1,300 potential start-ups across over 30 industries. It covers new and traditional business areas, including working from home and working via the internet. Each entry is rated according to the following criteria: ease of start-up; estimated cost and potential income; possibility of exploiting the idea online; skills required; whether the start-up could be run part-time; and licensing/franchising opportunities.

Understanding the Small Family Business

Denise Fletcher (editor)

London: Routledge, 2002
240pp, ISBN: 978-0-415-25053-5

This book offers an overview of current research in the small family business sector, with the main focus on the relationship between work and family and the tensions and contradictions that can arise. The contributions are organized in three sections relating to rationality discourse, resource-based discourse, and critical discourse.

What No One Ever Tells You about Starting Your Own Business: Real Life Start-Up Advice from 101 Successful Entrepreneurs, 2nd ed

Jan Norman

Chicago, Illinois: Upstart Publishing, 2004
240pp, ISBN: 978-0-7931-8596-2

Drawing on the experience of, and mistakes made by, 100 businesspeople, this book contains helpful and practical advice on how to start your own business without headaches.

Working Ethically: Creating a Sustainable Business … Without Breaking the Bank

Business on a Shoestring Series
London: A&C Black Publishers, 2007
168pp, ISBN: 978-0-7136-7548-1

There has never been more interest in working ethically, and many small business owners are leading the way in finding positive solutions that

  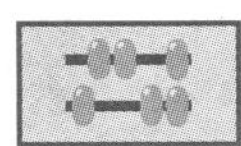      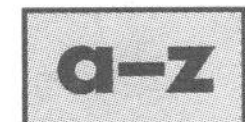

benefit them and their community. This book helps you to do the same, by covering key issues such as: creating an ethical strategy for your business; finding suppliers who share your aims; banking ethically; and respecting and protecting the environment.

MAGAZINES

Better Business

Active Information
Cribau Mill, Chepstow, Wales, NP16 6LN, UK
T: +44 (0) 1291 641222
F: +44 (0) 1291 641777
www.better-business.co.uk

This magazine appears 10 times a year and has a practical focus. The contents include case studies of successful businesses and updates on legal, tax, and technological topics.

Entrepreneur

Entrepreneur Incorporated
2445 McCabe Way, Irvine, CA 92614, USA
T: +1 949 261 2325
F: +1 949 261 0222
www.entrepreneur.com
ISSN: 0163-3341

This monthly magazine aims to give practical information to prospective entrepreneurs. It offers readers hands-on advice on many aspects of entrepreneurship, and covers the latest developments in technology, finance, management, and marketing. Products, services, and strategies are highlighted in order to help individuals run a better business, and readers can also learn from other entrepreneurs who have successfully improved their businesses.

Inc.

Gruner & Jahr USA Publishing
38 Commercial Wharf, Boston, MA 02110–3883, USA
T: +1 617 248 8000
F: +1 617 248 8090
www.inc.com
ISSN: 0162-8968

Inc. is a US publication for entrepreneurs, and is published 14 times a year. The magazine provides advice, case studies, and overviews on the subject of small business in the United States, and also provides prospective entrepreneurs with resources and road-tested strategies for managing people, finance, sales, marketing, and technology. The magazine also looks at the personal aspects of the entrepreneurial lifestyle.

JOURNALS

Journal of Small Business Management

Blackwell Publishing
9600 Garsington Road, Oxford, OX4 2DQ, UK
T: +44 (0) 1865 791100
F: +44 (0) 1865 791347
www.wiley.com/bw/journal.asp?ref=0047-2778
ISSN: 0047-2778

The *JSBM* is published for the International Council for Small Business and the Bureau of Business and Economic Research at West Virginia University College of Business and Economics. It is a quarterly refereed journal covering topics of interest to researchers and academics as well as practitioners.

INTERNET

BBC Business Basics—Small Business

news.bbc.co.uk/1/hi/in_depth/business/2003/small_business

The small business section of the BBC's main business pages offers articles clarifying the key issues and answering practical questions related to the running of a small business. These short articles are divided up into three subject areas: start-up support, environment issues, and bank and money matters. Many of the articles provide links to other related areas on the BBC website, such as Working Lunch (the award-winning daily business, personal finance, and consumer news program), or other organizations on the web where further information can be found.

Business.com

www.business.com

This is an extensive and helpful search engine and directory site. The home page offers over 20 topics for users to research, including small businesses, accounting, law and computing. Search results are presented as a series of useful click-through links.

Business Eye (Wales)

www.businesseye.org.uk

Launched in September 2003, Business Eye (Wales) replaces Business Connect as a free information service for all businesses in Wales. The service is managed by the Welsh Development Agency and has more than 25 offices throughout Wales. Business Eye does not provide business support or grants itself but instead aims to "signpost" users towards the best sources of help for their particular needs. The website offers a gateway to numerous resources for Welsh entrepreneurs, including links to useful sites across more than 20 key topics, a business forum, business news, information on courses and training, a support directory, and contact details of the local branches in North, Mid, West, and Southeast Wales.

Business Gateway (Scotland)

www.bgateway.com

Aimed at both start-ups and existing businesses in Scotland, Business Gateway (Scotland) operates in partnership with Scottish Enterprise, the Scottish Executive, and Scottish local authorities. There are local offices ("Gateways") in 13 regions across Scotland, but the website offers a range of help and advice to the reader, including a business information service, start-up and high-growth start-up services, and a business growth service.

Business Link

www.businesslink.gov.uk

This resource helps your business save time and money by providing instant access to clear, simple, and trustworthy information. It is developed in partnerships with subject experts within government and relevant business-support organizations to help you comply with regulations and improve your performance.

Business Owner's Toolkit

www.toolkit.cch.com

This site is packed with information for budding small business owners. Offering a series of brief guides to key aspects of starting up your own company, the site also features a selection of downloadable document templates, official government forms, and spreadsheet templates.

Community Interest Companies (CICs)

www.cicregulator.gov.uk

This site is of particular interest to anyone planning on starting a business with social, ethical, or environmental aims: a Community Interest Company (CIC). In order to register your company as a CIC you will need to gain approval by the regulator, which has a continuing monitoring and enforcement role. The CIC Regulator conducts a "community interest test" and "asset lock" to confirm that the company has indeed been established for community purposes.

Department for Business, Enterprise and Regulatory Reform

www.berr.gov.uk/bbf/smallbusiness

This site contains links to all relevant UK government departments and also offers a variety of helpful information, including taxation advice, sources of finance and legal requirements, and more generally useful "best practice" guides for small businesses from the Enterprise Directorate, formerly the Small Business Service.

Environment Agency

www.environment-agency.gov.uk/netregs

This UK government website aims to help small businesses get to grips easily with the environmental legislation with which they are legally obliged to comply.

Formationshouse.com

www.formationshouse.com

This online company-formation service guides you through the process of forming and registering a limited company.

Invest in Northern Ireland

www.investni.com

This site offers practical advice on how to establish a business in Northern Ireland. It has an excellent section of sources of further information made up of weblinks to key organizations and industries in the area. The site is colorful and well-designed, and features key facts about Northern Ireland.

IRS Small Business One Stop Resource

www.irs.gov/businesses/small/index.html

The US government's Internal Revenue Service offers a broad range of tax resources for the self-employed and those running small businesses, including online workshops, forms, and publications. In addition to this, the IRS provides more general advice to those starting, operating, or closing a business, in the form of articles, checklists, tips, and extensive web links to other sources of information and help.

Jordans UK

www.jordans.co.uk

An online company-formation service that also offers additional services such as search functions and debt recovery.

     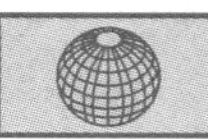   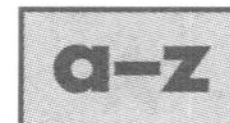

Redwoods Dowling Kerr

www.redwoodsdk.com

An agency that deals in businesses for sale, from retailers to nurseries. This site offers free access to lists of businesses as well as additional fee-based services, such as finding a business that meets your specification.

SCORE

www.score.org

This site bills itself as "Counselors to America's Small Business," and is a nonprofit organization that aims to give free support and advice to entrepreneurs, both face-to-face and remotely (via e-mail). SCORE has a team of more than 10,500 retired and working volunteer advisers who offer guidance on a wide variety of issues, passing on the benefit of their business experience.

Scottishbusinesswomen.com

www.scottishbusinesswomen.com

Part of the Scottish Enterprise Network initiative, this website is aimed at women in Scotland who either run their own business or who are thinking about establishing one. It offers support and advice on how to grow and develop existing businesses, and also offers practical help and valuable sources of information for start-ups.

Small Business Advice Service

www.smallbusinessadvice.org.uk

SmallBusinessAdvice.org.uk is a free and independent source of information and advice for entrepreneurs, owner-managers, and the self-employed starting or running a business with fewer than 10 staff and based in England. The website operates a business enquiry service which links users to over 200 accredited business advisers. It also offers online guides to various aspects of business planning, a resource centre, e-business advice, discussion boards, and help for students.

Small Business Research Portal

www.smallbusinessportal.co.uk

Intended for academics, policymakers, and support agencies, the portal provides a collection of links to small business sites under categories that include news, publications, research, institutes, and conferences.

SmallBusiness.co.uk

www.smallbusiness.co.uk

This website offers extensive help on variety of key small business issues. The site is divided into seven main areas (including starting up, finance, people, technology, legal, and property) that are then subdivided into more detailed sections.

UK Company Registration

www.uk-company-registration.co.uk

Another site which helps users set up companies online. The site is easy to navigate and has a helpful list of frequently asked questions.

UK National Work-Stress Network

www.workstress.net

An informative site that aims to educate users about the causes of work-stress and various ways of coping with it. While the site does not offer stress counseling, it does feature helpful sources of, and links to, sources of further information and support.

UK Online

www.ukonline.gov.uk

UK Online is a government-sponsored website run by the Office of the e-Envoy, which falls under the jurisdiction of the Cabinet Office. The UK Online site covers a variety of topics, and has a separate section on setting up and running a small business. It includes jargon-free explanations of taxes and other relevant regulations and also offers a series of checklists and sources of information about first steps.

Welcome Business USA

www.welcomebiz.com

This site is an extensive online resource for entrepreneurs and those thinking of starting their own business. It has an alliance with SCORE, who provide a team of advisers that users can contact free. The Welcome Business site offers a variety of services, including a start-up checklist, free business counseling, information on business plans, and information on tax issues for small businesses.

ORGANIZATIONS

Europe

Federation of Small Businesses

Sir Frank Whittle Way, Blackpool Business Park, Blackpool, Lancashire, FY4 2FE, UK
T: +44 (0) 1253 336 000
F: +44 (0) 1253 348 046
E: membership@fsb.org.uk
www.fsb.org.uk

The FSB, which has more than 195,000 members, represents the interests of small businesses with up to 200 employees. It organizes an annual conference, publishes a bimonthly magazine, *First Voice*, and lobbies on policy issues, while its local branches provide networking and research facilities in addition to general support services for members.

Forum of Private Business

Ruskin Chambers, Drury Lane, Knutsford, Cheshire, WA16 6HA, UK
T: +44 (0) 1565 634 467
F: +44 (0) 870 241 9570
E: info@fpb.org
www.fpb.co.uk

The FPB aims to influence laws and policies affecting private businesses in the United Kingdom and provide support for its members.

The Prince's Trust

18 Park Square East, London, NW1 4LH, UK
T: +44 (0) 800 842 842
F: +44 (0) 20 7543 1200
E: info@princes-trust.org.uk
www.princes-trust.org.uk

The Prince's Trust was established by the Prince of Wales in 1976 to help young people realize their full potential. Aimed at those aged between 14–30 (or 14–25 in Scotland), the Trust offers support and financial assistance across a range of core programs including business start-ups. Since 1983 the Trust has helped over 60,000 businesses, and its business program currently offers: a low-interest loan of up to £4,000 for a sole trader or £5,000 for a partnership; a test marketing grant of up to £250; advice lines and seminars; and access to a volunteer business mentor.

Small Business Bureau

Curzon House, Church Road, Windlesham, Surrey, GU20 6BH, UK
T: +44 (0) 1276 452 010
F: +44 (0) 1276 451 602
E: info@sbb.org.uk
www.smallbusinessbureau.org.uk

The Small Business Bureau was founded in 1976 to promote the interests of small businesses in the United Kingdom. Its activities include an annual conference and a magazine, *Small Business News*, which is published three times a year.
The organization has also set up Women into Business to encourage more women to choose business and business ownership as a career.

Small Firms Enterprise Development Initiative (SFEDI)

Business Incubation Centre, Durham Way South, Aycliffe Industrial Park, County Durham, DL5 6XP, UK
T: +44 (0) 845 224 5928
F: +44 (0) 845 224 5928
E: info@sfedi.co.uk
www.sfedi.co.uk

The SFEDI has been appointed by the UK government to identify standards of best practice for small businesses and to work with providers of small business training, education, and advice to raise standards of support.

USA

American Small Business Association

P.O. Box 300777, Chicago, IL 60630–0777, USA
T: +1 877 906 2722
E: info@asbaonline.org
www.asbaonline.org/about/about.htm

ASBA is a nonprofit organization dedicated to the needs of small business owners, and advocacy and education for men and women age 50 and above. They are a national association with over 500,000 members, that offers educational and consumer programs, and acts as a resource for its members and partners.

Independent Small Business Employers (ISBE)

Ground Floor, 137 Euston Road, London, NW1 2AA, UK
T: +44 (0) 20 7554 9941
F: +44 (0) 1423 500 046
E: info@isbe.org.uk

ISBE is a network for individuals and organizations driving small business and entrepreneurship research, enterprise support and advice, entrepreneurship education, and for those who formulate, deliver, and evaluate policy

  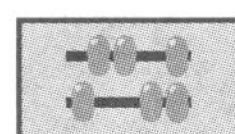      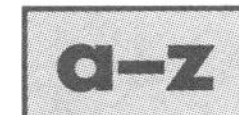

in this area. It promotes the advancement of knowledge, expertise, and best practice in the area of small business and entrepreneurship.

National Business Association

PO Box 700728, Dallas, TX 75370, USA
T: +1 800 456 0440 or 972 458 0900
F: +1 972 960 9149
E: info@nationalbusiness.org
www.nationalbusiness.org

Established in 1982, the National Business Association (NBA) is a nonprofit organization, designed and managed to assist the self-employed and small business community in achieving their professional goals. The NBA uses its group buying power to provide its members with support programs, cost and time-saving products, services, and valuable small business resource materials.

National Federation of Independent Business

53 Century Boulevard, Suite 300, Nashville, TN 37214, USA
T: +1 615 872 5800
F: +1 615 872 5353
www.nfib.org

The NFIB was founded by Wilson Harder in 1942. With 600,000 members it is the largest and probably the most influential small business lobbying group in the United States. It represents the interests of small business owners at national and state government levels and provides a range of services for its members.

Small Business Administration

409 3rd Street, SW, Washington, DC 20416, USA
T: +1 704 344 6563
F: +1 704 344 6769
E: answerdesk@sba.gov
www.sbaonline.sba.gov

The Small Business Administration was set up by the US government in 1953 to provide assistance to those starting and running their own businesses. It provides training, financial support, and advice through a network of offices in every state.

Small Business Institute Directors' Association

Miami University, Department of DSC/MIS, 311 Upham Hall, Oxford, OH 45056, USA
T: +1 513 529 4826
F: +1 513 529 4841
E: broidams@muohio.edu
www.sbida.org

The SBIDA promotes the development and improvement of educational programs for small businesses and acts as a coordinating body for Small Business Institute programs at universities and colleges in the United States. The latter were started in 1972 in cooperation with the US Small Business Administration, but became independent in 1996.

BRIC

Brazilian Micro & Small Business Support Service

SEPN 515 – Bloco C, Loja 32, Asa Norte, Brasília, Brazil
T: +55 61 348 7218
F: +55 61 347 4120
E: paulo.alvim@sebrae.com.br
www.sebrae.com.br

This is a private, nonprofit organization that supports the development and activity of small-sized businesses. It combines both public and private sectors and Brazil's main research bodies.

Enterprise Europe Network Russia

17B, Mosfilmovskaya Str, Moscow, 119330, Russia
T: +7 499 143 7320
F: +7 499 143 7321
E: eicc@siora.ru
www.euroinfocenter.ru

The Euro Info Centre Network is one of several business networks within EU that support the creation and development of an information environment for small and medium-sized enterprises (SMEs).

Secretariat for Industrial Assistance

Udyog Bhawan, New Delhi, 110011, India
T: +91 11 2306 2626
F: +91 11 2306 1222
E: cim@nic.in
dipp.gov.in

This organization promotes the industrial development of industrially emerging areas in the North Eastern region in India. It offers international cooperation for industrial partnerships, and monitors industrial growth.

Shanghai Small Enterprises Development Coordination Office

7F, 108 Da Mu Qiao Road, Shanghai, China
T: +86 21 5452 1128
www.ssme.gov.cn

The SSE administrates and regulates roles and functions in Shanghai, including research on policy and regulations relevant to small business development, as well as collecting and analyzing information and data on SMEs.

International

International Council for Small Business

GWU School of Business, 2201 G Street NW, Funger Hall, Suite 315, Washington, DC 20052, USA
T: +1 314 977 3628
F: +1 314 977 3627
E: icsb@slu.edu
www.icsb.org

The ICSB works to increase awareness and understanding of the role of small and medium businesses worldwide through education, research, publications, management development programs, conferences, and an international exchange program. Its membership includes educators, small business owners, consultants and advisers, government officials, and trade and business associations. It also publishes the *Journal of Small Business Management*, a bulletin, a newsletter, research papers, and conference proceedings.

World Association for Small and Medium Enterprises

Plot No. 4, Sector 16A, Noida, Uttar Pradesh, 201301, India
T: +91 118 451 5238
F: +91 118 451 5243
E: wasme@vsnl.com
www.wasmeinfo.org

WASME was founded in 1980 in New Delhi, India with the aim of providing support and advice to SMEs internationally and has members and associates in 112 countries. The organization promotes technology transfer, joint ventures, and cooperation between SMEs in industrialized, developing, and least-developed countries. It has set up a Technology and Trade Promotion Exchange Center (TPX) and an International Committee for Rural Industrialization (ICRI). WASME has consultative status with the Economic and Social Council of the United Nations and other UN bodies.

Social Responsibility of Management

BOOKS

The Answer to How Is Yes: Acting on What Matters

Peter Block
San Francisco, California: Berrett-Koehler, 2003
208pp, ISBN: 978-1-57675-271-5

The preponderance of the "how?" question in society, Block claims, is symptomatic of people living in accordance with an ethic of defense. We must strive to reclaim both our liberty and autonomy that have been radically sequestered from us. This position is to be attained for workers and managers by encouraging them to act on what they know, confronting passivity, and promoting a life where we can choose accountability and demand more compelling purpose from our work.

Awakening Social Responsibility: A Call to Action Guidebook for Global Citizens, Corporate and Nonprofit Organizations

Rossella Derickson, Krista Henley
Cupertino, California: Happy About, 2007
204pp, ISBN: 978-1-60005-065-7

The book addresses the implementation of corporate social responsibility (CSR), providing actionable steps and perspectives on how organizations can actively engage in eco initiatives, employee giving, volunteering, and savvy sustainable business practices. It acts as a guidebook to for engaging all employees in initiating CSR programs or making current programs more robust.

       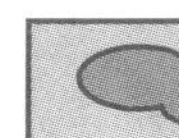 

Building Public Trust: The Future of Corporate Reporting

Samuel A. Di Piazza, Robert G. Eccles

New York: Wiley, 2002
192pp, ISBN: 978-0-471-26151-3

In response to the global crisis in corporate reporting and its associated fallout, the authors offer their recommendations for addressing the increased levels of accountability, transparency, and integrity that are necessary in order to rebuild public trust. A three-tier model for corporate reporting is proposed that encompasses GAAP, industry standards, and company-specific information into a framework, which in turn feeds into new enabling technologies such as the internet that will assist and accelerate the process.

Business and Society: Ethics and Stakeholder Management, 7th ed

Archie B. Carroll, Ann K. Buchholtz

Cincinnati, Ohio: South-Western College Publishing, 2009
992pp, ISBN: 978-0-324-56939-1

Though the book is intended as a textbook, its managerial perspective makes it relevant for businesspeople as well. It uses case studies to illustrate relationships between business and society stakeholders and emphasizes ethical considerations in decision-making.

Business as Unusual

Anita Roddick

Chichester, UK: Anita Roddick Publishing, 2005
304pp, ISBN: 978-0-9543959-5-7

This book contains the ideas for the philosophy of Anita Roddick's Body Shop chain, detailing the unique ethos of the company, which is to maintain an operation that can be at once profitable whilst not harming the environment or violating human rights.

Citizen Brands: Putting Society at the Heart of Your Business, 2nd ed

Michael Willmott

Chichester, UK: Wiley, 2003
272pp, ISBN: 978-0-470-85358-0

Citizen Brands reflects on the need for organizations to demonstrate corporate social responsibility. The book develops this concept further, evolving the idea of corporate citizenship, the practice of which should make a business more successful.

Counting What Counts: Turning Corporate Accountability to Competitive Advantage

Bill Birchard, Marc J. Epstein

Cambridge, Massachusetts: Perseus Books Group, 2000
320pp, ISBN: 978-0-7382-0313-3

Fraud, tax evasion etc. are what the authors of this book identify as practices which obstruct managers from working efficiently. The text argues that managers should adopt the ethic of accountability, and succeed by becoming responsive and responsible. Using over 25 years of research and the experiences of a number of managers, Epstein and Birchard show that managers frequently overlook accountability and are in need of reform.

The End of Shareholder Value

Allan Kennedy

London: Orion Business, 2001
256pp, ISBN: 978-0-7382-0484-0

The main premise of Kennedy's argument is that the shareholder value ethic has signally failed to produce anything of lasting value, with the result that the future of the company as we know it is under threat. The book outlines three eras of business evolution, from the family enterprises of the 19th century to the entrepreneurs of high technology, often unfavorably, and ends with Kennedy's proposed remedies to create real, sustainable wealth for all of a company's stakeholder groups, not just the stockholders.

The Heroic Enterprise: Business and the Common Good

John Hood

New York: Free Press, 2005
272pp, ISBN: 978-1-58798-246-0

Attacking the common assertion that businesses necessarily neglect the public good at the expense of short-term profits, Hood demonstrates numerous examples of how business works to enhance the wider social good. Detailing actual examples of this happening in today's world, Hood reveals how inner-city areas have been regenerated, and how the environment, workplace, and education have all been reformed in line with business initiatives.

Mainstreaming Corporate Responsibility: Cases and Text for Integrating Corporate Responsibility Across the Business School Curriculum

N. Craig Smith and Gilbert Lenssen

Hoboken, New Jersey: Wiley, 2009
512pp, ISBN: 978-0-470-75394-1

This practical overview of corporate responsibility and its impact on the business world assesses how it is now in the economic interest of corporates to address social and environmental impacts in a manner that is integrated with their operations. It explores issues such as sustainability, stakeholder management, and corporate governance, as well as corporate philanthropy.

Managing Values and Beliefs in Organisations

Tom McEwan

Harlow, UK: FT Prentice Hall, 2001
560pp, ISBN: 978-0-273-64340-1

This is book written as a student text that summarizes the origins of corporate responsibility, business ethics, and corporate governance, and reviews the similarities and differences between them. The specific issues covered include: moral meaning and applied ethics; values, beliefs, and ideologies; individual morality in organizations; unethical behavior by individuals; international business and the developing world; ethical investment; organization culture and stakeholder theory; and corporate social performance, ethical leadership, and reputation management.

The Oxford Handbook of Corporate Social Responsibility

Andrew Crane

Oxford Handbooks in Business & Management Series
Oxford: Oxford University Press, 2009
608pp, ISBN: 978-0-19-957394-3

This handbook is an authoritative review of the academic research that has both prompted, and responded to, issues involving corporate social responsibility. It examines questions about the changing relationship between business, society and government, environmental issues, corporate governance, the social and ethical dimensions of management, globalization, stakeholder debates, shareholder and consumer activism, changing political systems and values, and the ways in which corporations can respond to new social imperatives.

Perspectives on Corporate Citizenship

Jorg Andriof, Malcolm McIntosh

Sheffield, UK: Greenleaf Publishing, 2001
336pp, ISBN: 978-1-874719-39-7

Corporate citizenship is seen as one of the big issues of the 21st century. This book introduces the concept of corporate citizenship and explains the need for a fuller understanding of its impact. This collection of articles on corporate citizenship is divided into three broad sections: the evolution, context and concepts of corporate citizens; stakeholder engagement; and social accountability.

The Sustainable Company: How to Create Lasting Value through Social and Environmental Performance

Chris Laszlo

Washington, DC: Island Press, 2008
208pp, ISBN: 978-0-8047-5963-2

This illustrates how the competitive strategies of some of the world's largest businesses are changing as their leaders begin to take on a number of the world's most important social, environmental, and economic issues.

The Sustainable Company

Chris Laszlo

Washington, DC: Island Press, 2005
232pp, ISBN: 978-1-59726-018-3

Leading corporations are recognizing the changing role and expectations of business in the 21st century and the competitive advantage that can be gained in addressing the problems and challenges concerned. The gap between the interests of business and those of society and the environment have created a "triple bottom line" within organizations, resulting from associated yet conflicting sets of performance measures. This book aims to go beyond the triple bottom line. It aims to bridge the gap between shareholder concerns and stakeholder expectations, and presents an integrative business paradigm for both.

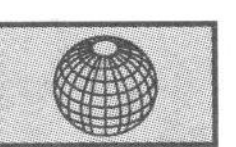

Take It Personally: How Globalization Affects You and Powerful Ways to Fight Back

Anita Roddick

London: Thorsons, 2001
256pp, ISBN: 978-0-00-712898-3

Like Naomi Klein, Roddick points to the need to concentrate on business accountability, focusing on human rights violations, environmental issues, the treatment of the developing world, and the growth of global markets. She forces her reader to ask the question: Who really controls the world—business or government?

Value Shift: Why Companies Must Merge Social and Financial Imperatives to Achieve Superior Performance

Lynn Sharp Paine

New York: McGraw-Hill, 2003
304pp, ISBN: 978-0-07-142733-3

This book argues the case for a new style of management that will align company performance with today's ethical standards. It argues that there is now a dichotomy between traditional management and the expectations of business in contemporary society. Acknowledging it is no longer enough simply to produce goods and services and create wealth, the author discusses today's corporate leaders' need to make a shift in management values to incorporate high ethical standards along with strong financial results.

What Matters Most: Business, Social Responsibility and the End of the Era of Greed

Jeffrey Hollender, Stephen Fenichell

London: Random House, 2004
320pp, ISBN: 978-1-84413-397-0

Jeffrey Hollender, CEO of Seventh Generation, a world leader in manufacturing environmentally friendly household products, is a frequent commentator on corporate responsibility. This book, which he has co-authored with Stephen Fenichell, puts forward an approach to corporate strategy that is designed to help integrate concerns related to social responsibility into an organization's culture, systems, and activities.

MAGAZINES

Journal of Corporate Citizenship

Greenleaf Publishing
Aizlewood Business Centre, Aizlewood's Mill, Nursery Street, Sheffield, S3 8GG, UK
T: +44 (0) 114 282 3475
F: +44 (0) 114 282 3475
www.greenleaf-publishing.com/default.asp?ContentID=7
ISSN: 1470-5001

The *Journal of Corporate Citizenship* focuses explicitly on integrating theory about corporate citizenship with management practice. It provides a forum in which the tensions and practical realities of making corporate citizenship real are addressed in a reader-friendly, yet conceptually and empirically rigorous format.

JOURNALS

Social Responsibility Journal

Emerald
60/62 Toller Lane, Bradford, West Yorkshire, BD8 9BY, UK
T: +44 (0) 1274 777 700
F: +44 (0) 1274 785 200
www.emeraldinsight.com/1747-1117.htm
ISSN: 1747-1117

The *Social Responsibility Journal*, the official journal of the Social Responsibility Research Network, is interdisciplinary in its scope and encourages submissions from any relevant discipline. It encompasses the full range of theoretical, methodological and substantive debates in the area of social responsibility, and encourages contributions which address the link between different disciplines and/or implications for societal, organizational or individual behavior.

Society and Business Review

Emerald
60/62 Toller Lane, Bradford, West Yorkshire, BD8 9BY, UK
T: +44 (0) 1274 777 700
F: +44 (0) 1274 785 200
www.emeraldinsight.com/1746-5680.htm
ISSN: 1746-5680

Society and Business Review aims to cultivate and share knowledge and ideas in order to assist businesses to enhance their commitment to society. Being international in outlook and interdisciplinary in scope, the journal seeks to provide a platform for diverse academic and practitioner communities to debate a broad spectrum of social issues and disciplinary perspectives.

INTERNET

Business Ethics

www.business-ethics.com

The online counterpart to *Business Ethics* magazine, the site offers articles, news, an events calendar, a marketplace, and a free e-mail newsletter.

Business for Social Responsibility

www.bsr.org

Sponsored by a membership organization, the site offers news, articles, a membership directory, conference and events information, and job listings.

Community Action Network

www.can-online.org.uk

This site gives access to a mutual learning and support network for social entrepreneurs.

The Corporate Social Responsibility Newswire

www.csrwire.com

This content-rich site bills itself as "the leading source of corporate responsibility and sustainability, press releases, reports, and news." It features CSR press releases, reports, an events calendar, useful resources (including an organization directory), and book recommendations.

Do-It

www.do-it.org.uk

This is a national database of voluntary work opportunities for both companies and individuals.

Ethical Corporation

www.ethicalcorp.com

Ethical Corporation is an independent media firm, launched in 2001 to encourage debate and discussion on responsible business. Ethical Corporation publishes a 60-page print magazine, a daily website, and hosts business ethics conferences all over the world.

ORGANIZATIONS

Europe

AccountAbility

250–252 Goswell Road, London, EC1V 7EB, UK
T: +44 (0) 20 7549 0400
F: +44 (0) 20 7253 7440
E: secretariat@accountability.org.uk
www.accountability21.net

Founded in 1996 as an international membership organization with the aim of improving the accountability and performance of organizations worldwide, AccountAbility (full name: the Institute of Social and Ethical Accountability) promotes best practice and ethical accounting, auditing, and reporting, and develops standards and certification for professionals in the field.

Corporate Social Responsibility (CSR) Europe

78–80 rue Defacqz, Brussels, B-1050, Belgium
T: +32 2 502 83 54
F: +32 2 502 84 58
E: info@csreurope.org
www.csreurope.org

CSR Europe helps companies achieve profitability, sustainable growth, and human progress by placing corporate social responsibility in the mainstream of business practice. It provides printed and online publications, best practices and tools, learning, benchmarking, and tailored capacity building programs.

The Prince of Wales International Business Leaders Forum (IBLF)

15–16 Cornwall Terrace, Regent's Park, London, NW1 4QP, UK
T: +44 (0) 20 7467 3600
F: +44 (0) 20 7467 3610
E: info@iblf.org
www.iblf.org

This nonprofit membership organization was established in 1990 by HRH The Prince of Wales and a group of CEOs from international companies to promote corporate social responsibility (CSR). CSR business practices are based on ethical values to help achieve socially, economically, and environmentally sustainable development.

USA

Center for Corporate Citizenship at Boston College

Wallace E. Carroll School of Management, 55 Lee Road, Chestnut Hill, MA 02467–3942, USA

T: +1 617 552 4545
F: +1 617 552 8499
E: ccc@bc.edu
www.bcccc.net

This membership organization was founded in 1985 to establish corporate citizenship as a business essential. It offers executive education, particularly the certificate program in community relations. It arranges conferences, meetings, and discussions, encourages research, oversees the standards of excellence and their companion diagnostic tools, and provides consulting services.

BRIC

Business and Social Development Institute Foundation (FIDES)

R. Santanésia, 528 – 1° ss., São Paulo, Brazil
T: +55 3726 3373
F: +55 3843 3770
E: fides@fides.org.br
www.fides.org.br

FIDES is a private, non-profit, cultural, and educational Brazilian organization dedicated to the humanization of business enterprises and to their integration with society.

Center for Business Ethics and Corporate Governance

Office 22, 2, Shvedsky pereulok, St. Petersburg, 191186, Russia
T: +7 812 324 6706
F: +7 812 327 3125
E: info@cfbe.ru
www.ethicsrussia.org

The mission of the Center for Business Ethics and Corporate Governance is to create social capital in the Russian Federation, the Independent States, and Eastern Europe by helping to institutionalize ethical and transparent business practices.

Centre for Social Markets (CSM)

3/5 Rani Jhansi Road, New Delhi, 110 055, India
T: +91 11 2352 6000
E: info@csmworld.org
www.csmworld.org

CSM promotes social, economic, political, and institutional transformation for the public interest. It is an independent, non-profit organization dedicated to making markets work for people, the planet, and for profit.

Chinese Federation for Corporate Social Responsibility

Room 801, Recourse Plaza, No.151 Zhongguancun North Street, Haidian District, Beijing, 10080, China
T: +86 10 5887 6801
F: +86 10 5887 6122
E: cfcsr@126.com
www.cfcsr.org/shehuien/index.asp

This federation aims promote the spirit and advance the development of corporate social responsibility in China.

Structured Finance

BOOKS

The Analysis of Structured Securities: Precise Risk Measurement and Capital Allocation
Sylvain Raynes, Ann Rutledge
Oxford, UK: Oxford University Press, 2003
449pp, ISBN: 978-0-19-515273-9

This is a technical assessment of this expanding part of the capital markets, for practitioners looking for greater precision, efficiency, and control in managing their structured exposures. It analyzes the credit quality of structured securities, the methods used to rate asset-backed securities, collateralized debt obligations, and asset-backed commercial paper, and offers guidance on using numerical methods in cash flow modeling.

Collateralized Debt Obligations and Structured Finance: New Developments in Cash and Synthetic Securitization
Janet Tavakoli
Wiley Finance Series
Hoboken, New Jersey: Wiley, 2003
338pp, ISBN: 978-0-471-46220-0

This provides an overview of the fast-growing CDO and structured credit products market. It examines new securitization topics, such as the increase in the CDO arbitrage created by synthetics, dumping securitizations on bank balance sheets, the abuse of offshore vehicles by companies such as Enron, and securitizations made possible by new securitization techniques and the introduction of the euro.

Credit Derivatives: CDOs and Structured Credit Products, 3rd ed
Satyajit Das
Wiley Finance Series
Singapore: Wiley, 2005
800pp, ISBN: 978-0-470-82159-6

This is a comprehensive reference on credit derivative products, applications, pricing and valuation approaches, and documentation, accounting, and taxation issues. It looks in detail at the collateralized debt obligations market, presents detailed examples of applications of credit derivatives by different market participants, and discusses trading, market structures, and the regulatory framework for credit derivatives.

A Fast Track to Structured Finance Modeling, Monitoring and Valuation: Jump Start VBA
William Preinitz
Wiley Finance Series
Hoboken, New Jersey: Wiley, 2009
768pp, ISBN: 978-0-470-39812-8

This is a new, technical treatment of structured finance, which focuses on implementing simple tasks into VBA code. It helps develop the skills in an accessible way, breaking complex tasks down into simple tasks, and covers all the key issues involved, such as designing the VBA model, the VBA language, controlling the model flow, building message capabilities, and writing the main program.

FX Options and Structured Products
Uwe Wystup
Wiley Finance Series
Chichester, UK: Wiley, 2006
323pp, ISBN: 978-0-470-01145-4

This is a technical guide to the nature, risks, applications, and strategies of the main FX options and structured products. It explains how they can be used for cost savings, risk controls, and yield enhancements, and provides a grounding in the quantitative fundamentals, the basics of FX products, principles, and concepts, and a structuring view and client perspective.

The Handbook of Structured Finance
Arnaud de Servigny, Norbert Jobst (editors)
New York: McGraw-Hill, 2007
785pp, ISBN: 978-0-07-146864-0

This provides a comprehensive guide to the key issues facing investors in the structured finance market. It describes new models for identifying, measuring, pricing, and monitoring deals, and how to take advantage of leverage and market incompleteness, as well as models for debt and equity modeling.

Introduction to Structured Finance
Frank J. Fabozzi, Henry A. Davis, Moorad Choudhry
Frank J. Fabozzi Series
Hoboken, New Jersey: Wiley, 2006
385pp, ISBN: 978-0-470-04535-0

This book examines the fundamentals of structured finance, and the growing role it plays in the financial markets. It also acts as a comprehensive guide to securitization, interest rate derivatives, credit derivatives, securitized and synthetic funding structures, cash and synthetic collateralized debt obligations, credit-linked notes and structured notes, complex leasing transactions, and project financing.

Modeling Structured Finance Cash Flows with Microsoft Excel: A Step-by-Step Guide
Keith A. Allman
Wiley Finance Series
Hoboken, New Jersey: Wiley, 2007
199pp, ISBN: 978-0-470-04290-8

This book provides a guide to building a cash flow model for structured finance and securitization deals. It outlines individual functions and formulas, as well as the theory behind the spreadsheets, for practical applications of the model. It can be used as a resource for training

  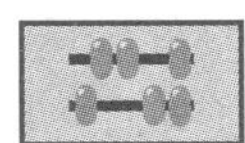   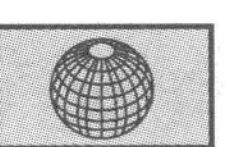   

new analysts, or help experienced cash flow modelers with their analysis of structured finance transactions.

Mortgage-Backed Securities: Products, Structuring, and Analytical Techniques

Frank J. Fabozzi, Anand K. Bhattacharya, William S. Berliner
Frank J. Fabozzi Series
Hoboken, New Jersey: Wiley, 2007
318pp, ISBN: 978-0-470-04773-6

This book provides a comprehensive introduction to the products, structures, and analytical techniques that have made such an impact on the fixed income market. Aimed primarily at investors and traders, it offers a guide to the investment characteristics, creation, and analysis of residential real estate-backed securities, and describes the methodologies and techniques used to value MBS products and assess interest-rate risk.

The Structured Credit Handbook

Arvind Rajan, Glen McDermott, Ratul Roy
Wiley Finance Series
Hoboken, New Jersey: Wiley, 2007
496pp, ISBN: 978-0-471-74749-9

This is a comprehensive introduction to all types of credit-linked financial instruments, such as collateralized debt obligations, collateralized loan obligations, credit derivatives such as credit default swaps and swaptions, and iBoxx indexes. It provides a solid grounding in the investment rationale, risks, and rewards associated with structured credit investments, with little financial jargon or mathematical complexity.

Structured Credit Portfolio Analysis, Baskets and CDOs

Christian Bluhm, Ludger Overbeck
Chapman & Hall/CRC Financial Mathematics Series
Boca Raton, Florida: Chapman & Hall/CRC, 2007
357pp, ISBN: 978-1-58488-647-1

This is a guide to the concepts and techniques for evaluating structured credit products, and presents a review of the basic concepts of credit risk modeling. It also addresses in detail more advanced topics such as the modeling and evaluation of basket products, credit-linked notes, collateralized debt obligations, and index tranches. It is aimed at practitioners who apply mathematical concepts to structured credit products.

Structure Finance: Techniques, Products and Market

Stefano Caselli, Stefano Gatti
Springer Finance Series
Berlin: Springer, 2005
206pp, ISBN: 978-3-540-25311-2

This analyzes the characteristics of structured finance deals, such as asset-backed securitization, project finance, structured leasing and leveraged acquisitions, and discusses the state of the international financial markets for these operations. It explains new ways of financing deals based on the capacity of the operations to generate sufficient cash for the repayment of loans or bonds, and compares it to more traditional sources of funding.

Structured Finance: The Object Oriented Approach

Umberto Cherubini, Giovanni Della Lunga
Wiley Finance Series
Chichester, UK: Wiley, 2007
288pp, ISBN: 978-0-470-02638-0

This explores structured finance issues relevant to the structured finance business, for both finance professionals engaged in building, pricing and hedging products, and IT professionals engaged in designing and updating the corresponding software. It strives to share common concepts and definition within the industry, and overcome the problems of communication between these different professional functions.

Structured Finance and Insurance: The ART of Managing Capital and Risk, 2nd ed

Chistopher L. Culp
Wiley Finance Series
Hoboken, New Jersey: Wiley, 2006
892pp, ISBN: 978-0-471-70631-1

This presents a comprehensive introduction to key financing and risk management innovations in both the alternative insurance and capital markets. It explores the economic and practical benefits of this new generation of products and solutions for managing market, credit, operational, legal, and other risks, and attempts to integrate these solutions and products into a unified theory of financial markets.

Structured Products and Related Credit Derivatives: A Comprehensive Guide for Investors

Brian P. Lancaster, Glenn M. Schultz, Frank J. Fabozzi
Frank J. Fabozzi Series
Hoboken, New Jersey: Wiley, 2008
523pp, ISBN: 978-0-470-12985-2

This examines the fundamentals of structured assets and credit derivatives, describing the opportunities and risks involved in this complex financial market. It examines various consumer asset-backed securities, offers an insight on collateralized debt obligations, analyzes structured finance operating companies, and the commercial real estate sector, including ABS issues such as aircraft securitization, intermodal equipment, and life insurance reserve securitization.

Structured Products in Wealth Management

Steffen Tolle, Boris Hutter, Patrik Rüthemann, Hanspeter Wohlwend
Wiley Finance Series
Singapore: Wiley, 2008
226pp, ISBN: 978-0-470-82330-9

This describes the range of structured products in the market, as well as their characteristics and practical applications. It shows how they can be incorporated to strategically optimize an investment portfolio, explains the use of derivatives and structured products in wealth management, and is aimed at retail private investors, wealth managers, client relationship managers, and advisers.

Synthetic and Structured Assets

Erik Banks
Wiley Finance Series
Chichester, UK: Wiley, 2006
266pp, ISBN: 978-0-470-01713-5

This book analyzes many of the original classes of structured assets, including mortgage and asset-backed securities and strips, as well as structured and synthetic instruments such as exchange-traded funds, collateralized debt obligations, and insurance-linked securities. It outlines the scope of the market, key definitions, and the financial building blocks used to create synthetic and structured assets, and reviews their risk, legal, regulatory, and accounting features.

A Wealth Manager's Guide to Structured Products

Robert Benson (editor)
London: Risk Books, 2004
257pp, ISBN: 978-1-904339-32-8

This is a comprehensive analysis of the challenges and issues that wealth managers face when using structured products into their investment strategies. It discusses the relevance of structured products for portfolio construction and risk management, the use of credit derivatives, and how the structure of products can create capital guarantees, and includes coverage of hedge funds.

MAGAZINES

SRP Magazine

Arete Consulting
12 Broadbent Close, 20–22 Highgate High Street, London, N6 5JL, UK
T: +44 (0) 20 8347 0203
F: +44 (0) 20 8347 7872
www.srpmagazine.com

This is a monthly electronic magazine for structured products professionals, which has access to a database of nearly one million products and a dedicated global news service.

Structured Products

Incisive Media
Haymarket House, 28–29 Haymarket, London, SW1Y 4RX, UK
T: +44 (0) 20 7484 9700
F: +44 (0) 20 7484 9932
www.structuredproductsonline.com
ISSN: 1745-4611

This monthly magazine on structured products provides news, features, regulatory updates, commentaries, profiles of leading companies, and analysis of new structured investment products. It covers the market for guaranteed investment products, structured notes, index products, alternative investments and funds of funds, and also produces a series of conferences and training courses.

JOURNALS

Journal of Structured Finance

Institutional Investor Journals
225 Park Avenue South, 8th Floor, New York, NY 10003, USA
T: +1 212 224 3570
F: +1 212 224 3197
www.iijournals.com/JPF
ISSN: 1082-3220

This quarterly journal offers research and commentary on all aspects of structured finance, with a detailed analysis of structuring and investing in products such as ABSs, MBSs, CDOs, CLOs, and life settlements. It focuses on a range of real-life securitization deals and their investment implications to provide a strategic understanding of the products, applications, and market.

INTERNET

Securitization.net

www.securitization.net

This resource for the structured finance industry provides news and information from industry organizations on all aspects of securitization. It offers free email updates, links to articles and commentaries, notification of upcoming industry events, and details of relevant accounting, banking, legal, regulatory issues.

SRPAdviser.com

www.srpadviser.com

This website is aimed at financial advisers in the structured products market. It provides access to a large database of structured retail products, and features a search function for product offerings, downloadable product literature, filters, score charts, and enables the tracking of closing offers and maturing products.

Structured Retail Products

www.structuredretailproducts.com

This website focuses on the structured products market, and features a news service, analysis and research reports, portfolio, product scoring and pricing tools, and downloadable product literature. It also provides access to a large database of structured retail investment products covering the major European markets, the Americas, and the Asia-Pacific markets.

StructuredFinanceNews.com

www.structuredfinancenews.com

This online industry resource provides news and commentary on topics such as asset-backed securities, covered bonds, mortgage-backed securities, and derivatives, and offers an extensive news archive and a proprietary people database for information on the industry's top players. It also features an Asset Securitization Report and Scorecards Database.

Total Securitization

www.totalsecuritization.com

This is a news service for the global securitization markets, which provides current news and analysis, as well as aggregated stories from other sources, on significant issues in the ABS, MBS, CMBS and CDOs markets.

ORGANIZATIONS

USA

The Structured Products Association

Chair: Keith Styrcula
USA
E: keith.styrcula@structuredproducts.org
www.structuredproducts.org

The SPA is a trade group whose mission is to position structured products as a distinct asset class, promote financial innovation among member firms, develop best practices for members and their firms, and identify legal, tax, compliance and regulatory challenges to the business. Its membership comes from exchanges, self-regulatory bodies, the legal compliance community, investor networks, and both buy-side and sell-side structured product firms.

Technical Analysis

BOOKS

The ART of Trading: Combining the Science of Technical Analysis with the Art of Reality-Based Trading

Bennet A. McDowell
Wiley Trading Series
Hoboken, New Jersey: Wiley, 2008
296pp, ISBN: 978-0-470-18772-2

This is a comprehensive introduction to technical analysis, money management, risk control, paper trading, and the psychology of trading, based on the author's own reality-based trading system. It details its benefits, use for executing trade entries and exits, identifying market direction, and ensuring consistent profits, and shows how to use price and volume to minimize distortions in financial decision-making, and select the best financial market timeframe.

Breakthroughs in Technical Analysis: New Thinking from the World's Top Minds

David Keller (editor)
New York: Bloomberg Press, 2007
227pp, ISBN: 978-1-57660-242-3

This exploration of new trends and developments in technical analysis by leading industry experts describes a number of new methods in trading. It examines their techniques and strategies, and covers key topics such as charting with candles and clouds, candlesticks, options-based technical analysis, indicators for stock trading, point-and-figure charting, deconstructing the market, and the application of market profile to global spreads.

Evidence-Based Technical Analysis: Applying the Scientific Method and Statistical Inference to Trading Signals

David R. Aronson
Hoboken, New Jersey: Wiley, 2007
544pp, ISBN: 978-0-470-00874-4

This is a focused treatment of the methodological, philosophical, and statistical foundations of evidenced-based technical analysis (EBTA), examining methods for its application, statistical tests, and the effectiveness of the data mining for evaluating technical trading signals. It shows how EBTA is based on objective rules, quantification, scrutiny, and statistical inference, and discusses the problems with interpretative methodologies, and the Efficient Market Hypothesis.

Fibonacci Analysis

Constance Brown
Bloomberg Market Essentials Series: Technical Analysis
New York: Bloomberg Press, 2008
182pp, ISBN: 978-1-57660-261-4

This is a practical overview and reference on Fibonacci analysis, and which also covers the basics of the most popular technical analysis tools. It describes trend and counter-trend movements within markets to identify the future market price, and explains how to use this analytical technique properly to achieve a higher probability of trading success.

Getting Started in Technical Analysis

Jack D. Schwager
Getting Started in Series
New York: Wiley, 1999
339pp, ISBN: 978-0-471-29542-6

This respected primer on technical analysis provides a framework for analyzing price activity to better understand market behavior and identify trading opportunities. It demystifies the subject for new investors, and details the essentials of trends such as trading ranges, types of charts, chart patterns, trading systems, charting and analysis software, the planned trading approach, with the assistance of numerous examples and explanations.

The Heretics of Finance: Conversations with the Leading Practitioners of Technical Analysis

Andrew W. Lo, Jasmina Hasanhodzic
New York: Bloomberg Press, 2009
464pp, ISBN: 978-1-57660-316-1

This is a series of extended interviews with pioneers and experts in technical analysis discuss the influence of creativity, emotion, and intuition in their work, as well as offering insights into the patterns, strategies, and applications that contributed to their success. Produced by a leading expert academic, it explains the rationale

  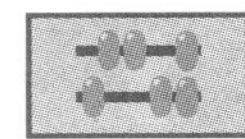      

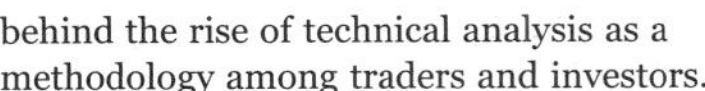

behind the rise of technical analysis as a methodology among traders and investors.

Japanese Candlestick Charting Techniques: A Contemporary Guide to the Ancient Investment, 2nd ed

Steve Nison

Paramus, New Jersey: Prentice Hall, 2001
320pp, ISBN: 978-0-7352-0181-1

This guide to Japanese candlestick charts examines their role as a technical analysis methodology that can be integrated with other tools to improve market analysis. It takes a comprehensive approach to its range of applications, and describes how they can also be used for speculation and hedging, for futures, and equities, or as a stand-alone charting method with uses in almost any market.

New Thinking in Technical Analysis: Trading Models from the Masters

Rick Bensignor (editor)

Bloomberg Professional Library Series
Princeton, New Jersey: Bloomberg Press, 2000
287pp, ISBN: 978-1-57660-049-8

This shows how to use technical analysis for predicting the price behavior of a stock, commodity, or any financial instrument, and offers advice on how create an effective trading strategy using its models based on tips from market experts. It also presents a number of tools for improving investment performance, and describes the importance of market timing for traders seeking to gain a competitive edge.

Technical Analysis: The Complete Resource for Financial Market Technicians

Charles D. Kirkpatrick, Julie R. Dahlquist

Upper Saddle River, New Jersey: FT Prentice Hall, 2007
672pp, ISBN: 978-0-13-153113-0

This comprehensive reference explains technical analysis theory, and the analysis of markets and individual issues, and presents a complete investment system and portfolio management plan. It describes how to use it for identifying trading opportunities, to test sentiment, momentum indicators, seasonal affects, flow of funds, risk mitigation, and many other techniques. It also analyzes which chart patterns and indicators have been most reliable.

Technical Analysis Explained: The Successful Investor's Guide to Spotting Investment Trends and Turning Points, 4th ed

Martin J. Pring

New York: McGraw-Hill Professional, 2002
641pp, ISBN: 978-0-07-138193-2

This is a guidebook to understanding and implementing the tools of technical analysis, explaining the methods for improving trading and investing profits by understanding, interpreting, and forecasting movements in markets and individual stocks. It describes how individual investors can forecast price movements with the same accuracy as professionals, and presents a program for incorporating technical analysis into an overall trading strategy.

Technical Analysis for the Trading Professional: Strategies and Techniques for Superior Returns

Constance Brown

McGraw-Hill Trader's Edge Series
New York: McGraw-Hill Professional, 1999
341pp, ISBN: 978-0-07-012062-4

This guide for professional traders examines new uses of key market indicators and techniques, combinations of indicators and formulas, and techniques for combining indicators with other indicators. It also focuses on specific formulas and chart applications to improve market timing, detection of false signals, and new uses of oscillators. The formulas and combinations of indicators can be applied across different markets and different time frames.

Technical Analysis from A to Z, 2nd ed

Steven B. Achelis

New York: McGraw-Hill Professional, 2001
380pp, ISBN: 978-0-07-136348-8

This is a concise directory of technical analysis that presents and analyzes the vast array of technical tools and techniques available. It also serves as a comprehensive reference of current technical analysis indicators used in trading in stocks, bonds, futures, and options.

Technical Analysis of Stock Trends, 9th ed

Robert D. Edwards, John Magee, W. H. C. Bassetti

Boca Raton, Florida: CRC Press, 2007
789pp, ISBN: 978-0-8493-3772-7

This guide to stock trends presents a methodology for interpreting the behavior of investors and markets for traders and investors wanting to achieve success regardless of type of market. It offers a practical overview and reference to technical investment approaches, from the basics to less well-known chart patterns, and presents simple indicators that can be easily applied to intraday movements.

Technical Analysis of the Financial Markets: A Comprehensive Guide to Trading Methods and Applications, 2nd ed

John J. Murphy

New York Institute of Finance Series
New York: NYIF, 1998
576pp, ISBN: 978-0-7352-0066-1

This is an updated version of the classic guide to technical analysis and its application to the financial markets. It describes the fundamentals, underlying concepts, and key techniques, recent techniques in charts and charting, how to understand indicators, and the role of technical analysis in investing, as well as price patterns, methods of analysis, Elliot Wave theory, and candlestick charting.

Technical Analysis Plain and Simple: Charting the Markets in Your Language, 2nd ed

Michael N. Kahn

Harlow, UK: FT Prentice Hall, 2006
309pp, ISBN: 978-0-13-134597-3

This concise guide to technical analysis presents a general overview of theory and practice, the core concepts of chart analysis and the various aspects of the investment process, as well as more advanced topics such as candlesticks, cycles, and Elliot waves. It also shows how to read charts, follow the market effectively, understand trendlines, and corrections, and assess potential risk and reward.

Technical Analysis Tools: Creating a Profitable Trading System

Mark Tinghino

New York: Bloomberg Press, 2008
295pp, ISBN: 978-1-57660-248-5

This practical guide examines how the assessment of price and volume factors to predict future price movements can be used for effective trading, and provides an assessment of the most common analytical tools available. It details the strength and weakness of each tool, which works best in which type of market, and how to integrate them into an effective trading system.

MAGAZINES

Technical Analysis of Stocks & Commodities

Technical Analysis
4757 California Avenue SW, Seattle, WA 98116-4499, USA
T: +1 206 938 0570
www.traders.com
ISSN: 0738-3355

This monthly magazine provides traders with information on how to apply charting, numerical, and computer trading methods to trade stocks, bonds, mutual funds, options, forex and futures, and examines both old and new trading methods, techniques and products.

Technical Analyst

Global Markets Media
Jeffries House, 1–5 Jeffries Passage, Guildford, GU1 4AP, UK
T: +44 (0) 1483 573 150
www.technicalanalyst.co.uk
ISSN: 1742-8718

This quarterly magazine is devoted to technical analysis for trading and investment professionals. It offers news, features, and commentary from industry players, and presents technical trading ideas to the global markets, supported by regular events, conferences, and training courses for institutional traders, fund managers and hedge funds.

JOURNALS

STA Market Technician

Society of Technical Analysts
Dean House, Vernham Dean, Hampshire, SP11 0JZ, UK
T: +44 (0) 20 7870 5950

  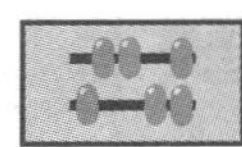   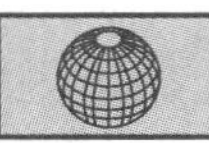   

F: +44 (0) 20 7900 2585
www.sta-uk.org/sta_journal.htm

This journal is published three times each year by the Society of Technical Analysts. It offers articles by expert members and guest writers on technical analysis, charting methods, book and software reviews, as well as speaker notes from some of their monthly meetings.

INTERNET

BarChart

www.barchart.com

This free resource offers a comprehensive selection of industry analysis on commodities, equities, delayed data, quotes, charts, technical analysis, and Internet applications. It also provides introductory trading newsletters, custom web content solutions, real-time charting applications, as well as access to futures prices, charts, and real-time quotes.

ChartFilter

www.chartfilter.com

This online resource for technical analysis provides a number of useful features for professional trades, such as information on technical indicators, financial content and articles, stock screeners, newsletters, e-books, educational material, and a glossary.

StockTA.com

www.stockta.com

This is a free technical analysis and stock screener website, which focuses on teaching and utilizing stock technical analysis to help optimize stock trades. It presents automated technical stock and mutual fund analysis, delayed charts, Fibonacci numbers, stock opinions, and stock profiles, as well as featuring analysis, picks, charts, a watch list, forum, book store, and educational material.

Traders Log

www.traderslog.com

The technical analysis section of this useful trading website offers detailed articles, forums, reviews, brokers, charts, newsletters, as well as featuring technical indicators, Fibonacci, trading pairs, trendlines, stochastics, and Japanese candlesticks.

ORGANIZATIONS

Europe

Society of Technical Analysts

Chair: Deborah Owen
Dean House, Vernham Dean, Hampshire,
SP11 0JZ, UK
T: +44 (0) 20 7870 5950
F: +44 (0) 20 7900 2585
E: info@sta-uk.org
www.sta-uk.org

The aims of the STA are to promote greater use and understanding of technical analysis as an investment tool, and serve all members of the investment community. It provides information on education, exams and professional qualifications, meetings, reference sources, useful links, recruitment links, and charts.

USA

American Association of Professional Technical Analysts

Chair: Peter Mauthe
USA
E: membership@aapta.com
www.aapta.com

AAPTA provides a forum for its members to share research and resources, exchange ideas on technical analysis and the markets, and facilitate professionalism in the industry. It allows professional technicians to engage in networking through online forums, an annual conference, and one-day brainstorming meetings. Its members include money managers, analysts, advisers, and traders.

Association for Technical Analysis

Chair: Marv Slater
PO Box 802504, Dallas, Texas 75380-2504, USA
www.afta-dfw.com

This is an active, non-profit volunteer organization aimed at providing education, fellowship, and community to traders and investors focused on technical and investment analysis.

Market Technicians Association

Chair: Larry Berman
61 Broadway, Suite 514, New York,
NY 10006, USA
T: +1 646 652 3300
F: +1 646 652 3322
www.mta.org

MTA is a global professional association devoted to those practicing technical analysis. Its CMT program and qualification is one of the industry's standards in technical analysis.

Technical Securities Analysts Association

Chair: Hank Pruden
5 Third Street, Suite 724, San Francisco,
CA 94103, USA
T: +1 415 543 2111
F: +1 415 543 2112
E: staff@tsaasf.org
www.tsaasf.org

This is a non-profit, independent association committed to fellowship and development in professional technical analysis and the markets. It encourages and supports its members, providing a forum for the exchange of ideas and methodologies, leadership opportunities, and educational resources, and offers regular meetings, an annual conference, and a newsletter three times a year on topics of current interest.

BRIC

The Association of Technical Analysts

Chair: Sudarshan Sukhani
103, Chiranjeev Towers, 43 Nehru Place, New Delhi
110019, Delhi, India
T: +91 11 2646 6090
E: india1.ta@gmail.com
www.taindia.org

ATA is a trade association in India for professionals working in the technical analysis of the stock and futures markets. It promotes the art and science of technical analysis for decision making in trading and investing in stocks, futures, currencies, commodities, interest rate futures and more, and provides regular interaction for education and application of technical analysis in the real world.

International

International Federation of Technical Analysts

Chair: Elaine Knuth
9707 Key West Avenue, Suite 100, Rockville,
MD 20850, USA
T: +1 240 404 6508
F: +1 301 990 9771
E: admin@ifta.org
www.ifta.org

IFTA is a non-profit affiliation of individual country societies dedicated to research, education, and dissemination of technical analysis of world markets. It supports the sharing of technical analytical methodology, high standards of professional conduct, international cooperation and scholarship, the exchange of information and data, and the standardization of education and testing.

Trading

BOOKS

Adventures of a Currency Trader: A Fable about Trading, Courage, and Doing the Right Thing

Rob Booker
Wiley Trading Series
Hoboken, New Jersey: Wiley, 2007
221pp, ISBN: 978-0-470-04948-8

An entertaining and educational guide to successful currency trading, told through the story of a fictional trader, Harry Banes. It tells of his start in the foreign currency market, learning how to trade, finding the best trading approach, avoiding the most common trading mistakes, and demonstrating in a readable way the strategies and pitfalls of currency trading.

Come into My Trading Room: A Complete Guide to Trading

Alexander Elder
Wiley Trading Series
New York: Wiley, 2002
320pp, ISBN: 978-0-471-22534-8

Practical advice on trading essentials, which outlines trading psychology, technical analysis, how to keep records and organize your time, with guidance on risk control and money management. It presents the author's own successful trading strategies, following him through several real trades, and giving an understanding of trading stocks, futures, options, and currencies.

The Disciplined Trader: Developing Winning Attitudes

Mark Douglas

New York Institute of Finance Series
New York: Prentice Hall, 1990
256pp, ISBN: 978-0-13-215757-5

This is an examination of the dynamics of trading psychology, which looks at how to analyze and limit your trading behavior, and develop the right mental approach. It argues that behavior in real life does not translate well into trading, and presents a series of insights into discipline, responsibility, and self-esteem, and the effect attitude has on potential trading success.

Exotic Options Trading

Frans de Weert

Wiley Finance Series
Chichester, UK: Wiley, 2008
188pp, ISBN: 978-0-470-51790-1

This is a practical assessment of the full range of exotic options available to the professional trader. It provides the skills for pricing and trading these complex products, and analyses the associated risks in terms of the economics and Greeks involved. It keeps the use of mathematics down to the essential pricing formulae, and explains key concepts in simple terms.

Fibonacci Trading: How to Master the Time and Price Advantage

Carolyn Boroden

New York: McGraw-Hill Professional, 2008
303pp, ISBN: 978-0-07-149815-9

A specialized book on Fibonacci trading and analyzing different patterns within the market. It explains how to identify numeric clusters and measure timing signals, to maximize profits and limit losses, using real-world trading situations. It helps a trader predict turning points in advance, improve stop–loss placement, and better identify critical support and resistance levels.

High Probability Trading Strategies: Entry to Exit Tactics for the Forex, Futures, and Stock Markets

Robert C. Miner

Wiley Trading Series
Hoboken, New Jersey: Wiley, 2009
272pp, ISBN: 978-0-470-18166-9

Shows how to recognize and profit from high-probability trading opportunities, analyze market behavior, and build a trading plan, based on four key factors that improve high-probability trade decisions. It also explains the best way to execute and managing the trades, and take them through to completion.

An Introduction to Options Trading

Frans de Weert

Securities Institute Series
Chichester, UK: Wiley, 2006
157pp, ISBN: 978-0-470-02970-1

This is a primer on options trading that presents the theory and practice of options from first principles, and provides the tools to trade options effectively. It analyzes where the profit of option traders actually comes from, the use of option structures, the hedging of options, and includes simple mathematical formulae to aid understanding, and a glossary of common terms.

Market Wizards: Interviews with Top Traders

Jack D. Schwager

Columbia, Maryland: Marketplace Books, 2008
512pp, ISBN: 978-1-59280-337-8

A series of interviews with some of the most successful traders in market history. It delves into their trading strategies, their different perspectives, and the mental approach they take to trading, and provides an insight into what it takes to become a great trader in a variety of markets.

Mastering the Trade: Proven Techniques for Profiting from Intraday and Swing Trading Setups

John F. Carter

McGraw-Hill Trader's Edge Series
New York: McGraw-Hill Professional, 2006
406pp, ISBN: 978-0-07-145958-7

Presents a practical approach to trading, focused on understanding the intricacies of the market and applying this knowledge to trading strategies and concepts. It provides chart setups, trading methodologies, money management principles, psychological guidelines, and advice on trading systems, and examines the underlying reasons price movements.

New Trading Systems and Methods, 4th ed

Perry J. Kaufman

Wiley Trading Series
Hoboken, New Jersey: Wiley, 2005
1,174pp, ISBN: 978-0-471-26847-5

Now in its 4th edition, this bestseller provides a guide to technical trading strategies and techniques, as well as information on the latest indicators, programs, spreadsheets, charts, algorithms, and systems, for choosing the right trading program. It also analyzes how much data to use, the key techniques of identifying the trend and momentum, and contains extensive risk analysis.

Quantitative Trading: How to Build Your Own Algorithmic Trading Business

Ernest P. Chan

Wiley Trading Series
Hoboken, New Jersey: Wiley, 2009
182pp, ISBN: 978-0-470-28488-9

A new guide to understanding and implementing algorithmic trading techniques—once the sole preserve of elite traders—as part of a quantitative trading strategy. It explains how to use specialized software to build algorithmic trading tools that are suited to individual needs, how to conduct quantitative research and analysis, and how to implement this highly effective approach.

Traders, Guns and Money: Knowns and Unknowns in the Dazzling World of Derivatives

Satyajit Das

Harlow, UK: FT Prentice Hall, 2006
334pp, ISBN: 978-0-273-70474-4

Recounts the author's career in financial derivatives, describing how derivatives originated, how they are used, their benefits, their dangers, and their impact on the financial markets. It is an insider's exposé of derivatives trading, which uncovers the theft, misrepresentation, and lies that can occur, written in a readable style.

Trading and Exchanges: Market Microstructure for Practitioners

Larry Harris

Financial Management Association Survey & Synthesis Series
Oxford, UK: Oxford University Press, 2003
643pp, ISBN: 978-0-19-514470-3

This is an overview of trading, those who trade securities and contracts, the marketplace, and the rules that govern trading operations. It examines the players such as investors, brokers, dealers, arbitrageurs, and retail traders, the different types of exchange, and looks in detail at the variety of trades, auctions, and orders available.

Trading Commodities and Financial Futures: A Step-by-Step Guide to Mastering the Markets, 3rd ed

George Kleinman

Boston: FT Prentice Hall, 2005
288pp, ISBN: 978-0-13-147654-7

Presenting a trading methodology based on the author's long experience in the markets, it assesses the fundamentals of trading commodities and futures, and offers a primer on how futures and options trading works. It also shows how traders' psychology can impact the markets, how to avoid common mistakes, and examines electronic trading, contracts, and trading techniques.

Trading for a Living: Psychology, Trading Tactics, Money Management

Alexander Elder

Wiley Finance Series
New York: Wiley, 1993
289pp, ISBN: 978-0-471-59224-2

Elder's classic book, which presents his successful trading strategy based on the three M's: mind, method, and money. It emphasizes the importance of developing discipline and avoiding emotional trading, of using analytic techniques in a trading system, and how to effectively manage money in your trading account, and shows how to trade using charts, computerized indicators, and other tools.

Trend Following: How Great Traders Make Millions in Up or Down Markets, 2nd ed

Michael W. Covel

Upper Saddle River, New Jersey: FT Prentice Hall, 2006
420pp, ISBN: 978-0-13-613718-4

An examination of the technique of following patterns and trends in the markets to create

 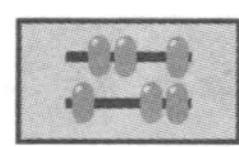   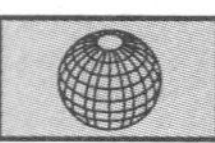   

improved trading returns. Based on a tested and successful trading strategy, it presents practical guidance on applying trend following in a portfolio, and real results from leading trend followers, as well as understandable charts to aid learning.

Volatility Trading
Euan Sinclair
Wiley Trading Series
Hoboken, New Jersey: Wiley, 2008
212pp, ISBN: 978-0-470-18199-7

Offers practical guidance on the basics of option pricing, volatility measurement, hedging, money management, and trade evaluation, and presents a quantitative model for measuring volatility. It discusses the psychological aspects of trading, and emphasizes the importance of identifying and evaluating the price of implied volatility, and finding trades with a distinct statistical edge.

Way of the Turtle: The Secret Methods that Turned Ordinary People into Legendary Traders
Curtis M. Faith
New York: McGraw-Hill Professional, 2007
286pp, ISBN: 978-0-07-148664-4

The author was the youngest and most successful member of the Turtles, a group started as a bet about whether great traders were born or made. Way of the Turtle recounts the whole experiment, how 23 ordinary people were recruited and trained into effective traders in only two weeks, and explaining the selection process, rules, strategies, and how to use their system in practice.

MAGAZINES

Active Trader
161 North Clark, Suite 4915, Chicago, IL 60601, USA
T: +1 312 775 5422
F: +1 815 734 5238
www.activetradermag.com
ISSN: 1542-9466

This monthly magazine provides information and analysis on trading strategy and risk control, the buying and selling of stocks, options, futures and currencies on a (mostly) short-term basis. It also covers different aspects of the market for short-term traders, including analysis of new trading rules or regulations, new trading instruments, the impact of after-hours trading, and using different ECNs.

Technical Analysis of Stocks & Commodities
Technical Analysis
4757 California Avenue SW, Seattle, WA 98116-4499, USA
T: +1 206 938 0570
www.traders.com
ISSN: 0738-3355

This monthly magazine provides traders with information on how to apply charting, numerical, and computer trading methods to trade stocks, bonds, mutual funds, options, forex and futures, and examines both old and new trading methods, techniques and products.

Trader Monthly
Doubledown Media
240 West 35th Street, 11th Floor, New York, NY 10001, USA
T: +1 212 719 9500
F: +1 212 507 9878
www.traderdaily.com/magazine
ISSN: 1935-0279

This monthly upmarket trading magazine provides news, strategies, career information, events, and profiles of successful traders from around the world, as well as covering luxury items that traders might want to purchase. Trader Monthly is available free to professional traders and hedge fund managers.

Traders Magazine
SourceMedia
1 State Street Plaza, 27th Floor, New York, NY 10004, USA
T: +1 212 803 8333
www.tradersmagazine.com
ISSN: 0894-7295

This monthly magazine for securities industry professionals is the official publication of the Security Traders Association (STA). It publishes coverage of the entire trading process, including equities and options, major trends, financial industry news, executive profiles, and cutting edge technology developments, and is aimed at C-Level executives, senior management, head traders, managing directors, partners, and portfolio managers.

Traders World
Halliker's
2508 West Grayrock Street, Springfield, MO 65810, USA
T: +1 417 882 9697
F: +1 417 885 5180
www.tradersworld.com
ISSN: 1045-7690

Traders World is a monthly magazine that offers a range of news, analysis, and information on the use of technical analysis by traders. It covers all the main issues in trading through stock charting, and provides detail on relevant books, software, computers, links, and conferences.

JOURNALS

Journal of Trading
Institutional Investor
225 Park Avenue South, New York, NY 10003, USA
T: +1 212 224 3570
F: +1 212 224 3197
www.iijournals.com/JOT
ISSN: 1559-3967

This quarterly journal provides analysis of new tools and strategies in institutional trading, focusing on algorithmic trading, execution options, trading platforms, liquidity, analytical models, and multi-asset trading. It examines a number of relevant issues, such as how to review and measure trade execution performance, conduct pre- and post-trade analysis and transaction cost analysis, and achieve best execution and avoid trading pitfalls.

INTERNET

The Technical Trader
www.thetechtrader.com

A site run by veteran trader and financial commentator Harry Boxer, who has many years of experience in investment and technical analysis, this is a popular real-time diary of his trading ideas and market analysis.

Trade2Win
www.trade2win.com

This is a community website for active traders, that aims to unite and support traders around the world. It provides information, analysis, and educational content, and a range of facilities to enable members to communicate with each another, and to share their trading knowledge and views.

Traders' Resource
technical.traders.com

A site run by Technical Analysis of Stocks & Commodities magazine, this is a useful industry search area for information about products, services, and companies related to trading. It lists and links to advisory services, books, brokerages, consultants, courses and seminars, data services, exchanges, hardware, mutual funds, online trading services, publications and newsletters, software, and trading systems.

Transport Finance

BOOKS

Air Transportation: A Management Perspective, 6th ed
John G. Wensveen (editor)
Aldershot, UK: Ashgate, 2007
568pp, ISBN: 978-0-7546-7171-8

This accessible textbook provides a comprehensive introduction to both the theory and practice of air transportation management. It explains the basics, past and present trends, and forecasts potential challenges and difficult decisions that the industry may face. It also details aspects of airline financing, as well as passenger marketing, labor relations, and security.

Airline Finance, 3rd ed
Peter S. Morrell
Aldershot, UK: Ashgate, 2007
259pp, ISBN: 978-0-7546-7000-1

This provides a fundamental understanding of airline finance, addressing each of the main techniques in financial analysis within the context of the air transport industry. It explores how these areas separately and in an integrated way, reinforcing key points with useful case studies. It also discusses financial trends and prospects for the industry, as well as topics such as low cost carriers, fuel hedging, and US Chapter 11 provisions.

Applied Transport Economics: Policy, Management and Decision Making, 3rd ed

Stuart Cole

London: Kogan Page, 2005
449pp, ISBN: 978-0-7494-3964-4

This focuses on the practical application of theoretical models, and managerial aspects of transport economics. It derives the main principles and theoretical concepts, discusses the latest developments in transport economics, and examines the application of economics techniques to commercial transport operations, public policy issues, and the role of transport in its wider economic context.

Essays on Transport Economics

Pablo Coto-Millán, Vicente Inglada (editors)

Contributions to Economics Series
New York: Physica, 2007
381pp, ISBN: 978-3-7908-1764-5

This collection of articles covers a wide range of topics in transport economics, from basic analytical methods and policy analysis, to more technical discussions of industrial organization, welfare economics, general equilibrium theory, and input-output analysis. It provides theoretical introductions in each area, and presents case studies using current statistical and econometric techniques.

The Future of Pricing: How Airline Ticket Pricing Has Inspired a Revolution

E. Andrew Boyd

Basingstoke, UK: Palgrave Macmillan, 2007
192pp, ISBN: 978-0-230-60019-5

This examines the science of pricing and revenue management, and the impact it has had on the way in which airline companies approach profitable growth. Using anecdotes, interviews, and examples from the airline industry, technology, technology companies, and the history of pricing and revenue management, it provides an insight into how airline price ticketing and other related practices are transforming pricing strategies in other industries.

The Handbook of Maritime Economics and Business

Costas T. Grammenos (editor)

Maritime & Transport Law Library Series
London: LLP Professional Publishing, 2002
930pp, ISBN: 978-1-84311-195-5

This practical guide presents a thorough examination of the current state of the shipping industry, and related economic theories. It combines the original writing of a team of leading academics from around the world, to analyze an array of major maritime economic issues, and assess the research in terms of real-life applications.

Introduction to Air Transport Economics: From Theory to Applications

Bijan Vasigh, Ken Fleming, Thomas Tacker

Aldershot, UK: Ashgate, 2008
358pp, ISBN: 978-0-7546-7081-0

This comprehensive textbook applies economic theory to all technical aspects of the aviation industry. It offers an introduction to the economics of aviation, by presenting a number of articles and institutional developments that have occurred over the last few years, as well as providing new analysis of the underlying economic forces that are currently shaping the industry.

Maritime Economics, 3rd ed

Martin Stopford

London: Routledge, 2008
562pp, ISBN: 978-0-415-27558-3

This provides both an historical and an analytical account of the development of the shipping industry, and an overview of current thinking in maritime economics. It analyzes the historical roots of the industry, presents a framework for understanding modern shipping operations, and explores key issues such as markets, trade theory, shipping costs, accounts, forecasting, ship finance, return on capital, and regulation.

Modelling Transport, 3rd ed

Juan de Dios Ortúzar, Luis G. Willumsen

Chichester, UK: Wiley, 2001
499pp, ISBN: 978-0-471-86110-2

This is a comprehensive and technical guide to mathematical techniques used in transport modeling, and their use for improved decision-making, planning, and design. It examines the main modeling techniques and applications, as well as the role of theory, data, model specification, estimation, validation, and application, data collection techniques, new modeling approaches, time-of-travel and assignment modeling, and the valuation of externalities.

Principles of Transport Economics

Emile Quinet, Roger Vickerman

Cheltenham, UK: Edward Elgar, 2004
385pp, ISBN: 978-1-84542-256-1

This textbook provides a comprehensive analysis of the main areas of transportation economics and policy, including demand, costs, market structure, externalities, and investment appraisal and regulation. It explains how economic principles can be applied to problem solving, and addresses the link between transport and issues of location, urban, and regional development, and economic growth.

Project Finance: The Guide to Financing Transport Projects

Macquarie Corporate Finance

London: Euromoney Books, 2000
95pp, ISBN: 978-1-85564-752-7

This is a focused, practical report on project financing in the transport sector, which examines private financing and development of transport infrastructure. It analyzes the unique challenges posed by the sector, through a study of particular project finance deals, and discusses key issues that are common to a large number of projects, innovative approaches to funding, and risks specific to developing economies and their mitigation.

Road Pricing: Theory and Evidence

Georgina Santos (editor)

Research in Transportation Economics Series
Oxford, UK: JAI Press, 2004
324pp, ISBN: 978-0-7623-0968-9

This examines the transformation in road economic policy brought about by recent advances in road pricing as a method for reducing congestion. It discusses its role as an effective traffic demand management tool, assesses the impact of the London congestion charge, and looks at other schemes in place around the world. It also focuses on second-best congestion pricing, including the impact on the performance of the road network, and optimal locations and charge levels.

Shipping Derivatives and Risk Management

Amir Alizadeh, Nikos Nomikos

Basingstoke, UK: Palgrave Macmillan, 2009
256pp, ISBN: 978-0-230-21591-7

This is a comprehensive examination of shipping derivatives and risk management, from both a theoretical and practical standpoint. It looks at key issues such as pricing and trading different shipping derivatives instruments, the use of forward freight agreements to manage freight rate risk, basis and settlement risk, real options, and other risks such as bunker risk, interest rate risk, ship price risk, and credit risk.

Shipping Finance, 3rd ed

Stephenson Harwood

London: Euromoney Books, 2006
568pp, ISBN: 978-1-84374-265-4

This examines the shipping finance sector, and provides an explanation of ship mortgage terms, conditions, and mortgagee's rights, with a description of documentation, legislation and registration procedures across the main maritime jurisdictions. It also covers key topics such as the financing of second-hand ships, the financing of new buildings, the assignment of insurances and earnings, guarantees, indemnities, charges, debentures, and the application of Islamic finance.

Transport Economics: Theory, Application, and Policy

Graham Mallard, Stephen Glaister

Basingstoke, UK: Palgrave Macmillan, 2008
315pp, ISBN: 978-0-230-51688-5

This introductory textbook explores the key areas of the transport sector economics, and provides a concise explanation of related economic theory, as well as detailed case studies from across the European Union. It focuses on the application of microeconomic theory, and cover topics such as

  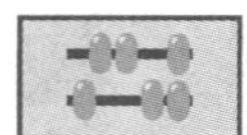      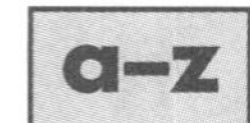

the theory of markets, market failure, transport policy, and future trends.

Transport Policy and Funding

Dai Nakagawa, Ryoji Matsunaka

Oxford, UK: Elsevier, 2006

208pp, ISBN: 978-0-08-044852-7

This takes an international perspective on transport policy and funding issues, comparing how different countries make capital provisions to achieve their transportation goals. It looks at a variety of funding resources and systems and how they relate to current policy, presents calculations about who is really paying transport costs, and discusses potential improvements to make transport investment and policy more effective.

Transportation Finance Review 2008/09

London: Euromoney Books, 2008

ISBN: 978-1-84374-518-1

This annual publication provides a current overview of the latest developments, trends, and funding issues in transportation and its infrastructure around the world. It offers analysis of large-scale projects for new roads, bridges, tunnels, ports and airports, and rail, and presents case studies, profiles, and discussions on the legal and risk challenges facing such projects.

Urban Transportation Economics, 2nd ed

Kenneth A. Small, Erik T. Verhoef

London: Routledge, 2006

276pp, ISBN: 978-0-415-28515-5

This textbook on the economics of transportation discusses the fundamental issues for an application of economics to transportation, including forecasting demand under alternative policies, measuring costs, price setting under practical constraints, how to choose and evaluate investments in facilities, and methods for ensuring that the private and public sectors work together in the provision of services.

Wheels Up: Airline Business Plan Development, 2nd ed

John G. Wensveen (editor)

Malabar, Florida: Krieger Publishing, 2007

130pp, ISBN: 978-1-57524-293-4

This examines airline business operations, identifying current and new trends, and exploring the importance of flexibility within the business plan. It looks at how vital this flexibility is for an airline in terms of competition, the impact of failure within the aviation environment, and how to develop an effective business plan that is suitable for airlines of any size.

MAGAZINES

Aircraft Value News

Access Intelligence

4 Choke Cherry Road, 2nd Floor, Rockville, MD 20850, USA

T: +1 301 354 2000

www.aviationtoday.com/avn

ISSN: 1071-0655

This biweekly magazine is dedicated to trends and the market analysis of aircraft values. It explores aircraft leasing and purchasing decisions, current and planned joint ventures and mergers, issues in the emerging markets, and provides useful aircraft value tabulation and analysis tables.

Airfinance Journal

Institutional Investor

Nestor House, Playhouse Yard, London, EC4V 5EX, UK

T: +44 (0) 20 7779 8999

www.airfinancejournal.com

ISSN: 0266-2132

This monthly magazine covers all the key financial aspects of commercial aviation industry, offering news on the financing of airline fleets and issues affecting commercial airlines, financiers, manufacturers, consultants, and aviation law firms. It also tracks and analyzes aircraft, airline, and aerospace finance techniques and deals, features interviews with leading industry figures, and presents relevant surveys and data tables.

Airline Fleet Management

Aviation Industry Press

2nd Floor, Ludgate House, 245 Blackfriars Road, London, SE1 9UY, UK

T: +44 (0) 20 7579 4840

F: +44 (0) 20 7579 4848

www.aviationindustrygroup.com/ME2/Audiences/Default.asp?AudID=8FB7A82C60B7404F842B557F22850190

ISSN: 1757-8833

AFM is a bimonthly, global magazine for aircraft owners, operators and lessors. It provides commentary and analysis of the main issues and challenges facing the airline industry, such as the selection, procurement, financing, operations, and management of airline fleets, and network planning, as well as forecasts and future trends.

Aviation Business Asia Pacific

Yaffa Publishing Group, Australia

T: +61 2 9281 2333

www.yaffa.com.au/btob/air.html

This bimonthly magazine is a source of news, analysis, information, and commercial intelligence for the region's airlines and airports, and the businesses that support their operations. It describes the issues and agendas of the aviation and aerospace industry, and focuses on business decision-making, and the policies that influence business investment and the business climate in the sector.

Jetrader

Naylor

401 North Michigan Avenue, Chicago, Illinois 60611, USA

www.istat.org/Media/Jetrader

This bimonthly magazine is published by the International Society of Transport Aircraft Trading and is distributed to its members. It highlights and analyzes industry news and case studies, and presents feature articles and a member focus, as well as acting as a forum for promoting communications among those involved in the aviation and supporting industries.

JOURNALS

Journal of Air Transport Management

Elsevier

www.elsevier.com/wps/find/journaldescription.cws_home/30438/description#description

ISSN: 0969-6997

This bimonthly journal publishes research articles and commentary on the major policy and management issues facing the air transport industry. It offers practitioners and academics an international forum for analysis and discussion of these issues, and covers all the major sectors of the industry. Analysis focuses on air transport policy and regulation, strategic issues, operations, management, finance and economics, air law, and environmental impact.

Journal of Transport, Economics and Policy

School of Management, University of Bath, Claverton Down, Bath, BA2 7AY, UK

T: +44 (0) 1225 386 302

F: +44 (0) 1225 386 767

www.bath.ac.uk/e-journals/jtep

ISSN: 0022-5258

JTEP is published three times a year, and covers all modes of transport and a wide variety of economic themes. It acts as a source of information and debate on the economics of transport and its interface with transport policy, and offer research on the latest policy developments, as well as topics such as transport infrastructure, planning and policy, costs and pricing, productivity, economies of scale, and regulation.

Research in Transportation Economics

Elsevier

www.elsevier.com/wps/find/journaldescription.cws_home/714194/description#description

ISSN: 0739-8859

Published three times each year, this journal is devoted to the dissemination of economics research in the field of transportation. It covers a wide variety of topics relating to the economics aspects of transportation, government regulatory policies regarding transportation, and issues of concern to transportation industry planners, with a focus on the application of economic theory and/or applied economic methodologies to transportation questions.

Transport Policy

Elsevier

T: +353 61 709 190

www.elsevier.com/wps/find/journaldescription.cws_home/30473/description#description

ISSN: 0967-070X

This bimonthly international journal analyzes how transport policy decisions are taken, monitors their impact, and makes suggestions regarding potential improvements. Emphasizing both theory and practice, and covering all modes of transport, it reflects the concerns of policymakers in government, industry, voluntary organizations, and the public, and examines policy topics such as traffic management and control, regulation, and economic and commercial pricing policy.

  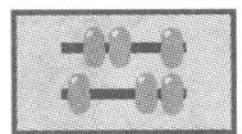      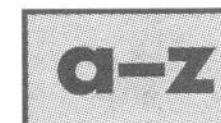

INTERNET

Innovative Finance for Surface Transportation

www.innovativefinance.org

This provides guidance on innovations in all areas of surface transportation finance, and information on technical topics, projects, legislation, publications, application guidance, and institutional issues relating to all transport modes of surface transport. It describes new sources of revenue, financing mechanisms, funds management techniques, and institutional arrangements, and features news, definitions, Q&As, a resource library, an events calendar, and a glossary.

Jane's Transport Finance

jtf.janes.com

This allows viewing of the contents of the Jane's site, with a subscription providing access to full articles, news and analysis, research, and finance intelligence on debt pricing, structure, arrangers and lenders for debt deals in the aircraft, airport, shipping and rail rolling-stock sectors, as well as information on mergers and acquisitions, and financing trends.

ORGANIZATIONS

USA

International Society of Transport Aircraft Trading

Chair: Michael Platt
401 North Michigan Avenue, Chicago, Illinois 60611, USA
T: +1 312 321 5169
F: +1 312 673 6579
E: istat@istat.org
www.istat.org

ISTAT provides a forum for improved communication among those involved in aviation and supporting industries who operate, manufacture, maintain, sell, purchase, finance, lease, appraise, insure, or otherwise engage in activities related to the commercial aviation trading industry. It provides news and information, develops standards, holds lectures and demonstrations, establishes and promotes standards, certifies professional appraisers, and offers an educational program.

Transportation Research Forum

Chair: Kenneth Button
NDSU Dept 2880, PO Box 6050, Fargo, ND 58108-6050, USA
T: +1 701 231 7766
F: +1 701 231 1945
www.trforum.org

TRF is an independent organization of transportation professionals, whose aim is to provide a meeting ground for carriers, shippers, government officials, consultants, university researchers, suppliers, and others seeking an exchange of information and ideas related to both passenger and freight transportation. It offers information for researchers, holds international, national, and local meetings, and publishes professional papers related to numerous transportation topics.

International

World Conference on Transport Research Society

Chair: Tony May
LET-ISH 14, avenue Berthelot, 69363 Lyon, France
T: +33 (0) 4 72 72 64 36
F: +33 (0) 4 72 72 64 48
E: wctrs@let.ish-lyon.cnrs.fr
www.wctrs.org

WCTRS provides a forum for the interchange of ideas among transportation researchers, managers, policy makers, and educators from all over the world. It also helps to identify emerging issues and opportunities of a policy, managerial, or technical nature that will influence transportation research, policy, management and education in the future.

Venture Capital

BOOKS

Angel Capital: How to Raise Early-Stage Private Equity Financing

Gerald A. Benjamin, Joel B. Margulis
Hoboken, New Jersey: Wiley, 2005
373pp, ISBN: 978-0-471-69063-4

The book offers real-world advice on how to find investors and take control of the private placement process. It explains all stages of raising capital, from valuation to negotiation to due diligence, and provides a comprehensive directory of alternative capital resources, based on research of over 2,000 organizations, and a legal appendix that serves as a short course in exempt offerings, and provides the skills needed to have success with any early-stage business venture or investment.

Angel Financing: How to Find and Invest in Private Equity

Gerald A. Benjamin, Joel B. Margulis
Wiley Investment Series
New York: Wiley, 1999
320pp, ISBN: 978-0-471-35085-9

This book draws on extensive experience of the private investor market in the United States. It stresses the importance of careful planning and preparation to ensure the success of financial deals. It provides practical advice and information for entrepreneurs, investors, and intermediaries in four sections: the first focuses on how entrepreneurs can address the challenge of raising capital and finding workable strategies; the second examines the angel investor market; the third deals with the search for an investor; and the fourth provides insight into the investor's perspective on prospective deals. Detailed advice on preparing an investor-oriented business plan and an overview of securities law issues for nonlawyers are provided in appendices.

Directory of Venture Capital, 2nd ed

Kate E. Lister, Thomas D. Harnish
New York: Wiley, 2000
400pp, ISBN: 978-0-471-36104-6

The directory lists venture capital firms by state and provides detailed information on their preferences with regard to industry, stage of funding, geography, and size of company. The authors also provide information on the returns required by private equity investors, selecting the right lawyer, and important aspects of a venture partnership. Entrepreneurs will find the directory a good resource for locating the right venture capital firm to approach for funding.

Raising Venture Capital

Rupert Pearce, Simon Barnes
Hoboken, New Jersey: Wiley, 2006
258pp, ISBN: 978-0-470-02757-8

Offering a deep insight into the venture capital deal making process, this also provides a valuable introduction to the subject. It is practical in approach, although based on sound academic theory, research, and teaching materials.

Raising Venture Capital Finance in Europe: A Practical Guide for Business Owners, Entrepreneurs and Investors

Keith Arundale
London: Kogan Page, 2007
308pp, ISBN: 978-0-7494-4849-3

This book provides an outline for developing and presenting a strategic business plan, with tips on how to selectively approach venture capital in Europe, negotiate to sell or build a business, prepare for due diligence, define the benefits for investors, and plan potential exit routes.

Venture Capital and Private Equity: A Casebook, 4th ed

Josh Lerner, Felda Hardymon, Ann Leamon
Hoboken, New Jersey: Wiley, 2009
576pp, ISBN: 978-0-470-22462-5

The book explains in detail the venture capital and private equity markets. Divided into four sections, the book covers the fundraising process required to start a venture capital fund, investment selection, and the relationship between the venture capitalist and entrepreneur, the various exit strategies available, and some key issues unique to the private equity market.

Venture Capital Funding: A Practical Guide to Raising Finance, 2nd ed

Stephen Bloomfield
London: Kogan Page, 2008
256pp, ISBN: 978-0-7494-5230-8

Written in an informal and jargon-free style, this book offers step-by-step advice on how to attract

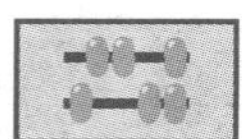

venture capital funding for your business. To make the process seem less daunting, the process is broken down into a number of manageable sections.

The Venture Capital Handbook

William D. Bygrave, Michael Hay, Jos B. Peeters (editors)
Harlow, UK: FT Prentice Hall, 1999
384pp, ISBN: 978-0-273-63899-5

This handbook, which consists of contributions from practitioners, provides an overview of the European venture capital industry and a detailed treatment of the investment process. The aspects of the process covered include fundraising and investor relations, deal generation, due diligence, deal structuring and pricing, and postinvestment venture management. Legal and ethical issues, going public, international syndication, and returns on venture capital are also dealt with.

Venture Capital Investing: The Complete Handbook for Investing in Private Businesses for Outstanding Profits, 2nd ed

David Gladstone, Laura Gladstone
Upper Saddle River, New Jersey: Prentice Hall, 2004
480pp, ISBN: 978-0-13-101885-3

This classic serves as a primer on venture capital investing. It outlines the key considerations for investing private capital, including an analysis of management, compensation, marketing and sales, financial statements and projections, and the production process. From due diligence and deal negotiation to the exit strategy, the author suggests a logical, step-by-step process that is filled with insights and actual examples from his experience as a venture capitalist. While most books are focused on how an entrepreneur can raise venture capital, this book provides an in-depth look at what it takes to be a successful investor in small private businesses.

Venture Catalyst: The Five Strategies for Explosive Corporate Growth

Don Laurie
Cambridge, Massachusetts: Perseus Books Group, 2001
288pp, ISBN: 978-0-7382-0407-9

This book presents a five-part framework for launching new initiatives, and illustrates each part with examples from industries as diverse as packaged goods and web marketing. Interviews with such pioneers as Roger Ackerman of Corning, David Wetherall of CMGI, and Mitch Kapoor of Accel provide the reader with an insider's perspective on the volatile world of corporate venturing.

MAGAZINES

Private Equity Analyst

Asset Alternatives
170 Linden Street, Wellesley, MA 02482–7919, USA
T: +1 781 304 1500
www.fis.dowjones.com/products/privateequityanalyst.html

This monthly newsletter covers the private equity market, dealing mainly with venture capital, LBOs, mezzanine investing, and turnarounds.

Private Equity Journal for India

Dickenson Intellinetics Private
266, Dr. Annie Besant Road, Worli, Mumbai 25, India
T: +91 22 2625 2282
F: +91 22 2625 2282
www.vcindia.com/pub_ind-v-c-j.asp
ISSN: 0973-1636

This quarterly journal offers research and analysis from its own editorial and research team, and by participants and academics who wish to share their knowledge and research.

Private Equity Week

Thomson Financial
195 Broadway, 10th Floor, New York, NY 10007, USA
T: +1 646 822 2000
F: +1 646 822 3230
www.pewnews.com
ISSN: 1099-341X

PEW is a weekly newsletter providing information on private equity deals in the venture capital market.

Real Deals Europe

National Federation of Independent Business
53 Century Boulevard, Suite 300, Nashville, TN 37214, USA
T: +1 615 872 5800
F: +1 615 872 5353
www.realdeals.eu.com

Real Deals is a private equity magazine for venture capitalists, advisers, and debt providers. Published every two weeks, it offers news, commentary, analysis, and independently compiled deal information on the European private equity and venture capital industry.

JOURNALS

European Venture Capital Journal

Venture Economics
195 Broadway, 10th Floor, NY 10007, USA
T: +1 646 822 2000
F: +1 646 822 3230
www.privateequityweek.com
ISSN: 0954-1675

This journal, published ten times a year, provides information on the European private equity market. The *UK Venture Capital Journal* merged with it in 1999.

Venture Capital Journal

Thomson Financial
195 Broadway, 10th Floor, New York, NY 10007, USA
T: +1 646 822 2000
F: +1 646 822 3230
www.vcjnews.com
ISSN: 0883-2773

VCJ is a monthly journal covering the private equity and venture capital industry. It provides news and analysis of deals, company profiles, and interviews.

INTERNET

PricewaterhouseCoopers MoneyTree Report

www.pwcmoneytree.com

This survey, sponsored by the accounting firm of PricewaterhouseCoopers, provides a comprehensive list of venture capital investing in the United States by industry, stage of funding, geography, and type of financing on a quarterly basis. The report tracks venture capital firm investments and the enterprises receiving capital by region/state and industry.

US Venture Partners (USVP)

www.usvp.com

Created in 1981, USVP aims to specifically help entrepreneurial ventures. In total, it has put over $1.8 billion into more than 370 companies, and their clients have gone on to become leaders in their respective fields.

vcapital

www.vcfodder.com

This is an action-packed site for entrepreneurs, with a distinct editorial voice. It features a "Dr VC" feature, whereby users can ask for specific advice, and encourages users to e-mail in their own stories of success and failure.

VentureSource

www.ventureone.com

VentureSource is a Dow Jones database that tracks the key developments of more the 30,000 venture-backed companies in every industry and every region in the US, Europe, Israel, and China. It also tracks the moves and people of over 8,000 private capital firms around the world.

Venturewire

fis.dowjones.com/products/venturewire.html

This website hosts a family of publications that are exclusively devoted to the private equity marketplace. *Venturewire Professional*, the site's flagship publication, features the latest news on fundings, acquisitions, venture capital firms, and key personnel changes in venture-backed businesses. Venturewire also publishes *Lifescience*, *Alert*, and *People* on a daily basis and provides the Research section as a source of in-depth coverage on specific industries.

vFinance Venture Capital Resource Library

www.vfinance.com

This site is aimed at investors, entrepreneurs, and company CEOs and provides access to databases of investors, angels, and business plans. Registration is required.

ORGANIZATIONS

Europe

British Business Angels Network

New City Court, 20 St Thomas Street, London, SE1 9RS, UK
T: +44 (0) 20 7089 2305
F: +44 (0) 20 7089 2301
E: liz@bbaa.org.uk
www.bbaa.org.uk

BBAA, formerly NBAN (National Business Angels Network), is a nonprofit association sponsored by financial institutions and the Department for Business, Enterprise and Regulatory Reform in

the United Kingdom. Through a network of associates across the country, it provides a service linking businesses seeking equity finance with investors seeking opportunities. A monthly bulletin of opportunities is sent to all registered investors, and an online service, BestMatch, is also provided.

British Venture Capital Association

3 Clements Inn, London, WC2A 2AZ, UK
T: +44 (0) 20 7025 2950
F: +44 (0) 20 7025 2951
E: bvca@bvca.co.uk
www.bvca.co.uk

The BVCA was founded in 1983 and is the representative body for the UK venture capital industry. It promotes private equity and venture capital for the benefit of entrepreneurs, investors, practitioners, and the economy as a whole. Its members are venture capital companies and professional firms involved in advising on venture capital transactions. Its wide variety of activities include training, workshops, lobbying, and research, and it produces publications.

European Private Equity and Venture Capital Association (EVCA)

Bastion Tower, Place du Champ de Mars 5, Brussels, 1050, Belgium
T: +32 2 715 00 20
F: +32 2 725 07 04
E: evca@evca.com
www.evca.com

EVCA was founded in 1983 and now has over 850 members. Its aim is to promote and facilitate the development of the European venture capital industry through lobbying and initiatives such as conferences, training, and networking opportunities. The organization was involved in the creation of EASD (European Association of Security Dealers) and the EASDAQ pan-European capital market.

USA

National Association of Investment Companies

1300 Pennsylvania Avenue NW, Suite 700, Washington, DC 20004, USA
T: +1 202 289 4336
F: +1 202 289 4329
E: naichqtrs@aol.com
www.naicvc.com

NAIC is an industry association for venture capital and private equity firms. Its members are privately owned equity investment firms, small business investment companies licensed by the United States Small Business Administration, and investment companies chartered by state and local governments.

National Association of Small Business Investment Companies

666 11th Street NW, Suite 750, Washington, DC 20001, USA
T: +1 202 628 5055
F: +1 202 628 5080
E: nasbic@nasbic.org
www.nasbic.org

NASBIC is a nonprofit industry association which has represented and served the SBIC industry for over 40 years. It provides educational programs for investment professionals through the Venture Capital Institute and cooperates with other business associations. Its policies and priorities are established by a board of governors.

National Venture Capital Association

1655 North Fort Myer Drive, Suite 850, Arlington, VI 22209, USA
T: +1 703 524 2549
F: +1 703 524 3940
E: lturner@nvca.org
www.nvca.org

NVCA is a trade association with a membership of over 400 venture capital firms. It aims to foster understanding of the venture capital industry in the United States, to stimulate the flow of equity capital to growth companies, to promote professional standards, facilitate networking, and provide research data for members. NVCA publishes: *NVCA Today*, a quarterly review of legislative and regulatory developments; *The Venture Capital Review*, a biannual journal which provides an overview of trends in the industry; and the *Venture Capital Yearbook*.

BRIC

Brazil Venture Capital

FINEP, Praia do Flamengo 200, 1, 2, 3, 4, 5, 7, 9, 13 e 24 andares, Rio de Janeiro, 22210-030, Brazil
T: +55 21 2555 0330
F: +55 21 2555 0402
www.venturecapital.gov.br

This site is part of the INOVAR project, launched by the Brazilian ministry of Science and Technology department FINEP, to promote the development of small- and medium-size businesses by designing instruments for their financing, especially venture capital.

China Venture Capital Association (CVCA)

Room 1002, 10/F, Office Tower C1, 1 East Chang An Avenue, Beijing 100738, China
T: +86 10 8515 0829
F: +86 10 8515 0835
E: cindy@cvca.com.cn
www.cvca.com.hk

CVCA is a member-based, trade organization established to promote the interest and the development of the venture capital and private equity industry in the Greater China Region.

China Venture Capital Research Institute (CVCRI)

TU427, The Hong Kong Polytechnic University, Hung Hom, Kowloon, Hong Kong
T: +852 2766 4264
F: +852 2764 2340
E: cvcri@cvcri.com
www.cvcri.com/english/index.asp

This institute is a joint venture between The Hong Kong Polytechnic University and the China Venture Capital Company, which promotes the development of China's venture capital and hi-tech industries by providing the best services for related theoretical and practical studies and policy making. It also publishes the China Venture Capital Journal and the China Venture Capital Yearbook.

Indian Venture Capital and Private Equity Association (IVCA)

301–302, Delhi Blue Apartments, Main Ring Road, Near Safdarjung Hospital, New Delhi 110 029, India
T: +91 11 4162 8566
F: +91 11 4162 8863
E: info@indiavca.org
www.indiavca.org

Indian Venture Capital and Private Equity Association (IVCA) is a member-based, national organization that represents venture capital and private equity firms, promotes the industry within India and throughout the world, and encourages investment in high-growth companies.

Russian Private Equity and Venture Capital Association (RVCA)

Office 209, 12B, pr. Engelsa 29, Saint-Petersburg, Russia
T: +7 812 326 6180
F: +7 812 326 6180
E: rvca@rvca.ru
www.rvca.ru/english

RVCA is a member-based platform that works to create a positive political and entrepreneurial environment for investment activities, represent its members interests at the government level, in press, in financial and industrial markets within the country and abroad, provide information and support, and build a cluster of highly qualified professionals for the venture business companies.

International

Australian Venture Capital Association

Level 41, Gateway Building, 1 Macquarie Place, Sydney, New South Wales, 2000, Australia
T: +61 2 9251 3888
F: +61 2 9251 3808
E: mbrs@avcal.com.au
www.avcal.com.au

AVCAL was founded in 1992 to act as a forum for the venture capital industry in Australia and to encourage investment in growing businesses. Its members, numbering over 100, include venture capital firms, banks, incubators, angels, advisers, and government bodies. It organizes networking events and training courses, and sponsors a twice-yearly survey of venture capital investment.

Hong Kong Venture Capital Association

4010 Jardine House, One Connaught Place, Central, Hong Kong
T: +852 2845 6100
F: +852 2526 2713
E: enquiry@hkvca.com.hk
www.hkvca.com.hk

The HKVCA was founded in 1987 to promote and protect the interests of, and provide a forum for, the venture capital industry in Hong Kong. It organizes meetings, conferences, and seminars, and conducts research studies.

  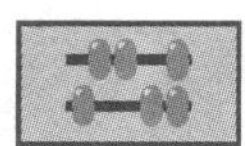      

Wealth Management

BOOKS

Behavioral Finance and Wealth Management: How to Build Optimal Portfolios that Account for Investor Biases

Michael M. Pompian
Wiley Finance Series
Hoboken, New Jersey: Wiley, 2006
317pp, ISBN: 978-0-471-74517-4

This is a comprehensive guide to irrational investor behavior, and how to build portfolios for individual investors that account for these behaviors. It focuses on improving decision-making by understanding behavioral finance research, examines an array of investor biases, and describes the impact of fear and greed in the markets, as well as good and bad investment decision-making.

Breaking Through: Building a World Class Wealth Management Business

John J. Bowen Jr., Patricia J. Abram, Jonathan Powell
San Martin, Calilfornia: CEG Worldwide, 2008
164pp, ISBN: 978-0-615-19928-3

This presents a comprehensive set of effective strategies for developing a wealth management business, with guidance on the opportunities available for financial advisers. It explains how to focus on the right affluent clients, and implement a consultative process, and explores techniques for acquiring assets and key clients, and developing useful strategic alliances.

Financial Planning and Wealth Management: An International Perspective

Louis Cheng, Tak Yan Leung, Yiu Hing Wong
New York: McGraw-Hill, 2008
520pp, ISBN: 978-0-07-124984-3

This international guide provides information and advice for those working in financial planning and wealth management. It assesses the latest developments and trends, and presents an implementable financial planning process, interviews with financial planners, and different approaches to investment management, as well as covering risk profiling and asset allocation strategies.

Global Private Banking and Wealth Management: The New Realities

David Maude
Wiley Finance Series
Chichester, UK: Wiley, 2006
346pp, ISBN: 978-0-470-85421-1

This is a comprehensive examination of the industry and the key challenges it is currently facing during a period of great change. It describes in detail the workings of the wealth management market, and the role of banks and other financial services, and covers issues such as the changing client profile, new products, pricing, and channels, competitor and business-model landscapes, and external challenges and opportunities.

Integrated Wealth Management: The New Direction for Portfolio Managers

Jean Brunel
London: Euromoney Books, 2002
335pp, ISBN: 978-1-85564-923-1

This is a thorough and authoritative examination of wealth management, which presents an integrated approach for helping portfolio managers become wealth managers. It focuses on the impact of investor psychology, maximizing tax efficiency, the implications of multiple asset locations, capital market opportunities and forecasting, strategic asset allocation, the importance of manager selection, and the multi-manager approach.

The Offshore Money Book: How to Move Assets Offshore for Privacy, Protection, and Tax Advantage

Arnold Cornez
Chicago, Illinois: Contemporary Books, 1998
280pp, ISBN: 978-0-8092-2880-5

This comprehensive and accessible resource on offshore tax havens offers practical guidance on using offshore investing as a method of asset protection. It details the practicalities of moving assets offshore, how to evaluate the best places to invest, and how to avoid offshore scams.

Private Wealth: Wealth Management in Practice

Stephen M. Horan (editor)
CFA Institute Investment Perspectives Series
Hoboken, New Jersey: Wiley, 2009
564pp, ISBN: 978-0-470-38113-7

This new collection presents the latest guidance and research on private wealth management issues, such as tax matters, lifecycle modeling, investment management for taxable private investors and the use of tax-deferred investment accounts, and after-tax performance measurement. It also presents a framework for various tax environments, and explores tax-efficient asset allocation and portfolio management techniques.

Structured Products in Wealth Management

Steffen Tolle, Boris Hutter, Patrik Rüthemann, Hanspeter Wohlwend
Wiley Finance Series
Singapore: Wiley, 2008
226pp, ISBN: 978-0-470-82330-9

This accessible guide to the use of structured products in private wealth management offers a detailed description of their emergence in the form of equity-linked derivatives, and their characteristics and practical applications. It describes how they can generate added value as part of an integrated investment process, their systematic use in portfolio management and optimization, and their overall use in achieving investment objectives.

Tax Havens Today: The Benefits and Pitfalls of Banking and Investing Offshore

Hoyt Barber
Hoboken, New Jersey: Wiley, 2007
324pp, ISBN: 978-0-470-05123-8

This is a practical guide to the effective placement of finances and investments in offshore tax havens, exploring the best investment strategies and the most common mistakes, for any type of investor. It describes 40 popular tax havens, and provides full contact details of the most important investment, banking, legal, and financial advisers, divided by tax haven or other jurisdiction, with a description of their areas of expertise.

Vault Career Guide to Private Wealth Management

John Ransom
Vault Career Library Series
New York: Vault, 2007
128pp, ISBN: 978-1-58131-448-9

This is a practical guide to finding a job or career in the private wealth management industry. It explains how the industry works, and the different job roles and career paths available, and covers the basics of equity and fixed income products, market and regulatory trends, and private wealth management at the both large and small firms.

Wealth: How the World's High-Net-Worth Grow, Sustain, and Manage Their Fortunes

Merrill Lynch, Cap Gemini
Mississauga, Ontario: Wiley, 2008
236pp, ISBN: 978-0-470-15303-1

This offers advice on wealth management based on the successful strategies and techniques used by high net worth individuals. Featuring interviews with prominent HNWI individuals and advisers, it analyzes how they acquired their wealth, how they manage it to attain high investment growth. It also presents new approaches to asset allocation and alternative investments, and emerging issues such as the role of philanthropy, and inter-generational wealth transfer.

Wealth Creation by Design: The Next Wave in Wealth Management for Financial Advisors

Goldman Sachs
Reinvented Wealth Manager Series
Hoboken, New Jersey: Wiley, 2009
320pp, ISBN: 978-0-470-28948-8

This resource for financial advisers assesses the main elements of investment and wealth management, and offers advice on how to increase value for clients and improve the effectiveness of their business. It explains prospecting, and dealing with conflicts of interest, and identifies the key challenges and opportunities open to wealth managers.

Wealth Management: A Concise Guide to Financial Planning and Investment Management for Wealthy Clients, 2nd ed

S. Timothy Kochis

Chicago, Illinois: CCH, 2006
320pp, ISBN: 978-0-8080-8949-0

This practical guide to personal wealth planning and investment management describes a wide range of strategies, and appropriate responses to decision-making issues, and examines emerging trends, such as alternative investment options. It is aimed at financial planners, accountants, lawyers, brokers, and portfolio managers serving high net worth individuals, who need assistance in effective planning and implementation.

Wealth Management: Private Banking, Investment Decisions, and Structured Financial Products

Dimitris N. Chorafas

Oxford, UK: Butterworth-Heinemann, 2006
376pp, ISBN: 978-0-7506-6855-2

This analyzes wealth management from a practical viewpoint, and examines structured products as suitable investments for retail and institutional investors. It looks at the real risks and returns of structured financial products offered by banks, relating them to the volatility of future value of an underlying, the uncertainty of future events, and the exposure of the product.

Wealth Management: The Financial Advisor's Guide to Investing and Managing Client Assets

Harold E. Evensky

Chicago, Illinois: McGraw-Hill, 1997
481pp, ISBN: 978-0-7863-0478-3

This provides applied guidance on wealth management for financial advisers, presenting a thorough overview of current investment theories, and a range of tools and techniques for effective financial planning. It also explores an optimal asset allocation policy that can be tailored to goals and constraints of different clients, and detailed reference material for further study.

Wealth Management in Any Market: Timeless Strategies for Building Financial Security

Bishara A. Bahbah

Hoboken, New Jersey: Wiley, 2009
300pp, ISBN: 978-0-470-40528-4

This provides accessible guidance on wealth management and financial security, which explains both the basic strategies involved, as well as more technical areas such as setting up an estate plan, managing debt, purchasing insurance, retirement planning, and employing tax-reduction techniques. It also examines how to protect assets and build wealth under different financial conditions, and how to select a wealth management team.

Wealth Management Planning: The UK Tax Principles

Malcolm James Finney

Chichester, UK: Wiley, 2008
588pp, ISBN: 978-0-470-72424-8

This presents a comprehensive summary of the UK tax rules affecting wealth management planning for UK domiciled and non-UK domiciled individuals. It describes the principles underpinning income tax, capital gains tax, and inheritance tax for financial planners, places UK tax rules in an international context, and explores topics such as the suitability of off shore financial centers, and the use of double-taxation agreements.

Wealth Management Teams

Steven Drozdeck, Lyn Fisher

Logan, Utah: Financial Forum Publishing, 2005
160pp, ISBN: 978-0-9745175-4-4

This is a practical investor guide to selecting and evaluating the best financial advisers and wealth management teams. It presents detailed case studies from a series of high-level financial industry teams that explore how they deliver superior levels of advice and service to their clients.

MAGAZINES

Private Wealth

Charter Financial Publishing Network
499 Broad Street, Shrewsbury, NJ 07702, USA
T: +1 732 450 8866
F: +1 732 450 8877
www.pw-mag.com

This bimonthly magazine is for professionals focused on meeting the financial, legal, and lifestyle demands of ultra-high-net-worth clients. It provides news and research on the target market, the competition, and the financial and legal strategies, and is structured around key topics such as investments, estate planning, insurance, wealth protection, lifestyle, business development, and philanthropy.

Professional Wealth Management

Financial Times
1 Southwark Bridge, London, SE1 9HL, UK
T: +44 (0) 20 7873 3000
www.pwmnet.com
ISSN: 1476-3001

This magazine is devoted to the growth in the use of third parties to distribute financial products to high-net-worth investors across Europe. It provides strategic advice and information to the key decision-makers at all levels of European distribution, and examines the new partnerships formed from banks and insurance companies contracting out the management of some of their core assets to external specialist asset management groups.

Wealth Management

Wealth Management Information Services
Buckingham Gate, London, SW1E 6LB, UK
T: +44 (0) 20 7674 0400
F: +44 (0) 20 7674 0404
ISSN: 1462-2807

This is a quarterly electronic magazine on all aspects of wealth management. It is an online publication laid out in a magazine format, that comes with virtual page turning.

Wealth Management

Cloughmore Media Group
Cunningham House, 130 Francis Street, Dublin 8, Ireland
T: +353 1 416 7800
F: +353 1 416 7899
www.businessandfinance.ie/publications/wealth.html

This quarterly magazine provides information and advice for the growing high-net-worth sector in Ireland. It offers news and analysis on Irish and international markets, and emerging markets, and the latest developments and trends in the investment and consumption markets.

Wealth Management Review

Sovereign Publications
32 Woodstock Grove, London, W12 8LE, UK
T: +44 (0) 20 7616 0800
F: +44 (0) 20 7724 1444
www.sovereign-publications.com/wealth-management.htm

This new monthly magazine provides news and information to the super-rich and professional intermediaries advising family groups and ultra-high-net-worth individuals. It covers wealth management opportunities, issues, planning, and implementation, and effective investment strategies, as well as the basics of acquiring, growing, protecting, and using wealth, and passing it on to others.

Wealth Manager

Summit Business Media
33–41 Newark Street, 2nd Floor, Hoboken, NJ 07030, USA
T: +1 201 526 1254
www.wealthmanagermag.com

This monthly magazine is a resource for investment advisers, brokers, and financial planners who manage assets for clients with high net worth. It offers guidance on investment strategies and opportunities, and news and analysis of relevant topics such as high-end investing, tax planning, practice management, legal compliance, and client relations.

Worth

Sandow Media
58 West 40th Street, 16th Floor, New York, NY 10018, USA
T: +1 212 665 6100
www.worth.com

This bimonthly magazine for high-net-worth individuals and their advisers reports on issues related to comprehensive wealth management, including investment opportunities, private banking and financial advisory services, business ownership and succession planning, and philanthropy and estate planning. It also offers features on advisers, investments/risk management, business/entrepreneurship, politics and policy, profiles, money and meaning, and cultural investments.

JOURNALS

Journal of Wealth Management

Institutional Investor
225 Park Avenue South, 8th Floor, New York, NY 10003, USA
T: +1 212 224 3800
F: +1 212 224 3197
www.iijournals.com/JPPM
ISSN: 1520-4154

 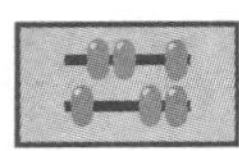      

This quarterly journal is dedicated to the practical analysis of financial tools and investment strategies for investment advisers, to best service and manage high-net-worth, taxable portfolios. It covers topics such as behavioral finance, investment policy formation, investment policy execution, tax-aware investing, interdisciplinary issues, and performance measurement, as well as new investment vehicles such as hedge funds and alternatives.

Review of Income and Wealth

Wiley
c/o Faculty of Economics and Business, University of Groningen, PO Box 800, 9700 AV Groningen, The Netherlands
T: +31 50 363 8455
F: +31 50 363 8454
www.wiley.com/bw/journal.asp?ref=0034-6586
ISSN: 0034-6586

This quarterly journal aims to advance the understanding of the definition, measurement, and interpretation of national income, wealth and distribution. It covers national and social accounting, systems of economic, financial, and social statistics, and comparisons of income, wealth, inequality, poverty, well-being, and productivity.

INTERNET

TheWealthNet

www.thewealthnet.com

This is an online resource for wealth management professionals. It provides industry information, news on the latest changes and developments, such as people moves, new product launches, and M&A activity, commentary and analysis, profiles of the leading players in the market, reviews of books and reports, an industry directory, and an events calendar that features major wealth management events.

Wealth Briefing

www.wealthbriefing.com

This provides online news and analysis for wealth managers, with daily updates, weekly briefings, and in-depth features, as well as a useful search facility that contains listing of news and features, articles by professional lawyers, accountants and consultants, conferences, training and exhibitions, organizations involved in wealth management, and people moves.

ORGANIZATIONS

Europe

Association of International Wealth Management

Feldstrasse 80, 8180 Bulach, Switzerland
T: +41 44 872 35 40
F: +41 44 872 35 32
E: info@aiwm.org
www.aiwm.org

AIWM is a global, non-profit association for wealth managers, portfolio managers, investment advisers, asset managers, and trust and estate practitioners. It promotes global education in the wealth management industry, provides a set of standards for the qualification of private banking professionals, and awards the private banking designation Certified International Wealth Manager Diploma.

Association of Private Client Investment Managers and Stockbrokers

Chair: David Bennett
22 City Road, Finsbury Square, London, EC1Y 2AJ, UK
T: +44 (0) 20 7448 7100
F: +44 (0) 20 7638 4636
E: info@apcims.co.uk
www.apcims.co.uk

APCIMS is a trade association of firms who act for the private investor. Its objectives include the advancement of the interests of members across the financial services community, communicating industry changes to members, leading the debate on the development of the European securities industry, and providing information and assistance to members across a wide range of regulatory, market, and business issues.

The International Money Management Institute

26 York Street, London, W1U 6PZ, UK
T: +44 (0) 20 7553 9742
intlmmi.org

IMMI is a non-profit association that facilitates the exchange of knowledge among a global network of industry executives, and promotes the use of managed solutions in a consultative environment. It serves as a forum for wealth management organizations to discuss issues of product and service development, and distribution globally, and works to identify and address operational and regulatory barriers to market entry and distribution.

USA

The Money Management Institute

Chair: Brian Jacobs
1140 Connecticut Avenue, NW Suite 1040, Washington, DC 20036-4001, USA
T: +1 202 822 4949
F: +1 202 822 5188
www.moneyinstitute.com

MMI is a national organization for the managed solutions industry, representing portfolio manager firms and sponsors of investment consulting programs. It serves as a forum for the industry's leaders, and is a leading advocate on regulatory and legislative issues. It also educates prospective investors about the benefits of financial consulting/managed solution services, and promotes the professionalism of financial consultants who work with managed solutions.

Wealth Management Institute

Chair: Gary A. Ferraro
1200 North Federal Highway, Suite 200, Boca Raton, Florida 33432, USA
T: +1 561 210 8504
F: +1 561 447 8724
E: info@w-m-i.org
www.w-m-i.org

This professional member and trade association offers information, education, professional resources, and expert guidance on domestic and international financial products and services for the wealth management industry. It also promotes and supports the industry in the provision of legal and ethical access to all wealth management and personal finance products, services, and subject matters for individuals and companies worldwide.

International

International Association for Research in Income and Wealth

Chair: Andrea Brandolini
IARIW Executive Director, 111 Sparks Street, Suite 500, Ottawa, Ontario K1P 5B5, Canada
T: +1 613 233 8891
F: +1 613 233 8250
E: info@iariw.org
www.iariw.org

This association is dedicated to the furthering of research on national and economic and social accounting, and focuses on international comparisons of income and wealth, the use of economic and social accounting for budgeting and policy analysis in different countries, and the experiences of different countries in the development of economic and social accounting systems.

Wealth Management Institute

Chair: Ng Kok Song
60B Orchard Road, #06–18 Tower 2, The Atrium@Orchard, Singapore 238891, Singapore
T: +65 6828 6988
F: +65 6821 1155
E: mwm@smu.edu.sg
www.wmi.com.sg

WMI is an educational institution dedicated to the wealth management industry in Asia. It caters for the rising demand for professional wealth management services, such as fund management and private banking, in the region, by providing education and research on institutional fund management, and financial and tax planning, and provides an opportunity for networking.

QUOTATIONS

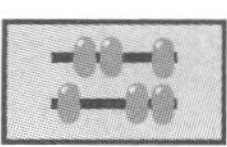

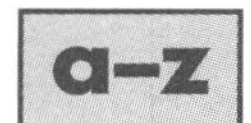

Quotations

The **Quotations** section includes over 2,000 quotations on finance, management, leadership, money, and business in general. It is indexed by both author and theme, and provides up-to-date quotations on subjects ranging from **Accounting** and **Change** to **Power** and **Wealth**.

The entries can be viewed as perfect to enliven meetings, presentations, or conversation, and include contributions from the likes of **W. W. Rostow**, **Milton Friedman**, **Peter F. Drucker**, and **Donald J. Trump**.

The Quotations section includes:

- **Index** of people quoted, including **biographical information**
- **Full quotation** with source and date
- **Thematic headings** enabling quick identification of relevance by theme

Contents

Ability

If you work hard enough, the maxim goes, you can do anything. This is one of those notions that is so stupid it has to embody a deeply held belief. If you work hard enough, you can be a poet ... If you work hard enough, you can become a brain surgeon, a model, the president. Obviously no one believes those things ... Meritocracy resists the fact of talent, because talent is not merited. Beauty, artistic ability, athletic gifts, big brains: these are all just things you're born with, however much you may be able to develop what you've been given. Talent is undemocratic. **William Deresiewicz**. *American Scholar* blog (August 2012)

If you can run one business well, you can run any business well. **Sir Richard Branson**. *New York Times* (2000)

I found that there were these incredibly great people at doing certain things, and you couldn't replace one of these people with 50 average people. They could just do stuff that no number of average people could do. **Steve Jobs**. Quoted in "Steve's Two Jobs," *Time* (Michael Krantz, October 18, 1999)

A human being should be able to change a diaper, plan an invasion, butcher a hog, conn a ship, design a building, write a sonnet, balance accounts, build a wall, set a bone, comfort the dying, take orders, give orders, cooperate, act alone, solve equations, analyse a new problem, pitch manure, program a computer, cook a tasty meal, fight efficiently, die gallantly. Specialization is for insects. **Robert A. Heinlein**. *Time Enough for Love* (1973)

Competence, like truth, beauty, and contact lenses, is in the eye of the beholder. **Laurence J. Peter**. *The Peter Principle: Why Things Always Go Wrong* (cowritten with Raymond Hull, 1969)

Ability and achievement are *bona fides* no one dares question, no matter how unconventional the man who presents them. **J. Paul Getty**. *How to Be Rich* (1965)

Intelligence is quickness to apprehend as distinct from ability which is capacity to act wisely on the thing apprehended. **Alfred North Whitehead**. *Dialogues* (1954)

Great ability develops and reveals itself increasingly with every new assignment. **Baltasar Gracián**. *The Oracle* (1647)

Behind an able man there are always other able men. **Anonymous**. Chinese proverb

Ability will never catch up with the demand for it. **Malcolm S. Forbes**. Attributed

Accounting

You have wondered, perhaps, why all real accountants wear hats? They are today's cowboys. As will you be. Riding the American range. Riding herd on the unending torrent of financial data. The eddies, cataracts, arranged variations, fractious minutiae. You order the data, shepherd it, direct its flow, lead it where it's needed ... You deal in facts, gentlemen, for which there has been a market since man first crept from the primeval slurry. **David Foster Wallace**. *The Pale King* (2011)

The older I get, the more interesting I find lawyers and accountants. **Alex James**. *Independent (London)* (April 21, 2010)

There are 300,000 accountants in Britain, which means that, as with rats, you're never less than a few feet from one. **Jolyon Jenkins**. "A brief history of double-entry book-keeping," BBC radio (March 8, 2010)

The bonus mania which caused the recession could never have happened without corrupted accounting rules. This is the great secret of the credit crunch—the one the world's financial writers have missed. **Nicholas Jones**. *Independent (London)* (July 22, 2009)

They are a special breed-like normal accountants, but without the soppy sentimentality. These are the oncologists of market capitalism. **Sean O'Grady**. *Independent (London)* (July 3, 2009)

What's the difference between Enron and Fannie Mae? The guys at Enron have been convicted. **Anonymous**. Comparing accounting practices at Fannie Mae with those of the collapsed energy giant Enron. *Wall Street Journal* (June 14, 2006)

Accountants are the witch-doctors of the modern world and willing to turn their hands to any kind of magic. **Sir Charles Eustace Harman**. Speech (February 1964)

One can't say that figures lie. But figures, as used in financial arguments, seem to have the bad habit of expressing a small part of the truth forcibly, and neglecting the other part, as do some people we know. **Fred Schwed**. *Where Are the Customers' Yachts?* (1940)

The system of book-keeping by double entry is, perhaps, the most beautiful one in the wide domain of literature or science. Were it less common, it would be the admiration of the learned world. **Edwin T. Freedley**. *A Practical Treatise on Business* (1853)

The pen is mightier than the sword, but no match for the accountant. **Jonathan Glancey**. Attributed

It sounds extraordinary, but it's a fact that balance sheets can make fascinating reading. **Mary, Lady Archer**. Attributed

Accuracy

If you don't get it right, what's the point? **Michael Cimino**. Kodak advertisement. Quoted in *Variety* (July 23, 1980)

It's time that financial types developed a greater tolerance for imprecision, because that's the way the world is. **John C. Burton**. *Time* (January 24, 1977)

Nothing is more central to an organization's effectiveness than its ability to transmit accurate, relevant, understandable information among its members. **Saul W. Gellerman**. *The Management of Human Resources* (1976)

Accuracy is to a newspaper what virtue is to a lady, but a newspaper can always print a retraction. **Adlai E. Stevenson**. Quoted in *The Stevenson Wit* (Bill Adler, 1966)

A little inaccuracy sometimes saves tons of explanation. **Saki (H. H. Munro)**. "Clovis on the Alleged Romance of Business," *The Square Egg* (1924)

I do not mind lying, but I hate inaccuracy. **Samuel Butler**. "Truth and Convenience," *Notebooks* (H. Festing-Jones, ed, 1912)

It is the nature of greatness not to be exact. **Edmund Burke**. Speech. "On American Taxation" (1774)

In all pointed sentences, some degree of accuracy must be sacrificed to conciseness. **Samuel Johnson**. "The Bravery of the English Common Soldier," *The British Magazine* (1760)

Achievement

That's what building a body of work is all about. It's about the daily labor, the many individual acts, the choices large and small that add up over time, over a lifetime to a lasting legacy. It's about not being satisfied with the latest achievement, the latest gold star, because the one thing I know about a body of work is that it's never finished. It's cumulative. It deepens and expands with each day you give your best. You may have setbacks and you may have failures, but you're not done. **Barack Obama**. Commencement address, Arizona State University (May 13, 2009)

It is necessary to be slightly under-employed if you want to do something significant. **James D. Watson**. Quoted in *Is There A Book In You?* (Alison Baverstock, 2006)

What the mind can believe, you can achieve. **Lorraine Moller**. Quoted in *Running with the Legends* (Michael Sandrock, 1996)

But what those critics don't know is that these same assets that excite me in the chase often, once they are acquired, leave me bored. **Donald J. Trump**. *Trump: Surviving at the Top* (cowritten with Charles Leerhsen, 1990)

If you do it right 51% of the time you will end up a hero. **Alfred P. Sloan**. Quoted in *Corporate Cultures* (Deal and Kennedy, 1982)

Well, we knocked the bastard off. **Sir Edmund Hillary**. Referring to his ascent of Everest. Press comment (1953)

Man grows beyond his work, walks up the stairs of his concepts, emerges ahead of his accomplishment. **John Steinbeck**. *The Grapes of Wrath* (1939)

Happiness ... lies in the joy of achievement, in the thrill of creative effort. The joy and moral stimulation of work no longer must be forgotten in the mad chase of evanescent profits. **Franklin D. Roosevelt**. Presidential inaugural address (March 4, 1933)

They have not any difficulties on the way up because they fly, but they have many when they reach the summit. **Niccolò Machiavelli**. *The Prince* (1513)

Action

Idleness is not just a vacation, an indulgence, or a vice; it is as indispensable to the brain as vitamin D is to the body, and deprived of it we suffer a mental affliction as disfiguring as rickets. The space and quiet that idleness provides is a necessary condition for standing back from life and seeing it whole, for making unexpected connections and waiting for the wild summer lightning strikes of inspiration—it is, paradoxically, necessary to getting any work done. **Tim Kreider**. *New York Times* (June 30, 2012)

In some situations, doing nothing—forever—is the right response ... Sometimes, not trying to fix something is precisely what's needed to fix it. **Peter Bregman**. *Harvard Business Review* blog (December 5, 2011)

Do what you can, where you are, with what you have. **Theodore Roosevelt**. Quoted in *The Military Quotation Book, Revised and Expanded* (James Charlton, 2002)

One's objective should be to get it right, get it quick, get it out, and get it over ... your problem won't improve with age. **Warren Buffett**. "Interview with Warren Buffett," *Harvard Business Review* (Norman Augustine, November–December 1995)

In politics if you want anything said, ask a man. If you want anything done, ask a woman. **Margaret, Baroness Thatcher**. Quoted in *People* (September 15, 1975)

The world can only be grasped by action, not by contemplation. The hand is the cutting edge of man. **Jacob Bronowski**. *The Ascent of Man* (1973)

Never confuse movement with action. **Ernest Hemingway**. Quoted in *Papa Hemingway* (A. E. Hotchner, 1966)

Action is at bottom a swinging and flailing of the arms to regain one's balance and keep afloat. **Eric Hoffer**. *The Passionate State of Mind* (1955)

I acted, and my action made me wise. **Thom Gunn**. "Incident on a Journey," *Fighting Terms* (1954)

Action springs not from thought, but from a readiness for responsibility. **Dietrich Bonhoeffer**. *Letters and Papers from Prison* (1953)

A man of action forced into a state of thought is unhappy until he can get out of it. **John Galsworthy**. *Maid in Waiting* (1932)

Freedom from activity is never achieved by abstaining from action. **Bhagavad Gita**. 3:4 (300? BC)

Chie Wen Tzu used to think thrice before acting. The Master hearing of it said, Twice is quite enough. **Confucius**. *Analects* (500? BC)

When fog prevents a small-boat sailor from seeing the buoy marking the course he wants, he turns his boat rapidly in small circles, knowing that the waves he makes will rock the buoy in the vicinity. Then he stops, listens and repeats the procedure until he hears the buoy clang. By making waves, he finds where his course lies. Often the price of finding these guides is a willingness to take a few risks, to "make a few waves." **Richard Armstrong**. Attributed

Follow effective action with quiet reflection. From the quiet reflection will come even more effective action. **Peter F. Drucker**. Attributed

There are people who make things happen, those who watch what happens, and those who wonder what happened. **Anonymous**.

Adversity

You don't ever want a crisis to go to waste: it's an opportunity to do important things that you would otherwise avoid. **Emanuel Rahm**. Urging radical reform of the financial system after the fall of Lehman Brothers. Quoted in *Epic Journey: The 2008 Elections and American Politics* (James W. Ceaser, 2009)

Dress your best on your execution day. Be extremely courteous to your assistant when you lose money. Try not to blame others for your fate, even if they deserve blame. Never exhibit any self-pity. Do not complain. **Nassim Nicholas Taleb**. On how to behave in adversity. *Fooled by Randomness* (2004)

In times like these, it helps to recall that there have always been times like these. **Paul Harvey**. Quoted in *A Business Tale* (Marianne M. Jennings, 2003)

Even when the universe made it quite clear to me that I was mistaken in my certainties ... I did not break. The shattering of my sureties did not shatter me. **Lucille Clifton**. Quoted in *The Black Woman's Gumbo Ya-Ya* (Terri L. Jewell, 1993)

Sometimes you're the bug, sometimes you're the windshield. **Mark Knopfler**. *The Bug* (1991)

Any idiot can face a crisis; it is this day-to-day living that wears you out. **Anton Chekhov**. Quoted in *Business Babble: A Cynic's Dictionary of Corporate Jargon* (David Olive, 1991)

I believe that if ever I had to practice cannibalism, I might manage if there were enough tarragon around. **James Beard**. Quoted in obituary, *New York Times* (January 23, 1985)

If you warn 100 men of possible forthcoming bad news, 80 will immediately dislike you. And if you are so unfortunate to be right, the other 20 will as well. **Anthony Gaubis**. Quoted in *The Wit and Wisdom of Wall Street* (Bill Adler, 1985)

Life is truly known only to those who suffer, lose, endure adversity, and stumble from defeat to defeat. **Ryszard Kapuściński**. "A Warsaw Diary," *Granta* (1985)

Hope is the power of being cheerful in circumstances which we know to be desperate. **G. K. Chesterton**. *Heretics* (1905)

There is no education like adversity. **Benjamin Disraeli (Earl of Beaconsfield)**. *Endymion* (1880), ch. 61

Adversity is sometimes hard upon a man; but for one man who can stand prosperity, there are a hundred that will stand adversity. **Thomas Carlyle**. "The Hero As Man of Letters," *On Heroes, Hero-Worship, and the Heroic in History* (1841)

Prosperity is a great teacher; adversity is a greater. **William Hazlitt**. "On the Conversation of Cards," *Essays* (1819)

He knows not his own strength who has not met adversity. **Ben Jonson**. "Explorata," *Timber, or Discoveries* (1640)

Advertising

Society once did a deal accepting advertising because it seemed occasionally useful and interesting and because it paid for lots of journalism and entertainment. It's not necessarily going to pay for those things for much longer, so we might start questioning whether we want to live in a Blade Runner world brought to us by Cillit Bang. **Sir Howard Davies**. *Observer (London)* (January 2, 2011)

Over the next few years we're going to be interrupted by advertising like never before. Video screens are getting so cheap and disposable that they'll be plastered everywhere we go. And they'll have enough intelligence and connectivity that they'll see our faces, do a quick search on Facebook to find out who we are and direct a message at us based on our purchasing history. At least, that'll be the idea. It probably won't work very well and when it does work it'll probably drive us mad. **Russell Davies**. *Observer (London)* (January 2, 2011)

The Mass Audience is made up of individuals, and good advertising is written always from one person to another. When it is aimed at millions it rarely moves anyone. **Fairfax Cone**. Quoted in *The Art and Science of Marketing* (Grahame Robert Dowling, 2004)

Whatever happens, you get your pet back. **Anonymous**. Slogan of a Manhattan firm founded by two brothers, one a vet, the other a taxidermist. Quoted in *Architect's Journal* (July 13, 2000)

Tell me quick and tell me true, what your product's going to do, or else, my love, to hell with you. **Anonymous**. Quoted in *Marketing* (July 2000)

Don't focus on the mink, but what's in it. **Jane Trahey**. Speaking about her famous advertising campaign for Blackglama fur. Quoted in the *New York Times* (2000)

I know half the money I spend on advertising is wasted, but I can never find out which half. **John Wanamaker**. Quoted in "How to Acquire Customers on the Web," *Harvard Business Review* (Donna L. Hoffman and Thomas P. Novak, 2000)

Good advertising can make people buy your product even if it sucks ... A dollar spent on brainwashing is more cost-effective than a dollar spent on product improvement. **Scott Adams**. *The Dilbert Principle* (1996)

Advertising is the ability to sense, interpret ... to put the very heart throbs of a business into type, paper, and ink. **Leo Burnett**. Quoted in *Leo Burnett: Star Reacher* (Joan Kufrin, 1995)

Society drives people crazy with lust and calls it advertising. **John Lahr**. *Guardian (London)* (August 1989)

When you have nothing to say, sing it. **David Ogilvy**. *Ogilvy on Advertising* (1983)

Time spent in the advertising business seems to create a permanent deformity like the Chinese habit of foot-binding. **Dean Acheson**. Quoted in *Among Friends* (David S. McLellan and David C. Acheson, 1980)

From Those Wonderful Folks Who Gave You Pearl Harbor. **Jerry Della Femina**. Book title, originally suggested as an advertising slogan for Panasonic Corporation. *From Those Wonderful Folks Who Gave You Pearl Harbor* (1970)

Of course advertising creates wants. Of course it makes people discontented, dissatisfied. Satisfaction with things as they are would defeat the American Dream. **Bernice Fitz-Gibbon**. *Macy's, Gimbels and Me* (1967)

What do you want from me? Fine writing? Or would you like to see the goddam sales curve stop going down and start going up? **Rosser Reeves**. Interview (1965)

What you say in advertising is more important than how you say it. **David Ogilvy**. *Confessions of an Advertising Man* (1963)

Ninety percent of advertising doesn't sell much of anything. **David Ogilvy**. *Confessions of an Advertising Man* (1963)

Advertising is only evil when it advertises evil things. **David Ogilvy**. *Confessions of an Advertising Man* (1963)

Never stop testing, and your advertising will never stop improving. **David Ogilvy**. *Confessions of an Advertising Man* (1963)

A desirable advertisement will be reasonable, but never dull ... original, but never self-conscious ... imaginative, but never misleading. **Fairfax Cone**. *Christian Science Monitor* (1963)

Until the rise of American advertising, it never occurred to anyone anywhere in the world that the teenager was a captive in a hostile world of adults. **Gore Vidal**. *Rocking the Boat* (1962)

It is pretty obvious that the debasement of the human mind caused by a constant flow of fraudulent advertising is not a trivial thing. There is more than one way to conquer a country. **Raymond Chandler**. Quoted in *Raymond Chandler Speaking* (Dorothy Gardiner and Katherine S. Walker, eds, 1962)

We read advertisements ... to discover and enlarge our desires. **Daniel J. Boorstin**. *The Image* (1961)

The modern corporation must manufacture not only goods but the desire for the goods it manufactures. **J. K. Galbraith**. *The Affluent Society* (1958), ch. 20

It is not necessary to advertise food to hungry people, fuel to cold people, or houses to the homeless. **J. K. Galbraith**. *American Capitalism* (1956)

Advertising is the very essence of democracy. **Bruce Barton**. *Reader's Digest* (1955)

An advertising agency is 85% confusion and 15% commission. **Fred Allen**. *Treadmill to Oblivion* (1954)

Don't sell the steak; sell the sizzle. It is the sizzle that sells the steak and not the cow, although the cow is, of course, mighty important. **Elmer Wheeler**. *Principles of Salesmanship* (1936?), no. 1

Advertising may be described as the science of arresting human intelligence long enough to get money from it. **Stephen Leacock**. *The Perfect Salesman* (1924)

It is far easier to write ten passably effective sonnets, good enough to take in the not too enquiring critic, than one effective advertisement that will take in a few thousand of the uncritical buying public. **Aldous Huxley**. *On the Margin* (1923)

Make a Fair Product for a Fair Price, then Tell the World. **William Wrigley, Jr.** "Make a Fair Product for a Fair Price, then Tell the World," *Illustrated World* (S. J. Duncan-Clark, March 1922)

The business that considers itself immune to the necessity for advertising sooner or later finds itself immune to business. **Derby Brown**. Attributed

Advertising is the greatest art form of the twentieth century. **Marshall McLuhan**. Attributed

I've written books on advertising—cheque books. **Sir Alan, Lord Sugar**. *The Apprentice (UK)*, BBC TV

Ambition

A simple problem of arithmetic: there are far more ambitions than there are grand destinies available. **Alain de Botton**. *Twitter (alaindebotton)* (December 6, 2010)

You can't just have ambition. You must have a *rage* to succeed. You must have a mad passion for success. **Larry Thompson**. Advice to would-be movie stars. Quoted in the *Independent (London)* (June 23, 2009)

Focusing your life solely on making a buck shows a certain poverty of ambition. It asks too little of yourself ... Because it's only when you hitch your wagon to something larger than yourself that you realize your true potential. **Barack Obama**. Commencement address, Knox College, Illinois (June 4, 2005)

When you reach for the stars, you may not quite get one, but you won't come up with a handful of mud either. **Leo Burnett**. Quoted in *Reader's Digest* (January 1985)

Ambition if it feeds at all, does so on the ambition of others. **Susan Sontag**. *The Benefactor* (1963), ch. 1

At the age of six I wanted to be a cook. At seven I wanted to be Napoleon. And my ambition has been growing steadily ever since. **Salvador Dali**. *The Secret Life of Salvador Dali* (1948)

If ambition doesn't hurt you, you haven't got it. **Kathleen Norris**. *Hands Full of Living* (1931)

The world continues to offer glittering prizes to those who have stout hearts and sharp swords. **Frederick E. Smith (Earl of Birkenhead)**. Rectorial address (November 7, 1923)

The man who starts out simply with the idea of getting rich won't succeed, you must have a larger ambition. **John D. Rockefeller**. *Random Reminiscenses of Men and Events* (1909)

Man's restlessness makes him strive. **Johann Wolfgang von Goethe**. *Faust* (1832), Part 2

Ambition often puts men upon doing the meanest offices; so climbing is performed in the same posture with creeping. **Jonathan Swift**. *Thoughts on Various Subjects* (1711)

To him that will, ways are not wanting. **George Herbert**. *Jacula Prudentum* (1651)

All my life, I've always wanted to be somebody, but I see now I should have been more specific. **Jane Wagner**. Comedy sketch written for Lily Tomlin

Attitude

Every organisation and every partnership should be carefully balanced to include both optimists and pessimists. A marriage also needs both ... it's good to have an optimist to come up with endless wild schemes for picnics and outings and a pessimist to squash the maddest ones and temper the rest with paracetamol and umbrellas. Businesses need both even more to have just the right mix of daring and caution. Diversity of optimists and pessimists is the most important sort there is and should be actively sought at board level and every level below. Corporate pessimists should be de-stigmatised and beckoned out of the closet. **Lucy Kellaway**. *Financial Times (London)* (July 3, 2011)

Optimism requires a touch of arrogance. **Steven Pinker**. *The Better Angels of Our Nature* (2011)

Care—about your customers, about your employees, about your brand—with everything you've got. **Gary Vaynerchuk**. *The Thank You Economy* (2011)

Without the right attitude, a business with everything going for it will fail. **Robert Heller**. Referring to research into company growth carried out by consulting firm Binder Hamlyn. *Goldfinger* (1998)

Your attitude determines your altitude. **Stephen Covey**. Quoted in *Woodbury Reports Archives* (October 1995)

Empty your mind, be formless, shapeless—like water. Now you put water into a cup, it becomes the cup. You put water into a bottle, it becomes the bottle. You put it in a teapot, it becomes the teapot. Now water can flow or it can crash! Be water my friend. **Bruce Lee**. Quoted in *Bruce Lee: Fighting Spirit* (Bruce Thomas, 1994)

If you can't change your fate change your attitude. **Amy Tan**. *The Joy Luck Club* (1989)

A professional is a man who can do his job when he doesn't feel like it. An amateur is a man who can't do his work when he does feel like it. **James Agate**. Diary (July 19, 1945)

You cannot control what happens to you, but you can control your attitude toward what happens to you, and in that, you will be mastering change rather than allowing it to master you. **Brian Tracy**. Attributed

Attitudes are more important than facts. **Karl Augustus Menninger**. Attributed

Banking

In Britain, we need to come up with a new word for this type of dysfunctional capitalism—where banks neither lend nor pay their way in taxes, yet retain a stranglehold on policy-making. We could try bankocracy: ruled by the banks, for the banks. **Aditya Chakrabortty**. *Guardian (London)* (December 12, 2011)

We were at the stage where in a very short period of time, one of the world's biggest banks would have to shut the door and switch off the electricity. **Alistair Darling**. On the near-collapse of Royal Bank of Scotland in October 2008. Interview, *Independent (London)* (March 18, 2011)

In a Bloomberg poll, 88% of respondents said that Wall Street bonuses should either be banned outright or taxed at 50%. Just 7% said they should remain an incentive. To put that 7% figure in perspective, 6% of Americans believe the moon landings were a hoax; 7% believe Elvis lives; 24% believe that Barack Obama is a secret Muslim; 41% believe in ESP; and 48% believe in creationism. Americans will believe anything, it seems—except the idea that incentivizing bankers at systemically important institutions to take big risks makes any sense at all. **Felix Salmon**. "Wall Street Bonus Datapoint of the Day," Reuters blog (December 13, 2010)

People want to say: look at those profligate governments, spending all that money. We've got to restore fiscal sanity. But it wasn't fiscal insanity that got us here. It was private-sector leverage and the insanity of banking that brought us to this point. So the bankers put it on the state, and the state turned around it put it on the taxpayer. It's the biggest bait-and-switch in human history. **Mark Blyth**. Interview on *Radio Open Source* blog (December 1, 2010)

Of all the many ways of organizing banking, the worst is the one we have today. Change is, I believe, inevitable. The question is only whether we can think our way through to a better outcome before the next generation is damaged by a future and bigger crisis. **Mervyn King**. Speech, New York (October 25, 2010)

No one ever felt sorry for a banker. **Dominic Lawson**. *Independent (London)* (August 3, 2010)

There are remuneration packages that will no longer be tolerated because they bear no relation to merit. That those who create jobs and wealth may earn a lot of money is not shocking. But that those who contribute to destroying jobs and wealth also earn a lot of money is morally indefensible. **Nicolas Sarkozy**. On bonuses paid to bankers. Address to the World Economic Forum (January 27, 2010)

It has been a masterful fight-back by the big banks. We the paying public can't do anything much except admit defeat and settle back for the next set of bills. In the meantime, perhaps, we should try and think of a name for the new economic system, which certainly isn't capitalism ... The most accurate term would probably be "bankocracy." **John Lanchester**. *London Review of Books* (November 5, 2009)

Think of the indispensable contribution bankers will make to Britain's recovery, on one condition: that they are allowed to become indecently rich. It is a small price to pay. **Bruce Anderson**. *Independent (London)* (October 26, 2009)

Politicians and policymakers became victims of a sort of Stockholm syndrome. Having been taken hostage by the bankers, they began to identify with their interests. **Ruth Sunderland**. On the lead-up to the financial crisis of 2008–09. *Observer (London)* (October 4, 2009)

Never in the field of financial endeavour has so much money been owed by so few to so many. **Mervyn King**. Referring to the British government's bank bail-out in the wake of the financial crisis of 2008–09. Speech to Edinburgh business leaders (October 2009)

It would be like Rome selling the Vatican to the Japanese to make it a hotel, and hiring the Pope as a bellboy. **Craig Warner**. On the prospect of the US government allowing Lehman Brothers investment bank to collapse. *The Last Days of Lehman Brothers*, BBC TV (September 9, 2009)

If you talk to 100 people, 102 will tell you they hate bankers. **Craig Warner**. *The Last Days of Lehman Brothers*, BBC TV (September 9, 2009)

No bank should be allowed to become so big that it can blackmail governments. **Angela Merkel**. Quoted in the *Financial Times (London)* (August 31, 2009)

Bonuses are back—and we're worth it. **Anonymous**. Comment by an anonymous banker. Quoted in *Grazia (London)* (August 2009)

They took bonuses for going bust, bonuses for getting bailed out, and bonuses for getting out of bed. They can do what they want because the government agrees that they are too big to fail. They are beyond the laws of God, man and gravity. **Simon Carr**. On bankers. *Independent (London)* (July 9, 2009)

The world's most powerful investment bank is a great vampire squid wrapped around the face of humanity, relentlessly jamming its blood funnel into anything that smells like money. **Matt Taibbi**. On Goldman Sachs. *Rolling Stone (New York)* (July 2009)

The Bank finds itself in a position rather like that of a church whose congregation attends weddings and burials but ignores the sermons in between. Warnings are unlikely to be effective when people are being asked to change behaviour which seems to them highly profitable. **Mervyn King**. On the Bank of England's lack of regulatory powers. Speech, Mansion House, City of London (June 17, 2009)

Sir Fred has become the epitome of the bankers who collectively occupy a place in public opinion significantly lower than cannibalistic paedophile global-warming deniers. **Boris Johnson**. On Sir Fred Goodwin, former chief executive of RBS. *Daily Telegraph (London)* (March 3, 2009)

The problem with the bank managers was not that they were malevolent but that they were mediocre. **Christopher Caldwell**. On the banking crisis of 2008. *Financial Times (London)* (February 13, 2009)

This is like people who hold up banks getting paid to stop holding up banks. It isn't good policy. **Peter Morici**. On the large "retention awards" given to executives of failed financial services companies. Quoted in the *Huffington Post* blog (February 11, 2009)

Please do not call it a bonus. It is not a bonus. It is an award. **James P. Gorman**. Instructing colleagues on how to discuss their "retention awards," given after the company was bailed out with $60 million of public money. Quoted in the *Huffington Post* blog (February 11, 2009)

You can blame it on me and close the book, but it doesn't come close to explaining what happened. **Sir Fred Goodwin**. On the failure of RBS. Speaking before the Treasury Select Committee (February 10, 2009)

You have to eventually nationalize US banks, you have to take the problem by the horns. In my view actually most of the US banking system is insolvent. **Nouriel Roubini**. Interview on Bloomberg TV (January 29, 2009)

Socialism for rich bankers and capitalism for everyone else. **Robert Reich**. On the Paulson bank bail-out scheme. Quoted in the *Guardian (London)* (January 21, 2009)

If I were a banker with RBS or Barclays or Lloyds, I would do exactly what they have done. Having made rotten business decisions in the past and now been offered limitless riches to cover them, I would take the money and say thank you. **Sir Simon Jenkins**. On the British government's attempts to influence the lending policy of the major banks in the wake of the credit crunch. *Guardian (London)* (January 21, 2009)

His obsession with bankers has become that of an infatuated teenager. He loves them and loathes them. They taunt and tease him, and he pouts and begs and cries and loses his temper. His body craves them, but each day finds him furiously beating their chests with his fists. They have their way with him and walk away. **Sir Simon Jenkins**. On Gordon Brown's attempts to influence the lending policy of the major banks in the wake of the credit crunch. *Guardian (London)* (January 21, 2009)

All banks are insolvent all of the time. Their liabilities exceed their assets ... If all banks are trading insolvently then the world economy is based on a hallucination, a mass deception, a general agreement to ignore reality. **Simon Carr**. *Independent (London)* (January 12, 2009)

Bankers were scapegoats for the whole Reagan–Thatcher era, which exalted finance and humbled industry, and which had allowed the fruits of progress to accrue disproportionately to the rich and super-rich. **Robert Skidelsky**. *Keynes—The Return of the Master* (2009)

If you were alive, they would give you a loan. Actually, I think if you were dead, they would still give you a loan. **Steven M. Knoebel**. On lax lending at the Washington Mutual Bank, which went into receivership in September 2008 (December 29, 2008)

They took 50 sheriffs off the beat at a time when lending was becoming the Wild West. **Roy Cooper**. On the decision to block state governments from using consumer protection laws to control predatory subprime lending. Quoted in the *New York Times* (December 20, 2008)

A bank is a bank and if the security of its depositors is not its main concern, it should be required to adopt another name. Members of the public are entitled to take this for granted. **Ronald Grierson**. Letter, *Financial Times (London)* (December 5, 2008)

This is not nationalization. **Geir Haarde**. On nationalizing the country's leading banks. Quoted in the *London Review of Books* (November 20, 2008)

Less of a negotiation, more of a drive-by shooting. **Sir Fred Goodwin**. On the UK government's forced recapitalization of the banking system. Quoted in the *Evening Standard (London)* (October 15, 2008)

Not since the First World War has our banking system been so close to collapse. The past few weeks have been somewhat too exciting ... So let me extend an invitation to the banking industry to join me in promoting the idea that a little more boredom would be no bad thing. The long march to boredom and stability starts tonight. **Mervyn King**. Speech (October 2008)

You can't overestimate what happens when you encourage regulators to believe that the goal of regulation is not to regulate. **Joseph Stiglitz**. Quoted in the *International Herald Tribune (Paris)* (September 20, 2008)

Then they should all be sent down the job centre. At first they'll complain, "There's nothing for me in there. I trained for two whole hours to get my qualifications as a parasite and there's no parasite jobs going at the moment anywhere." **Mark Steel**. On bankers losing their jobs in the 2008 financial crisis. *Independent (London)* (September 17, 2008)

We're not just going to see mid-sized banks go under in the next few months, we're going to see a whopper. **Kenneth Rogoff**. Lehman Brothers filed for bankruptcy two weeks later. Remark (August 2008)

It's a safe banking system, a sound banking system. Our regulators are on top of it. This is a very manageable situation. **Henry Paulson**. On the failure of the Indymac bank. CBS News broadcast (July 20, 2008)

We are used to a less dynamic environment than we have seen in the past few months and days. **Rod Kent**. Explaining Bradford & Bingley's financial troubles. The bank was rescued by the UK government in September. Quoted in the *Independent (London)* (June 3, 2008)

If banks feel they must keep on dancing while the music is playing and that at the end of the party the central bank will make sure everyone gets home safely, then over time, the parties will become wilder and wilder. When the party ends, some innocent bystanders may lose their homes altogether. **Mervyn King**. Speech to the British Bankers' Association (June 2008)

I have great, great confidence in our capital markets and in our financial institutions. Our financial institutions, banks and investment banks, are strong. Our capital markets are resilient. They're efficient. They're flexible. **Henry Paulson**. Remark (March 16, 2008)

We have a good deal of comfort about the capital cushions at these firms at the moment. **Christopher Cox**. On the big investment banks (March 11, 2008)

I expect there will be some failures ... I don't anticipate any serious problems of that sort among the large internationally active banks that make up a very substantial part of our banking system. **Ben Bernanke**. Testifying to the Senate Banking Committee (February 28, 2008)

Financial institutions have been merging into a smaller number of very large banks. Almost all banks are interrelated. So the financial ecology is swelling into gigantic, incestuous, bureaucratic banks—when one fails, they all fall ... We have moved from a diversified ecology of small banks, with varied lending policies, to a more homogeneous framework of firms that all resemble one another. True, we now have fewer failures, but when they occur ... I shiver at the thought. **Nassim Nicholas Taleb**. *The Black Swan* (2006)

When I was young, people called me a gambler. As the scale of my operations increased I became known as a speculator. Now I am called a banker. But I have been doing the same thing all the time. **Sir Ernest Cassel**. Quoted in *Fat Cats: The Strange Cult of the CEO* (Gideon Haigh, 2005)

I'm very happy to support it. And I keep my fingers crossed for the future. **Roel C. Campos**. On the Commission's decision to exempt the big investment banks from capital requirements rules. Meeting of the Securities and Exchange Commission (April 28, 2004)

It's one of life's ironies that the more you can prove that you don't need a loan, the better your chances usually are of getting one. This is especially true for start-up businesses. **Lillian Vernon**. Speech. "The Entrepreneur and the Professional Manager: Getting the Best of Both Worlds" (1998)

I hesitate to deposit money in a bank. I am afraid I shall never dare to take it out again. When you go to confession and entrust your sins to the safe-keeping of the priest, do you ever come back for them? **Jean Baudrillard**. *America* (1989)

It is no accident that banks resemble temples, preferably Greek, and that the supplicants who come to perform the rites of deposit and withdrawal instinctively lower their voices into the registers of awe. Even the most junior tellers acquire within weeks of their employment the officiousness of hierophants tending an eternal flame. **Lewis H. Lapham**. *Money and Class in America* (1988)

You know what the difference is between a dead skunk and a dead banker on the road? There's skid marks by the skunk. **Anonymous**. Quoted in *Final Harvest: An American Tragedy* (Andrew H. Malcolm, 1986)

Except for the con men borrowing money they shouldn't get and the widows who have to visit with the handsome young men in the trust department, no sane person ever enjoyed visiting a bank. **Martin Mayer**. *The Money Bazaars* (1984)

I doubt if there is any occupation which is more consistently and unfairly demeaned, degraded, denounced, and deplored than banking. **William Proxmire**. Quoted in *Fortune* (October 31, 1983)

It has been the bankers' destiny ... to find themselves on the dangerous edge of the world, pointing up the contradictions and cross-purposes. They are not often

 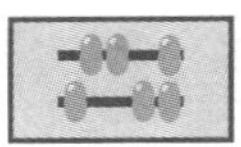     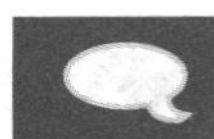 

loved for it. **Anthony Sampson**. *The Moneylenders: Bankers in a Dangerous World* (1981), ch. 22

Our banking system grew by accident; and whenever something happens by accident, it becomes a religion. **Walter Wriston**. *BusinessWeek* (January 20, 1975)

The process by which banks create money is so simple that the mind is repelled. **J. K. Galbraith**. *Money: Whence It Came, Where It Went* (1975)

A bank is a place that will lend you money if you can prove that you don't need it. **Bob Hope**. Quoted in "The Tyranny of Forms," *Life in the Crystal Palace* (Alan Harrington, 1959)

What is robbing a bank compared with founding a bank? **Bertolt Brecht**. *The Threepenny Opera* (1928)

Bankers regard research as most dangerous and a thing that makes banking hazardous due to the rapid changes it brings about in industry. **Charles Franklin Kettering**. Address (1927)

The business of banking ought to be simple. If it is hard it is wrong. The only securities which a banker, using money that he may be asked at short notice to repay, ought to touch, are those which are easily saleable and easily intelligible. **Walter Bagehot**. *Lombard Street: A Description of the Money Market* (1873)

Adventure is the life of commerce but caution, I had almost said timidity, is the life of banking. **Walter Bagehot**. *Lombard Street: A Description of the Money Market* (1873)

Blame

By blaming others, we fail to find the real solutions to our problems and we do not carry out our own responsibilities. **Jeb Bush**. *Foundation for Florida's Future* (1996)

An expert is someone called in at the last minute to share the blame. **Sam Ewing**. Quoted in *Reader's Digest* (December 1992)

Underneath runs the main current of preoccupation, which is keeping one's nose clean at all times. This means that when things go wrong you have to pass the blame along the line, like pass-the-parcel, till the music stops. **Sir Tom Stoppard**. *Neutral Ground* (1983)

Our culture peculiarly honors the act of blaming, which it takes as the sign of virtue and intellect. **Lionel Trilling**. *The Liberal Imagination* (1950)

Everyone threw the blame on me ... they nearly always do. I suppose ... they think I shall be able to bear it best. **Sir Winston Churchill**. *My Early Life* (1947), ch. 17

One must first learn to live oneself before one blames others. **Fyodor Dostoevsky**. *Notes from the Underground* (1864)

I find that pain of a little censure, even when it is unfounded, is more acute than the pleasure of much praise. **Thomas Jefferson**. Letter to F. Hopkinson (March 13, 1789)

Success is never blamed. **Thomas Fuller**. *Gnomologia* (1732), no. 4273

If we had no faults of our own, we should not take so much pleasure in noticing those of others. **François La Rochefoucauld**. *Reflections: or, Sentences and Moral Maxims* (5th ed, 1678)

Boasting

The only thing I have to do is look each day and see how much money came in. £50 million came in only last Friday! **Sigurjon Arnason**. Quoted in the *London Review of Books* (November 20, 2008)

Some of them think they have me by the balls, but their hands aren't big enough. **Bernie Ecclestone**. Referring to negotiations with Formula 1 racing teams, when planning to float Formula 1 on the Stock Exchange. Quoted in *Formula 1, The Business of Winning* (Russell Hotten, 1998)

It ain't bragging if you can do it. **Babe Ruth**. Quoted in *Woodbury Reports Archives* (December 1994)

I have helped to change society in a way that is beyond presidents and is going to make the world a better and happier place. **Hugh Hefner**. *Mail and Femail* (December 18, 1989)

If I only had a little humility, I'd be perfect. **Ted Turner**. *New York Times* (1980)

I don't meet competition. I crush it. **Charles Revson**. *Time* (June 16, 1958)

It is very vulgar to talk about one's business. Only people like stockbrokers do that, and then merely at dinner parties. **Oscar Wilde**. Said by Algernon. *The Importance of Being Earnest* (1895), Act 2

If you wish in this world to advance
Your merits you're bound to enhance;
You must stir it and stump it, And blow your own trumpet, Or trust me, you haven't a chance. **Sir W. S. Gilbert**. *Ruddigore* (1887), Act 1

Boldness

There are moments in our lives when we summon the courage to make choices that go against reason, against common sense and the wise counsel of people we trust. But we lean forward nonetheless because, despite all risks and rational argument, we *believe* that the path we are choosing is right and best thing to do. We refuse to be bystanders, even if we do not know exactly where our actions will lead. **Howard Schultz**. *Onward: How Starbucks Fought for Its Life without Losing Its Soul* (with Joanne Gordon, 2011)

We need a readiness to enter a room in the dark and stumble over unfamiliar furniture until the pain in our shins reminds us of where things are. **Fons Trompenaars**. *Financial Times (London)* (July 1996)

Anything worth doing is worth doing to excess. **Edwin Land**. *Boston Globe* (March 1991)

You can be very bold as a theoretician. Good theories are like good art. A practitioner has to compromise. **Warren Bennis**. *The Director* (October 1988)

All good fortune is a gift of the gods and you don't win the favour of the ancient gods by being good but by being bold. **Anita Brookner**. Quoted in *Writers at Work* (1988)

If you're going to be thinking only one thing, you might as well be thinking big. **Donald J. Trump**. Referring to the grand scale of his property deals. *Trump: The Art of the Deal* (1987)

Corporate courage is usually no greater than personal courage. **Edward Teller**. Interview, *Playboy* (August 1979)

If the creator had a purpose in equipping us with a neck, he surely meant us to stick it out. **Arthur Koestler**. *The Sleepwalkers* (1959)

Boldness, again boldness, and always boldness! **Georges Jacques Danton**. Speech to the Legislative Committee of General Defense (September 2, 1792)

Nothing will ever be attempted, if all possible objections must first be overcome. **Samuel Johnson**. *Rasselas, Prince of Abyssinia* (1759)

Boldness in business is the first, second, and third thing. **Thomas Fuller**. *Gnomologia* (1732)

It is better to be impetuous than circumspect. Experience shows that [fortune] is more often subdued by men who do this than by those who act coldly. **Niccolò Machiavelli**. *The Prince* (1513)

Boom and Bust

The greatest tragedy would be to accept the refrain that no one could have seen this coming, and thus nothing could have been done. If we accept this notion, it will happen again. **Financial Crisis Inquiry Commission**. On the financial crisis of 2008–09. "The Financial Crisis Inquiry Report" (January 2011)

If Greece is equivalent to Bear Sterns, which was rescued by the US authorities, which country is equivalent to Lehman Brothers, which wasn't? **Hamish McRae**. *Independent (London)* (April 30, 2010)

Wall Street is not being made a scapegoat for this crisis: they really did this. **Michael Lewis**. Interview, *Independent (London)* (April 23, 2010)

My daughter asked me when she came home from school, "What's the financial crisis?" and I said, it's something that happens every five to seven years. **Jamie Dimon**. Speaking to the Financial Crisis Inquiry Commission (January 13, 2010)

We've just had a financial crisis that bankers believed was impossible, whose economic damage has been incalculable. In response we must think the unthinkable. **Stephen Foley**. *Independent (London)* (January 2, 2010)

The only surprise about the economic crisis of 2008 was that it came as a surprise to so many. **Joseph Stiglitz**. *Freefall: America, Free Markets and the Sinking of the World Economy* (2010)

Our long, unaffordable global lunch is coming to an end and a headachey afternoon in the office beckons. We've spent the last 10 years downing extra digestifs to delay the arrival of the bill. But here it is, without so much as an accompanying mint, and it's massive. The trick now is to persuade the third world to pay an equal share even though they only had a soup. **David Mitchell**. *Observer (London)* (December 13, 2009)

Everyone is saying that we're on a tightrope, and we certainly are in mid-air over a gorge. But where is the rope? **Anonymous**. On the state of the British economy. Anonymous Tory MP quoted in the *Independent (London)* (December 7, 2009)

When the crash came, the free market had no answers, no self-correcting mechanisms and no solutions. **Ivon Fallon**. *Independent (London)* (November 27, 2009)

The lesson, surely, is that the recurring nature and the frequency of such follies, and their mutation into hitherto undreamt of forms, suggest that they are in fact an inherent cost of capitalism, or even human nature ... The delusion now would be to believe that any system of regulation could prevent such crises and busts happening again. **Sean O'Grady**. *Independent (London)* (November 20, 2009)

The commercial storm leaves its path strewn with ruin. When it is over there is calm, but a dull, heavy calm. **Alfred Marshall**. Quoted in the *Economist (London)* (October 1, 2009)

We will have more crises and none of them will look like this because no two crises have anything in common except human nature. **Alan Greenspan**. Interview on BBC TV (September 8, 2009)

It is a bit like trying to cure a cancer patient, while also training him for next year's marathon. **Bruce Anderson**. On attempts to lead the economy out of recession while also cutting government spending. *Independent (London)* (August 10, 2009)

By rescuing the financial system without reforming it, Washington has done nothing to protect us from a new crisis, and, in fact, has made another crisis more likely. **Paul R. Krugman**. *New York Times* (July 16, 2009)

Companies that weren't much more than pot-fueled ideas scrawled on napkins by up-too-late bong smokers were taken public via IPOs, hyped in the media, and sold to the public for mega-millions. It was as if banks like Goldman were wrapping ribbons around watermelons, tossing them out 50-story windows, and opening the phones for bids. In this game you were a winner only if you took your money out before the melon hit the pavement. **Matt Taibbi**. On the dot.com bubble of 1999–2000. *Rolling Stone (New York)* (July 2009)

When this crisis began, crucial decisions about what would happen to some of the world's biggest companies—companies employing tens of thousands of people and holding trillions of dollars in assets—took place in emergency meetings in the middle of the night. We should not be forced to choose between allowing a company to fall into a rapid and chaotic dissolution or to support the company with taxpayer money. That is unacceptable. **Barack Obama**. Speech introducing proposed regulatory reforms for the financial sector (June 17, 2009)

The panic appears to be over. Now is the time to get worried. **William Keegan**. On the recession of 2008–09. *Observer (London)* (June 14, 2009)

Give a small number of people the power to enrich themselves beyond everyone's wildest dreams, a philosophical rationale to explain all the damage they're causing, and they will not stop until they've run the world economy off a cliff. **Philipp Meyer**. *Independent (London)* (April 27, 2009)

In a boom, envy; in a bust, anger. **Dominic Lawson**. *Independent (London)* (April 7, 2009)

Gordon Brown promised to abolish boom and bust. He has kept half his promise. **William Hague**. Speech quoted in the *Independent (London)* (April 6, 2009)

The uncomfortable truth is that we all enjoyed the party far too much to query where all the booze was coming from. Now we seem intent on lynching the barman for letting us get drunk and attacking the Government for letting us get a hangover. **Sean O'Grady**. Referring to the financial crisis of 2008–09. *Independent (London)* (April 2, 2009)

My nightmare scenario is that the government saves Citibank once again, as well as the other banks, and business resumes as usual. Then, the next time the system breaks, it breaks much, much bigger. **Nassim Nicholas Taleb**. Interview, *Washington Post* (March 15, 2009)

We are chronicling something unprecedented: the billionaire bust. **Steve Forbes**. On *Forbes* magazine's revelation that the number of billionaires in the world had fallen by 30% over the previous 12 months. Quoted in the *Sunday Independent (Dublin)* (March 15, 2009)

You know, in every movie I've seen about the end of the world, civilization collapses because of something wicked cool happening—an asteroid hits, nuclear war, a supervirus, an ape revolution, whatever. If civilization collapses over credit default swaps I am going to be *pissed*. **Dan McEnroe**. Referring to the role of complex derivatives in the financial crisis of 2008–09. *A Blog Named Sue* blog (March 5, 2009)

An army of experts assured us on a daily basis that this boom couldn't possibly crash like previous booms because this boom was still going on whereas all previous booms had ended. **Mark Steel**. *Independent (London)* (February 11, 2009)

The reality is that this is becoming the most serious global recession for ... over 100 years. **Ed Balls**. Speech to Labour conference, Yorkshire (February 9, 2009)

We were on our own for years and we went too far, too fast, in too little time ... We're just like kids whose parents went away for the weekend and we trashed the whole house. **Hallgrimur Helgason**. On the implosion of Iceland's financial services industry. Quoted in the *Guardian (London)* (January 26, 2009)

This recession is not a failure of market economics. It is a reassertion of market economics after a decade in which we paid ourselves more than we were producing, and funded it precariously and temporarily by complicated credit instruments that it took a while for the market to rumble ... The collapse of confidence is not irrational; it's the correction to a long run of irrational confidence. **Matthew Parris**. *The Times (London)* (January 24, 2009)

Currently the prime minister is the equivalent of a doctor who is asked to save the same person's life several times. Originally the relatives are grateful but then start to wonder why his services are required so often. **Steve Richards**. On Gordon Brown's bank bailout plans. *Independent (London)* (January 20, 2009)

The government increasingly resembles somebody who is trying to give the kiss of life to a corpse. **Vince Cable**. On the British government's bank bailout plan. *Independent (London)* (January 20, 2009)

There's a rumour going around that states cannot go bankrupt. This rumour is not true. **Angela Merkel**. Speech, Frankfurt (January 2009)

That's our mirror. Every dip, every crash, every bubble that's burst, a testament to our brilliant stupidity. This one gave us the railroads. This one the Internet. This one the slave trade. And if we hope to do anything about saving the environment, or getting to other worlds, we'll need a bubble for that too. Everything I've ever done in my life worth anything has been done in a bubble: in a state of extreme hope and trust and stupidity. **Lucy Prebble**. Spoken by Jeffrey Skilling, CEO of Enron, as he points to a chart showing booms and bust in the US stock market. *Enron* (2009)

In that restaurant, crammed with self-satisfied know-nothings, we had gazed upon the amoral soul of the housing boom, the crux, the fulcrum, the place where so many dreams would begin, and where heartbreak and financial collapse would surely follow. **Larry McDonald**. On a restaurant frequented by mortgage salesmen at the height of the subprime lending boom. *A Colossal Failure of Common Sense: The Incredible Inside Story of the Collapse of Lehman Brothers* (2009)

Once you're in a bubble, it needs nerves of steel to stay out. Can you imagine the pressure? On any trader? Everyone around you is making money ... and you're the one who says I don't believe in securitised credit arrangements? **Sir David Hare**. *The Power of Yes* (2009)

There's a strange thing goes on inside a bubble. It's hard to describe. People who are in it can't see outside of it, don't believe there is an outside. **Lucy Prebble**. *Enron* (2009)

At present it is a bit like being in a country where a civil war is taking place. Away from the fighting, everything seems normal enough ... Open-air cafes are full, shops are busy and the best restaurants have no spare tables. But in the combat zones, perhaps not very far away, life is hellish. **Andreas Whittam Smith**. On the deepening recession. *Independent (London)* (December 5, 2008)

I and others were mistaken early on in saying that the subprime crisis would be contained. **Ben Bernanke**. "Anatomy of a Meltdown," *New Yorker* (December 1, 2008)

I looked at the screens. I was staring into the abyss. The end. I felt this shooting pain in my head. I don't get headaches ... I thought I was having an aneurysm. **Danny Moses**. On the stock-market crash of September 18, 2008. Quoted in *Condé Nast Portfolio (New York)* (December 2008)

When depression economics prevails, the usual rules of economic policy no longer apply: virtue becomes vice, caution is risky and prudence is folly. **Paul R. Krugman**. *New York Times* (November 14, 2008)

We are in the midst of a once-in-a-century credit tsunami. Central banks and governments are being required to take unprecedented measures. Those of us who have looked to the self-interest of lending institutions to protect shareholders' equity are in a state of shocked disbelief. **Alan Greenspan**. Speaking before the House Committee on Oversight (October 23, 2008)

This thaw took a while to thaw, it's going to take a while to unthaw. **George W. Bush**. Referring to frozen credit markets. Speech, Alexandria, Louisiana (October 20, 2008)

Consumer spending is now plunging at serious-recession rate ... even if the rescue now in train succeeds in unfreezing credit markets, the real economy has immense downward momentum. In addition to financial rescues, we need major stimulus programs. **Paul R. Krugman**. "Train Headed Downhill," *New York Times* blog (October 15, 2008)

Why did no one see it coming? **Elizabeth II**. On the financial crash of 2008. During a visit to the London School of Economics (October 2008)

When we're talking about a trillion dollars of taxpayer money, "trust me" just isn't good enough. **John McCain**. On the US Treasury secretary's Wall Street bailout plan. Quoted in *The Times (London)* (September 25, 2008)

This sucker could go down. **George W. Bush**. Referring to the entire US financial system at an emergency cabinet meeting. Quoted in the *New York Times* (September 25, 2008)

These are not normal circumstances. The market is not functioning properly. **George W. Bush**. Speech (September 24, 2008)

There are no atheists in foxholes and there are no libertarians in financial crises. **Paul R. Krugman**. Interview with Bill Maher on HBO TV (September 19, 2008)

Anyone who says we're in a recession, or heading into one—especially the worst one since the Great Depression—is making up his own private definition of "recession." **Donald Luskin**. This was the day before Lehman Brothers filed for bankruptcy, triggering a stock-market crash. *Washington Post* (September 14, 2008)

Last year this was a financial crisis that we thought with a bit of luck would be over by Christmas. **Charles Bean**. Quoted in the *Guardian (London)* (August 26, 2008)

What, pray, is all the fuss about? ... If this is the worst crisis since the Great Depression then we must have all been living pretty cushy, gilded lives since the 1930s. If this is all it takes to destroy capitalism ... then it is a wonder why the Soviet Union failed to do so during its seven decades of existence. For the past year has actually not been very bad at all—unless you are a banker, a bank shareholder or Gordon Brown; and few will shed tears for any of

  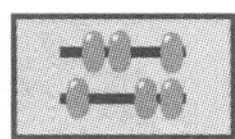   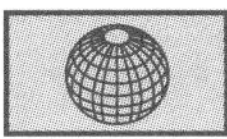   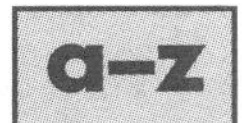

those. **Bill Emmott**. *Guardian (London)* (August 12, 2008)

We can have confidence in the long-term foundation of our economy ... I think the system basically is sound. I truly do. **George W. Bush**. The US financial system plunged into crisis in September. Speech (July 15, 2008)

I think this is a case where Freddie Mac and Fannie Mae are fundamentally sound. They're not in danger of going under ... I think they are in good shape going forward. **Barney Frank**. Fannie Mae and Freddie Mac were taken into government "conservatorship" in September 2008. Remark (July 14, 2008)

It's quite possible that at some point we may get an odd quarter or two of negative growth, but recession is not the central projection at all. **Mervyn King**. Speech (May 2008)

The fundamentals of America's economy are strong. **John McCain**. Interview on Bloomberg TV (April 17, 2008)

A very powerful and durable rally is in the works. But it may need another couple of days to lift off. Hold the fort and keep the faith! **Richard Band**. *Profitable Investing Letter* (March 27, 2008)

The current financial crisis in the US is likely to be judged in retrospect as the most wrenching since the end of the Second World War. **Alan Greenspan**. *Financial Times (London)* (March 16, 2008)

The market is in the process of correcting itself. **George W. Bush**. Speech (March 14, 2008)

History records no case where the bubble gracefully deflated, accompanied by a slight hiss of escaping optimism. The speculative episode always ends with a loud explosion. **Andreas Whittam Smith**. *Independent (London)* (January 28, 2008)

If the financial system has a defect, it is that it reflects and magnifies what we human beings are like ... money amplifies our tendency to overreact, to swing from exuberance when things are going well to deep depression when they go wrong. Booms and busts are products, at root, of our emotional volatility. **Niall Ferguson**. *The Ascent of Money* (2008)

The recession debate is over. It's not gonna happen ... The Bush boom is alive and well. It's finishing up its sixth splendid year with many more years to come. **Lawrence Kudlow**. *Kudlow's Money Politics* blog (December 5, 2007)

The world economy [is] more stable than for a generation ... Our hugely sophisticated financial markets match funds with ideas better than ever before. **David Cameron**. The first signs of the global financial crisis were already becoming apparent. Speech, London School of Economics (September 2007)

Over the ten years that I have had the privilege of addressing you as Chancellor, I have been able year by year to record how the City of London has risen by your efforts, ingenuity and creativity to become a new world leader ... So I congratulate you, Lord Mayor and the City of London, on these remarkable achievements, an era that history will record as the beginning of a new golden age for the City of London. **Gordon Brown**. The first signs of the global financial crisis became apparent the following month. Speech while chancellor of the exchequer, Mansion House, City of London (June 20, 2007)

It's a crisis if everybody calls it a crisis. **Morgan Downey**. Remark (2007)

The final chapter of Greenspan's legacy has not been written. Maybe it will work out fine, but maybe not. **Paul Kasriel**. On Alan Greenspan's retirement as chairman of the US Federal Reserve. Quoted on *Bloomberg.com* (January 26, 2006)

Unsustainable situations usually go on longer than most economists think possible. But they always end, and when they do, it's often painful. **Paul R. Krugman**. Address given in Bangkok (September 2005)

Real estate is still a great investment opportunity for households. Price appreciation will continue. It may not be at 20%. It may ... even go down to 5%. **David Lereah**. Between 2006 and 2008 US house prices fell faster than they fell during the Great Depression. Interview on *SmartMoney.com* (August 12, 2005)

We are in the biggest real-estate boom we've ever seen. Something is going to happen to end this. **Robert Shiller**. Between 2006 and 2008 US house prices fell faster than they fell during the Great Depression. Remark (August 2005)

Global capital markets pose the same kinds of problems that jet planes do. They are faster, more comfortable, and they get you where you are going better. But the crashes are much more spectacular. **Lawrence H. Summers**. Interview, *Time* (June 26, 2005)

Bull markets are born on pessimism, grow on skepticism, mature on optimism, and die on euphoria. **Sir John Templeton**. Quoted in *Short-term Trading in the New Stock Market* (Toni Turner, 2005)

The central problem of depression-prevention has been solved, for all practical purposes. **Robert Lucas, Jr**. Address to the American Economic Association (2003)

The four most expensive words in the English language are, "This time, it's different." **Sir John Templeton**. Quoted in *The Four Pillars of Investing* (William J. Bernstein, 2002)

If Wall Street crashes, does Main Street follow? Not necessarily. **Ben Bernanke**. Remark (September 2000)

Nothing sedates rationality like large doses of effortless money. After a heady experience of that kind, normally sensible people drift into behavior akin to that of Cinderella at the ball the giddy participants all plan to leave just seconds before midnight. There's a problem, though: they are dancing in a room in which the clocks have no hands. **Warren Buffett**. Letter to shareholders (2000)

Property and stock market crashes ... litter the history of capitalism. But at the same time there is no evidence that anyone has ever been successful in preventing such a crash. **Lester Thurow**. "Barking Up the Wrong Tree," *www.lthurow.com* (November 2, 1999)

A crash does not come knocking at the front door by appointment. **Jim Slater**. Quoted in *Treasury of Investment Wisdom* (Bernice Cohen, 1999)

Blaming speculators as a response to financial crisis goes back at least to the Greeks. It's almost always the wrong response. **Lawrence H. Summers**. On the financial crisis in South-East Asia. Remark (1997)

There is no evidence that the business cycle has been repealed. **Alan Greenspan**. *Wall Street Journal* (1997)

In a market like this, every story is a positive one. Any news is good news. It's pretty much taken for granted now that the market is going to go up. **Anonymous**. The market began to decline that day, plummeted nearly 1,000 points in October, and did not regain its August peak for nearly two years. *Wall Street Journal* (August 26, 1987)

In the next economic downturn there will be an outbreak of bitterness and contempt for the supercorporate chieftains who pay themselves millions. In every major economic downturn in US history the villains have been the heroes during the preceding boom. **Peter F. Drucker**.

Quoted in "Seeing Things As They Really Are," *Forbes* (Robert Lenzner and Stephen S. Johnson, 1987)

A depression is a situation of self-fulfilling pessimism. **Joan Robinson**. "The Short Period," *Economic Heresies* (1970)

Brands

If we are loyal to, say, Sainsbury's or Hob Nobs, it's usually in the same way a rabbit is loyal to a nine-year-old girl. We don't care that much. **Simon Usborne**. *Independent (London)* (April 20, 2012)

It's no coincidence that Woolworths and Jane Norman went bust—no one looked up to them. Nobody ever walked into Woolworths and felt like they weren't good enough. **Harriet Walker**. *Independent (London)* (August 18, 2011)

More than simply products, gadgets like the iPad and programmes like *The Wire* have become badges—ways to identify ourselves in a world in which the traditional ways of classifying us by social class and mainstream religion are losing their purchase. On social networks like Facebook, it's easy to get lost. Profiling ourselves according to the things we really like makes it easy to mark ourselves out from the crowd, and gives us a flock to fly with. **James Harkin**. *Independent (London)* (March 28, 2011)

The vision is of Durex as a brand people talk about at dinner parties. **Garry Watts**. Interview, *Independent (London)* (April 15, 2010)

Brands need identities ... I think you have only built a brand when you own two or three brain cells in 80% of the public's mind. **George Davies**. Quoted in the *Observer (London)* (September 27, 2009)

Brands are all about trust. You buy the brand because you consider it a friend. **Sir Michael Perry**. *Marketing* (March 2000)

With the strongest brands, the CEO owns the brand. It must be owned by someone, the higher in the company the better. **Shelly Lazarus**. *Marketing News* (2000)

You, me, all of us, must turn ourselves into distinctive one-person Brands. **Tom Peters**. "Work Matters! Movement Manifesto," *www.tompeters.com* (September 1999)

Truly great brands are far more than just labels for products; they are symbols that encapsulate the desires of consumers; they are standards that are held aloft under which the masses congregate. **Tony O'Reilly**. Speech, British Council of Shopping Centres. Quoted in *Granta* (Spring 1996)

Budgeting

For as long as I can remember the slogan has been ... the federal government ought to behave more like families, because families balance their budgets. It turns out that families looked around and said, "You know what? Let's behave more like the government!" **George Will**. On irresponsible borrowing. *This Week* (September 2008)

I just never got involved with the cash flow thing. My attitude was creativity will see me through. **Adrienne Landau**. *Forbes* (October 2000)

The budget is God. **Anonymous**. Slogan at Japanese optical company Topcom. Quoted in the *Economist (London)* (January 13, 1996)

Watch the costs and the profits will take care of themselves. **Andrew Carnegie**. Quoted in *The Entrepreneurs—An American Adventure* (R. Sobel and D. B. Silicia, 1986)

Whenever I think about the budgetary problems, I think about the problems of Errol Flynn ... reconciling net income with gross habits. **Sir Malcolm Rifkind**. Quoted in *Film Yearbook* (1986)

We didn't actually overspend our budget. The Health Commission allocation simply fell short of our expenditure. **Keith Davis**. Quoted in *Sydney Morning Herald* (November 14, 1981)

Annual income twenty pounds, annual expenditure nineteen nineteen six, result happiness. Annual income twenty pounds, annual expenditure twenty pounds ought and six, result misery. **Charles Dickens**. There were twenty shillings in a pound and twelve pence in a shilling. *David Copperfield* (1849–1850), ch. 12

Bureaucracy

Bureaucracies temporarily suspend the Second Law of Thermodynamics. In a bureaucracy, it's easier to make a process more complex than to make it simpler, and easier to create a new burden than kill an old one. **Clay Shirky**. "The Collapse of Complex Business Models," *shirky.com/weblog* (April 1, 2010)

Institutions will try to preserve the problem to which they are the solution. **Clay Shirky**. *Cognitive Surplus: Creativity and Generosity in a Connected Age* (2010)

The bureaucracies of the Industrial Age will appear to the new inter-corporate, transcontinental networks like old Royal typewriters do to PC owners. **Jessica Lipnack**. *St. Louis Post-Dispatch* (December 1991)

Bureaucratic time ... slower than geologic time but more expensive than time spent with Madame Claude's girls in Paris. **P. J. O'Rourke**. *Parliament of Whores* (1991)

It seems to me that there must be an ecological limit to the number of paper pushers the Earth can sustain. **Barbara Ehrenreich**. "Premature Pragmatism," *The Worst Years of Our Lives* (1991)

Corpocracy is large-scale corporate America's tendency to be like the government bureaucracy. **Richard G. Darman**. *New York Times* (November 9, 1986)

Bureaucracy, safely repeating today what it did yesterday, rolls on as ineluctably as some vast computer, which, once penetrated by error, duplicates it forever. **Barbara W. Tuchman**. *The March of Folly* (1984)

The only thing that saves us from the bureaucracy is inefficiency. An efficient bureaucracy is the greatest threat to liberty. **Eugene McCarthy**. *Time* (February 12, 1979)

A memorandum is written not to inform the reader but to protect the writer. **Dean Acheson**. Quoted in the *Wall Street Journal* (September 8, 1977)

A committee is an animal with four back legs. **John Le Carré**. *Tinker, Tailor, Soldier, Spy* (1974)

A committee is a cul-de-sac down which ideas are lured and then quietly strangled. **Barnett Cocks**. Quoted in *New Scientist* (1973)

Guidelines for bureaucrats: (1) When in charge, ponder. (2) When in trouble, delegate. (3) When in doubt, mumble. **James H. Boren**. *New York Times* (November 9, 1970)

However many people complain about the red tape, it would be sheer illusion to think for a moment that continuous administrative work can be carried out except by means of officials working in offices ... The choice is only that between bureaucracy and dilettantism in the field of administration. **Max Weber**. Quoted in *Economy and Society* (Guenther Roth and Claus Wittich, eds, 1968)

Muddle is the extra unknown personality in any committee. **Anthony Sampson**. *Anatomy of Britain Today* (1965)

Poor fellow, he suffers from files. **Aneurin Bevan**. Referring to the administrator Sir Walter Citrine. Quoted in *Aneurin Bevan* (Michael Foot, 1962), vol. 1

Few great men could pass Personnel. **Paul Goodman**. *Growing Up Absurd* (1960)

Bureaucracy, the rule of no one, has become the modern form of despotism. **Mary McCarthy**. "The Vita Activa," *New Yorker* (October 18, 1958)

An administrator in a bureaucratic world is a man who can feel big by merging his non-entity with an abstraction. A real person in touch with real things inspires terror in him. **Marshall McLuhan**. Letter to Ezra Pound (1951)

Officials are highly educated but one-sided; in his own department an official can grasp whole trains of thought from a single word, but let him have something from another department explained to him ... he won't understand a word of it. **Franz Kafka**. *The Castle* (1926)

A committee is a group of people who keep minutes and waste hours. **Milton Berle**. Attributed

Business Ethics

What would happen if employees of a London casino were found colluding to rig games for the benefit of the house, and particularly themselves? The police would arrive in force, the company would lose its operating licence and senior management would be excluded from the industry ... banks should operate to standards as high as those of casinos. **John Kay**. On revelations that banks had profited by manipulating the LIBOR interest rate. *Financial Times (London)* (July 4, 2012)

I will manage my enterprise with loyalty and care, and I will not advance my personal interests at the expense of my enterprise or society ... I will protect the human rights and dignity of all people affected by my enterprise, and I will oppose discrimination and exploitation ... I will protect the right of future generations to advance their standard of living and enjoy a healthy planet. **Anonymous**. Oath devised by MBA students at Harvard University. Quoted in the *Independent (London)* (July 8, 2010)

Consumerism has become a new religion, complete with its high priests at *Which?* and its fatwas against anyone with the temerity to try to sell anything at more than cost price ... It is a depressingly medieval outlook on economic life. **Sean O'Grady**. *Independent (London)* (November 26, 2009)

No one can lie about what the the future will bring because nobody knows what the future will bring. **Sisam Brune**. Defending Matt Tannin, a Bear Stearns hedge fund manager, against criminal charges of misleading investors in the run-up to the fund's collapse. Quoted in the *Independent (London)* (October 16, 2009)

In London, Washington, and Paris people talk of bonuses or no bonuses. In parts of Africa, South Asia, and Latin America, the struggle is for food or no food. **Robert Zoellick**. Quoted in the *Independent (London)* (April 1, 2009)

When I find a short-seller, I want to tear his heart out and eat it before his eyes while he's still alive. **Richard S. Fuld, Jr**. Quoted in the *Financial Times (London)* (December 30, 2008)

That Wall Street has gone down because of this is justice ... They built a castle to rip people off. Not once in all these years have I come across a person inside a big Wall Street firm who was having a crisis of conscience. **Steve Eisman**. Quoted in *Condé Nast Portfolio (New York)* (December 2008)

I'm going to ask the three executives here to raise their hand if they flew here commercial. Let the record show, no hands went up. Second, I'm going to ask you to raise your hand if you are planning to sell your jet in place now and fly back commercial. Let the record show, no hands went up. **Brad Sherman**. To the chief executive officers of Ford, Chrysler, and General Motors at a hearing of the House Financial Services Committee (November 18, 2008)

There is a delicious irony in seeing private luxury jets flying into Washington, DC, and people coming off of them with tin cups in their hand, saying that they're going to be trimming down and streamlining their businesses. It's almost like seeing a guy show up at the soup kitchen in high hat and tuxedo. It kind of makes you a little bit suspicious. **Gary Ackerman**. To the chief executive officers of Ford, Chrysler, and General Motors at a hearing of the House Financial Services Committee (November 18, 2008)

Your company is now bankrupt, our economy is now in a state of crisis, but you get to keep $480 million. I have a very basic question for you: Is this fair? **Henry Waxman**. Questioning Lehman Brothers CEO Richard S. Fuld Jr over the bank's collapse. Speaking at a Congressional hearing (October 5, 2008)

To a bystander like me, those who made 190 million pounds deliberately underselling the shares of HBOS, in spite of its very strong capital base, and drove it into the bosom of Lloyds TSB Bank, are clearly bank robbers and asset strippers. **Dr John Sentamu**. Adressing a meeting of bankers (September 24, 2008)

They are like looters after a hurricane. **Andrew Cuomo**. On short-selling of bank shares by traders during the financial crisis. Attributed (September 2008)

If it is not right, don't do it; if it is not true, don't say it. **John A. Byrne**. *Fast Company: The Rules of Business* (2005)

If you think you're too small to have an impact, try going to bed with a mosquito in the room. **Dame Anita Roddick**. Quoted in *4-D Branding* (Thomas Gad, 2001)

We have our values from the church, the temple, the mosque. Do not rob, do not murder. But our behaviour changes the minute we go into the corporate place. Suddenly all of this is irrelevant. **Dame Anita Roddick**. Interview, *Marketing Week* (February 24, 2000)

The latter-day robber barons are discovering that better conditions and rewards for workers pay off in a world where consumers increasingly demand ethical standards. **Clare Short**. *Management Today* (November 1999)

A business that makes nothing but money is a poor kind of business. **Henry Ford**. Quoted in *The Arizona Republic* (1999)

As an anonymous participant in financial markets, I never had to weigh the social consequences of my actions ... I felt justified in ignoring them on the grounds that I was playing by the rules. **George Soros**. *The Crisis of Global Capitalism* (1998)

I'll keep it short and sweet. Family. Religion. Friendship. These are the three demons you must slay if you wish to succeed in business. **John Swartzwelder**. Spoken by tycoon C. Montgomery Burns. *The Simpsons*, Fox TV (April 20, 1997)

If you can take advantage of a situation in some way, it's your duty as an American to do it. **John Swartzwelder**. Spoken by tycoon C. Montgomery Burns. *The Simpsons*, Fox TV (February 2, 1997)

I believe that nicotine is not addictive. **Thomas Sandefur**. Said at the 1994 US Congressional hearings on the tobacco industry. Quoted in the *New York Times* (1997)

Creative swiping provides energy to an organization. **Chuck Chambers**. Quoted in *Liberation Management* (Tom Peters, 1992)

If there was a market in mass-produced portable nuclear weapons, we'd market them too. **Sir Alan, Lord Sugar**. Quoted in *The Condition of Postmodernity* (David Harvey, 1989)

The market has no morality. **Michael, Lord Heseltine**. Interview on *Panorama*, BBC TV (June 1988)

We take society's capital, we take their people, we take their materials, yet without a good profit we are using precious resources that could be used better elsewhere. **Konosuke Matsushita**. *Quest for Prosperity* (1988)

I find it rather easy to portray a businessman. Being bland, rather cruel and incompetent comes naturally to me. **John Cleese**. Referring to appearing in industrial training videos. *Newsweek* (June 15, 1987)

There cannot be a situation where a businessman says, "I base all my business on moral considerations." Equally, you can't say you can run a business without morality. **Sir Timothy Bevan**. Said as Chairman of Barclays Bank Ltd, when asked about Barclays' withdrawal from South Africa. *Observer (London)* (November 30, 1986)

I ran the wrong kind of business, but I did it with integrity. **Sydney Biddle Barrows**. "Mayflower Madam Tells All," *Boston Globe* (1986)

The meek shall inherit the Earth, but not the mineral rights. **J. Paul Getty**. Quoted in *The Great Getty* (Robert Lenzner, 1985)

Commercialism is doing well that which should not be done at all. **Gore Vidal**. *Listener* (August 1975)

In business we cut each others' throats, but now and then we sit around the same table and behave—for the sake of the ladies. **Aristotle Onassis**. *Sunday Times (London)* (March 16, 1969)

Two half truths do not make a truth. **Arthur Koestler**. *The Ghost in the Machine* (1967)

Experience teaches you that the man who looks you straight in the eye, particularly if he adds a firm handshake, is hiding something. **Clifton Fadiman**. *Enter Conversing* (1962)

Armaments, universal debt, and planned obsolescence—these are the three pillars of Western prosperity. **Aldous Huxley**. *Island* (1962), ch. 9

Such is the brutalization of commercial ethics in this country no one can feel anything more delicate than the velvet touch of a soft buck. **Raymond Chandler**. Letter to his publisher. Quoted in *Raymond Chandler Speaking* (Dorothy Gardiner and Katherine S. Walker, eds, 1962)

We have always known that heedless self-interest was bad morals; we know now that it is bad economics. **Franklin D. Roosevelt**. Second presidential inaugural address (January 20, 1937)

Food comes first, then morals. **Bertolt Brecht**. *The Threepenny Opera* (1928)

Love your neighbour is not merely sound Christianity; it is good business. **David Lloyd George (Earl of Dwyfor)**. Quoted in "Sayings of the Week," *Observer (London)* (February 20, 1921)

Commerce, n. A kind of transaction in which A plunders from B the goods of C, and for compensation B picks the pocket of D of money belonging to E. **Ambrose Bierce**. *The Devil's Dictionary* (1911)

Most men are individuals no longer so far as their business, its activities, or its moralities are concerned. They are not units but fractions. **Woodrow Wilson**. Address to the American Bar Association (August 31, 1910)

Thieves respect property. They merely wish the property to become their property that they may more perfectly respect it. **G. K. Chesterton**. *The Man Who Was Thursday* (1908)

Always do right. This will gratify some people, and astonish the rest. **Mark Twain**. Speech to the Young People's Society, Greenpoint Baptist Church, Brooklyn, New York (1901)

If you can't pay for a thing, don't buy it. If you can't get paid for it, don't sell it. Do this, and you will have calm and drowsy nights, with all of the good business you have now and none of the bad. **Benjamin Franklin**. Quoted in *Fors Clavigera* (John Ruskin, 1873)

Thou shalt not steal; an empty feat when it's so lucrative to cheat. **Arthur Hugh Clough**. "The Latest Decalogue" (1862)

Oh God, that bread should be so dear And flesh and blood so cheap. **Thomas Hood**. "The Song of the Shirt" (1843)

Here's the rule for bargains: Do other men, for they would do you. That's the true business precept. **Charles Dickens**. *Martin Chuzzlewit* (1843–1844), ch. 11

A bargain is in its very essence a hostile transaction. Do not all men try to abate the price of all they buy? I contend that a bargain—even between brethren—is a declaration of war. **George Gordon, Lord Byron**. Letter (July 14, 1821)

Ministers and merchants love nobody. **Thomas Jefferson**. Letter to John Langdon (September 11, 1785)

The leader should know how to enter into evil when necessity commands. **Niccolò Machiavelli**. *The Prince* (1513)

If you allow men to use you for your own purposes, they will use you for theirs. **Aesop**. "The Horse, Hunter, and Stag" (6th century BC)

You can't get that sort of buying opportunity very often. It's important to take advantage of it, if you have the guts and temperament. **David Lui**. On the Tiananmen Square massacre

Capitalism

The domination of capitalism globally depends today on the existence of a Chinese Communist party that gives delocalized capitalist enterprises cheap labour to lower prices and deprive workers of the rights of self-organization. **Jacques Rancière**. Quoted in the *Guardian (London)* (July 4, 2012)

Economics as a discipline has in effect become the study of capitalism. The two are taken as the same subject. **John Lanchester**. *London Review of Books* (April 5, 2012)

Capitalism depends on people keeping their promises to one another, often over very long periods of time. **William Davies**. *New Statesman* (November 16, 2011)

A free market was never meant to be a free licence to take whatever you can get, however you can get it. **Barack Obama**. On the need for radical reform of the US financial industry. Speech (April 22, 2010)

Since the crisis, developing countries have lost interest in the old Washington consensus that promoted democracy and liberal economics ... The West must come up with a new model of capitalism that's consistent with our political values. Either we reinvent ourselves or we will lose. **Anonymous**. Anonymous US diplomat referring to the financial crisis of 2008–09. Quoted in *The Times (London)* (Anatole Kaletsky, February 4, 2010)

The free market doesn't exist. Every market has some rules and boundaries that restrict freedom of choice. A market looks free only because we so unconditionally accept its underlying restrictions that we fail to see them. **Ha-Joon Chang**. *23 Things They Don't Tell You About Capitalism* (2010)

There are different ways to organise capitalism. Free-market capitalism is only one of them—and not a very good one at that. **Ha-Joon Chang**. *23 Things They Don't Tell You About Capitalism* (2010)

Enterprise is a nightmare of red ink, final demands and columns that don't add up ... a biblical saga of missed deadlines, faulty documents, defective quality control and collapsing share prices. **Simon Carr**. *Independent (London)* (June 15, 2009)

If you bound the arms and legs of gold-medal swimmer Michael Phelps, weighed him down with chains, threw him in a pool and he sank, you wouldn't call it a "failure of swimming." So, when markets have been weighted down by inept and excessive regulation, why call this a "failure of capitalism"? **Peter Boettke**. On the financial crisis of 2008–09. *The Times (London)* (March 9, 2009)

Capitalism is a forest fire that is never extinguished, only contained. **Bryan Appleyard**. *Sunday Times (London)* (January 4, 2009)

This administration made decisions that allowed the free market to operate as a barroom brawl instead of a prize fight. **L. William Seidman**. On the Bush administration in the run-up to the financial crisis of 2008. Quoted in the *New York Times* (December 20, 2008)

The frantic scrambling that is going on in Washington marks the passing of only one type of capitalism—the peculiar and highly unstable variety that has existed in America over the last 20 years ... While the impact of the collapse will be felt everywhere, the market economies that resisted American-style deregulation will best weather the storm. Britain, which has turned itself into a gigantic hedge fund, but of a kind that lacks the ability to profit from a downturn, is likely to be especially badly hit. **John Gray**. *Observer (London)* (September 28, 2008)

After a recent trip to New York one French journalist remarked that leafing through a copy of Forbes or Fortune is like reading the operating manual of a strangely sanctimonious pirate ship. **Adam Gopnik**. *Paris to the Moon* (2001)

The chief business of the American people is business. **Calvin Coolidge**. Quoted in the *New York Times* (2000)

It is just as important that business keep out of government as that government keep out of business. **Herbert Hoover**. Quoted in the *East Valley Tribune* (2000)

Capitalism, as practiced, is a financially profitable, non-sustainable aberration in human development. **Paul Hawken**. *Natural Capitalism* (cowritten with Amory B. Lovins and L. Hunter Lovins, 1999)

The great challenge of the twentieth century ... is to create a new financial architecture in which private decisions produce a less degenerate capitalism. **Will Hutton**. *The State We're In* (1995)

Our belief in salvation through the market is very much in the Utopian tradition. The economists and managers are the servants of God. Like the medieval scholastics, their only job is to uncover the divine plan. They could never create or stop it. At most they might aspire to small alterations. **John Ralston Saul**. *The Unconscious Civilization* (1995)

Capitalism works better than any of us can conceive. It is also the only truly moral system of exchange. It encourages individuals to devote their energies ... to the satisfaction of others' wants and needs. **Steve Forbes**. "Three Cheers for Capitalism," *Imprimis* (September 1993)

To speak of limits to growth under a capitalistic market economy is as meaningless as to speak of limits of warfare under a warrior society. **Murray Bookchin**. *Remaking Society* (1990)

Capitalism without bankruptcy is like Christianity without hell. **Frank Borman**. Remark (April 21, 1986)

What breaks capitalism, all that will ever break capitalism, is capitalists. **Raymond Williams**. *Loyalties* (1985)

The prevailing theory of capitalism suffers from one central and disabling flaw, a profound distrust and incomprehension of capitalism. **George Gilder**. *The Spirit of Enterprise* (1984)

Mr Heath talks about the unacceptable face of capitalism, but intrinsically it doesn't have an unacceptable face. **Arnold, Lord Weinstock**. Referring to prime minister Edward Heath's description of Lonrho as the unacceptable face of capitalism. Quoted in the *Daily Telegraph (London)* (June 17, 1974)

The system of private property is the most important guarantee of freedom, not only for those who own property, but scarcely less for those who do not. **Friedrich August von Hayek**. *The Road to Serfdom* (1944), ch. 8

Private property is a necessary institution, at least in a fallen world; men work more and dispute less when goods are private than when they are in common. **Richard Tawney**. *Religion and the Rise of Capitalism* (1926), ch. 1, sect. 1

Capitalism, wisely managed, can probably be made more efficient for attaining economic ends than any alternative system yet in sight. **John Maynard Keynes**. *The End of Laissez-Faire* (1926)

We accept and welcome, therefore, as conditions to which we must accommodate ourselves, great inequality of environment, the concentration of business, industrial and commercial, in the hands of a few, and the law of competition between these, as being not only beneficial, but essential for the future progress of the race. **Andrew Carnegie**. "Wealth," *North American Review* (June 1889)

Capital must be propelled by self-interest; it cannot be enticed by benevolence. **Walter Bagehot**. *Economic Studies* (1880)

The man who accepts the laissez-faire doctrine would allow his garden to grow wild so that roses might fight it out with the weeds and the fittest might survive. **John Ruskin**. Attributed

Capitalism versus Socialism

China embraced capitalism to entrench its socialist elite. The US embraced socialism to entrench its capitalist elite. **Jim Chanos**. Referring to the US bank bailout of 2008–09. Presentation (February 2010)

The fact that global capitalism is flawed does not mean that we should turn to communism or withdraw into national isolation, just as the failure of communism does not mean that markets are perfect.

George Soros. Speech to the Council on Foreign Relations, New York. "The Crisis of Global Capitalism: Open Society Endangered" (December 10, 1998)

The natural counterpart of a free market economy is a politics of insecurity. **John Gray**. *False Dawn* (1998)

Communism has failed, but capitalism has not succeeded. **William Keegan**. *The Spectre of Capitalism* (1992)

Prosperity or egalitarianism—you have to choose. I favor freedom—you never achieve real equality anyway: you simply sacrifice prosperity for an illusion. **Mario Vargas Llosa**. *Independent on Sunday (London)* (May 5, 1991)

You cannot go to sleep with one form of economic system and wake up the next morning with another. **Mikhail Gorbachev**. *Guardian (London)* (December 7, 1990)

In the end we beat them with Levi 501 jeans. Seventy-two years of Communist indoctrination and propaganda was drowned out by a three-ounce Sony Walkman. **P. J. O'Rourke**. "The Death of Communism," *Rolling Stone* (November 1989)

Less than seventy-five years after it officially began, the contest between capitalism and socialism is over: capitalism has won. **Robert L. Heilbroner**. "Reflections: The Triumph of Capitalism," *New Yorker* (January 23, 1989)

Capitalism is at its liberating best in a noncapitalist environment. The crypto-businessman is the true revolutionary in a Communist country. **Eric Hoffer**. *Reflections on the Human Condition* (1973)

Capitalism inevitably and by virtue of the very logic of its civilization creates, educates and subsidizes a vested interest in social unrest. **Joseph Alois Schumpeter**. *Capitalism, Socialism and Democracy* (1942), ch. 13

The twentieth century marks the turning point from the old capitalism to the new, from the domination of capital in general to the domination of financial capital. **Vladimir Ilich Lenin**. *Imperialism, the Higher Stages of Capitalism* (1917)

If there is a man on this Earth who is entitled to all the comforts and luxuries of this life ... it is the man whose labor produces them ... Does he get them in the present system? **Eugene V. Debs**. Speech at Girard, Kansas. "The Issue" (May 23, 1908)

During its rule of scarce one hundred years, capitalism has created more massive and more colossal productive forces than have all preceding generations together. **Karl Marx**. *The Communist Manifesto* (cowritten with Friedrich Engels, 1848)

Careers

In the past, building a steady (if unspectacular) career by honing a craft was not looked down on. Professionals won the respect of their peers by a dedication to the task in hand. The modern career path of the fast-tracked executive looks completely different. They leap from one "stretch assignment" to another in an accelerated journey to the top. It is not obvious that this leads to more capable management or better leadership. **Stefan Stern**. *Independent (London)* (May 15, 2012)

Soon the emphasis will be on getting a life instead of a career, and work will be viewed as a series of gigs or projects. **Jonas Ridderstråle**. *Funky Business* (cowritten with Kjell Nordström, 2000)

I got my start by giving myself a start. **C. J. Walker**. Quoted in *On Her Own Ground: The Life and Times of Madam C. J. Walker* (A'Lelia Bundles, 2000)

Security no longer comes from being employed. It comes from being employable. **Rosabeth Moss Kanter**. *Changing Workplace Alert* (1997)

Your career is literally your business. **Theodore Levitt**. *Only the Paranoid Survive* (1996)

The emerging work paradox is that in a post-job world, the only viable long-term career is to be a temp. **Anonymous**. Quoted in *Management Today* (February 1995)

The stepladder is gone, and there's not even the implied structure of an industry's rope ladder. It's more like vines, and you bring your own machete. **Peter F. Drucker**. Referring to to the impact of rapid organizational change. Quoted in *How to Manage* (Ray Wild, 1995)

The world's best poker players don't hanker for jobs in casino management. **Tom Peters**. *Liberation Management* (1992)

In many corporations managers now work with one eye on their résumé. Assignments that used to be seen in terms of their political value in the promotion game are now assessed for their résumé value. **Rosabeth Moss Kanter**. *When Giants Learn to Dance: Mastering the Challenges of Strategy, Management and Careers in the 1990s* (1992), ch. 12

The traditional corporate career may soon share the fate of the dad-at-work-mom-at home-two-kids nuclear family: an oft-invoked ideal that applies to fewer and fewer people. **Rosabeth Moss Kanter**. *When Giants Learn to Dance: Mastering the Challenges of Strategy, Management and Careers in the 1990s* (1992), ch. 11

Tomorrow's typical career will be neither linear nor continuous, nor will it always be upwards. Instead, one's life work will take more of a zig-zag course. **Tom Horton**. *Management Review* (1990)

When you retire ... you go from who's who to who's that, like stepping off the pier [or] achieving statutory senility. **Walter Wriston**. On retiring as chairman of Citibank Corp. *New York Times* (1985)

I'm just a guy who probably should have been a semi-talented poet on the Left Bank. I got sort of side-tracked here. **Steve Jobs**. *Fortune* (October 1, 1984)

People don't choose their careers; they are engulfed by them. **John Dos Passos**. *New York Times* (October 25, 1959)

The best augury of a man's success in his profession is that he thinks it the finest in the world. **George Eliot**. *Daniel Deronda* (1876)

No man likes to acknowledge that he has made a mistake in the choice of his profession. **Charlotte Brontë**. *The Professor* (1857), ch. 4

Challenge

I am always doing things I can't do, that's how I get to do them. **Pablo Picasso**. Quoted in *Street-Smart Advertising* (Margo Berman, 2006)

The secret of life is to have a task—something you bring everything to. And the most important thing is—it must be something you cannot possibly do. **Henry Moore**. Quoted in *The Brand You 50; Reinventing Work* (Tom Peters, 1999)

We specialize in the wholly impossible. **Nannie Burroughs**. Motto of the National Training School for Girls in Washington. Quoted in *Black Women in White America* (1972)

If anything terrifies me, I must try to conquer it. **Sir Francis Charles Chichester**. *Life* (June 1967)

  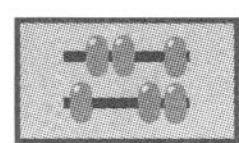   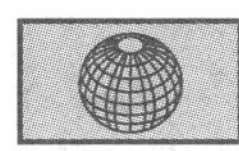   

You must do the thing you think you cannot do. **Eleanor Roosevelt**. *You Learn by Living* (1960)

The struggle itself toward the heights is enough to fill a human heart. **Albert Camus**. *The Myth of Sisyphus* (1942)

It is so tempting to try the most difficult thing possible. **Jennie Churchill**. Quoted in the *Daily Chronicle* (July 8, 1909)

Change

Unless the company becomes obsessed with constant change for the better, gradual change for the worse usually goes unnoticed. **Vineet Nayar**. *Employees First, Customer Second: Turning Conventional Management Upside Down* (2010)

So many companies adhere to the Zimbabwe school of change management—altering course only after ruin, by coup d'etat. **Simon Caulkin**. *Observer (London)* (February 15, 2009)

I skate to where the puck is going to be, not to where it has been. **Wayne Gretzky**. Quoted in *How to Work for an Idiot* (John Hoover, 2004)

The future is already upon us, it is just unevenly distributed. **William Gibson**. Quoted in the *Economist (London)* (June 23, 2000)

Technology changes. Economics does not. **Carl Shapiro**. *Information Rules* (cowritten with Hal L. Varian, 1999)

If the 1980s were about quality and the 1990s were about reengineering, then the 2000s will be about velocity. **Bill Gates**. *Business @ the Speed of Thought* (cowritten with Collins Hemingway, 1999)

This extraordinary arrogance that change must start at the top is a way of guaranteeing that change will not happen in most companies. **Gary Hamel**. Interview, *Strategy + Business* (October–December 1997)

It is extremely important that you show some insensitivity to your past in order to show the proper respect for the future. **Roberto Goizueta**. Speech. Quoted in *Fortune* (December 1995)

When the rate of change outside exceeds the rate of change inside, the end is in sight. **Jack Welch**. *Inc.* (March 1995)

When you are through changing, you are through. **Percy Barnevik**. Quoted in *Financial Times Handbook of Management* (Stuart Crainer, ed, 1995)

It is idle to speak of organizational transformation without individuals being transformed, especially the leader. **S. K. Chakraborty**. *Ethics in Management: Vedantic Perspectives* (1995)

Anyone in a large organization who thinks major change is impossible should probably get out. **John P. Kotter**. *The New Rules* (1995)

Notions of property, value, ownership, and the nature of wealth itself are changing more fundamentally than at any time since the Sumerians first poked cuneiform into wet clay and called it stored grain ... few people are aware of the enormity of this shift and fewer of them are lawyers or public officials. **John Perry Barlow**. Former songwriter for the Grateful Dead, Barlow was the first to use William Gibson's science-fiction term cyberspace to describe the global electronic social space. "The Economy of Ideas," *Wired* (March 1994)

Management that wants to change an institution must first show that it loves that institution. **Sir John Tusa**. *Observer (London)* (February 1994)

From now on, change will be the constant. The individuals best prepared to succeed are those who can learn, modify, and grow, regardless of age, experience, or ego. **Danny Goodman**. *Living at Light Speed: Your Survival Guide to Life on the Information Superhighway* (1994)

To succeed at re-engineering, you have to be a missionary, a motivator, and a leg breaker. **Michael Hammer**. *Fortune* (August 1993)

Unless companies change these rules, any superficial re-organizations they perform will be no more effective than dusting the furniture in Pompeii. **Michael Hammer**. *Re-engineering the Corporation* (cowritten with James Champy, 1993)

I want to put a ding in the universe. **Steve Jobs**. Quoted in *Made in the USA* (Phil Patton, 1992)

It isn't the changes that do you in, it's the transition. **Daniel Webster**. *Managing Transitions* (1991)

If it ain't broke, break it. **Richard Pascale**. *Managing on the Edge* (1990)

The incremental approach to change is effective when what you want is more of what you've already got. **Richard Pascale**. *Managing on the Edge* (1990)

Revitalizing General Motors is like teaching an elephant to tap dance. You find the sensitive spot and start poking. **H. Ross Perot**. *International Management* (February 1987)

All great change in business has come from outside the firm, not from inside. **Peter F. Drucker**. Quoted in "Seeing Things As They Really Are," *Forbes* (Robert Lenzner and Stephen S. Johnson, 1987)

Open the windows, let in the year we're living in. **Kitty D'Alessio**. Referring to the conflict between tradition and modernity after she succeeded company founder Coco Chanel to become president of Chanel, Inc. *New York Times* (1985)

Better never means better for everyone ... It always means worse, for some. **Margaret Atwood**. *The Handmaid's Tale* (1985)

Changing the direction of a large company is like trying to turn an aircraft carrier. It takes a mile before anything happens. And if it was a wrong turn, getting back on course takes even longer. **Al Ries**. *Positioning: The Battle for Your Mind* (cowritten with Jack Trout, 1980)

Most of us are about as eager to be changed as we were to be born, and go through our changes in a similar state of shock. **James Baldwin**. "Every Good-Bye Ain't Gone," *New York* (December 19, 1977)

If I were to give off-the-cuff advice to anyone trying to institute change, I would say, "How clear is the metaphor?" **Warren Bennis**. "Why Leaders Can't Lead," *Amacom* (1976)

Future shock is the disorientation that affects an individual, a corporation, or a country when he or it is overwhelmed by change and the prospect of change ... we are in collision with tomorrow. **Alvin Toffler**. *Observer (London)* (1972)

Change means movement. Movement means friction. **Saul Alinsky**. *Rules for Radicals* (1971)

Change is the process by which the future invades our lives. **Alvin Toffler**. *Future Shock* (1970)

Change is not merely necessary to life, it is life. **Alvin Toffler**. *Future Shock* (1970)

If we want everything to remain as it is, it will be necessary for everything to change. **Giuseppe di Lampedusa**. *The Leopard* (1955), ch. 1

I never think of the future. It comes soon enough. **Albert Einstein**. Interview (December 1930)

The inevitability of gradualness. **Sidney Webb (Lord Passfield)**. Speech, Labour Party Conference (1920)

The more things change, the more they are the same. **Alphonse Karr**. *Les Guêpes* (1849)

The reformer has enemies in all who profit by the old order, and only lukewarm defenders in all those who would profit by the new order. **Niccolò Machiavelli**. *The Prince* (1513)

It is only the very wisest and the very stupidest who cannot change. **Confucius**. *Analects* (500? BC)

The new environment dictates two rules: first, everything happens faster; second, anything that can be done will be done, if not by you, then by someone else, somewhere. **Andrew S. Grove**. Attributed

Let chaos reign, then rein in chaos. **Andrew S. Grove**. Attributed

If you do what you've always done, you'll get what you've always gotten. **Anonymous**.

To change and to improve are two different things. **Anonymous**. German proverb

When the wind of change blows, some build walls, others build windmills. **Anonymous**.

If you want truly to understand something, try to change it. **Kurt Lewin**. Attributed

Character

Be more concerned with your character than your reputation, because your character is what you really are, while your reputation is merely what others think you are. **John Wooden**. *They Call Me Coach* (2003)

My trouble is I lack what the English call character. By which they mean the power to refrain. **Alan Bennett**. "An Englishman Abroad," *Single Spies* (1989)

There are people whose external reality is generous because it is transparent, because you can read everything, accept everything, understand everything about them: people who carry their own sun with them. **Carlos Fuentes**. *The Old Gringo* (1985)

A woman is like a tea bag—only in hot water do you realize how strong she is. **Nancy Reagan**. *Observer (London)* (March 1981)

The analysis of character is the highest human entertainment. **Isaac Bashevis Singer**. *New York Times* (November 26, 1978)

To keep your character you cannot stoop to filthy acts. It makes it easier to stoop the next time. **Katharine Hepburn**. Quoted in the *Los Angeles Times* (November 1974)

The best index to a person's character is (a) how he treats people who can't do him any good, and (b) how he treats people who can't fight back. **Abigail Van Buren**. "Dear Abby," syndicated newspaper column (May 16, 1974)

The perfection preached in the Gospels never yet built an empire. Every man of action has a strong dose of egotism, pride, hardness, and cunning. **Charles de Gaulle**. Quoted in *New York Times Magazine* (May 12, 1968)

Though intelligence is powerless to modify character, it is a dab hand at finding euphemisms for its weaknesses. **Quentin Crisp**. *The Naked Civil Servant* (1968)

We don't love qualities, we love persons; sometimes by reason of their defects as well as of their qualities. **Jacques Maritain**. *Reflections on America* (1958), ch. 3

You know what charm is: a way of getting the answer yes without having asked any clear question. **Albert Camus**. *The Fall* (1956)

He looked like the kind of a guy that wouldn't talk to you much unless he wanted something off you. He had a lousy personality. **J. D. Salinger**. *The Catcher in the Rye* (1951), ch. 11

If you will think about what you ought to do for other people, your character will take care of itself. Character is a by-product, and any man who devotes himself to its cultivation in his own case will become a selfish prig. **Woodrow Wilson**. Speech, Pittsburgh, Pennsylvania (October 24, 1914)

Between ourselves and our real natures we interpose that wax figure of idealizations and selections which we call our character. **Walter Lippmann**. *A Preface to Politics* (1914), ch. 6

A man with so-called character is often a simple piece of mechanism; he has often only one point of view for the extremely complicated relationships of life. **J. August Strindberg**. *The Son of a Servant* (Claud Field, tr., 1913)

Character is the basis of happiness and happiness the sanction of character. **George Santayana**. "Reason in Common Sense," *The Life of Reason* (1906), ch. 9

One of the best strengtheners of character and developers of stamina ... is to assume the part you wish to play; to assert stoutly the possession of whatever you lack. **Orison Swett Marden**. *The Young Man Entering Business* (1903)

What is character but the determination of incident? What is incident but the illustration of character? **Henry James**. "The Art of Fiction," *Partial Portraits* (1888)

I think that, as life is action and passion, it is required of a man that he should share the passion and action of his time at peril of being judged not to have lived. **Oliver Wendell Holmes, Jr.** Memorial Day address (1884)

Talent is formed in quiet, character in the stream of human life. **Johann Wolfgang von Goethe**. *Torquato Tasso* (1790), Act 1, Scene 2

It is with narrow-souled people as with narrow-necked bottles: the less they have in them, the more noise they make in pouring it out. **Alexander Pope**. *Thoughts on Various Subjects* (1741)

If I cannot get men who steer a middle course to associate with, I would far rather have the impetuous and hasty. For the impetuous at any rate assert themselves. **Confucius**. *Analects* (500? BC)

Be polite. Write diplomatically. Even in a declaration of war one observes the rules of politeness. **Otto Edward Leopold von Bismarck**. Attributed

Choice

Why do I squander so much mental energy on the mundane purchases of everyday life? I think I've found a good answer ... Instead of realizing that picking a floss is an easy decision, I confuse the array of options and excess of information with importance, which then leads my brain to conclude that this decision is worth lots of time and attention. Call it the drug store heuristic: A cluttered store shelf leads us to automatically assume that a choice must really matter, even if it doesn't. (After all, why else would there be so many alternatives?) **Jonah Lehrer**. *Frontal Cortex* blog (*Wired* science blogs) (March 2, 2011)

Business is often about killing your favourite children to allow others to succeed. **Sir John Harvey-Jones**. *Troubleshooter*, BBC TV (1990)

From a narrow either/or society with a limited range of personal choices, we are exploding into a free-wheeling multiple-option society. **John Naisbitt**. *Megatrends* (1982)

Any color you like as long as it's black. **Henry Ford**. Slogan advertising the mass-produced Model-T Ford. Attributed in *Ford* (Allan Nevins, 1954), vol. 2, ch. 15

Things are in their essence what we choose to make them. **Oscar Wilde**. *De Profundis* (1905)

Commerce is the agency by which the power of choice is obtained. **John Ruskin**. *Munera Pulveris* (1872)

No choice among stinking fish. **Thomas Fuller**. *Gnomologia* (1732), no. 3554

Even children learn in growing up that both is not an admissible answer to a choice of which one? **Paul Samuelson**. Attributed

Civilization

The inability to make things is not merely a matter of imminent economic bankruptcy, it is cultural bankruptcy too. Civilisations are remembered by their artifacts, not by their credit default swaps or PSBRs. **Stephen Bailey**. *Independent (London)* (May 4, 2011)

If civilization has risen from the Stone Age, it can rise again from the Wastepaper Age. **Jacques Barzun**. *The House of Intellect* (1959)

Ours is not so much an age of vulgarity as of vulgarization; everything is tampered with or touched up, or adulterated or watered down, in an effort to make it palatable, in an effort to make it pay. **Louis Kronenberger**. "The Spirit of the Age," *Company Manners* (1954)

Every advance in civilisation has been denounced as unnatural while it was recent. **Bertrand Russell (Earl Russell)**. "An Outline of Intellectual Rubbish," *Unpopular Essays* (1950)

Civilization is the progress towards a society of privacy ... the process of setting man free from men. **Ayn Rand**. *The Fountainhead* (1943)

A few suits of clothes, some money in the bank, and a new kind of fear constitute the main differences between the average American today and the hairy men with clubs who accompanied Attila to the city of Rome. **Philip Gordon Wylie**. *Generation of Vipers* (1942)

Civilization has developed executive powers far beyond its understanding. **Maude Meagher**. *Fantastic Traveler* (1931)

To be able to fill leisure intelligently is the last product of civilization. **Bertrand Russell (Earl Russell)**. *The Conquest of Happiness* (1930)

Civilization advances by extending the number of important operations which we can perform without thinking about them. **Alfred North Whitehead**. *An Introduction to Mathematics* (1911)

A good civilisation spreads over us freely like a tree, varying and yielding because it is alive. A bad civilisation stands up and sticks out above us like an umbrella—artificial, mathematical in shape; not merely universal, but uniform. **G. K. Chesterton**. "Cheese," *Alarms and Discursions* (1910)

In a state of nature, the weakest go to the wall; in a state of over-refinement, both the weak and the strong go to the gutter. **Elbert Hubbard**. *The Philistine* (1895–1915)

Upon the sacredness of property civilization itself depends—the right of the laborer to his hundred dollars in the savings bank, and equally the legal right of the millionaire to his millions. **Andrew Carnegie**. "Wealth," *North American Review* (June 1889)

Bare-faced covetousness was the moving spirit of civilization from its first dawn to the present day; wealth, and again wealth, and for the third time wealth; wealth, not of society, but of the puny individual, was its only and final aim. **Friedrich Engels**. *The Origin of the Family* (1885)

Increased means and increased leisure are the two civilizers of man. **Benjamin Disraeli (Earl of Beaconsfield)**. Speech to the Conservatives of Manchester (April 3, 1872)

A decent provision for the poor is the true test of civilization. **Samuel Johnson**. Quoted in *The Life of Samuel Johnson* (James Boswell, 1791)

Commerce is the great civilizer. We exchange ideas when we exchange fabrics. **Robert Green Ingersoll**. Said to Indianapolis clergy. Attributed

I think it would be an excellent idea. **Mahatma Gandhi**. Said when asked what he thought of Western civilization. Attributed

Common Sense

Common Sense and Education: The more you think you have of one, the less you think you need of the other. **Tom Heehler**. *The Well-Spoken Thesaurus: The Most Powerful Ways to Say Everyday Words and Phrases* (2011)

Success is more a function of consistent common sense than it is of genius. **An Wang**. *Boston Magazine* (December 1986)

Common sense is the collection of prejudices acquired by age eighteen. **Albert Einstein**. Quoted in *Scientific American* (February 1976)

Common sense is a very tricky instrument; it is as deceptive as it is indispensable. **Susanne K. Langer**. *Philosophical Studies* (1962)

Nothing astonishes men so much as common sense and plain dealing. **Ralph Waldo Emerson**. "Art," *Essays: First Series* (1841)

Common sense (which, in truth, is very uncommon) is the best sense I know of. **Lord Chesterfield (Philip Dormer Stanhope)**. Letter (September 27, 1748)

We seldom attribute common sense except to those who agree with us. **François La Rochefoucauld**. *Reflections: or, Sentences and Moral Maxims* (1665)

Common sense is the best distributed commodity in the world, for every man is convinced that he is well supplied with it. **René Descartes**. *Le Discours de la méthode* (1637), pt. 1

Communication

It's not what you say, it's what people hear. **Frank Luntz**. *Words that Work* (2007)

At office-managerial level ... you do not read more than the first two sentences of any given report. You believe that anything which cannot be put into two sentences is not worth attending to. **Penelope Fitzgerald**. "The Axe," *The Means of Escape* (2000)

I say what I mean, you hear what I say. That is the end of it. **Barbara Cassani**. *Management Today* (August 1999)

Toilets are great ways of giving information, whether you put things on the wall or ask for comments. You can write things on the wall anonymously. **Dame Anita Roddick**. Quoted in *The Adventure Capitalists* (Jeff Grout and Lynne Curry, 1998)

A quotation is what a speaker wants to say, unlike a soundbite which is all that an interviewer allows you to say. **Tony Benn**. Letter (1996)

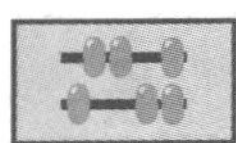

Electronic communication, as fast and efficient as it has become, does not automatically lead to better communication. **Dan Dimancescu**. *World-class New Product Development* (cowritten with Kemp Dwenger, 1996)

If figures of speech based on sports and fornication were suddenly banned, American corporate communication would be reduced to pure mathematics. **Jay McInerney**. *Brightness Falls* (1992)

It is ironic but true that in this era of electronic communications, personal interaction is becoming more important than ever. **Regis McKenna**. Quoted in *Thriving on Chaos* (Tom Peters, 1987)

Today, communication itself is the problem. We have become the world's first overcommunicated society. Each year we send more and receive less. **Al Ries**. *Positioning: The Battle for Your Mind* (cowritten with Jack Trout, 1980)

Even the frankest and bravest of subordinates do not talk with their boss the same way they talk with colleagues. **Robert Greenleaf**. *Servant Leadership: A Journey into the Nature of Legitimate Power and Greatness* (1977)

Through the picture I see reality; through the word I understand it. **Peter Kindersley**. Referring to the importance of both words and images in communication and publishing. Quoted in *Goldfinger* (Robert Heller, 1998)

The newest computer can merely compound, at speed, the oldest problem in the relations between human beings, and in the end the communicator will be confronted with the old problem, of what to say and how to say it. **Edward R. Murrow**. Speech (October 1964)

Let us write as if we were writing to a skeptical aunt. All the rest of the world can look over our aunt's shoulder. **Fairfax Cone**. *Christian Science Monitor* (1963)

The difference between the *almost* right word and the *right* word is really a large matter—it's the difference between the lightning bug and the lightning. **Mark Twain**. Letter to George Bainton (October 15, 1888)

Competition

It is easier to see the joy of competition if you are the one getting the prizes. **Lucy Kellaway**. *Financial Times (London)* (June 12, 2011)

Microsoft has had clear competitors in the past. It's a good thing we have museums to document that. **Bill Gates**. Speech, Computer History Museum (October 2001)

There is no gap in the market unless you have sharp elbows. **Andrew Neil**. *Sunday Times (London)* (September 2000)

You can't measure the value of being first. **Chris Moore**. *Marketing* (June 2000)

If we had just continued the way we were going, we would end up being nibbled to death. **Sir David Michels**. Referring to competition from smaller companies on the Internet. *Sunday Times (London)* (May 2000)

In a garage somewhere, an entrepreneur is forging a bullet with your company's name on it. **Gary Hamel**. *Digital Britain* (January 2000)

Never wrestle with a pig. You get dirty and only the pig enjoys himself. **Mark McCormack**. Quoting a proverb. *What You'll Never Learn on the Internet* (2000)

Running other companies out of business and gaining market share is what capitalistic competition is all about. Efficiency and lower prices flow from that all-out economic life-and-death struggle. **Lester Thurow**. "Microsoft Case Is About a Good Capitalist Practice: Running Your Competitor Out of Business," *www.lthurow.com* (November 3, 1999)

The goal of competitors is to prevail, not to preserve competition in the markets. **George Soros**. *Atlantic Monthly* (January 1998)

On the Internet ... competitive advantage has shrunk to a few months. If they don't keep innovating, they'll be overtaken. They have to keep adding digital value, adding services, building their brand. **William (Walid) Mougayar**. Interview, *UpsideToday* (1998)

What do you do when your competitor's drowning? Get a live hose and stick it in his mouth. **Ray Kroc**. *Wall Street Journal* (October 1997)

A prosperous competitor is often less dangerous than a desperate one. **Barry J. Nalebuff**. *Co-opetition* (cowritten with Adam M. Brandenburger, 1997)

Competition as most of us have routinely thought of it is dead. **James F. Moore**. *The Death of Competition* (1997)

I believe that if you're going to take someone on, you might as well take on the biggest brand in the world. **Sir Richard Branson**. "The Mavericks," *Fortune* (June 1995)

When the competition is moving at 200 miles an hour, every second you're in the pits matters a lot. **Doug Nelson**. "The Mavericks," *Fortune* (June 1995)

This is not an age of castles, moats, and armor where people can sustain a competitive advantage for very long. **Richard D'Aveni**. "The Mavericks," *Fortune* (June 1995)

I feel sorry for those who live without competition ... fat, dumb, and unhappy in cradle-to-grave security. **Donald M. Kendall**. Quoted in *How to Manage* (Ray Wild, 1995)

Business is becoming more and more akin to intellectual sumo wrestling. **Sir John Harvey-Jones**. *All Together Now* (1994)

Nothing focuses the mind better than the constant sight of a competitor who wants to wipe you off the map. **Wayne Calloway**. *Fortune* (March 11, 1991)

We feel the spear of the marketplace in our back. **Tony O'Reilly**. *Fortune* (April 9, 1990)

Men often compete with one another until the day they die; comradeship consists of rubbing shoulders jocularly with a competitor. **Edward Hoagland**. "Heaven and Nature," *Harper's Magazine* (March 1988)

In business, the competition will bite you if you keep running, if you stand still, they will swallow you. **William S. Knudsen**. Quoted in *The Fords: An American Epic* (Peter Collier and David Horowitz, 1987)

So far as power is concerned, does anyone believe the premiums of insurance companies are all almost uniform by accident? **Jimmy Hoffa**. Interview, *Playboy* (December 1975)

Perfect competition is a theoretical concept like the Euclidean line, which has no width and no depth. Just as we've never seen that line there has never been truly free enterprise. **Milton Friedman**. *There's No Such Thing as a Free Lunch* (1975), Introduction

Don't look back, something might be gaining on you. **Leroy Paige**. Personal saying (1952)

All business sagacity reduces itself in the last analysis to a judicious use of sabotage. **Thorstein Veblen**. *An Inquiry into the Nature of Peace and the Terms of Its Perpetuation* (1917)

  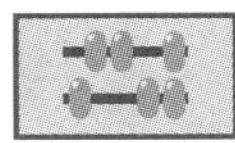   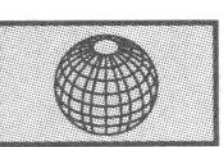   

Without vassal loyalty, or abject vassal fear, the monopolist's sleep can never be secure. **Joseph Furphy**. *Such Is Life* (1903)

Thou shalt not covet, but tradition Approves all forms of competition. **Arthur Hugh Clough**. "The Latest Decalogue" (1862), ll. 19–20

Computers

As computing and the internet become more ubiquitous over the coming decades and offline and online worlds blur, the very notion of being addicted to digital connectivity will seem as absurd and laughable as being addicted to electricity. **Rhodri Marsden**. *Independent (London)* (January 12, 2012)

If you have a child, you'll notice they have two states: asleep or online. **Eric Schmidt**. Speech, DLD Conference, Munich (January 25, 2011)

The Internet is the first thing that humanity has built that humanity doesn't understand, the largest experiment in anarchy that we've ever had. **Eric Schmidt**. Quoted in the *Independent (London)* (August 18, 2010)

Programming today is a race between software engineers striving to build bigger and better idiot-proof programs, and the Universe trying to produce bigger and better idiots. So far, the Universe is winning. **Rick Cook**. Quoted in *Applied Choice Analysis* (David A. Hensher, John M. Rose, and William H. Greene, 2005)

The Star Trek computer doesn't seem that interesting. They ask it random questions, it thinks for a while. I think we can do better than that. **Larry Page**. Interview, *Business Week* (May 3, 2004)

Computers are useless. They can only give you answers. **Pablo Picasso**. Quoted in *How Breakthroughs Happen* (Andrew Hargadon, 2003)

The value of e-commerce is not in the e, but in the commerce. **Octavio Paz**. Quoted in *Management Today* (June 2000)

We no longer think of chairs as technology, we just think of them as chairs. But there was a time when we hadn't worked out how many legs chairs should have, how tall they should be, and they would often "crash" when we tried to use them. Before long, computers will be as trivial and plentiful as chairs and we will cease to be aware of the things. In fact I'm sure we will look back on this last decade and wonder how we could ever have mistaken what we were doing with them for "productivity." **Douglas Adams**. "How to Stop Worrying and Learn to Love the Internet," *Sunday Times (London)* (August 29, 1999)

The one thing computers have done is let us make bigger mistakes. We have to be careful not to depend on our machines. **Michael Bloomberg**. Quoted in "Terminal Velocity," *Wired* (David S. Bennahum, February 1999)

The search button on the browser no longer provides an objective search, but a commercial one. **Sir Tim Berners-Lee**. Referring to the commercialization of the Internet. *Weaving the Web* (1999)

Take Wrigley's Chewing Gum. I don't think the Internet is going to change how people chew gum. **Warren Buffett**. Interview, *Fortune* (July 1998)

The Weightless World. **Diane Coyle**. Book title. Referring to an economy in which information is more important than physical products. *The Weightless World* (1997)

A sort of cognitive equivalent of a condom—it's a layer of contraceptive rubber between the direct experience and the cognitive system. **Sir Jonathan Miller**. Referring to reading from a computer screen. *Independent on Sunday (London)* (January 1996)

Buying the right computer and getting it to work properly is no more complicated than building a nuclear reactor from wristwatch parts in a darkened room using only your teeth. **Dave Barry**. *Dave Barry in Cyberspace* (1996)

I would say that hardware is the bone of the head, the skull. The semiconductor is the brain within the head. The software is the wisdom and data is the knowledge. **Masayoshi Son**. *Harvard Business Review* (January–February 1992)

A computer can tell you down to the dime what you've sold, but it can never tell you how much you could have sold. **Sam M. Walton**. *Made in America* (cowritten with John Huey, 1992)

A modern computer hovers between the obsolescent and the non-existent. **Sydney Brenner**. *Society* (January 1990)

Imagine if every Thursday your shoes exploded if you tied them the usual way. This happens to us all the time with computers, and nobody thinks of complaining. **Jeff Raskin**. Interview in Dr. Dobb's *Journal of Software Tools for the Professional Programmer* (1986)

Every program has (at least) two purposes: the one for which it was written, and another for which it wasn't. **Alan Jay Perlis**. *Epigrams in Programming* (1985)

The best book on programming for the layman is *Alice in Wonderland*; but that's because it's the best book on anything for the layman. **Alan Jay Perlis**. "Epigrams in Programming," *SIGPLAN Notices* (September 1982), no. 48

There are two ways to write error-free programs; only the third one works. **Alan Jay Perlis**. "Epigrams in Programming," *SIGPLAN Notices* (September 1982), no. 40

There is no reason for any individual to have a computer in his home. **Kenneth H. Olsen**. Speech to the convention of the World Future Society (1977)

The computer is a moron. **Peter F. Drucker**. Quoted in *Drucker, the Man Who Invented the Corporate Society* (John J. Tarrant, 1976)

Men are going to have to learn to be managers in a world where the organization will come close to consisting of all chiefs and one Indian. The Indian, of course, is the computer. **Thomas L. Whisler**. *Christian Science Monitor* (April 21, 1964)

Confidence and Self-Belief

Confidence is what you have before you understand the problem. **Woody Allen**. Quoted in *Leadership Virtuosity: A Trove of Virtuoso Ideas* (Lee Thayer, 2010)

Confidence is what you have before you understand the problem. **Woody Allen**. Quoted in *Leadership Virtuosity: A Trove of Virtuoso Ideas* (Lee Thayer, 2010)

We are the ones we have been waiting for. **Barack Obama**. Speech while campaigning for the Democratic Party's nomination for president (February 5, 2008)

Nothing has ever been achieved except by those who dared believe that something inside of them was superior to circumstances. **Bruce Barton**. Quoted in *Fearless Interviewing* (Marky Stein, 2002)

If you think you can, you can. And if you think you can't, you're right. **Mary Kay Ash**. *New York Times* (October 20, 1985)

One man that has a mind and knows it can always beat ten men who haven't and don't.

       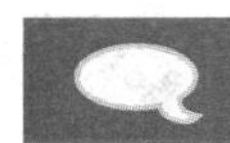 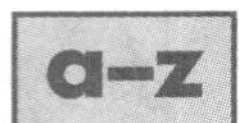

George Bernard Shaw. *The Apple Cart* (1929), Act 1

All you need in this life is ignorance and confidence; then success is sure. **Mark Twain**. Letter to Mrs Foote (December 2, 1887)

Ignorance more frequently begets confidence than does knowledge. **Charles Darwin**. *The Descent of Man* (1871)

Take the place and attitude to which you see your unquestionable right, and all men acquiesce. **Ralph Waldo Emerson**. *Journals* (1836)

Attempt easy tasks as if they were difficult, and difficult as if they were easy: in the one case that confidence may not fall asleep, in the other that it may not be dismayed. **Baltasar Gracián**. *The Art of Worldly Wisdom* (1647)

We should do everything both cautiously and confidently at the same time. **Epictetus**. *Discourses* (2nd century AD), bk. 2

For a man to achieve all that is demanded of him he must regard himself as greater than he is. **Johann Wolfgang von Goethe**. Attributed

Whether you believe you can, or whether you believe you can't, you're absolutely right. **Henry Ford**. Attributed

I don't really see the hurdles. I sense them like a memory. **Edwin Moses**. Attributed

Conscience

Be the master of your will but the servant of your conscience. **Robin S. Sharma**. *MegaLiving!: 30 Days to a Perfect Life* (1995)

Sufficient conscience to bother him, but not sufficient to keep him straight. **David Lloyd George (Earl of Dwyfor)**. Referring to Ramsay MacDonald. Quoted in *Life with Lloyd George* (A. J. Sylvester, 1975)

Conscience is the inner voice that warns us somebody may be looking. **H. L. Mencken**. *A Mencken Chrestomathy* (1948)

Most people sell their souls and live with a good conscience on the proceeds. **Logan Pearsall Smith**. "Other People," *Afterthoughts* (1931)

If we cannot be powerful and happy and prey on others, we invent conscience and prey on ourselves. **Elbert Hubbard**. *The Philistine* (1895–1915)

Conscience is the name which the orthodox give to their prejudices. **John Oliver Hobbes**. *A Bundle of Life* (1894)

Conscience and cowardice are really the same things. Conscience is the trade-name of the firm. **Oscar Wilde**. *The Picture of Dorian Gray* (1891), ch. 1

I've got just as much conscience as any man in business can afford to keep—just a little, you know, to swear by as 't were. **Harriet Beecher Stowe**. *Uncle Tom's Cabin* (1852), ch. 1

It is always term-time in the court of conscience. **Thomas Fuller**. *Gnomologia* (1732)

Conscience gets a lot of credit that belongs to cold feet. **Anonymous**. US proverb

A business must have a conscience as well as a counting house. **Sir Montague Burton**. Attributed

Consultants and Advisers

Want to find cost savings? Call in one of the big accountancy firms. Got a PR crisis? Hire an agency. Directors' pay—you've guessed it ... If there's something a company does, the chances are there will be a consultant out there to advise on it and protect executives by taking the hit if disaster strikes. The consultantification of British business, if not Western business, is complete. **James Moore**. *Independent (London)* (April 12, 2012)

The two most dreaded words in any office are the same—management consultants. Their arrival rumbles through a workplace like the approaching thwump-thwump of the T-Rex in *Jurassic Park*, rattling our desks and making us all fear we will be picked up and gored at random. **Johann Hari**. *Independent (London)* (July 8, 2011)

The British state will soon be spending more on management consultants than upgrading its nuclear weapons. **Johann Hari**. *Independent (London)* (August 20, 2010)

The Cranfield School of Management studied 170 companies who had used management consultants, and it discovered just 36% of them were happy with the outcome—while two-thirds judged them to be useless or harmful. A medicine with that failure-rate would be taken off the shelves. **Johann Hari**. *Independent (London)* (August 20, 2010)

As the shamans who poison chickens and the soothsayers who read entrails have long demonstrated, sometimes it is more important to build a consensus around a good decision than to make the best possible decision; sometimes it is more useful to believe that a decision is sanctioned by a higher authority than to acknowledge that it rests on mere conjecture ... Consultants, following in the footsteps of their pagan forebears, understand that they must adopt the holy mien of a priestly caste. **Matthew Stewart**. *The Management Myth: Management Consulting Past, Present and Largely Bogus* (2009)

I landed the job by providing a credible response to this question: How many pubs are there in Great Britain? The purpose of that question, I realised after the interview, was to see how easily I could talk about a subject of which I knew almost nothing, on the basis of facts that were almost entirely fictional. It was an excellent introduction to management consulting. **Matthew Stewart**. *The Management Myth: Management Consulting Past, Present and Largely Bogus* (2009)

Consulting is where product companies go to die. IBM is the most famous example. So starting as a consulting company is like starting out in the grave and trying to work your way up into the world of the living. **Paul Graham**. "How to Fund a Startup," *paulgraham.com* (November 2005)

We were proud of the way we used to make things up as we went along ... It's like robbing a bank but legal. We could take somebody straight off the street, teach them a few simple tricks in a couple of hours and easily charge them out to our clients for more than £7,000 per week. **David Craig**. On management consultancy. *Rip Off! The Scandalous Inside Story of the Management Consulting Money Machine* (2005)

Thinking must be the hardest job in the world. What people want to do is outsource it to a mantra or a methodology like reengineering. **Eileen C. Shapiro**. *Fad Surfing in the Boardroom* (1998)

Consultants eventually leave, which makes them excellent scapegoats for major management blunders. **Scott Adams**. *The Dilbert Principle* (1996)

A consultant is a person who takes your money and annoys your employees while tirelessly searching for the best way to extend the consulting contract. **Scott Adams**. *The Dilbert Principle* (1996)

I come from an environment where, if you see a snake, you kill it. At General Motors, if you see a snake, the first thing you do is hire a consultant on snakes. **H. Ross Perot**. Speech (December 1991)

Wall Street is the only place people ride to in a Rolls Royce to get advice from people who take the subway. **Warren Buffett**. *Newsday* (August 1991)

Timing; originality; forcefulness; a gift for self-promotion and perhaps above all else, the ability to encapsulate memorably what others recognize as true ... are the hallmarks of the modern management guru. **Carol Kennedy**. *Guide to the Management Gurus* (1991)

Techniques shrouded in mystery clearly have value to the purveyor of investment advice. After all, what witch doctor has ever achieved fame and fortune by simply advising "Take two aspirins"? **Warren Buffett**. Letter to shareholders (1987)

It is always easier to talk about change than to make it. It is easier to consult than to manage. **Alvin Toffler**. *The Adaptive Corporation* (1985)

They are the people who borrow your watch to tell you what time it is and then walk off with it. **Robert Townsend**. Referring to consultants. *Up the Organization* (1970)

The function of the expert is not to be more right than other people, but to be wrong for more sophisticated reasons. **Sir David Butler**. Quoted in the *Observer (London)* (1969)

Get the advice of everybody whose advice is worth having—they are very few—and then do what you think best yourself. **Charles Stewart Parnell**. Quoted in *Parnell* (Conor Cruise O'Brien, 1957)

What a difficult thing it is to ask someone's advice on a matter without coloring his judgment by the way in which we present our problem. **Blaise Pascal**. *Pensées* (1670)

My greatest strength as a consultant is to be ignorant and ask a few questions. **Peter F. Drucker**. Attributed

Consumption

All the senses can be manipulated to attempt to alter consumer mood, and in turn purchasing interest and perception of the quality of a product. Stimulate two senses and the brand impact increases by 30%, rising to 70% when a third is added ... US company Inscentivation, for example, owns a scent that increases betting on slot machines in casinos by 45%, while UK company Bodywise treats its bills with an odour that makes them 17% more likely to be paid. **Helen Soteriou**. BBC News (August 13, 2012)

We could live as we did in 1948 and have an additional six months off a year, or strike some better balance between time and more things. But this is never the choice presented to us. The option is never more time, it's always buying more. **Neal Lawson**. *All Consuming* (2009)

Whoever said money can't buy happiness didn't know where to go shopping. **Bo Derek**. Quoted in *The 10 Women You'll Be Before You're 35* (Alison James, 2005)

America is a vast conspiracy to make you happy. **John Updike**. *Problems* (1980)

What's great about this country is that America started the tradition where the richest consumers buy essentially the same things as the poorest. **Andy Warhol**. *The Philosophy of Andy Warhol (from A to B and Back Again)* (1975)

Buying is much more American than thinking and I'm as American as they come. **Andy Warhol**. *The Philosophy of Andy Warhol (from A to B and Back Again)* (1975)

People want economy and they will pay any price to get it. **Lee Iacocca**. *New York Times* (1974)

In a consumer society there are inevitably two kinds of slaves: the prisoners of addiction and the prisoners of envy. **Ivan Illich**. *Tools for Conviviality* (1973)

Work to survive, survive by consuming, survive to consume: the hellish cycle is complete. **Raoul Vaneigem**. *The Revolution of Everyday Life* (1967)

Teenagers travel in droves, packs, swarms. To the librarian, they're a gaggle of geese. To the cook, they're a scourge of locusts. To department stores they're a big beautiful exaltation of larks, all lovely and loose and jingly. **Bernice Fitz-Gibbon**. *New York Times* (1960)

Our gadget-filled paradise suspended in a hell of insecurity. **Reinhold Niebuhr**. *Pious and Secular America* (1957)

A society in which consumption has to be artificially stimulated in order to keep production going is a society founded on trash and waste, and such a society is a house built on sand. **Dorothy L. Sayers**. *Creed or Chaos* (1947)

Man wants but little here below but likes that little good—and not too long in coming. **Samuel Butler**. *Further Extracts from the Notebooks* (A. Bartholomew, ed, 1934)

Consumption is the sole end and purpose of production; and the interest of the producer ought to be attended to only so far as it may be necessary for promoting that of the consumer. **Adam Smith**. *An Inquiry into the Nature and Causes of the Wealth of Nations* (1776)

Too many of us are spending money we haven't earned to buy things we don't need to impress people we don't like. **Anonymous**.

Contracts

I had to get back to work. NBC has me under contract; the baby and I only have a verbal agreement. **Tina Fey**. On the birth of her first child. *Parade* (March 9, 2008)

Contracts are agreements made up of big words and little type. **Sam Ewing**. Quoted in the *Saturday Evening Post* (May 1993)

You'll have the legal authority to use my skin for lampshades so far as I can see. **Robert Bolt**. Referring to a punitive contract. Letter (July 1963)

A verbal contract isn't worth the paper it's written on. **Samuel Goldwyn**. Quoted in *The Great Goldwyn* (Alva Johnson, 1937)

He that payeth beforehand shall have his work ill done. **Thomas Fuller**. *Gnomologia* (1732), no. 2245

There is nothing more likely to start disagreement among people or countries than an agreement. **E. B. White**. Attributed

Make your bargain before beginning to plow. **Anonymous**. Arab proverb

Contract: an agreement that is binding on the weaker party. **Frederick Sawyer**. Attributed

Cooperation

The key to using the Internet to extend and build relationships is to view ownership of information differently—you need to bring customers inside your business to create information partnerships ... relationships become the differentiator, more than products or services. Businesses become intertwined. **Michael Dell**. Speech (March 3, 1999)

The speed of the Internet provides a fundamentally different perspective on how business relationships occur ... The approach relies on collaboration, not on competition ... on sharing information, and understanding what we as businesses do best. **Michael Dell**. Speech to the Executives' Club of Chicago. "NetSpeed: The Supercharged Effect of the Internet" (October 23, 1998)

Only recently have people begun to recognise that working with suppliers is just as important as listening to customers. **Barry J. Nalebuff**. *Co-opetition* (cowritten with Adam M. Brandenburger, 1997)

Virtually all economic activity in the contemporary world is carried out not by individuals but by organizations that require a high degree of social cooperation. **Francis Fukuyama**. *Trust: The Social Virtues and the Creation of Prosperity* (1995)

When you collaborate with other people, you tend to regard your own individual contribution as the most important. **Yang Jiang**. *A Cadre School Life* (1980)

Successful cooperation in or by formal organizations is the abnormal, not the normal, condition. **Chester Barnard**. *Organization and Management* (1948)

Corporations can have no soul but they can love each other. **Henry Demarest Lloyd**. *Wealth Against Commonwealth* (1894)

Men will find that they can ... avoid far more easily the perils which beset them on all sides by united action. **Baruch Spinoza**. *Ethics* (1677), pt. 4, proposition 35, note

Corporate Culture

Put a bunch of confident, aggressive men in the same room and reward them for taking risks, and you create a pressure cooker, from which probity and prudence evaporate like steam. **Ian Leslie**. *Guardian (London)* (June 30, 2012)

I knew it was time to leave when I realized I could no longer look students in the eye and tell them what a great place this was to work. **Greg Smith**. Letter to the *New York Times* (March 14, 2012)

That is what *The Office* was partly about: the gap between the managerialist rhetoric of modernisation and change, in which employees had to sit through suffocatingly well-meaning "training days" and identify "strategic goals" in their annual appraisals, and the mundane reality of typing away at a workstation in an anonymous out-of-town office park and then suddenly noticing that ten years have gone by. **Johann Hari**. *Guardian (London)* (July 9, 2011)

Just ask yourself: if you were to walk into any corporation, would you find faces brimming over with deep fulfillment and authentic delight—or stonily asking themselves, "If it wasn't for the accursed paycheck, would I really imprison myself in this dungeon of the human soul?" **Umair Haque**. *Harvard Business Review* blog (June 8, 2011)

In one section of the HMRC ... workers were prohibited from keeping personal items on their desks. Instead they were given red tape to mark out where they should put their pens and pencils, their computer keyboards and their phones. That is the office as factory. **Andreas Whittam Smith**. *Independent (London)* (September 25, 2009)

Too many people are on boards because they want to have nice-looking visiting cards. **Utz Felcht**. *Sunday Times (London)* (October 2000)

I don't want to feel responsible to outsiders with financial concerns that may differ from those of the welfare of IKEA. **Ingvar Kamprad**. *Forbes* (August 2000)

Companies ... are likely to find hierarchies turned upside down. Juniors teach seniors, subordinates lead teams with their bosses on them ... A decision-making hierarchy is replaced by an internal marketplace of ideas. **Rosabeth Moss Kanter**. "How E-Smart Are You?" *World Link* (January–February 2000)

Never pick up someone else's ringing phone. **Mark McCormack**. *What You'll Never Learn on the Internet* (2000)

Corporate totalitarianism ... rules through dispensability rather than exploitation. It treats communities, people, countries, ecosystems, species as disposable and dispensable. **Vandana Shiva**. *Globalisation: Gandhi and Swadeshi* (2000)

A company's culture is often buried so deeply inside rituals, assumptions, attitudes, and values that it becomes transparent to an organization's members only when, for some reason, it changes. **Rob Goffee**. *The Character of a Corporation* (cowritten with Gareth Jones, 1998)

The oppressive atmosphere in most companies resembles downtown Calcutta in summer. **Christopher Bartlett**. *The Individualised Corporation* (cowritten with Sumantra Ghoshal, 1997)

Constructive confrontation. **Christopher Bartlett**. *The Individualised Corporation* (cowritten with Sumantra Ghoshal, 1997)

I believe in provocative disruption. **Charlotte Beers**. *Fortune* (August 1996)

IBM is like the Stepford Wives. It takes the best people from the best universities and colleges and then snips out some part of the brain so that they become mindless clones. **Bill Campbell**. Quoted in *Giant Killers* (Geoffrey James, 1996)

The software industry as a whole tends to be slightly managed chaos. It was a giant group grope in the 1970s, when this whole thing started ... effectively there are no rules. **Ann Winblad**. Quoted in *Giant Killers* (Geoffrey James, 1996)

Every company has its own language, its own version of its own history (its myths), and its own heroes and villains (its legends), both historical and contemporary. **Michael Hammer**. *Beyond Re-engineering* (1996)

This system sounds chaotic, can be frustrating and is, in some ways, uncontrollable. It has destroyed any semblance of corporate security. And ... it has worked very well. **Ricardo Semler**. "The Mavericks," *Fortune* (June 1995)

Any engineer that doesn't need to wash his hands at least three times a day is a failure. **Shoichiro Toyoda**. Referring to the importance of manufacturing in Japanese industry. Quoted in *How to Manage* (Ray Wild, 1995)

To write down, frame, and publish your corporate values is all about self-deceit and ego. It is almost certainly bullshit. **Barry J. Gibbons**. Quoted in *How to Manage* (Ray Wild, 1995)

There is a misconception that small is always more beautiful than big. **Lou Gerstner**. *Fortune* (May 1993)

If you look at the companies where the CEO stayed on till he's 80, those are the people who confuse themselves with the company. **Walter Wriston**. *New York Times* (April 1993)

The corporation's edict to its members could be phrased as: While you are here, you will act as though you have no other responsibilities, no other life. **Rosabeth Moss Kanter**. *When Giants Learn to Dance: Mastering the Challenges of Strategy, Management and Careers in the 1990s* (1992), ch. 10

The clichés of a culture sometimes tell the deepest truths. **Faith Popcorn**. *The Popcorn Report* (1991)

Real commitment is rare in today's organization ... 90% of the time what passes for commitment is compliance. **Peter Senge**. *The Fifth Discipline: The Art and Practice of the Learning Organization* (1990)

If you're not scared, you're too stupid to work here. **Lee Iacocca**. Speech (1990)

I'm forcing more men into my company to get more sexual tension into the business ... I love the buzz and ... sexuality of verbal foreplay. **Dame Anita Roddick**. *Marketing* (August 3, 1989)

Nobody here cares which washroom you use. **Debi Coleman**. *US News & World Report* (September 1987)

I looked for those sharp, scratchy, harsh, almost unpleasant guys who see and tell you about things as they really are. **Thomas J. Watson, Jr**. *Fortune* (August 1987)

I believe in God, family, and McDonald's and, in the office, that order is reversed. **Ray Kroc**. Quoted in *McDonald's—Behind the Arches* (John F. Love, 1986)

If the washroom isn't good enough for the people in charge, then it's not good enough for the people in the store. **Marcus, Lord Sieff**. Quoted in *A Passion for Excellence* (Tom Peters and Mary Austin, 1985)

A corporation does seem like a family. Not necessarily that one big happy family they like to boast about ... but just like every family, a hotbed of passion, rivalry, and dreams that build or destroy careers. **Paula Bernstein**. *Family Ties, Corporate Bonds* (1985)

The way management treats their associates is exactly how the associates will then treat the customers. **Sam M. Walton**. "The Hot Ticket in Retailing," *New York Times* (Isadore Barmash, July 1984)

The soul of a business is a curious alchemy of needs, desires, greed, and gratifications mixed together with selflessness, sacrifices, and personal contributions far beyond material rewards. **Harold S. Geneen**. *Managing* (cowritten with Alvin Moscow, 1984)

Clothes don't make the man—but they go a long way towards making a businessman. **Thomas J. Watson, Sr**. Quoted in *IBM: Colossus in Transition* (Robert Sobel, 1981)

Modelers build intricate decision trees whose pretension to utility is exceeded only by the awe in which high-level managers hold the technocrats who constrain them. **Theodore Levitt**. "A Heretical View of Management Science," *Fortune* (December 1978)

I've often thought that after you get organized, you ought to throw away the organization chart. **David Packard**. "Lessons of Leadership," *The Nation's Business* (January 1974)

A company needs smart young men with the imagination and the guts to turn everything upside down if they can. It also needs old figures to keep them from turning upside down those things that ought to be rightside up. **Henry Ford II**. Speech (1966)

It is difficult to get a man to understand something when his salary depends upon his not understanding it. **Upton Sinclair**. *I, Candidate for Governor: And How I Got Licked* (1935)

Company cultures are like country cultures. Never try to change one. Try, instead, to work with what you've got. **Peter F. Drucker**. Attributed

Corporate Responsibility

I'm a little disappointed that the perpetrators of a crime that killed 11 people are still in charge of the crime scene. **Dr John**. Referring to the management of BP, in the light of the oil-rig explosion that killed 11 workers and precipitated the Gulf Coast oil-spill disaster. Quoted in *The Times (London)* (May 31, 2010)

On the face of it, shareholder value is the dumbest idea in the world. Shareholder value is a result, not a strategy ... Your main constituencies are your employees, your customers and your products. **Jack Welch**. Speech quoted in the *Financial Times (London)* (March 13, 2009)

Business has to be a force for social change. It is not enough to avoid hideous evil—it must, we must, actively do good. If business stays parochial, without moral energy or codes of behaviour, claiming there are no such thing as values, then God help us all. If you think morality is a luxury business can't afford, try living in a world without it. **Dame Anita Roddick**. Speech, International Forum on Globalization Teach-In, Seattle, Washington. "Trading with Principles" (November 27, 1999)

Increasingly, I have become concerned that the motivation to meet Wall Street earnings expectations may be overriding common sense business practices ... Managing may be giving way to manipulation; integrity may be losing out to illusion. **Arthur Levitt, Jr**. Speech to the New York University Center for Law and Business. "The Numbers Game" (September 28, 1998)

Companies have to be socially responsible or the shareholders pay eventually. **Warren Shaw**. "The Players," *Fortune* (Eileen Gunn, April 1997)

The market is a mechanism for sorting the efficient from the inefficient, it is not a substitute for responsibility. **Charles Handy**. *The Empty Raincoat: Making Sense of the Future* (1994), pt. 1, ch. 1

Only the little people pay taxes. **Leona Helmsley**. *New York Times* (July 1989)

I would never make a decision which might be damaging to Turin's local administration. A Texan capitalist couldn't care less about local government, he couldn't care less about the federal government. **Giovanni Agnelli**. Fiat's headquarters are based in Turin. Quoted in *Interview on Modern Capitalism* (Arrigo Levi, 1983)

Few trends could so thoroughly undermine the very foundations of our free society as the acceptance by corporate officials of a social responsibility other than to make as much money for their stockholders as possible. **Milton Friedman**. *Capitalism and Freedom* (1962)

The public be damned. I am working for my stockholders. **William Henry Vanderbilt**. Refusing to speak to a reporter. Quoted in a letter from A. W. Cole, *New York Times* (August 25, 1918)

CORPORATION, n. An ingenious device for obtaining individual profit without individual responsibility. **Ambrose Bierce**. *The Devil's Dictionary* (1911)

Corporate bodies are more corrupt and profligate than individuals because they have more power to do mischief and are less amenable to disgrace or punishment.

They feel neither shame, remorse, gratitude, nor goodwill. **William Hazlitt**. "On Corporate Bodies," *Table Talk* (1821–22), Essay 27

Corruption and Scandal

It is no exaggeration to say that since the 1980s, much of the global financial sector has become criminalised, creating an industry culture that tolerates or even encourages systematic fraud. The behaviour that caused the mortgage bubble and financial crisis of 2008 was a natural outcome and continuation of this pattern, rather than some kind of economic accident. **Charles H. Ferguson**. *Guardian (London)* (May 20, 2012)

Three years after our horrific financial crisis caused by financial fraud, not a single financial executive has gone to jail, and that's wrong. **Craig Ferguson**. Speech when accepting an Oscar for his 2010 movie *Inside Job*, a documentary about the financial crisis of 2008 (March 2011)

Yet another hedge fund manager explained Icelandic banking to me this way: you have a dog, and I have a cat. We agree that each is worth a billion dollars. You sell me the dog for a billion, and I sell you the cat for a billion. Now we are no longer pet owners but Icelandic banks, with a billion dollars in new assets. **Michael Lewis**. *Boomerang: Travels in the New Third World* (2011)

The SEC now is 3500 chickens, and we need to get some foxes in there. **Harry Markopolos**. On the SEC's failure to investigate the activities of Bernie Madoff. Testimony before a Congressional Committee (February 4, 2009)

I don't know how I could have been more explicit. I gave them a roadmap and a flashlight, but they didn't go where I told them to go, they didn't look where I told them to look, they didn't tell the people I told them to call. **Harry Markopolos**. On alerting the SEC to Bernie Madoff's fraudulent activities. Testimony before a Congressional Committee (February 4, 2009)

Surely I'm not the only person to ask the obvious question: How different, really, is Mr. Madoff's tale from the story of the investment industry as a whole? **Paul R. Krugman**. On the fraudulent investment fund run by Bernie Madoff. *New York Times* (December 19, 2008)

If this were a traditional bank robbery, the eyewitness reports would say that Mr Madoff walked out with billions of dollars as someone held the door open for him. **Jeffrey Zwerling**. Quoted in the *Independent (London)* (December 17, 2008)

The argument that rigorous oversight will somehow stifle Wall Street's "creativity" is no longer convincing. Any system that permits a scam artist like Madoff to deceive, not just widows and orphans, but also sophisticated investors ... isn't a market at all; it's a shooting gallery. **Tim Rutten**. *Los Angeles Times* (December 17, 2008)

All one great big lie. **Bernard Madoff**. Confessing that his $50 billion investment fund was a total fraud. Quoted in the *Independent (London)* (December 16, 2008)

It looked incredibly credible! **Nicola Horlick**. On her decision to invest £10M of clients' money in the Madoff fund, subsequently exposed as entirely fraudulent. Interview on *Today*, BBC Radio 4 (December 15, 2008)

My aim was to make money for the bank. You lose track of the amounts involved when you are engaged in this kind of work. **Jérôme Kerviel**. Referring to his loss of €4.8 billion through unauthorized futures trading. Quoted in the *Independent (London)* (February 6, 2008)

In today's regulatory environment, it's virtually impossible to violate rules ... but it's impossible for a violation to go undetected, certainly not for a considerable period of time. **Bernard Madoff**. In 2008 Madoff was charged with the biggest investment fraud in history. Remark in an interview (October 20, 2007)

Corruption is a cancer that steals from the poor, eats away at governance and moral fibre and destroys trust. **Robert Zoellick**. Quoted in the *New York Times* (June 26, 2007)

I've found that wherever there is one cockroach in plain sight, many more are lurking behind the corner out of view. **Harry Markopolos**. Document submitted to the Securities and Exchange Commission warning them about the Madoff fund. "The World's Largest Hedge Fund Is a Fraud" (November 2005)

A super-sized fraud of this magnitude was bound to happen given the lack of regulation of these off-shore entities. **Harry Markopolos**. Document submitted to the Securities and Exchange Commission warning them about the Madoff fund. "The World's Largest Hedge Fund Is a Fraud" (November 2005)

I have ... spoken to the heads of various Wall Street equity derivatives trading desks and every single one of the senior managers I spoke with told me that Bernie Madoff was a fraud. Of course no one wants to take an undue career risk by sticking their head up ... The fewer people who know who wrote this report the better. I am worried about the personal safety of myself and my family. **Harry Markopolos**. Document submitted to the Securities and Exchange Commission warning them about the Madoff fund. "The World's Largest Hedge Fund Is a Fraud" (November 2005)

I have no doubt that mothers in America use my name to frighten their children into finishing their vegetables. **Conrad, Lord Black**. Interview, *Fortune* (May 30, 2005)

The business pages of American newspapers should not read like a scandal sheet. **George W. Bush**. Referring to a series of high-profile accounting scandals. Speech (July 2002)

What was done was not in keeping with the values and heritage of this firm. It was wrong, there's no other word for it. **Joseph Berardino**. Referring to the part played by accountanting firm Arthur Andersen in the collapse of Enron. Quoted in the *Guardian (London)* (June 2002)

It argues no fault in the construction of the aqueduct that the water it conveys is often dirty. **Anonymous**. Financier referring to corruption in the City. Quoted in *The City of London, Vol IV: A Club No More* (David Kynaston, 2002)

If there is anything material and we're not reporting it, we'll be breaking the law. We don't break the law. **Kenneth Lay**. Referring to Enron's accounting practices. Quoted in *BusinessWeek* (August 24, 2001)

It's a proprietary strategy. I can't go into it in great detail. **Bernard Madoff**. On being asked to explain the secrets of his success. Remark (2001)

It's time to make things ship-shape, to get rid of the debt, to get a bit of a cash box to work from, to enjoy life a bit more. **Conrad, Lord Black**. Referring to disposals from his media group. *New York Times* (April 2000)

There are two parties involved in every corrupt transaction, typically a government official and a business person. Yet those who pay bribes are often depicted as innocent victims ... The reality is that both parties conspire to defraud the public.

Lynda, Baroness Chalker. Speech, University of Glasgow, UK. "Public Sector Corruption from an International Perspective" (February 19, 1999)

Money you haven't earned is not good for you. **Robert Maxwell**. Quoted in *Time* (November 28, 1988)

Greed is all right ... Greed is healthy. You can be greedy and still feel good about yourself. **Ivan Boesky**. After success as a trader on Wall Street, in 1987 he was convicted of securities fraud, imprisoned for two years, and fined US$100 million. Commencement address, University of California, Berkeley (May 18, 1986)

If things were half as bad as some people persist in believing, I'd have retired with a bottle of Scotch and a pistol a long time ago. **Robert Maxwell**. *Daily Mail (London)* (June 1973)

Like many businessmen of genius he learned that free competition was wasteful, monopoly efficient. And so he simply set about achieving that efficient monopoly. **Mario Puzo**. Referring to Don Vito Corleone. *The Godfather* (1969), bk. 3, ch. 14

He's a businessman ... I'll make him an offer he can't refuse. **Mario Puzo**. The offer referred to is a death threat. *The Godfather* (1969), bk. 1, ch. 1

If only 50 or more people were doing for the country what I have been doing, there would not be a pay freeze or a balance of payments problem. **Robert Maxwell**. Referring to his world trips to build an international scientific publishing business. Speech (December 1966)

Creativity

What made Leonardo da Vinci, Thomas Edison, and Albert Einstein such creative geniuses? It wasn't reading books or watching YouTube talks about How To Be More Creative, that's for sure ... If startling insights could be systematically arrived at, they wouldn't be startling. The best you can do is to create a conducive environment: put in the hours; take time to daydream; avoid mind-corroding substances. **Oliver Burkeman**. *Guardian (London)* (January 11, 2013)

There is a stigma attached to boredom—parents are always worried about their kids being bored—but it gives your mind a chance to wander. Our work shows that daydreaming could be potentially beneficial in the workplace, as it allows lateral thinking that could assist with problem solving ... Boredom at work has always been seen as something to be eliminated, but perhaps we should be embracing it in order to enhance our creativity. **Sandi Mann**. Quoted in the *Daily Mail (London)* (January 9, 2013)

I think "creativity" is better described as failing repeatedly until you get something right. **Seth Godin**. Interviewed on *The Great Discontent* blog (August 14, 2012)

There are clear benefits to boredom ... it can be a very productive emotion. Put simply, people who are bored and dissatisfied with accepted ways of doing things are liable to come up with new ways of doing them. Creativity is the antidote to boredom ... Essentially, boredom leads to some form of change. **Peter Toohey**. Quoted in the *Independent (London)* (August 25, 2011)

Experts say our brains need boredom so we can process thoughts and be creative. I think they're right. I've noticed that my best ideas always bubble up when the outside world fails in its primary job of frightening, wounding, or entertaining me. **Scott Adams**. *Wall Street Journal* (August 6, 2011)

Designers must be both conscious and unconscious at the same time. Clear thinking at the wrong moment can stifle talent. **Karl Lagerfeld**. *Twitter (Karl_Lagerfeld)* (June 17, 2010)

Creativity does not require invention. At its best, creativity is an effort to reveal the truth, no matter how elusive or complex it may seem. It's *12 Angry Men*, not Athena emerging from Zeus's head. **Mandy Brown**. *A Working Library* blog (June 18, 2008)

The best ideas come as jokes. Make your thinking as funny as possible. **David Ogilvy**. Quoted in *Don't Get Taken—Take Control* (Tom Sabella, 2006)

I think the enemy of creativity in the world today is that so much thinking is done for you. **J. G. Ballard**. Quoted in the *Observer (London)* (2002)

All the great work comes from people's obsession and imagination, not from focus groups. **Michael, Lord Grade**. *Marketing* (June 2000)

The wild, the absurd, the seemingly crazy: this kind of thinking is where new ideas come from ... The people capable of such playful thought carry forward their childish qualities and childhood dreams, applying them in areas where most of us get stuck, victims of our adult seriousness. Staying a child isn't easy. **Nicholas Negroponte**. "Toys of Tomorrow," *Wired* (March 6, 1998)

The majority of creative acts are unplanned, and each begins with awareness of an unexpected opportunity. **Alan G. Robinson**. *Corporate Creativity* (cowritten with Sam Stern, 1997)

When you ask creative people how they did something, they feel a little guilty because they didn't really *do* it, they just *saw* something ... That's because they were able to connect experiences they've had and synthesize new things. **Steve Jobs**. Interview, "The Next Insanely Great Thing," *Wired* (February 1996)

Creativity is allowing oneself to make mistakes. Art is knowing which ones to keep. **Scott Adams**. *The Dilbert Principle* (1996)

Planning, by its very nature, defines and preserves categories. Creativity, by its very nature, creates categories or re-arranges established ones. **Henry Mintzberg**. *The Rise and Fall of Strategic Planning* (1994)

In the middle of a hard project, I remind people to do something else. Sometimes people need to work on something completely different to get their best ideas. **Brad Fregger**. "On Achieving Excellence" (July 1991)

Tap the energy of the anarchist and he will be the one to push your company ahead. **Dame Anita Roddick**. *Body and Soul* (cowritten with Russell Miller, 1991)

Music is spiritual. The music business is not. **Van Morrison**. *The Times (London)* (July 1990)

Could Henry Ford produce the Book of Kells? Certainly not. He would quarrel initially with the advisability of such a project and then prove it was impossible. **Flann O'Brien**. *Myles Away from Dublin* (1990)

We created an environment in which a man was expected to sit and think for two years. **Edwin Land**. *Selected Papers in Industry* (Polaroid Corporation, 1983)

If it doesn't sell, it isn't creative. **David Ogilvy**. *Ogilvy on Advertising* (1983)

Creativity often consists of merely turning up what is already there. Did you know that right and left shoes were thought up only a little over a century ago? **Bernice Fitz-Gibbon**. Quoted in obituary, *New York Times* (1982)

Creativity is thinking new things. Innovation is doing new things. **Theodore Levitt**. "Ideas Are Useless Unless Used," *Inc.* (February 1981)

Creative people tend to pass the responsibility for getting down to brass tacks to others. **Theodore Levitt**. "Ideas Are Useless Unless Used," *Inc.* (February 1981)

Every creative act is a sudden cessation of stupidity. **Edwin Land**. *Forbes* (June 1975)

An artist is someone who produces things that people don't need to have but that he—for some reason—thinks it would be a good idea to give them. **Andy Warhol**. *The Philosophy of Andy Warhol (from A to B and Back Again)* (1975)

Creativity can be described as letting go of certainties. **Gail Sheehy**. *Speed Is of the Essence* (1971)

The majority of businessmen are incapable of original thought because they are unable to escape from the tyranny of reason. **David Ogilvy**. Quoted in *The Creative Organisation* (Gary A. Steiner, ed, 1965)

True creativity often starts where language ends. **Arthur Koestler**. *The Act of Creation* (1964)

Originality is deliberate and forced, and partakes of the nature of a protest. **Eric Hoffer**. *The Passionate State of Mind* (1955)

Many people are inventive, sometimes cleverly so. But real creativity begins with the drive to work on and on and on. **Margueritte Bro**. *Sarah* (1949)

Controlled accident. **Jackson Pollock**. Referring to his painting technique. Interview (1946)

One doesn't discover new lands without consenting to lose sight of the shore for a very long time. **André Gide**. *The Counterfeiters* (1926)

Minds are like parachutes. They only function when they are open. **Sir James Dewar**. Attributed

Criticism

The thought pattern that keeps most people poor: they criticize instead of analyse. **Robert Kiyosaki**. *Rich Dad, Poor Dad* (2000)

Criticism is one of the most important tasks a manager has. **Jacques Barzun**. *Emotional Intelligence* (1996)

If you have bright plumage, people will take pot shots at you. **Alan Clark**. *Independent (London)* (June 25, 1994)

A negative judgment gives you more satisfaction than praise, providing it smacks of jealousy. **Jean Baudrillard**. *Cool Memories* (1987)

A thick skin is a gift from God. **Konrad J. Adenauer**. *New York Times* (December 30, 1959)

No one can make you feel inferior without your consent. **Eleanor Roosevelt**. *This Is My Story* (1937)

Cheers hearten a man. But jeers are just as essential. They help maintain his sense of balance and proportion. **Jay E. House**. "On Second Thoughts," *On Second Thoughts* (1936)

Next to the joy of the egotist is the joy of the detractor. **Agnes Repplier**. "Writing an Autobiography," *Under Dispute* (1924)

I fancy it is just as hard to do your duty when men are sneering at you as when they are shooting at you. **Woodrow Wilson**. Speech (1914)

No man can tell another his faults so as to benefit him, unless he loves him. **Henry Ward Beecher**. *Proverbs from Plymouth Pulpit* (1887)

Damn with faint praise, assent with civil leer, And, without sneering, teach the rest to sneer. **Alexander Pope**. "An Epistle to Dr Arbuthnot" (1735)

Customers

The question is, then, do we try to make things easy on ourselves or do we try to make things easy on our customers, whoever they may be? **Erwin Frand**. Quoted in *Business Models* (David Watson, 2005)

There is only one boss. The customer. And he can fire everybody in the company, from the chairman on down, simply by spending his money somewhere else. **Sam M. Walton**. Quoted in *500 of the Most Witty, Acerbic and Erudite Things Ever Said About Money* (Philip Jenks, 2002)

Consumers are statistics. Customers are people. **Stanley Marcus**. *Quest for the Best* (2001)

A restaurant is great if there are people queuing to get into it. It doesn't matter what the critics say. **Sir David Michels**. *Sunday Times (London)* (September 2000)

You could not have got more knowledge about detergents anywhere in the world ... I asked, could anyone who has washed their own clothes in the past three months put their hands up. Not one hand went up. **Niall Fitzgerald**. Referring to Unilever's problems with a detergent. *Marketing* (July 2000)

If you look after the customers and look after the people who look after the customers, you should be successful. **Charles Dunstone**. *Sunday Times (London)* (June 2000)

Whatever the business model, it doesn't matter what anybody else thinks if customers don't like it. **Paul Gratton**. *Sunday Times (London)* (May 2000)

The most exciting thing happening in business is the rise of vigilante consumers. **Dame Anita Roddick**. Interview, *Marketing Week* (February 24, 2000)

Your most unhappy customers are your greatest source of learning. **Bill Gates**. *Business @ The Speed of Thought* (1999)

Customers do not care about industry boundaries; they want service and convenience. **Peter G. W. Keen**. "Basic Change," *The Process Edge* (1999)

Many people believe that we have entered the age of the Internet. Actually, it's more accurate to say that we're living in the age of the customer. **Anne Busquet**. "Next Stop—The 21st Century," *Fast Company* (Lucy McCauley, 1999)

It is a company's customers who effectively control what it can and cannot do. **Clayton M. Christensen**. *The Innovator's Dilemma* (1997)

If someone thinks they are being mistreated by us, they won't tell 5 people, they'll tell 5000. **Jeff Bezos**. *Wall Street Journal* (May 1996)

Everything changes when there is a real customer yelling at you from the other end of the phone. **Percy Barnevik**. Quoted in *Liberation Management* (Tom Peters, 1992)

The consumer is the most important part of the production line. **W. Edwards Deming**. *Out of the Crisis* (1992)

Good companies will meet needs; great companies will create markets. **Philip Kotler**. *Marketing Management* (1990)

The customer will become so integrated into the production process that we will find it more and more difficult to tell just who is actually the consumer and the producer. **Alvin Toffler**. *The Third Wave* (1980)

The consumer isn't a moron; she is your wife. **David Ogilvy**. *Confessions of an Advertising Man* (1963)

When you are skinning your customers you should leave some skin on to grow again so that you can skin them again. **Nikita Khrushchev**. Speech to British businessmen (May 1961)

There is only one valid definition of business: to create a customer. **Peter F. Drucker**. *The Practice of Management* (1954)

A manufacturer is not through with his customer when a sale is completed. He has then only started with his customer. **Henry Ford**. *My Life and Work* (cowritten with Samuel Crowther, 1922)

Goodwill is the one and only asset that competition cannot undersell or destroy. **Marshall Field**. Attributed

Debt

For decades mortgage dealers insisted that home buyers be able to produce a down payment of 10% or more, show a steady income and good credit rating, and possess a real first and last name. Then, at the dawn of the new millennium, they suddenly threw all that shit out the window and started writing mortgages on the backs of napkins to cocktail waitresses and ex-cons carrying five bucks and a Snickers bar. **Matt Taibbi**. On the origins of the subprime lending crisis. *Rolling Stone (New York)* (July 2009)

He is like some sherry-crazed old dowager who has lost the family silver at roulette, and who now decides to double up by betting the house as well. **Boris Johnson**. On Gordon Brown's decision to increase government borrowing to alleviate the effects of the 2008 recession. *Daily Telegraph (London)* (November 25, 2008)

Drive-in banks were established so most of the cars today could see their real owners. **E. Joseph Cossman**. Quoted in *The Truth About Money* (Ric Edelman, 2004)

Today, there are three kinds of people: the have's, the have-not's, and the have-not-paid-for-what-they-have's. **Earl Wilson**. Quoted in *Investing Under Fire* (Alan R. Ackerman, 2003)

I feel these days like a very large flamingo. No matter what way I turn, there is always a very large bill. **Joseph O'Connor**. *The Secret World of the Irish Male* (1994)

The debt is like a crazy aunt we keep down in the basement. All the neighbors know she's there, but nobody wants to talk about her. **H. Ross Perot**. *United We Stand: How We Can Take Back Our Country* (1992)

Give the Germans five deutschmarks and they will save it. But give the British £5 and they will borrow £25 and spend it. **Sir John Major**. Said while Chancellor of the Exchequer. Interview, *Daily Express (London)* (May 28, 1990)

Should we really let our people starve so we can pay our debts. **Julius Nyerere**. *Guardian (London)* (March 1985)

Christmas is a time when kids tell Santa Claus what they want and adults pay for it. Deficits are when adults tell the government what they want—and their kids pay for it. **Richard D. Lamm**. *US News & World Report* (1985)

We at Chrysler borrow money the old-fashioned way. We pay it back. **Lee Iacocca**. *New York Times* (1983)

A debt may get mouldy, but it never decays. **Chinua Achebe**. *No Longer at Ease* (1960)

One must have some sort of occupation now-a-days. If I hadn't my debts I shouldn't have anything to think about. **Oscar Wilde**. *A Woman of No Importance* (1893), Act 1

Creditors have better memories than debtors. **Benjamin Franklin**. The *Poor Richard's Almanack* series (1732–58) were originally published under the pseudonym Richard Saunders. *Poor Richard's Almanack* (1758)

Decisions

Disregarding information can make not only for cheaper but also for better decisions. Ignorance can be bliss ... Among physicians diagnosing heart attacks, simple decision trees beat a complex model. Among detectives locating serial criminals, simple locational rules trump complex psychological profiling. Among investors picking stocks, simple passive strategies outperform complex active ones. And among shopkeepers understanding spending patterns, repeat purchase data out-predict complex models. Applying complex decision rules in a complex environment may be a recipe not just for a cock-up but catastrophe. **Andy Haldane**. Speech to the Federal Reserve Bank of Kansas City. "The Dog and the Frisbee" (August 31, 2012)

Once we have a sense of how long a decision should take, we generally should delay the moment of decision until the last possible instant. If we have an hour, we should wait 59 minutes before responding. If we have a year, we should wait 364 days. Even if we have just half a second, we should wait as long as we possibly can ... Life might be a race against time but it is enriched when we rise above our instincts and stop the clock to process and understand what we are doing and why. A wise decision requires reflection, and reflection requires a pause. **Frank Partnoy**. *Wait: The Useful Art of Procrastination* (2012)

Part of the resistance against making decisions comes from our fear of giving up options. The word "decide" shares an etymological root with "homicide," the Latin word "caedere," meaning "to cut down" or "to kill." **John Tierney**. "Do You Suffer From Decision Fatigue?" *New York Times* (August 17, 2011)

Effective decision makers are distinguished, not so much by the superior extent of their knowledge, as by their recognition of the limitations of that knowledge. **John Kay**. *Obliquity: Why Our Goals Are Best Achieved Indirectly* (2010)

As prime minister you face a decision every hour which comes down to one question-do you want to cut your throat or slit your wrists? **Anonymous**. Comment by a senior adviser to Tony Blair. Quoted in the *Independent (London)* (September 4, 2009)

Most discussions of decision making assume that only senior executives make decisions or that only senior executives' decisions matter. This is a dangerous mistake. **Peter F. Drucker**. *Classic Drucker* (2006)

Business today is about making decisions amid ambiguity. **Geraldine Laybourne**. Quoted in "Next Stop—The 21st Century," *Fast Company* (Lucy McCauley, 1999)

Spend the optimal amount of time on each decision and pretty soon you run out of life. **Steven Waldman**. "The Tyranny of Choice," *New Republic (Washington, DC)* (January 27, 1992)

A real decision is measured by the fact that you've taken a new action. If there's no action, you haven't truly decided. **Anthony Robbins**. *Awaken the Giant Within* (1992)

Every decision is liberating, even if it leads to disaster. Otherwise, why do so many people walk upright and with open eyes into their misfortune. **Elias Canetti**. "1980," *The Secret Heart of the Clock: Notes, Aphorisms, Fragments 1973–1985* (1991)

A weak man has doubts before a decision, a strong man has them afterwards. **Karl Kraus**. *Half Truths and One-and-a-Half Truths* (1990)

Good decisions come from wisdom. Wisdom comes from experience. Experience comes from bad decisions. **Anonymous**. *Forbes* (August 10, 1987)

What is important is not the decision itself but rather how committed and informed people are. The best decisions can be bungled just as the worst decisions can work just fine. **William Ouchi**. *Theory Z: How American Business Can Meet the Japanese Challenge* (1981)

The man who is denied the opportunity of taking decisions of importance begins to regard as important the decisions he is allowed to take. **C. Northcote Parkinson**. *Parkinson's Law: The Pursuit of Progress* (1958)

A complex decision is like a great river, drawing from its many tributaries the innumerable premises of which it is constituted. **Herbert A. Simon**. *Administrative Behavior* (1947)

There is always a multitude of reasons both in favour of doing a thing and against doing it. The art of debate lies in presenting them; the art of life lies in neglecting ninety-nine hundreths of them. **Mark Rutherford**. *More Pages from a Journal* (1910)

Delegating

I've been blessed to find people who are smarter than I am, and they help me to execute the vision I have. **Russell Simmons**. Quoted in the *Independent (London)* (February 16, 2009)

Do not delegate an assignment and then attempt to manage it yourself—you will make an enemy of the overruled subordinate. **Wess Roberts**. *Leadership Secrets of Attila the Hun* (1991)

If you are having as much fun running a big corporation as you did running a piece of it, then you are probably interfering too much with the people who really make it happen. **James E. Burke**. *Fortune* (June 6, 1988)

Big things and little things are my job. Middle level management can be delegated. **Konosuke Matsushita**. *Quest for Prosperity* (1988)

Surround yourself with the best people you can find, delegate authority, and don't interfere. **Ronald Reagan**. Quoted in *Fortune* (September 1986)

You could not maintain any illusion of direct control over a general or provincial governor ... You appointed him, you watched his chariot and baggage train disappear over the hill in a cloud of dust, and that was that. **Sir Antony Jay**. Arguing that a key reason the Roman Empire grew so large and lasted so long was the delegation necessitated by poor communications. *Management Machiavelli* (1970)

He liked nobody to be in any way superior to him ... he chose his ministers, not for their knowledge, but for their ignorance; not for their capacity, but for their want of it. **Duc de Saint-Simon (Louis de Rouvroy)**. Referring to Louis XIV. *Memoires* (1694–1723), vol. 3

Not the least among the qualities in a great king is a capacity to permit his ministers to serve him. **Cardinal Richelieu**. *Testament Politique* (1641)

Never learn to do anything. If you don't learn, you'll always find someone else to do it for you. **Mark Twain**. Attributed

Details

The contribution which the human mind makes to work and business is very much one of picking up information from tiny, seemingly insignificant trifles, and relating them to new ideas or concepts. **Sir John Harvey-Jones**. *Managing to Survive* (1993)

Neglecting small things under the pretext of wanting to accomplish large ones is the excuse of a coward. **Alexandra David-Neel**. *Quest* (May–June 1978)

God is in the details. **Ludwig Mies van der Rohe**. *New York Times* (August 1969)

The mechanics of running a business are really not very complicated, when you get down to essentials. You have to make some stuff and sell it to somebody for more than it cost you. That's about all there is to it, except for a few million details. **John L. McCaffrey**. Speech (1953)

Pedantry is the dotage of knowledge. **Holbrook Jackson**. *Anatomy of Bibliomania* (1930), vol. 1

The art of being wise is the art of knowing what to overlook. **William James**. *The Principles of Psychology* (1890)

Our life is frittered away by detail ... Simplify, simplify. **Henry David Thoreau**. "Where I Lived and What I Lived For," *Walden, or Life in the Woods* (1854)

All knowledge is of itself of some value. There is nothing so minute or inconsiderable, that I would not rather know it than not. **Samuel Johnson**. Quoted in *The Life of Samuel Johnson* (James Boswell, 1791)

A handful of men have become very rich by paying attention to details that most others ignored. **Henry Ford**. Attributed

Determination

Dealing with failure is easy: Work hard to improve. Success is also easy to handle: You've solved the wrong problem. Work hard to improve. **Alan Jay Perlis**. Quoted in *If Ignorance Is Bliss, Why Aren't There More Happy People?* (John Mitchinson and John Lloyd, 2009)

Miracles can be made, but only by sweating. **Giovanni Agnelli**. *Corriere della Sera* (1994)

In some circumstances, a refusal to be defeated is a refusal to be educated. **Margaret Halsey**. *No Laughing Matter* (1977)

Sweat is the cologne of accomplishment. **Heywood Hale Broun**. Interview on CBS TV (July 21, 1973)

To gain that which is worth having, it may be necessary to lose everything else. **Bernadette Devlin**. *The Price of My Soul* (1969), Preface

Never give in, never give in, never, never, never, never—in nothing, great or small, large or petty—never give in except to convictions of honour and good sense. **Sir Winston Churchill**. Address given at Harrow School (October 29, 1941)

Fanaticism consists in redoubling your effort when you have forgotten your aim. **George Santayana**. *The Life of Reason* (1905)

I shall find a way or make one. **Robert Edwin Peary**. Inscription on an expedition hut (1902)

I wish to preach, not the doctrine of ignoble ease, but the doctrine of the strenuous life, the life of toil and effort, of labor and strife.

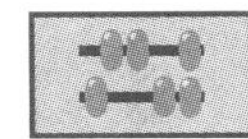

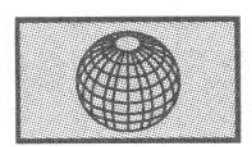

Theodore Roosevelt. Speech, The Hamilton Club, Chicago, Illinois. "The Strenuous Life," *The Strenuous Life: Essays and Addresses* (1900)

The people who get on in this world are the people who get up and look for the circumstances they want, and, if they can't find them, make them. **George Bernard Shaw**. *Mrs Warren's Profession* (1893), Act 2

Discrimination

Business shouldn't be like sports, separating the men from the women. **Barbara Ward (Baroness Jackson)**. Speech (October 2002)

This fellow said to me, "You know for a woman you make a lot of money. If I was you, I'd go back to my office and be happy just to have the job." **Grace Fey**. Quoted in *Women of the Street* (Sue Herera, 1997)

I regard affirmative action as pernicious—a system that had wonderful ideals when it started but was almost immediately abused for the benefit of white middle-class women. **Camille Paglia**. Interview, *Reason Magazine* (August–September 1995)

Top jobs are designed for people with wives. **Lucy Heller**. Quoted in the *Economist (London)* (March 28, 1992)

We don't so much want to see a female Einstein become an assistant professor. We want a woman schlemiel to get promoted as quickly as a male schlemiel. **Bella Abzug**. Quoted in *America Chronicle* (Lois Gordon and Alan Gordon, 1987)

Saying that a person cannot be kept out doesn't ensure that that person can get in, and more important, stay in. **Margaret Hennig**. Discussing corporate responses to antidiscrimination legislation. *The Managerial Woman* (cowritten with Anne Jardim, 1976)

There are very few jobs that actually require a penis or vagina. All other jobs should be open to everybody. **Florynce R. Kennedy**. "Freelancer with No Time to Write," *Writer's Digest* (February 1974)

The legend of the jungle heritage and the evolution of man as a hunting carnivore has taken root in man's mind ... He may even believe that equal pay will do something terrible to his gonads. **Elaine Morgan**. *The Descent of Woman* (1972)

The test for whether or not you can hold a job should not be the arrangement of your chromosomes. **Bella Abzug**. *Bella!* (1972)

The low wages at which women will work form the chief reason for employing them at all ... A woman's cheapness is, so to speak, her greatest economic asset. She can be used to keep down the cost of production. **Bureau of Labor**. "Report on the Condition of Woman and Child Wage-Earners in the United States" (1910), vol. 11

Men their rights and nothing more; women their rights and nothing less. **Susan B. Anthony**. *The Revolution* was the magazine of the women's suffrage movement in the United States. *The Revolution* (1868)

Doing Business in Africa

After Asia, Africa is the fastest-growing continent in the world right now, and it's largely due to China. **Thomas Barnett**. "When China Ruled the World," *Esquire* (January 2011)

Multinational organisations and those governments truly concerned about Africa should be directing all their efforts to creating and supporting a ... policy of real diplomatic sticks and large economic carrots untainted by protectionism. **Nicky Oppenheimer**. Speech, Southern Africa Business Association, London (June 26, 2000)

International finance is always looking for new opportunities. The challenge for Africa is not just to be attractive to traders and investors, but to offer opportunities which are more attractive than anywhere else in the world. **Peter Hain**. Speech, Challenges for Governance in Africa Conference, Wilton Park, England (September 13, 1999)

If you look at Malaysian companies, they are not investing in Europe or the United States, they are investing in African countries, high-potential countries, where they can transfer their expertise. **Raphael Auphan**. Quoted in the *International Herald Tribune (Paris)* (November 4, 1997)

Here, in this realm of the spices, a market price was being created—a set of fiscal frontiers within which to reach a consensus. It was the language of the stock exchange ... and it was the bourse which had obviously imitated the ways of the souk. **Douglas Kennedy**. Describing bartering for spices in the Casablanca souk. *Chasing Mammon: Travels in the Pursuit of Money* (1992)

One of the principal reasons why genuine industrialization cannot easily be realized in Africa today is that the market for manufactured goods in any single African country is too small. **Walter Rodney**. *How Europe Underdeveloped Africa* (1972)

We face neither East nor West; we face forward. **Kwame Nkrumah**. Speech (April 1960)

Doing Business in Asia-Pacific

India is the place where all generalisations are true, but so are the exceptions ... India is the land of synthesis. **Salil Tripathi**. "India: A Portrait, by Patrick French" [book review], *Independent (London)* (January 14, 2011)

China's economy is almost Dickensian in the freedom it offers robber barons, corrupt government officials, and all the schemers in between. The well-connected capitalist can destroy everything in his path, confident that the complaints of the downtrodden won't go anywhere—until they erupt in violence. And even then, our man can rest assured that when social push comes to government shove, some local official scapegoat will stand in front of the firing squad and not he. **Thomas Barnett**. *Esquire* (December 21, 2010)

Like most catch-up artists before it, including rising America of the nineteenth century, China has cheated its way to the pinnacle of the global economy, racking up hidden debts of unprecedented proportions. But heading a single-party state, Beijing remains insidiously adept at disguising that mortgaged future ... In the end, China's pervasive short-term thinking exacts a terrible moral price as everybody cheats everybody else with nary a pang of conscience, as lies upon lies are statistically amassed to achieve China's annual growth rate of 8% or better. **Thomas Barnett**. *Esquire* (December 21, 2010)

The largest burst of continuous economic growth in history has occurred without the benefit of free markets. Wealth has been created as never before, not as a result of evolutionary change, but as a product of revolution and dictatorship. **John Gray**. On the Chinese economic boom of the 2000s. *New Statesman* (August 2, 2010)

In 2040, the Chinese economy will reach US$123 trillion, or nearly three times the economic output of the entire globe in 2000. China's per capita income will hit US$85,000, more than double the forecast for the European Union, and also much higher than that of India and Japan. In other words, the average Chinese megacity dweller will be living twice as well as the average Frenchman ... Although it will not have overtaken the United States in per capita wealth, according to my forecasts, China's share of global GDP—40%—will dwarf that of the United States (14%) ... This is what economic hegemony will look like. **Robert Fogel**. *Foreign Policy* (January/February 2010)

We had better get used to Chinese and Indian ideas coming to influence ours: on the environment, on financial services, on corporate governance and so on. We had better get used to great scientific research coming not from Europe or North America but from Asia. We had better get used to ideas about society ... coming from other parts of the world. It will be thrilling but also frightening—and maybe for those of us in the comfortable West, just a little humbling. **Hamish McRae**. *Independent (London)* (December 24, 2009)

America needs China to buy her Treasury bills; and China needs America to buy her exports. They are like two drunken giants leaning on each other. Yet a sober reckoning of some sorts seems inevitable; and it is difficult to see how both can be winners. **Sean O'Grady**. *Independent (London)* (October 6, 2009)

China is becoming the world's second largest economy ... And within a generation it is on track to become the largest ... the renminbi will [then] become the world's most important currency. **Hamish McRae**. *Independent (London)* (June 12, 2009)

We in the West have a choice. Either we concede the argument that China, in the 5,000 years of recorded human history, has been a much more successful and durable culture than America or Western Europe and is now reclaiming its natural position of global leadership. Or we stop denying the rivalry between the Chinese and Western models and start thinking seriously about how Western capitalism can be reformed to have a better chance of winning. **Anatole Kaletsky**. *The Times (London)* (February 4, 2009)

There is still a widespread view in the West that China will eventually conform, by a process of natural and inevitable development, to the Western pradigm. This is wishful thinking. **Martin Jacques**. *When China Rules the World* (2009)

Asians save today's money for tomorrow while Americans spend tomorrow's money today. **Cheng Siwei**. Speech to the World Economic Forum (January 2008)

Indians in general have tended to under-market themselves. That comes because it's part of our culture ... you don't go and say I have created the world's greatest software. **Subeer Bhatia**. *BusinessWeek* (September 2000)

The velocity of decision making in government was extraordinarily slow. It took 18 to 24 months and 15 to 20 trips to Delhi to get a license to import computers. **Narayana Murthy**. *Forbes* (June 2000)

It says something about this new global economy that *USA Today* now reports every morning on the day's events in Asian markets. **Lawrence H. Summers**. Remark (1998)

In Sydney, you're in Asia, but not of Asia. Basing your Asian operations in Sydney is like basing your American operations in Rio. **Donald Saunders**. *Asia Inc.* (December 1996)

Given the economic growth and blossoming of billionaires in the region, Asia is likely to produce the world's first trillionaire. **Anonymous**. Quoted in *Asia, Inc.* (September 1996)

Five Rules for Doing Business in China: 1. Think small—focus on one region at a time. 2. Skip the manager, talk to the clerk. 3. Study the side streets. 4. Get the goods to market. 5. Above all be flexible. **Anonymous**. Quoted in the *New York Times Magazine* (February 18, 1996)

In Japan, the best and brightest young people aspire to become bureaucrats, not businessmen, and there is intense competition for bureaucratic jobs. **Francis Fukuyama**. *Trust: The Social Virtues and the Creation of Prosperity* (1995)

The dramatic modernization of the Asian economies ranks alongside the Renaissance and the Industrial Revolution as one of the most important developments in economic history. **Lawrence H. Summers**. Remark (1993)

Never visit a Japanese company without tons of business cards. Basically, no meishi (name cards) means no existence for you on this Earth. **Mark Gauthier**. *Making It in Japan: Work, Life, Leisure and Beyond* (1993)

Indian management has to pursue processes which conform to the underlying grain of the Indian temper. **S. K. Chakraborty**. *Management by Values: Towards Cultural Congruence* (1991)

Some people think that Japan's success is due to cartels and collaboration. It is not. In the industries in which Japan is internationally successful, it has many fiercely competitive local rivals. **Michael Porter**. *Economist (London)* (June 9, 1990)

Acts of marketing insanity such as the US firm that invested heavily in a campaign to sell cake mix to the Japanese—in profound and dismal ignorance of the fact that hardly any homes in Japan have ovens. **Robert Heller**. *The Supermarketers* (1987)

There is nothing Japan really wants to buy from foreign countries except, possibly, neckties with unusual designs. **Yoshihiro Inayama**. Quoted in "Sayings of the Week," *Sydney Morning Herald* (August 3, 1985)

This road of industrialization was not planned in advance by theoreticians. Rather, it has been created by the peasants on the basis of their experience in real life. **Fei Xiaotong**. Comparing China's industrialization favorably to that of the West, where modern industry had grown at the expense of the countryside. *Beijing Review* (1985), no. 21

Doing Business in Europe

Europe faces one of its toughest, perhaps the toughest hour since the Second World War. If the euro fails, then Europe fails. We want to prevent this and we will prevent this. **Angela Merkel**. Speech, Christian Democratic Union party conference, Leipzig (November 14, 2011)

The franc was like our mum. The euro is like our stepmother. **Anonymous**. Quoted in the *Independent (London)* (January 1, 2009)

Propose to an Englishman any principle, or any instrument, however admirable, and you will observe that the whole effort of the English mind is directed to find a difficulty, a defect, or an impossibility in it. **Charles Babbage**. Referring to the British inability to support inventors. Quoted in *The Code Book* (Simon Singh, 1999)

No one can bring together a country that has 265 kinds of cheese. **Charles de Gaulle**. Said after an electoral setback in 1953. Quoted in the *Economist (London)* (June 27, 1992)

Europe's strength is its diversity, not its uniformity. **Sir John Harvey-Jones**. Speech (1990)

Lifestyles around Europe are converging, but tastes are not. **Nicholas Colchester**. *Europe Relaunched* (cowritten with David Buchan, 1990)

Italy is a poor country full of rich people. **Richard Gardner**. Quoted in the *Observer (London)* (August 16, 1981)

Europe has never existed. One must genuinely create Europe. **Jean Monnet**. Quoted in *The New Europeans* (Anthony Sampson, 1968)

When an American heiress wants to buy a man, she at once crosses the Atlantic. The only really materialistic people I have ever met have been Europeans. **Mary McCarthy**. "America the Beautiful," *Commentary* (September 1947)

The rough broad difference between the American and the European business man is that the latter is anxious to leave his work, while the former is anxious to get to it. **Arnold Bennett**. *Those United States* (1926)

You can tell that our economy is improving at last. For the first time someone has been arrested for counterfeiting the Hungarian currency. **Geza Jeszenszky**. Attributed.

Doing Business in India

The consumerism of India is different to that in the West. Here we still repair things that get thrown away in the West. Here things are used for longer, they last longer. **Shashi Tharoor**. Quoted in the *Independent (London)* (August 6, 2009)

India copes with stress in the way that its roads cope with the traffic: constant chaos, surprisingly few casualties. **Bruce Anderson**. *Independent (London)* (March 9, 2009)

India will become the country of choice ... It's already starting to happen. **Narayana Murthy**. Referring to software development. *Forbes* (October 2000)

The question is does India need dot coms? If you were to ask me this question, the answer is no, India needs infrastructure. **Subeer Bhatia**. *BusinessWeek* (September 2000)

A company's reputation does not necessarily follow it into India, which has been a closed market for so long that established global brands have no meaning for the Indian consumer. **Rajiv Desai**. *Indian Business Culture* (1999)

Indian businesses often appear to be weak partners ... however, they are formidable opponents who can subvert the best-laid plans of international firms. **Rajiv Desai**. *Indian Business Culture* (1999)

Old India requires few tools, few skills, and many hands. **V. S. Naipaul**. *India: A Wounded Civilization* (1977)

Our private enterprise is more private than enterprising. **Indira Gandhi**. Speech (December 5, 1970)

Doing Business in Latin America

What's the chance that I'd want to own this Venezuelan company for a long time because I have confidence in the company and the country? Very, very small. **Anonymous**. Said by a US emerging markets fund manager. Quoted in the *Wall Street Journal* (November 21, 1996)

It is easier for a Chilean to buy a company in Argentina than it is to buy duty free. **Anonymous**. Quoted in the *New York Times* (November 17, 1996)

Multinationals are no longer immune from violence in Mexico. I personally know of seven American chief executives that have looked at the wrong end of a weapon in Mexico. **Morton Palmer**. Quoted in the *Wall Street Journal* (October 29, 1996)

We may not be a tiger yet but we are already a jaguar. **Anonymous**. Referring to the Chilean economy. Quoted in *Worth* (August 1995)

The United States is glad to manipulate cheap Mexican labor, chastising it in days of crisis, accepting it in boom times, and always maintaining the police fiction of an impregnable border. **Carlos Fuentes**. *A New Time for Mexico* (1994)

Since economies in the process of organization lack resources to dynamize themselves ... it is right to accept the aid of all who want to run with us the risks of the marvelous adventure that is progress. **Roberto Campos**. Speech, Mackenzie University, São Paulo, Brazil (December 22, 1966)

The Argentinians alter their currency almost as frequently as they change their finance ministers. No people on Earth has a keener interest in currency experimentation than the Argentinians. **Anonymous**. *Bankers Magazine* (1889)

Doing Business in North America

America is still a place where most people react to seeing a man in a Ferrari by redoubling their own efforts to be able to afford one, rather than by trying to let down his tires. **Anonymous**. Let down means deflate. *Economist (London)* (January 3, 1998)

If it's worth doing, California will do it to excess. **Anonymous**. Comment on National Public Radio in the United States (1996)

It seems to be a law in American life that whatever enriches us anywhere except in the wallet inevitably becomes uneconomic. **Russell Baker**. *New York Times* (March 24, 1968)

If there is anything of which American industry has a superfluity It is green lights, know-how, initiative, and ingenuity. **Ogden Nash**. "Ring Out the Old, Ring In the New, but Don't Get Caught In Between," *You Can't Get There from Here* (1957), 1: First Chime

Perhaps the most revolting character that the United States ever produced was the Christian business man. **H. L. Mencken**. *Minority Report—H. L. Mencken's Notebook* (1956)

As a rule, from what I've observed, the American captain of industry doesn't do anything out of business hours. When he has put the cat out and locked up the office for the night, he just relapses into a state of coma from which he emerges only to start being a captain of industry again. **P. G. Wodehouse**. "Leave It to Jeeves," *My Man Jeeves* (1919)

There is no business in America ... which will not yield a fair profit if it receives the unremitting, exclusive attention, and all the

  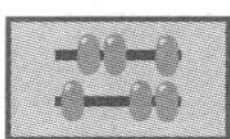   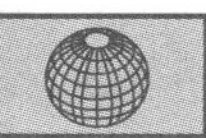   

capital of capable and industrious men. **Andrew Carnegie**. Speech at Curry Commercial College, Pittsburgh, Pennsylvania. "The Road to Business Success" (June 23, 1885)

E-Commerce

It's amazing how easy the Internet makes it to destroy a business without creating another one in its place. **Robert Levine**. *Free Ride: How the Internet Is Destroying the Culture Business and How the Culture Business Can Fight Back* (2011)

Digital network architectures naturally incubate monopolies. **Jaron Lanier**. *You Are Not a Gadget: A Manifesto* (2010)

I'm not sure we could have learnt how to really use the Internet without a dot.com bubble. **Tyler Cowen**. Quoted in the *Sunday Times (London)* (January 4, 2009)

Every industry that becomes digital will eventually become free. **Chris Anderson**. *Free: The Future of a Radical Price* (2009)

The Internet means you don't have to convince anyone else that something is a good idea before trying it. **Scott Bradner**. Quoted in *Here Comes Everybody: The Power of Organizing Without Organizations* (Clay Shirky, 2008)

The Long Tail is an expression of a network effect on a marketplace of infinite capacity that is unique to the Internet. Previously our culture was dominated by limited distribution channels; the Internet is the first unlimited distribution channel. **Chris Anderson**. *The Long Tail: Why the Future of Business Is Selling Less of More* (2006)

The Internet is about the free exchange and sale of other people's ideas. **Eric Kaplan**. Spoken by a Nappster executive. *Futurama*, Fox TV (May 13, 2001)

Pack lightly and carry a compass. **Raul Fernandez**. Website (September 2000)

Marketing is marketing. It's easy to drape new media in magic but it comes down to whether it's a good business or not. **Carl Lyons**. *Marketing* (August 2000)

I believe we can still be a footnote in the history of e-commerce. **Jeff Bezos**. *Sunday Telegraph (London)* (July 2000)

Thus, in the future, instead of buying bananas in a grocery store, you could go pick them off a tree in a virtual jungle. **Yasuhiro Fukushima**. *Wired Asia* (June 2000)

Any company, old or new, that does not see this technology as important as breathing could be on its last breath. **Jack Welch**. Referring to e-commerce. *Sunday Times (London)* (May 2000)

Fireflies throwing off sparks before the storm. **Lou Gerstner**. Referring to dot.com companies. *Sunday Times (London)* (May 2000)

The web site needs to be as sticky as a currant bun. **Carolyn McCall**. *Marketing* (April 2000)

The phrase click, click you're dead focuses the mind. **Sir Martin Sorrell**. Interview (March 2000)

We're fast approaching the point at which there is really no distinction between the dot.com companies and traditional businesses. The only distinction will be between the winners and losers, and of course, the pace of change at which companies become winners or losers. **Michael Dell**. Speech to the DirectConnect Customer Conference, Austin, Texas. "DirectConnect" (August 25, 1999)

Much as we talk about Internet companies today, in five years' time there won't be any Internet companies. All companies will be Internet companies or they will be dead. **Andrew S. Grove**. Speech, Los Angeles Times 3rd Annual Investment Strategies Conference, Los Angeles, California (May 22, 1999)

Secure web servers are the equivalent of heavy armoured cars. The problem is, they are being used to transfer rolls of coins and cheques written in crayon by people on park benches to merchants doing business in cardboard boxes from beneath highway bridges. Further, the roads are subject to random detours, anyone with a screwdriver can control the traffic lights, and there are no police. **Gene Spafford**. *Web Security and Commerce* (1997)

I am secretly looking forward to rediscovering the little pleasures of pre-electronic shopping: holding things in my hands, trying them on, and even taking them home with me after I have paid. **Anonymous**. Quoted in the *Economist (London)* (December 21, 1996)

The Internet is an elite organization; most of the population of the world have never made a phone call. **Noam Chomsky**. *Observer (London)* (February 1996)

Stop thinking about it as the information highway and start thinking about it as the marketing superhighway. Doesn't it sound better already? **Don Logan**. Speech to the Association of National Advertisers

The Internet is the Viagra of big business. **Jack Welch**. Attributed

Economics

Economists arguing about the economy: they're like angry astrologers arguing about the effects of Saturn. **Simon Carr**. *Independent (London)* (June 23, 2011)

Economics, as it has been practised in the last three decades, has been positively harmful for most people. **Ha-Joon Chang**. *23 Things They Don't Tell You About Capitalism* (2010)

Like other branches of the study of society, economics remains culturally parochial, and its underlying concepts based on a few centuries of Western experience. **John Gray**. *London Review of Books* (November 19, 2009)

There's a whole branch of economics devoted to proving that ... what most of us would consider humankind's cardinal virtues—love, honor, compassion—do not actually exist. **Philipp Meyer**. *Independent (London)* (April 27, 2009)

The Robert Mugabe school of economics provides a salutary warning about uncontrolled monetary expansion in generating hyper-inflation. The road to Harare is not as long as we might hope. **Vince Cable**. On the British government's anti-recessionary policies. *Independent (London)* (January 8, 2009)

Although there are shining exceptions, most ... practise a modern form of medieval scholasticism—of no use or interest to man or beast. **Roger Bootle**. On modern economists. *The Trouble With Markets* (2009)

Spread the truth—the laws of economics are like the laws of engineering. One set of laws works everywhere. **Lawrence H. Summers**. Quoted in *The Shock Doctrine* (Naomi Klein, 2007)

An economist is a man who states the obvious in terms of the incomprehensible. **Alfred A. Knopf**. Quoted in *Deflation: What Happens When Prices Fall* (Chris Farrell, 2004)

Waiting for supply-side economics to work is like leaving the landing lights on for Amelia Earhart. **Walter Heller**. Quoted in *500 of the Most Witty, Acerbic, and Erudite*

Things Ever Said About Money (Philip Jenks, 2002)

All the great economic ills the world has known this century can be directly traced back to the London School of Economics. **N. M. Perera**. Quoted in *500 of the Most Witty, Acerbic, and Erudite Things Ever Said About Money* (Philip Jenks, 2002)

We may be in a rapidly evolving international financial system with all the bells and whistles of the so-called new economy. But the old-economy rules of prudence are as formidable as ever. We violate them at our own peril. **Alan Greenspan**. Speech to the Financial Crisis Conference, Council on Foreign Relations, New York. "Global Challenges" (July 12, 2000)

We're a me-me-me generation. We're borrowing the savings of every nation in the world. We're ... piling up a big tab. Now, I may think we're too big to have a run on us. You may think that. But it's possible that God does not. **Paul Samuelson**. Interview, *The New Economy?* (Online NewsHour, January 13, 2000)

When the facts change, I change my mind. **John Maynard Keynes**. Quoted in *Treasury of Investment Wisdom* (Bernice Cohen, 1999)

The invisible hand is not perfect. Indeed, the invisible hand is a little bit arthritic ... I'm a believer in free markets, but I think we need to be less naïve. We need to accept that markets give us pretty good solutions, but occasionally they will lock in something inferior. **W. Brian Arthur**. Interview, *Strategy + Business* (April–June 1998)

Economists got away from really questioning how the world works, how decisions actually got made. If something doesn't conform to neoclassical models ... people are not somehow behaving themselves properly. **W. Brian Arthur**. Interview, *Strategy + Business* (April–June 1998)

Humans have trouble with economics, as you may have noticed, and not just because economic circumstances sometimes cause them to starve. Humans seem to have an innate inability to pay attention to economic principles. **P. J. O'Rourke**. *Eat the Rich* (1998), ch. 1

Neoclassical economics ... has uncovered important truths about the nature of money and markets because its fundamental model of rational self-interested human behavior is correct about 80% of the time. **Francis Fukuyama**. *Trust: The Social Virtues and the Creation of Prosperity* (1995)

Economics is as much a study in fantasy and aspiration as in hard numbers—maybe more so. **Theodore Roszak**. *The Making of a Counter Culture* (1995), Introduction

Unfortunately monetarism, like Marxism, suffered the only fate that for a theory is worse than death: it was put into practice. **Ian Gilmour**. *Dancing with Dogma* (1992)

Trickle-down theory—the less than elegant metaphor that if one feeds the horse enough oats, some will pass through to the road for the sparrows. **J. K. Galbraith**. *The Culture of Contentment* (1992)

I think there are two areas where new ideas are terribly dangerous—economics and sex. By and large, it's all been tried before, and if it's new, it's probably illegal or unhealthy. **Felix Rohatyn**. Quoted in *Business Babble: A Cynic's Dictionary of Corporate Jargon* (David Olive, 1991)

If freedom were not so economically efficient it certainly wouldn't stand a chance. **Milton Friedman**. Quoted in "Sayings of the Week," *Observer (London)* (March 1, 1987)

Economists are always recommending the elimination of this or that market imperfection ... no astrophysicist recommends the elimination of planets that he does not like. **Lester Thurow**. Referring to how economists relate to economic realities. *Dangerous Currents* (1983)

There are two things you are better off not watching in the making: sausages and econometric estimates. **Edward E. Leamer**. "Let's Take the Con Out of Econometrics," *American Economic Review* (1983)

Economics is extremely useful as a form of employment for economists. **J. K. Galbraith**. Quoted in *The Book of Incomes* (Gerald Krefetz and Philip Gittelman, 1982)

The modern history of economic theory is a tale of evasions of reality. **Thomas Balogh**. Referring to classical economics. *The Irrelevance of Conventional Economics* (1982)

Did you ever think that making a speech on economics is a lot like pissing down your leg? It seems hot to you but it never does to anyone else. **Lyndon B. Johnson**. Quoted in *A Life in Our Times* (J. K. Galbraith, 1981)

The experience of being disastrously wrong is salutary; no economist should be denied it, and not many are. **J. K. Galbraith**. *A Life in Our Times* (1981)

Having a little inflation is like being a little bit pregnant. **Leon Henderson**. Quoted in *Peter's Quotations: Ideas For Our Time* (Laurence J. Peter, 1977)

We hate inflation, but we love everything that causes it. **William Simon**. Speech (1974)

In economics, hope and faith coexist with great scientific pretension and also a deep desire for respectability. **J. K. Galbraith**. *New York Times Magazine* (June 1970)

An economist is a surgeon with an excellent scalpel and a rough-edged lancet, who operates beautifully on the dead and tortures the living. **Nicholas Chamfort**. *Products of the Perfected Civilization: Selected Writings* (1969)

Inflation might be called prosperity with high blood pressure. **Arnold H. Glasgow**. Quoted in *Readers Digest* (1966)

One speaks with great respect of economists, if only because they represent such a variety of opinions. **Robert Menzies**. *Sydney Morning Herald* (March 14, 1964)

Economists may not know how to run the economy, but they know how to create shortages or gluts simply by regulating prices below the market, or artificially supporting them from above. **Milton Friedman**. Attributed (1962)

Economics limps along with one foot in untested hypotheses and the other in untestable slogans. **Joan Robinson**. "Metaphysics, Morals and Science," *Economic Philosophy* (1962)

Everybody is always in favour of general economy and particular expenditure. **Anthony Eden (Earl of Avon)**. Quoted in "Sayings of the Week," *Observer (London)* (June 17, 1956)

Economists can be called the worldly philosophers for they sought to embrace in a scheme of philosophy the most worldly of man's activities—his drive for wealth. **Robert L. Heilbroner**. *The Worldly Philosophers* (1953), Introduction

The ideas of economists and political philosophers ... are more powerful than is commonly understood. Indeed the world is ruled by little else. Practical men who believe themselves to be quite exempt from any intellectual influences, are usually the slaves of some defunct economist. **John Maynard Keynes**. *The General Theory of Employment Interest and Money* (1936)

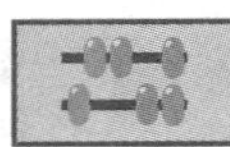

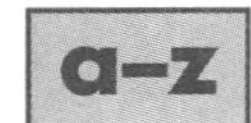

What a country calls its vital economic interests are not the things that enable its citizens to live, but the things that enable it to make war. **Simone Weil**. *The Need for Roots* (1935)

If economists could manage to get themselves thought of as humble, competent people on a level with dentists, that would be splendid. **John Maynard Keynes**. *Essays in Persuasion* (1931)

A commodity appears, at first sight, a very trivial thing, and easily understood. Its analysis shows that is is, in reality, a very queer thing, abounding in metaphysical subtleties and theological niceties. **Karl Marx**. *Das Kapital* (1867), vol. 1

As in the instances of alchemy, astrology, witchcraft, and other such popular creeds, political economy, has a plausible idea at the root of it. **John Ruskin**. "The Roots of Honour," *Unto This Last* (1862)

One of the soundest rules to remember when making forecasts in the field of economics is that whatever is to happen is happening already. **Sylvia Porter**. Attributed

Education

The purpose of a university is to make students safe for ideas—not ideas safe for students. **Clark Kerr**. Quoted in *Arizona Republic (Phoenix)* (1999)

Our schools must preserve and nurture the yearning for learning that everyone is born with. **W. Edwards Deming**. Quoted in *Woodbury Reports Archives* (February 1998)

I'd seen a lot of MBAs come down to the trading floors, and they were like sheep to the wolves ... They think the world will function like this nice little model or equation and nothing's further from the truth. **Linda Bradford Raschke**. Quoted in *Women of the Street* (Sue Herera, 1997)

In the Middle Ages, the rich tried to buy immortality by building cathedrals. These days they set up business schools instead. **Anonymous**. *Economist (London)* (July 20, 1996)

I think I'd rather have an English major than an economics major. **Michael Eisner**. Speech (June 1994)

The most important thing I would learn in school was that almost everything I would learn in school would be utterly useless. **Joseph O'Connor**. *The Secret World of the Irish Male* (1994)

It is the motto of the US universities that when a subject becomes totally obsolete, then a required course should be built around it. **Peter F. Drucker**. *Managing for the Future* (1992)

If Thomas Edison had gone to business school, we would all be reading by larger candles. **Anonymous**. Quoted in *What They Don't Teach You at Harvard Business School* (Mark H. McCormack, 1984)

Education is what survives when what has been learned has been forgotten. **B. F. Skinner**. *New Scientist* (May 21, 1964)

Real education must ultimately be limited to one who INSISTS on knowing, the rest is mere sheep-herding. **Ezra Pound**. *ABC of Reading* (1960)

An art can only be learned in the workshop of those who are winning their bread by it. **Samuel Butler**. *Erewhon* (1872)

If you think education is expensive, try ignorance. **Anonymous**.

Education is simply the soul of a society as it passes from one generation to another. **G. K. Chesterton**. Attributed

Efficiency

The principal weapon companies have to lift efficiency is to apply technology more thoughtfully. **Hamish McRae**. *Independent (London)* (October 21, 2009)

If the Wright brothers were alive today, Wilbur would have to fire Orvill to reduce costs. **Charles Horton Cooley**. Quoted in *USA Today* (June 1994)

The pyramid, the chief organizational principle of the modern organization, turns a business into a traffic jam. **Ricardo Semler**. *Maverick!* (1993)

I make no secret of the fact that I would rather lie on a sofa than sweep beneath it. But you have to be efficient if you're going to be lazy. **Shirley Conran**. "The Reason Why," *Superwoman* (1975)

If you have someone on a job, use him. If you can't, get rid of him. **Frederick Herzberg**. *Harvard Business Review* (January–February 1968)

It is possible for a business venture to be an island of efficiency in a sea of sloth. **Indira Gandhi**. Speech (December 9, 1967)

When two men always agree, one of them is unnecessary. **William Wrigley, Jr**. *American Magazine* (March 1920)

It's pretty hard to be efficient without being obnoxious. **Kin Hubbard**. Attributed

There is nothing so useless as doing efficiently that which should not be done at all. **Peter F. Drucker**. Attributed

Employees

American business long ago gave up on demanding that prospective employees be honest and hardworking. It has even stopped hoping for employees who are educated enough that they can tell the difference between the men's room and the women's room without having little pictures on the doors. **Dave Barry**. Quoted in *Really Bad Business Advice* (David Dallas and Arlen Foote, 2003)

You can't treat your people like an expense item. **Andrew S. Grove**. Quoted in *In the Company of Giants* (Rama Dev Jager, 1997)

Take our 20 best people away, and I will tell you that Microsoft would become an unimportant company. **Bill Gates**. *Fortune* (November 1996)

Empowerment: A magic wand management waves to help traumatized survivors of restructuring suddenly feel engaged, self-managed, and in control of their futures and their jobs. **Anonymous**. *Fortune* (February 15, 1995)

The average employee can deliver far more than his or her current job demands and far more than the terms employee empowerment, participative management, and multiple skills imply. **Tom Peters**. *The Tom Peters Seminar* (1994)

At nights and on weekends we cry out for human rights and freedom of speech, and then we go to work and become strategic and cautious about our every word for fear we will be seen as disloyal or uncommitted. **Peter Block**. *Stewardship* (1993)

Many organizations view people as things that are but one variable in the production equation. **David M. Noer**. *Healing the Wounds* (1993)

Few top executives can even imagine the hatred, contempt, and fury that has been created—not primarily among blue-collar workers who never had an exalted opinion of the bosses—but among their middle management and professional people. **Peter F. Drucker**. Quoted in "Seeing Things As They Really Are,"

Forbes (Robert Lenzner and Stephen S. Johnson, 1987)

You can't look the troops in the eye and say, "It's been a bad year, we can't do anything for you," but then say, "By the way, we're going to pay ourselves a $1 million bonus." **H. Ross Perot**. Referring to his resignation from the General Motors board following GM's decision to freeze profit-sharing payments to workers while going ahead with executive bonus payments. Quoted in *Thriving on Chaos* (Tom Peters, 1987)

A bad reference is as hard to find as a good employee. **Robert Half**. *Half on Hiring* (1985), ch. 9

The inventory goes down the elevator every night. **Fairfax Cone**. Quoted in *The Trouble with Advertising* (John O'Toole, 1981)

Don't be condescending to unskilled labor. Try it for a half a day first. **Brooks Atkinson**. *Theatre Arts* (1956)

I tell you, sir, the only safeguard of order and discipline in the modern world is a standardized worker with interchangeable parts. That would solve the entire problem of management. **Jean Giraudoux**. *The Madwoman of Chaillot* (1945)

How come when I want a pair of hands I get a human being as well? **Henry Ford**. *My Life and Work* (cowritten with Samuel Crowther, 1922)

Each employee should receive every day clear-cut definite instructions as to what he is to do and how he is to do it, and these instructions should be exactly carried out, whether they are right or wrong. **F. W. Taylor**. *The Principles of Scientific Management* (1911)

Employers

Companies ... have a hard time distinguishing between the cost of paying people and the value of investing in them. **Thomas A. Stewart**. *Intellectual Capital* (1997)

Just as an employer should believe it is his duty to promote good human relations, so too should he see it as his duty to pursue the best possible relationship with the community. **Marcus, Lord Sieff**. *Sieff on Management* (1990)

I am the proprietor. I am the boss ... There can only be one boss and that is me. **Robert Maxwell**. Speech to labor leaders. Quoted in *Maxwell: The Outsider* (Tom Bower, 1988)

It might be said that it is the ideal of the employer to have production without employees and the ideal of the employee is to have income without work. **Ernst Friedrich Schumacher**. Quoted in "Sayings of the Week," *Observer (London)* (May 4, 1975)

Dear, never forget one little point. It's my business. You just work here. **Elizabeth Arden**. Said to her husband. Quoted in *Miss Elizabeth Arden* (Alfred A. Lewis and Constance Woodworth, 1972)

There could be no worse friend to labour than the benevolent, philanthropic employer ... sooner or later he will be compelled to close. **Lord Leverhulme (William Hesketh Lever)**. Quoted in *The History of Unilever* (Charles Wilson, 1951)

A good paymaster never wants workmen. **Thomas Fuller**. *Gnomologia* (1732), no. 168

Enthusiasm

I don't know anyone who is passionate and unsuccessful. **Jean-Pierre Garnier**. *The Times (London)* (September 26, 2005)

If you aren't fired with enthusiasm, then you will be fired with enthusiasm. **Vince Lombardi**. Quoted in *The Instant Manager* (Cyril Charney, 2004)

To run this business ... you need ... optimism, humanism, enthusiasm, intuition, curiosity, love, humour, magic and fun, and that secret ingredient—euphoria. **Dame Anita Roddick**. *Body and Soul* (co-written with Russell Miller, 1991)

My advice to anyone in any field is to be faithful to your obsessions. Identify them and be faithful to them, let them guide you like a sleepwalker. **J. G. Ballard**. Quoted in *I-D (London)* (1987)

A mediocre idea that generates enthusiasm will go further than a great idea that inspires no one. **Mary Kay Ash**. *On People Management* (1984)

People who never get carried away, should be. **Steve Forbes**. *Town and Country* (November 1976)

Flaming enthusiasm, backed up by horse sense and persistence, is the quality that most frequently makes for success. **Dale Carnegie**. *How to Win Friends and Influence People* (1936)

Nothing great was ever achieved without enthusiasm. **Ralph Waldo Emerson**. "Circles," *Essays: First Series* (1841)

There is nothing so easy but that it becomes difficult when you do it reluctantly. **Terence**. *The Self-Tormenter* (163 BC), l. 805

We act as though comfort and luxury were the chief requirements of life, when all that we need to make us happy is something to be enthusiastic about. **Charles Kingsley**. Attributed

I find that when you have a real interest in life that sleep is not the most important thing. **Martha Stewart**. Attributed

Entrepreneurs

Entrepreneurs must love what they do to such a degree that doing it is worth sacrifice and, at times, pain. But doing anything else, we think, would be unimaginable. **Howard Schultz**. *Onward: How Starbucks Fought for Its Life without Losing Its Soul* (with Joanne Gordon, 2011)

In my experience "enterprise" should be put on the same shelf as "recreational heroin use." Only a few people can handle it, let alone benefit from it. The attrition is appalling. **Simon Carr**. *Independent (London)* (June 15, 2009)

There are very few self-made millionaires, if any, who have not taken risks which would make the rest of us unable to sleep at night, or keep our food down. **Dominic Lawson**. *Independent (London)* (December 16, 2008)

Entrepreneurs constantly confuse what they do with who they are. We're all certainly responsible for what we do, but failing doesn't make us bad people and succeeding doesn't make us omniscient. **Howard Tullman**. *You Need to Be a Little Crazy: The Truth about Starting and Growing Your Business* (Barry J. Moltz, 2003), Preface

Entrepreneurs start businesses because ... they have no choice. Passion and energy drive them on good days and sustain them on bad days **Barry J. Moltz**. *You Need to Be a Little Crazy: The Truth about Starting and Growing Your Business* (2003)

Successful entrepreneurs judge correctly the need for change, then do something about it. **James Edward, Lord Hanson**. Website (2000)

  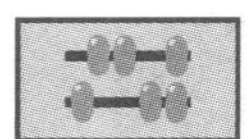      

Money isn't what motivates entrepreneurs; it is acknowledgement—a craving for your ideas to be acknowledged, **Reuben Singh**. *Management Today* (September 1999)

The truth is I started my own company because I could not fill out a job application. **Terri Bowersock**. *Phoenix Business Journal* (1999)

Around Britain, thousands of young people are working from bedrooms, workshops and run-down offices, hoping that they will come up with the next Hotmail or Netscape. **Charles Leadbeater**. Quoted in the *Independent (London)* (1999)

You can never be an entrepreneur if you're afraid to lose money. It's like being a pilot who is afraid of bad weather. **Peter de Savary**. Quoted in *The Adventure Capitalists* (Jeff Grout and Lynne Curry, 1998)

It sounds boring, but anything is easy to start—starting a novel, starting a business ... it's keeping the thing going that is difficult. **Prue Leith**. Quoted in *The Adventure Capitalists* (Jeff Grout and Lynne Curry, 1998)

It's better to be the head of a chicken than the tail of a cow. **Stan Shih**. Referring to a Taiwanese proverb and the preference of entrepreneurs for running their own small business. Quoted in *Giant Killers* (Geoffrey James, 1996)

If you want to understand entrepreneurs, you have to study the psychology of the juvenile delinquent. They don't have the same anxiety triggers that we have. **Abraham Zaleznik**. *US News & World Report* (October 1992)

Three components make an entrepreneur: the person, the idea and the resources to make it happen. **Dame Anita Roddick**. *Body and Soul* (cowritten with Russell Miller, 1991)

Where would the Rockefellers be today if old John D. had gone on selling short-weight kerosene ... to widows and orphans instead of wisely deciding to mulct the whole country. **S. J. Perelman**. Letter (October 25, 1976)

Environment

We in the West can do something that no people in history have done: we can show the world that we know when we have enough ... If the people who have everything are content to live with less, maybe the whole world will consider the virtues of knowing when to stop. We have no choice other than to learn this at some point, because the planet is not an eat-all-you-can buffet. It's going to run out. **John Lanchester**. Speech. "Enough" (December 12, 2010)

Green is the first socio-political movement in which every single leader and spokesperson is filthy rich. **Julie Burchill**. *Independent (London)* (August 18, 2010)

Accustomed to saving natural systems from civilization, Greens now have the unfamiliar task of saving civilization from a natural system—climate dynamics. **Stewart Brand**. *Whole Earth Discipline* (2010)

The financial crisis is nothing compared with the environmental crisis. **Jean-Christophe Vie**. On a report that 25% of the world's mammals face extinction. Quoted in *Time* (October 6, 2008)

Green protesters are our best passengers. They're always flying off to their demonstrations. **Michael O'Leary**. Quoted in *The Times (London)* (August 2, 2008)

Conservation is business too. **Gaston Vizcarra**. *Forbes* (April 2000)

Study how a society uses its land, and you can come to pretty reliable conclusions as to what its future will be. **Ernst Friedrich Schumacher**. *Small Is Beautiful* (1973)

Now there is one outstandingly important fact regarding Spaceship Earth, and that is that no instruction book came with it. **R. Buckminster Fuller**. *Operating Manual for Planet Earth* (1969)

I am I plus my surroundings, and, if I do not preserve the latter, I do not preserve myself. **Jose Ortega y Gasset**. *Meditaciones del Quijote* (1914)

Excellence

We don't get a chance to do that many things, and every one should be really excellent. Because this is our life. **Steve Jobs**. Interviewed in *Fortune* (February 2008)

If you do things well, do them better. Be daring, be first, be different, be just. **Dame Anita Roddick**. Quoted in *Best Practice: Process Innovation Management* (Mohamed Zairi, 1999)

Striving for excellence motivates you; striving for perfection is demoralizing. **Harriet Beryl Braiker**. *Type E Woman: How to Overcome the Stress of Being Everything to Everybody* (1987)

If you don't do it excellently, don't do it at all. Because if it's not excellent, it won't be profitable or fun, and if you're not in business for fun or profit, what the hell are you doing there? **Robert Townsend**. *Further Up the Organization* (1984)

The business world worships mediocrity. Officially we revere free enterprise, initiative, and individuality. Unofficially we fear it. **George Lois**. *The Art of Advertising* (1977)

The sad truth is that excellence makes people nervous. **Shana Alexander**. "Neglected Kids—The Bright Ones," *The Feminine Eye* (1967)

No one has a greater asset for his business than a man's pride in his work. **Mary Parker Follett**. *Freedom and Co-ordination* (1949), ch. 2

All things excellent are as difficult as they are rare. **Baruch Spinoza**. *Ethica Ordine Geometrico Demonstrata* (1677)

Executives

The nature of the job is you only hear problems—I guess that's what a CEO's job is. **William Clay Ford, Jr**. Interview, *Fortune* (November 2002)

Their problem is that they play a lot of golf, which is right up there with heroin abuse as a killer of our nation's productivity. The only difference is that golf is more expensive. **Dave Barry**. Referring to executives. Interview, *Fortune* (July 7, 1997)

The biggest change in the workplace of the future will be the widespread realization that having one idiot boss is a much higher risk than having many idiot clients. **Scott Adams**. *The Dilbert Principle* (1996)

Some years back, a CEO friend of mine—in jest, it must be said—described the pathology of many big deals ... With an impish look, he simply said: Aw, fellas, all the other kids have one. **Warren Buffett**. Chairman's letter to shareholders (March 7, 1995)

There is nothing more short term than a 60-year-old CEO holding a fistful of share options. **Gary Hamel**. *Competing for the Future* (cowritten with C. K. Prahalad, 1994)

Successful executives are great askers. **Warren Bennis**. *Beyond Leadership:*

  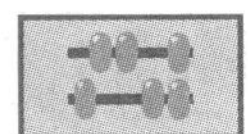      

Balancing Economics, Ethics and Ecology (cowritten with Jagdish Parikh and Ronnie Lessem, 1994)

From now on, choosing my successor is the most important decision I'll make. It occupies a considerable amount of thought almost every day. **Jack Welch**. Quoted in *The New GE* (Robert Slater, 1993)

The trouble with corporate America is that too many people with too much power live in a box (their home), travel the same road every day to another box (their office). **Faith Popcorn**. *The Popcorn Report* (1991)

An overburdened, stretched executive is the best executive, because he or she doesn't have time to meddle, to deal in trivia, to bother people. **Jack Welch**. "Quotes of the Year," *Financial Times (London)* (December 30, 1989)

I always say to executives that they should go and see *King Lear*, because they'll be out there one day, wandering on the heath without a company car. **Charles Handy**. Interview, *The Times (London)* (April 12, 1989)

Executives are like joggers. If you stop a jogger, he goes on running on the spot. If you drag an executive away from his business, he goes on running on the spot, pawing the ground, talking business. **Jean Baudrillard**. *Cool Memories* (1987)

Chief executives, who themselves own few shares of their companies, have no more feeling for the average stockholder than they do for baboons in Africa. **T. Boone Pickens**. *Harvard Business Review* (May–June 1986)

You can know a person by the kind of desk he keeps ... If the president of a company has a clean desk ... then it must be the executive vice president who is doing all the work. **Harold S. Geneen**. *Managing* (cowritten with Alvin Moscow, 1984)

I can tell more about how someone is likely to react in a business situation from one round of golf than I can from a hundred hours of meetings. **Mark McCormack**. *What They Don't Teach You at Harvard Business School* (1984)

The salary of the chief executive of the large corporation is not a market reward for achievement. It is frequently in the nature of a warm personal gesture by the individual to himself. **J. K. Galbraith**. *Annals of an Abiding Liberal* (1979)

One lesson a man learns from Harvard Business School is that an executive is only as good as his health. **Jeffrey, Lord Archer**. *Not a Penny More, Not a Penny Less* (1976)

The chief executive ... like a juggler keeps a number of projects in the air: periodically one comes down, is given a new burst of energy, and is sent back into orbit. **Henry Mintzberg**. "The Manager's Job: Folklore and Fact," *Harvard Business Review* (July–August 1975)

Nobody should be chief executive officer of anything for more than five or six years. By then he's stale, bored, and utterly dependent upon his own clichés. **Robert Townsend**. *Up the Organization* (1970)

When I've had a rough day, before I go to sleep I ask myself if there's anything more I can do right now. If there isn't, I sleep sound. **L. L. Colbert**. *Newsweek* (1955)

A molehill man is a pseudo-busy executive who comes to work at 9 a.m. and finds a molehill on his desk. He has until 5 p.m. to make this molehill into a mountain. An accomplished molehill man will often have his mountain finished before lunch. **Fred Allen**. *Treadmill to Oblivion* (1954)

Regarded as a means, the businessman is tolerable. Regarded as an end, he is not so satisfactory. **John Maynard Keynes**. *Essays in Persuasion* (1931)

Executive: A man who can make quick decisions and is sometimes right. **Frank McKinney Hubbard**. *The Roycroft Dictionary* (1923)

The heroic role of the captain of industry is that of a deliverer from an excess of business management. It is a casting out of businessmen by the chief of businessmen. **Thorstein Veblen**. *The Theory of Business Enterprise* (1904)

Executive ability is deciding quickly and getting somebody else to do the work. **John G. Pollard**. Attributed

Expectations

High expectations are the key to everything. **Sam M. Walton**. Quoted in *The Ten Rules of Sam Walton* (Michael Bergdahl, 2006)

Unhappiness is best defined as the difference between our talents and our expectations. **Edward de Bono**. Quoted in the *Observer (London)* (June 12, 1997)

Buy what's deliverable, not what could be. **Michael Bloomberg**. *Bloomberg by Bloomberg* (cowritten with Matthew Winkler, 1997)

When I build something for somebody ... My guys come in, they say it's going to cost $75 million. I say it's going to cost $125 million, and I build it for $100 million. Basically, I did a lousy job. But they think I did a great job. **Donald J. Trump**. Said to a meeting of US Football League owners. Quoted in the *New York Times* (July 1, 1986)

Expect nothing. Live frugally on surprise. **Alice Walker**. *Expect Nothing* (1973)

Always do one thing less than you think you can do. **Bernard Baruch**. Referring to maintaining good health. *Newsweek* (May 28, 1956)

The loss that is unknown is no loss at all. **Publilius Syrus**. *Moral Sayings* (1st century BC)

Experience

The way I was raised, if something wasn't tough it was not a valuable or enriching experience. **Lynn Forrester, Lady de Rothschild**. *Sunday Times (London)* (June 2000)

I try to avoid experience if I can. Most experience is bad. **E. L. Doctorow**. Interview, *Writers at Work* (1988)

In the business world, everyone is paid in two coins: cash and experience. Take the experience first; the cash will come later. **Harold S. Geneen**. *Managing* (cowritten with Alvin Moscow, 1984)

Education is when you read the fine print; experience is what you get when you don't. **Pete Seeger**. Quoted in *Loose Talk* (L. Botts, 1980)

I have learned the novice can often see things that the expert overlooks. **Tom Peters**. *Eupsychian Management* (1965)

You cannot acquire experience by making experiments. You cannot create experience. You must undergo it. **Albert Camus**. *Notebooks 1935–1942* (1962)

The process of maturing is an art to be learned, an effort to be sustained. By the age of fifty you have made yourself what you are, and if it is good, it is better than your youth. **Marya Mannes**. *More in Anger* (1958)

And the end of all our exploring Will be to arrive where we started And know the place for the first time. **T. S. Eliot**. "Little Gidding," *Four Quartets* (1943)

Experience isn't interesting until it begins to repeat itself—in fact, till it does that, it hardly is experience. **Elizabeth Bowen**. *The Death of the Heart* (1938), pt. 1, ch. 1

a man who is so dull that he can learn only by personal experience is too dull to learn anything important by experience **Don Marquis**. "archy on this and that," *archy does his part* (1935)

EXPERIENCE, n. The wisdom that enables us to recognise as an undesirable old acquaintance the folly that we have already embraced. **Ambrose Bierce**. *The Devil's Dictionary* (1911)

Men are wise in proportion, not to their experience, but to their capacity for experience. **George Bernard Shaw**. "Maxims for Revolutionists," *Man and Superman* (1903)

Experience is a good teacher, but she sends in terrific bills. **Minna Antrim**. *Naked Truth and Veiled Illusions* (1902)

Experience is the name everyone gives to their mistakes. **Oscar Wilde**. *Lady Windermere's Fan* (1892), Act 3

Experience is never limited, and it is never complete; it is an immense sensibility, a kind of huge spider-web ... suspended in the chamber of consciousness, and catching every air-borne particle in its tissue. **Henry James**. "The Art of Fiction," *Partial Portraits* (1888)

A moment's insight is sometimes worth a life's experience. **Oliver Wendell Holmes**. *The Professor at the Breakfast-Table* (1860), ch. 10

I do not see how any man can afford ... to spare any action in which he can partake. Drudgery, calamity, exasperation, want, are instructors in eloquence and wisdom. **Ralph Waldo Emerson**. Speech to the Phi Beta Kappa Society, Cambridge Divinity College, Harvard. "American Scholar" (August 31, 1837)

To most men, experience is like the stern lights of a ship, which illumine only the track it has passed. **Samuel Taylor Coleridge**. *Table Talk* (1836)

Nothing ever becomes real till it is experienced ... even a proverb is no proverb till your life has illustrated it. **John Keats**. Letter to George and Georgiana Keats (March 19, 1819)

Learn every day, but especially from the experiences of others. It's cheaper! **John Clifton Bogle**. Attributed

The only thing experience teaches us is that experience teaches us nothing. **André Maurois**. Attributed

Failure

If the argument is that failure helps you succeed, well, so does success and it's quicker. This suggests at least one reason for trying to succeed. **Norman Geras**. *Normblog* (July 23, 2012)

Exactly 5,126 attempts to make the first bagless vacuum cleaner were failures—some catastrophic disappointments, some minor defects. It took 15 years. Prototype 5,127 was the success ... Failure is painful, but it spurs on improvement like nothing else. **Sir James Dyson**. *Guardian (London)* (July 22, 2012)

I think failing is the best way to keep you grounded, curious, and humble. Success is dangerous because often you don't understand why you succeeded. You almost always know why you've failed. You have a lot of time to think about it. **Mark Pincus**. Interviewed in *Bloomberg Businessweek* (April 12, 2012)

I wake up every single night wondering what I could have done differently. This is a pain that will stay with me the rest of my life. **Richard S. Fuld, Jr**. Speaking before a congressional panel (October 5, 2008)

When the company did well, we did well. And when the company did not do well, we did not do well, sir. **Richard S. Fuld, Jr**. Speaking before a congressional panel (October 5, 2008)

Books proliferate, and occasionally sell in very large numbers, which claim to have found the rule, or small set of rules, which will guarantee business success. But business is far too complicated, far too difficult an activity to distil into a few simple commands ... It is failure rather than success which is the distinguishing feature of corporate life. **Paul Ormerod**. *Why Most Things Fail* (2007)

Failure is important because the first time you win (or lose), it could be luck, it could be timing, or it could be talent. It's only after you fail once or twice and learn to rely equally on thought, analysis, and anticipation—in addition to speed, talent, and execution—that you can really call yourself an entrepreneur ... In the long run, it's mind over muscle, strategy over strength, and a healthy perspective—not just a lot of perspiration—that make someone a real success in his or her business and in the equally important rest of his or her life. **Howard Tullman**. *You Need to Be a Little Crazy: The Truth about Starting and Growing Your Business* (Barry J. Moltz, 2003), Preface

At some point, we all have to decide how we are going to fail: by not going far enough, or by going too far. The only alternative for the most successful (maybe even the most fulfilled) people is the latter. **Harriet Rubin**. "How Will You Fail?" *Fast Company* (1999)

I set a rule that people weren't allowed to send good news unless they sent around an equal amount of bad news. We had to get a balanced picture. In fact, I kind of favored just hearing about the accounts we were losing because ... bad news is generally more actionable than good news. **Bill Gates**. Speech, Microsoft's Second Annual CEO Summit, Seattle, Washington (May 28, 1998)

I had a lot of successes, but what really made me fearless was my complete failure at Zidd-Davis. Once you've lived through that, you know you can survive, and you're not as scared ... There's nothing to build confidence like real achievement, but also like real failure. **Esther Dyson**. Referring to her experience of being hired to start a newspaper, which flopped. Interview, *Reason Magazine* (November 1996)

Failing is good as long as it doesn't become a habit. **Michael Eisner**. Speech (April 19, 1996)

We don't publicize our failures. When something doesn't work don't leave the corpse lying around. **Kenneth Iverson**. Speech (February 5, 1996)

If we do not succeed, then we run the risk of failure. **Dan Quayle**. Quoted in *Esquire* (August 1992)

Failures, repeated failures, are finger posts on the road to achievement. The only time you don't fail is the last time you try something, and it works. One fails forward toward success. **Charles Franklin Kettering**. Quoted in *Reader's Digest* (May 1989)

It would have been cheaper to lower the Atlantic. **Sir Lew, Lord Grade**. On the failure of his movie *Raise the Titanic*. *Sun (London)* (December 22, 1987)

There are few things more dreadful than dealing with a man who knows he is going under, in his own eyes and in the eyes of others. **James Baldwin**. *The Price of the Ticket* (1985), Introduction

One of the most important tasks of a manager is to eliminate his people's excuses for failure. **Robert Townsend**. *Further Up the Organization* (1984)

Bankruptcy is a sacred state, a condition beyond conditions ... attempts to investigate it are necessarily obscene like spiritualism. One knows only he has passed into it and lives beyond us, in a condition not ours. **John Updike**. "The Bankrupt Man," *Hugging the Shore* (1983)

Ever tried. Ever failed. No matter. Try again. Fail again. Fail better. **Samuel Beckett**. *Worstward Ho* (1983)

More strategies fail because they are overripe than because they are premature. **Kenichi Ohmae**. *The Mind of the Strategist* (1982)

In the long run, failure was the only thing that worked predictably. **Joseph Heller**. *Good As Gold* (1979)

It is not impossibilities which fill us with deepest despair, but possibilities which we have failed to realize. **Robert Mallet**. *Apostilles: ou, L'Utile et le Futile* (1972)

Success requires no explanations. Failure permits no alibi. **Napoleon Hill**. *Think and Grow Rich* (1937)

Three failures denote uncommon strength. A weakling has not enough grit to fail thrice. **Minna Antrim**. *At the Sign of the Golden Calf* (1905)

For everything you have missed, you have gained something else. **Ralph Waldo Emerson**. "Compensation," *Essays: First Series* (1841)

Companies do not go bankrupt the way they used to, and countries are not declared in default. We talk about restructuring instead. I think this is detrimental. We cannot abolish death. **Pehr Gyllenhammar**. Attributed

Whenever you fall, pick up something. **Oswald Theodore Avery**. Attributed

The difference between failure and success is doing a thing nearly right and doing it exactly right. **Edward Emerson Simmons**. Attributed

If at first you don't succeed, try, try again. Then quit. No use being a damn fool about it. **W. C. Fields**. Attributed

Fear

Fear nothing—failing that, fake it! **Felix Dennis**. *Guardian (London)* (May 8, 2010)

You cannot banish fear, but you can face it down, stomp on it, crush it, bury it, padlock it into the deepest recesses of your heart and soul and leave it there to rot. Refuse to acknowledge fear of failure, fear of losing your job, fear of your boss, fear of any kind. **Felix Dennis**. *How to Get Rich* (2006)

You know the saying, a horse always knows when the rider is afraid? That is true for business as well. **Dennis, Lord Stevenson**. *Management Today* (April 1999)

Our deepest fear is not that we are inadequate. Our deepest fear is that we are powerful beyond measure. **Marianne Williamson**. *A Return To Love* (1996)

We will continue to ignore political and economic forecasts, which are an expensive distraction for many investors ... we have usually made our best purchases when apprehensions about some macro event were at a peak. Fear is the foe of the faddist, but the friend of the fundamentalist. **Warren Buffett**. Chairman's letter to shareholders (March 7, 1995)

Most people live and die with their music still unplayed. They never dare to try. **Mary Kay Ash**. *New York Times* (1985)

If you aren't afraid to fail, then you probably don't care enough about success. **Mark McCormack**. *What They Don't Teach You at Harvard Business School* (1984)

We fear our highest possibilities (as well as our lowest ones). We are generally afraid to become that which we can glimpse in our most perfect moment, under the most perfect conditions, under conditions of greatest courage. We enjoy and even thrill to the godlike possibilities we see in ourselves in such peak moments. And yet we simultaneously shiver with weakness, awe, and fear before these very same possibilities. **Abraham Maslow**. *The Farther Reaches of Human Nature* (1971)

A few yes men may be born, but mostly they are made. Fear is a great breeder of them. **William Wrigley, Jr.** *American Magazine* (March 1920)

Always do what you are afraid to do. **Ralph Waldo Emerson**. *Essays* (1841)

Anything that I've ever done that ended up worthwhile, initially scared me to death. You have to risk everything sometimes or you risk even more. **Danny McCrossan**. Attributed

Finance

We need to move beyond the demonisation of overpaid traders ... In finance and economics, ill-designed policy is a more powerful force for harm than individual greed or error. **Adair, Lord Turner**. Speech, City of London (September 21, 2010)

When you work in bank trading you are trading other people's money; you learn a lot of bad habits. Some of the worst traders I know are bank traders ... There's nothing better than being able to dump your worst positions on your customers. We don't have that ability. **Yra Harris**. On the difference between bank trading and bond trading. Quoted in the *Independent (London)* (June 7, 2010)

There is an angry mob out there. Its shape is dimly perceived, but the terrifying shadows cast by its flaming torches are clear enough. This is the bond market in full cry. Its most aggressive participants even call themselves the "bond vigilantes." **Stephen Foley**. On the bond market's hostile reaction to rising government deficits. *Independent (London)* (June 7, 2010)

In Las Vegas, people know that the odds are stacked against them. On Wall Street, they manipulate the odds while you are playing the game. **John Ensign**. Speaking at a congressional hearing into the trading practices of Goldman Sachs (April 27, 2010)

An elected government making huge changes with the consent of its people, is being undermined by concentrated powers in unregulated markets—powers which go beyond those of any individual government. **George Papandreou**. Referring to the role of financial markets in the Greek debt crisis of 2010. Speech, Washington, DC (March 2010)

I've always been sceptical about the notion that the market is a person you can engage in an argument with, and that that person is an intelligent, rational, well-intentioned person: it is fantasy. We know that ... the market is subject to irrational optimism and pessimism, and is vindictive ... You're dealing with a crazy man ... Having got what he wants he will still kill you. **Joseph Stiglitz**. On government attempts to placate financial markets. Interview, *Independent (London)* (February 9, 2010)

If we are really serious about preventing another crisis like the 2008 meltdown we should simply ban complex financial instruments, unless they can be unambiguously shown to benefit society in the long run. This is what we do all the time with other products—drugs, cars, electrical products and many others. **Ha-Joon Chang**. *23 Things They Don't Tell You About Capitalism* (2010)

  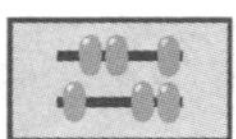      

It sounds to me like selling a car with faulty brakes, and then buying an insurance policy on those cars. **Phil Angelides**. On Goldman Sachs's policy of selling high-risk mortgage-linked derivatives while simultaneously betting against them in the market. Remark made when chairing the Financial Crisis Inquiry Commission (2010)

It's as if people used the invention of seat belts as an opportunity to take up drunk driving. **John Lanchester**. On the changing use of credit derivatives in the years leading up to the crisis of 2008–09. *I.O.U.: Why Everyone Owes Everyone and Noone Can Pay* (2010)

I wish someone would give me one shred of neutral evidence that financial innovation has led to economic growth—one shred of evidence. **Paul A. Volcker**. Speaking at a conference of senior bankers (December 8, 2009)

I want them poor and they deserve to be poor. You can't have capitalism without punishment. **Nassim Nicholas Taleb**. Comments made at the World Economic Forum, January 2009. Quoted in James Saft's Reuters blog (January 30, 2009)

Private equity has absolutely no reason to exist. The private equity holder has all the upside and the banks all the downside. **Nassim Nicholas Taleb**. Comments made at the World Economic Forum, January 2009. Quoted in James Saft's Reuters blog (January 30, 2009)

We should probably stop trading derivatives, anything more complex than regular options ... I am an options trader, and I don't understand options. How do you want a regulator to understand them? **Nassim Nicholas Taleb**. Interview on Bloomberg TV (January 29, 2009)

Blaming the hedge funds for the crisis is like blaming the passengers in a bus crash. **Paul Marshall**. Speaking to a Treasury Committee inquiry (January 28, 2009)

I don't think there is a sound UK bank now, at least, if there is one I don't know about it. The City of London is finished, the financial centre of the world is moving east. All the money is in Asia. Why would it go back to the West? You don't need London. **Jim Rogers**. Speaking on Bloomberg TV (January 20, 2009)

What kind of monster has been created here? It's like you raised a cute kid who then grew up and committed a horrible crime. **Anonymous**. Comment by a financier at JP Morgan Stern on complex derivatives. Quoted in *Fool's Gold* (Gillian Tett, 2009)

Financial hydrogen bombs built on personal computers by 26-year-olds with MBAs. **Felix Rohatyn**. On complex derivatives. Quoted in *Fool's Gold* (Gillian Tett, 2009)

When car crashes happen, people don't blame cars or stop driving them, they blame the drivers! Derivatives are the same. **Terri Duhon**. Quoted in *Fool's Gold* (Gillian Tett, 2009)

Remember this crisis began in regulated entities. This happened right under our noses. **Paul S. Atkins**. Quoted in the *Washington Post* (December 16, 2008)

The arrangement bore the same relation to actual finance as fantasy football bears to the NFL. **Michael Lewis**. On credit default swaps. *Condé Nast Portfolio* (December 2008)

The really scary part is that we don't have a clue. This has become essentially the dark matter of the financial universe. **Chris Wolf**. On the risk posed by credit default swaps. Quoted in *Fortune* (Nicholas Varchaver and Katie Benner, September 30, 2008)

The Treasury's plan has little for those outside of the financial industry. It is aimed at rescuing the same financial institutions that created this crisis with the sloppy underwriting and reckless disregard for the risk they were creating, taking or passing on to others. **Richard Shelby**. Senate Banking Committee hearing on the Paulson Plan (September 29, 2008)

In the past six months, our federal government has devised a dozen strategies to save America's financial markets. Each plan has been more costly, more risky, and less aligned with the principles of our country's free market economy than the last. I am disappointed to say that this latest plan puts all the rest of them to shame. **Mike Enzi**. Senate Banking Committee hearing on the Paulson Plan (September 29, 2008)

Henry Paulson is to finance what Donald Rumsfeld was to military strategy, Dick Cheney to geopolitics and Michael Chertoff to flood defence. **Anatole Kaletsky**. On the US Treasury Secretary's Wall Street bailout plan. *The Times (London)* (September 25, 2008)

Wall Street got drunk and now it's got a hangover. And the question is, how long will it sober up and not try to do those fancy financial instruments? **George W. Bush**. Speech (July 2008)

In an ideal world, one populated by vegetarians and Esperanto speakers, derivatives would be used for one thing only: reducing levels of risk. The list of individual traders who have lost more than a billion dollars at a time betting on derivatives is not short. **John Lanchester**. *London Review of Books* (January 3, 2008)

The City is, in terms of its basic functioning, a far-off country of which we know little. **John Lanchester**. *London Review of Books* (January 3, 2008)

It is hard for us ... to even see a scenario within any kind of realm of reason that would see us losing one dollar in any of those transactions. **Joseph J. Cassano**. On trading in credit derivatives. AIG received a federal bailout of $85 billion in September 2008. Comment (August 2007)

It seems superfluous to constrain trading in some of the newer derivatives and other innovative financial contracts of the past decade. The worst have failed; investors no longer fund them and are not likely to in the future. **Alan Greenspan**. *The Age of Turbulence* (2007)

Usually God favours the people who try to do good. So, when you find that the crowd is desperately trying to sell, help them and buy. When you find that the crowd is overenthusiastically trying to buy, help them and sell. It usually works out. **Sir John Templeton**. Interview on *Nightly Business Review* (February 2004)

Never ask a trader if he is profitable: you can easily see it in his gesture and gait. **Nassim Nicholas Taleb**. *Fooled by Randomness* (2004)

Finance is the art of passing currency from hand to hand until it finally disappears. **Robert W. Sarnoff**. Quoted in *An Introduction to International Political Economy* (Alison M. S. Watson, 2004)

Markets can remain irrational longer than you can remain solvent. **John Maynard Keynes**. Quoted in *Straight Talk on Investing* (Jack Brennan, 2004)

What we have found over the years in the marketplace is that derivatives have been an extraordinarily useful vehicle to transfer risk from those who shouldn't be taking it to those who are willing to and are capable of doing so. **Alan Greenspan**. Addressing the Senate Banking Committee (2003)

In our view, derivatives are financial weapons of mass destruction carrying dangers that, while latent, are potentially lethal. **Warren Buffett**. Letter to shareholders (2003)

     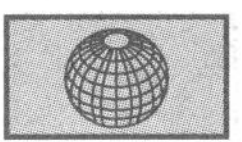   

The range of derivatives contracts is limited only by the imagination of man (or sometimes, so it seems, madmen). Say you want to write a contract speculating on the number of twins to be born in Nebraska in 2020. No problem—at a price, you will easily find an obliging counterparty. **Warren Buffett**. Letter to shareholders (2003)

Reversion to the mean is the iron rule of the financial markets. **John Clifton Bogle**. Speech, University of Missouri (October 22, 2002)

Trading has been, and always will be, a hard way to make an easy living. **Jeffrey Silverman**. Quoted in *500 of the Most Witty, Acerbic, and Erudite Things Ever Said About Money* (philip Jenks, 2002)

Remember, the price that people agree to in the pit is not the price that people think is going to exist in the future. It's the price that both sides vehemently agree won't be there. **Jeffrey Silverman**. Quoted in *500 of the Most Witty, Acerbic, and Erudite Things Ever Said About Money* (Philip Jenks, 2002)

Discipline allows you to trade effectively. You can take your ego out of it. You can go wrong 60, 70% of the time and still make a lot of money. If you ignore the discipline of managing risk, you have to be right 80% of the time or more, and I don't know anyone who's that good. **Larry Rosenberg**. Quoted in *500 of the Most Witty, Acerbic and Erudite Things Ever Said About Money* (Philip Jenks, 2002)

There is time to go long, time to go short and time to go fishing. **Jesse Livermore**. Quoted in *Come Into My Trading Room* (Alexander Elder, 2002)

Amateurs look for challenges; professionals look for easy trades. Losers get high from the action; the pros look for the best odds. **Alexander Elder**. *Come Into My Trading Room* (2002)

You only find out who is swimming naked when the tide goes out. **Warren Buffett**. Letter to shareholders (2001)

I made my money by selling too soon. **Bernard Baruch**. Quoted in *The Global Trader* (Barbara Rockefeller, 2001)

We should never lose sight of the underlying essence of a market—a place where buyers and sellers come together. Every other feature—whether crafted by tradition or technology—exists only to serve that primary purpose. **Arthur Levitt, Jr**. Speech to the Columbia Law School, New York. "Dynamic Markets, Timeless Principles" (September 23, 1999)

The time of maximum pessimism is the best time to buy and the time of maximum optimism is the best time to sell. **Sir John Templeton**. Quoted in *The Book of Investing Wisdom* (Peter Krass, 1999)

Nobody beats the market, they say. Except for those of those of us who do. **David N. Dreman**. *Contrarian Investment Strategies* (1999)

A group of lemmings looks like a pack of individuals compared with Wall Street when it gets a concept in its teeth. **Warren Buffett**. Quoted in *Treasury of Investment Wisdom* (Bernice Cohen, 1999)

Financial markets ... resent any kind of government interference but they hold a belief deep down that if conditions get really rough the authorities will step in. **George Soros**. *The Crisis of Global Capitalism* (1998)

To suppose that the value of a common stock is determined purely by a corporation's earnings discounted by the relevant interest rates and adjusted for the marginal tax rate is to forget that people have burned witches, gone to war on a whim, risen to the defense of Joseph Stalin and believed Orson Welles when he told them over the radio that the Martians had landed. **Jim Grant**. Quoted in *Value Investing Made Easy* (Janet Lowe, 1997)

There is no human feeling to the US securities markets and sometimes no discernible evidence of human intelligence either. But they work. **Robert J. Eaton**. Speech (March 18, 1996)

A market that slowly grinds higher is a good buy. A market that soars is usually a good sell. **Neal Weintraub**. *Tricks of the Floor Trader* (1995)

If you spend more than 14 minutes a year worrying about the market, you've wasted 12 minutes. **Peter Lynch**. Quoted in *Barron's Guide to Making Investment Decisions* (Donald R. Sease and John Prestbo, 1994)

The world of finance hails the invention of the wheel over and over again, often in a slightly more unstable form. **J. K. Galbraith**. *A Short History of Financial Euphoria* (1993)

Investing in the market without knowing what stage it is in is like selling life insurance to 20 year olds and 80 year olds at the same premium. **Victor Sperandeo**. Quoted in *The New Market Wizards* (John D. Schwager, 1992)

You can picture price fluctuations around an equilibrium level as a rubber band being stretched—if it gets pulled too far, eventually it will snap back. As a short-term trader, I try to wait until the rubber band is stretched to its extreme point. **Linda Bradford Raschke**. Quoted in *The New Market Wizards* (John D. Schwager, 1992)

Don't think about what the market's going to do; you have absolutely no control over that. Think about what you're going to do if it gets there. **William Eckhardt**. Quoted in *The New Market Wizards* (John D. Schwager, 1992)

It is not whether you are right or wrong that's important, but how much money you make when you're right and how much you lose when you're wrong. **Stanley Druckenmiller**. Quoted in *The New Market Wizards* (John D. Schwager, 1992)

One market paradigm that I take exception to is: Buy low and sell high. I believe far more money is made by buying high and selling at even higher prices. **Richard Driehaus**. Quoted in *The New Market Wizards* (John D. Schwager, 1992)

Patience is the hardest part of trading and investing, but also the most important, for it is in the waiting that we make bigger profits. **William F. Eng**. *Trading Rules: Strategies for Success* (1990)

Twenty years in this business convinces me that any normal person using the customary 3% of the brain can pick stocks as well as, if not better than, the average Wall Street expert. **Peter Lynch**. *One Up On Wall Street* (1990)

Although it's easy to forget sometimes, a share is not a lottery ticket. It's part-ownership of a business. **Peter Lynch**. *One Up On Wall Street* (1990)

I have noticed that everyone who has ever tried to tell me that markets are efficient is poor. **Larry Hite**. Quoted in *Market Wizards* (John D. Schwager, 1989)

Anybody who plays the stock market not as an insider is like a man buying cows in the moonlight. **Daniel Drew**. Quoted in *Boom and Bust* (Christopher Woo, 1989)

The best traders have no ego. You cannot let ego get in the way of a trade that is a loser; you have to swallow your pride and get out. **Tom Baldwin**. Quoted in *Market Wizards* (John D. Schwager, 1989)

The biggest public fallacy is that the market is always right. The market is nearly always wrong. I can assure you of that. **Jim Rogers**. Quoted in *Market Wizards* (John D. Schwager, 1989)

On Wall Street he and a few others—how many?—three hundred, four hundred, five hundred?—had become precisely that … Masters of the Universe. **Tom Wolfe**. *The Bonfire of the Vanities* (1987), ch. 1

I have probably purchased fifty "hot tips" in my career, maybe even more. When I put them all together, I know I am a net loser. **Charles Schwab**. *How To Be Your Own Stockbroker* (1986)

The little I know of it has not served to raise my opinion of what is vulgarly called the Monied Interest; I mean, that blood-sucker, that muckworm, that calls itself the friend of government. **William Pitt the Elder (Earl of Chatham)**. Speech, House of Lords (November 22, 1970)

A speculator is a man who observes the future, and acts before it occurs. **Bernard Baruch**. *Baruch: My Own Story* (1957)

All these financiers, all the little gnomes of Zürich and the other financial centres, about whom we keep on hearing. **Harold, Lord Wilson**. Speech, House of Commons (November 12, 1956)

In the short-run, the market is a voting machine but in the long run, the market is a weighing machine. **Benjamin Graham**. *The Intelligent Investor* (1949)

Take care to sell your horse before he dies. The art of life is passing losses on. **Robert Frost**. "The Ingenuities of Debt" (1946)

A successful trader studies human nature and does the opposite of what the general public does. **W. D. Gann**. *How to Make Profits Trading in Commodities* (1942)

The game of speculation is the most uniformly fascinating game in the world. But it is not a game for the stupid, the mentally lazy, the person of inferior emotional balance, or the get-rich-quick adventurer. They will die poor. **Jesse Livermore**. *How To Trade in Stocks* (1940)

Wall Street, runs the sinister old gag, is a street with a river at one end and a graveyard at the other. This is striking, but incomplete. It omits the kindergarten in the middle. **Fred Schwed**. *Where Are The Customers' Yachts?* (1940)

Investing is an activity of forecasting the yield over the life of the asset; speculation is the activity of forecasting the psychology of the market. **John Maynard Keynes**. Attributed (1938?)

If human nature felt no temptation to take a chance there might not be much investment merely as a result of cold calculation. **John Maynard Keynes**. *The General Theory of Employment, Interest and Money* (1936)

Market values are fixed only in part by balance sheets and income statements; much more by the hopes and fears of humanity; by greed, ambition, acts of God, invention, financial stress and strain, weather, discovery, fashion and numberless other causes impossible to be listed without omission. **Gerald M. Loeb**. *The Battle for Investment Survival* (1935)

The City is a machine miraculously organized for extracting gold from the seas, airs, clouds, from barren lands, holds of ships, mines, plantations, cottage hearth-stones, trees and rock. **Christina Stead**. "The Sensitive Goldfish," *The Salzburg Tales* (1934)

There are two times in a man's life when he should not speculate: when he can't afford it and when he can. **Mark Twain**. *Following the Equator* (1899)

A good technician gets it right maybe 60% of the time. And a great technician, maybe 61% of the time. **Gary B. Smith**. On technical analysis of financial markets. Attributed

A market is the combined behaviour of thousands of people responding to information, misinformation and whim. **Kenneth Chang**. Attributed

I used to think that if there was reincarnation, I wanted to come back as the President or the Pope or as a .400 baseball hitter, but now I would like to come back as the bond market. You can intimidate everybody. **James Carville**. Attributed

What is high finance? It's knowing the difference between one and ten, multiplying, subtracting and adding. You just add noughts. It's no more than that. **John Bentley**. Attributed

If you must play, decide on three things at the start: the rules of the game, the stakes, and the quitting time. **Anonymous**. Chinese proverb

Focus

There's a lot to be said for quitters. Those people who are extremely good at one thing got that way by quitting almost everything else. **Penelope Trunk**. *Twitter (penelopetrunk)* (December 12, 2012)

I try to learn from the past, but I plan for the future by focusing exclusively on the present. **Donald J. Trump**. Quoted in *101 Best Ways to Get Ahead* (Michael E. Angier, 2004)

I sometimes find, and I am sure you know the feeling, that I simply have too many thoughts and memories crammed into my mind. At these times I use the Pensieve. One simply siphons the excess thoughts from one's mind, pours them into the basin, and examines them at one's leisure. It becomes easier to spot patterns and links, you understand, when they are in this form. **J. K. Rowling**. Dumbledore speaking to Harry in *Harry Potter and the Goblet of Fire* (2000)

The quality of your attention determines the quality of other people's thinking. **Nancy Kline**. *Time to Think* (1999)

Focus on where you want to go, not on what you fear. **Anthony Robbins**. *Awaken the Giant Within* (1992)

Never waste your attention on matters that have nothing to do with your work … Remember that it is the family business that must not be neglected for a moment. **Mitsui Takafusa**. Quoted in *Premodern Japan: A Historical Survey* (Mikiso Hane, 1991)

When conscious activity is wholly concentrated on some one definite purpose, the ultimate result, for most people, is lack of balance accompanied by some form of nervous disorder. **Bertrand Russell (Earl Russell)**. Quoted in *Management by Objectives: An Integrated Approach* (S. K. Chakraborty, 1976)

Intense concentration for hour after hour can bring out resources in people that they didn't know they had. **Edwin Land**. *Forbes* (June 1975)

It is better to do thine own duty, however lacking in merit, than to do that of another, even though efficiently. **Bhagavad Gita**. 3:35 (300? BC)

Forecasting

Economists did something even better than predict the crisis. We correctly predicted that we would not be able to predict it. **William Easterly**. Referring to the financial crisis of 2008–09. *Aid Watch* blog (August 7, 2009)

Forecasting by bureaucrats tends to be used for anxiety relief rather than for adequate policy making. **Nassim Nicholas Taleb**. *The Black Swan: The Impact of the Highly Improbable* (2007)

People who forecast simply because "that's my job," knowing pretty well that their forecast is ineffectual, are not what I would call ethical. What they do is no different from repeating lies simply because "it's my job." **Nassim Nicholas Taleb**. *The Black Swan: The Impact of the Highly Improbable* (2007)

An economic forecaster is like a cross-eyed javelin thrower: they don't win many accuracy contests, but they keep the crowd's attention. **Anonymous**. Quoted in *Demystifying Wall Street* (Bruce Fleet, 2007)

The government-sponsored institution Fannie Mae, when I look at its risks, seems to be sitting on a barrel of dynamite, vulnerable to the slightest hiccup. But not to worry: their large staff of scientists deemed these events "unlikely." **Nassim Nicholas Taleb**. Fannie Mae and Freddie Mac were taken into government "conservatorship" in September 2008. *The Black Swan: The Impact of the Highly Improbable* (2007)

Business, more than any other occupation, is a continual dealing with the future; it is a continual calculation, an instinctive exercise in foresight. **Henry R. Luce**. Quoted in *The Leslie Pockell 101 Greatest Business Principles of All Time* (2004)

A general rule: if enough people predict something, it won't happen. **J. G. Ballard**. *New Statesman* (2000)

In a crowded room, you only have to see one inch above everyone else to notice things that others will miss. **Jim Slater**. Quoted in *Treasury of Investment Wisdom* (Bernice Cohen, 1999)

We have two classes of forecasters: Those who don't know—and those who don't know they don't know. **J. K. Galbraith**. Quoted in *Predicting the Future* (Nicholas Rescher, 1998)

In the mid 80s, *Fortune* magazine carried the prediction that, by the year 2010, North America would become the world's granary, the Pacific the world's manufacturing base and that Europe will become a discotheque. They could still be right. **Max Comfort**. *Portfolio People* (1997)

Economists are about as useful as astrologers in predicting the future (and, like astrologers, they never let failure on one occasion diminish certitude on the next). **Arthur Schlesinger, Jr**. Quoted in the *New York Times* (April 15, 1993)

We've long felt that the only value of stock forecasts is to make fortune tellers look good. Short-term market forecasts are poison and should be kept locked up in a safe place, away from children and also from grown-ups who behave in the market like children. **Warren Buffett**. Letter to shareholders (1992)

The future bears a resemblance to the past, only more so. **Faith Popcorn**. *The Popcorn Report* (1991)

An economist is an expert who will know tomorrow why the things he predicted yesterday didn't happen today. **Laurence J. Peter**. *Peter's Quotations: Ideas For Our Time* (1977)

The easiest way to predict the future is to invent it. **Anonymous**. Xerox Research Center, Palo Alto, California (1970)

Wall Street indexes predicted nine out of the last five recessions. **Paul Samuelson**. *Newsweek* (September 19, 1966)

Forecast: to observe that which has passed, and guess it will happen again. **Frank McKinney Hubbard**. *The Roycroft Dictionary* (1923)

Among all forms of mistake, prophecy is the most gratuitous. **George Eliot**. *Middlemarch* (1871–1872)

Trying to predict the future is like trying to drive down a country road at night with no lights while looking out the back window. **Peter F. Drucker**. Attributed

Getting Started

If you have an idea, just get on and do it. Get it out there in front of people so they can tell you whether or not it's good. **John Abbott**. Quoted in "Change Your Life: Meet the Austerity Entrepreneurs," *Independent (London)* (January 2, 2011)

You need a strategy, yes. You need a business plan, yes. But most of all you need to sell something, anything, to keep you going and give you cash and cash-flow. **George Freeman**. Quoted in "Change Your Life: Meet the Austerity Entrepreneurs," *Independent (London)* (January 2, 2011)

However whizzy the technology seems, however in touch with the zeitgeist the product feels, and however young and trendy your staff, you don't have a viable business until you have a credible business model. If you haven't yet dreamed up a a way to monetise your creation, then don't count on it earning you a living. **David Prosser**. *Independent (London)* (June 24, 2009)

Doing a startup is like running a high hurdles race early in the morning before the fog has burned off and before the setup crew has all of the hurdles positioned correctly. The starting gun goes off and you can see perhaps a dozen feet in front of you. You can hear the grunts of the other racers and the scuff of shoes on the track. You take off running and the first hurdle appears out of the fog. You clear it easily and then realize that you are slowing down slightly, expecting the next one, but the setup crew has not put it out. Then suddenly it's in front of you and you barely clear up. You can hear some of the other runners stumbling but ahead you hear others racing ahead of you. You have to set a pace to catch them but you cannot just put your head down and run because you have to keep a lookout for another hurdle to appear at the limit of your fogbound vision. **Anonymous**. Quoted in "Two Images of Startups," *SKMurphy* blog (Sean Murphy, December 21, 2006)

I can think of several heuristics for generating ideas for startups, but most reduce to this: look at something people are trying to do, and figure out how to do it in a way that doesn't suck. **Paul Graham**. "How to Start a Startup," *paulgraham.com* (March 2005)

That's the essence of a startup: having brilliant people do work that's beneath them. Big companies try to hire the right person for the job. Startups win because they don't—because they take people so smart that they would in a big company be doing "research," and set them to work instead on problems of the most immediate and mundane sort. Think Einstein designing refrigerators. **Paul Graham**. *Why Smart People Have Bad Ideas* (2005)

Reading the *Wall Street Journal* for a week should give anyone ideas for two or three new startups. **Paul Graham**. *Why Smart People Have Bad Ideas* (2005)

Remember that on day one, when you go in as the boss, you'll feel a mixture of exhilaration that you've made it and fatigue with all the effort. **Barbara, Lady Judge**. *Management Today* (October 1999)

Keep starting and the finishing will take care of itself. **Neil A. Fiore**. *The Now Habit* (1993)

One sees great things from the valley; only small things from the peak. **G. K. Chesterton**. *The Innocence of Father Brown* (1911)

  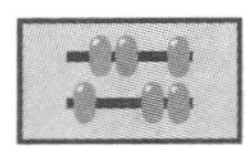      

The beginning is the most important part of any work. **Plato**. *The Republic* (370? BC), bk. 2, sect. 377

In a start-up company, you basically throw out all assumptions every three weeks. **Scott McNealy**. Attributed

Globalization

It is not too far-fetched to say that the "nice" era of non-inflationary growth in Western economies has been built, mainly, on Chinese labour; and that the structures of modern financial capitalism have depended on the continued cooperation and stability provided by the Chinese Communist party. **Vince Cable**. *The Storm* (2009)

The recent turbulence in the international markets reminds us what happens when an event in one part of the world can touch us all in just a few weeks. There was a time when a small bank in America got in trouble it was bad news for that town, or state, but nowhere else. But today, when a Florida householder defaults on his mortgage, the effects are felt, not just in America but across the world, in France, Germany, the rest of Europe and here in Britain. **Alistair Darling**. Speech, University of Stirling, UK (November 8, 2007)

The raw fact is that every successful example of economic development this past century—every case of a poor nation that worked its way up to a more or less decent, or at least dramatically better, standard of living—has taken place via globalization, that is, by producing for the world market rather than trying for self-sufficiency. **Paul R. Krugman**. *The Great Unraveling: Losing Our Way in the New Century* (2007)

The United States in particular and the West in general should be feeling a little embarrassed about all that lecturing we did to the Third World. **Paul R. Krugman**. Remark made at the World Economic Forum (February 2002)

These days Paris is a suburb of New York and vice-versa. **Jean-Marie Messier**. *Sunday Times (London)* (September 2000)

Sometimes, I'm more in the air than I am in a country. **Raoul Pinnell**. Referring to the volume of business travel for a global marketing executive. *Marketing* (June 2000)

Investing is a business that never tires. You have to work with every known thing in the world—the weather in Asia, or politics in East Europe, or the scandal of an American president. **Charles Brady**. *Sunday Times (London)* (May 2000)

Does it really make sense to operate on all continents? **Keiji Tachikawa**. *Forbes* (May 2000)

It is better to underpromise and overdeliver than vice versa. For this one need not break the law of the land. **Narayana Murthy**. "Employee Satisfaction Crucial to Success," *Hindu Business Line* (2000)

Globalisation has in effect made the citizen disappear, and it has reduced the state into being a mere instrument of global capital. **Vandana Shiva**. *Globalisation: Gandhi and Swadeshi* (2000)

Economic modernization ... spawns indigenous types of capitalism that owe little to any western model. **John Gray**. *False Dawn* (1998)

Global democratic capitalism is as unrealizable a condition as worldwide communism. **John Gray**. *False Dawn* (1998)

The Death of Distance. **Frances Cairncross**. Book title. Referring to the effects of increasing globalization. *The Death of Distance* (1997)

All things start in California and spread to New Jersey, then to London and then throughout Europe. **Sir Stelios Haji-Ioannou**. *Wall Street Journal* (December 1996)

If the whole world operates as one big market, every employee will compete with every person in the world who is capable of doing the same job. **Andrew S. Grove**. *Fortune* (September 1995)

All you need is the best product in the world, the most efficient production in the world and global marketing. **Akio Morita**. Quoted in *The Financial Times Handbook of Management* (Stuart Crainer, ed, 1995)

You can always buy something in English, you can't always sell something in English. **Rosabeth Moss Kanter**. *World Class* (1995)

Capital, technology, and ideas flow these days like quicksilver across national boundaries. **Robert H. Waterman, Jr**. *The Frontiers of Excellence* (1994)

We must not fall into the mistake of thinking that it is America that trades with Taiwan or Europe that trades with Asia. The truth is that it is American companies that trade with Taiwanese companies. **Margaret, Baroness Thatcher**. *Far Eastern Economic Review* (September 2, 1993)

Today's global economic dance is no Strauss waltz. It's break dancing accompanied by street rap. **Tom Peters**. *Liberation Management* (1992)

The United States is just one part of a global marketplace today. There isn't any offshore anymore; it's all onshore. **Walter Wriston**. *US News & World Report* (1987)

Think globally, act locally. **Friends of the Earth**. Slogan (1985)

The bigger the world economy, the more powerful its smallest player. **John Naisbitt**. *Megatrends* (1982)

Nationalism is an infantile sickness. It is the measles of the human race. **Albert Einstein**. Quoted in *The Human Side* (Helen Dukas and Banesh Hoffmann, 1979)

This going into Europe will not turn out to be the thrilling mutual exchange supposed. It is more like nine middle-aged couples with failing marriages meeting in a darkened bedroom in a Brussels hotel for a group grope. **E. P. Thompson**. *Sunday Times (London)* (April 1975)

The new electronic interdependence recreates the world in the image of a global village. **Marshall McLuhan**. *The Gutenberg Galaxy* (1962)

Merchants have no country. The mere spot they stand on does not constitute so strong an attachment as that from which they draw their gains. **Thomas Jefferson**. Letter to Horatio G. Spafford (March 17, 1814)

No nation was ever ruined by trade. **Benjamin Franklin**. *Essays* (1730s)

Goals and Objectives

I think if your goal is for everything to be okay, that's a mistake. To achieve that goal, the only obstacle you'd have to face tomorrow is to eliminate all risk ... I've made the decision that I'm never trying to make everything okay. I'm trying for there to be more loose ends, not fewer loose ends. **Seth Godin**. Interviewed on *The Great Discontent* blog (August 14, 2012)

What you measure affects what you do. If you don't measure the right thing, you don't do the right thing. **Joseph Stiglitz**. Quoted in the *New York Times* (October 4, 2009)

You don't run for second. I don't believe in that. **Barack Obama**. Interview with David Letterman on *The Late Show* (April 9, 2007)

Busy is good, isn't it? Busy means we're hard at it, achieving our ends or "goals." Haven't had time to stop, or look around or think. That's considered the sign of a life well lived ... Suppose, though, you're not sure that what you're doing is at all worthwhile. Suppose you blundered into it over a spoonful of lime pickle. It's easy, it pays quite well. But really it's a distraction. It stops you thinking about what you ought to be doing. **Sebastian Faulks**. *Engleby* (2007)

The mantra of execute, execute, execute, speed, speed, speed seems to preclude any consideration of what we are speeding toward. That's sort of like saying, Don't bother me with the facts—I'm busy executing them. **Jay S. Walker**. Interview, *Strategy + Business* (January–March 2000)

Goals too clearly defined can become blinkers. **Mary Catherine Bateson**. *Composing a Life* (1989)

Often it is the means that justify the ends: goals advance technique and technique survives even when goal structures crumble. **Alan Jay Perlis**. *Epigrams in Programming* (1985)

You read a book from beginning to end. You run a business the opposite way. You start with the end, and then you do everything you must to reach it. **Harold S. Geneen**. *Managing* (1984)

A good goal is like a strenuous exercise—it makes you stretch. **Mary Kay Ash**. *On People Management* (1984)

Economics are the method. The object is to change the soul. **Margaret, Baroness Thatcher**. *Sunday Times (London)* (April 1975)

If you don't know where you are going, you will probably end up somewhere else. **Laurence J. Peter**. *The Peter Principle: Why Things Always Go Wrong* (cowritten with Raymond Hull, 1969)

There are two things to aim at in life: first, to get what you want; and, after that, to enjoy it. Only the wisest of mankind achieve the second. **Logan Pearsall Smith**. "Life and Human Nature," *Afterthoughts* (1931)

If you would hit the mark, you must aim a little above it; Every arrow that flies feels the attraction of Earth. **Henry Wadsworth Longfellow**. "Elegaic Verse" (1880)

Ah, but a man's reach should exceed his grasp, Or what's a heaven for? **Robert Browning**. "Andrea del Sarto" (1855), l. 97

Government

Want to live in a place with no government? Try Somalia! **Anonymous**. Placard carried by demonstrator at the "Rally to Restore Sanity" in Washington, DC (October 30, 2010)

We ultimately witnessed the demise of an ideology that says the only rule for government is always to get out of the way. **Douglas Alexander**. On the financial crisis of 2008–09. *Independent (London)* (January 20, 2009)

Leave it up to the free market, and in a few generations Florida will be underwater. **Paul R. Krugman**. *New York Times* (October 15, 2008)

The private market has screwed itself up and they need the government to come help them unscrew it. **Barney Frank**. On the government's bailout of insurance giant AIG. Remark (September 16, 2008)

Washington today is a place where good ideas go to die. **Barack Obama**. Speech, Milwaukee, Wisconsin (February 2008)

Regulation should not be at a level set to achieve the impossible task of protecting fools from their own folly—it should be no greater than that required to protect reasonable people from being made fools of. **Jim Gower**. Quoted in the *Independent (London)* (January 4, 2008)

In Africa, you often see that the difference between a village where everybody eats and a village where people starve is government. One has a functioning government, and the other does not. Which is why it bothers me when I hear people say that government is the enemy. **Barack Obama**. *Independent (London)* (March 10, 2007)

There is most definitely a role for government in the innovative process. The market does not do everything well. **Anne K. Bingaman**. Speech, University of Kansas Law School (September 19, 1996)

The task of government policy is not to prejudge winners but to make sure that neither private nor public restraints narrow the potential sources of innovation. **Anne K. Bingaman**. Speech, University of Kansas Law School (September 19, 1996)

Governments of the Industrial World, you weary giants of flesh and steel, I come from Cyberspace ... On behalf of the future, I ask you of the past to leave us alone ... You have no sovereignty where we gather. **John Perry Barlow**. "A Declaration of the Independence of Cyberspace" (February 8, 1996)

It is a popular delusion that the government wastes vast amounts of money through inefficiency and sloth. Enormous effort and elaborate planning are required to waste this much money. **P. J. O'Rourke**. *Parliament of Whores* (1991)

The business of the Civil Service is the orderly management of decline. **William, Lord Armstrong**. Quoted in *Whitehall* (Peter Hennessey, 1990)

Government does not solve problems, it subsidizes them. **Ronald Reagan**. "The Wit and Wisdom of Ronald Reagan," *Speaking My Mind* (1989)

You can't expect a viable economy if the only object of government policy is to be re-elected every four years. **Arnold, Lord Weinstock**. *Independent (London)* (December 20, 1986)

Government's view of the economy could be summed up in a few short phrases: If it moves, tax it. If it keeps moving, regulate it. And if it stops moving, subsidise it. **Ronald Reagan**. Speech (1981)

A species of tetanus where one set of muscles goes rigid pulling against another—and the patient becomes paralysed. **Sir Terence Norman Beckett**. On government interference in industry. *Daily Mail (London)* (September 28, 1979)

There's only one place where inflation is made: that's in Washington. **Milton Friedman**. Attributed (1977)

A government which robs Peter to pay Paul can always depend on the support of Paul. **George Bernard Shaw**. *Everybody's Political What's What?* (1944)

Governments can err. Presidents do make mistakes, but ... better the occasional faults of a government that lives in a spirit of charity than the consistent omissions of a government frozen in the ice of its own indifference. **Franklin D. Roosevelt**. Speech accepting re-nomination for a second presidential term, Philadelphia (June 27, 1936)

With perfect citizens, any government is good. **Stephen Leacock**. *The Unsolved Riddle of Social Justice* (1920)

Trade and commerce, if they were not made of india-rubber, would never manage to bounce over obstacles which legislators are continually putting in their way. **Henry David Thoreau**. "Resistance to Civil Government" (1849)

It is with government as with medicine, its only business is the choice of evils. Every law is an evil, for every law is an infraction of liberty. **Jeremy Bentham**. *Principles of Legislation* (1789)

There is no art which one government sooner learns of another than that of draining money from the pockets of the people. **Adam Smith**. *An Inquiry into the Nature and Causes of the Wealth of Nations* (1776)

Government, like dress, is the badge of lost innocence ... man finds it necessary to surrender up a part of his property to furnish means for the protection of the rest. **Thomas Paine**. *Common Sense* (1776)

Greed

Suddenly I find myself feeling sorry for those greedy, needy people whose huge salaries are never quite enough, whose sense of worth is defined by their own personal wad. What a diminished, impoverished world they must inhabit ... We should feel sorry for them and their sadly limited lives. Then we should remember never to trust the judgement of those whose priorities are so idiotically skewed. **Terence Blacker**. *Independent (London)* (January 29, 2010)

Greed is gross. Greed is vile. Greed sucks. **Yasmin Alibhai-Brown**. *Independent (London)* (June 15, 2009)

It was the kind of blind, gulping, insensate greed that you associate with some milk-eyed creature in a volcanic fissure at the bottom of the Marianas Trench—an organism with no understanding of the existence, let alone the feelings, of other members of the ecosystem. **Boris Johnson**. On Sir Fred Goodwin, former chief executive of RBS. *Daily Telegraph (London)* (March 3, 2009)

For top executives to award themselves these kinds of compensation packages in the midst of this economic crisis is not only bad taste, it's bad strategy—and I will not tolerate it as president. **Barack Obama**. Press conference (February 4, 2009)

Nothing is enough for a person for whom enough is too little. **Anonymous**. *Contemporary Social Evils* (David Utting, ed, 2009)

If you take the greed out of Wall Street, you're left with pavement. **Anonymous**. Remark (Fall 2008)

Nothing defines human beings better than their willingness to do irrational things in the pursuit of phenomenally unlikely payoffs. **Scott Adams**. *The Dilbert Principle* (1996)

Greed is even more contagious than fear. **Bud Hadfield**. *Wealth within Reach: Winning Strategies for Success from the Unconventional Wisdom of Bud Hadfield* (1995)

My father said: You must never try to make all the money that's in a deal. Let the other fellow make some money too, because if you have a reputation for always making all the money ... you won't make many deals. **J. Paul Getty**. Referring to his father, George Franklin Getty, who was also a successful oil business executive. Quoted in *Getty on Getty* (Somerset de Chair, 1989), ch. 2

Greed—for lack of a better word—is good. Greed is right. Greed works. **Oliver Stone**. From the movie satirizing some of the excesses of the 1980s. *Wall Street* (1987)

The fact that people will be full of greed, fear, or folly is predictable. The sequence is not predictable. **Warren Buffett**. *Channels* (1986)

What kind of society isn't structured on greed? **Milton Friedman**. *There's No Such Thing as a Free Lunch* (1975)

Laissez-faire, supply and demand—one begins to be weary of all that. Leave all to egotism, to ravenous greed of money, of pleasure, of applause—it is the gospel of despair. **Thomas Carlyle**. *Past and Present* (1843)

Growth

An elephant is vastly more efficient, metabolically, than a mouse. It's the same for a megacity as opposed to a village. But an elephant can break a leg very easily, whereas you can toss a mouse out of a window and it'll be fine. Size makes you fragile. **Nassim Nicholas Taleb**. *Foreign Policy* (November 2012)

Most companies aim to get bigger. But beyond a certain point, bigness becomes synonymous with badness. Think of Big Pharma, Big Auto, Big Oil. Worse, if you are regularly described as one of the Big Four, Five, or Six in any business sector, you are probably already in the sights of regulators and lawmakers. **Andrew Hill**. *Financial Times (London)* blog (September 20, 2011)

Growth has failed on its own terms. You can't have infinite growth in a world of finite resources. **Andrew Simms**. Quoted in the *Observer (London)* (January 10, 2010)

Things that grow are not always benign. **Rt Revd James Jones**. *Observer (London)* (September 20, 2009)

The big will get bigger; the small will get wiped out. **Charles Revson**. Quoted in *The Quotable Billionaire* (Stephen D. Price, 2009)

Anyone who believes that exponential growth can go on forever in a finite world is either a madman or an economist. **Kenneth Boulding**. Quoted in *Jump the Curve* (Jack Uldrich, 2008)

There are as many foolhardy ways to grow as there are to downsize. **Gary Hamel**. *Digital Britain* (January 2000)

Is your company so small you have to do everything for yourself? Wait until you're so big that you can't. That's worse. **Michael Bloomberg**. *Bloomberg by Bloomberg* (cowritten with Matthew Winkler, 1997)

Think small and act small, and we'll get bigger. Think big and act big, and we'll get smaller. **Herb Kelleher**. *Sales and Marketing Management* (October 1996)

Growth does not always lead a business to build on success. All too often it converts a highly successful business into a mediocre large business. **Sir Richard Branson**. Speech to the Institute of Directors, London. "Growing Bigger While Still Staying Small" (May 1993)

You make the best products you can, and you grow as fast as you deserve to. **Kenneth H. Olsen**. Quoted in *Entrepreneurial Megabucks* (Aaron David Silver, 1985)

The strongest principle of growth lies in human choice. **George Eliot**. *Daniel Deronda* (1876)

Do you want to know my one-word secret of happiness? It's growth—mental, financial, you name it. **Harold S. Geneen**. Attributed

Hiring and Firing

When looking for a senior technical manager ... Amazon is believed to have asked candidates, "How would you fix the US economy?" ... The accounting firm Ernst & Young reportedly asked tax-analyst candidates, "Does life fascinate you?" ... and Citigroup supposedly asks prospects, "What is your strategy at table tennis?" ... Google used to ask job candidates to "design an evacuation plan for San Francisco" ... along with, "How many golf balls can fit in a school bus?" (Answer: about 500,000.) **Tim Walker**. *Independent (London)* (March 21, 2012)

The only three true job interview questions are: 1. Can you do the job? 2. Will you love the job? 3. Can we tolerate working with you? That's it. Those three ... every question, however it is phrased, is just a variation on one of these topics: Strengths, Motivation, and Fit. **George Bradt**. *Forbes* (April 27, 2011)

Always be smart enough to hire people brighter than yourself. **Caroline Marland**. *Management Today* (September 1999)

When I find an employee who turns out to be wrong for a job, I feel it is my fault because I made the decision to hire him. **Akio Morita**. Quoted in *In Search of European Excellence* (Robert Heller, 1997)

Employees throughout downsized companies do not have time to think about new growth opportunities. Nor are they inclined to suggest innovations because their implicit commitment contract with the company has been severed. **Kenneth Blanchard**. "Empowerment Is the Key," *Quality Digest* (April 1996)

You do not get good people if you lay off half your workforce just because one year the economy isn't very good and then you hire them back. **Kenneth Iverson**. Speech (February 5, 1996)

Restructuring: A simple plan instituted from above in which workers are right-sized, downsized, surplused, lateralized, or in the business jargon of the days of yore, fired. **Anonymous**. *Fortune* (February 15, 1995)

I believe you can go into any traditionally centralized corporation and cut its headquarters staff by 90% in one year. **Percy Barnevik**. *Harvard Business Review* (March–April 1991)

Nothing bad's going to happen to us. If we get fired, it's not failure; it's a midlife vocational assessment. **P. J. O'Rourke**. *Rolling Stone* (November 30, 1989)

You're fired! No other words can so easily and succinctly reduce a confident, self-assured executive to an insecure, groveling shred of his former self. **Frank P. Louchheim**. "The Art of Getting Fired," *Wall Street Journal* (July 16, 1984)

Well sometimes you just don't like somebody. **Henry Ford II**. Referring to his reasons for firing Lee Iacocca, then president of Ford, in 1978. Quoted in *Iacocca: An Autobiography* (Lee Iacocca, 1984)

In the end we are all sacked and it's always awful. It is as inevitable as death following life. If you are elevated there comes a day when you are demoted. **Alan Clark**. Diary (June 21, 1983)

If each of us hires people who are smaller than we are, we shall become a company of dwarfs. But if each of us hires people who are bigger than we are, we shall become a company of giants. **David Ogilvy**. *Ogilvy on Advertising* (1983)

Recession isn't the fault of the workers. If management takes the risk of hiring them, we have to take the responsibility for them. **Akio Morita**. *Daily Telegraph (London)* (February 24, 1982)

In a recession, people want to test me to see if I'm brave enough to have a lay-off. I'm willing to take that ridicule because it's paid off to hold on to our people. **Kenneth H. Olsen**. Speech (1982)

Trahey's Simple Rule: Would you hire you? **Jane Trahey**. *Women in Advertising* (1979)

People in the company are almost never fired ... they are encouraged to retire early or are eased aside into hollow, insignificant positions with fake functions and no authority, where they are sheepish and unhappy for as long as they remain. **Joseph Heller**. *Something Happened* (1974)

Fire the whole personnel department ... Fire the whole purchasing department. They'd hire Einstein and then turn down his requisition for a blackboard. **Robert Townsend**. *Up the Organization* (1970)

Honesty

If a brand screws up, honesty with the customer is the best way to recapture support. **Sir Michael Perry**. *Marketing* (March 2000)

Confronting reality—no matter how negative and depressing the process—is the first step toward coming to terms with it. **John Ralston Saul**. *The Unconscious Civilization* (1995)

Total commercial honesty always costs something, but total or partial dishonesty will cost more. **Robert Heller**. *The Supermarketers* (1987)

It is difficult but not impossible to conduct strictly honest business. What is true is that honesty is incompatible with the amassing of a large fortune. **Mahatma Gandhi**. *Non-Violence in Peace and War* (1948)

If you tell the truth you don't have to remember anything. **Mark Twain**. *Notebooks* (1935)

When in doubt tell the truth. **Mark Twain**. *Following the Equator* (1897)

It is always the best policy to speak the truth, unless of course you are an exceptionally good liar. **Jerome K. Jerome**. *The Idler* (February 1892)

Honour sinks where commerce long prevails. **Oliver Goldsmith**. *The Traveller* (1764)

It is not the crook in modern business that we fear, but the honest man who does not know what he is doing. **Owen D. Young**. Attributed

Ideas

Obvious almost always isn't. With the sheer number of different world views people have these days one person's obvious is another person's revelation. **Joshua Porter**. *Bokardo* blog (August 1, 2012)

To have a few good ideas, you need to have a hell of a lot of awful ideas. **Michael Acton Smith**. *Independent (London)* (April 19, 2012)

To be creative, what we're looking for is not one idea but dozens of ideas—some good, some average and some rubbish. We need to go through the wrong stuff to get to the right stuff. So no matter how wild and wacky an idea is, we need to learn to suspend judgement and get it to the table. **Michael Dunn**. Quoted in the *Independent (London)* (October 26, 2010)

The most reckless and treacherous of all theorists is he who professes to let facts and figures speak for themselves. **Alfred Marshall**. Quoted in the *Independent (London)* (November 20, 2009)

What matters is not ideas, but the people who have them. Good people can fix bad ideas, but good ideas can't save bad people.

Paul Graham. "How to Start a Startup," *paulgraham.com* (March 2005)

The newness of an idea matters less than its ease of use. **Mari Matsunaga**. *Fortune* (October 2000)

Unlike a straight academic career, you end up fully recognizing that hypotheses matter, that actions matter, and the ideas that you come up with matter. **Alan Greenspan**. Speech accepting appointment to fourth term as US Federal Reserve chairman, Washington, DC (January 4, 2000)

Sometimes the first step is the hardest: coming up with an idea. Coming up with an idea should be like sitting on a pin—it should make you jump up and do something. **Kemmons Wilson**. "What Makes for Success?" *Imprimis* (March 1997)

After the idea, there is plenty of time to learn the technology. **Sir James Dyson**. *Against the Odds* (1997)

Owning the intellectual property is like owning land: You need to keep investing in it again and again to get a payoff; you can't simply sit back and collect rent. **Esther Dyson**. *Release 1.0* (1994)

I can't understand why people are frightened of new ideas. I'm frightened of the old ones. **John Cage**. Quoted in *Conversing with Cage* (1988)

Don't worry about people stealing an idea. If it's original, you will have to ram it down their throats. **Howard Aiken**. Quoted in *Portraits in Silicon* (Robert Slater, 1987)

Unless your ideas are ridiculed by experts, they are worth nothing. **Reg Revans**. *Action Learning* (1979)

Never dump a good idea on a conference table. It will belong to the conference. **Jane Trahey**. *New York Times* (September 18, 1977)

We haven't got the money, so we've got to think. **Ernest, Lord Rutherford**. *Bulletin of the Institute of Physics* (1962)

It is a far, far better thing to have firm anchor in nonsense than to put out on the troubled sea of thought. **J. K. Galbraith**. *The Affluent Society* (1958)

Ours is the age of substitutes; instead of language, we have jargon; instead of principles, slogans; and, instead of genuine ideas, bright ideas. **Eric Bentley**. *New Republic (Washington, DC)* (December 1952)

There is nothing so practical as a good theory. **Kurt Lewin**. *Field Theory in Social Science: Selected Theoretical Papers* (D. Cartwright, ed, 1951)

The empires of the future are the empires of the mind. **Sir Winston Churchill**. Speech (September 1943)

Nothing is more dangerous than an idea, when you only have one idea. **Émile-August Chartier**. *Propos sur la Religion* (1938)

For an idea ever to be fashionable is ominous, since it must afterwards always be old-fashioned. **George Santayana**. *Winds of Doctrine* (1913)

If you are possessed by an idea, you find it expressed everywhere, you even smell it. **Thomas Mann**. *Death in Venice* (1913)

It is the customary fate of new truths to begin as heresies and to end as superstitions. **Thomas Huxley**. *Science and Culture* (1887)

One of the greatest pains to a human being is the pain of a new idea. **Walter Bagehot**. *Physics and Politics* (1872)

Every now and then a man's mind is stretched by a new idea and never shrinks back to its original dimensions. **Oliver Wendell Holmes**. *The Autocrat of the Breakfast Table* (1858)

The ancestor of every action is a thought. **Ralph Waldo Emerson**. *Essays* (1841)

It is as absurd to argue men, as to torture them into believing. **John Henry Newman**. Sermon (December 1831)

When an idea is not robust enough to stand expression in simple terms, it is a sign that it should be rejected. **Luc de Clapiers Vauvenargues**. *Reflections and Maxims* (1746)

It's not that we need new ideas, but we need to stop having old ideas. **Edwin Land**. Attributed

Image

According to research in America, the hairless male head now represents potency and decisiveness. Something called "the power buzz" is all the rage among shaven-headed business leaders, says the *Wall Street Journal*. One CEO said it made him appear more dynamic, another that it deflected questions about his age. A third revealed that shaving off his hair was "a highly leveraged marketing choice." **Terence Blacker**. *Independent* (London) (October 7, 2012)

Corporate identities must not be shortlived. **Clive Chajet**. "Why Corporate Identity Can't Be Designed," *The Manager* (David Uren, 2000)

We don't know how to sell products based on performance. Everything we sell, we sell based on image. **Roberto Goizueta**. *Wall Street Journal* (February 1997)

Beyond a certain point, personal media such as telephones, computers, and planners aren't just functional objects anymore, they're fashion accessories. **Michael Schrage**. Quoted in *Liberation Management* (Tom Peters, 1992)

Deep down, I'm pretty superficial. **Ava Gardner**. Quoted in *Ava* (Roland Flamini, 1983), ch. 8

Clothes are our weapons, our challenges, and our visible insult. **Angela Carter**. *Nothing Sacred* (1982)

It depends entirely upon the image of you that people have in their minds whether you will climb the ladder slowly, painfully, or with a rapidity that will surprise—and appal—your friends. **Gerald Sparrow**. *How to Become a Millionaire* (1960), ch. 2

Keep up appearances; there lies the test. The world will give thee credit for the rest. **Charles Churchill**. *Night* (1761)

To be successful, keep looking tanned, live in an elegant building (even if you're in the cellar), be seen in smart restaurants (even if you only nurse one drink) and if you borrow, borrow big. **Aristotle Onassis**. Attributed

Imagination

The imagination of nature is far, far greater than the imagination of man. **Richard P. Feynman**. *The Meaning of it All* (1998)

We are what and where we are because we have first imagined it. **Donald Curtis**. Quoted in *Awaken the Giant Within* (Anthony Robbins, 1992)

My imagination makes me human and makes me a fool; it gives me all the world and exiles me from it. **Ursula K. Le Guin**. "Winged the Adventures on My Mind," *Harper's* (August 1990)

Live out of your imagination, not your history. **Sir Arthur Bryan**. *Seven Habits of Highly-Effective People* (1990)

Skill without imagination is craftsmanship and gives us many useful objects such as wickerwork picnic baskets. Imagination

without skill gives us modern art. **Sir Tom Stoppard**. *Artist Descending a Staircase* (1988)

Imagination was given to man to compensate him for what he is not. A sense of humour was provided to console him for what he is. **Horace Walpole (Earl of Orford)**. Quoted in "The Artist," *A Kick in the Seat of the Pants* (Roger von Oech, 1986)

I dream for a living. **Steven Spielberg**. *Time* (July 1985)

The life of nations no less than that of men is lived largely in the imagination. **Enoch Powell**. Epigraph. Quoted in *English Culture and the Decline of the Industrial Spirit, 1850–1980* (Martin J. Weiner, 1981)

For people who live in the imagination, there is no lack of subjects. To seek for the exact moment at which inspiration comes is false. Imagination floods us with suggestions all the time, from all directions. **Federico Fellini**. *Autobiography* (1974)

Imagination and fiction make up more than three quarters of our real life. **Simone Weil**. *Gravity and Grace* (1952)

His imagination resembled the wings of an ostrich. It enabled him to run, though not to soar. **Thomas Babington, Lord Macaulay**. Referring to John Dryden. "John Dryden," *Essays and Biographies* (1828)

If a man carefully examine his thoughts he will be surprised to find out how much he lives in the future. **Ralph Waldo Emerson**. Attributed

Independence

Quit waiting to get picked; quit waiting for someone to give you permission; quit waiting for someone to say you are officially qualified—and pick yourself. It doesn't mean you have to be an entrepreneur or a freelancer, but it does mean you stand up and say, "I have something to say. I know how to do something. I'm doing it. If you want me to do it with you, raise your hand." **Seth Godin**. Interviewed on *The Great Discontent* blog (August 14, 2012)

Your time is limited, so don't waste it living someone else's life. Don't be trapped by dogma ... Don't let the noise of others' opinions drown out your own inner voice. And most important, have the courage to follow your heart and intuition. They somehow already know what you truly want to become. **Steve Jobs**. Commencement address, Stanford University, California (June 12, 2005)

A man who trims himself to suit everybody will soon whittle himself away. **Charles M. Schwab**. Quoted in *The Game of Life* (Lou Harry, 2004)

You can't win without being completely different. When everyone else says we are crazy, I say, gee we really must be on to something. **Larry D. Ellison**. *Forbes* (October 2000)

It's better to be a pirate than join the Navy. **Steve Jobs**. Quoted in *West of Eden* (Frank Rose, 1989)

Some people have so much respect for their superiors they have none left for themselves. **Peter McArthur**. *The Best of Peter McArthur* (1967)

No one can possibly achieve any real and lasting success or get rich in business by being a conformist. **J. Paul Getty**. *International Herald Tribune (Paris)* (1961)

I want to prevent as many men as possible from pretending that they have to do this or that because they must earn a living. *It is not true*. **Henry Miller**. The book was based on Miller's five years' experience working for Western Union; he walked out of the job in 1925 declaring, "My own master now.". *Tropic of Capricorn* (1939)

God makes the animals, man makes himself. **Georg C. Lichtenberg**. Notebook entry

Once you decide to work for yourself, you never go back to work for somebody else. **Sir Alan, Lord Sugar**. *The Apprentice (UK)*, BBC TV

Never sing in chorus, if you want to be heard. **Jules Archibald**. Attributed

Industrial Relations

The strike is the weapon of the oppressed, of men capable of appreciating justice and having the courage to resist wrong and contend for principle. **Eugene V. Debs**. Speaking during the strike of engineers and firefighters on the Chicago, Burlington, and Quincy Rail Line. Quoted in *The Arizona Republic* (2000)

Why do people focus ... on cash rewards? ... We seldom create opportunities to congratulate each other. It's hard to imagine union leaders storming into a meeting, smashing their fists on the desk and demanding, "We want more congratulations!" **Kenneth Blanchard**. "The Gift of the Goose," *Quality Digest* (December 1997)

I am just a hoary old bastard who wants to win. **Sir Ian McGregor**. *Observer (London)* (March 11, 1984)

The two sides of industry have traditionally always regarded each other in Britain with the greatest possible loathing, mistrust and contempt. They are both absolutely right. **Auberon Waugh**. *Private Eye* (December 16, 1983)

The fertility of happy invention denied its full fruit by the grimy rules of union demarcation. **Sir Harold Evans**. Referring to union opposition to new technology in the newspaper industry. *Good Times, Bad Times* (1983)

When you're negotiating for a 35 hour week, remember they have only just got 66 hours in Taiwan, and you're competing with Taiwan. **Victor Kiam**. *Daily Express (London)* (June 12, 1981)

All classes of society are trades unionists at heart, and differ chiefly in the boldness, ability, and secrecy with which they pursue their respective interests. **William Stanley Jevons**. *The State in Relation to Labour* (1882)

Industry

I have never yet come across an engineer who can turn his hands to business. **Sir Alan, Lord Sugar**. *The Apprentice (UK)*, BBC TV (June 15, 2011)

If you understand how to make something, you understand everything about it. You appreciate its beauty, its logic and its meaning. And its value. And you can pass on these pleasures and benefits. Never mind an aeroplane, designing and making, say, a stacking chair is at the outer levels of human intellectual capability. Abstract reasoning, spatial awareness, advanced motor skills, a keen aesthetic sense are all required. In comparison the attainments of a commercial lawyer or a fund manager seem crude and debased. **Stephen Bailey**. *Independent (London)* (May 4, 2011)

I was delighted to learn that in Britain today more people are employed in Indian restaurants than in your coal, steel and shipbuilding industries combined. **Shashi Tharoor**. Quoted in the *Independent (London)* (January 18, 2010)

  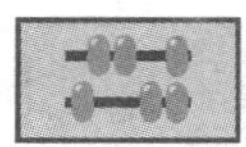      

Our bailout of Detroit will be remembered as the equivalent of pouring billions of taxpayers' money into the mail-order catalogue business on the eve of the birth of eBay. **Thomas Friedman**. *New York Times* (December 10, 2008)

While we're still the US sales leader, we acknowledge we have disappointed you. **General Motors**. On its financial troubles. Full-page ad in *Automotive News* (December 2008)

The task of industry is continuously, year on year, to make more and better things, using less of the world's resources. **Sir John Harvey-Jones**. *Making It Happen* (1988)

It takes five years to develop a new car in this country. Heck, we won World War II in four years. **H. Ross Perot**. Quoted in *Thriving on Chaos* (Tom Peters, 1987)

The difficulty is that we have an industrial base with so many characteristics of an industrial museum or of an industrial hospital. **Barry Owen Jones**. Quoted in "Sayings of the Week," *Sydney Morning Herald* (July 12, 1986)

What will Britain's service industry be servicing when there is no hardware, when no wealth is actually being produced. We will be servicing presumably the product of wealth by others. **Arnold, Lord Weinstock**. *International Management* (December 1985)

The most striking thing about modern industry is that it requires so much and accomplishes so little. **Ernst Friedrich Schumacher**. *Small Is Beautiful* (1973)

Modern industry seems to be inefficient to a degree that surpasses one's enduring powers of imagination. Its inefficiency therefore remains unnoticed. **Ernst Friedrich Schumacher**. *Small Is Beautiful* (1973)

Properly, urban-industrialization must be regarded an experiment. And if the scientific spirit has taught us anything of value, it is that honest experiments may well fail. **Theodore Roszak**. *Where the Wasteland Ends* (1972), Introduction

It is an axiom, enforced by all the experience of the ages, that they who rule industrially will rule politically. **Aneurin Bevan**. Quoted in *Aneurin Bevan* (Michael Foot, 1962), vol. 1

It takes more than industry to industrialize. **W. W. Rostow**. *The Stages of Economic Growth* (1960), ch. 3

For years I thought what was good for our country was good for General Motors and vice versa. The difference did not exist. Our company is too big. It goes with the welfare of the country. **Charles E. Wilson**. Quoted in "Statement to US Senate committee," *New York Times* (February 24, 1953)

We have created an industrial order geared to automation, where feeble-mindedness, native or acquired, is necessary for docile productivity in the factory; and where a pervasive neurosis is the final gift of the meaningless life which issues forth at the other end. **Lewis Mumford**. *The Conduct of Life* (1951)

The spark-gap is mightier than the pen. This is not the age of the pamphleteers, it is the age of the engineers. **Lancelot Hogben**. *Science for the Citizen* (1938)

Power and machinery, money and goods are useful only as they set us free to live. **Henry Ford**. *My Life and Work* (cowritten with Samuel Crowther, 1922)

Industry is the root of all ugliness. **Oscar Wilde**. *Phrases and Philosophies for the Use of the Young* (1894)

The successful conduct of an industrial enterprise requires two quite distinct qualifications: fidelity and zeal. **John Stuart Mill**. *Principles of Political Economy* (1848)

Man is a tool-using animal ... Without tools he is nothing, with tools he is all. **Thomas Carlyle**. *Sartor Resartus* (1834)

Since the introduction of inanimate mechanism into British manufactories, man, with few exceptions, has been treated as a secondary and inferior machine; and far more attention has been given to perfect the raw materials of wood and metals than those of body and mind. **Robert Owen**. *A New View of Society* (1813)

Information

I actually think most people don't want Google to answer their questions. They want Google to tell them what they should be doing next. **Eric Schmidt**. Speaking to journalists (August 13, 2011)

Information is the new atom or electron, the fundamental building block of the universe ... We now see the world as entirely made of information: it's bits all the way down. **Bryan Appleyard**. *Sunday Times (London)* (April 3, 2011)

I don't believe society understands what happens when everything is available, knowable and recorded by everyone all the time. **Eric Schmidt**. On the impact of the Internet and information technology. Interview, *Wall Street Journal* (August 14, 2010)

History shows a typical progression of information technologies: from somebody's hobby to somebody's industry; from jury-rigged contraption to slick production marvel; from a freely accessible channel to one strictly controlled by a single corporation or cartel—from open to closed system. **Tim Wu**. *The Master Switch: The Rise and Fall of Information Empires* (2010)

There's no such thing as information overload—only filter failure. **Clay Shirky**. Speech, Web 2.0 Expo NY (September 2008)

We can say with certainty—or 90% probability—that the new industries that are about to be born will have nothing to do with information. **Peter F. Drucker**. Quoted in *Great Writers on Organizations* (Derek S. Pugh and David J. Hickson, 2007)

The ultimate search engine would basically understand everything in the world, and it would always give you the right thing. And we're a long, long way from that. **Larry Page**. Interview, *Business Week* (May 3, 2004)

We don't believe it's possible to protect digital content. What's new is this amazingly efficient distribution system for stolen property called the Internet—and no one's gonna shut down the Internet. And it only takes one stolen copy to be on the Internet ... You'll never stop that. So what you have to do is compete with it. **Steve Jobs**. "Steve Jobs: The Rolling Stone Interview," *Rolling Stone* (December 2003)

A Harvard professor told me that if there was no Gallup poll there'd be no Bill Clinton. **Jim Clifton**. *Financial Times (London)* (October 2000)

Facts are available to everyone; it is interpretation and implementation that is key. **Ric Simcock**. *Marketing* (September 2000)

Nothing in business (or life) is more expensive than bad information. **Gary Halbert**. Quoted in *2,239 Tested Secrets For Direct Marketing Success* (Denny Hatch and Don Jackson, 1999)

Information is costly to produce, but cheap to reproduce. **Carl Shapiro**. *Information Rules* (cowritten with Hal L Varian, 1999)

The new economy favors intangible things—ideas, information, and relationships.

Kevin Kelly. *New Rules for the New Economy: 10 Radical Strategies for a Connected World* (1998)

If you file your waste basket for 50 years, you have a public library. **Tony Benn**. *Daily Telegraph (London)* (March 1994)

While hard data may inform the intellect, it is largely soft data that generates wisdom. **Henry Mintzberg**. *The Rise and Fall of Strategic Planning* (1994)

Data without generalization is just gossip. **Robert M. Pirsig**. *Lila* (1992)

I find more and more executives less and less well informed about the outside world, if only because they believe that the data on the computer printouts are ipso facto information. **Peter F. Drucker**. Quoted in "Seeing Things As They Really Are," *Forbes* (Robert Lenzner and Stephen S. Johnson, 1987)

An individual without information cannot take responsibility; an individual who is given information cannot help but take responsibility. **Wilbert Lee Gore**. Quoted in *Thriving on Chaos* (Tom Peters, 1987)

Information is a business in itself. It is also something that has made control impossible ... you cannot get customers to accept prices in one place when they know there's a better deal elsewhere. It's a whole new world. **Walter Wriston**. Quoted in *The Financial Revolution: The Big Bang Worldwide* (Adrian Hamilton, 1986), ch. 2

You can use the fanciest computers in the world and you can gather all the charts and numbers, but in the end you have to have to bring all your information together, set a timetable, and act. **Lee Iacocca**. *Iacocca: An Autobiography* (1984)

The highest art of professional management requires the literal ability to smell a real fact from all others. **Harold S. Geneen**. *Managing* (cowritten with Alvin Moscow, 1984)

The more the data banks record about each one of us, the less we exist. **Marshall McLuhan**. Interview, *Playboy* (March 1969)

Where is all the knowledge we lost with information? **T. S. Eliot**. *The Rock* (1934)

Innovation

Innovation is important, exciting, and necessary. But so is Refinement. We need to celebrate refinement more than we have. However, we shouldn't be asking ourselves which is more important. Innovation and refinement are not goals. They are methods and strategies. The question we should be asking: Is this Better? That's the only question that matters. **Don Lehman**. *The More Real Blog* (July 9, 2012)

The average individual innovator is having a smaller and smaller impact ... I've noticed that Nobel prizewinners are getting older. That's a sure sign it's taking longer to innovate. **Ben Jones**. Quoted in the *New Statesman* (October 27, 2011)

The average individual innovator is having a smaller and smaller impact ... I've noticed that Nobel prizewinners are getting older. That's a sure sign it's taking longer to innovate. **Ben Jones**. Quoted in *New Statesman* (October 27, 2011)

Out there, somewhere, maybe in India, maybe in China, there's a person in a garage, doing something neither you nor I can even imagine, but which they just know is insanely great. And it'll change everything. **Michael Bywater**. *Independent (London)* (October 7, 2011)

Our understanding of historical progress tends to be "innovation-centric" rather than "use-centred." We obsess about exciting new inventions and underestimate how much they will have to struggle against the forces of habit and inertia in our daily lives. Old-fashioned but serviceable technologies often prove surprisingly resilient ... The lessons from history are that technological progress is uneven, that consumers are often sceptical of techno-hype, and that new technologies do not supplant old ones in linear fashion. Look at the iPad's ebook reader: your book purchase is stored on a real-looking wooden bookcase and you take it off the shelf and flip its virtual pages over with your fingers. Why, it's exactly like ... reading a book! **Joe Moran**. *Guardian (London)* (October 2010)

Invaluable though innovation may be, our relentless focus on it may be obscuring the value of its much-maligned relative, imitation. Imitation has always had a faintly disreputable ring to it—presidents do not normally give speeches extolling the virtues of the copycat. But where innovation brings new things into the world, imitation spreads them; where innovators break the old mold, imitators perfect the new one; and while innovators can win big, imitators often win bigger. **Drake Bennett**. *Boston Globe* (April 18, 2010)

Innovation will always be a mixture of serendipity, genius, and sheer bull-mindedness. But while you can't bottle lightning, you can build lightning rods. Non-linear innovation can be legitimized, fostered, supported, and rewarded. **Gary Hamel**. Interview, *Barnes & Noble* (September 2000)

To invent, you need a good imagination and a pile of junk. **Thomas Edison**. Quoted in "Building an Innovation Factory," *Harvard Business Review* (Andrew Hargadon and Robert I. Sutton, 2000)

Sometimes I think we'll see the day when you introduce a product in the morning and announce the end of its life at the end of the day. **Al Shugart**. Quoted in *Goldfinger* (Robert Heller, 1998)

One possibility for difficulties innovating is that most people really don't care about innovation. **Peter Senge**. "The Practice of Innovation," *Leader to Leader* (1998)

Slack allows innovative projects to be pursued because it buffers organizations from the uncertain success of these projects, fostering a culture of experimentation. **Nitin Nohria**. *The Differentiated Network* (cowritten with Sumantra Ghoshal, 1997)

The most successful innovators are the creative imitators, the number two. **Peter F. Drucker**. Interview, *Hot Wired* (August 1996)

Everything that can be invented has been invented. **Charles H. Duell**. Quoted in *Maxi Marketing* (Stan Rapp and Thomas L. Collins, 1995)

Innovation is not just technical; it is also organizational and managerial. **Stewart Clegg**. "Business Values and Embryonic Industry: Lessons from Australia," *Whose Business Values? Some Asian and Cross-Cultural Perspectives* (Sally Stewart and Gabriel Donleavy, eds, 1995)

People are unlikely to know that they need a product which does not exist and the basis of market research in new and innovative products is limited in this regard. **Sir John Harvey-Jones**. *All Together Now* (1994)

Above all, innovation is not invention. It is a term of economics rather than of technology. **Peter F. Drucker**. Speech (April 1992)

A common mistake that people make when trying to design something completely foolproof is to underestimate the ingenuity of complete fools. **Hugh Davidson**. *Mostly Harmless* (1992)

In a small company, one person's hunch can be enough to launch a new product. In a big

 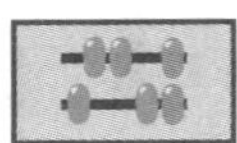      

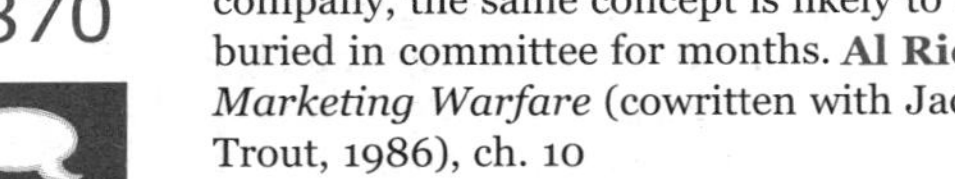

company, the same concept is likely to be buried in committee for months. **Al Ries**. *Marketing Warfare* (cowritten with Jack Trout, 1986), ch. 10

The public does not know what is possible, we do. **Akio Morita**. *Made in Japan* (1986)

By observing California's youngsters on roller skates, a Sony engineer came up with the concept of the Walkman. **Kenichi Ohmae**. *Industry Week* (July 1985)

Not a single, substantial, commercially-successful project had come from an adequately-funded team. They'd always come from the scrounging, scrapping, underfunded teams. **Kenneth H. Olsen**. Quoted in *A Passion for Excellence* (Tom Peters and Nancy Austin, 1985)

There is no shortage of creative people in American business. The shortage is of innovators. All too often people believe that creativity leads to innovation. It doesn't. **Theodore Levitt**. "Ideas Are Useless Unless Used," *Inc.* (February 1981)

The great discoveries are usually obvious. **Philip B. Crosby**. *Quality Is Free* (1979)

I don't think necessity is the mother of invention—invention, in my opinion arises directly from idleness, possibly also from laziness. To save oneself trouble. **Dame Agatha Christie**. *An Autobiography* (1977)

The artist brings something into the world that didn't exist before, and ... he does it without destroying something else. **John Updike**. Quoted in *Writers at Work* (George Plimpton, ed, 1977)

Everyone likes innovation until it affects himself, and then it's bad. **Walter Wriston**. Quoted in "Sayings of the Year," *Observer (London)* (December 29, 1974)

Innovation! One cannot be forever innovating. I want to create classics. **Coco Chanel**. Quoted in *Coco Chanel: Her Life, Her Secrets* (1971)

Discovery consists of seeing what everybody has seen and thinking what nobody has thought. **Albert Szent-Györgyi**. Quoted in *The Scientist Speculates* (I. J. Good, ed, 1962)

It is easy to overlook the absence of appreciable advance in an industry. Inventions that are not made, like babies that are not born, are rarely missed. **J. K. Galbraith**. *The Affluent Society* (1958), ch. 9

If you can measure it, it's not innovation. **Chad Stoller**. Attributed

Intelligence

But many intelligent people have a sort of bug: they think intelligence is an end in itself. They have one idea in mind: to be intelligent, which is really stupid. And when intelligence takes itself for its own goal, it operates very strangely. **Muriel Barbery**. *The Elegance of the Hedgehog* (2008)

A dozen more questions occurred to me. Not to mention twenty-two possible solutions to each one, sixteen resulting hypotheses and counter-theorems, eight abstract speculations, a quadrilateral equation, two axioms, and a limerick. That's raw intelligence for you. **Jonathan Stroud**. *Ptolemy's Gate* (2005)

I'm educated enough to talk myself out of any plan. To deconstruct any fantasy. Explain away any goal. I'm so smart I can negate any dream. **Chuck Palahniuk**. *Choke* (2001)

Even in a hierarchy people can be equal as thinkers. **Nancy Kline**. *Time to Think* (1999)

You put too much stock in human intelligence, it doesn't annihilate human nature. **Philip Roth**. *American Pastoral* (1997)

Intellectual capital is the sum of everything everybody in a company knows that gives it a competitive edge. **Thomas A. Stewart**. *Intellectual Capital* (1997)

Brains are becoming the core of organisations—other activities can be contracted out. **Charles Handy**. Interview (February 1994)

Intelligence ... is really a kind of taste: taste in ideas. **Susan Sontag**. "Notes on Camp," *Against Interpretation* (1966)

Anti-intellectualism has long been the anti-Semitism of the businessman. **Arthur Schlesinger, Jr**. *Partisan Review* (1953)

As a human being, one has been endowed with just enough intelligence to be able to see clearly how utterly inadequate that intelligence is when confronted with what exists. **Albert Einstein**. Letter (September 1932)

The brain is a wonderful organ. It starts working the moment you get up in the morning, and does not stop until you get into the office. **Robert Frost**. Attributed

Investment

As a general rule in financial matters, things take longer to happen than you would expect but when they do start to move they happen more quickly. **Hamish McRae**. *Independent (London)* (April 27, 2011)

If investing is entertaining, if you're having fun, you're probably not making any money. Good investing is boring. **George Soros**. Quoted in *The Winning Investment Habits of Warren Buffett & George Soros* (Mark Tier, 2006)

Successful investing is anticipating the anticipations of others. **John Maynard Keynes**. Quoted in *Isms* (Gregory Bergman, 2006)

More money is probably lost by people who attempt to invest their money conservatively and sanely, but ignorantly, than is lost by those who enter into frank speculations. **John Moody**. Quoted in *The Book of Investing Wisdom* (Peter Krass, 1999)

Go for a business that any idiot can run—because sooner or later, any idiot probably is going to run it. **Peter Lynch**. Quoted in *The Book of Investing Wisdom* (Peter Krass, 1999)

Make your company stock a consumer product. When consumers buy stock in your company, they'll never buy a competitive product. You've linked their financial future to yours. **Faith Popcorn**. "Q&A with Faith Popcorn," *www.brainreserve.com* (1999)

The historical data support one conclusion with unusual force: To invest with success, you must be a long-term investor. **John Clifton Bogle**. *Common Sense on Mutual Funds: New Imperatives for the Intelligent Investor* (1999), ch. 1

Bond investors are the vampires of the investment world. They love decay, recession—anything that leads to low inflation and the protection of the real value of their loans. **Bill Gross**. *Bill Gross on Investing* (1998)

I don't invest in anything I don't understand—it makes more sense to buy TV stations than oil wells. **Oprah Winfrey**. Quoted in *Oprah Winfrey Speaks* (Janet Lowe, 1998)

If you aren't willing to own a stock for ten years, don't even think about owning it for ten minutes. **Warren Buffett**. Chairman's Letter to Shareholders (February 28, 1997)

Rule no. 1: Never lose money. Rule no. 2: Never forget rule no. 1. **Warren Buffett**. Quoted in *Warren Buffett Speaks* (Janet Lowe, 1997)

The true investor *welcomes* volatility ... a wildly fluctuating market means that irrationally low prices will periodically be attached to solid businesses. **Warren Buffett**. Chairman's Letter to Shareholders (March 7, 1995)

Speculation is an effort, probably unsuccessful, to turn a little money into a lot. Investment is an effort, which should be successful, to prevent a lot of money from becoming a little. **Fred Schwed**. *Where Are the Customers' Yachts?* (1995)

Four hundred seventy-three million to one. Those are the odds against George Soros compiling the investment record he did as manager of the Quantum Fund from 1968 through 1993. **Paul Tudor Jones**. *The Alchemy of Finance: Reading the Mind of the Market* (1994)

I don't pay attention to what the stock does. If the business does well, the stock eventually follows. **Warren Buffett**. *BusinessWeek* (1994)

Those who invest only to get rich will fail. Those who invest to help others will probably succeed. **Art Fry**. Interview, *The Empty Raincoat: Making Sense of the Future* (Charles Handy, 1994)

Investing is not nearly as difficult as it looks. Successful investing involves doing a few things right and avoiding serious mistakes. **John Clifton Bogle**. *Bogle on Mutual Funds* (1993)

Never invest in any ideas you can't illustrate with a crayon. **Peter Lynch**. *Beating the Street* (1993)

Lethargy bordering on sloth remains the cornerstone of our investment style. **Warren Buffett**. *Newsweek* (May 1991)

I got positive feelings when I saw that Taco Bell's headquarters was stuck behind a bowling alley. When I saw those executives operating out of that grim little bunker, I was thrilled. Obviously they weren't wasting money on landscaping the office. **Peter Lynch**. On his decision to invest in Taco Bell restaurants. *One Up On Wall Street* (1990)

Investing in stocks is an art, not a science, and people who've been trained to rigidly quantify everything have a big disadvantage. **Peter Lynch**. *One Up On Wall Street* (1990)

You have to be intellectually honest with yourself and others. In my judgment, all great investors are seekers of truth. **Michael Steinhardt**. Quoted in *Market Wizards* (John D. Schwager, 1989)

Sometimes your best investments are the ones you don't make. **Donald J. Trump**. Quoted in *Trump: The Art of the Deal* (cowritten with Tony Schwartz, 1987)

The only reason to invest in the market is because you think you know something others don't. **R. Foster Winans**. *Newsweek* (December 1, 1986)

My advice to this investor is the same that I give to the young investors in my classes ... Devote the same earnest attention to investing that $50,000 as you devoted to earning it. **Ivan Boesky**. Quoted in the *Wall Street Journal* (January 2, 1985)

Never invest your money in anything that eats or needs repainting. **Billy Rose**. *New York Post* (October 26, 1957)

To achieve satisfactory investment results is easier than most people realize; to achieve superior results is harder than it looks. **Benjamin Graham**. *The Intelligent Investor* (1949)

As time goes on, I get more and more convinced that the right method in investment is to put fairly large sums into enterprises which one thinks one knows something about and in the management of which one thoroughly believes. It is a mistake to think that one limits one's risk by spreading too much between enterprises about which one knows little and has no reason for special confidence. **John Maynard Keynes**. Letter to F. C. Scott (August 15, 1934)

Whales only get harpooned when they come to the surface, and turtles can only move forward when they stick their neck out, but investors face risk no matter what they do. **Charles A. Jaffe**. Attributed

Investing is simple, but not easy. **Warren Buffett**. Attributed

Jobs

More and more people in this country no longer make or do anything tangible; if your job wasn't performed by a cat or a boa constrictor in a Richard Scarry book I'm not sure I believe it's necessary. **Tim Kreider**. *New York Times* (June 30, 2012)

My father advised me to get a job that didn't involve running into burning buildings. **Michael R. Lynch**. Quoted in *The Times (London)* (July 8, 2008)

Ninety percent of our jobs are in jeopardy, and corporations are in the middle of unprecedented change. If we simply do the job our bosses want us to do, we may soon find ourselves without any marketable skills. **Tom Peters**. "The Ominous Prediction of Tom Peters," *Small Manufacturing SIG Newsletter* (Ira Smolowitz, 2000)

In the past, business was the employer of all those who wanted to work. In the future, there will be lots of customers, but not lots of jobs. **Charles Handy**. *The Empty Raincoat: Making Sense of the Future* (1994)

It is just a job. Grass grows, birds fly, waves pound the sand. I beat people up. **Muhammad Ali**. Quoted in the *New York Times* (April 6, 1977)

You ask me what I do. Well, actually, you know, I'm partly a liaison man and partly PRO Essentially I integrate the export drive And basically I'm viable from ten o'clock till five. **Sir John Betjeman**. "The Executive," *A Nip in the Air* (1974)

Oh brave new world, said Robyn, where only the managing directors have jobs. **David Lodge**. *Nice Work* (1968)

I don't think anybody yet has invented a pastime that's as much fun, or keeps you as young, as a good job. **Frederick Hudson Ecker**. Quoted in obituary, *New York Times* (March 20, 1964)

You don't need to interpret tea leaves stuck in a cup To understand that people who work sitting down get paid more than those people who work standing up. **Ogden Nash**. "Will Consider Situation," *The Face Is Familiar* (1940)

If you have a job without any aggravations, you don't have a job. **Malcolm S. Forbes**. Attributed

Judgment

We made a professional judgement about the appropriate accounting treatment that turned out to be wrong. **Joseph Berardino**. Referring to Enron's accounting practices. Submission to a hearing on Enron (December 12, 2002)

A man with a surplus can control circumstances, but a man without a surplus is controlled by them, and often has no opportunity to exercise judgment.

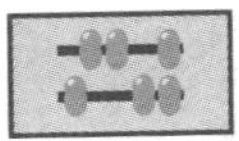

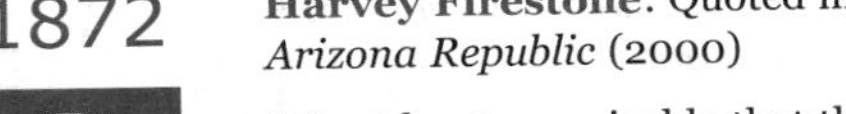

Harvey Firestone. Quoted in *The Arizona Republic* (2000)

It is at least conceivable that the 21st century business environment will be so fluid that it defies analysis, forcing executives to fall back upon hunch, or instinct. **John Elkington**. *Cannibals with Forks* (1997)

Discrimination is the capacity to discern what is important. **Warren Blank**. *The 9 Natural Laws of Leadership* (1995)

It takes little talent to see clearly what lies under one's nose, a good deal of it to know in what direction to point that organ. **W. H. Auden**. *The Dyers Hand* (1963)

Power in a corporation becomes residual and dwells in the background. It is the ability to exercise nice matters of judgment. **Viscount Chandos (Oliver Lyttelton)**. *Memoirs of Lord Chandos: An Unexpected View from the Summit* (1963)

I leave this rule for others when I'm dead. Be always sure you're right—then go ahead. **Davy Crockett**. His motto in the War of 1812. *Autobiography* (1834)

Your representative owes you, not his industry only, but his judgement; and he betrays instead of serving you if he sacrifices it to your opinion. **Edmund Burke**. Speech in Bristol, United Kingdom (November 3, 1774)

Knowledge

The best way to sound like you know what you're talking about is to know what you're talking about. **John Hockenberry**. Quoted in *The Science of Settlement: Ideas for Negotiators* (Barry Goldman, 2008)

There is no substitute for accurate knowledge. Know yourself, know your business, know your men. **Randall Jacobs**. Quoted in *How to Get from Cubicle to Corner Office* (Joel Weiss, 2005)

Now what is the message there? The message is that there are known knowns. There are things we know that we know. There are known unknowns. That is to say there are things that we now know we don't know. But there are also unknown unknowns. There are things we don't know we don't know. So when we do the best we can and we pull all this information together, and we then say well that's basically what we see as the situation, that is really only the known knowns and the known unknowns. And each year, we discover a few more of those unknown unknowns. **Donald Rumsfeld**. Press conference at NATO Headquarters, Brussels, Belgium (June 6, 2002)

Knowledge resides in the heads of people. Shareholders cannot own it since owning people is not considered moral. It is also not practical. Acquisitions of intellectual capital firms therefore often fail. **Charles Handy**. Speech at the Second Workshop on Inventing the Organization of the 21st Century, Munich, Germany. "The Age of Paradox" (April 1996)

Knowledge is the only meaningful resource today. **Peter F. Drucker**. *Post-capitalist Society* (1993)

The person who knows how will always have a job. The person who knows why will always be his boss. **Diane Ravitch**. *Time* (June 17, 1985)

What our competitive and careerist knowledge industry has produced already hopelessly exceeds our ability to make graceful use of it. **Theodore Roszak**. *Where the Wasteland Ends* (1972)

Knowledge is proportionate to being. You know in virtue of what you are. **Aldous Huxley**. *Time Must Have a Stop* (1944)

An expert is one who knows more and more about less and less. **Nicholas Murray Butler**. *Speed* (1901)

The secret of business is to know something that nobody else knows. **Aristotle Onassis**. Attributed

Law and Lawyers

In any business model you need someone to sue. That's the American way. **Bill Weinberg**. Quoted in "UpFRONT," *Linux Journal* (November 2000)

When the meek inherit the Earth, lawyers will be there to work out the deal. **Sam Ewing**. Quoted in the *Wall Street Journal* (May 22, 1997)

Lawyers are like rhinoceroses: thick-skinned, short-sighted, and always ready to charge. **David Mellor**. *Question Time*, BBC TV (December 3, 1992)

Trying to control corporate power and abuse by American corporate law has proven about as effective as drinking coffee with a fork. **Ralph Nader**. Quoted in *The Times (London)* (October 23, 1976)

Nothing is illegal if 100 businessmen decide to do it. **Andrew Jackson Young, Jr.** Press conference (1976)

No brilliance is needed in the law. Nothing but common sense, and relatively clean finger nails. **Sir John Mortimer**. *A Voyage Round My Father* (1970)

You might as well try to employ a boa constrictor as a tape-measure as to go to a lawyer for legal advice. **Oliver St. John Gogarty**. *Tumbling in the Hay* (1939)

There is no better way of exercising the imagination than the study of law. No poet ever interpreted nature as freely as a lawyer interprets truth. **Jean Giraudoux**. *Tiger at the Gates* (1935)

As in law so in war, the longest purse finally wins. **Mahatma Gandhi**. Lecture to the Bombay Provincial Conference (September 17, 1917)

A community that endures a contemptible law is itself contemptible. **Alfred G. Stephens**. *Bookfellow* (March 1, 1912)

LAWYER, n. One skilled in circumvention of the law. **Ambrose Bierce**. *The Devil's Dictionary* (1911)

Laws are like spider's webs: if some poor weak creature come up against them, it is caught; but a bigger one can break through and get away. **Solon**. Quoted in "Solon," *Parallel Lives* (Plutarch, 1st century AD)

Lawyers are the only persons in whom ignorance of the law is not punished. **Jeremy Bentham**. Attributed

Leadership

Leadership used to be about ideas, setting an example and doing the right thing. Today, if you make enough money for the firm (and are not currently an ax murderer) you will be promoted into a position of influence. **Greg Smith**. Resigning from executive director position at Goldman Sachs. *New York Times* (March 14, 2012)

Leadership comes through respect, and a large part of respect is liking someone. **Carol Leonard**. *The Times (London)* (September 26, 2005)

Charisma becomes the undoing of leaders. It makes them inflexible, convinced of their own infallibility, unable to change. **Peter F. Drucker**. *The Essential Drucker* (2003)

The function of leadership is to produce more leaders, not more followers. **Ralph Nader**. *Crashing the Party* (2002)

Challenge the mind and capture the heart. **Carly Fiorina**. *Forbes* (October 2000)

A company is an organic, living, breathing thing, not just an income sheet and balance sheet. You have to lead it with that in mind. **Carly Fiorina**. "Secrets of the Fastest Rising Stars," *Fortune* (Patricia Sellers, 2000)

The first lesson is: To hell with centralized strategic planning. If you don't have a good leader, it's all nothing; it's just a bunch of papers flying around. **Robert Townsend**. "Townsend's Third Degree in Leadership," *The Conference Board Challenge to Business: Industry Leaders Speak Their Minds* (Peter Krass and Richard E. Cavanagh, eds, 2000)

A leader is one who ventures and takes the risks of going out ahead to show the way and whom others follow, voluntarily, because they are persuaded that the leader's path is the right one—for them, probably better than they could devise for themselves. **Robert Greenleaf**. "Servant: Retrospect and Prospect," *The Power of Servant Leadership* (Larry Spears, ed, 1998)

Without some element of leadership, the many at the bottom will be paralyzed with choices. **Kevin Kelly**. *New Rules for the New Economy: 10 Radical Strategies for a Connected World* (1998)

Consensus is the negation of leadership. **Margaret, Baroness Thatcher**. Quoted in *Woodbury Reports Archives* (June 1997)

I think you have a rocket up your ass and I want to point it in the right direction. **Harry E. Figgie, Jr**. Exemplifying Figgie's aggressive management style. Quoted in *Dangerous Company* (James O'Shea and Charles Madigan, 1997)

The hierarchical manager of yesterday ran the Industrial Age company with "Yes Sir! Yes Sir!" ... When you're running an Information Age company, you've got to allow a lot of dissent. **Bill Campbell**. Quoted in *Giant Killers* (Geoffrey James, 1996)

Leaders with unruly, lowly minds will project and create turbulent and contaminated environments in their spheres of action. **S. K. Chakraborty**. *Ethics in Management: Vedantic Perspectives* (1995)

The difference between a leader and a boss is the difference between good and bad management. **Joe Klock**. *Like Klockwork: The Whimsy, Wit, and (Sometime) Wisdom of a Key Largo Curmudgeon* (1995)

The art of leadership is saying no, not yes. It is very easy to say yes. **Tony Blair**. *Daily Mail (London)* (October 1994)

Leadership is all hype. We've had three great leaders in this century—Hitler, Stalin, and Mao. **Peter F. Drucker**. *Fortune* (February 1994)

A leader is a person you will follow to a place you wouldn't go by yourself. **Joel A. Barker**. *Paradigms* (1994)

I'm the boss. I'm allowed to yell. **Ivan Boesky**. Quoted in *Den of Thieves* (James B. Stewart, 1991)

The manager does things right; the leader does the right thing. **Warren Bennis**. "Managing the Dream," *Training Management* (1990)

Managers have been brought up on a diet of power, divide and rule. they have been pre-occupied with authority, rather than making small things happen. **Charles Handy**. *The Age of Unreason* (1989)

You just have to be the kind of guy to get people to do things. **Donald J. Trump**. *US News & World Report* (April 1987)

Either lead, follow, or get out of the way. **Anonymous**. Sign on the desk of broadcasting executive Ted Turner. *Fortune* (January 5, 1987)

They have a particular drive, a desire to bring order out of chaos, or if something is too cosy, to create chaos in order to bring change. **Sir Michael Owen Edwardes**. On leaders. Quoted in *The New Elite* (Berry Ritchie and Walter Goldsmith, 1987)

If we're going to run this business on viscera, it's going to be my viscera. **Thomas J. Watson, Jr**. Quoted in *CEO* (Harry Levinson and Stuart Rosenthal, 1984)

Most people in big companies are administered, not led. They are treated as personnel, not people. **Robert Townsend**. *Further Up the Organization* (1984)

The most effective leader is the one who satisfies the psychological needs of his followers. **David Ogilvy**. *Ogilvy on Advertising* (1983)

The task of the leader is to get people from where they are to where they have not been. **Henry Kissinger**. *Time* (October 1980)

A leader is a man who has the ability to get other people to do what they don't want to do and like it. **Harry S. Truman**. Quoted in *Leadership Is Not a Bowler Hat* (P. Prior, 1977)

Teach me to smile if it kills me. Make me a better leader ... by helping develop larger and greater qualities of understanding, tolerance, sympathy, wisdom, perspective, equanimity, mind-reading, and second sight. **Anonymous**. Quoted in "A Leader's Prayer," *Understanding Organisations* (Charles Handy, 1976), pt. 1, ch. 4

I'll tell you what leadership is. It's persuasion and conciliation, and education, and patience. **Dwight D. Eisenhower**. Quoted in *Handbook of Leadership* (R. M. Stogdill, 1974)

In order for an ideal to become a reality, there must be a person, a personality to translate it. **Jesse Jackson**. Eulogy (October 1972)

The leader must know, must know that he knows, and must be able to make it abundantly clear to those about him that he knows. **Clarence B. Randall**. *Making Good in Management* (1964)

In essence leadership appears to be the art of getting others to want to do something you are convinced should be done. **Vance Packard**. *The Pyramid Climbers* (1962)

At a rehearsal I let the orchestra play as they like. At the concert I make them play as I like. **Sir Thomas Beecham, Bt**. Quoted in *Sir Thomas Beecham* (Neville Cardew, 1961)

The final test of a leader is that he leaves behind him in other men the conviction and the will to carry on. **Walter Lippmann**. "Roosevelt Has Gone," *New York Herald Tribune* (April 14, 1945)

I have never issued an order since I have been the operating head of the corporation. **Alfred P. Sloan**. Referring to the benefits of decentralized management. "The Most Important Things I Learned About Management," *System* (August 1924)

Here lies one who knew how to get around him men who were cleverer than himself. **Andrew Carnegie**. Epitaph (1919)

Drive thy business, let not that drive thee. **Benjamin Franklin**. The *Poor Richard's Almanack* series (1732–58) were originally published under the pseudonym Richard Saunders. *Poor Richard's Almanack* (1758)

When the effective leader is finished with his work, the people say it happened naturally. **Laozi**. *Daode Jing* (6th century BC), ch. 17

Learning

Questions are places in your mind where answers fit. If you haven't asked the question, the answer has nowhere to go. It hits your mind and bounces right off. You have to ask the question—you have to want to know—in order to open up the space for the answer to fit. **Clayton M. Christensen**. *Farnam Street* blog (August 9, 2012)

It's what you learn after you know it all that counts. **John Wooden**. *The Essential Wooden* (2006)

Learning is not compulsory. Neither is survival. **W. Edwards Deming**. Quoted in *Discover Your Hidden Talents* (Bill Lucas, 2005)

You know what a learning experience is? A learning experience is one of those things that says, "You know that thing you just did? Don't do that." **Douglas Adams**. *The Salmon of Doubt* (2004)

The learning person looks forward to failure or mistakes. The worst problem in leadership is basically early success. **Warren Bennis**. Quoted in *Guide to the Management Gurus* (C. Kennedy, 1998)

True learning begins with unlearning. **Fred Kofman**. *On Becoming a Leader* (1998)

Once a company has adapted to a new environment, it is no longer the organization it used to be; it has evolved. That is the essence of learning. **Arie de Geus**. "The Living Company," *Harvard Business Review* (1997)

We're not in cultures which support learning; we're in cultures that give us the message consistently: "Don't mess up, don't make mistakes, don't make the boss look bad, don't give us any surprises." So we're asking for a kind of predictability, control, respect, and compliance that has nothing to do with learning. **Walter Wriston**. Interview with Scott London, US National Public Radio (November 1996)

Many organizations are now trying to walk under the banner of The Learning Organization, realizing that knowledge is our most important product ... But the only place that I've seen it is in the Army. As one colonel said, "We realized a while ago that it's better to learn than be dead." **Walter Wriston**. Interview with Scott London, US National Public Radio (November 1996)

Never let formal education get in the way of your learning. **Mark Twain**. Quoted in *Jump Start Your Brain* (Doug Hall, 1996)

I'm not an educator ... I'm a learner. **Bill Gates**. *The Road Ahead* (cowritten with Nathan Myhrvold and Peter N. Rinearson, 1995)

Learning and performance will become one and the same thing. Everything you say about learning will be about performance. People will get the point that learning is everything. **Peter Block**. "The Future of Workplace Learning and Performance," *Training and Development* (1994)

Over the long run, superior performance depends on superior learning. **Peter Senge**. "The Leader's New Work: Building Learning Organizations," *Sloan Management Review* (1990)

Individual learning is a necessary but insufficient condition for organizational learning. **Chris Argyris**. *Organizational Learning: A Theory of Action Perspective* (cowritten with Donald A. Schon, 1978)

The man who views the world at fifty the same as he did at twenty has wasted thirty years of his life. **Muhammad Ali**. *Playboy* (1975)

Bromidic though it may sound, some questions don't have answers, which is a terribly difficult lesson to learn. **Katharine Graham**. "The Power That Didn't Corrupt," *Ms.* (Jane Howard, 1974)

The illiterate of the 21st century will not be those who cannot read and write but those who cannot learn, unlearn and relearn. **Alvin Toffler**. *Future Shock* (1970)

Listening

Powerful people do not have good listening skills. They hate to listen. They succeed by getting good at faking it ... If you're an extrovert, you think while you're talking. And it's impossible to listen to someone if you are thinking of the next thing you want to say. **Penelope Trunk**. *Brazen Careerist* blog (December 14, 2012)

I remind myself every morning: Nothing I say this day will teach me anything. So if I'm going to learn, I must do it by listening. **Larry King**. Quoted in the *Daily Telegraph (London)* (December 16, 2010)

Good listeners, like precious gems, are to be treasured. **Walter Anderson**. *The Confidence Course: Seven Steps to Self-Fulfillment* (1998)

I think we have to lead people by being good listeners. That is to say, we lead in a company such as ours by drawing out ideas from people ... We can't simply issue commands. **Minoru Makihara**. Interview, *Strategy + Business* (Joel Kurtzman, January–March 1996)

In the industrial age, the CEO sat on the top of the hierarchy and didn't have to listen to anybody ... In the information age, you have to listen to the ideas of people regardless of where they are in the organization. **John Sculley**. *Nation's Business Today* (1987)

Sometimes listening itself may not be enough—some people must be prodded if you are to find out what they're thinking. **Mary Kay Ash**. *On People Management* (1984)

Wisdom comes with talking less frivolously and listening more seriously. The latter implies a learning attitude; the former assumes an air of omniscience that does not exist. **S. K. Chakraborty**. *Management by Objectives: An Integrated Approach* (1976)

One never repents of having spoken too little but often of having spoken too much. **Philippe de Commines**. *Mémoires* (1524)

I have often heard that the outstanding man is he who thinks deeply about a problem, and the next is he who listens carefully to advice. **Livy**. *History of Rome* (26 BC–15 AD)

Losing

Losing and dying: it's the same thing. **Lance Armstrong**. Quoted in the *London Review of Books* (November 22, 2012)

I'm the only person I know that's lost a quarter of a billion dollars in one year ... It's very character building. **Steve Jobs**. Quoted in *Apple Confidential 2.0: The Definitive History of the World's Most Colorful Company* (Owen Linzmayer, 2004)

Stifle that ego and learn to love small losses. If you don't have small losses, it is positively guaranteed that you will have huge losses. **John R. Hill**. *The Ultimate Trading Guide* (2000)

There is no such thing as a paper loss. A paper loss is a very real loss. **Jim Rogers**. Quoted in *Treasury of Investment Wisdom* (Bernice Cohen, 1999)

     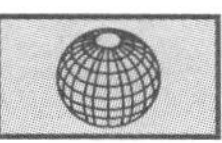   

If you think you are going to win, you'll lose. Moreover, if you think you are going to lose, you'll lose. **Toshihiko Seko**. Quoted in *Running with the Legends* (Michael Sandrock, 1996)

If the losses don't hurt, your financial survival is tenuous. **William Eckhardt**. Quoted in *The New Market Wizards* (John D. Schwager, 1992)

For me coming second is the same as coming last. **Sir Lew, Lord Grade**. Interview, *You Magazine* (October 25, 1987)

I never thought of losing, but now that it's happened, the only thing is to do it right. That's my obligation to all the people who believe in me. We all have to take defeats in life. **Muhammad Ali**. Said after losing his first fight to Ken Norton, March 31, 1973. Quoted in the *New York Times* (1973)

'Tis better to have fought and lost, Than never to have fought at all. **Arthur Hugh Clough**. "Peschiera," *Poems* (1862)

There is nothing worse than a battle won except a battle lost. **Duke of Wellington (Arthur Wellesley)**. Letter to Philip von Neumann (January 11, 1821)

If you want to know what a man is really like, take notice how he acts when he loses money. **Anonymous**.

Loyalty

The primary rule of business success is loyalty to your employer. That's all right as a theory. What is the matter with loyalty to yourself? **Mark Twain**. Quoted in *East Valley Tribune* (2000)

I walk into all these organizations, and I'm always puzzled when I realize that people still want to be there. Most people really want to love their organizations. We need that level of commitment ... Yet organizations have done very little to deserve that kind of staying-power. **Walter Wriston**. Interview with Scott London, US National Public Radio (November 1996)

Forget loyalty. Or at least loyalty to one's corporation. Try loyalty to your Rolodex—your network—instead. **Tom Peters**. *Economist (London)* (1996)

Today professionalism is almost a byword for loyalty towards personal mercenary aims. Yet no great achievement is ever possible without a focus of loyalty which transcends the individual self. **S. K. Chakraborty**. *Management by Values: Towards Cultural Congruence* (1991)

What job is worth the enormous psychic cost of following a leader who values loyalty in the narrowest sense. **Warren Bennis**. *On Becoming a Leader* (1989)

Loyalty saves the wear and tear of making daily decisions as to what is best to do. **Thomas J. Watson, Sr**. Quoted in *Think* (William Rogers, 1972)

Almost all our relationships begin and most of them continue as forms of mutual exploitation. **W. H. Auden**. *The Dyers Hand* (1963)

What I want is men who will support me when I am in the wrong. **Lord Melbourne (William Lamb)**. Quoted in *Lord M* (David Cecil, 1954), vol. 2

Men are more often bribed by their loyalties and ambitions than money. **Robert H. Jackson**. "United States v. Wunderlich" (1951)

Patriotism is a lively sense of collective responsibility. Nationalism is a silly cock crowing on a dunghill. **Richard Aldington**. *The Colonel's Daughter* (1931)

Make yourself necessary to someone. **Ralph Waldo Emerson**. *The Conduct of Life* (1860)

Luck

I've found that luck is quite predictable. If you want more luck, take more chances. Be more active. Show up more often. **Brian Tracy**. Quoted in *How to Succeed in Life* (Moses Michael, 2007)

With all due respect to Microsoft and Intel, there is no substitute for being in the right place at the right time. **Andrew S. Grove**. *Fortune* (June 1993)

What we call luck is the inner man externalized. We make things happen to us. **Robertson Davies**. *What's Bred in the Bone* (1985)

I think a lot more decisions are made on serendipity than people think. Things come across their radar screens and they jump at them. **Jay W. Lorsch**. *Wall Street Journal* (October 1, 1984)

Fortune knocks once, but misfortune has much more patience. **Laurence J. Peter**. *The Peter Principle: Why Things Always Go Wrong* (cowritten with Raymond Hull, 1969)

My batting average has been good, so people ask how much luck is involved. I tell them when I work 14 hours a day, 7 days a week, I get lucky. **Armand Hammer**. *International Management* (June 1966)

Some folk want their luck buttered. **Thomas Hardy**. *The Mayor of Casterbridge* (1886)

Where observation is concerned, chance favors only the prepared mind. **Louis Pasteur**. Address (December 1854)

It is a great skill to know how to guide your luck even while waiting for it. **Baltasar Gracián**. Attributed

We must believe in luck. For how else can we explain the success of those we don't like? **Jean Cocteau**. Attributed

Management

Most managers only measure outputs, not inputs, which is like telling a Little League team to score more runs, rather than actually explaining how to swing a bat and make contact with the ball. Similarly, most companies measure traffic, revenue or earnings, without considering how to improve the company at an atomic level: how to make a meeting better, or an engineer more productive. **James Slavet**. *Forbes* (December 13, 2011)

A book called *Marketing Lessons from the Grateful Dead*, written by a couple of high-flying experts in entrepreneurialism, is about to be published ... There is, it seems, a desperate hunger among business types for some code that will help them make more money. In recent years, an addiction to metaphor has been in evidence—businesses only understand how it works through the prism of an entirely different world. Before writers raided the hippie archive, there were management manuals based on Greek mythology, on classical history, on war. Next it will be the natural world ... This week a collection of lessons from nature will be published under the title *Smart Swarms*. **Terence Blacker**. *Independent (London)* (August 3, 2010)

Management theory is like Marxism in the last years of the Soviet Union—nobody believes it, but everybody must pretend that they do. **Bryan Appleyard**. *Sunday Times (London)* (July 19, 2009)

The management model that has run us for the past 30 years, like the discredited economic theories ... to which it cringes, is bust, dead, finished—a mortal danger to us and the planet. **Simon Caulkin**. *Observer (London)* (June 14, 2009)

The edifice of management had been turned upside down—it was shareholders who had become monarch, their courtiers lavishly rewarded managers whose MBA courses had taught them to manage deals and numbers, not things or people. Management had suffered a reverse takeover. Finance ousted reality, cost ousted value, the means became the end. **Simon Caulkin**. *Observer (London)* (June 14, 2009)

Locke defined a madman as someone "reasoning correctly from erroneous premises." For Einstein, madness was repeatedly doing the same thing and hoping for a different result. The worst of modern management—and, alas, that often seems most of it—manages to combine the two. **Simon Caulkin**. *Observer (London)* (April 26, 2009)

The truth is that much conventional management is central planning in Western disguise. This is why most companies are zombie-like in their structural and strategic similarity. This is why, too, they are unable to learn. **Simon Caulkin**. *Observer (London)* (February 15, 2009)

There are three secrets to managing. The first secret is have patience. The second is be patient. And the third most important secret is patience. **Chuck Tanner**. Quoted in *Tales from the 1979 Pittsburgh Pirates* (John McCollister, 2005)

Management means, in the last analysis, the substitution of thought for brawn and muscle, of knowledge for folklore and superstition, and of cooperation for force. **Peter F. Drucker**. Quoted in *The Financial Times Handbook of Management* (Stuart Crainer and Des Dearlove, 2004)

Good management to Wall Street means nothing more than a company with three consecutive quarters of rising earnings. Make it four quarters and you have great management. **Ralph Wanger**. Quoted in *500 of the Most Witty, Acerbic, and Erudite Things Ever Said About Money* (Philip Jenks, 2002)

The first steps to becoming a really great manager are simply common sense; but common sense is not very common. **Gerald M. Blair**. *What Makes a Great Manager* (2000)

Controlled unreasonableness. **Gerry Robinson**. Referring to his personal management style. *Management Today* (April 1999)

Responsibility without control is at the core of management. **Paul Corrigan**. *Shakespeare on Management* (1999)

Ultimately, the job of the manager is to get ordinary people to create extraordinary results. **Christopher Bartlett**. *The Individualised Corporation* (cowritten with Sumantra Ghoshal, 1997)

In large organizations, middle managers serve the purpose of relaying information up and down—orders down, numbers up. But with the new information technologies and more efficient forms of work, their purpose dwindles. **James Champy**. Quoted in the *New York Times* (January 7, 1996)

Traditional management structures were devised when information was a scarce commodity, so that knowledge about how to run the business could be communicated layer by layer. **Raymond W. Smith**. Speech (October 17, 1995)

This blight is management—the dreaded four Ms, male, middle class, middle-aged and mediocre. **Janet Street-Porter**. Referring to television management in the United Kingdom. MacTaggart Lecture, Edinburgh Television Festival, UK (August 1995)

Management, a science? Of course not, it's just a wastepaper basket full of recipes which provided the dish of the day during a few years of plenty and economic growth. Now the recipes are inappropriate and the companies which persist in following them will disappear. **Léon Courville**. Quoted in *The Unconscious Civilization* (John Ralston Saul, 1995)

We have a technique at Hewlett-Packard for helping managers and supervisors know their people and understand the work their people are doing ... Management by Walking About. **David Packard**. *The HP Way* (1995)

A couple of hours in a hot kitchen can teach you as much about management as the latest books on re-engineering or total quality management. **Tom Peters**. "The Way the Cookie Crumbles" (1995)

Management today is reactive behavior. You put your hand on a hot stove and yank it off. A cat would know to do as much. **W. Edwards Deming**. Quoted in *BusinessWeek* (January 10, 1994)

The manager's job is to thrive in a chaotic world he cannot control. He is at last reconciled to being, openly, an intermediary. **Theodore Zeldin**. *An Intimate History of Humanity* (1994)

He not only conducts his version of Beethoven and Bach, but scores it as he goes along. **Tom Peters**. Referring to the management style of Cable Network News. *Liberation Management* (1992)

I've spent 30 years going round factories. When you know something's wrong, nine times out of ten it's the management ... people aren't being led right. And bad leaders invariably blame the people. **Sir John Harvey-Jones**. Interview, *Daily Telegraph (London)* (March 24, 1990)

A manager is an assistant to his men. **Thomas J. Watson, Sr**. Quoted in *Father, Son & Co.: My Life at IBM and Beyond* (Thomas J. Watson, Jr, and Peter Petre, 1990)

Frightened, nervous managers use thick, convoluted planning books and busy slides filled with everything they've known since childhood. **Jack Welch**. *Harvard Business Review* (September–October 1989)

Society has become unmanageable as a result of management. **Henry Mintzberg**. *Mintzberg on Management* (1989)

Management is more fun, more creative, more personal, more political and more intuitive than any textbook. **Charles Handy**. *Gods of Management* (1986)

The conventional definition of management is getting work done through people, but real management is developing people through work. **Hasan Abedi**. *Leaders* (July 1984)

Management must manage! **Harold S. Geneen**. *Managing* (co-written with Alvin Moscow, 1984)

Top management is supposed to be a tree full of owls ... hooting when management heads into the wrong part of the forest. I'm still unpersuaded they even know where the forest is. **Robert Townsend**. *Further up the Organization* (1984)

The key managerial processes are enormously complex and mysterious, drawing on the vaguest of information and using the least articulated of mental processes. **Henry Mintzberg**. *Harvard Business Review* (July–August 1976)

Nobody is sure anymore who really runs the company (not even the people who are credited with running it), but the company does run. **Joseph Heller**. *Something Happened* (1974)

Most of what we call management consists of making it difficult for people to get their work done. **Peter F. Drucker**.

     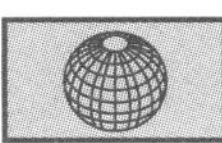   

Management: Tasks, Responsibilities and Practises (1973)

A good manager is a man who isn't worried about his own career but rather the careers of those who work for him. **H. S. M. Burns**. Quoted in *Men at the Top* (Osborn Elliott, 1959)

Bad administration, to be sure, can destroy good policy; but good administration can never save bad policy. **Adlai E. Stevenson**. Speech, Los Angeles (September 11, 1952)

No institution can possibly survive if it needs geniuses or supermen to manage it. It must be organized in such a way as to be able to get along under a leadership composed of average human beings. **Peter F. Drucker**. *Big Business* (1947)

At best we live by homely proverbs, at worst we live by pompous inanities. **Herbert A. Simon**. *Administrative Behavior* (1947)

Of all business activities, 99% are routine ... The entire 100% can be handled by managing the 1% of exceptions. **Alfred P. Sloan**. "The Most Important Things I Learned About Management," *System* (August 1924)

To be dilatory about giving orders, but to expect absolute punctuality, that is called being a tormentor. **Confucius**. *Analects* (500? BC)

Managing is getting paid for home runs someone else hits. **Casey Stengel**. Attributed

Marketing

There is more similarity in the marketing challenge of selling a precious painting by Degas and a frosted mug of root beer than you ever thought possible. **A. Alfred Taubman**. Quoted in *The Virtual Handshake* (David Teten and Scott Allen, 2005)

There are three things that you should spend you time doing: marketing, marketing, marketing. If you are not prepared to do that, then everything else is irrelevant. **Emma Harrison**. *Daily Mail (London)* (November 14, 2004)

Business has only two functions—marketing and innovation. **Peter F. Drucker**. *The Daily Drucker* (2004)

Marketing people talk about emotion. They present charts and diagrams, even raise their voices and wave their arms, but fundamentally they treat emotion as ... out-there, felt by someone else and able to be manipulated. Analyzing other people's emotions and refusing to acknowledge our own dumps us in the same old rut. What a waste. **Salil Tripathi**. *Lovemarks: The Future Beyond Brands* (2004)

One of the qualities I always seek in marketing people is curiosity. **Raoul Pinnell**. *Marketing* (June 2000)

There's no business without show business. **Michael J. Wolf**. *The Entertainment Economy* (1999)

Half the sponsors don't know if their money is wasted or not; the other half do it in order not to be left out. **Anonymous**. Quoted in *Formula 1, The Business of Winning* (Russell Hotten, 1998)

Focus Groups are people who are selected on the basis of their inexplicable free time and their common love of free sandwiches. **Scott Adams**. *The Dilbert Principle* (1996)

Every product has some element of service, and every service some element of product. **Aubrey Wilson**. *New Directions in Marketing* (1991)

The mass market has split into ever-multiplying, ever-changing sets of micromarkets that demand a continually expanding range of options. **Alvin Toffler**. *Powershift* (1990)

But markets today are moving targets. The only way to hit them is to launch your business like a cruise missile. **Harry V. Quadracci**. *Success* (June 1988)

The man who whispers down a well About the goods he has to sell Will not make as many dollars As the man who climbs the tree and hollers! **Lord Leverhulme (William Hesketh Lever)**. Leverhulme was a consummate salesman, pioneering US mass-marketing techniques in Britain. Quoted in *Enlightened Entrepreneurs* (Ian Campbell Bradley, 1987), ch. 10

Marketing should focus on market creation, not market share. **Regis McKenna**. *The Regis Touch* (1986)

No great marketing decisions have ever been made on qualitative data. **John Sculley**. Quoted in *The Intuitive Manager* (Roy Rowan, 1986)

Marketing takes a day to learn. Unfortunately, it takes a lifetime to master. **Philip Kotler**. *Marketing Management* (1967)

Your company does not belong in any market where it cannot be the best. **Philip Kotler**. *Marketing Management* (1967)

Manufacturers who don't test their products incur the colossal cost (and disgrace) of having their products fail on a national scale instead of dying inconspicuously and economically in test markets. **David Ogilvy**. *Confessions of an Advertising Man* (1963)

Marketing is not a function, it is the whole business seen from the customer's point of view. **Peter F. Drucker**. *The Practice of Management* (1954)

We're obviously going to spend a lot in marketing because we think the product sells itself. **Jim Allchin**. Attributed

Marketing is what you do when your product is no good. **Edwin Land**. Attributed

Media

We allowed the community to tell us what was entertaining them. **Chad Hurley**. BBC News (May 22, 2007)

I think editors are excellent marketers. They know their audience and produce copy to appeal to them—they just don't call it marketing. **David Robinson**. *Marketing* (June 2000)

There is not one shred of evidence that the Internet has had any downward influence on North American or European newspaper circulation. **Conrad, Lord Black**. Press conference (March 2000)

We're in the attention getting business. **Peter Chernin**. *Forbes* (June 1998)

When I started out, people were afraid of parish priests. Now they're afraid of newspaper editors. **Michael D. Higgins**. Attributed (1997)

Television has made dictatorship impossible, but democracy unbearable. **Shimon Peres**. *Financial Times (London)* (January 1995)

The information highway will transform our culture as dramatically as Gutenberg's press did the Middle Ages. **Bill Gates**. *The Road Ahead* (cowritten with Nathan Myhrvold and Peter N. Rinearson, 1995)

Someone once described the information business as exactly the opposite of sex. When it's good, it's still lousy. **Michael Bloomberg**. *New York Times* (November 1993)

No first world country has ever managed to eliminate so entirely from its media all objectivity—much less dissent.

  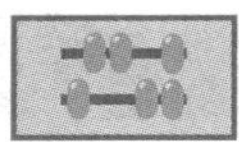      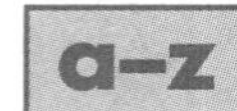

Gore Vidal. Referring to the United States. *A View from the Diner's Club* (1991)

The media … is like an oil painting. Close up, it looks like nothing on Earth. Stand back and you get the drift. **Sir Bernard Ingham**. Speech (February 1990)

One man saying that everything is wrong can command coast-to-coast attention in living color, a power not given to an absolute monarch a century ago. **Walter Wriston**. *Risk and Other Four Letter Words* (1986)

For a politician to complain about the press is like a ship's captain complaining about the sea. **Enoch Powell**. *Guardian (London)* (December 1984)

No self-respecting fish would be wrapped in a Murdoch newspaper. **Mike Royko**. *Chicago Sun Times* (1984)

Government always tends to want, not a really free press, but a managed and well-conducted one. **Cyril John, Lord Radcliffe**. Quoted in *What the Papers Never Said* (Peter Hennessey, 1983)

Television is simultaneously blamed, often by the same people, for worsening the world and for being powerless to change it. **Clive James**. *Glued to the Box* (1981)

I can do more in communications than any conqueror could have done. **Ted Turner**. *Newsweek* (June 16, 1980)

Gutenberg made everyone a reader. Xerox makes everybody a publisher. **Marshall McLuhan**. *Guardian (London)* (June 1977)

Freedom of the press in Britain means freedom to print such of the proprietor's prejudices as the advertisers don't object to. **Hannen Swaffer**. Quoted in *Swaff* (Tom Driberg, 1974)

The medium is the message. **Marshall McLuhan**. *Understanding Media* (1964)

A good newspaper, I suppose, is a nation talking to itself. **Arthur Miller**. *Observer (London)* (November 1961)

A continuous clash of egomaniacal monsters, wasting more energy than dinosaurs and pouring rivers of money into the sand. **Robert Bolt**. Referring to the movie industry. *Sunday Times (London)* (June 1961)

I hate television. I hate it as much as peanuts. But I can't stop eating peanuts. **Orson Welles**. *New York Herald Tribune* (October 1956)

Journalism—an ability to meet the challenge of filling the space. **Dame Rebecca West**. *New York Herald Tribune* (April 1956)

News is what a chap who doesn't care much about anything wants to read. **Evelyn Waugh**. *Scoop* (1938)

Meetings

Some CEOs … make the mistake of driving the board line by line through the agenda, cutting off meaty discussions in the name of staying on schedule. The purpose of board meetings is to have those meaty discussions. Most of the items should be strategic and thorny questions that the business must tackle to be successful. A technique I like a lot is when the CEO puts up a list of the three or four things that are "keeping me up at night" at the start of each meeting. **Fred Wilson**. *Bloomberg Businessweek* (April 12, 2012)

Start with small groups of smart people—and keep them small. Every time the body count goes higher, you're simply inviting complexity to take a seat at the table … The idea is pretty basic: everyone in the room should be there for a reason. There's no such thing as a "mercy invitation." Either you're critical to the meeting or you're not. It's nothing personal, just business. **Ken Segall**. *Insanely Simple: The Obsession that Drives Apple's Success* (2012)

My period of greatest creative output was during my corporate years, when every meeting felt like a play date with coma patients. I would sit in long meetings, pretending to pay attention while writing computer code in my mind and imagining the anatomically inspired nicknames I would assign to my boss after I won the lottery. **Scott Adams**. *Wall Street Journal* (August 6, 2011)

A manager's ability to turn meetings into a thinking environment is probably an organization's greatest asset. **Nancy Kline**. *Time to Think* (1999)

I find that no matter how long a meeting goes on, the best ideas always come during the final five minutes, when people drop their guard and I ask them what they really think. **Michael Eisner**. *International Management* (April 1988)

Whoever invented the meeting must have had Hollywood in mind. I think they should consider giving Oscars for meetings: Best Meeting of the Year, Best Supporting Meeting, Best Meeting Based on Material from Another Meeting. **William Goldman**. *Adventures in the Screen Trade* (1983), ch. 2

When committees gather, each member is necessarily an actor, uncontrollably acting out the part of himself, reading the lines that identify him, asserting his identity. **Lewis Thomas**. "On Committees," *The Medusa and the Snail* (1979)

Outside of traffic, there is nothing that has held this country back as much as committees. **Will Rogers**. Quoted in *Will Rogers, His Life and Times* (Richard M. Ketchum, 1973)

Any committee that is the slightest use is a committee of people who are too busy to want to sit on it for a second longer than they have to. **Katharine Whitehorn**. "Are You Sitting Comfortably?" *Observations* (1970)

A meeting is an arrangement whereby a large number of people gather together, some to say what they really do not think, some not to say what they really do. **Vladimir Voinovich**. *The Life and Extraordinary Adventures of Private Ivan Chonkin* (1969), pt. 2, ch. 6

Meetings are a great trap. Soon you find yourself trying to get agreement and then the people who disagree come to think they have a right to be persuaded … However, they are indispensable when you don't want to do anything. **J. K. Galbraith**. *Ambassador's Journal* (1969), ch. 5

The length of a meeting rises with the number of people present and the productiveness of a meeting falls with the square of the number of people present. **Eileen Shanahan**. *Times Talk* (1963)

My life has been a meeting … one long meeting. Even on the few committees I don't yet belong to, the agenda winks at me when I pass. **Gwyn Thomas**. *The Keep* (1961)

What is a committee? A group of the unwilling, picked from the unfit, to do the unnecessary. **Richard Harkness**. *New York Herald Tribune* (1960)

No grand idea was ever born in a conference, but a lot of foolish ideas have died there. **F. Scott Fitzgerald**. *The Crack-Up* (1945)

A conference is a gathering of important people who, singly, can do nothing but together can decide that nothing can be done. **Fred Allen**. W. M. Martin was the president of the New York Stock Exchange. Letter to W. M. Martin (January 25, 1940)

  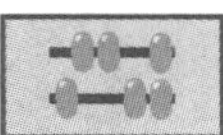   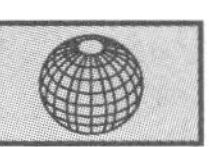 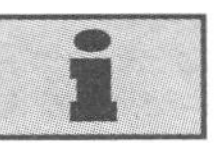  

Mergers and Demergers

A good first step towards selling your company is declaring that you'll never sell it. **Peter Thiel**. Quoted in *The Browser* (May 22, 2012)

When you sell 30% of a business, it is like taking two limbs off a body—it's not surprising there is a negative effect on the rest of the business. **Sir Clive Thompson**. *Sunday Times (London)* (October 2000)

The big danger in mega-mergers is that they are seen as a mating of dinosaurs. **Sir Peter Bonfield**. *Sunday Times (London)* (July 2000)

When it comes to mergers, hope triumphs over experience. **Irwin Stelzer**. Quoted in *Treasury of Investment Wisdom* (Bernice Cohen, 1999)

Chief executives seem no more able to resist their biological urge to merge, than dogs can resist chasing rabbits. **Philip Coggan**. Quoted in *Treasury of Investment Wisdom* (Bernice Cohen, 1999)

You might merge with another organization, but two drunks don't make a sensible person. **Gary Hamel**. *Competing for the Future* (cowritten with C. K. Prahalad, 1994)

Dividing an elephant in half does not produce two elephants. **Peter Senge**. *The Fifth Discipline: The Art and Practice of the Learning Organization* (1990)

The very best takeovers are thoroughly hostile. I've never seen a really good company taken over. I've only seen bad ones. **Sir James Goldsmith**. *Financial Times (London)* (March 21, 1989)

Leadership that's reliant on mergers and acquisitions is dangerous leadership. **John Varley**. Attributed

Mistakes

Keith Richards ... was once asked how he came up with all those amazing guitar riffs. His answer? He just starts playing until he makes the right mistake. In other words he's optimistic he will create something good by virtue of getting something "wrong." **Mark Stevenson**. *The School of Life* blog (January 16, 2013)

You will get something wrong today, and tomorrow, and every day of your life. So will I, and everybody you know. You don't have a choice about being wrong sometimes: mistakes will be your life-long companion. But you do have a choice about whether to approach your error in terror so you suppress, ignore, and repeat it—or to make it your honest, open ally in trying to get to the truth. **Johann Hari**. *Independent (London)* (August 13, 2010)

Of all the things we are wrong about, error might well top the list ... We are wrong about what it means to be wrong. Far from being a sign of intellectual inferiority, the capacity to err is crucial to human cognition. Far from being a moral flaw, it is inextricable from some of our most humane and honourable qualities: empathy, optimism, imagination, conviction, and courage. And far from being a mark of indifference or intolerance, wrongness is a vital part of how we learn and change. Thanks to error, we can revise our understanding of ourselves and amend our ideas about the world. **Kathryn Schulz**. *Being Wrong: Adventures in the Margin of Error* (2010)

Business is like war in one respect. If its grand strategy is correct, any number of tactical errors can be made and yet the enterprise proves successful. **Robert E. Wood**. Quoted in *What's Your Game Plan: Creating Business Strategies that Work* (Milton C. Lauenstein, 2004)

You can't live life without an eraser. **Tom Peters**. *The Circle of Innovation* (1998)

We became uncompetitive by not being tolerant of mistakes. **Roberto Goizueta**. *Fortune* (May 1995)

I've always been able to make erroneous decisions very quickly. **Herb Kelleher**. *The Nation's Business* (October 1991)

We are built to make mistakes, coded for error. **Lewis Thomas**. "To Err Is Human," *The Medusa and the Snail* (1979)

The better a man is, the more mistakes will he make—for the more new things he will try. I would never promote a man into a top level job who had not made mistakes, and big ones at that. Otherwise he is sure to be mediocre. **Peter F. Drucker**. *The Practice of Management* (1954)

Every great mistake has a halfway moment, a split second when it can be recalled and perhaps remedied. **Pearl S. Buck**. *What America Means to Me* (1943)

If a man is both wise and lucky, he will not make the same mistake twice. But he will make any one of ten thousand brothers or cousins of the original. **Jesse Livermore**. *Reminiscences of a Stock Operator* (writing as Edwin Lefèvre, 1923)

Give me fruitful error any time, full of seeds, bursting with its own corrections. **Vilfredo Pareto**. *Mind and Society* (1916)

The man who makes no mistakes does not usually make anything. **E. J. Phelps**. Speech, Mansion House, London (January 24, 1899)

Man errs as long as he strives. **Johann Wolfgang von Goethe**. *Faust* (1808), pt. 1

A man should never be ashamed to own he has been in the wrong, which is but saying, in other words, that he is wiser to-day than he was yesterday. **Alexander Pope**. *Thoughts on Various Subjects* (1741)

The first chance you have to avoid a loss from a foolish loan is by refusing to make it; there is no second chance. **Charlie Munger**. Attributed

You must learn from the mistakes of others. You can't possibly live long enough to make them all yourself. **Sam Levenson**. Attributed

If all else fails, immortality can always be achieved by a spectacular mistake. **J. K. Galbraith**. Attributed

It is a good thing to make mistakes so long as you're found out quickly. **John Maynard Keynes**. Attributed

Money

To be extraordinarily happy and to have no concern for money drives some people nuts. **Danny Baker**. *Desert Island Discs*, BBC Radio (July 31, 2011)

People would rather earn 60 grand in an area where their neighbours earn 40, than earn 80 in an area where their neighbours earn a hundred. **John Lanchester**. Speech. "Enough" (December 12, 2010)

It turns out there is a specific dollar number, or income plateau, after which more money has no measurable effect on day-to-day contentment. The magic income: $75,000 a year. **Anonymous**. Reporting the findings of a study by economist Angus Deaton and psychologist Daniel Kahneman. *Wall Street Journal* blog (September 7, 2010)

Above the Bear Stearns trading floor hung the slogan "Let's make nothing but money." Bear Stearns did indeed make nothing but money: not friends or loyal clients, not even many products that customers should have wanted to buy. And in the end the company lost all the money it had ever made. **John Kay**. *Obliquity: Why Our Goals Are Best Achieved Indirectly* (2010)

Money turns out to be whatever we agree it to be. It is a collective work of the imagination. **Simon Carr**. *Independent (London)* (January 12, 2009)

There's plenty of money out there. They print more and more of it every day. But that ticket? There are only five of them, and that's all there's ever going to be. Only a dummy would give this up for something as common as money. Are you a dummy? **John August**. Grandpa George persuading Charlie that he should not sell the golden ticket. Screenplay of the movie *Charlie and the Chocolate Factory* (2006)

Money isn't everything, but it keeps the kids in touch. **Anonymous**. Quoted in *Business Wit and Wisdom* (Richard S. Zera, 2005)

It isn't necessary to be rich and famous to be happy. It's only necessary be rich. **Alan Alda**. Quoted in *Really Bad Business Advice* (David Dallas and Arlen Foote, 2003)

I have never been in no situation where having money made it worse. **Clinton Jones**. Quoted in *How to License Your Million Dollar Idea* (Harvey Reese, 2002)

I cannot afford to waste my time making money. **Louis Agassiz**. Quoted in *The Lazy Person's Guide to Success* (Ernie J. Zelinski, 2002)

I'm not in Wall Street for my health. **J. P. Morgan**. Quoted in *Treasury of Investment Wisdom* (Bernice Cohen, 1999)

Money, of course, is never just money. It's always something else, and it's always something more, and it always has the last word. **Paul Auster**. *Hand to Mouth* (1997)

What good is money if you can't inspire terror in your fellow man? **Jon Vitti**. Spoken by tycoon C. Montgomery Burns. *The Simpsons*, Fox TV (December 5, 1991)

Americans want action for their money. They are fascinated by its self-reproducing qualities if it's put to work. Gold-hoarding goes against the American grain; it fits in better with European pessimism than with America's traditional optimism. **Paula Nelson**. *The Joy of Money: The Woman's Guide to Financial Freedom* (1986)

It's not how much you earn, it's how much you owe. **Ted Turner**. Speech (1986)

To turn $100 into $110 is work. To turn $100 million into $110 million is inevitable. **Edgar Bronfman, Jr.** *Newsweek* (December 2, 1985)

Money doesn't mind if we say it's evil, it goes from strength to strength. It's a fiction, an addiction, and a tacit conspiracy. **Martin Amis**. *Money* (1984)

Money is a singular thing. It ranks with love as man's greatest source of joy. And with death as his greatest source of anxiety. Over all history it has oppressed nearly all people in one of two ways: either it has been abundant and very unreliable, or reliable and very scarce. **J. K. Galbraith**. *The Age of Uncertainty* (1977)

Money is better than poverty, if only for financial reasons. **Woody Allen**. "The Early Essays," *Without Feathers* (1976)

Money couldn't buy you friends but you got a better class of enemy. **Spike Milligan**. *Puckoon* (1963)

Money is like manure. If you spread it around, it does a lot of good, but if you pile it up in one place, it stinks like hell. **Clint W. Murchison**. Quoted by his son Clint Murchison, Jr, in *Time* (June 16, 1961)

Money, it turned out, was exactly like sex: you thought of nothing else if you didn't have it and thought of other things if you did. **James Baldwin**. "Black Boy Looks at the White Boy," *Esquire* (May 1961)

The best things in life are free But you can give them to the birds and bees I need money. **Barrett Strong**. *Money (That's What I Want)* (1959)

You've heard money talking? Did you understand the message? **Marshall McLuhan**. *The Mechanical Bridge* (1951)

My hardest job has been to keep from being a millionaire. **Amadeo Giannini**. *American magazine* (January 1931)

The instinct of acquisitiveness has more perverts, I believe, than the instinct of sex. At any rate, people seem to me odder about money than about even their amours. **Aldous Huxley**. *Point Counter Point* (1928), ch. 22

We all know how the size of sums of money appear to vary in a remarkable way according as they are paid in or out. **Sir Julian Huxley**. *Essays of a Biologist* (1923)

Money is like a sixth sense without which you cannot make a complete use of the other five. **W. Somerset Maugham**. *Of Human Bondage* (1915)

The universal regard for money is the one hopeful fact in our civilization. **George Bernard Shaw**. *Major Barbara* (1905), Preface

Money's a horrid thing to follow, but a charming thing to meet. **Henry James**. *The Portrait of a Lady* (1881), ch. 35

I finally know what distinguishes man from the other beasts: financial worries. **Jules Renard**. Journal (1877–1910)

It has been said that the love of money is the root of all evil. The want of money is so quite as truly. **Samuel Butler**. *Erewhon* (1872), ch. 20

To mistake money for wealth, is the same sort of error as to mistake the highway which may be the easiest way of getting to your house or lands, for the house and lands themselves. **John Stuart Mill**. *Principles of Political Economy, with Some of Their Applications to Social Philosophy* (7th ed, 1871)

Money, which represents the prose of life, and which is hardly spoken of in parlors without an apology, is, in its effects and laws, as beautiful as roses. **Ralph Waldo Emerson**. "Nominalist and Realist," *Essays: Second Series* (1844)

In civilised society, personal merit will not serve you so much as money will. Sir, you may make the experiment. Go into the street, and give one man a lecture on morality, and another a shilling, and see which will respect you the most. **Samuel Johnson**. Quoted in *The Life of Samuel Johnson* (James Boswell, 1791)

Money is the seed of money. The first guinea is sometimes more difficult to aquire than the second million. **Jean-Jacques Rousseau**. *Discourse Upon the Origin and Foundation of the Inequality Among Mankind* (1754)

Money is neither my god nor my devil. It is a form of energy that tends to make us more of who we already are, whether it's greedy or loving. **Dan Millman**. Attributed

A billion here, a billion there. Sooner or later it adds up to real money. **Everett Dirksen**. Attributed

A fool and his money are soon invited everywhere. **Warren Buffett**. Notice hanging in his office

There is nothing so habit forming as money. **Don Marquis**. Attributed

Getting money is like digging with a needle; spending it is like water soaking into sand. **Anonymous**. Japanese proverb

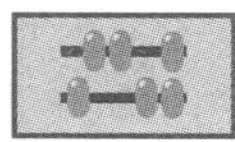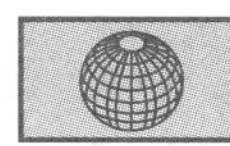

For the love of money is the root of all evil: which while some coveted after, they have erred from the faith, and pierced themselves through with many sorrows. **New Testament**. 1 Timothy 6:10

Motivation

It is possible to steer people towards better decisions by presenting choices in different ways ... Research into why people did not take up financial incentives to reduce energy consumption by insulating their homes found one possibility was the hassle of clearing out the attic. A nudge was designed whereby insulation firms would offer to clear the loft, dispose of unwanted items, and return the rest after insulating it. This example of what behavioural economists call "goal substitution"—replacing lower energy use with cleaning out the attic—led to a threefold increase in take-up of an insulation grant. **Anonymous**. *Economist (London)* (March 24, 2012)

What humans want is not just happiness ... if that were all people were interested in, we should have been extinguished a long time ago. **Martin Seligman**. Interviewed in *Psychologies* (April 2011)

The bonus system has proved to be wrong. Substantial cash bonuses do not reward the right kind of behaviour. **Andy Hornby**. Speaking before the Treasury Select Committee (February 10, 2009)

The man who does not work for the love of work but only for money is not likely to make money nor find much fun in life. **Charles M. Schwab**. Quoted in *The Best Damn Book About The Profession of Selling. Period!* (Howard B. Rutstein, 2006)

Success is not the result of spontaneous combustion. You must set yourself on fire. **Reggie Leach**. Quoted in *Wisdom for the Soul* (Larry Chang, 2006)

The world is full of people who are waiting for someone to come along and motivate them to be the kind of people they wish they could be. The problem is that no one is coming to the rescue. **Brian Tracy**. *Eat That Frog* (2002)

You cannot motivate the best people with money. Money is just a way to keep score. The best people in any field are motivated by passion. **Eric S. Raymond**. Interview, *Fast Company* (1999)

Every day I get up and look through the Forbes list of the richest people in America. If I'm not there, I go to work. **Robert Orben**. Quoted in *The Winning Manager* (Julius E. Eitington, 1997)

Forget socialism, capitalism, just-in-time deliveries, salary surveys, and the rest ... concentrate on building organizations that accomplish that most difficult of all challenges: to make people look forward to coming to work in the morning. **Ricardo Semler**. *Maverick!* (1993)

Make people believe that what they think and do is important—and then get out of their way while they do it. **Jack Welch**. Quoted in *Teaching the Elephant to Dance* (James A. Belasco, 1990)

I do not love the money. What I do love is the getting of it ... What other interest can you suggest to me? I do not read. I do not take part in politics. What can I do? **Philip D. Armour**. Quoted in *Forbes* (October 26, 1987)

The common wisdom is that ... managers have to learn to motivate people. Nonsense. Employees bring their own motivation. **Tom Peters**. *A Passion for Excellence* (cowritten with Nancy Austin, 1985)

I can charge a man's battery and then recharge it again. But it is only when he has his own generator that we can talk about motivation. He then needs no outside stimulation. He wants to do it. **Frederick Herzberg**. *Harvard Business Review* (January–February 1968)

A reward once given becomes a right. **Frederick Herzberg**. *The Motivation to Work* (1959)

A man always has two reasons for what he does—a good one and the real one. **J. P. Morgan**. Quoted in *Roosevelt: The Story of a Friendship* (Owen Wister, 1930)

Negotiation

Know what you want—and remember that whatever your bottom line is, there's always another line below that. **Anonymous**. Quoted in Charles Crawford's blog (May 12, 2012)

Be careful, be cautious, do not rush into negotiations ... be careful what you give away now, you may wish you had not done so should in future the balance of forces turn in your favour. **Oliver Tambo**. Advice on negotiating with the apartheid-supporting South African government. Quoted in *Mandela: The Authorised Biography* (Anthony Sampson, 2000)

Place a higher priority on discovering what a win looks like for the other person. **Harvey Robbins**. *TransCompetition* (cowritten with Michael Finley, 1998)

The trouble about bargaining ... is that when one loses in a particular competitive negotiation, one's chances of winning the next negotiation are frequently diminished. **Theodore Zeldin**. *An Intimate History of Humanity* (1994)

When money is at stake, never be the first to mention sums. **Ahmed Zaki Yamani**. Quoted in *Yamani* (Jeffrey Robinson, 1988)

The single and most dangerous word to be spoken in business is no. The second most dangerous word is yes. It is possible to avoid saying either. **Lois Wyse**. *Company Manners* (1987)

It's a well-known proposition that you know who's going to win a negotiation: it's he who pauses the longest. **Robert Holmes à Court**. *Sydney Morning Herald* (May 24, 1986)

A negotiator should observe everything. You must be part Sherlock Holmes, part Sigmund Freud. **Victor Kiam**. *Going For It* (1986)

Make a suggestion or assumption and let them tell you you're wrong. People also have a need to feel smarter than you are. **Mark McCormack**. *What They Don't Teach You at Harvard Business School* (1984)

Anger can be an effective negotiating tool, but only as a calculated act, never as a reaction. **Mark McCormack**. *What They Don't Teach You at Harvard Business School* (1984)

Let us never negotiate out of fear, but let us never fear to negotiate. **John F. Kennedy**. Presidential inaugural speech (January 20, 1961)

Never corner an opponent, and always assist him to save his face ... Avoid self-righteousness like the devil—there is nothing so self-blinding. **Sir Basil Henry Liddell Hart**. *Deterrent or Defence* (1960)

He knew the precise psychological moment when to say nothing. **Oscar Wilde**. *The Picture of Dorian Gray* (1891), ch. 2

Necessity never made a good bargain. **Benjamin Franklin**. The *Poor Richard's Almanack* series (1732–58) were originally published under the pseudonym Richard Saunders. *Poor Richard's Almanack* (1735)

Diplomacy is the art of letting someone else have your way. **Sir David Frost**. Attributed

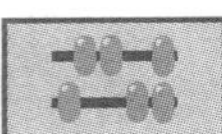

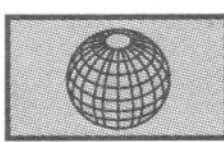

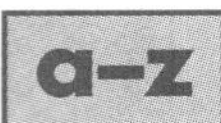

Nepotism

If you want to ruin your family business, give it to your eldest son. **Anonymous**. Report by social scientists at the London School of Economics. Quoted in the *Independent (London)* (January 14, 2008)

I have concluded that it is in the best interests of those whom this institution serves for that mission to be carried forward under new leadership. **Paul Wolfowitz**. Statement on resigning from the World Bank amid claims that his girlfriend, who worked for the Bank, received favourable treatment. Quoted in the *New York Times* (May 17, 2007)

In all industries, including the media, a few names are as common as muck. This isn't talent telling, it's unashamed favoritism. **Anonymous**. Referring to nepotism. *Guardian (London)* (July 27, 2000)

The presumption that because you share a surname with someone who is good at their job, you'll be good at it too, is patently nonsense. Yet nothing seems to help you more in life than your signature. **Anonymous**. Referring to nepotism. *Guardian (London)* (July 27, 2000)

You do not have to be the son of a rich man to be an entrepreneur. Today kids are far more willing to take risks because they've seen high rewards. **Narayana Murthy**. *Forbes* (June 2000)

I avoided the company because I wanted the opportunity to have a track record of starting a business where you are not the boss's son. **James Murdoch**. Referring to his father, Rupert Murdoch. *Forbes* (July 1998)

Office Politics

I realized that talent would get me as far as middle management, but beyond that point it would become a matter of politics and currying favor with bosses. **Masahiro Origuchi**. *Wired Asia* (June 2000)

I just had this conversation with a guy about a problem we're trying to fix, and he said to me, "Just put out a memo and tell them what to do." I told him, "If only life were that easy." **Shelly Lazarus**. "The 50 Most Powerful Women in American Business," *Fortune* (Patricia Sellers and Cora Daniels, October 1999)

Institutional life is only made possible, or even tolerable, by the shared pretence that everything we do is ... a matter of life and death ... I came to find the small hierarchies of office life and the ways in which, after a holiday, the office worker had to play himself back into his part, learning once more to feign rage or delight or indignation, both moving and extremely comic. **Jeremy Lewis**. *Playing for Time* (1987)

Weiler's Law: "Nothing is impossible for the man who doesn't have to do it himself." **Anonymous**. Quoted in *Murphy's Law and Other Reasons That Things Go Wrong* (Arthur Bloch, 1977)

There are but two means of locomotion to the top. Either people must like you so much that they push you there, or you, yourself, are so good that you push yourself there. **Gerald Sparrow**. *How to Become a Millionaire* (1960), ch. 2

The working of great institutions is mainly the result of a vast mass of routine, petty malice, self interest, carelessness, and sheer mistake. Only a residual fraction is thought. **George Santayana**. *The Crime of Galileo* (1958)

He draws the bonds of his new engagements closer and tighter about him. He loses sight, by degrees, of all common sense ... in the petty squabbles, intrigues, feuds, and airs of affected importance to which he has made himself accessory. **William Hazlitt**. Describing the corporate employee. "On Corporate Bodies," *Table Talk* (1821–22), Essay 27

Opinions

The web 2.0 generation may be shocked to learn that everyone's opinion is not equally valid on every subject. **Michael R. Lynch**. Quoted in the *Financial Times (London)* (June 30, 2008)

An opinion should be the result of thought, not a substitute for it. **Jef Mallett**. *Frazz* comic strip (August 26, 2005)

All opinions are not equal. Some are a very great deal more robust, sophisticated, and well supported in logic and argument than others. **Douglas Adams**. *The Salmon of Doubt* (2004)

The more opinions you have, the less you see. **Wim Wenders**. Quoted in the *Evening Standard (London)* (April 25, 1990)

It's not that I don't have opinions, rather that I'm not paid to think aloud. **Yitzhak Navon**. Quoted in the *Observer (London)* (January 16, 1983)

The Spirit of Liberty is the spirit which is not too sure that it is right. **Learned Hand**. *The Spirit of Liberty* (1952)

Markets are never wrong—opinions often are. **Jesse Livermore**. *How To Trade in Stocks* (1940)

The fact that an opinion has been widely held is no evidence whatever that it is not utterly absurd. **Bertrand Russell (Earl Russell)**. *Marriage and Morals* (1929)

Comment is free but facts are sacred. **C. P. Scott**. *Manchester Guardian* (May 1922)

Public opinion is a weak tyrant compared with our own private opinion. **Henry David Thoreau**. *Walden, or Life in the Woods* (1854)

Some praise at morning what they blame at night; But always think the last opinion right. **Alexander Pope**. *An Essay on Criticism* (1711)

Opportunity

My first rule is not to lose money. Losing an opportunity is minor in comparison, because there are always new opportunities around the corner. **Bert Dohmen**. *Wellington Letter* (February 1999)

One way of building private foresight out of public data is looking where others aren't ... if you want to see the future, go to an industry confab and get the list of what was talked about. Then ask, "What did people never talk about?" That's where you're going to find opportunity. **Gary Hamel**. Interview, *Strategy + Business* (October–December 1997)

I am far more interested in avoiding risk than I am in capturing every opportunity. My philosophy says that loss of opportunity is preferable to loss of capital. **Joseph DiNapoli**. Quoted in *Trading Systems* (Joe Krutsinger, 1997)

I just wait until there is money lying in the corner, and all I have to do is go over there and pick it up. I do nothing in the meantime. **Jim Rogers**. On his approach to financial trading. Quoted in *The New Market Wizards* (John D. Schwager, 1992)

Equal opportunity means everyone will have a fair chance at becoming incompetent. **Laurence J. Peter**. *Why Things Go Wrong: The Peter Principle Revisited* (1984)

Companies worry too much about the cost of doing something. They should worry about the cost of not doing it. **Philip Kotler**. *Marketing Management* (1967)

When written in Chinese, the word "crisis" is composed of two characters—one represents danger, and the other represents opportunity. **John F. Kennedy**. Speech, Indianapolis, Indiana (April 12, 1959)

Only through curiosity can we discover opportunities, and only through gambling can we take advantage of them. **Clarence Birdseye**. *American Magazine* (February 1951)

One can present people with opportunities. One cannot make them equal to them. **Rosamond Lehmann**. *The Ballad and the Source* (1944)

Next to knowing when to seize an opportunity, the most important thing in life is to know when to forgo an advantage. **Benjamin Disraeli (Earl of Beaconsfield)**. *The Infernal Marriage* (1834)

There is a tide in the affairs of men Which, taken at the flood, leads on to fortune; Omitted, all the voyage of their life Is bound in shallows and in miseries. **William Shakespeare**. *Julius Caesar* (1599), Act 4, Scene 3

A wise man will make more opportunities than he finds. **Sir Francis Bacon (Viscount St Alban)**. "Of Ceremonies and Respects," *Essays* (1597–1625)

You never need to chase a trade. The market has plenty of opportunities. The money runs out before the opportunities do. **John Saleeby**. Attributed

Opportunity doesn't knock. It presents itself when you beat down the door. **Kyle Chandler**. Attributed

Opportunities are usually disguised as hard work, so most people don't recognize them. **Ann Landers**. Attributed

Order

At the point where order and chaos most closely resemble one another, there exists the greatest possibility for broadening the human capacity to adapt to instability and uncertainty. **Daryl R. Conner**. *Leading at the Edge of Chaos* (1998)

Filing is concerned with the past; anything you actually need to see again has to do with the future. **Katharine Whitehorn**. *Sunday Best* (1976)

Since we cannot hope for order let us withdraw with style from the chaos. **Sir Tom Stoppard**. *Lord Malaquist and Mr Moon* (1966)

There is a quality even meaner than outright ugliness or disorder, and this meaner quality is the dishonest mask of pretended order, achieved by ignoring or suppressing the real order that is struggling to exist and to be served. **Jane Jacobs**. *The Death and Life of Great American Cities* (1961)

Life creates order, but order does not create life. **Antoine de Saint-Exupéry**. *Letter to a Hostage* (1942)

A. A violent order is disorder; and B. A great disorder is an order. These two things are one. **Wallace Stevens**. "Connoisseur of Chaos," *Notes Toward a Supreme Fiction* (1942)

Confusion is a word we have invented for an order which is not understood. **Henry Miller**. "Interlude," *Tropic of Capricorn* (1939)

Have a place for everything and keep the thing somewhere else. This is not advice, it is merely custom. **Mark Twain**. *Notebook* (1935)

Large organisation is loose organisation. Nay, it would be almost as true to say that organisation is always disorganisation. **G. K. Chesterton**. "The Bluff of the Big Shops," *Outline of Sanity* (1926)

There is a rage to organize which is the sworn enemy of order. **Georges Duhamel**. *Vie des Martyrs* (1917)

Chaos often breeds life, when order breeds habit. **Henry Brooks Adams**. *Education of Henry Adams* (1907)

A place for everything and everything in its place. Order is wealth. **Samuel Smiles**. *Thrift* (1875)

There are some enterprises in which a careful disorderliness is the true method. **Herman Melville**. *Moby-Dick* (1851)

Organizations

It can take just as much effort to run a small company as a much larger one. **Barbara, Lady Judge**. *Management Today* (October 1999)

There have been seven directors or acting directors in six years. That's not an organization. That's an institutional collapse. **Daniel P. Moynihan**. Referring to the problems of managing the CIA. *Independent on Sunday (London)* (March 1997)

For a large organization to be effective, it must be simple. **Jack Welch**. Quoted in *In Search of European Excellence* (Robert Heller, 1997)

In companies whose wealth is intellectual capital, networks, rather than hierarchies, are the right organizational design. **Thomas A. Stewart**. *Intellectual Capital* (1997)

Highly-adaptive, informal networks move diagonally and eliptically, skipping entire functions to get things done. **Jacques Barzun**. *Emotional Intelligence* (1996)

Whatever the country, whatever the culture, whatever the time, when you become a big enough organization, you start to collapse and slow down. **Masayoshi Son**. Quoted in *Giant Killers* (Geoffrey James, 1996)

The introduction of a new grammar, not just new words, is the key to organizational transformation. **Michael D. McMaster**. *The Intelligence Advantage* (1996)

In the future the optimal form of industrial organization will be neither small companies nor large ones but network structures that share the advantages of both. **Francis Fukuyama**. *Trust: The Social Virtues and the Creation of Prosperity* (1995)

Large, centralized organizations foster alienation like stagnant ponds breed algae. **Ricardo Semler**. *Maverick!* (1993)

It is sobering to reflect on the extent to which the structure of our business has been dictated by the limitations of the file folder. **Michael Hammer**. *Re-engineering the Corporation* (cowritten with James Champy, 1993)

America's business problem is that it is entering the twenty-first century with companies designed during the nineteenth century to work well in the twentieth. **Michael Hammer**. *Re-engineering the Corporation* (cowritten with James Champy, 1993)

We're controlled by ideas and norms that have outlived their usefulness, that are only ghosts but have as much influence on our behavior as if they were alive. **Robert H. Waterman, Jr**. *Adhocracy* (1993)

Most of our organization tends to be arranged on the assumption that people cannot be trusted ... that sort of attitude creates a paraphernalia of systems, checkers, and checkers checking checkers—expensive and deadening.

Charles Handy. "Trust and the Virtual Organization," *Harvard Business Review* (May–June 1991)

In the knowledge economy, bureaucracy will increasingly be replaced by adhocracy, a holding unit that co-ordinates the work of numerous temporary workers. **Richard Crawford**. *In the Era of Human Capital* (1991)

The core corporation is ... increasingly a façade, behind which teems an array of decentralized groups and subgroups continuously contracting with similarly diffuse working units all over the world. **Robert Reich**. *The Work of Nations* (1991)

Every company has two organizational structures: The formal one is written on the charts; the other is the everyday relationships of the men and women in the organization. **Harold S. Geneen**. *Managing* (cowritten with Alvin Moscow, 1984)

In Japan, organizations and people in the organization are synonymous. **Kenichi Ohmae**. "The Myth and Reality of the Japanese Corporation," *Chief Executive* (Summer 1981)

In a hierarchy every employee tends to rise to his level of incompetence. **Laurence J. Peter**. *The Peter Principle: Why Things Always Go Wrong* (cowritten with Raymond Hull, 1969)

TWIMBLE: I play it the company way Where the company puts me, there I'll stay. FINCH: But what is your point of view? TWIMBLE: I have no point of view, FINCH: Supposing the company thinks ... TWIMBLE: I think so too! **Frank Loesser**. Song lyric. "The Company Way," *How to Succeed in Business without Really Trying* (1961)

We talk about organizations in terms not unlike those used by an Ubongi medicine man to discuss diseases. **Herbert A. Simon**. *Administrative Behavior* (1947)

The trouble with organizing a thing is that pretty soon folks get to paying more attention to the organization than to what they're organized for. **Laura Ingalls Wilder**. *Little Town on the Prairie* (1941)

Originality

It's not where you take things from—it's where you take them to. **Jean-Luc Godard**. Quoted in *MovieMaker* (October 20, 2005)

Nothing is original. Steal from anywhere that ... fuels your imagination. Devour old films, new films, music, books, paintings, photographs, poems, dreams, random conversations, architecture, bridges, street signs, trees, clouds, bodies of water, light, and shadows. Select only things to steal from that speak directly to your soul. If you do this, your work (and theft) will be authentic. Authenticity is invaluable; originality is non-existent. **Jim Jarmusch**. *MovieMaker* (October 20, 2005)

Keep on the lookout for novel ideas that others have used successfully. Your idea has to be original only in its adaption to the problem you're working on. **Thomas Edison**. Quoted in *A Kick in the Seat of the Pants* (Roger von Oech, 1986)

Original thought is like original sin: both happened before you were born to people you could not have possibly met. **Fran Lebowitz**. *Social Studies* (1981)

Anyone who attempts anything original in the world must expect a bit of ridicule. **Alberto Juantorena**. Quoted in *Quick Frozen Foods* (March 1960)

When people are free to do as they please, they usually imitate each other. **Eric Hoffer**. *The Passionate State of Mind* (1955)

I have never avoided the influence of others. I would have considered this a cowardice and lack of sincerity toward myself. **Henri Matisse**. Interview (1907)

New opinions are always suspected, and usually opposed, without any other reason but because they are not already common. **John Locke**. *An Essay Concerning Human Understanding* (1690), Dedicatory epistle

If I have seen further, it is by standing on the shoulders of giants. **Sir Isaac Newton**. Letter to Robert Hooke (February 5, 1675)

People and Relationships

The network by itself is meaningless. Only the people were ever meaningful. **Jaron Lanier**. *You Are Not a Gadget: A Manifesto* (2010)

Anonymous blog comments, vapid video pranks and lightweight mashups may seem trivial and harmless, but, as a whole, this widespread practice of fragmentary, impersonal communication has demeaned personal interaction. **Jaron Lanier**. On the effects of Internet use. *You Are Not a Gadget: A Manifesto* (2010)

The best way to guarantee a steady stream of new ideas is to make sure that each person in your organization is as different as possible from the others. Under these conditions, and only these conditions, will people maintain varied perspectives and demonstrate their knowledge in different ways. **Nicholas Negroponte**. "Where Do New Ideas Come From," *Wired* (January 4, 1996)

People are now becoming the most expensive optional component of the production process and technology is becoming the cheapest. **Michael Dunkerley**. *The Jobless Economy* (1996)

If you were to hire household staff to cook, clean, drive, stoke the fire, and answer the door, can you imagine suggesting that they not talk to each other, not see what each other is doing, not coordinate their functions? **Nicholas Negroponte**. Referring to the pressure on work relationships in an office. *Being Digital* (1995)

There is practically no area of business where the difference between rhetoric and actuality is greater than in the handling of people. **Sir John Harvey-Jones**. *All Together Now* (1994)

Develop the business around the people; build it, don't buy it; and, then, be the best. **Sir Richard Branson**. Speech to the Institute of Directors, London. "Growing Bigger While Still Staying Small" (May 1993)

The best minute I spend is the one I invest in people. **Kenneth Blanchard**. *The One Minute Manager* (1993)

If future competitiveness depends on treating people as an important part of the institution, the least respectful thing I can imagine doing to a human being is asking him to urinate in a cup. **Tom Peters**. Said in testimony before the California state legislature, November 28, 1993. *New York Times* (1993)

The more time I spend with our people, the more I find out about our business. **Herb Kelleher**. *The Nation's Business* (October 1991)

Distinguish between the person and the behavior or performance. **Stephen Covey**. *Thirty Methods of Influence* (1991)

You can be totally rational with a machine. But, if you work with people, sometimes logic has to take a back seat to

        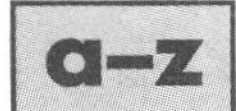

understanding. **Akio Morita**. *Made in Japan* (1986)

Get to know your people. What they do well, what they enjoy doing, what their weaknesses and strengths are, and what they want and need to get from their job. **Robert Townsend**. *Further Up the Organization* (1984)

You cannot love an employee into creativity, although you can … avoid his dissatisfactions with the way you treat him. **Frederick Herzberg**. *Work and the Nature of Man* (1966), ch. 6

No office anywhere on Earth is so puritanical, impeccable, elegant, sterile or incorruptible as not to contain the yeast for at least one affair … just let a yeast raiser into the place and first thing you know—bread! **Helen Gurley Brown**. *Sex and the Office* (1964)

Most men are individuals no longer, so far as their business, its activities, or its moralities are concerned. They are not units but fractions. **Woodrow Wilson**. Speech (August 1910)

If you are planning for one year, plant rice. If you are planning for ten years, plant trees. If you are planning for 100 years, plant people. **Anonymous**. Indian proverb

Perfection

The pleasure we found in working together made us exceptionally patient; it is much easier to strive for perfection when you are never bored. **Daniel Kahneman**. On working with his collaborator Amos Tversky (1937–96). *Thinking, Fast and Slow* (2011)

The delusion that you're perfect—or that if you just do the right thing, things will always work out OK—makes you resistant to change and fearful of failure … you'd rather not discover that you're imperfect, that maybe what you were doing was wrong. The more people can go through those discoveries the better. **Esther Dyson**. Interview, *Reason Magazine* (November 1996)

Perfectionism is the voice of the oppressor, the enemy of the people. It will keep you cramped and insane your whole life … perfectionism is based on the obsessive belief that if you run carefully enough, hitting each stepping stone just right, you won't have to die. The truth is that you will die anyway and that a lot of people who aren't even looking at their feet are going to do a whole lot better than you, and have a lot more fun while they're doing it. **Anne Lamott**. *Bird by Bird* (1994)

When you consider something ideal, you lose the opportunity to improve it. **Shoji Shiba**. Quoted in "Toyota's Fresh Look at JIT [Just-In-Time]," *Financial Times (London)* (September 10, 1990)

Perfection can be a fetish. **Bernard Leach**. *The Potter's Challenge* (1976)

Perfect numbers, like perfect people, are very rare. **René Descartes**. Quoted in *Mathematical Circles Squared* (H. Eves, 1972)

An environment which calls for perfection is not likely to be easy. But aiming for it is always good for progress. **Thomas J. Watson, Jr**. *A Business and Its Beliefs* (1963)

The indefatigable pursuit of an unattainable perfection … is what alone gives a meaning to our life on this unavailing star. **Logan Pearsall Smith**. "Art and Letters," *Afterthoughts* (1931)

Performance

There are no hidden genuises in large corporations. It's so obvious when someone is good and does well. **Jean-Pierre Garnier**. *The Times (London)* (September 26, 2005)

Best practices usually aren't. **Christopher Locke**. *The Cluetrain Manifesto* (2000)

The best judgment we can make about managerial competence does not depend on what people say, but simply what the record says. **Warren Buffett**. Quoted in *Treasury of Investment Wisdom* (Bernice Cohen, 1999)

Shoulda, coulda, and woulda won't get it done. **Pat Riley**. *The Winner Within* (1993)

Your legacy should be that you made it better than it was when you got it. **Lee Iacocca**. *Talking Straight* (1988)

Performance stands out like a ton of diamonds. Nonperformance can always be explained away. **Harold S. Geneen**. *Managing* (cowritten with Alvin Moscow, 1984)

It is an immutable law in business that words are words, explanations are explanations, promises are promises—but only performance is reality. **Harold S. Geneen**. *Managing* (cowritten with Alvin Moscow, 1984)

Resolve to perform what you ought. Perform without fail what you resolve. **Benjamin Franklin**. The fourth of his 13 precepts for moral living. *Benjamin Franklin's Autobiography* (1793), pt. 2

The best performance improvement is the transition from the nonworking state to the working state. **John Ousterhout**. Attributed

Persistence

You have to put in many, many, many tiny efforts that nobody sees or appreciates before you achieve anything worthwhile. **Brian Tracy**. Quoted in *101 Best Ways to Get Ahead* (Michael E. Angier, 2004)

Saving New York City from bankruptcy is like making love to a gorilla. You don't stop when you're tired; you stop when he's tired. **Felix Rohatyn**. Quoted in *500 of the Most Witty, Acerbic, and Erudite Things Ever Said About Money* (Philip Jenks, 2002)

Perseverance may be just as important as speed in the battle for the future. **Gary Hamel**. *Competing for the Future* (cowritten with C. K. Prahalad, 1994)

How you start is important, but it is how you finish that counts. In the race for success, speed is less important than stamina. The sticker outlasts the sprinter. **Bertie Charles Forbes**. Quoted in *Reader's Digest* (1993)

I just love it when people say I can't do something. **David Andrews**. Quoted in *CNN: The Inside Story* (Hank Whittemore, 1990)

I am extraordinarily patient, provided I get my own way in the end. **Margaret, Baroness Thatcher**. *Observer (London)* (April 1989)

There are no secrets to success: don't waste time looking for them. Success is the result of perfection, hard work, learning from failure, loyalty to those for whom you work, and persistence. **Colin Powell**. *Colin Powell* (1989)

We're gonna stay on until the end of the world. And when that day comes we'll cover it, play Nearer My God to Thee and sign off. **Ted Turner**. Referring to his ambitions for the then fledgling Cable News Network. Quoted in *The Corporate Warriors* (Douglas K. Ramsey, 1988)

We must just KBO. **Sir Winston Churchill**. KBO stands for Keep Buggering

On. Quoted in *Finest Hour* (Martin Gilbert, 1983)

You can eat an elephant one bit at a time. **Mary Kay Ash**. *Mary Kay* (1981)

The sea does not reward those who are too anxious, too greedy, or too impatient ... Patience, patience, patience, is what the sea teaches. **Anne Morrow Lindbergh**. *Gift from the Sea* (1955)

It's dogged as does it. It ain't thinking about it. **Anthony Trollope**. *The Last Chronicle of Barset* (1867), vol. 1, ch. 61

Irresolute men are sometimes very persistent in their undertakings, because if they give up their designs they would have to make a second resolution. **Giacomo Leopardi**. "Sayings of Filippo Ottonieri," *Essays, Dialogues, and Thoughts* (1827)

Perseverance is more prevailing than violence; and many things which cannot be overcome when they are together, yield themselves up when taken little by little. **Plutarch**. "Sertorius," *Parallel Lives* (1st century AD), sect. 16

Nothing in the world can take the place of persistence. Talent will not; nothing is more common than unsuccessful men of talent. Genius will not; unrewarded genius is almost a proverb. Education will not; the world is full of educated derelicts. Persistence and determination are omnipotent. **Calvin Coolidge**. Quoted at his memorial service (1933). Attributed

Personalities

Gerald Corrigan is the head of the world's most successful financial institution. Weighing in at—I'd say 450 lbs—he is, like his bank, too big to fail. Yes, he is fantastically rich. You couldn't fit his personal wealth into the dome of St Paul's. He could hang Istanbul off his charm bracelet. He's probably got golden bones—but he's sensitive to public opinion and we all noticed he didn't come to the Treasury in his chariot pulled by unicorns. He left at home his suit made from extinct animals. **Simon Carr**. *Independent (London)* (February 23, 2010)

I'm not retiring because I'm old and tired. I'm retiring because an organization has had 20 years of me. My success will be determined by how well my successor grows it in the next 20 years. **Jack Welch**. Referring to his planned retirement on December 31, 2000. Quoted in "The Ultimate Manager," *Fortune* (November 22, 1999)

Bill Gates follows somebody's tail lights for a while then zooms past. Soon there will be no tail lights left. **Andrew S. Grove**. *BusinessWeek* (June 1994)

Doing business with Alan Bond is like wrestling with a pig. You both get sprayed with mud and the pig loves it. **Anonymous**. An anonymous Texan banker on Bond's famously aggressive business strategy. *Sunday Times (London)* (February 12, 1989)

For exercise, I wind my watch. **Robert Maxwell**. Quoted in *Time* (November 28, 1988)

I consider that I am a revolutionary socialist. **Tiny Rowland**. Quoted in *My Life with Tiny* (Richard Hall, 1987)

Just look at him. He runs his company with five people in an office the size of a closet. **Katharine Graham**. Referring to Warren Buffett. *US News & World Report* (1986)

If a guy is over 25% jerk, he's in trouble. And Henry was 95%. **Lee Iacocca**. Referring to Henry Ford II. Said in a speech to market analysts in Detroit. Quoted in *Time* (April 1, 1985)

I've got a virtually limitless supply of bullshit. **Ted Turner**. Interview, *Playboy* (1978)

There's only room for one bigmouth in my organisation, and that's me. **Sir Alan, Lord Sugar**. *The Apprentice (UK)*, BBC TV

Philanthropy

Half the day he engages in the most ruthless financial exploitations, ruining the lives of hundreds of thousands, even millions. The other half he just gives part of it back. **Slavoj Žižek**. On George Soros's philanthropic activities. *The Reality of the Virtual* (2007)

If you show people the problems and you show people the solutions they will be moved to act. **Bill Gates**. Speech, Live 8 concert, London (July 2, 2005)

The big opportunity that I see now is shepherding this wealth that has been created into our philanthropic goals. Those goals have to do with rekindling a sense of the community, reminding people that it's important to be part of your community and there's a benefit that comes with being part of your community. **Pierre M. Omidyar**. Interview, *Academy of Achievement* (October 2000)

I've been learning how to give. It's something you have to keep working on, because people like money the way they do their homes and their dogs. **Ted Turner**. *New York Times* (September 20, 1997)

I believe it is my duty to make money and still more money and to use the money I make for the good of my fellow man according to the dictates of my conscience. **John D. Rockefeller**. Interview (1905)

The man who dies rich dies disgraced. **Andrew Carnegie**. "Wealth," *North American Review* (June 1889)

By this time two years I can so arrange all my business as to secure at least 50,000 per annum. Beyond this never earn—make no effort to increase fortune, but spend the surplus each year for benevolent purposes. **Andrew Carnegie**. Carnegie's spelling was not always very good—benovelent—and, indeed, he gave financial backing to the Simplified Spelling Board. Private memo to himself (December 1868)

Earn as much as you can. Save as much as you can. Invest as much as you can. Give as much as you can. **Revd John Wellesly**. Attributed

Planning

Plans are only good intentions unless they immediately degenerate into hard work. **Peter F. Drucker**. Quoted in *The Definitive Drucker* (Elizabeth Haas Edersheim, 2007)

It takes as much energy to wish as it does to plan. **Eleanor Roosevelt**. Quoted in *From Scratch and on a Shoestring* (Arthur A. Leidecker, 2006)

Grand business plans are all very well, but nothing beats dipping your toe in the water. **Karan, Lord Bilimoria**. *Sunday Times (London)* (October 2000)

Today, if someone showed me a five-year plan, I'd toss out the pages detailing Years Three, Four, and Five as pure fantasy ... Anyone who thinks he or she can evaluate business conditions five years from now, flunks. **Mark McCormack**. *Staying Street Smart in the Internet Age: What Hasn't Changed about the Way We Do Business* (2000), Introduction

There was no business plan, no model. It was just guts. **Peter Chernin**. Referring to the planning style of News Corporation. *Forbes* (June 1998)

Managers who extensively plan the future get the timing wrong. **Shona L. Brown**. *Competing on the Edge* (cowritten with Kathleen M. Eisenhardt, 1998)

Central planning didn't work for Stalin or Mao, and it won't work for an entrepreneur either. **Michael Bloomberg**. *Bloomberg on Bloomberg* (cowritten with Matthew Winkler, 1997)

You need to plan the way a fire department plans: it cannot anticipate where the next fire will be, so it has to shape an energetic and efficient team that is capable of responding to the unanticipated as well as to any ordinary event. **Andrew S. Grove**. *Only the Paranoid Survive: How to Exploit the Crisis Points That Challenge Every Company and Career* (1996), Preface

Basing our happiness on our ability to control everything is futile. **Stephen Covey**. *First Things First: To Live, To Love, To Learn, To Leave a Legacy* (1994)

A lot of companies ... find planning more interesting than getting out a saleable product. **H. Edward Wrapp**. *Dunn's Review* (September 1980)

Planning ahead is a matter of class. The rich and even the middle class plan for future generations, but the poor can plan ahead only a few weeks or days. **Gloria Steinem**. "The Time Factor," *Ms.* (March 1980)

Life is what happens to you while you're busy making other plans. **John Lennon**. *Beautiful Boy Double Fantasy* (1980)

There is nothing so disastrous as a rational policy in an irrational world. **John Maynard Keynes**. Quoted in *The Money Game* (Adam Smith, 1976)

In preparing for battle I have always found that plans are useless, but planning is indispensible. **Dwight D. Eisenhower**. Quoted in "Krushchev," *Six Crises* (Richard Nixon, 1962)

We can chart the path to the future clearly and wisely only when we know the path which has led to the present. **Adlai E. Stevenson**. Speech, Richmond, Virginia (September 20, 1952)

If we had had more time for discussion we should probably have made a great many more mistakes. **Leon Trotsky**. Referring to discussions of the Soviet Communist Party's Central Committee about the Red Army. *My Diary* (1930), ch. 36

To be practical, any plan must take account of the enemy's power to frustrate it. **Karl von Clausewitz**. *On War* (1831)

Hindsight is good, foresight is better; but second sight is best of all. **Evan Esar**. Attributed

Power

Being chairman of the Senate Commerce Committee is like being a mosquito in a nudist colony. **John McCain**. Quoted in *Fortune* (March 2003)

Women have so much power that even hearing the word power frightens them. **Harriet Rubin**. *www.tompeters.com* (2000)

Real power is creating stuff. **Geraldine Laybourne**. "The 50 Most Powerful Women in American Business," *Fortune* (Patricia Sellers and Cora Daniels, October 1999)

In the new organisation, power flows from expertise, not position. **Thomas A. Stewart**. *Intellectual Capital* (1997)

Power is the ability to get things done. **Rosabeth Moss Kanter**. *Getting It All Together: Communes Past, Present, Future* (1996)

You carry forever the fingerprint that comes from being under someone's thumb. **Nancy Banks-Smith**. *Guardian (London)* (January 30, 1991)

The exercise of power is determined by thousands of interactions between the world of the powerful and that of the powerless, all the more so because these worlds are never divided by a sharp line; everyone has a small part of himself in both. **Václav Havel**. *Disturbing the Peace* (1990), ch. 5

I was allowed to ring the bell for five minutes until everyone was in assembly. It was the beginning of power. **Jeffrey, Lord Archer**. Referring to his experience at school. Quoted in *Daily Telegraph (London)* (March 16, 1988)

Influence, position and wealth are not given for nothing and we must try to use them as we would wish at the last we had done. **Jeremiah James Colman**. Quoted in *Enlightened Entrepreneurs* (Ian Campbell Bradley, 1987), ch. 5

Men of power have no time to read; yet the men who do not read are unfit for power. **Michael Foot**. *Debts of Honour* (1980)

Monopoly is a terrible thing, till you have it. **Rupert Murdoch**. *The New Yorker* (1979)

Powerful men in particular suffer from the delusion that human beings have no memories. I would go so far as to say that the distinguishing trait of powerful men is the psychotic certainty that people forget acts of infamy as easily as their parents' birthdays. **Stephen Vizinczey**. "Commentary on a Poem," *Horizon* (October 1976)

Whenever you're sitting across from some important person, always picture him sitting there in a suit of long red underwear. That's the way I always operated in business. **Joseph P. Kennedy**. Quoted in *No Final Victories* (Lawrence O'Brien, 1974)

But the relationship of morality and power is a very subtle one. Because ultimately power without morality is no longer power. **James Baldwin**. Conversation between James Baldwin and Nikki Giovanni. *A Dialogue* (1973)

God must have loved the People in Power, for he made them so very like their own image of him. **Kenneth Patchen**. Quoted in the *Guardian (London)* (February 1, 1972)

Power is the ultimate aphrodisiac. **Henry Kissinger**. *New York Times* (January 19, 1971)

Power is not only what you have but what the enemy thinks you have. **Saul Alinsky**. "Tactics," *Rules for Radicals* (1971)

The quality of the will to power is, precisely, growth. Achievement is its cancellation. To be, the will to power must increase with each fulfillment, making the fulfillment only a step to a further one. The vaster the power gained the vaster the appetite for more. **Ursula K. Le Guin**. *The Lathe of Heaven* (1971), ch. 9

He did not care in which direction the car was travelling, so long as he remained in the driver's seat. **Lord Beaverbrook (Max Aitken)**. Referring to British prime minister David Lloyd George. *New Statesman* (June 14, 1963)

Power corrupts, but lack of power corrupts absolutely. **Adlai E. Stevenson**. Referring to Lord Acton's quotation about power corrupting and absolute power corrupting absolutely. Quoted in the *Observer (London)* (January 1963)

The appetite for power, even for universal power, is only insane when there is no possibility of indulging it; a man who sees the possibility opening before him and does not try to grasp it, even at the risk of destroying himself and his country, is either a saint or a mediocrity. **Simone Weil**. "Cold War Policy in 1939," *Selected Essays* (Richard Rees, ed, 1962)

The purpose of getting power is to be able to give it away. **Aneurin Bevan**. Quoted in *Aneurin Bevan* (Michael Foot, 1962), vol. 1, ch. 1

Power intoxicates men. It is never voluntarily surrendered. It must be taken from them. **James F. Byrnes**. Quoted in the *New York Times* (May 15, 1956)

Those in possession of absolute power can not only prophesy and make their prophecies come true, but they can also lie and make their lies come true. **Eric Hoffer**. *The Passionate State of Mind* (1955)

Power-worship blurs political judgement because it leads, almost unavoidably, to the belief that present trends will continue. Whoever is winning at the moment will always seem to be invincible. **George Orwell**. "Second Thoughts on James Burnham," *Shooting an Elephant* (1950)

Every Communist must grasp the truth. Political power grows out of the barrel of a gun. **Mao Zedong**. Speech to Central Committee, Communist Party (November 6, 1938)

The megalomaniac differs from the narcissist by the fact that he wishes to be powerful rather than charming, and seeks to be feared rather than loved. To this type belong many lunatics and most of the great men of history. **Bertrand Russell (Earl Russell)**. *The Conquest of Happiness* (1930), ch. 1

A big man has no time really to do anything but just sit and be big. **F. Scott Fitzgerald**. *This Side of Paradise* (1920)

A friend in power is a friend lost. **Henry Brooks Adams**. *Education of Henry Adams* (1907)

The need to exert power, when thwarted in the open fields of life, is the more likely to assert itself in trifles. **Charles Horton Cooley**. *Human Nature and the Social Order* (1902), ch. 5

Power tends to corrupt and absolute power corrupts absolutely. **John Dalberg-Acton, Lord Acton**. Letter to Bishop Mandell Creighton (April 5, 1887)

Life is a search after power. **Ralph Waldo Emerson**. "Power," *The Conduct of Life* (1860)

The good want power, but to weep barren tears. The powerful goodness want: worse need for them ... And all best things are thus confused with ill. **Percy Bysshe Shelley**. *Prometheus Unbound* (1819), l. 625

An honest man can feel no pleasure in the exercise of power over his fellow citizens. **Thomas Jefferson**. Letter to John Melish (January 13, 1813)

Those who have been once intoxicated with power and have derived any kind of emolument from it, even though but for one year, never can willingly abandon it. They may be distressed in the midst of all their power; but they will never look to anything but power for their relief. **Edmund Burke**. Letter to a member of the National Assembly (January 19, 1791)

You must either conquer and rule or serve and lose, suffer or triumph, be the anvil or the hammer. **Johann Wolfgang von Goethe**. *Der Gross-Cophta* (1791), bk. 2

The stronger man's argument is always the best. **Jean de La Fontaine**. "The Wolf and the Lamb," *Fables* (1668), bk. 1, fable 10

Avoid having your ego so close to your position that, when your position fails, your ego goes with it. **Colin Powell**. Kept on his desk at the Pentagon. Attributed

Behind the screen of the ballot, the real holders of power ... are the great industrial and monetary monopolies who own our national economic life. **Florence Luscomb**. Attributed

Praise and Recognition

Always establish a paper trail to make sure others can't take credit for what you do. **Dennis, Lord Stevenson**. *Management Today* (April 1999)

Congratulations offer more potential than cash. The amount of available cash is limited, but managers have an unlimited supply of congratulations. It's important to pay people fairly, but managers also should heap on congratulations and feed people's souls. **Kenneth Blanchard**. "The Gift of the Goose," *Quality Digest* (December 1997)

It is better to deserve honors and not have them than to have them and not deserve them. **Mark Twain**. Quoted in *Woodbury Reports Archives* (August 1995)

If you cannot communicate your many worthwhile achievements, no one will ever know what you have done. **Jac Fitz-Enz**. *How to Measure Human Resources Management* (1995)

They gave me star treatment when I was making a lot of money. But I was just as good when I was poor. **Bob Marley**. Quoted in *True Confessions* (Jon Winokar, 1992)

It goes back to all of us wanting to be in Hollywood. We're all dying to win an Oscar. **Jerry Della Femina**. *Wall Street Journal* (1987)

There is no end to what you can accomplish if you don't care who gets the credit. **Florence Luscomb**. Quoted in *Moving the Mountain* (E. Cantorow, 1980)

The world is divided into people who do things and people who get the credit. Try, if you can, to belong to the first class. There's far less competition. **Dwight Morrow**. Written in a letter to his son. Quoted in *Dwight Morrow* (Harold Nicolson, 1935)

Watch how a man takes praise and there you have the measure of him. **Thomas Burke**. *T. P.'s Weekly* (June 8, 1928)

We find it easy to believe that praise is sincere: why should anyone lie in telling us the truth? **Jean Rostand**. *De la vanité* (1925)

People ask you for criticism but they only want praise. **W. Somerset Maugham**. *Of Human Bondage* (1915)

Sandwich every bit of criticism between two layers of praise. **Mary Kay Ash**. Attributed

Principles

Ideals may tell us something important about what we would like to be. But compromises tell us who we are. **Avishai Margalit**. *On Compromise and Rotten Compromises* (2010)

I'm a man of principle, I like to know whether I'm lying to save the skin of a tosser or a moron. **Armando Iannucci**. *The Thick of It* (2005)

Strong men don't compromise, it is said, and principles should never be compromised. I shall argue that strong men, conversely, know when to compromise and that all principles can be compromised to serve a greater principle. **Charles Handy**. *The Age of Paradox* (1994)

Occasionally, a man must rise above principles. **Warren Buffett**. Annual report (1991)

It is easier to fight for one's principles than to live up to them. **Alfred Adler**. Quoted in *Alfred Adler* (Phyllis Bottome, 1939)

You can't learn too soon that the most useful thing about a principle is that it can always be sacrificed to expediency. **W. Somerset Maugham**. *The Circle* (1921)

The Great Principles on which we will build this Business are as everlasting as the Pyramids. **Gordon Selfridge**. Preliminary announcement, opening of Selfridge's store, London (1909)

Principles always become a matter of vehement discussion when practice is at an ebb. **George Gissing**. *Private Papers of Henry Ryecroft* (1903)

Priorities

I typically work 70–80 hours a week. I'm also married, raising two children, I work out 3–4 times per week and I make sure that I spend no less than 20 days a year on the ski slopes. I'm also on the boards of three not-for-profit organizations in healthcare, arts, and education, and I still have dinner with my parents every Sunday night. **Alison Mass**. Speech, Stern School of Business, New York University (May 13, 2010)

If the history of Homo sapiens so far were represented as a single day, an average human lifespan would represent a little over half a second ... So what you must do—being an intelligent, thinking creature—is make a very careful, well-informed judgement about how best you can spend your one and only half-second. You analyse yourself and your abilities; you match them to the world, its ways and possibilities, and you make a solemn decision to do what would most contribute to the well-being of the world and of yourself. Except you've got a deadline, Friday at noon. And your lover coming round on Tuesday. And there's football on. This "busy" thing isn't a commitment, it's an evasion. **Sebastian Faulks**. *Engleby* (2007)

Ownership is not the most important thing. IT IS THE ONLY THING THAT COUNTS. **Felix Dennis**. *How to Get Rich* (2006)

It's hard enough to make money that you can't do it by accident. Unless it's your first priority, it's unlikely to happen at all. **Paul Graham**. *Why Smart People Have Bad Ideas* (2005)

My #1 job here at Apple is to make sure that the top 100 people are A + players. And everything else will take care of itself. If the top 50 people are right, it just cascades down throughout the whole organization. **Steve Jobs**. Quoted in "Steve's Two Jobs," *Time* (Michael Krantz, October 18, 1999)

Having a sick child has put life into perspective for me. I would not care if I had no money and no material possessions if I could have Georgina's health. **Nicola Horlick**. Referring to the fact that her eldest child, Georgina, has leukemia. *Can You Have It All?* (1997)

Managing intellectual assets has become the single most important task of business. **Thomas A. Stewart**. *Intellectual Capital* (1997)

Survive first and make money afterwards. **George Soros**. *Soros on Soros* (1995)

First things first, second things never. **Shirley Conran**. *Superwoman* (1975)

Problems and Obstacles

Going for a walk, letting our minds wander and having a really good rummage around in our mind is a very good problem-solving technique. Don't go out with blinkers on. Walk around and see what captures your attention. It's a great way to help us bust out of our usual mindset. **Mark Millard**. Quoted in the *Independent (London)* (October 26, 2010)

I believe that the only important structural obstacles to world prosperity are the obsolete doctrines that clutter the minds of men. **Paul R. Krugman**. *The Return of Depression Economics and the Crisis of 2008* (2008)

Obstacles are things a person sees when he takes his eyes off his goal. **E. Joseph Cossman**. Quoted in *How to Turn Your Million-Dollar Idea into a Reality* (Pete Williams, 2007)

There is a time in the life of every problem when it is big enough you can see it, but small enough you can still solve it. **Mike Leavitt**. Speech (May 16, 2005)

If you eat a frog first thing in the morning, the rest of your day will be wonderful. **Mark Twain**. A "frog" being any unpleasant or difficult task that you would rather put off. Quoted in *Eat That Frog* (Brian Tracy, 2002)

The worst possible thing ... was to lie dead in the water with any problem. Solve it, solve it quickly ... If you solved it wrong, it would come back and slap you in the face, and then you could solve it right. **Thomas J. Watson, Jr**. Quoted in "The Businessmen of the Century," *Fortune* (November 22, 1999)

Problems are the price of progress. Don't bring me anything but trouble. Good news weakens me. **Charles Franklin Kettering**. Quoted in *Strategy + Business* (1997)

Satisfactory under-performance is a far greater problem than a crisis. **Christopher Bartlett**. *The Individualised Corporation* (cowritten with Sumantra Ghoshal, 1997)

The greatest risk lies in not knowing what you don't know. In a fast changing marketplace such as the Internet, this trap seems to be so open and so wide. **William (Walid) Mougayar**. Referring to the challenge to managers of traditional industries of the new economy. *Opening Digital Markets* (1997), Introduction to 2nd edition

We live in an information economy. The problem is that information's usually impossible to get, at least in the right place, at the right time. **Steve Jobs**. Interview, "The Next Insanely Great Thing," *Wired* (February 1996)

Problems can only be solved by the people who have them. You have to try and coax them and love them into seeing ways in which they can help themselves. **Sir John Harvey-Jones**. On his approach as a Mr Fix-It for troubled businesses. *Independent on Sunday (London)* (March 11, 1990)

I need problems. A good problem makes me come alive. **Tiny Rowland**. *Sunday Times (London)* (March 4, 1990)

My door is always open—bring me your problems. This is guaranteed to turn on every whiner, lackey, and neurotic on the property. **Robert F. Six**. Quoted in *Money Talks* (Robert W. Kent, ed, 1986)

Work only on problems that are manifestly important and seem to be nearly impossible to solve. That way you will have a natural market for your product and no competition. **Edwin Land**. *Physics Today* (January 1982)

It is characteristic of all deep human problems that they are not to be approached without some humor and some bewilderment. **Freeman Dyson**. *Disturbing the Universe* (1979)

One must think until it hurts. One must worry a problem in one's mind until it seems there cannot be another aspect of it that hasn't been considered. **Roy Herbert, Lord Thomson**. *After I Was Sixty* (1975)

I have yet to see any problem, however complicated, which, when you looked at it in the right way, did not become still more complicated. **Poul Anderson**. *New Scientist* (September 25, 1969)

Problems are only opportunities in work clothes. **Henry J. Kaiser**. Quoted in obituary, *New York Times* (August 24, 1967)

I suppose it is tempting, if the only tool you have is a hammer, to treat everything as if it were a nail. **Abraham Maslow**. *The Psychology of Science: A Reconnaissance* (1966)

Every solution of a problem raises new unsolved problems. **Sir Karl Raimund Popper**. *Conjectures and Refutations* (1963)

It isn't that they can't see the solution. It is that they can't see the problem. **G. K. Chesterton**. *The Scandal of Father Brown* (1935)

That is the trouble with prosperity—it hides the defects of a business. **Harvey Firestone**. *Men and Rubber* (cowritten with Samuel Crowther, 1926)

Success is to be measured not so much by the position that one has reached in life as by the obstacles which one has overcome while trying to succeed. **Booker T. Washington**. *Up from Slavery* (1901)

Any problem can be solved using the materials in the room. **Edwin Land**. Attributed

Beware of the danger signals that flag problems: silence, secretiveness, or sudden outburst. **Sylvia Porter**. Attributed

Procrastination

The only time I ever iron the sheets or make meringues is when there is an … urgent deadline in the offing. **Angela Carter**. Quoted in *A Card from Angela Carter* (Susannah Clapp, 2012)

I don't think of it as procrastination. I think of it as allowing my work to accumulate urgency. **Maud Newton**. *Twitter (maudnewton)* (December 13, 2011)

Resisting a task is usually a sign that it's meaningful—which is why it's awakening your fears and stimulating procrastination. You could adopt "Do whatever you're resisting the most" as a philosophy of life. **Oliver Burkeman**. *Help! How To Become Slightly Happier and Get a Bit More Done* (2011)

If you have to eat a frog, don't look at it for too long. **Mark Twain**. Quoted in *Eat That Frog* (Brian Tracy, 2002)

Hamlet had it wrong: he who hesitates is halfway home. **Peter Bernstein**. *Against the Gods: The Remarkable Story of Risk* (1998)

She felt weary and careworn, in the way one often does before the big job of work is tackled; that sense of premature or projected exhaustion that is the breeding-ground of all procrastination. **William Boyd**. *Brazzaville Beach* (1990)

A wrong decision isn't forever; it can always be reversed. The losses from a delayed decision *are* forever; they can never be retrieved. **J. K. Galbraith**. *A Life in Our Times* (1981)

Most executives have learned that what one postpones, one actually abandons … timing is a most important element in the success of any effort. To do five years later what would have been smart to do five years earlier, is almost a sure recipe for frustration and failure. **Peter F. Drucker**. *The Effective Executive* (1967), ch. 5

procrastination is the art of keeping up with yesterday **Don Marquis**. *certain maxims of archie* (1927)

Make me a beautiful word for doing things tomorrow; for that surely is a great and blessed invention. **George Bernard Shaw**. *Back to Methuselah* (1921)

There is no more miserable human being than the one in whom nothing is habitual but indecision. **William James**. *The Principles of Psychology* (1890), ch. 10

No task is a long one but the task on which one dare not start. It becomes a nightmare. **Charles Baudelaire**. *My Heart Laid Bare* (1869)

Procrastination is the thief of time. **Edward Young**. *The Complaint, or Night Thoughts on Life, Death, and Immortality* (1742–1745)

Business neglected is business lost. **Daniel Defoe**. *The Complete English Tradesman* (1726), vol. 1

Defer no time; delays have dangerous ends. **William Shakespeare**. *Henry VI, Part One* (1592), Act 3, Scene 3, l. 16

While we're talking, envious time is fleeing: seize the day, put no trust in the future. **Horace**. *Odes* (24–23 BC), bk. 1, no. 11, l. 7

The key to productivity is to rotate your avoidance techniques. **Shannon Wheeler**. *Too Much Coffee Man* comic strip

If I had eight hours to chop down a tree, I'd spend six sharpening the axe. **Abraham Lincoln**. Attributed

Tomorrow is often the busiest day of the week. **Anonymous**. Spanish proverb

Productivity

My goal is no longer to get more done, but rather to have less to do. **Francine Jay**. *Miss Minimalist: Inspiration to Downsize, Declutter, and Simplify* (2011)

Sometimes the biggest gain in productive energy will come from cleaning the cobwebs, dealing with old business, and clearing the desks—cutting loose debris that's impeding forward motion. **David Allen**. *Ready for Anything: 52 Productivity Principles for Getting Things Done* (2004)

Thanks to him, we have increased the productivity of manual work 3% to 4% compounded—which is 50-fold—and on that achievement rests all the prosperity of the modern world. **Peter F. Drucker**. Referring to Frederick W. Taylor, who inspired Henry Ford's mass-production revolution. Quoted in "The Businessman of the Century," *Fortune* (November 22, 1999)

The best balance of morale for employee productivity can be described this way: happy, but with low self-esteem. **Scott Adams**. *The Dilbert Principle* (1996)

I've never seen a job being done by a five-hundred person engineering team that couldn't be done better by fifty people. **C. Gordon Bell**. *Spectrum* (February 1989)

In an industrial society which confuses work and productivity, the necessity of producing has always been an enemy of the desire to create. **Raoul Vaneigem**. *The Revolution of Everyday Life* (1967)

Management productivity is a more appropriate term than labor productivity. Improved productivity means less human sweat, not more. **Henry Ford II**. Speech, *US News & World Report* (March 1959)

Production not being the sole end of human existence, the term unproductive does not necessarily imply any stigma. **John Stuart Mill**. *Principles of Political Economy* (1848)

When properly administered, vacations do not diminish productivity: for every week you're away and get nothing done, there's another when your boss is away and you get twice as much done. **Daniel B. Luten**. Attributed

No matter how great the talent or effort, some things just take time: you can't produce a baby in one month by getting nine women pregnant. **Warren Buffett**. Attributed

Products

However bad things get, people still have sex and they still walk. **Garry Watts**. Interview, *Independent (London)* (April 15, 2010)

You go to bed feeling very comfortable just thinking about two and a half billion males with hair growing while you sleep. No one at Gillette has trouble sleeping. **Warren Buffett**. Quoted in *Warren Buffett Speaks* (Janet Lowe, 2007)

Anybody can cut prices, but it takes brains to produce a better article. **Philip D. Armour**. Quoted in *The 101 Greatest Business Principles of All Time* (Leslie Pockell, 2004)

My theory is that good furniture could be priced so that the man with a flat wallet could be attracted to it. **Ingvar Kamprad**. *Forbes* (August 2000)

Both Apple and Pixar ... Their product is pure intellectual property. Bits on a disk. **Steve Jobs**. Quoted in "Steve's Two Jobs," *Time* (Michael Krantz, October 18, 1999)

We try never to forget that medicine is for the people. It is not for the profits. The profits follow, and if we have remembered that, they have never failed to appear. **George Merck**. Quoted in *Built to Last: Successful Habits of Visionary Companies* (Jim Collins, 1994)

A successful product merely gives us a head start in the race. **Sir John Harvey-Jones**. *Managing to Survive* (1993)

What makes this business difficult is that grown ups have to solve children's problems. **Horst Brandstätter**. Quoted in *Liberation Management* (Tom Peters, 1992)

All products must be seen as experiments. **David Lodge**. *Relationship Marketing* (1991)

If you can't smell it, you can't sell it. **Estée Lauder**. Interview (1976)

Every company should work hard to obsolete its own product line before its competitors do. **Philip Kotler**. *Marketing Management* (1967)

Twenty four out of twenty five new products never get out of test markets. **David Ogilvy**. *Confessions of an Advertising Man* (1963)

Junk is the ideal product—the ultimate merchandise. No sales talk necessary. The client will crawl through a sewer and beg to buy. **William S. Burroughs**. *The Naked Lunch* (1959)

No other man-made device since the shields and lances of ancient knights fulfills a man's ego like an automobile. **William, Lord Rootes**. Speech (1958)

I have no use for a motor car which has more spark plugs than a cow has teats. **Henry Ford**. *My Life and Work* (cowritten with Samuel Crowther, 1922)

Profits

The purpose of the market system ... is not to maximise profits but to produce goods and services that satisfy human needs and wants. Profits are a tool for achieving those objectives, a by-product of fulfilling human needs. If you view profits as the main objective, you will ultimately fail to create products and services that satisfy people, and so, because of the very logic of the market system, you will eventually lose your profits. **Anatole Kaletsky**. Interviewed in *FiveBooks* (June 2012)

We shall eliminate any undue profit-seeking. **Sony**. Founding statement. Quoted in *Obliquity: Why Our Goals Are Best Achieved Indirectly* (John Kay, 2010)

Profit is like health, necessary but not the reason why we live. **Anonymous**. Statement by the London-based St Luke's Advertising Agency. *Management Today* (April 1999)

My argument is: keep the bloody bottom line at the bottom. That's where it should be. **Dame Anita Roddick**. Quoted in *The Adventure Capitalists* (Jeff Grout and Lynne Curry, 1998)

Company directors always have to prove that things are going better. They are judged like politicians, only worse, because elections are held every three months. **André Leysen**. Quoted in *Euromanagement* (H. Bloom, R. Claori, and P. de Woot, 1998)

In the foundation and development of a successful enterprise there must be a single-minded pursuit of financial profit. **C. Northcote Parkinson**. Quoted in *Famous Financial Fiascoes* (J. Train, 1995)

Profit has to be a means to other ends rather than an end in itself. **Charles Handy**. *The Empty Raincoat: Making Sense of the Future* (1994)

If there is excitement in their lives, it is contained in the figures on the profit and loss sheet. What an indictment. **Dame Anita Roddick**. Referring to companies run by accountants. *Body and Soul* (cowritten with Russell Miller, 1991)

Business is many things, the least of which is the balance sheet. It is a fluid, ever changing, living thing, sometimes building to great peaks, sometimes falling to crumbled lumps. **Harold S. Geneen**. *Managing* (cowritten with Alvin Moscow, 1984)

Short-term can be terminal. **Mark McCormack**. Referring to error of commitment to short-term profitability. *What They Don't Teach You at Harvard Business School* (1984)

The bottom line is in heaven. **Edwin Land**. Shareholder meeting (1977)

Civilization and profits go hand in hand. **Calvin Coolidge**. Speech (November 1920)

I don't want to do business with those who don't make a profit, because they can't give the best service. **Lee Bristol**. Attributed

Where profit is, loss is hidden nearby. **Anonymous**. Japanese proverb

Progress

See everything. Overlook a great deal. Improve a little. **Pope John XXIII**. Quoted in *The Power of IT* (Jean De Sutter, 2004)

Much work remains to be done before we can announce our total failure to make any progress. **E. L. Kersten**. *The Art of Demotivation* (2003)

How we feel about the evolving future tells us who we are as individuals and as a civilization: Do we search for stasis—a regulated, engineered world? Or do we embrace dynamism—a world of constant creation, discovery, and competition? **Virginia Postrel**. *The Future and Its Enemies: The Growing Conflict over Creativity, Enterprise, and Progress* (1998)

You can only stumble if you're moving. **Roberto Goizueta**. *Fortune* (May 1995)

If economic progress means that we become anonymous cogs in some great machine, then progress is an empty promise. **Charles Handy**. *The Empty Raincoat: Making Sense of the Future* (1994)

Progress is mostly the product of rogues. **Tom Peters**. *Liberation Management* (1992)

It's the same each time with progress. First they ignore you, then they say you're mad, then dangerous, then there's a pause and you can't find anyone who disagrees with you. **Tony Benn**. Quoted in the *Observer (London)* (October 6, 1991)

To go fast, row slowly. **Brendan Kennelly**. *The Power of Positive Thinking* (1972)

In vulgar usage, progress has come to mean limitless movement in space and time, accompanied, necessarily, by an equally limitless command of energy: culminating in limitless destruction. **Lewis Mumford**. *The Pentagon of Power* (1970)

We have stopped believing in progress. What progress that is! **Jorge Luis Borges**. *Borges et Borges* (1969)

The test of our progress is not whether we add more to the abundance of those who have much; it is whether we provide enough for those who have too little. **Franklin D. Roosevelt**. Second presidential inaugural address (January 20, 1937)

All progress is based upon a universal innate desire on the part of every organism to live beyond its income. **Samuel Butler**. "Life," *Notebooks* (H. Festing-Jones, ed, 1912)

The reasonable man adapts himself to the world; the unreasonable one persists in trying to adapt the world to himself. Therefore all progress depends on the unreasonable man. **George Bernard Shaw**. "Reason," *Maxims for Revolutionists* (1905)

Progress, far from consisting in change, depends on retentiveness. Those who cannot remember the past are condemned to repeat it. **George Santayana**. *The Life of Reason* (1905)

Progress, therefore, is not an accident but a necessity ... a part of nature. **Herbert Spencer**. *Social Statics* (1851), pt. 1, ch. 2

Society never advances. It recedes as fast on one side as it gains on the other. Society acquires new arts, and loses old instincts. **Ralph Waldo Emerson**. "Self-Reliance," *Essays: First Series* (1841)

What we call progress is the exchange of one nuisance for another nuisance. **Havelock Ellis**. Attributed

Publicity

I had worked hard for 30 years, making millions of pounds for shareholders and creating thousands of jobs for a company I loved, and I suddenly had it all taken away from me. Not for doing anything criminal. I hadn't embezzled. I hadn't lied. All I had done was say a sherry decanter was crap. **Gerald Ratner**. *Gerald Ratner: The Rise and Fall and Rise Again* (2007)

PR cannot overcome things that shouldn't have been done. **Harold Burson**. *USA Today* (June 7, 1993)

With publicity comes humiliation. **Tama Janowitz**. Quoted in the *International Herald Tribune (Paris)* (September 8, 1992)

You can't shame or humiliate modern celebrities. What used to be called shame and humiliation is now called publicity. **P. J. O'Rourke**. *Give War a Chance* (1992)

The worst tragedy that could have befallen me was my success. I knew right away that I was through, cast out. **Jonas Salk**. Referring to other scientists' reactions to publicity surrounding his discovery of a polio vaccine. Interview (1992)

We must try to find ways to starve the terrorist and the hijacker of the oxygen of publicity on which they depend. **Margaret, Baroness Thatcher**. Speech (July 1985)

There's no such thing as bad publicity except your own obituary. **Brendan Behan**. Quoted in *My Brother Brendan* (Dominic Behan, 1965)

Some are born great, some achieve greatness, and some hire public relations officers. **Daniel J. Boorstin**. *The Image* (1961)

This famous store needs no name on the door. **Gordon Selfridge**. Referring to the fact that Selfridge removed the name from his famous London store in 1925. Quoted in *No Name on the Door* (A. H. Williams, 1957)

The price of justice is eternal publicity. **Arnold Bennett**. *The Title* (1918)

Quality

Bad ideas are so widespread because those who have good content don't take seriously the task of charming others into trusting in it. **Alain de Botton**. *Twitter (alaindebotton)* (May 23, 2012)

We have learned to live in a world of mistakes and defective products as if they were necessary to life. It is time to adapt to a new philosophy in America. **W. Edwards Deming**. *Out of the Crisis* (1992)

Don't just make it and try to sell it. But redesign it and then bring the process under control with ever-increasing quality. **W. Edwards Deming**. *Out of the Crisis* (1992)

We also do cut-glass sherry decanters complete with six glasses on a silver-plated tray that your butler can serve you drinks on, all for £4.95. People say, "How can you sell this for such a low price?" I say, because it's total crap. **Gerald Ratner**. Adverse publicity for Ratner's remarks effectively destroyed his company. Speech, Institute of Directors (April 23, 1991)

Quality control was treated as a fad here, but it's been part of the Japanese business philosophy for decades. That's why they laugh at us. **Peter Senge**. *The Fifth Discipline: The Art and Practice of the Learning Organization* (1990)

The funny thing is better TV shows don't cost that much more than lousy TV shows. **Warren Buffett**. *Channels* (November 1986)

The subtle accumulation of nuances, a hundred things done a little better. **Henry Kissinger**. Quoted in *In Search of Excellence* (Tom Peters and Robert H. Waterman, 1982)

Quality has to be caused, not controlled. **Philip B. Crosby**. *Quality Is Free* (1979)

Quality is not a thing. It is an event. **Robert M. Pirsig**. *Zen and the Art of Motorcycle Maintenance* (1974)

Standards are always out of date. That's what makes them standards. **Alan Bennett**. *Forty Years On* (1969)

More will mean worse. **Sir Kingsley Amis**. *Encounter* (July 1960)

Reputation

Reputation matters so much only because people so seldom think for themselves. **Alain de Botton**. *Twitter (alaindebotton)* (May 23, 2012)

It takes 20 years to build a reputation, and five minutes to ruin it. If you think about that, you'll do things differently. **Warren Buffett**. Quoted in the *Independent (London)* (October 28, 2009)

Would you rather be the world's greatest lover, but have everyone think you're the world's worst lover? Or would you rather be the world's worst lover but have everyone think you're the world's greatest lover? Now, that's an interesting question. **Warren Buffett**. Quoted in *The Snowball: Warren Buffett and the Business of Life* (Alice Schroeder, 2008)

You can't build a reputation on what you are going to do. **Henry Ford**. Quoted in *Woodbury Reports Archives* (December 1994)

In business a reputation for keeping absolutely to the letter and spirit of an agreement, even when it is unfavorable, is the most precious of assets, although it is not entered in the balance sheet. **Viscount Chandos (Oliver Lyttelton)**. *Memoirs of Lord Chandos: An Unexpected View from the Summit* (1963)

It took me fifteen years to discover that I had no talent for writing, but I couldn't give it up because by that time I was too famous. **Robert Benchley**. Quoted in *Robert Benchley* (Nathaniel Benchley, 1955)

The world is not unkind, and reprobates are worse than their reputations. **Logan Pearsall Smith**. *Afterthoughts* (1931)

Reputation, reputation, reputation—O, I ha' lost my reputation, I ha' lost the immortal part of myself, and what remains is bestial! **William Shakespeare**. *Othello* (1602–04), Act 2, Scene 3, ll. 256–258

Research

Not many appreciate the ultimate power and potential usefulness of basic knowledge accumulated by obscure, unseen investigators who, in a lifetime of intensive study, may never see any practical use for their findings but who go on seeking answers to the unknown without thought of financial or practical gain. **Eugenie Clark**. Quoted in *Research: What, Why and How?* (P. M. Kasi, 2009)

I have an simple algorithm which is, where ever you see paid researchers instead of grad students, that's not where you want to be doing research. **Larry Page**. Lecture to the American Association for the Advancement of Science (February 16, 2007)

Some people use research like a drunkard uses a lamppost: for support not illumination. **David Ogilvy**. Ogilvy's advocacy of the importance of sound research reflected the experience gained during his early career selling George Gallup's innovative sampling techniques to Hollywood studios. Quoted in "Anatomies of Desire: David Ogilvy," BBC Radio 4 (September 4, 2000)

It's really hard to design products by focus groups. A lot of times, people don't know what they want until you show it to them. **Steve Jobs**. Quoted in *BusinessWeek* (May 25, 1998)

The close relationships we form between researchers and product groups have already shown we can move the great ideas as they come along, without a schedule, into the products. **Bill Gates**. *Net News* (August 10, 1997)

My job is to help people see what I see. If it's of value, fine. And, if it's not of value, then at least I've done what I can do. **Jonas Salk**. Referring to his development of the Salk vaccine for polio. Interview (1992)

We don't believe in market research for a new product unknown to the public. So we never do any. **Akio Morita**. Referring to his rejection of in-house engineers' concerns regarding lack of research into his idea for the Sony Walkman. *Made in Japan* (1986)

Motto for a research laboratory: what we work on today, others will first think of tomorrow. **Alan Jay Perlis**. *Epigrams in Programming* (1985)

The trouble with research is that it tells you what people were thinking about yesterday, not tomorrow. It's like driving a car using a rearview mirror. **Bernard Loomis**. *International Herald Tribune (Paris)* (1985)

The way to do research is to attack the facts at the point of greatest astonishment. **Celia Green**. *The Decline and Fall of Science* (1977)

Basic research is what I am doing when I don't know what I am doing. **Wernher von Braun**. Quoted in *A Random Walk in Science* (R. L. Weber, 1973)

When action grows unprofitable, gather information; when information grows unprofitable, sleep. **Ursula K. Le Guin**. *The Left Hand of Darkness* (1969)

Research! A mere excuse for idleness; it has never achieved, and will never achieve any results of the slightest value. **Benjamin Jowett**. Quoted in *Unforgotten Years* (Logan Pearsall Smith, 1939)

I keep six honest serving men (They taught me all I know) Their names are What and Why and When And How and Where and Who. **Rudyard Kipling**. *Just So Stories* (1902)

Responsibility

Banks aren't neutral observers, they're … the people who caused the mess. It's like someone who's wet themselves in a public building insisting they choose which mop the librarian fetches to clear up the puddle. **Mark Steel**. *Independent (London)* (December 7, 2011)

I take responsibility. It wasn't the board. It wasn't my colleagues at Time Warner. It wasn't the bankers or the lawyers … I presided over the worst deal of the century, apparently, and it is time for those involved in companies to stand up and say, "You know what, I am solely responsible for it. I was the CEO, I was in charge." **Jerry Levin**. On Time Warner's disastrous merger with AOL in 2000. Interview on CNBC TV (January 5, 2010)

Human beings were held accountable long before there were corporate bureaucracies. If the knight didn't deliver, the king cut off his head. **Alvin Toffler**. "Breaking with Bureaucracy," *Across the Board* (February 1991)

We are responsible for actions performed in response to circumstances for which we are not responsible. **Allan Massie**. "Etienne," *A Question of Loyalties* (1989), pt. 3, ch. 22

Don't have good ideas if you aren't willing to be responsible for them. **Alan Jay Perlis**. *Epigrams in Programming* (1985)

Responsibility is what awaits outside the Eden of Creativity. **Nadine Gordimer**. "Lecture, University of Michigan," *The Tanner Lectures on Human Values* (Sterling M. McMurrin, ed, 1985)

The buck stops here. **Harry S. Truman**. Sign on his desk while president. Quoted in

Presidential Anecdotes (Paul F. Boiler, 1981)

I cannot believe that the purpose of life is to be "happy." I think the purpose of life is to be useful, to be responsible, to be honorable, to be compassionate. It is, above all, to matter: to count, to stand for something, to have made some difference, that you lived at all. **Leo C. Rosten**. *Passions and Prejudices* (1978)

The salvation of mankind lies only in making everything the concern of all. **Aleksander Solzhenitsyn**. Nobel lecture (1970)

There are plenty of recommendations on how to get out of trouble cheaply and fast. Most of them come down to the same thing. Deny your responsibility. **Lyndon B. Johnson**. Speech (September 1967)

People are responsible for their opinions, but Providence is responsible for their morals. **William Butler Yeats**. Quoted in *Edward Marsh, Patron of the Arts* (Christopher Hassall, 1959), ch. 6

Perhaps it is better to be irresponsible and right than to be responsible and wrong. **Sir Winston Churchill**. Party political broadcast, London (August 26, 1950)

I don't know whether you fellows ever had a load of hay fall on you, but when they told me yesterday what had happened, I felt like the moon, the stars, and all the planets had fallen on me. **Harry S. Truman**. Said on succeeding Franklin D. Roosevelt as president. Attributed (April 1944)

Responsibility is the great developer of men. **Mary Parker Follett**. *Dynamic Administration* (1941)

It is impossible to get the measure of what an individual can accomplish unless the responsibility is given him. **Alfred P. Sloan**. "Modern Ideas of the Big Business World," *Work* (October 1926)

Whatever you blame, that you have done yourself. **Georg Groddeck**. *The Book of the It* (1923), Letter 14

Those who enjoy responsibility usually get it; those who merely like exercising authority usually lose it. **Malcolm S. Forbes**. Attributed

Risk Taking

Any strategy that involves crossing a valley—accepting short-term losses to reach a higher hill in the distance—will soon be brought to a halt by the demands of a system that celebrates short-term gains and tolerates stagnation, but condemns anything else as failure. In short, a world where big stuff can never get done. **Neal Stephenson**. *World Policy Journal* (Fall 2011)

There is a simple way of avoiding excess risk-taking by the managers of our financial institutions. It is to make it a crime ... had a crime for reckless management of a financial institution been on the books, Northern Rock and RBS would not have blown up. **Paul Collier**. *Independent (London)* (December 18, 2009)

If we listened to our intellect, we'd never have a love affair. We'd never have a friendship. We'd never go into business. Well, that's nonsense. You've got to jump off cliffs all the time and build your wings on the way down. **Ray Bradbury**. Quoted in *Business Wit and Wisdom* (Richard S. Zera, 2005)

The more you seek security, the less of it you have. But the more you seek opportunity, the more likely it is that you will achieve the security that you desire. **Brian Tracy**. *Goals!: How to Get Everything You Want Faster Than You Ever Thought Possible* (2004)

People who don't take risks generally make about two big mistakes a year. People who do take risks generally make about two big mistakes a year. **Peter F. Drucker**. Quoted in *Don't Play in the Street* (George Thompson, 2003)

We are pioneers and the history of pioneers is not that good. **Jeff Bezos**. *Sunday Telegraph (London)* (July 2000)

You don't go to a poker table with no money in your pocket. **Barbara, Lady Judge**. *Management Today* (October 1999)

Risk comes from not knowing what you are doing. **Warren Buffett**. Quoted in *Treasury of Investment Wisdom* (Bernice Cohen, 1999)

A lot of people criticize Formula 1 as an unnecessary risk. But what would life be like if we only did what is necessary? **Niki Lauda**. Quoted in *Treasury of Investment Wisdom* (Bernice Cohen, 1999)

To be a leader in this new economy, you have to love risk—which means patterning your life on the heroic, not on the strategic. Acting boldly is better than acting knowingly. **Harriet Rubin**. "How Will You Fail?" *Fast Company* (1999)

Risk is what an entrepreneur eats for breakfast. It's what she slips into bed with at night. If you have no appetite for this stuff, or no ability to digest it, then get out of the game right now. **Heather Robertson**. *Taking Care of Business* (1997)

You want a valve that doesn't leak and you try everything possible to develop one. But the real world provides you with a leaky valve. You have to determine how much leakiness you can tolerate. **Arthur Rudolph**. Quoted in the *New York Times* (January 3, 1996)

By definition, risk-takers often fail. So do morons. In practice it's difficult to sort them out. **Scott Adams**. *The Dilbert Principle* (1996)

If you only take small risks, you are only entitled to a small life. **Robin S. Sharma**. *MegaLiving!: 30 Days to a Perfect Life* (1995)

Unless you're running scared all the time, you're gone. **Michael C. Lynch**. Quoted in *Playboy* (1994)

The easy way out usually leads back in. **Peter Senge**. *The Fifth Discipline: The Art and Practice of the Learning Organization* (1990)

How many millionaires do you know who have become wealthy by investing in savings accounts? I rest my case. **Robert G. Allen**. *Creating Wealth* (1986)

There are one hundred men seeking security to one able man who is willing to risk his fortune. **J. Paul Getty**. Quoted in *The Great Getty* (Robert Lenzner, 1985)

If you are scared to go to the brink you are lost. **John Foster Dulles**. *Life* (January 16, 1956)

A desperate disease requires a dangerous remedy. **Guy Fawkes**. Referring to the attempted destruction of Parliament. Speech (November 1605)

Eagles may soar but weasels don't get sucked into jet engines. **Anonymous**. On the dangers of ambition

Science

Perhaps the greatest pleasure in science comes from theories that derive the solution to some deep puzzle from a small set of simple principles in a surprising way. **John Brockman**. *This Explains Everything: Deep, Beautiful, and Elegant Theories of How the World Works* (2012)

We live in a society exquisitely dependent on science and technology, in which hardly anyone knows anything about science and technology. **Carl Sagan**. *The Sceptical Inquirer* (1990)

It is the tension between the scientist's laws and his own attempted breaking of them that powers the engines of science and makes it forge ahead. **W. V. O. Quine**. *Quiddities* (1987)

For a successful technology, reality must take precedence over public relations, for Nature cannot be fooled. **Richard P. Feynman**. Report into the crash of the space shuttle Challenger (1986)

The essence of science; ask an impertinent question, and you are on the way to a pertinent answer. **Jacob Bronowski**. *The Ascent of Man* (1973)

It is a good exercise for a research scientist to discard a pet hypothesis every day before breakfast. **Konrad Lorenz**. *On Aggression* (1966)

The aim of science is not to open the door to infinite wisdom, but to set a limit to infinite error. **Bertolt Brecht**. *The Life of Galileo* (1939)

In science, the credit goes to the man who convinces the world, not to the man to whom the idea first occurs. **Francis Darwin**. *Eugenics Review* (April 1914)

There are no such things as applied sciences, only applications of science. **Louis Pasteur**. Address (September 1872)

Science is a method to keep yourself from kidding yourself. **Edwin Land**. Attributed

Selling

What's the point in selling things that people need? There's no future in that: People Who Need buy less than People Who Want. One market has a glass ceiling, the other elastic potential. And in order to maintain Want, one has to aggressively patrol one's brand identity. **Harriet Walker**. *Independent (London)* (August 18, 2011)

You have to love the products if you are going to sell them. **Barbara, Lady Judge**. *Management Today* (October 1999)

If you don't listen, you don't sell anything. **Caroline Marland**. *Management Today* (September 1999)

We sell sex. It is never going to go out of style. **Bob Guccione**. *Wall Street Journal* (1996)

Our sales representatives are like race car drivers. They can't succeed without incredible co-operation from the support team back at HQ. **Doug Nelson**. "The Mavericks," *Fortune* (June 1995)

The person who agrees with everything you say either isn't paying attention or else plans to sell you something. **Sam Ewing**. Quoted in *Reader's Digest* (1989)

When you stop talking, you've lost your customer. When you turn your back, you've lost her. **Estée Lauder**. "As Gorgeous As It Gets," *New Yorker* (Kennedy Fraser, 1986)

If you don't sell, it's not the product that's wrong, it's you. **Estée Lauder**. "As Gorgeous As It Gets," *New Yorker* (Kennedy Fraser, 1986)

Inequality of knowledge is the key to a sale. **Deil O. Gustafson**. *Newsweek* (1974)

He's a man way out there in the blue, riding on a smile and a shoestring. **Arthur Miller**. *Death of a Salesman* (1949)

Real salesmen stick until the buyer has used up his last No. **William Wrigley, Jr.** "The Lowdown on Salesmanship," *American Magazine* (Neil M. Clark, October 1929)

The art of salesmanship can be stated in four words: Believing something and convincing others. **William Wrigley, Jr.** "The Lowdown on Salesmanship," *American Magazine* (Neil M. Clark, October 1929)

To found a great empire for the sole purpose of raising up a people of customers may at first sight appear a project fit only for a nation of shopkeepers. **Adam Smith**. *An Inquiry into the Nature and Causes of the Wealth of Nations* (1776)

I have heard of a man who had a mind to sell his house, and therefore carried a piece of brick in his pocket, which he showed as a pattern to encourage purchasers. **Jonathan Swift**. *The Drapier's Letters* (1724)

In selling as in medicine, prescription before diagnosis is malpractice. **Tony Allesandra**. Attributed

There's a sucker born every minute. **P. T. Barnum**. Attributed

Service

Zingerman's 3 Steps to Great Service: 1. Figure out what the customer wants. 2. Get it for them: accurately, politely, and enthusiastically. 3. Go the extra mile. **Ari Weinzweig**. *Zingerman's Guide to Giving Great Service* (2004)

I would advise young companies, particularly the small dot.com companies, to pay close attention to their service levels. **Lillian Vernon**. "Mentor FAQs," *Inc.* (2000)

The decision to do that extra bit must be embedded in the company's culture. **Sir Tom Farmer**. *Management Today* (July 1999)

That's what I say about restaurants—the back part is manufacturing, the front part is retailing, the theatre is what holds the whole thing together. **Sir Terence Conran**. Quoted in *The Adventure Capitalists* (Jeff Grout and Lynne Curry, 1998)

The only certain means of success is to render more and better service than is expected of you, no matter what the task may be. This is a habit followed by all successful people since the beginning of time. Therefore the surest way to doom yourself to mediocrity is to perform only the work for which you are paid. **Og Mandino**. *The Greatest Miracle in the World* (1978)

In the best institutions, promises are kept, no matter what the cost in agony and overtime. **David Ogilvy**. *Confessions of an Advertising Man* (1963)

A man without a smiling face must not open a store. **Anonymous**. Chinese proverb
Show me the business man or institution not guided by sentiment and service, by the idea that "he profits most who serves best," and I will show you a man or an outfit that is dead or dying. **B. F. Harris**. Attributed

Sincerity

The only work that spiritually purifies us is that which is done without personal motives. **Sri Aurobindo**. Quoted in *Ethics in Management: Vedantic Perspectives* (S. K. Chakraborty, 1995)

The secret of success is sincerity: once you can fake that, you've got it made. **Jean Giraudoux**. Quoted in *Murphy's Law Book Two: More Reasons Why Things Go Wrong* (Arthur Bloch, 1980)

Some of the worst men in the world are sincere and the more sincere they are the worse they are. **Lord Hailsham (Quintin Hogg)**. Quoted in "Sayings of the Week," *Observer (London)* (January 7, 1968)

Nothing in all the world is more dangerous than sincere ignorance and conscientious stupidity. **Martin Luther King**. *Strength to Love* (1963)

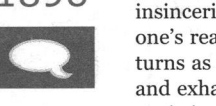

The great enemy of clear language is insincerity. When there is a gap between one's real and one's declared aims, one turns as it were instinctively to long words and exhausted idioms, like a cuttlefish squirting ink. **George Orwell**. "Politics and the English Language," *Shooting an Elephant* (1950)

Few people would not be the worse for complete sincerity. **F. H. Bradley**. *Collected Essays* (1935)

Men are always sincere. They change sincerities, that's all. **Tristan Bernard**. *Ce que l'on dit aux Femmes* (1922), Act 3

We ought to see far enough into a hypocrite to see even his sincerity. **G. K. Chesterton**. *Heretics* (1905)

A little sincerity is a dangerous thing, and a great deal of it is absolutely fatal. **Oscar Wilde**. "The Critic As Artist" (1890)

Profound sincerity is the only basis of talent as of character. **Ralph Waldo Emerson**. "Natural History of Intellect," *Essays: First Series* (1841)

Sincerity has to do with the connexion between our words and thoughts, and not between our beliefs and actions. **William Hazlitt**. "On Cant and Hypocrisy," *London Weekly Review* (December 6, 1828)

Weak people cannot be sincere. **François La Rochefoucauld**. *Reflections: or, Sentences and Moral Maxims* (5th ed, 1678)

Let us say what we feel, and feel what we say; let speech harmonize with life. **Seneca**. *Letters to Lucilius* (1st century AD)

Always be sincere, even if you don't mean it. **Harry S. Truman**. Attributed

Socialism and Communism

Your money does not cause my poverty. Refusal to believe this is at the bottom of most bad economic thinking. **P. J. O'Rourke**. *Eat the Rich* (1999)

A community in which power, wealth and opportunity are in the hands of the many not the few ... in which the enterprise of the market and the rigour of competition are joined with the forces of partnership and co-operation. **Labour Party**. This new version of the Labour Party Constitution's Clause Four compares with the 1918 (revised 1928) original: To secure for workers ... the full fruits of their industry and the most equitable distribution thereof that may be possible upon the basis. "Clause IV," *Labour Party Constitution* (April 29, 1995)

You can't get good Chinese takeout in China and Cuban cigars are rationed in Cuba. That's all you need to know about communism. **P. J. O'Rourke**. *Give War a Chance* (1992)

Later Marx was to recall his mother's shrewd words, "If only Karl had made capital, instead of writing about it." **Edna, Lady Healey**. *Wives of Fame: Mary Livingstone, Jenny Marx, Emma Darwin* (1986)

To the ordinary working man, the sort you would meet in any pub on Saturday night, Socialism does not mean much more than better wages and shorter hours, and nobody bossing you about. **George Orwell**. *The Road to Wigan Pier* (1937)

Marxian Socialism must always remain a portent to the historians of Opinion—how a doctrine so illogical and so dull can have exercised so powerful and enduring an influence over the minds of men. **John Maynard Keynes**. *The End of Laissez-Faire* (1926)

Socialism proposes no adequate substitute for the motive of enlightened selfishness that to-day is at the basis of all human labor and effort, enterprise and new activity. **William Howard Taft**. *Popular Government* (1913)

From each according to his ability, to each according to his needs. **Karl Marx**. *Critique of the Gotha Programme* (1875)

Society

The danger is not an ever-expanding socialist state, per Hayek's road to serfdom, but of a move to economic feudalism, in which a small set of wealthy masters dominate markets and the state and subvert or outsmart efforts to regulate their behavior or rein them in. **Richard B. Freeman**. Quoted in the *New York Times* (February 19, 2012)

There's class warfare, all right, but it's my class, the rich class, that's making war, and we're winning. **Warren Buffett**. *New York Times* (November 26, 2006)

The quality of a society will be judged by what the least privileged in it achieves. **Robert Greenleaf**. "Old Age: The Ultimate Test of the Spirit," *The Power of Servant Leadership* (Larry Spears, ed, 1998)

We have an underdeveloped democracy and overdeveloped plutocracy. **Ralph Nader**. *Economist (London)* (1996)

The trouble with a free market economy is that it requires so many policemen to make it work. **Dean Acheson**. Quoted in the *Observer (London)* (May 26, 1985)

Economic growth may one day turn out to be a curse rather than a good, and under no conditions can it either lead to freedom or constitute a proof for its existence. **Hannah Arendt**. *On Revolution* (1963)

The Affluent Society. **J. K. Galbraith**. Book title. *The Affluent Society* (1958)

No advance in wealth, no softening of manners, no reform or revolution has ever brought human equality a millimetre nearer. **George Orwell**. *Nineteen Eighty-Four* (1949), pt. 2, ch. 9

Idiots are always in favour of inequality of income (their only chance of eminence), and the truly great in favour of equality. **George Bernard Shaw**. *The Intelligent Woman's Guide to Socialism and Capitalism* (1928)

Years ago I recognized my kinship with all living things, and I made up my mind that I was not one bit better than the meanest on the Earth. I said then and I say now, that while there is a lower class, I am in it. **Eugene V. Debs**. Statement to the Court after being convicted for violating the Sedition Act, Cleveland, Ohio. (September 18, 1918)

Which of us ... is to do the hard and dirty work for the rest—and for what pay? who is to do the pleasant and clean work, and for what pay? **John Ruskin**. *Sesame and Lillies* (1865)

All men are created equal ... they are endowed by their Creator with inalienable rights ... among these are Life, Liberty, and the pursuit of happiness. **Thomas Jefferson**. "Declaration of Independence" (July 4, 1776)

Freedom is a more complex and delicate thing than force. It is not as simple to live under as force is. **Thomas Mann**. Attributed

Speeches

Prepare your heart and mind before you prepare your speech. **Stephen Covey**. *Thirty Methods of Influence* (1991)

A speech is poetry and cadence, rhythm, imagery, sweep! A speech reminds us that words, like children, have the power to make dance the dullest beanbag of a heart. **Peggy Noonan**. *What I Saw at the Revolution* (1990)

I feel like Zsa Zsa Gabor's fifth husband. I know what I'm supposed to do but I don't know if I can make it interesting. **Al Gore**. Said on being twenty-third speaker at a political dinner. Quoted in *Today* (March 1, 1989)

Oratory is just like prostitution: you must have little tricks. **Vittorio Emanuele Orlando**. Quoted in *Time* (December 8, 1952)

If I am to speak for ten minutes, I need a week for preparation; if fifteen minutes, three days; if half an hour, two days; if an hour, I am ready now. **Woodrow Wilson**. Quoted in *The Wilson Era* (Josephus Daniels, 1946)

Oratory is dying; a calculating age has stabbed it to the heart with innumerable dagger-thrusts of statistics. **W. Keith Hancock**. *Australia* (1930)

The finest eloquence is that which gets things done; the worst is that which delays them. **David Lloyd George (Earl of Dwyfor)**. Speech, Paris Peace Conference (1919)

He is one of those orators of whom it was well said, Before they get up, they do not know what they are going to say; when they are speaking, they do not know what they are saying; and when they have sat down, they do not know what they have said. **Sir Winston Churchill**. Referring to Lord Charles Beresford (1846–1919). Quoted in *Hansard* (December 20, 1912)

An orator can hardly get beyond commonplaces: if he does he gets beyond his hearers. **William Hazlitt**. *The Plain Speaker* (1826)

The object of oratory is not truth, but persuasion. **Thomas Babington, Lord Macaulay**. *The Athenian Orators* (1824)

Eloquence lies as much in the tone of the voice, in the eyes, and in the speaker's manner, as in his choice of words. **François La Rochefoucauld**. *Reflections: or, Sentences and Moral Maxims* (1665)

Nothing is so unbelievable that oratory cannot make it acceptable. **Cicero**. *Paradoxa Stoicorum* (46 BC?)

It is terrible to speak well and be wrong. **Sophocles**. *Electra* (430?–415? BC)

Speak when you're angry and you'll make the best speech you'll ever regret. **Henry Ward Beecher**. Attributed

It usually takes me more than three weeks to prepare a good impromptu speech. **Mark Twain**. Attributed

Statistics

Almost everyone in Sweden has more than the average number of legs. That's a statistic, and understanding why it's true delivers a crash course in how averages can sometimes divert from common sense, and how an understanding of the importance of distribution can bring them back in line again (essentially you need to remember that not one of Sweden's amputees is offset by a Swede with three legs). **Tom Sutcliffe**. Reviewing BBC TV documentary *The Joy of Stats* with Professor Hans Rosling. *Independent (London)* (December 8, 2010)

The Budget has been presented as a necessity ... backed up by piles of figures that sound apocalyptic but mean nothing by themselves, like "We now owe £800 for every insect in Britai," or "The debt burden is equivalent to 300 years on a premium rate girl-on-girl action chatline" or "The deficit is more than the value of the moon." **Mark Steel**. On the UK's 2010 "emergency Budget". *Independent (London)* (June 24, 2010)

I have been to sales seminars where the motivational speaker implied to 250 real estate professionals from the same company that all of them could be the firm's number one salesperson next year. **Steve Salerno**. *Sham: How the Gurus of the Self-help Movement Make Us Helpless* (2005)

Data, as used to map regularities, quantities, frequencies, probabilities, and so on, produces a landscape rich in surreal potential ... Facts about tea drinking and dog excreting are produced via a range of information: they coalesce as a composite form—one giant dog, one giant turd, one monstrous orchestrated chorus of tea drinking. **Ben Highmore**. *Day-to-Day Data* (2005)

Numbers in all their impersonality are democracy's ideal language, suited for gods, machines, and collectives ... The metaphysical status of numbers is profoundly ambiguous: They are concrete and imaginary, precise and intangible, mechanical and intellectual, human and inhuman. **John Durham Peters**. *Political Communication* (October 2001)

Employing data bases and statistical skills, academics compute with precision the beta of a stock ... then build arcane investment and capital-allocation theories around this calculation. In their hunger for a single statistic to measure risk they forget a fundamental principle: It is better to be approximately right than precisely wrong. **Warren Buffett**. Chairman's letter to shareholders (March 7, 1995)

Like dreams, statistics are a form of wish fulfilment. **Jean Baudrillard**. *Cool Memories* (1987)

The average family exists only on paper and its average budget is a fiction, invented by statisticians for the convenience of statisticians. **Sylvia Porter**. *Sylvia Porter's Money Book* (1975)

There are two kinds of statistics, the kind you look up and the kind you make up. **Rex Stout**. *Death of a Doxy* (1966)

Statistical figures referring to economic events are historical data. They tell us what happened in a nonrepeatable case. **Ludwig von Mises**. *Human Action* (1949)

Statistics are the triumph of the quantitative method and the quantitative method is the victory of sterility and death. **Hilaire Belloc**. *Silence of the Sea* (1941)

Never cross a river because it is on average four feet deep. **Nassim Nicholas Taleb**. Attributed

Strategy

I discovered ... that business was no great mystery. It's not something like physics or medicine that requires extensive study. You just try to get people to pay you for stuff. **Paul Graham**. "How to Start a Startup," *paulgraham.com* (March 2005)

Build something users love, and spend less than you make. How hard is that? **Paul Graham**. "How to Start a Startup," *paulgraham.com* (March 2005)

At Berkshire, our carefully-crafted acquisition strategy is simply to wait for the phone to ring. Happily, it sometimes does so, usually because a manager who sold to us earlier has recommended to a friend that he think about following suit. **Warren Buffett**. Chairman's letter to shareholders, *Berkshire Hathaway 1999 Annual Report* (March 1, 2000)

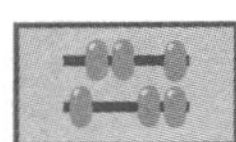

Whatever you shoot is dead for a while before it starts to stink. The same goes for strategies. How many organizations carry this dead thing around with them, unaware of its irrelevancy until it is too late? **Gary Hamel**. Lecture, "Pronking and Surviving in the Age of Gazelles" (October 26, 1999)

There is only one winning strategy. It is to carefully define the target market and direct a superior offering to that target market. **Philip Kotler**. Interview, *The Events & Awards Managers of Asia and Hamlin-Iturralde Corporation* (1999)

Swing for hits, not home runs. **Michael Dell**. *Direct from Dell* (1996)

A question that often comes up at times of strategic transformation is, should you pursue a highly focused approach, betting everything on one strategic goal, or should you hedge? ... Mark Twain hit it on the head when he said, Put all of your eggs in one basket and WATCH THAT BASKET. **Andrew S. Grove**. *Only the Paranoid Survive: How to Exploit the Crisis Points That Challenge Every Company and Career* (1996), ch. 8

Reengineering: The principal slogan of the Nineties, used to describe any and all corporate strategies. **Anonymous**. *Fortune* (February 15, 1995)

The prevailing wisdom is that markets are always right. I take the opposite position. I assume that markets are always wrong. **George Soros**. *Soros on Soros* (1995)

Strategy is not the consequence of planning but the opposite, its starting point. **Henry Mintzberg**. *The Rise and Fall of Strategic Planning* (1994)

Strategy-making is an immensely complex process involving the most sophisticated, subtle, and at times subconscious of human cognitive and social processes. **Henry Mintzberg**. *The Rise and Fall of Strategic Planning* (1994)

Mold-breaking strategies grow initially like weeds, they are not cultivated like tomatoes in a hothouse. **Henry Mintzberg**. *The Rise and Fall of Strategic Planning* (1994)

We like to believe we can break strategy down to Five Forces or Seven Ss. But you can't. Strategy is extraordinarily emotional and demanding. **Gary Hamel**. *Competing for the Future* (cowritten with C. K. Prahalad, 1994)

The strategist's method is very simply to challenge the prevailing assumptions with a single question: Why? **Kenichi Ohmae**. *The Mind of the Strategist* (1982)

Long-range planning does not deal with future decisions. It deals with the future of present decisions. **Peter F. Drucker**. *Managing in Turbulent Times* (1980)

To stay ahead, you must have your next idea waiting in the wings. **Rosabeth Moss Kanter**. *Men and Women of the Corporation* (1977)

I buy when other people are selling. **J. Paul Getty**. *International Herald Tribune (Paris)* (1961)

Stress

There are three categories of things: fragile things that break, like the financial system; robust things that don't break easily but don't improve, like the Brooklyn Bridge; and my new category, "antifragile" things that gain strength from stressors and get stronger from failure, like evolution. **Nassim Nicholas Taleb**. *Foreign Policy* (November 2012)

Contentment is too bland; worry is more stimulating. We don't say "She was gripped by contentment." The good news, though, is that worriers tend to be the smartest, most creative people we've got. It takes a lot of imagination to dream up all these worries. **Edward M. Hallowell**. Quoted in *Help! How to Become Slightly Happier and Get a Bit More Done* (Oliver Burkeman, 2011)

Mach-S, the speed at which stress can't keep up, is simply forward motion. But it has to be self-propelled. **Jef Mallett**. *Frazz* (April 4, 2007)

I try to only worry about things I have control over. **Steve Nash**. "Stevie Wonder," *FastBreak Magazine* (Brian Bujdos, April 1998)

Brain cells create ideas. Stress kills brain cells. Stress is not a good idea. **Doug Hall**. *Jump Start Your Brain* (1996)

At a certain speed, the speed of light, you lose even your shadow. At a certain speed, the speed of information, things lose their sense. **Jean Baudrillard**. *The Gulf War Did Not Take Place* (1995)

The trouble with being in the rat race is that even if you win, you're still a rat. **Lily Tomlin**. Quoted in *Slowing Down in a Speeded Up World* (Adair Lara, 1994)

If you can't stand the heat, get out of the kitchen. **Harry S. Truman**. *Mr. Citizen* (1960)

If you want to avoid worry, do what Sir William Osler did: Live in day-tight compartments. Don't stew about the future. Just live each day until bedtime. **Dale Carnegie**. *How to Stop Worrying and Start Living* (1948)

Business pressures are good for the soul: when it has unburdened itself of them, it plays all the more fully and enjoys life. **Johann Wolfgang von Goethe**. Attributed

Success

GDP just measures output; whether that is good output, like medical equipment, or bad, like cigarettes, and treats them just the same ... Time, love, compassion, co-operation, happiness and sustainability find no echo in this dry utilitarian measure of success. **Neal Lawson**. *Observer (London)* (September 20, 2009)

To be successful, you need leisure. You need time hanging heavily on your hands. **George Soros**. Quoted in *Becoming Rich* (Mark Tier, 2005)

A man is a success if he gets up in the morning and gets to bed at night, and in between he does what he wants to do. **Bob Dylan**. Quoted in *How to Survive and Succeed in the Music Industry* (Teri Saccone, 2003)

I am successful because I have always been a tortoise. I did not come from a rich family. I was not smart in school. I did not finish school. I am not particularly talented. Yet, I am far richer than most people simply because I did not stop. **Robert Kiyosaki**. *Rich Dad's Retire Young, Retire Rich* (2002)

People who are successful simply want it more than people who are not. **Ian Schrager**. *Sunday Times (London)* (May 2000)

I have worked without thinking of myself. This is the largest factor in whatever success I have attained. **Amadeo Giannini**. Quoted in "America's Banker," *Time 100: Heroes and Inspirations* (December 1999)

Success is made of 99% failure. **Sir James Dyson**. *Management Today* (July 1999)

It takes years to make an overnight success. **Eddie Cantor**. Quoted in *Treasury of Investment Wisdom* (Bernice Cohen, 1999)

I believe in the value of paranoia. Business success contains the seeds of its own destruction. The more successful you are, the more people want a chunk of your business and then another chunk and then another until there is nothing left.

  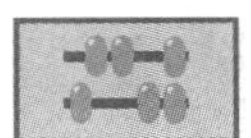      

Andrew S. Grove. *Only the Paranoid Survive: How to Exploit the Crisis Points That Challenge Every Company and Career* (1996), Preface

Success is a lousy teacher. It seduces smart people into thinking they can't lose. **Bill Gates**. *The Road Ahead* (1995)

God doesn't require us to succeed; he only requires that you try. **Mother Teresa**. Quoted in *Rolling Stone* (December 1992)

The secret of success is learning how to use pain and pleasure instead of having pain and pleasure use you. If you do that, you're in control of your life. If you don't, life controls you. **Anthony Robbins**. *Awaken the Giant Within* (1992)

The secret of the truly successful ... is that they learned early in life how *not* to be busy. **Barbara Ehrenreich**. "The Cult of Busyness," *The Worst Years of Our Lives* (1991)

I've always realised that if I'm doing well at business I'm cutting some other bastard's throat. **Kerry Packer**. *Daily Mail (London)* (November 1, 1988)

If you do anything just for the money you don't succeed. **Barry Hearn**. *Sunday Telegraph (London)* (April 10, 1988)

When you struggle hard and lose money, you're a hero. When you start making money you become a capitalist swine. **Sir Terence Conran**. Quoted in *The Risk Takers* (Jeffrey Robinson, 1985)

To be successful you have to be lucky, or a little mad, or very talented, or to find yourself in a rapid-growth field. **Edward de Bono**. *Tactics: The Art and Science of Success* (1984)

Eighty percent of success is showing up. **Woody Allen**. Quoted in *In Search of Excellence* (Thomas J. Peters and Robert H. Waterman, 1982)

It is not enough to succeed. Others must fail. **Gore Vidal**. Attributed (December 1976)

For a writer, success is always temporary, success is only a delayed failure. And it is incomplete. **Graham Greene**. *A Sort of Life* (1971)

If at first you don't succeed, you may be at your level of incompetence. **Laurence J. Peter**. *The Peter Principle: Why Things Always Go Wrong* (cowritten with Raymond Hull, 1969)

She knows there's no success like failure and that failure's no success at all. **Bob Dylan**. Song lyric. "Love Minus Zero, No Limits" (1965)

I am doomed to an eternity of compulsive work. No set goal achieved satisfies. Success only breeds a new goal. The golden apple devoured has seeds. It is endless. **Bette Davis**. *The Lonely Life* (1962)

The toughest thing about success is that you've got to keep on being a success. **Irving Berlin**. Quoted in *Theater Arts* (1958)

Success is relative: It is what we can make of the mess we have made of things. **T. S. Eliot**. *The Family Reunion* (1939)

The common idea that success spoils people by making them vain, egotistic and self-complacent is erroneous; on the contrary, it makes them for the most part humble, tolerant and kind. **W. Somerset Maugham**. *The Summing Up* (1938)

Whom the gods wish to destroy they first call promising. **Cyril Connolly**. *Enemies of Promise* (1938)

If you want to succeed, double your failure rate. **Samuel Butler**. *Men-Minutes-Money* (1934)

The conduct of successful business merely consists in doings things in a very simple way, doing them regularly, and never neglecting to do them. **Lord Leverhulme (William Hesketh Lever)**. Speech, Liverpool University (1922)

The test of a first-rate work, and a test of your sincerity in calling it a first-rate work, is that you finish it. **Arnold Bennett**. *Things That Have Interested Me* (1921–1925)

A minute's success pays the failure of years. **Robert Browning**. "Apollo and the Fates" (1886), st. 42

Success is a science; if you have the conditions, you get the result. **Oscar Wilde**. Letter (1883)

The secret of success is concentration ... Taste everything a little, look at everything a little; but live for one thing. **Olive Schreiner**. *The Story of an African Farm* (1883)

To burn always with this hard, gem-like flame, to maintain this ecstasy, is success in life. **Walter Pater**. *Studies in the History of the Renaissance* (1873)

The conduct of a losing party never appears right: at least it never can possess the only infallible criterion of wisdom to vulgar judgements—success. **Edmund Burke**. Letter to a member of the National Assembly (1791)

Tis not in mortals to command success But we'll do more, Sempronius, we'll deserve it. **Joseph Addison**. *Cato* (1713)

The man of virtue makes the difficulty to be overcome his first business, and success only a subsequent consideration. **Confucius**. *Analects* (500? BC)

To succeed in business it is necessary to make others see things as you see them. **Aristotle Onassis**. Attributed

Talent

Too many companies believe people are interchangeable. Truly gifted people never are. They have unique talents. Such people cannot be forced into roles they are not suited for, nor should they be. **Warren Bennis**. *Organizing Genius: The Secrets of Creative Collaboration* (cowritten with Patricia Ward Biederman, 1998)

The leader ... is rarely the brightest person in the group. Rather, they have extraordinary taste, which makes them more curators than creators. They are appreciators of talent and nurturers of talent and they have the ability to recognize valuable ideas. **Warren Bennis**. Interview, *Strategy + Business* (July–September 1997)

Talent is cheaper than table salt. What separates the talented individual from the successful one is a lot of hard work. **Stephen King**. Quoted in the *Independent on Sunday (London)* (March 10, 1996)

The world is filled with unsuccessful men of talent. **Ray Kroc**. Quoted in *The Fifties* (David Halberstan, 1993)

An idea can turn to dust or magic, depending on the talent that rubs against it. **William Bernbach**. *New York Times* (October 6, 1982)

Timing and arrogance are decisive factors in the successful use of talent. **Marya Mannes**. *Out of My Time* (1971)

All our talents increase in the using, and every faculty, both good and bad, strengthens by exercise. **Anne Brontë**. *The Tenant of Wildfell Hall* (1848)

Targets

Targets make organisations stupid. Because they are a simplistic response to a complex issue, they have unintended and unwelcome consequences ... so every target generates others to counter the perverse effects of the first one. **Simon Caulkin**. *Observer (London)* (March 22, 2009)

We build four of them a year—it's my job to sell four a year. **Robert Clifford**. Referring to the production of luxury yachts. *Australian Financial Review* (September 2000)

People are ambitious and unrealistic. They set targets for themselves that are higher than what you would set for them. And because they set them, they hit them. **Liisa Joronen**. *Fast Company* (1997)

Our view was, if we could measure it, we could manage it. **Dan England**. "The Mavericks," *Fortune* (June 1995)

It is much more difficult to measure nonperformance than performance. **Harold S. Geneen**. Referring to why managers sometimes accept underachievement. *Managing* (cowritten with Alvin Moscow, 1984)

A minor invention every ten days and a big thing every six months. **Thomas Edison**. Press conference (1876)

Think nothing done while aught remains to do. **Samuel Rogers**. *Human Life* (1819)

Taxes

Writing checks to the IRS that include strings of zeros does not bother me ... Overall, we feel extraordinarily lucky to have been dealt a hand in life that enables us to write large checks to the government rather than one requiring the government to regularly write checks to us—say, because we are disabled or unemployed. **Warren Buffett**. Chairman's letter to shareholders, *Berkshire Hathaway 1998 Annual Report* (March 1, 1999)

Taxes will eventually become a voluntary process, with the possible exception of real estate—the one physical thing that does not move easily and has computable value ... wait until that's all there is left to tax, when the rest of the things we buy and sell come from everywhere, anywhere, and nowhere. **Nicholas Negroponte**. Referring to the prospects for taxing Internet commerce. "Taxing Taxes," *Wired* (May 6, 1998)

Sex and taxes are in many ways the same. Tax does to cash what males do to genes. It dispenses assets among the population as a whole. **Steve Jones**. Speech, London (January 25, 1997)

President Herbert Hoover returned his salary to government. His idea caught on and now we're all doing it. **Sam Ewing**. Referring to taxation. Quoted in the *Wall Street Journal* (July 23, 1996)

Patrick Henry railed against taxation without representation. He should see it with representation. **Saul Landau**. *New York Times* (1995)

The Rich aren't like us—they pay less taxes. **Peter De Vries**. *Washington Post* (July 30, 1989)

Inflation is one form of taxation that can be imposed without legislation. **Milton Friedman**. *Observer (London)* (September 22, 1974)

All money nowadays seems to be produced with a homing instinct for the Treasury. **Prince Philip (Duke of Edinburgh)**. Quoted in the *Observer (London)* (May 26, 1963)

To tax and to please is no more given to man than to love and be wise. **John, Viscount Simon**. Budget speech, House of Commons, British Parliament (April 25, 1938)

Income tax has made more liars out of the American people than golf. **Will Rogers**. *The Illiterate Digest* (1924)

The hardest thing in the world to understand is income tax. **Albert Einstein**. Attributed

Teams

A camel is a horse invented by a committee. **Sir Alec Issigonis**. Quoted in *Guardian (London)* (January 14, 2001)

A good team is a great place to be, exciting, stimulating, supportive, successful. A bad team is horrible, a sort of human prison. **Charles Handy**. *Inside Organisations* (1999)

A team of dragons doesn't need a head. **Stan Shih**. *Forbes* (September 1998)

Team-building exercises come in many forms but they all trace their roots back to the prison system. **Scott Adams**. *The Dilbert Principle* (1996)

Team player: An employee who substitutes the thinking of the herd for his/her own good judgment. **Anonymous**. *Fortune* (February 15, 1995)

One man can be a crucial ingredient on a team, but one man cannot make a team. **Kareem Abdul-Jabbar**. *Star* (1986)

People can be themselves only in small comprehensible groups. **Ernst Friedrich Schumacher**. *Small Is Beautiful* (1973)

The desire to stand well with one's fellows, the so-called human instinct of association, easily outweighs the merely individual interest. **Elton Mayo**. *The Human Problems of an Industrial Civilization* (1933)

Dividing enemy forces to weaken them is clever, but dividing one's own team is a grave sin against the business. **Henri Fayol**. *General and Industrial Management* (1916)

Technology

For the first time in financial history, machines can execute trades far faster than humans can intervene. That gap is set to widen. **Andy Haldane**. Quoted in the *Daily Telegraph (London)* (July 8, 2012)

Technology alone is not enough ... it's technology married with the liberal arts, married with the humanities, that yields us the results that make our hearts sing. **Steve Jobs**. Speech launching the iPad 2 tablet computer (March 2011)

The cyborg is now the ideal to which all our most advanced technology is tending. **Bryan Appleyard**. *The Brain is Wider than the Sky* (2011)

The washing machine changed the world more than the Internet. **Ha-Joon Chang**. *23 Things They Don't Tell You About Capitalism* (2010)

The Internet for everyman, though slow and clunky, got going in 1989. The dotcom crash of 2000 asked two big questions. What's it for? How do we make money out of it? Then everybody got broadband and it all started to fall into place. The answer to the first question was porn and everything. The answer to the second was ... well, we're still not quite sure. **Bryan Appleyard**. *Sunday Times (London)* (December 27, 2009)

Technology is the principal engine of global growth, the main force that is transforming our lives. It is not politics; it is not the law; it is not the civil service; it is not even the business world, except in so far as this brings the fruits of technological advance to the rest of us. **Hamish McRae**. *Independent (London)* (October 21, 2009)

Egalitarianism is possible only in small social systems. Once a medium gets past a certain size fame is a forced move. **Clay Shirky**. On the development of the

Internet. *Here Comes Everybody: The Power of Organizing Without Organizations* (2008)

Few influential people involved with the Internet claim that it is good in and of itself. It is a powerful tool for solving social problems, just as it is a tool for making money, finding lost relatives, receiving medical advice, or, come to that, trading instructions for making bombs. **Esther Dyson**. Quoted in *IQuote: Brilliance and Banter from the Internet Age* (David L. Green, 2007)

It's a new medium, it's a universal medium and it's not itself a medium which inherently makes people do good things, or bad things. It allows people to do what they want to do more efficiently. **Sir Tim Berners-Lee**. Talking about the World Wide Web, which he founded. Interview with Mark Lawson, *Newsnight*, BBC TV (August 9, 2005)

I would trade all of my technology for an afternoon with Socrates. **Steve Jobs**. Quoted in *Newsweek* (October 29, 2001)

Technology is our word for something that doesn't work yet. **Douglas Adams**. *Sunday Times (London)* (June 2000)

Technology will move so fast that unfortunately, or fortunately for me, you will be required to buy a new phone quite often. **Charles Dunstone**. *Management Today* (August 1999)

We've all heard that a million monkeys banging on one million typewriters will eventually reproduce the entire works of Shakespeare. Now, thanks to the Internet, we know this is not true. **Robert Wilensky**. *Mail on Sunday* (February 1997)

Many executives continue to believe that they are not in the technology business and that they might just as well outsource their information technology needs. This is like an athlete saying that he is not in the strength business ... these naysayers might as well say that they are not in the business of being in business. **J. William Gurley**. *Above the Crowd: Productivity Paradox* (1997)

Machines need to talk easily to one another in order to better serve people. **Nicholas Negroponte**. *Being Digital* (1995)

If the technocratic class often invokes technology, it is because these inanimate objects can take on a trajectory of their own and so cover for the manager's inability to give leadership. **John Ralston Saul**. *The Unconscious Civilization* (1995)

The thing with high-tech is that you always end up using scissors. **David Hockney**. *Observer (London)* (July 1994)

An important technology first creates a problem and then solves it. **Alan Kay**. Quoted in *Reengineering the Corporation* (Michael Hammer and James Champy, 1993)

The trouble is that all-encompassing though information technology may be, it will always convey facts and numbers ... what it does not convey is perception, belief and motivation. **Sir John Harvey-Jones**. *Managing to Survive* (1993)

We bet the company on that basic technology and, in 23 years, nobody else has been able to match it. **Masaru Ibuka**. *Fortune* (February 1992)

A common mistake people make when trying to design something foolproof is to underestimate the ingenuity of complete fools. **Douglas Adams**. *Mostly Harmless* (1992)

If we hadn't put a man on the moon, there wouldn't be a Silicon Valley today. **John Sculley**. *US News & World Report* (1992)

Why did the Roman Empire collapse? What is Latin for office automation? **Alan Jay Perlis**. *Epigrams in Programming* (1985)

The technology of mass production is inherently violent, ecologically damaging, self-defeating in terms of non-renewable resources, and stultifying for the human person. **Ernst Friedrich Schumacher**. *Small Is Beautiful* (1973)

Any sufficiently advanced technology is indistinguishable from magic. **Sir Arthur C. Clarke**. *The Lost Worlds of 2001* (1972)

If the automobile had followed the same development as the computer, a Rolls Royce would cost $100, get a million miles per gallon, and explode once a year, killing everyone inside. **Robert X. Cringley**. *Infoworld* (March 6, 1969)

There are three roads to ruin; women, gambling and technicians. The most pleasant is with women, the quickest is with gambling, but the surest is with technicians. **George Pompidou**. Quoted in the *Sunday Telegraph (London)* (1968)

When this circuit learns your job, what are you going to do? **Marshall McLuhan**. *The Medium Is the Message* (1967)

Technology—the knack of so arranging the world that we need not experience it. **Max Frisch**. *Homo Faber* (1957)

If it keeps up, man will atrophy all his limbs but the push-button finger. **Frank Lloyd Wright**. Referring to advances in technology. *New York Times Magazine* (1953)

Machines are worshipped because they are beautiful, and valued because they confer power; they are hated because they are hideous and loathed because they impose slavery. **Bertrand Russell (Earl Russell)**. *Sceptical Essays* (1928)

It took 75 years for telephones to be used by 50 million customers, but it took only four years for the Internet to reach that many users. **Lori Valigra**. Attributed

Time Management

There is no longer much that divides up our working lives. Days and evenings merge into each other, as do workdays and weekends. It's supposed to be an age of flexibility and empowerment; actually it's a great, undifferentiated expanse of frantic inefficiency. **Lucy Kellaway**. *Financial Times (London)* (January 15, 2012)

When my children were young I had to get home at a fixed time every day to relieve the nanny. I had no choice in the matter, and so my work was miraculously always done in time. Now I have the option of working more flexibly—i.e. working longer and much more unwisely—and so I never fail to take it. **Lucy Kellaway**. *Financial Times (London)* (January 15, 2012)

The Law of Forced Efficiency: There is never enough time to do everything, but there is always enough time to do the most important thing. **Brian Tracy**. *The 100 Absolutely Unbreakable Laws of Business Success* (2000)

We are speeding up our lives and working harder in a futile attempt to buy the time to slow down and enjoy it. **Paul Hawken**. *The Ecology of Commerce* (1993)

What is the best use of my time right now? **Alan Lakein**. *How To Get Control of Your Time and Your Life* (1973)

Do not wait; the time will never be just right. **Napoleon Hill**. *Think and Grow Rich* (1937)

The clock not the steam engine is the key machine of the modern industrial age. **Lewis Mumford**. *Technics and Civilization* (1934)

Time waste differs from material waste in that there can be no salvage. **Henry Ford**. *My Life and Work* (cowritten with Samuel Crowther, 1922)

He who would make serious use of his life must always act as though he had a long time to live and must schedule his time as though he were about to die. **Émile Littré**. *Dictionnaire de la Langue Française* (1863–1873)

The man who can master his time can master nearly anything. **Bernard Baruch**. Attributed

If you did not look after today's business then you might as well forget about tomorrow. **Isaac Mophatlane**. Attributed

Travel

Travel, at least in the modern business sense, does not broaden the mind, it merely inflates the ego. **Jonathan Brown**. *Independent (London)* (December 3, 2009)

To constantly look for yourself even when you encounter the foreign is never to travel; while we know that it's in observing and overhearing others as we journey that we often discover unexpected dimensions of ourselves. **Amit Chaudhuri**. "In Search of India," *Guardian (London)* (April 18, 2009)

No one travelling on a business trip would be missed if he failed to arrive. **Thorstein Veblen**. Quoted in *Thorstein Veblen's Contribution to Environmental Sociology* (Ross E. Mitchell, 2007)

When you travel, remember that a foreign country is not designed to make you comfortable. It is designed to make its own people comfortable. **Clifton Fadiman**. Quoted in *Driving The Career Highway* (Janice Reals Ellig and William J. Morin, 2007)

Airplane travel is nature's way of making you look like your passport photo. **Al Gore**. Quoted in *The World According to Gore* (Bill Katovsky, 2007)

Airports have become a new kind of discontinuous city, whose vast populations, measured by annual passenger throughputs, are entirely transient, purposeful and, for the most part, happy. An easy camaraderie rules the departure lounges, along with the virtual abolition of nationality—whether we are Scots or Japanese is far less important than where we are going ... I suspect that the airport will be the true city of the next century. The great airports are already the suburbs of an invisible world capital, a virtual metropolis whose faubourgs are named Heathrow, Kennedy, Charles de Gaulle, Nagoya ... The concourses are the ramblas and agoras of the future city, time-freeze zones where all the clocks of the world are displayed, an atlas of arrivals and destinations forever updating itself, where briefly we become true world citizens. Air travel may well be the most important civic duty that we discharge today, erasing class and national distinctions and subsuming them within the unitary global culture of the departure lounge. **J. G. Ballard**. *Observer (London)* (September 14, 1997)

In the Middle Ages, people were tourists because of their religion, whereas now they are tourists because tourism is their religion. **Robert, Lord Runcie**. Speech (December 1988)

Commuter—one who spends his life In riding to and from his wife; A man who shaves and takes a train, And then rides it back to shave again. **E. B. White**. "The Commuter" (1982)

They say travel broadens the mind; but you must have the mind. **G. K. Chesterton**. "The Shadow of the Shark" (1921)

A man who leaves home to mend himself and others is a philosopher; but he who goes from country to country, guided by a blind impulse of curiosity, is a vagabond. **Oliver Goldsmith**. *The Citizen of the World* (1762)

Trust

Our trust in those who made the financial system work has been decimated—no less than we would lose faith in the water company if the taps started dripping cyanide. **Peggy Drexler**. *Huffington Post* blog (December 29, 2008)

I've learned the perimeter of my circle of confidence. **Warren Buffett**. Quoted in *Treasury of Investment Wisdom* (Bernice Cohen, 1999)

Trust comes back to the character, behaviour, and values of the company. You only achieve trust and retain it if you behave in a way which inspires trust. **Sir Dominic Cadbury**. Quoted in *The Winning Streak Mark II* (Walter Goldsmith and David Clutterbuck, 1997)

Management by trust, empathy, and forgiveness sounds good. It also sounds soft. It is in practice tough. Organizations based on trust have, on occasion, to be ruthless. **Charles Handy**. *Harvard Business Review* (November–December 1992)

I am very careful about bringing people into my confidence. I want to see the color of their eyes. **E. Gerald Corrigan**. Referring to becoming president of the Federal Reserve Bank in Minneapolis. *New York Times* (December 30, 1984)

The open bins and store rooms were symbols of trust, a trust that is central to the way HP does business. **David Packard**. "Lessons of Leadership," *The Nation's Business* (January 1974)

The superior confidence which people repose in the tall man is well merited. Being tall, he is more visible than other men and being more visible, he is much more closely watched. **J. K. Galbraith**. *The Scotch* (1964)

Confidence is a thing not to be produced by compulsion. Men cannot be forced to trust. **Daniel Webster**. Speech, US Senate (1834)

Confidence placed in another often compels confidence in return. **Livy**. *History of Rome* (26 BC–15 AD)

Value

As markets and market-oriented thinking reach into spheres of life traditionally governed by nonmarket norms—health, education, procreation, refugee policy, environmental protection—this dilemma arises more and more often. What should we do when the promise of economic growth or economic efficiency means putting a price on goods we consider priceless? **Michael J. Sandel**. *What Money Can't Buy: The Moral Limits of Markets* (2012)

If you're over 30, you think there's no such thing as a free lunch; if you're under 30, you assume all lunches are free. Look at your children: they know ways of getting movies, music, and television free. They make phone calls free. They set up social networks or blogs using expensive software systems handed out free. They have free word processors, free web browsers, they can search every web page in the world for free. **Bryan Appleyard**. *Sunday Times (London)* (June 28, 2009)

There are only four ways to create value in the New Economy, and they're really simple: information, entertainment, convenience, and savings. **Jay S. Walker**.

Interview, *Strategy + Business* (April–June 2000)

Creating value is an inherently cooperative process, capturing value is inherently competitive. **Barry J. Nalebuff**. *Co-opetition* (cowritten with Adam M. Brandenburger, 1997)

In hyperinflation, a kilo of potatoes was worth, to some, more than the family silver; a side of pork more than the grand piano. A prostitute in the family was better than an infant corpse; theft was preferable to starvation; warmth was finer than honour, clothing more essential than democracy, food more needed than freedom. **Adam Fergusson**. *When Money Dies: The Nightmare of the Weimar Collapse* (1975)

Nothing that costs only a dollar is worth having. **Elizabeth Arden**. Quoted in *In Cosmetics the Old Mystique Is No Longer Enough* (Eleanore Carruth, 1973)

The public should always be wondering how it is possible to give so much for the money. **Henry Ford II**. *My Life and Work* (cowritten with Samuel Crowther, 1922)

The value of a thing is the amount of laboring or work that its possession will save the possessor. **Henry George**. *The Science of Political Economy* (1897)

Value is the most invisible and impalpable of ghosts. **William Stanley Jevons**. *Investigations on Currency and Finance* (1884)

Vision

Good business leaders create a vision, articulate the vision, passionately own the vision, and relentlessly drive it to completion. **Jack Welch**. Quoted in *10 Simple Secrets of the World's Greatest Business Communicators* (Carmine Gallo, 2006)

The last thing IBM needs right now is a vision. **Lou Gerstner**. *Fortune* (1997)

Vision: Top management's heroic guess about the future, easily printed on mugs, T-shirts, posters, and calendar cards. **Anonymous**. *Fortune* (February 15, 1995)

Vision without action is merely a dream. Action without vision just passes the time. Vision with action can change the world. **Joel A. Barker**. *Future Edge* (1992)

Dreams have their place in management activity, but they need to be kept severely under control. **Arnold, Lord Weinstock**. *Financial Times (London)* (December 30, 1989)

Effective visions are lived in details, not broad strokes. **Tom Peters**. *Thriving on Chaos* (1987)

Whenever anything is being accomplished, it is being done, I have learned, by a monomaniac with a mission. **Peter F. Drucker**. *Adventures of a Bystander* (1979)

A zealous sense of mission is only possible where there is opposition to it. **D. W. Ewing**. "Tension Can Be an Asset," *Harvard Business Review* (September–October 1964)

A formal and orderly conception of the whole is rarely present, perhaps even rarely possible, except to a few men of exceptional genius. **Chester Barnard**. *The Functions of the Executive* (1938)

Vision is the art of seeing things invisible. **Jonathan Swift**. Attributed

Wages

Somebody told me ... that he overheard a banker's wife saying her husband was working for free this year—this was 2009. What she meant was, he was just getting his basic salary of £300,000, and no bonus. Their sense of entitlement is, in the proper sense of the word, psychotic. **John Lanchester**. Interviewed in the *Sunday Times (London)* (February 19, 2012)

The key thing that went wrong was that a culture was allowed to develop where the relationship between what people did and what they got went way out of alignment, especially at the top end. **Alistair Darling**. On pay and bonuses in the financial sector. Interview, *Daily Telegraph (London)* (March 3, 2009)

Wages are the measure of dignity that society puts on a job. **Johnnie Tillmon**. "Welfare Is a Woman's Issue," *The First Ms Reader* (Francine Klagsbrun, ed, 1972)

One man's wage increase is another man's price increase. **Harold, Lord Wilson**. Speech, Blackburn, UK (January 8, 1970)

Wages are determined by the bitter struggle between capitalist and worker. **Karl Marx**. *Early Writings* (T. B. Bottomore, ed, 1963)

The income men derive from producing things of slight consequence is of great consequence. The production reflects the low marginal utility of the goods to society. The income reflects the high total utility of a livelihood to a person. **J. K. Galbraith**. *The Affluent Society* (1958), ch. 21

The trouble with the profit system has always been that it was highly unprofitable to most people. **E. B. White**. *One Man's Meat* (1942)

No business which depends for existence on paying less than living wages to its workers has any right to continue in this country ... by living wages I mean more than a bare subsistence level—I mean the wages of decent living. **Franklin D. Roosevelt**. Address (1933)

The theory of the determination of wages in a free market is simply a special case of the general theory of value. Wages are the price of labour. **Sir John Richard Hicks**. *The Theory of Wages* (1932), pt. 1

All wages are based primarily on productive power. Anything else would be charity. **Elbert Hubbard**. *Notebook* (1927)

When a man says he wants to work, what he means is that he wants wages. **Richard Whately**. Quoted in *Principles of Political Economy* (Henry Sidgwick, 1883)

It is but a truism that labor is most productive where its wages are largest. Poorly paid labor is inefficient labor, the world over. **Henry George**. *Progress and Poverty* (1879), bk. 9

There is no way of keeping profits up but by keeping wages down. **David Ricardo**. *On Protection to Agriculture* (1820)

Men work but slowly, that have poor wages. **Thomas Fuller**. *Gnomologia* (1732), no. 3407

Economy: cutting down other people's wages. **J. B. Morton**. Attributed

We're overpaying him, but he's worth it. **Samuel Goldwyn**. Attributed

Wealth

Richness, the ideas of having plenty of money, is not ... an absolute state. Richness is about the amount of money you have compared to the people you see around you. It is about where you are in relation to others, and where they are in relation to you ... and whether you can have the things you want and other people have. **John Lanchester**. Speech. "Enough" (December 12, 2010)

Making rich people richer doesn't make the rest of us richer. **Ha-Joon Chang**.

23 Things They Don't Tell You About Capitalism (2010)

As recently as the 1970s, the idea that the point of life was to get rich and that governments existed to facilitate this would have been ridiculed: not only by capitalism's traditional critics but also by many of its staunchest defenders. **Tony Judt**. *Ill Fares the Land: A Treatise on Our Present Discontents* (2010)

Contrast 1968, when the CEO of General Motors took home, in pay and benefits, about sixty-six times the amount paid to a typical GM worker. Today the CEO of Wal-Mart earns nine hundred times the wages of his average employee. Indeed, the wealth of the Wal-Mart founder's family in 2005 was estimated at about the same ($90 billion) as that of the bottom 40% of the US population: 120 million people. **Tony Judt**. *Ill Fares the Land: A Treatise on Our Present Discontents* (2010)

A nation cannot prosper long when it favors only the prosperous. **Barack Obama**. Presidential inaugural address (January 21, 2009)

In short, it's a great economy if you're a high-level corporate executive or someone who owns a lot of stock. For most other Americans, economic growth is a spectator sport. **Paul R. Krugman**. *New York Times* (July 14, 2006)

Someday I want to be rich. Some people get so rich they lose all respect for humanity. That's how rich I want to be. **Rita Rudner**. Quoted in *Ten Commitments to Your Success* (Steve Chandler, 2005)

Nothing is more admirable than the fortitude with which millionaires tolerate the disadvantages of their wealth. **Rex Stout**. Quoted in *500 of the Most Witty, Acerbic, and Erudite Things Ever Said About Money* (Philip Jenks, 2002)

If you are not happy while getting rich, chances are that you will not be happy when you do get rich. **Robert Kiyosaki**. *Rich Dad's Rich Kid, Smart Kid* (2001)

Someone will always be getting richer faster than you. This is not a tragedy. **Charlie Munger**. Annual general meeting of Berkshire Hathaway (May 15, 2000)

The old foundations of success are gone ... The world's wealthiest man, Bill Gates, owns nothing tangible: no land, no gold or oil, no factories ... For the first time in history the world's wealthiest man owns only knowledge. **Lester Thurow**. *Building Wealth: New Rules for Individuals, Companies, and Countries in a Knowledge-Based Economy* (1999), Prologue

When I got my statement in January, I was worth $2.2 billion. Then I got another statement in August that said I was worth $3.2 billion. So I figure it's only nine months' earnings, who cares? **Ted Turner**. Referring to his decision to donate US$1 billion to the United Nations over a decade. Speech, United Nations Association of the USA, Marriott Marquis Hotel, New York (September 19, 1997)

It is inconceivable that anyone will divulge a truly effective get-rich scheme for the price of a book. There is ample opportunity to use wealth in this world, and neither I nor my friends, nor anyone else I have ever met, has so much of it that they are interested in putting themselves at a disadvantage by sharing their secrets. **Victor Niederhoffer**. *The Education of a Speculator* (1997)

Part of the loot went for gambling, part for horses, and part for women. The rest I spent foolishly. **George Raft**. Explaining how he spent $10 million. Quoted in *The Perfect Business* (Michael Lebeouf, 1997)

In our society, the best predictor of a man's wealth is his wife's looks, and the best predictor of a woman's looks is her husband's wealth. **Steven Pinker**. *How the Mind Works* (1997)

I have no interest in celebrities. If all the superrich disappeared, the world economy would not even notice. The superrich are irrelevant to the economy. **Peter F. Drucker**. Quoted in "Seeing Things As They Really Are," *Forbes* (Robert Lenzner and Stephen S. Johnson, 1987)

Having money is rather like being a blond. It is more fun but not vital. **Mary Quant**. Quoted in the *Observer (London)* (November 2, 1986)

If you can count your money, you don't have a billion dollars. **J. Paul Getty**. Quoted in *The Great Getty* (Robert Lenzner, 1985)

Purchasing power is a license to purchase power. **Raoul Vaneigem**. *The Revolution of Everyday Life* (1967)

In the affluent society, no useful distinction can be made between luxuries and necessities. **J. K. Galbraith**. *The Affluent Society* (1958)

Wealth is not without its advantages and the case to the contrary, although it has often been made, has never proved widely persuasive. **J. K. Galbraith**. *The Affluent Society* (1958), ch. 1

Short of genius, a rich man cannot imagine poverty. **Charles Pierre Péguy**. "Socialism and the Modern World," *Basic Verities* (1943)

Prosperity is only an instrument to be used, not a deity to be worshipped. **Calvin Coolidge**. Speech, Boston, Massachusetts (June 11, 1928)

A society which reverences the attainment of riches as the supreme felicity will naturally be disposed to regard the poor as damned ... if only to justify itself for making their life a hell. **Richard Tawney**. *Religion and the Rise of Capitalism* (1926), ch. 4, sect. 4

The millionaires are a product of natural selection ... the naturally selected agents of society for certain work. They get high wages and live in luxury, but the bargain is a good one for society. **William Graham Sumner**. Sumner was the leading US advocate of Herbert Spencer's Social Darwinism, the survival of the fittest. *The Challenge of Facts and Other Essays* (Albert Galloway Keller, ed, 1914)

In every well-governed state wealth is a sacred thing; in democracies it is the only sacred thing. **Anatole France**. *Penguin Island* (1908)

Not evil, but good, has come to the race from the accumulation of wealth by those who have the ability and energy that produce it. **Andrew Carnegie**. "Wealth," *North American Review* (June 1889)

There are three ways by which an individual can get wealth—by work, by gift, and by theft. And, clearly, the reasons why the workers get so little is that the beggars and thieves get so much. **Henry George**. *Social Problems* (1883)

What is really desired, under the name of riches, is essentially, power over men ... this power ... is in direct proportion to the poverty of the men over whom it is exercised, and in inverse proportion to the number of persons who are as rich as ourselves. **John Ruskin**. "The Veins of Wealth," *Unto This Last* (1862)

Superfluous wealth can buy superfluities only. **Henry David Thoreau**. *Walden, or Life in the Woods* (1854), Conclusion

Wealth is like sea-water; the more we drink, the thirstier we become; the same is true of fame. **Arthur Schopenhauer**. "What a Man Has," *Parerga and Paralipomena* (1851)

As long as there are rich people in the world, they will be desirous of distinguishing themselves from the poor.

  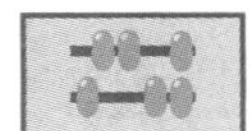      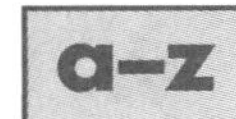

Jean-Jacques Rousseau. *Discours sur l'Économie Politique* (1758)

Prosperity tries the souls even of the wise. **Sallust**. *Bellum Catilinae* (41? BC), ch. 11

A man who has a million dollars is as well off as if he were rich. **John Jacob Astor**. Attributed

It is easier for a camel to go through the eye of a needle, than for a rich man to enter into the kingdom of God. **New Testament**. Matthew 19:24

Winners and Winning

Having been here before and lost ... I've got to tell you, winning is really a lot better than losing. Really a lot better. **Kate Winslet**. Oscar acceptance speech (February 22, 2009)

The winner is simply someone who gets up one more time than they fall over. **Robin Sieger**. *Natural Born Winners* (1999)

The best way to win an argument is to begin by being right. **Jill Ruckelshaus**. Quoted in *Words of Women: Quotations for Success* (1997)

Winning is everything. The only ones who remember you when you come second are your wife and your dog. **Damon Hill**. *Sunday Times (London)* (December 1994)

One of the things I learned long ago about auctions was that it's not about ego or talent. It's simply about raising your hand for the next bid. They won. We lost. Next. **Barry Diller**. *Business Week* (1994)

Everyone is a potential winner. Some people are disguised as losers, don't let their appearances fool you. **Kenneth Blanchard**. *The One Minute Manager* (1993)

He who owns the most when he dies, wins. **Ivan Boesky**. *The Times (London)* (November 20, 1986)

Winners are people who have fun—and produce results as a result of their zest. **Tom Peters**. *A Passion for Excellence* (cowritten with Nancy Austin, 1985)

He who does not hope to win has already lost. **José Joaquín Olmedo**. Quoted in *Reader's Digest* (June 1968)

Women in Business

Do you know why it's so difficult to find a female CEO? It's because most women are sexually frustrated. Men are not because they can fall back on call girls, go to erectile dysfunction clinics. If you have a CEO who's sexually frustrated, she can't act properly. **Graham Boustred**. Quoted in *Business Day (Johannesburg)* (July 8, 2009)

Running a business here in the UK, particularly being a woman, is just far too big a deal. The point at which some woman starts up a business and nobody cares about it, that's when we'll all know we made it. **Barbara Cassani**. "Mount Holyoke College: Barbara Cassani '82, Soaring to New Heights," *Vista* (2000)

Women are underserved and underestimated as consumers. **Geraldine Laybourne**. "The 50 Most Powerful Women in American Business," *Fortune* (Patricia Sellers and Cora Daniels, October 1999)

Women are opening businesses at twice the rate of men ... Forty percent of businesses will be owned by women. Women are saying, I don't belong in this company. I'm sick of fighting this battle. **Faith Popcorn**. Interview, *phenomeNEWS* (1999)

I don't play golf. I don't go to the men's room. I didn't have the ability to network the way men do. But I made myself visible. **Jill Barad**. *Wall Street Journal* (1997)

Women actually do quite well on Wall Street because so much of this business is intuitive. **Elizabeth MacKay**. Quoted in *Women of the Street* (Sue Herera, 1997)

Women are naturally good motivators, good at juggling different projects and issues at the same time, and more cooperative rather than aggressive and confrontational. **Bridget A. Macaskill**. Quoted in *Women of the Street* (Sue Herera, 1997)

One of the biggest mistakes women make in business is that they aren't friendly enough. **Charlotte Beers**. *Fortune* (1996)

It's so much easier for men. They don't have to paint their nails for a meeting. **Eve Pollard**. Quoted in the *Guardian (London)* (December 30, 1995)

Women do not win formula one races, because they simply are not strong enough to resist the G-forces. In the boardroom, it is different. I believe women are better able to marshal their thoughts than men and because they are less egotistical they make fewer assumptions. **Nicola Foulston**. Interview, *Independent (London)* (April 10, 1995)

People assume you slept your way to the top. Frankly, I couldn't sleep my way to the middle. **Joni Evans**. Conference speech to female executives, referring to her start in publishing as a manuscript reader. *New York Times* (July 22, 1986)

I have yet to hear a man ask for advice on how to combine marriage and a career. **Gloria Steinem**. Radio interview, LBC (April 2, 1984)

The men are always playing their own macho games. It's not really the money they want—it's beating their colleagues by making that extra phone call at night. **Anonymous**. A senior female banker on her male colleages and why women are still rare at the top of the profession. Quoted in *The Moneylenders: Bankers in a Dangerous World* (Anthony Sampson, 1981)

Total commitment to family and total commitment to career is possible, but fatiguing. **Muriel Fox**. Quoted in "Wait Late to Marry," *New Woman* (Barbara Jordan Moore, October 1971)

Men always try to keep women out of business so they won't find out how much fun it really is. **Vivien Kellems**. Quoted in *Women Can Be Engineers* (Alice Goff, 1946)

What kind of nation is this ... nation of silk knees, slender necks, narrow fingers, and ironic mouths which has established itself upon our boundaries? **Anonymous**. A complaint about the growing number of women in the modern business office. *Fortune* (1935)

Well-ventilated, well-lighted, and sanitarily kept workrooms, rest-rooms and other creature comforts provided in factories, stores, and office buildings are largely the results of women's presence in industry. **Edith Johnson**. *To Women of the Business World* (1923)

Men are troublesome. They complain about trifles a woman wouldn't notice. The office boys ... complain that the temperature of the building is too hot or too cold ... If they have a slight headache, they stay at home. **Clara Lanza**. "Women Clerks in New York," *Cosmopolitan* (1891)

If you want to push something ... you're accused of being aggressive, and that's not supposed to be a good thing for a woman. If you get upset and show it, you're accused of being emotional. **Mary Harney**. Attributed

Work and Employment

We're living in an economy where productivity is no longer the goal, employment is. That's because, on a very fundamental level, we have pretty much everything we need. America is productive enough that it could probably shelter, feed, educate, and even provide health care for its entire population with just a fraction of us actually working … Our problem is not that we don't have enough stuff—it's that we don't have enough ways for people to work and prove that they deserve this stuff. **Douglas Rushkoff**. "Are Jobs Obsolete?" *CNN* (September 7, 2011)

Work, work, work, but what mark do we leave, what point do we make? People who are too beholden to work become like erasers: as things move forward, they leave in their wake no trace of themselves. **Yann Martel**. Letter to Canadian prime minister Steven Harper (January 31, 2011)

Seeing work as the meaning of life is a human, metaphysical invention; it has little basis in biology. Play, not work, seems to be the defining essence of life on Earth. Elephants push over trees, penguins belly flop on the ice, birds chase each other or drop and catch sticks in the air, cranes leap up together like ballet dancers—and all just for the hell of it. **Joe Moran**. *Guardian (London)* (August 1, 2010)

Hard work often pays off after time, but laziness always pays off now. **E. L. Kersten**. *The Art of Demotivation* (2003)

I think many people just work as a way of not confronting themselves. **Gerry Robinson**. *Management Today* (April 1999)

Some people see things that are and ask, "Why?" Some people dream of things that never were and ask, "Why not?" Some people have to go to work and don't have time for all that shit. **George Carlin**. *Brain Droppings* (1998)

Nothing is really work unless you would rather be doing something else. **Sir James Barrie**. Quoted in *Woodbury Reports Archives* (June 1997)

We do not go to work only to earn an income, but to find meaning in our lives. What we do is a large part of what we are. **Alan Ryan**. Quoted in *If Aristotle Ran General Motors* (Tom Morris, 1997)

Retirement is an illusion. Not a reward but a mantrap. The bankrupt underside of success. A shortcut to death. Golf courses are too much like cemeteries. **Saul Bellow**. *The Actuel* (1997)

The greatest testimony to the human spirit that I'm witnessing now is the fact that people still come back to work, after all that has been done to them. They are still willing to participate for a more positive future if they would be sincerely invited. **Walter Wriston**. Interview with Scott London. US National Public Radio (November 1996)

One day is much like another for the desk-bound office worker: life ebbs away, almost imperceptibly, in a blur of meetings and memos and gossip, of coffee-drinking and conferences and sticky summer afternoons when a post-prandial slumber becomes almost de rigueur; and our passage from our thirties into our forties and beyond is accompanied, and given definition, by the complicated movement of pieces of paper from one place to another. **Jeremy Lewis**. *Kindred Spirits* (1995)

I have nothing against work, particularly when performed, quietly and unobtrusively, by someone else. I just don't happen to think it's an appropriate subject for an ethic. **Barbara Ehrenreich**. "Goodbye to the Work Ethic," *The Worst Years of Our Lives* (1991)

We're not built for free time as a species. We think we are but we aren't. **Douglas Coupland**. *Generation X* (1991)

It's true hard work never killed anyone but I figure why take the chance? **Ronald Reagan**. *Speaking My Mind* (1990)

The one thing I know through experience … is that people don't know why they come to work until they don't have to come to work. **H. Ross Perot**. *Inc.* (January 1989)

The bond between a man and his profession is similar to that which ties him to his country; it is just as complex, often ambivalent, and it is understood completely only when it is broken. **Primo Levi**. *Other People's Trades* (1989)

Japanese salarymen know that for pure relaxation, nothing beats a good long day in the office. **Peter Tasker**. *Inside Japan* (1987)

Without work, all life goes rotten, but when work is soulless, life stifles and dies. **Albert Camus**. Quoted in *Good Work* (E. F. Schumacher, 1979)

Business is like sex. When it's good, it's very, very good; when it's not so good, it's still good. **George Katona**. *Wall Street Journal* (April 9, 1969)

Anyone can do any amount of work provided it isn't the work he is supposed to be doing at the moment. **Robert Benchley**. Quoted in *The Algonquin Wits* (R. E. Drennan, 1968)

If I were a medical man, I should prescribe a holiday to any patient who considered his work important. **Edward O. Wilson**. *Autobiography* (1967)

I believe in hard work. It keeps the wrinkles out of the mind and spirit. **Helena Rubinstein**. *My Life for Beauty* (1965)

Work is much more fun than fun. **Sir Noël Coward**. Quoted in "Sayings of the Week," *Observer (London)* (June 21, 1963)

Work was like cats were supposed to be: if you disliked and feared it … it knew at once and sought you out and jumped on your lap and climbed all over you to show how much it loved you. **Sir Kingsley Amis**. *Take a Girl Like You* (1960), ch. 5

Labor is work that leaves no trace behind it when it is finished. **Mary McCarthy**. "The Vita Activa," *New Yorker* (October 18, 1958)

One of the saddest things is that the only thing a man can do for eight hours a day, day after day, is work. You can't eat … nor make love for eight hours. **William Faulkner**. Interview, *Writers at Work (first series)* (Malcom Cowley, ed, 1958)

Why should I let the toad *work* Squat on my life? … Six days of the week it soils With its sickening poison— Just for paying a few bills! That's out of proportion. **Philip Larkin**. "Toads," *The Less Deceived* (1955), ll. 1–2, 5–8

A man who has no office to go to—I don't care who he is—is a trial of which you can have no conception. **George Bernard Shaw**. *The Irrational Knot* (1950)

The master of the art of living makes little distinction between his work and his play, his labor and his leisure, his mind and his body, his education and his recreation, his love and his religion. He hardly knows which is which. He simply pursues his vision of excellence in whatever he does, leaving others to decide whether he is working or playing. To himself he always seems to be doing both. Enough for him that he does it well. **Lawrence Pearsall Jacks**. *Education Through Recreation* (1932)

  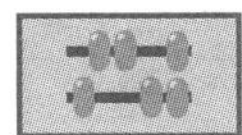   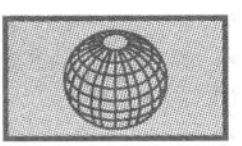   

Work is of two kinds: first, altering the position of matter at or near the earth's surface relative to other matter; second, telling other people to do so. The first kind is unpleasant and ill paid, the second is pleasant and highly paid. **Bertrand Russell (Earl Russell).** *In Praise of Idleness* (1932)

I would live my life in nonchalance and insouciance Were it not for making a living, which is really rather a nouciance. **Ogden Nash.** "Introspective Reflection," *Hard Lines* (1931)

That state is a state of slavery in which a man does what he likes to do in his spare time and, in his working time, that which is required of him. **Eric Gill.** *Art—Nonsense and Other Essays* (1929)

Work alone qualifies us for life. **Zoë Akins.** Attributed (1924)

A perpetual holiday is a good working definition of hell. **George Bernard Shaw.** *Parents and Children* (1914)

Nothing is more humiliating than to have to beg for work, and a system in which any man has to beg for work stands condemned. No man can defend it. **Eugene V. Debs.** Speech given at the founding of the Federal Council of Churches in Girard, Kansas. "The Issue" (May 23, 1908)

I don't like work—no man does—but I like what is in work—the chance to find yourself. Your own reality—for yourself, not for others—what no other man can ever know. **Joseph Conrad.** *Heart of Darkness* (1902)

One of the first things to be noted in business life is its imperialism. Business is exacting, engrossing, and inelastic. **Margaret Sangster.** *Winsome Womanhood* (1900)

I like work; it fascinates me. I can sit and look at it for hours. I love to keep it by me: the idea of getting rid of it nearly breaks my heart. **Jerome K. Jerome.** *Three Men in a Boat* (1889)

Work is the grand cure of all the maladies and miseries that ever beset mankind. **Thomas Carlyle.** Speech, Edinburgh, UK (April 2, 1866)

Everyone confesses in the abstract that exertion ... is the best thing for us all, but practically most people do all they can to get rid of it. **Harriet Beecher Stowe.** "The Lady Who Does Her Own Work," *Atlantic Monthly* (1864)

Every man's work, pursued steadily, tends to become an end in itself, and so to bridge over the loveless chasms of his life. **George Eliot.** *Silas Marner* (1861), ch. 2

If the artist does not fling himself, without reflecting, into his work as the soldier flings himself into the enemy's trenches, and if, once in this crater, he does not work like a miner on whom the walls of his gallery have fallen in; if he contemplates difficulties instead of overcoming them one by one he is simply looking on at the suicide of his own talent. **Honoré de Balzac.** *A Cousine Bette* (1846)

There is nothing like employment, active, indispensable employment, for relieving sorrow. **Jane Austen.** *Mansfield Park* (1814), vol. 3, ch. 15

Work keeps us from three great evils: boredom, vice, and poverty. **Voltaire (François-Marie Arouet).** *Candide* (1759)

What is work and what is not work is a question that perplexes the wisest of men. **Bhagavad Gita.** 4:16 (300? BC)

The world is full of willing people: some willing to work, the rest willing to let them. **Robert Frost.** Attributed

When a man tells you he got rich through hard work, ask him, "Whose?" **Don Marquis.** Attributed

I yield to no one in my admiration for the office as a social centre, but it's no place actually to get any work done. **Katharine Whitehorn.** Attributed

  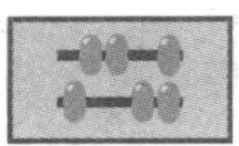   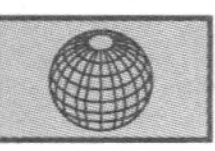   

Author Index

Abbott, John (*b.* 1977) BRITISH cofounder of Oobafit, an online fitness company **1861**

Abdul-Jabbar, Kareem (*b.* 1947) US basketball player **1900**

Abedi, Hasan (1922–1995) PAKISTANI banker and president of the Bank of Credit and Commerce International, Luxembourg **1876**

Abzug, Bella (1920–1998) US politician, lawyer, and campaigner **1847, 1847**

Achebe, Chinua (*b.* 1930) NIGERIAN novelist, poet, and essayist **1845**

Acheson, Dean (1893–1971) US statesman **1820, 1828, 1896**

Ackerman, Gary (*b.* 1942) US congressman **1829**

Acton, John Dalberg-Acton, Lord (1834–1902) BRITISH historian **1888**

Acton Smith, Michael (*b.* 1974) BRITISH entrepreneur, founder of Firebox and founder and CEO of Mind Candy **1865**

Adams, Douglas (1952–2001) BRITISH author **1837, 1874, 1882, 1901, 1901**

Adams, Henry Brooks (1838–1918) US historian **1883, 1888**

Adams, Scott (*b.* 1957) US cartoonist and humorist **1820, 1838, 1839, 1843, 1843, 1854, 1864, 1877, 1878, 1890, 1894, 1900**

Addison, Joseph (1672–1719) BRITISH statesman and author **1899**

Adenauer, Konrad J. (1876–1967) GERMAN chancellor **1844**

Adler, Alfred (1870–1937) AUSTRIAN psychologist and psychiatrist **1889**

Aesop (620?–560? BC) GREEK writer **1830**

Agassiz, Louis (1807–1873) SWISS-BORN US zoologist **1880**

Agate, James (1877–1947) BRITISH critic and essayist **1821**

Agnelli, Giovanni (1921–2003) ITALIAN business executive and president of Fiat **1841, 1846**

Aiken, Howard (1900–1973) US computer engineer and mathematician **1866**

Akins, Zoë (1886–1958) US poet and playwright **1907**

Alda, Alan (*b.* 1936) US actor **1880**

Aldington, Richard (1892–1962) BRITISH poet and novelist **1875**

Alexander, Douglas (*b.* 1967) BRITISH politician **1863**

Alexander, Shana (1925–2005) US writer and editor **1854**

Ali, Muhammad (*b.* 1942) US boxer **1871, 1874, 1875**

Alibhai-Brown, Yasmin (*b.* 1949) UGANDAN-BORN BRITISH journalist and author **1864**

Alinsky, Saul (1909–1972) US activist **1833, 1887**

Allchin, Jim (*b.* 1951) US computer scientist and former Microsoft executive **1877**

Allen, David (*b.* 1945) US time-management consultant and author **1890**

Allen, Fred (1894–1956) US comedian and satirist **1820, 1855, 1878**

Allen, Robert G. (*b.* 1948) CANADIAN financial writer **1894**

Allen, Woody (*b.* 1935) US actor, humorist, movie producer, and director **1837, 1837, 1880, 1899**

Allesandra, Tony US marketing strategist and motivational speaker **1895**

Amis, Sir Kingsley (1922–1995) BRITISH novelist and poet **1892, 1906**

Amis, Martin (*b.* 1949) BRITISH novelist **1880**

Anderson, Bruce BRITISH journalist **1822, 1825, 1849**

Anderson, Chris (*b.* 1961) US author and journalist, editor-in-chief of *Wired* **1850, 1850**

Anderson, Poul (1926–2001) US science fiction writer **1890**

Anderson, Walter (*b.* 1944) US writer and former CEO of Parade Publications **1874**

Andrews, David (*b.* 1936) IRISH politician **1885**

Angelides, Phil (*b.* 1953) US politician **1858**

Anonymous 1818, 1818, 1819, 1820, 1820, 1822, 1823, 1825, 1827, 1828, 1829, 1831, 1832, 1834, 1834, 1834, 1838, 1839, 1839, 1842, 1845, 1846, 1848, 1848, 1848, 1849, 1849, 1849, 1849, 1849, 1849, 1850, 1852, 1852, 1852, 1852, 1858, 1860, 1861, 1861, 1861, 1863, 1864, 1864, 1865, 1873, 1873, 1875, 1877, 1879, 1880, 1880, 1881, 1881, 1882, 1882, 1882, 1882, 1885, 1886, 1890, 1891, 1891, 1894, 1895, 1898, 1900, 1903, 1905, 1905

Anthony, Susan B. (1820–1906) US reformer and women's suffrage leader **1847**

Antrim, Minna (1856–1950) US writer **1856, 1857**

Appleyard, Bryan (*b.* 1951) BRITISH journalist **1831, 1868, 1875, 1900, 1900, 1902**

Archer, Jeffrey, Lord (*b.* 1940) BRITISH novelist and politician **1855, 1887**

Archer, Mary, Lady (*b.* 1944) BRITISH scientist **1818**

Archibald, Jules (1856–1919) AUSTRALIAN journalist **1867**

Arden, Elizabeth (1884–1966) US entrepreneur and cosmetics manufacturer **1853, 1903**

Arendt, Hannah (1906–1975) US political philosopher **1896**

Argyris, Chris (*b.* 1923) US academic and organizational behavior theorist **1874**

Armour, Philip D. (1832–1901) US business executive **1881, 1891**

Armstrong, Lance (*b.* 1971) US former racing cyclist, banned for drugs violations **1874**

Armstrong, Richard (1903–1986) BRITISH author and mariner **1819**

Armstrong, William, Lord (1915–1980) BRITISH civil servant **1863**

Arnason, Sigurjon ICELANDIC CEO of nationalized bank Landsbanki (operated as Icesave in the UK) **1824**

Arthur, W. Brian (*b.* 1945) US economist **1851, 1851**

Ash, Mary Kay (1915–2001) US entrepreneur, business executive, and founder of Mary Kay Cosmetics **1837, 1853, 1857, 1863, 1874, 1886, 1888**

Astor, John Jacob (1763–1848) US entrepreneur and financier **1905**

Atkins, Paul S. (*b.* 1958) US former member of the Securities and Exchange Commission **1858**

Atkinson, Brooks (1894–1984) US critic and essayist **1853**

Atwood, Margaret (*b.* 1939) CANADIAN poet and novelist **1833**

Auden, W. H. (1907–1973) US poet **1872, 1875**

August, John (*b.* 1970) US screenwriter **1880**

Auphan, Raphael FRENCH business executive **1847**

Aurobindo, Sri (1872–1950) INDIAN philosopher, mystic, and nationalist **1895**

Austen, Jane (1775–1817) BRITISH novelist **1907**

Auster, Paul (*b.* 1947) US novelist, short-story writer, and poet **1880**

Avery, Oswald Theodore (1877–1955) US bacteriologist **1857**

Babbage, Charles (1792–1871) BRITISH mathematician and inventor **1848**

Bacon, Sir Francis (Viscount St Alban) (1561–1626) ENGLISH philosopher and statesman **1883**

Bagehot, Walter (1826–1877) BRITISH economist and journalist **1824, 1824, 1831, 1866**

Bailey, Stephen (*b.* 1951) BRITISH design critic **1835, 1867**

Baker, Danny (*b.* 1957) BRITISH journalist and broadcaster **1879**

Baker, Russell (*b.* 1925) US journalist **1849**

Baldwin, James (1924–1987) US writer **1833, 1856, 1880, 1887**

Baldwin, Tom US financial trader **1859**

Ballard, J. G. (1930–2010) BRITISH novelist **1843, 1853, 1861, 1902**

Balls, Ed (*b.* 1967) BRITISH politician **1826**

Balogh, Thomas (1905–1985) BRITISH economist **1851**

Balzac, Honoré de (1799–1850) FRENCH novelist **1907**

Band, Richard US financial writer **1827**

Banks-Smith, Nancy (*b.* 1929) BRITISH journalist **1887**

Barad, Jill (*b.* 1951) US former CEO of Mattel **1905**

Barbery, Muriel (*b.* 1969) FRENCH novelist and philosopher **1870**

  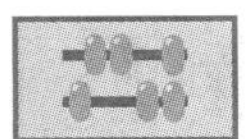   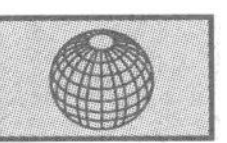   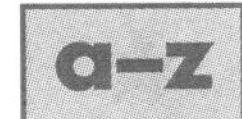

Barker, Joel A. US futurologist **1873, 1903**
Barlow, John Perry (*b.* 1947) US academic, lyricist, and writer **1833, 1863**
Barnard, Chester (1886–1961) US business executive and management theorist **1840, 1903**
Barnett, Thomas (*b.* 1962) US geostrategist and author **1847, 1847, 1847**
Barnevik, Percy (*b.* 1941) SWEDISH former CEO of ABB **1833, 1844, 1865**
Barnum, P. T. (1810–1891) US showman and circus entrepreneur **1895**
Barrie, Sir James (1860–1937) BRITISH novelist and playwright **1906**
Barrows, Sydney Biddle (*b.* 1952) US brothel owner **1830**
Barry, Dave (*b.* 1947) US humorist **1837, 1852, 1854**
Bartlett, Christopher (*b.* 1945) AUSTRALIAN business writer **1840, 1840, 1876, 1889**
Barton, Bruce (1886–1967) US advertising executive and author **1820, 1837**
Baruch, Bernard (1870–1965) US financier and economist **1855, 1859, 1860, 1902**
Barzun, Jacques (*b.* 1907) FRENCH-BORN US educator, historian, and writer **1835, 1844, 1883**
Bateson, Mary Catherine (*b.* 1939) US anthropologist **1863**
Baudelaire, Charles (1821–1867) FRENCH poet and critic **1890**
Baudrillard, Jean (1929–2007) FRENCH philosopher **1823, 1844, 1855, 1897, 1898**
Bean, Charles (*b.* 1953) BRITISH economist and deputy governor of the Bank of England **1826**
Beard, James (1903–1985) US chef and author **1819**
Beaverbrook, Lord (Max Aitken) (1879–1964) CANADIAN-BORN BRITISH newspaper owner and politician **1887**
Beckett, Samuel (1906–1989) IRISH playwright, novelist, and poet **1857**
Beckett, Sir Terence Norman (*b.* 1923) BRITISH business executive **1863**
Beecham, Sir Thomas, Bt (1879–1961) BRITISH conductor **1873**
Beecher, Henry Ward (1813–1887) US clergyman and reformer **1844, 1897**
Beers, Charlotte (*b.* 1935) US advertising executive and former under secretary of state for public diplomacy and public affairs **1840, 1905**
Behan, Brendan (1923–1964) IRISH playwright and author **1892**
Bell, C. Gordon (*b.* 1934) US inventor and computer pioneer **1890**
Belloc, Hilaire (1870–1953) BRITISH writer and politician **1897**
Bellow, Saul (1915–2005) US novelist **1906**
Benchley, Robert (1889–1945) US humorist **1893, 1906**
Benn, Tony (*b.* 1925) BRITISH politician **1835, 1869, 1892**
Bennett, Alan (*b.* 1934) BRITISH playwright **1834, 1892**
Bennett, Arnold (1867–1931) BRITISH novelist, playwright, and essayist **1849, 1892, 1899**
Bennett, Drake US journalist **1869**
Bennis, Warren (*b.* 1925) US educator and writer **1824, 1833, 1854, 1873, 1874, 1875, 1899, 1899**
Bentham, Jeremy (1748–1832) BRITISH philosopher, economist, and jurist **1864, 1872**
Bentley, Eric (*b.* 1916) BRITISH writer **1866**
Bentley, John (*b.* 1940) BRITISH entrepreneur **1860**
Berardino, Joseph (*b.* 1951) US business executive **1842, 1871**
Berle, Milton (1908–2002) US comedian **1829**
Berlin, Irving (1888–1989) US composer and songwriter **1899**
Bernanke, Ben (*b.* 1953) US economist and chairman of the US Federal Reserve **1823, 1826, 1827**
Bernard, Tristan (1866–1947) FRENCH novelist and dramatist **1896**
Bernbach, William (1911–1982) US advertising executive **1899**
Berners-Lee, Sir Tim (*b.* 1955) BRITISH computer scientist and inventor of the World Wide Web **1837, 1901**
Bernstein, Paula (*b.* 1933) US writer **1841**
Bernstein, Peter (1919–2009) US economist and author **1890**
Betjeman, Sir John (1906–1984) BRITISH poet **1871**
Bevan, Aneurin (1897–1960) BRITISH politician **1829, 1868, 1888**
Bevan, Sir Timothy (*b.* 1927) BRITISH banker **1830**
Bezos, Jeff (*b.* 1964) US founder and CEO of Amazon.com **1844, 1850, 1894**
Bhagavad Gita Hindu scripture **1819, 1860, 1907**
Bhatia, Subeer (*b.* 1967) INDIAN IT entrepreneur and founder of Hotmail **1848, 1849**
Bierce, Ambrose (1842–1914?) US journalist and writer **1830, 1841, 1856, 1872**
Bilimoria, Karan, Lord (*b.* 1962) INDIAN entrepreneur and founder of Cobra Beer **1886**
Bingaman, Anne K. (*b.* 1943) US lawyer **1863, 1863**
Birdseye, Clarence (1886–1956) US inventor, businessman, and founder of Birds Eye **1883**
Bismarck, Otto Edward Leopold von (1815–1898) PRUSSIAN chancellor **1834**
Black, Conrad, Lord (*b.* 1944) CANADIAN-BORN BRITISH newspaper proprietor and business executive **1842, 1842, 1877**
Blacker, Terence (*b.* 1948) BRITISH author and journalist **1864, 1866, 1875**
Blair, Gerald M. (*b.* 1959) US writer **1876**
Blair, Tony (*b.* 1953) BRITISH former prime minister **1873**
Blanchard, Kenneth (*b.* 1939) US management theorist and author **1865, 1867, 1884, 1888, 1905**
Blank, Warren (*b.* 1945) US writer **1872**
Block, Peter (*b.* 1935) US writer **1852, 1874**
Bloomberg, Michael (*b.* 1942) US entrepreneur, business executive, and mayor of New York **1837, 1855, 1864, 1877, 1887**
Blyth, Mark US political economist **1822**
Boesky, Ivan (*b.* 1937) US financier convicted of insider dealing in 1987 **1843, 1871, 1873, 1905**
Boettke, Peter (*b.* 1960) US economist **1831**
Bogle, John Clifton (*b.* 1929) US investment analyst, founder and CEO of the Vanguard Group **1856, 1859, 1870, 1871**
Bolt, Robert (1924–1995) BRITISH screenwriter and dramatist **1839, 1878**
Bonfield, Sir Peter (*b.* 1944) BRITISH former CEO of British Telecom **1879**
Bonhoeffer, Dietrich (1906–1945) GERMAN religious writer **1819**
Bookchin, Murray (1921–2006) US writer and environmentalist **1831**
Boorstin, Daniel J. (1914–2004) US Pulitzer Prize-winning historian **1820, 1892**
Bootle, Roger (*b.* 1952) BRITISH economist, financial analyst, and author **1850**
Boren, James H. (1925–2010) US lecturer and satirist **1828**
Borges, Jorge Luis (1899–1986) ARGENTINIAN writer **1892**
Borman, Frank (*b.* 1928) US astronaut and business executive **1831**
Boulding, Kenneth (1910–1993) BRITISH-BORN US economist and political activist **1864**
Boustred, Graham SOUTH AFRICAN businessman, former deputy chairman of Anglo-American mining **1905**
Bowen, Elizabeth (1899–1973) IRISH writer **1856**
Bowersock, Terri (*b.* 1956) US furniture company entrepreneur **1854**
Boyd, William (*b.* 1952) BRITISH novelist and scriptwriter **1890**
Bradbury, Ray (*b.* 1920) US writer **1894**
Bradley, F. H. (1846–1924) BRITISH philosopher **1896**
Bradner, Scott US computer scientist, secretary of the Internet Society **1850**
Bradt, George (*b.* 1958) US management guru and blogger **1865**
Brady, Charles (*b.* 1935) US investor **1862**
Braiker, Harriet Beryl (1948–2004) US psychologist **1854**
Brand, Stewart (*b.* 1938) US author **1854**
Brandstätter, Horst (*b.* 1933) GERMAN toy manufacturer and director of Playmobil **1891**
Branson, Sir Richard (*b.* 1950) BRITISH entrepreneur, founder and chairman of Virgin Group **1818, 1836, 1864, 1884**

Brecht, Bertolt (1898–1956) GERMAN playwright and poet **1824, 1830, 1895**
Bregman, Peter US strategic business adviser **1819**
Brenner, Sydney (*b.* 1927) SOUTH AFRICAN-BORN BRITISH scientist and winner of the 2002 Nobel Prize in Medicine **1837**
Bristol, Lee US pioneer of renewable energy systems **1891**
Bro, Margueritte (1894–1977) US writer **1844**
Brockman, John (*b.* 1941) US science writer and literary agent **1894**
Bronfman, Edgar, Jr (*b.* 1955) CANADIAN chairman of Warner Music Group **1880**
Bronowski, Jacob (1908–1974) POLISH mathematician and philosopher **1819, 1895**
Brontë, Anne (1820–1849) BRITISH novelist and poet **1899**
Brontë, Charlotte (1816–1855) BRITISH novelist and poet **1832**
Brookner, Anita (*b.* 1928) BRITISH novelist and art historian **1824**
Broun, Heywood Hale (1918–2001) US broadcast journalist, actor, and author **1846**
Brown, Derby US businessman **1821**
Brown, Gordon (*b.* 1951) BRITISH former prime minister **1827**
Brown, Helen Gurley (*b.* 1922) US writer and editor **1885**
Brown, Jonathan BRITISH journalist **1902**
Brown, Mandy US writer, designer, and blogger **1843**
Brown, Shona L. (*b.* 1966) CANADIAN writer **1887**
Browning, Robert (1812–1889) BRITISH poet **1863, 1899**
Brune, Sisam US lawyer **1829**
Bryan, Sir Arthur (1923–2011) BRITISH chairman of Wedgwood **1866**
Buchwald, Art (1925–2007) US journalist
Buck, Pearl S. (1892–1973) US writer **1879**
Buffett, Warren (*b.* 1930) US entrepreneur and financier **1819, 1827, 1837, 1839, 1839, 1854, 1857, 1858, 1859, 1859, 1859, 1861, 1864, 1870, 1871, 1871, 1871, 1871, 1871, 1880, 1885, 1889, 1891, 1891, 1892, 1893, 1893, 1894, 1896, 1897, 1897, 1900, 1902**
Burchill, Julie (*b.* 1959) BRITISH journalist **1854**
Bureau of Labor US former government department **1847**
Burke, Edmund (1729–1797) IRISH-BORN BRITISH philosopher and politician **1818, 1872, 1888, 1899**
Burke, James E. (*b.* 1925) US former CEO of Johnson & Johnson **1846**
Burke, Thomas (1886–1945) BRITISH writer **1888**
Burkeman, Oliver (*b.* 1975) BRITISH journalist and author **1843, 1890**
Burnett, Leo (1891–1971) US advertising executive and author **1820, 1821**
Burns, H. S. M. (1900–1971) BRITISH oil industry executive, geophysicist, and president of Shell Oil Company **1877**
Burroughs, Nannie (1883–1961) US educator and journalist **1832**
Burroughs, William S. (1914–1997) US novelist **1891**
Burson, Harold (*b.* 1921) US business executive and founder of Burson-Marsteller **1892**
Burton, John C. (1932–2010) US accountant and academic **1818**
Burton, Sir Montague (1885–1952) BRITISH tailor and founder of the Burton Group **1838**
Bush, George W. (*b.* 1946) US former president **1826, 1826, 1826, 1827, 1827, 1842, 1858**
Bush, Jeb (*b.* 1953) US politician, former governor of Florida **1824**
Busquet, Anne (*b.* 1951?) US business executive **1844**
Butler, Sir David (*b.* 1924) BRITISH psephologist **1839**
Butler, Nicholas Murray (1862–1947) US academic **1872**
Butler, Samuel (1835–1902) BRITISH writer **1818, 1839, 1852, 1880, 1892, 1899**
Byrne, John A. US journalist and writer **1829**
Byrnes, James F. (1879–1972) US politician **1888**
Byron, George Gordon, Lord (1788–1824) BRITISH poet **1830**
Bywater, Michael (*b.* 1953) BRITISH journalist and author **1869**
Cable, Vince (*b.* 1943) BRITISH politician **1826, 1850, 1862**
Cadbury, Sir Dominic (*b.* 1940) BRITISH business executive, former CEO and chairman of Cadbury Schweppes **1902**
Cage, John (1912–1992) US composer **1866**
Cairncross, Frances (*b.* 1944) BRITISH journalist and author **1862**
Caldwell, Christopher (*b.* 1962) US journalist **1822**
Calloway, Wayne (1935–1998) US CEO of PepsiCo **1836**
Cameron, David (*b.* 1966) BRITISH prime minister **1827**
Campbell, Bill (*b.* 1940) US chairman of Intuit **1840, 1873**
Campos, Roberto (1917–2001) BRAZILIAN politician and economist **1849**
Campos, Roel C. (*b.* 1949) US member of the Securities and Exchange Commission **1823**
Camus, Albert (1913–1960) FRENCH novelist and essayist **1833, 1834, 1855, 1906**
Canetti, Elias (1905–1994) BRITISH philosopher and writer **1846**
Cantor, Eddie (1892–1964) US entertainer **1898**
Carlin, George (1937–2008) US comedian and author **1906**
Carlyle, Thomas (1795–1881) BRITISH historian and essayist **1820, 1864, 1868, 1907**
Carnegie, Andrew (1835–1919) US industrialist and philanthropist **1828, 1831, 1835, 1850, 1873, 1886, 1886, 1904**
Carnegie, Dale (1888–1955) US consultant and author **1853, 1898**
Carr, Simon BRITISH journalist **1822, 1822, 1831, 1850, 1853, 1880, 1886**
Carter, Angela (1940–1992) BRITISH novelist, short-story writer, and essayist **1866, 1890**
Carville, James (*b.* 1944) US political consultant, presidential campaign manager to Bill Clinton **1860**
Cassani, Barbara (*b.* 1960) US former CEO of Go **1835, 1905**
Cassano, Joseph J. (*b.* 1955?) US former executive of AIG insurance **1858**
Cassel, Sir Ernest (1852–1921) BRITISH private banker to King Edward VII **1823**
Caulkin, Simon BRITISH business journalist **1833, 1876, 1876, 1876, 1876, 1900**
Chajet, Clive (*b.* 1937) US management consultant **1866**
Chakrabortty, Aditya BRITISH economics journalist **1821**
Chakraborty, S. K. (*b.* 1957) INDIAN academic **1833, 1848, 1873, 1874, 1875**
Chalker, Lynda, Baroness (*b.* 1942) BRITISH politician **1843**
Chambers, Chuck US CEO of Sara Lee Direct **1830**
Chamfort, Nicholas (1741–1794) FRENCH writer **1851**
Champy, James (*b.* 1942) US business executive **1876**
Chandler, Kyle (*b.* 1965) US actor **1883**
Chandler, Raymond (1888–1959) US writer **1820, 1830**
Chandos, Viscount (Oliver Lyttelton) (1893–1972) BRITISH statesman and industrialist **1872, 1893**
Chanel, Coco (1883–1971) FRENCH couturier **1870**
Chang, Ha-Joon (*b.* 1963) SOUTH KOREAN economist and author **1831, 1831, 1850, 1857, 1900, 1903**
Chang, Kenneth US journalist **1860**
Chanos, Jim (*b.* 1958) US hedge fund manager **1831**
Chartier, Émile-August (1868–1951) FRENCH philosopher **1866**
Chaudhuri, Amit (*b.* 1962) INDIAN author and academic **1902**
Chekhov, Anton (1860–1904) RUSSIAN playwright and short-story writer **1819**
Cheng Siwei (*b.* 1935) CHINESE vice chairman of the National People's Congress of China **1848**
Chernin, Peter (*b.* 1951) US former president and COO of News Corporation, and former CEO and chairman of the Fox Entertainment Group **1877, 1886**
Chesterfield, Lord (Philip Dormer Stanhope) (1694–1773) ENGLISH statesman, orator, and letter writer **1835**

Chesterton, G. K. (1874–1936) BRITISH novelist, poet, and critic **1820, 1830, 1835, 1852, 1861, 1883, 1890, 1896, 1902**

Chichester, Sir Francis Charles (1901–1972) BRITISH yachtsman and aviator **1832**

Chomsky, Noam (*b.* 1928) US linguist and political activist **1850**

Christensen, Clayton M. (*b.* 1952) US writer **1844, 1874**

Christie, Dame Agatha (1891–1976) BRITISH novelist **1870**

Churchill, Charles (1731–1764) BRITISH curate and satirist **1866**

Churchill, Jennie (1854–1921) US socialite and writer **1833**

Churchill, Sir Winston (1874–1965) BRITISH prime minister **1824, 1846, 1866, 1885, 1894, 1897**

Cicero (106–43 BC) ROMAN orator and statesman **1897**

Cimino, Michael (*b.* 1939) US movie director **1818**

Clark, Alan (1928–1999) BRITISH politician and diarist **1844, 1865**

Clark, Eugenie (*b.* 1922) US biologist **1893**

Clarke, Sir Arthur C. (1917–2008) BRITISH science fiction writer **1901**

Clausewitz, Karl von (1780–1831) PRUSSIAN general and military strategist **1887**

Cleese, John (*b.* 1939) BRITISH comedian, actor, and writer **1830**

Clegg, Stewart (*b.* 1947) AUSTRALIAN writer **1869**

Clifford, Robert (*b.* 1943) AUSTRALIAN business executive **1900**

Clifton, Jim (*b.* 1951) US CEO and chairman of Gallup **1868**

Clifton, Lucille (1936–2010) US poet and author **1819**

Clough, Arthur Hugh (1819–1861) BRITISH poet **1830, 1837, 1875**

Cocks, Barnett (1907–1989) BRITISH author **1828**

Cocteau, Jean (1889–1963) FRENCH poet, novelist, dramatist, and movie director **1875**

Coggan, Philip (*b.* 1959) BRITISH journalist **1879**

Colbert, L. L. (1905–1995) US chairman of Chrysler Corporation **1855**

Colchester, Nicholas (1949?–1996) BRITISH author and journalist **1849**

Coleman, Debi (*b.* 1953) US business executive and former CFO of Apple Computer **1841**

Coleridge, Samuel Taylor (1772–1834) BRITISH poet **1856**

Collier, Paul BRITISH economist **1894**

Colman, Jeremiah James (1830–1898) BRITISH food industry executive **1887**

Comfort, Max BRITISH business theorist **1861**

Commines, Philippe de (1445?–1511?) FRENCH historian and politician **1874**

Cone, Fairfax (1903–1977) US advertising executive **1820, 1820, 1836, 1853**

Confucius (551–479 BC) CHINESE philosopher, administrator, and writer **1819, 1834, 1834, 1877, 1899**

Conner, Daryl R. (*b.* 1946) US management author **1883**

Connolly, Cyril (1903–1974) BRITISH critic, essayist, and novelist **1899**

Conrad, Joseph (1857–1924) POLISH-BORN BRITISH novelist and seaman **1907**

Conran, Shirley (*b.* 1932) BRITISH designer, fashion editor, and author **1852, 1889**

Conran, Sir Terence (*b.* 1931) BRITISH designer, restaurateur, and founder of Habitat **1895, 1899**

Cook, Rick (*b.* 1944) US author **1837**

Cooley, Charles Horton (1864–1929) US sociologist **1852, 1888**

Coolidge, Calvin (1872–1933) US president **1831, 1886, 1891, 1904**

Cooper, Roy (*b.* 1957) US attorney general of North Carolina **1823**

Corrigan, E. Gerald (*b.* 1941) US investment banker and managing director of Goldman Sachs **1902**

Corrigan, Paul (*b.* 1948) BRITISH author **1876**

Cossman, E. Joseph (1918–2002) US salesman and entrepreneur **1845, 1889**

Coupland, Douglas (*b.* 1961) WEST GERMAN-BORN CANADIAN writer **1906**

Courville, Léon (*b.* 1945) CANADIAN banker **1876**

Covey, Stephen (*b.* 1932) US writer and psychologist **1821, 1884, 1887, 1896**

Coward, Sir Noël (1899–1973) BRITISH dramatist, actor, producer, and composer **1906**

Cowen, Tyler (*b.* 1962) US economist, journalist, and blogger **1850**

Cox, Christopher (*b.* 1952) US former chairman of the Securities and Exchange Commission **1823**

Coyle, Diane BRITISH economist and journalist **1837**

Craig, David BRITISH author and former management consultant **1838**

Crawford, Richard US investment banker **1884**

Cringley, Robert X. pen name of journalist Mark Stephens and others **1901**

Crisp, Quentin (1908–1999) BRITISH writer **1834**

Crockett, Davy (1786–1836) US frontiersman, pioneer, and politician **1872**

Crosby, Philip B. (1926–2001) US business executive and author **1870, 1892**

Cuomo, Andrew (*b.* 1957) US governor of New York State **1829**

Curtis, Donald (1915–1997) US actor, minister, and writer **1866**

D'Alessio, Kitty US business executive **1833**

Dali, Salvador (1904–1989) SPANISH artist **1821**

Danton, Georges Jacques (1759–1794) FRENCH lawyer and revolutionary leader **1824**

Darling, Alistair (*b.* 1953) BRITISH politician **1821, 1862, 1903**

Darman, Richard G. (1943–2008) US investment banker, academic, and presidential adviser **1828**

Darwin, Charles (1809–1882) BRITISH scientist and evolutionary theorist **1838**

Darwin, Francis (1848–1925) BRITISH botanist **1895**

D'Aveni, Richard (*b.* 1950) US strategist **1836**

David-Neel, Alexandra (1868–1969) FRENCH oriental scholar and explorer **1846**

Davidson, Hugh (*b.* 1935) BRITISH management consultant **1869**

Davies, George (*b.* 1941) BRITISH fashion entrepreneur **1828**

Davies, Sir Howard (*b.* 1951) BRITISH former chairman of the Financial Services Authority **1820**

Davies, Robertson (1913–1995) CANADIAN novelist, playwright, and essayist **1875**

Davies, Russell BRITISH advertising executive and journalist **1820**

Davies, William BRITISH academic and writer **1830**

Davis, Bette (1908–1989) US actor **1899**

Davis, Keith (*b.* 1926) AUSTRALIAN administrator and physician **1828**

de Bono, Edward (*b.* 1933) MALTESE-BORN BRITISH creative-thinking theorist, educator, and writer **1855, 1899**

de Botton, Alain (*b.* 1969) SWISS philosophical writer **1821, 1892, 1893**

Debs, Eugene V. (1855–1926) US politician and labor union leader **1832, 1867, 1896, 1907**

Defoe, Daniel (1660–1731) ENGLISH novelist and journalist **1890**

de Gaulle, Charles (1890–1970) FRENCH president and brigadier general **1834, 1849**

de Geus, Arie (*b.* 1938) DUTCH writer **1874**

Dell, Michael (*b.* 1965) US founder, CEO, and chairman of Dell, Inc. **1840, 1840, 1850, 1898**

Della Femina, Jerry (*b.* 1936) US advertising executive **1820, 1888**

Deming, W. Edwards (1900–1993) US consultant and author **1844, 1852, 1874, 1876, 1892, 1892**

Dennis, Felix (*b.* 1947) BRITISH entrepreneur and publisher **1857, 1857, 1889**

Derek, Bo (*b.* 1956) US actress **1839**

Deresiewicz, William US essayist and critic **1818**

Desai, Rajiv INDIAN journalist and public relations executive **1849, 1849**

de Savary, Peter (*b.* 1944) BRITISH entrepreneur **1854**

Descartes, René (1596–1650) FRENCH philosopher and mathematician **1835, 1885**

Devlin, Bernadette (*b.* 1947) IRISH politician **1846**

De Vries, Peter (1910–1993) US novelist and short-story writer **1900**

  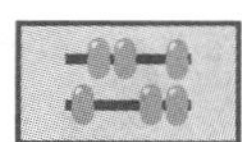      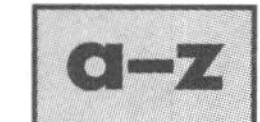

Dewar, Sir James (1842–1923) BRITISH physicist **1844**
Dickens, Charles (1812–1870) BRITISH novelist **1828, 1830**
Diller, Barry (*b.* 1942) US media mogul **1905**
Dimancescu, Dan (*b.* 1943) US consultant and writer **1836**
Dimon, Jamie (*b.* 1956) US CEO of JPMorgan Chase **1825**
DiNapoli, Joseph US financial analyst **1882**
Dirksen, Everett (1896–1969) US senator **1880**
Disraeli, Benjamin (Earl of Beaconsfield) (1804–1881) BRITISH prime minister and novelist **1820, 1835, 1883**
Doctorow, E. L. (*b.* 1931) US novelist **1855**
Dohmen, Bert US investor and financial commentator **1882**
Dos Passos, John (1896–1970) US novelist **1832**
Dostoevsky, Fyodor (1821–1881) RUSSIAN novelist **1824**
Downey, Morgan US commodities trader **1827**
Dreman, David N. (*b.* 1937) US investor **1859**
Drew, Daniel (1797–1879) US financier **1859**
Drexler, Peggy US psychologist and author **1902**
Driehaus, Richard (*b.* 1942) US fund manager **1859**
Dr John (*b.* 1940) US blues and jazz musician **1841**
Druckenmiller, Stanley (*b.* 1953) US financier **1859**
Drucker, Peter F. (1909–2005) US management consultant and academic **1819, 1827, 1832, 1833, 1837, 1839, 1841, 1845, 1845, 1852, 1852, 1852, 1861, 1868, 1869, 1869, 1869, 1872, 1872, 1873, 1876, 1876, 1877, 1877, 1877, 1879, 1886, 1890, 1890, 1894, 1898, 1903, 1904**
Duell, Charles H. (1905–1970) US commissioner of the US Patent Office **1869**
Duhamel, Georges (1884–1966) FRENCH writer **1883**
Duhon, Terri US financier **1858**
Dulles, John Foster (1888–1959) US statesman **1894**
Dunkerley, Michael BRITISH author **1884**
Dunn, Michael BRITISH business psychologist **1865**
Dunstone, Charles (*b.* 1964) BRITISH business executive and founder of Carphone Warehouse **1844, 1901**
Dylan, Bob (*b.* 1941) US singer-songwriter **1898, 1899**
Dyson, Esther (*b.* 1951) US knowledge entrepreneur and government adviser **1856, 1866, 1885, 1901**
Dyson, Freeman (*b.* 1923) BRITISH-BORN US physicist **1890**
Dyson, Sir James (*b.* 1947) BRITISH designer and entrepreneur **1856, 1866, 1898**
Easterly, William (*b.* 1957) US economist and author **1860**
Eaton, Robert J. (*b.* 1940) US automobile industry executive and engineer **1859**
Ecclestone, Bernie (*b.* 1930) BRITISH entrepreneur and CEO of Formula 1 motor racing **1824**
Ecker, Frederick Hudson (1867–1964) US insurance executive and chairman of Metropolitan Life **1871**
Eckhardt, William US mathematician and financial trader **1859, 1875**
Eden, Anthony (Earl of Avon) (1897–1977) BRITISH prime minister **1851**
Edison, Thomas (1847–1931) US inventor **1869, 1884, 1900**
Edwardes, Sir Michael Owen (*b.* 1930) SOUTH AFRICAN-BORN BRITISH company executive **1873**
Ehrenreich, Barbara (*b.* 1941) US writer, sociologist, and feminist **1828, 1899, 1906**
Einstein, Albert (1879–1955) GERMAN-BORN US physicist **1833, 1835, 1862, 1870, 1900**
Eisenhower, Dwight D. (1890–1969) US president and general of the army **1873, 1887**
Eisman, Steve US financial trader **1829**
Eisner, Michael (*b.* 1942) US former CEO and chairman of Disney **1852, 1856, 1878**
Elder, Alexander ESTONIAN-BORN US financial trader and psychiatrist **1859**
Eliot, George (1819–1880) BRITISH novelist **1832, 1861, 1864, 1907**
Eliot, T. S. (1888–1965) US-BORN BRITISH poet, dramatist, and critic **1855, 1869, 1899**
Elizabeth II (*b.* 1926) BRITISH Queen **1826**
Elkington, John (*b.* 1949) BRITISH author and ecologist **1872**
Ellis, Havelock (1859–1939) BRITISH psychologist **1892**
Ellison, Larry D. (*b.* 1944) US cofounder and CEO of Oracle Corporation **1867**
Emerson, Ralph Waldo (1803–1882) US essayist, lecturer, and poet **1835, 1838, 1853, 1856, 1857, 1857, 1866, 1867, 1875, 1880, 1888, 1892, 1896**
Emmott, Bill (*b.* 1956) BRITISH economics journalist **1827**
Eng, William F. US financial trader and author **1859**
Engels, Friedrich (1820–1895) GERMAN social philosopher and political economist **1835**
England, Dan (*b.* 1948) US chairman of C. R. England, Inc. **1900**
Ensign, John (*b.* 1958) US senator **1857**
Enzi, Mike (*b.* 1944) US senator **1858**
Epictetus (55?–135?) GREEK philosopher **1838**
Esar, Evan (1899–1995) US humorist **1887**
Evans, Sir Harold (*b.* 1928) BRITISH journalist and editor, editor-at-large of Reuters **1867**
Evans, Joni (*b.* 1942) US publishing executive **1905**
Ewing, D. W. (*b.* 1923) US writer and editor of *Harvard Business Review* **1903**
Ewing, Sam (1920–2001) US author **1824, 1839, 1872, 1895, 1900**
Fadiman, Clifton (1904–1999) US editor and author **1830, 1902**
Fallon, Ivon BRITISH journalist and author **1825**
Farmer, Sir Tom (*b.* 1940) BRITISH entrepreneur, founder and former chairman of Kwik-Fit **1895**
Faulkner, William (1897–1962) US novelist **1906**
Faulks, Sebastian (*b.* 1953) BRITISH novelist and writer **1863, 1889**
Fawkes, Guy (1570–1606) ENGLISH conspirator **1894**
Fayol, Henri (1841–1925) FRENCH management theorist and mining engineer **1900**
Fei Xiaotong (1910–2005) CHINESE social anthropologist **1848**
Felcht, Utz (*b.* 1947) GERMAN chairman of Degussa **1840**
Fellini, Federico (1920–1993) ITALIAN movie director **1867**
Ferguson, Charles H. (*b.* 1955) US documentary filmmaker and author **1842**
Ferguson, Craig (*b.* 1955) US movie director **1842**
Ferguson, Niall (*b.* 1964) BRITISH historian **1827**
Fergusson, Adam BRITISH author **1903**
Fernandez, Raul (*b.* 1966) MEXICAN IT entrepreneur **1850**
Fey, Grace US former vice president and director of Frontier Capital Management **1847**
Fey, Tina (*b.* 1970) US comedian and actress **1839**
Feynman, Richard P. (1918–1988) US physicist **1866, 1895**
Field, Marshall (1834–1906) US retailer **1845**
Fields, W. C. (1880–1946) US actor and comedian **1857**
Figgie, Harry E., Jr (1923?–2009) US founder of Figgie International **1873**
Financial Crisis Inquiry Commission (2009–2011) US government-appointed commission **1825**
Fiore, Neil A. US self-help writer **1861**
Fiorina, Carly (*b.* 1954) US former CEO of Hewlett-Packard **1873, 1873**
Firestone, Harvey (1868–1938) US founder of Firestone Tire and Rubber **1872, 1890**
Fitz-Enz, Jac (*b.* 1948) US writer **1888**
Fitzgerald, F. Scott (1896–1940) US writer **1878, 1888**
Fitzgerald, Niall (*b.* 1945) IRISH deputy chairman of Thomson Reuters, and former CEO and chairman of Unilever **1844**

  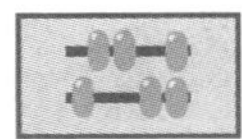   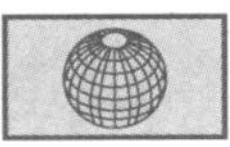   

Fitzgerald, Penelope (1916–2000) BRITISH novelist and biographer **1835**
Fitz-Gibbon, Bernice (1895?–1982) US advertising executive **1820, 1839, 1843**
Fogel, Robert (*b.* 1926) US economist and scientist **1848**
Foley, Stephen BRITISH journalist **1825, 1857**
Follett, Mary Parker (1868–1933) US management thinker and author **1854, 1894**
Foot, Michael (1913–2010) BRITISH politician and writer **1887**
Forbes, Bertie Charles (1880–1954) US publisher and writer **1885**
Forbes, Malcolm S. (1919–1990) US publisher **1818, 1871, 1894**
Forbes, Steve (*b.* 1947) US publishing executive **1825, 1831, 1853**
Ford, Henry (1863–1947) US industrialist, automobile manufacturer, and founder of Ford Motor Company **1829, 1835, 1838, 1845, 1846, 1853, 1868, 1891, 1893, 1902**
Ford, Henry II (1919–1987) US automobile manufacturer and CEO of Ford Motor Company **1841, 1865, 1890, 1903**
Ford, William Clay, Jr (*b.* 1957) US executive chairman and former CEO of Ford Motor Company **1854**
Forrester, Lynn, Lady de Rothschild (*b.* 1954) US business executive **1855**
Foster Wallace, David (1962–2008) US novelist and writer **1818**
Foulston, Nicola (*b.* 1958?) BRITISH former CEO of the Brands Hatch group **1905**
Fox, Muriel (*b.* 1928) US business executive **1905**
France, Anatole (1844–1924) FRENCH novelist **1904**
Frand, Erwin US businessman and journalist **1844**
Frank, Barney (*b.* 1940) US politician **1827, 1863**
Franklin, Benjamin (1706–1790) US politician, inventor, and journalist **1830, 1845, 1862, 1873, 1881, 1885**
Freedley, Edwin T. (1827–1904) US manufacturer **1818**
Freeman, George BRITISH biotech entrepreneur **1861**
Freeman, Richard B. (*b.* 1943) US labor economist **1896**
Fregger, Brad (*b.* 1940) US entrepreneur, publisher, and author **1843**
Friedman, Milton (1912–2006) US economist and winner of the 1976 Nobel Prize in Economics **1836, 1841, 1851, 1851, 1863, 1864, 1900**
Friedman, Thomas (*b.* 1953) US journalist and author **1868**
Friends of the Earth environmental campaign organization **1862**
Frisch, Max (1911–1991) SWISS author **1901**
Frost, Sir David (*b.* 1939) BRITISH broadcaster **1881**
Frost, Robert (1874–1963) US poet **1860, 1870, 1907**
Fry, Art (*b.* 1931) US entrepreneur and inventor of Post-it notes **1871**
Fuentes, Carlos (*b.* 1928) MEXICAN writer **1834, 1849**
Fukushima, Yasuhiro (*b.* 1948) JAPANESE business executive **1850**
Fukuyama, Francis (*b.* 1952) US economist and writer **1840, 1848, 1851, 1883**
Fuld, Richard S., Jr (*b.* 1946) US CEO and chairman of the collapsed Lehman Brothers investment house **1829, 1856, 1856**
Fuller, R. Buckminster (1895–1983) US inventor, architect, and philosopher **1854**
Fuller, Thomas (1654–1734) ENGLISH physician and writer **1824, 1825, 1835, 1838, 1839, 1853, 1903**
Furphy, Joseph (1843–1912) AUSTRALIAN journalist, novelist, and poet **1837**
Galbraith, J. K. (1908–2006) US economist and diplomat **1820, 1820, 1824, 1851, 1851, 1851, 1851, 1855, 1859, 1861, 1866, 1870, 1878, 1879, 1880, 1890, 1896, 1902, 1903, 1904, 1904**
Galsworthy, John (1867–1933) BRITISH novelist and playwright **1819**
Gandhi, Indira (1917–1984) INDIAN prime minister **1849, 1852**
Gandhi, Mahatma (1869–1948) INDIAN nationalist leader and philosopher **1835, 1865, 1872**
Gann, W. D. (1878–1955) US trader and financial forecaster **1860**
Gardner, Ava (1922–1990) US actress **1866**
Gardner, Richard (1927–2003) US diplomat, lawyer, and educator **1849**
Garnier, Jean-Pierre (*b.* 1947) FRENCH former CEO of GlaxoSmithKline **1853, 1885**
Gates, Bill (*b.* 1955) US entrepreneur, cofounder and chairman of Microsoft **1833, 1836, 1844, 1852, 1856, 1874, 1877, 1886, 1893, 1899**
Gaubis, Anthony (1902–1989) US financial analyst **1819**
Gauthier, Mark US travel writer **1848**
Gellerman, Saul W. (*b.* 1929) US psychologist and writer **1818**
Geneen, Harold S. (1910–1997) US telecommunications entrepreneur and CEO of ITT **1841, 1855, 1855, 1863, 1864, 1869, 1876, 1884, 1885, 1885, 1891, 1900**
General Motors (*b.* 1908) US automobile manufacturer **1868**
George, Henry (1839–1897) US economist **1903, 1903, 1904**
Geras, Norman (*b.* 1943) BRITISH political philosopher **1856**
Gerstner, Lou (*b.* 1942) US former CEO and chairman of IBM **1840, 1850, 1903**
Getty, J. Paul (1892–1976) US entrepreneur, oil industry executive, and financier **1818, 1830, 1864, 1867, 1894, 1898, 1904**
Giannini, Amadeo (1870–1949) US banker and founder of Bank of America **1880, 1898**
Gibbons, Barry J. (*b.* 1946) US former CEO and chairman of Burger King **1840**
Gibson, William (*b.* 1948) US-CANADIAN science-fiction writer **1833**
Gide, André (1869–1951) FRENCH novelist and essayist **1844**
Gilbert, Sir W. S. (1836–1911) BRITISH librettist and playwright **1824**
Gilder, George (*b.* 1939) US economist **1831**
Gill, Eric (1882–1940) BRITISH sculptor and engraver **1907**
Gilmour, Ian (1926–2007) BRITISH politician **1851**
Giraudoux, Jean (1882–1944) FRENCH diplomat, novelist, and playwright **1853, 1872, 1895**
Gissing, George (1857–1903) BRITISH novelist **1889**
Glancey, Jonathan BRITISH journalist **1818**
Glasgow, Arnold H. US psychologist **1851**
Godard, Jean-Luc (*b.* 1930) SWISS-FRENCH film director, screenwriter, and critic **1884**
Godin, Seth (*b.* 1960) US entrepreneur, author, and motivational speaker **1843, 1862, 1867**
Goethe, Johann Wolfgang von (1749–1832) GERMAN poet, playwright, novelist, and scientist **1821, 1834, 1838, 1879, 1888, 1898**
Goffee, Rob (*b.* 1952) US writer, consultant, and academic **1840**
Gogarty, Oliver St. John (1878–1957) IRISH poet and novelist **1872**
Goizueta, Roberto (1931–1997) US CEO of Coca-Cola **1833, 1866, 1879, 1892**
Goldman, William (*b.* 1931) US screenwriter and novelist **1878**
Goldsmith, Sir James (1933–1997) BRITISH entrepreneur, financier, and politician **1879**
Goldsmith, Oliver (1730–1774) IRISH-BORN BRITISH playwright, writer, and poet **1865, 1902**
Goldwyn, Samuel (1882–1974) US movie producer **1839, 1903**
Goodman, Danny (*b.* 1950) US writer **1833**
Goodman, Paul (1911–1972) US educator, psychoanalyst, and writer **1829**
Goodwin, Sir Fred (*b.* 1958) BRITISH former CEO of the Royal Bank of Scotland **1822, 1823**
Gopnik, Adam (*b.* 1956) US writer **1831**
Gorbachev, Mikhail (*b.* 1931) RUSSIAN former president **1832**
Gordimer, Nadine (*b.* 1923) SOUTH AFRICAN novelist and short-story writer **1893**
Gore, Al (*b.* 1948) US former vice president **1897, 1902**
Gore, Wilbert Lee (1912–1986) US founder of Goretex **1869**
Gorman, James P. (*b.* 1960?) US CEO of Morgan Stanley **1822**
Gower, Jim BRITISH law academic **1863**

  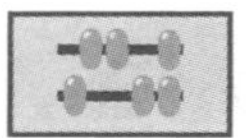      

Gracián, Baltasar (1601–1658) SPANISH writer and priest **1818, 1838, 1875**
Grade, Sir Lew, Lord (1906–1998) RUSSIAN-BORN BRITISH entertainment entrepreneur **1856, 1875**
Grade, Michael, Lord (*b.* 1943) BRITISH television executive **1843**
Graham, Benjamin (1894–1976) US economist and investor **1860, 1871**
Graham, Katharine (1917–2001) US newspaper publisher and owner of *Washington Post* **1874, 1886**
Graham, Paul (*b.* 1964) US computer programmer, writer, and venture capitalist **1838, 1861, 1861, 1861, 1866, 1889, 1897, 1897**
Grant, Jim US investor and financial commentator **1859**
Gratton, Paul (*b.* 1960) BRITISH former CEO of Egg **1844**
Gray, John (*b.* 1948) BRITISH academic and writer **1831, 1832, 1847, 1850, 1862, 1862**
Green, Celia (*b.* 1935) BRITISH psychophysicist **1893**
Greene, Graham (1904–1991) BRITISH novelist **1899**
Greenleaf, Robert (1904–1990) US director of Management Research for AT&T and author **1836, 1873, 1896**
Greenspan, Alan (*b.* 1926) US economist, former chairman of Federal Reserve **1825, 1826, 1827, 1827, 1851, 1858, 1858, 1866**
Gretzky, Wayne (*b.* 1961) CANADIAN ice-hockey player **1833**
Grierson, Ronald BRITISH banker **1823**
Groddeck, Georg (1866–1934) GERMAN psychoanalyst **1894**
Groening, Matt (*b.* 1954) US animator and writer
Gross, Bill (*b.* 1944) US cofounder and co-chief investment officer of PIMCO **1870**
Grove, Andrew S. (*b.* 1936) HUNGARIAN-BORN US entrepreneur, author, and former chairman of Intel Corporation **1834, 1834, 1850, 1852, 1862, 1875, 1886, 1887, 1898, 1899**
Guccione, Bob (1930–2010) US magazine publisher **1895**
Gunn, Thom (1929–2004) BRITISH poet **1819**
Gurley, J. William US venture capitalist and journalist **1901**
Gustafson, Deil O. (1932–1999) US real estate executive **1895**
Gyllenhammar, Pehr (*b.* 1935) SWEDISH businessman, former CEO and chairman of Volvo **1857**
Haarde, Geir (*b.* 1951) ICELANDIC former prime minister **1823**
Hadfield, Bud (1923–2011) US entrepreneur and founder of Kwik Kopy **1864**
Hague, William (*b.* 1961) BRITISH politician **1825**
Hailsham, Lord (Quintin Hogg) (1907–1990) BRITISH politician **1895**
Hain, Peter (*b.* 1950) BRITISH politician **1847**
Haji-Ioannou, Sir Stelios (*b.* 1967) GREEK founder of easyJet and easyGroup **1862**
Halbert, Gary (1942–2007) US copywriter and marketing guru **1868**
Haldane, Andy (*b.* 1967) BRITISH executive director of the Bank of England **1845, 1900**
Half, Robert (1918–2001) US founder of Robert Half International employment agency **1853**
Hall, Doug (*b.* 1959) US business writer **1898**
Hallowell, Edward M. US psychiatrist and author **1898**
Halsey, Margaret (1910–1997) US writer **1846**
Hamel, Gary (*b.* 1954) US academic, business writer, and consultant **1833, 1836, 1854, 1864, 1869, 1879, 1882, 1885, 1898, 1898**
Hammer, Armand (1898–1990) US industrialist, philanthropist, founder, and CEO of Occidental Petroleum **1875**
Hammer, Michael (1948–2008) US author and academic **1833, 1833, 1840, 1883, 1883**
Hancock, W. Keith (1898–1988) AUSTRALIAN academic **1897**
Hand, Learned (1872–1961) US judge **1882**
Handy, Charles (*b.* 1932) IRISH business executive and author **1841, 1855, 1870, 1871, 1872, 1873, 1876, 1884, 1888, 1891, 1892, 1900, 1902**
Hanson, James Edward, Lord (1922–2004) BRITISH business executive and entrepreneur **1853**
Haque, Umair US economist and author **1840**
Hardy, Thomas (1840–1928) BRITISH novelist and poet **1875**
Hare, Sir David (*b.* 1947) BRITISH playwright **1826**
Hari, Johann (*b.* 1979) BRITISH journalist **1838, 1838, 1838, 1840, 1879**
Harkin, James BRITISH writer and social forecaster **1828**
Harkness, Richard (1907–1977) US radio and television journalist **1878**
Harman, Sir Charles Eustace (1894–1970) BRITISH judge **1818**
Harney, Mary (*b.* 1953) IRISH politician **1906**
Harris, B. F. (1811–1905) US businessman **1895**
Harris, Yra US bond trader and blogger **1857**
Harrison, Emma BRITISH entrepreneur **1877**
Harvey, Paul (1918–2009) US broadcaster **1819**
Harvey-Jones, Sir John (1924–2008) BRITISH management adviser, author, and chairman of ICI **1834, 1836, 1846, 1849, 1868, 1869, 1876, 1884, 1889, 1891, 1901**
Havel, Václav (*b.* 1936) CZECH president and writer **1887**
Hawken, Paul (*b.* 1946) US entrepreneur and business author **1831, 1901**
Hayek, Friedrich August von (1899–1992) AUSTRO-HUNGARIAN-BORN BRITISH economist **1831**
Hazlitt, William (1778–1830) BRITISH essayist and journalist **1820, 1842, 1882, 1896, 1897**
Healey, Edna, Lady (1918–2010) BRITISH author **1896**
Hearn, Barry (*b.* 1948) BRITISH sports promoter **1899**
Heehler, Tom US linguist and writer on public speaking **1835**
Hefner, Hugh (*b.* 1926) US entrepreneur and publisher **1824**
Heilbroner, Robert L. (1919–2005) US economist **1832, 1851**
Heinlein, Robert A. (1907–1988) US science-fiction writer **1818**
Helgason, Hallgrimur (*b.* 1959) ICELANDIC novelist and journalist **1826**
Heller, Joseph (1923–1999) US novelist **1857, 1865, 1876**
Heller, Lucy (*b.* 1959) BRITISH business executive **1847**
Heller, Robert (*b.* 1932) BRITISH management writer **1821, 1848, 1865**
Heller, Walter (1915–1987) US economist **1850**
Helmsley, Leona (1920–2007) US hotelier **1841**
Hemingway, Ernest (1899–1961) US author **1819**
Henderson, Leon (1895–1986) US administrator **1851**
Hennig, Margaret (*b.* 1940) US business executive and writer **1847**
Hepburn, Katharine (1907–2003) US actress **1834**
Herbert, George (1593–1633) ENGLISH poet **1821**
Herzberg, Frederick (1923–2000) US psychologist **1852, 1881, 1881, 1885**
Heseltine, Michael, Lord (*b.* 1933) BRITISH politician **1830**
Hicks, Sir John Richard (1904–1989) BRITISH economist **1903**
Higgins, Michael D. (*b.* 1941) IRISH politician **1877**
Highmore, Ben BRITISH cultural theorist **1897**
Hill, Andrew BRITISH business journalist **1864**
Hill, Damon (*b.* 1960) BRITISH Formula 1 motor racing driver **1905**
Hill, John R. US financial trader **1874**
Hill, Napoleon (1883–1970) US motivational author **1857, 1901**
Hillary, Sir Edmund (1919–2008) NEW ZEALAND explorer and mountaineer **1819**
Hite, Larry US investment manager **1859**
Hoagland, Edward (*b.* 1932) US novelist, essayist, and naturalist **1836**

Keen, Peter G. W. (*b.* 1930) US information technology consultant **1844**
Kellaway, Lucy (*b.* 1959) BRITISH business journalist **1821, 1836, 1901, 1901**
Kelleher, Herb (*b.* 1931) US businessman, founder of Southwest Airlines **1864, 1879, 1884**
Kellems, Vivien (1896–1975) US industrialist, feminist, and lecturer **1905**
Kelly, Kevin (*b.* 1952) US cofounder and former editor of *Wired* magazine **1869, 1873**
Kendall, Donald M. (*b.* 1921) US former CEO of PepsiCo **1836**
Kennedy, Carol (*b.* 1952) BRITISH business executive, editor, and author **1839**
Kennedy, Douglas (*b.* 1955) BRITISH writer, journalist, and playwright **1847**
Kennedy, Florynce R. (1916–2000) US lawyer and political activist **1847**
Kennedy, John F. (1917–1963) US president **1881, 1883**
Kennedy, Joseph P. (1888–1969) US entrepreneur, government official, and diplomat **1887**
Kennelly, Brendan (*b.* 1936) IRISH poet and academic **1892**
Kent, Rod (*b.* 1947?) BRITISH former chairman of Bradford & Bingley Building Society **1823**
Kerr, Clark (1911–2003) US educator **1852**
Kersten, E. L. US satirist, former organizational communication academic **1891, 1906**
Kerviel, Jérôme (*b.* 1977) FRENCH trader **1842**
Kettering, Charles Franklin (1876–1958) US businessman and engineer **1824, 1856, 1889**
Keynes, John Maynard (1883–1946) BRITISH economist **1831, 1851, 1851, 1852, 1855, 1858, 1860, 1870, 1871, 1879, 1887, 1896**
Khrushchev, Nikita (1894–1971) SOVIET politician **1845**
Kiam, Victor (1926–2001) US CEO of Remington Corporation **1867, 1881**
Kindersley, Peter (*b.* 1941) BRITISH publisher, cofounder of Dorling-Kindersley **1836**
King, Larry (*b.* 1933) US television presenter **1874**
King, Martin Luther (1929–1968) US pastor and civil rights leader **1895**
King, Mervyn (*b.* 1948) BRITISH governor of the Bank of England **1822, 1822, 1822, 1823, 1823, 1827**
King, Stephen (*b.* 1947) US writer **1899**
Kingsley, Charles (1819–1875) BRITISH clergyman and novelist **1853**
Kipling, Rudyard (1865–1936) BRITISH novelist, poet, and short-story writer **1893**
Kissinger, Henry (*b.* 1923) GERMAN-BORN US diplomat and winner of the 1973 Nobel Peace Prize **1873, 1887, 1892**
Kiyosaki, Robert (*b.* 1947) US author **1844, 1898, 1904**
Kline, Nancy (*b.* 1946) US author, educator, and consultant **1860, 1870, 1878**
Klock, Joe (*b.* 1949) US writer **1873**
Knoebel, Steven M. US cofounder of a real-estate appraisal company **1823**
Knopf, Alfred A. (1892–1984) US publisher **1850**
Knopfler, Mark (*b.* 1949) BRITISH rock musician **1819**
Knudsen, William S. (1879–1948) US industrialist, president of General Motors **1836**
Koestler, Arthur (1905–1983) BRITISH writer and journalist **1824, 1830, 1844**
Kofman, Fred US writer **1874**
Kotler, Philip (*b.* 1931) US marketing management thinker **1844, 1877, 1877, 1883, 1891, 1898**
Kotter, John P. (*b.* 1947) US writer and academic **1833**
Kraus, Karl (1874–1936) AUSTRIAN writer **1846**
Kreider, Tim (*b.* 1967) US essayist and cartoonist **1819, 1871**
Kroc, Ray (1902–1984) US founder of McDonald's **1836, 1841, 1899**
Kronenberger, Louis (1904–1980) US writer **1835**
Krugman, Paul R. (*b.* 1953) US economist **1825, 1826, 1826, 1826, 1827, 1842, 1862, 1862, 1863, 1889, 1904**
Kudlow, Lawrence (*b.* 1947) US economist and right-wing commentator **1827**
Labour Party BRITISH political party **1896**
La Fontaine, Jean de (1621–1695) FRENCH writer and poet **1888**
Lagerfeld, Karl (*b.* 1933) GERMAN fashion designer **1843**
Lahr, John (*b.* 1941) US writer and critic **1820**
Lakein, Alan US self-help writer **1901**
Lamm, Richard D. (*b.* 1935) US politician **1845**
Lamott, Anne (*b.* 1954) US novelist and author **1885**
Lampedusa, Giuseppe di (1896–1957) ITALIAN writer **1833**
Lanchester, John (*b.* 1962) BRITISH journalist and novelist **1822, 1830, 1854, 1858, 1858, 1858, 1879, 1903, 1903**
Land, Edwin (1909–1991) US inventor and founder of Polaroid Corporation **1824, 1843, 1844, 1860, 1866, 1877, 1889, 1890, 1891, 1895**
Landau, Adrienne (*b.* 1950) US fashion designer **1828**
Landau, Saul (*b.* 1936) US moviemaker and writer **1900**
Landers, Ann (1918–2002) US columnist **1883**
Langer, Susanne K. (1895–1985) US philosopher **1835**
Lanier, Jaron (*b.* 1960) US computer scientist and author **1850, 1884, 1884**
Lanza, Clara (1859–1939) US journalist **1905**
Laozi (570?–490? BC) CHINESE philosopher, reputed founder of Daoism **1873**
Lapham, Lewis H. (*b.* 1935) US writer and editor **1823**
Larkin, Philip (1922–1985) BRITISH poet, critic, essayist, and librarian **1906**
La Rochefoucauld, François (1613–1680) FRENCH epigrammatist **1824, 1835, 1896, 1897**
Lauda, Niki (*b.* 1949) AUSTRIAN Formula 1 motor racing driver and airline entrepreneur **1894**
Lauder, Estée (1908–2004) US entrepreneur and cosmetics executive **1891, 1895, 1895**
Lawson, Dominic (*b.* 1956) BRITISH journalist **1822, 1825, 1853**
Lawson, Neal (*b.* 1963) BRITISH journalist and author **1839, 1898**
Lay, Kenneth (1942–2006) US CEO and chairman of Enron **1842**
Laybourne, Geraldine (*b.* 1947) US founder, and former CEO, and former chairman of Oxygen Media **1845, 1887, 1905**
Lazarus, Shelly (*b.* 1949) US chairman of Ogilvy & Mather Worldwide **1828, 1882**
Leach, Bernard (1887–1979) BRITISH potter **1885**
Leach, Reggie (*b.* 1950) CANADIAN ice-hockey player **1881**
Leacock, Stephen (1869–1944) CANADIAN humorist, essayist, economist, and historian **1820, 1863**
Leadbeater, Charles BRITISH government adviser, journalist, and author **1854**
Leamer, Edward E. (*b.* 1944) US economist **1851**
Leavitt, Mike (*b.* 1951) US politician **1889**
Lebowitz, Fran (*b.* 1950) US writer and columnist **1884**
le Carré, John (*b.* 1931) BRITISH novelist **1828**
Lee, Bruce (1940–1973) US-BORN HONG KONG martial arts expert **1821**
Le Guin, Ursula K. (*b.* 1929) US author **1866, 1887, 1893**
Lehman, Don US industrial designer and blogger **1869**
Lehmann, Rosamond (1901–1990) BRITISH novelist **1883**
Lehrer, Jonah (*b.* 1981) US neuroscientist and journalist **1834**
Leith, Prue (*b.* 1940) BRITISH cookbook writer and business executive **1854**
Lenin, Vladimir Ilich (1870–1924) RUSSIAN revolutionary leader and political theorist **1832**
Lennon, John (1940–1980) BRITISH rock musician and songwriter **1887**
Leonard, Carol BRITISH director of Whitehead Mann **1872**
Leopardi, Giacomo (1798–1837) ITALIAN poet and scholar **1886**
Lereah, David US economist and former spokesman for the National Association of Realtors **1827**

  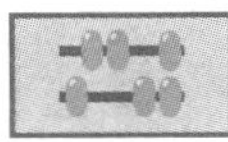   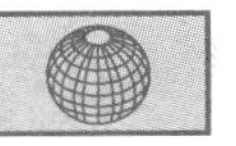   

Leslie, Ian BRITISH author and broadcaster **1840**
Levenson, Sam (1911–1980) US humorist **1879**
Leverhulme, Lord (William Hesketh Lever) (1851–1925) BRITISH entrepreneur, philanthropist, and cofounder of Unilever **1853, 1877, 1899**
Levi, Primo (1919–1987) ITALIAN novelist, essayist, and chemist **1906**
Levin, Jerry x(*b.* 1939) US former CEO of Time Warner **1893**
Levine, Robert US journalist and author **1850**
Levitt, Arthur, Jr (*b.* 1931) US author and former chairman of the Securities and Exchange Commission **1841, 1859**
Levitt, Theodore (1925–2006) US management theorist, writer, and editor **1832, 1841, 1844, 1844, 1870**
Lewin, Kurt (1890–1947) US author **1834, 1866**
Lewis, Jeremy BRITISH publisher and author **1882, 1906**
Lewis, Michael (*b.* 1960) US writer and former financial trader **1825, 1842, 1858**
Leysen, André (*b.* 1927) BELGIAN chairman of Agfa-Gevaert **1891**
Lichtenberg, Georg C. (1742–1799) GERMAN scientist and writer **1867**
Liddell Hart, Sir Basil Henry (1895–1970) BRITISH military historian and strategist **1881**
Lincoln, Abraham (1809–1865) US president **1890**
Lindbergh, Anne Morrow (1906–2001) US writer **1886**
Lipnack, Jessica (*b.* 1947) US journalist **1828**
Lippmann, Walter (1889–1974) US political commentator, editor, and writer **1834, 1873**
Littré, Émile (1801–1881) FRENCH philosopher and lexicographer **1902**
Livermore, Jesse (1877–1940) US stock trader **1859, 1860, 1879, 1882**
Livy (59 BC–AD 17) ROMAN historian **1874, 1902**
Lloyd, Henry Demarest (1847–1903) US journalist and reformer **1840**
Lloyd George, David (Earl of Dwyfor) (1863–1945) BRITISH prime minister **1830, 1838, 1897**
Locke, Christopher (*b.* 1947) US author and blogger **1885**
Locke, John (1632–1704) ENGLISH philosopher and political thinker **1884**
Lodge, David (*b.* 1935) BRITISH novelist and critic **1871, 1891**
Loeb, Gerald M. (1899–1975) US investor, author **1860**
Loesser, Frank (1910–1969) US composer, lyricist, and librettist **1884**
Logan, Don US former CEO and chairman of Time Inc. **1850**
Lois, George (*b.* 1931) US advertising executive **1854**
Lombardi, Vince (1913–1970) US football coach **1853**
Longfellow, Henry Wadsworth (1807–1882) US poet **1863**
Loomis, Bernard (1923–2006) US business executive **1893**
Lorenz, Konrad (1903–1989) AUSTRIAN zoologist **1895**
Lorsch, Jay W. (*b.* 1932) US sociologist **1875**
Louchheim, Frank P. (*b.* 1923) US business executive **1865**
Lucas, Robert, Jr (*b.* 1937) US economist **1827**
Luce, Henry R. (1898–1967) US publisher **1861**
Lui, David HONG KONG-BASED investment fund manager **1830**
Luntz, Frank (*b.* 1962) US political consultant **1835**
Luscomb, Florence (1887–1985) US campaigner for women's suffrage, architect, and pacifist **1888, 1888**
Luskin, Donald (*b.* 1954) US investment guru **1826**
Luten, Daniel B. US civil engineer **1891**
Lynch, Michael C. (*b.* 1946) BRITISH historian **1894**
Lynch, Michael R. (*b.* 1965) IRISH software entrepreneur **1871, 1882**
Lynch, Peter (*b.* 1944) US fund manager **1859, 1859, 1859, 1870, 1871, 1871, 1871**
Lyons, Carl (*b.* 1970) BRITISH former marketing director of OpenTable and Lastminute.com **1850**
Macaskill, Bridget A. (*b.* 1949) BRITISH business executive, former president and CEO of Oppenheimer Funds **1905**
Macaulay, Thomas Babington, Lord (1800–1859) BRITISH politician and historian **1867, 1897**
Machiavelli, Niccolò (1469–1527) ITALIAN historian, statesman, and political philosopher **1819, 1825, 1830, 1834**
MacKay, Elizabeth US political adviser, former investment strategist and managing director of Bear Stearns **1905**
Madoff, Bernard (*b.* 1938) US former fund manager and former governor of NASDAQ **1842, 1842, 1842**
Major, Sir John (*b.* 1943) BRITISH former prime minister **1845**
Makihara, Minoru (*b.* 1930) JAPANESE adviser to IBM, former chairman of Mitsubishi **1874**
Mallet, Robert (1915–2002) FRENCH poet and playwright **1857**
Mallett, Jef (*b.* 1962) US comic-strip artist **1882, 1898**
Mandino, Og (1923–1996) US motivational writer **1895**
Mann, Sandi BRITISH occupational psychologist **1843**
Mann, Thomas (1875–1955) GERMAN writer **1866, 1896**
Mannes, Marya (1904–1990) US essayist and journalist **1855, 1899**
Mao Zedong (1893–1976) CHINESE revolutionary leader **1888**
Marcus, Stanley (1905–2002) US businessman **1844**
Marden, Orison Swett (1848–1924) US author **1834**
Margalit, Avishai (*b.* 1939) ISRAELI political philosopher **1888**
Maritain, Jacques (1882–1973) FRENCH philosopher **1834**
Markopolos, Harry (*b.* 1956) US financial analyst **1842, 1842, 1842, 1842, 1842**
Marland, Caroline (*b.* 1946) IRISH former managing director of Guardian Newspapers **1865, 1895**
Marley, Bob (1945–1981) JAMAICAN musician **1888**
Marquis, Don (1878–1937) US journalist and humorist **1856, 1880, 1890, 1907**
Marsden, Rhodri (*b.* 1971) BRITISH writer and musician **1837**
Marshall, Alfred (1842–1924) BRITISH economist **1825, 1865**
Marshall, Paul (*b.* 1959) BRITISH hedge fund manager **1858**
Martel, Yann (*b.* 1963) CANADIAN novelist **1906**
Marx, Karl (1818–1883) GERMAN political and economic philosopher **1832, 1852, 1896, 1903**
Maslow, Abraham (1908–1970) US behavioral psychologist **1857, 1890**
Mass, Alison US executive at Goldman Sachs **1889**
Massie, Allan (*b.* 1938) BRITISH author **1893**
Matisse, Henri (1869–1954) FRENCH painter and sculptor **1884**
Matsunaga, Mari (*b.* 1954) JAPANESE IT designer **1866**
Matsushita, Konosuke (1894–1989) JAPANESE electronics executive, entrepreneur, and inventor **1830, 1846**
Maugham, W. Somerset (1874–1965) BRITISH novelist, short-story writer, and dramatist **1880, 1888, 1889, 1899**
Maurois, André (1885–1967) FRENCH biographer and critic **1856**
Maxwell, Robert (1923–1991) CZECHOSLOVAKIAN-BORN BRITISH publisher, business executive, and politician **1843, 1843, 1843, 1853, 1886**
Mayer, Martin (*b.* 1928) US author and journalist **1823**
Mayo, Elton (1880–1949) AUSTRALIAN-BORN US psychologist **1900**
McArthur, Peter (1866–1924) CANADIAN journalist and author **1867**
McCaffrey, John L. (1892–1982) US president of International Harvester **1846**
McCain, John (*b.* 1936) US senator and presidential candidate **1826, 1827, 1887**
McCall, Carolyn (*b.* 1962) BRITISH CEO of easyJet, former CEO of Guardian Newspapers **1850**
McCarthy, Eugene (1916–2005) US politician and writer **1828**

  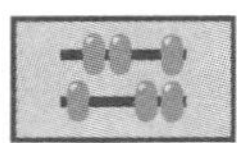   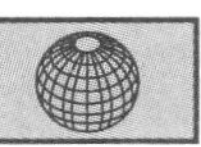   

McCarthy, Mary (1912–1989) US author and critic **1829, 1849, 1906**

McCormack, Mark (1930–2003) US entrepreneur, founder and CEO of International Management Group **1836, 1840, 1855, 1857, 1881, 1881, 1886, 1891**

McCrossan, Danny (*b.* 1980) BRITISH comedian **1857**

McDonald, Larry US former trader at Lehman Brothers **1826**

McEnroe, Dan US writer and blogger **1825**

McGregor, Sir Ian (1912–1998) BRITISH chairman of the National Coal Board **1867**

McInerney, Jay (*b.* 1955) US author **1836**

McKenna, Regis (*b.* 1939) US marketing entrepreneur **1836, 1877**

McLuhan, Marshall (1911–1980) CANADIAN sociologist and author **1821, 1829, 1862, 1869, 1878, 1878, 1880, 1901**

McMaster, Michael D. (*b.* 1943) US writer **1883**

McNealy, Scott (*b.* 1954) US software entrepreneur **1862**

McRae, Hamish BRITISH journalist **1825, 1848, 1848, 1852, 1870, 1900**

Meagher, Maude (1895–1977) US writer **1835**

Melbourne, Lord (William Lamb) (1779–1848) BRITISH prime minister **1875**

Mellor, David (*b.* 1949) BRITISH politician and broadcaster **1872**

Melville, Herman (1819–1891) US novelist **1883**

Mencken, H. L. (1880–1956) US journalist, essayist, and critic **1838, 1849**

Menninger, Karl Augustus (1893–1990) US psychiatrist **1821**

Menzies, Robert (1894–1978) AUSTRALIAN prime minister **1851**

Merck, George (1894–1957) US chairman of Merck & Co pharmaceuticals company **1891**

Merkel, Angela (*b.* 1954) GERMAN chancellor **1822, 1826, 1848**

Messier, Jean-Marie (*b.* 1956) FRENCH businessman, former CEO and chairman of Vivendi Universal **1862**

Meyer, Philipp (*b.* 1975?) US novelist and former financial trader **1825, 1850**

Michels, Sir David (*b.* 1946) BRITISH business executive, former CEO of Hilton Hotels **1836, 1844**

Mies van der Rohe, Ludwig (1886–1969) GERMAN architect **1846**

Mill, John Stuart (1806–1873) BRITISH economist and philosopher **1868, 1880, 1891**

Millard, Mark BRITISH psychologist **1889**

Miller, Arthur (1915–2005) US dramatist **1878, 1895**

Miller, Henry (1891–1980) US writer **1867, 1883**

Miller, Sir Jonathan (*b.* 1934) BRITISH theater director and writer **1837**

Milligan, Spike (1918–2002) IRISH comedian and writer **1880**

Millman, Dan (*b.* 1946) US former world trampoline champion and motivational writer **1880**

Mintzberg, Henry (*b.* 1939) CANADIAN academic and management theorist **1843, 1855, 1869, 1876, 1876, 1898, 1898, 1898**

Mises, Ludwig von (1881–1973) US economist **1897**

Mitchell, David (*b.* 1974) BRITISH comedian and writer **1825**

Moller, Lorraine (*b.* 1955) NEW ZEALAND former athlete **1819**

Moltz, Barry J. US entrepreneur and author **1853**

Monnet, Jean (1888–1979) FRENCH diplomat and founder of European Community **1849**

Moody, John (1868–1958) US investor and financial analyst **1870**

Moore, Chris (*b.* 1960) BRITISH CEO of Domino's Pizza UK & Ireland **1836**

Moore, Henry (1898–1986) BRITISH sculptor **1832**

Moore, James BRITISH business journalist **1838**

Moore, James F. (*b.* 1948) US writer and business consultant **1836**

Mophatlane, Isaac SOUTH AFRICAN business executive **1902**

Moran, Joe BRITISH social historian **1869, 1906**

Morgan, Elaine (*b.* 1920) BRITISH playwright, screenwriter, and nonfiction author **1847**

Morgan, J. P. (1837–1913) US financier **1880, 1881**

Morici, Peter US economist **1822**

Morita, Akio (1921–1999) JAPANESE business executive **1862, 1865, 1865, 1870, 1885, 1893**

Morrison, Van (*b.* 1945) IRISH musician **1843**

Morrow, Dwight (1873–1931) US lawyer, banker, and diplomat **1888**

Mortimer, Sir John (1923–2009) BRITISH lawyer, dramatist, and writer **1872**

Morton, J. B. (1893–1979) BRITISH writer and humorist **1903**

Moses, Danny US financial trader **1826**

Moses, Edwin (*b.* 1955) US athlete **1838**

Mougayar, William (Walid) (*b.* 1959) US consultant and management theorist **1836, 1889**

Moynihan, Daniel P. (1927–2003) US politician **1883**

Mumford, Lewis (1895–1990) US social thinker and writer **1868, 1892, 1901**

Munger, Charlie (*b.* 1924) US investor **1879, 1904**

Murchison, Clint W. (1885–1969) US entrepreneur, oil industry executive, and financier **1880**

Murdoch, James (*b.* 1973) BRITISH CEO and chairman of News Corporation, Europe, and Asia **1882**

Murdoch, Rupert (*b.* 1931) AUSTRALIAN-BORN US CEO of News Corporation **1887**

Murrow, Edward R. (1908–1965) US journalist and broadcaster **1836**

Murthy, Narayana (*b.* 1946) INDIAN cofounder of Infosys **1848, 1849, 1862, 1882**

Nader, Ralph (*b.* 1934) US lawyer, consumer-rights campaigner, and presidential candidate **1872, 1872, 1896**

Naipaul, V. S. (*b.* 1932) TRINIDADIAN writer and winner of the 2001 Nobel Prize in Literature **1849**

Naisbitt, John (*b.* 1929?) US business executive and author **1835, 1862**

Nalebuff, Barry J. (*b.* 1958) US author and management academic **1836, 1840, 1903**

Nash, Ogden (1902–1971) US humorist and writer **1849, 1871, 1907**

Nash, Steve (*b.* 1974) SOUTH AFRICAN-BORN CANADIAN basketball player **1898**

Navon, Yitzhak (*b.* 1921) ISRAELI former president **1882**

Nayar, Vineet (*b.* 1962) INDIAN businessman, CEO of HCL Technologies **1833**

Negroponte, Nicholas (*b.* 1943) US academic, cofounder of the MIT Media Lab, and founder of the One Laptop Per Child organization **1843, 1884, 1884, 1900, 1901**

Neil, Andrew (*b.* 1949) BRITISH publisher and broadcaster **1836**

Nelson, Doug (*b.* 1944) US regional vice president of Philip Morris USA **1836, 1895**

Nelson, Paula (*b.* 1944) US educator **1880**

Newman, John Henry (1801–1890) BRITISH theologian **1866**

New Testament second part of the Christian Bible **1881, 1905**

Newton, Sir Isaac (1642–1727) ENGLISH mathematician and physicist **1884**

Newton, Maud US writer, journalist, and blogger **1890**

Niebuhr, Reinhold (1892–1971) US theologian **1839**

Niederhoffer, Victor (*b.* 1943) US hedge fund manager and statistician **1904**

Nkrumah, Kwame (1909–1972) GHANAIAN president **1847**

Noer, David M. (*b.* 1939) US writer and human resources consultant **1852**

Nohria, Nitin (*b.* 1962) US writer and dean of Harvard Business School **1869**

Noonan, Peggy (*b.* 1950) US author and presidential speechwriter **1897**

Norris, Kathleen (1880–1966) US novelist **1821**

Nyerere, Julius (1922–1999) TANZANIAN president **1845**

Obama, Barack (*b.* 1961) US president **1819, 1821, 1825, 1830, 1837, 1863, 1863, 1863, 1864, 1904**

O'Brien, Flann (1911–1966) IRISH writer **1843**

O'Connor, Joseph (*b.* 1963) IRISH journalist and novelist **1845, 1852**

        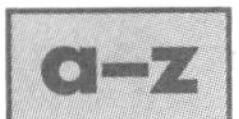

Ogilvy, David (1911–1999) BRITISH advertising executive, founder and chairman of Ogilvy & Mather **1820, 1820, 1820, 1820, 1820, 1843, 1843, 1844, 1845, 1865, 1873, 1877, 1891, 1893, 1895**
O'Grady, Sean BRITISH economics journalist **1818, 1825, 1825, 1829, 1848**
Ohmae, Kenichi (*b.* 1943) JAPANESE management consultant and theorist **1857, 1870, 1884, 1898**
O'Leary, Michael (*b.* 1961) IRISH CEO of Ryanair **1854**
Olmedo, José Joaquín (1780–1847) ECUADOREAN poet and politician **1905**
Olsen, Kenneth H. (1926–2011) US computer designer and cofounder of Digital Equipment Corporation **1837, 1864, 1865, 1870**
Olson, Kenneth H. US president of Digital Equipment Corporation
Omidyar, Pierre M. (*b.* 1967) FRENCH-BORN US founder and chairman of eBay **1886**
Onassis, Aristotle (1906–1975) GREEK shipowner and financier **1830, 1866, 1872, 1899**
Oppenheimer, Nicky (*b.* 1945) SOUTH AFRICAN chairman of De Beers **1847**
Orben, Robert (*b.* 1927) US writer **1881**
O'Reilly, Tony (*b.* 1936) IRISH former CEO of Independent News & Media and former CEO and chairman of Heinz **1828, 1836**
Origuchi, Masahiro (*b.* 1962) JAPANESE business executive **1882**
Orlando, Vittorio Emanuele (1860–1952) ITALIAN statesman **1897**
Ormerod, Paul BRITISH economist and statistician **1856**
O'Rourke, P. J. (*b.* 1947) US humorist and journalist **1828, 1832, 1851, 1863, 1865, 1892, 1896, 1896**
Ortega y Gasset, Jose (1883–1955) SPANISH author and philosopher **1854**
Orwell, George (1903–1950) BRITISH novelist, critic, and essayist **1888, 1896, 1896, 1896**
Ouchi, William (*b.* 1943) US writer **1846**
Ousterhout, John (*b.* 1954) US computer scientist **1885**
Owen, Robert (1771–1858) BRITISH industrialist and social reformer **1868**
Packard, David (1912–1996) US entrepreneur and cofounder of Hewlett-Packard **1841, 1876, 1902**
Packard, Vance (1914–1996) US journalist and writer **1873**
Packer, Kerry (1937–2005) AUSTRALIAN entrepreneur and chairman of Consolidated Press Holdings **1899**
Page, Larry (*b.* 1973) US cofounder and CEO of Google **1837, 1868, 1893**
Paglia, Camille (*b.* 1947) US academic, educator, and writer **1847**
Paige, Leroy (1906–1982) US baseball player **1836**
Paine, Thomas (1737–1809) BRITISH politician, philosopher, and writer **1864**
Palahniuk, Chuck (*b.* 1962) US novelist and journalist **1870**
Palmer, Morton US head of Palmer Associates security consultants **1849**
Papandreou, George (*b.* 1952) GREEK prime minister **1857**
Pareto, Vilfredo (1848–1923) ITALIAN economist and sociologist **1879**
Parkinson, C. Northcote (1909–1993) BRITISH political scientist and author **1846, 1891**
Parnell, Charles Stewart (1846–1891) IRISH politician **1839**
Parris, Matthew (*b.* 1949) BRITISH journalist and former politician **1826**
Partnoy, Frank US author and academic, former investment banker **1845**
Pascal, Blaise (1623–1662) FRENCH philosopher and mathematician **1839**
Pascale, Richard (*b.* 1938) US academic and author **1833, 1833**
Pasteur, Louis (1822–1895) FRENCH scientist **1875, 1895**
Patchen, Kenneth (1911–1972) US poet **1887**
Pater, Walter (1839–1894) BRITISH author and critic **1899**
Paulson, Henry (*b.* 1946) US banker, former Treasury Secretary, former chairman and CEO of Goldman Sachs **1823, 1823**
Paz, Octavio (1914–1998) MEXICAN writer **1837**
Peary, Robert Edwin (1856–1920) US Arctic explorer **1846**
Péguy, Charles Pierre (1873–1914) FRENCH writer **1904**
Perelman, S. J. (1904–1979) US humorist **1854**
Perera, N. M. (1905–1979) SRI LANKAN politician **1851**
Peres, Shimon (*b.* 1923) ISRAELI president and former prime minister **1877**
Perlis, Alan Jay (1922–1990) US computer scientist **1837, 1837, 1837, 1846, 1863, 1893, 1893, 1901**
Perot, H. Ross (*b.* 1930) US entrepreneur and presidential candidate **1833, 1839, 1845, 1868, 1906, 1853**
Perry, Sir Michael (*b.* 1934) BRITISH business executive **1828, 1865**
Peter, Laurence J. (1919–1990) CANADIAN academic and writer **1818, 1861, 1863, 1875, 1882, 1884, 1899**
Peters, John Durham (*b.* 1958) US historian and social theorist **1897**
Peters, Tom (*b.* 1942) US management consultant and author **1828, 1832, 1852, 1855, 1862, 1871, 1875, 1876, 1876, 1879, 1881, 1884, 1892, 1903, 1905**
Phelps, E. J. (1822–1900) US diplomat **1879**
Philip, Prince (Duke of Edinburgh) (*b.* 1921) BRITISH consort of Queen Elizabeth II **1900**
Picasso, Pablo (1881–1973) SPANISH artist and sculptor **1832, 1837**
Pickens, T. Boone (*b.* 1928) US oil company executive and financier **1855**
Pincus, Mark (*b.* 1966) US founder and CEO of Zynga **1856**
Pinker, Steven (*b.* 1954) CANADIAN-BORN US psychologist and author **1821, 1904**
Pinnell, Raoul (*b.* 1951) BRITISH former branding and marketing communications director of Shell **1862, 1877**
Pirsig, Robert M. (*b.* 1928) US author **1869, 1892**
Pitt the Elder, William (Earl of Chatham) (1708–1778) BRITISH prime minister **1860**
Plato (428?–347? BC) GREEK philosopher **1862**
Plutarch (46?–120?) GREEK writer and philosopher **1886**
Pollard, Eve (*b.* 1945) BRITISH journalist and newspaper editor **1905**
Pollard, John G. (1871–1937) US politician **1855**
Pollock, Jackson (1912–1956) US painter **1844**
Pompidou, George (1911–1974) FRENCH politician **1901**
Popcorn, Faith (*b.* 1947) US trend expert and founder of BrainReserve **1841, 1855, 1861, 1870, 1905**
Pope, Alexander (1688–1744) ENGLISH poet **1834, 1844, 1879, 1882**
Popper, Sir Karl Raimund (1902–1994) AUSTRO-HUNGARIAN-BORN BRITISH philosopher of science **1890**
Porter, Joshua US software designer and author **1865**
Porter, Michael (*b.* 1947) US strategist **1848**
Porter, Sylvia (1913–1991) US journalist and finance expert **1852, 1890, 1897**
Postrel, Virginia (*b.* 1960) US editor and author **1892**
Pound, Ezra (1885–1972) US poet, critic, editor, and translator **1852**
Powell, Colin (*b.* 1937) US general and secretary of state **1885, 1888**
Powell, Enoch (1912–1998) BRITISH politician **1867, 1878**
Prebble, Lucy (*b.* 1981) BRITISH playwright **1826, 1826**
Prosser, David BRITISH business journalist **1861**
Proxmire, William (1915–2005) US politician **1823**
Puzo, Mario (1920–1999) US novelist **1843, 1843**
Quadracci, Harry V. (1936–2002) US entrepreneur and founder of Quad Graphics **1877**
Quant, Mary (*b.* 1934) BRITISH fashion designer **1904**
Quayle, Dan (*b.* 1947) US former vice president **1856**
Quine, W. V. O. (1908–2000) US philosopher **1895**
Radcliffe, Cyril John, Lord (1899–1977) BRITISH lawyer **1878**

Raft, George (1895–1980) US film actor **1904**
Rahm, Emanuel (*b*. 1959) US mayor of Chicago, former White House chief-of-staff to President Obama **1819**
Rancière, Jacques (*b*. 1940) FRENCH Marxist philosopher **1830**
Rand, Ayn (1905–1982) US writer **1835**
Randall, Clarence B. (1891–1967) US industrialist and government adviser **1873**
Raschke, Linda Bradford US financial trader **1852, 1859**
Raskin, Jeff (1943–2005) US computer pioneer **1837**
Ratner, Gerald (*b*. 1949) BRITISH former CEO of Ratners Group **1892, 1892**
Ravitch, Diane (*b*. 1938) US educator and academic **1872**
Raymond, Eric S. (*b*. 1957) US computer programmer and hacker **1881**
Reagan, Nancy (*b*. 1921) US former actress and first lady **1834**
Reagan, Ronald (1911–2004) US president and actor **1846, 1863, 1863, 1906**
Reeves, Rosser (1910–1984) US advertising executive **1820**
Reich, Robert (*b*. 1946) US economist and politician **1822, 1884**
Renard, Jules (1864–1910) FRENCH writer **1880**
Repplier, Agnes (1858–1950) US writer and historian **1844**
Revans, Reg (1907–2003) BRITISH academic **1866**
Revson, Charles (1906–1975) US entrepreneur, business executive, and founder of Revlon **1824, 1864**
Ricardo, David (1772–1823) BRITISH economist **1903**
Richards, Steve (*b*. 1960) BRITISH journalist **1826**
Richelieu, Cardinal (1585–1642) FRENCH clergyman and politician, Louis XIII's chief minister **1846**
Ridderstråle, Jonas (*b*. 1966) SWEDISH academic and author **1832**
Ries, Al (*b*. 1926) US marketing strategist and author, founder and chairman of Ries & Ries consultancy **1833, 1836, 1870**
Rifkind, Sir Malcolm (*b*. 1946) BRITISH politician **1828**
Riley, Pat (*b*. 1945) US basketball coach and motivational speaker **1885**
Robbins, Anthony (*b*. 1960) US motivational writer and speaker **1845, 1860, 1899**
Robbins, Harvey US writer on business psychology **1881**
Roberts, Wess (*b*. 1946) US writer **1846**
Robertson, Heather (*b*. 1942) CANADIAN author **1894**
Robinson, Alan G. (*b*. 1958) US author **1843**
Robinson, David (*b*. 1959) AUSTRALIAN marketing executive **1877**
Robinson, Gerry (*b*. 1948) IRISH former chairman of Granada Television and of the Arts Council of England **1876, 1906**
Robinson, Joan (1903–1983) BRITISH economist **1828, 1851**
Rockefeller, John D. (1839–1937) US industrialist, philanthropist, and founder of Standard Oil **1821, 1886**
Roddick, Dame Anita (1942–2007) BRITISH entrepreneur and founder of The Body Shop **1829, 1829, 1835, 1841, 1841, 1843, 1844, 1853, 1854, 1854, 1891, 1891**
Rodney, Walter (1942–1980) GUYANESE historian and political activist **1847**
Rogers, Jim (*b*. 1942) US investor and author **1858, 1859, 1874, 1882**
Rogers, Samuel (1763–1855) BRITISH poet **1900**
Rogers, Will (1879–1935) US actor, columnist, and humorist **1878, 1900**
Rogoff, Kenneth (*b*. 1953) US economist **1823**
Rohatyn, Felix (*b*. 1928) US investment company executive **1851, 1858, 1885**
Roosevelt, Eleanor (1884–1962) US reformer, author, and first lady **1833, 1844, 1886**
Roosevelt, Franklin D. (1882–1945) US president **1819, 1830, 1863, 1892, 1903**
Roosevelt, Theodore (1858–1919) US president **1819, 1847**
Rootes, William, Lord (1894–1964) BRITISH car manufacturer **1891**
Rose, Billy (1899–1966) US theatrical impresario and composer **1871**
Rosenberg, Larry US financial trader **1859**
Rostand, Jean (1894–1977) FRENCH biologist and writer **1888**
Rosten, Leo C. (1908–1997) US author and humorist **1894**
Rostow, W. W. (1916–2003) US economist **1868**
Roszak, Theodore (1933–1981) US historian, writer, and editor **1851, 1868, 1872**
Roth, Philip (*b*. 1933) US novelist **1870**
Roubini, Nouriel (*b*. 1959) US financial analyst **1822**
Rousseau, Jean-Jacques (1712–1778) FRENCH philosopher and writer **1880, 1905**
Rowland, Tiny (1917–1998) BRITISH entrepreneur, co-CEO, and managing director of Lonrho **1886, 1889**
Rowling, J. K. (*b*. 1965) BRITISH writer **1860**
Royko, Mike (1932–1997) US journalist **1878**
Rubin, Harriet (*b*. 1952) US author **1856, 1887, 1894**
Rubinstein, Helena (1870–1965) US entrepreneur, cosmetics manufacturer, and philanthropist **1906**
Ruckelshaus, Jill (*b*. 1937) US public official **1905**
Rudner, Rita (*b*. 1953) US comedian and writer **1904**
Rudolph, Arthur (1906–1996) GERMAN-BORN US developer of the Saturn 5 rocket **1894**
Rumsfeld, Donald (*b*. 1932) US businessman and politician **1872**
Runcie, Robert, Lord (1921–2000) BRITISH archbishop of Canterbury **1902**
Rushkoff, Douglas (*b*. 1961) US media theorist **1906**
Ruskin, John (1819–1900) BRITISH art critic and writer **1831, 1835, 1852, 1896, 1904**
Russell, Bertrand (Earl Russell) (1872–1970) BRITISH philosopher and writer **1835, 1835, 1860, 1882, 1888, 1901, 1907**
Ruth, Babe (1895–1948) US baseball player **1824**
Rutherford, Ernest, Lord (1871–1937) NEW ZEALAND-BORN BRITISH physicist **1866**
Rutherford, Mark (1831–1913) BRITISH novelist **1846**
Rutten, Tim US critic and journalist **1842**
Ryan, Alan (*b*. 1940) BRITISH political philosopher **1906**
Sagan, Carl (1934–1996) US astronomer **1895**
Saint-Exupéry, Antoine de (1900–1944) FRENCH writer and aviator **1883**
Saint-Simon, Duc de (Louis de Rouvroy) (1675–1755) FRENCH writer and soldier **1846**
Saki (H. H. Munro) (1870–1916) BRITISH short-story writer **1818**
Saleeby, John US financial trader **1883**
Salerno, Steve US journalist and author **1897**
Salinger, J. D. (*b*. 1919) US novelist **1834**
Salk, Jonas (1914–1995) US medical researcher **1892, 1893**
Sallust (86–35? BC) ROMAN historian and politician **1905**
Salmon, Felix US financial journalist **1821**
Sampson, Anthony (1926–2004) BRITISH author and journalist **1824, 1829**
Samuelson, Paul (1915–2009) US economist and winner of the 1970 Nobel Prize in Economics **1835, 1851, 1861**
Sandefur, Thomas (1939–1996) US head of Brown & Williamson **1830**
Sandel, Michael J. (*b*. 1953) US political philosopher **1902**
Sangster, Margaret (1838–1912) US poet and writer **1907**
Santayana, George (1863–1952) US philosopher, novelist, and poet **1834, 1846, 1866, 1882, 1892**
Sarkozy, Nicolas (*b*. 1955) FRENCH president **1822**
Sarnoff, Robert W. (1918–1997) US media executive **1858**
Saul, John Ralston (*b*. 1947) CANADIAN writer **1831, 1865, 1901**
Saunders, Donald AUSTRALIAN business executive **1848**
Sawyer, Frederick (*b*. 1947) US writer **1839**

     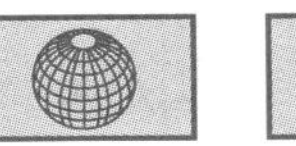   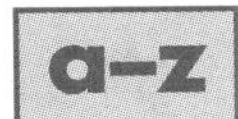

Sayers, Dorothy L. (1893–1957) BRITISH author **1839**
Schlesinger, Arthur, Jr (1917–2004) US historian, writer, and educator **1861, 1870**
Schmidt, Eric (*b.* 1955) US executive chairman of Google **1837, 1837, 1868, 1868**
Schopenhauer, Arthur (1788–1860) GERMAN philosopher **1904**
Schrage, Michael US commentator on innovation **1866**
Schrager, Ian (*b.* 1946) US entrepreneur **1898**
Schreiner, Olive (1855–1920) SOUTH AFRICAN novelist and social critic **1899**
Schultz, Howard (*b.* 1953) US businessman, chairman and CEO of Starbucks **1824, 1853**
Schulz, Kathryn US journalist and author **1879**
Schumacher, Ernst Friedrich (1911–1977) GERMAN-BORN BRITISH economist and conservationist **1853, 1854, 1868, 1868, 1900, 1901**
Schumpeter, Joseph Alois (1883–1950) US economist and social theorist **1832**
Schwab, Charles (*b.* 1937) US investment broker **1860**
Schwab, Charles M. (1862–1939) US industrialist **1867, 1881**
Schwed, Fred (1901–1966) US author **1818, 1860, 1871**
Scott, C. P. (1846–1932) BRITISH editor **1882**
Sculley, John (*b.* 1939) US businessman, former president of PepsiCo and former CEO of Apple Computer **1874, 1877, 1901**
Seeger, Pete (*b.* 1919) US singer and songwriter **1855**
Segall, Ken US advertising director **1878**
Seidman, L. William (1921–2009) US economist and financial commentator **1831**
Seko, Toshihiko (*b.* 1956) JAPANESE athlete **1875**
Selfridge, Gordon (1858–1947) US-BORN BRITISH retailer **1889, 1892**
Seligman, Martin (*b.* 1942) US psychologist and author **1881**
Semler, Ricardo (*b.* 1959) BRAZILIAN business executive and president of Semco **1840, 1852, 1881, 1883**
Seneca (4? BC–AD 65) ROMAN politician, philosopher, and writer **1896**
Senge, Peter (*b.* 1947) US academic and author **1841, 1869, 1874, 1879, 1892, 1894**
Sentamu, Dr John (*b.* 1949) UGANDAN-BORN archbishop of York **1829**
Shakespeare, William (1564–1616) ENGLISH poet and playwright **1883, 1890, 1893**
Shanahan, Eileen (1924–2001) US journalist and author **1878**
Shapiro, Carl (*b.* 1955) US academic and author **1833, 1868**
Shapiro, Eileen C. US business consultant and author **1838**
Sharma, Robin S. (*b.* 1965) CANADIAN self-help writer **1838, 1894**
Shaw, George Bernard (1856–1950) IRISH writer and critic **1838, 1847, 1856, 1863, 1880, 1890, 1892, 1896, 1906, 1907**
Shaw, Warren (*b.* 1950) US former CEO of Chancellor LGT Asset Management **1841**
Sheehy, Gail (*b.* 1937) US journalist and author **1844**
Shelby, Richard (*b.* 1934) US senator **1858**
Shelley, Percy Bysshe (1792–1822) BRITISH poet **1888**
Sherman, Brad (*b.* 1954) US congressman **1829**
Shiba, Shoji (*b.* 1933) JAPANESE academic and author **1885**
Shih, Stan (*b.* 1945) TAIWANESE cofounder and former CEO of Acer **1854, 1900**
Shiller, Robert (*b.* 1946) US economist and author **1827**
Shirky, Clay (*b.* 1964) US author and expert on new media **1828, 1828, 1868, 1900**
Shiva, Vandana (*b.* 1952) INDIAN philosopher and academic **1840, 1862**
Short, Clare (*b.* 1946) BRITISH politician **1829**
Shugart, Al (1930–2006) US entrepreneur and pioneer of disk drive technology **1869**
Sieff, Marcus, Lord (1913–2001) BRITISH president of Marks & Spencer **1841, 1853**
Sieger, Robin BRITISH business executive and author **1905**
Silverman, Jeffrey (*b.* 1946) US former director of the Chicago Mercantile Exchange **1859, 1859**
Simcock, Ric (*b.* 1965) BRITISH advertising executive **1868**
Simmons, Edward Emerson (1852–1931) US painter **1857**
Simmons, Russell (*b.* 1957) US founder of Def Jam records and Phat Farm clothes **1846**
Simms, Andrew BRITISH economist **1864**
Simon, Herbert A. (1916–2001) US political scientist and economist **1846, 1877, 1884**
Simon, John, Viscount (1873–1954) BRITISH foreign secretary and chancellor of the exchequer **1900**
Simon, William (1927–2000) US Treasury Secretary **1851**
Sinclair, Upton (1878–1968) US writer and political campaigner **1841**
Singer, Isaac Bashevis (1904–1991) US novelist and short-story writer **1834**
Singh, Reuben (*b.* 1976) BRITISH entrepreneur and author **1854**
Six, Robert F. (1907–1986) US airline executive **1889**
Skidelsky, Robert (*b.* 1939) BRITISH historian **1823**
Skinner, B. F. (1904–1990) US psychologist **1852**
Slater, Jim (*b.* 1929) BRITISH business executive and author **1827, 1861**
Slavet, James US venture capitalist **1875**
Sloan, Alfred P. (1875–1966) US president of General Motors **1819, 1873, 1877, 1894**
Smiles, Samuel (1812–1904) BRITISH social reformer and writer **1883**
Smith, Adam (1723–1790) BRITISH economist and philosopher **1839, 1864, 1895**
Smith, Andreas Whittam (*b.* 1937) BRITISH journalist **1826, 1827, 1840**
Smith, Gary B. US financial analyst and trader **1860**
Smith, Greg (*b.* 1978) US businessman, former executive director of Goldman Sachs **1840, 1872**
Smith, Logan Pearsall (1865–1946) BRITISH essayist and critic **1838, 1863, 1885, 1893**
Smith, Raymond W. (*b.* 1937) US former CEO and chairman of Bell Atlantic **1876**
Smith, Frederick E. (Earl of Birkenhead) (1872–1930) BRITISH politician **1821**
Solon (638?–559? BC) ATHENIAN statesman, legislator, and poet **1872**
Solzhenitsyn, Aleksander (1918–2008) RUSSIAN author and winner of the 1970 Nobel Prize in Literature **1894**
Son, Masayoshi (*b.* 1957) TAIWANESE CEO of Softbank Corporation **1837, 1883**
Sontag, Susan (1933–2004) US novelist and essayist **1821, 1870**
Sony (*b.* 1946) JAPANESE electronics and media conglomerate **1891**
Sophocles (496?–406 BC) GREEK tragedian **1897**
Soros, George (*b.* 1930) HUNGARIAN-BORN US financier, entrepreneur, and philanthropist **1829, 1832, 1836, 1859, 1870, 1889, 1898, 1898**
Sorrell, Sir Martin (*b.* 1945) BRITISH advertising executive **1850**
Soteriou, Helen BRITISH business journalist **1839**
Spafford, Gene (*b.* 1956) US computer security expert **1850**
Sparrow, Gerald (1903–1988) BRITISH business executive and writer **1866, 1882**
Spencer, Herbert (1820–1903) BRITISH social theorist **1892**
Sperandeo, Victor (*b.* 1945) US financial trader and author **1859**
Spielberg, Steven (*b.* 1946) US movie director **1867**
Spinoza, Baruch (1632–1677) DUTCH philosopher **1840, 1854**
Stead, Christina (1902–1983) AUSTRALIAN writer **1860**
Steel, Mark (*b.* 1960) BRITISH comedian and author **1823, 1826, 1893, 1897**
Steinbeck, John (1902–1968) US novelist **1819**
Steinem, Gloria (*b.* 1934) US entrepreneur, editor, and writer **1887, 1905**

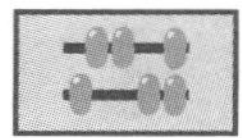

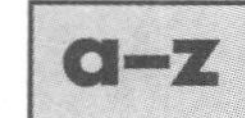

Steinhardt, Michael (*b.* 1940) US hedge fund manager **1871**
Stelzer, Irwin (*b.* 1932) US economist and writer **1879**
Stengel, Casey (1890–1975) US baseball player and manager **1877**
Stephens, Alfred G. (1865–1933) AUSTRALIAN journalist and literary critic **1872**
Stephenson, Neal (*b.* 1959) US science-fiction author **1894**
Stern, Stefan BRITISH management journalist and academic **1832**
Stevens, Wallace (1879–1955) US poet **1883**
Stevenson, Adlai E. (1900–1965) US statesman and author **1818, 1877, 1887, 1887**
Stevenson, Dennis, Lord (*b.* 1945) BRITISH company director **1857, 1888**
Stevenson, Mark (*b.* 1971) BRITISH author, comedian, and futurologist **1879**
Stewart, Martha (*b.* 1941) US businesswoman, TV personality, and founder of Martha Stewart Living Omnimedia **1853**
Stewart, Matthew US writer and former management consultant **1838, 1838**
Stewart, Thomas A. (*b.* 1948) US journalist and author **1853, 1870, 1883, 1887, 1889**
Stiglitz, Joseph (*b.* 1943) US economist **1823, 1825, 1857, 1862**
Stoller, Chad US digital marketing guru **1870**
Stone, Oliver (*b.* 1946) US movie director and screenwriter **1864**
Stoppard, Sir Tom (*b.* 1937) CZECHOSLOVAKIAN-BORN BRITISH playwright and screenwriter **1824, 1867, 1883**
Stout, Rex (1886–1975) US writer **1897, 1904**
Stowe, Harriet Beecher (1811–1896) US writer **1838, 1907**
Street-Porter, Janet (*b.* 1946) BRITISH broadcaster **1876**
Strindberg, J. August (1849–1912) SWEDISH playwright and novelist **1834**
Strong, Barrett (*b.* 1941) US singer and songwriter **1880**
Stroud, Jonathan (*b.* 1970) BRITISH fantasy novelist **1870**
Sugar, Sir Alan, Lord (*b.* 1947) BRITISH entrepreneur, TV personality, and founder of Amstrad electronics company **1821, 1830, 1867, 1867, 1886**
Summers, Lawrence H. (*b.* 1954) US economist and former president of Harvard University **1827, 1827, 1848, 1848, 1850**
Sumner, William Graham (1840–1910) US economist and sociologist **1904**
Sunderland, Ruth BRITISH financial journalist **1822**
Sutcliffe, Tom BRITISH journalist and broadcaster **1897**
Swaffer, Hannen (1879–1962) BRITISH journalist **1878**
Swartzwelder, John (*b.* 1950) US television writer and author **1829, 1830**
Swift, Jonathan (1667–1745) IRISH writer and satirist **1821, 1895, 1903**
Syrus, Publilius (*fl.* 1st century BC) ROMAN writer **1855**
Szent-Györgyi, Albert (1893–1986) US biochemist **1870**
Tachikawa, Keiji (*b.* 1939) JAPANESE president of the Japan Aerospace Exploration Agency and former IT executive **1862**
Taft, William Howard (1857–1930) US president and chief justice **1896**
Taibbi, Matt (*b.* 1970) US journalist **1822, 1825, 1845**
Takafusa, Mitsui (1684–1748) JAPANESE merchant **1860**
Taleb, Nassim Nicholas (*b.* 1960) LEBANESE-BORN US academic and writer, former derivatives trader **1819, 1823, 1825, 1858, 1858, 1858, 1858, 1860, 1861, 1861, 1864, 1897, 1898**
Tambo, Oliver (1917–1993) SOUTH AFRICAN political leader **1881**
Tan, Amy (*b.* 1952) US writer **1821**
Tanner, Chuck (1928–2011) US baseball player and manager **1876**
Tasker, Peter (*b.* 1955) BRITISH business author **1906**
Taubman, A. Alfred (*b.* 1924) US real estate developer and former owner of Sotheby's **1877**
Tawney, Richard (1880–1962) BRITISH economic historian and social critic **1831, 1904**
Taylor, F. W. (1856–1915) US engineer and author **1853**
Teller, Edward (1908–2003) US nuclear scientist **1824**
Templeton, Sir John (1912–2008) AMERICAN-BORN BRITISH investor and philanthropist **1827, 1827, 1858, 1859**
Terence (185?–159 BC) ROMAN comic playwright **1853**
Teresa, Mother (1910–1997) ALBANIAN missionary **1899**
Tharoor, Shashi (*b.* 1956) INDIAN politician, diplomat, and author **1849, 1867**
Thatcher, Margaret, Baroness (*b.* 1925) BRITISH former prime minister **1819, 1862, 1863, 1873, 1885, 1892**
Thiel, Peter (*b.* 1967) WEST GERMAN-BORN US entrepreneur, founder and former CEO of PayPal **1879**
Thomas, Gwyn (1913–1981) BRITISH dramatist and writer **1878**
Thomas, Lewis (1913–1993) US academic, physician, and writer **1878, 1879**
Thompson, Sir Clive (*b.* 1943) BRITISH former president of the Confederation of British Industry and former CEO and chairmain of Rentokil **1879**
Thompson, E. P. (1924–1993) BRITISH historian **1862**
Thompson, Larry US movie producer **1821**
Thomson, Roy Herbert, Lord (1894–1976) CANADIAN-BORN BRITISH media entrepreneur, founder and chairman of the Thomson Organisation **1890**
Thoreau, Henry David (1817–1862) US writer **1846, 1864, 1882, 1904**
Thurow, Lester (*b.* 1938) US economist, management theorist, and writer **1827, 1836, 1851, 1904**
Tierney, John (*b.* 1953) US science journalist **1845**
Tillmon, Johnnie (1926–1995) US welfare rights activist **1903**
Toffler, Alvin (*b.* 1928) US social commentator **1833, 1833, 1833, 1839, 1844, 1874, 1877, 1893**
Tomlin, Lily (*b.* 1939) US comedian and actress **1898**
Toohey, Peter US academic and author **1843**
Townsend, Robert (1920–1998) US business executive and author **1839, 1854, 1855, 1856, 1865, 1873, 1873, 1876, 1885**
Toyoda, Shoichiro (*b.* 1925) JAPANESE former chairman of Toyota **1840**
Tracy, Brian (*b.* 1944) CANADIAN businessman, author, and motivational speaker **1821, 1875, 1881, 1885, 1894, 1901**
Trahey, Jane (1923–2000) US copywriter and author **1820, 1865, 1866**
Trilling, Lionel (1905–1975) US academic, writer, and literary critic **1824**
Tripathi, Salil INDIAN journalist and campaigner **1847, 1877**
Trollope, Anthony (1815–1882) BRITISH novelist **1886**
Trompenaars, Fons (*b.* 1952) DUTCH author and management consultant **1824**
Trotsky, Leon (1879–1940) RUSSIAN revolutionary leader and Marxist theorist **1887**
Truman, Harry S. (1884–1972) US president **1873, 1893, 1894, 1896, 1898**
Trump, Donald J. (*b.* 1946) US real estate developer and TV personality **1819, 1824, 1855, 1860, 1871, 1873**
Trunk, Penelope (*b.* 1966) US businesswoman, author, and blogger **1860, 1874**
Tuchman, Barbara W. (1912–1989) US historian **1828**
Tullman, Howard (*b.* 1946) US multimedia entrepreneur **1853, 1856**
Turner, Adair, Lord (*b.* 1955) BRITISH chairman of the Financial Services Authority **1857**
Turner, Ted (*b.* 1938) US founder of Turner Broadcasting Systems and CNN **1824, 1878, 1880, 1885, 1886, 1886, 1904**
Tusa, Sir John (*b.* 1936) BRITISH broadcaster and former managing director of the Barbican **1833**

  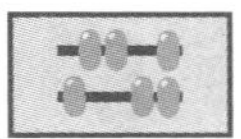   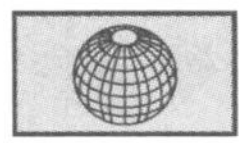   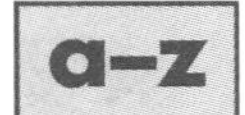

Twain, Mark (1835–1910) US writer **1830, 1836, 1838, 1846, 1860, 1865, 1865, 1874, 1875, 1883, 1888, 1889, 1890, 1897**
Updike, John (1932–2009) US novelist and critic **1839, 1857, 1870**
Usborne, Simon BRITISH journalist **1828**
Valigra, Lori US science writer **1901**
Van Buren, Abigail (*b.* 1956) US pen name of advice consultant Pauline Phillips and now her daughter Jeanne Phillips **1834**
Vanderbilt, William Henry (1821–1885) US industrialist **1841**
Vaneigem, Raoul (*b.* 1934) BELGIAN philosopher **1839, 1890, 1904**
Vargas Llosa, Mario (*b.* 1936) PERUVIAN novelist, playwright, and essayist **1832**
Varley, John (*b.* 1956) BRITISH banker and former CEO of Barclays Bank **1879**
Vauvenargues, Luc de Clapiers (1715–1747) FRENCH soldier and writer **1866**
Vaynerchuk, Gary (*b.* 1975) RUSSIAN-BORN US wine expert, author, and video blogger **1821**
Veblen, Thorstein (1857–1929) US economist and social scientist **1836, 1855, 1902**
Vernon, Lillian (*b.* 1927) GERMAN-BORN US entrepreneur and founder of Lillian Vernon Corporation **1823, 1895**
Vidal, Gore (*b.* 1925) US novelist and critic **1820, 1830, 1878, 1899**
Vie, Jean-Christophe FRENCH conservationist **1854**
Vitti, Jon US television writer **1880**
Vizcarra, Gaston (*b.* 1952) PERUVIAN ecological entrepreneur and president of Candela Peru **1854**
Vizinczey, Stephen (*b.* 1933) HUNGARIAN novelist and critic **1887**
Voinovich, Vladimir (*b.* 1932) RUSSIAN novelist **1878**
Volcker, Paul A. (*b.* 1927) US economist and former chairman of the Federal Reserve **1858**
Voltaire (François-Marie Arouet) (1694–1778) FRENCH writer, philosopher, and reformer **1907**
von Braun, Wernher (1912–1977) GERMAN-BORN US rocket engineer **1893**
Wagner, Jane (*b.* 1935) US writer **1821**
Waldman, Steven US journalist **1845**
Walker, Alice (*b.* 1944) US Pulitzer Prize-winning writer and poet **1855**
Walker, C. J. (1867–1919) US business executive **1832**
Walker, Harriet BRITISH fashion journalist **1828, 1895**
Walker, Jay S. (*b.* 1955) US entrepreneur, founder of Priceline.com, and chairman of Walker Digital **1863, 1902**
Walker, Tim BRITISH journalist **1865**
Walpole, Horace (Earl of Orford) (1717–1797) BRITISH writer **1867**
Walton, Sam M. (1918–1992) US entrepreneur and founder of Wal-Mart **1837, 1841, 1844, 1855**
Wanamaker, John (1838–1922) US businessman **1820**
Wang, An (1920–1990) US entrepreneur, business executive, electrical engineer, and founder of Wang Laboratories **1835**
Wanger, Ralph (*b.* 1925) US investor **1876**
Ward, Barbara (Baroness Jackson) (1914–1981) BRITISH economist, journalist, and educator **1847**
Warhol, Andy (1928–1987) US artist and producer **1839, 1839, 1844**
Warner, Craig (*b.* 1964) BRITISH screenwriter **1822, 1822**
Washington, Booker T. (1856–1915) US educator and political scientist **1890**
Waterman, Robert H., Jr (*b.* 1936) US consultant and author **1862, 1883**
Watson, James D. (*b.* 1928) US biologist and geneticist **1819**
Watson, Thomas J., Sr (1874–1956) US founder and president of IBM **1841, 1875, 1876**
Watson, Thomas J., Jr (1914–1993) US president of IBM and ambassador to the Soviet Union **1841, 1873, 1885, 1889**
Watts, Garry BRITISH CEO of SSL International, makers of Durex condoms and Scholl footware **1828, 1891**
Waugh, Auberon (1939–2001) BRITISH writer and journalist **1867**
Waugh, Evelyn (1903–1966) BRITISH novelist **1878**
Waxman, Henry (*b.* 1939) US politician **1829**
Webb, Sidney (Lord Passfield) (1859–1947) BRITISH economist, historian, and social reformer **1834**
Weber, Max (1864–1920) GERMAN economist and sociologist **1829**
Webster, Daniel (1782–1852) US statesman, orator, and lawyer **1833, 1902**
Weil, Simone (1909–1943) FRENCH philosopher and activist **1852, 1867, 1888**
Weinberg, Bill US software pioneer **1872**
Weinstock, Arnold, Lord (1924–2002) BRITISH managing director of General Electric Company **1831, 1863, 1868, 1903**
Weintraub, Neal US financial trader and author **1859**
Weinzweig, Ari US cofounder of Zingerman's delicatessan **1895**
Welch, Jack (*b.* 1935) US former CEO and chairman of General Electric **1833, 1841, 1850, 1850, 1855, 1855, 1876, 1881, 1883, 1886, 1903**
Welles, Orson (1915–1985) US actor and movie director **1878**
Wellesly, Revd John US minister **1886**
Wellington, Duke of (Arthur Wellesley) (1769–1852) BRITISH general and statesman **1875**
Wenders, Wim (*b.* 1945) GERMAN movie director and producer **1882**
West, Dame Rebecca (1892–1983) BRITISH writer and journalist **1878**
Whately, Richard (1787–1863) BRITISH archbishop and economist **1903**
Wheeler, Elmer (1903–1968) US writer **1820**
Wheeler, Shannon (*b.* 1966) US graphic artist and writer **1890**
Whisler, Thomas L. US academic **1837**
White, E. B. (1899–1985) US writer **1839, 1902, 1903**
Whitehead, Alfred North (1861–1947) BRITISH philosopher and mathematician **1818, 1835**
Whitehorn, Katharine (*b.* 1928) BRITISH journalist **1878, 1883, 1907**
Wilde, Oscar (1854–1900) IRISH writer and wit **1824, 1835, 1838, 1845, 1856, 1868, 1881, 1896, 1899**
Wilder, Laura Ingalls (1867–1957) US novelist **1884**
Wilensky, Robert (*b.* 1951) US academic **1901**
Will, George (*b.* 1941) US Pulitzer Prize-winning journalist **1828**
Williams, Raymond (1921–1988) BRITISH academic, critic, and novelist **1831**
Williamson, Marianne (*b.* 1952) US spiritual writer and activist **1857**
Wilson, Aubrey BRITISH marketing consultant and author **1877**
Wilson, Charles E. (1890–1961) US politician and president of General Motors **1868**
Wilson, Earl (1907–1987) US journalist and author **1845**
Wilson, Edward O. (*b.* 1929) US biologist and Pulitzer Prize-winning author **1906**
Wilson, Fred (*b.* 1961) US venture capitalist **1878**
Wilson, Harold, Lord (1916–1995) BRITISH prime minister **1860, 1903**
Wilson, Kemmons (1913–2003) US entrepreneur and founder of Holiday Inn **1866**
Wilson, Woodrow (1856–1924) US president **1830, 1834, 1844, 1885, 1897**
Winans, R. Foster (*b.* 1948) US journalist and author **1871**
Winblad, Ann (*b.* 1950) US venture capitalist **1840**
Winfrey, Oprah (*b.* 1954) US talk show host, actress, and business executive **1870**
Winslet, Kate (*b.* 1975) BRITISH film actress **1905**
Wodehouse, P. G. (1881–1975) US writer and humorist **1849**
Wolf, Chris US hedge fund manager **1858**
Wolf, Michael J. US consultant, author, and former president and COO of MTV Networks **1877**
Wolfe, Tom (*b.* 1931) US novelist and journalist **1860**
Wolfowitz, Paul (*b.* 1943) US diplomat and former head of the World Bank **1882**
Wood, Robert E. (1879–1969) US soldier and businessman, chairman of Sears Roebuck **1879**

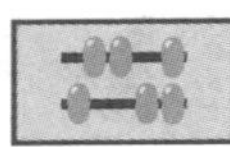

Wooden, John (1910–2010) US basketball player and coach **1834, 1874**
Wrapp, H. Edward (1917–2009) US academic **1887**
Wright, Frank Lloyd (1867–1959) US architect **1901**
Wrigley, William, Jr (1861–1932) US businessman and founder of Wrigley Company **1821, 1852, 1857, 1895, 1895**
Wriston, Walter (1919–2005) US banker **1824, 1832, 1840, 1862, 1869, 1870, 1874, 1874, 1875, 1878, 1906**
Wu, Tim US academic and communications expert **1868**
Wylie, Philip Gordon (1902–1971) US writer **1835**
Wyse, Lois (1926–2007) US advertising executive and writer **1881**
Yamani, Ahmed Zaki (*b.* 1930) SAUDI ARABIAN politician **1881**
Yang Jiang (*b.* 1911) CHINESE playwright and writer **1840**
Yeats, William Butler (1865–1939) IRISH poet and playwright **1894**
Young, Andrew Jackson, Jr (*b.* 1932) US diplomat and civil rights advocate **1872**
Young, Edward (1683–1765) ENGLISH poet **1890**
Young, Owen D. (1874–1962) US lawyer and corporate executive **1865**
Zaleznik, Abraham (*b.* 1924) US psychologist **1854**
Zeldin, Theodore (*b.* 1933) BRITISH academic, author, and historian **1876, 1881**
Žižek, Slavoj (*b.* 1949) SLOVENIAN sociologist and philosopher **1886**
Zoellick, Robert (*b.* 1953) US president of the World Bank **1829, 1842**
Zwerling, Jeffrey US lawyer **1842**

DICTIONARY

  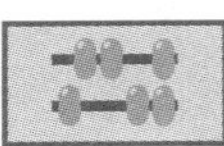   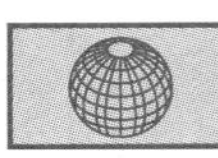    

Dictionary

Defining finance and business; the most up-to-date global business and finance English dictionary

The dictionary provides clear and simple definitions of more than 9,000 international finance and business terms. Updated and expanded for this edition, the dictionary has been compiled by an international team of expert researchers and information specialists. It is an up-to-date, practical resource that will help the user understand both basic and complex finance terms from around the world. Easy-to-use and full of helpful information, it aims to define the world of finance.

ORDER OF TERMS

All terms are listed in strict alphabetical order, ignoring spaces and punctuation, apart from when a term is part of a phrase. For example, **asking price** is listed before **ask price**. In the case of phrases, the definition is shown at the most valid element of the phrase.

ENTRY ANATOMY

Topic Areas

The terms have been drawn from 27 key topic areas, and each term labeled accordingly. The topic areas help to give extra context to each term, especially when the term can have more than one meaning depending on the situation in which it is used.

Quick Definitions

All terms are listed with a single-sentence definition, allowing the reader to quickly grasp a concept, before reading the fuller definition available immediately following this.

Cross-References

Cross-references are used in the dictionary to link terms that are closely related, or which expand on information given in the current entry.

Abbreviations

Finance is full of abbreviations and acronyms, and the dictionary features many of these. The definition is shown at either the full or abbreviated form depending on which is more commonly used, with the other form pointing to this.

Variant Names

Where different words or phrases are used to refer to the same concept, these are also shown in the dictionary. Again, the full definition is shown at the most commonly used form, with variants referring the reader to those common forms.

Informal Terms

Where terms are only used informally, as slang, or are dated, this is mentioned in the entry.

     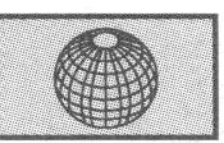   

A

AAA[1] *abbr* ACCOUNTING ***American Accounting Association***

AAA[2] STOCKHOLDING & INVESTMENTS top investment rating the maximum safety rating given to potential investments by ***Standard & Poor's*** or ***Moody's***, the two best-known ***rating agencies***. *Also called* ***triple A***

AAD *abbr* CURRENCY & EXCHANGE ***Arab Accounting Dinar***

AASB *abbr* ACCOUNTING ***Australian Accounting Standards Board***

AAT *abbr* ACCOUNTING ***Association of Accounting Technicians***

AB *abbr* BUSINESS ***Aktiebolag***

ABA *abbr* BANKING ***American Bankers Association***

abacus FINANCE frame holding rods strung with beads for calculating a counting device used for making basic arithmetic calculations, that consists of parallel rods strung with beads. Still widely used in education worldwide and for business and accounting in China and Japan, its origins can be traced back to early civilizations. Australia's oldest accounting journal bears the same name.

abandonment option STOCKHOLDING & INVESTMENTS early investment-termination option the option of terminating an investment before the time that it is scheduled to end

abandonment value STOCKHOLDING & INVESTMENTS value of investment terminated early the value that an investment has if it is terminated at a particular time before it is scheduled to end

ABA routing number BANKING number allocated to US financial institution in the United States, a nine-digit number allocated to a financial institution, such as a bank. It appears on US checks in the bottom-left corner. *Also called* ***routing number***. *See also* ***sort code***

abatement FINANCE decrease in debt obligation a reduction in an amount of a liability, for example, in the amount of a person's debts, or in a company's costs of paying employee benefits

ABB *abbr* TREASURY MANAGEMENT ***activity based budgeting***

abbreviated accounts ACCOUNTING abridged UK company accounts in the United Kingdom, a shortened version of a company's ***annual accounts*** that a company classified as small- or medium-sized under the ***Companies Act*** (1989) can file with the ***Registrar of Companies***, instead of having to supply a full version

ABC *abbr* ACCOUNTING ***activity based costing***

ABI *abbr* INSURANCE ***Association of British Insurers***

Abilene paradox GENERAL MANAGEMENT theory of group decisions based on mistaken impressions a theory stating that some decisions that seem to be based on consensus are in fact based on misperception and lead to courses of action that defeat original intentions. The Abilene paradox was proposed by management professor Jerry Harvey in 1974 following a trip made by his family to the town of Abilene. One person suggested the visit and the others agreed, each believing that everyone else wanted to go. On their return, everyone admitted that they would rather have stayed at home. Harvey used this experience to illustrate the mismanagement of agreement, and of decision making in organizations when apparent consensus is actually founded on poor communication.

ability-to-pay principle TAX theory of tax liability a theory which holds that taxes should be paid only by those who can best afford them

ABM *abbr* GENERAL MANAGEMENT ***activity based management***

ABN *abbr* TAX ***Australian Business Number***

abnormal loss ACCOUNTING loss exceeding normal allowance any loss which exceeds the normal loss allowance. Abnormal losses are generally accounted for as though they were completed products.

abnormal shrinkage ACCOUNTING shrinkage contributing to abnormal loss the unexpectedly high level of reduction in inventory that has contributed to an abnormal loss

abnormal spoilage ACCOUNTING shortfall contributing to abnormal loss the unexpectedly high level of shortfall that has contributed to an abnormal loss

abnormal waste ACCOUNTING waste contributing to abnormal loss the unexpectedly high level of waste that has contributed to an abnormal loss

above par STOCKHOLDING & INVESTMENTS trading above face value used to describe a security that trades above its ***nominal value*** or ***redemption value***

above-the-line **1.** ACCOUNTING indicating exceptional items in accounts used to describe entries in a company's profit and loss accounts that appear above the line separating those entries that show the origin of the funds that have contributed to the profit or loss from those that relate to its distribution. Exceptional and extraordinary items appear above the line. *See also* ***below-the-line*** *(sense 1)* **2.** ECONOMICS indicating country's revenue transactions in macroeconomics, used to describe a country's revenue transactions, as opposed to its ***below-the-line*** or capital transactions. *See also* ***below-the-line*** *(sense 2)* **3.** MARKETING relating to marketing costs for advertising used to describe marketing expenditure on advertising in media such as the press, radio, television, film, and the World Wide Web, on which a commission is usually paid to an agency. *See also* ***below-the-line*** *(sense 3)*

abridged accounts ACCOUNTING provisional UK company financial statement in the United Kingdom, financial statements produced by a company that fall outside the requirements stipulated in the ***Companies Act***. Abridged accounts are often made public through the media.

ABS *abbr* **1.** STOCKHOLDING & INVESTMENTS ***asset-backed security*** **2.** STATISTICS ***Australian Bureau of Statistics***

absolute advantage ECONOMICS favorable position of regions having low production costs an advantage enjoyed by a country or area of the world that is able to produce a product or provide a service more cheaply than any other country or area

absolute title LEGAL **1.** in UK, guaranteed right of ownership of land in the United Kingdom, an owner's guaranteed title to land, confirmed by registration with the Land Registry **2.** in UK, guaranteed right to lease in the United Kingdom, a proprietor's guaranteed valid lease on leasehold land

absorb ACCOUNTING merge production overhead costs to assign an overhead to a particular cost center in a company's production accounts so that its identity becomes lost. *See also* ***absorption costing***

absorbed account ACCOUNTING account merged with related accounts an account that has lost its separate identity by being combined with related accounts in the preparation of a financial statement

absorbed business MERGERS & ACQUISITIONS firm combined with another a company that has been merged into another company with which it is not on an equal footing

absorbed costs ACCOUNTING indirect manufacturing costs the indirect costs associated with manufacturing, for example, insurance or property taxes

absorbed overhead ACCOUNTING locally adjusted overhead an overhead attached to products or services by means of ***absorption rates***

absorption costing ACCOUNTING method allocating overhead costs to product an accounting practice in which fixed and variable costs of production are absorbed by different cost centers. Providing all the products or services can be sold at a price that covers the allocated costs, this method ensures that both fixed and variable costs are recovered in full. However, if sales are lost because the resultant price is too high, the organization may lose revenue that would have contributed to its overhead. *See also* ***marginal costing***

absorption rate ACCOUNTING rate of merging production overhead costs the rate at which overhead costs are absorbed into each unit of production

abusive tax shelter TAX illegal tax-reduction method a tax shelter that a person claims illegally to avoid or minimize tax

ACA **1.** ACCOUNTING ICAEW Associate Chartered Accountant an Associate (member) of the Institute of Chartered Accountants in England and Wales **2.** *abbr* REGULATION & COMPLIANCE ***Australian Communications Authority***

Academy of Accounting Historians ACCOUNTING US institution for accounting history a US organization founded in 1973 that promotes "research, publication, teaching, and personal interchanges in all phases of Accounting History and its interrelation with business and economic history"

ACAS *abbr* BUSINESS ***Advisory, Conciliation and Arbitration Service***

ACAUS *abbr* ACCOUNTING ***Association of Chartered Accountants in the United States***

ACCA *abbr* ACCOUNTING ***Association of Chartered Certified Accountants***

ACCC *abbr* REGULATION & COMPLIANCE ***Australian Competition and Consumer Commission***

accelerated cost recovery system ACCOUNTING use of asset depreciation to reduce US taxes in the United States, a system used for computing the depreciation of some assets acquired before 1986 in a way that reduces taxes. *Abbr* ***ACRS***

  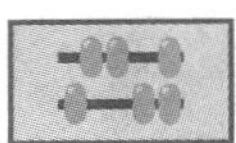      

accelerated depreciation ACCOUNTING assigning higher depreciation to new assets a system used for computing the depreciation of some assets in a way that assumes that they depreciate faster in the early years of their acquisition. The cost of the asset less its residual value is multiplied by a fraction based on the number of years of its expected useful life. The fraction changes each year and charges the highest costs to the earliest years. *Also called* ***declining balance method, sum-of-the-year's-digits depreciation***

acceleration clause LEGAL clause specifying conditions for early repayment of loan a section of a contract which details how a loan may be required to be repaid early if the borrower defaults on other clauses of the contract

acceptance FINANCE signature guaranteeing payment for bill of exchange the signature on a bill of exchange, indicating that the drawee (the person to whom it is addressed) will pay the face amount of the bill on the due date

acceptance bonus FINANCE bonus paid to new employee a bonus paid to a new employee on acceptance of a job. An acceptance bonus can be a feature of a golden hello and is designed both to attract and to retain staff.

acceptance credit BANKING facility for seller to draw bill of exchange a letter of credit granted by a bank to a buyer (the "applicant") against which a seller (the "beneficiary") can draw a bill of exchange

acceptance house *UK* BANKING institution guaranteeing financial instruments an institution that accepts financial instruments and agrees to honor them should the borrower default

acceptance region STATISTICS values for which null hypothesis is acceptable the set of values in a test statistic for which the null hypothesis can be accepted

acceptance sampling OPERATIONS & PRODUCTION method of checking subset to test whole group a decision-making technique for assuring quality used in a manufacturing environment, in which acceptance or rejection of a batch of parts is decided by testing a sample of the batch. The sample is checked against established standards and, if it meets those standards, the whole batch is deemed acceptable.

accepting bank BANKING bank accepting letter of credit a bank in an exporter's own country to which an issuing bank sends a ***letter of credit*** for the exporter

accepting house BANKING firm accepting bills of exchange a company, usually an investment bank, that accepts bills of exchange at a discount, in return for immediate payment to the issuer

Accepting Houses Committee BANKING banks linked to Bank of England for lending the main London ***investment banks*** that organize the lending of money with the ***Bank of England*** and receive favorable ***discount rates***

acceptor FINANCE addressee of signed bill of exchange a person who has accepted liability for a bill of exchange by signing its face

access BUSINESS right to sell into particular market the right to sell goods or services into a particular market without contravening related legislation

access bond MORTGAGES S. African mortgage accepting capital against other loans in South Africa, a type of mortgage that permits borrowers to take out loans against extra capital paid into the account, home-loan interest rates being lower than interest rates on other forms of credit

ACCI *abbr* BUSINESS ***Australian Chamber of Commerce and Industry***

accident insurance INSURANCE insurance against losses incurred in accidents insurance that will pay the insured person for loss or damages when an accident takes place

accommodation address BUSINESS address for receiving messages only an address used for receiving messages, which is not the address of the company's premises

accommodation bill FINANCE bill of exchange facilitating loan for another company a bill of exchange where the drawee who signs it is helping another company (the drawer) to raise a loan. The bill is given on the basis of trade debts owed to the borrower.

account 1. FINANCE arrangement for deferred payment a business arrangement involving the exchange of money or credit in which payment is deferred **2.** FINANCE record of financial dealings a record maintained by a financial institution itemizing its dealings with a particular customer **3.** ACCOUNTING record of monetary value of transactions a structured record of transactions in monetary terms, kept as part of an accounting system. This may take the form of a simple list or that of entries on a credit and debit basis, maintained either manually or as a computer record. **4.** MARKETING advertising firm's client a client of an advertising or public relations agency **on account** FINANCE used to describe a transaction where something is received that is to be paid for later

accountability CORPORATE GOVERNANCE responsibility for actions the allocation or acceptance of responsibility for one's own actions or those of others lower in the hierarchy

accountancy ACCOUNTING professional activities of accountants the work and profession of accountants

accountancy bodies *UK* ACCOUNTING = ***accounting bodies***

accountancy profession *UK* ACCOUNTING = ***accounting profession***

accountant ACCOUNTING somebody responsible for financial records a professional person who maintains and checks the business records of a person or organization and prepares forms and reports for financial purposes

accountant's letter ACCOUNTING independent statement about financial report a written statement by an independent accountant that precedes a financial report, describing the scope of the report and giving an opinion on its validity

accountant's opinion ACCOUNTING audit report on firm's accounts a report of the audit of a company's books, carried out by a certified public accountant

account day ACCOUNTING day of settlement of executed order the day on which an executed order is settled by the delivery of securities, payment to the seller, and payment by the buyer. This is the final day of the ***accounting period***.

account debtor ACCOUNTING body responsible for paying for something a person or organization responsible for paying for a product or service

account director MARKETING advertising firm employee in charge of client's business a senior person within an advertising agency responsible for overall policy on a client's advertising account

account executive MARKETING senior employee in charge of specific client's business an employee of an organization such as a bank, public relations firm, or advertising agency who is responsible for the business of a specific client

accounting ACCOUNTING range of activities undertaken by accountants a generic term for the activities such as bookkeeping and financial accounting conducted by accountants. Accounting involves the classification and recording of monetary transactions; the presentation and interpretation of the results of those transactions in order to assess performance over a period and the financial position at a given date; and the monetary projection of future activities arising from alternative planned courses of action. Accounting in larger businesses is typically carried out by financial accountants, who focus on formal, corporate issues such as taxation, and management accountants, who provide management reports and guidance.

Accounting and Finance Association of Australia and New Zealand ACCOUNTING organization for accountancy and financial professionals an organization for accounting and finance academics, researchers, and professionals. The Association has a variety of objectives, including the promotion of information on accounting to the public, and the provision of programs in continual professional development to both members and nonmembers. The Association's name was changed in 2002 to incorporate the Accounting Association of Australia and New Zealand and the Australian Association of University Teachers in Accounting. *Abbr* ***AFAANZ***

accounting bases ACCOUNTING fundamental accounting methods the methods used for applying fundamental accounting concepts to financial transactions and items; preparing financial accounts; determining the accounting periods in which revenue and costs should be recognized in the profit and loss account; and determining the amounts at which material items should be stated in the balance sheet

accounting bodies *US* ACCOUNTING professional organizations for accountants professional institutions and associations for accountants. These include such bodies as the ***Accounting Standards Board*** in the United Kingdom and the ***American Institute of Certified Public Accountants*** in the United States. *UK term* ***accountancy bodies***

accounting concept ACCOUNTING accepted basis for preparing accounts any of the general assumptions on which accounts are prepared. The main concepts are: that the business is a going concern; that revenue and costs are noted when they are incurred and not when cash is received or paid; that the present accounts are drawn up following the same principles as the previous accounts; and that the revenue or costs are only recorded if it is certain that they will be received or incurred.

accounting cost ACCOUNTING cost of proper financial records the cost of maintaining and checking the business records of a person or organization and of preparing forms and reports for financial purposes

  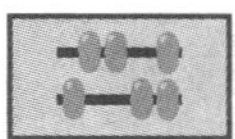      

accounting cycle ACCOUNTING process of regularly updating financial records the regular process of formally updating a firm's financial position by recording, analyzing, and reporting its transactions during the accounting period

accounting date ACCOUNTING end date of accounting period the date on which an accounting period ends. This can be any date, though it is usually 12 months after the preceding accounting date.

accounting department *US* ACCOUNTING company department dealing with finance the department in a company which deals with money paid, received, borrowed, or owed. *UK term* ***accounts department***

accounting equation ACCOUNTING formula relating assets, liabilities, and equity a formula in which a firm's assets must be equal to the sum of its liabilities and the owners' equity. *Also called* ***balance sheet equation***

accounting exposure ACCOUNTING risk from changing exchange rates the risk that foreign currency held by a company may lose value because of exchange rate changes when it conducts overseas business

accounting fees ACCOUNTING fees for preparing accounts fees paid to an accountant for preparing accounts. Such fees are tax-deductible.

accounting insolvency ACCOUNTING condition of liabilities exceeding assets the condition that a company is in when its liabilities to its creditors exceed its assets

accounting manager *US* ACCOUNTING manager of accounting department the manager of the accounting department in a business or institution. *UK term* ***accounts manager***

accounting manual ACCOUNTING set of instructions for keeping accounts a collection of accounting instructions governing the responsibilities of persons, and the procedures, forms, and records relating to the preparation and use of accounting data. There can be separate manuals for the constituent parts of the accounting system, for example, budget manuals or cost accounting manuals.

accounting period ACCOUNTING time between financial reports a length of time for which businesses may prepare internal accounts so as to monitor progress on a weekly, monthly, or quarterly basis. Accounts are generally prepared for external purposes on an annual basis.

accounting policies ACCOUNTING options for financial reporting the specific accounting methods selected and consistently followed by an entity as being, in the opinion of the management, appropriate to its circumstances and best suited to present fairly its results and financial position. For example, from the various possible methods of ***depreciation***, the accounting policy may be to use ***straight line depreciation***.

accounting principles ACCOUNTING rules of financial reporting the rules that apply to accounting practices and provide guidelines for dealing appropriately with complex transactions

Accounting Principles Board ACCOUNTING former US organization with oversight of accounting in the United States, the professional organization which issued opinions that formed much of ***Generally Accepted Accounting Principles*** until 1973, when the Financial Accounting Standards Board (FASB) took over that role. *Abbr* ***APB***

accounting procedure ACCOUNTING method of keeping financial records an accounting method developed by a person or organization to deal with routine accounting tasks

accounting profession *US* ACCOUNTING set of organizations overseeing accountants collectively, the professional bodies of accountants that establish and regulate training entry standards and professional examinations, as well as ethical and technical rules and guidelines. These bodies are organized on national and international levels. *UK term* ***accountancy profession***

accounting profit ACCOUNTING difference between revenue and costs the difference between total revenue and explicit costs. Accounting profits exclude costs such as ***opportunity costs***.

accounting rate of return ACCOUNTING ratio of unadjusted profit to capital employed the ratio of profit before interest and taxation to the percentage of capital employed at the end of a period. Variations include using profit after interest and taxation, equity capital employed, and average capital for the period. *Abbr* ***ARR***

accounting ratio ACCOUNTING ratio of one accounting result to another an expression of accounting results as a ratio or percentage, for example, the ratio of ***current assets*** to ***current liabilities***

accounting records ACCOUNTING materials for preparing financial statements all documentation and books used during the preparation of financial statements. *Also called* ***books of account***

accounting reference date ACCOUNTING last day included in financial record the nominal last day of a company's ***accounting reference period***, which ends on that date or on one no more than seven days on either side of it

accounting reference period ACCOUNTING 12 months that annual accounts cover the period covered by a company's annual accounts, which is usually one full year

accounting software ACCOUNTING programs for electronic accounts computer programs used to help maintain ***accounting records*** electronically. Such software can be used for a variety of tasks, including preparing statements and recording transactions.

accounting standard ACCOUNTING approved method of presenting financial information an authoritative statement of how specific types of transaction and other events should be reflected in financial statements. Compliance with accounting standards will usually be necessary for financial statements to give a true and fair view.

Accounting Standards Board ACCOUNTING UK standard-setting organization in the United Kingdom, a standard-setting organization established on August 1, 1990, to develop, issue, and withdraw accounting standards. Its objectives are "to establish and improve standards of financial accounting and reporting, for the benefit of users, preparers, and auditors of financial information." *Abbr* ***ASB***

accounting system ACCOUNTING everything used in producing accounting information the means, including staff and equipment, by which an organization produces its accounting information

accounting technician ACCOUNTING qualified person working in finance industry a qualified person who works in accounting and finance alongside ***certified public accountants***. Accounting technicians have a variety of jobs, including accounts clerk, credit controller, and financial manager. Their professional body is the ***Association of Accounting Technicians***.

accounting year *UK* ACCOUNTING TAX = ***fiscal year***

account reconciliation ACCOUNTING **1.** comparing balances of transactions a procedure for ensuring the reliability of accounting records by comparing balances of transactions **2.** comparing checkbook records with bank statement a procedure for comparing the register of a checkbook with an associated bank statement

accounts ACCOUNTING record of monetary value of transactions a structured record of transactions in monetary terms, kept as part of an accounting system. This may take the form of a simple list or that of entries on a credit and debit basis, maintained either manually or as a computer record.

accounts department *UK* ACCOUNTING = ***accounting department***

accounts manager *UK* ACCOUNTING = ***accounting manager***

accounts payable ACCOUNTING amount owed through credit the amount that a company owes for goods or services obtained on credit. *Abbr* ***AP***

accounts receivable ACCOUNTING amount owed by customers the money that is owed to a company by those who have bought its goods or services and have not yet paid for them. *Abbr* ***AR***

accounts receivable aging ACCOUNTING money owed grouped by month and customer a periodic report that classifies outstanding receivable balances according to customer and month of the original billing date

accounts receivable factoring ACCOUNTING buying of discounted invoiced debts the buying of ***accounts receivable*** at a discount with the goal of making a profit from collecting them

accounts receivable financing ACCOUNTING using money owed as collateral for loan a form of borrowing in which a company uses money that it is owed as collateral for a loan it needs for business operations

accounts receivable turnover ACCOUNTING ratio indicating length of time before customers pay a ratio that shows how long the customers of a business wait before paying what they owe. This can cause cash flow problems for small businesses.

The formula for accounts receivable turnover is straightforward. Simply divide the average amount of receivables into annual credit sales:

$$\frac{\text{Sales}}{\text{Receivables}} = \text{Receivables turnover}$$

If, for example, a company's sales are $4.5 million and its average receivables are $375,000, its receivables turnover is:

$$\frac{4,500,000}{375,000} = 12$$

A high turnover figure is desirable, because it indicates that a company collects revenues effectively, and that its customers pay bills promptly. A high figure also suggests that a firm's credit and collection policies are sound. In addition, the measurement is a reasonably good indicator of cash flow, and of overall operating efficiency.

  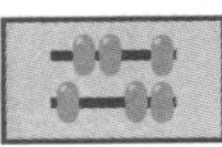      

accredited investor STOCKHOLDING & INVESTMENTS investor with income of specific size an investor whose wealth or income is above a specific amount. It is illegal for an accredited investor to be a member of a private limited partnership.

accreted value STOCKHOLDING & INVESTMENTS bond's value at present interest rate the theoretical value of a bond if interest rates remained at the current level

accretion MERGERS & ACQUISITIONS firm's asset growth the growth of a company through additions or purchases of plant or value-adding services

accrual ACCOUNTING unpaid charge in accounting results a charge that has not been paid by the end of an accounting period but must be included in the accounting results for the period. If no invoice has been received for the charge, an estimate must be included in the accounting results.

accrual basis *or* accrual concept *or* accrual method ACCOUNTING recording transactions for period they refer to an accounting method that includes income and expense items as they are earned or incurred irrespective of when money is received or paid out. *See also* ***cash accounting*** *(sense 1)*

accrual bond STOCKHOLDING & INVESTMENTS = ***zero coupon bond***

accrual of discount STOCKHOLDING & INVESTMENTS annual gain for bond bought below face value the annual gain in value of a bond owing to its having been bought originally for less than its ***nominal value***

accrual of interest FINANCE addition of interest to principal the automatic addition of interest to the original amount loaned or invested. Accrual of interest costs match the cost of capital with the provision of capital.

accruals basis *or* accruals concept ACCOUNTING see ***accrual basis***

accrue 1. FINANCE increase with time to increase and be due for payment at a later date, for example, interest 2. ACCOUNTING include item when earned or incurred to include an income or expense item in transaction records at the time it is earned or incurred

accrued dividend STOCKHOLDING & INVESTMENTS dividend earned since previous dividend payment a dividend earned since the date when the last dividend was paid

accrued expense ACCOUNTING expense incurred but not paid an expense that has been incurred within a given accounting period but not yet paid

accrued income FINANCE income due income that has been earned or accumulated over a period of time but not yet received

accrued interest STOCKHOLDING & INVESTMENTS interest accumulated since previous interest payment the amount of interest earned by a bond or similar investment since the previous interest payment

accrued liabilities FINANCE recorded but unpaid liabilities liabilities which are recorded, although payment has not yet been made. This can include liabilities such as rent and utility payments.

accruing FINANCE increasing with time added as a periodic gain, for example, as interest on an amount of money

accumulated depreciation ACCOUNTING cumulative depreciation claimed as expense the cumulative annual depreciation of an ***asset*** that has been claimed as an expense since the asset was acquired. *Also called* ***aggregate depreciation***

accumulated dividend STOCKHOLDING & INVESTMENTS dividend earned since previous dividend payment the amount of money in dividends earned by a stock or similar investment since the previous dividend payment

accumulated earnings tax TAX tax in place of dividends the tax that a company must pay because it chose not to pay dividends that would subject its owners to higher taxes

accumulated profit ACCOUNTING profit carried over into next year profit which is not paid as dividend but is taken over into the accounts of the following year

accumulated reserves FINANCE annual reserves put aside reserves which a company has put aside over a period of years

accumulating shares STOCKHOLDING & INVESTMENTS common stock issued in place of dividend common stock issued by a company equivalent to and in place of the net dividend payable to holders of common stock

accumulation unit STOCKHOLDING & INVESTMENTS unit with dividends used for more units a share in a mutual fund for which dividends accumulate and form more units, as opposed to an ***income unit***, where the investor receives the dividends as ***income***

accuracy STATISTICS closeness of data match the degree to which data conforms to a recognized standard value

ACH *abbr* E-COMMERCE, BANKING ***automated clearing house***

acid test 1. ACCOUNTING test of organization's liquidity a test used to measure an organization's ***liquidity***. *See also* ***acid-test ratio*** 2. GENERAL MANAGEMENT decisive test a stringent test of the worth or reliability of something

acid-test ratio ACCOUNTING measure of organization's liquidity an accounting ratio used to measure an organization's ***liquidity***. The most common expression of the ratio is:

$$\text{Acid-test ratio} = \frac{(\text{Current assets} - \text{Inventory})}{\text{Current liabilities}}$$

If, for example, current assets total $7,700, inventory amounts to $1,200, and current liabilities total $4,500, then:

$$\frac{(7,700 - 1,200)}{4,500} = 1.44$$

A variation of this formula ignores inventories altogether, distinguishes assets as cash, receivables, and short-term investments, then divides the sum of the three by the total current liabilities, or:

$$\text{Acid-test ratio} = \frac{(\text{Cash} + \text{Accounts receivable} + \text{Short-term investments})}{\text{Current liabilities}}$$

If, for example, cash totals $2,000, receivables total $3,000, short-term investments total $1,000, and liabilities total $4,800, then:

$$\frac{(2,000 + 3,000 + 1,000)}{4,800} = 1.25$$

In general, the ratio should be 1:1 or better. It means a company has a unit's worth of easily convertible assets for each unit of its current liabilities.

ACP *abbr* INTERNATIONAL TRADE ***African Caribbean and Pacific States***

acquirer 1. FINANCE buyer an organization or individual that buys a business or asset 2. BANKING, E-COMMERCE institution handling credit card transactions a financial institution, commonly a bank, that processes a merchant's credit card authorizations and payments, forwarding the data to a credit card association, which in turn communicates with the issuer. *Also called* ***acquiring bank, clearing house*** *(sense 3)*

acquiring bank BANKING, E-COMMERCE = ***acquirer*** *(sense 2)*

acquisition MERGERS & ACQUISITIONS when one organization buys another the process of one organization taking control of another, by the direct purchase of the net assets or liabilities of the other. *See also* ***merger***

acquisition accounting MERGERS & ACQUISITIONS, ACCOUNTING = ***purchase acquisition***

acquisition integration MERGERS & ACQUISITIONS merging of new company into existing company the process by which a company plans for and implements a successful integration of a newly acquired company

ACRS *abbr* ACCOUNTING ***accelerated cost recovery system***

ACT *abbr* TAX ***advance corporation tax***

action-centered leadership GENERAL MANAGEMENT model of actions of effective leaders a leadership model that focuses on what leaders actually have to do in order to be effective. The action-centered leadership model is illustrated by three overlapping circles representing the three key activities undertaken by leaders: achieving the task, building and maintaining the team, and developing the individual.

action research GENERAL MANAGEMENT study of results of researcher's own changes research that involves conducting experiments by making changes while simultaneously observing the results. The researcher takes an involved role as a participant in planning and implementing change.

active account BANKING account regularly used for transactions an account such as a bank account or investment account that is used to deposit and withdraw money frequently

active asset FINANCE asset in daily use an asset that is used in the daily operations of a business

active fund management STOCKHOLDING & INVESTMENTS proactive managing of mutual fund the managing of a mutual fund by making judgments about stock valuations instead of relying on automatic adjustments such as indexation. *See also* ***passive investment management***

active partner HR & PERSONNEL working partner in partnership firm a partner who gives a significant amount of working time to a company that is a partnership

active portfolio strategy STOCKHOLDING & INVESTMENTS proactive managing of investment portfolio the managing of an investment portfolio by making judgments about stock valuations instead of relying on automatic adjustments such as indexation

activist fiscal policy TREASURY MANAGEMENT institutional intervention to affect exchange rate the policy of a government or national bank that tries to affect the value of its country's money by such measures as changing interest rates for loans to banks and buying or selling foreign currencies

activity based budgeting TREASURY MANAGEMENT allocation of resources to individual activities the determination of which activities incur costs within an organization, establishing the relationships between them, and then deciding how much of the total budget should be allocated to each activity. *Abbr* ***ABB***

activity based costing ACCOUNTING calculating business's cost from cost of activities a method of calculating the cost of a business by focusing on the actual cost of activities, thereby producing an estimate of the cost of individual products or services.

An ABC cost-accounting system requires three preliminary steps: converting to an ***accrual method*** of accounting; defining cost centers and cost allocation; and determining process and procedure costs.

Businesses have traditionally relied on the cash basis of accounting, which recognizes income when received and expenses when paid. ABC's foundation is the accrual-basis income statement. The numbers this statement presents are assigned to the various procedures performed during a given period. Cost centers are a company's identifiable products and services, but also include specific and detailed tasks within these broader activities. Defining cost centers will of course vary by business and method of operation. What is critical to ABC is the inclusion of all activities and all resources.

Once cost centers are identified, management teams can begin studying the activities each one engages in and allocating the expenses each one incurs, including the cost of employee services.

The most appropriate method is developed from time studies and direct expense allocation. Management teams who choose this method will need to devote several months to data collection in order to generate sufficient information to establish the personnel components of each activity's total cost.

Time studies establish the average amount of time required to complete each task, plus best- and worst-case performances. Only those resources actually used are factored into the cost computation; unused resources are reported separately. These studies can also advise management teams how best to monitor and allocate expenses that might otherwise be expressed as part of general overheads, or go undetected altogether. *Abbr* ***ABC***

activity based management TREASURY MANAGEMENT management based on cost of activities a management control technique that focuses on the resource costs of organizational activities and processes, and the improvement of quality, profitability, and customer value. This technique uses ***activity based costing*** information to identify strategies for removing resource waste from operating activities. Main tools employed include: ***strategic analysis***, ***value analysis***, ***cost analysis***, ***life-cycle costing***, and ***activity based budgeting***.

activity cost pool TREASURY MANAGEMENT total cost of activity a grouping of all of the cost elements associated with an activity

activity driver analysis TREASURY MANAGEMENT assessing financial demands of activity the identification and evaluation of the activity drivers used to trace the cost of activities to cost objects. It may also involve selecting activity drivers with potential to contribute to the cost management function, with particular reference to cost reduction.

activity indicator ECONOMICS measure of economic productivity a calculation used to measure labor productivity or manufacturing output in an economy

act of God INSURANCE unforeseen event not covered by insurance an unexpected and unavoidable event or occurrence such as a storm or a flood that is not covered by an insurance policy

actual cash value INSURANCE cost of replacing something damaged beyond repair the amount of money, less ***depreciation***, that it would cost to replace something damaged beyond repair with a comparable item

actual price MARKETS price for immediate delivery a price for a commodity that is to be delivered immediately

actuals **1.** FINANCE commodities immediately available commodities that can be bought and used, as contrasted with commodities traded on a ***futures contract*** **2.** ACCOUNTING past earnings and expenses earnings and expenses that have occurred rather than being only projected

actual to date ACCOUNTING cumulative value already realized the cumulative value realized by something between an earlier date and the present

actual turnover FINANCE times person spends average available sum the number of times during a specific period that somebody spends the average amount of money that he or she has available to spend during that period

actuarial age INSURANCE person's statistically derived life expectancy the statistically derived life expectancy for any given person's age, used, for example, to calculate the periodic payments from an annuity

actuarial analysis INSURANCE calculation carried out by actuary a life expectancy or risk calculation carried out by an actuary

actuarial science INSURANCE statistics for calculating risk and life expectancy the branch of statistics used in calculating risk and life expectancy for the administration of pension funds and life insurance policies

actuarial tables INSURANCE lists of life expectancy by age lists showing how long people of specific ages are likely to live, used in calculating life assurance premiums

actuary INSURANCE statistician calculating life expectancy a statistician who calculates probable life spans so that the insurance premiums to be charged for various risks can be accurately determined

ACU *abbr* CURRENCY & EXCHANGE ***Asian Currency Unit***

adaptive control OPERATIONS & PRODUCTION automatic changes to industrial process a system of automatic monitoring and adjustment, usually by computer, of an industrial process. Adaptive control allows operating parameters to be changed continuously in response to a changing environment in order to achieve optimum performance.

adaptive learning GENERAL MANAGEMENT method of modifying behavior to repeat successes a style of organizational learning that focuses on prior successes and the use of these as the basis for developing future strategies and successes. Organizations use adaptive learning to make incremental improvements to existing products, services, and processes in response to the changing business environment. ***Generative learning*** is a contrasting approach to organizational learning.

adaptive measure STATISTICS choosing best statistical method a means of choosing the most appropriate method for a statistical analysis

ADB *abbr* BANKING **1.** ***African Development Bank*** **2.** ***Asian Development Bank***

ad click rate E-COMMERCE = ***click-through rate***

ADDACS *abbr* BANKING ***Automated Direct Debit Amendment and Cancellation Service***

added value **1.** GENERAL MANAGEMENT = ***value added*** **2.** MARKETING addition to product that increases attractiveness an increase in the attractiveness to customers of a product or a service achieved by adding something to it

addend FINANCE number added to complete sum the initial number added to an ***augend*** in order to complete an ***addition***

addition FINANCE adding together numbers to make sum an arithmetical operation consisting of adding together two or more numbers to make a sum

additional premium INSURANCE payment for extra insurance cover a payment made to cover extra items added on to existing insurance

additional principal payment *US* ACCOUNTING making larger than necessary loan payment the payment of a lump sum to reduce the capital borrowed on a mortgage or other loan, thereby reducing the term of the loan and saving a large amount of interest expense, or the amount paid. *UK term* ***overpayment***

additional voluntary contributions PENSIONS beneficiary's extra payments into company pension extra money that an individual chooses to pay into an ***occupational pension*** plan to improve the benefits he or she will receive on retirement. *Abbr* ***AVCs***

address verification E-COMMERCE matching credit card customer's stated address to records a procedure used by the processor of a credit card to verify that a customer's ordering address matches the address in the customer's record

ADF *abbr* PENSIONS ***Approved Deposit Fund***

adhocracy GENERAL MANAGEMENT organizational system with no set rules a system of organization that emphasizes informality and flexibility and does not employ fixed rules or standard procedures for dealing with problems

adjudication of bankruptcy LEGAL legal statement of bankruptcy a legal order officially stating that somebody is bankrupt

adjustable rate mortgage MORTGAGES mortgage with fluctuating interest rate a mortgage where the interest rate changes according to the current market rates. *Abbr* ***ARM***

adjustable rate preferred stock STOCKHOLDING & INVESTMENTS preferred stocks linked to Treasury interest rate preferred stocks on which dividends are paid in line with the interest rate on Treasury bills. *Abbr* ***ARPS***

adjusted book value ACCOUNTING current value of firm's assets and liabilities the value of a company in terms of the current market values of its assets and liabilities. *Also called* ***modified book value***

adjusted futures price STOCKHOLDING & INVESTMENTS current value of futures contract the current value of a futures contract to buy a commodity at a fixed future date

adjusted gross income ACCOUNTING income after adjustments for tax purposes the amount of annual income that a person or company has after various adjustments for income or corporation tax purposes. *Abbr* ***AGI***

adjusted present value ACCOUNTING separated discounted cash flows for operations and finance where the capital structure of a company is complex, or expected to vary over time, discounted cash flows may be separated into (i) those that relate to operational items, and (ii) those associated with financing. This treatment enables assessment to be made of the separate features of each area. *Abbr* ***APV***

adjuster *US* INSURANCE assessor of insurance claims a professional person acting on behalf of an insurance company to assess the value of an insurance claim. *UK term* ***loss adjuster***

adjustment FINANCE change in financial condition a change, often a significant downward turn, in the financial condition of a business, business sector, stock market, economy, etc.

adjustment credit BANKING short-term loan from US Federal Reserve a short-term loan from the US Federal Reserve to a commercial bank and the most common borrowing method to meet reserve requirements

adjustment trigger CURRENCY & EXCHANGE factor triggering adjustment in exchange rates a factor such as a specific level of inflation that triggers an adjustment in exchange rates

adminisphere GENERAL MANAGEMENT part of firm dealing with administration the part of an organization that deals with administrative matters, often perceived negatively by employees because of the apparently unnecessary nature of decisions made by its members (slang)

administered price OPERATIONS & PRODUCTION retail price fixed by manufacturer the price of a good or service which is fixed by a manufacturer and which cannot be varied by a retailer

administration 1. FINANCE = ***receivership*** **2.** GENERAL MANAGEMENT management of firm's operations the management of the affairs of a business, especially the planning and control of its operations

administration costs TREASURY MANAGEMENT management costs costs of management, not including production, marketing, or distribution costs

administration school GENERAL MANAGEMENT attitude to business management a school of thought that defines management activities as a set of processes: organizing, coordinating, commanding, and controlling. *See also* ***business administration***

administrative receiver FINANCE receiver representing long-term creditor a receiver appointed by a ***debenture*** holder to liquidate the assets of a company on his or her behalf

administrator GENERAL MANAGEMENT, HR & PERSONNEL somebody appointed to return firm to solvency a licensed ***insolvency practitioner*** who is appointed by a court, the company itself, or somebody owed money to bring the company back to solvency

admissibility STATISTICS when procedure performs better than all others the property of a procedure if, and only if, there is no other of its class that performs as well or better in at least one case

ADR *abbr* STOCKHOLDING & INVESTMENTS ***American depository receipt***

ADS *abbr* STOCKHOLDING & INVESTMENTS ***American depository share***

adspend MARKETING = ***advertising expenditure***

ad valorem duty *or* ad valorem tax TAX sum based on something's value a tax such as Value Added Tax or duty that is calculated on the value of the products or services provided, rather than on their number or size

advance FINANCE **1.** money loaned or paid before due date money paid as a loan or as a part of a payment scheduled to be made later **2.** rise in price or rate an increase in the price, rate, or value of something **3.** pay money as loan or part payment to pay an amount of money to somebody as a loan or as a part of a payment scheduled to be made later **4.** become higher in price or rate to increase in price, rate, or value

advance corporation tax TAX former UK company tax formerly, in the United Kingdom, a tax paid by a company equal to a percentage of its dividends or other distributions of profit to its stockholders. It was abolished in 1999. *Abbr* ***ACT***

advance-decline ratio MARKETS ratio of rising stocks to falling stocks a ratio used for indicating the strength of a stock market, calculated by dividing the number of securities whose price rose by the number whose price fell. A positive result indicates a rising market and a negative result, a falling market.

advance payment FINANCE prepaid amount an amount paid before it is earned or incurred, for example, a prepayment by an importer to an exporter before goods are shipped, or a cash advance for travel expenses

advance payment bond FINANCE made under a contract or order if the supplier fails to fulfill its contractual obligations.

advance payment guarantee *or* advance payment bond FINANCE guarantee for recovery of advance payment a guarantee that enables a buyer to recover an advance payment made under a contract or order if the supplier fails to fulfill its contractual obligations

adverse action FINANCE refusal of credit the action of refusing somebody credit or of canceling somebody's credit

adverse balance ACCOUNTING deficit on account a deficit on an account

adverse balance of trade INTERNATIONAL TRADE level of imports higher than exports a situation where a country has more visible imports than it has exports

adverse opinion ACCOUNTING auditor's statement that accounts are misleading a statement in the auditor's report of a company's annual accounts indicating a fundamental disagreement with the company to such an extent that the auditor considers the accounts misleading

adverse selection MARKETING poor quality items sell faster the theory that poor quality goods are more likely to sell than good, because some sellers want to get rid of products, and buyers are unable to judge whether the quality or price is too low. This applies in many spheres, such as the stock market or insurance industry, as well as in the buying and selling of merchandise. Three factors come into play: (i) the variable quality of similar products on the market; (ii) the fact that buyers and sellers do not possess the same information about the product (usually the seller knows more than the buyer); (iii) sellers are more likely to want to get rid of bad quality products than good quality products.

advertisement MARKETING firm's paid announcement to sell product a public announcement by a company in a newspaper, on television or radio, or over the Internet, intended to attract buyers for a product or service

advertising MARKETING using paid announcements to try to sell products the promotion of goods, services, or ideas, through paid announcements. Advertising aims to persuade or inform the general public and can be used to induce purchase, increase brand awareness, or enhance product differentiation. An advertisement has two main components: the message, and the medium by which it is transmitted. Advertising forms just one part of an organization's total marketing strategy.

advertising agency MARKETING firm that creates paid product announcements for clients an organization that, on behalf of clients, drafts and produces advertisements, places advertisements in the media, and plans advertising campaigns. Advertising agencies may also perform other marketing functions, including market research and consulting.

advertising campaign MARKETING planned series of paid product announcements a planned program using advertising aimed at a particular target market or audience over a defined period of time for the purpose of increasing sales or raising awareness of a product or service

advertising department MARKETING part of firm that creates paid product announcements the department within an organization which is responsible for advertising its products or services. The advertising department is also the name given to the section of a publishing house that coordinates the placing of advertisements in its magazines, newspapers, or other publications. It is involved in the sale of advertising space to clients.

advertising expenditure MARKETING money spent by firm on paid product announcements the amount spent by an organization on advertising, usually per year. Advertising expenditure is analyzed by breaking it down into the main advertising channels used by companies, such as newspapers, magazines, television, radio, movie theaters, and outdoor advertising. Expenditure can show the total spending nationally, by sector, or by type and size of company, or may relate to one company's spend on advertising, including the proportion spent on specific brands. *Also called* ***adspend***

advertising manager MARKETING employee in charge of firm's paid product announcements an employee of a business who is responsible for planning and controlling its advertising activities and budgets

advertising media MARKETING TV, radio, newspapers, etc. used for product announcements

  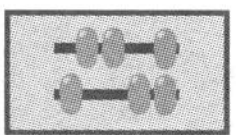      

the communication channels used for advertising, including television, radio, the printed press, and outdoor advertising

advertising research MARKETING gathering information about effectiveness of product announcements research carried out before or after advertising to ensure or test its effectiveness

advertorial MARKETING article influenced by advertisers a combination of an advertisement and an editorial article. The content of an advertorial is significantly influenced, and may even be entirely written, by the advertisers. Examples of advertorials include travel or leisure supplements in newspapers or magazines that are designed to attract advertisements from suppliers of relevant goods or services. A criticism of advertorials is that it is sometimes difficult to distinguish between an advertising article and ordinary journalistic articles, particularly when they appear in the same typeface as the other contents of the newspaper or magazine. To overcome this, some advertorials are headed "Advertisement."

advice of fate BANKING notification as to whether check will be honored immediate notification from a drawer's bank as to whether a check is to be honored or not

advid MARKETING promotional video a video used to promote a product or service

advising bank BANKING, INTERNATIONAL TRADE bank facilitating firm's overseas credit a bank in an exporter's own country to which an issuing bank sends a letter of credit. *Also called* ***notifying bank***

Advisory, Conciliation and Arbitration Service BUSINESS UK organization resolving workplace disputes in the United Kingdom, a public body, funded by taxpayers, that aims to prevent and resolve problems between employers and their workforces. The government established the first voluntary conciliation service in 1896, but the modern ACAS was founded in 1974 when the organization moved away from government control and became independent. It hosted talks between opposing sides in many of the high-profile labor disputes in the 1970s and 1980s, including the miners' strike in 1984. *Abbr* ***ACAS***

advisory funds STOCKHOLDING & INVESTMENTS funds invested at intermediary's discretion funds placed with a financial institution to invest on behalf of a client as the institution sees fit

advisory management STOCKHOLDING & INVESTMENTS stockbroker's provision of investment advice an advisory service offered by some stockbrokers through which clients are able to discuss a variety of investment options with their broker and receive appropriate advice. No resulting action may be taken, however, without a client's express approval.

AEO *abbr* INTERNATIONAL TRADE ***Authorized Economic Operator***

AER *abbr* FINANCE ***Annual Equivalent Rate***

AEX *abbr* MARKETS, STOCKHOLDING & INVESTMENTS Amsterdam Exchange = ***Euronext Amsterdam***

AEX Index MARKETS, STOCKHOLDING & INVESTMENTS main Dutch stock market index an index of the 25 most-actively traded stocks on the ***Euronext Amsterdam*** exchange. It was established on January 3, 1983, with a base value of 45.38.

AFAANZ *abbr* ACCOUNTING ***Accounting and Finance Association of Australia and New Zealand***

AFBD *abbr* MARKETS ***Association of Futures Brokers and Dealers***

AfDB *abbr* BANKING ***African Development Bank***

affiliate BUSINESS **1.** firm legally linked to another a company that is controlled by another or is a member of a larger group **2.** firm owning some voting stock of another either of two companies where one owns a minority of the voting stock of the other

affiliated enterprise BUSINESS firm partly owned by another a company that is partly owned, though less than 50%, by another, and in which the stock-owning company exerts some management control or has a close trading relationship with the associate. *Also called* ***associate company***

affiliate directory E-COMMERCE, MARKETING list of websites with affiliate programs a directory that indexes sites belonging to ***affiliate programs***. Affiliate directories offer information for companies seeking to subscribe to a program, as well as for those wanting to establish affiliate programs of their own.

affiliate marketing E-COMMERCE, MARKETING advertising through Internet partnerships the use of ***affiliate programs*** providing advertising links on websites

affiliate partner E-COMMERCE, MARKETING firm that advertises another firm's products on Internet a company that markets a product or service on the Internet for another company

affiliate program E-COMMERCE, MARKETING Internet advertising partnership between firms an advertising program in which one merchant induces others to place their banners and buttons on its website in return for a commission on purchases made by their customers.

There is no better example of the success of affiliate marketing than that of Amazon.com. The company has links on literally hundreds of thousands of external websites, linking through to its own site, from where it offers books and other products. It is a win-win situation: the external vendors can offer their visitors extra services that are easy to establish, and receive revenue from Amazon. At the same time, Amazon opens up a new channel for marketing each time a new visitor links through to its website. *Also called* ***associate program***

affinity card MARKETING credit card offering benefits a credit or debit card co-issued by a bank and another organization whose logo appears on the card. The other organization may be a charity or a commercial enterprise. If it is a charity, the issuing bank makes a donation each time the card is used. A commercial enterprise may get a portion of the revenues that the card generates and may offer benefits in the form of discounts or frequent flyer miles to the cardholder to encourage use of the card.

affirmative action *US* HR & PERSONNEL favoring appointments from disadvantaged groups preferential treatment, usually through a quota system, to prevent, or correct, discriminatory employment practices, particularly relating to recruitment and promotion. *UK term* ***positive discrimination***

affluent society wealthy community a community in which material wealth is widely distributed

affluenza bad feelings associated with being rich feelings of unhappiness, stress, and guilt induced by the pursuit and possession of wealth (slang)

AFP *abbr* FINANCE ***Association for Financial Professionals***

African Caribbean and Pacific States INTERNATIONAL TRADE nations grouped for trade purposes a set of independent states that are treated in a similar way for the purposes of trade preferences. *Abbr* ***ACP***

African Development Bank BANKING bank supporting development in African countries a bank set up by African countries to provide long-term loans to help agricultural development and improvement of infrastructure. *Abbr* ***ADB***

Afrikaanse Handelsinstituut GENERAL MANAGEMENT S. African business organization the South African national chamber of commerce for Afrikaans businesses. *Abbr* ***AHI***

AFTA *abbr* INTERNATIONAL TRADE ***ASEAN Free Trade Area***

after-acquired collateral FINANCE collateral obtained after loan agreed collateral for a loan that a borrower obtains after making the contract for the loan

after date FINANCE after date stated on bill after the date specified on a bill of exchange. Wording on a bill will state when payment has to be made, for example, "60 days after date, we promise to pay..." means 60 days after the date of the bill. *See also* ***bill of exchange***

after-hours buying MARKETS deals done after close of stock exchange buying, selling, or dealing in stock after a stock exchange has officially closed for the day, such deals being subject to normal stock exchange rules. In this way, dealers can take advantage of the fact that, because of time differences and the various stock exchanges around the world, there is almost always at least one stock exchange open throughout 24 hours.

aftermarket MARKETS trade in newly launched stock a market in new shares of stock that starts immediately after trading in the shares begins

after-sales service MARKETING help for customers after buying product customer support following the purchase of a product or service. In some cases, after-sales service can be almost as important as the initial purchase. The manufacturer, retailer, or service provider determines what is included in any warranty or guarantee package. This will include the duration of the warrant, traditionally one year from the date of purchase but increasingly two or more years, maintenance and/or replacement policy, items included/excluded, labor costs, and speed of response. In the case of a service provider, after-sales service might include additional training or help desk availability. Of equal importance is the customer's perception of the degree of willingness with which a supplier deals with a question or complaint, speed of response, and action taken.

after sight FINANCE after bill's acceptance after acceptance of a bill of exchange. Wording on a bill will state when payment has to be made, for example, "60 days after sight, we promise to pay..." means 60 days after acceptance of the bill. *See also* ***bill of exchange***

after-tax TAX after deduction of tax relating to earnings or income from which tax has already been deducted

AG FINANCE public limited company in German-speaking country used after the name of a German, Austrian, or Swiss business to identify it as a

  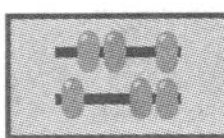      

public limited company. *Full form* ***Aktiengesellschaft***

against actuals STOCKHOLDING & INVESTMENTS relating to futures trade in cash relating to a trade between owners of futures contracts that allows both to reduce their positions to cash instead of commodities

aged debt FINANCE debt that is overdue a debt that is overdue by one or more given periods, usually increments of 30 days

aged debtor FINANCE somebody with overdue debt a person or organization responsible for a debt that is overdue

agency GENERAL MANAGEMENT authority to represent somebody else a relationship between two people or organizations in which one is empowered to act on behalf of the other in dealings with a third party

agency bank BANKING bank that is foreign bank's agent a bank that does not accept deposits, but acts as an agent for another, usually foreign, bank

agency bill BANKING bill of exchange drawn on local bank a bill of exchange drawn on the local branch of a foreign bank

agency broker STOCKHOLDING & INVESTMENTS dealer trading in shares for commission a dealer who acts for a client, buying and selling stock for a commission

agency commission MARKETING money given to advertising firm for delivering business a percentage of advertising expenditure rebated to an advertising agency, media buyer, or client organization by a media owner

agency markup MARKETING additional management fee charged by advertising firm a management fee charged by an advertising agency in addition to the cost of external services that it buys on behalf of a client

agenda GENERAL MANAGEMENT list of subjects to deal with at meeting a list of topics to be discussed or business to be transacted during the course of a meeting, usually sent prior to the meeting to those invited to attend

agent GENERAL MANAGEMENT representative for somebody else a person or organization empowered to act on behalf of another when dealing with a third party

agent bank BANKING **1.** bank participating in partner bank's credit card program a bank that takes part in another bank's credit card program, acting as a depository for merchants **2.** bank acting on foreign bank's behalf a bank that acts on behalf of a foreign bank

agent's commission FINANCE money paid for agent's services money, often a percentage of sales, paid to an agent

age pension *ANZ* PENSIONS government money received by retired person a sum of money paid regularly by the government to people who have reached the age of retirement

agflation ECONOMICS rapidly rising food prices an economic situation occurring when the cost of food rises rapidly

aggregate demand ECONOMICS total money spent or invested in economy the sum of all expenditures in an economy that makes up its ***GDP***, for example, consumers' expenditure on goods and services, investment in ***capital stock***, and government spending

aggregate depreciation ACCOUNTING = ***accumulated depreciation***

aggregate income FINANCE total of all incomes in economy the total of all incomes in an economy without adjustments for inflation, taxation, or types of ***double counting***

aggregate output ECONOMICS all goods and services produced in economy the total value of all the goods and services produced in an economy. *Also called* ***aggregate supply***

aggregate planning OPERATIONS & PRODUCTION planning for manufacture of related products medium-range capacity planning, typically covering a period of 3 to 18 months. Aggregate planning is used in a manufacturing environment and determines not only the overall output levels planned but the appropriate resource input mix to be used for related groups of products. Generally, planners focus on overall or aggregate capacity rather than on individual products or services. Aggregate planning can be used to influence demand as well as supply, in which case variables such as price, advertising, and the product mix are taken into account.

aggregate supply ECONOMICS = ***aggregate output***

aggregator **1.** FINANCE firm selling product packages a company that combines similar products or services into larger packages, making a profit by cost savings, by reaching a larger market, or by charging more for the combined package. In the secondary mortgage market, aggregators buy individual mortgages from financial institutions and turn them into ***mortgage-backed securities***, pooling them and selling them on at a higher price. **2.** E-COMMERCE middleman between producers and online customers an organization that acts as an intermediary between producers and customers in an Internet business web. The aggregator selects products, sets prices, and ensures fulfillment of orders.

aggressive STOCKHOLDING & INVESTMENTS describing high-risk investment strategy used to describe an investment strategy marked by willingness to accept high risk while trying to realize higher than average gains. Such a strategy involves investing in rapidly growing companies that promise capital appreciation but produce little or no income from dividends and de-emphasizes income-producing instruments such as bonds.

aggressive accounting ACCOUNTING deliberately inaccurate accounting to improve firm's position inaccurate or unlawful accounting practices used by an organization in order to make its financial position seem healthier than it is in reality (slang)

aggressive growth fund STOCKHOLDING & INVESTMENTS mutual fund pursuing large profits riskily a mutual fund that takes considerable risks in the hope of making large profits

AGI *abbr* ACCOUNTING ***adjusted gross income***

agile manufacturing OPERATIONS & PRODUCTION flexible method for producing goods to meet demand a manufacturing method that focuses on meeting the demands of customers by adopting flexible manufacturing practices. Agile manufacturing emerged as a reaction to ***lean production***. It differs by focusing on meeting the demands of customers without sacrificing quality or incurring added costs. Based on the idea of the ***virtual organization***, agile manufacturing aims to develop flexible, often short-term, relationships with suppliers, as market opportunities arise. Stock control is considered less important than satisfying the customer, and so customer satisfaction measures become more important than output measures. Agile manufacturing requires an adaptable, innovative, and empowered work force.

agility GENERAL MANAGEMENT ability to quickly respond and adapt to change the organizational capability to be flexible, responsive, adaptive, and show initiative in times of change and uncertainty. Agility has origins in manufacturing and has been cited as a source of competitive advantage by many management gurus. For others, the key to agility lies in what the organization is, as opposed to what it does. Agility grew as a reaction against the slowness of bureaucratic organizations to respond to changing market conditions. The ***virtual organization*** has been quoted as one extreme example of an agile organization.

agio **1.** FINANCE difference between two related values the difference between two values, for example, between the interest charged on loans made by a bank and the interest paid by the bank on deposits, or between the values of two currencies **2.** CURRENCY & EXCHANGE charge for exchanging currency a charge made for changing money of one currency into another, or for changing paper money into coins

AGM *UK* CORPORATE GOVERNANCE = ***annual meeting***

agreed price OPERATIONS & PRODUCTION price agreed on by buyer and seller a price for a product or service that has been accepted by both the buyer and seller

agreement among underwriters STOCKHOLDING & INVESTMENTS document forming syndicate of underwriters a document which forms a syndicate of underwriters, linking them to the issuer of a new stock issue

agreement of sale LEGAL formal contract between buyer and seller a written contract specifying the terms under which the buyer agrees to buy particular real estate and the seller agrees to sell it

agreement to sell LEGAL contract to sell at future date a contract between two parties in which one agrees to sell something to the other at a date in the future

agricultural produce ACCOUNTING slaughtered animals and harvested plants farm animals and plants once they have been slaughtered or harvested. Before this they are classified as ***biological assets***

AHI *abbr* BUSINESS ***Afrikaanse Handelsinstituut***

AIA *abbr* ACCOUNTING ***Association of International Accountants***

AIB *abbr* BANKING ***American Institute of Banking***

AIC *abbr* STOCKHOLDING & INVESTMENTS ***Association of Investment Companies***

AICPA *abbr* ACCOUNTING ***American Institute of Certified Public Accountants***

AIFA *abbr* FINANCE ***Association of Independent Financial Advisers***

aim GENERAL MANAGEMENT goal of effort an end toward which effort is directed and on which resources are focused, usually to achieve an organization's strategy. There is considerable discussion on whether aim, goal, target, and

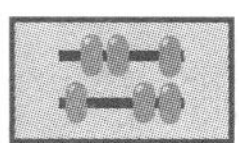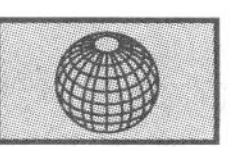

objective are the same. In general usage, the terms are often interchangeable, so it is important that, if an organization has a particular meaning for one of these terms, it must define it in its documentation. Sometimes an aim is seen as the desired final end result, while a goal is a smaller step on the road to it.

AIM *abbr* MARKETS ***Alternative Investment Market***

air bill *US* FINANCE documents accompanying shipments by air the documentation issued by an airline for the shipment of goods by air freight. *UK term* ***air waybill***

air cover GENERAL MANAGEMENT support and protection from high-ranking employee support from a senior member of staff, usually during a time of change, upheaval, or unpopular decisions (slang)

airtime MARKETING amount of time that advertisement is broadcast the amount of time given to an advertisement on television, radio, or in movie theaters

air waybill *UK* FINANCE = ***air bill***

AITC *abbr* FINANCE Association of Investment Trust Companies. *See* ***Association of Investment Companies***

Aktb *abbr* BUSINESS ***Aktiebolag***

Aktiebolag *or* Aktiebolaget BUSINESS Incorporated the Swedish equivalent of Inc. *Abbr* ***Aktb***

Aktiengesellschaft FINANCE *see* ***AG***

alien corporation BUSINESS firm registered in another country a company that is based in one country, but registered in another

all equity rate FINANCE interest rate charged for high-risk project the interest rate that a lender charges because of the apparent risks of a project that are independent of the normal market risks of financing it

alligator spread MARKETS unprofitable spread in good market conditions in the US options market, a ***spread*** that remains unprofitable even with good market conditions, usually as the result of high commissions paid to brokers or agents (slang)

All Industrials Index MARKETS Australian index of non-mining companies a subindex of the Australian ***All Ordinaries Index*** which includes all the companies from that index that are not involved in resources or mining

All Mining Index MARKETS Australian index of mining companies a subindex of the Australian ***All Ordinaries Index*** which includes all the companies from that index that are involved in the mining industry

allocate 1. FINANCE assign item to single cost unit to assign a whole item of ***cost***, or of ***revenue***, to a single cost unit, center, account, or time period **2.** STOCKHOLDING & INVESTMENTS choose between different investments to assign assets to different investment types such as equities, bonds, or cash

allonge FINANCE attachment to bill of exchange allowing more signatures a piece of paper attached to a bill of exchange, so that more endorsements can be written on it

All Ordinaries Accumulation Index MARKETS measure of change in Australian stock prices a measure of the change in stock prices on the Australian Stock Exchange, based on the ***All Ordinaries Index***, but assuming that all dividends are reinvested

All Ordinaries Index MARKETS major index of Australian stocks the major index of Australian stocks, comprising more than 300 of the most active Australian companies listed on the Australian Stock Exchange. *Abbr* ***All Ords***, ***AO***

all-or-none underwriting MARKETS option of canceling undersubscribed stock issue the option of canceling a public offering of stock if the underwriting is not fully subscribed. *Abbr* ***AON***

allotment STOCKHOLDING & INVESTMENTS UK issue of new company's stock to applicants in the United Kingdom, the act of selling shares of stock in a new company to people who have applied for them

allowable deductions TAX legitimate deductions from UK taxable income in the United Kingdom, deductions from income that are allowed by HM Revenue & Customs, reducing the total on which tax is payable

allowable expenses TAX business expenses offset against tax business expenses that can be used to reduce the amount of income on which tax is paid

allowable losses ACCOUNTING losses rightly offset against gains losses such as those on the sale of assets that can be used to reduce the amount of income on which tax is paid

allowance for bad debt ACCOUNTING accounting arrangement covering unpaid debt a provision made in a company's accounts for potentially unrecoverable debts

All Resources Index MARKETS Australian index of companies in resources industry a subindex of the Australian ***All Ordinaries Index*** which includes all the companies from that index that are involved in the resources industry

all-risks policy INSURANCE insurance policy covering all likely claims an insurance policy that covers risks of any kind, with no exclusions

alpha STOCKHOLDING & INVESTMENTS number measuring price increase a number representing an estimate of the anticipated price increase of a stock. A high alpha suggests a stock is likely to produce a good return. *See also* ***beta***

alpha rating STOCKHOLDING & INVESTMENTS expected return when market's rate is zero the return a security or a portfolio would be expected to earn if the market's rate of return were zero. Alpha expresses the difference between the return expected from a stock or mutual fund, given its beta rating, and the return actually produced. A stock or trust that returns more than its beta would predict has a positive alpha, while one that returns less than the amount predicted by beta has a negative alpha. A large positive alpha indicates a strong performance, while a large negative alpha indicates a dismal performance.

To begin with, the market itself is assigned a beta of 1.0. If a stock or trust has a beta of 1.2, this means its price is likely to rise or fall by 12% when the overall market rises or falls by 10%; a beta of 7.0 means the stock or trust price is likely to move up or down at 70% of the level of the market change.

In practice, an alpha of 0.4 means the stock or trust in question outperformed the market-based return estimate by 0.4%. An alpha of − 0.6 means the return was 0.6% less than would have been predicted from the change in the market alone.

Both alpha and beta should be readily available upon request from investment firms, because the figures appear in standard performance reports. It is always best to ask for them, because calculating a stock's alpha rating requires first knowing a stock's beta rating, and beta calculations can involve mathematical complexities. *See also* ***beta rating***

alpha value STOCKHOLDING & INVESTMENTS money given to departing employee for investment in Australia and New Zealand, a sum paid to an employee when he or she leaves a company that can be transferred to a concessionally taxed investment account such as an ***Approved Deposit Fund***

alternate director CORPORATE GOVERNANCE absent director's representative at board meeting a person who is allowed to act for an absent named director of a company at a board meeting

alternative investment STOCKHOLDING & INVESTMENTS investment not in bonds or stock an investment other than in bonds or stock of a large company or one listed on a stock exchange

Alternative Investment Market MARKETS London market trading in smaller firms' stock the market on the ***London Stock Exchange*** trading in stock of emerging or small companies not eligible for listing on the LSE's main market. It replaced the Unlisted Securities Market (USM) in 1995. *Abbr* ***AIM***

alternative minimum tax TAX US system to ensure that wealthy pay tax in the United States, a way of calculating income tax that is intended to ensure that wealthy individuals, corporations, trusts, and estates pay at least some tax regardless of deductions, but that is increasingly targeting the middle class because the threshold was never indexed for inflation. This has turned the AMT into an important political issue, with the possibility that the threshold will either be raised substantially or the AMT eliminated altogether in future. *Abbr* ***AMT***

alternative mortgage instrument MORTGAGES open-ended non-amortizing mortgage any form of mortgage other than a fixed-term amortizing loan

alternative order STOCKHOLDING & INVESTMENTS instruction for either of two specified actions an order given to a broker to do one of two things, for example, to sell a stock either when it goes up to a specified price or down to a specified price, thereby limiting gains and losses

AM *abbr* STOCKHOLDING & INVESTMENTS ***asset management***

amalgamation MERGERS & ACQUISITIONS joining of organizations for mutual benefit the process of two or more organizations joining together for mutual benefit, either through a ***merger*** or ***consolidation***

amanah FINANCE trust arrangement between parties in Islamic financing, an arrangement in which one person holds funds or property in trust for another

ambit claim *ANZ* FINANCE excessive arbitration claim anticipating compromise a claim made to an arbitration authority for higher pay or improved conditions that is deliberately exaggerated because the claimants know that they will subsequently have to compromise

American Accounting Association ACCOUNTING organization promoting accounting research a voluntary organization for those with an interest in accounting research and best practice. Its mission is "to foster worldwide excellence in the creation, dissemination, and application of accounting knowledge and skills." The association was founded in 1916. *Abbr* ***AAA***

        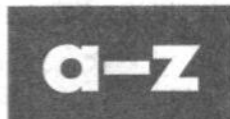

American Bankers Association BANKING US association representing banks an association that represents banks in the United States and promotes good practice. *Abbr* ***ABA***

American depository receipt STOCKHOLDING & INVESTMENTS document indicating ownership of foreign stock a document that indicates a US investor's ownership of stock in a foreign corporation. *Abbr* ***ADR***

American depository share STOCKHOLDING & INVESTMENTS foreign stock owned by US investor a share of stock in a foreign corporation, whose ownership by a US investor is represented by an ***American depository receipt***. *Abbr* ***ADS***

American Institute of Banking BANKING US association training bankers the part of the American Bankers Association that organizes training for people who work in the banking industry. *Abbr* ***AIB***

American Institute of Certified Public Accountants ACCOUNTING US association for certified public accountants in the United States, the national association for certified public accountants, founded in New York in 1887. *Abbr* ***AICPA***

American option *or* American style option STOCKHOLDING & INVESTMENTS option contract running to expiration date an option contract that can be exercised at any time up to and including the expiration date. Most exchange-traded options are of this style. *See also* ***European option***

American Stock Exchange *or* AMEX MARKETS = ***NYSE Amex Equities***

AMF *abbr* MARKETS ***Autorité des Marchés Financiers***

amortization FINANCE **1.** method of recovering costs of assets a method of recovering (deducting or writing off) the capital costs of intangible assets over a fixed period of time.

For tax purposes, the distinction is not always made between amortization and depreciation, yet amortization remains a viable financial accounting concept in its own right.

It is computed using the straight-line method of depreciation: divide the initial cost of the intangible asset by the estimated useful life of that asset.

$$\frac{\text{Initial cost}}{\text{Useful life}} = \text{Amortization per year}$$

For example, if it costs $10,000 to acquire a patent and it has an estimated useful life of 10 years, the amortized amount per year is $1,000.

The amount of amortization accumulated since the asset was acquired appears on the organization's balance sheet as a deduction under the amortized asset.

While that formula is straightforward, amortization can also incorporate a variety of noncash charges to net earnings and/or asset values, such as depletion, write-offs, prepaid expenses, and deferred charges. Accordingly, there are many rules to regulate how these charges appear on financial statements. The rules are different in each country, and are occasionally changed, so it is necessary to stay abreast of them and rely on expert advice.

For financial reporting purposes, an intangible asset is amortized over a period of years. The amortizable life, or "useful life," of an intangible asset is the period over which it gives economic benefit.

Intangibles that can be amortized can include:

Copyrights, based on the amount paid either to purchase them or to develop them internally, plus the costs incurred in producing the work (wages or materials, for example). At present, a copyright is granted to a corporation for 75 years, and to an individual for the life of the author plus 50 years. However, the estimated useful life of a copyright is usually far less than its legal life, and it is generally amortized over a fairly short period.

Cost of a franchise, including any fees paid to the franchiser, as well legal costs or expenses incurred in the acquisition. A franchise granted for a limited period should be amortized over its life. If the franchise has an indefinite life, it should be amortized over a reasonable period not to exceed 40 years.

Covenants not to compete: an agreement by the seller of a business not to engage in a competing business in a certain area for a specific period of time. The cost of the not-to-compete covenant should be amortized over the period covered by the covenant unless its estimated economic life is expected to be less.

Easement costs that grant a right of way may be amortized if there is a limited and specified life.

Organization costs incurred when forming a corporation or a partnership, including legal fees, accounting services, incorporation fees, and other related services. Organization costs are usually amortized over 60 months.

Patents, both those developed internally and those purchased. If developed internally, a patent's "amortizable basis" includes legal fees incurred during the application process. A patent should be amortized over its legal life or its economic life, whichever is the shorter.

Trademarks, brands, and trade names, which should be written off over a period not to exceed 40 years.

Other types of property that may be amortized include certain intangible drilling costs, circulation costs, mine development costs, pollution control facilities, and reforestation expenditures.

Certain intangibles cannot be amortized, but may be depreciated using a straight-line approach if they have "determinable" useful life. Because the rules are different in each country and are subject to change, it is essential to rely on specialist advice. **2.** equal payment of principal and interest the payment of the principal and interest on a loan in equal amounts over a period of time

amortize FINANCE gradually repay debt or reduce value of assets to reduce the value of an ***asset*** gradually by systematically writing off its cost over a period of time, or to repay a ***debt*** in a series of regular installments or transfers

amortized mortgage *US* MORTGAGES mortgage with combined principal and interest payments a long-term loan, usually for the purchase of real estate, in which the borrower makes monthly payments, part of which cover the interest on the loan and part of which cover the repayment of the principal. In the early years, the greater proportion of the payment is used to cover the interest charged but, as the principal is gradually repaid, the interest portion diminishes and the repayment portion increases. *UK term* ***repayment mortgage***

amortized value FINANCE value of amortized financial instrument the value at a specific time of a financial instrument that is being amortized

amortizing swap STOCKHOLDING & INVESTMENTS interest rate swap with decreasing notional principal amount an ***interest rate swap*** in which the ***notional principal amount*** declines over the period of the contract

amount paid up MARKETS money paid for new stock an amount paid for a new issue of shares of stock, either the total payment or the first installment, if the shares are offered with installment payments

AMPS *abbr* STOCKHOLDING & INVESTMENTS ***auction market preferred stock***

Amsterdam Stock Exchange MARKETS, STOCKHOLDING & INVESTMENTS = ***Euronext Amsterdam***

AMT *abbr* TAX ***alternative minimum tax***

analysis STOCKHOLDING & INVESTMENTS evaluation of markets a systematic examination and evaluation of the financial markets and the performance of securities

analysis of variance STATISTICS isolation of one cause of statistical variation the process of separating the statistical variation caused by a particular factor from that caused by other factors

analysis of variance table STATISTICS table showing variation in statistical data a table that shows the total variation in the observations in a statistical data set

analyst STOCKHOLDING & INVESTMENTS somebody who evaluates investments a person whose job is to analyze the performance of securities and make recommendations about buying and selling

analytical review TREASURY MANAGEMENT examination of trends between financial periods the examination of ratios, trends, and changes in balances from one period to the next, to obtain a broad understanding of the financial position and results of operations and to identify any items requiring further investigation

Andersen effect ACCOUNTING overcautious checking of data the tendency to be more careful than usual in scrutinizing data, especially when carrying out financial ***audits***, in order to avoid errors being found later. The term comes from the name of the firm Arthur Andersen which was involved in a major accounting scandal.

angel investing FINANCE investing in unproven business venture willingness of an individual or network of individuals to invest in an unproven but well-researched startup business, taking an advisory role without making demands

angel investor *or* angel FINANCE investor in unproven business venture an individual or group of individuals willing to invest in an unproven but well-researched startup business. Angel investors are typically the first port of call for Internet startups looking for financial backing, because they are more inclined to provide early funding than ***venture capital*** firms are. After investing in a company, angel investors take an advisory role without making demands.

angel network *or* angel investment group FINANCE network of potential investors for entrepreneurs a network of backers, organized through a central office which keeps a database of suitable investors and puts them in touch with entrepreneurs who need financial backing

angular histogram STATISTICS circular chart showing data a histogram that represents data in a circular form. *Also called* ***pie chart***

ANN *abbr* E-COMMERCE ***artificial neural network***

  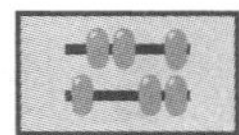   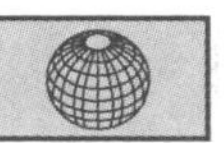   

announcement STOCKHOLDING & INVESTMENTS statement of company's trading prospects a statement that a company makes to provide information on its trading prospects, which will be of interest to its existing and potential investors

announcement date STOCKHOLDING & INVESTMENTS = ***declaration date***

annual accounts CORPORATE GOVERNANCE, ACCOUNTING document showing company's financial performance a profit and loss account and balance sheet, and, where a company has subsidiaries, the company's group accounts, included in the ***annual report and accounts*** for stockholders. *See also* ***annual report***

annual charge STOCKHOLDING & INVESTMENTS management fee covering administrative costs a management fee paid yearly to a stockbroker or collective fund manager by a client to cover a variety of administrative costs and ***commission***

annual depreciation ACCOUNTING reduction in book value of asset a reduction in the book value of a fixed asset at a specific rate per year, based on the estimated useful life of that asset. *See also* ***straight line depreciation***

annual depreciation provision ACCOUNTING allocation of cost of asset to specific year the allocation of the cost of an asset to a single year of the asset's expected lifetime

Annual Equivalent Rate FINANCE UK notional annual compound interest rate in the United Kingdom, a way of expressing different interest rates charged over different periods as an annual rate equivalent to a single payment of interest made on the anniversary of the loan and each subsequent year to repayment. *Abbr* ***AER***. See also ***compound annual return***

annual general meeting *UK* CORPORATE GOVERNANCE = ***annual meeting***

annual income FINANCE money received in one year the money received from earnings or investments during a calendar year

annualized percentage rate FINANCE monthly rate times twelve the percentage rate over a year, calculated by multiplying the monthly rate by twelve. It is not as accurate as the ***annual percentage rate***, which includes fees and other charges. *Abbr* ***APR***

annual management charge STOCKHOLDING & INVESTMENTS charge made for managing investment account a charge made by the financial institution that is managing an investment account

annual meeting *US* CORPORATE GOVERNANCE stockholders' yearly business meeting a yearly meeting at which a company's management reports the year's results and stockholders have the opportunity to vote on company business, for example, the appointment of directors and auditors. Other business, for example, voting on dividend payments and board/stockholder-sponsored resolutions, may also be transacted. *Also called* ***annual stockholders' meeting***. *UK term* ***AGM***

annual percentage rate FINANCE hypothetical rate based on simple interest the interest rate that would exist if it were calculated as simple rather than compound interest.

Different investments typically offer different compounding periods, usually quarterly or monthly. The APR allows them to be compared over a common period of time: one year. This enables an investor or borrower to compare like with like, providing an excellent basis for comparing mortgage or other loan rates.

APR is calculated by applying the formula:

$$\text{APR} = \left[\frac{(1+i)}{m}\right]^{m-1}$$

In the formula, i is the interest rate quoted, expressed as a decimal, and m is the number of compounding periods per year.

The APR is usually slightly higher than the quoted rate, and should be expressed as a decimal, that is, 6% becomes 0.06. When expressed as the cost of credit, other costs should be included in addition to interest, such as loan closing costs and financial fees. *Abbr* ***APR***

annual percentage yield FINANCE effective annual return on investment the effective or true annual rate of return on an investment, taking into account the effect of ***compounding***. For example, an annual percentage rate of 6% compounded monthly translates into an annual percentage yield of 6.17%. *Abbr* ***APY***

annual report *or* annual report and accounts CORPORATE GOVERNANCE, ACCOUNTING document reporting company's business performance a document prepared each year to give a true and fair view of a company's state of affairs.

Annual reports are issued to shareholders and filed at the ***Securities and Exchange Commission*** in accordance with the provisions of company legislation. Contents include a ***profit and loss account*** and ***balance sheet***, a ***cash flow statement***, ***auditor's report***, ***directors' report***, and, where a company has subsidiaries, the company's group accounts. The ***financial statements*** are the main purpose of the annual report, and usually include notes to the accounts. These amplify numerous points contained in the figures and are critical for anyone wishing to study the accounts in detail.

annual rest system MORTGAGES system crediting overpayments once a year a system in which extra payments or overpayments made to reduce the amount borrowed on a mortgage are credited to the account only once a year

annual return ACCOUNTING in UK, firm's report to Registrar of Companies in the United Kingdom, an official report that a registered company has to make each year to the Registrar of Companies

annual stockholders' meeting *US* CORPORATE GOVERNANCE = ***annual meeting***

annuitant PENSIONS recipient of annuity income a person who receives income from an ***annuity***

annuity PENSIONS contract for regular payments from one-off investment a contract under which a person pays a lump-sum premium to an insurance company and in return receives periodic payments, usually yearly, often beginning on retirement.

There are several types of annuities. They vary both in the ways they accumulate funds and in the ways they dispense earnings. A ***fixed annuity*** guarantees fixed payments to the individual receiving it for the term of the contract, usually until death; a ***variable annuity*** offers no guarantee but has potential for a greater return, usually based on the performance of a stock or ***mutual fund***; a ***deferred annuity*** delays payments until the individual chooses to receive them; and a ***hybrid annuity***, also called a combination annuity, combines features of both fixed and variable annuities.

annuity certain PENSIONS contract paying for set period an ***annuity*** that provides payments for a specific number of years, regardless of whether the annuitant remains alive

annuity contract INSURANCE contract providing lifelong regular payments an ***annuity*** that provides payments of a fixed sum regularly while the annuitant is alive

annuity in arrears INSURANCE annuity with delayed first payment an ***annuity*** whose first payment is due at least one payment period after the start date of the annuity's contract

anonymizer E-COMMERCE website that hides user's identity a website through which a person browsing can visit the World Wide Web without leaving any identity traces

ANSI X.12 standard E-COMMERCE accepted method of electronic business transactions an American National Standards Institute-supported protocol for the electronic interchange of business transactions. *Also called* ***X.12***

antedate *UK* GENERAL MANAGEMENT = ***predate***

anticipation note STOCKHOLDING & INVESTMENTS bond repaid with future receipts or borrowings a bond that a borrower intends to pay off with money from taxes due or money to be borrowed in a later and larger transaction

anticipatory hedging STOCKHOLDING & INVESTMENTS hedging before relevant transaction occurs hedging conducted before the transaction to which the ***hedge*** applies has taken place. *See also* ***hedge*** *(sense 2)*

anti-dumping INTERNATIONAL TRADE preventing cheap sale of products overseas intended to prevent the sale of goods on a foreign market at a price lower than is usually charged in the home market

anti-dumping duty TAX, INTERNATIONAL TRADE import tax offsetting subsidized price of import a tax imposed by a country on imported goods, when the price of the goods includes a subsidy from the government in the country of origin. *Also called* ***countervailing duty***

anti-inflationary ECONOMICS restricting inflation restricting or trying to restrict an increase in inflation

anti-trust laws LEGAL US laws preventing monopolies in the United States, laws that prevent the formation of monopolies. Antitrust laws also attempt to curb ***trusts*** and ***cartels*** and to keep them from employing monopolistic practices to make unfair profits. They are intended to encourage competitive behavior.

ANZCERTA *abbr* INTERNATIONAL TRADE ***Australia and New Zealand Closer Economic Relations Trade Agreement***

AO *abbr* MARKETS ***All Ordinaries Index***

AON MARKETS *see* ***all-or-none underwriting***

AP *abbr* ACCOUNTING ***accounts payable***

APACS *abbr* BANKING ***Association for Payment Clearing Services***

APB *abbr* ACCOUNTING ***Accounting Principles Board***

APEC *abbr* INTERNATIONAL TRADE ***Asia-Pacific Economic Cooperation***

application server E-COMMERCE host computer network allowing dynamic information exchange an advanced type of server used to run programming languages that help websites to deliver dynamic information such as the latest news headlines,

        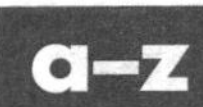

stock quotes, personalized information, or shopping carts

applied economics ECONOMICS use of economic theories for practical policies the practical application of theoretical economic principles, especially in formulating national and international economic policies

apportionment ACCOUNTING distribution of costs the sharing of costs between different internal parties, cost centers, etc.

appreciation **1.** ACCOUNTING value that asset accrues over time the value that some assets such as land and buildings accrue over time. Directors of companies are obliged to reflect this in their accounts. **2.** CURRENCY & EXCHANGE relative increase in currency value the increase in value of a currency with a ***floating exchange rate*** relative to another

appropriation ACCOUNTING sum set aside a sum of money that has been allocated for a specific purpose

appropriation account ACCOUNTING section of account showing treatment of profits the part of a ***profit and loss account*** that shows how a company's profit has been dealt with, for example, how much has been given to the stockholders as dividends and how much is being put into the reserves

approved accounts ACCOUNTING accounts agreed on by company directors accounts that have been formally accepted by a company's board of directors

Approved Deposit Fund PENSIONS fund accepting payments from superannuation fund in Australia and New Zealand, a concessionally taxed fund managed by a financial institution into which ***eligible termination payments*** can be transferred from a superannuation fund. *Abbr* ***ADF***

approved securities STOCKHOLDING & INVESTMENTS state bonds as bank reserves state bonds that can be held by banks to form part of their reserves

APR *abbr* FINANCE **1.** hypothetical rate based on simple interest ***annual percentage rate*** **2.** ***annualized percentage rate***

APRA *abbr* REGULATION & COMPLIANCE ***Australian Prudential Regulation Authority***

APS *abbr* BANKING, INSURANCE ***Asset Protection Scheme***

APV *abbr* ACCOUNTING ***adjusted present value***

APY *abbr* FINANCE ***annual percentage yield***

AR *abbr* FINANCE ***accounts receivable***

Arab Accounting Dinar CURRENCY & EXCHANGE accounting unit of Arab Monetary Fund a bookkeeping unit used between member states of the Arab Monetary Fund, equal to three IMF ***Special Drawing Rights***. *Abbr* ***AAD***

arbitrage MARKETS trade profiting from variations in market price the buying and selling of foreign currencies, products, or financial securities between two or more markets in order to make an immediate profit by exploiting the differences in market prices quoted

arbitrage fund MARKETS fund capitalizing on variations in market price a fund which tries to take advantage of price discrepancies for the same ***asset*** in different ***markets***

arbitrage pricing theory MARKETS model used for assessing return and risk a model of financial instrument and portfolio behavior that provides a benchmark of return and risk for capital budgeting and securities analysis. It can be used to create portfolios that track a market index, estimate the risk of an asset allocation strategy, or estimate the response of a portfolio to economic developments.

arbitrage syndicate MARKETS group raising capital for arbitrage deals a group of people formed to raise the capital to invest in arbitrage deals

arbitrageur MARKETS somebody buying stock for windfall profit a firm or individual who purchases stock or financial securities to make a windfall profit

arbitration GENERAL MANAGEMENT, HR & PERSONNEL process of resolving disagreement by unbiased person the settlement of a dispute by an independent third person, rather than by a court of law. Arbitration allows for claims or grievances to be settled quickly, cost-effectively, privately, and by somebody who is suitably qualified. A contract may include an arbitration clause to be invoked in the case of a dispute. *See also* ***mediation***

arbitrator GENERAL MANAGEMENT unbiased person who resolves other people's disagreements an impartial person accepted by both parties in a dispute to hear both sides and make a judgment

arbun FINANCE nonrefundable deposit allowing buyer right to cancel in Islamic financing, a nonrefundable down payment paid by a buyer to a seller upon the signing of a sale contract in which the buyer has the right to cancel the contract at any time

ArcaEx MARKETS = ***NYSE Arca***

Archipelago MARKETS = ***NYSE Arca***

area sampling STATISTICS randomly selecting subregions for inspection a form of sampling in which a region is subdivided and some of the divisions are then selected at random for a complete survey

arithmetic mean STATISTICS simple average a simple average calculated by dividing the sum of two or more items by the number of items

ARM *abbr* MORTGAGES ***adjustable rate mortgage***

armchair economics ECONOMICS casual economic opinion economic forecasting or theorizing based on insufficient data or knowledge of a subject (informal)

arm's-length price OPERATIONS & PRODUCTION price agreed by unrelated seller and buyer a price at which an unrelated seller and buyer agree to deal on an asset or a product

ARPS *abbr* STOCKHOLDING & INVESTMENTS ***adjustable rate preferred stock***

ARR *abbr* ACCOUNTING ***accounting rate of return***

arrangement fee BANKING bank charge for arranging credit a charge made by a bank to a client for arranging credit facilities

arrears FINANCE money owed but unpaid money that is owed, but that has not been paid at the time when it was due **in arrears** FINANCE still owing money that should have been paid, especially in a series of payments

articles of association *UK* CORPORATE GOVERNANCE = ***bylaws***

articles of incorporation CORPORATE GOVERNANCE legal document creating US corporation in the United States, a legal document that creates a corporation and sets forth its purpose and structure according to the laws of the state in which it is established. *Also called* ***charter***

articles of partnership CORPORATE GOVERNANCE = ***partnership agreement***

artificial intelligence GENERAL MANAGEMENT computer systems thinking like humans a branch of computer science concerned with the development of computer systems capable of performing functions that normally require human intelligence, for example, reasoning, problem solving, learning from experience, and speech recognition. Artificial intelligence research combines aspects of computer science and cognitive psychology. Artificial intelligence has applications in business and management, for example, in ***expert systems***.

artificial neural network GENERAL MANAGEMENT information processing system allowing computers to learn an information processing system with interconnected components analogous to neurons, based on mathematical models that mimic some features of biological nervous systems and the ability to learn through experience. *Abbr* ***ANN***

ASB *abbr* ACCOUNTING ***Accounting Standards Board***

ascending tops MARKETS market chart pattern showing series of ascending peaks a term used to refer to an upward trend in the market as shown on a chart, in which each peak in the chart is higher than the preceding one

ASEAN Free Trade Area INTERNATIONAL TRADE conceptual agreement fostering trade around Singapore a conceptual regional free trade agreement supported by Singapore to foster trade within the region covered by the Association of Southeast Asian Nations. *Abbr* ***AFTA***

A share STOCKHOLDING & INVESTMENTS share issued to raise additional capital in the United States, a share of stock in a company issued to raise additional capital without diluting control of the company. *Also called* ***nonvoting share***. *See also* ***B share***

Asian Currency Unit ACCOUNTING unit for recording transactions in Asian Dollar market a bookkeeping unit used for recording transactions made by approved financial institutions operating in the Asian Dollar market. *Abbr* ***ACU***

Asian Development Bank BANKING bank supporting development in Asia a bank set up by various Asian countries, with other outside members, to assist countries in the region with money and technical advice. *Abbr* ***ADB***

Asian dollar BANKING, CURRENCY & EXCHANGE US dollar deposited in Asian bank a dollar deposited in a bank in Asia or the Pacific region

Asian option STOCKHOLDING & INVESTMENTS, RISK = ***average option***

Asia-Pacific Economic Cooperation INTERNATIONAL TRADE forum promoting trade in Pacific region a forum designed to promote trade and economic cooperation among countries bordering the Pacific Ocean. It was established in 1989. Members include Australia, Indonesia, Thailand, the Philippines, Singapore, Brunei, and Japan. *Abbr* ***APEC***

ASIC *abbr* REGULATION & COMPLIANCE ***Australian Securities and Investments Commission***

ask **1.** *US* MARKETS security's selling price the price at which a security is offered for sale. *UK term* ***asked price*** **2.** STOCKHOLDING & INVESTMENTS value of mutual fund the net asset value of a mutual fund plus any sales charges

asked price *UK* MARKETS = ***ask*** *(sense 1)*

asking price OPERATIONS & PRODUCTION original price the price that a seller puts on something before any negotiation

ask price *US* MARKETS = ***ask*** *(sense 1)*

assay precious metal purity test a test used for determining the purity of a precious metal such as gold or silver

assembly OPERATIONS & PRODUCTION putting product parts together the process of joining components together to make a complete product

assembly line OPERATIONS & PRODUCTION system for putting parts together in specific order a line of production in which a number of assembly operations are performed in a set sequence. The speed of movement of an assembly line has to be matched with the skills and abilities of the workers and the complexity of the assembly process to be performed. The assembly line emerged from the ideas of ***scientific management*** and was popularized by a number of entrepreneurs, including Henry Ford in the car production industry.

assembly plant OPERATIONS & PRODUCTION factory for assembling products the factory building in which an ***assembly line*** is housed

assessed loss TAX in S. Africa tax-deductible expenses exceeding taxable income the excess of tax-deductible expenses over taxable income as confirmed by the South African Revenue Service. It may be carried forward and deducted in determining the taxpayer's taxable income in subsequent years of assessment.

assessed value FINANCE value calculated by professional adviser a value for something that is calculated officially by somebody such as an investment adviser

assessor FINANCE somebody who establishes something's worth a person who determines the value of something such as real estate for tax or insurance purposes

asset ACCOUNTING item to which value is assigned any tangible or intangible item to which a value can be assigned. Assets can be physical, such as machinery and consumer durables, or financial, such as cash and accounts receivable, or intangible, such as brand value and goodwill.

Assets are typically broken down into five different categories. ***Current assets*** include cash, cash equivalents, marketable securities, inventories, and prepaid expenses that are expected to be used within one year or a normal operating cycle. All cash items and inventories are reported at historical value. Securities are reported at market value. ***Noncurrent assets***, or long-term investments, are resources that are expected to be held for more than one year. They are reported at the lower of cost and current market value, which means that their values will vary. ***Fixed assets*** include property, plant and facilities, and equipment used to conduct business. These items are reported at their original value, even though current values might well be much higher. ***Intangible assets*** include legal claims, patents, franchise rights, and accounts receivable. These values can be more difficult to determine. ***Accounts receivable***, for example, reflect the amount a business expects to collect, such as, say, $9,000 of the $10,000 owed by customers. Deferred charges include prepaid costs and other expenditures that will produce future revenue or benefits.

asset allocation STOCKHOLDING & INVESTMENTS strategy maximizing return while minimizing risk an investment strategy that distributes investments in a portfolio so as to achieve the highest investment return while minimizing risk. Such a strategy usually apportions investments among cash equivalents, stock in domestic and foreign companies, fixed-income investments, and real estate.

asset-backed security STOCKHOLDING & INVESTMENTS security backed by loans a security based on the collateral of outstanding loans for which the investor receives the payments

asset backing STOCKHOLDING & INVESTMENTS assets supporting stock price support for a stock price provided by the value of the company's assets

asset base STOCKHOLDING & INVESTMENTS tangible assets of firm or person the ***tangible assets*** held by a company or individual investor at any point in time

asset-based lending FINANCE loans repaid with proceeds from acquired assets the lending of money with the expectation that the proceeds from an asset or assets will allow the borrower to repay the loan

asset class STOCKHOLDING & INVESTMENTS investment category a category into which an investment falls, for example, stocks, bonds, commodities, or real estate

asset conversion loan FINANCE loan repaid with proceeds from sale of asset a loan that the borrower will repay with money raised by selling an asset

asset cover *or* asset coverage FINANCE ratio showing company's solvency a ratio, derived from the net assets of a company divided by its debt, that indicates the company's solvency

asset demand ECONOMICS assets held in cash the amount of assets held as cash, which will be low when interest rates are high and high when interest rates are low

asset financing FINANCE borrowing that uses assets as collateral the borrowing of money by a company using its assets as collateral

asset for asset swap FINANCE exchange of bankrupts' debts an exchange of one bankrupt debtor's debt for that of another

asset management STOCKHOLDING & INVESTMENTS investment service combining banking and brokerage an investment service offered by some financial institutions that combines banking and brokerage services. *Abbr* ***AM***—**asset manager**

asset play STOCKHOLDING & INVESTMENTS stock purchase assuming unknown assets the purchase of a company's stock in the belief that it has assets that are not properly documented and therefore unknown to others

asset pricing model FINANCE pricing model determining asset's future profit a pricing model that is used to determine the profit that an asset is likely to yield

Asset Protection Scheme BANKING, INSURANCE UK insurance plan supporting banks in the United Kingdom, a government program established in 2009 that, for a fee, supports banks which have many bad loans and whose capital base is therefore compromised. It provides insurance against further losses, on the security of agreed assets, so that banks can continue to lend money. *Abbr* ***APS***

asset protection trust FINANCE trust protecting funds from creditors a trust, often established in a foreign country, used to make the trust's principal inaccessible to creditors

asset restructuring FINANCE purchase or sale of valuable assets the purchase or sale of assets worth more than 50% of a listed company's total or net assets

asset side ACCOUNTING side of balance sheet showing assets the side of a balance sheet that shows the economic resources a firm owns, for example, cash in hand or in bank deposits, products, or buildings and fixtures

assets requirements FINANCE assets needed to trade the tangible and intangible assets needed for a business to continue trading

asset stripping MERGERS & ACQUISITIONS practice of selling acquired firm's assets piecemeal the purchase of a company whose market value is below its asset value, usually so that the buyer can sell the assets for immediate gain. The buyer usually has little or no concern for the purchased company's employees or other ***stakeholders***, so the practice is generally frowned upon. —**asset stripper**

asset substitution FINANCE purchase of risky assets undisclosed to lender the purchase of assets that involve more risk than those a lender expected the borrower to buy

asset swap **1.** FINANCE exchange of assets allowing easy diversification an exchange of assets between companies so that they may dispose of parts no longer required and enter another product area **2.** STOCKHOLDING & INVESTMENTS exchange of fixed for varying payment in capital markets, the exchange of a fixed coupon payment associated with a bond for a floating rate payment, usually based on LIBOR

asset turnover ACCOUNTING measure of firm's business efficiency the ratio of a company's sales revenue to its total assets, used as a measure of the firm's business efficiency

asset valuation ACCOUNTING total value of firm's assets the aggregated value of the assets of a firm, usually the capital assets, as entered on its balance sheet

asset value MERGERS & ACQUISITIONS firm's value as combined value of assets the value of a company calculated by adding together all its assets

assign FINANCE transfer ownership of asset to transfer ownership of an ***asset*** to another person or organization

assignable cause of variation OPERATIONS & PRODUCTION apparent reason that something is different an evident reason for deviation from the norm. An assignable cause exists when variation within a process can be attributed to a particular cause that is a fundamental part of the process. Once identified, the assignable cause of the errors must be investigated and the process adjusted before other possible causes of variation are examined.

assignation *UK* LEGAL = ***assignment***

assigned risk INSURANCE poor risk that company must insure for a poor insurance risk that a company is required by law to insure itself against

  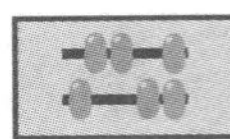      

assignee LEGAL somebody receiving property or rights a person to whom property or the rights to something have been transferred

assignment *US* LEGAL transfer of property or rights a legal transfer of property or the rights to something. *UK term* ***assignation***

assignor LEGAL person transferring property or rights a person who transfers property or the rights of something to somebody else

associate *ANZ* MARKETS stock exchange member without seat a member of a stock exchange who does not have a seat on it

associate company BUSINESS = ***affiliated enterprise***

associated company BUSINESS firm partly owned and controlled by another a company in which another company owns less than 50% and either has some management control over it or has a close trading relationship with it

associate director CORPORATE GOVERNANCE unelected director attending board meetings a director who attends board meetings, but has not been elected by the stockholders

associate program E-COMMERCE, MARKETING = ***affiliate program***

Association for Financial Professionals FINANCE US organization for professionals in finance industry in the United States, an organization for corporate financial managers that provides training and certification to members and represents their interests to government. *Abbr* ***AFP***

Association for Payment Clearing Services BANKING UK organization for payments industry the professional organization for providers of payment services to customers in the United Kingdom. *Abbr* ***APACS***

Association of Accounting Technicians ACCOUNTING UK accounting organization a professional organization founded in the United Kingdom in 1980 and offering qualifications in subjects related to accounting. It now has members and students worldwide. *Abbr* ***AAT***

Association of British Insurers INSURANCE association representing UK insurance companies an association that represents over 400 UK insurance companies to the government, the regulators, and other agencies, as well as providing a wide range of services to its members. *Abbr* ***ABI***

Association of Chartered Accountants in the United States ACCOUNTING association representing US chartered accountants a nonprofit professional and educational organization that represents over 5,000 chartered accountants based in the United States. The Association was founded in 1985. *Abbr* ***ACAUS***

Association of Chartered Certified Accountants ACCOUNTING international organization representing accountants an international accounting organization with over 300,000 members in more than 160 countries. It was formed in 1904 as the London Association of Accountants. *Abbr* ***ACCA***

Association of Futures Brokers and Dealers MARKETS former UK organization overseeing futures and options trading a now-defunct self-regulating organization that oversaw the activities of dealers in the UK futures and options markets. It merged with the Securities Association to become the Securities and Futures Authority, and its activities have now been taken over by the ***Financial Services Authority***. *Abbr* ***AFBD***

Association of Independent Financial Advisers FINANCE UK trade association for financial advisers a UK trade association that represents the interests of independent financial advisers to the UK government and in the European Union. *Abbr* ***AIFA***

Association of International Accountants ACCOUNTING organization for accountants a professional accounting organization founded in the United Kingdom in 1928 and offering qualifications in international accounting. *Abbr* ***AIA***

Association of Investment Companies STOCKHOLDING & INVESTMENTS UK organization for investment industry the professional organization for UK investment trust companies. It was founded in 1932 and until 2006 was called the Association of Investment Trust Companies. *Abbr* ***AIC***

Association of Unit Trusts and Investment Funds STOCKHOLDING & INVESTMENTS *see* ***Investment Management Association***

assumable mortgage MORTGAGES mortgage that buyer can take over from seller a mortgage that the buyer of a property can take over from the seller

assumed bond STOCKHOLDING & INVESTMENTS bond for which new firm takes responsibility a bond for which a company other than the issuer takes over responsibility

assumption STATISTICS condition for statistical method to work accurately the conditions under which valid results can be obtained from a statistical technique

assurance *UK* INSURANCE *see* ***life insurance***

assure *UK* INSURANCE = ***insure*** *(sense 2)*

assured shorthold tenancy *UK* REAL ESTATE tenancy for fixed short period a tenancy for a fixed period of at least six months during which the tenant cannot be evicted other than by court order. Any new tenancy without a written agreement is an assured shorthold tenancy.

assured tenancy *UK* REAL ESTATE tenancy for indefinite period a tenancy for an indefinite period in which the tenant cannot be evicted other than by court order

assurer *or* assuror *UK* INSURANCE = ***insurer***

AST *abbr* MARKETS ***automated screen trading***

ASX *abbr* MARKETS ***Australian Securities Exchange***

ASX 200 MARKETS = ***S&P/ASX 200***

asymmetrical distribution STATISTICS uneven distribution of data around central point a frequency or probability distribution of statistical data that is not symmetrical about a central value in the data

asymmetric information BUSINESS information that differs between parties to transaction a situation in which consumers, suppliers, and producers do not all have the same information on which to base their decisions

asymmetric risk RISK investment risk where gains and losses differ widely the risk an investor faces when the gain realized from the move of an ***underlying asset*** in one direction is significantly different from the loss incurred from its move in the opposite direction

asymmetric taxation TAX difference in tax status between parties to transaction a difference in tax status between parties to a transaction, typically making the transaction attractive to both parties because of taxes that one or both can avoid

asynchronous transmission E-COMMERCE method of sending intermittent data the transmission of data in which the end of the transmission of one unit denotes the start of the next, rather than transmission at fixed intervals

at best MARKETS instruction to buy or sell immediately an instruction to a stockbroker to buy or sell securities immediately at the best possible current price in the market, regardless of adverse price movements. It is also applicable to the commodity or currency markets. *See also* ***at limit***

at call FINANCE repayable on demand used to describe a short-term loan that is repayable immediately upon demand

at limit MARKETS instruction to buy or sell security within limits an instruction to a stockbroker to buy or sell a security within specific limits, usually not to sell below or to buy above a set price. A time limit is stipulated by the investor, and, if there has been no transaction within that period, the instruction lapses. It is also applicable to the commodity or currency markets. *See also* ***at best***

ATM BANKING electronic machine for withdrawing money an electronic machine at which bank customers can withdraw money or access an account using an encoded plastic card. *Full form* ***automated teller machine***. *UK terms* ***cash machine, cashpoint***

ATM card *US* BANKING plastic card used in ATM a plastic card used to withdraw money or access an account at an ATM. *UK term* ***cash card***

ATO *abbr* TAX ***Australian Taxation Office***

atomize GENERAL MANAGEMENT subdivide firm to split a large organization into smaller operating units

at par MARKETS, STOCKHOLDING & INVESTMENTS describing security sold at face value used to describe a security that sells at a price equal to its face value

ATS *abbr* BANKING ***automatic transfer service***

at sight FINANCE immediately as soon as presented. A negotiable instrument which is payable at sight is called a ***sight draft***. *See also* ***bill of exchange***

attachment LEGAL process enabling creditor to secure debtor's repayment a legal process that enables a creditor to secure dues from a debtor. A debtor's earnings and/or funds held at his or her bankers may be attached.

attachment order LEGAL court order preventing sale of debtor's property an order from a court to hold a debtor's property to prevent it from being sold until debts are paid

attention economy ECONOMICS theory that website viewing is tradable commodity a view of the economy in the late 20th century that suggests that people's attention to websites is a valuable and tradable commodity

attention management GENERAL MANAGEMENT making sure employees focus on work and goals a method of ensuring that employees are focused on their work and on organizational goals, as inattentiveness results in wasted time. An important factor in winning and sustaining attention is tapping into people's emotions.

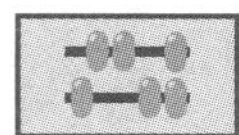

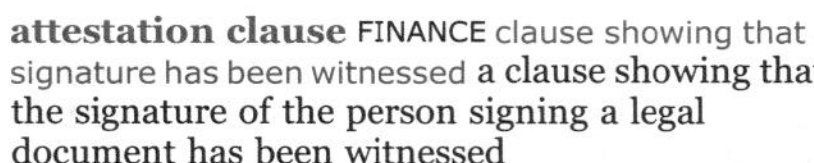

attestation clause FINANCE clause showing that signature has been witnessed a clause showing that the signature of the person signing a legal document has been witnessed

at-the-money STOCKHOLDING & INVESTMENTS describing option where trading price matches stock price used to describe an option with a ***strike price*** roughly equivalent to the price of the underlying stock

attitude GENERAL MANAGEMENT feeling or belief about situation a mental position consisting of a feeling, emotion, or opinion evolved in response to an external situation. An attitude can be momentary or can develop into a habitual position that has a long-term influence on somebody's behavior. Attempts can be made to modify attitudes that have a negative effect in the workplace, for example, through education and training.

attitude survey MARKETING questions about people's feelings toward firm or product a piece of research carried out to assess the feelings of a target audience toward a product, brand, or organization

attributable profit ACCOUNTING profit generated by specific business activity a profit that can be shown to come from a specific area of the company's operations

attribute sampling OPERATIONS & PRODUCTION method of quality testing through random samples a random testing method for determining the quality of a finished product by inspecting a sample number of the items in each batch. The items selected are examined for a selected attribute, which is usually an abnormal or negative characteristic—for example, a sample of cars from one production run might be inspected for poor paintwork, and the number of sampled cars found with this attribute used to calculate the number of defective items in the whole batch.

auction FINANCE sale of goods by competitive bidding a sale of goods or property by competitive bidding on the spot, by mail, by telecommunications, or over the Internet

auction market preferred stock STOCKHOLDING & INVESTMENTS UK stock with dividends tracking money-market index stock in a company owned in the United Kingdom that pays dividends which track a money-market index. *Abbr* ***AMPS***

AUD *abbr* CURRENCY & EXCHANGE Australian dollar The currency of Australia, introduced on February 14, 1966, replacing the Australian pound.

audience MARKETING everyone who reads, sees, or hears advertisement the total number of readers, viewers, or listeners who are exposed to an advertisement

audience research MARKETING research concerning target group of advertising research carried out to measure the size or composition of the target audience for a piece of advertising

audit ACCOUNTING systematic examination of firm's activities and records a systematic examination of the activities and status of an entity, based primarily on investigation and analysis of its systems, controls, and records

audit committee ACCOUNTING, GENERAL MANAGEMENT committee monitoring firm's finances a committee of a company's board of directors, from which the company's executives are excluded, that monitors the company's finances

audited accounts ACCOUNTING accounts passed by auditor a set of accounts that have been thoroughly scrutinized, checked, and approved by a team of auditors

auditing ACCOUNTING official examination of firm's accounts the work of officially examining the books and accounts of a company to see that they follow generally accepted accounting practices

audit of management GENERAL MANAGEMENT = ***operational audit***

auditor ACCOUNTING person auditing accounts a person who audits companies' accounts or procedures

Auditor-General FINANCE official responsible for legality of Australian government expenditure an officer of an Australian state or territory government who is responsible for ensuring that government expenditure is made in accordance with legislation

auditors' fees ACCOUNTING approved payment to firm's auditors fees paid to a company's auditors, which are approved by the stockholders at an annual meeting

auditors' qualification ACCOUNTING auditors' statement that firm's financial position is misrepresented a form of words in a report from the auditors of a company's accounts, stating that in their opinion the accounts are not a true reflection of the company's financial position. *Also called* ***qualification of accounts***

auditor's report ACCOUNTING auditor's confirmation of firm's financial records a certification by an auditor that a firm's financial records give a true and fair view of its profit and loss for the period

audit report ACCOUNTING official summary of audit the summary submission made by auditors of the findings of an ***audit***. An audit report is usually of the financial records and accounts of a company. An auditor's report normally takes one of the forms approved by the accountancy professional organizations to cover all requirements imposed by law on the auditor. If reports do not support the company's records, they may be termed "qualified." A report is qualified if it contains any indication that the auditor has failed to satisfy himself or herself on any of the points that the law requires. The qualification may, for example, add a rider stating that the appointed auditor has had to rely on secondary information supplied by other auditors under circumstances in which it has been inappropriate to do otherwise. Qualifications may also refer to the inadequacy of information or explanations supplied, or to the fact that the auditor is not satisfied that proper books or other records are being kept.

audit risk ACCOUNTING, RISK danger of auditors' mistaken view the risk that auditors may give an inappropriate audit opinion on financial statements

audit trail ACCOUNTING record of steps in transaction the records of all the sequential stages of a transaction. An audit trail may trace the process of a purchase, a sale, a customer complaint, or the supply of goods. Tracing what happened at each stage through the records can be a useful method of problem solving. In financial markets, audit trails may be used to ensure fairness and accuracy on the part of the dealers.

augend FINANCE number added to complete sum the number added to an ***addend*** in order to complete an addition

Aussie Mac MORTGAGES Australian security backed by mortgages a mortgage-backed certificate issued in Australia by the National Mortgage Market Corporation. The corporation has been issuing such certificates since 1985.

austerity budget TREASURY MANAGEMENT budget to discourage consumer spending a budget imposed on a country by its government with the goal of reducing the national deficit by way of cutting consumer spending

Austrade FINANCE Australian government organization promoting trade Australian Trade Commission, a federal government body responsible for promoting Australian products abroad and attracting business to Australia. It currently has 108 offices in 63 countries.

Australia and New Zealand Closer Economic Relations Trade Agreement INTERNATIONAL TRADE intergovernmental agreement to foster trade an accord between Australia and New Zealand designed to facilitate the exchange of goods between the two countries. It was signed on January 1, 1983. *Abbr* ***ANZCERTA***

Australian Accounting Standards Board ACCOUNTING agency overseeing accounting standards the body that is responsible for setting and monitoring accounting standards in Australia. It was established under Corporations Law in 1988, replacing the Accounting Standards Review Board. *Abbr* ***AASB***

Australian Bureau of Statistics STATISTICS Australian government agency collecting data on population an Australian federal government body responsible for compiling national statistics and conducting regular censuses. It was established in 1906. *Abbr* ***ABS***

Australian Business Number TAX tax code of Australian business a numeric code that identifies an Australian business for the purpose of dealing with the Australian Tax Office and other government departments. ABNs are part of the new tax system that came into operation in Australia in 1998. *Abbr* ***ABN***

Australian Chamber of Commerce and Industry BUSINESS national organization for businesses a national council of business organizations in Australia. It represents around 350,000 businesses and its members include state chambers of commerce as well as major national employer and industry associations. *Abbr* ***ACCI***

Australian Communications Authority REGULATION & COMPLIANCE government organization overseeing communications industries the government body responsible for regulating practices in the communications industries. It was established in 1997 as a result of the merger of the Australian Telecommunications Authority and the Spectrum Management Agency. *Abbr* ***ACA***

Australian Competition and Consumer Commission REGULATION & COMPLIANCE body monitoring Australian trade practices in Australia, an independent statutory body responsible for monitoring trade practices. It was established in November 1995 as a result of the merger of the Trade Practices Commission and the Prices Surveillance Authority. *Abbr* ***ACCC***

Australian Prudential Regulation Authority REGULATION & COMPLIANCE organization overseeing solvency of financial institutions a federal government body responsible for ensuring that financial institutions are able to meet their commitments. *Abbr* ***APRA***

  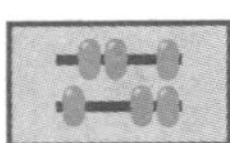   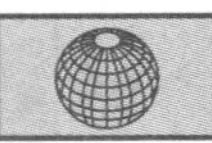   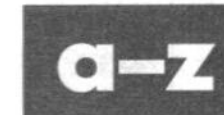

Australian Securities and Investments Commission REGULATION & COMPLIANCE organization overseeing financial dealings of businesses an Australian federal government body responsible for regulating Australian businesses and the provision of financial products and services to consumers. It was established in 1989, replacing the Australian Securities Commission. *Abbr **ASIC***

Australian Securities Exchange *or* Australian Stock Exchange MARKETS principal Australian stock exchange the principal market for trading stock and other securities in Australia. The Australian Stock Exchange was formed in 1987 as a result of the amalgamation of six state stock exchanges and has offices in most state capitals. It became the first exchange in the world to have a listing on its own market on October 14, 1998. It merged with the ***Sydney Futures Exchange*** on July 7, 2006, to become the Australian Securities Exchange. The main index of stocks on the exchange is the ***S&P/ASX 200***. *Abbr **ASX***

Australian Taxation Office TAX organization overseeing federal tax system a statutory body responsible for the administration of the Australian federal government's taxation system. It is based in Canberra and is also responsible for the country's superannuation system. *Abbr **ATO***

AUT *abbr* STOCKHOLDING & INVESTMENTS ***authorized unit trust***

authentication E-COMMERCE procedure for verifying authenticity of online sales messages a software security verification procedure to acknowledge or validate the source, uniqueness, and integrity of an e-commerce message to make sure data is not being tampered with. The verification is typically achieved through the use of an electronic signature in the form of a key or algorithm that is shared by the trading partners.

authority GENERAL MANAGEMENT right to be in charge the right to act or command. People willingly obey a person in authority, because they believe he or she has a legitimate entitlement to exercise power.

authority chart CORPORATE GOVERNANCE diagram of organization's hierarchical relationships a diagram showing the hierarchical lines of authority and reporting within an organization. ***Organization charts*** are similar.

authority to purchase FINANCE bill bearing authorization for bank to buy it a bill drawn up and presented with shipping documentation to the purchaser's bank, allowing the bank to purchase the bill

authorization FINANCE giving approval for financial transaction the process of assessing a financial transaction, confirming that it does not raise the account's debt above its limit, and allowing the transaction to proceed. This would be undertaken, for example, by a credit card issuer. A positive authorization results in an authorization code being generated and the relevant funds being set aside. The available credit limit is reduced by the amount authorized.

authorized capital FINANCE firm's money raised from selling shares the money made by a company from the sale of authorized shares of common and preferred stock. It is measured by multiplying the number of authorized shares by their par value.

Authorized Economic Operator INTERNATIONAL TRADE internationally recognized EU trader an internationally recognized certification that an EU trader's role in the international supply chain is secure and that customs controls and procedures are compliant. *Abbr **AEO***

authorized share STOCKHOLDING & INVESTMENTS share issued legitimately a share that a company issued with the authority to do so

authorized share capital *UK* STOCKHOLDING & INVESTMENTS stock firm has approval to issue the type, class, number, and amount of the stocks that a company may issue, as empowered by its memorandum of association. *See also **nominal share capital***

authorized signatory STOCKHOLDING & INVESTMENTS issuer of documents approving financial transactions the most senior issuer of authorization certificates in an organization, recognized by a signatory authority and designated in a signatory certificate

authorized stock *US* STOCKHOLDING & INVESTMENTS stock firm has approval to issue the number of shares of stock that a corporation is allowed to issue, as stated in its articles of incorporation. *See also **authorized share***

authorized unit trust STOCKHOLDING & INVESTMENTS UK mutual fund in the United Kingdom, a mutual fund that complies with the regulations of the Financial Services Authority. Different rules apply to different categories of mutual fund. *Abbr **AUT***

AUTIF STOCKHOLDING & INVESTMENTS *see **Investment Management Association***

autocorrelation STATISTICS = ***serial correlation***

automated clearing house BANKING, E-COMMERCE computerized network for interbank transactions ***ATM*** systems for interbank clearing and settlement of financial transactions. The network is also used for electronic fund transfers from a checking or savings account. *Abbr **ACH***

Automated Direct Debit Amendment and Cancellation Service BANKING UK computerized system for changing direct debits in the United Kingdom, a ***BACS*** service that allows paying banks to inform direct debit payees of a change of instruction, for example, an amendment to the customer's account details or a request to cancel the instructions. *Abbr **ADDACS***

automated handling OPERATIONS & PRODUCTION using computers to move goods in warehouses the use of computers to control the moving and positioning of materials in a warehouse or factory. Automated handling may involve the use of robots.

Automated Order Entry System MARKETS US system of direct access to exchange floor in the United States, a system that allows small orders to bypass the floor brokers and go straight to the specialists on the exchange floor

automated screen trading MARKETS computerized system for trading securities an electronic trading system for the sale and purchase of securities. Customers' orders are entered via a keyboard; a computer system matches and executes the deals; and prices and deals are shown on monitors, thus dispensing with the need for face-to-face contact on a trading floor. *Abbr **AST***

automated storage and retrieval systems OPERATIONS & PRODUCTION using computers to manage storage in warehouses the use of computerized vehicles to store, select, and move pallets around a large warehouse

automated teller machine BANKING *see **ATM***

automatic debit *US* BANKING bank customer's instruction for regular payments an instruction given by an account holder to a bank to make regular payments on given dates to the same payee. *Also called **banker's order**. UK term **standing order***

automatic execution MARKETS computerized matching of buy and sell orders a trade of a security that is executed electronically by a computerized trading system that matches buy and sell orders

automatic rollover MARKETS in UK, automatic repetition of fixed-term investment on the London Money Market, the automatic reinvestment of a maturing fixed term deposit for a further identical fixed term, an arrangement that can be canceled at any time

automatic transfer service BANKING automatic funds transfer protection an arrangement by which money from a depositor's savings account can be transferred automatically to his or her checking account to cover an overdraft or maintain a minimum balance. *Abbr **ATS***

Auto Pact INTERNATIONAL TRADE Canadian and US agreement about automobile imports an agreement between Canada and the United States, by which duties were reduced on imported cars for US automakers assembling vehicles in Canada. Subsequent provisions of the North American Free Trade Agreement reduced its effect. (informal)

autopoiesis E-COMMERCE process of replacing own parts a process whereby a system, organization, or organism produces and replaces its own components and distinguishes itself from its environment

Autorité des Marchés Financiers MARKETS French financial markets regulator the regulator of financial markets in France. Its responsibilities include regulation, authorization, supervision, and enforcement of corporate finance activities, funds, markets, and investment services. It was established by the merger of the ***Commission des Opérations de Bourse*** and the ***Conseil des Marchés Financiers*** on August 1, 2003. *Abbr **AMF***

availability float ACCOUNTING money representing checks written but not cashed money that is available to a company because checks that it has written have not yet been charged against its accounts

aval FINANCE guarantee of payment of bill or note in Europe, an endorsement by a third party guaranteeing the payment of a bill or promissory note

AVCs *abbr* PENSIONS ***additional voluntary contributions***

average 1. STATISTICS arithmetic mean the arithmetic mean of a sample of observations **2.** STOCKHOLDING & INVESTMENTS purchase stock regularly over period of changing prices to purchase additional shares of a stock whose price is rising or falling at intervals during the period of changing prices, in order to affect the average price paid for the stock

average accounting return ACCOUNTING percentage return of asset based on recorded value the percentage return realized on an asset, as measured by its ***book value***, after taxes and depreciation

average adjuster INSURANCE insurer determining shared losses a person who calculates how much of an insurance is to be borne by each party

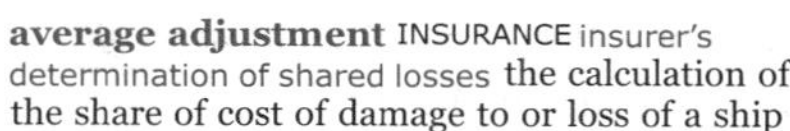

average adjustment INSURANCE insurer's determination of shared losses the calculation of the share of cost of damage to or loss of a ship

average collection period ACCOUNTING average time for cashing accounts receivable the mean time required for a firm to liquidate its accounts receivable, measured from the date each receivable is posted until the last payment is received.

Its formula is:

$$\frac{\text{Accounts receivable}}{\text{Average daily sales}} = \text{Average collection period}$$

For example, if accounts receivable are $280,000, and average daily sales are 7,000, then:

$$\frac{280,000}{7,000} = 40$$

average cost of capital FINANCE average cost of getting money the average of what a company is paying for the money it borrows or raises by selling stock

average deviation STATISTICS difference between actual and average values the spread of a sample of observations, measured by calculating their mean, specifying the distance between each observation and that mean, then calculating the mean of these distances

average down STOCKHOLDING & INVESTMENTS purchase stock regularly over period of falling prices to purchase additional shares of a security whose price is falling at intervals during the price drop period, in order to lower the average price paid for the stock

average due date FINANCE date around which several payments are due the average date when several different payments fall due

average nominal maturity FINANCE average time for mutual fund to provide return the average length of time until the ***financial instruments*** of a mutual fund mature

average option *or* average price option STOCKHOLDING & INVESTMENTS, RISK option determined by commodity's average price an option whose value depends on the average price of a commodity during a specific period of time. *Also called* ***Asian option***

average up STOCKHOLDING & INVESTMENTS purchase stock regularly over period of rising prices to purchase additional shares of a security whose price is rising at intervals during the price rise period, in order to raise the average price paid for the stock

Average Weekly Earnings STATISTICS in Australia, official measure of wages a measure of wage levels in the Australian workforce that is calculated regularly by the Australian Bureau of Statistics. The measure is considered one of Australia's key ***economic indicators***. *Abbr* ***AWE***

Average Weekly Ordinary Time Earnings STATISTICS in Australia, official measure of wages without overtime a measure of wage levels in the Australian workforce that excludes overtime payments, published by the Australian Bureau of Statistics

averaging STOCKHOLDING & INVESTMENTS stock trading at intervals to get average price the buying or selling of stocks at different times and at different prices to establish an average price

AWB *abbr UK* FINANCE ***air waybill*** = ***air bill***

AWE *abbr* STATISTICS ***Average Weekly Earnings***

"aw shucks" REGULATION & COMPLIANCE US strategy for denying responsibility for financial irregularities in the United States, a defense strategy adopted by senior executives involved in financial scandals before the ***Sarbanes-Oxley Act***, affecting corporate governance, came into effect in 2005. Under this strategy the accused maintained that they were simply not aware of the distortion of financial reporting that took place on their watch. The new law aimed to overhaul corporate financial reporting by improving its accuracy and reliability. Accountability standards have also been considerably tightened, and chief executives are to take full responsibility for the accuracy of all financial results by signing a statement to that effect. (informal) *See also* ***Sarbanes-Oxley Act***

ax STOCKHOLDING & INVESTMENTS expert in a particular investment a financial adviser who is the current expert on a particular security or market sector

B

B2B E-COMMERCE relating to Internet commerce between businesses used to describe an advertising or marketing program aimed at companies doing business with other companies as opposed to consumers. The term is most commonly used in reference to commerce or business that is conducted over the Internet between commercial enterprises. *Full form* ***business-to-business***

B2B advertising MARKETING advertising directed at firms advertising that is aimed at buyers for organizations rather than domestic consumers

B2B agency MARKETING advertising firm for businesses selling to other businesses an advertising agency that specializes in planning, creating, and buying advertising aimed at buyers for organizations rather than domestic consumers

B2B auction E-COMMERCE Internet site where suppliers compete for sales a Web marketplace that provides a mechanism for negotiating prices and bidding for services. Web-based B2B auctions reverse the traditional auction formula in which the goal is to help the seller get the best price. B2B Web auctions involve suppliers competing with one another by bidding down the price of their service. This inevitably benefits the buyer, as, instead of having to bid higher for a specific service or product, he or she can wait until the suppliers have bid themselves down to a reasonable price. Typically, online auctions require companies to follow a registration process in order to take part. During this process, users have to provide their credit card information and shipping preferences as well as agree to the site's code of conduct. Some sites also manage secure auctions, which restrict potential bidders to specific firms or individuals.

B2B commerce BUSINESS business involving firms only, not individual customers the business conducted between companies, rather than between a company and individual consumers

B2B exchange BUSINESS place for businesses to trade with each other the business-to-business marketplace that enables suppliers, buyers, and intermediaries to come together and offer products to each other according to a set of criteria

B2B marketing MARKETING = ***industrial marketing***

B2B web exchange E-COMMERCE marketplace adjusting prices the business-to-business marketplace that provides constant price adjustments in line with fluctuations of supply and demand

B2C E-COMMERCE connected with Internet commerce between businesses and consumers relating to an advertising or marketing program aimed at businesses doing business directly with consumers as opposed to other businesses. The term is most commonly used in reference to commerce or business that is conducted over the Internet between a commercial enterprise and a consumer. *Full form* ***business-to-consumer***

BAA *abbr* ACCOUNTING ***British Accounting Association***

baby bonds *US* STOCKHOLDING & INVESTMENTS bonds with low values bonds in small denominations, usually less than $1,000, which small investors can afford to buy (informal)

backdate GENERAL MANAGEMENT **1.** put earlier date on document to put an earlier date than the current date on a document such as a check or an invoice **2.** make something apply from earlier date to make something effective from an earlier date than the current date

backdoor selling FRAUD **1.** illegal wholesaler selling directly to consumers the practice by wholesalers of selling products directly to consumers in violation of contracts with retailers **2.** selling tactic bypassing competitive bid requirement the practice by salespeople of persuading buyers who are required to obtain competitive bids to purchase goods and services without them

back duty TAX tax unpaid because information was withheld tax relating to a past period that has not been paid because of the taxpayer's failure to disclose relevant information through negligence or fraud. If back duty is found to be payable, the relevant authorities may instigate an investigation and penalties or interest may be charged on the amount.

back-end loading STOCKHOLDING & INVESTMENTS sales fee paid by investor a management charge or commission that is levied when an investor sells some types of investments such as funds and annuities. *See also* ***front-end loading***

backer FINANCE provider of financial or moral support a person or company that gives somebody financial or moral support

back interest FINANCE interest not yet paid interest that is due but has not yet been paid

backlink checking E-COMMERCE way of discovering which websites are linked a means of finding out which web pages are linked to a specific website. Backlink checking enables e-business and website managers to keep track of their own and their competitors' online popularity.

backlog OPERATIONS & PRODUCTION list of orders not yet filled the buildup of unfulfilled orders for a product or process that is behind schedule.
A backlog can result from bad scheduling, production delays, an unanticipated demand for a product or process, or where the capacity of the process is not able to keep up with demand. Some large products, for example, aircraft and ships, have to be built to a backlog of orders, as it is not feasible to supply them on demand.

  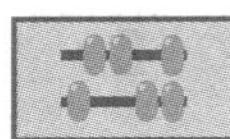      

backlog depreciation ACCOUNTING extra depreciation on revalued asset the additional depreciation required when an asset is revalued to make up for the fact that previous depreciation had been calculated on a now out-of-date valuation

back office GENERAL MANAGEMENT staff without direct dealings with customers the administrative staff of a company who do not have face-to-face contact with the company's customers. *See also* ***front office, middle office***

back pay FINANCE overdue pay from earlier time period pay that is owed to an employee for work carried out before the current payment period and is either overdue or results from a backdated pay increase

back payment FINANCE payment due but not yet paid a payment that is due to somebody but has not yet been paid

back tax TAX tax due but not yet paid tax that is owed to a government and that is overdue

back-to-back loan FINANCE, CURRENCY & EXCHANGE arrangement for two matching loans in different currencies an arrangement in which two companies in different countries borrow offsetting amounts in each other's currency and each repays their loan at a specific future date in its domestic currency. Such a loan, often between a company and its foreign subsidiary, eliminates the risk of loss from fluctuations in exchange rates.

backup MARKETS **1.** when yields rise and prices fall a period in which the yields from bonds rise and prices fall, moving inversely to each other **2.** when market trends reverse a sudden reversal in a stock market trend, so that a ***bear market*** becomes a ***bull market*** or vice versa

backup credit BANKING secondary source of credit a ***line of credit*** to be used as a standby should the primary credit source become unavailable. *Also called* ***standby credit*** *(sense 1)*

backup facility GENERAL MANAGEMENT substitute copy to be used if original fails a secondary system, record, or contract intended to take the place of another that fails

backup withholding TAX tax payable on miscellaneous income in the United States, a withholding tax that a payer sends to the Internal Revenue Service so that somebody who has received certain types of income such as dividends or interest, or who has not provided a correct taxpayer identification number, cannot avoid all taxes on that income

backwardation MARKETS **1.** penalty paid for late delivery of stock a penalty paid by the seller when postponing delivery of stock to the buyer **2.** when cash price exceeds forward price a situation in which the ***spot price*** is higher than the ***forward price***. *See also* ***forwardation***

backward compatible E-COMMERCE usable with previous software or computers describes a computer hardware or software product that is compatible with its predecessors to the extent that it can use interfaces and data from earlier versions

backward integration OPERATIONS & PRODUCTION forming alliance with supplier to protect supply the building of relationships with suppliers in order to secure the supply of raw materials. Backward integration can involve taking control of supply companies.

backward scheduling OPERATIONS & PRODUCTION determining scheduling plan based on due date a technique for scheduling production, planning work on the basis of when the completed work is due. By using backward scheduling, managers are able to assign work to particular workstations so that the overall task is completed exactly when it is due. The technique allows potential bottlenecks and idle time for particular workstations to be identified in advance.

BACS BANKING UK electronic clearing system for straightforward payments in the United Kingdom, an electronic bulk clearing system generally used by banks and building societies for low-value and/or repetitive items such as standing orders, direct debits, and automated credits such as salary payments. It was formerly known as the Bankers Automated Clearing Service.

bad bank BANKING government bank accepting other banks' risky loans a government-owned bank created to buy and hold risky assets from other banks, in order to re-activate lending and stimulate economic activity

BADC *abbr* REGULATION & COMPLIANCE ***Business Accounting Deliberation Council***

bad check *or* bad cheque BANKING check returned unpaid a check that is returned uncashed for any reason to the person who wrote it

bad debt FINANCE debt that has to be written off a debt that is or is considered to be uncollectable and is, therefore, written off either as a charge to the ***profit and loss account*** or against an existing doubtful debt provision

bad debt provision ACCOUNTING estimate of uncollectable debts an accounting estimate of the amount of debts thought likely to have to be written off

bad debt reserve FINANCE firm's money set aside for uncollectable debts an amount of money that a company sets aside to cover bad debts

bad debts recovered FINANCE money written off then recovered money formerly written off as uncollectable debt that has since been recovered either wholly or in part

badwill FINANCE negative goodwill a situation in which the value of the ***separable net assets*** of a company is greater than the total value of the business (slang)

BaFin *abbr* MARKETS, REGULATION & COMPLIANCE ***Bundesanstalt für Finanzdienstleistungsaufsicht***

bai al-bithaman ajil FINANCE installment sale of goods arranged by bank in Islamic financing, a sale of goods in which a bank purchases the goods on behalf of the buyer from the seller and sells them to the buyer at a profit, allowing the buyer to make installment payments. *Also called* ***bai muajjal***

bailment FINANCE delivery of something on loan the delivery of goods from the owner to another person on the condition that they will eventually be returned

bail out FINANCE give help to firm in financial difficulty to provide sufficient financial support to a company that is having financial difficulties to ensure its survival

bailout FINANCE financial backing for firm in crisis the provision of sufficient financial support to a company that is having financial difficulties to ensure its survival

bai muajjal FINANCE = ***bai al-bithaman ajil***

bait and switch MARKETING advertising one product but selling more expensive one a marketing practice whereby customers are encouraged to enter a store by an advertisement for one product and are then persuaded to buy another more expensive product (slang)

balance 1. BANKING money in bank account the state of a bank account at any one time, indicating whether money is owed (a debit) or owing (a credit balance) **2.** ACCOUNTING discrepancy between debit and credit figures in double-entry bookkeeping, the amount required to make the debit and credit figures in the books equal each other **3.** ACCOUNTING difference between money paid and received the difference between the totals of the debit and credit entries in an account

balance billing FINANCE charging person for own insurance shortfall the practice of requesting payment from a receiver of a service such as medical treatment for the part of the cost not covered by the person's insurance

balance brought down ACCOUNTING figure in account to balance income and expenditure an amount entered in an account at the end of a period to balance income and expenditure

balanced budget ACCOUNTING spending plan in which income equals expenses a budget in which planned expenditure on goods and services and debt interest can be met by current income

balanced design STATISTICS experimental design with equal observations for each combination an experimental design in which the same number of observations is used for each combination of the experimental factors

balanced fund STOCKHOLDING & INVESTMENTS mutual fund with diversified investments a mutual fund that invests in a variety of types of companies and financial instruments to reduce the risk of loss through poor performance of any one type

balanced investment strategy STOCKHOLDING & INVESTMENTS spreading types of investment the practice of investing in a variety of types of companies and financial instruments to reduce the risk of loss through poor performance of any one type

balanced line OPERATIONS & PRODUCTION production system with equalized workstation times an assembly line in which the cycle time for all the workstations is equal. A balanced line is achieved by allocating the right amount of work and the correct amount of operators and machinery to produce a given flow of product over a set period, taking into account the fact that each workstation will have a different capacity and that each process involved has a different cycle time.

balanced quantity OPERATIONS & PRODUCTION materials needed by workstation to produce agreed amount an inventory measure of the quantity of materials and parts required by a workstation to achieve a planned level of output

balanced scorecard approach GENERAL MANAGEMENT emphasis on providing management with strategic information an approach to the provision of information to management in order to assist strategic policy formulation and implementation to build the long-term value of the business. It emphasizes the need to provide the user with information that addresses all relevant areas of performance in an objective and unbiased fashion. The information provided may include financial and non-financial items and

  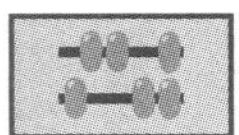   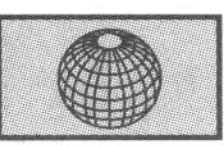   

cover areas such as profitability, customer satisfaction, internal efficiency, and innovation. The term originates from the best-selling business book, *The Balanced Scorecard*, written by Robert Kaplan and David Norton and published by Harvard Business School Press in 1996. Their approach applies the concept of ***shareholder value analysis***, and is based on the premise that the traditional measures used by managers to see how well their organizations are performing, such as business ratios, productivity, unit costs, growth, and profitability, are only a part of the picture. Traditional measures are seen as providing a narrowly focused snapshot of how an organization performed in the past, and give little indication of likely future performance. In contrast, the balanced scorecard offers a measurement and management system that links strategic objectives to comprehensive performance indicators.

balance off ACCOUNTING find balance by adding up totals to add up and enter the totals for both sides of an account at the end of an accounting period in order to determine the balance

balance of payments INTERNATIONAL TRADE country's trade transactions over time period a list of a country's credit and debit transactions with international financial institutions and foreign countries over a specific period. *Abbr* ***BOP***

balance of payments capital account INTERNATIONAL TRADE non-domestic items in country's balance of payments items in a country's balance of payments which refer to capital investments made in or by other countries

balance of payments current account INTERNATIONAL TRADE record of trade between countries a record of imports and exports of goods and services and the flow of money between countries arising from investments

balance of payments deficit INTERNATIONAL TRADE extent to which imports exceed exports the shortfall in income that arises when a country buys more from other countries than it sells as exports

balance of payments on capital account INTERNATIONAL TRADE record of country's non-domestic investment transactions a system of recording a country's investment transactions with the rest of the world during a given period, usually one year. Among the included transactions are the purchase of physical and financial assets, intergovernmental transfers, and the provision of economic aid to emerging nations.

balance of payments on current account INTERNATIONAL TRADE record of imports and exports a system of recording a country's imports and exports of goods and services during a given period, usually one year

balance of payments surplus INTERNATIONAL TRADE extent to which exports exceed imports the increase in income that arises when a country sells more to other countries than it buys as imports

balance of trade INTERNATIONAL TRADE gap between imports and exports the difference between a country's imports and exports of goods and services. *Abbr* ***BOT***

balance sheet ACCOUNTING statement of total assets, liabilities, and owners' equity a financial report stating the total assets, liabilities, and owners' equity of an organization at a given date, usually the last day of the accounting period. The credit side of the balance sheet states assets, while the debit side states liabilities and equity, and the two sides must be equal, or balance.

Assets include cash in hand and cash anticipated (receivables), inventories of supplies and materials, properties, facilities, equipment, and whatever else the company uses to conduct business. Assets also need to reflect depreciation in the value of equipment such as machinery that has a limited expected useful life.

Liabilities include pending payments to suppliers and creditors, outstanding current and long-term debts, taxes, interest payments, and other unpaid expenses that the company has incurred.

Subtracting the value of aggregate liabilities from the value of aggregate assets reveals the value of owners' equity. Ideally, it should be positive. Owners' equity consists of capital invested by owners over the years and profits (net income) or internally generated capital, which is referred to as "retained earnings"; these are funds to be used in future operations. *Abbr* ***B/S***

balance sheet audit ACCOUNTING partial audit to check compliance with rules a limited audit of the items on a company's balance sheet in order to confirm that it complies with the relevant standards and requirements. Such an audit involves checking the value, ownership, and existence of assets and liabilities and ensuring that they are correctly recorded.

balance sheet date ACCOUNTING annual date for balance sheet preparation the date, usually the end of a financial or accounting year, when a company's balance sheet is drawn up

balance sheet equation ACCOUNTING = ***accounting equation***

balance sheet total ACCOUNTING total at bottom of UK firm's balance sheet in the United Kingdom, the total of assets shown at the bottom of a balance sheet and used to classify a company according to size

balancing item *or* balancing figure ACCOUNTING number making one total equal another a number added to a series of numbers to make the total the same as another total. For example, if a debit total is higher than the credit total in the accounts, the balancing figure is the amount of extra credit required to make the two totals equal.

ball take the ball and run with it GENERAL MANAGEMENT to take an idea and implement it

balloon FINANCE **1.** = ***balloon loan*** **2.** = ***balloon payment***

balloon loan FINANCE loan with large final payment a loan repaid in regular installments with a single larger final payment including interest

balloon mortgage MORTGAGES mortgage with large final payment a mortgage for which the final payment including interest, called a ***balloon payment***, is larger than the others

balloon payment FINANCE large final payment on loan a large final payment including interest on a loan, after a number of periodic smaller payments have been made

ballpark *or* ballpark figure FINANCE rough total a rough, estimated figure. The term was derived from the approximate assessment of the number of spectators at a sporting event that might be made on the basis of a glance around. (slang)

BALO FINANCE French financial publication a French government publication that includes financial statements of public companies. *Full form* ***Bulletin des Annonces Légales Obligatoires***

BAN *abbr* STOCKHOLDING & INVESTMENTS ***bond anticipation note***

bang for the/your buck FINANCE financial benefit the leverage provided by an investment (slang)

bangtail MARKETING order form attached to envelope an order form for a new product that is attached by a perforated line to an envelope flap (slang)

bank BANKING institution holding and lending money a commercial institution that keeps money in accounts for individuals or organizations, makes loans, exchanges currencies, provides credit to businesses, and offers other financial services

bankable BANKING acceptable as security for loan acceptable by a bank as security for a loan

bankable paper BANKING document accepted by bank as security a document that a bank will accept as security for a loan

bank account BANKING facility for depositing and withdrawing money at bank an arrangement that a customer has with a bank, by which the customer can deposit and withdraw money

bank advance BANKING = ***bank loan***

bank balance BANKING money in bank account the state of a bank account at any one time, indicating whether money is owed (a debit) or owing (a credit balance)

bank base rate BANKING interest rate determining bank's rate to customers the basic rate of interest on which the actual rate a bank charges on loans to its customers is calculated

bank bill BANKING **1.** *US* = ***banknote*** **2.** = ***banker's bill***

bank book BANKING booklet recording deposits and withdrawals a small booklet formerly issued by banks and some other financial institutions to record deposits, withdrawals, interest paid, and the balance on savings and deposit accounts. In most cases, it has now been replaced by statements. *Also called* ***passbook***

bank card BANKING payment card issued by bank a plastic card issued by a bank and accepted by merchants in payment for transactions. The most common types are ***credit cards*** and ***debit cards***. Bank cards are governed by an internationally recognized set of rules for the authorization of their use and the clearing and settlement of transactions.

bank certificate BANKING confirmation of firm's bank balance a document, often requested during an audit, that is signed by a bank official and confirms the balances due to or from a company on a specific date

bank charge BANKING = ***service charge***

bank confirmation BANKING verification of firm's bank balances verification of a company's balances requested by an auditor from a bank

bank credit BANKING maximum credit the maximum credit available to somebody from a specific bank

bank deposits BANKING money deposited in banks all money placed in banks by private or corporate customers

bank discount basis BANKING income from US Treasury bills expressed over 360 days the expression of yield that is used for US Treasury bills, based on a 360-day year

bank draft BANKING = ***banker's draft***

bank-eligible issue BANKING US Treasury bonds available to commercial banks US Treasury obligations with a remaining maturity of ten years or less, eligible for purchase at any time by commercial banks

banker BANKING owner or senior executive of bank somebody who owns or is an executive of a bank or group of banks

banker's acceptance BANKING = ***banker's credit***

Bankers Automated Clearing Service BANKING *see* ***BACS***

banker's bill BANKING bank's order to another bank to pay money an order by one bank telling another bank, usually in another country, to pay money to somebody. *Also called* ***bank bill***

banker's check BANKING = ***banker's draft***

banker's credit BANKING financial instrument guaranteed by bank a financial instrument, typically issued by an exporter or importer for a short term, that a bank guarantees. *Also called* ***banker's acceptance***

banker's draft BANKING check drawn by bank on itself a ***bill of exchange*** payable on demand and drawn by one bank on another. Regarded as being equivalent to cash, the draft cannot be returned unpaid. *Also called* ***bank draft, banker's check***. *Abbr* ***B/D***

bankers' hours BANKING short working day short hours of work. The term refers to the relatively short time that a bank is open to customers in some countries. (informal)

banker's lien BANKING bank's right to hold client's property as security the right of a bank to hold some property of a customer as security against payment of a debt

banker's order BANKING = ***automatic debit***

banker's reference BANKING bank's report on customer's creditworthiness a report issued by a bank regarding a particular customer's creditworthiness

bank fee BANKING administrative charge for transaction a charge that is either paid in advance or is included in the gross capitalized cost, usually covering administrative costs such as the costs of obtaining a credit report, verifying insurance coverage, and checking documentation

Bank for International Settlements BANKING bank dealing with international finance a bank that promotes cooperation between central banks, provides facilities for international financial operations, and acts as agent or trustee in international financial settlements. The 17-member board of directors consists of the governors of the central banks of Belgium, Canada, France, Germany, Italy, Japan, the Netherlands, Sweden, Switzerland, the United Kingdom, and the United States. *Abbr* ***BIS***

bank giro BANKING = ***giro***

bank guarantee BANKING bank's undertaking to pay debt a commitment that a bank will pay a debt if the debtor defaults, for example, a bank may guarantee to pay an exporter for goods shipped if the buyer defaults

bank holding company BANKING firm owning bank or banks a company that owns one or more banks as part of its assets

bank holiday *UK* BANKING public holiday on weekday a weekday, especially a Monday, that is a public holiday when the banks are closed

bank identification number BANKING international number identifying individual bank n internationally agreed six-digit number that formerly identified a bank for credit card purposes. *Abbr* ***BIN***. See also ***issuer identification number***

banking account BANKING facility for depositing and withdrawing money at bank an arrangement that a customer has with a bank, by which the customer can deposit and withdraw money

Banking Code BANKING UK banks' voluntary code of practice a voluntary code of best practice for the banking and financial services industry, which is developed and revised by the ***British Bankers' Association***

banking house BANKING financial institution providing banking services a financial organization such as a bank or ***credit union*** that is in the business of providing banking services to the public

banking insurance fund INSURANCE US fund insuring banks' deposits in the United States, a fund maintained by the Federal Deposit Insurance Corporation to provide deposit insurance for banks other than savings banks and savings and loan associations

Banking Ombudsman BANKING Australian or New Zealand official handling banking complaints an official of the Australian or New Zealand government responsible for dealing with complaints relating to banking practices

banking passport BANKING passport for holding assets abroad a second passport in another name used to hold assets confidentially and for banking transactions in another country

banking products BANKING items provided by banks for customers goods and services that banks provide for their customers, for example, statements, direct debits, and automatic debits

banking syndicate BANKING investment banks jointly offering new security a group of investment banks that jointly underwrite and distribute a new security offering

banking system BANKING network of banks providing financial services a network of commercial, savings, and specialized banks that provide financial services, including accepting deposits and providing loans and credit, money transmission, and investment facilities

bank investment contract BANKING contract between bank and investors a contract that specifies what a bank will pay its investors

bank line FINANCE = ***line of credit***

bank loan BANKING loan made to bank's customer a loan made by a bank to a customer, usually against the security of a property or asset. *Also called* ***bank advance***

bankmail BANKING agreement by bank not to finance customer's rival an agreement by a bank not to finance any rival's attempt to take over the same company that a particular customer is trying to buy (slang)

bank mandate BANKING written order for opening bank account a written order to a bank that asks the bank to open an account, names the person(s) allowed to sign checks on behalf of the account holder, and provides specimen signatures, etc.

banknote BANKING **1.** item of paper money a piece of paper money printed by a bank and approved as legal tender. *Also called* ***bank bill*** **2.** note from Federal Reserve Bank usable as cash in the United States, a non-interest bearing note, issued by a Federal Reserve Bank, that can be used as cash

Bank of England BANKING UK central bank the ***central bank*** of the United Kingdom, established in 1694. Originally a private bank, it became public in 1946 and increased its independence from government in 1997, when it was granted sole responsibility for setting the base rate of interest.

bank rate BANKING **1.** central bank's discount rate the discount rate offered by a country's ***central bank*** **2.** formerly, Bank of England's lending rate formerly, the rate at which the ***Bank of England*** lent to other banks, now replaced by the ***base rate***. *Also called* ***minimum lending rate***

bank reconciliation BANKING comparison of bank statement with firm's ledger the process of comparing a bank statement with a company's ledger to verify that the balances are the same

bank reserve ratio BANKING = ***required reserve ratio***

bank reserves BANKING bank's ready money the money that a bank has available to meet the demands of its depositors

bankroll FINANCE **1.** finance for project the money used for financing a project or business **2.** give money to support something to provide the financing for a project or business

bankrupt LEGAL **1.** entity legally recognized as unable to pay debts a person or corporation that has been declared by a court of law as unable to meet their financial obligations **2.** unable to pay debts legally declared unable to meet financial obligations

bankruptcy LEGAL when unable to pay debts the condition of being unable to pay debts, with liabilities greater than assets. There are two types of bankruptcy: involuntary bankruptcy, where one or more creditors bring a petition against the debtor; and voluntary bankruptcy, where the debtor files a petition claiming inability to meet his or her debts.

bankruptcy-remote RISK not likely to risk bankruptcy used to describe a strategy or business structure designed to isolate a valuable asset or entity from financial risk

bank statement BANKING statement of transactions on customer's bank account a written statement from a bank showing the balance of an account and transactions over a period of time

bank term loan BANKING bank loan lasting at least one year a loan from a bank that has a term of at least one year

bank transfer BANKING transference of money to another account an act of moving money from one bank account to another

Banque Centrale de Compensation MARKETS French clearing house ***clearing house*** based in Paris, France, established in 1969 to clear commodities contracts. It added other clearing services and operations in other European countries, and was renamed Clearnet, before merging with the ***London Clearing House*** in 2003 to form ***LCH.Clearnet***. *Also called* ***Clearnet***

bar *UK* CURRENCY & EXCHANGE £1,000,000 one million pounds sterling, used by traders (slang)

  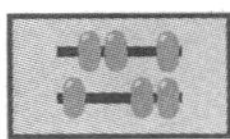      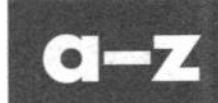

barbell STOCKHOLDING & INVESTMENTS portfolio with no medium-term bonds a portfolio that concentrates on very long-term and very short-term bonds only

bar chart GENERAL MANAGEMENT informational graph using colored bars the presentation of data in the form of a graph using blocks or bars of color or shading. A bar chart is especially useful for showing the impact of one factor against another, for example, income over time, or customer calls against sales.

barefoot pilgrim *US* STOCKHOLDING & INVESTMENTS inexperienced and unsuccessful investor an unsophisticated investor who has lost everything trading in securities (slang)

bargain MARKETS stock-market transaction a transaction on a stock market, especially the London Stock Exchange (slang)

bargaining chip FINANCE useful factor in negotiation something that can be used as a concession or inducement in negotiation

bargain tax date MARKETS date of stock-market transaction the date of a transaction on a stock market, especially the London Stock Exchange

barometer FINANCE indicator of trend an economic or financial indicator that forecasts a trend in the economy or in financial markets

barometer stock MARKETS popular security typical of market a widely held security such as a ***blue chip*** that is regarded as an indicator of the state of the market

barren money STOCKHOLDING & INVESTMENTS = ***idle capital***

barrier option STOCKHOLDING & INVESTMENTS option with trigger for trading in others an option that includes automatic trading in other options when a commodity reaches a specific price

barrier to entry MARKETS obstacle to free entry into market any impediment to the free entry of new competitors into a market

barrier to exit MARKETS obstacle to withdrawal from market any impediment to the exit of existing competitors from a market

barter FINANCE exchange of goods or services the direct exchange of goods or services between two parties without the use of money as a medium

BAS *abbr* TAX ***Business Activity Statement***

base currency CURRENCY & EXCHANGE way of expressing income from investment the currency used for measuring the return on an investment, usually the currency of the country in which the investment is made

base date MARKETS benchmark date for index calculations the reference date from which an index number such as the ***retail price index*** is calculated

base interest rate FINANCE US minimum expected interest rate in the United States, the minimum interest rate that investors will accept for investing in a non-Treasury security. *Also called* ***benchmark interest rate***

base pay *US* FINANCE basic salary before additional benefits a guaranteed sum of money given to an employee in payment for work, disregarding any fringe benefits, allowances, or extra rewards from an ***incentive plan***. *UK term* ***basic pay***

base period FINANCE period against which current financial period is measured a period of time against which financial or economic comparisons are made

base rate BANKING **1.** US Federal Reserve's interest rate the ***interest rate*** set by the US ***Federal Reserve*** that dictates the rate at which money is lent to other banks and which they in turn charge their customers **2.** Bank of England's interest rate the ***interest rate*** at which the ***Bank of England*** lends to other UK banks and which they in turn charge their customers

base rate tracker mortgage MORTGAGES mortgage with varying interest rate a mortgage whose interest rate varies periodically, usually annually, so as to remain a specific percentage above a standard rate

base-weighted index ECONOMICS price index comparing prices against standard time period a price index that is weighted according to prices from the base period

base year ECONOMICS benchmark year for index calculations the reference year from which an index is calculated

basic balance FINANCE relationship of current and long-term capital accounts the balance of current and long-term capital accounts in a country's balance of payments, which by implication must be financed with short-term ***capital flows*** such as short-term securities, money funds, and bank deposits

basic pay *UK* FINANCE = ***base pay***

basic rate TAX lower UK rate of income tax in the United Kingdom, the lower of the two bands of income tax, paid by the majority of people. ***Her Majesty's Revenue & Customs*** is responsible for the administration of income tax and publishes information on current tax rates and allowances on its website. *See also* ***higher rate***

basic wage FINANCE in Australia, minimum allowable pay for particular job in Australia, the minimum rate of pay set by an industrial court or tribunal for a specific occupation

basic wage rate FINANCE minimum pay in UK job in the United Kingdom, the wages paid for a specific number of hours' work per week, excluding overtime payments and any other incentives

basis FINANCE starting point for calculations a point, price, or number from which calculations are made. For example, the purchase price of a security would be used as the basis for calculating gains or losses.

basis of assessment TAX way of deciding time of tax assessment a method of deciding in which year financial transactions should be assessed for taxation

basis period TAX time when transactions are assessed for taxation the period during which financial transactions occur, used for the purpose of deciding when they should be assessed for taxation

basis point STOCKHOLDING & INVESTMENTS in bond interest rates, one hundredth of 1% one hundredth of 1%, used in relation to changes in bond interest rates. Thus a change from 7.5% to 7.4% is 10 basis points.

basis price STOCKHOLDING & INVESTMENTS **1.** price on which investment return is based the price used for calculating the gain on any investment when selling it, based on purchase price and any other costs **2.** price of bond given as yield to maturity the price of a bond shown as its annual percentage yield to maturity rather than being quoted in a currency **3.** over-the-counter securities price the price agreed between a buyer and seller on the over-the-counter market

basis risk MARKETS danger from price or interest-rate changes the risk that price variations in the cash or futures market will diminish revenue when a futures contract is liquidated, or the risk that changes in interest rates will affect the repricing of interest-bearing liabilities

basis swap MARKETS exchange of financial instruments with different interest rates the exchange of two financial instruments, each with a variable interest calculated at a different rate

basket case BUSINESS firm or person beyond recovery a company or individual considered to be in such dire circumstances as to be beyond help (slang)

basket of currencies CURRENCY & EXCHANGE group of currencies providing benchmark a group of currencies, each of which is weighted, calculated together as a single unit in establishing a standard of value for another unit of currency. *Also called* ***currency basket***

basket of prices FINANCE group of prices used as benchmark a group of prices used as a standard for measuring value over time

basket of securities STOCKHOLDING & INVESTMENTS set of securities traded together a group of securities that is treated as a single unit and traded together

basket of shares *US* STOCKHOLDING & INVESTMENTS set of shares of stock sold together a fixed number of shares of stock that is treated as a single unit and traded together. *UK term* ***parcel of shares***

batch E-COMMERCE credit card transactions submitted together a collection of credit card transactions including authorizations, payments, and credits saved for electronic submission to an ***acquirer*** for settlement. The merchant is encouraged to submit one large batch rather than several small ones by being charged a fee for each batch submitted.

batch production OPERATIONS & PRODUCTION producing goods in groups through individual stages a production system in which a process is broken down into distinct operations that are completed on a batch or group of products before moving to the next production stage. As batch sizes can vary from very small to extremely large quantities, batch production offers greater flexibility than other production systems.

bath take a bath FINANCE to experience a serious financial loss

Bayesian theory *or* Bayes's theorem STATISTICS statistical technique for predicting future based on past a statistical theory and method for drawing conclusions about the future occurrence of a given parameter of a statistical distribution by calculating from prior data on its frequency of occurrence. The theory is useful in the solution of theoretical and applied problems in science, industry, and government, for example, in econometrics and finance.

BBA *abbr* BANKING ***British Bankers' Association***

BC *abbr* TREASURY MANAGEMENT ***budgetary control***

BCA *abbr* BUSINESS ***Business Council of Australia***

  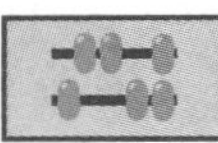      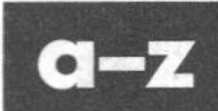

BCC *abbr* BUSINESS ***British Chambers of Commerce***

BCCS *abbr* CURRENCY & EXCHANGE ***Board of Currency Commissioners***

B/D *abbr* BANKING ***banker's draft***

bean counter ACCOUNTING accountant an accountant, used to refer in a derogatory way especially to an accountant who works in a large organization (slang)

bear STOCKHOLDING & INVESTMENTS exploiter of unfavorable business conditions somebody who anticipates unfavorable business conditions, especially somebody who practices ***short selling***, or selling stocks or commodities expecting their prices to fall, with the intention of buying them back cheaply later. *See also* ***bull***

bear CD STOCKHOLDING & INVESTMENTS CD paying more in falling market a ***certificate of deposit*** that pays a higher interest rate when an underlying market index falls in value

bear covering MARKETS buying back stock at lower prices the point in a market at which dealers who sold stock short now buy back at lower prices to cover their positions

bearer BANKING person holding check or certificate a person who holds a check or certificate that is redeemable for payment

bearer bond STOCKHOLDING & INVESTMENTS bond owned by physical possessor of it a negotiable bond or security whose ownership is not registered by the issuer, but is presumed to lie with whoever has physical possession of the bond

bearer check *US* BANKING blank check a check with no name written on it, so that the person who holds it can cash it. *Also called* ***check to bearer***. *UK term* ***cheque to bearer***

bearer instrument FINANCE financial document entitling its presenter to payment a financial instrument such as a check or bill of exchange that entitles the person who presents it to receive payment

bearer security STOCKHOLDING & INVESTMENTS security owned by physical possessor of it a stock or bond that is owned by the person who possesses it.

bearish MARKETS of markets with falling prices relating to unfavorable business conditions or selling activity in anticipation of falling prices. *See also* ***bullish***

bear market MARKETS market with falling prices a market in which prices are falling and in which a dealer is more likely to sell securities than to buy them. *See also* ***bull market***

bear market rally MARKETS fast improvement in falling market a fast rise in prices, which may be temporary, after a general downward trend in a financial market

bear raid STOCKHOLDING & INVESTMENTS = ***raid***

bear spread MARKETS transactions to make profit when price falls a combination of purchases and sales of options for the same commodity or stock with the intention of making a profit when the price falls. *See also* ***bull spread***

bear tack MARKETS downward market movement a downward movement in the value of a stock, a part of the market, or the market as a whole

bear trap MARKETS reversing trends in market a situation in which a market reverses its upward trend, leading ***short investors*** to believe the trend will then continue downward and encouraging them to get into the market, at which time the market reverses again, forcing short investors to cover their positions and lose money

beauty contest *US* GENERAL MANAGEMENT situation where competing firms try to attract business a situation in which several organizations in turn compete in order to persuade another organization to use their services. *UK term* ***beauty parade***

beauty parade *UK* GENERAL MANAGEMENT = ***beauty contest***

bed get into bed with somebody GENERAL MANAGEMENT to begin a business association with a person or organization

bed and breakfast deal STOCKHOLDING & INVESTMENTS selling and buying back security overnight a transaction in which somebody sells a security at the end of one trading day and repurchases it at the beginning of the next. This is usually done to formally establish the profit or loss accrued to this security for tax or reporting purposes.

bed and spouse STOCKHOLDING & INVESTMENTS method for couples to reduce capital gains tax in the United Kingdom, a method used by married taxpayers to reduce capital gains tax. A spouse who has a capital gain and has not used all their capital gains tax allowance may sell a security, and the other spouse may buy the same security back the next day, thereby allowing the spouse who sold to offset all or part of the gain with their tax allowance, while still holding onto the stock.

before-tax profit margin TAX income before tax minus expenditure the amount by which the net income of a company before tax exceeds its expenditure

beginning inventory *US* ACCOUNTING inventory carried over to next balance sheet the closing inventory at the end of the balance sheet from one accounting period that is transferred forward and becomes the opening inventory in the one that follows. *UK term* ***opening stock***

behavioral accounting *US* ACCOUNTING accounting emphasizing psychological and social aspects an approach to the study of accounting that emphasizes the psychological and social aspects of the profession in addition to the more technical areas

behavioral science *US* HR & PERSONNEL science studying how people act academic disciplines such as sociology and psychology that relate to the study of the way in which humans conduct themselves. In the field of management, the behavioral sciences are used to study the behavior of organizations.

bells and whistles (slang) **1.** FINANCE features appealing to investors or producers special features attached to a derivatives instrument or securities issue that are intended to attract investors or reduce issue costs **2.** MARKETING extra unnecessary features peripheral features of a product that are unnecessary but desirable

bellwether STOCKHOLDING & INVESTMENTS security with representative price a security whose price is viewed by investors as an indicator of future developments or trends

belly go belly up FINANCE to fail financially or go bankrupt

below par STOCKHOLDING & INVESTMENTS selling at less than face value describes a stock with a market price that is lower than its par value

below-the-line **1.** ACCOUNTING showing profit distribution or sources of bottom line used to describe entries in a company's ***profit and loss account*** that show how the profit is distributed, or where the funds to finance the loss originate. *See also* ***above-the-line*** *(sense 1)* **2.** ECONOMICS showing country's capital transactions in macroeconomics, used to describe a country's capital transactions, as opposed to its ***above-the-line*** or revenue transactions. *See also* ***above-the-line*** *(sense 2)* **3.** MARKETING connected with marketing costs for everything but advertising relating to the proportion of marketing expenditure allocated to activities that are not related to advertising, such as public relations, sales promotion, printing, presentations, sponsorship, and sales force support. *See also* ***above-the-line*** *(sense 3)*

belt and braces man FINANCE lender wanting extra safeguards a very cautious lender who asks for extra collateral as well as guarantees for a loan (slang)

BEL 20 MARKETS, STOCKHOLDING & INVESTMENTS main Belgian stock market index an index of the 20 most-highly capitalized companies on the ***Euronext Brussels*** exchange. It was established on December 30, 1990, with a base value of 1,000.

benchmark GENERAL MANAGEMENT standard used for measuring performance a point of reference or standard against which to measure performance. Originally used for a set of computer programs to measure the performance of a computer against similar models, benchmark is now used more generally to describe a measure identified in the context of a ***benchmarking*** program against which to evaluate an organization's performance in a specific area.

benchmark accounting policy ACCOUNTING one of two possible approved policies one of a choice of two possible policies within an International Accounting Standard. The other policy is marked as an "allowed alternative," although there is no indication of preference.

benchmark index MARKETS significant index an influential index for a particular market or activity

benchmarking GENERAL MANAGEMENT establishment of baselines and targets for assessing performance the establishment, through data gathering, of targets and comparators, through whose use relative levels of performance, and particularly areas of underperformance, can be identified. By the adoption of identified best practices it is hoped that performance will improve.

There are various types of benchmarking. ***Internal benchmarking*** is a method of comparing one operating unit or function with another within the same industry. Functional benchmarking compares internal functions with those of the best external practitioners of those functions, regardless of the industry they are in (also known as operational benchmarking or generic benchmarking). Competitive benchmarking gathers information about direct competitors, through techniques such as reverse engineering. Strategic benchmarking is a type of competitive benchmarking aimed at strategic action and organizational change.

benchmark interest rate FINANCE = ***base interest rate***

beneficial interest FINANCE benefiting from house as if its owner an arrangement whereby somebody is allowed to occupy or receive rent from a house without owning it

     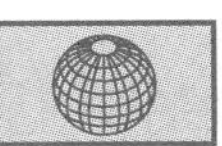   

beneficial occupier REAL ESTATE occupier not owning property a person who occupies a property but does not own it fully

beneficial owner STOCKHOLDING & INVESTMENTS receiver of benefits of another's stock a person who receives all the benefits of a stock such as dividends, rights, and proceeds of any sale but is not the registered owner of the stock

beneficiary FINANCE somebody who will receive assets or proceeds a person who is designated to receive assets or proceeds from, for example, an estate or insurance policy

beneficiary bank BANKING bank dealing with gift a bank that handles a gift such as a bequest

benefit **1.** FINANCE something extra offering improvement or reward something that improves the profitability or efficiency of an organization or reduces its risk **2.** HR & PERSONNEL nonmonetary reward for employee any nonmonetary reward such as a paid vacation or employer contribution to a pension that is given to employees

benefit–cost ratio ACCOUNTING = ***cost–benefit analysis***

benefit in kind *UK* HR & PERSONNEL = ***fringe benefits***

BEP *abbr* OPERATIONS & PRODUCTION ***break-even point***

bequest FINANCE item left in will a gift that has been left to somebody in a will

Berhad BUSINESS Malay equivalent of plc a Malay term for "private." Companies can use "Sendirian Berhad" or "Sdn Bhd" in their name instead of "plc." *Abbr* ***Bhd***

Berne Union FINANCE = ***International Union of Credit and Investment Insurers***

BERR *abbr* Department for Business, Enterprise and Regulatory Reform

Besloten venootschap BUSINESS limited company the Dutch term for a limited liability company. *Abbr* ***BV***

best-in-class GENERAL MANAGEMENT leading in best practice leading a market or industrial sector in efficiency. A best-in-class organization exhibits exemplary ***best practice***. Such an organization is clearly singled out from the pack and is recognized as a leader for its procedures for dealing with the acquisition and processing of materials and the delivery of end products or services to its customers. The concept of best in class is closely allied with ***total quality management***, and one tool that can help in achieving this status is ***benchmarking***.

best-of-breed MARKETING best available among computer products in marketing, sales, and competitive analysis, a computer product that is the best available software, hardware, or system in its class

best practice GENERAL MANAGEMENT most effective way of doing something the most effective and efficient method of achieving any objective or task. What constitutes best practice can be determined through a process of ***benchmarking***. An organization can move toward achieving best practice, either across the whole organization or in a specific area, through ***continuous improvement***. In production-based organizations, ***world class manufacturing*** is a related concept. More generally, a market or sector leader may be described as best-in-class.

best value GENERAL MANAGEMENT UK program encouraging local government efficiency a UK government initiative intended to ensure cost efficiency and effectiveness in the delivery of public services by local authorities. The best value initiative was announced in early 1997 to replace compulsory competitive tendering, and pilot schemes in selected local authorities began in April 1998. The Local Government Act 1999 requires councils, as part of the best value process, to review all services over a five-year period, setting standards and performance indicators for each service, comparing performance with that of other bodies, and undertaking consultation with local taxpayers and service users.

beta *or* beta coefficient STOCKHOLDING & INVESTMENTS number measuring changes in value a number representing an estimate of the fluctuations in value of a stock in relation to the market as a whole. A high beta indicates that a stock is likely to be more sensitive to market movements and therefore has a higher risk. *See also* ***alpha, beta rating***

beta rating STOCKHOLDING & INVESTMENTS means of measuring market risk a means of measuring the volatility (or risk) of a stock or fund in comparison with the market as a whole.

The beta of a stock or fund can be of any value, positive or negative, but usually is between +0.25 and +1.75. Stocks of many utilities have a beta of less than 1. Conversely, most high-tech NASDAQ-based stocks have a beta greater than 1; they offer a higher rate of return but are also risky. Both alpha and beta ratings should be readily available upon request from investment firms, because the figures appear in standard performance reports. *See also* ***alpha rating***

b/f *abbr* ACCOUNTING ***brought forward***

BFH *abbr* TAX ***Bundesfinanzhof***

Bhd *abbr* BUSINESS ***Berhad***

bias STATISTICS distortion of statistical results inaccuracy or deviation in inferences, results, or a statistical method

bid **1.** FINANCE highest realistic price the highest price a prospective buyer for a good or service is prepared to pay **2.** STOCKHOLDING & INVESTMENTS offer for most of firm's capital shares an offer to buy all or the majority of the capital shares of a company in an attempted takeover **3.** OPERATIONS & PRODUCTION statement outlining acceptable price for job a statement of what a person or company is willing to accept when selling a product or service. *Also called* ***quote***. *See also* ***tender***

bid-ask price MARKETS price charged for security in some markets, the price charged to buyers and sellers of a security, based on the ***bid-offer spread***. *See also* ***bid-offer price***

bid-ask quote MARKETS statement of amounts being offered and asked a statement of the prices that are being offered and asked for a security or option contract

bid bond FINANCE guarantee of finance for international tender offer a guarantee by a financial institution of the fulfillment of an international tender offer

bid costs MERGERS & ACQUISITIONS professional fees paid during takeover costs incurred during the takeover of a company as a result of professional advice to the purchasing company from, for example, lawyers, accountants, and bankers

bidder OPERATIONS & PRODUCTION person submitting quote a person or company that submits a quotation. *UK term* ***tenderer***

bidding war MARKETS when buyers compete for same stock or security a competition between prospective buyers for the same stock or security, during which it rises in price

bid form MARKETS form detailing offer to underwrite US municipal bonds in the United States, a form containing details of an offer to underwrite municipal bonds

bid market MARKETS market for price of stocks a market for bids (the price at which a dealer will buy stocks)

bid-offer price MARKETS price charged for security in some markets, the price charged to buyers and sellers of a security, based on the ***bid-offer spread***. *See also* ***bid-ask price***

bid-offer spread MARKETS gap between buyer's offer and seller's price the difference between the highest price that a buyer of a security is prepared to offer and the lowest price that a seller is prepared to accept

bid price MARKETS what stock exchange dealer will pay the price a stock exchange dealer will pay for a security or option contract

bid rate FINANCE, CURRENCY & EXCHANGE interest rate on Eurocurrency deposits a rate of interest paid on Eurocurrency deposits

bid-to-cover ratio MARKETS ratio of would-be and actual purchasers a number that shows how many more people wanted to buy Treasury bills than actually did buy them

bid up MARKETS **1.** make offer to raise price to bid for something merely to increase its price, not with the intention of acquiring it **2.** repeatedly increase bid price to make successive increases to the ***bid price*** for a security so that unopened orders do not remain unexecuted

Big Bang MARKETS 1980s restructuring of London Stock Exchange radical changes to practices on the ***London Stock Exchange*** implemented in October 1986. Fixed commission charges were abolished, leading to an alteration in the structure of the market, and the right of member firms to act as market makers as well as agents was also abolished. (slang)

big bath ACCOUNTING deliberately making bad income statement worse the practice of making a particular year's poor income statement look even worse by increasing expenses and selling assets. Subsequent years will then appear much better in comparison. (slang)

big beast *UK* powerful person or firm a person or a company that has a lot of financial or political power and is able to influence events (informal)

Big Board MARKETS (informal) = ***New York Stock Exchange***

big business BUSINESS large firms with a lot of power powerful business interests or companies in general. The term is particularly used when referring to ***large-sized businesses*** or ***multinational businesses***.

Big Four **1.** BANKING largest UK banks the United Kingdom's four largest commercial banks: Barclays, HSBC, Lloyds Banking Group, and NatWest (owned by Royal Bank of Scotland) **2.** ACCOUNTING largest accounting firms the four largest international auditors: PricewaterhouseCoopers, Deloitte Touche Tohmatsu, Ernst & Young, and KPMG **3.** BANKING largest Australian banks Australia's four largest banks: the Commonwealth Bank of Australia,

Westpac Banking Corporation, National Australia Bank, and the Australia and New Zealand Banking Group Limited

Big GAAP ACCOUNTING in US, accounting principles for large firms in the United States, the ***Generally Accepted Accounting Principles*** that apply to large companies. It is sometimes felt that they are unnecessarily complex for smaller companies. (slang)

big money lots of money a very large amount of money

big picture GENERAL MANAGEMENT overview of situation and context a broad perspective on an issue that encompasses its surrounding context and long-term implications (slang)

Big Three BUSINESS largest US automobile manufacturers before 1998 before the merger of Chrysler and Mercedes in 1998, the three largest automobile manufacturers in the United States: Chrysler, Ford, and General Motors

big-ticket FINANCE expensive used to describe something that costs a lot of money (slang)

big uglies BUSINESS established manufacturing and industrial firms traditional manufacturing and industrial companies, thought to be unglamorous but good long-term investments (informal)

Bilanzrichtliniengesetz ACCOUNTING German law covering accounting the 1985 German accounting directives law. *Abbr* ***BiRiLiG***

bilateral clearing BANKING central banks' settling of accounts between countries the system of annual settlements of accounts between some countries, where accounts are settled by the central banks

bilateral credit BANKING credit to banks during clearing of checks credit allowed by banks to other banks in a clearing system to cover the period while checks are being cleared

bilateral facility BANKING arrangement for lending to single borrower a facility for making loans from one bank to one borrower, especially a corporate borrower

bilateral monopoly ECONOMICS market with one seller and one buyer a market in which there is a single seller and a single buyer

bilateral netting BANKING significant settling of contracts between banks the settling of contracts between two banks to give a new position

bilateral trade INTERNATIONAL TRADE special trade arrangement between two countries trade between two countries which give each other specific privileges such as favorable import quotas that are denied to other trading partners

bill 1. FINANCE document promising payment a written paper promising to pay money **2.** *US* FINANCE piece of paper money a piece of paper currency printed by a bank and approved as legal tender. *UK term* ***note*** **3.** LEGAL draft of new law a draft of a new law that will be discussed in a legislature **4.** OPERATIONS & PRODUCTION list of charges payable to supplier a written list of charges to be paid by a customer to a supplier **5.** OPERATIONS & PRODUCTION give bill to customer for payment to present a bill to a customer so that it can be paid

bill broker FINANCE dealer in bills of exchange an agent who buys and sells ***promissory notes*** and ***bills of exchange***

bill discount BANKING Federal Reserve's interest rate to banks the interest rate that the Federal Reserve charges banks for short-term loans. This establishes a de facto floor for the interest rate that banks charge their customers, usually a little above the ***discount rate***.

bill discounting rate FINANCE reduction in cost of US Treasury bill the amount by which the price of a Treasury bill is reduced to reflect expected changes in interest rates

billing cycle FINANCE time between requests for payment the period of time, often one month, between successive requests for payment

billion FINANCE **1.** thousand millions a sum equal to one thousand millions **2.** *UK* million millions a sum equal to one million millions (dated)

billionaire FINANCE person with income over one billion a person whose net worth or income is more than one billion dollars, pounds, or other unit of currency

bill of entry INTERNATIONAL TRADE statement about imports or exports for customs a statement of the nature and value of goods to be imported or exported, prepared by the shipper and presented to a customhouse

bill of exchange FINANCE negotiable instrument a negotiable instrument, drawn by one party on another, for example, by a supplier of goods on a customer, who, by accepting (signing) the bill, acknowledges the debt, which may be payable immediately (a ***sight draft***) or at some future date (a ***time draft***). The holder of the bill can thereafter use an accepted time draft to pay a bill to a third party, or can discount it to raise cash.

bill of goods FINANCE **1.** in US, batch of goods in the United States, a consignment of merchandise for transportation and delivery **2.** in US, statement about batch of goods in the United States, a statement of the nature and value of a consignment of goods to be transported and delivered

bill of lading FINANCE document acknowledging shipment of goods a document prepared by a consignor by which a carrier acknowledges the receipt of goods and which serves as a document of title to the goods consigned

bill of sale FINANCE document confirming purchase a document confirming the transfer of goods or services from a seller to a buyer

bills payable FINANCE bills that firm must pay to creditors bills, especially bills of exchange, that a company will have to pay to its creditors. *Abbr* ***B/P***

bills receivable FINANCE bills that firm's debtors will pay bills, especially bills of exchange, that are due to be paid by a company's debtors. *Abbr* ***B/R***

BIN *abbr* FINANCE ***bank identification number***

binary thinker GENERAL MANAGEMENT somebody who thinks "it's all or nothing" a person who thinks only in absolute, black-and-white terms and is incapable of appreciating the subtleties and complexities of a situation (slang)

binder *US* INSURANCE temporary insurance certificate a document that an insurance company issues to a customer to serve as a temporary insurance certificate until the issue of the policy itself. *UK term* ***cover note***

biological assets ACCOUNTING live animals and growing plants farm animals and plants classified as assets. International Accounting Standards require that they are recorded on balance sheets at market value. Once they have been slaughtered or harvested, the assets become ***agricultural produce***.

bionomics ECONOMICS economics considered as ecosystem a theory suggesting that economics can usefully be thought of as similar to an evolving ecosystem

BiRiLiG *abbr* ACCOUNTING ***Bilanzrichtliniengesetz***

birth-death ratio STATISTICS birth count compared to death count the ratio of the number of births to the number of deaths in a population over a specific period of time

BIS *abbr* BANKING ***Bank for International Settlements***

bivariate data STATISTICS information involving two variables data in which two variables are involved in each subject

bivariate distribution STATISTICS distribution involving two variables a form of distribution in which two random variables are involved

black in the black FINANCE making a profit, or having more assets than debt

black chip *S. AFRICA* BUSINESS firm with black owners or stockholders a South African company that is owned or managed by black people, or is controlled by black stockholders (slang)

black economic empowerment ECONOMICS encouraging S. African black economic participation the promotion of black ownership and control of South Africa's economic assets

black economy ECONOMICS unofficial, untaxed economic activity economic activity that is not declared for tax purposes and is usually carried out in exchange for cash

black hole GENERAL MANAGEMENT project using resources without producing profit a project that consumes unlimited amounts of resources without yielding any profit (slang)

black knight MERGERS & ACQUISITIONS former friendly firm involved in takeover a former ***white knight*** that has disagreed with the board of the company to be acquired and has established its own hostile bid. *See also* ***knight***

black market MARKETS illegal market for scarce goods an illegal ***market***, usually for goods that are in short supply, but also for currency. Black market trading breaks government regulations or legislation and is particularly prevalent during times of shortage or rationing, or in industries such as pharmaceuticals or armaments that are highly regulated. *Also called* ***shadow market***

black market economy 1. ECONOMICS illegal trading a system of illegal trading in officially controlled goods **2.** CURRENCY & EXCHANGE illicit parallel currency market an illicit secondary currency market that has rates markedly different from those in the official market

Black Monday MARKETS 10.28.1929 or 10.19.1987 when financial markets dropped either of two Mondays, October 28, 1929, or October 19, 1987, that were marked by the largest stock market declines of the 20th century. Although both market crashes originated in the United States, they were immediately followed by similar market crashes around the world.

black money ECONOMICS untaxed money earned unofficially or illegally money circulating in the ***black economy*** in payment for goods and services

Black-Scholes model STOCKHOLDING & INVESTMENTS formula for determining option call price a complex mathematical formula for

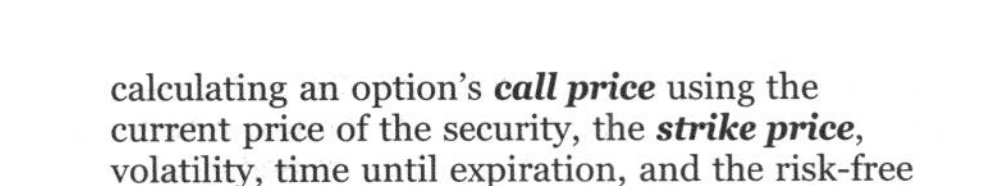

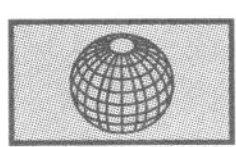

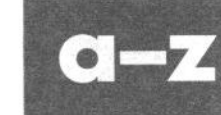

calculating an option's ***call price*** using the current price of the security, the ***strike price***, volatility, time until expiration, and the risk-free interest rate

Black Tuesday MARKETS 10.29.1929 when financial markets dropped Tuesday, October 29, 1929, a day on which values of stocks fell precipitously

Black Wednesday ECONOMICS 09.16.1992 when sterling crashed Wednesday, September 16, 1992, when the pound sterling left the European Exchange Rate Mechanism and was devalued against other currencies

blame culture GENERAL MANAGEMENT group's tendency to blame others for mistakes a set of attitudes, for example, within a business or organization, characterized by an unwillingness to take risks or accept responsibility for mistakes because of a fear of criticism or prosecution

blank check *or* blank cheque BANKING signed check with amount left blank a check with the amount of money and the name of the payee left blank, but signed by the drawer

blanket bond INSURANCE insurance against losses caused by employees an insurance policy that covers a financial institution for losses caused by the actions of its employees

blanket lien LEGAL right to somebody's property a legal right to all a person's property, including their personal effects

blended rate FINANCE intermediate interest rate an interest rate charged by a lender that is between an old rate and a new one

blind certificate E-COMMERCE computer file with user's name omitted a cookie from which the user's name is omitted so as to protect his or her privacy while making collected data available for marketing studies

blind entry 1. ACCOUNTING uninformative bookkeeping entry a bookkeeping entry that records a debit or credit but fails to show other essential information **2.** *ANZ* FINANCE statement of cost of goods and tax a document issued by a supplier that stipulates the amount charged for goods or services as well as the amount of ***Goods and Services Tax*** payable

blind pool BUSINESS limited partnership without details of purposes a limited partnership in which the investment opportunities the general partner plans to pursue are not specified

blindside MARKETING attack somebody without warning to attack somebody in a way that he or she cannot anticipate (slang)

blind trust STOCKHOLDING & INVESTMENTS trust without participation of beneficiary a trust that manages somebody's business interests, with contents that are unknown to the beneficiary. People assuming public office use such trusts to avoid conflicts of interest.

block STOCKHOLDING & INVESTMENTS 10,000 or more shares of stock a very large number of shares of stock, typically 10,000 or more

block diagram STATISTICS presentation of statistical data in blocks a diagram that represents ranges of statistical data by vertical rectangular blocks

blocked account BANKING frozen bank account a bank account from which funds cannot be withdrawn for any of a number of reasons, for example, bankruptcy proceedings, liquidation of a company, or government order when freezing foreign assets

blocked currency CURRENCY & EXCHANGE currency hard to exchange a currency that people cannot easily trade for other currencies because of foreign ***exchange controls***

blocked funds CURRENCY & EXCHANGE money frozen in one place money that cannot be transferred from one place to another, usually because of foreign ***exchange controls*** imposed by the government of the country in which the funds are held

block grant FINANCE **1.** in US, federal money for local government in the United States, money that the federal government gives to a local government to spend in ways that the recipient determines **2.** in UK, government money for local authorities in the United Kingdom, money that the government gives to local authorities to fund local services

blockholder STOCKHOLDING & INVESTMENTS investor with large stake in firm an individual or institutional investor who holds a large number of shares of stock or a large dollar amount of bonds in a given company

block investment *ANZ* STOCKHOLDING & INVESTMENTS taking or having large stake in firm the purchase or holding of a large number of shares of stock or a large dollar amount of bonds in a given company

block trade STOCKHOLDING & INVESTMENTS sale of many stocks or bonds the sale of a large round number of stocks or large amount of bonds

block trading MARKETS bulk trading in securities buying and selling in very large numbers of securities

blow-off top MARKETS rapid price rise then fall a rapid increase in the price of a financial stock followed by an equally rapid drop in price (slang)

blowout *US* MARKETS immediate sale of complete stock issue the rapid sale of the whole of a new stock issue (slang)

Blue Book FINANCE UK national statistics of incomes and expenditure national statistics of personal incomes and spending patterns in the United Kingdom, published annually

blue chip STOCKHOLDING & INVESTMENTS profitable and low risk used to describe an equity or company which is of the highest quality and in which an investment would be considered as low risk with regard to both dividend payments and capital values

blue-chip stocks STOCKHOLDING & INVESTMENTS common stock in safe firm common stock in a company that is considered to be well established, highly successful, and reliable, and is traded on a stock market

blue-collar job HR & PERSONNEL job involving manual labor a position that involves mainly physical labor. With the decline in manufacturing and an increase in ***harmonization*** agreements, the term blue collar is now rarely used. Blue collar refers to the blue overalls traditionally worn in factories in contrast to the white shirt and tie supposedly worn by an office worker, known as a ***white-collar worker***.

blue-collar worker HR & PERSONNEL manual laborer a person whose job involves mainly physical labor

Blue Dogs FINANCE fiscally conservative democrats in US Congress members of a coalition of fiscally conservative Democrats in the House of Representatives of the US Congress

Blue List MARKETS information about municipal bonds in the United States, a daily list of ***municipal bonds*** and their ratings, published by ***Standard & Poor's***

blue-sky ideas GENERAL MANAGEMENT unrealistically optimistic plans extremely ambitious, idealistic, or unrealistic proposals, apparently unconfined by conventional thinking

blue-sky laws FRAUD, REGULATION & COMPLIANCE US state laws protecting investors from fraudulent deals in the United States, state laws designed to protect investors against fraudulent traders in securities

blue-sky securities STOCKHOLDING & INVESTMENTS worthless stocks and bonds stocks and bonds that have no value, being worth the same as a piece of "blue sky" (slang)

blur GENERAL MANAGEMENT when big changes in firm happen quickly a period of transition for a business in which changes occur at great speed and on a large scale

BO *abbr* BANKING ***branch office***

board CORPORATE GOVERNANCE = ***board of directors***

board dismissal CORPORATE GOVERNANCE removal of firm's whole board the dismissal and removal from power of an entire board or ***board of directors***

board meeting CORPORATE GOVERNANCE directors' meeting a meeting of the board of directors of a company

Board of Currency Commissioners CURRENCY & EXCHANGE issuer of Singaporean currency the sole currency issuing authority in Singapore, established in 1967. *Abbr* ***BCCS***

Board of Customs and Excise INTERNATIONAL TRADE *see* ***Her Majesty's Revenue & Customs***

board of directors CORPORATE GOVERNANCE firm's highest management board the people selected to sit on an authoritative standing committee or governing body, taking responsibility for the management of an organization. Members of the board of directors are officially chosen by stockholders, but in practice they are usually selected on the basis of the current board's recommendations. The board usually includes major stockholders as well as directors of the company. *Also called* ***board***

Board of Inland Revenue TAX *see* ***Her Majesty's Revenue & Customs***

board of trustees STOCKHOLDING & INVESTMENTS group managing funds, assets, or property for others a committee or governing body that takes responsibility for managing—and holds in trust—funds, assets, or property belonging to others, for example, charitable or pension funds or assets

boardroom CORPORATE GOVERNANCE room for board meetings a room in which board meetings are held. A boardroom may be a room used only for board meetings or can be a multiuse room that becomes a boardroom for the duration of a board meeting.

boardroom battle CORPORATE GOVERNANCE struggle between board members a conflict or power struggle between individual board members or between groups of board members

board seat CORPORATE GOVERNANCE position on firm's board a position of membership of a board, especially a ***board of directors***

board secretary CORPORATE GOVERNANCE organization's senior administrative officer a senior employee in a public organization, with a role similar to that of a ***company secretary***

body corporate CORPORATE GOVERNANCE group acting as individual an entity such as a company or institution that is legally authorized to act as if it were one person

body of creditors BUSINESS creditors regarded as single unit the creditors of a company or individual treated as a single creditor in dealing with the debtor

body of shareholders STOCKHOLDING & INVESTMENTS shareholders regarded as single unit the shareholders of a company treated as a single shareholder in dealing with the company

bogey *US* MARKETS performance benchmark for fund managers a benchmark, often the Standard and Poor's 500 Index, against which mutual fund managers or portfolio managers measure their performance (slang)

boilerplate LEGAL reusable contract language standard language that can be used for the same purpose from contract to contract (slang)

boiler room MARKETING room for selling financial products by phone a room from which sales personnel using high-pressure sales tactics try to sell financial products or real estate of questionable value, usually by telephone and often using illegal tactics

boiler room fraud FRAUD illegal selling of worthless stock the illegal practice of calling people and pressing them to buy worthless stock in companies that do not exist or are virtually bankrupt

Bolivarism ECONOMICS socialist vision of Venezuelan president the new socialist and pan-South American vision of President Hugo Chávez of Venezuela, named for Simón Bolívar, the South American revolutionary leader who fought against Spanish colonial rule

bolsa MARKETS stock exchange a ***stock exchange*** in a Spanish-speaking country

Bolsa de Valores de Lisboa e Porto MARKETS, STOCKHOLDING & INVESTMENTS = ***Euronext Lisbon***

bona fide FINANCE undertaken in good faith used to describe a sale or purchase that has been conducted in good faith, without collusion or fraud

bona vacantia FINANCE goods of intestate person with no heirs the goods of somebody who has died intestate and has no traceable living relatives. In the United Kingdom, these goods become the property of the state.

bond **1.** FINANCE money given as deposit a sum of money paid as a deposit, especially on rented premises **2.** STOCKHOLDING & INVESTMENTS contract promising loan repayment with interest a certificate issued by a company or government that promises repayment of borrowed money at a set rate of interest on a particular date **3.** *S. AFRICA* MORTGAGES = ***mortgage bond***

bond anticipation note STOCKHOLDING & INVESTMENTS loan repaid through bonds issued later a loan that a government agency receives to provide capital that will be repaid from the proceeds of bonds that the agency will issue later. *Abbr* ***BAN***

bond covenant STOCKHOLDING & INVESTMENTS promise by lender to limit activities part of a bond contract whereby the lender promises not to do some things such as borrow beyond a specified limit

bond discount STOCKHOLDING & INVESTMENTS gap between price and higher face value the difference between the face value of a bond and the lower price at which it is issued

bonded warehouse INTERNATIONAL TRADE warehouse for dutiable or taxable goods a warehouse that holds goods awaiting duty or tax to be paid on them

bond equivalent yield STOCKHOLDING & INVESTMENTS compound interest conversion for bond comparison the interest rate on a Treasury bill, commercial paper, or discount note, usually quoted as simple interest, converted to compound interest in order to compare it with the interest on a bond. *Also called* ***equivalent bond yield***. *See also* ***compound annual return***

bond fund STOCKHOLDING & INVESTMENTS mutual fund with bonds a mutual fund with an investment ***portfolio*** made up of bonds

bondholder STOCKHOLDING & INVESTMENTS entity owning bonds an individual or institution owning bonds issued by a government or company. Bondholders are entitled to payments of the interest as due and the return of the ***principal*** when the bond matures.

bond indenture STOCKHOLDING & INVESTMENTS document describing bond a document that specifies the terms and conditions of a bond

bond indexing STOCKHOLDING & INVESTMENTS matching yield from bonds and specific index the practice of investing in bonds in such a way as to match the yield of a designated index

bond issue STOCKHOLDING & INVESTMENTS sale of bonds to investors an occasion when a company or government offers ***bonds*** to investors in order to raise funding

bond market MARKETS market for government or municipal bonds a financial market in which participants trade in government or municipal bonds

bond premium STOCKHOLDING & INVESTMENTS gap between price and lower face value the difference between the face value of a bond and a higher price at which it is issued

bond quote STOCKHOLDING & INVESTMENTS up-to-date statement of bond's price a statement of the current price of a bond when traded on the open market

bond rating STOCKHOLDING & INVESTMENTS assessment of bond-issuer's reliability the rating of the reliability of a company, government, or local authority that has issued a bond. The highest rating is AAA (triple A).

bond swap STOCKHOLDING & INVESTMENTS simultaneous sale and purchase of bonds an exchange of some bonds for others, usually to gain a tax advantage or to diversify a portfolio

bond value ACCOUNTING value stated in accounts the value of an ***asset*** or ***liability*** as recorded in the accounts of a person or organization

bond-washing STOCKHOLDING & INVESTMENTS avoidance of tax on dividend income the practice of selling a bond before its dividend is due and buying it back later in order to avoid paying tax on the dividend

bond yield STOCKHOLDING & INVESTMENTS yield of bond in relation to market price the annual return on a bond (the rate of interest) expressed as a percentage of the current market price of the bond. Bonds can tie up investors' money for periods of up to 30 years, so knowing their yield is a critical investment consideration.

bonus FINANCE extra money given as reward to employee a financial incentive given to employees in addition to their ***base pay*** in the form of a one-time payment or as part of a ***bonus plan***

bonus dividend STOCKHOLDING & INVESTMENTS irregular additional dividend a one-time extra dividend in addition to the usual payment

bonus issue STOCKHOLDING & INVESTMENTS proportionate issue of new shares to stockholders the capitalization of the reserves of a company by the issue of additional shares to existing stockholders, in proportion to their holdings. Such shares are usually fully paid up with no cash called for from the stockholders.

bonus offer MARKETING sales offer of extra product for same price a sales promotion technique offering consumers an additional amount of product for the basic price

bonus plan *US* FINANCE program for rewarding employees with extra money a form of ***incentive plan*** under which a ***bonus*** is paid to employees in accordance with rules concerning eligibility, performance targets, time period, and size and form of payments. A bonus plan may apply to some or all employees and may be determined on organization, business unit, or individual performance, or on a combination of these. A bonus payment may be expressed as a percentage of salary or as a flat-rate sum. *UK term* ***bonus scheme***

bonus scheme *UK* FINANCE = ***bonus plan***

bonus shares STOCKHOLDING & INVESTMENTS **1.** increased number of shares not affecting total value shares issued to stockholders in a ***stock split***, with at least one more share for every share owned, without affecting the total value of each holding. *See also* ***stock split*** **2.** UK government reward to loyal founding stockholders in the United Kingdom, extra shares paid by the government as a reward to founding stockholders who did not sell their initial holding within a specific number of years

book STOCKHOLDING & INVESTMENTS record of trader's investments and amounts owed a statement of all the holdings of a trader and the amount he or she is due to pay or has borrowed **cook the books** FRAUD to use accounting methods to hide aspects of a company's financial dealings such as losses or illegal activities **do the books** ACCOUNTING to keep records of expenditure and income

book-building STOCKHOLDING & INVESTMENTS gathering information to determine offering price the research done among potential institutional investors to determine the optimum offering price for a new issue of stock

book cost STOCKHOLDING & INVESTMENTS total cost of stocks the price paid for a stock, including any payments to intermediaries such as brokers

book entry ACCOUNTING account entry unsupported by documentation an accounting entry indicated in a record somewhere but not represented by any document

book-entry security STOCKHOLDING & INVESTMENTS security without paper certificate a

  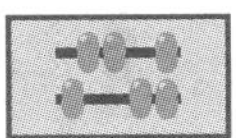   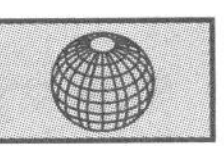   

security that is recorded as a ***book entry*** but is not represented by a paper certificate

book inventory ACCOUNTING stock level recorded in accounts the number of items in stock according to accounting records. This number can be validated only by a physical count of the items.

bookkeeper ACCOUNTING maintainer of business's financial records a person who is responsible for maintaining the financial records of a business

bookkeeping ACCOUNTING recording income and expenditure the activity or profession of recording the money received and spent by an individual, business, or organization

bookkeeping barter ACCOUNTING exchange of goods treated as money transaction the direct exchange of goods between two parties without the use of money as a medium, but using monetary measures to record the transaction

book of original entry *or* book of prime entry ACCOUNTING chronological and classified record of transactions a chronological record of a business's transactions arranged according to type, for example, cash or sales. The books are then used to generate entries in a double-entry bookkeeping system.

books ACCOUNTING record of sales and receipts the set of records that a business keeps, showing what has been spent and earned

book sales OPERATIONS & PRODUCTION recorded sales sales as recorded in a company's sales book

books of account *UK* ACCOUNTING = ***accounting records***

book-to-bill ratio ACCOUNTING relationship between orders received and bills issued the ratio of the value of orders that a company has received to the amount for which it has billed its customers

book transfer STOCKHOLDING & INVESTMENTS recorded change in security's ownership without transfer documents a transfer of ownership of a security without physical transfer of any document that represents the instrument

book value **1.** ACCOUNTING recorded value of asset the value of an asset as recorded in a company's balance sheet, usually the original cost with an allowance made for depreciation. Book value is not usually the same as ***market value*** (the amount it could be sold for). **2.** STOCKHOLDING & INVESTMENTS, ACCOUNTING firm's own valuation of its stock the value of a company's stock according to the company itself, which may differ considerably from the ***market value***. Book value is calculated by subtracting a company's liabilities and the value of its debt and ***preferred stock*** from its total assets. All of these figures appear on a company's balance sheet. For example:

$	
Total assets	1,300
Current liabilities	– 400
Long-term liabilities, preference shares	– 250
Book value	**= 650**

Book value represents a company's net worth to its stockholders. When compared with its market value, book value helps reveal how a company is regarded by the investment community. A market value that is notably higher than the book value indicates that investors have a high regard for the company. A market value that is, for example, a multiple of book value suggests that investors' regard may be unreasonably high. *Also called* ***carrying amount, carrying value***

book value per share STOCKHOLDING & INVESTMENTS, ACCOUNTING firm's own valuation of each share the value of one share of a stock according to the company itself, which may differ considerably from the market value. It is calculated by dividing the ***book value*** by the number of shares in issue.

boom FINANCE significant increase in business a period of time during which business activity increases significantly, with the result that demand for products grows, as do prices, salaries, and employment

boom and bust *or* boom or bust FINANCE extreme economic or market upswings and downswings a regular pattern of alternation in an economy or market between extreme growth and collapse and recession

BOP *abbr* INTERNATIONAL TRADE ***balance of payments***

border tax adjustment INTERNATIONAL TRADE taxing imported but not exported goods the application of a domestic tax on imported goods while exempting exported goods from the tax in an effort to make the exported goods' price competitive both nationally and internationally

borrow **1.** FINANCE arrange to use another's assets for a time to be given money by a person or financial institution for a fixed period of time, usually paying it back in installments and with interest **2.** STOCKHOLDING & INVESTMENTS buy at delivery price and sell forward simultaneously to buy a commodity or security at the present spot price and sell forward at the same time

borrower FINANCE somebody borrowing money from lender a person who receives money from a lender with the intention of paying it back, usually with interest

borrowing FINANCE receipt of money from lender the act of borrowing money from a lender

borrowing capacity *or* borrowing power FINANCE amount firm can borrow in loans the amount of money available as a loan to a company at a particular time, based on the company's financial situation

borrowing costs FINANCE expense of taking out loan expenses such as interest payments incurred from taking out a loan or any other form of borrowing. In the United States, such costs are included in the total cost of the asset whereas in the United Kingdom, and in International Accounting Standards, this is optional.

borrowings FINANCE money borrowed money borrowed, usually in the form of long-term loans

Borsa Italiana MARKETS Italian stock exchange stock exchange based in Milan, Italy, established as the Borsa di Commercio in 1808. It was privatized and became Borsa Italiana in 1998 and merged with the ***London Stock Exchange*** in 2007. The main index of stocks on the exchange is the ***FTSE MIB***.

boss GENERAL MANAGEMENT person managing group or process the person in charge of a job, process, department, or organization, more formally known as a manager or supervisor

Boston Box *or* Boston matrix BUSINESS plotting market share against growth rate a model used for analyzing a company's potential by plotting market share against growth rate. The Boston Box was conceived by the Boston Consulting Group in the 1970s to help in the process of determining which businesses a company should invest in and which it should divest itself of. A business with a high market share and high growth rate is a ***star***, and one with a low market share and low growth rate is a ***dog***. A high market share with low growth rate is characteristic of a ***cash cow***, which could yield significant but short-term gain, and a low market share coupled with high growth rate produces a ***question mark company***, which offers a doubtful return on investment. To be useful, this model requires accurate assessment of a business's strengths and weaknesses, which may be difficult to obtain.

BOT *abbr* INTERNATIONAL TRADE ***balance of trade***

bottleneck **1.** FINANCE process that holds up others an activity within an organization which has a lower capacity than preceding or subsequent activities, thereby limiting throughput. Bottlenecks are often the cause of a buildup of work in progress and of idle time. **2.** OPERATIONS & PRODUCTION somebody or something that slows down process a limiting factor on the rate of an operation. A workstation operating at its maximum capacity becomes a bottleneck if the rate of production elsewhere in the plant increases but throughput at that workstation cannot be increased to meet demand. An understanding of bottlenecks is important if the efficiency and capacity of an assembly line are to be increased. The techniques of ***fishbone charts, flow charts***, and Pareto charts can be used to identify where and why bottlenecks occur.

bottom fisher MARKETS financial bargain hunter an investor who searches for bargains among stocks that have recently dropped in price (slang)

bottom line ACCOUNTING firm's net profit or loss the net profit or loss that a company makes at the end of a specific period of time, used in the calculation of the earnings-per-share business ratio

bottom-of-the-harbor scheme *ANZ* TAX tax avoidance involving asset-stripping a tax avoidance strategy that involves stripping a company of assets and then selling the company a number of times so that it is hard to trace

bottom out MARKETS stabilize at low level to reach the lowest level in the downward trend of the market price of securities or commodities before the price begins an upward trend again

bottom-up approach **1.** STOCKHOLDING & INVESTMENTS describing investment on individual potential independent of trends used to describe an approach to investing that seeks to identify individual companies that are fundamentally sound and whose stock will perform well regardless of general economic or industry-group trends **2.** GENERAL MANAGEMENT involving employee participation at all levels used to describe a consultative leadership style that promotes employee participation at all levels in decision making and problem solving. A bottom-up approach to leadership is associated with ***flat*** organizations and the empowerment of employees. It can encourage creativity and flexibility. *See also* ***top-down approach***

bottom-up budgeting TREASURY MANAGEMENT = ***participative budgeting***

bought day book ACCOUNTING record of items bought on credit a book used to record purchases for which cash is not paid immediately

bought deal STOCKHOLDING & INVESTMENTS purchase of new issue for resale to investors a method of selling stock in a new company or selling an issue of new shares in an existing

  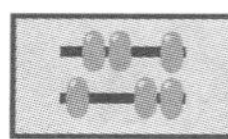   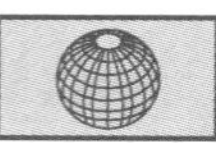   

company, in which an underwriter purchases all the shares at a fixed price for resale to investors

bought-in goods FINANCE goods from outside supplier components and subassemblies that are purchased from an outside supplier instead of being made within the organization

bought ledger ACCOUNTING firm's book recording expenditure a book in which all of a company's expenditure is logged

bought ledger clerk *UK* HR & PERSONNEL employee dealing with bought ledger an office employee who deals with the bought ledger or the sales ledger

bounce BANKING **1.** fail to honor check to refuse payment of a check because the account for which it is written holds insufficient money (slang) *Also called* ***dishonor*** **2.** be refused by bank (of a check) to be returned by a bank because there are insufficient funds in the account to meet the demand (informal)

bounced check BANKING check that bank fails to honor a draft on an account that a bank will not honor, usually because there are insufficient funds in the account

boundaryless organization GENERAL MANAGEMENT organizational model whose goal is flexibility a model that views organizations as having permeable boundaries. An organization has external boundaries that separate it from its suppliers and customers, and internal boundaries that provide demarcation to departments. This rigidity is removed in boundaryless organizations, where the goal is to develop greater flexibility and responsiveness to change and to facilitate the free exchange of information and ideas. The boundaryless organization behaves more like an organism encouraging better integration between departments and closer partnerships with suppliers and customers. The concept was developed at General Electric and described in the book *The Boundaryless Organization: Breaking the Chains of Organizational Structure* by Ron Ashkenas and others, which was published in 1995.

bourse MARKETS European stock exchange a European stock exchange, especially ***Euronext Paris***

boutique **1.** STOCKHOLDING & INVESTMENTS small specialist firm a small firm that offers a limited number of investments or services. *See also* ***boutique investment house*** **2.** BANKING small investment bank a small investment banking firm

boutique investment house STOCKHOLDING & INVESTMENTS specialist broker a brokerage that deals in securities of only one industry. *Also called* ***niche player*** *(sense 2)*

Bowie bond STOCKHOLDING & INVESTMENTS, RISK bond backed by intellectual property an ***asset-backed security*** for which the right to royalties from intellectual property is the collateral

box think outside the box GENERAL MANAGEMENT to think imaginatively about a problem

box spread MARKETS trading in single thing an arbitrage strategy that eliminates risk by buying and selling the same thing

B/P *abbr* FINANCE ***bills payable***

BPR *abbr* GENERAL MANAGEMENT, OPERATIONS & PRODUCTION ***business process reengineering***

B/R *abbr* FINANCE ***bills receivable***

bracket creep *US* TAX incremental movement into higher tax bracket the movement of a taxpayer into increasingly higher tax brackets in a progressive tax system, usually as a result of incremental pay increases to keep pace with inflation

Brady bond STOCKHOLDING & INVESTMENTS emerging country's bond backed by Treasury bonds a bond issued by an emerging nation that has US Treasury bonds as collateral. It is named for Nicholas Brady, banking reformer and former Secretary of the Treasury.

brain drain GENERAL MANAGEMENT relocation of experts overseas for better working environment the overseas migration of specialists, usually highly qualified scientists, engineers, or technical experts, in pursuit of higher salaries, better research funding, and a perceived higher quality of working life

brainstorming GENERAL MANAGEMENT activity for generating free flow of ideas a technique for generating ideas, developing creativity, or problem solving in small groups, through the free-flowing contributions of participants. To encourage the free flow of ideas, brainstorming sessions operate according to a set of guidelines, and the production and evaluation of ideas are kept separate. Several variations of brainstorming and related techniques have emerged such as ***brainwriting***, where ideas are written down by individuals, and ***buzz groups***.

brainwriting GENERAL MANAGEMENT writing down flow of ideas a variation of ***brainstorming*** in which ideas are written down by individuals

branch accounts ACCOUNTING financial records for firm's subsidiary operations the ***accounting records*** or ***financial statements*** for the component parts of a business, especially those that are located in a different region or country from the main enterprise

branch office BANKING organization in different location from headquarters a bank or other financial institution that is part of a larger group and is located in a different geographic area from the parent organization. *Abbr* ***BO***

branch tax TAX S. African tax on some foreign companies a South African tax imposed on nonresident companies that register a branch rather than a separate company

brand MARKETING name or symbol identifying product or service the distinguishing proprietary name, symbol, or ***trademark*** that differentiates a particular product or service from others of a similar nature

brand architecture MARKETING strategy for using brand on products and services the naming and structuring of ***brands*** within the product portfolio of an organization. Brand architectures may be monolithic (the corporate name is used on all products and services), endorsed (subordinate brands are linked to the corporate brand by means of either a verbal or visual endorsement), or freestanding (each product or service is individually branded for its target market). Brand architecture is influenced by the overall brand management and brand positioning strategy of the organization.

brand awareness MARKETING measure of consumers' familiarity with specific brand name the level of ***brand recognition*** that consumers have of a specific brand and its specific product category. Brand awareness examines three levels of recognition: whether the brand name is the first to come to mind when a consumer is questioned about a specific product category; whether the brand name is one of several that come to mind when a consumer is questioned about a specific product category; and whether or not a consumer has heard of a specific brand name.

brand building MARKETING efforts to gain consumer confidence in brand the establishment and improvement of a brand's identity, including giving the brand a set of values that the consumer wants, recognizes, identifies with, and trusts. Values developed in the process of brand building include psychological, physical, and functional properties that consumers desire and should always identify a property that is unique to that brand.

brand champion MARKETING employee responsible for developing and marketing brand an employee of an organization who is responsible for the development, performance, and communication of a particular brand

brand equity MARKETING brand's perceived value the estimated value that a particular brand name brings

brand extension MARKETING using known brand name to enter new market the exploitation, diversification, or stretching of a brand to revive or reinvigorate it in the marketplace. Products developed in the brand extension process may be directly recognizable derivatives or may look and feel completely different.

brand image MARKETING consumer's opinion of brand the perception that consumers have of a brand. Brand image is usually carefully developed by the brand owner through marketing campaigns or product positioning. Occasionally, the image of a brand may develop spontaneously through customer responses to a product. The image of a brand can be seriously tarnished through inappropriate advertising or association with somebody or something that has fallen from public favor.

branding MARKETING process of creating identity for brand a means of distinguishing one firm's products or services from another's and of creating and maintaining an image that encourages confidence in the quality and performance of that firm's products or services

brand leader MARKETING best-selling brand the brand that has the largest ***market share***

brand life cycle MARKETING stages from brand introduction to withdrawal from market the three phases through which brands pass as they are introduced, grow, and then decline. The three stages of the brand life cycle are the introductory period, during which the brand is developed and is introduced to the market; the growth period, when the brand faces competition from other products of a similar nature; and, finally, the maturity period, in which the brand either extends to other products or its image is constantly updated. Without careful ***brand management***, the maturity period can lead to decline and result in the brand being withdrawn. Similar stages can be observed in the ***product life cycle***.

brand loyalty MARKETING customer's inclination to stay with specific brand a long-term customer preference for a specific product or service. Brand loyalty can be produced by factors such as customer satisfaction with the performance or price of a specific product or service, or through identifying with a brand image. It can be encouraged by advertising.

brand management MARKETING responsibility for advertising, promoting, and selling product the marketing of one or more proprietary products. Brand managers have responsibility for the promotion and marketing of one or more commercial brands. This includes setting targets, advertising, and retailing, as well as coordinating all related activities to achieve those targets. In the case of multiple brand management, consideration needs be to given to questions relating to the treatment of the brands as equal or as having some differentiating value. This may affect the amount of resources committed to each brand. —**brand manager**. *See also* ***product management***

brand positioning MARKETING Identifying place in market to compete effectively the development of a brand's position in the market by heightening customer perception of the brand's superiority over other brands of a similar nature. Brand positioning relies on the identification of a real strength or value that has a clear advantage over the nearest competitor and is easily communicated to the consumer.

brand recognition MARKETING measurement of consumer's awareness of brand a measurement of the ability of consumers to recall their experience or knowledge of a particular brand. Brand recognition forms part of ***brand awareness***.

brand value MARKETING benefit to firm of brand the amount that a brand is worth in terms of income, potential income, reputation, prestige, and market value. Brands with a high value are regarded as considerable assets to a company, so that when a company is sold a brand with a high value may be worth more than any other consideration.

brand wagon MARKETING increasing use of branding the trend toward using branding in marketing concepts and techniques (slang)

brandwidth MARKETING measurement of awareness of product the degree to which a brand of product or service is recognized (slang)

breach of contract LEGAL not performing according to contract a refusal or failure to fulfill an obligation imposed by a ***contract***

breach of trust LEGAL instance of betraying people's trust a situation in which somebody does not act correctly or honestly when people expect him or her to

breadth-of-market theory MARKETS significance of relationship of rising and falling prices the theory that the health of a market is measured by the relative volume of items traded that are going up or down in price

break 1. MARKETS sharp price drop in stocks a sudden or sharp fall in prices on a financial market **2.** LEGAL fail to honor contract to fail to carry out the duties of a contract **3.** LEGAL end contract to cancel a contract

breakdown GENERAL MANAGEMENT list of individual items a detailed list or analysis of something item by item

break even ACCOUNTING make neither profit nor loss to balance income and expense, so as to show neither a net gain nor a loss

break-even MARKETING when revenue equals costs the point at which revenue from a product or project cancels out its costs

break-even analysis OPERATIONS & PRODUCTION establishing point of profit and loss balance a method for determining the point at which fixed and variable production costs are equaled by sales revenue and where neither a profit nor a loss is made. Usually illustrated graphically through the use of a ***break-even chart***, break-even analysis can be used to aid decision making, set product prices, and determine the effects of changes in production or sales volume on costs and profits.

break-even chart 1. GENERAL MANAGEMENT chart showing break-even point a management aid used in conjunction with ***break-even analysis*** to calculate the point at which fixed and variable production costs are met by incoming revenue. Lines are plotted to indicate expected sales revenue and production costs. The point at which the lines intersect marks the ***break-even point***, where no profit or loss is made. **2.** OPERATIONS & PRODUCTION chart comparing sales volumes and income a chart that indicates approximate profit or loss at different levels of sales volume within a limited range

break-even point OPERATIONS & PRODUCTION balance of profit and loss the point or level of financial activity at which expenditure equals income, or the value of an investment equals its cost, so that the result is neither a profit nor a loss. *Abbr* ***BEP***

breakout 1. MARKETS significant movement in security's price a rise in a security's price above its previous highest price, or a drop below its former lowest price, taken by technical analysts to signal a continuing move in that direction **2.** GENERAL MANAGEMENT analysis of collected data a summary or breakdown of data that has been collected

breakpoint 1. FINANCE investment size that triggers reduced charges the size of investment at which the ***front-end loading*** on larger investments in a mutual fund starts to be reduced **2.** BANKING account balance that causes interest rate change a balance reached in an account that triggers the payment of either a higher or lower interest rate

breakthrough strategy GENERAL MANAGEMENT successful new strategy a strategy that achieves significant new results in business or management

break-up value MERGERS & ACQUISITIONS value of company's assets sold individually the combined market value of a firm's assets if each were sold separately, as contrasted with selling the firm as an ongoing business. Analysts look for companies with a large break-up value relative to their market value to identify potential takeover targets.

Bretton Woods ECONOMICS agreement establishing IMF and IBRD an agreement signed at a conference at Bretton Woods, in the United States, in July 1944, that established the ***IMF*** and the ***IBRD***

bribery FRAUD offer of gift or cash to gain advantage the act of persuading somebody to exercise his or her business judgment in your favor by offering cash or a gift and thereby gaining an unfair advantage. Many organizations have ***codes of conduct*** that expressly forbid the soliciting or payment of bribes.

BRIC *or* **BRIC countries** *or* **BRICs** INTERNATIONAL TRADE Brazil, Russia, India, China the countries Brazil, Russia, India, and China, which have rapidly developing economies and are large in land mass and population

brick hit the bricks GENERAL MANAGEMENT to go out on strike

bricks-and-mortar E-COMMERCE relating to firms not operating online used to describe a traditional business not involved in e-commerce and incurring the cost of physical structures such as retail stores

bridge financing FINANCE borrowing in expectation of later loans short-term borrowing that the borrower expects to repay with the proceeds of later, larger loans. *See also* ***takeout financing***

bridge loan *US* FINANCE temporary loan while waiting for money a short-term loan providing funds until further money is received, for example, for buying one property while trying to sell another. *UK term* ***bridging loan***

bridging FINANCE borrowing short-term until finance is arranged the obtaining of a short-term loan to provide a continuing source of financing in anticipation of receiving an intermediate or long-term loan. Bridging is routinely employed to finance the purchase or construction of a new building or property until an old one is sold.

bridging loan *UK* FINANCE = ***bridge loan***

bring forward ACCOUNTING carry sum to next column or page to carry a sum from one column or page to the next, or from one account to the next

Brisch system OPERATIONS & PRODUCTION coding system for all firm's resources a coding system, developed principally for the engineering industry by E. G. Brisch and Partners, in which a code is assigned to every item of resources, including materials, labor, and equipment.

British Accounting Association ACCOUNTING UK association for accountancy education and research an organization for the promotion of accounting education and research in the United Kingdom. The BAA has more than 800 members, a large proportion of which work in higher education institutions. Founded in 1947, the BAA also organizes conferences and publishes the *British Accounting Review*. *Abbr* ***BAA***

British Bankers' Association BANKING nonprofit financial organization a not-for-profit trading association for the financial services and banking industries. The Association was established in 1919 and has 260 members, including 57 associate members. It addresses a variety of industry issues, including the development and revision of the voluntary ***Banking Code***, which aims to set standards of best practice. *Abbr* ***BBA***

British Chambers of Commerce BUSINESS association of accredited chambers of commerce a national network of accredited ***chambers of commerce***. The BCC represents over 135,000 businesses in the United Kingdom. *Abbr* ***BCC***

British pound (informal) = ***pound sterling***

British Private Equity and Venture Capital Association FINANCE UK organization for equity and venture firms the official organization representing UK-based private equity and venture capital firms and their advisers. *Abbr* ***BVCA***

broad tape MARKETS news service reporting financial information a news service that reports general information about securities and commodities

broken lot MARKETS = ***odd lot***

broker 1. FINANCE, GENERAL MANAGEMENT intermediary in transaction an agent who arranges a deal, sale, or contract **2.** STOCKHOLDING & INVESTMENTS = ***stockbroker*** **3.** FINANCE, GENERAL MANAGEMENT act as intermediary in transaction to

  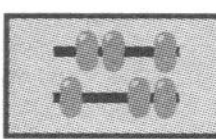   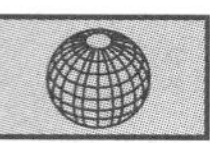  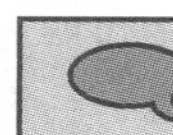 

act as an agent in arranging a deal, sale, or contract

brokerage **1.** FINANCE fee for arranging deal a fee paid to somebody who acts as an agent for somebody else. For example, brokers who arrange deals for the purchase and sale of real estate, those who execute orders for securities, and those who sell insurance receive commissions. *Also called* ***broker's commission*** **2.** STOCKHOLDING & INVESTMENTS broker's business the business of being a broker, trading on a stock exchange on behalf of clients **3.** *US* STOCKHOLDING & INVESTMENTS firm trading in securities for others a company whose business is buying and selling stocks and other securities for its clients. *Also called* ***brokerage firm, brokerage house****. UK term* ***broking house***

broker-dealer STOCKHOLDING & INVESTMENTS broker who also holds stocks for resale a dealer who buys stocks and other securities and holds them for resale, and also deals on behalf of investor clients

brokered market MARKETS where brokers introduce traders a financial market in which brokers bring buyers and sellers together

brokering *US* MARKETS securities the business or job of dealing in securities. *UK term* ***broking***

broker loan rate BANKING interest charged for buying derivatives the interest rate that banks charge brokers on money that they lend for purchases ***on margin***

broker recommendation STOCKHOLDING & INVESTMENTS advice to trade or hold security a recommendation to buy, hold, or sell a stock, made by an analyst who is employed by a brokerage firm to research specific companies' strengths and weaknesses

broker's commission STOCKHOLDING & INVESTMENTS = ***brokerage*** *(sense 1)*

broking *UK* STOCKHOLDING & INVESTMENTS = ***brokering***

broking house *UK* STOCKHOLDING & INVESTMENTS firm trading in stocks and bonds for others a company whose business is buying and selling stocks and bonds for its clients. *US term* ***brokerage***

brought forward ACCOUNTING carried to next column or page indicating a sum carried from one column or page to the next, or from one account to the next. *Abbr* ***b/f****.* See also ***bring forward***

brownfield *US* REAL ESTATE unused urban development site an urban development site that has been previously built on but is currently unused. *UK term* ***brownfield site***

brownfield site *UK* REAL ESTATE = ***brownfield***

brown goods *UK* MARKETING audio, video, computing, and telecommunications consumer goods electronic consumer goods such as televisions, radios, and CD players, used primarily for home entertainment. *See also* ***white goods***

Brussels Stock Exchange MARKETS, STOCKHOLDING & INVESTMENTS = ***Euronext Brussels***

B/S *abbr* ACCOUNTING ***balance sheet***

BSC *abbr* GENERAL MANAGEMENT ***balanced scorecard***

B share STOCKHOLDING & INVESTMENTS **1.** US share with limits on voting in the United States, a share that has limited voting power. *See also* ***A share*** **2.** Australian mutual fund share with fee payable on redemption in Australia, a share in a mutual fund that has no front-end sales charge but carries a redemption fee, or ***back-end loading***, payable only if the share is redeemed. This load, called a ***contingent deferred sales charge***, declines every year until it disappears, usually after six years.

BTI *abbr* MARKETS ***Business Times Industrial index***

bubble MARKETS rapid rise followed by fall in asset price a rapid rise in the price of any type of asset, due mainly to people's belief that the price will continue to rise. When it rises above the real value of the asset, the price falls rapidly, analogous to a bubble bursting. *Also called* ***speculative bubble***

bubble economy ECONOMICS booming economic activity before crash an unstable boom based on speculation in any market, often followed by a financial crash

buck *US* CURRENCY & EXCHANGE (slang) **1.** US dollar a United States dollar **2.** one million one million of any currency unit, used by traders

bucket shop MARKETS broker engaging in delayed trades to customer's disadvantage in the United States, a firm of brokers or dealers that accepts customers' orders but does not execute the transactions until it is financially advantageous to the broker, at the customers' expense

bucket trading MARKETS broker's illegal delay of transactions for own benefit in the United States, an illegal practice in which a broker or dealer accepts customers' orders but does not execute the transactions until it is financially advantageous to the broker, at the customers' expense

budget TREASURY MANAGEMENT statement of predicted income and expenditure a quantitative statement, for a defined period of time, that may include planned revenues, expenses, assets, liabilities, and cash flows. A budget provides a focus for an organization, as it aids the coordination of activities, allocation of resources, and direction of activity, and facilitates control. Planning is achieved by means of a fixed master budget, whereas control is generally exercised through the comparison of actual costs with a flexible budget.

Budget FINANCE UK government's annual statement of financial plans in the United Kingdom, the government's annual spending plan, which is announced to the House of Commons by the Chancellor of the Exchequer. The government is legally obliged to present economic forecasts twice a year, and since the 1997 general election the main Budget has been presented in the spring while a ***pre-Budget report*** is given in the autumn. This outlines government spending plans prior to the main Budget, and also reports on progress since the last Budget.

budget account *UK* BANKING bank account for regular expenses a bank account established to control a person's regular expenditure, such as the payment of insurance premiums, mortgage, utilities, or telephone bills. The annual expenditure for each item is paid into the account in equal monthly installments, bills being paid from the budget account as they become due.

budgetary TREASURY MANAGEMENT of future financial plans relating to a detailed plan of financial operations, with estimates of both revenue and expenditure for a specific future period

budgetary control TREASURY MANAGEMENT regulation of spending regulation of spending according to a planned budget

budget committee TREASURY MANAGEMENT committee that prepares budgets the group within an organization responsible for drawing up budgets that meet departmental requirements, ensuring they comply with policy, and then submitting them to the board of directors

budget deficit ACCOUNTING amount expenditure exceeds income the extent by which expenditure exceeds revenue, especially that of a government. *Also called* ***deficit***

budget director TREASURY MANAGEMENT person responsible for budget preparation the person in an organization who is responsible for running the budget system

budgeted capacity TREASURY MANAGEMENT output level in budget an organization's available output level for a budget period according to the budget. It may be expressed in different ways, for example, in machine hours (the number of hours for which a machine is in production) or standard hours.

budgeted revenue TREASURY MANAGEMENT expected income in budget the income that an organization expects to receive in a budget period according to the budget

budgeting TREASURY MANAGEMENT preparation of budget the preparation of a budget in planning the management of income and expenditure

budget management TREASURY MANAGEMENT adjusting activities to meet budgets the comparison of actual financial results with the estimated expenditures and revenues for the given time period of a budget and the taking of corrective action as necessary

budget surplus ACCOUNTING amount income exceeds expenditure the extent by which revenue exceeds expenditure, especially that of a government. *Also called* ***surplus***

budget variance ACCOUNTING difference between budget estimate and reality the difference between the financial value of something estimated in the budget, such as costs or revenues, and its actual financial value

buffer inventory OPERATIONS & PRODUCTION items available to cope with changes the products or supplies of an organization maintained on hand or in transit to stabilize variations in supply, demand, production, or lead time

buffer stock OPERATIONS & PRODUCTION items available to cope with supply failure a stock of materials, or of work in progress, maintained in order to protect user departments from the effect of possible interruptions to supply

building and loan association BANKING = ***savings and loan association***

Building Societies Ombudsman REGULATION & COMPLIANCE UK official protecting customers of building societies a UK official whose duty is to investigate complaints by members of the public against building societies

building society BANKING UK financial institution supporting real estate purchases in the United Kingdom, a financial institution that offers interest-bearing savings accounts, the deposits being reinvested by the society in long-term loans, primarily mortgage loans for the purchase of real estate

  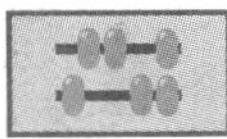   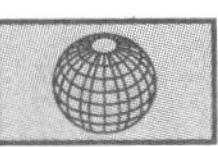   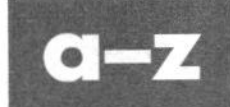

bulge MARKETS sudden trend of rising prices a rapid increase in prices in the commodities market

bulk buying OPERATIONS & PRODUCTION purchase of goods cheaply in quantity the act of buying large quantities of goods at low prices

bulk handling FINANCE financing of moneys due in bulk the financing of a group of receivables together to reduce processing costs

bull STOCKHOLDING & INVESTMENTS exploiter of favorable business conditions somebody who anticipates favorable business conditions, especially somebody who buys specific stocks or commodities in anticipation that their prices will rise, often with the expectation of selling them at a large profit at a later time. *See also* ***bear***

bull CD STOCKHOLDING & INVESTMENTS CD paying more in rising market a ***certificate of deposit*** that pays a higher interest rate when an underlying market index rises in value. *See also* ***bear CD***

bulldog bond STOCKHOLDING & INVESTMENTS foreign sterling bond in UK market a bond issued in sterling in the UK market by a non-British corporation

bullet FINANCE final large loan repayment a single large repayment of the outstanding ***principal*** of a loan at maturity

bullet bond STOCKHOLDING & INVESTMENTS bond repaid with single payment a bond that can be redeemed only when it reaches its maturity date

Bulletin des Annonces Légales Obligatoires FINANCE *see* ***BALO***

bullet loan FINANCE loan with only interest payments until maturity a loan that involves specific payments of interest until maturity, when the ***principal*** is repaid

bullion FINANCE precious metal in bars gold, silver, or platinum produced and traded in the form of bars

bullish **1.** MARKETS of markets with rising prices conducive to or characterized by buying stocks or commodities in anticipation of rising prices. *See also* ***bearish*** **2.** GENERAL MANAGEMENT optimistic about business anticipating favorable business conditions and optimistic about taking advantage of them

bull market MARKETS market with rising prices a market in which prices are rising and in which a dealer is more likely to be a buyer than a seller. *See also* ***bear market***

bull spread MARKETS transactions to make profit when price rises a combination of purchases and sales of options for the same commodity or stock, intended to produce a profit when the price rises. *See also* ***bear spread***

bunching MARKETS combining orders for same security from different clients a process by which brokers combine orders for the same security, so that the orders can be executed together and save clients who have placed orders for ***odd lots*** of fewer than 100 shares of stock from paying extra fees

Bund STOCKHOLDING & INVESTMENTS, RISK German government bond a bond issued by the German government with a maturity of 8.5 to 10 years

Bundesanstalt für Finanzdienstleistungsaufsicht MARKETS, REGULATION & COMPLIANCE organization overseeing German financial system in Germany, since 2002, the independent body responsible for the supervision of the financial system, including banks, providers of financial services, and traders in securities. *Abbr* ***BaFin***

Bundesfinanzhof TAX German tax court in Germany, the supreme court for issues concerning taxation. *Abbr* ***BFH***

bundle FINANCE combination of products or services a package of financial products or services offered to a customer

buoyant MARKETS showing a continuous rise in prices describes a financial market or a security with continuously rising prices

buoyant market MARKETS market with rising prices a market that experiences plenty of trading activity and on which prices are rising, rather than falling

bureaucracy GENERAL MANAGEMENT rigid organizational structure an organizational structure with a rigid hierarchy of personnel, regulated by set rules and procedures. The term bureaucracy has gradually become a pejorative synonym for excessive and time-consuming paperwork and administration. Bureaucracies fell subject to ***delayering*** and ***downsizing*** from the 1980s onward, as the flatter organization became the target structure to ensure swifter market response and organizational flexibility.

burn rate FINANCE rate at which firm's capital is used the rate at which a new business spends its initial capital before it becomes profitable or needs additional funding, used by investors as a measure of a company's ability to survive, or the rate at which a mature business spends its accumulated cash and liquid securities. *Also called* ***cash burn***

bush telegraph GENERAL MANAGEMENT quick informal communication method a method of communicating information or rumors swiftly and unofficially by word of mouth or other means

business BUSINESS **1.** activity carried out for profit work such as buying, selling, or producing goods or services that a person or organization does to make a profit **2.** commercial organization a company or other organization that buys, sells, or produces goods or services to make a profit **3.** commercial transactions commercial dealings or discussions carried on between people or organizations

Business Accounting Deliberation Council REGULATION & COMPLIANCE Japanese body making accounting rules in Japan, a committee controlled by the Ministry of Finance that is responsible for drawing up regulations regarding the consolidated financial statements of listed companies. *Abbr* ***BADC***

Business Activity Statement TAX Australian document giving firm's tax details in Australia, a standard document used to report the amount of ***GST*** and other taxes paid and collected by a business. *Abbr* ***BAS***

business address BUSINESS address of firm's premises the details of number, street, and city or town where a company is located

business administration GENERAL MANAGEMENT procedures involved in operating successful business the establishment and maintenance of procedures, records, and regulations in the pursuit of a commercial activity. Business administration involves the conduct of activities leading to, and resulting from, the delivery of a product or service to the customer. Administration is often seen as paperwork and form-filling, but it reaches more widely than that to encompass the coordination of all the procedures that enable a product or service to be delivered, together with the keeping of records that can be checked to identify errors or opportunities for improvement.

business angel FINANCE investor in new company an individual who is prepared to invest money in a startup company. The amount offered by angels is typically much less than that offered by ***venture capitalists***, but angels are often willing to take greater risks.

business case GENERAL MANAGEMENT proposal showing tangible value to organization the essential value to an organization of a proposal. A business case is made through the preparation and presentation of a business plan and is used to prevent blue-sky ideas taking root without justifiable or provable value to an organization.

business center BUSINESS **1.** area where city's main businesses are the part of a city or town where the main banks, stores, and offices are located **2.** independent office providing business services an office that provides business services such as Internet access, photocopying, meeting rooms, etc., for example, to travelers in a hotel

business cluster BUSINESS cooperative of small related firms a group of small firms from similar industries that team up and act as one body. Creating a business cluster enables firms to enjoy economies of scale usually only available to bigger competitors. Marketing costs can be shared and goods can be bought more cheaply. There are also networking advantages, allowing small firms to share experiences and discuss business strategies.

business combinations MERGERS & ACQUISITIONS acquisitions or mergers in the United States, acquisitions or mergers involving two or more business enterprises

Business Council of Australia BUSINESS organization of chief executives a national association of chief executives, designed as a forum for the discussion of matters pertaining to business leadership in Australia. *Abbr* ***BCA***

business cycle ECONOMICS regular repeating pattern of economic activity a regular pattern of fluctuation in national income, moving from upturn to downturn in about five years

business day BUSINESS normal weekday a weekday when banks, businesses, and stock exchanges are open for business

business efficiency GENERAL MANAGEMENT maximizing output while minimizing input a situation in which an organization maximizes benefit and profit, while minimizing effort and expenditure. Maximization of business efficiency is a balance between two extremes. Managed correctly, it reduces costs, waste, and duplication. The greater the efficiency, the more impersonal, rational, and emotionally detached a bureaucracy becomes. The flatter organizations more prevalent today attempt to be more customer-responsive than efficient in this sense, and the notion of such an ordered and impersonal efficiency has lost favor in an era when creativity and innovation are valued as a competitive advantage.

business expenses ACCOUNTING money spent on firm's running costs money spent on running a business, not on stock or assets

business failure GENERAL MANAGEMENT bankrupt organization an organization that has gone bankrupt. A business that is at risk of failure may

  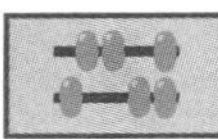      

be saved by ***turnaround management***, which identifies and deals with the reasons for decline. *Also called* ***failure***

business gift MARKETING gift presented to customer a present, usually from a supplier to a customer, often used to maintain good relations. Business gifts may range from a pen to a gift basket and are often a form of ***merchandising***. The acceptance of a business gift is often governed by an organization's ***code of conduct*** and is often forbidden on the grounds that business gifts, particularly high value ones, may be seen as an attempt to bribe.

business hours BUSINESS period when most firms are open the time during which a business is available to be in contact with customers, usually 9:00 a.m. to 5:00 p.m.

business intelligence GENERAL MANAGEMENT collection of business data the information and information gathering techniques used by businesses

business interruption insurance INSURANCE insurance protection against interruptions to business a policy indemnifying an organization for loss of profits and continuing fixed expenses when some insurable disaster, for example, a fire, causes the organization to stop or reduce its activities. *Also called* ***consequential loss policy***

business manager GENERAL MANAGEMENT somebody responsible for firm's operations a person who is responsible for implementing the policies and procedures of a business or part of a business

business model GENERAL MANAGEMENT description of business operations a description of the way in which a specific business or type of business operates, including its structure, policies, products, services, customers, and market strategies

business name BUSINESS in UK, name that organization uses in the United Kingdom, the legal term for the name under which an organization operates

business objective GENERAL MANAGEMENT organization's goal as basis for operational policies a goal that an organization sets for itself, for example, profitability, sales growth, or return on investment. These goals are the foundation upon which the strategic and operational policies adopted by the organization are based.

business plan GENERAL MANAGEMENT outline of firm's intentions for achieving goals a document describing the current activities of a business, setting out its goals and objectives and how they are to be achieved over a set period of time.
A business plan may cover the activities of an organization or a group of companies, or it may deal with a single department within the organization. In the former case, it is sometimes referred to as a corporate plan. The sections of a business plan usually include a market analysis describing the target market, customers, and competitors, an operations plan describing how products and services will be developed and produced, and a financial section providing profit, budget, and cash flow forecasts, annual accounts, and financial requirements. Businesses may use a business plan internally as a framework for implementing strategy and improving performance or externally to attract investment or raise capital for development plans. A business plan may form part of the overall corporate planning process within an organization and be used for the implementation of a company's strategy.

business process reengineering GENERAL MANAGEMENT, OPERATIONS & PRODUCTION review and change to benefit organization the initiation and control of the change of processes within an organization, in order to derive competitive advantage from improvement in the quality of products. Business process reengineering requires a review and imaginative analysis of the processes currently used by the organization. BPR, therefore, has similarities to ***benchmarking***, as this review of processes can reveal critical points where significant improvements in quality can be made. Business process reengineering was at the height of its popularity in the early to mid-1990s. It has been criticized as one of the root causes of the bouts of ***downsizing*** and ***delayering*** that have affected many parts of industry. It has also received a negative press because few BPR projects have delivered the benefits expected of them. *Abbr* ***BPR***

business property relief TAX reduction in UK inheritance tax on business property in the United Kingdom, a reduction in the amount liable to inheritance tax on some types of business property

business rate TAX UK tax on business premises in the United Kingdom, a tax on businesses calculated on the value of the property occupied. Although the rate of tax is set by central government, the tax is collected by the local authority.

business risk RISK possible risk to firm's standing the uncertainty associated with the unique circumstances of a particular company which might affect the price of that company's securities, for example, the introduction of a superior technology by a competitor

business segment ACCOUNTING distinct part of business or enterprise a distinguishable part of a business or enterprise which is subject to a different set of risks and returns from any other part. Listed companies are required to declare in their annual reports information such as sales, profits, and assets, for each segment of an enterprise.

business strategy GENERAL MANAGEMENT firm's intended means of achieving long-term goals a long-term approach to implementing a firm's business plans to achieve its business objectives

Business Times Industrial index MARKETS Asian index of stocks an index of 40 Singapore and Malaysian stocks, sponsored by the *Business Times*. *Abbr* ***BTI***

business-to-business E-COMMERCE *see* ***B2B***

business-to-consumer E-COMMERCE *see* ***B2C***

business transaction OPERATIONS & PRODUCTION instance of buying or selling an act of buying or selling goods or services in order to make a profit

business transfer relief TAX UK tax benefit in takeovers the UK tax advantage gained when selling a business for shares of stock in the company that buys it

business unit ACCOUNTING distinct part of business organization a part of an organization that operates as a distinct function, department, division, or stand-alone business. Business units are usually treated as a separate ***profit center*** within the overall business.

bust go bust FINANCE to become bankrupt (informal)

bust up MERGERS & ACQUISITIONS divide or subdivide firm to split up a company or a division of a company into smaller units

bust-up proxy proposal MERGERS & ACQUISITIONS approach to stockholders for leveraged buyout an overture to a company's stockholders for a ***leveraged buyout*** in which the acquirer will sell some of the company's assets in order to repay the debt used to finance the takeover

butterfly spread STOCKHOLDING & INVESTMENTS simultaneously buying and selling variety of options a complex option strategy based on simultaneously purchasing and selling calls at different exercise prices and maturity dates, the profit being the premium collected when the options are sold. Such a strategy is most profitable when the price of the underlying security is relatively stable.

buy FINANCE **1.** pay to get something to get something in exchange for money **2.** something you pay for something that you pay for relative to its being worth or not worth the amount you pay

buy and hold STOCKHOLDING & INVESTMENTS investment for long term an investment strategy based on retaining securities for a long time

buy and write STOCKHOLDING & INVESTMENTS buying stock and selling options as safeguard an investment strategy involving buying stock and selling options to eliminate the possibility of loss if the value of the stock goes down

buyback **1.** MARKETS purchase by firm of its own stock an arrangement whereby a company buys its own stock on the stock market. *Also called* ***stock buyback*** **2.** STOCKHOLDING & INVESTMENTS agreed repurchase of bonds or stock the repurchase of bonds or stock, as agreed by contract. The seller is usually a ***venture capitalist*** who helped finance the forming of the company.

buydown **1.** FINANCE initial payment to secure favorable interest rate an initial lump-sum payment made on a loan in order to get a more favorable ongoing rate, especially a loan secured by a mortgage **2.** MORTGAGES partial repayment of principal on mortgage the payment of principal amounts which reduces the monthly payments due on a mortgage

buyer **1.** BUSINESS person buying or intending to buy somebody who is in the process of buying something or who intends to buy something **2.** OPERATIONS & PRODUCTION professional acquirer of items needed somebody whose job is to choose and buy goods, merchandise, services, or media time or space for a company, factory, store, or advertiser

buyer expectation MARKETING = ***customer expectation***

buyer's guide MARKETING information helping consumer choose from variety of products a document that offers information on a variety of related products, usually from a number of different organizations

buyer's market MARKETS when supply exceeds demand a situation in which supply exceeds demand, prices are relatively low, and buyers therefore have an advantage

buy in STOCKHOLDING & INVESTMENTS acquire controlling interest in firm to buy stock in a company so as to have a controlling interest. This is often done by or for executives from outside the company.

buying department *UK* OPERATIONS & PRODUCTION = ***purchasing department***

buying economies of scale FINANCE lower cost involved in large transactions a reduction in the cost of purchasing raw materials and components or of borrowing money due to the increased size of the purchase

buying manager OPERATIONS & PRODUCTION = ***purchasing manager***

buying power FINANCE assessment of ability to purchase products and services the assessment of a person's or organization's disposable income, regarded as determining the quantity and quality of products and services that person or organization can afford to buy

buy on close MARKETS purchase late in day a purchase of securities or insurance policies made at the end of the trading day

buy on margin STOCKHOLDING & INVESTMENTS, RISK borrow to pay for part of security purchase to purchase securities by paying cash for part of the purchase and borrowing, using the security as collateral, for the remainder

buy on opening MARKETS purchase early in day a purchase of securities or insurance policies made at the beginning of the trading day

buy or make OPERATIONS & PRODUCTION = ***purchasing versus production***

buy out MERGERS & ACQUISITIONS **1.** buy and take over business to purchase the entire stock of, or controlling financial interest in, a company **2.** buy all somebody's share to pay somebody to relinquish his or her interest in a property or other enterprise

buyout 1. MERGERS & ACQUISITIONS buying and taking over of business the purchase and ***takeover*** of an ongoing business. It is more formally known as an ***acquisition***. If a business is purchased by managers or staff, it is known as a ***management buyout***. **2.** MERGERS & ACQUISITIONS buying all of somebody's stock ownership the purchase of somebody else's entire stock ownership in a firm. It is more formally known as an ***acquisition***. **3.** PENSIONS leaver's ability to move pension assets an option to transfer benefits of a pension plan on leaving a company

buy stop order MARKETS instruction to buy stock at specific price an order to buy stock when its price reaches a specific level, above the current offering level

buy-to-let *UK* FINANCE = ***buy-to-rent***

buy-to-let mortgage *UK* MORTGAGES = ***buy-to-rent mortgage***

buy-to-rent *US* FINANCE purchase of property for rental purposes an investment in property with the intention of renting it to produce income, often to pay the original mortgage used to purchase it. *UK term* ***buy-to-let***

buy-to-rent mortgage *US* MORTGAGES mortgage to purchase property for rental a mortgage used to buy property that you intend to rent. It differs from a mortgage on property that you intend to live in, in that the mortgagee takes into consideration the income the property will produce in deciding how much to lend. *UK term* ***buy-to-let mortgage***

buzz group GENERAL MANAGEMENT small group for discussing specific issue a small discussion group formed for a specific task such as generating ideas, solving problems, or reaching a common viewpoint on a topic within a specific period of time. Large groups may be divided into buzz groups after an initial presentation in order to cover different aspects of a topic or maximize participation. Each group appoints a spokesperson to report the results of the discussion to the larger group. Buzz groups are a form of brainstorming.

BV *abbr* BUSINESS ***Besloten venootschap***

BVCA *abbr* FINANCE ***British Private Equity and Venture Capital Association***

BVLP MARKETS, STOCKHOLDING & INVESTMENTS = ***Euronext Lisbon***

by-bidder FINANCE somebody bidding at auction to benefit seller somebody who bids at an auction solely to raise the price for the seller

bylaws *US* CORPORATE GOVERNANCE rules for corporation's internal procedures rules governing the internal running of a corporation, such as the number of meetings, the appointment of officers, and so on. *UK term* ***articles of association***

bypass trust TAX trust saving tax by increasing beneficiaries a trust that leaves money in a will in trust to people other than the prime beneficiary in order to gain tax advantage

byproduct OPERATIONS & PRODUCTION secondary product sold for profit a secondary product, made as a result of manufacturing a main product, that can be sold for profit

C

CA *abbr* ACCOUNTING **1.** ***chartered accountant*** **2.** ***certified accountant***

C/A *abbr* FINANCE ***capital account***

c/a *abbr* BANKING ***checking account***

cable CURRENCY & EXCHANGE exchange rate between US dollar and pound a spot exchange rate between the US dollar and the pound sterling

CAC 40 MARKETS, STOCKHOLDING & INVESTMENTS main French stock market index an index of 40 stocks selected from those traded on the ***Euronext Paris*** exchange based on capitalization and turnover. It was established on December 31, 1987, with a base value of 1,000.

CAD *abbr* OPERATIONS & PRODUCTION ***computer-aided design***

cafeteria plan *or* cafeteria employee benefit plan HR & PERSONNEL US employee benefit plan allowing choice of benefits in the United States, an employee benefit plan that allows employees to select a number of benefits such as contributions to a retirement plan, insurance, or cash to pay for medical expenses not covered by insurance, all or some of which may be exempt from payroll tax. *Also called* ***flexible benefit plan***

cage *US* MARKETS department of brokerage firm handling paperwork the part of a brokerage firm where the paperwork involved in the buying and selling of stocks is processed (slang)

calendar spread STOCKHOLDING & INVESTMENTS, RISK = ***horizontal spread***

calendar variance ACCOUNTING accounting difference from calendar months versus working days a variance that occurs if a company uses calendar months for the financial accounts but uses the number of actual working days to calculate overhead expenses in the cost accounts

calendar year January 1 to December 31 a year between the calendar dates January 1 and December 31

call STOCKHOLDING & INVESTMENTS **1.** option to buy stock an ***option*** to buy stock at an agreed price or before a particular date. *Also called* ***call option*** **2.** demand for agreed partial payment of share capital a request made to the holders of partly paid-up share capital for the payment of a predetermined sum due on the share capital, under the terms of the original subscription agreement. Failure on the part of the stockholder to pay a call may result in the forfeiture of the relevant holding of partly paid shares. *Also called* ***call up***

callable STOCKHOLDING & INVESTMENTS able to be repurchased before maturity used to describe a security that the issuer has the right to buy back before its maturity date. *See also* ***noncallable***

callable bond STOCKHOLDING & INVESTMENTS bond able to be bought back a bond that may be bought back by the issuer prior to its maturity date

callable capital FINANCE capital from unpaid sale of stock the part of a company's capital from the sale of stock for which the company has not yet received payment

callable preferred stock *US* STOCKHOLDING & INVESTMENTS = ***redeemable preferred stock***

call center GENERAL MANAGEMENT department or business providing information by telephone a department or business wholly focused on telephone inquiries. Call centers usually provide a centralized point of contact for an organization and support telemarketing, after-sales service, telephone helplines, or information services, either for a parent organization or on a contract basis for other businesses.

call date STOCKHOLDING & INVESTMENTS pre-maturity deadline for repurchase of bond the date before maturity on which the issuer of a ***callable bond*** has the right to buy it back

called-up share capital STOCKHOLDING & INVESTMENTS stock not paid for by stockholders the proportion of stock issued by a company that has not yet been paid for. *See also* ***fully paid share capital***

call in BANKING request payment of debt to ask for a debt to be paid at once

call loan BANKING bank loan repayable on demand a bank loan that must be repaid as soon as repayment is requested

call option STOCKHOLDING & INVESTMENTS = ***call*** *(sense 1)*

call payment STOCKHOLDING & INVESTMENTS sum in partial payment for stock an amount that a company demands in partial payment for stock such as a rights issue that is not paid for at one time

call price STOCKHOLDING & INVESTMENTS early redemption cost of US bond a price to be paid by an issuer for the early redemption of a US bond

call provision STOCKHOLDING & INVESTMENTS clause allowing bond to be redeemed early a clause in an ***indenture*** that lets the issuer of a bond redeem it before the date of its maturity

call purchase FINANCE purchase where either party can establish price a transaction where either

  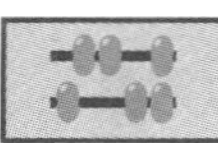      

the seller or purchaser can fix the price for future delivery

call risk STOCKHOLDING & INVESTMENTS, RISK risk of premature repurchase of bond the possibility that the issuer of a ***callable bond*** will buy back the bond and the bondholder will be forced to reinvest at a lower interest rate

call rule MARKETS fixing of commodity price at end of trading a commodities exchange rule whereby the price of a commodity is fixed at the end of a day's trading and remains valid until the next trading day begins

calls in arrears STOCKHOLDING & INVESTMENTS outstanding money for shares money called up for shares, but not paid at the correct time. The shares may be forfeited or a special calls in arrears account is established to debit the sums owing.

call up STOCKHOLDING & INVESTMENTS = ***call*** *(sense 2)*

CAM *abbr* OPERATIONS & PRODUCTION ***computer-aided manufacturing***

campaign MARKETING advertising and marketing plan a program of advertising and marketing activities with a specific objective

Canadian Institute of Chartered Accountants ACCOUNTING main professional body for accountants in Canada, the principal professional accountancy body that is responsible for setting accounting standards. *Abbr* ***CICA***

cancellation price STOCKHOLDING & INVESTMENTS price at which mutual fund will redeem securities the lowest value possible in any one day of a mutual fund. In the United Kingdom, it is regulated by the ***Financial Services Authority***.

cap FINANCE upper limit an upper limit such as on a rate of interest for a loan

CAPA *abbr* ACCOUNTING ***Confederation of Asian and Pacific Accountants***

capacity OPERATIONS & PRODUCTION measure of production capability the measure of the capability of a workstation or a plant to produce output. Capacity measures can focus on a variety of factors, which typically include quantity (the number of items produced over a given period) and scope (the range of items produced by type or size).

capacity planning OPERATIONS & PRODUCTION estimation of organization's requirements to meet workload the process of measuring the amount of work that can be completed within a given time and determining the necessary physical and human resources needed to accomplish it. Capacity planning uses ***capacity utilization*** to ensure that the maximum amount of product is made and sold. The planning involves a regulation process that identifies deviations from the plan, allowing corrective action to be taken. A ***capacity requirements planning*** program can aid in the process of capacity planning.

capacity requirements planning OPERATIONS & PRODUCTION computerized system for planning resource requirements a computerized tracking process that translates production requirements into practical implications for manufacturing resources. Capacity requirements planning is part of ***manufacturing resource planning*** and is carried out after a manufacturing resource planning program has been run. This produces an ***infinite capacity plan***, as it does not take account of the capacity constraints of each workstation. Where the process is extended to cover capacity requirements, a ***finite capacity plan*** is produced. This enables ***loading*** at each workstation to be smoothed and determines the need for additional resources.

capacity usage variance FINANCE difference in result caused by working hours the difference in gain or loss in a given period compared to budgeted expectations, caused because the hours worked were longer or shorter than planned

capacity utilization 1. OPERATIONS & PRODUCTION measure of equipment actually used for production a measure of the plant and equipment of a company or an industry that is actually being used to produce goods or services. Capacity utilization is usually measured over a specific period of time, for example, the average for a month, or at a given point in time. It can be expressed as a ratio, where utilization = actual output divided by design capacity. This measure is used in both ***capacity planning*** and ***capacity requirements planning*** processes. **2.** ECONOMICS degree of production capability being used the output of an economy, firm, or plant divided by its output when working at full capacity

Caparo case ACCOUNTING English ruling on auditors' responsibilities in England, a court decision made by the House of Lords in 1990 that auditors owe a duty of care to present, not prospective, stockholders as a body but not as individuals

CAPEX *abbr* ACCOUNTING ***capital expenditure***

capital FINANCE investment money money that is available to be invested by a person, business, or organization in order to make a profit

capital account FINANCE firm's total capital the sum of a company's ***capital*** at a specific time. *Abbr* ***C/A***

capital adequacy ratio FINANCE percentage of bank's assets represented by capital an amount of money which a bank has to hold in the form of stockholders' equity, shown as a proportion of its risk-weighted assets, agreed internationally not to fall below 8%. *Abbr* ***CAR***. Also called ***capital to risk-weighted assets ratio***

capital allowance TAX tax allowance for new plant and machinery in the United Kingdom and Ireland, an allowance against income or corporation tax available to businesses or sole traders who have purchased plant and machinery for business use. The rates are set annually and vary according to the type of fixed asset purchased, for example, whether it is machinery or buildings. This system effectively removes subjectivity from the calculation of depreciation for tax purposes.

capital appreciation FINANCE increase in wealth the increase in a company's or individual's wealth at market values

capital appreciation fund STOCKHOLDING & INVESTMENTS mutual fund concentrating on capital not income a mutual fund that aims to increase the value of its holdings without regard to the provision of income to its owners

capital asset ACCOUNTING real estate owned but not traded real estate that a company owns and uses but that the company does not buy or sell as part of its regular trade

capital asset pricing model STOCKHOLDING & INVESTMENTS theory about relationship between cost and expected return a model of the market used to assess the cost of capital for a company based on the rate of return on its assets.

The capital asset pricing model holds that the expected return on a security or portfolio equals the rate on a risk-free security plus a risk premium. If this expected return does not meet or beat a theoretical required return, the investment should not be undertaken. The formula used for the model is:

$$\text{Risk-free rate} + (\text{Market return} - \text{Risk-free rate}) \times \text{Beta value} = \text{Expected return}$$

The risk-free rate is the quoted rate on an asset that has virtually no risk. In practice, it is the rate quoted for 90-day US Treasury bills. The market return is the percentage return expected of the overall market, typically a published index such as Standard & Poor's. The beta value is a figure that measures the volatility of a security or portfolio of securities compared with the market as a whole. A beta of 1, for example, indicates that a security's price will move with the market. A beta greater than 1 indicates higher volatility, while a beta less than 1 indicates less volatility.

Say, for instance, that the current risk-free rate is 4%, and the S&P 500 index is expected to return 11% next year. An investment club is interested in determining next year's return for XYZ Software, a prospective investment. The club has determined that the company's beta value is 1.8. The overall stock market always has a beta of 1, so XYZ Software's beta of 1.8 signals that it is a more risky investment than the overall market represents. This added risk means that the club should expect a higher rate of return than the 11% for the S&P 500. The CAPM calculation, then, would be:

$$4\% + (11\% - 4\%) \times 1.8 = 16.6\% \text{ expected return}$$

What the results tell the club is that, given the risk, XYZ Software has a required rate of return of 16.6%, or the minimum return that an investment in XYZ should generate. If the investment club does not think that XYZ will produce that kind of return, it should probably consider investing in a different company. *Abbr* ***CAPM***

capital base FINANCE funding structure as basis of firm's worth the funding structure of a company (***stockholders' equity*** plus loans and retained profits) used as a way of assessing the company's worth

capital bonus INSURANCE extra payment arising from capital gain a bonus payment by an insurance company that is produced by ***capital gain***

capital budget ACCOUNTING part of firm's budget concerned with capital expenditure a subsection of a company's master budget that deals with expected capital expenditure within a defined period. *Also called* ***capital expenditure budget, capital investment budget***

capital budgeting TREASURY MANAGEMENT preparing budget for capital expenditure the process concerned with decision making with respect to the following issues: the choice of specific investment projects, the total amount of ***capital expenditure*** to commit, and the method of financing the investment portfolio

capital buffer FINANCE sufficient capital to counter risk the amount of capital a financial institution needs to hold above minimum requirements, calculated on an assessment of forecast risk

capital commitments ACCOUNTING authorized but unspent capital expenditure expenditure on assets which has been authorized by directors, but not yet spent at the end of a financial period

     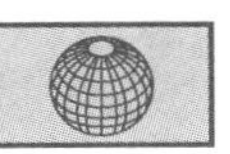   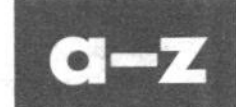

capital consumption FINANCE depreciation of fixed assets in a given period, the total depreciation of the fixed assets of a company or national economy, based on replacement costs

capital controls REGULATION & COMPLIANCE government restrictions on asset ownership regulations placed by a government on the amount of capital people may hold. Sometimes there are restrictions only on share ownership, at other times on bank accounts; also controls may apply to non-residents as well as residents.

capital cost allowance TAX Canadian tax benefit for capital depreciation in Canada, a tax advantage given for the depreciation in value of ***capital assets***

capital costs ACCOUNTING expenses on buying fixed assets expenses associated with the purchase of fixed assets such as land, buildings, and machinery

capital deepening ECONOMICS increase in country's capital-to-labor ratio the process whereby capital increases but the number of employed people falls or remains constant

capital employed FINANCE stockholders' funds plus long-term loans an amount of ***capital*** consisting of ***stockholders' equity*** plus the long-term loans taken out by a business. *See also* ***return on assets***

capital equipment ACCOUNTING equipment used for everyday operations the equipment that a factory or office uses in operating its business

capital expenditure ACCOUNTING spending on fixed assets the cost of acquiring, producing, or enhancing fixed assets such as land, buildings, and machinery. *Abbr* ***CAPEX***. Also called ***capital investment***

capital expenditure budget ACCOUNTING = ***capital budget***

capital expenditure proposal ACCOUNTING application for capital expenditure a formal request for authority to undertake ***capital expenditure***. This is usually supported by the case for expenditure in accordance with capital investment appraisal criteria. Levels of authority must be clearly defined and the reporting structure of actual expenditure must be to the equivalent authority level.

capital flight STOCKHOLDING & INVESTMENTS withdrawal of investments from country the transfer of large sums of money between countries to seek higher rates of return or to escape a political or economic disturbance

capital flow STOCKHOLDING & INVESTMENTS international movement of money the movement of investments from one country to another. *Also called* ***capital movement***

capital formation STOCKHOLDING & INVESTMENTS adding to capital by investment the creation of long-term assets, such as long-dated bonds or shares

capital funding planning TREASURY MANAGEMENT determining of means to finance capital expenditure the process of selecting suitable funds to finance long-term assets and ***working capital***

capital gain ACCOUNTING money made from disposing of asset the financial gain made upon the disposal of an asset. The gain is the difference between the cost of its acquisition and the net proceeds upon its sale.

capital gains distribution STOCKHOLDING & INVESTMENTS allocation of capital gains to investors a sum of money that a body such as a mutual fund pays to its owners in proportion to the owners' share of the organization's capital gains for the year

capital gains expenses ACCOUNTING cost of buying or selling assets expenses incurred in buying or selling assets, which can be deducted when calculating a capital gain or loss

capital gains reserve TAX Canadian tax benefit for customers' unpaid bills in Canada, a tax advantage given for money not yet received in payment for something that has been sold

capital gains tax TAX tax on difference between buying and selling price a tax on the difference between the gross acquisition cost and the net proceeds when an asset is sold. *Abbr* ***CGT***

capital gearing STOCKHOLDING & INVESTMENTS firm's debt per share the amount of debt of all kinds that a company has for each share of its common stock

capital goods ECONOMICS assets used for producing other goods physical assets that are used in the production of other goods

capital growth FINANCE increase in value of assets an increase in the value of assets in a fund, or of the value of stock

capital inflow FINANCE money entering country from services overseas the amount of capital that flows into an economy from services rendered abroad

capital instrument FINANCE means of raising money a security such as stocks or ***debentures*** that a business uses to raise finance

capital-intensive FINANCE requiring money rather than labor used to describe economic activities that primarily require a high proportion of ***capital*** as opposed to needing labor. *See also* ***labor-intensive***

capital investment ACCOUNTING = ***capital expenditure***

capital investment budget ACCOUNTING = ***capital budget***

capitalism ECONOMICS economic system where citizens own means of production an economic and social system in which individuals can maximize profits because they own the means of production

capitalist FINANCE investor in business a person who invests ***capital*** in trade and industry, for profit

capitalist economy ECONOMICS economy giving great commercial and financial freedom an economy in which each person has the right to invest money, to work in business, and to buy and sell products and services, without major government restrictions

capitalization 1. FINANCE raising funds through stock split the conversion of a company's reserves into ***capital*** through a stock split **2.** STOCKHOLDING & INVESTMENTS amount invested in firm the amount of money that is invested in a company **3.** STOCKHOLDING & INVESTMENTS firm's worth the worth of the bonds and stocks issued by a company

capitalization issue *UK* STOCKHOLDING & INVESTMENTS = ***stock split***

capitalization rate FINANCE rate of raising capital through stock split the rate at which a company's ***reserves*** are converted into ***capital*** by way of a ***stock split***

capitalization ratio FINANCE proportion of firm's value in capital the proportion of a company's value represented by debt, stock, assets, and other items.

By comparing debt to total capitalization, these ratios provide a glimpse of a company's long-term stability and ability to withstand losses and business downturns.

A company's capitalization ratio can be expressed in two ways:

$$= \frac{\text{Long-term debt}}{(\text{Long-term debt} + \text{Owners' equity})}$$

and

$$= \frac{\text{Total debt}}{(\text{Total debt} + \text{Preferred} + \text{Common equity})}$$

For example, a company whose long-term debt totals $5,000 and whose owners hold equity worth $3,000 would have a capitalization ratio of:

$$\frac{5,000}{(5,000 + 3,000)} = \frac{5,000}{8,000} = 0.625$$

Both expressions of the ratio are also referred to as ***component percentages***, since they compare a firm's debt with either its total capital (debt plus equity) or its equity capital. They readily indicate how reliant a firm is on debt financing. Capitalization ratios need to be evaluated over time, and compared with other data and standards. Care should be taken when comparing companies in different industries or sectors. The same figures that appear to be low in one industry can be very high in another.

capitalize 1. FINANCE invest money in business to provide investment money for a business, in expectation of making a profit **2.** ACCOUNTING enter cost of asset in balance sheet to include money spent on the purchase of an ***asset*** as an element in a ***balance sheet***

capital lease *US* REAL ESTATE lease treated as though leased assets were purchased a lease that is treated as though the lessee had borrowed money and bought the leased assets.

If a lease agreement does not meet any of the criteria below, the lessee treats it as an ***operating lease*** for accounting purposes. If, however, the agreement meets one of the following criteria, it is treated as a capital lease:

(i) The lease agreement transfers ownership of the assets to the lessee during the term of the lease.

(ii) The lessee can purchase the assets leased at a bargain price (also called a bargain purchase option), such as $1, at the end of the lease term.

(iii) The lease term is at least 75% of the economic life of the leased asset.

(iv) The present value of the minimum lease payments is 90% or greater of the asset's value.

Capital leases are reported by the lessee as if the assets being leased were acquired and the monthly rental payments as if they were payments of principal and interest on a debt obligation. Specifically, the lessee capitalizes the lease by recognizing an asset and a liability at the lower of the present value of the minimum lease payments or the value of the assets under lease. As the monthly rental payments are made, the corresponding liability decreases. At the same time, the leased asset is depreciated in a manner that is consistent with other owned assets having the same use and economic life. *UK term* ***finance lease***

  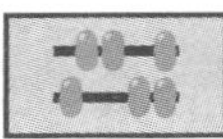      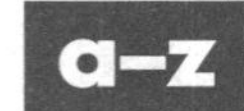

capital levy TAX tax on fixed assets a tax on fixed assets or property, rather than income. Capital levies are usually collected only once.

capital loss ACCOUNTING loss on sale of fixed asset a loss made through selling a ***capital asset*** for less than its market price

capital maintenance concept ACCOUNTING principle underpinning inflation accounting a concept used to determine the definition of profit, which provides the basis for different systems of ***inflation accounting***

capital market MARKETS market for longer-term securities a financial market dealing with securities that have a life of more than one year

capital movement STOCKHOLDING & INVESTMENTS = ***capital flow***

capital outlay ACCOUNTING = ***capital expenditure***

capital profit ACCOUNTING profit from sale of asset a profit that a company makes by selling a ***capital asset***

capital project OPERATIONS & PRODUCTION project requiring capital investment a project that involves expenditure of an organization's monetary resources for the purpose of creating capacity for production. Capital projects are usually large scale, complex, need to be completed quickly, and involve ***capital expenditure***. *See also* ***capital project management***

capital project management GENERAL MANAGEMENT control of project requiring capital expenditure control of a project that involves expenditure of an organization's monetary resources for the purpose of creating capacity for production. Capital project management often involves the organization of major construction or engineering work. Different techniques have evolved for capital project management from those used for normal ***project management***, including methods for managing the complexity of such projects and for analyzing return on investment afterward.

capital property ACCOUNTING, TAX type of asset under Canadian tax law under Canadian tax law, assets that can depreciate in value or be sold for a capital gain or loss

capital ratio ACCOUNTING firm's income as fraction of fixed assets a company's income expressed as a fraction of its ***tangible assets***. These assets include leases and company stock, as well as physical assets such as land, buildings, and machinery.

capital rationing FINANCE **1.** firm's limiting of new investment the restriction of new investment by a company because of a shortfall in its capital budget **2.** imposition of limit on capital expenditure a restriction on an organization's ability to invest capital funds, caused by an internal budget ceiling being imposed by management (***soft capital rationing***), or by external limitations being applied to the company, as when additional borrowed funds cannot be obtained (***hard capital rationing***)

capital reconstruction MERGERS & ACQUISITIONS closing down then reconstituting firm the act of placing a company into voluntary liquidation and then selling its assets to another company with the same name and same stockholders, but with a larger capital base

capital redemption reserve ACCOUNTING in UK, firm's account underpinning trade in own stock in the United Kingdom, an account required by law to prevent a reduction in capital, where a company purchases or redeems its own stock out of ***distributable profits***

capital reduction FINANCE withdrawal of capital funds the ***retirement*** or redemption of capital funds by a company

capital reorganization STOCKHOLDING & INVESTMENTS restructuring firm's share holdings the act of changing the capital structure of a company by amalgamating or dividing existing shares to form shares of a higher or lower nominal value

capital reserves FINANCE **1.** *UK* funds unavailable for dividend payments reserves not legally available for distribution to stockholders as dividends according to the Companies Act (1985) **2.** *US* funds for future investment money that a company holds in reserve for future investment or expense

capital resource planning TREASURY MANAGEMENT assessing assets for strategic purposes the process of evaluating and selecting long-term assets to meet established strategies

capital shares STOCKHOLDING & INVESTMENTS shares with increasing value but no income shares in a mutual fund that rise in value as the capital value of the individual stocks rises, but do not receive any income

capital stock STOCKHOLDING & INVESTMENTS stock authorized by US firm's charter in the United States, the stock authorized by a company's charter, including ***common stock*** and ***preferred stock***. *See also* ***share capital***

capital structure ACCOUNTING relationship of equity capital and debt capital the relative proportions of ***equity capital*** and ***debt capital*** in a company's ***balance sheet***

capital sum INSURANCE lump sum from insurance an amount of money that an insurer pays as a ***lump sum*** on the death of an insured person or some other agreed occurrence

capital surplus STOCKHOLDING & INVESTMENTS difference between current and nominal value of stock the value of all of the stock in a company that exceeds the ***nominal value*** of the stock

capital tax TAX tax on firm's capital a tax levied on the capital owned by a company, rather than on its spending. *See also* ***capital gains tax***

capital-to-asset ratio *or* capital/asset ratio FINANCE = ***capital adequacy ratio***

capital to risk-weighted assets ratio FINANCE = ***capital adequacy ratio***

capital transaction FINANCE transaction bearing on non-current items a transaction affecting non-current items such as fixed assets, long-term debt, or share capital, rather than revenue transactions

capital transfer tax TAX former UK tax on asset transfers in the United Kingdom, a tax on the transfer of assets, which was replaced in 1986 by inheritance tax

capital turnover FINANCE annual sales in relation to stock value the value of annual sales as a multiple of the value of a company's stock

capital widening ECONOMICS increase in country's capital per person employed the process whereby capital is increased as a result of an increase in the number of people being employed

CAPM *abbr* **1.** OPERATIONS & PRODUCTION ***computer-aided production management*** **2.** STOCKHOLDING & INVESTMENTS ***capital asset pricing model***

capped floating rate note FINANCE floating rate note with limited interest rate a ***floating-rate note*** that has an agreed maximum rate of interest

capped rate FINANCE variable interest rate with upper limit an interest rate on a loan that may change, but cannot be greater than an amount fixed at the time when the loan is taken out by a borrower

captive finance company FINANCE provider of credit for customers of parent company an organization that provides credit and is owned or controlled by a commercial or manufacturing company, for example, a retailer that owns its store card operation or a car manufacturer that owns a company for financing the vehicles it produces

captive insurance company INSURANCE provider of insurance for customers of parent company an insurance company that has been established by a parent company to underwrite all its insurance risks and those of its subsidiaries. The benefit is that the premiums paid do not leave the organization. Many captive insurance companies are established offshore for tax purposes.

captive market MARKETS market with one supplier operating monopoly a market in which one supplier has a monopoly and the buyer has no choice over the product that he or she must purchase

capture E-COMMERCE transfer of funds in credit card transaction the submission of a credit card transaction for processing and settlement. Capture initiates the process of moving funds from the ***issuer*** to the ***acquirer***.

CAR *abbr* FINANCE ***capital adequacy ratio***

cardholder BANKING named user of credit card an individual or company that has an active credit card account with an ***issuer*** with which transactions can be initiated

card-issuing bank BANKING = ***issuer***

card-not-present merchant account E-COMMERCE account permitting online processing of credit card transactions an account that permits e-merchants to process credit card transactions without the purchaser being physically present for the transaction

cards get your cards *UK* HR & PERSONNEL (informal) = ***get your pink slip***

careline MARKETING customer assistance telephone service a telephone service allowing customers to obtain information, advice, or assistance from retailers

caring economy ECONOMICS friendly relationships between firms and individuals an economy based on amicable and helpful relationships between businesses and people

carriage free *UK* OPERATIONS & PRODUCTION sent without charge to customer sent without making a charge to the customer for shipping

carriage inward OPERATIONS & PRODUCTION cost of having purchase delivered delivery expenses incurred through the purchase of goods. These may be separately itemized in financial statements.

carriage outward OPERATIONS & PRODUCTION cost of delivering purchase delivery expenses incurred through the sale of goods. These may be separately itemized in financial statements.

carriage paid UK OPERATIONS & PRODUCTION with shipping charge paid by seller sent by a seller who has paid for the shipping

carried interest FINANCE profit paid to private equity partners the profit that partners in a private equity enterprise receive for the services they provide

carrier OPERATIONS & PRODUCTION provider of network services to customers a telecommunications company that provides network infrastructure services and charges customers for carrying their communications over the network. Carriers do not necessarily own their own network, but may rent time on a number of networks.

carry FINANCE = ***carrying charge***

carry forward ACCOUNTING use as opening balance for next accounting period to use an account balance at the end of the current period or page as the starting point for the next period or page

carrying amount STOCKHOLDING & INVESTMENTS = ***book value*** *(sense 2)*

carrying charge FINANCE interest paid on money borrowed the interest expense on money borrowed to finance a purchase. *Also called* ***carry***

carrying cost OPERATIONS & PRODUCTION cost of temporarily holding stock any expense associated with holding stock for a given period, for example, from the time of delivery to the time of dispatch. Carrying costs will include storage and insurance.

carrying value STOCKHOLDING & INVESTMENTS = ***book value*** *(sense 2)*

carryover STOCKHOLDING & INVESTMENTS amount of commodity at beginning of fiscal year the amount of a commodity that is being held at the beginning of a new fiscal year, to be added to the next year's supply. The amount of carryover may have an impact on price.

carryover day MARKETS new account's first day on London Stock Exchange the first day of trading on a new account on the London Stock Exchange

carry trade MARKETS, CURRENCY & EXCHANGE borrowings in one currency purchasing assets in another the practice of borrowing at low interest rates in one currency and using the loan to buy assets offering higher yields in another country

cartel BUSINESS association to regulate competition an alliance of business companies formed to control production, competition, and prices

cartogram STATISTICS map showing statistical data a diagrammatic map on which statistical information is represented by shading and symbols

carve-out STOCKHOLDING & INVESTMENTS = ***equity carve-out***

cash BANKING **1.** exchange check for cash to present a check and receive banknotes and coins in return **2.** banknotes and coins money in the form of banknotes and coins that are legal tender. This includes cash in hand, deposits repayable on demand with any bank or other financial institution, and deposits denominated in foreign currencies.

cash account **1.** ACCOUNTING record of money transactions a record of receipts and payments of cash, checks, or other forms of money transfer **2.** STOCKHOLDING & INVESTMENTS type of brokerage account an account with a broker that does not allow ***buying on margin***

cash accounting **1.** ACCOUNTING recording money transactions as they occur an accounting method in which receipts and expenses are recorded in the period when they actually occur. *See also* ***accrual basis*** **2.** TAX UK system giving automatic VAT relief on debts in the United Kingdom, a system for ***value-added tax*** that enables the taxpayer to account for tax paid and received during a given period, thus allowing automatic relief for bad debts

cash advance BANKING **1.** loan of cash against future payment a loan given in cash as early part payment of a larger sum to be received in the future **2.** loan on credit card a sum of money taken as a loan on a credit card account

cash at bank BANKING money in bank accounts the total amount of money held at the bank by a person or company

cash available to invest STOCKHOLDING & INVESTMENTS total amount available for investment with broker the amount, including cash on account and balances due soon for outstanding transactions, that a client has available for investment with a broker

cashback FINANCE **1.** giving purchaser cash refund a sales promotion technique offering customers a cash refund after they buy a product **2.** service allowing debit card payment to include cash a facility that allows consumers who pay for items by debit card in a supermarket or some other stores to add a small amount of money to the amount of their purchase and receive that amount in cash

cash balance ACCOUNTING account balance representing held cash only an account balance that represents cash alone, as distinct from an account balance that includes money owed but as yet unpaid

cash basis ACCOUNTING recording money in account only for actual transactions the bookkeeping practice of accounting for money only when it is actually received or spent

cash bonus STOCKHOLDING & INVESTMENTS extra dividend payment an unscheduled dividend that a company declares because of unexpected income

cashbook ACCOUNTING account book for cash transactions a book in which all cash payments and receipts are recorded. In a double-entry bookkeeping system, the balance at the end of a given period is included in the trial balance and then transferred to the balance sheet itself.

cash budget TREASURY MANAGEMENT estimate of cash transactions a detailed budget of estimated cash inflows and outflows incorporating both revenue and capital items. *Also called* ***cash flow projection***

cash burn FINANCE = ***burn rate***

cash card UK BANKING = ***ATM card***

cash contract OPERATIONS & PRODUCTION contract for delivery of product a contract for actual delivery of a commodity, by which the seller receives the ***spot price*** on the day of delivery

cash conversion cycle ACCOUNTING period between buying materials and selling product the time between the acquisition of a raw material and the receipt of payment for the finished product. *Also called* ***cash cycle***

cash cow **1.** FINANCE mature product generating cash a product characterized by a high market share but low sales growth, whose function is seen as generating cash for use elsewhere within the organization **2.** MARKETING very profitable product requiring little investment a product that sells well and makes a substantial profit without requiring much advertising or investment (slang) **3.** GENERAL MANAGEMENT slow-growing firm with high market share in the ***Boston Box*** model, a business with a high market share with low growth rate, which could yield significant but short-term gain. *See also* ***Boston Box***

cash crop ECONOMICS plants grown in quantity and sold for cash a crop such as tobacco, that is typically sold for cash rather than used by the producer

cash cycle ACCOUNTING = ***cash conversion cycle***

cash deficiency agreement FINANCE agreement to supply cash shortfall a commitment to supply whatever additional cash is needed to complete the financing of a project

cash discount FINANCE discount for paying promptly or in cash a discount offered to a customer who pays for goods or services with cash, or who pays an invoice within a particular period

cash dispenser UK BANKING = ***ATM***

cash dividend STOCKHOLDING & INVESTMENTS dividend in cash not shares a share of a company's current earnings or accumulated profits distributed to stockholders in cash, not in the form of ***bonus shares***

cash economy ECONOMICS sector of economy avoiding tax an unofficial or illegal part of the economy, where goods and services are paid for in cash, and therefore not declared for tax

cash equivalents STOCKHOLDING & INVESTMENTS investments convertible into cash immediately short-term investments that can be converted into cash immediately and that are subject to only a limited risk. There is usually a limit on their duration, for example, three months.

cash float FINANCE banknotes and coins for giving change banknotes and coins held by a retailer for the purpose of supplying customers with change

cash flow ACCOUNTING money from sales the movement through an organization of money that is generated by its own operations, as opposed to borrowing. It is the money that a business actually receives from sales (the cash inflow) and the money that it pays out (the cash outflow).

cash flow accounting ACCOUNTING accounting that considers only cash receipts and payments the practice of measuring the financial activities of a company in terms of cash receipts and payments, without recording ***accruals***, advance payments, debtors, creditors, and stocks

cash flow coverage ratio ACCOUNTING ratio of cash received and required the ratio of income to outstanding obligations which must be paid in cash

cash flow forecast TREASURY MANAGEMENT estimate of money coming in and going out a prediction of the amount of money that will move through an organization. This is an important tool for monitoring its solvency. *See also* ***cash budget***

cash flow life HR & PERSONNEL lifestyle dependent on income from project fees a lifestyle characterized by working for individual project fees rather than a regular salary

cash flow per common share STOCKHOLDING & INVESTMENTS cash generated for each share of common stock the amount of cash that a company derives from its activities, less any dividends paid, for each share of its common stock

cash flow projection TREASURY MANAGEMENT = ***cash budget***

cash flow risk RISK danger of receiving less cash than required the risk that a company's available cash will not be sufficient to meet its financial obligations

cash flow statement ACCOUNTING account of cash transactions a record of a company's cash inflows and cash outflows over a specific period of time, typically a year.

It reports funds on hand at the beginning of the period, funds received, funds spent, and funds remaining at the end of the period. Cash flows are divided into three categories: cash from operations; cash investment activities; and cash-financing activities. Companies with holdings in foreign currencies use a fourth classification: effects of changes in currency rates on cash.

cash fraction STOCKHOLDING & INVESTMENTS cash sum for allocation of part of share a small amount of cash paid to a stockholder to make up the full amount of part of a share which has been allocated in a ***stock split***

cash-generating unit FINANCE smallest set of assets involved in cash transactions the smallest identifiable group of assets generating cash inflows and outflows that can be measured

cash hoard FINANCE, MERGERS & ACQUISITIONS (informal) = ***cash reserves***

cashier *UK* BANKING = ***teller***

cashier's check BANKING check drawn by bank on itself a bank's own check, drawn on itself and signed by the cashier or other bank official

cash in STOCKHOLDING & INVESTMENTS sell investments for cash to sell stock or other property for cash

cash in hand FINANCE, ACCOUNTING available money money that is held in coins and banknotes, not in a bank account

cash ISA STOCKHOLDING & INVESTMENTS UK tax-free account for savings in the United Kingdom, a savings account for which tax is not paid on interest earned. The maximum that can be invested per ***tax year*** is capped, at £5,640 for 2012–13. ***Stocks and shares ISAs*** are also available, instead of or alongside cash ISAs. *See also* ***stocks and shares ISA, ISA***

cashless pay HR & PERSONNEL payment directly into bank account the payment of a weekly or monthly wage through the electronic transfer of funds directly into the bank account of an employee

cashless society ECONOMICS community in which all payments are electronic a society in which all bills and debits are paid by electronic money media such as bank and credit cards, direct debits, and online payments

cash limit **1.** FINANCE fixed sum available to spend a fixed amount of money that can be spent during a specific period or on a specific project **2.** BANKING limit on single ATM withdrawal a maximum amount somebody can withdraw at one time from an ATM using an ATM card

cash loan company FINANCE S. African provider of unsecured short-term loans in South Africa, a ***microcredit*** business that provides short-term loans without collateral, usually at high interest rates

cash machine *UK* BANKING = ***ATM***

cash management OPERATIONS & PRODUCTION strategy for having cash available to produce income a strategy used by businesses to manage their cash flow in order to have more cash available for short-term investment. The strategy would include such things as accelerating cash receipts, prioritizing cash disbursements, and maintaining a cash balance to cover emergencies.

cash market MARKETS securities market based on immediate payment the market in ***gilt-edged securities*** where purchases are paid for almost as soon as they are made

cash offer FINANCE **1.** offer to buy firm for cash an offer to buy a company for cash rather than for stock **2.** offer of cash payment an offer to pay for something in cash

cash payments journal BANKING chronological record of payments from firm's bank account a chronological record of all the money paid out from a company's bank account

cashpoint *UK* BANKING = ***ATM***

cash position **1.** ACCOUNTING amount of cash currently available to firm a statement of the amount of cash that a company currently has available to spend **2.** STOCKHOLDING & INVESTMENTS holdings in short-term debt the extent to which a portfolio of assets includes short-term debt securities

cash price FINANCE **1.** better deal offered to customer paying cash a lower price or better terms that apply to a sale if the customer pays cash rather than using credit **2.** = ***spot price***

cash ratio FINANCE liquid assets divided by total liabilities the ratio of a company's liquid assets such as cash and securities divided by total liabilities. *Also called* ***liquidity ratio***

cash receipts journal BANKING chronological record of deposits into firm's bank account a chronological record of all the receipts that have been paid into a company's bank account

cash reserves FINANCE, MERGERS & ACQUISITIONS available cash a large amount of cash that a company holds in order to facilitate an expected project. Cash reserves are often attractive to a company looking to make an acquisition. *Also called* ***cash hoard***

cash sale FINANCE sale paid for in cash a sale in which payment is made immediately in cash rather than put on credit

cash settlement STOCKHOLDING & INVESTMENTS **1.** early payment on options contract an immediate payment on an options contract without waiting for expiration of the normal, usually five-day, settlement period **2.** paying for securities bought the completion of a transaction by paying for securities, rather than physical delivery of them

cash surrender value INSURANCE sum received on cancellation of insurance policy the amount of money that an insurance company will pay to terminate a policy at a specific time if the policy does not continue until its normal expiration date

cash transaction FINANCE dealing involving cash payment a transaction in which the method of payment is cash, as distinct from a transaction paid for by means of a transfer of a ***financial instrument***

cash voucher FINANCE document exchangeable for cash a piece of paper that can be exchanged for cash

casino bank BANKING bank taking large investment risks a bank that is regarded as pursuing an unreasonably high-risk investment strategy

casino banking BANKING high-risk investment practices by banks the activity of pursuing a high-risk investment strategy for profit rather than providing a balanced range of banking services

casino capitalism FINANCE high-risk financial dealings a global phenomenon of increased financial risk-taking and instability, as an outcome of financial markets becoming very large and introducing many new investment products, and financial institutions being self-regulated, among other factors

casual worker HR & PERSONNEL worker who is not regular employee somebody who provides labor or services under an irregular or informal working arrangement. A casual worker is usually considered as an independent contractor rather than as an employee. Consequently, there is no obligation on the part of an employer to provide work, and there is no obligation on the part of the casual worker to accept all offers of work made by an employer.

catastrophe bond STOCKHOLDING & INVESTMENTS bond with lower value in event of disaster a bond with a very high interest rate which may be worth less or give a lower rate of interest if a disaster occurs, whether it be natural or otherwise

catastrophe future STOCKHOLDING & INVESTMENTS, RISK futures contract covering insurance losses from catastrophes a futures contract used by insurers to hedge their risk for low-probability catastrophic losses due to natural causes

catastrophe swap STOCKHOLDING & INVESTMENTS, RISK option contract covering insurance losses from catastrophes an option contract in which an investor exchanges a fixed periodic payment for part of the difference between an insurance company's premiums and its losses caused by claims due to a catastrophe

catch-up contribution PENSIONS extra payment to US pension in the United States, an additional contribution that somebody over the age of 50 is allowed to contribute to a personal retirement plan such as a ***401(k) plan*** or an ***IRA***

category killer BUSINESS large business destroying competition a major organization that puts out of business smaller or more specialized companies in a given field by offering goods or services at a lower price, or by using its brand to attract more consumer interest (slang)

category management MARKETING product development involving both manufacturers and retailers the process of manufacturers and retailers working together to maximize profits and enhance customer value in any given product category. Category management has developed from ***brand management*** and the techniques of efficient consumer response, and is most prevalent in the fast moving consumer goods sector. It is founded on the assumption that consumer purchase decisions are made from a variety of products within a category and not merely by brand. It has gained in prominence, as it is believed to meet customer needs better than standard brand management. *Abbr* ***CM***

cats and dogs *US* STOCKHOLDING & INVESTMENTS stocks with doubtful origins speculative stocks with dubious sales histories (slang)

  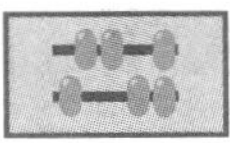    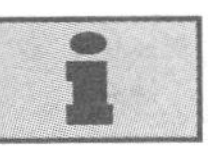  

cause and effect diagram GENERAL MANAGEMENT **1.** aid to identifying causes of variation a diagram that aids the generation and sorting of the potential causes of variation in an activity or process **2.** = ***fishbone chart***

caveat emptor BUSINESS buyer should check condition of goods purchased a Latin phrase meaning "let the buyer beware," which indicates that the buyer is responsible for checking that what he or she buys is in good condition

CBI *abbr* BUSINESS ***Confederation of British Industry***

CBO *abbr* STOCKHOLDING & INVESTMENTS, RISK ***collateralized bond obligation***

CC *abbr* BUSINESS ***close corporation*** *(sense 2)*

CCA *abbr* ACCOUNTING ***current cost accounting***

ccc *UK* FINANCE public limited company the Welsh term for a public limited company *Full form* ***cwmni cyfyngedig cyhoeddus***

CD *abbr* BANKING ***certificate of deposit***

CDO *abbr* STOCKHOLDING & INVESTMENTS ***collateralized debt obligation***

CDS *abbr* STOCKHOLDING & INVESTMENTS ***credit default swap***

CDSC *abbr* STOCKHOLDING & INVESTMENTS ***contingent deferred sales charge***

CEIC *abbr* BUSINESS ***closed-end investment company***

ceiling upper limit the highest point that something can reach, for example, the highest rate of a pay increase

ceiling effect STATISTICS when statistical data groups near upper limit in a statistical study, the occurrence of clusters of scores near the upper limit of the data

cellular organization GENERAL MANAGEMENT independently functioning members of single organization a form of organization consisting of a collection of self-managing firms or cells held together by mutual interest. A cellular organization is built on the principles of self-organization, member ownership, and entrepreneurship. Each cell within the organization shares common features and purposes with its sister cells but is also able to function independently.

center *US* ACCOUNTING chargeable unit of organization a department, area, or function to which costs and/or revenues are charged

central bank ECONOMICS, BANKING bank controlling country's monetary system a bank that controls the credit system and money supply of a country

central bank discount rate BANKING central bank's rate for discounting bills the rate at which a central bank discounts bills such as ***Treasury bills***

centralization FINANCE concentration of shared functions at main office the gathering together, at a corporate headquarters, of specialist functions such as finance, personnel, centralized purchasing, and information technology. Centralization is usually undertaken in order to effect economies of scale and to standardize operating procedures throughout the organization. Centralized management can become cumbersome and inefficient, and may produce communications problems. Some organizations have shifted toward ***decentralization*** to try to avoid this.

centralized purchasing OPERATIONS & PRODUCTION concentration of purchasing in single department the control by a central department of all the purchasing undertaken within an organization. In a large organization centralized purchasing is often located in the headquarters. Centralization has the advantages of reducing duplication of effort, pooling volume purchases for discounts, enabling more effective inventory control, consolidating transport loads to achieve lower costs, increasing skills development in purchasing personnel, and enhancing relationships with suppliers.

central planning ECONOMICS economy planned by government the use of an economic system in which the government plans all business activity, regulates supply, sets production targets, and itemizes work to be done

Central Provident Fund PENSIONS Singapore's retirement benefit plan in Singapore, a retirement benefit plan to which all employees and employers make compulsory contributions each month. *Abbr* ***CPF***

central purchasing OPERATIONS & PRODUCTION purchasing through firm's main office purchasing organized by a company's main office on behalf of all its departments or branches

Central Registration Depository STOCKHOLDING & INVESTMENTS US searchable database of investment advisers and brokers a computerized database of brokers, investment advisers, and brokerage firms that is maintained by the US Securities and Exchange Commission and is accessible to the public. *Abbr* ***CRD***

CEO *abbr* CORPORATE GOVERNANCE ***chief executive officer***

CEO churning GENERAL MANAGEMENT, HR & PERSONNEL speed at which chief executive officers lose jobs the rapid rate at which chief executive officers are often removed from their positions (slang)

certain annuity PENSIONS annuity payable for limited number of years an annuity that will be paid for a specific number of years only

certificate STOCKHOLDING & INVESTMENTS document of share ownership a document representing partial ownership of a company which states the number of shares that the document is worth and the names of the company and the owner of the shares

certificate authority E-COMMERCE organization verifying identities of parties in online transactions an independent organization that verifies the identity of a purchaser or merchant and issues a ***digital certificate*** attesting to this for use in e-commerce transactions

certificate of deposit BANKING document giving guaranteed interest rate for deposit a document from a bank showing that money has been deposited at a guaranteed interest rate for a specific period of time. *Abbr* ***CD***

certificate of incorporation LEGAL registration document of new company in UK in the United Kingdom, a written statement by the Registrar of Companies confirming that a new company has fulfilled the necessary legal requirements for incorporation and is now legally constituted

certificate of origin INTERNATIONAL TRADE document declaring origin of imported goods a document showing where imported goods come from or were made

certificate of tax deducted TAX UK statement of tax paid on interest in the United Kingdom, a document issued by a financial institution showing that tax has been deducted from interest payments on an account

certificate to commence business LEGAL authorizing document for UK public limited company in the United Kingdom, a written statement issued by the Registrar of Companies confirming that a public limited company has fulfilled the necessary legal requirements regarding its authorized minimum share capital

certified accountant ACCOUNTING UK accountant qualified by practical training in the United Kingdom, an accountant trained in industry, the public service, or in the offices of practicing accountants, who is a member of the ***Association of Chartered Certified Accountants***. Such an accountant fulfills much the same role as a ***chartered accountant*** and is qualified to audit company records. *Abbr* ***CA***

certified check BANKING check bank guarantees to pay a check that a bank guarantees is good and will be paid out of money put aside from the payer's bank account.

certified public accountant ACCOUNTING US professional licensed accountant in the United States, an accountant who has passed the exam administered by the American Institute of Certified Public Accountants and has met all other educational and experience requirements to be licensed by the state in which he or she practices. Certified public accountants fulfill much the same role as ***chartered accountants*** in the United Kingdom and are qualified to audit company records. *Abbr* ***CPA***

cessation LEGAL closing down of business the discontinuation of a business for tax purposes or of its trading on the stock market

ceteris paribus STATISTICS indicator of effect of one variable on another a Latin phrase meaning "all other things being equal", used to indicate that when considering the effect of one economic variable on another, all other factors that may affect the second variable remain constant

CFD *abbr* **1.** STOCKHOLDING & INVESTMENTS ***contract for difference*** *(sense 1)* **2.** CURRENCY & EXCHANGE ***contract for difference*** *(sense 2)*

CFO *abbr* TREASURY MANAGEMENT ***chief financial officer***

CFR *abbr* OPERATIONS & PRODUCTION ***cost and freight***

CFTC *abbr* REGULATION & COMPLIANCE ***Commodity Futures Trading Commission***

CGT *abbr* TAX ***capital gains tax***

CH *abbr* REGULATION & COMPLIANCE ***Companies House***

chain of command GENERAL MANAGEMENT hierarchical structure for passing down instructions the line of authority in a hierarchical organization through which instructions pass. The chain of command usually runs from the most senior personnel, through all reporting links in an organization's or department's structure, to a targeted person or to frontline employees. ***Line management*** relies on the chain of command in order for instructions to pass throughout an organization.

chair CORPORATE GOVERNANCE *see* ***chairman***

chairman CORPORATE GOVERNANCE organization's highest executive the most senior executive in an organization, responsible for running the ***annual meeting*** and meetings of the ***board of directors***. He or she may be a figurehead, appointed for prestige or power, and may have no role in the day-to-day running of the organization. Sometimes the roles of chairman and ***chief executive officer*** are combined, and the chairman then has more control over daily operations; sometimes the chairman is a retired chief executive. In the United States, the person who performs this function is often called a president. Historically, the term chairman was more common. The terms ***chairwoman*** and ***chairperson*** are later developments, although ***chair*** is now the most generally acceptable. Chairman, however, remains in common use, especially in the corporate sector.

chairman's report *or* chairman's statement CORPORATE GOVERNANCE chair's review of year's performance and prospects a statement included in the annual report of most large companies in which the chair of the board of directors gives an often favorable overview of the company's performance and prospects

chairperson CORPORATE GOVERNANCE *see* ***chairman***

chairwoman CORPORATE GOVERNANCE woman who is organization's highest executive a woman who is the most senior executive in an organization, responsible for running the ***annual meeting***, and meetings of the ***board of directors***. *See also* ***chairman***

chamber of commerce BUSINESS association of local businesspeople an organization of local businesspeople who work together to promote trade in their area and protect common interests

Chancellor of the Exchequer FINANCE UK's chief finance minister the United Kingdom's senior finance minister, based at ***HM Treasury*** in London. The office of Chancellor dates back to the 13th century. Some of the most famous names in British politics have served in this very senior government position, including William Gladstone and David Lloyd George.

change agent GENERAL MANAGEMENT administrator of major and minor changes in organization a person in an organization who is a leader in the process of change. *See also* ***change management***

change management GENERAL MANAGEMENT administration of major and minor changes in organization the coordination of a structured period of transition from situation A to situation B in order to achieve lasting change within an organization. Change management can be of varying scope, from ***continuous improvement***, which involves small ongoing changes to existing processes, to radical and substantial change involving organizational strategy. Change management can be reactive or proactive. It can be instigated in reaction to something in an organization's external environment, for example, in the realms of economics, politics, legislation, or competition, or in reaction to something within the processes, structures, people, and events of the organization's internal environment. It may also be instigated as a proactive measure, for example, in anticipation of unfavorable economic conditions in the future. Change management usually follows five steps: recognition of a trigger indicating that change is needed; clarification of the end point, or "where we want to be"; planning how to achieve the change; accomplishment of the transition; and maintenance to ensure the change is lasting. Effective change management involves alterations on a personal level, for example, a shift in attitudes or work routines, and thus personnel management skills such as motivation are vital to successful change. Other important influences on the success of change management include leadership style, communication, and a unified positive attitude to the change among the workforce. ***Business process reengineering*** is one type of change management, involving the redesign of processes within an organization to raise performance. With the accelerating pace of change in the business environment in the 1990s and 2000s, change has become accepted as a fact of business life and is the subject of books on management.

channel MARKETING way of selling products directly or through others a method of selling and distributing products to customers, directly or through intermediaries. Channels include direct sales, retail outlets, the Internet, and wholesalers.

channel communications MARKETING communications targeting customer sales organizations communications aimed at organizations that sell and distribute products to customers, for example, retailers, sales teams, or wholesalers

channel management MARKETING process of identifying, reaching, and satisfying customers the organization of the ways in which companies reach and satisfy their customers. Channel management involves more than just distribution, and has been described as management of how and where a product is used and of how the customer and the product interact. Channel management covers processes for identifying key customers, communicating with them, and continuing to create value after the first contact.

channel of distribution OPERATIONS & PRODUCTION = ***distribution channel***

channel strategy MARKETING plan for effectively getting products to customers a management technique for determining the most effective method of selling and distributing products to customers

channel stuffing FINANCE making special offers at end of fiscal year the artificial boosting of sales at the end of a fiscal year by offering distributors and dealers incentives to buy a greater quantity of goods than they actually need (slang)

channel support MARKETING marketing or financial support for customer sales organizations marketing or financial support aimed at improving the performance of organizations that sell and distribute products to customers, for example, retailers, sales teams, or wholesalers

chaos GENERAL MANAGEMENT situation in which change happens quickly and unexpectedly a situation of unpredictability and rapid change

chaos theory GENERAL MANAGEMENT belief in randomness of change the theory that behavior is essentially random. It emerged in the 1970s as a mathematical concept that defied the theory of cause and effect. Writers have applied the theory to management, arguing that attempts to plan and control management processes are fundamentally doomed to failure and that, instead, managers should embrace change and flexibility in order to cope with an environment that is altering at an ever-increasing rate.

CHAPS BANKING means of rapid electronic transfer of substantial funds Clearing House Automated Payment System: a method for the rapid electronic transfer of funds between participating banks on behalf of large commercial customers, where transfers tend to be of significant value. *Full form* ***Clearing House Automated Payment System***

Chapter 7 LEGAL part of US Bankruptcy Act regulating liquidation process a section of the US Bankruptcy Reform Act 1978, that sets out the rules for liquidation, a choice available to individuals, partnerships, and corporations

Chapter 11 LEGAL US act protecting potential bankrupts the US Bankruptcy Reform Act (1978) that entitles enterprises experiencing financial difficulties to apply for protection from creditors and thus have an opportunity to avoid bankruptcy

Chapter 11 bankruptcy FINANCE bankruptcy protected from creditors a bankruptcy declared under the US Bankruptcy Reform Act (1978) which entitles enterprises experiencing financial difficulties to apply for protection from creditors

charge LEGAL legal interest in land as surety to creditor a legal interest in land or real estate created in favor of a creditor to ensure that the amount owing is paid off

chargeable asset TAX type of asset liable to capital gains tax an asset that will produce a ***capital gain*** when sold. Assets that are not chargeable include family homes, cars, and some types of investments such as government stocks.

chargeable gain *UK* TAX = ***taxable gain***

chargeable transfer TAX gifts liable to UK inheritance tax in the United Kingdom, gifts that are liable to ***inheritance tax***

charge account FINANCE arrangement for customer to buy on credit a facility with a retailer that enables the customer to buy goods or services on credit rather than pay in cash. The customer may be required to settle the account within a month to avoid incurring interest on the credit. *Also called* ***credit account***

charge and discharge accounting ACCOUNTING former bookkeeping system formerly, a bookkeeping system in which a person charges himself or herself with receipts and credits himself or herself with payments. This system was used extensively before the advent of double-entry bookkeeping.

charge card FINANCE card used for buying store items on account a card issued to customers by a store, bank, or other organization, used to charge purchases to an account for later payment. *See also* ***credit card***

chargee FINANCE **1.** creditor with legal interest in land a person who holds a ***charge*** over a property, and who therefore has first claim on proceeds from the sale of the property **2.** person with enforcement rights a person who has the right to force a debtor to pay

charge off ACCOUNTING unrepeated expense or bad debt an uncollectable debt or a one-time expense that appears on a company's income statement

charitable contribution ACCOUNTING firm's gift to charity a donation by a company to a charity, deductible against tax

charity accounts ACCOUNTING records of charity's financial activities the accounting records of a charitable institution, which include a statement of financial activities rather than a profit and loss account. In the United Kingdom,

  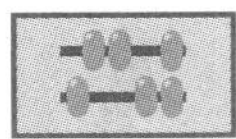   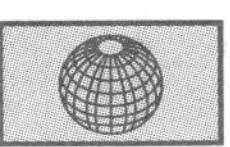 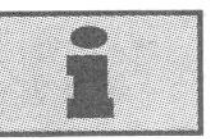  

the accounts should conform to the requirements stipulated in the Charities Act (1993).

charter LEGAL legal document creating US corporation in the United States, a legal document that creates a corporation and sets forth its purpose and structure according to the laws of the state in which it is established. *Also called* ***articles of incorporation***

chartered accountant ACCOUNTING UK accountant qualified by professional examination in the United Kingdom, a qualified professional accountant who is a member of an Institute of Chartered Accountants. Chartered accountants are qualified to audit company accounts and some hold management positions in companies. *Abbr* ***CA***

Chartered Association of Certified Accountants ACCOUNTING formerly, UK certified accountants' association the former name of the ***Association of Chartered Certified Accountants*** in the United Kingdom

chartered bank BANKING N. American bank established by government charter in the United States and Canada, a bank that has been set up by government charter

chartered company *or* chartered entity BUSINESS UK organization founded by royal charter in the United Kingdom, an organization formed by the grant of a royal charter. The charter authorizes the entity to operate and states the powers specifically granted.

Chartered Institute of Management Accountants ACCOUNTING *see* ***CIMA***

Chartered Institute of Public Finance and Accountancy ACCOUNTING *see* ***CIPFA***

Chartered Institute of Taxation TAX UK organization for tax professionals in the United Kingdom, an organization for professionals in the field of taxation

charter value BANKING worth of bank's capacity to continue operating the value of a bank being able to continue to do business in the future, reflected as part of its share price

charting MARKETS stock market analysis based on charts the use of charts to analyze stock market trends and to forecast future rises or falls

chartist MARKETS stock market analyst employing charts an analyst who studies past stock market trends, the movement of stock prices, and changes in the accounting ratios of individual companies. The chartist's philosophy is that history repeats itself: using charts and graphs, he or she uses past trends and repetitive patterns to forecast the future. Although the chartist approach is considered narrower than that of a traditional analyst, it nevertheless has a good following.

chase demand plan OPERATIONS & PRODUCTION plan for matching output to customer demand a production control plan that attempts to match capacity to the varying levels of forecast demand. Chase demand plans require flexible working practices and place varying demands on equipment requirements. Pure chase demand plans are difficult to achieve and are most commonly found in operations where output cannot be stored or where the organization is seeking to eliminate stores of finished goods.

chattel mortgage MORTGAGES money borrowed using personal items as security money that is borrowed using an item of personal property, not land or buildings, as collateral

cheap money FINANCE money lent at low interest money that is lent at low interest rates, used as a government strategy to stimulate an economy either at the initial signs of, or during, a recession. *Also called* ***easy money***. *See also* ***dear money, expansionary monetary policy***

check *US* BANKING written instruction to bank to pay money an order in writing requiring the banker to pay on demand a specific sum of money to a specified person or bearer. Although a check can theoretically be written on anything (in a P. G. Woodhouse story, one was written on the side of a cow), banks issue preprinted, customized forms for completion by an account holder who inserts the date, the name of the person to be paid (the payee), the amount in both words and figures, and his or her signature. The customer is the drawer. *UK term* ***cheque***

checkbook *US* BANKING book of blank cheques a booklet with new blank checks for a bank's customer to complete. *UK term* ***cheque book***

check card *US* BANKING = ***debit card***

check digit BANKING reference number for validating transactions the last digit of a string of computerized reference numbers, used to validate a transaction

checking account *US* BANKING flexible bank account with easy withdrawal a bank account in which deposits can be withdrawn at any time by writing checks but do not usually earn interest, except in the case of some online accounts. It is the most common type of bank account. *Abbr* **c/a**. UK term ***current account***

check register *US* BANKING record of check transactions a control record of checks issued or received, maintained by a person or organization. *UK term* ***cheque register***

check routing symbol BANKING number on US check identifying Federal Reserve district a number shown on a US check that identifies the Federal Reserve district through which the check will be cleared

check stub *US* BANKING part of check left in checkbook a piece of paper left in a checkbook after a check has been written and taken out. *UK term* ***cheque stub***

check to bearer *US* BANKING = ***bearer check***

cheque *UK* BANKING = ***check***

cheque book *UK* BANKING = ***checkbook***

cheque card BANKING UK card guaranteeing payment of check a plastic card from a UK bank that guarantees payment of a check up to some amount, even if the user has no money in his or her account

cheque register *UK* BANKING = ***check register***

cheque stub *UK* BANKING = ***check stub***

cheque to bearer *UK* BANKING = ***bearer check***

cherry picking GENERAL MANAGEMENT selecting the best of available options the selection of what is perceived to be the best or most valuable from a series of ideas or options

Chicago Mercantile Exchange MARKETS Chicago exchange trading in futures a leading exchange for futures contracts based in Chicago. Its main product areas are interest rates, stock indexes, foreign exchange, and commodities. *Abbr* ***CME***

Chicago School ECONOMICS school of conservative economic thought a school of conservative economic thought, promoting free markets and capitalism and relying heavily on mathematical analysis. It is associated with the University of Chicago and was for many years led by Professor Milton Friedman.

chief executive officer *or* chief executive CORPORATE GOVERNANCE executive ultimately responsible for firm's management the person with overall responsibility for ensuring that the daily operations of an organization run efficiently and for carrying out strategic plans. The chief executive of an organization normally sits on the ***board of directors***. In a limited company, he or she is usually known as a managing director. *Abbr* ***CEO***

chief financial officer TREASURY MANAGEMENT executive responsible for firm's financial management the officer in an organization responsible for handling funds, signing checks, the keeping of financial records, and financial planning for the company. *Abbr* ***CFO***

chief information officer GENERAL MANAGEMENT executive responsible for firm's internal information systems the officer in an organization responsible for its internal information systems and sometimes for its e-business infrastructure. *Abbr* ***CIO***

chief operating officer GENERAL MANAGEMENT executive responsible for firm's day-to-day operations the officer in a corporation responsible for its day-to-day management, usually reporting to the chief executive officer. *Abbr* ***COO***

Chief Secretary to the Treasury FINANCE UK government minister controlling public expenditure in the United Kingdom, a government minister responsible to the Chancellor of the Exchequer for the control of public expenditure

Chinese wall STOCKHOLDING & INVESTMENTS obstacle to exchange of inside information the procedures enforced within a securities firm to prevent the exchange of confidential information between the firm's departments so as to avoid the illegal use of inside information

CHIPS BANKING US international wire transfer system in the United States, the computerized domestic and international wire transfer system that also serves to convert all pending payments into a single transaction *Full form* ***Clearing House Interbank Payments System***

CHIS *abbr* FRAUD ***covert human intelligence source***

chit GENERAL MANAGEMENT **1.** official note an official note or document, usually signed by somebody in authority **2.** receipt a receipt for something or a statement of money owed

chose in action FINANCE personal right treated like property a personal right such as a patent, copyright, debt, or check that can be enforced or claimed as if it were property

chose in possession FINANCE object that can be owned a physical item such as a piece of furniture that can be owned

churn 1. STOCKHOLDING & INVESTMENTS encourage investor to change portfolio frequently to encourage an investor to change stock frequently because the broker is paid every time there is a change in the investor's portfolio (slang) **2.** INSURANCE encourage somebody to change insurance policy to encourage a client to change his or her insurance policy solely to earn the salesperson a commission **3.** GENERAL MANAGEMENT successive purchases of different brands of products to purchase a quick

  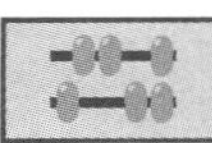      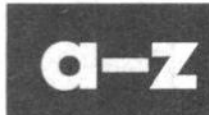

succession of products or services without displaying loyalty to any of them, often as a result of competitive marketing strategies that continually undercut rival prices, thus encouraging customers to switch brands constantly in order to take advantage of the cheapest or most attractive offers **4.** HR & PERSONNEL experience high employee turnover to suffer a high turnover rate of executives or other employees

churn rate **1.** STOCKHOLDING & INVESTMENTS measure of change in investment portfolio a measure of the frequency and volume of trading of stocks and bonds in a brokerage account **2.** GENERAL MANAGEMENT rate at which customers abandon new product the rate at which new customers try a product or service and then stop using it

CICA *abbr* ACCOUNTING ***Canadian Institute of Chartered Accountants***

CIF *abbr* OPERATIONS & PRODUCTION ***cost, insurance, and freight***

CIFAS *abbr* FRAUD ***Credit Industry Fraud Avoidance System***

CIMA ACCOUNTING UK institution awarding financial degree to businesspeople a UK organization that is internationally recognized as offering a financial degree for business, focusing on strategic business management. Founded in 1919 as the Institute of Cost and Works Accountants, it has offices worldwide, supporting over 128,000 members and students in 156 countries. *Full form* ***Chartered Institute of Management Accountants***

CIO *abbr* GENERAL MANAGEMENT ***chief information officer***

CIPFA ACCOUNTING UK professional accountancy organization in the United Kingdom, one of the leading professional accountancy bodies and the only one that specializes in the public services, for example, local government, public service bodies, and national audit agencies, as well as major accounting firms. It is responsible for the education and training of professional accountants and for their regulation through the setting and monitoring of professional standards. CIPFA also provides a variety of advisory, information, and consulting services to public service organizations. It is the leading independent commentator on managing accounting for public money. *Full form* ***Chartered Institute of Public Finance and Accountancy***

circuit breaker MARKETS US provision for stopping trading a rule created by the major US stock exchanges and the ***Securities and Exchange Commission*** by which trading is halted during times of extreme price fluctuations (slang)

circular file GENERAL MANAGEMENT office wastebasket a wastebasket in an office (slang)

circular flow of income ECONOMICS model of relationship between income and spending a model of a country's economy showing the flow of resources when consumers' wages and salaries are used to buy goods and so generate income for manufacturing firms

circularization of debtors ACCOUNTING auditors' approach to debtors to identify assets the sending of letters by a company's auditors to debtors in order to verify the existence and extent of the company's assets

circular letter of credit BANKING bank's authorization of payment to every branch a letter of credit sent to all branches of the bank which issues it

circular merger MERGERS & ACQUISITIONS joining of firms sharing distribution channels a merger involving firms that have different products but similar distribution channels. *See also* ***merger***

circulating capital FINANCE = ***working capital***

circulation MARKETING number of copies of newspaper or magazine sold the number of copies sold or distributed of a single issue of a newspaper or magazine

circulation of capital FINANCE transfer of capital between investments the movement of ***capital*** from one investment to another, or between one country and another

City *or* City of London FINANCE area of London containing UK financial center the United Kingdom's financial center found in the historic center of London, where most banks and many large companies have their main offices. *Also called* ***Square Mile***. *See also* ***Wall Street***

City bonus FINANCE annual financial reward for UK employee a very large sum of money, in addition to salary, paid to an employee in London's financial industry for effective performance in increasing his or her company's profits. *See also* ***Wall Street bonus***

City Code on Takeovers and Mergers MERGERS & ACQUISITIONS UK code for fairness in takeovers in the United Kingdom, a code issued on behalf of the ***City Panel on Takeovers and Mergers*** that is designed principally to ensure fair and equal treatment of all stockholders in relation to ***takeovers***. The Code also provides an orderly framework within which takeovers are conducted. It is not concerned with the financial or commercial advantages or disadvantages of a takeover, nor with issues such as competition policy which are the responsibility of the government. The Code represents the collective opinion of those professionally involved in the field of takeovers on how fairness to stockholders can be achieved in practice.

City Panel on Takeovers and Mergers MERGERS & ACQUISITIONS independent UK group supervising takeovers in the United Kingdom, an independent nonstatutory group whose job is to supervise and regulate ***takeovers*** according to the ***City Code on Takeovers and Mergers***. *Also called* ***Takeover Panel***

City watchdog REGULATION & COMPLIANCE (informal) = ***Financial Services Authority***

claim LEGAL statement of entitlement to money an official request for money, usually in the form of compensation, from a person or organization

claimant FINANCE somebody who makes benefit claim to government a person who claims a government benefit such as an unemployment or disability benefit

claim form INSURANCE form completed to make insurance claim a form that has to be filled in giving details of the reason for making an insurance claim

claims adjuster *US* INSURANCE assessor of insurance claims somebody who determines the value of a claim made under an insurance policy. *UK term* ***loss adjuster***

claims manager INSURANCE person responsible for insurance claims the person responsible for dealing with claims in an insurance company

class STOCKHOLDING & INVESTMENTS classification for common stock a type of common stock issued by a company, usually with the designations A and B, and conferring different voting rights

class action LEGAL joint civil law action a civil law action taken by a group of individuals who have a common grievance against an individual, organization, or legal entity

classical economics ECONOMICS economic theory stressing importance of free enterprise a theory focusing on the functioning of a market economy and providing a rudimentary explanation of consumer and producer behavior in particular markets. The theory postulates that, over time, the economy would tend to operate at full employment because increases in supply would create corresponding increases in demand.

classical system of corporation tax TAX system doubly taxing firm's income a system in which companies and their owners are liable for ***corporation tax*** as separate entities. A company's taxed income is therefore paid out to stockholders, who are in turn taxed again. This system operates in the United States and the Netherlands. It was replaced in the United Kingdom in 1973 by an ***imputation system***.

classified stock STOCKHOLDING & INVESTMENTS US firm's common stock divided into classes in the United States, a company's ***common stock*** divided into classes such as Class A and Class B

class interval STATISTICS division of statistical frequency distribution in a set of statistical observations, any of the intervals of the frequency distribution

class of assets ACCOUNTING categorization of assets the grouping of similar assets into categories. This is done because, under International Accounting Standards Committee rules, ***tangible assets*** and ***intangible assets*** cannot be revalued on an individual basis, only within a class of assets.

claw back FINANCE take back money previously allocated to recover money that has already been assigned to a specific use, especially money given in grants or tax incentives

clawback **1.** FINANCE money reclaimed money taken back, especially money taken back by the government from grants or tax incentives which had previously been made **2.** MARKETS allocation of new stock to existing stockholders the allocation of new shares of stock to existing stockholders, so as to maintain the value of their holdings

clean float CURRENCY & EXCHANGE exchange rate unrestricted by government a ***floating exchange rate*** that is allowed to vary without any intervention from the country's monetary authorities

clean opinion *or* clean report ACCOUNTING auditor's report without reservations an auditor's report that is not qualified because of concern about the scope or treatment of some matter

clean price MARKETS bond price not including interest the price of a bond excluding accrued interest

clean surplus concept FINANCE advocating statements showing all gains and losses the idea that a company's income statement should show

  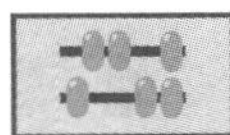      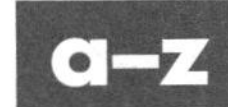

the totality of gains and losses, without any of them being taken directly to equity

clear OPERATIONS & PRODUCTION sell cheaply to get rid of merchandise to sell goods at a discounted price in order to dispose of inventory

clearance certificate INTERNATIONAL TRADE document giving goods customs clearance a document showing that goods have been passed by customs

clearing **1.** BANKING process of passing check through banking system an act of passing of a check through the banking system, including the transfer of money from one account to another **2.** MARKETS completion of transactions and payments the process of verifying and settling orders between buyers and sellers in securities transactions

clearing bank BANKING in UK, bank employing clearing house in the United Kingdom, a bank that deals with other banks through a ***clearing house***

clearing house *or* clearing firm *or* clearing corporation **1.** BANKING institution handling bank transactions an institution that settles accounts between banks, using the ***clearing system*** **2.** MARKETS institution handling securities transactions an organization that coordinates the confirmation, delivery, and settlement of securities transactions on behalf of exchanges **3.** BANKING, E-COMMERCE = ***acquirer*** *(sense 2)*

Clearing House Automated Payment System BANKING *see* ***CHAPS***

Clearing House Interbank Payments System BANKING *see* ***CHIPS***

clearing system BANKING system for handling bank transactions the system of settling accounts among banks through ***clearing houses***. It allows member banks to offset claims against each other.

Clearnet MARKETS French clearing house ***clearing house*** based in Paris, France, established as the Banque Centrale de Compensation in 1969 to clear commodities contracts. It added other clearing services and operations in other European countries, before merging with the ***London Clearing House*** in 2003 to form ***LCH.Clearnet***. *Also called* ***Banque Centrale de Compensation***

clear profit FINANCE profit after paying expenses the profit remaining after all expenses have been paid

clear title LEGAL = ***good title***

clerical error mistake in preparing documents a mistake made in the preparation of documents such as reports or financial accounts

clickable corporation E-COMMERCE firm operating online a company that operates on the Internet. The term was popularized by a 1999 book by Jonathan Rosenoer, Douglas Armstrong, and J. Russell Gates.

click rate E-COMMERCE = ***click-through rate***

clicks-and-bricks *or* clicks-and-mortar E-COMMERCE organization with physical facility that also operates online combining a traditional ***bricks-and-mortar*** organization with the click technology of the Internet. Such an organization has both a virtual and a physical presence. Examples include retailers with physical stores and also websites where their goods can be bought online.

clickstream E-COMMERCE record of activity left by user surfing Web the virtual trail that a user leaves behind while surfing the Internet. A clickstream is a record of a user's activity on the Internet, including every Web page visited, how long each page is visited for, and the order in which the pages are visited. Both Internet service providers and individual websites are able to track an Internet user's clickstream.

click-through rate E-COMMERCE using click-throughs as measure of success of ad the percentage of viewings of an advertisement that result in a click on an on-screen device to take the user to the advertiser's website, which is a measure of the success of the advertisement. *Also called* ***ad click rate, click rate***

click wrap agreement *or* click wrap license E-COMMERCE contract agreed to online a contract presented entirely over the Internet, the purchaser indicating assent to be bound by the terms of the contract by clicking on an "I agree" button. The term stems from "shrink wrap" agreements, licenses that become enforceable when the user removes designated packaging containing a copy of the agreement. *Also called* ***point and click agreement***

client MARKETING **1.** somebody hiring professional services a person or organization that employs the services of a professional person or organization **2.** customer a person or organization to whom goods or services are provided or sold

client base MARKETING professional's steady clients the group of regular clients of a professional person or organization

clientele effect STOCKHOLDING & INVESTMENTS influence of investors on choice of securities the preference of an investor or group of investors for buying a particular type of security

Clintonomics ECONOMICS Clinton's policy of economic intervention the policy of former US President Clinton's Council of Economic Advisers to intervene in the economy to correct market failures and redistribute income

CLO *abbr* STOCKHOLDING & INVESTMENTS ***collateralized loan obligation***

CLOB International MARKETS Singaporean facility for trading in foreign stocks in Singapore, a mechanism for buying and selling foreign stocks, especially Malaysian stocks

clone fund STOCKHOLDING & INVESTMENTS mutual fund matching established fund by using derivatives a mutual fund that, by the use of derivatives, is able to duplicate the strategy and performance of a successful established mutual fund

close **1.** MARKETS end of stock trading for day the end of a day's trading on a stock exchange **2.** MARKETS have a particular price at end of trading of a stock, to end the day's trading at a particular price **3.** *US* REAL ESTATE pay balance on real estate to pay off the balance owed on real estate in exchange for a deed showing ownership of the real estate. *UK term* ***complete*** **close a position** MARKETS to arrange affairs so that there is no longer any liability to pay, for example, by selling all securities held **close the accounts** FINANCE to come to the end of an accounting period and make up the profit and loss account

close company *or* closed company *UK* BUSINESS = ***close corporation*** *(sense 1)*

close corporation *or* closed corporation BUSINESS **1.** *US* public corporation controlled by few shareholders a public corporation in which all of the voting stock is held by a few stockholders, for example, management or family members. Although it is a public company, stock would not normally be available for trading because of a lack of liquidity. *UK term* ***close company*** **2.** S. African business controlled by 10 or fewer in South Africa, a business registered in terms of the Close Corporations Act of 1984, consisting of not more than 10 members who share its ownership and management. *Abbr* ***CC***

closed economy ECONOMICS economic system isolated from international trade an economic system in which little or no external trade takes place

closed-end credit FINANCE credit with fixed date for full repayment a loan, plus any interest and finance charges, that is to be repaid in full by a specific future date. Loans that have real estate or motor vehicles as collateral are usually closed-end. *See also* ***open-end credit***

closed-end fund *or* closed-end investment company STOCKHOLDING & INVESTMENTS investment company with fixed number of shares an investment company such as an investment trust that has a fixed number of shares that can be bought and sold in the marketplace. *See also* ***open-end fund***

closed-end mortgage MORTGAGES mortgage that cannot be paid off early a mortgage with an ***indenture*** disallowing repayment before it comes to maturity. *See also* ***open-end mortgage***. *Also called* ***closed mortgage***

closed fund STOCKHOLDING & INVESTMENTS mutual fund in US closed to new investors in the United States, a mutual fund that is no longer accepting new investors, because it has become too large

closed-loop production system OPERATIONS & PRODUCTION system of recycling industrial output into new product an environmentally friendly production system in which any industrial output is capable of being recycled to create another product

closed-loop system GENERAL MANAGEMENT management control system allowing correction a management control system which includes a provision for corrective action, taken on either a feed forward or a feedback basis

closed market OPERATIONS & PRODUCTION market with supplier dealing exclusively with agent or distributor a market in which a supplier deals only with one agent or distributor and does not supply any others direct

closed mortgage MORTGAGES = ***closed-end mortgage***

closely held corporation BUSINESS US public company with few stockholders in the United States, a company whose stock is publicly traded but held by very few people

closely held shares STOCKHOLDING & INVESTMENTS publicly traded US stock with few holders in the United States, stock that is publicly traded but held by very few people

Closer Economic Relations agreement INTERNATIONAL TRADE = ***Australia and New Zealand Closer Economic Relations Trade Agreement***

closing *US* REAL ESTATE act of transferring ownership in real estate the point at which a buyer pays off the balance owed on real estate in

  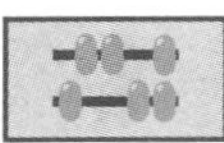      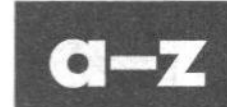

exchange for a deed showing ownership of the real estate. *UK term* ***completion***

closing balance 1. ACCOUNTING amount carried forward to next accounting period the difference between credits and debits in a ledger at the end of one accounting period that is carried forward to the next 2. BANKING bank balance at end of business day the amount in credit or debit in a bank account at the end of a business day

closing bell MARKETS end of period of trading the end of a trading session at a stock or commodities exchange when a bell is rung

closing costs REAL ESTATE expenses of transferring real estate ownership the charges and fees paid by buyers and sellers in a real estate or mortgage transaction at the time of closing

closing-down sale OPERATIONS & PRODUCTION sale of goods by store closing down a sale of goods that follows a store's decision to cease trading

closing entries ACCOUNTING entries at very end of accounting period in a double-entry bookkeeping system, entries made at the very end of an ***accounting period*** to balance the expense and revenue ledgers

closing out 1. MARKETS sale of commodity that ends futures contract the ending of a ***futures contract*** by the sale of the relevant commodity 2. OPERATIONS & PRODUCTION sale of goods cheaply to offload them the act of selling goods cheaply to try to get rid of them, usually because they have not been selling well or because the seller is going out of business

closing price MARKETS last price paid during trading session the price of the last transaction for a specific security or commodity at the end of a trading session

closing quote MARKETS last price bid or offered during trading session the last bid and offer prices for a specific security or commodity recorded at the close of a trading session

closing rate CURRENCY & EXCHANGE exchange rate at end of accounting period the exchange rate of two or more currencies at the close of business at the end of an accounting period, for example, at the end of the fiscal year

closing rate method CURRENCY & EXCHANGE currency conversion method in accounts a technique for translating the figures from a set of financial statements into a different currency using the ***closing rate***. This method is often used for the accounts of a foreign subsidiary of a parent company.

closing sale FINANCE sale that reduces seller's risk a sale that reduces the risk that the seller has through holding a greater number of shares or a longer term contract

closing statement REAL ESTATE statement of expenses of transferring real estate ownership a statement of all charges and fees paid by buyers and sellers in a real estate or mortgage transaction at the time of closing

closing stock ACCOUNTING inventory at end of accounting period a business's remaining stock at the end of an ***accounting period***. It includes finished products, raw materials, or work in progress and is deducted from the period's costs in the balance sheets.

cluster analysis STATISTICS statistical analysis using groupings that share characteristics a statistical method used to analyze complex data and identify groupings that share common features. Cluster analysis is a form of ***multivariate analysis*** that attempts to explain variability in a set of data. It involves finding unifying elements that enable identification of groups or clusters displaying common characteristics. It could be used, for example, to analyze results of market research and delineate groups of respondents that share specific attitudes.

clustered data STATISTICS statistical information grouped according to shared features data in which sampling units in a study are grouped into clusters sharing a common feature, or longitudinal data in which clusters are defined by repeated measures on the unit

cluster sampling STATISTICS *see* ***random sampling***

CM *abbr* GENERAL MANAGEMENT ***category management***

CMBS *abbr* STOCKHOLDING & INVESTMENTS, MORTGAGES ***commercial mortgage-backed securities***

CME *abbr* MARKETS ***Chicago Mercantile Exchange***

CMF *abbr* MARKETS *see* ***Autorité des Marchés Financiers***

CML *abbr* MORTGAGES ***Council of Mortgage Lenders***

CMO *abbr* MORTGAGES ***collateralized mortgage obligation***

CN *or* **C/N** *abbr* FINANCE ***credit note***

CNCC *abbr* REGULATION & COMPLIANCE ***Compagnie Nationale des Commissaires aux Comptes***

CNS *abbr* MARKETS ***continuous net settlement***

COB *abbr* MARKETS *see* ***Autorité des Marchés Financiers***

co-branding MARKETING, E-COMMERCE display of multiple logos to suggest joint venture the display of two or more corporate logos on a product or website in order to give the impression that the product or site is a joint enterprise

CoCo *or* **COCO** REGULATION & COMPLIANCE Canadian framework for internal regulation a system for evaluating the internal controls over financial reporting. The Criteria of Control Board (CoCo) is charged by the Board of Governors of the Canadian Institute of Chartered Accountants with issuing guidance on designing, assessing, and reporting on the control systems of organizations.

co-creditor FINANCE one of several people to whom firm owes money one of two or more people or organizations that are owed money by the same company

code of conduct GENERAL MANAGEMENT standard of ethical and social behavior and responsibility a statement and description of required behaviors, responsibilities, and actions expected of employees of an organization or of members of a professional body. A code of conduct usually focuses on ethical and socially responsible issues and applies to individuals, providing guidance on how to act in cases of doubt or confusion.

code of practice GENERAL MANAGEMENT statement of preferred organizational procedures a policy statement and description of preferred methods for organizational procedures.

Codes of practice may govern procedures for industrial relations, health and safety, and, more recently, customer service and professional development. An agreed code of practice enables activities to be carried out to a required organizational standard and provides a basis for dispute resolution.

co-director CORPORATE GOVERNANCE person involved in controlling firm one of two or more people who direct the same company

coefficient of variation STATISTICS measure of dispersion of statistical information a measure of the spread of a set of statistical data, such as a set of investment returns, calculated as the mean or standard deviation of the data multiplied by 100

co-financing FINANCE joint provision of finance the provision of money for a project jointly by two or more parties

COGS *abbr* OPERATIONS & PRODUCTION ***cost of goods sold***

cohesion fund FINANCE EU fund to equalize members' economies in the European Union, the main financial instrument for reducing economic and social disparities within by providing financial help for projects in the fields of the environment and transport infrastructure

cohort STATISTICS group of study participants with shared characteristic a group of individuals in a statistical study who have a common characteristic such as age or income

cohort study STATISTICS long-term study of people with shared characteristic a study in which a group of individuals who have a common characteristic such as age or income are observed over several years

coincident indicator ECONOMICS indicator of current economic activity a factor that provides information on economic activity taking place at the current time

COLA *abbr* FINANCE ***cost-of-living adjustment***

cold call MARKETING call strangers to sell something to make unsolicited calls to customers or consumers in an attempt to sell products or services. Cold calling is disliked, particularly by individual consumers, and is an inefficient way of selling, as the take-up rate is very low. *Also called* ***dial and smile***

cold start OPERATIONS & PRODUCTION new operation unsupported by previous turnover the act of beginning a new business or opening a new store with no previous turnover to base it on

Collaborative Planning, Forecasting, and Replenishment OPERATIONS & PRODUCTION *see* ***CPFR®***

collar STOCKHOLDING & INVESTMENTS, RISK preset limit a contractually imposed lower limit on a ***financial instrument***

collateral FINANCE resources providing security against loan property or goods used as security against a loan and forfeited to the lender if the borrower defaults

collateralize FINANCE provide loan with security to secure a loan by pledging assets. If the borrower defaults on loan payments, the pledged assets can be taken by the lender. —***collateralization***

collateralized bond obligation STOCKHOLDING & INVESTMENTS, RISK investment grade pool of bonds carrying risk an ***investment grade asset-backed security*** that consists of a portfolio of bonds, some of which may carry high risk. Pooling bonds with different degrees of risk is thought to

     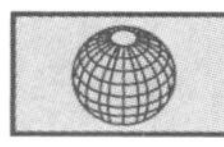   

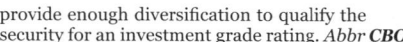

provide enough diversification to qualify the security for an investment grade rating. *Abbr* ***CBO***

collateralized debt obligation STOCKHOLDING & INVESTMENTS investment combining bonds and loans a complex investment vehicle based on a portfolio of bonds and loans, which may include assets with an underlying risk. *Abbr* ***CDO***. Also called ***debt obligation***

collateralized loan obligation STOCKHOLDING & INVESTMENTS asset-backed security formed when loan is repackaged an asset-backed security that is created by repackaging loans, usually commercial loans made by a bank, at an attractive rate of interest. *Abbr* ***CLO***

collateralized mortgage obligation STOCKHOLDING & INVESTMENTS, MORTGAGES instrument with mortgages on property a financial instrument that has mortgages on property given as security in case of default. CMOs are issued against the collective value of pooled mortgages, offering interest payments based on the overall cash flow. *Abbr* ***CMO***

collateral trust certificate STOCKHOLDING & INVESTMENTS bond with stock in another firm as security a bond for which stock in another company, usually a subsidiary, is used as collateral

collecting bank BANKING bank receiving check for processing a bank into which a person has deposited a check, and which has the duty to collect the money from the account of the writer of the check

collection FINANCE collecting payments on unpaid debts the process of collecting payments on unpaid loans or bills

collection agency FINANCE business collecting outstanding payments a business that collects payments on unpaid loans or on bills

collection ratio ACCOUNTING average time for invoice to be paid the average number of days it takes a firm to convert its accounts receivable into cash.

Ideally, this period should be decreasing or constant. A low figure means the company collects its outstanding receivables quickly. Collection ratios are usually reviewed quarterly or yearly.

Calculating the collection ratio requires three figures: total accounts receivable, total credit sales for the period analyzed, and the number of days in the period (annual, 365; six months, 182; quarter, 91). The formula is:

$$\frac{\text{(Accounts receivable}}{\text{(Total credit sales for the period)}} \times \text{Number of days in the period}$$

For example: if total receivables are $4,500,000, total credit sales in a quarter are $9,000,000, and number of days is 91, then:

$$\frac{(4,500,000}{9,000,000)} \times 91 = 45.5$$

Thus, it takes an average of 45.5 days to collect receivables.

Properly evaluating a collection ratio requires a standard for comparison. A traditional rule of thumb is that it should not exceed a third to a half of selling terms. For instance, if terms are 30 days, an acceptable collection ratio would be 40 to 45 days.

Companies use collection ratio information with an ***accounts receivable aging*** report. This lists aged categories of receivables, for example, 0–30 days, 30–60 days, 60–90 days, and over 90 days. The report also shows the percentage of total accounts receivable that each group represents, allowing for an analysis of delinquencies and potential bad debts. *Also called* ***days' sales outstanding***

collusive tendering FINANCE when job offerers share inside information the illegal practice among companies making offers for a job of sharing privileged information between themselves, with the objective of fixing the end result

colocation E-COMMERCE sharing of hosting center with other Internet clients the sharing of the facilities of a hosting center with other Internet clients

combination annuity INSURANCE = ***hybrid annuity***

combination bond STOCKHOLDING & INVESTMENTS bond secured by project's revenue and government credit a government bond for which the collateral is both revenue from the financed project and the government's credit

combined financial statement FINANCE summary of financial position of related firms a written record covering the assets, liabilities, net worth, and operating statement of two or more related or affiliated companies

COMEX *abbr* MARKETS ***commodity exchange***

comfort letter 1. FINANCE parent company's support for subsidiary's loan a letter from the parent company of a subsidiary that is applying for a loan, stating the intention that the subsidiary should remain in business **2.** ACCOUNTING in US, endorsement of financial statement in the United States, a statement from an accounting firm provided to a company preparing for a public offering, which confirms that the unaudited financial information in the ***prospectus*** follows ***Generally Accepted Accounting Principles***

command economy ECONOMICS economic system controlled by government an economy in which all economic activity is regulated by the government, as formerly in China or the Soviet Union

commerce FINANCE trading on large scale the large-scale buying and selling of goods and services, usually applied to trading between different states or countries

commerce integration FINANCE marrying of old and new ways of trading the blending of Internet-based commerce capabilities with the ***legacy systems*** of a traditional business to create a seamless transparent process

commerce server E-COMMERCE **1.** computer storing e-commerce data for website a computer in a network that maintains all transactional and back-end data for an e-commerce website **2.** computer containing programs for processing online transactions a networked computer that contains the programs required to process transactions via the Internet, including dynamic inventory databases, shopping cart software, and online payment systems

commerce service provider E-COMMERCE organization providing service to firm involved in e-commerce an organization or company that provides a service to a company to facilitate some aspect of electronic commerce, for example, by functioning as an Internet ***payment gateway***. *Abbr* ***CSP***

commercial FINANCE of trading relating to the buying and selling of goods and services

commercial bank BANKING privately owned bank offering range of facilities a bank that provides financial services such as checking and savings accounts and loans to individuals and businesses. *See also* ***investment bank***

commercial bill FINANCE bill of exchange not issued by government a ***bill of exchange*** issued by a company (a ***trade bill***) or accepted by a bank (a ***banker's bill***), as opposed to a ***Treasury bill***, which is issued by a government

commercial directory BUSINESS book listing local businesses a book that lists all the businesses and businesspeople in a town

commercial hedger STOCKHOLDING & INVESTMENTS producer investing in commodities it needs a company that holds ***options*** in the commodities it uses or produces, usually in order to ensure the price stability of the commodity

commercialization FINANCE conversion of something into business the application of business principles to something in order to run it as a business

commercial law LEGAL law dealing with trade the body of law that deals with the rules and institutions of commercial transactions, including banking, commerce, contracts, copyrights, insolvency, insurance, patents, trademarks, shipping, storage, transportation, and warehousing

commercial loan FINANCE short-term renewable loan to firm a short-term renewable loan or line of credit used to finance the seasonal or cyclical working capital needs of a company

commercial mortgage-backed securities MORTGAGES stocks with cash flow from commercial mortgage stocks that are backed by the security of a mortgage on commercial rather than residential property. *Abbr* ***CMBS***

commercial paper FINANCE unsecured short-term loan note an unsecured loan note issued by a company for a short period, generally maturing within nine months

commercial property REAL ESTATE buildings and land used by business buildings and land used for the performance of business activities. Commercial property can include single offices, buildings, factories, and hotels.

commercial report FINANCE background financial report on applicant an investigative report made by an organization such as a ***credit bureau*** that specializes in obtaining information regarding a person or organization applying for something such as credit or employment

commercial substance FINANCE economic reality behind piece of business the economic reality that underlies a transaction or arrangement, regardless of its legal or technical denomination. For example, a company may sell an office block and then immediately lease it back: the commercial substance may be that it has not been sold.

commercial year FINANCE 12 months of 30 days an artificial year treated as having 12 months of 30 days each, used for calculating such things as monthly sales data and inventory levels

commission 1. FINANCE sum paid to intermediary a payment made to an intermediary, often calculated as a percentage of the value of goods or services provided. Commission is most often paid to sales staff, brokers, or agents. **2.** *US* MARKETS broker's fee for sale a fee that a broker receives for a sale of securities. *Also called* ***placement fee***

  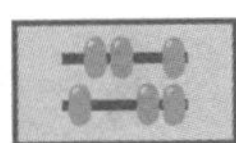      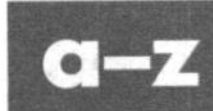

commission agent FINANCE agent paid percentage of sales an agent whose payment is based on a specific percentage of the sales made

Commission des Opérations de Bourse MARKETS *see* ***Autorité des Marchés Financiers***

commission house FINANCE firm charging commission on futures contracts a business that buys or sells ***futures contracts*** for clients and charges a commission for this service

Commission of the European Community = ***European Commission***

commitment STOCKHOLDING & INVESTMENTS agreement to underwrite credit an agreement by an underwriting syndicate to underwrite a ***note issuance facility*** or other credit facility

commitment document LEGAL document with contractual force confirming transaction a contract, change order, purchase order, or letter of intent pertaining to the supply of goods and services that commits an organization to legal, financial, and other obligations

commitment fee FINANCE payment to fix interest rate on forthcoming loan a fee that a lender charges to guarantee a rate of interest on a loan a borrower is soon to make. *Also called* ***establishment fee***

commitment letter FINANCE official confirmation of US loan in the United States, an official notice from a lender to a borrower that the borrower's application has been approved and confirming the terms and conditions of the loan

commitments basis FINANCE way of recording expenditure before outlay the method of recording the expenditure of a public sector organization at the time when it commits itself to it rather than when it actually pays for it

commitments for capital expenditure FINANCE amount committed to fixed assets in future the amount a company has committed to spend on fixed assets in the future. In the United Kingdom, companies are legally obliged to disclose this amount, and any additional commitments, in their ***annual report***.

committee GENERAL MANAGEMENT group of people delegated to consider particular matter a group of people appointed and authorized to study, investigate, or make recommendations on a particular matter

Committee on Accounting Procedure ACCOUNTING former US committee establishing accounting principles in the United States, a committee of the American Institute of Certified Public Accountants that was responsible between 1939 and 1959 for issuing accounting principles, some of which are still part of the ***Generally Accepted Accounting Principles***

Committee on Uniform Securities Identification Procedures REGULATION & COMPLIANCE committee that codes US securities a committee set up by the American Bankers Association to assign a code to all securities approved for trading in the United States. *Abbr* ***CUSIP***

commodities exchange MARKETS market for bulk raw materials a market in which raw materials are bought and sold in large quantities as ***actuals*** or ***futures***

commodities market MARKETS = ***commodity market***

commodity MARKETS product that can be traded an item that can be bought or sold, especially a raw material or something that has been manufactured

commodity-backed bond STOCKHOLDING & INVESTMENTS bond linked to price of commodity a bond tied to the price of an underlying commodity such as gold or silver, often used as a hedge against inflation

commodity contract MARKETS contract for transferring commodity a legal document for the delivery or receipt of a commodity

commodity exchange MARKETS exchange where commodity futures are traded an exchange where futures are traded, for example, the commodity exchange for metals. *Abbr* ***COMEX***

commodity future MARKETS fixed contract to buy or sell commodity a contract to buy or sell a commodity at a predetermined price and on a specific delivery date

Commodity Futures Trading Commission REGULATION & COMPLIANCE US agency monitoring futures trading an independent agency set up by the US government to monitor trading in ***futures contracts***. *Abbr* ***CFTC***

commodity market MARKETS market for bulk raw materials a market in which raw materials are bought and sold in large quantities as ***actuals*** or ***futures***. *Also called* ***commodities market***

commodity paper FINANCE loan secured by commodities a loan or advance for which commodities or financial documents relating to them are collateral

commodity pool FINANCE group trading in commodity options a group of people who join together to trade in ***options*** on commodities

commodity-product spread FINANCE trading in commodity and product coordinated trades in both a commodity and a product made from it

commodity trader MARKETS somebody buying and selling commodities a person whose business is buying and selling commodities

common cost 1. ACCOUNTING cost recorded in more than one center a cost that is allocated to two or more cost centers within a company **2.** OPERATIONS & PRODUCTION cost associated with multiple items cost relating to more than one product or service and unable to be allocated to any individual one

common equity STOCKHOLDING & INVESTMENTS common stock in a company the ownership interest in a company that consists only of the common stock

common market INTERNATIONAL TRADE group of trading partners with few trade barriers an economic association, typically between nations, with the goal of removing or reducing trade barriers

common ownership BUSINESS ownership by employees collectively a situation in which a business is owned by the employees who work in it

common pricing OPERATIONS & PRODUCTION illegal price-fixing the illegal fixing of the price of a good or service by several businesses so that they all charge the same price

common seal LEGAL = ***company seal***

common-size financial statements ACCOUNTING statements with everything in percentages statements in which all the separate parts are expressed as percentages of the total. Such statements are often used for making performance comparisons between companies.

common stock *US* STOCKHOLDING & INVESTMENTS stock without first call on dividends a stock that provides voting rights but only pays a dividend after dividends for preferred stock have been paid. *UK term* ***ordinary share***

common stock ratio STOCKHOLDING & INVESTMENTS in US, proportion of capital represented by share in the United States, a measure of the interest each stockholder has in the company's capital

commorientes LEGAL people who die at same time the legal term for two or more people who die at the same time. For the purposes of inheritance law, in the event of two people dying at the same time, it is assumed that the older person died first.

communication GENERAL MANAGEMENT exchange of messages, information, ideas, etc. the exchange of messages conveying information, ideas, attitudes, emotions, opinions, or instructions between individuals or groups with the objective of creating, understanding, or coordinating activities. Communication is essential to the effective operation of an organization. It may be conducted informally through a grapevine or formally by means of letters, reports, briefings, and meetings. Communication may be verbal or nonverbal and include spoken, written, and visual elements.

communications GENERAL MANAGEMENT systems or technologies used for communicating systems or technologies such as postal, telephone, and e-mail networks, used for the communication of messages or for communicating within an organization

communications channel GENERAL MANAGEMENT methods by which people communicate a medium through which a message is passed in the process of ***communication***. Communications channels include the spoken, written, and printed word, and electronic or computer-based media such as radio and television, telephones, videoconferencing, and e-mail. The most effective channel for a specific message depends on the nature of the message and the audience to be reached, as well as the context in which the message is to be transmitted.

communications envelope E-COMMERCE = ***electronic envelope***

communication skills HR & PERSONNEL skills required for effective communication skills that enable people to communicate effectively with one another. Effective communication involves the choice of the best ***communications channel*** for a specific purpose, the technical knowledge to use the channel appropriately, the presentation of information in an appropriate manner for the target audience, and the ability to understand messages and responses received from others. The ability to establish and develop mutual understanding, trust, and cooperation is also important. More specifically, communication skills include the ability to speak in public, make presentations, write letters and reports, chair committees and meetings, and conduct negotiations.

communications management GENERAL MANAGEMENT job of ensuring effective communications the management, measurement, and control activities undertaken to ensure the effectiveness of communications

communications strategy MARKETING deciding best way to communicate with marketplace a management technique for determining the most effective method of communicating with the marketplace

communication technology GENERAL MANAGEMENT electronic systems for communicating electronic systems used for communication between individuals or groups. Communication technology facilitates communication between individuals or groups who are not physically present at the same location. Systems such as telephones, telex, fax, radio, television, and video are included, as well as more recent computer-based technologies, including ***electronic data interchange*** and e-mail.

community E-COMMERCE group of people with shared interest communicating online a group of Internet users with a shared interest or concept who interact with each other in newsgroups, mailing-list discussion groups, and other online interactive forums

community of interest GENERAL MANAGEMENT diverse group united for common cause a group of diverse people or organizations with a shared concern who have united to campaign for a common cause

community property FINANCE asset to be shared equally on divorce any asset that is acquired during marriage by either spouse and that, in some states of the United States, must be divided equally between them if they should divorce. *Also called* ***marital property***

Compagnie Nationale des Commissaires aux Comptes REGULATION & COMPLIANCE French regulatory body in France, an organization that regulates auditing by external, independent auditors. *Abbr* ***CNCC***

Companies Act REGULATION & COMPLIANCE UK legislation governing activities of firms in the United Kingdom, an Act of Parliament that regulates the working of companies. Although the first one was passed in 1844, the Acts of 1985 and 1989 consolidated previous legislation and incorporated directives from the European Union.

Companies House REGULATION & COMPLIANCE building where UK firms are registered in the United Kingdom, the office of the ***Registrar of Companies***. It has three main functions: the incorporation, re-registration, and dissolving of companies; the registration of documents that must be filed under company, insolvency, and related legislation; and the provision of company information to the public. *Abbr* ***CH***

Companies Registration Office REGULATION & COMPLIANCE office where UK firms are registered the office of the Registrar of Companies, an official UK organization at which companies' records must be deposited so that they can be inspected by the public. *Abbr* ***CRO***

companion bond STOCKHOLDING & INVESTMENTS US bond secured by mortgages in the United States, a class of a ***collateralized mortgage obligation*** that is paid off first when interest rates fall, leading to the underlying mortgages being prepaid. Conversely, the ***principal*** on these bonds will be repaid more slowly when interest rates rise and fewer mortgages are prepaid.

company BUSINESS organized group trading goods or providing services a group of people organized to buy or sell goods or to provide a service, usually for profit

company director CORPORATE GOVERNANCE somebody appointed to help run company a person appointed by the stockholders to help run a company

company law CORPORATE GOVERNANCE legislation governing firms the body of legislation that relates to the formation, status, conduct, and ***corporate governance*** of companies as legal entities

company limited by guarantee BUSINESS incorporated organization whose members have pre-agreed liability a type of organization, normally formed for nonprofit purposes, in which each member of the company agrees to be liable for a specific sum in the event of liquidation

company limited by shares BUSINESS UK organization with share holdings determining liability in the United Kingdom, a type of organization in which each member of the company is liable only for the fully paid value of the shares they own

company pension PENSIONS = ***occupational pension***

company policy CORPORATE GOVERNANCE firm's guidelines for behavior or procedure a statement of desired standards of behavior or procedure applicable across an organization. Company policy defines ways of acting for staff in areas where there appears to be latitude in deciding how best to operate. This may concern areas such as time off for special circumstances, drug or alcohol abuse, workplace bullying, personal use of Internet facilities, or business travel. Company policy may also apply to customers, for example, policy on complaints, customer retention, or disclosure of information. Sometimes a company policy may develop into a ***code of practice***.

company promoter BUSINESS somebody establishing new firm a person who organizes the setting up of a new company

company registrar CORPORATE GOVERNANCE person maintaining firm's share register the person who is responsible for maintaining the share register records of a company

company report CORPORATE GOVERNANCE statement of firm's activities and performance a document giving details of the activities and performance of a company. Companies are legally required to produce specific reports and submit them to the competent authorities in the country of their registration. These include ***annual reports*** and financial reports. Other reports may cover specific aspects of an organization's activities, for example, environmental or social impact.

company seal LEGAL firm's authenticating stamp or signature the impression of a company's official signature on paper or wax. Certain documents, such as stock certificates, have to bear this seal. *Also called* ***common seal***

company secretary CORPORATE GOVERNANCE UK firm's senior administrative officer a senior employee in an organization with director status and administrative and legal authority. The appointment of a company secretary is a legal requirement for most limited companies, except the smallest. A company secretary can also be a ***board secretary*** with appropriate qualifications. In the United Kingdom, many company secretaries are members of the Institute of Chartered Secretaries and Administrators.

comparative advantage ECONOMICS, BUSINESS benefit of higher, more efficient production an instance of higher, more efficient production in a particular area. A country that produces far more cars than another, for example, is said to have the comparative advantage in car production. It has been suggested that specialization in activities in which individuals or groups have a comparative advantage will result in gains in trade.

comparative advertising MARKETING advertising comparing firm's product with competitors' products a form of advertising that gives carefully selected details of competitor products for comparison with a company's own product, usually to the detriment of competitors. Comparative advertising is frequently used to advertise cars, where the availability of features such as a sun roof, air conditioning, advanced braking systems, fuel efficiency, safety features, and warranty terms in similarly priced cars is given.

comparative balance sheet TREASURY MANAGEMENT financial statement compared with one of different date one of two or more financial statements prepared on different dates that lend themselves to a comparative analysis of the financial condition of an organization

comparative credit analysis RISK assessment of financial risk an analysis of the risk associated with lending to different companies

compensating balance BANKING **1.** money required in bank account the amount of money a bank requires a customer to maintain in a non-interest-bearing account, in exchange for which the bank provides free services **2.** money required in bank account allowing credit the amount of money a bank requires a customer to maintain in an account in return for holding credit available, thereby increasing the true rate of interest on the loan

compensating errors ACCOUNTING mistakes after which accounts still balance two or more errors that are set against each other so that the accounts still balance

compensation FINANCE **1.** payment for work pay given to somebody in recompense for work performed **2.** money paid to unfairly dismissed employee in the United Kingdom, money paid by an employer on the order of an employment tribunal to an employee who has been unfairly dismissed

compensation fund STOCKHOLDING & INVESTMENTS fund compensating investors when stock exchange members default a fund operated by a stock exchange to compensate investors for losses incurred when members of the stock exchange default (lose more on their trading positions than they hold in capital)

compensation package HR & PERSONNEL overall employee pay and benefits offered by US employer in the United States, a bundle of rewards including pay, financial incentives, and ***fringe benefits*** offered to, or negotiated by, an employee

compensatory financing FINANCE IMF financial assistance financing from the ***International Monetary Fund*** to help a country in economic difficulty

competence GENERAL MANAGEMENT, HR & PERSONNEL ability to perform duties at level required an acquired personal skill that is demonstrated in an employee's ability to provide a consistently adequate or high level of performance in a specific job function. Competence should be distinguished from ***competency***, although in general usage the terms are used interchangeably. Early attempts to define the qualities of effective managers were based on lists of the personality traits and skills of the ideal manager. This is an input model approach, focusing on the skills that are needed to do the job. These skills are competencies and reflect potential ability to do something. With the advent of scientific management, people turned their attention more to the behavior of effective managers and to the outcomes of successful management. This approach is an output model, in which a manager's effectiveness is defined in terms of actual achievement. This achievement manifests itself in competences, which demonstrate that somebody has learned to do something well. There tends to be a focus in the United Kingdom on competence, whereas in the United States, the concept of competency is more popular. Competences are used in the workplace in a variety of ways. Training is often competence based, and the United Kingdom National Vocational Qualification system is based on competence standards. Competences are also used in reward management, for example, in competence-based pay. The assessment of competence is a necessary process for underpinning these initiatives by determining what competences an employee shows. At an organizational level, the idea of ***core competence*** is gaining in popularity.

competency GENERAL MANAGEMENT, HR & PERSONNEL innate personal ability an innate skill or ability that somebody has. *See also* ***competence***

competition ECONOMICS, BUSINESS struggle between firms to win business rivalry between companies to achieve greater ***market share***. Competition between companies for customers will lead to product innovation and improvement and, ultimately, lower prices. The opposite of market competition is either a ***monopoly*** or a ***controlled economy***, where production is governed by quotas. A company that is leading the market is said to have achieved ***competitive advantage***.

Competition Commission REGULATION & COMPLIANCE UK regulator of competition in the United Kingdom, an independent public body with the role of ensuring healthy competition between companies. It conducts in-depth inquiries into mergers, markets, and the regulation of the major regulated industries. It replaced the Monopolies and Mergers Commission in April 1999.

competitive advantage ECONOMICS, BUSINESS benefit of being more competitive a factor giving an advantage to a nation, company, group, or individual in competitive terms

competitive analysis BUSINESS evaluation of competitors' ability to compete analysis carried out for marketing purposes, which can include industry, customer, and ***competitor analysis***. A thorough competitive analysis done within a strategic framework can provide in-depth evaluation of the capabilities of key competitors.

competitive bid STOCKHOLDING & INVESTMENTS selling new securities at competing prices or terms a method of auctioning new securities whereby various underwriters offer the stock at competing prices or terms

competitive devaluation CURRENCY & EXCHANGE currency devaluation to increase competitiveness the devaluation of a currency to make a country's goods more competitive on the international markets

competitive equilibrium price BUSINESS price resulting in balance of buyers and sellers the price at which the number of buyers willing to buy a good equals the number of sellers prepared to sell it

competitive forces ECONOMICS, BUSINESS external factors forcing organization to become more competitive the external business and economic factors that compel an organization to improve its competitiveness

competitive intelligence BUSINESS information gathered that improves organization's competitive ability data gathered to improve an organization's competitive capacity. Competitive intelligence may include, for example, information about competitors' plans, activities, or products, and may sometimes be gained through ***industrial espionage***. Such information can have a significant impact on a company's own plans: it could limit the effectiveness of a new product launch, or identify growing threats to important accounts, for example. Unless organizations monitor competitor activity and take appropriate action, their business faces risk.

competitive local exchange carrier BUSINESS telecommunications provider competing with established provider a company that offers an alternate service to the established telephone service provider in a particular area

competitiveness index ECONOMICS, BUSINESS ranking of countries in order of competitive advantage an international ranking of states which uses economic and other information to list countries in order of their competitive performance. A competitiveness index can show which countries have overall or industry sector ***competitive advantage***.

competitive position BUSINESS situation in relation to competitors the market share, costs, prices, quality, and accumulated experience of an entity or product relative to competition

competitive pricing BUSINESS determining price by checking others setting a price by reference to the prices of comparable competitive products

competitive trader MARKETS = ***floor trader***

competitor BUSINESS person, company, or product competing with another a person, company, or product that is in commercial competition with another

competitor analysis *or* competitor profiling BUSINESS comparing firm's products with competitors' in developing strategy the identification and quantification of the relative strengths and weaknesses of a product or service compared with those of competitors or potential competitors that could be of significance in the development of a successful competitive strategy

complaint GENERAL MANAGEMENT customer's expression of dissatisfaction an expression of dissatisfaction with a product or service, either orally or in writing, from an internal or external customer. A customer may have a genuine cause for complaint, although some complaints may be made as a result of a misunderstanding or an unreasonable expectation of a product or service. How a complaint is handled will affect the overall level of ***customer satisfaction*** and may affect long-term customer loyalty. It is important for providers to have clear procedures for dealing rapidly with any complaints, to come to a fair conclusion, and to explain the reasons for what may be perceived by the customer as a negative response. *Also called* ***customer complaint***

complaints management GENERAL MANAGEMENT technique for handling complaints a management technique for assessing, analyzing, and responding to customer complaints

complementary goods MARKETING products depending on each other for sales goods sold separately, but dependent on each other for sales. Examples of complementary goods include toothbrushes and toothpaste or computers and computer desks.

complementor BUSINESS firm selling product that complements another firm's product a company that supplies a product that complements a product supplied by another company, for example, computers and software

complete *UK* REAL ESTATE = ***close***

completion *UK* REAL ESTATE = ***closing***

completion date BUSINESS date when something will finish the date when a financial or business transaction is due to be finalized

complex adaptive system GENERAL MANAGEMENT self-regulating system without controls a system that overrides conventional human controls because those controls will subdue inevitable change and development within that system. Complex adaptive systems are a product of the application of ***chaos theory*** and ***complexity theory*** to the world of organizations. It has been suggested that organizations that are subject to too much control are at risk of failure. Bureaucracy and the ***top-down approach*** to management have been cited as examples of extreme control. However, if a bureaucracy is left to adapt naturally, it could become capable of self-organization and of creating new methods of operating.

complexity costs OPERATIONS & PRODUCTION business costs relating to changing economy the costs of operating a business which are difficult to quantify and relate to remaining competitive in a rapidly changing and increasingly complex economic environment. *Also called* ***costs of complexity***

complexity theory GENERAL MANAGEMENT theory that events will develop in random and complex fashion the theory that random events, if left to happen without interference, will settle into a complicated pattern rather than a simple one. Complexity theory is a development of ***chaos theory***. In a business context, it suggests that events within organizations and in the wider economic and social spheres cannot be predicted by simple models but will develop in a seemingly random and complex manner.

compliance REGULATION & COMPLIANCE fulfillment of requirements action to do what is required to meet official or agreed standards or regulations, or to do what is ordered by a court

compliance audit REGULATION & COMPLIANCE check to establish if obligations are being met an audit of specific activities in order to determine whether performance conforms with a predetermined contractual, regulatory, or statutory requirement

compliance department 1. STOCKHOLDING & INVESTMENTS, REGULATION & COMPLIANCE department in stockbroking firm enforcing stock exchange rules a department in a stockbroking firm that makes sure that the stock exchange rules are followed and that confidentiality is maintained in cases when the same firm represents rival clients **2.** REGULATION & COMPLIANCE department in firm enforcing business regulations a department that ensures that the company it is part of is adhering to any relevant laws and regulations relating to its business

  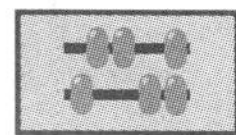  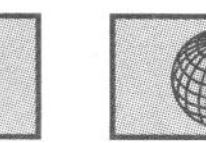   

compliance documentation STOCKHOLDING & INVESTMENTS, REGULATION & COMPLIANCE documents required for stock issues documents that a stock-issuing company publishes in line with regulations on stock issues

compliance officer REGULATION & COMPLIANCE officer ensuring that financial regulations are observed an employee of a financial organization who ensures that regulations governing its business are observed

component percentage FINANCE proportion of firm's value in capital the proportion of a company's value represented by debt, stock, assets, and other items. *See also* ***capitalization ratio***

composite index MARKETS index combining equities, indices, or averages an index of various equities, indices, or averages, mainly used as an indicator of the performance of the market or a specific sector of the market

compound FINANCE **1.** pay part of debt in the United Kingdom, to agree with creditors to settle a debt by paying part of what is owed **2.** calculate compound interest to calculate compound interest, based on the initial sum plus any interest that has accrued

compound annual return *or* compounded annual return STOCKHOLDING & INVESTMENTS return on investment including reinvestment returns the annual return on an investment after allowing for the return on reinvested intermediate ***cash flows***

compounding FINANCE **1.** calculating compound interest the calculation of ***compound interest***, based on the initial sum plus any interest that has accrued **2.** using compound interest the making of a transaction involving the payment or receipt of ***compound interest***

compound interest FINANCE interest calculated after inclusion of accrued interest interest calculated on the sum of the original borrowed amount and the accrued interest. *See also* ***simple interest***

compound option STOCKHOLDING & INVESTMENTS, RISK option with underlying asset another option an option that has a second option as the underlying asset. If the first option is exercised, the second option acts like an ordinary option.

compound rate FINANCE rate using compound interest the interest rate of a loan based on its ***principal***, the amount remaining to be paid, or any interest payments already received

comprehensive auditing ACCOUNTING = ***value for money audit***

comprehensive income FINANCE firm's income reflecting any changes in owner equity a company's total income for a given accounting period, including all gains and losses, not only those included in a normal income statement but also any that reflect a change in the value of an owner's interest in the business. In the United States, comprehensive income must be declared, whereas in the United Kingdom it appears in the statement of total recognized gains and losses.

comprehensive insurance *or* comprehensive policy INSURANCE insurance policy covering all likely risks an insurance policy that covers you against all risks that are deemed likely to happen

comptroller ACCOUNTING organization's senior accountant an accountant who is responsible for maintaining an organization's accounts

Comptroller of the Currency BANKING US official responsible for federal banks an official of the government responsible for the regulation of banks that are members of the Federal Reserve

compulsory acquisition STOCKHOLDING & INVESTMENTS purchasing last 10% of stocks at original price in the United Kingdom, the purchase by a bidder of the last 10% of stocks in an issue by right, at the offer price

compulsory liquidation BUSINESS enforced sale of assets to pay liabilities the closing of a business and selling its assets to pay off its liabilities, which is ordered by a court. *UK term* ***compulsory winding up***

compulsory purchase annuity PENSIONS annuity purchased from UK personal pension plan in the United Kingdom, an annuity that must be purchased with the fund built up in a personal pension plan before age 75

compulsory winding up *UK* BUSINESS = ***compulsory liquidation***

computational error ACCOUNTING calculation mistake a mistake that was made in doing a calculation

computer-aided design *or* computer-assisted design OPERATIONS & PRODUCTION product design using computers the use of a computer to assist with the design of a product. Computer graphics, modeling, and simulation are used to represent a product on screen, so that designers can produce more accurate drawings than is possible on paper alone, and to perform calculations easily, thereby optimizing designs for production. *Abbr* ***CAD***

computer-aided manufacturing *or* computer-assisted manufacturing OPERATIONS & PRODUCTION product manufacturing controlled by computer a system in which the manufacture and assembly of a product are directed by a computer. Computer-aided manufacturing can be integrated with ***computer-aided design*** to create a CAD/CAM system. *Abbr* ***CAM***

computer-aided production management OPERATIONS & PRODUCTION use of computers to direct production management functions a system that enables all functions within an organization that are associated with production management to be directed by computer. ***MRP II*** is a well-known form of computer-aided production management. *Abbr* ***CAPM***

computer-assisted design OPERATIONS & PRODUCTION = ***computer-aided design***

computer-assisted manufacturing OPERATIONS & PRODUCTION = ***computer-aided manufacturing***

computer model STOCKHOLDING & INVESTMENTS training using Internet, intranet, or standalone computer a system for calculating investment opportunities, used by fund managers to see the right moment to buy or sell

computer telephony integration BUSINESS combining of telephone technology and computer technology the combining of computer and telephone technology to allow a computer to dial telephone numbers, route calls, and send and receive messages. One product of computer telephony integration is the process of caller identification, or caller ID. Caller ID identifies the telephone number a customer is calling from, searches the customer database to identify the caller, and pops up the customer account on the receiver's computer screen, using the facility known as screen popping, before the call is answered. *Abbr* ***CTI***

concealment of assets FRAUD hiding of assets from creditors the dishonest act of hiding assets so that creditors do not know they exist

concentration ratio MARKETS ratio indicating composition of market a ratio showing the proportion of a market that is dominated by a few large companies. This is calculated according to information about the size distribution of firms.

concentration risk RISK risk related to lack of variety in lending the risk of loss to a financial institution as a result of having too many outstanding loans concentrated in a particular instrument, with a particular type of borrower, or in a particular country

concentration services BANKING moving money into single account the placing of money from various accounts into a single account

concept board MARKETING large board for displaying advertising ideas a board used for presenting creative advertising ideas, usually a large one that members of a group can see easily

concept product MARKETING innovative product not yet on market a highly advanced and innovative product that is not yet in commercial production

concepts ACCOUNTING principles of accounting principles and abstract ideas underpinning the preparation of accounting information. *See also* ***fundamental accounting concepts***

concept search E-COMMERCE online search returning documents relating to word an online search for documents related conceptually to a word, rather than specifically containing the word itself

concept statement MARKETING summary of project's goals or nature an explanation or summary of the overall goals or nature of a project

concept testing MARKETING test of effectiveness of advertising idea research carried out to test the effectiveness of a creative advertising idea

concern BUSINESS firm and its staff a business or company and the people involved in it

concert party MERGERS & ACQUISITIONS secret plan to acquire company an arrangement by which several people or companies work together in secret, usually to acquire another company through a takeover bid

concession **1.** FINANCE price reduction for selected group a reduction in price for a specific group of people, not for everyone **2.** BUSINESS right to operate in another's premises the right of a retail outlet to operate within the premises of another establishment **3.** GENERAL MANAGEMENT agreement to ignore product's nonconformity to specification an agreement to ignore the failure of a product or service to conform to its specification, with a possible resultant deterioration in the quality of the product or service **4.** GENERAL MANAGEMENT compromise a compromise in opinion or action by a party to a dispute

concessionaire BUSINESS somebody with exclusive right to sell product a person or business that has the right to be the only seller of a product in a place

concessionally taxed TAX taxed at low rate being liable to tax at a preferential rate. Savings or benefits, for example, may be concessionally taxed.

  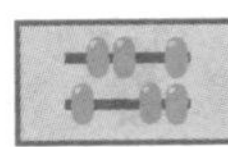      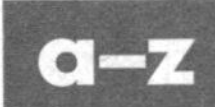

conciliation HR & PERSONNEL dispute resolution by independent negotiator action taken by an independent negotiator to bring disputing sides together with the goal of restoring trust or goodwill and reaching an agreement or bringing about a reconciliation

concurrent engineering OPERATIONS & PRODUCTION product development by teams working in parallel a team-based cooperative approach to product design and development, in which all parties involved in ***new product development*** work in parallel. Concurrent engineering reduces or removes the time lag between the different stages of a product's development, and earlier entry into a market is therefore possible. Product quality is improved, development and product costs are minimized, and competitiveness is increased. *Also called* ***parallel engineering, simultaneous engineering***

conditional distribution STATISTICS probability distribution of specific random variable the probability distribution of a random variable while the values of one or more random variables are fixed

conditions of employment HR & PERSONNEL contract containing terms of employment terms agreed to by an employer and employee, which are legally enforceable through a ***contract of employment***. Conditions of employment include conditions that may be unique to the individual, such as notice period, remuneration, fringe benefits, and hours of work, as well as those that form organization-wide policies, such as discipline and grievance procedures and those dictated by legislation.

conditions of sale OPERATIONS & PRODUCTION agreements about how something is sold agreed ways in which a sale may take place, including information on discounts and credit terms

condominium REAL ESTATE combination of private and joint real estate ownership in the United States, a type of real estate ownership in which the owner has title to a dwelling unit, especially an apartment or town house, in a building or on land that is owned jointly with the owners of the other units

conduit IRA PENSIONS = ***rollover IRA***

Confederation of Asian and Pacific Accountants ACCOUNTING Asia-Pacific organization for accountants an umbrella organization for a number of accounting associations. *Abbr* ***CAPA***

Confederation of British Industry BUSINESS organization supporting UK businesses a corporate membership organization that aims to promote the interests of UK business. The CBI's headquarters are in London, but it has regional offices throughout the United Kingdom, a European office in Brussels, and a US base in Washington, DC. *Abbr* ***CBI***

conference GENERAL MANAGEMENT meeting for members of organizations with shared interests a type of meeting held between members of often disparate organizations to discuss matters of mutual interest. Conferences are held for a variety of reasons, including resolving problems, making decisions, developing cooperation, and publicizing ideas, products, and services. They may take place within an organization but often draw people together regionally, nationally, or internationally, and involve a large number of speakers and delegates. Many conferences are organized for commercial profit.

conference call GENERAL MANAGEMENT telephone call connecting three or more people a telephone call that connects three or more lines so that people in different locations can communicate and exchange information by voice. Conference calls reduce the cost of meetings by eliminating travel time and expenditure. Public switched telephone networks or dedicated private networks and a centrally located device called a bridge are used to connect the participants. Microphones and loudspeakers may also be used to make group-to-group communication possible. Conference calls are a type of ***teleconferencing***.

confidence indicator ECONOMICS, MARKETS number that shows how economic market will perform a number that gives an indication of how well a market or an economy will fare

confidence interval STATISTICS expected range of possible outcomes in a statistical study, the range of values of sample observations that contain the true parameter value within a given probability

confidentiality agreement GENERAL MANAGEMENT agreement to treat information as private and confidential an agreement whereby an organization that has access to information about the affairs of another organization makes an undertaking to treat the information as private and confidential. A potential buyer of a company who requires further information in the process of due diligence may be asked to sign a confidentiality agreement stating that the information will only be used for the purpose of deciding whether to go ahead with the deal and will only be disclosed to employees involved in the negotiations. Such agreements are also used where information is shared in the context of a partnership or ***benchmarking*** program.

confirmation STOCKHOLDING & INVESTMENTS, OPERATIONS & PRODUCTION document confirming transaction or agreement a written acknowledgment of a transaction or agreement, for example, from a broker confirming and detailing a securities transaction

conflict management GENERAL MANAGEMENT discovering and controlling conflict within organization the identification and control of conflict within an organization. There are three main philosophies of conflict management: all conflict is bad and potentially destructive; conflict is inevitable and managers should attempt to harness it positively; conflict is essential to the survival of an organization and should be encouraged.

conflict of interest *or* conflict of interests GENERAL MANAGEMENT situation in which somebody's opposing interests prejudice objectivity a situation in which a person or institution is caught between opposing concerns, loyalties, or objectives that prejudice impartiality. A conflict of interest may be between self-advantage and the benefit of an organization for which somebody works, or it could arise when somebody is connected with two or more companies that are competing. The correct course of action in such cases is for the person concerned to declare any interests, to make known the way in which those interests conflict, and to abstain from participating in the decision-making process involving those interests. A conflict of interest may also arise when an institution acts for parties on both sides of a transaction and could derive an advantage from a specific outcome.

conglomerate company BUSINESS organization owning different types of companies an organization that owns a diverse range of companies in different industries. Conglomerates are usually ***holding companies*** with subsidiaries in wide-ranging business areas, often built up through mergers and takeovers and operating on an international scale.

conglomerate diversification MERGERS & ACQUISITIONS starting different types of subsidiaries the ***diversification*** of a ***conglomerate company*** through the setting-up of ***subsidiary companies*** with activities in various areas

conglomerate merger MERGERS & ACQUISITIONS merger of companies in unrelated industries a merger of organizations that belong to different types of industry

connectivity GENERAL MANAGEMENT ability of devices or people to connect electronically the ability of electronic products to connect with others, or of individuals, companies, and countries to be connected with one another electronically

connexity GENERAL MANAGEMENT being electronically connected worldwide the condition of being closely and intricately connected by worldwide communications networks

Conseil des Marchés Financiers MARKETS *see* ***Autorité des Marchés Financiers***

consequential loss policy INSURANCE = ***business interruption insurance***

consideration FINANCE payment for service a sum of money paid in return for a service

consignee OPERATIONS & PRODUCTION somebody receiving goods a person who receives goods from somebody for their own use or to sell for the owner

consignment OPERATIONS & PRODUCTION goods to be sold or returned a quantity of goods given to somebody for sale, with the provision that any unsold goods will be returned

consignment stock STOCKHOLDING & INVESTMENTS stock held by dealer for somebody stock held by one party (the "dealer") but legally owned by another (the "manufacturer") on terms that give the dealer the right to sell the stock in the normal course of its business, or, at its option, to return it unsold to the legal owner

consignor OPERATIONS & PRODUCTION somebody handing goods over a person who gives goods to somebody else for sale, safekeeping, or disposal

consistency ACCOUNTING using same accounting rules every year the concept that a company should apply the same rules and standards to its accounting procedures for similar items and from one year to the next. In the United Kingdom, deviation from consistency must be noted in the company's ***annual report***.

consolidate ACCOUNTING combine accounts of holding company and its subsidiaries to combine the accounts of several subsidiary companies as well as their ***holding company*** in a single financial statement

consolidated accounts ACCOUNTING = ***consolidated financial statement***

consolidated balance sheet ACCOUNTING outline of firm's finances a balance sheet containing the most significant details of a company's finances, including those of subsidiaries

consolidated debt FINANCE debt incorporating smaller debts a single large debt into which smaller ones have been subsumed

  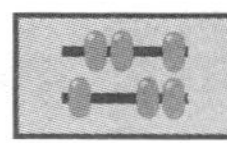      

consolidated financial statement ACCOUNTING outline of finances of parent company and subsidiaries a listing of the most significant details of the finances of a company and of all its subsidiaries. *Also called* ***consolidated accounts***

consolidated fund TAX public money for paying national debt a fund of public money, especially from taxes, used by the government to make interest payments on the national debt and other regular payments

consolidated invoice OPERATIONS & PRODUCTION combined invoice for items sent to buyer separately an invoice that covers all items shipped by one seller to one buyer during a particular period

consolidated loan FINANCE large loan for paying off smaller loans a large loan, the proceeds of which are used to eliminate smaller ones

consolidated stock STOCKHOLDING & INVESTMENTS *see* ***consols***

consolidated tape MARKETS ticker tape listing all US stock exchange activity a ticker tape that lists all transactions of the New York and other US stock exchanges

consolidated tax return TAX joint tax return for several firms a tax return that covers several companies, typically a parent company and all of its subsidiaries

consolidation **1.** MERGERS & ACQUISITIONS joining several firms together the uniting of two or more businesses into one company **2.** STOCKHOLDING & INVESTMENTS creating fewer but costlier shares the combination of a specific number of lower-priced shares into one higher-priced one

consolidation accounting ACCOUNTING combining financial statements for parent firm and subsidiaries the process of adjusting and combining financial information from the individual financial statements of a parent undertaking and its subsidiary undertakings to prepare consolidated financial statements that present financial information for the group as a single economic entity

consols STOCKHOLDING & INVESTMENTS UK government bonds with no maturity date in the United Kingdom, government bonds that pay interest but do not have a maturity date *Full form* ***consolidated stock***

consortium BUSINESS group of independent organizations allied for specific goal a group of independent organizations that join forces to achieve a particular goal, for example, to bid for a project or to conduct cooperative purchasing. A consortium goes on to complete the project if its bid is successful and is often dissolved on completion. This form of temporary alliance allows diverse skills, capabilities, and knowledge to be brought together.

consultant GENERAL MANAGEMENT specialist brought in to give advice to organization an expert in a specialized field brought in to provide independent professional advice to an organization on some aspect of its activities. A consultant may advise on the overall management of an organization or on a specific project, such as the introduction of a new computer system. Consultants are usually retained by a client for a set period of time, during which they will investigate the matter in hand and produce a report detailing their recommendations. Consultants may be established in business independently or be employed by a large consulting firm. Specific types of consultants include ***management consultants*** and ***internal consultants***.

consulting actuary PENSIONS actuary advising pension funds an independent actuary who gives mathematical and statistical advice to large pension funds

consumer ECONOMICS somebody using product or service somebody who uses a product or service. A consumer may not be the purchaser of a product or service and should be distinguished from a customer, who is the person or organization that purchased the product or service.

consumer advertising MARKETING advertising aimed at consumer market advertising aimed at individuals and the domestic and family market as opposed to industrial advertising, which is aimed at businesses

consumer behavior MARKETING consumer buying behavior the factors that affect people's decision-making on whether to buy something and what to buy. *See also* ***consumer demand***

consumer confidence ECONOMICS how people feel about economic future a measure of how people feel about the future of the economy and their own financial situation, obtained through polling

consumer council BUSINESS group representing consumers' interests a group that represents the interests of consumers

consumer credit FINANCE credit provided for purchase of goods credit given by stores, banks, and other financial institutions to consumers so that they can buy goods

Consumer Credit Act, 1974 FINANCE UK legislation regulating provision of loans in the United Kingdom, an Act of Parliament that licenses lenders and requires them to state clearly the full terms of loans that they make, including the APR

consumer demand MARKETING consumer buying behavior the patterns of ***consumer behavior*** that affect buying decisions. Consumer demand is influenced in various ways. Psychologists and marketers have identified three important factors affecting buying decisions: needs, which are things we must have, such as food; wants, which are nice to have but not essential, such as a new car; and motives, such as keeping up appearances. These factors form part of a profile which includes motivations, personality, perceptions, cognition, attitudes, and values. Other factors that influence demand include gender, age, social grouping, education, location, income, culture, and the seasons. Consumers can therefore be divided into discrete segments, each of which has a specific pattern of buying behavior. Products and services can then be targeted at specific segments of the market.

consumer durables BUSINESS purchased items intended for long-term use items that are bought and used by the public and intended to last a long time, for example, washing machines, refrigerators, or stoves

consumer-facing GENERAL MANAGEMENT **1.** engaging directly with consumers involved with or involving direct contact with consumers **2.** directly accessible by consumers able to be directly accessed by consumers, and often being the first point of contact

consumer goods marketing MARKETING promotion of products to end users the promotion of products to members of the public. Consumer goods marketing is aimed at individuals rather than organizations and promotes products directly to the end user rather than to intermediaries. Marketing strategies will be different from those used in ***industrial goods marketing***.

consumerism MARKETING influence of consumers on product manufacturing and sale the influence of the general public, as end users of products and services, on the way companies manufacture and sell their goods. Consumers exert considerable power over companies as organizations become more customer-focused. Demand is rising for products that are of high quality, ethically produced, well priced, and safe, and consumerism pressures companies to operate and produce goods and services in accordance with the public's wishes. In fact, the goals of consumerism are not at odds with those of marketing, as both have the end goal of pleasing the consumer. In practice, however, marketing does not always succeed, and there is still a need for legislation to back up the right of consumers to demand products that are of good quality and for consumer protection bodies that influence the commercial world on consumers' behalf. A particular form of consumer pressure, motivated by environmental concerns, is green consumerism, which campaigns for environmentally friendly goods, services, and means of production.

consumer market research MARKETING market research focusing on consumers ***market research*** that focuses on gathering and analyzing data on individual or domestic consumers, as opposed to industrial or business customers. *Also called* ***consumer research***

consumer panel MARKETING selected consumers whose purchasing habits are tracked a carefully selected group of people whose purchasing habits are regularly monitored. A consumer panel usually consists of a large cross-section of the population so as to provide meaningful data. There are two types of panel: diary panels, where members fill in a regular detailed diary of purchases, and, less commonly, home audit panels, where visits are made to the homes of members to check purchases, packaging, and used cartons. These panels run over a period of time to gain a broad overview of purchasing habits. A ***focus group*** is similar to a consumer panel, but is usually used to determine customers' views of a specific product or range of products. Members of a group meet together under the guidance of a facilitator to discuss their opinions on a face-to-face basis.

consumer price index ECONOMICS benchmark of basic retail prices an index of the prices of goods and services purchased by consumers, used to measure the cost of living or the rate of inflation in an economy. *Abbr* ***CPI***

consumer profile MARKETING detailed analysis of similar consumers for market research a detailed analysis of the purchasing habits of a group of ***consumers***, assessing influences such as age, gender, education, occupation, income, and personal and psychological characteristics. Consumer profiles are built up from extensive ***market research*** and are used for ***market segmentation*** purposes.

consumer protection MARKETING regulations protecting consumers' interests the safeguarding of consumers' interests in terms of quality, price, and safety, usually within a statutory framework. The growing purchasing power of consumers and the rise in ***consumerism*** from the late 1950s onward led to increased demands for protection against unsafe goods and services and unscrupulous trading practices.

consumer research MARKETING = ***consumer market research***

consumer services marketing MARKETING promotion and sale of services to domestic consumers the marketing of services to domestic consumers. Consumer services marketing may promote such services as banking, insurance, travel and tourism, leisure, telecommunications, and services provided by local authorities. Strategies to market these services to business constitute ***industrial services marketing***.

consumer spending MARKETING total amount of household and personal expenditure the total value of household and personal expenditure measured at macro and micro levels. At the macro level, consumer confidence can be measured by the overall levels of consumer spending; if earnings have increased at a faster rate than prices, then disposable income, or spending power, increases. At a micro level, there are market reports on the value of actual and predicted spend on a large range of consumer goods, including food, pharmaceuticals, clothing, cars, and vacations. ***Consumer demand*** is a related concept.

consumer-to-consumer commerce E-COMMERCE electronic transactions between consumers e-business transactions conducted between two individuals. The auction site eBay is a facilitator of consumer-to-consumer commerce.

consumption ECONOMICS amount of products and services used the quantity of resources used by consumers to satisfy their current needs and wants, measured by the sum of the current expenditure of the government and individual consumers

consumption tax TAX tax to encourage less use of something a tax used to encourage people to buy less of a particular good or service by increasing its price. This type of tax is often levied in times of national hardship.

contact card E-COMMERCE card that physically touches card reader a ***smart card*** in which the microprocessor chip is visible and can make physical contact with the reading device

contactless card E-COMMERCE card with chip read by radio signals a ***smart card*** in which the microprocessor chip is not visible and is accessed by the reading device by radio signals rather than by physical contact. An increasingly common use of this technology is in such applications as toll collection, where the card is accessed as the motorist displays it to the reading device in passing.

contagion ECONOMICS spreading effect of downturn across economies a situation in which a weakening economy in one country causes economies in other countries to weaken

contango MARKETS future delivery costing more than delivery now a situation where the price of commodities is higher for future delivery than it is for immediate delivery

content management E-COMMERCE dealing with words and pictures on website the means and methods of managing the textual and graphical content of a website

contestable market MARKETS economic market that any firm can participate in a market in which there are no barriers to entry, as when there is ***perfect competition***

contested takeover bid MERGERS & ACQUISITIONS takeover bid resisted by board of target firm a takeover bid where the board of the target company does not recommend it to the stockholders and tries to fight it. *Also called* ***hostile bid***

contingency LEGAL condition to be met in contract a condition in a contract which must be met before the contract becomes legally binding

contingency fund ACCOUNTING money held for unplanned expenditure money set aside from normal expenditure in case it is needed for unplanned expenses

contingency management GENERAL MANAGEMENT skill of adapting to changing situation the capacity for flexibility in varying responses and attitudes to meet the needs of different situations. Contingency management may be practiced by both individuals and organizations. Within the latter, it may be formalized through a ***contingency plan*** linked to ***risk*** or ***crisis management*** strategies, or be derived from the results of ***scenario planning***.

contingency plan GENERAL MANAGEMENT **1.** secondary plan prepared in case of situational changes a plan, drawn up in advance, to ensure a positive and rapid response to a changing situation. A contingency plan often results from ***scenario planning*** and may form part of an organization's strategy for coping with disasters. **2.** plan if situation does not progress as hoped action to be implemented only upon the occurrence of anticipated future events other than those in the accepted forward plan

contingency table STATISTICS table classifying data by variables a table in which observations on data are classified according to a number of variables

contingency tax TAX new tax to deal with particular problem a one-time tax levied by a government to deal with a particular economic problem, for example, too high a level of imports coming into the country

contingency theory GENERAL MANAGEMENT idea that management method should match situation in management, the theory that there is no single best way to organize or manage and that each firm should be organized and structured to suit the technology used and the environment around it

contingent beneficiary LEGAL person who inherits if main beneficiary is dead a person who is designated to receive assets or proceeds such as those from an insurance policy or estate, if the primary beneficiary has died

contingent deferred sales charge STOCKHOLDING & INVESTMENTS fee payable on redemption a redemption fee, or ***back-end loading***, payable on a share in a mutual fund only if the share is redeemed. It declines every year until it disappears, usually after six years. *Abbr* ***CDSC***. See also ***B share***

contingent liability ACCOUNTING potential liability provided for in company's accounts a liability that may or may not occur, but for which provision is made in a company's accounts, as opposed to "provisions," for which money is set aside for an anticipated expenditure

continuous budget TREASURY MANAGEMENT = ***rolling budget***

continuous compounding ACCOUNTING continuous calculation and addition of interest a system in which interest is continuously calculated and added to the initial sum plus any interest that has already accrued on a debt

continuous disclosure STOCKHOLDING & INVESTMENTS in Canada, providing full information about public firm in Canada, the practice of ensuring that complete, timely, accurate, and balanced information about a public company is made available to shareholders

continuous improvement GENERAL MANAGEMENT making frequent small changes to improve quality the seeking of small improvements in processes and products, with the objective of increasing quality and reducing waste. Continuous improvement is one of the tools that underpin the philosophies of ***total quality management*** and ***lean production***. Through constant study and revision of processes, a better product can result at reduced cost.

continuous inventory *or* continuous stocktaking ACCOUNTING comparing actual inventory to accounting records throughout year regular and consistent stocktaking throughout the fiscal year in order to ensure that the physical reality of the stock situation at any given time tallies with the accounting records. Any discrepancies will highlight errors or losses of stock and the accounts are adjusted to reflect this. Continuous inventory may preclude the need for an annual inventory.

continuous net settlement MARKETS automated system of tracking securities and cash balances an automated accounting system that uses a central clearing house to clear and settle securities transactions, maintaining complete records of companies' money balances. *Abbr* ***CNS***

continuous operation costing *or* continuous process costing OPERATIONS & PRODUCTION basing costs on process not product a costing method in which costs are first charged to the process of production, then averaged over the units produced during the relevant period. It is used where production consists of a sequence of continuous or repetitive operations.

contra account ACCOUNTING account offsetting another account an account that offsets another account, for example, when a company's supplier is not only a creditor in that company's books but also a debtor because it has purchased goods on credit

contract **1.** MARKETS securities transaction an agreement to buy or sell ***securities*** or other ***financial instruments*** **2.** GENERAL MANAGEMENT legal agreement a mutually agreed, legally binding agreement between two or more parties

contract broker MARKETS broker trading for other brokers a broker who buys or sells stock on behalf of other brokers

contract costing ACCOUNTING attributing costs to individual contracts a form of ***specific order costing*** in which costs are attributed to individual contracts

contract for difference **1.** STOCKHOLDING & INVESTMENTS swapping of fixed-price assets for floating-price assets an exchange of a fixed-price asset for one that has a price that varies **2.** CURRENCY & EXCHANGE currency exchange contract a ***forward exchange rate*** contract for currency. *Abbr* ***CFD***

contract hire GENERAL MANAGEMENT when firm leases resources from another firm an arrangement whereby an organization enters into a ***contract*** for the use of assets owned by another organization, as an alternative to purchasing the

     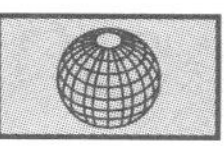   

assets itself. Contract hire agreements usually cover a period shorter than the useful economic life of the assets concerned and often include arrangements for maintenance and replacement. Organizations frequently use contract hire arrangements for the provision of company cars or office equipment.

contracting GENERAL MANAGEMENT process of making legal supply agreement the process of making an agreement governed by a ***contract*** for the provision of goods or services to an organization

contracting out **1.** PENSIONS moving employees from former UK state pension plan formerly in the United Kingdom, the withdrawal of employees by an employer or voluntarily from ***SERPS*** and their enrollment in a government-approved employer-sponsored pension plan **2.** GENERAL MANAGEMENT = ***outsourcing***

contracting party LEGAL party to formal agreement a person or organization that signs a formal agreement to do or not do something

contract manufacturing OPERATIONS & PRODUCTION having another firm produce product or part the ***outsourcing*** of a requirement to manufacture a particular product or component to a third party. Contract manufacturing enables companies to reduce the level of investment in their own capabilities to manufacture, while retaining a product produced to a high quality, at a reasonable price, and delivered to a flexible schedule.

contract month MARKETS month when goods must be delivered the month in which an option expires and goods covered by it must be delivered. *Also called* ***delivery month***

contract note MARKETS full description of transaction a document with the complete description of a stock transaction

contract of employment LEGAL, HR & PERSONNEL legal agreement between employer and employee a legally enforceable agreement, either oral or written, between an employer and an employee which defines terms and ***conditions of employment*** to which both parties must adhere. Express terms of the contract are agreed between the two parties and include the organization's normal terms and conditions in addition to those that relate specifically to the individual. These terms can only be changed by employee agreement, if the contract itself allows for variation, or by terminating the contract. Terms are also implied in the contract by custom and practice or by common law. *Also called* ***employment contract***

contract purchasing OPERATIONS & PRODUCTION process of buying product through leasing a mechanism for buying leased goods. In contract purchasing, a purchaser agrees to buy goods or equipment to be paid for in a series of installments, each comprising a proportion of the capital and an interest element. After a final payment, legal ownership passes to the user.

contractual liability LEGAL legal responsibility stated in contract a legal responsibility for something as set out formally in a written agreement

contractual obligation LEGAL course of action required by contract the legal duty to take a specific course of action, as imposed by a commercial ***contract*** or a ***contract of employment***

contractual savings STOCKHOLDING & INVESTMENTS money saved regularly in long-term investments savings in the form of regular payments into long-term investments such as pension plans

contract work HR & PERSONNEL work done under contract work done according to the terms of a written agreement

contra entry ACCOUNTING account entry offsetting earlier entry an entry made in the opposite side of an account to offset an earlier entry, for example, a debit against a credit

contrarian STOCKHOLDING & INVESTMENTS investing against market trends used to describe an investor who purchases securities in opposition to the current market trend, buying when most others are selling and vice versa

contrarian research STOCKHOLDING & INVESTMENTS investigation of purchases against market trends research on market trends resulting in advice to potential buyers to purchase stocks against the current trend

contrarian stockpicking STOCKHOLDING & INVESTMENTS choosing stocks against market trends the practice of purchasing stocks against the current market trend

contributed surplus FINANCE money from sources other than earnings the part of company profits that comes from sources other than earnings, for example, from selling stock above its ***nominal value***

contribution **1.** FINANCE, PENSIONS money paid into fund an amount of money placed in a fund of any kind, for example, money paid regularly into a pension **2.** FINANCE amount extra unit gains or loses the amount of money gained or lost from selling an additional unit of a product

contribution center FINANCE profitable section of business a ***profit center*** in which marginal or direct costs are equal to or less than revenue

contribution margin FINANCE profit from individual product the amount of money that an individual product or service contributes to net profit

contribution of capital FINANCE money paid as additional capital money paid to a company as additional capital

contributions holiday PENSIONS period when firm stops payments to pension plan a period during which a company stops making contributions to its pension plan because the plan is considered to be sufficiently well funded

contributory pension plan *US* PENSIONS pension provision requiring employees' contribution a pension plan into which employees must pay a portion of their salary on a regular basis. *UK term* ***contributory pension scheme***

contributory pension scheme *UK* PENSIONS = ***contributory pension plan***

control CORPORATE GOVERNANCE power to run organization the authority to direct an organization's operations and activities

control environment CORPORATE GOVERNANCE organization's management style the corporate culture of the directors and senior management of an organization

controlled company BUSINESS firm where one stockholder holds majority of voting stock a company in which a decisive proportion of the stock belongs to one owner. In the United States this is more than 25%, and in the United Kingdom, more than 50%.

controlled disbursement FINANCE payment once daily the practice of presenting checks for payment only once each day

controlled economy ECONOMICS economy with production quotas an economy in which production is governed by quotas. Controlled economies and ***monopolies*** are the opposite of market competition. *See also* ***competition***

controller ACCOUNTING organization's senior accountant an accountant who is responsible for maintaining an organization's accounts

control procedures CORPORATE GOVERNANCE rules for running organization the policies and procedures in addition to the ***control environment*** which are established to achieve an organization's specific objectives. They include procedures designed to prevent or to detect and correct errors.

control risk RISK likelihood of firm's control system allowing errors the part of an ***audit risk*** that relates to a client's internal control system

control security STOCKHOLDING & INVESTMENTS security held by somebody with management power a security held by a person who has an affiliation with the issuing company and the power to direct its management and policies, and whose resale must meet US Securities and Exchange Commission conditions

convergence **1.** ECONOMICS movement toward similarity in countries' economies a situation in which the economic factors in two countries become more alike, for example, when basic interest rates or budget deficits become more similar **2.** MARKETS coming together of futures and spot prices a situation in which the price of a commodity on the futures market moves toward the ***spot price*** as settlement date approaches

conversion **1.** MARKETS trading one investment product for another a trade of one convertible financial instrument for another, for example, a bond for shares of stock **2.** MARKETS trading one mutual fund's shares for another's a trade of shares of one mutual fund for shares of another in the same family **3.** PENSIONS transfer of assets to Roth IRA the process of transferring assets to a ***Roth IRA*** from another type of ***IRA***

conversion costs FINANCE expense of changing raw materials into products the cost of changing raw materials into finished or semi-finished products. Conversion costs include wages, other direct production costs, and the production overhead.

conversion discount *or* conversion premium STOCKHOLDING & INVESTMENTS price difference between convertible and common stock the difference between the price of convertible stock and the common stock into which it is to be converted

conversion issue STOCKHOLDING & INVESTMENTS offer of new bonds as older bonds expire the issue of new bonds, timed to coincide with the date of maturity of older bonds, with the intention of persuading investors to reinvest

conversion of funds FRAUD improper use of somebody else's money the act of using money that does not belong to you for a purpose for which it is not supposed to be used

conversion period STOCKHOLDING & INVESTMENTS period for converting loan stock into common stock a time during which convertible loan stock may be changed into common stock

  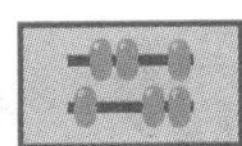      

conversion price **1.** CURRENCY & EXCHANGE exchange rate for currency the price at which a currency is changed into a foreign currency. *Also called* ***conversion rate*** *(sense 2)* **2.** STOCKHOLDING & INVESTMENTS price offered for converting preferred stock the price at which preferred stock is converted into common stock

conversion rate **1.** STOCKHOLDING & INVESTMENTS = ***conversion price*** *(sense 2)* **2.** CURRENCY & EXCHANGE = ***conversion price*** *(sense 1)* **3.** MARKETING how many people buy after consideration the percentage of inquiries by potential customers or sales calls by sales staff that results in actual sales

conversion ratio **1.** STOCKHOLDING & INVESTMENTS relative value of two convertible investment products an expression of the quantity of one security that can be obtained for another, for example, shares for a ***convertible bond***.

The conversion ratio may be established when the convertible is issued. If that is the case, the ratio will appear in the indenture, the binding agreement that details the convertible's terms.

If the conversion ratio is not set, it can be calculated quickly by dividing the nominal value of the convertible security (typically $1,000) by its conversion price.

$$\frac{\$1{,}000}{\$40 \text{ per share}} = 25$$

In this example, the conversion ratio is 25:1, which means that every bond held with a $1,000 nominal value can be exchanged for 25 shares of common stock.

Knowing the conversion ratio enables an investor to decide whether convertibles (or a group of them) are more valuable than the shares of common stock they represent. If the stock is currently trading at 30, the conversion value is $750, or $250 less than the nominal value of the convertible. It would therefore be unwise to convert.

A convertible's indenture can sometimes contain a provision stating that the conversion ratio will change over the years. **2.** MERGERS & ACQUISITIONS number of shares traded for others during merger the number of shares of one common stock to be issued for each outstanding ordinary share of a different type when a merger takes place

conversion value STOCKHOLDING & INVESTMENTS value of investment if changed for another type the value that a security would have if converted into another type of security

convertibility CURRENCY & EXCHANGE ease of currency exchange the ability of one currency to be easily exchanged for another currency

convertible ARM MORTGAGES adjustable-rate mortgage that can be made fixed-rate an adjustable-rate mortgage that the borrower can convert into a fixed-rate mortgage under specific terms

convertible bond STOCKHOLDING & INVESTMENTS bond that can be traded for another investment a bond that the owner can convert into another asset, especially common stock

convertible currency CURRENCY & EXCHANGE easily exchanged currency a currency that can easily be exchanged for another

convertible debenture STOCKHOLDING & INVESTMENTS debenture exchangeable for stock a debenture or ***loan stock*** that can be exchanged for stock at a later date

convertible loan stock STOCKHOLDING & INVESTMENTS in UK, money loaned and redeemable as stock in the United Kingdom, money lent to a company which can be converted into shares at a later date

convertible preference shares *UK* STOCKHOLDING & INVESTMENTS = ***convertible preferred stock***

convertible preferred stock *US* STOCKHOLDING & INVESTMENTS stock that can be traded for another investment stocks that give the holder the right to exchange them at a fixed price for another security, usually common stock.

Preferred stocks and other convertible securities offer investors a hedge: fixed-interest income without sacrificing the chance to participate in a company's capital appreciation.

When a company does well, investors can convert their holdings into common stock that is more valuable. When a company is less successful, they can still receive interest and principal payments, and also recover their investment and preserve their capital if a more favorable investment appears.

Conversion ratios and prices are important facts to know about preferred stocks. This information is found on the indenture statement that accompanies all issues. Occasionally the indenture will state that the conversion ratio will change over time. For example, the conversion price might be $50 for the first five years, $55 for the next five years, and so forth. Stock splits can affect conversion considerations.

In theory, convertible preferred stocks (and convertible exchangeable preferred stocks) are usually perpetual. However, issuers tend to force conversion or induce voluntary conversion for convertible preferred stocks within ten years. Steadily increasing common stock dividends is one inducement tactic used. As a result, the conversion feature for preferred stocks often resembles that of debt securities. Call protection for the investor is usually about three years, and a 30 to 60-day call notice is typical.

About 50% of convertible equity issues also have a "soft call provision." If the common stock price reaches a specified ratio, the issuer is permitted to force conversion before the end of the normal protection period. *UK term* ***convertible preference shares***

convertibles STOCKHOLDING & INVESTMENTS securities convertible to common stock corporate bonds or shares of preferred stock that can be converted into common stock at a set price on set dates

convertible security STOCKHOLDING & INVESTMENTS investment product that can be converted to another a bond, warrant, or share of preferred stock that can be converted into another type of security, especially common stock

convertible term assurance *UK* INSURANCE = ***convertible term insurance***

convertible term insurance *US* INSURANCE extendable life insurance life insurance with an agreed termination date that the policyholder can convert to insurance until death under specific conditions

convexity ECONOMICS, FINANCE relationship of values the convex shape of a curve. The theory is that if points in a set are connected and the line between any two points is included in the set, then the set is convex. In economics, this corresponds to diminishing ***marginal utility***. In finance it can represent a convex curve in the price yield relationship of a bond or any non-linear price function, for example, that of an option.

conveyance *US* REAL ESTATE transfer of title to real estate the legal transfer of real estate from the seller to the buyer. *UK term* ***conveyancing***

conveyancing *UK* REAL ESTATE = ***conveyance***

COO *abbr* GENERAL MANAGEMENT ***chief operating officer***

cooling-off period **1.** LEGAL time allowed for reconsidering agreement a period during which somebody who is about to enter into an agreement may reflect on all aspects of the arrangement and change his or her mind if necessary **2.** HR & PERSONNEL break in negotiations allowing parties to calm down an agreed pause in a dispute, especially a labor dispute, to allow the tempers of the negotiating parties to cool before the resumption of negotiations **3.** *UK* INSURANCE period allowing cancellation of insurance a period of ten days during which somebody who has signed a life insurance policy may cancel it

cooperative BUSINESS jointly owned organization a business that is jointly owned by the people who operate it, with all profits shared equally

cooperative advertising MARKETING joint advertising by different groups with same goals a joint advertising campaign between groups with a shared objective, for example, retailer groups, or manufacturer and retailer

cooperative movement BUSINESS organized effort to share profits from joint business a movement that aims to share profits and benefits from jointly owned commercial enterprises among members. The movement was begun in Rochdale, Lancashire, England, in 1844 by 28 weavers and developed to include manufacturing and wholesale businesses as well as insurance and financial services. The Co-op in the United Kingdom and the Mondragon cooperative in Spain are two of the best-known examples.

cooperative society BUSINESS organization with customers and employees as joint partners an organization in which customers and employees are partners and share the profits

coproperty BUSINESS co-ownership of property the ownership of property by two or more people together

coproprietor BUSINESS sharer in ownership of property a person who owns a property with one other person or more

copyright LEGAL legal protection for creative material the legal protection for creative ideas, trademarks, and other brand-related material

copy testing MARKETING investigating effectiveness of advertising content research carried out to test the effectiveness of creative advertising material

copywriter MARKETING somebody who writes advertising material a person who devises the wording of an advertisement or promotional material. A copywriter may be employed by an advertising agency or, in scientific or technical areas, directly by a manufacturing or distribution company. Many copywriters also work freelance.

core business BUSINESS firm's most important activities the central, and usually the original, focus of an organization's activities which differentiates it from others and makes a vital contribution to its success. The concept of core business became prominent in the 1980s when ***diversification*** by large companies failed to generate the anticipated degree of commercial success. It was later suggested that organizations

  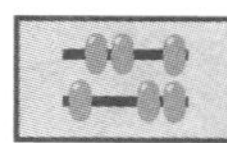      

should avoid diversifying into areas beyond their field of expertise. An organization's core business should be defined by its ***core competences***.

core capability GENERAL MANAGEMENT = ***core competence***

core competence GENERAL MANAGEMENT, HR & PERSONNEL firm's important ability that makes it different a key ability or strength that an organization has acquired that differentiates it from others, gives it ***competitive advantage***, and contributes to its long-term success. Core competence is a resource-based approach to corporate strategy. The terms core competence and core capability are often used interchangeably, but some writers make distinctions between the two concepts. *Also called* ***core capability***

core values **1.** GENERAL MANAGEMENT firm's important guiding principles the guiding principles of an organization, espoused by senior management, and accepted by employees, often reflected in the ***mission statement*** of the organization. Core values often influence the culture of an organization and are usually long-standing beliefs. *Also called* ***shared values*** **2.** HR & PERSONNEL person's important guiding principles a small set of key concepts and ideals that guide somebody's life and help him or her to make important decisions

corner MARKETS control market and price to control enough of a specific good or service to be able to manipulate the price

corporate action STOCKHOLDING & INVESTMENTS firm's action that affects its shares a measure that a company takes that has an effect on the number of shares outstanding or the rights that apply to shares

corporate bond STOCKHOLDING & INVESTMENTS bond issued by firm a long-term bond with fixed interest issued by a corporation

corporate culture GENERAL MANAGEMENT shared values of organization the combined beliefs, values, ethics, procedures, and atmosphere of an organization. The culture of an organization consists of largely unspoken values, norms, and behaviors that become the natural way of doing things. An organization's culture may be more apparent to an external observer than an internal practitioner. There can be several subcultures within an organization, for example, defined by hierarchy, e.g. shop floor or executive, or by function, e.g. sales, design, or production. Changing or renewing corporate culture in order to achieve the organization's strategy is considered one of the major tasks of organization leadership, as it is recognized that such a change is hard to achieve without the will of the leader.

corporate finance FINANCE financial affairs of businesses the financial affairs of companies and institutions

corporate fraud FRAUD dishonest behavior at company level a type of fraud committed by large organizations rather than individuals, for example, auditing irregularities. Since the collapse of Enron and WorldCom in 2001 and 2002, respectively, auditing practice around the world, but especially in the United States, has come under much scrutiny. Both companies had overstated their profits, but the auditors, Arthur Andersen, had approved accounts in each case.

corporate giving GENERAL MANAGEMENT donations by firm to community monetary or in-kind donations by organizations as part of the process of community involvement

corporate governance CORPORATE GOVERNANCE system for running firm the system by which companies are directed and controlled. Boards of directors are responsible for the governance of their companies. The stockholders' role in governance is to appoint the directors and the auditors and to satisfy themselves that an appropriate governance structure is in place. The responsibilities of the board include setting the company's strategic goals, providing the leadership to put them into effect, supervising the management of the business, and reporting to the stockholders on their stewardship. The board's actions are subject to laws, regulations, and the wishes of the stockholders in the general meeting.

corporate hospitality GENERAL MANAGEMENT meals and entertainment paid for by firm entertainment provided by an organization. Corporate hospitality was originally designed to help sales people build relationships with customers, but it is now increasingly used as a staff incentive and in employee team building and training exercises.

corporate identity CORPORATE GOVERNANCE firm's distinctive features as expressed to outsiders the distinctive characteristics or personality of an organization, including corporate culture, values, and philosophy as perceived by those within the organization and presented to those outside. Corporate identity is expressed through the name, symbols, and logos used by the organization, and the design of communication materials, and is a factor influencing the ***corporate image*** of an organization. The creation of a strong corporate identity also involves consistency in the organization's actions, behavior, products, and brands, and often reflects the ***mission statement*** of an organization. A positive corporate identity can promote a sense of purpose and belonging within the organization and encourage employee commitment and involvement.

corporate image CORPORATE GOVERNANCE public's ideas about what firm is like the perceptions and impressions of an organization by the public as a result of interaction with the organization and the way the organization presents itself. Organizations have traditionally focused on the design of communication and advertising materials, using logos, symbols, text, and color to create a favorable impression on target groups, but a variety of additional activities contribute to a positive corporate image. These include public relations programs such as community involvement, sponsorship, and environmental projects, participation in quality improvement schemes, and good practice in industrial relations.

corporate planning CORPORATE GOVERNANCE process of making plans to achieve firm's objectives the process of drawing up detailed action plans to achieve an organization's goals and objectives, taking into account the resources of the organization and the environment within which it operates. Corporate planning represents a formal, structured approach to achieving objectives and to implementing the corporate strategy of an organization. It has traditionally been seen as the responsibility of senior management. The use of the term became predominant during the 1960s but has now been largely superseded by the concept of ***strategic management***.

corporate raider MERGERS & ACQUISITIONS somebody buying stake prior to hostile takeover a person or company that buys a stake in another company with a view to making a ***hostile takeover*** bid

corporate resolution CORPORATE GOVERNANCE document saying who can manage firm's money a document signed by the officers of a corporation naming those persons who can sign checks, withdraw cash, and have access to the corporation's bank account

corporate restructuring GENERAL MANAGEMENT major change in firm's activities a fundamental change in direction and strategy for an organization, which affects the way in which the organization is structured. Corporate restructuring may involve increasing or decreasing the layers of personnel between the top and the bottom of an organization, or reassigning roles and responsibilities. Invariably, corporate restructuring has come to mean reorganizing after a period of unsatisfactory performance and poor results, and is often manifested in the divestment or closure of parts of the business and the outplacement, or shedding, of personnel. In this case, corporate restructuring is used as a euphemism for delayering, rationalization, downsizing, or rightsizing.

corporate spinoff BUSINESS small firm formed from larger parent firm a small company that has been split off from a larger, parent organization

corporate strategy GENERAL MANAGEMENT firm's plans for future the direction an organization takes with the objective of achieving business success in the long term. Recent approaches have focused on the need for companies to adapt to and anticipate changes in the business environment. The formulation of corporate strategy involves establishing the purpose and scope of the organization's activities and the nature of the business it is in, taking the environment in which it operates, its position in the marketplace, and the competition it faces into consideration.

corporation *US* BUSINESS firm owned by stockholders an organization in which a number of people provide financing in return for stock. The principle of ***limited liability*** limits the maximum loss a stockholder can make if the company fails. *UK term* ***limited liability company***

corporation tax TAX tax on profits and gains a tax on profits and capital gains made by companies, calculated before dividends are paid. *Abbr* ***CT***

correction FINANCE adjustment in valuation of something a change in the valuation of something that is thought to be overvalued or undervalued which results in its being more realistically valued

correlation STATISTICS relatedness of variables the interdependence between pairs of variables in data

correlation coefficient STATISTICS measure of relatedness of variables an index of the linear relationship between two variables in data

correspondent bank BANKING bank operating as foreign bank's agent a bank that acts as an agent for a foreign bank

cost FINANCE **1.** money paid for product the amount of money that is paid to secure a good or service. Cost is the amount paid from the purchaser's standpoint, whereas the price is the amount paid from the vendor's standpoint. **2.** calculate cost of something to ascertain what must be paid to acquire a specific thing or engage in a specific activity

cost account ACCOUNTING accounting record of section of business a record of revenue and/or expenditure of a cost center or cost unit

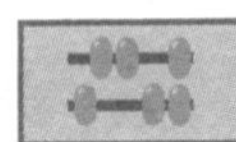

cost accountant ACCOUNTING accountant advising on business costs an accountant who gives managers information about their business costs

cost accounting ACCOUNTING preparation of accounts detailing business costs the process of preparing special accounts of manufacturing and sales costs

cost allocation ACCOUNTING assignment of fixed expenses to cost centers the way in which overhead expenses are assigned to different cost centers

cost analysis OPERATIONS & PRODUCTION calculation of cost of new product the process of calculating in advance how much a new product will cost

cost and freight OPERATIONS & PRODUCTION including product and shipping costs, but not insurance indicates that a quoted price includes the costs of the merchandise and the transportation but not the cost of insurance. *Abbr* ***CFR***

cost audit ACCOUNTING check on cost records and accounts the verification of cost records and accounts, and a check on adherence to prescribed ***cost accounting*** procedures and their continuing relevance

cost basis ACCOUNTING price paid including purchase costs the price paid for an asset plus any expenses such as commissions associated with it at the time of purchase

cost–benefit analysis ACCOUNTING comparison of activity's costs against results a comparison between the cost of the resources used, plus any other costs imposed by an activity, for example, pollution or environmental damage, and the value of the financial and non-financial benefits derived, to establish whether there is a positive outcome. *Also called* ***benefit–cost ratio***

cost center ACCOUNTING section of business that costs firm money a department, function, section, or individual whose cost, overall or in part, is an accepted overhead of a business in return for services provided to other parts of the organization. A cost center is usually an ***indirect cost*** of an organization's products or services.

cost cutting OPERATIONS & PRODUCTION actions to reduce organization's expenses the reduction of the amount of money spent on the operations of an organization or on the provision of products and services. Cost-cutting measures such as budget reductions, salary freezes, and layoffs may be taken by an organization at a time of recession or financial difficulty or in situations where inefficiency has been identified. Alternative approaches to cost cutting include modifying organizational structures and redesigning organizational processes for greater efficiency. Excessive cost cutting may affect ***productivity*** and quality or the organization's ability to add value.

cost driver ACCOUNTING something that affects cost of activity a factor that determines the cost of an activity. Cost drivers are analyzed as part of ***activity based costing*** and can be used in ***continuous improvement*** programs. They are usually assessed together as multiple drivers rather than singly. There are two main types of cost driver: the first is a ***resource driver***, which refers to the contribution of the quantity of resources used to the cost of an activity; the second is an ***activity driver***, which refers to the costs incurred by the activities required to complete a specific task or project.

cost-effective OPERATIONS & PRODUCTION giving best results for least expense offering the maximum benefit for a given level of expenditure. When limited resources are available to meet specific objectives, the cost-effective solution is the best that can be achieved for that level of expenditure and the one that provides good value for money. The term is also used to refer to a level of expenditure that is perceived to be commercially viable.

cost-effectiveness analysis TREASURY MANAGEMENT measurement of how much positive results cost a method for measuring the benefits and effectiveness of a particular item of expenditure. Cost-effectiveness analysis requires an examination of expenditure to determine whether the money spent could have been used more effectively or whether the resulting benefits could have been attained through less financial outlay.

cost factor ACCOUNTING activity or item incurring business cost an activity or item of material, equipment, or personnel that incurs a cost

cost function ECONOMICS ratio of total cost to quantity produced a mathematical function relating a firm's or an industry's total cost to its output and factor costs

cost inflation ECONOMICS = ***cost-push inflation***

costing OPERATIONS & PRODUCTION calculating total expenses related to product the determination of the total cost of a product, from the purchase of ***raw materials*** to delivery to the consumer. There are a large number of costing techniques, including ***life-cycle costing***, ***activity based costing***, and ***operating costing***.

cost, insurance, and freight OPERATIONS & PRODUCTION including product, shipping, and insurance costs indicates that a quoted price includes the costs of the merchandise, transportation, and insurance. *Abbr* ***CIF***

cost of appraisal OPERATIONS & PRODUCTION money spent to check quality of products the costs incurred in order to ensure that outputs produced meet required quality standards

cost of capital TREASURY MANAGEMENT interest paid on operating capital interest paid on the capital used in operating a business

cost of conformance OPERATIONS & PRODUCTION money spent on quality requirements the costs of achieving specific quality standards for a product or service. *See also* ***cost of appraisal***, ***cost of prevention***

cost of entry OPERATIONS & PRODUCTION expense of bringing out new product the costs of introducing a new product to the market. Cost of entry calculations include the cost of all research, development, production, testing, marketing, advertising, and distribution of the new product.

cost of external failure OPERATIONS & PRODUCTION cost of correcting quality of products after sale the costs arising from inadequate quality which are identified after the transfer of ownership from supplier to purchaser. *See also* ***cost of internal failure***

cost of goods sold OPERATIONS & PRODUCTION **1.** money spent on products to sell for a retailer, the cost of buying and acquiring the goods it sells to its customers **2.** money spent on supplying services for a service firm, the cost of the employee services supplied **3.** money spent manufacturing products to sell for a manufacturer, the cost of buying the raw materials and manufacturing finished products. *Abbr* ***COGS***

cost of internal failure TREASURY MANAGEMENT cost of correcting quality of products before sale the costs arising from inadequate quality which are identified before the transfer of ownership from supplier to purchaser. *See also* ***cost of external failure***

cost of living FINANCE money spent on housing, food, and basics the average amount spent by somebody on accommodations, food, and other basic necessities. In the United States, a broad definition might sometimes include education and healthcare. Salaries are usually increased annually to cover rises in the cost of living.

cost-of-living adjustment *US* FINANCE HR & PERSONNEL = ***cost-of-living increase***

cost-of-living allowance *UK* FINANCE HR & PERSONNEL = ***cost-of-living increase***

cost-of-living increase FINANCE, HR & PERSONNEL extra pay to cover price rises a small increase in salaries made to account for rises in the ***cost of living***

cost-of-living index FINANCE, HR & PERSONNEL information on changes in prices over time an index that shows changes in the cost of living by comparing current prices for a variety of goods with the prices paid for them in previous years

cost of nonconformance OPERATIONS & PRODUCTION money lost by not meeting quality requirements the cost of failure to deliver the required standard of quality for a product or service. *See also* ***cost of external failure***, ***cost of internal failure***

cost of prevention OPERATIONS & PRODUCTION money spent to avoid producing low-quality products the costs incurred prior to or during production in order to prevent substandard or defective products or services from being produced

cost of sales OPERATIONS & PRODUCTION = ***cost of goods sold*** *(sense 3)*

cost per click-through E-COMMERCE system paying online advertiser for each ad click a pricing model for online advertising, where the seller gets paid whenever a visitor clicks on an ad

cost-plus pricing OPERATIONS & PRODUCTION deciding price by adding amount to product's cost a standard ***markup*** added to the cost of a product or service to establish a selling price. Many companies simply add a percentage of production costs to arrive at a selling price. The degree of markup depends on the level of anticipated sales. It may incorporate a desired return on investment. Low volume luxury goods may have a high markup; high volume goods may have a relatively lower markup.

cost price OPERATIONS & PRODUCTION selling price yielding no profit to seller a selling price that is the same as the price paid by the seller, which results in no profit being made

cost-push inflation ECONOMICS price increases caused by rise in production costs inflation in which price rises result from increased production costs or similar factors rather than from customer demand

cost reduction OPERATIONS & PRODUCTION cutting costs to increase profits the process of identifying and eliminating unnecessary costs to improve the profitability of a business

  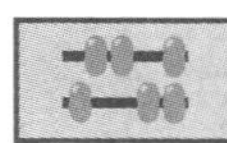   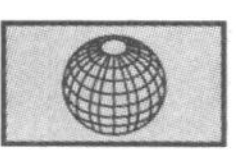   

costs ACCOUNTING amounts of money paid out for something amounts of money that are paid out for something, especially on a regular basis

cost savings OPERATIONS & PRODUCTION benefits from reducing costs the benefits to an organization derived from reducing expenditures

costs of complexity OPERATIONS & PRODUCTION = ***complexity costs***

cottage industry BUSINESS commercial activity performed by individuals or small businesses an industry made up of small businesses, often run from the home of the proprietor

Council of Mortgage Lenders MORTGAGES UK association for mortgage industry in the United Kingdom, the trade association for the mortgage industry, whose members account for about 98% of UK residential mortgage lending. *Abbr* ***CML***

council tax TAX local tax paid in UK in the United Kingdom, a tax paid by individuals or companies to a local authority. Introduced in April 1993, the rate of council tax depends on the estimated value of the residential or commercial property occupied.

counterbid FINANCE **1.** higher bid competing with another bid a higher bid made in reply to a previous bid by another bidder **2.** make counterbid to make a higher bid in reply to a previous bid

counter-claim LEGAL **1.** claim for damages responding to another a claim for damages made in reply to a previous claim **2.** make counter-claim to put in a counter-claim for something

countercyclical ECONOMICS falling when other factor rises tending to increase as another factor decreases and decreasing as it increases. *See also* ***procyclical***

countercyclical stock STOCKHOLDING & INVESTMENTS stock price moving against economic trend a stock that tends to rise as the economy weakens and fall as it strengthens

counterfeit FRAUD illegally produce imitation goods or money to produce forged or imitation goods or money intended to deceive or defraud. Counterfeited goods of inferior quality are often sold at substantially lower prices than genuine products and may bear the ***brand*** or ***trade name*** of the company. Counterfeiting violates ***trademark*** and ***intellectual property*** rights and may damage the reputation of producers of authentic goods. National and international legislation provides some recourse to companies against counterfeiters, but strategies such as consumer warnings and labeling methods are also used to minimize the impact of counterfeiting. Efforts to eliminate counterfeiting are coordinated by the International Anti-Counterfeiting Coalition. **counterfeited** relating to illegally produced imitations used to describe goods or money illegally produced but appearing authentic

counterfoil BANKING small paper record of transaction a slip of paper kept after writing a check, an invoice, or a receipt, as a record of the deal that has taken place

countermand GENERAL MANAGEMENT cancel order given earlier to say that an order must not be carried out

counter-offer BUSINESS higher or lower offer responding to another a higher or lower offer made in reply to another offer

counterparty LEGAL other person in legal agreement a person or organization with whom the person or organization in question is entering into a contract

counterparty risk RISK risk associated with other party to contract the possibility that the person or persons with whom a contract exists will fail to fulfill the terms of their side of the contract

counterpurchase INTERNATIONAL TRADE import bartered for exporter's commitment to further trade a reciprocal trading practice involving a traditional export transaction plus the commitment of the exporter to buy additional goods or services from that country. *See also* ***countertrade***

countersign FINANCE sign document after other signatory to sign a document that has already been signed by somebody else

countertrade INTERNATIONAL TRADE system of trade between two parties a variety of reciprocal trading practices. This umbrella term encompasses practices ranging from the direct exchange of goods for goods where no cash changes hands (***barter***) to more complex variations: ***counterpurchase***, which involves a traditional export transaction plus the commitment of the exporter to buy additional goods or services from that country; and ***buyback***, in which the supplier of a plant or equipment is paid from the future proceeds resulting from the use of the plant. Countertrade conditions vary widely from country to country and can be costly and administratively cumbersome.

countervailing duty TAX, INTERNATIONAL TRADE = ***anti-dumping duty***

country risk INTERNATIONAL TRADE risk of doing business in particular country the risk associated with undertaking transactions with, or holding assets in, a particular country. Sources of risk might be political, economic, or regulatory instability affecting overseas taxation, repatriation of profits, nationalization, currency stability, etc.

coupon STOCKHOLDING & INVESTMENTS **1.** paper requesting bond payment a piece of paper attached to a government bond certificate which a bondholder presents to request payment **2.** interest rate of bond the rate of interest paid on a bond issued at a fixed rate. *Also called* ***coupon rate*** **3.** interest payment on bond an interest payment made to a bondholder, originally on presentation of a dated coupon to the company or an agent of the issuer **clip coupons** FINANCE to collect periodic interest on a bond

coupon rate STOCKHOLDING & INVESTMENTS = ***coupon*** *(sense 2)*

coupon security STOCKHOLDING & INVESTMENTS government security carrying coupon and paying interest a government security that carries a coupon and pays interest, as opposed to a ***zero-coupon security***, that pays no interest but is sold at a discount from its face value. *See also* ***zero-coupon security***

covariance STATISTICS measure of two variables' tendency to change together the value that is predicted from the product of the deviations of two variables from each of their means

covariate STATISTICS less important variable affecting important variable a variable that is not crucial in an investigation but may affect the crucial variables from which a model is being built

covenant FINANCE legal financial agreement a financial agreement conditional on future events, for example, changes in the capital structure and rating of a firm, or fundamental changes in business strategy such as to divest of a major asset or to acquire another company. Covenants are frequently included in bond offerings or bank loan/syndication terms. In the United Kingdom, when payments are made by an individual under covenant to a charity, the charity can reclaim the tax paid by the donor.

cover *UK* INSURANCE = ***coverage*** *(sense 2)*

coverage **1.** MARKETING how many customers reached the percentage of a target audience reached by different media **2.** *US* INSURANCE level of insurance protection the amount or type of protection guaranteed by an insurance policy. *UK term* ***cover***

covered bond STOCKHOLDING & INVESTMENTS bond with loan as security a bond that has mortgage or other loans given as security in case of default

covered option STOCKHOLDING & INVESTMENTS option backed by actual stock an ***option*** whose owner holds the stock for the option. A covered option can be either a ***call option*** or a ***put option***.

covered warrant STOCKHOLDING & INVESTMENTS futures contract a type of ***futures contract*** issued by a financial institution allowing the holder to buy or sell a quantity of its ***financial instruments***

cover note *UK* INSURANCE = ***binder***

covert human intelligence source FRAUD somebody providing information about illegal activity in the United Kingdom, a person who supplies information about somebody being investigated, for example, for fraud, without the knowledge of the person being investigated. *Abbr* ***CHIS***

CP *abbr* FINANCE ***commercial paper***

CPA *abbr* ACCOUNTING ***certified public accountant***

CPF *abbr* PENSIONS ***Central Provident Fund***

CPFR® OPERATIONS & PRODUCTION business practice encouraging collaboration between buyers and sellers a business practice that uses information sharing among buyers and sellers throughout the supply chain to make products available to customers when they need them, while reducing suppliers' costs such as inventory and transportation. *Full form* ***Collaborative Planning, Forecasting, and Replenishment***

CPI *abbr* ECONOMICS ***consumer price index***

CPI inflation ECONOMICS inflation rate of economy using consumer price index the rate of ***inflation*** in an economy calculated using data from a ***consumer price index***

CPIX *ANZ* ECONOMICS consumer price index the ***consumer price index*** excluding interest costs, on the basis that these are a direct outcome of monetary policy

crack E-COMMERCE disable copy protection on software, CD, or DVD to defeat the copy protection that is intended to prevent somebody from illegally copying and distributing a software product, music CD, or DVD

crash **1.** MARKETS very large drop in stock price a precipitous drop in value, especially of the stocks traded in a market **2.** ECONOMICS large and sudden economic decline a sudden and catastrophic downturn in an economy. While there were several in the 20th century, the crash in the United States in 1929 is one of the most famous. However, the events of 2008 have had even more severe global consequences.

crawling peg CURRENCY & EXCHANGE incremental control on exchange rates a method of controlling exchange rates, allowing them to move up or down slowly

CRD *abbr* STOCKHOLDING & INVESTMENTS ***Central Registration Depository***

creative accounting FRAUD accounting methods used to conceal firm's true state the use of accounting methods to hide aspects of a company's financial dealings in order to make the company appear more or less successful than it is in reality (slang) *See also* ***corporate fraud***

creative destruction MERGERS & ACQUISITIONS process of new firms and products replacing old a way of describing the endless cycle of innovation, which results in established goods, services, or organizations being replaced by new models. The term was first mentioned by Joseph Schumpeter in *Capitalism, Socialism and Democracy* (1942), but used heavily during the dot-com boom of the late 1990s and early 2000s.

creative thinking *or* creativity GENERAL MANAGEMENT coming up with original interesting ideas the generation of new ideas by approaching problems or existing practices in innovative or imaginative ways. Psychologists have disagreed on the nature of creative thinking. Until about 1980, research concentrated on identifying the personality traits of creative people, but more recently psychologists have focused on the mental processes involved. Creative thinking involves reexamining assumptions and reinterpreting facts, ideas, and past experience. A growing interest in creative thinking as a source of ***competitive advantage*** has developed in recent years, and creative thinking is considered important, not just for the development of new products and services, but also for its role in organizational decision making and problem solving. Many organizations actively seek a corporate culture that encourages creative thinking. There are a number of techniques used to foster creative thinking, including brainstorming. Creative thinking is linked to innovation, the process of taking a new idea and turning it into a market offering.

credit FINANCE **1.** positive amount of assets after liabilities are deducted the amount of money left over when a person or organization has more ***assets*** than ***liabilities***, and those liabilities are subtracted from the total of the assets **2.** lender's belief that borrower will repay loan the trust that a lender has in a borrower's ability to repay a loan, or a loan itself **3.** arrangement to pay later for product bought now a financial arrangement between the vendor and the purchaser of a good or service by which the purchaser may buy what he or she requires, but pay for it at a later date **post a credit** ACCOUNTING in bookkeeping, to enter a credit item in a ledger

credit account FINANCE = ***charge account***

credit availability FINANCE ease of borrowing the ease with which money can be borrowed at a given time

credit balance FINANCE sum owed on credit account the amount of money that a customer owes on a ***charge account***

credit bureau FINANCE US firm evaluating people's ability to repay loans a company that assesses the creditworthiness of people for businesses or banks. *See also* ***mercantile agency***

credit capacity FINANCE total amount somebody can borrow and repay the amount of money that a person or organization can borrow and be expected to repay

credit card BANKING card from bank used to pay for things a card issued by a bank or financial institution and accepted by a merchant in payment for a transaction for which the cardholder must subsequently reimburse the issuer. *See also* ***charge card***

credit ceiling FINANCE = ***credit limit***

credit column ACCOUNTING accounting column recording money received the right-hand column in accounts showing money received

credit committee RISK group assessing creditworthiness a committee that evaluates a potential borrower's credit status and ability to repay loans

credit company FINANCE firm that lends money a company that extends credit to people. It may be an independent company or a subsidiary of a parent company such as an automobile manufacturer whose products are being bought.

credit control RISK monitoring of customers' credit management a system of checks designed to ensure that customers pay on time and do not owe more than their credit limit

credit controller FINANCE employee who manages payment of overdue invoices a member of staff whose job is to expedite the payment of overdue invoices

credit cooperative FINANCE group borrowing together an organization of people who join together to gain advantage in borrowing

credit creation FINANCE ability of banks to lend more money the collective ability of finance companies, banks, and other lenders of money to make money available to borrowers. While a central bank can create money, it cannot create credit.

credit crunch FINANCE inability or reluctance of banks to lend money the collective inability or unwillingness of finance companies, banks, and other lenders to make money available to borrowers (informal) *Also called* ***credit squeeze, liquidity squeeze***

credit default swap STOCKHOLDING & INVESTMENTS, RISK assumption of credit risk in return for payments a ***derivative instrument*** similar in structure to an insurance policy, in which the buyer of the instrument agrees to make payments to the seller in return for a guarantee that the seller will assume the credit risk of a third party. *Abbr* ***CDS***

credit deposit E-COMMERCE credit card transaction amount put in seller's bank the value of the credit card purchases deposited in a merchant's bank account after the acquirer's fees are deducted

credit derivative STOCKHOLDING & INVESTMENTS, RISK contract transferring lender's risk a ***financial instrument*** or ***derivative*** by which the lender's risk is devolved to a third party and separately traded

credit entity FINANCE person borrowing or lending a borrower from a finance company, bank, or other lender of money, or the lender of the funds

credit entry ACCOUNTING entry for income or value an item in a financial statement recording money received or the value of an asset

credit exposure RISK lender's risk that borrower will not repay the risk to a lender that a borrower will default and not fulfill their contractual payment

credit facility BANKING arrangement to supply credit an arrangement with a bank or supplier that enables a person or organization to be given credit or borrow money when it is needed, for example, a ***letter of credit, revolving credit*** or a ***term loan.*** *Also called* ***lending facility***

credit freeze FINANCE period when government limits banks' lending a period during which lending by banks is restricted by government

credit granter FINANCE lender a person or organization that lends money

credit history FINANCE record of somebody's repayment of loans a potential borrower's record of debt repayment. Individuals or organizations with a poor credit history may find it difficult to find lenders who are willing to give them a loan.

Credit Industry Fraud Avoidance System FRAUD UK fraud prevention service in the United Kingdom, a nonprofit membership organization established for the purpose of preventing financial crime. *Abbr* ***CIFAS***

crediting rate STOCKHOLDING & INVESTMENTS interest rate on insurance policy the interest rate paid on an insurance policy which is an investment

credit limit FINANCE total amount somebody is allowed to borrow the highest amount that a lender will allow somebody to borrow, for example, on a credit card. *Also called* ***credit ceiling***

credit line FINANCE = ***line of credit***

credit-linked note RISK fixed-income security with embedded credit default swap a fixed-income security with an embedded ***credit default swap*** which is sold to investors willing to take the risk of default in return for a high yield on their investment

credit market MARKETS market trading in debt securities the market in which debt securities such as loans, corporate bonds, commercial paper, and ***credit default swaps*** are bought and sold

credit note *CANADA, UK* FINANCE = ***credit slip***

creditor FINANCE somebody you owe money for goods or services a person or an entity to whom money is owed as a consequence of the receipt of goods or services in advance of payment

creditor days FINANCE number of days firm takes to pay creditors the number of days on average that a company requires to pay its creditors.

To determine creditor days, divide the cumulative amount of unpaid suppliers' bills (also called trade creditors) by sales, then multiply by 365. If suppliers' bills total $800,000 and sales are $9,000,000, the calculation is:

$$\frac{800,000}{9,000,000} \times 365 = 32.44 \text{ days}$$

The company takes 32.44 days on average to pay its bills.

Creditor days is an indication of a company's creditworthiness in the eyes of its suppliers and creditors, since it shows how long they are willing to wait for payment. Within reason, the higher the number the better, because all companies want to conserve cash. At the same time, a company that is especially slow to pay its bills (100 or more days, for example) may be a company having trouble generating cash, or one trying to finance its operations with its suppliers' funds. *See also* ***debtor days***

creditor nation INTERNATIONAL TRADE country with balance of payments surplus a country where

  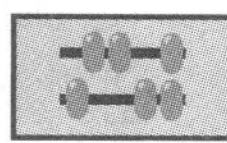   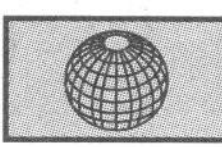   

payments received exceed those made over the same period

creditors' committee FINANCE lenders' group seeking money from bankrupt borrower a group that directs the efforts of creditors to receive partial repayment from a bankrupt person or organization. *Also called* ***creditors' steering committee***

creditors' meeting FINANCE meeting of bankrupt's creditors a meeting of those to whom a bankrupt person or organization owes money

creditors' settlement FINANCE agreement for partial repayment by bankrupt borrower an agreement on partial repayment to those to whom a bankrupt person or organization owes money

creditors' steering committee FINANCE = ***creditors' committee***

credit rating *or* credit ranking FINANCE **1.** evaluation of creditworthiness an assessment of a person's or an organization's ability to pay back money that they owe according to the terms on which it was borrowed, based on a broad assessment of financial health including previous loans and other outstanding financial obligations **2.** process of evaluating creditworthiness the process of assessing a person's or an organization's ability to pay back money that they owe according to the terms on which it was borrowed

credit rating agency *US* FINANCE firm evaluating creditworthiness a company that assesses a person's or an organization's ability to pay back money that they owe according to the terms on which it was borrowed, on behalf of businesses or banks. *UK term* ***credit-reference agency***

credit rationing FINANCE, RISK process of making it harder to borrow money the process of making credit less easily available or subject to high interest rates

credit receipt *US* FINANCE = ***credit slip***

credit-reference agency *UK* FINANCE = ***credit rating agency***

credit references FINANCE list of previous lenders when opening credit account details of individuals, companies, or banks who have given credit to a person or company in the past, supplied as references when somebody is opening a credit account with a new supplier

credit report FINANCE information concerning person's or organization's creditworthiness information about the ability of a person or organization to pay back money that they owe, used by financial institutions in determining decisions relevant to granting credit

credit risk RISK possibility that debtor will default the possibility that a person or an organization will not be able to pay back money that they owe according to the terms on which it was borrowed

credit sale FINANCE sale for which buyer can pay later a sales transaction by which the buyer is allowed to take immediate possession of the purchased goods and pay for them at a later date

credit scoring FINANCE calculation during credit rating a calculation done in the process of assessing a person's or an organization's ability to pay back money that they owe according to the terms on which it was borrowed

credit side ACCOUNTING part of financial statement with assets the section of a financial statement that lists assets. In ***double-entry bookkeeping***, the right-hand side of each account is designated as the credit side. *See also* ***debit side***

credit slip *US* FINANCE statement that store owes customer money a receipt saying that a store owes a customer an amount of money for returned goods and entitling the person to goods of that value. *Also called* ***credit receipt***. *UK term* ***credit note***

credit spread RISK difference between debt yield of firm and benchmark the difference between the yield on the debt of a particular company and the yield on a risk-free asset such as a US ***Treasury bond*** having the same maturity

credit spread option STOCKHOLDING & INVESTMENTS, RISK option contract based on firm's credit spread an option contract on the ***credit spread*** of the debt of a particular company whose payoff is based on changes in the credit spread

credit spread swap STOCKHOLDING & INVESTMENTS, RISK exchange of fixed for credit-spread payment a ***swap*** in which one party makes a fixed payment to the other on the swap's settlement date and the second party pays the first an amount based on the actual credit spread

credit squeeze FINANCE = ***credit crunch***

credit standing FINANCE somebody's reputation for repaying debt the reputation that somebody has with regard to meeting financial obligations

credit system FINANCE means of making loans a set of rules and organizations involved in making loans on a commercial basis

credit union BANKING financial institution providing banking services to members a cooperative financial organization that provides banking services, including loans, to its members at relatively low rates of interest

creditworthiness FINANCE reliability in repaying debt the extent to which a person or organization is financially reliable enough to borrow money or be given credit

creditworthy FINANCE reliable in repaying debt regarded as being reliable in terms of ability to pay back money owed according to the terms on which it was borrowed

creeping takeover MERGERS & ACQUISITIONS takeover through gradual acquisition a takeover of a company achieved by the gradual acquisition of small amounts of stock over an extended period of time (slang)

creeping tender offer MERGERS & ACQUISITIONS gradual acquisition of firm's stock an acquisition of many shares in a company by gradual purchase, especially to avoid US restrictions on tender offers

CREST MARKETS UK electronic transaction system in the United Kingdom, the paperless system used for settling stock transactions electronically

crisis management GENERAL MANAGEMENT firm's methods of dealing with unexpected negative situation actions taken by an organization in response to unexpected events or situations with potentially negative effects that threaten resources and people or the success and continued operation of the organization. Crisis management includes the development of plans to reduce the risk of a crisis occurring and to deal with any crises that do arise, and the implementation of these plans so as to minimize the impact of crises and assist the organization to recover from them. Crisis situations may occur as a result of external factors such as the development of a new product by a competitor or changes in legislation, or internal factors such as a product failure or faulty ***decision making***, and often involve the need to make quick decisions on the basis of uncertain or incomplete information. *See also* ***risk management, disaster management***

Criteria of Control Board REGULATION & COMPLIANCE Canadian financial regulator a group that issues guidance on designing, assessing, and reporting on the control systems of organizations, under the aegis of the the Canadian Institute of Chartered Accountants. *Abbr* ***CoCo***

criticality OPERATIONS & PRODUCTION evaluation of ways something can fail a ranking of the severity of the various ways in which a system, device, or process can fail, their frequency of occurrence, and the consequences of their failure

critical mass GENERAL MANAGEMENT when firm or project becomes clearly worth continuing the point at which an organization or project has gained sufficient momentum or ***market share*** to be either self-sustaining or worth the input of extra investment or resources

critical-path method *or* critical-path analysis GENERAL MANAGEMENT, OPERATIONS & PRODUCTION way of determining activities necessary for success a planning technique used especially in project management to identify the activities within a project that are critical for its success. In critical-path method, individual activities within a project and their duration are recorded in a diagram or flow chart. A critical path is plotted through the diagram, showing the sequence in which activities must be completed in order to complete the project in the shortest amount of time, incurring the least cost.

critical region STATISTICS set of test results causing rejection of hypothesis the range of values of a test statistic that lead a researcher to reject the null hypothesis

critical restructuring GENERAL MANAGEMENT very large changes in firm's organization major economic or social changes that fundamentally reshape traditional patterns of organization

critical success factor GENERAL MANAGEMENT aspect essential to firm's success any of the aspects of a business that are identified as vital for successful targets to be reached and maintained. Critical success factors are usually identified in such areas as production processes, employee and organization skills, functions, techniques, and technologies. The identification and strengthening of such factors may be similar to identifying ***core competences***, and is considered an essential element in achieving and maintaining ***competitive advantage***.

critical value STATISTICS standard against which hypothesis is rejected the value with which a researcher compares a statistic from sample data in order to determine whether or not the null hypothesis should be rejected

CRM *abbr* MARKETING ***customer relationship management***

CRO *abbr* REGULATION & COMPLIANCE ***Companies Registration Office***

crony capitalism ECONOMICS system in which well-connected people control wealth a form of capitalism in which business contracts are awarded to the family and friends of the government in power rather than by open-market tender

        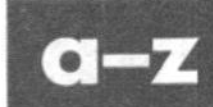

cross MARKETS transaction with shared broker a transaction in securities in which one broker acts for both parties

crossborder services ACCOUNTING accounting services for client in another country accounting services provided by an accounting firm in one country on behalf of a client based in another country

crossborder trade INTERNATIONAL TRADE trade between neighboring countries the buying and selling of goods and services between two countries that have a common frontier

cross currency swap CURRENCY & EXCHANGE = ***currency swap*** *(sense 1)*

cross-docking OPERATIONS & PRODUCTION immediately matching items between incoming and outgoing shipments a procedure used in ***logistics*** to reduce handling and warehousing costs by immediately matching items from incoming shipments on the loading dock with outgoing shipment requirements and transferring them to the outgoing vehicles

crossed cheque *UK* BANKING check that can only be deposited a check with two lines across it showing that it can only be deposited at a bank and not exchanged for cash

crossed market MARKETS where price to buy exceeds price to sell a situation in which a bid to buy a stock or option is higher than the offer to sell

cross-functional OPERATIONS & PRODUCTION working as team with different functions toward goal used to describe a group of employees who have different functions within an organization and who work together as a team to achieve an objective

cross-hedging MARKETS hedging with related futures contract a form of hedging using an option on a different but related commodity, especially a currency

cross holdings STOCKHOLDING & INVESTMENTS, MERGERS & ACQUISITIONS reciprocal stockholdings designed to combat takeovers a situation in which two companies own stock in each other in order to stop either from being taken over

cross listing OPERATIONS & PRODUCTION trying to sell same thing in multiple places the practice of offering the same item for sale in more than one place

cross rate CURRENCY & EXCHANGE exchange rate of two currencies against third currency the rate of exchange between two currencies expressed in terms of the rate of exchange between them and a third currency, for example, sterling and the peso in relation to the dollar. *Also called* ***exchange cross rate***

cross-sectional study STATISTICS survey collecting various information at once a statistical study in which a variety of information is collected at the same time, for example, in a single telephone call

cross-sell OPERATIONS & PRODUCTION sell range of complementary products at same time to sell customers a range of products or services offered by an organization at the same time, for example, offering insurance services while selling somebody a mortgage

crowding out *or* crowding out effect MARKETS effect of major borrowing by government on credit markets the effect on credit markets produced by extremely large borrowing by a national government, causing an increase in interest rates and a reduction in some areas of investment

Crown Agent INTERNATIONAL TRADE UK government representative on international board a person appointed by the UK government to sit on a board that provides financial, commercial, and other services to some foreign governments and international organizations

crown jewels FINANCE company's most valuable properties an organization's most valuable ***assets***, often the motivation behind ***takeover bids***

cryptography E-COMMERCE method of restricting who can access website a powerful means of restricting access to part or all of a website, whereby only a user with an assigned "key" can request and read the information

CSP *abbr* E-COMMERCE ***commerce service provider***

CT *abbr* TAX ***corporation tax***

CTI *abbr* BUSINESS ***computer telephony integration***

culture shock GENERAL MANAGEMENT confusion on exposure to unfamiliar situation the effects on an employee or organization when faced with new, unfamiliar, or rapidly changing circumstances. Symptoms of culture shock include uncertainty, stress, confusion, disorientation, or simply not knowing how to act in the circumstances. Culture shock can occur in a number of scenarios, for example, when expatriates come across new cultures and customs in a foreign country; when new staff are thrown into the deep end of a busy department; when two organizations merge with poor strategic, operational, or cultural synergy; or when public sector organizations adopt private sector practices. The degree of shock can be reduced through careful analysis, planning, training, and consequent preparedness.

cum FINANCE with the Latin word for "with." Its opposite is "ex-."

cum-all STOCKHOLDING & INVESTMENTS including all normal benefits of stock ownership including all of the entitlements that are attached to owning a share of stock. *See also* ***ex-all***

cum coupon STOCKHOLDING & INVESTMENTS with coupon attached or before payment of interest with a coupon attached or before interest due on a security is paid

cum dividend *or* cum div STOCKHOLDING & INVESTMENTS including unpaid dividend including the next dividend still to be paid

cum rights STOCKHOLDING & INVESTMENTS including rights an indication that the buyer of the stock is entitled to participate in a forthcoming ***rights issue***

cumulative increasing over time added to regularly and becoming increasingly larger over a period of time

cumulative interest FINANCE total interest the total interest added to capital originally invested

cumulative method GENERAL MANAGEMENT system of adding things together a system in which items are added together, used, for example, in some forms of electing officers to a number of posts

cumulative preference share *UK* STOCKHOLDING & INVESTMENTS = ***cumulative preferred stock***

cumulative preferred stock *US* STOCKHOLDING & INVESTMENTS preferred stock whose dividends accumulate if not paid a type of ***preferred stock*** that will have the dividend paid at a later date even if the company is not able to pay a dividend in the current year. *UK term* ***cumulative preference share***

cumulative voting CORPORATE GOVERNANCE system of election of directors a voting system that allows a stockholder one vote per share of stock owned multiplied by the number of directors to be elected. Stockholders may distribute these votes among the candidates in any way they choose.

currency CURRENCY & EXCHANGE money of particular country the system of money in general circulation in a particular country

currency backing CURRENCY & EXCHANGE gold or securities supporting currency gold, other valuable metal, or government securities, that support the strength of a country's currency

currency band CURRENCY & EXCHANGE allowable range of variation in exchange rate exchange rate levels between which a ***currency*** is allowed to move without full revaluation or devaluation

currency basket CURRENCY & EXCHANGE = ***basket of currencies***

currency clause CURRENCY & EXCHANGE clause fixing exchange rate for contract a clause in a contract that avoids problems of payment caused by exchange rate changes by fixing in advance the exchange rate for the various transactions covered by the contract

currency future STOCKHOLDING & INVESTMENTS option on currency a contract for buying or selling currency at a particular exchange rate within a set period

currency hedging STOCKHOLDING & INVESTMENTS, RISK reducing risk by diversifying currency holdings a method of reducing ***exchange rate risk*** by diversifying currency holdings and adjusting them according to changes in exchange rates

currency mismatching CURRENCY & EXCHANGE depositing low-interest loan in country with high-interest the practice of borrowing money in the currency of a country where interest rates are low and depositing it in the currency of a country with higher interest rates. The potential profit from the interest rate margin may be offset by changes in the exchange rates, which increase the value of the loan in the company's balance sheet.

currency note CURRENCY & EXCHANGE paper money a piece of paper money, representing a promise to pay the bearer a specific sum on demand

currency reserves CURRENCY & EXCHANGE government's reserves of foreign currency foreign money held by a government to support its own currency and to pay its debts

currency risk CURRENCY & EXCHANGE, RISK likelihood of adverse exchange rate the possibility of a loss due to future changes in exchange rates

currency swap CURRENCY & EXCHANGE **1.** agreement to use one currency for another an arrangement between two parties to exchange an amount of one currency for another currency, later returning the original amounts. This is useful, for instance, where both parties hold a currency other than the one they need at a specific time. *Also called* ***cross currency swap*** **2.** selling and buying same amount of foreign currency

the selling or buying of a particular amount of a foreign currency for immediate delivery, accompanied by selling or buying the same amount of the same currency on the ***futures market***

currency unit CURRENCY & EXCHANGE coin or bill in specific monetary system each of the notes and coins that are the medium of exchange in a country

current account BANKING **1.** record of transactions between two parties a record of transactions between two parties, for example, between a bank and its customer, or a branch and head office, or two trading nations. *Abbr* ***c/a*** **2.** *UK* = ***checking account***

current account equilibrium INTERNATIONAL TRADE balance of country's imports and exports a country's economic circumstances when its expenditure equals its income from trade and ***invisible earnings***

current account mortgage MORTGAGES long-term real estate loan a long-term loan, usually for the purchase of real estate, in which the borrower pays interest on the sum loaned in monthly installments and repays the principal in one lump sum at the end of the term. When calculating the interest payments, the lender takes into account the balance in the borrower's checking and/or savings accounts. It is the borrower's responsibility to make provisions to accumulate the required capital during the period of the mortgage, usually by contributing to tax efficient investment plans or by relying on an anticipated inheritance. *See also* ***mortgage***

current assets FINANCE cash, or asset to be converted to cash cash or other assets, such as stock and long-term investments, held for conversion into cash in the normal course of trading

current assets financing FINANCE using current assets to back loan the use of current assets such as cash, debtors, and stock as collateral for a loan

current cash balance STOCKHOLDING & INVESTMENTS money that broker's client has available to invest the amount, which excludes balances due soon for outstanding transactions, that a client has available for investment with a broker

current cost accounting ACCOUNTING accounting based on current replacement cost of assets a method of accounting that notes the cost of replacing assets at current prices, rather than valuing assets at their original cost. *Abbr* ***CCA***. See also ***historical cost accounting***

current earnings FINANCE firm's most recent annual earnings the annual earnings most recently reported by a company, which exclude interest and tax

current liabilities FINANCE debt to be repaid within one year liabilities which fall due for payment within one year. They include that part of any long-term loan due for repayment within one year.

current principal factor FINANCE part of original loan left to be paid the portion of the initial amount of a loan that remains to be paid

current ratio FINANCE ratio of current assets to current liabilities a ratio of ***current assets*** to ***current liabilities***, used to measure a company's liquidity and its ability to meet its short-term debt obligations.

The current ratio formula is a simple one:

$$\frac{\text{Current assets}}{\text{Current liabilities}} = \text{Current ratio}$$

Current assets are the ones that a company can turn into cash within 12 months during the ordinary course of business. Current liabilities are bills due to be paid within the coming 12 months.

For example, if a company's current assets are $300,000 and its current liabilities are $200,000, its current ratio would be:

$$\frac{300,000}{200,000} = 1.5$$

As a rule of thumb, the 1.5 figure means that a company should be able to get hold of $1.50 for every $1.00 it owes.

The higher the ratio, the more liquid the company. Prospective lenders expect a positive current ratio, often of at least 1.5. However, too high a ratio is cause for alarm too, because it indicates declining receivables and/or inventory, which may mean declining liquidity. *Also called* ***working capital ratio***

current stock value STOCKHOLDING & INVESTMENTS value of all stock held the value of all stock in an investor's set of holdings, including stock in transactions that have not yet been settled

current value FINANCE current assets minus current liabilities a ratio indicating the amount by which ***current assets*** exceed ***current liabilities***

current yield STOCKHOLDING & INVESTMENTS interest on bond divided by market price the interest being paid on a bond divided by its current market price, expressed as a percentage. *Also called* ***income yield***

curriculum vitae *UK* HR & PERSONNEL document summarizing job history and skills = ***résumé***

cushion FINANCE firm's surplus money money left after a company has serviced its debts and therefore available to meet unexpected demands

cushion bond STOCKHOLDING & INVESTMENTS high-interest bond a bond that pays a high rate of interest and so depreciates less when interest rates rise but is at risk of being ***called*** if interest rates fall

CUSIP *abbr* REGULATION & COMPLIANCE ***Committee on Uniform Securities Identification Procedures***

custodial account BANKING bank account for child in the United States, a bank account opened, normally by a parent or guardian, in the name of a minor who is too young to control it

custodian BANKING manager of trust funds a legal guardian, whether a person or an institution, whose principal function is to maintain and grow the assets contained in a trust

customer MARKETING somebody who buys product or service a purchaser of a product or service. A customer is a person or organization that purchases or obtains goods or services from other organizations such as manufacturers, retailers, wholesalers, or service providers. A customer is not necessarily the same person as the ***consumer***, as a product or service can be paid for by one party, the customer, and used by another, the consumer.

customer capital FINANCE value of firm's customer relationships the value of an organization's relationships with its customers, which involves factors such as market share, customer retention rates, and profitability of customers

customer care MARKETING = ***customer relations***

customer-centric model GENERAL MANAGEMENT emphasis on customers a business model organized around the needs of the customer

customer complaint GENERAL MANAGEMENT *see* ***complaint***

customer demand MARKETING amount of product customers will and can buy the quantity of a product or service that customers are willing and able to purchase at a given price during a given period of time

customer equity FINANCE value of firm's customer relationships the total asset value of the relationships that an organization has with its customers. The term was coined by Robert C. Blattberg and John Deighton in their article "Manage marketing by the customer equity test," *Harvard Business Review* 74:4 (Jul/Aug 1996), pp. 136–144. Customer equity is based on ***customer lifetime value***, and an understanding of customer equity can be used to optimize the balance of investment in the acquisition and retention of customers. It is also known as ***customer capital*** and forms one component of the ***intellectual capital*** of an organization.

customer expectation MARKETING what potential buyer thinks or feels about product the needs, wants, and preconceived ideas of a customer about a product or service. Customer expectation will be influenced by his or her perception of the product or service and can be created by previous experience, advertising, hearsay, awareness of competitors, and brand image. The level of customer service is also a factor, and a customer might expect to encounter efficiency, helpfulness, reliability, confidence in the staff, and a personal interest in his or her patronage. If customer expectations are met, then customer satisfaction results. *Also called* ***buyer expectation***

customer flow MARKETING how many customers pass through store, airport, etc. the number and pattern of customers coming into a store or passing through a train or bus station, airport, or other large service, retail, or leisure area. Customer flow can be monitored by observation, time lapse or normal closed circuit television, or, less satisfactorily, by analysis of purchase data. This provides useful information about the number of customers, flow patterns, bottlenecks, areas not visited, and other aspects of consumer behavior.

customer focus GENERAL MANAGEMENT firm's attention to what customers want or need an organizational orientation toward satisfying the needs of potential and actual ***customers***. Customer focus is considered to be one of the keys to business success. Achieving customer focus involves ensuring that the whole organization, and not just frontline service staff, puts its customers first. All activities, from the planning of a new product to its production, marketing, and after-sales care, should be built around the customer. Every department and every employee should share the same customer-focused vision. This can be aided by practicing good ***customer relationship management*** and maintaining a ***customer relations*** program.

customer knowledge management GENERAL MANAGEMENT use of information from customers to improve firm the acquisition and use of customer-

  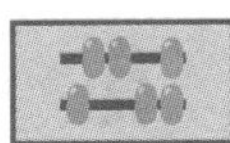      

related knowledge to create value for both the organization and the purchasers of its products and services. Customer knowledge management is a form of ***knowledge management*** which focuses on the human aspects of customer knowledge acquired through direct interaction with the customer as well as quantitative transactional data. Some writers restrict the concept to the use of knowledge residing in, or acquired from, customers as opposed to information *about* customers collected by ***customer relationship management*** systems. Interactive technologies, conversations with customers, and user groups may be used to create knowledge-sharing and partnership between the organization and its customers.

customer lifetime value FINANCE expected profit from customer over time the ***net present value*** of the profit an organization expects to realize from a customer for the duration of their relationship. Customer lifetime value focuses on customers as assets rather than sources of revenue; the volume of purchases made, customer retention rates, and profit margins are factors taken into account in calculations. Strategies for increasing customer lifetime value aim to improve customer retention and lengthen the life of the relationship with the customer. It is a key factor in the customer equity of an organization.

customer profitability FINANCE amount of firm's profits due to customers the degree to which a ***customer*** or segment of customers contributes toward an organization's profits. Customer profitability has been shown to be produced primarily by a small proportion of customers, perhaps 10% to 20%, who generate up to 80% of a company's profits. Up to 40% of customers may generate only moderate profits, and the other 40% may be loss making. Such data enables companies to focus efforts on the most profitable segments.

customer recovery MARKETING attempts to win back firm's customers activities intended to win back customers who no longer buy from an organization

customer relations MARKETING how firm deals with buyers of its products the approach of an organization to winning and retaining customers. The most critical activity of any organization wishing to stay in business is its approach to dealing with its customers. Putting customers at the center of all activities is seen by many as an integral part of quality, pricing, and product differentiation. On one level, customer relations means keeping customers fully informed, turning complaints into opportunities, and genuinely listening to customers. On another level, being a customer-focused organization means ensuring that all activities relating to trading—for example, planning, design, production, marketing, and after-sales of a product or service—are built around the customer, and that every department and individual employee understands and shares the same vision. Only then can a company deliver continuous ***customer satisfaction*** and experience good customer relations. *Also called* ***customer care***

customer relationship management MARKETING development of connections with buyers of firm's products the cultivation of meaningful relationships with actual or potential purchasers of goods or services. Customer relationship management aims to increase an organization's sales by promoting customer satisfaction, and can be achieved using tools such as relationship marketing.

CRM is particularly important in the sphere of e-commerce, as there is no personal interaction between the vendor and the customer. A website therefore has to work hard to develop the relationship with customers and demonstrate that their business is valued. A CRM system generally includes some or all of the following components: customer information systems, ***personalization*** systems, ***content management*** systems, ***call center*** automation, ***data warehousing***, ***data mining***, sales force automation, and campaign management systems. All these elements combine to provide the essentials of CRM: understanding customer needs; anticipating their information requirements; answering their questions promptly and comprehensively; delivering exactly what they order; making deliveries on time; and suggesting new products that they will be genuinely interested in. *Abbr* ***CRM***

customer retention MARKETING maintaining connections with buyers of firm's products the maintenance of the patronage of people who have purchased a company's goods or services once and the gaining of repeat purchases. Customer retention occurs when a customer is loyal to a company, a brand, or a specific product or service, expressing long-term commitment and refusing to purchase from competitors. A company can adopt a number of strategies to retain its customers. Of critical importance to such strategies are the wider concepts of customer service, customer relations, and relationship marketing. Companies can build loyalty and retention through the use of a number of techniques, including ***database marketing***, the issue of loyalty cards redeemable against a variety of goods or services, preferential discounts, free gifts, special promotions, newsletters or magazines, members' clubs, or customized products in limited editions. It has been argued that customer retention is linked to employee loyalty, since loyal employees build up long-term relationships with customers.

customer satisfaction MARKETING how happy buyers are with firm's products the degree to which ***customer expectations*** of a product or service are met or exceeded. Corporate and individual customers may have widely differing reasons for purchasing a product or service and therefore any measurement of satisfaction will need to be able to take into account such differences. The quality of after-sales service can also be a crucial factor in influencing any purchasing decision. More and more companies are striving, not just for customer satisfaction, but for customer delight, that extra bit of added value that may lead to increased customer loyalty. Any extra added value, however, will need to be carefully costed.

customer service MARKETING how firm helps buyers of its products the way in which an organization deals with its ***customers***. Customer service is most evident in sales and ***after-sales service***, but should infuse all the processes in the ***value chain***. Good customer service is the result of adopting ***customer focus***. Poor customer service can be a product of poor ***customer relations***.

customization GENERAL MANAGEMENT changing products for individual customers the process of modifying products or services to meet the requirements of individual customers

customs barrier INTERNATIONAL TRADE measure designed to restrict trade a provision intended to make trade more difficult, for example, a high level of duty

customs broker INTERNATIONAL TRADE shipper's agent clearing goods through customs a person or company that takes goods through customs for a shipping company

customs clearance INTERNATIONAL TRADE **1.** passage granted to imports or exports by customs the act of passing goods through customs so that they can enter or leave the country **2.** document proving payment of customs duty a document given by customs to a shipper to show that customs duty has been paid and the goods can be shipped

customs declaration INTERNATIONAL TRADE form stating dutiable imports a statement showing goods being imported on which duty will have to be paid

customs duty INTERNATIONAL TRADE tax on imports and exports tax paid on goods brought into or taken out of a country

customs entry point INTERNATIONAL TRADE border point for declaring goods to customs a place at a border between two countries where goods are declared to customs

customs formalities INTERNATIONAL TRADE procedures followed by customs officials a declaration of goods by the shipper and examination of them by the customs authorities

customs seal INTERNATIONAL TRADE seal showing contents not examined by customs officials a seal attached by a customs officer to a box, to show that the contents have not passed through customs

customs tariff INTERNATIONAL TRADE list of import taxes a list of taxes to be paid on imported goods

customs union INTERNATIONAL TRADE agreement allowing goods to cross borders without duties an agreement between several countries that goods can travel between them without ***duty*** being paid, while goods from other countries are subject to duties

cutthroat BUSINESS extremely competitive aggressively ruthless, especially in dealing with competitors

cutting-edge GENERAL MANAGEMENT technologically advanced at the forefront of new technologies or markets

CV *abbr* *UK* HR & PERSONNEL document summarizing job history and skills ***curriculum vitae*** = ***résumé***

cwmni cyfyngedig cyhoeddus *UK* ***see ccc***

cybermarketing E-COMMERCE advertising via the Internet the use of Internet-based promotions of any kind. This may involve targeted e-mail, bulletin boards, websites, or sites from which the customer can download files.

cybersales E-COMMERCE electronic sales sales made electronically through computers and information systems

cyberspace E-COMMERCE Internet as imagined world of electronic data the online world and its communication networks

cyberterrorism E-COMMERCE terrorist methods to disrupt information systems the use of techniques that disrupt or damage computer-based information systems to cause fear, injury, or economic loss

cyberwar E-COMMERCE using Internet to damage other's computer networks the use of information systems such as the Internet to exploit or damage an adversary's computer-based network processes

cycle time OPERATIONS & PRODUCTION **1.** time taken to get product to market the total time taken from the start of the production of a product or service to its completion. Cycle time includes processing time, move time, wait time, and inspection time, only the first of which creates value. **2.** = ***lead time*** *(sense 3)*

cyclical factors BUSINESS effects of trade cycle on businesses the way in which a ***trade cycle*** affects businesses

cyclical stock STOCKHOLDING & INVESTMENTS stock affected by business cycles a stock whose value rises and falls in line with economic cycles

cyclical unemployment ECONOMICS recurring temporary lack of employment unemployment, usually temporary, caused by a lack of ***aggregate demand***, for example, during a downswing in the business cycle

cyclic variation STATISTICS regular recurrence of change the repeatable systematic variation of a variable over time

D/A *abbr* BANKING ***deposit account***

daily price limit MARKETS daily allowable change in option price the amount by which the price of an ***option*** is allowed to rise or fall during a single trading day

daily trading limit MARKETS permitted daily futures or options price range the highest and lowest prices that are allowed for a futures or options contract during a single trading day

Daimyo bond CURRENCY & EXCHANGE Japanese bond for European investors a Japanese ***bearer bond*** that can be cleared through European clearing houses

daisy chaining MARKETS illegal practice to inflate price of security an illegal financial practice whereby traders create artificial transactions in order to make a particular security appear more active than it is in reality (slang)

daman FINANCE contract whereby one person underwrites obligation of another in Islamic financing, a contract of guarantee in which the guarantor agrees to be responsible for a debt or obligation of another. *Also called* ***dhaman***

D&B *abbr* BUSINESS ***Dun and Bradstreet***

data STATISTICS information from statistical survey the measurements made and observations collected during a statistical investigation

database GENERAL MANAGEMENT organized collection of information a structured collection of related information held in any form, especially on a computer. The creation of a database assists organizations in keeping records and facilitates the retrieval of specific facts or different categories of information as and when required. Databases of various kinds may form part of an organization's ***MIS***.

database management system STATISTICS computer program for managing information a dedicated computer program designed to manipulate a collection of information

database marketing MARKETING collecting information about customers to target advertising the collection and analysis of information about customers and their buying habits, lifestyles, and other such data. Database marketing is used to build profiles of individual customers, who are then targeted with customized mailings, special offers, and other incentives to encourage spending.

data capture MARKETING collecting customer information through response forms the acquisition of information through advertisement coupons, inquiry forms, or other means that require a customer response

data cleansing MARKETING making sure information is accurate the process of ensuring that data is up to date and free of duplication or error

data dredging STATISTICS using information from outside study to draw conclusions the process of making comparisons with, and drawing conclusions from, data which was not part of the original basis of a study

data fusion E-COMMERCE merging information from different sources into consistent system the integration of data and knowledge collected from disparate sources by different methods into a consistent, accurate, and useful whole

data mining 1. E-COMMERCE using software to find patterns in online databases the process of using sophisticated software to identify commercially useful statistical patterns or relationships in online databases **2.** MARKETING pulling information from firm's databases for management decisions the extraction of information from a ***data warehouse*** to assist managerial decision making. The information obtained in this way helps organizations gain a better understanding of their customers and can be used to improve customer support and marketing activities.

data protection MARKETING methods of keeping personal information in databases safe the safeguards that govern the storage and use of personal data held on computer systems and in paper-based filing systems. The growing use of computers to store information about individuals has led to the enactment of legislation in many countries designed to protect the privacy of individuals and prevent the disclosure of information to unauthorized persons.

data reduction STATISTICS summarizing large data sets the process of summarizing large data sets into histograms or frequency distributions so that calculations such as means can be made

data screening STATISTICS checking data for significant anomalies the process of assessing a set of observations to detect significant deviations such as ***outliers***

data set STATISTICS collection of statistical information all of the measurements or observations collected in a statistical investigation

data smoothing algorithm STATISTICS method for removing meaningless data a procedure for removing meaningless data from a sequence of observations so that a pattern can be detected

Datastream MARKETS online financial data system a data system available online that gives financial information, for example, about securities, prices, and stock exchange transactions

data transfer E-COMMERCE how much information is downloaded from website the amount of data downloaded from a website. This information can be useful, particularly for measuring the number of visitors to a website.

data warehouse GENERAL MANAGEMENT information database used for business analysis a collection of subject-orientated data collected over a period of time and stored on a computer to provide information in support of managerial decision making. A data warehouse contains a large volume of information selected from different sources, including operational systems and organizational databases, and brought together in a standard format to facilitate retrieval and analysis. ***Data mining*** techniques are used to access the information in a data warehouse.

dated date STOCKHOLDING & INVESTMENTS start date for calculation of interest the date on which interest begins to accrue on a fixed-income security, which is also the date the security is issued

date of maturity STOCKHOLDING & INVESTMENTS = ***maturity date***

dawn raid STOCKHOLDING & INVESTMENTS large morning purchase of firm's stock a sudden, planned purchase of a large amount of a company's stock at the beginning of a day's trading. Up to 15% of a company's stock can be bought in this way, and the purchaser must wait for seven days before buying more. A dawn raid may sometimes be the first step toward a ***takeover***.

DAX MARKETS main German stock market index an index of the 30 largest and best-performing companies on the ***Frankfurt Stock Exchange***. It was established in July 1988 with a base value of 1,000 at December 31, 1987. *Full form* ***Deutscher Aktienindex***

day book ACCOUNTING book for recording daily sales and purchases a book in which an account of sales and purchases made each day can be recorded

dayn FINANCE debt obligation in Islamic financing, a debt incurred as the result of any contract or financial transaction

Day of the Jackal Fraud FRAUD UK identity fraud using dead child's birth certificate in the United Kingdom, a form of identity fraud in which a person obtains the birth certificate of a dead child and uses it to acquire a false identity and passport

day order CURRENCY & EXCHANGE in dollar trading, order with one day's validity an order that is valid only during one trading day

days' sales outstanding ACCOUNTING = ***collection ratio***

day trader MARKETS trader operating by the day a trader who turns holdings into cash at the end of each day

day trading MARKETS operating by the day the practice of turning holdings into cash at the end of each day

DC *abbr* BANKING ***documentary credit***

D/C *abbr* BANKING ***documentary credit***

DCF *abbr* FINANCE ***discounted cash flow***

DCM *abbr* MARKETS ***Development Capital Market***

DD *abbr* **1.** BANKING ***direct debit*** **2.** ACCOUNTING ***due diligence***

dead account BANKING inactive account an account that is no longer used

dead cat bounce MARKETS brief rise in stock price after large drop a short-term increase in the value of a stock following a precipitous drop in value (slang)

deadweight loss ECONOMICS inefficiency caused by imbalance economic inefficiency caused by a fall in quantities of a product produced, for example, when a monopoly producer keeps production low to maintain high prices, or by a tax

deal 1. BUSINESS business transaction a business arrangement or agreement between two or more people, usually to their mutual benefit 2. BUSINESS trade in something as business to buy and sell something as a business 3. MARKETING bargain something offered for sale on favorable terms **cut somebody a deal** BUSINESS to agree on terms for a business arrangement with somebody

dealer 1. BUSINESS person who buys and sells something a person engaged in the purchase and sale of goods or services 2. MARKETS person trading for self, not clients a person or firm that buys or sells on their own account, not as a broker on behalf of clients

dealership MARKETING business selling products for specific manufacturer a retail outlet distributing, selling, and servicing products such as cars on behalf of a manufacturer

deal flow STOCKHOLDING & INVESTMENTS presentation of new investments the rate at which new offers of investments are being presented to underwriters

dealing room MARKETS area in stock exchange used for trading securities a room at a stock exchange where the buying and selling of stocks takes place

dealings BUSINESS business between people or organizations business activities conducted between people or organizations

dear money FINANCE money lent at high interest to restrict spending money that is lent at a high interest rate and will therefore restrict a borrower's expenditure. *See also* ***cheap money***

death benefit INSURANCE payment made when insured person dies insurance benefit paid to the family of somebody who dies in an accident at work

death by committee GENERAL MANAGEMENT termination of proposal by committee inertia the prevention of serious consideration of a proposal by assigning a committee to look at it

death duty *UK* TAX = ***estate tax***

death tax *US* TAX (informal) = ***estate tax***

debenture BUSINESS acceptance by firm of debt obligation the written acknowledgment of a debt by a company, usually given under its seal and containing provisions as to payment of interest and principal. A debenture may be secured on some or all of the assets of the company or its subsidiaries.

debenture bond FINANCE 1. documentation of unsecured bond a certificate showing that a ***debenture*** has been issued, and giving its terms and conditions 2. US loan without security in the United States, a long-term unsecured loan, a common type taken out by companies

debenture capital FINANCE loan that company secures with assets money borrowed by a company, using its fixed assets as security

debenture holder FINANCE somebody holding a bond a person who holds a bond or certificate of debt for money lent

debenture stock FINANCE stock paying fixed interest on fixed schedule a form of debt instrument in which a company guarantees payments on a fixed schedule or at a fixed rate of interest

debit ACCOUNTING charge against account in bookkeeping a bookkeeping entry that shows an increase in assets or expenses, or a decrease in liabilities, revenue, or capital. It is entered in the left-hand side of an account in ***double-entry bookkeeping***.

debit balance ACCOUNTING balance showing more money owed than received the difference between debits and credits in an account where the value of ***debits*** is greater

debit card BANKING bank card that functions like check a card issued by a bank or financial institution and accepted by a merchant in payment for a transaction. Unlike the procedure with a ***credit card***, purchases are deducted from the cardholder's account at the time when the transaction takes place. *Also called* ***check card***

debit column ACCOUNTING left side of double-entry bookkeeping system the left-hand side of an account, showing increases in a company's assets or decreases in its liabilities

debit entry ACCOUNTING entry for expenditure an item in a financial statement recording money spent

debit note FINANCE document showing that customer owes money a document that shows how much money a person or company owes. *Abbr* ***D/N***

debits and credits ACCOUNTING record of firm's financial transactions figures entered in a company's accounts to record increases and decreases in ***assets***, expenses, liabilities, revenues, or capital

debit side ACCOUNTING accounting column for money owed or paid out the section of a financial statement that lists payments made or owed. In ***double-entry bookkeeping***, the left hand side of each account is designated as the debit side. *See also* ***credit side***

debt FINANCE 1. money owed an amount of money owed to a person or organization 2. money borrowed money borrowed by a person or organization to finance personal or business activities

debt bomb ECONOMICS economic volatility caused by default of major institution instability in an economy as a result of a major financial institution defaulting on its obligations

debt capital FINANCE money raised as loan capital that is raised that carries an obligation to pay back the principal together with interest

debt collection agency FINANCE business specializing in getting debts repaid a business that secures the repayment of debts for third parties on a commission or fee basis

debt-convertible bond STOCKHOLDING & INVESTMENTS bond convertible from variable to fixed interest a floating-rate bond that can be converted to a fixed rate of interest. *See also* ***droplock bond***

debt counseling FINANCE guidance for people in financial difficulty a service offering advice and support to individuals who are financially stretched

debt/equity ratio MARKETS relationship between firm's debts and value the ratio of what a company owes to the value of all of its outstanding shares of stock

debt factoring FINANCE purchase of firm's accounts receivable at discount the business of buying debts at a discount. A factor collects a company's debts when due, and pays the creditor in advance part of the sum to be collected, thus "buying" the debt.

debt finance *UK* FINANCE = ***debt financing***

debt financing *US* FINANCE raising of capital by long-term borrowing the activity of raising capital from long-term borrowing such as the sale of bonds or notes. *UK term* ***debt finance***

debt forgiveness FINANCE lender's canceling of debt the writing off of all or part of a nation's debt by a lender

debt instrument FINANCE written agreement between borrower and lender any document used or issued for raising money, for example, a bill of exchange, bond, or promissory note

debt market FINANCE market trading in debts a market in which corporate or municipal, government, or public debts are bought and sold

debtnocrat BANKING person in position to make very large loans a senior bank official who specializes in lending extremely large sums, for example, to emerging nations (slang)

debt obligation STOCKHOLDING & INVESTMENTS = ***collateralized debt obligation***

debtor FINANCE person owing money a person or organization owing money to another. *Also called* ***obligor***

debtor days FINANCE average time it takes to collect payment the number of days on average that it takes a company to receive payment for what it sells.

To determine debtor days, divide the cumulative amount of accounts receivable by sales, then multiply by 365. If accounts receivable total $600,000 and sales are $9,000,000, the calculation is:

$$\frac{600,000}{9,000,000} \times 365 = 24.33 \text{ days}$$

The company takes 24.33 days on average to collect its debts.

Debtor days is an indication of a company's efficiency in collecting monies owed. Obviously, the lower the number the better. An especially high number is a telltale sign of inefficiency or worse. *See also* ***creditor days***

debtor nation INTERNATIONAL TRADE country owing more money than it is owed a country whose foreign debts are larger than money owed to it by other countries

debtors' control FINANCE systems for prompt repayment strategies used to ensure that borrowers pay back loans on time

debt ratio FINANCE relationship between firm's debts and assets the debts of a company shown as a percentage of its ***equity*** plus loan capital

debt rescheduling FINANCE negotiation of new terms for debt repayment the renegotiation of debt payments. Debt rescheduling is necessary when a company can no longer meet its debt payments. It can involve deferring debt payments, deferring payment of interest, or negotiating a new loan. It is usually undertaken as part of ***turnaround management*** to avoid ***business failure***. Debt rescheduling is also undertaken in less developed countries that encounter national debt difficulties. Such arrangements are usually overseen by the ***International Monetary Fund***.

debt security STOCKHOLDING & INVESTMENTS security issued as evidence of debt to purchaser a security issued by a company or government which represents money borrowed from the security's purchaser and which must be repaid at a specified maturity date, usually at a specified interest rate

debt service FINANCE combined interest and principal due on money borrowed the payments due under a loan agreement, i.e. interest payable and payments of principal

debt/service ratio ECONOMICS measurement of debt against gross income the ratio of a country's or company's borrowing to its equity or ***venture capital***

debt swap FINANCE exchange of country's debt for local currency a method of reducing exposure to long-term debt of nations with undeveloped economies by purchasing the debt at a discount and exchanging it with the central bank for local currency

decentralization GENERAL MANAGEMENT giving decision-making power to larger group the dispersal of decision-making control. Decentralization involves moving power, authority, and decision-making control within an organization from a central headquarters or from high managerial levels to subsidiaries, branches, divisions, or departments. As an organizational concept, decentralization implies delegation of both power and responsibility by top management in order to promote flexibility through faster decision making and improved response times. Decentralization is, therefore, strongly related to the concept of empowerment, though the latter is perhaps more focused on direct working front-line staff.

decile STATISTICS value representing one-tenth of frequency distribution one of the nine values that divide the total number of items in a ***frequency distribution*** into ten groups, each containing an equal number of items

decision analysis GENERAL MANAGEMENT = ***decision theory***

decision maker GENERAL MANAGEMENT somebody authorized to make important decisions for firm somebody with the responsibility and authority to make decisions within an organization, especially those that determine future direction and strategy. ***Decision theory*** is used to assist decision makers in the process of ***decision making***.

decision making GENERAL MANAGEMENT process of determining what to do the process of choosing between alternate courses of action. Decision making may take place at an individual or organizational level. The process may involve establishing objectives, gathering relevant information, identifying alternatives, setting criteria for the decision, and selecting the best option. The nature of the decision-making process within an organization is influenced by its culture and structure, and a number of theoretical models have been developed. ***Decision theory*** can be used to assist in the process of decision making. Specific techniques used in decision making include heuristics and decision trees. Computer systems designed to assist managerial decision making are known as decision support systems.

decision-making unit MARKETING group of employees responsible for purchase decisions a group of people within an organization who directly or indirectly influence the purchase of a product or service

decision support system GENERAL MANAGEMENT computer system containing information used for management decisions a computer system designed to collect, store, process, and provide access to information to support managerial decision making. Decision support systems were developed in the 1970s to facilitate unstructured and one-off decision making, as the standard reporting capabilities of ***MIS***s were perceived to be more suitable for routine day-to-day decisions. Data on an organization's external operating environment, as well as internal operational information, is included and an interactive interface allows managers to retrieve and manipulate data. Modeling techniques are used to examine the results of alternative courses of action.

decision theory GENERAL MANAGEMENT analysis of how people determine course of action a body of knowledge that attempts to describe, analyze, and model the process of ***decision making*** and the factors influencing it. Decision theory encompasses both formal mathematical and statistical approaches to solving decision problems, using quantitative techniques such as probability and ***game theory***, and more informal behavioral approaches. It is used to inform and assist decision making in organizations. *Also called* ***decision analysis***

decision tree GENERAL MANAGEMENT chart helping people determine course of action a diagram designed to help decision makers by representing available options and possible outcomes as branches of a tree. Decision trees provide an overview of multiple-stage ***decision making*** by showing successive decision points arising from previous choices. Values representing the relative probability of individual outcomes may be assigned to each branch of the tree in order to compare strategies and select the most favorable.

declaration date STOCKHOLDING & INVESTMENTS day when firm sets next dividend in the United States, the date when the directors of a company meet to announce the proposed dividend per share that they recommend be paid

declaration of dividend STOCKHOLDING & INVESTMENTS firm's official announcement of next dividend a formal announcement by a company's directors of the proposed dividend per share that they recommend be paid. It is subsequently put to a stockholders' vote at the company's annual meeting.

declaration of income TAX = ***income tax return***

declaration of solvency BUSINESS official notice of UK firm's creditworthiness in the United Kingdom, a document, filed with the ***Registrar of Companies***, that lists the assets and liabilities of a company seeking voluntary liquidation to show that the company is capable of repaying its debts within 12 months

declared value TAX figure on customs form the value of goods as entered on a customs declaration

declining balance method ACCOUNTING = ***accelerated depreciation***

deconstruction GENERAL MANAGEMENT breaking up old-fashioned business systems the breaking up of traditional business structures to meet the requirements of the modern economy

decreasing term life insurance *or* decreasing term life assurance INSURANCE life insurance with death benefit decreasing over time life insurance that is in effect for a specified period of time and provides a death benefit that decreases incrementally during the period the policy is in effect

de-diversify BUSINESS sell off firm's marginal interests to sell off parts of a company or group that are not considered directly relevant to its main area of interest

deductible *US* INSURANCE portion of insurance claim paid by policyholder the part of a commercial insurance claim that has to be met by the policyholder rather than the insurance company. A deductible of $1,000 means that the company pays all but $1,000 of the claim for loss or damage. *UK term* ***excess***

deduction FINANCE deducting from total, or amount deducted a subtraction of money from a total, or an amount of money subtracted from a total

deduction at source TAX taking taxes directly from salary in the United Kingdom, the collection of taxes from an organization or individual paying an income, rather than from the recipient of the income, for example, from an employer paying wages, a bank paying interest, or a company paying dividends

deed LEGAL legal evidence of real estate sale a legal document, most commonly one that details the transfer or sale of real estate

deed of arrangement LEGAL agreement to terms of repayment by insolvent debtor in the United Kingdom, a legal document that sets out the agreement between an insolvent person and his or her ***creditors***

deed of assignment LEGAL document transferring real estate to creditor in the United Kingdom, a legal document detailing the transfer of real estate from a ***debtor*** to a ***creditor***

deed of covenant LEGAL legal promise to make payments in the United Kingdom, a legal document in which a person or organization promises to pay a third party a sum of money on an annual basis, with tax advantages. A deed of covenant was often used for making regular payments to a charity before the introduction of ***Gift Aid***.

deed of partnership LEGAL legal agreement for partnership in the United Kingdom, a legal document formalizing the agreement and financial arrangements between the parties that make up a partnership

deed of transfer STOCKHOLDING & INVESTMENTS documentation of transfer of stock ownership in the United Kingdom, a legal document that attests to the transfer of stock ownership

deed of variation LEGAL procedure for changing deceased person's will in the United Kingdom, an arrangement that allows the will of a deceased person to be amended, provided specific conditions are met and the amendment is signed by all the original beneficiaries

deep-discount bond STOCKHOLDING & INVESTMENTS bond selling at far less than value a bond offered at a large discount on the face value of the debt so that a significant proportion of the return to the investor comes by way of a capital gain on redemption, rather than through interest payments

deep-discounted rights issue STOCKHOLDING & INVESTMENTS new shares priced below market value a rights issue where the new shares are priced at a very low price compared to their current market value to ensure that stockholders take up the rights

deep-in-the-money call option STOCKHOLDING & INVESTMENTS profitable contract to buy securities a ***call option*** that has an exercise price below the market price of the underlying asset and has therefore become very profitable. *See also* ***deep-out-of-the-money call option***

deep-in-the-money put option STOCKHOLDING & INVESTMENTS profitable contract to sell securities a ***put option*** that has an exercise price above the market price of an underlying asset and has therefore become very profitable. *See also* ***deep-out-of-the-money put option***

deep market MARKETS market in which volume will not affect price a commodity, currency, or stock market in which the volume of trade is such that a considerable number of transactions will not influence the market price

deep-out-of-the-money call option STOCKHOLDING & INVESTMENTS unprofitable contract to buy securities a ***call option*** that has an exercise price above the market price of the underlying asset and has little intrinsic value. *See also* ***deep-in-the-money call option***

deep-out-of-the-money put option STOCKHOLDING & INVESTMENTS unprofitable contract to sell securities a ***put option*** that has an exercise price below the market price of an underlying asset and has little intrinsic value. *See also* ***deep-in-the-money put option***

deep pocket BUSINESS firm giving financial assistance to another a company that provides much-needed funds for another company (slang)

de facto standard GENERAL MANAGEMENT successful product's recognized standing in market a standard set in a given market by a highly successful product or service

defalcation FINANCE misuse of money entrusted to somebody's care the improper and illegal use of funds by a person who does not own them, but who has been charged with their care

default 1. STOCKHOLDING & INVESTMENTS be unable to cover loss on trades as a member of an exchange, to lose more on a trading position than is held in capital **2.** LEGAL not do what you have contracted to do to fail to comply with the terms of a contract, especially to fail to pay back a debt

defaulter FINANCE person failing to make scheduled payments a person who defaults, for example, somebody who fails to make scheduled payments on a loan

default notice LEGAL = ***notice of default***

default risk STOCKHOLDING & INVESTMENTS, RISK risk of non-payment the possibility that the issuer of a bond will be unable to make payments of principal and interest when they are due

defeasance LEGAL clause specifying how contract might be broken a clause in a collateral deed that says a contract or bond will be revoked if something happens or if some act is performed

defended takeover bid MERGERS & ACQUISITIONS offer to buy firm that opposes being sold a bid for a company takeover in which the directors of the target company oppose the action of the bidder

defensive security STOCKHOLDING & INVESTMENTS security providing earnings despite falling market a security that has very little risk and provides a return even when the stock market is weak

defensive stock STOCKHOLDING & INVESTMENTS stock not affected by external factors stock that prospers predictably regardless of external circumstances such as an economic slowdown, for example, the stock of a company that markets a product everyone must have

deferment FINANCE putting off of something a postponement of something, for example, taxes or interest on a loan, until a later date

deferred annuity STOCKHOLDING & INVESTMENTS investment offering return 12 + months after last premium an investment that does not pay out until at least one year after the final premium has been paid

deferred common stock *US* STOCKHOLDING & INVESTMENTS stock paying dividends only after others are paid a type of stock usually held by founding members of a company, often with a higher dividend that is only paid after other shareholders have received their dividends and, in some cases, only when a specific level of profit has been achieved. This type of stock is rarely issued in the United States. *Also called* ***deferred share****. UK term* ***deferred ordinary share***

deferred consideration BUSINESS purchase in which final payment has conditions attached installment payments for the acquisition of new subsidiaries, usually made in the form of cash and stock, where the balance due after the initial deposit depends on the performance of the business acquired

deferred coupon STOCKHOLDING & INVESTMENTS bond that delays interest payments a ***coupon*** that pays no interest at first, but pays relatively high interest after a specific date

deferred credit *or* deferred income ACCOUNTING money received but not yet recorded as income revenue received but not yet reported as income in the profit and loss account, for example, payment for goods to be delivered or services provided at a later date, or government grants received for the purchase of assets. The deferred credit is treated as a credit balance on the balance sheet while waiting to be treated as income. *See also* ***accrual basis***

deferred creditor FINANCE creditor paid after all others a person who is owed money by a bankrupt person or organization but who is paid only after all other creditors

deferred interest bond STOCKHOLDING & INVESTMENTS bond that delays interest payments a bond that pays no interest at first, but pays relatively high interest after a specific date

deferred month STOCKHOLDING & INVESTMENTS distant month for option a month relatively late in the term of an ***option***

deferred ordinary share *UK* STOCKHOLDING & INVESTMENTS **1.** stock paying no dividend in early years a type of stock that pays no dividend for a specific number of years after its issue date but then is treated the same as the company's common stock **2.** = ***deferred common stock***

deferred payment 1. FINANCE money to be repaid later money owed that will be repaid at a later date **2.** OPERATIONS & PRODUCTION payment in installments payment for goods by installments over a period of time

deferred revenue ACCOUNTING income carried into next accounting period revenue carried forward to future accounting periods

deferred share STOCKHOLDING & INVESTMENTS = ***deferred common stock***

deferred tax TAX tax payable later a tax that may become payable at some later date

deficiency FINANCE amount of shortfall the amount by which something such as a sum of money is less than it should be

deficit ACCOUNTING = ***budget deficit***

deficit financing FINANCE covering shortfall the borrowing of money because expenditure will exceed receipts

deficit spending FINANCE spending financed by borrowing government spending financed through borrowing rather than through taxation or other current revenue

defined contribution pension plan PENSIONS employer's retirement plan with specific investments in the United States, a retirement plan arranged by an employer in which the money contributed by both the employer and employee is invested, so that the retirement benefit is not fixed but is dependent on how well the investments do

deflation ECONOMICS long-term decline in prices a reduction in the general level of prices sustained over several months, usually accompanied by declining employment and output

deflationary ECONOMICS causing drop in prices causing a decline in the prices of goods and services

deflationary fiscal policy ECONOMICS government policy of raising taxes and reducing spending a government policy that raises taxes and reduces public expenditure in order to reduce the level of ***aggregate demand*** in the economy

deflationary gap ECONOMICS failure in exploiting economic potential a gap between ***GDP*** and the potential output of the economy

deflator ECONOMICS inflation-related reduction in national income the amount by which a country's ***GDP*** is reduced to take into account ***inflation***

degearing BUSINESS reduction in firm's long-term debt a reduction in a company's loan capital in relation to the value of its common stock plus reserves. *See also* ***leverage***

degressive tax TAX tax decreasing as taxable amount increases a tax for which the amount to be paid decreases as the amount that is liable for taxation increases. *See also* ***progressive tax***

delayed settlement processing E-COMMERCE storing credit card transactions online until shipment a procedure for storing authorized transaction settlements online until after the merchant has shipped the goods to the purchaser

delayering GENERAL MANAGEMENT removing layers of firm's management the removal of supposedly unproductive layers of middle management to make organizations more efficient and customer-responsive. The term came into vogue during the 1980s.

del credere FINANCE extra charge to protect against nonpayment an amount added to a charge to cover the possibility of its not being paid

del credere agent FINANCE sales agent who guarantees purchaser's payment an agent who agrees to sell goods on commission and pay the principal even if the buyer defaults on payment. To cover the risk of default, the commission is marginally higher than that of a general agent.

delegatee GENERAL MANAGEMENT person being allocated task a person who is given the responsibility and authority to undertake a specific activity

delegation GENERAL MANAGEMENT putting somebody else in charge of activity the process of entrusting somebody else with the appropriate responsibility and authority for the accomplishment of a specific activity. Delegation involves briefing somebody else to perform a task for which the delegator holds individual responsibility, but which need not be executed by him or her. There are various degrees of delegation: for example, a manager may delegate responsibility, but not necessarily full authority, and continue to supervise the activity. Delegation should be a positive activity, for example, as an aid to employee development, rather than a negative one, for example, passing on an unpopular task. It should be accompanied by support and encouragement from the delegator to the delegatee. An extension of delegation is empowerment, in which complete authority for a task is passed to somebody else, who takes full responsibility for its objectives, execution, and results.

delegator GENERAL MANAGEMENT person allocating task a person who gives somebody else the responsibility and authority to undertake a specific activity

deleverage FINANCE pay off debt to reduce the size of a company's debt, possibly by selling off some assets

delinquent BUSINESS late in repaying money owed used to describe a person or organization that is late in paying an account, or a debt that remains unpaid

delisting REGULATION & COMPLIANCE removal of firm from stock exchange the action of removing a company from being traded on a recognized stock exchange —***delist***

delivered price OPERATIONS & PRODUCTION price that includes shipping and handling a price that includes any expenses incurred during packing and transportation of the item to its final destination

delivery **1.** FINANCE handing over of bill of exchange for payment the transfer of a bill of exchange or other negotiable instrument to the bank that is due to make payment **2.** OPERATIONS & PRODUCTION act of delivering commodity to buyer the transportation of a commodity by a seller to a purchaser as set out in a futures contract

delivery date MARKETS date for delivery of commodity the date on which a commodity bought or sold in a futures contract must be delivered

delivery month MARKETS = ***contract month***

delivery notice MARKETS notification of details of handover a written notice to the buyer of a commodity on a ***futures contract*** of its delivery and terms of settlement

Delphi technique GENERAL MANAGEMENT forecasting method avoiding group pressure a qualitative forecasting method in which a panel of experts respond individually to a questionnaire or series of questionnaires, before reaching a consensus. The Delphi technique requires individual submission of, and response to, the questionnaire on the topic under investigation, in order to avoid the effect of a dominant personality influencing a group discussion. A summary of the written replies is then distributed so that responses can be revised in the light of the views expressed. This cycle is repeated until the coordinator of the group is satisfied that the best possible consensus has been reached. The Delphi technique was developed at the Rand Corporation during the late 1940s and 1950s and owes its name to the Greek oracle at Delphi, which was believed to make predictions about the future.

delta STOCKHOLDING & INVESTMENTS option price change compared with associated asset the amount of change in the price of an option as compared to a corresponding change in the price of its underlying asset

demand **1.** FINANCE request for payment an act of asking somebody for payment of money owed **2.** MARKETING measure of consumers' willingness to buy the need that consumers have for a product or their eagerness and ability to buy it

demand bill FINANCE bill of exchange payable on demand a ***bill of exchange*** that must be paid when payment is asked for

demand deposit BANKING account balance available for writing checks money in a deposit account that the holder can withdraw at any time by writing a check

demand forecasting FINANCE estimation of consumer demand for product or service the activity of estimating the quantity of a product or service that consumers will purchase. Demand forecasting involves techniques including both informal methods such as educated guesses and quantitative methods such as the use of historical sales data or current data from test markets. Demand forecasting may be used in making pricing decisions, in assessing future capacity requirements, or in making decisions on whether to enter a new market.

demand management OPERATIONS & PRODUCTION predicting and meeting customer demand the ***supply chain*** activity of ***forecasting***, effectively planning for, and meeting ***customer demand*** for a product

demand note FINANCE promissory note that is payable on demand a promissory note that has no specific date for payment but instead must be paid when it is presented

demand price FINANCE price buyer is willing to pay the price that purchasers are willing to offer to pay for a given quantity of goods

demand-pull inflation ECONOMICS inflation caused by increased demand inflation caused by rising demand that cannot be met

demand risk RISK risk of customer demand not matching firm's forecast the risk for a company that demand for a product will either exceed their expectations and ability to meet the demand or fall short of their expectations and leave them with product they cannot sell

demassifying GENERAL MANAGEMENT tailoring mass medium to customers' needs the process of changing a mass medium to a medium that is customized to meet the requirements of individual consumers

demerge MERGERS & ACQUISITIONS separate parts of firm to split up an organization into a number of separate parts

demerger MERGERS & ACQUISITIONS separation of company into independent parts the separation of a company into several distinct entities, especially used of companies that have grown by acquisition

demographics STATISTICS characteristics and statistics of human population the characteristics of the size and structure of a human population, including features such as its distribution and age range

demography STATISTICS study of human population statistics the study of the size and structural characteristics of human populations

demonetize CURRENCY & EXCHANGE discontinue coin or note to withdraw a coin or note from a country's currency

demurrage BUSINESS payment made to compensate for late shipment compensation paid to a customer when shipment of a good is delayed at a port or by customs

demutualization BANKING conversion of mutual society to public corporation the process by which a mutual society becomes a publicly owned corporation

Denial of Service Attack E-COMMERCE attempt to prevent Internet use an attempt to limit or prevent a user or users from accessing the Internet, a network, or using their e-mail, for example, by flooding it with more requests than it can handle

denomination CURRENCY & EXCHANGE value on coin, banknote, or stamp a unit of money imprinted on a coin, banknote, or stamp

department GENERAL MANAGEMENT section of firm responsible for particular function a section of an organization, usually centered on a specialized function, under the responsibility of a head of department or team leader

departmental budget ACCOUNTING budget for department a budget of income and/or expenditure applicable to a specific department. *See also* ***functional budget***

departmentalization GENERAL MANAGEMENT dividing firm into sections the division of an organization into sections. Departmentalization is usually based on operating function, and organizations will commonly have departments for, for example, finance, personnel, or marketing. Such organizational structure is typical of a ***bureaucracy***. It may be used in ***centralization***, when a particular activity is undertaken by one department in one location on behalf of the whole organization, but may equally be a feature of a decentralized organization, in which departments are used as individual operating units responsible for their own management.

Department for Business, Enterprise and Regulatory Reform British government department a British government department dealing with areas such as enterprise, business law, markets, energy policy, and business regulation. It was created in 2007 to bring together the functions of the Department of Trade and Industry **and regulatory functions formerly performed within the Cabinet Office.** ***Abbr BERR***

Department of Trade and Industry former British government department the former British government department that dealt with areas such as commerce, international trade, and the stock exchange. Its functions are now taken over by the Department for Business, Enterprise and Regulatory Reform. ***Abbr DTI***

dependency ratio ECONOMICS proportion of society economically dependent on work force a measure of the proportion of a population that is too young or too old to work and is therefore economically dependent on that part of the population that is productively working. *Also called* ***support ratio***

dependent variable STATISTICS variable that changes in response to another a variable or factor whose value changes as a result of a change in another (the ***independent variable***)

     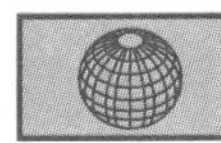   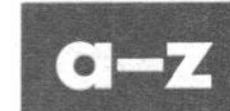

deposit **1.** BANKING money added to bank account money placed in a bank for safekeeping or to earn interest **2.** BUSINESS partial payment to reserve something part of the price of an item given by a customer in advance so that the item will not be sold to somebody else before the full price is paid **3.** OPERATIONS & PRODUCTION add money to bank account to pay money into a bank account

deposit account BANKING **1.** interest-paying account requiring prior notice for withdrawal a bank account that pays interest on deposited funds but on which prior notice must be given in order to withdraw money. *Abbr* ***D/A*** **2.** interest-paying UK building society account in the United Kingdom, a building society account that is held by somebody who is not a member of the society. Deposit accounts are generally paid a lower rate of interest, but in the event of the society going into liquidation deposit account holders are given preference. See also ***share account***

depositary BUSINESS somebody who entrusts valuable items to institution a person or organization that has placed money or documents for safekeeping with a ***depository***

depositor BANKING somebody who deposits money in financial institution a person or business that places money in a bank, savings and loan, or other type of financial institution

depository BANKING institution responsible for keeping valuable items safe a bank or organization with whom money or documents can be placed for safekeeping

Depository Trust and Clearing Corporation BUSINESS US company for handling securities transactions in the United States, a holding company with several subsidiaries, which is set up to efficiently handle clearance, settlement, and depository services for the securities industry. *Abbr* ***DTCC***

deposit protection INSURANCE insurance against loss of deposits insurance that depositors have against loss by a financial institution. In the United States, the Federal Deposit Insurance Corporation (FDIC) provides this.

deposit slip *or* deposit receipt *US* BANKING receipt for deposits made in bank account the slip of paper that accompanies money or checks being paid into a bank account. *UK term* ***paying-in slip***

deposit-taking institution BANKING banking institution serving general public an institution that is licensed to receive money on deposit from private individuals and to pay interest on it, for example, a bank or savings and loan

depreciable cost ACCOUNTING expense spread over several accounting periods an expense that may be set against the profits of more than one accounting period

depreciate **1.** FINANCE lose value over time to lose value, or decrease the value of something, usually over a period of time **2.** ACCOUNTING make allowance for asset's progressive loss of value to make an allowance in business accounts for the loss of value of an asset over time

depreciation **1.** ACCOUNTING loss of value an allocation of the ***cost*** of an ***asset*** over a period of time for accounting and tax purposes. Depreciation is charged against earnings, on the basis that the use of capital assets is a legitimate cost of doing business. Depreciation is also a non-cash expense that is added into net income to determine cash flow in a given accounting period.

To qualify for depreciation, assets must be items used in the business that wear out, become obsolete, or lose value over time from natural causes or circumstances, and they must have a useful life beyond a single tax year. Examples include vehicles, machines, equipment, furnishings, and buildings, plus major additions or improvements to such assets. Some intangible assets also can be included under certain conditions. Land, personal assets, stock, leased or rented property, and a company's employees cannot be depreciated.

Straight line depreciation is the most straightforward method. It assumes that the net cost of an asset should be written off in equal amounts over its life. The formula used is:

$$\frac{\text{(Original cost} - \text{Scrap value)}}{\text{Useful life in years}}$$

For example, if a vehicle cost $30,000 and can be expected to serve the business for seven years, its original cost would be divided by its useful life:

$$\frac{(30{,}000 - 2{,}000)}{7} = 4{,}000 \text{ per year}$$

The $4,000 becomes a depreciation expense that is reported on the company's year-end income statement under "operation expenses."

In theory, an asset should be depreciated over the actual number of years that it will be used, according to its actual drop in value each year. At the end of each year, all the depreciation claimed to date is subtracted from its cost in order to arrive at its ***book value***, which would equal its market value. At the end of its useful business life, any portion not depreciated would represent the salvage value for which it could be sold or scrapped.

For tax purposes, some accountants prefer to use the ***declining balance method*** to record larger amounts of depreciation in the asset's early years in order to reduce tax bills as soon as possible. In contrast to the straight-line method, this assumes that the asset depreciates more in its earlier years of use. The table below compares the depreciation amounts that would be available, under these two methods, for a $1,000 asset that is expected to be used for five years and then sold for $100 as scrap.

The depreciation method to be used for a particular asset is fixed at the time that the asset is first placed in service. Whatever rules or tables are in effect for that year must be followed as long as the asset is owned.

Depreciation laws and regulations change frequently over the years as a result of government policy changes, so a company owning property over a long period may have to use several different depreciation methods. **2.** CURRENCY & EXCHANGE decrease in value of currency a reduction of a currency's value in relation to the value of other currencies

depreciation rate ACCOUNTING annual rate at which asset loses value the rate at which the value of an asset decreases each year in business accounts

depressed market MARKETS market where supply outweighs demand a market in which there are more goods available than there are customers who are willing to buy them, leading to lower prices. A stock market that is depressed, with falling prices, is called a ***bear market***.

depression ECONOMICS long-term decline in economic activity a prolonged slump or downturn in the business cycle, marked by a high level of unemployment

deprival value FINANCE = ***value to the business***

deregulation REGULATION & COMPLIANCE lessening of government controls a reduction in government controls over a specific business activity with the intention of stimulating competition

deregulatory model REGULATION & COMPLIANCE belief in less government regulation the theory that less government regulation in the economy will result in more competition and a more efficient marketplace

derivative STOCKHOLDING & INVESTMENTS security with price link to underlying asset a ***security*** such as an ***option***, the price of which has a strong correlation with an underlying commodity, currency, or ***financial instrument***

derivative instruments *or* derivatives STOCKHOLDING & INVESTMENTS securities based on other securities or market conditions forms of traded securities, such as option contracts, which are derived from ordinary bonds and shares, exchange rates, or stock market indices.

Derivative Trading Facility MARKETS Australian computer system for trading options a computer system and associated network operated by the ***Australian Securities Exchange*** to facilitate the purchase and sale of exchange-traded options. *Abbr* ***DTF***

descending tops MARKETS chart pattern with each successive peak lower a term used to refer to a chart pattern that shows falling market, in which each high is lower than the previous one

designated account BANKING account requiring second person for extra identification an account opened and held in one person's name, but that also includes another person's name for extra identification purposes

design for manufacturability *or* design for assembly *or* design for production OPERATIONS & PRODUCTION designing products for ease of

Straight-line method of depreciation

Year	Annual depreciation	Year-end book value
1	$900 × 20% = $180	$1,000 − $180 = $820
2	$900 × 20% = $180	$820 − $180 = $640
3	$900 × 20% = $180	$640 − $180 = $460
4	$900 × 20% = $180	$460 − $180 = $280
5	$900 × 20% = $180	$280 − $180 = $100

Declining-balance method of depreciation

Year	Annual depreciation	Year-end book value
1	$1,000 × 40% = $400	$1,000 − $400 = $600
2	$600 × 40% = $240	$600 − $240 = $360
3	$360 × 40% = $144	$360 − $144 = $216
4	$216 × 40% = $86.40	$216 − $86.40 = $129.60
5	$129.60 × 40% = $51.84	$129.60 − $51.84 = $77.76

  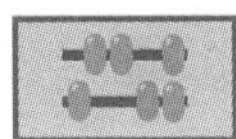      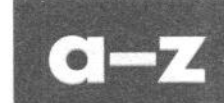

manufacture the process of designing products to optimize the manufacturing process while assuring the product's highest quality, performance, and reliability for the price

design for supply OPERATIONS & PRODUCTION designing desirable products that keep costs low the process of designing products that will meet ***customer demand*** without sacrificing quality or customer service, while minimizing costs throughout the ***supply chain***

design protection MARKETING = ***copyright***

de-skilling HR & PERSONNEL replacing need for particular job skills with technology the removal of the need for skill or judgment in the performance of a task, often because of new technologies. While it can be argued that de-skilling has adversely affected some manual workers in traditional manufacturing industries, the technologies used in modern production systems require a wider range and higher level of skill among the workforce as a whole.

desk research MARKETING investigation conducted from office research carried out in an office, using documents, telephone interviews, or the Internet

Deutsche Börse MARKETS = ***Frankfurt Stock Exchange***

Deutscher Aktienindex MARKETS *see* ***DAX***

devaluation ECONOMICS reduction of official currency exchange rate a reduction in the official fixed rate at which one currency exchanges for another under a fixed-rate regime, usually to correct a balance of payments deficit

developing country ECONOMICS poor nation with little industrial development a country, often a producer of primary goods such as cotton or rubber, that cannot generate investment income to stimulate growth and that possesses a national income that is vulnerable to change in commodity prices

development area *or* development zone BUSINESS area receiving government aid to attract commercial development a geographic area that has been given special help from a government to encourage businesses and factories to be set up there

development capital FINANCE money for expansion financing acquired or provided for the expansion of an established business

Development Capital Market MARKETS closed sector of Johannesburg exchange for developing companies a sector on the ***Johannesburg Stock Exchange*** for listing smaller developing companies which was closed to new listings in 2004 due to low liquidity. *Abbr* ***DCM***. See also ***Venture Capital Market***

development cycle MARKETING *see* ***new product development***

dhaman FINANCE = ***daman***

Diagonal Street *S. AFRICA* FINANCE financial district of Johannesburg the financial center of Johannesburg or, by extension, South Africa (informal)

dial and smile *US* MARKETING call strangers to sell something to call potential customers of a product or service to try to make a sale (slang)

DIAMONDs STOCKHOLDING & INVESTMENTS shares in selected firms on American Stock Exchange shares in a fund, traded on ***NYSE Amex Equities***, that is made up of the 30 companies represented in the ***Dow Jones Industrial Average***

dicing and slicing MARKETING analyzing information in different ways the analysis of raw data to extract information under different categories (slang)

dictum meum pactum MARKETS my word is my bond Latin for the phrase "My word is my bond," the motto of the London Stock Exchange

differential costing FINANCE way to determine costs based on production levels a costing method that shows the difference in costs that results from different levels of activity such as making one thousand or ten thousand extra units of a product

differential pricing MARKETING selling product at different prices in different places a method of pricing that offers the same product at different prices, for example, in different markets, countries, or retail outlets

differential tariff TAX charge that varies by class or source a tax on goods or services which varies according to their class or source

differentiation MARKETING = ***product differentiation***

digital cash E-COMMERCE form of electronic cash carrying no user information an anonymous form of ***digital money*** which can be linked directly to a bank account or exchanged for physical money. As with physical cash, there is no way to obtain information about the buyer from it, and it can be transferred by the seller to pay for subsequent purchases. *Also called* ***e-cash, electronic cash***

digital certificate E-COMMERCE electronic document that shows buyer is authentic an electronic document issued by a recognized authority which validates a purchaser. It is used much as a driver's license or passport is used for identification purposes in a traditional business transaction.

digital coins E-COMMERCE form of electronic cash for small payments a form of electronic payment authorized for instant transactions which facilitates the purchase of items priced in small denominations of ***digital cash***. Digital coins are transferred from customer to merchant for a transaction such as the purchase of a newspaper using a ***smart card*** for payment.

digital coupon E-COMMERCE online form used for obtaining lower product price a voucher or similar form that exists electronically, for example, on a website, and can be used to reduce the price of goods or services

digital divide E-COMMERCE inequality of access to information technology the difference in opportunities available to people who have access to modern information technology and those who do not. Factors such as urban living, education level, economic class, and industrialization affect the digital divide.

digital economy ECONOMICS economic system based on online business transactions an economy in which the main productive functions are in electronic commerce, for example, trade on the Internet

digital goods E-COMMERCE products sold and delivered electronically merchandise that is sold and delivered electronically, for example, over the Internet

digital hygienist GENERAL MANAGEMENT employee who inspects other employees' Internet usage somebody within a company who is responsible for checking employees' e-mails and surfing habits for non-work-related activity (slang)

digital money E-COMMERCE electronic cash related to real-world currency a series of numbers with an intrinsic value in some physical currency. Online digital money requires electronic interaction with a bank to conduct a transaction; offline digital money does not. Anonymous digital money is synonymous with ***digital cash***. Identified digital money carries with it information revealing the identities of those involved in the transaction. *Also called* ***e-money, electronic money***

digital strategy GENERAL MANAGEMENT plan based on information technology a business strategy that is based on the use of information technology

digital wallet E-COMMERCE shopper's software used for making online payments software stored on the hard drive of an online shopper's computer allowing the user to pay for purchases electronically. The wallet can hold in encrypted form such items as credit card information, digital cash or coins, a digital certificate to identify the user, and standardized shipping information. *Also called* ***electronic wallet***

digitizable E-COMMERCE able to be converted to electronic form capable of being converted to digital form for distribution via the Internet or other networks

dilution levy FINANCE charge to compensate for effect of investors' transactions an extra charge levied by fund managers on investors buying or selling units in a fund, designed to offset any potential effect on the value of the fund of such purchases or sales

dilution of equity *US* STOCKHOLDING & INVESTMENTS sale of additional stock resulting in reduced value a situation in which a company makes more shares of common stock available without an increase in its assets, with the end result that each share is worth less than before. *UK term* ***dilution of shareholding***

dilution of shareholding *UK* STOCKHOLDING & INVESTMENTS = ***dilution of equity***

dip MARKETS small temporary fall in securities prices a slight temporary fall in the price of securities after a long-term gain

direct action marketing MARKETING = ***direct response marketing***

direct channel MARKETING way of selling and delivering directly to buyers a method of selling and distributing products direct to customers. Direct channels include direct selling, mail order, and the Internet.

direct cost OPERATIONS & PRODUCTION cost relating to production a variable cost directly attributable to production. Items that are classed as direct costs include materials used, labor deployed, and marketing budget. Amounts spent will vary with output. *See also* ***indirect cost***

direct debit BANKING arrangement for charging customer's account automatically a system by which a customer allows a company to make charges to his or her bank account automatically and where the amount charged can be increased or decreased with the agreement of the customer. *Abbr* ***DD***. See also ***automatic debit***

directive LEGAL **1.** official order an official or government instruction that something should happen **2.** new law in EU in the EU, a decision made centrally that is applied through the domestic law of member states

  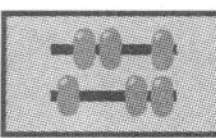      

direct labor HR & PERSONNEL employees who actually make products or perform services personnel directly involved in the manufacturing of products or the provision of services. Direct labor includes ***blue-collar workers***.

direct labor cost percentage rate FINANCE product overhead attributed to labor costs an ***overhead absorption rate***, based on labor costs, which can readily be allocated to individual units of production

direct labor hour rate FINANCE product overhead attributed to labor hours an ***overhead absorption rate***, based on labor hours, which can readily be allocated to individual units of production

direct mail MARKETING sending advertising directly to potential customers the sending by mail, fax, or e-mail of advertising communications addressed to specific prospective customers. Direct mail is one tool that can be used as part of a marketing strategy. The use of direct mail is often administered by third-party companies that own databases containing not only names and addresses, but also social, economic, and lifestyle information. It is sometimes seen as an invasion of personal privacy, and there is some public resentment of this form of advertising. This is particularly true of e-mailed direct mail, known as spam. By enabling advertisers to target a specific type of potential customer, however, direct mail can be more cost-efficient than other advertising media. It is frequently used as part of a relationship marketing strategy.

direct mail preference service MARKETING arrangement for removing name from firm's mailing list an arrangement that allows individuals and organizations to refuse direct mail by having participating organizations remove them from their mailing lists

direct marketing MARKETING = ***direct response marketing***

director HR & PERSONNEL **1.** person elected by stockholders to help run company a person appointed by the stockholders to be one of the people with the responsibility of running the company. A director is usually in charge of one or other of its main functions, for example, sales or human resources, and is usually a member of the board of directors. **2.** person in charge of something the person who is in charge of a project, an official institute, or other organization

directorate CORPORATE GOVERNANCE group directing firm's course the governing or controlling body of an organization responsible for the organization's corporate strategy and accountable to its stakeholders for business results. A directorate may also be known as a ***board of directors*** or council, or, at an inner level, the executive or management committee.

director's dealing STOCKHOLDING & INVESTMENTS stock transactions by firm's director the purchase or sale of a company's stock by one of its directors

director's fees FINANCE money paid to company director money paid to a director of a company for attendance at board meetings

directors' report CORPORATE GOVERNANCE board of directors' annual report the annual report prepared by the board of directors and distributed to the company's stockholders

direct response marketing *or* direct response advertising MARKETING methods for trying to sell directly to consumers the use of direct forms of advertising to elicit inquiries or sales from potential customers directly to producers or service providers. Direct response marketing aims to bypass intermediaries such as wholesalers or retailers. Forms of communication used include ***direct mail***, home shopping channels, and television and press advertisements. *Also called* ***direct action marketing, direct marketing***

direct selling MARKETING selling products to consumers without intermediate steps the selling of products or services directly to customers without the use of intermediaries such as wholesalers, retailers, or brokers. Direct selling offers many advantages to the customer, including lower prices and shopping from home. Potential disadvantages include lack of after-sales service, an inability to inspect products prior to purchase, lack of specialist advice, and difficulties in returning or exchanging goods. Methods of direct selling include mail order catalogs and door-to-door and telephone sales. Direct selling has increased with the growth of the Internet, which enables producers to make direct contact with potential customers.

direct share ownership *UK* STOCKHOLDING & INVESTMENTS = ***direct stock ownership***

direct stock ownership *US* STOCKHOLDING & INVESTMENTS ownership of stock by private individuals the ownership of stock by private individuals, buying or selling through brokers, and not via holdings in mutual funds. *UK term* ***direct share ownership***

direct tax TAX tax paid directly by producer or provider a tax on income or capital that is paid directly rather than added to the price of goods or services

dirty float CURRENCY & EXCHANGE exchange rate influenced by central bank's actions abroad a floating exchange rate that cannot float freely because a country's central bank intervenes on foreign exchange markets to alter its level

dirty price FINANCE cost of debt plus unpaid interest the price of a debt instrument that includes the amount of accrued interest that has not yet been paid

disaggregation MERGERS & ACQUISITIONS breaking up group of allied firms the breaking apart of an alliance of companies to review their strengths and contributions as a basis for rebuilding an effective business web

disaster management GENERAL MANAGEMENT firm's response to major unexpected negative events the actions taken by an organization in response to unexpected events that are adversely affecting people or resources and threatening the continued operation of the organization. Disaster management includes the development of ***disaster recovery plans***, for minimizing the risk of disasters and for handling them when they do occur, and the implementation of such plans. Disaster management usually refers to the management of natural catastrophes such as fire, flooding, or earthquakes. Related techniques include ***crisis management***, ***contingency management***, and ***risk management***.

disaster recovery plan GENERAL MANAGEMENT plan for firm's response to disaster a plan for minimizing the risk of disasters and for handling them when they do occur. It usually refers to natural catastrophes such as fire, flooding, or earthquakes. *See also* ***disaster management***

disbursement FINANCE paying out of money the payment of money, for example, as an expense or to get rid of a debt

disbursing agent FINANCE = ***paying agent***

discharged bankrupt LEGAL person released from bankruptcy a person who has been released from being bankrupt because his or her debts have been paid

discipline HR & PERSONNEL rules of expected behavior or performance standards of required behavior or performance. Good practice requires an organization to establish a disciplinary procedure in order to ensure just decisions. A disciplinary procedure should consist of a formal system of documented warnings and hearings, with rights of representation and appeal at each stage.

disclaimer LEGAL statement denying legal responsibility for something a statement expressing a refusal to accept legal responsibility for something such as the outcome of an event or the validity of a claim

disclosure REGULATION & COMPLIANCE legal obligation to reveal pertinent facts the act of declaring facts that were previously unknown, such as share ownership which might affect business decisions, especially to comply with legal requirements

disclosure of information LEGAL giving potentially confidential information to outsiders the release of information to a third party or parties which may be considered confidential. The disclosure of information in the public interest may be prohibited, permitted, or required, by legislation in a variety of contexts. For example: ***data protection*** legislation restricts the disclosure of personal data held by organizations; ***company law*** requires the publication of certain financial and company data; and ***whistleblowing*** legislation entitles employees to divulge information relating to unethical or illegal conduct in the workplace. ***Restrictive covenants*** and ***confidentiality agreements*** also regulate the information that may be disclosed to third parties.

disclosure of shareholding STOCKHOLDING & INVESTMENTS public disclosure of holdings in firm a public announcement of a shareholding in a company, required by the regulatory authorities and stock exchanges if a shareholding exceeds a given percentage

discount 1. FINANCE price reduction to encourage buying a reduction in the price of goods or services in relation to the standard price. A discount is a selling technique that is used, for example, to encourage customers to buy in large quantities or to make payments in cash. It can also be used to improve sales of a slow-moving line. The greater the purchasing power of the buyer, the greater the discounts that can be negotiated. Some companies inflate original list prices to give the impression that discounts offer value for money; conversely too many genuine discounts may harm profitability. **2.** STOCKHOLDING & INVESTMENTS reduced share price offered by investment trust the difference between the share price of an investment trust and its ***net asset value***

discount allowed BUSINESS amount of seller's price reduction the amount by which the seller agrees to reduce his or her price to the customer

discount broker STOCKHOLDING & INVESTMENTS broker with lower fees offering fewer services a broker who charges relatively low fees because he or she provides restricted services

discount brokerage *US* FINANCE finance firm offering fewer, cheaper services a brokerage that

    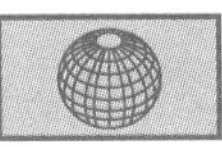   

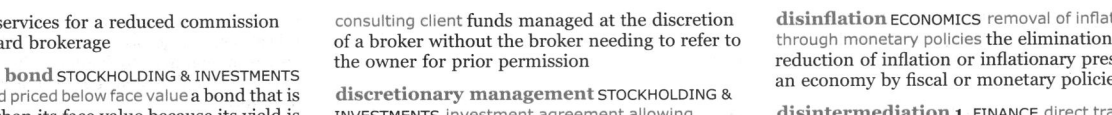

offers fewer services for a reduced commission than a standard brokerage

discounted bond STOCKHOLDING & INVESTMENTS low-yield bond priced below face value a bond that is sold for less than its face value because its yield is not as high as that of other bonds

discounted cash flow FINANCE forecast return on investment subject to cost-of-funds adjustment a calculation of the forecast return on capital investment by discounting future cash flows from an investment, usually at a rate equivalent to the company's minimum required rate of return. *Abbr* ***DCF***

discounted dividend model STOCKHOLDING & INVESTMENTS calculation of stock's value by discounting future dividends a method of calculating a stock's value by reducing future dividends to the present value. *Also called* ***dividend discount model***

discounted value STOCKHOLDING & INVESTMENTS = ***present value***

discount house FINANCE firm trading in discounted bills of exchange in the United Kingdom, a financial company that specializes in buying and selling ***bills of exchange*** at a reduced price

discount loan FINANCE loan issued with interest payments deducted a loan that amounts to less than its face value because payment of interest has been subtracted

discount market MARKETS market for borrowing and lending money a market for borrowing and lending money, through certificates of deposit, Treasury bills, etc.

discount rate **1.** BANKING interest rate banks pay for loans the rate charged by a central bank on any loans it makes to other banks **2.** E-COMMERCE fee seller pays for credit card transaction settlement a percentage fee that an e-commerce merchant pays to an account provider or independent sales organization for settling an electronic transaction

discount received BUSINESS amount of customer's price reduction the amount by which the purchaser receives a reduction in price from the seller

discount security FINANCE low-priced security not paying interest a security that is sold for less than its face value in lieu of bearing interest

discount window BANKING Federal Reserve loans to member banks in the United States, the system by which the Federal Reserve grants loans to a member bank by giving advances on the security of Treasury bills that the bank is holding

discrete variable STATISTICS statistical variable with whole-number value in a statistical study, a variable such as the number of deaths in a population which has only a whole-number value

discretionary account STOCKHOLDING & INVESTMENTS account allowing broker to make trading decisions a securities account in which the broker has the authority to make decisions about buying and selling without the customer's prior permission. *Also called* ***managed account***

discretionary client STOCKHOLDING & INVESTMENTS client who lets broker manage funds without consultation a client whose funds are managed at the discretion of a broker without the broker needing to refer to the client for prior permission

discretionary funds STOCKHOLDING & INVESTMENTS funds broker can manage without consulting client funds managed at the discretion of a broker without the broker needing to refer to the owner for prior permission

discretionary management STOCKHOLDING & INVESTMENTS investment agreement allowing broker to make decisions an arrangement between a stockbroker and his or her client whereby the stockbroker makes all investment decisions. It is the opposite of an ***advisory management*** arrangement.

discretionary order STOCKHOLDING & INVESTMENTS transaction handled by broker alone a security transaction in which a broker controls details such as the time of execution

discretionary spend *UK* FINANCE = ***discretionary spending***

discretionary spending *US* FINANCE money for things you want but don't need the amount of money available after direct taxation to an individual or family to spend on items other than necessities such as food, clothing, and homes. *UK term* ***discretionary spend***

discretionary trust FINANCE trust arrangement giving trustee full decision-making power a trust where the trustees decide how to invest the income and when and how much income should be paid to the beneficiaries

discriminant analysis STATISTICS statistical method of identifying variables that differentiate groups a statistical technique designed to predict the groups or categories into which individual cases will fall on the basis of a number of independent variables. Discriminant analysis attempts to identify which variables or combinations of variables accurately discriminate between groups or categories by means of a scatter diagram or classification table called a "confusion matrix." Discriminant analysis has applications in finance, for example, credit risk analysis, or in the prediction of company failure, and in the field of marketing, for market segmentation purposes.

discriminating monopoly ECONOMICS sole producer tailoring prices to markets a company able to charge different prices for its output in different markets because as the only producer it has power to influence prices for its goods

discrimination HR & PERSONNEL unfairly treating people differently because of prejudice unfavorable treatment in employment based on prejudice. Major forms of outlawed discrimination include those based on sex, race, disability, and, in some countries, age.

diseconomies of scale OPERATIONS & PRODUCTION increased unit cost with increased production a situation in which increased production increases, rather than decreases, unit costs

disequilibrium FINANCE imbalance in economy, as between supply and demand an imbalance in the economy when supply does not equal demand, or when a country's balance of payments is in deficit

disequilibrium price ECONOMICS product price causing supply and demand imbalance the price of a good set at a level at which demand and supply are not in balance

dishonor BANKING not pay check because funds are inadequate to refuse payment of a check because the account for which it is written does not contain enough money. *Also called* ***bounce*** *(sense 1)*

disinflation ECONOMICS removal of inflation through monetary policies the elimination or reduction of inflation or inflationary pressures in an economy by fiscal or monetary policies

disintermediation **1.** FINANCE direct trading in money market the process of savers and borrowers making transactions directly in the money market rather than by making deposits and taking loans from banks **2.** E-COMMERCE removing middlemen to sell directly to customer the elimination of intermediaries, for example, the wholesalers found in traditional retail channels, in favor of direct selling to the consumer. *See also* ***reintermediation***

disinvest **1.** FINANCE reduce investment by non-replacement of capital assets to reduce investment by not replacing capital assets when they wear out **2.** STOCKHOLDING & INVESTMENTS reduce investment by selling stock to reduce investment overall or in a specific area by selling stock

disinvestment FINANCE **1.** reduction in investment through non-replacement of capital assets a process of reducing investment by not replacing capital assets when they wear out **2.** reduction in investment by selling stock a process of reducing investment overall or in a specific area by selling stock

dismissal HR & PERSONNEL firing employee the termination of somebody's employment by his or her employer

dispensation TAX UK employer's tax allowance for business expenses in the United Kingdom, an arrangement between an employer and ***Her Majesty's Revenue & Customs*** in which business expenses paid to an employee are not declared for tax

dispersion STATISTICS degree of deviation from mean the amount by which a set of observations deviates from its mean

disposable income *or* disposable personal income TAX income after tax and other deductions income that is left for spending after taxes and other deductions have been made from the income of a person or organization. *See also* ***net pay***

dispute HR & PERSONNEL disagreement between parties a disagreement. A ***labor dispute*** is a disagreement between an employer and an employees' representative, usually a ***labor union***, over pay and conditions and can result in a ***job action***. A commercial dispute is a disagreement between two businesses, usually over a ***contract***. There are three main types of dispute resolution: ***litigation***, ***arbitration***, and alternative dispute resolution.

disqualification LEGAL court decision disallowing person from becoming company director a court order that prevents somebody from being a director of a company. A variety of offenses, even those termed as "administrative," can result in some people being disqualified for up to five years.

distrain BUSINESS take control of assets to pay debt to seize ***assets*** belonging to a person or organization in order to pay off a debt

distressed property FINANCE property subject to repossession property originally purchased with the aid of a loan on which payments have stopped and the borrower has defaulted

distress merchandise OPERATIONS & PRODUCTION goods sold cheaply to pay company's debts goods that are sold at sharply reduced prices in order to settle a company's debts

  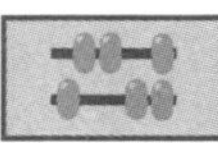      

distress sale OPERATIONS & PRODUCTION sale of goods cheaply to pay company's debts a sale of goods at sharply reduced prices in order to settle a company's debts

distributable profit STOCKHOLDING & INVESTMENTS profit usable as dividends profit that can be distributed to stockholders as dividends if the directors decide to do so

distributed profit STOCKHOLDING & INVESTMENTS profit passed on as dividends profit passed to stockholders in the form of dividends

distribution OPERATIONS & PRODUCTION supplying of manufactured goods to retailers the act of sending goods from the manufacturer to the wholesaler and then to retailers

distribution center OPERATIONS & PRODUCTION place for holding products to be sent out a warehouse or storage facility where the emphasis is on processing and moving goods on to wholesalers, retailers, or consumers rather than on storage

distribution channel OPERATIONS & PRODUCTION means of moving products from suppliers to customers the route by which a product or service is moved from a producer or supplier to customers. A distribution channel usually consists of a chain of intermediaries, including wholesalers, retailers, and distributors, which is designed to transport goods from the point of production to the point of consumption in the most efficient way. *Also called* ***channel of distribution***

distribution list E-COMMERCE named group of e-mail addresses a list of e-mail addresses given one collective name. Internet users can send a message to all the addresses on the list simultaneously by referring to the list name.

distribution management OPERATIONS & PRODUCTION handling movement of goods from production to sale the management of the efficient transfer of goods from the place of manufacture to the point of sale or consumption. Distribution management encompasses such activities as warehousing, materials handling, packaging, stock control, order processing, and transportation.

distribution of income 1. STOCKHOLDING & INVESTMENTS payment of dividends to stockholders the payment of accumulated dividends to stockholders on record, usually on an annual basis **2.** ECONOMICS wealth range in society the way income is spread across society as a whole, as a measure of the equality or inequality of wealth

distribution resource planning OPERATIONS & PRODUCTION computerized system managing needs for finished products a computerized system that integrates distribution with manufacturing by identifying requirements for finished goods and producing schedules for ***inventory*** and its movement within the distribution process. Distribution resource planning systems receive data on sales forecasts, customer order and delivery requirements, available inventory, ***logistics***, and manufacturing and purchasing ***lead times***. This data is analyzed to produce a time-phased schedule of resource requirements that is matched against existing supply sources and production schedules to identify the actions that must be taken to synchronize supply and demand. The effective integration of material requirements planning and distribution resource planning systems leads to the more effective and timely delivery of finished goods to the customer, and to reduced inventory levels and lower material costs. *Abbr* ***DRP***

distributions STOCKHOLDING & INVESTMENTS income from investment any income arising from a bond fund or an equity

distributive network E-COMMERCE interconnected system for moving products a system or infrastructure that enables products and services to move around. Offline distributive networks include roads, telephone companies, electrical power grids, and the mail service. In the new economy, distributive networks include online banks and Web-enabled mobile telephones.

distributor MARKETING intermediary between manufacturer and seller an organization that distributes products to retailers on behalf of a manufacturer

distributor support MARKETING aid from manufacturer to firm that distributes products marketing or financial support by manufacturers aimed at improving the performance of organizations that distribute their products

District Bank BANKING member bank of Federal Reserve in the United States, one of the 12 banks that make up the ***Federal Reserve***. Each District Bank is responsible for all banking activity in its assigned region.

divergence MARKETS contradictory indications of trends a situation in which two or more indicators such as a stock price and an index move in opposite directions, showing a shift in a trend

diversification GENERAL MANAGEMENT, MERGERS & ACQUISITIONS developing new areas for growth or risk reduction a strategy to increase the variety of business, service, or product types within an organization. Diversification can be a growth strategy, taking advantage of market opportunities, or it may be aimed at reducing risk by spreading interests over different areas. It can be achieved through ***acquisition*** or through internal research and development, and it can involve managing two, a few, or many different areas of interest. Diversification can also be a corporate strategy of investment in acquisitions within a broad portfolio range by a large ***holding company***. One distinct type is ***horizontal diversification***, which involves expansion into a similar product area, for example, a domestic furniture manufacturer producing office furniture. Another is ***vertical diversification***, in which a company moves into a different level of the ***supply chain***, for example, a manufacturing company becoming a retailer.

diversified investment company FINANCE varied mutual fund a mutual fund with a range of types of investments

divestiture FINANCE firm's sale of asset the sale by a company of an asset, for example, to get money to pay off a debt

divestment 1. MERGERS & ACQUISITIONS selling or closing part of firm the sale or closure of one or several businesses, or parts of a business. Divestment often takes place as part of a rationalization effort to cut costs or to enable an organization to concentrate on core business or competences, and may take the form of a ***management buyout***. **2.** STOCKHOLDING & INVESTMENTS giving up ownership in firm the proportional or complete reduction in an ownership stake in an organization

dividend STOCKHOLDING & INVESTMENTS profits paid to stockholders part of a company's net profits paid out to qualified stockholders at a fixed amount per share

dividend check *US* STOCKHOLDING & INVESTMENTS check in payment of dividend a check issued to qualified stockholders that makes payment of a dividend. *UK term* ***dividend warrant***

dividend clawback STOCKHOLDING & INVESTMENTS arrangement for reinvestment of dividends an agreement that dividends will be reinvested as part of the financing of a project

dividend cover STOCKHOLDING & INVESTMENTS ability of net profit to pay firm's dividend the number of times a company's dividends to ordinary stockholders could be paid out of its net after-tax profits. This measures the likelihood of dividend payments being sustained, and is a useful indication of sustained profitability.

If the figure is 3, a firm's profits are three times the level of the dividend paid to stockholders.

Dividend cover is calculated by dividing earnings per share by the dividend per share:

$$\frac{\text{Earnings per share}}{\text{Dividend per share}} = \text{Dividend cover}$$

If a company has earnings per share of $8, and it pays out a dividend of 2.1, dividend cover is

$$\frac{8}{2.1} = 3.80$$

An alternative formula divides a company's net profit by the total amount allocated for dividends. So a company that earns $10 million in net profit and allocates $1 million for dividends has a dividend cover of 10, while a company that earns $25 million and pays out $10 million in dividends has a dividend cover of 2.5:

$$\frac{10,000,000}{1,000,000} = 10$$

and

$$\frac{25,000,000}{10,000,000} = 2.5$$

A dividend cover ratio of 2 or higher is usually adequate, and indicates that the dividend is affordable. A dividend cover ratio below 1.5 is risky, and a ratio below 1 indicates a company is paying the current year's dividend with retained earnings from a previous year's, a practice that cannot continue indefinitely. On the other hand, a high dividend cover figure may disappoint an investor looking for income, since the figure suggests directors could have declared a larger dividend. *See also* ***payout ratio***

dividend discount model STOCKHOLDING & INVESTMENTS = ***discounted dividend model***

dividend forecast STOCKHOLDING & INVESTMENTS predicted amount of next dividend a prediction of the amount that an expected dividend will pay per share

dividend limitation STOCKHOLDING & INVESTMENTS restriction on dividend payments for bond a provision in a bond limiting the dividends that may be paid

dividend mandate STOCKHOLDING & INVESTMENTS permission to directly deposit dividends in bank account an authorization by a stockholder to the company in which he or she has a holding to pay dividends directly into his or her bank account

dividend payout STOCKHOLDING & INVESTMENTS money paid as dividends to stockholders money distributed by a company in the form of dividends to qualified stockholders

dividend payout ratio STOCKHOLDING & INVESTMENTS = ***payout ratio***

dividend per share STOCKHOLDING & INVESTMENTS amount of dividend per share of stock held an amount of money paid by a company as dividend for each share of stock held

dividend reinvestment plan STOCKHOLDING & INVESTMENTS arrangement for reinvesting dividends in firm's stock a plan that provides for the reinvestment of dividends in the stock of the company paying the dividends. *Abbr* ***DRIP***

dividend rights STOCKHOLDING & INVESTMENTS rights to receive dividends the entitlement of a stockholder to receive a share of the company's profits

dividends-received deduction STOCKHOLDING & INVESTMENTS, TAX tax break on dividends from subsidiary company a tax advantage on dividends that a company receives from a company it owns

dividend warrant *UK* STOCKHOLDING & INVESTMENTS = ***dividend check***

dividend yield STOCKHOLDING & INVESTMENTS relative size of dividend dividends paid out expressed as a percentage of a stock's price

D/N *abbr* FINANCE ***debit note***

documentary credit *or* documentary letter of credit BANKING provision for payment in international transactions an arrangement, used in the finance of international transactions, whereby a bank undertakes to make a payment to a third party on behalf of a customer. *Abbr* ***D/C***

dog GENERAL MANAGEMENT firm with low market share and growth in the ***Boston Box*** model, a business with a low market share and low growth rate. *See also* ***Boston Box***

dog-eat-dog MARKETING extremely competitive ruthlessly willing to harm competitors, especially in the marketplace (slang)

dogs of the Dow MARKETS stocks with smallest yield according to Dow Jones in the United States, the stocks in the ***Dow Jones Industrial Average*** that pay the smallest dividends as a percentage of their prices (informal)

dollar CURRENCY & EXCHANGE currency unit in US and some other countries a unit of currency used in the United States and other countries such as Australia, Bahamas, Barbados, Bermuda, Brunei, Canada, Fiji, Hong Kong, Jamaica, New Zealand, Singapore, and Zimbabwe

dollar area CURRENCY & EXCHANGE region using US dollar for trading an area of the world where the US dollar is the main trading currency

dollar cost averaging *US* FINANCE regular repeating of investment the regular periodic purchase of the same amount in dollars of the same security regardless of its price. *UK term* ***pound cost averaging***

dollar gap CURRENCY & EXCHANGE shortage of US dollars a situation in which the supply of US dollars is not enough to satisfy the demand for them from overseas buyers

dollar roll MARKETS arrangement to sell then repurchase stock in the United States, an agreement to sell a stock and buy it back later for a specified price

dollars-and-cents *US* FINANCE influenced by money used to describe a situation in which cost and return are considered the determining factors

dollar stocks STOCKHOLDING & INVESTMENTS stocks in US companies stocks issued by companies incorporated in the United States

domestecutive BUSINESS woman working from home a woman who works or runs a business from her home

domestic consumer ECONOMICS user of product for personal purposes a ***consumer*** who uses a product for personal, domestic, or household purposes

domestic currency CURRENCY & EXCHANGE money legally accepted in home country the legal ***currency*** of the jurisdiction that issued it

domestic economy ECONOMICS economy of home country the production, consumption, and distribution of wealth within a specific country

domestic market MARKETS market in home country the market for goods and services in the country where a company is based

domestic production OPERATIONS & PRODUCTION production of goods for home country use the production of goods and services for internal consumption in the producer country rather than for export

domestic tax TAX tax on residents and businesses in home country tax levied on companies doing business and individuals living in a specific country

domestic trade BUSINESS trade inside firm's home country trade by a company within the country in which it is based. *Also called*

domicile LEGAL country of somebody's residence or firm's registration the country in which somebody has his or her permanent residence or where a company's office is registered

domicilium citandi et executandi *S. AFRICA* FINANCE address for delivering legal documents the address where a summons or other official notice should be served if necessary, which must be supplied by somebody applying for credit or entering into a contract

dominant influence TREASURY MANAGEMENT undisputed influence over financial policy influence that can be exercised to achieve the operating and financial policies designed by the holder of the influence, notwithstanding the rights or influence of any other party

donor FINANCE giver of gift a person who gives a gift, especially money

dormant account BANKING inactive bank account a bank account that is no longer used by the account holder

dormant company ACCOUNTING firm not doing business for a while a company that has not made any transactions during a specific ***accounting period***

dot.com E-COMMERCE firm selling on Internet an e-commerce enterprise, marketing its products only through the Internet

double bottom MARKETS bullish chart pattern with "W" shape a chart pattern in which the price of a security drops, recovers moderately, drops again, then recovers a second time and continues its upward trend, regarded as an indicator of a bullish market

double counting ACCOUNTING using same cost or benefit twice in calculation the counting of a cost or benefit element twice when carrying out analysis. This can happen when the total sales in a market is calculated as the sum of all sales made by companies, without deducting the purchases companies make from other firms in the market.

double-digit growth ECONOMICS rapid growth of firm or economy an increase of between 10% and 99% in the productivity or size of a company, business activity, or economy within a specific period of time

double-digit inflation ECONOMICS rapid growth of inflation rate a rate of inflation between 10% and 99%, usually calculated on an annual basis

double dipping FRAUD fraudulently receiving two incomes from government in the United States, the illegal practice of receiving income from a government pension as well as social security payments, or of holding a government job while receiving a government pension

double-dip recession ECONOMICS brief recovery preceding further recession a pattern in an economic cycle that shows two periods of recession separated by a brief period of growth. *Also called* ***W-shaped recession***

double-entry bookkeeping ACCOUNTING type of bookkeeping system used by most businesses the most commonly used system of ***bookkeeping***, based on the principle that every financial transaction involves the simultaneous receiving and giving of value, and is therefore recorded twice

double indemnity INSURANCE commitment to pay double insurance for accidental death a provision in an insurance policy that guarantees payment of double its face value on the accidental death of the holder

double-one-touch option STOCKHOLDING & INVESTMENTS option paying at one of two preset levels an ***option*** that gives an investor a payment if the price of the underlying asset reaches or exceeds one of two preset levels. *See also* ***no-touch option, one-touch option***

double taxation TAX having to pay tax twice on same income the taxing of something twice, usually the combination of corporation tax and tax on the dividends that stockholders earn

double taxation relief TAX tax break between countries on taxes already paid a reduction of tax payable in one country by the amount of tax on income, profits, or capital gains already paid in another country

double top MARKETS bearish chart pattern with "M" shape a chart pattern in which the price of a security rises, drops moderately, rises again, then drops a second time and continues its downward trend, regarded as an indicator of a bearish market

Dow Jones 1. BUSINESS, FINANCE Dow Jones & Company US publishing and financial information corporation, Dow Jones & Company. It was established in 1882 by reporters Charles Dow, Edward Jones, and Charles Bergstresser, and is now a subsidiary of News Corporation. It publishes the ***Wall Street Journal***. **2.** MARKETS Dow Jones Indexes US index provider Dow Jones Indexes, established as a spin-off from Dow Jones & Company in 1997, it is now 90% owned by CME Group. Its best-known product is the ***Dow Jones Industrial Average***, which was created in 1896. **3.** MARKETS Dow Jones Industrial Average abbreviated name sometimes used for the ***Dow Jones Industrial Average*** stock market index produced by Dow Jones Indexes the company

  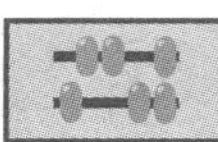   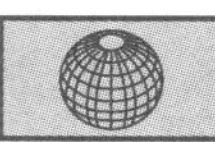   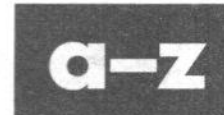

Dow Jones Industrial Average MARKETS stock market index of 30 major US firms an index of 30 leading US stocks actively traded on the ***New York Stock Exchange***, used as an indicator of the overall performance of stocks in the United States. Roughly two-thirds of the companies in the index are manufacturers, but the word is historical and companies trading in entertainment, financial services, and IT are also included.

downgrade MARKETS **1.** reduce projection for stock price to change the forecast for a stock price to a lower one **2.** reduce bond rating to change the credit rating for a ***bond*** to a lower one

down payment FINANCE partial payment at time of purchase a part of the full price of something paid at the time it is bought, with the remaining part to be paid later

downshifting GENERAL MANAGEMENT reducing work and income for simpler, better life the concept of giving up all or part of your work commitment and income in exchange for improved quality of life Downshifting is integral to the idea of ***portfolio working***, in which individuals opt out of a formal employee relationship to sell their services at a pace and at a price to suit themselves

downside factor *or* downside potential STOCKHOLDING & INVESTMENTS possibility of loss in value the possibility of incurring a loss when an investment declines in value

downside risk STOCKHOLDING & INVESTMENTS risk of loss in value the risk that an investment will decline in value. *See also* ***upside potential***

downsizing **1.** BUSINESS expense cuts to make organization more efficient organizational restructuring involving outsourcing activities, replacing permanent staff with contract employees, and reducing the number of levels within the organizational hierarchy, with the intention of making the organization more flexible, efficient, and responsive to its environment **2.** HR & PERSONNEL reducing number of firm's employees the reduction of the size of a business, especially by laying staff off. Downsizing may be part of a rationalization process, or corporate restructuring, with the removal of hierarchies or the closure of departments or functions either after a period of unsatisfactory results or as a consequence of strategic review. The terms "upsizing" and "resizing" are applied when an organization increases the number of staff employed.

downstream OPERATIONS & PRODUCTION at later stage at a point later in the production process

downstream progress GENERAL MANAGEMENT easy advancement toward goals movement by a company toward achieving its objectives which is easy because it involves riding a wave or trend and benefiting from favorable conditions. *See also* ***upstream progress***

downswing MARKETS decline in stock prices a downward movement in stock prices following a period of steady or rising prices

downtick MARKETS trade at price lower than in previous trade a transaction in which the price of a particular security is lower than the price in the transaction immediately preceding it

downtime OPERATIONS & PRODUCTION period when machinery is not working a period of time during which a machine is not available for use because of maintenance or breakdown

downturn FINANCE, MARKETS downward trend a downward trend in sales, profits, a stock market, or an economy

Dow Theory MARKETS idea that movements in selected stocks predict prices the theory that stock market prices can be forecast on the basis of the movements of selected industrial and transportation stocks

draft BANKING document ordering payment a written order to pay a particular sum from one account to another, or to a person. *See also* ***sight draft, time draft***

drawback TAX tax rebate on imports that produce exports a rebate on customs duty for imported goods that are used in producing exports

drawdown FINANCE decision to use money made available earlier the act of obtaining money that has previously been made available under a credit agreement

drawee BANKING payer of bill of exchange or check the individual or institution to whom a bill of exchange or check is addressed, who will pay the sum indicated

drawer BANKING person who writes check or bill the person who writes a check or a bill asking an individual or institution to pay money to the payee indicated

drawing account BANKING account for tracking money withdrawn an account that permits the tracking of withdrawals, used, for example, by a ***sole proprietor*** or ***partner***

drawing rights FINANCE member country's right to borrow from IMF fund a right of a member country of the ***International Monetary Fund*** to borrow money from the fund in a foreign currency. *See also* ***Special Drawing Right***

drilling down MARKETING investigating more detailed subject information a technique for managing data by arranging it in hierarchies that provide increasing levels of detail

DRIP *abbr* STOCKHOLDING & INVESTMENTS ***dividend reinvestment plan***

drip feed **1.** FINANCE gradual provision of capital a method of providing capital to a small startup company in which investors contribute capital as needed over a period of time **2.** STOCKHOLDING & INVESTMENTS regular increase in investment a method of investing in securities in which investors invest a specific amount of money on a regular basis

drip method MARKETING calling potential customers repeatedly until they buy a marketing method that involves calling potential customers at regular intervals until they agree to make a purchase (slang)

drive time MARKETING time when people drive to or from work the time of the day when most people are likely to be in their cars, usually early in the morning or late in the afternoon, considered to be the optimum time to broadcast a radio commercial (slang)

drop a bundle MARKETS spend or lose large sum of money to spend or lose a lot of money, especially on the stock market (slang)

drop lock FINANCE change from floating to fixed interest rate the automatic conversion of a debt instrument with a floating rate to one with a fixed rate when interest rates fall to an agreed percentage

droplock bond STOCKHOLDING & INVESTMENTS bond becoming fixed rate if interest rate falls a floating-rate bond that will convert to a fixed rate of interest if interest rates fall to a specific level. *See also* ***debt-convertible bond***

DRP *abbr* OPERATIONS & PRODUCTION ***distribution resource planning***

dry goods textiles and housewares textiles, clothing, and general housewares

DTCC *abbr* BUSINESS ***Depository Trust and Clearing Corporation***

DTF *abbr* MARKETS ***Derivative Trading Facility***

DTI *abbr* Department of Trade and Industry

dual currency bond CURRENCY & EXCHANGE bond issued and paying interest in different currencies a bond that pays interest in a currency other than the one used to buy it

dual economy ECONOMICS different growth rates for manufacturing and services an economy in which the manufacturing and service sectors are growing at different rates

dual listing MARKETS listing of stock on two exchanges the listing of a stock on two or more stock exchanges, often including a regional exchange in addition to a nationwide exchange

dual pricing MARKETS selling product at different prices in different markets the practice of setting different prices for the same product in the different markets in which it is sold

dual trading FINANCE working as agent for buyer and seller the practice of acting as agent for both a broker's firm and its customers

duck **get your ducks in a row** *or* line up your ducks GENERAL MANAGEMENT1. to get everything properly organized2. to get all concerned parties to agree to a plan of action

dud check BANKING check not honored because of insufficient funds a check that cannot be cashed because the person writing it does not have enough money in the account to pay it

due bill STOCKHOLDING & INVESTMENTS notice of transfer from seller to buyer a notification that a security has been transferred from the seller to the buyer, giving details of the amounts such as cost, dividends, or interest owed either the seller or buyer

due date FINANCE deadline for payment of debt the date on which a debt is required to be paid

due diligence **1.** ACCOUNTING detailed check of firm's accounts before sale the examination of a company's accounts prior to a potential ***takeover*** by another organization. This assessment is often undertaken by an independent third party. *Abbr* ***DD*** **2.** GENERAL MANAGEMENT investigation of firm before purchase or investment the collection, verification, analysis, and assessment of information about the operations and management of a company undertaken by a potential purchaser or investor. Due diligence aims to confirm that the purchaser or investor has an accurate picture of the target company and to identify risks and benefits associated with the prospective deal. Due diligence usually starts after the signing of a letter of intent by both parties and information disclosed during the process is normally protected by the signing of a ***confidentiality agreement***. Due diligence often leads on to negotiations on the detailed terms of the agreement. The process may cover the financial, legal, commercial, technical, cultural, and environmental aspects of the organization's operations as well as its ***assets*** and ***liabilities***, and may be conducted with the assistance of professional advisers.

  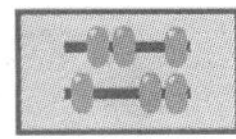   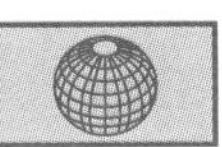   

due-on-sale clause MORTGAGES obligation to pay off mortgage upon property sale a provision requiring a homeowner to pay off a mortgage upon sale of the property

dumping INTERNATIONAL TRADE selling commodity abroad at greatly reduced price the selling of a commodity on a foreign market at a price below its ***marginal cost***, either to dispose of a temporary surplus or to achieve a monopoly by eliminating competition —***dump***

Dun and Bradstreet BUSINESS organization that collects and provides credit information an international organization that sources credit information from companies and their creditors which it then makes available to subscribers. *Abbr* ***D&B***

duopoly ECONOMICS market with only two sellers of product a market in which only two sellers of a good exist. If one decides to alter the price, the other will respond and influence the market's response to the first decision.

durable power of attorney LEGAL power to act for another a ***power of attorney*** that allows one person to act on behalf of another if that person should become unable to act on their own behalf, for example, because of mental incompetence

duration STOCKHOLDING & INVESTMENTS time to receive current value of payments the time in years that it will take to receive the present value of all the payments from a fixed-income investment, calculated using the effect that a 1% change in the interest rate will have on the investment. This calculation is mainly used to measure the sensitivity of changes in bond prices to changes in interest rates.

Dutch auction FINANCE auction in which price bidding goes down an auction in which the lot for sale is offered at an initial price that, if there are no bidders, is then reduced until there is a bid

duty TAX tax on goods, especially imports and exports a tax that must be paid on goods, especially on imported and exported goods

duty-free TAX exempt from customs duty sold without the requirement for any customs duties to be paid

dynamic pricing FINANCE pricing from demand pricing that changes in line with patterns of demand

dynamic programming GENERAL MANAGEMENT mathematical approach to solving production and inventory problems a mathematical technique used to solve complex problems in the fields of production planning and inventory control. Dynamic programming divides the problem into steps or decision stages that can be addressed sequentially, usually by working backward from the last stage. Applications of the technique include maintenance and replacement of equipment, resource allocation, and process design and control.

E

EAA *abbr* ACCOUNTING ***European Accounting Association***

EAI *abbr* OPERATIONS & PRODUCTION ***enterprise application integration***

e-alliance E-COMMERCE union of organizations for Internet commerce a partnership forged between organizations in order to achieve business objectives for enterprises conducted over the web. There has been a surge in such alliances since the Internet took off in the mid-1990s, and studies show that the most successful have been those involving traditional offline businesses and online entities, known as the clicks-and-mortar strategy, for example, that between Amazon.com and Toys 'R' Us. Toys 'R' Us had the physical infrastructure and brand, while Amazon.com had the online infrastructure and experience of making e-commerce work.

E&O *abbr* ACCOUNTING ***errors and omissions***

early adopter GENERAL MANAGEMENT one of first users of new technology an individual or organization that is among the first to make use of a new technique, strategy, technology, etc.

early withdrawal BANKING taking money out of time deposit account early the removal of money from a deposit account before the due date. Early withdrawal often incurs a penalty that the account holder must pay.

earned income FINANCE money earned for work performed money generated by a person's or organization's labor, for example, wages, salaries, fees, royalties, and business profits. *See also* ***unearned income***

Earned Income Credit TAX US tax credit for low paid in the United States, a federal income tax credit for low-income individuals and families with income generated from employment. *Abbr* ***EIC***

earning potential 1. BUSINESS amount person can earn the amount of money somebody should be able to earn in his or her professional capacity **2.** STOCKHOLDING & INVESTMENTS potential dividend earnings the amount of dividend that a share potentially can produce

earnings 1. ACCOUNTING money available to business after expenses income or profit from a business, quoted gross or net of tax, which may be retained and distributed in part to the stockholders **2.** FINANCE money obtained through work a sum of money gained from paid employment, usually quoted before tax, including any extra rewards such as ***fringe benefits***, allowances, or incentives

earnings before interest and taxes ACCOUNTING *see* ***EBIT***

earnings before interest, tax, depreciation, and amortization ACCOUNTING *see* ***EBITDA***

earnings cap PENSIONS in UK, maximum earnings for pension purposes in the United Kingdom, the top limit of earnings that can be used in calculating a retirement pension paid from an ***occupational pension*** plan

earnings credit BANKING in US, amount offsetting bank charges in the United States, an allowance that reduces bank charges on checking accounts

earnings drift FINANCE pay increases outstripping official rates a situation in which an increase in pay is greater than that of officially negotiated rates

earnings growth STOCKHOLDING & INVESTMENTS increase in profit per share of stock an increase in the profit a company earns as expressed on a per-share basis

earnings momentum STOCKHOLDING & INVESTMENTS change in profit per share of stock an increase or decrease in a company's earnings per share as compared to the same period of time in the previous year, used by investors as a measure of how its stock will perform

earnings performance STOCKHOLDING & INVESTMENTS dividend-yielding pattern of stock a measure of how well a specific stock does in providing dividends

earnings per share STOCKHOLDING & INVESTMENTS profit allotted to each share of common stock a financial ratio that measures the portion of a company's profit allocated to each outstanding share of common stock. It is the most basic measure of the value of a share, and also is the basis for calculating several other important investment ratios.

EPS is calculated by subtracting the total value of any preferred stock from net income (earnings) for the period in question, then dividing the resulting figure by the number of shares outstanding during that period.

$$\frac{\text{(Net income – Dividends on any preferred stock)}}{\text{Averagenumberofsharesoutstanding}}$$

Companies usually use a weighted average number of shares outstanding over the reporting period, but shares outstanding can either be "primary" or "fully diluted." Primary EPS is calculated using the number of shares that are currently held by investors in the market and able to be traded. Diluted EPS is the result of a complex calculation that determines how many shares would be outstanding if all exercisable warrants and options were converted into shares at the end of a quarter.

Suppose, for example, that a company has granted a large number of share options to employees. If these options are capable of being exercised in the near future, that could significantly alter the number of shares in issue and thus the EPS, even though the net income is the same. Often in such cases, the company might quote the EPS on the existing shares and the fully diluted version. *Abbr* ***EPS***

earnings-related contributions FINANCE payments into social security fund based on earnings contributions to social security that rise as the person's earnings rise, especially ***National Insurance*** contributions in the United Kingdom

earnings-related pension PENSIONS in UK, pension linked to salary in the United Kingdom, a pension that is linked to the size of the beneficiary's salary

earnings report *US* STOCKHOLDING & INVESTMENTS published financial report of US firm a company's financial statements, which must be published according to US law. *UK term* ***published accounts***

earnings retained ACCOUNTING = ***retained profits***

earnings season STOCKHOLDING & INVESTMENTS time when firms announce earnings the time of year when major companies declare their results for the previous period

earnings surprise STOCKHOLDING & INVESTMENTS gap between actual and expected earnings a considerable difference in size between a company's actual and anticipated earnings

earnings yield FINANCE earnings as percentage of stock price money earned by a company during a year, expressed as a percentage of the price of one of its shares

EASDAQ MARKETS former European stock exchange for technology and growth companies stock exchange based in Brussels, Belgium, for technology and growth companies, modeled on ***NASDAQ*** in the United States. It was acquired by

  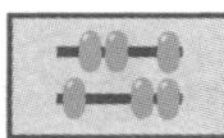      

NASDAQ in 2001 and closed down in 2003. *Full form* ***European Association of Securities Dealers Automated Quotations***

eased *UK* MARKETS describes stock market that is slightly down used in stock market reports to describe a market that has experienced a slight fall in prices

easy market MARKETS stock market with few buyers a market in which fewer people are buying, with the effect that prices are lower than hoped

easy money FINANCE = ***cheap money***

easy money policy FINANCE government policy to encourage borrowing a government policy that aims to expand the economy by making money more easily accessible to the public. This is done by strategies such as lowering interest rates and offering easy access to credit.

easy terms *UK* FINANCE = ***installment plan***

EBIT ACCOUNTING income minus costs revenue minus the cost of goods sold and normal operating expenses. *Full form* ***earnings before interest and taxes***

EBITDA ACCOUNTING use of earnings to measure firm's performance the earnings generated by a business's fundamental operating performance, frequently used in accounting ratios for comparison with other companies. Interest on borrowings, tax payable on those profits, depreciation, and amortization are excluded on the basis that they can distort the underlying performance.

It is calculated as follows:

EBITDA = Revenue − Expenses (excluding tax and interest, depreciation, etc.)

It is important to note that EBITDA ignores many factors that impact on true cash flow, such as working capital, debt payments, and other fixed expenses. Even so, it may be useful for evaluating firms in the same industry with widely different capital structures, tax rates, and depreciation policies. *Full form* ***earnings before interest, tax, depreciation, and amortization***

EBQ OPERATIONS & PRODUCTION size cheapest and easiest to produce the optimum batch size for the manufacture of an item or component, at the lowest cost. The batch size is a tradeoff between unit costs that increase with batch size and those that decrease. The point of lowest combined or total cost indicates the most economic batch size for production. *Full form* ***economic batch quantity***. *Also called* ***economic lot quantity***. *See also* ***economic order quantity***

EBRD BANKING European bank helping to develop market economies a bank, established in 1991, to develop programs to tackle a variety of issues. These included the creation and strengthening of infrastructure; industry privatization; the reform of the financial sector, including the development of capital markets and the privatization of commercial banks; the development of productive competitive private sectors of small and medium-sized enterprises in industry, agriculture, and services; the restructuring of industrial sectors to put them on a competitive basis; and the encouragement of foreign investment and cleaning up the environment. The EBRD had 41 original members: the European Commission, the European Investment Bank, all the then EU countries, and all the countries of Eastern Europe except Albania, which finally became a member in October 1991, followed by all the republics of the former USSR in March 1992. *Full form* ***European Bank for Reconstruction and Development***

e-business E-COMMERCE **1.** carrying out of business over Internet the conduct of business on the Internet, including the electronic purchasing and selling of goods and services, servicing customers, and communications with business partners. *Also called* ***electronic business*** **2.** firm operating over Internet a company that conducts the main part of its business on the Internet

EC *abbr* INTERNATIONAL TRADE ***European Community***

e-cash E-COMMERCE = ***digital cash***

ECB BANKING bank responsible for EU monetary policy the financial institution that replaced the European Monetary Institute in 1998 and that is responsible for carrying out EU monetary policy and administering the euro. *Full form* ***European Central Bank***

ECBC *abbr* FINANCE ***European Covered Bond Council***

ECGD *abbr* INTERNATIONAL TRADE ***Export Credit Guarantee Department***

ECML *abbr* E-COMMERCE ***electronic commerce modeling language***

ECN *abbr* MARKETS ***Electronic Communications Network***

ECOA *abbr* FINANCE US law ensuring equal treatment for borrowers ***Equal Credit Opportunity Act***

e-collaboration E-COMMERCE cooperation using Internet collaboration among people or organizations made possible by means of electronic technologies such as the Internet, videoconferencing, and wireless devices

e-commerce E-COMMERCE business conducted electronically, especially via Internet the exchange of goods, information products, or services via an electronic medium such as the Internet. Originally limited to buying and selling, it has evolved to include such functions as customer service, marketing, and advertising. *Also called* ***electronic commerce, web commerce***

e-commerce processes E-COMMERCE stages of trading over Internet the flow of information through planning, design, manufacture, sales, order processing, distribution, and quality in an e-business

e-company E-COMMERCE e-commerce business a company engaged in e-commerce or that conducts the main part of its business on the Internet

econometric model ECONOMICS set of mathematical equations representing economic relationships a way of representing the relationship between economic variables as an equation or set of equations with statistically precise parameters linking the variables

econometrics ECONOMICS study of mathematical equations for representing economic relationships the branch of economics concerned with using mathematical models to describe relationships in an economy, for example, between wage rates and levels of employment

economic assumption ECONOMICS belief on which economic model is based an assumption built into an economic model, for example, that output will grow at 2.5% in the next tax year

economic batch quantity OPERATIONS & PRODUCTION *see* ***EBQ***

economic benefit FINANCE benefit measurable in money a benefit to a person, business, or society that can be measured in financial terms

economic cycle ECONOMICS recurrent expansion and slowdown of trade a repeated sequence of business activity expanding, then slowing down, and then expanding again

economic development ECONOMICS rise in country's living standards improvements in the living standards and wealth of the citizens of a country

Economic Development Board BUSINESS organization promoting foreign investment in Singapore's economy an organization established in 1961 that works to promote investment in Singapore by providing various services and assistance programs to foreign and local companies. *Abbr* ***EDB***

economic efficiency BUSINESS *see* ***efficiency***

economic forecaster ECONOMICS person predicting future economic performance a person whose job is to predict how a country's economy will perform in the future

economic goods ECONOMICS products or services sold in market services or physical objects that can command a price in the market

economic growth ECONOMICS increase in country's economic activity and income an increase in the national income of a country created by the long-term productive potential of its economy

economic indicator ECONOMICS statistical measurement of country's economy a statistic that may be important for a country's long-term economic health, for example, rising prices or falling exports

economic life ECONOMICS country's manufacturing and trade conditions the conditions of trade and manufacture in a country that contribute to its prosperity or poverty

economic lot quantity OPERATIONS & PRODUCTION *see* ***EBQ***

economic miracle ECONOMICS dramatic rebuilding of economies after World War II the rapid growth after 1945 in countries such as Germany and Japan, where in ten years economies shattered by World War II were regenerated

economic model ECONOMICS computerized forecast of economic trends a computerized plan of a country's economic system, used for forecasting economic trends

economic order quantity OPERATIONS & PRODUCTION amount for best inventory control the most economic inventory replenishment order size, which minimizes the sum of inventory ordering costs and holding costs. *Abbr* ***EOQ***

economic paradigm ECONOMICS fundamental economic belief a basic unchanging economic principle, one that governs the way economists view the world

economic planning ECONOMICS government's plans for future of economy plans made by a government for the financial state of a country over different future time periods

Economic Planning and Advisory Council REGULATION & COMPLIANCE advisory group for Australia's economic policies a committee of businesspeople and politicians appointed to advise the Australian government on economic issues

economic pressure ECONOMICS country's negative economic conditions a condition in a country's economy in which economic indicators are unfavorable

  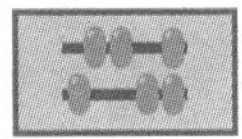      

economic profit ACCOUNTING total revenue less total cost the difference between the total revenue and total cost associated with a specific business

economic relations INTERNATIONAL TRADE trade and finance interactions between countries the arrangements for cooperation in international trade, finance, and investment existing between individual countries and sets of countries

economics ECONOMICS study of society's wealth the study of the consumption, distribution, and production of wealth in societies

economic sanctions INTERNATIONAL TRADE trade restrictions to bring about political changes restrictions on trade with a country in order to influence its political situation or to make its government change its policy

economic surplus ECONOMICS positive balance of costs against output the positive difference between an economy's output and the costs incurred in factors such as wages, raw materials, and depreciation

economic theory of the firm ECONOMICS idea that firm's responsibility is to serve stockholders the theory that the only duty that a company has to those external to it is financial. The economic theory of the firm holds that stockholders should be the prime beneficiaries of an organization's activities. The theory is associated with ***top-down leadership*** and ***cost cutting*** through rationalization and ***downsizing***. With immediate stock price dominating management activities, the economic theory of the firm has been criticized as being too short-term, as opposed to the longer-term thinking behind ***stakeholder theory***.

economic value added FINANCE evaluating performance by comparing earnings to capital investment a way of judging financial performance by measuring the amount by which the earnings of a project, an operation, or a corporation exceed or fall short of the total amount of capital that was originally invested by its owners.

EVA is conceptually simple: from net operating profit, subtract an appropriate charge for the opportunity cost of all capital invested in an enterprise (the amount that could have been invested elsewhere). It is calculated using this formula:

$$\text{Net operating profit less applicable taxes} - \text{Cost of capital} = \text{EVA}$$

If a company is considering building a new plant, and its total weighted cost over ten years is \$80 million, while the expected annual incremental return on the new operation is \$10 million, or \$100 million over ten years, then the plant's EVA would be positive, in this case \$20 million:

$$\$100\text{million} - \$80\text{million} = \$20\text{million}$$

An alternative but more complex formula for EVA is:

$$(\%\text{Return on invested capital} - \%\text{Cost of capital}) \times \text{Original capital invested} = \text{EVA}$$

EVA is frequently linked with shareholder value analysis, and an objective of EVA is to determine which business units best utilize their assets to generate returns and maximize shareholder value; it can be used to assess a company, a business unit, a single plant, office, or even an assembly line. This same technique is equally helpful in evaluating new business opportunities. *Abbr* ***EVA***

economic welfare ECONOMICS society's well-being in economic terms the level of prosperity in an economy, as measured by employment and wage levels

economies of scale ECONOMICS savings achieved by mass production the cost advantages of a company producing a product in larger quantities so that each unit costs less to make. *See also* ***diseconomies of scale***

economies of scope ECONOMICS savings achieved when multiple products share same technology the cost advantages of a company producing a number of products or engaging in a number of profitable activities that use the same technology

economist ECONOMICS somebody who studies society's wealth a person who studies the consumption, distribution, and production of wealth in societies

economy ECONOMICS production, consumption, and distribution of society's wealth the distribution of wealth in a society and the means by which that wealth is produced and consumed

economy drive BUSINESS effort to save money or materials a concerted effort to save money or materials, as by reducing expenditures or avoiding waste

economy efficiency principle ECONOMICS theory about relationships in efficient economy the principle that if an economy is efficient, no one can be made better off without somebody else being made worse off

ecopreneur BUSINESS environmentalist entrepreneur an entrepreneur who is concerned with environmental issues

ECP *abbr* MARKETS ***Eurocommercial paper***

EDB *abbr* BUSINESS ***Economic Development Board***

EDC *abbr* E-COMMERCE ***electronic data capture***

EDI *abbr* E-COMMERCE ***electronic data interchange***

EDI envelope E-COMMERCE = ***electronic envelope***

EEA *abbr* INTERNATIONAL TRADE ***European Economic Area***

EEC *abbr* INTERNATIONAL TRADE ***European Economic Community***

e-economy ECONOMICS economy based largely on online business transactions an economy that is characterized by extensive use of the Internet and information technology

effect STATISTICS result of change of statistical variable the change in a response that is created by a change in one or more of the explanatory ***variables*** in a statistical study

effective annual interest rate FINANCE average annual interest rate on deposit the average interest rate paid on a deposit for a period of a year. It is the total interest received over 12 months expressed as a percentage of the principal at the beginning of the period.

effective capacity OPERATIONS & PRODUCTION output under normal operating conditions the volume that a workstation or process can produce in a given period under normal operating conditions. Effective capacity can be influenced by the age and condition of the machine, the skills, training, and flexibility of the workforce, and the availability of ***raw materials***.

effective date FINANCE, OPERATIONS & PRODUCTION actual starting date the date when an action such as the issuing of new stock is effective

effective demand FINANCE demand for product by those able to buy demand for a product made by people and organizations with sufficient wealth to pay for it

effective exchange rate CURRENCY & EXCHANGE exchange rate of one currency against others a rate of exchange for a currency calculated against a group of currencies whose values have been weighted

effectiveness BUSINESS *see* ***efficiency***

effective price STOCKHOLDING & INVESTMENTS stock price adjusted for rights issue the price of a stock adjusted to take into account the effects of existing stockholders being offered a rights issue. *See also* ***rights issue***

effective rate FINANCE true interest rate including all factors the real interest rate to be paid on a loan or deposit, which includes compounding and other factors

effective sample size STATISTICS size of sample with extraneous factors removed the remaining size of a sample after irrelevant or excluded factors have been removed

effective spread STOCKHOLDING & INVESTMENTS difference between new issue price and underwriter's price the difference between the price of a newly issued stock and what the underwriter pays, adjusted for the effect of the announcement of the offering

effective strike price STOCKHOLDING & INVESTMENTS actual price paid when option is exercised the price of an option at a specific time, adjusted for fluctuation since the initial offering

effective tax rate TAX actual tax rate paid by taxpayer after adjustments the average tax rate applicable to a given transaction, whether it is income from work undertaken, the sale of an asset, or a gift, taking into account personal allowances and scales of tax. It is the amount of money generated by the transaction divided by the additional tax payable because of it.

effective yield *UK* STOCKHOLDING & INVESTMENTS = ***yield to maturity***

efficiency BUSINESS meeting goals economically the achievement of goals in an economic way. Efficiency involves seeking a good balance between economy in terms of resources such as time, money, space, or materials, and the achievement of an organization's goals and objectives. A distinction is often made between technical and economic efficiency. Technical efficiency means producing maximum output with minimum input, while ***economic efficiency*** means the production and distribution of goods at the lowest possible cost. In management, a further distinction is often made between efficiency and ***effectiveness***, with the latter denoting performance in terms of achieving objectives.

efficiency ratio FINANCE measure of relationship between income and overhead expenses a way of measuring the proportion of operating revenues or fee income spent on overhead expenses.

Often identified with banking and financial sectors, the efficiency ratio indicates a management's ability to keep overhead costs low. In banking, an acceptable efficiency ratio was once in the low 60s. Now the goal is 50, while better-performing banks boast ratios in the mid-40s. Low ratings usually indicate a higher return on equity and earnings.

  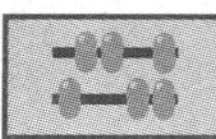      

This measurement is also used by mature industries, such as steel manufacture, chemicals, or car production, that must focus on tight cost controls to boost profitability because growth prospects are modest.

The efficiency ratio is defined as operating overhead expenses divided by turnover. If operating expenses are $100,000, and turnover is $230,000, then

$$\frac{100,000}{230,000} = 0.43 \text{ efficiency ratio}$$

However, not everyone calculates the ratio in the same way. Some institutions include all non-interest expenses, while others exclude certain charges and intangible asset amortization.

A different method measures efficiency simply by tracking three other measures: accounts payable to sales, days' sales outstanding, and stock turnover. This indicates how fast a company is able to move its merchandise. A general guide is that if the first two of these measures are low and the third is high, efficiency is probably high; the reverse is likewise true.

To find the stock turnover ratio, divide total sales by total stock. If net sales are $300,000, and stock is $140,000, then

$$\frac{300,000}{140,000} = 2.14 \text{ stock turnover ratio}$$

To find the accounts payable to sales ratio, divide a company's accounts payable by its annual net sales. A high ratio suggests that a company is using its suppliers' funds as a source of cheap financing because it is not operating efficiently enough to generate its own funds. If accounts payable are $50,000, and total sales are $300,000, then

$$\frac{50,000}{300,000} = 0.14 = 14\% \text{ accounts payable to sales ratio}$$

efficiency variance FINANCE disparity between actual and standard cost of production the difference between the standard cost of making a product and actual costs of production. A separate variance can be calculated for materials, labor, and overhead.

efficient capital market MARKETS stock market in which prices quickly reflect information a market in which stock prices reflect all the information available to the market about future economic trends and company profitability

efficient markets hypothesis ECONOMICS theory on limitations of financial information the hypothesis that exploiting stock market information cannot bring an investor unexpected returns because stock prices already reflect all the information available to the market about future economic trends and company profitability. *Abbr* ***EMH***

EFT *abbr* E-COMMERCE ***electronic funds transfer***

EFTA *abbr* INTERNATIONAL TRADE ***European Free Trade Association***

EFTPOS *abbr* E-COMMERCE ***electronic funds transfer at point of sale***

EGM *abbr* CORPORATE GOVERNANCE ***extraordinary general meeting***

EIB BANKING organization that finances EU development a financial institution whose main task is to further regional development within the EU by financing capital projects, modernizing or converting undertakings, and developing new activities. *Full form* ***European Investment Bank***

EIC *abbr* TAX ***Earned Income Credit***

EIS *abbr* GENERAL MANAGEMENT **1.** ***environmental impact statement*** **2.** ***electronic information system***. *See also* ***MIS***

either-way market CURRENCY & EXCHANGE currency market buying and selling at same price a currency market with identical prices for buying and selling, especially for the euro

elastic ECONOMICS sensitive to price changes responsive to changes in the price of a product

elasticity ECONOMICS relationship between supply, demand, and price a measurement of the relationship between supply, demand, and price.

In practical terms, elasticity indicates the degree to which consumers respond to changes in price. It is obviously important for companies to consider such relationships when contemplating changes in supply, demand, and price.

Demand elasticity measures how much the quantity demanded by a customer changes when the price of a product or service is increased or lowered. This measurement helps companies to find out whether the quantity demanded will remain constant despite price changes. Supply elasticity measures the impact on supply when a price is changed. The reverse can also be calculated, that is, how much the market clearing price for a good or service changes in response to changes in the supply or demand function. This is called the price elasticity, or demand or supply elasticity, respectively.

The general formula for elasticity is:

$$\text{Elasticity} = \frac{\%\ \text{change in x}}{\%\ \text{change in y}}$$

In theory, x and y can be any variable. However, the most common application measures price and demand. If the price of a product is increased from $20 to $25, or 25%, and demand in turn falls from 6,000 to 3,000, elasticity would be calculated as:

$$\frac{-50\%}{25\%} = -2$$

A value greater than 1 means that demand is strongly sensitive to price, while a value of less than 1 means that demand is not price-sensitive.

elected officers HR & PERSONNEL officials chosen in election officials such as directors or union representatives who are chosen by a vote of the members or stockholders of an organization and who hold a ***decision making*** position on a committee or board

electronic banking BANKING remote bank transactions by computer the use of computers to carry out banking transactions such as withdrawals through ATMs or transfer of funds at point of sale

electronic business E-COMMERCE = ***e-business***

electronic cash E-COMMERCE = ***digital cash***

electronic check *US* E-COMMERCE means of paying electronically a payment system in which fund transfers are made electronically from the buyer's checking account to the seller's bank account. *UK term* ***electronic cheque***

electronic cheque *UK* E-COMMERCE = ***electronic check***

electronic commerce E-COMMERCE = ***e-commerce***

electronic commerce modeling language E-COMMERCE standardized format for electronic purchases a standardization of field names to streamline the process by which e-merchants electronically collect information from consumers about order shipping, billing, and payment. *Abbr* ***ECML***

Electronic Communications Network MARKETS system for direct securities trading a computerized securities trading system that allows investors who have accounts with brokers with access to the system to trade directly and anonymously. *Abbr* ***ECN***

electronic data capture E-COMMERCE use of computers for card transactions the use of a point-of-sale terminal or other data-processing equipment to validate and submit credit or debit card transactions. *Abbr* ***EDC***

electronic data interchange E-COMMERCE standardized way of transmitting business documents a standard for exchanging business documents such as invoices and purchase orders in a standard form between computers through the use of electronic networks such as the Internet. *Abbr* ***EDI***

electronic envelope E-COMMERCE opening and closing data in electronic transmission the header and trailer information that precedes and follows the data in an electronic transmission to provide routing information and security. *Also called* ***communications envelope, EDI envelope, envelope***

electronic funds transfer E-COMMERCE payment system using electronic medium a payment system that processes financial transactions between two or more parties or institutions. *Abbr* ***EFT***

electronic funds transfer at point of sale E-COMMERCE payment by card swipe, immediately transferring funds the payment for goods or services by a bank customer using a card that is swiped through an electronic reader on the register, thereby transferring the cash from the customer's account to the retailer's or service provider's account. *See also* ***debit card***

electronic information system GENERAL MANAGEMENT information collection system supporting decision making a management information system designed specifically to collect and store information from both internal and external sources for use by senior managers in making strategic decisions. *Abbr* ***EIS***. See also ***MIS***

electronic money E-COMMERCE = ***digital money***

electronic payment system E-COMMERCE method for payments over Internet a means of making payments over an electronic network such as the Internet

electronic point of sale E-COMMERCE automated checkout system a computerized checkout system in stores that records sales by scanning bar codes, automatically updates the retailer's inventory lists, and provides a printout of the customer's purchases. *Abbr* ***epos***

electronic procurement E-COMMERCE = ***e-procurement***

electronic retailer E-COMMERCE = ***e-retailer***

electronic shopping E-COMMERCE making purchases over Internet the process of selecting, ordering, and paying for goods or services over an electronic network such as the Internet. *Also called* ***online shopping***

electronic software distribution E-COMMERCE making computer programs available over Internet a

  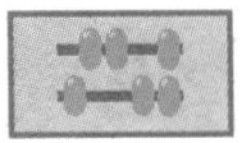      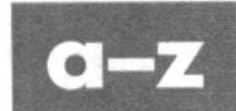

form of electronic shopping in which computer programs can be purchased and downloaded directly from the Internet

electronic store E-COMMERCE website for selling goods a website that is specifically designed to provide product information and handle transactions, including accepting payments

electronic trading STOCKHOLDING & INVESTMENTS securities trading using computers the buying and selling of investment instruments using computer systems

electronic wallet E-COMMERCE = ***digital wallet***

elephant FINANCE financial institution whose high-volume trading increases prices a very large financial institution such as a bank that makes trades in high volumes, thereby increasing prices (slang)

eligible liabilities BANKING liabilities considered when calculating bank's reserves liabilities that must be taken into account in the calculation of a bank's reserves

eligible paper FINANCE **1.** US financial instruments accepted for rediscounting in the United States, first class paper, such as a bill of exchange or a check, acceptable for rediscounting by the Federal Reserve System **2.** UK financial instruments accepted as loan security in the United Kingdom, bills of exchange or securities accepted by the ***Bank of England*** as security for loans to discount houses. *See also* ***lender of last resort***

eligible reserves BANKING total amount of money held by US bank the sum of the cash held by a US bank plus the money it holds at its local Federal Reserve Bank

eligible termination payment TAX in UK, termination pay eligible for concessional tax in the United Kingdom, a sum paid to an employee when he or she leaves a company, that can be transferred to a concessionally taxed investment account, such as an ***Approved Deposit Fund***. *Abbr* ***ETP***

e-mail blast MARKETING e-mail appeal to large group a single instance of sending out an e-mail to a large group to reach potential customers

e-marketplace E-COMMERCE place on Internet for trading an Internet-based environment that brings together business-to-business buyers and sellers so that they can trade more efficiently online.

The key benefits for users of an e-marketplace are reduced purchasing costs, greater flexibility, saved time, better information, and better collaboration. However, the drawbacks include costs in changing procurement processes, cost of applications, set-up, and integration with internal systems, and transaction/subscription fees.

There are three distinct types of e-marketplace: independent, in which public environments seek simply to attract buyers and sellers to trade together; consortium-based, in which sites are established on an industry-wide basis, typically when a number of key buyers in a particular industry get together; and private, in which e-marketplaces are established by a particular organization to manage its purchasing alone.

embargo INTERNATIONAL TRADE government order stopping trade with foreign country a government order that stops a type of trade, such as exports to, or imports from, a specific country

embezzlement FRAUD illegal use of money for personal benefit the illegal use of somebody else's money for personal benefit by the person to whom it has been entrusted

emergency credit FINANCE special credit given by US Federal Reserve in the United States, credit given by the ***Federal Reserve*** to an organization that has no other means of borrowing capital

emerging country *or* emerging nation ECONOMICS country experiencing development and economic growth a country in the early stages of becoming industrialized and undergoing economic growth and foreign investment

emerging economy ECONOMICS *see* ***emerging market*** *(sense 1)*

emerging market **1.** ECONOMICS country experiencing development and economic growth a country that is becoming industrialized and undergoing economic growth. *Also called* ***emerging economy*** **2.** MARKETS financial market in emerging nation a financial market in a newly industrialized country, often with a high growth rate but with some risks

EMH *abbr* ECONOMICS ***efficient markets hypothesis***

emoluments FINANCE payments from employment wages, salaries, fees, or any other monetary benefit derived from employment

e-money E-COMMERCE = ***digital money***

emotional capital GENERAL MANAGEMENT interaction of employees the intangible organizational asset created by employees' cumulative emotional experiences that give them the ability to successfully communicate and form interpersonal relationships. Emotional capital is increasingly being seen as an important factor in company performance. Low emotional capital can result in conflict between staff, poor teamwork, and poor ***customer relations***. By contrast, high emotional capital is evidence of emotional intelligence and an ability to think and feel in a positive way, which results in good interpersonal communication and self-motivation. A related concept is ***intellectual capital***.

employability HR & PERSONNEL possession of useful skills the potential for obtaining and keeping fulfilling work through the development of skills that are transferable from one employer to another. Employability is affected by market demand for a particular set of skills and by personal circumstances. Employees may take responsibility for developing their own employability through learning and training, or, as part of the ***psychological contract***, employers may assist their employees in enhancing their employability. An important factor in employability is the concept of learning throughout life.

employee HR & PERSONNEL person contracted to work for another somebody hired by an employer under a ***contract of employment*** to perform work on a regular basis at the employer's behest. An employee works either at the employer's premises or at a place otherwise agreed, is paid regularly, and enjoys ***fringe benefits*** and employment protection.

employee ownership STOCKHOLDING & INVESTMENTS when shares are in employees' hands the possession of shares in a company, in whole or in part, by the workers. There are various forms of employee ownership that give employees a greater or lesser stake in the business. These include: ***employee stock ownership plans***, employee ***buyouts***, ***cooperatives***, and employee trusts. Ownership does not necessarily lead to greater ***employee participation*** in decision making, although the evidence suggests that where employees are involved in this, the company is more successful.

employee participation HR & PERSONNEL inclusion of employees in decision making the involvement of employees in decision making. Employee participation can take either a representational or direct form. Representation takes place through bodies such as consultative committees. Direct participation can be achieved through communication methods such as letters, employee attitude surveys, and team briefing, or through initiatives such as self-managed teams and suggestion programs.

Employee Retirement Income Security Act LEGAL US law setting benefit plan standards in the United States, a federal law that sets the minimum requirements for retirement and health benefit plans in the private sector. *Abbr* ***ERISA***

employee share ownership plan *UK* STOCKHOLDING & INVESTMENTS = ***employee stock ownership plan***

employee share scheme STOCKHOLDING & INVESTMENTS making stock available to employees in the United Kingdom, a plan to give, or encourage employees to buy, a stake in the company that employs them by awarding free or discounted stock. Such plans may be available to some or all employees, and plans approved by HM Revenue & Customs enjoy tax advantages. Types of plan include ***employee share ownership plans***, ***stock options***, ***Save as You Earn***, and employee share ownership trusts. Among the potential benefits are improved employee commitment and productivity, but the success of a plan may depend on linking it to employee performance and the performance of the price of stock.

employee stock fund STOCKHOLDING & INVESTMENTS US firm's fund for buying stock for employees in the United States, a fund from which money is taken to buy shares of a company's stock for its employees

employee stock ownership plan *US* STOCKHOLDING & INVESTMENTS system of allocating stock to employees a plan sponsored by a company by which a trust holds stock in the company on behalf of ***employees*** and distributes that stock to employees. In the United States, stock can only be sold when an employee leaves the organization, and is thus thought of as a form of pension provision. In the United Kingdom, stock can be disposed of at any time. There are two types of employee stock ownership plans in the United Kingdom: the case-law employee stock ownership plan, which can benefit all or some employees but may not qualify for tax benefits; and the employee stock ownership trust. *UK term* ***employee share ownership plan***. *Abbr* ***ESOP***

employee stock purchase plan STOCKHOLDING & INVESTMENTS making stock available to employees in the United States, a plan to encourage employees to buy a stake in the company that employs them by awarding free or discounted stock. Such plans may be available to some or all employees, and plans approved by the Internal Revenue Service enjoy tax advantages. Among the potential benefits are improved employee commitment and productivity, but the success of a plan may depend on linking it to employee performance and the performance of the price of stock. *Abbr* ***ESPP***

employer HR & PERSONNEL person or organization with employees a person or organization that pays people to perform specific activities. An employer usually contracts an ***employee*** to fill a permanent

  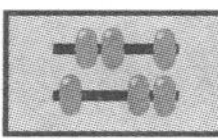   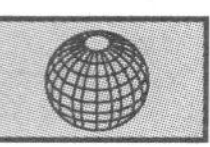  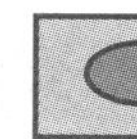 

or temporary position to perform work on a regularly paid basis within the relevant legal framework of the country of residence.

employers' association BUSINESS organization assisting employers a body that regulates relations between employers and employees, represents members' views on public policy issues affecting their business to national and international policymakers, and supplies support and advice. An employers' association represents companies within one or many sectors at regional, national, or international level and is usually a nonprofit, nonparty political organization, funded by subscriptions paid by its members.

employer's contribution PENSIONS employer's payments into employee's pension money paid regularly by an employer toward an employee's retirement pension

employers' liability insurance INSURANCE insurance covering employee accidents insurance to cover accidents that may happen to employees at work, and for which the company may be responsible

employment contract HR & PERSONNEL = ***contract of employment***

employment equity *S. AFRICA* HR & PERSONNEL offering opportunities to qualified people from disadvantaged groups the policy of giving preference in employment opportunities to qualified people from sectors of society that were previously discriminated against, for example, black people, women, and physically challenged people

employment law LEGAL, HR & PERSONNEL rules regulating employers and employees the collection of statutes, common law rules, and decisions in court or employment tribunal cases that govern the rights and duties of employers and employees. The ***contract of employment*** forms the cornerstone of employment law, which also embraces ***discrimination*** and ***severance*** rights, collective bargaining, health and safety, union membership, and industrial action.

employment pass HR & PERSONNEL in S. Africa, work permit for professionals in South Africa, a visa issued to a foreign national who is a professional with a qualifying salary level

empowerment GENERAL MANAGEMENT, HR & PERSONNEL conferring authority on employees the redistribution of power and decision-making responsibilities, usually to employees, where such authority was previously a management prerogative. Empowerment is based on the recognition that employee abilities are frequently underused, and that, given the chance, most employees can contribute more. Empowered workplaces are characterized by managers who focus on energizing, supporting, and coaching their staff in a blame-free environment of trust.

EMS CURRENCY & EXCHANGE first stage in European monetary union the first stage of economic and monetary union of the EU, which came into force in March 1979, giving stable, but adjustable, exchange rates. *Full form* ***European Monetary System***

EMU ECONOMICS movement toward common European currency a program for the integration of European economies and the introduction of a common currency. The timetable for European monetary union was outlined in the Maastricht Treaty in 1991. The criteria were that national debt must not exceed 60% of GDP; budget deficit should be 3% or less of GDP; inflation should be no more than 1.5% above the average rate of the three best performing economies of the EU in the previous 12 months; and applicants must have been members of the ***ERM*** for two years without having realigned or devalued their currency. The ERM was abandoned with the introduction of the ***euro*** in 12 countries in 2002. *Full form* ***European Monetary Union***

encash *UK* CURRENCY & EXCHANGE = ***cash*** *(sense 1)*

encryption E-COMMERCE putting information in code for transmission over Internet a means of encoding information, especially financial data, so that it can be transmitted over the Internet without being read by unauthorized parties.

Within an Internet security system, a secure server uses encryption when transferring or receiving data from the Web. Credit card information, for example, that could be targeted by a hacker, is encrypted by the server, turning it into special code that will then be decrypted only when it is safely within the server environment. Once the information has been acted on, it is either deleted or stored in encrypted form.

encryption key E-COMMERCE system for encoding and decoding information a sequence of characters known to both or all parties to a communication, used to initiate the ***encryption*** process

encumbrance MORTGAGES debt using real estate as collateral a liability such as a mortgage or charge that is attached to a property or piece of land

end consumer MARKETING somebody using product or service a person who uses a product or service. An end consumer may not be the purchaser of a product or service and should be distinguished from a customer.

endogenous variable STATISTICS dependent variable in an econometric study, the dependent variable, such as the stock price of a company, that is acted on by an independent variable, such as the company's earnings growth rate

endorse BANKING sign reverse side of check to sign a bill or check on the back to show that its ownership is being passed to another person or company

endorsement MARKETING explicit approval of product the public approval of a product by a person or organization. The endorsement can be used to promote the product to other organizations that may be more cautious in their approach to adopting new products.

endowment FINANCE donation of money for specified purpose a gift of money, especially to a nonprofit organization, to be used for a specific purpose

endowment assurance *UK* INSURANCE = ***endowment insurance***

endowment fund FINANCE fund for nonprofit organization a mutual fund established to provide income for a nonprofit institution

endowment insurance *US* INSURANCE insurance paying on policy's maturity or death an insurance policy that pays a set amount to the policyholder when the policy matures, or to a beneficiary if the policyholder dies before it matures. Part of the premium paid is for the life coverage element, while the remainder is invested in real estate and stocks (either a "with-profits" or "without-profits" policy) or, in the case of a share-linked policy, is used to purchase shares in a life fund. The sum the policyholder receives at the end of the term depends on the size of the premiums and the performance of the investments. *See also* ***term insurance***. *UK term* ***endowment assurance***

endowment mortgage MORTGAGES loan with both interest and endowment policy payments a long-term loan, usually for the purchase of real estate, in which the borrower makes two monthly payments, one to the lender to cover the interest on the loan, and the other as a premium paid into an endowment insurance policy. At the end of the loan's term, the proceeds from the endowment policy are used to repay the principal. *See also* ***mortgage***

endowment policy INSURANCE *see* ***endowment insurance***

endpoint STATISTICS when final event in study happens a point at which a definable event in a study takes place

energy audit GENERAL MANAGEMENT investigation of sourcing and employment of energy a review, inspection, and evaluation of sources and uses of energy within an organization to ensure efficiency and lack of waste

energy conservation GENERAL MANAGEMENT prevention of overuse of fuel the minimization of fuel consumption. Energy conservation, through the monitoring and control of the amounts of electricity, gas, and other fuels used in the workplace, can help reduce costs and damage to the environment. An energy management plan provides a systematic method of assessing, evaluating, and improving an organization's energy usage. This forms part of an organization's approach to environmental management.

engagement letter BUSINESS letter formalizing business relationship between professional and client a letter, usually required by professional standards, sent by a professional such as an accountant to a client, setting out the work the accountant is to do and further administrative matters such as any limit on the accountant's liability

entail LEGAL restriction on somebody inheriting real estate a legal condition that passes ownership of a property to specific persons only

enterprise **1.** GENERAL MANAGEMENT bold undertaking a venture characterized by innovation, creativity, dynamism, and risk. An enterprise can consist of one project, or may refer to an entire organization. It usually requires several of the following attributes: flexibility, initiative, problem-solving ability, independence, and imagination. Enterprises flourish in the environment of delayered, nonhierarchical organizations but can be stifled by bureaucracy. **2.** BUSINESS firm a commercial business or company

enterprise application integration OPERATIONS & PRODUCTION sharing of information and proceedings using software the unrestricted sharing of data and business processes via integrated and compatible software programs. As businesses expand and recognize the need for their information and applications to be shared between systems, they are investing in enterprise application integration in order to streamline processes and keep all the parts of their organizations, for example, human resources and inventory control, connected. *Abbr* ***EAI***

enterprise culture GENERAL MANAGEMENT attitudes and behavior fostering bold undertakings an organizational or social environment that encourages and makes possible initiative and innovation. An organization with an enterprise culture is usually more competitive and more profitable than a bureaucracy. Such an organization is believed to be more rewarding and stimulating to work in. A society with an

enterprise culture facilitates individuality and requires people to take responsibility for their own welfare. Conservative governments in the United Kingdom during the 1980s and 1990s promoted an enterprise culture by introducing market principles into all areas of economic and social life. These included policies of deregulation of financial services, privatization of utilities and national monopolies, and commercialization of the public sector. The enterprise culture is now supported by both main political parties.

enterprise investment scheme TAX tax incentives for investors in unquoted UK firms in the United Kingdom, a plan to promote investment in unquoted companies by which qualifying gains are exempt from capital gains tax

enterprise portal E-COMMERCE website collating useful information a website that assembles a wide range of content and services for employees of a particular organization, with the goal of bringing together all the key information they need to do a better job. The key difference between an enterprise portal and an intranet is that an enterprise portal contains not just internal content, but also external content that may be useful, such as specialized news feeds, or access to industry research reports. Ensuring that content is relevant, current, and frequently refreshed is essential for such sites to succeed, and enterprise portals are thus expensive to maintain.

enterprise risk management RISK procedure for reducing risk to organization the process of planning and establishing control systems in order to minimize the risks that an organization faces, including financial, strategic, operational, and hazard risks. *Abbr* ***ERM***

enterprise zone FINANCE, BUSINESS district where government gives incentives for economic development an area in which the government offers financial incentives such as tax relief to encourage new business activities. *Abbr* ***EZ***

entertainment expenses HR & PERSONNEL reclaimable money spent on customers or suppliers costs, reimbursable by an employer, that are incurred by an employee in hosting social events for clients or suppliers in order to obtain or maintain their patronage or goodwill

entitlement GENERAL MANAGEMENT assumption of deserving reward the expectation that an organization or individual will make large profits regardless of their contribution to the economy or company

entitlement offer FINANCE nontransferable offer an offer that cannot be transferred to anyone else

entrepot port OPERATIONS & PRODUCTION international port dealing in re-exports a town with a large international commercial port dealing in re-exports

entrepreneur BUSINESS somebody who starts and operates new business somebody who sets up a business or enterprise. An entrepreneur typically demonstrates effective application of a number of enterprising attributes, such as creativity, initiative, risk taking, problem-solving ability, and autonomy, and will often risk his or her own capital to establish a business.

entropy STATISTICS measure of system's information transfer rate a measure of the rate of transfer of the information that a system such as a computer program or factory machine receives or outputs

entry ACCOUNTING item written in accounts ledger an item of written information put in an accounts ledger

entry barrier MARKETING hindrance to entering market a perceived or real obstacle preventing a competitor from entering a market

envelope E-COMMERCE = ***electronic envelope***

environmental accounting ACCOUNTING including costs to environment in decision making the practice of including the indirect costs and benefits of a product or activity, for example, its environmental effects on health and the economy, along with its direct costs when making business decisions. *Also called* ***full cost accounting***, ***green accounting***

environmental audit GENERAL MANAGEMENT assessment of success of environmental policies the regular systematic gathering of information to monitor the effectiveness of environmental policies. An environmental audit is concerned with checking conformity with legislative requirements and environmental standards, as well as with company policy. The audit may also cover potential improvements in environmental performance and systems.

environmental impact assessment GENERAL MANAGEMENT study of effect on environment of proposed project a study, undertaken during the planning phase before an investment is made or an operation started, to consider any potential environmental effects

environmental impact statement GENERAL MANAGEMENT findings of environmental impact assessment a report on the results of a particular environmental impact assessment. *Abbr* ***EIS***

environmental management GENERAL MANAGEMENT control of organization's impact on environment a systematic approach to minimizing the damage created by an organization to the environment in which it operates. Environmental management has become an issue in organizations because consumers now expect them to be environmentally aware, if not environmentally friendly. Senior managers and directors are increasingly being held liable for their organizations' environmental performance, and the onus is on them to adopt a ***corporate strategy*** that balances economic growth with environmental protection. Environmental management involves reducing pollution, waste, and the consumption of natural resources by implementing an environmental action plan. This plan brings together the key elements of environmental management, including an organization's ***environmental policy*** statement, an ***environmental audit***, environmental management system, and external standards.

environmental policy GENERAL MANAGEMENT intentions regarding minimizing harm to environment a statement of organizational intentions regarding the safeguarding of the environment

EOQ *abbr* FINANCE, OPERATIONS & PRODUCTION ***economic order quantity***

epos *or* EPOS *or* EPoS *abbr* E-COMMERCE ***electronic point of sale***

e-procurement E-COMMERCE purchasing of products over Internet the business-to-business sale and purchase of goods and services over an electronic network such as the Internet. *Also called* ***electronic procurement***

EPS *abbr* STOCKHOLDING & INVESTMENTS ***earnings per share***

Equal Credit Opportunity Act FINANCE US law ensuring equal treatment for borrowers in the United States, a federal law that gives all consumers an equal opportunity to obtain credit by requiring creditors to follow specific rules regarding the information they can obtain from applicants. *Abbr* ***ECOA***

equal opportunities HR & PERSONNEL provision of same chances to all the granting of equal rights, privileges, and status regardless of gender, age, race, religion, disability, or sexual orientation. Equality in employment is regulated by law in most Western countries. An organizational equal opportunities policy works to go farther than the regulatory framework demands. Such a policy should focus on preventing discriminatory or harassing behavior in the workplace and achieving equal access to training, job, and promotion opportunities. ***Affirmative action***, referred to as positive discrimination in the United Kingdom, is a controversial approach to encouraging the advancement of minorities. Diversity management builds on and goes beyond equal opportunities by looking at the rights of individuals rather than groups.

equal pay HR & PERSONNEL paying men and women at same rate the principle and practice of paying men and women in the same organization at the same rate for like work, or work that is rated as of equal value. Work is assessed either through an organization's job evaluation plan or by the judgment of an independent expert appointed by an industrial committee. Although many countries have legislation on equal pay, a gap still exists between men's pay and women's pay and is attributed to sexual discrimination in job evaluation and payment systems.

equal treatment HR & PERSONNEL avoidance of discrimination at work a principle of the European Union that requires member states to ensure that there is no ***discrimination*** with regard to employment, vocational training, and working conditions. The principle of equal treatment is applied through Europe-wide directives and national legislation of the member states.

equilibrium ECONOMICS balance in economy the state of balance in the economy where supply equals demand or a country's balance of payments is neither in deficit nor in excess

equilibrium price ECONOMICS product price causing balanced supply and demand the price at which the supply of and the demand for a good are equal. Suppliers increase prices when demand is high and reduce prices when demand is low.

equilibrium quantity ECONOMICS amount regulating supply and demand the quantity that needs to be bought for supply to match demand at a specific price. Suppliers increase quantity when demand, and therefore the price, is high and reduce quantity when demand or price is low.

equilibrium rate of interest ECONOMICS when expected and actual interest rates match the rate at which the expected interest rate in a market equals the actual rate prevailing

equipment trust certificate STOCKHOLDING & INVESTMENTS US bond issued to pay for equipment in the United States, a bond sold for a 20% down payment and collateralized by the equipment purchased with its proceeds

equities STOCKHOLDING & INVESTMENTS stock in corporation a stockholder's holdings in a corporation

equity **1.** FINANCE value of asset minus outstanding loans the value of an asset minus any loans outstanding on it **2.** FINANCE value of company

  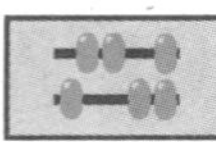      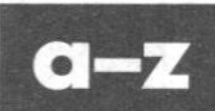

owned by stockholders the value of a company that is the property of its stockholders, calculated as the value of the company's assets minus the value of its liabilities, not including the ordinary share capital **3.** STOCKHOLDING & INVESTMENTS ownership of company's stock ownership in a company in the form of stock **4.** STOCKHOLDING & INVESTMENTS stockholder's right to share in company's profit the right of a stockholder to receive dividends from the profit of a company in which the shares of stock are owned

equity accounting ACCOUNTING listing subsidiary's profits on parent company's books a method of accounting that puts part of the profits of a subsidiary into the parent company's books

equity capital STOCKHOLDING & INVESTMENTS stock owned by stockholders the part of the nominal value of the stock owned by the stockholders of a company. *See also* ***share capital***

equity carve-out STOCKHOLDING & INVESTMENTS sale of shares of stock to fund spin-off a situation in which an established company sells off shares of stock to investors in order to create an independent company from a subsidiary part of the business. *Also called* ***carve-out***

equity claim FINANCE claim on residual earnings a claim on earnings that remain after debts are satisfied

equity contribution agreement FINANCE agreement to contribute equity an agreement to buy a proportion of the ***capital stock*** of a company in order to provide funds for a project

equity derivative STOCKHOLDING & INVESTMENTS derivative instrument based on stock a ***derivative instrument*** whose ***underlying asset*** is a stock. The most common equity derivative is an ***option***.

equity dilution STOCKHOLDING & INVESTMENTS decrease in percentage of ownership in firm the reduction in the percentage of a company represented by each share for an existing stockholder who has not increased his or her holding in the issue of new common stock

equity dividend cover *UK* ACCOUNTING calculation of firm's ability to pay dividend an accounting ratio, calculated by dividing the distributable profits during a given period by the actual dividend paid in that period, that indicates the likelihood of the dividend being maintained in future years.

equity finance *UK* FINANCE = ***equity financing***

equity financing *US* FINANCE money contributed for share in business the money introduced into a business by its owners. If it is a for-profit company, then the equity is introduced in exchange for shares and investors can expect a share of any profit. In the case of limited companies, it takes the form of dividends. *UK term* ***equity finance***

equity floor MARKETS payment agreement based on market drop an agreement for one party to pay another whenever some indicator of a stock market's value falls below a specific limit

equity fund STOCKHOLDING & INVESTMENTS mutual fund that is invested in equities a mutual fund that is invested mainly in stocks, not in government securities or other funds

equity gearing FINANCE relationship of borrowings to equity the ratio between a company's borrowings and its ***equity***

equity kicker MARKETS investment incentive promising share of future revenue an incentive given to people to lend a company money, in the form of a warrant to share in future earnings

equity multiplier FINANCE US firm's worth as multiple of stock price in the United States, a measure of a company's worth, expressed as a multiple of each dollar of its stock's price

equity risk premium STOCKHOLDING & INVESTMENTS extra return expected on equities compared to bonds an extra return on equities over the return on bonds, because of the risk involved in investing in equities

equity swap STOCKHOLDING & INVESTMENTS, RISK agreement between parties to exchange cash flows an agreement in which one party agrees to exchange its cash flow, which is linked to a benchmark such as the ***London Interbank Offered Rate*** or the rate of return on an ***index***, for another party's fixed or floating rate of interest

equity sweetener FINANCE incentive for people to lend firm money an incentive to encourage people to lend a company money. The sweetener takes the form of a warrant that gives the lender the right to buy stock at a later date and at a specific price.

equivalent annual cash flow FINANCE return on annuity compared to other investment the value of an annuity required to provide an investor with the same return as some other form of investment

equivalent bond yield STOCKHOLDING & INVESTMENTS = ***bond equivalent yield***

equivalent taxable yield TAX return on taxable investment compared to other investment the value of a taxable investment required to provide an investor with the same return as some other form of investment

ERDF *abbr* FINANCE ***European Regional Development Fund***

e-retailer E-COMMERCE retail business operating over Internet a business that uses an electronic network such as the Internet to sell its goods or services. *Also called* ***electronic retailer, e-tailer***

ergonomics GENERAL MANAGEMENT, HR & PERSONNEL study of efficient working environments the study of workplace design and the physical and psychological impact it has on workers. Ergonomics is about the fit between people, their work activities, equipment, work systems, and environment to ensure that workplaces are safe, comfortable, efficient, and that productivity is not compromised. Ergonomics may examine the design and layout of buildings, machines, and equipment, as well as aspects such as lighting, temperature, ventilation, noise, color, and texture. Ergonomic principles also apply to working methods such as systems and procedures, and the allocation and scheduling of work.

ERISA *abbr* LEGAL ***Employee Retirement Income Security Act***

ERM 1. CURRENCY & EXCHANGE former system for stabilizing European Community exchange rates a system to maintain exchange rate stability used in the past by member states of the European Community. *Full form* ***Exchange Rate Mechanism*** **2.** *abbr* RISK ***enterprise risk management***

ERR *abbr* STOCKHOLDING & INVESTMENTS ***expected rate of return***

error account BANKING account for recording transactions made in error an account for the temporary placement of funds involved in a financial transaction known to have been executed in error

error rate ACCOUNTING proportion of errors made the number of mistakes per thousand entries or per page

errors and omissions ACCOUNTING bookkeeping mistakes mistakes arising from incorrect record keeping or accounting. *Abbr* ***E&O***

ESC *abbr* GENERAL MANAGEMENT, HR & PERSONNEL ***European Social Charter***

escalator clause LEGAL contract clause permitting price increases a clause in a contract that allows for regular price increases for a product or service to cover projected cost increases

escape clause LEGAL clause specifying conditions under which contract is void a clause in a contract that allows one of the parties to avoid carrying out the terms of the contract under specific conditions

escheat LEGAL government claim on property in absence of heirs the reversion of real or personal property to the government upon the death of a person who has no legal heirs

escrow LEGAL safe keeping by third party of valuable item an agreement between two parties that holds that something such as a good, document, or amount of money should be held for safe keeping by a third party until specific conditions are fulfilled

escrow account BANKING account holding money until contract conditions are met an account where money is held until specific conditions, such as a contract being signed, or a consignment of goods being safely delivered, are met

e-shock E-COMMERCE unstoppable advance of e-commerce the forward momentum of electronic commerce, considered as powerful and irresistible

ESOP *abbr* STOCKHOLDING & INVESTMENTS ***employee stock ownership plan***

ESPP *abbr* STOCKHOLDING & INVESTMENTS ***employee stock purchase plan***

essential industry ECONOMICS industry necessary to nation's economy an industry regarded as crucial to a country's economy and often supported financially by a government by way of tariff protection and tax breaks

establishment fee FINANCE = ***commitment fee***

estate FINANCE deceased person's assets the net assets of somebody who has died

estate duty TAX former tax paid on estate before distribution in the United Kingdom until 1975, a tax paid on the property left by a dead person before it is passed to the heirs. *See also* ***inheritance tax***

estate tax TAX tax paid on estate before distribution to heirs in the United States, a tax paid on the property left by a dead person before it is passed to the heirs

estimate FINANCE **1.** approximation of something's value an approximate calculation of an uncertain value. An estimate may be a reasonable guess based on knowledge and experience or it may be calculated using more sophisticated techniques designed to forecast projected costs, profits, losses, or value. **2.** approximation of cost of work a written statement of an approximate price for work to be undertaken by a business

  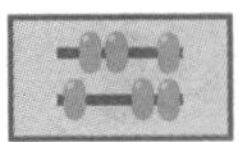      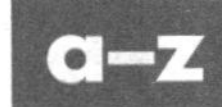

estimation STATISTICS predicted numerical value the provision of a numerical value for a parameter of a population that has been sampled

estimator FINANCE person who calculates expected job costs a person whose job is to calculate the likely cost for carrying out work

estoppel LEGAL ruling denying somebody right to give evidence a rule of evidence whereby somebody is prevented from denying or asserting a fact in legal proceedings

e-tailer E-COMMERCE = ***e-retailer***

e-tailing E-COMMERCE operating retail business over Internet the practice of doing business over an electronic network such as the Internet

ETF *abbr* MARKETS ***exchange-traded fund***

ethical fund FINANCE fund providing money to firms having moral practices a fund that invests in companies that operate by moral standards approved of by their investors, such as not manufacturing or selling weapons, not trading with countries with poor human rights records, or using only environmentally acceptable sources of raw materials

ethical index STOCKHOLDING & INVESTMENTS list of stock in conscientious firms a published index of stock in companies that operate by moral standards approved of by their investors

ethical investment STOCKHOLDING & INVESTMENTS investing only in socially responsible firms investment only in companies whose policies meet the ethical criteria of the investor. *Also called* ***socially conscious investing***

Ethical Investment Research Service STOCKHOLDING & INVESTMENTS organization determining which firms have moral practices an organization that does research into companies and recommends those that follow specific ethical standards

ETP *abbr* TAX ***eligible termination payment***

EU *abbr* ECONOMICS ***European Union***. *See also* ***single market***

Euribor *abbr* MARKETS ***Euro Interbank Offered Rate***

euro *or* Euro CURRENCY & EXCHANGE currency of nations belonging to EU the currency of 12 member nations of the European Union. The euro was introduced in 1999, when the first 11 countries to adopt it joined together in an Economic and Monetary Union and tied their currencies' exchange rate to the euro. Notes and coins were brought into general circulation in January 2002, although banks and other financial institutions had before that time carried out transactions in euro. The official plural of euro is "euro," although "euros" is widely used.

euro account BANKING account operated in euro a checking account or savings account in euro

Eurobank BANKING, CURRENCY & EXCHANGE US bank dealing in Eurocurrency a bank that handles transactions in ***Eurocurrency***

Eurobond STOCKHOLDING & INVESTMENTS bond issued and traded in different currencies a bond issued in the currency of one country and sold to investors from another country. *Also called* ***global bond***

Eurocheque BANKING check good in any European bank a check that can be cashed at any bank in the world displaying the European Union crest. The Eurocheque system is based in Brussels.

Euroclear MARKETS European payment system for securities a user-owned system for routing and settling securities transactions throughout Europe

Eurocommercial paper MARKETS unsecured short-term loan in foreign currency ***commercial paper*** issued by a company in a different currency to that in which the company normally operates. *Abbr* ***ECP***

Eurocredit BANKING, CURRENCY & EXCHANGE credit in currency of another country a loan made in a currency other than that of the lending institution

Eurocurrency BANKING, CURRENCY & EXCHANGE deposits in currency of another country money deposited in one country but denominated in the currency of another country, for example, dollars deposited in a British bank

Eurodeposit BANKING, CURRENCY & EXCHANGE deposit in Eurocurrency a short-term deposit of ***Eurocurrency***. Eurodeposits have a variable interest rate based on the ***Euro Interbank Offered Rate***.

Eurodollar BANKING, CURRENCY & EXCHANGE US dollar deposited in foreign bank a dollar deposited in a European bank or other bank outside the United States

Euroequity MARKETS European stock not traded domestically a stock in an international company that is traded outside its country of origin

Euroequity issue MARKETS security for foreign country a capital issue in a currency and a country other than that of the issuer

Euro Interbank Offered Rate MARKETS lending rate for euro the ***Interbank Offered Rate*** for loans in euros. *Abbr* ***Euribor***

euroland ECONOMICS = ***eurozone***

euro LIBOR MARKETS LIBOR denominated in euros the ***London Interbank Offered Rate*** denominated in euros rather than US dollars

Euronext MARKETS, STOCKHOLDING & INVESTMENTS pan-European stock exchange the stock exchange formed by the merger of the Amsterdam, Brussels, and Paris stock exchanges on September 22, 2000. It expanded in 2002 to include the ***Lisbon Stock Exchange*** and ***London International Financial Futures and Options Exchange***, before merging with the ***New York Stock Exchange*** in 2007 to form the ***NYSE Euronext*** group.

Euronext Amsterdam MARKETS, STOCKHOLDING & INVESTMENTS Dutch stock exchange considered the world's first stock exchange, the Amsterdam Stock Exchange has its origins in 1602 with the first stocks issued by the Dutch East India Company. It merged with the Hague and Rotterdam stock exchanges in 1972. It then merged with the Brussels and Paris stock exchanges on September 22, 2000, to create ***Euronext***, the first pan-European exchange, and is now part of the ***NYSE Euronext*** group. The main index of stocks on the exchange is the ***AEX Index***. *Also called* ***AEX, Amsterdam Stock Exchange***

Euronext Brussels MARKETS, STOCKHOLDING & INVESTMENTS Belgian stock exchange stock exchange based in Brussels, Belgium, established in 1801. The Brussels Stock Exchange merged with the Antwerp Stock Exchange in 1993 and with the Belgian Futures and Options Exchange in 1999. It then merged with the Amsterdam and Paris stock exchanges on September 22, 2000, to create ***Euronext***, the first pan-European exchange, and is now part of the ***NYSE Euronext*** group. The main index of stocks on the exchange is the ***BEL 20***. *Also called* ***Brussels Stock Exchange***

Euronext Lisbon MARKETS, STOCKHOLDING & INVESTMENTS Portuguese stock exchange stock exchange based in Lisbon, Portugal, established as the Business Man's Assembly in 1769. The Lisbon Stock Exchange merged with the Porto Derivatives Exchange in 1999 to form BVLP, then with the ***Euronext*** stock exchange in 2002, and is now part of the ***NYSE Euronext*** group. The main index of stocks on the exchange is the ***PSI 20***. *Also called* ***Bolsa de Valores de Lisboa e Porto, BVLP, Lisbon Stock Exchange***

Euronext Paris MARKETS, STOCKHOLDING & INVESTMENTS French stock exchange stock exchange based in Paris, France, established in 1724. The Paris Stock Exchange merged with the Amsterdam and Brussels stock exchanges on September 22, 2000, to create ***Euronext***, the first pan-European exchange, and is now part of the ***NYSE Euronext*** group. The main index of stocks on the exchange is the ***CAC 40***. *Also called* ***Paris Bourse, Paris Stock Exchange***

Euro-note CURRENCY & EXCHANGE security in Eurocurrency market a form of ***Eurocommercial paper*** in the ***Eurocurrency*** market

Euro-option MARKETS option to buy European bonds an option to buy European bonds at a later date

European Accounting Association ACCOUNTING European organization for accounting academics an organization for accounting academics. Founded in 1977 and based in Brussels, the EAA aims to be a forum for European research in accounting. It holds an annual congress and since 1992 has published a journal, *European Accounting Review*. *Abbr* ***EAA***

European Association of Securities Dealers Automated Quotations MARKETS *see* ***EASDAQ***

European Bank for Reconstruction and Development BANKING *see* ***EBRD***

European Central Bank BANKING *see* ***ECB***

European Commission EU executive body the main executive body of the European Union, made up of members nominated by each member state. ***Also called Commission of the European Community***

European Community INTERNATIONAL TRADE former organization of European nations the name of the immediate precursor of the ***EU***. *Abbr* ***EC***

European Covered Bond Council FINANCE representative organization for various financial institutions the official organization bringing together bond issuers, analysts, investment bankers, rating agencies, and a wide range of interested market participants. *Abbr* ***ECBC***

European Economic Area INTERNATIONAL TRADE EU and EFTA member countries an area comprising the countries of the European Union and the members of EFTA, formed by an agreement on trade between the two organizations. *Abbr* ***EEA***

European Economic Community INTERNATIONAL TRADE former organization of European nations the name of the precursor of the ***European Community*** before it became the ***EU***. *Abbr* ***EEC***

  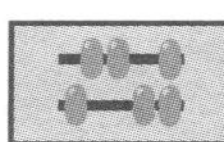      

European Free Trade Association INTERNATIONAL TRADE free-trade group linked with EU a group of countries (Iceland, Liechtenstein, Norway, and Switzerland) formed to encourage free trade between its members, and linked with the European Union in the European Economic Area. *Abbr* ***EFTA***

European Investment Bank BANKING *see* ***EIB***

European Monetary System CURRENCY & EXCHANGE *see* ***EMS***

European Monetary Union CURRENCY & EXCHANGE *see* ***EMU***

European option STOCKHOLDING & INVESTMENTS option exercisable only on expiration date an option that the buyer can exercise only on the day that it expires. *See also* ***American option***

European Private Equity and Venture Capital Association FINANCE group providing information for investors an organization that provides information and networking opportunities for investors, entrepreneurs, and policymakers in the ***equity financing*** industry. *Abbr* ***EVCA***

European Regional Development Fund FINANCE fund supporting less developed European areas a fund set up to provide grants to less industrially developed parts of Europe. *Abbr* ***ERDF***

European Social Charter ECONOMICS charter containing rights of EU members a charter adopted by the European Council of the EU in 1989. The 12 rights it contains are: freedom of movement, employment, and remuneration; social protection; improvement of living and working conditions; freedom of association and collective bargaining; worker information; consultation and participation; vocational training; equal treatment of men and women; health and safety protection in the workplace; pension rights; integration of those with disabilities; and protection of young people. *Abbr* ***ESC***

European Union ECONOMICS organization of European nations a social, economic, and political organization involving 27 European countries. It came into effect in 1993 as a result of the signing of the Maastricht Treaty by 15 countries; other countries joined later. Precursors were the ***European Community*** (EC) and the ***European Economic Community*** (EEC). *Abbr* ***EU***. See also ***single market***

Euroyen CURRENCY & EXCHANGE yen deposited in bank abroad a Japanese yen deposited in a bank outside Japan

Euroyen bond STOCKHOLDING & INVESTMENTS Eurobond in yen a Eurobond denominated in yen but issued outside of Japan by a non-Japanese company

eurozone ECONOMICS countries using euro the area of Europe comprising those countries that have adopted the euro as a common currency. *Also called* ***euroland***

EVA *abbr* FINANCE ***economic value added***

EVCA *abbr* FINANCE ***European Private Equity and Venture Capital Association***

event marketing MARKETING promotion of social functions the promotion and marketing of a specific event such as a conference, seminar, exhibition, or trade fair. Event marketing may encompass ***corporate hospitality*** activities, business or charity functions, or sporting occasions. The planning, marketing, and managing of the function on the day are sometimes entirely ***outsourced*** to companies specializing in event management.

event risk STOCKHOLDING & INVESTMENTS chance of loss on bond the possibility that a bond rating will drop because of an unexpected event such as a takeover or restructuring

evergreen loan FINANCE loan supplying flow of capital a series of loans providing a continuing stream of capital for a project

exact interest ACCOUNTING annual interest calculated over 365 days annual interest calculated on the basis of a full 365 days, as opposed to ordinary interest that is calculated on 360 days

ex-all STOCKHOLDING & INVESTMENTS without rights to anything pending having no right with respect to stocks in any pending transaction such as a split or the issuance of dividends. *Abbr* ***xa***. See also ***cum-all***

excellence GENERAL MANAGEMENT, OPERATIONS & PRODUCTION attainment of highest standards a state of organizational performance achieved through the successful integration of a variety of operational and strategic elements which enables an organization to become one of the best in its field. Excellence is initially evident when an organization rises above its competitors, and it is usually measured by the ability to sustain a leading or significant market share. The strategic and operational elements contributing to excellence include the organization's approach to ***total quality management***, core competency, ***benchmarking***, ***customer service***, the ***balanced scorecard approach***, and ***leadership***. Taken all together, these components should produce an organizational approach to the generation, development, and delivery of products and services which is better, cheaper, and smarter than that of the competition. Attempts at becoming an excellent organization have spawned terms such as ***best practice*** and ***world class manufacturing*** and are usually associated with a holistic approach to ***competitive advantage***.

exceptional items ACCOUNTING **1.** ordinary business costs of unusual size or nature costs that arise from normal business dealings, but that must be recorded because of their unusual size or nature **2.** unusual items included in pre-tax balance sheet items in a balance sheet that do not appear there each year and that are included in the accounts before the pre-tax profit is calculated, as opposed to ***extraordinary items*** that are calculated after the pre-tax profit

exception reporting GENERAL MANAGEMENT providing only significant information the passing on of information only when it breaches or transcends agreed norms. Exception reporting is intended to reduce information overload by minimizing the circulation of repetitive or old information. Under this system, only information that is new and out of the ordinary will be transmitted.

excess **1.** FINANCE assets less liabilities in a financial institution, the amount by which assets exceed liabilities **2.** *UK* INSURANCE = ***deductible***

excess capacity OPERATIONS & PRODUCTION underutilized manufacturing capability spare manufacturing capability that is not being used

excess liquidity BANKING cash in bank exceeding required amount cash held by a bank above what is required by the regulatory authorities

excess profit FINANCE unusually high profit a level of profit that is higher than a level regarded as usual

excess profits tax TAX tax levied in unusual situation a tax levied by a government on a company that makes extraordinarily large profits in times of unusual circumstances, for example, during a war. An excess profits tax was imposed in both the United States and the United Kingdom during World War II.

excess reserves BANKING reserves in financial institution exceeding required amount reserves held by a financial institution that are higher than those required by the regulatory authorities. As such reserves may indicate that demand for loans is low, banks often sell their excess reserves to other institutions.

excess return FINANCE profit from investment the amount received from an investment in excess of the basic interest rate or the cost of capital by which an activity is financed

exchange **1.** MARKETS place for buying and selling a ***market*** where goods, services, or financial instruments are bought and sold **2.** STOCKHOLDING & INVESTMENTS converting one form of security to another the conversion of one type of security for another, for example, the exchange of a bond for stock **3.** E-COMMERCE environment for conducting business the main type of business-to-business marketplace. The ***B2B exchange*** enables suppliers, buyers, and intermediaries to come together and offer products to each other according to a set of criteria. ***B2B web exchanges*** provide constant price adjustments in line with fluctuations of supply and demand. In E2E or **"exchange-to-exchange" e-commerce, buyers and sellers conduct transactions not only within exchanges but also between them.** **4.** FINANCE barter to trade goods and services for other goods and services **5.** CURRENCY & EXCHANGE trade one country's currency for another to trade the currency of one country or economic zone for that of another

exchange controls CURRENCY & EXCHANGE regulations governing foreign exchange dealings the regulations by which a country's banking system controls its residents' or resident companies' dealings in foreign currencies and gold

exchange cross rate CURRENCY & EXCHANGE = ***cross rate***

exchange dealer CURRENCY & EXCHANGE foreign currency trader a person who buys and sells foreign currency

exchange equalization account CURRENCY & EXCHANGE bank account for regulating value of British pound the ***Bank of England*** account that sells and buys ***sterling*** for gold and foreign currencies to smooth out fluctuations in the exchange rate of the British pound

exchange offer STOCKHOLDING & INVESTMENTS offer of one security for another an offer to trade one security for another, usually to stockholders of a company in financial trouble and at less favorable terms

exchange option STOCKHOLDING & INVESTMENTS option allowing holder to exchange assets an option that allows the holder to trade one asset for another. The option may be either a ***European option***, which can be exercised only on the expiration date, or an ***American option***, which can be exercised at any time up to and including the expiration date. *Also called* ***Margrabe option***

exchange premium CURRENCY & EXCHANGE surcharge for buying foreign currency an extra cost above the usual rate for buying a foreign currency

  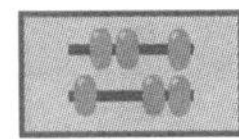      

exchange rate CURRENCY & EXCHANGE rate for converting one currency to another the rate at which one country's currency can be exchanged for that of another country

Exchange Rate Mechanism CURRENCY & EXCHANGE *see* ***ERM***

exchange rate movements CURRENCY & EXCHANGE changes in value between currencies the fluctuations in value between currencies that can result in losses to businesses that import and export goods and to investors

exchange rate parity CURRENCY & EXCHANGE relative value of currencies the relationship between the value of one currency and another

exchange rate risk CURRENCY & EXCHANGE, RISK chance of incurring loss on converting currencies the risk of suffering loss on converting another currency to the currency of a company's own country.

Exchange rate risks can be arranged into three primary categories. (i) Economic exposure: operating costs will rise due to changes in rates and make a product uncompetitive in the world market. Little can be done to reduce this routine business risk that every enterprise must endure. (ii) Translation exposure: the impact of currency exchange rates will reduce a company's earnings and weaken its balance sheet. To reduce translation exposure, experienced corporate fund managers use a variety of techniques known as ***currency hedging***. (iii) Transaction exposure: there will be an unfavorable move in a specific currency between the time when a contract is agreed and the time it is completed, or between the time when a lending or borrowing is initiated and the time the funds are repaid. Transaction exposure can be eased by ***factoring*** (transferring title to foreign accounts receivable to a third-party factoring house).

Although there is no definitive way of forecasting exchange rates, largely because the world's economies and financial markets are evolving so rapidly, the relationships between exchange rates, interest rates, and inflation rates can serve as leading indicators of changes in risk. These relationships are as follows. Purchasing Power Parity theory (PPP): while it can be expressed differently, the most common expression links the changes in exchange rates to those in relative price indices in two countries:

Rate of change of exchange rate
= Difference in inflation rates

International Fisher Effect (IFE): this holds that an interest-rate differential will exist only if the exchange rate is expected to change in such a way that the advantage of the higher interest rate is offset by the loss on the foreign exchange transactions. Practically speaking, the IFE implies that while an investor in a low-interest country can convert funds into the currency of a high-interest country and earn a higher rate, the gain (the interest rate differential) will be offset by the expected loss due to foreign exchange rate changes. The relationship is stated as:

Expected rate of change of the exchange rate
= Interest-rate differential

Unbiased Forward Rate Theory: this holds that the forward exchange rate is the best unbiased estimate of the expected future spot exchange rate.

Expected exchange rate = Forward exchange rate

exchange rate spread CURRENCY & EXCHANGE difference in buying and selling price of currencies the difference between the price at which a broker or other intermediary buys and sells foreign currency

exchange-traded MARKETS traded on exchange bought and sold on an exchange, as opposed to over-the-counter

exchange-traded fund MARKETS fund traded like stocks a group of stocks that can be traded on a stock exchange like a single stock and is linked to a specific market index. *Abbr* ***ETF***

Exchequer BANKING UK government's bank account in the United Kingdom, the government's account at the ***Bank of England*** into which all revenues from taxes and other sources are paid

Exchequer stocks STOCKHOLDING & INVESTMENTS UK government stocks UK government stocks used to finance government expenditure. They are regarded as a very safe investment.

excise duty TAX tax on specific goods a tax on goods such as alcohol or tobacco produced and sold within a specific country

excise license TAX license permitting sale of specific products a license issued against payment to allow somebody to trade in products such as wine that are subject to excise duty

excise tax TAX tax on specific goods a tax levied for a particular purpose

exclusion clause LEGAL clause listing items not covered by agreement a clause in an insurance policy or warranty that states which items or events are not included in the cover provided

exclusive agency *US* BUSINESS exclusive agreement to operate an agreement to be the only person to represent a company or to sell a product in a particular area. *UK term* ***sole agency***

exclusive agent *US* BUSINESS somebody with exclusive agency for company a person who has the ***exclusive agency*** for a company in an area. *UK term* ***sole agent***

exclusive agreement MARKETING sole right to sell product an agreement by which a person or company is made sole agent for selling a product in a market

exclusive economic zone ECONOMICS area in country with special economic conditions a zone in a country in which specific economic conditions apply. The Special Economic Zone in China, where trade is conducted free of state control, is an example.

ex coupon STOCKHOLDING & INVESTMENTS without interest coupons without the interest coupons or after interest has been paid

ex dividend STOCKHOLDING & INVESTMENTS giving buyer no dividend right used to describe bonds or stocks that, when they are sold, do not provide the buyer with the right to a forthcoming dividend

execution **1.** STOCKHOLDING & INVESTMENTS completion of securities trade the process of completing an order to buy or sell securities **2.** LEGAL carrying out contract the process of carrying out the terms of a legal order or contract

execution only MARKETS handling security transaction without giving advice used to describe a stock market transaction undertaken by an intermediary who acts on behalf of a client without providing advice. *See also* ***active fund management, discretionary management***

executive CORPORATE GOVERNANCE **1.** person in senior management an employee in a position of senior responsibility in an organization. An executive is involved in planning, strategy, policy making, and ***line management***. **2.** any person with responsible job a person with a significant role in an organization or project, for example, a ***manager***, ***consultant***, ***executive officer***, or ***agent***

executive chairman CORPORATE GOVERNANCE organization's highest executive the most senior executive in an organization when the roles of chair and chief executive are combined, and the executive chairman has some control over daily operations. *See also* ***chairman***

executive director CORPORATE GOVERNANCE director in senior management position a senior employee of an organization, usually with responsibility for a specific function and usually, but not always, a member of the ***board of directors***

executive officer CORPORATE GOVERNANCE = ***executive*** *(sense 2)*

executive pension plan PENSIONS UK pension plan for firm's top executives in the United Kingdom, a pension plan for senior executives of a company. The company's contributions are a tax-deductible expense but are subject to a cap. The plan does not prevent the executive from being a member of the company's group pension plan although the executive's total contributions must not exceed a specific percentage of his or her salary.

executive share option scheme *UK* STOCKHOLDING & INVESTMENTS = ***executive stock option plan***

executive stock option plan *US* STOCKHOLDING & INVESTMENTS stock purchase arrangement for top employees an arrangement whereby some directors and employees are given the opportunity to purchase stock in the company at a fixed price at a future date. In some jurisdictions, such arrangements can be tax efficient if specific local tax authority conditions are met. *UK term* ***executive share option scheme***

executive summary GENERAL MANAGEMENT statement outlining main points of business plan a concise summary at the beginning of a business plan of the objectives, products and/or services, marketing plans, operations, etc. of the proposed business, designed to attract investors

executor LEGAL person responsible for distribution of deceased person's assets a person appointed under a will to ensure the deceased's estate is distributed according to the terms of the will

exempt gift TAX in US, untaxed gift in the United States, a gift that is not subject to ***gift tax***

exempt investment fund TAX UK investment for people having certain tax advantages in the United Kingdom, a collective investment, usually a mutual fund, for investors, such as charities or contributors to pension plans, who have tax privileges

exemption TAX allowance per person subtracted from taxable income an amount per family member that somebody can subtract when reporting income to be taxed

exempt purchaser STOCKHOLDING & INVESTMENTS institutional investor exempt from securities commission filing requirements an institutional investor who may buy newly issued securities without filing a prospectus with a securities commission

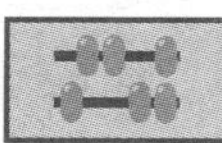

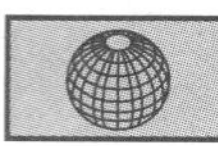

exempt security STOCKHOLDING & INVESTMENTS security exempt from legal requirement a security that is not subject to a provision of law such as margin or registration requirements

exempt supply TAX in UK, item exempt from VAT in the United Kingdom, an item or service on which ***VAT*** is not levied, for example, the purchase of, or rent on, real estate and financial services

exercise STOCKHOLDING & INVESTMENTS to use the right to act to put into effect a right to carry out a transaction with previously agreed terms, especially in trading ***options***

exercise date STOCKHOLDING & INVESTMENTS date when option may be taken the date on which the holder of an option can put its terms into effect

exercise notice STOCKHOLDING & INVESTMENTS option holder's notice of wish to exercise option an option holder's notification to the option writer of his or her desire to exercise the option

exercise of warrants STOCKHOLDING & INVESTMENTS using warrant to buy stock the process of activating the right given by a warrant to purchase stock at a specific date

exercise price STOCKHOLDING & INVESTMENTS **1.** price at which option is taken the price at which an option will be put into effect **2.** = ***strike price***

exercise value STOCKHOLDING & INVESTMENTS profit from cashing in option the amount of profit that can be realized by cashing in an ***option***

ex-gratia payment HR & PERSONNEL exceptional extra payment a one-time extra payment in addition to normal pay, made out of gratitude or courtesy, or in recognition of a special contribution

exhibition MARKETING large event for displaying goods an event organized to bring together buyers and sellers at a single venue

Eximbank BANKING US bank lending money to foreign importers a bank founded in 1934 that provides loans direct to foreign importers of US goods and services *Full form* **Export-Import Bank**

existential culture GENERAL MANAGEMENT attitudes and behavior fostering individuals a form of corporate culture in which the organization exists to serve the individual, rather than individuals being servants of the organization. Existential culture was identified by Charles Handy. It typically consists of a group of professionals who work together, but have no leader.

exit STOCKHOLDING & INVESTMENTS termination of investment the way in which an investor can realize the gains or losses of an investment, for example, by selling the company they have invested in

exit charge *or* exit fee STOCKHOLDING & INVESTMENTS fee charged to sell out of investment a charge sometimes made by a trust when selling shares in a ***mutual fund***

exit P/E ratio FINANCE final price/earnings ratio the ***price/earnings ratio*** when a company changes hands, as by a takeover or sale

exit price MARKETS price at which investment is sold the price at which an investor sells an investment or at which a firm sells all its merchandise and leaves a market

exit strategy BUSINESS planned disposal of business a plan for disposing of a business and realizing the value of the investment made in it. The development of an exit strategy involves establishing the value of the business, identifying and selecting exit options, identifying and removing obstacles, and preparing and implementing a plan. Exit options include the sale of the business, ***merger***, flotation or public listing, ***management buyout***, ***franchising***, family succession, ceasing to trade, or ***liquidation***.

ex-legal STOCKHOLDING & INVESTMENTS US bond not displaying legal opinion in the United States, a municipal bond that is issued without the legal opinion of a law firm printed on it

ex officio CORPORATE GOVERNANCE by virtue of one's office because of an office held. An officeholder such as a treasurer may attend a committee meeting "ex officio" because of the office held in the wider organization, even if they are not otherwise a member of that committee.

exogenous variable STATISTICS variable from outside study in an econometric study, any variable that has an impact on it from outside

exotic option STOCKHOLDING & INVESTMENTS, RISK complicated option traded in over-the-counter market a complex option contract whose underlying asset or terms of payoff differ from those of either a standard ***American option*** or ***European option***. Exotic options are usually traded in the ***over-the-counter market***.

expansionary monetary policy FINANCE lending at low interest to stimulate economy a government strategy of lending money at low interest rates to stimulate an economy that is entering or experiencing a recession

expected rate of return *or* expected return STOCKHOLDING & INVESTMENTS probable return on investment the projected percentage return on an investment, based on the weighted probability of all possible rates of return.

It is calculated by the following formula:

$$ERR = \sum_{i=1}^{n} = (P(i) \times r_i)$$

where P(*i*) is the probability of outcome *i* and r*i* is the return for outcome *i*.

The following example illustrates the principle that the formula expresses:

The current price of ABC, Inc. stock is trading at $10. At the end of the year, ABC shares are projected to be traded:

25% higher if economic growth exceeds expectations-a probability of 30%;

12% higher if economic growth equals expectations-a probability of 50%;

5% lower if economic growth falls short of expectations-a probability of 20%.

To find the expected rate of return, simply multiply the percentages by their respective probabilities and add the results:

$$(30\% \times 25\%) + (50\% \times 12\%) + (25\% \times -5\%)$$
$$= 7.5 + 6 + -1.25 = 12.25\ \%\ \text{ERR}$$

A second example:

if economic growth remains robust (a 20% probability), investments will return 25%;

if economic growth ebbs, but still performs adequately (a 40% probability), investments will return 15%;

if economic growth slows significantly (a 30% probability), investments will return 5%;

if the economy declines outright (a 10% probability), investments will return 0%.

Therefore:

$$(20\% \times 25\%) + (40\% \times 15\%) + (30\% \times 5\%) + (10\% \times 0\%)$$
$$= 5\% + 6\% + 1.5\% + 0\% = 12.5\ \%\ \text{ERR}$$

Abbr ***ERR***. See also ***capital asset pricing model***

expected return FINANCE probable return on investment

expected value FINANCE future value based on probability of an occurrence the future value of a course of action, weighted according to the probability that the course of action will actually occur. If the possible course of action produces income of $10,000 and has a 10% chance of occurring, its expected value is 10% of $10,000 or $1,000.

expenditure FINANCE amount spent an amount of money spent on a particular thing, or the total amount spent

expenditure switching ECONOMICS switching government spending from one area to another government action to divert domestic spending from one sector to another, for example, from imports to home-produced goods

expense ACCOUNTING **1.** cost required a cost incurred in buying goods or services **2.** money spent a charge against a company's profit

expense account HR & PERSONNEL **1.** money allowed for business travel and entertainment money that businesspeople are allowed by their companies to spend on traveling and entertaining clients in connection with business **2.** facility to draw or reclaim money for expenses an amount of money that an employee or group of employees can draw on to reclaim personal ***expenses*** incurred in carrying out activities for an organization

expense ratio STOCKHOLDING & INVESTMENTS percentage of management costs passed on the percentage of the assets held in a mutual fund that includes management fees and other costs of operating the fund and that are passed on to stockholders

expenses HR & PERSONNEL money spent by employee as part of work personal costs that are reimbursed by the employer to any employee carrying out activities for an organization

experience curve GENERAL MANAGEMENT = ***learning curve***

experiential learning HR & PERSONNEL learning through experience and analysis a model that views learning as a cyclical process in four stages: concrete experience, reflective observation, abstract conceptualization, and active experimentation. Experiential learning relates to participants' activities and reactions to a training event, in contrast to passive learning. Proposed by David A. Kolb in 1971, the model was later expanded by other practitioners including Peter Honey and Alan Mumford.

experimental design STATISTICS how experiment is set up the planning of the procedures to be used in an experimental study

expert system GENERAL MANAGEMENT computer program providing expert knowledge and procedures a computer program that emulates the reasoning and decision making of a human expert in a particular field. The main components of an expert system are the knowledge base, which consists of facts and rules about appropriate courses of action based on the knowledge and experience of human experts; the inference

engine, which simulates the inductive reasoning of a human expert; and the user interface, which enables users to interact with the system. Expert systems may be used by nonexperts to solve well-defined problems when human expertise is unavailable or expensive, or by experts seeking to find solutions to complex questions. They are used for a wide variety of tasks, including medical diagnostics and financial decision making, and are an application of ***artificial intelligence***.

expiration cycle MARKETS system showing stock option's expiration date in options trading, a way of designating the month on which a stock option expires. An option is assigned to one of three cycles, January (with expiration dates in January, April, July, and October), February (with expiration dates in February, May, August, and November), and March (with expiration dates in March, June, September, and December).

expiration date *US* STOCKHOLDING & INVESTMENTS last day on which to exercise an option the last day on which somebody who holds an option to buy or sell an asset can exercise that option. *UK term* ***expiry date***

expiry date *UK* STOCKHOLDING & INVESTMENTS = ***expiration date***

explicit cost FINANCE cost of using resources not owned by producer the cost of resources that are bought from outside the company producing the good or service. *See also* ***implicit cost***

exploding bonus FINANCE potential recruits' bonus that diminishes with time a bonus offered to recent graduates that encourages them to sign for a job as quickly as possible as it reduces in value with every day of delay (slang)

exponential smoothing STATISTICS statistical method of identifying long-term trends a statistical technique used in quantitative ***forecasting***, particularly in the areas of inventory control and ***sales forecasting***, that adjusts data to give a clearer view of trends in the long term. In exponential smoothing, values are calculated using a formula that takes all previous values into account but assigns greatest weight to the most recent data.

exponential trend STATISTICS trend in statistics over time a statistical trend that is revealed as observations are collected at uniformly spaced intervals over a period of time

export INTERNATIONAL TRADE **1.** sending goods abroad for sale the practice or business of sending goods from one country to another to be sold. *See also* ***exports*** **2.** send goods abroad for sale to send goods from one country to another to be sold

export agent INTERNATIONAL TRADE facilitator of trade abroad an intermediary who acts on behalf of a company to open up or develop a market in a foreign country. Export agents are often paid a commission on all sales and may have exclusive rights in a particular geographic area. A good agent will know or get to know local market conditions and will have other valuable information that can be used to mutual benefit.

exportation INTERNATIONAL TRADE act of sending goods abroad for sale the act of sending goods to foreign countries for sale

Export Credit Guarantee Department INTERNATIONAL TRADE UK government department helping exporters with finances a UK government department that provides financial and insurance assistance for exporters. The Export Credit Guarantee Department works to benefit organizations exporting UK goods and services and sets up insurance for UK companies investing overseas. *Abbr* ***ECGD***

exporter INTERNATIONAL TRADE firm sending goods abroad for sale a company that sends goods from one country to another to be sold

Export-Import Bank BANKING, INTERNATIONAL TRADE *see* ***Eximbank***

exporting INTERNATIONAL TRADE selling products abroad the process of selling goods to other countries. Exporting provides access to nondomestic markets and can be coordinated by an export manager. As with all business activities, careful market research needs to be undertaken. This can be conducted by the company itself or through an experienced export agent. Many companies produce goods almost entirely for export. Services also can be exported, but require different delivery mechanisms through subsidiary offices, or local ***franchise*** or ***licensing agreements***.

export-led growth ECONOMICS increase in economy based on exports growth in which a country's main source of income is from its export trade

export license LEGAL government permit allowing exportation of something a government permit allowing goods to be sent to another country for sale

exports INTERNATIONAL TRADE goods sent abroad for sale goods sent to another country to be sold. *See also* ***export***

ex-rights STOCKHOLDING & INVESTMENTS sold without rights for sale without rights such as voting or conversion rights. The term can be applied to transactions such as the purchase of new shares.

ex-rights date MARKETS date of first ex-rights trade the date when a stock first trades ex-rights, with the rights remaining with the seller rather than transferring to the buyer

extendable bond STOCKHOLDING & INVESTMENTS bond whose maturity can be postponed a bond whose maturity can be delayed by either the issuer or the holder

extendable note STOCKHOLDING & INVESTMENTS note whose maturity can be postponed a note whose maturity can be delayed by either the issuer or the holder

extended credit FINANCE **1.** credit with long repayment terms credit that allows the borrower a long time before payment is required **2.** long repayment term offered by US Federal Reserve in the United States, an extra long period of credit offered to commercial banks by the Federal Reserve

extended fund facility ECONOMICS time allowance for repaying IMF a credit facility operated by the ***International Monetary Fund*** that allows a country up to eight years to repay money it has borrowed from the fund

Extensible Business Reporting Language FINANCE *see* ***XBRL***

extension GENERAL MANAGEMENT extra time granted for something an additional period of time allowed for something, for example, the repayment of a debt or the filing of a tax return

external account BANKING account of overseas resident in UK bank an account held at a United Kingdom-based bank by a customer who is an overseas resident

external audit ACCOUNTING periodic independent audit of firm's accounts a periodic examination of the books of account and records of an entity conducted by an independent third party (an auditor) to ensure that they have been properly maintained; are accurate and comply with established concepts, principles, and accounting standards; and give a true and fair view of the financial state of the entity. *See also* ***internal audit***

external communication GENERAL MANAGEMENT informal exchange of information the exchange of information and messages between an organization and other organizations, groups, or individuals outside its formal structure. The goals of external communication are to facilitate cooperation with groups such as suppliers, investors, and stockholders, and to present a favorable image of an organization and its products or services to potential and actual customers and to society at large. A variety of channels may be used for external communication, including face-to-face meetings, print or broadcast media, and electronic communication technologies such as the Internet. External communication includes the fields of PR, media relations, advertising, and marketing management.

external debt ECONOMICS country's debts to nonresidents the part of a country's debt that is owed to creditors who are not residents of the country

external finance FINANCE investors' money money that a company obtains from investors, for example, by loans or by issuing stock

external funds FINANCE third-party money money that a business obtains from a third party rather than from its own resources

external growth BUSINESS growth as result of joining with another firm business growth as a result of a merger, a takeover, or through a partnership with another organization

external market INTERNATIONAL TRADE international market for securities issued outside single country a securities market in which securities issued outside the jurisdiction of any one country are offered simultaneously to investors in a number of countries

external trade INTERNATIONAL TRADE trade with other countries commercial activity carried out with foreign countries. *See also* ***internal trade***, ***crossborder trade***

extraordinary general meeting CORPORATE GOVERNANCE general meeting other than regular annual meeting any general meeting of an organization other than the ***annual meeting***. Directors can usually call an extraordinary general meeting at their discretion, as can company members who either hold not less than 10% of the paid-up voting shares, or who represent not less than 10% of the voting rights. Directors are obliged to call an EGM if there is a substantial loss of capital. Fourteen days' written notice must be given, or 21 days' written notice if a special resolution is to be proposed. Only special business can be transacted at the meeting, the general nature of which must be specified in the convening notice. *Abbr* ***EGM***

extraordinary item ACCOUNTING exceptional inclusion in firm's accounts an item, such as an acquisition or a sale of assets, that is included in a company's accounts but is not likely to occur again. These items are not taken into account when a company's ***operating profit*** is calculated.

extraordinary resolution CORPORATE GOVERNANCE vote held on exceptional issue in the United Kingdom, an exceptional issue that is put to the vote at a company's general meeting, for example, a change to the company's articles of association, requiring 14 days' notice

extrapolate STATISTICS estimate value beyond set of known values to estimate from a set of values that lies beyond the range of the data collected

extreme value STATISTICS smallest or largest values in statistical study either of the smallest or largest variate values in a sample of observations from a statistical study

EZ *abbr* FINANCE, BUSINESS ***enterprise zone***

F

face value 1. FINANCE amount on banknote the amount printed on a banknote, showing its value **2.** STOCKHOLDING & INVESTMENTS value displayed the value shown on a ***financial instrument*** such as bonds or stocks, often different than the actual value

facilitation HR & PERSONNEL making it easier for others to do something the process of helping groups, or individuals, to learn, find a solution, or reach a consensus, without imposing or dictating an outcome. Facilitation works to empower individuals or groups to learn for themselves or find their own answers to problems without control or manipulation. Facilitators need good communication skills, including listening, questioning, and reflecting. Facilitation is used in a variety of contexts including training, conflict resolution, and negotiation.

facility FINANCE total credit offered the total amount of credit that a lender will allow a borrower under a specific agreement

facility fee FINANCE charge for arranging credit a charge made by a lender to a borrower for arranging credit facilities

facility takeover *UK* FRAUD type of identity theft a type of fraud in which a person impersonates another person and falsely claims a change of address in order to gain access to and control that person's financial accounts

factor 1. FINANCE collector of corporate debt a business that purchases or lends money on ***accounts receivable*** based on an evaluation of the ***creditworthiness*** of prospective customers of the business, for a small percentage of the debt amount **2.** STATISTICS statistical variable in a statistical study, a variable such as one affecting the price of an asset which can be isolated and modeled separately

factor analysis STATISTICS study of relationships between variables the examination of the relationships existing between the variables observed in a statistical study

factor four OPERATIONS & PRODUCTION quadrupling productivity to reduce waste a concept of environmentally friendly production based on increasing the productivity of resources by a factor of four to reduce waste

factoring FINANCE **1.** transferring of foreign debts the practice of transferring title to foreign ***accounts receivable*** to a third-party ***factor*** that assumes responsibility for collections, administrative services, and any other services requested. Major exporters use factoring as a way of reducing exchange rate risk. The fee for this service is a percentage of the value of the receivables, anywhere from 5% to 10% or higher, depending on the currencies involved. Companies often include this percentage in selling prices to recoup the cost. **2.** selling firm's debts at discount the sale of ***accounts receivable*** to a third party (the ***factor***) at a discount, in return for cash. A factoring service may be "with recourse," in which case the supplier takes the risk of the debt not being paid, or "without recourse," when the factor takes the risk. *See also* ***invoice discounting*** **3.** buying of debts the practice of buying up a business's ***accounts receivable***, providing it with ***working capital***

factoring charges FINANCE cost of selling debts to third party the cost of selling ***accounts receivable*** to an agent for a commission

factor market ECONOMICS place where capital or labor is traded a market in which ***factors of production*** are bought and sold, for example, the capital market or the labor market

factors of production OPERATIONS & PRODUCTION land, labor, and capital the three things needed to produce a product: land, labor, and capital

factory OPERATIONS & PRODUCTION place for manufacturing goods a building or set of buildings housing workers and equipment for the sole purpose of manufacturing goods, often on a large scale

factory gate price OPERATIONS & PRODUCTION manufacturing cost of goods the actual cost of manufacturing goods before any additional charges are added to give a profit. The factory gate price includes direct costs such as labor, raw materials, and energy, and indirect costs such as interest on loans, plant maintenance, or rent.

failure GENERAL MANAGEMENT = ***business failure***

Failure Mode and Effects Analysis RISK way of identifying and dealing with potential failures a method for identifying and ranking the seriousness of ways in which a product, process, or service could fail, and finding ways in which to minimize the risk of those potential failures. *Abbr* ***FMEA***

fair dealing MARKETS legal trading in stock the buying and selling of stock in a legal and open manner

fair market value *or* fair value FINANCE asset's or liability's worth in arm's length transaction the amount for which an asset or liability could be exchanged in an arm's length transaction between informed and willing parties, other than in a forced or liquidation sale.

fair price OPERATIONS & PRODUCTION good price for both buyer and seller a price that is favorable for both buyer and seller

fair trade INTERNATIONAL TRADE agreement waiving duties on some imports an international business system by which countries agree not to charge import duties on some items imported from their trading partners

fair value accounting *UK* ACCOUNTING = ***historical cost accounting***

fair wear and tear OPERATIONS & PRODUCTION, INSURANCE damage caused by normal use the acceptable and expected level of damage caused by normal use

fallen angel STOCKHOLDING & INVESTMENTS highly rated security whose value has dropped a stock that was once very desirable but has now dropped in value (slang)

falling knife STOCKHOLDING & INVESTMENTS stock whose price has taken steep drop a stock whose price has fallen at a rapid rate over a short time period

false accounting ACCOUNTING, FRAUD criminal accounting practices the criminal offense of changing, destroying, or hiding accounting records for a dishonest purpose

false market MARKETS, FRAUD market influenced by illegal manipulation of stock prices a market in stocks caused by persons or companies conspiring to buy or sell and so influence the stock price to their advantage

falsification FRAUD making false accounting entries the activity of making false entries in financial accounts

family business BUSINESS business owned and run by family a ***small or medium-sized enterprise*** that is controlled and operated by members of a family. It may be organized as a sole proprietorship, partnership, corporation, or limited liability company.

family of funds STOCKHOLDING & INVESTMENTS related group of mutual funds a selection of mutual funds with different objectives that is offered by one investment company, allowing investors to easily transfer money from one fund to another with little cost. *Also called* ***fund family***

Fannie Mae MORTGAGES US institution financing housing the largest source of financing for housing in the United States, which funds mortgages by issuing debt securities in US and international securities markets. Fannie Mae was created in 1938 as a federal agency and chartered in 1968 by the US Congress as a stockholder-owned private company. On September 7, 2008, after Fannie Mae reported billions of dollars in losses from ***subprime loans***, its government regulatory agency, the Federal Housing Finance Agency put Fannie Mae under its conservatorship. In addition, the US Treasury agreed to provide up to $100 billion of capital as needed to ensure Fannie Mae's continued operation. *Full form* ***Federal National Mortgage Association***. *See also* ***Freddie Mac***

FAQ E-COMMERCE commonest questions about something FAQ pages are often included on websites to provide first-time visitors with answers to the most likely questions they may have. FAQ pages are also used in newsgroups and software applications. *Full form* ***frequently asked question***

far month MARKETS most distant month in futures trading the latest month for which there is a futures contract for a particular commodity. *See also* ***nearby month***

FAS ACCOUNTING US accounting standards in the United States, the standards of financial reporting and accounting established by the FASB. *Full form* ***Financial Accounting Standards***

FASB ACCOUNTING US accounting organization in the United States, an institution responsible for establishing the standards of financial reporting and accounting for companies in the private sector. The ***Securities and Exchange Commission*** performs a comparable role for public companies. *Full form* ***Financial Accounting Standards Board***

FASTER MARKETS New Zealand Exchange's computerized trading system a computer-based

  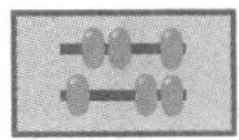      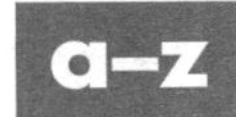

clearing, settlement, registration, and information system operated by the ***New Zealand Exchange***. *Full form* ***Fully Automated Screen Trading and Electronic Registration***

fast track GENERAL MANAGEMENT route providing rapid results a rapid route to success or advancement. The fast track involves competition and a race to get ahead, and is associated with high ambition and great activity. An employee can be on a fast track, for example, to promotion, but an activity also can be said to take the fast track, for example, to rapid product development.

fat cat BUSINESS highly paid chief executive a derogatory term used to describe a chief executive of a large company or organization who secures extremely large pay, pension, and termination packages, and may receive large bonuses

FCA ACCOUNTING ICAEW Fellow Chartered Accountant a Fellow (long-term member) of the Institute of Chartered Accountants in England and Wales

FCCA ACCOUNTING ACCA Fellow, Chartered Certified Accountant a Fellow (long-term member) of the Association of Chartered Certified Accountants

FCM *abbr* STOCKHOLDING & INVESTMENTS ***futures commission merchant***

FCMA ACCOUNTING CIMA Fellow Chartered Management Accountant a Fellow (long-term member) of the Chartered Institute of Management Accountants

FDI *abbr* STOCKHOLDING & INVESTMENTS ***foreign direct investment***

FDIC *abbr* INSURANCE ***Federal Deposit Insurance Corporation***

feasibility study GENERAL MANAGEMENT assessment of ease of doing something an investigation into a proposed plan or project to determine whether and how it can be successfully and profitably carried out. Frequently used in ***project management***, a feasibility study may examine alternative methods of reaching objectives or be used to define or redefine the proposed project. The information gathered must be sufficient to make a decision on whether to go ahead with the project, or to enable an investor to decide whether to commit finances to it. This will usually require analysis of technical, financial, and market issues, including an estimate of resources required in terms of materials, time, personnel, and finance, and the expected return on investment.

Fed BANKING = ***Federal Reserve***

Federal Deposit Insurance Corporation INSURANCE US agency insuring deposits in commercial banks the US federal agency that manages insurance funds that insure deposits in commercial banks and in savings and loans associations. *Abbr* ***FDIC***

Federal Funds FINANCE US reserves deposits held in reserve at the ***Federal Reserve*** by the US banks. The Federal Funds rate, the rate that the Federal Reserve charges banks for borrowing reserves, is the key US monetary policy rate.

Federal Home Loan Mortgage Corporation MORTGAGES, RISK *see* ***Freddie Mac***

federal income tax TAX deductions from employees' pay funding US government in the United States, money deducted from employees' salaries in order to fund Federal services and projects

Federal Insurance Contributions Act HR & PERSONNEL *see* ***FICA***

Federal National Mortgage Association MORTGAGES, RISK *see* ***Fannie Mae***

Federal Open Market Committee ECONOMICS committee that oversees US monetary policy the 12-member committee of the ***Federal Reserve Board*** that meets eight times a year to determine US monetary policy by setting interest rates or by buying and selling government securities. *Abbr* ***FOMC***

federal organization GENERAL MANAGEMENT combining of subsidiaries for benefits of scale a form of organization structure in which subsidiaries federate to gain benefits of scale. In a federal organization, the leader provides coordination and vision, and initiatives are generated from the component subsidiary organizations. Federal organization is one of the many ways in which organizations restructure in order to deal with the dilemmas of power and control. Federal organization offers an enabling framework for autonomy to release corporate energy for people to do things in their own way, provided that it is in the common interest, and for people to be well informed so as to be able to interpret that common interest. Royal Dutch Shell, Unilever, and ABB are exemplars of federalism.

Federal Reserve BANKING system of federal government control of US banks the central banking system of the United States, founded in 1913 by an Act of Congress. The board of governors, made up of seven members, is based in Washington, DC, and 12 ***Federal Reserve Banks*** are located in major cities across the United States. It regulates money supply, prints money, fixes the ***discount rate***, and issues bonds for government debt. *Also called* ***Fed***, ***Federal Reserve System***

Federal Reserve Bank BANKING major US bank any of the 12 banks that are members of the US ***Federal Reserve***, based in Atlanta, Boston, Chicago, Cleveland, Dallas, Kansas City, Minneapolis, New York, Philadelphia, Richmond, St. Louis, and San Francisco

Federal Reserve Board BANKING supervisory board of the US Federal Reserve the seven-member Board of Governors, appointed by the President of the United States and confirmed by the Senate, that supervises the ***Federal Reserve*** and formulates monetary policy. Appointees to the Board of Governors serve for 14 years. *Abbr* ***FRB***

Federal Reserve note CURRENCY & EXCHANGE US paper money a piece of paper money issued by the Federal Reserve Bank and approved as the legal tender of the United States

Federal Reserve System BANKING = ***Federal Reserve***

Federation of Small Businesses BUSINESS organization representing UK small businesses in the United Kingdom, a not-for-profit membership organization representing the interests of small businesses. The FSB was established in 1974 and has over 174,000 members. *Abbr* ***FSB***

Fed funds rate BANKING interest rate on interbank loans in Federal Reserve the rate charged by US banks for lending money deposited with the ***Federal Reserve*** to other banks

Fed pass BANKING US Federal Reserve's easing of credit the addition of reserves to the ***Federal Reserve*** in order to increase availability of credit

Fedwire BANKING US electronic transfer system the US ***Federal Reserve***'s electronic system for transferring funds

fee FINANCE payment to professional for services money paid for work carried out by a professional person such as an accountant

feedback GENERAL MANAGEMENT information about performance to facilitate improvement the communication of responses and reactions to proposals and changes, or of the findings of appraisals of performance, with the goal of enabling improvements to be made. Feedback can be either positive or negative.

feedback control GENERAL MANAGEMENT identification and regulation of outputs the measurement of differences between planned outputs and actual outputs achieved, and the modification of subsequent action and/or plans to achieve future required results

feeding frenzy MARKETS frantic buying in a financial market, a period of extremely active buying (slang)

fee work FINANCE work done for organization by non-employees work on a project carried out by independent workers or contractors, rather than employees of an organization

fempreneur BUSINESS = ***lipstick entrepreneur***

femterprise BUSINESS firm with woman owner a business that has been started or is owned by a woman

FHLMC MORTGAGES *see* ***Freddie Mac***

fiat money FINANCE government-recognized money coins or banknotes that have little intrinsic value in the material of which they are made but that are recognized by a government or other issuing authority, such as the European Central Bank, as having value

FICA HR & PERSONNEL in US money deducted for Social Security and Medicare in the United States, a federal law that requires employers to deduct a percentage of their employees' income for payment into the trust fund that provides Social Security and Medicare benefits. Employers and employees are each responsible for half the payment, while self-employed individuals are responsible for the entire payment but are allowed a tax deduction for half. *Full form* ***Federal Insurance Contributions Act***

FICO score FINANCE US system for assessing credit rating a score used by lenders in the United States to assess a person's ability to pay back a loan, based on the person's payment history, current debt, types of credit used, length of credit history, and new credit. Scores range from 300 to 850. The system was devised by the Fair Isaac Corporation (FICO).

fictitious assets ACCOUNTING book assets with no resale value assets such as pre-payments that do not have a resale value but are entered as assets on a company's ***balance sheet***

FID *abbr* TAX ***Financial Institutions Duty***

fiduciary LEGAL **1.** person acting for another a person who controls property or acts on behalf of or for the benefit of another person **2.** on behalf of another controlled or managed for another person

fiduciary deposit BANKING bank-managed deposit a bank deposit that is managed for the depositor by the bank

field research MARKETING direct contact with customers to gain information the collection of data

        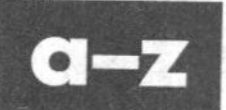

directly from contact with customers and potential customers through surveys, interviews, and other forms of ***market research***

field trial MARKETING test of product in actual use a limited pilot test of a product under real conditions. A field trial is undertaken to test the physical or engineering properties of a product in order to identify and iron out any technical shortcomings prior to marketing. Customers may be involved in some trials, for example, in testing a new laundry detergent. Field trials should not be confused with test marketing, which is used to determine the likely market for, and likely consumer response to, a new product or service.

field work MARKETING work in real environment practical work, study, or research carried out in the real world away from the desk. In a marketing context, field work forms primary ***market research*** and involves obtaining customers' views and opinions on a face-to-face basis or through mail questionnaires or telephone surveys.

FIFO OPERATIONS & PRODUCTION inventory control system a method of inventory management in which the stock of a given product first placed in store is used before more recently produced or acquired goods or materials. *Full form* ***first in first out***

FIF Tax *abbr* TAX ***Foreign Investment Funds Tax***

figures ACCOUNTING financial results a company's financial results calculated for a particular period of time

filing date *UK* TAX = ***filing deadline***

filing deadline *US* TAX due date for income tax returns the date by which income tax returns must be filed with the relevant taxation authority. *UK term* ***filing date***

fill STOCKHOLDING & INVESTMENTS buy or sell an investment upon client's order to carry out a client's instructions to buy or sell a security or commodity

filter GENERAL MANAGEMENT extracting useful information from large amounts of data a process for analyzing large amounts of incoming information to identify any material that might be of interest to an organization

FIMBRA *abbr* REGULATION & COMPLIANCE ***Financial Intermediaries, Managers and Brokers Regulatory Association***

final average monthly salary PENSIONS earnings on which most US pensions are based the earnings on which most defined benefit pensions are based. *UK term* ***pensionable earnings***

final closing date MERGERS & ACQUISITIONS final day for acceptance of takeover the last date for the acceptance of a ***takeover bid***, when the bidder has to announce how many stockholders have accepted the offer

final demand FINANCE last reminder before legal action of debt a last reminder from a supplier to a customer to pay an outstanding debt. Suppliers often begin legal proceedings if a final demand is ignored.

final discharge FINANCE last debt payment the final payment on the amount outstanding on a debt

final dividend STOCKHOLDING & INVESTMENTS year-end dividend payment the ***dividend*** paid at the end of a year's trading. The final dividend must be approved by a company's stockholders.

final salary pension PENSIONS in UK, benefit on retirement based on earnings in the United Kingdom, a retirement benefit regularly paid to employees or their survivors by an employer, based on salary at or near retirement. Employers set up pension plans by depositing an amount of money in the employee's name into a pension fund, which may be contributed to by the employer or both the employer and the employee. The fund is invested and benefits are paid to the employee from the fund upon retirement. Either the employer or employee may assume the risk of investment failure depending upon the type of pension.

final sale *US* FINANCE sale of nonreturnable items a sale that does not allow the purchaser to return the goods. *UK term* ***firm sale***

finance FINANCE **1.** supply money for business or project to provide an amount of money for a particular purpose. *See also* ***fund* 2.** *UK* = ***financing***

Finance Act TAX legislation granting British government power of taxation an annual Act of the British Parliament that gives the government the power to obtain money from taxes as proposed in the ***Budget***

Finance and Leasing Association FINANCE financing and leasing firms' UK organization in the United Kingdom, an organization representing firms engaged in business financing and the leasing of equipment and cars

finance bill TAX public-spending bill a proposal for legislation giving a government the power to obtain money from taxes

finance company FINANCE business lending money for purchases a business that lends money to people or companies against ***collateral***, especially to make purchases of some kind. *UK term* ***finance house***

finance house *UK* FINANCE = ***finance company***

finance lease *UK* FINANCE = ***capital lease***

finance market MARKETS = ***money market***

finances FINANCE money available for spending the financial status of a person or organization

financial FINANCE of finance relating to the management of money

financial accountant TREASURY MANAGEMENT UK accountant acting as adviser or financial director a qualified accountant, a member of the Institute of Financial Accountants, who advises on accounting matters or who works as the financial director of a company

financial accounting 1. TREASURY MANAGEMENT financial reports for investors and external parties the form of accounting in which financial reports are produced to provide investors or others outside a company with information on a company's financial status. *See also* ***management accounting*** **2.** ACCOUNTING process of producing financial statements the process of classifying and recording a company's transactions and presenting them in the form of profit and loss accounts, balance sheets, and cash flow statements, for a given ***accounting period***

Financial Accounting Standards ACCOUNTING *see* ***FAS***

Financial Accounting Standards Board ACCOUNTING *see* ***FASB***

financial adviser FINANCE investment adviser somebody whose job is to give advice about investments

financial aid FINANCE money provided to help somebody or something monetary assistance given to an individual, organization, or nation. International financial aid, from one country to another, is often used to fund educational, health-related, or other humanitarian activities.

financial analyst STOCKHOLDING & INVESTMENTS = ***investment analyst***

financial capital FINANCE funds for buying physical assets funds that can be used for the purchase of assets such as buildings and equipment. *See also* ***real capital***

financial control TREASURY MANAGEMENT management of firm's finances the policies and procedures established by an organization for managing, documenting, and reporting its financial transactions

financial correspondent FINANCE reporter who covers money matters a reporter who writes articles on money matters or reports on them on television or radio

financial distress FINANCE situation close to bankruptcy the condition of being in severe difficulties over money, especially being close to ***bankruptcy***

financial economies of scale FINANCE benefits gained by increasing scale of activity financial advantages gained by being able to do things on a large scale

financial engineering STOCKHOLDING & INVESTMENTS converting or creating financial instruments the conversion of one form of financial instrument into another, such as the swap of a fixed-rate instrument for a floating-rate one, or the creation of a new type of financial instrument —**financial engineer**

financial futures *or* financial futures contract MARKETS contract to purchase financial instrument for future delivery a contract for the purchase of a specific ***basket of securities***, such as interest rates, exchange rates, share prices, or indices, for delivery at a date in the future. *Also called* ***financials***

financial futures market MARKETS market in financial instruments for future delivery the market in ***basket of securities***, such as interest rates, exchange rates, share prices, or indices, for delivery at a date in the future

financial incentive scheme FINANCE in UK, money rewarding improved performance in the United Kingdom, a program offering employees a cash bonus, share options or other monetary reward for improved commitment and performance and as a means of motivation. *See also* ***non-financial incentive scheme***

Financial Industry Regulatory Authority MARKETS, REGULATION & COMPLIANCE regulator of US securities firms established in 2007 by the merger of the ***National Association of Securities Dealers*** and regulatory functions of NYSE Regulation, FINRA is a ***self-regulatory organization*** that oversees the activities of member ***brokerage firms*** as well as performing market regulation under contract for US stock markets including the ***New York Stock Exchange*** and ***NASDAQ***. *Abbr* ***FINRA***

financial institution FINANCE organization investing large sums of money an organization, such as a bank, savings and loan, pension fund, or insurance company, that invests large amounts of money in securities

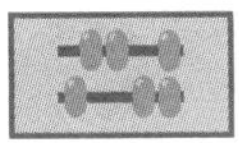

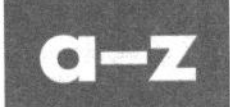

Financial Institutions Duty TAX Australian tax on money deposited in financial institutions a tax on monies paid into financial institutions imposed by all state governments in Australia except for Queensland. Financial institutions usually pass the tax on to customers. *Abbr* ***FID***

financial instrument STOCKHOLDING & INVESTMENTS contract that is evidence of financial transaction any contract that gives rise to both a financial asset of one entity and a financial liability or equity instrument of another entity. Financial instruments include both primary financial instruments such as bonds, currency, and stocks, and derivative financial instruments, whose value derives from the underlying assets.

Financial Intermediaries, Managers and Brokers Regulatory Association REGULATION & COMPLIANCE former UK financial regulator a former UK financial regulatory authority, now incorporated into the ***Financial Services Authority***. *Abbr* ***FIMBRA***

financial intermediary FINANCE financial institution handling deposits and/or loans an institution that accepts deposits or loans from individuals and lends money to clients. Banks, ***savings and loan associations***, and finance companies are all financial intermediaries.

financial leverage FINANCE relationship between firm's borrowings and stockholders' funds the relationship between a company's borrowings (which includes both prior charge capital and long-term debt) and its stockholders' funds (common share capital plus reserves). Calculations can be made in a number of ways, and may be based on capital values or on earnings/interest relationships. Overdrafts and interest paid thereon may also be included:

$$\frac{\text{Profit before interest and tax}}{\text{Profit before tax}}$$

shows the effect of interest on the operating profit.

$$\frac{\text{Profit before interest and tax}}{\text{Interest expense}}$$

shows the number of times that profit will cover interest expense.

$$\frac{\text{Total long-term debt}}{\text{(Shareholders' funds + long-term debt)}}$$

shows the proportion of long-term financing which is being supplied by debt.

$$\frac{\text{Total long-term debt}}{\text{Total assets}}$$

a measure of the capacity to redeem debt obligations by the sale of assets.

$$\frac{\text{(Operating cash flows − Taxation paid − Returns on investment and servicing of finance)}}{\text{Repayments of debt due within one year}}$$

measures ability to redeem debt.

A company with a high proportion of prior charge capital to shareholders' funds is highly leveraged, and is lowly or lightly leveraged if the reverse situation applies. *Also called* ***gearing***

financial market MARKETS market for buying and selling financial instruments a market in which financial instruments are traded. The financial markets are stock exchanges, commodity exchanges, bond markets, and the foreign exchange market.

financial obligation FINANCE something you must pay a sum of money that you are committed to pay, especially a debt. *See also* ***collateralized debt obligation***

financial obligations FINANCE things you must spend money on things that you must use your money to pay for, such as rent, household expenses, dependent family members, etc.

Financial Ombudsman REGULATION & COMPLIANCE UK organization handling complaints against financial institutions in the United Kingdom, an organization responsible for investigating and resolving complaints involving money from members of the public against a company, institution, or other organization. The Ombudsman is not a governmental body, but it does operate under an Act of Parliament in the form of the Financial Services and Markets Act 2000.

financial performance FINANCE firm's ability to generate revenue a measure of a company's ability to generate income over a given period of time

financial planner FINANCE somebody giving advice about money a professional investment adviser who analyzes a person's financial situation and goals and prepares a plan to meet those goals. *See also* ***independent financial adviser***

financial planning FINANCE money management for future the activity of producing strategies for the acquisition of funds to finance activities and meet established goals

Financial Planning Association of Australia FINANCE Australian organization for financial planners a national organization representing companies and individuals working in the Australian financial planning industry. Established in 1992, the Association is responsible for monitoring standards among its members. *Abbr* ***FPA***

financial position FINANCE value of firm's assets and liabilities the amount of money that a person or organization has in terms of assets and liabilities

financial pyramid STOCKHOLDING & INVESTMENTS, RISK investment pattern tapering from safe to risky an investment strategy, typically having four levels of risk. The first and largest percentage of assets are in safe, liquid investments; the second, in investments that provide income and long-term growth; the third, in riskier investments with a chance of greater return; and the fourth and smallest percentage, in the riskiest investments with the chance of greatest return.

financial report ACCOUNTING document detailing firm's financial position a document that gives the financial position of a company or other organization

Financial Reporting Council REGULATION & COMPLIANCE UK regulator for corporate reporting in the United Kingdom, an independent regulator responsible for setting standards for corporate reporting and actuarial practice, as well as monitoring and enforcing accounting and auditing standards. They also oversee the regulatory activities of the professional accounting bodies and operate independent disciplinary arrangements for public interest cases involving accountants and actuaries. *Abbr* ***FRC***

Financial Reporting Review Panel ACCOUNTING UK group for examining questionable accounting practices in the United Kingdom, a review panel established to examine contentious departures from accounting standards by large companies. It is a subsidiary body of the ***Financial Reporting Council***.

Financial Reporting Standards Board ACCOUNTING New Zealand accounting organization in New Zealand, an organization that is responsible for setting and monitoring accounting standards. *Abbr* ***FRSB***

financial resources FINANCE money available for spending the money that is available for a person or organization to spend

financial review FINANCE examination of organization's finances an examination of the state of an organization's finances

financial risk FINANCE, RISK investors' chance of loss the possibility of financial loss in an investment or speculation

financials MARKETS = ***financial futures***

Financial Services Act REGULATION & COMPLIANCE UK legislation regulating providers of financial services in the United Kingdom, an Act of Parliament that regulates the offering of financial services to the general public and to private investors

Financial Services Authority REGULATION & COMPLIANCE UK organization overseeing financial system in the United Kingdom, an independent non-governmental organization formed in 1997 following reforms in the regulation of financial services. Banking and investment services supervision was merged into the remit of the previous regulator, the ***Securities and Investments Board***, which then changed its name to become the Financial Services Authority. The FSA's four statutory objectives were specified by the Financial Services and Markets Act 2000: maintaining market confidence; increasing public knowledge of the finance system; ensuring appropriate protection for consumers; and reducing financial crime. *Abbr* ***FSA***. Also called ***City watchdog***

Financial Services Compensation scheme FINANCE fund compensating customers of insolvent UK financial firm in the United Kingdom, an independent organization set up by law to pay compensation to customers who have made claims against an authorized financial services firm in the event that the firm is unable, or likely to be unable, to pay the claims

financial services industry FINANCE financial institutions dealing in money management the business activity of the financial institutions that offer money management services such as banking, investment, brokerage, and insurance

financial statements ACCOUNTING documents reporting company's financial performance summaries of accounts to provide information for interested parties. The most important financial statements are the balance sheet, income statement, statement of cash flows, and the shareholders' equity statement. *See also* ***annual report***

financial supermarket FINANCE firm providing many different financial services a company that offers a variety of financial services. For example, a bank may offer loans, mortgages, retirement plans, and insurance alongside its existing range of normal banking services.

Financial Times BUSINESS, FINANCE British financial newspaper a respected British financial daily newspaper, first published on January 9,

  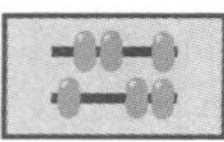      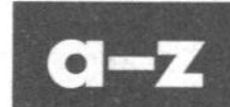

1888. It is published in London but printed in 24 cities and available worldwide, as well as online. It jointly owns the index company ***FTSE*** with the ***London Stock Exchange***. *Abbr* ***FT***

Financial Times Index MARKETS = ***FT 30***

financial year *UK* **1.** ACCOUNTING, TAX = ***fiscal year*** **2.** TAX for UK corporations, April 1–March 31 in the United Kingdom, for corporation tax purposes, the period from 1 April of a given year to 31 March of the following year

financier FINANCE somebody who provides financing a person who specializes in the provision of financing to other people or organizations

financing *US* FINANCE money required to pay for something the money needed by an individual or company to pay for something, for example, a project or inventory. *UK term* ***finance***

financing gap **1.** FINANCE difference between money available and money needed a shortfall between the funds available and the funds needed for a project. For example, a company planning expansion is able to finance some of this activity from internally generated cash and some from existing finance agreements but any shortfall requires the raising of new funds. **2.** ECONOMICS funding shortfall from canceling poorer countries' debts a gap in funding for institutions such as the ***International Monetary Fund*** caused by canceling the debts of poorer countries such as those in West Africa

financing vehicle FINANCE product providing funds for activity a method or product used to provide the funds for an activity

finder's fee FINANCE fee for finding new client a fee paid to somebody who finds a client for another person or company, for example, somebody who introduces a new client to a brokerage firm

fine-tuning ECONOMICS making small changes to improve economic position the process of making small adjustments in areas such as interest rates, tax bands, or the money supply, to improve a nation's economy

finish MARKETS end of stock trading for day the end of a day's trading on a stock exchange

finished goods OPERATIONS & PRODUCTION items ready for sale completed goods that are available for distribution or sale to customers

finite capacity plan OPERATIONS & PRODUCTION plan for resource requirements a plan produced where ***capacity requirements planning*** covers capacity requirements, enabling ***loading*** at each workstation to be smoothed and determining the need for additional resources. *See also* ***capacity requirements planning***

finite population STATISTICS fixed-size group a statistical population that has a limited size

FINRA *abbr* MARKETS, REGULATION & COMPLIANCE ***Financial Industry Regulatory Authority***

FIRB *abbr* REGULATION & COMPLIANCE ***Foreign Investment Review Board***

fire sale **1.** FINANCE sale of anything at a large discount a sale of anything at a very low price, usually because the seller is facing ***bankruptcy*** **2.** OPERATIONS & PRODUCTION sale of fire-damaged goods a sale of goods that have been damaged during a fire

firm BUSINESS **1.** company a business or company. This wide sense is the one in which the word is used in this dictionary. **2.** partnership a business run by ***partners***

firm order MARKETS order to broker to sell or buy an order to a broker to sell or buy a security on a specific date or at a specific price

firm quote MARKETS bid to trade with time limit a bid to buy or offer to sell a security that a ***market maker*** is obligated to meet within a specified period of time

firm sale *UK* FINANCE = ***final sale***

first call MARKETS firm processing earnings forecasts a company that gathers and reports brokerage analysts' earnings forecasts for use by brokers and investors in making investment recommendations and decisions

first in first out OPERATIONS & PRODUCTION *see* ***FIFO***

first mover MARKETING innovating firm the company that first introduces a new type of product or service to a market. Those organizations that follow a first mover to market are known as ***followers*** or ***laggards***—terms that also describe companies that are not the recognized leaders in a sector.

first mover advantage GENERAL MANAGEMENT advantage of being first with new product the benefit produced by being the first to enter a market with a new product or service. First mover advantages include: becoming a ***market leader*** in a new area; establishing a new leading ***brand***; being able to charge a premium until competitor products appear; enhanced reputation, design, and copyright protection; and possibly setting an industry standard to which other competitors may have to aspire. Disadvantages include: cheaper, and possibly better, ***follower*** products; the possibility of having to reduce prices or continuously having to add value to stay ahead; first mover development costs; a possible shift in consumer tastes away from the product; obsolescence; and a follower product being accepted as the industry standard.

first quarter ACCOUNTING first part of fiscal year the period of three months from January to the end of March, or the period of three months at the start of any fiscal year. *Abbr* ***Q1***

first-round financing FINANCE initial funding the first infusion of capital into a project

fiscal TAX relating to finance, especially to tax relating to financial matters, especially in respect of governmental collection, use, and regulation of money through taxation

fiscal agent BANKING agent in finance matters a bank or trust that takes over the fiscal responsibilities of another party

fiscal balance ECONOMICS balance of income and expenditure the extent to which government receipts differ from government outlay. If outlays exceed receipts then the fiscal balance is negative or in deficit; if receipts exceed outlays then the balance is positive or in surplus.

fiscal consolidation ECONOMICS policy for controlling government shortfall a set of measures designed to reduce government deficits and the accumulation of debts

fiscal drag *UK* TAX increase in tax paid as inflation rises the effect that inflation has on taxation in that, as earnings rise, the amount of tax collected increases without a rise in tax rates

fiscal measures TAX tax changes introduced for economic reasons tax changes made by a government to improve the working of the economy

fiscal policy ECONOMICS, TAX government's methods for managing economy the central government's policy on lowering or raising taxation or increasing or decreasing public expenditure in order to stimulate or depress ***aggregate demand***

fiscal year *US* ACCOUNTING TAX firm's 12-month accounting period a twelve-month period used by a company for accounting and in some jurisdictions tax purposes. A fiscal year is not necessarily the same as a calendar year. *Abbr* ***FY***. UK terms ***accounting year***, ***financial year***. See also ***accounting period***

fishbone chart GENERAL MANAGEMENT diagram for investigation of causes of problems a diagram that is used to identify and categorize the possible causes of problems. Within such a chart, which resembles the shape of the skeleton of a fish, the topic or problem to be discussed is placed in a box at the right-hand side that corresponds to the fish's head, and the major items to be investigated are shown as branches at an angle to the horizontal spine. Questions are asked to identify possible causes of problems in each area and the results are added to the diagram as additional layers of branches. This ensures that all aspects of the problem are considered systematically. It is frequently used in brainstorming and problem solving. *Also called* ***cause and effect diagram***

fixation MARKETS setting of commodity's price on options market the act by a government of stating the price of a commodity on an options market

fixed annuity INSURANCE *see* ***annuity***

fixed asset ACCOUNTING asset that firm keeps long-term a long-term business asset such as a machine or building that will not usually be traded

fixed assets register ACCOUNTING register of tangible assets a record of individual tangible fixed assets belonging to a company or organization

fixed-asset turnover ratio ACCOUNTING measure of how firm uses its assets a measure of the use a business makes of its capital assets. It is calculated by dividing sales by net fixed assets.

fixed capital FINANCE durable assets such as buildings and machinery assets in the form of buildings and machinery, that are long-lasting and can be used repeatedly for production

fixed charge FINANCE creditor's right to specific asset the right of a creditor to a claim on a specific asset, as opposed to a ***floating charge*** that applies to all a company's assets. *Also called* ***specific charge***

fixed cost ACCOUNTING cost that remains fixed when sales fluctuate a cost that does not change according to sales volumes, for example, overhead such as rent or production costs

fixed deduction TAX agreed UK tax deduction for general expenses in the United Kingdom, a deduction agreed by HM Revenue & Customs and a group of employees which covers general expenditure on clothes or tools used in the course of employment

fixed deposit BANKING deposit paying fixed interest over set period a deposit that pays a fixed rate of interest over a defined period

fixed exchange rate CURRENCY & EXCHANGE set rate of exchange between currencies a rate of exchange of one currency against another that cannot fluctuate, and can only be changed by devaluation or revaluation

  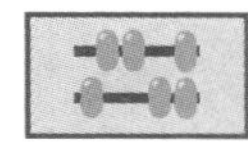   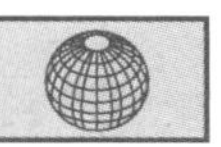   

fixed exchange rate system CURRENCY & EXCHANGE currency exchange system with unchanging rates a system of currency exchange in which there is no change of rate

fixed expenses FINANCE unvarying overhead costs costs that do not vary with different levels of production, for example, rent, staff salaries, and insurance

fixed income FINANCE income that remains unchanged each year income that does not change from year to year, for example, from an annuity

fixed interest FINANCE **1.** with unvarying interest rate used to describe a loan or financial product that has an interest rate that does not go up or down **2.** interest rate that stays the same interest that is paid at a rate that does not vary over a period of time

fixed-interest loan FINANCE loan with unchanging interest rate a loan whose rate of interest stays the same over the whole period of the loan

fixed-interest security STOCKHOLDING & INVESTMENTS investment paying constant interest an investment such as a government bond that produces an amount of interest that does not change with changes in short-term interest rates. *Also called* ***fixed-rate security***

fixed interval re-order system OPERATIONS & PRODUCTION = ***periodic inventory review system***

fixed-price agreement OPERATIONS & PRODUCTION contract setting prices for period of time an agreement whereby a company provides a service or a product at a price that stays the same for the whole period of the agreement

fixed rate FINANCE unchanging interest rate an interest rate for loans that does not change with fluctuating conditions in the market and stays the same for the whole period of the loan

fixed-rate loan FINANCE loan with unchanging interest rate a loan with an interest rate that is set at the beginning of the term and remains the same throughout

fixed-rate mortgage MORTGAGES mortgage with unchanging interest rate a mortgage for which the interest rate on the loan it secures is set at the beginning of the term and remains the same throughout

fixed-rate security STOCKHOLDING & INVESTMENTS = ***fixed-interest security***

fixed scale of charges FINANCE range of standard charges a set of charges that does not vary according to individual circumstances but is applied consistently in all cases of the same kind

fixed yield FINANCE constant percentage return on investment a percentage return on an investment which does not change over a period of time

fixtures and fittings REAL ESTATE items sold along with property the objects in a property that are sold with the property, both those which cannot be removed and those which can. Fixtures and fittings are a category of ***fixed assets***.

flag MARKETS chart pattern that confirms price trend a pattern on a chart showing a period during which securities prices consolidate a previous advance or fall

flat 1. MARKETS steady market price due to low demand used to describe market prices that do not fall or rise, because of low demand **2.** GENERAL MANAGEMENT without hierarchy used to describe a management structure that is not strongly hierarchical

flat rate FINANCE unvarying standard rate a price, payment or interest rate that remains the same regardless of other factors which may change

flat tax TAX tax unrelated to income a tax levied at one unchanging rate regardless of the level of somebody's income. *See also* ***progressive tax***

flat yield STOCKHOLDING & INVESTMENTS interest rate as percentage of fixed-interest security price an interest rate that is a percentage of the price paid for a ***fixed-interest security***

flat yield curve FINANCE graph using unified interest rate for bonds a visual representation of relative interest rates that shows the same interest rates for long-term bonds as for short-term bonds. As investors are assumed to prefer shorter maturities to longer ones, other factors being equal, a flat yield curve is normally assumed to imply that investors can expect lower short-term rates in future.

flexed budget FINANCE budget responsive to changes in trade a budget that changes in response to changes in sales turnover and output

flexible benefit plan HR & PERSONNEL = ***cafeteria plan***

flexible exchange rate system CURRENCY & EXCHANGE currency exchange system with fluctuating rates a system of currency exchange in which rates change from time to time

flexible manufacturing system OPERATIONS & PRODUCTION **1.** various stages of production under central computer control an integrated system of computer-controlled machine tools and transport and handling systems under the control of a larger computer. Flexibility is achieved by having an overall method of control that coordinates the functions of both the machine tools and the handling systems. **2.** computer-controlled system producing variety of parts an integrated, computer-controlled production system that is capable of producing any of a variety of parts, and of switching quickly and economically between them *Abbr* ***FMS***

flexible spending account HR & PERSONNEL US employee benefit based on voluntary salary deductions in the United States, an employee benefit plan, a type of ***cafeteria plan***, funded by voluntary salary reduction, that the employee may use for specific expenses that are exempt from payroll taxes. *Also called* ***salary reduction plan***

flight of capital FINANCE removal of investment money because of economic uncertainty the rapid movement of investment money out of one country because of lack of confidence in that country's economic future

flight to quality STOCKHOLDING & INVESTMENTS movement of investors to low-risk securities a tendency of investors to buy safe well-established securities when the economic outlook is uncertain

flip 1. BUSINESS new company run for short-term success a startup company that works to build market share quickly and generate short-term personal wealth for its founders through flotation or sell-off **2.** REAL ESTATE develop property for quick profit to buy a property, fix it up, and then resell it in a short period in order to make a profit

float 1. FINANCE delay between presentation of check and actual payment the period between the presentation of a check as payment and the actual payment to the payee or the financial advantage provided by this period to the drawer of a check **2.** FINANCE cash held for small transactions a small cash balance maintained to facilitate low-value cash transactions. Records of these transactions should be maintained as evidence of expenditure, and periodically a float or petty cash balance will be replenished to a predetermined level. **3.** STOCKHOLDING & INVESTMENTS sell stocks or bonds to sell stocks or bonds. *See also* ***new issue***

floater FINANCE variable-rate loan a loan with an interest rate that varies over time

floating asset FINANCE short-term asset replaced by another an asset that it is assumed will be consumed during the company's normal trading cycle and then replaced by the same type of asset

floating capital FINANCE amount of company's money invested in current assets the portion of a company's money that is invested in current assets, as distinct from that invested in ***fixed assets*** or ***capital assets***

floating charge FINANCE charge linked to company's assets overall a charge linked to any of the company's assets in a category, but not to a specific item

floating debenture FINANCE debenture running for lifetime of firm a ***debenture*** secured on all of a company's assets which runs until the company is closed down

floating debt FINANCE loan frequently renewed a borrowing for less than one year that is repeatedly renewed

floating exchange rate CURRENCY & EXCHANGE currency exchange rate that is allowed to vary an exchange rate for a specific currency that can vary according to market demand, and is not fixed by a government

floating rate FINANCE interest rate fluctuating as market fluctuates an interest rate that is not fixed and which changes according to fluctuations in the market

floating-rate note FINANCE, CURRENCY & EXCHANGE Eurocurrency loan with variable interest rate a Eurocurrency loan that is not given at a fixed rate of interest. *Abbr* ***FRN***

floor 1. FINANCE lower limit a lower limit on an interest rate, price, or the value of an asset **2.** MARKETS = ***trading floor***

floor broker MARKETS = ***pit broker***

floor effect STATISTICS when statistical data groups approach lower limit in a statistical study, the occurrence of clusters of scores near the lower limit of the data

floor limit BANKING limit on credit card sale without bank authorization the highest sale through a credit card that a retailer can accept without having to obtain authorization from the issuing bank

floor price MARKETS lowest possible price the lowest possible price that something can be sold for

floor trader MARKETS exchange member trading for own account a member of an exchange who buys and sells securities mainly for their own account on the ***trading floor*** of an exchange. *Also called* ***competitive trader***

flotation MARKETS funds raised by sale of stock the financing of a company by selling stock in it or a new debt issue, or the offering of stock and bonds

for sale on the stock exchange. *See also* ***initial public offering***

flow chart *or* flow diagram GENERAL MANAGEMENT diagrammatic representation of stages a graphic representation of the stages in a process or system, or of the steps required to solve a problem. A flow chart is commonly used to represent the sequence of functions in a computer program or to model the movement of materials, money, or people in a complex process. Two primary symbols used in flow charts are the ***process box***, indicating a process or action taking place, and the decision lozenge, indicating the need for a decision.

flow line production *or* flow production OPERATIONS & PRODUCTION processing in stages in single direction a production method in which successive operations are carried out on a product in such a way that it moves through the factory in a single direction. Flow line production is most widely used in ***mass production*** on production lines. More recently, it has been linked with ***batch production***. Under flow line production, inventory is often kept to the minimum necessary to ensure continued activity. Stoppages and interruptions to the flow indicate a fault, and corrective action can be taken. Assembly line production is an extreme version of flow line production.

flow on BUSINESS pay raise awarded to match another a pay increase awarded to one group of employees as a result of a pay raise awarded to another group working in the same field

flow theory GENERAL MANAGEMENT idea about people's reaction to change a theory of the way in which people become engaged with, or disengaged from, change. Flow theory suggests that people harmonize in change situations, and open, honest, trusting relationships emerge. The theory recognizes the unpredictability and rigidity of human nature when faced with change. *See also* ***change management***

flow trader MARKETS person trading for client a trader in an organization such as an investment bank who buys and sells products for the bank's clients rather than trading aggressively on behalf of the bank itself. *See also* ***proprietary trading***

fluff it and fly it MARKETING make product look good, then sell it to enhance a product's appearance and then put it on the market (slang)

FMA *abbr* STOCKHOLDING & INVESTMENTS ***Fund Managers' Association***

FMEA *abbr* RISK ***Failure Mode and Effects Analysis***

FMS *abbr* OPERATIONS & PRODUCTION ***flexible manufacturing system***

FNMA MORTGAGES *see* ***Fannie Mae***

FOB *or* f.o.b. *abbr* OPERATIONS & PRODUCTION ***free on board***

focus group MARKETING group giving reactions and opinions a carefully selected representative variety of consumers or employees used for the purposes of providing feedback on preferences and responses to a selected range of issues. A focus group usually operates with a facilitator to guide discussion.

folio ACCOUNTING numbered page in account book a page with a number, especially two facing pages in an account book which have the same number

followback survey STATISTICS follow-up check on statistical population a further survey of a statistical population carried out a period of years after an original survey

follower MARKETING firm moving into area created by another a company that follows the first company to introduce a new type of product or service to a market. *Also called* ***laggard***. *See also* ***first mover***

FOMC *abbr* ECONOMICS ***Federal Open Market Committee***

footfall MARKETING how many people walk past store a measure of the number of people who walk past a store

Footsie MARKETS (informal) = ***FTSE 100***

Forbes 500 FINANCE list of largest US public companies a list of the 500 largest public companies in the United States, ranked according to various criteria by *Forbes* magazine

forced sale BUSINESS sale enforced by court order a sale that takes place as the result of a court order or because it represents the only reasonable way for a company or individual to avoid a financial crisis

force field analysis GENERAL MANAGEMENT means of making change more acceptable a technique for promoting change by identifying positive and negative factors and by working to lessen the negative forces while developing the positive ones

force majeure LEGAL incident that contractual parties cannot predict or control something that happens that is out of the control of the parties who have signed a contract, for example, a strike, war, or storm

forecast STATISTICS estimation of value of variable a prediction of the value of a variable in a statistical study

forecast dividend STOCKHOLDING & INVESTMENTS expected year-end dividend a dividend that a company expects to pay at the end of the current trading year. *Also called* ***prospective dividend***

forecasting GENERAL MANAGEMENT estimation or prediction of future the prediction of outcomes, trends, or expected future behavior of a business, industry sector, or the economy through the use of statistics. Forecasting is an ***operational research*** technique used as a basis for management planning and decision making. Common types of forecasting include trend analysis, ***regression analysis***, ***Delphi technique***, ***time series*** analysis, ***correlation***, and ***exponential smoothing***.

foreclose *US* FINANCE acquire mortgaged property when owner defaults to acquire a property because the owner cannot or will not repay money that he or she has borrowed to buy the property.

foreclosure *US* FINANCE act of recovering security on unpaid loan the acquisition of property when an owner cannot or will not repay the loan that was taken out to buy the property. *UK term* ***repossession***

foreign bill FINANCE bill of exchange payable only overseas a bill of exchange that is not payable in the country where it is issued

foreign currency CURRENCY & EXCHANGE other country's money the currency or interest-bearing bonds of a foreign country

foreign currency account BANKING, CURRENCY & EXCHANGE bank account operated in foreign currency a bank account in the currency of another country, for example, a dollar account in a bank in the United Kingdom

foreign currency reserves CURRENCY & EXCHANGE foreign money held by government foreign money held by a government to support its own currency and pay its debts. *Also called* ***foreign exchange reserves, international reserves***

foreign debt CURRENCY & EXCHANGE debt owed to other country hard-currency debt owed to a foreign country in payment for goods and services

foreign direct investment STOCKHOLDING & INVESTMENTS investment in firm by foreign company or government investment in a company outside the country of the investor, who sets up subsidiaries or acquires usually about 10% of the stock with voting rights, thus gaining influence in the foreign company's management. *Abbr* ***FDI***

foreign dividend STOCKHOLDING & INVESTMENTS in UK, dividend paid from overseas in the United Kingdom, a dividend paid from another country, possibly subject to special rules under UK tax codes

foreign draft CURRENCY & EXCHANGE check drawn and payable in different countries a check that is drawn in one country and payable in another

foreign equity market MARKETS market equities of overseas companies the market in one country for equities of companies in other countries

foreign exchange CURRENCY & EXCHANGE **1.** foreign currencies currencies and financial instruments used to buy goods abroad or as investments. *Also called* ***forex*** **2.** dealings in foreign currencies dealings in the currencies of other countries, on foreign-exchange markets

foreign exchange broker *or* foreign exchange dealer CURRENCY & EXCHANGE trader in foreign currencies a person whose business is to buy and sell foreign currencies

foreign exchange dealing CURRENCY & EXCHANGE trade in foreign currencies the business of buying and selling currencies of other countries

foreign exchange market CURRENCY & EXCHANGE **1.** market for trading foreign currencies a market where people buy and sell foreign currencies **2.** dealings in foreign currencies dealings in the currencies of other countries

foreign exchange option CURRENCY & EXCHANGE contract guaranteeing minimum rate in currency exchange a contract that, for a fee, guarantees a worst-case exchange rate for the future purchase of one currency for another. Unlike a ***forward transaction***, the option does not obligate the buyer to deliver a currency on the settlement date unless the buyer chooses to. These options protect against unfavorable currency movements while preserving the ability to participate in favorable movements.

foreign exchange reserves CURRENCY & EXCHANGE = ***foreign currency reserves***

foreign exchange transfer CURRENCY & EXCHANGE sending of money abroad the process of sending money from one country to another

foreign income dividend STOCKHOLDING & INVESTMENTS dividend from earnings abroad a dividend paid from earnings in countries other than the one in which the investment was made

Foreign Investment Funds Tax TAX Australian tax on offshore investments a tax imposed by the Australian government on ***unrealized capital***

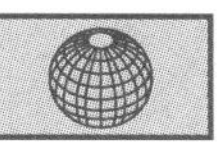

gains made by Australian residents from offshore investments. It was introduced in 1992 to prevent overseas earnings from being taxed at low rates and never brought to Australia. *Abbr* ***FIF Tax***

Foreign Investment Review Board REGULATION & COMPLIANCE Australian institution regulating foreign investment in Australia, a non-statutory body that regulates and advises the federal government on foreign investment. It was established in 1976. *Abbr* ***FIRB***

foreign investments STOCKHOLDING & INVESTMENTS money invested abroad money invested in countries other than your own

foreign money order CURRENCY & EXCHANGE money order for somebody abroad a money order in a foreign currency that is payable to somebody living in a foreign country

foreign reserve CURRENCY & EXCHANGE centrally held foreign currency the currency of other countries held by an organization, especially a country's central bank

foreign subsidiary company BUSINESS *see* ***subsidiary company***

foreign tax credit TAX tax benefit for taxes paid abroad a tax advantage for taxes that are paid to or in another country

forensic accounting **1.** ACCOUNTING, FRAUD accounting that assists in identifying financial fraud an accounting practice that specializes in investigating and presenting expert court testimony concerning crimes involving financial matters **2.** ACCOUNTING reference to accounts to check legality of activities the use of accounting records and documents in order to determine the legality or otherwise of past activities

forex *or* Forex CURRENCY & EXCHANGE = ***foreign exchange***

forfaiting INTERNATIONAL TRADE purchase of exporter's goods by third party the purchase of an exporter's goods by a third party at a discount. This party then collects payment from the importer with the shipped goods serving as collateral.

forfeit clause LEGAL contractual clause stating forfeit if contract not fulfilled a clause in a contract which states that goods or a deposit will be taken if the contract is not fulfilled by one of the signers

forfeiture LEGAL punitive loss of property or right loss of property or the right to something, usually because of an unlawful act

form 3 STOCKHOLDING & INVESTMENTS US form for reporting first securities transactions in the United States, a form that must be filed with the Securities and Exchange Commission within 10 days of the first securities transaction by officers, directors, or 10% shareholders in a company reporting their holdings in the company

form 4 STOCKHOLDING & INVESTMENTS US form for reporting changes in securities holdings in the United States, a form that must be filed with the Securities and Exchange Commission reporting any changes in the securities holdings of officers, directors, or 10% shareholders in a company

formal documents MERGERS & ACQUISITIONS documents detailing takeover bid documents that provide the full details of a takeover bid

form letter GENERAL MANAGEMENT identical letter sent to different people a letter that can be sent without any change to several correspondents

form T STOCKHOLDING & INVESTMENTS US form for reporting transactions after market close in the United States, a required form used by brokers to report to the National Association of Securities Dealers all securities transactions that have taken place after the markets have closed

Fortune 500 FINANCE list of largest US industrial companies a list of the 500 largest industrial companies in the United States, compiled annually by *Fortune* magazine

Forum of Private Business BUSINESS UK small-business support group in the United Kingdom, a business support and lobby group representing more than 25,000 small businesses. *Abbr* ***FPB***

forwardation MARKETS when cash price is lower than forward price a situation in which the spot price of a futures product is lower than the ***forward price***

forward contract MARKETS contract for future delivery a private contract for delivery of a commodity at a later date

forward cover FINANCE cash purchase of commodity fulfilling futures contract the purchase for cash of the quantity of a commodity needed to fulfill a futures contract

forward delivery MARKETS, OPERATIONS & PRODUCTION delivery at agreed future date a delivery at some date in the future that has been agreed to by the buyer and seller

forwarder OPERATIONS & PRODUCTION agent who handles shipping and customs for clients a person or company that arranges shipping and customs documents for several shipments from different companies, putting them together to form one large shipment

forward exchange rate CURRENCY & EXCHANGE rate for future foreign currency purchase a rate for purchase of foreign currency at a fixed price for delivery at a later date. *Also called* ***forward rate*** *(sense 2)*

forwarding agent BUSINESS somebody preparing shipping and customs documents a person or company that arranges shipping and customs documents for clients

forward integration OPERATIONS & PRODUCTION way to ensure products will be distributed a means of guaranteeing ***distribution channels*** for products and services by building relationships with, or taking control of, ***distributors***. Forward integration can free the supplier from the threat or influence of major buyers and can also provide a barrier to market entry by potential rivals. ***Backward integration*** can provide similar guarantees on the supply side.

forward interest rate FINANCE interest rate set for future loan an interest rate specified for a loan to be made at a future date

forward-looking study STATISTICS ongoing statistical survey a survey of a statistical population carried out for a period such as a year after an original survey

forward margin MARKETS difference between current and future price the difference between the current price (***spot price***) and the future price (***forward price***)

forward market MARKETS market for purchases delivered at future date a market for the buying of foreign currency, stocks, or commodities for delivery at a later date at a prearranged price

forward price MARKETS contracted price for future delivery the price set in an ***option*** contract for a security or commodity to be delivered at a future date

forward pricing STOCKHOLDING & INVESTMENTS setting of investment price using future valuation the establishment of the price of a share in a mutual fund based on the next asset valuation

forward rate **1.** FINANCE rate for loan the rate at which there is no economic arbitrage between receiving an interest rate today and receiving an interest rate starting at some point in the future **2.** CURRENCY & EXCHANGE = ***forward exchange rate***

forward rate agreement STOCKHOLDING & INVESTMENTS, RISK contract trading fixed interest for variable interest a contract traded in the ***over-the-counter market*** in which parties agree to exchange a fixed interest rate or currency exchange rate for a variable rate on an agreed amount of money for an obligation beginning at a future time

forward sales MARKETS sale for future delivery sales of stock, commodities, or foreign exchange for delivery at a later date

forward scheduling OPERATIONS & PRODUCTION way of establishing when each stage must start a method for determining the start times for the various operations involved in a particular ***job***. Forward scheduling is most often used when the operations department sets the delivery date for a job, rather than the sales or marketing departments. Jobs are scheduled for the various operations as the workstations are expected to become available. The customer can then be informed of the projected delivery date. *See also* ***backward scheduling***

forward trading MARKETS buying or selling for future delivery the activity of buying or selling stock, commodities, or foreign exchange for delivery at a later date

forward transaction MARKETS agreement to buy and sell currency in future an agreement to buy one currency and sell another on a date some time beyond two business days. This allows an exchange rate on a given day to be specified for a future payment or receipt, thereby eliminating exchange rate risk.

founders' shares *UK* STOCKHOLDING & INVESTMENTS stock issued to firm's founders stock held by founding members of a company, often with a higher dividend that is only paid after other stockholders have received their dividends and, in some cases, only when a specific level of profit has been achieved. *See also* ***deferred common stock***

401(k) plan PENSIONS type of US retirement plan in the United States, a personal retirement plan arranged by an employer for an employee, invested in bonds, mutual funds, or stock. The employee contributes a proportion of salary, on which tax can be deferred; the employer can also make contributions.

fourteen hundred MARKETS warning of stranger in London Stock Exchange formerly, an exclamation used as a warning when a stranger walked onto the ***trading floor*** of the London Stock Exchange

fourth level of service GENERAL MANAGEMENT high level of increased value a very high rating in a system of measuring the value added to a product or service

fourth market MARKETS direct trading, without brokers trading conducted directly without brokers, usually by large institutions

        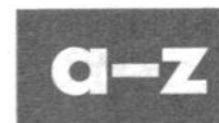

fourth quarter ACCOUNTING last period of fiscal year the period of three months from October to the end of the year, or the period of three months at the end of a fiscal year. *Abbr* ***Q4***

FPA *abbr* FINANCE ***Financial Planning Association of Australia***

FPB *abbr* BUSINESS ***Forum of Private Business***

fractional certificate STOCKHOLDING & INVESTMENTS certificate relating to part of share a certificate for less than a full share (***fractional share***)

fractional currency CURRENCY & EXCHANGE paper money in very small denominations the paper money that is in denominations smaller than one unit of a standard national currency

fractional share STOCKHOLDING & INVESTMENTS less than full share of stock one part of a full share of stock, usually created as the result of a dividend reinvestment plan or a ***stock split***

franchise MARKETING authorization to provide another's products an agreement enabling a third party to sell or provide products or services owned by a manufacturer or supplier. A franchise is granted by the manufacturer, or ***franchisor***, to a ***franchisee***, who then retails the product. The franchise is regulated by a franchise contract, or franchise agreement, that specifies the terms and conditions of the franchise. These may include an obligation for the franchisor to provide national advertising or training for sales staff in return for the meeting of agreed sales targets by the franchisee. The franchisee usually retains a percentage of sales income. In other cases, a franchise may involve the ***licensing*** of a franchisee to manufacture a product to the franchisor's specification, and the sale of this product to retailers. Franchises can also be organized by issue of a ***master franchise***.

franchise agreement *or* franchise contract MARKETING *see* ***franchise***

franchise chain MARKETING group of stores with same franchise a number of retail outlets operating the same ***franchise***. A franchise chain may vary in size from a few to many thousands of outlets and in coverage from a small local area to worldwide.

franchisee MARKETING holder of franchise a third party with a contract to sell or provide products or services owned by a manufacturer or supplier. The franchisee usually retains a percentage of sales income. *See also* ***franchise***

franchisor MARKETING granter of franchise a manufacturer or supplier who has made an agreement enabling a third party to sell or provide products or services that it owns. *See also* ***franchise***

franco FINANCE free available at no cost

franked payment STOCKHOLDING & INVESTMENTS **1.** dividends with tax credits dividends carrying tax credits paid by a company to stockholders **2.** dividend free of UK corporation tax in the United Kingdom, a dividend received by a company from another UK company, exempt from corporation tax

Frankfurt Stock Exchange *or* Frankfurter Wertpapierbörse MARKETS German stock exchange stock exchange based in Frankfurt, Germany. It has its origins in the first meeting to establish uniform exchange rates in 1585, becoming known as the Frankfurter Wertpapierbörse (Frankfurt Stock Exchange). The company running the exchange changed its name to Deutsche Börse on December 16, 1992, and demutualized on February 5, 2001. The headline index of stocks on the exchange is the ***DAX***. *Abbr* ***FWB***. Also called ***Deutsche Börse***

fraud FRAUD dishonest methods used for personal benefit the use of dishonesty, deception, or false representation in order to gain a material advantage or to injure the interests of others. Types of fraud include false accounting, theft, third party or investment fraud, employee collusion, and computer fraud. *See also* ***corporate fraud***

fraud ring FRAUD group organized to defraud others an organized group of people or companies who defraud others, for example, by stealing identities to gain access to financial information, by forging mortgage documents, or by filing false insurance claims

fraudulent misrepresentation LEGAL making false statements to deceive the action of making a false statement with the intention of deceiving a customer

FRB *abbr* BANKING ***Federal Reserve Board***

FRC *abbr* REGULATION & COMPLIANCE ***Financial Reporting Council***

Freddie Mac MORTGAGES, RISK US institution financing housing a stockholder-owned private company chartered in 1970 by the US Congress to fund home mortgages by issuing debt securities in US and international securities markets. On September 7, 2008, after Freddie Mac reported more than $2 billion in losses from ***subprime loans***, its government regulatory agency, the Federal Housing Finance Agency, put Freddie Mac under its conservatorship. *Full form* ***Federal Home Loan Mortgage Corporation***. *See also* ***Fannie Mae***

freebie MARKETING something given away free a product or service that is given away, often as a business promotion

free coinage CURRENCY & EXCHANGE minting from donated metals a government's minting of coins from precious metals provided by citizens

free competition BUSINESS unregulated competition for business between companies a situation in which companies are allowed to compete with each other to win business without government intervention or restrictions

free currency CURRENCY & EXCHANGE currency that can be traded without restriction a currency that is allowed by the government to be bought and sold without restriction

free enterprise ECONOMICS freedom to trade without government control the trade carried on in a free-market economy, where resources are allocated on the basis of supply and demand

free gold FINANCE government gold not part of national reserve gold held by a government but not pledged as a reserve for the government's currency

freeholder REAL ESTATE person who owns property a person who owns a property legally and unconditionally, with rights to grant leases

freehold property REAL ESTATE property held free and clear property that the owner holds legally and unconditionally, with rights to grant leases

free issue STOCKHOLDING & INVESTMENTS = ***bonus issue***

freelance GENERAL MANAGEMENT, HR & PERSONNEL self-employed working on the basis of being self-employed, and possibly working for several employers at the same time, perhaps on a temporary basis. Freelance workers have been described as ideally suited to ***portfolio working***.

freelancer HR & PERSONNEL self-employed person somebody who works on a ***freelance*** basis, offering skills and expertise to different employers anywhere in the world. A freelancer works independently and may follow a pattern of ***portfolio working***.

free market ECONOMICS system of trade without government controls a market in which supply and demand are unregulated, except by the country's competition policy, and rights in physical and intellectual property are upheld

free market economy ECONOMICS economic system operating without government controls an economic system in which the government does not intervene or unduly regulate business activity

free on board OPERATIONS & PRODUCTION **1.** including all costs till goods are on carrier including in the price all the seller's costs until the goods are on the ship for transportation **2.** including all costs to point of delivery including in the price all the seller's costs until the goods are delivered to a place *Abbr* ***FOB***

free period BANKING permitted delay between credit card purchase and payment the period allowed to credit card holders before payment for credit card purchases is requested

free port INTERNATIONAL TRADE port without customs duties a port where no customs duties are charged

free reserves BANKING bank reserves without restrictions the part of a bank's reserves that are above the statutory level and so can be used for various purposes as the bank wishes

free-standing additional voluntary contributions plan PENSIONS additional personal pension a separate pension plan taken out by somebody in addition to an ***occupational pension***

free trade INTERNATIONAL TRADE unrestricted trade between nations a system in which trading of goods between one country and another takes place without any restrictions or customs barriers

free trade area *or* free trade zone INTERNATIONAL TRADE group of countries trading without restrictions a group of countries engaged in trading between themselves without restrictions or customs barriers

free trader INTERNATIONAL TRADE person favoring free trade a person who is in favor of free trade

freeze-out STOCKHOLDING & INVESTMENTS compulsory purchase of minor stockholdings in acquired company the exclusion of minority stockholders in a company that has been taken over. A freeze-out provision may exist in a ***takeover*** agreement, which permits the acquiring organization to buy the noncontrolling shares held by small stockholders. A fair price is usually set, and the freeze-out may take place at a specific time, perhaps two to five years after the takeover. A freeze-out can still take place, even if provision for it is not made in a corporate charter, by applying pressure to minority stockholders to sell their shares to the acquiring company.

freight OPERATIONS & PRODUCTION goods being transported goods loaded for onward transport, most often by sea or by air

freight forwarder OPERATIONS & PRODUCTION firm consolidating shipments of freight an organization that collects shipments from a number of businesses and consolidates them into larger shipments for economies of scale. A freight forwarder often also deals with route selection, price negotiation, and documentation of distribution, and can act as a distribution agent for a business. By consolidating loads, a freight forwarder can negotiate cheaper rates of transportation than the individual businesses and can prebook space to ensure a more rapid delivery schedule.

frequency analysis MARKETING way of comparing chances of reaching target audience a technique for comparing the number of opportunities to reach the same target audience in different media

frequency distribution STATISTICS classifying statistical data and recording frequencies in a statistical study, the process of dividing a sample of observations into classes and listing the number of observations in each class

frequency polygon STATISTICS representation of frequency a diagrammatic representation showing the values in a ***frequency distribution***

frequently asked question E-COMMERCE *see* ***FAQ***

frictional unemployment ECONOMICS temporarily between jobs a situation in which people are temporarily out of the labor market. They could be seeking a new job, incurring search delays as they apply, attending interviews, and relocating.

friction-free market MARKETS market in which competing products are very similar a market in which there is little differentiation between competing products, so that the customer has exceptional choice

friendly society BANKING in UK, association whose dues help members in need in the United Kingdom, a group of people forming an association to pay regular subscriptions to a fund that is used to help members of the group when they are in financial difficulties

fringe benefits HR & PERSONNEL supplements to main pay from employer rewards given or offered to employees in addition to their wages or salaries and included in their employment contract. Fringe benefits range from share options, company cars, expense accounts, cheap loans, medical insurance, and other types of ***incentive plan*** to discounts on company products, subsidized meals, and membership of social and health clubs. Many of these benefits are liable for tax. In the United States, a ***cafeteria plan*** permits employees to select from a variety of such benefits, although usually some are deemed to be core and not exchangeable for others. Minor benefits, sometimes appropriated rather than given, are known as ***perks***.

FRN *abbr* FINANCE, CURRENCY & EXCHANGE ***floating-rate note***

front company BUSINESS, FRAUD firm hiding illegal activities of controlling firm a company established as a legitimate business to conceal the illegal activities of the business controlling it

front end GENERAL MANAGEMENT section of firm dealing directly with customers the part of an organization that deals with customers on a face-to-face basis

front-end loading FINANCE early deduction of charges and commission the practice of taking the commission and administrative expenses from the early payments made to an investment or insurance plan. *See also* ***back-end loading***

front office GENERAL MANAGEMENT staff that interacts with customers and clients the members of staff in a financial institution or brokerage who deal directly with customers and clients. *See also* ***back office, middle office***

frozen account BANKING bank account made inoperable by court order a bank account whose funds cannot be used or withdrawn because of a court order

frozen credits BANKING credits that are not movable credits in an account which cannot be moved, usually owing to a legal dispute

FRSB *abbr* ACCOUNTING ***Financial Reporting Standards Board***

FSA *abbr* REGULATION & COMPLIANCE ***Financial Services Authority***

FSB *abbr* BUSINESS ***Federation of Small Businesses***

FT *abbr* BUSINESS, FINANCE ***Financial Times***

FT 30 MARKETS historical UK stock market index of 30 companies an index based on the stock prices of 30 influential companies on the ***London Stock Exchange***. It was established on July 1, 1935, and is the oldest continuous index in the UK. It is now less popular but its long history makes it of value to some analysts. In contrast to ***FTSE*** indices, the index constituents are equally weighted and are only removed on a company merger or failure, with final decisions being made by the editor of the ***Financial Times***. *Also called* ***Financial Times Index, FT Ordinary Index***

FTASI *abbr* MARKETS ***FTSE Actuaries Share Indices***

FT Ordinary Index MARKETS = ***FT 30***

FTSE MARKETS **1.** index company an independent company established in 1995, jointed owned by the ***Financial Times*** and the ***London Stock Exchange***, which specializes in producing indices, including stock market indices such as the ***FTSE 100***. It is based in London but has offices in the United States, Europe, and Asia. **2. (informal)** = ***FTSE 100***

FTSE 100 MARKETS stock market index of 100 largest UK companies an index of the 100 most-highly capitalized companies on the ***London Stock Exchange***. It represents over 85% of UK and 7% of global capitalization. It was established on January 3, 1984, with a base value of 1,000.

FTSE 250 MARKETS stock market index of 250 medium-capitalized UK companies an index of the 250 most-highly capitalized companies on the ***London Stock Exchange*** which are not included in the ***FTSE 100***. It represents over 12% of UK capitalization and was established on October 12, 1992, with a base value of 1,412.6 at December 31, 1985.

FTSE 350 MARKETS stock market index of 350 large and medium-capitalized UK companies an index of the 350 most-highly capitalized companies on the ***London Stock Exchange***. It is an aggregation of the ***FTSE 100*** and ***FTSE 250*** indices.

FTSE Actuaries Share Indices MARKETS several indices based on London stock prices several indices based on prices on the London Stock Exchange, which are calculated by and published in the *Financial Times* in conjunction with the Actuaries Investment Research Committee. *Abbr* ***FTASI***

FTSE All-Share MARKETS broad stock market index of UK companies an index of companies on the ***London Stock Exchange***. Often used as a performance measure of the overall London equity market, it is an aggregation of the ***FTSE 100, FTSE 250***, and ***FTSE SmallCap***. It was established as the FT Actuaries All-Share Index on November 26, 1962, with a base value of 100 at April 10, 1962.

FTSE/JSE Top 40 MARKETS main South African stock market index a stock market index that tracks the 40 largest companies on the ***Johannesburg Stock Exchange*** ranked by full market value. It was established on June 24, 2002, with a base value of 10,300.31. *Also called* ***JSE Top 40***

FTSE MIB MARKETS main Italian stock market index an index of the 40 most-highly capitalized companies on the ***Borsa Italiana*** exchange. It was established on October 31, 2003, as the S&P/MIB index with a base value of 10,644, replacing the MIB 30 index. It was renamed the FTSE MIB index after ***FTSE*** took over running the index from ***S&P***. *Also called* ***S&P/MIB***

FTSE SmallCap MARKETS stock market index of small-capitalized UK companies an index of the companies listed on the main market of the ***London Stock Exchange*** which are outside the ***FTSE 350*** due to their small capitalization

FTSE TMT MARKETS stock market index of UK technology, media, and telecom companies an index which indicates the performance of companies in the United Kingdom in three key business areas: technology, media, and telecommunications.

fulfillment MARKETING dealing with approaches from customers the process of responding to customer inquiries, orders, or sales promotion offers

fulfillment house MARKETING firm handling approaches from customers for others an organization that specializes in responding to inquiries, orders, or sales promotion offers on behalf of a client

full bank BANKING bank offering full domestic and international services a local or foreign bank permitted to engage in the full range of domestic and international services

full cost accounting ACCOUNTING = ***environmental accounting***

full coupon bond STOCKHOLDING & INVESTMENTS bond with competitive interest rate a bond whose interest rate is competitive in the current market

full cover *UK* INSURANCE = ***full coverage***

full coverage *US* INSURANCE insurance for most risks insurance that provides coverage against a wide range of risks. *UK term* ***full cover***

full employment HR & PERSONNEL situation in which all capable workers have jobs a situation in which all the people who are fit to work have jobs

full faith and credit FINANCE US government debt repayment guarantee an unconditional guarantee by the US government to repay the principal and interest on all its debt

full price OPERATIONS & PRODUCTION standard price with no discounts the regular price for a product, with no special discounts applied

full rate OPERATIONS & PRODUCTION standard charge with no discounts the standard charge for a service, with no special discounts applied

full-service banking BANKING provision of banking and financial services a type of banking that offers a whole range of services including mortgages, loans, and pension plans

  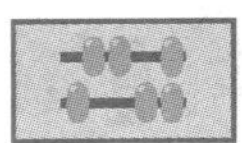   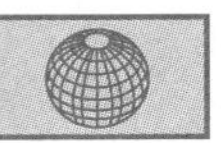   

full-service broker FINANCE broker managing portfolios and giving financial advice a broker who manages portfolios for clients, and gives advice on stocks and financial questions in general

full time HR & PERSONNEL standard working hours the standard hours of attendance expected in an organization. *See also* ***part time***

Fully Automated Screen Trading and Electronic Registration MARKETS *see* ***FASTER***

fully connected world GENERAL MANAGEMENT population in touch by networks a world in which most people and organizations are linked by networks such as the Internet

fully diluted earnings per (common) share STOCKHOLDING & INVESTMENTS earnings including commitments to issue more stocks the amount earned per share taking into account commitments to issue more shares, for example, as a result of convertibles, stock options, or warrants

fully diluted earnings per share STOCKHOLDING & INVESTMENTS earnings per share taken over all ordinary shares the amount earned per share calculated over the whole number of shares on the assumption that convertible shares and options have been converted to ordinary shares

fully diluted shares STOCKHOLDING & INVESTMENTS total shares, including convertible shares and stock options total number of shares that would be outstanding assuming that convertible shares have been converted to ordinary shares and that stock options have been exercised

fully distributed issue STOCKHOLDING & INVESTMENTS issue fully sold out to investors an issue of stocks sold entirely to investors rather than being held by dealers

full year ACCOUNTING 12 months a 12-month period, especially with reference to financial information such as earnings, sales, profits, and outlook for the future

full-year forecast ACCOUNTING prediction of future 12 months' earnings or losses a prediction of the expected earnings or losses of a business for the future over a 12-month period

full-year results ACCOUNTING past 12 months of financial data the financial information of a business, especially its profits or losses, calculated for the preceding 12-month period

fully paid share capital *or* fully paid-up capital STOCKHOLDING & INVESTMENTS total paid by investors for capital holdings the amount of the share capital when all calls have been paid on all issued shares. *See also* ***called-up share capital, paid-up capital***

functional budget TREASURY MANAGEMENT budget for activity or department a budget of income and/or expenditure applicable to a specific function. A function may refer to a process or a department. Functional budgets frequently include the following: production cost budget (based on a forecast of production and plant utilization); marketing cost budget; sales budget; personnel budget; purchasing budget; and research and development budget. *See also* ***departmental budget***

functional relationship STATISTICS relationship between statistical variables the relationship between variables in a statistical study in which there is no bias or any other distorting factor

fund FINANCE **1.** money earmarked for something an amount of money set aside for a particular purpose **2.** money invested money invested in an investment trust as part of a mutual fund, or given to a financial adviser to invest on behalf of a client. *See also* ***funds*** **3.** supply money for purpose to provide an amount of money for a particular purpose. *See also* ***finance***

fundamental accounting concepts ACCOUNTING basic assumptions for accounts broad basic assumptions that underlie the periodic financial accounts of business enterprises. *See also* ***concepts***

fundamental analysis STOCKHOLDING & INVESTMENTS assessment of influences affecting firm's performance an assessment of how the external and internal influences on a company's activities should affect investment decisions. *See also* ***technical analysis***

fundamentals BUSINESS, MARKETS most basic business components the basic components such as assets, profitability, and dividends of a company or a stock market

funded FINANCE **1.** backed by long-term loans supported by money in the form of long-term loans **2.** based on a fund a future financial commitment, such as the payment of a pension, that is supported by an existing fund of money

funded debt FINANCE long- or medium-term debt long-term debt or debt that has a maturity date in excess of one year. Funded debt is usually issued in the public markets or in the form of a private placement to qualified institutional investors.

fund family STOCKHOLDING & INVESTMENTS = ***family of funds***

funding FINANCE **1.** finance for business or project the financial support that is available for a business or project **2.** changing short-term debt into long-term loan the conversion of a short-term debt into a loan that has a maturity date in excess of one year

funding risk RISK likelihood of difficulty in raising funds the risk that it might be difficult to realize assets or otherwise raise funds to meet commitments associated with ***financial instruments***. *See also* ***liquidity risk***

fund management STOCKHOLDING & INVESTMENTS business of investing clients' money the business of dealing with the investment of sums of money on behalf of clients

fund manager STOCKHOLDING & INVESTMENTS manager of investments somebody who manages the investments of a mutual fund or other financial institution. *Also called* ***investment manager***

Fund Managers' Association STOCKHOLDING & INVESTMENTS UK organization for fund managers an association representing the interests of UK-based institutional fund managers. It now forms part of the ***Investment Management Association***. *Abbr* ***FMA***

fund of funds STOCKHOLDING & INVESTMENTS mutual fund investing in several underlying mutual funds a registered mutual fund that invests in a variety of underlying mutual funds. Subscribers own units in the fund of funds, not in the underlying mutual funds.

funds FINANCE money available to spend money that is available to a person, business, or organization for spending. *See also* ***insufficient funds***

fungibility BUSINESS, FINANCE interchangeability of product the ability to be easily substituted for or combined with another similar product

fungible **1.** FINANCE substitutable indistinguishable for business purposes from other items of the same type. Such products may be easily combined in making up shipments. **2.** STOCKHOLDING & INVESTMENTS interchangeable used to describe an asset, especially a security, that can be exchanged for a similar asset

funny money **1.** CURRENCY & EXCHANGE forged currency money that is counterfeit or forged **2.** FRAUD questionable money money obtained from a legally or morally suspect source

future STOCKHOLDING & INVESTMENTS contract for future delivery a contract to deliver a commodity at a future date at a fixed price. *Also called* ***futures contract***

future delivery OPERATIONS & PRODUCTION delivery at prearranged future date a delivery at some date in the future that has been arranged by the buyer and seller

future option STOCKHOLDING & INVESTMENTS contract for future trade at set price a contract in which somebody agrees to buy or sell an option for purchasing or selling a commodity, currency, or security at a prearranged price for delivery in the future. *Also called* ***futures option***

futures STOCKHOLDING & INVESTMENTS items traded now for later delivery stock, currency, or commodities that are bought or sold now for delivery at a later date

futures commission merchant STOCKHOLDING & INVESTMENTS broker for futures somebody who acts as a broker for ***futures contracts***. *Abbr* ***FCM***

futures contract STOCKHOLDING & INVESTMENTS *see* ***future***

futures exchange CURRENCY & EXCHANGE exchange for futures an exchange on which ***futures contracts*** are traded

futures market MARKETS market for trade in items with fluctuating prices a market for buying and selling securities, commodities, or currencies that tend to fluctuate in price over a period of time. The market's goal is to reduce the risk of uncertainty about prices in the period ahead.

futures option STOCKHOLDING & INVESTMENTS *see* ***future option***

futures research GENERAL MANAGEMENT consideration of what could happen in future the identification of possible future ***scenarios*** with the goal of anticipating and perhaps influencing what the future holds. Futures research is important to the process of ***issues management***. It usually identifies several possible scenarios for any set of circumstances, and enables an informed decision to be made.

future value FINANCE projected value of sum of money the value that a sum of money will have in the future, taking into account the effects of inflation, interest rates, or currency values.

Future value calculations require three figures: the sum in question, the percentage by which it will increase or decrease, and the period of time. In this example, these figures are $1,000, 11%, and two years.

At an interest rate of 11%, the sum of $1,000 will grow to $1,232 in two years:

$1,000 × 1.11 = $1,110 (first year) × 1.11

= $1,232 (second year, rounded to whole dollars)

Note that the interest earned in the first year generates additional interest in the second year, a practice known as compounding. When large sums are in question, the effect of compounding can be significant.

At an inflation rate of 11%, by comparison, the sum of $1,000 will shrink to $812 in two years:

$1,000 × 1.11 = $901 (first year) × 1.11

= $812 (second year, rounded to whole dollars)

In order to avoid errors, it is important to express the percentage as 1.11 and multiply and divide by that figure, instead of using 11%; and to calculate each year, quarter, or month separately. *See also* ***present value***

futuristic planning GENERAL MANAGEMENT planning for potentially radically different future planning for a period that extends beyond the planning horizon in the form of future expected conditions that may exist in respect of the entity, products/services, and environment, but that cannot usefully be expressed in quantified terms. An example would be working out the actions needed in a future with no automobiles.

futurize GENERAL MANAGEMENT keep technologically up to date to ensure that an organization is taking full advantage of the latest technologies

fuzzy accounting ACCOUNTING, FRAUD accounting practices that mislead investors company accounting practices designed to inflate earnings or earnings estimates in order to attract investors

fuzzy search E-COMMERCE computer search giving near and exact matches a computer search that returns not only exact matches to the search request, but also close matches that include possibilities and allow for such things as spelling errors

FWB *abbr* MARKETS ***Frankfurter Wertpapierbörse***

FY *abbr* ACCOUNTING ***fiscal year***

G

G7 FINANCE group of seven major industrial nations the group of seven major industrial nations established in 1985 to discuss the world economy, consisting of Canada, France, Germany, Italy, Japan, the United Kingdom, and the United States. *Full form* ***Group of Seven***

G8 FINANCE G7 countries plus Russia the group of eight major industrial nations consisting of the ***G7*** plus Russia. *Full form* ***Group of Eight***

G10 FINANCE nations contributing to General Arrangements to Borrow fund the group of ten countries who contribute to the General Arrangements to Borrow fund: Belgium, Canada, France, Germany, Italy, Japan, the Netherlands, Sweden, the United States, and the United Kingdom. Switzerland joined in 1984. *Full form* ***Group of Ten***. *Also called* ***Paris Club***

G20 ECONOMICS group of industrial and emerging countries a forum for discussion between 20 industrialized and emerging-market countries on issues related to global economic stability. *Full form* ***Group of Twenty***

GAAP *abbr* ACCOUNTING ***Generally Accepted Accounting Principles***

GAB FINANCE international fund providing large loans to countries a fund financed by the ***G10*** that is used when the IMF's own resources are insufficient, for example, when there is a need for large loans to one or more industrialized countries. *Full form* ***General Arrangements to Borrow***

gain FINANCE increase in amount or value an increase in the amount or level of something, for example, in a company's profit or in the value of stocks on a stock exchange

gain sharing FINANCE sharing profits from efficiency improvements with employees a group-based ***bonus plan*** to share profits from improvements in production efficiency between employees and the company

galloping inflation ECONOMICS very rapid inflation inflation that increases rapidly by large amounts

game theory GENERAL MANAGEMENT technique for investigating consequences of strategies and conflicts a mathematical technique used in ***operational research*** to analyze and predict the outcomes of games of strategy and conflicts of interest. Game theory is used to represent conflicts and problems involved in formulating marketing and organizational strategy, with the goal of identifying and implementing optimal strategies. It involves assessing likely strategies to be adopted by players in a given situation under a particular set of rules.

gamma STOCKHOLDING & INVESTMENTS rate of change in option price the rate of change in the ***delta*** of an option for a unit change in the price of the underlying asset. It is a measure of ***convexity***.

gap analysis **1.** FINANCE analyzing shortfall between current results and ultimate goals a method of improving a company's financial performance by analyzing the reasons for the gap between current results and long-term objectives **2.** MARKETING investigation of gaps in market or availability a marketing technique used to identify gaps in market or product coverage. In gap analysis, consumer information or requirements are tabulated and matched to product categories in order to identify product or service opportunities or gaps in product planning.

gap financing FINANCE short-term loan arrangement the process of arranging an extra loan such as a ***bridge loan*** in order to make a purchase not fully covered by an existing loan

garage **1.** MARKETS part of New York Stock Exchange the annex to the main floor of the ***New York Stock Exchange*** **2.** *UK* TAX move assets or liabilities for tax advantage to transfer assets or liabilities from one financial center to another to take advantage of a tax benefit

garbatrage *US* STOCKHOLDING & INVESTMENTS stocks benefiting from unrelated takeover stocks that rise because of a ***takeover*** but that are not connected to the target company (slang)

garden leave GENERAL MANAGEMENT full pay without working in a ***contract of employment***, a clause that allows the employer to keep an employee on full pay, but not require him or her to work, during the employee's contractual ***notice period***. Garden leave thereby prevents the employee from working for another employer until the notice period has expired, by which time any confidential information the employee holds is likely to have become commercially out of date.

garnishee FINANCE person ordered to redirect debt payment to another a person who owes money to a creditor and is ordered by a court to pay that money to a creditor of the original creditor, and not to the actual creditor

garnishee order LEGAL order requiring debt payment to third party a court order, making somebody pay money not directly to a creditor, but to a third party. For example, a court may order an employer to take money from an employee's pay and pay it to somebody to whom the employee owes money. *Also called* ***garnishment*** *(sense 2)*

garnishment **1.** FINANCE withholding of income to repay debt a procedure by which wages or salary are withheld from an employee in order to pay off the employee's debt **2.** LEGAL = ***garnishee order***

GAS *abbr* ACCOUNTING ***Government Accountancy Service***

gatekeeper GENERAL MANAGEMENT controller of dissemination of information somebody within an organization who controls the flow of information and therefore influences policy

gateway E-COMMERCE where computer networks meet and exchange data a point where two or more computer networks meet and can exchange data

GATT INTERNATIONAL TRADE international treaty promoting multilateral trade a treaty signed in Geneva in 1947 that aimed to foster multilateral trade and settle trading disputes between adherent countries. Initially signed by 23 nations, it started to reduce trade tariffs and, as it was accepted by more and more countries, tackled other barriers to trade. It was replaced on January 1, 1995, by the World Trade Organization. *Full form* ***General Agreement on Tariffs and Trade***

gazump *UK* REAL ESTATE accept higher offer, negating earlier verbal agreement to agree verbally to sell to one buyer, but before the agreement becomes legally binding, to accept a higher offer from another buyer. Gazumping is usually associated with the real estate market, although it can occur in any market where the prices are rising rapidly.

gazunder *UK* REAL ESTATE undercut price verbally agreed earlier to agree verbally to buy at one price, but before the agreement becomes legally binding, to offer a lower price. Gazundering is usually associated with the real estate market, although it can occur in any market where the prices are falling rapidly.

GBE *abbr* GENERAL MANAGEMENT ***Government Business Enterprise***

GB pound CURRENCY & EXCHANGE = ***pound sterling***

GDP ECONOMICS all goods and services produced by economy the total flow of goods and services produced by an economy over a quarter or a year, measured by the aggregate value of goods and services at market prices. *Full form* ***gross domestic product***

GDP per capita ECONOMICS total economic output divided by population ***GDP*** divided by the country's population so as to achieve a figure per person in the population

GEAR ECONOMICS redistributive economic program in S. Africa the macroeconomic reform program of the South African government, intended to foster

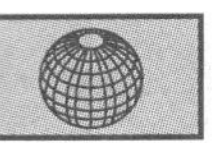

economic growth, create employment, and redistribute income and opportunities in favor of the poor. *Full form* ***Growth, Employment, and Redistribution***

geared investment trust *UK* STOCKHOLDING & INVESTMENTS = ***leveraged investment company***

gearing FINANCE, RISK = ***financial leverage***

gearing ratios FINANCE = ***leverage ratios***

geisha bond STOCKHOLDING & INVESTMENTS = ***shogun bond***

general account MARKETS account with investment broker who lends money the US Federal Reserve Board's term for a ***margin account*** set up for a brokerage customer

General Agreement on Tariffs and Trade INTERNATIONAL TRADE *see* ***GATT***

General Arrangements to Borrow FINANCE *see* ***GAB***

general audit ACCOUNTING comprehensive examination of firm's accounts an examination of all books and accounts belonging to a company

general average INSURANCE sharing of insured loss by all policyholders a process by which the cost of lost goods is shared by all parties to an insurance policy, as in cases when some goods have been lost in an attempt to save the rest of the cargo

General Commissioners TAX in UK, officials appointed to hear tax appeals in the United Kingdom, an independent group of people from a variety of backgrounds appointed by the Lord Chancellor to hear appeals from taxpayers against Her Majesty's Revenue & Customs. In Scotland, Commissioners are appointed by Scottish ministers.

general expenses ACCOUNTING routine costs of running business minor expenses of various kinds incurred in the running of a business

general fund FINANCE mutual fund with wide-ranging investments a mutual fund that has investments in a variety of stocks

general insurance INSURANCE insurance against losses excluding life insurance insurance relating to various potential losses such as theft or damage, but excluding life insurance

general ledger ACCOUNTING book listing firm's financial transactions a book that lists all of the financial transactions of a company

general lien LEGAL **1.** right to hold property until debt paid a right to hold the goods or property of a debtor until a debt has been paid **2.** right to hold debtor's personal property only a right to hold the personal possessions of a debtor until a debt is paid, but not his or her house or land. *See also* ***banker's lien***

Generally Accepted Accounting Principles ACCOUNTING guidelines relating to fair accounting practices a summary of best practice in respect to the form and content of financial statements and auditors' reports, and of accounting policies and disclosures adopted for the preparation of financial information. GAAP has statutory or regulatory authority in the United States and Canada and some other countries, but not in the United Kingdom. *Abbr* ***GAAP***

general manager GENERAL MANAGEMENT manager involved in all aspects of organization a ***manager*** whose work encompasses all areas of an organization. A general manager is traditionally a nonspecialist, has a working knowledge of all aspects of an organization's activities, and oversees all operating functions. In large companies and the public sector, specialist managers with expert knowledge may control departments, while a general manager provides unifying ***leadership*** from the top.

general meeting CORPORATE GOVERNANCE meeting of company's stockholders a meeting of all the stockholders of a company or of all the members of an organization

General National Mortgage Association MORTGAGES *see* ***Ginnie Mae***

general obligation bond STOCKHOLDING & INVESTMENTS municipal bond financing public undertakings a municipal or state bond that is repaid out of general funds. *Abbr* ***GO bond***

general partner BUSINESS partner in firm who has no limited liability a partner in a business whose responsibility for its debts is not limited and whose personal assets may be at risk if the company's assets are not sufficient to discharge its debts

general partnership BUSINESS business where all partners share profits and liabilities a business in which each partner has a share in the administration, profits, and losses of the operation

general undertaking REGULATION & COMPLIANCE directors' undertaking to obey Stock Exchange regulations an agreement, signed by all the directors of a company applying for Stock Exchange listing, that promises that they will work within the regulations of the Stock Exchange

generative learning GENERAL MANAGEMENT learning that fosters experimentation and open-mindedness a style of organizational learning that encourages experimentation, risk taking, openness, and system-wide thinking. Organizations have successfully used this style of learning to transform themselves in the face of technological, social, and market change. ***Adaptive learning*** is a contrasting approach.

generic strategy MARKETING marketing strategy any of three strategies for marketing products or services: cost leadership, differentiation, and focus. The first implies supplying products in a more cost-effective way than competitors; the second refers to adding value to products or services; and the third focuses on a specific product market segment with the goal of establishing a monopoly.

gensaki STOCKHOLDING & INVESTMENTS bond sale incorporating repurchase agreement the Japanese term for a bond sale incorporating a repurchase agreement at a later date

gentleman's agreement GENERAL MANAGEMENT reliable unwritten agreement a verbal agreement between two people who trust each other to keep the agreement without a formal contract

Gesellschaft mit beschränkter Haftung BUSINESS *see* ***GmbH***

gharar FINANCE uncertainty prohibited in Islamic business dealings in Islamic financing, excessive uncertainty in a business transaction of any type. It is one of three prohibitions in Islamic law, the others being ***maysir*** and ***riba***.

ghosting MARKETS, FRAUD illegal price fixing of stock an illegal practice in which two or more market makers, who are required by law to compete, join to influence the price of a stock

Giffen good ECONOMICS = ***inferior good***

Gift Aid TAX in UK, tax advantage on gifts to charity in the United Kingdom, a system through which a charity receiving a gift of money from a taxpayer can also directly receive the tax that had been paid on the sum at the standard rate

gift inter vivos TAX gift between living persons a gift that is made to another living person. *Abbr* ***GIV***

gift-leaseback TAX leasing back of gifted property the practice of giving somebody a property and then leasing it back, usually for tax advantage or charitable purposes

gift tax TAX in US, tax paid by giver on gift in the United States, a tax on money or property given to another living person, which is to be paid by the giver. Exemptions exist for gifts below a specific value, gifts between spouses, etc.

gift with reservation FINANCE gift that benefits donor in some way in the United Kingdom, a gift with some benefit retained for the donor, for example, the legal transfer of a dwelling when the donor continues in residence

gilt STOCKHOLDING & INVESTMENTS = ***gilt-edged security***

gilt-edged STOCKHOLDING & INVESTMENTS issued by blue-chip company used to describe a security issued by a blue-chip company, which is therefore considered very secure (informal)

gilt-edged security STOCKHOLDING & INVESTMENTS UK government security paying regular fixed interest in the United Kingdom, a ***security*** issued by the government that pays a fixed rate of interest on a regular basis for a specific period of time until the ***redemption date***, when the principal is returned. Their names, for example, Exchequer $10\frac{1}{2}$% 2005 (abbreviated to Ex $10\frac{1}{2}$% '05) or Treasury $11\frac{3}{4}$% 2003–07 (abbreviated to Tr $11\frac{3}{4}$% '03–'07) indicate the rate and redemption date. Thought to have originated in the 17th century to help fund the war with France, today they form a large part of the ***national debt***. *Also called* ***gilt***. *See also* ***index-linked gilt, short-dated gilts***

gilt repos MARKETS UK market in trading gilts in the United Kingdom, the market in prearranged sales and repurchase of ***gilt-edged securities***, launched in 1996 by the ***Bank of England*** to make gilts more attractive to overseas investors

gilt strip STOCKHOLDING & INVESTMENTS UK bond yielding single cash payment at maturity in the United Kingdom, a ***zero coupon bond*** created by splitting the interest payments from a gilt-edged security so that it produces a single cash payment at maturity

gilt unit trust STOCKHOLDING & INVESTMENTS UK mutual fund investing in gilts in the United Kingdom, a mutual fund where the underlying investments are ***gilt-edged securities***

Ginnie Mae MORTGAGES US securities agency in the United States, a government agency that issues mortgage-backed bonds. *Full form* ***General National Mortgage Association***

giro 1. BANKING UK bank transfer in the United Kingdom, a system of transferring money from one bank account to another. *Also called* ***bank giro*** **2.** FINANCE UK state benefit in the United Kingdom, a benefit paid by the state (slang)

GIV *abbr* TAX ***gift inter vivos***

give up MARKETS three-way trade a transaction involving three brokers in which broker A, who is busy, asks broker B to execute a trade for a client with broker C. The trade is recorded as broker A's transaction, so broker A receives a commission, and broker B, who actually executed the trade, gives up the transaction.

glamour stock STOCKHOLDING & INVESTMENTS fashionable investment a currently fashionable and popular security (slang)

Glass–Steagall Act REGULATION & COMPLIANCE US law separating banking and brokerage industries in the United States, a law enacted in 1933 that enforces the separation of the banking and brokerage industries. Some provisions have since been repealed, most notably: (i) allowing the Federal Reserve to regulate interest rates in savings accounts, and (ii) prohibiting a bank holding company from owning other financial companies.

global bank BANKING bank with worldwide business a bank that is active in the international markets and has a presence in several continents

global bond STOCKHOLDING & INVESTMENTS = ***Eurobond***

global bond issue STOCKHOLDING & INVESTMENTS bond issue allowing transfer of titles between markets an issue of a bond that incorporates a settlement mechanism allowing for the transfer of titles between markets

global brand MARKETING brand name known everywhere the brand name of a product that has worldwide recognition. A global brand has the advantage of economies of scale in terms of production, recognition, and packaging. *Also called* ***global product***

global coordinator STOCKHOLDING & INVESTMENTS overall manager of global stock issue the lead manager of a global offering who is responsible for overseeing the entire issue and is usually supported by regional and national coordinators

global custody FINANCE bundle of financial services for institutional investors a financial service, usually available to institutional investors only, that includes the safekeeping of securities certificates issued in markets across the world, the collection of dividends, dealing with tax, valuation of investments, foreign exchange, and the settlement of transactions

global depositary receipt STOCKHOLDING & INVESTMENTS certificate for shares of stock traded abroad a certificate held by a bank in one country representing shares of stock that are traded on an exchange in a foreign country but can be purchased through various banks worldwide

global economy ECONOMICS, INTERNATIONAL TRADE international trade relations the economic relations between countries in a world where markets in individual countries have now spread beyond national boundaries and are more integrated with those of other countries. *Also called* ***world economy***

global hedge STOCKHOLDING & INVESTMENTS = ***macrohedge***

globalization GENERAL MANAGEMENT expanding operations worldwide the creation of international strategies by organizations for overseas expansion and operation on a worldwide level. The process of globalization has been precipitated by a number of factors, including rapid technology developments that make global communications possible, political developments such as the fall of communism, and transportation developments that make traveling faster and more frequent. These produce greater development opportunities for companies with the opening up of additional markets, allow greater customer harmonization as a result of the increase in shared cultural values, and provide a superior competitive position with lower operating costs in other countries and access to new raw materials, resources, and investment opportunities.

global marketing MARKETING marketing to sell products worldwide a marketing strategy used mainly by multinational companies to sell goods or services internationally. Global marketing requires that there be harmonization between the marketing policies for different countries and that the marketing mix for the different countries can be adapted to the local market conditions. Global marketing is sometimes used to refer to overseas expansion efforts through ***licensing***, ***franchises***, and ***joint ventures***.

global marketplace ECONOMICS, INTERNATIONAL TRADE market encompassing whole world a worldwide trading system that has grown up since the 1970s, in which goods can be produced wherever the production costs are cheapest wherever they are ultimately sold

global offering STOCKHOLDING & INVESTMENTS worldwide offering of securities the offering of securities in several markets simultaneously, for example, in Europe, the Far East, and North America

global pricing contract OPERATIONS & PRODUCTION contract for single worldwide price a contract between a customer and a supplier whereby the supplier agrees to charge the customer the same price for the delivery of parts or services anywhere in the world. As ***globalization*** increases, more customers are likely to press their suppliers for global pricing contracts. Through such contracts suppliers can benefit by gaining access to new markets and growing their business, achieving economies of scale, developing strong relationships with customers, and thereby gaining a ***competitive advantage*** that is difficult for competitors to break. There are risks involved, too, for example, being in the middle of a conflict between a customer's head office and its local business units, or being tied to one customer when there are more attractive customers to serve.

global product MARKETING *see* ***global brand***

glocalization GENERAL MANAGEMENT expanding and adapting operations worldwide the process of tailoring products or services to different local markets around the world. Glocalization is a combination of globalization and localization. Improved communications and advances in technology have made worldwide markets accessible to even small companies but, rather than being homogenous, the global market is in fact made up of many different localities. Success in a globalized environment is more likely if products are not globalized or mass marketed, but glocalized and customized for individual local communities that have different needs and different cultural approaches.

glue GENERAL MANAGEMENT unifying factor a common factor such as information that unifies organizations, supply chains, and other commercial groups (informal)

GM *abbr* **1.** FINANCE ***gross margin*** *(sense 1)* **2.** ACCOUNTING ***gross margin*** *(sense 2)* **3.** OPERATIONS & PRODUCTION ***gross margin*** *(sense 3)*

GmbH BUSINESS corporation the German term for a corporation. *Full form* ***Gesellschaft mit beschränkter Haftung***

GNMA MORTGAGES *see* ***Ginnie Mae***

gnomes of Zurich BANKING Swiss bankers bankers and currency dealers based in Switzerland, who have a reputation for secrecy. The term is often used to refer in a derogatory way to unknown currency speculators who cause upheavals in the currency markets (informal)

GNP ECONOMICS country's total economic output plus foreign investment income the ***GDP*** plus domestic residents' income from investment abroad less income earned in the domestic market accruing to noncitizens abroad. *Full form* ***gross national product***

GNP per capita ECONOMICS GNP divided by population the ***GNP*** divided by the country's population so as to achieve a figure per person in the population

goal GENERAL MANAGEMENT target of effort an end toward which effort is directed and on which resources are focused, usually to achieve an organization's strategy. There is considerable discussion on whether objective, goal, target, and aim are the same. In general usage, the terms are often interchangeable, so it is important that, if an organization has a particular meaning for one of these terms, it must define it in its documentation. Sometimes an objective is seen as the desired final end result, while a goal is a smaller step on the road to it.

GO bond STOCKHOLDING & INVESTMENTS = ***general obligation bond***

go-go fund STOCKHOLDING & INVESTMENTS, RISK high-risk mutual fund a mutual fund that trades heavily and predominantly in high-return, high-risk investments

going concern BUSINESS company currently trading a company that is actively trading and making a profit

going short FINANCE selling asset for repurchase at lower price borrowing and then selling an asset one does not own with the intention of acquiring it at a later date at a lower price for delivery to the purchaser. *See also* ***bear***

gold bond STOCKHOLDING & INVESTMENTS bond with gold as collateral a bond for which gold is collateral, often issued by mining companies

gold bug STOCKHOLDING & INVESTMENTS investor who believes gold prices will rise a person who believes that gold is the best investment

gold bullion FINANCE gold bars gold in the form of bars

gold card BANKING credit card for wealthy customer a gold-colored credit card, generally issued to customers with above average incomes, that may include additional benefits such as an overdraft at an advantageous interest rate. It may require an annual fee.

gold certificate LEGAL document stating ownership of gold a document that shows ownership of gold that the owner may not be storing

golden handcuffs FINANCE financial incentive to remain in organization a financial incentive paid to encourage employees to remain in an organization and dissuade them from leaving for a rival business or to start their own company (informal)

  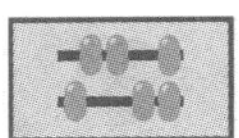   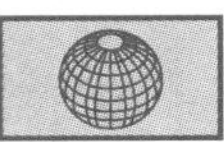   

golden handshake *or* golden goodbye FINANCE generous payment for departing senior executive a sum of money given to a senior executive on his or her involuntary departure from an employing organization as a form of severance pay. A golden handshake can be offered when an executive is required to leave before the expiration of his or her contract, for example, because of a ***merger*** or corporate restructuring. It is intended as compensation for loss of office. It can be a very large sum of money, but often it is not related to the perceived performance of the executive concerned (informal)

golden hello FINANCE **1.** generous financial arrangement for new employee a welcome package for a new employee which may include a bonus and stock options. A golden hello is designed as an incentive to attract employees. Some of the contents of the welcome package may be contingent on the performance of the employee. **2.** support for employer hiring new employee a payment from a government to an employer who takes on new staff when jobs are hard to find in a recession

golden parachute *or* golden umbrella FINANCE generous financial package on dismissal from employment a clause inserted in the contract of employment of a senior employee that details a financial package payable if the employee is dismissed. A golden parachute provides an executive with a measure of financial security and may be payable if the employee leaves the organization following a ***takeover*** or ***merger***, or is dismissed as a result of poor performance.

golden share STOCKHOLDING & INVESTMENTS government's controlling interest in newly privatized company a controlling interest retained by a government in a company that has been privatized after having been in public ownership

gold fix *or* gold fixing FINANCE twice-daily setting of gold price a system by which the world price for gold is set twice a day in US dollars on the London Gold Exchange and in Paris and Zurich

gold point CURRENCY & EXCHANGE price variation in gold-backed currency an amount by which a currency that is linked to gold can vary in price

gold reserve CURRENCY & EXCHANGE central bank's gold holdings gold coins or bullion held by a central bank to support a paper currency and provide security for borrowing

gold standard CURRENCY & EXCHANGE system valuing currency against gold a system in which a currency unit is defined in terms of its value in gold

good faith deposit FINANCE sum given to confirm deal a deposit made by a buyer to a seller to show a firm intention to complete the transaction

good for the day STOCKHOLDING & INVESTMENTS describing instructions valid only on specific day used to describe instructions to a broker that are valid only for the specific day indicated

good for this week *or* good for this month *UK* STOCKHOLDING & INVESTMENTS = ***good this week, good this month***

goods OPERATIONS & PRODUCTION things that are bought and sold items, materials, and products that can be transported and are for sale

goods and chattels FINANCE movable personal property movable personal possessions, as opposed to land and buildings

Goods and Services Tax TAX **1.** Australian tax on goods and services in Australia, a government-imposed consumption tax of 10% introduced on July 1, 2000, added to the retail cost of goods and services **2.** Canadian national tax on goods and services in Canada, a national ***value-added tax*** levied by the federal government on goods and services. In some provinces it is charged alongside ***Provincial Sales Tax*** or combined with this as ***Harmonized Sales Tax***. *Abbr* ***GST***

goods received note OPERATIONS & PRODUCTION receipt for goods a record of goods issued at the point of receipt

good this week *or* good this month *US* STOCKHOLDING & INVESTMENTS valid only during specific week/month used to describe instructions to a broker that are valid only for the duration of the week/month given. *Abbr* ***GTW***, ***GTM***. UK terms ***good for this week***, ***good for this month***

good 'til cancel MARKETS order effective until canceled used to describe an order to buy or sell a security that is effective until an investor cancels it, up to a maximum of 60 days. *Abbr* ***GTC***

good title LEGAL unquestionable property ownership ownership of a property that cannot be legally challenged successfully. *Also called* ***clear title***

goodwill ACCOUNTING business assets such as reputation and expertise an ***intangible asset*** of a company which includes factors such as reputation, contacts, and expertise, for which a buyer of the company may have to pay a premium.

Goodwill becomes an intangible asset when a company has been acquired by another. It then appears on a balance sheet in the amount by which the price paid by the acquiring company exceeds the net tangible assets of the acquired company. In other words

Purchase price – Net assets = Goodwill

If an airline is bought for $12 billion and its net assets are valued at $9 billion, $3 billion of the purchase would be allocated to goodwill on the balance sheet.

go private STOCKHOLDING & INVESTMENTS change to private status without stock market listing to revert from being a public limited company quoted on a stock exchange to a private company without a stock market listing

go public STOCKHOLDING & INVESTMENTS become public corporation to place stock of a private company for sale on a stock exchange in order to raise funds

gourde CURRENCY & EXCHANGE Haitian currency unit a unit of currency used in Haiti

governance CORPORATE GOVERNANCE management of firm the process of managing a company, especially with respect to the soundness or otherwise of its management

Government Accountancy Service ACCOUNTING body monitoring accounting practice in UK Civil Service in the United Kingdom, a part of ***HM Treasury*** whose remit is to ensure that best accounting practice is observed and conducted across the whole of the Civil Service. *Abbr* ***GAS***

government bond STOCKHOLDING & INVESTMENTS investment product issued by government a bond or other security issued by a government on a regular basis as a method of borrowing money for government expenditure

government borrowing FINANCE money government borrows to fund public spending the total amount of money that a country's central government has borrowed to fund its spending on public services and benefits. *See also* ***national debt***

Government Business Enterprise GENERAL MANAGEMENT partly nationalized Australian business an Australian business that is fully or partly owned by the state. *Abbr* ***GBE***

Government National Mortgage Association MORTGAGES *see* ***Ginnie Mae***

government securities/stock STOCKHOLDING & INVESTMENTS securities or stock issued by government securities or stock such as US Treasury bonds or UK gilt-edged securities that are issued by a government

GPM *abbr* MORTGAGES ***graduated payments mortgage***

graduated payments mortgage MORTGAGES US mortgage with initial low payments in the United States, a mortgage with a fixed interest rate but with low payments that gradually increase over the first few years. *Abbr* ***GPM***

graduated pension scheme PENSIONS former UK government pension linking benefits to individual salaries in the United Kingdom, a government pension arrangement where the benefit was calculated as a percentage of a person's salary. Former contributors still receive payments but there are no new contributors.

graduated tax TAX = ***progressive tax***

grand total FINANCE sum of all subtotals the final total, which is a result of adding several subtotals

granny bond *UK* STOCKHOLDING & INVESTMENTS savings type for older people a long-term savings opportunity for older people, with a tax advantage or a return linked to the rate of inflation (informal) *See also* ***index-linked savings certificate***

grant **1.** FINANCE money given to fund something money given by a government or other organization to help pay for something such as education or research **2.** LEGAL transfer something legally to somebody else to transfer money, property, or rights to somebody in a legal transaction

grant of probate LEGAL in UK, document certifying validity of will in the United Kingdom, a document that states the validity of a will and upholds the appointment of the executor(s)

grantor STOCKHOLDING & INVESTMENTS seller of option a person who sells an ***option*** to another person

grapevine GENERAL MANAGEMENT unofficial means of communication an informal communication network within an organization that conveys information through unofficial channels independent of management control. Information travels much more quickly through the grapevine than through formal channels and may become distorted. A grapevine may reinterpret official corporate messages or spread gossip and rumor in the absence of effective organization channels. It can, however, also complement official communication, provide feedback, and strengthen social relationships within the organization.

graph STATISTICS representation of relationship between variables a diagram depicting the relationship between dependent and independent variables through the use of lines, curves, or figures on horizontal and vertical axes. Time is the most common independent variable, showing how the dependent variable has altered over a defined period.

graveyard market MARKETS **1.** market for infrequently traded stocks a market for stock that is infrequently traded either through lack of interest or because of little or no value **2.** market where sellers face large losses a ***bear market*** where investors who dispose of their holdings are faced with large losses, as potential investors prefer to stay liquid until the market shows signs of improving

gravy train BUSINESS business activity yielding large profits easily any type of business activity in which a person or organization makes a large profit without much effort

gray knight *US* MERGERS & ACQUISITIONS unreliable friendly firm involved in takeover a ***white knight*** that does not have the confidence of the company to be acquired in a ***takeover***. *UK term* ***grey knight***. *See also* ***knight***

gray market *US* **1.** MARKETS unofficial market for stock before official trading an unofficial market run by dealers, in which new issues of stock are bought and sold before they officially become available for trading on a stock exchange, even before the stock allocations become known **2.** MARKETS market for imported goods a ***market*** in which goods are sold that have been manufactured abroad and imported. A gray market product is one that has been imported legally, in contrast to one on the ***black market***, which is illegal. Such markets arise when there is a supply shortage, usually for exclusive goods, and the goods are offered for sale at lower prices than the equivalent goods manufactured in the home country. **3.** MARKETING older people's shopping preferences the market segment occupied by older members of a population *UK term* ***grey market***

gray marketing *US* MARKETING targeting older people marketing aimed at older age groups such as the middle-aged and elderly. *UK term* ***grey marketing***

gray wave *US* BUSINESS describing companies with good prospects for distant future used to describe a company that is thought likely to have good prospects in the distant future. It gets its name from the fact that investors are likely to have gray hair before they see their expectations fulfilled (slang) *UK term* ***grey wave***

Great Depression ECONOMICS 1930s global economic crisis the world economic crisis that began after the US stock market collapsed in 1929 and continued through the 1930s, resulting in mass unemployment and poverty, especially in North America

greater fool theory STOCKHOLDING & INVESTMENTS strategy assuming overpriced stock will attract buyer the investing strategy that assumes it is wise to buy a stock that is not worth its current price. The assumption is that somebody will buy it from you later for an even greater price.

green accounting ACCOUNTING = ***environmental accounting***

greenback CURRENCY & EXCHANGE US paper money a piece of US paper money of any denomination

green card HR & PERSONNEL work permit for noncitizens in US an identity card and work permit issued by the US government to a person living and working in the United States who is not a US citizen. It is officially known as a "United States Permanent Resident Card."

green chips BUSINESS promising small companies small companies considered to have potential for growth

green currency CURRENCY & EXCHANGE former EU currency for agricultural prices in the European Union, currency formerly used for calculating agricultural payments. Each country had an exchange rate fixed by the Commission, so before the introduction of the euro there were currencies such as "green francs" and "green marks."

green dollar *US* FINANCE spending and investment based on environmental awareness money spent on environmentally sound products and services and investing in companies with environmentally sound policies and practices. *UK term* ***green pound***

green investing STOCKHOLDING & INVESTMENTS investment in green technologies investing in companies developing environmentally sound technologies and products to counter the economic effects of climate change

greenmail MARKETS stock purchase threatening takeover to prompt profitable resale the purchase of enough of a company's stock to threaten it with ***takeover***, so that the company is forced to buy back the stock at a higher price to avoid the takeover (slang)

Green Paper UK government report on proposed law in the United Kingdom, a report from the government on proposals for a new law to be discussed in Parliament. ***See also White Paper***

green pound **1.** *UK* FINANCE = ***green dollar*** **2.** CURRENCY & EXCHANGE monetary unit used for converting EU agricultural prices in the European Union, a currency unit formerly used for converting agricultural prices into pounds sterling

green shoe *or* greenshoe option STOCKHOLDING & INVESTMENTS option in stock issue covering potential shortfall an option offered by a company raising the capital for the issue of further shares of stock to cover a shortfall in the event of overallocation. It gets its name from the Green Shoe Manufacturing Company, which was the first to include the feature in a public offering. (slang)

green taxes TAX taxes that discourage environmental damage taxes levied to discourage behavior that will be harmful to the environment

Gresham's Law ECONOMICS theory that cheaper money replaces more valuable money the principle that "bad money will drive out good." If two forms of money with the same denomination exist in the same market, the form with the higher metal value will be driven out of circulation because people hoard it and use the lower-rated form to spend.

grey knight *UK* MERGERS & ACQUISITIONS = ***gray knight***

grey market *UK* MARKETS = ***gray market***

grey marketing *UK* MARKETING = ***gray marketing***

grey wave *UK* BUSINESS = ***gray wave***

gross ACCOUNTING without deductions before taxes and other deductions have been taken into account

gross borrowings ACCOUNTING total of firm's loans and overdrafts the total of all money borrowed by a company including items such as overdrafts and long-term loans but without deducting cash in bank accounts and on deposit

gross domestic product ECONOMICS *see* ***GDP***

gross earnings FINANCE total pay before deductions a person's salary or wage before subtracting payroll deductions such as taxes and retirement savings

gross income FINANCE total income before deductions a person's salary or wage plus any other money received from other sources, before subtracting payroll deductions, such as taxes and retirement savings, and any other taxes

gross income yield ACCOUNTING yield before tax the yield of an investment before tax is deducted

gross interest ACCOUNTING interest earned before tax is deducted the interest earned on a deposit or security before the deduction of tax. *See also* ***net interest***

gross lease FINANCE lease that exempts lessee from some payments a lease that does not require the lessee to pay for things the owner usually pays for. *See also* ***net lease***

gross margin **1.** FINANCE difference between borrower's interest payments and lender's costs the difference between the interest rate paid by a borrower and the cost of the funds to the lender **2.** ACCOUNTING percentage difference between income and costs the difference between revenue and cost of revenue expressed as a percentage **3.** OPERATIONS & PRODUCTION difference between unit's manufacturing cost and sale price the difference between the manufacturing cost of a unit of output and the price at which it is sold. *Abbr* ***GM***

gross national product ECONOMICS *see* ***GNP***

gross negligence GENERAL MANAGEMENT failure to act responsibly a breach of a duty to act with expected care in conducting activities. *See also* ***negligence***

gross profit ACCOUNTING difference between total sales revenue and production costs the difference between an organization's sales revenue and the cost of goods sold. Unlike ***net profit***, gross profit does not include distribution, administration, or finance costs. *Also called* ***trading profit***

gross profit margin ACCOUNTING *see* ***profit margin***

gross receipts ACCOUNTING total revenue the total revenue received by a business, before tax and other deductions have been taken into account. *See also* ***net receipts***

gross redemption yield *UK* STOCKHOLDING & INVESTMENTS = ***yield to maturity***

gross sales ACCOUNTING sales before discounts the total of all sales before discounts

gross spread MARKETS difference between public's and underwriter's price for security the difference between the price of a security offered to the public and the price the underwriter pays

gross turnover ACCOUNTING total turnover all of a business's income less statutory allowances, and other taxes on this income

gross yield STOCKHOLDING & INVESTMENTS income derived from securities before tax the income return derived from securities before the deduction of tax

gross yield to redemption *UK* STOCKHOLDING & INVESTMENTS = ***gross redemption yield***

ground rent REAL ESTATE **1.** rent paid to owner of land under building a rent paid by the main tenant to the owner of the ground on which a building sits **2.** rent paid on vacant land in the United States,

  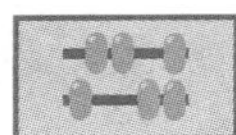      

a rent paid on land by a tenant to the owner of the land

group BUSINESS firm with subsidiaries a commercial organization consisting of a parent company and subsidiaries under common ownership

group balance sheet ACCOUNTING = ***consolidated balance sheet***

group investment STOCKHOLDING & INVESTMENTS shared investment an investment made by more than one person

group life assurance *UK* INSURANCE = ***group life insurance***

group life insurance *US* INSURANCE life insurance policy covering several individuals a life insurance policy that covers a number of people such as members of an association or club, or employees at a company. *UK term* ***group life assurance***

Group of Eight FINANCE *see* ***G8***

Group of Seven FINANCE *see* ***G7***

Group of Ten FINANCE *see* ***G10***

Group of Twenty FINANCE *see* ***G20***

groupthink GENERAL MANAGEMENT desire for agreement that compromises judgment a phenomenon that occurs during ***decision making*** or ***problem solving*** when a team's desire to reach an agreement overrides its ability to appraise the problem properly. It is similar to the ***Abilene paradox*** in that it is based on people's desire to conform and please others.

growth 1. FINANCE firm's economic increase an increase in productivity, sales, or earnings that an organization experiences **2.** OPERATIONS & PRODUCTION increase in demand for product the second stage in a product life cycle, following the launch, when demand for the product increases rapidly

growth and income fund STOCKHOLDING & INVESTMENTS mutual fund seeking capital increase with large dividends a mutual fund that tries to maximize growth of capital while paying significant dividends

growth capital FINANCE funding that firm uses to expand funding that allows a company to accelerate its growth. For new startup companies, growth capital is the second stage of funding after ***seed capital***.

growth company BUSINESS firm increasing in size or output a company whose contribution to the economy is growing because it is increasing its workforce or earning increased foreign exchange for its exported goods

growth curve STATISTICS line on graph showing increase over time a line plotted on a graph that shows a statistical increase over a period of time

Growth, Employment, and Redistribution INTERNATIONAL TRADE *see* ***GEAR***

growth equity STOCKHOLDING & INVESTMENTS promising investment product an equity that is thought to have good prospects of growth, usually with a high price/earnings ratio. *Also called* ***growth stock***

growth fund STOCKHOLDING & INVESTMENTS mutual fund focusing on capital increase a mutual fund that tries to maximize growth of capital without regard to dividends

growth index BUSINESS numerical scale representing firm's economic increase an index showing the growth in a company's revenues, earnings, dividends, or other figures

growth industry FINANCE area of business expanding quickly an industry that is developing and expanding at a faster rate than other industries

growth prospects FINANCE potential for economic increase the likelihood that something such as a specific stock or a country's economy will considerably improve its performance

growth rate ECONOMICS how much and how fast economy is growing the rate of an economy's growth as measured by its technical progress, the growth of its labor force, and the increase in its ***capital stock***

growth stock STOCKHOLDING & INVESTMENTS = ***growth equity***

GST *abbr* TAX ***Goods and Services Tax***

GTC *abbr* STOCKHOLDING & INVESTMENTS ***good 'til cancel***

GTM *abbr* STOCKHOLDING & INVESTMENTS **good this month**

GTW *abbr* STOCKHOLDING & INVESTMENTS ***good this week***

guarantee FINANCE promise to cover another person's contractual duties a promise made by a third party, or guarantor, that he or she will be liable if one of the parties to a contract fails to fulfill their contractual obligations. A guarantee may be acceptable to a bank as security for borrowing, provided the guarantor has sufficient financial means to cover his or her potential liability.

guaranteed bond STOCKHOLDING & INVESTMENTS bond with guaranteed principal and interest a bond on which the principal and interest are guaranteed by an institution other than the one that issues it, or a stock in which the dividends are similarly guaranteed. *Also called* ***guaranteed stock***

guaranteed fund STOCKHOLDING & INVESTMENTS investment whose losses third party promises to cover a fixed term investment where a third party promises to repay the investor's principal in full should the investment fall below the initial sum invested

guaranteed income bond INSURANCE UK life insurance bond providing fixed income a bond issued by a UK life insurance company designed to provide an investor with a fixed rate of income for a specific period of time. Only those policies with an independent third party guarantee can receive this denomination.

guaranteed investment certificate *UK* INSURANCE = ***guaranteed investment contract***

guaranteed investment contract *US* INSURANCE investment guaranteeing interest but not principal an investment instrument issued by an insurance company that guarantees interest but not principal. *UK term* ***guaranteed investment certificate***

guaranteed renewable policy INSURANCE policy valid as long as payments continue an insurance policy that remains in effect as long as the premiums are paid

guaranteed stock STOCKHOLDING & INVESTMENTS = ***guaranteed bond***

guarantor BUSINESS somebody promising to repay borrower's loan if necessary a person or organization that guarantees repayment of a loan if the borrower defaults or is unable to pay

guarantor of last resort FINANCE person or entity guaranteeing bad debt repayment a person, organization, or government that guarantees repayment of a debt that cannot otherwise be repaid

guardian LEGAL court-appointed person managing affairs of another a person appointed by law to act on behalf of somebody, especially a child, who cannot act on his or her own behalf

guardian ad litem LEGAL somebody representing child in court case a person who acts on behalf of a minor who is a defendant in a court case

gun jumping FINANCE profitable trading based on inside information trading that takes place on the basis of privileged information (slang)

gunslinger STOCKHOLDING & INVESTMENTS investment manager investing in high-risk stocks a portfolio manager who invests in high-risk stocks hoping that they will yield high returns (slang)

GW *abbr* E-COMMERCE ***payment gateway***

haggle FINANCE discuss to agree on price of item to reach a price with a buyer or seller by the gradual raising of offers and lowering of the price asked until a mutually accepted figure is obtained

haircut 1. FINANCE difference between loan amount and value of collateral the difference between the market value of a security and the amount lent to the owner using the security as collateral **2.** STOCKHOLDING & INVESTMENTS estimate of investment loss an estimate of possible loss in investments

half-life MORTGAGES years it takes to repay half of mortgage the number of years needed to repay half the principal borrowed on a mortgage

half-normal plot STATISTICS plot of statistical data to identify anomalies a way of plotting statistical data which is used to check for the presence of values in the data that fall outside the expected range

half-stock STOCKHOLDING & INVESTMENTS $50 stock a stock that has a nominal value of fifty US dollars

half-year ACCOUNTING half of accounting period six months for which accounts are presented

hammer MARKETS take firm off London Stock Exchange to remove a business from trading on the ***London Stock Exchange*** because it has failed
hammering the market MARKETS the practice of ***short selling*** by speculators who think prices are about to drop so they can buy back before delivery and make a profit

handle 1. BUSINESS to deal in particular product, service, or market to buy, sell, or trade in a particular product, service, or market **2.** STOCKHOLDING & INVESTMENTS whole-number price of share of stock or currency the price of a stock or foreign currency, quoted as a whole number

handling charge OPERATIONS & PRODUCTION money charged for preparing goods for dispatch money to be paid for packing, invoicing, or dealing with goods which are being shipped

  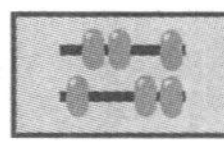      

hand off *US, CANADA* GENERAL MANAGEMENT transfer responsibility for project to give responsibility for a project to another person or organization

hand signals MARKETS signs made with hands in stock exchange the signs used by ***traders*** on the ***trading floors*** at exchanges for futures and options to overcome the problem of noise

hands-off GENERAL MANAGEMENT without constant supervision characterized by an absence of close and constant management attention

hands-on GENERAL MANAGEMENT closely involved characterized by first-hand personal involvement in the management of an activity

hang out loan FINANCE outstanding amount on loan the amount of a loan that is still outstanding after the termination of the loan

Hang Seng Index MARKETS Hong Kong stock market index an index of the prices of selected stocks on the Hong Kong Stock Exchange, used as an indicator of overall Hong Kong Stock Exchange performance. It was established on November 24, 1969.

hara-kiri swap FINANCE exchange of interest rates with no profit margin an interest rate swap made without a profit margin

hard capital rationing FINANCE *see* ***capital rationing*** *(sense 2)*

hard cash CURRENCY & EXCHANGE money in bills money in the form of bills and coins, as opposed to checks or credit cards

hard commodities MARKETS nonperishable raw materials metals such as copper, zinc, mercury, tin, aluminum, and lead, and other solid raw materials. *See also* ***commodity, soft commodities***

hard currency CURRENCY & EXCHANGE money traded in foreign exchange market a currency that is traded in a foreign exchange market and for which demand is persistently high relative to its supply. *See also* ***soft currency***

hardening FINANCE **1.** stabilizing after changes becoming stable after a period of fluctuation **2.** describing prices that are slowly rising used to describe prices that are slowly moving upward

hard landing ECONOMICS sudden economic recession after growth period the rapid decline of an economy into recession and business stagnation after a sustained period of growth

harmonization **1.** FINANCE equality of financial and social regulation the convergence of financial and social regulation in the countries of the European Union **2.** GENERAL MANAGEMENT equalizing pay and conditions the resolution of inequalities in the pay and conditions of employment between different categories of employees **3.** GENERAL MANAGEMENT equalizing benefits of related companies the alignment of the systems of pay and benefits of two companies that become one by merger, acquisition, or takeover **4.** GENERAL MANAGEMENT equalizing treatment of full- and part-time employees the process of removing differences between groups of employees, such as full- and part-time staff, with regard to terms and conditions of employment such as rates of pay, pension rights, and vacation entitlement

Harmonized Sales Tax TAX Canadian tax on goods and services in Canada, a ***value-added tax*** levied on goods and services that is a combination of the national ***Goods and Services Tax*** *(sense 2)* and a ***Provincial Sales Tax***. *Abbr* ***HST***

harvesting strategy MARKETING slowing marketing activity before sale of product ends a reduction in or cessation of marketing for a product prior to it being withdrawn from sale, resulting in an increase in profits on the back of previous marketing and advertising campaigns

head and shoulders MARKETS graph showing three rallies in firm's stock price a pattern in a graph plotting a company's stock price which resembles the silhouette of a person's head and shoulders (three rises and falls, with the most pronounced rise and fall in the middle). Analysts see this pattern as an indication of an impending larger fall in price.

headcount reduction HR & PERSONNEL reducing number of employees a reduction in the number of people employed by a company in circumstances such as a drop in the amount of sales

headline rate of inflation ECONOMICS inflation measure including wide range of costs a measure of inflation that attempts to take account of most costs and services. In the United States, the headline rate is based on the Consumer Price Index. In the United Kingdom, it is based on the Retail Price Index, which takes account of homeowners' mortgage costs.

head of household TAX US tax status for somebody with dependents in the United States, a federal tax filing status that qualifies a person to pay less income tax if they are unmarried or considered unmarried on the last day of the year, have paid more than half of the cost of keeping a home for the year, and have had a dependent child or other qualified dependent such as a parent living with them for more than half the year

headquarters *or* head office BUSINESS firm's main office the main office of an organization where most of the administrative work is done and where the board of directors meets

heads of agreement GENERAL MANAGEMENT key items agreed on the most important subjects or items dealt with in a commercial agreement

head tax TAX tax on each adult a tax paid by all adult inhabitants of a country, regardless of their income

health saving account FINANCE US savings plan for medical expenses in the United States, a savings plan with tax benefits that is designed to help individuals accumulate money for qualified medical expenses. *Abbr* ***HSA***

health warning STOCKHOLDING & INVESTMENTS message on UK advertisements about risks of investing in the United Kingdom, a legally required warning message printed on advertisements for investments, stating that the value of investments can fall as well as rise (slang)

heavy **1.** MARKETS experiencing more activity than usual used to describe a market in which trading is more active than usual **2.** STOCKHOLDING & INVESTMENTS investing too much in one type of stock having too many investments in related industries or stock **3.** STOCKHOLDING & INVESTMENTS high-priced used to describe a stock that has such a high price that small investors are reluctant to buy it. In this case the company may decide to split the stock so as to make it more attractive.

heavy industry OPERATIONS & PRODUCTION manufacturing sector making large products a manufacturing industry that requires a lot of resources, uses heavy raw materials such as coal, and makes large products such as ships or engines

hedge STOCKHOLDING & INVESTMENTS **1.** method of protecting against possible loss a protection against a possible loss on an investment which involves taking an action that is the opposite of an action taken earlier **2.** take action to reduce risk of investment loss to take measures to offset risk of loss on an investment, especially by investing in counterbalancing securities as a guard against price fluctuations

hedge fund STOCKHOLDING & INVESTMENTS, RISK risky type of investment fund an investment fund that takes considerable risks, including investment in unconventional instruments, in the hope of generating great profits. There are many types of hedge funds, using very different strategies. Some are highly geared and some use arbitrage, futures, and options to achieve their objectives.

hedging STOCKHOLDING & INVESTMENTS, RISK strategy for protecting against possible financial losses financial transactions intended to protect against possible losses from existing financial activities or investments, for example, buying investments at a fixed price for delivery later or investing in counterbalancing securities **hedging against inflation** STOCKHOLDING & INVESTMENTS investing in order to avoid the impact of inflation, thus protecting the purchasing power of capital. Historically, equities have generally outperformed returns from savings accounts in the long term and beaten the ***retail price index***. They are thus considered as one of the best hedges against inflation, although no stock market investment is without risk.

held order STOCKHOLDING & INVESTMENTS large order that seller waits to process an order that a dealer does not process immediately, often because of its large size

hereditament LEGAL property that can be inherited any property, including personal, land, and buildings, that somebody can inherit

Her Majesty's Revenue & Customs TAX, INTERNATIONAL TRADE UK government department that collects tax in the United Kingdom, the government department responsible for the administration and collection of all forms of tax, including VAT, income tax, and excise duties. HMRC combines the duties of two formerly separate departments, the Inland Revenue and HM Customs and Excise. *Abbr* ***HMRC***

Herstatt Risk CURRENCY & EXCHANGE, RISK risk of delivery failure in foreign currency transaction the risk in foreign currency exchange transactions that one party to the exchange will fail to make payment after having received payment from the other party

heuristics GENERAL MANAGEMENT exploration of possible solutions in problem solving a method for problem solving or decision making that arrives at solutions through exploratory means such as experimentation, trial and error, or evaluation

hidden asset ACCOUNTING firm's property recorded at lower than actual value an asset that is shown in a company's accounts as being worth much less than its true market value

hidden economy ECONOMICS = ***black economy***

hidden reserves ACCOUNTING firm's unrecorded reserves funds that are set aside but not declared in the company's balance sheet

hidden tax TAX tax that not everyone is aware of a tax that is not immediately apparent. For

  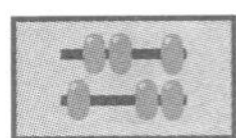      

example, while a consumer may be aware of a tax on retail purchases, a tax imposed at the wholesale level, which consequently increases the cost of items to the retailer, will not be apparent.

high concept GENERAL MANAGEMENT succinct idea a compelling idea that is expressed clearly and concisely

high-end GENERAL MANAGEMENT of most expensive, advanced, or powerful kind relating to the most expensive, most advanced, or most powerful in a variety of products such as computers

higher rate TAX upper UK income tax rate in the United Kingdom, the higher of the two bands of income tax. ***Her Majesty's Revenue & Customs*** is responsible for the administration of income tax and publishes information on current tax rates and allowances on its website. *See also* ***basic rate***

high finance FINANCE dealing with very large amounts of money the lending, investing, and borrowing of very large sums of money organized by financiers

high-flier *or* high-flyer STOCKHOLDING & INVESTMENTS stock that increases quickly in price a heavily traded stock that increases in value considerably over a short period

high gearing FINANCE when firm borrows a lot of money a situation in which a company has a high level of borrowing compared to its stock price

high-income STOCKHOLDING & INVESTMENTS describing fund yielding high returns used to describe a fund that yields a high rate of return

highly geared company *UK* BUSINESS = ***highly leveraged company***

highly leveraged company *US* BUSINESS firm with relatively large debts a company that has a large amount of debt in proportion to its equity. *UK term* ***highly geared company***

high net worth individual FINANCE somebody with at least $4 million a person whose net assets, excluding the value of a home, are worth more than $4 million, by some classifications. It is estimated that some 10 million worldwide fall into this category. *Abbr* ***HNWI***

high-powered GENERAL MANAGEMENT able and dynamic having, showing, or requiring great dynamism and ability

high-premium convertible debenture STOCKHOLDING & INVESTMENTS bond unlikely to be converted a convertible bond with an exercise price that makes it unlikely to be converted in the foreseeable future. It therefore has a low option premium.

high-pressure MARKETING forceful and persistent used to describe a selling technique in which the sales representative attempts to persuade a buyer forcefully and persistently

high-risk company BUSINESS, RISK firm running high business risks a company that is exposed to high levels of business risk

High Street bank BANKING major UK bank with local offices a UK bank that provides ***retail banking*** services and has many local offices for customers to visit, as distinguished from an ***investment bank*** or a bank that provides services only on the Internet

high-tech crime FRAUD crime committed using computer technologies illegal activities using the Internet or other computer technologies. *Also called* ***hi-tech crime***

high yield STOCKHOLDING & INVESTMENTS, RISK higher than usual yield a higher rate of return than is usual for a particular type of investment or company

high-yield bond STOCKHOLDING & INVESTMENTS, RISK = ***junk bond***

high yielder STOCKHOLDING & INVESTMENTS, RISK high-performing but risky investment product a security that has a higher than average rate of return and is consequently often a higher risk investment

hire 1. HR & PERSONNEL give job to somebody to employ somebody new to work for you or your organization **2.** *UK* FINANCE = ***rent***

hire purchase *UK* FINANCE = ***installment plan***

historical cost *or* historic cost ACCOUNTING original cost of item bought in past the record of the value of a firm's asset reflecting its original price when it was purchased

historical cost accounting ACCOUNTING record keeping based on original cost of items the preparation of accounts on the basis of historical cost, with assets valued at their original cost of purchase. *UK term* ***fair value accounting***. *See also* ***current cost accounting***

historical cost depreciation ACCOUNTING discounting asset's value based on original cost the accounting practice of depreciating a firm's asset based on its original cost

historical figures ACCOUNTING figures or values correct at the time figures or values that were correct at the time of purchase or payment, as distinct from a current value

historical summary ACCOUNTING UK report of firm's results in past in the United Kingdom, an optional synopsis of a company's results over a period of time, often five or ten years, featured in the annual accounts

historical trading range MARKETS = ***trading range***

historic pricing STOCKHOLDING & INVESTMENTS basing mutual fund prices on most recent holdings the establishment of the price of a share in a mutual fund on the basis of the most recent values of its holdings

hi-tech crime FRAUD = ***high-tech crime***

HMCE INTERNATIONAL TRADE *see* ***Her Majesty's Revenue & Customs***

HM Customs and Excise INTERNATIONAL TRADE *see* ***Her Majesty's Revenue & Customs***

HMRC *abbr* TAX, INTERNATIONAL TRADE ***Her Majesty's Revenue & Customs***

HM Revenue & Customs TAX, INTERNATIONAL TRADE = ***Her Majesty's Revenue & Customs***

HM Treasury FINANCE UK government department that manages public funds the UK government department responsible for managing the country's public revenues. While the incumbent prime minister holds the title of First Lord of the Treasury, the department is run on a day-to-day basis by the ***Chancellor of the Exchequer***.

HNWI *abbr* FINANCE ***high net worth individual***

hockey stick BUSINESS performance curve that falls then rises sharply a performance curve, typical of businesses in their early stages, that descends then rises sharply in a straight line, creating a shape similar to that of a hockey stick

hold STOCKHOLDING & INVESTMENTS own security for long time to own a security over a long period of time

holdback E-COMMERCE reserve funds covering possible disputed charges funds from a merchant's credit card transactions held in reserve for a predetermined time by the merchant account provider to cover possible disputed charges. *Also called* ***reserve account***

holder FINANCE owner of financial obligation the person who is in possession of a ***bill of exchange*** or ***promissory note***

holder of record STOCKHOLDING & INVESTMENTS official owner of stock the person who is registered as the owner of stock in a company

holding *or* holdings STOCKHOLDING & INVESTMENTS investment owned by somebody an investment, or set of investments, that a person owns at a specific time

holding company BUSINESS parent firm that owns other firms a parent organization that owns the majority of share capital in other companies in order to gain control of them. A holding company may have no other business than the holding of stock in other companies.

holding period STOCKHOLDING & INVESTMENTS period between purchase and sale of asset the length of time an asset was held from the time of purchase to the time of sale, used for determining whether a capital gain or loss is taxed as short-term (less than one year) or long-term (one year or more)

home banking BANKING using computer at home for banking services a system of banking using a personal computer at home to carry out various financial transactions such as paying invoices or checking transactions in a bank account

home loan MORTGAGES money used for house purchase a loan of money to enable the purchase of a house

homeowner's insurance policy *US* INSURANCE insurance for house and contents an insurance policy that protects homeowners against loss of or damage to a home or its contents and provides coverage for personal liability if somebody is injured while on the premises. *UK terms* ***home policy***, ***household policy***

home policy *UK* INSURANCE = ***homeowner's insurance policy***

home run FINANCE investment with rapid returns an investment that produces a high rate of return in a short time

home trade *UK* BUSINESS = ***domestic trade***

homogenization INTERNATIONAL TRADE imposition of uniformity on separate markets and cultures the removal of characteristic differences between separate markets and cultures. Globalization is frequently blamed for homogenization.

honorarium FINANCE modest payment for simple duties a payment made to somebody for performing a specific service, often a token amount

horizontal diversification BUSINESS developing new but related areas expansion into a related but different product area, for example, a

  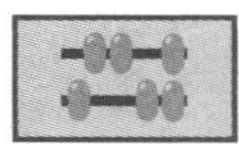      

domestic furniture manufacturer producing office furniture. *See also* ***diversification***

horizontal equity ECONOMICS belief in similar taxation for similar incomes the theory that individuals in similar financial situations should be taxed at the same rate

horizontal integration BUSINESS merging of similar functions or organizations the merging of functions or organizations that operate on a similar level. Horizontal integration involves the amalgamation of companies producing the same types of goods or operating at the same stage of the supply chain. It may also describe the merging of departments within an organization that perform similar tasks. *See also* ***vertical integration***

horizontal merger MERGERS & ACQUISITIONS combining of firms in same industry the amalgamation of two or more organizations from the same industry under single ownership, through the direct ***acquisition*** by one organization of the ***net assets*** or ***liabilities*** of the other. *See also* ***merger***

horizontal spread STOCKHOLDING & INVESTMENTS, RISK simultaneous buying and selling of two options a purchase of one ***option*** accompanied by the sale of another with the same ***exercise price*** but a different date of maturity. *Also called* ***calendar spread***

horse-trading GENERAL MANAGEMENT shrewd bargaining bargaining in which the goods are not directly comparable and the valuations are frequently subjective

hostile bid MERGERS & ACQUISITIONS = ***contested takeover bid***

hostile takeover MERGERS & ACQUISITIONS unwelcome acquisition of firm the acquisition by a company of a controlling interest in the voting share capital of another company whose directors or stockholders are opposed to the action. *See also* ***takeover***

hot card BANKING stolen credit card a credit card that has been stolen and might be used fraudulently

hot issue STOCKHOLDING & INVESTMENTS new investment product expected to perform well a new security that is expected to trade at a significant premium to its issue price. *See also* ***hot stock***

hot money **1.** FRAUD stolen money money that has been obtained by dishonest means. *See also* ***money laundering*** **2.** STOCKHOLDING & INVESTMENTS funds transferred for short-term gain money that is moved on short notice from one financial center to another to secure the best possible return

hot stock MARKETS stock whose price rises rapidly a stock, usually a new issue, that rises quickly on the stock market. *See also* ***hot issue***

house FINANCE finance firm a business organization, especially a financial institution that handles the purchase and sale of securities to investors

house call STOCKHOLDING & INVESTMENTS warning by brokerage firm of low margin account notice from a brokerage firm that the amount of money in a client's margin account is less than the required amount

household policy *UK* INSURANCE = ***homeowner's insurance policy***

house journal GENERAL MANAGEMENT periodic bulletin giving internal information an informal publication issued periodically by an organization or agency to aid the internal communication process

house poor FINANCE with all money invested in house a situation in which the cost of owning a home is too high in proportion to the homeowner's income

HSA *abbr* FINANCE ***health saving account***

HST *abbr* TAX ***Harmonized Sales Tax***

human asset accounting HR & PERSONNEL = ***human capital accounting***

human capital HR & PERSONNEL staff the ***employees*** of an organization. The term builds on the concept of capital as an asset of an organization, implying recognition of the importance and monetary worth of the skills and experience of its employees. It is measured through ***human capital accounting***.

human capital accounting HR & PERSONNEL attempted valuation of employee knowledge and skills an attempt to place a financial figure on the knowledge and skills of an organization's ***employees*** or ***human capital***. *Also called* ***human asset accounting***, ***human resource accounting*** *(sense 1)*

human resource accounting HR & PERSONNEL **1.** = ***human capital accounting*** **2.** record keeping of value of firm's employees the identification, recording, and reporting of the investment in, and return from the employment of, the personnel of an organization

human resource forecasting GENERAL MANAGEMENT estimates of future employment needs and supply the prediction of future levels of demand for, and supply of, workers and skills at organizational, regional, or national level. A variety of techniques are used in manpower forecasting, including the statistical analysis of current trends and the use of mathematical models. At national level, these include the analysis of census statistics; at organizational level, projections of future requirements may be made from sales and production figures. Human resource forecasting forms part of the human resource planning process. *Also called* ***manpower forecasting***

human resource management HR & PERSONNEL management of employees as individuals a model of ***personnel management*** that focuses on the individual rather than taking a collective approach. It is characterized by an emphasis on strategic integration, employee commitment, workforce flexibility, and quality of goods and services.

human resource planning GENERAL MANAGEMENT efforts to balance employment needs with supply the development of strategies to match the supply of workers to the availability of jobs at organizational, regional, or national level. Human resource planning involves reviewing current personnel resources, forecasting future requirements and availability, and taking steps to ensure that the supply of people and skills meets demand. At a national level, this may be conducted by government or industry bodies, and at an organizational level, by human resource managers. *Also called* ***manpower planning***

hurdle rate **1.** BANKING rate above which loan is profitable for bank a minimum ***rate of return*** needed by a bank to fund a loan, representing the rate below which a loan is not profitable for the bank **2.** STOCKHOLDING & INVESTMENTS minimum return before fees due the minimum rate of return required on a fund before the fund manager can begin taking fees **3.** *UK* STOCKHOLDING & INVESTMENTS growth rate needed to repay stock's redemption price the rate of growth in a portfolio required to repay the final fixed redemption price of zero dividend preference shares

hurricane bond STOCKHOLDING & INVESTMENTS, RISK catastrophe bond for hurricane insurance risk a type of ***catastrophe bond*** that transfers some of the insurance risk from insurers to investors in the event of a hurricane

hybrid STOCKHOLDING & INVESTMENTS combination of investment types a combination of financial instruments, for example, a bond with warrants attached, or a variety of cash and derivative instruments designed to mirror the performance of a financial market

hybrid annuity INSURANCE part fixed part variable annuity a type of ***annuity*** that combines features of both a fixed annuity (guaranteeing fixed payments to the individual receiving it for the term of the contract, usually until death) and a variable annuity (offering no guarantee but having potential for a greater return, usually based on the performance of a stock or mutual fund). *Also called* ***combination annuity***

hybrid financial instrument STOCKHOLDING & INVESTMENTS investment type with features of other types a ***financial instrument*** such as a convertible bond that has characteristics of multiple types of instruments, often convertible from one to another

hyperinflation ECONOMICS extremely high rate of inflation a very rapid growth in the rate of inflation so that money loses value and physical goods replace currency as a medium of exchange. This happened, for example, in Latin America in the early 1990s and in Zimbabwe in the 2000s.

hyperpartnering E-COMMERCE temporary commercial partnerships using Internet technology a form of commerce in which companies use Internet technology to form partnerships and execute transactions at high speed and low cost in order to take advantage of business opportunities as soon as they appear

hypothecate FINANCE **1.** use real estate to back loan to use the mortgage on real estate as collateral for a loan **2.** use money for defined purpose to designate money, especially public funds, to be used for a specific purpose only

hypothecation FINANCE **1.** using assets as loan collateral without transferring ownership an arrangement in which assets such as securities are used as collateral for a loan but without transferring legal ownership to the lender **2.** designating money for specific purpose the process of earmarking money derived from specific sources for related expenditure, for example, using taxes collected on gasoline sales solely on public transportation

hypothesis testing STATISTICS checking sample data against knowledge of sample the process of testing sample data from a statistical study to determine whether it is consistent with what is known about the sample population

hysteresis ECONOMICS dependency of equilibrium on change the way in which equilibrium is dependent on the changes that take place as an economy experiences change

 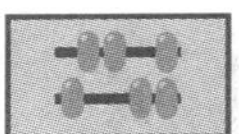   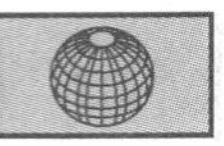   

I

IAS *abbr* TAX, STOCKHOLDING & INVESTMENTS ***installment activity statement***

IASB *abbr* ACCOUNTING ***International Accounting Standards Board***

IASC *abbr* ACCOUNTING ***International Accounting Standards Committee***

IB *abbr* BANKING ***investment bank***

IBOR *abbr* MARKETS ***Interbank Offered Rate***

IBR *abbr* MARKETS *see* ***Interbank Offered Rate***

IBRC INSURANCE former association of UK insurance brokers in the United Kingdom, a statutory body established under the Insurance Brokers Registration Act of 1977 which was deregulated following the establishment of the Financial Services Authority and the General Insurance Services Council. Its complaints and administration functions passed to the Institute of Insurance Brokers. *Full form* ***Insurance Brokers Registration Council***

IBRD BANKING UN bank that helps poorest nations a United Nations organization that provides funds, policy guidance, and technical assistance to facilitate economic development in its poorer member countries. *Full form* ***International Bank for Reconstruction and Development***

ICA *abbr* INSURANCE ***Insurance Council of Australia***

ICAEW *abbr* ACCOUNTING ***Institute of Chartered Accountants in England and Wales***

ICAI *abbr* ACCOUNTING ***Institute of Chartered Accountants in Ireland***

ICANZ *abbr* ACCOUNTING ***Institute of Chartered Accountants of New Zealand***

ICAS *abbr* ACCOUNTING ***Institute of Chartered Accountants of Scotland***

ICC BUSINESS association to support private business an organization that represents business interests to governments, working to improve trading conditions and foster private enterprise. *Full form* ***International Chamber of Commerce***

ICMA *abbr* MARKETS ***International Capital Market Association***

ICSA *abbr UK* FINANCE ***Institute of Chartered Secretaries and Administrators***

ICSID *abbr* BANKING ***International Centre for Settlement of Investment Disputes***

IDA *abbr* FINANCE ***International Development Association***

identity theft FRAUD use of another's identity for criminal purpose the use of another person's personal and financial information, such as credit card numbers, Social Security numbers, or passport information, without their knowledge, to commit a crime

idle capital *or* idle cash FINANCE firm's unused money and property the money and assets of a business that are not being invested productively. *Also called* ***barren money, sideline cash***

IDR *abbr* STOCKHOLDING & INVESTMENTS ***International Depository Receipt***

IFA *abbr* **1.** FINANCE ***independent financial adviser*** **2.** ACCOUNTING ***Institute of Financial Accountants***

IFAD *abbr* FINANCE ***International Fund for Agricultural Development***

IFC *abbr* FINANCE ***International Finance Corporation***

IFRS *abbr* ACCOUNTING ***International Financial Reporting Standards***

IHT *abbr* TAX ***inheritance tax***

IIB *abbr* INSURANCE ***Institute of Insurance Brokers***

IIN *abbr* BANKING ***issuer identification number***

ijara *or* ijarah FINANCE agreement by bank to purchase then lease item in Islamic financing, a leasing arrangement in which a bank or financier purchases an item for a customer, then leases it to the customer at a profit

ijara wa-iqtina FINANCE agreement by customer to buy item after leasing it in Islamic financing, a leasing arrangement with a bank similar to ijara in which the customer agrees to purchase the item at a prearranged price at the end of the lease term

ILG *abbr* STOCKHOLDING & INVESTMENTS ***index-linked gilt***

illegal parking STOCKHOLDING & INVESTMENTS, FRAUD concealing true ownership an illegal stock market practice of using another company's name when purchasing securities (slang)

illiquid FINANCE **1.** lacking easy access to cash used to describe a person or business that lacks cash or assets such as securities that can readily be converted into cash **2.** not easily convertible to cash used to describe an asset that cannot be easily converted into cash

illiquid market STOCKHOLDING & INVESTMENTS securities market with low trading volume a securities market in which very little trading is taking place

IMA *abbr* STOCKHOLDING & INVESTMENTS
1. ***investment management agreement***
2. ***Investment Management Association***

imaginization GENERAL MANAGEMENT business approach encouraging creativity and innovation an approach to creativity concerned with improving our ability to see and understand situations in new ways, with finding new ways of organizing, with creating shared understanding and personal empowerment, and with developing a capability for continuing self-organization

IMF FINANCE international lending organization an international organization based in Washington, DC, that was established by industrialized nations to monitor economic and financial developments, lend to countries with balance of payments difficulties, and provide expert policy advice and technical assistance. *Full form* ***International Monetary Fund***

immediate annuity PENSIONS single-premium annuity with immediate payments a type of ***annuity*** that is purchased with a single premium and whose payments begin immediately

immediate holding company BUSINESS subsidiary UK firm with its own subsidiaries in the United Kingdom, a company with one or more subsidiaries that is itself a subsidiary of another company (the holding company)

immovable property REAL ESTATE land and buildings land and permanent structures such as buildings

impact day MARKETS first day of trading the day when the terms of a new issue of stock are announced

impaired capital FINANCE firm's total capital lower than stock value a company's capital that is worth less than the nominal value of its stock

impaired credit FINANCE when somebody's credit rating is reduced a situation in which a person becomes less creditworthy than before

impairment of capital FINANCE how much firm's stock value exceeds total capital the extent to which the value of a company is less than the nominal value of its stock

imperfect competition MARKETS = ***monopolistic competition***

impersonation of the deceased fraud FRAUD fraud using deceased person's identity in the United Kingdom, a situation in which a person uses the identity of somebody who has recently died to commit a crime such as accessing financial information or obtaining a passport. *Abbr* ***IOD fraud***

implicit cost FINANCE cost of using resources owned by producer the cost of using resources that are owned by a company that is producing a good or service. *See also* ***explicit cost***

import INTERNATIONAL TRADE product or service introduced from abroad a product or service brought into another country from its country of origin either for sale or for use in manufacturing

import duty INTERNATIONAL TRADE, TAX tax on imported products a tax on goods imported into a country. Although it may simply be a measure for raising revenue, it can also be used to protect domestic manufacturers from overseas competition.

importer INTERNATIONAL TRADE firm bringing goods into country for sale a company that brings goods from one country to another to be sold

import license INTERNATIONAL TRADE government-issued document allowing importation of goods a document issued by a government which allows goods that are to be sold to be brought into the country from another country

import penetration INTERNATIONAL TRADE proportion of foreign goods in domestic market the degree to which one country's imports dominate the ***market share*** of those from other industrialized countries

import quota INTERNATIONAL TRADE set amount of product allowed into country a fixed quantity of a particular type of goods, which the government allows to be brought into the country from another country

import restriction INTERNATIONAL TRADE government action limiting goods brought into country an action by a government to reduce the level of imported goods, for example, by setting quotas and imposing duties

import surcharge INTERNATIONAL TRADE, TAX extra tax on imported goods to discourage imports an extra duty levied on imported goods in an attempt to limit imports in general and to encourage local manufacture

imprest account ACCOUNTING type of petty cash record in the United Kingdom, a record of the transactions of a type of petty cash system. An employee is given an advance of money, an imprest, for incidental expenses and, when most of it has been spent, he or she presents receipts for

     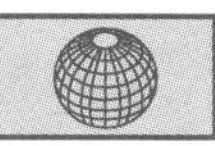   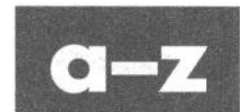

the expenses to the accounts department and is then reimbursed with cash to the total value of the receipts.

imprest system ACCOUNTING petty cash system involving written receipts in the United Kingdom, a system of controlling a petty cash fund, in which cash is paid out against a written receipt, and the receipt is used to get more cash to bring the fund up to the original level

improvement curve GENERAL MANAGEMENT = ***learning curve***

imputation system TAX dividend tax credit for tax paid by firm a system in which recipients of dividends gain tax advantage for taxes paid by the company that paid the dividends

imputed interest FINANCE, TAX taxable interest considered paid but not paid interest that is considered to be paid and may be taxed, even though it has not yet been paid

IMRO *abbr* REGULATION & COMPLIANCE ***Investment Management Regulatory Organisation***

inactive account BANKING bank account that is not in use a bank account that is not used over a particular period of time

inactive market MARKETS market with little trading taking place a stock or commodities market in which there is little interest shown by potential investors, resulting in few trades

'inan BUSINESS business partnership where partners contribute money and work in Islamic financing, a type of partnership in which the partners contribute both capital and work to a business

Inc. *abbr* BUSINESS ***incorporated***

incentive plan *US* FINANCE program rewarding improved performance a program set up to give benefits to employees to reward them for improved commitment and performance and as a means of motivation. An incentive plan is designed to supplement ***base pay*** and ***fringe benefits***. A financial incentive plan may offer stock options or a cash bonus, whereas a nonfinancial incentive plan offers benefits such as additional paid vacations. Awards from incentive plans may be made on an individual or team basis. *UK term* ***incentive scheme***

incentive scheme *UK* FINANCE = ***incentive plan***

incentive stock option STOCKHOLDING & INVESTMENTS US plan allowing employees to buy stock in the United States, an employee stock option plan that gives each qualifying employee the right to purchase a specific number of the corporation's shares at a set price during a specific time period. Tax is only payable when the stocks are sold.

incestuous share dealing STOCKHOLDING & INVESTMENTS stock trading among firms in same group stock trading by companies within a group in the stock of the other companies within that group. The legality of such transactions depends on the objective of the deals.

inchoate instrument FINANCE incomplete monetary contract a ***negotiable instrument*** that is incomplete because, for example, the date or amount is missing. The person to whom it is delivered has the authority to complete it in any way he or she considers fit.

incidence of tax TAX indicating who must pay tax used to indicate where the final burden of a tax lies. For example, although a retailer pays any sales tax to the tax collecting authority, the tax itself is ultimately paid by the customer.

incidental expenses FINANCE small amounts spent on unplanned items small amounts of money spent at various times in addition to the usual larger budgeted amounts

income 1. FINANCE money received money received by a company or individual **2.** FINANCE money created money generated by a business **3.** STOCKHOLDING & INVESTMENTS interest or dividends received from investments money received from savings or investments, for example, interest on a bank account or dividends from stock

income bond STOCKHOLDING & INVESTMENTS bond repaid from profits a bond that a company repays only from its profits

income distribution 1. FINANCE, HR & PERSONNEL levels of earnings across group or area the distribution of income across a specific group such as a company or specific area such as a region or country, showing the various wage levels and the percentage of individuals earning at each level **2.** *UK* STOCKHOLDING & INVESTMENTS = ***income dividend***

income dividend *US* STOCKHOLDING & INVESTMENTS money paid to investors from group investment earnings payment to investors of the income generated by a collective investment, less management charges, tax, and expenses. It is distributed in proportion to the number of shares held by each investor. *UK term* ***income distribution*** *(sense 2)*

income elasticity of demand FINANCE demand changing with income a proportional change in demand in response to a change in income

income fund STOCKHOLDING & INVESTMENTS fund focused on high income a fund that attempts to provide high income rather than capital growth

income gearing FINANCE ratio of firm's loan interest payments to profits the ratio of the interest a company pays on its borrowing shown as a percentage of its pre-tax profits

income redistribution ECONOMICS government policy to balance income levels through taxation a government policy to redirect income to a targeted sector of a country's population, for example, by lowering the rate of tax paid by low-income earners

income shares *UK* STOCKHOLDING & INVESTMENTS = ***income stock***

income smoothing ACCOUNTING accounting method to make income appear steady a form of ***creative accounting*** that involves the manipulation of a company's financial statements to show steady annual profits rather than large fluctuations

incomes policy ECONOMICS UK government policy to limit wage and price increases in the United Kingdom, any government policy that seeks to restrain increases in wages or prices by regulating the permitted level of increase

income statement ACCOUNTING = ***profit and loss account***

income stock *US* **1.** STOCKHOLDING & INVESTMENTS stock expected to pay high dividends common stock sought because of its relatively high yield as opposed to its potential to produce capital growth **2.** MARKETS split fund shares receiving income, not capital appreciation certain funds, for example, investment trusts, that issue split level funds where holders of the income element receive all the income (less expenses, charges, and tax), while holders of the capital element receive only the capital gains (less expenses, charges, and tax). *UK term* ***income shares***

income stream FINANCE money received from product or activity the income received by a company from a particular product or activity

income support FINANCE UK government subsidy for people with low incomes in the United Kingdom, a government benefit paid to low-income earners who are working less than 16 hours per week, and may be disabled or have family care responsibilities. *Abbr* ***IS***

income tax TAX tax on money received a tax levied directly on the income of a person or a company and paid to a local, state, or federal government. *Abbr* ***IT***

income tax allowance TAX untaxed part of person's income in the United Kingdom, a proportion of somebody's income that is not subject to tax. Allowances are announced each year by the ***Chancellor of the Exchequer*** in the ***Budget***. *See also* ***income tax***

income tax return TAX report of earnings for tax purposes a standard format used for reporting income and computing the tax due on it. *Also called* ***declaration of income***

income unit STOCKHOLDING & INVESTMENTS in UK, share in mutual fund in the United Kingdom, a share in a mutual fund that makes regular dividend payments to its stockholders

income yield STOCKHOLDING & INVESTMENTS = ***current yield***

inconvertible CURRENCY & EXCHANGE describing currency not easily converted used to describe a currency that cannot be easily converted into other currencies

incorporated BUSINESS set up as corporation in the United States, legally established as a corporation. *Abbr* ***inc.***

incorporation LEGAL process of forming corporation the legal process of creating a corporation or company. Incorporated entities have a legal status distinct from that of their owners, and limited liability.

incorporeal chattels LEGAL intellectual properties intangible properties such as patents or copyrights

incremental scale *UK* HR & PERSONNEL system of salaries increasing by regular yearly amounts a scale that includes standard increases, especially a salary scale that increases by regular annual amounts

indebted FINANCE owing money to somebody else used to describe a person, company, or country that owes money to another person, a financial institution, or another country

indebtedness FINANCE amount of debt the degree to which a person, organization, or country owes money. High levels of domestic and public indebtedness have an effect on economic growth. ***Mortgage indebtedness*** was major factor in the global financial crisis of 2007–8.

indemnity FINANCE agreement to pay compensation an agreement by one party to make good the losses suffered by another. *See also* ***indemnity insurance***, ***letter of indemnity***

indemnity insurance INSURANCE insurance paid to reimburse damages or losses an insurance contract in which the insurer agrees to cover the cost of losses suffered by the insured party. Most insurance contracts take this form except personal accident and life insurance policies, where fixed sums are paid as compensation, rather than reimbursement, for a loss that cannot be quantified in monetary terms.

indenture STOCKHOLDING & INVESTMENTS agreement about bond a formal document showing the terms of agreement on a ***bond issue***

independent authenticator BUSINESS firm that guarantees other firms are genuine a company that has the authority, either from the government or a controlling body, to issue certificates of authentication when they are sure that a company is who it claims to be

independent company BUSINESS firm not owned by another firm a company that is not owned or controlled by any another company

independent financial adviser FINANCE somebody giving unbiased advice about money a person who gives impartial advice to clients on financial matters and who is not employed by any financial institution, although commission for the sale of products may be received. *Abbr* ***IFA***. See also ***financial planner***

independent variable STATISTICS factor whose change in value affects other factors a factor whose value, when it changes, influences one or more other variables

index 1. FINANCE amount representing value of group an amount calculated to represent the relative value of a group of things **2.** MARKETS number indicating value of stocks in market a standard that represents the value of stocks in a market, for example, the ***Dow Jones Industrial Average***, ***FTSE 100***, or ***Hang Seng Index***. *Also called* ***stock market index***. *UK term* ***share index***

index arbitrage MARKETS simultaneously trading stocks and stock index futures the buying or selling of a basket of stocks against an index option or future

indexation FINANCE connecting rate to standard price index the linking of a rate to a standard index of prices, interest rates, stock prices, or similar items

indexed portfolio STOCKHOLDING & INVESTMENTS stock in all firms in stock exchange index a portfolio of stock in all the companies that form the basis of a specific stock exchange index

index fund STOCKHOLDING & INVESTMENTS mutual fund linked to stock exchange index a mutual fund composed of companies listed in an important stock market index in order to match the market's overall performance. *Also called* ***index tracker***, ***tracker fund***. *See also* ***managed fund***

index futures STOCKHOLDING & INVESTMENTS futures contract on stock exchange index a ***futures contract*** trading in one of the major stock market indices such as the ***S&P 500***

index-linked FINANCE changing in relation to numerical scale varying in value in relation to an index, especially the ***consumer price index***, or the ***retail price index*** for index-linked securities in the United Kingdom

index-linked bond STOCKHOLDING & INVESTMENTS investment product with index tied to index a security where the income is linked to an index such as a financial index. *See also* ***index-linked gilt***, ***index-linked savings certificate***

index-linked gilt STOCKHOLDING & INVESTMENTS UK bond with payments linked to retail prices in the United Kingdom, an inflation-proof government bond, first introduced for institutional investors in 1981 and then made available to the general public in 1982. It is inflation-proof in two ways: the dividend is raised every six months in line with the ***retail price index*** and the original capital is repaid in real terms at redemption, when the indexing of the repayment is undertaken.
The nominal value of the stock, however, does not increase with inflation. Like other gilts, ILGs are traded on the market. Price changes are principally dependent on investors' changing perceptions of inflation and real yields. *Abbr* ***ILG***

index-linked savings certificate STOCKHOLDING & INVESTMENTS UK savings type with payments linked to inflation rate a certificate issued by the UK ***National Savings & Investments*** organization, with a return linked to the ***retail price index***. *See also* ***granny bond***

index-linked security *UK* STOCKHOLDING & INVESTMENTS = ***sinflation-proof security***

index number ECONOMICS number indicating relative economic change a weighted average of a number of observations of an economic attribute, for example, retail prices expressed as a percentage of a similar weighted average calculated at an earlier period

index of leading economic indicators ECONOMICS predictor of future economic performance a statistical measure that uses a set of economic variables to predict the future performance of an economy

index option STOCKHOLDING & INVESTMENTS option to purchase shares in market index an option to purchase shares in a stock market index. This allows an investor to trade within a particular sector and eliminates some of the risk of investing in individual stocks.

index tracker STOCKHOLDING & INVESTMENTS = ***index fund***

index tracking MARKETS managing stocks to match stock exchange performance an investment technique whereby a portfolio is maintained in such a way as to match the growth in a stock market index

indicated dividend STOCKHOLDING & INVESTMENTS predicted annual dividends if current rate stays same the forecast total of all dividends in a year if the amount of each dividend remains as it is

indicated yield STOCKHOLDING & INVESTMENTS predicted annual income the forecast yield at the current dividend rate

indication price *UK* MARKETS approximate price of investment product an approximation of the price of a security as opposed to its firm price

indicative price MARKETS investment product price as shown on trading screen the price shown on a screen-based system for trading securities such as the UK Stock Exchange Automated Quotations system. The price is not firm, as the size of the bargain will determine the final price at which market makers will actually deal.

indicator STATISTICS something that shows situation's trend over time a variable that, followed over time, gives an indication of a trend with regard to a particular situation

indifference curve ECONOMICS curve on graph representing customers' product satisfaction a line on a graph showing how consumers view different combinations of products. The line joins various points, each point representing a combination of two products, and each combination giving the customer equal satisfaction.

indirect channel MARKETING selling and distribution via intermediary the selling and distribution of products to customers through intermediaries such as wholesalers, distributors, agents, dealers, or retailers

indirect cost ACCOUNTING unchanging expense not directly related to production a fixed or overhead cost that cannot be attributed directly to the production of a particular item and is incurred even when there is no output. Indirect costs may include the ***cost center*** functions of finance and accounting, information technology, administration, and personnel. *See also* ***direct cost***

indirect labor costs OPERATIONS & PRODUCTION pay for staff not directly involved in production the cost of paying employees such as cleaners or cafeteria staff who are not directly involved in making a product. Such costs cannot be allocated to a ***cost center***.

indirect tax TAX tax not paid directly to government a tax such as sales tax that is not paid directly to the government that levies it but is collected and paid by a third party

indirect taxation TAX process of collecting taxes paid through third party the process of levying taxes that are not paid directly to a government, but are paid through a third party. A sales tax, for example, is paid by the purchaser of a product to the seller, who then pays the tax to the government.

individual retirement account PENSIONS *see* ***IRA***

Individual Savings Account STOCKHOLDING & INVESTMENTS *see* ***ISA***

Individual Voluntary Arrangement LEGAL UK payment agreement between debtors and lenders in the United Kingdom, a legally binding arrangement between debtors and creditors by which debtors offer the creditors the best deal they can afford by realizing their assets, thus avoiding the expense of bankruptcy proceedings

induction *UK* HR & PERSONNEL = ***orientation***

industrial action *UK* GENERAL MANAGEMENT = ***job action***

industrial dispute *UK* GENERAL MANAGEMENT = ***labor dispute***

industrial espionage GENERAL MANAGEMENT underhand methods of obtaining rival's commercial secrets the practice of spying on a business competitor in order to obtain its trade or commercial secrets. Information sought through industrial espionage will often refer to new products, designs, formulas, manufacturing processes, marketing surveys, research, or future plans. The goal of industrial espionage is either to injure the business prospects or market share of the target company, or to use the secrets discovered for another organization's commercial benefit.

industrial goods OPERATIONS & PRODUCTION goods produced for industry goods used in industrial processes, including processed or raw materials, machinery, components, and equipment

     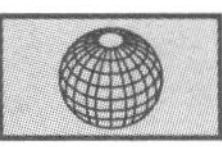   

industrial goods marketing MARKETING marketing of goods to organizations marketing directed at organizations, businesses, and other institutions, rather than at the individual end user of a product. It may require different marketing strategies from those used in ***consumer goods marketing*** to be effective.

industrial marketing MARKETING marketing of goods or services to organizations the marketing of goods or services to companies, as opposed to individual consumers. Industrial marketing involves a number of key differences from selling to consumers. These include a smaller customer base with higher value or larger unit purchases, more technically complex or specially tailored products, professionally qualified purchasers, closer buyer–seller relationships, and possible group-purchasing decision making. *Also called* ***B2B marketing***

industrial market research MARKETING research into marketing of products to organizations research into the marketing of services and goods to industry, businesses, and other institutions. Industrial market research is used as an aid to ***decision making*** and concerns the manufacture, selling, and distribution of products with the goal of reducing costs and increasing profits. It considers factors such as the available labor force, location of the firm, export market potential, and use of resources.

industrial production ECONOMICS total output of factories and mines the output of a country's productive industries. Until the 1960s, this commonly related to iron and steel or coal, but since then lighter engineering in automobile or robotics manufacture has taken over.

industrial revenue bond STOCKHOLDING & INVESTMENTS bond to pay for building a bond that a private company uses to finance construction

industrial services marketing MARKETING marketing of services to organizations the marketing of services such as maintenance contracts, insurance, training, transportation, office cleaning, and advertising to industry, businesses, and other institutions. Many services offered to industry are also offered to the consumer, but promoting them to consumers requires strategies derived from ***consumer services marketing***.

industrial tribunal HR & PERSONNEL UK court deciding employment disagreements in the United Kingdom, a court that can hear and decide disputes involving employment. These include disputes relating to discrimination, unfair dismissal, breach of contract, and pay.

industry BUSINESS **1.** all components of manufacturing process all factories, companies, or processes involved in the manufacturing of products **2.** companies providing similar products or services a group of companies making the same type of product or offering the same type of service

ineligible bills FINANCE bills unacceptable for discounting those ***bills of exchange*** that cannot be ***discounted*** by a central bank

inertia selling MARKETING selling by sending unsolicited goods in the United Kingdom, a method of selling, regarded by some as unethical, that involves the sending of unsolicited goods on a sale or return policy. Inertia selling relies on the passive reaction of a potential purchaser to choose to pay for the goods received rather than undertake the effort to send them back. The receiver of the goods is not bound by law to pay for them but must keep them in good condition until they are collected or returned.

infant industry BUSINESS new area of business an industry in the early stages of development

inference STATISTICS conclusion about statistical population based on observation a conclusion drawn by a researcher about a statistical population after observing individuals in the population

inferior good ECONOMICS item demanded less as income rises a good that a consumer buys in decreasing quantities as his or her income rises. *Also called* ***Giffen good***

infinite capacity plan OPERATIONS & PRODUCTION plan for resource requirements disregarding workstation limitations a plan produced where ***capacity requirements planning*** does not take account of the capacity constraints of each workstation. *See also* ***capacity requirements planning***

inflation ECONOMICS increase in prices over time a sustained increase in a country's general level of prices which devalues its currency, often caused by excess demand in the economy

inflation accounting ACCOUNTING record-keeping method including effects of inflation the adjustment of a company's accounts to reflect the effect of inflation and provide a more realistic view of the company's position

inflationary ECONOMICS tending to cause increase in prices characterized by excess demand or high costs creating an excessive increase in the country's money supply

inflationary gap ECONOMICS situation where demand is greater than production capacity a gap that exists when an economy's resources are utilized and ***aggregate demand*** is more than the full-employment level of output. Prices will rise to remove the excess demand.

inflationary spiral ECONOMICS cycle of rising prices and wages a situation in which, repeatedly, in inflationary conditions, excess demand causes producers to raise prices and employees to demand wage rises to sustain their living standards. *Also called* ***wage-price spiral***

Inflation linked bond STOCKHOLDING & INVESTMENTS, RISK government bond with inflation protection a bond issued by a government that is indexed to protect against inflation

inflation-proof ECONOMICS indexed to inflation so as to preserve value used to describe a pension, wage, or investment that is indexed to inflation so that its value is preserved in times of inflation

inflation-proof security *US* STOCKHOLDING & INVESTMENTS security growing with inflation a security that is indexed to inflation or a cost-of-living index. *UK term* ***index-linked security***

inflation rate ECONOMICS rate at which prices increase over time the rate at which general price levels increase over a period of time

inflation target ECONOMICS central bank's goal for increase in prices a range or figure for the rate of increase in prices that the central bank of a country aims to reach at a specific date in the future

inflation tax TAX **1.** government gain from inflation the decrease in buying power imposed by inflation on holders of currency and fixed-return assets, to the government's gain as it inflates the money supply **2.** tax on firms that give large pay raises an income policy that taxes companies that grant pay raises above a specific level

infomediary E-COMMERCE website providing industry information for companies a website that provides and aggregates relevant customer or industry information for other companies

infomercial MARKETING commercial including helpful information a television or cinema commercial that includes helpful information about a product as well as advertising content

info rate MARKETS provisional rate a money market rate quoted by dealers for information only

informal economy ECONOMICS untaxed, unofficial economic activity the economy that runs in parallel to the formal economy but outside the reach of the tax system, most transactions being paid for in cash or goods

information management GENERAL MANAGEMENT acquisition and organization of information the acquisition, recording, organizing, storage, dissemination, and retrieval of information. Good information management has been described as getting the right information to the right person in the right format at the right time.

information space E-COMMERCE Web as information source the abstract concept of all the knowledge, expertise, and information accessible on the Web

infrastructure GENERAL MANAGEMENT basic support system the basic parts of a system that function together to support something, for example, the network and systems that support computing or the public services and facilities that support business activity

ingot CURRENCY & EXCHANGE gold or silver bar a bar of gold or silver

inheritance FINANCE property received from somebody who has died property that is received from somebody through a will or by legal succession

inheritance tax TAX **1.** US tax paid on inherited property in some states of the United States, tax paid on property received by inheritance or legal succession, calculated according to the value of the property received **2.** UK tax paid on estate before distribution to heirs in the United Kingdom, tax payable on wealth or property worth above a specific amount and inherited after somebody's death. The threshold introduced on April 6, 2009, was £325,000, with the estate liable for 40% tax on the excess amount. *Abbr* ***IHT***

initial capital FINANCE money used for starting firm the money that is used to start a business. Sources of initial capital might include personal funds, bank loans, grants, or credit from suppliers.

initial margin STOCKHOLDING & INVESTMENTS required deposit on open positions the deposit required of members of the ***London Clearing House*** on all open positions, long or short, to cover short-term price movements. It is returned to members when the position is closed. *See also* ***variation margin***

initial offer STOCKHOLDING & INVESTMENTS in UK, first offer on another firm's stock in the United Kingdom, the first offer that a company makes to buy the stock of another company

initial public offering STOCKHOLDING & INVESTMENTS first time firm's stock are sold the first

instance of making particular stock available for sale to the public. *Abbr* ***IPO***. See also ***flotation***

initial sales OPERATIONS & PRODUCTION product sales when product is new to market the sales of a new product or service immediately after its introduction to the market

initial yield STOCKHOLDING & INVESTMENTS expected yield of new investment fund the yield that an investment fund is estimated to provide at its launch

injunction LEGAL court ruling preventing specific action a court order preventing a person or organization from doing something

inland bill CURRENCY & EXCHANGE in UK, bill belonging to one country in the United Kingdom, a bill of exchange that is payable and drawn in the same country

inland freight charge OPERATIONS & PRODUCTION fee for transporting products within country a charge for transporting goods from one part of a country to another part of the same country

Inland Revenue TAX, INTERNATIONAL TRADE *see* ***Her Majesty's Revenue & Customs***

Inland Revenue Department TAX New Zealand government agency responsible for taxes the New Zealand government body responsible for the administration of the national taxation system. *Abbr* ***IRD***

innovation GENERAL MANAGEMENT creation of new product or service the creation, development, and implementation of a new product, process, or service with the goal of improving efficiency, effectiveness, or ***competitive advantage***. Innovation may apply to products, services, manufacturing processes, managerial processes, or the design of an organization. It is most often viewed at a product or process level, where product innovation satisfies a customer's needs, and process innovation improves efficiency and effectiveness. Innovation is linked with creativity, and involves taking new ideas and turning them into reality through invention, research, and new product development.

inputs OPERATIONS & PRODUCTION things needed for producing products and services resources such as materials, staff, equipment, and funds that are required to produce a product or service

input tax TAX *see* ***VAT***

input tax credit TAX refund of Canadian Goods and Services Tax in Canada, an amount paid as ***Goods and Services Tax*** on supplies purchased for business purposes, which can be offset against Goods and Services Tax collected

inside director CORPORATE GOVERNANCE full-time director of firm a director who works full-time in a corporation. *See also* ***outside director***

inside information *or* insider information STOCKHOLDING & INVESTMENTS secret knowledge about firm information that is of advantage to investors but is only available to people who have personal contact with a company

inside quote MARKETS range of buyers' and sellers' prices a range of prices for a security, from the highest offer to buy to the lowest offer to sell

insider BUSINESS somebody with secret information about firm somebody who has access to information that is privileged and unavailable to most members of the public

insider dealing *or* insider trading MARKETS, FRAUD trading stock using secret information profitable, usually illegal, trading in securities carried out using information not available to the public

insolvency FINANCE lacking money to pay debt the inability to pay debts when they become due. Insolvency will apply even if total assets exceed total liabilities, if those assets cannot be readily converted into cash to meet debts as they mature. Even then, insolvency may not necessarily mean ***business failure***. ***Bankruptcy*** may be avoided through ***debt rescheduling*** or ***turnaround management***.

insolvency practitioner FINANCE UK insolvency specialist in the United Kingdom, a licensed professional who advises on or acts in all formal insolvency procedures

insolvent FINANCE unable to pay debts used to describe a person or business that is unable to pay debts, because the debts are more than the amount of assets that can be readily turned into cash

insourcing GENERAL MANAGEMENT use of internal staff, not external contractor or consultant the use of in-house personnel or an internal department to meet an organization's need for specific services. Insourcing is seen as a reaction to the growing popularity of ***outsourcing***, a practice that has not always met expectations.

inspector of taxes TAX UK government tax official in the United Kingdom, an official who reports to HM Revenue & Customs and is responsible for issuing tax returns and assessments, determining tax liabilities, and conducting appeals on tax matters

installment FINANCE one of several payments for initial public offering one of two or more payments made for the purchase of an initial public offering

installment activity statement TAX, STOCKHOLDING & INVESTMENTS Australian form for reporting payments on investment income a standard form used in Australia to report ***pay-as-you-go*** installment payments on investment income. *Abbr* ***IAS***

installment loan *US* FINANCE fixed-interest loan with regular payments a loan that is repaid with fixed regular installments, and with a rate of interest fixed for the duration of the loan. *UK term* ***instalment credit***

installment plan *US* FINANCE method of paying for purchase with regular payments a method of buying something by paying for it in regular equal amounts over a period of time. *UK terms* ***hire purchase***, ***easy terms***

instalment credit *UK* FINANCE = ***installment loan***

instant access account BANKING UK savings account with easily accessible funds in the United Kingdom, a savings account that pays interest, but from which the account holder can withdraw money immediately whenever he or she needs it

Institute of Chartered Accountants in England and Wales ACCOUNTING UK accounting organization the largest professional accounting body in Europe, providing certification by examinations, ensuring high standards of education and training, and supervising professional conduct. *Abbr* ***ICAEW***

Institute of Chartered Accountants in Ireland ACCOUNTING Ireland-wide accounting organization the oldest and largest professional body for accountants in Ireland, the ICAI was founded in 1888. Its many objectives include promoting best practice in chartered accountancy and maintaining high standards of professionalism among its members. It publishes a journal, *Accountancy Ireland*, and has offices in Dublin and Belfast. *Abbr* ***ICAI***

Institute of Chartered Accountants of New Zealand ACCOUNTING New Zealand accounting organization the only professional accounting body in New Zealand, representing over 26,000 members in that country and abroad. ICANZ has overseas branch offices in Fiji, London, Melbourne, and Sydney. *Abbr* ***ICANZ***

Institute of Chartered Accountants of Scotland ACCOUNTING Scottish accounting organization the world's oldest professional body for accountants, based in Edinburgh. *Abbr* ***ICAS***

Institute of Chartered Secretaries and Administrators *UK* FINANCE association of administrators and administrative assistants an organization that works to promote the efficient administration of commerce, industry, and public affairs. Founded in 1891 and granted a royal charter in 1902, it represents the interests of its members to government, publishes journals and other materials, promotes the standing of its members, and provides educational support and qualifying programs. *Abbr* ***ICSA***

Institute of Directors CORPORATE GOVERNANCE UK organization for directors of firms in the United Kingdom, an individual membership association whose stated objective is to "serve, support, represent, and set standards for directors." Founded in 1903 by Royal Charter, the IoD it is an independent, nonpolitical body. It is based in London, but also has offices in Belfast, Birmingham, Bristol, Edinburgh, Manchester, and Nottingham. *Abbr* ***IoD***

Institute of Financial Accountants ACCOUNTING UK organization for accountants a UK professional organization, established in 1916, that works to set technical and ethical standards in financial accounting. *Abbr* ***IFA***

Institute of Financial Services BANKING UK organization for financial education in the United Kingdom, the trading name of the Chartered Institute of Bankers, especially when involved with education

Institute of Insurance Brokers INSURANCE UK association of insurance brokers in the United Kingdom, the professional body for insurance brokers and the caretaker for the deregulated Insurance Brokers Registration Council's complaints program. *Abbr* ***IIB***

institutional buyout MERGERS & ACQUISITIONS purchase of firm by financial institution the ***takeover*** of a company by a financial institution that backs a group of managers who will run it

institutional investor STOCKHOLDING & INVESTMENTS organization that invests an institution such as an insurance company, bank, or labor union that makes investments

institutional survey STATISTICS statistical analysis of firms a statistical investigation in which an institution such as a company is the unit of analysis

instrument **1.** FINANCE way of achieving something a means to an end, for example, a government's expenditure and taxation in its quest for reducing unemployment

  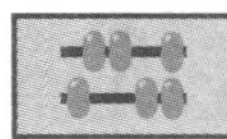      

2. STOCKHOLDING & INVESTMENTS investment product a generic term for either securities or derivatives. Instruments can be negotiable or nonnegotiable. *See also* ***financial instrument***, ***negotiable instrument*** **3.** LEGAL legal document an official or legal document

insufficient funds FINANCE too little money in bank account for check a lack of enough money in a bank account to pay a check drawn on that account

insurable interest INSURANCE personal interest in insured property a relationship between a person insuring something and the thing insured that would cause the person financial loss if the thing insured were damaged or destroyed

insurable risk INSURANCE quantifiable risk a risk that can be accurately assessed on the basis of past experience and for which insurance policy may be acquired. *See also* ***risk***

insurance **1.** INSURANCE contract to pay for others' losses a legally binding arrangement in which individuals or companies pay another company to guarantee them compensation if they suffer loss resulting from risks such as fire, theft, or accidental damage **2.** MARKETS any method of reducing investment risk in financial markets, hedging or any other strategy that reduces risk while permitting participation in potential gains

Insurance and Superannuation Commission INSURANCE Australian government insurance agency an Australian federal government body responsible for regulating the superannuation and insurance industries. *Abbr* ***ISC***

insurance broker INSURANCE somebody who sells insurance a person or company that acts as an intermediary between companies providing insurance and individuals or companies that need insurance

Insurance Brokers Registration Council INSURANCE *see* ***IBRC***

insurance company INSURANCE firm that pays for damage or injury a company whose business is guaranteeing people compensation if they suffer financial loss as a result of events such as death, fire, and accidental damage

Insurance Council of Australia INSURANCE Australian organization supporting insurance firms an independent body representing the interests of businesses involved in the insurance industry. It was established in 1975 and currently represents around 110 companies. *Abbr* ***ICA***

insurance coverage *or* insurance cover INSURANCE guaranteed compensation for specified risks the type and amount of compensation against specific risks that is guaranteed by an ***insurance policy***

insurance intermediary INSURANCE somebody that gives insurance advice and arranges policies a person or company that provides advice on insurance and can arrange policies. *See also* ***IIB***, ***IBRC***

insurance policy INSURANCE contract specifying terms of insurance a document that sets out the terms and conditions for providing compensation against specific risks

insurance premium INSURANCE regular payment to insurance firm a regular payment made by a person or a company to a company for a specific ***insurance policy***

insurance premium tax TAX UK tax on general insurance in the United Kingdom, a tax on household, motor vehicle, travel, and other general insurance

insurance reserves *US* INSURANCE insurance firm's funds in reserve the assets that an insurance company maintains to meet future claims or losses. *UK term* ***technical reserves***

insure INSURANCE **1.** agree to compensate in declared circumstances to make a contract to pay compensation if a particular loss or event occurs **2.** *US* insure somebody's life to insure somebody's life, so that the insurance company will pay compensation when that person dies. *UK term* ***assure***

insured INSURANCE protected by insurance covered by a contract of insurance for specific risks such as loss, damage, illness, or death

insured account INSURANCE US bank account protected by insurance in the United States, an account with a bank or savings institution that belongs to a federal or private insurance organization

insured bond STOCKHOLDING & INVESTMENTS bond protected by insurance a bond whose principle and interest payments are insured against default

insurer INSURANCE insurance provider a company that provides insurance for a variety of risks *UK term* ***assurer***

intangible asset FINANCE non-material resource an asset such as intellectual property or ***goodwill***. *Also called* ***invisible asset***. *See also* ***tangible asset***

intangibles FINANCE non-material costs and benefits to business the benefits to a business such as customer goodwill and employee loyalty, and costs such as training time and lost production, that cannot easily be quantified

integrated implementation model GENERAL MANAGEMENT product development with simultaneous stages a model of ***new product development*** that strives to achieve both flexibility and acceleration of development. All activities such as design, production planning, and test marketing are performed in parallel rather than going through a sequential linear progression. *See also* ***new product development***

integration BUSINESS joining business under central authority the act of bringing several businesses together under a central control

intellectual assets FINANCE knowledge, experience, and skills of workers the knowledge, experience, and skills of its staff that an organization can make use of

intellectual capital FINANCE firm's combined intangible assets the combined intangible assets owned or controlled by a company or organization that provide ***competitive advantage***. Intellectual capital assets can include the knowledge and expertise of employees, brands, customer information and relationships, contracts, ***intellectual property*** such as patents and copyright, and organizational technologies, processes, and methods. Intellectual capital can be implicit and intangible, stored in people's heads, or explicit and documented in written or electronic format.

intellectual property FINANCE ownership of items such as copyrights and patents the ownership of rights to ideas, designs, and inventions, including ***copyrights***, ***patents***, and ***trademarks***. Intellectual property is protected by law in most countries, and the World Intellectual Property Organization is responsible for harmonizing the law across different countries and promoting the protection of intellectual property rights.

intellectual property crime FRAUD crime involving counterfeiting and copyright piracy illegal activities involving the manufacture and distribution of counterfeit and copyrighted products

intellectual property rights LEGAL rights to ownership of intellectual property the legal rights a person or company has to the ownership of their ideas, designs, and inventions, including ***copyrights***, ***patents***, and ***trademarks***. *Abbr* ***IPRs***

interactive planning GENERAL MANAGEMENT process allowing participation in futures design and achievement a process that promotes participation in both the design of a desirable future and the developments that enable this future to be achieved rather than waiting for it to happen. Interactive planning is associated with Russell Ackoff, and was outlined in *Creating the Corporate Future* (1981).

interbank loan BANKING loan made to another bank a loan that one bank makes to another bank

interbank market MARKETS, BANKING lending of money amongst banks a market in which banks lend money to or borrow money from each other for short periods

Interbank Offered Rate *or* Interbank Rate MARKETS interest rate that banks charge each other the rate of interest at which banks lend to each other on the ***interbank market***. *Abbr* ***IBOR***, ***IBR***

interchange E-COMMERCE, BANKING transaction between issuing and acquiring banks a transaction between an ***acquirer*** and an ***issuer***

interchangeable bond STOCKHOLDING & INVESTMENTS bond whose form can be changed a bond whose owner can change it at will between registered and coupon form, sometimes for a fee

interchange fee E-COMMERCE, BANKING charge on interchange, paid by acquiring bank the charge on a transaction between the acquiring bank and the issuing bank, paid by the acquirer to the issuer

intercommodity spread STOCKHOLDING & INVESTMENTS options for purchase and sale of related goods a combination of purchase and sale of options for related commodities with the same delivery date

intercompany pricing OPERATIONS & PRODUCTION setting prices for product sales between firms the setting of prices by companies within a group to sell products or services to each other, rather than to external customers

inter-dealer broker STOCKHOLDING & INVESTMENTS intermediary between dealers a broker who arranges transactions between dealers in government securities

interest FINANCE borrowing charge or payment the rate that a lender charges for a loan or ***credit facility***, or a payment made by a financial institution for the use of money deposited in an account

interest arbitrage *UK* FINANCE switching funds between countries for higher interest rates transactions in two or more financial centers in order to make an immediate profit by exploiting differences in interest rates. *See also* ***arbitrage***

interest assumption FINANCE predicted amount of interest the expected rate of return on a portfolio of investments

  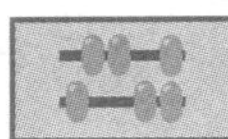      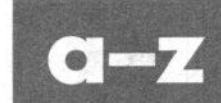

interest-bearing FINANCE paying or requiring interest used to describe a deposit, account, shares, etc., that pay interest, or a loan that requires interest

interest-bearing account *or* interest-bearing deposit BANKING money in bank account that earns interest a deposit of money, or a bank account, that receives interest

interest charge BANKING fee paid for borrowing money an amount of money paid by a borrower as interest on a loan

interest cover FINANCE amount of money available for payment of interest the amount of earnings available to make interest payments after all operating and nonoperating income and expenses, except interest and income taxes, have been accounted for.

Interest cover is regarded as a measure of a company's creditworthiness because it shows how much income there is to cover interest payments on outstanding debt.

It is expressed as a ratio, comparing the funds available to pay interest (earnings before interest and taxes, or EBIT) with the interest expense. The basic formula is

$$\frac{\text{EBIT}}{\text{Interest expense}} = \text{Interest coverage ratio}$$

If interest expense for a year is $9 million, and the company's EBIT is $45 million, the interest coverage would be

$$\frac{45\text{ million}}{9\text{ million}} = 5:1$$

The higher the number, the stronger a company is likely to be. A ratio of less than 1 indicates that a company is having problems generating enough cash flow to pay its interest expenses, and that either a modest decline in operating profits or a sudden rise in borrowing costs could eliminate profitability entirely. Ideally, interest coverage should at least exceed 1.5; in some sectors, 2.0 or higher is desirable.

Variations of this basic formula also exist. For example, there is:

$$\frac{(\text{Operating cash flow} + \text{Interest} + \text{Taxes})}{\text{Interest}} = \text{Cash flow interest coverage ratio}$$

This ratio indicates the firm's ability to use its cash flow to satisfy its fixed financing obligations. Finally, there is the fixed-charge coverage ratio, that compares EBIT with fixed charges:

$$\frac{(\text{EBIT} + \text{Lease expenses})}{(\text{Interest} + \text{Lease expenses})} = \text{Fixed-charge coverage ratio}$$

"Fixed charges" can be interpreted in many ways, however. It could mean, for example, the funds that a company is obliged to set aside to retire debt, or dividends on preferred stock.

interested party BUSINESS somebody with financial relationship to firm a person or company that has a financial interest in a company

interest-elastic investment STOCKHOLDING & INVESTMENTS investment with variable rate of return an investment with a rate of return that varies with the rise and fall of interest rates

interest expense FINANCE cost of borrowing money the cost of the interest payments on borrowed money

interest-free credit FINANCE loan for which no fee is charged credit or a loan on which no interest is paid by the borrower

interest group GENERAL MANAGEMENT group promoting members' interests a group that is concerned with promoting the economic interests of its members, for example, a business association, professional association, or labor union

interest-inelastic investment STOCKHOLDING & INVESTMENTS investment with fixed rate of return an investment with a rate of return that does not vary with the rise and fall of interest rates

interest in possession trust FINANCE UK trust whose income can be distributed immediately in the United Kingdom, a trust that gives one or more beneficiaries an immediate right to receive any income generated by the trust's assets. It can be used for real estate, enabling the beneficiary either to enjoy the rent generated by the property or to reside there, or as a life policy, a common arrangement for inheritance tax planning.

interest-only mortgage MORTGAGES loan on which interest is paid before principal a long-term loan, usually for the purchase of real estate, in which the borrower only pays interest to the lender during the term of the mortgage, with the principal being repaid at the end of the term. It is thus the borrower's responsibility to make provisions to accumulate the required capital during the period of the mortgage. *See also* ***mortgage***

interest payment FINANCE borrowing or lending charge an amount of money paid by a financial institution for the use of money deposited in an account, or money paid by a borrower as interest on a loan

interest rate FINANCE percentage of money charged for borrowing the amount of interest charged for borrowing a sum of money over a specific period of time

interest rate cap MORTGAGES highest allowed interest rate an upper limit on a rate of interest, for example, in an adjustable-rate mortgage

interest rate effect ECONOMICS interest rate change leading to increased investment the increase in investment that takes place when companies take advantage of lower interest rates to invest more

interest rate exposure *UK* FINANCE possible loss related to changes in interest rates the risk of a loss associated with movements in the level of interest rates. *See also* **bond**

interest rate floor MORTGAGES lowest allowed interest rate a lower limit on a rate of interest, for example, in an adjustable-rate mortgage

interest rate future MARKETS futures contract for interest a ***futures contract*** with an underlying asset that bears interest. *See also* ***future***

interest rate guarantee FINANCE **1.** limit on fluctuation a limit that is set to prevent interest rates moving outside a specific range **2.** legal protection from interest-rate changes a tailored indemnity protecting the purchaser against future changes in interest rates

interest rate option STOCKHOLDING & INVESTMENTS contract for interest a contract conferring the right but not an obligation to pay or receive a specific interest rate under stated terms. *See also* **option**

interest rate risk FINANCE risk of investment loss due to rising interest the risk that the value of a fixed-income investment will decrease if interest rates rise

interest rate swap FINANCE trade of loans with different interest rates an exchange of two debt instruments with different rates of interest, made to tailor cash flows to the participants' different requirements. Most commonly a longer-term fixed rate is swapped for a shorter-term floating one.

interest-sensitive FINANCE affected by changes in interest rates used to describe assets, generally purchased with credit, that are in demand when interest rates fall but considered less attractive when interest rates rise

interest yield FINANCE set rate of return paid on investment a rate of gain generated by an investment that pays a fixed rate of return, usually a percentage of the amount invested

interfirm cooperation GENERAL MANAGEMENT agreement between firms to collaborate commercially a formal or informal agreement between organizations to collaborate in achieving common or new goals more efficiently or effectively. Interfirm cooperation may take the form of a ***joint venture.***

interim certificate LEGAL document showing partial stock ownership a ***certificate of deposit*** certifying partial ownership of stock that is not totally paid for at one time

interim dividend STOCKHOLDING & INVESTMENTS dividend for part of tax year a dividend whose value is determined on the basis of a period of time of less than a full ***fiscal year***

interim financial statement FINANCE financial statement for part of tax year only a financial statement that covers a period other than a full ***fiscal year***. Although UK companies are not legally obliged to publish interim financial statements, those listed on the London Stock Exchange are obliged to publish a half-yearly report of their activities and a profit and loss account that may either be sent to stockholders or published in a national newspaper. In the United States, the practice is to issue quarterly financial statements. *Also called* ***interim statement***

interim financing FINANCE providing of temporary finance financing by means of bridge loans, between the purchase of one asset and the sale of another

interim payment STOCKHOLDING & INVESTMENTS partial payment of dividend early in year a distribution to stockholders of part of a dividend in the first part of a financial year

interim statement FINANCE = ***interim financial statement***

intermarket spread MARKETS trading in similar options in different markets a combination of purchase and sale of options for the same commodity with the same delivery date on different markets

intermediary FINANCE agent for financial transactions a person or organization that arranges financing, insurance, or investments for others

intermediate goods OPERATIONS & PRODUCTION items for producing other items goods bought for use in the production of other products

intermediation FINANCE acting as agent in financial transaction the process of arranging financing through an intermediary. Financial institutions act as intermediaries when they lend depositors' money to borrowers.

internal audit RISK audit by firm's own employees an audit of a company undertaken by its employees, usually to check on its internal controls. *See also* ***external audit***

internal benchmarking GENERAL MANAGEMENT *see* ***benchmarking***

internal consultant GENERAL MANAGEMENT expert within company advising colleagues an employee who uses knowledge and expertise to offer advice or business solutions to another department or business unit within an organization

internal consulting GENERAL MANAGEMENT advising colleagues elsewhere in firm the activity of offering advice or business solutions to another department or business unit within an organization. *See also* ***internal consultant***

internal control GENERAL MANAGEMENT management system for controlling firm's activities a system set up by the management of a company to monitor and control the company's activities

internal cost analysis ACCOUNTING investigation into organization's activities to establish profitable areas an examination of an organization's value-creating activities to determine sources of profitability and to identify the relative costs of different processes. Internal cost analysis is a tool for analyzing the ***value chain***. Principal steps include identifying those processes that create value for the organization, calculating the cost of each value-creating process against the overall cost of the product or service, identifying the cost components for each process, establishing the links between the processes, and working out the opportunities for achieving relative cost advantage.

internal differentiation analysis GENERAL MANAGEMENT assessment of what makes product or service distinctive an examination of processes in the ***value chain*** to determine which of them create differentiation of the product or service in the customer's eyes, and thus enhance its value. Internal differentiation analysis enables an organization to focus on improving the identified processes to maximize ***competitive advantage***. Steps involve identification of value-creating activities, evaluation of strategies that can enhance value for the customer, and assessment of which differentiation strategies are the most sustainable.

internal growth BUSINESS growth by developing existing business organic growth created within a business, for example, by inventing new products and so increasing its market share, producing products that are more reliable, offering a more efficient service than its competitors, or being more aggressive in its marketing. *See also* ***external growth***

internal marketing MARKETING implementation of marketing principles within organization the application of the principles of marketing within an organization. Internal marketing involves the creation of an internal market by dividing departments into business units, with control over their own operations and expenditure, with attendant impacts on corporate culture, politics, and power. Internal marketing also involves treating employees as internal customers with the goal of increasing employees' motivation and focus on customers.

internal rate of return FINANCE interest rate indicating worthwhile profit in a discounted cash flow calculation, the rate of interest that reduces future income streams to the cost of the investment; practically speaking, the rate that indicates whether or not an investment is worth pursuing.

Let's assume that a project under consideration costs $7,500 and is expected to return $2,000 per year for five years, or $10,000. The IRR calculated for the project would be about 10%. If the cost of borrowing money for the project, or the return on investing the funds elsewhere, is less than 10%, the project is probably worthwhile. If the alternative use of the money will return 10% or more, the project should be rejected, since from a financial perspective it will break even at best.

Typically, managements require an IRR equal to or higher than the cost of capital, depending on relative risk and other factors.

The best way to compute an IRR is by using a spreadsheet (such as Excel) or financial calculator.

If using Excel, for example, select the IRR function. This requires the annual cash flows to be set out in columns and the first part of the IRR formula requires the cell reference range of these cash flows to be entered. Then a guess of the IRR is required. The default is 10%, written 0.1.

If a project has the following expected cash flows, then guessing IRR at 30% returns an accurate IRR of 27%, indicating that if the next best way of investing the money gives a return of -20%, the project should go ahead.

Now	−2,500
Year 1	1,200
Year 2	1,300
Year 3	1,500

IRR can be misleading, especially as significant costs will occur late in the project. The rule of thumb "the higher the IRR the better" does not always apply. For the most thorough analysis of a project's investment potential, some experts urge using both IRR and net present value calculations, and comparing their results. *Abbr* ***IRR***

Internal Revenue Code TAX US federal tax laws the complex series of federal tax laws in the United States

Internal Revenue Service TAX *see* ***IRS***

internal trade BUSINESS trade within one country commercial activity that is carried out within a specific country. *Also called* ***home trade***. *See also* ***external trade***

internal versus external sourcing OPERATIONS & PRODUCTION = ***purchasing versus production***

International Accounting Standards Board ACCOUNTING organization that sets accounting standards an independent and privately funded standard-setting organization for the accounting profession, based in London. The Board, whose members come from nine countries and a variety of backgrounds, is committed to developing a single set of high quality, understandable, and enforceable global standards that require transparent and comparable information in general purpose financial statements. It also works with national accounting standard setters to achieve convergence in accounting standards around the world. *Abbr* ***IASB***

International Accounting Standards Committee ACCOUNTING former organization promoting international agreement on accounting standards formerly, an organization based in London that worked toward achieving global agreement on accounting standards, replaced by the ***International Accounting Standards Board***. *Abbr* ***IASC***

International Bank for Reconstruction and Development BANKING *see* ***IBRD***

International Capital Market Association MARKETS association concerned with international capital market the self-regulatory organization and trade association for the international capital market. Its primary role is to ensure the international capital market works as efficiently as possible and to promote best practice. Established in 1969 as the Association of International Bond Dealers, it changed its name to the International Securities Market Association, before merging with the International Primary Market Association to become the International Capital Market Association. The organization has approximately 390 members from 47 countries. *Abbr* ***ICMA***

International Centre for Settlement of Investment Disputes BANKING part of World Bank Group one of the five institutions that comprise the World Bank Group, based in Washington, DC. It was established in 1966 to undertake the role previously undertaken in a personal capacity by the president of the World Bank in assisting in mediation or conciliation of investment disputes between governments and private foreign investors. The overriding consideration in its establishment was that a specialist institution could help to promote increased flows of international investment. Although ICSID has close links to the World Bank, it is an autonomous organization. *Abbr* ***ICSID***

International Chamber of Commerce BUSINESS *see* ***ICC***

international depository receipt STOCKHOLDING & INVESTMENTS outside US, document indicating ownership of stock the equivalent of an ***American depository receipt*** in the rest of the world, an IDR is a negotiable certificate issued by a bank that indicates ownership of stock. *Abbr* ***IDR***

International Development Association FINANCE agency helping poorest nations an agency administered by the International Bank for Reconstruction and Development to provide assistance on concessionary terms to the poorest countries. Its resources consist of subscriptions and general replenishments from its more industrialized and developed members, special contributions, and transfers from the net earnings of the International Bank for Reconstruction and Development. *Abbr* ***IDA***

International Finance Corporation FINANCE UN agency encouraging private investment in developing nations a United Nations organization promoting private sector investment in developing countries to reduce poverty and improve the quality of people's lives. It finances private sector projects that are profit-oriented and environmentally and socially sound, and helps to foster development. The International Finance Corporation has a staff of 2,000 professionals around the world who seek profitable and creative solutions to complex business issues. *Abbr* ***IFC***

International Financial Reporting Standards ACCOUNTING standards for preparing financial statements a set of rules and guidelines established by the ***International Accounting Standards Board*** for standardizing the preparation of financial statements so that investors, organizations, and governments have a basis for comparison. *Abbr* ***IFRS***

international fund FINANCE mutual fund with domestic and foreign investments a mutual fund

  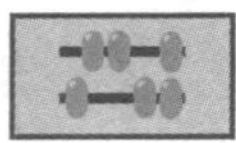   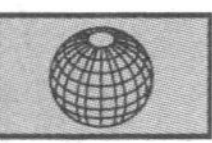   

that invests in securities both inside and outside a country

International Fund for Agricultural Development FINANCE UN agency in poor countries a specialized United Nations agency with a mandate to combat hunger and rural poverty in countries with developing economies. Established as an international financial institution in 1977 following the 1974 World Food Conference, it has financed projects in over 100 countries and independent territories, to which it has committed US$7.7 billion in grants and loans. It has three sources of finance: contributions from members, loan payments, and investment income. *Abbr* ***IFAD***

International Monetary Fund FINANCE *see* ***IMF***

international money market MARKETS, CURRENCY & EXCHANGE exchange of foreign currencies a market in which currencies can be borrowed and lent and converted into other currencies

International Organization of Securities Commissions REGULATION & COMPLIANCE institution overseeing international securities transactions an organization of securities commissions from around the world, based in Madrid. Its objectives are to promote high standards of regulation, exchange information, and establish standards for, and effective surveillance of, international securities transactions. *Abbr* ***IOSCO***

international reserves CURRENCY & EXCHANGE = ***foreign currency reserves***

International Swaps and Derivatives Association STOCKHOLDING & INVESTMENTS organization for derivative traders a professional association for international traders in derivatives, founded in 1985. *Abbr* ***ISDA***

international trade INTERNATIONAL TRADE buying and selling activity between countries the sale and purchase of goods and services that takes place between trading partners in different countries

International Union of Credit and Investment Insurers INSURANCE association concerned with exports and foreign investments an organization that works for international acceptance of sound principles of export credit and foreign investment insurance. Founded in 1934, the London-based Union has 51 members in 42 countries that play a role of central importance in world trade, both as regards exports and foreign direct investments. *Also called* ***Berne Union***

Internet merchant E-COMMERCE businessperson selling over Internet a businessperson who sells a product or service over the Internet

Internet payment system E-COMMERCE fund transfer system using Internet any mechanism for fund transfer from customer to merchant or business to business via the Internet. There are many payment options available, including credit card payment, credit transfer, electronic checks, direct debit, smart cards, prepaid plans, loyalty plan points-based approaches, person-to-person payments, and cellphone plans.

Getting the online payment system right is critical to the success of e-commerce. Currently, the most common form of online consumer payment is by credit card (90% in the United States; 70% in Europe). The most common business-to-business payments, however, are still offline, probably because such transactions often involve large sums of money.

Good online payment systems share key characteristics: ease of use; robustness and reliability; proper authentication (to combat fraud); efficient integration with the vendor's own internal systems; and security and assurance procedures that check that the seller gets the money and the buyer gets the goods.

Internet security E-COMMERCE protection of computer files from unauthorized access the means used to protect websites and other electronic files from attack by hackers and viruses. The Internet is, by definition, a network; networks are open, and are thus open to attack. A poor Internet security policy can result in a substantial loss of productivity and a drop in consumer confidence.

interpolation STATISTICS way of calculating approximate value a method of estimating an unknown value such as a return on an investment using values that are known

interquartile range STATISTICS difference between first and third quartiles the difference between the first and third quartiles of a statistical sample, used to measure the spread of variables in the data

interstate commerce BUSINESS trade between US states in the United States, commerce that involves more than one state and is therefore subject to regulation by Congress. *See also* ***intrastate commerce***

intervention ECONOMICS government action to influence market forces government action to manipulate market forces for political or economic purposes

intervention mechanism CURRENCY & EXCHANGE central banks' means of maintaining fixed exchange rates a method such as buying or selling of foreign currency used by central banks in maintaining equivalence between exchange rates

inter vivos trust FINANCE trust set up between living people a legal arrangement for managing somebody's money or property, set up by one living person for another living person

in the money STOCKHOLDING & INVESTMENTS having intrinsic value used to describe an option that, if it expired at the current market price, would have significant ***intrinsic value***. *See also* ***out of the money***

intraday MARKETS during one trading day within a single day of trading

intrapreneur GENERAL MANAGEMENT worker deploying entrepreneurial skills within firm an employee who uses the approach of an entrepreneur within an organizational setting. An intrapreneur must have freedom of action to explore and implement ideas, although the outcome of such work will be owned by the organization rather than the intrapreneur, and it is the organization that will take the associated risk. Managers of organizations in which intrapreneurs are allowed to operate subscribe to the view that innovation can be achieved by encouraging creative and exploratory activity in semiautonomous units.

intrastate commerce BUSINESS trade within US state in the United States, commerce that occurs within a single state. *See also* ***interstate commerce***

intrinsic value STOCKHOLDING & INVESTMENTS gap between share price and option price with reference to an option or convertible, the value at which a security would trade if there were no ***option premium***, i.e. the share price less the option price

introducing broker STOCKHOLDING & INVESTMENTS broker not paid directly by customers a person or organization acting as a broker but not able to accept payment from customers

introduction 1. MARKETING making product available for first time an act of bringing something into existence or operation for the first time, for example, bringing a new product onto the market for sale for the first time **2.** MARKETS initially listing established company on stock exchange the act of bringing an established company to the Stock Exchange. It is done by getting permission for the shares to be traded on the Stock Exchange, and is used when a company is formed by splitting from an existing larger company and no new shares are being offered for sale.

inventory 1. BUSINESS all commercial assets owned in the United States, the sum total of the commercial assets of an organization **2.** OPERATIONS & PRODUCTION firm's supply of finished and unfinished products the supply of finished goods, raw materials, and work in progress held by a company. *UK term* ***stock***

inventory control OPERATIONS & PRODUCTION keeping optimal level of merchandise on hand the process of making sure that the correct level of inventory is maintained, to be able to meet demand while keeping the costs of holding inventory to a minimum

inventory depreciation ACCOUNTING reduction in value of stored stock a reduction in value of inventory that is held in a warehouse for some time

inventory financing FINANCE obtaining loans against product inventory a method by which manufacturers of consumer products obtain a loan by using their inventory as collateral

inventory level OPERATIONS & PRODUCTION quantity of goods in inventory the quantity of goods kept in inventory. *Also called* ***stock level***

inventory record OPERATIONS & PRODUCTION firm's record of inventory a record of the ***inventory*** held by an organization. An inventory record forms an important part of material requirements planning systems. Such records usually make use of some form of part numbering or classification system, and include a description of the part, the quantity held, and the location of all the holdings. A ***transaction file*** keeps track of inventory use and replenishment.

inventory turnover 1. ACCOUNTING replacement rate of commercial assets an accounting ratio of the number of times ***inventory*** is replaced during a given period. The ratio is calculated by dividing net sales by average inventory over a given period. Values are expressed as times per period, most often a year, and a higher figure indicates a more efficient manufacturing operation.

It is calculated as follows:

$$\frac{\text{Cost of goods sold}}{\text{Inventory}}$$

If COGS is $2 million, and inventory at the end of the period is $500,000, then

$$\frac{2,000,000}{500,000} = 4$$

Also called ***stock turns*** **2.** *US* STOCKHOLDING & INVESTMENTS measure of how quickly inventory

     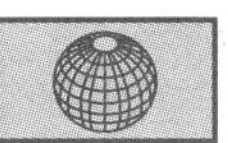   

needs replacing the total value of inventory sold in a year divided by the average value of goods held in stock. This checks that cash is not tied up in inventory for too long, losing its value over time. *UK term* ***stock turnover***

inventory valuation *US* ACCOUNTING estimation of stock value an estimation of the value of inventory at the end of an accounting period. *UK term* ***stock valuation***

inverse floating rate note STOCKHOLDING & INVESTMENTS security with interest varying inversely with base rate a security whose interest rate varies inversely with a ***base interest rate***, rising as it falls and vice versa

inverted market MARKETS when near-term futures are dearest a situation in which near-term ***futures contracts*** cost more than long-term futures for the same commodity. *See also* ***backwardation***

inverted yield curve STOCKHOLDING & INVESTMENTS showing lower interest rates for long-term bonds a visual representation of relative interest rates that shows lower interest rates for long-term bonds than for short-term bonds. *See also* ***yield curve***

invested capital FINANCE firm's stock, retained earnings plus debt the total amount of a company's stock, retained earnings, and long-term debt

investment 1. FINANCE expenditure on assets and securities the spending of money on stocks and other securities, or on assets such as plant and machinery **2.** FINANCE something invested in something such as stocks, real estate, or a project in which money is invested in the expectation of making a profit **3.** STOCKHOLDING & INVESTMENTS money invested an amount of money invested in something in the expectation of making a profit

investment analyst STOCKHOLDING & INVESTMENTS researcher into investment possibilities an employee of a stock exchange company who researches other companies and identifies investment opportunities for clients. *Also called* ***financial analyst***

investment appraisal STOCKHOLDING & INVESTMENTS assessment of future value of new assets analysis of the future profitability of capital purchases as an aid to good management

investment bank BANKING **1.** bank for corporate borrowers a bank that specializes in providing funds to corporate borrowers for startup or expansion **2.** *US* bank for investors and their backers a bank that does not accept deposits but provides services to those who offer securities to investors, and to those investors. *Abbr* ***IB***. UK term ***merchant bank***. *See also* ***commercial bank***

investment bond INSURANCE UK investment in life insurance policy in the United Kingdom, a product where the investment is paid as a single premium into a life insurance policy with an underlying asset-backed fund. The bondholder receives a regular income until the end of the bond's term when the investment (the current value of the fund) is returned to the bondholder. *Also called* ***life insurance bond***

investment borrowing ECONOMICS borrowing money to promote economic growth the borrowing of funds intended to encourage a country's economic growth or to support the development of particular industries or regions by adding to physical or human capital

investment center STOCKHOLDING & INVESTMENTS section responsible for profitable investment a profit center with additional responsibilities for capital investment, and possibly for financing, whose performance is measured by its return on investment

investment club STOCKHOLDING & INVESTMENTS group combining to invest in securities a group of people who join together to make investments in securities

investment committee BANKING bank employees assessing proposals for investment in the United States, a group of employees of an investment bank who evaluate investment proposals

investment company STOCKHOLDING & INVESTMENTS firm investing money of several investors a company that pools for investment the money of several investors. *See also* ***investment fund***

investment dealer *CANADA* STOCKHOLDING & INVESTMENTS securities broker a broker dealing in stock, bonds, debentures, and other securities. *Also called* ***broker***

investment fund STOCKHOLDING & INVESTMENTS savings plan that makes investments a savings plan that invests its clients' funds in, for example, corporate start-up or expansion projects. *See also* ***investment company***

investment grade STOCKHOLDING & INVESTMENTS refers to highly rated bond relating to a bond issued by a company, government, or local authority with a rating of BBB or higher, carrying relatively little risk. Trusts or pension funds may be restricted to investing in investment grade securities.

investment grade rating STOCKHOLDING & INVESTMENTS opinion of quality of bond as safe investment an assessment by a ***rating agency*** that a bond carries little risk for the investor. Bonds with ratings between AAA and BBB are considered investment grade.

investment grant STOCKHOLDING & INVESTMENTS government money given to firms for capital assets a government grant to a company to help it invest in capital assets such as buildings, equipment, or new machinery

investment horizon STOCKHOLDING & INVESTMENTS period of time for holding investment the length of time an investor expects to hold an investment, or the holding period over which an investment is analyzed

investment income STOCKHOLDING & INVESTMENTS money earned on investments revenue paid to investors that is derived from their investments, for example, dividends and interest on securities. *See also* ***earned income***

investment management agreement STOCKHOLDING & INVESTMENTS contract between investor and fund manager a contract between an investor and an investment manager. *Abbr* ***IMA***

Investment Management Association STOCKHOLDING & INVESTMENTS association for UK investment professionals the trade body for the UK investment industry, formed in February 2002 following the merger of the Association of Unit Trusts and Investment Funds and the Fund Managers' Association. *Abbr* ***IMA***. See also ***Fund Managers' Association***

Investment Management Regulatory Organisation REGULATION & COMPLIANCE UK group regulating investment fund managers in the United Kingdom, an organization that regulated managers of investment funds such as retirement funds, now part of the Financial Services Authority. *Abbr* ***IMRO***

investment manager STOCKHOLDING & INVESTMENTS = ***fund manager***

investment objective STOCKHOLDING & INVESTMENTS long-term financial goal of investments the financial goal that determines how an individual or institution invests its assets, for example, for long-term growth or income

investment portfolio STOCKHOLDING & INVESTMENTS = ***portfolio***

investment professional STOCKHOLDING & INVESTMENTS somebody legally qualified to give investment advice a person who is licensed to offer advice on, and sell, investment products

investment properties FINANCE buildings bought to rent out either commercial buildings such as stores, factories, or offices, or residential dwellings such as houses or apartments, that are purchased by businesses or individuals for renting to third parties

investment revaluation reserve *UK* FINANCE reserve created by firm investing in property the capital reserve where changes in the value of a business's investment properties are disclosed when they are revalued

Investment Services Directive STOCKHOLDING & INVESTMENTS former EU regulations governing investment and market conduct formerly, an EU directive regulating the conduct and operation of investment companies and markets, replaced by the ***Markets in Financial Instruments Directive***. *Abbr* ***ISD***

investment tax credit TAX former US tax advantage in the United States, a tax advantage for investment that was available until 1986

investment trust STOCKHOLDING & INVESTMENTS investment firm with limited shares an investment company with a fixed number of shares available. Investment trusts are ***closed-end investment companies***.

investment vehicle STOCKHOLDING & INVESTMENTS product or firm to invest in a financial product such as stocks, bonds, funds, or futures, or a company, in which somebody can invest money

investomer BUSINESS combined customer and investor a customer of a business who is also an investor (slang)

investor STOCKHOLDING & INVESTMENTS person or organization spending money for financial return a person or organization that invests money in something, especially in the stock of publicly owned corporations

investor relations research STOCKHOLDING & INVESTMENTS research into how financial markets view firm research carried out on behalf of an organization in order to gain an understanding of how financial markets regard the organization, its stock, and its sector

invisible asset FINANCE = ***intangible asset***

invisible earnings INTERNATIONAL TRADE foreign currency from services not commodities foreign currency earned by a country in providing services such as banking and tourism, rather than in selling goods

invisible exports INTERNATIONAL TRADE money generated by selling services overseas the profits, dividends, interest, and royalties received from selling a country's services abroad

invisible hand ECONOMICS power of market forces according to the 18th century British economist Adam Smith, the force of the market which drives the economy

invisible imports INTERNATIONAL TRADE money paid to foreign service firms the profits, dividends, interest, and royalties paid to foreign service companies based in a country

invisibles INTERNATIONAL TRADE services that are traded items such as financial and leisure services that are traded by a country, rather than physical goods

invisible trade INTERNATIONAL TRADE buying and selling services between countries trade in items such as financial and other services that are listed in the current account of the ***balance of payments***

invoice FINANCE document requesting payment a document that a supplier sends to a customer detailing the cost of products or services supplied and asking for payment

invoice date FINANCE official date of sending of invoice the date on which an invoice is issued. The invoice date may be different from the delivery date.

invoice discounting FINANCE sale of invoices for less than stated value the selling of invoices at a discount for collection by the buyer, or the payment of invoices at a discount by an intermediary with the customer's eventual payment routed through the intermediary, who takes a fee

invoice price OPERATIONS & PRODUCTION total price as listed on bill the price as given on an invoice, including any discount and sales tax

invoice register ACCOUNTING record of invoices for things bought a list of purchase invoices recording the date of receipt of the invoice, the supplier, the invoice value, and the person to whom the invoice has been passed to ensure that all invoices are processed by the accounting system

invoicing FINANCE requesting payment the process of sending out invoices to customers

involuntary bankruptcy LEGAL bankruptcy petitioned for by creditors a situation in which a petition is filed with the creditors to have a person or corporation declared bankrupt

involuntary liquidation preference STOCKHOLDING & INVESTMENTS payment to particular stockholders before liquidation a payment that a company must make to holders of its preferred stock if it is forced to sell its assets when facing bankruptcy

inward bill INTERNATIONAL TRADE list of merchandise being brought into country a bill of lading for goods arriving in a country from a foreign country

inward investment STOCKHOLDING & INVESTMENTS investment in local area investment by a government or company in its own country or region, often to stimulate employment or develop a business infrastructure

IoD *abbr* CORPORATE GOVERNANCE ***Institute of Directors***

IOD fraud *abbr* FRAUD ***impersonation of the deceased fraud***

IOSCO *abbr* REGULATION & COMPLIANCE ***International Organization of Securities Commissions***

IOU FINANCE note of money borrowed personally a representation of "I owe you" that can be used as legal evidence of a debt, although it is most commonly used as an informal reminder of a minor transaction

IP-backed STOCKHOLDING & INVESTMENTS, RISK describes securities backed by intellectual property used to describe securities whose underlying assets are intellectual property such as patents, copyrights, and trademarks

IPO *abbr* STOCKHOLDING & INVESTMENTS ***initial public offering***

IPRs *abbr* LEGAL ***intellectual property rights***

IRA PENSIONS personal pension plan allowing tax-free deposits in the United States, a pension plan, designed for individuals without a company pension plan, that allows annual sums, subject to limits dependent upon employment income, to be set aside from earnings tax-free. Individuals with a company pension may invest in an IRA, but only from their net income. IRAs, including the Education IRA, designed as a way of saving for children's education, may invest in almost any financial security except real estate. *Full form* ***individual retirement account***

IRA rollover PENSIONS transfer of assets between retirement plans in the United States, a transfer of assets from a tax-deferred qualified retirement plan to a tax-deferred IRA managed by the plan's owner

IRD *abbr* TAX ***Inland Revenue Department***

IRD number TAX New Zealand income tax code for employees a numeric code assigned to all members of the New Zealand workforce for the purpose of paying income tax

IRR *abbr* FINANCE ***internal rate of return***

irrecoverable debt FINANCE loan that will never be repaid a debt that will never be paid to the person to whom it is owed and must be written off, either as a charge to the profit and loss account or against an existing doubtful debt provision

irredeemable bond STOCKHOLDING & INVESTMENTS indefinite government bond a government bond that has no date of maturity but provides interest

irrevocable letter of credit BANKING permanent credit authorization a ***letter of credit*** that cannot be canceled

irrevocable trust FINANCE unalterable trust a trust that cannot be canceled or revised without the agreement of its beneficiary

IRS TAX US government agency for tax collection in the United States, the branch of the federal government charged with collecting the majority of federal taxes. *Full form* ***Internal Revenue Service***

IS *abbr* FINANCE ***income support***

ISA STOCKHOLDING & INVESTMENTS UK tax-free account for savings and investment in the United Kingdom, a tax-free savings or investment account. Both ***cash ISAs*** and ***stocks and shares ISAs*** are available. The maximum that can be invested per ***tax year*** is capped, at £11,280 for 2012–13, up to £5,640 of which can be saved in cash. Formerly, ***Mini ISAs*** allowed investment in either cash or stocks, and ***Maxi ISAs*** investment in both together. *Full form* ***Individual Savings Account***

ISC *abbr* INSURANCE ***Insurance and Superannuation Commission***

ISD *abbr* STOCKHOLDING & INVESTMENTS ***Investment Services Directive***

ISDA *abbr* STOCKHOLDING & INVESTMENTS ***International Swaps and Derivatives Association***

Islamic law LEGAL Muslim religious law the law as interpreted by trained Islamic legal scholars. In strict Islamic countries, all businesses, financial institutions, and products must meet the requirements of Islamic law. *Also called* ***shariah***

issuance costs FINANCE money spent issuing debt the underwriting, legal, and administrative fees required to issue a debt. These fees are significant when issuing debt in the public markets, such as the bond market. However, other types of debt, such as private placements or bank loans, are cheaper to issue because they require less underwriting, legal, and administrative support.

issue STOCKHOLDING & INVESTMENTS stocks or bonds for sale at one time a set of stocks or bonds that a company offers for sale at one time

issue by tender STOCKHOLDING & INVESTMENTS = ***sale by tender***

issued capital STOCKHOLDING & INVESTMENTS = ***share capital***

Issue Department BANKING part of Bank of England issuing currency the department of the ***Bank of England*** that is responsible for issuing currency

issued price STOCKHOLDING & INVESTMENTS price of firm's first stock issue the price of shares of stock in a company when they are offered for sale for the first time

issued share capital STOCKHOLDING & INVESTMENTS amount representing shares the type, class, number, and amount of the shares held by stockholders. *See also* ***stockholders' equity***

issued shares STOCKHOLDING & INVESTMENTS shares held by investors those shares that comprise a company's authorized capital that has been distributed to investors. They may be either fully paid or partly paid shares.

issue price STOCKHOLDING & INVESTMENTS original price of securities the price at which securities are first offered for sale

issuer E-COMMERCE organization providing payment cards a financial institution that issues payment cards such as credit or debit cards, pays out to the merchant's account, and bills the customer or debits the customer's account. The issuer guarantees payment for authorized transactions using the payment card. *Also called* ***card-issuing bank, issuing bank***

issuer bid STOCKHOLDING & INVESTMENTS offer to buy own securities an offer made by an issuer for its own securities when it is disappointed by the offers of others

issuer identification number BANKING international number identifying individual bank an internationally agreed six-digit number that uniquely identifies a bank in electronic transactions. *Abbr* ***IIN***

issues management GENERAL MANAGEMENT process of anticipating trends for commercial gain the anticipation and assessment of key trends and

  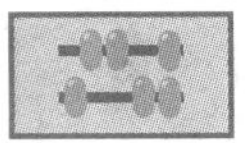      

themes of the next decade, and the relation of these to the organization. Issues management is informed by ***futures research*** in order to formulate strategic plans and actions.

issuing bank E-COMMERCE = ***issuer***

issuing house FINANCE UK financial institution that launches private companies in the United Kingdom, a financial institution that specializes in the flotation of private companies. *See also* ***investment bank, merchant bank***

istisna'a *or* istisnah OPERATIONS & PRODUCTION product manufacturing contract with agreed delivery and price in Islamic financing, a contract for manufacturing a product in which the manufacturer agrees to produce a specified product to be delivered at a specified time for a specified price

IT *abbr* TAX ***income tax***

item ACCOUNTING unit of accounting information a single piece of information included in a company's accounts

itemized deductions TAX expenses allowed to reduce US income tax in the United States, amounts paid by individual taxpayers for expenses that can be deducted to reduce taxable income, for example, medical and dental expenses, charitable contributions, mortgage interest, and losses due to theft

J

jawboning BUSINESS using status to affect decisions using influence, especially the influence of a public position or office, to try to affect the decisions of leaders in the business world

J curve CURRENCY & EXCHANGE line representing falling exchange rate's effect on trade a line on a graph shaped like a letter "J," with an initial short fall, followed by a longer rise, used to describe the effect of a falling exchange rate on a country's balance of trade

Jensen's measure FINANCE = ***risk-adjusted return on capital***

JEPI *abbr* E-COMMERCE ***joint electronic payment initiative***

jikan MARKETS Japanese rule for choosing between identical instructions in Japan, the priority rule relating to transactions on the Tokyo Stock Exchange whereby the earlier of two buy or sell orders received at the same price prevails

JIT *abbr* OPERATIONS & PRODUCTION ***just-in-time***

job BUSINESS assignment a customer order or other piece of work

job action *US* GENERAL MANAGEMENT action to force resolution of dispute a temporary action such as a strike or lockout taken by one side in a ***labor dispute*** in an attempt to bring pressure on the other side to settle. *UK term* ***industrial action***

jobber's turn MARKETS UK dealer's profit on transaction formerly, a term used on the London Stock Exchange for a ***spread***, the difference between the buying and selling price that a dealer arranges and takes as profit

jobbing backward *UK* STOCKHOLDING & INVESTMENTS review of actions the analysis of an investment transaction with the benefit of hindsight

job cost ACCOUNTING describes accounting allowing determination of profit per job used to describe a method of accounting whereby a project-oriented business allocates costs to a specific project, thereby having the ability to determine the profitability of individual projects

job lot FINANCE varied items bought or sold together a miscellaneous assortment of items, including securities, that are offered as a single deal

Johannesburg Stock Exchange MARKETS South African stock exchange the largest stock exchange in Africa, located in Johannesburg, South Africa, established in 1887. It demutualized in 2005 to become JSE Limited. The main index of stocks on the exchange is the ***FTSE/JSE Top 40***. *Abbr* ***JSE***

joint account BANKING account shared by two or more people an account, such as one held at a bank or by a broker, that two or more people own in common and can access

joint and several liability LEGAL obligation to meet payment together or individually a legal liability that applies to a group of individuals as a whole and each member individually, so that if one member does not meet his or her liability, the shortfall is the shared responsibility of the others. Most guarantees given by two or more individuals to secure borrowing are joint and several. It is a typical feature of most partnership agreements.

joint bond STOCKHOLDING & INVESTMENTS bond guaranteed by third party a bond that is guaranteed by a party other than the company or government that issued it

joint electronic payment initiative E-COMMERCE proposed protocol for electronic payment a proposed industry standard protocol for electronic payment in e-commerce transactions. *Abbr* ***JEPI***

joint float CURRENCY & EXCHANGE shared exchange relationship within set of currencies a group of currencies that maintains a fixed internal relationship and moves jointly in relation to another currency

joint life annuity INSURANCE annuity lasting until death of both parties an annuity that continues until both parties have died. They are attractive to married couples as they ensure that the survivor has an income for the rest of his or her life.

joint management GENERAL MANAGEMENT running of firm by more than one person the overseeing and control of the affairs of an organization shared by two or more people

joint ownership BUSINESS ownership by several people or organizations ownership by more than one party, each with equal rights in the item owned. Joint ownership is often applied to property or other assets.

joint return TAX single tax return covering spouses in the United States, a tax return filed jointly by a husband and wife

joint stock bank BANKING formerly, commercial bank a term that was formerly used for a commercial bank that is a partnership, as opposed to one that is a ***publicly held corporation***

joint-stock company BUSINESS formerly, public limited company in UK formerly in the United Kingdom, a public company whose stock was owned by many people. Now such a company is called a public limited company or Plc. *See also* ***company limited by shares***

joint venture BUSINESS enterprise undertaken by two or more firms a business project in which two or more independent companies collaborate and share the risks and rewards. *Abbr* ***JV***

journal ACCOUNTING consolidated record of transactions a record of original entry, into which transactions are usually transferred from source documents. The journal may be subdivided into: sales journal/day book for credit sales; purchases journal/day book for credit purchases; cash book for cash receipts and payments; and the journal proper for transactions which could not appropriately be recorded in any of the other journals.

JSE *or* JSE Limited *or* JSE Securities Exchange MARKETS ***Johannesburg Stock Exchange***

JSE Top 40 MARKETS = ***FTSE/JSE Top 40***

ju'alal FINANCE contract for payment for services performed in Islamic financing, a contract for performing a specified act for a specified fee

judgment creditor LEGAL plaintiff in court case for debt in a legal action, the individual or business who has brought the action and to whom the court orders the judgment debtor to pay the money owed. In the event of the judgment debtor not conforming to the court order, the judgment creditor must return to the court to request that the judgment be enforced.

judgment debtor LEGAL defendant in court case for debt in a legal action, the individual or business ordered to pay the judgment creditor the money owed

jumbo mortgage MORTGAGES US mortgage too large for favorable terms in the United States, a mortgage that is too large to qualify for favorable treatment by a government agency

junior capital STOCKHOLDING & INVESTMENTS capital representing stockholders' equity capital in the form of stockholders' equity which is repaid only after the secured loans forming the senior capital have been paid if the firm goes into liquidation

junior debt FINANCE debt with low priority for repayment a debt that has no claim on a debtor's assets, or less claim than another debt. *See also* ***senior debt***. *Also called* ***subordinated debt***

junior mortgage MORTGAGES mortgage with low priority for repayment a mortgage whose holder has less claim on a debtor's assets than the holder of another mortgage. *See also* ***senior mortgage***

junior partner BUSINESS member of business partnership with limited involvement a person whose participation in management and share in the profits of a partnership are very limited

junior security STOCKHOLDING & INVESTMENTS security that is subordinate to another a security whose interest or dividend payment has a lower priority than that of another security issued by the same company

junk bond STOCKHOLDING & INVESTMENTS, RISK high-interest but high-risk bond a high-yielding bond issued on a low-grade security. The issue of junk bonds has most commonly been linked with takeover activity.

junk-rated STOCKHOLDING & INVESTMENTS, RISK describes bond that is risky investment used to describe a bond that is considered by a ***rating agency*** to not be ***investment grade*** and therefore has a higher than average risk. Junk-rated bonds have a rating of BB or less.

  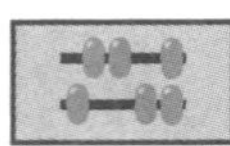      

just-in-time OPERATIONS & PRODUCTION production method reducing inventory stockpiling a production method that requires necessary materials to be at the place of manufacture or assembly at the appropriate time to minimize holding excess inventory, reducing wastage and expense. *Abbr* ***JIT***

JV *abbr* BUSINESS ***joint venture***

K

K FINANCE 1,000 one thousand: used especially after numbers expressing a sum of money. It derives from kilo-.

kafalah FINANCE agreement to pay debt of another who defaults in Islamic financing, an agreement in which one party assumes responsibility for the debt of another if the debtor should fail to pay

kakaku yusen MARKETS Japanese rule for choosing between differing instructions in Japan, the price priority system operated on the Tokyo Stock Exchange whereby a lower price takes precedence over a higher price for a sell order, and vice versa for a buy order. *See also* ***jikan***

kangaroo MARKETS Australian stock an Australian stock traded on the London Stock Exchange (slang)

Kansas City Board of Trade MARKETS specialized US commodities exchange a commodities exchange, established in 1856, that specializes in futures and options contracts for hard red winter wheat

kappa STOCKHOLDING & INVESTMENTS relationship between option price change and asset's volatility a ratio between the expected change in the price of an option and a one percent change in the expected volatility of the underlying asset. *Also called* ***lambda, vega***

Keidanren BUSINESS Japan Federation of Economic Organizations the Japanese abbreviation for the Japan Federation of Economic Organizations. Established in 1946, it works toward a resolution of the major problems facing the Japanese and international business communities and the sound development of their economies. Its members include over 1,000 of Japan's leading corporations, including over 50 foreign companies, and over 100 industry-wide groups representing such major sectors as manufacturing, trade, distribution, finance, and energy.

Keough Plan PENSIONS US pension benefiting specific groups in the United States, a pension subject to tax advantage for somebody who is self-employed or has an interest in a small company. *See also* ***stakeholder pension***

kerb market *UK* MARKETS unofficial stock market a stock market that exists outside the stock exchange. The term originates from markets held in the street.

ker-ching FINANCE expression suggesting financial success an expression suggesting that something will be very successful financially (slang)

key account management MARKETING management of most important customer relationships the management of the customer relationships that are most important to a company. Key accounts are those held by customers who produce most ***profit*** for a company or have the potential to do so, or those who are of strategic importance. Development of these ***customer relations*** and ***customer retention*** is important to business success. Particular emphasis is placed on analyzing which accounts are key to a company at any one time, determining the needs of these particular customers, and implementing procedures to ensure that they receive premium ***customer service*** and to increase ***customer satisfaction***.

Keynesian economics ECONOMICS economic philosophy of John Maynard Keynes the economic teachings and doctrines associated with John Maynard Keynes, a British economist who lived from 1883 to 1946. He is best known for his theories regarding ***macroeconomics***. He believed that in a ***recession***, the only way to reduce unemployment and improve the economy was for the government to increase spending, even if it meant running a ***deficit***, and to reduce ***interest rates*** to encourage borrowing.

key rate FINANCE interest rate on which other rates are based an interest rate that gives the basic rate on which other rates are calculated, for example, the Bank of England's bank rate or the Federal Reserve's discount rate in the United States

kickback FRAUD illicit payment to facilitator in transaction a sum of money paid illegally to somebody in order to gain concessions or favors (slang)

kicker STOCKHOLDING & INVESTMENTS attractive extra to standard security an addition to a standard security that makes it more attractive, for example, options and warrants (slang) *See also* ***bells and whistles, sweetener***

kiddie tax TAX US tax on youth income in the United States, a tax on the investment income of children and young people up to the age of 24. The amount of the tax is calculated based on their student status and/or earned income.

kill FINANCE stop instruction to stop an instruction or order from being carried out (slang)

killer bee BUSINESS facilitator in averting takeover somebody, especially a banker, who helps a company avoid being taken over

killing make a killing FINANCE to make a lot of money very quickly

kimono open the kimono GENERAL MANAGEMENT to inspect something that has not been open for examination before, especially a company's accounts

kitchen sink bond STOCKHOLDING & INVESTMENTS, RISK bond created from collection of collateralized mortgage obligations a high-risk bond created by combining ***tranches*** of existing collateralized mortgage obligations

kite 1. FRAUD fraudulent check, bill, or receipt a fraudulent financial transaction, for example, a bad check that is dated to take advantage of the time interval required for clearing **2.** FINANCE sign fraudulent checks to write bad checks in order to take advantage of the time interval required for clearing **fly a kite1.** FRAUD to use a fraudulent financial document such as a bad check2. GENERAL MANAGEMENT to make a suggestion in order to test people's opinion of it

kiwibond CURRENCY & EXCHANGE Eurobond in NZ dollars a ***Eurobond*** denominated in New Zealand dollars

knight MERGERS & ACQUISITIONS firm involved in takeover a term borrowed from chess strategy to describe a company involved in the politics of a ***takeover*** bid. There are three main types of knights. A ***white knight*** is a company that is friendly to the board of the company to be acquired. If the white knight gains control, it may retain the existing ***board of directors***. A ***black knight*** is a former white knight that has disagreed with the board of the company to be acquired and has established its own hostile bid. A ***gray knight*** is a white knight that does not have the confidence of the company to be acquired.

knock-for-knock *UK* INSURANCE with each insurer paying own customer's repair bill used to describe a practice between insurance companies whereby each will pay for the repairs to the vehicle it insures in the event of an accident

knockout option STOCKHOLDING & INVESTMENTS option with condition attached an option to which a condition relating to the underlying security's or commodity's present price is attached so that it effectively expires when it goes ***out of the money***

knowledge capital FINANCE knowledge applicable for profit knowledge that a company possesses and can put to profitable use

knowledge management GENERAL MANAGEMENT use of organization's knowledge for competitive advantage the coordination and exploitation of an organization's knowledge resources, in order to create benefit and competitive advantage

Korea Composite Stock Price Index MARKETS index of traded Korean stocks the index of all the common stocks traded on the Korean stock exchanges. *Abbr* ***KOSPI***

KOSPI *abbr* MARKETS ***Korea Composite Stock Price Index***

krona CURRENCY & EXCHANGE Swedish and Icelandic currency unit a unit of currency used in Sweden and Iceland

Krugerrand CURRENCY & EXCHANGE South African gold coin a South African coin consisting of one ounce of gold, first minted in 1967, bearing the portrait of 19th-century South African president Paul Kruger on the obverse

kurtosis STATISTICS distribution around mean a statistical measure of the distribution of data around a mean, as used in charts that assess the volatility of an investment

L

L ECONOMICS measurement of money supply a measure of the money supply, calculated as the broad money supply plus short-term Treasury securities, savings bonds, and commercial paper

labor HR & PERSONNEL all workers considered as group all the people employed in work, especially those doing manual labor, in a country, company, or industry considered as a group

labor dispute *US* GENERAL MANAGEMENT conflict between workers and management a disagreement or conflict between an ***employer*** and ***employees*** or between the ***employers' association*** and ***labor union***. *UK term* ***industrial dispute***

labor force survey STATISTICS quarterly survey of UK workforce a survey carried out every quarter in the United Kingdom, covering such topics as unemployment and hours of work

labor-intensive OPERATIONS & PRODUCTION requiring many people involving large numbers of

workers or high labor costs. *See also* ***capital-intensive***

labor-intensive industry OPERATIONS & PRODUCTION business requiring many workers an industry that needs large numbers of employees and in which labor costs are high in relation to other costs

labor union *US* GENERAL MANAGEMENT organization representing employees' interests an organization of ***employees*** within a trade or profession that has the objective of representing its members' interests, primarily through improving pay and conditions, and provides a variety of services. *UK term* ***trade union***

laddering 1. STOCKHOLDING & INVESTMENTS selling after raising stock price by continued buying the investment strategy of repeatedly buying shares in a newly launched corporation so as to force up the price, then selling the whole investment at a profit **2.** STOCKHOLDING & INVESTMENTS, RISK timed purchase, sale, and reinvestment strategy reducing risk the action of making a series of investments that mature at different times, cashing each one at maturity, then reinvesting the proceeds, thereby reducing the risk of losing large amounts all at once

ladder option STOCKHOLDING & INVESTMENTS, RISK option whose profit is locked in set level an option whose ***strike price*** is reset when the underlying asset breaks through a specified level, locking in the profit between the old and new strike price

Lady Macbeth strategy BUSINESS change in which white knight becomes black knight a change of approach on the part of a presumed white knight, in which it becomes a black knight. A Lady Macbeth strategy is usually associated with ***takeover*** battles and has connotations of treachery.

Laffer curve ECONOMICS, TAX graph showing effects of tax rate changes a graph showing that cuts in tax rates increase output in the economy and thus increase overall tax revenues

laggard MARKETING firm that does not innovate an organization that follows a ***first mover*** to market, or a company that is not the recognized leader in a sector. *Also called* ***follower***. *See also* ***first mover***

lagging indicator ECONOMICS economic factor confirming change in economic trend a measurable economic factor, for example, corporate profits or unemployment, that changes after the economy has already moved to a new trend, which it can confirm but not predict

laissez-faire economy ECONOMICS economic system in which government does not intervene an economy in which the government does not interfere because it believes that market forces should determine the course of the economy

lambda STOCKHOLDING & INVESTMENTS relationship of option price to underlying asset's volatility a ratio between the expected change in the price of an option and a one percent change in the expected volatility of the underlying asset. *Also called* ***kappa, vega***

lame duck BUSINESS firm with financial problems a company that is in financial difficulties

land bank FINANCE undeveloped land owned by builder or developer the land that a builder or developer has that is available for development

land banking FINANCE acquiring land for future development the practice of buying land that is not needed immediately, but with the expectation of using it in the future

landed costs INTERNATIONAL TRADE costs of shipping and customs clearance costs of goods that have been delivered to a port, unloaded, and passed through customs

landing order INTERNATIONAL TRADE permit to hold goods in bonded warehouse a permit that allows goods to be unloaded into a bonded warehouse without paying customs duty

landlord BUSINESS owner of rented property a person or company that owns a property that is rented

land register REAL ESTATE record of UK property and its owners in the United Kingdom, a list of pieces of land, showing who owns each and what buildings are on it

land tax TAX Australian tax on residential land a form of ***wealth tax*** imposed in Australia on the value of residential land. The level and conditions of the tax vary from state to state.

lapping *US* ACCOUNTING way of concealing missing funds an attempt to hide missing funds by delaying the recording of cash receipts in a business's books. *UK term* ***teeming and lading***

lapse STOCKHOLDING & INVESTMENTS expiry of option without trading the termination of an option without trade in the underlying security or commodity

lapsed option STOCKHOLDING & INVESTMENTS expired right to buy or sell investment an option to buy or sell a security or commodity that is no longer valid because it has expired

lapse rights STOCKHOLDING & INVESTMENTS rights of somebody allowing offer to lapse rights, such as those to a prearranged premium, owned by the person who allows an offer to lapse

large-sized business BUSINESS organization with 250 or more employees an organization that has grown beyond the limits of a ***medium-sized business*** and has 250 or more employees. This definition of a large-sized enterprise is the one adopted by the United Kingdom's Department for Business Enterprise and Regulatory Reform for statistical purposes. It is usually from the ranks of large-sized businesses that ***multinational businesses*** arise.

last quarter ACCOUNTING final period of fiscal year a period of three months from October to the end of the year, or the period of three months at the end of the fiscal year

last survivor policy INSURANCE life insurance policy for two or more an insurance policy covering the lives of two or more people. The sum insured is not paid out until all the policyholders are deceased. *See also* ***joint life annuity***

last trading day MARKETS final trading day in futures or options contract the last day in which trading takes place in a futures or options contract relating to a certain delivery month, after which the contract must be settled

latency MARKETS delay in transmission the delay between the sending of information electronically and its receipt; low latency refers to the rapid execution of a transaction

latent market MARKETING group of potential consumers of proposed product a group of people who have been identified as potential consumers of a product that does not yet exist

launch MARKETING making new product available the process of introducing a new product to the market

laundering FRAUD concealing illegal origins of money the process of passing the profits of illegal activities such as tax evasion into the normal banking system via apparently legitimate businesses

LAUTRO REGULATION & COMPLIANCE former UK regulator a former UK financial authority regulating life insurance and mutual funds. It was brought to an end in 1995. *Full form* ***Life Assurance and Unit Trust Regulatory Organisation***

law of diminishing marginal utility ECONOMICS increased consumption of product decreases consumer's satisfaction a general theory in economics stating that each unit of a product consumed adds less satisfaction to the consumer than the previous one, i.e., the ***marginal utility*** of any good or service diminishes as each new unit of it is consumed

law of diminishing returns ECONOMICS increase in one area has limited effect a rule stating that as one factor of production is increased, while others remain constant, the extra output generated by the additional input will eventually fall. The law of diminishing returns therefore means that extra workers, extra capital, extra machinery, or extra land may not necessarily raise output as much as expected. For example, increasing the supply of raw materials to a production line may allow additional output to be produced by using any spare capacity workers have. Once this capacity is fully used, however, continually increasing the amount of raw material without a corresponding increase in the number of workers will not result in an increase of output.

law of supply and demand ECONOMICS *see* ***supply and demand***

lay-away *US* FINANCE paying for product in installments before taking ownership the reservation of an article for purchase by the payment of an initial deposit followed by regular interest-free installments, on completion of which the article is claimed by the buyer

lay off HR & PERSONNEL **1.** terminate somebody's employment because of too little work to dismiss an employee or employees permanently because there is insufficient work to occupy them **2.** temporarily stop somebody's employment to suspend an employee or employees temporarily because there is insufficient work to occupy them

layoff *US* HR & PERSONNEL termination of employment because of too little work dismissal, often temporarily, from work because a job ceases to exist or because of lack of work. Employees who are laid off may qualify for severance pay. If the layoff process is handled incorrectly, the employer may be faced with claims for unfair dismissal. *UK term* ***redundancy***

LBO *abbr* MERGERS & ACQUISITIONS ***leveraged buyout***

LC *or* L/C *abbr* BANKING ***letter of credit***

LCH *abbr* MARKETS ***London Clearing House***

LCH.Clearnet MARKETS European clearing house the ***clearing house*** formed by the merger of the ***London Clearing House*** and Paris-based ***Clearnet*** in 2003. It serves major international exchanges and platforms, as well as a range of ***over-the-counter markets***, clearing a range of asset classes including: securities, exchange-traded derivatives, commodities, energy, freight, interest rate swaps, credit default swaps, and euro and sterling-denominated bonds and repos.

LCM *abbr* ACCOUNTING ***lower of cost or market***

LDC *abbr* ECONOMICS **1.** ***less developed country*** **2.** ***least developed country***

LDT *abbr* FINANCE ***licensed deposit-taker***

lead INSURANCE first underwriter of Lloyd's policy in an insurance policy from Lloyd's, the first named underwriting syndicate

lead bank BANKING main bank in loan syndicate the primary bank in a loan syndicate, which organizes the transaction in question

leader **1.** GENERAL MANAGEMENT, HR & PERSONNEL firm's executive who motivates others well a business executive who possesses exceptional leadership qualities as well as management skills **2.** MARKETING top performing thing the most successful product or company in a marketplace

leadership GENERAL MANAGEMENT, HR & PERSONNEL ability to guide and motivate others well the capacity to establish direction and to influence and align others toward a common goal, motivating and committing them to action and making them responsible for their performance. Leadership theory is one of the most discussed areas of management, and many different approaches are taken to the topic. Some notions of leadership are related to types of ***authority*** delineated by Max Weber. It is often suggested that leaders possess innate personal qualities that distinguish them from others. Other theories, such as Behaviorist theories of leadership, suggest that leadership is defined by action and behavior, rather than by personality. A related idea is that leadership style is not fixed but should be adapted to different situations, and this is explored in ***contingency theory***. Perhaps the most simple model of leadership is action-centered leadership, which focuses on what an effective leader actually does. These many approaches and differences of opinion illustrate the complexity of the leadership role and the intangibility of the essence of good leadership.

leading economic indicator *or* leading indicator ECONOMICS early indication of change in economic trends an economic variable, such as private-sector wages, that tends to show the direction of future economic activity earlier than other indicators. *See also* ***lagging indicator***

leading edge BUSINESS most modern and innovative situated at the forefront of ***innovation***. A leading edge company is ahead of others in such areas as inventing or implementing new technologies, and in entering new markets.

lead manager *UK* STOCKHOLDING & INVESTMENTS = ***lead underwriter***

lead partner BUSINESS dominant partner the organization that takes the lead role in an alliance

leads and lags CURRENCY & EXCHANGE adjusting speed of transactions with exchange rates in businesses that deal in foreign currencies, the practice of speeding up the receipt of payments (leads) if a currency is going to weaken, and slowing down the payment of costs (lags) if a currency is thought to be about to strengthen, in order to maximize gains and reduce losses

lead time **1.** FINANCE, OPERATIONS & PRODUCTION time between starting and finishing the time interval between the start of an activity or process and its completion, for example, the time between ordering goods and their receipt, or between starting manufacturing of a product and its completion **2.** OPERATIONS & PRODUCTION period between order placement and delivery in inventory control, the time between placing an order and its arrival on site. Lead time differs from delivery time in that it also includes the time required to place an order and the time it takes to inspect the goods and receive them into the appropriate store. Inventory levels can afford to be lower and orders smaller when purchasing lead times are short. **3.** OPERATIONS & PRODUCTION, MARKETING period from new product idea to sales readiness in ***new product development*** and manufacturing, the time required to develop a product from concept to market delivery. Lead time increases as a result of the poor sequencing of dependent activities, the lack of availability of resources, poor quality in the component parts, and poor plant layout. The technique of ***concurrent engineering*** focuses on the entire concept-to-customer process with the goal of reducing lead time. Companies can gain a ***competitive advantage*** by achieving a lead time reduction and so getting products to market faster. *Also called* ***cycle time*** *(sense 2)*

lead underwriter *US* STOCKHOLDING & INVESTMENTS institution in charge of new issue the financial institution with overall responsibility for a new issue of shares of stock including its coordination, distribution, and related administration. *UK term* ***lead manager***

lean enterprise OPERATIONS & PRODUCTION efficient business structure with little waste an organizational model that strategically applies the key ideas behind ***lean production***. A lean enterprise is viewed as a group of separate individuals, functions, or organizations that operate as one entity. The goal is to apply lean techniques that create individual breakthroughs in companies and to link these up and down the supply chain to form a continuous value stream to raise the whole chain to a higher level.

lean manufacturing OPERATIONS & PRODUCTION = ***lean production***

lean operation OPERATIONS & PRODUCTION business with little waste a company following the methodology of ***lean production***, with low ***inventories***. *See also* ***lean production***

lean production OPERATIONS & PRODUCTION efficient manufacturing method with little waste a methodology aimed at reducing waste in the form of overproduction, excessive ***lead time***, or product defects in order to make a business more effective and more competitive. Lean production originates in the production systems established by Toyota in Japan in the 1950s. In the early 1980s there was a significant increase in the application of lean production in Western companies. Lean production is characterized by ***lean operations*** with low ***inventories***; ***quality management*** through prevention of errors; small batch runs; ***just-in-time*** production; high commitment human resource policies; team-based working; and close relations with suppliers. Concepts that can help an organization move toward lean production include ***continuous improvement*** and ***world class manufacturing***. *Also called* ***lean manufacturing***

LEAPS STOCKHOLDING & INVESTMENTS options with one to three-year expiry dates options that expire between one and three years in the future *Full form* ***long-term equity anticipation securities***

learning by doing GENERAL MANAGEMENT finding out about job by performing it the acquisition of knowledge or skills through direct experience of carrying out a task. Learning by doing often happens under supervision, as part of a training or ***orientation*** process, and is closely associated with the practical experience picked up by "sitting with Nellie." It is an outcome of the research into learning of David Kolb and Reg Revans. A more formalized approach to learning by doing is ***experiential learning***.

learning curve **1.** GENERAL MANAGEMENT rate at which new information must be acquired a graphic representation of the acquisition of knowledge or experience over time. A steep learning curve reflects a substantial amount of learning in a short time, and a shallow curve reflects a slower learning process. The curve eventually levels out to a plateau, during which time the knowledge gained is being consolidated. **2.** OPERATIONS & PRODUCTION proportional reduction in effort when production doubles the proportional decrease in effort when production is doubled. The learning curve has its origin in productivity research in the airplane industry of the 1930s, when T. P. Wright discovered that in assembling an aircraft, the time and effort decreased by 20% each time the cumulative number of planes produced doubled. *Also called* ***experience curve***

learning opportunity GENERAL MANAGEMENT mistake to learn from a positive way of referring to a mistake that somebody has made at work, presenting it as a chance to gain new knowledge

learning organization GENERAL MANAGEMENT customer-focused firm with little hierarchy an organizational model characterized by a flat structure and ***customer-focused*** teams, that engenders the collective ability to develop shared visions by capturing and exploiting employees' willingness, commitment, and curiosity. The concept of the learning organization was proposed by Chris Argyris and Donald Schön as part of their work on organizational learning, but was brought back to public attention in the 1990s by Peter Senge. For Senge, a learning organization is one with the capacity to shift away from views inherent in a traditional hierarchical organization, toward the ability of all employees to challenge prevailing thinking and gain a balanced perspective. Senge believes the five major characteristics of a learning organization are mental models, personal mastery, systems thinking, shared vision, and team learning. Because of the requirement for an open, risk-tolerant culture, which is the opposite of the corporate culture of most organizations today, the learning organization remains, for many, an unattainable ideal.

learning style GENERAL MANAGEMENT way that somebody best acquires knowledge and skills the way in which somebody approaches the acquisition of knowledge and skills. Learning styles have been divided into four main types by Peter Honey and Alan Mumford, in their *Manual of Learning Styles* (1982). The types of learners are the activist, who likes to get involved in new experiences and enjoys the challenges of change; the theorist, who likes to question assumptions and methodologies and learns best when there is time to explore links between ideas and situations; the pragmatist, who prefers practicality and learns best when there is a link between the subject matter and the job in hand and when he or she can try out what he or she has learned; and the reflector, who likes to take his or her time and think things through, and who learns best from activities where he or she can observe and conduct research. One person can demonstrate more than one learning style, and the category or categories that best describe somebody can be determined through use of a learning styles questionnaire.

lease LEGAL **1.** written contract for renting something a written contract for renting a building, a piece of land, or a piece of equipment for a fixed period of time in return for payment of a fee **2.** rent offices, land, or equipment to somebody to rent offices, land, or equipment to a person or business for a fixed period of time specified in a written contract **3.** rent offices, land, or equipment from somebody to use offices, land, or equipment for a fixed period of time specified in a written contract and pay a fee

leaseback LEGAL, FINANCE *see* ***sale and leaseback***

leasehold LEGAL, REAL ESTATE **1.** right to rent property for fixed period the right to possess a property on a lease, for a fixed period of time **2.** piece of property that is rented a property held on a lease granted by the legal owner of the property

leaseholder LEGAL, REAL ESTATE somebody renting piece of property under lease a person who is in possession of a property by way of a lease

least developed country ECONOMICS very poor country with little economic development a country that is not economically advanced, especially a country that borrowed heavily from commercial banks in the 1970s and 1980s to finance its industrial development, and so helped to create an international debt crisis. *Abbr* ***LDC***

leave HR & PERSONNEL paid time away from work work time when an employee is paid, but is not required to be at work. Leave takes several forms and includes time off for vacation. The number of days of vacation is set out in the contract of employment and may be dependent on the employee's length of service. It may also take the form of sick leave, educational leave, or maternity or paternity leave.

ledger ACCOUNTING **1.** book for accounts a book in which account transactions are recorded **2.** book with record of account transactions a collection of accounts, or book of accounts. Credit sales information is recorded, for example, by debtor, in the sales ledger. **3.** book of consolidated accounts a collection of accounts, maintained by transfers from the books of original entry. The ledger may be subdivided as follows: the sales ledger/debtors' ledger contains all the personal accounts of customers; the purchases ledger/creditors' ledger contains all the personal accounts of suppliers; the private ledger contains accounts relating to the proprietor's interest in the business such as capital and drawings; the general ledger/nominal ledger contains all other accounts relating to assets, expenses, revenue, and liabilities.

leg STOCKHOLDING & INVESTMENTS price for security either the highest price offered for a security or the lowest price a seller will accept for a security

legacy system BUSINESS computer system with long-term function an existing computer system that provides a strategic function for a specific part of a business. Inventory management systems, for example, are legacy systems.

legal charge LEGAL legal document showing ownership of UK property in the United Kingdom, a legal document held by the Land Registry showing who has a claim on a property

legal charges LEGAL = ***legal costs***

legal claim LEGAL lawful right or statement of ownership a legally recognized right to the ownership of something, or a statement of such a right

legal costs LEGAL money spent on lawyers' fees the amount of money spent on legal matters, particularly lawyers' fees. *Also called* ***legal charges, legal expenses***

legal currency LEGAL, CURRENCY & EXCHANGE legally accepted money money that is recognized by a government to be legally acceptable for payment of a debt

legal expenses LEGAL = ***legal costs***

legal list LEGAL, STOCKHOLDING & INVESTMENTS securities that financial institutions can legally invest in a list of blue-chip securities in which banks and financial institutions are allowed to invest by the state in which they are based

legal loophole LEGAL legal flaw allowing people to get around law an area in the law that is insufficiently explicit or comprehensive and allows the law to be circumvented

legal tender LEGAL, CURRENCY & EXCHANGE legally accepted paper money and coins paper money and coins that have to be accepted within a given jurisdiction when offered as payment of a debt. *See also* ***limited legal tender***

lemon BUSINESS unsatisfactory product a product that is defective in some way, for example, an investment that is performing poorly (slang)

lender FINANCE somebody who lends money a person or financial institution that lends money

lender of last resort BANKING bank lending to troubled commercial banks a ***central bank*** that lends money to banks that cannot borrow elsewhere

lending facility BANKING = ***credit facility***

lending limit BANKING maximum amount of money bank can lend a restriction placed on the amount of money a bank can legally lend

lending margin BANKING spread above base rate borrowers agree to pay an agreed spread for lending paid by borrowers, based on a reference rate such as the London Interbank Offered Rate

length of service HR & PERSONNEL how long employee has worked for firm the period in which somebody has been continually employed in an organization, without breaks in the ***contract of employment***. Length of service may determine entitlement to employment rights or ***fringe benefits***, for example, the amount of annual leave allocated.

less developed country ECONOMICS poorer country with limited economic development a country whose economic development is held back because it lacks the technology and capital to make use of its natural resources to produce goods demanded on world markets. *Abbr* ***LDC***

lessee LEGAL user of something leased the person who has the use of a leased asset

lessor LEGAL provider of something on lease the person who provides an asset being leased

let *UK* REAL ESTATE = ***rent***

letter of acknowledgment GENERAL MANAGEMENT letter saying something has been received a letter written to somebody to say that something that he or she sent has been received

letter of agreement LEGAL simple contract a document that constitutes a simple form of contract

letter of comfort *UK* BANKING = ***letter of moral intent***

letter of credit BANKING letter of authorization from one bank to another a letter issued by a bank that can be presented to another bank to authorize the issue of credit or money. *Abbr* ***LC***

letter of indemnity LEGAL statement accepting loss from replaced stock certificate a statement that a stock certificate has been lost, destroyed, or stolen and that the stockholder will indemnify the company for any loss that might result from its reappearance after the company has issued a replacement to the stockholder

letter of intent BUSINESS written commitment to do something a document that indicates an intention to do something such as buy a business, grant somebody a loan, or participate in a project. The intention may or may not depend on specific conditions being met and the document is not legally binding. *See also* ***letter of moral intent***

letter of license LEGAL, FINANCE letter giving debtor more time for repayment a letter from a creditor to a debtor who is having problems repaying money owed, giving the debtor a specific period of time to raise the money and an undertaking not to bring legal proceedings to recover the debt during that period

letter of moral intent *US* BANKING parent company's support for subsidiary's loan a letter from a holding company addressed to a bank where one of its subsidiaries wishes to borrow money. The purpose of the letter is to support the subsidiary's application to borrow funds and offer reassurance—although not a guarantee—to the bank that the subsidiary will remain in business for the foreseeable future, often with an undertaking to advise the bank if the subsidiary is likely to be sold. *UK term* ***letter of comfort***

letter of renunciation STOCKHOLDING & INVESTMENTS document transferring new stock a form used to transfer an allotment of shares in a ***rights issue*** to another person

letter security STOCKHOLDING & INVESTMENTS unregistered security salable under certain conditions in the United States, a security that has not been registered with the ***SEC*** but can be sold privately if the buyer signs a letter of intent stating that the security is for investment, not resale, or can be traded publicly if the owner files a Form 144 with the SEC showing that the sale meets conditions that exempts it from registration with the SEC

letters patent LEGAL official document conferring commercial rights on inventor an official document giving somebody the exclusive right to make and sell something that he or she has invented

level load STOCKHOLDING & INVESTMENTS decreasing annual fee an annual fee that is deducted from the assets in a mutual fund to cover management costs and that decreases gradually over time

level term insurance INSURANCE life insurance policy for fixed period a life insurance policy in which an agreed lump sum is paid if the policyholder dies before a specific date. A joint form of this life cover is popular with couples who have children.

leverage FINANCE corporate funding mainly through borrowing a method of corporate funding in which a higher proportion of funds is raised through borrowing than through stock issue. *Also called* ***gearing***. *See also* ***financial leverage***

leveraged bid MERGERS & ACQUISITIONS takeover bid with borrowed finance a takeover bid financed by borrowed money, rather than by a stock issue

  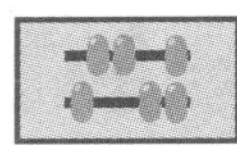      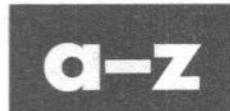

leveraged buyout MERGERS & ACQUISITIONS takeover with borrowed finance a takeover using borrowed money, with the purchased company's assets as collateral. *Abbr* ***LBO***

leveraged investment company *US* STOCKHOLDING & INVESTMENTS investment company using borrowed money to expand an investment company that borrows money in order to increase its portfolio. When the market is rising, stocks in a leveraged investment trust rise faster than those in an unleveraged trust, but they fall faster when the market is falling. *UK term* ***geared investment trust***

leveraged required return STOCKHOLDING & INVESTMENTS income from investment exceeding cost of loan the rate of return from an investment of borrowed money needed to make the investment worthwhile

leverage ratios FINANCE, RISK means of quantifying risk from capital ratios that indicate the level of risk taken by a company as a result of its capital structure. A number of different ratios may be calculated, for example, debt ratio (total debt divided by total assets), debt-to-equity or leverage ratio (total debt divided by total equity), or interest cover (earnings before interest and tax divided by interest paid). *Also called* ***gearing ratios***

levy TAX tax that raises money for specific purpose a type of tax on a specific product or service by which a government raises money for a specific purpose

liabilities FINANCE firm's debts the debts of a business, including dividends owed to stockholders

liability FINANCE money lent without guarantee of repayment a debt that has no claim on a debtor's assets, or less claim than another debt

liability insurance INSURANCE insurance against incurring costs insurance against legal liability that the insured might incur, for example, from causing an accident

liability management FINANCE investigation of impact of liabilities on profitability any exercise carried out by a business with the objective of controlling the effect of liabilities on its profitability. This will typically involve controlling the amount of risk undertaken, and ensuring that there is sufficient liquidity and that the best terms are obtained for any funding needs.

LIBID *abbr* MARKETS ***London Interbank Bid Rate***

LIBOR *abbr* MARKETS ***London Interbank Offered Rate***

license *US* LEGAL contract to do or use something for payment a contractual arrangement, or a document representing this, in which one organization gives another the rights to produce, sell, or use something in return for payment

licensed deposit-taker FINANCE UK institution that took deposits and paid interest formerly in the United Kingdom, a type of ***deposit-taking institution*** that was licensed to receive money on deposit from private individuals and to pay interest on it, for example, a bank or savings and loan. *Abbr* ***LDT***

licensed institution FINANCE = ***licensed deposit-taker***

licensing LEGAL making contract to do or use something the transfer of rights to manufacture or market a particular product to another individual or organization through a legal arrangement or contract. Licensing usually requires that a fee, commission, or royalty is paid to the licensor.

licensing agreement LEGAL permission for firm to do or use something an agreement permitting a company to market or produce a product or service owned by another company. A licensing agreement grants a license in return for a fee or royalty payment. Items licensed for use can include patents, trademarks, techniques, designs, and expertise. This kind of agreement is one way for a company to penetrate overseas markets in that it provides a middle path between direct export and investment overseas.

lien LEGAL legal right to hold property against debt a legal right to hold somebody's goods or property until a debt that is secured by the goods or property has been repaid

life annuity INSURANCE annuity with fixed monthly payment until death an annuity that pays a fixed amount per month until the holder's death

life assurance *UK* INSURANCE = ***life insurance***

Life Assurance and Unit Trust Regulatory Organisation REGULATION & COMPLIANCE *see* ***LAUTRO***

life assured INSURANCE = ***life insured***

lifeboat 1. FINANCE = ***lifeboat scheme* 2.** *S. AFRICA* BANKING loan to rescue commercial bank a low-interest emergency loan made by a central bank to rescue a commercial bank in danger of becoming insolvent

lifeboat scheme FINANCE rescue measure for business or fund a measure designed to protect or rescue a failing business or fund. *Also called* ***lifeboat*** *(sense 1)*

life cover INSURANCE = ***life insurance***

life cycle MARKETING course of product's development and sales over time the sales pattern of a product or service over a period of time. Typically, a life cycle falls into four stages: introduction, growth, maturity, and decline.

life-cycle costing ACCOUNTING way of assessing asset's cost over time a method of calculating the total cost of a physical asset throughout its life. Life-cycle costing is concerned with all costs of ownership and takes account of the costs incurred by an asset from its acquisition to its disposal, including design, installation, operating, and maintenance costs.

life-cycle fund STOCKHOLDING & INVESTMENTS mutual fund linked to investor's age a mutual fund whose investments vary according to the age of the investor

life-cycle savings motive ECONOMICS reason for saving money over lifetime a reason that a household or individual has for saving at specific times in life so as to have sufficient funds available to spend on anticipated expenses, for example, when starting a family or nearing retirement

life expectancy INSURANCE, PENSIONS how long average person lives the number of years that somebody of a given age is expected to live

life insurance *US* INSURANCE insurance paying others on insured's death insurance that pays a specified sum to the insured person's beneficiaries after the person's death. *Also called* ***life cover***. *UK term* ***life assurance***

life insurance bond INSURANCE = ***investment bond***

life insured *US* INSURANCE person with life insurance policy the person or persons covered by a life insurance policy. The insurance company pays out on the death of the policyholder. *UK term* ***life assured***

life interest REAL ESTATE lifetime right to benefit from property a situation where somebody benefits from a property for the entirety of his or her lifetime

life office INSURANCE, PENSIONS firm offering life insurance in the United Kingdom, a company that provides life insurance and sometimes pension plans

life policy INSURANCE, PENSIONS life insurance contract a contract for insurance that pays a specific sum to the insured person's beneficiaries after the person's death

lifestyle audit TAX comparison of taxpayer's living standards to reported income a study of a taxpayer's living standards and spending to determine if it is consistent with that person's reported income

lifestyle business BUSINESS business run by enthusiasts a typically small business run by individuals who have a strong interest in the product or service offered, for example, handmade greeting cards or jewelry, antique dealing or restoring. Such businesses tend to operate during hours that suit the owners, and generally provide them with a comfortable living.

life table STATISTICS table listing expected life spans by age a table that shows the probabilities of death, survival, and remaining years of life for people of given ages

lifetime customer value BUSINESS = ***lifetime value***

lifetime transfer TAX = ***chargeable transfer***

lifetime value BUSINESS person's accumulated expenditure on brand a measure of the total value to a supplier of a customer's business over the duration of their transactions.

In a consumer business, customer lifetime value is calculated by analyzing the behavior of a group of customers who have the same recruitment date. The revenue and cost for this group of customers is recorded, by campaign or season, and the overall contribution for that period can then be worked out. Industry experience has shown that the benefits to a business of increasing lifetime value can be enormous. A 5% increase in customer retention can create a 125% increase in profits; a 10% increase in retailer retention can translate to a 20% increase in sales; and extending customer life cycles by three years can treble profits per customer. *Also called* ***lifetime customer value***

LIFFE *abbr* MARKETS ***London International Financial Futures and Options Exchange*** = ***NYSE Liffe***

lightning strike HR & PERSONNEL strike that happens with little warning in the United Kingdom, a stoppage of work as protest that occurs at very short notice. It may be of short duration and may not be sanctioned by a labor union.

LIMEAN *abbr* MARKETS ***London Interbank Mean Rate***

limit STOCKHOLDING & INVESTMENTS specified minimum or maximum price for transaction an amount above or below which a broker is not to conclude the purchase or sale of a security for the client who specifies it

  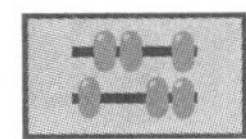   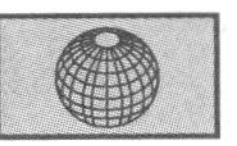   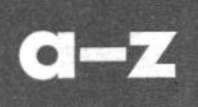

limit down MARKETS maximum daily price fall in option the most that the price of an option may fall in one day on a particular market

Limited BUSINESS part of name of UK limited company when placed at the end of the company's name, used to indicate that a UK company is a limited company

limited company BUSINESS UK firm with individual liability related to investment a British-registered company in which each stockholder is responsible for the company's debts only to the amount that he or she has invested in the company. Limited companies must be formed by at least two directors. *See also* ***private company, publicly held corporation***. *Abbr Ltd*

limited legal tender LEGAL, CURRENCY & EXCHANGE bills and coins only usable in small transactions in some jurisdictions, low denomination bills and all coins that may only be submitted up to a specific sum as legal tender in any one transaction

limited liability BUSINESS obligation to pay limited to size of investment the restriction of an owner's loss in a business to the amount of capital he or she has invested in it

limited liability company *UK* BUSINESS = ***corporation***

limited market MARKETS market with few of each security a market in which dealings for a specific security are difficult to transact, for example, because it has only limited appeal to investors or, in the case of stock, because institutions or family members are unlikely to sell it

limited partnership BUSINESS firm with partners responsible for proportion of debts a registered business in which the liability of the partners is limited to the amount of capital they have each provided for the business, and in the running of which the partners may not take part

limit order STOCKHOLDING & INVESTMENTS order to buy or sell security an order to a broker to sell a security at or above an agreed price, or to buy a security at or below an agreed price

limit up MARKETS maximum daily price rise in option the most that the price of an option may rise in one day on a particular market

linear programming GENERAL MANAGEMENT method for optimizing production a mathematical technique used to identify an optimal solution for the deployment of resources to meet organizational objectives. Linear programming uses graphic and algebraic means to calculate which combination of resources, subject to predicted constraints, is most likely to fulfill a given objective.

line management GENERAL MANAGEMENT hierarchy where each employee reports to single manager a hierarchical ***chain of command*** from executive to front-line level. Line management is the oldest and least complex management structure, in which top management have total and direct authority and employees report to only one supervisor. Managers in this type of organizational structure have direct responsibility for giving orders to their subordinates. Line management structures are usually organized along functional lines, although they increasingly undertake a variety of cross-functional duties such as employee development or strategic direction. The lowest managerial level in an organization following a line management structure is supervisory management.

line manager GENERAL MANAGEMENT employee's direct boss an employee's immediate superior, who oversees and has responsibility for the employee's work. A line manager at the lowest level of a large organization is a supervisor, but a manager at any level with direct responsibility for employees' work can be described as a line manager.

line of credit FINANCE means of borrowing money an agreed finance facility that allows a company or individual to borrow money. *Also called* ***bank line, credit line***

line organization GENERAL MANAGEMENT hierarchy with line managers an organizational structure that is based on ***line management***

lipstick entrepreneur BUSINESS independent businesswoman a woman who starts or owns a business. *Also called* ***fempreneur***

liquid FINANCE easy to convert to cash describes an asset that is easily converted to cash

liquid asset ratio FINANCE ratio of liquid to total assets the ratio of liquid assets to total assets. This is an indicator of a company's solvency.

liquid assets FINANCE possible sources of cash cash, and other assets readily convertible into cash without significant loss of capital

liquidate 1. BUSINESS end existence of firm to close a company by selling its assets, paying off any outstanding debts, distributing any remaining profits to the stockholders, and then ceasing trading **2.** STOCKHOLDING & INVESTMENTS convert into cash to sell assets in order to be able to have cash

liquidated damages LEGAL penalty for breaking contract an amount of money somebody pays for breaching a ***contract***

liquidated damages clause LEGAL clause stating penalty for breaking contract a clause in a ***contract*** that sets out the compensation to be paid in the event of a breach or a default of the terms of the contract. The compensation set out in a liquidated damages clause should be a genuine preestimate of the loss suffered as a result of the noncompletion of the contract. An example would be an amount payable per day in the event of the noncompletion of a building project. If the amount specified is not considered a genuine estimate of the losses incurred, and the clause is perceived to be solely an incentive for the completion of the contract, the clause is deemed a penalty clause and is not legally enforceable. However, liquidated damages clauses are often inaccurately referred to as penalty clauses. *See also* ***breach of contract***

liquidation BUSINESS process of ending existence of firm the winding-up of a company, a process during which assets are sold, liabilities settled as far as possible, and any remaining cash returned to the members. Liquidation may be voluntary or compulsory.

liquidation value BUSINESS yield from quick sale of firm's assets the amount of money that a quick sale of all of a company's assets would yield

liquidator BUSINESS seller of insolvent firm's assets the person appointed by a company, its creditors, or its stockholders to sell the assets of an insolvent company. The proceeds of the sale are used to discharge debts to creditors, with any surplus distributed to stockholders.

liquidity FINANCE ability to obtain cash from assets an assessment of the ease with which assets can be converted to cash

liquidity agreement FINANCE agreement to cash in asset an agreement to allow a company to convert an asset into cash

liquidity event FINANCE exit strategy of startup business the means by which founders and initial investors in a new company are able to obtain the money the business has earned by changing their ***equity*** into cash. The company may be sold or there may be a public offering of stock.

liquidity preference FINANCE desire for cash over other investments a choice made by people to hold their wealth in the form of cash rather than bonds or stocks. A general increase in liquidity preference is symptomatic of a financial crisis whereas a general decrease is associated with increased appetite for risk.

liquidity ratio FINANCE = ***cash ratio***

liquidity risk RISK danger of inability to cash in assets the risk that an entity will encounter difficulty in realizing assets or otherwise raising funds to meet commitments associated with financial instruments. *See also* ***funding risk***

liquidity squeeze FINANCE time when money is hard to borrow a situation or period in which money for borrowing is unavailable from finance companies, banks, and other lenders of money. *Also called* ***credit squeeze***

liquidity trap BANKING inability to push interest rates lower a central bank's inability to lower interest rates once investors believe rates can go no lower

liquid market MARKETS market with brisk trading a market in which a large number of trades are being made

liquid savings FINANCE money saved money held in deposit and savings accounts that is easily available if needed and not usually subject to large fluctuations in value

Lisbon Stock Exchange MARKETS, STOCKHOLDING & INVESTMENTS = ***Euronext Lisbon***

list broker BUSINESS intermediary arranging shared mailing lists a person or organization that makes the arrangements for one company to use another company's direct mail list

listed company BUSINESS firm with stock trading on exchange a company whose stock is quoted on a recognized stock exchange. *Also called* ***quoted company***

listed security STOCKHOLDING & INVESTMENTS, MARKETS security traded on exchange a security that is quoted on a recognized stock exchange

listing agreement MARKETS agreement when firm's stock are listed a document that a company signs when being listed on a stock exchange, in which the company promises to abide by stock exchange regulations

listing details MARKETS **1.** information published before firm's UK stock exchange listing in the United Kingdom, detailed information about a company, which is published when the company applies for a listing on a stock exchange. The US equivalent is the ***registration statement***. **2.** information about institutions backing issue detailed information published about the institutions that are backing a stock issue

listing requirements MARKETS conditions for security to be traded on exchange the conditions that have to be met before a security can be traded on a recognized stock exchange. Although exact requirements vary from one exchange to another, the two main ones are that the issuing company's assets should exceed a minimum amount and that the required information about its finances and business should have been published.

list price BUSINESS product price given by supplier the price of goods or services published by a supplier. The list price of an item may be discounted to regular customers or for bulk purchases.

list renting BUSINESS making firm's direct mail list available for fee an arrangement in which a company that owns a direct mail list lets another company use it for a fee

litigation LEGAL process of dealing with lawsuit the process of bringing a lawsuit against a person or organization

Little Board MARKETS (informal) = ***NYSE Amex Equities***

lively market MARKETS stock market with brisk trading an active stock market in which many stocks are being bought or sold

livery MARKETING symbol on corporate property a mark of corporate identity used on something belonging to a company

living wage FINANCE amount of pay needed for normal life a level of pay that provides enough income for normal day-to-day basic requirements

living will LEGAL instructions for allowing death a legal document that specifies the measures you want or do not want taken to prolong your life in the event of a terminal illness or injury. It may also designate a person to make healthcare decisions on your behalf.

Lloyd's INSURANCE = ***Lloyd's of London***

Lloyd's broker INSURANCE agent arranging insurance through Lloyd's an agent who represents a client who wants insurance, and who arranges this insurance for him through a ***Lloyd's underwriting syndicate***

Lloyd's of London INSURANCE London-based insurance market an insurance market based in London made up of a group of member underwriting syndicates that underwrite most types of insurance policy. *Also called* ***Lloyd's***. *See also* ***Lloyd's underwriting syndicate***

Lloyd's underwriting syndicate INSURANCE London-based syndicate underwriting insurance an underwriting syndicate in membership with ***Lloyd's of London***

LME *abbr* MARKETS ***London Metal Exchange***

load STOCKHOLDING & INVESTMENTS administration charge for investment a charge in some investment funds to cover administration, profit, and incidentals. When the primary cost is paid at the beginning this is ***front-end loading***; at the end it is ***back-end loading***. *See also* ***load fund***

load fund STOCKHOLDING & INVESTMENTS mutual fund requiring payment for transactions a mutual fund that charges a fee for the purchase or sale of shares. *See also* ***no-load fund***

loading **1.** *ANZ* FINANCE extra pay for exceptional skills or work environment a payment made to employees over and above the basic wage in recognition of special skills or unfavorable conditions, for example, for overtime or shiftwork **2.** OPERATIONS & PRODUCTION giving particular jobs to workstation the assignment of tasks or jobs to a workstation. The loading of jobs is worked out through the use of ***master production scheduling***.

loan FINANCE borrowing arrangement with fixed schedule a borrowing either by a business or a consumer where the amount borrowed is repaid according to an agreed schedule at an agreed interest rate, typically by regular installments over a set period of years. However, the principal may be repayable in one installment. *See also* ***balloon loan, fixed-rate loan, interest-only mortgage, variable interest rate***

loanable funds theory ECONOMICS interest rates are determined by supply and demand the theory that interest rates are determined solely by supply and demand. It assumes that consumers must be offered interest on their savings to induce them not just to spend their income and to make funds available for investment.

loanback **1.** FINANCE in US, return of money to lender in the United States, the return to somebody of money that has been given as a loan, often as a way of illegally masking the money's true owner **2.** PENSIONS in UK, arrangement to borrow from pension fund in the United Kingdom, the ability of a holder of a pension fund to borrow money from it

loan capital FINANCE money firm borrows for operations a part of a company's capital that is a loan to be repaid at a later date

loan committee FINANCE group considering nonstandard loan applications a committee that examines applications for special loans, such as higher loans than usually allowed by a bank

loan constant ratio FINANCE ratio of annual payments to original balance the total of annual payments due on a loan as a fraction of the amount of the principal

Loan Council FINANCE Australian federal committee overseeing borrowing by states an Australian federal body, made up of treasurers from the states and the Commonwealth of Australia, that monitors borrowing by state governments

loan loss reserves BANKING sum held by bank to cover bad debts the money a bank holds to cover losses through defaults on loans that it makes

loan note FINANCE written details of loan a written agreement between parties describing the terms of repayment, interest if applicable, and due date of a loan

loan participation BANKING collaboration by banks to make single large loan the grouping together by several banks to share a very large loan to one single customer

loan production cycle FINANCE time between loan application and lending of money the period that begins with an application for a loan and ends with the lending of money

loan schedule FINANCE details of loan payments a list of the payments due on a loan and the balance outstanding after each has been made

loan shark FINANCE lender charging excessively high interest rates somebody who lends money at excessively, often illegally, high rates of interest (informal)

loan stock STOCKHOLDING & INVESTMENTS bonds and debentures a fixed-income security given in exchange for a loan

loan to value ratio FINANCE ratio of worth of loan to collateral the ratio of the amount of a loan to the value of the collateral for it. *Abbr* ***LTV ratio***

loan value FINANCE sum available to borrower the amount that a lender is willing to lend a borrower

lobby GENERAL MANAGEMENT group trying to influence decisions of politicians a group that seeks to influence government or legislators on behalf of a specific cause or interest

local MARKETS independent trader in futures or options a trader in futures or options, who occasionally makes trades on behalf of clients, but usually trades on his or her own account

local authority bond STOCKHOLDING & INVESTMENTS UK local government's fixed-interest bond in the United Kingdom, a loan raised by a local authority in the form of a fixed-interest bond, repayable at a specific date. Local authority bonds are similar to US ***Treasury bonds***.

local authority deposits FINANCE money lent to UK local government in the United Kingdom, money deposited with a local authority to earn interest for the depositor

localization MARKETING customizing to geographic audience adapting products, websites, and marketing to the needs of target users in different parts of the world. Studies have shown that if a vendor is serious about selling to foreign marketplaces, localizing is essential. Without localization, sales will be minimal, and returns very high.

lockbox BANKING banking service for checks sent by mail a banking system in which checks sent to a Post Office box rather than to a company are picked up by a bank and deposited in a bank account

lock limit MARKETS market limit on price change per session an occasion in which the trading price of a contract in a ***futures market*** reaches an exchange's specified upward or downward limit during a trading session, causing trading to halt. Lock limits are set to protect investors from large losses in a volatile market.

lockup period MARKETS time when investors cannot sell a specified period of time during which investors, especially insiders and employees of an initial public offering, are unable to sell their shares of stock

logistics OPERATIONS & PRODUCTION controlling flow of materials through firm's processes the management of the movement, storage, and processing of materials and information in the ***supply chain***. Logistics encompasses the acquisition of raw materials and components, manufacturing or processing, and the distribution of finished products to the end user. Each organization focuses on a different aspect of logistics, depending on its area of interest. For example, one might apply logistics to find a way of linking ***physical distribution management*** with earlier events in the supply chain, another to plan its acquisition and storage, while a third might use logistics as a support operation.

logistics management OPERATIONS & PRODUCTION handling of delivery the management of the distribution of products to the market

logo GENERAL MANAGEMENT firm's recognizable symbol a graphic device or symbol used by an organization as part of its corporate identity. A logo is used to facilitate instant recognition of an organization and to reinforce ***brand*** expectations and public image.

Lombard loan RISK loan with securities pledged as collateral a loan granted by a financial institution against pledged collateral in the form of securities

  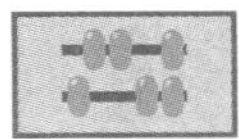   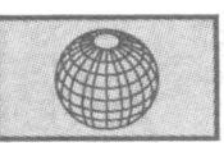   

London Bullion Market MARKETS market for gold and silver the world's largest market for gold, where silver is also traded. It is a wholesale market, where the minimum trades are generally 1,000 ounces for gold and 50,000 ounces for silver. Members typically trade with each other and their clients on a principal-to-principal basis so that all risks, including those of credit, are between the two parties to the transaction.

London Chamber of Commerce and Industry BUSINESS UK's largest chamber of commerce in the United Kingdom, the largest chamber of commerce, that strives "to help London businesses succeed by promoting their interests and expanding their opportunities as members of a worldwide business network." *See also* ***ICC***

London Clearing House MARKETS British clearing house ***clearing house*** based in London, established in 1888 to clear commodities contracts. It added other clearing services, before merging with ***Clearnet*** in 2003 to form ***LCH.Clearnet***. *Abbr* ***LCH***

London Commodity Exchange MARKETS *see* ***NYSE Liffe***

London Interbank Bid Rate MARKETS UK rate for banks' bidding for deposits on the UK money markets, the rate at which banks will bid to take deposits in Eurocurrency from each other. The deposits are for terms from overnight up to five years. *Abbr* ***LIBID***

London Interbank Mean Rate MARKETS average of two interbank interest rates the average of the ***London Interbank Bid Rate*** and the ***London Interbank Offered Rate***, occasionally used as a reference rate. *Abbr* ***LIMEAN***

London Interbank Offered Rate MARKETS UK rate for bank's offering to take deposits on the UK money markets, the rate at which banks will offer to make deposits in ***Eurocurrency*** from each other, often used as a reference rate. The deposits are for terms from overnight up to five years. *Abbr* ***LIBOR***

London International Financial Futures and Options Exchange MARKETS = ***NYSE Liffe***

London Metal Exchange MARKETS market for nonferrous metals one of the world's largest nonferrous metal exchanges, based in London. Its origins can be traced back to the opening of the Royal Exchange in 1571, though in its present form it dates from 1877. It now deals in aluminum, copper, lead, nickel, tin, and zinc, as well as other, minor metals. The primary roles of the exchange are hedging, providing official international reference prices, and appropriate storage facilities. *Abbr* ***LME***

London Stock Exchange MARKETS British stock exchange stock exchange based in London. It has its origins in the late 17th century coffee shops in Change Alley, but the first regulated exchange was established in 1801. It merged with 11 British and Irish regional exchanges in 1973 and with ***Borsa Italiana*** in 2007. The headline index of stocks on the exchange is the ***FTSE 100*** and the ***FTSE All-Share*** covers all stocks on the exchange.

London Traded Options Market MARKETS *see* ***NYSE Liffe***

long STOCKHOLDING & INVESTMENTS having more shares than wanted having a positive holding as a trader in a security

long bond *or* long coupon bond STOCKHOLDING & INVESTMENTS bond that matures after 10 years or more a bond which will mature in more than ten years' time, usually a 30-year bond issued by the US Department of the Treasury

long credit FINANCE loan that borrower can repay over long time credit terms which allow the borrower a long time to pay back the money he or she has borrowed

long-dated STOCKHOLDING & INVESTMENTS maturing after 15 years or more used to describe securities such as bonds that mature after fifteen years or more. *See also* ***short-dated***

long-dated bill STOCKHOLDING & INVESTMENTS bill payable after three or more months a bill that is payable at a date that is not less than three months away

long-dated gilt STOCKHOLDING & INVESTMENTS UK government security maturing in 15 years or more a security issued by the UK government that pays a fixed rate of interest on a regular basis until the redemption date, in 15 years or more, when the principal is returned. *See also* ***gilt-edged security***

long-dated stocks STOCKHOLDING & INVESTMENTS = ***longs***

long firm fraud FRAUD crime of business buying on credit, then disappearing in the United Kingdom, a criminal activity in which somebody sets up an apparently legitimate wholesaling business, obtains fake credit references, trades on credit with wholesale suppliers with no intention of paying for the goods, and then disappears

longitudinal study STATISTICS statistical investigation over period of time a statistical study that produces data gathered over a period of time

long lease REAL ESTATE over 21-year lease in UK in the United Kingdom, a rental agreement that runs at least 21 years

long position MARKETS when dealers avoid selling a situation in which dealers hold securities, commodities, or contracts, expecting prices to rise. *See also* ***short position***

longs STOCKHOLDING & INVESTMENTS long-term government stocks government stocks that will mature more than 15 years after the date of purchase

long-term balance of payments INTERNATIONAL TRADE record of money used in overseas investments a record of movements of capital relating to overseas investments and the purchase of companies overseas

long-term bond STOCKHOLDING & INVESTMENTS bond maturing in 7 years or more a bond that has at least seven years before its redemption date, or, in some markets, a bond with more than seven years until its redemption date

long-term borrowings FINANCE borrowings repayable in several years' time money that is borrowed that does not have to be repaid for a number of years

long-term care insurance INSURANCE insurance against need for costly care insurance that provides coverage for a person who needs ongoing care in a nursing home or their own home

long-term debt FINANCE loans for more than one year loans and debentures that are not due until after at least one year

long-term equity anticipation securities STOCKHOLDING & INVESTMENTS *see* ***LEAPS***

long-term financing FINANCE provision of funding with extended credit forms of funding, such as loans or stock issue, that do not have to be repaid immediately

long-term lease REAL ESTATE lease of 10 years plus a lease that does not expire for at least ten years

long-term liabilities FINANCE debts with extended credit forms of debt such as loans that do not have to be repaid immediately

lookback option MARKETS option with price selected from past prices an option whose price the buyer chooses from all of the prices that have existed during the option's life

loose change CURRENCY & EXCHANGE coins of little value money in the form of coins, especially when the value is small

loose credit ECONOMICS easily available credit to encourage growth a central banking policy to make borrowing easier by lowering interest rates in order to stimulate economic activity

loss ACCOUNTING when costs of activity exceed income from it a financial position in which the ***costs*** of an activity exceed the ***income*** derived from it

loss adjuster *UK* INSURANCE = ***adjuster***

loss assessor INSURANCE in UK, person who assists with insurance claims in the United Kingdom, somebody appointed by an insurance policyholder to assist with his or her claim. *See also* ***claims adjuster***

loss carryback ACCOUNTING application of current-year loss to prior year the process of applying a net operating loss to a previous accounting year in order to reduce tax liability in that year

loss carryforward ACCOUNTING application of current-year loss to future year the process of applying a net operating loss to a following accounting year in order to reduce tax liability in that year

loss control FINANCE, RISK methods of limiting impact of loss of asset the implementation of safety procedures to prevent or limit the impact of a complete or partial loss of an organization's physical assets. Loss control is based on safety audit and prevention techniques. It is concerned with reduction or elimination of losses caused by accidents and occupational ill health. The extent to which it is implemented is usually decided by calculating the total organizational asset cost and weighing this against the likelihood of failure and its worst possible effects on the organization. Loss control was developed in the 1960s as an approach to ***risk management***.

loss leader MARKETING product sold cheaply to attract customers for others a product or service that is sold below the cost of producing it in order to attract more customers to other associated products for purchase

lossmaker BUSINESS product or firm that loses money a product or company that fails to make a profit or break even

loss-making BUSINESS losing money used to describe a business or business activity that is losing money

loss relief TAX in UK, tax relief on previous year's loss in the United Kingdom, an amount of tax not to be paid on one year's profit to offset a loss in the previous year

lot 1. MARKETS smallest quantity traded on exchange the minimum quantity of a commodity that may be purchased on an exchange, for example, 1,000 ounces of gold on the London Bullion Market **2.** BUSINESS unit for sale at auction an item or a collection of related items being offered for sale at an auction **3.** MARKETS group of shares treated together in the United States, a group of shares held or traded together, usually in units of 100 **4.** *US, CANADA* REAL ESTATE land for sale a piece of land assigned to be sold. *UK term* ***plot***

lottery GENERAL MANAGEMENT random selection of successful applicants the random method of selecting successful applicants for something, occasionally used when a new stock issue is oversubscribed

lower level domain E-COMMERCE sublevel name at beginning of Internet address the main part of a domain name. For most e-business sites this is usually the company or brand name.

lower of cost or market ACCOUNTING accounting method treating stocks at lower value a method used by manufacturing and supply firms when accounting for their homogenous stocks which involves valuing them either at their original cost or the current market price, whichever is lower. *Abbr* ***LCM***

low gearing *UK* FINANCE low ratio of firm's debt to assets a situation in which a company has only a small amount of debt in proportion to its assets

low latency MARKETS minimal delay relating to an electronic financial network or trading system that offers near-zero delay between transmission and receipt of an electronic signal

low start mortgage MORTGAGES loan with only interest repayment at first a long-term loan, usually for the purchase of real estate, in which the borrower only pays the interest on the loan for the first few years, usually three. After that, the payments increase to cover the interest and part of the original loan, as in an ***amortized mortgage***. Low start mortgages are popular with first-time buyers, as the lower initial costs may free up funds for furnishings or home improvements. *See also* ***mortgage***

loyalty bonus STOCKHOLDING & INVESTMENTS extra shares given after UK privatizations in the United Kingdom in the 1980s, a number of extra shares, calculated as a proportion of the shares originally subscribed, given to original subscribers of privatization issues providing the shares were held continuously for a given period of time

Ltd *abbr UK* BUSINESS ***limited company***

LTV ratio *abbr* FINANCE ***loan to value ratio***

lump sum FINANCE **1.** repaid in one installment used to describe a loan that is repayable with one installment at the end of its term. *See also* ***balloon loan, interest-only mortgage*** **2.** money received in single payment an amount of money received in one payment, for example, the sum payable to the beneficiary of a life insurance policy on the death of the policyholder

luxury tax TAX tax on inessential items a tax on goods or services that are considered nonessential

M

M0 ECONOMICS money available to public for spending an estimate of the amount of money in public circulation, available for use as a means of exchange. *Also called* ***narrow money*** *(sense 2)*

M1 ECONOMICS cash plus bank accounts an estimate of the amount of money held by the public in coins, banknotes, and checking accounts. *Also called* ***narrow money*** *(sense 1)*

M2 ECONOMICS cash plus easily available deposits an estimate of the amount of money held by the public in coins, currency, checking and savings accounts, and deposits

M3 ECONOMICS M1, M2 plus international money an estimate of the amount of money in M1, M2 and large denomination repurchase agreements, institutional money market accounts, and some Eurodollar time deposits

ma and pa shop *UK* BUSINESS = ***mom-and-pop operation***

Macaulay duration MARKETS, RISK measure of interest-rate risk in owning bonds a measure of a bond's sensitivity to changes in interest rates. It is calculated by dividing the present value of the cash flows received by the current market value of the bond. *See also* ***modified duration***

machine hour rate FINANCE proportion of overhead costs an ***overhead absorption rate*** based on the number of hours a machine is used in production

macroeconomics ECONOMICS study of national economic systems the study of national income and the economic systems of nations. *See also* ***microeconomics***

macroeconomy ECONOMICS national economy as whole the broad sectors of a country's economic activity, for example, the financial or industrial sectors, that are aggregated to form its economic system as a whole. *See also* ***microeconomy***

macrohedge RISK reduction of risk on whole portfolio a ***hedge*** that aims to cover the overall risk to an entire investment ***portfolio***. *Also called* ***global hedge***. *See also* ***microhedge***

macroprudential regulation REGULATION & COMPLIANCE overall control of financial systems oversight that focuses on the stability of a financial system as a whole, rather than on its components. The need for macroprudential regulation of the system arises because the actions of individual companies acting prudently within guidelines may collectively result in the instability of a financial system, for example, if all lenders restrict lending or all companies sell assets at the same time. *See also* ***microprudential regulation***

macroprudential risk RISK risk of collective action causing instability the risk that individual companies acting prudently will nevertheless cause instability in a financial system by their collective action in a particular area, for example, all lenders restricting lending or all companies selling assets at the same time

mail ballot *US* FINANCE election accepting votes returned by mail an election of officers of a company in which the voters send in their ballot papers by mail. *UK term* ***postal vote***

mail form E-COMMERCE webpage for inputting data sent as e-mail a webpage that requires the user to input data such as name, address, or order or shipping information, that is transmitted to an e-merchant via e-mail

mailing *US* MARKETING appeal to specific group through mail a speculative targeting of a specific group of people by mail. A mailing normally contains information, advertising, fundraising requests, or press releases. *Also called* ***mail-out, mailshot***

mailing house MARKETING firm dealing in direct mail projects an organization that specializes in planning, creating, and implementing direct mail campaigns for clients

mailing list MARKETING names and addresses for marketing purposes the names and addresses of a specific group of people compiled for marketing purposes. A mailing list may be compiled internally or bought or rented from an outside agency, and can be used for advertising, fundraising, news releases, or for direct mail or a mailshot. A mailing list is usually compiled for a selected group using one or more criteria, such as men between the ages of 25 and 30, or retired people.

mail order MARKETING method of requesting products from catalog for delivery a form of retailing in which consumers order products from a catalog for delivery to their home

mail-out MARKETING = ***mailing***

mailshot MARKETING = ***mailing***

mailsort MARKETING UK sorting service for direct mail in the United Kingdom, a sorting service offered to organizations by the Post Office, intended to reduce the cost and time spent on direct mail

mainstream corporation tax TAX main UK tax on corporations the principal UK tax on resident companies, paid on profits after deduction of allowable expenses. This was formerly reduced by the amount of ***advance corporation tax*** already paid.

maintenance bond STOCKHOLDING & INVESTMENTS guarantee for period after complete transaction a bond that provides a guarantee against defects for some time after a contract has been fulfilled

majority decision *or* majority vote GENERAL MANAGEMENT decision of most people made by voting a decision that represents the wishes of the largest group as shown by a vote, for example, in a board meeting or a shareholders' meeting

majority shareholder STOCKHOLDING & INVESTMENTS stockholder with controlling interest a shareholder with a controlling interest in a company. *See also* ***minority interest***

majority shareholding STOCKHOLDING & INVESTMENTS stockholding in excess of 50% a group of shares of stock that are more than half the total and enough to give control to the person or entity holding them

make or buy GENERAL MANAGEMENT *see* ***purchasing versus production***

maladministration GENERAL MANAGEMENT incompetent management of public affairs failure on the part of an administration to act in a competent manner, especially in public affairs

managed account STOCKHOLDING & INVESTMENTS = ***discretionary account***

managed currency fund CURRENCY & EXCHANGE managed fund investing in currencies a managed mutual fund that makes considered investments in foreign exchange

managed derivatives fund STOCKHOLDING & INVESTMENTS fund investing in derivatives a fund that uses mainly ***futures*** and ***options*** instead of investing in the underlying securities

managed economy ECONOMICS economy controlled by government an economy directed by a government rather than the free market

managed float ECONOMICS exchange rate affected by government action the position when the exchange rate of a country's currency is influenced by government action in the foreign exchange market

managed fund STOCKHOLDING & INVESTMENTS mutual fund investing after research a mutual fund with professional managers who make considered investments, as opposed to an ***index fund***. *Also called* ***managed mutual fund***

managed mutual fund *US* STOCKHOLDING & INVESTMENTS = ***managed fund***

managed rate BANKING financial institution's independently established interest rate a rate of interest charged by a financial institution for borrowing that it sets itself from time to time, rather than following a prescribed margin over base rate

managed unit trust STOCKHOLDING & INVESTMENTS = ***managed fund***

management GENERAL MANAGEMENT, HR & PERSONNEL using firm's resources effectively to achieve goals the use of professional skills for identifying and achieving organizational objectives through the deployment of appropriate resources. Management involves identifying what needs to be done, and organizing and supporting others to perform the necessary tasks. A manager has complex and ever-changing responsibilities, the focus of which shifts to reflect the issues, trends, and preoccupations of the time. At the beginning of the 20th century, the emphasis was both on supporting the organization's administration and managing ***productivity*** through increased efficiency. At the beginning of the 21st century, those original drivers are still much in evidence, although the emphasis has moved to key areas of competence such as people management. Although management is a profession in its own right, its skill set often applies to professionals of other disciplines.

management accountant TREASURY MANAGEMENT financial adviser on management decisions a person who contributes to management's decision-making processes by, for example, collecting and processing data relating to a business's costs, sales, and the profitability of individual activities

management accounting TREASURY MANAGEMENT use of accounting principles to benefit organization the application of the principles of accounting and financial management to create, protect, preserve, and increase value so as to deliver that value to the stakeholders of profit and nonprofit enterprises, both public and private. Management accounting is an integral part of management, requiring the identification, generation, presentation, interpretation, and use of information relevant to formulating business strategy; planning and controlling activities; decision making; efficient resource usage; performance improvement and value enhancement; safeguarding tangible and intangible assets; and corporate governance and internal control.

management accounts TREASURY MANAGEMENT financial report prepared for manager financial information prepared for a manager so that decisions can be made, including monthly or quarterly financial statements, often in great detail, with analysis of actual performance against the budget

management audit GENERAL MANAGEMENT = ***operational audit***

management buyin MERGERS & ACQUISITIONS purchase of business by external managers the purchase of an existing business by an individual manager or management group outside that business. *Abbr* ***MBI***

management buyout MERGERS & ACQUISITIONS takeover of business by its management the purchase of an existing business by an individual manager or management group from within that business. *Abbr* ***MBO***

management by objectives *or* management by results GENERAL MANAGEMENT method for achieving goals through series of objectives a method of managing an organization by setting a series of ***objectives*** that contribute toward the achievement of its goals. *Abbr* ***MBO***

management charge *UK* STOCKHOLDING & INVESTMENTS = ***annual management charge***

management company BUSINESS firm that manages aspects of another firm's business a company that takes over responsibility from internal staff for managing facilities such as computer systems, telecommunications, or maintenance. The process is known as ***outsourcing***.

management consultancy *UK* GENERAL MANAGEMENT = ***management consulting***

management consultant GENERAL MANAGEMENT person who gives advice about management methods a person professionally engaged in advising on, and providing, a detached, external view of a company's management techniques and practices.
A management consultant may be self-employed, a partner, or employed in a specialist firm. Consultants can be called in for many reasons, but are employed particularly for projects involving business improvement, ***change management***, information technology, and long-term planning.

management consulting *US* GENERAL MANAGEMENT giving advice about management methods the activity of advising on management techniques and practices. Management consulting usually involves the identification of a problem, or the analysis of a specific area of one organization, and the reporting of any resulting findings. The consulting process can sometimes be extended to help put into effect the recommendations made. *UK term* ***management consultancy***

management consulting firm GENERAL MANAGEMENT firm giving management advice a firm of ***management consultants***, offering professional advice on ways to improve efficiency

management fee STOCKHOLDING & INVESTMENTS fee for managing mutual fund a fee paid to a mutual fund manager by a client to cover their services and a variety of administrative costs

management information system OPERATIONS & PRODUCTION *see* ***MIS***

management process GENERAL MANAGEMENT management of human, financial, and material resources the process of planning, implementing, and controlling activities that involve human, financial, and material resources

management team GENERAL MANAGEMENT, HR & PERSONNEL = ***senior management***

management trainee HR & PERSONNEL low-ranking manager learning management methods an employee who holds a low-level management position while undergoing formal training in management techniques

management training HR & PERSONNEL courses teaching management methods planned activities for developing management skills. Management training methods include public or in-company training courses and on-the-job training designed to improve managerial ***competences***.
Management training tends to be practical and to focus on specific management techniques. It does not result in a formal degree.

manager GENERAL MANAGEMENT, HR & PERSONNEL employee responsible for part of firm's activities a person who identifies and achieves organizational objectives through the deployment of appropriate resources. A manager can have responsibilities in one or more of five key areas: managing activities; managing resources; managing information; managing people; and managing him- or herself while working within the context of the organizational, political, and economic business environments. There are managers in all disciplines and activities, although some may not bear the title of manager. Some specialize in areas such as personnel, marketing, production, finance, or project management, while others are ***general managers***, applying management skills across all business areas. Very few jobs are entirely managerial, and very few exist without any management responsibilities. It is the capability to harness resources that largely distinguishes a manager from a non-manager.

managerialism GENERAL MANAGEMENT firm's focus on effective management emphasis on efficient management, and the use of systems, planning, and management practice.
Managerialism is often used in a critical sense, especially from the perspective of the public sector, to imply overenthusiasm for efficiency, or private sector management techniques and systems, possibly at the expense of service or quality considerations. The term is also used to describe confrontational attitudes, or actions displayed by management toward labor unions.

managing agent INSURANCE administrator of Lloyd's syndicate a person who runs the day-to-day activities of a Lloyd's syndicate

managing director CORPORATE GOVERNANCE limited company's director in charge of daily business the ***chief executive officer*** of a ***limited company*** in the United Kingdom and other countries, who has overall responsibility for its day-to-day operations. *Abbr* ***MD***

managing for value GENERAL MANAGEMENT focusing on long-term value of business an approach to building the long-term value of a business. The term is most frequently used by businesses that are implementing the ***balanced scorecard approach*** and emphasizes the need to make financial and commercial decisions that build the value of the business for its stockholders.

M&A *abbr* MERGERS & ACQUISITIONS ***mergers and acquisitions***

mandarin GENERAL MANAGEMENT important government adviser a high-ranking and influential adviser, especially in government circles

mandatory bid STOCKHOLDING & INVESTMENTS compulsory bid for remaining stock an offer to purchase the remaining shares of a company that a stockholder has to make if he or she acquires at least 30% of that company's stock

mandatory quote period MARKETS time when security prices must be displayed on the London Stock Exchange, the period of time during which prices of securities must be displayed

  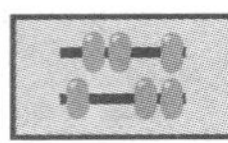      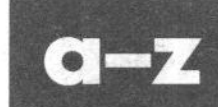

manpower forecasting GENERAL MANAGEMENT = ***human resource forecasting***

manpower planning GENERAL MANAGEMENT = ***human resource planning***

manufacture OPERATIONS & PRODUCTION making products in factory the large-scale production of goods from raw materials or parts

manufacturer OPERATIONS & PRODUCTION maker of factory products a person or organization involved in the large-scale production of goods from raw materials or parts

manufacturer's agent OPERATIONS & PRODUCTION representative of product-maker for getting contracts a person or organization with authority to act for a ***manufacturer*** in obtaining a ***contract*** with a third party

manufacturing OPERATIONS & PRODUCTION process by which product is made the processes and techniques used in making a product from raw materials or parts

manufacturing account ACCOUNTING accounts showing only production costs a financial statement that shows production costs only, as opposed to a ***profit and loss account***, which shows sales and costs of sales. A manufacturing account will include direct materials and labor costs and the production overhead.

manufacturing cost OPERATIONS & PRODUCTION money needed to make products the expenditure incurred in carrying out the production processes of an organization. The manufacturing cost includes ***direct costs***, for example, labor, materials, and expenses, and indirect costs, for example, subcontracting and overhead.

manufacturing information system OPERATIONS & PRODUCTION computer system for production process a management information system designed specifically for use in a production environment

manufacturing resource planning OPERATIONS & PRODUCTION *see* ***MRP II***

manufacturing system OPERATIONS & PRODUCTION organization of firm's production process a method of organizing production. Manufacturing systems include assembly and ***batch production***, ***flexible manufacturing systems***, ***lean production***, and ***mass production***.

manufacturing to order OPERATIONS & PRODUCTION producing goods to fill requests not for stockpile a production management technique in which goods are produced to meet firm orders, rather than being produced for inventory

Marché à Terme International de France MARKETS *see* ***MATIF***

Marché des Options Négociables de Paris MARKETS *see* ***MONEP***

margin FINANCE **1.** gap between cost and selling price the difference between the cost and the selling price of a product or service **2.** *ANZ* extra pay for employees' special skills a payment made to workers over and above the basic wage in recognition of special skills

margin account FINANCE account with investment broker who lends money an account with a broker who lends money for investments, held in the name of an investor who pays only a percentage of the price of purchases

marginal **1.** FINANCE not worth money spent producing very little benefit in relation to the amount of money spent (informal) **2.** OPERATIONS & PRODUCTION barely covering production cost nearly unable to cover the cost of production when selling goods or when goods are being sold

marginal analysis ECONOMICS investigation into economic effects of small changes the study of how small changes in an economic variable will affect an economy

marginal cost OPERATIONS & PRODUCTION extra cost of producing additional item the part of the cost of one unit of product or service that would be avoided if that unit were not produced, or that would increase if one extra unit were produced

marginal costing ACCOUNTING accounting system treating variable and fixed costs differently the accounting system in which variable costs are charged to cost units and fixed costs of the period are written off in full against the aggregate contribution. Its special value is in recognizing cost behavior, and hence assisting in decision making. *Also called* ***variable costing***

marginal costs and benefits ECONOMICS losses and gains resulting from incremental changes the losses or gains to a person or household arising from a small change in a variable, such as food consumption or income received

marginalization ECONOMICS process of becoming less important in world economy the process by which countries lose importance and status because they are unable to participate in mainstream activities such as industrialization or the Internet economy

marginal lender FINANCE lender with lower limit on interest rate a lender who will make a loan only at or above a particular rate of interest

marginal pricing OPERATIONS & PRODUCTION setting prices between variable cost and full cost the practice of basing the selling price of a product on its variable costs of production plus a margin, but excluding fixed costs

marginal revenue OPERATIONS & PRODUCTION money from producing more the revenue generated by additional units of production

marginal tax rate TAX tax rate on income after business expenses the rate of tax payable on a person's income after business expenses have been deducted

marginal utility ECONOMICS satisfaction in using one additional unit satisfaction gained from using one more unit of a product or service

margin call STOCKHOLDING & INVESTMENTS request for additional deposit to margin account a request for a purchaser of a futures contract or an option to deposit more money in his or her ***margin account***, since the fall in the price of the securities or commodity has brought the value of the original deposit below the minimum required

margining STOCKHOLDING & INVESTMENTS, RISK way London Clearing House controls risk the system by which the London Clearing House controls the risk associated with the position of a member of the London International Financial Futures and Options Exchange on a daily basis. To achieve this, members deposit cash or collateral with the London Clearing House in the form of initial and variation margins. The initial margin is the deposit required on all open positions, long or short, to cover short-term price movements and is returned to members by the London Clearing House when the position is closed. The variation margin is the members' profits or losses, calculated daily from the marked-to-market-close value of their position, whereby contracts are revalued daily for the calculation of variation margin and credited to or debited from their accounts.

margin of error GENERAL MANAGEMENT amount allowed for miscalculation an allowance made for the possibility that something has been miscalculated or that conditions change

margin of safety TREASURY MANAGEMENT level of firm's performance above break-even point the difference between the level of activity at which an organization breaks even and the level of activity greater than this point. For example, a margin of safety of $300,000 is achieved when the break-even point is $900,000 and sales reach $1,200,000. This measure can be expressed as a proportion of sales value, as a number of units sold, or as a percentage of ***capacity***.

Margrabe option STOCKHOLDING & INVESTMENTS, RISK = ***exchange option***

marital deductions TAX spouse's nontaxable part of inheritance the part of an estate which, after a death, is not subject to estate tax because it goes to the spouse of the deceased

marital property FINANCE = ***community property***

mark down OPERATIONS & PRODUCTION reduce price of something to make the price of something lower

mark-down OPERATIONS & PRODUCTION **1.** reduction in price an act of reducing the price of something to less than its usual price **2.** percentage reduction in price the percentage amount by which a price has been reduced

marked cheque *UK* BANKING (slang) = ***certified check***

marked price OPERATIONS & PRODUCTION price displayed on product for sale the original displayed price of a product in a store. In a sale, customers may be offered a savings on the marked price.

market **1.** FINANCE rate of financial sales the rate at which financial commodities or securities are being sold **2.** ECONOMICS, MARKETING group of consumers with shared need a group of people or organizations unified by common requirements **3.** ECONOMICS group of buyers and sellers trading goods a gathering of sellers and purchasers to exchange commodities **make a market** MARKETS to be prepared as a dealer to buy or sell a particular security at the quoted bid or ask price

marketable MARKETING able to be sold successfully possessing the potential to be commercially viable. To determine whether a new product or service is marketable, an assessment needs to be conducted to see if it is likely to make a profit. The assessment is often based on detailed ***market research*** analyzing the potential market, and the projected financial returns and any other benefits for the company.

marketable security STOCKHOLDING & INVESTMENTS security easily sold or exchanged a security that can easily be sold and converted into cash, or exchanged for a different type of security

market analysis MARKETING study of particular market the study of a market to identify and quantify business opportunities

market area MARKETING where market is the geographic location of a particular group of consumers with shared needs

market-based pricing OPERATIONS & PRODUCTION charging what customer will pay

setting a price based on the value of the product in the perception of the customer. *Also called* ***perceived value pricing***

market bubble MARKETS short period of inflated prices a stock market phenomenon in which values in a particular sector become inflated for a short period. If the bubble bursts, stock prices in that sector collapse.

market capitalization MARKETS full market value of firm the total market value of a company, calculated by multiplying the price of its shares on the stock exchange by the number of shares outstanding. *Abbr* ***market cap***. Also called ***market valuation*** *(sense 1)*

market coverage MARKETING how well product satisfies customers' needs the degree to which a product or service meets the needs of a market

market cycle MARKETS sequence of market expansion, contraction, and expansion a period during which a market expands, then slows down, and then expands again

market development MARKETING activities to expand demand for particular product type marketing activities designed to increase the overall size of a market through education and awareness

market-driven MARKETING strongly influenced by needs of potential customers using market knowledge to determine the corporate strategy of an organization. A market-driven organization has a customer focus, together with awareness of competitors, and an understanding of the market.

market economist MARKETS specialist in investment a person who specializes in the study of financial structures and the return on investments in the stock market

market economy ECONOMICS economic system not controlled by government an economy in which a ***free market*** in goods and services operates

marketeer MARKETING small firm competing with larger firms a small company that competes in the same market as larger companies. Examples of marketeers are restaurants, travel agents, computer software providers, garages, and insurance brokers.

marketer MARKETING promoter of sales a person who is responsible for developing and implementing marketing policy

marketface BUSINESS where suppliers and customers meet the interface between suppliers of goods or services and their customers

market-facing enterprise BUSINESS firm focusing on marketplace and customers an organization that aligns itself with its markets and customers and makes them its priority concern

market-focused organization BUSINESS organization responsive to market needs an organization whose strategies are determined by market requirements rather than organizational demands

market forces BUSINESS factors affecting prices influences on sales which bring about a change in prices

market fragmentation BUSINESS market consisting of small-scale buyers and sellers a situation in which the buyers or sellers in a market consist of a large number of small organizations

market gap BUSINESS situation where no producer is meeting market need an opportunity in a market where no supplier provides a product or service that buyers need

market if touched STOCKHOLDING & INVESTMENTS instruction to trade at specific price an order to trade a security if it reaches a specific price. *Abbr* ***MIT***

marketing MARKETING efforts to promote products the process of building long-term relationships with customers and with other interested parties and to provide value to them. This begins with ***market research***, which analyzes needs and wants in society, and continues with attracting customers and the cultivation of mutually beneficial exchange processes with them. Tools used in this process are diverse and include ***market segmentation***, ***brand management***, PR, ***logistics***, ***direct response marketing***, ***sales promotion***, and ***advertising***. **4 Ps of marketing** MARKETING the variety of integrated decisions made by a marketing manager to ensure successful marketing, in four key areas—product, price, place, and promotion—covering issues such as the type of product to be marketed, brand name, pricing, advertising, publicity, geographic coverage, retailing, and distribution

marketing agreement MARKETING agreement to market another firm's product a contract by which one company agrees to market another company's products

marketing audit MARKETING evaluation of firm's marketing approach an analysis of either the external marketing environment or a company's internal marketing goals, objectives, operations, and efficiency. An external marketing audit covers issues such as economic, political, infrastructure, technological, and consumer perspectives; market size and market structure; and competitors, suppliers, and distributors. An internal marketing audit covers aspects such as the company's mission statement, goals, and objectives; its structure, corporate culture, systems, operations, and processes; product development and pricing; profitability and efficiency; advertising; and deployment of the sales force.

marketing consultancy MARKETING firm creating marketing plan for other firms an organization that plans and develops marketing strategies and programs on behalf of clients

marketing information system MARKETING computer system for managing firm's marketing program an information system concerned with the collection, storage, and analysis of information and data for marketing decision-making purposes. Information for use in marketing information systems is gathered from customers, competitors, and their products, and from the market itself.

marketing management MARKETING responsibility for firm's efforts to promote products one of the main management disciplines, encompassing all the strategic planning, operations, activities, and processes involved in achieving organizational objectives by delivering value to customers. Marketing management focuses on satisfying customer requirements by identifying needs and wants, and developing products and services to meet them.

marketing manager MARKETING person responsible for promoting firm's products somebody who is responsible for planning and controlling marketing activities and budgets for a company

marketing mix MARKETING mixture of techniques for promoting products the variety of integrated decisions made by a marketing manager to ensure successful marketing. These decisions are made in four key areas known as the ***4 Ps of marketing***—product, price, place, and promotion—and cover issues such as the type of product to be marketed, brand name, pricing, advertising, publicity, geographic coverage, retailing, and distribution.

marketing myopia MARKETING mistake of forgetting customers' needs the theory that some organizations ignore the fact that to be successful, the wants of customers must be their central consideration

marketing planning MARKETING process of deciding plan for promoting firm's products the process of producing a marketing plan incorporating overall marketing objectives and the strategies and programs of action designed to achieve those objectives. Marketing planning requires a careful examination of all strategic issues, including the business environment, the markets themselves, competitors, the corporate ***mission statement***, and organizational capabilities. The resulting marketing plan should be communicated to appropriate staff through an oral briefing to ensure it is fully understood.

market intelligence MARKETING information about particular area of commercial activity a collection of internal and external data on a given market. Market intelligence focuses particularly on competitors, customers, consumer spending, market trends, and suppliers.

market leader BUSINESS, MARKETING one with highest market share the product, service, or company that has a dominant ***market share***

market logic MARKETS circumstances governing firm's stock market performance the prevailing forces or attitudes that determine a company's success or failure on the stock market

market maker MARKETS **1.** provider of market for unlisted security a broker or bank that maintains a market for a security that does not trade on any exchange **2.** securities dealer who both buys and sells a securities dealer who offers either to buy or sell stock on the stock market at a guaranteed price **3.** *UK* promoter of trading in one particular firm somebody who works in a stock exchange to facilitate trades in one particular company

market-neutral funds STOCKHOLDING & INVESTMENTS hedge funds exploiting temporary fluctuations ***hedge funds*** that are not related to general market movements but that are used to find opportunities to take advantage of temporary slight changes in the relative values of particular financial assets

market order MARKETS instruction to trade security at best available price an order to trade a security at the best price the broker can obtain

market penetration BUSINESS percentage of potential sales that firm has made a measure of the percentage or potential percentage of the market that a product or company is able to capture, expressed in terms of total sales or turnover. Market penetration is often used to measure the level of success a new product or service has achieved.

market penetration pricing MARKETING practice of setting prices low to increase sales the policy of pricing a product or service very competitively, and sometimes at a loss to the producer, in order to increase its ***market share***

market position BUSINESS, MARKETING product's portion of total sales in market the place held by a product or service in a ***market***, usually

  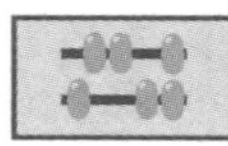      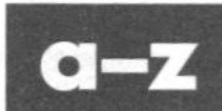

determined by its percentage of total sales. An ideal market position is often predefined for a product or service. Analysis of potential customers and competing products can be used with product differentiation techniques to formulate a product to fill the desired market position.

market potential BUSINESS predictions about product's sales and earning possibilities a forecast of the size of a market in terms of revenue, numbers of buyers, or other factors

market power BUSINESS buyers' or sellers' ability to control market the dominance of a market either by customers, who create a buyer's market, or by a particular company, which creates a seller's market. Individuals or companies retain control of the market by fixing the pricing and number of products available.

market price **1.** MARKETS price consumers are paying the price that buyers are currently paying for a good, service, commodity, etc. **2.** ECONOMICS price at which supply equals demand the theoretical price at which supply equals demand

market quote MARKETS current best stock market price the most up-to-date highest price being offered for a security on a stock exchange

market research MARKETING investigation of commercial activity research conducted to assess the size and nature of a market

market risk MARKETS, RISK risk inherent in securities market or economy investment risk that is attributable to the performance of the stock market or of the economy and cannot be removed by diversification

market risk premium RISK, STOCKHOLDING & INVESTMENTS return needed to compensate for risk the extra return required from a high-risk investment to compensate for its higher-than-average risk

market sector *or* market segment MARKETING distinctive subsection of consumers a subdivision of a ***market*** with distinctive characteristics. Market sectors are usually determined by ***market segmentation***, which divides a market into different categories. Car buyers, for example, could be put into sectors such as car fleet buyers, private buyers, buyers under 20 years old, and so on. The smaller the sector, the more its members will have in common. Sellers may decide to compete in the whole market or only in segments that are attractive to them or where they have an advantage.

market segmentation MARKETING categorization of buyers by buying habits the division of the market or consumers into categories according to their buying habits

market sentiment MARKETS general feeling among brokers and traders the mood of those participating in exchange dealings that can range from absolute euphoria to downright gloom and despondency and tends to reflect recent company results, economic indicators, and comments by politicians, analysts, or opinion formers. Optimism increases demand and therefore prices, while pessimism has the opposite effect.

market share BUSINESS firm's or product's proportion of total sales the proportion of the total market value of a product or group of products or services that a company, service, or product holds. Market share is shown as a percentage of the total value or output of a market, usually expressed in US dollars, pounds sterling, or euros, by weight (tons or tonnes), or as individual units, depending on the commodity. The product, service, or company with a dominant market share is referred to as the ***market leader***.

Markets in Financial Instruments Directive MARKETS, REGULATION & COMPLIANCE EU directive governing conduct of investment companies an EU directive that sets out detailed requirements governing the organization and conduct of business of investment companies, and how regulated markets and multilateral trading facilities should operate. It came into force on November 1, 2007, replacing the ***Investment Services Directive*** (ISD), and made significant changes to the regulatory framework to reflect developments in financial services and markets since the ISD was implemented. *Abbr* ***MiFID***

market site E-COMMERCE website shared by several Internet firms a website shared by multiple e-commerce vendors, each having a different specialty, to conduct business over the Internet

market size **1.** MARKETS maximum number of shares traded together the largest number of shares that a market will handle in one trade of a specific security **2.** MARKETING number of consumers in specific group the size of a group of consumers with shared needs and their buying power

market structure BUSINESS organization of particular area of commercial activity the makeup of a particular ***market***. Market structure can be described with reference to different characteristics of a market, including its size and value, the number of providers and their ***market share***, consumer and business purchasing behavior, and growth forecasts. The description may also include a demographic and regional breakdown of providers and customers and an analysis of pricing structures, likely technological impacts, and domestic and overseas sales.

market targeting MARKETING promoting products to specific group of consumers the selection of a particular market sector toward which all marketing effort is directed. Market targeting enables the characteristics of the chosen sector to be taken into account when formulating a product or service and its advertising.

market timing MARKETS trading determined by market trends an investing strategy of buying and selling securities based on indicators of market trends over relatively short periods of time

market trend MARKETS rising or falling price movements a period during which stock market prices are moving in a particular direction

market valuation **1.** MARKETS = ***market capitalization*** **2.** STOCKHOLDING & INVESTMENTS worth of portfolio on selling the value of a portfolio if all its investments were to be sold at current market prices **3.** REAL ESTATE professional assessment of current value of real estate the opinion of an expert professional as to the current worth of a piece of real estate

market value FINANCE worth of asset if sold the value of an asset based on what price would be received for it if it were sold

market value added MARKETS difference between market and book value the difference between a company's ***market value*** (derived from the stock price), and its economic ***book value*** (the amount of capital that stockholders have committed to the firm throughout its existence, including any retained earnings). *Abbr* ***MVA***

marking down MARKETS lowering of price required the reduction by market makers in the price at which they are prepared to deal in a security, for example, because of an adverse report by an analyst, or the announcement or anticipated announcement of a profit warning by a company

mark to market MARKETS securities valuation that reflects current prices daily valuation of the price of securities held in an account at the closing price, or the ***market quote*** if the last sale falls outside the market quote, so that the equity fully reflects current prices

mark up BUSINESS increase price of something to make the price of something higher, especially in order to provide the seller with a profit

markup BUSINESS amount added to make selling price the addition to the cost of goods or services which results in a selling price. The markup may be expressed as a percentage or as an absolute monetary amount.

massaging ACCOUNTING presentation to suggest better performance the adjustment of financial figures to create the impression of better performance (slang)

mass market MARKETING area of commercial activity involving much of population a market that covers substantial numbers of the population. A mass market may consist of a whole population or just a segment of that population. Mass customization of products has allowed a greater number of single products to satisfy a mass market.

mass production OPERATIONS & PRODUCTION manufacturing large numbers of same product at once large-scale manufacturing, often designed to meet the demand for a particular product. Mass production methods were developed by Henry Ford, founder of the Ford Motor Company. Mass production involves using a moving production or assembly line on which the product moves while operators remain at their stations carrying out their work on each passing product. Mass production is now challenged by methods including ***just-in-time*** and ***lean production***.

master franchise MARKETING arrangement allowing franchisee to permit further franchises a license issued by the owner of a product or service to another party or master franchisee allowing them to issue further ***franchise*** licenses. A master franchise can benefit the original franchisor, as the master franchisee effectively develops the ***franchise chain*** on their behalf. A master franchise usually grants further licenses within a defined geographic area, and several master franchises may cover a country.

master limited partnership BUSINESS partnership with benefits in tax and liquidity a partnership of a type that combines tax advantages and advantages of liquidity

Master of Business Administration GENERAL MANAGEMENT *see* ***MBA***

master production scheduling OPERATIONS & PRODUCTION method of developing detailed manufacturing plan a technique used in material requirements planning systems to develop a detailed plan for product manufacturing. The master production schedule, compiled by a master scheduler, takes account of the requirements of various departments, including sales (delivery dates), finance (inventory minimization), and manufacturing (minimization of setup times), and it schedules production and the purchasing of materials within the capacity of and resources available to the production system.

  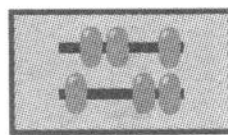   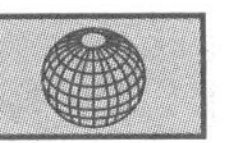   

matador bond STOCKHOLDING & INVESTMENTS foreign bond in Spain a foreign bond issued into the Spanish domestic market by a non-Spanish company (slang)

matched bargain *UK* STOCKHOLDING & INVESTMENTS connected sale and rebuying the linked sale and repurchase of the same quantity of the same security. *See also* ***bed and breakfast deal***

matching convention ACCOUNTING accounts basis with matching of sales with costs the basis for preparing accounts that says that profits can only be recognized if sales are fully matched with costs accrued during the same period

material cost OPERATIONS & PRODUCTION price paid for product's raw materials the cost of the raw materials that go into a product. The material cost of a product excludes any ***indirect costs***, for example, overhead or wages, associated with producing the item.

material facts MARKETS **1.** compulsory information for prospectus information about a company that has to be disclosed in a ***prospectus***. *See also* ***listing requirements*** **2.** information insurer must be told in an insurance contract, information that the insured has to reveal at the time that the policy is taken out, for example, that a house is located on the edge of a crumbling cliff. Failure to reveal material facts can result in the contract being declared void.

material information *US* MARKETS information firm must tell exchange price-sensitive developments in a company, for example, proposed acquisitions, mergers, profit warnings, and the resignation of directors, that most stock exchanges require a company to announce immediately to the exchange. *UK term* ***material news***

material news *UK* MARKETS = ***material information***

materials returned note OPERATIONS & PRODUCTION record of unused material a record of the return to stores of unused material

MATIF *abbr* MARKETS French futures market in France, a market that deals in ***futures***, established in 1986. It merged with the ***Paris Bourse*** in 1999 and is now part of the ***NYSE Euronext*** group. *Full form* ***Marché à Terme International de France***

matrix management GENERAL MANAGEMENT managing through both horizontal and vertical reporting structures management based on two or more reporting systems that are linked to the vertical organization hierarchy, and to horizontal relationships based on geographic, product, or project requirements

matrix organization GENERAL MANAGEMENT way of structuring firm both horizontally and vertically organization by both vertical administrative functions and horizontal tasks, areas, processes, or projects. Matrix organization originated in the 1960s and 1970s, particularly within the US aerospace industry, when ***organization charts*** showing how the management of a given project would relate to ***senior management*** were often required to win government contracts. A two-dimensional matrix chart best illustrates the dual horizontal, and vertical, reporting relationships. Matrix organization is closely linked to ***matrix management***.

matrix structure GENERAL MANAGEMENT firm's organization with both horizontal and vertical relationships a form of organizational structure based on horizontal and vertical relationships. The matrix structure is linked closely to ***matrix management***, and is related to ***project management***. It emerged on an improvised rather than a planned basis as a way of showing how people work with or report to others in their organization, project, geographic region, process, or team.

matrix trading STOCKHOLDING & INVESTMENTS trading taking advantage of differences in yields a ***bond swap*** strategy that takes advantages of discrepancies in yields of bonds of different classes

mature FINANCE due for payment having reached maturity

mature economy ECONOMICS economy that has slowed down an economy that is no longer developing or growing rapidly. Such economies tend to have increased consumer spending rather than industrial and manufacturing investment.

maturity STOCKHOLDING & INVESTMENTS period before repayment date of financial instrument the period that will elapse before a financial instrument such as a bond becomes due for repayment or an option expires

maturity date STOCKHOLDING & INVESTMENTS expiration date of option the date on which a financial instrument such as a bond becomes due for repayment or an option expires

maturity value STOCKHOLDING & INVESTMENTS amount payable on mature financial instrument the amount payable when a bond or other financial instrument matures

maturity yield STOCKHOLDING & INVESTMENTS = ***yield***

Maxi ISA STOCKHOLDING & INVESTMENTS former UK tax-free account for savings and investment formerly, in the United Kingdom, an ***ISA*** in which savers invested tax-free mainly in stocks with a limited cash component. Savers could own only one Maxi ISA. *See also* ***Mini ISA, ISA***

maximize FINANCE increase financial gain as much as possible to take measures to increase something such as your gain on an investment or profit in a business as much as possible

maximum **1.** greatest possible amount the largest number, price, quantity, or degree possible or allowed **2.** greatest possible of the largest possible or allowed amount or value

maximum inventory level *US* OPERATIONS & PRODUCTION size above which inventory must not increase an inventory level, set for control purposes, which actual holdings should never exceed. It is calculated as follows:

Reorder level + Economic order quantity
− Minimum rate of usage × Minimum lead time

UK term ***maximum stock level***

maximum stock level *UK* OPERATIONS & PRODUCTION = ***maximum inventory level***

maysir FINANCE gambling or speculation prohibited by Islamic law in Islamic financing, gambling with the intention of making an easy profit. It is one of three prohibitions in Islamic law, which is extended to such financial practices as speculation, insurance, futures, and options; the others are ***gharar*** and ***riba***.

MBA GENERAL MANAGEMENT master's degree in business administration a postgraduate degree awarded after a period of study of topics relating to the strategic management of businesses. A Master of Business Administration course can be taken at a business school or university, and covers areas such as finance, personnel, and resource management, as well as the wider business environment and skills such as information technology use. The course is mostly taken by people with experience of managerial work, and is offered by universities worldwide. Part-time or distance learning MBAs are available, so that students can study while still working. There is an increasing number of MBA graduates, as an MBA is seen as a passport to a better job and higher salary. For many positions at a higher level within organizations, an MBA is now a prerequisite. *Full form* ***Master of Business Administration***

MBI *abbr* MERGERS & ACQUISITIONS ***management buyin***

MBIA INSURANCE US firms insuring high-rated municipal bonds a large US-based insurance company whose core business is in high-rated municipal bonds. *Full form* ***Municipal Bond Insurance Association***

MBO *abbr* **1.** MERGERS & ACQUISITIONS ***management buyout*** **2.** GENERAL MANAGEMENT ***management by objectives***

MBS *abbr* MORTGAGES, STOCKHOLDING & INVESTMENTS ***mortgage-backed security***

m-commerce E-COMMERCE sales transactions conducted with portable electronic devices electronic transactions between buyers and sellers using mobile communications devices such as cellphones, personal digital assistants (PDAs), or laptop computers

MD *abbr* CORPORATE GOVERNANCE ***managing director***

mean STATISTICS average statistical value a central value or location for a continuous variable in a statistical study

mean reversion STATISTICS pattern of returning to average value the tendency of a variable such as price to return toward its average value after approaching an extreme position

means **1.** resources required to accomplish something the amount of money or resources that are needed to achieve something **2.** way of accomplishing something a method, action, or thing that makes it possible for somebody to do something

means test FINANCE **1.** examination of somebody's eligibility for government aid an inquiry into how much money somebody earns or has in savings to see if they are eligible for government benefits **2.** bankruptcy test in US courts a test used by US courts to see whether somebody wishing to file for bankruptcy has enough income to repay some of the debt, determining which type of bankruptcy that person is eligible for

means-test FINANCE determine if somebody is eligible for government aid to find out how much money somebody earns or has in savings and assets to see if they are eligible for government benefits

measurement error STATISTICS numerical mistake in statistical analysis an error in the recording, calculating, or reading of a numerical value in a statistical study

media independent MARKETING firm that buys advertising for clients an organization that specializes in planning and buying advertising for clients or advertising agencies

  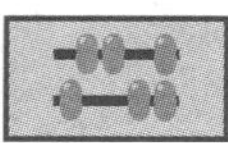   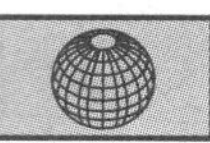   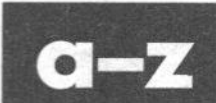

median STATISTICS midpoint in set of statistical values the value that divides a set of ranked observations into two parts of equal size

media plan MARKETING evaluation of communication channels for advertising an assessment and outline of the various advertising media to be used for a campaign

media planner MARKETING employee who organizes advertising an employee of an advertising agency or media independent who chooses the media, timing, and frequency of advertising

media schedule MARKETING document detailing advertising plan a document that sets out the choice of media, timing, and frequency of advertising

mediation GENERAL MANAGEMENT effort by outsider to solve disagreement intervention by a third party in a dispute in order to try to reach agreement between the disputing parties. Where a commitment or award is imposed on either party the process is known as ***arbitration***. *Also called* ***conciliation***

medical insurance INSURANCE insurance covering medical expenses arrangement by which a firm promises to pay all or part of the cost of medical treatment

Medicare INSURANCE **1.** US government health insurance for seniors a US health insurance program in which the government pays part of the cost of medical care and hospital treatment for people over 65 **2.** Australia's public health insurance system the Australian public health insurance system. It was created in 1983 and is funded by a levy on income.

medium-dated STOCKHOLDING & INVESTMENTS maturing in 5–10 years used to describe securities such as bonds that mature in five to ten years. *See also* ***long-dated, short-dated***

medium-dated gilt STOCKHOLDING & INVESTMENTS UK government security with 5–10 years' maturity a security issued by the UK government that pays a fixed rate of interest on a regular basis for at least five but no more than ten years until the redemption date, when the principal is returned. *See also* ***gilt-edged security***

medium of exchange FINANCE means of paying for goods anything that is used to pay for goods. Nowadays, this usually takes the form of money (banknotes and coins), but in ancient societies it included anything from cattle to shells.

medium-sized business BUSINESS *see* ***small and medium-sized enterprise***

medium-term bond STOCKHOLDING & INVESTMENTS bond redeemed in 5–10 years a bond that has at least five but no more than ten years before its redemption date. *See also* ***long-term bond***

medium-term note FINANCE borrowing repaid within 5 years borrowing arranged over a period of up to five years. *Abbr* ***MTN***

medium-term noteholder FINANCE investor repaying borrowings within 5 years an investor who borrows money over a period of up to five years

megacorporation *or* megacorp *US* BUSINESS extremely large, powerful firm an extremely large and powerful business organization (informal)

meltdown MARKETS stock market crash an incidence of substantial losses on the stock market. Black Monday, October 19, 1987, was described as Meltdown Monday in the press the following day.

member **1.** STOCKHOLDING & INVESTMENTS shareholder in firm somebody who owns stock in a limited liability company **2.** BUSINESS organization belonging to larger group a business organization that is part of a larger group

member bank BANKING bank in US Federal Reserve System a bank that is a member of the US Federal Reserve System

member firm MARKETS member of London Stock Exchange a firm of brokers or market makers that is a member of the London Stock Exchange

member of a company STOCKHOLDING & INVESTMENTS in UK, registered stockholder in the United Kingdom, a stockholder whose name is recorded in the register of members

members' voluntary liquidation BUSINESS in UK, decision to close down solvent firm in the United Kingdom, a special resolution passed by the members of a solvent company for the closing-down of the organization. Prior to the resolution the directors of the company must make a declaration of solvency. Should the appointed liquidator have grounds for believing that the company is not solvent, the winding-up will be treated as compulsory liquidation. *See also* ***voluntary liquidation***

memorandum of association LEGAL document officially registering UK firm in the United Kingdom, an official company document, registered with the ***Registrar of Companies***. A memorandum of association sets out company name, status, address of the registered office, objectives of the company, statement of ***limited liability***, amount of guarantee, and the amount of authorized share capital. The ***articles of association*** is a related document.

mentee GENERAL MANAGEMENT somebody being helped to develop professionally a person who, with the help of a ***mentor***, develops their skills and improves their performance so that they can achieve their goals

mentor GENERAL MANAGEMENT experienced person helping another to develop professionally a person experienced in a particular area who helps and encourages a less experienced person to learn and develop

mentoring GENERAL MANAGEMENT more-experienced employees' training of less-experienced employee a form of employee development whereby a trusted and respected person, the ***mentor***, uses his or her experience to offer guidance, encouragement, career advice, and support to another person, the ***mentee***. The aim of mentoring is to facilitate the mentee's learning and development and to enable him or her to discover more about his or her potential. Mentoring can occur informally or it can be arranged by means of an organizational program.

Mentor/mentee relationships can take any form that suits the individuals involved, but in practice there are a few rules that apply to most such arrangements, the most important of which is that anything discussed remains confidential. The relationship also needs to be based on trust and candid communication. A mentor does not have to belong to the same organization as the mentee, but can come from any sphere of the mentee's life (professional association, a community center, your alumni organization, for example) just as long as he or she is not the mentee's direct supervisor or working in the same department. Mentoring does not have to be paid for; in fact it is usually seen as an honor by the mentor. Many accomplished individuals consider it good professional citizenship to participate in the process of helping those coming up after them. It can also frequently be beneficial to volunteer to be a mentor, as many organizations consider mentoring a valuable hallmark of leadership material.

mercantile ECONOMICS relating to trading relating to trade or commercial activity

mercantile agency BUSINESS firm assessing credit status a company that evaluates the creditworthiness of potential corporate borrowers on behalf of other companies. *See also* ***credit bureau***

mercantile paper STOCKHOLDING & INVESTMENTS = ***commercial paper***

mercantilism ECONOMICS economic theory based on importance of international trade the body of economic thought developed between the 1650s and 1750s, based on the belief that a country's wealth depended on the strength of its foreign trade

merchandising MARKETING **1.** activities promoting quick sale of products the process of increasing the market share of a product in retail outlets using display, stocking, and sales promotion techniques **2.** promoting products in connection with movie, celebrity, etc. the promotion and display of goods associated with a specific ***brand***, movie, or celebrity. Merchandising based on a specific movie, for example, may significantly add to its total revenues through appropriate ***licensing*** opportunities. Merchandising may include clothing, toys, food products, or music and often extends well beyond the ***core business*** of the producer of the original product.

merchantable quality OPERATIONS & PRODUCTION UK standard of acceptable product quality in UK law, a minimum standard to which goods being sold must conform. It requires that the goods be reasonably priced given their description, be fit for the purpose for which they were purchased, and be free of defects.

merchant account E-COMMERCE seller's bank account for credit card transactions an account established by a trader to receive the proceeds of credit card transactions

merchant bank **1.** E-COMMERCE bank accepting proceeds from seller's credit card transactions a financial institution at which a trader has opened a ***merchant account*** into which the proceeds of credit card transactions are credited after the institution has subtracted its fee **2.** *UK* BANKING = ***investment bank***

merchant number E-COMMERCE identification number for credit card merchant a number that identifies a merchant, printed at the top of the report slip when depositing credit card payments

merger MERGERS & ACQUISITIONS when one organization buys and combines with another the amalgamation of two or more organizations under single ownership, through the direct acquisition by one organization of the net assets or liabilities of the other. A merger can be the result of a friendly ***takeover***, which results in the combining of companies on an equal footing. After a merger, the legal existence of the acquired organization is terminated. There is no standard definition of a merger, as each is different, depending on what is expected from the merger, and on the negotiations, strategy, stock and assets, human resources, and stockholders of the players. Four

  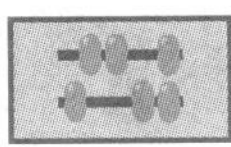      

broad types of mergers are recognized. A ***horizontal merger*** involves firms from the same industry, while a ***vertical merger*** involves firms from the same supply chain. A ***circular merger*** involves firms with different products but similar distribution channels. A ***conglomerate company*** is produced by the union of firms with few or no similarities in production or marketing but that come together to create a larger economic base and greater profit potential. *See also* ***acquisition, consolidation, joint venture, partnership***

merger accounting ACCOUNTING accounting treating combined firm as result of merger a method of accounting that regards a business combination as the acquisition of one company by another. The identifiable assets and liabilities of the company acquired are included in the consolidated balance sheet at their fair value at the date of acquisition, and its results included in the profit and loss account from the date of acquisition. The difference between the fair value of the consideration given and the fair values of the net assets of the entity acquired is accounted for as ***goodwill***.

merger arbitrage MERGERS & ACQUISITIONS trading securities of merging companies simultaneously in a merger, a hedge fund trader sells short the high-priced securities of the target company and buys the underpriced ones of the acquiring company, and then at a time when prices have reverted to true value, the trade can be liquidated at a profit

merger arbitrageur MERGERS & ACQUISITIONS trader in securities of merging firms a trader or fund dealing in ***merger arbitrage***

mergers and acquisitions MERGERS & ACQUISITIONS ways in which organizations change ownership a blanket term covering the main ways in which organizations change hands. *Abbr* ***M&A***

merit rating *or* merit pay HR & PERSONNEL system for increasing pay based on employees' performance a payment system in which the personal qualities of an employee are rated according to organizational requirements, and a pay increase or bonus is made against the results of this rating. Merit rating has been in use since the 1950s, and examines an employee's input to the organization (for example, their attendance, adaptability, or aptitude) as well as the quality or quantity of work produced. In merit rating programs, these factors may be weighted to reflect their relative importance and the resultant points score determines whether the employee earns a bonus or pay increase.

method study GENERAL MANAGEMENT evaluation of existing techniques to find best one the systematic recording, examination, and analysis of existing and proposed ways of conducting work tasks in order to discover the most efficient and economical methods of performing them. The basic procedure followed in method study is as follows: select the area to be studied; record the data; examine the data; develop alternative approaches; install the new method; maintain the new method. The technique was initially developed to evaluate manufacturing processes but has been used more widely to evaluate alternative courses of action.

metrics GENERAL MANAGEMENT measures of organization's effectiveness the standards used to measure or quantify the activities and success of an organization

mezzanine capital FINANCE = ***mezzanine financing***

mezzanine debt FINANCE additional borrowing debt that derives from a ***mezzanine financing*** arrangement

mezzanine finance *UK* FINANCE = ***mezzanine financing***

mezzanine financing FINANCE firm's additional borrowing capital provided to a company that cannot borrow more from banks. Mezzanine financing usually gives the lender the right to either ownership of the company or an equity interest in the company if the loan is not repaid. *UK term* ***mezzanine finance***

MFN *abbr* INTERNATIONAL TRADE ***most favored nation***

microbusiness BUSINESS firm with 1–9 employees a very ***small business*** that directly employs fewer than ten people. This definition of small and medium-sized enterprises is the one adopted by the United Kingdom's Department for Business Enterprise and Regulatory Reform for statistical purposes.

microcash E-COMMERCE type of electronic money allowing sub-denomination payments a form of electronic money with no denominations, permitting sub-denomination transactions of a fraction of, for example, a cent

microcredit BANKING financing those not eligible for standard bank loans the extension of credit to entrepreneurs and ***microbusinesses*** that are too poor to qualify for conventional bank loans. *Also called* ***microlending***

microeconomic incentive ECONOMICS financial encouragement to improve market performance a tax benefit or subsidy given to a business to achieve a specific objective such as increased sales overseas

microeconomics ECONOMICS study of consumers' and firms' roles in economy the branch of economics that studies the contribution of groups of consumers or firms, or of individual consumers, to a country's economy. *See also* ***macroeconomics***

microeconomy ECONOMICS individual areas of economy that influence whole economy the narrow sectors of a country's economic activity that influence the behavior of the economy as a whole, for example, consumer choices. *See also* ***macroeconomy***

microfinance *UK* FINANCE = ***microfinancing***

microfinancing *US* FINANCE providing variety of financial services to poor the provision of a range of financial resources such as small loans, insurance, and savings to low-income families in order to help them build businesses and increase their income. *UK term* ***microfinance***. *See also* ***microcredit***

microhedge STOCKHOLDING & INVESTMENTS hedge for one asset or liability a ***hedge*** that relates to a single asset or liability in an investment ***portfolio***. *See also* ***macrohedge***

microlending BANKING = ***microcredit***

microloan FINANCE small loan to low-income borrower a very small loan made to somebody who has a low or no income and nothing to offer as collateral, or to the owner of a small unprofitable business

micromanagement GENERAL MANAGEMENT too close control of subordinate employees' work a style of management where a manager becomes over-involved in the details of the work of subordinates, resulting in the manager making every decision in an organization, no matter how trivial. Micromanagement is a euphemism for meddling, and has the opposite effect to ***empowerment***. Micromanagement can retard the progress of organizational development, as it robs employees of their self-respect.

micromarketing MARKETING promoting products to very small groups marketing to individuals or very small groups. It targets the specific interests and needs of individuals by offering customized products or services. Rather than targeting one large niche market, a micromarketing company targets a large number of very small niches. *See also* ***mass market, niche market***

micromerchant E-COMMERCE online seller accepting microcash a provider of goods or services on the Internet in exchange for electronic money, including ***microcash***

micromort RISK measure of risk of death a one-in-a-million risk of dying

micropayment E-COMMERCE means of paying small sums electronically a payment protocol for small amounts of electronic money, ranging from a fraction of a cent to no more than ten US dollars or euros

micro-profits FINANCE profits after microfinancing the profits made by businesses that have been financed by ***microfinancing***

microprudential regulation REGULATION & COMPLIANCE control of components of financial systems supervision that focuses on the stability of the component parts of a financial system. *See also* ***macroprudential regulation***

middleman GENERAL MANAGEMENT go-between in interactions between others an intermediary in a transaction. With direct sales models, manufacturers cut out the middleman by dealing directly with end customers.

middle management HR & PERSONNEL level of managers neither at top nor bottom the position held by managers who are considered neither senior nor junior in an organization. Middle managers were subject to ***delayering*** and ***downsizing*** in the 1980s as organizations sought to reduce costs by removing the layer of managers between those who had direct interface with customers and senior decision-makers.

middle office GENERAL MANAGEMENT staff that works with front and back offices staff who do not interact directly with customers but are involved in making business decisions. Risk management is an example of a middle office function. *See also* ***back office, front office***

middle price *or* mid-price *UK* STOCKHOLDING & INVESTMENTS price between bid price and offer price a price, halfway between the bid price and the offer price, that is generally quoted in the press and on information screens

mid-range STATISTICS average of maximum and minimum values the mean of the largest and smallest values in a statistical sample

MiFID *abbr* MARKETS, REGULATION & COMPLIANCE ***Markets in Financial Instruments Directive***

MIGA *abbr* BANKING ***Multilateral Investment Guarantee Agency***

million FINANCE thousand thousands a sum equal to one thousand thousands

millionaire FINANCE person with income over one million a person whose net worth or income is more than one million dollars, pounds, or other unit of currency

mindshare MARKETING public goodwill the attitude toward a product or organization that has been generated among the general public

Mini-Case BUSINESS technique for training business and finance students a set of circumstances used as the basis for solving a business or financial problem, used as a technique for training college students in business and finance

Mini ISA STOCKHOLDING & INVESTMENTS former UK tax-free account for savings or investment formerly, in the United Kingdom, an ***ISA*** in which savers held either cash or stocks tax-free. Savers could have up to two Mini ISAs, one for cash and one for stocks. *See also* ***Maxi ISA, ISA***

minimax regret criterion GENERAL MANAGEMENT choosing course with minimum regret or loss an approach to decision making under uncertainty in which the opportunity cost (regret) associated with each possible course of action is measured, and the decision-maker selects the activity that minimizes the maximum regret, or loss. Regret is measured as the difference between the best and worst possible payoff for each option.

minimum **1.** least possible amount the smallest number, price, quantity, or degree possible or allowed **2.** least possible of the smallest possible or allowed amount or value

minimum balance BANKING least amount of money required in account the smallest amount of money which must be kept in an account to qualify for the services provided

minimum inventory level *US* OPERATIONS & PRODUCTION size below which inventory must not decrease an inventory level, set for control purposes, below which holdings should not fall without being highlighted. It is calculated as follows:

Reorder level − Average rate of usage × Average lead time

UK term ***minimum stock level***

minimum lending rate BANKING lowest UK central bank interest rate formerly, the rate at which the ***Bank of England*** lent to other banks, now replaced by the ***base rate***. *Abbr* ***MLR***. Also called ***bank rate*** *(sense 2)*

minimum quote size MARKETS minimum number of shares for one transaction the smallest number of shares that a market must handle in one trade of a particular security

minimum reserves BANKING least amount that bank must have in reserve the smallest amount of reserves which a commercial bank must hold with a central bank

minimum stock level *UK* OPERATIONS & PRODUCTION = ***minimum inventory level***

minimum subscription STOCKHOLDING & INVESTMENTS minimum bid for new issue the smallest number of shares or securities that may be applied for in a new issue

minimum wage FINANCE least hourly pay rate legally allowed the lowest hourly rate of pay, usually set by government, to which all ***employees*** are legally entitled

minority interest *or* minority ownership CORPORATE GOVERNANCE holding less than half of firm's common stock ownership of less than 50% of a company's common stock, which is not enough to control the company

minority shareholder STOCKHOLDING & INVESTMENTS stockholder with less than 50% of firm's stock a person who owns a group of shares of stock but less than half of the stock in a company. *Also called* ***minority stockholder***

minority shareholding STOCKHOLDING & INVESTMENTS less than 50% of firm's stock a group of shares of stock that somebody has which account for less than half the total shares in a firm

minority stockholder STOCKHOLDING & INVESTMENTS = ***minority shareholder***

minus factor GENERAL MANAGEMENT negative aspect of situation a factor that is unfavorable in some way, for example, because it reduces profitability

minutes CORPORATE GOVERNANCE official notes from meeting an official written record of the proceedings of a meeting. Minutes usually record points for action, and indicate who is responsible for implementing decisions. Good practice requires that the minutes of a meeting be circulated well in advance of the next meeting, and that those attending that meeting read the minutes in advance. Registered companies are required to keep minutes of meetings and make them available at their registered offices for inspection by company members and shareholders.

mirror fund STOCKHOLDING & INVESTMENTS investment trust and mutual fund under same control an investment trust where the manager also runs a mutual fund with the same objectives

MIS OPERATIONS & PRODUCTION computer system with information for management decisions management information system: a computer-based system for collecting, storing, processing, and providing access to information used in the management of an organization. Management information systems evolved from early electronic data processing systems. They support managerial decision making by providing regular structured reports on organizational operations. Management information systems may support the functional areas of an organization such as finance, marketing, or production. ***Decision support systems*** and ***EISs*** are types of MIS developed for more specific purposes. *Full form* ***management information system***

misappropriation FRAUD fraudulent use of somebody else's money the illegal use of money by somebody who is not the owner but who has been trusted to look after it

mismanagement GENERAL MANAGEMENT incompetent or illegal handling of firm's resources functional or ethical dereliction of duty due to ignorance, negligence, incompetence, avoidance, or criminality

missing value STATISTICS expected statistical observation that is missing an observation that is absent from a set of statistical data, for example, because a member of a population to be sampled was not at home when the researcher called

mission statement GENERAL MANAGEMENT formal statement of firm's goals a short memorable statement of the reasons for the existence of an organization. *See also* ***vision statement***

MIT *abbr* STOCKHOLDING & INVESTMENTS ***market if touched***

Mittelstand BUSINESS mid-sized German companies a German term that incorporates the meaning of "medium-sized enterprise"

mixed economy ECONOMICS combination of government and private business ownership an economy in which both public and private enterprises participate in the production and supply of goods and services

MLR *abbr* BANKING ***minimum lending rate***

MMC *abbr* REGULATION & COMPLIANCE ***Monopolies and Mergers Commission***

MMDA *abbr* BANKING ***money market deposit account***

MNC *abbr* BUSINESS ***multinational corporation***

mobile money FINANCE use of cell phones for financial transactions a facility that allows people to use their cell phones and other hand-held devices to handle financial transactions

mobile office GENERAL MANAGEMENT setup of portable office equipment a set of conditions allowing working on the move. Mobile office equipment would typically include a cell phone, laptop computer, and a modem to link the computer to the Internet or a company's main office.

mode STATISTICS most frequent statistical observation in a statistical study, the most frequently occurring value in a set of ranked observations

model building STATISTICS creating structure for statistical observations the process of providing an adequate fit to the data in a set of observations in a statistical study

model risk MARKETS danger of inadequacy of computer modeling the possibility that a computer model on which investment decisions are based may be unreliable in extreme market conditions

modernization GENERAL MANAGEMENT replacing outdated equipment with new investing in new equipment or upgrading existing equipment to bring resources up to date or improve efficiency

modern portfolio theory STOCKHOLDING & INVESTMENTS = ***portfolio theory***

modified accounts ACCOUNTING = ***abbreviated accounts***

modified ACRS TAX US method of assessing asset depreciation in the United States, a system used for computing the depreciation of some assets acquired after 1985 in a way that reduces taxes. The ACRS applies to older assets. *See also* ***accelerated cost recovery system***

modified book value ACCOUNTING = ***adjusted book value***

modified cash basis ACCOUNTING different accounting for short- and long-term assets the bookkeeping practice of accounting for short-term assets on a cash basis and for long-term assets on an accrual basis

modified duration MARKETS, RISK measure of interest-rate risk in owning bonds a measure of a bond's sensitivity to changes in interest rates, based on the assumption that interest rates and bond prices move in opposite directions

mom and pop investors *US* STOCKHOLDING & INVESTMENTS inexperienced investors people who hold or wish to purchase stock but have little experience with or knowledge of the stock market (slang)

  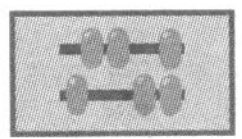   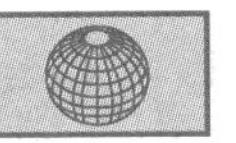   

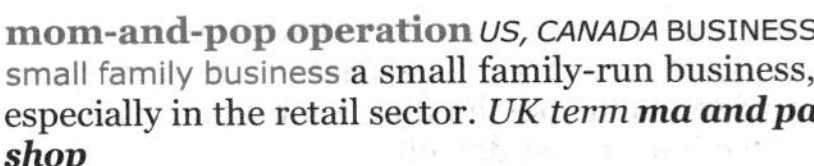

mom-and-pop operation *US, CANADA* BUSINESS small family business a small family-run business, especially in the retail sector. *UK term* ***ma and pa shop***

momentum investor STOCKHOLDING & INVESTMENTS buyer of stock rising in price an investor who buys stock that seems to be moving upward in price

MONEP *abbr* MARKETS French options market in France, a market that deals in ***options***, established in 1987. It merged with the ***Paris Bourse*** in 1999 and is now part of the ***NYSE Euronext*** group. *Full form* ***Marché des Options Négociables de Paris***

monetarism ECONOMICS belief that increased money causes inflation an economic theory that states that inflation is caused by increases in a country's money supply

monetarist ECONOMICS **1.** believer in monetarism a person who believes that inflation is caused by increases in a country's money supply and that the money supply should remain fairly steady **2.** according to monetarism according to the economic theory of ***monetarism***

monetary FINANCE of money, cash, or liquid assets relating to or involving cash, currency, or assets that are readily convertible into cash

monetary assets ACCOUNTING assets corresponding to amounts in accounts assets such as accounts receivable, cash, and bank balances that are realizable at the amounts stated in the accounts. Other assets such as facilities and machinery, inventories, and marketable securities will not necessarily realize the sum stated in a business's balance sheet.

monetary base ECONOMICS nation's total cash supply the stock of a country's coins, notes, and bank deposits held by the central bank

monetary base control ECONOMICS government restrictions on cash availability the restricting of the amount of ***liquid assets*** in an economy through government controls

monetary items ACCOUNTING items worth the same regardless of inflation monetary assets, such as cash and debtors, and monetary liabilities, such as overdrafts and creditors, whose values stay the same in spite of inflation

monetary policy ECONOMICS government policy regarding money and currency government economic policy concerning a country's rate of interest, its exchange rate, and the amount of money in the economy

Monetary Policy Committee ECONOMICS Bank of England committee that sets interest rates a committee of the ***Bank of England***, chaired by the Governor of the Bank, that has responsibility for setting UK ***interest rates*** independently of the British government. Its goal is to set rates with a view to keeping ***inflation*** at a defined level and avoiding ***deflation***. *Abbr* ***MPC***

monetary reserve BANKING currency and bullion in central bank the foreign currency and precious metals that a country holds, that provide a cushion for central banking functions

monetary standard CURRENCY & EXCHANGE value on which currency system is based the value underlying the currency in a specific country's monetary system, for example, the ***gold standard***, which in the past many countries used to set the value of their currencies

monetary system ECONOMICS set of government rules controlling nation's money the set of government regulations concerning a country's monetary reserves and its holdings of notes and coins

monetary targets FINANCE government financial targets figures that are given as targets by the government when setting out its budget for the forthcoming year

monetary unit CURRENCY & EXCHANGE standard unit of nation's currency the standard unit of a country's currency, such as the dollar in the United States, the pound sterling in the United Kingdom, or the euro in many other countries of the European Union

monetary working capital adjustment ACCOUNTING adjustment in accounts for inflation an adjustment in ***current cost accounting*** to the historical cost balance sheet to take account of the effect of inflation on the value of debtors, creditors, and stocks of finished goods. *Abbr* ***MWCA***

monetize **1.** FINANCE change securities into money If a government monetizes its debt, it converts interest-bearing securities into money, therefore expanding the money supply and reducing the value of money in circulation. **2.** CURRENCY & EXCHANGE designate as official currency to establish a currency as a country's legal tender

money CURRENCY & EXCHANGE current medium of exchange a medium of exchange that is accepted throughout a country as payment for services and goods and as a means of settling debts **at the money** MARKETS, RISK a situation in which the price an option holder must pay to exercise an option is the same as the current ***market price*** of the underlying security or commodity **at the money forward** MARKETS, RISK a situation in which the price an option holder must pay to exercise an option is the same as the ***forward price*** of the underlying security or commodity

money at call and short notice BANKING **1.** in UK, advances repayable on demand or soon in the United Kingdom, advances made by banks to other financial institutions, or corporate and personal customers, that are repayable either upon demand (call) or within 14 days (short notice) **2.** in UK, balances available on demand or soon in the United Kingdom, balances in an account that are either available upon demand (call) or within 14 days (short notice)

money broker MARKETS in UK, arranger of loans in the United Kingdom, an intermediary who works on the money market, arranging loans between banks, discount houses, and dealers in government securities

moneyer CURRENCY & EXCHANGE coiner of money an archaic term for somebody who is authorized to mint money

money laundering LEGAL concealing illegal origins of money the process of making money obtained illegally appear legitimate by passing it through banks or businesses

moneylender FINANCE lender of money at interest a person whose business is lending money to others for interest

money lying idle FINANCE uninvested money producing no interest money that is not being used to produce interest and that is not invested in business

money management FINANCE, STOCKHOLDING & INVESTMENTS business of investing clients' money the activity of making decisions about income and expenditure, including budgeting, banking arrangements, making investments, and tax payments, either for yourself or on behalf of clients

money manager STOCKHOLDING & INVESTMENTS specialist in investment management a person or company that manages an investment ***portfolio***, usually of ***money market instruments***, on behalf of investors. *See also* ***portfolio manager***

money market MARKETS market for buying and selling financial instruments a market in which short-term financial instruments such as certificates of deposit, Treasury bills, commercial papers, and bank deposits are traded. New York is the major money market, followed by London and Tokyo. *Also called* ***finance market***

money market account BANKING account with high interest rate an account with a financial institution that requires a minimum deposit, and pays a rate of interest, related to the wholesale money market rates, generally higher than retail rates. Most institutions offer a variety of term accounts, with either a fixed rate or variable rate, and notice accounts, with a variety of notice periods at variable rates.

money market deposit account BANKING US savings account in the United States, a type of savings account with deposits invested in the money market and having a high yield. There is often a high minimum deposit and withdrawals require notice. *Abbr* ***MMDA***

money market fund STOCKHOLDING & INVESTMENTS mutual fund investing in short-term securities a mutual fund that invests in short-term debt securities. In the United States these are strictly regulated by the ***Securities and Exchange Commission***.

money market instruments STOCKHOLDING & INVESTMENTS financial products traded on money markets short-term assets and securities, usually maturing within 12 months, that are traded on money markets, for example, certificates of deposit, commercial papers, and Treasury bills

money men FINANCE people working in finance industry the people who provide finance for a venture, campaign, etc.

money national income ECONOMICS unadjusted value of nation's annual output ***GDP*** measured using money value, not adjusted for the effect of inflation

money of account ACCOUNTING unit for accounting purposes a monetary unit that is used in keeping accounts but is not necessarily an actual currency unit

money order BANKING instruction to make payment to someone a written order to pay somebody a sum of money, issued by a bank or post office

money purchase pension *or* money purchase scheme PENSIONS UK pension plan to buy annuity in the United Kingdom, a pension plan where the fund that is built up is used to purchase an annuity. The retirement income that the beneficiary receives therefore depends on his or her contributions, any employer contributions, the performance of the investments those contributions are used to buy, the annuity rates, and the type of annuity purchased at retirement.

money purchase plan PENSIONS US pension plan with employer and employee contributing in the United States, a pension plan (a defined benefit plan) in which the participant contributes part and the firm contributes at the same or a different rate

 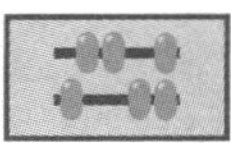      

money substitute CURRENCY & EXCHANGE trading goods used to replace currency any goods used as a medium of exchange because of the degree of devaluation of a country's currency

money supply ECONOMICS nation's cash available for purchases the stock of ***liquid assets*** in a country's economy that can be given in exchange for services or goods

monies *or* moneys CURRENCY & EXCHANGE sums of money amounts of money, especially those that come from a specific place or have a specific purpose

Monopolies and Mergers Commission REGULATION & COMPLIANCE former UK commission for competition in the United Kingdom, a commission that was replaced by the Competition Commission in April 1999. *Abbr* ***MMC***

monopolistic competition MARKETS situation blocking new competition in market a situation that exists in a market in which there are strong barriers to the entry of new competitors. *Also called* ***imperfect competition***

monopoly ECONOMICS economic situation in which one firm controls market a ***market*** in which there is only one producer or one seller. A company establishes a monopoly by entering a new market or eliminating all competitors from an existing market. A company that holds a monopoly has control of a market and is able to fix prices. For this reason, governments usually try to avoid monopoly situations. However, some monopolies such as government-owned utilities are seen as beneficial to ***consumers***.

monopsony MARKETS situation where only one customer needs product a situation in which there is only one buyer for a specific product or service

Monte Carlo method *or* Monte Carlo simulation STATISTICS statistical method of deciding based on uncertainties a statistical method of reducing the uncertainty in estimating future outcomes by running repeated calculations using current and historical data, used in business decision-making that involves a number of uncertain variables such as capital investment and resource allocation. The name of the Monte Carlo method derives from the use of random numbers as generated by a roulette wheel. The numbers are used in repeated simulations, often performed by spreadsheet programs on computers, to calculate a range of possible outcomes, using current and historical data. The technique was developed by mathematicians in the early 1960s for use in nuclear physics and ***operational research*** but has since been used more widely.

month-end ACCOUNTING of end of month relating to the end of each month when financial transactions for the current month are finalized

Moody's STOCKHOLDING & INVESTMENTS US firm that rates credit risk of investments a US organization that rates the reliability of a debtor organization on a scale from AAA to C. It also issues ratings on municipal bonds, running from MIG1, the highest rating, to MIG4. *See also* ***Standard & Poor's***

moonlighting HR & PERSONNEL doing second job in addition to main job undertaking a second job, often for cash and in the evenings, in addition to a full-time permanent job

moral hazard RISK danger through protection from consequences of actions a risk that somebody will behave immorally because insurance, the law, or some other agency protects them against loss that the immoral behavior might otherwise cause

moratorium FINANCE postponement a period of delay, for example, additional time agreed on by a creditor and a debtor for recovery of a debt

more bang for your buck *US* FINANCE greater financial benefit greater leverage provided by an investment (slang)

Morgan Stanley Capital International Indexes MARKETS worldwide stock market indexes a group of indexes that track stocks traded on stock markets worldwide and are considered benchmarks for international investment portfolios

mortality and expense risk charge INSURANCE charge for annuity guaranteeing benefit and compensating insurer an extra charge paid on some annuities to guarantee that if the policyholder dies, his or her heirs will receive a benefit, and also that the insurance company will be compensated for an annuitant who lives longer than he or she should according to the mortality tables

mortgage MORTGAGES **1.** agreement to lend money for property a financial lending arrangement enabling somebody to borrow money from a bank or other lending institution in order to buy property or land. The original amount borrowed, the ***principal***, is then repaid with interest to the lender over a fixed number of years. *See also* ***amortized mortgage, current account mortgage, endowment mortgage, interest-only mortgage, low start mortgage*** **2.** grant of right to asset of defaulting borrower a borrowing arrangement whereby the lender is granted a legal right to an asset, usually a piece of real estate, should the borrower default on the payments. *See also* ***second mortgage***

mortgage-backed security STOCKHOLDING & INVESTMENTS, MORTGAGES security backed by mortgages a security for which the collateral is the principal and interest on a set of mortgages

mortgage bank BANKING bank dealing in mortgages a financial institution that trades in mortgages

mortgage bond STOCKHOLDING & INVESTMENTS, MORTGAGES debt backed by real estate especially in the United States, a debt secured by real estate

mortgage broker MORTGAGES intermediary between seekers and offerers of mortgages a person or company that acts as an agent between people seeking mortgages and organizations that offer them

mortgage debenture MORTGAGES long-term loan secured against firm's fixed assets a debenture in which the loan is secured against a company's ***fixed assets***

mortgagee MORTGAGES lender in mortgage agreement a person or organization that lends money to a borrower under a mortgage agreement. *See also* ***mortgagor***

mortgage equity analysis MORTGAGES calculation of value of property minus mortgages owed a computation of the difference between the value of a property and the amount owed on it in the form of mortgages

mortgage famine MORTGAGES when house buyers unable to get mortgages a situation where there is not enough money available to offer mortgages to house buyers

mortgage indebtedness FINANCE money borrowed against property money owed on loans using a property, especially a residence, as ***collateral***

mortgage insurance INSURANCE mortgagee's insurance against borrower's default insurance that provides somebody holding a mortgage with protection against default

mortgage lien MORTGAGES claim against mortgaged property a claim against a property that is mortgaged. Mortgagees often own the mortgage lien to secure the loan.

mortgage note MORTGAGES record of mortgage a note that documents the existence and terms of a mortgage

mortgage pool MORTGAGES mortgages on sale together a group of mortgages with similar characteristics packaged together for sale

mortgage portfolio MORTGAGES in US, bank's holdings in mortgages in the United States, the group of mortgages held by a ***mortgage bank***

mortgage rate MORTGAGES interest rate on mortgage the interest rate charged on a mortgage by a lender

mortgage securitizer STOCKHOLDING & INVESTMENTS firm creating and selling groups of mortgage loans as securities a company that collects residential mortgage loans into a package for sale to investors

mortgage tax TAX US tax on mortgage in the United States, a one-time tax paid when a mortgage is taken out

mortgagor MORTGAGES borrower in mortgage agreement somebody who has taken out a mortgage to borrow money. *See also* ***mortgagee***

most distant futures contract MARKETS futures option with longest term a futures option with the latest delivery date of those being considered. *See also* ***nearby futures contract***

most favored nation INTERNATIONAL TRADE foreign country given very good trade terms a foreign country allowed very favorable trade terms by another country. *Abbr* ***MFN***

motion study GENERAL MANAGEMENT evaluation of efficiency of physical work patterns the observation of physical movements involved in the performance of work, and investigation of how these can be made more effective and cost efficient

motivation GENERAL MANAGEMENT giving employees reason to perform their best the creation of stimuli, incentives, and working environments which enable people to perform to the best of their ability in pursuit of organizational success. Motivation is commonly viewed as the magic driver that enables managers to get others to achieve their targets. In the 20th century, there was a shift, at least in theory, away from motivation by dictation and discipline toward motivation by creating an appropriate corporate climate and addressing the needs of individual employees. Although it is widely agreed to be one of the key management tasks, it has frequently been argued that one person cannot motivate others but can only create conditions for others to self-motivate.

mousetrap build a better mousetrap MARKETING to create a new or better product

mover and shaker GENERAL MANAGEMENT powerful person who initiates things an influential and dynamic person within an organization or group of people

moving average MARKETS average of stock prices that is continually recalculated an average of stock

  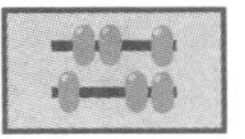      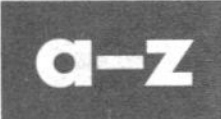

prices on a stock market, in which the calculation is made over a period which moves forward regularly

MPC *abbr* ECONOMICS ***Monetary Policy Committee***

MRP II OPERATIONS & PRODUCTION computer-based system used in manufacturing a computer-based manufacturing, inventory planning, and control system that broadens the scope of production planning by involving other functional areas that influence production decisions. Manufacturing resource planning evolved from material requirements planning to integrate other functions in the planning process. These functions may include engineering, marketing, purchasing, production scheduling, business planning, and finance. *Full form* ***manufacturing resource planning***

MSB *abbr* BANKING ***mutual savings bank***

MTF *abbr* MARKETS ***multilateral trading facility***

MTN *abbr* FINANCE ***medium-term note***

mudaraba *or* mudarabah BUSINESS Islamic partnership between investor and entrepreneur in Islamic financing, a type of partnership in which one partner provides the capital while the other provides expertise and management. Each gets a prearranged percentage of the profits, but the partner providing the capital bears any losses.

mudarib BUSINESS entrepreneur in mudaraba partnership in Islamic financing, the entrepreneurial partner in a ***mudaraba*** partnership who provides the expertise and management

multichannel E-COMMERCE using Internet and traditional methods using a combination of online and offline communication methods to conduct business

multicurrency FINANCE offering number of currencies used to describe a loan that gives the borrower a choice of currencies

multifunctional card BANKING plastic card with more than one use a plastic card that may be used for two or more purposes, for example, as an ATM card, a check card, and a debit card

Multilateral Investment Guarantee Agency BANKING part of World Bank Group one of the five institutions that constitute the World Bank Group. MIGA was created in 1988 to promote foreign direct investment into emerging economies by insuring against political risk, with the objective of improving people's lives and reducing poverty. Apart from offering political risk insurance to investors and lenders, MIGA assists emerging countries to attract and retain private investment. *Abbr* ***MIGA***

multilateral netting CURRENCY & EXCHANGE consolidating sums from various sources into one currency a method of putting together sums from various international sources to reduce currency transaction costs, used by groups of companies or banks trading in several currencies at the same time

multilateral trading facility MARKETS system combining third-party commercial interests under the provisions of the ***Markets in Financial Instruments Directive***, a system of bringing together multiple third-party buying and selling interests in financial instruments. *Abbr* ***MTF***

multilevel marketing MARKETING = ***network marketing***

multinational business *or* multinational *or* multinational company *or* multinational corporation BUSINESS firm operating in more than one country a company that operates internationally, usually with subsidiaries, offices, or production facilities in more than one country *Also called* ***transnational, transnational business***

multiparty auction E-COMMERCE Internet selling with buyers making online bids a method of buying and selling on the Internet in which prospective buyers make electronic bids

multiple application STOCKHOLDING & INVESTMENTS more than one application for new share issue the submission of more than one share application for a new issue that is expected to be oversubscribed. In most jurisdictions, this practice is illegal.

multiple exchange rate CURRENCY & EXCHANGE exchange rate varying with transaction's purpose a two-tier rate of exchange used in some countries where the more advantageous rate may be for tourists or for businesses proposing to build a factory

multiple ownership BUSINESS when group owns something together a situation in which something is owned by several parties jointly

multiple regression analysis STATISTICS *see* ***regression analysis***

multiple sourcing OPERATIONS & PRODUCTION using more than one supplier a ***purchasing*** policy of using two or more suppliers for products or services. Multiple sourcing prevents reliance on any one supplier. It encourages competition between suppliers, and ensures access to a wide variety of goods or services. Dealing with more than one supplier can improve access to market information but can also entail more administration.

multiple time series STATISTICS sets of data observed together over time two or more sets of data that are observed simultaneously

multiplier FINANCE factor that multiplies another number or value a number that multiplies another, or a factor that tends to multiply something, for example, the effect of new expenditure on total income and reserves

multiplier effect ECONOMICS effect of increased investment or spending on income a situation in which a small initial change in investment or spending produces a proportionately larger change in national income

multiskilling HR & PERSONNEL training in a variety of skills a process of training employees to do a variety of tasks rather than focusing on single tasks. Employees are therefore available to undertake a number of different jobs and have better general employability.

multitasking E-COMMERCE conducting several tasks together the practice of doing more than one activity or task at a time

multivariate analysis STATISTICS investigation of characteristics of multiple variables any of a number of statistical techniques used in ***operational research*** to examine the characteristics and relationships between multiple variables. Multivariate analysis techniques include ***cluster analysis***, ***discriminant analysis***, and multiple ***regression analysis***.

multivariate data STATISTICS statistical observations involving multiple variables data for which each observation involves values for more than one random variable

mum and dad investors *ANZ* STOCKHOLDING & INVESTMENTS = ***mom and pop investors***

mumpreneur BUSINESS mother who is independent businesswoman a mother who starts or owns a business

municipal bond *or* muni *or* muni-bond STOCKHOLDING & INVESTMENTS US government security in the United States, a security issued by states, local governments, and municipalities

municipal bond fund STOCKHOLDING & INVESTMENTS fund investing in municipal bonds a fund that is invested in municipal bonds

Municipal Bond Insurance Association INSURANCE *see* ***MBIA***

murabaha *or* murabahah FINANCE when Islamic bank purchases item for customer in Islamic financing, an arrangement in which a bank purchases an item for a customer provided the customer agrees to purchase it from the bank at a prearranged higher price. *See also* ***tawarruq***

Murphy's Law GENERAL MANAGEMENT anything that can go wrong will the principle that if something can go wrong, it will

musharaka *or* musharakah BUSINESS Islamic partnership in which all partners invest money in Islamic financing, a type of partnership in which all partners contribute capital to an enterprise, share profits in a prearranged way, and share losses equally

mutual BUSINESS relating to financial organization with members not stockholders used to describe an organization that is run in the interests of its members and that does not have to pay dividends to its stockholders, so surplus profits can be plowed back into the business. In the United Kingdom, building societies and friendly societies were formed as mutual organizations, although in recent years many have demutualized, either by becoming public limited companies or by being bought by other financial organizations, resulting in members receiving cash or share windfall payments. In the United States, mutual associations, a type of savings and loan association, and state-chartered mutual savings banks are organized in this way.

mutual company BUSINESS firm owned by its customers a company that is owned by its customers who share in the profits

mutual fund *US* STOCKHOLDING & INVESTMENTS firm trading in investments for clients an investment company that holds a range of stocks in which investors can buy units. *UK term* ***unit trust***

mutual insurance INSURANCE insurance firm owned by policyholders an insurance company that is owned by its policyholders who share the profits and cover claims with their pooled premiums

mutual recognition directive REGULATION & COMPLIANCE EU directive about recognizing other members' practices a directive of the European Union that each country's accounting firms and cross-border services should be recognized by other member states

mutual savings bank BANKING US savings bank run by trustees in the United States, a state-chartered savings bank run in the interests of its members. It is governed by a local board of trustees, not necessarily the legal owners. Most of these banks offer accounts and services that are typical of full-service banks. *Abbr* ***MSB***

        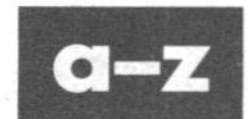

muzara'a *or* muzara'ah FINANCE payment for land rent by crop share in Islamic financing, an agreement in which a landowner lets somebody farm an area of land in return for part of the crop

MVA *abbr* MARKETS ***market value added***

MWCA *abbr* ACCOUNTING ***monetary working capital adjustment***

N

NAIC *abbr* **1.** INSURANCE, REGULATION & COMPLIANCE ***National Association of Insurance Commissioners*** **2.** STOCKHOLDING & INVESTMENTS ***National Association of Investors Corporation***

naked debenture BUSINESS unsecured debt obligation a debt acknowledged by a company that is without security for the interest or the amount of principal. *See also* ***debenture***

naked option STOCKHOLDING & INVESTMENTS = ***uncovered option***

naked position STOCKHOLDING & INVESTMENTS holding with unhedged securities a situation in which an investor holds securities some of which are not ***hedged***

naked shorting *or* naked short selling MARKETS selling security not in possession the practice of selling commodities, currencies, or securities without first having borrowed them, as in a conventional ***short sale***. It is illegal in the United States.

naked writer STOCKHOLDING & INVESTMENTS offerer of option on another's shares a person selling an option who does not own the underlying shares

name INSURANCE member of Lloyd's insurance group an individual who is a member of the ***Lloyd's underwriting syndicate***, an insurance group based in London

named perils insurance INSURANCE insurance for specific types of risk a type of insurance that provides coverage for only those losses that occur as a result of specifically named risks

NAO *abbr* REGULATION & COMPLIANCE ***National Audit Office***

narrow bank BANKING bank with safely invested deposits a proposed type of bank that has all its deposits invested in safe assets, and which does not involve itself in ***investment banking***

narrowcasting E-COMMERCE targeting information to restricted group targeting information to a niche audience. Owing to its ability to personalize information to the requirements of individual users, the Internet is generally viewed as a narrowcast rather than a broadcast medium.

narrow market MARKETS market with little trading a market where the trading volume is low. A characteristic of such a market is a wide spread of bid and offer prices.

narrow money ECONOMICS **1.** *US* = ***M1*** **2.** *UK* = ***M0***

NASD *abbr* MARKETS, REGULATION & COMPLIANCE ***National Association of Securities Dealers***

NASDAQ MARKETS stock exchange in New York stock exchange based in New York, established in 1971 by the ***National Association of Securities Dealers*** (who sold their last stock in 2001). The name NASDAQ originally stood for National Association of Securities Dealers Automated Quotations and also referred to the computerized trading platform used. Traditionally high-technology companies listed on the NASDAQ. In 2008 it acquired ***OMX*** and formed the ***NASDAQ OMX*** group. The main indices of stocks on the exchange are the ***NASDAQ-100*** and the ***NASDAQ Composite***.

NASDAQ-100 MARKETS stock market index of 100 largest NASDAQ companies an index of 100 most-highly capitalized nonfinancial companies on the ***NASDAQ*** stock exchange. It was established in January 1985.

NASDAQ Composite MARKETS stock market index of all NASDAQ companies an index of all companies on the NASDAQ stock exchange. It was established in 1971.

NASDAQ OMX MARKETS Euro-American stock exchange group corporation formed in 2008 by the merger of the ***NASDAQ*** and ***OMX*** exchanges. Headquartered in New York, it runs NASDAQ and eight European exchanges.

National Association of Insurance Commissioners INSURANCE, REGULATION & COMPLIANCE US group of insurance regulators in the United States, an organization that brings together the state regulators of insurance. *Abbr* ***NAIC***

National Association of Investors Corporation STOCKHOLDING & INVESTMENTS US organization promoting investment clubs in the United States, an organization that fosters the creation and development of ***investment clubs***. *Abbr* ***NAIC***

National Association of Securities Dealers MARKETS, REGULATION & COMPLIANCE former US organization for traders in securities the ***self-regulatory organization*** that was responsible for regulation of US securities dealers and the ***NASDAQ*** stock exchange. Established in 1938, its functions are now carried out by the ***Financial Industry Regulatory Authority***. *Abbr* ***NASD***

National Audit Office REGULATION & COMPLIANCE UK organization monitoring public spending an independent nongovernmental body in the United Kingdom that examines public spending. The NAO audits the accounts of government agencies and departments, reporting back to Parliament with the results. An officer of the House of Commons, the Comptroller and Auditor General, runs the NAO. It has offices in London, Newcastle, Cardiff, and Blackpool. *Abbr* ***NAO***

national bank BANKING **1.** central bank of state a bank owned or controlled by the state that acts as a bank for a government and implements its monetary policies **2.** US bank in Federal Reserve in the United States, a bank that operates under federal charter and is legally required to be a member of the ***Federal Reserve***

National Credit Union Administration REGULATION & COMPLIANCE US government organization overseeing credit unions in the United States, a federal agency that charters and supervises federal ***credit unions*** and insures savings in federal and most state-chartered credit unions through a fund backed by the US government. *Abbr* ***NCUA***

national debt ECONOMICS amount of government borrowing the total amount of money that a country's central government has borrowed and is still unpaid

national demand ECONOMICS overall need for products in country's economy the total demand for goods and services made by consumers in an economy

National Guarantee Fund MARKETS insurance fund of Australian Securities Exchange a supply of money held by the ***Australian Securities Exchange*** which is used to compensate investors for losses incurred when an exchange member fails to meet its obligations

national income ECONOMICS country's total earnings from goods and services the total earnings from a country's production of goods and services in a specific year

national income accounts FINANCE statistical information on country's economy economic statistics that show the state of a nation's economy over a given period of time, usually a year. *See also* ***GDP, GNP***

National Insurance PENSIONS UK social insurance plan for all adults in the United Kingdom, a compulsory state social insurance plan to which employees and employers contribute. *Abbr* ***NI***. See also ***Social Security***

National Insurance contributions PENSIONS money paid into UK social insurance plan in the United Kingdom, payments made by both employers and employees to the government. The contributions, together with other government receipts, are used to finance pensions given by the government and other benefits such as welfare. *Abbr* ***NIC***

National Insurance number PENSIONS person's identifying number for UK social insurance plan a unique number allocated to each UK citizen at the age of 16. It allows HM Revenue & Customs and the Department for Work and Pensions to record contributions and credit them to each person's account. *See also* ***Social Security number***

nationalization GENERAL MANAGEMENT transferring of private firms to state ownership the taking over of privately owned companies by government. Nationalization has strong political connotations. Recent global political trends had moved away from nationalization by introducing more competition and liberalization into markets before the banking crisis of 2008 caused governments to take considerable holdings in financial institutions to save them from collapse. *See also* ***privatization***

National Market System MARKETS system encouraging competition between US stock exchanges in the United States, an inter-exchange network system designed to foster greater competition between domestic stock exchanges. Legislated for in 1975, it was implemented in 1978 with the Intermarket Trading System that electronically links eight markets: American, Boston, Cincinnati, Chicago, New York, Pacific, Philadelphia, and NASDAQ. It allows traders at any exchange to seek the best available price on all other exchanges that a specific security is eligible to trade on. *Abbr* ***NMS***

National Savings & Investments STOCKHOLDING & INVESTMENTS UK government agency for savings and investment in the United Kingdom, a government agency accountable to the Treasury that offers a variety of savings and investment products directly to the public or through post offices. The funds raised finance government borrowing (the ***national debt***).

  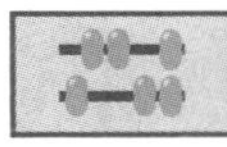      

National Savings Bank BANKING UK savings plan in the United Kingdom, a savings plan established in 1861 as the Post Office Savings Bank and now operated by ***National Savings & Investments***. *Abbr* ***NSB***

National Savings Certificate STOCKHOLDING & INVESTMENTS UK investment providing tax-free income in the United Kingdom, either a fixed-interest or an index-linked certificate issued for two- or five-year terms by ***National Savings & Investments*** with returns that are free of ***income tax***. *Abbr* ***NSC***

National Society of Accountants ACCOUNTING US association of financial professionals in the United States, a non-profit organization of some 17,000 professionals who provide accounting, tax preparation, financial and estate planning, and management advisory services to an estimated 19 million individuals and business clients. Most of the NSA's members are individual practitioners or partners in small to mid-size accounting and tax firms. *Abbr* ***NSA***

natural capitalism ECONOMICS capitalism incorporating environmentalism an approach to capitalism in which protection of the Earth's resources is a strategic priority

natural disaster INSURANCE disaster caused by forces of nature a catastrophe that occurs as a result of forces of nature. Natural disasters include hurricanes, tornados, severe storms, floods, tsunamis, earthquakes, and volcanic eruptions.

NAV *abbr* STOCKHOLDING & INVESTMENTS ***net asset value***

NBV *abbr* ACCOUNTING ***net book value***

NCUA REGULATION & COMPLIANCE US government organization overseeing credit unions ***National Credit Union Administration***

NDA *abbr* HR & PERSONNEL **1.** ***nondisclosure agreement*** **2.** ***nondisparagement agreement***

NDP *abbr* ECONOMICS ***net domestic product***

nearby futures contract STOCKHOLDING & INVESTMENTS option with closest delivery date a futures option with the earliest delivery date of those being considered. *See also* ***most distant futures contract***

nearby month STOCKHOLDING & INVESTMENTS next month with futures contract available the earliest month for which there is a ***futures contract*** for a specific commodity. *Also called* ***spot month***. *See also* ***far month***

near-cash STOCKHOLDING & INVESTMENTS easy to convert to cash used to describe an investment that can be quickly converted to cash

near money STOCKHOLDING & INVESTMENTS assets easily cashed in assets such as some types of bank deposit, short-dated bonds, and certificates of deposit that can quickly be turned into cash. *See also* ***quick asset***

negative amortization FINANCE addition to principal following incomplete interest payments an increase in the ***principal*** of a loan due to the inadequacy of payments to cover the interest

negative carry FINANCE when interest payments exceed income on loan interest that is so high that the borrowed money does not return enough profit to cover the cost of borrowing

negative cash flow FINANCE higher expenditures than income a cash flow in which expenditures are higher than income

negative equity FINANCE when property is worth less than it cost a situation in which a fall in prices leads to a property being worth less than was paid for it

negative gearing FINANCE, TAX borrowing money that earns less than interest payments the practice of borrowing money to invest in property or stocks and claiming a tax deduction on the difference between the income and the interest payments

negative goodwill MERGERS & ACQUISITIONS value of company's assets above price paid the gain that a company has when a company it acquires has assets with a market value greater than the price the acquiring company paid for them

negative income tax TAX US tax credits to raise income levels in the United States, payments such as tax credits made to households or individuals to increase their income to a guaranteed minimum level

negative pledge clause STOCKHOLDING & INVESTMENTS condition preventing bond issuer from disadvantaging holders a provision in a bond agreement that prohibits the issuer from doing something that would give an advantage to holders of other bonds

negative yield curve STOCKHOLDING & INVESTMENTS graph plotting interest rates against different maturities a visual representation of relative interest rates showing that they are higher for short-term bonds than they are for long-term bonds

negligence GENERAL MANAGEMENT failure to act responsibly a breach of a duty to act with expected care in conducting activities, resulting in harm to one or more people. Negligence occurs when an organization causes harm or injury through carelessness or inattention to the needs of the groups to which it owes a duty of care. These can include its customers, consumers of its product or service, shareholders, or the local community. Victims of negligence are entitled to claim compensation. Negligence is considered to be ***gross negligence*** if it is the result of excessively careless behavior.

negotiable FINANCE transferable or cashable able to be transfered from one person to another or exchanged for cash

negotiable certificate of deposit FINANCE certificate of deposit that can change hands freely a certificate of deposit with a very high value that can be freely traded

negotiable instrument *or* negotiable paper FINANCE document promising to pay cash to holder a document that can be exchanged for cash, for example, a bill of exchange or a check

negotiable order of withdrawal BANKING in US, check drawn on savings account in the United States, a check drawn on a type of savings account that bears interest but allows withdrawals

negotiable order of withdrawal account BANKING = ***NOW account***

negotiable security STOCKHOLDING & INVESTMENTS security that can change ownership a security that can be freely traded to bring its owner some benefit

negotiate FINANCE **1.** sell financial instruments to transfer ownership of financial instruments such as bearer securities, bills of exchange, checks, and promissory notes to somebody else in exchange for money **2.** discuss to agree price of item to reach an agreed price with a buyer or seller by the gradual raising of offers and lowering of the price asked until a mutually agreeable price is reached

negotiated commission FINANCE brokers' commission discussed and agreed with customers a commission that results from bargaining between brokers and their customers, typically large institutions

negotiated issue STOCKHOLDING & INVESTMENTS = ***negotiated offering***

negotiated market MARKETS market where buyers and sellers bargain over prices a market in which each transaction results from negotiation between a buyer and a seller

negotiated offering STOCKHOLDING & INVESTMENTS offer at price negotiated with underwriting syndicate a ***public offering*** of stock, the price of which is determined by negotiations between the issuer and an ***underwriting syndicate***. *Also called* ***negotiated issue***

negotiated sale FINANCE offer at price negotiated with one underwriter a ***public offering*** of stock, the price of which is determined by negotiations between the issuer and a single underwriter

negotiation GENERAL MANAGEMENT attempt to reach agreement a discussion with the goal of resolving a difference of opinion or dispute, or to settle the terms of an agreement or transaction

neoclassical economics ECONOMICS economic theory emphasizing free markets an economic theory that emphasizes the need for the free operation of market forces through supply and demand

nest egg FINANCE savings for retirement savings, usually other than a pension plan or retirement account, that have been set aside for use in somebody's retirement (informal)

nester MARKETING person not easily affected by advertising in advertising or marketing, a consumer who is not influenced by advertising hype but prefers value for money and traditional products (slang)

net 1. FINANCE remaining after deductions have been made used to describe the amount of something such as a price or salary remaining after all deductions have been made **2.** ACCOUNTING earn amount as profit to make a profit after all expenses have been taken into account

net advantage of refunding ACCOUNTING money raised by replacing debt the amount gained by renewing the funding of debt after interest rates have fallen

net advantage to leasing ACCOUNTING cost difference between leasing and borrowing to buy the amount by which leasing something is financially better than borrowing money and purchasing it

net advantage to merging MERGERS & ACQUISITIONS value gained after merging firms the amount by which the value of a merged enterprise exceeds the value of the preexisting companies, minus the cost of the merger

net assets ACCOUNTING value of assets minus liabilities the amount by which the value of a company's assets exceeds its liabilities, representing its capital

net asset value STOCKHOLDING & INVESTMENTS firm's net market value the value of a company's stock assessed by subtracting any liabilities from the market value. *Abbr* ***NAV***

net asset value per share ACCOUNTING, STOCKHOLDING & INVESTMENTS firm's net market

value divided by share number the value of a company's stock assessed by subtracting any liabilities from the market value and dividing the remainder by the number of shares of stock issued

NetBill® E-COMMERCE means of buying digital goods over Internet a micropayment system developed at Carnegie Mellon University for purchasing digital goods over the Internet. After the goods are delivered in encrypted form to the purchaser's computer, the money is debited from the purchaser's prefunded account and the goods are decrypted for the purchaser's use.

net book value ACCOUNTING original cost of asset minus depreciation the historical cost of an asset less any accumulated depreciation or other provision for diminution in value, for example, reduction to net realizable value, or asset value which has been revalued downward to reflect market conditions. *Abbr* ***NBV***. Also called ***written-down value***

net borrowings ACCOUNTING borrowings minus cash available the total of all borrowings less the cash in bank accounts and on deposit

net capital ACCOUNTING net assets minus noncash assets the amount by which net assets exceed the value of assets not easily converted to cash

net cash balance ACCOUNTING value of ready cash on a balance sheet, the amount of cash recorded as on hand

net cash flow ACCOUNTING difference between cash inflows and outflows the difference between the amount of money coming in and going out of an organization

net change MARKETS difference between prices on successive days the difference between the price of a security at the close of business from one day to the next

net change on the day MARKETS difference between opening and closing prices the difference between the opening price of a stock at the beginning of a day's trading and the closing price at the end

NetCheque™ E-COMMERCE means of exchanging electronic checks a trademark for an electronic payment system developed at the University of Southern California to allow users to write electronic checks to one another

net current assets ACCOUNTING assets minus liabilities the amount by which the value of a company's current assets exceeds its current liabilities. *Also called* ***net working capital***

net dividend STOCKHOLDING & INVESTMENTS worth of dividend after tax the value of a dividend after the recipient has paid tax on it

net domestic product ECONOMICS total national economic output with factors deducted the figure produced after factors such as depreciation have been deducted from ***GDP***. *Abbr* ***NDP***

net errors and omissions ACCOUNTING size of discrepancies in accounting the net amount of the discrepancies that arise in the calculation of a balance of payments

net exports FINANCE total exports minus total imports a figure showing the total value of exports less the total value of imports

net fixed assets ACCOUNTING worth of fixed assets after depreciation the value of fixed assets after depreciation as shown on a balance sheet

net foreign factor income FINANCE gross national minus gross domestic product income from outside a country, constituting the amount by which a country's gross national product exceeds its gross domestic product

net income ACCOUNTING **1.** income minus expenditures an organization's income less the costs incurred to generate it **2.** income after tax gross income less tax that has been deducted **3.** earnings after tax and other deductions a salary or wage less tax and other statutory deductions such as Social Security contributions. *See also* ***disposable income***

net interest FINANCE interest after tax gross interest less tax that has been deducted

net investment STOCKHOLDING & INVESTMENTS capital invested minus estimated capital consumption an increase in the total capital invested. It is calculated as gross capital invested less an estimated figure for capital consumption or depreciation.

net lease REAL ESTATE lease where lessee pays operating costs a lease that requires the lessee to pay for things that the owner usually pays for. *See also* ***gross lease***

net liquid funds ACCOUNTING money plus salable investments minus short-term borrowings an organization's cash plus its marketable investments less its short-term borrowings such as overdrafts and loans

net loss ACCOUNTING loss taking all expenses into consideration a loss calculated after the deduction of overhead and other expenses

net margin ACCOUNTING percentage of income that is profit the percentage of revenues that is profit, often used an an indicator of cost control

net national product FINANCE national income a country's ***GNP*** adjusted to deduct capital depreciation during the period in question. *Abbr* ***NNP***

net operating income ACCOUNTING income minus expenses the amount by which income exceeds expenditure, before considering taxes, interest, and other expenses

net operating margin ACCOUNTING income minus expenses as percentage of revenues ***net operating income*** as a percentage of revenues. It is an indicator of profitability.

net pay FINANCE total pay minus deductions the amount of pay an employee receives after all deductions such as income tax, social security, or pension contributions. *Also called* ***take-home pay***. *See also* ***disposable income***

net position STOCKHOLDING & INVESTMENTS balance of long and short positions the difference between an investor's long and short ***positions*** in the same security

net present value ACCOUNTING cash inflows minus cash outflows the value of an investment calculated as the sum of its initial cost and the ***present value*** of expected future cash flows

A positive NPV indicates that the project should be profitable, assuming that the estimated cash flows are reasonably accurate. A negative NPV indicates that the project will probably be unprofitable and therefore should be adjusted, if not abandoned altogether.

NPV enables management to consider the time-value of money it will invest. This concept holds that the value of money increases with time because it can always earn interest in a savings account. When the time-value-of-money concept is incorporated in the calculation of NPV, the value of a project's future net cash receipts in "today's money" can be determined. This enables proper comparisons between different projects.

For example, if Global Manufacturing Inc. is considering the acquisition of a new machine, its management will consider all the factors: initial purchase and installation costs; additional revenues generated by sales of the new machine's products, plus the taxes on these new revenues. Having accounted for these factors in its calculations, the cash flows that Global Manufacturing projects will generate from the new machine are:

Year 1	– 100,000 (initial cost of investment)
Year 2	30,000
Year 3	40,000
Year 4	40,000
Year 5	35,000
Net Total	145,000

At first glance, it appears that cash flows total 45% more than the $100,000 initial cost, a sound investment indeed. But the time-value of money shrinks the return on the project considerably, since future dollars are worth less than present dollars in hand. NPV accounts for these differences with the help of present-value tables, which list the ratios that express the present value of expected cash flow dollars, based on the applicable interest rate and the number of years in question.

In the example, Global Manufacturing's cost of capital is 9%. Using this figure to find the corresponding ratios on the present value table, the $100,000 investment cost and expected annual revenues during the five years in question, the NPV calculation looks like this:

Year	Cash flow	Table factor (at 9%)	Present value
1	($100,000) ×	1.000000 =	($100,000)
2	$30,000 ×	0.917431 =	$27,522.93
3	$40,000 ×	0.841680 =	$33,667.20
4	$40,000 ×	0.772183 =	$30,887.32
5	$35,000 ×	0.708425 =	$24,794.88
NPV =	$16,873.33		

NPV is still positive. So, on this basis at least, the investment should proceed. *Abbr* ***NPV***

net price OPERATIONS & PRODUCTION price actually paid the price paid for goods or services after all relevant discounts have been deducted

net proceeds ACCOUNTING gains from transaction minus its cost the amount received from a transaction minus the cost of making it

net profit ACCOUNTING income after expenses an organization's income as shown in a ***profit and loss account*** after all relevant expenses have been deducted. *Also called* ***profit after tax***

net profit margin ACCOUNTING, OPERATIONS & PRODUCTION *see* ***profit margin***

net profit ratio ACCOUNTING ratio of net profit to net sales the ratio of an organization's net profit to its total net sales. Comparing the net profit ratios of companies in the same sector shows which are the most efficient.

  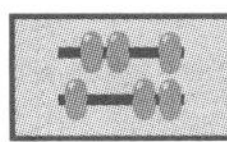   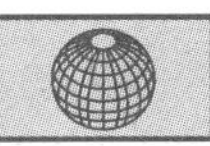   

net realizable value ACCOUNTING selling price minus costs the value of an asset if sold, allowing for costs

net receipts ACCOUNTING income after all deductions have been made receipts calculated after the deduction of commission, tax, discounts, and other associated expenses. *See also* ***gross receipts***

net relevant earnings TAX income for pension-contribution purposes earnings which qualify for calculating pension contributions and against which relief against tax can be claimed. Such earnings can be income from employment which is not pensionable, for example, the profits of a self-employed sole trader.

net residual value ACCOUNTING value of asset being disposed of the anticipated proceeds of an asset at the end of its useful life, less the costs such as transportation and the commission associated with selling it. It is used when calculating the annual charge for ***straight line depreciation***. *Abbr* ***NRV***

net return ACCOUNTING profit from investment after expenditures the amount received from an investment, taking taxes and transaction costs into account

net salary FINANCE earnings after all deductions have been made the salary remaining after deductions for taxes, social security, medicare, and any employee share of insurance premiums. *See also* ***disposable income***

net sales ACCOUNTING actual value of sales a company's total sales less any relevant discounts such as those given to retailers

net salvage value ACCOUNTING value of project being abandoned, after tax the amount of money remaining after a project has been terminated, taking tax consequences into consideration

net tangible assets ACCOUNTING firm's total assets minus intangible assets the total assets of a company less its intangible assets such as goodwill or intellectual property. *Abbr* ***NTA***

netting MARKETS carrying only net result forward a method of settling financial transactions in which only the net result in a transaction is carried forward

network culture GENERAL MANAGEMENT attitudes and behavior of global networks cultural patterns that are heavily influenced by communication using global networks

net working capital ACCOUNTING = ***net current assets***

network management GENERAL MANAGEMENT supervision of functioning of computer network the coordinated control of computer systems and programs to allow access to and delivery of information to a number of users

network marketing MARKETING trading through independent agents the selling of goods or services through a network of self-employed agents or representatives. Network marketing usually involves several levels of agents, each level on a different commission rate. Each agent is encouraged to recruit other agents. In genuine network marketing, in contrast to ***pyramid selling***, there is an end product or service sold to customers. Another version of network marketing is the loose cooperative relationship between a company, its competitors, collaborators, suppliers, and other organizations affecting the overall marketing function. *Also called* ***multilevel marketing***

network organization GENERAL MANAGEMENT loose association of teams a company or group of companies that has a minimum of formal structures and relies instead on the formation and dissolution of teams to meet specific objectives. A network organization utilizes information and communications technologies extensively, and makes use of knowledge across and within companies along the ***value chain***. *See also* ***virtual organization***

network revolution GENERAL MANAGEMENT dramatic change arising from global networks the fundamental change in business practices triggered by the growth of global networks

network society GENERAL MANAGEMENT society dependent on global networks a society in which patterns of work, communication, and government are characterized by the use of global networks

net worth ACCOUNTING assets minus liabilities the difference between the assets and liabilities of a person or company

net yield ACCOUNTING rate of return after costs and tax the amount produced by an investment after deducting all costs and taxes

new economy ECONOMICS economic system based on e-commerce a term used in the late 1990s and 2000s to describe the e-commerce sector and the ***digital economy***, in which firms mostly trade online rather than in the bricks and mortar of physical premises

new entrant MARKETING new arrival in market or sector an organization or product that has recently come into a market or sector

new issue STOCKHOLDING & INVESTMENTS **1.** new security on sale for first time a new security, such as a bond or stock, being offered to the public for the first time. *See also* ***float, initial public offering*** **2.** issue of new security an additional issue of an existing security, for example, a ***rights issue***

new issue market *or* new issues market MARKETS market into which new stock is launched a market where companies can raise finance by issuing additional shares or by a flotation. *See also* ***float, initial public offering, primary market***

newly acquired business BUSINESS business recently bought by another a business in the early stages of the changes caused by having been bought by another company

newly industrialized economy ECONOMICS nation benefiting from industrialization a country whose industrialization has recently started to develop. Mexico and Malaysia are examples of newly industrialized economies.

new metrics GENERAL MANAGEMENT nontraditional standards for measuring business performance standards for measuring or quantifying the activities and success of an organization that incorporate nontraditional approaches

new money FINANCE financing from a new source financing provided by an issue of new shares of stock or by the transfer of money from one account to another

new product development MARKETING stages of bringing something new to market the processes involved in getting a new product or service to market. The traditional product development cycle, the ***stage-gate model***, embraces the conception, generation, analysis, development, testing, marketing, and commercialization of new products or services. Alternative models of new product development fall into two broad categories: accelerating time to market models and ***integrated implementation models***. These strive to achieve both flexibility and acceleration of development. All activities such as design, production planning, and test marketing are performed in parallel rather than going through a sequential linear progression. *Abbr* ***NPD***

new time MARKETS when stock exchange sales are carried over the period on a stock exchange when sales in the last few days of the previous account are credited to the following account

New York Mercantile Exchange MARKETS US exchange for energy and precious metals the world's largest physical commodity exchange and North America's most important trading exchange for energy and precious metals. It deals in crude oil, gasoline, heating oil, natural gas, propane, gold, silver, platinum, palladium, and copper. *Abbr* ***NYMEX***

New York Stock Exchange MARKETS stock exchange in New York the leading stock exchange in New York, which is self-regulatory but has to comply with the regulations of the US ***Securities and Exchange Commission***. It has its origins in the Buttonwood Agreement of 1792. It merged with ***Archipelago*** in 2006, and then with ***Euronext*** in 2007 to form the ***NYSE Euronext*** group. *Abbr* ***NYSE***. Also called ***Big Board***

New Zealand Exchange *or* New Zealand Stock Exchange MARKETS New Zealand's main market for securities stock exchange based in Wellington, New Zealand, established in 1974. The New Zealand Stock Exchange replaced the Stock Exchange Association of New Zealand and a number of regional trading floors. It demutualized in 2002 and became simply the New Zealand Exchange in 2003. The main index of stocks on the exchange is the ***NZX 50***. *Abbr* ***NZX***

New Zealand Trade Development Board FINANCE New Zealand agency promoting exports and inward investment a government body responsible for promoting New Zealand exports and facilitating foreign investment in New Zealand. *Also called* ***TRADENZ***

next futures contract STOCKHOLDING & INVESTMENTS option for following month an ***option*** to buy or sell for the month after the current month

NI *abbr* PENSIONS ***National Insurance***

NIC *abbr* PENSIONS ***National Insurance contributions***

niche bank *or* niche banker BANKING specialist banker a bank or banker specializing in a specific field such as management buyouts

niche company BUSINESS specialist firm a company that produces a product or service that fills a specialized gap in the overall provision of a market

niche market MARKETING specialized market segment a very specialized market segment within a broader segment. A niche market involves specialist goods or services with relatively few or no competitors. Customers may look for exclusiveness or some other differentiating factor such as high status. Alternatively, they may have a specific requirement not satisfied by standard products. *See also* ***micromarketing***

niche player (informal) **1.** BANKING = ***niche bank*** **2.** STOCKHOLDING & INVESTMENTS = ***boutique investment house***

nickel *US* FINANCE small margin five hundredths of one percent, expressing a fine margin (slang)

  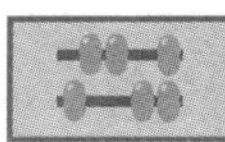      

NIF *abbr* FINANCE ***note issuance facility***

Nifty Fifty *US* MARKETS institutional investors' favorite stocks the 50 most popular stocks among institutional investors on the ***New York Stock Exchange*** from the 1960s until the early 1970s (informal)

Nikkei 225 *or* Nikkei Index MARKETS Japanese stock price index an index of stock prices on the Tokyo Stock Exchange, the largest stock exchange in Japan

nil paid STOCKHOLDING & INVESTMENTS nothing paid yet with no money yet paid. In the United Kingdom, the term is used in reference to the purchase of newly issued stocks, or to the stocks themselves, when the stockholder entitled to buy new stocks has not yet made a commitment to do so and may sell the rights instead.

nil return *UK* TAX report of no taxable income a report filed with a tax authority showing no transactions or income on which tax is owed

ninja loan FINANCE loan made to somebody with poor credit rating a loan made to somebody who has No INcome, No Job, and no Assets (slang) *See also* ***subprime loan***

NMS *abbr* MARKETS ***National Market System***

NNP *abbr* FINANCE ***net national product***

no-claims bonus *or* no-claims discount INSURANCE reduced insurance price because no claims are made a reduction of premiums on an insurance policy because no claims have been made

noise GENERAL MANAGEMENT distracting unimportant data irrelevant or insignificant data which overload a feedback process. The presence of noise can confuse or divert attention from relevant information; efficiency in a system is enhanced as the ratio of information to noise increases.

noise trader MARKETS uninformed market participant a participant in the stock market who does not have much knowledge about the securities being traded (slang)

no-load fund STOCKHOLDING & INVESTMENTS mutual fund with no fee for trading a mutual fund that does not charge a fee for the purchase or sale of shares. *See also* ***load fund***

nominal **1.** FINANCE very much lower than usual level very small when compared with what would be considered usual, especially with reference to a sum of money **2.** ACCOUNTING relating to current prices considered in terms of the stated or original value only, without adjustment for inflation and other changes **3.** GENERAL MANAGEMENT assigned by name assigned to a specific name or category

nominal account ACCOUNTING account recording items according to category a record of revenues and expenditures, liabilities and assets classified by their nature, for example, sales, rent, rates, electricity, wages, or share capital

nominal annual rate FINANCE = ***annual percentage rate***

nominal capital STOCKHOLDING & INVESTMENTS = ***nominal share capital***

nominal cash flow ACCOUNTING cash flow disregarding inflation cash flow in terms of currency, without adjustment for inflation

nominal exchange rate CURRENCY & EXCHANGE stated exchange rate the exchange rate as specified, without adjustment for transaction costs or differences in purchasing power

nominal interest rate FINANCE stated interest rate the interest rate as specified, without adjustment for compounding or inflation

nominal ledger *UK* ACCOUNTING ledger recording money values a record of revenue, operating expenses, assets, and capital

nominal price OPERATIONS & PRODUCTION price disregarding value the price of an item being sold when the price is lower than the full value

nominal share capital STOCKHOLDING & INVESTMENTS maximum amount of firm's share capital the total value of all of a corporation's stock at ***nominal value***. *Also called* ***nominal capital***. *See also* ***authorized share capital***

nominal value STOCKHOLDING & INVESTMENTS original value of new stock the original value officially given to a newly issued stock. *Also called* ***par value***. *See also* ***capitalization, reserves***

nominal yield STOCKHOLDING & INVESTMENTS dividend as percentage of face value the dividend paid on a share of stock expressed as a percentage of its face value

nominee **1.** FINANCE in US, somebody acting for another in the United States, a person who is appointed to deal with financial matters on your behalf **2.** *US* STOCKHOLDING & INVESTMENTS holder of security on another's behalf a financial institution, or an individual employed by such an institution, that holds a security on behalf of the actual owner. While this may be to hide the owner's identity, for example, in the case of a celebrity, it is also to allow an institution managing any individual's portfolio to conduct transactions without the need for the owner to sign the required paperwork. *UK term* ***nominee name***

nominee account BANKING account not in owner's name an account held not in the name of the real owner of the account, but instead in the name of another person, organization, or financial institution. Stocks can be bought and held in nominee accounts so that the owner's identity is not disclosed.

nominee name *UK* STOCKHOLDING & INVESTMENTS = ***nominee***

nonacceptance BANKING rejection of bill of exchange on presentation a refusal to accept a bill of exchange when it is presented, by the person on whom it is drawn

nonbranded goods MARKETING items from unidentified source generic goods such as food produce, pharmaceuticals, or computer keyboards that are not linked to a specific ***brand*** name, manufacturer, or producer. Nonbranded goods are often widely available in street markets or by mail order and are often perceived to be of low quality.

nonbusiness days BANKING days when banks are closed those days when banks are not open for business, for example, public holidays, or Saturdays and Sundays in Western countries

noncallable STOCKHOLDING & INVESTMENTS not able to be repurchased before maturity used to describe a security that the issuer cannot buy back before its maturity date. *See also* ***callable***

noncash item **1.** ACCOUNTING entry in income statement not representing cash an item, such as a gain or loss from an investment or depreciation expenses, that occurs on an income statement and is not a receipt of actual money **2.** BANKING financial instruments representing money checks, drafts, and similar items that have money value but are not money themselves

noncompetitive bid MARKETS purchasing US Treasury security at average competitive bid price a method of purchasing US Treasury securities through member banks of the ***Federal Reserve*** in which a buyer agrees to pay a price equal to the average of all competitive bids for that particular week's issue of securities

nonconformance costs OPERATIONS & PRODUCTION = ***quality costs***

nonconforming loan TAX loan not meeting usual conditions a loan that does not conform to the lender's standards, especially those of a US government agency

noncontributory pension plan *US* PENSIONS pension plan financed by employer a pension plan to which the employee makes no payments. *UK term* ***non-contributory pension scheme***

non-contributory pension scheme *UK* PENSIONS = ***noncontributory pension plan***

noncurrent assets FINANCE long-term investments resources that are expected to be held for more than one year. They are reported at the lower of cost and current market value, which means that their values will vary.

nondeductible ACCOUNTING not admissible as deduction not allowed to be deducted from a payment, especially not acceptable as an allowance against income tax

nondisclosure agreement HR & PERSONNEL agreement not to give away company secrets a legally enforceable agreement preventing present or past employees from disclosing commercially sensitive information belonging to the employer to any other party. A nondisclosure agreement can remain in force for several years after an employee leaves a company. In the event of a dispute, a company may be required to prove that the information in question belongs to the company itself, is not in the public domain, or cannot be obtained elsewhere. *Abbr* ***NDA***

nondisparagement agreement HR & PERSONNEL agreement not to criticize employer an agreement that prevents present or past employees from criticizing an employing organization in public. Nondisparagement agreements are a relatively new type of agreement and have arisen primarily to prevent employees putting comments about their employing organization onto the Internet. Case law has yet to determine whether such agreements are legally binding. *Abbr* ***NDA***

nondom *or* non-domicile TAX person not paying tax on earnings abroad a person who is exempt from paying tax on foreign earnings because his or her permanent home is in another country

nonexecutive director CORPORATE GOVERNANCE board member without day-to-day involvement a part-time, nonsalaried member of the ***board of directors***, involved in the planning, strategy, and policy making of an organization but not in its day-to-day operations. The appointment of a nonexecutive director to a board is usually made in order to provide independence and balance to that board, and to ensure that good ***corporate governance*** is practiced. A nonexecutive director may be selected for the prestige they bring or for their experience, contacts, or specialist knowledge. *Also called* ***part-time director***. *See also* ***outside director***

  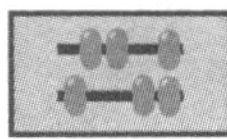   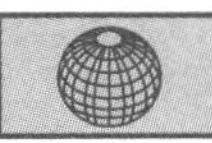   

nonfinancial asset ACCOUNTING not money or financial contract an asset such as real estate or personal property that is neither money nor a financial instrument

non-financial incentive scheme FINANCE UK program rewarding performance other than with money in the United Kingdom, a program offering benefits such as additional paid vacations, set up to reward employees for improved commitment and performance and as a means of motivation. *See also **financial incentive scheme***

noninterest-bearing bond STOCKHOLDING & INVESTMENTS bond with discount rather than interest a bond that is sold at a discount instead of with a promise to pay interest

nonjudicial foreclosure LEGAL in US, reclamation of property without using court in the United States, a foreclosure on real estate without recourse to a court. The mortgage lender issues a notice of mortgage default to the owner, along with a notice of intent to sell the property.

nonline E-COMMERCE not online not provided with an Internet connection, or not done via the Internet

nonlinear programming STATISTICS using some nonlinear equations a process in which the equations expressing the interactions of variables are not all linear but may, for example, be in proportion to the square of a variable

nonline community E-COMMERCE people not using e-mail or Internet the people who do not use e-mail or the Internet for communications, information, or purchasing

nonnegotiable instrument FINANCE financial contract that cannot change hands a financial instrument that cannot be signed over to anyone else. These include ***bills of exchange*** and ***crossed cheques***.

nonoperational balances BANKING Bank of England deposits that cannot be withdrawn accounts that banks maintain at the ***Bank of England*** without the power of withdrawal

nonparticipating preferred stock STOCKHOLDING & INVESTMENTS preferred stock paying fixed dividend the most common type of preferred stock that pays a fixed dividend regardless of the profitability of the company. *See also **participating preferred stock***

nonperforming asset STOCKHOLDING & INVESTMENTS asset providing no income an asset that is not producing income, for example, one that is no longer accruing interest

nonperforming loan FINANCE loan made to borrower likely to default a loan made to a borrower who is not likely to pay any interest nor to repay the principal

nonprofit organization *or* nonprofit BUSINESS organization not operated solely for profit an ***organization*** that does not have financial profit as a main strategic objective. Nonprofit organizations include charities, professional associations, labor unions, and religious, arts, community, research, and campaigning bodies. These organizations are not situated in either the ***public*** or ***private sectors***, but in what has been called the ***third sector***. Many have paid staff and working capital but their main purpose is not to provide a product or service, but to effect change. They are led by values rather than financial commitments to shareholders. *Abbr* ***NPO***. See also ***third sector***

nonqualified annuity PENSIONS US annuity bought with taxed income in the United States, a type of annuity that can be purchased with after-tax income to provide retirement income. Taxes on earnings from the annuity are deferred until money is withdrawn.

nonrandom sampling OPERATIONS & PRODUCTION sampling with unequal chances of selection a ***sampling*** technique that is used when it cannot be ensured that each item has an equal chance of being selected, or when selection is based on expert knowledge of the population. *See also **random sampling***

nonrecourse debt FINANCE debt with no liability a debt for which the borrower has no personal responsibility, typically a debt of a limited partnership

nonrecoverable FINANCE that will never be paid back used to describe a debt that will never be paid, for example, because of the borrower's bankruptcy

nonrecurring charge ACCOUNTING unique charge a charge that is made only once

nonrecurring item ACCOUNTING unique item in account in a set of accounts an item that is included on only one occasion

nonresident TAX working abroad used to describe somebody who has left his or her native country to work overseas for a period. Nonresidency has tax advantages, such as exemption from tax on overseas earning. While a US citizen is working overseas for a period of 11 out of 12 months, a limited amount of his or her earned income generated overseas is exempt from US income tax. During a period of nonresidency, many expatriates choose to bank offshore.

Non-Resident Withholding Tax TAX New Zealand levy on nonresidents' investment income a duty imposed by the New Zealand government on interest and dividends earned by a nonresident from investments. *Abbr* ***NRWT***

nonstore retailing E-COMMERCE selling over Internet without building to visit the selling of goods and services electronically without actually establishing a physical store

nonstrategic BUSINESS not related to achievement of long-term goals not related to the long-term objectives of an organization or the resources used to achieve those objectives

non-sufficient funds *UK* BANKING = ***insufficient funds***

nonsystematic risk RISK risk related to particular firm investment risk that is attributable to the performance of a specific company, not to the performance of the stock market or economy, and can be reduced by diversification

nontariff barrier INTERNATIONAL TRADE regulations that make imports more difficult a country's economic regulation on something such as safety standards that impedes imports, often from emerging markets. *Abbr* ***NTB***

nontaxable TAX not liable for tax not subject to tax. In the United Kingdom, interest from ***ISAs***, prize winnings, and statutory redundancy pay are among nontaxable sources of income.

nonvoting share STOCKHOLDING & INVESTMENTS common stock receiving dividend but not voting rights common stock that is paid a dividend from the company's profits, but that does not entitle the stockholder to vote at any meeting of stockholders. Such stock is unpopular with institutional investors. *Also called* ***A share***

norm STATISTICS expected range of values for set in a statistical study, a range of values that is normal for a population or other set

normal distribution STATISTICS expected distribution of random variable in a statistical study, the probability distribution of a random variable

normal profit ECONOMICS minimum profit required for business the minimum level of profit that will attract an entrepreneur to begin a business or remain trading

normal yield curve STOCKHOLDING & INVESTMENTS showing lower yields for short-term bonds a visual representation of interest rates showing higher yields for long-term bonds than for short-term bonds. *See also **yield curve***

no-strike agreement HR & PERSONNEL arrangement with union not to call strike a formal understanding between an employer and a labor union that the union will not call its members out on strike. A no-strike agreement is usually won by the employer in exchange for improved terms and conditions of employment, including pay, and sometimes guaranteed employment.

nostro account BANKING account with bank abroad an account that a bank has with a ***correspondent bank*** in another country

notary public LEGAL somebody with authority to officially witness documents a person who has been authorized by a state to witness documents, making them legally accepted, and to administer oaths

notch *S. AFRICA* HR & PERSONNEL point on scale a position on a scale such as an incremental salary scale

note 1. CURRENCY & EXCHANGE item of paper money a piece of paper money printed by a bank and approved as legal tender. *Also called* ***banknote*** *(sense 1)*, ***bill*** *(sense 2)* **2.** FINANCE document promising to repay borrowed money a written promise to repay money that has been borrowed

note issuance facility FINANCE facility for buying and reselling Eurocurrency notes a credit facility where a company obtains a loan underwritten by banks and can issue a series of short-term ***Eurocurrency*** notes to replace others that have expired. *Abbr* ***NIF***

note of hand FINANCE = ***promissory note***

notes to the accounts *or* notes to the financial statements ACCOUNTING information supporting account entries an explanation of specific items in a set of accounts

not-for-profit FINANCE not operated to generate income organized typically for a charitable, humanitarian, or educational purpose and not generating profits for shareholders. In the United States, not-for-profit corporations can apply for tax-exempt status at both the federal and state levels of government. *See also **nonprofit organization***

notice of coding TAX information about another's tax code a notice that informs a third party of the code number given to indicate the amount of tax allowances to which somebody is entitled

notice of default *US* LEGAL official notification to defaulter a formal document issued by a lender to a borrower who is in default. *UK term* ***default notice***

notice period HR & PERSONNEL time between resignation or dismissal and leaving the amount of time specified in the terms and ***conditions of employment*** that an ***employee*** must work between resigning from an organization and leaving the employment of that organization

notifying bank BANKING, INTERNATIONAL TRADE = ***advising bank***

notional income ACCOUNTING income not physically received invisible benefit that is not actual money, goods, or services

notional principal amount FINANCE value of loan the value used to represent a loan in calculating ***interest rate swaps***

notional rent ACCOUNTING theoretical rent for firm's own premises an amount of money noted in accounts as rent where the company owns the building it is occupying and so does not pay an actual rent

not negotiable FINANCE not able to change hands absolutely used to describe a check or bill of exchange that cannot be transferred to somebody else. If such a document is given by one person to another, the recipient obtains no better title to it than the signatory. *See also* ***negotiable instrument***

no-touch option STOCKHOLDING & INVESTMENTS option paying if preset level not reached an ***option*** that gives an investor a payment only if the price of the underlying asset has not reached or exceeded a preset level. *See also* ***double-one-touch option, one-touch option***

not sufficient funds *UK* BANKING = ***insufficient funds***

novation LEGAL agreed replacement of one party to contract an agreement to change a contract by substituting a third party for one of the two original parties

NOW account BANKING interest-paying US account with checks in the United States, an interest-bearing account with a bank or savings and loan association, on which checks (called ***negotiable orders of withdrawal***) can be drawn. *Full form* ***negotiable order of withdrawal account***

NPD *abbr* MARKETING ***new product development***

NPO *abbr* BUSINESS ***nonprofit organization***

NPV *abbr* ACCOUNTING ***net present value***

NRV *abbr* ACCOUNTING ***net residual value***

NRWT *abbr* TAX ***Non-Resident Withholding Tax***

NSA *abbr* ACCOUNTING ***National Society of Accountants***

NS&I *abbr* STOCKHOLDING & INVESTMENTS ***National Savings & Investments***

NSB *abbr* BANKING ***National Savings Bank***

NSC *abbr* STOCKHOLDING & INVESTMENTS ***National Savings Certificate***

NSF *abbr* BANKING ***non-sufficient funds*** *or* ***not sufficient funds***

NTA *abbr* ACCOUNTING ***net tangible assets***

NTB *abbr* INTERNATIONAL TRADE ***nontariff barrier***

nuisance parameter STATISTICS unimportant but necessary variable in a statistical model, a parameter that is insignificant in itself but whose unknown value is needed to make inferences about significant variables in a study

null hypothesis STATISTICS lack of significant effect the assumption that there is no relationship between variables that has produced a significant difference

numbered account BANKING bank account without holder's name a bank account identified by a number to allow the holder to remain anonymous

numbers FINANCE financial data financial results or forecasts calculated for a particular period of time or project

numerical control OPERATIONS & PRODUCTION automation using numerical data the use of numerical data to influence the operation of equipment. It allows the operation of machinery to be automated and usually involves the use of computer systems. Data is generated, stored, manipulated, and retrieved while a process is in operation.

nuncupative will LEGAL oral will a will that is made orally in the presence of a witness, rather than in writing

NYMEX *abbr* MARKETS ***New York Mercantile Exchange***

NYSE *abbr* MARKETS ***New York Stock Exchange***

NYSE Alternext US MARKETS = ***NYSE Amex Equities***

NYSE Amex Equities MARKETS New York exchange listing smaller firms a New York stock exchange listing smaller and less mature companies than those listed on the larger ***New York Stock Exchange***. It was established in 1908 as the New York Curb Market and in 1953 was renamed as the American Stock Exchange. It was acquired by ***NYSE Euronext*** on October 1, 2008, and is now known as NYSE Amex Equities. *Also called* ***American Stock Exchange, Little Board, NYSE Alternext US***

NYSE Arca MARKETS US stock exchange stock exchange based in the US, established in 2001 as the Archipelago Stock Exchange, a regulated facility of the Pacific Stock Exchange. It then acquired the Pacific Exchange in 2005 before merging with the ***New York Stock Exchange*** in 2006. It is now part of the ***NYSE Euronext*** group. *Also called* ***ArcaEx, Archipelago***

NYSE Composite MARKETS NYSE stock market index an index of all common stocks listed on the ***New York Stock Exchange***, it serves as a broad-based benchmark and uses a transparent, rule-based methodology which includes free-float market capitalization weighting. It was reestablished in January 2003 with a base value of 5,000.

NYSE Euronext MARKETS Euro-American stock exchange group corporation formed in 2007 by the merger of the ***New York Stock Exchange*** and ***Euronext***. It also includes ***ArcaEx*** and ***LIFFE***.

NYSE Liffe MARKETS exchange for financial futures and options an exchange for trading financial futures and options. Established in 1982 as the London International Financial Futures Exchange, it offered contracts on interest rates denominated in most of the world's major currencies until 1992, when it merged with the ***London Traded Options Market***, adding equity options to its product range. In 1996 it merged with the ***London Commodity Exchange***, adding a variety of soft commodity and agricultural commodity contracts to its financial portfolio. From November 1998, trading gradually migrated from the floor of the exchange to screen-based trading. It was acquired by the ***Euronext*** exchange in 2002 and is now part of the ***NYSE Euronext*** group. *Also called* ***LIFFE, London International Financial Futures and Options Exchange***

NZSE *abbr* MARKETS New Zealand Stock Exchange = ***New Zealand Exchange***

NZX *abbr* MARKETS ***New Zealand Exchange***

NZX 50 MARKETS main New Zealand stock market index an index of the 50 largest and most liquid securities traded on the ***New Zealand Exchange***. It was established on March 3, 2003, with a base value of 1,880.85, replacing the NZX 40 index.

O

OBI *abbr* E-COMMERCE ***open buying on the Internet***

object and task technique GENERAL MANAGEMENT budgeting by costing each task in the United States, a method of budgeting that involves assessing a project's objectives, determining the tasks required for their accomplishment, and then estimating the cost of each task

objective GENERAL MANAGEMENT goal of effort an end toward which effort is directed and on which resources are focused, usually to achieve an organization's strategy. There is considerable discussion on whether objective, goal, target, and aim are the same. In general usage, the terms are often interchangeable, so it is important that, if an organization has a particular meaning for one of these terms, it must define it in its documentation. Sometimes an objective is seen as the desired final end result, while a goal is a smaller step on the road to it.

obligation LEGAL legal agreement, especially to pay debt a binding legal agreement, by which somebody is bound to do something, especially to pay an amount of money

obligor FINANCE = ***debtor***

OBSF *abbr* FINANCE ***off-balance-sheet financing***

obsolescence **1.** FINANCE loss through becoming out of date the loss of value of a fixed asset due to advances in technology or changes in market conditions **2.** MARKETING becoming out of date the decline of products in a market due to the introduction of better competitor products or rapid technology developments. Obsolescence of products can be a planned process, controlled by introducing deliberate minor cosmetic changes to a product every few years to encourage new purchases. It can also be unplanned, however, and in some sectors the pace of technological change is so rapid that the rate of obsolescence is high Obsolescence is part of the product life cycle, and if a product cannot be turned around, it may lead to product abandonment.

occupational pension PENSIONS in UK, pension plan maintained by employer in the United Kingdom, a pension plan run by an organization for its employees. Occupational pensions are regarded as deferred pay and form part of the total compensation package. Until recently, most plans were based on final salary but there has been a shift toward ***money purchase pensions***, particularly among smaller companies. Alternatively, employers may choose to contribute to an employee's ***personal pension***. *Also called* ***company pension***

OCF *abbr* ACCOUNTING ***operating cash flow***

OCR *abbr* BANKING ***official cash rate***

O/D *abbr* BANKING ***overdraft***

odd lot MARKETS fewer than 100 shares traded together a group of fewer than 100 shares of stock bought or sold together. *Also called* **broken lot, uneven lot**

OECD INTERNATIONAL TRADE association of nations promoting democracy and free market a group of 30 member countries, with a shared commitment to democratic government and the market economy, that has active relationships with some 70 other countries via nongovernmental organizations. Formed in 1961, its work covers economic and social issues from macroeconomics to trade, education, development, and scientific innovation. Its goals are to promote economic growth and employment in member countries in a climate of stability; to assist the sustainable economic expansion of both member and nonmember countries; and to support a balanced and even-handed expansion of world trade. *Full form* ***Organisation for Economic Co-operation and Development***

OEIC *abbr* STOCKHOLDING & INVESTMENTS ***open-ended investment company***

OEM *abbr* OPERATIONS & PRODUCTION ***original equipment manufacturer***

off-balance-sheet financing FINANCE raising money through items not on balance sheet financing obtained by means other than debt and equity instruments, for example, by partnerships, joint ventures, and leases. *Abbr* ***OBSF***

off-board MARKETS of trading between dealers used to describe the trade of listed securities that does not take place on the stock exchange, or that takes place in the ***over-the-counter market***

offer STOCKHOLDING & INVESTMENTS **1.** *see* ***offering price*** **2.** net value of mutual fund the ***net asset value*** of a mutual fund plus any sales charges. It is the price investors pay when they buy a security.

offer by prospectus STOCKHOLDING & INVESTMENTS UK means of selling securities to public in the United Kingdom, one of the ways available to a ***lead underwriter*** of offering securities to the public. *See also* ***float, initial public offering, new issue, offer for sale***

offer document STOCKHOLDING & INVESTMENTS = ***prospectus***

offered market *UK* MARKETS market with more sellers than buyers a market in which sellers outnumber buyers, giving an advantage to buyers

offer for sale STOCKHOLDING & INVESTMENTS invitation to buy stock an invitation to apply for stock in a company, based on information contained in a prospectus

offering MARKETS security offered for sale an issue of a security that is offered for sale

offering circular STOCKHOLDING & INVESTMENTS = ***prospectus***

offering date MARKETS first day of stock sale the date on which a company offers its stock for sale to the public for the first time

offering price *US* STOCKHOLDING & INVESTMENTS selling price of share of stock the price at which somebody offers a share of a stock, especially a new issue, for sale. *UK term* ***offer price***

offeror STOCKHOLDING & INVESTMENTS maker of bid somebody who makes a bid to buy a ***financial obligation*** such as a debt

offer period MERGERS & ACQUISITIONS time span when takeover bid is open the time after a ***takeover bid*** for a company is first announced until the deal is closed or the offer lapses

offer price *UK* STOCKHOLDING & INVESTMENTS = ***offering price***

Office of Fair Trading REGULATION & COMPLIANCE UK government department protecting consumers a department of the UK government that protects consumers against unfair or illegal business practices. *Abbr* ***OFT***

Office of Management and Budget REGULATION & COMPLIANCE US government office that helps prepare federal budget the US government office, part of the executive branch of the government, that helps the President to prepare the federal budget. *Abbr* ***OMB***

Office of Thrift Supervision REGULATION & COMPLIANCE US agency regulating savings and loan associations an agency within the United States Department of the Treasury that regulates the savings and loan associations to ensure that they operate in a way that protects people's savings. *Abbr* ***OTS***

officer GENERAL MANAGEMENT = ***executive***

official books of account ACCOUNTING institution's financial records the official financial records of an organization set up for educational, professional, religious, or social purposes

official cash rate BANKING government interest rate the current interest rate as set by a central bank. *Abbr* ***OCR***

official development assistance FINANCE money made available to emerging country money that the ***OECD***'s Development Assistance Committee gives or lends to an emerging country

official intervention CURRENCY & EXCHANGE government action to affect exchange rate an attempt by a government to influence the exchange rate by buying or selling foreign currency

official list MARKETS list of securities traded on London Stock Exchange in the United Kingdom, the list maintained by the ***Financial Services Authority*** of all the securities traded on the London Stock Exchange

official receiver LEGAL UK court agent managing bankruptcy in the United Kingdom, an officer of the court who is appointed to wind up the affairs of an organization that goes bankrupt. An official receiver is appointed by the Department for Business, Enterprise & Regulatory Reform and often acts as a ***liquidator***. The job involves realizing any assets that remain to repay debts, for example, by selling property. *Abbr* ***OR***

official return ACCOUNTING legally required financial report a financial report or statement required by law and made by a person or company, for example, a tax return

off-line transaction processing E-COMMERCE recording of credit or debit card transactions the receipt and storage of order and credit or debit card information through a computer network or point-of-sale terminal for subsequent authorization and processing

offset STOCKHOLDING & INVESTMENTS counterbalancing transaction in security a transaction that balances all or part of an earlier transaction in the same security

offset clause INSURANCE insurance condition allowing counterbalancing of credits and debits a provision in an insurance policy that permits the balancing of credits against debits so that, for example, a company can reduce or omit payments to another company that owes it money and is bankrupt

offshore INTERNATIONAL TRADE **1.** send jobs overseas to get cheaper labor to hire workers in foreign countries in order to take advantage of a supply of skilled but relatively cheap labor **2.** located in another country based outside a specific country, especially in a place where taxes are low

offshore account TAX account located in low-tax country an account maintained in a place where taxes are low, to reduce a person's or company's liability to tax where their income originates

offshore banking BANKING banking in foreign banks banking in a foreign country, especially one that has favorable taxation regulations and is considered as a ***tax haven***

offshore company BUSINESS firm registered abroad for financial benefits a company that is registered in a country other than the one in which it conducts most of its business, usually for tax purposes. For example, many ***captive insurance companies*** are registered in the Cayman Islands.

offshore finance subsidiary *UK* BUSINESS = ***offshore financial subsidiary***

offshore financial center FINANCE finance hub in foreign country a country or other political unit that has banking laws intended to attract business from industrialized nations

offshore financial subsidiary *US* BUSINESS firm abroad handling parent company's finances a company created in another country to handle financial transactions, giving the owning company tax and legal advantages in its home country. *UK term* ***offshore finance subsidiary***

offshore fund STOCKHOLDING & INVESTMENTS fund based abroad a fund that is based in a foreign country, usually a country that has favorable taxation regulations

offshore holding company BUSINESS firm abroad owning firms at home a company created in another country to own other companies, giving the owning company legal advantages in its home country

offshore production INTERNATIONAL TRADE making goods abroad for import the manufacture of goods abroad for import to the home market

offshore trading company BUSINESS firm abroad handling parent company's commercial transactions a company created in another country to handle commercial transactions, giving the owning company legal advantages in its home country

offshoring INTERNATIONAL TRADE moving service operations abroad the transfer of service operations to foreign countries in order to take advantage of a supply of skilled but relatively cheap labor

off-the-shelf company BUSINESS UK firm available for purchase in the United Kingdom, a company for which all the legal formalities, except the appointment of directors, have been completed so that a purchaser can transform it into a customized new company with relative ease and low cost

OFT *abbr* REGULATION & COMPLIANCE ***Office of Fair Trading***

OI ACCOUNTING *see* ***EBIT***

oil economy ECONOMICS **1.** economy based on oil revenues an economy that is funded by the revenues from oil resources **2.** economy based on oil an economy that depends on oil supplies for its transportation, agricultural, and energy needs

Old Lady of Threadneedle Street *UK* BANKING Bank of England the ***Bank of England***, which is located in Threadneedle Street in the City of London (informal)

oligarch FINANCE rich powerful businessman one of a small group having financial and political power, especially nowadays somebody with extreme personal wealth (slang)

oligarchy GENERAL MANAGEMENT control by small group an organization in which a small group of managers exercises control. Within an oligarchy, the controlling group often directs the organization for its own purposes, or for purposes other than the best interests of the organization.

oligopoly MARKETS market with few major sellers a market that is controlled by a few, very large, suppliers

oligopsony MARKETS market with few customers a market in which there are only a few buyers for a specific product or service

OMB *abbr* REGULATION & COMPLIANCE ***Office of Management and Budget***

ombudsman REGULATION & COMPLIANCE independent investigator of complaints a public official who investigates complaints against public departments, large organizations, or business sectors

omitted dividend STOCKHOLDING & INVESTMENTS unpaid regular dividend a regularly scheduled dividend that a company does not pay

omnibus account STOCKHOLDING & INVESTMENTS combined account for broker's convenience an account of one broker with another that combines the transactions of multiple investors for the convenience of the brokers

omnibus survey MARKETING wide-ranging survey a survey covering a number of topics, usually undertaken on behalf of several clients who share the cost of conducting the survey

OMX MARKETS European stock exchange group the stock exchange group formed by the merger of OM and HEX in 2003. Initially OMHEX, it changed its name to OMX in 2004. It expanded to include eight stock exchanges in Nordic and Baltic Europe, before being taken over by NASDAQ in 2008 and is now part of the ***NASDAQ OMX*** group.

on account FINANCE by advance payment used to describe an amount of money paid that represents part of a sum of money due to be paid in the future

oncost ACCOUNTING general cost of running business a business cost that cannot be charged directly to a particular good or service and must be apportioned across the business

on demand **1.** BANKING allowing immediate withdrawals used to describe an account from which withdrawals may be made without giving a period of notice **2.** FINANCE allowing demand for immediate repayment used to describe a loan, usually an overdraft, that the lender can request the borrower to repay immediately **3.** FINANCE payable immediately to holder used to describe a bill of exchange that is paid upon presentation

one-stop shopping FINANCE provision of complete variety of financial services the ability of a single financial institution to offer a full variety of financial services

one-to-one marketing MARKETING emphasis on individual customers a marketing technique using detailed data, personalized communications, and customized products or services to match the requirements of individual customers

one-touch option STOCKHOLDING & INVESTMENTS option paying at preset level an ***option*** that gives an investor a payment if the price of the underlying asset reaches or exceeds a preset level. *See also* ***double-one-touch option, no-touch option***

one-way trade INTERNATIONAL TRADE when seller does not buy in return an economic situation in which one country sells to another, but does not buy anything in return

one-year money STOCKHOLDING & INVESTMENTS investment for fixed period of one year money placed on a money market for a fixed period of one year, with either a fixed or variable rate of interest. It can be removed during the fixed term only upon payment of a penalty.

on-hold advertising MARKETING advertising to telephone callers waiting for service telephone advertising aimed at consumers who are being kept on hold while waiting to speak to somebody

online banking E-COMMERCE, BANKING banking service accessible by computer over Internet a system by which customers have bank accounts that they can access directly from their home computers, using the Internet, and can carry out operations such as checking on their account balances, paying invoices, and receiving their salaries electronically

online capture E-COMMERCE means of initiating payment after shipment a payment transaction generated after goods have been shipped, in which funds are transferred from the issuing bank to the acquiring bank and into the merchant account

online catalog E-COMMERCE consolidated catalog on Internet a business-to-business marketplace that collects the catalog data of every supplier in a specific industry and places it on one central Web resource. *Also called* ***procurement portal***

online community E-COMMERCE user network for Internet communication a means of allowing Web users to engage with one another and with an organization through use of interactive tools such as e-mail, discussion boards, and chat systems. They are a means by which a website owner can take the pulse of consumers to find out what they are thinking, and to generate unique content. As stand-alone businesses, online communities have been found to be weak; they work best when they are supporting the need for an organization to collect ongoing feedback.

online shopping E-COMMERCE = ***electronic shopping***

online trading MARKETS trading securities via Internet the process of buying and selling securities over the Internet

onshore FINANCE located in home country based in the home country, especially referring to a company that is registered in the country in which it conducts most of its business, or to funds or activities that are held or located in the home country. *See also* ***offshore***

on-target earnings FINANCE commission equaling amount aimed at the amount earned by somebody working on ***commission*** who has achieved the targets set. *Abbr* ***OTE***

OPEC INTERNATIONAL TRADE association of oil-producing countries an international organization of 11 countries, each one largely reliant on oil revenues as its main source of income, that tries to ensure there is a balance between supply and demand by adjusting the members' oil output. OPEC's headquarters are in Vienna. The current members, Algeria, Indonesia, Iran, Iraq, Kuwait, Libya, Nigeria, Qatar, Saudi Arabia, the United Arab Emirates, and Venezuela, meet at least twice a year to decide on output levels and discuss recent and anticipated oil market developments. *Full form* ***Organization of the Petroleum Exporting Countries***

open account FINANCE **1.** credit offered to buyer without requiring security a credit account offered by a supplier to a purchaser for which the supplier does not require security **2.** unpaid credit an account offered by a business to a customer that is as yet unpaid

open buying on the Internet E-COMMERCE protocol for Internet trading a standard built around a common set of business requirements for electronic communication between buyers and sellers that, when implemented, allows different e-commerce systems to talk to one another. *Abbr* ***OBI***. See also ***open trading protocol***

open check *US* BANKING blank signed check a signed check where the amount payable has not been indicated

open cheque *UK* BANKING uncrossed check a check that is not crossed and so may be cashed by the payee at the branch of the bank where it is drawn. *See also* ***crossed cheque***

open credit FINANCE credit offered without requiring security credit given by a supplier to a good customer without requiring security

open economy INTERNATIONAL TRADE economic system with unrestricted international trade an economy that places few restrictions on the movement of capital, labor, foreign trade, and payments into and out of the country

open-end credit *US* FINANCE arrangement allowing borrowing and repaying at will a credit facility that allows the borrower, within an overall credit limit and for a set period, to borrow or repay debt as required. *Also called* ***revolving credit***. *UK term* ***open-ended credit***

open-ended credit *UK* FINANCE = ***open-end credit***

open-ended fund *UK* STOCKHOLDING & INVESTMENTS = ***open-end fund***

open-ended investment company *UK* STOCKHOLDING & INVESTMENTS **1.** = ***open-end fund*** **2.** = ***open-end investment company***

open-ended management company *UK* STOCKHOLDING & INVESTMENTS = ***open-end management company***

open-ended mortgage *UK* MORTGAGES = ***open-end mortgage***

open-end fund *US* STOCKHOLDING & INVESTMENTS mutual fund with varying share numbers a mutual fund that has a variable number of shares. *UK term* ***open-ended fund***. *See also* ***closed-end fund***

  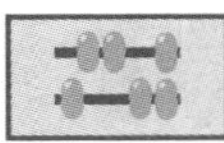      

open-end investment company *US* STOCKHOLDING & INVESTMENTS firm pooling funds for mutual funds a company with a variable number of shares that it sells to investors and pools for investment in mutual funds. *UK term* ***open-ended investment company***. *See also* ***open-end fund***

open-end management company *US* STOCKHOLDING & INVESTMENTS firm selling mutual funds a company that sells mutual funds. *UK term* ***open-ended management company***

open-end mortgage *US* MORTGAGES mortgage permitting prepayment a mortgage that can be paid off before the closing date originally agreed on. *UK term* ***open-ended mortgage***

opening balance ACCOUNTING amount at beginning of record the value of a financial quantity at the beginning of an accounting period

opening balance sheet ACCOUNTING record of opening balances a record giving details of an organization's financial balances at the beginning of an accounting period

opening bell MARKETS start of day's trading the beginning of a day of trading on a market

opening entry ACCOUNTING first record in account the first entry recorded in an account, for example, the first entry when starting a new business

opening price MARKETS price at start of day's trading the price for a security at the beginning of a day of trading on a market

opening purchase STOCKHOLDING & INVESTMENTS first in series of option purchases the first of a series of purchases to be made in options of a specific type for a specific commodity or security

opening stock *UK* ACCOUNTING = ***beginning inventory***

open interest STOCKHOLDING & INVESTMENTS total of options not yet closed the number of ***options*** contracts that have not yet been exercised, offset, or allowed to expire

open loop system GENERAL MANAGEMENT system with no facility for intervention a management control system that includes no provision for corrective action to be applied to the sequence of activities

open market MARKETS market with unlimited competition a market in which anyone is allowed to buy or sell and compete without restrictions

open market operation MARKETS government transaction in public market a transaction conducted by a central bank in a public market

open market value MARKETS potential price if available to all the price that an asset or security would realize if it was offered on a market open to all

open order MARKETS order remaining open until executed or canceled an order to buy or sell a security that is effective until it is executed or an investor cancels it. *See also* ***good 'til cancel***

open outcry MARKETS verbal exchanges to complete sale the method of making verbal bids and offers used by buyers and sellers on the ***trading floor*** of some exchanges such as the London Metal Exchange

open trading protocol E-COMMERCE e-commerce standard a standard designed to support Internet-based retail transactions, that allows different systems to communicate with each other for a variety of payment-related activities. The ***open buying on the Internet*** protocol is a competing standard. *Abbr* ***OTP***. See also ***open buying on the Internet***

operating budget ACCOUNTING plan for firm's income and expenses a forecast of income and expenses that result from the day-to-day activities of a company over a period of time

operating cash flow ACCOUNTING money used and generated in firm's operations the amount used to represent the money moving through a company as a result of its operations, as distinct from its purely financial transactions. *Abbr* ***OCF***

operating costing OPERATIONS & PRODUCTION way of costing output of continuous operation a costing system that is applied to continuous operations in mass production or in the service industries. In the simplest form of operating costing, the costing period is set at a specific length of time, usually a calendar month or four weeks. The costs incurred over the period are related to the number of units produced, and the division of the first by the second gives the average unit cost for the period.

operating costs *or* operating expenses ACCOUNTING expenses for firm's ordinary business activities the costs arising from the day-to-day activities of running a company. *Also called* ***running costs***

operating cycle OPERATIONS & PRODUCTION process between investment and income from product the cycle of business activity in which cash is used to buy resources that are converted into products or services and then sold for cash

operating environment OPERATIONS & PRODUCTION combination of external factors affecting business the combination of economic, social, and political factors that affect an organization's activities

operating income ACCOUNTING = ***EBIT***

operating lease GENERAL MANAGEMENT lease treated as rent in accounts a lease that is regarded by accountants as rental rather than as a ***capital lease***. The monthly lease payments are simply treated as rental expenses and recognized on the income statement as they are incurred. There is no recognition of a leased asset or liability.

operating leverage ACCOUNTING ratio of fixed to total costs the ratio of a business's fixed costs to its total costs. Fixed costs have to be paid regardless of output, the higher the ratio, the higher the risk of losses in an economic downturn.

operating loss ACCOUNTING firm's loss during ordinary business activities a loss incurred by a company during the course of its usual business

operating margin ACCOUNTING = ***profit margin***

operating profit ACCOUNTING standard income minus standard costs the difference between a company's revenues and any related costs and expenses, not including income or expenses from any sources other than its normal methods of providing a good or service

operating risk ACCOUNTING poor ratio of fixed to total costs the risk of a high ***operating leverage***, when each sale makes a significant contribution to fixed costs

operational audit GENERAL MANAGEMENT assessment of systems and procedures of organization a structured review of the systems and procedures of an organization in order to evaluate whether they are being conducted efficiently and effectively. An operational audit involves establishing performance ***objectives***, agreeing the standards and criteria for assessment, and evaluating actual performance against targeted performance. *Also called* ***management audit, operations audit***

operational costs ACCOUNTING costs of running business the costs incurred by a company during the course of its usual business

operational disciplines OPERATIONS & PRODUCTION activities supporting ongoing operation of business the activities and systems within an organization that ensure that the daily operations required to produce goods and services are running smoothly

operational gearing ACCOUNTING ratio of fixed to total costs the relationship between a company's fixed costs and its total costs. Fixed costs have to be paid before profit can be made, so high operational gearing increases a company's risk.

operational manager OPERATIONS & PRODUCTION manager of goods and services production the person in an organization who is in charge of the activities required to produce goods and services

operational research GENERAL MANAGEMENT analysis of managerial and administrative procedures the application of scientific methods to the solution of managerial and administrative problems, involving complex systems or processes. Operational research strives to find the optimum plan for the control and operation of a system or process. It was originally used during World War II as a means of solving logistical problems. It has since developed into a planning, scheduling, and ***problem solving*** technique applied across the industrial, commercial, and public sectors.

operational risk OPERATIONS & PRODUCTION, RISK risk of loss from internal or external failures the risk of economic loss that an organization faces, resulting from failed or inadequate controls, processes, or systems, or from human or external events

operations OPERATIONS & PRODUCTION production processes activities that are required to produce goods or services for consumers. *See also* ***operations management***

operations audit GENERAL MANAGEMENT = ***operational audit***

operations management OPERATIONS & PRODUCTION overseeing of production processes the maintenance, control, and improvement of organizational activities that are required to produce goods or services for consumers. Operations management has traditionally been associated with manufacturing activities but can also be applied to the service sector.

opinion leader MARKETING influencer of public opinion a high-profile person or organization that can significantly influence public opinion. An opinion leader can be a politician, a religious, business or community leader, a journalist, or an educator. Show business and sports personalities can exert a great deal of influence on young people's leisure lifestyles and buying habits and are consequently frequently used in advertising campaigns.

opinion leader research MARKETING inquiry into top people's views the investigation of the perceptions of ***corporate image*** and reputation

        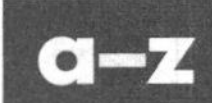

among the people at the top of a company, industry, or profession

opinion survey GENERAL MANAGEMENT set of questions to discover people's attitudes a survey conducted to determine what members of a population think about a specific topic

opportunity cost STOCKHOLDING & INVESTMENTS loss through choice of investment an amount of money lost as a result of choosing one investment rather than another

opportunity score MARKETING measure of salability of product before production a measure of the potential marketability of a product or service while it is still in the development stage

optimal portfolio STOCKHOLDING & INVESTMENTS best possible investments a theoretical set of investments that would be the most profitable for an investor

optimize GENERAL MANAGEMENT use resources in best way to allocate such things as resources or capital as efficiently as possible

optimum best best or most desirable out of a number of possible options or outcomes

optimum capacity OPERATIONS & PRODUCTION cheapest quantity to produce the level of output at which the minimum cost per unit is incurred

option **1.** STOCKHOLDING & INVESTMENTS contract for trading rights a contract for the right to buy or sell an asset, typically a commodity, under agreed terms. *Also called* ***option contract, stock option*** **2.** BUSINESS opportunity to buy or sell on agreed terms an agreement that somebody may buy or sell a specific asset on predetermined terms on or before a future date

option account STOCKHOLDING & INVESTMENTS account for buying and selling options an account that an investor holds with a broker and uses for trading in ***options***

optionaire STOCKHOLDING & INVESTMENTS millionaire in terms of stock options a millionaire whose wealth consists of or is derived from stock ***options*** (slang)

optional redemption provision STOCKHOLDING & INVESTMENTS bond early redemption clause the terms in a bond agreement that allow the issuer (usually) or the lender (less frequently) to redeem it before the final redemption date

option buyer STOCKHOLDING & INVESTMENTS buyer of option an investor who acquires an ***option*** to buy or sell a security, currency, or commodity

option class STOCKHOLDING & INVESTMENTS group of options of same type a set of ***options*** that are identical with respect to type and underlying asset

option contract STOCKHOLDING & INVESTMENTS = ***option***

option dealing MARKETS trading in stock options the activity of buying and selling stock ***options***

option elasticity STOCKHOLDING & INVESTMENTS relative changing values of option and underlying asset the relative change in the value of an ***option*** as a function of a change in the value of the underlying asset

option income fund STOCKHOLDING & INVESTMENTS mutual fund with options a mutual fund that derives income from investing in ***options***

option premium STOCKHOLDING & INVESTMENTS cost of each share in option the amount per share that a buyer pays for an ***option*** to buy or sell a security, currency, or commodity above the exercise price

option price STOCKHOLDING & INVESTMENTS price of option the price of an ***option*** to buy or sell a security, currency, or commodity

option pricing model STOCKHOLDING & INVESTMENTS means of establishing value of options a model that is used to determine the fair value of ***options***. *See also* ***Black-Scholes model***

options clearing corporation REGULATION & COMPLIANCE US organization overseeing trades in options in the United States, an organization responsible for the listing of ***options*** and clearing trades in them

option seller STOCKHOLDING & INVESTMENTS = ***option writer***

option series STOCKHOLDING & INVESTMENTS group of options representing same thing a collection of options that are identical in terms of class, ***exercise price***, and date of maturity

options market MARKETS **1.** trading options the trading in ***options*** to buy or sell securities, currencies, or commodities **2.** place for trading options a venue where traders engage in buying and selling ***options***

options on physicals STOCKHOLDING & INVESTMENTS options on physical assets a type of ***option*** that is on real assets rather than financial assets

option trading MARKETS trading in stock options the business of buying and selling stock ***options***

option writer STOCKHOLDING & INVESTMENTS seller of option a person, institution, or other organization that sells an ***option*** to buy or sell a security, currency, or commodity. *Also called* ***option seller***

OR *abbr* LEGAL ***official receiver***

order **1.** STOCKHOLDING & INVESTMENTS instruction to trade for investor's own account an occasion when a broker is told to buy or sell a financial product for an investor's own account **2.** OPERATIONS & PRODUCTION arrangement between customer and supplier a ***contract*** made between a customer and a supplier for the supply of a variety of goods or services in a determined quantity and quality, at an agreed price, and for delivery at or by a specific time

order book OPERATIONS & PRODUCTION record of orders waiting to be fulfilled a record of the outstanding orders that an organization has received. An order book may be physical, with the specifications and delivery times of orders recorded in it, or the term may be used generally to describe the health of a company. A full order book implies a successful company, while an empty order book can indicate an organization at risk of business failure.

order confirmation E-COMMERCE e-mail acknowledgment of order an e-mail message informing a purchaser that an order has been received

order-driven system *or* order-driven market MARKETS system where stock prices change according to orders on a stock exchange, a price system where prices vary according to the level of orders. *See also* ***quote-driven system***

order imbalance MARKETS backlog in trading of security a situation in which there are more orders to buy or sell a security than can be executed, sometimes resulting in a halt to trading until the situation is resolved

order picking OPERATIONS & PRODUCTION extraction of items requested selecting and withdrawing goods or components from a store or warehouse to meet production requirements or to satisfy customer orders

order point OPERATIONS & PRODUCTION amount triggering reordering the quantity of an item that is on hand when more units of the item are to be ordered

order processing OPERATIONS & PRODUCTION keeping track of orders the tracking of orders made with suppliers and received from customers

orders pending STOCKHOLDING & INVESTMENTS, OPERATIONS & PRODUCTION unfulfilled orders orders that have not yet resulted in transactions

ordinary interest FINANCE interest based on 360-day year interest calculated on the basis of a year having only 360 days

ordinary resolution CORPORATE GOVERNANCE general issue put to vote at annual meeting a resolution put before an annual meeting, usually referring to some general procedural matter, that requires a simple majority of votes to be accepted

ordinary share *UK* STOCKHOLDING & INVESTMENTS = ***common stock***

ordinary share capital *UK* MARKETS capital from sale of ordinary shares the capital of a company raised by selling common stock

organic growth BUSINESS = ***internal growth***

organigram GENERAL MANAGEMENT = ***organization chart***

Organisation for Economic Co-operation and Development INTERNATIONAL TRADE *see* ***OECD***

organization GENERAL MANAGEMENT collection of people and resources with specific purpose an arrangement of people and resources working in a planned manner toward specific strategic goals. An organization can be any structured body such as a business, company, or firm in the private or public sector, or in a nonprofit association.

organization chart GENERAL MANAGEMENT diagram of organization's structure a graphic illustration of an organization's structure, showing hierarchical authority and relationships between departments and jobs. The horizontal dimension of an organization chart shows the nature of job function and responsibility and the vertical dimension shows how jobs are coordinated in reporting or authority relationships. *Also called* ***organigram, org chart***

Organization of the Petroleum Exporting Countries INTERNATIONAL TRADE *see* ***OPEC***

org chart GENERAL MANAGEMENT = ***organization chart***

orientation *US* HR & PERSONNEL formal introduction to new job a process through which a new employee is integrated into an organization, learning about its ***corporate culture***, policies and procedures, and the specific practicalities of his or her job. An orientation program should not consist of a one-day introduction, but should be planned and paced over a few days or weeks. There is a growing use of boot camps, which work to assimilate a new employee rapidly into the culture of the employing organization. *UK term* ***induction***

  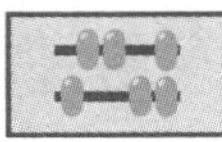      

original cost ACCOUNTING total cost of asset the total cost of acquiring an asset

original equipment manufacturer OPERATIONS & PRODUCTION firm making product from bought-in parts a company that assembles components from other suppliers to produce a complete product. *Abbr* ***OEM***

original face value MORTGAGES amount originally borrowed the amount of the principal of a mortgage on the day it is created

original issue discount STOCKHOLDING & INVESTMENTS discount at bond's first sale the discount offered on the day of sale of a debt instrument

original maturity STOCKHOLDING & INVESTMENTS date for payment of bond a date on which a ***debt instrument*** is due to mature

origination fee MORTGAGES charge for providing mortgage a fee charged by a lender for providing a mortgage, usually expressed as a percentage of the principal

orthogonal STATISTICS statistically unrelated statistically independent

OTC *abbr* FINANCE ***over-the-counter***

OTCBB *abbr* MARKETS ***OTC Bulletin Board***

OTC Bulletin Board MARKETS electronic system for quoting unlisted securities an electronic real-time quoting system for unlisted securities that are traded in the ***over-the-counter market*** but not traded on the ***NASDAQ***. *Abbr* ***OTCBB***

OTC market *abbr* MARKETS ***over-the-counter market***

OTE *abbr* FINANCE ***on-target earnings***

other capital ACCOUNTING uncategorized capital capital that is not listed in specific categories

other current assets ACCOUNTING non-cash assets maturing within year assets that are not cash and are due to mature within a year

other long-term capital ACCOUNTING uncategorized long-term assets long-term capital that is not listed in specific categories in accounts

other long-term liabilities FINANCE obligations with no interest charge in next year obligations such as deferred taxes and employee benefits with terms greater than one year and on which there is no charge for interest in the next year

other prices FINANCE unlisted prices prices that are not listed in a catalog

other short-term capital ACCOUNTING uncategorized short-term assets a residual category in the balance of payments that includes financial assets of less than one year such as currency, deposits, and bills

OTP *abbr* E-COMMERCE ***open trading protocol***

OTS *abbr* REGULATION & COMPLIANCE ***Office of Thrift Supervision***

outgoings *UK* ACCOUNTING = ***costs***

outlay ACCOUNTING money spent for specific purpose money spent on something such as capital assets or operating costs

outlier STATISTICS statistic that is very different from others a statistical observation that deviates significantly from other members of a sample

out-of-pocket expenses ACCOUNTING amount of employee's own money spent on business an amount of an employee's personal money that he or she has spent on company business, especially when considered for reimbursement

out of the money STOCKHOLDING & INVESTMENTS having no intrinsic value used to describe an ***option*** that, if it expired at the current market price, would have no intrinsic value. *See also* ***in the money***

outperform MARKETS do better than other companies to achieve better results in the stock market than other similar companies

output OPERATIONS & PRODUCTION goods produced anything that a company produces, usually referring to physical products but also to services

output gap ECONOMICS difference between economy's production capacity and actual production the difference between the amount of activity that is sustainable in an economy and the amount of activity actually taking place

output method ACCOUNTING accounting technique categorizing costs by output purpose an accounting system that classifies costs according to the outputs for which they are incurred, not the inputs they have bought

output per hour OPERATIONS & PRODUCTION how much is produced each hour the amount of something produced in one hour, especially the amount of a company's product or service

output tax TAX tax due from trader in Australia and New Zealand, the amount of Goods and Services Tax paid to the tax office after the deduction of ***input tax credits***

outside director CORPORATE GOVERNANCE director not employed by firm a member of a company's ***board of directors*** neither currently nor formerly in the company's employment. An outside director is sometimes described as being synonymous with a ***nonexecutive director***, and as usually being employed by a holding or associated company. In the United States, an outside director is somebody who has no relationships at all to a company. In US public companies, compensation and audit committees are generally made up of outside directors, and use of outside directors to select board directors is becoming more common.

outsourcing GENERAL MANAGEMENT **1.** switching from in-house personnel to outside supplier the transfer of the provision of services previously performed by in-house personnel to an external organization, usually under a ***contract*** with agreed standards, costs, and conditions. Areas traditionally outsourced include legal services, transport, catering, and security. An increasing variety of activities, including IT services, training, and public relations are now being outsourced. Outsourcing, or ***contracting out***, is often introduced with the goal of increasing efficiency and reducing costs, or to enable the organization to develop greater flexibility or to concentrate on core business activities. The term ***subcontracting*** is sometimes used to refer to outsourcing. **2.** obtaining goods or services from outside suppliers the use of external suppliers as a source of finished products, components, or services

outstanding check ACCOUNTING check issued but not cashed a check which has been written and therefore has been entered in the company's ledgers, but which has not been presented for payment and so has not been debited from the company's bank account

outstanding share STOCKHOLDING & INVESTMENTS share allotted to applicant a share that a company has issued and somebody has bought

outstanding share capital STOCKHOLDING & INVESTMENTS value of stock available to trade the value of all of the stock of a company minus the value of retained shares

outwork GENERAL MANAGEMENT in UK, work done away from premises in the United Kingdom, work performed for a company away from its premises

outworker HR & PERSONNEL in UK, person working away from premises in the United Kingdom, a subcontractor or employee carrying out work for a company away from its premises

overall capitalization rate FINANCE income minus most costs divided by value ***net operating income*** other than debt service divided by value

overall market capacity ECONOMICS amount of product that market can absorb the amount of a service or good that can be absorbed in a market without affecting the price

overall rate of return *or* overall return STOCKHOLDING & INVESTMENTS return relative to investment the aggregate of all the dividends received over an investment's life together with its capital gain or loss at the date of its realization, calculated either before or after tax. It is one of the ways an investor can look at the performance of an investment.

overbid FINANCE **1.** bid too much to bid more than necessary to make a successful purchase **2.** too high a bid an amount that is offered that is unnecessarily high for a successful purchase to be made

overborrowed FINANCE having too much debt in comparison to assets used to describe a company that has very high borrowings compared to its assets, and has difficulty in meeting its interest payments

overbought MARKETS inflated by too many buyers used to describe a market or security considered to have risen too rapidly as a result of excessive buying

overbought market MARKETS market with overinflated prices a market where prices have risen beyond levels that can be supported by fundamental analysis. The market for Internet companies in 2001 was overbought and subsequently collapsed when it became clear that their trading performance could not support such price levels.

overcapacity OPERATIONS & PRODUCTION more capacity than needed an excess of capability to produce goods or provide a service over the level of demand

overcapitalized FINANCE having surplus capital used to describe a business that has more capital than can profitably be employed. An overcapitalized company could buy back some of its own stock in the market; if it has significant debt capital it could repurchase its bonds in the market; or it could make a large one-time dividend to stockholders.

overdraft BANKING **1.** deficit in bank account the amount by which the money withdrawn from a bank account exceeds the balance in the account. *Abbr* ***O/D*** **2.** = ***overdraft facility***

overdraft facility BANKING agreement for deficit in bank account a credit arrangement with a bank, allowing a person or company with an account to

        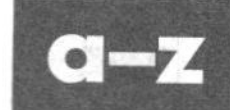

use borrowed money up to an agreed limit when nothing is left in the account

overdraft line BANKING agreed amount of overdraft an amount in excess of the balance in an account that a bank agrees to pay in honoring checks on the account

overdraft protection BANKING guarantee of payment from overdrawn account a bank service, amounting to a ***line of credit***, that assures that the bank will honor overdrafts, up to a limit and for a fee

overdraw BANKING create deficit in bank account to withdraw more money from a bank account than it contains or than was agreed could be withdrawn

overdrawn BANKING having deficit in bank account in debt to a bank because the amount withdrawn from an account exceeds its balance

overdue FINANCE still owing still to be paid after the date due

overfunding ECONOMICS when UK government sells more stock than necessary in the United Kingdom, a situation in which the government borrows more money than it needs for expenditure, as a result of selling too much government stock

overgeared FINANCE with greater financial commitments than common stock capital describing a company with debt capital and preferred stock that outweigh its **common stock capital**

overhang MARKETS **1.** large remaining block of one investment, depressing price a large quantity of shares of unsold stock or of a commodity available for sale, which has the effect of depressing the market price **2.** to depress market prices to put downward pressure on stock or commodity prices

overhead *US* ACCOUNTING = ***overhead costs***

overhead absorption rate ACCOUNTING proportion of overhead attributed to product or service a means of attributing overhead to a product or service, based for example on direct labor hours, direct labor cost, or machine hours (the number of hours for which a machine is in production). The choice of overhead absorption base may be made with the objective of obtaining "accurate" product costs, or of influencing managerial behavior; for example, overhead applied to labor hours or part numbers appears to make the use of these resources more costly, thus discouraging their use.

overhead capacity variance ACCOUNTING gap between budgeted and required overhead the difference between the overhead absorbed, based on budgeted hours, and actual hours worked

overhead costs ACCOUNTING costs incurred in upkeep or running the indirect costs of the day-to-day running of a business, i.e. not money spent on producing goods, but money spent on such things as renting or maintaining buildings and machinery. *Also called* ***overhead, overheads***

overhead expenditure variance ACCOUNTING misjudgment of indirect costs the difference between the budgeted ***overhead costs*** and the actual expenditure

overheads *UK* ACCOUNTING = ***overhead costs***

overindebtedness FINANCE unsustainable debt the situation in which borrowers, including individuals, companies and countries, have borrowed more money than they are able to pay back

overinsuring INSURANCE obtaining excessive insurance cover insuring an asset for a sum in excess of its market or replacement value. It is unlikely that an insurance company will pay out more in a claim for loss than the asset is worth or than the cost of replacing it.

overinvested **1.** STOCKHOLDING & INVESTMENTS with too much invested having a higher than desired amount invested in a security, or having a higher amount committed to tracking an index or matching a model portfolio than the index or model suggests **2.** BUSINESS with investment predicated on higher demand used to describe a business that invests heavily during an economic boom only to find that when it starts to produce an income, the demand for the product or service has fallen

overlap profit ACCOUNTING profit assignable to two accounting periods profit that arises in two overlapping accounting periods and on which tax relief can be claimed

overnight position MARKETS trader's commitments at end of trading day a trader's holdings in a security or option at the end of a trading day

overnight rate MARKETS, RISK interest rate on interbank overnight loans the interest rate charged by financial institutions on overnight loans to each other

overnight repo BANKING arrangement for temporary sale for cash a repurchase agreement where banks sell securities for cash and repurchase them the next day at a higher price. This type of agreement is used by central banks as a means of regulating the ***money markets***.

overpayment **1.** FINANCE paying too much an act of paying more than is required or reasonable, or the sum paid in such a situation **2.** *UK* ACCOUNTING = ***additional principal payment***

overprice MARKETING charge too high price for something to set the price of a product or service too high, with the result that it is unacceptable to the market

overrated FINANCE with value set too high used to describe something that is valued more highly than it should be

overriding commission *or* override *or* overrider FINANCE further additional commission a special extra commission which is above all other commissions

overseas company BUSINESS part of firm incorporated abroad a branch or subsidiary of a business that is incorporated in another country

overseas funds FINANCE investment products in foreign countries investment funds that are based in other countries and are not subject to regulation in the home country

Overseas Investment Commission REGULATION & COMPLIANCE New Zealand organization overseeing investment from abroad in New Zealand, an independent body reporting to the government that regulates foreign investment. It was established in 1973 and is funded by the Reserve Bank of New Zealand.

oversold MARKETS depressed by too many sellers used to describe a market or security that is considered to have fallen too rapidly as a result of excessive selling. *See also* ***bear market***

overspend ACCOUNTING **1.** spend more than planned to spend more money than was budgeted or planned or than can be afforded **2.** excess amount spent an amount that is more than was budgeted for spending

overstocked OPERATIONS & PRODUCTION having surplus inventory used to describe a business that has more inventory than it needs

oversubscription MARKETS when investors want more stock than are available a situation in which investors are interested in buying more shares of stock in a new issue than are being made available

over-the-counter FINANCE of trading between dealers used to describe the trade of securities directly between licensed dealers, rather than through an auction system. *Abbr* ***OTC***

over-the-counter market MARKETS market conducted directly between dealers a market in which trading takes place directly between licensed dealers, rather than through an auction system as used in most organized exchanges. *Abbr* ***OTC market***

over-the-counter security STOCKHOLDING & INVESTMENTS security traded directly between dealers a security that is traded directly between licensed dealers on the ***over-the-counter market***

overtrading OPERATIONS & PRODUCTION when firm increases sales and production too rapidly a situation in which a company increases sales and production too much and too quickly, so that it runs short of cash

overvalue FINANCE, GENERAL MANAGEMENT give something too high a value to give a higher value to something or somebody than is justified

own brand *UK* MARKETING = ***private label***

owner **1.** LEGAL possessor of legal title to something a person or organization that has legal title to products or services **2.** BUSINESS person having own firm the person who has legal control of a private company

owner-occupier REAL ESTATE somebody who owns home a person who owns the property in which he or she lives

owner-operator BUSINESS = ***sole proprietor***

owner's equity ACCOUNTING total assets minus total liabilities a business's total assets less its total liabilities, being the funds provided by the owners. *See also* ***capital, common stock***

ownership of companies BUSINESS holding of stock in firms the possession of stock in companies. Company ownership structures can differ widely. Owners of public companies may be institutions, or individuals, or a mixture of both. Directors are often offered company stock as incentives and more participative companies may offer stock to employees through ***employee ownership*** plans. Private companies are usually owned by individuals, families, or groups of individual stockholders. Nationalized industries are publicly owned. Cooperatives are wholly owned by employees. A separation between the ownership and control of companies became a widely discussed issue during the 20th century, especially in the United States and the United Kingdom where stockholders have tended to be more passive. Managers were viewed as having come to occupy controlling positions as the scale of industry grew. From the 1980s, this position changed to some extent as ***privatization***, ***management buyouts***, restructuring, and ***stock incentive plans*** led to greater stock ownership among managers and produced less passive stockholders.

own label *UK* MARKETING = ***private label***

  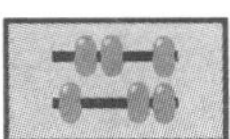   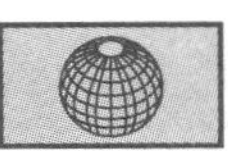   

P

paced line OPERATIONS & PRODUCTION production line moving at steady speed a production line that moves at a constant speed

package and sell STOCKHOLDING & INVESTMENTS sell combined loans to combine a number of loans and sell them to investors as ***mortgage-backed securities***

package deal GENERAL MANAGEMENT agreement including several aspects simultaneously an agreement that covers several different things at the same time

packaging MARKETS combining securities for trade the practice of combining different securities in a single trade

Pac Man defense MERGERS & ACQUISITIONS offer to purchase buyer to avoid firm's takeover a strategy by a company seeking to avoid a hostile takeover, in which the target company makes an offer to purchase the prospective buyer

paid-in capital STOCKHOLDING & INVESTMENTS firm's capital received from investors for stock capital in a business that has been provided by its stockholders

paid up FINANCE fully paid having paid all the money owed

paid-up capital *or* paid-up share capital STOCKHOLDING & INVESTMENTS stock issued and paid for an amount of money paid for the issued capital shares of stock, which does not include ***called-up share capital***. *See also* ***fully paid share capital, partly paid capital***

paid-up policy INSURANCE **1.** policy providing life insurance after policyholder stops paying in the United Kingdom, an ***endowment insurance*** policy that continues to provide life insurance while the cost of the premiums is covered by the underlying fund after the policyholder has decided not to continue paying premiums. If the fund is sufficient to pay the premiums for the remainder of the term, the remaining funds will be paid to the policyholder at maturity. **2.** insurance policy with premiums paid in the United States, an insurance policy on which all the premiums have been paid

paid-up share STOCKHOLDING & INVESTMENTS stock paid for in full a stock for which stockholders have paid the full contractual amount. *See also* ***call, called-up share capital, paid-up capital, share capital***

painting the tape MARKETS illegal splitting of orders into smaller units an illegal practice in which traders break large orders into smaller units in order to give the illusion of heavy buying activity. This encourages investors to buy, and the traders then sell as the price of the stock goes up. (slang)

panda CURRENCY & EXCHANGE Chinese gold or silver collector coin one of a series of Chinese gold and silver bullion collector coins, each featuring a panda, that were first issued in 1982. Struck with a highly polished surface, the smallest gold coin weighs 0.05 ounces, the largest 12 ounces.

P&L *abbr* ACCOUNTING ***profit and loss***

Panel on Takeovers and Mergers MERGERS & ACQUISITIONS UK group overseeing fairness in takeovers in the United Kingdom, the group that issues the ***City Code on Takeovers and Mergers***, a code designed principally to ensure fair and equal treatment of all stockholders in relation to takeovers. *See also* ***City Code on Takeovers and Mergers***

panel study MARKETING study of small group's opinions over time a study that surveys a selected group of people over a period of time

panic buying FINANCE exceptional buying because of fear of shortages an unusual level of buying caused by fear or rumors of product shortages or by severe price rises

panic dumping CURRENCY & EXCHANGE selling currency because of devaluation fears a rush to sell a currency at any price because of fears of a possible devaluation

paper 1. FINANCE record of holdings a certificate of deposits and other securities **2.** STOCKHOLDING & INVESTMENTS issue of stock or bonds to raise capital a rights issue or an issue of bonds launched by a company to raise additional capital **3.** FINANCE all debt issued by firm all funding instruments issued by a company, other than ***equity***

paper company BUSINESS firm without physical presence a company that only exists on paper and has no ***physical assets***

paper gain STOCKHOLDING & INVESTMENTS = ***paper profit***

paper loss STOCKHOLDING & INVESTMENTS drop in value of unsold investment a loss made when an asset has fallen in value but has not been sold. *Also called* ***unrealized loss***

paper millionaire STOCKHOLDING & INVESTMENTS person owning stock valued currently at one million an individual who owns stock that is worth in excess of a million in currency at a specific date, but which may fall in value. In 2001 many of the founders of dot-com companies were paper millionaires. *See also* ***paper profit***

paper money 1. CURRENCY & EXCHANGE bills currency that is not coins **2.** BANKING checks payments in paper form such as checks

paper offer MERGERS & ACQUISITIONS takeover bid with stock rather than cash a takeover bid in which the purchasing company offers its stock in exchange for stock in the company being taken over, as opposed to a cash offer

paper profit ACCOUNTING increase in value on investment not yet sold an increase in the value of an investment that the investor has no immediate intention of realizing

PAR *abbr* BANKING ***prime assets ratio***

paradigm shift GENERAL MANAGEMENT fundamental change a basic change in an accepted pattern of thought or behavior

paradox of saving *or* paradox of thrift ECONOMICS cutbacks in expenditure lead to increased expenditure elsewhere the observation that savings made by individuals in their consumption lead to a drop in overall demand which in turn leads to increased spending by a business or government

parafiscal tax TAX tax levied for specific purpose a tax on a specific product or service by which a government raises money for a specific purpose. The money raised is usually paid to a body other than the national tax authority.

parallel economy ECONOMICS = ***black economy***

parallel engineering OPERATIONS & PRODUCTION = ***concurrent engineering***

parallel loan FINANCE = ***back-to-back loan***

parallel pricing OPERATIONS & PRODUCTION competitors' changing of prices together the practice of varying prices in a similar way and at the same time as competitors

paralysis by analysis GENERAL MANAGEMENT substitution of background work for decision making the inability of managers to make decisions as a result of a preoccupation with attending meetings, writing reports, and collecting statistics and analyses. Paralysis of effective ***decision making*** in organizations can occur in situations where there is horizontal conflict, disagreement between different hierarchical levels, or unclear objectives.

parameter STATISTICS quantity relating to entire statistical set a quantity that is numerically characteristic of a whole model or population

parameter design STATISTICS method of limiting variability a process aimed at reducing variation in processes or products

parcel STOCKHOLDING & INVESTMENTS set of securities sold together a group of related securities that are sold at one time

parcel of shares *UK* STOCKHOLDING & INVESTMENTS = ***basket of shares***

parent company BUSINESS firm with subsidiaries a main company in a group that also has one or more subsidiary undertakings

Pareto's Law ECONOMICS idea that income will be distributed similarly everywhere a theory of income distribution that states that regardless of political or taxation conditions, income will be distributed in the same way across all countries

pari passu GENERAL MANAGEMENT ranking equally a Latin phrase that means being of equal rank

Paris Bourse MARKETS, STOCKHOLDING & INVESTMENTS = ***Euronext Paris***

Paris Club FINANCE = ***G10***

Paris Interbank Offered Rate BANKING bank releasing money against check the French equivalent of the ***London Interbank Offered Rate***. *Abbr* ***PIBOR***

Paris Stock Exchange MARKETS, STOCKHOLDING & INVESTMENTS = ***Euronext Paris***

parity MARKETS price equivalence in different markets a situation when the price of a commodity, foreign currency, or security is the same in different markets. *See also* ***arbitrage***

parity bit E-COMMERCE digit used as check an odd or even digit used to check binary computer data for errors

parity value STOCKHOLDING & INVESTMENTS = ***conversion value***

park STOCKHOLDING & INVESTMENTS (slang) **1.** illegally disguise ownership of stock to place owned stock with third parties to disguise their ownership, usually illegally **2.** invest money safely for short time to put money into safe investments while deciding where to invest it in the longer term

parking STOCKHOLDING & INVESTMENTS (slang) **1.** illegal transfer of stock to nominee the transfer of stock in a company to a third party such as a nominee or the name of an associate, often illegally **2.** temporarily keeping money in safe investments the practice of putting money into safe investments while deciding where to invest it in the longer term

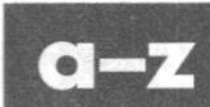

Parkinson's Law HR & PERSONNEL work expands to fill time available the facetious assertion that work will expand to fill the time available

Parquet MARKETS Paris stock exchange historical name for the ***Euronext Paris*** stock exchange, the name originating from the special raised floor traders operated on (slang)

part exchange *UK* FINANCE = ***trade-in***

participating bond STOCKHOLDING & INVESTMENTS bond yielding dividends and interest a bond that pays the holder dividends as well as interest

participating insurance INSURANCE insurance offering dividends a form of insurance in which policyholders receive a dividend from the insurer's profits

participating preference share *UK* STOCKHOLDING & INVESTMENTS = ***participating preferred stock***

participating preferred stock *US* STOCKHOLDING & INVESTMENTS stock yielding dividend and share of surplus profit a type of ***preferred stock*** that entitles the holder to a fixed dividend and, in addition, to the right to participate in any surplus profits after payment of agreed levels of dividends to holders of ***common stock*** has been made. *See also* ***nonparticipating preferred stock***. *UK term* ***participating preference share***

participative budgeting TREASURY MANAGEMENT system allowing budget holders to draft own budgets a budgeting system in which all budget holders are given the opportunity to participate in setting their own budgets. *Also called* ***bottom-up budgeting***

partly paid capital *or* partly paid share capital STOCKHOLDING & INVESTMENTS capital not paid in full capital composed of shares for which the stockholders have not paid the full value at once, but have paid in installments. *See also* ***fully paid share capital, paid-up capital***

partly paid share STOCKHOLDING & INVESTMENTS stock not paid in full a stock for which stockholders have not paid the full value at once, but have paid in installments. *See also* ***call, partly paid capital***

partner BUSINESS member of business partnership a person who works in a business partnership and shares with one or more other people in the profits or losses of the business

partnership BUSINESS legal relationship between business partners the relationship which exists between persons carrying on business in common with a view to profit. In the United Kingdom, this is regulated by the Partnership Act of 1890, and the liability of the individual partners is unlimited unless provided for by the partnership agreement. The Limited Partnership Act of 1907 allows a partnership to contain one or more partners with limited liability so long as there is at least one partner with unlimited liability. A partnership consists of not more than 20 persons.

partnership accounts **1.** BANKING accounts of business partners the capital and checking accounts of each partner in a partnership **2.** ACCOUNTING record of financial activities accounts that record the business activities of each partner in a partnership

partnership agreement LEGAL legal basis for partnership the document that establishes a partnership, detailing the capital contributed by each partner; whether an individual partner's liability is limited; the apportionment of the profit; salaries; and possibly procedures to be followed, for example, in the event of a partner retiring or a new partner joining. *Also called* ***articles of partnership***

part-owner BUSINESS somebody owning something jointly with others a person who owns something jointly with one or more other people

part-ownership BUSINESS shared ownership of business or property a situation in which two or more people share in the ownership of a business or property

part payment FINANCE amount paid to cover part of debt a partial payment that leaves a balance to pay at some future time

part time HR & PERSONNEL some of standard working hours a proportion of the standard working hours expected in an organization. *See also* ***full time***

part-time director CORPORATE GOVERNANCE = ***nonexecutive director***

party LEGAL somebody involved in legal dispute or agreement a person or organization involved in a legal dispute or legal agreement

par value STOCKHOLDING & INVESTMENTS = ***nominal value***

passbook BANKING = ***bank book***

passing off FRAUD intentionally making one product appear to be another a form of fraud in which a company tries to sell its own product by deceiving buyers into thinking it is another product

passive investment management STOCKHOLDING & INVESTMENTS managing investment portfolio by automatic adjustments the managing of a ***mutual fund*** or other investment portfolio by relying on automatic adjustments such as tracking an index instead of making personal judgments. *See also* ***active fund management***

passive portfolio strategy STOCKHOLDING & INVESTMENTS relying on automatic adjustments to manage investments a plan for managing an investment portfolio that relies on automatic adjustments such as tracking an index

passportable BUSINESS describing financial activities permitted in another European state used to describe activities set out in the relevant EU directives for banking, insurance, insurance mediation, management, and investment services that permit a company registered in the European Economic Area to carry on business in another EEA state

passporting BUSINESS doing business in another European state the exercise by a company registered in the European Economic Area of a right to carry on business in another EEA state

passport in/out BUSINESS do business in another European state to exercise the right to carry on business in another state of the European Economic Area

pass-through security STOCKHOLDING & INVESTMENTS security made up of pool of securities a security that represents an interest in a pool of securities, most commonly ***mortgage-backed securities***, in which the earnings are passed through to investors

patent LEGAL government licence giving sole right to something a type of ***copyright*** granted as a fixed-term monopoly to an inventor by a government to prevent others copying an invention or improvement to a product or process.

The granting of a patent requires the publication of full details of the invention or improvement. The use of the patented information is restricted to the patent holder or any organizations licensed by them.

A patent's value is usually the sum of its development costs, or its purchase price if acquired from someone else. It is generally to a company's advantage to spread the patent's value over several years. If this is the case, the critical time period to consider is not the full life of the patent (17 years in the United States), but its estimated useful life.

For example, in January 2000 a company acquired a patent issued in January 1995 at a cost of $100,000. It concludes that the patent's useful commercial life is ten years, not the 12 remaining before the patent expires. In turn, patent value would be $100,000, and it would be spread (or amortized in accounting terms) over 10 years, or $10,000 each year.

patent attorney LEGAL specialist in law of patents a lawyer who specializes in patents

path analysis STATISTICS method of showing relationships between statistical variables in a statistical study, a method for showing the correlation between variables

pathfinder prospectus *UK* STOCKHOLDING & INVESTMENTS preliminary prospectus to test market a preliminary prospectus used in initial public offerings to gauge the reaction of investors. *US term* ***red eye***

pawnbroker FINANCE person lending money against personal items a person who lends money against the security of a wide variety of chattels, from jewelry to cars. The borrower may recover the goods by repaying the loan and interest by a specific date. Otherwise, the items pawned are sold and any surplus after the deduction of expenses, the loan, and interest is returned to the borrower.

pay FINANCE money paid for work done a sum of money given in return for work done or services provided. Pay, in the form of salary or wages, is generally provided in weekly or monthly fixed amounts, and is usually expressed in terms of the total sum earned per year. It may also be allocated using a ***piece rate*** system, where employees are paid for each unit of work they perform.

payables ledger *US* ACCOUNTING record of accounts to be paid a ledger in which a company records its ***accounts payable***. *UK term* ***purchase ledger***

payable to order FINANCE indicating that payee may be changed the statement on a bill of exchange or check, used to indicate that the payee is able to endorse it to a third party

Pay As You Earn TAX in UK, payment of employees' taxes through employer in the United Kingdom, a system for collecting direct taxes that requires employers to deduct taxes from employees' pay before payment is made. *Abbr* ***PAYE***

pay-as-you-go PENSIONS financing of current pensions by current employees in Canada, a means of financing a pension system whereby benefits of current retirees are financed by current workers

Pay-As-You-Go TAX Australian payment system for business and investment taxes in Australia, a system used for paying income tax installments on business and investment income. PAYG is part of the new tax system introduced by the Australian government on July 1, 2000. *Abbr* ***PAYG***

payback FINANCE **1.** repayment of borrowed money the act of paying back money that has been borrowed **2.** time taken for investment project to break even the time required for the cash revenues from a capital investment project to equal the cost

payback clause LEGAL rules in contract about loan repayment a clause in a contract that states the terms which govern the repayment of a loan

payback period ACCOUNTING time needed to recover project investment costs the length of time it will take to earn back the money invested in a project.

The straight payback period method is the simplest way of determining the investment potential of a major project. Expressed in time, it tells a management how many months or years it will take to recover the original cash cost of the project. It is calculated using the formula:

$$\frac{\text{Cost of project}}{\text{Annual cash revenues}} = \text{Payback period}$$

Thus, if a project cost $100,000 and was expected to generate $28,000 annually, the payback period would be:

$$\frac{100,000}{28,000} = 3.57 \text{ years}$$

If the revenues generated by the project are expected to vary from year to year, add the revenues expected for each succeeding year until you arrive at the total cost of the project.

For example, say the revenues expected to be generated by the $100,000 project are:

Revenue	Total	Cum. total
Year 1	$19,000	$19,000
Year 2	$25,000	$44,000
Year 3	$30,000	$74,000
Year 4	$30,000	$104,000
Year 5	$30,000	$134,000

Thus, the project would be fully paid for in Year 4, since it is in that year the total revenue reaches the initial cost of $100,000. The precise payback period would be calculated as:

$$\frac{((100,000 - 74,000)}{(1000,000 - 74,000))} \times 365 = 316 \text{ days} + 3 \text{ years}$$

The picture becomes complex when the time-value-of-money principle is introduced into the calculations. Some experts insist this is essential to determine the most accurate payback period. Accordingly, the annual revenues have to be discounted by the applicable interest rate, 10% in this example. Doing so produces significantly different results:

Revenue	Present value	Total	Cum. total
Year 1	$19,000	$17,271	$17,271
Year 2	$25,000	$20,650	$37,921
Year 3	$30,000	$22,530	$60,451
Year 4	$30,000	$20,490	$80,941
Year 5	$30,000	$18,630	$99,571

This method shows that payback would not occur even after five years.

Generally, a payback period of three years or less is desirable; if a project's payback period is less than a year, some contend it should be judged essential.

pay down FINANCE reduce loan amount through payments to reduce the amount of the ***principal*** on a loan by making payments

paydown FINANCE partial repayment of loan a repayment of part of a sum which has been borrowed

PAYE *abbr* TAX ***Pay As You Earn***

payee **1.** FINANCE person being paid the person or organization to whom a payment has to be made **2.** BANKING person to whom check is payable the person or organization to whom a check is specified as payable. *Also called* ***drawee***

payer BANKING person paying the person or organization making a payment

PAYG *abbr* TAX ***Pay-As-You-Go***

paying agent FINANCE institution paying interest or repaying capital the institution responsible for making interest payments on a security and repaying capital at redemption. *Also called* ***disbursing agent***

paying banker *UK* BANKING bank releasing money against check the bank on which a bill of exchange or check is drawn

paying-in book *UK* BANKING book of slips for listing bank deposits a book of detachable slips that accompany money or checks being paid into a bank account

paying-in slip *UK* BANKING = ***deposit slip***

payload OPERATIONS & PRODUCTION cargo capacity the amount of cargo that a form of transport can carry

paymaster FINANCE person issuing pay the person responsible for paying an organization's employees or the members of a country's armed services

payment FINANCE **1.** giving of money for goods or services the act of giving an amount of money in exchange for goods or services **2.** money paid for goods or services an amount of money paid in exchange for goods or services

payment by results FINANCE making pay dependent on work output a system of pay that directly links an employee's salary to his or her work output

payment gateway E-COMMERCE intermediary in card payment system a company or organization that provides an interface between a merchant's point-of-sale system, ***acquirer*** payment systems, and ***issuer*** payment systems. *Abbr* ***GW***

payment in advance FINANCE payment made before goods are delivered a payment made for goods when they are ordered and before they are delivered. *See also* ***prepayment***

payment in due course FINANCE payment on fixed future date the payment of a bill of exchange on a fixed date in the future

payment in kind FINANCE something of equivalent value instead of money an alternative form of pay given to employees in place of monetary reward but considered to be of equivalent value. A payment in kind may take the form of use of a car, purchase of goods at cost price, or other nonfinancial exchange that benefits the employee. It forms part of the total pay package rather than being an extra benefit. *See also* ***PIK note***

payment-in-kind note FINANCE *see* ***PIK note***

payment-in-lieu FINANCE money as substitute payment that is given in place of an entitlement

payment terms OPERATIONS & PRODUCTION firm's conditions for reimbursement for goods and services the stipulation by a business as to when it should be paid for goods or services supplied, for example, cash with order, payment on delivery, or within a particular number of days of the invoice date

payoff FINANCE **1.** final repayment a final payment for something that is owed, for example, the outstanding balance of principal and interest on a mortgage or loan **2.** profit or reward of some sort a profit or reward, for example, from a plan or project that is financially successful

payout FINANCE **1.** money given to somebody in difficulties money that is given to help a company or person experiencing difficulties **2.** amount paid a particular sum of money offered, for example, in compensation, or from an insurance policy

payout ratio STOCKHOLDING & INVESTMENTS amount of firm's earnings paid as dividends an expression of the total dividends paid to stockholders as a percentage of a company's net profit in a specific period of time. This measures the likelihood of dividend payments being sustained, and is a useful indication of sustained profitability. The lower the ratio, the more secure the dividend, and the company's future.

The payout ratio is calculated by dividing annual dividends paid on common stock by earnings per share:

$$\frac{\text{Annual dividend}}{\text{Earnings per share}} = \text{Payout ratio}$$

Take the company whose earnings per share are $8 and its dividend payout is 2.1. Its payout ratio would be:

$$\frac{2.1}{8} = 0.263 \text{ or } 26.3\%$$

A high payout ratio clearly appeals to conservative investors seeking income. When coupled with weak or falling earnings, however, it could suggest an imminent dividend cut, or that the company is short-changing reinvestment to maintain its payout. A payout ratio above 75% is a warning. It suggests the company is failing to reinvest sufficient profits in its business, that the company's earnings are faltering, or that it is trying to attract investors who otherwise would not be interested. *Also called* ***dividend payout ratio***. *See also* ***dividend cover***

PayPal™ E-COMMERCE means of paying over Internet a Web-based service that enables Internet users to send and receive payments electronically. To open a PayPal™ account, users register and provide their credit card or checking account details. When they decide to make a transaction via PayPal™, their card or account is charged for the transfer.

payroll ACCOUNTING record of pay and deductions for each employee a record showing for each employee his or her gross pay, deductions, and net pay. The payroll may also include details of the employer's associated employment costs.

payroll giving plan *US* TAX system for deducting money from salary for charity a plan by which an employee pays money to a charity directly out of his or her salary. The money is deducted by the employer and paid to the charity, and the employee gets tax relief on such donations. *UK term* ***payroll giving scheme***

payroll giving scheme *UK* TAX = ***payroll giving plan***

payroll tax TAX tax on money paid to employees a tax on salary and wages of the people employed by a company

  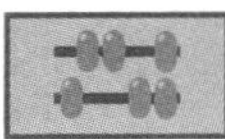      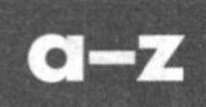

payslip HR & PERSONNEL statement of employee's pay a document given to employees when they are paid, providing a statement of pay for that period. A payslip includes details of deductions such as income tax, social security contributions, pension contributions, and labor union dues.

PBR *abbr* FINANCE ***pre-Budget report***

PBT *abbr* ACCOUNTING ***profit before tax***

P/C *abbr* ACCOUNTING ***petty cash***

PDR *abbr* STOCKHOLDING & INVESTMENTS ***price/dividend ratio***

P/E STOCKHOLDING & INVESTMENTS *see* ***price/earnings multiple, price/earnings ratio***

peak MARKETS highest point or rate the highest price, value, or point reached in a cycle

pecuniary FINANCE of money relating to or involving money

peg **1.** CURRENCY & EXCHANGE fix exchange rate of currency against others to fix the exchange rate of one currency against that of another or of a basket of other currencies **2.** FINANCE fix wages and salaries to control inflation to fix wages and salaries during a period of inflation to help prevent an inflationary spiral

P/E multiple *abbr* STOCKHOLDING & INVESTMENTS ***price/earnings multiple***

penalty FINANCE money paid for breaking contract an arbitrary prearranged sum that becomes payable if one party breaks a term of a contract or an undertaking. A common penalty is a high rate of interest on an unauthorized ***overdraft***. *See also* ***overdraft***

penalty clause LEGAL clause stating exaggerated penalty for breaking contract a clause in a ***contract*** that sets out the compensation to be paid in the event of a breach or a default of the terms of the contract when the amount specified is not considered a genuine estimate of the losses incurred, and the clause is perceived to be solely an incentive for the completion of the contract. However, genuine ***liquidated damages clauses*** are often inaccurately referred to as penalty clauses. *See also* ***liquidated damages clause***

penalty rate *ANZ* FINANCE high rate of overtime pay a higher than normal rate of pay awarded for work performed outside normal working hours

penetrated market MARKETING existing customers the customers who already exist within a well-established market

penetration pricing OPERATIONS & PRODUCTION setting low prices to break into market setting prices low, especially for new products, in order to maximize ***market penetration***

pennant MARKETS chart pattern showing converging high and low prices a triangular chart pattern that is formed when a stock's high and low points begin to converge

penny share *UK* STOCKHOLDING & INVESTMENTS = ***penny stock***

penny stock *US* STOCKHOLDING & INVESTMENTS very low-priced stock very low-priced stock, typically under one dollar, that is a speculative investment. *UK term* ***penny share***

pension PENSIONS money received regularly after retirement from paid work money received regularly after retirement, from a government or through a ***personal pension*** or ***occupational pension***. *Also called* ***retirement pension***

pensionable earnings *UK* PENSIONS = ***final average monthly salary***

pension benefit guaranty corporation PENSIONS, INSURANCE US corporation insuring pension benefits for retirees in the United States, a corporation set up by the federal government to insure the retirement benefits of employees of private-sector companies that have established pension plans

pension entitlement PENSIONS amount of retirement income due the amount of income that someone has the right to receive when he or she retires

pension fund PENSIONS **1.** organization investing money to provide future pensions an organization that receives money from employers and employees in order to provide pensions at a later date. The pension funds of large companies and organizations are significant investors in the financial markets. **2.** *UK* = ***retirement fund***

Pension Protection Fund PENSIONS UK fund compensating people when pension providers fail in the United Kingdom, a fund set up by government to compensate people whose pension providers fail. It is funded by a levy on all pension funds. *Abbr* ***PPF***

pension provider PENSIONS firm selling pension products a company ***pension fund***, or company that sells different investment plans that will build up savings for retirement

PEP *abbr* STOCKHOLDING & INVESTMENTS former UK stock-based investment in the United Kingdom, a stock-based tax-effective investment replaced by ***ISAs*** in 1999. *Full form* ***Personal Equity Plan***

PER *abbr* STOCKHOLDING & INVESTMENTS ***price/earnings ratio***

per annum FINANCE in a year in one year

P/E ratio *abbr* STOCKHOLDING & INVESTMENTS ***price/earnings ratio***

per capita FINANCE per person average for each person

per capita income ECONOMICS average income of group of people the average income of each of a specific group of people, for example, the citizens of a country

perceived value pricing OPERATIONS & PRODUCTION = ***market-based pricing***

percentage increase STATISTICS increase expressed as percentage an increase calculated on the basis of a rate for one hundred

percentile STATISTICS one of 99 equal divisions of total one of a series of ninety-nine figures below which a percentage of the total falls

perception of risk RISK = ***risk perception***

per diem FINANCE, HR & PERSONNEL rate allowed for each day an amount of money paid per day, for example, for expenses when an employee is working away from the office

perfect capital market ECONOMICS when buying and selling do not affect prices a situation in which the decisions of buyers and sellers have no effect on market price in a ***capital market***

perfect competition ECONOMICS when no single buyer or seller affects price a situation in which no individual buyer or seller can influence prices. In practice, perfect markets are characterized by few or no barriers to entry and by many buyers and sellers.

perfect hedge STOCKHOLDING & INVESTMENTS investment with balanced risks an investment that exactly balances the risk of another investment

performance bond BANKING guarantee against third party failure to perform a guarantee given by a bank or insurance company to a third party stating that it will pay a sum of money if its customer, the account holder, fails to complete a specific contract

performance criteria GENERAL MANAGEMENT standards for judgment the standards used to evaluate a product, service, or employee

performance fund STOCKHOLDING & INVESTMENTS higher-risk investment fund expecting high returns an investment fund designed to produce a high return, reflected in the higher risk involved

performance indicator GENERAL MANAGEMENT criterion for assessing firm's performance a key measure designed to assess an aspect of the qualitative or quantitative performance of a company. Performance indicators can relate to operational, strategic, confidence, behavioral, and ethical aspects of a company's operation and can help to pinpoint its strengths and weaknesses. They are periodically monitored to ensure the company's long-term success.

performance management GENERAL MANAGEMENT helping employees to be successful the facilitation of high achievement by employees. Performance management involves enabling people to perform their work to the best of their ability, meeting and perhaps exceeding targets and standards. For successful performance management, a culture of collective and individual responsibility for the continuing improvement of business processes needs to be established, and individual skills and contributions need to be encouraged and nurtured Where organizations are concerned, performance management is usually known as company performance and is monitored through business appraisal.

performance rating MARKETS, GENERAL MANAGEMENT assessment of stock or firm's performance a judgment of how well a stock or a company has performed

performance-related pay FINANCE payment related to the quality of work a payment system in which the level of pay is dependent on the employee's performance. Performance-related pay can be entirely dependent or only partly dependent on performance. There are usually three stages to a performance-related pay system: determining the criteria by which the employee is assessed, establishing whether the employee has met the criteria, and linking the employee's achievements to the pay structure. Performance measures can incorporate skills, knowledge, and behavioral indicators. The system can be compared to ***payment by results***, which is based solely on quantitative productivity measures.

performance share *UK* STOCKHOLDING & INVESTMENTS = ***performance stock***

performance stock *US* STOCKHOLDING & INVESTMENTS higher-risk stock showing capital growth a stock which is likely to show capital growth rather than income, which is a characteristic of stocks with a higher risk. *UK term* ***performance share***

period bill *UK* FINANCE bill of exchange with specific payment date a bill of exchange payable on a specific date rather than on demand. *Also called* ***term bill***

  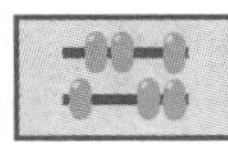      

period-end ACCOUNTING of end of accounting period relating to the end of an accounting period when financial transactions for that period are finalized

periodic inventory review system OPERATIONS & PRODUCTION means of regularly re-ordering inventory a system for placing orders of varying sizes at regular intervals to replenish inventory up to a specified or target level. A periodic inventory review system sets a specific re-order period, but the re-order quantity can vary according to need. The quantity re-ordered is calculated by subtracting existing inventory and on-order inventory from the target level. *Also called* ***fixed interval re-order system***

period of account ACCOUNTING time span covered by UK firm's accounts the period covered by a UK firm's accounts, sometimes coinciding with the firm's ***accounting period***

period of qualification time required to become qualified the time that has to pass before somebody becomes eligible or suitable for something

perk HR & PERSONNEL small supplement to pay a minor benefit that an employee receives in addition to pay, such as the opportunity to buy products cheaply or an interest-free loan for a season ticket (informal) *See also* ***fringe benefits***

permanent interest-bearing shares STOCKHOLDING & INVESTMENTS UK stock issued by credit union in the United Kingdom, stock issued by the UK equivalent of a credit union to raise capital because the law prohibits it from raising capital in more conventional ways. *Abbr* ***PIBS***

perpetual bond STOCKHOLDING & INVESTMENTS bond without maturity date a ***bond*** that has no date of maturity and pays interest in perpetuity

perpetual debenture FINANCE debenture without maturity date a ***debenture*** that has no date of maturity and pays interest in perpetuity

perpetual inventory OPERATIONS & PRODUCTION daily inventory check the daily tracking of inventory in order to keep its recorded amount and value up to date

perpetuity PENSIONS annuity that continues indefinitely a form of annuity that entitles the person holding it to receive payments without setting an end date

perquisites HR & PERSONNEL = ***fringe benefits***

per se GENERAL MANAGEMENT as such a Latin phrase meaning by itself or in itself

personal account **1.** ACCOUNTING record of amounts for or from individual a record of amounts receivable from or payable to a person or an entity. In the United Kingdom, a collection of these accounts is known either as a sales/debtor ledger or a purchases/creditors ledger, or, more simply, as a ***revenue ledger*** or a ***purchase ledger***. In the United States, the terms ***receivables ledger*** and ***payables ledger*** are used. **2.** BANKING bank account for individual a bank account designed for a private individual rather than a business entity

personal allowance *UK* TAX = ***personal exemption***

personal brand GENERAL MANAGEMENT distinctive way somebody wishes to be seen the public expression and projection of a person's identity, personality, values, skills, and abilities. It aims to influence the perceptions of others, emphasizing personal strengths and differentiating the individual from others.

personal contract HR & PERSONNEL individualized contract of employment a ***contract of employment*** that is negotiated on an employee by employee basis, rather than using a traditional structured system that gives identical contracts to groups of workers

Personal Equity Plan STOCKHOLDING & INVESTMENTS *see* ***PEP***

personal exemption *US* TAX amount somebody can earn without paying income tax the amount of money that an individual can earn without having to pay income tax. *UK term* ***personal allowance***

personal financial planning FINANCE person's short- and long-term financial arrangements short- and long-term financial planning by somebody, either independently or with the assistance of a professional adviser. It will include the use of tax-efficient plans such as Individual Retirement Accounts, ensuring adequate provisions are being made for retirement, and examining short- and long-term borrowing requirements such as overdrafts and mortgages.

Personal Identification Number BANKING *see* ***PIN***

personal income FINANCE money person receives from earnings and other payments the income received by somebody from various sources such as earnings, retirement funds, disability benefits, and dividends from investments

Personal Investment Authority REGULATION & COMPLIANCE UK organization regulating financial service providers in the United Kingdom, a self-regulatory organization that regulates the activities of financial advisers, insurance brokers, and others who give financial advice or arrange financial services for small clients. *Abbr* ***PIA***

personalization E-COMMERCE individualized selection of information by website the process by which a website presents customers with selected information on their specific needs. To do this, personal information is collected on the individual user and employed to customize the website for that person.

personal loan FINANCE loan used for personal purpose a loan from a financial institution to somebody for a personal use such as making home improvements or purchasing an automobile

personal pension PENSIONS pension independent of employer a pension taken out by somebody with a private sector insurance company or bank. A personal pension usually takes the form of a program in which money is paid regularly to a pension provider, who invests it in a pension fund. On retirement, a lump sum is available for the purchase of an annuity that provides weekly or monthly payments.

personal pension plan PENSIONS pension provision covering one person not group a pension plan that is set up for one specific person rather than covering a group of employees

personal property FINANCE things belonging to somebody property other than real estate that a person owns

personnel management HR & PERSONNEL appointment, training, and welfare of employees the part of management that is concerned with people and their relationships at work. Personnel management is the responsibility of all those who manage people, as well as a description of the work of specialists. Personnel managers advise on, formulate, and implement personnel policies such as recruitment, conditions of employment, performance appraisal, training, industrial relations, and health and safety. There are various models of personnel management, of which ***human resource management*** is the most recent.

person-to-person lending FINANCE = ***social lending***

per stirpes LEGAL distribution of estate between remaining heirs a method of distributing the assets of an estate, in which the share of assets that would have gone to an heir who predeceases the maker of the will are divided equally among that heir's descendants

PERT *abbr* OPERATIONS & PRODUCTION ***program evaluation and review technique***

petites et moyennes entreprises GENERAL MANAGEMENT small and medium-sized businesses the French for small and medium-sized businesses. *Abbr* ***PME***

petroleum revenue tax TAX UK tax on North Sea oil firms in the United Kingdom, a tax on revenues from companies extracting oil from the North Sea. *Abbr* ***PRT***

petty cash ACCOUNTING amount kept for small payments a small accessible store of cash used for minor business expenses. *Abbr* ***P/C***

petty cash account ACCOUNTING record of small cash receipts and payments a record of relatively small cash receipts and payments, the balance representing the cash in the control of an individual, usually dealt with under an ***imprest system***

petty cash voucher ACCOUNTING document recording petty cash payments a document supporting payments of small amounts of cash to employees under a petty cash system

petty expenses ACCOUNTING small amounts spent on small items small sums of money spent on such items as postage, taxi fares, or copying charges

phantom bid MERGERS & ACQUISITIONS rumored company purchase a reported but nonexistent attempt to buy a company

phantom income TAX income subject to tax though never received income that is subject to tax even though the recipient never actually gets control of it, for example, income from a limited partnership

pharming E-COMMERCE, FRAUD fraudulent poaching of online bank customers the hijacking of online bank customers by infecting web browsers and redirecting them to fake websites, where they are asked to disclose their account details

Phillips curve STATISTICS relationship between unemployment and inflation rate a visual representation of the relationship between unemployment and the rate of inflation

phishing E-COMMERCE, FRAUD fraud to obtain financial information the fraudulent use of e-mail and fake websites to obtain financial information such as credit card numbers, passwords, and bank account information

phoenix activity *or* phoenix practices BUSINESS recreating liquidated firm under new name evasion of official responsibilities by the directors of a company that has had to cease doing business, by leaving liabilities in the liquidated business so that the underlying business activity can be immediately resumed under another name free of such liabilities

        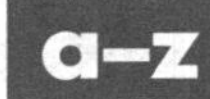

phoenix company BUSINESS firm formed from identical failed firm a company formed by the directors of a company that has gone into ***receivership***, trading in the same way as the first company and, except in name, appearing to be exactly the same

physical asset ACCOUNTING asset that is not cash or securities an asset such as a building or equipment that has a physical presence, as opposed to cash or securities

physical distribution management OPERATIONS & PRODUCTION overseeing of distribution of manufactured goods the planning, monitoring, and control of the distribution and delivery of manufactured goods

physical market MARKETS futures market involving delivery of commodities a market dealing in ***futures contracts*** that involves physical delivery of the commodities traded, rather than purchases that will be set off against sales in cash transactions and never actually delivered

physical price MARKETS price of commodity for immediate delivery the price of a commodity that is available for immediate delivery, rather than just representing a purchase that will be set off against a sale in a cash transaction and never actually delivered

physicals MARKETS commodities that can be bought and used commodities that are bought and delivered, rather than commodities traded on a ***futures contract***

PIA *abbr* REGULATION & COMPLIANCE ***Personal Investment Authority***

PIBOR *abbr* BANKING ***Paris Interbank Offered Rate***

PIBS *abbr* STOCKHOLDING & INVESTMENTS ***permanent interest-bearing shares***

picture MARKETS details of particular Wall Street stock the price and trading quantity of a specific stock on Wall Street used, for example, in the question to a specialist dealer "What's the picture on ABC?" The response would give the bid and offer price and number of shares for which there would be a buyer and seller (slang)

piece rate FINANCE payment according to units completed payment of a predetermined amount for each unit of output by an employee. The rate of pay is usually fixed subjectively, rather than by more objective techniques. Rates are said to be tight when it is difficult for an employee to earn a bonus and loose when bonuses are easily earned. Piece-rate systems are a form of ***payment by results*** or ***performance-related pay***.

piecework FINANCE work paid according to items produced work for which employees are paid in accordance with the number of products produced or pieces of work done and not at an hourly rate

pie chart STATISTICS circle graph divided into sections a chart drawn as a circle divided into proportional sections like portions of a pie

piggyback advertising MARKETING free secondary advertising with another campaign an offer or promotion that runs in parallel with another campaign and incurs no costs

piggyback loan FINANCE loan against same security as existing loan a loan that is raised against the same security as an existing loan

piggyback rights STOCKHOLDING & INVESTMENTS permission to sell existing shares with new shares permission to sell existing shares in conjunction with the sale of similar shares in a new offering

PIIGS INTERNATIONAL TRADE Portugal, Ireland, Italy, Greece, Spain the countries Portugal, Ireland, Italy, Greece, and Spain, regarded collectively as having poorly performing economies within the European Union

PIK note FINANCE debt finance paying interest on note redemption a form of ***debt financing*** that pays interest only when the note is redeemed, although the interest rate is usually much higher than on ordinary debt. The issue of PIK notes constitutes the payment of interest for tax purposes, so if the notes are issued in the accounting period in which the interest accrues, the interest is tax deductible on an ***accrual basis*** and does not affect cash flow. *Full form* ***payment-in-kind note***

pilot *or* pilot scheme *or* pilot survey MARKETING trial to test methodology a preliminary piece of work conducted before full implementation of an activity or process to test its effectiveness

PIN BANKING number verifying card transaction a set of numbers that is used to access an account at an ATM, a computer, or a telephone system, or to verify a credit or debit card at an electronic point of sale. *Full form* ***Personal Identification Number***

pink dollar *US* FINANCE money spent by gays and lesbians money spent by gays and lesbians on goods and services that appeal to them. *UK term* ***pink pound***

pink form STOCKHOLDING & INVESTMENTS in the UK, stock application form for employees in the United Kingdom, a preferential application form for an ***initial public offering*** that is reserved for the employees of the company being floated. *Also called* ***preferential form***

pink paper *UK* FINANCE (informal) = ***Financial Times***

pink pound *UK* FINANCE = ***pink dollar***

pink sheets MARKETS publication giving unlisted securities prices a daily publication of the prices of unlisted securities traded in the ***over-the-counter market*** but that are not traded on the NASDAQ exchange

pink slip **get your pink slip** *US* HR & PERSONNEL to be dismissed from employment (informal) *UK terms* ***get your cards***, ***get the sack***

Pink 'Un *UK* FINANCE Financial Times an informal name for the London-based newspaper the *Financial Times*. It is printed on pink paper. (informal)

pip CURRENCY & EXCHANGE smallest unit in currency price the smallest unit of change in the bid or ask price of a currency

pipeline MARKETS SEC procedure for new security issue the procedure required by the US Securities and Exchange Commission before a new security can be issued for sale to the public

piracy FRAUD illegal copying illegal copying of a product such as software or music

pit MARKETS trading area of financial exchange the area of an exchange where trading takes place. It was traditionally an octagonal stepped area with terracing so as to give everyone a good view of the proceedings during the verbal trading called ***open outcry***. *See also* ***ring*** *(sense 1)*

pit broker MARKETS trader in pit of financial exchange a broker who transacts business in the ***pit*** of a futures or options exchange. *Also called* ***floor broker***

pitch MARKETING attempt to persuade somebody to buy an attempt to win business from a customer, especially a presentation by a sales person

PITI MORTGAGES four items in monthly mortgage payment the four items included in a monthly mortgage payment. Lenders use PITI to determine the amount they will lend based on the relationship between monthly income and PITI. *Full form* ***principal***, ***interest***, ***taxes***, *and* ***insurance***

placement *US* STOCKHOLDING & INVESTMENTS = ***private placement***

placement fee *UK* STOCKHOLDING & INVESTMENTS = ***commission***

placing *UK* MARKETS = ***private offering***

plain vanilla FINANCE standard form of financial product a basic or standard form of a ***financial instrument*** such as an ***option***, ***bond***, or ***swap*** (slang)

plank **make somebody walk the plank** HR & PERSONNEL to dismiss somebody from employment

planned economy ECONOMICS economic system completely controlled by government an economic system in which the government plans all business activity, regulates supply, sets production targets, and itemizes work to be done. *Also called* ***command economy***. *See also* ***central planning***

planned obsolescence OPERATIONS & PRODUCTION deliberate designing of products to require replacing a policy of designing products to have a limited life span so that customers will have to buy replacements regularly

plan participant HR & PERSONNEL employee in benefit plan an employee enrolled in a employer-sponsored benefit plan

plant ACCOUNTING fixed assets producing goods the capital assets used to produce goods, typically factories, production lines, and large equipment

plastic *or* plastic money BANKING debit or credit card a payment system using a debit or credit card, not cash or checks (informal) *See also* ***credit card***, ***debit card***, ***multifunctional card***

platform GENERAL MANAGEMENT product supporting others a product used as a basis for building more complex products or delivering services, for example, a communications network is a platform for delivering knowledge or data

platinum MARKETS precious metal traded as commodity a rare precious metal traded on bullion markets

plc *or* PLC *abbr* BUSINESS ***public limited company***

plenitude ECONOMICS hypothetical situation with abundant supply of products a hypothetical condition of an economy in which manufacturing technology has been perfected and scarcity is replaced by an abundance of products

plot *UK* REAL ESTATE = ***lot*** *(sense 4)*

plough back *UK* FINANCE = ***plow back***

ploughed back profits *UK* FINANCE = ***plowed back profits***

plow back *US* FINANCE reinvest earnings instead of paying dividends to reinvest a company's earnings in the business instead of paying them out as dividends. *UK term* ***plough back***

plowed back profits *US* FINANCE retained profits the amount of profit kept within the company for reinvestment, not distributed. *UK term* ***ploughed back profits***

plug MARKETING advertise something to publicize or advertise a product or service

plum *UK* STOCKHOLDING & INVESTMENTS successful investment an investment that yields a good return (slang)

plus tick MARKETS = ***uptick***

PME *abbr* GENERAL MANAGEMENT ***petites et moyennes entreprises***

PN *abbr* FINANCE ***promissory note***

PO *abbr* OPERATIONS & PRODUCTION ***purchase order***

point FINANCE **1.** unit used in calculating a value a unit used for calculation of a value, such as a hundredth of a percentage point for interest rates **2.** unit on scale a single unit on any scale of measurement, such as a salary scale or range of prices

point and click agreement E-COMMERCE = ***click wrap agreement***

poison pill MERGERS & ACQUISITIONS deterrent measure taken to avoid hostile takeover a measure taken by a company to avoid a hostile takeover, for example, the purchase of a business interest that will make the company unattractive to the potential buyer (slang) *Also called* ***show stopper***

policyholder INSURANCE person or organization with insurance policy a person or business that has taken out a specific insurance policy

political economy ECONOMICS study of government and economics the study of the ways in which the politics and economic organization of a country interact

political price ECONOMICS bad effect on government of decision the negative impact on a government of a policy decision such as raising interest rates

political risk ECONOMICS possible bad effect on government of decision the potential negative impact on a government of a policy decision such as raising interest rates

Ponzi scheme FRAUD banking fraud a fraudulent pyramid selling activity that offers investors high returns which are paid directly from the money deposited by new investors. When new deposits cannot match payments, the organization fails. The fraud is named after Charles Ponzi, who first set up such a scheme in the United States in 1920.

pool FINANCE collateral underpinning loan a group of mortgages and other collateral that is used to back a loan

poop *US* FINANCE somebody with privileged information a person who has ***inside information*** on a financial deal (slang)

pooping and scooping *US* MARKETS illegally spreading rumor to lower stock price an illegal financial practice in which a person or group of individuals attempts to drive down the price of a stock by spreading false unfavorable information. The advent of the Internet has allowed pooping and scooping to become more widespread. (slang)

population STATISTICS set of people, things, or events in a statistical study, the entire collection of units such as events or people from which a sample may be observed

population pyramid STATISTICS representation of group by sex and age a graphical presentation of data in the form of two histograms with a common base, showing a comparison of a human population in terms of sex and age

pork bellies FINANCE meat of pigs traded as commodity meat from the underside of pig carcasses used to make bacon, traded as ***futures*** on some US commodities exchanges

portable pension *UK* PENSIONS pension savings transferring with employee to new job a ***personal pension*** that moves with an employee when he or she changes employer, as opposed to an ***occupational pension*** that usually does not. *See also* ***stakeholder pension***

portfolio STOCKHOLDING & INVESTMENTS investments held by one owner a set of investments, such as stocks and bonds, owned by one person or organization. *Also called* ***investment portfolio***

portfolio career HR & PERSONNEL work pattern of several employments followed simultaneously an employment pattern that involves working part-time on several different jobs at any one time, rather than on a succession of single full-time jobs. *See also* ***portfolio working***

portfolio immunization STOCKHOLDING & INVESTMENTS measures to maintain investment value measures taken by traders to protect their holdings against loss or undue risk

portfolio insurance STOCKHOLDING & INVESTMENTS options protecting portfolio the use of ***options*** that provide ***hedges*** against the set of investments held

portfolio investment STOCKHOLDING & INVESTMENTS investment seeking spread of assets a form of investment that attempts to achieve a mixture of securities in order to minimize risk and maximize return

portfolio management STOCKHOLDING & INVESTMENTS trading to maximize investor's profit the professional management of investment portfolios with the goal of minimizing risk and maximizing return

portfolio manager STOCKHOLDING & INVESTMENTS specialist in investment management a person or company that specializes in managing an investment portfolio on behalf of investors. *See also* ***money manager***

portfolio theory STOCKHOLDING & INVESTMENTS idea that variety of investments bring best results a strategy for managing a portfolio of investments in order to minimize risk and maximize return by having a variety of types of investments. *Also called* ***modern portfolio theory***. *See also* ***CAPM***

portfolio working HR & PERSONNEL having several employments simultaneously a way of working in which a person follows several simultaneous career pursuits at any one time rather than working full-time for one employer. *See also* ***downshifting***, ***portfolio career***

position STOCKHOLDING & INVESTMENTS size of holding of one owner the number of shares of a security that are owned by a person or organization

position limit STOCKHOLDING & INVESTMENTS maximum holding for individual or group the largest amount of a security that any group or individual may own

positive carry STOCKHOLDING & INVESTMENTS when investment return is greater than cost a situation in which the cost of financing an investment is less than the return obtained from it

positive cash flow FINANCE when firm's income is greater than outflow a situation in which more money is coming into a company than is going out

positive discrimination *UK* HR & PERSONNEL favoring appointments from disadvantaged groups preferential treatment, usually through a quota system, to prevent or correct discriminatory employment practices, particularly relating to recruitment and promotion. *US term* ***affirmative action***

positive economics ECONOMICS study of verifiable economic theories the study of economic propositions that can be verified by observing the real economy

positive yield curve STOCKHOLDING & INVESTMENTS when long-term investment return exceeds short-term a visual representation of a situation in which the yield on a short-term investment is less than that on a long-term investment. In a long-term investment, an investor expects a higher return because his or her money is tied up and at risk for a longer period of time.

possessor in bad faith REAL ESTATE holder of land not asserting legal right somebody who occupies land even though they do not believe they have a legal right to do so

possessor in good faith REAL ESTATE holder of land asserting legal right somebody who occupies land believing they have a legal right to do so

possessory action REAL ESTATE legal action about land rights a lawsuit over the right to own a piece of land

postal account BANKING account operated only by mail an account for which all dealings are done by post, thereby reducing ***overhead costs*** and allowing a higher level of ***interest*** to be paid

postal vote *UK* FINANCE = ***mail ballot***

post-balance sheet event ACCOUNTING incident affecting accounts after balance sheet completed something that happens after the date when a balance sheet is completed but before it is officially approved by the directors, that affects a company's financial position

Post Big Bang MARKETS describing current London Stock Exchange trading system used to describe the trading mechanism on the ***London Stock Exchange*** after the market liberalization changes effected in October 1986. *See also* ***Big Bang***

post-completion audit GENERAL MANAGEMENT independent appraisal of success of project an objective and independent appraisal of the measure of success of a capital expenditure project in progressing the business as planned. The appraisal should cover the implementation of the project from authorization to commissioning and its technical and commercial performance after commissioning. The information provided is also used by management as feedback, which helps the implementation and control of future projects.

postdate GENERAL MANAGEMENT date document or check later than date signed to put a later date on a document or check than the date when it is signed, with the effect that it is not valid until the later date

postindustrial society ECONOMICS economy not reliant on heavy industry a society in which the

  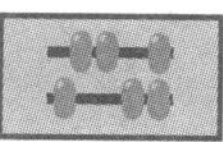     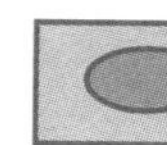 

resources of labor and capital are replaced by those of knowledge and information as the main sources of wealth creation. The postindustrial society involves a shift in focus from manufacturing industries to service industries and is enabled by technological advances.

pot **1.** STOCKHOLDING & INVESTMENTS unreleased portion of stock issue the part of a new stock issue that is not released to the public and is only available for purchase by institutional investors **2.** *US* FINANCE amount collected for specific use an amount of money collected from the members of a group for a specific purpose **pot of gold** FINANCE a large amount of money, especially one that is achieved by accident or good luck **pot of money** FINANCE an amount of money assigned to a specific purpose **pots of money** FINANCE an extremely large amount of money

potential GDP ECONOMICS full value of country's production capacity a measure of the real value of the services and goods that can be produced when a country's factors of production are fully employed. *See also* ***GDP***

potentially exempt transfer TAX gift conditionally exempt from UK inheritance tax in the United Kingdom, an outright gift made during a lifetime to a person or to some types of trusts that does not affect the standard of living of the donor. There is no ***inheritance tax*** to be paid on such a gift, but a liability arises if the donor dies within seven years, with that liability decreasing the longer the donor survives. *See also* ***chargeable transfer***

pot trust FINANCE trust for group of people a trust, typically created in a will, for a group of beneficiaries

pound CURRENCY & EXCHANGE main currency unit in UK and other countries a unit of currency used in the United Kingdom and many other countries including Cyprus, Egypt, Lebanon, Malta, Sudan, and Syria

pound cost averaging *UK* STOCKHOLDING & INVESTMENTS = ***dollar cost averaging***

pound sterling CURRENCY & EXCHANGE official UK currency the official term for the currency used in the United Kingdom

poverty trap TAX disadvantage occurring when pay rise reduces total income a situation whereby low-income families are penalized by a progressive tax system: an increase in income is either counteracted by a loss of social benefit payments or by an increase in taxation

power center GENERAL MANAGEMENT most influential section of organization the part of an organization that has the strongest influence on policy

power of appointment LEGAL power of trustee to dispose of real estate the power of a trustee to dispose of interests in real estate to another person

power of attorney LEGAL legal agreement for acting for another a legal document granting one person the right to act on behalf of another in legal and financial matters and, in the United Kingdom since 2007, in decisions on healthcare and welfare

power structure GENERAL MANAGEMENT relative location of influence the way in which power is distributed among different groups or individuals in an organization

pp GENERAL MANAGEMENT on behalf of derived from the Latin "per pro," used beside a signature at the end of a letter, meaning "on behalf of"

PPF *abbr* PENSIONS ***Pension Protection Fund***

PPP *abbr* **1.** CURRENCY & EXCHANGE ***purchasing power parity*** **2.** BUSINESS ***public private partnership***

preauthorized electronic debit *US* BANKING agreed transfer between bank accounts a system in which a payer agrees to let a bank make payments from an account to somebody else's account. *UK term* ***direct debit***

prebilling OPERATIONS & PRODUCTION submitting bill before delivery the practice of submitting a bill for a product or service before it has actually been delivered

pre-Budget report FINANCE fall forecast of UK government's economic plans in the United Kingdom, an economic forecast the government has to present in the fall of each year, reporting on progress since the Budget in the spring and outlining government spending plans prior to the next Budget. *Abbr* ***PBR***

preceding year ACCOUNTING previous fiscal year the year before the ***fiscal year*** in question

preceding year basis ACCOUNTING using previous year's accounts the principle of assessing income or profits based on the figures for the year before the ***fiscal year*** in question. *Abbr* ***PYB***

precious metals FINANCE high value metals rare metals with a high economic value, especially gold, silver, and platinum

predate *US* GENERAL MANAGEMENT **1.** put earlier date on document to put an earlier date than the current date on a document **2.** make something apply from earlier date to make something effective from an earlier date than the current date *UK term* ***antedate***

predatory lending FINANCE unfair lending practices the practice of encouraging people to borrow in an unfair or unprincipled way, especially if the loan is greater than a borrower can reasonably be expected to repay, or is based on personal property such as a house or car which will be lost if the borrower defaults

predatory pricing OPERATIONS & PRODUCTION setting prices lower than competitors the practice of setting prices for products that are designed to win business from competitors or to damage competitors

pre-emption right *UK* STOCKHOLDING & INVESTMENTS = ***pre-emptive right***

pre-emptive right *US* STOCKHOLDING & INVESTMENTS right of stockholder to first purchase of new stock the right of a stockholder who already owns stock in a company to maintain proportional ownership by being first to purchase stock in a new issue. *UK term* ***pre-emption right***

preference share *UK* STOCKHOLDING & INVESTMENTS = ***preferred stock***

preferential creditor FINANCE creditor who must be paid before others a creditor who is entitled to payment, especially from a bankrupt, before other creditors

preferential form STOCKHOLDING & INVESTMENTS = ***pink form***

preferential issue STOCKHOLDING & INVESTMENTS stock for specific buyers an issue of stock available only to designated buyers

preferential payment FINANCE payment to priority creditor a payment to a ***preferential creditor***, whose debt has first claim on a bankrupt or company that is winding up

preferred risk INSURANCE somebody not regarded as a poor insurance risk somebody considered by an insurance company to be less likely to collect on a policy than the average person, for example, a nonsmoker

preferred stock *US* STOCKHOLDING & INVESTMENTS stock receiving dividend or repayment before others stock that entitles the owner to preference in the distribution of dividends and the proceeds of liquidation in the event of bankruptcy. *UK term* ***preference share***

pre-financing FINANCE securing funding before project begins the practice of arranging funding in advance of the start date of a project

prelaunch MARKETING preparation for product launch the activities that precede the introduction of a new product to the market

preliminary announcement ACCOUNTING initial announcement of firm's financial results an announcement of a company's full-year financial results, which are given out to the press before the detailed annual report is released

preliminary prospectus STOCKHOLDING & INVESTMENTS details about firm given before initial public offering a document issued prior to an ***initial public offering*** that provides details about the company and its financial situation. *Also called* ***red herring***

premarket MARKETS describing transactions before official opening of market used to describe transactions between market members conducted prior to the official opening of the market. *Also called* ***pretrading***

Premiers' Conference FINANCE annual meeting of Australian federal and state heads an annual meeting at which the premiers of the states and territories of Australia meet with the federal government to discuss their funding allocations

premium **1.** FINANCE extra cost for scarcity a higher price paid for a scarce product or service **2.** FINANCE extra charge for high quality a pricing method that uses high price to indicate high quality **3.** STOCKHOLDING & INVESTMENTS price paid for option the price a purchaser of a traded ***option*** pays to its seller **4.** STOCKHOLDING & INVESTMENTS difference between futures price and cash price the difference between the futures price and the cash price of an underlying asset **5.** INSURANCE price of insurance contract the amount paid for an insurance contract, which is needed before the contract is valid **at a premium1.** FINANCE of a fixed interest security, at an issue price above its nominal value2. FINANCE at a price that is considered expensive in relation to others3. STOCKHOLDING & INVESTMENTS of a new issue, at a trading price above the one offered to investors

Premium Bond STOCKHOLDING & INVESTMENTS non-interest-bearing UK security eligible for prize draw in the United Kingdom, a nonmarketable security issued by ***National Savings & Investments*** at £1 each that pays no interest but is entered into a draw every month to win prizes from £25 to £1 million. There are many lower value prizes, but only one £1 million prize. The bonds are repayable upon demand.

premium income INSURANCE insurance firm's income from premiums the income earned by an insurance company from the money paid for its contracts

premium offer MARKETING offer of free gift with sale a sales promotion technique in which customers are offered a free gift

  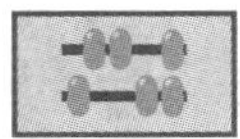      

premium pay plan FINANCE higher pay scale for top employees an enhanced pay scale for high performing employees. A premium pay plan can be offered as an incentive to motivate employees, rewarding such achievements as high productivity, long service, or completion of training with an increased pay package.

premium pricing MARKETING charging high price for high quality the deliberate setting of high prices for a product or service to emphasize its quality or exclusiveness. *Also called* ***prestige pricing***

premoney valuation *or* premoney value FINANCE firm's value before capital investors contribute the assessed value of a business before ***venture capital*** or other capital investors make their investment

prepack *or* prepack administration *or* prepackaged administration BUSINESS UK firm recreated via administration process in the United Kingdom, a business that goes into administration and, having shed its debts, legally emerging as an almost identical company

prepaid interest FINANCE interest paid early interest paid in advance of the date on which it is due

prepayment FINANCE payment of debt before due date the payment of a debt before it is due to be paid

prepayment penalty FINANCE charge made for early payment a charge that may be levied if a payment, such as one on a mortgage or loan, is made before it is due to be paid. The penalty compensates the lender or seller for potential lost interest.

prepayment privilege FINANCE payment before due date without penalty the right to make a payment, such as one on a loan or mortgage, before it is due to be paid, without penalty

prepayment risk FINANCE, RISK risk that prepayment will reduce interest income the risk that a debtor will avoid interest charges by making partial or total payment in advance on a mortgage or loan, especially when interest rates fall

prequalification **1.** FINANCE, MORTGAGES evaluation of likely borrower the process of establishing the financial circumstances of a borrower or mortgage customer before a loan is formally applied for **2.** MARKETING evaluation of likely customer a sales technique in which the potential value of a prospect is carefully evaluated through research

prerefunding STOCKHOLDING & INVESTMENTS using funds from new bond to repay another the process of issuing a longer-term bond in order to take advantage of a drop in interest rates and use the funds to pay off another bond issued earlier

prescribed payments system TAX deduction of tax from Australian casual workers' payments in Australia, a system under which employers are obliged to deduct a specific amount of tax from cash payments made to casual workers

present value FINANCE **1.** future value of asset, discounted for inflation the amount that a future interest in a financial asset is currently worth, discounted for inflation. *Also called* ***discounted value*** **2.** current value of future income, minus accruing interest the value now of an amount of money that somebody expects to receive at a future date, calculated by subtracting any interest that will accrue in the interim

preservation of capital STOCKHOLDING & INVESTMENTS cautious investment strategy an approach to financial management that protects a person's or company's capital by arranging additional forms of finance

pressure group GENERAL MANAGEMENT group formed to lobby for something a body of people who have banded together to campaign on one or more issues of importance to them. A pressure group usually has a formal constitution and coordinates its activities to influence the attitudes or activities of business or government.

prestige pricing MARKETING = ***premium pricing***

pre-syndicate bid STOCKHOLDING & INVESTMENTS advance bid on NASDAQ exchange in the ***NASDAQ*** system, a bid made before a public offering in order to stabilize the price of the stock on offer

pretax TAX before tax before taxes are deducted

pretax profit TAX profit before tax the amount of profit a company makes before taxes are deducted

pretax profit margin TAX profit as a percentage of sales, before tax the profit made by a company, calculated as a percentage of sales and before taxes are considered

pretrading MARKETS = ***premarket***

prevalence STATISTICS how many individuals show same feature in a statistical study, a measure of the number of individuals involved who have a specific characteristic

previous balance ACCOUNTING closing balance of previous accounting period a balance in an account at the end of the ***accounting period*** before the current one

price OPERATIONS & PRODUCTION amount charged to customer an amount of money that a seller charges a customer for a good or service

price-book ratio STOCKHOLDING & INVESTMENTS = ***price-to-book ratio***

price cartel OPERATIONS & PRODUCTION set of firms illegally coordinating prices a group of businesses who make an agreement, often illegally, to maintain prices for a product at a specific level

price ceiling OPERATIONS & PRODUCTION highest price on offer the highest price that a buyer is willing to pay

price change MARKETS price movement of specific stock over a given period of time an amount by which the price of a specific share of stock changes during a specified time period

price competition OPERATIONS & PRODUCTION competition on price only a form of competition that is based only on price rather than factors such as quality or design

price controls ECONOMICS government limits on prices to control inflation measures used by a government to set prices in order to protect consumers from rapidly rising prices. Many economists believe that price controls actually hurt the economy by creating shortages and should only be used in an emergency.

price cutting OPERATIONS & PRODUCTION reducing prices to encourage sales a sudden lowering of prices below normal levels in order to boost sales and outsell competitors

price-cutting war OPERATIONS & PRODUCTION = ***price war***

price differential OPERATIONS & PRODUCTION difference in price between similar products a difference in price between products in a range. A basic digital camera, for example, will have a relatively low price compared to the same camera with additional features.

price differentiation OPERATIONS & PRODUCTION pricing same product differently in different markets a pricing strategy in which a company sells the same product at different prices in different markets

price discovery ECONOMICS establishment of price in free market the process by which price is determined by negotiation in a free market

price discrimination OPERATIONS & PRODUCTION selling to different buyers at different prices the practice of selling the same product to different buyers at different prices

price/dividend ratio STOCKHOLDING & INVESTMENTS price of stock divided by annual dividend paid a ratio derived from the price of a stock divided by the annual dividend paid on a share, which gives an indication of how much has to be paid to receive $1 of dividends. *Abbr* ***PDR***

price/earnings multiple STOCKHOLDING & INVESTMENTS stock price divided by its earnings the number of times by which the price of stock is greater than the ***earnings per share***. *Abbr* ***P/E multiple***. See also ***price/earnings ratio***

price/earnings ratio STOCKHOLDING & INVESTMENTS price of stock divided by earnings per share a company's stock price divided by earnings per share.

While earnings per share (EPS) is an actual amount of money, usually expressed in cents per share, the P/E ratio has no units, it is just a number. Thus if a quoted company has a stock price of $100 and EPS of $12 for the last published year, then it has a historical P/E ratio of 8.3. If analysts are forecasting for the next year EPS of, say, $14, then the forecast P/E ratio is 7.1.

The P/E ratio is predominantly useful in comparisons with other stocks rather than in isolation. For example, if the average P/E ratio in the market is 20, there will be many stocks with P/E ratios well above and well below this, for a variety of reasons. Similarly, in a particular sector, the P/E ratios will frequently vary from the sector average, even though the constituent companies may all be engaged in similar businesses. The reason is that even two businesses doing the same thing will not always be doing it as profitably as each other. One may be far more efficient, as demonstrated by a history of rising EPS compared with the flat EPS picture of the other over a series of years, and the market might recognize this by awarding the more profitable stock a higher P/E ratio. *Abbr* ***PER***

price effect ECONOMICS how price changes affect economy the impact of price changes on a market or economy

price elasticity of demand ECONOMICS how demand responds to price changes the percentage change in demand divided by the percentage change in price of a good

price elasticity of supply ECONOMICS how supply responds to price changes the percentage change in supply divided by the percentage change in price of a good

price escalation clause LEGAL provision permitting seller to cover increased costs a contract provision that permits the seller to raise prices in response to increased costs

price fixing OPERATIONS & PRODUCTION illegal agreement by producers to coordinate prices an

  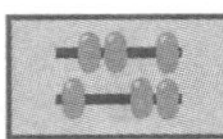      

often illegal agreement between producers of a good or service in order to maintain prices at a particular level

price floor OPERATIONS & PRODUCTION lowest price acceptable the lowest price at which a seller is prepared to do business

price index ECONOMICS index measuring inflation an index such as the consumer price index that measures inflation

price indicator ECONOMICS measure of general price trends a measurable variable that can be used as an indicator of the price of something, for example the number of home loans arranged can be an indicator for rising or falling house prices

price-insensitive ECONOMICS describing essential goods or services with unvarying sales used to describe a good or service for which sales remain constant no matter what its price because it is essential to buyers

price instability ECONOMICS situation in which prices change frequently a situation in which the prices of goods alter daily or even hourly

price leadership OPERATIONS & PRODUCTION setting of prevailing market price the establishment of price levels in a market by a dominant company or brand

price ring OPERATIONS & PRODUCTION set of traders illegally coordinating prices a group of individual traders who make an agreement, often illegally, to maintain the price of a product at a specific level

prices and incomes policy ECONOMICS government regulations on prices and wages a policy that limits price or wage increases through government regulations

price-sensitive ECONOMICS describing goods or services with price-dependent sales used to describe a good or service for which sales fluctuate depending on its price, often because it is a nonessential item

price-sensitive information MARKETS information affecting firm's stock price if published as yet unpublished information that will affect a company's stock price. For example, the implementation of a new manufacturing process that will substantially cut production costs would have a positive impact, whereas the discovery of harmful side effects from a recently launched drug would have a negative impact.

price slashing OPERATIONS & PRODUCTION making very large price reduction sudden extreme lowering of a price in order to boost sales

price stability ECONOMICS insignificant changes in prices a situation in which there is little fluctuation in the price of goods or services overall

price support ECONOMICS government spending to keep prices from falling government assistance designed to keep market prices from falling below a minimum level

price-to-book ratio STOCKHOLDING & INVESTMENTS ratio of firm's market value to theoretical value the ratio of the value of all of a company's stock to its ***book value***. *Also called* ***price-book ratio***

price-to-cash-flow ratio STOCKHOLDING & INVESTMENTS ratio of firm's market value to cash flow the ratio of the value of all of a company's stock to its cash flow for the most recent complete fiscal year

price-to-sales ratio STOCKHOLDING & INVESTMENTS ratio of firm's market value to sales the ratio of the value of all of a company's stock to its sales for the previous twelve months, a way of measuring the relative value of a stock when compared with others.

The P/S ratio is obtained by dividing the ***market capitalization*** by the latest published annual sales figure. So a company with a capitalization of $1 billion and sales of $3 billion would have a P/S ratio of 0.33.

P/S will vary with the type of industry. You would expect, for example, that many retailers and other large-scale distributors of goods would have very high sales in relation to their market capitalizations—in other words, a very low P/S. Equally, manufacturers of high-value items would generally have much lower sales figures and thus higher P/S ratios.

A company with a lower P/S is cheaper than one with a higher ratio, particularly if they are in the same sector so that a direct comparison is more appropriate. It means that each share of the lower P/S company is buying more of its sales than those of the higher P/S company.

It is important to note that a stock which is cheaper only on P/S grounds is not necessarily the more attractive stock. There will frequently be reasons why it has a lower ratio than another similar company, most commonly because it is less profitable.

price war OPERATIONS & PRODUCTION cycle of cost cutting to undercut competitors a situation in which two or more companies each try to increase their own share of the market by lowering prices. A price war involves companies undercutting each other in an attempt to encourage more customers to buy their goods or services. In the long term, this can devalue a market and lead to loss of profits, but it can sometimes have short-term success.

price-weighted index ECONOMICS index adjusted for price changes an index of production or market value that is adjusted for changes that occur in prices

pricing model OPERATIONS & PRODUCTION computerized multifactorial system for calculating prices a computerized system for calculating prices, based on a variety of factors including costs and anticipated margins

pricing policy *or* pricing strategy OPERATIONS & PRODUCTION way in which businesses determine prices the method of ***decision making*** used for setting the prices for a company's products or services. A pricing policy is usually based on the costs of production or provision with a margin for profit, for example, ***cost-plus pricing***.

primary account number BANKING credit card identifier an identifier for a credit card used in secure electronic transactions

primary commodities MARKETS agricultural bulk produce farm produce that is grown in large quantities, for example corn, rice, or cotton

primary data *or* primary information MARKETING information from original research original data derived from a new research study and collected at source, as opposed to previously published material

primary earnings per (common) share STOCKHOLDING & INVESTMENTS profit from each current share of common stock a measure of earnings per share calculated on the basis of the number of shares of ***common stock*** actually held by investors, not including exercisable warrants and options. *See also* ***fully diluted earnings per (common) share, earnings per share***

primary industry BUSINESS type of business involved in obtaining natural resources an industry that deals with obtaining basic raw materials such as coal, wood, or farm products

primary liability FINANCE, INSURANCE responsibility as first payer of financial claims a responsibility to pay before anyone else who also has financial responsibility for financial claims such as damages covered by insurance

primary market MARKETS market for securities offered to investors by issuer the part of the market on which securities are first offered to investors by the issuer. The money from this sale goes to the issuer, rather than to traders or investors as it does in the secondary market. *See also* ***secondary market***

primary product MARKETS natural resource, often used in other products a product which is a basic raw material, for example, wood, milk, or fish

primary sector ECONOMICS part of economy involved in production businesses operating in the sector of a country's economy that is involved in producing goods

prime BANKING = ***prime rate***

prime assets ratio BANKING Australian banks' obligatory holding in secure assets in Australia, the proportion of total liabilities that banks are obliged by the Reserve Bank to hold in highly secure assets such as cash and government securities. *Abbr* ***PAR***

prime bill FINANCE risk-free bill of exchange an agreement that involves no risk of default, setting out an instruction to pay a particular person a fixed sum of money on a particular date or when the person requests payment

prime broker STOCKHOLDING & INVESTMENTS investment bank servicing hedge fund an investment bank that provides borrowing, lending, and settlement services to a ***hedge fund***. Such financial services are often considered the most profitable activity for a major bank but great losses can be incurred if the hedge fund fails.

prime cost OPERATIONS & PRODUCTION cost of producing product, not including overhead the cost involved in producing a product, excluding the general recurring costs of running a business

prime lending BANKING safe lending to creditworthy borrower lending to borrowers who have no delinquencies or defaults and no historical or current financial problems. *Also called* ***vanilla lending***

prime loan BANKING safe loan to creditworthy borrower a loan to a borrower who is regarded as being highly creditworthy, has no obvious financial difficulties and a good payment record, and is therefore very likely to repay the loan. *Also called* ***vanilla loan***

prime rate *or* prime interest rate BANKING in US, best interest rate on offer in the United States, the lowest interest rate that commercial banks offer on loans to well-regarded customers. It is analogous to the ***base rate*** in the United Kingdom. *Also called* ***prime***

priming FINANCE = ***pump priming***

principal FINANCE original amount lent the original amount of a loan or investment, not including any ***interest***. *See also* ***mortgage***

principal shareholders *UK* STOCKHOLDING & INVESTMENTS = ***principal stockholders***

principal stockholders *US* STOCKHOLDING & INVESTMENTS owners of majority of stock the people who own the largest percentage of stock in a business or organization. *UK term* ***principal shareholders***

principles-based regulation REGULATION & COMPLIANCE financial industry regulation relying on good practice regulation of the financial industry that relies more on desired regulatory outcomes and principles and less on detailed rules

prior charge percentage STOCKHOLDING & INVESTMENTS = ***priority percentage***

priority percentage STOCKHOLDING & INVESTMENTS share of profit paid to priority stockholders the proportion of a business's net profit that is paid in interest to holders of ***debt capital*** and ***preferred stock***. *Also called* ***prior charge percentage***

prior lien bond STOCKHOLDING & INVESTMENTS bond giving priority claim on debtor's assets a bond whose holder has more claim on a debtor's assets than holders of other types of bonds

prior year adjustment ACCOUNTING alteration to accounts of previous years an adjustment made to accounts for previous years, because of changes in accounting policies or because of errors

private bank BANKING **1.** bank owned by individual or small group a bank that is owned by a single person or a limited number of private stockholders **2.** bank for wealthy clients a bank that provides banking facilities to high net worth individuals. *See also* ***private banking*** **3.** independent bank in country with state-owned institutions a bank that is not state-owned in a country where most banks are owned by the government

private banking BANKING banking services offered to wealthy clients a service offered by some financial institutions to high net worth individuals. In addition to standard banking services, it will typically include portfolio management and advisory services on taxation, including estate planning.

private company BUSINESS company whose stock is not publicly traded a company that is privately owned and whose stock is not offered for sale to the public

private cost ECONOMICS cost to individual consumer or firm of consumption the cost incurred by individuals or companies when they consume resources

private debt FINANCE nongovernmental borrowings money owed by individuals and organizations other than governments

private enterprise ECONOMICS businesses not controlled by government business or industry that is controlled by companies or individuals rather than the government

private equity company BUSINESS private firm funding profitable projects a company not quoted on a public stock market that provides long-term equity finance to unquoted companies by investing money in the form of shares of stock or shares and shareholder loans. Private equity companies provide money for both ***venture capital funds*** and ***buyout*** or ***growth funds***.

private equity financing FINANCE = ***venture capital***

private income FINANCE income separate from salary income from dividends, interest, or rent which is not part of a salary

private investor STOCKHOLDING & INVESTMENTS ordinary person investing money an ordinary person who makes investments and who is not in the business of investing other people's money

private label *US* MARKETING generic product sold under retailer's name a product or range of products offered by a retailer under its own name in competition with branded goods. Private label products, like ***nonbranded goods***, are normally cheaper than branded items but are often perceived to be of lower quality. *Also called* ***own label***. *UK term* ***own brand***

private label MBS BUSINESS US finance company creating and selling bonds in the United States, a finance company other than Fannie Mae, Ginnie Mae, and Freddie Mac that creates and sells mortgage-backed securities or other bonds and is often collateralized by loans which are not eligible for purchase by Freddie Mac

private limited company BUSINESS private UK firm with small number of stockholders in the United Kingdom and some other countries, a company that has a small number of stockholders and whose stock is not traded on the stock exchange

private mortgage insurance INSURANCE insurance to cover default on mortgage an insurance policy that will cover the risk of a mortgagee defaulting on payments, in the case of loss of job, long-term illness, or other financial difficulty

private offering *US* MARKETS finding buyer for many shares in new firm the act of finding a single buyer or a group of institutional buyers for a large number of shares in a new company or a company that is going public. *UK term* ***placing***

private ownership BUSINESS ownership by citizens not by government a situation in which a company is owned by private stockholders, as opposed to being owned by a government

private placement *US* STOCKHOLDING & INVESTMENTS sale of securities directly to investors the sale of securities directly to institutions for investment rather than resale. *UK term* ***private placing***

private placing *UK* STOCKHOLDING & INVESTMENTS = ***private placement***

private property FINANCE property not for general public use property or assets that are owned by a person or group and not for use by the general public

private sector ECONOMICS part of economy not controlled by government the section of the economy that is financed and controlled by individuals or private institutions such as companies, stockholders, or investment groups. *See also* ***public sector***

private sector investment ECONOMICS non-government investment investment by the private enterprise sector of an economy

private treaty FINANCE land sale without auction the sale of land arranged by seller and buyer without a public auction

privatization GENERAL MANAGEMENT transfer from state to private ownership the transfer of a company from ownership by either a government or a few individuals to the public via the issuance of stock

probability STATISTICS how likely it is something will happen the quantitative measure of the likelihood that a given event will occur

probability distribution STATISTICS formula representing probability of values of variables in a statistical study, a mathematical formula showing the probability for each value of a variable

probability measure RISK, STATISTICS evaluation of chance of event occurring in a statistical study, a calculation of the likelihood that a given event will occur

probability plot STATISTICS graph comparing two probability distributions in a statistical study, a graphic plot of data that compares two probability distributions

probability sampling STATISTICS creating statistical sample that could include any individual in a statistical study, a way of sampling in which every individual in a finite population has a known, but not necessarily equal, chance of being included in the sample, which is known as a ***probability sample***

probate LEGAL legal acceptance of validity of will the legal process by which a will is accepted as valid

problem child **1.** *US* BUSINESS troublesome subsidiary company a subsidiary company that is not performing well or is damaging the ***parent company*** in some way (slang) **2.** MARKETING underperforming product with high potential a product with a low market share but high growth potential. Problem children often have good long-term prospects, but high levels of investment may be needed to realize the potential, thereby draining funds that may be needed elsewhere. *See also* ***Boston Box***

problem solving GENERAL MANAGEMENT methodology for dealing with management problems a systematic approach to overcoming obstacles or problems in the management process. Problems occur when something is not behaving as it should, when something deviates from the norm, or when something goes wrong. A number of problem-solving methodologies exist, but the most widely used includes these steps: recognizing a problem exists and defining it; generating a variety of solutions; evaluating the possible solutions and choosing the best one; implementing the solution and evaluating its effectiveness in solving the problem.

proceeds FINANCE income from sale the money derived from a sale or other commercial transaction

process box GENERAL MANAGEMENT symbol representing action a primary symbol used in a ***flow chart*** that indicates a process or action taking place. *See also* ***flow chart***

process costing OPERATIONS & PRODUCTION costing method dividing manufacturing cost by units produced a method of costing something that is manufactured from a series of continuous processes, where the total costs of those processes are divided by the number of units produced

processor E-COMMERCE = ***acquirer***

procurement OPERATIONS & PRODUCTION = ***purchasing***

procurement exchange OPERATIONS & PRODUCTION group of companies with combined buying power a group of companies that act together to buy products or services they need at lower prices

  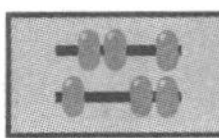      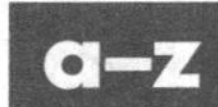

procurement manager OPERATIONS & PRODUCTION = ***purchasing manager***

procurement portal E-COMMERCE = ***online catalog***

procyclical ECONOMICS **1.** increasing in line with other factor tending to increase and decrease in tandem with another factor. *See also* ***countercyclical*** **2.** promoting instability likely to increase instability or fluctuation

procyclicality ECONOMICS positive feedback in linked factors a pattern of positive reinforcement in the behavior of linked factors that can intensify fluctuations in a system. For example, credit expands as the financial climate improves, but in a subsequent period of economic contraction credit shrinks and financial constraint increases

producer price index ECONOMICS statistical measure of wholesale prices the ***weighted average*** of the prices of commodities that firms buy from other firms

product OPERATIONS & PRODUCTION, MARKETING marketable good or service anything that is offered to a market that customers can acquire, use, interact with, experience, or consume, to satisfy a want or need. Early ***marketing*** tended to focus on tangible physical goods and these were distinguished from ***services***. More recently, however, the distinction between products and services has blurred, and the concept of the product has been expanded so that in its widest sense it can now be said to cover any tangible or intangible thing that satisfies the consumer. Products that are marketed can include services, people, places, and ideas.

product abandonment OPERATIONS & PRODUCTION, MARKETING discontinuation of particular good or service the ending of the manufacture and sale of a product. Products are abandoned for many reasons. The market may be saturated or declining, the product may be superseded by another, costs of production may become too high, or a product may simply become unprofitable. Product abandonment usually occurs during the decline phase of the ***product life cycle***.

product assortment OPERATIONS & PRODUCTION, MARKETING = ***product mix***

product churning OPERATIONS & PRODUCTION, MARKETING launch of multiple products hoping one will succeed the flooding of a market with new products in the hope that one of them will become successful. Product churning is especially prevalent in Japan, where prelaunch test marketing is often replaced by multiple product launches. Most of these products will decline and disappear, but one or more of the new products churned out may become profitable.

product development OPERATIONS & PRODUCTION, MARKETING modification of product for renewed consumer appeal the revitalization of a product through the introduction of a new concept or consumer benefit. Product development is part of the ***product life cycle***. The concepts or benefits that can be implemented range from modification of the product to simply introducing new packaging.

product development cycle OPERATIONS & PRODUCTION, MARKETING *see* ***new product development***

product differentiation MARKETING promotion of product as different from competition a marketing technique that promotes and emphasizes a product's difference from other products of a similar nature. *Also called* ***differentiation***

product family MARKETING group of similar goods or services a group of products or services that meet a similar need in the market

production versus purchasing OPERATIONS & PRODUCTION = ***purchasing versus production***

productive capacity OPERATIONS & PRODUCTION maximum output achievable at any one time the maximum amount of output that an organization or company can generate at any one time

productive capital FINANCE assets producing income the part of a company's assets that generate an income

productivity OPERATIONS & PRODUCTION measure of production efficiency a measurement of the efficiency of production, taking the form of a ratio of the output of goods and services to the input of factors of production. Labor productivity takes account of inputs of employee hours worked; capital productivity takes account of inputs of machines or land; and marginal productivity measures the additional output gained from an additional unit of input. Techniques to improve productivity include greater use of new technology, altered working practices, and improved training of the workforce.

productivity measurement OPERATIONS & PRODUCTION *see* ***productivity***

product launch MARKETING introduction of new product to market the introduction of a new product to a market. A product launch progresses through a number of important stages: internal communication, which encourages high levels of awareness and commitment to the new product; prelaunch activity, which secures distribution and makes sure that retailers have the resources and knowledge to market the product; launch events at national, regional, or local level; post-event activity, which helps sales forces and retailers make the most of the event; and launch advertising and other forms of customer communication.

product leader MARKETING = ***brand leader***

product liability OPERATIONS & PRODUCTION obligation to accept responsibility for defects in products a manufacturer's, producer's, or service provider's obligation to accept responsibility for defects in their products or services. Faulty products may result in personal injury or damage to property, in which case product liability may result in the payment of compensation to the purchaser.

product life cycle OPERATIONS & PRODUCTION, MARKETING time from development through decline of product the life span of a product from development, through testing, promotion, growth, and maturity, to decline and perhaps regeneration. A new product is first developed and then introduced to the market. Once the introduction is successful, a growth period follows with wider awareness of the product and increasing sales. The product enters maturity when sales stop growing and demand stabilizes. Eventually, sales may decline until the product is finally withdrawn from the market or redeveloped.

product line OPERATIONS & PRODUCTION family of related products a family of related products. Products within a line may be the same type of product, they may be sold to the same type of customer or through similar outlets, or they may all be within a specific price range.

product management OPERATIONS & PRODUCTION control of manufacturing process the process of producing a specification or chart of the manufacturing operations to be carried out by different functions and workstations over a specific time period. Production scheduling takes account of factors such as the availability of plant and materials, customer delivery requirements, and maintenance schedules.

product manager OPERATIONS & PRODUCTION, MARKETING person with oversight of product at all stages a person in charge of ***product management***, who focuses on the marketing of the product but may also be responsible for pricing, packaging, branding, research and development, production, distribution, sales targets, and product performance appraisal

product market OPERATIONS & PRODUCTION, MARKETING selling to business rather than consumer the market in which products are sold to companies rather than directly to consumers. The product market is concerned with purchasing by organizations for their own use, and includes such items as raw materials, machinery, and equipment, which may in turn be used to manufacture items for the consumer market.

product mix OPERATIONS & PRODUCTION, MARKETING variety of products sold by business the variety of product lines that a company produces, or that a retailer stocks. Product mix usually refers to the length (the number of products in the product line), breadth (the number of product lines that a company offers), depth (the different varieties of product in the product line), and consistency (the relationship between products in their final destination) of product lines. *Also called* ***product assortment***

product portfolio OPERATIONS & PRODUCTION, MARKETING products that company handles the range of products manufactured or supplied by an organization

product positioning MARKETING = ***brand positioning***

product range *UK* OPERATIONS & PRODUCTION MARKETING complete list of products all of the types of products made by one company

product recall OPERATIONS & PRODUCTION removal of defective product from market the removal from sale of products that may constitute a risk to consumers because of contamination, sabotage, or faults in the production process. A product recall usually originates from the product manufacturer but retailers may act autonomously, especially if they believe their outlets are at risk. *See also* ***brand positioning***

profile BUSINESS description of firm a description of the activities of a company, including information on its products or business activities and its finances

profit FINANCE **1.** difference between higher selling price and lower purchase price the difference between the selling price and the purchase price of a product when the selling price is higher. In the case of a security or financial instrument the profit will include any accrued interest. **2.** income exceeding expenditure in business transactions, the amount by which income is greater than expenditure **3.** money made by activity the amount of money that is made from a business undertaking or transaction **turn a profit** to make a profit from a business activity

profitability FINANCE **1.** extent of profit the degree to which an individual, company, or single

  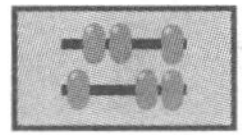      

transaction achieves financial gain **2.** generation of profit the ability to achieve financial gain from a sale or other commercial transaction

profitability index FINANCE current value of investment divided by original investment the present value of the amount of money an investment will earn divided by the amount of the original investment

profitability threshold FINANCE start point of making profit the point at which a business begins to make profits from its activities or from a specific product

profitable FINANCE producing a profit used to refer to a product, service, or business that achieves financial gain

profit after tax ACCOUNTING = ***net profit***

profit and loss ACCOUNTING difference between income and costs the difference between a company's income and its costs as shown in its accounts. *Abbr* ***P&L***

profit and loss account *or* profit and loss statement ACCOUNTING record of firm's external financial transactions the summary record of a company's sales revenues and expenses over a period, providing a calculation of profits or losses during that time. *Also called* ***trading account***

profit before tax ACCOUNTING amount of profit before tax the amount that a company or investor has made, before tax is deducted. *Abbr* ***PBT***

profit center ACCOUNTING business unit responsible for own costs and profits a person, unit, or department within an organization that is considered separately when calculating profit. Profit centers are used as part of management control systems. They operate with a degree of autonomy with regard to marketing and pricing, and have responsibility for their own costs, revenues, and profits.

profit distribution STOCKHOLDING & INVESTMENTS, FINANCE allocation of profits the allocation of profits to different categories of recipients such as stockholders and owners, or for different purposes such as research or investment

profiteering BUSINESS making high profit unethically the practice of making an excessive profit, often in a way that is thought to be unethical or dishonest, or has a detrimental effect on others

profit from ordinary activities ACCOUNTING profits gained from usual business profits earned in the normal course of business, as opposed to profits from extraordinary sources such as windfall payments

profit margin ACCOUNTING, OPERATIONS & PRODUCTION amount by which revenues exceed expenses the amount by which income is greater than expenditure. The profit margin of an individual product is the sale price minus the cost of production and associated costs such as distribution and advertising. The ***net profit margin*** or ***return on sales*** is net income after taxes divided by total sales. On a larger scale, the profit margin is an accounting ratio of company income compared with sales. The profit margin ratio can be used to compare the efficiency and profitability of a company over a number of years, or to compare different companies. The ***gross profit margin*** or ***operating margin*** of a company is its operating, or gross, profit divided by total sales. The level of profit reported is also influenced by the extent of the application of accounting conventions, and by the method of product costing used, for example, ***marginal costing*** or ***absorption costing***.

profit motive BUSINESS desire to make a profit the desire of a business or service provider to make a profit

profit sharing FINANCE allocation of some profit to employees the allocation of a proportion of a company's profit to employees by an issue of stock or other means

profit-sharing debenture STOCKHOLDING & INVESTMENTS employee debenture linking payouts to company performance a ***debenture*** held by an employee, the payments from which depend on the employing company's financial success

profit squeeze BUSINESS reduced profitability compared with the past the inability to maintain a person's or business's profit in a venture, in comparison to previous ventures

profits tax *UK* TAX tax on firm's profit any tax on a company's profits, for example, UK corporation tax (informal)

profits warning STOCKHOLDING & INVESTMENTS firm's prediction of low profits an announcement by a company of lower than expected profits for a specific period. *Also called* ***profit warning***

profit-taking STOCKHOLDING & INVESTMENTS sale of investments the act of selling investments in order to receive money for the profit they have made

profit warning STOCKHOLDING & INVESTMENTS = ***profits warning***

pro-forma GENERAL MANAGEMENT preliminary document issued before final version a document issued before all relevant details are known, usually followed by a final version

pro forma balance sheet ACCOUNTING statement of projected financial position after planned transaction in the United States, a projection showing a business's financial statements after the completion of a planned transaction

pro-forma financial statement *UK* ACCOUNTING statement of projected financial position after planned transaction a projection showing a business's likely financial statements after the completion of a planned transaction

pro-forma invoice ACCOUNTING initial basic invoice an invoice that does not include all the details of a transaction, often sent before goods are supplied and followed by a final detailed invoice

program evaluation and review technique *US* OPERATIONS & PRODUCTION way of managing major project a way of planning and controlling a large project, concentrating on scheduling individual activities and completing the project on time. *Abbr* ***PERT***. UK term ***programme evaluation and review technique***

programme evaluation and review technique *UK* OPERATIONS & PRODUCTION = ***program evaluation and review technique***

program trading STOCKHOLDING & INVESTMENTS electronic trading of securities the trading of securities electronically, by sending messages from the investor's computer to a market

progressive tax TAX tax with rate rising with income a tax with a rate that increases proportionately with taxable income. *See also* ***proportional tax, regressive tax, flat tax***

progress payment FINANCE payment of project work in stages a payment of a portion of the total contracted price of a project that is made at a agreed stage of completion

project creep GENERAL MANAGEMENT gradual extension of deadlines and targets the gradual alteration of deadlines and expansion of targets as a project progresses

project finance FINANCE funds raised for specific venture money raised for a specific self-contained venture such as a construction or development project

projection FINANCE financial forecast a forecast of conditions that will occur in the future, especially the ways in which they are likely to affect business operations

project management GENERAL MANAGEMENT management of operation and outcome of project the integration of all aspects of a project in order to ensure that the proper knowledge and resources are available when and where needed, and above all to ensure that the expected outcome is produced in a timely, cost-effective manner. The primary function of a project manager is to manage the trade-offs between performance, timeliness, and cost.

project risk analysis *or* project risk assessment GENERAL MANAGEMENT, RISK assessment of risks to activities the identification of ***risks*** to which a project is exposed, and the assessment of the potential impact of those risks on the project. Project risk analysis forms part of the process of ***project management*** and is a specialized type of ***risk analysis***.

promissory note FINANCE agreement to pay for something received a written contract to pay money to a person or organization for a good or service received. *Abbr* ***PN***

promotion MARKETING = ***sales promotion***

property FINANCE asset owned by somebody ***assets***, such as real estate or goods, that a person or organization owns

property bond STOCKHOLDING & INVESTMENTS bond with property as collateral a bond for which real estate is collateral

property damage insurance INSURANCE insurance for real property insurance against the risk of damage to or on one's real estate

property developer *UK* REAL ESTATE = ***real estate developer***

property tax REAL ESTATE, TAX local tax on real estate a tax that is based on the value of a piece of real estate and paid to a local government

proportional tax TAX tax proportional to value of taxed item a tax that is strictly proportional in amount to the value of the item being taxed, especially income. *See also* ***progressive tax, regressive tax***

proprietary company *ANZ, S. AFRICA* BUSINESS private limited liability company in Australia and South Africa, a private limited liability company. *Abbr* ***Pty***

proprietary drug OPERATIONS & PRODUCTION patented drug marketed exclusively under brand name a patented drug that is made by a specific company and marketed only by that company under a brand name

proprietary trading MARKETS trading on financial institution's own account trading by a

  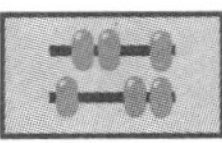      

trader in an organization such as an investment bank whose job is to trade on behalf of the bank in order to make large profits for the bank itself, rather than on behalf of the bank's clients

proprietors' interest FINANCE owners' investment in business an amount of money which the owners of a business have invested in the business

pro rata FINANCE at a proportional rate at a rate that is in proportion to something. For example, several investors in a company may share the profits of that company in proportion to their ownership interest.

ProShare MARKETS group representing private investors on London Stock Exchange a group that acts in the interests of private investors in securities on the ***London Stock Exchange***

prospect MARKETING potential client or customer a person or organization considered likely to buy a product or service

prospecting MARKETING identification of potential clients or customers the process of identifying people or organizations that are likely to buy a product or service

prospective dividend STOCKHOLDING & INVESTMENTS = ***forecast dividend***

prospective P/E ratio STOCKHOLDING & INVESTMENTS P/E ratio forecast on expected dividends an assessment of the ***price/earnings ratio*** that can be expected for the future on the basis of forecast dividends

prospect theory GENERAL MANAGEMENT analysis of why individuals make nonrational decisions a branch of decision theory that attempts to explain why individuals make decisions that deviate from rational decision making by examining how the expected outcomes of alternative choices are perceived. The theory is based on the premise that people treat risks associated with perceived losses differently from risks associated with perceived gains. Prospect theory has applications in a wide range of fields, including marketing management, where it is relevant to the way in which choices are presented to the consumer.

prospectus STOCKHOLDING & INVESTMENTS document accompanying sale of securities a description of a company's operations, financial background, prospects, and the detailed terms and conditions relating to an offer for sale or placing of its stock by notice, circular, advertisement, or any form of invitation which offers securities to the public

protectionism INTERNATIONAL TRADE government protection of domestic firms by limiting imports a government economic policy of restricting the level of imports by using measures such as ***tariffs*** and ***nontariff barriers*** in order to protect a country's domestic industries

protective put buying STOCKHOLDING & INVESTMENTS purchase of options to sell something already owned the purchase of ***options*** to sell ***financial instruments*** that are the same as some the purchaser already owns

protective tariff INTERNATIONAL TRADE tax on imports to protect domestic firms a tariff imposed to restrict imports into a country

protest FINANCE proof that bill of exchange is unpaid an official document that proves that a bill of exchange has not been paid

protocol GENERAL MANAGEMENT rules regulating a process a set of rules that govern and regulate a process

prototype GENERAL MANAGEMENT working model of new product or invention an initial version or working model of a new product or invention. A prototype is constructed and tested in order to evaluate the feasibility of a design and to identify problems that need to be corrected. Building a prototype is a key stage in ***new product development***.

provident INSURANCE paying benefits for illness or other need providing benefits in case of illness, old age, or other cases of need

Provincial Sales Tax TAX Canadian provincial tax on goods and services in Canada, a ***value-added tax*** levied by individual provinces on goods and services. The rate varies between provinces and it is not charged in Alberta, the Northwest Territories, Nunavut, or Yukon. In some provinces it is combined with ***Goods and Services Tax (sense 2)*** as ***Harmonized Sales Tax***. *Abbr* ***PST***

provision ACCOUNTING money earmarked for potential future expense a sum set aside in the accounts of an organization in anticipation of a future expense, often for doubtful debts. *See also* ***bad debt***

provisional tax TAX tax payment based on previous year's income tax paid in advance on the following year's income, the amount being based on the actual income from the preceding year

proxy CORPORATE GOVERNANCE surrogate voter at company meeting somebody who votes on behalf of another person at a company meeting

proxy fight CORPORATE GOVERNANCE consideration of proxy votes in settling disagreement the use of ***proxy votes*** to settle a contentious issue at a company meeting

proxy form *or* proxy card CORPORATE GOVERNANCE form that stockholders use to appoint proxy a form that stockholders receive with their invitations to attend an ***annual meeting***, and that they fill in if they want to appoint somebody to vote for them on a ***resolution***

proxy statement CORPORATE GOVERNANCE firm's notification to stockholders of voting rights a notice that a company sends to stockholders, allowing them to vote and giving them all the information they need to vote in an informed way

proxy vote CORPORATE GOVERNANCE vote made by somebody authorized by absent person a vote given by somebody who is present at a company meeting and has been authorized by a person who is not present to vote on his or her behalf

PRT *abbr* TAX ***petroleum revenue tax***

prudence TREASURY MANAGEMENT *see* ***prudence concept***

prudence concept TREASURY MANAGEMENT principle of not anticipating profits in accounts the principle that revenue and profits are not anticipated but are included in the ***profit and loss account*** only when realized in the form either of cash or of other assets, the ultimate cash realization of which can be assessed with reasonable certainty. Provision is made for all known liabilities (expenses and losses) whether the amount of these is known with certainty or is a best estimate in the light of the information available.

prudent FINANCE careful and sensible about money careful and exercising good judgment, especially in financial matters

prudential ratio BANKING, REGULATION & COMPLIANCE in EU, ratio of capital to assets in the European Union, the regulations covering the ratio of capital to assets that a bank should have

prudent man rule FINANCE rule requiring trustees to act carefully the assumption that trustees who make financial decisions on behalf of other people will act carefully, as any prudent person usually would

PSBR *abbr* FINANCE ***public sector borrowing requirement*** (*see* ***public sector cash requirement***)

PSI 20 MARKETS, STOCKHOLDING & INVESTMENTS main Portuguese stock market index an index of the 20 most-actively traded stocks on the ***Euronext Lisbon*** exchange. It was established on December 31, 1992, with a base value of 3,000.

PST *abbr* TAX ***Provincial Sales Tax***

psychic income HR & PERSONNEL job satisfaction independent of salary the level of satisfaction derived from a job rather than the salary earned doing it (slang)

psychological contract HR & PERSONNEL tacit understanding between employee and employer the set of unwritten expectations concerning the relationship between an employee and an employer. The psychological contract addresses factors that are not defined in a written contract of employment such as levels of commitment, productivity, quality of working life, job satisfaction, attitudes to working flexibly, and the provision and take-up of suitable training. Expectations of both employer and employee can change, so the psychological contract must be reevaluated at intervals to minimize misunderstandings.

Pty *abbr* *ANZ, S. AFRICA* BUSINESS ***proprietary company***

Public Accounts Committee FINANCE UK House of Commons committee monitoring government spending in the United Kingdom, a committee of the House of Commons that examines the spending of each department and ministry

public company BUSINESS = ***publicly held corporation***

public corporation BUSINESS government-owned organization especially in the United Kingdom, a state-owned organization established to provide a specific service, for example, the British Broadcasting Corporation

public debt FINANCE money owed by government the money that a government or a group of governments owes

public deposits FINANCE money of UK government departments in the United Kingdom, the balances to the credit of the government held at the ***Bank of England***

public expenditure FINANCE government spending on citizens' needs spending by the government of a country on items such as pension provision and infrastructure enhancement

public finance law REGULATION & COMPLIANCE financial legislation regulating public-sector organizations legislation relating to the financial activities of government or public-sector organizations

public financing FINANCE money that governments raise and spend the money raised by means of taxation and borrowing, and spent by governments, or the process of raising and spending this money

public funds FINANCE money that government spends money that a government has available for expenditure

public issue STOCKHOLDING & INVESTMENTS offer of stock to public offering a new issue of stock for sale to the public. An issue of this type is often advertised in the press. *See also* ***offer for sale, offer by prospectus***

public-liability insurance INSURANCE insurance against financial liability for injury insurance against the risk of being held financially liable for injury to somebody

public limited company *UK* BUSINESS *Abbr* **plc.** = ***publicly held corporation***

publicly held corporation *US* BUSINESS organization listed on exchange an organization with common stock listed on a stock exchange. *UK terms* ***public company, public limited company***

public monopoly BUSINESS when government is sole supplier of good a situation of limited competition in the public sector, usually relating to nationalized industries

public offering STOCKHOLDING & INVESTMENTS raising of funds via offer of stock a method of raising money used by a company in which it invites the public to apply for shares

public ownership BUSINESS ownership by national government a situation in which a government owns and operates a business

public placement *US* STOCKHOLDING & INVESTMENTS restricted selling of stock in public company the selling of stock in a ***publicly held corporation*** to a limited number of designated buyers. *UK term* ***public placing***. *See also* ***private placement***

public placing *UK* STOCKHOLDING & INVESTMENTS = ***public placement***

public private partnership BUSINESS private-sector involvement in traditionally public-sector service a partnership between government and the private sector for the purpose of more effectively providing services and infrastructure traditionally provided by the public sector. *Abbr* ***PPP***

public sector BUSINESS organizations financed and controlled by government the organizations in the section of the economy that is financed and controlled by central government, local authorities, and publicly funded corporations. *See also* ***private sector***

public sector borrowing requirement FINANCE *see* ***public sector cash requirement***

public sector cash requirement FINANCE difference between revenue and expenses of public sector the difference between the income and the expenditure of the public sector. It was formerly called the ***public sector borrowing requirement***.

public spending ECONOMICS government expenditure spending by the government of a country on publicly provided goods and services

public utility BUSINESS company providing basic service to community a company that provides a service such as electricity, gas, telecommunications, or water that is used by the whole community

published accounts *UK* ACCOUNTING = ***earnings report***

puff MARKETING exaggerate merits of something to overstate the virtues of a product or a service (informal)

puffery MARKETING exaggerated claims regarding product or service exaggerated claims made for a product or service. In general, puffery does not constitute false advertising under law. (slang)

puff piece MARKETING press item for promotional purposes an article in a newspaper or magazine promoting a product or service (slang)

pullback MARKETS price drop after rise a fall in the price of a security after it has reached a high

pull strategy MARKETING *see* ***push and pull strategies***

pull system OPERATIONS & PRODUCTION production of goods only as needed by customer a production planning and control system in which the specification and pace of output of a delivery, or supplier, workstation is set by the receiving, or customer, workstation. In pull systems, the customer acts as the only trigger for movement. The supplier workstation can only produce output on the instructions of the customer for delivery when the customer is ready to receive it. Demand is therefore transferred down through the stages of production from the order placed by an end customer. Pull systems are far less likely to result in work-in-progress inventory, and are favored by just-in-time or ***lean production*** systems. *See also* ***push system***

pump-and-dump STOCKHOLDING & INVESTMENTS illegal exaggeration of value of stock for profit an illegal practice in which the owner of a stock makes false claims about the stock, exaggerating its value, then sells it at a profit (slang)

pump priming FINANCE injection of funds to boost business the injection of further investment in order to revitalize a company or economy in stagnation, or to help a ***startup*** business over a critical period. Pump priming has a similar effect to the provision of ***seed capital***.

punter STOCKHOLDING & INVESTMENTS speculator in stock market a person who hopes to make a quick profit in a stock market (slang)

purchase FINANCE **1.** something bought a product or service that somebody is going to buy or has bought **2.** to buy something to buy a product or service

purchase acquisition MERGERS & ACQUISITIONS, ACCOUNTING accounting procedures for mergers the standard accounting procedures that must be followed when one company merges with another. *Also called* ***acquisition accounting***

purchase contract OPERATIONS & PRODUCTION agreement to buy at stated price a form of agreement to buy specific products at an agreed price

purchase ledger *UK* ACCOUNTING = ***payables ledger***

purchase money mortgage MORTGAGES mortgage used to buy property that is collateral in the United States, a mortgage whose proceeds the borrower uses to buy the property that is collateral for a loan

purchase order OPERATIONS & PRODUCTION document specifying terms of purchase of goods or services a written order for goods or services specifying quantities, prices, delivery dates, and contract terms. *Abbr* ***PO***

purchase price OPERATIONS & PRODUCTION price paid the price that somebody pays to buy a good or service

purchase requisition OPERATIONS & PRODUCTION internal request to purchase goods or services an internal instruction to a buying office to purchase goods or services, stating their quantity and description and generating a ***purchase order***

purchase tax TAX in UK, forerunner of VAT in the United Kingdom, a former tax paid when purchasing nonessential items that was replaced by VAT

purchasing OPERATIONS & PRODUCTION acquisition of goods and services by organization the acquisition of goods and services needed to support the various activities of an organization, at the optimum cost and from reliable suppliers. Purchasing involves defining the need for goods and services; identifying and comparing available supplies and suppliers; negotiating terms for price, quantity, and delivery; agreeing contracts and placing orders; receiving and accepting delivery; and authorizing the payment for goods and services. *Also called* ***procurement***

purchasing by contract OPERATIONS & PRODUCTION = ***contract purchasing***

purchasing department OPERATIONS & PRODUCTION department of firm responsible for purchasing the department in a company that buys raw materials or goods for use in the company. *Also called* ***buying department***

purchasing manager OPERATIONS & PRODUCTION employee responsible for purchasing an individual with responsibility for all activities concerned with purchasing. The responsibilities of a purchasing manager can include ordering, commercial negotiations, and delivery chasing. *Also called* ***buying manager***

purchasing power FINANCE measure of ability to buy goods and services a measure of the ability of a person, organization, or sector to buy goods and services

purchasing power parity CURRENCY & EXCHANGE theory linking exchange rate to purchasing power a theory that the ***exchange rate*** between two currencies is in equilibrium when the ***purchasing power*** of currency is the same in each country. If a basket of goods costs £100 in the United Kingdom and $150 for an equivalent in the United States, for equilibrium to exist, the exchange rate would be expected to be £1 = $1.50. If this were not the case, ***arbitrage*** would be expected to take place until equilibrium was restored. *Abbr* ***PPP***

purchasing routine OPERATIONS & PRODUCTION stages in purchase of product or service the various stages involved in organizing the purchase of a product or service

purchasing versus production OPERATIONS & PRODUCTION choice between making or buying needed item a decision on whether to produce goods internally or to buy them in from outside the organization. The goal of purchasing versus production is to secure needed items at the best possible cost, while making optimum use of the resources of the organization. Factors influencing the decision may include: cost, spare ***capacity*** within the organization, the need for tight quality and scheduling control, flexibility, the enhancement of skills that can then be used in other ways, volume and economies of scale, utilization of existing personnel, the need for secrecy, capital and financing requirements, and the potential reliability of supply. *Also called* ***buy or make, make or buy, internal versus external sourcing***

pure competition MARKETS situation in which many sellers compete in market a situation in which there are many sellers in a market and there is free flow of information

pure endowment FINANCE gift with conditions attached a gift that can only be used in the way laid down by its donor

purpose credit STOCKHOLDING & INVESTMENTS credit for purchasing securities credit obtained with the intention of buying and selling securities

push and pull strategies MARKETING contrasting marketing strategies targeting either distributor or customer approaches used as part of a marketing strategy to encourage customers to purchase a product or service. Push and pull strategies are contrasting approaches and tend to target different types of consumers. A *pull strategy* targets the end consumer, using advertising, sales promotions, and direct response marketing to pull the customer in. This approach is common in consumer markets. A *push strategy* targets members of the distribution channel, such as wholesalers and retailers, to push the promotion up through the channel to the consumers. This approach is more common in industrial markets.

push system OPERATIONS & PRODUCTION production of goods to be sold from inventory a production control and planning system in which demand is predicted centrally and each workstation pushes work out without considering if the next station is ready for it. While the central control aspect of a push system can achieve a balance across workstations, in practice a specific station can experience any one of a number of problems that delay work flow, so affecting the whole system. Push systems are characterized by work-in-progress inventory, lines, and idle time. *See also* ***pull system***

push the envelope GENERAL MANAGEMENT take risk of overstepping normal limits to exceed normal limits, implying a sense of risk at transcending the normal safe limits of operation

put *or* put option STOCKHOLDING & INVESTMENTS option to sell stock an option to sell stock within an agreed time at a specific price

put bond STOCKHOLDING & INVESTMENTS bond redeemable at specific date before maturity a bond that can be redeemed at face value at a specified time before its maturity date

put-call ratio MARKETS volume of puts divided by calls a ratio of the volume of ***puts*** to ***calls***, often used as an indicator of the best time to buy or sell stocks

PV *abbr* FINANCE ***present value***

PYB *abbr* ACCOUNTING ***preceding year basis***

pyramiding 1. FINANCE illegal payment of interest from new deposits the illegal practice of using new investors' deposits to pay the interest on the deposits made by existing investors **2.** MERGERS & ACQUISITIONS process of acquiring increasingly large companies the process of building up a major group by acquiring controlling interests in many different companies, each larger than the original company

pyramid selling MARKETING chain selling of goods from distributor to distributor the sale of the right to sell products or services to distributors who in turn recruit other distributors. Sometimes ending with no final buyer, pyramid selling is a form of multilevel marketing, and often involves a system of franchises. It is similar to ***network marketing***, but in many cases no end products are actually sold. Unscrupulous sellers of a pyramid marketing plan profit from the initial fees paid to them by distributors in advance of promised sales income. Pyramid selling is illegal in the United Kingdom.

Q

Q1 *abbr* ACCOUNTING ***first quarter***

Q2 *abbr* ACCOUNTING ***second quarter***

Q3 *abbr* ACCOUNTING ***third quarter***

Q4 *abbr* ACCOUNTING ***fourth quarter***

qard *or* qard hassan FINANCE interest-free loan in Islamic financing, a loan, which under Islamic law is always free of profit. A qard may also be a bank deposit, which is considered a loan to a bank for its use but which must be returned to the depositor upon request.

qualification of accounts ACCOUNTING = ***auditors' qualification***

qualification payment FINANCE financial reward for academic qualification an additional payment sometimes made to employees of New Zealand companies who have gained an academic qualification relevant to their job

qualified auditor's report ACCOUNTING = ***adverse opinion***

qualified domestic trust FINANCE trust giving benefits to non-US spouse in the United States, a trust established by a US citizen for a noncitizen spouse that affords tax advantages to the spouse at the time of the citizen's death

qualified lead MARKETING good potential customer a prospective customer whose potential value has been carefully researched

qualified listed security STOCKHOLDING & INVESTMENTS security that can be purchased by regulated entity a security that is eligible for purchase by a regulated entity such as a trust

qualified plan PENSIONS IRS-approved retirement or benefit plan in the United States, a retirement plan or employee benefit plan that meets the requirements of the IRS for special tax consideration

qualified valuer FINANCE professional person conducting valuation a person conducting a valuation who holds a recognized and relevant professional qualification. The person must also have recent post-qualification experience and sufficient knowledge of the state of the market with reference to the location and category of the tangible fixed asset being valued.

qualifying distribution STOCKHOLDING & INVESTMENTS former UK dividend payment formerly in the United Kingdom, the payment to a stockholder of a dividend on which ***advance corporation tax*** was paid

qualifying period FINANCE period needed for eligibility a period of time that has to pass before somebody is eligible for something, for example, a grant or subsidy

qualifying ratio MORTGAGES calculation of mortgage affordability a calculation of how much mortgage a borrower can afford, by comparing his or her monthly income against monthly outgoings

qualifying shares STOCKHOLDING & INVESTMENTS stockholding required before rights are granted the number of shares of stock somebody needs to hold to be eligible for something such as a bonus issue

qualitative analysis GENERAL MANAGEMENT appraisal of project with no quantifiable data the subjective appraisal of a project or investment for which there is no quantifiable data. *See also* ***chartist, quantitative analysis, technical analysis***

qualitative research GENERAL MANAGEMENT research using data that is not measurable research that focuses on "soft" data, for example, attitude research or focus groups. *See also* ***quantitative research***

quality bond STOCKHOLDING & INVESTMENTS bond issued by safe firm a bond issued by an organization that has an excellent credit rating

quality costs OPERATIONS & PRODUCTION costs associated with failure to meet standards costs associated with the failure to achieve conformance to requirements. Quality costs accrue when organizations waste large sums of money because of carrying out the wrong tasks, or failing to perform the right tasks correctly the first time. *Also called* ***nonconformance costs***

quality equity STOCKHOLDING & INVESTMENTS equity with good performance history an equity with a good track record of earnings and dividends. *See also* ***blue chip***

quango *UK* GENERAL MANAGEMENT semi-governmental organization an acronym derived from quasi-autonomous nongovernmental organization, a body outside the civil service but established by the government, answerable to a government minister, and with responsibility in a specific area

quant FINANCE **1.** = ***quantitative analyst*** **2.** = ***quantitative analysis***

quantitative analysis FINANCE numerical assessment of financial variables the use of mathematical and statistical models in the evaluation of financial data of all kinds. *Also called* ***quant*** *(sense 2). See also* ***chartist, qualitative analysis, technical analysis***

quantitative analyst FINANCE somebody assessing financial variables numerically a person who uses econometric, mathematical, or statistical models to evaluate a project or investment. *Also called* ***quant*** *(sense 1)*

quantitative easing FINANCE central bank's issue of money to other banks the release by a central bank of sufficient funds to stimulate activity in a banking system that has become sluggish and generate an improvement in the economy. This sometimes means printing money in order to give banks more capital.

quantitative research GENERAL MANAGEMENT analysis of numerical data the gathering and analysis of data that can be expressed in numerical form. Quantitative research involves data that is measurable and can include statistical results, financial data, or demographic data. *See also* ***qualitative research***

quantity discount OPERATIONS & PRODUCTION price reduction for bulk buying a reduction in price given to people who buy large quantities of a product

quantum meruit FINANCE as much as has been earned a Latin phrase meaning "as much as has been earned." A claim for quantum meruit can be for reasonable payment for work that has been done without a full estimate.

        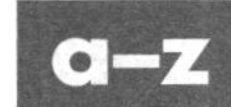

quarter 1. ACCOUNTING three-month period a three-month calendar period, often used as a period for reporting earnings, paying taxes, or calculating dividends 2. CURRENCY & EXCHANGE US coin worth 25 cents a US coin worth one-fourth of a dollar or 25 cents

quarter day *UK* OPERATIONS & PRODUCTION day when some payments become due a day at the end of a quarter, when rents, fees, and other payments become due

quarter-end ACCOUNTING of end of three-month period relating to the end of a three-month ***accounting period*** when financial transactions for that period are finalized

quarterly 1. GENERAL MANAGEMENT happening every three months taking place once in every period of three months 2. ACCOUNTING company's financial results the results of a corporation, produced each quarter

quarterly report ACCOUNTING financial statement for quarter of tax year a financial statement that covers a quarter of a full fiscal year. In the United States the general practice is to issue quarterly reports. *See also* ***interim financial statement***

quartile STATISTICS one of four equal ranges of values any of the values in a frequency or probability distribution that divide it into four equal parts

quasi-contract LEGAL in UK, court order stipulating legal obligation a decree by a UK court stipulating that one party has a legal obligation to another, even though there is no legally binding contract between the two parties

quasi-loan FINANCE arrangement to pay somebody else's debt an arrangement whereby one party pays the debts of another, on the condition that the sum of the debts will be reimbursed by the indebted party at some later date

quasi-money *UK* STOCKHOLDING & INVESTMENTS = ***near money***

quasi-public corporation BUSINESS firm partly owned by government in the United States, an organization that is owned partly by private or public stockholders and partly by the government

quasi-rent FINANCE difference between production cost and selling cost excess earnings made by a company representing the difference between production cost (the cost of labor and materials) and selling cost

qubes STOCKHOLDING & INVESTMENTS fund tracking NASDAQ-100 an exchange-traded fund that tracks the stocks in the NASDAQ-100 index, which consists mainly of the largest nonfinancial companies traded on the NASDAQ

question mark company STOCKHOLDING & INVESTMENTS uncertain investment prospect a company that offers a doubtful return on investment

quick asset FINANCE asset easily cashed in cash or any asset that can quickly be turned into cash, for example, a bank deposit of some types, a short-dated bond, or a certificate of deposit. *See also* ***near money***

quick ratio FINANCE 1. measure of somebody's short-term borrowing potential a measure of the amount of cash a potential borrower can acquire in a short time, used in evaluating creditworthiness 2. ratio of liquid assets to current debts the ratio of a company's liquid assets to its current liabilities, used as an indicator of ***liquidity***

quid pro quo FINANCE something in exchange a Latin phrase meaning "something for something," something given or done in exchange for something else. To be valid, a contract must involve a quid pro quo.

quorum CORPORATE GOVERNANCE minimum number of attendees required for decision-making the minimum number of people required in a meeting for it to be able to make decisions that are binding on the organization. For a company, this number is stated in its ***bylaws***; for a partnership, in its partnership agreement.

quota 1. FINANCE limit of investment by party in joint venture the maximum sum to be contributed by each party in a joint venture or joint business undertaking 2. STOCKHOLDING & INVESTMENTS ceiling on investment in given situation or market the maximum number of investments that may be purchased and sold in a specific situation or market, as in a US Treasury auction, where bidders may not apply for more than a specific percentage of the securities being offered 3. INTERNATIONAL TRADE limit of imports or exports the maximum amount of a specific commodity, product, or service that can be imported into or exported out of a country

quota system 1. OPERATIONS & PRODUCTION, INTERNATIONAL TRADE system that limits imports or supplies a system in which imports or supplies of a commodity, for example, are limited to fixed maximum amounts 2. OPERATIONS & PRODUCTION distribution system allocating items evenly among distributors an arrangement for distribution which allows each distributor only a specific number of items

quote *or* quotation FINANCE estimate of price a statement of what a person or company is willing to accept when selling a product or service. *Also called* ***bid***

quoted company BUSINESS, MARKETS = ***listed company***

quote-driven system MARKETS system fixing initial stock price by quotes a price system on a stock exchange in which prices are generated by dealers' and market makers' quotes before market forces come into play and prices are determined by the interaction of supply and demand. The London Stock Exchange's dealing system, as well as those of many ***over-the-counter markets***, have quote-driven systems. *See also* ***order-driven system***

quoted securities MARKETS securities listed on exchange securities or stocks that are listed on a recognized stock exchange

R

racket FRAUD illegal money-making deal an illegal business deal that makes a lot of money, involving such activities as bribery or intimidation

raid MARKETS illegal selling of stock the illegal practice of taking a ***short position*** in a large number of shares of stock of a particular company in order to drive the price down. *Also called* ***bear raid***

raider MERGERS & ACQUISITIONS maker of hostile takeover bids a person or company that makes hostile takeover bids, wanted neither by directors nor stockholders

rake it in BUSINESS make large amount of money to make a great deal of money relatively easily (slang)

rake-off BUSINESS commission a payment made to an intermediary, often calculated as a percentage of the value of goods or services provided (slang)

rally MARKETS price rise after fall a rise in stock prices after a significant fall

ramp MARKETS buy stock to raise price to buy stock with the objective of raising its price rather than as an investment. *See also* ***rigged market***

ramp up GENERAL MANAGEMENT greatly increase efforts or interest to increase significantly your interest or efforts in a particular area

rand CURRENCY & EXCHANGE S. African currency unit the standard unit of currency of the Republic of South Africa, equal to 100 cents

Randlord BUSINESS wealthy businessman in Johannesburg originally a Johannesburg-based mining magnate or tycoon of the late 19th or early 20th centuries, now used informally for any wealthy or powerful Johannesburg businessman

random STATISTICS equally likely to occur relating to a set in which all the members have the same probability of occurrence

random sampling STATISTICS statistical technique for sampling individuals at random an unbiased ***sampling*** technique in which every member of a population has an equal chance of being included in the sample. Based on probability theory, random sampling is the process of selecting and canvassing a representative group of individuals from a specific population in order to identify the attributes or attitudes of the population as a whole. Related sampling techniques include: *stratified sampling*, in which the population is divided into classes, and random samples are taken from each class; *cluster sampling*, in which a unit of the sample is a group such as a household; and *systematic sampling*, which refers to samples chosen by any system other than random selection. *See also* ***nonrandom sampling***

random walk 1. MARKETS unpredictable movement in stock prices a movement that cannot be predicted, used to describe movements in stock prices that cannot be forecast 2. STATISTICS sampling method producing random selection a sampling technique that allows for random selection within specific limits set up by a non-random technique

range STATISTICS spread from smallest to largest value the difference between the smallest and the largest observations in a data set

range pricing BUSINESS logical pricing of products in range the pricing of individual products so that their prices fit logically within a variety of connected products offered by one supplier, differentiated by a factor such as weight of pack or number of product attributes offered

ranking STATISTICS order in which values are arranged the ordered arrangement of a set of variable values

ratchet effect ECONOMICS adjusting more easily to income increases than decreases the result when households adjust more easily to rising incomes than to falling incomes, as, for example, when their consumption drops by less than their income in a recession

  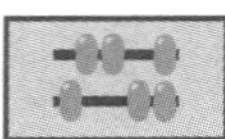      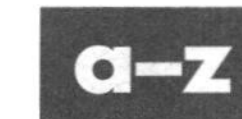

rate FINANCE assess value to calculate or assess the value of something, for example, real estate for tax purposes

rateable value FINANCE value calculated according to rule the value of something calculated with reference to a rule. An example is the value of a commercial property taken as a basis for calculating local taxes.

rate cap FINANCE = ***cap***

rate of exchange CURRENCY & EXCHANGE = ***exchange rate***

rate of inflation ECONOMICS percentage increase in prices over year the percentage increase in the price of goods and services calculated over a twelve-month period

rate of interest FINANCE percentage charged on loan or paid on investment a percentage charged on a loan or paid on an investment for the use of the money

rate of return ACCOUNTING, STOCKHOLDING & INVESTMENTS ratio of investment profit to investment cost an accounting ratio of the income from an investment to the amount of the investment, used to measure financial performance.

There is a basic formula that will serve most needs, at least initially:

$$\frac{\text{(Current value of amount invested} - \text{Original value of amount invested)}}{\text{Original value of amount invested}} \times 100\% = \text{Rate of return}$$

If $1,000 in capital is invested in stock, and one year later the investment yields $1,100, the rate of return of the investment is calculated like this:

$$\frac{(1,100 - 1,000)}{1,000} \times 100\% = \frac{100}{1,000} \times 100\% = 10\%$$

Now, assume $1,000 is invested again. One year later, the investment grows to $2,000 in value, but after another year the value of the investment falls to $1,200. The rate of return after the first year is:

$$\frac{(2,000 - 1,000)}{1,000} \times 100\% = 100\%$$

The rate of return after the second year is:

$$\frac{(1,200 - 2,000)}{2,000} \times 100\% = -40\%$$

The average annual return for the two years (also known as average annual arithmetic return) can be calculated using this formula:

$$\frac{\text{(Rate of return for year 1 + Rate of return for year 2)}}{2} = \text{Average annual return}$$

Accordingly:

$$\frac{(100\% + -40\%)}{2} = 30\%$$

The average annual rate of return is a percentage, but one that is accurate over only a short period, so this method should be used accordingly.

The geometric or compound rate of return is a better yardstick for measuring investments over the long term, and takes into account the effects of compounding. This formula is more complex and technical.

The real rate of return is the annual return realized on an investment, adjusted for changes in the price due to inflation. If 10% is earned on an investment but inflation is 2%, then the real rate of return is actually 8%. *Also called* ***return***

rates TAX in UK, forerunner of council tax in the United Kingdom, local UK taxes formerly levied on property and now replaced by ***council tax***

rate tart FINANCE somebody often changing to accounts with better rates somebody who changes loan providers or savings accounts regularly to benefit from better interest rates (slang)

rating FINANCE relative assigned value the value or quality that something is assessed as having, for example, the status of a person or company in terms of creditworthiness, or a company or product in terms of suitability for investment. *See also* ***credit rating***

rating agency STOCKHOLDING & INVESTMENTS organization rating firms issuing bonds an organization that gives a ***rating*** to companies or other organizations issuing bonds

ratio analysis FINANCE using ratios in financial analysis the use of ratios to measure a company's financial performance, for example, the ***current ratio*** or the ***leverage ratios***

rationalization GENERAL MANAGEMENT measures taken to increase organization's efficiency the application of efficiency or effectiveness measures to an organization. Rationalization can occur at the onset of a downturn in an organization's performance or results. It usually takes the form of cutbacks intended to bring the organization back to profitability and may involve layoffs, plant closures, and cutbacks in supplies and resources. It often involves changes in organization structure, particularly in the form of ***downsizing***. The term is also used in a cynical way as a euphemism for mass layoffs.

raw materials OPERATIONS & PRODUCTION materials from which products are manufactured items bought for use in the manufacturing or development processes of an organization. While most often referring to bulk materials, raw materials can also include components, subassemblies, and complete products.

RBA *abbr* BANKING ***Reserve Bank of Australia***

RBNZ *abbr* BANKING ***Reserve Bank of New Zealand***

RD *or* R/D *abbr* UK BANKING ***refer to drawer***

RDG *abbr* ECONOMICS ***regional development grant***

RDP FINANCE government policies addressing economic aftermath of apartheid a policy framework by means of which the South African government intends to correct the socioeconomic imbalances caused by apartheid. *Full form* ***Reconstruction and Development Program***

RDPR *abbr* BANKING ***refer to drawer please re-present***

ready money FINANCE money immediately available cash or money that is immediately available for use

Reaganomics ECONOMICS 1980s economic policies of Ronald Reagan the economic policy of former US President Reagan in the 1980s, who reduced taxes and social security support and increased the national budget deficit to an unprecedented level

real FINANCE after considering inflation after the effects of inflation are taken into consideration

real asset FINANCE physical asset an asset with a physical presence such as land or a building. *See also* ***tangible asset***

real balance effect ECONOMICS results of falling prices and increased consumption the effect on income and employment when prices fall and consumption increases

real capital FINANCE assets with monetary value assets such as buildings or equipment that are used in creating products and can be assigned a monetary value. *See also* ***financial capital***

real earnings FINANCE available income after deductions income that is available for spending after tax and other contributions have been deducted, adjusted for inflation. *Also called* ***real income, real wages***

real economy ECONOMICS goods, services, and jobs the production of goods and services on which jobs, incomes, and consumer spending depend

real estate REAL ESTATE land and improvements in the United States, property that consists of land and anything attached to it, for example, trees and buildings. *Also called* ***realty***

real estate developer *US* REAL ESTATE somebody who develops land or buildings a person or company that develops land or buildings to increase their value. *UK term* ***property developer***

real estate investment trust REAL ESTATE, STOCKHOLDING & INVESTMENTS trust investing in properties and mortgages a publicly traded ***investment trust*** that uses investors' money to invest in properties and mortgages. *Abbr* ***REIT***

real exchange rate CURRENCY & EXCHANGE exchange rate adjusted for inflation a current exchange rate that has been adjusted for inflation

real GDP ECONOMICS GDP adjusted for prices a measure of ***GDP*** adjusted for changes in prices

real growth ECONOMICS economic growth adjusted for prices the increase in productivity, sales, or earnings of a country or a household adjusted for changes in prices

real income FINANCE = ***real earnings***

real interest rate FINANCE interest rate adjusted for inflation an interest rate after a deduction for inflation has been made

real investment FINANCE purchase of real estate or plant, not securities the purchase of assets such as land, real estate, and plant and machinery, as opposed to the acquisition of securities

realize FINANCE sell asset for cash to change an ***asset*** into an amount of money by selling it

realized profit FINANCE profit from sale of something profit made when something has been sold, as opposed to ***paper profit***

real money FINANCE **1.** capital from investors who have not borrowed investment capital provided by investors such as pension funds, some insurance companies, retail mutual funds, and high net worth individuals who are not borrowing it from other sources **2.** bills and coins money available as bills and coins to spend, rather than existing only as items on financial accounts **3.** lots of money a very large amount of money (informal)

real option STOCKHOLDING & INVESTMENTS, RISK choice available to investor in tangible investment

the opportunity to choose a course of action that an investor has when investing in something tangible such as a business project

real property REAL ESTATE land and permanent improvements in the United States, land and the permanent structures on it

real purchasing power ECONOMICS how much consumer is able to buy the purchasing power of a country or a household adjusted for changes in prices

real rate of return FINANCE rate of return allowing for inflation the rate of return received after a deduction for inflation

real return after tax FINANCE, TAX net income or profit the income or profit made after deductions for taxes and inflation

real time company BUSINESS firm providing immediate response to customers over Internet a company that uses the Internet and other technologies to respond immediately to customer demands

real time credit card processing E-COMMERCE immediate authorization of credit card during online transaction the online authorization of a credit card indicating that the credit card has been approved or rejected during the transaction

real time EDI E-COMMERCE online transactions between businesses and customers online ***electronic data interchange***: the online transfer and processing of business data, for example, purchase orders, customer invoices, and payment receipts, between suppliers and their customers

real time manager E-COMMERCE service manager for Internet customers a manager who is responsible for delivering the immediate service that customers expect, using the Internet and other technologies

real time transaction E-COMMERCE online payment immediately approved or rejected an Internet payment transaction that is approved or rejected immediately when the customer completes the online order form

Realtor REAL ESTATE real estate agent belonging to professional body in the United States, a licensed real estate agent who is a member of the National Association of Realtors

realty REAL ESTATE land and buildings property that consists of land and anything attached to it, for example, trees and buildings. *Also called* ***real estate***

real value FINANCE value of investment in real terms a value of an investment that is maintained at the same level, for example, by making it ***index-linked***

real wages FINANCE = ***real earnings***

rebadge MARKETING sell another company's product under your name to buy a product or service from another company and sell it as part of your own product range

rebate 1. FINANCE money returned when payment is excessive money returned because a payment exceeded the amount required, for example, a tax rebate **2.** FINANCE discount a reduction in the price of goods or services in relation to the standard price **3.** STOCKHOLDING & INVESTMENTS reduce client's commission charge of a broker, to reduce part of the commission charged to the client as a promotional offer

recapitalization FINANCE reorganization of firm's capital the process of changing the way a company's capital is structured, in terms of the balance between debt and equity, usually in response to a major financial problem such as ***bankruptcy***

recapture 1. FINANCE sale with right to buy back a situation in which a seller of an asset retains the right to buy back part or all of the asset **2.** TAX, ACCOUNTING treatment of past deduction as income a situation in which a deduction taken in a previous tax year must be reported as income, for example, when a depreciated asset is sold at a gain

recd *or* rec'd *abbr* FINANCE ***received***

receipt BUSINESS acknowledgment of transfer a document acknowledging that something has been received, for example, a payment

receipts FINANCE money from sales the total amount a retailer takes from sales. *Also called* ***takings***. *See also* ***gross receipts, net receipts***

receivables ACCOUNTING money owing but not paid money that has been billed to customers or clients but has not yet been received

receivables ledger *US* ACCOUNTING record of accounts receivable a ledger in which a company records its ***accounts receivable***. *See also* ***payables ledger***. *UK term* ***purchase ledger***

received FINANCE referring to money taken in used in recording payments or sums of money. *Abbr* ***recd***

receiver LEGAL person selling firm's assets in insolvency a person appointed to sell the assets of a company that is insolvent. The proceeds of the sale are used to discharge debts to creditors, with any surplus distributed to ***shareholders***.

Receiver of Revenue TAX **1.** S. African tax office a local office of the South African Revenue Service (***SARS***) **2.** S. African Revenue Service the South African Revenue Service (***SARS***) as a whole (informal)

receivership FINANCE, LEGAL management of insolvent company by court-appointed official a state of ***insolvency*** prior to ***liquidation***. During receivership, receivers may attempt to undertake ***turnaround management*** or decide that the company must go into liquidation. *Also called* ***administration*** *(sense 1)*

recession ECONOMICS slowdown of economic activity a stage of the ***business cycle*** in which economic activity is in slow decline. Recession usually follows a boom, and precedes a ***depression***. It is characterized by rising unemployment and falling levels of output and investment.

recessionary gap ECONOMICS shortfall of demand needed to ensure full employment a shortfall in the amount of ***aggregate demand*** in an economy needed to create full employment

recharacterization PENSIONS movement of US retirement contributions in the United States, the process of transferring a contribution made to one type of Individual Retirement Account (***IRA***) to another type, or reversing a prior conversion such as from a ***traditional IRA*** to a ***Roth IRA***

reciprocal holdings STOCKHOLDING & INVESTMENTS mutual stockholdings that prevent takeover bids a situation in which two companies own stock in each other to prevent takeover bids

reciprocal trade INTERNATIONAL TRADE trade between countries trade between two countries, usually based on an agreement that benefits both countries

recognized investment exchange MARKETS in UK, financial exchange recognized by FSA in the United Kingdom, a stock exchange, futures exchange, or commodity exchange recognized by the ***Financial Services Authority***. *Abbr* ***RIE***

recognized professional body BUSINESS in UK, organization recognized by FSA in the United Kingdom, a professional organization that regulates its members and is recognized by the ***Financial Services Authority***. *Abbr* ***RPB***

recommended retail price *UK* BUSINESS = ***suggested retail price***

reconciliation ACCOUNTING accounting adjustment in line with authoritative information adjustment of a record, such as somebody's own record of bank account transactions, to match more authoritative information

reconciliation statement ACCOUNTING document verifying date of independently recorded transaction a document used to verify that two independent records of the same financial transactions agree as of a particular date

Reconstruction and Development Program FINANCE *see* ***RDP***

record date GENERAL MANAGEMENT date of computer data entry the date when a computer data entry or record is made

recourse FINANCE right of lender to demand repayment of loan a right of a lender to compel a borrower to repay money borrowed, or, in some cases, to take assets belonging to the borrower if the money is not repaid

recourse agreement FINANCE installment plan agreement allowing retailer to repossess an agreement in an installment plan whereby the retailer repossesses the goods being purchased in the event that the purchaser fails to make regular payments

recoverable ACT TAX former part of UK corporation tax formerly in the United Kingdom, ***advance corporation tax*** that could be set against the ***corporation tax*** payable for the period

recoverable amount ACCOUNTING value of asset if sold or when used the value of an asset, either the price it would bring if sold, or its value to the company when used, whichever is the larger figure

recovery ECONOMICS return to normal economic activity after downturn the return of a country to economic health after a crash or a depression

recovery fund STOCKHOLDING & INVESTMENTS fund investing in recovery stock a fund that invests in ***recovery stock*** that it considers likely to return to a previous higher price

recovery stock STOCKHOLDING & INVESTMENTS underperforming stock now recovering a stock that has fallen in price because of poor business performance, but is now expected to climb as a result of an improvement in the company's prospects

rectification note OPERATIONS & PRODUCTION authorization to improve poor product the authorization for more work to be done to improve a product that did not originally meet the required standard

recurring billing transaction E-COMMERCE automatic rebilling of customer's credit card a means of electronic payment based on the automatic

  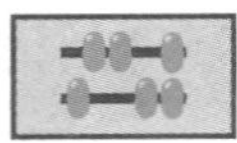      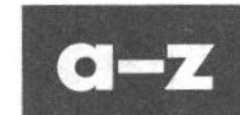

charging of a customer's credit card in each payment period

recurring payments E-COMMERCE series of automatic payments preauthorized by customer a means of electronic payment that permits a merchant to process multiple authorizations by the same customer either as multiple payments for a fixed amount or recurring billings for varying amounts

red BANKING color for debits the color of debit or overdrawn balances in some bank statements **in the red** FINANCE, BANKING, ACCOUNTING in debt, or losing money

Red Book FINANCE copy of UK finance minister's Budget speech a copy of the Chancellor of the Exchequer's speech published on the day of the Budget. It can be regarded as the United Kingdom's financial statement and report.

Red chips STOCKHOLDING & INVESTMENTS good Chinese companies Chinese companies that are considered risk-free and worth investing in

red day *US* FINANCE unprofitable day a day on which no profit has been made (slang)

redeem 1. FINANCE pay off loan or debt to carry out the repayment of a loan or a debt **2.** BUSINESS exchange voucher for something to exchange a voucher, coupon, or stamp for a gift or a reduction in price **3.** STOCKHOLDING & INVESTMENTS exchange security for cash to exchange a security for cash

redeemable bond STOCKHOLDING & INVESTMENTS bond that will be repaid a bond that is redeemable

redeemable gilt STOCKHOLDING & INVESTMENTS gilt that will be repaid a gilt that is redeemable

redeemable government stock STOCKHOLDING & INVESTMENTS stock redeemable for cash government stock that can be redeemed for cash at some time in the future

redeemable preference share *UK* STOCKHOLDING & INVESTMENTS = ***redeemable preferred stock***

redeemable preferred stock *US* STOCKHOLDING & INVESTMENTS preference share that firm may buy back a type of preferred stock that a company has the right to buy back at a specific date and for a specific price. *Also called* ***callable preferred stock***. *UK term* ***redeemable preference share***

redeemable security STOCKHOLDING & INVESTMENTS security redeemable at face value a security that can be redeemed at its face value at a specific date in the future

redeemable shares STOCKHOLDING & INVESTMENTS shares of stock that may be repurchased stock that is issued on terms that may require it to be bought back by the issuer at some future date, at the discretion either of the issuer or of the holder

redemption STOCKHOLDING & INVESTMENTS ending of financial obligation repayment of a financial obligation, frequently used in connection with preferred stock, debentures, and bonds

redemption date STOCKHOLDING & INVESTMENTS date for repayment of redeemable security the date on which a redeemable security is due to be repaid

redemption value STOCKHOLDING & INVESTMENTS value of security at redemption the value of a security at the time it is redeemed

redemption yield STOCKHOLDING & INVESTMENTS yield on security up to redemption a yield on a security including interest and its value up to the time it is redeemed. *See also* ***yield to maturity***

red eye *US* STOCKHOLDING & INVESTMENTS preliminary prospectus to test market information in the form of a ***preliminary prospectus*** used in ***initial public offerings*** to gauge the reaction of investors (slang) *UK term* ***pathfinder prospectus***

red herring STOCKHOLDING & INVESTMENTS = ***preliminary prospectus***

rediscount FINANCE discount bill of exchange for second time to discount a bill of exchange that has already been discounted by a commercial bank

redistribution of wealth ECONOMICS sharing of wealth across population the process of sharing wealth among the entire population, often through taxation

redistributive effect ECONOMICS, TAX wealth equalization resulting from taxes and benefits the tendency toward equalization of people's wealth that results from a ***progressive tax*** or selective benefit

redlining FINANCE, LEGAL discrimination against borrowers because of neighborhood of residence the illegal practice by financial institutions of discriminating against prospective borrowers because of the area of the town or city in which they live

red screen market MARKETS in UK, market with low prices in the United Kingdom, a market where the prices are down and are being shown as red on the dealing screens

red tape GENERAL MANAGEMENT excessive bureaucracy excessive bureaucracy or unwillingness to depart from rules and regulations

reducing balance depreciation CURRENCY & EXCHANGE *see* ***depreciation***

reducing balance method ACCOUNTING = ***accelerated depreciation***

redundancy *UK* HR & PERSONNEL = ***severance***

redundancy package *UK* HR & PERSONNEL = ***severance package***

redundancy payment *UK* FINANCE HR & PERSONNEL = ***severance pay***

redundant capacity OPERATIONS & PRODUCTION = ***surplus capacity***

reengineering GENERAL MANAGEMENT *see* ***business process reengineering***

reference BANKING = ***banker's reference***

reference population STATISTICS standard set for statistical comparison a standard against which a statistical population under study can be compared

reference rate FINANCE rate used as benchmark a benchmark interest rate, for example, a bank's own set rate or the ***London Interbank Offered Rate***. Lending rates are often expressed as a margin over a reference rate.

reference site E-COMMERCE customer website showcasing new technology a customer website where a new technology is being used successfully

referred share STOCKHOLDING & INVESTMENTS ex dividend stock a stock that is ***ex dividend***, the right to dividends remaining with the vendor

refer to drawer *UK* BANKING refuse to pay check from underfunded account to refuse to pay a check because the account from which it is drawn has too little money in it. *Abbr* ***RD***, **R/D**

refer to drawer please re-present BANKING shown on refused UK check in the United Kingdom, marked on a check by the paying banker to indicate that there are currently insufficient funds to meet the payment, but that the bank believes sufficient funds will be available shortly. *See also* ***refer to drawer***. *Abbr* ***RDPR***

refinance FINANCE replace loan to replace one loan with another, especially at a lower rate of interest or at a longer maturity

refinancing FINANCE **1.** replacing one loan with another the process of taking out a loan to pay off other loans **2.** new loan that repays old loan a loan taken out for the purpose of repaying another loan or loans

reflation ECONOMICS increasing employment by increasing demand a method of reducing unemployment by increasing an economy's ***aggregate demand***. *See also* **recession**

refugee capital FINANCE resources entering country through necessity people and other financial resources that come into a country because they have been forced to leave their own country for economic or political reasons

refund BUSINESS return of purchase price to buyer the reimbursement of the purchase price of a good or service, for reasons such as manufacturing flaws or dissatisfaction with the service provided

refundable BUSINESS able to be repaid able or liable to be paid back

refunding FINANCE issuance of new bonds to replace old the process of a government's renewing of the funding of a debt by issuing new bonds to replace those that are about to mature

regeneration ECONOMICS revitalization of rundown industrial or business areas the redevelopment of industrial or business areas that have suffered decline, in order to increase employment and business activity

regional development grant ECONOMICS grant encouraging business in UK regions in the United Kingdom, a grant given to encourage a business to establish itself in a specific part of the country. *Abbr* ***RDG***

regional fund STOCKHOLDING & INVESTMENTS mutual fund investing in geographic region a mutual fund that invests in the markets of a particular geographic region

regional stock exchange MARKETS stock exchange outside country's main financial center a stock exchange that is not in the main financial center of a country

registered bond STOCKHOLDING & INVESTMENTS bond with ownership recorded by issuer a bond the ownership of which is recorded on the books of the issuer

registered broker MARKETS broker registered on exchange a broker who is registered as a member of a particular stock exchange

registered capital FINANCE = ***authorized capital***

registered check BANKING check written on temporary bank account a check written on a bank's account on behalf of a customer who does not have a bank account but who gives the bank funds to hold to cover the check

registered company REGULATION & COMPLIANCE UK firm registered with Companies House in the United Kingdom, a company that has filed official documents with the ***Registrar of Companies*** at Companies House. A registered company is obliged to conduct itself in accordance with company law. All organizations must register in order to become companies.

registered investment adviser STOCKHOLDING & INVESTMENTS professionally recognized US financial manager a person or company that is registered with the US ***Securities and Exchange Commission*** and usually manages the portfolios of others

registered name REGULATION & COMPLIANCE name of UK firm registered with Companies House in the United Kingdom, the name of a company as it is registered at Companies House. It must appear, along with the company's registered number and office, on all its letterheads and orders. *See also* ***company, corporation***

registered number REGULATION & COMPLIANCE number assigned to registered UK firm in the United Kingdom, a unique number assigned to a company registered at Companies House. It must appear, along with the company's registered name and office, on all its letterheads and orders. *See also* ***company, corporation***

registered office REGULATION & COMPLIANCE in UK, company's official mailing address in the United Kingdom, the official address of a company, which is reproduced on its letterheads and registered with Companies House, to which all legal correspondence and documents must be delivered

registered representative STOCKHOLDING & INVESTMENTS qualified US seller of securities a person who is licensed by the US Securities and Exchange Commission to sell securities, after having passed the required examinations

registered security *or* registered share STOCKHOLDING & INVESTMENTS security with holder's name recorded by issuer a security for which the holder's name is recorded in the books of the issuer. *See also* ***nominee***

registered share capital STOCKHOLDING & INVESTMENTS = ***authorized share capital***

registered trademark LEGAL unique mark identifying product with producer a unique legally registered mark on a product, that may be a symbol, words, or both, connecting the product to the trader or producer of that product

register of companies REGULATION & COMPLIANCE in UK, list of registered firms in the United Kingdom, the list of companies maintained at Companies House. *See also* ***company, corporation***

register of directors and secretaries REGULATION & COMPLIANCE firm's record of directors and secretaries a record that every ***registered company*** in the United Kingdom must maintain of the names and residential addresses of directors and the company secretary together with their nationality, occupation, and details of other directorships held. Public companies must also record the date of birth of their directors. The record must be kept at the company's registered office and be available for inspection by stockholders without charge and by members of the public for a nominal fee.

register of directors' interests REGULATION & COMPLIANCE, STOCKHOLDING & INVESTMENTS firm's record of directors' holdings a record that every ***registered company*** in the United Kingdom must maintain of the stocks and other ***securities*** that have been issued by the company and are held by its directors. It has to be made available for inspection during the company's ***annual meeting***.

registrar CORPORATE GOVERNANCE keeper of official records a person or organization responsible for keeping official records, for example, the person who keeps a record of stockholders in a company

Registrar of Companies LEGAL, CORPORATE GOVERNANCE official holding record of registered UK companies the person charged with the duty of holding and registering the official startup and constitutional documents of all ***registered companies*** in the United Kingdom

registration REGULATION & COMPLIANCE **1.** official listing or recording of information the process of recording something such as names, data, or other required information on an official list **2.** provision of required documentation before selling company stock in the United States, the process by which a company files documents with the ***SEC*** prior to offering stock for sale to the public. The document must contain detailed financial information that has been certified by an outside accountant, information about the company's management, and details of the public offering.

registration fee **1.** REGULATION & COMPLIANCE money paid to have something registered money paid to cover the cost of having something, such as a company, registered **2.** GENERAL MANAGEMENT fee for attending event money paid to take part in an event or activity, for example, a conference or training session

registration statement REGULATION & COMPLIANCE document produced by US corporation issuing securities in the United States, a document that corporations planning to issue securities to the public have to submit to the ***SEC***. It features details of the issuer's management, financial status, and activities, and the purpose of the issue. *See also* ***shelf registration***

regression analysis STATISTICS method of determining relationships between variables a ***forecasting*** technique used to establish the relationship between quantifiable variables. In regression analysis, data on dependent and independent variables is plotted on a scatter graph or diagram, and trends are indicated through a line of best fit. The use of a single independent variable is known as *simple regression analysis*, while the use of two or more independent variables is called *multiple regression analysis*.

regressive tax TAX tax where rate falls as income increases a tax with a rate that decreases proportionally as the value of the item being taxed, especially income, rises. Social security taxes are regressive. *See also* ***progressive tax, proportional tax***

regulated superannuation fund TAX Australian superannuation fund regulated by legislation an Australian superannuation fund that is regulated by legislation and therefore qualifies for tax concessions. To attain this status, a fund must either show that its main function is the provision of pensions, or adopt a corporate trustee structure.

regulation REGULATION & COMPLIANCE control of activities using laws and rules the use of laws or rules stipulated by a government or regulatory body, such as the ***Securities and Exchange Commission*** in the United States or the ***Financial Services Authority*** in the United Kingdom, to provide orderly procedures and to protect consumers and investors

regulation D REGULATION & COMPLIANCE rule allowing sale of securities without SEC registration in the United States, a regulation that allows some smaller companies to offer their securities for sale without having to register them with the ***Securities and Exchange Commission***

regulation S-X REGULATION & COMPLIANCE US rules on financial reports in the United States, a regulation that controls the form and content of financial reports filed with the ***Securities and Exchange Commission***

regulation T REGULATION & COMPLIANCE rule on extensions of credit in the United States, a federal law that regulates extensions of credit by brokers and dealers and specifies initial margin requirements and payment rules on some securities transactions

regulation Z REGULATION & COMPLIANCE rule requiring transparency in loans in the United States, a federal law requiring that all lenders and credit card issuers disclose in writing all the costs and terms associated with obtaining the loan or credit

regulator REGULATION & COMPLIANCE government official who monitors businesses and markets a government official or body that monitors the behavior of companies and the level of competition in particular markets, for example, telecommunications or energy

regulatory body *or* regulatory agency REGULATION & COMPLIANCE organization regulating firms' activities an independent organization, usually established by government, that regulates the activities of companies in an industry

regulatory framework REGULATION & COMPLIANCE system of regulations and enforcement a system of regulations and the means to enforce them, usually established by a government to regulate a specific activity. *Also called* ***regulatory regime***

regulatory pricing risk INSURANCE, RISK risk that government will regulate insurance company's prices the risk an insurance company faces that a government will regulate the prices it can charge

regulatory regime REGULATION & COMPLIANCE = ***regulatory framework***

rehypothecation FINANCE pledge of client's securities as loan collateral an arrangement in which a broker pledges securities in a client's margin account as collateral for a loan from a bank

reimbursement FINANCE repayment of expense incurred repayment of money spent for an agreed or official purpose or taken as a loan, or money paid as compensation for a loss

reinsurance INSURANCE reduction of insurance risk by transferring policy a method of reducing risk by transferring all or part of an insurance policy to another insurer

reinsurer INSURANCE provider of insurance to insurers an insurer to whom another insurer transfers all or part of an insurance policy to reduce risk

reintermediation E-COMMERCE reintroduction of intermediaries in traditional retail channels the reintroduction of intermediaries found in traditional retail channels. *See also* ***disintermediation***

reinvestment STOCKHOLDING & INVESTMENTS **1.** investing of money again the act of investing money again in the same securities **2.** firm's investing of earnings in own business the act of investing a company's earnings in its own business by using them to create new products for sale

reinvestment rate FINANCE interest rate available for reinvested income the interest rate at which an investor is able to reinvest income received from an investment

reinvestment risk FINANCE, RISK risk that reinvestment will be at lower rate the risk that an investor will be unable to earn the same rate of return on the proceeds of an investment as he or she earns on the investment as a result of declining interest rates

reinvestment unit trust STOCKHOLDING & INVESTMENTS mutual fund using dividends to buy more stock in the United Kingdom, a mutual fund that uses dividends to buy more shares in the company issuing them. *See also* ***accumulation unit***

REIT *abbr* REAL ESTATE, STOCKHOLDING & INVESTMENTS ***real estate investment trust***

rejects OPERATIONS & PRODUCTION inferior products or merchandise units of output that fail a set quality standard and are subsequently rectified, sold as substandard, or disposed of as scrap

related company BUSINESS firm that other firm invests in a company in which another company makes a long-term capital investment in order to gain control of it or influence its decisions

relationship management MARKETING effort to maintain good customer relations the process of fostering good relations with customers to build loyalty and increase sales

relative income hypothesis ECONOMICS belief that people care about others' incomes the theory that consumers are concerned less with their absolute living standards than with consumption relative to other consumers

relevant interest *ANZ* STOCKHOLDING & INVESTMENTS legal position enabling investor to buy and sell the legal status held by stock investors who can legally dispose of, or influence the disposal of, stocks

relocation GENERAL MANAGEMENT transfer of business to new location the transfer of a business from one location to another. Relocation occurs for a variety of reasons, including the need for more space, the desire to centralize operations, or to be nearer to suppliers, customers, or raw materials.

reminder BUSINESS, FINANCE letter reminding of obligation to pay invoice a letter to remind a customer that he or she has not paid an invoice

remittance BUSINESS, FINANCE money sent as payment money that is sent to pay a debt or to pay an invoice

remittance advice *or* remittance slip BUSINESS, FINANCE detailed document accompanying payment a document sent with payment, giving details of what invoices are being paid and credits, if any, being taken

remitting bank BANKING = ***collecting bank***

remuneration FINANCE, HR & PERSONNEL = ***earnings***

remuneration package HR & PERSONNEL employee's total pay, including bonuses and benefits the salary, pension contributions, bonuses, and other forms of payment or benefits that an employer gives an employee

renewal notice INSURANCE document advising of need to renew insurance a document, usually in the form of an invoice, sent by an insurance company asking the insured person to renew the insurance for a particular period of time

renewal premium INSURANCE payment to renew insurance a payment to an insurance company to renew insurance for a particular period of time

renounceable document LEGAL evidence of temporary ownership in the United Kingdom, written proof of ownership for a limited period, for example, a letter of allotment of shares of stock in a ***rights issue***. *See also* ***letter of renunciation***

rent 1. FINANCE arrangement to use equipment for money an arrangement whereby customers pay money to be able to use a car, boat, or piece of equipment owned by another person or firm for a period of time **2.** REAL ESTATE arrangement to use buildings or land for money money paid to use an office, building, or piece of farmland, for example, owned by another person for a period of time **3.** FINANCE allow somebody use of something for money to use or allow somebody to use, an office, building, or piece of farmland, for example, in return for a regular payment. *Also called* ***let***

rental value REAL ESTATE level of rent at current market rate a full value of the rent for a property if it were charged at the current market rate, usually calculated between rent reviews

rent control LEGAL, REAL ESTATE limit on amount chargeable as residential rent regulation by a government restricting the amount somebody can charge to rent a residential property

renting back FINANCE = ***sale and leaseback***

rent review LEGAL, REAL ESTATE increase in rent during term of lease an increase in rents that is carried out during the term of a lease. Most leases allow for rents to be reviewed every three or five years.

renunciation STOCKHOLDING & INVESTMENTS = ***letter of renunciation***

reorder level OPERATIONS & PRODUCTION fixed limit triggering new order of inventory a level of inventory at which a replenishment order should be placed. Traditional "optimizing" systems use a variation on the computation of maximum usage multiplied by maximum lead, which builds in a measure of safety.

reorganization bond STOCKHOLDING & INVESTMENTS US bond for creditors of firm being reorganized in the United States, a bond issued to creditors of a business that is undergoing a form of ***Chapter 11*** reorganization. Interest is normally only paid when the company can make the payments from its earnings.

repatriation FINANCE return of foreign investment earnings to home country the act of sending money earned on foreign investments to the home country of their firm or owner

repayable FINANCE to be repaid used to describe money that is to be paid back, usually in a particular way, for example, in monthly installments

repayment FINANCE **1.** repaying of money the act of paying money back, usually in a particular way, for example, in monthly installments **2.** money repaid money that is paid back, usually in a particular way, for example, in monthly installments

repayment mortgage *UK* MORTGAGES = ***amortized mortgage***

repeat business BUSINESS, MARKETING continuing orders from same supplier the placing of order after order with the same supplier. Repeat business can be implemented by an agreement between the customer and supplier for purchase on a regular basis. It is often used where there are small numbers of customers, or high volumes per product and low product variety. There is market competition for the first order only, and customization is usually available for the initial purchase only. Sales and marketing have a diminished role once the business has been gained.

replacement cost *or* replacement price ACCOUNTING today's cost of replacing something the cost of replacing an asset or service with its current equivalent

replacement cost accounting ACCOUNTING means of evaluating firm's assets a method of valuing company assets based on their replacement cost

replacement cost depreciation ACCOUNTING depreciation based on current replacement cost depreciation based on the actual cost of replacing the asset in the current year

replacement ratio ECONOMICS difference between wages and unemployment benefits the ratio of the total resources received when unemployed to those received when in employment

replacement value INSURANCE today's cost of replacing something the cost of replacing an insured asset with its current equivalent

repo 1. FINANCE, MARKETS = ***repurchase agreement*** **2.** BANKING, MARKETS open-market buying and selling by US Federal Reserve in the United States, an ***open market operation*** undertaken by the ***Federal Reserve*** to purchase securities and agree to sell them back at a stated price on a future date **3.** BANKING, MARKETS Bank of England's repurchase agreement in the United Kingdom, a ***Bank of England*** repurchase agreement with ***market makers*** in ***gilt-edged securities***. It is used to provide securities for ***short positions***.

reporting entity CORPORATE GOVERNANCE organization providing financial information to stockholders any organization such as a limited company that reports its accounts to its stockholders

repositioning MARKETING marketing old product in new ways a marketing strategy that changes aspects of a product or brand in order to change ***market position*** and alter consumer perceptions

repossession FINANCE return of merchandise after default on time payments the return of goods purchased through an installment plan when the purchaser fails to make the required regular payments. *See also* ***recourse agreement***

repudiation FINANCE refusing to honor debt a refusal to pay or acknowledge a debt or similar contract

repurchase FINANCE buy back shares in mutual fund to buy back shares, for example, when a fund manager buys back the shares in a mutual fund after an investor sells, or when companies

  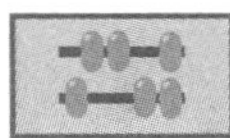      

repurchase shares instead of or in addition to paying a dividend to shareholders

repurchase agreement MARKETS agreement to both sell and buy back security in the bond and money markets, a ***spot transaction*** sale of a security combined with its repurchase at a later date and pre-agreed price. In effect, the buyer is lending money to the seller for the duration of the transaction and using the security as collateral. Dealers finance their ***positions*** by using repurchase agreements. *Also called* ***repo*** *(sense 1)*

request form E-COMMERCE Web page with blanks for user data an interactive Web page that accepts user-provided data—for example, name, address, or shipping information—that can be saved for recurring use or sent by e-mail to the page owner

required beginning date PENSIONS, TAX date to start pension payments in the United States, the date on which the ***IRS*** requires that distributions to a participant in a ***qualified retirement plan*** begin

required rate of return FINANCE lowest acceptable return the minimum return for a proposed project investment to be acceptable. *See also* ***discounted cash flow***

required reserve ratio *or* required reserves BANKING ratio of bank's reserves to deposits the proportion of a bank's deposits that must be kept in reserve.

In the United Kingdom and in certain other European countries, there is no compulsory ratio, although banks will have their own internal measures and targets to be able to repay customer deposits as they forecast they will be required. In the United States, specified percentages of deposits—established by the ***Federal Reserve Board***—must be kept by banks in a non-interest-bearing account at one of the twelve ***Federal Reserve Banks*** located throughout the country.

In Europe, the reserve requirement of an institution is calculated by multiplying the reserve ratio for each category of items in the reserve base, set by the ***European Central Bank***, with the amount of those items in the institution's balance sheets. These figures vary according to the institution.

The required reserve ratio in the United States is set by federal law, and depends on the amount of checkable deposits a bank holds. Effective from December 29, 2011, up to $11.5M the required reserve ratio is 0%, from $11.5M to $71M it is 3% and above $71M it is 10%. These breakpoints are reviewed annually in accordance with ***money supply*** growth. No reserves are required against ***certificate of deposit*** or ***savings accounts***.

The reserve ratio requirement limits a bank's lending to a certain fraction of its demand deposits. The current rule allows a bank to issue loans in an amount equal to 90% of such deposits, holding 10% in reserve. The reserves can be held in any combination of till money and deposit at a Federal Reserve Bank. *Also called* ***bank reserve ratio, reserve ratio, reserve requirement***

requisition OPERATIONS & PRODUCTION firm's purchase order an official order form used by companies when purchasing a product or service

resale price maintenance MARKETING UK agreement with supplier restricting retail price formerly in the United Kingdom, an agreement between suppliers or manufacturers and retailers, restricting the price that retailers can ask for a product or service. Resale price maintenance was designed to enable all retailers to make a profit. The Resale Prices Act now prevents this practice on the grounds that it is uncompetitive. Now, unless they can prove that resale price maintenance is in the public interest, manufacturers can only recommend a retail price. *Abbr* ***RPM***

reschedule FINANCE arrange new payment schedule for debt to arrange a new payment schedule and new conditions for the repayment of a debt

rescission LEGAL cancellation of contract an act of rescinding or annulling a contract

research STOCKHOLDING & INVESTMENTS evaluation of information to aid investing the examination of statistics and other information regarding past, present, and future trends or performance that enables analysts to recommend to investors which stocks to buy or sell in order to maximize their return and minimize their risk. It may be used either in the top-down approach (where the investor evaluates a market, then an industry, and finally a specific company) or the bottom-up approach (where the investor selects a company and confirms his or her findings by evaluating the company's sector and then its market). Careful research is likely to help investors find the best deals, in particular ***value shares*** or ***growth equities***. *See also* ***technical analysis***

reserve FINANCE business profits withheld to cover unexpected costs profits in a business that have not been paid out as dividends but have been set aside in the business to cover any unexpected costs. *Also called* ***reserve fund***

reserve account E-COMMERCE = ***holdback***

reserve bank BANKING bank that holds money for other banks in the United States, a bank such as a Federal Reserve bank that holds the reserves of other banks

Reserve Bank of Australia BANKING central bank of Australia Australia's central bank, which is responsible for managing the Commonwealth's monetary policy, ensuring financial stability, and printing and distributing currency. *Abbr* ***RBA***

Reserve Bank of New Zealand BANKING central bank of New Zealand New Zealand's central bank, which is responsible for managing the government's monetary policy, ensuring financial stability, and printing and distributing currency. *Abbr* ***RBNZ***

reserve currency CURRENCY & EXCHANGE foreign currency kept for international trading foreign currency that a central bank holds for use in international trade

reserve for fluctuations CURRENCY & EXCHANGE money to absorb exchange rate differences money set aside to allow for changes in the values of currencies

reserve fund FINANCE = ***reserve***

reserve price FINANCE minimum price in auction a price for a particular lot, set by the vendor, below which an auctioneer may not sell

reserve ratio BANKING = ***required reserve ratio***

reserve requirement BANKING = ***required reserve ratio***

reserves **1.** FINANCE money held for contingencies and opportunities a sum of money held by a person or organization to finance unexpected business opportunities. *See also* ***war chest*** **2.** BANKING money that bank holds for withdrawals the money that a bank holds to ensure that it can satisfy its depositors' demands for withdrawals **3.** ACCOUNTING, STOCKHOLDING & INVESTMENTS profit not distributed plus stock subscriptions in a company balance sheet, the total of profits not yet distributed to shareholders and the amount subscribed for stock in excess of the ***nominal value***

residential property REAL ESTATE dwellings houses, apartments, or other dwellings in which people and their families live

residual value ACCOUNTING value of asset after depreciation a value of an asset after it has been depreciated in the company's accounts

residuary legatee LEGAL person inheriting after specific bequests the person to whom a testator's estate is left after specific bequests have been made

residue FINANCE money left over money that has not been spent or paid out

resizing HR & PERSONNEL = ***upsizing***

resolution CORPORATE GOVERNANCE proposal to be voted on at meeting a proposal put to a meeting, for example, an ***annual meeting*** of shareholders, on which those present and eligible can vote. *See also* ***extraordinary resolution, special resolution***

resource driver ACCOUNTING **1.** *see* ***cost driver*** **2.** unit for measuring usage and assignment of resources a measurement unit that is used to assign resource costs to ***activity cost pools*** based on some measures of usage. For example, it may be used to assign office occupancy costs to purchasing or accounting services within a company.

resources OPERATIONS & PRODUCTION total means by which organization achieves its purpose anything that is available to an organization to help it achieve its purpose. Resources are often categorized into finance, property, premises, equipment, people, and raw materials.

response bias STATISTICS difference between answer given and actual fact the disparity between information that a survey respondent provides and data analysis, for example, a person claiming to watch little television but giving answers showing 30 hours' weekly viewing

response rate STATISTICS how many people respond to survey the proportion of subjects in a statistical study who respond to a researcher's questionnaire

responsibility accounting ACCOUNTING record-keeping that shows individual responsibilities the keeping of financial records with an emphasis on who is responsible for each item

responsibility center GENERAL MANAGEMENT organizational center for which manager is completely accountable a department or organizational function whose performance is the direct responsibility of a specific manager

restated balance sheet ACCOUNTING accounts reorganized to emphasize selected feature a balance sheet reframed to serve a specific purpose such as highlighting depreciation on assets

restatement ACCOUNTING revised financial statement a revision of a company's earlier financial statement

restraint of trade GENERAL MANAGEMENT, HR & PERSONNEL restriction of right to compete against former employer a term in a contract of employment that restricts a person from carrying on their trade or profession if they leave an organization. Generally illegal, it is usually

       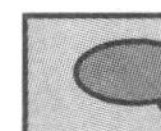 

intended to prevent key employees from leaving an organization to establish a competing organization.

restricted security STOCKHOLDING & INVESTMENTS security bought in unregistered sale a security acquired in an unregistered private resale from the issuer or an affiliate of the issuer, and whose sale must meet certain conditions laid down by the ***Securities and Exchange Commission***

restricted surplus *US* FINANCE funds unavailable for dividend payments reserves that are not legally available for distribution to stockholders as dividends. *UK term* ***undistributable reserves***

restricted tender STOCKHOLDING & INVESTMENTS conditional offer for stock an offer to buy stock only under specific conditions

restrictive covenant FINANCE agreement to retain loan collateral an agreement by a borrower not to sell an asset that he or she has used as collateral for a loan

restructure BUSINESS reorganize firm's financial basis to reorganize the financial basis of a company

result ACCOUNTING account produced at end of trading period a profit or loss account for a company at the end of a trading period

result-driven GENERAL MANAGEMENT focused on outcome rather than process used to describe a type of corporate strategy focused on outcomes and achievements. A result-driven organization concentrates on meeting objectives, delivering to the required time, cost, and quality, and holds performance to be more important than procedures.

résumé *US* HR & PERSONNEL document summarizing job history and skills a document that provides a summary of personal career history, skills, and experience. A résumé is usually prepared to aid in a job application. A job advertisement may ask either for a résumé or instead may require a candidate to complete an application form.

Every résumé should include the following: the jobseeker's name and contact details; a clear and concise description of his or her career objective; some kind of outline of work experience; and a list of education and degrees. It is important to customize a résumé to the type of job or career being applied for, and to make sure it has impact: a hiring manager receives an average of over 120 résumés for every job opening.

There are four basic types of résumé: the chronological, the functional, the targeted, and the capabilities résumé. A chronological résumé is useful for people who stay in the same field and do not make major career changes. They should start with and focus on the most recent positions held. A functional résumé is the preferred choice for those seeking their first professional job, or those making a major career change. It is based around 3–5 paragraphs, each emphasizing and illustrating a particular skill or accomplishment. A targeted résumé is useful for jobseekers who are very clear about their job direction and need to make an impressive case for a specific job. Like a functional résumé, it should be based around several capabilities and accomplishments that are relevant to the target job, focusing on action and results. A capabilities résumé is used for people applying for a specific job within their current organization. It should focus on 5–8 skills and accomplishments achieved with the company.

The format of a résumé should also be considered—whether it is to be printed out, incorporated into an e-mail, posted on a website, or burned onto a CD-ROM. Different layout and design elements, such as the choice of fonts or inclusion of multimedia, are suitable for each medium, and should be thought through carefully. *UK term* ***curriculum vitae***

retail BUSINESS **1.** sale of goods to general public the sale of small quantities of goods to the general public **2.** sell goods to general public to sell goods in small quantities to the general public

retail banking BANKING financial services for individuals services provided by commercial banks to individuals as opposed to business customers that include current accounts, deposit and savings accounts, as well as credit cards, mortgages, and investments. In the United Kingdom, although this service was traditionally provided by high street banks, separate organizations, albeit offshoots of established financial institutions, more recently began to provide Internet and telephone banking services, though the credit crunch of 2008 has set back their operations. *See also* ***wholesale banking***

retail cooperative BUSINESS retailers who cut costs by purchasing collectively an organization for the collective purchase and sale of goods by a group who share profits or benefits. Retail cooperatives were the first offshoot of the ***cooperative movement*** and profits were originally shared among members through dividend payments proportionate to a member's purchases.

retail deposit BANKING money held in bank on somebody's behalf a sum of money held in a bank on behalf of an individual

retail depositor BANKING individual bank customer an individual who deposits money in a bank, as opposed to a business customer

retailer BUSINESS store selling directly to customer an outlet through which products or services are sold to customers. Retailers can be put into three broad groups: independent traders, multiple stores, or ***retail cooperatives***.

retailer number BANKING retailer's identification number for depositing credit card payments the identification number of the retailer, printed at the top of the report slip when depositing credit card payments

retail investor STOCKHOLDING & INVESTMENTS small investor a private investor who buys and sells stock

retail price BUSINESS price for small quantity a price charged to customers who buy in limited quantities *Also called* ***shop price***

retail price index ECONOMICS list of average prices charged to consumers a listing of the average levels of prices charged by retailers for goods or services. The retail price index is calculated on a set variety of items, and usually excludes luxury goods. It is updated monthly, and provides a running indicator of changing costs. *Abbr* ***RPI***

retained earnings *US* ACCOUNTING = ***retained profits***

retained profits ACCOUNTING firm's profits kept as reserves, expansion, or investment the amount of profit remaining after tax and distribution to stockholders that is retained in a business and used as a reserve or as a means of financing expansion or investment. *Also called* ***retained earnings, retentions***

retainer FINANCE money advanced to retain somebody's services money paid in advance to somebody so that they will work for you and not for someone else

retention **1.** FINANCE withholding of payment the holding back of money due until a condition has been fulfilled **2.** HR & PERSONNEL keeping existing employees the process of keeping the loyalty of existing employees and persuading them not to work for another company

retentions ACCOUNTING = ***retained profits***

retire **1.** FINANCE pay off loan to pay the balance owed on a loan **2.** HR & PERSONNEL stop working at end of career to leave a job or career voluntarily at the usual age or time for doing so

retirement **1.** FINANCE payment of loan balance the act of paying the balance owed on a loan **2.** HR & PERSONNEL act of retiring the act of leaving a job or career voluntarily at the usual age or time for doing so **3.** HR & PERSONNEL time after retiring the time that follows the end of a person's working life

retirement annuity PENSIONS pension paid as annuity to retired person an annuity paid to a person when they reach a specific age, derived from a fund built up over time

retirement benefits PENSIONS pension payments to retired person benefits that are payable by a pension plan to somebody who retires

retirement fund *US* PENSIONS money set aside to pay pensions of retirees a large sum of money made up of contributions from employees and their employer which provides pensions for retired employees. *UK term* ***pension fund***

retirement pension PENSIONS = ***pension***

retrenchment FINANCE cost reductions to improve profitability the reduction of costs or spending in order to maintain or improve profitability, especially in response to changed economic circumstances

return **1.** ACCOUNTING, STOCKHOLDING & INVESTMENTS = ***rate of return*** **2.** TAX = ***tax return***

return date ACCOUNTING in UK, date for required annual return in the United Kingdom, a date by which a company's annual return has to be made to the ***Registrar of Companies***

return on assets ACCOUNTING net income as percentage of total assets a measure of profitability calculated by expressing a company's net income as a percentage of total assets. *Abbr* ***ROA***

return on capital *or* return on capital employed ACCOUNTING ratio used for measuring profitability by UK firms in the United Kingdom, a ratio of the net profit made in a fiscal year in relation to the ***capital employed***. It is used as a measure of business profitability. *Abbr* ***ROC, ROCE***

return on equity FINANCE relationship between net income and stockholders' funds the ratio of a company's net income as a percentage of shareholders' funds.

Return on equity is easy to calculate and is applicable to the majority of industries. It is probably the most widely used measure of how well a company is performing for its shareholders.

It is calculated by dividing the net income shown on the income statement (usually of the past year) by shareholders' equity, which appears on the balance sheet:

  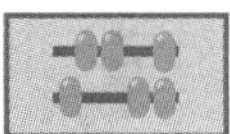      

$$\frac{\text{Net income}}{\text{Owners' equity}} = \text{Return on equity}$$

For example, if net income is $450 and equity is $2,500, then:

$$\frac{450}{2,500} = 0.18 \times 100\% = 18\% \text{ return on equity}$$

Return on equity for most companies should be in double figures; investors often look for 15% or higher, while a return of 20% or more is considered excellent. Seasoned investors also review five-year average ROE, to gauge consistency. *Abbr* ***ROE***

return on invested capital *or* return on investment FINANCE profit as percentage of investment a ratio of the profit made in a financial year as a percentage of an investment.

The most basic expression of ROI can be found by dividing a company's net profit (also called net earnings) by the total investment (total debt plus total equity), then multiplying by 100 to arrive at a percentage:

$$\text{ROI} = \frac{\text{Net profit}}{\text{Total investment}}$$

If, say, net profit is $30 and total investment is $250, the ROI is:

$$\frac{30}{250} = 0.12 \times 100\% = 12\%$$

A more complex variation of ROI is an equation known as the Du Pont formula:

$$\frac{\text{Net profit after taxes}}{\text{Total assets}} = \frac{\text{Net profit after taxes}}{\text{Sales}} \times \frac{\text{Sales}}{\text{Total assets}}$$

If, for example, net profit after taxes is $30, total assets are $250, and sales are $500, then:

$$\frac{30}{250} = \frac{30}{500} \times \frac{500}{250} = 12\% = 6\% \times 2 = 12\%$$

Champions of this formula, which was developed by the Du Pont Company in the 1920s, say that it helps reveal how a company has both deployed its assets and controlled its costs, and how it can achieve the same percentage return in different ways.

For shareholders, the variation of the basic ROI formula used by investors is:

$$\text{ROI} = \frac{(\text{Net income} + \text{Current value} - \text{Original value})}{\text{Original value}}$$

If, for example, somebody invests $5,000 in a company and a year later has earned $100 in dividends, while the value of the shares is $5,200, the return on investment would be:

$$\frac{(100 + 5,200 - 5,000)}{5,000} = \frac{300}{5,000} = 0.06 \times 100\% = 6\%$$

It is vital to understand exactly what a return on investment measures, for example, assets, equity, or sales. Without this understanding, comparisons may be misleading. It is also important to establish whether the net profit figure used is before or after provision for taxes. *Abbr* ***ROI, ROIC***

return on net assets FINANCE profit as percentage of firm's assets a ratio of the profit made in a fiscal year as a percentage of the assets of a company. *Abbr* ***RONA***

return on sales ACCOUNTING profit or loss as percentage of sales a company's operating profit or loss as a percentage of total sales for a given period, typically a year. *Abbr* ***ROS***. See also ***profit margin***

returns to scale ECONOMICS increase in output related to increases in inputs the proportionate increase in a country's or company's output as a result of increases in all its inputs

revaluation CURRENCY & EXCHANGE increase in value of nation's currency a rise in the value of a country's currency in relation to other currencies

revaluation method ACCOUNTING asset depreciation using change in value over year a method of calculating the depreciation of assets by which the asset is depreciated by the difference in its value at the end of the year over its value at the beginning of the year

revaluation of assets ACCOUNTING asset depreciation using change in value since acquisition the revaluation of a company's ***assets*** to take account of inflation or changes in value since the assets were acquired. The change in value is credited to the ***revaluation reserve account***.

revaluation of currency CURRENCY & EXCHANGE altering currency value to affect balance of payments an increase in the value of a currency in relation to others. In situations where there is a ***floating exchange rate***, a currency will usually find its own level automatically but this will not happen if there is a ***fixed exchange rate***. Should a government have persistent ***balance of payment*** surpluses, it may exceptionally decide to revalue its currency, making imports cheaper but its exports more expensive.

revaluation reserve CURRENCY & EXCHANGE money held to cover fluctuations in foreign currencies money set aside to account for the fact that the value of assets may vary as a result of accounting in different currencies

revaluation reserve account ACCOUNTING account for asset depreciation an account to which the change in value of a company's assets is credited during a ***revaluation of assets***

revalue ACCOUNTING reassess value of something to value something again, usually setting a higher value on it than before

revenue FINANCE income from product or service the income generated by a product or service over a period of time

revenue account ACCOUNTING business account for recording income an account in a business used for recording receipts from sales, services, commissions, and other income associated with the business's activities

revenue anticipation note STOCKHOLDING & INVESTMENTS, TAX government means of raising money a government-issued ***debt instrument*** for which expected income from taxation is collateral

revenue bond STOCKHOLDING & INVESTMENTS US government bond a bond that a US state or a local government issues, to be repaid from the money made from the project financed with it

revenue center FINANCE center for generating income without costs a part of a business that raises revenue but has no responsibility for costs, for example, a sales center

revenue expenditure ACCOUNTING money spent on inventory purchases for current-year sale expenditure on purchasing stock, but not on capital items, which is then sold during the current accounting period

revenue ledger ACCOUNTING record of total income a record of all the income received by an organization. *Also called* ***sales ledger***

revenue officer TAX employee in tax office a person working in the government tax offices

revenue recognition ACCOUNTING determination of when income becomes revenue an accounting principle that determines when income is recognized as revenue. In ***cash accounting***, revenue is recognized not when services were performed or products delivered but when payment is actually received. Following the ***accrual concept***, revenue is recognized when payment is earned no matter when it is actually received.

revenue reserves FINANCE, ACCOUNTING undistributed earnings held as stockholders' funds ***retained profits*** that are shown in the company's balance sheet as part of the stockholders' funds

revenue sharing 1. TAX distribution of US federal taxes to states distribution to states by the federal government of money that it collects in taxes **2.** BUSINESS income sharing within limited partnerships the distribution of income within ***limited partnerships***, where there are both general and limited partners

revenue stamp TAX stamp certifying receipt of tax payment a stamp that a government issues to certify that somebody has paid a tax

revenue tariff TAX national tax on imports or exports a tax levied on imports or exports to raise revenue for a national government

reversal FINANCE change in status a change to the opposite, for example, from being profitable to unprofitable, or, in the case of a stock price from rising to falling

reversal stop MARKETS price that triggers change between buying and selling a price at which a trader stops buying and starts selling a security, or vice versa

reverse leverage FINANCE **1.** higher expenditures than income a cash flow in which expenditures are higher than income **2.** borrowing at higher interest rate than investments pay the borrowing of money at a rate of interest higher than the expected rate of return on investing the money borrowed

reverse mortgage MORTGAGES arrangement using mortgage as collateral for annuity payment a financial arrangement in which a lender such as a bank takes over a mortgage and then pays an annuity to the homeowner

reverse split STOCKHOLDING & INVESTMENTS exchange of fewer new shares for old shares the issuing to stockholders of a fraction of one share for every share that they own. *See also* ***stock split***

reverse takeover MERGERS & ACQUISITIONS takeover by lesser company the ***takeover*** of a large company by a smaller one, or the takeover of a public company by a private one

reverse yield gap FINANCE, STOCKHOLDING & INVESTMENTS amount by which expenditure exceeds yield or income the amount by which bond yield exceeds equity yield, or interest rates on loans exceed rental values as a percentage of the costs of properties

reversing entry ACCOUNTING final debit or credit entry reversing earlier entry a debit or credit entry in a chart of accounts that is made at the end of an accounting period to reverse an entry

reversionary annuity PENSIONS annuity paid on person's death an annuity paid to somebody on the death of another person

reversionary bonus INSURANCE annual bonus on life assurance policy an annual bonus on a life assurance policy, declared by the insurer

revocable trust FINANCE trust that can be revoked a trust whose provisions can be amended or canceled

revolving charge account FINANCE account with renewable credit for buying goods a charge account with a company for use in buying that company's goods with ***revolving credit***

revolving credit FINANCE = ***open-end credit***

revolving fund FINANCE fund receiving revenue from projects it finances a fund the resources of which are replenished from the revenue of the projects that it finances

revolving loan BANKING loan allowing money repaid to be borrowed again a loan facility whereby the borrower can choose the number and timing of withdrawals against their bank loan and any money repaid may be reborrowed at a future date. Such loans can be made available to both businesses and personal customers.

riba FINANCE interest charge or unfair profit in Islamic financing, interest or any unjust profit made by a lender in a financial transaction. It is one of three prohibitions in Islamic law, the others being ***gharar*** and ***maysir***.

rider INSURANCE additional provision added to contract an additional clause or provision added to an insurance policy, which becomes part of the policy

RIE *abbr* MARKETS ***recognized investment exchange***

rigged market MARKETS illegal trading practice to attract investors a market where two or more parties are buying and selling securities among themselves to give the impression of active trading with the intention of attracting investors to purchase the stocks. This practice is illegal in most jurisdictions.

right of survivorship LEGAL joint owner's right after death of other the right of a surviving joint owner of property to acquire the interest of a deceased joint owner

rights issue STOCKHOLDING & INVESTMENTS raising capital by offering existing stockholders additional stock the raising of new capital by giving existing stockholders the right to subscribe to new shares or ***debentures*** in proportion to their current holdings. These shares of stock are usually issued at a discount to market price. A stockholder not wishing to take up a rights issue may sell the rights. *Also called* ***rights offer***

rightsizing GENERAL MANAGEMENT restructuring of company to most effective size corporate restructuring, or rationalization, with the goal of reducing costs and improving efficiency and effectiveness. Rightsizing is often used as a euphemism for ***downsizing***, or ***delayering***, with the suggestion that it is not as far-reaching. Rightsizing can also be used to describe increasing the size of an organization, perhaps as an attempt to correct a previous downsizing, or delayering, exercise.

rights offer STOCKHOLDING & INVESTMENTS = ***rights issue***

rights offering STOCKHOLDING & INVESTMENTS offering additional stock to existing stockholders an offering for sale of a ***rights issue***, in proportion to the holdings of existing stockholders

ring MARKETS **1.** trading floor a trading area at an exchange, especially a commodity exchange. *See also* ***pit*** **2.** session on London Metal Exchange a trading session on the ***London Metal Exchange***, which deals in copper, lead, zinc, aluminum, tin, and nickel

ring-fence **1.** FINANCE separate profitable elements to safeguard business to separate valuable assets or profitable businesses from others in a group that are unprofitable and may make the whole group collapse **2.** FINANCE use money for specific projects to identify money from specific sources and only use it in agreed areas or for specific projects. *See also* ***hypothecation*** **3.** BUSINESS not let firm's liquidation affect others in group to allow one company within a group to go into liquidation without affecting the viability of the group as a whole or any other company within it

ring member MARKETS member of London Metal Exchange a member of the ***London Metal Exchange***, dealing in copper, lead, zinc, aluminum, tin, and nickel

ring trading MARKETS business conducted on trading floor business conducted in the trading area of a commodity exchange

rising bottoms MARKETS graph showing stock's rising price following low prices a pattern on a graph of the price of a security or commodity against time that shows an upward price movement following a period of low prices (slang) *See also* ***chartist***

risk RISK **1.** possibility of suffering harm or loss the possibility of suffering damage or loss in the face of uncertainty about the outcome of actions, future events, or circumstances. Organizations are exposed to various types of risk, including damage to property, injury to personnel, financial loss, and legal liability. These may affect profitability, hinder the achievement of objectives, or lead to business interruption or failure. Risk may be deemed high or low, depending on the probability of an adverse outcome. Risks that can be quantified on the basis of past experience are insurable and those that cannot be calculated are uninsurable. **2.** potential for negative outcome a condition in which there exists a quantifiable dispersion in the possible outcomes from any activity

risk-adjusted return on capital STOCKHOLDING & INVESTMENTS, RISK return on capital evaluated in terms of risks return on capital calculated in a way that takes into account the risks associated with income. *Also called* ***Jensen's measure***, ***Treynor ratio***

risk analysis RISK determination of how risks might affect organization the identification of risks to which an organization is exposed and the assessment of the potential impact of those risks on the organization. The goal of risk analysis is to identify and measure the risks associated with different courses of action in order to inform ***decision making***. In the context of business decision making, risk analysis is especially used in investment decisions and capital investment appraisal. Risk analysis may be used to develop an organizational ***risk profile***, and also may be the first stage in a ***risk management*** program.

risk arbitrage MARKETS, RISK trading without guaranteed profit simultaneous buying and selling without certainty of profit, though at relatively low risk. It is particularly employed by ***hedge fund*** managers.

risk arbitrageur RISK somebody engaged in risk arbitrage a person whose business is ***risk arbitrage***

risk assessment RISK determination of how risky something is the determination of the level of risk in a specific course of action. Risk assessments are an important tool in areas such as health and safety management and environmental management. Results of a risk assessment can be used, for example, to identify areas in which safety can be improved. Risk assessment can also be used to determine more intangible forms of risk, including economic and social risk, and can inform the scenario planning process. The amount of risk involved in a specific course of action is compared to its expected benefits to provide evidence for decision making.

risk asset ratio BANKING, RISK proportion of assets that carry risk the proportion of a bank's total capital assets that carry risk. *See also* ***risk-weighted asset***

risk-averse STOCKHOLDING & INVESTMENTS, RISK having desire to avoid risk in investment wanting to achieve the best return that can be had on an investment while taking the least possible risk

risk aversion STOCKHOLDING & INVESTMENTS, RISK desire to avoid risk in investment a desire to achieve the best return that can be had on an investment while taking the least possible risk

risk-based capital assessment BANKING, RISK bank's value based on risk attached to assets an internationally approved system of calculating a bank's capital value by assessing the risk attached to its assets. Cash deposits and gold, for example, have no risk, while loans to less-developed countries have a high risk.

risk-bearing economy of scale BUSINESS, RISK employing diversification to reduce risk conducting business on such a large scale that the risk of loss is reduced because it is spread over so many independent events, as in the issuance of insurance policies

risk capital FINANCE, RISK = ***venture capital***

risk factor RISK degree of risk in enterprise the degree of risk in a project or other business activity

risk-free return STOCKHOLDING & INVESTMENTS, RISK money from safe investment the profit made from an investment that involves no risk

risk management RISK **1.** actions intended to reduce or eliminate risks the variety of activities undertaken by an organization to control and minimize threats to the continuing efficiency, profitability, and success of its operations. The process of risk management includes the identification and analysis of risks to which the organization is exposed, the assessment of potential impacts on the business, and deciding what action can be taken to eliminate or reduce risk and deal with the impact of unpredictable events causing loss or damage. Risk management strategies include taking out insurance against financial loss or legal liability and introducing safety or security measures. **2.** understanding and dealing with inevitable risks the process of understanding and managing the risks that an organization is inevitably subject to in attempting to achieve its corporate objectives. For management purposes, risks are usually divided

  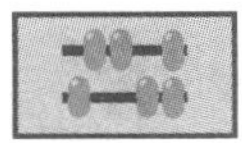      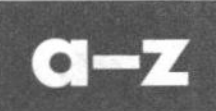

into categories such as operational, financial, legal compliance, information, and personnel.

risk manager GENERAL MANAGEMENT, HR & PERSONNEL, RISK employee managing business risk the person in an organization who is in charge of assessing and managing business risks

risk perception RISK nonobjective view of risk the way in which people and organizations view risk, based on their concerns and experiences, but not necessarily on objective data. Risk perceptions can influence such things as business policies and investment decisions. *Also called* ***perception of risk***

risk premium FINANCE, RISK extra payment received by somebody taking risks an extra payment, for example, increased dividend or higher than usual profits, for taking risks

Risk Priority Number RISK number used to quantify risk a measure used in ***Failure Mode and Effects Analysis*** to quantify risk. It is a product of the severity, probability of occurrence, and ability to detect failure. *Abbr* ***RPN***

risk profile RISK **1.** description of risks facing organization an outline of the risks to which an organization is exposed. An organizational risk profile may be developed in the course of ***risk analysis*** and used for ***risk management***. It examines the nature of the threats faced by an organization, the likelihood of adverse effects occurring, and the level of disruption and costs associated with each type of risk. **2.** analysis of willingness to take risks an analysis of the willingness of individuals or organizations to take risks. A risk profile describes the level of risk considered acceptable by an individual or by the leaders of an organization, and considers how this will affect decision making and corporate strategy.

risk tolerance STOCKHOLDING & INVESTMENTS, RISK ability to withstand stress of investing the ability of an investor to handle the uncertainty and money losses inherent to investing

risk-weighted asset FINANCE, RISK asset weighted by its riskiness an asset weighted by factors relating to its riskiness, used by financial institutions in managing their capital requirements. *See also* ***risk asset ratio***

ROA *abbr* ACCOUNTING ***return on assets***

road show STOCKHOLDING & INVESTMENTS events to interest potential investors a series of presentations to potential investors and brokers given by the management of a company prior to issuing securities, especially in an ***initial public offering***, intended to create interest in the offering

ROC *abbr* ACCOUNTING ***return on capital***

ROCE *abbr* ACCOUNTING ***return on capital employed***

rocket scientist FINANCE innovative finance worker an employee of a financial institution who creates innovative securities that usually include derivatives (slang)

rodo kinko FINANCE Japanese provider of loans to small businesses in Japan, a financial institution that specializes in providing credit for small businesses

ROE *abbr* FINANCE ***return on equity***

rogue trader MARKETS stock dealer acting illegally a dealer in stocks who uses illegal methods to make profits

ROI *abbr* FINANCE ***return on investment***

ROIC *abbr* FINANCE ***return on invested capital***

roll down MARKETS close then open option position at lower price to close a position on one option and open another at a lower ***strike price***

rolled-up coupon *UK* STOCKHOLDING & INVESTMENTS interest coupon added to capital value of security an interest coupon on a security that is not paid out, but added to the capital value of the security

rolling account MARKETS stock exchange system with no fixed settlement days a system in which there are no fixed settlement days, but stock exchange transactions are paid at a fixed period after each transaction has taken place, as opposed to the UK system, in which a settlement day is fixed each month

rolling budget ACCOUNTING budget that moves with time a budget that moves forward on a regular basis, for example, a budget covering a twelve-month period that moves forward each month or quarter

roll-out MARKETING launch of program the full-scale implementation of an advertising campaign or marketing program

rollover FINANCE extension of credit or period of loan an extension of credit or of the period of a loan, though not necessarily on the same terms as previously

rollover IRA PENSIONS US personal retirement plan transferred to individual control in the United States, an ***IRA*** that is created when the assets of a ***qualified retirement plan*** arranged by an employer are transferred out of the employer-sponsored plan into an IRA managed by the owner of the plan. *Also called* ***conduit IRA***. *See also* ***traditional IRA***

roll up FINANCE loan payments including interest the addition of interest amounts to principal in loan payments

Romalpa clause LEGAL clause withholding title to goods pending full payment a clause in a contract whereby the seller provides that title to the goods does not pass to the buyer until the buyer has paid for them

RONA *abbr* FINANCE ***return on net assets***

rort *ANZ* GENERAL MANAGEMENT (slang) **1.** dishonest practice an illegal or underhand strategy **2.** work a system to manipulate or break the rules of a system for personal gain

ROS *abbr* ACCOUNTING ***return on sales***

Roth 401(k) PENSIONS employee plan with taxed contributions and untaxed payments in the United States, a qualified employee retirement plan, to which the employee contributes after-tax dollars but whose distributions are tax-exempt

Roth IRA PENSIONS personal plan with taxed contributions and untaxed payments in the United States, an ***IRA*** whose contributions unlike ***traditional IRAs*** are not tax-deductible, but whose distributions are tax-exempt

round figures FINANCE numbers adjusted to nearest 10, 100, 1,000, etc. figures that have been adjusted up or down to the nearest 10, 100, 1,000, and so on

rounding STATISTICS expressing number as simpler estimated value the practice of reducing the number of significant digits in a number, for example, expressing a figure that has four decimal places with only two decimal places

round lot MARKETS 100 shares of stock traded together a group of 100 shares of stock bought or sold together in one transaction

round-trip trading MARKETS frequent trading of assets an arrangement made between two companies continuously to trade an asset that is not being used or to trade a security at a set price, in order to create the impression of great demand. *See also* ***churning***

routing number BANKING = ***ABA routing number***

royalties FINANCE share of income paid to creator of product a proportion of the income from the sale of a product paid to its creator, for example, an inventor, author, or composer

RPB *abbr* BUSINESS ***recognized professional body***

RPI *abbr* ECONOMICS ***retail price index***

RPIX ECONOMICS indicator of inflation excluding mortgages in the United Kingdom, an index based on the ***retail price index*** that excludes mortgage interest payments and is regarded as an indication of ***underlying inflation***

RPIY ECONOMICS indicator of inflation excluding indirect tax and mortgages in the United Kingdom, an index based on the ***retail price index*** that excludes mortgage interest payments and indirect taxation

RPM *abbr* MARKETING ***resale price maintenance***

RPN *abbr* RISK ***Risk Priority Number***

RRP *abbr* BUSINESS ***recommended retail price***

R-squared STOCKHOLDING & INVESTMENTS benchmarked measure of investment performance a measure of how much of the performance of an investment can be explained by the performance of a ***benchmark index***

rubber check BANKING check returned because of insufficient funds a check that cannot be cashed because the person writing it does not have enough money in the account to pay it (slang)

rule 144 REGULATION & COMPLIANCE rule on selling certain securities an ***SEC*** rule that specifies the conditions under which somebody holding ***restricted*** or ***control securities*** can sell them to the public

rule of 72 STOCKHOLDING & INVESTMENTS method of calculating growth of investment a calculation that an investment will double in value at compound interest after a period shown as 72 divided by the interest percentage, so interest at 10% compounded will double the capital invested in 7.2 years

rule of 78 STOCKHOLDING & INVESTMENTS calculation of interest rebate on loan repaid early a method used to calculate the rebate on a loan with front-loaded interest that has been repaid early. It takes into account the fact that as the loan is repaid, the share of each monthly payment related to interest decreases, while the share related to principal increases.

rumortrage *US* MARKETS securities trading based on rumor of takeover speculation in securities issued by companies that are rumored to be the target of an imminent takeover attempt (slang)

run 1. BANKING, CURRENCY & EXCHANGE simultaneous withdrawal of money by bank customers an incidence of bank customers, or owners of holdings in a specific currency, simultaneously withdrawing their entire funds

  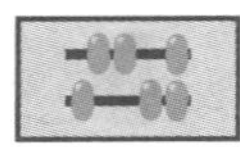      

because of a lack of confidence in the institution **2.** STATISTICS unbroken sequence in statistical series an uninterrupted sequence of the same value in a statistical series

running account credit BANKING UK arrangement for borrowing and reborrowing limited sum in the United Kingdom, an overdraft facility, credit card, or similar system that allows customers to borrow up to a specific limit and reborrow sums previously repaid by either writing a check or using their card

running costs ACCOUNTING = ***operating costs***

running total ACCOUNTING total carried over to next column a total carried from one column or set of figures to the next

running yield STOCKHOLDING & INVESTMENTS = ***current yield***

runoff MARKETS display of closing prices the process of displaying the closing prices of every stock on an exchange on the ***ticker***

run-off STOCKHOLDING & INVESTMENTS reduction in value of mortgage-backed securities a decline in the value of ***mortgage-backed securities***, caused by borrowers refinancing at lower interest rates or defaulting on their loans, resulting in losses by investors in the securities

SA *abbr* BUSINESS **1.** ***Sociedad Anónima*** **2.** ***Sociedade Anónima*** **3** ***Société Anonyme***

sack get the sack *UK* HR & PERSONNEL (informal) = ***get your pink slip***

SADC *or* **SADEC** INTERNATIONAL TRADE organization for economic development in southern Africa an organization that aims to harmonize economic development in southern Africa. The member countries are Angola, Botswana, the Democratic Republic of the Congo, Lesotho, Malawi, Mauritius, Mozambique, Namibia, Seychelles, South Africa, Swaziland, Tanzania, Zambia, and Zimbabwe. *Full form* ***Southern African Development Community***

safe custody STOCKHOLDING & INVESTMENTS = ***safe keeping***

safe hands STOCKHOLDING & INVESTMENTS **1.** investors buying securities to hold for longer term investors who buy securities and are unlikely to sell in the short- to medium-term **2.** securities held by friendly investors securities held by investors who are not likely to sell them

safe investment STOCKHOLDING & INVESTMENTS investment unlikely to lose value an investment such as a bond that is not likely to fall in value

safe keeping STOCKHOLDING & INVESTMENTS holding by financial institutions of customers' valuable documents a service provided by a financial institution in which stock certificates, deeds, wills, or a locked deed box are held by it on behalf of customers. Securities are often held under the customer's name in a locked cabinet in the vault so that if the customer wishes to sell, the bank can forward the relevant certificate to the broker. A will is also usually held in this way so that it may be handed to the executor on the customer's death. Deed boxes are always described as "contents unknown to the bank." Most institutions charge a fee for this service. *Also called* ***safe custody***

safety margin OPERATIONS & PRODUCTION extra time or space allowed for safety an extra amount of time or space allowed to make sure that something can be done safely

SAIF *abbr* INSURANCE ***Savings Association Insurance Fund***

salam FINANCE agreement to pay now for goods delivered later in Islamic financing, a contract for the purchase of goods to be delivered at a specified time in the future. Payment for the goods is made in advance.

salaried partner BUSINESS partner paid regular salary a partner, often a junior one, who receives a regular salary that is detailed in the partnership agreement

salary FINANCE payment for work a form of pay given to employees at regular intervals in exchange for the work they have done. Traditionally, a salary is a form of remuneration given to professional employees on a monthly basis. In modern usage, the word refers to any form of pay that employees receive on a regular basis. A salary is usually paid straight into an employee's account.

salary ceiling HR & PERSONNEL **1.** top of relevant pay range the highest level in a pay range that an employee can achieve under his or her contract **2.** restriction on size of pay an upper limit on pay imposed by government or fixed according to labor union and employer agreements

salary reduction plan HR & PERSONNEL = ***flexible spending account***

salary reduction simplified employee pension PENSIONS voluntary pay deductions for pension in the United States, a ***simplified employee pension plan*** that is funded by voluntary employee salary reductions

salary review HR & PERSONNEL regular reconsideration of employee's pay a reassessment of an individual employee's rate of pay, usually conducted on an annual basis

salary sacrifice scheme HR & PERSONNEL exchange of future pay rise for other benefit in the United Kingdom, an agreement between ***employer*** and ***employees*** by which the employees relinquish a right to future cash in exchange for a noncash benefit of some sort

sale and leaseback FINANCE seller's leasing of previously sold asset the leasing back by the former owner of an asset, usually buildings, that has been sold to a third party. *Also called* ***leaseback, renting back***

sale by tender FINANCE sale to party invited to make offer the sale of an asset to interested parties who have been invited to make an offer. The asset is sold to the party that makes the highest offer. *See also* ***tender***

sales MARKETING **1.** selling the activity of selling a company's products or services **2.** income from selling the income generated by selling a company's products or services **3.** department for selling the department within a company that deals with selling its products or services

sales analysis MARKETING examination of reports of poor sales an examination of the reports of sales to discover why items have or have not sold well

sales charge STOCKHOLDING & INVESTMENTS purchase fee on some mutual funds a fee charged to the purchaser of some types of mutual funds

sales figures MARKETING total amount of money spent by consumers the total amount of money spent by consumers, for example, in a particular product category, a particular region of the country, or within a particular time period. Sales figures are often used by analysts to judge how well an economy is doing.

sales force MARKETING team responsible for selling a group of salespeople or sales representatives responsible for the sales of either a single product or the entire range of an organization's products. *Also called* ***sales team***

sales forecast MARKETING estimation of future sales a prediction of future sales, based mainly on past sales performance. Sales forecasting takes into account the economic climate, current sales trends, company capacity for production, company policy, and ***market research***. A sales forecast can be a good indicator of future sales in stable market conditions, but may be less reliable in times of rapid market change.

sales ledger ACCOUNTING = ***revenue ledger***

sales mix profit variance FINANCE varying profitability of products in range the differing profitability of different products within a product range

sales promotion MARKETING concentrated activities to sell product activities, usually short-term, designed to attract attention to a particular product and to increase its sales, using advertising and publicity. Sales promotion usually runs in conjunction with an advertising campaign that offers free samples or money-off coupons. The product may be offered at a reduced price and the campaign may be supported by additional telephone or door-to-door selling or by competitions. *Also called* ***promotion***

sales revenue FINANCE income from sales the income generated by sales of goods or services

sales tax *US* TAX tax on item sold, collected at purchase a tax that is paid on each item sold and is collected when the purchase is made. *UK term* ***VAT***. *Also called* ***turnover tax***

sales team MARKETING = ***sales force***

sales turnover FINANCE amount of sales in specific period the total amount sold within a specific time period, usually a year. Sales turnover is often expressed in monetary terms but can also be expressed in terms of the total amount of stock or products sold.

sales volume FINANCE number of items sold the number of units of a product sold

sales volume profit variance FINANCE difference between actual and forecast profits the difference between the profit on the number of units actually sold and the forecast figure

Sallie Mae FINANCE US company investing in student loans the largest source of student loans and administrator of college savings plans in the United States. Created in 1972 as a government-sponsored entity, it became completely privatized in 2004 and is a stockholder-owned company traded on the ***New York Stock Exchange***. Sallie Mae purchases loans from lenders, pools them, and sells them to investors. *Full form* ***Student Loan Marketing Association***

salvage value ACCOUNTING = ***scrap value***

sample STATISTICS representative subgroup of larger group to be investigated a subset of a population in a statistical study chosen so that selected properties of the overall population can be investigated

sample size STATISTICS number of individuals in subgroup to be investigated the number of individuals included in a statistical survey

sample survey STATISTICS statistical analysis of subgroup of larger population a statistical study of a sample of individuals designed to collect information on specific subjects, such as buying habits or voting behavior

sampling 1. MARKETING providing free samples a sales promotion technique in which customers and prospects are offered a free sample of a product **2.** STATISTICS selecting representative subgroup from population under investigation the selection of a small proportion of a set of items being studied, from which valid inferences about the whole set or population can be made. Sampling makes it possible to obtain valid research results when it is impracticable to survey the whole population. The size of the sample needed for valid results depends on a number of factors, including the uniformity of the population being studied and the level of accuracy required. The technique is based on the laws of probability, and a number of different sampling methods can be used, including ***random sampling*** and ***nonrandom sampling***.

sampling design STATISTICS plan for selecting representative subgroup the procedure by which a particular sample is chosen from a population

sampling error STATISTICS discrepancy between whole population and subgroup investigated the difference between the population characteristic being estimated in a statistical study and the result produced by the sample investigated

sampling units STATISTICS items chosen from whole population for investigation the items chosen for sampling from a larger population by a sampling design

sampling variation STATISTICS differences between various subgroups of same population variation between different samples of the same size taken from the same population

samurai bond STOCKHOLDING & INVESTMENTS bond sold by foreign institution in Japan a bond issue denominated in yen and issued in Japan by a foreign institution. *See also* ***shibosai bond, shogun bond***

sandbag MERGERS & ACQUISITIONS prolong negotiations in hostile takeover in a hostile ***takeover*** situation, to enter into talks with the bidder and attempt to prolong them as long as possible, in the hope that a ***white knight*** will appear and rescue the target company (slang)

S&L *abbr* BANKING ***savings and loan association***

S&P *abbr* STOCKHOLDING & INVESTMENTS ***Standard & Poor's***

S&P 500 *abbr* MARKETS stock market index of largest 500 US companies an index of 500 leading companies in the United States, it is regarded as a benchmark of the US equities market as a whole. It is calculated by ***Standard & Poor's*** and was established on March 4, 1957.

S&P/ASX 200 MARKETS main Australian stock market index benchmark stock market index that tracks 200 stocks selected from those traded on the ***Australian Securities Exchange*** by the ***Standard & Poor's*** Australian Index Committee. It is comprised of the S&P/ASX 100 plus an additional 100 stocks. It was established on March 31, 2000, with a base value of 3,133.3. *Also called* ***ASX 200***

S&P/MIB MARKETS = ***FTSE MIB***

Santa Claus rally MARKETS year-end stock price rise a rise in stock prices in the last week of the year (slang) *Also called* ***year-end bounce***

Sarbanes–Oxley Act REGULATION & COMPLIANCE US law covering financial reporting and accountability a corporate governance law that came into effect in the United States in 2005. Created in the aftermath of a series of high-profile financial scandals, including Enron and WorldCom, Sarbanes–Oxley seeks to overhaul corporate financial reporting by improving its accuracy and reliability. Though it is an American law, its reach is global and has affected the way that large companies and audit firms do business. Chief executives are to take full responsibility for the accuracy of all financial results by signing a statement to that effect, thereby putting paid to the so-called ***"aw shucks"*** defense strategy adopted by senior executives involved in earlier financial scandals. Under this strategy, the accused maintained that they were simply not aware of the distortion of financial reporting that took place under their governance. *Abbr* ***SOX***

sarf CURRENCY & EXCHANGE currency trading in Islamic financing, the buying and selling of currencies

SARL *abbr* BUSINESS ***société à responsabilité limitée***

SARS *abbr* TAX ***South African Revenue Service***

saucer MARKETS chart shape showing stock price rising from low a dish-shaped chart that indicates that the price of a stock has reached its low and is beginning to rise

Save as You Earn STOCKHOLDING & INVESTMENTS method of saving attracting tax relief in the United Kingdom, a system for employees to save on a regular basis toward buying shares in their company that is encouraged by the government through tax concessions. *Abbr* ***SAYE***

savings FINANCE money reserved for future use money set aside by consumers for various purposes such as meeting contingencies or providing an income during retirement. Savings (money in deposit and savings accounts) differ from investments such as stocks in that they are not usually subject to price fluctuations and are thus considered safer. *Also called* ***liquid savings***

savings account BANKING account paying interest an account with a bank or savings and loan association that pays interest. *See also* ***fixed rate, gross interest, net interest***

savings and loan association BANKING chartered bank offering services for consumers in the United States, a ***chartered bank*** that offers savings accounts, pays dividends, and invests in new mortgages. *Abbr* ***S&L***. Also called ***building and loan association***. *See also* ***thrift institution***

Savings Association Insurance Fund INSURANCE insurance for federal and state savings in the United States, an insurer of deposits in federal savings banks and federal and state savings and loan associations operated by the Federal Deposit Insurance Corporation. *Abbr* ***SAIF***

savings bank BANKING bank managing small investments a bank that specializes in managing small deposits from customers with personal savings. *See also* ***thrift institution***

savings bond STOCKHOLDING & INVESTMENTS = ***US savings bond***

savings certificate STOCKHOLDING & INVESTMENTS = ***National Savings Certificate***

savings function ECONOMICS measurement of how much people will save an expression of the extent to which people save money instead of spending it

savings ratio ECONOMICS measurement of proportion of income saved the proportion of the income of a country or household that is saved in a particular period

savings-related share option scheme STOCKHOLDING & INVESTMENTS arrangement allowing UK employees to buy stock in the United Kingdom, an arrangement that allows employees of a company to buy company shares of stock with money which they have contributed to a savings scheme

SAYE *abbr* STOCKHOLDING & INVESTMENTS ***Save as You Earn***

SC *abbr* REGULATION & COMPLIANCE ***Securities Commission***

scale GENERAL MANAGEMENT system of graded levels a system that is graded into various levels

scalp MARKETS make profits on many quick trades to make many quick trades in a single day for many small gains

scarce currency CURRENCY & EXCHANGE money traded in foreign exchange market a currency that is traded in a foreign exchange market and for which demand is persistently high relative to its supply

scarcity ECONOMICS situation in which demand exceeds supply a situation in which the demand for something exceeds the supply. This can apply to anything from consumer goods to raw materials.

scarcity value FINANCE value of rare item in great demand the value something has because it is rare and a large demand exists for it

scatter STATISTICS how much observations differ from average observation the amount by which a set of observations deviates from its mean

scatter chart *or* scatter diagram *or* scatter plot STATISTICS graph showing relationship between variables a chart or diagram that plots a sample of values for two variables for a set of data, in two dimensions

scenario GENERAL MANAGEMENT postulated state of affairs or sequence of events a possible future state of affairs or sequence of events. Scenarios are imagined or projected on the basis of current circumstances and trends and expectations of change in the future.

scenario planning GENERAL MANAGEMENT imagining future conditions or events for planning strategy a technique that requires the use of a scenario in the process of strategic planning to aid the development of corporate strategy in the face of uncertainty about the future The process of identifying alternative scenarios of the future, based on a variety of differing assumptions, can help managers anticipate changes in the business environment and raise awareness of the frame of reference within which they are operating. The scenarios are then used to assist in both the development of strategies for dealing with unexpected events and the choice between alternative strategic options.

schedule 1. FINANCE long-term plan a plan of how an activity will be carried out over a period of time, drawn up in advance. For example, a

  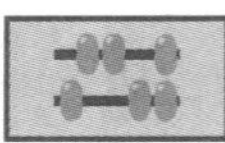   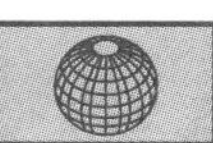   

repayment schedule sets out how debts will be paid. **2.** FINANCE list of interest rates a list of rates of interest that apply to a range of investments **3.** LEGAL list attached to contract a list, especially a list forming an additional document attached to a contract **4.** TAX form relating to UK income tax in the United Kingdom, a form relating to a particular kind of income liable for income tax **5.** INSURANCE details of insurance cover details of the items covered by insurance, sent with the policy

Schedule A TAX UK tax schedule governing income from property in the United Kingdom, a schedule under which tax is charged on income from land or buildings

Schedule B TAX UK tax schedule governing income from woodlands in the United Kingdom, a schedule under which tax was formerly charged on income from woodlands

Schedule C TAX UK schedule taxing income from public sources in the United Kingdom, a schedule to the Finance Acts under which tax was charged on income from public sources such as government stock

Schedule D TAX UK tax schedule governing income from trades in the United Kingdom, a schedule under which tax is charged on income from trades or professions, interest, and other earnings not derived from being employed

Schedule E TAX UK tax schedule governing income from salaries in the United Kingdom, a schedule under which tax is charged on income from salaries, wages, or retirement funds

Schedule F TAX UK tax schedule governing income from dividends in the United Kingdom, a schedule under which tax is charged on income from dividends

scheme *UK* arrangement or method a plan, arrangement, or way of working

scheme of arrangement FINANCE UK plan for avoiding bankruptcy proceedings in the United Kingdom, a plan offering ways of paying debts, drawn up by a person or company to avoid bankruptcy proceedings

scientific management GENERAL MANAGEMENT, HR & PERSONNEL managing using systematic approaches an analytical approach to managing activities by optimizing efficiency and productivity through measurement and control. Scientific management theories were dominant in the 20th century, and many management techniques such as ***benchmarking***, ***total quality management***, and ***business process reengineering*** result from a scientific management approach.

scrap value ACCOUNTING value of asset if scrapped the value of an asset if it is sold for scrap. *Also called* ***salvage value***

screening study STATISTICS statistical investigation of prevalence of particular disease a medical statistical study of a population, conducted to investigate the prevalence of a disease

scrip MARKETS security or certificate for it a security, for example, a share or bond, or the certificate issued to show that somebody has been allotted such a security

scrip dividend STOCKHOLDING & INVESTMENTS dividend paid with stock a dividend paid by the issue of additional company shares, rather than by cash

scrip issue *UK* STOCKHOLDING & INVESTMENTS = ***stock split***

scripophily STOCKHOLDING & INVESTMENTS collecting of old stocks and bonds the collecting of stock or bond certificates that have been canceled, for their historical, aesthetic, or rarity value

Sdn *abbr* BUSINESS ***Sendirian***

SDR *abbr* CURRENCY & EXCHANGE ***Special Drawing Right***

SEAQ MARKETS London Stock Exchange's system for UK securities transactions the London Stock Exchange's system for UK securities. It is a continuously updated computer database of quotations that also records prices at which transactions have been struck. *Full form* ***Stock Exchange Automated Quotations system***

SEAQ International MARKETS London Stock Exchange's system for overseas securities transactions the London Stock Exchange's system for overseas securities. It is a continuously updated computer database of quotations that also records prices at which transactions have been struck. *Full form* ***Stock Exchange Automated Quotations system International***

seasonal adjustment ACCOUNTING accounts adjustment for seasonal distortion of figures an adjustment made to accounts to allow for any short-term seasonal factors such as Christmas sales that may distort the figures

seasonal business BUSINESS trade influenced by time of year trade that is affected by seasonal factors, for example, trade in goods such as suntan products or Christmas trees

seasonality OPERATIONS & PRODUCTION situation in which business varies between seasons variations in production or sales that occur at different but predictable times of the year

seasonal products MARKETING items sold at particular time of year products that are only marketed at particular times of the year, for example, Christmas trees or fireworks

seasonal unemployment HR & PERSONNEL unemployment that changes with seasons unemployment that rises and falls according to the season

seasonal variation STATISTICS changes in data based on time of year the variation of data according to specific times of the year such as the winter months or a tourist season

seasoned equity STOCKHOLDING & INVESTMENTS stocks traded for 90 days stocks that have traded for more than 90 days on a regulated market, long enough to be purchased by ***retail investors***

seasoned issue STOCKHOLDING & INVESTMENTS offering from established company a stock issue that has traded for more than 90 days on a regulated market, long enough to be purchased by ***retail investors***. *See also* ***unseasoned issue***

seat MARKETS stock exchange membership membership in a stock exchange

SEATS MARKETS Australian Stock Exchange's electronic trading system the electronic screen-trading system operated by the Australian Stock Exchange. It was introduced in 1987. *Full form* ***Stock Exchange Automatic Trading System***

SEC *abbr* MARKETS, REGULATION & COMPLIANCE ***Securities and Exchange Commission***

SEC fee STOCKHOLDING & INVESTMENTS US SEC trading fee in the United States, a small fee that the Securities and Exchange Commission charges for the sale of securities listed on a stock exchange

secondary bank BANKING finance company funding installment-plan deals a finance company that provides money for installment-plan deals

secondary industry OPERATIONS & PRODUCTION industry manufacturing goods from raw materials an industry that uses basic raw materials to produce manufactured goods

secondary issue STOCKHOLDING & INVESTMENTS offer of already traded stock an offer of listed stocks that have previously been publicly traded

secondary market MARKETS market buying and selling other than new issues a market that trades in existing stocks rather than new stock issues, for example, a stock exchange. The money earned from these sales goes to the dealer or investor, not to the issuer. *See also* ***primary market***

secondary offering MARKETS offering of securities already on market an offering of securities of a kind that is already on the market

secondary product OPERATIONS & PRODUCTION product made from raw materials a product that has been processed from raw materials. *See also* ***primary product***

Secondary Tax on Companies TAX *see* ***STC***

second half ACCOUNTING second 6-month period in fiscal year the period of six months that is the second part of any fiscal year

secondment HR & PERSONNEL temporary assignment to work elsewhere in the United Kingdom, the temporary transfer of a member of staff to another organization for a defined length of time, usually for a specific purpose. Secondment has grown in popularity in recent years, primarily for career development purposes. Secondments between the public and private sectors have been used as a mechanism to share management techniques and to disseminate best practice.

second mortgage MORTGAGES loan using already-mortgaged property as collateral a loan that uses the equity on a mortgaged property as security and is taken out with a different lender from the first mortgage. The second mortgagee has to record its interest and cannot be paid off on foreclosure until the first mortgagee is paid off.

second quarter ACCOUNTING second of four divisions of fiscal year the period of three months from April to the end of June, or the period of three months following the first quarter of the fiscal year. *Abbr* ***Q2***

second-tier market MARKETS more informal financial market than main market a market in stocks where the listing requirements are less onerous than for the main market, as in, for example, London's ***Alternative Investment Market***

secretary of the board CORPORATE GOVERNANCE *see* ***company secretary***

Secretary of the Treasury FINANCE US government official overseeing finance a senior member of the US government in charge of financial affairs

secret reserves FINANCE = ***hidden reserves***

Section 21 company BUSINESS S. African nonprofit organization in the Republic of South Africa, a company established as a nonprofit organization

sector 1. ECONOMICS businesses in economy providing similar products or services a part of the economy in which businesses produce the same

  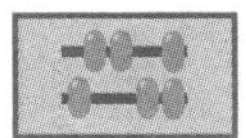      

type of product or provide the same type of service **2.** STOCKHOLDING & INVESTMENTS securities in particular industry or market a group of securities in one type of industry or market, for example, the banking sector or the industrial sector

sector fund STOCKHOLDING & INVESTMENTS fund invested in a particular sector a fund that is invested in only one sector of the stock market

sector index MARKETS list of firms specializing in specific markets an index of companies specializing in specific markets whose stocks are listed on a general or specialist stock exchange

secular STOCKHOLDING & INVESTMENTS developing over many years underlying movement over a long period, usually a number of years

secular trend STATISTICS pattern of change in data collected over time the underlying development of a series of measurements collected over a time period of several years to assess long-term trends and seasonal fluctuations

secured FINANCE *see* ***collateral, security***

secured bond STOCKHOLDING & INVESTMENTS bond with asset as collateral a bond for which real estate or goods have been pledged as collateral

secured creditor FINANCE creditor with legal claim on defaulting debtor's assets a person or organization that is owed money and has a legal claim to some or all of the borrower's assets if the borrower fails to repay the money owed

secured debt FINANCE debt backed by assets a debt that is guaranteed by assets that have been pledged. *See also* ***unsecured debt***

secured loan FINANCE loan guaranteed by borrower's assets as security a loan that is guaranteed by the borrower giving assets as security

secure server E-COMMERCE computer system protecting card transactions over Internet a combination of hardware and software that secures e-commerce credit card transactions so that there is no risk of unauthorized people gaining access to credit card details online

securities account TREASURY MANAGEMENT account record of financial assets an account that shows the value of financial assets held by a person or organization

securities analyst FINANCE professional studying effectiveness of firms and their securities a professional person who studies the performance of securities and the companies that issue them

Securities and Exchange Commission MARKETS, REGULATION & COMPLIANCE US agency overseeing securities markets in the United States, the government agency responsible for overseeing and regulating securities exchanges, brokers, dealers, advisers, and mutual funds. It promotes the disclosure of market-related information, fair dealing, and protection against fraud, and undertakes enforcement activities. *Abbr* ***SEC***

Securities and Futures Authority REGULATION & COMPLIANCE US organization for supervising financial advisers and facilitators in the United States, a self-regulatory organization responsible for supervising the activities of institutions advising on corporate finance activity, or dealing or facilitating deals in securities or derivatives. *Abbr* ***SFA***

Securities and Investments Board REGULATION & COMPLIANCE former UK organization regulating securities markets in the United Kingdom, the organization that formerly had the responsibility of regulating the securities markets, now superseded by the FSA. *Abbr* ***SIB***

Securities Commission REGULATION & COMPLIANCE New Zealand monitoring organization for securities market a statutory body responsible for monitoring standards in the New Zealand securities markets and for promoting investment in New Zealand. *Abbr* ***SC***

securities deposit account BANKING electronic deposit account for securities a brokerage account in which deposits of securities are registered electronically, without receipt of an actual certificate

Securities Institute of Australia FINANCE organization of Australian financial industry professionals a national professional body that represents people involved in the Australian securities and financial services industry. *Abbr* ***SIA***

Securities Investor Protection Corporation INSURANCE US corporation insuring clients of securities firms in the United States, a corporation created by Congress in 1970 that is a mutual insurance fund established to protect clients of securities firms. In the event of a firm being closed because of bankruptcy or financial difficulties, the corporation will step in to recover clients' cash and securities held by the firm. Its reserves are available to satisfy cash and securities that cannot be recovered up to a maximum of $500,000, including a maximum of $100,000 on cash claims. *Abbr* ***SIPC***

securities lending FINANCE lending of securities between brokers the loan of securities from one broker to another in the process of ***selling short***

securitization MORTGAGES, STOCKHOLDING & INVESTMENTS changing debt into securities the process of changing financial assets such as mortgages and loans into securities. The practice of selling mortgages to investors by repackaging the loans as ***loan notes*** paying a rate of interest that international banks and fund managers found attractive became widespread and eventually contributed to the financial difficulties experienced by banks and other financial institutions worldwide in 2008.

securitized mortgage STOCKHOLDING & INVESTMENTS mortgage exchanged for securities a mortgage that has been converted into securities. *See also* ***securitization***

securitized paper STOCKHOLDING & INVESTMENTS documents representing securitization the ***bond*** or ***promissory note*** resulting from changing financial ***assets*** such as mortgages and loans into ***securities***

security **1.** STOCKHOLDING & INVESTMENTS financial asset that can be bought and sold a tradable financial asset, for example, a bond, stock, or a warrant **2.** FINANCE guarantee of payment of debt an asset pledged as collateral for a loan or other borrowing

security deposit FINANCE deposit forfeited in transaction if buyer backs out an amount of money paid before a transaction occurs to compensate the seller in the event that the transaction is not concluded because the buyer defaults

security investment company MARKETS firm engaged in securities trading a financial institution that specializes in the analysis and trading of securities

security printer FINANCE printer of valuable documents a printer who prints paper money, stock prospectuses, and confidential government documents

seed capital *or* seed money FINANCE money needed to start new business a usually modest amount of money used to convert an idea into a viable business. Seed capital is a form of ***venture capital***.

segmentation STATISTICS separating statistical data into categories the division of the data in a study into categories

seigniorage CURRENCY & EXCHANGE difference between money's production cost and its value the difference between the cost of producing a currency and the face value of the currency. If the money is worth more than it cost to produce, the government makes a profit.

selection bias STATISTICS distortion of data by unmeasured variables in a statistical study, the distorting effect on variables of the methods that have been used to collect the data

selective pricing FINANCE pricing according to market setting different prices for the same product or service in different markets. This practice can be broken down as follows: category pricing, which involves cosmetically modifying a product such that the variations allow it to sell in a number of price categories; customer group pricing, which involves modifying the price of a product or service so that different groups of consumers pay different prices; peak pricing, setting a price which varies according to the level of demand; and service level pricing, setting a price based on the specific level of service chosen from a range.

self-assessment TAX UK system allowing taxpayers to estimate taxes owed in the United Kingdom, a system that enables taxpayers to assess their own income tax and capital gains tax payments for the fiscal year

self-certification FINANCE borrower's unconfirmed statement of income a statement by a borrower of their income, without confirmation by an employer or accountant, made in order to obtain a loan

self-certified mortgage MORTGAGES mortgage granted based on borrower's statement of income a mortgage granted on the basis of a borrower's statement of their income rather than an employer's or accountant's statement. Self-certified mortgages are usually granted to self-employed people whose income varies during the year but who have good credit ratings.

self-employed HR & PERSONNEL working but not on any firm's payroll working for yourself, or not on the payroll of a company

self-financing FINANCE financing of project from own resources the process by which a company finances a project or business activity from its own resources, rather than by applying for external financing

self-insurance INSURANCE setting money aside for possible loss the practice of saving money to pay for a possible loss rather than taking out an insurance policy against it

Self Invested Personal Pension Plan PENSIONS UK pension plan with great freedom of investment in the United Kingdom, a pension plan that allows the holder a much wider choice of investments than a conventional plan, and allows the investments to be held directly rather than by a third party. The plan holder can control the investment strategy or can appoint a fund

  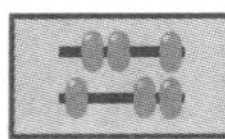      

manager or stockbroker to manage the fund. *Abbr* ***SIPP***

self-liquidating FINANCE paying for itself providing enough income to pay off the amount borrowed for financing

self-liquidating premium MARKETING self-financing promotional technique a sales promotion technique that pays for itself, in which customers send money and vouchers or proof of purchase to obtain a premium gift

self-liquidating promotion MARKETING self-financing sales activity a sales promotion in which the cost of the campaign is covered by the incremental revenue generated by the promotion

self-regulation REGULATION & COMPLIANCE regulation of industry by own members the regulation of an industry by its own members, usually by means of a committee that issues guidance and sets standards that it then enforces

self-regulatory organization REGULATION & COMPLIANCE **1.** in US, organization that is its own authority in the United States, an organization that polices its own members, for example, a stock exchange **2.** in UK, professional body responsible for financial activities in the United Kingdom, a professional body licensed by the ***Financial Services Authority*** and responsible for policing the range of investment activities undertaken by its members, ensuring that compensation is available in cases of negligence or fraud, and ensuring that there is sufficient professional indemnity. *Abbr* ***SRO***

self-tender STOCKHOLDING & INVESTMENTS US firm's offer to buy back stock in the United States, the repurchase by a corporation of its stock by way of a tender

sell and build GENERAL MANAGEMENT practice of only producing when order paid for an approach to manufacturing in which the producer creates a product only when a customer has placed an order and paid for it, rather than creating and stocking products that have not been ordered

seller's market MARKETS market in which sellers can get top price a market in which sellers can dictate prices, typically because demand is high or there is a product shortage

selling costs *or* selling overhead OPERATIONS & PRODUCTION expenses involved in selling something the amount of money needed for the advertising, sales representatives' commissions, and other expenses involved in selling something

selling price OPERATIONS & PRODUCTION price at which something is sold the price at which somebody is willing to sell something

selling price variance OPERATIONS & PRODUCTION discrepancy between actual and planned selling prices the difference between the actual selling price and the budgeted selling price

selling season MARKETS good time for selling a period in which market conditions are favorable to sellers

sell-off MARKETS wave of selling that lowers security's price rapid or widespread selling that causes a sudden drop in the price of a security or a drop in a market

sell short MARKETS sell borrowed security anticipating price drop to sell commodities, currencies, or securities that have been borrowed from a third party in the expectation that prices will fall, expecting to be able to buy them back at a lower price before the loan is redeemed, so ensuring a profit. *Also called* ***short*** *(sense 3)*

semiannual FINANCE paying or payable twice a year paying, or requiring payment, every six months

semi-variable cost *or* semi-fixed cost OPERATIONS & PRODUCTION production costs that vary somewhat according to quantity the amount of money paid to produce a product, which increases, though less than proportionally, with the quantity of the product made

Sendirian BUSINESS "Limited," in company name the Malay term for "limited." Companies can use "Sendirian Berhad" or "Sdn Bhd" in their name instead of "plc." *Abbr* ***Sdn***

senior capital FINANCE loan capital with priority for payment capital in the form of ***secured loans*** to a company that, in the event of liquidation, is repaid before ***junior capital*** such as stockholders' equity

senior debt FINANCE debt with higher claim on assets than others a debt whose holder has more claim on the debtor's assets than the holder of another debt. *See also* ***junior debt***

senior management GENERAL MANAGEMENT, HR & PERSONNEL those at top level of organization the managers and executives at the highest level of an organization. Senior management includes the ***board of directors***. Senior management has responsibility for ***corporate governance***, ***corporate strategy***, and the interests of all the organization's ***stakeholders***. *Also called* ***management team***

senior mortgage MORTGAGES mortgage with higher claim on assets than others a mortgage whose holder has more claim on the debtor's assets than the holder of another mortgage with the same mortgagee. *See also* ***junior mortgage***

sensitivity analysis ACCOUNTING analysis of effect of small adjustments to calculation the analysis of the effect of a small change in a calculation on the final result

SEP *abbr* PENSIONS ***simplified employee pension plan***

separable net assets ACCOUNTING assets that can be sold separately assets that can be separated from the rest of the assets of a business and sold off

sequestration LEGAL act of seizing property by court order the act of taking and keeping property on the order of a court, especially of seizing property from somebody who is in contempt of court

sequestrator LEGAL person seizing property by court order a person who takes and keeps property on the order of a court

serial correlation STATISTICS correlation of variable over period of time the correlation of a variable with itself over different points in time, used as an indicator of the future performance of something such as a security or economy. *Also called* ***autocorrelation***

serial entrepreneur BUSINESS person who repeatedly starts new enterprises an ***entrepreneur*** who sets up a string of new ventures, one after the other

seriation STATISTICS arrangement of objects in series the process of arranging a set of objects in a series on the basis of similarities or dissimilarities

series STOCKHOLDING & INVESTMENTS bonds or savings certificates issued over time a group of bonds or savings certificates, issued over a period of time but all bearing the same interest

Serious Fraud Office FRAUD, REGULATION & COMPLIANCE UK government department investigating major commercial fraud in the United Kingdom, a government department in charge of investigating major fraud in companies. *Abbr* ***SFO***

SERPS PENSIONS UK plan for earnings-related pensions State Earnings-Related Pension Scheme: in the United Kingdom, a state program that was designed to pay retired employees an additional pension to the standard state pension. It was replaced by the ***State Second Pension***. *Full form* ***State Earnings-Related Pension Scheme***

service MARKETING system or activity meeting need any activity with a mix of tangible and intangible outcomes that is offered to a market with the goal of satisfying a customer's need or desire. Early marketing tended to distinguish a service from a physical good, but more recently these two have been seen as interrelated because service delivery frequently has physical aspects. For example, in a restaurant, service is provided by a waiter but physical goods, such as the food and the dining room, are also involved. In modern marketing, all forms of services and goods can be seen as products.

service charge **1.** FINANCE, BANKING sum or additional sum paid for service a fee for any service provided, or an additional fee for any improvements to an existing service. For example, residents in apartment buildings may pay an annual maintenance fee, or banks may charge a fee for operating an account or obtaining foreign currency for customers (also called a ***bank charge***). **2.** MARKETING payment to serving staff a gratuity usually paid in restaurants and hotels. A service charge may be voluntary or may be added as a percentage to the bill.

service contract HR & PERSONNEL employment contract for senior executive a contract of employment for executive directors that lays down the conditions of employment and details of any bonus that may be paid, and outlines the procedure for ending employment

service cost center FINANCE cost center serving other cost centers in organization a cost center providing services to other cost centers. When the output of an organization is a service rather than goods, an alternative name is usually used, for example, support cost center or utility cost center.

service/function costing ACCOUNTING cost accounting for services within organization ***cost accounting*** for services or functions, for example, canteens, maintenance, or personnel

service industry BUSINESS industry specializing in service not products an industry that does not make products, but instead offers a service such as banking, insurance, or transport

service level agreement LEGAL contract giving details of service to be performed a contract between a service provider and a customer that specifies in detail the level of service (quality, frequency, flexibility, charges, etc.) to be provided over the contract period, as well as the procedures to implement in the case of default

servicing borrowing FINANCE paying interest the process of paying the interest that is due on a loan

set-aside ACCOUNTING = ***reserves***

set-off FINANCE offset of debts or loss against gain an agreement between two parties to balance one debt against another or a loss against a gain

  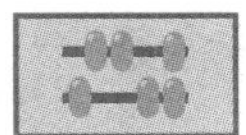      

settle STOCKHOLDING & INVESTMENTS finalize security sale to transfer property such as securities from a seller to a buyer in return for payment

settlement **1.** FINANCE payment the payment of an outstanding debt, invoice, account, or charge **2.** STOCKHOLDING & INVESTMENTS finalizing security sale the transfer of property such as securities from a seller to a buyer in return for payment **3.** E-COMMERCE transfer of payment to account of e-business the portion of an electronic transaction during which the customer's credit card is charged for the transaction and the proceeds are deposited into the ***merchant account***

settlement date FINANCE due date for paying debt or charge the date on which an outstanding debt or charge is due to be paid, or when cash offered for securities or derivatives of them must be delivered

settlement day MARKETS **1.** in UK, final day for paying for stock in the United Kingdom, the day on which shares of stock bought must be paid for. On the London Stock Exchange the account period is three business days from the day of trade. **2.** in US, day when securities become purchaser's property in the United States, the day on which securities bought actually become the property of the purchaser

setup costs ACCOUNTING amount spent to make equipment usable the costs associated with making a workstation or equipment available for use. Setup costs include the personnel needed to set up the equipment, the cost of downtime during a new setup, and the resources and time needed to test the new setup to achieve the specification of the parts or materials produced.

setup fees E-COMMERCE amount spent arranging to accept Internet payments the costs associated with establishing a ***merchant account***, for example, application and software licensing fees and point-of-sale equipment purchases

setup time OPERATIONS & PRODUCTION time spent to make equipment fully productive the time it takes to prepare, calibrate, and test a piece of equipment to produce a required output

seven-day money MARKETS money-market funds with seven-day term funds that have been placed on the money market for a term of seven days

severally LEGAL not jointly as separate individuals or entities, not jointly

severance *US* HR & PERSONNEL dismissal or discharge from employment dismissal from employment because the job or worker is considered no longer necessary. *UK term* ***redundancy***

severance package *US* HR & PERSONNEL benefits for dismissed or discharged employee a package of benefits that an employer gives to an employee who is dismissed. *UK term* ***redundancy package***

severance pay *US* FINANCE payment to dismissed or discharged employee a payment made by an employer to an employee when the employee who has been dismissed or discharged leaves the organization. *Also called* ***unemployment compensation***. *UK term* ***redundancy payment***

SFA *abbr* REGULATION & COMPLIANCE ***Securities and Futures Authority***

SFAS *abbr* REGULATION & COMPLIANCE ***Statement of Financial Accounting Standards***

SFE *abbr* MARKETS ***Sydney Futures Exchange***

SFO *abbr* FRAUD, REGULATION & COMPLIANCE ***Serious Fraud Office***

SGX *abbr* MARKETS ***Singapore Exchange***

shadow economy ECONOMICS = ***black economy***

shadow market MARKETS = ***black market***

shadow price ECONOMICS estimated cost of new economic activity the amount that engaging in a new economic activity is likely to cost a person or an economy. *See also* ***opportunity cost***

shakeout MARKETS exiting of timid investors during financial crisis the elimination of weak or cautious investors during a crisis in the financial market (slang)

share STOCKHOLDING & INVESTMENTS = ***stock***

share account **1.** BANKING member's account in UK building society in the United Kingdom, an account at a building society where the account holder is a member of the society. Account holders who are not members are offered a deposit account. *See also* ***deposit account*** **2.** STOCKHOLDING & INVESTMENTS account with credit union paying dividends in the United States, an account with a credit union that pays dividends rather than interest

share at par STOCKHOLDING & INVESTMENTS stock valued at face value a share whose value on the stock market is the same as its face value

share buyback STOCKHOLDING & INVESTMENTS = ***buyback***

share capital STOCKHOLDING & INVESTMENTS capital from sale of stock the amount of ***nominal share capital*** that a company raises by issuing shares of stock. Share capital does not reflect any subsequent increase or decrease in the value of stock sold; it is capital raised, irrespective of changes in stock value in the secondary markets. *Also called* ***issued capital***. *See also* ***stockholders' equity, reserves***

share certificate *UK* STOCKHOLDING & INVESTMENTS = ***stock certificate***

shared drop MARKETING delivery of simultaneous promotional offers a sales promotion technique in which a number of promotional offers are delivered by hand to ***prospects*** at the same time

shared values GENERAL MANAGEMENT = ***core values***

share exchange STOCKHOLDING & INVESTMENTS exchange of individual stockholdings for shares in fund a service provided by some collective investment plans whereby they exchange investors' existing individual stockholdings for shares in their funds. This saves the investor the expense of selling holdings, which can be uneconomical when dealing with small stockholdings.

share-for-share offer STOCKHOLDING & INVESTMENTS bidder's offer of shares as payment for company a type of ***takeover bid*** where the bidder offers its own shares, or a combination of cash and shares, for the target company

shareholder STOCKHOLDING & INVESTMENTS **1.** somebody owning stock in corporation a person or organization that owns shares in a limited company or partnership. A shareholder has a stake in the company and becomes a member of it, with rights to attend the ***annual meeting***. Since shareholders have invested money in a company, they have a vested interest in its performance and can be a powerful influence on company policy; they should consequently be considered ***stakeholders*** as well as shareholders. Some pressure groups have sought to exploit this by becoming shareholders in order to get a particular viewpoint or message across. At the same time, in order to maintain or increase the company's market value, managers must consider their responsibility to shareholders when formulating strategy. It has been argued that on some occasions the desire to make profits to raise returns for shareholders has damaged companies, because it has limited the amount of money spent in other areas (such as the development of facilities, or health and safety). *Also called* ***stockholder*** **2.** participant in pooled investment a person who owns shares of a fund or ***investment trust***

shareholders' equity *or* shareholders' funds STOCKHOLDING & INVESTMENTS = ***stockholders' equity***

shareholders' perks STOCKHOLDING & INVESTMENTS benefits for stockholders besides dividends benefits offered to stockholders in addition to dividends, often in the form of discounts on the company's products and services. *Also called* ***stockholder perks***

shareholder value STOCKHOLDING & INVESTMENTS total return to stockholders including dividends and appreciation the total return to the stockholders in terms of both dividends and share price growth, calculated as the present value of future free cash flows of the business discounted at the weighted average cost of the capital of the business less the market value of its debt. *Also called* ***stockholder value***

shareholder value analysis STOCKHOLDING & INVESTMENTS firm's value based on return to stockholders a calculation of the value of a company made by looking at the returns it gives to its stockholders. *Abbr* ***SVA***. Also called ***stockholder value analysis***

shareholding *UK* STOCKHOLDING & INVESTMENTS = ***stockholding***

share incentive scheme *UK* HR & PERSONNEL = ***stock incentive plan***

share index *UK* MARKETS = ***index*** *(sense 2)*

share issue STOCKHOLDING & INVESTMENTS offer to sell shares in business the offering for sale of shares in a business. The capital derived from share issues can be used for investment in the core business or for expansion into new commercial ventures.

share of voice MARKETING comparative amount spent on advertising an individual company's proportion of the total advertising expenditure in a sector

share option *UK* STOCKHOLDING & INVESTMENTS = ***stock option***

share option scheme *UK* STOCKHOLDING & INVESTMENTS = ***stock option plan***

shareowner STOCKHOLDING & INVESTMENTS = ***shareholder***

share premium STOCKHOLDING & INVESTMENTS amount paid for share above declared value the amount payable for a share above its ***nominal value***. Most shares are issued at a ***premium*** to their nominal value. Share premiums are credited to the company's ***share premium account***.

share premium account ACCOUNTING account where firms credit share premiums the special reserve in a company's balance sheet to which ***share premiums*** are credited. Expenses associated with the issue of shares may be written off to this account.

share register STOCKHOLDING & INVESTMENTS list of stockholders a list of the stockholders in a particular company

share shop STOCKHOLDING & INVESTMENTS office where stock is traded the name given by some financial institutions to an office open to the public where stock may be bought and sold

shares of negligible value STOCKHOLDING & INVESTMENTS worthless shares in defunct firm shares that are considered as having no value in income tax terms because the company has ceased to exist. The shares of companies in receivership are not deemed to be of negligible value, although they may eventually end up as such.

share split STOCKHOLDING & INVESTMENTS = ***scrip issue stock split***

share tip *UK* STOCKHOLDING & INVESTMENTS = ***stock tip***

Share Transactions Totally Electronic MARKETS *see* ***STRATE***

shareware E-COMMERCE program available free but chargeable for continued use software distributed free of charge, but usually with a request that users pay a small fee if they like the program

share warrant STOCKHOLDING & INVESTMENTS document stating right to hold stock a document stating that somebody has the right to a number of shares of stock in a company

shariah *or* sharia LEGAL = ***Islamic law***

shariah-compliant FINANCE in accordance with Islamic law used to describe financial activities and investments that comply with ***Islamic law***, which prohibits the charging of interest and involvement in any enterprise associated with activities or products forbidden by Islamic law

shark watcher *US* MARKETS firm that identifies takeover targets a firm that specializes in monitoring the stock market for potential takeover activity (slang)

Sharpe ratio STOCKHOLDING & INVESTMENTS formula for calculating relationship between risk and return a method of determining the relationship between investment risk and return, calculated by subtracting the return on a risk-free investment from the rate of return on a portfolio of investments and dividing the result by the standard deviation of the return

sharp practice FRAUD underhand business methods business methods that are not illegal but are not entirely open and honest

shelf registration STOCKHOLDING & INVESTMENTS in US, statement registering future securities sale in the United States, a ***registration statement*** filed with the ***Securities and Exchange Commission*** two years before a corporation issues securities to the public. The statement, which has to be updated periodically, allows the corporation to act quickly when it considers that the market conditions are right without having to start the registration procedure from scratch.

shelfspace MARKETING area available for product in store the amount of space allocated to a product in a retail outlet

shell company BUSINESS registered firm whose shares no longer trade a company that has ceased to trade but is still registered, especially one sold to enable the buyer to begin trading without having to establish a new company

shibosai STOCKHOLDING & INVESTMENTS sale of securities direct to investors the Japanese term for a ***private placement***, which is the sale of securities direct to institutions for investment rather than resale

shibosai bond STOCKHOLDING & INVESTMENTS yen-denominated bond sold direct by issuing company a bond denominated in yen sold direct to investors by the foreign issuing company. *See also* ***samurai bond, shogun bond***

shift differential FINANCE extra pay for working unpopular shift payment made to employees over and above their basic rate to compensate them for the inconvenience of working in shifts. A shift differential usually takes account of the time of day when the shift is worked, the duration of the shift, the extent to which weekend working is involved, and the speed of rotation within the shift.

shingle hang out your shingle GENERAL MANAGEMENT to start a business or announce the startup of a new business

shinyo kinku BANKING Japanese bank financing small businesses in Japan, a financial institution that provides financing for small businesses

shinyo kumiai BANKING Japanese credit union financing small businesses in Japan, a credit union that provides financing for small businesses

shirkah FINANCE contract between people going into business for profit in Islamic financing, a contract between two or more people who launch a business or financial enterprise in order to make a profit. *Also called* ***musharaka***

shogun bond STOCKHOLDING & INVESTMENTS non-yen bond sold in Japan by non-Japanese institution a bond denominated in a currency other than the yen that is sold on the Japanese market by a non-Japanese financial institution. *Also called* ***geisha bond***. *See also* ***samurai bond, shibosai bond***

shop price OPERATIONS & PRODUCTION = ***retail price***

short 1. FINANCE asset behind security benefiting from asset's fall an asset underlying a security in which a dealer has a ***short position*** and so gains by a fall in the asset's value **2.** MARKETS investor selling short an investor who is holding a ***short position*** **3.** MARKETS = ***sell short***

short bill FINANCE bill payable at short notice a bill of exchange that becomes payable at short notice

short-change FRAUD give customer too little change to give a customer less change than is right, either by mistake or in the hope that it will not be noticed, or to treat somebody less than fairly

short covering MARKETS purchase of security benefiting from asset's fall the buying back of foreign exchange, commodities, or securities by a firm or individual that has been ***selling short***. Such purchases are undertaken when the market has begun to move upward, or when it is thought to be about to do so.

short credit FINANCE credit terms demanding repayment soon terms of borrowing that allow the customer only a little time to pay

short-dated STOCKHOLDING & INVESTMENTS maturing in 5 years or less used to describe securities such as bonds that mature in five years or less. *See also* ***long-dated, medium-dated***

short-dated bill FINANCE bill payable almost immediately a bill that is payable within a few days

short-dated gilts STOCKHOLDING & INVESTMENTS UK government security maturing within 5 years fixed-interest securities issued by the UK government that mature in less than five years from the date of purchase. *Also called* **shorts**. *See also* ***gilt-edged security***

shortfall FINANCE amount missing from expected total an amount that is missing that would make the total expected sum

shorting MARKETS = ***short selling***

short interest STOCKHOLDING & INVESTMENTS quantity of security sold and not repurchased the total number of shares of a specific security that investors have sold short and have not repurchased in anticipation of a price decline

short investor MARKETS seller of securities expecting to repurchase them somebody who sells shares they have borrowed in order to buy expecting to be able to buy them back later at a lower price

short position STOCKHOLDING & INVESTMENTS selling unbought security hoping price will decline a situation in which somebody sells commodities, currencies, or securities they have borrowed for a fee in the expectation that they will be able to buy them back and return the loan at a lower price, so making a profit. *See also* **long position**

shorts STOCKHOLDING & INVESTMENTS = ***short-dated gilts***

short sale STOCKHOLDING & INVESTMENTS sale of borrowed security anticipating cheap repurchase a sale of borrowed commodities, currencies, or securities in the expectation that prices will fall before they have to be bought back and then returned to the original owner

short selling MARKETS selling borrowed security anticipating cheap repurchase the practice of selling borrowed commodities, currencies, or securities in the expectation that prices will fall before they have to be bought back and then returned to the original owner. *Also called* ***shorting***

short-term bond STOCKHOLDING & INVESTMENTS bond maturing within 2 years a bond on the corporate bond market that has an initial maturity of less than two years

short-term capital FINANCE money on short-term loan funds raised for a period of less than 12 months, for example, by a bank loan, to cover a short-term shortage. *See also* ***working capital***

short-term debt FINANCE debt due within year debt that has a term of one year or less

short-term economic policy ECONOMICS economic planning for near future an economic policy with objectives that can be met within a period of months or a few years

short-term forecast MARKETS forecast covering few months only a forecast that covers a period of a few months

short-termism GENERAL MANAGEMENT emphasis on quick results not long-term goals an approach to business that concentrates on short-term results rather than long-term objectives

short-term loan FINANCE loan repayable in weeks a loan that has to be repaid within a year, usually within a few weeks

  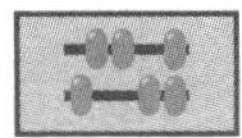      

short-term security STOCKHOLDING & INVESTMENTS security maturing within 5 years a security that matures in less than five years

show stopper MERGERS & ACQUISITIONS (slang) = ***poison pill***

shrinkage OPERATIONS & PRODUCTION **1.** reduction in firm's inventories a reduction in the amount of inventory held by a company, often caused by production processes **2.** goods lost to theft or damage a term used to describe goods that leave a retail outlet but are not logged as sales. Shrinkage can include goods that are stolen by shoplifters, or are damaged or broken.

SI *abbr* LEGAL ***statutory instrument***

SIA *abbr* FINANCE ***Securities Institute of Australia***

SIB *abbr* REGULATION & COMPLIANCE ***Securities and Investments Board***

SIC *abbr* BUSINESS ***Standard Industrial Classification***

SICAV *abbr* BUSINESS ***société d'investissement à capital variable***

sickness and accident insurance INSURANCE policy paying creditors during sickness or injury a form of insurance for ill health that may be sold with some form of credit, for example, a credit card or personal loan. In the event of the borrower being unable to work because of accident or illness, the policy covers the regular payments to the credit card company or lender.

sideline cash FINANCE = ***idle capital***

sight bill FINANCE bill of exchange payable immediately a bill of exchange payable when it is presented, rather than at a given length of time after presentation or after a date indicated on the bill

sight deposit BANKING bank deposit withdrawable immediately a bank deposit against which the depositor can immediately make a withdrawal

sight draft FINANCE bill of exchange payable immediately a bill of exchange that is payable on delivery. *See also* ***time draft***

sight letter of credit FINANCE letter of credit presented along with required documents a ***letter of credit*** that is paid when the necessary documents have been presented

signatory LEGAL somebody signing contract or document a person who signs a contract or other legal document

signature guarantee BANKING stamp or seal validating signature a stamp or seal, usually from a bank or a broker, that vouches for the authenticity of a signature

signature loan FINANCE = ***unsecured loan***

silent partner *US* BUSINESS investment partner with no active management role a person or organization that invests money in a company but takes no active part in the management of the business. Although silent partners are inactive in the operation of the business, they have legal obligations and benefits of ownership, and are therefore fully liable for any debts. *UK term* ***sleeping partner***

silly money FINANCE excessively high or low sum an amount of money that is regarded as excessively large or, occasionally, small (informal)

silver MARKETS precious metal traded as commodity a precious metal traded on commodity markets such as the London Metal Exchange

simple interest FINANCE interest paid on principal only interest charged simply as a constant percentage of the principal and not compounded. *See also* ***compound interest***

simple moving average STATISTICS method of sampling giving every unit equal chance the selection of units from a population in such a way that every possible combination of selected units is equally likely to be in the sample chosen

simplified employee pension plan PENSIONS IRA funded by employer a type of ***qualified plan*** that provides employers with a way of making contributions toward their employees' and their own retirement. Contributions are paid directly into an ***IRA*** set up for each person. *Abbr* ***SEP***

simulation GENERAL MANAGEMENT representation of possible situation or system the construction of a mathematical model to imitate the behavior of a real-world situation or system in order to test the outcomes of alternative courses of action. Simulation techniques are used in situations where real-life experimentation would be impossible, costly, or dangerous, and for training purposes.

simultaneous engineering OPERATIONS & PRODUCTION = ***concurrent engineering***

Singapore dollar CURRENCY & EXCHANGE Singapore's unit of currency Singapore's unit of currency, whose exchange rate is quoted as S$ per US$

Singapore Exchange MARKETS Singapore stock and monetary exchange the institution resulting from the merger in 1999 of the Stock Exchange of Singapore and the Singapore International Monetary Exchange. It provides securities and derivatives trading, securities clearing and depository, and derivatives clearing services. The headline index of stocks on the exchange is the ***Straits Times Index***. *Abbr* ***SGX***

single-currency CURRENCY & EXCHANGE denominated in same currency used to describe an international transaction denominated entirely in one currency

single customs document INTERNATIONAL TRADE standardized customs form a standard, universally used form for the passage of goods through customs

single entry ACCOUNTING book-keeping system using only one entry per transaction a type of bookkeeping where only one entry, reflecting both a credit to one account and a debit to another, is made for each transaction

single-figure inflation ECONOMICS inflation below 10% inflation that is rising at less than 10% per annum

single market ECONOMICS organization of European nations the European Union in its role as an economic organization. *See also* ***European Union***

single-payment bond STOCKHOLDING & INVESTMENTS bond redeemed with single payment at maturity a bond redeemed with a single payment combining principal and interest at maturity

single premium assurance *UK* INSURANCE = ***single premium insurance***

single premium deferred annuity TAX deferred annuity funded with single initial payment an annuity that is paid for with a single payment at inception and pays returns regularly after a set date. It gives a tax advantage.

single premium insurance *US* INSURANCE life insurance paid for with single initial premium life coverage where the premium is paid in one lump sum when the policy is taken out, rather than in installments. *UK term* ***single premium assurance***

single tax TAX tax to cover everything one major tax that supplies all revenue, especially on land

sinker STOCKHOLDING & INVESTMENTS bond paid from debt repayment reserve a bond whose principal and interest payments are paid out of the issuer's ***sinking fund***

sinking fund FINANCE money set aside for debt payments money put aside periodically to settle a liability or replace an asset. The money is invested to produce a required sum at an appropriate time.

SIPC *abbr* INSURANCE ***Securities Investor Protection Corporation***

SIPP *abbr* PENSIONS ***Self Invested Personal Pension Plan***

sister company BUSINESS company belonging to same group a company that belongs to the same group of companies as another

SIV *abbr* STOCKHOLDING & INVESTMENTS ***structured investment vehicle***

six-month money MARKETS money invested for 6 months funds invested on the money market for a period of six months

size of firm BUSINESS relative size of company for government records a method of categorizing companies according to size for the purposes of government statistics. Divisions are typically ***microbusiness***, ***small business***, ***medium-sized business***, and ***large-sized business***.

skewness STATISTICS lack of statistical symmetry a lack of symmetry in a ***probability distribution***

skimming FRAUD stealing small amounts from customer accounts the unethical and usually illegal practice of taking small amounts of money from accounts that belong to other individuals or organizations

skin in the game FINANCE amount of entrepreneur's money invested in business the amount of an entrepreneur's own money that they have invested in their business, considered by ***venture capitalists*** as an indication of the entrepreneur's commitment to making the business successful

sleeper **1.** STOCKHOLDING & INVESTMENTS stock with potential to rise in value a stock that has not risen in value for some time, but may suddenly do so in the future **2.** BUSINESS product that sells after period of sluggish sales a product that does not sell well for some time, then suddenly becomes very popular

sleeping partner *UK* BUSINESS = ***silent partner***

slippage STOCKHOLDING & INVESTMENTS discrepancy between estimated and actual costs the difference between the estimated costs of buying or selling a security and the actual costs of the transaction

slowdown ECONOMICS minor decrease in economic activity a fall in demand that causes a lowering of economic activity, less severe than a ***recession*** or ***slump***

slow payer FINANCE somebody slow to pay debts a person or company that does not pay debts on time

slump ECONOMICS major decrease in economic activity a severe downturn phase in the business cycle

slumpflation ECONOMICS decrease in economic activity with increased inflation a collapse in all economic activity accompanied by wage and price inflation. This happened, for example, in the United States and Europe in 1929. (slang)

slush fund FINANCE fund used for bribery or corruption a fund used by a company for illegal purposes such as bribing officials to obtain preferential treatment for planned work or expansion

small and medium-sized enterprise BUSINESS firm with under 250 employees an organization that is in the ***startup*** or growth phase of development and has fewer than 250 employees. This definition of a small and medium-sized enterprise is the one adopted by the United Kingdom's Department for Business Enterprise and Regulatory Reform for statistical purposes. *Abbr* ***SME***

small business BUSINESS firm with under 50 employees managed by owner an organization that is small in relation to the potential market size, is managed by its owners, and has fewer than 50 employees. This definition of a small business is the one adopted by the United Kingdom's Department for Business Enterprise and Regulatory Reform for statistical purposes.

small change FINANCE money in coins a small quantity of coins of mixed value that somebody might carry, often used to suggest a sum of no significance

small claim LEGAL in UK, claim for less than £5,000 in the United Kingdom, a claim for less than £5,000 in the County Court

Small Order Execution System MARKETS NASDAQ system for trading small lots automatically on the NASDAQ, an automated execution system for bypassing brokers when processing small order agency executions of NASDAQ securities up to 1,000 shares

small print GENERAL MANAGEMENT details and conditions printed smaller than main text details in an official document such as a contract that are usually printed in a smaller size than the rest of the text and, while often important, may be overlooked. Items often referred to as "small print" may include deliberately hidden charges, unfavorable terms, or loopholes.

smart card E-COMMERCE plastic card with built-in microprocessor a small plastic card containing a microprocessor that can store and process transactions and maintain a bank balance, thus providing a secure, portable medium for electronic money. Financial details and personal data stored on the card can be updated each time the card is used.

smart market E-COMMERCE market only using electronic communications a market in which all transactions are performed electronically using network communications

SME *abbr* BUSINESS ***small and medium-sized enterprise***: an organization that is in the ***startup*** or growth phase of development and has fewer than 250 employees.

smoothing methods STATISTICS ways of removing irregularities in statistical data procedures used in fitting a set of observations in a study into a statistical model, often by creating a graph of the data

smurf FRAUD somebody involved in money-laundering someone who passes money obtained illegally through banks or businesses in order to make it appear legitimate

snake CURRENCY & EXCHANGE currencies formerly in European Exchange Rate Mechanism formerly, the group of currencies within the European Exchange Rate Mechanism whose exchange rates were allowed to fluctuate against each other within specific bands or limits

snowball sampling STATISTICS method of creating samples based on existing samples a form of sampling in which existing sample members suggest potential new sample members, for example, personal acquaintances

snowflake STATISTICS graph of multiple variables a graph that shows ***multivariate data***

social business *or* social enterprise BUSINESS business run for positive social change a business whose main objective is to make positive social change in areas such as poverty, education, health, the environment, etc.

social lending FINANCE direct lending between people the practice of one person offering to lend money to another, without the involvement of a bank or other institution, especially through the Internet. *Also called* ***person-to-person lending***. *See also* ***ZOPA***

socially conscious investing STOCKHOLDING & INVESTMENTS = ***ethical investment***

social marginal cost ECONOMICS cost to society of change in economic variable the additional cost to a society of a change in an economic variable, for example, the price of gas or bread

social security INSURANCE, PENSIONS government financial support system a system of financial support in a variety of areas of personal need provided by a government, for example for retired people, those with young children, or those unemployed or unable to work

Social Security INSURANCE, PENSIONS US government assistance program for elderly and disabled in the United States, the federal insurance program that provides income for retirees and their dependents and survivors, disability income, and healthcare for seniors. The program is funded by required contributions from employers and working individuals.

Social Security number INSURANCE, PENSIONS, TAX person's identifying number for US social insurance plan in the United States, a unique nine-digit number assigned to each person within the Social Security system, which is used for taxation and identification purposes and does not change throughout the person's life. *Abbr* ***SSN***

Sociedad Anónima BUSINESS Spanish publicly held corporation a Spanish company with a status comparable to a ***publicly held corporation***. *Abbr* ***SA***

Sociedade Anónima BUSINESS Portuguese publicly held corporation a Portuguese company with a status comparable to a ***publicly held corporation***. *Abbr* ***SA***

Società a responsabilità limitata BUSINESS Italian private corporation an Italian unlisted company with a status comparable to a private corporation. *Abbr* ***Srl***

Società per Azioni BUSINESS Italian public corporation an Italian company with a status comparable to a public corporation. *Abbr* ***SpA***

Société Anonyme BUSINESS French publicly held corporation a French company with a status comparable to a ***publicly held corporation***. *Abbr* ***SA***

société à responsabilité limitée BUSINESS French unlisted corporation a French unlisted company with a status comparable to a private corporation. *Abbr* ***SARL***

société d'investissement à capital variable BUSINESS French investment company a French company managing an investment fund with capital varying according to the number of investors at any one time. *Abbr* ***SICAV***

Society for Worldwide Interbank Financial Telecommunication BANKING *see* ***SWIFT***

socioeconomic ECONOMICS relating to social and economic factors involving both social and economic factors. Structural unemployment, for example, has socioeconomic causes.

socioeconomic segmentation MARKETING separation of market into socioeconomic groups the division of a market according to the different socioeconomic categories within it

Sod's Law *UK* GENERAL MANAGEMENT = ***Murphy's Law***

soft capital rationing ACCOUNTING management's imposition of limit on capital investment a restriction on an organization's ability to invest capital funds caused by an internal budget ceiling being imposed by management. *See also* ***capital rationing***

soft commissions FINANCE brokerage commissions rebated to institutional customer brokerage commissions that are rebated to an institutional customer in the form of, or to pay for, research or other services

soft commodities MARKETS commodities other than solid raw materials commodities such as foodstuffs that are neither metals nor other solid raw materials. *Also called* ***softs***. *See also* ***future***, ***hard commodities***

soft-core radicalism MARKETING exploitation of customers' environmental and ethical concerns a marketing technique that plays on people's concerns about environmental and ethical issues in order to sell them a product (slang)

soft currency CURRENCY & EXCHANGE currency that is weak or expected to fall a currency that is weak, usually because there is an excess of supply and a belief that its value will fall in relation to others. *See also* ***hard currency***

soft dollars MARKETS payment by brokers for management firms' business rebates given by brokers to money management firms in return for funds' transaction business

soft landing ECONOMICS slowdown of economic activity without recession the situation when a country's economic activity has slowed down but demand has not fallen far enough or rapidly enough to cause a recession

soft loan FINANCE loan on highly favorable terms a loan on exceptionally favorable terms, for example, for a project that a government considers worthy

soft market MARKETS market with falling prices a market in which prices are falling because there are more sellers than buyers

  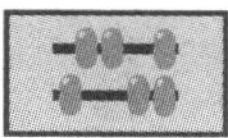      

softs MARKETS = ***soft commodities***

sold short STOCKHOLDING & INVESTMENTS borrowed and sold anticipating price drop used to refer to commodities, currencies, or securities that somebody borrows and sells, then buys back and repays in the expectation that prices will have fallen. *See also* ***sell short***

sole agency *UK* BUSINESS = ***exclusive agency***

sole agent *UK* BUSINESS = ***exclusive agent***

sole distributor BUSINESS retailer with exclusive right to sell something a retailer who is the only one in an area who is allowed by the manufacturer to sell a specific product or service

sole practitioner BUSINESS professional practicing alone the proprietor of a professional practice, who is personally responsible for all its debts

sole proprietor BUSINESS person operating business alone somebody who owns and runs an unincorporated business by himself or herself. Sole proprietors are taxed at the personal income level and are personally liable for all business losses or debts; in the event of bankruptcy personal possessions may be forfeited. *Also called* ***sole trader, owner-operator***

sole proprietorship BUSINESS business of one person a business operated by a sole proprietor, who is personally responsible for all its debts

sole trader BUSINESS = ***sole proprietor***

solicit FINANCE request money to ask another person or company for money

solvency FINANCE situation of being able to pay all debts situation in which a person or organization is able to pay all debts on their due date. *See also* ***insolvency***

solvency margin FINANCE business's assets minus liabilities a business's ***liquid assets*** that exceed the amount required to meet its liabilities

solvency ratio **1.** FINANCE ratio of assets to liabilities a ratio of assets to liabilities, used to measure a company's ability to meet its debts **2.** INSURANCE in UK, measure of insurance company's financial condition in the United Kingdom, the ratio of an insurance company's net assets to its non-life premium income

solvent FINANCE able to pay all one's debts used to refer to a situation in which the assets of an individual or organization are worth more than their liabilities

sort code *UK* BANKING number identifying UK bank branch a combination of numbers that identifies a bank branch on official documentation such as bank statements and checks. *See also* ***ABA routing number***

source and application of funds statement ACCOUNTING = ***cash flow statement***

sources and uses of funds statement ACCOUNTING = ***cash flow statement***

South African Revenue Service TAX S. African tax authority the government body that is responsible for collecting taxes and ensuring compliance with tax law in South Africa. *Abbr* ***SARS***

Southern African Development Community INTERNATIONAL TRADE *see* ***SADC***

sovereign bond STOCKHOLDING & INVESTMENTS government bond in foreign currency a bond issued by a national government denominated in a foreign currency

sovereign debt FINANCE borrowing by government borrowing that has been undertaken by a government

sovereign default FINANCE government not repaying debt the inability or refusal of a government to pay back money it has borrowed

sovereign loan FINANCE bank loan to foreign government a loan by a financial institution to an overseas government, usually of an emerging country. *See also* ***sovereign risk***

sovereign money STOCKHOLDING & INVESTMENTS money in sovereign wealth funds the money that is invested in ***sovereign wealth funds***

sovereign risk FINANCE risk that government defaults on loan the risk that a government may refuse to repay or be unable to repay money it has borrowed

sovereign wealth fund STOCKHOLDING & INVESTMENTS very wealthy state investment fund an investment fund owned by a government with very large amounts of money at its disposal. There is concern that such a fund would be able to buy stakes in another country's strategic industries. *Abbr* ***SWF***

SOX *abbr* REGULATION & COMPLIANCE ***Sarbanes–Oxley Act***

SpA *abbr* BUSINESS ***Società per Azioni***

spam MARKETING unwanted e-mailed advertising e-mailed direct mail regarded as an invasion of personal privacy. *See also* ***direct mail***

special clearing BANKING = ***special presentation***

Special Commissioner TAX UK Treasury official who hears income tax appeals in the United Kingdom, an official appointed by the Treasury to hear cases where a taxpayer is appealing against an income tax assessment

special damages FINANCE damages awarded for calculable loss damages awarded by a court to compensate for a loss that can be calculated, for example, the expense of repairing something

special deposit **1.** MORTGAGES in US, mortgage money for home improvements in the United States, an amount of money set aside for the renovation or improvement of a property as part of a mortgage **2.** BANKING commercial bank's required deposit in Bank of England a large sum of money that a ***commercial bank*** has to deposit with the ***Bank of England***

Special Drawing Right CURRENCY & EXCHANGE country's entitlement to receive IMF loans an accounting unit used by the ***International Monetary Fund***, allocated to each member country for use in loans and other international operations. The value is calculated daily on the weighted values of a group of currencies shown in dollars. *Abbr* ***SDR***

Special Economic Zone INTERNATIONAL TRADE Chinese free trade region in China, an area where trade is conducted under special conditions and largely free of state control

specialist **1.** BUSINESS person or company specializing in one thing a person or company that deals with one particular type of product, or with one subject **2.** MARKETS stock exchange member acting as market maker a member of a stock exchange who maintains an inventory of particular stocks, selling to or buying from brokers in order to maintain a stable market for those stocks

special notice STOCKHOLDING & INVESTMENTS late announcement of proposal for stockholder meeting notice of a proposal to be put before a meeting of the stockholders of a company that is issued less than 28 days before the meeting

special presentation BANKING direct delivery of check to paying banker the sending of a check directly to the paying banker rather than through the clearing system. *Also called* ***special clearing***. *See also* ***advice of fate***

special purpose bond STOCKHOLDING & INVESTMENTS bond for one particular project a bond for one particular project, financed by levies on the people who benefit from the project

special resolution CORPORATE GOVERNANCE vote held on exceptional issue in the United Kingdom, an exceptional issue that is put to the vote at a company's general meeting, for example, a change to the company's articles of association, requiring 21 days' notice

special situation STOCKHOLDING & INVESTMENTS expectation of stock price rise the expectation that a stock will increase in value as a result of a change in the company such as a merger

specie CURRENCY & EXCHANGE coins that are legal tender coins, as opposed to pieces of paper money, that are legal tender

specific charge FINANCE = ***fixed charge***

specific order costing ACCOUNTING way to track costs billed by separate contractors the basic cost accounting method used where work consists of separately identifiable contracts, jobs, or batches

speculation FINANCE purchase made on basis of large anticipated gain a purchase made solely to make a profit when the price or value of something increases

speculative bubble MARKETS = ***bubble***

speculator MARKETS somebody taking risks to make quick profit somebody who buys goods, stock, or foreign currency with a higher-than-average risk in the hope that it will rise quickly in value

spending money CURRENCY & EXCHANGE personal money money that is available for small ordinary personal expenses

spinning MARKETS offering stock to preferred customers a practice of questionable legality in which brokerage firms offer stock in ***initial public offerings*** that are in high demand to preferred customers, in order to obtain or keep their business

spin-off GENERAL MANAGEMENT firm formed from larger one a company or subsidiary formed by splitting away from a parent company. A spin-off company can, for example, be created when research and development yields a new product that does not fit into the company's current portfolio, or when a company wants to explore a new venture related to its current activities. It can also be formed from a demerger, in which acquired companies or parts of a business are separated in order to create a more streamlined parent organization. A spin-off is often entrepreneurial in spirit, but the backing of the parent company can provide financial stability.

split STOCKHOLDING & INVESTMENTS = ***stock split***

split annuity INSURANCE combined immediate and deferred annuity product a combination of two

  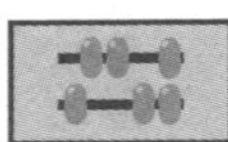      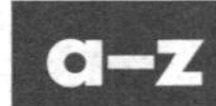

products, an immediate annuity and a deferred annuity, each having a single premium. The immediate annuity provides monthly income over a set period and the deferred annuity provides capital growth to replace the original principal, on a fixed interest basis.

split-capital investment trust *or* split-capital trust STOCKHOLDING & INVESTMENTS = ***split-level investment trust***

split commission FINANCE transaction fee divided among multiple parties commission that is divided between two or more parties in a transaction

split coupon bond STOCKHOLDING & INVESTMENTS = ***zero coupon bond***

split-level investment trust *or* split-level trust STOCKHOLDING & INVESTMENTS investment trust combining income shares and capital shares an investment trust with two categories of shares: ***income shares***, which receive income from the investments, but do not benefit from the rise in their capital value, and ***capital shares***, which increase in value as the value of the investments rises. Income shareholders receive all or most of the income generated by the trust and a predetermined sum at liquidation, while capital shareholders receive no interest but the remainder of the capital at liquidation. *Also called* ***split trust, split-capital investment trust, split-capital trust***

split payment FINANCE payment greatly subdivided a payment that is divided into small units

split trust STOCKHOLDING & INVESTMENTS = ***split-level investment trust***

sponsor 1. FINANCE person or company giving money for venture a person or company that pays money to help with an activity or to pay for a business venture **2.** FINANCE firm giving money to sport for advertising rights a company that pays to help a sport, in return for advertising rights **3.** STOCKHOLDING & INVESTMENTS backer of an initial public offering an organization such as an investment bank that backs an initial public offering **4.** BUSINESS somebody giving job recommendation somebody who recommends another person for a job **5.** MARKETING company purchasing advertising on TV program a company that pays part of the cost of making a television program by taking advertising time on the program

sponsorship 1. FINANCE financial support financial backing for an activity or business venture **2.** MARKETING financial support as means of advertising a form of advertising in which an organization provides funds for something such as a television program or sports event in return for exposure to a target audience

spot MARKETING broadcast advertisement a commercial broadcast on television or radio

spot cash CURRENCY & EXCHANGE cash paid on the spot cash paid immediately for something bought

spot currency market CURRENCY & EXCHANGE, MARKETS market for currency deliverable at time of sale a market that deals in foreign exchange for immediate rather than future delivery. *See also* ***spot market***

spot exchange rate CURRENCY & EXCHANGE, MARKETS current exchange rate the exchange rate used for immediate currency transactions

spot goods MARKETS commodity deliverable immediately a commodity traded on the ***spot market***, for immediate delivery

spot interest rate MARKETS current interest rate an interest rate that is determined when a loan is made

spot market MARKETS market for items deliverable at time of sale a market that deals in commodities or foreign exchange for immediate rather than future delivery. *See also* ***spot currency market***

spot month MARKETS = ***nearby month***

spot price MARKETS current price the price for immediate delivery of a commodity or currency

spot rate MARKETS current rate of interest to maturity on security the rate of interest to maturity currently offered on a particular type of security

spot transaction MARKETS transaction for immediate delivery a transaction in commodities or foreign exchange for immediate delivery

spread 1. MARKETS difference between buying and selling price for security the difference between the buying and selling price of a security achieved by a ***market maker*** on a stock exchange **2.** STOCKHOLDING & INVESTMENTS mix of investments the range of the investments in a particular portfolio

spread betting STOCKHOLDING & INVESTMENTS betting on stock movements within specified range betting on the movement of a stock price in relation to a range of high and low values. If the price moves outside the range on a specific day, the bettor wins a multiple of the original stake times the number of points outside the range.

spreadsheet GENERAL MANAGEMENT software organizing data in columns a computer program that provides a series of ruled columns in which data can be entered, manipulated, and analyzed

sprinkling trust STOCKHOLDING & INVESTMENTS trust in which trustees have discretion over distributions a trust with multiple beneficiaries where the trustees have discretion over how the trust's income is distributed

Square Mile FINANCE = ***the City***

squeeze ECONOMICS government restriction of available credit a government policy of restriction, commonly affecting the availability of credit in an economy

Srl *abbr* BUSINESS ***Società a responsabilità limitata***

SRO *abbr* REGULATION & COMPLIANCE ***self-regulatory organization***

SSAPs *abbr* REGULATION & COMPLIANCE, ACCOUNTING ***Statements of Standard Accounting Practice***

SSN *abbr* INSURANCE, PENSIONS, TAX ***Social Security number***

stabilization fund ECONOMICS government reserve for international financial support a fund created by a government for use in maintaining its official exchange rate when necessary

stag STOCKHOLDING & INVESTMENTS somebody buying new stock for immediate resale somebody who buys ***initial public offerings*** at the offering price and sells them immediately to make a profit

staged payments FINANCE payments made in stages payments that are made in stages over a period of time

stage-gate model MARKETING way of bringing something new to market the traditional model of ***new product development***, comprising the conception, generation, analysis, development, testing, marketing, and commercialization of new products or services. *See also* ***new product development***

stagflation ECONOMICS situation with high unemployment and inflation a situation in which both inflation and unemployment exist at the same time in an economy. There was stagflation in the United Kingdom and the United States in the 1970s, for example.

stagnation ECONOMICS situation with no economic progress a situation in which no progress is being made, especially in economic matters

stakeholder BUSINESS party with vested interest in firm's success a person or organization with a legitimate interest in the successful operation of a company or organization. A stakeholder may be an employee, customer, supplier, partner, or even the local community within which an organization operates.

stakeholder pension PENSIONS in UK, low-cost pension supplementing state plan a pension bought from a private company in which the retirement income depends on the level of contributions made during a person's working life. Stakeholder pensions are designed for people without access to a pension from their employment, and are intended to provide a low-cost supplement to a pension from the government. A stakeholder pension plan can either be trust-based, like an occupational pension plan, or contract-based, similar to a personal pension. Employers must provide access to a stakeholder pension plan for employees, subject to some exceptions, although they are not required to establish a stakeholder pension plan themselves. Membership of a stakeholder pension plan is voluntary. *See also* ***Keough Plan***

stakeholder theory STOCKHOLDING & INVESTMENTS theory that stockholders' interests needn't harm stakeholders the theory that an organization can enhance the interests of its stockholders without damaging the interests of its wider ***stakeholders***. Stakeholder theory grew in response to the ***economic theory of the firm***. One of the difficulties of stakeholder theory is allocating importance to the values of different groups of stakeholders, and a solution to this is proposed by ***stakeholder value analysis***.

stakeholder value analysis STOCKHOLDING & INVESTMENTS assessment of stakeholders' views for corporate planning purposes a method of determining the values of the ***stakeholders*** in an organization for the purposes of making strategic and operational decisions. Stakeholder value analysis is one method of justifying an approach based on ***stakeholder theory*** rather than the ***economic theory of the firm***. It involves identifying groups of stakeholders and eliciting their views on particular issues in order that these views may be taken into account when making decisions.

stale bull STOCKHOLDING & INVESTMENTS investor seeking to sell nonperforming security an investor who bought stocks hoping that they would rise, and now finds that they have not risen and wants to sell them

stamp duty LEGAL in UK, duty verified with postage stamp in the United Kingdom, a duty that is payable on some legal documents and is shown to have been paid by a stamp being affixed to the document

standard OPERATIONS & PRODUCTION benchmark measurement a benchmark measurement of

  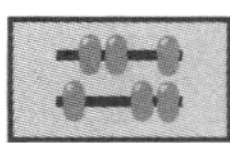      

resource usage, set in defined conditions on the basis of expected, potentially attainable, prior or comparable performance standards. Standards may be set at attainable levels, which assume efficient levels of operation but include allowances for normal loss, waste, and machine downtime, or at ideal levels, which make no allowance for the above losses and are only attainable under the most favorable conditions.

standard agreement *or* standard contract LEGAL contract containing usual language a printed contract form that contains the usual language applicable to a particular situation

Standard & Poor's STOCKHOLDING & INVESTMENTS major US bond-rating corporation in the United States, a corporation that rates bonds according to the creditworthiness of the organizations issuing them. Standard & Poor's also issues stock market indices, for example, the ***S&P 500***. *Abbr* ***S&P***. See also ***Moody's***

Standard & Poor's rating STOCKHOLDING & INVESTMENTS US stock rating service a stock rating service provided by the US agency Standard & Poor's

standard cost FINANCE calculated future cost as basis of estimates a future cost that is calculated in advance and against which estimates are measured

standard costing ACCOUNTING comparison of standard and actual costs a control procedure that compares standard costs and revenues with actual results to obtain variances, which are used to stimulate improved performance

standard deduction TAX untaxed part of person's income in the United States, a proportion of personal income that is not subject to tax for people who do not itemize their deductions. It is calculated based on marital status, number of children or dependents, and whether or not a person is aged 65 or older. *See also* ***itemized deductions***

standard deviation STATISTICS quantity expressing difference from mean a measure of how dispersed a set of numbers are around their mean

standard hour OPERATIONS & PRODUCTION amount of work expected per hour the amount of work achievable, at standard efficiency levels, in an hour

Standard Industrial Classification BUSINESS US system for identifying businesses with their activity in the United States, a system used for categorizing and coding businesses according to the type of activity in which they are engaged. *Abbr* ***SIC***

standard letter GENERAL MANAGEMENT letter sent to several correspondents a letter that is sent without change to a number of correspondents

standard of living ECONOMICS people's ability to buy desired goods and services a measure of economic well-being based on the ability of people to buy the goods and services they desire

standard rate TAX in UK, usual rate of VAT in the United Kingdom, the rate of ***VAT*** usually payable on goods or services

standby credit **1.** BANKING = ***backup credit*** **2.** ECONOMICS credit that can be used by emerging countries credit drawing rights given to an emerging country by an international financial institution, to fund industrialization or other growth policies

standby fee FINANCE fee for additional loan a fee paid to obtain ***standby credit***

standby loan ECONOMICS loan to emerging country for specific purposes a loan given to an emerging country by an international financial institution, to fund technology hardware purchase or other growth policies

standing instructions GENERAL MANAGEMENT procedural instructions normally in effect instructions, which may be revoked at any time, for a specific procedure to be undertaken in the event of a specific occurrence; for example, an instruction that money in a savings account for a fixed term should be placed on deposit for a further period when the term expires

standing order *UK* BANKING = ***automatic debit***

standing room only MARKETING illusion of high demand to encourage sales a sales technique whereby customers are given the impression that there are many other people waiting to buy the same product at the same time (slang)

staple commodity FINANCE basic item of trade any basic food or a raw material that is important in a country's economy

star **1.** STOCKHOLDING & INVESTMENTS outstanding investment an investment that is performing extremely well **2.** BUSINESS fast-growing business with high market share in the ***Boston Box*** model, a business with a high market share and high growth rate. *See also* ***Boston Box***

startup BUSINESS new business, especially in technology sector a relatively new, usually small business, particularly one supported by venture capital and within those sectors closely linked to new technologies

startup costs FINANCE money required to launch new business the initial sum required to establish a business or to get a project under way. The costs will include the capital expenditure and related expenses before the business or project generates revenue.

startup financing *or* start-up financing FINANCE first stage in financing new project the first stage in financing a new project, which is followed by several rounds of investment capital as the project gets under way

state bank BANKING bank chartered by US state in the United States, a commercial bank chartered by one of the states rather than having a federal charter

state capitalism ECONOMICS capitalistic system where government controls most production a way of organizing society in which the state controls most of a country's means of production and capital

State Earnings-Related Pension Scheme PENSIONS *see* ***SERPS***

state enterprise BUSINESS nationalized or largely nationalized firm an organization in which the government or state has a controlling interest

statement BANKING list of bank account transactions a summary of all transactions, for example, deposits or withdrawals, that have occurred in an account at a bank or savings and loan association over a given period of time

statement of account ACCOUNTING **1.** list of recent transactions a summary of transactions that have occurred between two parties over a given period of time **2.** list of commercial transactions a list of sums due, usually comprising unpaid invoices, items paid on account but not offset against particular invoices, credit notes, debit notes, and discounts

statement of affairs ACCOUNTING list of assets and liabilities showing financial condition a statement in a prescribed form, usually prepared by a receiver, showing the estimated financial position of a debtor or a company that may be unable to meet its debts. It contains a summary of the debtor's assets and liabilities, with the assets shown at their estimated realizable values. The various classes of creditors, such as preferential, secured, partly secured, and unsecured, are shown separately.

statement of cash flows ACCOUNTING list of cash transactions a statement that documents actual receipts and expenditures of cash

statement-of-cash-flows method ACCOUNTING accounting system based on business's cash flow a method of accounting that is based on flows of cash rather than balances on accounts

statement of changes in financial position ACCOUNTING list of business's income and expenditures a financial report of a company's incomes and outflows during a period, usually a year or a quarter

Statement of Financial Accounting Standards REGULATION & COMPLIANCE in US, declaration of standards governing financial reporting in the United States, a statement detailing the standards to be adopted for the preparation of financial statements. *Abbr* ***SFAS***

statement of source and application of funds ACCOUNTING = ***cash flow statement***

statement of total recognized gains and losses ACCOUNTING list of changes in stockholders' equity a financial statement showing changes in stockholders' equity during an accounting period

Statements of Standard Accounting Practice REGULATION & COMPLIANCE, ACCOUNTING UK rules for preparation of financial statements rules laid down by the UK Accounting Standards Board for the preparation of financial statements. *Abbr* ***SSAPs***

state of indebtedness FINANCE situation of owing money the situation that exists when somebody owes money

state ownership BUSINESS ownership of industry by government a situation in which an industry is taken over from private ownership and run by a government

state pension PENSIONS UK government pension in the United Kingdom, the basic pension entitlement provided by the government for a retired person

State Second Pension PENSIONS additional UK government pension in the United Kingdom, an additional pension entitlement over and above the basic pension provided by the government, available to people who had caring responsibilities or long-term illness or disability as well as to those who were employed

statistic STATISTICS item of numerical data a piece of information in numerical form, obtained from analysis of a large quantity of numerical data

statistical discrepancy STATISTICS discrepancy arising from different calculation methods the amount by which sets of figures differ, usually because of a difference in the methods of calculation

statistical expert system STATISTICS computer program for performing statistical analysis a computer program used to conduct a statistical analysis of a set of data

  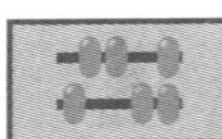      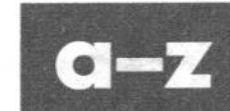

statistical model STATISTICS techniques for analyzing data in statistical study the particular methods used to investigate the data in a statistical study

statistical quality control OPERATIONS & PRODUCTION, STATISTICS methods for checking consistency of statistical samples the process of inspecting samples of a product to check for consistent quality according to given parameters

statistical significance STATISTICS status as statistical pointer in a statistical study, a value assigned to the likelihood that something has occurred by chance

statistics STATISTICS **1.** numerical data information in numerical form, obtained from analysis of a large quantity of numerical data **2.** study of numerical data the collection, analysis, and presentation of large quantities of numerical data

status inquiry FINANCE credit check the act of checking on a customer's credit rating

statute-barred debt FINANCE debt that is uncollectable after time limit a debt that cannot be pursued as the time limit laid down by law has expired

statute of limitations LEGAL time limit for bringing lawsuit a law that allows only a fixed period of time during which somebody can start legal proceedings to claim property or compensation for damage

statutory auditor ACCOUNTING, REGULATION & COMPLIANCE in UK, officially qualified auditor in the United Kingdom, a professional person qualified to conduct an audit required by the Companies Act

statutory body BUSINESS group created by law an organized group with a particular function that has been established by government legislation

statutory instrument LEGAL in UK, legislation not needing full Parliamentary approval in UK law, a form of legislation that allows the provision of an Act of Parliament to be brought into force or altered without full Parliamentary approval. *Abbr* ***SI***

statutory regulations REGULATION & COMPLIANCE UK financial regulations based on Parliamentary acts in the United Kingdom, regulations covering financial dealings that are based on Acts of Parliament, for example, the Financial Services Act, as opposed to the rules of self-regulatory organizations, which are non-statutory

statutory voting CORPORATE GOVERNANCE system granting one vote per share a system of voting in which stockholders in a company have one vote per share of stock owned

STC TAX S. African tax on dividends in South Africa, a tax that is levied on corporate dividends. *Full form* ***Secondary Tax on Companies***

stealth tax TAX initially unnoticed tax a new tax or tax increase, especially an indirect tax, that is introduced without much public attention, or an additional charge that is effectively a tax although not officially classed as one

sterling CURRENCY & EXCHANGE UK currency the standard currency (pounds and pence) used in the United Kingdom

sterling area CURRENCY & EXCHANGE formerly, countries using sterling as trading currency formerly, the area of the world where the pound sterling was the main trading currency

sterling balances CURRENCY & EXCHANGE trade balances expressed in sterling a country's trade balances expressed in pounds sterling

sterling index CURRENCY & EXCHANGE index measuring sterling against other currencies an index that shows the current value of sterling against a group of other currencies

stipend FINANCE regular payment to office-holder a regular remuneration or allowance paid as a salary to an office-holder such as a member of the clergy

stock **1.** STOCKHOLDING & INVESTMENTS fixed interest investment a form of security issued in fixed units at a fixed rate of interest. The technical difference between stocks and shares is that a company that fixes its capital in terms of a monetary amount and then sells different proportions of it to investors creates stock, while a company that creates a number of shares of equal nominal value and sells different numbers of them to investors creates shares. For all practical purposes they are the same. In the United States, all equity instruments are called stocks, whereas in the United Kingdom, they are called shares. **2.** *UK* OPERATIONS & PRODUCTION = ***inventory***

stockalypse STOCKHOLDING & INVESTMENTS collapse in stock prices a sudden and dramatic drop in the price of stock (slang)

stockbroker STOCKHOLDING & INVESTMENTS professional agent for securities a person or company that arranges the sale and purchase of stocks and other securities, usually for a commission. *Also called* ***broker***

stockbroking STOCKHOLDING & INVESTMENTS dealing in stock the business of dealing in stocks and other securities for clients

stock buyback STOCKHOLDING & INVESTMENTS = ***buyback***

stock certificate *US* STOCKHOLDING & INVESTMENTS document representing ownership in firm a document that certifies ownership of stock in a company. *UK term* ***share certificate***

stock control *UK* OPERATIONS & PRODUCTION = ***inventory control***

stock depreciation *UK* ACCOUNTING = ***inventory depreciation***

stock dividend STOCKHOLDING & INVESTMENTS dividend paid as additional shares of stock a dividend paid to a stockholder in the form of additional stock rather than cash

stock exchange MARKETS market for securities a registered place where securities are bought and sold. *Also called* ***stock market*** *(sense 2)*

Stock Exchange Automated Quotations system MARKETS *see* ***SEAQ***

Stock Exchange Automated Quotations system International MARKETS *see* ***SEAQ International***

Stock Exchange Automatic Trading System MARKETS *see* ***SEATS***

stock exchange listing MARKETS presence on official stock list the fact of being on the official list of stocks that can be bought or sold on a stock exchange

stockholder *US* STOCKHOLDING & INVESTMENTS somebody with shares in company a person or organization that owns one or more shares of stock in a company. *UK term* ***shareholder*** *(sense 1)*

stockholder perks *US* STOCKHOLDING & INVESTMENTS = ***shareholders' perks***

stockholders' equity *US* FINANCE firm's share capital and reserves the part of a company's financial assets consisting of ***share capital*** and ***retained profits***. *Also called* ***shareholders' equity, shareholders' funds***

stockholder value *US* STOCKHOLDING & INVESTMENTS = ***shareholder value***

stockholder value analysis *US* STOCKHOLDING & INVESTMENTS = ***shareholder value analysis***

stockholding *US* STOCKHOLDING & INVESTMENTS ownership of shares in firm the stock in a ***corporation*** owned by a stockholder. *UK term* ***shareholding***

stock incentive plan *US* HR & PERSONNEL offering shares in firm to employees a type of financial ***incentive plan*** in which employees can acquire shares in the company in which they work and so have an interest in its financial performance. A stock incentive plan is a type of ***employee stock ownership plan***, in which employees may be given stock by their employer, or stock may be offered for purchase at an advantageous price, as a reward for personal or group performance. *UK term* ***share incentive scheme***

stockjobber MARKETS former UK dealer in securities the equivalent of a ***market maker*** on the London Stock Exchange before the ***Big Bang*** of October 1986. Stockjobbers could not deal directly with private investors. *See also* ***market maker***

stockjobbing MARKETS former trading activities on stock exchange formerly, the business of buying and selling shares from other traders on a stock exchange

stock level OPERATIONS & PRODUCTION = ***inventory level***

stock market MARKETS **1.** trading in securities the activity or profession of trading in securities **2.** = ***stock exchange***

stock market crash MARKETS = ***crash***

stock market index MARKETS = ***index*** *(sense 2)*

stock market manipulation MARKETS efforts to influence stock prices an attempt or series of attempts to influence the price of stocks by buying or selling in order to give the impression that the stocks are widely traded

stock market rating MARKETS stock price indicating firm's value the price of a stock on the stock market, which shows how investors and financial advisers generally consider the value of the company

stock market valuation MARKETS firm's value based on stock price the value of a company based on the current market price of its stock

stock option STOCKHOLDING & INVESTMENTS right to buy or sell on agreed terms the right of an option holder to buy or sell a specific stock on predetermined terms on, or before, a future date. *Also called* ***option***. *UK term* ***share option***

stock option plan *US* STOCKHOLDING & INVESTMENTS employees' right to buy company stock a program in which an employee is given the option to buy a specific number of shares of stock at a future date, at an agreed price. Stock options provide a financial benefit to the recipient only if the stock price rises over the period the option is available. If the stock price falls over the period,

  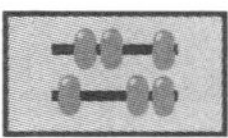      

the employee is under no obligation to buy. There may be a tax advantage to the employees who participate in such a program. Share options may be available to all employees or operated on a discretionary basis. *UK term* ***share option scheme***

stockout OPERATIONS & PRODUCTION unavailability of part from stock the situation where the stock of a particular component or part has been used up and has not yet been replenished. Stockouts result from poor stock control or the failure of a ***just-in-time*** supply system. They can result in delays in the delivery of customer orders and can damage the reputation of the business.

stockpicker STOCKHOLDING & INVESTMENTS buyer choosing stock somebody who is choosing which stock to buy. *See also* ***bottom-up approach***

stock quote MARKETS current price of stock trading on stock exchange the highest ***bid price*** or lowest ***ask price*** of a share of stock at any point in time during a trading day

stocks and shares STOCKHOLDING & INVESTMENTS firms' capital owned by public the units of ownership in public companies. The technical difference between stocks and shares is that a company that fixes its capital in terms of a monetary amount and then sells different proportions of it to investors creates stock, while a company that creates a number of shares of equal nominal value and sells different numbers of them to investors creates shares. For all practical purposes they are the same. In the United States, all equity instruments are called stocks, whereas in the United Kingdom, they are called shares.

stocks and shares ISA STOCKHOLDING & INVESTMENTS UK tax-free account for investment in the United Kingdom, an investment account for which interest is not paid on dividends, and ***capital gains tax*** is not paid on any profits. The maximum that can be invested per ***tax year*** is capped, at £11,280 for 2012–13, although this is reduced by the amount invested in any ***cash ISA*** also held. *See also* ***cash ISA, ISA***

stock split *US* STOCKHOLDING & INVESTMENTS numerical increase of shares without affecting total value an act of issuing stockholders with at least one more share for every share owned, without affecting the total value of each holding. A stock split usually occurs because the stock price has become too high for easy trading. *Also called* ***share split, split***. *See also* ***bonus shares, reverse split***. *UK term* ***scrip issue***

stock symbol MARKETS short form of firm's name a shortened version of a company's name, usually made up of two to four letters, used in screen-based trading systems and newspaper listings

stocktaking OPERATIONS & PRODUCTION counting items held in stock the process of measuring the quantities of stock held by an organization. Inventory can be held both in stores and within the processes of the operation.

stock tip *US* STOCKHOLDING & INVESTMENTS expert's recommendation on stock a recommendation about a stock published in the financial press, usually based on research published by a financial institution. *UK term* ***share tip***

stock turnover *UK* STOCKHOLDING & INVESTMENTS = ***inventory turnover***

stock turns ACCOUNTING = ***inventory turnover***

stock valuation *UK* ACCOUNTING = ***inventory valuation***

stokvel BANKING S. African savings association in South Africa, an informal, widely used cooperative savings program that provides small-scale loans

stop-go ECONOMICS alternately tightening and loosening economic policies the alternate tightening and loosening of fiscal and monetary policies, characteristic of the UK economy in the 1960s and 1970s

stop limit order MARKETS order to trade stock above specific price an order to trade only if and when a security reaches a specified price

stop-loss order *or* stop-loss *or* stop order MARKETS instruction to sell stock if price falls an instruction to a stockbroker to sell a stock if the price falls to a specified level.

stop price MARKETS specified trading price the price at which to sell or buy a security specified in a ***stop-loss order***

store card FINANCE credit card used exclusively in department store a credit card issued by a large department store, which can only be used for purchases in that store

story stock STOCKHOLDING & INVESTMENTS stock reported on in press a stock that is the subject of a press or financial community story that may affect its price

straddle STOCKHOLDING & INVESTMENTS simultaneous security purchase of put and call options the act of buying a ***put option*** and a ***call option*** for the same number of shares of the same security at the same time with the same ***strike price*** and expiration date. This allows the buyer to make a profit if the price rises or falls. *See also* ***strangle***

straight line depreciation ACCOUNTING reducing value of asset evenly over its lifetime a form of ***depreciation*** in which the cost of a fixed asset is spread equally over each year of its anticipated lifetime

Straits Times Index MARKETS main Singaporean stock market index an index of 30 most-highly capitalized companies on the ***Singapore Exchange***. It is jointly calculated by Singapore Press Holdings (the publishers of the *Straits Times*), the Singapore Exchange, and ***FTSE***. It was established on January 10, 2008, with a base value of 3344.53, as a continuation of the Straits Times Industrials Index.

strangle MARKETS simultaneously trading differently priced put and call options a strategy in which a ***put option*** and a ***call option*** with the same expiration date but different ***strike prices*** on the same asset are either bought or sold. *See also* ***straddle***

STRATE MARKETS S. African electronic exchange system the electronic stock transactions system of the ***Johannesburg Stock Exchange***. *Full form* ***Share Transactions Totally Electronic***

strategic analysis GENERAL MANAGEMENT assessment of business procedures and environment the process of evaluating the business environment within which an organization operates and the organization itself as part of a process of formulating long-term objectives

strategic business unit GENERAL MANAGEMENT section with own marketing strategy a division within a large organization that shares the organization's market and customer focus but has responsibility for the development of its own marketing strategy. A single overall strategic approach is often inappropriate in large diversified organizations or multinational companies.

strategic financial management FINANCE handling firm's money to achieve firm's goals the identification of the strategies capable of maximizing an organization's net present value, the allocation of scarce capital resources, and the implementation and monitoring of a particular strategy

strategic management GENERAL MANAGEMENT management for longer-term objectives the development of corporate strategy, and the management of an organization according to that strategy. Strategic management focuses on achieving and maintaining a strong competitive advantage. It involves the application of corporate strategy to all aspects of the organization, and especially to decision making. As a discipline, strategic management developed in the 1970s, but it has evolved in response to changes in organization structure and corporate culture. With greater empowerment, strategy has become the concern not just of directors but also of employees at all levels of the organization.

strategic marketing MARKETING direct selling to customers a method of selling products directly to customers, bypassing traditional retailers or distributors

strategy GENERAL MANAGEMENT structured course of action for longer-term objectives a planned course of action undertaken to achieve the goals and objectives of an organization. The overall strategy of an organization is known as corporate strategy, but strategy may also be developed for any aspect of an organization's activities such as environmental management or manufacturing strategy.

stratified random sampling STATISTICS selecting random subgroups from stratified statistical population sampling carried out at random from each stratum of a stratified population. *See also* ***random sampling***

stratified sampling STATISTICS *see* ***random sampling***

street[1] *US* MARKETS describing person with market awareness used to describe somebody who is considered to be well informed about the market (slang)

Street[2] MARKETS = ***Wall Street***

street name MARKETS brokerage house holding customer's investments in the United States, a way of registering a customer's security in which a broker or brokerage holds the security in the brokerage house's name to facilitate transactions

stress test BANKING review of system's stability a stringent set of checks on the stability and security of a system or of an organization such as a bank

strike price STOCKHOLDING & INVESTMENTS price fixed by seller the price for a security or commodity that underlies an ***option***. *Also called* ***exercise price*** *(sense 2)*

strip STOCKHOLDING & INVESTMENTS separation of coupons from bond for sale individually the separation of the coupons from the principal of a bond in order to sell them separately as a package of interest coupons and a bond that repays principal without interest. *See also* ***strips***

strippable bond STOCKHOLDING & INVESTMENTS bond separable into principal and interest payments a bond that can be divided into separate zero-coupon bonds, representing its principal and

  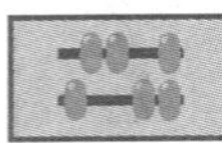      

interest payments, which can be traded independently

stripped bond STOCKHOLDING & INVESTMENTS bond separated into principal and interest payments a bond that has been divided into separate zero-coupon bonds, representing its principal and interest payments, which can be traded independently

stripped stock STOCKHOLDING & INVESTMENTS stock without dividend rights stock for which the rights to dividends have been split off and sold separately

stripping STOCKHOLDING & INVESTMENTS splitting bond into two parts for separate trading the process of separating the coupons from the principal of a bond in order to sell them separately as a package of interest coupons and a bond that repays principal without interest. *See also* ***strips***

strips STOCKHOLDING & INVESTMENTS bond parts allowing interest or principal payments only the parts of a ***stripped bond*** that entitle the owner to interest payments only, or to the payment of principal only

strong currency CURRENCY & EXCHANGE currency with relatively high value a currency that has a high value against other currencies

structural adjustment ECONOMICS change in basic framework of economy the reallocation of resources in response to alterations in the composition of the output of an economy as it experiences changes between the contribution of different business sectors. *Also called* ***structural change***

structural change ECONOMICS = ***structural adjustment***

structural fund STOCKHOLDING & INVESTMENTS mutual fund invested in EU economic development a type of ***mutual fund*** that invests in projects that contribute to the economic development of poorer nations in the European Union

structural inflation ECONOMICS inflation with no specific cause inflation that naturally occurs in an economy, without any particular triggering event

structural reform FINANCE improve and strengthen system reorganization of a system by which something such as the financial services industry is managed in order to strengthen it

structural unemployment ECONOMICS unemployment caused by change in basic economic framework unemployment resulting from a change in demand or technological advances, which cause a surplus of labor in a particular location or skills area

structured finance FINANCE nonstandard form of borrowing complex financial arrangements individually designed to support a client's needs for which the normal sources of financing are not suitable

structured investment vehicle STOCKHOLDING & INVESTMENTS product with short-term borrowing funding high-yielding securities a product that borrows money in the short-term credit market to invest in high-yielding, longer-dated securities. *Abbr* ***SIV***

structured note FINANCE debt with derivative component typically, a senior unsecured debt obligation with a derivative component, reflecting the terms of the transaction and specifying payments, normally including the return of the principal amount at maturity (for principal protected notes), or possibly some principal loss (in the case of nonprincipal protected notes), depending on the performance of the underlying investment

structured product STOCKHOLDING & INVESTMENTS customized financial contract a legally binding financial contract between a client and an investment bank, designed to meet a client's specific needs and stating the specific terms that have been agreed. The legal form of the transaction is called a ***wrapper***.

stub equity STOCKHOLDING & INVESTMENTS **1.** money from high risk bond sales the money raised through the sale of large quantities of high risk bonds, as in a ***leveraged buyout*** **2.** stock with greatly reduced price a stock whose price has seriously fallen due to major financial problems. Stub stock is a risky investment with great potential if the company regains its strength.

Student Loan Marketing Association FINANCE *see* ***Sallie Mae***

subcontracting GENERAL MANAGEMENT, OPERATIONS & PRODUCTION employing another to fulfill part of contract the delegation to a third party of some or all of the work that somebody has contracted to do. Subcontracting usually occurs where the contracted work such as the construction of a building requires a variety of skills. Responsibility for the fulfillment of the original contract remains with the original contracting party. Where the fulfillment of a contract depends on the skills of the person who has entered into the contract, as in the painting of a portrait, then the work cannot be subcontracted to a third party. The term subcontracting is sometimes used to describe ***outsourcing*** arrangements.

subject to collection FINANCE depending on repayment dependent upon the ability to collect the amount owed

subordinated debt FINANCE = ***junior debt***

subordinated loan FINANCE debt whose repayment ranks after all others a loan that ranks below all other borrowings with regard to both the payment of interest and principal. *See also* ***pari passu***

subprime loan FINANCE loan made to borrower unlikely to repay a loan made to somebody who does not meet the usual or standard qualifications for borrowing the amount in question. In 2007–8, a world financial crisis was precipitated by defaults on subprime mortgage loans.

subscribed capital *or* subscribed share capital STOCKHOLDING & INVESTMENTS = ***issued share capital***

subscriber **1.** STOCKHOLDING & INVESTMENTS somebody who buys stocks in new firm a buyer, especially one who buys stocks in a new company or new issues **2.** BUSINESS original stockholder a person who signs a company's ***memorandum of association***

subscription price STOCKHOLDING & INVESTMENTS price of new stock offered for sale the price at which new shares of stock in an existing company are offered for sale

subscription share STOCKHOLDING & INVESTMENTS share of stock in new firm a stock purchased by a subscriber when a new company is formed

subsidiary BUSINESS = ***subsidiary company***

subsidiary account BANKING individual account for one owner of joint account an account for one of the individual people or organizations that jointly hold another account

subsidiary company BUSINESS firm controlled by another a company that is controlled by another. A subsidiary company operates under the control of a parent or ***holding company***, which may have a majority on the subsidiary's ***board of directors***, or a majority shareholding in the subsidiary—giving it majority voting rights—or it may be named in a contract as having control of the subsidiary. If all of the stock in a company is owned by its parent, it is known as a ***wholly-owned subsidiary***. A subsidiary that is located in a different country from the parent is a ***foreign subsidiary company***.

subsidized FINANCE having financial assistance for which a ***subsidy*** has been paid

subsidy FINANCE financial assistance for activity or firm financial assistance to a company or group of people, usually given by a government, to encourage new developments of benefit to the public or to support an industry for a period of time. Subsidies are regarded as restrictive in international trade if by supporting a domestic industry they make imports more expensive.

subsistence allowance FINANCE money for living expenses away from home ***expenses*** paid by an employer, usually within preset limits, to cover the cost of accommodations, meals, and incidental expenses incurred by employees when away on business

subtreasury FINANCE subordinate treasury a place where some of a nation's money is held

sub-underwriter MARKETS firm underwriting stock issue a company that underwrites an issue, taking shares of stock from the main underwriters

subvention FINANCE financial support given officially money given by a government or official body to support an activity

suggested retail price *US* BUSINESS sale price suggested by manufacturer the price at which a manufacturer suggests a product should be sold on the retail market, though this may be reduced by the retailer. *UK term* ***recommended retail price***

suit GENERAL MANAGEMENT employee in formal role a business executive who works for a large corporation, especially in a relatively faceless management role (slang)

suitability rules REGULATION & COMPLIANCE rules ensuring that client can afford an investment guidelines that brokers and others selling or recommending investments are required to follow to ensure that investors are financially able to handle the risks involved in investing

sukuk FINANCE asset-backed interest-free bond in Islamic financing, the equivalent of a bond, which represents undivided shares in ownership of tangible assets. Under Islamic law it cannot earn interest.

sum FINANCE **1.** money a particular amount of money **2.** total amount of something the total amount of any given item, such as stocks or securities **3.** total of added numbers the total arising from the addition of two or more numbers

sum at risk FINANCE, RISK how much of something investors might lose an amount of any given item, such as money, stocks, or securities, that an investor might lose

sum insured INSURANCE largest amount insurance firm will pay the maximum amount that

  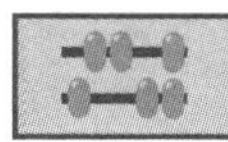   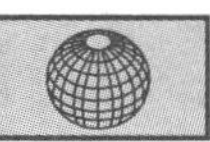   

an insurance company will pay out in the event of a claim

sum of digits method *or* sum-of-the-year's-digits depreciation ACCOUNTING = ***accelerated depreciation***

sums chargeable to the reserve ACCOUNTING sums debited to company's reserves sums that can be debited to a company's reserves

sunk cost ACCOUNTING completed cost unrelated to future decisions a cost that has been irreversibly incurred or committed prior to a decision point, and cannot therefore be considered relevant to subsequent decisions

sunshine law REGULATION & COMPLIANCE US law requiring openness in the United States, a law that requires public disclosure of a government act or government proceedings

superannuation PENSIONS money yielding income, usually in retirement money providing an income for somebody who no longer works, usually because they are older than the normal age for retirement

superannuation plan PENSIONS Australian pension plan in Australia, a pension plan that may be personal or operated by an employer

superannuation scheme PENSIONS New Zealand pension plan in New Zealand, a pension plan that may be personal or operated by an employer

supertax TAX **1.** high tax on high earnings a high rate of tax levied on the income of the highest earners **2.** former UK tax in the United Kingdom, a tax rate levied from 1919 to 1973 on the income of the highest earners. *Also called* ***surtax*** *(sense 2)*

supplementary benefit HR & PERSONNEL formerly in UK, government payments for poor people formerly, in the United Kingdom, payments from the government to people with very low incomes. It was replaced by ***income support***.

supplementary capital BANKING = ***Tier 2 capital***

supplier OPERATIONS & PRODUCTION firm providing what another firm needs a company that provides materials, components, goods, or services for another company

supply and demand ECONOMICS quantity of available goods and desire for them the quantity of goods available for sale at a given price, and the level of consumer need for those goods. The balance of supply and demand fluctuates as external economic factors—for example, the cost of materials and the level of competition in the marketplace—influence the level of demand from consumers and the desire and ability of producers to supply the goods. Supply and demand is recognized as an economic force, and is often referred to as the ***law of supply and demand***.

supply chain GENERAL MANAGEMENT, OPERATIONS & PRODUCTION network of firms involved in production process the network of manufacturers, wholesalers, distributors, and retailers, who turn raw materials into ***finished goods*** and services and deliver them to consumers. Supply chains are increasingly being seen as integrated entities, and closer relationships between the organizations throughout the chain can bring competitive advantage, reduce costs, and help to maintain a loyal customer base.

supply chain management OPERATIONS & PRODUCTION overseeing of relationships between firms in supply chain the management of the movement of goods and flow of information between an organization and its suppliers and customers, to achieve strategic advantage. Supply chain management covers the processes of managing materials, physical distribution, purchasing, information, and logistics.

supply price OPERATIONS & PRODUCTION price at which something is provided the price at which goods or services are supplied

supply shock ECONOMICS event causing reduced supply of necessity an event that causes a sudden reduction, or perceived reduction, in the production or availability of a product or resource necessary to an economy

supply-side economics ECONOMICS economic theory stressing incentives for suppliers a branch of economics that emphasizes the production of goods through incentives as a means of stimulating economic growth

support price ECONOMICS product price subsidized by government the price of a product that is fixed or stabilized by a government so that it cannot fall below a specific level

support ratio ECONOMICS = ***dependency ratio***

surcharge OPERATIONS & PRODUCTION charge added to standard charge a charge added to the standard charge for a specific product or service

surety FINANCE **1.** guarantor somebody who promises to cover another person's obligations **2.** guarantee for loan the ***collateral*** given as security when a person, business, or organization takes out a loan

surplus ACCOUNTING = ***budget surplus***

surplus capacity OPERATIONS & PRODUCTION ability to produce more than customers require the capability of a factory or workstation to produce output over and above the level required by consumers or subsequent processes. Surplus capacity is a product of materials, personnel, and equipment that are superfluous, or not working to maximum ***capacity***. Some surplus capacity is required in any production system to deal with fluctuations in demand, and as a backup in case of failure. Excessive surplus capacity, however, adds to the cost of the production process as work-in-process inventory or finished-goods storage increases, and can result in ***overcapacity***. If a workstation has no surplus capacity its workloads cannot be increased, so it is at risk of becoming a ***bottleneck***. *Also called* ***redundant capacity***

surrender INSURANCE relinquish insurance policy before maturity to cancel an insurance policy before the contracted date for maturity

surrender charge FINANCE penalty for early withdrawal of invested money a charge levied when somebody withdraws money invested before the date allowed

surrender value INSURANCE money paid by insurance firm for canceled policy the sum of money offered by an insurance company to somebody who cancels a policy before it has completed its full term

surtax TAX **1.** tax paid on top of other taxes a tax paid in addition to another tax, typically levied on a corporation with very high income **2.** = ***supertax*** *(sense 2)*

survey MARKETING, STATISTICS collection of data from group on particular topic the collection of data from a given population for the purpose of analysis of a particular issue. Data is often collected from only a sample of a population, and this is known as a ***sample survey***. Surveys are used widely in research, especially in ***market research***.

survivalist enterprise *S. AFRICA* BUSINESS small firm with no paid workers a business that has no paid employees, generates income below the poverty line, and is considered the lowest level of microbusiness

sushi bond STOCKHOLDING & INVESTMENTS Japanese bond a bond that is not denominated in yen and is issued in any market by a Japanese financial institution. This type of bond is often bought by Japanese institutional investors. (slang)

suspended trading MARKETS halt in trading of stock a period when trading in a specific stock or on an exchange is stopped, usually in response to information about a company, or concern about rapid movement of the stock price. *See also* ***trading halt***

suspense account BANKING temporary holding account an account in which debits or credits are held temporarily until sufficient information is available for them to be posted to the correct accounts

sustainable advantage GENERAL MANAGEMENT lasting competitive advantage a competitive advantage that can be maintained over the long term, as opposed to one resulting from a short-term tactical promotion

sustainable development GENERAL MANAGEMENT development that does not disadvantage future generations development that meets the needs of the present without compromising the ability of future generations to meet their own needs. The concept of sustainable development was introduced by the Brundtland Report, the first report of the World Commission on Environment and Development, established by the United Nations in 1983. It advocates the integration of social, economic, and environmental considerations into policy decisions by business and government. Particular emphasis is given to social, cultural, and ethical implications of development. Sustainable development can be achieved through ***environmental management*** and is a feature of a socially responsible business.

SVA *abbr* STOCKHOLDING & INVESTMENTS ***shareholder value analysis***

swap **1.** FINANCE, STOCKHOLDING & INVESTMENTS trade of payment terms between two firms an arrangement whereby two organizations contractually agree to exchange payments on different terms, for example, in different currencies, or one at a fixed rate and the other at a floating rate. *See also* ***asset swap, bond swap, interest rate swap*** **2.** FINANCE exchange an exchange of credits or liabilities

swap book STOCKHOLDING & INVESTMENTS list of exchanges wanted a broker's list of stocks or securities that clients wish to swap

swaption STOCKHOLDING & INVESTMENTS right to exchange an ***option*** giving the right but not the obligation to enter into a ***swap*** contract (slang)

sweat equity FINANCE unpaid work by firm's founder work done for little or no pay by the owner or partners of a new company in the early stages of the company's activities

sweep facility BANKING automatic service moving money to different account the automatic transfer of sums from a checking account to a deposit account, or from any low interest account to a higher one. For example, a personal customer may have the balance transferred just before receipt of their monthly salary, or a business may stipulate that when a balance exceeds a specific sum, the excess is to be transferred.

sweetener 1. STOCKHOLDING & INVESTMENTS high-yield investment added to lower yield collection a security with a high yield that has been added to a portfolio to improve its overall return. *See also* ***kicker*** **2.** GENERAL MANAGEMENT incentive an incentive offered to somebody to take a particular course of action **3.** STOCKHOLDING & INVESTMENTS attractive extra feature on investment product a feature added to a security to make it more attractive to investors

SWF *abbr* STOCKHOLDING & INVESTMENTS ***sovereign wealth fund***

SWIFT BANKING society supporting common global financial transactions network a nonprofit cooperative organization with the mission of creating a shared worldwide data processing and communications link and a common language for international financial transactions. Established in Brussels in 1973 with the support of 239 banks in 15 countries, it now has over 7,000 live users in 192 countries, exchanging millions of messages valued in trillions of dollars every business day. *Full form* ***Society for Worldwide Interbank Financial Telecommunication***

swing trading MARKETS buying and selling stock after sudden price changes the trading of stock in order to take advantage of sudden price movements that occur especially when large numbers of traders have to cover short sales

switch 1. STOCKHOLDING & INVESTMENTS replace one investment product in set with another to exchange a specific security with another within a portfolio, usually because the investor's objectives have changed **2.** STOCKHOLDING & INVESTMENTS swap involving exchange rates a type of ***swap*** that involves different currencies and interest rates. *See also* ***swap*** **3.** OPERATIONS & PRODUCTION move goods elsewhere to move a commodity from one location to another

Switch BANKING UK debit card a debit card formerly used in the United Kingdom

switching STOCKHOLDING & INVESTMENTS buying and selling different futures contracts simultaneously the simultaneous sale and purchase of contracts in futures with different expiration dates, as, for example, when a business decides that it would like to take delivery of a commodity earlier or later than originally contracted

switching discount STOCKHOLDING & INVESTMENTS lower charge to existing customers for exchanging funds the discount available to holders of collective investments who move from one fund to another offered by the same fund manager. The discount is usually a lower initial charge compared to the one made to new investors, or to existing investors who make a further investment.

SWOT analysis GENERAL MANAGEMENT, MARKETING assessment of strengths, weaknesses, opportunities, and threats an assessment of the "Strengths, Weaknesses, Opportunities, and Threats" in an organization. SWOT analysis is used in the early stages of strategic and ***marketing planning***, in ***problem solving*** and ***decision making***, or for making staff aware of the need for change. It can be used at a personal level when determining possible career development.

SYD *abbr* ACCOUNTING ***sum-of-the-year's-digits depreciation*** = ***accelerated depreciation***

Sydney Futures Exchange MARKETS Australian commodity exchange exchange based in Sydney, Australia, established in 1962 as a wool futures market, the Sydney Greasy Wool Futures Exchange, but adopted its current name in 1972 to reflect its widening role. It merged with the Australian Stock Exchange on July 7, 2006, to become the ***Australian Securities Exchange***. *Abbr* ***SFE***

symmetrical distribution STATISTICS even distribution of statistical data around central value a distribution of statistical data that is symmetrical about a central value

syndicate 1. BUSINESS group joining together for business activity a group of people or companies that come together for a specific business activity, especially when they jointly contribute capital to a project **2.** GENERAL MANAGEMENT distribute item to several outlets to agree to distribute an article, a cartoon, a television show, or other work to several different outlets, publications, or broadcasting companies **3.** BANKING get large loan underwritten by international banks to arrange for a large loan to be underwritten by several international banks

syndicated research MARKETING data on commercial trends trend data supplied by research agencies from their regularly operated retail audits or consumer panels

synthetic CDO FINANCE investment backed by derivatives a ***collateralized debt obligation*** that is based on credit derivatives rather than bonds or loans

systematic risk RISK risk related to securities market or economy investment risk that is attributable to the performance of the stock market or the economy

systematic sampling STATISTICS *see* ***random sampling***

systematic withdrawal STOCKHOLDING & INVESTMENTS regular payment from mutual fund to shareholder an arrangement in which a mutual fund pays out a specific amount to the shareholder at regular intervals. *See also* ***withdrawal plan***

systems analysis GENERAL MANAGEMENT assessment of efficiency of business operation the examination and evaluation of an operation or task in order to identify and implement more efficient methods, usually through the use of computers. Systems analysis can be broken down into three main areas: the production of a statement of objectives; determination of the best methods of achieving these objectives in a cost-effective and efficient way; and the preparation of a ***feasibility study***. *Also called* ***systems planning***

systems approach GENERAL MANAGEMENT use of computers in business organization a technique employed for organizational ***decision making*** and ***problem solving*** involving the use of computer systems. The systems approach uses ***systems analysis*** to examine the extent to which a system's components are interrelated and interdependent. When working together, these components produce an effect greater than the sum of the parts. System components might comprise departments or functions of an organization or business which work together for an overall objective.

systems audit GENERAL MANAGEMENT auditing approach an approach to ***auditing*** that utilizes a ***systems approach***. By using a systems audit to assess the internal control system of an organization, it is possible to assess the quality of the accounting system and the level of testing required from the financial statements. One shortcoming of systems audit is that it does not consider audit risk.

systems planning GENERAL MANAGEMENT = ***systems analysis***

T

T + FINANCE number of days for completing business deal an expression of the number of days allowed for settlement of a transaction

tactical plan GENERAL MANAGEMENT short-term plan a short-term plan for achieving the objectives of a person, business, or organization

tail 1. MARKETS difference between acceptable yields in US Treasury auction the spread between the average yield accepted in an auction of US government securities and the highest yield accepted **2.** STOCKHOLDING & INVESTMENTS numbers after decimal point in bond price the figures that come after the decimal point in the quoted price of a bond

tailgating MARKETS broker trading stock immediately after client does the practice by a broker of buying or selling a security immediately after a client's transaction, in order to take advantage of the impact of the client's deal

takaful INSURANCE insurance comprised of pool of funds Islamic insurance in which all participants are members and contribute to a pool of funds that provide assistance in the event of loss on the part of any of the participants. An Islamic insurance arrangement avoids the prohibitions against gambling and interest in Islamic law.

take a flier FINANCE guess to speculate about what might happen (slang)

take a hit FINANCE lose money to make a loss on an investment (slang)

take a view MARKETS form expectation of how market will perform to form an opinion on the likely direction a market will take, and take a position that will be of benefit if the opinion proves correct

takeaway MARKETING customer's impressions of product the impressions that a consumer forms about a product or service

take-home pay FINANCE (informal) = ***net pay***

takeout STOCKHOLDING & INVESTMENTS selling stock in firm the act of removing capital that was originally invested in a new company by selling stock

takeout financing FINANCE long-term borrowing long-term loans taken out to replace short-term financing

takeover MERGERS & ACQUISITIONS **1.** when one firm takes control of another the acquisition by a company of a controlling interest in the voting share capital of another company, usually achieved by the purchase of a majority of the voting stocks **2.** = ***takeover bid***

takeover approach *UK* MERGERS & ACQUISITIONS price offered for takeover the price at which a prospective buyer offers to purchase a controlling interest in a business or corporation. *US term* ***tender offer***

takeover battle MERGERS & ACQUISITIONS result of firm's resistance to acquisition the activities surrounding a ***contested takeover bid***. The bidder may raise the offer price and write to the stockholders extolling the benefits of the takeover. The board may contact other companies in the same line of business, hoping that a ***white knight*** may appear. It could also take action to make the company less desirable to the bidder. *See also* ***poison pill***

takeover bid MERGERS & ACQUISITIONS firm's attempt to buy another an attempt by one company to acquire another. A takeover bid can be made either by a person or an organization, and usually takes the form of an approach to shareholders with an offer to purchase. The bidding stage is often difficult and fraught with politics, and various forms of ***knight*** may be involved.

Takeover Panel MERGERS & ACQUISITIONS, REGULATION & COMPLIANCE = ***City Panel on Takeovers and Mergers***

takeover ratio *UK* MERGERS & ACQUISITIONS indicator of likelihood that firm is acquisition target the ***book value*** of a company divided by its market capitalization. If the resulting figure is greater than one, then the company is a candidate for a takeover. *See also* ***appreciation, asset stripping***

takeover target MERGERS & ACQUISITIONS firm another company wants to purchase a company that another company has chosen to acquire by buying enough of its stock to control it

taker 1. STOCKHOLDING & INVESTMENTS buyer of option the buyer of an ***option*** to buy or sell at a particular price and time **2.** FINANCE borrower somebody who takes out a loan

take-up rate STOCKHOLDING & INVESTMENTS percentage of stockholders agreeing to buy more stock the percentage of acceptances of an offer to existing stockholders to buy more stock in a specific company

takings FINANCE = ***receipts***

talon STOCKHOLDING & INVESTMENTS form for ordering bond coupons a form attached to a ***bearer bond*** that the holder of the bond uses to order new coupons when those attached to the bond have been depleted

tangible asset ACCOUNTING firm's material resource an asset that has a physical presence, for example, buildings, cash, and stock. Leases and securities, although not physical in themselves, are classed as tangible assets because the underlying assets are physical. *See also* ***intangible asset***

tangible asset value *or* tangible net worth ACCOUNTING asset value expressed per share the value of all the assets of a company less its intangible assets such as goodwill, shown as a value per share

tangible book value ACCOUNTING value of all firm's material resources the book value of a company after intangible assets, patents, trademarks, and the value of research and development have been subtracted

tank STOCKHOLDING & INVESTMENTS drop steeply in price to fall suddenly and steeply, especially with reference to stock prices (slang)

tap CD FINANCE certificate of deposit issued on demand an issue of a ***certificate of deposit***, normally in a large denomination, at the request of a specific investor

tape don't fight the tape STOCKHOLDING & INVESTMENTS don't go against the direction of the market

taper relief TAX UK system for adjusting capital gains tax payable in the United Kingdom, a system of reduction in the capital gains tax payable on the disposal of assets by relating the proportion of the capital gain charged to tax to the length of time the asset has been owned. The reduction differs for business assets and non-business assets.

tap stock STOCKHOLDING & INVESTMENTS UK government stock issued over time in the United Kingdom, a government stock that is made available over a period of time in varying amounts

target 1. GENERAL MANAGEMENT goal of effort an end toward which effort is directed and on which resources are focused, usually to achieve an organization's strategy. **2.** MERGERS & ACQUISITIONS = ***target company***

target audience MARKETING likely consumers of product or service a group of people considered likely to buy a product or service

target cash balance FINANCE amount of money firm wants available the amount of cash that a company would like to have readily available

target company MERGERS & ACQUISITIONS firm subject to acquisition a company that is the object of a ***takeover bid***

targeted repurchase MERGERS & ACQUISITIONS buying back stock from firm's potential buyer a company's purchase of its own stock from somebody attempting to buy the company

target population STATISTICS group to be investigated in statistical study in a statistical study, a sample set of units such as events or people that is to be observed

target savings motive ECONOMICS desire to save money for particular goal the wish to have a specific item or to achieve a specific goal that gives people a reason to save

target stock level OPERATIONS & PRODUCTION supply of stored goods that meets likely customer demand the level of inventory that is needed to satisfy all demand for a product or component over a specific period

tariff 1. INTERNATIONAL TRADE government tax on imports or exports a government duty imposed on imports or exports to stimulate or dampen economic activity **2.** OPERATIONS & PRODUCTION list of prices a list of prices at which goods or services are supplied

Tariff Concession Scheme TAX Australian program for reduced duties on some imports a system operated by the Australian government in which imported goods that have no locally produced equivalent attract reduced duties. *Abbr* ***TCS***

tariff office INSURANCE UK insurance firm charging regulated premiums in the United Kingdom, an insurance company whose premiums are based on a scale set collectively by several companies

TARP *abbr* FINANCE ***Troubled Asset Relief Program***

tawarruq FINANCE sale for cash of item purchased by installments in Islamic financing, an arrangement in which somebody purchases an item from a bank on a deferred payment plan, then sells it immediately to obtain money. *See also* ***murabaha***

tax TAX government charge on people and firms a charge levied by a government on individuals and companies to pay for public services. Tax may be taken directly from income or indirectly through a sales tax or other indirect tax.

tax abatement TAX temporary reduction in tax owed a reduction in the amount of tax owed, usually for a short period of time

taxability TAX liability to tax the extent to which a good or individual is subject to a tax

taxable base TAX amount that can be taxed the amount of income that is subject to taxation, after allowances and deductions have been made

taxable gain *US* TAX profit liable to capital gains tax a profit from the sale of an asset that is subject to ***capital gains tax***. *UK term* ***chargeable gain***

taxable income TAX income that can be taxed the proportion of the income of a person, business, or organization that is subject to taxes

taxable matters TAX products that can be taxed goods or services that fall into a category of things that is subject to a tax

taxable supply TAX goods subject to VAT a supply of goods that are subject to tax in countries that have ***VAT***

tax adjustment TAX change to amount of tax owed a change made to the amount of tax owed

tax adviser TAX = ***tax consultant***

tax allowance TAX portion of UK income not taxed in the United Kingdom, a part of somebody's income that is not taxed. There are different reasons for receiving a tax allowance and they vary according to age and personal circumstances.

tax and price index ECONOMICS, TAX UK measure of household buying power in the United Kingdom, an index number showing the percentage change in gross income that taxpayers need if they are to maintain their real ***disposable income***

tax assessment TAX calculation of property value for tax an official calculation of the value of property for the purposes of taxation

taxation TAX **1.** system of raising public revenue the system of raising revenue for public funding by taxing individuals and organizations **2.** amount raised by tax the amount of money raised by imposing a tax

tax auditor *US* TAX official checking tax returns a government employee who investigates taxpayers' returns. *UK term* ***tax inspector***

tax avoidance TAX way of managing finances to pay less tax the organization of a taxpayer's affairs so that the minimum tax liability is incurred. Tax avoidance involves making the maximum use of all legal means of minimizing liability to taxation. *See also* ***tax break, tax evasion***

tax base TAX value of things taxed the taxable value of all property, goods, and activities taxed by a government

tax bracket TAX group of incomes with same tax rate a range of income levels subject to marginal tax at the same rate

tax break TAX special reduction in taxes an investment that is tax-efficient or a legal arrangement that reduces the liability to tax. *See also* ***tax avoidance, tax shelter***

tax code TAX **1.** number indicating UK tax allowance in the United Kingdom, a number given to indicate the amount somebody can earn before

  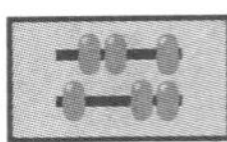      

tax has to be paid **2.** US laws on tax in the United States, the system of laws and regulations regarding taxation

tax concession *UK* TAX tax reduction encouraging investment a tax reduction allowed, for example, to encourage investment in a particular type of industry

tax consultant TAX professional adviser on taxes a professional who advises on all aspects of taxation from tax avoidance to estate planning. *Also called* ***tax adviser***

tax court TAX US court deciding cases involving federal taxes in the United States, a court that deals with disputes between taxpayers and the Internal Revenue Service

tax credit TAX **1.** sum offset against tax a sum of money that can be offset against tax **2.** portion of UK dividend already taxed in the United Kingdom, the part of a dividend on which the company has already paid tax, so that the stockholder is not taxed on it **3.** deduction from individual's income tax liability an amount that can be subtracted directly to reduce somebody's income tax liability

tax-deductible TAX subtracted before tax calculation allowed to be removed from the total of income that will be subject to tax

tax-deferred TAX taxed later not to be taxed until a later time

tax deposit certificate TAX UK certificate showing advance payment of tax in the United Kingdom, a certificate showing that a taxpayer has deposited money in advance of an expected tax payment. The money earns interest while on deposit.

tax dodge TAX illegal way of avoiding taxes any illegal method of paying less tax than a person or company is obliged to pay (informal)

tax dollars TAX US taxes funding government the income taxes paid in the United States to fund the government

tax domicile TAX somebody's legal home for tax purposes a place that a government levying a tax considers to be somebody's home

tax-efficient TAX reducing tax due financially advantageous by leading to a reduction of the taxes that have to be paid

tax evasion TAX illegally not paying taxes the illegal practice of paying less money in taxes than is due. *See also* ***tax avoidance***

tax evasion amnesty TAX official forgiveness by government for not paying taxes a government measure that gives freedom from punishment to people who have evaded a tax

tax-exempt TAX **1.** not subject to expected tax not subject to tax though falling into a category of things that are usually subject to tax **2.** tax-free falling into a category of things that is legally exempted from a tax

tax exemption TAX **1.** freedom from specific tax liability freedom from having to pay specific taxes that would ordinarily be collected **2.** portion of income not taxed a part of somebody's income on which tax does not have to be paid

Tax-Exempt Special Savings Account STOCKHOLDING & INVESTMENTS *see* ***TESSA***

tax exile TAX **1.** living abroad to avoid tax residence in another country in order to avoid paying taxes in the home country **2.** person or firm moving abroad to avoid taxes a person or business that leaves a country to avoid paying taxes

tax-favored asset TAX resource taxed at lower rate an asset that receives more favorable tax treatment than some other asset

tax file number TAX Australian taxpayer's number in Australia, a unique identification number assigned to each taxpayer. *Abbr* ***TFN***

Tax File Number Withholding Tax TAX *see* ***TFN Withholding Tax***

tax-free TAX not subject to tax not subject to an expected tax

tax harmonization TAX making tax laws in different areas similar the enactment of taxation laws in different jurisdictions, such as neighboring countries, provinces, or states of the United States, that are consistent with one another

tax haven TAX place with attractively low tax rates a country that has generous tax laws, especially one that encourages noncitizens to base operations in the country to avoid higher taxes in their home countries

tax holiday *UK* TAX period when tax is waived an exemption from tax granted for a specific period of time, for example, when just starting out in business (informal) *See also* ***tax subsidy***

tax incentive TAX lowering of taxes on specific activities a tax reduction given to encourage or support specific courses of action

tax inspector *UK* TAX = ***tax auditor***

tax invoice TAX in Australia and New Zealand, invoice specifying tax in Australia and New Zealand, a document issued by a supplier which stipulates the amount charged for goods or services as well as the amount of ***Goods and Services Tax*** payable

tax law TAX legislation regulating taxation the body of laws on taxation, or a specific law on an aspect of taxation

tax liability TAX tax payable by person or organization the amount of tax that a person or organization has to pay

tax lien TAX legal notice to recover tax a legal order to hold somebody's goods or property until a debt that is secured by the goods or property has been repaid

tax loophole TAX flaw in law allowing tax avoidance an ambiguity in a tax law that enables some individuals or companies to avoid or reduce taxes

tax loss TAX financial loss claimable against tax a transaction that results in a reduced tax liability, even though it may not be associated with an actual cash loss, for example, a loss associated with depreciation

tax loss carry back TAX using current losses to lower past year's taxes the reduction of taxes in a previous year, by subtraction from income for that year of losses suffered in the current year

tax loss carry forward TAX using current losses to lower future taxes the reduction of taxes in a future year, by subtraction from income for that year of losses suffered in the current year

tax obligation TAX how much tax is owed the amount of tax that a person, business, or organization owes

tax on capital income TAX tax on selling assets a tax on a business's income from sales of capital assets

tax payable TAX how much tax is due the amount of tax a person or company has to pay

taxpayer TAX somebody paying tax a person, business, or organization that pays a tax

tax planning TAX planning of tax avoidance the process of planning how to avoid paying too much tax, for example by investing in tax-exempt bonds

tax rate TAX percentage of income due in tax the rate at which a tax is payable, usually expressed as a percentage

tax refund TAX overpaid tax money returned to taxpayer an amount that a government gives back to a taxpayer who has paid more taxes than were due

tax relief TAX reduction in taxes deductions and exemptions allowed taxpayers for specific expenses or losses they may have incurred, or because of their age or status as a caregiver, etc.

tax return TAX form for calculating and reporting taxes owed an official form on which a company or individual enters details of income and expenses, used to assess tax liability. *Also called* ***return***

tax revenue FINANCE, TAX money from taxes the money that a government receives in taxes from any source

tax sale TAX government's sale of property for unpaid tax in the United States, the sale of an item by a government to recover overdue taxes on a taxable item

tax shelter TAX arrangement to avoid tax a financial arrangement designed to avoid or reduce tax liability. *See also* ***abusive tax shelter, tax break***

tax subsidy TAX special lowering of taxes for business a tax reduction that a government gives a business for a particular purpose, usually to create jobs. *See also* ***tax holiday***

tax system TAX processes for taxation an organized and integrated method for imposing and collecting taxes

tax threshold *UK* TAX point at which tax rate changes a point at which another percentage of tax is payable

tax treaty TAX agreement between nations concerning taxes an international agreement that deals with taxes, especially taxes by several countries on the same individuals

tax year TAX period for which taxes are calculated a 12-month period covered by a statement for taxation purposes about income, spending, and allowable deductions

T-bill *abbr* STOCKHOLDING & INVESTMENTS ***Treasury bill***

T-bond *abbr* STOCKHOLDING & INVESTMENTS ***Treasury bond***

TCO *abbr* GENERAL MANAGEMENT ***total cost of ownership***

T-commerce E-COMMERCE business via TV business that is conducted by means of interactive television

TCS *abbr* TAX ***Tariff Concession Scheme***

TDB *abbr* FINANCE ***Trade Development Board***

  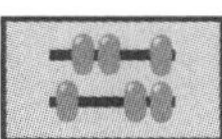      

teaser MARKETING advertising that interests customers in learning more an advertisement that gives a little information about a product in order to attract customers by making them curious to know more

teaser rate MORTGAGES special temporary interest rate to attract customers a temporary concessionary interest rate offered on mortgages or credit cards in order to attract new customers (informal)

technical analysis STOCKHOLDING & INVESTMENTS examination of changes in investment prices the analysis of past movements in the prices of financial instruments, currencies, commodities, etc., with a view to predicting future price movements by applying analytical techniques. *See also* ***fundamental analysis, qualitative analysis, quantitative analysis***

technical correction MARKETS when stock price changes to match true value a situation where a stock price or a currency moves up or down because it was previously too low or too high, due to technical factors

technical rally MARKETS short-term price increase against prevailing market decrease a temporary rise in security or commodity prices while the market is in a general decline. This may be because investors are seeking bargains, or because analysts have noted a support level.

technical reserves *UK* INSURANCE = ***insurance reserves***

Technology and Human Resources for Industry Programme FINANCE *see* ***THRIP***

technology stock STOCKHOLDING & INVESTMENTS shares in technology firms stock issued by a company that is involved in new technology

TED spread MARKETS yield difference between LIBOR and US Treasury bills the difference in yield between commercial ***LIBOR*** rates and US ***Treasury bills***. *Full form* ***Treasury Eurodollar spread***

teeming and lading *UK* ACCOUNTING = ***lapping***

telebanking BANKING = ***telephone banking***

telecommuter GENERAL MANAGEMENT, HR & PERSONNEL = ***teleworker***

teleconferencing GENERAL MANAGEMENT meetings conducted via telephones or TV channels the use of telephone or television channels to connect people in different locations in order to conduct group discussions, meetings, conferences, or courses

telegraphic transfer BANKING means of moving money abroad a method of transferring funds from a bank to a financial institution overseas, using telephone or cable. *Abbr* ***TT***

teleimmersion GENERAL MANAGEMENT advanced teleconferencing creating impression of physical immediacy an enhanced teleconferencing technology that uses banks of video cameras linked to computers, enabling users in remote locations to collaborate as if they were in the same room

telephone banking BANKING accessing bank account by telephone a system in which customers can access their accounts and a variety of banking services 24 hours a day by telephone. *Also called* ***telebanking***

telephone number salary FINANCE very high salary a six- or seven-figure salary, especially one aspired to or considered undeserved (informal)

teleworker GENERAL MANAGEMENT, HR & PERSONNEL employee who works largely remotely an employee who spends a substantial amount of working time away from the employer's main premises and communicates with the organization through the use of computing and telecommunications equipment. *Also called* ***telecommuter***

teller *US* BANKING bank employee dealing with customers face to face an employee in a bank or savings and loan association who deals in person with customers' deposits and withdrawals. *UK term* ***cashier***

tenancy in common LEGAL joint ownership without right to inherit other's share a type of ownership in property in which two or more people each have the right to enjoy the entire property but have no right to automatically inherit other owners' shares

tenant REAL ESTATE somebody renting place to live or work a person or company that rents a house, apartment, or office to live or work in

tenbagger STOCKHOLDING & INVESTMENTS investment with big increase in value an investment that increases in value ten times over its purchase price (slang)

tender 1. STOCKHOLDING & INVESTMENTS make offer for investment product at auction to bid for securities at auction. The securities are allocated according to the method adopted by the issuer. In the standard auction style, the investor receives the security at the price they tendered. In a Dutch style auction, the issuer announces a strike price after all the tenders have been examined. This is set at a level where all the issue is sold. Investors who submitted a tender above the strike price just pay the strike price. The Dutch style of auction is increasingly being adopted in the United Kingdom. US Treasury bills are also sold using the Dutch system. *See also* ***offer for sale, sale by tender*** **2.** GENERAL MANAGEMENT submit price to do work to offer to undertake work or supply goods at a specific price, usually in response to an invitation to bid for a work contract in competition with other suppliers **3.** OPERATIONS & PRODUCTION statement outlining acceptable price for job a statement of what a person or company is willing to accept when offering to undertake a major piece of work or supply goods, given in response to request to bid competitively for the work. *See also* ***quote***

tenderer *UK* OPERATIONS & PRODUCTION = ***bidder***

tender offer *US* MERGERS & ACQUISITIONS price offered for takeover the price at which a prospective buyer offers to purchase a controlling interest in a business or corporation. *UK term* ***takeover approach***

10-K ACCOUNTING US firm's official yearly financial statement the filing of a US company's annual accounts with the ***New York Stock Exchange***

tenor FINANCE period before bill of exchange can be paid the period of time that has to elapse before a bill of exchange becomes payable

10-Q ACCOUNTING US firm's official quarterly financial statement the filing of a US company's quarterly accounts with the ***New York Stock Exchange***

term STOCKHOLDING & INVESTMENTS period before investment product is fully payable the period of time that has to elapse from the date of the initial investment before a security or other investment such as a term deposit or endowment insurance becomes redeemable or reaches its maturity date

term assurance *UK* INSURANCE = ***term insurance***

term bill FINANCE = ***period bill***

term deposit BANKING savings held for a specified period in the United Kingdom, a deposit account held for a fixed period. Withdrawals are either not allowed during this period, or they involve a fee payable by the depositor.

terminal bonus INSURANCE bonus received at policy maturity date in the United Kingdom, a bonus received when insurance comes to an end

terminal date *UK* STOCKHOLDING & INVESTMENTS end date for futures contract the day on which a ***futures contract*** expires and the buyer must take delivery. *Also called* ***delivery date***

terminal market MARKETS place for trading futures contracts an exchange on which futures contracts or spot deals for commodities are traded

termination clause LEGAL clause detailing termination of contract a clause that explains how and when a contract can be terminated

term insurance INSURANCE insurance that is valid for specified period insurance, especially life insurance, that is in effect for a specified period of time. *UK term* ***term assurance***

term loan FINANCE debt arrangement for specified period a loan for a fixed period, usually called a ***personal loan*** when it is for non-business purposes. While a personal loan is usually at a fixed rate of interest, a term loan to a business may be at either a fixed or variable rate. Term loans may be either secured or unsecured. An early payment fee is usually payable when such a loan is repaid before the end of the term. *See also* ***balloon loan, bullet loan***

terms STOCKHOLDING & INVESTMENTS conditions attached to new issue the conditions that apply to an issue of shares of stock

term share BANKING building society account for specified period in the United Kingdom, a share account in a building society that is for a fixed period of time. Withdrawals are usually not allowed during this period. However, if they are, then a fee is usually payable by the account holder.

terms of sale OPERATIONS & PRODUCTION agreed conditions attached to sale the conditions attached to a sale and agreed to by buyer and seller, for example, payment due dates, method of payment, and delivery date

term structure of interest rates STOCKHOLDING & INVESTMENTS discount pattern for each year to maturity a set of interest rates for each year to maturity of fixed-rate securities such as bonds of differing ***term***. *See also* ***yield to maturity***

terotechnology OPERATIONS & PRODUCTION techniques designed to optimize life of assets a multidisciplinary technique that combines the areas of management, finance, and engineering with the goal of optimizing life-cycle costs for physical assets and technologies. Terotechnology is concerned with acquiring and caring for physical assets. It covers the specification and design for the reliability and maintainability of plant, machinery, equipment, buildings, and structures, including the installation, commissioning, maintenance, and replacement of this plant, and also incorporates the feedback of information on design, performance, and costs.

tertiary industry BUSINESS business providing a service an industry that does not produce raw

  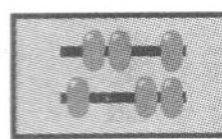      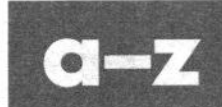

materials or manufacture products but offers a service such as banking, retailing, or accountancy

tertiary sector ECONOMICS part of economy involving nonprofit organizations the part of the economy made up of nonprofit organizations such as consumer associations

TESSA STOCKHOLDING & INVESTMENTS former untaxed UK bank account a former UK savings account in which investors could save up to £9,000 over a period of five years and not pay any tax, provided they made no withdrawals over that time. TESSAs were replaced by ***ISAs*** in 1999. *Full form* ***Tax-Exempt Special Savings Account***

test STOCKHOLDING & INVESTMENTS assessment of likely stock price movements in technical analysis, a way of determining whether to buy or sell a stock by observing if it is likely to rise above or drop below specific price levels that it has had difficulty breaking through in the past

testacy LEGAL possession of valid will at death the legal position of somebody who has died leaving a valid will

testate LEGAL having valid will at death used to refer to somebody who has died leaving a valid will

testator LEGAL somebody with valid will a person who has made a valid will or left a legacy

testatrix LEGAL woman with valid will a woman who has made a valid will or left a legacy

test level STOCKHOLDING & INVESTMENTS barrier price level a specific price level that a stock has had difficulty breaking through in the past. In technical analysis, it is used in determining whether to buy or sell a stock.

TFN *abbr* TAX ***tax file number***

TFN Withholding Tax TAX Australian tax when information missing in Australia, a levy imposed on financial transactions involving somebody who has not disclosed his or her tax file number. *Full form* ***Tax File Number Withholding Tax***

theta STOCKHOLDING & INVESTMENTS ratio of option's decreasing value to decreasing time a ratio between the rate of decrease in the value of an option and the decrease in time as it approaches expiration. *Also called* ***time decay***

thin market MARKETS exchange where little trading is happening a market where the trading volume is low. A characteristic of such a market is a wide spread of bid and offer prices.

third market MARKETS secondary stock exchange a market other than the main stock exchange in which stocks are traded

third party LEGAL person other than two main parties to contract a person other than the two main parties involved in a contract, for example, in an insurance contract, anyone who is not the insurance company nor the person who is insured

third-party network *or* third-party service provider E-COMMERCE = ***value-added network***

third quarter ACCOUNTING third of four divisions of fiscal year the period of three months from July to the end of September, or the period of three months following the second quarter of the fiscal year. *Abbr* ***Q3***

third sector ECONOMICS part of economy involving nonprofit organizations the part of the economy made up of ***nonprofit organizations*** such as charities, professional associations, labor unions, and religious, arts, community, research, and campaigning bodies

three-dimensional management *or* 3D management GENERAL MANAGEMENT theory of management styles a theory outlining eight styles of management that differ in effectiveness, four that are effective and four that are less effective. Different styles may be used in different types of work settings and managers modify their style to suit different circumstances.

360 degree branding LEGAL, STOCKHOLDING & INVESTMENTS supporting brand identity by all marketing activity taking an inclusive approach in branding a product by bringing the brand to all points of consumer contact

3i BANKING bank-owned group providing company finance a finance group owned by the big British commercial banks which provides finance to other companies, especially small ones

three steps and a stumble MARKETS if interest rates increase three times, stocks fall a rule of thumb used on the US stock market that if the Federal Reserve increases interest rates three times consecutively, stock market prices will go down

threshold GENERAL MANAGEMENT starting point the point at which something begins or changes

threshold agreement FINANCE UK contract promising pay raise in specific situation in the United Kingdom, a contract that says that if the cost of living goes up by more than an agreed amount, pay will go up to match it

threshold company BUSINESS emerging company a company that is on the verge of becoming well established in the business world

threshold price OPERATIONS & PRODUCTION lowest sale price for imports into EU in the European Union, the lowest price at which farm produce imported into the EU can be sold

thrift **1.** FINANCE care in managing money a cautious attitude toward the management of money, shown by saving, or spending it carefully and looking for good value **2.** BANKING private local US bank for small investors in the United States, a private local bank, savings and loan association, or credit union, that accepts and pays interest on deposits from small investors

thrift institution BANKING US institution acting like savings bank in the United States, an institution that is not a bank but accepts savings deposits and makes loans to savers. *See also* ***savings and loan association, savings bank***

THRIP FINANCE S. African program supporting industry research and development in South Africa, a collaborative program involving industry, government, and educational and research institutions, which supports research and development in technology, science, and engineering. *Full form* ***Technology and Human Resources for Industry Programme***

TIBOR *abbr* MARKETS ***Tokyo Interbank Offered Rate***

tick STOCKHOLDING & INVESTMENTS smallest amount price or rate can change the least amount by which a value such as the price of a stock or a rate of interest can rise or fall, for example, a hundredth of a percentage point or an eighth of a dollar **have ticks in all the right boxes** GENERAL MANAGEMENT to be on course to meet a series of objectives

ticker *or* ticker tape MARKETS continuous display of stock prices the electronic display of stock prices that stream across a computer or television screen. The information was formerly produced on continuous paper tape.

ticker symbol MARKETS letters representing stocks traded on stock exchange letter or letters used to identify the stocks or funds listed for trade on a stock exchange

tied loan FINANCE loan to foreign country to buy lender's products a loan made by one national government to another on the condition that the funds are used to purchase goods from the lending nation

Tier 1 capital BANKING bank's core capital funds the core capital of a bank, mainly consisting of stockholders' funds, which is used by regulators as a measure of a bank's stability

Tier 1 capital ratio BANKING ratio of bank's core to supplementary funds the relationship between the amount of ***Tier 1 capital*** and other capital held by a bank. *See also* ***capital adequacy ratio***

Tier 2 capital BANKING bank's supplementary funds funds such as undisclosed reserves, held by a bank in addition to its core capital of stockholders' funds. *Also called* ***supplementary capital***

tiger MARKETS Hong Kong, S. Korea, Singapore, or Taiwan any of the key markets in the Pacific Basin region except Japan, i.e. Hong Kong, South Korea, Singapore, and Taiwan

tight money ECONOMICS situation where borrowing money is difficult a situation where it is expensive to borrow because of restrictive government policy or high demand

tight money policy ECONOMICS government policy restricting money supply a government policy to restrict money supply, usually by raising interest rates, making it more difficult to borrow and spend money

TILA *abbr* LEGAL ***Truth in Lending Act***

time and material pricing FINANCE determining price based on work and materials a form of ***cost-plus pricing*** in which price is determined by reference to the cost of the labor and material inputs to the product or service

time bargain MARKETS stock exchange trade for future date a stock market transaction in which the securities are deliverable at a future date beyond the exchange's normal settlement day

time decay STOCKHOLDING & INVESTMENTS = ***theta***

time deposit BANKING US savings arrangement for specified period a US savings account or a certificate of deposit, issued by a financial institution. While the savings account is for a fixed term, deposits are accepted with the understanding that withdrawals may be made subject to a period of notice. Banks are authorized to require at least 30 days' notice. While a certificate of deposit is equivalent to a term account, passbook accounts are generally regarded as funds readily available to the account holder.

time draft BANKING type of US bill of exchange a bill of exchange drawn on and accepted by a US bank. It is either an ***after date*** bill or ***after sight*** bill.

times covered STOCKHOLDING & INVESTMENTS ability of net profit to pay firm's dividend the number of times a company's dividends to ordinary stockholders could be paid out of its net after-tax profits. This measures the likelihood of dividend payments being sustained, and is a useful indication of sustained profitability. *Also called* ***dividend cover***

time series STATISTICS collection of data at intervals a series of measurements collected at uniformly spaced intervals of time, sometimes over a period of several years, used to assess long-term trends and seasonal fluctuations

time spread MARKETS simultaneously buying and selling options with different maturities the purchase and sale of options in the same commodity or security with the same price and different ***maturities***

time value MARKETS market value minus face value the premium at which an option is trading relative to its ***intrinsic value***

time value of money FINANCE potential growth in value over time the principle that a specific amount of money is worth more now than it will be at a date in the future, because the sum available now can be invested and will have grown in value by the date in the future

tip STOCKHOLDING & INVESTMENTS recommendation given by expert a piece of useful expert information, for example, a recommendation about a product or a ***stock tip***

tip-off STOCKHOLDING & INVESTMENTS confidential information a piece of confidential information about something that is going to happen, or a warning based on confidential financial or commercial information. *See also* ***insider dealing, money laundering***

title LEGAL right of ownership a legal right to the ownership of property. If somebody has good title to a property, proof of ownership is beyond doubt.

title deed LEGAL document showing real estate ownership a document showing who is the owner of real estate

title insurance INSURANCE protection from problems in legal title an insurance policy that protects a purchaser or lender from loss of real property due to defects in the ***title***

toasted FINANCE having suffered financial losses used to refer to someone or something that has lost money (slang)

Tobin tax TAX **1.** levy on foreign currency dealings a tax imposed on foreign transactions with the aim of securing greater economic stability and protecting currencies from speculators. It was proposed by US economist James Tobin (1918–2002). **2.** levy on financial transactions a tax imposed on a financial transaction of any kind

toehold purchase *or* toehold MERGERS & ACQUISITIONS small stake in corporation in the United States, the acquisition of less than 5% of the outstanding stock in a company that is targeted for a takeover. At the 5% level, the acquiring company must notify the Securities and Exchange Commission and the targeted company of its plans.

token charge OPERATIONS & PRODUCTION small charge levied as token gesture a small charge that does not cover the real costs of providing the goods or services

token payment FINANCE small payment made as token gesture a small payment made only so that a payment of some sort is seen to be made

Tokyo Interbank Offered Rate MARKETS in Japan, rate for banks' offers of deposits on the Japanese money markets, the rate at which banks will offer to make deposits in yen with each other, often used as a reference rate. The deposits are for terms from overnight up to five years. *Abbr* ***TIBOR***

tombstone FINANCE newspaper notice detailing large loan for business a notice in the financial press giving details of a large lending facility, or large equity or debt securities offerings, to a business. It may relate to a management buyout or to a package that may include an ***interest rate cap*** and ***collars*** to finance a specific package. More than one bank may be involved. Although it may appear to be an advertisement, technically in most jurisdictions it is regarded as a statement of fact and therefore falls outside the advertisement regulations. The borrower generally pays for the advertisement, though it is the financial institutions that derive the most benefit.

top-down approach GENERAL MANAGEMENT leadership style with managers driving changes an autocratic style of leadership in which strategies and solutions are identified by senior management and then cascaded down through an organization. The top-down approach can be considered a feature of large bureaucracies. A number of management gurus have criticized it as an out-of-date style that leads to stagnation and business failure. *See also* ***bottom-up approach***

top management HR & PERSONNEL senior members of firm the upper-level managers of an organization or company, especially the ***senior management*** or a ***board of directors*** (informal)

top slicing **1.** STOCKHOLDING & INVESTMENTS sale of holding yielding original cost of investment selling part of a stockholding that will realize a sum that is equal to the original cost of the investment. What remains therefore represents potential pure profit. **2.** TAX in UK, assessment of tax on mature investments in the United Kingdom, a complex method used by HM Revenue & Customs for assessing what tax, if any, is paid when some investment bonds or endowment policies mature or are cashed in early

total absorption costing ACCOUNTING accountant's method of pricing goods and services a method used by a cost accountant to price goods and services, allocating both direct and indirect costs. Although this method is designed so that all of an organization's costs are covered, it may result in opportunities being missed because of high prices. Consequently sales may be lost that could contribute to overheads. *See also* ***marginal costing***

total assets FINANCE sum of assets owned by person or organization the total value of all current and long-term assets owned by a person or organization

total cost OPERATIONS & PRODUCTION sum of costs of producing amount of something all the costs of producing a specific amount of something, including fixed costs and variable costs

total cost of ownership GENERAL MANAGEMENT cost including all aspects of ownership a structured approach to calculating the ***costs*** associated with buying and using a product or service. Total cost of ownership takes the purchase cost of an item into account but also considers related costs such as ordering, delivery, subsequent usage and maintenance, supplier costs, and after-delivery costs. Originally designed as a process for measuring IT expense after implementation, total cost of ownership considers only financial expenses and excludes any ***cost-benefit analysis***. *Abbr* ***TCO***

total overhead cost variance ACCOUNTING difference between actual and absorbed overhead costs the difference between the overhead costs absorbed and the actual overhead costs incurred, both fixed and variable

total quality management GENERAL MANAGEMENT integrated system of business planning an integrated and comprehensive system of planning and controlling all business functions so that products or services are produced which meet or exceed customer expectations. TQM is a philosophy of business behavior, embracing principles such as employee involvement, continuous improvement at all levels, and customer focus, as well as being a collection of related techniques, such as full documentation of activities, clear goal-setting, and performance measurement from the customer perspective, that are aimed at improving quality. *Abbr* ***TQM***

total responsibility management GENERAL MANAGEMENT procedures ensuring responsible business practices systems and procedures to ensure responsible business practices and management. It is used to describe the codes of practice and systems that organizations are developing to manage their social, environmental, and ethical responsibilities in response to pressures from stakeholders, emerging global standards, general social trends, and institutional expectations. Some issues, linked to labor, ecology, and community, are included because they are subject to increasing assessment or regulation, while others are raised intermittently as a result of public controversies.

total return STOCKHOLDING & INVESTMENTS percentage change in overall value of investment the total percentage change in the value of an investment over a specified time period, including capital gains, dividends, and the investment's appreciation or depreciation.

The total return formula reflects all the ways in which an investment can earn or lose money, resulting in an increase or decrease in the investment's ***net asset value*** (NAV):

$$\frac{(\text{Dividends} + \text{Capital gains distributions} \pm \text{Change in NAV})}{\text{Beginning NAV}} = \text{Total return}$$

If, for instance, you buy a stock with an initial NAV of $40, and after one year it pays an income dividend of $2 per share and a capital gains distribution of $1, and its NAV has increased to $42, then the stock's total return would be:

$$\frac{(2+1+2)}{40} = \frac{5}{40} = 0.125 \times 100\% = 12.5\%$$

The total return time frame is usually one year, and it assumes that dividends have been reinvested. It does not take into account any sales charges that an investor paid to invest in a fund, or taxes they might owe on the income dividends and capital gains distributions received.

total revenue FINANCE total income from all sources all income from all sources

total utility ECONOMICS consumer's total satisfaction from good or service the overall satisfaction that a consumer receives from consuming a particular quantity of a specific good or service

touch MARKETS difference between best bid and offer prices the difference between the best bid and the best offer price quoted by all market makers for a specific security

touch barrier *or* touch level STOCKHOLDING & INVESTMENTS preset price point triggering option

  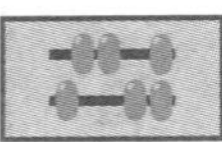      

payment the preset point that the price of an underlying asset must reach, exceed, or fail to reach before a ***touch option*** will pay an investor

touch option STOCKHOLDING & INVESTMENTS option paying at different preset levels a type of ***option*** that gives an investor a payment dependent on the price of the underlying security reaching, exceeding, or not reaching a preset level. *See also* ***double-one-touch option, no-touch option, one-touch option***

touch price MARKETS best gap between bid and offer prices the largest available difference between the bid and offer prices of a security

toxic FINANCE, STOCKHOLDING & INVESTMENTS adversely affecting financial status damaging to financial health. The term as applied to loans, debt, assets, and financial instruments such as mortgages, bonds and other securities refers to finance that is risky and potentially seriously damaging not only to the owner but to the financial system as a whole (informal)

toxic waste STOCKHOLDING & INVESTMENTS high-risk securities new securities with unusually high risk, often notes that have as collateral the riskiest portions of numerous issues of otherwise relatively low-risk debt (slang)

TQM *abbr* GENERAL MANAGEMENT ***total quality management***

tracker fund STOCKHOLDING & INVESTMENTS = ***index fund***

tracking 1. STOCKHOLDING & INVESTMENTS investing to match a market index the practice of buying investments in order to achieve the same or a similar return to a market index **2.** MARKETING research into changing perception of product or organization research designed to monitor changes in the public perception of a product or organization over a period of time

tracking error STOCKHOLDING & INVESTMENTS degree to which fund fails to track index the deviation by which an ***index fund*** fails to replicate the index it is aiming to mirror

tracking stock STOCKHOLDING & INVESTMENTS stock with dividends linked to performance of subsidiary a stock whose dividends are tied to the performance of a subsidiary of the corporation that owns it

trade OPERATIONS & PRODUCTION **1.** carry on a business to buy and sell products, or carry on a business **2.** buying and selling the business of buying and selling goods or, in some situations, bartering goods **3.** particular type of business a particular type of business, or the people or companies dealing in the same type of product **4.** one transaction a single activity of buying or selling that is carried out

trade agreement INTERNATIONAL TRADE trading agreement between countries an international agreement between countries over general terms of trade

trade association OPERATIONS & PRODUCTION organization promoting interests of particular trade a membership organization of businesses in the same trade that promotes the interests of the businesses

trade balance INTERNATIONAL TRADE = ***balance of trade***

trade barrier INTERNATIONAL TRADE government-imposed impediment to international trade a condition imposed by a government to limit the free exchange of goods internationally. Nontariff barriers, safety standards, and tariffs are typical trade barriers.

trade bill FINANCE bill of exchange between trading partners a bill of exchange between two businesses that trade with each other. *See also* ***acceptance credit***

trade credit FINANCE credit offered to trading partner credit offered by one business when trading with another. Typically this is for one month from the date of the invoice, but it could be for a shorter or longer period.

trade cycle INTERNATIONAL TRADE period of cyclical fluctuations in trade a period during which trade expands, then slows down, then expands again

trade date STOCKHOLDING & INVESTMENTS date of a purchase or sale the date on which a buyer and seller reach an agreement for the purchase and sale of an asset

trade debt FINANCE debt from normal trading a debt that originates during the normal course of trade

trade debtor FINANCE debtor with debt incurred through normal trading a person or company that owes money to a company as a result of the normal activities of trading

trade deficit INTERNATIONAL TRADE extent to which imports exceed exports the difference in value between a country's imports and exports when its imports exceed its exports. *Also called* ***balance of payments deficit***. *See also* ***trade gap***

trade description REGULATION & COMPLIANCE legal description of product a description of a product provided by the manufacturer and controlled for accuracy by the ***Trade Descriptions Act***

Trade Descriptions Act REGULATION & COMPLIANCE UK legislation governing product description in the United Kingdom, an act that limits the way in which products can be described so as to protect customers from wrong descriptions made by manufacturers

Trade Development Board INTERNATIONAL TRADE agency promoting trade with Singapore companies a Singapore government agency that was established in 1983 to promote trade and explore new markets for Singapore products, and offers various programs of assistance to companies. *Abbr* ***TDB***

trade discount OPERATIONS & PRODUCTION price reduction for person in same trade a reduction in price given to a customer in the same trade

traded option STOCKHOLDING & INVESTMENTS option bought and sold on exchange an option that can be continuously traded on an exchange

trade gap INTERNATIONAL TRADE gap between imports and exports the difference between the value of a country's imports and that of its exports. *See also* ***trade deficit***

trade-in *US* FINANCE using old product as partial payment for new the act of giving an old product as part of the payment for a new one. *UK term* ***part exchange***

trade investment STOCKHOLDING & INVESTMENTS investment of one business in another the action or process of one business making a loan to another, or buying stock in another. The latter may be the first stages of a friendly ***takeover bid***.

trademark GENERAL MANAGEMENT unique mark identifying product with producer an identifiable mark on a product that may be a symbol, words, or both, that connects the product to the trader or producer of that product and gives the producer or trader protection from fraudulent use. Any use of the trademark without permission gives the owner the right to sue for damages. In the United States, trademarks are controlled by the United States Patent and Trademark Office. In the United Kingdom, a trademark can be registered at the Register of Trademarks maintained by the Intellectual Property Office.

trade mission INTERNATIONAL TRADE foreign visit for purpose of discussing trade a visit by businesspeople from one country to another for the purpose of discussing trade between their respective nations

trade name MARKETING proprietary name of product or service the proprietary name given by the producer or manufacturer to a product or service. A trade name occasionally becomes the generic name for products of a similar nature, for example, "Thermos" is often applied to all insulated flasks, and "Kleenex" to all tissues.

TRADENZ *abbr* BUSINESS ***New Zealand Trade Development Board***

tradeoff OPERATIONS & PRODUCTION exchange of items or concessions in business deal an act of exchanging one thing for another as part of a business deal

trade point MARKETS informal, minor stock exchange a stock exchange that is less formal than the major exchanges

trader MARKETS **1.** = ***floor trader*** **2.** = ***market maker***

trader's index MARKETS *see* ***TRIN***

trade surplus INTERNATIONAL TRADE extent to which exports exceed imports the difference in value between a country's imports and exports when its exports exceed its imports. *Also called* ***balance of payments surplus***

trade union *UK* GENERAL MANAGEMENT HR & PERSONNEL = ***labor union***

trade war INTERNATIONAL TRADE competition between countries for market share a competition between two or more countries for a share of international or domestic trade

trade-weighted index CURRENCY & EXCHANGE measure of country's currency against trading partners' currencies an index that measures the value of a country's currency in relation to the currencies of its trading partners

trading MARKETS buying and selling goods the business of buying and selling goods or assets

trading account ACCOUNTING = ***profit and loss account***

trading area BUSINESS area where business is concentrated the area in which a company does most of its business, or the area around a city that is the main center of a region

trading company BUSINESS firm that buys and sells goods a company that specializes in buying and selling goods

trading floor MARKETS where dealers trade face to face an area in a stock exchange or similar market where dealers meet to trade with each other personally

trading halt MARKETS cessation of trade in firm's stock a stoppage of trading in a stock on an exchange, usually in response to information about a company, or concern about rapid

  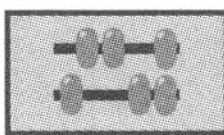   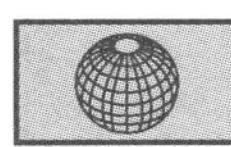   

movement of the stock price. *See also* ***suspended trading***

trading limit MARKETS maximum amount allowed to single trader the maximum amount of a product that can be traded by a single trader

trading loss FINANCE sales income lower than expenditure a situation in which the amount of money an organization receives in sales is less than its expenditure

trading partner **1.** BUSINESS, INTERNATIONAL TRADE firm or country doing business with another one of two or more businesses or countries that engage in trade with each other **2.** E-COMMERCE partner in electronic data interchange transaction the merchant, customer, or financial institution with whom an EDI (***electronic data interchange***) transaction takes place. Transactions can be either between senders and receivers of EDI messages or within distribution channels in an industry, for example, financial institutions or wholesalers.

trading pit MARKETS *see* ***pit***

trading profit ACCOUNTING = ***gross profit***

trading range MARKETS difference between highest and lowest prices the difference between the highest and lowest price for a stock or bond over a period of time. *Also called* ***historical trading range***

trading session MARKETS one trading day in stock or commodities market a period of one day of buying and selling at a stock or commodities exchange from the opening bell to the closing bell

trading stamp OPERATIONS & PRODUCTION stamp exchanged for goods in store a special stamp given away by a store, which the customer can collect and exchange later for free goods

traditional IRA PENSIONS retirement savings facility in the United States, the original ***IRA***, that allows individuals to set up retirement accounts, contributions to which are tax-deductible up to a specific amount depending on income. *See also* ***rollover IRA, Roth IRA***

training levy TAX UK tax funding government's training programs in the United Kingdom, a tax to be paid by companies to fund the government's training programs

tranche STOCKHOLDING & INVESTMENTS one installment in series one of a series of installments, used, for example, when referring to loans to companies, government securities that are issued over a period of time, or money withdrawn by a country from the IMF

tranche CD BANKING certificate of deposit sold in series over time a ***certificate of deposit*** that is part of a set that is sold by the issuing bank over a period of time. Each of the CDs in a tranche has the same maturity date.

transaction **1.** BUSINESS business negotiation an act of negotiating something or carrying out a business deal **2.** MARKETS instance of trading an instance of buying or selling a security, currency, or commodity **3.** E-COMMERCE item of business transmitted electronically any item or collection of sequential items of business that are enclosed in encrypted form in an electronic envelope and transmitted between trading partners

transaction costs STOCKHOLDING & INVESTMENTS direct costs of buying or selling asset incremental costs that are directly attributable to the buying or selling of an asset. Transaction costs include commissions, fees, and direct taxes.

transaction e-commerce E-COMMERCE electronic selling the electronic sale of goods and services, either business-to-business or business-to-customer

transaction exposure CURRENCY & EXCHANGE, RISK risk in international trade from changing exchange rates the risk that an organization may incur major losses from the effects of foreign exchange rate changes during the time it takes to arrange the export or import of goods or services. Transaction exposure is present from the time a price is set.

transaction file OPERATIONS & PRODUCTION means of tracking inventory a file for keeping track of inventory use and replenishment. *See also* ***inventory record***

transaction history STOCKHOLDING & INVESTMENTS record of trades with broker a record of all of an investor's transactions with a broker

transaction message *or* transaction set E-COMMERCE electronic document exchanged in e-commerce transaction the EDI (***electronic data interchange***) equivalent of a paper document, exchanged as part of an e-commerce transaction, comprising at least one data segment representing the document sandwiched between a header and a trailer. It is called a transaction message in the UN/EDIFACT protocol and a transaction set in the ANSI X.12 protocol.

transactions motive ECONOMICS desire to keep cash for upcoming purchases the motive that consumers have to hold money for their likely purchases in the immediate future

transfer **1.** BANKING movement of money between banks the movement of money through the domestic or international banking system, between banks in a ***clearing system***, or between particular bank accounts. *See also* ***BACS, Fedwire, SWIFT*** **2.** STOCKHOLDING & INVESTMENTS change of ownership the change of ownership of an asset or security

transferable LEGAL **1.** legally able to be passed on able to be legally passed into somebody else's ownership **2.** document eligible to be passed on a document such as a bearer bond that can be passed legally into somebody else's ownership

transfer agent STOCKHOLDING & INVESTMENTS agent handling transfers of ownership an agent employed by a corporation to keep a record of the owners of securities and handle transfers of ownership

transferee LEGAL somebody to whom an asset is transferred a person who receives ownership of an asset that is being transferred

transferor LEGAL somebody transferring asset to another a person who transfers the ownership of an asset or security to another person

transfer out fee STOCKHOLDING & INVESTMENTS fee for closing broker's account a fee payable when an investor closes an account with a broker

transfer price OPERATIONS & PRODUCTION price for goods or services within firm the price at which goods or services are transferred between different units of the same company. If those units are located in different countries, the term international transfer pricing is used.

The extent to which the transfer price covers costs and contributes to (internal) profit is a matter of policy. A transfer price may, for example, be based upon marginal cost, full cost, market price, or negotiation. Where the transferred products cross national boundaries, the transfer prices used may have to be agreed with the governments of the countries concerned.

transfer pricing OPERATIONS & PRODUCTION pricing method used between departments of organization a pricing method used when supplying products or services from one part of an organization to another. The transfer pricing method can be used to supply goods either at cost or at profit if profit targets are to be achieved. This can cause difficulties if an internal customer can buy more cheaply outside the organization. Multinational businesses have been known to take advantage of this pricing policy by transferring products from one country to another in order for profits to be higher in the country where corporation tax is lower.

transfer stamp REAL ESTATE, TAX mark on UK deeds showing payment of stamp duty in the United Kingdom, the mark embossed onto ***title deeds*** when property is transferred to signify that ***stamp duty*** has been paid

transfer value PENSIONS in UK, value of somebody's pension rights in the United Kingdom, the value of a person's rights in a pension when they are given up on acquiring rights in a new pension, for example, when somebody changes the company providing the pension. *See also* ***vested rights***

transit time OPERATIONS & PRODUCTION delay after completing operation the period between the completion of an operation and the availability of the material at the next workstation

translation exposure CURRENCY & EXCHANGE, RISK risk on business from changing exchange rates the risk that the balance sheet and income statement may be adversely affected by foreign exchange rate changes

transmission E-COMMERCE electronic data sent between trading partners digital data sent electronically from one trading partner to another, or from a trading partner to a ***value-added network***

transmission control standards E-COMMERCE format for exchanging electronic business data the defined format by which to address the ***electronic envelopes*** used by trading partners to exchange business data

transnational business *or* transnational company *or* transnational corporation *or* transnational BUSINESS = ***multinational business***

transparency MARKETS when information is freely available the condition in which nothing is hidden. This is an essential condition for a free market in securities. Prices, the volume of trading, and factual information must be available to all.

trash and cash MARKETS driving stock price down to repurchase more cheaply a trade of a security in which a trader sells a stock, then spreads negative information about the company whose stock they just sold, causing the stock's price to decline and enabling the trader to buy it back at a low price and make a profit

travel accident insurance INSURANCE travel insurance provided by credit card company a form of insurance coverage offered by some credit card companies when the whole or part of a travel arrangement is paid for with the card. In the event of death resulting from an accident in the course of travel, or the loss of eyesight or a limb, the credit card company will pay the cardholder, or his or her estate, a pre-stipulated sum. *See also* ***travel insurance***

  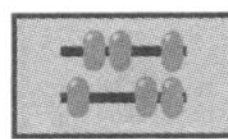      

traveler's checks BANKING checks for cashing in foreign country checks bought by a traveler that are valid for use at home or abroad, but are generally cashed in a foreign country. Only a countersignature is required from the holder for verification. *UK term* ***traveller's cheques***

travel insurance INSURANCE insurance for various risks associated with travel a form of insurance coverage that provides medical cover while abroad as well as covering the policyholder's possessions and money while traveling. Many travel insurance policies also reimburse the policyholder if a holiday has to be canceled and pay compensation for delayed journeys. *See also* ***travel accident insurance***

traveller's cheques BANKING = ***traveler's checks***

treasurer TREASURY MANAGEMENT officer responsible for money a person who is responsible for the funds and other assets of an organization

Treasurer FINANCE Australian government minister responsible for financial and economic matters in Australia, the minister responsible for financial and economic matters in a national, state, or territory government

treasuries STOCKHOLDING & INVESTMENTS US government securities negotiable debt instruments issued by the US government. *See also* ***Treasury bill, Treasury bond, Treasury note***

treasury TREASURY MANAGEMENT section of firm responsible for financial matters the department of a company or corporation that deals with all financial matters

Treasury FINANCE government department responsible for finance and economy in some countries, the government department responsible for the nation's financial policies as well as the management of the economy

Treasury bill STOCKHOLDING & INVESTMENTS discounted short-term security a short-term security issued by the US or UK government that is sold at a discount from face value and pays no interest but can be redeemed for full face value at maturity. *Abbr* ***T-bill***

Treasury bill rate STOCKHOLDING & INVESTMENTS effective interest earned from holding Treasury bill the rate of interest obtainable by holding a ***Treasury bill***. Although Treasury bills are non-interest bearing, by purchasing them at a discount and holding them to redemption, the discount is effectively the interest earned by holding these instruments. The Treasury bill rate is the discount expressed as a percentage of the issue price. It is annualized to give a rate per annum.

Treasury bond STOCKHOLDING & INVESTMENTS US government bond a bond issued by the US government that bears fixed interest. *Abbr* ***T-bond***

treasury direct STOCKHOLDING & INVESTMENTS trading system for US Treasury bills in the United States, a system offered through Federal Reserve banks that allows investors to buy and sell ***Treasury bills*** directly from the Federal Reserve

Treasury Eurodollar spread MARKETS *see* ***TED spread***

treasury inflation protected security STOCKHOLDING & INVESTMENTS US government security protected from inflation a security issued by the US government with principal and coupon payments that are increased automatically to protect against inflation

treasury management TREASURY MANAGEMENT firm's handling of all financial matters the corporate handling of all financial matters, the generation of external and internal funds for business, the management of currencies and cash flows, and the complex strategies, policies, and procedures of corporate finance

Treasury note STOCKHOLDING & INVESTMENTS **1.** US 2–10-year government security a fixed-interest security issued by the US government that can mature within two to ten years **2.** short-term debt instrument issued by Australian government a short-term debt instrument issued by the Australian federal government. Treasury notes are issued on a tender basis for periods of 13 and 26 weeks.

treasury stock STOCKHOLDING & INVESTMENTS shares of firm's stock bought back by firm shares of a company's stock that have been bought back by the company and not canceled. In the United States, these shares are shown as deductions from equity; in the United Kingdom, they are shown as assets in the balance sheet.

treaty 1. LEGAL written agreement between nations a written agreement between nations, such as the Treaty of Rome (1957), that was the foundation of the ***European Union*** **2.** INSURANCE contract in which reinsurer accepts insurer's risks a contract between an insurer and the reinsurer whereby the latter is to accept risks from the insurer **3.** REAL ESTATE = ***private treaty***

trend STATISTICS regular movement of variable values over time the movement in a specific direction of the values of a variable over a period of time

trendline STATISTICS pattern of change in variable values over time a visual representation of the direction of change shown by variables over a period of time

Treynor ratio ECONOMICS = ***risk-adjusted return on capital***

trial balance ACCOUNTING draft balance in bookkeeping in a double-entry bookkeeping system, a draft calculation of debits and credits to see if they balance

trickle-down theory ECONOMICS belief that benefits spread downward in economy the theory that financial and other benefits received by big businesses and wealthy people eventually spread down through an economy to the rest of society

trillion one million millions a sum equal to one million millions (1 plus 12 zeros). An older use in the United Kingdom was a larger number, 1 plus 18 zeros.

TRIN MARKETS measure of rising to falling stocks a market indicator calculated by dividing the advancing stocks by declining stocks and comparing it to the volume of advances to declines. A result less than one is considered bullish, and a result greater than one is considered bearish. *Full form* ***trader's index***

tripartite authority REGULATION & COMPLIANCE UK system of financial regulators in the United Kingdom, the financial regulatory system composed of ***HM Treasury***, the ***Financial Services Authority***, and the ***Bank of England***

triple A STOCKHOLDING & INVESTMENTS = ***AAA***

triple bottom line GENERAL MANAGEMENT firm's environmental and social behavior, together with profitability environmental sustainability and social responsibility used as criteria when judging the overall performance of a company, in addition to purely financial considerations

triple I organization GENERAL MANAGEMENT corporate culture focusing on information, intelligence, and ideas a type of ***corporate culture*** in which the focus is on three areas: information, intelligence, and ideas. The triple I organization recognizes the value of information and learning. It minimizes the distinction between managers and workers, concentrating instead on people and the need to pursue learning, including personal, lifelong, and organizational learning, in order to keep up with the pace of change.

triple tax exempt TAX exempt from US tax at all levels in the United States, used to describe bonds, interest payments, and other sources of income that are exempt from federal, state, and local taxes

triple witching hour MARKETS joint maturity date for futures and options a time when stock options, stock index futures, and options on such futures all mature at once. Triple witching hours occur quarterly and are usually marked by highly volatile trading.

Troubled Asset Relief Program FINANCE federal government support for lenders in the United States, a federal government program established in response to the credit crunch of 2007–08 by which the Treasury was authorized to buy mortgage-backed securities from financial institutions in an attempt to provide them with funds that would enable them to return to lending. *Abbr* ***TARP***

troubleshooter FINANCE consultant employed by firm in difficulty an independent person, often a consultant, who is called in by a company in difficulties to help formulate a strategy for recovery

trough ECONOMICS low point in economic cycle the lowest point or period in an economic cycle before the situation begins to improve

troy ounce FINANCE unit of weight for precious metals the traditional unit used when weighing precious metals such as gold or silver. It is equal to approximately 1.097 ounces avoirdupois or 31.22 grams.

true and fair view *UK* ACCOUNTING auditor-confirmed statement of firm's financial position a correct statement of a company's financial position as shown in its accounts and confirmed by the auditors

true copy LEGAL copy of legal document attested by notary an exact copy of a legal document, as declared before a ***notary public***

true interest cost FINANCE real interest rate paid on debt security the effective rate of interest paid by the issuer on a debt security that is sold at a discount

trump MARKETING make competitor's product appear useless by comparison to make something such as a competitor's product appear useless because what you have is so much better (slang)

trust 1. *US* BUSINESS cartel a group of companies that act together with the effect of reducing competition and controlling prices **2.** FINANCE assets held for somebody else money or property held by one person or a group of people (the trustees) with a legal obligation to administer them for another person's benefit. *See also* ***blind trust***

trust account BANKING account held for somebody else money held by one person (the trustee), often a professional, on behalf of the owner of the funds in it, for example, a minor

trust bank BANKING Japanese bank offering banking and trustee services a Japanese bank that acts commercially in the sense of accepting deposits and making loans and also in the capacity of a trustee

trust company BUSINESS firm administering trusts a company whose business is administering trusts on behalf of trustees

trust corporation BANKING US institution sometimes performing banking activities a US state-chartered institution that may undertake banking activities

trust deed LEGAL document outlining trust a document that sets out the regulations governing a trust

trustee FINANCE somebody holding assets in trust a person who, either individually or as a member of a board, has a legal obligation to administer assets for another person's benefit

trustee in bankruptcy FINANCE somebody managing bankrupt's finances somebody appointed by a court to manage the finances of a bankrupt person or company

trustee investment STOCKHOLDING & INVESTMENTS investment made by trustee an investment that is made by a trustee and is subject to legal restrictions

trusteeship FINANCE **1.** status of trustee the position of a ***trustee*** with a legal obligation to administer assets for another person's benefit **2.** time as trustee the term during which somebody acts as a ***trustee***

trust fund FINANCE set of assets held in trust assets held in trust by a ***trustee*** or board of trustees for the trust's beneficiaries

trust officer FINANCE manager of assets of trust somebody who manages the assets of a trust, especially for a bank that is acting as a ***trustee***

Truth in Lending Act LEGAL US law requiring transparent disclosure of credit terms in the United States, a law requiring lenders to disclose the terms of their credit offers accurately so that consumers are not misled and are able to compare the various credit terms available. The Truth in Lending Act requires lenders to disclose the terms and costs of all loan plans, including the following: annual percentage rate, points, and fees; the total of the principal amount being financed; payment due date and terms, including any balloon payment where applicable and late payment fees; features of variable-rate loans, including the highest rate the lender would charge, how it is calculated and the resulting monthly payment; total finance charges; whether the loan is assumable; the existence of any application fees or any annual or one-time service fees; and whether there are any pre-payment penalties. Where applicable, it also requires the lender to confirm the address of the property securing the loan. *Abbr* ***TILA***

TT *abbr* BANKING ***telegraphic transfer***

turbulence GENERAL MANAGEMENT sudden changes affecting performance unpredictable and swift changes in an organization's external or internal environments, or in an economy, that affect its performance. The late 20th century was considered a turbulent environment for business because of the rapid growth in technology and globalization, and the frequency of restructuring and merger activity. 2008 was an especially turbulent period for financial markets, when banks worldwide could not meet their loans and had to receive government support.

turkey FINANCE poor performer an investment or business that is performing badly (informal)

turn MARKETS market maker's profit the difference between the bid and offer prices of a ***market maker***

turnaround *US* **1.** FINANCE return of profitability a term for the act of making a company profitable again **2.** OPERATIONS & PRODUCTION value of sales divided by value of inventory a term for the value of goods sold during a year divided by the average value of goods held in stock **3.** OPERATIONS & PRODUCTION preparation of vehicle for another commercial trip a term for the process of emptying a ship, plane, etc., and getting it ready for another commercial trip **4.** OPERATIONS & PRODUCTION processing and dispatching of orders a term for the time it takes to process orders and send out the goods. *UK term* ***turnround***

turnaround management GENERAL MANAGEMENT implementation of rescue measures for failing organization the implementation of a set of actions required to save an organization from business failure and return it to operational normality and financial solvency. Turnaround management usually requires strong leadership and can include restructuring and job losses, an investigation of the root causes of failure, and long-term programs to revitalize the organization.

Turnbull REGULATION & COMPLIANCE UK internal control guidance in the United Kingdom, a best-practice framework for internal control in UK listed companies, originally established in 1999 and subsequently updated

turnkey contract GENERAL MANAGEMENT agreement to control project until handover to client an agreement in which a contractor designs, constructs, and manages a project until it is ready to be handed over to the client and operation can begin immediately

turnover **1.** ACCOUNTING firm's total sales revenue the total sales ***revenue*** of an organization for an accounting period. This is shown net of ***VAT***, trade discounts, and any other taxes based on the revenue in a ***profit and loss account***. **2.** MARKETS total value of stocks traded during year the total value of stocks bought and sold on an exchange during the year. This covers both sales and purchases, so each transaction is counted twice. **3.** HR & PERSONNEL rate of change of staff the rate at which staff leave and are replaced in an organization

turnover ratio OPERATIONS & PRODUCTION frequency of firm's changes in inventory during year a measure of the number of times in a year that a business's inventory changes completely. It is calculated as the cost of sales divided by the average book value of inventory.

turnover tax TAX **1.** *US* = ***sales tax*** **2.** *UK* = ***VAT***

turnround *UK* = ***turnaround***

20-F BUSINESS document giving detailed information about non-US companies a document compiled by non-US companies listed on the ***New York Stock Exchange*** for the ***Securities and Exchange Commission*** that gives detailed corporate information

twenty-four hour trading MARKETS constant financial trading the possibility of trading in currencies or securities at any time of day or night, because there are always trading floors open at different locations in different time zones. A financial institution with offices in the Far East, Europe, and the United States can offer its clients 24-hour trading-either by the client contacting their offices in each area, or by the customer's local office passing the orders on to another center.

two-tier tender offer MERGERS & ACQUISITIONS offering premium for initial stock in acquisition attempt in the United States, a ***takeover bid*** in which the acquirer offers to pay more for shares bought early than for those acquired at a later date, in order to encourage stockholders to accept the offer, thus gaining control quickly. This form of bidding is outlawed in some jurisdictions, including the United Kingdom.

U

UBR *abbr* TAX ***uniform business rate***

UCC *abbr* REGULATION & COMPLIANCE ***uniform commercial code***

UCITS STOCKHOLDING & INVESTMENTS EU rules for mutual funds a set of directives that regulate mutual funds throughout all the countries of the European Union. *Full form* ***Undertakings for Collective Investment in Transferable Securities***

UGMA *abbr* REGULATION & COMPLIANCE ***Uniform Gifts to Minors Act***

UHNWI *abbr* FINANCE ***ultra high net worth individual***

UIF *abbr* INSURANCE ***Unemployment Insurance Fund***

UIT *abbr* STOCKHOLDING & INVESTMENTS ***unit investment trust***

UKFI *abbr* FINANCE ***UK Financial Investments Ltd***

UK Financial Investments Ltd FINANCE firm managing UK government's banking investments a company that manages the UK government's investments in the Royal Bank of Scotland plc, Lloyds Banking Group, Bradford & Bingley, Northern Rock plc and Northern Rock Asset Management plc. It was set up in 2008 after the government had to step in to overcome serious difficulties in independent banks. *Abbr* ***UKFI***

ultra high net worth individual FINANCE person with $30 million plus a person whose net assets, excluding the value of a home, are worth more than $30 million. About 100,000 people worldwide fall into this category. *Abbr* ***UHNWI***

ultra vires LEGAL beyond scope of organization's authority a Latin phrase meaning "beyond the powers," used to refer to an activity that normally falls beyond the scope of the instrument from which an organization's authority is derived, and thus may be challenged by the courts. A corporation's powers are limited by the objectives in its charter. Most objectives tend to be wide-ranging, but, should a corporation's directors act outside of these objectives, any resulting agreement may be unenforceable.

ultra vires activity FINANCE something disallowed by rules an act that is not permitted by applicable rules such as those of a corporate charter. Such acts may lead to contracts being void.

  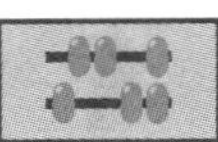      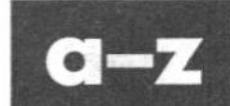

umbrella fund STOCKHOLDING & INVESTMENTS offshore investment in other offshore concerns a collective investment based offshore that invests in other offshore collective investments

umbrella organization BUSINESS organization embracing several member organizations a large organization that includes a number of member organizations and works to protect their shared interests

unbalanced growth ECONOMICS different parts of economy growing at different rates the situation that occurs when some sectors of an economy grow at different rates from others

unbundling 1. MERGERS & ACQUISITIONS dividing of firm before selling it off the dividing of a company into separate constituent companies, often to sell all or some of them after a takeover **2.** STOCKHOLDING & INVESTMENTS splitting returns on security for separate sale the separation of the components of a security in order to sell them separately

uncalled share capital STOCKHOLDING & INVESTMENTS unpaid proportion of stock value the amount of the ***nominal value*** of shares for which the company has not requested payment. It may not be intended that this payment should be requested unless the company goes into ***liquidation***.

uncollectable FINANCE describing debt that is written off used to describe a debt that must be written off, either as a charge to the ***profit and loss account*** or against an existing doubtful debt provision

uncollected funds BANKING value residing in deposit that bank cannot negotiate money deriving from the deposit of an instrument that a bank has not been able to negotiate

unconditional bid MERGERS & ACQUISITIONS takeover bid offering payment irrespective of stock volume in a takeover battle, a situation in which a bidder will pay the offered price irrespective of how many shares are acquired, typically after the acquisition of a majority of the shares

unconsolidated STOCKHOLDING & INVESTMENTS not grouped together used to describe shares, holdings, loans, or subsidiaries that are not combined into a single unit

uncontested bid GENERAL MANAGEMENT offer of contract to single bidder the offering of a contract by a government or other organization to one bidder only, without competition

uncovered bear STOCKHOLDING & INVESTMENTS person selling stock not yet acquired a person who sells stock which he or she does not hold, hoping to be able to buy stock back at a lower price when it is time to settle

uncovered option STOCKHOLDING & INVESTMENTS option whose seller does not own associated asset a type of ***option*** in which the underlying asset is not owned by the seller, who risks considerable loss if the price of the asset falls. *Also called* ***naked option***

UNCTAD INTERNATIONAL TRADE UN department dealing with development and finance a part of the United Nations system dealing with the integrated treatment of development and interrelated issues in trade, finance, technology, and investment. *Full form* ***United Nations Conference on Trade and Development***

undated bond STOCKHOLDING & INVESTMENTS bond without maturity date a bond to which no maturity date has been assigned

underbanked STOCKHOLDING & INVESTMENTS describing new issue with few sellers used to describe a new issue without enough brokers to sell it

undercapitalized FINANCE with insufficient capital used to describe a business that has insufficient capital for its requirements

underemployed capital FINANCE capital not producing enough income capital that is not being used effectively to produce income

underlying asset STOCKHOLDING & INVESTMENTS asset with option an asset that is associated with an ***option*** or other derivative or structured note

underlying inflation *or* underlying rate of inflation MORTGAGES inflation rate not considering mortgage costs a measure of inflation that does not take mortgage costs into account

underlying security STOCKHOLDING & INVESTMENTS security with option a security that is associated with an ***option***

undermargined account BANKING account with funds insufficient for margin requirements an account that does not have enough funds to cover its margin requirements, resulting in a ***margin call***

underspend FINANCE **1.** spend less than intended or allowed to spend less than the amount that was budgeted for spending **2.** smaller amount spent than expected an amount that is less than the amount that was budgeted for spending

undersubscribed STOCKHOLDING & INVESTMENTS describing stock issue with some stock unsold used to describe a new issue in which not all shares are sold, and part of the issue remains with the underwriters

undertaking 1. BUSINESS business a commercial business or company **2.** LEGAL formal promise a promise, especially a legally binding one

Undertakings for Collective Investment in Transferable Securities STOCKHOLDING & INVESTMENTS *see* ***UCITS***

underused liquidity FINANCE cash not being optimally used available capital that is not being put to effective use in developing a business

undervaluation FINANCE valuation at less than true worth the assessment of an asset as having a value that is less than its expected value or worth

undervalued FINANCE describing asset available for less than value used to describe an asset that is offered for sale at a price lower than its expected value or worth

undervalued currency CURRENCY & EXCHANGE currency available cheaply a currency that costs less to buy with another currency than it is worth in goods

underwrite STOCKHOLDING & INVESTMENTS, INSURANCE, RISK be liable for potential losses to assume risk, especially for a new issue or an insurance policy. *Also called* ***write***

underwriter 1. STOCKHOLDING & INVESTMENTS guarantor of public offering an institution or group of institutions who, for a fee, guarantee a public offering from a corporation and, if it fails to find enough buyers, will purchase the remaining shares **2.** INSURANCE insurance risk assessor a person who establishes insurance risk and issues insurance policies for an ***insurance company*** or syndicate, paying the insured party if a specified loss occurs. *Also called* ***writer*** *(sense 1). See also* ***Lloyd's underwriting syndicate***

underwriters' syndicate STOCKHOLDING & INVESTMENTS group guaranteeing public offering a group of institutions who, for a fee, guarantee a public offering from a corporation and, if it fails to find enough buyers, will purchase the remaining shares

underwriting STOCKHOLDING & INVESTMENTS guaranteeing of public offering the activity of guaranteeing a public offering from a corporation for a fee, agreeing to buy any shares that remain unsold

underwriting commission *or* underwriting fee STOCKHOLDING & INVESTMENTS fee guaranteeing purchase of new stock a fee paid by a company to the ***underwriters*** for guaranteeing the purchase of new shares in that company.

underwriting income INSURANCE profit from insurance premiums the money that an insurance company makes because the premiums it collects exceed the claims it pays out

underwriting spread STOCKHOLDING & INVESTMENTS difference between stock costs and income from sale an amount that is the difference between what an organization pays for an issue and what it receives when it sells the issue to investors

underwriting syndicate STOCKHOLDING & INVESTMENTS group of institutions selling new securities to investors a group of financial institutions who join to sell new securities to investors, and agree to buy any that are unsold themselves

undischarged bankrupt LEGAL somebody still officially classed as bankrupt a person who has been declared bankrupt and has not yet been released from that status by a court

undistributable reserves *UK* FINANCE = ***restricted surplus***

undistributed profit STOCKHOLDING & INVESTMENTS profit not paid out as dividend profit that has not been distributed as dividends to stockholders

UNDP ECONOMICS UN agency providing human development grants a part of the United Nations system with goals that include the elimination of poverty, environmental regeneration, job creation, and advancement of women. It is the world's largest source of grants for sustainable human development. *Full form* ***United Nations Development Programme***

unearned income FINANCE money not received from employment income received from sources such as investments or interest on savings rather than from employment. *See also* ***earned income***

unearned increment REAL ESTATE increase in property value not created by owner an increase in the value of a property that arises from causes other than the owner's improvements or expenditure

unearned premium INSURANCE money repaid from terminated insurance policy the amount of money repaid by an insurance company when a policy is terminated

uneconomic FINANCE not producing profits not profitable for a country, firm, or investor in the short or long term

unemployment ECONOMICS people wanting to work but not finding jobs the situation in which some members of a country's labor force are willing to work but cannot find employment

  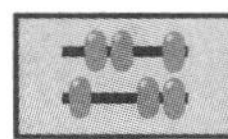      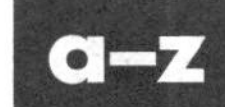

unemployment compensation US HR & PERSONNEL = ***severance pay***

Unemployment Insurance Fund INSURANCE employee insurance against potential unemployment in South Africa, a system administered through payroll deductions that insures employees against loss of earnings through being made unemployed by such causes as retrenchment, illness, or maternity. *Abbr* ***UIF***

unencumbered REAL ESTATE property with no mortgage used to describe a property that is not subject to a mortgage

uneven lot MARKETS = ***odd lot***

unfair competition BUSINESS dubious way of gaining competitive advantage the practice of trying to do better than another company by using underhand techniques such as importing foreign goods at very low prices or wrongly criticizing a competitor's products

unfunded debt FINANCE debt to be repaid within a year short-term debt requiring repayment within a year of being issued

ungeared UK FINANCE = ***unleveraged***

ungluing MERGERS & ACQUISITIONS splitting up established networks the process of breaking up traditional supply chains or groups of cooperating organizations after taking control of the element of mutual interest that holds them together

uniform business rate TAX tax on UK local businesses in the United Kingdom, the rate of tax set by central government that is to be collected from businesses by local government. *Abbr* ***UBR***

uniform commercial code REGULATION & COMPLIANCE US laws regulating commercial transactions in the United States, a set of laws governing commercial transactions that has been adopted totally or in part by all 50 states. *Abbr* ***UCC***

uniform costing OPERATIONS & PRODUCTION identical approach to costing the use by several businesses of the same costing methods, principles, and techniques

Uniform Gifts to Minors Act REGULATION & COMPLIANCE US standards protecting assets given to children in the United States, a set of standards for protecting financial assets that have been given to minors. *Abbr* ***UGMA***

Uniform Transfers to Minors Act REGULATION & COMPLIANCE US regulations protecting noncash gifts to children in the United States, a set of standards for protecting noncash assets that have been given to minors. *Abbr* ***UTMA***

unincorporated BUSINESS describing business without status of company used to describe a business that is operating as a partnership or sole trader and has not been made into a company

uninsurable risk INSURANCE risk for which insurance is unavailable an event that is met with so rarely that it is impossible to calculate a probability of occurrence and therefore impossible to calculate a suitable price for insurance. *See also* ***insurable risk, risk***

unique selling point *or* unique selling proposition MARKETING *see* ***USP***

unissued share capital *or* unissued capital UK STOCKHOLDING & INVESTMENTS = ***unissued stock***

unissued stock US STOCKHOLDING & INVESTMENTS capital stock not yet issued the proportion of a company's ***capital stock*** that is authorized but has not been issued. *UK term* ***unissued share capital***

unit STOCKHOLDING & INVESTMENTS **1.** securities traded together a collection of securities traded together as a single item **2.** single mutual fund share of stock a share in a mutual fund

unitary taxation TAX taxing of international firm based on worldwide income a method of taxing a corporation based on its worldwide income rather than on its income in the country of the tax authority

unit cost OPERATIONS & PRODUCTION cost of producing single item the cost of one item, calculated on the basis of production and overhead costs for a number of such items produced together

United Nations Conference on Trade and Development INTERNATIONAL TRADE *see* ***UNCTAD***

United Nations Development Programme ECONOMICS *see* ***UNDP***

unit investment trust STOCKHOLDING & INVESTMENTS investment company offering units in unmanaged portfolio an investment company that offers an unmanaged portfolio of securities to investors through brokers, typically in units of $1,000 each. *Abbr* ***UIT***

unit-linked insurance INSURANCE insurance policy linked to unit trust in the United Kingdom, an insurance policy that is linked to the security of units in a unit trust or fund

unit of account CURRENCY & EXCHANGE currency unit used for payments a unit of a country's currency that can be used in payment for goods or in a firm's accounting

unit of trade STOCKHOLDING & INVESTMENTS smallest amount that can be traded the smallest quantity that can be bought or sold of a share of stock, or a contract included in an ***option***

unit price OPERATIONS & PRODUCTION price of single item the price of one item, calculated on the basis of the cost of production and overhead costs for a number of such items produced together

unit trust UK STOCKHOLDING & INVESTMENTS = ***mutual fund***

universal life insurance INSURANCE life insurance that accrues savings a type of life insurance policy that builds up savings and allows the insurer to change the amount of premiums and the coverage

unleveraged US FINANCE describing firm with no borrowings used to describe a company that has no borrowed money. *UK term* ***ungeared***

unlimited liability FINANCE full responsibility for debts full responsibility for the obligations of a ***general partnership***. This may include the use of personal assets to pay debts.

unlimited risk RISK risk with unlimited potential loss a risk whose potential loss is unlimited, for example, in futures trading

unlisted company BUSINESS, MARKETS company with stock not listed on exchange a company whose shares are not listed on an exchange

unlisted securities STOCKHOLDING & INVESTMENTS stocks not listed on exchange stocks that are not listed on an exchange. *Also called* ***unquoted investments, unquoted shares***

unlisted securities market MARKETS market for minor stocks a market for stocks that are not listed on a recognized exchange. *Abbr* ***USM***

unprofitable FINANCE not profitable not producing a profit

unquoted MARKETS having no publicly stated price used to describe a security that has no publicly stated price because it is not listed on an exchange

unquoted investments STOCKHOLDING & INVESTMENTS = ***unlisted securities***

unquoted shares STOCKHOLDING & INVESTMENTS = ***unlisted securities***

unrealized capital gain ACCOUNTING profitable investment not yet sold a profit from the holding of an asset worth more than its purchase price, but not yet sold

unrealized loss ACCOUNTING = ***paper loss***

unrealized profit ACCOUNTING = ***paper profit***

unreason GENERAL MANAGEMENT unorthodox approaches that bring business success the process of thinking the unlikely and doing the unreasonable that can be a means by which an organization or individual achieves success

unremittable gain ACCOUNTING in UK, capital gain that cannot be imported in the United Kingdom, a capital gain that cannot be imported into the taxpayer's country, especially because of currency restrictions

unseasoned issue STOCKHOLDING & INVESTMENTS issue of stocks to SEC-approved investors an issue of stocks that a dealer may only sell to specific qualifying investors as agreed by the US Securities and Investment Commission. *See also* ***seasoned issue***

unsecured creditor FINANCE creditor making unsecured loans a creditor who is owed money, but has no security from the debtor for the debt. Unsecured creditors are at risk of losing everything, as official procedures may absorb most of the money remaining after a business failure and small creditors may not be paid.

unsecured debt FINANCE money borrowed without collateral an amount of money borrowed without the borrower providing ***collateral*** to the lender

unsecured loan FINANCE loan provided without collateral a loan made without ***collateral*** provided to the lender by the borrower. *Also called* ***signature loan***

unstable equilibrium ECONOMICS easily disrupted balance of supply and demand a market situation in which, if there is a movement of price or quantity away from the equilibrium, existing forces will push the price even further away

unsubsidized FINANCE without financial assistance for which no ***subsidy*** has been paid. *See also* ***subsidized***

up market MARKETS rising stock market a stock market that is rising or is at its highest level

upside potential STOCKHOLDING & INVESTMENTS potential for value of security to go up the possibility that a security will increase in value. *See also* ***downside risk***

upsizing HR & PERSONNEL increase in activities and staff expansion and restructuring of business activities, including an increase in the number of staff employed. *Also called* ***resizing***. *See also* ***downsizing***

upstairs market MARKETS area of exchange where major institutions trade the place where traders for major brokerages and institutions do business at an exchange

upstream OPERATIONS & PRODUCTION at earlier stage at a point earlier in the production process. *See also* ***downstream***

upstream progress GENERAL MANAGEMENT commercial progress in difficult conditions advancement against opposition or in difficult conditions. A company or project can make upstream progress if it moves toward achieving its objectives despite impediments. *See also* ***downstream progress***

upswing MARKETS rise in stock prices following fall an upward movement in stock prices following a period of steady or falling prices

uptick MARKETS trade at price higher than in previous trade a transaction in which the price of a specific security is higher than the price in the transaction immediately preceding it. *Also called* ***plus tick***

upturn ECONOMICS upward trend an upward trend in sales, profits, a stock market, or an economy

urbun FINANCE forfeitable deposit paid by buyer to seller in Islamic financing, money paid by a buyer to a seller at the time of execution of a contract that will be forfeited if the contract is canceled by the buyer

used credit FINANCE used part of offered credit the portion of a ***line of credit*** that is no longer available for use

use of proceeds FINANCE details of intended investment use detailed information for investors on how money invested in an undertaking will be put to use

U-shaped recovery ECONOMICS slow exit from recession a pattern of recovery after a recession shaped like the letter U, showing a gradual improvement of conditions. *See also* ***V-shaped recovery***

USM *abbr* MARKETS ***unlisted securities market***

USP MARKETING feature distinguishing specific product a specific feature that differentiates a product from similar products. *Full form* ***unique selling point***

US savings bond STOCKHOLDING & INVESTMENTS US Federal government savings product in the United States, a bond that can be bought from the Federal government. *Also called* ***savings bond***

usury FINANCE lending money at high rates the practice of lending money at a rate of interest that is either unlawful or considered to be excessively high

utility 1. BUSINESS company that provides a service to community a public service company, for example, one that supplies water, gas, or electricity or that runs public transportation **2.** ECONOMICS customer satisfaction the usefulness or satisfaction that a consumer gets from a product

UTMA *abbr* REGULATION & COMPLIANCE ***Uniform Transfers to Minors Act***

V

valuation FINANCE estimate of worth an estimate of how much something is worth

value FINANCE **1.** worth measured in money the amount of money that something is worth **2.** estimate worth of something in money to estimate how much money something is worth

value added GENERAL MANAGEMENT **1.** difference between cost of materials and selling price the difference between the cost of bought-in materials and the eventual selling price of the finished product **2.** valuable distinguishing features of product or service the features that differentiate one product or service from another, and thus create value for the customer. Value added is a customer perception of what makes a product or service desirable over others and worth a higher price. Value added is more difficult to measure without a physical end product, but value can be added to services as well as physical goods, through the process of ***value engineering***. *Also called* ***added value*** *(sense 1)*

value-added network E-COMMERCE organization providing messaging and communications services an organization that provides messaging-related functions and EDI (***electronic data interchange***) communications services, for example, protocol matching and line-speed conversion, between trading partners. *Abbr* ***VAN***. Also called ***third-party network, third-party service provider***

value-added reseller BUSINESS trader selling repackaged items bought at retail a merchant who buys products at retail and packages them with additional items for sale to customers. *Abbr* ***VAR***

value-added tax TAX *see* ***VAT***

value-adding intermediary GENERAL MANAGEMENT distributor adding value to product before sale a distributor who adds value to a product before selling it to a customer, for example, by installing software or a modem in a computer

value analysis OPERATIONS & PRODUCTION technique of eliminating unnecessary costs a cost reduction and problem-solving technique that analyzes an existing product or service in order to reduce or eliminate any costs that do not contribute to value or performance. Value analysis usually focuses on design issues relating to the function of a product or service, looking at the properties that make it work, or which are ***USPs***.

value-at-risk STOCKHOLDING & INVESTMENTS, RISK *see* ***Var***

value chain BUSINESS business activities adding value to products or services the sequence of business activities by which, in the perspective of the end user, value is added to products or services produced by an organization

value date FINANCE transfer date a date on which a transaction takes place

value driver FINANCE something adding value to product or service an activity or organizational focus that enhances the value of a product or service in the perception of the consumer and which therefore creates value for the producer. Advanced technology, reliability, or reputation for customer relations can all be value drivers.

value engineering OPERATIONS & PRODUCTION activity that aids design of product an activity that helps to design products that meet customer needs at the lowest cost while assuring the required standards of quality and reliability

value for customs purposes only INTERNATIONAL TRADE declared value of item imported into US what somebody importing something into the United States declares that it is worth

value for money audit ACCOUNTING examination of firm's effectiveness in using resources an investigation into whether proper arrangements have been made for securing economy, efficiency, and effectiveness in the use of resources. *Abbr* ***VFM***. Also called ***comprehensive auditing***

value innovation GENERAL MANAGEMENT approach to business growth concentrating on new markets a strategic approach to business growth, involving a shift away from a focus on the existing competition to one of trying to create entirely new markets. Value innovation can be achieved by implementing a focus on innovation and creation of new market possibilities.

value investing STOCKHOLDING & INVESTMENTS investing based on company's value an investment strategy based on the value of a company rather than simply on its stock price

value map MARKETING extra value differentiating product or service the level of value that the market recognizes in a product or service and that helps to differentiate it from competitors

value proposition FINANCE proposed profit-making plan a proposed plan for making a profit, presented, for example, to a potential investor

value share *or* value stock STOCKHOLDING & INVESTMENTS currently underpriced stock a stock that is considered to be currently underpriced by the market, and therefore an attractive investment prospect

value to the business *or* value to the owner FINANCE asset's minimum assessable value the lower of the figures for the ***recoverable amount*** and the ***replacement cost*** of an asset. *Also called* ***deprival value***

VAN *abbr* E-COMMERCE ***value-added network***

vanilla lending FINANCE = ***prime lending***

vanilla loan FINANCE = ***prime loan***

VaR *or* VAR STOCKHOLDING & INVESTMENTS, RISK assessment of likely depreciation of asset or investment a risk assessment measure that is used to establish how much the market value of an asset or a portfolio is likely to decrease over a specific period of time. *Full form* ***value-at-risk***

VAR *abbr* BUSINESS ***value-added reseller***

variable STATISTICS piece of data studied in statistical analysis an element of data whose changes are the object of a statistical study

variable annuity INSURANCE annuity without fixed payments an ***annuity*** that offers no guarantee but has potential for a greater return, usually based on the performance of a stock or mutual fund. *See also* ***annuity***

variable costing ACCOUNTING = ***marginal costing***

variable interest rate FINANCE interest rate that fluctuates during loan period an interest rate that changes, usually in relation to a standard index, during the period of a loan

variable life assurance *UK* INSURANCE = ***variable life insurance***

variable life insurance *US* INSURANCE life insurance where benefits vary with investment performance a type of whole-life insurance policy providing a death benefit that varies according to

  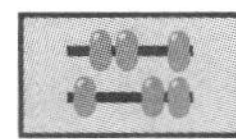      

the performance of an investment portfolio managed by the insurance company. *UK term* ***variable life assurance***

variable rate FINANCE interest rate that fluctuates a rate of interest on a loan that is not fixed, but can change with the current bank interest rates. *Also called* ***floating rate***

variable rate note FINANCE note with interest rate linked to index a note whose interest rate is tied to an index, such as the prime rate in the United States or the London Interbank Offering Rate in the United Kingdom. *Abbr* ***VRN***

variance 1. GENERAL MANAGEMENT difference between actual and predicted performance a measure of the difference between actual performance and forecast, or standard, performance **2.** ACCOUNTING difference between planned and actual cost the difference between a planned, budgeted, or standard cost and the actual cost incurred. The same comparisons may be made for revenues.

variation margin STOCKHOLDING & INVESTMENTS, RISK daily profits or losses the profits or losses of members of the ***London Clearing House***, calculated daily from the marked-to-market-close value of their position. *See also* ***initial margin***

VAT TAX tax added at each manufacturing stage a tax added at each stage in the manufacture of a product. It acts as a replacement for a ***sales tax*** in almost every industrialized country outside North America. It is levied on selected goods and services, paid by organizations on items they buy, and then charged to customers. *Full form* ***value-added tax***

VAT declaration TAX in UK, statement of VAT income in the United Kingdom, a statement to ***Her Majesty's Revenue & Customs*** declaring that proportion of a business's income that is liable to ***VAT***

VAT inspector TAX UK government official checking payment of VAT a UK government official who examines VAT returns and checks that VAT is being paid

VAT paid TAX in UK, with VAT paid in the United Kingdom, indicating an item on which ***VAT*** has already been paid

VAT receivable TAX with VAT not yet collected with the VAT for an item not yet collected by a taxing authority

VAT registration TAX listing as firm eligible for some refunding of VAT the process of listing with a European government as a company eligible for the return of VAT in some cases

vault cash BANKING cash used for bank's everyday needs cash held by a bank in its vaults, used for day-to-day needs

VC *abbr* FINANCE ***venture capitalist***

VCM *abbr* MARKETS ***Venture Capital Market***

VCT *abbr* BUSINESS ***venture capital trust***

vega STOCKHOLDING & INVESTMENTS relationship of option price to underlying asset's volatility a ratio between the expected change in the price of an option and a 1% change in the expected volatility of the underlying asset. *Also called* ***kappa, lambda***

velocity of circulation of money ECONOMICS how quickly money moves around economy the rate at which money circulates in an economy

vendor FINANCE seller a person or organization that sells goods, services, shares, or property

vendor placing STOCKHOLDING & INVESTMENTS business vendor's exchanging of acquired stock for cash the practice of issuing stock to acquire a business, where an agreement has been made to allow the vendor of the business to place the stock with investors for cash

venture capital FINANCE finance for new businesses or projects money used to finance new companies or projects, especially those with high earning potential and high risk. *Also called* ***risk capital***

venture capital fund FINANCE fund providing venture capital a fund that invests in finance houses providing ***venture capital***

venture capitalist FINANCE firm or individual providing venture capital a finance company or private individual specializing in providing venture capital. *Abbr* ***VC***

Venture Capital Market MARKETS closed sector of Johannesburg exchange for developing companies a sector on the ***Johannesburg Stock Exchange*** for listing smaller developing companies that was closed to new listings in 2004 due to low liquidity. *Abbr* ***VCM***. See also ***Development Capital Market***

venture capital trust BUSINESS in UK, trust investing in smaller firms in the United Kingdom, a trust that invests in smaller firms that need capital to grow. *Abbr* ***VCT***

venture funding FINANCE second round of funding for new firm the round of funding for a new company that follows the provision of seed capital by venture capitalists

venture management GENERAL MANAGEMENT collaboration encouraging entrepreneurism and innovation the collaboration of various sections within an organization to encourage an ***entrepreneurial*** spirit, increase innovation, and produce successful new products more quickly. Venture management is used within large organizations to create a small-firm, entrepreneurial atmosphere, releasing innovation and talent from promising employees. It cuts out bureaucracy and bypasses traditional management systems. The collaboration is generally between research and development, corporate planning, marketing, finance, and purchasing functions.

venturer FINANCE partner in joint venture one of two or more parties involved in a ***joint venture***

verbal contract GENERAL MANAGEMENT oral, not written, agreement an agreement that is oral and not written down. It remains legally enforceable by the parties who have agreed to it.

verification ACCOUNTING in-depth examination of firm's assets and liabilities in an audit, a substantive test of the existence, ownership, and valuation of a company's assets and liabilities

vertical diversification GENERAL MANAGEMENT, MERGERS & ACQUISITIONS developing new areas in supply chain ***diversification*** in which a company moves into a different level of the ***supply chain***, for example, a manufacturing company becoming a retailer. *See also* ***diversification***

vertical equity TAX principle that tax rates vary with income the principle that people with different incomes should pay different rates of tax

vertical form ACCOUNTING presentation of debits and credits in single column the presentation of a financial statement in which the debits and credits are shown in one column of figures

vertical integration GENERAL MANAGEMENT combining of operations in supply chain the practice of combining some or all of the sequential operations of the ***supply chain*** between the sourcing of ***raw materials*** and sale of the final product. Vertical integration can be pursued as a strategy through the acquisition of ***suppliers***, ***wholesalers***, and ***retailers*** to increase control and reliability. It can also be achieved when a company gains strong control over suppliers or distributors, usually by exercising purchasing power.

vertical market MARKETS market geared toward one product type a market that is oriented to one particular specialty, for example, plastics manufacturing or transportation engineering

vertical merger MERGERS & ACQUISITIONS combining of firms in same supply chain the amalgamation of two or more organizations from the same ***supply chain*** under single ownership, through the direct ***acquisition*** by one organization of the net assets or liabilities of the other. *See also* ***merger***

vested employee benefits HR & PERSONNEL benefits not linked to job employee benefits that are not conditional on future employment by the company in question, for example, a pension plan

vested interest FINANCE personal interest in maintaining status quo a special interest in keeping an existing state of affairs for personal gain

vested rights PENSIONS in US, value of pension on leaving job the value of somebody's rights in a pension if he or she leaves a job

vesting HR & PERSONNEL in US, continuing right to receive employer contributions the right of an employee participating in a benefit plan to employer contributions to the plan, whether or not the employee continues working for the company

VFM *abbr* ACCOUNTING ***value for money audit***

v-form FINANCE graph line showing value falling then rising a graphic representation of something that had been falling in value and is now rising

viatical settlement INSURANCE proceeds from sale of terminal patient's insurance policy the proceeds received from the sale of a life insurance policy to a third party by somebody who is terminally ill

virement *UK* ACCOUNTING transfer of money between accounts or budgets a transfer of money from one account to another or from one section of a budget to another

virtual bank BANKING, E-COMMERCE bank only accessible electronically a financial institution that offers banking services via the Internet, ATMs, and telephone but does not have a physical location for customers to visit

virtual hosting E-COMMERCE hosting option with user responsible for software a type of hosting suitable for small and medium-sized businesses, in which the customer uses space on a network vendor's server that is also used by other organizations. The hosting company agrees to deliver minimum access speeds and data transfer rates, and to conduct basic hardware maintenance, but the customer is responsible for managing the content and software.

virtualization E-COMMERCE creation of product or service with electronic existence the creation of a product, service, or organization that has an electronic rather than a physical existence

virtual organization E-COMMERCE temporary partnerships between firms via communications technologies a temporary network of companies, suppliers, customers, or employees, linked by information and communications technologies, with the purpose of delivering a service or product. A virtual organization can bring together companies in partnering or outsourcing arrangements, enabling them to share expertise, resources, and cost savings until objectives are met and the network is dissolved. Such organizations are virtual not only in the sense that they exist largely in cyberspace, but also in that they are unconstrained by the traditional barriers of time and place. A greater level of trust is required between employer and employee or coworkers, or partner organizations, because they will be working out of one another's sight for most of the time. *See also* ***network organization, virtual team***

virtual team GENERAL MANAGEMENT remote employees collaborating via communications technologies a group of employees using information and communications technologies to collaborate from different work bases. Members of a virtual team may work in different parts of the same building or may be scattered across a country or around the world.

visible INTERNATIONAL TRADE describing tangible goods imported or exported used to describe real products or goods that are imported or exported

visible trade INTERNATIONAL TRADE buying and selling physical goods trade in physical goods and merchandise

vision statement GENERAL MANAGEMENT statement of organization's aims a statement giving a broad, aspirational image of the future that an organization is aiming to achieve

voetstoots FINANCE in S. Africa, at buyer's risk in South Africa, used to describe a sale or purchase for which there is no warranty or guarantee

Volcker rule BANKING US restriction on banks' investment activities in the United States, a federal government proposal, in response to the global banking crisis of 2007–08, that no bank or financial institution that contains a bank can own, invest in, or sponsor, for its own profit, hedge funds, private equity funds, or proprietary trading operations that are unrelated to serving customers. The effect of this is to separate banking operations from trading activities.

volume discount OPERATIONS & PRODUCTION discount to customer for quantity purchase the discount given to a customer who buys a large quantity of goods

volume of retail sales BUSINESS how much consumers buy the amount of trade in goods conducted in the retail sector of an economy in a particular period

volume of trade MARKETS number of stocks sold during trading day the number of shares sold on a stock exchange during a day's trading

volume variances ACCOUNTING monetary differences when actual and budgeted activity diverges differences in costs or revenues compared with budgeted amounts, caused by differences between the actual and budgeted levels of activity

voluntary arrangement FINANCE agreement with terms not legally binding an agreement the terms of which are not legally binding on the parties

voluntary bankruptcy LEGAL bankruptcy declared by debtor ***bankruptcy*** in which the debtor files a petition claiming inability to meet his or her debts, as opposed to involuntary bankruptcy, where one or more creditors bring a petition against the debtor. *See also* ***bankruptcy***

voluntary liquidation BUSINESS unforced liquidation supported by stockholders liquidation of a solvent company that is supported by the stockholders

voluntary registration TAX in UK, optional VAT registration by small company in the United Kingdom, registration for ***VAT*** by a trader whose turnover is below the registration threshold. This is usually done in order to reclaim tax on inputs.

vostro account BANKING local bank account held for foreign bank an account held by a local bank on behalf of a foreign bank

votes on account FINANCE extra money for UK government department in the United Kingdom, money granted by Parliament to allow government departments to continue spending in a fiscal year before final authorization of the totals for the year

voting shares *UK* STOCKHOLDING & INVESTMENTS = ***voting stock***

voting stock *US* STOCKHOLDING & INVESTMENTS stock giving voting rights stock whose owners have the right to vote at the company's annual meeting and any extraordinary meetings. *UK term* ***voting shares***

voting trust STOCKHOLDING & INVESTMENTS group with voting rights from stockholders a group of individuals who have collectively received voting rights from stockholders

voucher ACCOUNTING evidence for accounting entry a document supporting an entry in a company's accounts

vouching ACCOUNTING auditor's matching of vouchers with accounting entries an auditing process in which documentary evidence is matched with the details recorded in an accounting record in order to check for validity and accuracy

Vredeling Directive GENERAL MANAGEMENT proposal requesting multinational firms to consult employees a proposal, presented to the European Council of Ministers in 1980, for obligatory information, consultation, and participation of employees at headquarters level in multinational enterprises

VRN *abbr* FINANCE ***variable rate note***

V-shaped recovery ECONOMICS rapid exit from recession a pattern of recovery after a recession shaped like the letter V, showing rapid smooth improvement in conditions. *See also* ***U-shaped recovery***

vulture capitalist FINANCE venture capitalist benefiting investors, not entrepreneur client a ***venture capitalist*** who exploits entrepreneurs by structuring deals on their behalf in such a way that the investors benefit rather than the entrepreneurs (slang)

vulture fund STOCKHOLDING & INVESTMENTS investment fund specializing in discounted items a mutual fund that specializes in acquiring investments such as bonds that have been downgraded or ***distressed property***

W

wage FINANCE money regularly paid for work done the money paid to an employee in return for work done, especially when it is based on an hourly rate and is paid weekly

wage drift FINANCE = ***earnings drift***

wage freeze ECONOMICS government restraints on wage increases a government policy of preventing pay raises in order to combat inflation

wage incentive FINANCE monetary reward for employee's performance a monetary benefit offered as a reward to those employees who perform well in an agreed way

wage indexation ECONOMICS linking of pay raises to cost of living the linking of increases in wages to the percentage rise in the cost of living

wage policy *US* ECONOMICS government policy on wage levels a government policy setting wages and wage increases for workers, for example, setting minimum wage requirements. *UK term* ***wages policy***

wage-price spiral ECONOMICS = ***inflationary spiral***

wage restraint FINANCE curbs on pay raises the act of keeping increases in wages under control and in proportion to increases in workers' productivity

wages FINANCE money in return for work a form of pay given to employees in exchange for the work they have done. Traditionally, the term wages applied to the weekly pay of manual, or nonprofessional workers. In modern usage, the term is often used interchangeably with salary.

wages costs ACCOUNTING costs of paying employees the costs of paying employees for their work. Along with other costs such as pension contributions, these costs typically form the largest single cost item for a business.

wages payable account ACCOUNTING in UK, account showing expenditure on employees in the United Kingdom, an account showing the gross wages and employer's ***National Insurance*** contributions paid during a specific period

wages policy *UK* ECONOMICS = ***wage policy***

waiting time OPERATIONS & PRODUCTION period of inactivity enforced by machine breakdown the period for which an operator is available for production but is prevented from working by shortage of material or tooling, or by machine breakdown

waiver LEGAL avoidance of legal condition an act of giving up a right or removing the conditions of a rule

waiver of premium INSURANCE policy provision to suspend premium payments a provision of an insurance policy that suspends payment of premiums, for example, if the insured receives a disabling injury

wakalah FINANCE contract appointing agent in Islamic financing, a contract in which one person appoints another person to act as an agent on their behalf in a transaction

wallet technology E-COMMERCE software facilitating payment by digital cash a software package providing ***digital wallets*** or purses on

     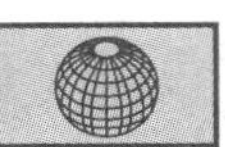   

the computers of merchants and customers to facilitate payment by digital cash

wallflower STOCKHOLDING & INVESTMENTS unappealing investment an investment that does not attract a lot of interest from potential investors (slang)

wall of worry MARKETS stock market moving up with fallbacks a stock market that moves generally upward but that also has many losing sessions is said to be "climbing the wall of worry"

wallpaper STOCKHOLDING & INVESTMENTS major stock issue financing takeovers a disparaging term used to describe a situation where a company issues and sells many new shares in order to finance a series of takeovers (slang)

Wall Street MARKETS **1.** US financial markets a collective name for the financial industry in the United States **2.** financial district of New York a street in Manhattan in and around which the ***New York Stock Exchange*** and other important financial institutions are located

Wall Street bonus FINANCE large financial reward for US employee a very large sum of money, in addition to annual salary, paid to an employee in New York's financial industry for effective performance in increasing his or her company's profits. *See also* ***City bonus***

Wall Street Journal FINANCE US financial newspaper a respected US daily newspaper, first published on July 8, 1889. It is published in New York by Dow Jones & Company, now a subsidiary of News Corporation, with Asian and European editions.

war babies STOCKHOLDING & INVESTMENTS defense industry securities securities in companies that work as contractors in the defense industry (slang)

war chest MERGERS & ACQUISITIONS reserves for financing takeovers a large amount of money held by a person or a company in ***reserves*** that can be used to finance the ***takeover*** of other companies (slang)

warehouse capacity OPERATIONS & PRODUCTION available storage space in warehouse the space available in a warehouse for storing goods

war loan STOCKHOLDING & INVESTMENTS UK government bond paying fixed interest a UK government bond that pays a fixed rate of ***interest*** and has no final ***redemption date***. War loans were originally issued to finance military expenditure.

warrant STOCKHOLDING & INVESTMENTS contract to buy stocks in future a contract that gives the right to buy a predetermined number of shares of stock in the future

warrantee LEGAL somebody given warranty a person who is given a warranty by a ***warrantor***

warrantor LEGAL somebody giving warranty a person who gives a warranty to a ***warrantee***

warrant premium STOCKHOLDING & INVESTMENTS extra paid for buying and exercising warrant a premium paid to buy and exercise a warrant, above the price of buying the shares of stock directly without the warrant

warrants risk warning notice STOCKHOLDING & INVESTMENTS broker's statement of risks of options trading a statement that a broker in the United Kingdom gives to clients to alert them to the risks inherent in trading in options

warranty **1.** INSURANCE insured person's statement that information provided is correct a statement made by somebody who is being insured that the facts stated by that person are true **2.** LEGAL legal document promising quality of goods a legal document that promises that a machine will work properly or that an item is of good quality **3.** LEGAL promise in contract a promise explicitly stated in a contract

wash sale STOCKHOLDING & INVESTMENTS sale and repurchase of same stock the sale and then immediate repurchase of a block of stock. In the United States it may be used as a means of creating fictitious trading volume. *See also* ***bed and breakfast deal***

wasting asset ACCOUNTING asset that is consumed to earn income a ***fixed asset*** that is consumed or exhausted in the process of earning income, for example, a mine or a quarry

watchdog REGULATION & COMPLIANCE organization regulating particular industry an independent organization set up to police a particular industry, ensuring that member companies do not act illegally

watch list MARKETS list of securities to be monitored a list of securities that a brokerage firm, exchange, or regulatory agency is watching closely. These may be securities of firms targeted for takeovers, those planning to issue new securities, or those suspected of rules violations.

waterbed effect FINANCE linked fall and rise the effect of a reduction in one area creating an increase in another area. For example, if the price for one service provided by a company is fixed at a particular level, the price for another of its services rises.

watered stock STOCKHOLDING & INVESTMENTS stock with value lower than capital invested stock in a company that is worth less than the total ***capital*** invested

watermark LEGAL symbol in document proving authenticity a design inserted into documents to prove their authenticity. For example, banknotes all carry watermarks to prevent forgery.

WC *abbr* FINANCE ***working capital***

WDA *abbr* ACCOUNTING, TAX ***writing-down allowance***

WDV *abbr* ACCOUNTING ***written-down value*** = ***net book value***

weak market MARKETS stock market with falling prices a stock market in which prices tend to fall because there are no buyers

wealth ECONOMICS real estate or investments physical assets such as a house or financial assets such as stocks and bonds that can yield an income for their holder

wealth tax TAX tax on accumulated wealth a tax on somebody's accumulated wealth, as opposed to their income

wear and tear ACCOUNTING degeneration of asset owing to normal use the deterioration of a tangible ***fixed asset*** as a result of normal use. This is recognized for accounting purposes by ***depreciation***.

web commerce E-COMMERCE = ***e-commerce***

web marketplace E-COMMERCE online community for commercial trade a business-to-business web community that brings business buyers and sellers together. Although their exact nature can vary considerably, there are essentially three types of web-based B2B marketplace: online catalogs, auctions, and exchanges.

wedge MARKETS representation of converging highs and lows in market analysis, a chart pattern in which the lines that connect the highs and lows are gradually converging while moving in the same direction

weekend effect MARKETS low market tendency on Mondays the theory that stocks tend to perform better on Fridays than on Mondays. Some analysts say this is the result of companies waiting until the close of trading on Friday to release bad news. Others attribute it to Mondays' auctions of US Treasury securities, and others say there is no weekend effect.

WEF *abbr* ECONOMICS ***World Economic Forum***

weighted average STATISTICS average reflecting relative importance of individual values an average of quantities that have been adjusted by the addition of a statistical value to allow for their relative importance in a set of items

weighted average cost of capital FINANCE average cost of firm's capital the average cost of a company's financing (equity, debentures, bank loans) weighted according to the proportion each element bears to the total pool of capital. Weighting is usually based on market valuations, current yields, and costs after tax. The weighted average cost of capital is often used as the ***hurdle rate*** for investment decisions, and as the measure to be minimized in order to find the optimal capital structure for the company.

weighted average cost price FINANCE cost of each item in inventory a value for the cost of each item of a specific type in an inventory, taking into account what quantities were bought at what prices

weighted average number of ordinary shares *UK* STOCKHOLDING & INVESTMENTS = ***weighted average number of shares outstanding***

weighted average number of shares outstanding *US* STOCKHOLDING & INVESTMENTS figure used for calculating earnings per share the number of shares of common stock at the beginning of a period, adjusted for shares canceled, bought back, or issued during the period, multiplied by a time-weighting factor. This number is used in the calculation of ***earnings per share***. *UK term* ***weighted average number of ordinary shares***

weighted index ECONOMICS index with importance affecting value an index in which some important items are given more value than less important ones

weighting STATISTICS giving more importance to some values the assigning of greater importance to particular items in a data set

weightlessness GENERAL MANAGEMENT quality ascribed to knowledge economy a quality considered to characterize an economy that is based on knowledge or other intangibles rather than on physical assets

Wheat Report ACCOUNTING report examining principles and methods of US accounting a report produced by a committee in 1972 that set out to examine the principles and methods of accounting in the United States. Its publication led to the establishment of the ***FASB***.

whisper number *or* whisper estimate FINANCE rumored earnings an estimate of a company's earnings that is based on rumors.

whisper stock STOCKHOLDING & INVESTMENTS stock predicted to rise in value a stock about which there is talk of a likely change in value, usually upward and often related to a takeover

whistle blow the whistle on somebody or something GENERAL MANAGEMENT to engage in ***whistleblowing*** with regard to some malpractice, misconduct, corruption, or mismanagement

whistleblowing GENERAL MANAGEMENT exposure of misconduct within organization speaking out to the media or the public on malpractice, misconduct, corruption, or mismanagement witnessed in an organization. Whistleblowing is usually undertaken on the grounds of morality or conscience, or because of a failure of business ethics on the part of the organization being reported.

white-collar crime FRAUD crime by white-collar worker a crime committed by somebody in the course of doing a ***white-collar job***, for example, embezzlement

white-collar job HR & PERSONNEL job involving no physical labor a position of employment that does not involve physical labor, for example, a job in an office. The term refers to the white shirt and tie supposedly worn by office workers. *See also* ***blue-collar job***

white-collar worker HR & PERSONNEL office worker a person whose job involves working in an office

white elephant BUSINESS product or service underperforming against development costs a product or service that has not sold well, despite large amounts of money being pumped into its development

white goods MARKETING large household appliances large household electrical appliances such as ranges, refrigerators, and freezers. *See also* ***brown goods***

white knight MERGERS & ACQUISITIONS preferred buyer whose action thwarts takeover a person or company liked by a company's management, who buys the company when a hostile company is trying to buy it. *See also* ***knight***

whitemail MERGERS & ACQUISITIONS issue of cheap shares of stock to prevent takeover a method used by a company that is the target of a takeover bid to prevent the takeover, in which the target company issues a large number of shares of stock below the market price to friendly investors. The company wanting to acquire the target must buy the shares in order to be successful.

White Paper BUSINESS report stating UK government's policy a report issued by the UK government as a statement of government policy on a particular problem. *See also* ***Green Paper***

white squire MERGERS & ACQUISITIONS shareholder whose stock purchases prevent takeover bid somebody who purchases a significant, but not controlling, number of shares of stock in order to prevent a ***takeover bid*** from succeeding. A white squire is often invited to purchase the shares by the company to be acquired, and may be required to sign an agreement to prevent him or her from later becoming a ***black knight***.

whiz kid BUSINESS young person enjoying huge business success a young, exceptionally successful person, especially one who makes a lot of money in large financial transactions, including takeovers (informal)

whole-life assurance *UK* INSURANCE = ***whole-life insurance***

whole-life insurance *or* whole-life policy *US* INSURANCE insurance policy paying out on death an insurance policy in which the insured person pays a fixed premium each year and the insurance company pays a sum when he or she dies. *UK term* ***whole-life assurance***

whole loan MORTGAGES mortgage sold in entirety a mortgage loan that is sold to an investor along with all of its rights and responsibilities

wholesale BUSINESS describing business of selling goods to retailers relating to the business of buying goods from manufacturers and selling them in large quantities to retailers who then sell in smaller quantities to the general public

wholesale banking BANKING banking services provided by merchant banks banking services between investment banks and other financial institutions. *See also* ***retail banking, commercial bank***

wholesale funded BANKING funded by short-term borrowing used to describe a bank whose funds come from other banks and financial institutions in the form of short-term loans rather than from long-term deposits

wholesale funding BANKING funding of banks through short-term borrowing a method of funding banks by short-term borrowing from other banks and financial institutions

wholesale market MARKETS, BANKING = ***interbank market***

wholesale price BUSINESS price for bulk purchases of items for resale a price charged to customers who buy large quantities of an item for resale in smaller quantities to others

wholesale price index ECONOMICS government indicator of inflation level a government-calculated index of wholesale prices, indicative of inflation in an economy

wholesaler OPERATIONS & PRODUCTION intermediary between producer and retailer a business that purchases goods from a manufacturer or producer and sells them to a retailer or distributor

wholly-owned subsidiary BUSINESS firm completely owned by another a company that is completely owned by another company. A wholly-owned subsidiary is a ***registered company*** with board members who all represent one ***holding company*** or corporation. Board members may be directly from the holding company or acting as its nominees, or they may be from other wholly-owned subsidiaries of the holding company.

whoops *US* FINANCE disparaging name for Washington state power company a disparaging way of referring to the Washington Public Power Supply System, a municipal corporation in the US state of Washington that built and operated power plants. Delays, cost overruns, and mismanagement in the construction of nuclear power plants caused the company to default on the $2.25 billion in bonds, the largest bond default in US history before the events of 2008.

widow-and-orphan stock *US* STOCKHOLDING & INVESTMENTS dependable stock a stock considered extremely safe as an investment

will LEGAL document stating distribution of property after death a legal document in which a person says what should happen to his or her property after he or she dies

wimbledonization *UK* BUSINESS migration of ownership of British industry the process of the ownership of British industry gradually moving out of the country. The term derives from the major tennis tournament of Wimbledon, where the contest is still played in the UK but the high-profile players are from other countries. (slang)

windfall gains and losses FINANCE unforeseen gains and losses large financial gains and losses that occur unexpectedly

windfall profit FINANCE large unexpected profit a large profit that is made unexpectedly and may be subject to extra tax

windfall tax *UK* TAX = ***excess profits tax***

winding-up LEGAL dissolving firm the legal process of closing down a company

winding-up petition LEGAL petition to court to liquidate company a formal request to a court for the compulsory liquidation of a company

window dressing GENERAL MANAGEMENT artificial inflation of firm's success the practice of making a business seem more profitable or more efficient than it really is

wind up LEGAL close business down to close down a business or organization and sell its assets

WIP *abbr* OPERATIONS & PRODUCTION ***work in process*** *UK term* ***work in progress***

wire house MARKETS brokerage with electronically connected branch offices a brokerage firm whose branch offices are linked by a communications system that allows them to rapidly share data relating to financial markets and individual securities

wire room 1. BANKING bank department dealing with payment orders the department in a financial institution that originates, receives, and transmits payment orders **2.** MARKETS brokerage department dealing with securities orders the department in a brokerage firm that receives and transmits securities orders to the floor of the exchange or the trading department

wire transfer E-COMMERCE electronic transfer of funds a transfer of money from one account to another electronically

witching hour *US* MARKETS time when financial instrument becomes due the time when a type of derivative financial instrument such as a ***put***, a ***call***, or a contract for advance sale becomes due (slang)

withdraw 1. BANKING take money from account to remove money from an account **2.** FINANCE rescind offer to retract an offer that has been made

withdrawal STOCKHOLDING & INVESTMENTS income disbursement from open-end mutual fund the regular disbursement of dividend or capital gain income from an open-end mutual fund

withdrawal plan STOCKHOLDING & INVESTMENTS regular payment to shareholder from mutual fund an arrangement in which a mutual fund pays out a specific amount to a shareholder at regular intervals. *See also* ***systematic withdrawal***

withholding *or* withholding tax TAX **1.** US employee's income tax deducted at source in the United States, the money that an employer pays directly to the government as a payment of the income tax of the employee **2.** tax on dividend or interest paid directly to government the money deducted from a dividend or interest payment that a financial institution pays directly to the government as a payment of the income tax on the recipient **3.** tax in place of dividends the tax that a company must pay because it chose not to pay

dividends that would subject its owners to higher taxes

with profits INSURANCE describing insurance policy paying share of profits used to describe an insurance policy that guarantees the policyholder a share in the profits of the fund in which the premiums are invested

working capital FINANCE firm's money available for trading the funds that are readily available to operate a business.

Working capital comprises the total net ***current assets*** of a business minus its ***current liabilities***.

$$\text{Current assets} - \text{Current liabilities}$$

Current assets are cash and assets that can be converted to cash within one year or a normal operating cycle; current liabilities are monies owed that are due within one year.

If a company's current assets total $300,000 and its current liabilities total $160,000, its working capital is:

$$\$300,000 - \$160,000 = \$140,000$$

Abbr ***WC***

working capital productivity FINANCE measure of firm's productivity a way of measuring a company's efficiency by comparing working capital with sales or turnover.

It is calculated by first subtracting ***current liabilities*** from ***current assets***, which is the formula for working capital, then dividing this figure into sales for the period.

$$\frac{\text{Sales}}{(\text{Current assets} - \text{Current liabilities})} = \text{Working capital productivity}$$

If sales are $3,250, current assets are $900, and current liabilities are $650, then:

$$\frac{3250}{(900 - 650)} = \frac{3250}{250} = 13 \text{ working capital productivity}$$

In this case, the higher the number the better. Sales growing faster than the resources required to generate them is a clear sign of efficiency and, by definition, productivity.

The working capital to sales ratio uses the same figures, but in reverse:

$$\frac{\text{Working capital}}{\text{Sales}} = \text{Working capital to sales ratio}$$

Using the same figures in the example above, this ratio would be calculated:

$$\frac{250}{3250} = 0.077 \times 100\% = 7.7\%$$

For this ratio, obviously, the lower the number the better.

Some experts recommend doing quarterly calculations and averaging them for a given year to arrive at the most reliable number.

working capital ratio ACCOUNTING = ***current ratio***

working capital turnover FINANCE sales divided by average working capital a figure equal to sales divided by average working capital

Working Time Directive *or* Working Hours Directive HR & PERSONNEL EU directive concerning maximum working hours a European Union directive concerning the maximum number of hours an employee can work. The directive currently limits weekly working hours to a maximum of 48, but employees can choose to opt out and work more hours than this.

work in process *US* OPERATIONS & PRODUCTION products currently being made any product that is in the process of being made. Such items are included in inventories and usually valued according to their production costs. *Abbr* ***WIP***. UK term ***work in progress***

work in progress *UK* OPERATIONS & PRODUCTION = ***work in process***

work simplification GENERAL MANAGEMENT elimination of nonessential tasks the streamlining of business practices that attempts to eliminate tasks that do not add value to an idea or process. Tasks in a procedure are analyzed to see if unnecessary steps can be eliminated, thereby reducing complexity as much as possible, enabling workers to complete tasks more quickly. Work simplification is most suited to manufacturing processes and low-skilled jobs. It can lead to cost savings and better use of resources, but it has been criticized for resulting in workers specializing in only one task and for making work repetitive and monotonous.

World Bank BANKING group of institutions funding less developed countries one of the largest sources of funding for the less industrially developed countries in the world. It is made up of five organizations: the International Bank for Reconstruction and Development, the International Development Association, the International Finance Corporation, the Multilateral Investment Guarantee Agency, and the International Centre for Settlement of Investment Disputes. The World Bank was founded at the 1944 Bretton Woods Conference and has over 180 member countries. Its head office is located in Washington, DC, but the Bank has field offices in over 100 countries. Its focus has shifted dramatically since the 1980s, when over one-fifth of its lending was made up of investment in the energy industry. Its current priorities are education, health, and nutrition in the most economically challenged countries of the world.

world class manufacturing GENERAL MANAGEMENT level of manufacturing excellence recognized internationally a position of international manufacturing excellence, achieved by developing a culture based on factors such as continuous improvement, problem prevention, zero defect tolerance, customer-driven ***just-in-time*** production, and ***total quality management***

World Economic Forum ECONOMICS organization seeking to effect global economic improvement an independent economic organization whose goal is to "improve the state of the world." Based in Switzerland, the WEF was formed in the 1970s by Professor Klaus Schwab, who set out to bring together the CEOs of leading European companies in order to discuss strategies that would enable Europe to compete in the global marketplace. Since then, over 1,000 companies around the world have become members of the WEF and its interests have diversified to cover health, corporate citizenship, and peace-building activities. However, it has attracted criticism from some quarters, and antiglobalization protesters gather regularly at its meetings. *Abbr* ***WEF***

world economy ECONOMICS = ***global economy***

World Trade Organization INTERNATIONAL TRADE international organization established to reduce trade restrictions an international organization set up with the goal of reducing restrictions in trade between countries. *Abbr* ***WTO***

wrap account STOCKHOLDING & INVESTMENTS brokerage account charging periodic fee a client account with a broker in which the broker charges a set quarterly or annual fee covering transaction and management costs instead of charging per transaction

wrap fund STOCKHOLDING & INVESTMENTS fund investing in various underlying mutual funds a registered fund that, while not itself a mutual fund, has similar status to that of a stockbroker's portfolio and invests in a variety of underlying mutual funds, each of which is treated as a discrete holding, often in the form of an insurance bond. *Also called* ***wrapper***

wrapper 1. FINANCE financial contract a legally binding financial contract between a client and an investment bank, stating the specific terms that have been agreed. Common wrappers are ***structured notes***, ***swaps***, and ***over-the-counter*** transactions. **2.** STOCKHOLDING & INVESTMENTS = ***wrap fund***

writ LEGAL document starting legal process an official document issued by a judge requiring a specific action

write STOCKHOLDING & INVESTMENTS, RISK = ***underwrite***

write-down ACCOUNTING assignment of lower value to asset the recording of an asset at a lower value than previously

write-off 1. ACCOUNTING reduction in recorded value of asset a reduction in the recorded value of an asset, usually to zero **2.** INSURANCE cancellation of debt the total loss or cancellation of a bad debt **3.** INSURANCE something damaged beyond repair for insurance claims, something that is so badly damaged that it cannot be repaired and will have to be replaced

writer 1. INSURANCE = ***underwriter***
2. STOCKHOLDING & INVESTMENTS seller of traded option somebody who is selling a ***traded option***

write-up ACCOUNTING increase in book value of asset an increase made to the book value of an asset to adjust for an increase in market value

writing-down allowance ACCOUNTING, TAX tax relief on acquired assets that lose value in the United Kingdom, a form of capital allowance giving tax relief to companies acquiring ***fixed assets*** that are then depreciated. This allowance forms part of the system of ***capital allowances***. *Abbr* ***WDA***

written-down value ACCOUNTING = ***net book value***

wrongful trading LEGAL continued trading by directors aware of impending insolvency in the United Kingdom, the continuation of trading when a company's directors know that it cannot avoid insolvent liquidation

W-shaped recession ECONOMICS = ***double-dip recession***

WTO *abbr* INTERNATIONAL TRADE ***World Trade Organization***

X

X STOCKHOLDING & INVESTMENTS with no dividend right a symbol used in newspapers to designate a stock or bond that is trading ***ex dividend***

X.12 E-COMMERCE = ***ANSI X.12 standard***

  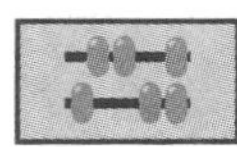      

xa *abbr* STOCKHOLDING & INVESTMENTS ***ex-all***

XBRL FINANCE computer language for financial reporting a computer language used for financial reporting. It allows companies to publish, extract, and exchange financial information through the Internet and other electronic means. *Full form* ***Extensible Business Reporting Language***

xd *abbr* STOCKHOLDING & INVESTMENTS ***ex dividend***

xr *abbr* STOCKHOLDING & INVESTMENTS ***ex-rights***

xw STOCKHOLDING & INVESTMENTS trading without a warrant to buy shares a symbol used in newspapers to designate a stock that is trading without a ***warrant*** to buy shares of stock

Y

Yankee bond STOCKHOLDING & INVESTMENTS foreign bond in US market a bond issued in the US domestic market by a non-US company

yard CURRENCY & EXCHANGE one billion currency units used by traders for one billion units of any currency (slang)

year end ACCOUNTING end of fiscal year the end of the financial year, when a company's accounts are prepared

year-end ACCOUNTING of end of fiscal year relating to the end of a fiscal year

year-end bounce MARKETS (slang) = ***Santa Claus rally***

year-end closing ACCOUNTING statements at end of firm's fiscal year the financial statements issued at the end of a company's fiscal year

year to date ACCOUNTING period from start of fiscal year to now the period from the start of a fiscal year to the current time. A variety of financial information, such as a company's profits, losses, or sales, may be displayed on this basis. *Abbr* ***YTD***

yen CURRENCY & EXCHANGE Japanese currency the basic unit of currency used in Japan

yield STOCKHOLDING & INVESTMENTS percentage that is annual income from investment a percentage of the amount invested that is the annual income from an investment.

Yield is calculated by dividing the annual cash return by the current share price and expressing that as a percentage.

Yields can be compared against the market average or against a sector average, which in turn gives an idea of the relative value of the share against its peers. Other things being equal, a higher yield share is preferable to that of an identical company with a lower yield.

An additional feature of the yield (unlike many of the other share analysis ratios) is that it enables comparison with cash. Cash placed in an interest-bearing source like a bank account or a government stock produces a yield—the annual interest payable. This is usually a safe investment. The yield from this cash investment can be compared with the yield on shares, which are far riskier. This produces a valuable basis for share evaluation.

Share yield is less reliable than bank interest or government stock interest yield, because, unlike banks paying interest, companies are under no obligation at all to pay dividends. Frequently, if they go through a bad patch, even the largest companies will cut dividends or abandon paying them altogether.

yield curve STOCKHOLDING & INVESTMENTS graph showing comparable interest on bonds a visual representation of relative interest rates of short- and long-term bonds. It can be normal, flat, or inverted.

yield gap STOCKHOLDING & INVESTMENTS difference in return between equities and bonds an amount representing the difference between the yield on a safe equity investment and the yield on a riskier bond investment. *See also* ***reverse yield gap***

yield management FINANCE price adjustment that secures maximum profits securing maximum profits from available capacity by manipulating pricing to gain business at different times, and from differing market segments. Yield management is used particularly in service industries such as the airline, hotel, and equipment rental industries, where there are heavy fixed overheads and additional revenue has a big impact on bottom line profitability. Increasing computing power has enabled organizations to integrate complex information from different sources (for example, customer travel histories and current information on bookings) and use mathematical models to analyze the possibility of increasing profitability. Hotel businesses, for example, can use price offers to increase "revenue per available room," or "RevPAR," on the basis of yield management analysis.

yield to call STOCKHOLDING & INVESTMENTS yield on bond at potential call date the yield on a bond at a date when the bond can be called

yield to maturity *US* STOCKHOLDING & INVESTMENTS investor's total return if security held to maturity the total return to an investor if a fixed interest security is held to maturity, in other words, the aggregate of gross interest received and the capital gain or loss at redemption, annualized. *Abbr* ***YTM***. UK term ***gross redemption yield***

yield to worst MARKETS lowest possible bond yield the lowest possible yield from a bond, calculated using the lower of the yield to maturity or any ***yield to call***

YK *abbr* BUSINESS ***yugen kaisha***

YTD *abbr* ACCOUNTING ***year to date***

YTM *abbr* STOCKHOLDING & INVESTMENTS ***yield to maturity***

yugen kaisha BUSINESS private limited liability corporation in Japan in Japan, a private limited liability corporation. Usually, the number of stockholders must be under 50. The minimum capital of a limited liability corporation is 3 million yen. The nominal value of each share must be 50,000 yen or more. *Abbr* ***YK***

Z

ZBB *abbr* ACCOUNTING ***zero-based budgeting***

Z bond STOCKHOLDING & INVESTMENTS bond paying interest after paying all other holders a bond whose holder receives no interest until all of the holders of other bonds in the same series have received theirs

zero-balance account BANKING bank account for outgoings, holding no residual funds a bank account that does not hold funds continuously, but has money automatically transferred into it from another account when claims arise against it

zero-based budgeting ACCOUNTING budgeting method requiring costs to be justified a method of budgeting that requires each cost element to be specifically justified, as though the activities to which the budget relates were being undertaken for the first time. Without approval, the budget allowance is zero. *Abbr* ***ZBB***

zero coupon bond STOCKHOLDING & INVESTMENTS discounted bond paying no interest a bond that pays no interest and is sold at a large discount. *Also called* ***accrual bond, split coupon bond***

zero-coupon security STOCKHOLDING & INVESTMENTS government security without interest a government security that pays no interest but is sold at a discount from its face value

zero-fund FINANCE provide no money for project to assign no money to a business project without actually canceling it (slang)

zero growth ECONOMICS no increase in output a lack of increase in the output of a business or economy between one period, such as one quarter, and the next. *See also* ***recession***

zero-rated TAX on which no sales tax is paid used to describe an item on which a buyer pays no sales tax

zero-rated supplies *or* zero-rated goods and services TAX goods or services not liable for VAT in the United Kingdom, taxable items or services on which ***VAT*** (Value Added Tax) is charged at zero rate, for example, food, books, public transport, and children's clothes.

zero-rating TAX sales tax rating of 0% the rating of a product or service at 0% sales tax

zero-sum game FINANCE gain by one results in loss by another a situation in which a gain by one participant results in another participant's equivalent loss

zombie *US* BUSINESS firm still trading although insolvent a business that continues to trade supported by its bank even though it is insolvent and unlikely to recover (slang)

ZOPA BANKING, E-COMMERCE website facilitating loans between users a personal loan exchange website that allows web users to lend to and borrow from each other directly. *Full form* ***Zone of Possible Agreement***

Z score STATISTICS, FINANCE measure of bankruptcy risk a statistical measure used to determine the likelihood of bankruptcy from a company's credit strength

Index

  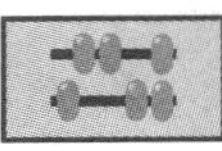   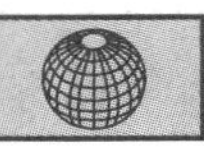   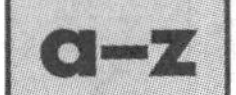

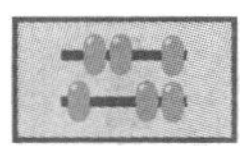

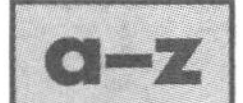

  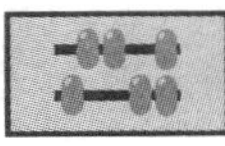      
a–z

  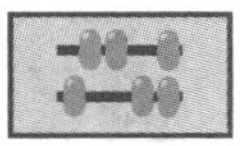      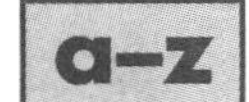

  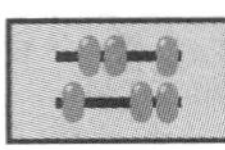   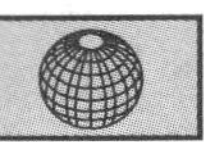   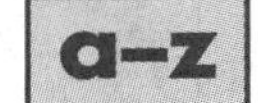

  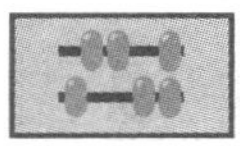      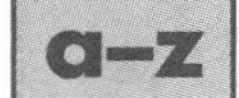

  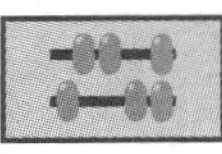      

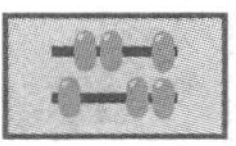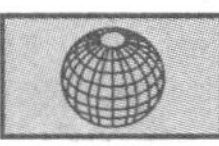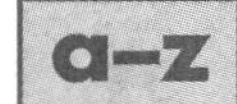
a–z

  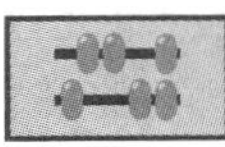   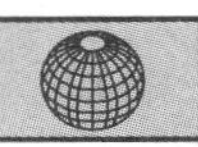   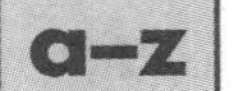

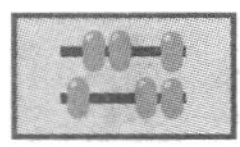

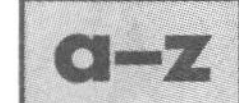

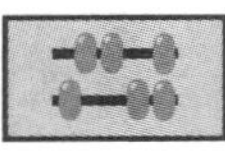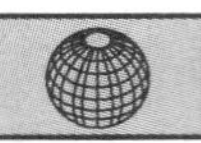
a–z

  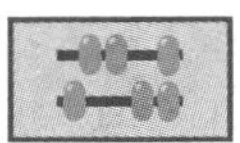      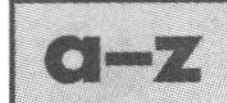
a–z

  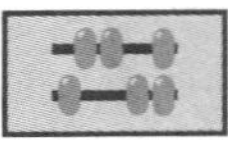      

  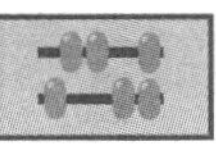      

  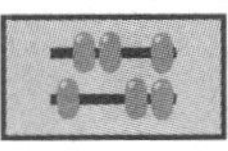      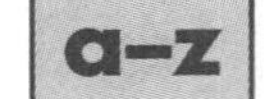

  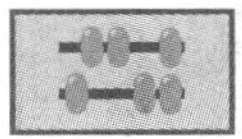      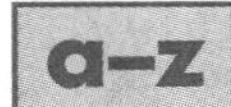

  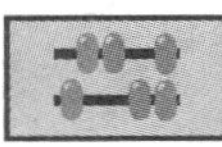      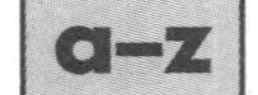

  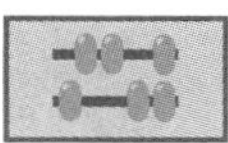      
a–z

Credits

Best Practice

pp. 42–47, "Formulating a Contingency Funding Plan to Manage Liquidity Risks" copyright © Gary Deutsch
pp. 107–112, "Tools for Measuring Interest Rate Risk" copyright © Steven V. Mann
pp. 125–129, "ALM in Financial Intermediation: The Derivatives Business" copyright © Krzysztof M. Ostaszewski
pp. 130–134, "Analyzing a Bank's Financial Performance" copyright © Jyothi Manohar
pp. 292–296, "Auditor Sensitivity to Source Reliability" copyright © Denise Cicchella and Stuart Gardner
pp. 297–302, "An Auditor's Approach to Risk-Based Auditing: What to Audit and When" copyright © Paul J. Sanchez
pp. 327–332, "Cultural Changes in External Auditing" copyright © Jyothi Manohar
pp. 397–401, "Pros and Cons of Using External Auditors for Internal Auditing and Other Services" copyright © Curtis C. Verschoor
pp. 402–406, "Sarbanes–Oxley After Nearly 10 Years" copyright © Curtis C. Verschoor
pp. 411–417, "Threats to Auditor Independence and Possible Remedies" copyright © Gilad Livne
pp. 549–552, "Passive Portfolio Management and Fixed-Income Investing" copyright © Andrew Ainsworth
pp. 570–572, "Raising Capital in the United Kingdom" copyright © Lauren Mills
pp. 579–584, "Risk Management Revisited" copyright © Duncan Hughes
pp. 622–625, "Venture Capital Funds as an Alternative Class of Investment" copyright © Michael D. McKenzie and Bill Janeway
pp. 777–781, "An Approach to Understanding Reputation Risk in Financial Services" copyright © Philip Whittingham
pp. 792–796, "The Case for Continuous Auditing of Management Information Systems" copyright © Robert E. Davis
pp. 797–800, "The CEO's Role in Reputation Management" copyright © Leslie Gaines-Ross
pp. 808–811, "The Cost of Reputation: The Impact of Events on a Company's Financial Performance" copyright © Daniel Diermeier
pp. 817–820, "Crisis Management and Strategies for Dealing with Crisis" copyright © Jon White
pp. 821–825, "Digital Reputation Management" copyright © Shireen Smith
pp. 826–831, "Digital Strategies for Enhancing Reputation" copyright © Paul Argenti and Georgia Aarons
pp. 837–840, "Engaging Your Stakeholders: How to Make Allies of Investors and Activists" copyright © Peter Firestein
pp. 861–865, "How Firms Should Fight Rumors" copyright © Andrew Hiles
pp. 893–896, "Managing Reputational Risk: Business Journalism" copyright © Jonathan Silberstein-Loeb
pp. 933–938, "Smart Use of Reputation Capital: How to Benefit from Different Reputation Investment Strategies" copyright © Joachim Klewes and Robert Wreschniok

Calculations and Ratios

61 Calculations and Ratios copyright © A&C Black Publishers Ltd

Country and Sector Profiles

All content except "Financial Outlook" from *Whitaker's Almanack 2013*, copyright © Bloomsbury Publishing plc

Finance Information Sources

29 Finance Information Sources copyright © Chartered Management Institute

Dictionary

Management terms copyright © Chartered Management Institute

Photographs

Prince Al-Walid bin Talal copyright © AFP Photo/Gerard Cerles
Gary Becker copyright © Ralf-Finn Hestoft/CORBIS
Peter L. Bernstein copyright © Peter Bernstein
Fischer Black copyright © The MIT Museum
Warren Buffet copyright © Paul White/AP/Press Association Images
Andrew Carnegie copyright © AP/Press Association Images
Ronald Harry Coase copyright © Coase Institute
John C. Cox copyright © MIT Sloan
Herman Daly copyright © University of Maryland
Joseph de la Vega copyright © Sonsbeek Publishers
W. Edwards Deming copyright © Bettmann/CORBIS
Marc Faber copyright © Marc Faber
Eugene Fama copyright © Eugene Fama
Irving Fisher copyright © Robert Kradin/AP/Press Association Images
John Kenneth Galbraith copyright © AP/Press Association Images
Benjamin Graham copyright © AP/Press Association Images
Alan Greenspan copyright © AP/Press Association Images
Friedrich Hayek copyright © HL/AP/Press Association Images
Daniel Kahneman copyright © Daniel Hulshizer/AP/Press Association Images
John Maynard Keynes copyright © Walter Sanders/Time Life Pictures/Getty Images

  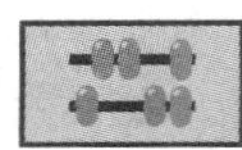   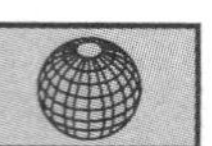   

Edwin Lefèvre copyright © Condé Nast Archive/CORBIS
Burton Malkiel copyright © Don Heiny/AP/Press Association Images
Harry Markowitz copyright © AP/Press Association Images
Robert Merton copyright © KUNI/AP/Press Association Images
Merton Miller copyright © Charles Bennett/AP/Press Association Images
Hyman Minsky copyright © Levy Economics Institute of Bard College
Franco Modigliani copyright © Mark Lennihan/AP/Press Association Images
J. P. Morgan copyright © AP/Press Association Images
Paul O'Neill copyright © Paul Goguen/LANDOV/Press Association Images
Michael Eugene Porter copyright © Lou Krasky/AP/Press Association Images
David Ricardo copyright © Hulton Archive/Stringer/Getty Images. From an engraving by Hodgetts after a portrait by T. Phillips
John D. Rockefeller copyright © AP/Press Association Images
Stephen A. Ross copyright © Daniel Acker/LANDOV/Press Association Images
Nouriel Roubini copyright © Mark Lennihan/AP/Press Association Images
Paul Samuelson copyright © Daniel Lippitt/AP/Press Association Images
Jean-Baptiste Say copyright © The Warren J. Samuels Portrait Collection at Duke University
Myron Scholes copyright © Daniel Acker/LANDOV/Press Association Images
Ernst Friedrich Schumacher copyright © The Schumacher Society
Joseph Schumpeter copyright © Imagno/Getty Images
William F. Sharpe copyright © AP/Press Association Images
Jeremy Siegel copyright © Matt Rourke/AP/Press Association Images
Adam Smith copyright © Hulton-Deutsch Collection/CORBIS. From an engraving by Robert Graves
George Soros copyright © Koji Sashara/AP/Press Association Images
Joseph Stiglitz copyright © Virginia Mayo/AP/Press Association Images
Richard Thaler copyright © Ralf-Finn Hestoft/CORBIS
James Tobin copyright © Joel Page/AP/Press Association Images
Amos Tversky copyright © Barbara Tversky
Arnold, Lord Weinstock copyright © PA/PA Archive/Press Association Images
Jack Welch copyright © Elise Amendola/AP/Press Association Images
Mohammed Yunus copyright © Franka Bruns/AP/Press Association Images
Robert Zoellick copyright © Gregorio Borgia/AP/Press Association Images

We extend our grateful thanks to all of the following who donated photographs for use in *QFINANCE*:
Amjid Ali, Philipp Bagus, Wim Bartels, Jeremy Beckwith, Barruch Ben-Zekry, Björn Bloching, Paul Brain, David Bresch, Janet Campagna, Laurie Carroll, James Chadwick, Yves Choueifaty, Tony Clare, Eddie Cochrane, Angelos Damaskos, Rod Davidson, Hernando de Soto, Thibault de Tersant, Rajiv Dogra, Sudhir Singh Dungarpur, Simon Earp, Richard Ellis, Peter Elston, Javier Estrada, James Gifford, Annette Godart-van der Kroon, Erik Gosule, Michelle Greene, Ben Gunnee, Keith Guthrie, Renée Haugerud, Tim Hindle, Dan Hird, Sir Christopher Hogg, Mark Hogg, Catherine Howarth, Andrew Howie, Jesús Huerta de Soto, Christopher Johnson, Andrew Kakabadse, Jonathan M. Karpoff, Mark Kenber, Brendan LeBlanc, Peter, Lord Levene, Jay W. Lorsch, Aldo Mareuse, Robert Marquardt, John Mauldin, Alex McNeil, Marcus Mollan, James Montier, Pau Morilla-Giner, Arun Motianey, Richard Murphy, Russell Napier, Ravi Nedungadi, Stephen Penman, Lawrence Phillips, Riccardo Rebonato, James Roberts, Shahzada Omar Saeed, Richard Sambrook, David Schofield, Leonard Seabrooke, Robert, Lord Skidelsky, Stuart Thomson, Valentijn van Nieuwenhuijzen, John Vail, Jayanth R. Varma, Theo Vermaelen, Hans Vrensen, Paul Wharton, Gervais Williams, Neil Williams, Toby Willson, Richard Wilson, and Muhammad Yunus.